The Longman Anthology of Drama and Theater

A GLOBAL PERSPECTIVE

REVISED FIRST EDITION

Michael L. Greenwald
Texas A&M University

Roger Schultz
Texas A&M University

Roberto D. Pomo
California State University at Sacramento

PEARSON
Longman

New York Boston San Francisco
London Toronto Sydney Tokyo Singapore Madrid
Mexico City Munich Paris Cape Town Hong Kong Montreal

Vice President and Editor-in-Chief: Joseph Terry
Managing Editor: Erika Berg
Development Editor: Marlane Miriello
Senior Marketing Manager: Melanie Craig
Senior Supplements Editor: Donna Campion
Managing Editor: Valerie Zaborski
Project Coordination, Text Design, and Electronic Page Makeup: Nesbitt Graphics, Inc.
Cover Designer/Manager: Wendy Ann Fredericks
Cover Photo: © R. Chen/Superstock
Photo Researcher: Photosearch, Inc.
Manufacturing Manager: Mary Fischer
Printer and Binder: Hamilton Printing
Cover Printer: Lehigh Press, Inc.

For permission to use copyrighted material, grateful acknowledgment is made to the copyright holders on pp. 1787-1791, which are hereby made part of this copyright page.

Library of Congress Cataloging-in-Publication Data

Greenwald, Michael L. 1945–
     The Longman anthology of drama and theater: a global perspective/Michael L.
Greenwald, Roger Schultz, Roberto D. Pomo
          p.   cm.
     Includes bibliographical references and index.
     ISBN 0-321-01559-2 (pbk.)
     1. Theater—History. 2. Drama—History and criticism. 3. Drama—Collections. I.
     Schultz, Roger. II. Dario Pomo, Roberto. III. Title.
     PN1655 .G74   2000
792'.09-dc21

Please visit our website at http://www.ablongman.com

ISBN 0-321-29138-7

     8 9 10—HT--15 14 13 12

CONTENTS

Contents

Contents

Contents

PREFACE

In *The Longman Anthology of Drama and Theater: A Global Perspective* we offer students of theater and dramatic literature a collection of plays that is truly international. While acknowledging the presence of other fine drama anthologies, we have chosen to go beyond the traditional Western canon and also offer readers works from Asia, Africa, Latin America, and the Caribbean. In doing so, we hope to better meet the needs of students who both represent and are interested in exploring the diversity of the world as it is mirrored in dramatic works.

Flexible organization

The Longman Anthology of Drama and Theater provides the most comprehensive textbook coverage of theater conventions and history available today. We have organized it to accommodate the broad variety of teaching and learning approaches used in courses such as Introduction to Theater, Theater History, Comparative and/or Dramatic Literature, and World Theater.

The text is divided into two parts. Part I, The Theoretical and Practical Foundations of Theater (Chapters 1 to 3), examines the roots of theater, the theoretical and critical foundations of theater and drama, and the role of the various artists who bring plays to life before an audience. This section provides a particularly useful introduction to theater and drama to students who may be just beginning their exploration of one of the most important and ubiquitous arts developed by humans. Part II, An Anthology of the World's Drama (Chapters 4 to 9), is divided into six historical and geographical sections:

Chapter 4   The Theater of Greece and Rome
Chapter 5   The Theater of India, China, and Japan, with an emphasis on Sanskrit and modern drama (India), Yuan and Peking Opera (China), and Noh, Kabuki, and contemporary drama (Japan)
Chapter 6   The Early Modern Theater, including the Middle Ages, the European Renaissance, Mesoamerica and its conquest drama, and the Late-Seventeenth and Eighteenth Centuries
Chapter 7   The Modern Theater and its various movements (Romanticism, Realism, Expressionism and the Epic Theater, and Absurdism)
Chapter 8   The Theater of Africa and the African Diaspora in America and the Caribbean
Chapter 9   The Contemporary Theater, featuring works since 1960 and Pirandello's *Six Characters in Search of an Author*, the prototype of the postmodern drama.

Each chapter in Part II opens with a brief overview of the cultural, historical, and especially the performance contexts that shaped the plays. A map and timeline of key historical, cultural, and artistic events accompany the geographic and historic sections within chapters. Photos and diagrams also appear within chapters to support the discussion. The individual plays can be taught by themselves or with as much of the supporting historical and cultural material as time and inclination allow.

Because the history of the theater presents many complex issues and an overlapping of thoughts and styles, it is difficult to categorize events with true precision. The framework we have chosen provides a useful starting point for an exploration of the drama and theater, whether chronological (the primary organization of the text), geographic, or thematic.

Breadth of Selections

With 61 plays, many of them full-length, *The Longman Anthology of Drama and Theater* affords teachers and students maximum flexibility, whether they are pursuing a traditional course of study, exploring the diversity of voices in the world's theater, or a combination of the two. Approximately one-third of the plays are less than ten pages, which, when performed, would probably run less than one hour. Some of these "short plays" include Harold Pinter's *One for the Road* and Griselda Gambaro's *Personal Effects*, which can be readily examined in a single class period. In addition, a number of the text's plays complement one another. For instance, the Japanese Noh play, *Komachi at Sekidera*, and Beckett's *Rockaby* share thematic and stylistic similarities that encourage discussion and understanding. Students can also explore two versions of the Medea legend: that written by Euripides as well as a postmodern treatment by Germany's Heiner Müller.

The plays are nearly evenly split between the traditional classical and modern canon and the nontraditional selections. We present a broad range of drama from around the globe, including works from:

- **India:** *The Recognition of Śakuntulā*, a Sanskrit romance written at the royal court over 1500 years ago, and *The Post Office*, a play by the patriarch of the modern Indian theater, Rabindranath Tagore.
- **China:** *Autumn in the Palace of Han*, a classical Yuan play, and *The Qing Ding Pearl*, a work from the Peking Opera that influenced Brecht's theater.
- **Japan:** *Komachi at Sekidera*, a Noh drama; *Kanjinchō (The Subscription List)*, a Kabuki-Bunraku play; and, representing the contemporary Japanese theater, Kobo Abe's inventive *The Man Who Turned into a Stick*.
- **Africa:** *Woza Albert!*, a South African township political comedy, appears alongside the more widely published *"MASTER HAROLD"...and the boys* by Fugard, and *Death and the King's Horseman* by Soyinka.
- **Mexico:** *The Divine Narcissus*, Mexico's first conquest drama, by Sor Juana Inés de la Cruz, and *A Solid Home*, by Elena Garro, a modern play employing the magic realism of Mexico.
- **Latin America:** *The Man Who Turned into a Dog* by Osvaldo Dragún, and *Personal Effects* by Griselda Gambarro, two Argentine comedies in the absurdist tradition, and *Paper Flowers* by Egon Wolff, a surrealistic drama from Chile.
- **The Caribbean:** *Ti-Jean and His Brothers*, a political folk-tale by Nobel Laureate Derek Walcott.

We have purposefully chosen a number of western plays that are indebted to other cultures for both their thematic material and performance style, including:

- Bertolt Brecht's *The Good Woman of Setzuan* and David Henry Hwang's *The Dance and the Railroad*, both of which employ Chinese theater techniques.
- *The Great Celestial Cow*, a contemporary feminist play by England's Sue Townsend that draws from the mythology and dance drama of India.
- Luis Valdez's *No saco nada de la escuela*, which celebrates the Aztec heritage of contemporary Chicanos.
- Lorraine Hansberry's *A Raisin in the Sun*, Amiri Baraka's *Slave Ship*, and August Wilson's *Fences*, which address the African Diaspora within the context of contemporary American social drama.

The classical dramas of the West are also well represented with the inclusion of plays by each of the four acknowledged masters of Greek drama and a comedy by Rome's finest playwright:

- Aeschylus (*Prometheus Bound*)
- Sophocles (*Oedipus the King*)
- Euripides (*Medea*)
- Aristophanes (*Lysistrata*)
- Terence (*Brothers*)

We include examples of five secular and liturgical dramas from the Middle Ages:

- the farcical *Master Pierre Pathelin*
- a mystery play, *Abraham and Isaac* (taken from the famous Brome manuscript)
- two liturgical moralities (the stately *Everyman* and the ribald *Mankind*)
- a secular morality from the Netherlands (*The Apple Tree*)

Significant works by major playwrights of the European Renaissance (Shakespeare and Calderón) and the Enlightenment (Molière, Aphra Behn, and Oliver Goldsmith) are also included.

The text contains historically significant Romantic melodramas (*Hernani* and *Uncle Tom's Cabin*) as well as plays by the founders of Social Realism (Ibsen, Strindberg, Chekhov, Shaw, and O'Neill).

The most critically acclaimed contemporary playwrights are also represented: Williams, Miller, Albee, Beckett, Shepard, Pinter, Fugard, and August Wilson. In addition, important voices, heretofore underrepresented, are heard: Susan Glaspell, Caryl Churchill, Sue Townsend, Maria Irene Fornes (major feminist playwrights), and Amiri Baraka, Luis Valdez, and David Henry Hwang (minority playwrights).

And finally innovative new dramatists of the 90s (Tony Kushner and Anna Deavere Smith) address current issues as the world redefines itself.

Pedagogical Support

Rituals, Ceremonies, and Folk Customs

In addition to an unequalled offering of international plays, we describe rituals, ceremonies, and folk customs to enhance our readers' understanding of the human need to create theater and then present plays that incorporate these traditions. For example, our discussions of:

- The Yoruban Obatala relates to Wole Soyinka's *Death and the King's Horseman*
- The Japanese Tanabata Festival is integral to the action of *Komachi at Sekidera*
- Mexico's festive Día de los Muertos, which laughs at death, accompanies Elena Garro's *A Solid Home*
- Summer solstice celebrations prepare readers for Shakespeare's *A Midsummer Night's Dream* and Strindberg's *Miss Julie,* which are both set against the backdrop of this major European festival. The ritual origins of theater are further addressed as we examine the birth of theater in Greece, Mesoamerica, Africa, and Asia. The role of the storyteller (bard, *sūtradhara, griot, cha,* or *cancionero*) is also examined to provide an appreciation of the impulses that prompt humans to create theater.

Headnotes

We introduce each play with a thorough headnote that provides a biography of its playwright, its context in history, and a discussion of its themes. Because we are practicing theater artists who have acted in, directed, or reviewed many of these plays, we enthusiastically explore the performance dimensions of the plays so that students may better appreciate their theatrical as well as their dramatic appeal.

Center Stage Boxes

Throughout the text, we have included brief boxed essays that supplement the play or commentary where they appear. Nineteen Center Stage boxes present dramatic descriptions of special performances, in many cases the first performance of a well-known play. For instance, students can read about *Oedipus the King* as it was performed at the Theatre of Dionysus in ancient Athens, in Italy's Teatro Olýmpico in 1585, and by Tyrone Guthrie's company in 1955. Productions of *A Midsummer Night's Dream*, *Tartuffe*, *Uncle Tom's Cabin*, and *Death of a Salesman* are similarly featured. Many Center Stage boxes are devoted to a description of rituals and folk customs, such as Ireland's mid-winter Wren Festival. Each Center Stage box is accompanied by a photo that invites students to experience the event through their visual imaginations.

Spotlight Boxes

The 17 Spotlight boxes identify and discuss the staging conventions of particular theaters. Students read about the conventions of the Hellenistic theater, Greek Old Comedy, the colorful style of the Kabuki theater, Shakespeare's two theaters, popular theater in Latin America, South African township theater, and many others.

Forum Essays

Under the general title "Forum," 41 essays and extracts from important works by critics, theoreticians, and theater artists themselves illuminate plays and discussions throughout the text. Students may read a review of the first production of *Death of a Salesman*, written by a professional critic; Jo Mielziner's discussion of his scenic design for that play; and Arthur Miller's discussion of tragedy and the common man. Elsewhere, they can learn about theater from such diverse thinkers as Aristotle, Brazil's Augusto Boal, and the Chinese scholar, Tao Ching-hsu.

Maps and Timelines

Because students may not be familiar with world geography, and because scores of dates can become cumbersome within a text, we have included 20 maps with key cities and historical sites clearly marked and timelines with selected theatrical and historical/cultural events highlighted by eye-catching icons. These introduce each section in the anthology and in many cases allow students to see how historical events (e.g., the defeat of the Spanish Armada by the English) correspond to major theatrical events (e.g., the flowering of the Elizabethan theater). The maps and timelines should prove especially useful as students study regions with which they may be unfamiliar (e.g., Latin America, the Caribbean, and Mesoamerica). Our collective experience as teachers has taught us that students find such devices useful as they review material for examinations and papers. Better yet, they make attractive and memorable learning aids.

Photos and Illustrations

Because "theater" derives from the Greek word meaning "the seeing place," we have also included a comprehensive collection of photos and illustrative material. There are approximately 125 illustrations that help students visualize the possibilities for theatrical production. There is a production photo—or other useful illustration (e.g., a medieval illumination to illustrate Abraham's sacrifice of Isaac)—to stimulate students as they "see" the plays they read.

Appendixes

To supplement the text, we offer the following appendixes: A two-part primer on critical writing for students: the first dealing with production reviews and the second on critical analysis of a play script; a glossary of principal terms used in the text; and a bibliography of essential works for each chapter and section of the text. (In the interest of creating a clean, uncluttered text, we have placed the bibliography at the end of the book.)

Supplements

Website. *The Longman Anthology of Drama and Theater* offers students and instructors a lavish website at www.awl.com/greenwald. Featuring additional information on playwrights, plays, and related works, as well as an abundance of links, the site extends and enhances the text and brings its contents to life in real-world contexts.

Instructor's Manual. An outline summary of each section and questions for discussion and writing are included in the *Instructor's Manual*, as well as a comprehensive list of films and videos that illustrate ideas in the text.

Acknowledgments

We are indebted to many people who have contributed their expertise to the completion of this volume. To them we offer Shakespeare's words from *Twelfth Night*:

[We] can no other answer make but thanks,
And thanks; and ever oft good turns
Are shuffled off with such uncurrent pay.

We begin with Lisa Moore, who encouraged this project from the outset and issued the original contract; to our editors at Addison Wesley Longman, Janice Wiggins Clark and Laura McKenna, for steering the final manuscript to press. Lois Lombardo's expertise and patience helped to organize this gigantic manuscript in its many forms and to expedite the production process. Viqi Wagner's astute final edit refined and polished content and style. Mark Naccarelli's stewardship as production manager was truly Promethean. Most importantly, we are grateful to Marlane Miriello, our development editor, whose knowledge, encouragement, advice, and warmth were as treasured as they were useful.

We also thank the many external reviewers whose comments and especially whose suggestions have helped make this a better and more accurate text: Cora Agatucci, Central Oregon Community College; Jean Heard Bazemore, Humboldt State University; Anne Brannen, Duquesne University; David Boudreaux, Nicholls State University; Rhett Bryson, Furman University; Joyce Cavarozzi, Wichita State University; Maria Carrig, Loyola University, Chicago; Barbara Clayton, University of Wisconsin-Madison; Mark Cosdon, Colby College; David Denny, De Anza College; Larry Fink, The Ohio State University; Glorianne Engel, Arizona State University; Robert Everding, University of Central Arkansas; Anthony Fichera, University of North Carolina; Melissa Gibson, University of Pittsburgh; Michael Gillespie, Oakland University; L. W. Harrison, Santa Rosa Junior College; Melissa Hillman, University of California, Berkeley; Robert Jackson, Bellevue Community College; Harvey Kassebaum, Cuyahoga Community College; Josephine Lee, University of Minnesota; Michael Longrie, University of Wisconsin-Whitewater; Lurana D. O'Malley, University of Hawaii; Meenakshi Ponnuswami, Bucknell University; George Plakidas, York University and Seneca College (Ontario, Canada); Brian Richardson, University of Maryland; Frances Dodson Rhome, Indiana University-Purdue University at Indiana; Leslie Riedel, University of Delaware; Jyotsna G. Singh, Southern Methodist University; Rita Smilkstein, North Seattle Community College; Fritz Szabo, Iowa State University; Linda Wells, Boston University; and Joyce Wszalek, James Madison University.

As is often the case, we learned and benefited most from our severest critics, and we trust you will see your input in the completed project.

Others contributed their scholarship to this project, and to them we offer our deepest gratitude. Contributors: Allen Alford, Temple Community College; Lisajo Epstein; Bernardine Banning, Radford University; C. L. Etheridge; Robert Everding, University of Central Arkansas; Ayumi Kazama, Sayaka Sudo, and Robert W. Wenck, Texas A&M University.

Thanks also to the secretarial and office help: Susan Williams, Amanda Watkins, Judy Wade; and student workers: Amber Bellchere, Tricia Hale, Abby Johnson, Amanda Mitchell, Allisia Montalvo, Eric Montalvo, Beau Pihlaja, Doug Sandlin, Leslie Spieks, and Kelly Zayas.

And a special thanks to Ann Marie Welsh, theater critic at *The San Diego Union-Tribune*, for her provocative observations and enthusiasm; and Peter Schwab, the math guru at the Bishop's School, whose computer savvy helped enormously.

Finally, though most importantly, we thank our families for their saintly patience and support: our wives, Demetra and Ruthie; and our children, Sean, Jennifer, Eric, Peter, Elizabeth, Anna, and William—to whom we dedicate this book with our love.

Only in Plato's Republic does the ideal textbook exist. With that reservation in mind, we offer *The Longman Anthology of Drama and Theater: A Global Perspective* as another necessary step in the evolution of drama anthologies, and we do so with a sense of awe at the rich variety of plays and performance styles produced by artists throughout the world.

Michael L. Greenwald

Roger Schultz

Roberto D. Pomo

PART I

The Theoretical and Practical Foundations of Theater

All the world's a stage,

And all the men and women

merely players . . .

WILLIAM SHAKESPEARE

Masked Sandaran warriors guard the Barong as part of a sacred trance rite in Bali. The costumes and masks attest to a universal impulse to invest special events with theatrical artifice.

CHAPTER 1

STORIES, RITUALS, AND THEATER

A Foundation for the Theatrical Arts

The Theatrical Impulse

Of all the arts, the theater is among the oldest and the most instinctive. Though you may have never read or attended a play, you demonstrate an innate theatricality when you embellish your activities with symbolic words and gestures, or with such visual symbols as costumes and decorations. You choose the perfect attire for a date or an interview because it will help establish the image (or character) you wish your audience to perceive. A teacher slings a sheet about the shoulders to play Socrates for an audience of students. Children play games to learn about their emerging roles in the world, as well as for their amusement. Flowers are ordered, musicians are hired, and a white gown is designed for a magnificent ritual performed before an audience to signify the union of two people in love. Flowers are ordered, musicians are hired, a casket is draped in black, and an audience returns to mourn the passing of one of its own.

Our daily English vocabulary is filled with the language of the theater. We talk about "acting" properly in a given situation. Headlines proclaim the "tragedy" of a plane crash, the "drama" of a trial, or a "comedy of errors" involving the local athletic team. CEOs think in terms of best- or worst-case *scenarios*. Parents command their children not to make "a scene." We accuse a two-faced person of being a hypocrite (a word actually derived from the Greek word *hypokrites*, or "actor," i.e., someone who pretends to be something he is not).

Little wonder, then, that we should devise theater as one of our principal means of communication. Though we live in a high-tech age with many electronic diversions to instruct and entertain us, live theater remains an integral part of people's lives throughout the world. Before beginning a formal study of the theater as an art, consider some of the creative impulses that prefigure it. Because theater depends on the power of the imagination, transport yourself back in time as you imagine yourself in each of the following situations.

The Storyteller

As shadows dance against the wall of a cliff in West Africa, an old *griot* entrances the Dogon people with a heroic tale about a blacksmith who stole a piece of the sun from the gods so that the Dogon might live more fruitfully. The storyteller suddenly rises and transforms himself, almost magically, from mere man into the mighty blacksmith. His voice deepens and his body seems to grow as he defiantly shakes his fist at the gods. The Dogon shout as one to encourage his bravery and their voices echo through the night.

Thousands of miles to the east, a Brahman *sūtradhara* retells the much-loved story of Gautama, the sacred Buddha, who sacrifices himself to a hungry tigress so that she might feed her seven starving cubs. For his noble act, Gautama is rewarded in his next life as he returns to a life of luxury as Prince Siddhartha. To illustrate how a beautiful girl enchants the prince, the priest sways rhythmically to the accompaniment of drums and a stringed instrument. His audience no longer sees him as a man, but as a dancer radiant in the glow of the smiling Buddha.

Among the Pueblo of North America, a *shaman*—part healer, part prophet, and conjurer of many stories—hunches to show his young disciples how Coyote, the mischief maker in Amerindian lore, stalks its prey. The boys admire the shaman's mime, for they have often seen Coyote's offspring on the mesas. Entranced by the magic of the moment, the boys also imitate Coyote as they become a chorus of cavorting dancers. The shaman, wearing the pelt of an actual coyote, laughs at the boys, satisfied that they have surrendered themselves to the power of Coyote this night.

In the agora, the marketplace of a Greek village, a blind poet-singer describes the deadly battle between Achilles, warrior-hero of the Argive army, and Hector, prince of Troy. As Hector suffers a deathblow from Achilles, the storyteller falls to the ground to show the agony of the dying prince. The Greek villagers are at once entertained and instructed by this man they call a *rhapsode*—literally, a "song-stitcher." Over the centuries other rhapsodes add to his story, and they, too, enliven their stories by imitating the actions of the epic heroes.

In Africa, Asia, the Americas, and Europe, we see the roots of an art we call theater in the tales of the griot and rhapsode. In China, Ireland, and Chile, they were called the *wu*, the bard, and the *cancionero*; they too invented stories and myths to help people understand their place in the world. At some point *mimesis*—the art of imitation—was introduced to physically and vocally re-create the characters of the story. And would they not likely have added costumes and perhaps a mask? And may we not imagine that at some point others in the audience rose to help tell the story through mime, voice, and costumes? Robert Edmund Jones, the admired American scene designer, has written an imaginative account of this process (see Forum, "The Theatre As It Was and As It Is").

You, too, are a storyteller—and an actor. You have embellished a story while telling a friend about an event as you gestured broadly, changed your voice, and—if only for an instant—became the person in your story. If you have not done so recently, you surely did so as a child. In a very real sense you were acting, and you were creating theater just as the griot or the rhapsode did centuries ago.

Over 2,200 years ago the Greek philosopher Plato suggested that the Greek rhapsodes were as much actors as poets. In the *Ion*—a dialogue between Socrates and General Ion—Plato noted that "rhapsodes and actors are wise" because they are inspired by the gods themselves to instruct people even as they entertain them.

Storytelling and the instinct to act out the story are but two of the cornerstones of the theatrical arts. Among others are rituals, ceremonies, pageantry, and carnivals—we have many words for activities that use theatrical elements. Coincidentally, Plato's student, Aristotle, suggested that theater in Greece might have grown from religious rites in honor of the god Dionysus; the Natyashastra, the sacred book of Hindu dramaturgy, begins with an account of a ritual performed by the gods themselves in the celestial theater of the goddess Indra. Such matters are dealt with elsewhere, but first consider the link between storytelling, rituals, and modern theater. As a starting point, consider the annual retelling of an ancient story about a terrifying witch from the island of Bali in the western Pacific.

The Barong or Trance Dance of Bali

Behind the sacred temple of Poera Panataran on Bali, a rice farmer named Ida Njoman puts on a huge mask to become the principal actor in a cosmic drama that has been performed for centuries. The dragonlike mask represents Rangda, an evil witch (perhaps derived from the Hindu goddess Durga) who opposes the Barong, a life-giving lion who defends the village against her destructive powers. In this universal battle between good and evil, between creation and destruction, local farmers, dressed in the traditional plaid sarong, carry short swords (kris) to dispel Rangda's evil powers. The entire village gathers under an enormous banyan tree in front of the temple honoring Banaspati Radja, king of the benevolent spirits. This ritual drama is un-

FORUM

"The Theatre As It Was and As It Is"

ROBERT EDMUND JONES

Robert Edmund Jones, one of the United States' preeminent scene designers, imagines one of the first theatrical performances in human history.

I am going to ask you to do the most difficult thing in the world—to imagine. Let us imagine ourselves back in the Stone Age, in the days of the cave man and the mammoth and the Altamira frescoes. It is night. We are all sitting together around a fire—Ook and Pow and Pung and Glup and Little Zowie and all the rest of us. We sit close together. We like to be together. It is safer that way, if wild beasts attack us. And besides, we are happier when we are together. We are afraid to be alone. Over on that side of the fire the leaders of the tribe are sitting together—the strongest men, the men who can run fastest and fight hardest and endure longest. They have killed a lion today. We are excited about this thrilling event. We are all talking about it. We are always afraid of silence. We feel safer when somebody is talking. There is something strange about silence, strange like the black night around us, something we can never understand.

The lion's skin lies close by, near the fire. Suddenly the leader jumps to his feet. "I killed the lion! I did it! I followed him! He sprang at me! I struck at him with my spear! He fell down! He lay still!"

He is telling us. We listen. But all at once an idea comes to his dim brain. "I know a better way to tell you. See! It was like this! *Let me show you!*"

In that instant drama is born.

The leader goes on. "Sit around me in a circle—you, and you, and you—right here, where I can reach out and touch you all." And so with one inclusive gesture he makes—a theatre . . .

The leader continues: "You, Ook, over there—you stand up and be the lion. Here is the lion's skin. You put it on and be the

lion and I'll kill you and we'll show them how it was." Ook gets up. He hangs the skin over his shoulders. He drops on his hands and knees and growls. How terrible he is! Of course, he isn't the real lion. We know that. The real lion is dead. We killed him today. Of course, Ook isn't a lion. Of course not. He doesn't even look like a lion. "You needn't try to scare us, Ook. We know you. We aren't afraid of you!" And yet, in some mysterious way, Ook *is* the lion. He isn't like the rest of us any longer. He is Ook all right, but he is a lion, too.

And now these two men—the world's first actors—begin to show us what the hunt was like. They do not tell us. They *show* us. They *act* it for us. The hunter lies in ambush. The lion growls. The hunter poises his spear. The lion leaps. We all join in with yells and howls of excitement and terror. The first community chorus! The spear is thrown. The lion falls and lies still.

The drama is finished.

Now Ook takes off the lion's skin and sits beside us and is himself again. Just like you. Just like me. Good old Ook. No, not quite like you or me. Ook will be, as long as he lives, the man who can be a lion when he wants to. Pshaw! A man can't be a lion! How can a man be a lion? But Ook can make us believe it, just the same. Something strange happens to that man Ook sometimes. The lion's spirit gets into him. And we shall always look up to him and admire him and perhaps be secretly a little afraid of him. Ook is an actor. He will always be different from the rest of us, a little apart from us. For he can summon spirits.

Many thousands of years have passed since that first moment of inspiration when the theatre sprang into being. But we still like to get together, we still dread to be alone, we are still a little awed by silence, we still like to make believe, . . . we are still lost in wonder before this magical are of the theatre. It is really a kind of magic, this art. We call it glamour or poetry or romance, but that doesn't explain it. In some mysterious way these old, simple, ancestral moods still survive in us, and an actor can make them live again for a while. We become children once more. We believe.

derscored by the hypnotic beat of drums and bamboo xylophones played by the gamelan, the sacred musicians.

The climax of this drama is riveting: Rangda casts a spell on the attacking dancers, whose swords are turned violently toward their chests. However, those who believe in the goodness of the Barong are not harmed, and the sharp swords bend grotesquely against the men's breastbones. The dancers fall into in a deep trance and eventually awaken, exhausted from their encounter with the Evil One. Ida Njoman remains entranced hours after this performance in which he willingly sacrifices himself by portraying Rangda for the good of his neighbors. The village celebrates its liberation from evil as girls, each named after a flower, dance the *sang hyang* to celebrate life. An old priest pours a libation on the ground to purify it, while smoke from a sacred brazier is wafted into the faces of the congregation as they return to their homes, purified by their experience at the Barong (or "trance") dance.

A Broadway Musical

Meanwhile, in New York City a spectacular musical, *The Lion King*, plays nightly at the venerable New Amsterdam Theater on Broadway, as it has since September 1997. An audience pays $80 a ticket to watch a company of professional actor-dancers portray an assortment of animal characters to the accompaniment of musicians seated near the stage. The director, Julie Taymor, has significantly adapted theater techniques she learned in Southeast Asia to this tale about Africa. The performers who transform themselves into lions and other creatures of the African veldt entrance the audience. True, the costuming, the makeup, and Taymor's inventive puppetry aid this illusion, but it is still the performers' mime and dance that charm the audience into accepting this "magical lie." The play reaches its climax when the Lion Prince defeats his murderous uncle in a battle every bit as thrilling as that between Rangda and the Barong. (More than a few stories in the theater involve princes who defeat murderous uncles: see *Hamlet*.) The spectators cheer enthusiastically and return to their homes, refreshed by the "magic" of the evening. They feel that they, too, have participated in the triumph of the good in this entertaining diversion.

Rituals Versus Theater

Though the dance of the Barong and *The Lion King* share common traits such as music, costumes, and storytelling, there are significant differences between the two. The Balinese drama is a *ritual*. Rituals are:

Director Julie Taymor used puppetry and theatrical techniques she learned in Indonesia as she staged The Lion King *on Broadway; see the Forum box in Chapter 3 for her discussion of* The Lion King.

- symbolic actions developed by and performed for a community, usually to satisfy its spiritual or cultural needs;
- arranged in patterns that eventually—often over many generations—become precise in their execution;
- believed to have originally been performed to achieve "magical" effects, such as controlling the weather or the success of a hunt.

Note that "ritual" and "ceremony" are not necessarily synonymous terms. Ceremonies are formalized actions meant to sanction a political, social, or religious concept. A graduation is a social ceremony, whereas the inauguration of a president is a political ceremony. In many cultures, rituals and ceremonies are often sources of formal theater and drama, which are deliberate artistic mediums.

While it employs elements we identify with ritual (chanting, the rite in which Rafiki anoints Simba), *The Lion King* is an entertainment that melds a variety of arts: theater, dance, music, literature, and the visual arts. Theater as an art form can be distinguished from rituals in several ways:

- It is deliberately created by (usually) professional writers, directors, musicians, performers, and designers, and it is meticulously planned and rehearsed.
- Most contemporary commercial theater is created primarily to entertain, though *The Lion King* has an instructive value in the lessons it teaches and the culture it portrays.
- Modern theatrical art depends on commercial success to sustain itself.
- Contemporary theater addresses various sociological, political, psychological, and aesthetic needs of its audience.
- Theater depends upon an audience that chooses to attend the play.

Rituals and ceremonies often contribute to the theater. Appended to selected plays throughout this text you will find descriptions of rituals, ceremonies, and folk customs around the world that may help us understand the plays. Though the particulars of these events differ from place to place because of cultural influences, the impulses to use theatrical means to engage both participants and audiences are universal:

- The Yoruban Obatala Festival (Nigeria, West Africa), a two-week reenactment of a cosmic battle between a Yoruban hero-god and his captor. Wole Soyinka's *Death and the King's Horseman* uses elements of Yoruban ritual (see Chapter 8).
- *Día de los Muertos* (Mexico), an autumnal festival in which people dressed as skeletons mock death even as they recognize it as an essential part of life's experience. Elena Garro's *A Solid Home* is a short play that also laughs at death (see Chapter 9).
- The Yaqui Easter (Southwestern United States), a fascinating rite that combines pre-Columbian rituals with those of the Christian tradition as a young man performs a mysterious deer dance on Easter morning. Sor Juana Inés de la Cruz's *The Divine Narcissus* also merges the rituals of indigenous people in Mesoamerica with Christian theology (see Chapter 6).
- The Wren Festival of Dingle (Ireland), in which young men called Wrenboys dress in huge straw costumes as they woo village maidens in a midwinter festival. In contrast, John Millington Synge's one-act *Riders to the Sea* shows Irish women mourning the death of their husbands and sons (see Chapter 7).
- The Tannabata Festival (Japan), which commemorates the fate of mythical lovers as young people tie love poems to bamboo shoots as pledges of fidelity. Zeami's Noh drama about a famous poet, *Komachi at Sekidera* is set against the background of the Tannabata (see Chapter 5).
- Carnival (Trinidad), like Mardi Gras, a pre-Lenten Caribbean street festival in which thousands of performers wear colorful costumes to liberate themselves from the doldrums of daily life. Carnival originated in 1830 to celebrate the liberation of slaves. Derrick Wal-

cott's *Ti-Jean and His Brothers* also addresses some of the political issues that spawned the Trinidad Carnival (see Chapter 8).

- The Midsummer Festivals of Europe, in which people dance around bonfires and enact short plays about lovers lost in a mysterious forest, suggest some of the impulses behind Shakespeare's famous comedy *A Midsummer Night's Dream* (see Chapter 6).

An Autumnal Ritual in America

Some may dismiss such rituals, ceremonies, and folk customs as remnants of bygone days that were developed by superstitious peoples and maintained by tradition-loving moderns. Imagine cultural anthropologists in the year 2500 examining the communal activities of an American town in the late twentieth century. They might note that thousands gather on an autumn afternoon in a huge amphitheater to watch a battle between young warriors with names like Wildcats and Golden Bears. The combatants, esteemed for their strength, speed, and bravery, wear colorful headpieces bearing icons of the animals they emulate. Ecstatic followers also appear in gaudy dress, and some even paint their faces or chests in colors sacred to the community. Many gather at midnight to chant before a towering bonfire to insure success in battle.

Musicians dressed in matching livery parade around the arena as maidens dance vigorously. The observers of this autumnal rite chant strange incantations: "Hold 'em Tigers, Hold 'em Tigers!" Some are known only to the initiated: "Hullabaloo, Canek! Canek! . . ." One tribe, the Eli, chant from an ancient Athenian comedy by Aristophanes: "Brekekkekex, Coax. Co-ax, Co-ax, Co-ax." The warriors enter the arena by running a ceremonial phalanx formed by the musicians and maidens. A masked being dressed as the animal or other totem with which the community identifies leads them. The sage elders who maintain order in this contest emerge from a dark tunnel, dressed in identical zebralike clothing to manifest their authority. An elder produces a sacred talon (often a coin of the realm) to determine the order of the proceedings. Symbolic gestures inform the spectators that one group of warriors will take possession of the contested object—made from the skin of a pig—while the other will "defend the north goal."

As the battle unfolds, the faithful have an appropriate supplication for every situation: "First and ten, do it again! We like it, we like it!" Eventually one tribe advances the sacred pigskin into its antagonist's territory and a great celebration ensues. The hero who has penetrated the forbidden land improvises a triumphant dance as he hurls the pigskin into the earth while his worshippers chant ecstatically.

Halfway through the contest—as the warriors rest in the dark recesses of the stadium— the audience is treated to a spectacle as the musicians create huge artworks on the amphitheater floor. Festive floats—vestiges of medieval theatricals—are paraded about while beautiful maidens, wearing jeweled headdresses and carrying greenery, salute the audience.

The battle continues into the fading light during this, "the dying time" of year. At the conclusion of the contest, the opposing forces sing their most sacred hymns: "When the twilight shadows gather out upon the campus green. . . ." The winners exit chanting mantras to celebrate their victory ("We're Number One!"), while the vanquished meditate on their failure, chins buried in their chests. As night settles on the land, the spectators head for meetinghouses where quantities of food and drink are consumed to celebrate and console.

This description of the modern American football game suggests that, for all our technology, we are not unlike our ancestors. The game has elements common to rituals, though the football game is not a ritual, per se. Its audience lacks "ritual expectancy" because football fans are not consciously aware of the ritual purpose of the event, which for them is primarily an entertainment. Nonetheless, it reflects the core values of the competitive, commercial society that supports it, while also addressing such essential needs of humans who seek order, spectacle, and communal celebration. (See Forum, "Acting in Everyday Life and Everyday Life in Acting.")

FORUM

"Acting in Everyday Life and Everyday Life in Acting"

Victor Turner

Victor Turner, a scholar at the University of Virginia, has written extensively on the phenomenon of human rituals, theater, and drama. In this essay he traces many of the impulses (and the vocabulary that describes them) that have prompted humans to devise rituals—and ultimately theater and drama—throughout the world.

Acting, like all "simple" Anglo-Saxon words, is ambiguous—it can mean doing things in everyday life, or performing on the stage or in a temple. It can take place in ordinary time or in extraordinary time. It may be a way of working or moving, like a body's or machine's "action"; or it may be the art or occupation of performing in plays. It may be the essence of sincerity—the commitment of the self to a line of action for ethical motives perhaps to achieve "personal truth," or it may be the essence of pretence—when one "plays a part" in order to conceal or dissimulate. The former is the ideal of Jerzy Grotowski's "Poor Theatre"; the latter happens every day "at work." A spy, conman, an *agent provocateur*—each of these has skill in "acting." The same person, in different situations, in a single day, can "put on" an act, or "act divinely." Yet these opposites coincide in our common parlance; we speak of "playing a role," when we intend a reference to some civically *serious* activity, such as an advisory role to a president. On the other hand, we talk of "great acting" on the stage as the source of some of our deepest "truest" understandings of the human condition. Acting is therefore both work and play, solemn and ludic, pretence or earnest, our mundane trafficking and commerce and what we do or behold in ritual or theatre. The very word "ambiguity" is derived from the Latin *agere* to "act" for it comes from the verb *ambigere*, to "wander," *ambi*, "about, around" + *agere*, "to do," resulting in the sense of having two or more possible meanings, "moving from side to side," "of doubtful nature." In both major senses, doing deeds and performing, it is indispensable to mental health; as William Blake said: "He who nourishes Desires but *Acts* not, breeds Pestilence," a doublet "Proverb of Hell" to, "Expect Poison from the standing Water." In Western languages, action has also the flavor of contestation. Action is "agonistic." *Act, agon, agony,* and *agitate* are all derived from the same Indo-European base **ag-*, "to drive," from which came the Latin *agere*, to do, and the Greek *agein*, to lead. In Western (Euro-American) culture, work and play both have this driving,

conflictive character, which long precedes Max Weber's famed Protestant ethic. In those genres of *cultural* performance which predated Greek theatre—for example, myth-recitation, ritual, oral epic or saga, and the telling and acting of lays and *märchen*—wars and feuds between groups of deities or clans and lineages headed by well-armed heroes, as well as competition for position, power, or scarce resources, men's conflict over women, and divisions between close kin were vividly portrayed, carried out in mimicry.

Phyllis Hartnoll (*The Concise History of Theater*, n.d.: p.8) writes of the development of Greek tragedy from the dithyramb (or unison hymn) sung around the altar of Dionysus during certain religious feasts. The dithyramb, originally in lyric form, a praise song for Dionysus, came to deal with his life and mythos in much the same way as early medieval European liturgical plays about the birth, life, and resurrection of Christ, narratives loaded with conflict, grew from the lyrical portion of the Easter morning mass. The Mass, the Eucharist, itself was, of course, a drama with a scriptural script long before it gave rise to "Passion Plays." The Greek dithyramb expanded to embrace not only Dionysian tales, but also those of gods, demigods, and heroes, some of whom were regarded as the founding ancestors of the Hellenes and their Mediterranean neighbors. "The deeds of these heroes, good or bad," writes Hartnoll (*ibid*: 8–9), "their wars, feuds, marriages and adulteries, and the destinies of their children, who so often suffered for the sins of their parents, are a source of dramatic tension, and gives rise to the essential element of conflict—between man and god, good and evil, child and parent, duty and inclination. This may lead to comprehension and reconciliation between the conflicting elements—since a Greek tragedy need not necessarily end unhappily—or to incomprehension and chaos. The plots of all Greek plays were already well known to the audience. They formed part of its religious and cultural heritage, for many of them dated from Homeric times. The interest for the spectator lay, therefore, not in the novelty of the story, but in seeing how the dramatist had chosen to deal with it, and no doubt, in assessing the quality of the acting, and the work of the chorus, both in singing and dancing, about which unfortunately we know very little."

Hartnoll's summary is correct—as far as it goes. But it does not mention the important fact that the plays—Aristophanes' comedies as much as Aeschylus' and Sophocles' tragedies—in Geertz's terms are "social metacommentaries" on contemporaneous Greek society, that is, whatever the nature of their plot, whether drawn from myths or reputed historical accounts, they were intensely "reflexive." If they were "mirrors held up to nature" (or rather to society and culture) they were *active* (that

(continued)

propulsive word again!) mirrors, mirrors that probed and analyzed the axioms and assumptions of the social structure, isolated the building blocks of the culture, and sometimes used them to construct novel edifices, Cloud Cuckoolands or Persian courts that never were on land or sea, but were, nevertheless, possible variants based on rules underlying the structures of familiar sociocultural life or experienced social reality.

Theatre is perhaps the most forceful, *active*, if you like, genre of cultural performance, but there are many others, some of which I have mentioned. No society is without some mode of metacommentary—Geertz's illuminating phrase for a "story a group tells itself about itself" or in the case of theatre, a play a society acts about itself—not only a reading of its experience but an interpretive reenactment of its experience. In the simpler, preindustrial societies, there are often complex systems of ritual—initiatory, seasonal, curative, and divinatory—which act, so to speak, not only as means of "reanimating sentiments of social solidarity" as an older generation of anthropologists would put it, but also as scanning devices whereby the difficulties and conflicts of the present are articulated and given meaning through contextualization in an abiding cosmological scheme. The anger of gods or ancestors may be proposed as the cause of present misfortune, anger aroused by some blatant or persistent transgression of customs handed down from high antiquity and vouched for by revered origin myths. In complex, large-scale societies, in which the sphere of leisure is clearly separated from that of work, innumerable genres of cultural performance arise in accordance with the principle of the division of labor. These may be labeled art, entertainment, sport, play, games, recreation, theatre, light or serious reading, and many more. They may be collective or private, amateur or professional, slight or serious. Not all of them have the reflexive character of many Greek plays. Not all of them have universal reference, for many are limited to specific to specific constituencies (men, women, children, rich, poor, intellectual, middlebrow, and so on). But in this prolixity of genres, now given wider scope by the electronic media, some seem more effective than others in giving birth to self-regulatory or self-critical works, which catch the attention, or fire the imagination, of an entire society or even of an epoch, transcending national frontiers. In a complex culture it might be possible to regard the ensemble of performative and narrative genres, active and acting modalities of expressive culture as a hall of mirrors, or better magic mirrors (plane, convex, concave, convex cylinder, saddle or matrix mirrors to borrow metaphors from the study of reflecting surfaces) in which social problems, issues, and crises (from *causes célèbres* to changing macrosocial categorial relations between the sexes and age groups) are reflected as diverse images, transformed, evaluated, or diagnosed in works typical of each genre, then shifted to another genre better able to scrutinize certain of their aspects, until many facets of the problem have been illuminated and made accessible to conscious remedial action. In this hall of mirrors the reflections are multiple, some magnifying, some diminishing, some distorting the faces peering into them, but in such a way as to provoke not merely thought, but also powerful

feelings and the will to modify everyday matters in the minds of the gazers. For no one likes to see himself as ugly, ungainly, or dwarfish. Mirror distortions of reflection provoke reflexivity. In a fascinating article entitled "Mirror Images," (*Scientific American*, 1980:206–228) David Emil Thomas discusses how the mirror image is not always a faithful reflection; it can be inverted, reversed in handedness, or distorted in other ways. Thomas analyzes the transformations through a few basic curved mirrors, from which compound matrix mirrors are constructed: "by introducing various curvatures into reflecting surfaces, it is possible to create mirrors that change the shape, size, orientation, and handedness of the objects they reflect in dramatic and disturbing ways" (p. 206).

Theatre is perhaps closer to life than most performative genres, in that, despite its conventions and spatial restraints on physical possibility, it is as Marjorie Boulton wrote, (*The Anatomy of Drama*, 1971:3) "literature that *walks* and *talks* before our eyes, meant to be performed, 'acted' we might say, rather than seen as marks on paper and sights, sounds, and action in our heads." Richard Schechner, in "Performers and Spectators Transported and Transformed" published in the *Kenyon Review* (1981:84) reminds us, however, that "performance behavior isn't free and easy. Performance behavior is known and/or practiced behavior or 'twice-behaved behavior,' 'restored behavior'—either rehearsed, previously known, learned by osmosis since early childhood, revealed during the performance by masters, guides, gurus, elders, or generated by rules that govern the outcomes as in improvisatory theatre or sports." Performance, then, is always doubled, the doubleness of acting as earlier discussed—it cannot escape reflection and reflexivity. This proximity of theatre to life, while remaining at a mirror distance from it, makes of it the form best fitted to comment or "meta-comment" on conflict, for life is conflict, of which contest is only a species. . . .

The stage drama, when it is meant to do more than entertain—though entertainment is always one of its vital aims—is a metacommentary, explicit or implicit, witting or unwitting, on the major social dramas of its social context (wars, revolutions, scandals, institutional changes). Not only that, but its message and its rhetoric feed back into the *latent* processual structure of the social drama and partly account for its ready ritualization. Life itself now becomes a mirror held up to art, and the living now *perform* their lives, for the protagonists of a social drama, a "drama of living," have been equipped by aesthetic drama with some of their most salient opinions, imageries, tropes, and ideological perspectives. Neither mutual mirroring, life by art, art by life, is exact for each is not a planar mirror but a matricial mirror; at each exchange something new is added, something old is lost or discarded. Human beings learn through experience, though all too often they repress painful experience, and perhaps the deepest experience is through drama; *not* through social drama, or stage drama (or its equivalent) *alone*, but in the circulatory or oscillatory process of their mutual and incessant modification. . . .

The Origins of Theater

Exactly when rituals passed into the realm of theater varies from culture to culture. But there are some striking similarities when we consider examples of the evolution of theater throughout the world, each of which is covered in greater depth in Part II:

- Aristotle tells us that Greek theater grew from springtime rituals honoring Dionysus, the god of wine, fertility, and both the creative and irrational forces in humans. Other scholars suggest that Greek theater grew from rites in honor of the dead, sacred mysteries, or harvest dances.
- The theater of India is said to have originated from the Hindu gods Brahma, Vishnu, and Siva ("the lord of the dance"), who inspired the priest Bharata to write and perform plays. An entire book in the sacred Vedas is dedicated to theatrical presentation.
- The first professional actors in China were monks hired by farmers to perform sacred rites during the planting and harvest seasons.
- The Yorubans of Africa believe that Ogun—the Creative Essence in the universe—created theater to bridge the gap between humans and the cosmos. Ogun himself is said to have been the first actor when he assumed human form to save humans from their exile.
- The Noh theater of Japan began in religious and agricultural festivals sponsored by Buddhist monks. Specifically, the *surugaku* ("monkey dance") and the *dengaku* ("field dance") are cited as sources of the Noh.
- In medieval Europe, a major strain of theater was born in the great cathedrals as church ministers reenacted the mystery of Christ's resurrection on Easter morning.
- Among the Maya of Mesoamerica, professional entertainers called *tlaquetzque* performed cosmic dramas in spectacular costumes to honor sun gods. These provide us with one of the great myths of creation (*The Popul Vuh*) and the only extant play (*The Rabinal Achi*) from the pre-Columbian Americas.

In most instances, theater seems to have evolved from seasonal and agricultural rites acknowledging the power of some metaphysical force. Consequently, the first "actors" were often priests or shamans responsible for the well-being of the community. Many of the impulses that generated theater around the world may be found in the *Abydos Passion Play,* which was performed in Egypt for almost two thousand years. (See Center Stage box, The *Abydos Passion Play.*)

Common Ground for Uncommon Cultures

Though specific cultural forces such as power, ideology, economic status, race, gender, and historical circumstances shape particular rituals, ceremonies, and theatrical events, shared factors suggest why we, whatever our culture, often rely on—or invent—theatrical means to communicate:

1. We are mimetic beings. Aristotle began his famous treatise on theater with the observation that "the instinct for imitation is implanted in man from childhood." On its simplest level we learn by imitating how others walk, talk, dress, behave, and so on. This is *nonperformative* imitation because we are not imitating for the benefit of others. More consciously, we also frequently embellish our conversations by imitating the words, vocal patterns, and gestures of others, though we never relinquish our own personality while doing so. Though this is *performative,* it is not theater, as such, but it typifies our predisposition to imitate those about us. Actors begin with this instinct and elevate it to art. In 1402 Zeami, who (with his father, Kan-ami) founded Noh theater in Japan, wrote "Role Playing involves imitation, in every particular, with nothing left out."

2. We seek order. Whether an ancient Hindu rite or modern wedding ceremony, a Midsummer's Eve festival or a collegiate bonfire, rituals exist to give order to an often chaotic

CENTER STAGE   THE *ABYDOS PASSION PLAY*

That Egypt, among the first great Mediterranean civilizations, should develop a sophisticated theatricalized ritual is not surprising. It had a complex mythology, a ruling class viewed as powerful deities (the pharaohs), and a strong dependence on the cycle of the seasons to sustain life in the arid Nile valley. What we know about actual theatrical practice, as well as a more formal drama, in ancient Egypt is severely limited to hieroglyphs collectively known as the Pyramid Texts. These artifacts date to about 2500 B.C.E. and are the source of considerable scholarly debate about their meaning and the extent to which drama actually existed in Egypt. Some argue that priests enacted events from the lives of the pharaohs as a means of keeping their spirits (and therefore their power) alive, while others suggest that the glyphs merely illustrate poems and other literary forms.

The *Memphite Drama* and especially the *Abydos Passion Play* are generally regarded as the two most representative forms of Egyptian theater. Keep in mind that both titles were coined by archaeologists who discovered the fragmentary texts upon which our limited knowledge rests. The *Memphite Drama* was likely performed on the first day of spring and recounts the resurrection of Osiris, son of the earth and the sky, who was killed, dismembered, and buried by his jealous brother, Set. Osiris was resurrected by his sister and wife, Isis. Where his body had been buried, the land was especially fertile and produced rich crops. Horus, the son of Osiris, eventually destroyed Set in a cosmic battle. Again we see the traditional themes of death and resurrection, good confronting evil, and the need for plentitude to sustain the tribe providing rich

The Abydos Passion Play was performed in honor of the Egyptian sun god, Osiris, for 2,000 years; note the sunburst on the headdress in this bronze statue from the Ptolemaic Period.

material for early dramas. The *Memphite Drama* celebrates not only the resurrection of Osiris, the slain god-king, but the coronation of Horus. It is possible that the pharaoh himself played Horus in this yearly drama to associate himself with the god.

The *Abydos Passion Play* is regarded as the most important of the Egyptian drama-rituals. Abydos, the most sacred spot in Egypt, was associated with Osiris, and each spring the faithful gathered to reenact his story of resurrection and redemption. We know little about the particulars of this dramatization (which might have been performed over a number of weeks), but we do possess fragments written by Ikernofret about 1860 B.C.E. They suggest that the *Abydos Passion Play* was a spectacle that included battles, magnificent river barges, burial ceremonies, and coronations. According to Ikernofret's account (perhaps the first piece of recorded "performance criticism" in the world), mime and dance, music and song, recitations of great speeches, and even audience participation were ingredients in this ritual. Ikernofret, himself a participant, tells us that he reenacted "the Feast of the Going Forth" of Upwawet by repelling

   . . . the foe from the sacred barque. I overthrew the enemies of Osiris.

   I celebrated the "Great Going-Forth," following the god at his gong. . . .

   I led the way of the god to his tomb before Peker, I championed Wennofer

   at "That Day of the Great Conflict;" I slew all the enemies of Nedyt.

The *Abydos Passion Play* might have been performed annually (or at least regularly) from about 2500 B.C.E. until about 550 B.C.E. (very close to the time when, most scholars agree, formal theater began in Greece), which would make it the longest-running drama in world history. However fragmented the information we possess about it, this Nile River drama provides more evidence about the theatrical impulses of our ancestors.

world. By carefully structuring a ritual, by controlling the elements that define it (e.g., words, dress, gestures, and visual elements), and by performing it in the presence of the community, there evolves a sense that we can—or would like to—control our destinies. Tragedy, discussed in Chapter 2, reminds us that this is not always possible. The preparation for a ritual can itself become a means of diminishing anxieties. For example, the Wrenboys of Dingle, Ireland, prepare their festivities as a means of overcoming the midwinter "blahs." The repetition of the event fosters a familiarity that also calms. Passing the lore of the ritual from generation to generation establishes traditions while it promotes communal unity.

We know that many rituals, ceremonies, and even the theater itself evolved from either the agricultural calendar or spiritual-religious impulses—or both, since nature and gods were often one to early peoples. Literary critics such as Northrop Frye and Suzanne Langer (a biologist who became an art theorist) have written about plays in terms of their seasonal elements. Tragedies are autumnal plays about dying, while comedies are springtime plays about new life. Recall that the most memorable song in *The Lion King* celebrates this "circle of life."

Because it is an art form, formal theater also gives order. To make art is to select, to plan, to control, to determine an outcome. Our ancestors were, it has been argued, trying to become godlike in their early rituals; their masks often suggested spirit-world beings such as gods and ancestors. Even the modern artist is a creator-god, as Daniel Boorstin writes in *The Creators* (1992), a history of the artistic achievements of humans throughout the world:

> Mystified by the power to create, it is no wonder that man should imagine the artist to be god-like. . . . Across the world, the urge to create needed no express reason and conquered all obstacles. Man's power to make the new was the power to outlive himself in his creations. . . . He dared to make images of himself and of the life around him. He made his words into worlds, to relive his past and reshape his future.

3. We are communal beings. Tadashi Suzuki, a contemporary theater artist from Japan, defines a primary appeal of the theater when he writes that

> the works of novelists, painters, and composers are provided their essence by their sole creators. Such is not the case with theater. The theater is what it is because various performers occupy the same space, living at that precise moment in a collaborative creation.

Suzuki's observation is even more significant when we add that the audience also occupies the same space and is as much a part of the "collaborative creation" as are the performers.

Most of us crave social alliances for our well-being, and social interaction is inherent in the theatrical act. In the modern world of commerce, going to the theater is often an expensive activity that requires planning, dressing up, travel, and other special preparations. Why then do we still attend the theater in large numbers? Why aren't we simply content to go to a movie or, less expensively, rent a video? Why leave the comfort of our homes, and their readily accessible refrigerator and bathroom, to pay $10 to $100 to go to a play? The answers are complex because art and theater are complex subjects; however, two reasons merit consideration.

First, part of theater's lasting appeal has to do with the live contact between actor and audience. Movies can give audiences vicarious thrills and stunning action, but they cannot give us a live being taking the risks that are central to the theater experience. Actors walk a tightrope as they work their way through a script each night, however many times they've performed it. Such elements of "danger" are important to live theater, and those who watch also share that danger. Actors and audiences undertake a collective journey.

More importantly, theater depends very much on the contributions of the audience. A painting by Michelangelo is frozen for eternity; once a film goes into "the can" it is fixed forever and an audience cannot affect the film. Every performance in theater, however, is a new event, even a musical, such as *Cats*, that has been running for over 5,000 performances. Because actors are human, they can adjust their performance to fit the responses of the audience. "How's the house tonight?" is the universal actor's question. In a very real sense, the audience

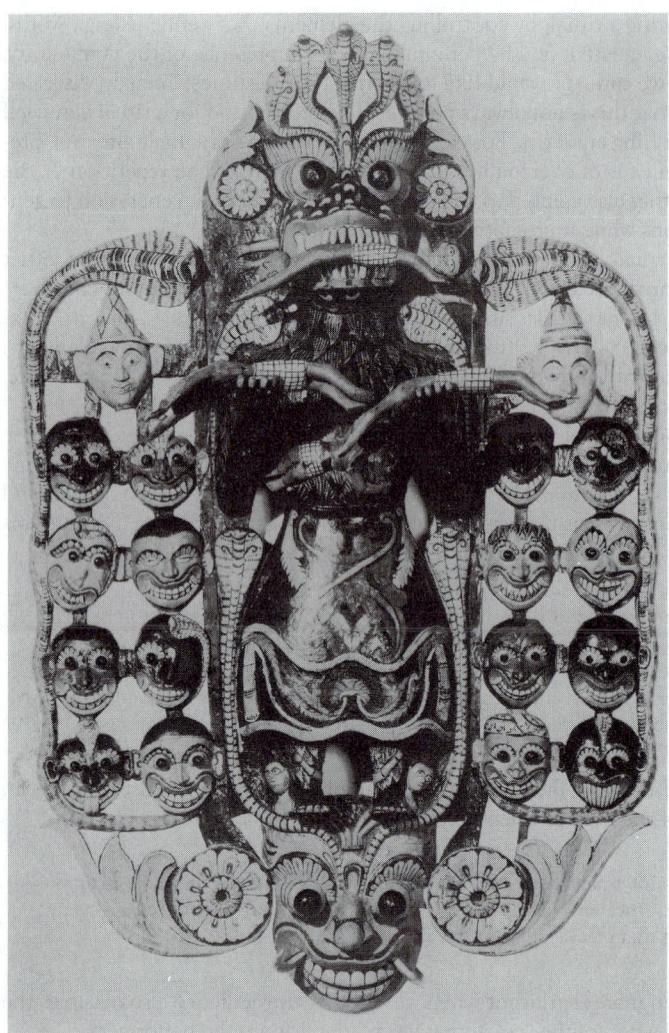

The face of evil may be found in an ancient mask of Mvaha-kola, a demon in the mythology of Ceylon, and more recently in the mask of Darth Vader, the dark spirit of the universe in George Lucas' 1983 film The Empire Strikes Back *(see photo opposite).*

contributes to the event as much as the performers, and together actors and audience create theater.

4. We use "masks" throughout our lives. Given their importance to life-sustaining rituals, it is not surprising that masks have been found in virtually every culture throughout human history. Masks are, of course, the quintessential symbol of the theater. "Mask" here is used in both its specific and literal sense (i.e., a face covering) and in its most general and figurative senses (any form of disguise, such as costume, makeup, or hairpieces). In our evolution, we have passed from "spiritual masks," rooted in religion, to "psychological masks," as defined in T. S. Eliot's poem "The Love Song of J. Alfred Prufrock," which asks, "Shall I prepare a face to meet the faces that I meet?"

Consider the ways in which masks serve many functions:

- *Masks transform,* that is, they make individuals into something more than they are in their ordinary world. They take on a magical quality that can make a mere mortal superhuman,

The mask of Darth Vader.

even godlike. The Chinese theater scholar Tao-Ching Hsu argues that "a mask may fail to terrify or to amuse but it never fails to mystify. We are instinctively afraid of the unknown, hence even the most absurd mask can inspire religious awe." In a similar vein, anthropologists describe the positive flow of energy between the spiritual and material worlds that is generated by masks.

- *Masks liberate* because they embolden us and permit us to do things we might not ordinarily do. A mugger wears a mask both to protect his identity and to abet his courage. People often wear masks at festivals, such as that in Trinidad, because masks allow them to behave more boldly—even break social taboos—without censure.

- *Masks encourage imagination.* Samuel Taylor Coleridge, the nineteenth-century critic and poet, wrote eloquently about the "willing suspension of disbelief"—that is, the audience's ability to accept the "lie" that is central to an act of theater. Coleridge's observation manifests itself most readily in masked drama. Few styles of theater are as imaginative as that of China and Japan, both of which make liberal use of masks or painted faces in their performances.

- *Masks are metaphors* because they symbolize something else. A play is not life itself, but a metaphor for life from which we may derive understanding and enjoyment. Masks enhance the metaphorical aspect of the dramatic experience. In many forms of theater (e.g., the Italian *commedia dell'arte* and the Javanese *Wayang Topeng*) masks immediately establish the symbolic nature of a character.

- *Masks are aesthetic.* That masks are collected as objets d'art attests to their appeal as both art and as a source of fascination. It is worth noting that much "modern art" (e.g., that of Picasso, Henry Moore, the Cubists, and other avant-garde artists) was inspired by masks from Africa.

5. We enjoy and need entertainment. Because rituals, and later the theater, confront life's most elemental issues—creation and destruction, birth and death, decay and resurrection—one might assume that the only worthwhile plays are profound or mystic. We must also acknowledge that at heart we retain a childlike fascination with storytelling, imaginative games, and fantasy. It is no accident that so much of the vocabulary of the theater is shared with children's activities: "play," "pretend," and "make believe." Like children's games, plays are learning events that provide a safe, entertaining means of experiencing life's challenges without actually suffering the discomfort of the real thing. We may cry in the theater; we may experience great fear and suspense; and we may be shocked by outrageous acts. Like a good roller-coaster ride, in the theater we experience the thrills and even the dangers of our journey, all the while knowing we cannot really be hurt. That's part of the entertainment.

Reading a Play

Now entertain yourself by reading a short play, *Master Pierre Pathelin*. Though it was written during the Middle Ages, it seems modern because it may properly be regarded as a "sitcom" similar to the lighthearted entertainment found on television. In fact, most of the characters are models for succeeding generations of comic characters. Here you'll meet:

- a conniving lawyer who must fast-talk his way out of a lawsuit;
- his boisterous wife;
- a crooked merchant with an inflated ego;
- a pompous judge;
- a simple shepherd with a trick or two up his own sleeve.

Though you can certainly enjoy this play without much background, consider a couple of points that the play reinforces about rituals, the human instinct to imitate, and the universal appeal of certain character types.

One of the most popular celebrations throughout medieval Europe was the Feast of Fools. This was a day, usually around Christmas, when the social hierarchy was reversed, and commoners were allowed to play the lord or lady for a day. The highborn even played at being common folk. Such customs actually can be traced to a church festival in which minor clergy spoofed the actions of their bishops and pastors. Presiding over the Feast of Fools was a much-loved figure called the Lord of Misrule (originally he was the Boy Bishop). He—and frequently his Lady of Misrule (invariably played by a man)—represented the spirit of anarchy that is central to comedy. Under his reign confusion and chaos are celebrated to remind humans of their folly. The Lord of Misrule is a cultural variation on the Trickster, the ubiquitous creator of mischief that you will encounter in many plays from around the world. His cousins are popular in the Japanese *kyōgen* (farce) and as the Chinese *ch'ou* (clown), Puck in *A Midsummer Night's Dream*, and many other characters.

Disguisings—the use of costumes, masks, and imitation—were integral to the Feast of Fools. Pierre does a little role-playing to further the comic action of the play. In fact, Pierre himself gets a bit of his own medicine when—but you must discover who dupes whom.

Read this comedy, which is as appealing today as it was in 1469 when it was performed on a simple platform in town squares, and in Chapter 2 we will refer to *Pierre Pathelin* often as we discuss those elements that make theater "drama."

A medieval woodcut suggests how audiences in the late fifteenth century may have viewed Pierre Pathelin and his wife.

MASTER PIERRE PATHELIN

—ANONYMOUS—

Translated by Alan E. Knight

CHARACTERS
PATHELIN (*a lawyer*)
GUILLEMETTE (*his wife*)
GUILLAUME JOCEAULME (*a clothier*)
THIBAULT AIGNELET (*a shepherd*)
THE JUDGE (*whom no man dare judge*)

SCENE ONE

PATHELIN. Holy Mary, Guillemette, for all the trouble I take to scrimp and save we just can't get ahead. I've seen the day, though, when I was a real attorney.

GUILLEMETTE. By Our Lady of the Law Trade! I was just thinking about that. But now people don't think you're nearly as clever as they used to. I remember when everybody wanted you to take his case. Now they all call you a prattling pettifogger.

PATHELIN. And I don't mean to brag, of course, but there's not a sharper fellow in the whole circuit, except maybe the mayor.

GUILLEMETTE. Yes, but he's studied his Latin grammar and he knows how to conjure his verbs.

PATHELIN. Whose case don't I expedite if I decide to take it on? It's true I don't know much Latin, but when I chant

17

with our priest from the mass-book, it sounds like I've studied for as long as Charlemagne stayed in Spain.

GUILLEMETTE. But what's it worth to us? Not a thing! We're starving to death, our clothes have as many holes as a sieve, and we have no idea how we can get new ones. So, what's all your knowledge worth to us?

PATHELIN. Hold your tongue! I swear, if I really put my mind to it, I'll find out where to get some clothes—and some headgear too. God willing, we'll pull out of this and be back on our feet in no time. "God does a deed with all due speed," they say. If I really have to apply myself to further my practice, you won't be able to find my equal.

GUILLEMETTE. By Saint James, certainly not in swindling. At that you're a past master.

PATHELIN. By God, you mean a master of proper lawyering.

GUILLEMETTE. By my faith, you're a master deceiver. I know, because, despite your little learning and less common sense, you're taken for one of the slyest wits in the parish.

PATHELIN. Nobody knows the finer points of the law the way I do.

GUILLEMETTE. Or the finer points of cheating, by God. At least that's the reputation you have.

PATHELIN. And so have those who wear fine clothes of silk and velvet, who claim to be lawyers, but aren't. Enough of this chatter, I'm off to the fair.

GUILLEMETTE. To the fair?

PATHELIN. Yes, by Saint John! (*He sings.*) "To the fair, my pretty maid . . ." Would it displease you if I bought some cloth or some other little thing that we need? Our clothes are nothing but rags.

GUILLEMETTE. But you don't have a penny to bless yourself with. What'll you do there?

PATHELIN. Don't ask too many questions, my lady. But if I don't bring back enough cloth to outfit us both, then call me a liar to my face. What color would you like? A gray-green, a Brussels black, or what? I need to know.

GUILLEMETTE. Whatever you can get. Beggars can't be choosers.

PATHELIN (*counting on his fingers*). Two and a half yards for you and three for me, or maybe four. That makes . . .

GUILLEMETTE. You count off the yards very generously, but who the Devil will give you that much cloth on credit?

PATHELIN. What do you care who? Somebody will give it to me and with payment due on Judgment Day, because it won't be paid for any sooner.

GUILLEMETTE. Very well then. In that case, no matter what happens, we'll be covered.

PATHELIN. I'll buy some gray or green, Guillemette, and for a waistcoat I'll need three quarters of a yard of fine black cloth . . . or maybe a yard.

GUILLEMETTE. Indeed! God help me! Go ahead then and don't forget to drink on the bargain if you find a gullible creditor.

PATHELIN. Take care of things here. (*He leaves.*)

GUILLEMETTE. Oh God! But what merchant . . . ? Whoever it is, I just pray he's blind as a bat.

SCENE TWO

PATHELIN (*approaching the Clothier's shop*). Isn't that the one there? No, I don't think so. Yes it is, by Saint Mary. He deals in cloth goods. (*To the Clothier.*) God be with you.

GUILLAUME JOCEAULME, CLOTHIER. And God give you joy.

PATHELIN. So help me, you're just the person I wanted to see. How's your health, Guillaume? Are you hale and hearty?

THE CLOTHIER. Yes, thank God.

PATHELIN. Here, shake. How are things going?

THE CLOTHIER. Pretty well. (*They shake.*) At your service. And how are you?

PATHELIN. By Saint Peter, I'm as well as ever. So, you're enjoying life?

THE CLOTHIER. Yes, but believe me, merchants can't always do as they please.

PATHELIN. And how's business? Are you able to keep the wolf from the door?

THE CLOTHIER. So help me God, Master Pierre, it's hard to say. It's always work, work, work.

PATHELIN. Ah, what a wise man your father was! God rest his soul. By Our Lady, it seems to me that you're like him in every way. What a good and clever merchant he was. (*He stares at the Clothier.*) Your face resembles his, by God, like a perfect picture. If God ever had mercy on one of his creatures, may he grant true pardon to his soul.

THE CLOTHIER. Amen! And to us too if it please him.

PATHELIN. By my faith, he often predicted in great detail the times we live in now; and I often think of what he said, for he was considered one of the best.

THE CLOTHIER. Please sit down, sir. It's high time I remembered my manners.

PATHELIN. I'm fine like this. By heaven, your father had . . .

THE CLOTHIER. Truly, you must sit down.

PATHELIN. Very well. (*He sits down.*) "Ah," he used to say to me, "you will see great marvels." (*He stares at the Clothier again.*) Look at those eyes, those ears, that nose, that mouth! So help me God, never did a son more closely resemble his father! And look at that dimpled chin; you're really a chip off the old block. If anyone should say to your mother that you're not your father's son, he'd just be itching for a quarrel. Truly I can't imagine how nature in all her works formed two faces so much alike that one is blemished exactly like the other. Why, it's as if somebody had spit you both out in the same way, like two gobs against a wall. You're the very spit and image of your father. By the way, what about the good Laurence, your lovely aunt? Did she pass away?

THE CLOTHIER. No, certainly not.

PATHELIN. How beautiful she was when I saw her, tall and straight and graceful. By the precious Mother of God, you resemble her in shape as if someone had made you both of snow. I think there's not a family in the whole region whose members look so much alike. (*He gets up and stares more intently at the Clothier.*) By God, the more I look at you, the more I see your father. You're more alike than two drops of water, without a doubt. What a gentleman he was, what an honest man, who would sell his goods on credit to anyone who asked. May God have mercy on him. He always used to give me a hearty laugh. Would to Christ the worst in the world were like him; then people wouldn't rob and steal from one another the way they do. (*He feels a piece of cloth.*) What a fine piece of cloth this is, so soft and smooth, and so attractive.

THE CLOTHIER. I had it specially made from the wool of my own sheep.

PATHELIN. Ah, what a good business man you are! But you wouldn't be your father's son, if you weren't. You just never stop working.

THE CLOTHIER. So what do you expect? If a man wants to make a living, he's got to toil and sweat.

PATHELIN (*feeling another piece of cloth*). And this cloth, is it dyed in the wool? It's as strong as leather.

THE CLOTHIER. It's a very good fabric from Rouen, and well made I assure you.

PATHELIN. Well, I'm really tempted. By the Lord's passion, I had no intention of buying cloth when I came. I've saved up 80 gold pieces to pay off a debt, but I can see you're going to get 20 or 30 of them. I like that color so much it hurts.

THE CLOTHIER. Gold pieces? Indeed! Is it possible that the people you're indebted to would take some other coinage instead?

PATHELIN. Oh yes, if I wanted them to. It doesn't matter to me how it's paid. (*He feels another piece of cloth.*) And what cloth is this? The more I look at it, the crazier I am about it. I'll have to have a coat made of it, and another for my wife.

THE CLOTHIER. As you know, cloth is very expensive these days. I'll sell you some if you wish, but 10 or 20 francs won't buy very much.

PATHELIN. That doesn't matter; it's worth the price. Besides, I have a few sous put away that have never seen the light of day.

THE CLOTHIER. God be praised! By Saint Peter, that doesn't displease me a bit.

PATHELIN. To be brief, I'm so taken with this cloth that I just have to have some of it.

THE CLOTHIER. All right. First you must decide how much you need. Take as much as you want. In fact, I could let *you* take the entire bolt even if you didn't have a sou.

PATHELIN. That's kind of you. Thanks very much.

THE CLOTHIER. Do you want some of this light blue?

PATHELIN. First, how much will a yard cost me? Wait, here's a penny. God's share should be paid first; it's only right. "Let no bargain be made before God's share is paid." (*He puts the coin in a collection box.*)

THE CLOTHIER. By God, that's the talk of an honest man: you've really cheered me up. Do you want my last word on the price?

PATHELIN. Yes.

THE CLOTHIER. It will cost *you* only 24 sous per yard.

PATHELIN. Never! 24 sous? Holy Mother!

THE CLOTHIER. That's just what it cost me, by my soul! I'll have to charge at least that, if you take it.

PATHELIN. The Devil take it! It's too much.

THE CLOTHIER. But you don't realize how much cloth has gone up. All the sheep died last winter in the great freeze.

PATHELIN. Twenty sous! Twenty sous!

THE CLOTHIER. I swear to you I have to charge 24. Just wait till market day on Saturday and you'll see what it costs. A fleece that used to cost 20 pence when they were plentiful, cost me 40 pence last July.

PATHELIN. By God, if that's the way it is, then without more haggling I'll buy. Come on, measure it.

THE CLOTHIER. How much do you need?

PATHELIN. That's easy to figure out. What's the width?

THE CLOTHIER. The standard Brussels width.

PATHELIN. Three yards for me and two and a half yards for my wife—she's tall. That makes six yards, doesn't it? . . . No it doesn't. How stupid of me!

THE CLOTHIER. It only lacks half a yard of being six exactly.

PATHELIN. Then I'll round it off at six. Anyway, I need a hat.

THE CLOTHIER. Take that end and we'll measure it. I'm sure we've got a good six yards here. One . . . two . . . three . . . four . . . five . . . and six.

PATHELIN. Saint Peter's gut! It's six on the nose.

THE CLOTHIER. Shall I measure it again?

PATHELIN. No, for Pete's sake! There's always a little gain or loss in business deals. How much is that altogether?

THE CLOTHIER. Let's see. At 24 sous a yard and six yards, it comes to nine francs.

PATHELIN. That makes six gold pieces, right?

THE CLOTHIER. That's right, by God.

PATHELIN. Then, Sir, will you give me that much credit for the short time it takes to come to my house? It's not really credit. You'll have your money, in gold or in francs, as soon as you reach the door.

THE CLOTHIER. By our Lady! I'd have to go far out of my way to get there.

PATHELIN. I swear to God, not a word has passed your lips since you failed to speak the gospel truth. You say it's far out of your way. The thing is, you've never wanted to find an occasion to come drink at my house. But this time you will have a drink there.

THE CLOTHIER. By Saint James, I hardly do anything but drink to seal the bargain with my customers. I'll go, but it's bad luck, you know, to give credit on the first sale of the day.

PATHELIN. Isn't it worth it if I pay you in gold coins instead of the common currency? By God, we'll even eat the goose that my wife is roasting.

THE CLOTHIER (*aside*). This man is driving me crazy! (*To Pathelin.*) Go ahead then. I'll come later and bring the cloth.

PATHELIN. There's no need for that. Will it burden me if I just tuck it under my arm? Not in the least.

THE CLOTHIER. No, don't bother. It would be more fitting and proper if I carried it.

PATHELIN. May Mary Magdalene send me misfortune if I put you to that trouble. As I said, under the arm. It'll give me a nice hump. (*He puts the cloth under his arm inside his robe.*) There, that's perfect. You'll have plenty of drink and good cheer before you leave my house.

THE CLOTHIER. Please give me my money as soon as I arrive.

PATHELIN. Of course I will. No, I won't, by God, not until you've been well fed. And I'm glad I didn't have any money on me. At least you'll come sample my wine. Your late father, when he passed my house, used to call out: "Hi there, friend," or "What do you say?" or "What's new?" but now you rich people don't care a straw about us poor people.

THE CLOTHIER. God in heaven, I'm a lot poorer than you are.

PATHELIN. Well, so long; goodbye. Come to my house as soon as you can and we'll drink well, I promise you.

THE CLOTHIER. I'll do that. Go on ahead, but see that I get the gold.

PATHELIN. Gold? I give you my word. And the Devil take me if I ever broke my word. (*He leaves the shop.*) Gold, indeed! Well, hang him! He wouldn't sell to me at my price, only his. But he'll be paid at mine. He needs gold, does he? Fool's gold he'll get. By God, if he had to run from now till he's paid, he'd get to the end of the world first.

THE CLOTHIER. Those gold pieces he gives me won't see daylight for a whole year, I swear, unless somebody steals them. Well, there's no buyer so clever that he won't find a seller who can outwit him. That would-be trickster was stupid enough to pay 24 sous a yard for cloth that's not even worth 20!

SCENE THREE

PATHELIN. Well, did I get it?

GUILLEMETTE. What?

PATHELIN. What happened to your old worn-out dress?

GUILLEMETTE. That's just what it was. What do you want with that?

PATHELIN. Nothing. Nothing. So did I get it? I told you I would. (*He takes the cloth from beneath his robe.*) How's that for a piece of cloth?

GUILLEMETTE. Holy Mother! I'll stake my salvation there's been a swindle. Oh, God! What have you gotten us into now? Alas! Alas! Who'll pay for it?

PATHELIN. Who'll pay for it, you ask. By Saint John, it's paid for. The draper that sold it to me wasn't as crazy as all that, my love. May I be hanged if I didn't bleed him white as a sack of plaster. The thieving ragpicker got what he deserved.

GUILLEMETTE. How much did it cost?

PATHELIN. I owe nothing. He's been paid, so don't worry.

GUILLEMETTE. He's been paid? But you didn't have a penny. What did you use for money?

PATHELIN. I swear to you, woman. I did have money. I had one Paris penny.

GUILLEMETTE. You either signed a note or used a magic formula; that's how you got it. And when the note comes due, they'll come and seize all our goods. Everything we have will be taken away.

PATHELIN. I swear to God, the whole thing cost only a penny.

GUILLEMETTE. *Benedicite Maria!* Only a penny? That can't be.

PATHELIN. You can pluck out this eye if he got more than that or ever does get more, no matter what tune he sings.

GUILLEMETTE. Who's the merchant?

PATHELIN. It's a certain Guillaume whose last name is Joceaulme, if you must know.

GUILLEMETTE. But how did you get it for one penny? What was the trick?

PATHELIN. It was God's penny that sealed the bargain. If I had asked him to drink on it instead, I could have kept the penny. Still, it was a pretty good deal. He and God can divide that penny if they want to, because it's all they'll get from me, no matter how much they rant and rave.

GUILLEMETTE. How did he decide to let you have the cloth on credit? He's so bullheaded.

PATHELIN. By Saint Mary, I flattered him and his whole family tree so much that he almost gave it to me. I told him that his late father was such a worthy man. "Oh, my friend," says I, "what good stock you come from! Your lineage," says I, "is the purest in the whole district." But I swear to God that guy comes from the scurviest lot of scoundrels and the vilest riffraff in the country. "Guillaume, my friend," says I, "how much you resemble your good father in looks and in every other way!" God knows I piled on the flattery, and all the while I was throwing in remarks about his cloth. "Holy Mary," says I, "how easily he gave his merchandise on credit, and without pretense! I can see," says I, "that you're his spit and image." But you could pull all the teeth of that sea-hog of a father and that baboon of a son before they'd give you anything on credit or even give you the time of day. Anyway, I talked so fast that he finally gave me six yards on credit.

GUILLEMETTE. Really? And you never have to return it?

PATHELIN. That's right. If I return anything to him, it'll be the Devil.

GUILLEMETTE. That reminds me of the fable of the crow, who was sitting up on a high cross with a piece of cheese in his beak. A fox came by and, seeing the cheese, thought to himself, "How can I get that?" Then he sat directly beneath the crow and said, "Ah, you have such splendid feathers and your song is so melodious." The vain and foolish crow, hearing his song praised like that, opened his beak to sing. His cheese fell to the ground and Master Fox grabbed it in his teeth and ran. That's just the way it was, I'm sure, with this cloth. You got it by flattery and sweet-talk, the same way the fox got the cheese. You really put one over on him.

PATHELIN. He's supposed to come eat goose with us, so here's what we have to do. I know he'll come whining to have his money immediately and I've planned a good reception for him. I'll go get into bed and pretend to be sick and when he comes you'll say, "Shh! Speak softly," and you'll moan and put on a long face. "Alas!," you'll say, "he's been sick for the past six or eight weeks." And if he says to you, "That's a lot of nonsense! He just left my shop a few minutes ago," you'll say, "Alas! This is a poor time to be making jokes." Then I'll make him think he's on a wild goose chase, because that's the only kind of goose or anything else he'll ever get here.

GUILLEMETTE. I swear I'll play the role to perfection. But if you get caught again and brought to justice, I'm afraid it'll be twice as bad as it was before.

PATHELIN. Quiet. I know what I'm doing; we have to do exactly what I said.

GUILLEMETTE. But, for God's sake, think of that Saturday they put you in the pillory. You know how everybody jeered at you for your shady dealings.

PATHELIN. Enough of such talk. He'll be here any minute now and we've got to keep this cloth. I'm gong to get into bed.

GUILLEMETTE. Go ahead.

PATHELIN. Now don't laugh.

GUILLEMETTE. Of course I won't. I'll be crying hot tears.

PATHELIN. We both have to be serious so he won't suspect anything.

SCENE FOUR

THE CLOTHIER (in his shop). I think it's time for me to have a little drink before I leave. Oh, no I won't. I'll soon be drinking and eating goose at Master Pierre Pathelin's house. By the patron saint of fools, I'll get my money there

and the special treat they're preparing, and it won't cost me a sou. I can't sell anything more here, so I'll be going.

SCENE FIVE

THE CLOTHIER (shouts in front of Pathelin's house). Hey There! Master Pierre!

GUILLEMETTE (opening the door). Please sir, for the love of God, if you have something to say, speak softly.

THE CLOTHIER. God be with you, Madame.

GUILLEMETTE. Shh! Softer.

THE CLOTHIER. What's the matter?

GUILLEMETTE. Bless my soul . . .

THE CLOTHIER. Where is he?

GUILLEMETTE. Alas! Where should he be?

THE CLOTHIER. Who . . . ?

GUILLEMETTE. Ah, that was ill-spoken, my good sir. "Where is he," indeed! May God in his mercy have pity on him. The poor suffering man is in the same place he's been without budging for eleven weeks now.

THE CLOTHIER. But who . . . ?

GUILLEMETTE. Pardon me, but I don't dare speak louder. I think he's resting now; he was a little drowsy. Alas, he's so sick, the poor man.

THE CLOTHIER. Who?

GUILLEMETTE. Master Pierre.

THE CLOTHIER. What? Didn't he come to my shop to get six yards of cloth just now?

GUILLEMETTE. Who? Him?

THE CLOTHIER. He just left there, not ten minutes ago. Hurry up! Devil take me, I've stayed too long already. Quick, give me my money and no more foolishness.

GUILLEMETTE. Hey! No more of your foolishness! This is no time to joke around.

THE CLOTHIER. Are you crazy? My money! Now! You owe me nine francs.

GUILLEMETTE. Ah, Guillaume, are you making fun of me? This is no asylum for lunatics. Go tell your nonsense to fools like yourself and play your tricks on them.

THE CLOTHIER. May I renounce God, if I don't get my nine francs!

GUILLEMETTE. Alas, Sir, not everyone is as eager to laugh and gossip as you are.

THE CLOTHIER. Please, I beg you, no more joking. Just have Master Pierre come here, for the love of . . .

GUILLEMETTE. Misfortune strike you down! Will this go on all day?

THE CLOTHIER. But isn't this the house of Master Pierre Pathelin?

GUILLEMETTE. Of course! May the patron saint of lunatics (crosses herself) addle your brain! Speak low!

THE CLOTHIER. The Devil take your "speak low"! Shouldn't I ask for what's mine?

GUILLEMETTE. God help me! Speak low, if you don't want him to wake up.

THE CLOTHIER. How "low" do you want? In the ear? In the cellar? Or in the bottom of the well?

GUILLEMETTE. My God, how you drivel on! But that's always been your way.

THE CLOTHIER. The Devil it has! (*Calming down.*) Now that I think about it, if you want me to speak low, just say so. I'm really not used to arguments like this. The truth is that Master Pierre took six yards of cloth today.

GUILLEMETTE. What is this? Will this go on all day? The Devil take it! Now, just what do you mean by "took"? Oh, may the one who's lying be hanged! That poor man is in such a pitiful state that he hasn't left his bed in eleven weeks. Then you come along with your wild ideas. Now is that right? By God's passion, you'll leave my house at once. Oh, what misery!

THE CLOTHIER. You asked *me* to speak so low. Now, by the Holy Virgin, you're screaming.

GUILLEMETTE. So help me, you're the one who can't speak without quarreling.

THE CLOTHIER. Look, so I can go, just give me . . .

GUILLEMETTE (*shouting*). Are you going to speak low?

THE CLOTHIER. But you're going to wake him yourself. Damn it all, you're yelling four times louder than I am. I insist that you pay me.

GUILLEMETTE. What is this? Are you drunk or just out of your mind? God in heaven!

THE CLOTHIER. Drunk! Saint Peter curse you! What a question!

GUILLEMETTE. Please! Speak lower!

THE CLOTHIER. By Saint George, I demand payment for six yards of cloth!

GUILLEMETTE. You must have been dreaming. And just who did you give it to?

THE CLOTHIER. To him.

GUILLEMETTE. He's in fine shape to be buying cloth. Alas, he can't even move. He has no need for new clothes. He'll never get dressed again, except in graveclothes; and he'll never leave his room again, except feet first.

THE CLOTHIER. Then this happened since early this morning, because I spoke to him for sure.

GUILLEMETTE (*in a loud voice*). Your voice is so loud. For the love of God, speak lower!

THE CLOTHIER. You're the one shouting, damn it all, you and nobody else. God help me, this is agony. Will somebody pay me so I can go! By God, every time I've given credit, I've had nothing but trouble.

PATHELIN (*from his bed*). Guillemette, a little rose water. Prop me up. Tuck me in behind. Damn! Who was I talking to? The water jar! Give me a drink! Rub my feet!

THE CLOTHIER. I hear him in there.

GUILLEMETTE. Yes.

PATHELIN (*delirious*). Ah, wicked woman! Come here! Did I tell you to open these windows? Come cover me up. Get rid of these people in black! *Marmara carimari carimara!* Take them away from me, away!

GUILLEMETTE. What's the matter? You're tossing about so. Have you lost your senses?

PATHELIN. You don't see what I see. There's a monk in black flying around the room. Catch him. Get a stole to exorcise him! The cat! Get the cat! Look how he rises up!

GUILLEMETTE. What is all this? Aren't you ashamed? This is too much stirring about, for heaven's sake.

PATHELIN. Those doctors are killing me with all the vile potions they make me drink. And yet we have to believe them; we're like putty in their hands.

GUILLEMETTE (*to the Clothier*). Alas! Come and see him, good sir. He's suffering terribly.

THE CLOTHIER. Was he taken so ill on returning from the fair?

GUILLEMETTE. The fair?

THE CLOTHIER. Yes, by Saint John! I'm sure he was there. Master Pierre! I need the money for the cloth I gave you on credit.

PATHELIN (*pretending to take the Clothier for a doctor*). Ah, Doctor John! I shat two tiny black turds, round as balls and hard as rocks. Should I take another enema?

THE CLOTHIER. How should I know? What've I got to do with enemas? I want my nine francs or six gold pieces.

PATHELIN. Those three black sharp things—you call those pills? They nearly busted my jaws. For God's sake don't make me take any more of them, Doctor John. There's nothing in the world more bitter, and they made everything come up again.

THE CLOTHIER. No they didn't, by God. My nine francs haven't appeared yet.

GUILLEMETTE. Hang such tiresome people. (*To the Clothier.*) Go away, by all the devils, since it can't be on God's part.

THE CLOTHIER. I swear to God, I'll get my cloth before I leave, or my nine francs.

PATHELIN (*pretending the Clothier is a doctor*). And my urine specimen, doesn't it show that I'm dying? For God's sake, whatever happens, don't let me die.

GUILLEMETTE (*to the Clothier*). Be off with you! It's terrible to torment him like this.

THE CLOTHIER. Lord God in heaven! Six yards of cloth! Tell me, do you think it's right that I should lose it?

PATHELIN. Oh, Doctor John! Do you think you could loosen my bowels? I'm so constipated I don't know how I stand to sit on the throne.

THE CLOTHIER. I want my nine francs now or by Saint Peter of Rome . . .

GUILLEMETTE. Alas! You're tormenting this man so. How can you be so cruel? You can see plain as day that he thinks you're his doctor. Alas! The poor soul has had such misfortune. He's been in that bed for eleven straight weeks, the poor man!

THE CLOTHIER. By God, I don't know how this sickness came about, because today he was in my shop and we did

business together—at least it seems we did. Otherwise I don't know what could have happened.

GUILLEMETTE. By Our Lady, I think your memory is slipping, my friend. If you take my advice, you'll go get some rest. Besides there are a lot of gossips around who'll think you came in here to see me. Go on now; his doctors will be here soon.

THE CLOTHIER. I don't care if others do think evil of it, because I have no such thoughts. Damn it all, how'd I get into this mess? I swear to God, I thought . . .

GUILLEMETTE. Again?

THE CLOTHIER. And don't you have a goose cooking?

GUILLEMETTE. What a question! Sir, that's not a dish for sick people. Go chase your own goose and don't come here making fun of us. You've got some nerve to do that.

THE CLOTHIER. Please excuse me, but I really thought . . .

GUILLEMETTE. Still?

THE CLOTHIER. By the sacrament! Goodbye! (He leaves the house.) Now I've got to figure this out. I know I should have six yards of cloth in one piece. But that woman addles my brain so much I can't think. He really did take the cloth. . . . No, he couldn't have, damn it! It just doesn't fit. I saw Death coming to strike him down—at least he so pretended. . . . Yes he did! He did take the cloth and he put it under his arm, by Saint Mary! . . . No, he didn't. Maybe I'm dreaming. But even in my sleep I'd never give my cloth away to anybody, no matter how much I liked him. I just wouldn't have given credit . . . By God, he did take the cloth! . . . No damn it all, he didn't. I know he didn't. But where does that leave me! . . . Yes he did, by Our Lady's passion! . . . Misfortune take me, body and soul, if I know who could decide who got the best of this deal, them or me. I just can't figure it out.

PATHELIN. Is he gone?

GUILLEMETTE. Quiet, I'm listening. I don't know what he was muttering, but he left grumbling so much that he was almost hysterical.

PATHELIN. Isn't it time for me to get up? We sure pulled that one off.

GUILLEMETTE. I don't know if he's coming back or not. (Pathelin starts to get up.) No, don't get up yet! Everything would be ruined if he found you out of bed.

PATHELIN. He's always so suspicious of others, but by God he met his match this time. The joke was on him and it fit like a cross on a steeple.

GUILLEMETTE. No greedy shark ever took the bait quicker than he did. It serves him right. He never gives a thing in church on Sundays. (She laughs.)

PATHELIN. For God's sake, don't laugh. If he came back and heard you, it would spoil everything. I'm sure he'll be back.

GUILLEMETTE. Hold in your laughter if you can, but I swear I can't help myself.

THE CLOTHIER (at his shop). By the sacred sun that shines, I'm going back to that backwoods barrister, I don't care

what anybody says. Oh, God! That phoney financial fraud would fleece his own family. Now, by St. Peter, I know he has my cloth, the sneaky swindler. I gave it to him right on this spot.

GUILLEMETTE. When I think of the face he made looking at you, I can't help laughing. He was so greedy in asking you for . . .

PATHELIN. Peace, you cackler! I swear to God, if he came back and heard you, we might as well start running. He's such a sour old bastard.

THE CLOTHIER (returning to Pathelin's house). That addlepated advocate, that bilbulous barrister, does he take us all for fools? By damn, the only doctor he needs is a good hangman. I'll renounce God if he doesn't have my cloth. And he played this trick on me, too. (At the door.) Hey, in there! Where are you hiding?

GUILLEMETTE. On my oath, he heard me and now he seems to be raving mad.

PATHELIN. I'll pretend to be delirious. Go to the door.

GUILLEMETTE (to the Clothier). My, how you're shouting.

THE CLOTHIER. By God, you were laughing! My money, now!

GUILLEMETTE. Holy Mary! What do you think I have to laugh about? There's no sadder person in town. He's fading fast. Never did you hear such an uproar or such raving. He's still delirious. His mind wanders, he sings, he jabbers in so many languages and jumbles them all together. He won't live half an hour longer. I swear, I laugh and cry at the same time.

THE CLOTHIER. I don't know what you mean about laughing and crying. But to put it bluntly, I must be paid now!

GUILLEMETTE. For what? Are you insane? Are you going to start that again?

THE CLOTHIER. I'm not used to being paid with words when I sell my cloth. Would you have me believe the moon is made of green cheese?

PATHELIN (delirious). Arist! Make way for the Queen of Guitars. Let her approach without delay. I know she gave birth to four and twenty guitarlings, sired by the Abbot of Iverneaux. I'll have to be the godfather.

GUILLEMETTE. Alas! Think about God the father, my dear, not about guitars.

THE CLOTHIER. What a pair of con artists you are! Quick, now, give me my money in gold or silver for the cloth you took.

GUILLEMETTE. Good God! You were mistaken once, isn't that enough?

THE CLOTHIER. Do you know what's going on, woman? So help me, I don't know what you mean by "mistaken." But never mind, you'll either pay up or be strung up. How do I wrong you by coming here to ask for what's mine? By Saint Peter of Rome . . .

GUILLEMETTE. Alas! How you torment this poor man! Truly, I can see in your face that you're losing your wits. If only I had help, sinner that I am, I'd have you tied up. You're a raving lunatic.

THE CLOTHIER. I'm raving because I don't have my money.

GUILLEMETTE. Oh, what madness! Cross yourself. *Benedicite!* Make the sign of the cross.

THE CLOTHIER. May I renounce God if I ever again sell cloth on credit. (*Pathelin stirs.*) What an invalid!

PATHELIN.

> Mere de Dieu, la coronade,
> Par ma fye, y m'en vuol anar,
> Or regni biou, oultre la mar!
> Ventre de Diou! z'en dis gigone!
> (*He points to the Clothier.*)
> Çastuy ça rible et res ne done.
> Ne carrilaine! fuy ta none!
> Que de l'argent il ne me sone![1]

(*To the Clothier.*) Did you understand, cousin?

GUILLEMETTE. He had an uncle from Limousin, the brother of his aunt by marriage. I'll bet that's what makes him babble in the Limousin dialect.

THE CLOTHIER. Damn it, he stole out of my shop with the cloth under his arm.

PATHELIN.

> Venez ens, doulce damiselle.
> Et que veult ceste crapaudaille?
> Alex en arriere, merdaille!
> (*He wraps himself in his blanket.*)
> Sa! tost! je vueil devenir prestre.
> Or sa! que le dyable y puist estre,
> En chelle vielle prestre rie!
> Et faut il que le prestre rie
> Quant il dëust chanter sa messe?[2]

GUILLEMETTE. Alas! Alas! The hour draws near when he'll need the last sacraments.

THE CLOTHIER. But how does he speak the Picard dialect so well? And why all this silliness?

GUILLEMETTE. His mother was from Picardy. That's why he speaks it now.

PATHELIN (*to the Clothier*). Where did you come from, you carnival clown?

> Vuacarme, liefe gode man!
> Etlbelic beq igluhe golan.
> Henrien! Henrien! conselapen.
> Ych salgneb nede que maignen.
> Grile, grile, scohehonden!
> Zilop, zilop, en mon que bouden!
> Disticlien unen desen versen.

Mat groet festal ou truit denhersen;
> En vuacte vuile! Comme trie!
> Cha! a dringuer, I beg of you.
> Quoy act semigot yaue.
> And put some water in it for me.
> Vuste vuille, because of the frost.[3]
> Quick, call Father Thomas so I can be shriven.

THE CLOTHIER. What's going on? Will he never stop jabbering in different languages? If he'd just give me my money, or even a deposit, I'd be on my way.

GUILLEMETTE. By God's passion, I'm tired of this. You're the weirdest man I ever met. Just what do you want? I don't know how you can be so obstinate.

PATHELIN.

> Or cha! Renouart au Tiné!
> (*He looks into his gown.*)
> Bé dea, que ma couille est pelouse!
> El semble une cate pelouse,
> Ou a une mousque a mïel.
> Bé! Parlez a moy, Gabriel.
> Les play's Dieu! Qu'esse qui s'ataque
> A men cul? Esse ou une vaque,
> Une mousque, ou ung escarbot?
> (*He puts his hand into his gown.*)
> Bé dea! J'é le mau saint Garbot!
> Suis je des foureux de Baieux?
> Jehan du Quemin sera joyeulz,
> Mais qu'i' sache que je le see.
> Bee! Par saint Miquiel, je beree
> Voulentiers a luy une fes.[4]

THE CLOTHIER. How can he stand to talk so much? He's going stark raving mad.

GUILLEMETTE. His schoolmaster was from Normandy. Now at the end he's remembering him. He's sinking fast.

THE CLOTHIER. Holy Mary! This is the craziest mess I've ever gotten myself into. Never would I have doubted that he was at the fair today.

GUILLEMETTE. You really believed it?

THE CLOTHIER. I did, by Saint James. But now I see it wasn't so.

PATHELIN. Is that an ass I hear braying? (*To the Clothier.*) Alas and alack, good cousin, they all shall bray in great

---

[1] (Limousin dialect.) Mother of God, crowned [queen of Heaven], by my faith, I want to go, or I'll renounce God, to the other side of the sea. God's belly, I say *gigone!* (*He points to the Clothier.*) That one there steals and gives nothing. Toll not the bell. Take your nap. Let him not speak to me of money!

[2] (Picard dialect.) Come in, sweet damsel. What does that pack of scoundrels want? Get back, you shitten knaves! (*He wraps himself in his blanket.*) Quick, I want to become a priest. Now, may the Devil be part of that ancient priesthood! And must the priest laugh when he should be chanting his mass?

[3] (The meaning of this garbled Flemish is not entirely clear.) Awake, to arms, dear good man! Fortunately I know several books. Henry! Henry! Come to sleep. I shall be well armed. Foolishness, foolishness, crazy inventions! A run, a run, a nun is bound! There are distichs in these verses. But great feasting disturbs the brain. Wait a while! Come quick! Something to drink, I beg of you! Come, look; a gift of God. And put some water in it for me. But wait a while because of the frost.

[4] (Norman dialect.) Come here! Renouart au Tiné! (*He looks into his gown.*) What the Devil! How hairy my balls are! They're furry as a caterpillar or a honeybee! Hey! Speak to me, Gabriel. God's wounds! What's biting my ass? Is it a fly, a dungbeetle, or a cockchafer? (*He puts his hand into his gown.*) What the Devil! I've got dysentery! Am I one of the loose-boweled of Bayeaux? Jean du Quemin would be glad to know that I am. Well, by St. Michael, I'll gladly drink to his health.

sorrow the day that I see thee no more. And yet I must needs detest thee, for thou hast played false with me. Thy work is naught but deceit.

> Ha oul danda oul en ravezeie
>
> Corfha en euf!

GUILLEMETTE (*to Pathelin*). May God have mercy on you.

PATHELIN.

> Huis oz bez ou dronc nos badou
>
> Digaut an tan en hol madou
>
> Empedif dich guicebnaun
>
> Quez queuient ob dre douch aman
>
> Men ez cahet hoz bouzelou
>
> Eny obet grande canou
>
> Maz rehet crux dan hol con
>
> So ol oz merueil grant nacon
>
> Aluzen archet epysy
>
> Har cals amour ha courteisy.[5]

THE CLOTHIER. Alas! For God's sake, listen to him. He's going fast. How he rattles on! But what the Devil is he jabbering about? Holy Mary, how he mutters! God's bodkin, he babbles and quacks his words so you can't understand a thing. It's no Christian tongue he's speaking, nor any that makes sense.

GUILLEMETTE. His father's mother came from Brittany. But he's dying, and all this indicates that it's time for the last sacraments.

PATHELIN.

> Hé, par saint Gigon, tu te mens.
>
> Voit a Deu! Couille de Lorraine!
>
> Dieu te mette en bote sepmaine!
>
> Tu ne vaulx mie une vielz nate.
>
> Va, sanglante bote savate;
>
> Va foutre! Va, sanglant paillart!
>
> Tu me refais trop le gaillart.
>
> Par la mort bieu! Sa! Vien t'en boire,
>
> Et baille moy stan grain de poire,
>
> Car vrayment je le mangera
>
> Et, par saint George, je bura
>
> A ty. Que veulx tu que je die?
>
> Dy, viens tu nient de Picardie?
>
> Jaques nient se sont ebobis.[6]
>
> Et bona dies sit vobis,

> Magister amantissime,
>
> Pater reverendissime.
>
> Quomodo brulis? Que nova?
>
> Parisius non sunt ova.
>
> Quid petit ille mercator?
>
> Dicat sibi quod trufator,
>
> Ille qui in lecto jacet,
>
> Vult ei dare, si placet,
>
> De oca ad comedendum.
>
> Si sit bona ad edendum,
>
> Pete tibi sine mora.[7]

GUILLEMETTE. I swear, he's going to die making speeches. My, how he Latinizes! Don't you see how highly he esteems the divinity? His humanity is ebbing away. Now I'll remain poor and miserable.

THE CLOTHIER. It would be better for me to go before he breathes his last. If he has some secret things to confide in you before he dies, I doubt that he would want to say them in front of me. Please forgive me, but I swear to you that I truly believed he had taken my cloth. Farewell, good woman. I beg you in God's name to forgive me.

GUILLEMETTE. May this day be blessed for you and also for me in my sorrow.

THE CLOTHIER (*leaving the house*). By the gracious Virgin, I'm more confused now than ever. The Devil, in his shape, took my cloth to tempt me. (*Crosses himself.*) *Benedicite.* May he leave me in peace. But since that's the way it is, I give the cloth, in God's name, to whoever took it.

PATHELIN (*getting up*). Now then, didn't I instruct you well? There he goes, the gullible simpleton. Now he's really got some confused ideas under that bonnet of his. I bet he'll have nightmares when he goes to bed tonight.

GUILLEMETTE. We really put him in his place. Didn't I play my part well?

PATHELIN. By God, you played it to perfection. Now at least we have enough cloth to make some clothes.

SCENE SIX

THE CLOTHIER (*in his shop*). Damn it all! Everybody feeds me lies; everybody steals from me and takes all he can get. I feel like I'm the king of the wretched. Even the shepherds of the field defraud me. And my own shepherd, to whom I've always been generous, will not get away with cheating me. He'll be begging for mercy, by the Blessed Virgin!

THIBAULT AIGNELET, THE SHEPHERD (*entering the shop*). God grant you a blessed day and a good evening, gentle Master.

---

[5](The translation of the Breton passage is based on the conjectural reconstruction of J. Loth.) P: May he go to the Devil, body and soul! G: May God have mercy on you. P: May you have dizzy spells all night with much lamenting and with all your relatives praying for you, for fear that you'll vomit your guts out. There will be such weeping and wailing that even the starving dogs will take pity on you. May you receive a coffin as alms out of much love and courtesy.

[6](Lorraine dialect.) Hey, by St. Gengoux, you're lying! I swear to God! Great balls, may God send you misfortune! You're not worth an old doormat. Get out of here, you bloody old boot; fuck off! Leave, you low-life lecher! You're too malicious, by God! You there! Come have a drink and give me a peppercorn; I'll really eat it and, by St. George, I'll drink to you. What do you expect me to say? Say, are you by chance from Picardy? The peasants there are dumbfounded.

[7](Latin.) Good day to you, beloved master, most reverend father. How are you burning? What's new? There are no eggs in Paris. What does that merchant want? Let him say to himself that the swindler, the one lying in bed, wants to give him, if he will, some goose to eat. If it's good, ask for some without delay.

THE CLOTHIER. Aha! There you are, you dung-covered scoundrel! What a good fellow you are! Good for nothing!

THE SHEPHERD. Begging your pardon, Sir, but some guy, I don't know who, with stripes on his sleeve, and all kind of excited, and carrying a whip handle without a cord, came up and said to me . . . But I don't rightly recollect what it was he said. He talked about you, Master, and some kind of summons, but, Holy Mary, I couldn't make heads or tails out of it. He mixed me up so with his talk about "sheep" and "afternoon session," and he made a great fuss about things you had said against me, Sir.

THE CLOTHIER. If I don't haul you before the judge in two shakes, I pray God to strike me with storm and flood. Never again will you get away with killing my sheep, I swear. And no matter what happens, you'll pay me for those six yards . . . I mean, for killing my sheep and for all the losses you've caused me in the last ten years.

THE SHEPHERD. You shouldn't believe those poison tongues, good Master, for by my soul . . .

THE CLOTHIER. And by Our Lady you'll pay me on Saturday for my six yards of cloth . . . I mean, for what you stole of my sheep.

THE SHEPHERD. What cloth? Ah, Sir, I believe you're upset about something else. By Saint Lupus, Master, I'm afraid to say anything when I see you like this.

THE CLOTHIER. Go and leave me in peace. And answer your summons, if you know what's good for you.

THE SHEPHERD. But Sir, let's settle this now. For God's sake, don't take me to court.

THE CLOTHIER. Go! The matter is in good hands. Go on, now! I won't make a settlement, by God, and I won't agree to anything but what the judge decides. Damn it all, everybody will cheat me from now on if I don't put a stop to it.

THE SHEPHERD. Goodbye, Sir. May God give you joy. (*He leaves.*) So now I have to defend myself.

SCENE SEVEN

THE SHEPHERD (*knocking at Pathelin's door*). Is anybody here?

PATHELIN (*to Guillemette*). I'll be hanged if he hasn't come back.

GUILLEMETTE. No it can't be! Saint George preserve us. That would be the end.

THE SHEPHERD. God be with you and keep you.

PATHELIN. God save you, my good fellow. What is it you want?

THE SHEPHERD. They're going to fine me for not showing up, if I don't answer my summons, Sir, this afternoon, and if you please, would you, good Master, plead my case for me, 'cause I don't know nothing about it, and I can pay you good, even though I'm dressed so poor.

PATHELIN. Come here and speak up. Which are you, plaintiff or defendant?

THE SHEPHERD. Well, Sir, I work for a certain merchant, you know, and for a long time I've taken his sheep out to graze and I guard 'em, and I swear when I think about him paying me next to nothing . . . Do I have to tell everything?

PATHELIN. Certainly. A client should hide nothing from his counsel.

THE SHEPHERD. It's true, Sir, it's the truth, I struck 'em down, so that many of 'em were knocked out and fell down dead, even though they were strong and healthy, and then I made him think, so's he wouldn't punish me, that they died of the scab. "Oh," he'd say, "don't leave a diseased one with the others, get rid of it." "I'll be glad to," I'd say; and I'd get rid of it all right, but not the way he thought, for, by Saint John, I ate every one of 'em, 'cause I knew what they really died of. What else can I tell you? I kept doin' this so long and struck down and killed so many that he noticed it, and when he found out he had been deceived, so help me God, he sent somebody to spy on me 'cause you could hear 'em cry out, you know, when you hit 'em. So I was caught red-handed. I can never deny it, and now I come to ask if there ain't some way we can put the old hound off the scent, and don't worry about money, I got enough to pay you good. I know he's got a good case, but you can find some loop-hole, if you will, to make it worthless.

PATHELIN. I promise you'll be satisfied with the results. What will you give me if I overturn the claim of your accuser and get you a full pardon?

THE SHEPHERD. Instead of payin' in sous, I'll pay you in solid gold crowns.

PATHELIN. Then you'll have an unbeatable case even if it's twice as weak as you say. The stronger the case I argue against, the quicker I can render it null, when I put my mind to it. You'll hear how well I can spiel it off after he's presented his argument. Come over here. By God, you're wily enough to understand the trick. Now tell me, what's your name?

THE SHEPHERD. By Saint Maurus, it's Thibault Aignelet.

PATHELIN. Aignelet, did you appropriate many lambs from your master?

THE SHEPHERD. On my oath, I may have eaten thirty or more in three years.

PATHELIN. That makes an income of ten a year—the equivalent of a few games at the tavern. (*He thinks for a moment.*) I believe I have a good ruse here. Do you think he can readily find a witness to prove his allegation? That's the most important part of the trial.

THE SHEPHERD. Prove, Sir? Holy Mary! By all the saints in paradise, instead of one, he'll find ten to testify against me.

PATHELIN. That's almost enough to ruin your case. Here's what I had in mind. I'll pretend that I'm not on your side and that I've never seen you before.

THE SHEPHERD. For God's sake, don't do that!

PATHELIN. No, that's no good. But here's what we have to do. If you speak, they'll trap you one by one on all counts

of the indictment, and in such cases confessions are as prejudicial and harmful as the Devil himself. So here's what will make our case: as soon as they call you to appear before the court, you'll answer only with "baa," no matter what they say to you. And if they should curse you, saying, "Hey, you stinking yokel! May God plunge you into misery! Are you making fun of the court?" just answer "baa." "Ha!" I'll say, "he's a poor simpleton who thinks he's talking to his sheep." But even if they knock themselves out yelling at you, make sure no other word comes out of your mouth.

THE SHEPHERD. Seein' as how this touches me close, I'll make sure I don't say nothin' else and I'll do it right, I promise.

PATHELIN. Now make sure you stick to your promise. And even to me, no matter what I say or ask, don't answer any other way.

THE SHEPHERD. Me? Never, by the sacrament! You can cry out that I'm crazy, if I say another word today, to you or anybody else, no matter what they say to me, except "Baa," just like you told me.

PATHELIN. If you do that, by Saint John, your accuser will be caught in our trap. But also make sure when it's over that I get a payment I'll be proud of.

THE SHEPHERD. Sir, if I don't pay you at your word, then never believe me again. But please work hard on my case.

PATHELIN. By Our Lady, I'll bet the judge is already on the bench; he always holds court around six o'clock. Now you come along after me; we won't both go together.

THE SHEPHERD. That's a good idea, so nobody sees you're my lawyer.

PATHELIN. And God help you if you don't pay generously.

THE SHEPHERD. I swear I'll pay at your word; really, Sir, have no fear.

PATHELIN (alone). Well now, it may not be raining money, but it's sprinkling. At least I'll get a little something out of this. If everything falls into place, I'll have a gold piece or two for my trouble.

SCENE EIGHT

PATHELIN (removing his hat to salute the Judge). Your Honor, God grant you success and whatever your heart desires.

THE JUDGE. Welcome, Sir. Please don your hat and take your place over there.

PATHELIN (seeing the Clothier). Damn! (To the Judge.) I'm fine here, Your Honor; I'll have more room to maneuver.

THE JUDGE. If there is business before the court, let it be done quickly so I can adjourn.

THE CLOTHIER. My lawyer is coming, Your Honor. He's finishing up some other business. If the court please, we had better wait for him.

THE JUDGE. Wait? I have cases to hear elsewhere. If the offending party is present, then state the case yourself without delay. Are you not the plaintiff?

THE CLOTHIER. I am.

THE JUDGE. Where is the defendant? Is he here in person?

THE CLOTHIER. Yes, there he is, not saying a word. God only knows what he's thinking.

THE JUDGE. Since you're both here, state your case.

THE CLOTHIER. Then here's my complaint against him, Your Honor. The truth is that for the love of God and in charity I fed and clothed him in his childhood; and, to be brief, when I saw that he was strong enough to go to the fields, I made him my shepherd and set him to watching my flock. But as sure as you're sitting there, Your Honor, he wrought such carnage among my wethers and ewes that without a doubt . . .

THE JUDGE. Just a minute! Wasn't he hired by you?

PATHELIN. That's a good point! Because if he had finagled to employ him without a contract . . .

THE CLOTHIER (recognizing Pathelin). May I disavow God if it isn't you! You, without a doubt!

THE JUDGE. Why are you holding your hand to your face, Master Pierre? Do you have a toothache?

PATHELIN. Yes, the pain is so excruciating that never before have I been in such agony. I can't even look up. For God's sake, make him get on with it.

THE JUDGE. Proceed! Finish your deposition. Come on, be brief about it.

THE CLOTHIER. It's him and nobody else! By God's cross, it really is! Master Pierre, it was you that I sold six yards of cloth to.

THE JUDGE. What's he saying about cloth?

PATHELIN. He's rambling. He thinks he's getting to his opening statement, but he doesn't know how because he isn't used to this.

THE CLOTHIER. May I be hanged by the bloody neck if anybody else took my cloth.

PATHELIN. Look how this unworthy man goes to extremes to build his case. He means, and he's very stubborn about it, that his shepherd had sold the wool—that's what I understood—from which the cloth of my robe was made. He seems to be saying that the shepherd's a thief and has been stealing the wool of his sheep.

THE CLOTHIER. God send me misfortune if you haven't got it!

THE JUDGE. Silence! The Devil take you for running off at the mouth! Can't you get back to your deposition without delaying the court with such drivel?

PATHELIN (laughing). Oh, my tooth aches, but I can't help laughing. He's already so rushed he doesn't know where he left off. We'll have to lead him back to the subject.

THE JUDGE. Come now, let's get back to those sheep. What happened next?

THE CLOTHIER. He took six yards of it, worth nine francs.

THE JUDGE. Do you take us for fools or simpletons? Where do you think you are?

PATHELIN. I swear to God, he's trying to make an ass of you! And he looks like such a decent man. But I suggest you examine his adversary.

THE JUDGE. That's a good idea. He sees him often, so he must know him. (*To the Shepherd.*) Step forward! Speak!

THE SHEPHERD. Baa!

THE JUDGE. Another vexation! What do you mean, "baa"? Am I a goat? Speak to me!

THE SHEPHERD. Baa!

THE JUDGE. The bloody pox take you! Are you trying to make a fool of me?

PATHELIN. He must be either crazy or pigheaded; or maybe he thinks he's among his sheep.

THE CLOTHIER. I'll renounce God if you aren't the one that got my cloth—you and nobody else! (*To the Judge.*) Oh, you don't know, Your Honor, by what malice . . .

THE JUDGE. What! Hold your tongue! Are you dense? Set aside this accessory matter and let's get back to the principal.

THE CLOTHIER. Very well, Your Honor, but the case concerns me. Nevertheless, I promise I won't say another word about it for the rest of the day. Some other time it may be different; right now I'll just have to swallow it. Now, I was saying in my complaint that I had given six yards . . . I should say, my sheep . . . Please forgive me, Your Honor. . . . This good Master . . . I mean, my shepherd, when he was supposed to be in the fields . . . He told me I would get six gold pieces when I came . . . I mean to say, three years ago my shepherd made an agreement that he would faithfully guard my sheep and would cause me no loss nor do me any wrong, and then . . . Now he brazenly refuses to give me either cloth or money. (*To Pathelin.*) Ah, Master Pierre, I swear . . . (*To the Judge.*) This scoundrel here was stealing the wool from my sheep, and he was killing healthy ones by clubbing them on the head. . . . When he put my cloth under his arm, he took off in a great hurry, saying that I should go collect my six gold pieces at his house.

THE JUDGE. There's neither rime nor reason in any of your railing and ranting. What is this? You mix in one thing and then another. In short, by God, I can't make heads or tails of it. (*To Pathelin.*) He prattles about cloth, then he jabbers about sheep and jumbles it all up. Nothing he says makes sense.

PATHELIN. I'll bet anything he's keeping this poor shepherd's wages for himself.

THE CLOTHIER. You can shut your mouth, by God. It's the gospel truth that my cloth . . . I know better than you or anybody else where my shoe pinches, and by God in heaven, I know you have it!

THE JUDGE. What does he have?

THE CLOTHIER. Nothing, Your Honor. But I swear he's the biggest swindler . . . OK. I'll try to control my tongue and I won't say another word about it today, no matter what happens.

THE JUDGE. Very well, but remember your promise. Now conclude quickly.

PATHELIN. This shepherd cannot answer the charges against him without counsel, and he's afraid or doesn't know how to ask for it. I would be willing to counsel him, Your Honor, if you so ordered.

THE JUDGE. Him? I should think that would be wasted effort. He's as poor as a churchmouse.

PATHELIN. I swear I have no thought of gain. Let it be for love of God. Now I'll try to find out from the poor lad what he has to say, and I'll see if he can instruct me as to how to reply to the charges against him. He'd have a hard time getting out of this, if nobody helped him. (*To the Shepherd.*) Come over here, my friend. Now if we could find . . . Do you understand?

THE SHEPHERD. Baa!

PATHELIN. What is this "baa"? By the Holy Blood, are you crazy? Tell me about your case.

THE SHEPHERD. Baa!

PATHELIN. What is this "baa"? Do you hear the ewes bleating? Try to understand, this is for your own good.

THE SHEPHERD. Baa!

PATHELIN. Come on! Answer yes or no. (*Softly.*) That's good. Keep it up. (*Aloud.*) Will you do that?

THE SHEPHERD. Baa!

PATHELIN. Speak up, or you'll find yourself in real trouble, I'm afraid.

THE SHEPHERD. Baa!

PATHELIN. It takes a real ass to bring such a poor fool to trial. Your Honor, send him back to his sheep. He's just a natural-born fool.

THE CLOTHIER. You call him a fool? By Saint Savior of Asturias, he's smarter than you are.

PATHELIN (*to the Judge*). Send him back to watch his sheep, *sine die*, never to return. A plague on him who brings charges against such natural-born fools.

THE CLOTHIER. Will he be sent back before I can be heard?

THE JUDGE. So help me, since he's a born fool, yes. Why shouldn't he be?

THE CLOTHIER. But Your Honor, at least allow me to sum up my case first. This isn't something I dreamed up or just idle discourse.

THE JUDGE. Nothing but vexation comes of bringing suit against fools and simpletons. Now hear this: to stop this senseless babble, the court will be adjourned.

THE CLOTHIER. Will they go without obligation to return?

THE JUDGE. And why not?

PATHELIN. Return! You never saw a greater fool in word or in deed. (*Pointing to the Clothier.*) And this other one isn't an ounce better. They're both brainless boneheads. By the Blessed Virgin, their brains together wouldn't weigh a carat.

THE CLOTHIER. You took my cloth by deceit, Master Pierre, without paying. As I'm a poor sinner, that wasn't the deed of an honest man.

PATHELIN. May I renounce Saint Peter of Rome if he isn't an insidious fool, or well on his way to being one.

THE CLOTHIER. I recognize you by your speech, by your clothes, and by your face. And I'm not crazy! I'm sane enough to know what's good for me. (*To the Judge.*) I'll tell you the whole story, Your Honor, upon my conscience. (*The Judge grimaces. Laughter in the audience.*)

PATHELIN (*pointing to the audience*). Please, Your Honor, bring them to order. (*To the Clothier.*) Aren't you ashamed to haul this poor shepherd into court for three or four grubby old sheep that aren't worth two buttons. (*To the Judge.*) His litany gets longer and more tedious.

THE CLOTHIER. What sheep? It's always the same old song! It's you I'm talking to and, by God, you'll give me back my cloth.

THE JUDGE (*to the audience*). You see that? I really get the cases, don't I? He won't stop braying for the rest of the day.

THE CLOTHIER. I'll bring suit . . .

PATHELIN. Make him shut up! (*To the Clothier.*) You prattle too much, by God. Let's say he did knock off six or seven sheep, or even a dozen, and ate them—Holy Christmas, you weren't crippled by it. You still earned a lot more than that in the time he's been watching your flock.

THE CLOTHIER. Look at that, Your Honor, just look! I talk to him about cloth and he answers me in sheep. (*To Pathelin.*) Those six yards of cloth that you stuck under your arm, where are they? Don't you intend to give them back to me?

PATHELIN. Oh, Sir, would you have him hanged for six or seven sheep? At least think it over. Don't be so harsh on this poor, unfortunate shepherd, who hasn't a thing to his name.

THE CLOTHIER. You're an expert in changing the subject. The Devil himself made me sell cloth to such a customer. Please, Your Honor, I charge him . . .

THE JUDGE (*thinking the Clothier is charging the Shepherd*). I absolve him of your charges and forbid you to proceed. A fine thing it is to bring suit against a fool. (*To the Shepherd.*) Go back to your sheep.

THE SHEPHERD. Baa!

THE JUDGE (*to the Clothier*). By our Lady, you've certainly shown what kind of person you are, Sir.

THE CLOTHIER. But Your Honor, I swear I want him to . . .

PATHELIN. Can't he shut up?

THE CLOTHIER. But it's you I have a case against. You tricked me with your eloquent speeches and carried my cloth away like a thief.

PATHELIN. Your Honor, I solemnly appeal! Are you going to listen to this?

THE CLOTHIER. So help me God, you're the biggest swindler . . . Your Honor, let me say . . .

THE JUDGE. It's a three-ring circus with you two—nothing but wrangling and squabbles. So help me, I've got to be going. (*To the Shepherd.*) Go, my son, and don't ever come back, even if an officer serves you with a warrant. The court grants you full pardon.

PATHELIN. Say "thank you."

THE SHEPHERD. Baa!

THE JUDGE. Is that clear? Go now and don't worry about a thing. It's all right.

THE CLOTHIER. But is it right for him to go like that?

THE JUDGE. Bah! I have business elsewhere. You're both outrageous mockers and you won't detain me a moment longer. I'm leaving. Will you come to supper with me, Master Pierre?

PATHELIN (*raising his hand to his cheek*). I can't. (*The Judge leaves.*)

SCENE NINE

THE CLOTHIER. You're an outright thief! Tell me, will I ever be paid?

PATHELIN. For what? Are you crazy? Who do you think I am anyway? By God, I've been trying to figure out who it is you take me for.

THE CLOTHIER. Indeed!

PATHELIN. No just a minute, my good man. I'll tell you right now who it is you take me for. It's the town fool, isn't it? But look! (*He lifts his hat.*) That can't be because he's not bald on top of his head like me.

THE CLOTHIER. Do you think I'm an imbecile? It was you in person; you, yourself, and nobody but you. Your voice proves it and don't think it doesn't.

PATHELIN. Me myself, and I? No it wasn't, I swear. Get that out of your head. It was probably John from Noyon; he's about my size.

THE CLOTHIER. The Devil it was! He doesn't have that besotted, witless face of yours. Didn't I leave you sick a while ago at your house?

PATHELIN. Now there's a fine bit of evidence! Me, sick? And what was I sick with? Come on, admit your stupidity; it's quite clear now.

THE CLOTHIER. I'll renounce Saint Peter if it wasn't you— you and nobody else. I know that to be absolutely true.

PATHELIN. Well don't you believe it, because it positively wasn't me. I never took a yard or even half a yard of cloth from you. I don't have that kind of reputation.

THE CLOTHIER. Damn it all. I'm going back to your house to see if you're there. We won't have to squabble here any more if I find you there.

PATHELIN. By Our Lady, that's a good idea! That way you'll know for sure. (*The Clothier leaves.*)

SCENE TEN

PATHELIN. Hey, Aignelet!

THE SHEPHERD. Baa!

PATHELIN. Come here. Was your case well disposed of?

THE SHEPHERD. Baa!

PATHELIN. Your accuser has gone, so you don't have to say "baa" anymore. I really cooked his goose, didn't I? And didn't I counsel you just right?

THE SHEPHERD. Baa!

PATHELIN. Hey, don't worry. Nobody'll hear you. Speak up.

THE SHEPHERD. Baa!

PATHELIN. It's time for me to go now, so pay me.

THE SHEPHERD. Baa!

PATHELIN. To tell you the truth, you played your part very well; you looked good. But what really fooled him was that you kept from laughing.

THE SHEPHERD. Baa!

PATHELIN. Why "baa"? You musn't say it any more. Just pay me generously.

THE SHEPHERD. Baa!

PATHELIN. Why do you keep saying "baa"? Speak normally and pay me so I can go.

THE SHEPHERD. Baa!

PATHELIN. You know what? I'll tell you. I'm asking you, please, without any more bleating around the bush to think about paying me. I've had enough of your baa's. Pay up quickly.

THE SHEPHERD. Baa!

PATHELIN. Is this some kind of joke? Is this all you're going to do? I swear to God, if you don't escape, you're going to pay me, understand? The money! Now!

THE SHEPHERD. Baa!

PATHELIN. You've got to be kidding. Is this all I'm going to get from you?

THE SHEPHERD. Baa!

PATHELIN. You're running this into the ground. And just who are you trying to fool? Do you know who you're deal-ing with? Don't babble your baa's to me anymore today; just pay me.

THE SHEPHERD. Baa!

PATHELIN. Is this the only pay I'll get? Who do you think you're playing games with? I was taking such pride in your performance; now really make me proud of you.

THE SHEPHERD. Baa!

PATHELIN. Are you trying to pull the wool over my eyes? God's curse! Have I lived so long that a shepherd, a sheep in human clothing, a churlish knave can make a fool of me?

THE SHEPHERD. Baa!

PATHELIN. Will I get no other word? If you're doing this for a joke, say so and don't make me argue any more. Come and have supper at my house.

THE SHEPHERD. Baa!

PATHELIN. By Saint John, you're right; the goslings lead the geese to pasture. (*To himself.*) I thought I was the master in these parts of all the cheaters and swindlers and those who give their word in payment, collectible on Judgment Day; and now a shepherd of the fields outwits me. (*To the Shepherd.*) By Saint James, if I could find an officer, I'd have you arrested.

THE SHEPHERD. Baa!

PATHELIN. Baa, yourself! May I be hanged if I don't go find me a good policeman! and misfortune seize him if he doesn't throw you in jail.

THE SHEPHERD (*running away*). If he finds me, I'll give him a full pardon.

Arthur Miller, among the modern era's finest playwrights, sits in an ancient Greek theater at Epidaurus.

CHAPTER **2**

FROM THEATER TO DRAMA

The Dramatic Impulse

Although rituals and ceremonies involve theatrical artistry, theater, in its fullest sense, becomes one of the arts when it is fused with drama. Although the two terms are often used interchangeably, there is a crucial distinction between *theater* and *drama*. Theater derives from the ancient Greek word for the space in which plays were performed, *theatron,* or "seeing place." Drama also derives from a Greek word, *drao,* which means "to do" or "to act." Drama depicts human actions, conveyed in story form, which are performed by actors, singers, dancers, or mimes. Those things that are seen—scenery, costumes, lighting, gestures, movement—enhance the story by giving it a concrete reality, though not always realistically. This is theater.

While the telling of epic tales to ancient peoples provided material for dramas such as *Oedipus the King* or *The Recognition of Śakuntalā*, the stories in themselves are not "dramatic," though they surely contain dramatic elements. What separates a play from an epic story like that of Ulysses, a ritualized enactment such as the Yoruban Obatala, or a novel? Because a play is usually bound by restrictions not normally confronting the storyteller, dramatists must be selective in the events they portray. Homer may devote lengthy passages to a minute description of Achilles' shield; the Yorubans may take two weeks to commemorate the battles of their ancestors; and Steinbeck may write an entire chapter about a turtle crossing a road in *The Grapes of Wrath*. But the playwright must, in most cases, create a script that can be told—as Shakespeare puts it—in "two hours traffic" on the stage. There are, of course, exceptions; it is not uncommon for plays in Asia, especially in Japan and India, to take many hours to perform. And the performance of Tony Kushner's two-part *Angels in America* requires about seven hours.

Furthermore, a play is written in the present tense—it takes place now. Playwright Thornton Wilder provides a helpful distinction between drama and other forms of narrative writing: "A novel [narrative form] is what one person tells us *took* place; a play [dramatic form] is what *takes* place" (emphases ours).

Thus, a play is a specialized, concise, and calculated form of storytelling that makes unusual demands on the writer. Look carefully at the spelling of *playwright*. The word is not spelled "playwrite," that is, one who writes plays. *Playwright* stems from an ancient Saxon word, *wyrhta,* meaning a worker or craftsman, such as a "boatwright" or "wheelwright." Surely a playwright is one who crafts, shapes, and purposefully constructs the story for maximum effect. In *The Poetics*, Aristotle makes a crucial distinction between the *mythos* (or story) and the *praxis* (or action, i.e., the careful arrangement of the events of the story).

Perhaps the most notable means by which the playwright focuses a story is through *conflict,* the clash of opposing forces. The Greeks often referred to a play as an *agon* ("contest" or "debate"). Its central character was the *protagonist* or "first contestant," and the *antagonist* was the opposing character. In Western drama we still use these terms to identify the primary characters in a play. Virtually all stories are based on conflict because it gets an audience involved in the action: we want to know how the conflict will be resolved. Every scene in a play is propelled by conflict, either by external or internal forces. The finest dramas are about people who ultimately must resolve inner conflicts that have been exacerbated by external forces. For instance, Oedipus may be in conflict with Creon or Teiresias, but he ultimately struggles with himself to learn who he truly is. *Kanjinchō*, one of the eighteen great Kabuki plays (see Chapter 5), depicts the warrior Benkei's dilemma. Benkei must choose between his need to respect Prince Yamamoto, whom he must protect (an interior conflict), and his duty to beat the prince before an enemy, whom he must trick so that the prince may escape (exterior conflict).

Film and television are generally much better equipped to portray external conflicts such as wars, "shoot-'em-ups," high-speed chases, and natural catastrophes. Despite the advantage of the close-up in film, the older, stately stage is actually better suited to the careful exploration of an intense personal dilemma because it is presented live and close to a living audience.

While rituals and ceremonies influence our lives and give order in an uncertain world, drama further organizes our experience into a manageable, perceptible form that instructs us, preserves our values, enhances our sense of community, and gives us pleasure. That is a function of all art. Let us consider how drama performs these functions.

The Poetics of Aristotle

In the West we customarily turn to Aristotle's *The Poetics*, written about 335 B.C.E., as a guide to our understanding of drama, just as the Japanese look to Zeami's *Kadensho* or the Indians seek the wisdom of Bharata's *Nātyaśātra*. Aristotle wrote *The Poetics* because his mentor, Plato, disparaged the theatrical arts. At the risk of oversimplifying the argument, Plato believed that a play was essentially a "lie" that portrayed humanity's basest actions. Furthermore, Plato felt that summoning up powerful emotions impeded clear thought. Aristotle countered Plato's arguments by systematically analyzing a number of plays, most written in the century before he lived, to illustrate:

- why the theater could be an effective teaching tool;
- what made plays effective works of art.

Importantly, Aristotle's comments were never meant to be rules about how plays must be written or performed. Rather, they were thoughtful observations that suggested, "All things being equal, *this* will make a play work more effectively, *that* will not." Unfortunately, Aristotle's comments were raised to dogma in Renaissance Italy and France, and a disservice was done to *The Poetics* (see Forum, pages 35–36).

Because it remains the standard tool for the discussion of drama in our Western culture, we use Aristotle's tract as a starting point for our exploration of the dramatic arts, but with two caveats:

- Much contemporary Western drama has significantly deviated from the ideas espoused in *The Poetics*. We shall identify important examples throughout this text.
- Because it derived from other cultures and their belief systems, legitimate variations of and additions to dramatic methodology are found in non-Western drama. Again, we shall note these where appropriate.

Before we examine some significant theatrical and dramatic terms and concepts, take a moment to read the Forum, "General Considerations of Theatrical Entertainment in China." In this Forum, Tao-Ching Hsu's advice to a Western audience new to the Chinese theater is applicable to other non-Western cultures. And, as much as Aristotle wrote over 2,000 years ago, Professor Hsu's comments are even appropriate to our understanding of the Greeks.

FORUM

"From *The Poetics*"

ARISTOTLE

The following excerpts from The Poetics *contain Aristotle's essential analysis of the tragic impulse and the elements of drama. The classic definition of Western tragedy may be found in part two. Parts 4–10 contain an analysis of plot, character is discussed at the end of part 10, and the role of the Chorus is addressed in part 11.*

1. Epic poetry and Tragedy, Comedy also and Dithyrambic poetry, and the music of the flute and of the lyre in their forms, are all in their general conception modes of imitation.

2. Tragedy, then, is an imitation of an action that is serious, complete, and of a certain magnitude; in language embellished with each kind of artistic ornament, the several kinds being found in separate parts of the play; in the form of action, not of narrative; through pity and fear affecting the proper purgation of these emotions.

3. Every Tragedy, therefore, must have six parts, which parts determine its quality—namely, Plot, Character, Diction, Thought, Spectacle, Song.

4. The Plot, then, is the first principle, and as it were, the soul of a tragedy: Character holds the second place. A similar fact is seen in painting. The most beautiful colours, laid on confusedly, will not give as much pleasure as the chalk outline of a portrait. Thus Tragedy is the imitation of an action, and of the agents mainly with a view of the action.

5. Unity of plot does not, as some persons think, consist in the unity of the hero. For infinitely various are the incidents in one man's life which cannot be reduced to unity; and so, too, there are many actions of one man out of which we cannot make one action, hence the error, as it appears, of all poets who have composed a Heracleid, Theseid, or other poems of the kind. They imagine that as Heracles was one man, the story of Heracles must also be a unity. But Homer, as in all else he is of surpassing merit, here too—whether from art or natural genius—seems to have happily discerned the truth. In composing *The Odyssey* he did not include all the adventures of Odysseus—such as his wound on Parnassus, or his feigned madness at the mustering or the host—incidents between which there was no necessary or probable connexion: but he made *The Odyssey*, and likewise *The Iliad*, to centre round and action that in our sense of the word is one. As therefore, in the other imitative arts, the imitation is one when the object action and that a

whole, the structural union of the parts being such that, if any one of them is displaced or removed, the whole will be disjointed and disturbed. For a thing whose presence or absence makes no visible difference, is not an organic part of the whole.

6. It is, moreover, evident from what has been said, that it is not the function of the poet to relate what has happened, but what may happen—what is possible according to the law of probability or necessity. The poet and the historian differ not by writing in verse or in prose. The work of Herodotus might be put into verse, and it would still be a species of history, with metre no less than without it. The true difference is that one relates what has happened, the other what may happen. Poetry, therefore, is a more philosophical and a higher thing than history: for poetry tends to express the universal, history the particular. By the universal I mean how a person of a certain type will on occasion speak or act, according to the law of probability or necessity; and it is this universality at which poetry aims in the names she attaches to the personages. The particular is—for example—what Alcibiades did or suffered.

7. Plots are either Simple or Complex, for the actions in real life, of which the plots are an imitation, obviously show a similar distinction. An action which is one and continuous in the sense above defined, I call Simple, when the change of fortune takes place without Reversal of the Situation and without Recognition. A Complex action is one in which the change is accompanied by such Reversal, or by Recognition, or by both. These last should arise from the internal structure of the plot, so that what follows should be the necessary or probable result of the preceding action. It makes all the difference whether any given event is a case of *propter hoc* or *post hoc*. Reversal of the Situation is a change by which the action veers round to its opposite, subject always to our rule of probability or necessity. Thus in the Oedipus, the messenger comes to cheer Oedipus and free him from his alarms about his mother, but by revealing who he is, he produces the opposite effect.

8. Recognition, as the name indicates, is a change from ignorance to knowledge, producing love or hate between the persons destined by the poet for good or bad fortune. The best form of recognition is coincident with a Reversal of the Situation, as in the Oedipus.

9. A perfect tragedy would, as we have seen, be arranged not on the simple but on the complex plan. It should, moreover, imitate actions which excite pity and fear, this being the distinctive mark of tragic imitation. It follows plainly, in the first place, that the change of fortune presented must not be

(continued)

From *Aristotle's Theory of Poetry and Fine Art*, translated by Samuel Henry Butcher. New York: MacMillan, 1895.

the spectacle of a virtuous man brought from prosperity to adversity: for this moves neither pity nor fear: it merely shocks us. Nor, again, that of a bad man passing adversity to prosperity: for nothing can be more alien to the spirit of Tragedy: it possesses no single tragic quality; it neither satisfies the moral sense nor calls forth pity and fear. Nor, again, should the downfall of the utter villain be exhibited. A plot of this kind would, doubtless, satisfy the moral sense, but it would inspire pity nor fear; for pity is aroused by unmerited misfortune, fear by the misfortune of a man like ourselves. Such an event, therefore, will neither be pitiful nor terrible. There remains, then, the character between these two extremes—that of a man who is not eminently good and just, yet whose misfortune is brought about not by vice or depravity, but by some error of frailty. He must be one who is highly renowned and prosperous—a personage like Oedipus, Thyestes, or other illustrious men of such families. A well-constructed plot should therefore be single in its issue, rather than double as some maintain. The change of fortune should not be from bad to good, but reversely, from good to bad. It should come about as the result not of vice, but of some error of frailty, in a character either such as we have described, or better rather than worse.

10. Fear and pity may be aroused by spectacular means; but they may also result from the inner structure of the piece, which is the better way, and indicates a superior poet. For the plot ought to be so constructed that, even without aid of the eye, he who hears the tale told will thrill with horror and melt to pity at what takes place. This is the impression we should receive from hearing the story Oedipus. But to produce this effect by the mere spectacle is a less artistic method, and dependent on extraneous aids. Those who employ spectacular means to create a sense not of terrible but only of the monstrous, are strangers to the purpose of tragedy; for we must not only demand of tragedy any and every kind of pleasure, but only that which is proper to it. And since the pleasure which the poet should afford is that which comes through pity and fear through imitation, it is evident that this quality must be impressed upon the incidents.

In respect of Character there are four things to be aimed at. First, and most important, it must be good. Now any speech or action that manifests moral purpose of any kind will be expressive of character: the character will be good if the purpose is good. This rule is relative to each class. Even a woman may be good, and also a slave; though the woman may be said to be an inferior being, and the slave quite worthless. The second thing to aim at is propriety. There is a type of manly valor; but valor in a woman, or unscrupulous cleverness, is inappropriate. Thirdly, character must be true to life: for this is a distinct thing from goodness and propriety, as here described. The fourth point is consistency; for though the subject of the imitation, who suggested the type, be inconsistent, still he must be consistently inconsistent.

11. The Chorus too should be regarded as one of the actors: it should be an integral part of the whole, and share in the action, in the manner not of *Euripides* but of *Sophocles*. As for the later poets, their choral songs pertain little to the subject of the piece as to that of any other tragedy. They are, therefore, sung as mere interludes—a practice first begun by Agathon. Yet what difference is there between introducing such choral interludes, and transferring a speech, of even a whole act, from one play to another?

The Elements of Drama

Applying a scientist's analytical skills to Greek drama, Aristotle identified six elements that enhance not only the storytelling, but also the instructive and aesthetic values of a play. Though he was specifically discussing Greek tragedy, his comments are useful for analyzing the makeup of most dramatic works, including those written as alternatives to Aristotelian drama. The first four elements—plot, character, thought, and diction—relate to drama, the remaining two—music and spectacle—to theater. Combined they constitute the essence of the theatrical arts and provide us with a useful starting point in our exploration of world drama. As you have now read *Master Pierre Pathelin*, we will refer to it (as well as some plays that you may read) to illustrate key points about the elements of drama. The *Master Pierre Pathelin* sections have been highlighted for easy reference.

Plot

Aristotle refers to plot as the "soul" of dramatic poetry. While we tend to think of plot as the story line, it actually refers to the arrangement of the incidents—the calculated structure that achieves maximum intellectual, emotional, and aesthetic effect.

There are essentially three types of plot:

1. The climactic plot: The most traditional form of plotting, the climactic (or linear) plot begins with the exposition of a problem, builds on a series of minor crises to a major cli-

FORUM

"General Considerations of Theatrical Entertainment in China"

TAO-CHING HSU

. . . Lack of understanding in the West of Chinese fine arts, especially of music, calligraphy and theatre, is probably partly due to the difficulty of acquiring new tastes and accepting new standards and partly to the lack of an equivalent form in the western culture—for instance, in calligraphy, as the Chinese understand it—which could serve as a point of reference for western students. The wide difference between the Chinese and European theatre of today is a case in point.

The Chinese have not shown much eagerness to advertise their theatre to the West: those who know western languages and are interested in the western peoples are often unappreciative of their own culture including the theatre and those who understand the Chinese theatre are mostly unfamiliar with western arts and tend to remain silent with cynical complacency. The difficulty of transporting the theatre physically over large distances further widens the gulf between the East and the West in this sphere. Foreigners in China who are interested in cultural matters can be easily discouraged by the forbidding approach to the Chinese arts which, as compared with the western, are more for the connoisseur. Those who are undaunted tend to be overconfident and too often judge the Chinese theatre with western standards and thereby overlook its distinctive merits.

The emphasis of the earliest European writings on the Chinese theatre was, as can be expected, placed on its strangeness. This point of view was that of the traveller for whom anything different from his own land is worth recording. Such writings are exemplified by Antonio Paglicci Brozzi's *Téatri e Spettacoli dei Popoli Orientali* (1887), Henry Borel's *Weisheit und Schonheit aus China* (1898) as well as Karl Mantzius' *A History of Theatrical Art* (1903) (translated by Louise von Cossel and C. Archer) in which the information on the Chinese theatre is apparently based on travellers' reports. Among the later works by European writers, although many are distinguished by the earnestness in purpose not all of them are free from misconceptions due to lack of genuine appreciation. It appears that in art even though an observer may be conscientious he does not *see* accurately without a certain degree of sympathy with the object of his observation. Western writers who have no direct knowledge of the Chinese theatre rely on the secondary information which these first-hand observers provide, and thus misunderstandings and distortions filter through the more popular, but by no means the most reliable, references into histories of World Theatre and World Drama and even into encyclopedias.

From *The Chinese Conception of the Theatre* by Tao-Ching Hsu. Copyright © 1985 by University of Washington Press. Reprinted by permission.

It is doubtful whether a foreigner's appreciation of Chinese art can ever be the same as the natives'. However, to understand a new style in art it is usually necessary to leave one's preconceptions first, to unlearn one's taste, to give up one's unconscious aesthetics. This statement applies with special force to the Europeans interested in the Chinese theatre, because the characteristics of the Chinese and modern western theatre are not only different but mostly opposite, and any attempt, deliberate or unconscious, to fit the former into the standards of the latter is doomed to failure. To those unfamiliar with the Chinese theatrical conventions watching Chinese dramas is like listening to music in a different scale, and just as the only way to understand such music is to learn the new scale, so the only way to learn to understand Chinese dramas is to try to appreciate them as the Chinese do. Adjustments of basic concepts, admittedly difficult, have to be made, otherwise appreciation, which could start in a small area, will remain crippled and become eventually smothered.

Most people are inclined to think that only one form of theatre—the form they know—is natural because their appreciation of that form appears to be effortless and natural. The ability to appreciate art is of course acquired, though in most cases the process of learning is so gradual as to be hardly perceptible even to the learner himself especially if the greater part of it is accomplished in childhood. By the time appreciation has become a habit, the process of acquiring it is forgotten. When confronted with a form of theatre belonging to a different period or country which one has not learned to enjoy, the mental adjustment for new ways of appreciation is usually so great and the success at the beginning so small that one is tempted to feel convinced that it is awkward and stylized, though to its own audience it appears perfectly natural.

In the European theatre itself dramatic values have by no means been stable: what was natural to the audience of the seventeenth century is not considered as natural now. Even the theatrical practices a century ago appear absurd now. Historians of the theatre realize that the mental habits of the theatregoers of the the past are vastly different from those of today and that reconstructions of theatrical conditions based on modern ideas of propriety in theatrical matters can lead to serious mistakes. As the study of the European theatrical history is now being freed from that of dramatic literature and as it is being recognized now that the modern European theatre is only one of many possible forms of theatre the study of the Chinese stage should become less forbidding and more significant, less forbidding because it is no more different from the European theatre of today than, for example, the Greek theatre and more significant because it can add a geographical dimension to the historical breadth of view.

max and its resolution. Causality is paramount in climactic plotting; that is, one event precipitates another. *Oedipus the King* is the prototype of the climactic plot, and most plays written prior to the late-nineteenth century use such plots. It is possible to have several linear plots (or *subplots*) existing simultaneously; usually they interconnect in the final act. Shakespeare is especially adept at subplotting in such comedies as *A Midsummer Night's Dream*.

> *Pierre Pathelin* is a climactic plot because it deals with a single story that builds to its payoff in the trial scene.

2. The episodic plot: Many Asian plays, Shakespeare's history plays, South African township plays, and particularly works by the modern dramatist Bertolt Brecht (such as *The Good Woman of Setzuan*) employ an episodic plot. They consist of numerous events that are related thematically if not always by a single dramatic action. Most novels and the great myths such as *The Iliad* and *The Mahabharata* of India are episodic.

3. The cyclic plot: Plot structures usually reflect the values and philosophy of the societies that produce them. As an outgrowth of a modern philosophy that suggests that there seem to be no answers for life's dilemmas and that our problems cannot be neatly resolved, some dramas employ the cyclic plot. They are intentionally unresolved; instead, they end much the way they began, suggesting the futility of life. Modern writers of the theater of the absurd, such as Samuel Beckett and Eugene Ionesco, employ cyclic plots in such works as *The Bald Soprano*, the last line of which is exactly the same as its first.

Is it possible to have a "plotless" play? Because they are often meditations on life, many Noh plays seem to have little plot, as Western audiences understand the term (see *Komachi at Sekidira*). Many recent Western plays adhere to the theory that conventional artistic forms—for example, the traditional plot—no longer reflect the reality of human experience. Beckett's *Waiting for Godot*, for instance, has no discernible plot. One critic even argued that it is a play in which nothing happens—twice! In Tom Stoppard's witty retelling of the Hamlet myth, *Rosencrantz and Guildenstern Are Dead* (1967), one of the characters exclaims, "Incidents! All we get are incidents. Is it too much to ask for a little sustained action?" Stoppard's line reflects the trend toward incidental plotting in much contemporary drama, which often portrays people living multiple realities that may not be comprehensibly connected.

Regardless of how we classify their plots, plays do have structures that organize experience, and even contemporary scripts retain elemental devices you should know as you read or watch plays. Technically, the elements noted in the following discussion compose the "well-made play," a form that was especially popular in the nineteenth century. Still, these elements may be found, however subtly, in most plays, Western and Eastern, classical and modern:

- The *exposition* provides the necessary background of time, place, plot, character, and social context for understanding the play and its issues. Necessarily, there is considerable exposition early in a play, but playwrights also distribute the exposition throughout.

> Virtually the entire first scene of *Pierre Pathelin* serves as exposition. We learn about the comically troubled relationship between Pierre and his wife, about Pierre's devious ways and his disdain for the merchants.

- The *point of attack* (or the *inciting incident*) clearly marks the moment at which the play's principal conflict begins. Think of it as a "point of no return" at which the protagonist and the antagonist begin the battle that constitutes the majority of the play's action.

> The point of attack occurs during Pierre's fourth speech as he swears, "[I]f I put my mind to it, I'll find where to get some clothes." When his wife protests that no one will give him credit for the clothing, Pierre brags that he will indeed get a loan that need not be paid until Judgment Day. This exchange initiates the primary action of the play: Pierre must get the clothes without paying for them.

- The *complication* (or *rising action*) depicts the struggle between the opposing forces through a series of crises, which move the action forward. In a multiact play, each scene usually mirrors the construction of the entire play. It has its own exposition, point of attack, and complication.

> Scenes 2 through 5 create a series of complications:
>
> *Scene 2:* Pierre, after some comic give-and-take, actually gets some cloth from the Clothier; "getting the cloth" is the first minor climax of the play.
>
> *Scene 5:* The Clothier tries to retrieve the cloth at Pierre's house but is conned by both Pierre and Guillemette, who pretend that Pierre has been bedridden for eleven weeks; the scene climaxes when the Pathelins succeed in getting the Clothier to leave without his cloth.
>
> *Scenes 6 and 7:* The plot is complicated when the Shepherd becomes involved and both the Clothier and Pierre plan to use him to further their ends.
>
> *Scene 8 (The Trial):* Pierre's trickery and the Shepherd's duplicity ("Baa") constantly thwart the Clothier's claims to the Judge. Pierre's trickery is checked, but only in part, by the Judge's numerous rulings, which help create suspense.

- The *climax* usually occurs late in the play and marks the moment in which the protagonist's imminent triumph or defeat is clearly decided. This moment is sometimes referred to as the *obligatory scene* because we expect a final confrontation between the protagonist and the antagonist and its resolution. Most climactic scenes offer the protagonist a moment of discovery (or recognition) to enhance the instructive power of the drama.

> Obviously, the climax in *Pierre Pathelin* occurs when Pierre wins his case as the Judge dismisses the Clothier's complaint and sends the Shepherd back to his pasture. Pierre gloats in his triumph in the short scene 9.

- The *denouement* (or *falling action*) "ties up" the loose ends of the plot. The fate of the characters is revealed, harmony is restored, and the future is determined. Modern playwrights often avoid denouements to maintain ambiguity and mystery.

> In a comic twist in scene 10, the Shepherd turns the tables on Pierre and "out-cheats the cheater." Remember, in the first scene his wife praised Pierre as "a master deceiver." Thus Pierre's downfall becomes the most fitting denouement, as he notes in his final two speeches.

Character

As pleasurable as it may be to hear a good tale well told, it is ultimately the human element that engages us at the highest level in the theater. Though plays are about ideas, we respond to a play emotionally because it portrays human beings for which we have some feeling. In 1839 the German writer Friedrich Hebbel cautioned that "bad playwrights with good heads give us their scheme instead of characters and their system instead of passions." Aristotle reminds us that character is "that which reveals moral purpose." Even notorious villains such as Tartuffe or Shakespeare's Richard III intrigue us because we see in them the darker side of human nature.

There may be a finite number of plots, but there are infinite possibilities in the creation of character. Given our modern fascination with psychology, character has in many ways supplanted plot as drama's primary element, particularly in Western drama, which characteristically emphasizes the individual. Eastern drama, by contrast, tends to focus on the more general aspects of human behavior. The *Nātyaśātra*, in fact, counsels Indian dramatists to portray the generality of humanity, while the actor-dancers in the theater of China, Japan, and India train arduously to learn the gestures and movements of particular kinds of characters such as the warrior, the maiden, or the beggar.

While classical writers have rendered fascinating portraits of the human mind under duress (e.g., the 700-year-old Yuan play, *Autumn in the Palace of Han*), in the West the "psychological drama" is primarily a product of the modern age, though *Hamlet* surely qualifies as a psychological drama. Anton Chekhov's Russian dramas did much to advance the way we perceive dramatic character. His plays are a particular challenge because there is little overt action in them; as we listen to their seemingly mundane conversations, we realize that his characters *are* the drama.

Two particular categories of characters have served the theater well for thousands of years:

- *Stock characters* are instantly recognizable types, such as the bragging soldier, the sassy servant, the conniving trickster, the wise elder, the ingenue (or youth), and the grumpy old man. Such types are frequently servants to the plot; that is, they exist to advance the story efficiently because they do not need great psychological depth. They are often secondary to the principal characters, though many plays are entirely devoted to stock characters alone. For instance, the ancient Greek comic playwright Menander wrote a play about the grumpy old man (*The Grouch*) that serves as the prototype of the character we associate with Walter Matthau in such films as *Grumpy Old Men*. Molière favored sassy serving maids (a role the Chinese would refer to as a *hua tan*); Dorine in *Tartuffe* is the epitome of such a character. Serious plays, even tragedies, also rely on stock characters. Teiresias, the blind prophet who could "see" what others could not, was a staple of many Greek tragedies. Prior to the twentieth century, plays were often written for specific acting troupes, called "stock companies," comprising performers who had perfected certain types. You will have little trouble recognizing stock characters, as much television fare depends on them.

> Each of the primary characters in *Pierre Pathelin* is a well-known stock character: Pierre is the conniving trickster (who gets tricked himself); his wife is the long-suffering, nagging spouse; the Clothier is the unscrupulous merchant who merits his comeuppance; and the Shepherd is the fool who outsmarts his betters.

- *Archetypal characters* are recurring figures that speak to all peoples of all times. They reside in our "collective unconscious," according to Swiss psychologist Carl Jung, who calls them "primordial images." Archetypal characters transcend the particulars of a given story and its culture to become universal symbols of virtues, vices, and human dilemmas. For instance, Prometheus is the archetype of the individual who sacrifices himself for the benefit of a greater good; that we often refer to such figures as Promethean suggests their archetypal nature. Hamlet, Sigismund in *Life's a Dream*, Olunde in *Death and the King's Horseman*, and even Simba in *The Lion King* are similar in many ways: each is a young prince struggling to mature while at odds with his elders, his society, and particularly himself. Oedipus is the archetype of the sighted man who cannot see the truth until he loses his sight. Throughout this anthology you will read about many characters who are blind to truths about themselves and others when they are most prosperous: Jason, Emperor Han, King Dushyanta, King Carlos, Nora Helmer, and Willy Loman.

In most plays we look for growth and change in principal characters. Characters usually change because something profound happens to them. Aristotle referred to this moment of change as a *reversal* of fortune, which usually precipitates or results from a *recognition* (or, to put it in archetypal terms, a moment when the blindness is lifted).

> Pierre Pathelin experiences both a reversal (the Shepard cons him even as he celebrates his triumph over the Clothier) and recognition ("I thought I was the master in these parts of all the cheaters . . . and now a shepard of the fields outwits me").

As you read these plays, be alert for those characters who change most dramatically in the course of the play (invariably it is the protagonist), and the precise moment that prompts the change. In the contemporary theater, characters often change little because playwrights depict people trapped by their own inertia. Their plight is that they cannot change. Chekhov, Beckett, and Tennessee Williams provide significant examples of such characters.

Today playwrights often explore the manner in which we live multifaceted lives defined by those with whom we come in contact. To our lover we may be one thing, to a neighbor another, and to an employer yet another. Accordingly, playwrights now frequently portray characters as fragmented beings, the many parts of which suggest the whole. Thus several actors may portray a single character or, conversely, a single actor may portray several characters within the same play. Caryl Churchill (*Top Girls*) and Maria Irene Fornes (*Mud*) have been especially influential as they explore the multiple roles women play in society. Note that *Woza Albert!* asks its two actors to play numerous roles as it explores the problems of apartheid in South Africa.

One must also consider the phenomenon of the "anticharacter," another contemporary device meant to illustrate that the industrial world has stripped humans of their identity and individualism. Characters may now appear as generic ciphers, often bearing such nondescript names as "He" or "the Woman," or even worse, "A" or "B." As with plot and the other elements of drama, characterization can be an indicator of the way a society sees itself. Osvaldo Dragún's bitter satire on the contemporary workplace, "The Man Who Turned into a Dog," typifies characterization as it is rendered by many contemporary writers.

Thought

For Aristotle, thought (sometimes referred to as "idea" or "theme") was a means of testing the idea the play posited through "proof and refutation," a reminder that plays were contests of conflicting ideas. Today, of course, most plays use words to argue their ideas. The witty debates between Andrew Undershaft and Adolphus Cusins in Bernard Shaw's *Major Barbara* celebrate verbal expression at its finest.

Thought, beliefs, values—there are many terms to be used here—vary from culture to culture and are subject to change and reevaluation. Because most of us are products of Western culture, there is a tendency to evaluate the "thoughts" raised by plays from other cultures in terms of our own experience. This is certainly one of the issues raised in Wole Soyinka's Nigerian drama, *Death and the King's Horseman,* as British colonialists attempt to impose their value system on a Yoruban tribal leader. The introductions to the plays in this collection attempt to provide some historical and cultural contexts that help you understand non-Western dramatists—and, of course, those from the West whose culture we may not readily understand.

The Roman orator and artist Horace advised a would-be dramatist that it was the function of the poet-dramatist to "instruct and delight" (*docere et dulcere*). (See Forum, "The Art of Poetry" in Chapter 4.) At the heart of his argument was the very issue under consideration here: theater exists to provide learning experiences while entertaining us. In earliest times, instruction most often centered on religion or the life cycle. Today plays from both the East and the West often attempt to influence audiences concerning political and social issues; indeed, a play can serve as an instrument of social criticism. Tony Kushner's *Angels in America, Part One: Millennium Approaches* addresses the AIDS crisis and American politics, while Griselda Gambaro's *Personal Effects* is both a critique of Argentinean social problems and a commentary on the alienation modern people often feel. As a general rule we can say plays that only teach are usually heavy-handed, and plays that only entertain are ultimately less satisfying than those that achieve a balance between thought and diversion. Plays that lack profundity can still be good, even great, theater. The slapstick farce, for instance, has little time for philosophy and only the most elemental moralizing. Yet the very nature of farce has much to say about our place in the world, random accidents of chance, and our ability to triumph over chaos.

The moral of *Pierre Pathelin* might be stated: "Cheaters never profit." Its "thought," however, deals with the pitfalls of egoism, greed, and other excessive behaviors.

One of the healthiest aspects of the contemporary theater is the rich diversity of human thought. Never has drama been so truly global in both its content (thought) and expression. Notice, for instance, the mix of African and Eastern thought and performance techniques and contemporary Western social problems as you read Amiri Baraka's *Slave Ship*, Sue Townsend's *The Great Celestial Cow*, and David Henry Hwang's *The Dance and the Railroad*.

Diction

By "diction" Aristotle meant language, and although theater, in its literal sense is about "seeing," the verbal dimension is central to the dramatic arts. Hamlet tells us that "tonight we'll hear a play," an expression that was in common usage well into the nineteenth century. Ironically, as we enter a new millennium, we are a much more visually oriented society than almost any other since the invention of the printing press. We are constantly bombarded with visual stimuli, most commonly in film and on television. In the era of MTV the image reigns, and thus "hearing" or reading a play, especially a classic, may be a challenge to those accustomed to quick cuts, wipes, and montages. Well-crafted writing still retains the power to spark an audience's imagination. A Prakrit verse from ancient India celebrates the power of diction in the theater:

> *Glory to speech!*
>
> *For she sits in the mouth of poets*
>
> *And creates whole worlds anew,*
>
> *Laughing at the ancient creator!*

In most cultures plays were first written in verse, for several reasons. First, music was an integral part of the theatrical experience, and so it remains in most non-Western drama. Thus, playwrights wrote plays in verse because it best suited the musical dimension of the theater. Furthermore, most early plays dealt with larger-than-life characters that required heightened language. Audiences, then as now, enjoyed the sound of a well-crafted, majestic line, as in Shakespeare's *Hamlet*:

> What a piece of work is a man, how noble in reason, how infinite in faculties, in form and moving how express and admirable, in action how like an angel, in apprehension how like a god: the beauty of the world, the paragon of animals . . .

In the early twentieth century, Bernard Shaw captivated audiences with witty, well-written lines, such as these from *Man and Superman*:

> Are we agreed that Life is a force which has made of innumerable experiments in organizing itself; that the mammoth and the man, the mouse and the megatherium, the flies and the fleas and the Fathers of the Church, are more or less successful attempts to build that raw force into higher and higher individuals, the ideal individual being omnipotent, omniscient, infallible, and withal completely, unilludedly self-conscious: in short, a god?

Modern realistic drama, on the other hand, often attempts to replicate the rhythms, cadences, and especially the vocabulary of everyday speech, as seen in this passage from David Mamet's *American Buffalo*, an award-winning play of the 1970s:

> We're talking about money for chrissake, huh? We're talking about cards. Friendship is friendship, and a wonderful thing, and I am all for it. I have never said different, and you know me on this point. Okay. But let's just keep it separate huh, let's just keep the two apart, and maybe we can deal with each other like some human beings.

The point here is not to disparage modern drama, but to illustrate that it is a function of drama to show, in Shakespeare's words, "the age and body of the time his form and pressure," an elegant way of saying that the theater reflects the manners, mores, and speech of the audience for whom the plays are written.

In the late twentieth century some brilliantly innovative writers have transformed the language of the street into a theatrical vocabulary that is as poetic as that of the great writers of the past. Read Sam Shepard's inventive, richly poetical use of the "hip" language of rock 'n' roll in *Tooth of Crime* (1972) as two rock stars "slug it out" with words:

> You could use a little cow flop on yer shoes, boy. Yo' music's in yo' head. You a blind minstrel with a phony shuffle. You got a wound gapin' 'tween the chords and the pickin.' Chuck Berry can't even mend you up. You doin' a pantomime in the eye of a hurricane. Ain't even got the sense to signal for help. You lost the barrelhouse, you lost the honkey-tonk. You lost your feelings in a suburban country club the first time they ask you to play "Risin' River Blues" for the debutante ball. You ripped your own self off and now all you got is yo' poison to call yo' gift. You a punk chump with a sequin nose and you'll need more'n a Les Paul Gibson to bring you home.

More recently, Suzan-Lori Parks draws on the colloquial speech of African Americans to extraordinary effect in such plays as *The Death of the Last Black Man in the Whole Entire World* (1990):

> I kin tell whats mines by whets gots my looks. Ssmymethod. Try it by testin it and it turns out true. Every time. Fool proofly. Look down at my foot and wonder if its mine. Foot mine? I kin

ask it and foot answers back with uh "yes Sir"—not like you and me Say "yes Sir" but us "yes Sir" peculiar tuh thuh foot.

As you read or see a play, keep in mind the purpose of the language employed by the playwright. Whether the language is lofty and poetic, colloquial or mundane, there is invariably a dramatic reason for it. Even the natural speech of contemporary drama is as calculated and painstakingly written as the most florid poetry in classical drama because language reflects character. Successful playwrights find a "voice" for each character in the play. Beware the play in which everyone speaks alike.

The anonymous medieval playwright of *Pierre Pathelin* has great fun with language. Pierre manipulates words—in several languages—to his own benefit as he puts on airs in the trial; the Clothier is reduced to a babbling fool when he has lost his cloth and his case; and, best of all, the humble Shepherd uses a single, nonsensical word ("Baa") to win his victory. While no one would claim that *Pierre Pathelin* is brilliant literature, language is inventively used to advance both plot and character.

Plays are not usually written for reading audiences, but for professional actors, sometimes for particular actors. A playwright knows that an intelligent, talented actor can wrench extraordinary meaning out of a word. Thus, when you read a play it is crucial that you try to hear the lines in your mind's ear, or try reading it aloud. There are actually three "texts" that you must confront. You will be reading a *text*—words on a page. From that you will derive the *context*— the social situation, the character relationships, the ideas being contested. Out of this grows the *subtext* of the play—the underlying meaning of the words the characters choose to use. In classical plays subtext is less subtle: these are people who wear their hearts on their sleeves and we can often take what they say at face value. In the modern theater, where characters often hide (or are unsure of) their true feelings and thoughts, subtext becomes far more important.

Dramatic speech takes many forms. Our earliest plays, contain long, poetic passages, a reminder that much drama may have developed from hymns to the gods or songs to mark an event central to the life of a community. Eventually *dialogue*—the exchange of lines between two or more characters—dominated the play script, though *monologues* (in which a character speaks a lengthy passage to other characters) and *soliloquies* (in which a character, usually alone onstage, speaks to the audience) are still a part of the theater. The monologue and soliloquy became less prominent in early modern plays that attempted to portray life realistically. Yet playwrights, realists and otherwise, have always appreciated that the monologue (like the soliloquy) is a conduit to an individual's consciousness. Beckett's *Rockaby* perhaps best captures this phenomenon among the many plays in this collection: a single character sits in a rocking chair listening to her own monologue about impending death. Many playwrights specialize in the dramatic monologue: Jane Martin, Eric Bogosian, and John Leguizamo are among the best known. Anna Deavere Smith's *Twilight: Los Angeles, 1992* comprises more than 60 monologues. In many ways, the resurgence of the monologic drama brings the theater full cycle; we have again entered the domain of the ancient storyteller.

While play scripts consist almost exclusively of dialogues and monologues, *stage direction* has become an integral part of the playwright's diction (although Aristotle never read a stage direction). The ancient Greek playwrights, like Shakespeare and Molière, like Kālidāsa in the courts of India and Zeami in feudal Japan, had no need for stage directions, as they worked directly with the actors when their plays were first staged. Stage directions today are important pieces of exposition that can describe setting, costume, appearance, psychological states, and other things that enable you to imagine the play in your mind's eye.

Stage directions that have become commonplace in the modern theater are *pause* and *silence*. Judiciously used, silence can be a powerful means of communication in the theater, and therefore it is an important element of a play's diction. Harold Pinter, the much-imitated

British playwright, has said, "It is in the silence that my characters are most evident to me." Be sure to "listen" for the silences as you read such scripts as Chekhov's *The Cherry Orchard* or Pinter's *One for the Road*.

Music

Aristotle included music among his six elements largely because the only plays he knew employed music, song, and dance. He recognized that music also manifests the human desire for harmony in the world, and thus it held "chief place among the embellishments" of a drama. In the West music became less prominent in the realistic theater and, in many cases, disappeared completely. It remains among the most characteristic elements of Asian drama. The Peking opera, the Japanese Noh and Kabuki theaters, and much Indian theater can rightfully be classified as forms of musical theater. South African township theater invariably uses popular *mbaquanga* music to underscore its action.

Actually, actors, directors, and designers constantly use musical terminology as they prepare even the most realistic plays. They talk of "tempo" and "rhythm" in speeches and scenes, and they cite the "orchestration" of voices as they work. Mamet's monosyllabic dialogue establishes mesmerizing rhythms that are as central to the experience of his plays as iambic pentameter was to Shakespeare's. Actors, especially comedians, are obsessed with getting their "timing" down, as are lighting designers who use "fade counts" to dim the lights. Directors cast shows for the musicality of the actors' voices and the harmonious (or perhaps dissonant) blend of their vocal qualities. The "music" of a play is perhaps the most difficult of drama's six elements to appreciate while reading, but it is there, and an awareness of a play's music enriches our experience.

> Though there is no music scripted into *Pierre Pathelin*, we do know that historically it was traditional for acting companies to end their plays with a song and dance (often as they "passed the hat" to earn their wages), a custom that continued well into Shakespeare's time. The mix of voices, especially those of Pierre and his wife, creates a musical effect in the blend and clash of tones, variations in volume, and changes in rhythm.

Spectacle

Spectacle refers to those elements of a production that appeal to the eye. While scenery, costume, makeup, masks, and lighting are the principal elements of spectacle, the presence of the actors, their movements, and their body language also contribute to the visual appeal of a play. Aristotle actually dismissed spectacle as the "least artistic" of the six elements of drama because it depends "more on the art of the stage machinist than the poet." However, he also recognized that spectacle has "an emotional attraction of its own." You are no doubt aware of the importance of costume, scenery, and lighting in a play, but also consider gesture, movement, and the physical relationship of the actors to each other and to the audience. The very size, shape, and configuration of the theater space affect the way we react to a play. The discussion of the artists involved in producing a play considers some of these issues in more detail (see Chapter 3). As you read the plays in this collection, try to picture the scenery and costumes, consider where lighting might enhance a dramatic moment, and imagine the movements and gestures of the characters.

> *Pierre Pathelin* would most likely have been performed on a bare stage backed by a simple curtain, using only a chair or a bench as props. Nevertheless, there is spectacle in the costuming, the colorful length of cloth, Pierre's pompous posturing during the trial, and the mere presence of "the judge whom no man dare judge" (that is as much a "spectacle" clue as it is a character clue. A clever designer would relish transforming this line into spectacular costume).

Is it possible to have effective theater without spectacle? Yes. It can also exist without playwrights, directors, designers, and others. In reality, there are only four things necessary to create theater:

- An *idea* to be communicated, though it need not be scripted; there is a rich history of improvised theater.
- A *performer* such as an actor, a singer, a dancer, a mime, or a storyteller.
- An *audience*; the audience may consist of one person, without whom there cannot truly be a theater event. That is how important you are to the making of theater.
- A *space* in which the previous three elements come together. (See the diagram on the essential elements of theater.)

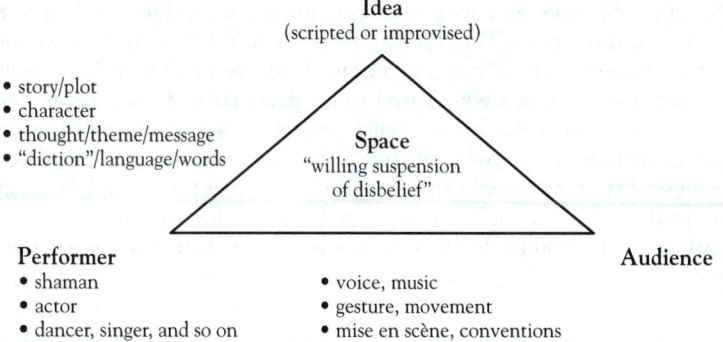

Idea
(scripted or improvised)

- story/plot
- character
- thought/theme/message
- "diction"/language/words

Space
"willing suspension
of disbelief"

Performer
- shaman
- actor
- dancer, singer, and so on

- voice, music
- gesture, movement
- mise en scène, conventions

Audience

The space need not be a formal theater or a stage. Peter Brook has said, "I can take any space, an empty space, and create theater." And he has—on the deserts of Iran, in the market square of an African village, and in an abandoned railway depot in Paris. A cliché reminds us that all an actor needs to create theater are "two boards and a passion."

The Principal Genres of Drama

Genre is a Western literary term that classifies a work into a distinctive type according to the treatment of the subject matter and the perspective of the writer. Like Polonius, the counselor to King Claudius in *Hamlet*, one can overclassify plays into "tragedy, comedy, history, pastoral, pastoral-comical, historical-pastoral, tragical-historical, tragical-comical-historical-pastoral. . . ." For expediency, let us limit the major kinds of Western plays to three primary genres—tragedy, comedy, and tragicomedy. Subgenres such as the comedy of manners and satire will be discussed with specific plays. And it bears noting that in the late twentieth century, playwrights frequently subvert traditional genres by parodying them, melding them for shock effect, or otherwise negating standard principles to extend the boundaries of drama. We shall, however, begin with the orthodox before proceeding to some striking alternatives.

Non-Western drama, especially in Asia, which was (until recently) less influenced by Western drama, has distinctive genres based largely on traditional modes of performance, as opposed to the West's classification of genres according to the serious or comic treatment of the themes. In India, for instance, plays are divided into ten major types, according to subject matter. The *nataka*, the most important, is a play in four to ten acts that portrays mythological beings (such as Śakuntalā and King Dushyanta), and that appeals primarily to the erotic and/or heroic sentiments (*rasas*) in the audience. Given our cultural experience, most of us in the West would likely classify *Śakuntalā* as a romance (a subset of tragicomedy), and one can make the case that it is indeed a romance. However, we ought to be open to the aesthetics of other cultures as we learn about and discuss their theater and drama. Specific non-Western genres will be discussed in conjunction with particular plays.

Actors can perform in many spaces, including a proscenium arch theater, as shown in this photo of the Royal Opera House in London, a theater-in-the-round (see photo below), a thrust stage (see photo on next page), and even on the streets of Nigeria (see photo on next page).

A theater-in-the-round: Krasnaya Presnya Theater, Moscow.

A thrust stage: Guthrie Theater, Minneapolis.

Street theater: Oshogbo Center for the Arts, Nigeria.

Tragedy Versus Comedy

Tragedy and comedy, the oldest and most elemental dramatic genres, reflect the way in which playwrights wish to examine human endeavors. Horace Walpole, the British philosopher, observed that tragedy is for "those who feel," while comedy is "for those who think," a distinction that suggests the degree to which the audience is involved in or detached from the theater experience. Tragedy, or at least serious drama, asks us to engage ourselves more fully in the emotional life of the central character, while comedy asks us to stand back and judge the folly of a play's characters.

Paradoxically, tragedy, for all its gravity and depiction of suffering and death, begins with an optimistic premise: as human beings, we possess nearly unlimited potential. Tragedy cautions, however, that we are only "godlike" and not gods ourselves. Comedy, for all the laughter and pleasure it brings, stems from the darker notion that we are fallible and foible-ridden. The mischievous Puck best invokes this comic premise in *A Midsummer Night's Dream* when he exclaims, "Lord, what fools these mortals be!"

Whatever their views of humanity, both genres share two common premises: things do go wrong and we are accountable for our actions. Causality, the recognition that actions lead to other actions, is central to the telling of a story, be it serious or comic. In tragedy actions have serious consequences that lead to suffering and death; in comedy, though there may be momentary threats of dire consequences, transgressions are ultimately forgiven and misfortune gives way to celebration. In some modern dramas, on the other hand, traditional notions of causality are challenged; the theater of the absurd (see Chapter 7), for instance, suggests that human actions—and misery—cannot necessarily be ascribed to the cause-and-effect principle. In the absurdist world, randomness reigns.

Tragedy

We offer here an essentially Western theory of tragedy. Because tragedy (and much comedy) is grounded in a culture's belief systems, it may be perceived differently in other cultures. Wole Soyinka, the Nigerian playwright and dramatic theorist, writes that

> the artist labors from an in-built, intuitive responsibility not only to himself but his roots. The test of the narrowness or the breadth of his vision however is whether it is his accidental situations which he tries to stretch to embrace his race and society or the fundamental truths of his community which inform his vision and enable him to acquire even a prophetic insight into the evolution of that society.

Soyinka's insight extends to readers and audiences as well: an audience's appreciation of a work is tempered by its roots. However, a knowledge of other cultures and the art they produce increases an appreciation of their work.

Again Aristotle's *Poetics* is the traditional starting point for an understanding of Western tragedy. Even those, such as Bertolt Brecht and Agusto Boal, who have refuted Aristotle's precepts, have had to acknowledge that he provided the foundation on which Western dramatic theory is built. Aristotle defined *tragedy* as "an imitation of an action that is serious, complete, and of a certain magnitude; in language embellished with each kind of artistic ornament, the several kinds being found in separate parts of the play; in the form of action, not of narration; through pity and fear effecting the proper purgation of these emotions." Consider two key components of this definition, the first and last phrases:

". . . an imitation of an action . . ."
Noting that we are innately mimetic, Aristotle argued that the "imitation" (i.e., the play) is not life itself but only a metaphor for life in which an actor plays another being. Though "action" (*praxis*) refers to a play's narrative line, Aristotle observed that the artistic and selective arrangement of the events (*mythos*) affect an audience's intellectual and emotional responses. Tragic action traces the "fall" of an individual from prosperity to misery, usually through an

Although the traditional Greek masks of comedy and tragedy are well known in the West, a comic mask from India (above) and a tragic mask from Japan (opposite) symbolize the universality of drama's two major genres.

error in judgment. The tragic impulse may be seen in King Dushyanta's lament in the Sanskrit drama *The Recognition of Śakuntalā*:

> Each day of our own life we slip and fall into error
> Through negligence that we are unaware of;
> How then can we fully know what paths
> The life of each one of our subjects takes?

Even as tragic heroes fall, there is a corresponding counterthrust in which they move from ignorance to knowledge. This schematic portrays the tragic action:

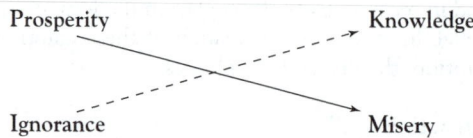

Two major principles are at work in this diagram: *reversal* and *recognition*. The downward (falling) movement from prosperity to misery is, in effect, a reversal (*peripeteia*) as things turn out differently and more disastrously for the tragic protagonist than anticipated. At the same time there is a recognition in the upward movement from ignorance to knowledge that brings understanding to both the protagonist and to the audience that watches the calamitous fall. Aristotle was careful to note that "the fall" must not happen to a thoroughly "virtuous man"

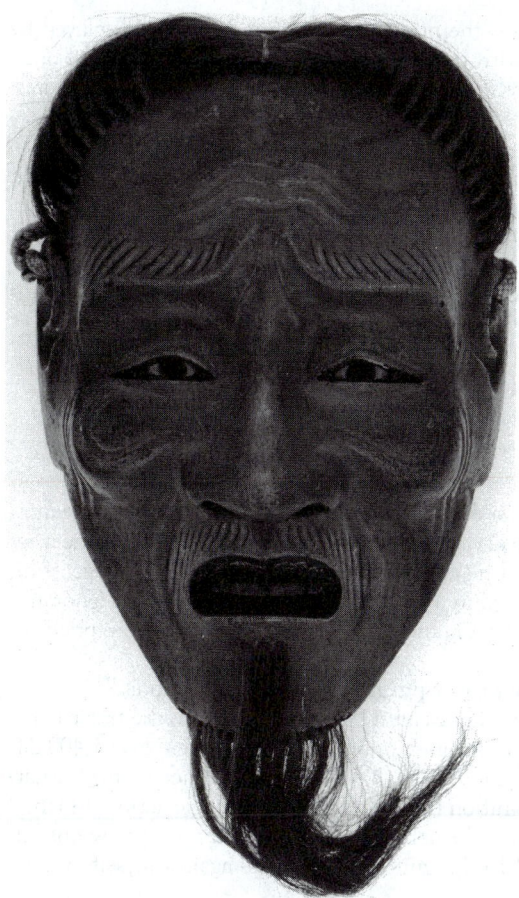

Tragic mask from Japan.

because this would "merely shock us." In life we know that good people are often the victims of terrible accidents, but tragedy as an art form does not deal with random accidents. It makes misfortune probable, even necessary. Nor does tragedy deal with the demise of "the utter villain." Though this satisfies our sense of morality and justice, it does not inspire pity and fear. The tragic hero, Aristotle says, ought to be one who is "not eminently good and just," yet one whose "misfortune is brought about not by vice and depravity, but by some error or frailty." In short the hero is one like ourselves and one in whom we can invest sympathy. Aristotle's observation that tragic heroes ought to be "highborn" may be attributed to the hierarchical society in which he lived. Arthur Miller's essay "Tragedy and the Common Man" (See Chapter 7) makes an eloquent case for democratizing the genre.

Whether highborn or common, the tragic hero makes a fateful "error in judgment." The term "tragic flaw" is often used to denote the protagonist's error, but flaw may be too strong a term. To describe the error of a tragic character, the Greeks borrowed an archer's term, *hamartia*, which means "missing the mark." It is less judgmental than "flaw" as it merely implies the tragic figure attempted to do something and was off the target. Often tragic heroes are motivated by the best of intentions but fail in their mission. As nineteenth-century German philosopher Georg W. F. Hegel pointed out, tragedy is most compelling when it involves the opposition of conflicting goods. In *Death and the King's Horseman*, for example, Pilkington's need to preserve the law of the state is pitted against Elesin's desire to observe Yoruban sacred law by accompanying the dead king in death.

Still, tragic heroes are human and thus susceptible to failure. *Hubris* (*hybris*) is most often applied to this defect of character, and it is frequently defined as "excessive pride," though this phrase is used too narrowly. To the Greeks hubris was applied to any form of excess, as it meant "swollen"; it was most often used to describe nature run amok (as in a swollen or flooded river). A popular Greek motto was "*medan agan,*" or "nothing in excess," a reminder that excessive behaviors often lead to catastrophe. Pride is the most common form of excess displayed by tragic characters. It is often synonymous with the attempt to be godlike, to transcend one's mortal limitations. The idea is not exclusively Greek, of course; one finds it in myriad cultures, most famously in the biblical warning that "pride goeth before a fall." Though it is a melodrama, the Chinese opera *The Qing Ding Pearl,* depicts the fall of a haughty tax collector. Tragic characters are by their very nature excessive, a mark of both their greatness and their humanity. Timid people are not likely to be tragic; heroes and heroines must be big enough to shake the universe. Like Prometheus, they must be bold enough to steal the fire of the gods, and like Oedipus they must pursue the truth whatever the price.

Ultimately, tragedy occurs not because the tragic protagonist is defeated or dies. Death is a natural part of the life process. As Hamlet says,

> If it [death] be now, 'tis not to come; if it be not to come, it will be now; if it be not now, yet it will come; the readiness is all. Since no man has aught of what he leaves, what is't to leave betimes? Let be.

The tragedy is that the heroes are defeated or die precisely at the moment when they are most "alive," that is, when they have an absolute knowledge of the great design of life. Imagine what a king an Oedipus or a Hamlet would be if he could rule with the certain knowledge of his strength and limitations. The action imitated in a tragedy brings heroes from that ignorance about themselves and their world to a profound knowledge, but only at an enormous price.

". . . through pity and fear effecting the proper purgation of these emotions."

This move from ignorance to knowledge inspires *catharsis,* and it is central to the tragic experience. (Scholars have debated this term for centuries: prior to 1931 there were over 1,400 different interpretations of catharsis, and, of course, many have been added since then.) Catharsis invariably accompanies the hero's recognition that is central to the tragic action. Much of the dignity we award tragic heroes stems from the nobility with which they accept responsibility for their actions. When Oedipus says "To this guilt I bore witness against myself" we are hearing a moment of catharsis.

Can true tragedy happen without recognition and its attendant catharsis? This is a debated point; contemporary tragicomedy involves characters who cannot (or will not) recognize their shortcomings and continue to live in ignorance. American critic Robert Brustein argues that modern "tragic heroes" are victims of psychology and sociology. Their plight may be pitiable, or more accurately pathetic. There is not the same ennobling uplift we experience in the presence of bona fide tragic heroes who face the worst life has to offer.

This passage concerning pity and fear may well be among Aristotle's most useful observations about the persuasive power of theater. He observes that in a tragedy two primary emotions are summoned. Pity implies an attraction to one, like us, who is suffering, while fear suggests a retreat from an impending evil or doom. These polar feelings complement one another to form a holistic response in which:

- we are moved by the suffering of tragic heroes;
- we are sufficiently distanced so that we may judge their actions.

This dual response thus cleanses—or purges—us, and thus the audience achieves its catharsis. Aristotle, a practitioner of the healing arts, knew that a cathartic agent cleansed the body of its impurities. A tragedy was, for Aristotle, a purging device for our spirits. Gerald Else argues that purgation enhances our ability to pity the tragic "doer" rather than condemning him. Catharsis "issues a license, so to speak, which says, 'you may pity this man for he is . . . like us, a good man rather than a bad and he is free of pollution.'"

Are pity, fear, and catharsis present in plays that are not tragedies? Absolutely. In fact, the melodrama, especially in films such as *Titanic,* thrives on summoning up powerful emotions, pity and fear in particular. They then provide a cathartic ending in which the good are (usually) rewarded while the villainous are soundly and spectacularly punished. In contrast to tragedy, however, melodramas most often deal with moral issues that can be too simply reduced to "good" versus "evil." Such melodramas are invariably driven by a villainous force, rarely by the protagonist's character. In truth, the vast majority of serious plays, especially those written after the Renaissance, are not tragedies in the classical sense, even though many end with the defeat or death of the protagonist. (See Spotlight box, Melodrama and Farce.)

In many Asian countries, people believe that catastrophe in this life provides enlightenment to prepare one for a future life. (E.g., Śakuntalā believes that her misfortunes are "the consequences of some wrongdoing on my part in a former birth.") In the East, death is often viewed as a passageway to a new life and that the "fallen heroes" will enter their next lives better prepared to confront life's challenges. And in some Eastern cultures, notably India and China, tragedy—as we understand it in the West—does not exist because playwrights are expected (under the codes of Hindu and Confucian thought) to render "just" endings in which the good are rewarded and the wicked punished. Transgressors in Japanese Noh and Kabuki dramas frequently become monks who wander the earth doing good works in reparation for their misdeeds.

Comedy

According to eighteenth-century literary critic Samuel Johnson, "comedy has been unpropitious to definers" because scholars and theorists have reached little accord on the topic of what makes people laugh. Comedy, even more so than tragedy, is dependent on the mores and customs of a particular culture. This is why we can refer to "British humor" and "French farce" as identifiable entities. To further complicate the issue, there are numerous subsets of comedy (the comedy of manners, slapstick, bawdry, the grotesque, the absurd, benign comedy, sentimental comedy, and so on), often appealing to particular people at a given time in history.

The classical definition of Western comedy derives from an anonymous work, the *Tractatus Coislinianus*, composed about the second century B.C.E. It neatly parallels Aristotle's description of tragedy and may be a remnant of his teachings. If tragedy deals with actions that are "serious" and of "a certain magnitude," comedy deals with those that are "ludicrous" and "imperfect." While tragedy provokes "pity" and "fear," comedy induces "laughter" and "pleasure" (notoriously ambiguous phrases) that also "purge" the emotions of the spectators. If tragedy deals with individuals at odds with the cosmos, comedy depends on a social world in which the comic hero (or buffoon) is at odds with the norms of society.

Comedy is very much about the here and now, and as such does not always translate well for subsequent generations. In some comedies the norms of society are strictly upheld, while in others they may be exposed and overthrown as an anarchic younger generation forges a new society. The women of *Lysistrata* challenge the destructive norms espoused by the men, while the young lovers in *A Midsummer Night's Dream* rebel against the tyranny of Theseus's court, escape into the Athenian woods, and return to build a new society. Many classical comedies end with a marriage (or two or three), a dance, or a banquet. The Greeks referred to this as a *komos* ("joyful union") that marks a new beginning for those who have survived the chaos of the play's action. Invariably, the *komos* suggests fertility (marriages), long life (banquets), and the restoration of the community's social order (dances). Such endings likely evolved from ancient agricultural festivals, and we find variations on the *komos* in virtually all cultures. The "wine dance" that concludes the Kabuki drama *Kanjinchō* reminds us that theater in Japan might have derived from such festivals. (See Forum, "The Mythos of Spring: Comedy.")

Whereas only a select few have the nobility of spirit to achieve tragic heroism, comedy is fundamentally democratic in that virtually all people, by nature of their folly, are candidates for comedy. As Thornton Wilder wrote in *Our Town*, "Whenever you come near the human race, there's layers and layers of nonsense." The television show *America's Funniest Home Videos* illustrates that even the most dignified person can be, under the right circumstances, wonderfully, howlingly comic.

So what is the difference between comedy and tragedy if both spring from human ignorance? On its simplest level, tragic heroes seek knowledge and play for much higher stakes to obtain it; they take on nothing less than the gods themselves on their journey of discovery. The stakes are rarely as high in comedy. In *A Midsummer Night's Dream* Egeus threatens his

SPOTLIGHT — MELODRAMA AND FARCE

While we can usually place a particular play within one of the three primary genres of drama, there are significant subsets of each, such as high comedy, satiric comedy, the romance, and sentimental dramas. Examples of the most common types and their particular characteristics are covered in the discussion of the specific plays. Melodrama and farce, in particular, complement our understanding of tragedy and comedy.

Melodrama

Melodrama often carries a negative connotation and suggests tawdry dramas in which mustache-twirling villains tie damsels-in-distress to the railroad tracks while square-jawed heroes ride to the rescue. This is "mellerdramer," a nineteenth-century variant on the much older, more respected melodrama. In truth many plays, including some of our most esteemed tragedies, have melodramatic elements. Stripped of its cosmic implications, *Hamlet* is a pretty lurid melodrama filled with ghosts skulking about castles, cloak-and-dagger espionage, and shocking, violent deaths.

Originally, a *melo drame* was a serious play accompanied by music to heighten its emotional impact. The Chinese refer to their operas by the generic term *melodrama*, which is quite fitting given the ubiquitous use of music that underscores every action in a Chinese play. In 1775 the French political philosopher Jean-Jacques Rousseau coined the term to describe his short play *Pygmalion* (a monologue set to music). Eventually, *melodrama* was applied to a sensational play in which:

- ingenious plots produce moments of danger for the protagonists;
- characters are thinly drawn symbols of singular virtues and vices pitted against one another;
- morality is reduced to its most simple elements;
- the emotional appeal surpasses any intellectual pretensions;
- poetic justice triumphs by the final curtain.

Like tragedy, the melodrama asks us to feel for the protagonists, to experience pity and fear, and to come away from the experience cleansed. But in melodrama the conflicts are almost always external, and the protagonists are frequently victims of villains. Tragedy demands that the hero's own personality contains the seeds of his or her downfall and that the hero ultimately recognizes this truth. While melodrama may flirt with tragedy by putting its heroes in life-threatening situations, its reliance on purely external circumstances diminishes the possibility of tragedy.

Uncle Tom's Cabin, the most popular stage play in America in the nineteenth century, typifies melodrama at both its best and at its most excessive. Many social dramas, especially those with an undercurrent of propaganda, are steeped in melodramatic techniques because they rely on oppressive villains (bankers, landowners, and bosses) to stir their audiences to action. *A Raisin in the Sun*, an outstanding play by any criterion, is—at heart—a melodrama. The term need not be pejorative, as there are numerous respected plays that are properly classified as melodramas.

Farce

Farce is the comedic equivalent of the melodrama. It also depends on an ingenious plot, a series of sticky situations in which broadly drawn characters must extricate themselves (usually by bounding at breakneck speed through any one of the doors that traditionally dominate farce's landscape!). Traditionally, there is a manipulated ending that resolves the confusion. Comedy has long been used as a social corrective as aberrant behaviors are laughed out of existence. There is an implied moral foundation to comedy. But farce is amoral. The audience does not laugh at immoral behavior (such as adultery) but rather at the situations in which the miscreants find themselves. Farce does not ask us to judge human behaviors; it is satisfied only that we laugh at the ingenious situations and the dexterity of the farceurs. Consider your reactions to *Master Pierre Pathelin*. Did you seriously believe that Pierre was "wrong" for duping the Clothier? More likely, you actually enjoyed his ingenious ruses. Imagine how much more fun it would be if you had actually seen a brilliant comedian such as Robin Williams play Pierre.

Farce is derived from a medieval French word, *farcir*, which means "to stuff." Like their Italian and ancient Roman counterparts, early French comedies relied on physical humor to "stuff" or fill out the plots. Thus farce is occasionally confused with *slapstick comedy*, which is grounded in the physical humor of pratfalls, beatings, and variations on pie-in-the-face routines. While farce may employ much physical humor, it transcends mere slapstick in the cleverness of its plotting and in its spirit of anarchy. Eric Bentley, whose analysis of the psychological appeal of farce is among the finest essays on the genre, argues that farce is ultimately about fulfilling repressed desires. It allows us to punch our boss in the nose or tread our way through the adventures of an adulterous love affair vicariously. We laugh from the safety of our theater seat. Though farce may lack profundity, it remains among the most difficult forms for actors to play, as reflected in the story of the old vaudevillian on his deathbed who is asked if dying is difficult. "Dying is easy," he wheezes, "it's comedy that's hard." He no doubt had played in a farce or two!

One means of achieving the tragicomic effect in the late twentieth century has been to fuse elements of farce with serious intent. The Europeans have a glorious history of clowning in their circuses and popular entertainments such as mime and puppetry. They have produced a number of playwrights (Romania's Eugene Ionesco, Belgium's Michel de Ghelderode, Switzerland's

Friedreich Duerrenmatt, England's Joe Orton and Tom Stoppard, and Italy's Dario Fo) who have successfully blended farce and existential philosophy. The Middle Europeans have used the laughter of farce to distance more serious political messages in their struggle against totalitarian regimes. The Poles, long the victims of subjugation, have been especially effective in this realm. Slawomir Mrozek (1930–), contemporary Poland's leading dramatist, even wrote a play he billed as a "melofarce" (*The Turkey*, 1960). Tewfik al-Hakim, Egypt's most notable playwright in the twentieth century, is also remembered for his fusion of farce and social commentary in such plays as *The Donkey Market* and *Fate of a Cockroach*.

daughter with death, but the conventions of romantic comedies are such that we know that death is improbable. Comedy is indeed "much ado about nothing," although the characters involved may feel hopelessly trapped and threatened by the proceedings. But we—on our thrones outside the action—have a greater perspective and know intuitively, like Puck, that by the final act "Naught shall go ill . . . and all shall be well."

Comic characters are frequently inflexible beings whose dilemmas are brought on by their unwillingness to accept change or the predictability with which they react to a situation. In 1900 Henri Bergson, a French philosopher, observed that laughter is induced by "mechanical inelasticity," which means that the more humans behave like machines, the funnier they are. Recall Charlie Chaplin's famous walk, especially as he rounded corners, for a classic example of physical mannerisms reduced to mechanisms. Chinese folk opera features a popular character called "the hobbler" with a similarly funny, mechanical walk. Tragic figures, such as Prometheus, can also be rigid and inflexible but there is nobility in their resoluteness as they confront momentous issues. The comic hero's rigidity is out of proportion to the seriousness of the situation and is thereby laughable. Some comic characters, Young Marlowe in *She Stoops to Conquer*, for instance, are reformed through the process of reversal and recognition, while others staunchly refuse to change, even as the society about them goes merrily on its way to a better world.

The principles of reversal and recognition are also applicable to comedy, but often in quite different ways. Comedy thrives on reversals (though not catastrophic ones) to move its intricate plots along at a brisk pace. As a general rule, comedy demands rapid pacing, both in its plotting and in its playing. A cardinal rule of the comedian is "Don't give the audience too much time to think about the improbabilities." Serious drama invites a more deliberate pace as we, like the tragic figures, reflect on the significance of the action.

Recognition is often a more nebulous element in comedy, as some characters never recognize their folly. Often recognition is imposed on the characters by an external force—a long-lost uncle, a timely letter, the disclosure of a secret, even the gods themselves stepping into the action to sort out the bumblings of the characters. To illustrate this point, consider speeches from two of Shakespeare's plays, likely written within a year of each other. Early in *Twelfth Night* the heroine, Viola, becomes aware of her dilemma: while dressed as a young man (cross-dressing is a popular convention of comedy) she has fallen in love with a duke who loves another young woman, Olivia, who—alas—has fallen in love with Viola's male countenance. At the end of act 2, scene 1 she expresses her dismay:

> *Time, thou must untangle this—not I;*
>
> *It is too hard a knot for me t'untie.*

In contrast, when Hamlet learns at the end of act 1 that his father has been murdered by his uncle and that he, alone, must right this wrong, he cries out:

> *The Time is out of joint, O cursed spite*
>
> *That ever I was born to set it right.*

These speeches epitomize a fundamental difference between comedy and tragedy. In comedy there is the implicit notion that humans may be incapable of resolving their dilemmas, that an

FORUM

"From 'The Mythos of Spring: Comedy'"

NORTHROP FRYE

Northrop Frye, a Canadian, is among the most influential literary critics of the twentieth century. After systematically examining the myths and literary output of a variety of cultures, he noticed recurring thematic patterns and character types. His analysis of the phenomenon of comedy, portions of which are included here, has increased our understanding of comic archetypes and stock character.

. . . The plot structure of Greek New Comedy, as transmitted by Plautus and Terence, in itself less a form than a formula, has become the basis for most comedy, especially in its more highly conventionalized dramatic form, down to our own day. It will be most convenient to work out the theory of comic construction from drama, using illustrations from fiction only incidentally. What normally happens is that a young man wants a young woman, that his desire is resisted by some opposition, usually paternal, and that near the end of the play some twist in the plot enables the hero to have his will. In this simple pattern there are several complex elements. In the first place, the movement of comedy is usually a movement from one kind of society to another. At the beginning of the play the obstructing characters are in charge of the play's society, and the audience recognizes that they are usurpers. At the end of the play the device in the plot that brings hero and heroine together causes a new society to crystallize around the hero, and the moment when this crystallization occurs is the point of resolution in the action, the comic discovery, *anagnorisis* or *cognitio*.

The appearance of this new society is frequently signalized by some kind of party or festive ritual, which either appears at the end of the play or is assumed to take place immediately afterward. Weddings are most common, and sometimes so many of them occur, as in the quadruple wedding at the end of *As You Like It*, that they suggest also the wholesale pairing off that takes place in a dance, which is another common conclusion, and the normal one for the masque. The banquet at the end of *The Taming of the Shrew* has an ancestry that goes back to Greek Middle Comedy; in Plautus the audience is sometimes jocosely invited to an imaginary banquet afterwards; Old Comedy, like the modern Christmas pantomime, was more generous, and occasionally threw bits of food to the audience. As the the final society reached by comedy is the one that the audience has recognized all along to be the proper and desirable state of affairs, an act of communion with the audience is in order. Tragic actors expect

to be applauded as well as comic ones, but nevertheless the word "plaudite" at the end of a Roman comedy, the invitation to the audience to form part of the comic society, would seem rather out of place at the end of a tragedy. The resolution of comedy comes, so to speak, from the audience's side of the stage; in a tragedy it comes from some mysterious world on the opposite side. In the movie, where darkness permits a more erotically oriented audience, the plot usually moves toward an act which, like death in Greek tragedy, takes place offstage, and is symbolized by a closing embrace.

The obstacles to the hero's desire, then, form the action of the comedy, and the overcoming of them the comic resolution. The obstacles are usually parental, hence comedy often turns on a clash between a son's and a father's will. Thus the comic dramatist as a rule writes for the younger men in his audience, and the older members of almost any society are apt to feel that comedy has something subversive about it. This is certainly one element in the social persecution of drama, which is not peculiar to Puritans or even Christians, as Terence in pagan Rome met much the same kind of social opposition that Ben Johnson did. There is one scene in Plautus where a son and father are making love to the same courtesan, and the son asks his father pointedly if he really does love mother. One has to see this scene against the background of Roman family life to understand its importance as psychological release. Even in Shakespeare there are startling outbreaks of baiting older men, and in contemporary movies the triumph of youth is so relentless that the moviemakers find some difficulty in getting anyone over the age of seventeen into their audiences.

The opponent to the hero's wishes, when not the father, is generally someone who partakes of the father's closer relation to established society: that is, a rival with less youth and more money. In Plautus and Terence he is usually either the pimp who owns the girl, or a wandering soldier with a supply of ready cash. The fury with which these characters are baited and exploded from the stage shows that they are father-surrogates, and even if they were not, they would still be usurpers, and their claim to possess the girl must be shown up as somehow fraudulent. They are, in short, impostors, and the extent to which they have real power implies some criticism of the society that allows them their power. In Plautus and Terence this criticism seldom goes beyond the immorality of brothels and professional harlots, but in Renaissance dramatists, including Jonson, there is some sharp observation of the rising power of money and the sort of ruling class it is building up.

The tendency of comedy is to include as many people as possible in its final society: the blocking characters are more often reconciled or converted than simply repudiated. Comedy often includes a scapegoat ritual of expulsion which gets rid of some irreconcilable character, but exposure and disgrace make for pathos, or even tragedy. *The Merchant of Venice* seems almost an experiment in coming as close as possible to upsetting the comic balance. If the dramatic role of Shylock is ever so slightly exaggerated, as it generally is when the leading actor of the company takes the part, it is upset, and the play becomes the tragedy of the Jew of Venice with a comic epilogue. *Volpone* ends with a great bustle of sentences to penal servitude and the galleys, and one feels that the deliverance of society hardly needs so much hard labor; but then *Volpone* is exceptional in being a kind of comic imitation of a tragedy, with the point of Volpone's hybris carefully marked.

The principle of conversion becomes clearer with characters whose chief function is the amusing of the audience. The original *miles gloriosus* in Plautus is a son of Jove and Venus who has killed an elephant with his fist and seven thousand men in one day's fighting. In other words, he is trying to put on a good show: the exuberance of his boasting helps to put the play over. The convention says that the braggart must be exposed, ridiculed, swindled, and beaten. But why should a professional dramatist, of all people, want so to harry a character who is putting on a good show—*his* show at that? When we find Falstaff invited to the final feast in *The Merry Wives*, Caliban reprieved, attempts made to mollify Malvolio, and Angelo and Parolles allowed to live down their disgrace, we are seeing a fundamental principle of comedy at work. The tendency of the comic society to include rather than exclude is the reason for the traditional importance of the parasite, who has no business to be at the final festival but is nevertheless there. The word "grace," with all its Renaissance overtones from the graceful courtier of Castiglione to the gracious God of Christianity, is a most important thematic word in Shakespearean comedy.

The action of comedy in moving from one social center to another is not unlike the action of a lawsuit, in which plaintiff and defendant construct different versions of the same situation, one finally being judged as real and the other as illusory. . . .

Comedy usually moves toward a happy ending, and the normal response of the audience to a happy ending is "this should be," which sounds like a moral judgement. So it is, except that it is not moral in the restricted sense, but social. Its opposite is not the villainous but the absurd, and comedy finds the virtues of Malvolio as absurd as the vices of Angelo. Molière's misanthrope, being committed to sincerity, which is a virtue, is morally in a strong position, but the audience soon realizes that his friend Philinte, who is ready to lie quite cheerfully in order to enable other people to preserve their self-respect, is the more genuinely sincere of the two. It is of course quite possible to have a moral comedy, but the result is often the kind of melodrama that we have described as comedy without humor, and which achieves its happy ending with a self-righteous tone that most comedy avoids. It is hardly possible to imagine a drama without a conflict, and it is hardly possible to imagine a conflict without some kind of enmity. But just as love, including sexual love, is a very different thing from lust, so enmity is a very different thing from hatred. In tragedy, of course, enmity almost al-

ways includes hatred; comedy is different, and one feels that the social judgement against the absurd is closer to the comic norm than the moral judgement against the wicked . . . .

The society emerging at the conclusion of comedy represents . . . a kind of moral norm, or pragmatically free society. . . . We are simply given to understand that the newly married couple will live happily ever after, or that at any rate they will get along in a relatively unhumorous and clear-sighted manner. That is one reason why the character of the successful hero is so often left undeveloped: his real life begins at the end of the play, and we have to believe him to be potentially a more interesting character than he appears to be. In Terence's *Adelphoi*, Demea, a harsh father, is contrasted with his brother Micio, who is indulgent. Micio being more liberal, he leads the way to the comic resolution, and converts Demea, but then Demea points out the indolence inspiring a good deal of Micio's liberality, and releases him from a complementary humorous bondage. . . .

The comic ending is generally manipulated by a twist in the plot. In Roman comedy the heroine, who is usually a slave or courtesan, turns out to be the daughter of somebody respectable, so that the hero can marry her without loss of face. The *cognitio* in comedy, in which the characters find out who their relatives are, and who is left of the opposite sex not a relative, and hence available for marriage, is one of the features of comedy that have never changed much: *The Confidential Clerk* indicates that it still holds the attention of dramatists. There is a brilliant parody of a *cognitio* at the end of *Major Barbara* (the fact that the hero of this play is a professor of Greek perhaps indicates an unusual affinity to the conventions of Euripides and Menander), where Undershaft is enabled to break the rule that he cannot appoint his son-in-law as successor by the fact that the son-in-law's own father married his deceased wife's sister in Australia, so that the son-in-law is his own first cousin as well as himself. It sounds complicated, but the plots of comedy often are complicated because there is something inherently absurd about complications. As the main character interest in comedy is so often focussed on the defeated characters, comedy regularly illustrates a victory of arbitrary plot over consistency of character. Thus, in striking contrast to tragedy, there can hardly be such a thing as inevitable comedy, as far as the action of the individual play is concerned. That is, we may know that the convention of comedy will make some kind of happy ending inevitable, but still for each play the dramatist must produce a distinctive "gimmick" or "weenie," to use two disrespectful Hollywood synonyms for *anagnorisis*. Happy endings do not impress us as true, but as desirable, and they are brought about by manipulation. The watcher of death and tragedy has nothing to do but sit and wait for the inevitable end; but something gets born at the end of comedy, and the watcher of birth is a member of a busy society.

The manipulation of plot does not always involve metamorphosis of character, but there is no violation of comic decorum when it does. Unlikely conversions, miraculous transformations, and providential assistance are inseparable from comedy. Further, whatever emerges is supposed to be there for good: if the curmudgeon becomes lovable, we understand that he will

(continued)

not immediately relapse again into his ritual habit. Civilizations which stress the desirable rather than the real, and the religious as opposed to the scientific perspective, think of drama almost entirely in terms of comedy. In the classical drama of India, we are told, the tragic ending was regarded as bad taste, much as the manipulated endings of comedy are regarded as bad taste by novelists interested in ironic realism.

The total *mythos* of comedy, only a small part of which is ordinarily presented, has regularly what in music is called a ternary form: the hero's society rebels against the society of the *senex* and triumphs, but the hero's society is a Saturnalia, a reversal of social standards which recalls a golden age in the past before the main action of the play begins. Thus we have a stable and harmonious order disrupted by folly, obsession, forgetfulness, "pride and prejudice," or events not understood by the characters themselves, and then restored. Often there is a benevolent grandfather, so to speak, who overrules the action set up by the blocking humor and so links the first and third parts. An example is Mr. Burchell, the disguised uncle of the wicked squire, in *The Vicar of Wakefield*. A very long play, such as the Indian *Sakuntala*, may present all three phases; a very intricate one, such as many of Menander's evidently were, may indicate their outlines. But of course very often the first phase is not given at all: the audience simply understands an ideal state of affairs which it knows to be better than what is revealed in the play, and which it recognizes as like that to which the action leads. This ternary action is, ritually, like a contest of summer and winter in which winter occupies the middle action; psychologically, it is like the removal of a neurosis or blocking point and the restoring of an unbroken current of energy and memory. The Jonsonian masque, with the antimasque in the middle, gives a highly conventionalized or "abstract" version of it.

We pass now to the typical characters of comedy. In drama, characterization depends on function; what a character is follows from what he has to do in the play. Dramatic function in its turn depends on the structure of the play; the character has certain things to do because the play has such and such a shape. The structure of the play in its turn depends on the category of the play; if it is a comedy, its structure will require a comic resolution and a prevailing comic mood. Hence when we speak of typical characters, we are not trying to reduce lifelike characters to stock types, though we certainly are suggesting that the sentimental notion of an antithesis between the lifelike character and the stock type is a vulgar error. All lifelike characters, whether in drama or fiction, owe their consistency to the appropriateness of the stock type which belongs to their dramatic function. That stock type is not the character but it is as necessary to the character as a skeleton is to the actor who plays it.

With regard to the characterization of comedy, the *Tractatus* lists three types of comic characters: the *alazons* or impostors, the *eirons* or self-deprecators, and the buffoons (*bomolochoi*). This list is closely related to a passage in the *Ethics* which contrasts the first two, and then goes on to contrast the buffoon with a character whom Aristotle calls *agroikos* or churlish, literally rustic. We may reasonably accept the churl as a fourth character type, and so we have two opposed pairs. The contest of *eiron* and *alazon* forms the basis of the comic action, and the buffoon and the churl polarize the comic mood.

We have previously dealt with the terms *eiron* and *alazon*. The humorous blocking characters of comedy are nearly always impostors, though it is more frequently a lack of self-knowledge than simple hypocrisy that characterizes them. The multitudes of comic scenes in which one character complacently soliloquizes while another makes sarcastic asides to the audience show the contest of *eiron* and *alazon* in its purest form, and show too that the audience is sympathetic to the *eiron* side. Central to the *alazon* group is the *senex iratus* or heavy father, who with his rages and threats, his obsessions and his gullibility, seems closely related to some of the demonic characters of romance, such as Polyphemus. Occasionally a character may have the dramatic function of such a figure without his characteristics: an example is Squire Allworthy in *Tom Jones*, who as far as the plot is concerned behaves almost as stupidly as Squire Western. Of heavy-father surrogates, the *miles gloriosus* has been mentioned: his popularity is largely due to the fact that he is a man of words rather than deeds, and is consequently far more useful to a practising dramatist than any tight-lipped hero could ever be. The pedant, in Renaissance comedy often a student of the occult sciences, the fop or coxcomb, and similar humors, require no comment. The female *alazon* is rare: Katharina the shrew represents to some extent a female *miles gloriosus*, and the *précieuse ridicule* a female pedant, but the "menace" or siren who gets in the way of the true heroine is more often found as a sinister figure of melodrama or romance than as a ridiculous figure in comedy.

The *eiron* figures need a little more attention. Central to this group is the hero, who is an *eiron* figure because, as explained, the dramatist tends to play him down and make him rather neutral and unformed in character. Next in importance is the heroine, also often played down: in Old Comedy, when a girl accompanies a male hero in his triumph, she is generally a stage prop, a *muta persona* not previously introduced. A more difficult form of *cognitio* is achieved when the heroine disguises herself or through some other device brings about the comic resolution, so that the person whom the hero is seeking turns out to be the person who has sought him. The fondness of Shakespeare for this "she stoops to conquer" theme needs only to be mentioned here, as it belongs more naturally to the *mythos* of romance.

Another central *eiron* figure is the type entrusted with hatching the schemes which bring about the hero's victory. This character in Roman comedy is almost always a tricky slave (*dolosus servus*), and in Renaissance comedy he becomes the scheming valet who is so frequent in Continental plays, and in Spanish drama is called the *gracioso*. Modern audiences are most familiar with him in Figaro and in the Leporello of *Don Giovanni*. Through such intermediate nineteenth-century figures as Micawber and the Touchwood of Scott's *St. Ronan's Well*, who, like the gracioso, have buffoon affiliations, he evolves into the amateur detective of modern fiction. The Jeeves of P. G. Wodehouse is a more direct descendant. Female confidantes of the same general family are often brought in to oil the machinery of the well-made play. Elizabethan comedy had another type of trickster, represented by the Matthew Merrygreek of *Ralph Roister Doister*, who is generally said to be developed from the vice or iniquity of the morality plays: as usual, the analogy is sound enough, whatever historians decide about origins. The vice, to give him that name, is very useful to a comic dramatist because he acts from pure love of mischief, and can set a comic action going with the minimum of motivation. The vice may be as light-hearted as Puck or as malignant as Don John in *Much Ado*, but as a rule the vice's activity is, in spite of his name, benevolent. One of the tricky slaves in Plautus, in a soliloquy, boasts that he is the *architectus* of the comic action: such a character carries out the will of the author to reach a happy ending. He is in fact the spirit of comedy, and the two clearest examples of the type in Shakespeare, Puck and Ariel, are both spiritual beings. The tricky slave often has his own freedom in mind as the reward of his exertions: Ariel's longing for release is in the same tradition.

The role of the vice includes a great deal of disguising, and the type may often be recognized by disguise. A good example is the Brainworm of Jonson's *Every Man in His Humour*, who calls the action of the play the day of his metamorphoses. Similarly Ariel has to surmount the difficult stage direction of "Enter invisible." The vice is combined with the hero whenever the latter is a cheeky, improvident young man who hatches his own schemes and cheats his rich father or uncle into giving him his patrimony along with the girl.

Another *eiron* type has not been much noticed. This is a character, generally an older man, who begins the action of the play by withdrawing from it, and ends the play by returning. He is often a father with the motive of seeing what his son will do. The action of *Every Man in His Humour* is set going in this way by Knowell Senior. The disappearance and return of Lovewit, the owner of the house which is the scene of *The Alchemist*, has the same dramatic function, though the characterization is different. The clearest Shakespearean example is the Duke in *Measure for Measure*, but Shakespeare is more addicted to the type than might appear at first glance. In Shakespeare the vice is rarely the real *architectus*: Puck and Ariel both act under orders from an older man, if one may call Oberon a man for a moment. In *The Tempest* Shakespeare returns to a comic action established by Aristophanes, in which an older man, instead of retiring from the action, builds it up on the stage. When the heroine takes the vice role in Shakespeare, she is often significantly related to her father, even when the father is not in the play at all, like the father of Helena, who gives her his medical knowledge, or the father of Portia, who arranges the scheme of the caskets. A more conventionally treated example of the same benevolent Prospero figure turned up recently in the psychiatrist of *The Cocktail Party*, and one may compare the mysterious alchemist who is the father of the heroine of *The Lady's Not for Burning*. The formula is not confined to comedy: Polonius, who shows so many of the disadvantages of a literary education, attempts the role of a retreating paternal *eiron* three times, once too often. *Hamlet* and *King Lear* contain subplots which are ironic versions of stock comic themes, Gloucester's story being the regular comedy theme of the gullible *senex* swindled by a clever and unprincipled son.

We pass now to the buffoon types, those whose function it is to increase the mood of festivity rather than to contribute to the plot. Renaissance comedy, unlike Roman comedy, had a great variety of such characters, professional fools, clowns, pages, singers, and incidental characters with established comic habits like malapropism or foreign accents. The oldest buffoon of this incidental nature is the parasite, who may be given something to do, as Jonson gives Mosca the role of a vice in *Volpone*, but who, *qua* parasite, does nothing but entertain the audience by talking about his appetite. He derives chiefly from Greek Middle Comedy, which appears to have been very full of food, and where he was, not unnaturally, closely associated with another established buffoon type, the cook, a conventional figure who breaks into comedies to bustle and order about and make long speeches about the mysteries of cooking. In the role of cook the buffoon or entertainer appears, not simply as a gratuitous addition like the parasite, but as something more like a master of ceremonies, a center for the comic mood. There is no cook in Shakespeare, though there is a superb description of one in the *Comedy of Errors*, but a similar role is often attached to a jovial and loquacious host, like the "mad host" of *The Merry Wives* or the Simon Eyre of *The Shoemakers Holiday*. In Middleton's *A Trick to Catch the Old One* the mad host type is combined with the vice. In Falstaff and Sir Toby Belch we can see the affinities of the buffoon or entertainer type both with the parasite and with the master of revels. If we study this entertainer or host role carefully we shall soon realize that it is a development of what in Aristophanic comedy is represented by the chorus, and which in its turn goes back to the *komos* or revel from which comedy is said to be descended.

Finally, there is a fourth group to which we have assigned the word *agroikos*, and which usually means either churlish or rustic, depending on the context. This type may also be extended to cover the Elizabethan gull and what in vaudeville used to be called the straight man, the solemn or inarticulate character who allows the humor to bounce off him, so to speak. We find churls in the miserly, snobbish, or priggish characters whose role is that of the refuser of festivity, the killjoy who tries to stop the fun, or, like Malvolio, locks up the food and drink instead of dispensing it. The melancholy Jaques of *As You Like It*, who walks out on the final festivities, is closely related. In the sulky and self-centered Bertram of *All's Well* there is a most unusual and ingenious combination of this type with the hero. More often, however, the churl belongs to the *alazon* group, all miserly old men in comedies, including Shylock, being churls. In *The Tempest* Caliban has much the same relation to the churlish type that Ariel has to the vice or tricky slave. But often, where the mood is more light-hearted, we may translate *agroikos* simply by rustic, as with the innumerable country squires and similar characters who provide amusement in the urban setting of drama. Such types do not refuse the mood of festivity, but they mark the extent of its range. In a pastoral comedy the idealized virtues of rural life may be represented by a simple man who speaks for the pastoral ideal, like Corin in *As You Like It*. Corin has the same *agroikos* role as the "rube" or "hayseed" of more citified

(continued)

comedies, but the moral attitude to the role is reversed. Again we notice the principle that dramatic structure is a permanent and moral attitude a variable factor in literature.

In a very ironic comedy a different type of character may play the role of the refuser of festivity. The more ironic the comedy, the more absurd the society, and an absurd society may be condemned by, or at least contrasted with, a character that we may call the plain dealer, an outspoken advocate of a kind of moral norm who has the sympathy of the audience. Wycherley's Manly, though he provides the name for the type, is not a particularly good example of it: a much better one is the Cléante of *Tartuffe*. Such a character is appropriate when the tone is ironic enough to get the audience confused about its sense of the social norm: he corresponds roughly to the chorus in a tragedy, which is there for a similar reason. When the tone deepens from the ironic to the bitter, the plain dealer may become a malcontent or railer, who may be morally superior to his society, as he is to some extent in Marston's play of that name, but who may also be too motivated by envy to be much more than another aspect of his society's evil, like Thersites, or to some extent Apemantus.

In tragedy, pity and fear, the emotions of moral attraction and repulsion, are raised and cast out. Comedy seems to make a more functional use of the social, even the moral judgement, than tragedy, yet comedy seems to raise the corresponding emotions, which are sympathy and ridicule, and cast them out in the same way. Comedy ranges from the most savage irony to the most dreamy wish-fulfilment romance, but its structural patterns and characterization are much the same throughout its range. This principle of the uniformity of comic structure through a variety of attitudes is clear in Aristophanes. Aristophanes is the most personal of writers, and his opinions on every subject are written all over his plays. We know that he wanted peace with Sparta and that he hated Cleon, so when his comedy depicts the attaining of peace and the defeat of Cleon we know that he approved and wanted his audience to approve. But in *Ecclesiazusae* a band of women in disguise railroad a communistic scheme through the Assembly which is a horrid parody of a Platonic republic, and proceed to inaugurate its sexual communism with some astonishing improvements. Presumably Aristophanes did not altogether endorse this, yet the comedy follows the same pattern and the same resolution. In *The Birds* the Peisthetairos who defies Zeus and blocks out Olympus with his Cloud-Cuckoo-Land is accorded the same triumph that is given to the Trygaios of the *Peace* who flies to heaven and brings a golden age back to Athens.

external agent—Time or Fortune—must intervene to set things straight. Only Hamlet himself, however, can "set it right" because tragic figures must embrace their fates without flinching. Fate is not the product of peevish gods who "kill us for their sport," as Shakespeare says in *King Lear*. Oliver Taplin argues in *Greek Tragedy in Action* (1988) that Fate is a combination of the will of the gods and the will of the tragic figure. To summarize, benevolent Fortune hovers over the world of comedy waiting to restore harmony, while Fate looms large in the tragic world as it follows the hero's quest for certainty.

Tragicomedy

The German novelist Thomas Mann remarked that the great triumph of modern art is that "it has ceased to recognize the categories of tragic and comic . . . and views life as tragicomedy." Though the term is attributed to the Roman playwright Plautus in the second century B.C.E., and though we can find examples of it in the works of Euripides, Kālidāsa, Shakespeare, and other pre-twentieth-century dramatists, tragicomedy is associated most with the modern era. Bernard Shaw credits Henrik Ibsen as being "the dramatic poet who firmly established tragicomedy as a much deeper and grimmer entertainment than tragedy."

Tragicomedy is more than a mere fusion of tragic events that threaten the lives of characters and the comic resolution that saves them. Melodrama often thrives on such plotting. Contemporary tragicomedy is born of a philosophy that denies a discernible order in the cosmos. Neither Fate nor Fortune plays a hand in human activity, which dramatists often judge to be futile and inconsequential. This pessimistic view was born of the chaos of the century's great wars, the Great Depression, and the threat of nuclear annihilation. The result is tragicomedy, which paradoxically arouses pity and fear through laughter. Modern dramatists such as Beckett, Pinter, Albee, Dragún, Kushner, Ngema, and Churchill have made a specialty of grimly comic plays in which laughter is an antidote for the conundrums of life.

Reversal and recognition are not always present in tragicomedy, at least overtly. Characters are often too shackled by their own inertia to allow for a reversal of fortune. Chekhov's characters, trapped physically on isolated Russian estates and mentally by their inability to adjust to changes, are the prototypes of this phenomenon. Beckett, who wrote that "habit is the great deadener," has invented an apt metaphor, however disturbing, for the malaise of contemporary life. In his play *Happy Days*, the central character, Winnie, is buried to her neck in a waste heap throughout the play. In *Rockaby* Beckett's heroine is as chained to her rocking chair as Prometheus was to his mountain, though for quite different reasons. Beckett's character sits there solely because she sat there yesterday, as she will sit there tomorrow. Amusing? Perhaps. Pathetic? Certainly. In tragicomedy we often invest much the same emotional energy in the dilemma of the character as we do in tragedy, yet there is no corresponding purgation derived from our encounter with one "better than we are." Too often our laughter in a tragicomedy stems from the realization that the characters are too much like we are.

In much modern tragicomedy the traditional elements of drama have been reshaped. Causality—and thereby plotting—has been replaced by "the action of inaction." Characters are less prone to act and more inclined to discuss dilemmas rather than confront them. "There are no brave causes anymore," laments Jimmy Porter in *Look Back in Anger* (1956), John Osborne's assault on modern life.

Just as there exists ambiguity in a world without certainty, there is a corresponding ambiguity in characterization. Aristotle's argument that characters must be "consistent even in their inconsistency" has found new meaning in tragicomedy. Contradictions are now the norm rather than the exception. In his essay *L'Umorismo* (1920), Luigi Pirandello notes that the concept of humor in Italy is far different from England's, where humor is a species of wit. For Pirandello, a pioneer of tragicomic drama, humor is a darker enterprise in which the artist is acutely aware of the contraries of life, the suffering and the comedy. "The humorist," says Pirandello, whose comments are particularly appropriate to the tragicomedian, "pays attention to the body and the shadow, sometimes more to the shadow than the body." Coincidentally, Pirandello's ideas are not uniquely Western; similar beliefs about the simultaneity of the serious and the comic are found in many Eastern philosophies, which embrace the dualities of life. The drama of Mexico (e.g., Elena Garro's *A Solid Home*) and Latin America (Osvaldo Dragún's *The Man Who Turned into a Dog*) is especially notable for its fusion of these seemingly disparate moods.

The playwright invites the audience to see life's many ironies. But modern characters are unable, often unwilling, to recognize their complicity in their dilemmas. And, if they do have a glimmer of insight, they are unable, perhaps unwilling, to act on it. This may be illustrated by the final moment of Beckett's *Waiting for Godot* (1953). The two tramps who have waited futilely for someone called "Godot" agree that they cannot continue their hopeless vigil. The play ends with an apparent resolution:

> VLADIMIR. *Well? Shall we go?*
> ESTRAGON. *Yes, let's go.*

But the final stage direction captures simultaneously the tragedy and comedy of their lives: "*They do not move. Curtain.*" We laugh at the incongruity between aspiration and realization, yet we are shaken by the futility of it all because it is a disturbingly true imitation of human nature.

Ultimately, tragicomedy is darker, less hopeful than tragedy or comedy. Although tragedy begins with the premise of potential greatness in humanity and ends with defeat, there is nevertheless a sense of triumph in the tragic protagonist's willingness to confront human shortcomings. Although comedy begins with the premise that we are folly-bound, it concludes with the promise of a better society as seen in its reconciliations, dances, feasts, and weddings. But in tragicomedy there is rarely the release of spirit observed in the other genres. There are only two tramps who "do not move" in a cosmos where inertia reigns.

Styles and Conventions

Whereas genre is indicative of a distinctive type of drama according to the treatment of the subject matter and the perspective of the writer, *style* is indicative of the manner of presentation. Tragedies, comedies, tragicomedies—and the myriad other subgenres—can be performed in a variety of styles.

Among the most appealing aspects of going to the theater on a regular basis is seeing the many ways in which a play can be written, performed, staged, and designed. You might visit ten different Shakespeare festivals in a summer, see a production of *A Midsummer Night's Dream* at each, and come away from your ten experiences viewing the play and the productions quite differently. A familiarity with styles and conventions will help you further appreciate live theater.

Styles

Style is the manner in which a play is written, directed, designed, and performed. Because it implies the degree of artificiality involved in the performance, perhaps it is easier to see style in nonrealistic works. Both the classical Greek style and Kabuki, for instance, use masks, padded costumes, and elevated shoes. And in both, the writing employs heightened language, much of it sung and danced. By contrast, the style demanded by American realists such as David Mamet and Marsha Norman is as far removed from a Greek or Kabuki performance as one can imagine. The actors wear clothing that seems "everyday." They talk in conversational, intimate tones, while movement, gestures, and body attitudes seem entirely natural, even antitheatrical. Some critics propose that modern realism is "antistyle," though realism does have a definable style.

Theater productions in all cultures can be divided into two principal performance styles: *presentational* and *representational*. The latter, with which Western audiences may be more familiar, asks the audience to accept as "real" that which they see onstage. It is most closely associated with modern Western theater. Presentational theater acknowledges the presence of spectators who know they are watching a theatrical event. Thus it uses such conventions as direct address to the audience through asides, soliloquies, and songs. The actors are as apt to play to the audience as to each other. Shakespeare opens his history play *Henry V* with an actor stepping forward to address the audience in a speech that is a prescription for presentational theater:

> *Piece out our imperfections with your thoughts;*
>
> *Into a thousand parts divide one man*
>
> *And make imaginary puissance.*
>
> *Think, when we talk of horses, that you see them*
>
> *Printing their proud hoofs i' th' receiving earth;*
>
> *For 'tis your thoughts that now must deck our kings . . .*

In presentational theater, the design elements are overtly theatrical—or, at the other extreme, nonexistent—with little pretense of realism. In fact, this style is often referred to as *theatrical* because it reminds us that what we see onstage is an imaginative "lie" that is only a metaphor for life, not life itself.

With the representational style, the "lie" exists in the auditorium because it suggests that the audience is not really in a theater, but that it is eavesdropping upon actual life through an invisible "fourth wall" into a private room. In *A Doll's House*, Henrik Ibsen describes the realistic detail of the Helmer household in his opening stage direction: *A comfortably and tastefully, but not expensively furnished room. . . . Engravings on the wall. A what-not with china and other bric-a-brac; a small bookcase with leather-bound books. A carpet on the floor; a fire in the stove.* In the representational theater there is often less call for the audience's "imaginary forces" to work.

Furthermore, the actors do not openly acknowledge the presence of the audience, though they are always carefully gauging its response. They play to one another onstage, though they usually "cheat out" so that they remain more visible to the audience. The design elements attempt to convince the audience that everything it sees and hears is "the real thing."

Is it possible to blend the presentational and representational styles in one production? It happens frequently. *Death of a Salesman*, an essentially realistic play, is overlaid with a theatrical style. Willy's "visions" are nonrealistic conventions that allow the audience to see inside his troubled mind. Bertolt Brecht frequently achieves his "alienation effect" by changing styles abruptly to provoke the audience into thinking about the play's issues. Some Latino theater artists favor a style known as *magical realism*, which allows a play to shift between realism and

The classic lines of a Greek temple (The Hephaisteion [Theseion] shown here) contrast with the more complex architecture of the Brighton Pavilion, which opened in England during the Romantic era.

The Brighton Pavilion.

the fantastical in a heartbeat. Chilean playwright Egon Wolff's *Paper Flowers* employs this style for both thematic and theatrical purposes.

Directors may tell their designers that they want to do a "stylized" version of a play, and the designers understand that they are being asked for a nonrealistic approach. For instance, Giles Havergill "stylized" Chekhov's *The Seagull* for the Glasgow Citizens' Theater by having each actor sit facing the audience as he or she recited the lines of the first act as a poem. Conversely, John Barton's 1979 production of *The Merchant of Venice* for the Royal Shakespeare Company was both acted and designed as if it were a modern realistic play.

Styles often reflect the time or philosophy of the society that produces them. The deliberate movement and chanting of the Noh theater has its roots in Buddhist meditation, while the classic theater of India uses dance because drama was shaped by Siva, the Lord of the Dance. In contrast, Western realism is largely a synthesis of nineteenth-century scientific empiricism and the democratic revolution that swept Europe and America. Hence, its style mirrors the daily activities of ordinary people who are observed in a laboratory-like setting that meticulously recreates their environment. One can more fully appreciate a theater piece, printed or performed, by knowing some of the cultural contexts of both the age that produced it and the age in which it is currently performed.

The "Isms" are another way of categorizing various theatrical styles. "Ism" is a much-used suffix that denotes both a distinctive doctrine and the characteristic features associated with it. For instance, the Greeks believed in the ideal of a harmonious, well-ordered cosmos; therefore, they placed a premium on simplicity, balance, proportion, and symmetry—characteristics we associate with Classicism. Conversely, Romanticism embraces extremes, contrast, freedom of form and experimentation, all an outgrowth of the Romantic belief that humans should be free from restraint and rules. Compare the Greek temple with the picture of the Pavilion at Brighton, England, which was built at the height of the Romantic era. Specific Isms, such as Expressionism or Theatricalism, will be examined within the context of particular plays and in the discussion of historical contexts preceding each group of plays.

In addition to the so-called Isms, many movements within the theater have characteristic styles. They include the theater of the absurd, the epic theater, and the theater of cruelty. Many of these movements freely combine other forms. Brecht's epic theater, for instance, grew out of German Expressionism during World War I, yet it also employs Theatricalism, Realism, and Romanticism to achieve its ends.

Conventions

Conventions are theater's rules of the game. Think of a deck of playing cards, its various suits, face cards, number cards, and possibly jokers. Many kinds of games can be played with those same 52 cards. So, too, with theater. It begins with the same "cards": an idea (usually scripted), performers, a space, and an audience. The performers may or may not wear formal costumes, makeup, or masks. They may act in front of spectacular scenery or on a bare floor. They may address the audience directly or they may ignore the audience altogether. They may speak in prose or poetry, or they may not speak at all, choosing instead to sing, dance, or mime the idea. The performance space may be a multi-million-dollar theater or it may be a "black box" in a church basement. Curiously, the audience will accept the performers and the story they present no matter which of these options is exercised, if the performers are good at what they do and if the idea engages the audience. Recall that Coleridge defined the "willing suspension of disbelief" as the audience's ability to accept the illusion inherent in the theater event. It is the first convention of the theater and all others stem from it.

A convention is the agreement between the performers and the audience to accept whatever happens in the theater space as "believable"—though not necessarily realistic—for the duration of the play. Although he writes about conventions in the Chinese theater, Tao-Ching Hsu aptly summarizes the purpose and appeal of conventions in theaters throughout the world: "Conventions, once accepted, are no longer felt as such; they appear natural and do not distract the mind from other matters of the play."

Often we do not think about conventions as they happen: a brightly lit auditorium suddenly dims to blackness, a curtain rises, and we forget we are in a theater. We accept that we are suddenly in the court of the Chinese emperor Han, in a market in Nigeria, or in a hovel in South Africa. A play ends, the lights fade to black and suddenly Dustin Hoffman, not Willy Loman, is standing before us to receive our applause. At other times, the conventions are so startling that they force us to stop and consider their import. Many theater companies throughout Latin America encourage actors to engage their audiences in discussion of social issues within the context of a play; audiences are challenged to provide resolutions to problems.

The Japanese theater is especially rich in its use of nonrealistic conventions. For instance, in Kabuki an actor enters through the audience via a long runway (the *hanimichi*); he suddenly stops, elevates himself on one leg, and strikes an exaggerated pose (*mie*) for several seconds to allow the audience to reflect on his character and costume. (The use of the male pronoun here is deliberate: a convention of the Kabuki theater is that only men act, though there is now a women's Kabuki in Tokyo). To Westerners steeped in the conventions of realism, Kabuki's conventions might seem "hammy." Similarly, while experiencing their first realistic Western play, Japanese playgoers—accustomed to singing and a persistent musical accompaniment in their theater—might find it disconcerting that the actors speak only to each other in rather hushed tones. To study theater and its rich history throughout the world is to study its many conventions. As virtually every period we will consider has its own set of conventions, be it the Greek chorus or Indian *mudras* (hand gestures), we will include a brief summary of the most important "ground rules" for each.

Much of the most interesting experimental work undertaken in this century has applied the conventions of one culture to the theater works of another. Bertolt Brecht's work in the German theater in the 1930s borrowed techniques from the Chinese theater. Arianne Mnouchkine and her Paris-based *Théâtre du Soleil* often adopts conventions of Asian theater in its production of European classics; for example, Aeschylus's *The Oresteia* featured conventions from India's Kathakali dance theater. Conversely, Chinese actors, influenced by Miller's production of *Death of a Salesman* in Beijing in 1982, now avidly study American "method" acting and its realistic conventions.

Not all acts of theater are created alike, and a few trips to the theater will quickly acquaint you with the many performance styles available to theater artists. They are as rich and diverse as the people creating and viewing them are.

Biff confronts Willy and his "woman in Boston" in the Beijing production of Death of a Salesman, *directed by Arthur Miller in 1982. Read a review of this production in Chapter 7.*

Juliet Stevenson relied on her expressive face and physical presence as she performed the principal role in Federico García Lorca's Yerma at the National Theater of Great Britain in 1987.

CHAPTER 3

FROM THE PAGE TO THE STAGE

Theater Artists at Work

A theater production is the result of a collaboration of artists drawn from such disciplines as literature, performance, painting, architecture, fashion, dance, athletics, music, and technology. Together they produce an experience that is—in the ideal—superior to any single art. In this chapter we will consider the work of the actor, the playwright, the director, and the designers (scenic, costume, lighting, and sound). In each case their contributions to the theater will be examined in a historical context. And because they assess the quality of the artists' choices, the work of the critic is also discussed here. Most of the examples cited are, of necessity, taken from the Western theater, as their work is more readily accessible to us. Also, much theater in Asia is performed in a traditional manner that has been preserved for often hundreds of years. In Japan's Kabuki theater, for instance, actors are judged on their ability to re-create the performance of their predecessors rather than—as in the West—for their innovative choices.

Choices

When theater artists talk to each other, they often use phrases such as "I like your choices there." Stage directors exhort actors to "make bold choices," a costume designer researches fashion history to choose the right silhouette for a show, and a lighting designer sorts through sheets of gels (colored light filters) to select the right hue for a scene. Thus, *choice* is a crucial term for theater artists, just as plays are about human choices and their consequences.

Clear, innovative choices can heighten the theater experience, while predictable or ill-conceived ones can produce a long evening for everyone. These comments apply to a performed play, but what of the play on the page? Reading can be a richer experience if you think along with the artists who produce the play. Remember, a play script is only a blueprint for a production. In most cases dramatists write for professional artists who can take a script and produce something richer perhaps than the playwright imagined.

The Actor

Any discussion of theater artists begins with actors, not only because they are the most visible, but because they are the first artists of the theater. Actors were performing long before there were playwrights, designers, and directors. More importantly, the actor is the least dispensable artist in the theater. While playwrights, designers, and directors contribute to most productions, a solo performer improvising on a bare floor or street corner can create memorable theater.

Put simply, an actor is "one who performs or impersonates." (Note that the "-or" suffix is gender neutral and is used here to denote both male and female performers. Most women who act prefer to be called actors rather than actresses. As one put it, "If I were a physician you wouldn't call me a 'doctress!'") But "performs" and "impersonates" do not begin to define the reality of what the actor does. Charles Marowitz, a director and critic, writes that, "an actor is one who remembers" all of the emotions, sensory experiences, triumphs and defeats known to humanity. Ellen Burstyn, recalling her work at the Actors Studio in New York, has said, "Our work is much more dangerous than even that of an astronaut because we relive other people's pain."

Such comments remind us that the first actors were priests or shamans. To them fell the duty of healing their people. "Magic," in a very real way, was integral to their work, and perhaps we have retained some of that sense of the magical and mysterious as we watch actors transform themselves into other beings. But we must be careful not to overromanticize the actor. Despite the adulation and fortune that some actors enjoy, the truth is that acting is a rigorous, mostly frustrating, lonely, and poorly paid profession. About 90 percent of all professional actors in America are unemployed at any given time. When actors do work after weeks in the unemployment line, it is typically under trying conditions: long hours in dingy rehearsal halls, cramped dressing rooms, and separation from loved ones.

Still, there is no shortage of actors. Acting, as both a professional and amateur enterprise, holds an undeniable attraction for many people. We are "the most imitative of living creatures," declared Aristotle, which is to say that each of us brings a wealth of intuitive experience to the theater. Or as Marlon Brando puts it: "Acting is something people think they are incapable of, but they do it from morning to night."

Actor training—and therefore acting style—has changed considerably over the roughly twenty-six centuries since Thespis established the profession in ancient Greece. Traditionally, most approaches to acting fall into one of two broad categories: *external* (vocal and physical) technique and *internal* (emotion-centered) technique. Today a third designation is evolving: *integrated* actors who fuse the external and internal approaches. Whatever their technique, the goal remains constant for actors: to create memorable characters that engage audiences.

External actors work largely "from the outside in," that is, they begin with rigorous physical and vocal training, as the body and especially the voice are the actor's primary tools. Some actors are famous for their obsession with external details. Sir Laurence Olivier felt he must find the right "nose" for his character before he could come to grips with his inner reality. Virtually all of pre-twentieth-century drama necessitated an external approach. Enormous theaters, scripts whose poetry and song demanded an exceptional vocal range, conventions such as males playing women's roles, few or no rehearsals, an oratorical acting tradition, and many other factors demanded an external, or "technical," style. Voice, breathing, and elocution exercises were compulsory, as was training in dance, mime, acrobatics, juggling, swordplay, posture, and balance. Today many Western actors have added to their physical regimen martial arts and yoga, longtime staples of Asian training. Some theater traditions, such as the Japanese Kabuki and Peking opera, are exclusively external in their style, and it takes years for a performer to achieve proficiency. As storytelling remains an integral part of their theater, actors in Africa and Latin America still favor an external approach. However, the popularity of American film and television has encouraged actors around the world to include realistic, more internal performance methods in their training.

If the accounts of eyewitnesses are reasonably accurate, a basically external approach to acting in the West produced two thousand years of admirable actors, from Thespis in ancient Greece to Henry Irving in the late nineteenth century. However, there were times when external technique approached the ludicrous. Consider these instructions from *The Thespian Preceptor, or, A Full Display of the Scenic Art,* an 1810 acting text that promised "ample and easy instructions for treading the stage." When playing anger a male actor produces "a violent and sudden shake" and then he

opens the eyes and mouth very wide, draws down the eye brows, gives the countenance an air of wildness, draws back the elbows parallel with the sides, lifts up the open hand (his fingers together) to the height of the breast so that the palms face the dreadful object, as shields opposed against it. The heart beats violently; the breath is fetched quick and short, and the whole is thrown in a general tremor.

For women anger was simply indicated "by a violent shriek, which produces fainting." Strangely, this advice was intended to insure truthfulness and naturalness in performance. "Truthful," "natural," and especially "lifelike" are always relative terms when applied to acting and must be considered in light of the age in which they are used. Do you think that the acting style of a 1920s silent movie is as "natural" as that of a recent film with Tom Hanks or Gwyneth Paltrow?

External acting does not preclude strongly felt inner emotion or truth. Aristotle believed that "those who feel emotion are most convincing through natural sympathy with the characters they represent." Hamlet counsels his actors to "use all gently . . . let your own discretion be your tutor: suit the action to the word, the word to the action, with this special observance, that you o'erstep not the modesty of nature."

These comments by Aristotle and Shakespeare point the way toward *internal* acting, largely a modern and Western approach to performance. The plays of Ibsen and Chekhov demanded an intimacy in playing style (as well as playing spaces). Thus a subtler, internally based style emerged, largely under the teaching of Constantin Stanislavsky, cofounder of the Moscow Art Theater in 1897. Stanislavsky's theories—commonly known as "the System"—excited a young generation of American actors in the 1930s, first with the Group Theater (1931–1941) and later with the Actors Studio (1947) where the System became known as "the Method." Brando, Dustin Hoffman, and Meryl Streep are among the best-known Method actors. Although there are significant differences between the System (which relies on "total training") and the Method (which is almost exclusively internally based), both encourage actors to tap their inner resources by using *emotion memory*, among other things, to project themselves into the characters they play. Though the process is complex and often misunderstood, emotion memory asks actors to summon up memories of personal experiences and attendant emotions comparable to those of the scripted characters. For instance, an actor who plays Hamlet recalls the pain he experienced when a close relative or friend died. Theoretically, this triggers the appropriate response when he must grieve for the death of Old Hamlet. Internal actors can place too much emphasis on inner feeling, which can lead to self-indulgence and a breakdown of the vocal and physical demands of performance. In truth, both Stanislavsky and Lee Strasberg, who mentored both the Group Theater and the Actors Studio, stressed that actors must first develop the voice and body before advancing to the internal aspects of performance. The Russian master told his pupils that "you must have a strong, well-trained voice of pleasant, expressive timbre, perfect diction, plasticity of movement—without being a poseur—a face that is beautiful and mobile, a good figure, and expressive hands." (See Forum, "When Acting Is an Art.")

For centuries acting theorists have debated the degree to which actors themselves should "feel" the emotions of the characters they play. In 1770 the French philosopher and playwright Denis Diderot (1713–1784) argued that actors need not feel the emotions of their characters but only *seem* to feel them. For him, playing extreme emotion makes "middling actors." Paradoxically, he wrote that "in complete absence of sensibility [feeling] is the possibility of the sublime actor" because actors overcome by emotion—or, to use a popular phrase, "living their roles"—cannot effectively gauge the quality of their performances, much less control their voice and bodies.

Though it is neither necessary nor realistic for you to seek formal actor training, a familiarity with fundamental technique can enliven your reading and viewing experiences. Recall that actors must confront three texts: the *scripted text*, the *context* in which the characters find themselves, and ultimately the *subtext* (what the text actually implies). Consider also the *intentional text*; that is, the reason a character must say those lines at that point in time. For an instant acting lesson, say the simple line "Don't go." Now repeat the line as if:

1. Your lover is about to walk out the door after an argument.
2. Your roommate wants to drive to the store in the midst of a terrible storm.
3. Your child is trying to sneak off to play with friends before the chores are done.

Without much thought or training you probably came up with a good subtext for each situation. Your subtext ("the text beneath the text") for the first was probably "I love you, don't

FORUM

"When Acting Is an Art"

CONSTANTIN STANISLAVSKY

*Without question Constantin Stanislavsky (1863–1938) was the preeminent acting teacher of the twentieth century. Co-founder of the Moscow Art Theatre, he became its principal director and a leading actor. At the MAT, Stanislavsky developed his "System" for actor training over a number of years. His theories have been set down in a series of books—*An Actor Prepares, Building a Character, *and* Creating a Role—*which, collectively, represent one of the most comprehensive treatises on acting ever written. The books are written in the form of personal diaries by Kostya, an aspiring actor. Here, the director, Tortsov (Stanislavsky's fictional ego) responds to some scenes by young actors; his comments provide the foundation of the Stanislavsky System.*

Today we were called together to hear the Director's criticism of our performance. He said:

"Above all look for what is fine in art and try to understand it. Therefore, we shall begin by discussing the constructive elements of the test. There are only two moments worth noting; the first, when Maria threw herself down the staircase with the despairing cry of 'Oh, help me!' and the second, more extended in time, when Kostya Nazvanov said 'Blood, Iago, blood!' In both instances, you who were playing, and we who were watching, gave ourselves up completely to what was happening on the stage. Such successful moments, by themselves, we can recognize as belonging to the art of living a part."

"And what is this art?" I asked.

"You experienced it yourself. Suppose you state what you felt."

"I neither know nor remember," said I, embarrassed by Tortsov's praise.

"What! You do not remember your own inner excitement? You do not remember that your hands, your eyes and your whole body tried to throw themselves forward to grasp something; you do not remember how you bit your lips and barely restrained your tears?"

"Now that you tell me about what happened, I seem to remember my actions," I confessed.

"But without me you could not have understood the ways in which your feelings found expression?"

"No, I admit I couldn't."

"You were acting with your subconscious, intuitively?" he concluded.

"Perhaps. I do not know. But is that good or bad?"

"Very good, if your intuition carries you along the right path, and very bad if it makes a mistake," explained Tortsov. "During the exhibition performance it did not mislead you, and what you gave us in those few successful moments was excellent."

"Is that really true?" I asked.

"Yes, because the very best that can happen is to have the actor completely carried away by the play. Then regardless of his own will he lives the part, not noticing *how* he feels, not thinking about *what* he does, and it all moves of its own accord, subconsciously and intuitively. Salvini said: 'The great actor should be full of feeling, and especially he should feel the thing he is portraying. He must feel an emotion not only once or twice while he is studying his part, but to a greater or lesser degree every time he plays it, no matter whether it is the first or the thousandth time.' Unfortunately this is not within our control. Our subconscious is inaccessible to our consciousness. We cannot enter into that realm. If for any reason we do penetrate into it, then the subconscious becomes conscious and dies.

"The result is a predicament; we are supposed to create under inspiration; only our subconscious gives us inspiration; yet we apparently can use this subconscious only through our consciousness, which kills it.

"Fortunately there is a way out. We find the solution in an oblique instead of a direct approach. In the soul of a human being there are certain elements which are subject to consciousness and will. These accessible parts are capable in turn of acting on psychic processes that are involuntary.

"To be sure, this calls for extremely complicated creative work. It is carried on in part under the control of our consciousness, but a much more significant proportion is subconscious and involuntary.

"To rouse your subconscious to creative work there is a special technique. We must leave all that is in the fullest sense subconscious to nature, and address ourselves to what is within our reach. When the subconscious, when intuition, enters into our work we must know how not to interfere.

"One cannot always create subconsciously and with inspiration. No such genius exists in the world. Therefore our art teaches us first of all to create consciously and rightly, because that will best prepare the way for the blossoming of the subconscious, which is inspiration. The more you have of conscious creative moments in your role the more chance you will have of a flow of inspiration.

"'You may play well or you may play badly; the important thing is that you should play truly,' wrote Shchepkin to his pupil Shumski.

"To play truly means to be right, logical, coherent, to think, strive, feel and act in unison with your role.

"If you take all these internal processes, and adapt them to the spiritual and physical life of the person you are representing, we call that living the part. This is of supreme significance in creative work. Aside from the fact that it opens up avenues for inspiration, living the part helps the artist to carry out one of his main objectives. His job is not to present merely the external life of his character. He must fit his own human qualities to the life of this other person, and pour into it all of his own soul. The fundamental aim of our art is the creation of this inner life of a human spirit, and its expression in an artistic form.

"That is why we begin by thinking about the inner side of a role, and how to create its spiritual life through the help of the internal process of living the part. You must live it by actually experiencing feelings that are analogous to it, each and every time you repeat the process of creating it."

"Why is this subconscious so dependent on the conscious?" said I.

"It seems entirely normal to me," was the reply. "The use of steam, electricity, wind, water and other involuntary forces in nature is dependent on the intelligence of an engineer. Our subconscious power cannot function without its own engineer— our conscious technique. It is only when an actor feels that his inner and outer life on the stage is flowing naturally and normally, in the circumstances that surround him, that the deeper sources of his subconscious gently open, and from them come feelings we cannot always analyse. For a shorter or longer space of time they take possession of us whenever some inner instinct bids them. Since we do not understand this governing power, and cannot study it, we actors call it simply nature.

"But if you break the laws of normal organic life, and cease to function rightly, then this highly sensitive subconscious becomes alarmed, and withdraws. To avoid this, plan your role consciously at first, then play it truthfully. At this point realism and even naturalism in the inner preparation of a part is essential, because it causes your subconscious to work and induces outbursts of inspiration."

"From what you have said I gather that to study our art we must assimilate a psychological technique of living a part, and that this will help us to accomplish our main object, which is to create the life of a human spirit," Paul Shustov said.

"That is correct but not complete," said Tortsov. "Our aim is not only to create the life of a human spirit, but also to 'express it in a beautiful, artistic form.' An actor is under the obligation to live his part inwardly, and then to give to his experience an external embodiment. I ask you to note especially that the dependence of the body on the soul is particularly important in our school of art. *In order to express a most delicate and largely subconscious life it is necessary to have control of an unusually responsive, excellently prepared vocal and physical apparatus.* This apparatus must be ready instantly and exactly to reproduce most delicate and all but intangible feelings with great sensitiveness and directness. *That is why an actor of our type is obliged to work so much more than others,* both on his inner equipment, which creates the life of the part, and also on his outer physical apparatus, which should reproduce the results of the creative work of his emotions with precision.

"Even the externalizing of a role is greatly influenced by the subconscious. In fact no artificial, theatrical technique can even compare with the marvels that nature brings forth.

"I have pointed out to you today, in general outlines, what we consider essential. Our experience has led to a firm belief that only our kind of art, soaked as it is in the living experiences of human beings, can artistically reproduce the impalpable shadings and depths of life. Only such art can completely absorb the spectator and make him both understand and also inwardly experience the happenings on the stage, enriching his inner life, and leaving impressions which will not fade with time.

"Moreover, and this is of primary importance, *the organic bases of the laws of nature on which our art is founded will protect you in the future from going down the wrong path.* Who knows under what directors, or in what theatres, you will work? Not everywhere, not with everyone, will you find creative work based on nature. In the vast majority of theatres the actors and producers are constantly violating nature in the most shameless manner. But if you are sure of the limits of true art, and of the organic laws of nature, you will not go astray, you will be able to understand your mistakes and correct them. That is why a study of the foundations of our art is the beginning of the work of every student actor."

---

leave me, I can't live without you!" Perhaps your subtext for the second was "Don't be a fool, you could get killed," for the third possibly "You're in big trouble!" In each case there was a very specific reason (intention, objective, motivation, goal) for saying the line, that is, to salvage a love affair, to protect a friend, to admonish a child. It was Stanislavsky who advocated breaking scripts into a series of "beats" in which actors defined the moment-to-moment intentions of their characters, the external and internal obstacle(s) that might keep them from achieving the goal, and the tactics characters might use to overcome them. (*Beats*, by the way, actually derived from Stanislavsky's mispronunciation of the word *bit*, meaning "a little piece of the whole.")

Consider—as an actor might—a beat (the smallest unit of a scene) from *Death of a Salesman*. These lines open act 2; at first glance, there appears to be little conflict in the dialogue between Willy Loman and his wife:

WILLY. Wonderful coffee. Meal in itself.
LINDA. Can I make you some eggs?
WILLY. No. Take a breath.
LINDA. You look so rested, dear.

Early morning chitchat, no conflict, nothing happening, right? True, this is a moment of repose in the otherwise tempestuous Loman household. It signals the start of what Willy hopes
will be a brighter day, and it suggests precisely the kind of home life Linda wants. But consider
the given circumstances: the previous night ended in a noisy argument between Willy and his
son Biff; Willy has cursed Linda; Biff has discovered a length of rubber hose with which Willy
perhaps intends to kill himself. Given this context the small talk is loaded with subtext.
Willy's intentions are to placate Linda, to apologize for his gruff behavior. The compliment
about the coffee is his way of saying "Listen, I was out of line last night." As we see elsewhere
in the play, he is a proud man and apologies don't come easily. Thus his text ("Wonderful coffee") implies a subtext: "You're a good wife, I know it's been hard for you." In these lines Willy
must overcome not only Linda's hurt feelings but his own self-doubts. The kind words are his
tactics for doing so. Linda is motivated to save the Loman household. Her obstacles? His despondent behavior, his low self-esteem, her status as "only" a woman in a male-dominated
household. Her tactics? To get his mind off the problems, to make his favorite breakfast, to feed
his ego ("You look rested"). The subtext here is, "Everything will be all right. No need for you
to kill yourself." There is enormous urgency in Linda's tactics, as there must be in all well-written scenes. Many actors, acting teachers, and directors prefer the phrase "fight for" instead of
intentions and motivations because it imparts urgency. Directors challenge actors, "What are
you fighting for and what will you do to get it?" One of the challenges of acting is that there are
so many possible answers to these questions. This is where actors must finally make "choices"
to define their characters.

Beats evolve into "units" (usually a section of a scene), units become scenes, and scenes
become acts, the whole of which is defined by an overall intention. Stanislavsky called this
"the super objective," which he defined as "the whole stream of individual, minor objectives,
all the imaginative thoughts, feelings and actions of an actor." Director Harold Clurman uses
an anatomical metaphor—"the spine"—to denote the super objective. Willy Loman's spine
could be "to preserve my dignity" or "to make my sons love me," while Linda's may be "to save
Willy." You'll find reading a play a richer experience if you become sensitive to these divisions
and, more importantly, the intentions and obstacles confronting every character in the play.

The Playwright

If actors were the theater's first artists, playwrights were its first "stars," at least in classical
Greece, where the winning dramatist at the theater festivals was accorded honors normally reserved for state leaders and generals. In the Middle Ages playwrights were often members of
the clergy and thus enjoyed the sanction of the church, while in the Renaissance writers were
often subsidized by royalty. Under the patronage of James I, Shakespeare's acting company was
known as the King's Men, and Molière's actors were known as *Les Comédiens du Roi* because
Louis XIV so admired his plays. Asian monarchs also were benefactors to playwrights. Kalidasa
wrote in the court at Ujjian in India, and the emperors of the Yuan dynasty (1280–1368 B.C.E.)
housed artists who produced China's finest literary drama.

With some notable exceptions, playwrights have become less prominent in the modern
theater. The star system for actors, the ascendancy of the director, the current emphasis on
technological spectacle, not to mention competition from film and television, have conspired
to relegate the playwright to a less visible role in the theater. When was the last time you saw
a playwright on a TV talk show?

Although theater is a collaborative art, the playwright works alone, at least in the earliest
stages of creation. Even when the play is in rehearsals, the playwright is customarily a solitary
figure, seated in the dark, taking copious notes. When developing a new script, the playwright
often works closely with the director, but much of this is done away from the hurly-burly of re-

hearsal. Playwrights are indispensable for more than the obvious reason of providing a script; they are the very lifeblood of the theater because they create fresh material and offer new challenges for actors.

Franco Zeffirelli, the renowned film and stage director, identified the playwright's most elemental task in the credits of his film of *Romeo and Juliet:* "We would like to thank William Shakespeare, without whom we would have been at a loss for words." Providing "the words" is the playwright's most basic task. Some playwrights offer other "words" about their function. For Shakespeare the playwright is an inventor who

> in a fine frenzy rolling,
>
> Doth glance from heaven to earth, from earth to heaven;
>
> And as imagination bodies forth
>
> The forms of things unknown, the poet's pen
>
> Turns them into shapes, and gives to airy nothing
>
> A local habitation and a name.
>
> *A Midsummer Night's Dream,* 5.1.12–17

The playwright is first a teller of stories, one who creates a world, peoples it, and decides fates and fortunes. Little wonder that playwrights have been portrayed as gods—literally or metaphorically—in some plays such as Calderón's *The Great Theater of the World.*

For some playwrights, the exposition of the idea is the artist's primary task. Shaw defined the intellectual function of the playwright as he argued that the writer must "pick out the significant incidents from the chaos of daily happenings, and arrange them so their relation to one another becomes significant, thus changing us from bewildered spectators of a monstrous confusion to men intelligently conscious of the world and its destinies. This is the highest function that man can perform." For Spain's Federico García Lorca, arousing passion is the artist's paramount duty. Of the dramatist, Lorca would ask, "Are you incapable of expressing a person's anguish at the sea? Daren't you show the despair of soldiers who hate war?" Poland's Stanislaw Witkiewicz maintains the playwright must use the freedom of the artist "to create a whole whose meaning would be defined only by its purely scenic internal construction, and not by the demands of consistent psychology and action according to assumptions from real life." For Luis Valdez, patriarch of the Chicano theater, the playwright has the political duty to "inspire the audience to social action. Illuminate specific points about social problems." Kawamura Takeshi, an avant-garde playwright in Japan, argues that "there is now a strongly held conviction among artists that contemporary reality cannot be expressed in terms of a human subject. They examine the present, not through some uneasy alliance with the past, but through a fabricated notion of the future." At the other extreme, many modern playwrights, like Joyce Carol Oates, are returning to the theater's roots:

> In my writing for the theater, I always have in mind, as an undercurrent shaping and guiding the surface action, the ancient structure of drama as sacrificial rite. Stories are told not by us [i.e., playwrights] but by way of us—"drama" is our formal acknowledgement of this paradox, which underscores our common humanity. Obviously, this phenomenon involves not only the performers on stage but an audience as well, for there is no ritual without community, and, perhaps no community without ritual.

The playwright faces, of course, the purely pragmatic task, articulated here by John Osborne, who revolutionized the British theater in 1956 when he wrote *Look Back in Anger:* "Part of my job is to try and keep people interested and in their seats for about two and half hours." This is not an easy task, and if the playwright does not accomplish this goal, the more lofty aspirations expressed by Osborne's colleagues are moot.

There is no formula by which playwrights begin to create a script, though almost all are driven by what playwright Sam Smiley calls the "creative compulsion." "Inspiration" is too

simple an explanation for this impulse. Usually something more concrete beckons the play-wright, such as:

- an observed incident (Chekhov kept notebooks full of such things);
- a preexisting story (Bernard Shaw said of Shakespeare, "He told great stories—providing someone told them to him first");
- a news clipping (*Equus* evolved from a two-paragraph story that made Peter Shaffer want to know what could have prompted a bizarre act by a young man);
- an image (Milcha Scott Sanchez was shown a picture of a friend's family, the faces of whom so haunted her that she eventually wrote *Roosters*);
- a conversation (Mbongeni Ngema heard someone ask, "What if Christ were black and he returned to South Africa for 'the Second Coming'?" The question inspired *Woza Albert!*).

Of course, many plays stem from autobiographical experiences: Tennessee Williams's *The Glass Menagerie* and Eugene O'Neill's *Long Day's Journey into Night* are among the most prominent examples. Other works evolve from actor improvisations based on their experiences, as did the Broadway musical *A Chorus Line*.

Whatever the source of their inspiration, playwrights have a multitude of choices as they shape their scripts. External realities such as current tastes and conventions often dictate a playwright's choices. Sophocles had little option but to write in the classical style while em-ploying the conventions of his time. Today playwrights have over 2,500 years of theater tradi-tion to guide them, though Aristotle's six elements of drama still constitute the playwright's essential tools. *Death and the King's Horseman* fuses Sophoclean dialectics, the thesis play, and traditional African storytelling and rituals. Luis Valdez's short play, "*No saco nada de la escuela*" is equal parts *commedia dell'arte*, Aristophanic satire, political harangue, and Mexican folk play. And there are plays, such as Heiner Müller's *Medeaplay*, written without regard to tradi-tional forms to expand the boundaries of theater through experimentation. Never in the his-tory of the theater have playwrights enjoyed such a rich variety of options as they prepare to write.

A finished script is usually the product of a lengthy period of note taking, character sketches, and jotting down scraps of dialogue. Once these suggest a pattern, the playwright usu-ally writes a scenario, or outline, of the plot. Aristotle's advice that the playwright "first sketch [the story's] general outline, and then fill in the episodes and amplify the detail" is as appropri-ate now as it was 2,300 years ago. The first draft is often given a reading—sometimes a staged reading in which actors move about—so that the playwright can hear the words spoken aloud, and so that audience reactions can be measured. Actors are usually quite adept at giving feed-back about the "speakability" of dialogue. But ultimately it is the solitary playwright who shapes and reshapes the script before it is produced. And then the process begins anew in rehearsals when the director, cast, and designers may contribute to the text that the audience hears open-ing night. The response of the audience and critics may dictate further revisions in the script.

Among the demands that make playwriting so challenging are the necessities of the medium itself. Thornton Wilder, who won Pulitzer Prizes for both drama (*Our Town*, 1938; *The Skin of Our Teeth*, 1941) and fiction (*The Bridge of San Luis Rey*, 1927), identifies several "fundamental conditions" that not only distinguish drama from other forms of writing, but which prescribe the playwright's choices. (See Forum, "Some Thoughts on Playwriting.")

First, **theater is a collaborative art** and therefore demands that the playwright produce a work that is "playable." While modern technology can accommodate the most extraordinary visions of a playwright—for example, the descent of a helicopter onstage in *Miss Saigon*—there is still the necessity of inventing a world, a story, and characters that will first inspire actors, di-rectors, and designers, then an audience. In addition to giving actors strong motivations for their characters, the playwright must offer each character a distinctive voice. Yet a playwright must be more than a "human tape recorder." Drama is not merely life reproduced (cameras and recorders can do that), but life interpreted more intensely. Finding the balance between the lifelike and the theatrical is among the playwright's most formidable tasks.

Wilder says that **drama must appeal to the "group-mind,"** which does not mean that one must appeal to the lowest common denominator. The dramatist must acknowledge that the

FORUM

"Some Thoughts on Playwriting"

THORNTON WILDER

Thornton Wilder (1897–1975), a Professor of Philosophy at the University of Chicago, was one of America's most decorated writers, winning Pulitzer Prizes for the novel, The Bridge of San Luis Rey, *and drama,* Our Town *and* The Skin of Our Teeth. *This essay, written in 1941, addresses the concerns of both the narrative and the dramatic writer.*

Four fundamental conditions of the drama separate it from the other arts. Each of these conditions has its advantages and disadvantages, each requires a particular aptitude from the dramatist, and from each there are a number of instructive consequences to be derived. These conditions are:

1. The theatre is an art which reposes upon the work of many collaborators.
2. It is addressed to the group-mind.
3. It is based upon a pretense and its very nature calls out a multiplication of pretenses.
4. Its action takes place in a perpetual present time.

I. THE THEATER IS AN ART WHICH REPOSES UPON THE WORK OF MANY COLLABORATORS

We have been accustomed to think that a work of art is by definition the product of one governing selecting will.

A landscape by Cézanne consists of thousands of brushstrokes, each commanded by one mind. *Paradise Lost* and *Pride and Prejudice*, even in cheap frayed copies, bear the immediate and exclusive message of one intelligence.

It is true that in musical performance we meet with intervening executants, but the element of intervention is slight compared to that which takes place in drama. Illustrations:

1. One of the finest productions of *The Merchant of Venice* in our time showed Sir Henry Irving as Shylock, a noble, wronged, and indignant being, of such stature that the Merchants of Venice dwindled before him into irresponsible schoolboys. He was confronted in court by a gracious, even queenly, Portia, Miss Ellen Terry. At the Odéon in Paris, however, Gémier played Shylock as a vengeful and hysterical buffoon, confronted in court by a Portia who was a *gamine* from the Paris streets with

a lawyer's quill three feet long over her ear; at the close of the trial scene Shylock was driven screaming about the auditorium, behind the spectators' backs and onto the stage again, in a wild Elizabethan revel. Yet for all their divergences both were admirable productions of the play.

2. If there were ever a play in which fidelity to the author's requirements were essential in the representation of the principal rôle, it would seem to be Ibsen's *Hedda Gabler*, for the play is primarily an exposition of her character. Ibsen's directions read: "Enter from the left Hedda Gabler. She is a woman of twenty-nine. Her face and figure show great refinement and distinction. Her complexion is pale and opaque. Her steel-gray eyes express an unruffled calm. Her hair is of an attractive medium brown, but is not particularly abundant; and she is dressed in a flowing loose-fitting morning gown." I once saw Eleonora Duse in this rôle. She was a woman of sixty and made no effort to conceal it. Her complexion was pale and transparent. Her hair was white, and she was dressed in a gown that suggested some medieval empress in mourning. And the performance was very fine.

One may well ask: why write for the theatre at all? Why not work in the novel where such deviations from one's intentions cannot take place?

There are two answers:

1. The theatre presents certain vitalities of its own so inviting and stimulating that the writer is willing to receive them in compensation for this inevitable variation from an exact image.

2. The dramatist through working in the theatre gradually learns not merely to take account of the presence of the collaborators, but to derive advantage from them; and he learns, above all, to organize the play in such a way that its strength lies not in appearances beyond his control, but in the succession of events and in the unfolding of an idea, in narration.

The gathered audience sits in a darkened room, one end of which is lighted. The nature of the transaction at which it is gazing is a succession of events illustrating a general idea—the stirring of the idea; the gradual feeding out of information; the shock and countershock of circumstances; the flow of action; the interruption of action; the moments of allusion to earlier events; the preparation of surprise, dread, or delight—all that is the author's and his alone.

For the reasons to be discussed later—the expectancy of the group-mind, the problem of time on the stage, the absence of the narrator, the element of pretense—the theatre carries the art of narration to a higher power than the novel or the epic poem. The theatre is unfolding action and in the disposition of events the authors may exercise a governance so complete that the distortions effected by the physical appearance of actors, by

(continued)

the fancies of scene-painters and the misunderstandings of directors, fall into relative insignificance. It is just because the theatre is an art of many collaborators, with the constant danger of grave misinterpretation, that the dramatist learns to turn his attention to the laws of narration, its logic and its deep necessity of presenting a unifying idea stronger than its mere collection of happenings. The dramatist must be by instinct a storyteller.

There is something mysterious about the endowment of the storyteller. Some very great writers possessed very little of it, and some others, lightly esteemed, possessed it in so large a measure that their books survive down the ages, to the confusion of severer critics. Alexandre Dumas had it to an extraordinary degree; while Melville, for all his splendid quality, had it barely sufficiently to raise his work from the realm of nonfiction. It springs, not, as some have said, from an aversion to general ideas, but from an instinctive coupling of idea and illustration; the idea, for a born storyteller, can only be expressed imbedded in its circumstantial illustration. The myth, the parable, the fable are the fountainhead of all fiction and in them is seen most clearly the didactic, moralizing employment of a story. Modern taste shrinks from emphasizing the central idea that hides behind the fiction, but it exists there nevertheless, supplying the unity to fantasizing, and offering a justification to what otherwise we would repudiate as mere arbitrary contrivance, pretentious lying, or individualistic emotional association-spinning. For all their magnificent intellectual endowment, George Meredith and George Eliot were not born storytellers; they chose fiction as the vehicle for their reflections, and the passing of time is revealing their error in that choice. Jane Austen was pure storyteller and her works are outlasting those of apparently more formidable rivals. The theatre is more exacting than the novel in regard to this faculty and its presence constitutes a force which compensates the dramatist for the deviations which are introduced into his work by the presence of his collaborators.

The chief of these collaborators are the actors.

The actor's gift is a combination of three separate faculties or endowments. Their presence to a high degree in any one person is extremely rare, although the ambition to possess them is common. Those who rise to the height of the profession represent a selection and a struggle for survival in one of the most difficult and cruel of the artistic activities. The three endowments that compose the gift are observation, imagination, and physical coordination.

1. An observant and analyzing eye for all modes of behavior about us, for dress and manner, and for the signs of thought and emotion in one's self and in others.

2. The strength of imagination and memory whereby the actor may, at the indication in the author's text, explore his store of observations and represent the details of appearance and the intensity of the emotions—joy, fear, surprise, grief, love, and hatred, and through imagination extend them to intenser degrees and to differing characterizations.

3. A physical coordination whereby the force of these inner realizations may be communicated to voice, face, and body.

An actor must *know* the appearances and the mental states; he must *apply* his knowledge to the rôle; and he must physically *express* his knowledge. Moreover, his concentration must be so great that he can effect this representation under conditions of peculiar difficulty—in abrupt transition from the nonimaginative conditions behind the stage; and in the presence of fellow actors who may be momentarily destroying the reality of the action.

A dramatist prepares the characterization of his personages in such a way that it will take advantage of the actor's gift.

Characterization in a novel is presented by the author's dogmatic assertion that the personage was such, and by an analysis of the personage with generally an account of his or her past. Since in the drama, this is replaced by the actual presence of the personage before us and since there is no occasion for the intervening all-knowing author to instruct us as to his or her inner nature, a far greater share is given in a play to (1) highly characteristic utterances and (2) concrete occasions in which the character defines itself under action and (3) a conscious preparation of the text whereby the actor may build upon the suggestions in the rôle according to his own abilities.

Characterization in a play is like a blank check which the dramatist accords to the actor for him to fill in—not entirely blank, for a number of indications of individuality are already there, but to a far less definite and absolute degree than in the novel.

The dramatist's principal interest being the movement of the story, he is willing to resign the more detailed aspects of characterization to the actor and is often rewarded beyond his expectation.

The sleepwalking scene from *Macbeth* is a highly compressed selection of words whereby despair and remorse rise to the surface of indirect confession. It is to be assumed that had Shakespeare lived to see what the genius of Sarah Siddons could pour into the scene from that combination of observation, self-knowledge, imagination, and representational skill, even he might have exclaimed, "I never knew I wrote so well!"

II. THE THEATRE IS AN ART ADDRESSED TO A GROUP-MIND

Painting, sculpture, and the literature of the book are certainly solitary experiences; and it is likely that most people would agree that the audience seated shoulder to shoulder in a concert hall is not an essential element in musical enjoyment.

But a play presupposes a crowd. The reasons for this go deeper than (1) the economic necessity for the support of the play and (2) the fact that the temperament of actors is proverbially dependent on group attention.

It rests on the fact that (1) the pretense, the fiction, on the stage would fall to pieces and absurdity without the support accorded to it by a crowd, and (2) the excitement induced by pretending a fragment of life is such that it partakes of ritual and festival, and requires a throng.

Similarly the fiction that royal personages are of a mysteriously different nature from other people requires audiences, levées, and processions for its maintenance. Since the beginnings of society, satirists have occupied themselves with the descriptions of kings and queens in their intimacy and delighted in showing how the prerogatives of royalty become absurd when the crowd is not present to extend to them the enhancement of an imaginative awe.

The theatre partakes of the nature of festival. Life imitated is life raised to a higher power. In the case of comedy, the vitality of these pretended surprises, deceptions, and *contretemps* becomes so lively that before a spectator, solitary or regarding himself as solitary, the structure of so much event would inevitably expose the artificiality of the attempt and ring hollow and unjustified; and in the case of tragedy, the accumulation of woe and apprehension would soon fall short of conviction. All actors know the disturbing sensation of playing before a handful of spectators at a dress rehearsal or performance where only their interest in pure craftsmanship can barely sustain them. During the last rehearsals the phrase is often heard: "This play is hungry for an audience."

Since the theatre is directed to a group-mind, a number of consequences follow:

1. A group-mind presupposes, if not a lowering of standards, a broadening of the fields of interest. The other arts may presuppose an audience of connoisseurs trained in leisure and capable of being interested in certain rarefied aspects of life. The dramatist may be prevented from exhibiting, for example, detailed representations of certain moments in history that require specialized knowledge in the audience, or psychological states in the personages which are of insufficient general interest to evoke self-identification in the majority. In the Second Part of Goethe's *Faust* there are long passages dealing with the theory of paper money. The exposition of the nature of misanthropy (so much more drastic than Molière's) in Shakespeare's *Timon of Athens* has never been a success. The dramatist accepts this limitation in subject matter and realizes that the group-mind imposes upon him the necessity of treating material understandable by the larger number.

2. It is the presence of the group-mind that brings another requirement to the theatre—forward movement.

Maeterlinck said that there was more drama in the spectacle of an old man seated by a table than in the majority of plays offered to the public. He was juggling with the various meanings in the word "drama." In the sense whereby drama means the intensified concentration of life's diversity and significance he may well have been right; if he meant drama as a theatrical representation before an audience he was wrong. Drama on the stage is inseparable from forward movement, from action.

Many attempts have been made to present Plato's dialogues, Gobineau's fine series of dialogues, *La Renaissance*, and the *Imaginary Conversations* of Landor; but without success. Through some ingredient in the group-mind, and through the sheer weight of anticipation involved in the dressing-up and the assumption of fictional rôles, an action is required, and an action that is more than a mere progress in argumentation and debate.

III. THE THEATRE IS A WORLD OF PRETENSE

It lives by conventions: a convention is an agreed-upon falsehood, a permitted lie.

Illustrations: Consider at the first performance of the *Medea*, the passage where Medea meditates the murder of her children. An anecdote from antiquity tells us that the audience was so moved by this passage that considerable disturbance took place.

The following conventions were involved:

1. Medea was played by a man.
2. He wore a large mask on his face. In the lip of the mask was an acoustical device for projecting the voice. On his feet he wore shoes with soles and heels half a foot high.
3. His costume was so designed that it conveyed to the audience, by convention: woman of royal birth and oriental origin.
4. The passage was in metric speech. All poetry is an "agreed-upon falsehood" in regard to speech.
5. The lines were sung in a kind of recitative. All opera involves this "permitted lie" in regard to speech.

Modern taste would say that the passage would convey much greater pathos if a woman "like Medea" had delivered it—with an uncovered face that exhibited all the emotions she was undergoing. For the Greeks, however, there was no pretense that Medea was on the stage. The mask, the costume, the mode of declamation, were a series of signs which the spectator interpreted and reassembled in his own mind. Medea was being recreated within the imagination of each of the spectators.

The history of the theatre shows us that in its greatest ages the stage employed the greatest number of conventions. The stage is fundamental pretense and it thrives on the acceptance of that fact and in multiplication of additional pretenses. When it tries to assert that the personages in the action "really are," really inhabit such and such rooms, really suffer such and such emotions, it loses rather than gains credibility. The modern world is inclined to laugh condescendingly at the fact that in the plays of Racine and Corneille the gods and heroes of antiquity were dressed like the courtiers under Louis XIV; that in the Elizabethan age scenery was replaced by placards notifying the audience of the location; and that a whip in the hand and a jogging motion of the body indicated that a man was on horseback in the Chinese theatre; these devices did not spring from naïveté, however, but from the vitality of the public imagination in those days and from an instinctive feeling as to where the essential and where the inessential lay in drama.

The convention has two functions:

1. It provokes the collaborative activity of the spectator's imagination; and
2. It raises the action from the specific to the general.

This second aspect is of even greater importance than the first.

If Juliet is represented as a girl "very like Juliet"—it was not merely a deference to contemporary prejudices that assigned this rôle to a boy in the Elizabethan age—moving about in "real" house with marble staircases, rugs, lamps, and furniture, the impression is irresistibly conveyed that these events happened to this one girl, in one place, at one moment in time. When the play is staged as Shakespeare intended it, the bareness of the stage releases the events from the particular and the experience of Juliet partakes of that of all girls in love, in every time, place, and language.

(continued)

The stage continually strains to tell this generalized truth and it is the element of pretense that reinforces it. Out of the lie, the pretense, of the theatre proceeds a truth more compelling than the novel can attain, for the novel by its own laws is constrained to tell of an action that "once happened"—"once upon a time."

IV. THE ACTION ON THE STAGE TAKES PLACE IN A PERPETUAL PRESENT TIME

Novels are written in the past tense. The characters in them, it is true, are represented as living moment by moment their present time, but the constant running commentary of the novelist ("Tess slowly descended into the valley"; "Anna Karenina laughed") inevitably conveys to the reader the fact that these events are long since past and over.

The novel is a past reported in the present. On the stage it is always now. This confers upon the action an increased vitality which the novelist longs in vain to incorporate into his work.

This condition in the theatre brings with it another important element:

In the theatre we are not aware of the intervening storyteller. The speeches arise from the characters in an apparently pure spontaneity.

A play is what takes place.

A novel is what one person tells us took place.

A play visibly represents pure existing. A novel is what one mind, claiming to omniscience, asserts to have existed.

Many dramatists have regretted this absence of the narrator from the stage, with his point of view, his powers of analyzing the behavior of the characters, his ability to interfere and supply further facts about the past, about simultaneous actions not visible on the stage, and above *all* his function of pointing the moral and emphasizing the significance of the action. In some periods of the theatre he has been present as chorus, or prologue and epilogue, or as raisonneur. But surely this absence constitutes an additional force to the form, as well as an additional tax upon the writer's skill. It is the task of the dramatist so to coordinate his play, through the selection of episodes and speeches, that though he is himself not visible, his point of view and his governing intention will impose themselves on the spectator's attention, not as dogmatic assertion or motto, but as self-evident truth and inevitable deduction.

Imaginative narration—the invention of souls and destinies—is to a philosopher an all but indefensible activity.

Its justification lies in the fact that the communication of ideas from one mind to another inevitably reaches the point where exposition passes into illustration, into parable, metaphor, allegory, and myth.

It is no accident that when Plato arrived at the height of his argument and attempted to convey a theory of knowledge and a theory of the structure of man's nature he passed over into storytelling, into the myths of the Cave and the Charioteer; and the great religious teachers have constantly had recourse to the parable as a means of imparting their deepest intuitions.

The theatre offers to imaginative narration its highest possibilities. It has many pitfalls and its very vitality betrays it into service as mere diversion and the enhancement of insignificant matter; but it is well to remember that it was the theatre that rose to the highest place during those epochs that aftertime has chosen to call "great ages" and that the Athens of Pericles and the reigns of Elizabeth, Philip II, and Louis XIV were also the ages that gave to the world the greatest dramas it has known.

theater—largely by economic necessity—must appeal to a broader spectrum of society than, say, a novelist who can find a niche among a relatively small number of readers. The playwright who chooses too esoteric a subject, who renders characters with whom the majority cannot identify, or whose language obscures communication, risks oblivion. Consider the fate of Luis Valdez's *Zoot Suit*. Based on its phenomenal success in California, the play, about Mexican-Americans in Los Angeles, was taken to New York in 1980. It soon closed, largely because Broadway audiences, including Hispanics, did not identify with the particulars of Mexican-American life and language across the continent. Many small theaters target selective audiences with the specialized types of work they produce—a healthy and necessary thing. But both commercial and regional not-for-profit theaters still must build broadly based support for their work. Playwrights are aware of this fact-of-theater-life, though some argue that accommodating the middle ground diminishes risk taking. Helene Keyssar discusses this dilemma in *Feminist Theatre* (1985). Her remarks apply to other minority voices in the theater:

> The relationship of feminist drama to commerce and public attention in many ways follows a predictable pattern. While some of the most innovative and challenging plays by feminists are produced in obscure venues and are heralded by a relatively small group of supporters, the dramas by women that have achieved commercial success . . . tend to take fewer theatrical risks and to be less threatening to middle-class audiences than those performed on the fringe of the theater establishment.

No wonder that writing plays in our modern society is often a frustrating experience.

Luis Valdez's Zoot Suit *was the first Broadway play written by a Mexican-American. Edward James Olmos played El Pachuco, a mythological figure in Chicano lore.*

Wilder's final point is perhaps his most important: **in the theater action "takes place in a perpetual present time."** Although "perpetual present time" in theater may foster greater urgency than the novel, which may be read leisurely over a longer period, that time is quite finite. While there are successful lengthy plays—uncut, *Hamlet* runs over four hours—audiences rarely tolerate more than about two and a half hours in the theater. According to their cultural traditions, Asian audiences are more amenable to longer works. The ten-act play is popular in India, and Japanese audiences often spend eight hours at Kabuki plays.

As if the internal demands of playwriting were not enough, external pressures also challenge dramatists. Today it is very expensive to produce a play. A two-character play with a single set can cost hundreds of thousands of dollars to mount on Broadway. Playwrights know that many producers will not consider a play unless it has a limited number of characters and sets. Unfortunately, this can dictate many choices playwrights make, as does the knowledge that most American actors are trained in some variation of Method acting; hence, the current emphasis on the small cast, and realistic plays. In many countries in Europe and Asia, theater is often heavily subsidized by state funds, which allows for greater risk taking. Playwrights can write for established companies who employ a number of actors and designers. They can thus "think bigger." England's Royal Shakespeare Company, which is government subsidized, could afford to develop its famed nine-hour adaptation of Charles Dickens's novel *Nicholas Nickleby*, a project that used almost thirty actors. Fortunately, the growth of regional theater companies in America since the 1960s has helped address this problem. Because production costs are considerably lower in regional theaters, which often employ a stable of actors, directors, and designers working in a single theater, they can afford to develop more ambitious projects that commercial producers cannot consider. Most regional theaters develop at least one new script a year, and some—for instance, the Actors Theater of Louisville (Kentucky)—make the production of new plays their highest priority. Consequently, America's current generation of playwrights are aligned with theaters beyond New York: Sam Shepard with the Magic Theater in San Francisco, David Mamet with the Goodman Theater in Chicago, and Beth Henley with the Dallas Theater Center. Universities and colleges also foster the development of new plays by both established and emerging playwrights because they can offer inexpensive productions in an atmosphere where the playwright receives useful feedback on the play. It is no longer the case that commercial producers audition their work in the provinces; today, not-for-profit theaters produce new works that then may transfer to commercial houses on Broadway. This is among the healthiest developments in the contemporary American theater and its new generation of playwrights.

The Director

Although stage directors were, historically, among the last artists to enter the theater, they have become a potent force in shaping a production. In theory, directors are meant to be the intermediaries between the script and the audience. However, they often rival writers, to the point that we glibly speak of "Brook's *Dream*," when we actually mean Peter Brook's production of Shakespeare's *A Midsummer Night's Dream* by the Royal Shakespeare Company. Thoughtful directorial interpretation, which may border on invention, can be so illuminating that audiences feel as if they are seeing a new play and therefore append the director's name to the title. At another extreme, directors may impose their vision on a script to the point that it is something other than what the playwright wrote. This directorial bent runs the gamut from putting a spiked-hair Hamlet on roller skates to restructuring or rewriting the play, as Charles Marowitz did with *Othello* in 1972. He incorporated material from the writings of the radical Black Panthers, cast a black man as Iago, and used a script comprising only one-third of Shakespeare's writing. He billed his production as *An Othello* to emphasize that it was an experiment. In this case, Marowitz functioned as an *auteur*, that is, an author-director who creates a new work and has complete control over its realization in production.

Stage direction has evolved slowly throughout the history of the theater. In ancient Greece, playwrights themselves worked with the actors, though a *didaskalos* ("instructor") was often employed to teach specific skills. Aeschylus himself was a respected actor and choreographer, and Sophocles was admired for his ability to coach his choruses' interpretation of the lines. In the Middle Ages the great cycle plays were often staged under the watchful eye of a *maître de jeu* ("play master") who was likely more a logistics coordinator than a director. Shakespeare and Molière not only advised the actors in their companies, but also performed with them. In the eighteenth and nineteenth centuries acting companies were led by an "actor-manager," usually a star who organized the company and oversaw the few rehearsals given a play. Most "directing" consisted of working out entrances and exits, as well as stage positions. A few actor-managers are noteworthy because they attempted to bring a unified interpretation and ensemble acting to their companies. England's David Garrick (1717–1779) and Germany's Caroline Neuber (1697–1760) were visionaries; Garrick asked his actors to read the entire play before it was performed, and Neuber required strict rehearsal discipline. At the Weimar Court Theater in Germany, Johann Wolfgang von Goethe (1789–1832) led casts in discussions of the script and rehearsed them on a "checkerboard" stage to improve movement and composition.

By the mid–nineteenth century the theater clearly needed an artist whose sole responsibility was to coordinate the many artistic elements that composed the production. The so-called father of stage directors was a bona fide duke, Georg II, who ruled the German duchy of Saxe-Meiningen. As head of state he commanded its artistic resources while pursuing his passion to create theater. Nothing went onstage that did not emanate from his vision of a play. When the duke staged Shakespeare's *Julius Caesar*, he visited Italy to research architecture and Roman apparel to insure the proper look for the play. The duke meticulously drilled his actors, from leads to extras, in lengthy rehearsals to ensure a unified interpretation of the play. The result was an ensemble effort, by both the actors and the support artists, which the theater world had rarely seen.

In May 1874 the Meiningen Company performed in Berlin and forever changed the way in which plays were presented in the West. Fifteen years later the company traveled to Russia, where it was seen by Stanislavsky, who applied many of the Meiningen techniques to his productions of the Moscow Art Theater. By 1900 theater production was firmly in the hands of such directors as Augustine Daly and David Belasco in America, André Antoine and Jacques Copeau in France, Harley Granville-Barker and Frank Benson in England, and, of course, Stanislavsky in Russia. Directing was formerly a male-dominated position, but Margaret Webster, Eva Le Gallienne, and Cheryl Crawford did much to open the doors for women in the 1940s when they founded the American Repertory Theater. Today the names of such directors as Trevor Nunn, Ariane Mnouchkine, Anne Bogart, Peter Stein, Lloyd Richards, Joanne Akalaitis, Liviu Ciulai, and Julie Taymor can attract Western theater patrons as easily as the names of top playwrights and actors. (See Forum, "Julie Taymor on Directing *The Lion King*.")

The stage director has also become a potent force in non-Western theater. In Asia, the "master teacher" functioned as a director for hundreds of years, but in this century a number of influential directors have emerged who have revitalized not only their native theater, but in many cases that of the West. Japan's Tadashi Suzuki is perhaps the best known of these, but we can turn to India, where Ebrahim Alkazi directed both classical Indian texts (*Andha Yug*) and Western masterpieces (*King Lear*) in Hindi and Urdu at the Bombay Unit Theater and later at National School of Drama in Delhi. In South Africa playwrights such as Athol Fugard and Mbongeni Ngema have also established reputations as directors; Gibson Kente, the country's first black independent director (1967), was unrivaled as a theatrical entrepreneur for twenty-five years. Nigeria's Zulu Sofala, also a playwright, is perhaps Africa's preeminent female director. She fuses magic, myth, and ritual to explore conflicts between traditionalism and modernism (and, coincidentally, she is noted for a memorable staging of *Pierre Pathelin*). Ludwick Margulies (Mexico), Oscar Ferrigno (Argentina), Sergio Corrieri (Cuba), Rene Márqúes (Puerto Rico), and Earl Warner (Barbados) are respected, and particularly innovative, directors from Latin America and the Caribbean.

Despite their considerable influence on the stage, theater directors do not necessarily enjoy the absolute power of film directors, who can choose exactly every image and sound they wish the audience to see and hear. Once the curtain rises in the theater, stage directors relinquish their power to the actors and the audience (which might choose to look at the spear-carrier in the back row).

Though directors wear many hats, they have four primary tasks as they guide a play to opening night:

1. Devising the Directorial Concept   Directors may or may not choose the plays they stage. In the commercial theater financial producers most often select the script and then hire a director to stage it. Permanent companies usually employ an *artistic director*, who is responsible for selecting the plays in a given season. In many cases, however, directors propose a play because they have a strong attraction to its message, writing style, period, or a particular challenge the play presents. Even when directors are hired to stage a play someone else has chosen, they usually accept the offer because they have some affinity for the play.

Long before the play is cast, the director studies the play. In some ways the director must know the play better than the playwright does. This necessitates considerable research on the play; the playwright and his or her style; the period in which it was written; the period in which it is set; the philosophical, historical, social, political and perhaps religious attitudes that shaped it; its production history; and commentaries by critics and scholars. Some plays demand a particular expertise. For instance, when directors work on a period play, such as Aphra Behn's *The Rover*, they must know as much as possible about life in the Restoration era. Not only must they know how a gentleman took snuff or how a lady flirted with a fan, they must know why these things were strategies in the romantic games people played. Again, we are talking about context and "given circumstances," terms that are as important to the director as to the actor.

Once directors have considered the myriad possibilities a play offers, they develop a *concept* for the production, that is, an interpretation of the play and the means to express it. The concept usually works on two levels, internal and external. Internally, the director—like the actor—looks for the central idea that holds the play together. One director might say that the super objective for *A Midsummer Night's Dream* is "humans act foolishly in their pursuit of love and power," another might believe that it exists "to celebrate the human imagination," while a third might conclude that as "an enchanted fairy tale it must only amuse." The directorial concept narrows the field of choices for the performers and designers, thereby allowing them to

F O R U M

"Julie Taymor on Directing *The Lion King*"

Julie Taymor, director and designer of the Broadway production of The Lion King, *gives the following account of casting procedure and rehearsals for that production.*

CASTING

As director, casting the show became my primary concern. Of the thirteen principal roles, seven of the actors who had participated in the August or February worskshops were asked to be in the production. Obviously this was a terrific advantage. We would know, to a degree, what we would be getting, and the actors would have a jump-start on their parts. They would also know what they were getting into. The last six roles took four to five months to cast. The criteria for the principals was to look for actors who act, sing, and move well—not a small order. During auditions, it is also vital for me to imagine what an actor will look like wearing a mask. Is the shape of the head powerful enough to carry the design?

I also brought puppets to auditions to see how performers would look in relation to specific puppets and how they would respond when asked to animate an inanimate object. And though performers would not be totally immersed within the puppets nor hidden behind the masks, they would have to be willing to accept that the audience is not going to be looking at them alone. Attitude is a very important part of my casting decision. I want an actor who is going to enjoy the challenge and not view it as a burden.

Rather than expressly hiring puppeteers, I look for inventive actors who move well. A strong actor gives an idiosyncratic performance, because he infuses the puppet character with his own personality instead of relying on generic puppetry technique. The thrill of working with a good actor who is new to this medium, and who loves the puppet he is working with, is that he will take the form further than I ever imagined.

Of the 27-member chorus, we sought 12 dancers and 15 singers. Once again a few of the singers who had done the workshop were invited into the company but the majority was left to cast. It was a very tricky affair. Lebo M [one of the composers and the Choral Director] wanted at least half of the chorus to be South African. A number of the songs were in Zulu or had a strong South African chant underscore. This style of singing is so distinct that it cannot be learned but only imitated and all of us were determined to have an authentic sound for our musical. Actor's Equity conceded to six South African performers whom Lebo handpicked. Added to the South African contingent were Lebo and his wife, Nandi, leaving seven choral spots open. Even trickier at this point was the hard fact that understudies for all of the principal roles would have to come from the chorus. This is

no easy task even for the most straightforward musical, but it is particularly challenging in *The Lion King* because the principal roles require a completely different set of skills from the chorus. We agreed to hire two full-time covers for the roles of Scar, Timon, Pumbaa, and Zazu. And the two child roles would each have his and her own understudy.

While casting the dancers I caught my first glimpse at the type of choreography Garth [Fagan] would bring to the piece. What I saw was athletic, sexy, rhythmically complex, and perfect for what I had envisioned. Four hundred dancers showed up for the open female dance call in New York. Quite clearly Mr. Fagan was a draw. Garth's auditions were murderous. His two terrific assistants, performers from his own company, would demonstrate a routine and the dancers would do their best to learn it. Sometimes these routines were two or three minutes long and had to be instantly memorized. I asked Garth why he made the audition so difficult and he said that he wanted not only to see if a dancer had good technique but also to see how fast he or she could learn. He wanted to let them know what they would be in for.

NEW YORK REHEARSALS

We planned to rehearse five weeks in New York and spend three weeks in technical rehearsals, on stage, in Minneapolis for our out-of-town tryout. The first day of rehearsal is totally nerve-racking and thrilling. We had about a hundred people in the room for the reading and presentation of the scenic, puppet and costume designs. Everyone from the Disney theatrical office and the puppet shop was invited. Gathered around an immense table, the actors read through the script and stumbled their way through the songs. The concept was laid out for the company, the goal set before them, and we were ready to begin.

At our studio at 890 Broadway we had four large rooms in which to do our work: one for music and choral rehearsals with Lebo and Joe [Church, the Musical Director]; one for dance with Garth; the main room for scene rehearsals with me; and a puppet hospital where the masks and puppets could be stored, repaired, and actors could work and experiment individually on their own in front of mirrors or with the aid of videotape. Every day the assistant directors and artistic team would spend our lunch hour agonizing and organizing the most complicated rehearsal schedule designed to take advantage of everyone at every moment. With more than two hundred intricate costume designs, the individual fittings also had to be worked into the daily schedule.

PRINCIPAL REHEARSALS

During the first rehearsal days I worked improvisationally with the principal actors. We would move back and forth between reading and analyzing the text and getting up on our feet and improvising with both the text and physical relationships of the characters. The masks and puppets were built, if not completely painted, by the time we went into rehearsal, and I urged the performers to wear or use them as much as possible. It is misleading for an actor to think he can find his or her character without the puppet or mask, especially in the case of Timon or Zazu, where the character is actually a complete puppet that is manipulated by the actor. Quite often, though, in discovering the natural flow of a scene or the more human gestures and inner nuances that might arise from the unencumbered performer, I would ask the actors to play the scenes without their "extended parts." The fun began when they then had to find the corresponding animal gestures through the vocabulary of the puppets and masks.

At this early stage I asked performers to find "ideographs" for their characters. An ideograph is a concept that I was first exposed to during the late 1960s, while I was studying mime with Jacques LeCoq at his L'Ecole de Mime in Paris. The concept was applied again during the 1970s, when I was a member of The Oberlin Group in Ohio, an experimental theater troupe led by avant-garde director Herbert Blau. In the visual arts, an example of an ideograph would be a Japanese brush painting of a bamboo forest: Just three or four quick brush strokes capture the whole. In the theater, an ideograph is also a pared-down form— a kinetic, abstract essence of an emotion, an action, or a character. At L'Ecole de Mime, LeCoq enjoined us to create ideographs of colors and materials, to "do red," "do blue," "be ice," or "be steel." We used our bodies to create ideographic images of the sun setting or of melting snow fields. We also explored ideographs of emotions. The idea was not to imitate ice or steel or joy but to reveal the essential kernel of the subject without the distracting details. A haiku.

I use ideographs in various ways in all aspects of my theater work. Once in rehearsal, I use the technique to help an actor find and express the essence of a character. The actor playing Pumbaa suggested during rehearsal that the ideograph for the fat, waddling warthog was "contentment," and he expressed this physically by just standing in one spot and breathing in a full, relaxed way. Timon, on the other hand, is a nervous, street-wise meerkat, and so his ideograph might be related to canniness or toughness. Again, the performer would not act out toughness, but rather find an essential, abstract series of movements which embody that character trait. These exercises lead the actor toward finding a physical, spatial, and rhythmic score for his character.

I often use ideographs to open up a text's visual motifs and themes. For my staging of *Titus Andronicus*, Shakespeare's most graphically bloody tragedy, actors explored ideographs for violence, racism, the meaning of the sacred and profane. In any theater piece requiring heightened style, ideographs can be used to find the physical vocabulary that matches the language, or in the case of *The Lion King*, that matches the style of the music and the overall nature of the production.

The dialogue in *The Lion King* is conversational, but from the design to the score, the piece is highly stylized. Each actor had to find the duality of the animal and the human within their performance. An actress cannot put on Nala's mask and costume and talk with Simba as though she had just run into him on the street. As lioness/young woman she has to find a way

of standing, walking and gesturing that fulfills the demands of the production's conceit. The tension inherent in the juxtaposition of the highly stylized gestural moves with the more naturalistic ones was my main thrust in the direction of the actors. Complete stylization would have been too formal and distancing for the audience, and would not service the script. The audience needs to identify with the chararcters, to recognize in them their selves, and therefore the familiar landscapes of emotion, dialogue, and interaction needed to be partially expressed in a familiar way. If the entire piece were performed naturalistically these moments would not stand out. In fact, the audience would take the most recognizable gestures for granted. What makes these simple human moments powerful is the selected isolation of them and the contrast and interplay with the heightened or stylized forms of expression.

Once the actors have their masks, they use their bodies to complete the sculpture. The architectural flow of the mask is the map or guide. Scar's mask is twisted and angular. John Vickery had to continue that angularity with his body. The stylized costume I designed obviously helps, but the actor must find his own rhythmic and spatial complement. When wearing a mask, an actor's head movements must be precise, strong, and clean As the mask has no interior facial expression it is the way the actor isolates the head and body that gives the illusion of change.

One of the keys to puppetry is stillness. Too much movement from a puppet forces the physicality to become general and unfocused. The actor must learn to make quick, small moves that contrast with long, luxurious ones, and to alternate motion with stasis. The individual movements become the pauses, the commas and the exclamation points in the character's phrasing. At the same time, energy levels must remain high and consistent. If an actor's kinetic intensity drops, the puppet loses energy. As the puppet Timon was explored we found that we needed to develop different mechanisms to keep every limb vital. While Max Cassela had his right hand articulating the mouth of the puppet and his left hand manipulating the left arm of the puppet, a holder was strapped to his right thigh which, when moved, allowed him to animate the right arm of the puppet. The challenge for the actor was to bring his puppet to life—to get "blood" flowing into every digit, into the legs, into the head, so that the audience sees and feels the life force inside this inanimate object.

When a figure made of wood or fabric moves like a living thing, the visual and emotional impact is magical. Watching puppetry at its best is a cubistic event, because an audience experiences the art from several perspectives at once. One can either focus solely on the puppet or enjoy the direct and transparent art of the actor motivating that puppet. At rest, a puppet is just a facsimile of a human being or an animal. But when Zazu's wings flutter excitedly or Timon cocks his head at a quizzical angle, the pleasure of watching that facsimile turn into a being with recognizable emotions is the pinnacle of this type of theater experience.

CHOREOGRAPHY

Prior to rehearsals Garth and I had laid out when dance would serve as the main event of a scene, or in a musical number, and

(continued)

at what points I would need him to work with the principals on their choreography. Herds and flocks of animals needed to lope, leap, fly, and stampede. The flora needed to blossom and blow in the wind. Songs simply needed kinetic respite from the lyrical sections. Some of these stagings were a joyous collaboration between Garth, the actors, and myself, but most of the dance choreography was created in Garth's workroom. In reality, Garth had the least amount of time to rehearse because everything he was creating was from scratch, while the music and text had already been written and had been tried out in prior workshops. Amongst the large pieces that Garth was to rehearse on his own and present to me once somewhat formed were the lioness hunt, the hyena march, and the male hyena breakout dance for "Be Prepared," the ballet interlude for "Can You Feel the Love Tonight," the trickster dance for "I Can't Wait to be King," and the fight choreography for the grand finale. The flying sections for the ballet as well as the other flying moments in the show had to be tried out and rehearsed on a stage on 42nd Street where Foy had set up the rigging.

Because Garth's choreography can be very difficult to learn and master, I would periodically check into his rehearsals to see if we were on the same wavelength. It's frustrating to have the dancers learn a piece to perfection only to have it thrown out because it's not what the director had in mind. For Garth this process was positively challenging, but also quite trying, as he is used to answering to no one but himself as the director of his own modern dance company. What was most difficult for Garth to get used to was the short amount of time alloted for many of the dance pieces. He would create these marvelous numbers that could have lived on their own in any dance concert. But in context of this book musical, some of his numbers were way too long in juxtaposition to the acting scenes that surrounded them. The rhythm of The Lion King script had been established in the film. The scenes were short and fast and moved along, unlike most plays. I liked this and wanted to maintain that pacing, but at the same I wanted to give Garth enough time to create developed dances that could tell a story and exploit the tremendous talents that we had engaged. There was much trial and error for all of us to find that balance and, until we finally had the show on its feet and running in Minneapolis, we wouldn't really nail the ultimate structure and pacing.

MUSIC REHEARSALS

For the first two weeks of rehearsals, the choral singers concentrated solely on learning their vocal arts with Lebo as choral director and arranger and Joe as overall music director. It was hard at the start for the two men to find a compatible working style. Lebo is extremely spontaneous and works out his complex harmonies and rhythms on the spot. Joe comes from a more traditional Western style of teaching and conducting and usually works from a completed score. The chorus had to learn to respond to the direction of both men and that took the usual getting used to. The individual principals would learn their music on a one-to-one basis with Joe and then they would come to me to work on integrating their songs into scenes.

Lebo's lioness and grasslands chants were created in rehearsal and, because they were linked to choreography, they

were not fixed musically until all the elements came together. Usually Garth choreographs to a finished piece of music and needs the counts to be absolutely specific, so this was a bit trying at first. Ultimately, though, the back-and-forth process of music inspiring dance, and then the dance moves inspiring new twists in the music, turned out to be the best and only method in what was a truly collaborative process. Throughout the rehearsal period, Bob Elhai, one of the main orchestrators, would take down the new material and start to design the orchestrations. Mark Mancina [one of the composers] was able to join us during the last ten days or so and helped to codify and finalize some of the musical questions.

PUTTING THE PIECES TOGETHER

Once the singers and dancers had learned their music and dance choreography, they joined me in the large rehearsal room to work out their blocking and integration into the show. A number of the animal puppets for the opening "Circle of Life," such as the life-size elephant, or the twenty-foot giraffes, were too large to fit into the space, so we had to leave those scenes for Minneapolis. We also were unable to fit a full-scale mock-up of the Pride Rock set piece in the room, as well as a number of other crucial set pieces that would determine spacing. The fact that the scenery was designed to be constantly shifting meant we had to use our imaginations in thinking through the staging and scene shifts in these first five weeks.

Even so, a number of thrilling moments came to life in that relatively small room. The first time all 27 hyenas broke into their frenzied dance, or the huge wildebeest masks were thrust high into the air by the stomping male dancers we all felt a rush of excitement. Every day felt like Christmas as some new creature or vision came into being. As exciting as the puppets and masks were, we were all as equally impressed and moved by the spontaneity, freshness, and truth that was coming from the acting, singing, and dance moves of Scott Irby-Ranniar, our twelve-year-old Simba. It was great to watch the chorus enjoying the acting performances of the principals and the actors enjoying the virtuosity of the dancers. Junior "Gabu" Wedderburn and Valerie Naranjo, two of our African percussionists, joined the rehearsals in the third week which brought the energy up to an even higher notch. The bonding of the company started to take shape as they began to sense the creativity and vitality at work.

By the fifth week in New York we were ready to take a stab at a run-through. With only a few assistants to help dress the company into their various head gear and puppet parts, we did manage to bring in the first run-through at under three hours. We were shocked at how smoothly it all flowed. There is a life to these first run-throughs that can never be replaced. The fact that it is all happening up close and in your face, and without the full complement of sets, lights, sound, makeup, and costumes, is a profoundly moving experience. The chorus is unamplified and will never sound better. The danger of a dancer leaping into your lap adds so much to an already highly visceral experience. Each muscle move of an actor's face is deliciously expressive and can't be seen across the orchestra pit in a 2,000-seat theater. One can only hope at this point in the process that what we were experiencing would translate onto the large stage and have the intimate, human, and emotional impact that only the rehearsal hall can give.

Our last day of rehearsal in New York was our second run-through. . . . All went smoothly and after the rehearsal, the team met to discuss the status of the book, music, choreography, and performances. Varying opinions flew back and forth. Some I registered, some I dismissed, and some I felt were extremely helpful critiques that only a fresh perspective could contribute. Everyone was very enthusiastic and we all felt ready to make the next move, onto the stage of the Orpheum Theater in Minneapolis.

MINNEAPOLIS—THE OUT-OF-TOWN TRYOUT

By the time *The Lion King* company arrived in Minneapolis for the last three weeks of rehearsal, the scenery had been loaded into the Orpheum Theater and set up on stage, lights had been hung, and the sound system installed. Jeff Lee, our production stage manager had come a week earlier to join Richard Hudson [the set designer] and his team to begin what is called a "dry tech." The idea is to move technically through the show, roughing out the scene setups and shifts, and to sketch in preliminary lighting cues. During the fifth week of rehearsals, Don Holder [the lighting designer] was flying back and forth between New York City and Minneapolis to observe our run-throughs and simultaneously focus the lights on stage. The daily reports sent to New York City from Jeff were generally positive, but there seemed to be problems with the computer functioning of the Pride Rock set piece. The last thing I was looking forward to was having to stop rehearsals for set pieces that refused to budge.

On June 14, my assistant directors and I traveled to Minneapolis, the actors to follow the next day. We spent the afternoon meeting the crew, inspecting and walking the set, and reviewing some of the major cues. It's always an overwhelming experience to see the set for the first time. Through what is probably intense trepidation and fear of everything that can go wrong, it's not unnatural to have an instant love-hate relationship with your new challenge. With my total enthusiasm, Richard had designed a set of infinite options as to the look, and Don had a blank cyc (a blank canvas) and six surrounding light boxes that also offered myriad choices as to the color of the lighting. We now had three weeks to develop and complete the total picture.

TECHNICAL REHEARSALS

With a host of computers sitting on large boards spread out over the seats, and headsets to communicate backstage, we were able to begin tracking the cues. While I, the designers, the production stage manager, and choreographer operate from the auditorium, the crew, stage managers, and performers are getting used to the idiosyncrasies of the stage deck, the mountains and traps they have to ascend and descend, and the limited backstage space they have to conquer for the numerous costume changes that occur. Wardrobe stations in the wings and under the stage are designated as there will not be enough time for the actors to get to their dressing rooms for the quick changes.

During tech rehearsals, Michael Ward [hair and makeup designer] works with the actors in the makeup room, doing tests and teaching them how to apply their own elaborate makeup. Mary [Nemecek Peterson, associate costume designer], Tracy [Dorman, assistant costume designer], and the wardrobe staff led by Kjeld Anderson continue to have fittings, make alterations, and organize the tracking sheets for the eighteen dressers who will work backstage during the show. Michael Curry [along with Taymor, the mask and puppet designer] and the carpenters figure out the elaborate storage system for the puppets in the wings that, when finished, looks like either the most wonderful flying zoo, or a bizarre slaughterhouse with gazelles hung upside down on suspended racks.

Tech time, especially on my shows, can prove quite frustrating for the actors because the pace is tedious, the attention is to the technical matters and not the acting, and the hours are long—up to twelve hours a day. Actually for the crew and the artistic team, especially the lighting designer, the day starts at 8:00 A.M. and ends at midnight. Each scene has some obstacle to overcome. Among our crises were:

- The elephant is too big to enter the door into the auditorium. A stage manager will have to guide it in as the actors inside the legs bow down and walk single file down the narrow aisle. Still works as a great image for the top of the show.
- The actress playing Sarabi is afraid of heights. She has to ascend Pride Rock with Mufasa. It is fifteen feet high with no railings and it moves. Give her time, she will overcome it. She did.
- The shadow puppet of little Simba that is supposed to appear in the tree looks terrible, is hard to light, and we couldn't hide the puppeteer. Solution? Cut it. Richard Hudson paints the image on a piece of muslin. We backlight it. Simpler. Elegant. And why didn't we just do that in the first place?
- The ground rows, which looked so great in the model, eat up too much space off stage. Cut them. Richard designs smaller ones. All is not lost.

(A quick note about the art of cutting scenic items. I'm not big on it. It's too expensive. I believe that with good planning you can avoid the shocking truth that things might not work. On the other hand you can't always know everything in advance and one needs to take risks and try for the best. But if your best isn't working, cut it. Fast.)

- The two kids are supposed to fly during the production number for "I Can't Wait to Be King." Scott keeps getting snagged on the tree branch in the wings and both kids keep spinning around in circles because of the type of flying rig and the limited flying space above. . . . Cut the flying in this scene. Scott will stay on the floor, Kujuana, young Nala, will remain on the back of the ostrich. Scott's a great dancer and now the scene can really focus around him. A very good cut. Except that that means the giant suspended giraffes have to go, too. We'll put them in the lobby of the New Amsterdam, when we go to New York.

(continued)

- The giant moving bone staircase in the elephant graveyard is killing the backs of our dancers who have to move it during the hyena chase scene. Too heavy. Bad casters. Bumps in the deck that can't be avoided. Solution? Put it on a central pivot point so that the dancers don't have to work so hard and there is no danger of it crashing into the side light-boxes.
- Biggest problem in Act One: The scene and costume change from the end of the hyena bacchanal in "Be Prepared" to the start of the stampede of the wildebeests. We always knew that this was going to be tough. Based on the given estimate of three minutes. I had designed a nonverbal transition scene that could happen downstage in front of a full-stage shadow screen. . . . We need a new scene to cover the transition. Solution for the first week of previews: a scheduled pause, as in opera. After that a new scene was created for Mufasa and Zazu which, surprisingly, did not turn out to be just filler but, instead, a rather comical and moving scene that adds to the development of these characters.

Every night, after a long day of tech. the artistic and stage managerial team would get together to assess how far we had progressed, what the problems were, and what would be the next day's plan of attack. As tech had been delayed a few days it seemed as if we would never make the appointed dress rehearsals, which would be our only rehearsals with full orchestra before the first preview. At these moments there is always pressure to move faster and to take less time with each light cue. The myth that everything can be fixed in previews raises its deceptive head and the tension rises. The fact is, at least in my experience and in my style of theater, that without getting overly fussy, it is absolutely essential that you not skip over cues that you know have to be there because, in reality, you never get back there again. Preview rehearsals should be for fine tuning the light cues and, more important, should be time for the focus to return to the performers. Given the complications and ambitions of the piece, Don, Jeff, and I felt that we were moving as fast as we could. Even though I had no serious doubts that we would be ready, it did seem miraculous when we finally arrived at our first dress rehearsal.

PREVIEWS

Two days later our first audience had taken their seats in high anticipation. By this time our whole crew, including producers and performers were a little frazzled, exhausted, and not quite sure how it all would play. We'd become inured to the beautiful pictures, the delicate nuances of performances, and the lowbrow jokes. Anything could happen with the functioning of the computer which operated the set; it seemed to have a mind of its own. So, with headset on, Michele [Steckler, assistant director] sits on my left, notepad in hand, ready to take the technical notes. And Dan [Fields, assistant director] sits on my right, ready to take the sound and actor notes. Butterflies.

The curtain rises and Rafiki starts her chant. From the balcony Lebo and Faca, under their antelope headdresses, chant

back. Clouds float upward one at a time to reveal the sun rising. Two giraffes emerge and slowly move across the stage, silhouetted by the large golden globe. The audience starts to clap and cheer. The large elephant lumbers down the aisle followed by the wildebeests and bird ladies. Heads are turning madly all around us. More applause. And again for the gazelles that leap across the stage. Another wave of applause from the balcony as they finally are able to see the elephant as he climbs up onto the deck. Rafiki starts to sing the familiar refrain "Circle of Life" and they cheer again. We can hardly hear the song through the racket of the audience. It is overwhelming after two years of work and anticipation. I turn to Dan and Michele. We are stunned.

There are plenty of technical notes that night but we knew that the basic performance was there. Our goal over the next three weeks of previews was to make certain cuts in some of the dance numbers, to work on the balance of sound, to reorchestrate some of the songs in order to achieve the desired climax, to fiddle with dialogue, and to rehearse the new scene that would eventually replace the pause in Act One. There were also technical glitches during those early performances that needed to be worked out. A few examples of these stomach-churning events:

- The mountain wouldn't rise (due to computer malfunction) causing Pride Rock to look like a mole hill that night.
- Mufasa had to climb the canyon wall using his own strength because the fly lines which support him had gotten tangled.
- The cactuses wouldn't inflate on cue.
- The king curtain, which is supposed to drop from the flies, got caught halfway and a stagehand, unbeknownst to the audience, had to climb out onto the grid during the show to untangle it.

And so on. These are the normal crises that eventually work themselves out. But the hardest challenge for everyone was the flow backstage. For a week or so, I declined the invitation to watch the chaos from the wings. I suspected that if I was confronted with all the misery up close it would be hard to keep pushing everyone to achieve the desired quick costume changes or complicated set changes. I knew that eventually they would get the rhythm down.

When the dust seemed settled and the look of confusion and despair had disappeared from the dressers' faces, I ventured backstage to see the "other show." In an odd way I was more moved by that experience than in watching the musical from the house. It was so utterly real. So dangerous. An intensely beautiful ballet of human and mechanical interaction without an inch of space unoccupied. While the children sang their "I Just Can't Wait to Be King" song downstage, in front of the black drop, the stagehands would, in time to the music, would be setting up the huge bones of the elephant graveyard. The absurd juxtaposition was startling but the incongruity had created another performance all of its own. From the audience's perspective, a perfect illusion was being performed, but from backstage the reality of making that illusion work was palpably raw, happening-in-the-moment, fundamentally live theater.

At the conclusion of the performance, I felt I had to go to the intercom to tell the company, both crew and performers, how moved I was by how they had surmounted the mechanics of running such an extremely difficult show. I'm sure I got quite maudlin over that intercom as I thanked them for helping to bring all of our visions to fruition, but that night was one of the most profoundly moving theater experiences I have ever had.

OPENING NIGHT

We were ready to open. That's a rare statement for me. This was the first time I truly felt that, even if every little detail wasn't perfect, the company, the crew, and myself had rehearsed enough. Under our belts were a month of preview performances and endless hours of rehearsals. There is a point where the exhaustion starts to set in and it can be dangerous to the health of the performers. We had experienced the trauma and excitement of understudies suddenly having to go on for injured dancers. Spirits remained high. Costumes were finally finished, makeup designs finalized, and the set was behaving well. The show was running smoothly and we could all breathe a little bit easier.

July 31, 1997. Minneapolis. Opening night.

Glorious.

OFF TO BROADWAY

At the end of August we will close the show in Minneapolis and set our sights to the New Amsterdam Theater on 42nd Street. The cast is chomping at the bit to go home and looking forward to the three-week hiatus while the set is being loaded into the theater. There's a big production meeting to finalize the changes in the set, script, music, and choreography. I don't believe there will be many changes but there are definite ideas that need to wait for New York to be re-rehearsed. The first order of business on the regathering of the troupe will be the cast album. Then we'll have a few days in the rehearsal rooms to review and make any acting and dancing alterations. Then back into tech with a whole new backstage crew. And this time the backstage is even smaller. Much smaller. A number of adjustments will have to be made, and the crew and cast will get to know each other really well.

As I come to the end of this often technical account of the making of *The Lion King* I want to add a few words about the company. In a collaboration as immense as this one, it is rare to have a unity that sizzles with such support, enthusiasm, and spirit. As hard as the work was, and will continue to be, it has been one of the most thoroughly gratifying experiences for all of us. The South African contingent of our performing cast, led by Lebo M, has made our piece an international, cross-cultural collaboration. Through their passion, talent, and unique artistic contributions, they have brought the work to another level that has widened all of our horizons.

From my direction of Shakespeare plays to international opera productions in multiple languages, to my five years in Indonesia and the Far East, I have spent my theatrical life devoted to theater that crosses age, race, class, and cultural boundaries. *The Lion King*, as a story, is archetypal, and as a production includes techniques and inspirations drawn from the world theater. It aspires to speak to the experience of anyone, any family, or any tribe.

---

work more efficiently within the director's parameters. In an ideal world, of course, all of the artists involved in a production would contribute to the discovery of the concept, but the exigencies of "getting the show up" preclude this practice, especially in the commercial theater, where time is indeed money. Some companies—for example, the Berliner Ensemble and New York's Wooster Group—are noted for the democratic way in which they let a production evolve.

After grappling with the intellectual and emotional center of the play, directors consider the visual and aural elements that may best realize the concept. Much of this may be done in conferences with the designers, though often a director will advance a strong personal image from the outset. Like designers, directors think in terms of graphic metaphors. In the Living Theater's 1965 production of Kenneth Brown's *The Brig*, for instance, Julian Beck and Judith Malina enclosed the playing area in a chain-link fence as a reminder to both the actors and the audience that the world is a prison. Even contemporary realistic plays in naturalistic settings can benefit from a well-conceived directorial concept. Anne Rooney staged Ibsen's *Hedda Gabler* at Dublin's Abbey Theater and, in opposition to the usual Victorian clutter one finds in this play, conceived a setting stripped of furniture and other props. The bare room, encased in faded, cracked wallpaper, symbolized the sterile relationship between Hedda and her husband.

When dealing with plays written before the age of realism, the choice of a period in which to "dress" the play can be an important step towards realizing the directorial concept. There are times when the setting actually *is* the concept, as when John Houseman directed *Much Ado About Nothing* at Stratford, Connecticut in 1955. To make the play instantly accessible to American audiences, Houseman set the play in the Wild West. The postmodern theater is especially noted for its ingenious, often willfully outrageous recontextualizations of classic plays. For instance, one West Coast theater-company recently refashioned Sophocles' *Oedipus the King* as a television talk show (in which the audience itself played a vital role) under the title *The Whole World Is Watching*.

Why do directors occasionally play fast and loose with the classics? There are several rationales. In his provocative assessment of the modern theater, *The Empty Space*, Brook questions directors who claim to let a play speak for itself because, in his estimation, a play may not make a sound. If the play is to be heard, Brook insists the director must often "conjure its sound." At its best "conjuring the sound" can provide us with perceptive insights into a script, much the way a good essay by a literary critic can. At its worst, "conjuring" can become indulgent, anarchic, confusing, and unfair to the playwright's intentions. Samuel Beckett sued the American Repertory Theater when a director set *Endgame* in a post–nuclear war subway car. Beckett believed the concept violated the integrity of his script.

A second rationale is the "*regardez-moi*" ("look at me!") syndrome, a phrase used by Ron Daniels, the former artistic director of the American Repertory Theater, to describe the tendency of modern directors, especially young ones, to make a name for themselves through audacious concepts. In some cases directorial invention is merely a bright idea wrapped in the cloak of art. There are few topics as controversial among theater scholars and critics in the contemporary theater as the liberties taken by the director.

Finally, today the theater must compete with other visual media, notably film and television. In this MTV age audiences are accustomed to a rich array of visual stimuli, quick cuts, and montages. The stage picture is fixed because the space does not change and the audience is usually in a permanent position for the duration of the play. Thus the modern director is faced with the dilemma of creating as much visual excitement as possible. Gregory Boyd, the artistic director of Houston's Alley Theater, addresses this issue: "If MTV has taught our audiences that the attention span is only eleven seconds and that the image must change every three to four seconds, that seems to me an existential fact and you don't ignore that."

2. Coordinating the Artists' Contributions The director provides the artistic leadership for a given production. Ideally the collaboration between the director and the designers and technicians, as well as the performers, is somewhat democratic. In practice, however, many directors are autocratic; they know exactly what they want and will accept nothing less. Much of the director's time is spent in conferences with designers and technicians in production meetings and in one-on-one discussions. Yet in the rehearsal hall or around the conference table, the director's task is rife with paradox, as Brook notes in *The Empty Space:*

> It is a strange role, that of the director: he does not ask to be God and yet his role implies it. He wants to be fallible, and yet an instinctive conspiracy of the actors [and designers?] is to make him the arbiter, because an arbiter is so desperately wanted all the time. In a sense the director is always an imposter, a guide at night who does not know the territory, and yet has no choice—he must guide, learning the route as he goes.

3. Creating an Aesthetic Experience An audience perceives a play aesthetically as well as intellectually and emotionally. Visually and aurally, directors attempt to make the theater experience pleasant by composing stage pictures and establishing the rhythm of the play. Some directors meticulously choreograph the movement of the actors in the privacy of their studios. Shaw, for instance, used chess pieces to work out the movement patterns of his actors. Others allow the blocking to evolve organically from the actors' instincts and then "tighten" it shortly before opening. Directors need the eye of a master painter to group actors onstage; indeed, a popular exercise for directing students is to look at the paintings of the masters to learn about groupings and body attitudes. Directors provide visual variety by using different areas of the stage, height levels, linear and curved patterns, and other techniques to produce a pleasing picture. If a play seems dull or static, it may not be entirely the actors' fault; perhaps the director has not provided a variety of visual stimuli.

Just as a good musical piece changes tempos and volume, so too does a play, and the director must guide not only the actors but also the technicians through the subtle variations. A director must acquire a sense of whether a three-second light fade will most effectively end a scene or whether it will benefit from an instant blackout. Lighting designers can surely contribute their expertise in such choices, but ultimately the director makes the call that heightens or diminishes the aesthetics of the piece.

4. Helping the Actors Tyrone Guthrie once labeled the director "an audience of one," that is, the director functions as an impartial observer who audits, evaluates, and adjusts the actors' work to develop truth and clarity. Early on the director frequently meets with actors for some "table talk," at which the individual characters are dissected. In rehearsal the director helps the actors make choices, always with an eye toward the whole. As the play takes shape and the individual actors bring their characters to life, the director helps them coalesce into an ensemble. As the actors advance beyond the exploratory stages, some directors sit back and react to scenes. Many of the reactions are strictly technical: "I can't hear you there" or "You're speaking too quickly." Others get to the psychological and emotional life of the character: "Why is he always so angry—aren't there other ways to react to a situation?" The director raises many of the same questions and criticisms that an audience member might; this is not always an easy task, particularly as the director gets to know the play better and better. Paradoxically, often the director is least prepared to help the actors when they need it most: just before opening. In many theater companies, other directors attend late rehearsals to bring fresh eyes and ears to the production.

The Designer

The very term *theater*—"the seeing place"—implies that the visual dimension is an important part of the audience's experience. Often our memories in the theater are most colored by what we have seen:

- a glorious angel descending over the bed of a dying man in *Angels in America;*
- the parade of ingeniously created animals and birds attending Simba's christening in *The Lion King;*
- the glitzy top hat and tails on the many dancers who strut through the finale of *A Chorus Line;*
- the barrage of swirling lights in the rock musical *Tommy.*

In Japan the Kabuki theater delights crowds with extraordinary battles, flying ghosts, disappearing spirits, and beautiful ladies who turn into enormous spiders. In Soweto, South Africa, discarded objects are given new life in township plays such as *Poppy Nongena:* a sheet of rusty corrugated metal is used first to symbolize a hut, and then, almost magically, it becomes a machine gun as an actor drags a broom handle across it for a "rat-a-tat-tat" effect.

Scenery, costumes, makeup, masks, props, sound, and even lighting effects have been central to theater events since an ancient hunter first donned an animal skin for a tribal dance. Visual elements and symbolic objects, like a totem or sunburst, were indispensable to early rituals and ceremonies, and theater artists appropriated them as formal drama developed.

The Emergence of the Designers: Scenery

In the West playwrights themselves were among the first scenic artists and costumers. Aeschylus devised costumes that so frightened the first audience for *The Eumenides* that, according to an ancient biographer, "children died and women suffered miscarriage." He also credits Aeschylus with introducing such scenic elements as "painting, machinery, altars, tombs, trumpets, Furies." Their splendor "delighted the eyes of the audience" and thus insured that *scenography* (a European term) would remain popular in theatrical art. The comedies of Aristophanes furthered both scenery and costuming as his choruses appeared as frogs, clouds, and giant horses.

The Middle Ages produced some extraordinary scenic effects. A 1547 drawing of the *Passion Play* in Valenciennes, France, confirms the visual appeal of medieval theater;

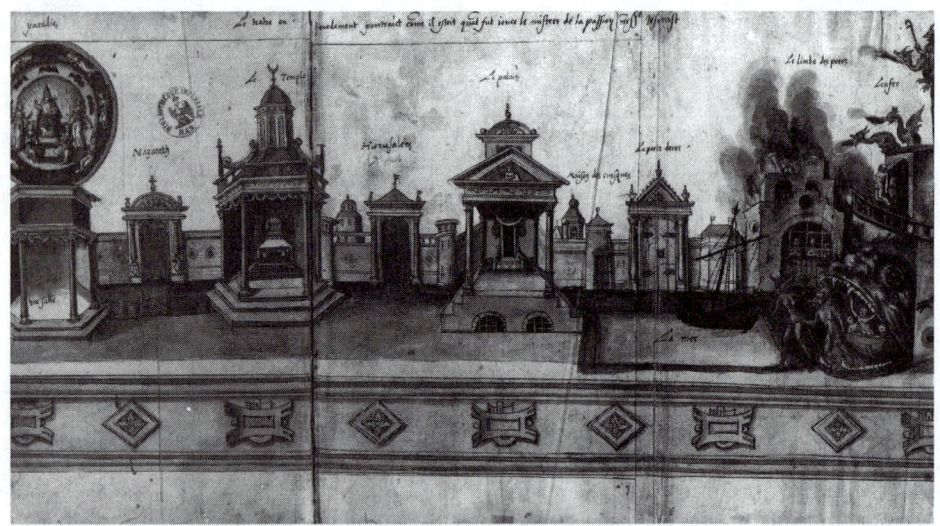

The stage for the Valenciennes Passion Play *(1547) used multiple locales, including Heaven, Jerusalem, and perhaps most famously, Hell itself, as depicted by the Hellmouth at right.*

contemporary records describe the walls as being 40 feet high. Note especially the large head at the right: this so-called Hellmouth graphically symbolized the horrors of eternal damnation. There are records of another French Hellmouth so complex that it took no less than 17 men to operate its machinery. Feats of illusion were also popular: Moses' rod magically sprouted flowers and fruits, while a fig tree cursed by the Almighty withered before the audience's eyes.

At the same time the Chinese and Japanese were laying the foundations of their theatrical arts. Unlike their Western counterparts, however, the court theaters of China and the early Noh theater of Japan minimized scenic splendor to maximize focus on the actor and the audience's imagination. The Chinese theater has for centuries relied on the simplest scenery, usually a table and two chairs, which inventive actors can transform into mountains, carriages, or prison cells. The Noh theater has always featured a bare stage, adorned only by four posts, three small pine trees, and a large backdrop with an evergreen painted on it. Both the Chinese and Japanese derive their spectacle from the use of masks and painted faces, sumptuous costumes, and especially the beauty of an actor's body in motion. But with the birth of the Kabuki theater in the seventeenth century, the Japanese turned to extraordinary scenic effects.

The Renaissance, Europe's golden age of painting, sculpture, and architecture, brought the scene designer to the forefront of theatrical activity, especially in Italy. With the rediscovery of perspective drawing, which allowed the illusion of multidimensionality and a more realistic reproduction of the world, such artists as Sebastiano Serlio (1475–1554) and Giacomo Torrelli (1608–1678) advanced scene design. Their British contemporary, Inigo Jones (1573–1652) visited Italy and brought formal scene design to England, which had relied on an essentially bare stage. Three-dimensional scenery made it possible to put characters *within* an environment, as opposed to in front of it. Realism (or, to be more accurate, illusionism) took another step forward. The new scenography furthered the secularization of the drama by focusing on the things of this world. The eighteenth and nineteenth centuries are noted eras of magnificent scenery. In fact, scenery was the principal reason people in Europe and America attended the theater at this time. In 1852 audiences flocked to see Eliza and her baby traverse the ice floes of the Ohio River in *Uncle Tom's Cabin*, just as late-twentieth-century audiences fill movie theaters to marvel at the special effects in *Titanic*. To accommodate the new and larger scenery and its machinery, nineteenth-century theaters were cavernous, their most striking distinguishing feature the enormous "picture frame" (or proscenium) that encased the stage.

The early realists and naturalists at the end of the nineteenth century demanded authentic settings because they believed one's environment often determined behavior. The scene designer now had to create faithful reproductions of life onstage, much the way the newly invented photocamera did. In the Théâtre Libre of André Antoine (1858–1943) Parisian audiences saw actual animal carcasses on stage during a production of *The Butchers*. In New York David Belasco (1854–1931) gave rise to the term "Belasco realism" when he bought the furnishings and wallpaper of a prominent restaurant because a play he was producing was set there.

Given such taste for lifelike detail, one might have predicted a new generation of scenic artists reacting to the excesses of the realists. The "new scenography," as typified by Switzerland's Adolph Appia and Britain's Edward Gordon Craig, returned the theater to abstraction, to evocative rather than actual environments. The modern scene designer also incorporates other media such as projections, cinema, and laser art into the setting. Middle Europeans, such as the Czech Josef Swoboda (1905–), are especially adept at this, as is Ming Cho Lee, the Shanghai-born artist who is currently one of the leading scene designers in the United States.

Because the various designers work in a similar manner, we will examine the specific responsibilities of each of the principal artists, then consider the process by which they work.

Costumes

Although Renaissance designers, such as Inigo Jones, produced spectacular costumes, usually meant to be worn by royalty and their entourages at court entertainments, costuming in the noncourt theaters developed more slowly. Pictures of seventeenth- and eighteenth-century actors suggest that actors wore contemporary dress, even when doing revivals of period plays such as Shakespeare's. In fact, it was the custom for actors to provide clothing from their own wardrobes. Not until the nineteenth century did historically accurate costuming come into vogue, when the English actor-manager Charles Kemble produced Shakespeare's *King John* in 1823 and created an authentic thirteenth-century setting. The production was enormously popular with audiences who filled Kemble's theater to see the "precise habits of the period"— that is, faithful reproductions of the dress and armor of the thirteenth century. As designers do today, Kemble's costumer, James Robinson Planché, methodically researched the period and produced apparel that was "never equaled on the English stage." Kemble's financial success inspired imitation, and soon authentic costuming became the norm. As with scenery, costuming became more a reproductive art than a creative one as the realists clamored for everyday clothing on their actors.

Today costumers also veer from realism when the occasion permits. José Carlos Serroni (Brazil) and Desmond Heeley (Great Britain) are noted for their unconventional costuming, while in America the designs of Patricia Zipprodt and Theoni V. Aldredge have won numerous awards for their distinctively glittery, theatrical costumes. In China and Japan, audiences expect traditional costumes that are bright, colorful, and spectacularly theatrical, particularly those of the Kabuki theater. Conversely, a major characteristic of township theater in South Africa (see Chapter 8) is the conspicuous use of everyday or "found" clothing, yet its stark simplicity takes on a theatricality within the improvisational nature of the performances.

Lighting

The first lighting effect in the West may have been devised by Aeschylus, who timed the opening lines of *Agamemnon*—in which a watchman seeks light amid the darkness—to coincide with daybreak over the Theater of Dionysus. Renaissance artists, including Leonardo da Vinci, experimented with colored glass to produce what appear to have been truly spectacular lighting effects (similar effects were actually tried in the Sanskrit dramas of India centuries earlier). However, lighting as an integral medium did not occur until theater technicians could control light sources. Until well into the eighteenth century, actors and audience shared the same light, usually a large candelabrum suspended over the forestage. Wicks floating in oil troughs placed in the floor (footlights) also illuminated the actors from below, producing a rather grotesque effect. There were early attempts to create color through light by placing glass containers filled with colored water in front of the light source. Between 1815 and 1880 carbon arc lights, gaslight, and eventually electric lighting entered the theater. Not only were they safer than flame, but they could be dimmed, focused on specific areas, and controlled by lighting

As an anecdote to realism, Swiss designer Adolph Appia created symbolic spaces and evocative lighting for such plays as Orpheus and Eurydice.

operators. As lighting became more sophisticated, theories of lighting for mood, atmosphere, and scenic effect emerged. Adolph Appia was not only a leader in the scenographic revolution, but is widely considered the progenitor of modern lighting design. Quite rightly, he noted that lighting has "an infinite range of variation" and that it is the only medium that can continually create the proper emotional pitch of a play. "The actor, in space, lit" was Appia's motto as he devised ways to accent the dimensionality of the performers. For the early realists, actors had to be lit by natural sources such a desk lamp, a lantern, or the glow of a fireplace.

Today lighting often replaces scenery as the primary visual element in a show, partly because it is relatively inexpensive, but mostly because it is versatile and strikingly dramatic. Shafts of colored light, highlighted by smoke or fog effects, cutting through a black space may elicit as many "oohs and ahhs" from an audience as mammoth sets. An open space can instantly be transformed into a forest, a prison, or a moonlit beach by the use of gobos (patterned metal disks that are inserted into a lighting instrument). The Chinese favor simple settings backed by silk curtains; they define the mood of a scene by coloring the curtains with lights.

Though some scene designers, such as Boris Aronson, double as lighting designers, most theater companies employ artists whose sole responsibility is to create the lighting design for a play. Jennifer Tipton, Jules Fisher, and Tharon Musser are among the leading contemporary lighting designers in America; in England, Terry Hands is not only one of the RSC's leading directors but also an accomplished lighting designer. Because stage lighting is a technology as well as an art, designers must be knowledgeable electricians and computer literate, as computers now control most lighting systems.

Sound

Like the lighting designer, the sound designer is mostly a twentieth-century phenomenon in the theater, although there are records of sound effects throughout the history of the theater. Elizabethan actors, for instance, rolled cannon balls across the wooden floor of their theaters to suggest thunder, while nineteenth-century melodramas were punctuated by effects from wind machines, thunder sheets, and "crash boxes." In the West such effects—as well as recorded sound effects—are usually further attempts at realism. The work of the sound designer has been improved by sophisticated digital stereo systems to suggest a variety of sound locations. The Chinese theater has for centuries used complex sound effects created by off-stage musicians who punctuate virtually every action with a bang of a drum or gong, the clack of wood on wood, or the mournful sound of the two-stringed fiddle. Paradoxically, such consciously artificial sound can contribute more to the vitality of a production than purely realistic sound.

How Designers Work

Though each designer has objectives particular to a specific area of expertise, there are common requirements for scenic, costume, and lighting designs:

- They should be consistent with the directorial concept as well as complement one another as they reinforce the production's visual metaphor.
- They support the actors functionally and aesthetically by providing focus on them.
- They help establish the degree of reality or theatricality of the production.
- They reinforce the emotional atmosphere of the production.
- They provide the audience with relevant information about the historical period, the locale, the characters, and their relationships with one another and their environment.

To put it succinctly, good designs work together to create exactly the right ambience for *this* production of *this* play. Theoni V. Aldredge once suggested that "good design is design you are not aware of." Strange talk from an artist in such a visual medium as costume design. She means, of course, that a good design does not compete with a production, but enhances it.

Once a concept has been agreed on, the designers begin informally sketching potential sets and costumes. They also thoroughly research the play and the period in which it is set through a wealth of resources including history books, museums, paintings, etchings, woodcuts, photographs, even vintage Sears Roebuck catalogues (among the best sources of 1920s clothing). Such research informs the sketches, which increasingly get more specific. The director and designers evaluate the sketches, selecting things that work and rejecting those that do not. As the several artistic minds become one in this process, the designers produce more formal drawings and models of the set and costumes. The scene designer drafts a floor plan of the set to help the actors and director as they rehearse. Perhaps a model of the set is constructed to suggest its dimensionality and spatial relationships; it may be lit by miniature stage lights to approximate the finished product. The costume designer often affixes swatches of cloth to the renderings to suggest texture, color, and sheen. The lighting designer watches, listens, and examines the evolving designs, thinking ahead to lighting areas, color media, and the emotional pitch of the play. When there is true collaboration among these artists, the process by which a play's design evolves is one of the most invigorating aspects of making theater.

While actors talk about subtext and motivation to describe their craft, designers refer to line, mass, form, color, palette, silhouette, balance, symmetry, asymmetry, intensity, texture, and much more to define their concerns. Each play dictates the manner in which a component is used. For instance, line—straight, curved, geometrically shaped, irregular—might suggest conflict if predominantly curved lines converge on sharply angled ones. Mass—the comparative size of objects—can suggest oppression. Jo Mielziner's acclaimed design for *Death of a Salesman* featured skyscrapers about to topple onto the Lomans' small house. There are silhouettes for comedy (oversized, rounded, horizontal, and out-of-balance) just as there are for weightier plays (proportioned, straight lines, vertical). Color and intensity affect mood and perceptions. *A Raisin in the Sun* and *Fences* are both about African American families in crisis in the 1950s, and both are set in realistic environments. But a designer would not use the same color palette or textures in the former (which ends more optimistically) and the latter (a bleaker work). It is possible for designers to use design elements ironically. Peter Nichols' play *Poppy* was designed as a playful fairy tale out of the Chinese opera, but its subject matter portrayed atrocities by

Jo Mielziner designed Death of a Salesman *for a proscenium theater in New York, while Eigisti designed the same play for a circular space at the Arena Theater in Washington, D.C. Both captured the play's expressionistic elements.*

British colonists during China's bloody Opium Wars. Texture can subtly, even subliminally, affect an audience's perception of the play. Rough textures, such as coarse cloth, pocked stones, or decaying metalwork, can add weight to a serious play. Lighting designers prefer heavily textured sets and costumes because they produce interesting effects by creating sharper contrasts between light and shadow.

Set designers know that scenery must be more than a mere backdrop for the action. Because the audience often sees the scenery before the play begins, the scene design is often the first element to affect an audience's response. And just as the playwright must intrigue the audience, so too must the scene designer arouse the audience's expectations when it first views the setting. An aptly chosen visual metaphor may suggest the thematic concerns of the play. The Guthrie Theater's 1985 production of *A Midsummer Night's Dream* featured an enormous moon as its primary set piece, which seemed to say "moonstruck" people do bizarre things.

The scene designer's first task is to transform a bare space into an environment where the actors can work. Though the design should have aesthetic appeal, it must be practical by providing entrances and exits, playing levels that encourage a variety of stage pictures, and places to sit, stand, or recline. Furthermore, a good set design provides focal points for key moments of action; downstage center may be a traditional "hot spot" onstage, but designers seek alternatives. The scenery must support the actors but must not dominate them, even in plays in which the environment overwhelms the characters. If audiences are distracted by an overly massive or cluttered scenic environment, they tend to stop listening and merely look at the setting. Splendid though it was, Norma Desmond's enormous Gothic staircase in the musical *Sunset Boulevard* competed with the stage action for the audience's attention.

A word about realistic settings may be helpful. Given a choice, most contemporary scene designers would avoid completely realistic settings, partly because it reduces their task to mere reproduction. They have learned that there are more interesting alternatives. Perhaps they have heeded Robert Edmund Jones's advice to "omit the details, the prose of nature, and give us only the spirit and the splendor." Thus, realistic settings can run the gamut from ultrarealism (sometimes called "kitchen-sink realism") to "impressionistic" scenery. Here the designer merely suggests the reality by selectively choosing only those elements necessary to suggest locale: partial walls, doors suspended in space, skeletal outlines of architectural features. Mielziner's design for *Death of a Salesman,* is a model of impressionistic scenery (see Forum, "Designing a Play: *Death of a Salesman*"). Examine the pictures throughout this book and decide at what level of realism the designers have chosen to work.

Costume designers also must address particular concerns. "Dressing" the actors, the first task, is complicated by the fact that stage clothing, even in realistic plays, is not the same thing as everyday apparel. Polonius's observation that "the apparel oft proclaims the man" is particularly true of stage costumes. A thoughtfully conceived and executed costume design is among the most expedient ways to define a character, almost instantaneously. This was the premise of the colorful *commedia dell'arte* costumes in the Renaissance. The brightly colored, diamond-shaped patches of Arlecchino and the vivid red cape of Pantalone immediately told audiences that the trickster and the lecherous old man were present. In Chinese opera, specific character types (the flirt, the warrior) wear the same style and color of costume from play to play. Some satiric theater companies, such as the San Francisco Mime Troupe, frequently reduce a character type to a single costume piece such as a particular hat, a loud tie, a mink stole.

Costumes not only quickly indicate one's social status, profession, and other facts, but can also hint at the character's personality. For instance, a too-tight jacket on the youthful Hally in Fugard's "*MASTER HAROLD*" . . . *and the boys* might show his frustration with the constraints placed on him. The "boys" of the title, Sam and Willie, might be distinguished by the fit of their clothes, although they wear identical waiter's uniforms. Sam, invariably cool, in control, and self-assured, can be dressed more smartly than Willie, whose oversized shirt and pants suggest that he is still immature in his behavior and understanding.

Well-designed costumes greatly enhance the work of actors by easing the transformation from "self" to "other." Aldredge, among the commercial theater's most respected designers, cautions that "a performance will suffer if an actor doesn't love his costume, and it's your job to make him love it." Noh actors traditionally meditate on their masks for hours before a performance because they believe it helps them merge with their characters. Dustin Hoffman dressed as a woman for two months before making the film *Tootsie* because he believed that wearing feminine attire helped him understand the psychology of a woman.

Not only do costumes tell us much about the individual characters, they also show relationships among the characters. Major characters are distinguished from minor ones and groups are contrasted with one another through a costume plot, a term that suggests that the designer must calculate effects carefully. The feuding families in *Romeo and Juliet* are quickly distinguished from each other by costumes. The Capulets might be clothed in red with constricting lines to suggest the severity of the world in which Juliet must live. The Montagues, by contrast, might wear clothing with softer lines to indicate the liberty Romeo enjoys as he moves about Verona. Romeo and Benvolio are kinsmen, but the costumer would give Romeo

FORUM

"Designing a Play: *Death of a Salesman*"

JO MIELZINER

My four months of living with *Death of a Salesman* began with a telephone call. . . .

Bloomgarden was sitting back from his desk, his feet up, deep in a manuscript. He removed a cigar from his mouth and said that he was rereading the script of an extraordinary play just completed by Arthur Miller. He called it a real "toughie." "At the end of his forty-odd scenes Miller says, 'The scenic solution to this production will have to be an imaginative and simple one. I don't know the answer, but the designer must work out something which makes the script flow easily.'"

Bloomgarden went on to say that they hoped to go into rehearsal in two weeks; Elia Kazan, who had read the script, had just called from Boston, where he was directing a new musical, *Love Life*, to say that he was anxious to take on the direction as soon as he was free. I took the script and went home to read.

I had previously had a fine time designing Tennessee Williams's *A Streetcar Named Desire* for Kazan, so I knew that if *Death of a Salesman* proved to be a tough job, I would have the support of a director with a strong visual imagination and a mind of his own. . . .

I started reading the Miller manuscript late that afternoon, and after supper I picked it up again. Script reading is always a slow process for me, but this time it was particularly laborious. It was not that the manuscript was overlong; I simply found it difficult to stick to the rule I had established many years before. This was to read a manuscript as if I were a member of an audience sitting out front, not as a scenic artist or as a director or even as a theatre man. I often go so far as to skip descriptions of scenes or business in these first readings. With *Death of a Salesman* I couldn't stick to my rule; the stage action was too complicated, and to follow the story line demanded an understanding of the sequence of scenes.

I began to understand what Bloomgarden had meant when he called it a "toughie." It was not only that there were so many different scenic locations but that the action demanded instantaneous time changes from the present to the past and back again. Actors playing a contemporaneous scene suddenly went back fifteen years in exactly the same setting—the Salesman's house. . . .

. . . a good scenic artist, without lacking respect for his author's contribution, should first make his own "breakdown" of the action, either in his mind or on paper. I always do mine on paper, as I did in rough form this night for *Death of a Salesman*. The designer should discover for himself what the author is saying in terms of the flow of action; he must examine the story as

it unfolds and determine on his own where the most important scenes should be played. After these key scenes are fully identified, an intelligent design can begin to develop.

SEPTEMBER 25, 1948

Early the next morning I glanced through the breakdown I had made. One thought came to me: in the scenes where the Salesman mentally goes back to the early years of his marriage, when his boys were young and the house was surrounded by trees and open country, I had to create something visually that would make these constant transitions in time immediately clear to the audience. My next thought was that, even if we ended up with a big stage, with plenty of stagehands, and I was able to design some mechanism for handling the large number of individual scenes, the most important visual symbol in the play—the real background of the story—was the Salesman's house. Therefore, why should that house not be the main set, with all the other scenes—the corner of a graveyard, a hotel room in Boston, the corner of a business office, a lawyer's consultation room,[1] and so on—played on a forestage? If I designed these little scenes in segments and fragments, with easily moved props and fluid lighting effects, I might be able, without ever lowering the curtain, to achieve the easy flow that the author clearly wanted.

By ten o'clock I had Bloomgarden on the telephone and we arranged to meet with Miller and Kazan later in the day. My calendar worried me. Kermit wanted *Death of a Salesman* to go into rehearsal in two weeks. This would leave me only six weeks in which to design and execute an extremely complex production. . . . But it wasn't other jobs that made me uneasy as much as it was my instinct that the new script would require a great deal of work by everyone if my basic idea for the setting proved to be acceptable. From long experience I knew that to delay an opening is usually too expensive for a producer even to consider; in addition, it sometimes means losing the services of important actors or of a top-notch director like Kazan.

Just the same, after we had gathered in Bloomgarden's office, I described the way I envisioned the production design and the method of its operation. When I finished, there was a long—a

---

[1]There is no scene in "Salesman" that takes place in a lawyer's consultation room. Perhaps Mielziner is thinking of the scene between Willy and Bernard that takes place in Charley's outer office. Since Mielziner began work with an early version of Miller's play, it is possible that he is referring to a scene that was later discarded. Similarly, his reference to a nonexistent character, Mr. Heizer, may stem from an early script.

much too long—pause. Then Kazan spoke up and said to Miller, "Art, this means a hell of a lot of work for me, and even more for you." And Kermit broke in with, "It means we can't possibly go into rehearsal in two weeks. I'll have to cancel my bookings out of town and in New York. It's up to you fellows to make the decisions. I'll go along if you feel you really need the time."

A long discussion followed. To Arthur Miller, a design scheme allowing him as author to blend scenes at will without even the shortest break for physical changes was a significant decision. To Kazan, with his strong sense of movement, stimulated by his already proven genius as a film director, the scheme would permit use of some of the best cinematic techniques. The decision to be made was not just a visual one; it would set the style in direction and performance, as well as in design.

Kazan had immediate commitments: he had to fly back to Boston that afternoon to a tryout of his musical. Miller had a great deal of rewriting to do, and felt that he didn't want to go ahead without constant conference with his director. Bloomgarden had complex financial and booking adjustments to make. But they all finally agreed to postpone and, provided my ideas worked out, to rewrite. . . .

SEPTEMBER 29, 1948

. . . In the five days that followed, I prepared about twenty sketches for *Death of a Salesman*. I decided to dispense with color at this time because it was more important to get the mood—the light and dark—and the feeling of isolation that lighting only a small segment of the setting would evoke. John Harvey[2] and his assistant went to work with my little ground plans, enlarging them to one half an inch to the foot. They were also going to build a model: the skeletonized version of the Salesman's house—the focal point of the whole design— was of the utmost importance and had to be developed three-dimensionally in a model, even if no one but the director ever looked at it. I was careful to start each sketch with the figures of Willy Loman, the Salesman, of his sons, or his wife, not only to intensify the dramatic mood of the sketch, but to control the interrelation of all the elements of the stage picture including the all-important human figure.

OCTOBER 4, 1948

. . . The greatest conundrum was in the scene in which the Salesman's two sons, as adults, go to bed in their attic bedroom in full view of the audience and then must appear elsewhere on the set a moment later as they were in their youth, entering downstage dressed in football togs. How were we going to get them out of bed and offstage without their being seen, when both the beds and their own bodies under the covers were completely visible to the audience, and also provide for an instantaneous costume change?

I said, "Let me try this out: We can build an inner frame in the beds that can act as an elevator. It can lower the boys quietly

---

[2]Mielziner's assistant.

from the attic bedroom down some seven feet to the stage in a spot hidden from the audience by the set. From there they can sneak backstage, make their changes, and appear in time." "But," someone asked, "what's going to happen if the audience sees their pillows and blankets suddenly flatten out?"

. . . I finally found the solution: the heads of the beds in the attic room were to face the audience; the pillows, in full view since there were to be no solid headboards, would be made of papier mâché. A depression in each pillow would permit the heads of the boys to be concealed from the audience, and they would lie under the blankets that had been stiffened to stay in place. We could then lower them and still retain the illusion of their being in bed.

Whenever I use a special mechanism of this sort, I always demonstrate it in full light at one of the early technical rehearsals. When I tried out this device, John Harvey was the demonstrator; he is a good six feet one and probably weighed more than either Arthur Kennedy or Cameron Mitchell, who were to play the sons. He got into position in one of the beds, and we signaled the master property man, Joe Lynn, to lower the elevator. Engineers had recommended that the mechanism be electrically driven, but both Joe and John advised me that it would be safer to have a hand-driven winch that could be instantly stopped or reversed if anything went wrong. We had already determined that signals would be necessary: a red light, controlled by a button under the pillow on each bed, enabled each boy to indicate when he was in position, ready for the stagehand below to turn the crank of the winch that would lower the inner frame of the bed.

The mechanism worked perfectly in the first demonstration. Then Arthur Kennedy asked to try it. He climbed into the bed and, on cue, flashed his red light. As Joe Lynn worked the winch, we suddenly heard a frightening crunching and grinding noise. Kazan cried, "My God, I hope that isn't Kennedy's skull!" Fortunately for both the actor and the play, it turned out to be the papier-mâché pillow, which was half an inch too large and had jammed in the elevator. This was soon fixed, and on the next try we did it with stage lighting. The effect worked magnificently. Theatrical illusion had been achieved. . . .

OCTOBER 15, 1948

. . . Anticipating the many lighting difficulties in *Death of a Salesman*, particularly in the scenes that used projections, I decided to have a preliminary check-up with my friend [Edward] Kook [of Century Lighting Company]. I outlined my problem: There must be a transformation of the Salesman's home from a house closely encircled by tenement buildings, which cut out all sunlight and view of the sky, to a vista of the same house years earlier, surrounded by open air and sunlit trees giving a feeling of leafy airiness. I showed him my design for the backdrop; instead of the customary rather opaque linen, I planned to use unbleached muslin, a much lighter material. On it I intended to have the surrounding buildings painted in translucent colors, particularly the windows, which would appear rather bright when lit from the rear. When the transformations to earlier

(continued)

times were to occur, I planned to use a number of projection units, like magic lanterns, both from the auditorium and from backstage, throwing leaf patterns on the backdrop and on parts of the house. As the lights behind the backdrop were faded out, the painted buildings on the front would, I hoped, virtually disappear as images of light, spring-like leaves and fresh greens were superimposed, liberating the house from the oppression of the surrounding structures and giving the stage a feeling of the free outdoors. This was an integral part of the Salesman's life story and had to be an easily recognized symbol of the springtime of that life. . . .[3]

OCTOBER 19, 1948

. . . I had reduced the Salesman's home to a series of three levels, with the frame outline of the house forming an open skeleton. Some of the doors were simply open framework; arches and windows were cut-outs of wood, but were drawn and painted with a good deal of quality in their line. Given this rather stark background, whatever props there would have to be highly significant in character. One thing in particular loomed large: the icebox.

One of the best references in my library is not a work on theatre history or the fine arts; it is a torn and tattered collection of old Sears, Roebuck catalogues. One of the difficulties of research into period costumes or furnishings is that the illustrators of most of the books show what the upper crust was wearing or sitting on; when a designer wants to know about *hoi polloi*, it usually takes some concentrated digging. In 1929, which was the year I needed for the icebox, Sears, Roebuck was not attracting customers from Fifth Avenue or Newport, and so, in looking through the catalogues for that year, I found a picture of what I had remembered as a refrigerator typical of the time—cast-iron Chippendale-type legs that were rather thin and ridiculous-looking, and condensation coils covered in white enamel and perched on top of the cabinet, looking for all the world like a mechanistic wedding cake.

Joe said he remembered the type very well, but added that they were hard to find, even in the best junkyards. However, he told me not to worry: "We'll allow ourselves enough time so that if we can't find one, we can make it. . . ."

NOVEMBER 1, 1948

. . . [Kazan's] chief concern after studying my model for "Salesman" was whether his actors would have enough room on the forestage to play the considerable number of scenes that we had placed there. We had agreed that the scenic effects for these episodes would be simple, but they would obviously involve a prop or two, and props have a way of taking up valuable playing space. Each scene would have to have enough of them

to make it identifiable. The model showed only five feet of space between the footlight area and the beginning of the Salesman's house. This worried Kazan.

I had previously discussed, and was still seriously working on, the idea of extending the working stage beyond the footlights. This, of course, meant losing valuable seats in the first two rows, and both the producer and the general manager were concerned about the economics of the suggestion. . . .

DECEMBER 8, 1948

I was still to face the possible battle over the lighting equipment, but, first, the time had come to pin down exactly what we were going to do about the forestage. Bloomgarden, Kazan, Miller, Max Allentuck, the general manager, and I met at the Morosco.

Del Hughes, the production stage manager, had been given my blueprint of the ground plan and had marked the stage floor with tape, indicating the location of the steps, platforms, exits, and entrances in relation to the footlight area. Kazan spent a silent half-hour moving thoughtfully around the stage, taking various positions, his head held down much of the time as he examined the marks on the floor; occasionally he would take a quick glance toward the forestage, mentally estimating where other actors would be when an actor was standing in the position that he, Kazan, was holding at the moment.

Suddenly he said, "Fine. But the real headache is out here," and he pointed to the space far downstage that I had asked for. He jumped over the footlights and landed in the aisle. He said, "Kerm, I'm afraid I'm going to kill at least a row and a half of doomed seats." I could see Max Allentuck concernedly counting the doomed seats. We experimented back and forth, and then Kazan offered a compromise. He decided that we would have to eliminate only the center section of the first row, a total of eleven seats. This meant a loss of $323.40 per week in receipts, which can mount up over a year. But the request was urgent, and Bloomgarden readily agreed. I was to build a forestage in this area.

With some nervousness I next brought up the high costs of the lighting equipment. After an hour of talk we settled on two special follow-spots and, necessarily, two extra men to operate them. As Bloomgarden pointed out, it was like a director saying, "I need two more good actors for this scene." And his reply to my request was the same as it would have been to his hypothetical director: "If it's important, you shall have them."

DECEMBER 10, 1948

. . . Bloomgarden asked me if I would meet with Alex North, the composer who had been engaged to do the music for *Death of a Salesman*. Everyone had agreed that the sound must be controlled with as much subtlety and care as the lights, increasing and diminishing almost imperceptibly. Since we had already planned to cover the orchestra pit with the forestage, where would the music be played, and what would the controlling mechanism be?

Using the blueprint of the ground plan, I reviewed the limitations with North and we concluded that we would use a dressing

---

[3]For Mielziner's conception of the house, before and after the transformation, see the color paintings in *Designing for the Theatre*, pp. 146–147. The volume also contains (pp. 28–29) reproductions of some of Mielziner's black-and-white sketches.

room as a control center and pipe the sound into the auditorium mechanically. Using headphones and a control speaker, the stage manager could then coordinate lighting cues with sound cues, for these two elements had to be in perfect harmony.

DECEMBER 15, 1948

. . . During the previous weeks I had been receiving from Arthur Miller, scene by scene, the final version of the rehearsal script. Although he had done the basic rewriting, he had made no attempt to say how the transitions from one scene to another would be made. This was a problem for the director and the designer to work out together as we studied the model, the ground plan, and the cut-out cardboard symbols representing the props.

I pointed out to Kazan how difficult it would be in an office scene, for instance, to remove two desks, two chairs, and a hatrack (which the present script called for) and at the same time have an actor walk quickly across the stage and appear in "a hotel room in Boston where he meets a girl." I urged him to do even more cutting, not in the text but in the props called for in this latest version of the script. We finally got the office pared down to one desk and one chair. Then I suggested going so far as to use the same desk for both office scenes—first in Heiser's[4] office and then, with a change of other props, in Charley's office. As usual, Kazan's imagination rose to the suggestion. He replied, "Sure, let's cut this down to the bone—we can play on practically anything." This is effective abstraction, giving the spectator the opportunity to "fill in."

I had felt from the outset that the cemetery scene at the end of the play would be done on the forestage, and I had actually drawn up a design for a trick trapdoor out of which would rise the small gravestone that we thought necessary for this scene. I had shown Kazan the working drawing for the gravestone, explained how it would operate, and mentioned that because of union rules the man operating this mechanism would be doing this and nothing else, thereby adding a member to the crew for the sake of one effect. I had also mentioned that since the trap would be very close to the audience the sound of its opening might disturb the solemnity of the scene.

With some malice aforethought, I had also done a drawing showing the Salesman's widow sitting on the step leading to the forestage, with her two sons standing behind her, their heads bowed; on the floor at her feet was a small bouquet of flowers. The whole scene was bathed in a magic-lantern projection of autumn leaves. Here, again, leaves were symbolic. With this kind of lighting I thought I could completely obliterate the house in the background and evoke a sense of sadness and finality that might enable us to eliminate the gravestone itself.

---

[4]Heiser may simply be a slip of Mielziner's pen, but it may also be a name given at one stage of the writing to Howard Wagner, the only character other than Charley who has an office in the play.

My hints were not lost. "I get your point," Kazan said. "Let's do it without the gravestone. No matter how quietly you move it into place, everybody nearby is going to be so busy thinking, 'How is that done?' that they'll miss the mood of the scene."

. . . When we came to the scene in the Boston hotel room, Kazan said, "I don't need anything; just give me the feeling of a hotel room." I showed him a sketch of a panel of cheap wallpaper which I planned to project from the theatre balcony onto a background that was really a section of the trellis at one side of the Salesman's house. Projected images used in conjunction with scenery can be very valuable. In this case, the associations evoked by faded old wallpaper gave the audience a complete picture. Both the house and the exterior trellis faded away. The audience saw the Salesman in the cheap hotel room with that woman. I stress the phrase "in that room." Actors should never play against a scenic background but within the setting.

Kazan felt that the right actress cast in the role of the girl who visits Willy Loman in the hotel room, dressed in the right costume, plus the visual image of the wallpaper, would be enough to make this short scene come alive. There is no question that when a good actor is backed up by simple scenic treatment, his strong qualities are stressed. Of course, this can work in reverse, but Arthur Miller was lucky in the casting of "Salesman"; even the bit roles were played by vivid actors. . . .

DECEMBER 24, 1948

. . . One example was the kitchen table for the Loman house. It would have been cheaper to buy one at a department store or a secondhand shop, but its color had to be right. I felt that in the Salesman's kitchen an old-fashioned oilcloth would have covered this table. But oilcloth is impossible to use on the stage because its shiny surface reflects too much light; and the moment the surface is sprayed down to kill the glare, the look of the oilcloth is lost. I knew from experience that glazed chintz with the right pattern plus a little over-painting by hand gives the impression of oilcloth. . . .

FEBRUARY 10, 1949

I was relaxed at the Broadway opening of *Death of a Salesman*. Here was a strong play. Audiences in Philadelphia had been tremendously enthusiastic. To me it was simply a question of how big a success the play would achieve. More than four months had passed since the initial phone call from Bloomgarden, and I felt I had done everything I was capable of doing to make the production visually effective and mechanically smooth-running. The performance *was* technically perfect. Artistically, the cast was superb, and they received a thunderous ovation. This type of reception is sometimes followed the next morning by cool reviews; but in this case the press was enthusiastic too. Contrary to custom, I even stayed up that night and went to a party. . . .

more flair in his costume to accent his importance. Cecil Beaton won many awards for his designs for *My Fair Lady*, largely for the brilliant "Ascot Gavotte" sequence in which the huge chorus was dressed in various shades of gray, black, and muted whites. When the newly transformed Eliza entered, she was gowned in brilliant white. Although there were dozens of actors onstage, the audience looked only at her.

Lighting designers usually begin their work after the scenery and costume designers have submitted their renderings for final approval by the director. They must know the ground plan, the height of platforms, and the location of entryways before devising the lighting plot. Usually designers observe a few rehearsals to learn where key actions are played, the mood of a scene, and where to focus "specials" (particular lighting instruments designated for a particular effect). The lighting designer also wants a strong feel for the colors and silhouette of the costumes. Much of the lighting designer's work is mechanical and is undertaken solely to make sure the actors are visible. The artistic dimension involves planning intensities, back and side lighting, and fade times, work that can be done in final rehearsals when the other components are brought together. The lighting design is the glue that binds all of the visual embellishments of the production.

Sound cues must also be meticulously planned and rehearsed. At technical rehearsals, much time is spent finding the right volume levels, placement of sound, and fade times. Not only do sound designers create the aural support for a play, they also develop amplification systems to insure that actors can be heard, especially in musicals and in large outdoor theaters.

Prior to technical rehearsals many artisans contribute to the execution of the designs. The scenery is built under the supervision of a technical director, who oversees carpenters, electricians, scene painters, and other specialized craftspeople. A costumer (or *costumier*) supervises cutters, stitchers, and tailors to construct the designer's renderings. Actors are fit for costumes, footwear, and even wigs when necessary. Shortly before "tech week" a costume parade may be organized to give the director and design team an opportunity to see how the garments look onstage under light. During technical rehearsals designers take notes concerning corrections, additions, deletions, and touchups. On opening night, if the design team has done its job well months in advance of the opening, the audience sees a fully integrated production that appears to have arrived effortlessly on the stage.

The Critic

Though they stand outside the production, critics nonetheless are an integral part of the process of giving a play life in the theater. Unfortunately, the very words *critic* and *criticism* have negative connotations. Even reliable, unbiased Webster defines *criticism* as "the act of criticizing, *usu. unfavorably*." Later, Webster does get to the heart of criticism in the arts: "the art of evaluating or analyzing with knowledge and propriety works of art and literature." On one hand, criticism is an "act" we each perform daily as we judge the food we eat, the music we listen to, the lectures we hear, and the TV shows we watch. Most of our criticism is simple: "I liked it," "It was awesome," "It was boring," "I hated it." When dealing with things artistic, we also respond critically, usually with some variant on "I may not know much about art, but I know what I like."

Criticism involves much more than giving "thumbs up" or "thumbs down" to a work. As Webster indicates, there is indeed an art to critical commentary, and the arts have been enriched by both professional and amateur critics. C. C. Colton, a music critic, defines the potential of criticism when he writes that it is "like champagne, nothing more execrable if bad, nothing more excellent when good; if meager, muddy, vapid, and sour, both are fit to engender colic and wind; if rich and generous and sparkling, they communicate a genial glow to the spirits, improve the taste and expand the heart."

Not everyone has written as elegantly about critics. The poet Samuel Taylor Coleridge, a critic himself, once wrote, "Critics—murderers!" Mark Twain dismissed them as members of "the most degraded of all trades." The Irish playwright Brendan Behan denounced critics because "they are there every night, they see it done every night, they see how it should be done, but they can't do it themselves." A witty critic might respond to Behan, "You don't have to know how to lay an egg to know when you've been served a bad one." Clearly, the battle between artists and critics is perpetual.

Theater artists, especially playwrights, can learn much from perceptive criticism. Because critics are outsiders and presumably objective and educated, their commentary may prompt improvements in a script, a performance, or a production concept. When the musical *Fiddler on the Roof* previewed in Washington, D.C., critics noted that an upbeat song about Motel the tailor's sewing machine in act 2 undercut the mood of the act; the composers weighed this commentary and cut the number.

In the theater there are essentially two types of adjudicators: the *reviewer* and the *critic*. These terms are often used interchangeably, but there is a practical difference between them. Reviewers are usually journalists who attend a play, most often on opening night, and evaluate their experience in writing for newspapers, magazines, or the electronic media. They assess the strengths of the play (especially if it is a new one), the quality of the performances, and the artistry of the director and designers. Reviews tend to be fairly short and are written quickly to meet deadlines and space limitations. Though reviewers in most cases are knowledgeable about theater and drama, they offer primarily a "gut reaction" to the production, a valuable thing because reviewers are much like the audience: they see a play, respond to it immediately, and judge the quality of their experience. Gotthold Lessing is generally considered the prototype of the reviewer. While serving as the dramaturge at Germany's Hamburg State Theater from 1767 to1769, Lessing wrote short essays about his reactions to the plays he saw. These have been collected under the title of *The Hamburg Dramaturgy* and stand as the model for reviewers.

Some reviews are written well after the theatrical event, often by scholars and critics who have considerable expertise. Their work is usually found in journals and perhaps the Sunday Arts section of major papers. The late Walter Kerr, for years the principal reviewer for the *New York Times*, wrote a weekly column in which he considered a production in greater detail, perhaps after a second viewing. Scholarly journals, such as *Theater Quarterly* and *Shakespeare Studies*, contain in-depth analyses of productions written by experts who have had considerable time to evaluate the strengths and weaknesses of a production.

Critics usually go to greater depth than reviewers and are able to base their opinions on lengthy reflection. Aristotle's *Poetics*, the model of this form of criticism, was written a half-century after the decline of golden age of Greek theater. Professional and scholarly critics often read and re-read a play to judge its structure, the quality of its dialogue, its depth of characterization, and its themes. Perhaps they have time to reflect on other productions, compare their reactions with those of other critics, and discuss the play with the artists who produced it. Ideally, such critics provide more profound insight into the play. This is not to say that reviewers cannot write exceptional criticism: see John Mason Brown's essay on *Death of a Salesman* (see Chapter 7).

The "critic-theorist" is a specialist whose primary interest is not so much in an individual play or production. They may consider a number of issues concerning theater and drama, such as the dramatic structure, genres, styles, conventions, the phenomenology of the theater, semiotics (the study of signs and symbols), gender, multicultural issues, history and popular culture. Hence, you may read essays, or perhaps entire books, such as Gerald Else's analysis of tragedy, Bert O. State's study of the phenomenon of the actor onstage, or Sue Ellen Case's discussion of the changing roles of women in the theater. Theorists may cite specific examples from particular plays or productions, but their focus is on the larger picture, and they provide a broader perspective from which we may view the theater experience. Importantly, they provide us with a common language with which we may discuss theater.

Among the most valuable functions of good criticism is that it educates audiences and makes the theater experience more rewarding. They do this by fulfilling the following tasks:

- They encourage excellence in art by providing, even raising, standards for artists and audiences.
- They attempt to weed out incompetence.
- They promote originality and encourage artists to stretch themselves and their art.

- They provide insight into and understanding of art in general, and of a specific work.
- They provide a context within which to appreciate a particular work.

By what standards ought we to judge critics? While criticism is inherently a subjective act, there are means by which critics can objectify their opinions. These are applicable to both professional and academic critics, and they give you some criteria that you might consider as you "critique the critics":

- A knowledge of the technical and theoretical principles of theater and drama;
- A familiarity with the history of the theater around the world;
- A broadly based education in subjects related to theater and drama;
- An ability to think analytically and to write clearly and vividly;
- An understanding of the creative impulse and imagination;
- An integrated personal philosophy of life;
- An open mind, inquisitiveness, and a willingness to learn;
- An awareness and acceptance of one's own limitations.

At its most fundamental level, criticism is opinion, not dogma; it is not irrefutable fact. But the stronger the foundation on which the opinion is formed, the more respect it carries. Thoughtful criticism, well conceived, well written, and motivated by a passion for the art, serves the theater and drama no less nobly than strong scripts, engaging actors, and memorable scenography.

Samples of the works of reviewers, critics, and theorists have been included throughout this text; some are whole, others have been abridged. Collectively they offer a range of insights about creating theater. As you read them, consider the various criteria by which they judge theater and drama. Also, in the appendix you will find some suggestions that may help you as you write about the plays you read and see.

PART II

An Anthology of the World's Drama

> "*I'm going to have a copy of this play put in that cornerstone, so that people a thousand—two thousand—years from now will know a few simple facts about us. . . . This is the way we were, in our growing up, in our marrying, in our living, and in our dying.*"
>
> Thornton Wilder, *Our Town*

Sir Peter Hall merged classical and modern sensibilities in his production of Aeschylus's The Oresteia *at the National Theater of Great Britain (1981); Orestes is pursued by the chorus of Furies in the trilogy's final play.*

CHAPTER 4

THE THEATER OF GREECE AND ROME

It is fitting we begin our survey of world theater by returning to Greece and Rome, the civilizations that laid the foundation for Western civilization and its arts. Without minimizing the significant artistic contributions made by various Mediterranean cultures—notably the Egyptians, whose drama was discussed in Chapter 1—it was first the Greeks, then the Romans, who built the foundation for the development of drama in the West.

From the Greeks and Romans, we have inherited a rich legacy of democracy, laws, and social organization. And as importantly, these two civilizations—which dominated the Western world for over a thousand years—provided us with models for architecture, sculpture, poetry, painting, and, of course, theater and drama. The latter group—the Arts—was intended to ensure an order sought by the former. Socrates, the venerable philosopher, declared that "the unexamined life is not worth living," and the theater, the great meeting place of the Greeks (and, admittedly, to a lesser degree the Romans), emerged as a locus for the collective examination of humanity's place and purpose in this world. Significantly, the examination was conducted against the backdrop of the cosmos itself in the great outdoor theatrons of the Hellenic world.

Today we commonly use words bequeathed us by Greek and Roman theater artists: tragedy, drama, hypocrite, prologue, catharsis, histrionic, and ludicrous (from the Roman word for "play"). These remind us that life and art were not things set apart from one another; rather, they were interdependent. Perhaps the greatest legacy, however, of the Greco-Roman theaters was the focus on the individual who is brought to a moment of self-examination and self-awareness. Subsequent Western literature has continued this emphasis on the individual caught in moments of crisis.

We commonly refer to Greco-Roman age as "classical" because their arts often achieved a perfection we still use as a standard by which we judge the worthiness of a work. Furthermore, they created models for future generations of artists to emulate or reject, but not to ignore. As we discuss the evolution of drama from fifth century B.C.E. through the twentieth century C.E., you may be surprised at how often we must return to Greece and Rome as points of reference. So let us return to Greece, where it all began.

GREECE

Artistic and Cultural Events

534:
First tragic competitions at City Dionysia

c. 550:
Thespis introduces "the first speaker"

471:
Aeschylus adds second actor to tragedy

c. 468:
Sophocles adds third actor to tragedy

c. 431:
Euripides' *Medea*

c. 430:
Sophocles' *Oedipus the King*

c. 411:
Aristophanes' *Lysistrata*

400–c. 320:
Middle comedy

336–300:
New comedy

c. 335:
Aristotle's *The Poetics*

c. 320:
Menander's *The Grouch*

Homeric Age: the great epics

Records of dithyrambic choruses

800 B.C.E.	700 B.C.E.	600 B.C.E.	500 B.C.E.	400 B.C.E.	300 B.C.E.

Historical and Political Events

600–300:
Classical Age

509–265:
The Republic

Peisistratus rules Athens

462–429:
Age of Pericles, Athens Golden Age

399:
Socrates executed

404:
Athens falls to Sparta

431–404:
Peloponnesian War

336–146:
Hellenistic Age

Adriatic Sea

ASIA MINOR

Mt. Olympus ▲

● Troy

GREECE

*Aegean
Sea*

Delphi ●

● Thebes

Corinth ●

● Athens

Epidauros ●

*Ionian
Sea*

Sparta ●

Crete

Mediterranean Sea

The Origins of the Theater in Greece

There is considerable debate about the precise beginnings of theater in the Western world, largely because the evidence is incomplete and often contradictory. Many historians, however, cite the Dionysian *dithyramb* as the origin of European theater and its subsequent drama. No less a figure than Aristotle supports this theory in his *The Poetics* (c. 335 B.C.E.), although in recent years Aristotle's commentary has been challenged. In 1964 Gerald Else theorized that drama (specifically tragedy) originated in the fertile minds of two Athenian playwrights, Thespis and Aeschylus, about whom more will be said. Aristotle's account of the dithyrambic origins of theater and Else's theory on the origins of tragedy are not necessarily incompatible. The traditional account is presented here with the caveat that scholars have not reached accord on the issue. Else rightly points out that his argument (like that of Aristotle's) is "a theory. With the evidence that we have available, no one can honestly claim to offer anything more." It should be noted that the Greek word for "ritual" was *dromenon*, meaning "something performed" or "to perform rites"; it was often used with the phrase *ta hiera*, "holy sacrifice." By the fifth century *dromenon* was applied to the performance of plays ("a thing done or performed"), which suggests that the early Greeks understood the evolutionary relationship between ritual and drama.

Early in his treatise Aristotle refers to *dithyrambs*, which were originally improvised hymns and dances performed in honor of Dionysus, a lesser agrarian deity associated with fertility and wine, and by extension with the passionate, irrational forces that wine induces. Dionysus, a patron of the creative force in humans, also could be fiercely destructive, as we see in *The Bacchae*, the only extant tragedy about him. Dionysus was the offspring of an illicit union between Zeus and a mortal, Semele. Each year he was buried in the earth at harvest time to protect him from jealous gods who resented his power. In the spring he came to life again (his name means "twice born") and blessed the land where he slept for the winter with plenty. The guardians of Dionysus were *satyrs*, a race of half-men, half-goats (with the tails of horses). The word *tragedy*— denoting a particular form of drama that developed much later—derives from *trago-dia* ("song of the goats"), perhaps a reference to the dithyrambic worshippers who dressed in goatskins. There is evidence that winners of the dithyrambic contests were given goats as prizes, and goats may have been sacrificed at the sacred altar (*thymele*) during these rites.

To ensure that Dionysus would bless the land, animals, and humans with healthy offspring, a public celebration in the god's honor was held each spring (about the time Christians celebrate the Resurrection of Christ, their god-king, at Easter). This cult of Dionysus can be traced as far back as the fifteenth century B.C.E., roughly a thousand years before formal theater developed in Greece. Much wine was consumed, as it was believed to be the blood of the god himself. Dithyrambs were performed in his honor, as were ecstatic dances, vestiges of the older agrarian matriarchy. This excerpt from Euripides' *The Bacchae* echoes the ancient dithyrambs sung to Dionysus (or Bacchus, as the Romans referred to him):

> Hither, O fragrant of Timolus the Golden,
>> Come with the voice of the timbrel and drum;
> Let the cry of your joyance uplift and embolden
>> The God of the joy-cry; O Bacchanals, come!

Aristotle says that processions in honor of Dionysus were held throughout Greece and the Mediterranean, notably in the Peloponnese and Megara. But the cult of Dionysus is most closely associated with Athens, where the ruler (*tyrannos*) Peisistratus declared Dionysus his particular deity. Men dressed as satyrs led the procession, while the nuns of Dionysus (*maenads*, the "mad ones") carried the bough of an evergreen (*thrysus*) to remind the people of Dionysus's return to life. The priests of Dionysus officiated at these *City Dionysia*, which eventually became more social and political than religious events. The 10 (later 15) tribes that ruled Athens each provided a dithyrambic chorus for the *Dionysia*, thereby adding a political dimension to what was originally purely religious. John Winkler and Froma Zeitlin provide a useful analogue to the experience of these ancient *Dionysia* for modern audiences:

> Even to come close to the authentic experience [of the Dionysia], and hence in some part to the meaning, of attending a "play" in ancient Athens, we would have to imagine that Arthur Miller, Tennessee Williams, and Sam Shepard had each written three serious plays and a farce for a one-time performance on a national holiday—say, the Fourth of July—in honor of an ancient god-hero, perhaps a cross between George Washington and Johnny Appleseed, and that these were preceded by a parade of congressional representatives and cabinet secretaries and federal judges and governors and mayors, that the plays were performed after ceremonies honoring the war dead and our national allies, that bishops and generals and mothers superior had prominent places in the front rows, and that the choruses who sang and danced were composed . . . of West Point cadets, dressed sometimes as old veterans, sometimes as servants or refugees or prisoners of war, occasionally (but only rarely) as young men.
>
> John Winkler and Froma Zeitlin, *Nothing to Do with Dionysus?* (1990, p. 5)

To improve the quality of the dithyrambs, and because humans enjoy competition (remember, the Greeks gave us the Olympic Games), contests became integral to the *Dionysia*. Both the composers of the best dithyrambs and the choruses that sang and danced them were rewarded. Dithyrambic competitions continued well into the fourth century, though the songs themselves carried a much weaker association with the cult of Dionysus.

We surmise that eventually someone was inspired to call for one member of the chorus to step aside and assume the role of Dionysus. This actor, known as a *hypokrites* ("the answerer," or literally "from under the mask"), engaged the dithyrambic chorus in dialogue. Later, the chorus questioned other gods and heroes of mythology; eventually, the great mythic tales so loved by the Greeks were "acted out" and "plays" evolved. Tradition suggests a young dithyrambic performer, Thespis, emerged from the chorus of 50 at the *City Dionysia* in Athens about the middle of the sixth century to become the first solo actor. Thespis ("inspired by god") covered his face with white paint and hung flowers about his face, thus giving us the first known "mask" in the Greek theater. Else believes that it was Thespis who reshaped the old Homeric myths into "action," as opposed to a "telling," as an early attempt at tragedy. Whatever his contributions, Thespis is revered as the first Western actor and his followers are known as thespians. Aeschylus, often called the father of tragedy because his genius raised the genre to an art form distinct from other kinds of plays, created the second actor and thus made true dialogue and conflict possible. Sophocles, whose dramas epitomize the greatness of Greece's golden age, used a third speaking role to provide greater contrast among characters. Euripides emphasized individual characters by diminishing the role of the chorus, though *The Bacchae* is an exception. These three tragedians produced the greatest drama of the fifth century, and established standards by which subsequent playwrights in the West would be judged.

Those who question the dithyrambic origins of theater in ancient Greece have suggested other possibilities based on some form of ritualistic or ceremonial activity:

- ecstatic rites of passage involving the seasons or puberty (e.g., Gilbert Murray and Jane Harrison)
- tomb and hero-cult worship (William Ridgeway)
- shamanistic practices by Dionysian priests (E. T. Kirby)
- dances performed by women while threshing grain.

It is not our purpose here to offer a complete history of the evolution of theater in ancient Greece. For now, you need only be aware that Western theater apparently developed about 2,500 years ago from rites similar in impulse to those described in Chapter 1. At its roots are a recognition of forces superior to humans, communal celebrations of triumphs, lamentations about death, and the ritualization of common beliefs through the use of storytelling, music, dance, gesture, masks, and costumes. (See Spotlight box, The Hellenistic Theater.)

SPOTLIGHT   THE HELLENISTIC THEATER

Because the *Dionysia* were communal events in which the free male populace of the city-state (*polis*) was expected to participate, it became necessary to build permanent spaces for the performance of the dithyrambs and, much later, plays. The architecture of the classical Greek theater, which evolved over many years, reminds us of the spiritual roots of theater. Significantly, the theaters were outdoor affairs; thus dramas about mythic heroes and their gods were played against the natural backdrop of the universe itself. Because the chorus was always central to the *Dionysia*, the place where it sang and danced became the premiere architectural feature of the early Greek theaters. A sacred circle, measuring between 60 to 90 feet in diameter, was the focal point for the singing and dancing chorus. Appropriately, it was named the *orchestra*, or "the dancing place." At its center was the *thymele* (or altar; there

were two in some theaters) at which sacrifices were offered, a remnant of the spiritual beginnings of the Greek theater. To improve both visibility and acoustics, the individual actors may have performed on a platform, or *logeion*. (You can still purchase orchestra or loge seats in large theaters today.) The actors donned padded costumes and masks to make them more readily visible to the enormous audiences, which may have numbered 15,000. A small dressing hut or tent, which the Greeks called a *skene*, originally stood some distance from the playing area, but eventually was moved directly behind the *logeion* to mask entrances and to provide both scenic backdrops and acoustical support. One of the theater's most frequently used terms, "scene," comes from this architectural feature of the early Greek theaters. To improve sight lines, the audience was elevated above the playing area by sculpting

seats into hillsides. Special seats for the priests of Dionysus were placed closest to the orchestra; as the *Dionysia* became more civic than religious affairs, seating for public officials became more prominent. The audience area was known as the *theatron*, or "seeing place." Today we customarily refer to the audience area as "the auditorium," or "hearing place," which suggests that the spoken word gradually supplanted dancing and choral singing as the primary means of communication. Still, *theatron* provides us with the terms *theatre* (the art of making spectacle and drama) and *theater* (most often used to denote the architectural space in which the plays are performed). We now use the generic term "theater" (and this Americanized spelling) to denote a wide variety of activities in which spectacle (e.g., costumes, masks, scenery) and physical action is integral to the event.

The Greek Mind

Whether its origins were in ancient dithyrambic rites, ceremonies such as burials and agricultural fetes, or even the genius of Thespis and Aeschylus, three elements of the Greek mind inform Greek drama. First, the Greeks were humanists who believed that human beings are "the measure of all things." To the Greeks humans were godlike in their unlimited potential for greatness. Indeed, tragedy was devised to remind the Greeks that they were only god*like* and not gods themselves.

Second, the Greeks understood that even exceptional beings were accountable to the natural order of things. *Dikē* represented a universal justice that insured that everything in creation behaved according to a master plan that humans might not understand. When *dikē* was upset—either through human or divine error—*anankē* ("necessity") demanded that the resultant chaos be harnessed to restore harmony and order; often this could only be accomplished through the death of the perpetrator. The *Erinyes*—sometimes called the Furies—acted as a type of cosmic police force deployed to restore *dikē*. Aeschylus's magnificent trilogy, *The Oresteia*, illustrates how the *Erinyes* were transformed into the *Eumenides* ("the kindly ones"), a more benevolent force that maintained harmony through reconciliation rather than retribution. The Greeks believed their vast pantheon of gods cooperated with humans to maintain *dikē*. That, at least, was the theory. The plays were written to depict the consequences of a mutual inability to adhere to *dikē*'s plan.

Third, the Greeks appreciated the complexity of life, as the dichotomy between the ideal of the perfect human and the reality of human error suggests. They enjoyed debate (*agon*) and in most Greek communities one could find an area of the agora (marketplace) set aside for discussions of social, political, and philosophical issues. The great Socratic questions—"What is man?" and "What is the highest good?"—were central to these lively discussions. Furthermore, debate fostered Greece's greatest legacy to subsequent generations: democracy and the free exchange of ideas. Greek dramas, which may have begun as religious affairs, became political events that promoted the general good. Predictably, they are filled with debates such as those between Oedipus and Teiresias or Lysistrata and the Athenian commissioner. The words we use to identify the principal characters in a play—protagonist and antagonist—derive from debate. A protagonist was the "first contestant," and the one who opposed her or him was the antagonist.

Because the dramatic festivals glorified the *polis* (city-state) and its ideals, the theaters were built to house the entire free, male population of the *polis*. The Theater of Dionysus in Athens held perhaps 14,000, while the great theaters at Epidaurus and Ephesus seated 17,000 and 25,000, respectively. Women and slaves could attend the theater, but all free men were expected to attend. Such male-centered attitudes raise questions about the role of women in classical Greek drama. Women held a curious, even contradictory, place in Greek society that is reflected in the plays. They were not considered citizens of the *polis*. Solon, Greece's most famous lawgiver, relegated them to the home, while Aristotle argued in *The Poetics* that as a class women were "inferior" (though he allowed that "a woman can be good"). Women were treated as chattel to be owned by men who valued them primarily as incubators for healthy offspring. For example, in *The Oresteia* Apollo argues that Agamemnon is the true parent of Orestes and that Clytemnestra was merely the carrier of his seed. Thus Orestes had every right—even a sacred duty under the patriarchal system—to kill his "mother." While men certainly could love women (a common theme in many myths), it was generally accepted that an ideal love could take place only between equals—that is, men. Thus some Greeks practiced homosexuality (an issue in the Achilles-Patroclus relationship in the *Iliad*). Though society relegated women to second-class status, in the plays they were frequently portrayed as wellsprings of common sense and civility. Antigone becomes the defender of divine law in Sophocles' play, while Aristophanes' heroine Lysistrata devises the plan to save Greece from the devastating effects of the Pelopennesian War. This paradoxical view of women may be explained in various ways: first, the propensity to debate encouraged the Greeks to accept both sides of an issue, even when presented by a female character. Sue Ellen Case and other feminist critics, however, argue that the depiction of women in Athenian theater was actually a product of a male-dominated social system and that women were portrayed, both as written and as performed by men, as men wished them to act.

Playwrights and Acting

Three playwrights are largely responsible for the greatest of the Greek tragedies. Though many men wrote plays, we have only the works of Aeschylus (525–456 B.C.E.), Sophocles (c. 496–406 B.C.E.), and Euripides (c. 480–406 B.C.E.). Because he wrote as tragedy was being created, Aeschylus's plays are most concerned with issues of theology and the shaping of a moral order in Greek society. *The Oresteia*, the only extant trilogy, traces the evolution of justice among gods and humans as it shows how we "must suffer, suffer into truth." Sophocles, by contrast, focused on the dilemma of the individual at a moment of intense crisis (see the introduction to *Oedipus the King*, later in this chapter). Sophoclean drama elevated tragedy in its depiction of the hero's journey to self-knowledge after a catastrophic reversal of fortune. Euripides is said to have diminished Greek tragedy with cynical works that challenged the power of the gods themselves. Such assessments of Euripides' purpose—as represented in the writings of the comic playwright Aristophanes (448–380 B.C.E.) and by the German philosopher Friedrich Nietzsche (1844–1900)—fail to account for the complexity of the last of the great Greek tragedians, whose works are perhaps the most accessible to late-twentieth-century audiences.

Greek acting was also a product of the cultural and social influences that shaped the dramas. Because their drama evolved from choric song and subsequently became political and moral debates, Greek actors relied on declamation. Furthermore, because of the vast size of

---

The Greek ideal promoted a world-view that was ordered, harmonious, and beautiful. In fact, the Greek word for "universe," which included the totality of their experience, was *cosmos*, a synonym for beauty (as in "cosmetics"). To the Greeks, the universe was indeed a beautiful place, and their tragedies were reminders of the consequences when human arrogance upset the natural order of things, which they called *dikē*. The virtues of order, harmony, unity, and beauty became signatures of what we now call *Classicism*; in the Renaissance, an era that imitated Greco-Roman ideals, a rebirth of Classicism (*Neoclassicism*) had a profound effect on theater and drama.

Because playwriting, theater architecture, and performance methods reflect the current culture, the style and conventions of Greek theater and drama are founded on the classical ideal. To enhance your reading of Greek drama, familiarize yourself with the play structure, the theater space, and the acting style. Keep in mind that these conventions developed to complement the subject matter of the plays themselves. Marshall McLuhan's observation that "the medium *is* the message" is as applicable to Greek theater in the fifth century B.C.E. as it is to contemporary television.

The Structure of a Greek Play

Because Greek drama descended from ancient rituals, the plays retain a structure that is as carefully ordered as a church service. The principal parts of a Greek play (both tragedy and comedy), in the order in which they appear, are:

The *prologue*: Like the preface to this book, the prologue prepares the audience for what follows. The prologue customarily consists of a dialogue between two or three characters who provide us with exposition about the conflict that the play must resolve. Euripides, who experimented with the forms of drama, often used a single character (such as Dionysus in *The Bac-*

chae) to present his prologues. In *Oedipus the King*, Oedipus is confronted by a priest who begs the monarch to liberate the Thebans from the terrible plague.

The *parados*: Because the chorus existed long before the emergence of formal, scripted dramas, it retained its prominence and was accorded a ceremonial entrance. The *parados* usually introduced the thematic concerns of the play, as well as creating its emotional atmosphere. Like the choric odes, it was sung and danced, much like the older *dithyrambs* that preceded formal drama.

Episodes are the "acts" of a Greek play. Here, the actual story of Prometheus or Oedipus is told through a series of scenes, usually about five. The episodes focus on what happens in a play. Here are found the structural units described in Chapter 2: complication, rising action, crisis, climax, reversal, recognition, and resolution. Some episodes were dedicated to particular conventions of Greek drama. Because the Greeks enjoyed debate, there was invariably an *agon*, or contest, in which conflicting characters argued their positions; see the heated discussion between Oedipus and Teiresias. Coinciding with the recognition and its attendant reversal was the *komos*, which—in tragedy—was a great outpouring of emotion, usually grief. In comedy, the *komos* was a joyful celebration, the culmination of the action of the play. One episode, usually occurring quite late in the action, often was allotted to the appearance of a "messenger" whose sole purpose was to describe offstage action, usually the violent death or mutilation of a character; both *Oedipus the King* and especially *Medea* provide notable examples of such speeches. Greek tragedies, with very few exceptions (e.g., Sophocles' *Ajax*), do not show violent acts onstage, although they are about calamitous violence. Exhibiting violence violated the Greek sense of decorum and diminished the role of the audience's imagination.

Odes (*Stasiman*): Throughout the middle section of the play, episodes alternate with the choric odes. After each episode the chorus commented on the action and heightened the mood. This was accomplished by a lengthy song, complemented by a dance. The odes were usually divided into *strophes* and *antistrophes*, or "turns" and "counterturns," which suggests something about the dance movements of the chorus. Just as the episodes tell us what is happening in a play, the odes frequently tell us why something happens. The chorus customarily speaks for the community and reflects on the consequences of human action. Furthermore, the odes often link the present action with the mythic past and thus bolster the cosmic implications of the plays. Though the odes may seem strange to us because apparently nothing is "happening," they are invaluable guides to the thematic purpose and emotional pitch of the play. They function very much like song-and-dance numbers in the modern musical (which actually derived from Greek drama when Renaissance scholars attempted to re-create Greek drama—opera, then operetta, and eventually musical comedy were born of this effort).

The *exodos*: After the final episode, in which the fate of the protagonist is made known, the principal characters leave the stage. The chorus exits with a final hymn in which the lesson of the tragedy is stated, much the way a fairy tale or Aesop's fable ends with "and the moral of the story is. . . ." Compared with the parados and other odes, the exodos is quite short because a prolonged speech would be anticlimactic.

Greek comedy also employed two particular features, the *agon* and the *parabisis*, which are discussed in conjunction with Greek Old Comedy.

The Physical Theater and Scenery

As the shape of the Greek theater suggests, everything about its design reflects the Greek preoccupation with

order and harmony. Note the graceful rings that form the *theatron* where the audience sat, as well as the great circle of the *orchestra* where the chorus sang and danced. To the right and left of the orchestra were the *paradoi*—pathways or ramps which provided the chorus and spectators access to the orchestra and theatron. The raised *logeion*, on which the principal characters may have stood, was backed by a *skene*, itself a model of harmony and balance with its three perfectly spaced doors. The doors traditionally signified locale to the audience: the center door was invariably "the palace" door, while the side doors usually suggested a way to the seaport or to a rural area (depending on the geographical orientation of the theater); thus when the Shepherd enters from the right door, they assumed he had arrived from the countryside.

Because of their enormous size and the construction problems they presented, the theaters were built outdoors, usually at the base of a hillside to facilitate the construction of the *theatron*. The stories the Greeks told, the characters that enacted them, and the cosmic themes they illustrated were all larger than life, and could be performed in the Greek mind only against the backdrop of the universe itself. Just as so much of contemporary drama needs small, intimate spaces to examine the interior lives of the ordinary people who cross its stages, the Greeks needed vast, open spaces large enough to contain characters who could, in H. D. F. Kitto's words, "shake their fists at the gods."

The Greeks used little scenery and thus relied on the evocative power of language to create time and place. Because their stories were universal, the particulars of place were insignificant. Three visual elements invite discussion, however. *Periaktoi* were triangular prisms on which suggestions of locale—forest, seacoast, or palace—were painted. Sophocles is reputed to have invented these ingenious devices, which could be rotated to suggest a change in locale. Although violence

was rarely shown on Greek stages, the *ekkyklema*, a small platform mounted on wheels, was apparently used to display the bodies of the dead. In Aeschylus's *Agamemnon*, the bodies of Agamemnon and his concubine, Cassandra, were wheeled onstage through the center door via the *ekkyklema*. On those very rare occasions when interior scenes were necessary, the *ekkyklema* may have been used to suggest the "indoors." Perhaps the most famous piece of Greek stage technology was the *mēchane*, an elaborate rope-and-pulley device that allowed supernatural beings to be lowered from the roof of the *skene* to suggest that heavenly intervention was necessary in human affairs. Euripides used the *mēchane* in a rather cynical fashion to intimate that gods were capricious and entirely fallible as interlopers in human affairs. Aristophanes employed the device to great effect in many of his comedies. As a literary term, a *deus ex machina* (a Latin phrase for "god from a machine") is an external agent who appears suddenly (and often mysteriously) to help resolve the plot. The King's Officer in Molière's *Tartuffe* and Sir Oliver Surface in Sheridan's *The School for Scandal* are popular examples of the *deus ex machina,* a term directly ascribable to one of the more spectacular conventions of Greek theater.

Acting Styles

Acting styles throughout the history of the theater have been dictated by several factors, including the language of the script, the playing space, and other accoutrements, such as costume, masks, and makeup, with which an actor must deal. This is especially true of the Greeks, who necessarily developed some of the most distinctive conventions of Western theater. Little wonder that the emblem of Western theater today is a Greek mask! Because the tragic plays depicted heroic characters whose passions and deeds exceeded those of ordinary mortals, the actors necessarily had to project themselves

physically and vocally. Furthermore, the enormous size of the theaters promoted an acting style, almost operatic by our standards, that depended on large gestures and declamatory speech when song was not used. The costumes helped the actors in their quest to measure up to the characters they portrayed. The actors wore a large headpiece (*onkos*) that increased their stature. To this was affixed a mask made of thin cloth, cork, and light wood; the mask suggested the dominant passion that enveloped a character, though characters could switch masks to indicate a change of personality. The masks also made it possible for an actor to play more than one character, as the traditional Greek acting company usually consisted of 3 actors, the chorus leader (the *koryphaies*), and the chorus, which numbered from 12 to 15. To insure proportion, the body was enlarged by padded robes and thick-soled footwear (*kothornoi*), though some argue that these boots were actually a Roman addition. The principal characters wore masks and robes that distinguished them by sex, social rank, and personality; the chorus was dressed alike and wore simpler robes and footwear that would not interfere with their lively dances. There is evidence that the Greeks used a more realistic acting style than we might surmise. Psychological detail, genuine human emotions, and true-to-life situations abound in the plays (especially in those of Euripides, whom Sophocles referred to as a "realist"). And there is the story of the actor Polus of Aegina. When he played Electra, Polus used an urn containing the ashes of his own son to motivate him in the scene in which Electra weeps over Orestes' remains—the world's first "Method actor"! Psychological truths and motivational techniques aside, Greek acting demanded much physical and vocal skill, especially when we consider that the actors had to perform four plays, a *tetralogy* of three tragedies and a satyr comedy, in a single day at the Dionysia.

Greek theaters, they were obligated to use sweeping gestures, a resonant voice, and stylized movement to make themselves heard and seen. They wore a large headpiece (*onkos*) and masks, padded robes, and (possibly) elevated shoes (*kothornoi*), which also necessitated stylized performance. Given the larger-than-life quality of the characters they played, as well as their unbridled passions, the style was appropriate. Actors customarily played more than one role in a play (including those of women) which further precluded naturalistic acting. (See Spotlight box, The Conventions of Greek Theater.)

After nearly a century-long Golden Age, Greek idealism was severely challenged by the Pelopennesian War (431–404 B.C.E.), which pitted Athens and Sparta in a destructive civil war. By the end of the fifth century, a bankrupt, decimated, and cynical Athens severely curtailed debate and freedom of expression. The new cynicism is reflected in the tragedies of Euripides and the comedies of Aristophanes. (See Spotlight box, Greek Old Comedy, which follows the text of *Lysistrata*.) By the fourth century, tragedy had deteriorated into melodrama, and comedy shifted from the satires of Aristophanes to the safer comedy of Menander (c. 342-c. 291 B.C.E.), which depicted common people in everyday situations, speaking more lifelike dialogue. Though we would never mistake his plays as realistic, they were an important step in the evolution of this distinctly Western style of performance. Moreover, Menander created a variety of stock characters—the giddy young lover, the conniving manservant—who would become staples of Western comedy to this day. Menander's sole surviving comedy, *Dyskalos* (*The Grouch*, 320 B.C.E.), is about the "grumpy old man" we associate with Walter Matthau's screen persona. It was Menander who, in effect, developed the prototype for television sitcoms.

PROMETHEUS BOUND

AESCHYLUS

AESCHYLUS (C. 525–C. 455 B.C.E.)

Although he wrote the first masterpieces of Western drama and is considered its patriarch, Aeschylus wished to be remembered for having fought in the Battle of Marathon (490 B.C.E.), where the Greeks defeated the invading Persian army. The victory made Greece the Mediterranean's leading power, and for the next century it flourished in virtually all phases of human endeavor. As author and civic leader Aeschylus contributed much to this golden age, yet his self-composed epitaph simply reads:

> Here lies the Athenian, Aeschylus, son of Euphorion, who died on grain-bearing Gala [now Sicily]. The plain of Marathon can tell of his proven might, and the long-haired Mede [i.e., the Persians] who learned of it there.

Aeschylus learned a valuable lesson at Marathon: greatness emerges from a severe test. This seems to be the recurring theme throughout the 90 plays he wrote, of which only 7 remain. Though his plays deal with suffering, they also reflect the optimism that permeated Greek life throughout most of the fifth century. Pain and loss ultimately lead to triumph, just as the wounds of Marathon produced one of the world's glorious cultures.

Aeschylus's greatest work, *The Oresteia*, is the single extant trilogy from the early Greek theater (Sophocles' Theban trilogy was written over many years and was not intended as a unified work). In *Agamemnon*, *The Libation Bearers*, and *The Eumenides* Aeschylus traces humanity's growth from barbarism to civility. Vengeance, that most primal of human urges, eventually gives way to reason as mortals and gods unite to create laws and courts to mediate grievances. The trilogy's movement from darkness to light, from slaughter to reconciliation, from ignorance to knowledge, celebrates humanity's maturation and is perhaps the greatest rite of passage in Western literature.

Aeschylus contributed much to the development of Western theater and may rightly be called "the Great Innovator." He is credited with inventing the second actor and thereby making true stage dialogue possible. His interlinked trilogies provided the structure for the multiact play. He devised costuming, footwear, scenic effects, and stage machinery. According to an early biographer, Aeschylus "was the first to give poses to his choruses, employing no dancing masters, but devising for himself the entire management of the piece." He also was admired as a superb actor. Most significantly, however, it was Aeschylus who invested Western drama with its essentially realistic nature. Though the conventions with which he had to work were theatrical, Aeschylus nonetheless rendered his characters in psychologically real strokes. We see it in the lament of the old Watchman who initiates *The Oresteia*, in the guilt-ridden madness of Orestes, and in the defiant suffering of Prometheus. Though it took Western theater well over 2,000 years to achieve complete realism, the seeds were sown by Aeschylus.

In addition to his artistic triumphs (he won festival prizes thirteen times), Aeschylus was involved in the civic life of Athens; he served as an officer in its navy and was an elected official. His family produced several theater artists; his nephew wrote the play (now lost) that won the festival prize over Sophocles' *Oedipus the King*. He retired to the island of Sicily, where he died most extraordinarily: an eagle, while attempting to drop a turtle on rocks to smash its shell, accidentally struck Aeschylus with the turtle and killed him, thus fulfilling the prophecy of an oracle that "a heavenly missile" would slay him.

PROMETHEUS BOUND (DATE UNCERTAIN)

Of late, the authorship of *Prometheus Bound* has generated substantial inquiry among scholars. Oliver Taplin, an outstanding scholar of Greek drama, surmises that Aeschylus began the play, left it unfinished, and an admirer completed the work (or perhaps even wrote the entire piece himself). "The case against the play is far from proven," argues Taplin, "but it is also far from negligible." In the absence of conclusive evidence that proves authorship, we will adhere to the traditional belief that the play is Aeschylus's and that it was composed sometime between c. 468 and 450 B.C.E. For years *Prometheus Bound* was believed to be among Aeschylus's earliest works and therefore the first surviving playscript in Western civilization, but recent scholarship now gives *The Persians* (472 B.C.E.) that distinction. *The Persians* is particularly noteworthy because it is a sympathetic portrait of the enemy Aeschylus himself helped defeat at the Battle of Marathon.

Prometheus Bound might have been the first in a trilogy of plays Aeschylus wrote about the fall and subsequent resurrection of the Titan who incurred the wrath of Zeus for stealing the fire of the gods (i.e., intelligence) and bestowing it on humans. For his cunning and arrogance, Prometheus was nailed to a mountain in the Caucasus, where an eagle gnawed his liver daily; the liver grew back each night as a sign of his resilience. We know that Aeschylus wrote a second play (*Prometheus Unbound*, of which only fragments survive) to show the hero's liberation by the mighty Heracles. A third play (*Prometheus the Fire-Bringer*) might have completed the trilogy on a triumphant note (as Aeschylus does in *The Oresteia*) or it might have been a satyr-play appended to the trilogy.

Because Aeschylus was writing at the dawn of dramatic literature, *Prometheus Bound*, though a legitimate masterpiece, is a flawed play. Aeschylus was experimenting with dramatic form and had not quite found the ideal vessel in which to pour his ideas. A comparison of this play with *Oedipus the King* indicates how much the Greek playwrights learned about dramatic structure in a short time. In Aeschylus's defense, at the time Greek drama characteristically featured only two speaking roles in a scene; note that Violence is silent during the opening sequence. Sophocles provided the third actor to enlarge the possibilities of dramatic writing.

Prometheus Bound has two major flaws. First, it is largely narrative and much closer to epic poetry than true drama. The play tends to unravel rather than build as most of the characters, notably Io, describe offstage action. The lengthy speeches, a characteristic of Aeschylean playwriting, remind us that drama likely evolved from the storyteller's art. More importantly, the major external conflict between Prometheus and his chief antagonist, Zeus, is portrayed only indirectly. All of the characters save Hermes are sympathetic to Prometheus's plight. The Chorus of Oceanads strikes a recurring note when they sing "I cry aloud, Prometheus, and lament your bitter fate." Prometheus and Io, his partner in suffering, never confront Zeus directly with their grievances. Nor is there significant internal conflict and its attendant discovery in the play. Prometheus changes little from the opening scene to the last. He remains the defiant rebel, ever proud of his deeds:

> *there is no disgrace in suffering*
>
> *at an enemy's hand, when you hate mutually.*
>
> *So let the curling tendril of the fire*
>
> *from the lightning bolt be sent against me . . .*

If we look at the play as the first act of a larger design by Aeschylus, then these apparent weaknesses in dramatic structure are tolerable.

What *Prometheus Bound* may lack in dramatic excellence is compensated for by its grand theatricality. From the opening scene, in which the Titan is pinned to the mountain by the blacksmith Hephaestus, to the explosive finale, with lightning and thunder cutting through the swirling clouds, the play is steeped in superb theatrical moments. Some theater historians suggest that Prometheus was portrayed by a huge effigy affixed to the *skene* wall, his lines delivered by an unseen actor. The entrance of Oceanos astride the sea monster, surrounded by the chorus of his daughters costumed in fanciful birdlike costumes, was surely as much a crowd pleaser in fifth-century Athens as the latest special effect in a Spielberg film. The Greeks possessed the machinery and imagination (a gift of Prometheus!) to realize Aeschylus's fantastic visions. Likewise, the appearance of lonely Io, the maiden transformed into a heifer by Zeus, represents another coup de theatre. We know that humans wore animal masks long before formal drama emerged as an art, so it is not surprising that the West's first great dramatist used an animal mask in this story of humanity's earliest civilization.

What remains most compelling about Aeschylus's play, however, is its central figure, among the most archetypal figures in world literature. Many cultures have comparable stories of mortals who steal some symbol of intelligence from the gods: the Dogon tribe of West Africa and the Winnebago Indians of North America provide examples. The Winnebago variant on Prometheus was a Trickster; recall that Prometheus himself is noted for his exceptional cunning. Other literary figures, for example, Milton's Satan and Melville's Captain Ahab, are often cited as Promethean in nature. Sigismund, the hero of Calderón's *Life's a Dream*, is first seen chained in a mountain cave by his despotic father. The nineteenth-century Romantic poets and playwrights saw in Prometheus the perfect symbol of the isolated rebel fighting a tyrant. It has been suggested that Aeschylus, like Shelley two millennia after him, used the Prometheus myth as a subtle criticism of Peisistratus, the Athenian tyrant.

There may be a political dimension to *Prometheus Bound*, but at its heart the play is an exploration of the relationship between humans and their gods. Prometheus is the martyr who takes on suffering for the greater good of humanity. His very pose onstage, pinned with arms outstretched against the mountain, resonates with Christian imagery. Job and Jeremiah are but two of his biblical counterparts.

But unlike the Judeo-Christian sufferers, Prometheus owes his suffering to that most human of all vices: pride, the desire to be godlike. Recall that Greek tragedy was conceived to remind humans that they are only god*like*, not gods themselves. True, Prometheus is a Titan, among the lesser deities in the Greek Pantheon, but Aeschylus's depiction of his protagonist is so recognizable that we think of him in human terms. Oceanos, a voice of moderation, warns Prometheus that his tongue "talked so high and haughty: you are not yet humble," a manifestation of hubris that is central to Greek tragedy.

Prometheus's ultimate crime, however, is not o'erweening pride. He tells us: "I dared." That is the essential flaw of the great heroes of dramatic literature: they dare to aspire to godhead, to control their own destiny. In an ordered cosmos they must accept the consequences of their actions. Defeat and suffering are common by-products of daring. Prometheus's heroism extends beyond his theft of the fire that illuminated the human mind; it rests in his resilience amid his suffering. That humans can, like Prometheus, triumph in their suffering provides the hope that is inherent in the tragic paradox: hope and knowledge grow out of suffering ("You must suffer into truth," says Aeschylus in *The Oresteia*). And "hope"—the virtue that transcends death and defeat—was Prometheus's most lasting gift to humanity. As Prometheus tells the chorus: "I caused mortals to cease foreseeing doom. I placed in them blind hope." As we watch Prometheus's heroic struggle in the face of unbearable pain, we must agree with the chorus: "That was a great gift you gave to men." One of the ways that hope is transmitted to subsequent generations is through theater and drama, which are among the "arts that mortals have, come from Prometheus".

Prometheus, alone atop a mountain, is the archetype of the alienated individual, a recurring theme in Western literature. (Round House Theater, London, 1979)

PROMETHEUS BOUND

AESCHYLUS

Translated by David Grene

CHARACTERS

MIGHT
VIOLENCE (*muta persona*)
HEPHAESTUS
PROMETHEUS
OCEANOS
IO
HERMES
CHORUS OF DAUGHTERS OF OCEANOS

SCENE: *A bare and desolate crag in the Caucasus. Enter Might and Violence, demons, servants of Zeus, and Hephaestus, the smith.*

MIGHT.

This is the world's limit that we have come to; this is the Scythian country, an untrodden desolation. Hephaestus, it is you that must heed the commands the Father laid upon you to nail this malefactor to the high craggy rocks in fetters unbreakable of adamantine chain. For it was 5 your flower, the brightness of fire that devises all, that he stole and gave to mortal men; this is the sin for which he must pay the Gods the penalty—that he may learn to endure and like the sovereignty of Zeus and quit his man-loving disposition. 10

HEPHAESTUS.

Might and Violence, in you the command of Zeus has its perfect fulfilment: in you there is nothing to stand in its way. But, for myself, I have not the heart to bind violently a God who is my kin here on this wintry cliff. Yet there is constraint upon me to have the heart for just 15 that, for it is a dangerous thing to treat the Father's words lightly.

High-contriving Son of Themis of Straight Counsel: this is not of your will nor of mine; yet I shall nail you in

20 bonds of indissoluble bronze on this crag far from men. Here you shall hear no voice of mortal; here you shall see no form of mortal. You shall be grilled by the sun's bright fire and change the fair bloom of your skin. You shall be glad when Night comes with her mantle of stars and
25 hides the sun's light; but the sun shall scatter the hoar-frost again at dawn. Always the grievous burden of your torture will be there to wear you down; for he that shall cause it to cease has yet to be born.

Such is the reward you reap of your man-loving disposi-
30 tion. For you, a God, feared not the anger of the Gods, but gave honors to mortals beyond what was just. Wherefore you shall mount guard on this unlovely rock, upright, sleepless, not bending the knee. Many a groan and many a lamentation you shall utter, but they shall not serve
35 you. For the mind of Zeus is hard to soften with prayer, and every ruler is harsh whose rule is new.

MIGHT.
Come, why are you holding back? Why are you pitying in vain? Why is it that you do not hate a God whom the Gods hate most of all? Why do you not hate him, since it
40 was your honor that he betrayed to men?

HEPHAESTUS.
Our kinship has strange power; that, and our life together.

MIGHT.
Yes. But to turn a deaf ear to the Father's words—how can that be? Do you not fear that more?

HEPHAESTUS.
You are always pitiless, always full of ruthlessness.

MIGHT.
45 There is no good singing dirges over him. Do not labor uselessly at what helps not at all.

HEPHAESTUS.
O handicraft of mine—that I deeply hate!

MIGHT.
Why do you hate it? To speak simply, your craft is in no way the author of his present troubles.

HEPHAESTUS.
50 Yet would another had had this craft allotted to him.

MIGHT.
There is nothing without discomfort except the overlord-ship of the Gods. For only Zeus is free.

HEPHAESTUS.
I know. I have no answer to this.

MIGHT.
Hurry now. Throw the chain around him that the Father
55 may not look upon your tarrying.

HEPHAESTUS.
There are the fetters, there: you can see them.

MIGHT.
Put them on his hands: strong, now with the hammer: strike. Nail him to the rock.

HEPHAESTUS.
It is being done now. I am not idling at my work.

MIGHT.
Hammer it more; put in the wedge; leave it loose 60 nowhere. He's a cunning fellow at finding a way even out of hopeless difficulties.

HEPHAESTUS.
Look now, his arm is fixed immovably!

MIGHT.
Nail the other safe, that he may learn, for all his clever-ness, that he is duller witted than Zeus. 65

HEPHAESTUS.
No one, save Prometheus, can justly blame me.

MIGHT.
Drive the obstinate jaw of the adamantine wedge right through his breast: drive it hard.

HEPHAESTUS.
Alas, Prometheus, I groan for your sufferings.

MIGHT.
Are you pitying again? Are you groaning for the enemies 70 of Zeus? Have a care, lest some day you may be pitying yourself.

HEPHAESTUS.
You see a sight that hurts the eye.

MIGHT.
I see this rascal getting his deserts. Throw the girth around his sides. 75

HEPHAESTUS.
I am forced to do this; do not keep urging me.

MIGHT.
Yes, I will urge you, and hound you on as well. Get below now, and hoop his legs in strongly.

HEPHAESTUS.
There now, the task is done. It has not taken long.

MIGHT.
Hammer the piercing fetters with all your power, for the 80 Overseer of our work is severe.

HEPHAESTUS.
Your looks and the refrain of your tongue are alike.

MIGHT.
You can be softhearted. But do not blame my stubborn-ness and harshness of temper.

HEPHAESTUS.
Let us go. He has the harness on his limbs. 85

MIGHT (*to Prometheus*).
Now, play the insolent; now, plunder the Gods' privileges and give them to creatures of a day. What drop of your sufferings can mortals spare you? The Gods named you wrongly when they called you Forethought; you yourself *need* Forethought to extricate yourself from this con- 90 trivance.

(*Prometheus is left alone on the rock.*)

PROMETHEUS.
Bright light, swift-winged winds, springs of the rivers, numberless

laughter of the sea's waves, earth, mother of all, and the all-seeing

circle of the sun: I call upon you to see what I, a God,
    suffer
at the hands of Gods—
95   see with what kind of torture
worn down I shall wrestle ten thousand
years of time—
such is the despiteful bond that the Prince
has devised against me, the new Prince
100   of the Blessed Ones. Oh woe is me!
I groan for the present sorrow,
I groan for the sorrow to come, I groan
questioning when there shall come a time
when He shall ordain a limit to my sufferings.
105   What am I saying? I have known all before,
all that shall be, and clearly known; to me,
nothing that hurts shall come with a new face.
So must I bear, as lightly as I can,
the destiny that fate has given me;
110   for I know well against necessity,
against its strength, no one can fight and win.

I cannot speak about my fortune, cannot
hold my tongue either. It was mortal man
to whom I gave great privileges and
115   for that was yoked in this unyielding harness.
I hunted out the secret spring of fire,
that filled the narthex stem, which when revealed
became the teacher of each craft to men,
a great resource. This is the sin committed
120   for which I stand accountant, and I pay
nailed in my chains under the open sky.

Ah! Ah!
What sound, what sightless smell approaches me,
God sent, or mortal, or mingled?
125   Has it come to earth's end
to look on my sufferings,
or what does it wish?
You see me a wretched God in chains,
the enemy of Zeus, hated of all
130   the Gods that enter Zeus's palace hall,
because of my excessive love for Man.
What is that? The rustle
of birds' wings near? The air whispers
with the gentle strokes of wings.
135   Everything that comes toward me is occasion for fear.
(The Chorus, composed of the daughters of
Oceanos, enters, the members wearing
some formalized representation
of wings, so that their general
appearance is birdlike.)
CHORUS.
    Fear not: this is a company of friends
    that comes to your mountain with swift
    rivalry of wings.

Hardly have we persuaded our Father's
mind, and the quick-bearing winds   140
speeded us hither. The sound
of stroke of bronze rang through our cavern
in its depths and it shook from us
shamefaced modesty; unsandaled
we have hastened on our chariot of wings.   145
PROMETHEUS.
    Alas, children of teeming Tethys and of him
    who encircles all the world with stream unsleeping,
    Father Ocean,
    look, see with what chains
    I am nailed on the craggy heights   150
    of this gully to keep a watch
    that none would envy me.
CHORUS.
    I see, Prometheus: and a mist of fear and tears
    besets my eyes as I see your form
    wasting away on these cliffs   155
    in adamantine bonds of bitter shame.
    For new are the steersmen that rule Olympus:
    and new are the customs by which Zeus rules,
    customs that have no law to them,
    but what was great before he brings to nothingness.   160
PROMETHEUS.
    Would that he had hurled me
    underneath the earth and underneath
    the House of Hades, host to the dead—
    yes, down to limitless Tartarus.
    yes, though he bound me cruelly   165
    in chains unbreakable,
    so neither God nor any other being
    might have found joy in gloating over me.
    Now as I hang, the plaything of the winds,
    my enemies can laugh at what I suffer.   170
CHORUS.
    Who of the Gods is so hard of heart
    that he finds joy in this?
    Who is that that does not feel
    sorrow answering your pain—
    save only Zeus? For he malignantly,   175
    always cherishing a mind
    that bends not, has subdued the breed
    of Uranos, nor shall he cease
    until he satisfies his heart,
    or someone take the rule from him—that hard-to-
        capture rule—   180
    by some device of subtlety.
PROMETHEUS.
    Yes, there shall come a day for me
    when he shall need me, me that now am tortured
    in bonds and fetters—he shall need me then,
    this president of the Blessed—   185
    to show the new plot whereby he may be spoiled
    of his throne and his power.

190 Then not with honeyed tongues
of persuasion shall he enchant me;
he shall not cow me with his threats
to tell him what I know,
until he free me from my cruel chains
and pay me recompense for what I suffer.

CHORUS.

195 You are stout of heart, unyielding
to the bitterness of pain.
You are free of tongue, too free.
It is my mind that piercing fear has fluttered;
your misfortunes frighten me.
Where and when is it fated
200 to see you reach the term, to see you reach
the harbor free of trouble at the last?
A disposition none can win, a heart
that no persuasions soften—these are his,
the Son of Kronos.

PROMETHEUS.

205 I know that he is savage: and his justice
a thing he keeps by his own standard: still
that will of his shall melt to softness yet
when he is broken in the way I know,
and though his temper now is oaken hard
210 it shall be softened: hastily he'll come
to meet my haste, to join in amity
and union with me—one day he shall come.

CHORUS.

Reveal it all to us: tell us the story of what the charge was
on which Zeus caught you and punished you so cruelly
215 with such dishonor. Tell us, if the telling will not injure
you in any way.

PROMETHEUS.

To speak of this is bitterness. To keep silent
bitter no less; and every way is misery.

When first the Gods began their angry quarrel,
220 and God matched God in rising faction, some
eager to drive old Kronos from his throne
that Zeus might rule—the fools!—others again
earnest that Zeus might never be their king—
I then with the best counsel tried to win
225 the Titans, sons of Uranos and Earth,
but failed. They would have none of crafty schemes
and in their savage arrogance of spirit
thought they would lord it easily by force.
But she that was my mother, Themis, Earth—
230 she is but one although her names are many—
had prophesied to me how it should be,
even how the fates decreed it: and she said
that "not by strength nor overmastering force
the fates allowed the conquerors to conquer
235 but by guile only": This is what I told them,
but they would not vouchsafe a glance at me.
Then with those things before me it seemed best

to take my mother and join Zeus's side:
he was as willing as we were:
240 thanks to my plans the dark receptacle
of Tartarus conceals the ancient Kronos,
him and his allies. These were the services
I rendered to this tyrant and these pains
the payment he has given me in requital.
245 This is a sickness rooted and inherent
in the nature of a tyranny:
that he that holds it does not trust his friends.

But you have asked on what particular
charge he now tortures me: this I will tell you.
250 As soon as he ascended to the throne
that was his father's, straightway he assigned
to the several Gods their several privileges
and portioned out the power, but to the unhappy
breed of mankind he gave no heed, intending
255 to blot the race out and create a new.
Against these plans none stood save I: I dared.
I rescued men from shattering destruction
that would have carried them to Hades' house;
and therefore I am tortured on this rock,
260 a bitterness to suffer, and a pain
to pitiful eyes. I gave to mortal man
a precedence over myself in pity: I
can win no pity: pitiless is he
that thus chastises me, a spectacle
265 bringing dishonor on the name of Zeus.

CHORUS.

He would be iron-minded and made of stone, indeed,
Prometheus, who did not sympathize with your sufferings.
I would not have chosen to see them, and now that I
see, my heart is pained.

PROMETHEUS.

270 Yes, to my friends I am pitiable to see.

CHORUS.

Did you perhaps go further than you have told us?

PROMETHEUS.

I caused mortals to cease foreseeing doom.

CHORUS.

What cure did you provide them with against that sickness?

PROMETHEUS.

I placed in them blind hopes.

CHORUS.

275 That was a great gift you gave to men.

PROMETHEUS.

Besides this, I gave them fire.

CHORUS.

And do creatures of a day now possess bright-faced fire?

PROMETHEUS.

Yes, and from it they shall learn many crafts.

CHORUS.

Then these are the charges on which—

PROMETHEUS.
280   Zeus tortures me and gives me no respite.
CHORUS.
    Is there no limit set for your pain?
PROMETHEUS.
    None save when it shall seem good to Zeus.
CHORUS.
    How will it ever seem good to him? What hope is there?
    Do you not see how you have erred? It is not pleasure for
285   me to say that you have erred, and for you it is a pain to
    hear. But let us speak no more of all this and do you seek
    some means of deliverance from your trials.
PROMETHEUS.
    It is an easy thing for one whose foot
    is on the outside of calamity
290   to give advice and to rebuke the sufferer.
    I have known all that you have said: I knew,
    I knew when I transgressed nor will deny it.
    In helping man I brought my troubles on me;
    but yet I did not think that with such tortures
295   I should be wasted on these airy cliffs,
    this lonely mountain top, with no one near.
    But do not sorrow for my present suffering;
    alight on earth and hear what is to come
    that you may know the whole complete: I beg you
300   alight and join your sorrow with mine: misfortune
    wandering the same track lights now upon one
    and now upon another.
CHORUS.
                    Willing our ears,
    that hear you cry to them, Prometheus,
    now with light foot I leave the rushing car
305   and sky, the holy path of birds, and light
    upon this jutting rock: I long
    to hear your story to the end.
        (Enter Oceanos, riding on a hippocamp, or sea-monster.)
OCEANOS.
                    I come
    on a long journey, speeding past the boundaries,
    to visit you, Prometheus: with the mind
310   alone, no bridle needed, I direct
    my swift-winged bird; my heart is sore
    for your misfortunes; you know that. I think
    that it is kinship makes me feel them so.
    Besides, apart from kinship, there is no one
315   I hold in higher estimation: that
    you soon shall know and know beside that in me
    there is no mere word-kindness: tell me
    how I can help you, and you will never say
    that you have any friend more loyal to you
320   than Oceanos.
PROMETHEUS.
    What do I see? Have you, too, come to gape
    in wonder at this great display, my torture?
    How did you have the courage to come here

to this land, Iron-Mother, leaving the stream
called after you and the rock-roofed, self-established   325
caverns? Was it to feast your eyes upon
the spectacle of my suffering and join
in pity for my pain? Now look and see
the sight, this friend of Zeus, that helped set up
his tyranny and see what agonies   330
twist me, by his instructions!
OCEANOS.
                    Yes, I see,
Prometheus, and I want, indeed I do,
to advise you for the best, for all your cleverness.
Know yourself and reform your ways to new ways,
for new is he that rules among the Gods.   335
But if you throw about such angry words,
words that are whetted swords, soon Zeus will hear you,
even though his seat in glory is far removed,
and then your present multitude of pains
will seem like child's play. My poor friend, give up   340
this angry mood of yours and look for means
of getting yourself free of trouble. Maybe
what I say seems to you both old and commonplace;
but this is what you pay, Prometheus, for
that tongue of yours which talked so high and haughty: 345
you are not yet humble, still you do not yield
to your misfortunes, and you wish, indeed,
to add some more to them; now, if you follow
me as a schoolmaster you will not kick
against the pricks, seeing that he, the King,   350
that rules alone, is harsh and sends accounts
to no one's audit for the deeds he does.
Now I will go and try if I can free you:
do you be quiet, do not talk so much.
Since your mind is so subtle, don't you know   355
that a vain tongue is subject to correction?
PROMETHEUS.
    I envy you, that you stand clear of blame,
    yet shared and dared in everything with me!
    Now let me be, and have no care for me.
    Do what you will, Him you will not persuade;   360
    He is not easily won over: look,
    take care lest coming here to me should hurt you.
OCEANOS.
    You are by nature better at advising
    others than yourself. I take my cue
    from deeds, not words. Do not withhold me now   365
    when I am eager to go to Zeus. I'm sure,
    I'm sure that he will grant this favor to me,
    to free you from your chains.
PROMETHEUS.
    I thank you and will never cease; for loyalty
    is not what you are wanting in. Don't trouble,   370
    for you will trouble to no purpose, and no help
    to me—if it so be you want to trouble.
    No, rest yourself, keep away from this thing;

because I am unlucky I would not,
375 for that, have everyone unlucky too.
No, for my heart is sore already when
I think about my brother's fortunes—Atlas,
who stands to westward of the world, supporting
the pillar of earth and heaven on his shoulders,
380 a load that suits no shoulders; and the earthborn
dweller in caves Cilician, whom I saw
and pitied, hundred-headed, dreadful monster,
fierce Typho, conquered and brought low by force.
Once against all the Gods he stood, opposing,
385 hissing out terror from his grim jaws; his eyes
flashed gorgon glaring lightning as he thought
to sack the sovereign tyranny of Zeus;
but upon him came the unsleeping bolt
of Zeus, the lightning-breathing flame, down rushing,
390 which cast him from his high aspiring boast.
Struck to the heart, his strength was blasted dead
and burnt to ashes; now a sprawling mass
useless he lies, hard by the narrow seaway
pressed down beneath the roots of Aetna: high
395 above him on the mountain peak the smith
Hephaestus works at the anvil. Yet one day
there shall burst out rivers of fire, devouring
with savage jaws the fertile, level plains
of Sicily of the fair fruits; such boiling wrath
400 with weapons of fire-breathing surf, a fiery
unapproachable torrent, shall Typho vomit,
though Zeus's lightning left him but a cinder.
But all of this you know: you do not need me
to be your schoolmaster: reassure yourself
405 as you know how: this cup I shall drain myself
till the high mind of Zeus shall cease from anger.

OCEANOS.
Do you not know, Prometheus, that words are healers of
the sick temper?

PROMETHEUS.
Yes, if in season due one soothes the heart with them, not
410 tries violently to reduce the swelling anger.

OCEANOS.
Tell me, what danger do you see for me in loyalty to you,
and courage therein?

PROMETHEUS.
I see only useless effort and a silly good nature.

OCEANOS.
Suffer me then to be sick of this sickness, for it is a prof-
415 itable thing, if one is wise, to seem foolish.

PROMETHEUS.
This shall seem to be my fault.

OCEANOS.
Clearly your words send me home again.

PROMETHEUS.
Yes, lest your doings for me bring you enmity.

OCEANOS.
His enmity, who newly sits on the all-powerful throne?

PROMETHEUS.
His is a heart you should beware of vexing. 420

OCEANOS.
Your own misfortune will be my teacher, Prometheus.

PROMETHEUS.
Off with you, then! Begone! Keep your present mind.

OCEANOS.
These words fall on very responsive ears. Already my
four-legged bird is pawing the level track of Heaven with
his wings, and he will be glad to bend the knee in his own 425
stable.

CHORUS

STROPHE

I cry aloud, Prometheus, and lament your bitter fate,
my tender eyes are trickling tears:
their fountains wet my cheek.
This is a tyrant's deed; this is unlovely, 430
a thing done by a tyrant's private laws,
and with this thing Zeus shows his haughtiness
of temper toward the Gods that were of old.

ANTISTROPHE

Now all the earth has cried aloud, lamenting:
now all that was magnificent of old 435
laments your fall, laments your brethren's fall
as many as in holy Asia hold
their established habitation, all lament
in sympathy for your most grievous woes.

STROPHE

Dwellers in the land of Colchis, 440
maidens, fearless in the fight,
and the host of Scythia, living
round the lake Maeotis, living
on the edges of the world.

ANTISTROPHE

And Arabia's flower of warriors 445
and the craggy fortress keepers
near Caucasian mountains, fighters
terrible, crying for battle,
brandishing sharp pointed spears.

STROPHE

One God and one God only I have seen 450
before this day, in torture and in bonds
unbreakable: he was a Titan,
Alas, whose strength and might
ever exceeded; now he bends his back
and groans beneath the load of earth and heaven. 455

ANTISTROPHE

The wave cries out as it breaks into surf;
the depth cries out, lamenting you; the dark
Hades, the hollow underneath the world,

460 sullenly groans below; the springs
of sacred flowing rivers all lament
the pain and pity of your suffering.

PROMETHEUS.

Do not think that out of pride or stubbornness I hold my
peace; my heart is eaten away when I am aware of myself,
when I see myself insulted as I am. Who was it but I who
465 in truth dispensed their honors to these new gods? I will
say nothing of this; you know it all; but hear what troubles there were among men, how I found them witless
and gave them the use of their wits and made them masters of their minds. I will tell you this, not because I would
470 blame men, but to explain the goodwill of my gift. For
men at first had eyes but saw to no purpose; they had ears
but did not hear. Like the shapes of dreams they dragged
through their long lives and handled all things in bewilderment and confusion. They did not know of building
475 houses with bricks to face the sun; they did not know how
to work in wood. They lived like swarming ants in holes
in the ground, in the sunless caves of the earth. For them
there was no secure token by which to tell winter nor the
flowering spring nor the summer with its crops; all their
480 doings were indeed without intelligent calculation until I
showed them the rising of the stars, and the settings, hard
to observe. And further I discovered to them numbering,
pre-eminent among subtle devices, and the combining of
letters as a means of remembering all things, the Muses'
485 mother, skilled in craft. It was I who first yoked beasts for
them in the yokes and made of those beasts the slaves of
trace chain and pack saddle that they might be man's substitute in the hardest tasks; and I harnessed to the carriage, so that they loved the rein, horses, the crowning
490 pride of the rich man's luxury. It was I and none other
who discovered ships, the sail driven wagons that the sea
buffets. Such were the contrivances that I discovered for
men—alas for me! For I myself am without contrivance
to rid myself of my present affliction.

CHORUS.

495 What you have suffered is indeed terrible. You are astray
and bewildered in your mind, and like a bad doctor that
has fallen sick himself, you are cast down and cannot find
what sort of drugs would cure your ailment.

PROMETHEUS.

Hear the rest, and you will marvel even more at the crafts
500 and resources I contrived. Greatest was this: in the former
times if a man fell sick he had no defense against the sickness, neither healing food nor drink, nor unguent; but
through the lack of drugs men wasted away, until I
showed them the blending of mild simples wherewith
505 they drive out all manner of diseases. It was I who
arranged all the ways of seercraft, and I first adjudged
what things come verily true from dreams; and to men I
gave meaning to the ominous cries, hard to interpret. It
was I who set in order the omens of the highway and the
510 flight of crooked-taloned birds, which of them were pro-

pitious or lucky by nature, and what manner of life each
led, and what were their mutual hates, loves, and com-
panionships; also I taught of the smoothness of the vitals
and what color they should have to pleasure the Gods
and the dappled beauty of the gall and the lobe. It was I 515
who burned thighs wrapped in fat and the long shank
bone and set mortals on the road to this murky craft. It
was I who made visible to men's eyes the flaming signs of
the sky that were before dim. So much for these. Beneath
the earth, man's hidden blessing, copper, iron, silver, and 520
gold—will anyone claim to have discovered these before
I did? No one, I am very sure, who wants to speak truly
and to the purpose. One brief word will tell the whole
story: all arts that mortals have come from Prometheus.

CHORUS.

Therefore do not help mortals beyond all expediency 525
while neglecting yourself in your troubles. For I am of
good hope that once freed of these bonds you will be no
less in power than Zeus.

PROMETHEUS.

Not yet has fate that brings to fulfilment determined
these things to be thus. I must be twisted by ten thousand 530
pangs and agonies, as I now am, to escape my chains at
last. Craft is far weaker than necessity.

CHORUS.

Who then is the steersman of necessity?

PROMETHEUS.

The triple-formed Fates and the remembering Furies.

CHORUS.

Is Zeus weaker than these? 535

PROMETHEUS.

Yes, for he, too, cannot escape what is fated.

CHORUS.

What is fated for Zeus besides eternal sovereignty?

PROMETHEUS.

Inquire of this no further, do not entreat me.

CHORUS.

This is some solemn secret, I suppose, that you are hiding.

PROMETHEUS.

Think of some other story: this one is not yet the season 540
to give tongue to, but it must be hidden with all care; for
it is only by keeping it that I will escape my despiteful
bondage and my agony.

CHORUS.

STROPHE

May Zeus never, Zeus that all
the universe controls, oppose 545
his power against my mind:
may I never dallying
be slow to give my worship at
the sacrificial feasts
when the bulls are killed beside 550
quenchless Father Ocean:
may I never sin in word:

may these precepts still abide
in my mind nor melt away.

ANTISTROPHE

555 It is a sweet thing to draw out
a long, long life in cheerful hopes,
and feed the spirit in the bright
benignity of happiness:
but I shiver when I see you
560 wasted with ten thousand pains,
all because you did not tremble
at the name of Zeus: your mind
was yours, not his, and at its bidding
you regarded mortal men
565 too high, Prometheus.

STROPHE

Kindness that cannot be requited, tell me,
where is the help in that, my friend? What succor
in creatures of a day? You did not see
the feebleness that draws its breath in gasps,
570 a dreamlike feebleness by which the race
of man is held in bondage, a blind prisoner.
So the plans of men shall never
pass the ordered law of Zeus.

ANTISTROPHE

This I have learned while I looked on your pains,
575 deadly pains, Prometheus.
A dirge for you came to my lips, so different
from the other song I sang to crown your marriage
in honor of your couching and your bath,
upon the day you won her with your gifts
580 to share your bed—of your own race she was,
Hesione—and so you brought her home.
(*Enter Io, a girl wearing horns like an ox.*)

Io.

What land is this? What race of men? Who is it
I see here tortured in this rocky bondage?
What is the sin he's paying for? Oh tell me
to what part of the world my wanderings have brought
585   me.
O, O, O,
there it is again, there again—it stings me,
the gadfly, the ghost of earth-born Argos:
keep it away, keep it away, earth!
590 I'm frightened when I see the shape of Argos,
Argos the herdsman with ten thousand eyes.
He stalks me with his crafty eyes: he died,
but the earth didn't hide him; still he comes
even from the depths of the Underworld to hunt me:
595 he drives me starving by the sands of the sea.

The reed-woven pipe drones on in a hum

and drones and drones its sleep-giving strain:
O, O, O,
Where are you bringing me, my far-wandering
wanderings?   600
Son of Kronos, what fault, what fault
did you find in me that you should yoke me
to a harness of misery like this,
that you should torture me so to madness
driven in fear of the gadfly?   605
Burn me with fire: hide me in earth: cast me away
to monsters of the deep for food: but do not
grudge me the granting of this prayer, King.
Enough have my much wandering wanderings
exercised me: I cannot find   610
a way to escape my troubles.
Do you hear the voice of the cow-horned maid?
PROMETHEUS.
Surely I hear the voice, the voice of the maiden, gadfly-
haunted, the daughter of Inachus? She set Zeus's heart on
fire with love and now she is violently exercised running 615
on courses overlong, driven by Hera's hate.
Io.
How is it you speak my father's name?
Tell me, who are you? Who are you? Oh
who are you that so exactly accosts me by name?
You have spoken of the disease that the Gods have sent
    to me   620
which wastes me away, pricking with goads,
so that I am moving always
tortured and hungry, wild bounding,
quick sped I come,
a victim of jealous plots.   625
Some have been wretched
before me, but who of these
suffered as I do?
But declare to me clearly
what I have still to suffer: what would avail   630
against my sickness, what drug would cure it:
Tell me, if you know:
tell me, declare it to the unlucky, wandering maid.
PROMETHEUS.
I shall tell you clearly all that you would know, weaving
you no riddles, but in plain words, as it is just to open the 635
lips to friends. You see before you him that gave fire to
men, even Prometheus.
Io.
O spirit that has appeared as a common blessing to all
men, unhappy Prometheus, why are you being punished?
PROMETHEUS.
I have just this moment ceased from the lamentable tale 640
of my sorrows.
Io.
Will you then grant me this favor?
PROMETHEUS.
Say what you are asking for: I will tell you all.

Io.

Tell who it was that nailed you to the cliff.

PROMETHEUS.

645   The plan was the plan of Zeus, and the hand the hand of Hephaestus.

Io.

And what was the offense of which this is the punishment?

PROMETHEUS.

It is enough that I have told you a clear story so far.

Io.

650   In addition, then, indicate to me what date shall be the limit of my wanderings.

PROMETHEUS.

Better for you not to know this than know it.

Io.

I beg you, do not hide from me what I must endure.

PROMETHEUS.

It is not that I grudge you this favor.

Io.

655   Why then delay to tell me all?

PROMETHEUS.

It is no grudging, but I hesitate to break your spirit.

Io.

Do not have more thought for me than pleases me myself.

PROMETHEUS.

Since you are so eager, I must speak; and do you give ear.

CHORUS.

Not yet: give me, too, a share of pleasure. First let us ques-
660   tion her concerning her sickness, and let her tell us of her
desperate fortunes. And then let you be our informant for
the sorrows that still await her.

PROMETHEUS.

It is your task, Io, to gratify these spirits, for besides other
considerations they are your father's sisters. To make wail
665   and lament for one's ill fortune, when one will win a tear
from the audience, is well worthwhile.

Io.

I know not how I should distrust you: clearly
you shall hear all you want to know from me.
Yet even as I speak I groan in bitterness
670   for that storm sent by God on me, that ruin
of my beauty; I must sorrow when I think
who sent all this upon me. There were always
night visions that kept haunting me and coming
into my maiden chamber and exhorting
675   with winning words, "O maiden greatly blessed,
why are you still a maiden, you who might
make marriage with the greatest? Zeus is stricken
with lust for you; he is afire to try
the bed of love with you: do not disdain him.
680   Go, child, to Lerna's meadow, deep in grass,
to where your father's flocks and cattle stand
that Zeus's eye may cease from longing for you."

With such dreams I was cruelly beset
night after night until I took the courage
to tell my father of my nightly terror.   685
He sent to Pytho many an embassy
and to Dodona seeking to discover
what deed or word of his might please the God,
but those he sent came back with riddling oracles
dark and beyond the power of understanding.   690
At last the word came clear to Inachus
charging him plainly that he cast me out
of home and country, drive me out footloose
to wander to the limits of the world;
if he should not obey, the oracle said,   695
the fire-faced thunderbolt would come from Zeus
and blot out his whole race. These were the oracles
of Loxias, and Inachus obeyed them.
He drove me out and shut his doors against me
with tears on both our parts, but Zeus's bit   700
compelled him to do this against his will.
Immediately my form and mind were changed
and all distorted; horned, as you see,
pricked on by the sharp biting gadfly, leaping
in frenzied jumps I ran beside the river   705
Kerchneia, good to drink, and Lerna's spring.
The earth-born herdsman Argos followed me
whose anger knew no limits, and he spied
after my tracks with all his hundred eyes.
Then an unlooked-for doom, descending suddenly,   710
took him from life: I, driven by the gadfly,
that god-sent scourge, was driven always onward
from one land to another: that is my story.
If you can tell me what remains for me,
tell me, and do not out of pity cozen   715
with kindly lies: there is no sickness worse
for me than words that to be kind must lie.

CHORUS.

Hold! Keep away! Alas!
never did I think that such strange
words would come to my ears: 720
never did I think such intolerable
sufferings, an offense to the eye,
shameful and frightening, so
would chill my soul with a double-edged point.
Alas, Alas, for your fate!   725
I shudder when I look on Io's fortune.

PROMETHEUS.

You groan too soon: you are full of fear too soon: wait till
you hear besides what is to be.

CHORUS.

Speak, tell us to the end. For sufferers it is sweet to know
beforehand clearly the pain that still remains for them.   730

PROMETHEUS.

The first request you made of me you gained
lightly: from her you wished to hear the story

of what she suffered. Now hear what remains,
what sufferings this maid must yet endure
735 from Hera. Do you listen, child of Inachus,
hear and lay up my words within your heart
that you may know the limits of your journey.
First turn to the sun's rising and walk on
over the fields no plough has broken: then
740 you will come to the wandering Scythians
who live in wicker houses built above
their well-wheeled wagons; they are an armed people,
armed with the bow that strikes from far away:
do not draw near them; rather let your feet
745 touch the surf line of the sea where the waves moan,
and cross their country: on your left there live
the Chalybes who work with iron: these
you must beware of; for they are not gentle,
nor people whom a stranger dare approach.
750 Then you will come to Insolence, a river
that well deserves its name: but cross it not—
it is no stream that you can easily ford—
until you come to Caucasus itself,
the highest mountains, where the river's strength
755 gushes from its very temples. Cross these peaks,
the neighbors of the stars, and take the road
southward until you reach the Amazons,
the race of women who hate men, who one day
shall live around Thermodon in Thermiscyra
760 where Salmydessos, rocky jaw of the sea,
stands sailor-hating, stepmother of ships.
The Amazons will set you on your way
and gladly: you will reach Cimmeria,
the isthmus, at the narrow gates of the lake.
765 Leave this with a good heart and cross the channel,
the channel of Macotis: and hereafter
for all time men shall talk about your crossing,
and they shall call the place for you Cow's-ford.*
Leave Europe's mainland then, and go to Asia.

(*To the Chorus*)

770 Do you now think this tyrant of the Gods
is hard in all things without difference?
He was a God and sought to lie in love
with this girl who was mortal, and on her
he brought this curse of wandering: bitter indeed
775 you found your marriage with this suitor, maid.
Yet you must think of all that I have told you
as still only in prelude.

   Io.
      O, O

*Cow's-ford: Bosporus

PROMETHEUS.
   Again, you are crying and lamenting: what will you do
   when you hear of the evils to come?   780
CHORUS.
   Is there still something else to her sufferings of which you
   will speak?
PROMETHEUS.
   A wintry sea of agony and ruin.
IO.
   What good is life to me then? Why do I not throw myself
   at once from some rough crag, to strike the ground and 785
   win a quittance of all my troubles? It would be better to
   die once for all than suffer all one's days.
PROMETHEUS.
   You would ill bear my trials, then, for whom Fate reserves
   no death. Death would be a quittance of trouble: but for
   me there is no limit of suffering set till Zeus fall from 790
   power.
IO.
   Can Zeus ever fall from power?
PROMETHEUS.
   You would be glad to see that catastrophe, I think.
IO.
   Surely, since Zeus is my persecutor.
PROMETHEUS.
   Then know that this shall be.   795
IO.
   Who will despoil him of his sovereign scepter?
PROMETHEUS.
   His own witless plans.
IO.
   How? Tell me, if there is no harm to telling.
PROMETHEUS.
   He shall make a marriage that shall hurt him.
IO.
   With god or mortal? Tell me, if you may say it.   800
PROMETHEUS.
   Why ask what marriage? That is not to be spoken.
IO.
   Is it his wife shall cast him from his throne?
PROMETHEUS.
   She shall bear him a son mightier than his father.
IO.
   Has he no possibility of escaping this downfall?
PROMETHEUS.
   None, save through my release from these chains.   805
IO.
   But who will free you, against Zeus's will?
PROMETHEUS.
   Fate has determined that it be one of your descendants.
IO.
   What, shall a child of mine bring you free?
PROMETHEUS.
   Yes, in the thirteenth generation.

Io.

810 Your prophecy has now passed the limits of understanding.

PROMETHEUS.

Then also do not seek to learn your trials.

Io.

Do not offer me a boon and then withhold it.

PROMETHEUS.

I offer you then one of two stories.

Io.

815 Which? Tell me and give me the choice.

PROMETHEUS.

I will: choose that I tell you clearly either what remains
for you or the one that shall deliver me.

CHORUS.

Grant her one and grant me the other and do not deny us
the tale. Tell her what remains of her wanderings: tell us

820 of the one that shall deliver you. That is what I desire.

PROMETHEUS.

Since you have so much eagerness, I will not
refuse to tell you all that you have asked me.
First to you, Io, I shall tell the tale
of your sad wanderings, rich in groans—inscribe

825 the story in the tablets of your mind.
When you shall cross the channel that divides
Europe from Asia, turn to the rising sun,
to the burnt plains, sun-scorched; cross by the edge
of the foaming sea till you come to Gorgona

830 to the flat stretches of Kisthene's country.
There live the ancient maids, children of Phorcys:
these swan-formed hags, with but one common eye,
single-toothed monsters, such as nowhere else
the sun's rays look on nor the moon by night.

835 Near are their winged sisters, the three Gorgons,
with snakes to bind their hair up, mortal-hating:
nor mortal that but looks on them shall live:
these are the sentry guards I tell you of.
Hear, too, of yet another gruesome sight,

840 the sharp-toothed hounds of Zeus, that have no bark,
the vultures—them take heed of—and the host
of one-eyed Arimaspians, horse-riding,
that live around the spring which flows with gold,
the spring of Pluto's river: go not near them.

845 A land far off, a nation of black men,
these you shall come to, men who live hard by
the fountain of the sun where is the river
Aethiops—travel by his banks along
to a waterfall where from the Bibline hills

850 Nile pours his holy waters, pure to drink.
This river shall be your guide to the triangular
land of the Nile and there, by Fate's decree,
there, Io, you shall find your distant home,
a colony for you and your descendants.

855 If anything of this is still obscure
or difficult ask me again and learn
clearly: I have more leisure than I wish.

CHORUS.

If there is still something left for you to tell her of her ruinous wanderings, tell it; but if you have said everything,
grant us the favor we asked and tell us the story too. 860

PROMETHEUS.

The limit of her wanderings complete
she now has heard: but so that she may know
that she has not been listening to no purpose
I shall recount what she endured before
she came to us here: this I give as pledge, 865
a witness to the good faith of my words.
The great part of the story I omit
and come to the very boundary of your travels.
When you had come to the Molossian plains
around the sheer back of Dodona where 870
is the oracular seat of Zeus Thesprotian,
the talking oaks, a wonder past belief,
by them full clearly, in no riddling terms,
you were hailed glorious wife of Zeus that shall be:
does anything of this wake pleasant memories? 875
Then, goaded by the gadfly, on you hastened
to the great gulf of Rhea by the track
at the side of the sea: but in returning course
you were storm-driven back: in time to come
that inlet of the sea shall bear your name 880
and shall be called Ionian, a memorial
to all men of your journeying: these are proofs
for you, of how far my mind sees something farther
than what is visible: for what is left,
to you and you this I shall say in common, 885
taking up again the track of my old tale.
There is a city, furthest in the world,
Canobos, near the mouth and issuing point
of the Nile: there Zeus shall make you sound of mind
touching you with a hand that brings no fear, 890
and through that touch alone shall come your healing.
You shall bear Epaphos, dark of skin, his name
recalling Zeus's touch and his begetting.
This Epaphos shall reap the fruit of all
the land that is watered by the broad flowing Nile. 895
From him five generations, and again
to Argos they shall come, against their will,
in number fifty, women, flying from
a marriage with their kinsfolk: but these kinsfolk
their hearts with lust aflutter like the hawks 900
barely outdistanced by the doves will come
hunting a marriage that the law forbids:
the God shall grudge the men these women's bodies,
and the Pelasgian earth shall welcome them
in death: for death shall claim them in a fight 905
where women strike in the dark, a murderous vigil.
Each wife shall rob her husband of his life

dipping in blood her two-edged sword: even so
may Love come, too, upon my enemies.

910 But one among these girls shall love beguile
from killing her bedfellow, blunting her purpose:
and she shall make her choice—to bear the name
of coward and not murder: this girl,
she shall in Argos bear a race of kings.

915 To tell this clearly needs a longer story,
but from her seed shall spring a man renowned
for archery, and he shall set me free.
Such was the prophecy which ancient Themis
my Titan mother opened up to me;

920 but how and by what means it shall come true
would take too long to tell, and if you heard
the knowledge would not profit you.

Io.

Eleleu, eleleu
It creeps on me again, the twitching spasm,
925 the mind-destroying madness, burning me up
and the gadfly's sting goads me on—
steel point by no fire tempered—
and my heart in its fear knocks on my breast.
There's a dazing whirl in my eyes as I run
930 out of my course by the madness driven,
the crazy frenzy; my tongue ungoverned
babbles, the words in a muddy flow strike
on the waves of the mischief I hate, strike wild
without aim or sense.

CHORUS.

STROPHE

935 A wise man indeed he was
that first in judgment weighed this word
and gave it tongue: the best by far
it is to marry in one's rank and station:
let no one working with her hands aspire
940 to marriage with those lifted high in pride
because of wealth, or of ancestral glory.

ANTISTROPHE

Never, never may you see me,
Fates majestic, drawing nigh
the bed of Zeus, to share it with the kings:
945 nor ever may I know a heavenly wooer:
I dread such things beholding
Io's sad virginity
ravaged, ruined; bitter wandering
hers because of Hera's wrath.

EPODE

950 When a match has equal partners
then I fear not: may the eye
inescapable of the mighty
Gods not look on me.
That is a fight that none can fight: a fruitful

source of fruitlessness: I would not   955
know what I could do: I cannot
see the hope when Zeus is angry
of escaping him.

PROMETHEUS.

Yet shall this Zeus, for all his pride of heart
be humble yet: such is the match he plans,   960
a marriage that shall drive him from his power
and from his throne, out of the sight of all.
So shall at last the final consummation
be brought about of Father Kronos' curse
which he, driven from his ancient throne, invoked   965
against the son deposing him: no one
of all the Gods save I alone can tell
a way to escape this mischief: I alone
know it and how. So let him confidently
sit on his throne and trust his heavenly thunder   970
and brandish in his hand his fiery bolt.
Nothing shall all of this avail against
a fall intolerable, a dishonored end.
So strong a wrestler Zeus is now equipping
against himself, a monster hard to fight.   975
This enemy shall find a plan to best
the thunderbolt, a thunderclap to best
the thunderclap of Zeus: and he shall shiver
Poseidon's trident, curse of sea and land.
So, in his crashing fall shall Zeus discover   980
how different are rule and slavery.

CHORUS.

You voice your wishes for the God's destruction.

PROMETHEUS.

They are my wishes, yet shall come to pass.

CHORUS.

Must we expect someone to conquer Zeus?

PROMETHEUS.

Yes; he shall suffer worse than I do now.   985

CHORUS.

Have you no fear of uttering such words?

PROMETHEUS.

Why should I fear, since death is not my fate?

CHORUS.

But he might give you pain still worse than this.

PROMETHEUS.

Then let him do so; all this I expect.

CHORUS.

Wise are the worshipers of Adrasteia.   990

PROMETHEUS.

Worship him, pray; flatter whatever king
is king today; but I care less than nothing
for Zeus. Let him do what he likes,
let him be king for his short time: he shall not
be king for long.

      Look, here is Zeus's footman,   995
this fetch-and-carry messenger of him,

the New King. Certainly he has come here
with news for us.
HERMES.
          You, subtle-spirit, you
bitterly overbitter, you that sinned
1000   against the immortals, giving honor to
the creatures of a day, you thief of fire:
the Father has commanded you to say
what marriage of his is this you brag about
that shall drive him from power—and declare it
1005   in clear terms and no riddles. You, Prometheus,
do not cause me a double journey; these
                      (*Pointing to the chains.*)
will prove to you that Zeus is not softhearted.
PROMETHEUS.
    Your speech is pompous sounding, full of pride,
as fits the lackey of the Gods. You are young
1010   and young your rule and you think that the tower
in which you live is free from sorrow: from it
have I not seen two tyrants thrown? the third,
who now is king, I shall yet live to see him
fall, of all three most suddenly, most dishonored.
1015   Do you think I will crouch before your Gods,
—so new—and tremble? I am far from that.
Hasten away, back on the road you came.
You shall learn nothing that you ask of me.
HERMES.
    Just such the obstinacy that brought you here,
1020   to this self-willed calamitous anchorage.
PROMETHEUS.
    Be sure of this: when I set my misfortune
against your slavery, I would not change.
HERMES.
    It is better, I suppose, to be a slave
to this rock, than Zeus's trusted messenger.
PROMETHEUS.
1025   Thus must the insolent show their insolence!
HERMES.
    I think you find your present lot too soft.
PROMETHEUS.
    Too soft? I would my enemies had it then,
and you are one of those I count as such.
HERMES.
    Oh, you would blame me too for your calamity?
PROMETHEUS.
1030   In a single word, I am the enemy
of all the Gods that gave me ill for good.
HERMES.
    Your words declare you mad, and mad indeed.
PROMETHEUS.
    Yes, if it's madness to detest my foes.
HERMES.
    No one could bear you in success.
PROMETHEUS.
                  Alas!

HERMES.
    Alas! Zeus does not know that word.   1035
PROMETHEUS.
    Time in its aging course teaches all things.
HERMES.
    But you have not yet learned a wise discretion.
PROMETHEUS.
    True: or I would not speak so to a servant.
HERMES.
    It seems you will not grant the Father's wish.
PROMETHEUS.
    I should be glad, indeed, to requite his kindness! 1040
HERMES.
    You mock me like a child!
PROMETHEUS.
                And are you not
a child, and sillier than a child, to think
that I should tell you anything? There is not
a torture or an engine wherewithal
Zeus can induce me to declare these things,   1045
till he has loosed me from these cruel shackles.
So let him hurl his smoky lightning flame,
and throw in turmoil all things in the world
with white-winged snowflakes and deep bellowing
thunder beneath the earth: me he shall not   1050
bend by all this to tell him who is fated
to drive him from his tyranny.
HERMES.
    Think, here and now, if this seems to your interest.
PROMETHEUS.
    I have already thought—and laid my plans.
HERMES.
    Bring your proud heart to know a true discretion— 1055
O foolish spirit—in the face of ruin.
PROMETHEUS.
    You vex me by these senseless adjurations,
senseless as if you were to advise the waves.
Let it not cross your mind that I will turn
womanish-minded from my fixed decision   1060
or that I shall entreat the one I hate
so greatly, with a woman's upturned hands,
to loose me from my chains: I am far from that.
HERMES.
    I have said too much already—so I think—
and said it to no purpose: you are not softened: 1065
your purpose is not dented by my prayers.
You are a colt new broken, with the bit
clenched in its teeth, fighting against the reins,
and bolting. You are far too strong and confident
in your weak cleverness. For obstinacy   1070
standing alone is the weakest of all things
in one whose mind is not possessed by wisdom.
Think what a storm, a triple wave of ruin
will rise against you, if you will not hear me,
and no escape for you. First this rough crag   1075

with thunder and the lightning bolt the Father
shall cleave asunder, and shall hide your body
wrapped in a rocky clasp within its depth;
a tedious length of time you must fulfill
1080 before you see the light again, returning.
Then Zeus's winged hound, the eagle red,
shall tear great shreds of flesh from you, a feaster
coming unbidden, every day: your liver
bloodied to blackness will be his repast.
1085 And of this pain do not expect an end
until some God shall show himself successor
to take your tortures for himself and willing
go down to lightless Hades and the shadows
of Tartarus' depths. Bear this in mind
1090 and so determine. This is no feigned boast
but spoken with too much truth. The mouth of Zeus
does not know how to lie, but every word
brings to fulfilment. Look, you, and reflect
and never think that obstinacy is better
than prudent counsel.

CHORUS.
1095   Hermes seems to us
to speak not altogether out of season.
He bids you leave your obstinacy and seek
a wise good counsel. Hearken to him. Shame
it were for one so wise to fall in error.

PROMETHEUS.
1100 Before he told it me I knew this message:
but there is no disgrace in suffering
at an enemy's hand, when you hate mutually.
So let the curling tendril of the fire
from the lightning bolt be sent against me: let
1105 the air be stirred with thunderclaps, the winds
in savage blasts convulsing all the world.
Let earth to her foundations shake, yes to her root,
before the quivering storm: let it confuse
the paths of heavenly stars and the sea's waves
1110 in a wild surging torrent: this my body
let Him raise up on high and dash it down
into black Tartarus with rigorous
compulsive eddies: death he cannot give me.

HERMES.
These are a madman's words, a madman's plan:
is there a missing note in this mad harmony?   1115
is there a slack chord in his madness? You,
you, who are so sympathetic with his troubles,
away with you from here, quickly away!
lest you should find your wits stunned by the thunder
and its hard defending roar.

CHORUS.
                          Say something else   1120
different from this: give me some other counsel
that I will listen to: this word of yours
for all its instancy is not for us.
How dare you bid us practice baseness? We
will bear along with him what we must bear.   1125
I have learned to hate all traitors: there is no
disease I spit on more than treachery.

HERMES.
Remember then my warning before the act:
when you are trapped by ruin don't blame fortune:
don't say that Zeus has brought you to calamity   1130
that you could not foresee: do not do this:
but blame yourselves: now you know what you're doing:
and with this knowledge neither suddenly
nor secretly your own want of good sense
has tangled you in the net of ruin, past   1135
all hope of rescue.

PROMETHEUS.
Now it is words no longer: now in very truth
the earth is staggered: in its depths the thunder
bellows resoundingly, the fiery tendrils
of the lightning flash light up, and whirling clouds   1140
carry the dust along: all the winds' blasts
dance in a fury one against the other
in violent confusion: earth and sea
are one, confused together: such is the storm
that comes against me manifestly from Zeus   1145
to work its terrors. O Holy mother mine,
O Sky that circling brings the light to all,
you see me, how I suffer, how unjustly.

OEDIPUS THE KING

SOPHOCLES

SOPHOCLES (c. 496–406 B.C.E.)

The second of the great Greek tragedians, Sophocles authored some 120 dramas, including *Oedipus the King*, *Antigone*, and *Oedipus at Colonus*, and won at least eighteen first prizes for playwriting in the *City Dionysia*. Born in Colonus, Sophocles received an excellent education and at age 16 led the boys' chorus in a celebration of the victory over Persia. In his maturity he was a model Greek citizen, serving as imperial treasurer and state commissioner; he was twice elected to the office of general and was a priest of Asclepias. Among his contributions to the development of theater are the introduction of the third actor, the invention of painted scenery, and the introduction of a new style of music. He is also credited with reducing the role of the chorus, thereby placing greater emphasis on individual characters. Unlike Aeschylus, he rarely acted in his own plays, reputedly because of his weak voice. As a playwright, he was a master craftsman who carefully planned exposition and intricately developed complications to create moving recognition scenes and heartrending, often ironic, reversals. Both Sophocles' diction and his use of irony are unmatched by his contemporaries. His characters are unique. Unlike those of Aeschylus, who are often characterized as "superhuman" or "godlike," and those of Euripides, who are described as "realistic," Sophocles' idealized characters are drawn neither as gods nor as they are, but, in his own words, "as they ought to be." Invariably they face choices and make decisions that lead them through suffering to self-realization. They represent the most noble achievements of the human spirit. The presence of the strong hand of fate and the undeniable existence and power of the gods is often present in Sophocles' plays.

OEDIPUS THE KING (428 B.C.E.)

Not only is *Oedipus the King* the most well known Greek tragedy, it is, according to Aristotle, the best of the canon. On no less than ten occasions in *The Poetics*, Aristotle uses *Oedipus the King* as an illustration when referring to "the perfect tragedy" or the "best means" of creating the tragic effect. For example, he cites *Oedipus the King* when he prescribes the preferred form of recognition as one that is coincident with *peripeteia* (the reversal). Likewise, when he identifies the qualities of a tragic hero, describes the type of action that arouses the pity and fear that lead to catharsis, and illustrates the need for probable and necessary action, *Oedipus the King* is his model. Given his admiration for the play, it is indeed easy to understand how many critics have ascribed to Aristotle the description of *Oedipus the King* as "the perfect tragedy."

What is it about the play that has captured and held the attention of playgoers for over 2000 years? To begin with, it is based on a fascinating story. The Greeks who saw the original production may have known the story as well as we know the stories of George Washington and Abe Lincoln, but familiarity with the story facilitates understanding of the play. *Oedipus the King* gives us one chapter in the story of the house of Thebes, an elaborate and intricately involved tale about the ancient Greek city and its leaders and the struggle for an understanding of life and the roles of the gods and fate in the lives of its citizens. Specifically this play por-

SPOTLIGHT — THE CURSE ON THE HOUSE OF THEBES

Long before the play begins, the young Cadmus (son of Agenor, king of Tyre and father of Semele, Dionysus's mother), searched the world for his sister, Europa, who had been seduced and carried off by Zeus. While on his quest, Cadmus founded the city of Thebes, populating it with warriors who sprang from the planted teeth of a monster he had slain. Cadmus ruled Thebes until his death and was succeeded by his son Polydoros, who was succeeded by his son, Labdacos. When Labdacos died, his brother Lycos served as regent for the infant Laius and ruled Thebes until he was overthrown by Amphion.

When Amphion died, the Thebans invited the exiled Laius, who had found refuge in Pisa, to reclaim his throne. Laius's joyful return soon soured as his marriage to Jocasta deteriorated. The marriage had been one of political convenience, for Jocasta was a daughter of one of the "sown men." To make matters worse, she appeared to be sterile. While secretly visiting the oracle of Apollo at Delphi, Laius learned of the curse that was placed upon him—any child of his born to Jocasta would be his murderer. The lack of an heir and the secret curse on the house of Thebes, coupled with his preference for the bed of Chrysippus, a young man from the court of Pelops in Pisa, motivated Laius to divorce Jocasta. Before that happened, however, Jocasta, feigning acquiescence, succeeded in enticing Laius one last time to her bed, where the seeds of Oedipus and the eventual destruction of Thebes were sown. In time Jocasta bore a son and, thinking that she had succeeded in tying Laius to her,

she presented her husband with the child, Oedipus. Outraged, Laius revealed the curse to her and gave the child, its ankles riveted together, to a trusted servant who was told to abandon it on the slopes of Mount Kithaeron. Fearing that any child born to Jocasta might fulfill the curse, Laius put Jocasta away and, to her great shame, spent his time dallying with Chrysippus.

True to their nature, the gods, especially Ares, Apollo, and Hera, were not pleased with the course of events in Thebes. Ares, the god of war, was still angered by the death of his sacred dragon at the hands of Cadmus; Apollo, the god of light, truth, and order, was displeased by the irrationality of the humans; and Hera, goddess of married women, already twice wounded by Zeus's assignations with Europa and Semele, was offended by Laius's banishment of Jocasta. With the support of Ares and Apollo, she sent the Sphinx to plague the city, devouring all who failed to answer her riddle.

In the meantime, Oedipus (which means "swollen foot"), supposedly abandoned on the slopes of Kithaeron, had been passed on to a shepherd who in turn gave the boy to the childless Polybus and Merope, the king and queen of Corinth. The young Oedipus grew to manhood as their royal heir. Then, after having been taunted and called a bastard by a drunken acquaintance, Oedipus began to question his origins and, dissatisfied with his parents' affirmation of his lineage, he journeyed to Apollo's shrine at Delphi, where he queried the oracle regarding his origins. In place of an answer, he

was confronted with the prophecy that he would one day kill his father and marry his mother. Appalled, Oedipus left Delphi and headed not back "home" but in the opposite direction, hoping to foil the prophecy. As he fled Delphi he encountered Laius and, in a fit of rage at being forced off the road by the king, killed Laius and his entourage. He continued toward Thebes and was confronted by the Sphinx, whose riddle he successfully answered.[1] Bested by Oedipus, the Sphinx threw herself off the cliff; unimpeded, Oedipus entered Thebes, where he was welcomed as a hero and, not unlike his father before him, given the hand of Jocasta in marriage as he ascended the Theban throne.

After years of successful reign and a happy marriage, which was blessed with four children—sons Etiocles and Polynices and daughters Antigone and Ismene—it appeared that the prophecy regarding Oedipus and the house of Thebes might prove to be inaccurate. However, a blight fell on the land and neither plant nor animal nor human being was well; in fact, all were sterile. Apparently the power of the gods was still a force with which to be reckoned. It is at this point that Sophocles begins his play.

---

[1]"What goes on four legs in the morning, two legs in the afternoon, three legs at night; is of one voice, and is the strongest when it has the least?" Man! He crawls on all fours as a baby, walks upright as an adult, and needs the help of a staff in old age; he has always the one voice and is most powerful when he uses the fewest legs.

trays the results of the curse that declares that Oedipus is destined to kill his father and marry his mother. (See Spotlight box, The Curse on the House of Thebes.)

Intriguing as this story may be, the key to Sophocles' brilliance is not his subject matter but his superb skill as a playwright. He takes an age-old story and carefully arranges the incidents to cleverly, but subtly, motivate the action of the agents. Through a strong sense of character, he imbues this action with the eternal human quest for cosmic knowledge and self-realization.

In plotting the play, Sophocles carefully rearranges the incidents of the myth to hold our interest and build suspense. By beginning the play at the end of the story, he allows Oedipus to live his final day in Thebes and simultaneously relive the major events of his life. As he moves slowly and painfully toward the end of his day of destiny, Oedipus also moves backward, swiftly but equally painfully, through the various crises of his life until the play's climax, when the mysteries of his own birth and his father's death are revealed. As each forward step leads him closer to identifying the slayer of Laius, a backward leap leads him closer to his own identity. Each new discovery about the present reveals more information about the past, and, conversely, each new scrap of evidence concerning the past sheds light on the present.

Sophocles carefully creates characters as individuals of depth and understanding whose behavior is logical and believable, whose actions are probable and necessary responses to the actions that precede them. In each scene, Sophocles presents Oedipus locked in conflict with both himself and another character. Throughout he displays great hubris—excessive pride—which had been the motivating force throughout Oedipus's life; it led him to question the legitimacy of his birth, drove him to consult the oracle at Delphi, and ultimately prompted the attack on his father. From his earliest comments, when he blatantly identifies himself as "Oedipus whom all men call the great," through the final scene, in which in his anguish he sees himself as "the greatly miserable, / the most accursed, whom God too hates / above all men on earth," it is apparent that Oedipus's *hamartia* (tragic flaw) is his pride. Tragically, it leads to errors in judgement and his precipitous fall from kingship.

However, it is also clear in each scene that, despite his pride, Oedipus is also motivated by his great concern for Thebes. From his early lamentation that his "spirit groans / for the city" to his final pleas to "drive me from [Thebes] with all the speed you can," he is commited to doing what is right for the city. Thus, he becomes that "intermediate kind of personage," neither all good nor all bad, identified by Aristotle as the ideal tragic hero. Perhaps more intriguing than this dialectic in his character is the sense of personal responsibility Sophocles instills in Oedipus. How easy it might have been for him to claim innocence by way of ignorance. After all, he did not know Laius was his father or that Jocasta was his mother or that Thebes was his birthplace. How easy it might have been for him to plead for mercy upon discovering the truth. This he does not do. Instead, he takes responsibility for each of his actions and stands ready to accept the consequences. It is from this sense of character that Sophocles depicts the human quest for cosmic knowledge and self-realization.

Our initial reaction to Oedipus might easily be a clichéd view—that he was caught between the proverbial rock and a hard place, that he was damned if he did and damned if he didn't, that he was a victim of circumstances, that he was not responsible for his actions. After all, it was preordained that he would kill his father and marry his mother—"the gods had spoken." Such a reaction, however, is based on our modern-day understanding of the deity and religion. We are children of the modern Western world and, as such, we perceive god in a monotheistic sense. We picture a single god who is omnipotent, omniscient, and omnipresent. It is from such a perspective that we hear the oracle's curse and assume that it is preordained. However, Sophocles and his audience had a different theology. As children of the ancient Greek world, they perceived their gods in a polytheistic sense; they pictured many gods, none omnipotent, omniscient, or omnipresent. Their sense of the gods was that of superhuman beings who were subject to the same passions and desires as humans. They believed that no god was in complete control and that, in fact, they often warred among themselves for the control of humans. To the Greeks all life, including that of the gods, was controlled by *ananke* ("necessity" or "what has to be") or *moira* ("the sharer-out" or "fate"). Therefore, it was not possible for any one god to preordain or predetermine the life of a human being. Thus, Sophocles created not a picture of predetermined life but a picture of an individual with a great sense of character who, though indeed caught between the rock and the hard place understood that he was damned if he did and damned if he didn't. He saw himself, not as a victim of circumstances but as an independent agent who, in spite of the consequences, was willing to accept responsibility for his actions. By the end of the play, Oedipus has come to an understanding not only of himself but of human nature and our place in the world. Thus the play transcends the particulars of Greek mythology and stands forever as a parable of the relationship each of us must make with the metaphysical world.

This production attempted to capture the ritualistic spirit of Oedipus the King at Stratford, Ontario, in 1955; Douglas Campbell, wearing an onkos, played the tragic king and appeared here with members of the Stratford Festival Acting Company. Directed by Sir Tyrone Guthrie and designed by Tanya Moiseiwitsch, this production was called King Oedipus.

OEDIPUS THE KING

SOPHOCLES

Translated by David Grene

CHARACTERS
OEDIPUS, *King of Thebes*
JOCASTA, *His Wife*
CREON, *His Brother-in-Law*
TEIRESIAS, *an Old Blind Prophet*
A PRIEST
FIRST MESSENGER
SECOND MESSENGER
A HERDSMAN
A CHORUS OF OLD MEN OF THEBES

SCENE: *In front of the palace of Oedipus at Thebes. To the right of the stage near the altar stands the Priest with a crowd of children. Oedipus emerges from the central door.*

OEDIPUS.
Children, young sons and daughters of old Cadmus,
why do you sit here with your suppliant crowns?
The town is heavy with a mingled burden
of sounds and smells, of groans and hymns and incense;

I did not think it fit that I should hear   5
of this from messengers but came myself,—
I Oedipus whom all men call the Great.

(*He turns to the Priest.*)

You're old and they are young; come, speak for them.
What do you fear or want, that you sit here
suppliant? Indeed I'm willing to give all   10
that you may need; I would be very hard
should I not pity suppliants like these.

PRIEST.
O ruler of my country, Oedipus,
you see our company around the altar;
you see our ages; some of us, like these,   15
who cannot yet fly far, and some of us
heavy with age; these children are the chosen
among the young, and I the priest of Zeus.
Within the market place sit others crowned
with suppliant garlands, at the double shrine   20
of Pallas and the temple where Ismenus
gives oracles by fire. King, you yourself
have seen our city reeling like a wreck

already; it can scarcely lift its prow
out of the depths, out of the bloody surf.
A blight is on the fruitful plants of the earth,
a blight is on the cattle in the fields,
a blight is on our women that no children
are born to them; a God that carries fire,
a deadly pestilence, is on our town,
strikes us and spares not, and the house of Cadmus
is emptied of its people while black Death
grows rich in groaning and in lamentation.
We have not come as suppliants to this altar
because we thought of you as of a God,
but rather judging you the first of men
in all the chances of this life and when
we mortals have to do with more than man.
You came and by your coming saved our city,
freed us from tribute which we paid of old
to the Sphinx, cruel singer. This you did
in virtue of no knowledge we could give you,
in virtue of no teaching; it was God
that aided you, men say, and you are held
with God's assistance to have saved our lives.
Now Oedipus, Greatest in all men's eyes,
here falling at your feet we all entreat you,
find us some strength for rescue.
Perhaps you'll hear a wise word from some God,
perhaps you will learn something from a man
(for I have seen that for the skilled of practice
the outcome of their counsels live the most).
Noblest of men, go, and raise up our city,
go,—and give heed. For now this land of ours
calls you its savior since you saved it once.
So, let us never speak about your reign
as of a time when first our feet were set
secure on high, but later fell to ruin.
Raise up our city, save it and raise it up.
Once you have brought us luck with happy omen;
be no less now in fortune.
If you will rule this land, as now you rule it,
better to rule it full of men than empty.
For neither tower nor ship is anything
when empty, and none live in it together.

OEDIPUS.

I pity you, children. You have come full of longing,
but I have known the story before you told it
only too well. I know you are all sick,
yet there is not one of you, sick though you are,
that is as sick as I myself.
Your several sorrows each have single scope
and touch but one of you. My spirit groans
for city and myself and you at once.
You have not roused me like a man from sleep;
know that I have given many tears to this,
gone many ways wandering in thought,
but as I thought I found only one remedy

and that I took. I sent Menoeceus' son
Creon, Jocasta's brother, to Apollo,
to his Pythian temple,
that he might learn there by what act or word
I could save this city. As I count the days,
it vexes me what ails him; he is gone
far longer than he needed for the journey.
But when he comes, then, may I prove a villain,
if I shall not do all the God commands.

PRIEST.

Thanks for your gracious words. Your servants here
signal that Creon is this moment coming.

OEDIPUS.

His face is bright. O holy Lord Apollo,
grant that his news too may be bright for us
and bring us safety.

PRIEST.

It is happy news,
I think, for else his head would not be crowned
with sprigs of fruitful laurel.

OEDIPUS.

We will know soon,
he's within hail. Lord Creon, my good brother,
what is the word you bring from the God?

(Creon enters.)

CREON.

A good word,—for things hard to bear themselves
if in the final issue all is well
I count complete good fortune.

OEDIPUS.

What do you mean?
What you have said so far
leaves me uncertain whether to trust or fear.

CREON.

If you will hear my news before these others
I am ready to speak, or else to go within.

OEDIPUS.

Speak it to all;
the grief I bear, I bear it more for these
than for my own heart.

CREON.

I will tell you, then,
what I heard from the God.
King Phoebus in plain words commanded us
to drive out a pollution from our land,
pollution grown ingrained within the land;
drive it out, said the God, not cherish it,
till it's past cure.

OEDIPUS.

What is the rite
of purification? How shall it be done?

CREON.

By banishing a man, or expiation
of blood by blood, since it is murder guilt
which holds our city in this destroying storm.

OEDIPUS.
Who is this man whose fate the God pronounces?
CREON.
My lord, before you piloted the state
we had a king called Laius.
OEDIPUS.
120   I know of him by hearsay. I have not seen him.
CREON.
The God commanded clearly: let some one
punish with force this dead man's murderers.
OEDIPUS.
Where are they in the world? Where would a trace
of this old crime be found? It would be hard
to guess where.
CREON.
125   The clue is in this land;
that which is sought is found;
the unheeded thing escapes:
so said the God.
OEDIPUS.
            Was it at home,
or in the country that death came upon him,
130   or in another country travelling?
CREON.
He went, he said himself, upon an embassy,
but never returned when he set out from home.
OEDIPUS.
Was there no messenger, no fellow traveller
who knew what happened? Such a one might tell
135   something of use.
CREON.
They were all killed save one. He fled in terror
and he could tell us nothing in clear terms
of what he knew, nothing, but one thing only.
OEDIPUS.
What was it?
140   If we could even find a slim beginning
in which to hope, we might discover much.
CREON.
This man said that the robbers they encountered
were many and the hands that did the murder
were many; it was no man's single power.
OEDIPUS.
145   How could a robber dare a deed like this
were he not helped with money from the city,
money and treachery?
CREON.
             That indeed was thought.
But Laius was dead and in our trouble
there was none to help.
OEDIPUS.
150   What trouble was so great to hinder you
inquiring out the murder of your king?
CREON.
The riddling Sphinx induced us to neglect

mysterious crimes and rather seek solution
of troubles at our feet.
OEDIPUS.
I will bring this to light again. King Phoebus   155
fittingly took this care about the dead,
and you too fittingly.
And justly you will see in me an ally,
a champion of my country and the God.
For when I drive pollution from the land   160
I will not serve a distant friend's advantage,
but act in my own interest. Whoever
he was that killed the king may readily
wish to dispatch me with the murderous hand;
so helping the dead king I help myself.   165
Come, children, take your suppliant boughs and go;
up from the altars now. Call the assembly
and let it meet upon the understanding
that I'll do everything. God will decide
whether we prosper or remain in sorrow.   170
PRIEST.
Rise, children—it was this we came to seek,
which of himself the king now offers us.
May Phoebus who gave us the oracle
come to our rescue and stay the plague.
                (*Exeunt all but the Chorus.*)
CHORUS.

STROPHE

What is the sweet spoken word of God from the shrine
    of Pytho rich in gold   175
that has come to glorious Thebes?
I am stretched on the rack of doubt, and terror and trem-
    bling hold
my heart, O Delian Healer, and I worship full of fears
for what doom you will bring to pass, new or renewed in
    the revolving years.
Speak to me, immortal voice,   180
child of golden Hope.

ANTISTROPHE

First I call on you, Athene, deathless daughter of Zeus,
and Artemis, Earth Upholder,
who sits in the midst of the market place in the throne
    which men call Fame,
and Phoebus, the Far Shooter, three averters of Fate,   185
come to us now, if ever before, when ruin rushed upon
    the state,
you drove destruction's flame away
out of our land.

STROPHE

Our sorrows defy number;
all the ship's timbers are rotten;   190
taking of thought is no spear for the driving away of the
    plague.

There are no growing children in this famous land;
there are no women bearing the pangs of childbirth.
You may see them one with another, like birds swift on
    the wing,
195   quicker than fire unmastered,
speeding away to the coast of the Western God.

ANTISTROPHE

In the unnumbered deaths
of its people the city dies;
those children that are born lie dead on the naked earth
unpitied, spreading contagion of death; and gray haired
200   mothers and wives
everywhere stand at the altar's edge, suppliant, moaning;
the hymn to the healing God rings out but with it the
    wailing voices are blended.
From these our sufferings grant us, O golden Daughter of
    Zeus,
glad-faced deliverance.

STROPHE

There is no clash of brazen shields but our fight is with
205   the War God,
a War God ringed with the cries of men, a savage God
    who burns us;
grant that he turn in racing course backwards out of our
    country's bounds
to the great palace of Amphitrite or where the waves of
    the Thracian sea
deny the stranger safe anchorage.
210   Whatsoever escapes the night
at last the light of day revisits;
so smite the War God, Father Zeus,
beneath your thunderbolt,
for you are the Lord of the lightning, the lightning that
    carries fire.

ANTISTROPHE

And your unconquered arrow shafts, winged by the
215   golden corded bow,
Lycean King, I beg to be at our side for help;
and the gleaming torches of Artemis with which she
    scours the Lycean hills,
and I call on the God with the turban of gold, who gave
    his name to this country of ours,
the Bacchic God with the wind flushed face,
220   Evian One, who travel
with the Maenad company,
combat the God that burns us
with your torch of pine;
for the God that is our enemy is a God unhonoured
    among the Gods.

                              (Oedipus returns.)

OEDIPUS.

For what you ask me—if you will hear my words,   225
and hearing welcome them and fight the plague,
you will find strength and lightening of your load.

Hark to me; what I say to you, I say
as one that is a stranger to the story
as stranger to the deed. For I would not   230
be far upon the track if I alone
were tracing it without a clue. But now,
since after all was finished, I became
a citizen among you, citizens—
now I proclaim to all the men of Thebes: 235
who so among you knows the murderer
by whose hand Laius, son of Labdacus,
died—I command him to tell everything
to me,—yes, though he fears himself to take the blame
on his own head; for bitter punishment   240
he shall have none, but leave this land unharmed.
Or if he knows the murderer, another,
a foreigner, still let him speak the truth.
For I will pay him and be grateful, too.
But if you shall keep silence, if perhaps   245
some one of you, to shield a guilty friend,
or for his own sake shall reject my words—
hear what I shall do then:
I forbid that man, whoever he be, my land,
my land where I hold sovereignty and throne;   250
and I forbid any to welcome him
or cry him greeting or make him a sharer
in sacrifice or offering to the Gods,
or give him water for his hands to wash.
I command all to drive him from their homes,   255
since he is our pollution, as the oracle
of Pytho's God proclaimed him now to me.
So I stand forth a champion of the God
and of the man who died.
Upon the murderer I invoke this curse—   260
whether he is one man and all unknown,
or one of many—may he wear out his life
in misery to miserable doom!
If with my knowledge he lives at my hearth
I pray that I myself may feel my curse.   265
On you I lay my charge to fulfill all this
for me, for the God, and for this land of ours
destroyed and blighted, by the God forsaken.

Even were this no matter of God's ordinance
it would not fit you so to leave it lie,   270
unpurified, since a good man is dead
and one that was a king. Search it out.
Since I am now the holder of his office,
and have his bed and wife that once was his,
and had his line not been unfortunate   275
we would have common children—(fortune leaped

upon his head)—because of all these things,
I fight in his defence as for my father,
and I shall try all means to take the murderer
280 of Laius the son of Labdacus
the son of Polydorus and before him
of Cadmus and before him of Agenor.
Those who do not obey me, may the Gods
grant no crops springing from the ground they plough
285 nor children to their women! May a fate
like this, or one still worse than this consume them!
For you whom these words please, the other Thebans,
may Justice as your ally and all the gods
live with you, blessing you now and for ever!

CHORUS.
290 As you have held me to my oath, I speak:
I neither killed the king nor can declare
the killer; but since Phoebus set the quest
it is his part to tell who the man is.

OEDIPUS.
Right; but to put compulsion on the Gods
295 against their will—no man can do that.

CHORUS.
May I then say what I think second best?

OEDIPUS.
If there's a third best, too, spare not to tell it.

CHORUS.
I know that what the Lord Teiresias
sees, is most often what the Lord Apollo
300 sees. If you should inquire of this from him
you might find out most clearly.

OEDIPUS.
Even in this my actions have not been sluggard.
On Creon's word I have sent two messengers
and why the prophet is not here already
I have been wondering.

CHORUS.
305   His skill apart
there is besides only an old faint story.

OEDIPUS.
What is it?
I look at every story.

CHORUS.
It was said
that he was killed by certain wayfarers.

OEDIPUS.
310 I heard that, too, but no one saw the killer.

CHORUS.
Yet if he has a share of fear at all,
his courage will not stand firm, hearing your curse.

OEDIPUS.
The man who in the doing did not shrink
will fear no word.

CHORUS.
Here comes his prosecutor:

led by your men the godly prophet comes   315
in whom alone of mankind truth is native.

(Enter Teiresias, led by a little boy.)

OEDIPUS.
Teiresias, you are versed in everything,
things teachable and things not to be spoken,
things of the heaven and earth-creeping things.
You have no eyes but in your mind you know   320
with what a plague our city is afflicted.
My lord, in you alone we find a champion,
in you alone one that can rescue us.
Perhaps you have not heard the messengers,
but Phoebus sent in answer to our sending   325
an oracle declaring that our freedom
from this disease would only come when we
should learn the names of those who killed King
    Laius,
and kill them or expel from our country.
Do not begrudge us oracles from birds,   330
or any other way of prophecy
within your skill; save yourself and the city,
save me; redeem the debt of our pollution
that lies on us because of this dead man.
We are in your hands; pains are most nobly taken   335
to help another when you have means and power.

TEIRESIAS.
Alas, how terrible is wisdom when
it brings no profit to the man that's wise!
This I knew well, but had forgotten it,
else I would not have come here.

OEDIPUS.
What is this?   340
How sad you are now you have come!

TEIRESIAS.
Let me
go home. It will be easiest for us both
to bear our several destinies to the end
if you will follow my advice.

OEDIPUS.
You'd rob us
of this your gift of prophecy? You talk   345
as one who had no care for law nor love
for Thebes who reared you.

TEIRESIAS.
Yes, but I see that even your own words
miss the mark; therefore I must fear for mine.

OEDIPUS.
For God's sake if you know of anything,   350
do not turn from us; all of us kneel to you,
all of us here, your suppliants.

TEIRESIAS.
All of you here know nothing. I will not
bring to the light of day my troubles, mine—
rather than call them yours.

OEDIPUS.

355   What do you mean?
You know of something but refuse to speak.
Would you betray us and destroy the city?

TEIRESIAS.
I will not bring this pain upon us both,
neither on you nor on myself. Why is it
360 you question me and waste your labour? I
will tell you nothing.

OEDIPUS.
You would provoke a stone! Tell us, you villain,
tell us, and do not stand there quietly
unmoved and balking at the issue.

TEIRESIAS.
365 You blame my temper but you do not see
your own that lives within you; it is me
you chide.

OEDIPUS.
Who would not feel his temper rise
at words like these with which you shame our city?

TEIRESIAS.
Of themselves things will come, although I hide them
and breathe no word of them.

OEDIPUS.
370   Since they will come
tell them to me.

TEIRESIAS.
                   I will say nothing further.
Against this answer let your temper rage
as wildly as you will.

OEDIPUS.
                        Indeed I am
so angry I shall not hold back a jot
375 of what I think. For I would have you know
I think you were complotter of the deed
and doer of the deed save in so far
as for the actual killing. Had you had eyes
I would have said alone you murdered him.

TEIRESIAS.
380 Yes? Then I warn you faithfully to keep
the letter of your proclamation and
from this day forth to speak no word of greeting
to these nor me; you are the land's pollution.

OEDIPUS.
How shamelessly you started up this taunt!
How do you think you will escape?

TEIRESIAS.
385   I have.
I have escaped; the truth is what I cherish
and that's my strength.

OEDIPUS.
                And who has taught you truth?
Not your profession surely!

TEIRESIAS.
                  You have taught me,
for you have made me speak against my will.

OEDIPUS.
Speak what? Tell me again that I may learn it better.   390

TEIRESIAS.
Did you not understand before or would you
provoke me into speaking?

OEDIPUS.
                       I did not grasp it,
not so to call it known. Say it again.

TEIRESIAS.
I say you are the murderer of the king
whose murderer you seek.

OEDIPUS.
                      Not twice you shall   395
say calumnies like this and stay unpunished.

TEIRESIAS.
Shall I say more to tempt your anger more?

OEDIPUS.
As much as you desire; it will be said
in vain.

TEIRESIAS.
           I say that with those you love best
you live in foulest shame unconsciously   400
and do not see where you are in calamity.

OEDIPUS.
Do you imagine you can always talk
like this, and live to laugh at it hereafter?

TEIRESIAS.
Yes, if the truth has anything of strength.

OEDIPUS.
It has, but not for you; it has no strength   405
for you because you are blind in mind and ears
as well as in your eyes.

TEIRESIAS.
                   You are a poor wretch
to taunt me with the very insults which
every one soon will heap upon yourself.

OEDIPUS.
Your life is one long night so that you cannot   410
hurt me or any other who sees the light.

TEIRESIAS.
It is not fate that I should be your ruin,
Apollo is enough; it is his care
to work this out.

OEDIPUS.
                Was this your design
or Creon's?

TEIRESIAS.
               Creon is no hurt to you,   415
but you are to yourself.

OEDIPUS.
Wealth, sovereignty and skill outmatching skill
for the contrivance of an envied life!
Great store of jealousy fill your treasury chests,
if my friend Creon, friend from the first and loyal,   420

thus secretly attacks me, secretly
desires to drive me out and secretly
suborns this juggling, trick devising quack,
this wily beggar who has only eyes
425 for his own gains, but blindness in his skill.
For, tell me, where have you seen clear, Teiresias,
with your prophetic eyes? When the dark singer,
the sphinx, was in your country, did you speak
word of deliverance to its citizens?
430 And yet the riddle's answer was not the province
of a chance comer. It was a prophet's task
and plainly you had no such gift of prophecy
from birds nor otherwise from any God
to glean a word of knowledge. But I came,
435 Oedipus, who knew nothing, and I stopped her.
I solved the riddle by my wit alone.
Mine was no knowledge got from birds. And now
you would expel me,
because you think that you will find a place
440 by Creon's throne. I think you will be sorry,
both you and your accomplice, for your plot
to drive me out. And did I not regard you
as an old man, some suffering would have taught you
that what was in your heart was treason.

CHORUS.
445 We look at this man's words and yours, my king,
and we find both have spoken them in anger.
We need no angry words but only thought
how we may best hit the God's meaning for us.

TEIRESIAS.
If you are king, at least I have the right
450 no less to speak in my defence against you.
Of that much I am master. I am no slave
of yours, but Loxias', and so I shall not
enroll myself with Creon for my patron.
Since you have taunted me with being blind,
455 here is my word for you.
You have your eyes but see not where you are
in sin, nor where you live, nor whom you live with.
Do you know who your parents are? Unknowing
you are an enemy to kith and kin
460 in death, beneath the earth, and in this life.
A deadly footed, double striking curse,
from father and mother both, shall drive you forth
out of this land, with darkness on your eyes,
that now have such straight vision. Shall there be
465 a place will not be harbour to your cries,
a corner of Cithaeron will not ring
in echo to your cries, soon, soon,—
when you shall learn the secret of your marriage,
which steered you to a haven in this house,—
470 haven no haven, after lucky voyage?
And of the multitude of other evils
establishing a grim equality
between you and your children, you know nothing.

So, muddy with contempt my words and Creon's!
Misery shall grind no man as it will you.   475

OEDIPUS.
Is it endurable that I should hear
such words from him? Go and a curse go with you!
Quick, home with you! Out of my house at once!

TEIRESIAS.
I would not have come either had you not called me.

OEDIPUS.
I did not know then you would talk like a fool—   480
or it would have been long before I called you.

TEIRESIAS.
I am a fool then, as it seems to you—
but to the parents who have bred you, wise.

OEDIPUS.
What parents? Stop! Who are they of all the world?

TEIRESIAS.
This day will show your birth and will destroy you.   485

OEDIPUS.
How needlessly your riddles darken everything.

TEIRESIAS.
But it's in riddle answering you are strongest.

OEDIPUS.
Yes, Taunt me where you will find me great.

TEIRESIAS.
It is this very luck that has destroyed you.

OEDIPUS.
I do not care, if it has saved this city.   490

TEIRESIAS.
Well, I will go. Come, boy, lead me away.

OEDIPUS.
Yes, lead him off. So long as you are here,
you'll be a stumbling block and a vexation;
once gone, you will not trouble me again.

TEIRESIAS.
                                        I have said
what I came here to say not fearing your   495
countenance: there is no way you can hurt me.
I tell you, king, this man, this murderer
(whom you have long declared you are in search of,
indicting him in threatening proclamation
as murderer of Laius)—he is here.   500
In name he is a stranger among citizens
but soon he will be shown to be a citizen
true native Theban, and he'll have no joy
of the discovery: blindness for sight
and beggary for riches his exchange,   505
he shall go journeying to a foreign country
tapping his way before him with a stick,
He shall be proved father and brother both
to his own children in his house; to her
that gave him birth, a son and husband both;   510
a fellow sower in his father's bed
with that same father that he murdered.
Go within, reckon that out, and if you find me

mistaken, say I have no skill in prophecy.

(Exeunt separately Teiresias and Oedipus.)

CHORUS.

STROPHE

515 Who is the man proclaimed
by Delphi's prophetic rock
as the bloody handed murderer,
the doer of deeds that none dare name?
Now is the time for him to run
520 with a stronger foot
than Pegasus
for the child of Zeus leaps in arms upon him
with fire and the lightning bolt,
and terribly close on his heels
525 are the Fates that never miss.

ANTISTROPHE

Lately from snowy Parnassus
clearly the voice flashed forth,
bidding each Theban track him down,
the unknown murderer.
530 In the savage forests he lurks and in
the caverns like
the mountain bull.
He is sad and lonely, and lonely his feet
that carry him far from the navel of earth;
535 but its prophecies, ever living,
flutter around his head.

STROPHE

The augur has spread confusion,
terrible confusion;
I do not approve what was said
540 nor can I deny it.
I do not know what to say;
I am in a flutter of foreboding;
I never heard in the present
nor past of a quarrel between
545 the sons of Labdacus and Polybus,
that I might bring as proof
in attacking the popular fame
of Oedipus, seeking
to take vengeance for undiscovered
550 death in the line of Labdacus.

ANTISTROPHE

Truly Zeus and Apollo are wise
and in human things all knowing;
but amongst men there is no
distinct judgment, between the prophet
555 and me—which of us is right.
One man may pass another in wisdom

but I would never agree
with those that find fault with the king
till I should see the word
proved right beyond doubt. For once   560
invisible from the Sphinx
came on him and all of us
saw his wisdom and in that test
he saved the city. So he will not be condemned by my
  mind.

(Enter Creon.)

CREON.

Citizens, I have come because I heard   565
deadly words spread about me, that the king
accuses me. I cannot take that from him.
If he believes that in these present troubles
he has been wronged by me in word or deed
I do not want to live on with the burden   570
of such a scandal on me. The report
injures me doubly and most vitally—
for I'll be called a traitor to my city
and traitor also to my friends and you.

CHORUS.

Perhaps it was a sudden gust of anger   575
that forced that insult from him, and no judgment.

CREON.

But did he say that it was in compliance
with schemes of mine that the seer told him lies?

CHORUS.

Yes, he said that, but why, I do not know.

CREON.

Were his eyes straight in his head? Was his mind right   580
when he accused me in this fashion?

CHORUS.

I do not know; I have no eyes to see
what princes do. Here comes the king himself.

(Enter Oedipus.)

OEDIPUS.

You, sir, how is it you come here? Have you so much
brazen-faced daring that you venture in   585
my house although you are proved manifestly
the murderer of that man, and though you tried,
openly, highway robbery of my crown?
For God's sake, tell me what you saw in me,
what cowardice or what stupidity,   590
that made you lay a plot like this against me?
Did you imagine I should not observe
the crafty scheme that stole upon me or
seeing it, take no means to counter it?
Was it not stupid of you to make the attempt,   595
to try to hunt down royal power without
the people at your back or friends? For only
with the people at your back or money can
the hunt end in the capture of a crown.

CREON.

Do you know what you're doing? Will you listen   600
to words to answer yours, and then pass judgment?

OEDIPUS.
You're quick to speak, but I am slow to grasp you,
for I have found you dangerous,—and my foe.
CREON.
First of all hear what I shall say to that.
OEDIPUS.
605 At least don't tell me that you are not guilty.
CREON.
If you think obstinacy without wisdom
a valuable possession, you are wrong.
OEDIPUS.
And you are wrong if you believe that one,
a criminal, will not be punished only
because he is my kinsman.
CREON.
610   This is but just—
but tell me, then, of what offense I'm guilty?
OEDIPUS.
Did you or did you not urge me to send
to this prophetic mumbler?
CREON.
           I did indeed,
and I shall stand by what I told you.
OEDIPUS.
615 How long ago is it since Laius. . .
CREON.
What about Laius? I don't understand.
OEDIPUS.
Vanished—died—was murdered?
CREON.
           It is long,
a long, long time to reckon.
OEDIPUS.
           Was this prophet
in the profession then?
CREON.
           He was, and honoured
620 as highly as he is today.
OEDIPUS.
At that time did he say a word about me?
CREON.
Never, at least when I was near him.
OEDIPUS.
You never made a search for the dead man?
CREON.
We searched, indeed, but never learned of anything.
OEDIPUS.
625 Why did our wise old friend not say this then?
CREON.
I don't know; and when I know nothing, I
usually hold my tongue.
OEDIPUS.
           You know this much,
and can declare this much if you are loyal.
CREON.
What is it? If I know, I'll not deny it.

OEDIPUS.
That he would not have said that I killed Laius   630
had he not met you first.
CREON.
           You know yourself
whether he said this, but I demand that I
should hear as much from you as you from me.
OEDIPUS.
Then hear,—I'll not be proved a murderer.
CREON.
Well, then. You're married to my sister.
OEDIPUS.
           Yes,   635
that I am not disposed to deny.
CREON.
           You rule
this country giving her an equal share
in the government?
OEDIPUS.
           Yes, everything she wants
she has from me.
CREON.
           And I, as thirdsman to you,
am rated as the equal of you two?   640
OEDIPUS.
Yes, and it's there you've proved yourself false friend.
CREON.
Not if you will reflect on it as I do.
Consider, first, if you think any one
would choose to rule and fear rather than rule
and sleep untroubled by a fear if power   645
were equal in both cases. I, at least,
I was not born with such a frantic yearning
to be a king—but to do what kings do.
And so it is with every one who has learned
wisdom and self-control. As it stands now,   650
the prizes are all mine—and without fear.
But if I were the king myself, I must
do much that went against the grain.
How should despotic rule seem sweeter to me
than painless power and an assured authority?   655
I am not so besotted yet that I
want other honours than those that come with profit.
Now every man's my pleasure; every man greets me;
now those who are your suitors fawn on me,—
success for them depends upon my favour.   660
Why should I let all this go to win that?
My mind would not be traitor if it's wise;
I am no treason lover, of my nature,
nor would I ever dare to join a plot.
Prove what I say. Go to the oracle   665
at Pytho and inquire about the answers,
if they are as I told you. For the rest,
if you discover I laid any plot
together with the seer, kill me, I say,
not only by your vote but by my own.   670

But do not charge me on obscure opinion
without some proof to back it. It's not just
lightly to count your knaves as honest men,
nor honest men as knaves. To throw away
675 an honest friend is, as it were, to throw
your life away, which a man loves the best.
In time you will know all with certainty;
time is the only test of honest men,
one day is space enough to know a rogue.

CHORUS.
680 His words are wise, king, if one fears to fall.
Those who are quick of temper are not safe.

OEDIPUS.
When he that plots against me secretly
moves quickly, I must quickly counterplot.
If I wait taking no decisive measure
685 his business will be done, and mine be spoiled.

CREON.
What do you want to do then? Banish me?

OEDIPUS.
No, certainly; kill you, not banish you[1]

CREON.
I do not think that you've your wits about you.

OEDIPUS.
For my own interests, yes.

CREON.
                              But for mine, too,
you should think equally.

OEDIPUS.
690   You are a rogue.

CREON.
Suppose you do not understand?

OEDIPUS.
                              But yet
I must be ruler.

CREON.
                Not if you rule badly.

OEDIPUS.
O, city, city!

CREON.
              I too have some share
in the city; it is not yours alone.

CHORUS.
695 Stop, my lords! Here—and in the nick of time
I see Jocasta coming from the house;
with her help lay the quarrel that now stirs you.

                              (Enter Jocasta.)

1. Two lines omitted here owing to the confusion in the dialogue
consequent on the loss of a third line. The lines as they stand in
Jebb's edition (1902) are:
OED.: That you may show what manner of thing is envy.
CREON: You speak as one that will not yield or trust.
[OED. lost line.]

JOCASTA.
For shame! Why have you raised this foolish
    squabbling
brawl? Are you not ashamed to air your private
griefs when the country's sick? Go in, you, Oedipus,   700
and you, too, Creon, into the house. Don't magnify
your nothing troubles.

CREON.
                    Sister, Oedipus,
your husband, thinks he has the right to do
terrible wrongs—he has but to choose between
two terrors: banishing or killing me.   705

OEDIPUS.
He's right, Jocasta; for I find him plotting
with knavish tricks against my person.

CREON.
That God may never bless me! May I die
accursed, if I have been guilty of
one tittle of the charge you bring against me!   710

JOCASTA.
I beg you, Oedipus, trust him in this,
spare him for the sake of this his oath to God,
for my sake, and the sake of those who stand here.

CHORUS.
Be gracious, be merciful,
we beg of you   715

OEDIPUS.
In what would you have me yield?

CHORUS.
He has been no silly child in the past.
He is strong in his oath now.
Spare him.

OEDIPUS.
Do you know what you ask?   720

CHORUS.
Yes.

OEDIPUS.
Tell me then.

CHORUS.
He has been your friend before all men's eyes; do not cast
him away dishonoured on an obscure conjecture.

OEDIPUS.
I would have you know that this request of yours   725
really requests my death or banishment.

CHORUS.
May the Sun God, king of Gods, forbid! May I die
without God's blessing, without friends' help, if I had any
such thought. But my spirit is broken by my unhappiness
for my wasting country; and this would but add troubles   730
amongst ourselves to the other troubles.

OEDIPUS.
Well, let him go then—if I must die ten times for it,
or be sent out dishonoured into exile.
It is your lips that prayed for him I pitied,
not his; wherever he is, I shall hate him.   735

CREON.

I see you sulk in yielding and you're dangerous
when you are out of temper; natures like yours
are justly heaviest for themselves to bear.

OEDIPUS.

Leave me alone! Take yourself off, I tell you.

CREON.

740 I'll go, you have not known me, but they have,
and they have known my innocence.

(*Exit.*)

CHORUS.

Won't you take him inside, lady?

JOCASTA.

Yes, when I've found out what was the matter.

CHORUS.

There was some misconceived suspicion of a story, and
on the other side the sting of injustice.

JOCASTA.

745 So, on both sides?

CHORUS.

Yes.

JOCASTA.

What was the story?

CHORUS.

I think it best, in the interests of the country, to leave it
where it ended.

OEDIPUS.

750 You see where you have ended, straight of judgment
although you are, by softening my anger.

CHORUS.

Sir, I have said before and I say again—be sure that I would
have been proved a madman, bankrupt in sane council, if I
should put you away, you who steered the country I love
755 safely when she was crazed with troubles. God grant that
now, too, you may prove a fortunate guide for us.

JOCASTA.

Tell me, my lord, I beg of you, what was it
that roused your anger so?

OEDIPUS.

Yes, I will tell you.
I honour you more than I honour them.
760 It was Creon and the plots he laid against me.

JOCASTA.

Tell me—if you can clearly tell the quarrel—

OEDIPUS.

Creon says
that I'm the murderer of Laius.

JOCASTA.

Of his own knowledge or on information?

OEDIPUS.

He sent this rascal prophet to me, since
765 he keeps his own mouth clean of any guilt.

JOCASTA.

Do not concern yourself about this matter;
listen to me and learn that human beings
have no part in the craft of prophecy.
Of that I'll show you a short proof.
There was an oracle once that came to Laius,— 770
I will not say that it was Phoebus' own,
but it was from his servants—and it told him
that it was fate that he should die a victim
at the hands of his own son, a son to be born
of Laius and me. But, see now, he, 775
the king, was killed by foreign highway robbers
at a place where three roads meet—so goes the story;
and for the son—before three days were out
after his birth King Laius pierced his ankles
and by the hands of others cast him forth 780
upon a pathless hillside. So Apollo
failed to fulfill his oracle to the son,
that he should kill his father, and to Laius
also proved false in that the thing he feared,
death at his son's hands, never came to pass. 785
So clear in this case were the oracles,
so clear and false. Give them no heed, I say;
what God discovers need of, easily
he shows to us himself.

OEDIPUS.

O dear Jocasta,
as I hear this from you, there comes upon me 790
a wandering of the soul—I could run mad.

JOCASTA.

What trouble is it, that you turn again
and speak like this?

OEDIPUS.

I thought I heard you say
that Laius was killed at a crossroads.

JOCASTA.

Yes, that was how the story went and still 795
that word goes round.

OEDIPUS.

Where is this place, Jocasta,
where he was murdered?

JOCASTA.

Phocis is the country
and the road splits there, one of the two roads from Delphi,
another comes from Daulia.

OEDIPUS.

How long ago is this?

JOCASTA.

The news came to the city just before 800
you became king and all men's eyes looked to you.
What is it, Oedipus, that's in your mind?

OEDIPUS.

What have you designed, O Zeus, to do with me?

JOCASTA.

What is the thought that troubles your heart?

OEDIPUS.

Don't ask me yet—tell me of Laius— 805
How did he look? How old or young was he?

JOCASTA.
> He was a tall man and his hair was grizzled
> already—nearly white—and in his form
> not unlike you.

OEDIPUS.
> O God, I think I have
810 called curses on myself in ignorance.

JOCASTA.
> What do you mean? I am terrified
> when I look at you.

OEDIPUS.
> I have a deadly fear
> that the old seer had eyes. You'll show me more
> if you can tell me one more thing.

JOCASTA.
> I will.
815 I'm frightened—but if I can understand,
> I'll tell you all you ask.

OEDIPUS.
> How was his company?
> Had he few with him when he went this journey,
> or many servants, as would suit a prince?

JOCASTA.
> In all there were but five, and among them
820 a herald; and one carriage for the king.

OEDIPUS.
> It's plain—it's plain—who was it told you this?

JOCASTA.
> The only servant that escaped safe home.

OEDIPUS.
> Is he at home now?

JOCASTA.
> No, when he came home again
> and saw you king and Laius was dead,
825 he came to me and touched my hand and begged
> that I should send him to the fields to be
> my shepherd and so he might see the city
> as far off as he might. So I
> sent him away. He was an honest man,
830 as slaves go, and was worthy of far more
> than what he asked of me.

OEDIPUS.
> O, how I wish that he could come back quickly!

JOCASTA.
> He can. Why is your heart so set on this?

OEDIPUS.
> O dear Jocasta, I am full of fears
835 that I have spoken far too much; and therefore
> I wish to see this shepherd.

JOCASTA.
> He will come;
> but, Oedipus, I think I'm worthy too
> to know what it is that disquiets you.

OEDIPUS.
> It shall not be kept from you, since my mind
840 has gone so far with its forebodings. Whom
> should I confide in rather than you, who is there
> of more importance to me who have passed
> through such a fortune?
> Polybus was my father, king of Corinth,
> and Merope, the Dorian, my mother. 845
> I was held greatest of the citizens
> in Corinth till a curious chance befell me
> as I shall tell you—curious, indeed,
> but hardly worth the store I set upon it.
> There was a dinner and at it a man, 850
> a drunken man, accused me in his drink
> of being bastard. I was furious
> but held my temper under for that day.
> Next day I went and taxed my parents with it;
> they took the insult very ill from him, 855
> the drunken fellow who had uttered it.
> So I was comforted for their part, but
> still this thing rankled always, for the story
> crept about widely. And I went at last
> to Pytho, though my parents did not know. 860
> But Phoebus sent me home again unhonoured
> in what I came to learn, but he foretold
> other and desperate horrors to befall me,
> that I was fated to lie with my mother,
> and show to daylight an accursed breed 865
> which men would not endure, and I was doomed
> to be murderer of the father that begot me.
> When I heard this I fled, and in the days
> that followed I would measure from the stars
> the whereabouts of Corinth—yes, I fled 870
> to somewhere where I should not see fulfilled
> the infamies told in that dreadful oracle.
> And as I journeyed I came to the place
> where, as you say, this king met with his death.
> Jocasta, I will tell you the whole truth. 875
> When I was near the branching of the crossroads,
> going on foot, I was encountered by
> a herald and a carriage with a man in it,
> just as you tell me. He that led the way
> and the old man himself wanted to thrust me 880
> out of the road by force. I became angry
> and struck the coachman who was pushing me.
> When the old man saw this he watched his moment,
> and as I passed he struck me from his carriage,
> full on the head with his two pointed goad. 885
> But he was paid in full and presently
> my stick had struck him backwards from the car
> and he rolled out of it. And then I killed them
> all. If it happened there was any tie
> of kinship twixt this man and Laius, 890
> who is then now more miserable than I,
> what man on earth so hated by the Gods,
> since neither citizen nor foreigner
> may welcome me at home or even greet me,
> but drive me out of doors? And it is I, 895
> I and no other have so cursed myself.

And I pollute the bed of him I killed
by the hands that killed him. Was I not born evil?
Am I not utterly unclean? I had to fly
900 and in my banishment not even see
my kindred nor set foot in my own country,
or otherwise my fate was to be yoked
in marriage with my mother and kill my father,
Polybus who begot me and had reared me.
905 Would not one rightly judge and say that on me
these things were sent by some malignant God?
O no, no, no—O holy majesty
of God on high, may I not see that day!
May I be gone out of men's sight before
910 I see the deadly taint of this disaster
come upon me.
CHORUS.
Sir, we too fear these things. But until you see this man
face to face and hear his story, hope.
OEDIPUS.
Yes, I have just this much of hope—to wait until the
915 herdsman comes.
JOCASTA.
And when he comes, what do you want with him?
OEDIPUS.
I'll tell you; if I find that his story is the same as yours, I at
least will be clear of this guilt.
JOCASTA.
Why what so particularly did you learn from my story?
OEDIPUS.
920 You said that he spoke of highway *robbers* who killed
Laius. Now if he uses the same number, it was not I who
killed him. One man cannot be the same as many. But if
he speaks of a man travelling alone, then clearly the burden of the guilt inclines towards me.
JOCASTA.
925 Be sure, at least, that this was how he told the story. He
cannot unsay it now, for every one in the city heard it—
not I alone. But, Oedipus, even if he diverges from what
he said then, he shall never prove that the murder of
Laius squares rightly with the prophecy—for Loxias de-
930 clared that the king should be killed by his own son. And
that poor creature did not kill him surely,—for he died
himself first. So as far as prophecy goes, henceforward I
shall not look to the right hand or the left.
OEDIPUS.
Right. But yet, send some one for the peasant to bring
935 him here; do not neglect it.
JOCASTA.
I will send quickly. Now let me go indoors. I will do nothing except what pleases you.
(*Exeunt.*)
CHORUS.

STROPHE

May destiny ever find me
pious in word and deed

prescribed by the laws that live on high: 940
laws begotten in the clear air of heaven,
whose only father is Olympus;
no mortal nature brought them to birth,
no forgetfulness shall lull them to sleep;
for God is great in them and grows not old. 945

ANTISTROPHE

Insolence breeds the tyrant, insolence
if it is glutted with a surfeit, unseasonable, unprofitable,
climbs to the roof-top and plunges
sheer down to the ruin that must be,
and there its feet are no service. 950
But I pray that the God may never
abolish the eager ambition that profits the state.
For I shall never cease to hold the God as our protector.

STROPHE

If a man walks with haughtiness
of hand or word and gives no heed 955
to Justice and the shrines of Gods
despises—may an evil doom
smite him for his ill-starred pride of heart!—
if he reaps gains without justice
and will not hold from impiety 960
and his fingers itch for untouchable things.
When such things are done, what man shall contrive
to shield his soul from the shafts of the God?
When such deeds are held in honour,
why should I honour the Gods in the dance? 965

ANTISTROPHE

No longer to the holy place,
to the navel of earth I'll go
to worship, nor to Abae
nor to Olympia,
unless the oracles are proved to fit, 970
for all men's hands to point at.
O Zeus, if you are rightly called
the sovereign lord, all-mastering,
let this not escape you nor your ever-living power!
The oracles concerning Laius 975
are old and dim and men regard them not.
Apollo is nowhere clear in honour; God's service per-
ishes.
(*Enter Jocasta, carrying garlands.*)
JOCASTA.
Princes of the land, I have had the thought to go
to the Gods' temples, bringing in my hand
garlands and gifts of incense, as you see. 980
For Oedipus excites himself too much
at every sort of trouble, not conjecturing,
like a man of sense, what will be from what was,
but he is always at the speaker's mercy,
when he speaks terrors. I can do no good 985
by my advice, and so I came as suppliant

to you, Lycaean Apollo, who are nearest.
These are the symbols of my prayer and this
my prayer: grant us escape free of the curse.

990 Now when we look to him we are all afraid;
he's pilot of our ship and he is frightened.

(Enter Messenger.)

MESSENGER.

Might I learn from you, sirs, where is the house of Oedipus? Or best of all, if you know, where is the king himself?

CHORUS.

This is his house and he is within doors. This lady is his
995 wife and mother of his children.

MESSENGER.

God bless you, lady, and God bless your household! God
bless Oedipus' noble wife!

JOCASTA.

God bless you, sir, for your kind greeting! What do you
want of us that you have come here? What have you to
1000 tell us?

MESSENGER.

Good news, lady. Good for your house and for your husband.

JOCASTA.

What is your news? Who sent you to us?

MESSENGER.

I come from Corinth and the news I bring will give you
1005 pleasure. Perhaps a little pain too.

JOCASTA.

What is this news of double meaning?

MESSENGER.

The people of the Isthmus will choose Oedipus to be
their king. That is the rumour there.

JOCASTA.

But isn't their king still old Polybus?

MESSENGER.

1010 No. He is in his grave. Death has got him.

JOCASTA.

Is that the truth? Is Oedipus' father dead?

MESSENGER.

May I die myself if it be otherwise!

JOCASTA.

(to a servant.)

Be quick and run to the king with the news! O oracles of
the Gods, where are you now? It was from this man Oedi-
1015 pus fled, lest he should be his murderer! And now he is
dead, in the course of nature, and not killed by Oedipus.

(Enter Oedipus.)

OEDIPUS.

Dearest Jocasta, why have you sent for me?

JOCASTA.

Listen to this man and when you hear reflect what is the
outcome of the holy oracles of the Gods.

OEDIPUS.

1020 Who is he? What is his message for me?

JOCASTA.

He is from Corinth and he tells us that your father Polybus is dead and gone.

OEDIPUS.

What's this you say, sir? Tell me yourself.

MESSENGER.

Since this is the first matter you want clearly told: Polybus has gone down to death. You may be sure of it.   1025

OEDIPUS.

By treachery or sickness?

MESSENGER.

A small thing will put old bodies asleep.

OEDIPUS.

So he died of sickness, it seems,—poor old man!

MESSENGER.

Yes, and of age—the long years he had measured.

OEDIPUS.

Ha! Ha! O dear Jocasta, why should one   1030
look to the Pythian hearth? Why should one look
to the birds screaming overhead? They prophesied
that I should kill my father! But he's dead,
and hidden deep in earth, and I stand here
who never laid a hand on spear against him,—   1035
unless perhaps he died of longing for me,
and thus I am his murderer. But they,
the oracles, as they stand—he's taken them
away with him, they're dead as he himself is,
and worthless.

JOCASTA.

That I told you before now.   1040

OEDIPUS.

You did, but I was misled by my fear.

JOCASTA.

Then lay no more of them to heart, not one.

OEDIPUS.

But surely I must fear my mother's bed?

JOCASTA.

Why should man fear since chance is all in all
for him, and he can clearly foreknow nothing?   1045
Best to live lightly, as one can, unthinkingly.
As to your mother's marriage bed,—don't fear it.
Before this, in dreams too, as well as oracles,
many a man has lain with his own mother.
But he to whom such things are nothing bears   1050
his life most easily.

OEDIPUS.

All that you say would be said perfectly
if she were dead; but since she lives I must
still fear, although you talk so well, Jocasta.

JOCASTA.

Still in your father's death there's light of
comfort?   1055

OEDIPUS.

Great light of comfort; but I fear the living.

MESSENGER.
Who is the woman that makes you afraid?
OEDIPUS.
Merope, old man, Polybus' wife.
MESSENGER.
What about her frightens the queen and you?
OEDIPUS.
1060   A terrible oracle, stranger, from the Gods.
MESSENGER.
Can it be told? Or does the sacred law
forbid another to have knowledge of it?
OEDIPUS.
O no! Once on a time Loxias said
that I should lie with my own mother and
1065   take on my hands the blood of my own father.
And so for these long years I've lived away
from Corinth; it has been to my great happiness;
but yet it's sweet to see the face of parents.
MESSENGER.
This was the fear which drove you out of Corinth?
OEDIPUS.
1070   Old man, I did not wish to kill my father.
MESSENGER.
Why should I not free you from this fear, sir,
since I have come to you in all goodwill?
OEDIPUS.
You would not find me thankless if you did.
MESSENGER.
Why, it was just for this I brought the news,—
1075   to earn your thanks when you had come safe home.
OEDIPUS.
No, I will never come near my parents.
MESSENGER.
                            Son,
it's very plain you don't know what you're doing.
OEDIPUS.
What do you mean, old man? For God's sake, tell me.
MESSENGER.
If your homecoming is checked by fears like these.
OEDIPUS.
1080   Yes, I'm afraid that Phoebus may prove right.
MESSENGER.
The murder and the incest?
OEDIPUS.
                  Yes, old man;
that is my constant terror.
MESSENGER.
               Do you know
that all your fears are empty?
OEDIPUS.
              How is that,
if they are father and mother and I their son?
MESSENGER.
1085   Because Polybus was no kin to you in blood.

OEDIPUS.
What, was not Polybus my father?
MESSENGER.
No more than I but just so much.
OEDIPUS.
                   How can
my father be my father as much as one
that's nothing to me?
MESSENGER.
           Neither he nor I
begat you.
OEDIPUS.
        Why then did he call me son?   1090
MESSENGER.
A gift he took you from these hands of mine.
OEDIPUS.
Did he love so much what he took from another's
    hand?
MESSENGER.
His childlessness before persuaded him.
OEDIPUS.
Was I a child you bought or found when I
was given to him?
MESSENGER.
          On Cithaeron's slopes   1095
in the twisting thickets you were found.
OEDIPUS.
               And why
were you a traveller in those parts?
MESSENGER.
               I was
in charge of mountain flocks.
OEDIPUS.
          You were a shepherd?
A hireling vagrant?
MESSENGER.
         Yes, but at least at that time
the man that saved your life, son.   1100
OEDIPUS.
What ailed me when you took me in your arms?
MESSENGER.
In that your ankles should be witnesses.
OEDIPUS.
Why do you speak of that old pain?
MESSENGER.
              I loosed you;
the tendons of your feet were pierced and fettered,—
OEDIPUS.
My swaddling clothes brought me a rare disgrace.   1105
MESSENGER.
So that from this you're called your present name.
OEDIPUS.
Was this my father's doing or my mother's?
For God's sake, tell me.

MESSENGER.

           I don't know, but he
1110 who gave you to me has more knowledge than I.
OEDIPUS.
    You yourself did not find me then? You took me
    from someone else?
MESSENGER.

           Yes, from another shepherd.
OEDIPUS.
    Who was he? Do you know him well enough
    to tell?
MESSENGER.

       He was called Laius' man.
OEDIPUS.
1115 You mean the king who reigned here in the old days?
MESSENGER.
    Yes, he was that man's shepherd.
OEDIPUS.

         Is he alive
    still, so that I could see him?
MESSENGER.

         You who live here
    would know that best.
OEDIPUS.

        Do any of you here
    know of this shepherd whom he speaks about
1120 in town or in the fields? Tell me. It's time
    that this was found out once for all.
CHORUS.
    I think he is none other than the peasant
    whom you have sought to see already; but
    Jocasta here can tell us best of that.
OEDIPUS.
1125 Jocasta, do you know about this man
    whom we have sent for? Is he the man he mentions?
JOCASTA.
    Why ask of whom he spoke? Don't give it heed;
    nor try to keep in mind what has been said.
    It will be wasted labour.
OEDIPUS.

        With such clues
1130 I could not fail to bring my birth to light.
JOCASTA.
    I beg you—do not hunt this out—I beg you,
    if you have any care for your own life.
    What I am suffering is enough.
OEDIPUS.

        Keep up
    your heart, Jocasta. Though I'm proved a slave,
1135 thrice slave, and though my mother is thrice slave,
    you'll not be shown to be of lowly lineage.
JOCASTA.
    O be persuaded by me, I entreat you;
    do not do this.

OEDIPUS.
    I will not be persuaded to let be
    the chance of finding out the whole thing clearly. 1140
JOCASTA.
    It is because I wish you well that I
    give you this counsel—and it's the best counsel.
OEDIPUS.
    Then the best counsel vexes me, and has
    for some while since.
JOCASTA.

        O Oedipus, God help you!
    God keep you from the knowledge of who you are! 1145
OEDIPUS.
    Here, some one, go and fetch the shepherd for me;
    and let her find her joy in her rich family!
JOCASTA.
    O Oedipus, unhappy Oedipus!
    that is all I can call you, and the last thing
    that I shall ever call you. 1150

                           (*Exit.*)
CHORUS.
    Why has the queen gone, Oedipus, in wild
    grief rushing from us? I am afraid that trouble
    will break out of this silence.
OEDIPUS.
    Break out what will! I at least shall be
    willing to see my ancestry, though humble. 1155
    Perhaps she is ashamed of my low birth,
    for she has all a woman's high-flown pride.
    But I account myself a child of Fortune,
    beneficent Fortune, and I shall not be
    dishonoured. She's the mother from whom I spring; 1160
    the months, my brothers, marked me, now as small,
    and now again as mighty. Such is my breeding,
    and I shall never prove so false to it,
    as not to find the secret of my birth.
CHORUS.

STROPHE

If I am a prophet and wise of heart 1165
you shall not fail, Cithaeron,
by the limitless sky, you shall not!—
to know at tomorrow's full moon
that Oedipus honours you,
as native to him and mother and nurse at once; 1170
and that you are honoured in dancing by us, as finding
    favour in sight of our king.
Apollo, to whom we cry, find these things pleasing!

ANTISTROPHE

Who was it bore you, child? One of
the long-lived nymphs who lay with Pan—

1175   the father who treads the hills?
   Or was she a bride of Loxias, your mother? The grassy
       slopes
   are all of them dear to him. Or perhaps Cyllene's king
   or the Bacchants' God that lives on the tops
   of the hills received you a gift from some
   one of the Helicon Nymphs, with whom he mostly
1180   plays?

             (*Enter an old man, led by Oedipus' servants.*)

OEDIPUS.
   If someone like myself who never met him
   may make a guess,—I think this is the herdsman,
   whom we were seeking. His old age is consonant
   with the other. And besides, the men who bring him
1185   I recognize as my own servants. You
   perhaps may better me in knowledge since
   you've seen the man before.

CHORUS.
              You can be sure
   I recognize him. For if Laius
   had ever an honest shepherd, this was he.

OEDIPUS.
1190   You, sir, from Corinth, I must ask you first,
   is this the man you spoke of?

MESSENGER.
           This is he
   before your eyes.

OEDIPUS.
           Old man, look here at me
   and tell me what I ask you. Were you ever
   a servant of King Laius?

HERDSMAN.
           I was,—
1195   no slave he bought but reared in his own house.

OEDIPUS.
   What did you do as work? How did you live?

HERDSMAN.
   Most of my life was spent among the flocks.

OEDIPUS.
   In what part of the country did you live?

HERDSMAN.
   Cithaeron and the places near to it.

OEDIPUS.
1200   And somewhere there perhaps you knew this man?

HERDSMAN.
   What was his occupation? Who?

OEDIPUS.
           This man here,
   have you had any dealings with him?

HERDSMAN.
           No—
   not such that I can quickly call to mind.

MESSENGER.
   That is no wonder, master. But I'll make him remember

what he does not know. For I know, that he well knows 1205
the country of Cithaeron, how he with two flocks, I with
one kept company for three years—each year half a year
—from spring till autumn time and then when winter
came I drove my flocks to our fold home again and he to
Laius' steadings. Well—am I right or not in what I said 1210
we did?

HERDSMAN.
   You're right—although it's a long time ago.

MESSENGER.
   Do you remember giving me a child
   to bring up as my foster child?

HERDSMAN.
           What's this?
   Why do you ask this question?

MESSENGER.
           Look old man,   1215
   here he is—here's the man who was that child!

HERDSMAN.
   Death take you! Won't you hold your tongue?

OEDIPUS.
           No, no,
   do no find fault with him, old man. Your words
   are more at fault than his.

HERDSMAN.
           O best of masters,
   how do I give offense?

OEDIPUS.
           When you refuse   1220
   to speak about the child of whom he asks you.

HERDSMAN.
   He speaks out of his ignorance, without meaning.

OEDIPUS.
   If you'll not talk to gratify me, you
   will talk with pain to urge you.

HERDSMAN.
           O, please, sir,
   don't hurt an old man, sir.

OEDIPUS.
           (*to the servants.*)
           Here, one of you,   1225
   twist his hands behind him.

HERDSMAN.
           Why, God help me, why?
   What do you want to know?

OEDIPUS.
           You gave a child
   to him,—the child he asked you of?

HERDSMAN.
           I did.
   I wish I'd died the day I did.

OEDIPUS.
           You will
   unless you tell me truly.

HERDSMAN.

1230   And I'll die
far worse if I should tell you.

OEDIPUS.

                              This fellow
is bent on more delays, as it would seem.

HERDSMAN.

O no, no! I have told you that I gave it.

OEDIPUS.

Where did you get this child from? Was it your own or
did you get it from another?

HERDSMAN.

1235   Not
my own at all; I had it from some one.

OEDIPUS.

One of these citizens? or from what house?

HERDSMAN.

O master, please—I beg you, master, please
don't ask me more.

OEDIPUS.

                              You're a dead man if I
ask you again.

HERDSMAN.

1240   It was one of the children
of Laius.

OEDIPUS.

              A slave? Or born in wedlock?

HERDSMAN.

O God, I am on the brink of frightful speech.

OEDIPUS.

And I of frightful hearing. But I must hear.

HERDSMAN.

The child was called his child; but she within,
1245   your wife would tell you best how all this was.

OEDIPUS.

She gave it to you?

HERDSMAN.

                       Yes, she did, my lord.

OEDIPUS.

To do what with it?

HERDSMAN.

                       Make away with it.

OEDIPUS.

She was so hard—its mother?

HERDSMAN.

                              Aye, through fear
of evil oracles.

OEDIPUS.

              Which?

HERDSMAN.

                       They said that he
should kill his parents.

OEDIPUS.

1250   How was it that you
gave it away to this old man?

HERDSMAN.

                              O master,
I pitied it, and thought that I could send it
off to another country and this man
was from another country. But he saved it
for the most terrible troubles. If you are   1255
the man he says you are, you're bred to misery.

OEDIPUS.

O, O, O, they will all come,
all come out clearly! Light of the sun, let me
look upon you no more after today!
I who first saw the light bred of a match   1260
accursed, and accursed in my living
with them I lived with, cursed in my killing.

                       (*Exeunt all but the Chorus.*)

CHORUS.

STROPHE

O generations of men, how I
count you as equal with those who live
not at all!   1265
What man, what man on earth wins more
of happiness than a seeming
and after that turning away?
Oedipus, you are my pattern of this,
Oedipus, you and your fate!   1270
Luckless Oedipus, whom of all men
I envy not at all.

ANTISTROPHE

In as much as he shot his bolt
beyond the others and won the prize
of happiness complete—   1275
O Zeus—and killed and reduced to nought
the hooked taloned maid of the riddling speech,
standing a tower against death for my land:
hence he was called my king and hence
was honoured the highest of all   1280
honours; and hence he ruled
in the great city of Thebes.

STROPHE

But now whose tale is more miserable?
Who is there lives with a savager fate?
Whose troubles so reverse his life as his?   1285

O Oedipus, the famous prince
for whom a great haven
the same both as father and son
sufficed for generation,
how, O how, have the furrows ploughed   1290
by your father endured to bear you, poor wretch,
and hold their peace so long?

ANTISTROPHE

Time who sees all has found you out
against your will; judges your marriage accursed,
1295　begetter and begot at one in it.

O child of Laius,
would I had never seen you.
I weep for you and cry
a dirge of lamentation.
1300　To speak directly, I drew my breath
from you at the first and so now I lull
my mouth to sleep with your name.

(Enter a second Messenger.)

SECOND MESSENGER.
O Princes always honoured by our country,
what deeds you'll hear of and what horrors see,
1305　what grief you'll feel, if you as true born Thebans
care for the house of Labdacus's sons.
Phasis nor Ister cannot purge this house,
I think, with all their streams, such things
it hides, such evils shortly will bring forth
1310　into the light, whether they will or not;
and troubles hurt the most
when they prove self-inflicted.
CHORUS.
What we had known before did not fall short
of bitter groaning's worth; what's more to tell?
SECOND MESSENGER.
1315　Shortest to hear and tell—our glorious queen
Jocasta's dead.
CHORUS.
　　　　　Unhappy woman! How?
SECOND MESSENGER.
By her own hand. The worst of what was done
you cannot know. You did not see the sight.
Yet in so far as I remember it
1320　you'll hear the end of our unlucky queen.
When she came raging into the house she went
straight to her marriage bed, tearing her hair
with both her hands, and crying upon Laius
long dead—Do you remember, Laius,
1325　that night long past which bred a child for us
to send you to your death and leave
a mother making children with her son?
And then she groaned and cursed the bed in which
she brought forth husband by her husband, children
1330　by her own child, an infamous double bond.
How after that she died I do not know,—
for Oedipus distracted us from seeing.
He burst upon us shouting and we looked
to him as he paced frantically around,
1335　begging us always: Give me a sword, I say,
to find this wife no wife, this mother's womb,
this field of double sowing whence I sprang

and where I sowed my children! As he raved
some god showed him the way—none of us there.
Bellowing terribly and led by some　　　　1340
invisible guide he rushed on the two doors,—
wrenching the hollow bolts out of their sockets,
he charged inside. There, there, we saw his wife
hanging, the twisted rope around her neck.
When he saw her, he cried out fearfully　　1345
and cut the dangling noose. Then, as she lay,
poor woman, on the ground, what happened after,
was terrible to see. He tore the brooches—
the gold chased brooches fastening her robe—
away from her and lifting them up high　　1350
dashed them on his own eyeballs, shrieking out
such things as: they will never see the crime
I have committed or had done upon me!
Dark eyes, now in the days to come look on
forbidden faces, do not recognize　　　　1355
those whom you long for—with such imprecations
he struck his eyes again and yet again
with the brooches. And the bleeding eyeballs gushed
and stained his beard—no sluggish oozing drops
but a black rain and bloody hail poured down.　1360

So it has broken—and not on one head
but troubles mixed for husband and for wife.
The fortune of the days gone by was true
good fortune—but today groans and destruction
and death and shame—of all ills can be named　1365
not one is missing.
CHORUS.
Is he now in any ease from pain?
SECOND MESSENGER.
　　　　　　　　He shouts
for some one to unbar the doors and show him
to all the men of Thebes, his father's killer,
his mother's—no I cannot say the word,　　1370
it is unholy—for he'll cast himself,
out of the land, he says, and not remain
to bring a curse upon his house, the curse
he called upon it in his proclamation. But
he wants for strength, aye, and someone to guide him;　1375
his sickness is too great to bear. You, too,
will be shown that. The bolts are opening.
Soon you will see a sight to waken pity
even in the horror of it.

(Enter the blinded Oedipus.)

CHORUS.
This is a terrible sight for men to see!　　1380
I never found a worse!
Poor wretch, what madness came upon you!
What evil spirit leaped upon your life
to your ill-luck—a leap beyond man's strength!
Indeed I pity you, but I cannot　　　　1385
look at you, though there's much I want to ask

and much to learn and much to see.
I shudder at the sight of you.

OEDIPUS.

O, O,

1390 where am I going? Where is my voice
borne on the wind to and fro?
Spirit, how far have you sprung?

CHORUS.

To a terrible place whereof men's ears
may not hear, nor their eyes behold it.

OEDIPUS.

1395 Darkness!
Horror of darkness enfolding, resistless, unspeakable
        visitant sped by an ill wind in haste!
madness and stabbing pain and memory
of evil deeds I have done!

CHORUS.

In such misfortunes it's no wonder
1400 if double weighs the burden of your grief.

OEDIPUS.

My friend,
you are the only one steadfast, the only one that attends
        on me;
you still stay nursing the blind man.
Your care is not unnoticed. I can know
1405 your voice, although this darkness is my world.

CHORUS.

Doer of dreadful deeds, how did you dare
so far to do despite to your own eyes?
what spirit urged you to it?

OEDIPUS.

It was Apollo, friends, Apollo,
that brought this bitter bitterness, my sorrows to comple-
1410   tion.
But the hand that struck me
was none but my own.
Why should I see
whose vision showed me nothing sweet to see?

CHORUS.

1415 These things are as you say.

OEDIPUS.

What can I see to love?
What greeting can touch my ears with joy?
Take me away, and haste—to a place out of the way!
Take me away, my friends, the greatly miserable,
1420 the most accursed, whom God too hates
above all men on earth!

CHORUS.

Unhappy in your mind and your misfortune,
would I had never known you!

OEDIPUS.

Curse on the man who took
1425 the cruel bonds from off my legs, as I lay in the field.
He stole me from death and saved me,
no kindly service.
Had I died then

I would not be so burdensome to friends.

CHORUS.

I, too, could have wished it had been so. 1430

OEDIPUS.

Then I would not have come
to kill my father and marry my mother infamously.
Now I am godless and child of impurity,
begetter in the same seed that created my wretched self.
If there is any ill worse than ill, 1435
that is the lot of Oedipus.

CHORUS.

I cannot say your remedy was good;
you would be better dead than blind and living.

OEDIPUS.

What I have done here was best done—don't tell me
otherwise, do not give me further counsel. 1440
I do not know with what eyes I could look
upon my father when I die and go
under the earth, nor yet my wretched mother—
those two to whom I have done things deserving
worse punishment than hanging. Would the sight 1445
of children, bred as mine are, gladden me?
No, not these eyes, never. And my city,
its towers and sacred places of the Gods,
of these I robbed my miserable self
when I commanded all to drive *him* out, 1450
the criminal since proved by God impure
and of the race of Laius.
To this guilt I bore witness against myself—
with what eyes shall I look upon my people?
No. If there were a means to choke the fountain 1455
of hearing I would not have stayed my hand
from locking up my miserable carcase,
seeing and hearing nothing; it is sweet
to keep our thoughts out of the range of hurt.
Cithaeron, why did you receive me? why 1460
having received me did you not kill me straight?
And so I had not shown to men my birth.

O Polybus and Corinth and the house,
the old house that I used to call my father's—
what fairness you were nurse to, and what foulness 1465
festered beneath! Now I am found to be
a sinner and a son of sinners. Crossroads,
and hidden glade, oak and the narrow way
at the crossroads, that drank my father's blood
offered you by my hands, do you remember 1470
still what I did as you looked on, and what
I did when I came here? O marriage, marriage!
you bred me and again when you had bred
bred children of your child and showed to men
brides, wives and mothers and the foulest deeds 1475
that can be in this world of ours.

Come—it's unfit to say what is unfit
to do.—I beg of you in God's name hide me

somewhere outside your country, yes, or kill me,
1480 or throw me into the sea, to be forever
out of your sight. Approach and deign to touch me
for all my wretchedness, and do not fear.
No man but I can bear my evil doom.

CHORUS.
Here Creon comes in fit time to perform
1485 or give advice in what you ask of us.
Creon is left sole ruler in your stead.

OEDIPUS.
Creon! Creon! What shall I say to him?
How can I justly hope that he will trust me?
In what is past I have been proved towards him
an utter liar.

                              (*Enter Creon.*)

CREON.
1490   Oedipus, I've come
not so that I might laugh at you nor taunt you
with evil of the past. But if you still
are without shame before the face of men
reverence at least the flame that gives all life,
1495 our Lord the Sun, and do not show unveiled
to him pollution such that neither land
nor holy rain nor light of day can welcome.

                              (*To a servant.*)

Be quick and take him in. It is most decent
that only kin should see and hear the troubles
of kin.

OEDIPUS.
1500   I beg you, since you've torn me from
my dreadful expectations and have come
in a most noble spirit to a man
that has used you vilely—do a thing for me.
I shall speak for your own good, not for my own.

CREON.
1505 What do you need that you would ask of me?

OEDIPUS.
Drive me from here with all the speed you can
to where I may not hear a human voice.

CREON.
Be sure, I would have done this had not I
wished first of all to learn from the God the course
of action I should follow.

OEDIPUS.
1510   But his word
has been quite clear to let the parricide,
the sinner, die.

CREON.
              Yes, that indeed was said.
But in the present need we had best discover
what we should do.

OEDIPUS.
              And will you ask about
a man so wretched?

CREON.
              Now even you will trust
1515

the God.

OEDIPUS.
        So. I command you—

                              and will beseech you—
to her that lies inside that house give burial
as you would have it; she is yours and rightly
you will perform the rites for her. For me—
never let this my father's city have me   1520
living a dweller in it. Leave me live
in the mountains where Cithaeron is, that's called
my mountain, which my mother and my father
while they were living would have made my tomb.
So I may die by their decree who sought   1525
indeed to kill me. Yet I know this much:
no sickness and no other thing will kill me.
I would not have been saved from death if not
for some strange evil fate. Well, let my fate
go where it will.

              Creon, you need not care   1530
about my sons; they're men and so wherever
they are, they will not lack a livelihood.
But my two girls—so sad and pitiful—
whose table never stood apart from mine,
and everything I touched they always shared—   1535
O Creon, have a thought for them! And most
I wish that you might suffer me to touch them
and sorrow with them.

                    (*Enter Antigone and Ismene,
                      Oedipus' two daughters.*)

O my lord! O true noble Creon! Can I
really be touching them, as when I saw?   1540
What shall I say?
Yes, I can hear them sobbing—my two darlings!
and Creon has had pity and has sent me
what I loved most?
Am I right?   1545

CREON.
You're right: it was I gave you this
because I knew from old days how you loved them
as I see now.

OEDIPUS.
              God bless you for it, Creon,
and may God guard you better on your road
than he did me!
              O children,   1550
where are you? Come here, come to my hands,
a brother's hands which turned your father's eyes,
those bright eyes you knew once, to what you see,
a father seeing nothing, knowing nothing,
begetting you from his own source of life.   1555
I weep for you—I cannot see your faces—
I weep when I think of the bitterness
there will be in your lives, how you must live
before the world. At what assemblages
of citizens will you make one? to what   1560
gay company will you go and not come home

in tears instead of sharing in the holiday?
And when you're ripe for marriage, who will he be,
the man who'll risk to take such infamy
1565 as shall cling to my children, to bring hurt
on them and those that marry with them? What
curse is not there? "Your father killed his father
and sowed the seed where he had sprung himself
and begot you out of the womb that held him."
1570 These insults you will hear. Then who will marry you?
No one, my children; clearly you are doomed
to waste away in barrenness unmarried.
Son of Menoeceus, since you are all the father
left these two girls, and we, their parents, both
1575 are dead to them—do not allow them wander
like beggars, poor and husbandless.
They are of your own blood.
And do not make them equal with myself
in wretchedness; for you can see them now
1580 so young, so utterly alone, save for you only.
Touch my hand, noble Creon, and say yes.
If you were older, children, and were wiser,
there's much advice I'd give you. But as it is,
let this be what you pray: give me a life
1585 wherever there is opportunity
to live, and better life than was my father's.

CREON.
Your tears have had enough of scope; now go within the
house.

OEDIPUS.
I must obey, though bitter of heart.

CREON.
In season, all is good.

OEDIPUS.
Do you know on what conditions I obey?

CREON.
1590 You tell me them,
and I shall know them when I hear.

OEDIPUS.
That you shall send me out
to live away from Thebes.

CREON.
That gift you must ask of the Gods.

OEDIPUS.
But I'm now hated by the Gods.

CREON.
So quickly you'll obtain your prayer.

OEDIPUS.
You consent then?

CREON.
What I do not mean, I do not use to say.

OEDIPUS.
Now lead me away from here.

CREON.
Let go the children, then, and come. 1595

OEDIPUS.
Do not take them from me.

CREON.
Do not seek to be master in everything,
for the things you mastered did not follow you throughout your life.

(*As Creon and Oedipus go out.*)

CHORUS.
You that live in my ancestral Thebes, behold this
Oedipus,—
him who knew the famous riddles and was a man most
masterful; 1600
not a citizen who did not look with envy on his lot—
see him now and see the breakers of misfortune swallow
him!
Look upon that last day always. Count no mortal happy
till
he has passed the final limit of his life secure from pain.

Not unlike our own religious festivals such as Christmas, Easter, Hanukkah, and Ramadan, the *City Dionysia* was a time of great celebration in Athens. Since Peisistratus moved the rural Dionysian Festival of the Fruits of the Earth to Athens in 534 B.C.E., this springtime festival was one of the highlights of the Athenian year.

On a beautiful March morning in 428 B.C.E., Athenians prepared to celebrate the City Dionysia, among the most exciting events of their year. For the moment, the burdens of everyday life and the transactions of civic and legal affairs were put aside as they gathered to celebrate and worship Dionysus.

The first two days of the City Dionysia were richly ceremonial, much like the opening of the Olympic Games. There was a huge parade, numerous religious and civic ceremonies, sacrifices to the gods, and much singing and dancing. On the first day Athenian audiences watched the *proagon,* (or "previews") of the dramas that they would witness over the next six days. Next, they were introduced to the three honored playwrights, each of whom presented his cast and said something about his plays. On the second day they heard the sacred dithyrambs, and on the following day they viewed the performances of five comedies. However, their real joy sprang from the anticipation of yet another entry by a favorite playwright, Sophocles. The people of Athens eagerly anticipated the awards ceremony on the final day of the festival when the winning plays would be announced. They had heard that Philocles, the nephew of Aeschylus, had entered an excellent tetralogy.

Four new plays by Sophocles, including *Oedipus the King*, would be performed that day. Although Athenians were familiar with the story of Oedipus—it was among the best known in their mythology—they were eager to know how Sophocles would retell the story and what new insights he might provide. After packing a lunch of cheese, olives, and bread and filling their wineskins with the blood of Dionysus himself, thousands of spectators made the long trek on the Eleusian Way, which led through the center of the city and eastward to the southern slope of the Acropolis to the Theater of Dionysus.

As they enter the *theatron* through the *parados,* they saw the small *skene* directly in front of them. This scene building served as a changing room for the principal actors who usually played several roles in a single play. As they looked up into the *theatron,* they saw wooden benches that held about 15,000 spectators, with a section designated for each of the Attic tribes. In the years to come the city fathers would build permanent stone seating and a more ornate marble *skene*, which would last for centuries. Across the *orchestra*, where the chorus sang and danced throughout the day, stood a large throne reserved for the priest of Dionysus, who presided over the performances. On either side of this throne were five smaller seats for the leaders of each of the ten Attic tribes. The elected city officials and important civic leaders sat in the rows immediately behind the priest and the tribal leaders.

Though the performance of Sophocles' plays was anticipated with great interest, an important ceremony—the selection of the judges—must be completed before they commenced. Prior to the Dionysia, the many nominations from each tribe were placed in urns. The *archon*—the wealthy citizen who sponsored the festival—selected one name from each tribal urn and the ten judges, fairly chosen, were installed after promising to deliver an impartial judgment. After the three tetralogies were performed, each judge placed the name of the winning playwright in a large urn. To allow the gods to have their vote, the archon drew only five ballots and the winning playwright was determined by a majority of those five fated votes.

The priests of Dionysus lit a sacred fire in the *thymele,* the sacred altar at the center of the orchestra; the Athenians rose to sing prayers of supplication to Dionysus, asking him to bless their soil and the seeds they have planted, their herds, and themselves—that they may enjoy good crops and healthy offspring. As the first of Sophocles' plays began, the audience sat quietly, even as the sacred smoke from the *thymele* drifted over the theater. As the prologue unfolded, the people of Thebes themselves were burning offerings to the gods as they begged for an end to the terrible plague that has ravaged their city. The *skene* door opened ominously and Tlepolemus, who played Oedipus, entered to address the Priest, played by Nicostratus, an especially versatile actor who would also portray Jocasta, the Second Messenger, and the Old Herdsman. A third actor, Cleidemides, played Creon, as well as the First Messenger and Teiresias. While these actors may have been well known to the Athenian audience, it was impossible to recognize them because of the masks and *onkoi* (large headpieces) they wore. To assume a new character, they simply changed costumes, headpieces, and masks, which told audiences the age, gender, social status, and especially the emotional state of each character they portrayed.

Because the actors wore large, padded costumes, including large, thick-soled boots called *kothornoi,* and because of the majestic dialogue, they performed in a grand and rhetorical acting style. Sometimes they used declamation to approximate everyday speech; at other times they employed recitative, a type of chanting. Of course, they also sang many passages. Their movements were sweeping and exaggerated so that even those who sat in the farthest reaches of the *theatron* missed neither a word nor a gesture. The actors and chorus spoke directly to the spectators to make them feel as though they were in the midst of the action.

After the initial exchange of dialogue among Oedipus and the Priest, the *orchestra* was vacated and the Cho-

(continued)

Oedipus confronts the Sphinx in this drawing taken from an ancient Athenian vessel: it is one of the few contemporary graphic representations of Greece's most famous tragic hero.

rus of Theban Elders entered through the *paradoi*. They sang and danced their first *stasimon*, or "standing song," a translation that does not begin to suggest the lively spectacle it produced. During this first choral ode, 15 actors, all male, were divided into two groups to dance in *strophes* and *antistrophes* ("turns" and "counterturns"). Their intricate dance steps, which Sophocles himself taught the chorus, were as important to the enjoyment of the play as the drama itself.

After the song, the next *episode* began, and the audience listened intently, as did the chorus, which stood quietly about the *orchestra*, as Cleidemides reentered as Teiresias to engage Oedipus in the first *agon* of the play.

The pace of the dialogue quickened to suggest the intensity of the debate. Perceptive Athenians smiled wryly as they watched Oedipus—he who defeated the dreadful Sphinx by answering her riddle—refuse to answer Teiresias's riddle. "By Zeus," they thought, "doesn't he know that Teiresias speaks for the gods themselves?" As the play unfolded the 15,000 Athenians found themselves caught up in Sophocles' bold plotting and the gradual intertwining of Oedipus's search for both the slayer of Laius and for his own identity. As each *episode* concluded, they were enlightened by the chorus's *stasimon*, which not only entertained them with songs and dances, but also provided the communal standards against which Oedipus's

actions were judged. Sophocles cleverly used this chorus of elders as participants in the action and as common people—like those sitting in the *theatron*—who stood outside the action to observe Oedipus's struggle. They spoke for all present when they sang "Count no mortal happy till he has passed the final limit of his life secure from pain."

After Oedipus discovered that he was indeed the killer of Laius in the scene with the Old Herdsman, he disappeared into the *skene*. He returned moments later—his royal robes spattered with blood—wearing another *onkos* and mask. Two gaping, black holes, each oozing blood, symbolized the terror of Oedipus's dreadful act. Although the audience was prepared for this pitiful sight by the Messenger's horrifying description of Jocasta's suicide and Oedipus's blinding, the image of this lonely and once-proud king terrified them. Creon reentered, leading Oedipus's two infant daughters, and the silent crowd was moved to tears when the blinded, disgraced monarch embraced them for the last time. These two sights—the bloody mask and a father clinging to his innocent girls—were Sophocles' triumph as a playwright.

The audience sat in the *theatron* emotionally drained. They felt pity and fear as they suffered with Oedipus; but through that experience they learned—like Oedipus himself—about themselves, their lives, and their gods. They discussed this quietly as they awaited the two tragedies yet to be performed that morning. And they thanked their gods that the day would end with the satyr play and an opportunity for laughter.

CENTER STAGE — *OEDIPUS THE KING* AT THE TEATRO OLYMPICO, 1585

Vicenza, a small town near Venice, gave the theater world perhaps its most elaborate production of Sophocles' *Oedipus the King* on March 3, 1585. It was, in the words of Filippo Pigafetta, an aristocrat in attendance, a spectacle of "theatrical pomp and magnificence." *Oedipus*—"the noblest tragedy ever written," in Pigafetta's estimation—was chosen to open the new Teatro Olympico, which had been designed by one of Italy's greatest architects, Andrea Palladio (1518–1580). The new theater, which stands today as the oldest surviving Renaissance theater, was the centerpiece of the Olympic Academy, founded by aristocrats in 1556 as a center for the study of Greek theater.

However, the theater Palladio and his assistant, Vincenzo Scamozzi (1552–1616), designed was actually patterned after a Roman theater. It held about 3,000 spectators who, although they sat indoors, were treated to the illusion that they were in an ancient outdoor theater. The semielliptical auditorium (as opposed to the Roman semicircle) was adorned with almost 80 statues of the academicians, friezes, and frescoes. A small orchestra pit fronted the wide (88 feet) yet shallow (22 feet) playing area. The stage was backed by a richly ornamented permanent facade, which remains the prototype of the proscenium arch. Five doors were cut into this facade, behind which Scamozzi added perspective vistas of a Roman street scene. The effect suggested the narrow walks and alleyways of an ancient city, and all audience members could look down at least one of these streets from seats in the auditorium. Actors could not, of course, venture up one of these curious roadways without destroying the illusion created by the perspective; speeches were delivered strictly from the stage in front of the facade. Still, the new theater was unparalleled in the world and richly clothed Italians gathered at the Teatro Olympico early in the afternoon to see this marvel. The sense of occasion was heightened by the presence of Empress Maria of Austria, a guest of academy president Leonardo Valmarana. The French ambassador and his family were also in the audience that evening.

At 7:30 *Oedipus the King* began with a resounding fanfare of trumpets and drums; fireworks erupted as the great curtain of the Teatro Olympico was lowered into a slot in the forestage to reveal Scamozzi's spectacular vista. Perfume wafted through the auditorium, as Pigafetta tells us, "to indicate that in the city in Thebes, according to the ancient legend, incense was burned to placate the wrath of the gods." The prologue began, and the actors spoke Sophocles' text in an Italian translation by the scholarly Orsato Giustiniani. Music and songs were composed for the

The Teatro Olympico opened at Vicenza, Italy, in 1585 with Angelo Ingegneri's elaborate production of Oedipus the King.

(continued)

production by the organist at St. Mark's, the great cathedral of Venice. Scamozzi's settings were complemented by the costumes of Alesandro Maganza, who dressed Oedipus's guards in Turkish attire. All was lit to suggest bright sunlight in Thebes, an effect created by placing bottles of colored water in front of banks of candles.

The three-and-a-half-hour production was performed by "actors of the best sort . . . dressed neatly and lavishly according to each one's station." Actually, we know little about the quality or style of the acting, save for Pigafetta's general comments quoted here. Of the size and spectacle of the production, however, there can be little doubt. Over 80 actors filled the Olympico's stage. Oedipus had a retinue of 32 (24 archers alone!), Jocasta was surrounded by "matrons, ladies in waiting, and pages," and Creon enjoyed a similar entourage. The chorus consisted of 15, much like Sophocles', seven on each side of the stage with the leader in the center; the chorus spoke, rather than sang, "in pleasing unison." Remember that Sophocles wrote the play for 3 actors who played 9 speaking roles and a chorus of 15. Though the academy was dedicated to preserving the work of the Greeks, its production of Oedipus at the Olympico transformed Sophocles' design into something far more elaborate. To be fair, the Italians were motivated by Aristotle's comments about the "magnitude" of tragedy, attributes best realized in the Renaissance mind through the sheer size of the spectacle. Though this production of Oedipus the King might have fallen short of its goal of re-creating the power of Greek tragedy, it succeeded in making visual splendor an integral part of theater. It also prepared theater audiences for that theatrical diversion we now call "grand opera."

FORUMS

"Ode to Oedipus"

Tyrone Guthrie

Tyrone Guthrie directed Oedipus Rex *at the Stratford, Ontario Festival in 1956. Because of its acclaim, it was subsequently filmed. In conjunction with the opening of the film in January 1957, Guthrie was asked to write about his treatment of the play for both stage and film. He wrote the following article for the* New York Times.

Oedipus Rex *was written more than two thousand years ago. Since then it has been revived thousands and thousands of times in many languages and in every part of the world.*

Its persistent appeal to audiences is the more remarkable when you remember how differently people have regarded the theatre in different epochs and different parts of the world; how not merely the architecture of theatres and techniques of theatrical presentation have varied, but how the ideas and intentions both of producers and playgoers change.

In this connection it would nice to feel that our own attitude is more intelligent, sophisticated and wise than that of the Athenian public two thousand years ago. But such a feeling can hardly be justified.

We regard the theatre as an entertainment. It may occasionally be serious; but to justify its seriousness it has to give evidence of compensating qualities. Light entertainment bears no such burden of proof. To admit to being serious in the theatre is almost—not quite, but almost—to admit to being a bore. The quality of a modern play is judged in terms of "success"; and success is judged in terms of the number of people who pay for admission.

Those of us who regard ourselves as professionals—and it is significant that this term now connotes that we draw our living out of the theatre rather than devoting our lives to it—have to be extremely careful how we talk about our professional aims and ideals. It is legitimate to talk in technical terms about conventions or styles of acting, direction, design and so on; it is certainly legitimate to talk in economic terms about the profits and the losses, successes and failures, how, and how not, to "promote" theatrical works.

When people start to talk about moral purposes, when they suggest that the purpose of art in general, and the theatre in particular, might possibly be to make mankind a little bit wiser or happier, or even just better adapted to his environment . . . they seem to be getting too big for their boots.

In Athens in 400 B.C.E. there was no "professional" theatre. Every year the spring festival, in celebration of the return of warmth and fertility to mother earth, was the occasion for the performance of—I will not say plays, because that word already implies decadence—dramas. The word signifies no more than actions, or doings or goings-on, which recapitulated in poetic form (which signifies no more than that the goings-on were carefully planned) certain myths or stories which seemed to the Greeks then, and have seemed so since to anybody who thought about them carefully, to have some important bearing on man's past, present, and future.

These dramas were "religious" in the sense that they were truly serious. But they certainly did not take the Party Line as regards Olympus. Sophocles in *Oedipus Rex* was, in my opinion, offering a calculated and dangerous criticism of Apollo in a manner infinitely more undermining to faith than anything to which a prince of any church might now object—in, for instance, *Baby Doll* [a film script by Tennessee Williams].

In Athens the festival plays were "produced," most sumptuously, by wealthy members of the community as an act of piety and of public service. In the time of Sophocles the actors did not get paid. Later they did; but history does not record whether the performances were on that account more, or less, efficient; more, or less, devout; more, or less, interesting.

In filming *Oedipus Rex* we have used the translation of the great Irish poet, William Butler Yeats. We have not attempted to fiddle with the text and turn it into a screen play. We assumed that one of the reasons for the play's survival was because, as well as being about something interesting, the material was well presented; its form, as well as its content, was impor-

tant. Therefore we based the film on a stage production, made for the Shakespeare Festival at Stratford, Ontario, which had proved itself able to grip and to move an audience.

The film is not, of course, just a photographic record of that performance. It makes some attempt to use the advantages of the mechanical eye and ear; some attempts to obviate their drawbacks. It makes no attempt to persuade the audience that what is seen and heard is "really" happening. Throughout emphasis is placed on the ritual character of the drama: the actors commemorate and comment upon the sacrifice of Oedipus—one man whose destruction was expedient that his people might live—in a manner analogous to Christian priests' commemoration and comment on Christ's sacrifice.

This may sound pretentious; and, if to be serious is pretentious, then it is so—very. But while all of us connected with this film did take our work seriously, we have not so lost our heads as to doubt that, if our effort is any good at all, it is only because we tried hard to interpret a good script.

"Guthrie Directs 'Ritual' Performance of *Oedipus Rex* at Edinburgh Fête"

PATRICK GIBBS

The following review of Oedipus Rex, *as directed by Tyrone Guthrie for the Stratford, Ontario Festival appeared in the* New York Times *on September 4, 1956. It was based on a performance at the Edinburgh Festival, one of Europe's premiere theater events. The review suggests the liabilities of using Greek theater conventions in a modern theater.*

"We endeavor to present the tragedy as a Ritual," writes Tyrone Guthrie, in a program note to *Oedipus Rex* given tonight by the Stratford, Ontario Festival Company at the Assembly Hall.

To this end the actors are masked as in ancient Greek times. They also wore the buskin or elevated boots, adding a few inches to their height. Even so, their masks, which are elaborate affairs leaving only the mouth uncovered, are so large that the characters, otherwise conventionally attired, seem dwarfed rather than superhuman.

As for the chorus, its masks are grotesque, coming near to caricature with the exaggerated features. Wearing monkish

cowls in drab colors, the chorus recalled giant slugs as they draped themselves over the steps of the apron stage.

Visually, therefore, it was not exactly the impression of an Attic ritual that Mr. Guthrie achieved. The declamatory methods of his actors recalled the chanting of responses in a Church of England service or the pulpit manner of some old-fashioned preacher.

The performance indeed is stylized throughout and makes a purely formal approach to the intellect alone. At the play's greater moments—Oedipus' realization of his guilt, his appearance with his eyes out, or the farewell to his little daughters—one's feelings were completely disengaged.

This might well be an effective production in an open-air theater seating 20,000 persons—the conditions of performance in ancient Greece. In the confines of this little hall, it had little more than the interest of a fresh and thoughtful approach.

Douglas Campbell's Oedipus, with his measured and mannered delivery, his stylized shrieks and groans, and his symbolic gestures, fitted well into the production.

The translation based on the works of Sophocles was by William Butler Yeats; it can seldom have sounded quite so bleak. All being considered, the reception was remarkably warm.

MEDEA

EURIPIDES

EURIPIDES (C. 480–406 B.C.E.)

A much younger contemporary of Sophocles, Euripides was born of well-to-do parents, probably on the island of Salamis. Little is known of his life, but he is said to have lived reclusively in a cave, a supposition that may have arisen from his reluctance to take an active part in the social and civic life of Athens. Unlike Aeschylus and Sophocles, he apparently devoted all his time to writing, which makes him unique as an individualist in an age when civic duty, such as holding public office, was the honorable ideal.

Euripides is reputed to have written 92 plays, of which 16 tragedies and 1 satyr drama survive. *Cyclops*, a burlesque of Odysseus's adventures in Sicily, is the single remaining example of Greek satyr drama. His broad range of interests is also represented by a large number of fragments from his writings. The best of his plays are *Medea* (431 B.C.E.), *The Trojan Women* (415 B.C.E.), and *The Bacchae* (404 B.C.E.).

Whereas Sophocles affirmed the traditional outlook of an aristocratic society, Euripides did not. His use of new and emotional music, his view of women in love, his interest in abnormal psychology, and his use of argumentation all aroused much interest. Although he was critical of society, his plays deal more with personal feelings and thoughts than with the attitudes of society. What distinguishes Euripides from Aeschylus and Sophocles is his keen acceptance of the fact that we humans are controlled by a superior awareness and that our existence is a part of a biological and historical evolution. Euripides' lack of popularity among his contemporaries, especially Aristophanes, greatly affected his career. Whereas Sophocles won 18 victories at the Dionysia, Euripides won only 5. After Euripides' death in Macedonia, Sophocles is said to have put his chorus in mourning as a sign of respect. Even his antagonist, Aristophanes, regarded his death as the end of an era in Greek culture.

Euripides is considered the great experimenter among the Greek tragic playwrights. Greater realism is evident throughout his works as he formulated the basic tenets of what has become the melodrama. Some of his plays—*Helen* and especially *Alcestis*—are much closer to the spirit of comedy. His use of the *deus ex machina*, as in *Orestes*, culminates the dramatic action without a torrent of choral explanations. His characters, such as Medea and Electra, are less heroic than those of Sophocles; indeed, they may not be heroes at all. The language of his characters teeters between tragedy and comedy. Thematically, Euripides places greater emphasis on human emotions, such as abnormal behavior (*Electra*), sexual passion (*Medea*), and madness (*Orestes*). He examines the role of women in the Greek world, particularly their manner of thinking. Despite his obvious sympathy with women's rights and their problems, he was thought to be a misogynist. Euripides is also the most realistic of the three great tragic playwrights in Greece, as he makes ordinary life more relevant to the plot. For instance, in his version of the Electra myth, he invents a farmer-husband for Electra and removes the action from the court to the workaday world of the countryside.

If Euripides was the auger of modern drama, or even of the postmodern sensibility, his influence is still detected in contemporary cinema and television. He continues to intrigue us since our thirst for human pain and suffering is still a part of our existence. As Edith Hamilton writes, Euripides feels "as no other writer has felt, the pitifulness of human life.... No poet's ear has ever been so sensitively attuned as his to the still, sad music of humanity, a strain little heeded by that world long ago."

MEDEA (431 B.C.E.)

If the surviving Euripidean canon speaks of a disjointed Greek world in which democratic fervor had become a weapon against women, foreigners, and the underclass, *Medea* clearly illustrates the concepts of suffering and sheer human agony. Furthermore, this dramatic and theatrical tour de force is the author's personal testament that human choices radically alter an entire societal structure. For Euripides, there is a clear and direct relationship between humanity and the inclination of the gods. The human will always be an instrument for carrying out the command of the gods, regardless of the consequences. Euripides' characters realize that there is something greater than humanity as they attempt to remain logical and in control while pursuing internal and external action. The gods intercept, and suddenly the human being is inert, frozen in time, and unable to control the environment any further. For instance, in the concluding moments of *Medea*, Jason crumbles to his knees while Medea's chariot ascends into the heavens.

Medea is a rapid and frenzied descent into the depths of human despair, where rational and irrational human choices, coupled with the title character's superstitious beliefs, meet as one in the arena of argumentation and confrontation. The plot is relatively simple: a lonely and spurned wife with magical prowess is betrayed by a husband who attempts to marry the king's daughter for power and social recognition. In his quest to climb the ladder of political success, his desperate wife seeks revenge. The play's tragic structure and theme differ radically from those of Aeschylus and Sophocles. To begin with, the prologue does not serve as a map of things to follow, but rather as an explanation of the character's distraught state of mind. As the Nurse attempts to guide the viewer, Medea's screams are heard offstage—doom and darkness are immediately established. The plot is fragmented; the chorus is no longer the manifestation of the universe in relationship to the individual, but remains secondary to the action of the play. The use of *stichomythia*, dialogue delivered by two actors alternating lines, particularly in the scenes between Jason and Medea, is prevalent and enhances the possibility for repartee and psychological motivation among the characters. Greater realism is evident as Euripides begins to formulate the basic ideas for what was to become the genre of present-day melodrama. Thematically, Euripides places greater emphasis on abnormal behavior and such potent human emotions as sexual passion and madness. He investigates the societal roles and thought processes of women, and he makes ordinary daily life more relevant to the plot.

Overall, Euripides' characters are individuals willing to push the limits of their mortal reality. They believe themselves to be responsible for their actions and therefore in control of their destinies. Medea's choice to violently murder Creon's daughter and annihilate her own children typifies the playwright's quest to question human motivation by reaching deep into the characters' psyches.

There are no tragic heroes in *Medea*; rather, we experience a terrifyingly tragic environment. In this bold experiment, is Euripides rejecting the notion of the Sophoclean hero in favor of the modern existential being? Is the playwright crafting a new type of dramatic persona? the antihero? Decrepit and unsavory as Medea and Jason may appear, nevertheless, they remain the author's mouthpieces for social and political commentaries on Athenian empiricism. Medea is capable of the most horrifying act, that of destroying her own flesh and blood. It is she, not Jason, who suffers unequivocally while losing all that is precious to her—her own children, her family, her former home, her adopted land. Is Medea, in the final analysis, the author's new-fashioned tragic figure?

In *Medea*, as in his other tragedies, Euripides creates an external, divinelike authority surrounding (even dictating?) human choices, but it cannot be realized by human perception. Ultimately, this divine resoluteness culminates the action of *Medea*—her revenge has purged her soul.

Aeschylus and Sophocles were able to pierce the spectators' hearts and minds at the discovery of a tragic change of events. However, as *Medea* illustrates so vividly, neither could equal Euripides' powerful and personal immersion into the psychological, spiritual, and physical torment of his characters.

In 1972, La Mama, one of New York's most respected experimental theaters, produced a multicultural interpretation of Euripides' Medea; the casting is appropriate, as Medea was brought to Corinth from the East by Jason.

MEDEA

E U R I P I D E S

Translated by Paul Roche

C H A R A C T E R S
NURSE
TUTOR *to Medea's sons*
MEDEA, *Asiatic princess*
CHORUS *of Corinthian women*
CREON, *king of Corinth*
JASON, *husband of Medea*
AEGEUS, *king of Athens*
MESSENGER
TWO BOYS, *sons of Medea*
HANDMAIDS *of Medea*
ATTENDANTS AND GUARDS *for Creon and Aegeus*

TIME AND SETTING: *It is midmorning outside Jason's house in Corinth. Ten years have passed since the Argonauts sailed home after finding the Golden Fleece. During that time, Jason and Medea [the Asian bride he brought back with him] have been living modestly in Corinth: models of an unassailable married life of devotion*

to each other and their children. But the news has just broken that Jason is to marry the daughter of the king of Corinth. [The exit on stage left leads to the town and royal palace, that on the right to the country.]

[Enter the Nurse from the house. She is an old woman who has looked after Medea from babyhood. Her face, the only part of her showing from the dark, heavy clothes that envelop her, is puckered with age and distress]

PROLOGUE

NURSE. Why did the winged oars of the Argo°
    ever weave between those gnashing blue

N.B. The line numbers in the margins are those of the original Greek text. [1]**Argo** the ship in which Jason and his companions sailed on the quest for the Golden Fleece

fjords toward the land of Colchis?
Why did the pines in the dells of Pelion°
ever fall to the axe and fill
the rowing hands of heroes sent by Pelias°
to fetch the Golden Fleece?
My mistress, Medea, then
never would have sailed to Iolcus with its towers
or been struck to the heart with love of Jason.
She never would have baited Pelias' daughters
to the murder of their father°
and be living here in Corinth° now
with her husband and her children . . .
Ah, she has merited this city's good opinion,
exile though she came,
and was in everything Jason's perfect foil,
being in marriage that saving thing:
a wife who does not go against her man.

[With a despairing glance toward the house]

Now everything has turned to hate,
her passion to a plague.
Jason has betrayed his sons and her,
takes to bed a royal bride,
Creon's daughter—the king of Corinth's.
Medea, spurned and desolate,
breaks out in oaths,
invokes the solemnest vows,
calls the gods to witness
how Jason has rewarded her.
She does not eat,
lies prostrate, slumped in anguish,
wastes away in day-long tears.
Ever since she heard of Jason's perfidy
she has not raised her eyes
or looked up from the floor.
She might be a rock or wave of the sea,
for all she heeds of sympathy from friends,
except sometimes to tilt her pale head away
and moan to herself about her father—
whom she loved—
and her country and the home she sacrificed°
to journey here

with a man—oh—who so disdains her now.
Yes, now she knows
at a terrible first hand
what it is to miss one's native land.

[She pauses; almost whispers the next words]

She hates her sons.
Takes no pleasure in their sight.
I dread to think
of what is hatching in her mind.
She is a fierce spirit:
takes no insult lying down.
I know her well. She frightens me:°
a dangerous woman, and
anyone who crosses her
will not easily sing a song of triumph.
But here come the boys after their run:
suspecting nothing of a mother's tragedy . . .
Oh, it is true—
unhappy thoughts and youth never go together.

[Enter Tutor with Two Boys, aged about eight and ten.
Tutor is an old man, dressed loosely in an ocher-colored
cloak. The boys are squeezed into shorts and have close-
fitting woolen caps on their heads. They hang about in the
background, laughing and talking, while the old man ad-
vances]

TUTOR. [With a half-teasing familiarity] Ah, Nurse!
Faithful old appendage of my Lady's home,
what are you doing here all forlorn,
standing moaning to yourself outside the gates?
Does Medea really want to be left alone?
NURSE. Ah, dogged old pedagogue of Jason's sons,
when a master's fortunes are struck down
the heart of a faithful slave is stricken too.
I am plunged in such a depth of grief
I came out here to tell the earth and sky
Medea's catastrophe.
TUTOR. What! Has the poor woman not stopped her
crying yet?
NURSE. Stopped! You amaze me.
Her ordeal, far from halfway done,
hardly has begun.
TUTOR. Poor innocent fool—to be quite frank about
our mistress—
she knows little of the latest blow.
NURSE. Latest? What's that, old man?
Don't keep it from me.
TUTOR. Nothing, nothing . . . I'm sorry I even spoke.

---

⁴**Pelion** a mountain in northern Greece ⁵**Pelias** When Jason came
to claim the kingdom of Iolcus, from which Pelias had expelled
Jason's father, Pelias sent him to get the Golden Fleece. ⁹**She never
. . . murder of their father** Medea, a sorceress by reputation, tricked
Pelias' daughters into cutting their father into pieces and boiling
them, on the pretext that this would magically restore him to youth.
Her revenge on Pelias, who had murdered Jason's father Aeson during Jason's absence on the quest for the Golden Fleece, was successful. ¹¹Jason and Medea were expelled from the kingdom, and they
took refuge in Corinth, a wealthy city and rival of Athens, located
on the isthmus between the Péloponnese and Attica. ³²**home she
sacrificed** Medea had helped Jason take the Golden Fleece away
from her own father's kingdom.

---

³⁹ Lines 40-43 are bracketed by many editors as doubtful. Dramatically they are certainly a mistake: *I am frightened she will slip / into the
palace unawares, / and in the nuptial bedroom / run a sharp knife into
Jason's side, / or even kill the King as well as bridegroom / and get herself
a far worse doom.*

NURSE. Come on now, we're both slaves here, are we not?

65   By your own gray beard, do not hold it back . . .
        I can keep a secret if I must.
TUTOR. Well, I'd gone to where the old dice-players sit,
        near Pirene's sacred fountain,
        and there I overheard (pretending not to listen)
        someone say:
            "Creon, this country's king,
70   is making plans to drive these boys from Corinth—
        their mother too"—
        I don't know if the story's true.
            I hope that it is not.
NURSE. No, surely no?
        Jason would not let his sons be treated so,
75   however far he's parted from their mother.
TUTOR. [Grimly] Old loves are left behind by new.
        That man is not this house's friend.
NURSE. We're all finished, then—
        If we ship this second wave
        before we've bailed the first.
TUTOR. Now listen—
80   This is not the time to let our mistress know.
        Just keep quiet about it—not a word.
NURSE. [With an anguished glance over her shoulder, in a
        whisper] Poor little boys,
        do you hear how much your father's worth to you?
            I wish he were . . .

        [Checks herself]

            no, not dead, he is my master still . . .
        but, oh, what an enemy he's proved
        to those he should have loved!
85   TUTOR. What human being is not?
            Is this news to you,
        that every person's dearest neighbor is himself:
        some rightly so, some out of greed and selfishness.
            This father does not love his sons, but—
        his new wedding bed.
NURSE. Come along, boys, into the house.
        Everything is going to be all right.

        [Dropping her voice]

90   Keep them away as much as you can.
            Do not let them near their mother
        so long as she is in this deadly mood.
            Already I have caught her eyes on them:
        the eyes of a mad bull.
            There's something she is plotting
        and her fury won't lie down—this I know—
        until the lightning strikes and someone's felled.
95   Let us hope it's enemies, not friends.

        [A long-drawn-out sob—Medea's—is heard from the
        house]°

⁹⁵ The next 116 lines in the Greek are cast in a different meter,
transposed into the nearest English equivalent.

MEDEA. I am so unhappy—oh!
        the misery of it! I wish I were dead.
NURSE. [Hustling the children toward the door]
        Listen—there . . . poor children, your mother,
        Raking her heart up, raking her rage.
        Quick, inside: into the house.   100
        Don't come anywhere near her sight.
        Don't approach. Beware, watch out
        For her savage mood, destructive spleen:
        Yes and her implacable will.
        Off with you now; hurry inside.   105
        Soon, I know, her fury will flare
        Out from the slowly gathering cloud
        What will she perpetrate then, I fear—
        Proud, importunate willful soul—
            So bitterly spurned.   110

[Exeunt Tutor and Boys]

[A long-suppressed shout is heard from inside: Medea's
voice]

MEDEA. Oh, what misery! Oh, what pain!
        Cursed sons, and a mother for cursing!
        Death take you all—you and your father:
            The whole house wither.
NURSE. [Sobbing] Oh, how it grieves me!   115
        Why make the sons
            share in their father's
        Guilt? Oh, why
            should they be hated?
        Poor young children, your danger appals me.
        Ruthless is the temper of royalty:
        Often commanding, seldom commanded;   120
        Terribly slow to forgive and forget.
        How much better to live among equals.
        I want no part of greatness and glory:
        Let me decline in a safe old age.
        The very name of the "middle way"   125
        Has health in it: is best for man.
        Good never comes from overreaching,
        And when it provokes the gods, it destroys   130
            All the more thoroughly.

PARADOS OR ENTRY SONG

[The Chorus of Corinthian women enters, full of apprehension and concern for Medea]

CHORUS. I heard her voice, I heard her shout,
            It was the most unhappy
        Woman from Colchis—far from calm yet—
            But tell me, old Nurse.
        From the porch of the house, it moaned outside.   135
            O women, I cannot delight
        In the pain of Jason's house:
        A house I have loved very well.
NURSE. House there is none: life of it gone.
        The master is had . . . by a princess's bed.   140

The mistress in her boudoir pines.
There are no words her friends can find
    To touch her disconsolate heart.
MEDEA. [*In another spasm*] Ahhh!
    Cleave my brain with a flash from the sky.
145 What good is left for me in living?
    Alas! Alas! Come Death, unloose
        My life from a life I loathe.

STROPHE

CHORUS.
    Listen, O Zeus and Earth and Light
150   To the stricken tune of this plangent° wife.
        And you, loveless lady,
    What yearning for love on a bed of delight
    Could make you hurry to death, the night?
155   Pray not for that.
        If your husband has gone to adore
        A new bride in his bed, why, this
        Has often happened before.
    Do not harrow your soul. For Zeus
        Will succor your cause. What use
    To lessen your life with grief
        For a lost lord?
MEDEA. [*From inside*] Oh mighty Themis°, and
160   Artemis, Queen,°
    For all the fine vows I bound him with,
    See what my hated husband has done.
    Grant me to watch him, at last, with his bride,
    Palace and all, crumble in ruin.
165 How dare they do to me what they have done!
    O Father, my country, the land I abandoned,
        Flagrantly killing my brother.°
NURSE. Hear what she says
        with her cry from the heart
    To Themis and Zeus:
        (goddess of rights
    And he whom mankind
170   makes keeper of vows.)
    Certainly soon
        in no small way
    Her fury will play itself out.

ANTISTROPHE

CHORUS.
    If she would come out and, face to face,
175   Listen to what we have to say,
        She might let go

This rampant anger, spite of soul.
I hope I never fail my friends.
So go, Nurse, entice her to come: 180
Say we are *with* her: we are her friends.
Hurry, before she does any harm
    To those inside . . .
Grief can swell to enormity.
NURSE. [*Walking to the door*] I'll do my best, but am
        afraid   185
May *not* be able to persuade
        My Lady; and yet
    I am glad to shoulder the burden;
Although she glares with a bull-mad gaze
(Or is it a lioness with her whelps)
When anyone comes or speaks or helps.

[*She turns at the door*]

    Oh, botchers and blunderers! Yes,   190
That's what they were, those artists of old:
Makers of music for life and joy,
For grand celebrations and groaning boards;
But, oh, nothing for sorrow and pain: 195
No music or song or hand-plucked lyre
    For the thing that brings death
And terrible endings to many a home.
    Oh, what a blessing is missed
        by having no music for this!   200
    What a waste of it, then
        by singing in vain,
    When fullness at feasts
        is its own joy and gain.

[*Exit Nurse into the house*]

CHORUS. Deep is her sobbing from depths of pain:
    Shrill the news her suffering brings   205
Of marriage betrayed, a love gone wrong.
    Outraged, she
        importunate prays
    To Themis, the daughter of Zeus:
Keeper of vows, who sailed her through
    Those dangerous straits and the night
To Hellas° across the salt of the sea.   210

FIRST EPISODE

[*Medea enters from the house, colorfully, even opulently,
dressed. She is wan and her eyes red with weeping, but she
is surprisingly calm and in control*]

MEDEA. Women of Corinth, be indulgent, please: 215
    I have obeyed you and come out.
        The charge of aloofness—as I know too well—
    is something often leveled
    at both the retiring and the busy man.

---

150 **plangent** lamenting ¹⁶⁰**Themis** justice. **Artemis** Guardian of
women. Called Diana by the Latins. ¹⁶⁷**killing my brother** Medea
slew her brother Absyrtus when she escaped with Jason, and tossed
him piecemeal over the side of the ship, knowing that their pursuers
would stop to pick the pieces up.

²¹⁰ **Hellas** Greece

He who chooses a quiet life
has this alleged against him too:
laziness and lack of spirit.

220   Yes, public opinion has most shallow eyes.
    People hate at sight
a harmless human being,
knowing nothing of the real man.
    I agree, of course,
that a foreigner should conform,
adapt to his society . . .
and a citizen is censurable no less
when too self-centered or uncouth
to avoid offending his companions.
    Nevertheless, I . . .

[She breaks off with a pang]

I . . . out of a clear sky
225 have been struck a blow that breaks my heart.
    My friends, it is over.
    I want to die.
    Life has lost all point.
    The man who was my life
—and he knows it too—
has become for me beneath contempt.

[She surveys the women]

230   Of all the creatures that can feel and think,
we women are the worst-treated things alive.
    To begin with,
we bid the highest price in dowries
just to buy some man
to be dictator of our bodies . . .
    How that compounds the wrong!
235   Then there is the terrifying risk:
Shall we get a good man or a bad?
    Divorce is a disgrace
(at least for women),
to repudiate the man, not possible.
    So, plunged into habits new to her,
conventions she has never known at home,
she has to guess like some clairvoyant
240 how to handle the man who shares her bed.
    And if we learn our lesson well
in this exacting role,
and our husband does not kick against the marriage yoke,
oh, ours is an enviable life!
    Otherwise, we are better dead.
    When a man gets bored with wife and home,
245 he simply roams abroad,
relieves the tedium of his spirit:
turns to a friend or finds his cronies.
    We women, on the other hand,
turn only to a single man.
    We live safe at home, they say.
    They do battle with the spear.

How superficial!   250
I had rather stand my ground three times among
    the shields
than face a childbirth once.
    Anyway,
your case and mine are not the same.
    You have your city.
    You have your father's home.
    Life offers you the sweet fellowship of friends.
    I am alone,   255
without a city, wronged by a husband,
uprooted from a foreign land.
    I have no mother, brother, cousin;
am without a haven from this storm.
    So, please, I ask you this:
if I can find a way to pay my husband back—   260
your silence.
    Woman, on the whole, is a timid thing:
the din of war, the flash of steel, unnerves her;
but, wronged in love,   265
there is no heart more murderous.

LEADER. As you wish, Medea.
    You have a score to settle with your lord.
    I do not wonder that you smart . . .
    But, look, I see Creon coming:
this country's king—
bristling, I dare say, with new decisions.   270

[Enter Creon with attendants. He is a bearded man of
about sixty; royally but modestly dressed. His face wears a
look of troubled resolution]

CREON. Go, Medea. Remove yourself.
    Get packing from this land.
    I order you—
you with your black-faced fury
lowering against your lord.
    And take your brace of offspring with you;
no dallying either.
    I am here to see this order done,
and until I've pushed you out and over the border,
I'll not go home.   275
MEDEA. So.
I am lost—crushed utterly.
    My enemies let out the sail,
while I have no place to disembark from doom.
    Nevertheless, hard-pressed as I am,   280
I ask you this:
    For what reason, Creon, do you drive me out?
CREON. Fear:
no need to camouflage the fact;
I am afraid you'll deal my child some lethal blow
    . . .
and many things conspire to make me fear.
    You are a woman of some knowledge,   285
versed in many an unsavory skill.

Your husband's gone:
your soul is raw with loss of love . . .
and now it is reported that you threaten me:
mean to hurt the father of the bride
and of course the bride and groom.
    That is what I want to guard against—
an accident.
290   Madam, better to be hated now by you
than soften and pay later with regrets.
MEDEA. [*Exchanging a look with the Chorus*]
Heaven help me!
    My reputation is a curse:
This is not the only time it has done me lasting harm.
    Oh, let the perspicacious man
295 keep his children from enlightenment—
above the general run.
    It will earn them only
the sneer of uselessness
and the spiteful jealousy of fellow men.
    Bring education to the dolt
and, far from being accounted wise,
you will yourself be cast as dolt.
300   Outshine a pundit of established fame
and you become a byword of distaste.
    This precisely
is what I have to face.
    Because I have a little knowledge,
some are filled with jealousy,
others think me secretive, and crazy.
    In point of fact, my knowledge
305 does not amount to much.

[*She turns upon Creon, eyes pathetic with innocence*]

    But now I frighten *you*:
do you think I'll strike some death-knell on your
    house?
    No, no: I am not like that.
    Creon, forget your fear:
I have no criminal intent against a king.
    For how have *you* wronged me?
    You simply gave your virgin child
310 to a suitor of your bent.
    No, it is my husband that I hate.
    You, I think, have acted prudently
and even now I don't begrudge your enterprise
    success.
    Marry them both and blessings on you,
only let me go on living in this land.
    Ill-used though I am, I shall keep quiet:
315 I am overruled.
CREON. Reassuring talk,
but it chills me to the marrow.
What are you really hatching in your mind?
I trust you, Madam,
less even than I did before.

The impassioned woman,
like the impassioned man,   320
is easier to watch than the crafty and the quiet.
    So, leave, I say, at once,
and no speeches, please.
    My mind's made up.
    You are dangerous.
    All your cleverness
shall not keep you here.
MEDEA. Please, I beg you—on my knees—
by your fresh young daughter-bride . . .
CREON. You waste your words.
    I am adamant.   325
MEDEA. Will you expel me—
heedless of my prayers?
CREON. I will. For I love you less
than I love my home.
MEDEA. Ah, home! My own beloved country.
    What memories crowd upon me now!
CREON. Exactly: next to my own children,
my country is *my* dearest love as well.
MEDEA. Love, did you say?   330
    It is a mighty curse.
CREON. In my opinion . . . that depends . . .
MEDEA. O Zeus, remember
the author of this crime.
CREON. Go away—you poor deluded thing—
rid me of my troubles.
MEDEA. The troubles are all mine:
    I have a glut of them.
CREON. [*Turning on his heel*] I'll call the servants:
    They'll put you out by force.   335
MEDEA. [*Clinging to him*] No, not that . . . Creon,
    I have something else . . .
CREON. You seem determined, Madam,
to make a nuisance of yourself.
MEDEA. No, I'll go into banishment . . .
    That is not what I beg you now.
CREON. Then, why not *go*, and let this land be rid of
    you?
MEDEA. Just let me stay this single day   340
to arrange my exodus from here
and make provision for my little sons—
whose father cannot bring himself to care.
    Be kind to them.
    You are a father too: 345
you know what kindly feelings are.
    As for me,
it means nothing to me
whether I stay or go.
    It's them I shed my tears for:
their lot is hard.
CREON. [*After a tussle with himself*]
    My soul is not tyrannical enough.
    My heart has often let me down . . .

So now, Medea,
350   though I know I take a false step:
have it your own way.
    But let me warn you solemnly,
if tomorrow's holy light
sees you and your two children
still inside the borders of this realm,
you die.
    Every word of this I mean.
355   Now, stay if you must; but one day only . . .
not long enough for you to perpetrate anything I
  dread.

[*Exit Creon*]

CHORUS. Ill-starred woman,
  Oh, what a nightmare of anguish is on you!
  Whom will you turn to? Where will you turn?
  What country, what stranger, what home for a
360   haven?
    Who will receive you?
  God has certainly steered you—
  Oh, my poor Medea—
  Into a sea-race of sorrows.

MEDEA. [*Turning on them with the gleam of revenge*]
  In the center of disasters, yes,
365   but all is far from lost—make no mistake—
  a test awaits the newlyweds,
  no little ordeal for the happy pair.

[*With a laugh of derision*]

  Do you think I ever would have toadied to this
    man
if nothing could be got from it, no gain, no tool?
No, not one syllable,
370   not a touch with my little finger.
    The fool!
    He could have scotched me with one stroke,
flung me out;
instead he lets me stay one extra day,
to make three enemies three corpses:
375   ha! father, daughter, and my husband.

[*She leans toward the Chorus*]

  Friends,
I can think of several ways to bring their death about.
    Which one shall I choose?
    Shall I set their house of honeymoon alight,
or creep into the nuptial bower
380   and plunge a sharp knife through their vitals?
    One thing makes me pause:
    if I am caught entering the palace, or red-handed,
I die . . . and give my enemies the last laugh.
    No, there is a surer way,
one more direct;

for which I have a natural bent:
death by poison.   385
Yes, that is it.

[*She walks, thinking*]

  Well, suppose they are dead:
will any city take me in,
will any man afford me home in a country safe
    for living
and shield me from reprisals?
    No, there is none.
    I must postpone it, therefore, for a while
until some tower of strength appears for me;   390
then, through trickery and stealth,
I shall proceed with death by poison.
    What if I'm forced to go before it's done?
    Ah, then I shall seize a sword,
face certain death,
and with my own hands run them through.
    I shall not shrink from such a step,   395
by Hecate,° no: the goddess who abides
in the shrine of my inner hearth—
the one I reverence most of all the gods
and have chosen to abet me.
    Nobody breaks my heart—
with impunity.
    Their wedding I'll reduce
to agony and grief:
agony for having met and married,
and grief for having banished me.   400
    Good!
    Use your magic to the hilt.
    Plot, Medea, devise your recipes:
advance to the deadly act that tests your courage.
    See your present plight:
laughed at by the seed of Sisyphus°
because of Jason's match?   405
    Never.
    Your father was a king:
his father, Helios the Sun . . .
be aware of *that*.
    Besides, you are a born woman:
feeble when it comes to the sublime,
marvelously inventive over crime.

FIRST CHORAL ODE

[*The Chorus sings an ode about the topsy-turvy changing standards of the world. Out of the turmoil will come a new*

396**Hecate** Identified with Artemis, and sometimes called Persephone (Roman name: Proserpine), she was supposed to preside over magic and witchcraft. 404 **Sisyphus** To be a descendant of Sisyphus was considered disgraceful by the ancients.

importance for women, and a new reverence. Meanwhile, Medea is a harbinger of female independence and vitality]

410 Back to their fountains
    the sacred rivers are falling;
The cosmos and all mortality
    turning to chaos.
The mind of a man is nothing but fraud
415   and his faith in the gods a delusion.
One day the story will change:
    then shall the glory
    of women resound,
And reverence will come to the race of woman,
    Reversing at last the sad
420   reputation of ladies.

ANTISTROPHE 1

The ballads of ages gone by
    that harped on the falseness
Of women, will cease to be sung . . .
    If only Apollo,
Prince of the lyric, had put
    in *our* hearts the invention
425 Of music and songs for the lyre,
Wouldn't I then have raised
    up a feminine paean
To answer the epic of men?
Time in the roll of the ages has much to unfold
Of the fortunes of women no less
430   than the fortunes of men.

STROPHE 2

So you, Medea, sailing away
    from your father's house,
Threading a passage with heart on fire
    through the jowls of the Euxine
Cliffs° to inhabit a strange
435   land where your bed is empty of man
(The lover you lost, O heartbroken lady!)
Now are chased from the realm,
    shamed and banned.

ANTISTROPHE 2

The joy of a bond is gone;
440   and wide the world of Hellas,
All shame has flown—
    high in the sky and away.
Bereft of a fatherly home,
Where can you sail for a haven against
The storm, unfortunate woman—

434**Euxine Cliffs** on the Black Sea

Your bed
Royally quelled by another
    who queens it in your home?   445

SECOND EPISODE

[Jason enters from the road that leads to the palace. He is a young-looking man, dressed in the swashbuckling cloak and plumed helmet of a captain in the King's Guards]

JASON. *[Embarrassed and exasperated]*
    So . . . this is not the first time
I have seen irrevocable damage done
by a barbarous rage.
    You could have stayed here,
in this land, in this house,
had you submitted quietly to your ruler's plans.
    Instead, you ranted like a lunatic . . .   450
so now are banished.
    To me your tirade does not mean a thing:
go on declaiming what a monster Jason is.
    But when it comes to royalty,
the princess and the king,
count yourself lucky to be only banished.
    I have tried continuously to calm things down; 455
for I should like you to remain.
    But you, Madam,
obstinate in folly,
have continuously reviled our royalty.
    And so you are banished.
    Yet, in spite of everything, I come, Medea,
patient to the last with someone I am fond of,
to do what I can do to help.   460
    You and the children
need not leave the country penniless
and unprovided for . . .
exile drags with it a chain of troubles.
    And hate me though you may,
I cannot bring myself to wish you harm.
MEDEA. You criminal—   465
    an epithet too good for you . . . such inhumanity . . .
so you come to me, do you,
you byword of aversion both in heaven and on
        earth,°
to me your own worst enemy?
    This is not courage.
    This is not being brave:
to look a victim in the eyes whom you've
        betrayed—   470
somebody you loved—
    This is a disease,
and the foulest that a man can have:
you are shameless.

468Editors bracket this line as doubtful.

[*With the thinnest of smiles*]

But you have done well to come:
I can unload some venom from my heart
and you can smart to hear it.
475　　To begin at the beginning,
yes, first things first:
I saved your life—
as every son of Greece who stepped on board the
　　Argo knows.
You were sent to yoke
the fire-breathing bulls
and sow the plot of death.
Yes, I saved you, lit up life for you,
when I slew the guardian of the Golden Fleece,
480　　that giant snake which hugged it, sleepless,
coil on coil.
I deserted my own father and my home
to come away with you to Iolcus by Mount
　　Pelion,
485　　full of zeal and very little sense.
King Pelias, I killed,
a most horrid death—
perpetrated through his daughters—
and overturned their home.
All this for you,
I even bore you sons—you most reprobate man—
just to be discarded for a new bride.
490　　Had you been childless,
this craving for another bedmate
might have been forgiven.
But no: all faith in vows is shattered.
I am baffled:
Do you suppose the gods of old no longer rule?
Or is it that mankind
now has different principles—
495　　because your every vow to me, I'm sure you know,
is null and void.
Curse this right hand of mine,
so often held by yours;
and these knees of mine—
sullied to no purpose
by the grasp of a rotten man.
You turned my hopes to lies.
Come now, tell me frankly—
as if we were two friends,
500　　as if you really were prepared to help
(and I hope the question makes you feel
　　ashamed)—
where do I go from here?

[*With a bitter laugh*]

Home to my father, perhaps,
and my native land,
both of whom I sacrificed for *you*?

Or to the poor deprived daughters of Pelias?
They would be overjoyed to entertain　　505
their father's murderer.
Yes: this is how things stand.
Among my own friends
I am an execrated woman.
There was no call for me to hurt *them*,
but now I have a death-feud on my hands—
and all for you.
What a reward!
What a heroine you have made me
among the daughters of Hellas!　　510
Lucky Medea, having *you*:
such a wonderful husband . . . and so loyal!
I leave this land displaced, expelled,
deprived of friends,
only my children with me, and alone.
What a charming record for our new bridegroom this:
"His own sons and the wife who saved him　　515
are wayside beggars."

[*She breaks off and looks upward*]

O Zeus, what made you give us
clear signs for telling
mere glitter from true gold,
but when we need to know
the base metal of a man
no stamp upon his flesh for telling counterfeit?
LEADER. How frightening is resentment　　520
　　　　how difficult to cure,
　　When lovers hurl past love
　　　　at one another's hate.
JASON. I'll have to choose my words
with no uncommon skill, it seems . . .
like a good sailor riding out a storm,
if I am to sail close-sheeted, Madam,
through your lashing, dangerous tongue.　　525

[*Folding his arms*]

So, you pile up what you did for me
into pinnacles of grace.
Well, as far as I am concerned,
it was Aphrodite° and no one else in heaven or earth
who saved me on my voyage.
Your cleverness played a part, of course,
but I could underline, if I wanted to be ungenerous,
how it was infatuation, sheer shooting passion,　　530
that drove you to save my life.
I shall not stress the point.
After all, your service did no harm.
But this I shall maintain:

___

527**Aphrodite** goddess of love, called by the Latins *Venus*

that what you gained by saving me
535 was far more than you gave.

[*Holds up a hand to stop Medea from interrupting*]

In the first place,
you have a home in Hellas
instead of some barbarian land.
    You have known justice:
the benefit of laws which never yield to might;
have had your talents recognized all over Greece
and won renown.
540   For, were you living at the world's ends,
your name would not be known . . .
    Oh, to me, houses crammed with gold,
and a sweeter song than Orpheus sang,
are nothing with no name.
545   But, enough discussion of my dangerous voyage:
an argument which *you* provoked.
    Now to your vindictive challenge
of my royal marriage.
    I'll show you, first, it was an act of common sense,
secondly, unselfish,
and, finally, a mark of my devotion
550 to you and all my family.

[*Medea gives a gasp of incredulity*]

No, be still.
    When I came here from the land of Iolcus,
frustrations crowding on my trail,
could I, a wretched fugitive,
have hit upon a greater stroke of luck
than marriage to the daughter of the king?
    It was not—which cuts you to the quick—
555 that I was tired of your attractions
and smitten with a longing for a new wife;
still less that I was out to multiply my offspring
(I am quite satisfied with the sons we have);
no, it was simply that I wanted above all
560 to let us live in comfort, not be poor . . .
    I know too well
how the pauper is avoided by his friends.
    I wanted our children to be reared
in a manner worthy of my ancestry,
and, begetting others, brothers for your sons,
knit them all together
into one close and happy family.
    What point was there for you to have more
565 children?
    My intention was—and it seemed real gain—
to help the ones I have,
through those I hope to have.
    Was this such a wicked plan?
    You would not say so,
except through jealousy—that stinging jealousy of
bed.

You women are all the same.
    If your love life goes all right,   570
everything is fine;
but once crossed in bed,
the liveliest and best that life can offer
might as well be wormwood.
    What we poor males really need
is a way of having babies on our own—
no females, please.
    Then the world would be
completely trouble free.   575
LEADER. [*Sternly*] Jason, this speech of yours is plausible,
    But say what you like, it is not right
    To sacrifice your wife.
MEDEA. [*With cold disdain*]
    My outlook must be very different, then, from others.
        To my mind a hypocrite who is too glib   580
    only multiplies the danger that it puts him in:
    the more he glozes° falsehood with his tongue,
    the more confident and rash he grows.
        He ends by not being very clever.
        So, you, toward me—
    you'd better drop your specious pleading.   585
        One simple observation
    lays the whole thing flat:
    were you not a coward, it was your duty
    to convince *me*; not go sneaking off to marry.
JASON. And you would have welcomed the suggestion,
        I am sure.
    Why, even now you can't contain your blazing rage. 590
MEDEA. *That* was not what governed you:
    you felt your glory tarnished by an aging oriental
        wife.
JASON. Please, please believe me:
    it was nothing to do with women—
    my desire to make this match—
    but as I have already said   595
    to safeguard you and rear young princes
    to be brothers to my sons . . .
    so make our family solid.
MEDEA. [*With a bitter laugh*]
    Haha! Solid happiness on the grave of love;
    Prosperity with a secret sting . . .
    O you gods—not for me—ever.
JASON. [*Earnestly*] Please change your prayer to this
    and make it reasonable: 600
    "May success not seem to me sad failure,
    nor good fortune ever a disaster."
MEDEA. You go on mocking me: *you* have roof and
        shelter.
    I am deserted, flying for my life, alone.
JASON. *You* chose it. Blame no one else.   605

<hr>

582**glozes** glosses over

MEDEA. Did I? I was the one who wed and then
    betrayed?
JASON. No: you just swore a heap of filthy curses on
    the king.
MEDEA. Yes, and you shall find that *I* am the curse
    that Fate has made to haunt you.
610 JASON. There's no point in talking any more with you.

[*Preparing to go*]

    Anything that you or the children want in exile,
let me know; I'd gladly furnish it,
or send letters of introduction for you
to friends abroad who will be kind.
    To turn this offer down, Medea,
is nothing short of madness.
615   Forget your feelings of resentment:
let yourself be helped.
MEDEA. [*Spitting out the words*]
    Not your friends, not your things:
I would not touch anything of yours—
how dare you offer it!
    The presents of the wicked are pure poison.
JASON. [*Flinging his cloak about him*]
    In that case, heaven be my witness:
620 all my design to help you and your sons
is thwarted by your preference for evil.
    Your self-will cuts you off.
    Suffer then accordingly.

[*He begins to go*]

MEDEA. Go then. Don't waste your passion here:
go to the fresh young virgin you can't wait for . . .
    Have her.

[*As Jason exits, furious and embarrassed*]

625   And God grant
the match you make, you'll long to have unmade.

SECOND CHORAL ODE

[*The women of the Chorus, appalled by what has happened to Medea, speak of the dangers of love and the sufferings of exile*]

STROPHE 1

    Love is a dangerous thing:
    Loving without any limit.
    Discredit and loss it can bring . . .
630   But, oh, if the goddess should visit
    A love that is modest and right,
    No god is so exquisite.
    Great lady, aim not at me
    Your gold and infallibly
    Passion-tipped, poisoned delight.

ANTISTROPHE 1

    Stay me with innocent living: 635
    Most beautiful gift of the gods.
    Never let Cypris° the fierce
    Queen of desire propel
    My heart to a dissolute lust
    From old to a new and another
    Bed and a dissonant longing,
    But test with a sweet eye for peace   640
    The love-bonds of reverent women.

STROPHE 2

    O my country, my home, never let
    Me lose my state and my city—
    Living that desperate loss
    so helpless and hard, without pity.   645
    Death: I would bargain with death,
    To die such a day to a finish.
    For nothing is like the sorrow
    Or supersedes the sadness   650
    Of losing your native land.

ANTISTROPHE 2

LEADER. The thing is before my eyes.
    Learned from no rumor or lies:
    Medea without city or friends
    Nowhere where pity extends—   655
    Oh, how you must suffer! . . .
    Let a man rot in a charmless lot
    If he never unshutters his heart
    To the cleansing esteem of another.   660
    He'll not be my friend: no, never.

THIRD EPISODE

[*Enter Aegeus from the country. He is a man in his early
middle years and dressed in traveling clothes. His open features—kindly but unimaginative—seem preoccupied. In
his retinue are Noblemen and Servants*]

AEGEUS. [*Stretching out his hands*]
    Medea, all health and happiness . . .
and can one say a fairer thing when greeting friends?
MEDEA. [*Wanly*] Health and happiness to you, good
    Aegeus,   665
wise Panidon's son . . . But where do you stem from?
AEGEUS. I have just left Apollo's ancient oracle at Delphi.
MEDEA. What—a pilgrim there—the nub of the
    world of prophecy?
AEGEUS. I went to ask for progeny—for a fruitful seed.
MEDEA. [*Suddenly interested*]
    In the name of heaven! Have you been childless   670
    all this time.
AEGEUS. Childless, yes—by some design of heaven.

636**Cypris** Aphrodite, goddess of love. Roman *Venus*

MEDEA. But with a wife . . . or have you never married?

AEGEUS. I am married. Yes, I have a wife who shares
my bed.

MEDEA. And what did Apollo say about your having
children?

AEGEUS. Something far too deep for me, a mere
675   mortal, to unravel.

MEDEA. Am I allowed to know the god's reply?

AEGEUS. Certainly. It would take a mind like yours
to fathom.

MEDEA. Tell me . . . what did he say . . . since you are
allowed?

AEGEUS. Why, just this:
"Do not unstopper the wine-skin till . . ."°

MEDEA. Till you've done something—been
680   somewhere—special?

AEGEUS. [Baffled] Until I'm back at home again.

MEDEA. Then why did you sail in here?

AEGEUS. There is a man called Pittheus, king of
Troezen . . .

MEDEA. Yes, a son of Pelops: a very pious man, they
say.

685 AEGEUS. I want to ask his help about this oracle.

MEDEA. Yes, a clever man, and an expert in such
things.

AEGEUS. And of all my old battle cronies, my favorite.

MEDEA. Well, I hope that all your dreams come true.

AEGEUS. Medea, you look so pale, so sad. What is it?

MEDEA. My husband, Aegeus; he is the world's most
690   wicked man.

AEGEUS. You don't say? . . . Come, tell me all about your
troubles.

MEDEA. He's set up a mistress to queen it in my home.

AEGEUS. Dear me! Would he really do a thing like
695   that?

MEDEA. Yes, yes . . . And I am deposed—the one he
loved.

AEGEUS. Did he fall in love . . . or is he just tired of *you*?

MEDEA. In love—Ha—head over heels . . . flinging
all fidelity to the winds.

AEGEUS. Let him get on with it . . . since he's as
wicked as you say he is.

700 MEDEA. But it was with royalty he fell in love:
a king's daughter.

AEGEUS. Eh? What king's daughter? Please go on.

MEDEA. Creon's, king of Corinth.

AEGEUS. In that case, Madam, it *is* serious.
You have my sympathies.

MEDEA. It is the end. What is more, I am being banished.

705 AEGEUS. Banished? This is indeed a crowning blow—
but by whom?

MEDEA. Creon: he wants to banish me from Corinth.

679"**Do not . . . wine-skin**" probably, "Do not have sexual intercourse."

AEGEUS. And Jason agrees? I find that monstrous.

MEDEA. [With fierce irony] Oh, he says he doesn't—
but he'll bear it bravely.

[On her knees]

Aegeus, I beg you,
by your beard,
by these knees of yours I clasp,   710
pity me, pity my unhappiness.
Do not see me banished and alone,
let me come to Athens, shelter me,
accept me in your home.
The gods will pay you back,
give you the children you so long to have,
surround your death with happiness.   715
You do not guess how Providence has blessed
you, meeting
me.
I mean to end your childlessness
and make your seed bear sons.

[Almost in a whisper]

I promise it. I know the drugs.

AEGEUS. [Impressed] Medea, many reasons make me
ready
to acquiesce in your request,
not least of all the gods;   720
then because you've given me—a promise:
promise of children . . .
oh, left to myself, I had all but given up.

[Gently raising her]

My proposition, then is this:
get yourself to Athens
and there, as is incumbent on me,
I shall do my utmost to protect you.
However, I must tell you clearly,   725
I cannot take you with me out of Corinth,
but if you reach my palace on your own,
there you shall have full sanctuary
and to no one shall I give you up.
So, by your own means you must leave this land:
I cannot risk offending the Corinthians—
who are also friends of mine.   730

MEDEA. As you say . . . but . . .
if only you could promise it on oath,
it would make it all so . . . settled between us.

AEGEUS. Do you not trust me? What is the matter now?

MEDEA. [Glancing nervously over her shoulders]

I do trust you . . . but . . .
but I have my enemies.
It isn't only Creon,   735
there is the house of Pelias too:
They'll want to prize me from your territories.
If you are bound by oath

you will not give me up.
  But if you have only made a promise,
not sworn it to the gods,
there is always the chance that sheer diplomacy
will win you to their wishes.
  I have no weapons on my side,
740   on theirs is wealth and all the weight of royalty.
AEGEUS. You are very provident, Medea.
  However, if that is what you want,
I shall not go against it.
  In point of fact,
to swear an oath protects me too:
I can counter those who wish you ill
with a clear excuse;
and you of course, are well secured.
745   So, name your deities.
MEDEA. [In crystal-cold syllables]
Swear by the Earth on which you tread.
Swear by the Sun, my father's father dread.
Swear by every god and godhead.
AEGEUS. Yes, but what to do or not to do? Please say.
MEDEA. Never yourself to drive me from your land,
750   and if an enemy of mine tries to drag me off,
never while you live to let me go.
AEGEUS. I swear by the Earth and sacred light of the
  Sun
to abide by the words you have just pronounced.
MEDEA. [Relentlessly]
Good . . . but if you break your word—what
755   penalty?
AEGEUS. The penalty for sacrilege.

[They clasp hands in silence]

MEDEA. Go now and be glad. All is well.
  I shall come to Athens as quickly as I can,
but first I have some work to do, to carry out a
  plan.

[As Aegeus is leaving]

LEADER. We hope that Hermes, master of journeys,
760   Will hasten you home safely to Athens:
Home to the hope of your heart's desire,
  For Aegeus, you are
  A most magnanimous man.
MEDEA. [Wheels round and faces the Chorus]
O Zeus and lady daughter, Justice,
O resplendent Sun!
765   And you my friends,
  At last we are on the road to vengeance
and to our song of triumph. At last there is hope:
we shall see my enemies put down.
  At the very point my plot could founder,
770   this man opens up a port, an anchorage.
  So to Athens I shall go
and moor to her fast towers.

[She beckons the women closer]

  Now I can unfold to you my whole design:
there is nothing sweet in it, as you will see.
I send a servant of my house to Jason
asking him to come to me.   775
  He arrives
I tell him in the softest accents;
how I now agree;
how it all seems for the best:
his royal marriage, his sacrifice of me;
everything that he has planned is for the best.
  But I ask him to let my children stay . . .   780
with no intention—you understand—
of leaving any child of mine in a hostile place
for those who hate me to maltreat.
  No, this is just a device
for murdering the daughter of the king.
  I send them there with presents in their hands,
presents for the bride—as a kind of plea   785
against their banishment—
yes, a gown of gossamer and a diadem made of
  beaten gold.
  If she takes this finery and puts it on,
the girl will die in agony
and anyone who touches her;
so deadly are the poisons I shall steep the presents
  in.
  But now my whole tone changes: 790
a sob of pain for the next thing I must do.
  I kill my sons—my own—
no one shall snatch them from me.
  And when I have desolated Jason's house
  beyond recall,
I shall escape from here:
fly from the murder of my little ones,   795
my mission done.
  People that one hates, my friends,
must never have the last laugh.
  Well, so be it.
  What good is life to me?
I have no father, home, defense from danger.
  Oh, the mistake I made was when I left his house, 800
trusting the word of a man from Greece . . .
but he is going to pay the price.
  Never again alive
shall he see the sons he had by me,
nor any child by this new bride of his—
poor girl, who has to die a wretched death,   805
poisoned by me.
  Let no man think me insignificant or weak:
I am no meek martyr, no—quite the contrary—
relentless an enemy I make;
though kind enough to friends.
  Such is the genius of my life.   810

LEADER. [*Imploringly*]
    Though you have shared all this in confidence
        with us, Medea,
    and though I long to be of help,
    we must uphold the laws of life:
    and so I say to you: "You must not do it."
MEDEA. There is no other way.
    And though I understand your sentiments,
815   *you* have not been through my agony.
LEADER. But, my lady, to kill your own two sons . . . ?
MEDEA. It is the supreme way to hurt my husband.
LEADER. And it makes you the most desolate of
        women.
MEDEA. Be that as it may.
    Argument is now superfluous.

[*She turns to the Nurse, who has entered during the previous dialogue*]

    Nurse, when I need real loyalty
    you are the one I always turn to.
820   Go now and fetch Jason here.
    But as you are a woman
    and a faithful servant of this house,
    whisper no syllable of what I plan.

[*Exit Nurse, dragging her feet*]

THIRD CHORAL ODE

[*The Women of Corinth desperately try to move Medea from her purpose. Does she imagine Athens, that blessed land, will welcome a murderess? Surely, she herself will flinch from the cold-blooded killing of her sons*]

STROPHE 1

825   The people of Athens are blest through the ages,
            Seeds of the all-hallowed gods,
        Born on a soil unravaged and holy,
            They feed on the wide
            Bright pastures of knowledge.
830   Lightly they walk through the crystal air
        In a land where Harmonia,
            Goldenly fair,
        Once gave birth, they say, to the nine
            Muses, the pure
            Maids of Pieria.°

ANTISTROPHE 1

835   And out of the sweetly flowing currents
        Of Cephisus,° they declare,

834**where Harmonia . . . Maids of Pieria** Harmonia, the balance of nature, and the genius of the people resulted in the cultivation of the arts. Pieria was a holy fountain in Boetia where the nine Muses were supposed to live.
836**Cephisus** an Athenian river

Aphrodite sprinkles the land
    And fragrantly breathes
    Delicate breezes.
Forever she sheds from the stream of her hair,   840
    Plaited with roses,
Scented petals; and sends the Loves—the
    Erotes—
To preside with Wisdom over the heart
    And together prepare
    The glories of art.   845

STROPHE 2

How then shall a glorious city,
    City of sacred rivers,
    Host of the salutary guest,
Kindly take to the killer of children,
Harbor among them a murderess?   850
Think of how you are stabbing your sons.
Think, too, of the blood you assume.
Do not, please, we beg by your knees,
By everything and every means—
    Murder your children.   855

ANTISTROPHE 2

Where, when, will you find the mind,
    The hand or the callous heart
    Hardened enough to strike
These, yours—oh, heartless enough?—
How then will you see through your gaze   860
Swollen with tears as you sight your aim?
No, no, when your little ones kneel
Crying for mercy, you will not
Find the nerve, never be able,
    To bloody your hands.   865

FOURTH EPISODE

[*Jason enters with the Nurse behind him. On his face is written apprehension mixed with hope; on hers, despair*]

JASON. I have come, Medea, because you asked me.
    I put myself at your disposal
even though you are against me.
    What, Madam, can I do for you?
MEDEA. [*In a small, contrite voice*]
    Jason please forgive me for all the things I said.   870
    Bear lightly with my outbursts, will you,
if only in remembrance of our great love together.
    I have been arguing with myself,
have taxed myself severely.
    "You raving fool," I said,
"To antagonize those who want to do you good,
setting yourself against your rulers and your
        husband.   875
    His royal marriage
and his design to bring up brothers for your sons

does you the greatest service that he could.
    Why not calm yourself?
    Are *you* suffering because the gods are good?
880   Have you no children of your own?
    And are you not aware
you came as fugitive with not too many friends?"
    Such reflections made me realize
I have been out of my mind, hysterical.
    Now I thank you.
    Now I am convinced
885   that in securing us this benefit
you are the wise one, *I* the fool—
I who should have been your ally
and encouraged you.
    Yes, I should have been at hand to help,
decked the bed, dressed the bride—
and been glad to do it . . .
    But we women—
well, we are what we are: let's leave it at that!
890   Do not copy us in our perverseness
or try to get your own back, giving tit for tat.
    I ask your pardon.
    I admit to being wrong.
    I've thought better of it now.

[*With an upsurge of put-on happiness*]

    Children, children, come out here,
out of the house.

[*The two Boys appear with their Tutor*]

895   Come greet your father, hug him, join with me
in loving, not resenting him.
    Your mother's rancor's over.
    There's peace between us: the fighting's done.
    Come, take his hand.

[*As the children run into their father's arms*]

    O God, what a presentiment!
900   What an image looming in the dark!
JASON. My sons, my sons,°
    if only you could go on living, go on loving,
    with your arms stretched out like that to me forever
    . . .
MEDEA. [*Choking*] It breaks my heart;
    I am far too prone to tears, too full of tears . . .
    it is the sudden ending of my quarrel with your
      father
    which makes them flow.
    A sight so touching . . .
905   it overflows.

°901No doubt this line and half the next (in the Greek) go to Jason,
and not Medea. Otherwise, Medea's remark in 930 makes no sense.

LEADER. My eyes, too, are stinging,
    but may this be the worst that is to come.
JASON. [*Gently releasing the Boys*] I praise you now,
    Medea,
    and I did not blame you then.
    It is natural for a woman to be enraged
when her husband goes off making second
    marriages.   910
    But now
    you are in a better frame of mind
and, even if it took a little time,
realize the good points of this plan . . .
    the decision is a level-headed woman's.

[*Turning to the children*]

    As for you, my boys,
your father has been far from idle
and, heaven willing, he has made
good settlements for you.   915
    In time I shouldn't wonder
if you were not first citizens in Corinth—
along with your new brothers.

[*Laying his hands on their shoulders*]

    Grow up now fine fellows.
    Your father and a kindly providence
have the rest in hand.   920
    How I look toward the time
when you will be two strapping grown young men,
trampling down my enemies.

[*Medea has averted her head and is sobbing. Her feelings,
though genuine, are being used by her to further her next
move*]

    But, Medea, what is this—
these dewy eyes, these tears;
your white face turned away
as if my words struck pain, not joy?   925
MEDEA. It is nothing.
    I was just thinking of our sons.
JASON. Well, be of good heart now:
    I shall see them through.
MEDEA. I will do my best . . . it isn't that I don't
    believe you,
    but you know how women weep.
JASON. I know, but don't be sad for *them* . . . why
    should you?
MEDEA. [*Watching the tender look on Jason's face*]
    I am their mother.
    When you prayed just now   930
for a long life for your sons,
a sudden sadness whispered: "Will this be?"
    Well, that's one item only
of what I had to say.
    The other thing is this:

Since the king has set his mind
on sending me away from Corinth,
935 and since I've come to recognize that this is best
(for I'd only be an obstacle to you,
living with the royal family here—
who think I am a menace to their house),
I shall take myself away, go into banishment.
But the children, please, I should like *them*
to grow up under your own hand.
940 Persuade Creon to let them stay.

JASON. [*Taken off his guard, but flattered*]
I—I am not certain that I can:
it'll take a little trying.

MEDEA. But you could ask your wife to beg her
father
to let the two boys stay.

JASON. [*Reflecting*]
Why not? I think I can get her to
agree.

MEDEA. Of course you can:
945 if she's the slightest bit like any woman.
And here *I* can play a useful part.
I shall send her a present
more ravishingly beautiful, believe me,
than anything this age has seen:
a gown of gossamer and a diadem of beaten gold.
950 These the boys shall carry them to her.

[*She claps her hands and two Maids appear*]

Go quickly, one of you,
and bring the gorgeous presents here.

[*One of the Maids hurries into the house*]

What a double delight
What a shower of happiness for her
to have you for a hero husband
and now these treasures which were handed down
955 by my father's father—the glorious Sun.

[*The Maid comes back with two boxes. Medea turns to the
Boys*]

Boys, take hold of this wedding gift.
Carry it to the happy princess-bride.
Place it in her hands.
It is not the kind of present she'll despise.

JASON. [*As the Boys step forward*]
You foolish woman—why empty your hands?
960 Do you think a royal wardrobe is in want,
or a palace short of gold?
Keep these things. Don't give them up.
If my wife values me at all,
my mere wish will have more weight than *things*.
I'm sure of that.

MEDEA. [*With an onrush of conviction*] Do not deny me.
Even the gods, they say, succumb to gifts,

and gold is stronger than the strongest wits. 965
She is lucky, *she* is blessed, *she* increases.
This exile I would barter for my babies
not just with gold but with my life.

[*Forcing the boxes into the Boys' hands*]

Go, my sons, into the halls of wealth;
down on your knees and beg her—
this new wife of your father's, and my mistress— 970
to let you stay in Corinth.
Most important of all,
see that she takes the precious things
into her own hands.

[*Packing them off*]

Quick, now, go. Success be yours.
Come and tell me the good news. 975
Your mother waits with all ears.

[*Exeunt the Boys with their Tutor, followed by Jason*]

FOURTH CHORAL ODE

[*The Chorus deplores the multimurders*]

STROPHE 1

Now has the last hope gone of the children living,
Gone and forever: they walk already to murder.
The bride is taking the golden diadem,
    Is taking the poison and doom.
Over her yellow hair her hands are fitting
    The decorated dying. 980

ANTISTROPHE 1

The gorgeousness of the gossamer gown will win,
And the beaten gold of the diadem embrace her.
The bride is decked and ready to meet the dead. 985
    The trap is lethally set:
Doomed miserable woman, doomed to fall in—
    Ineluctably caught by Fate.

STROPHE 2

And you who are groomed for a murder: 990
    Son-in-law of a king,
    Jason unsuspecting—
Are to bring on your sons a demise, and a death
    On your bride of a hideous kind.
        Unhappy man, how far
        You are falling. 995

ANTISTROPHE 2

And you the unenviable mother,
    How I weep for your pain!
    Killer of children for
A vengeance of love that has gone, betrayed 1000
    By your man for another

Bride whom he sleeps beside
In his wrong.

FIFTH EPISODE

[*The Tutor hurries in from the palace with the two Boys*]

TUTOR. [*Breathless with excitement*] My lady, your
    boys—
they won't be banished.
    And the princess, the bride—
with her own hands—
she took your presents, oh, so gladly . . .
1005   Now the children's danger is over!

[*Baffled by Medea's grim reaction*]

    Well I never! Isn't this good news?
    What so transfixes you?

[*Medea draws in her breath in a muffled cry of pain*]

MEDEA. What I hear is out of tune with what I say.

[*Medea sighs deeply*]

1010 TUTOR. I thought I brought good news.
    What kind of news, I wonder, have I brought?
MEDEA. What you have brought, you have brought:
    the fault is not with you.
TUTOR. Why, my Lady, these shuttered eyes:
    these tears falling?
MEDEA. Oh, I am pressed, old friend—hard pressed:
    the gods and my own evil counsels.
1015 TUTOR. Courage, dear mistress:
    Your sons will always bring you home.
MEDEA. [*In a kind of trance*]
    Home? . . . First I must send others there . . .
      Mercy!
TUTOR. You are not the only mother to be severed
      from her sons.
We have to bear our own humanity—humanely.
MEDEA. [*Pressing his hand*]
    I shall try . . . Now go inside
1020 and see to what the children need today.

[*Exit Tutor, worried*]

MEDEA. [*Throwing out her arms toward the two Boys*]
    My sons, my sons,
you will have a city and a home
far from me.
    I shall be left lonely,
and you will live without your mother always.
    For I must go in exile to another land:
never have my joy in you,
1025 or see your bright young progress;
never deck your brides, your marriage beds,
or light you radiant to your wedding day.

[*The Boys are now in her arms*]

    Oh, what a blight my ruthlessness has been!
    How useless, little ones,
my nursing all your growing up!
    How useless all the cares endured: 1030
The wearying solicitudes,
the shooting agony of giving you your lives.
    And now, how miserably have dwindled
my innumerable dreams of you:
your loving comfort when I'm old,
your own hands dressing me when I am dead—
a passing every person might desire.   1035
    Such sweet fancy vanishes
and, wrenched from you instead,
I shall drag my sad life out alone.

[*She cups their faces in her hands in turn*]

    Your own dear eyes shall miss forever
your poor mother's face—
your way of life and hers utterly apart.
    Oh, children,
do you let those eyes now stare their fill,   1040
and your last smiles linger to the last?

[*She turns to the Chorus, panting*]

    Oh! What shall I do?
    My heart dissolves
when I gaze into their bright irises . . .
    No, I cannot do it.
    Goodbye to my determination.
    I shall take my boys away with me.   1045
    Why damage *them* in trying to hurt their father,
and only hurt myself twice over?
    No, I cannot.
    Goodbye to my decisions.

[*A pause, then she suddenly breaks away from the Boys*]

    What—what undermines me now?
    Do I really mean to let my enemies go,   1050
to laugh at me?
    Steel yourself, Medea:
away with this cowardice, these arguments that melt.

[*Almost pushing them*]

    Go, Boys, into the house.

[*She turns to the Chorus grimly*]

    Anyone whose conscience will not let him stay
let him look to it: avoid my sacrifice . . .
this hand of mine shall never falter.   1055

[*Another spasm of emotion grips her, and she runs to the
Boys as they reach the door*]

No, no! Stop me, my heart:
we must not do this thing.
　　Let them go, you stricken woman,
spare your sons.
　　Let them live with you in Athens:
they will be your joy.

[*Throwing her arms round them again*]

　　Ah! Not by all the haunting spirits of the
　　　underworld,
shall I leave my children for my enemies to
　　　trample down.
1060　　No, never.°

[*With a sharp realization*]

But—they have to die—
the whole thing is settled anyway . . .
1065　　Yes . . . the diadem is on her head . . .
the royal bride at this moment rots,
dying in her gown—I know it.

[*She turns to the Chorus as if to explain her second impulsive embrace*]

　　You see: the path I have to tread
is unutterably sad,
but the one I set these children on
is sadder still . . .
　　Therefore I desire to speak with them.

[*Seizing their hands*]

　　Give me your right hands to kiss,
each of you, my little ones—
1070　　give them to your mother.

[*Covering their hands, their faces, their bodies, in kisses*]

　　How adorable—this hand—and this . . .
　　These lips—how very much adored!
　　And this face and form of childhood's
ingenuous nobility . . . how I bless you both . . .
not here—beyond . . .
every blessing here your father has despoiled.
1075　　So sweet . . . the mere touch of you:
the bloom of children's skin—so soft . . .
their breath—a perfect balm.

[*Gently releasing them: then almost savagely turning her back*]

　　Go, go . . . I cannot look at you.
　　I am in an agony, and lost.

[*The two Boys, weeping, hurry into the house*]

1060Some editors omit lines 1062 and 1063 as a melodramatic interpolation: "But they have to die, and since they must, / let it be by the hands of her who gave them life."

The evil that I do, I understand full well,
But a passion drives me greater than my will.
　　Passion is the curse of man:
　　It wreaks the greatest ill.　　　　　　　　1080

FIFTH CHORAL ODE

[*The Chorus wonders if there can be a feminine philosophy of parenthood, is its honest judgment likely to be that children are worth it after all?*]

　　So often before
Have I gone toward concepts far too tenuous
And come upon questions far too deep
For the race of woman to try to unravel.
Nevertheless, even we women
Have a muse of our own, that ushers us in.　　1085
(Though, alas, not all) to the world of wisdom.
Perhaps you might find it one in a thousand.
It serves to inspire the talent of ladies,
And makes me able now to proclaim　　　　　1090
That people without the function of parent
Are happier than begetters of offspring.
The childless man has no way of telling
Whether he misses a curse or a blessing.　　1095
Nevertheless, the childless person
Certainly misses many a burden.
I mark how the man with children growing
Sweetly at home is worn with worrying:　　　1100
How to make sure they are properly fed,
How to leave them a livelihood.
And then after all to be in the dark:
Were all the worries worth it or not?　　　　1105
Were they a worthy or worthless lot?
　　But now let me tell
Of the worst and saddest trait of all.
Suppose the children have quite a good life,
Reach their teenhood honest and fine,　　　　1110
What if a fate like Death the cruel
Carries them downward body and soul?
What is the use if after all
(On top of all those other ones)
The gods let loose this grief as well . . .　　1115
Just for the joy of having sons?

SIXTH EPISODE

[*Medea has been sitting during the Chorus. Now she leaps up as she catches sight of a man lunging breathlessly toward them from the street: the Messenger*]

MEDEA. Somebody with news at last, my friends,
　　And from the right direction.
　　　Yes, I see him:
one of Jason's men—panting as he hurries—
With some tremendous news of bad.　　　　　1120

[*The Messenger—an official of the Bride's house—bursts in: hardly able to get his words out*]

MESSENGER. Run, Medea, run!
> What—you have done . . . is . . . too unthinkable . . .
too awful . . .
> Seize whatever means you can . . .
sailing boat or chariot . . . Escape!

MEDEA. Run? Escape? Is it then so vital?

MESSENGER. Dead . . . They are this minute dead . . .
> the princess royal with her father—

1125 and through your poisons.

MEDEA. What a pretty word you bring—
> my benefactor, my friend forever!

MESSENGER. [*Recoiling*] What are you saying,
> Madam?
> Are you in your right mind—not unhinged?

1130 A king's home a charnel house—
and you rejoice? . . . Are you not afraid?

MEDEA. I have my ready answer too,
> so don't be hasty, friend,
but tell me how they perished.
An appalling death

1135 would give me double joy.

MESSENGER. [*Supports himself against a pillar as he begins to recollect an agonizing experience*]
> We were so pleased to see your brace of boys
come hand in hand to the bride's house with their
father:
for your ordeal had upset us servants greatly.
> The rumor went racing through the house
that all was well again between your husband

1140 and yourself.
> Some of us kissed the children's hands,
kissed their golden tops;
and I in my enthusiasm even followed them
to the women's wing.
> There, the mistress—
I mean the one we have to honor now—
had eyes so taken up with Jason

1145 she did not even see at first
the two boys hand in hand.
> But when she did,
a veil of scorn dropped over her eyes,
she turned her lovely face away,
bristling at your sons' intrusion.
> Your husband then began to woo her

1150 from her petulance and girlish tantrums, saying:
> "You must not hate your friends.
> Stop being hurt and turn your head around.
> Consider yours your husband's loved ones.
> Come, won't you take their presents
and beseech your father

1155 to let these boys off banishment—just for me?"

[*Pauses and sits down hopelessly on a step*]

When she saw how exquisite the presents were,
far from holding out on him,
there was nothing she withheld:
but gave in completely to her groom.
> And hardly had your husband and your children
left the house
when she took the gorgeous robe and put it on,
and placed the golden circlet on her curls,   1160
arranging the ringlets in the brightness of a mirror
and smiling at her own dead image there.
> Then rising from her stool
she minced off through the halls
on dainty milk white toes,
wildly pleased with what she had received,   1165
over and over again
running her eyes down the clear sweep to her
heels.
> But all at once
a hideous spectacle took place.
> Her color changed. She tottered back;
shuddered in every limb; was able just in time
to fall into a chair and not upon the floor.   1170
> An old woman there, attending her
thinking that perhaps the fierce possession of
Pan°
or some other power was on her,
broke into a chant of wonder,
then saw the white froth spuming at her lips,
her eyeballs bulging all askew,
her skin quite leached of blood,   1175
and changed her chanting to a yelp:
a wail of horror.
> A maid went dashing to the palace for her father,
another went to tell the fresh-wed groom
what was happening to his bride.
> The whole house rang with footsteps running.   1180
> It took no longer than a sprinter takes
to go the hundred yards,
before the poor girl lay unconscious with her eyelids shut.
> Then suddenly she rallied
and gave a curdling shriek,
fighting off a double nightmare.   1185

[*He pauses, gulps, takes a deep breath*]

The golden diadem that clasped her head
burst into a voracious and uncanny flow of fire,
while the robe of gossamer your children gave her

1171**Pan** the god of wild nature, who was supposed to be the cause of seizures and sudden madness. Hence, "panic."

began to eat her tender flesh away.
    Streaming with flame,
1190   she leapt up from her chair and fled,
tossing her mane of hair from side to side,
in a frantic bid to shake the diadem off.
    But its grip was adamant
and the golden circlet held.
    The more she tossed,
the more the fire flowed,
1195   till, overwhelmed with pain,
she sank down to the floor—
unrecognizable to all except her father—
her calm regard grotesquely twisted,
her sweet symmetry all shattered;
and from the crown of her head in molten clots
fire and blood dripped down together.
1200   The flesh curdled off her bones
like the teardrops congealing out of pines,
inexplicably dissolved by those ravening venoms.
    It was curious and horrible to see.
No one dared to touch her body:
the warning was too obvious.
    But her father, unawares, poor man,
1205   rushed headlong through the room,
flung himself lamenting on the body,
hugged and kissed it, sobbing out:
    "My stricken darling,
what evil power has done this to you,
who has made you dead
and left me, like some ancient tombstone,
    derelict?
1210   O gods! . . . let me die with you, my daughter."
    But . . . but when he stopped . . .
from these outpourings—
these melancholy sobs . . .
and tried to lift his aged carcass up,
he found himself stuck fast—
clamped to the flimsy robe
like ivy to a laurel bole.
    A ghastly wrestling match ensued.
1215   He would try to raise a knee,
she would drag him back;
and when he took to force,
his own decrepit flesh
pulled off from the bone.
    At last, exhausted,
pathetically unable
to lift himself above the shambles,
he gave his spirit up.
1220   There they lie, corpse by corpse,
father and young daughter—
fit objects for our tears.

[*He rises, swaying*]

To you, Medea . . . from me . . .
there are no words to say.
    Retribution? You yourself will know
the best escape . . .
though in my esteem—and not just for today—
the whole of life is shadow,   1225
and I would even say:
the people who know best or seem to know,
the subtlest professors,
are the very ones who pay the dearest price.

[*Flinging his cloak about him*]

    A happy human being? Ha, there's no such
    thing . . .
more prosperity, more success in one maybe:
but happier? . . . It does not make one happy.   1230

[*Exit Messenger*]

LEADER. Justice personified this day
has brought on Jason's head
    —oh, we have seen it!—
the richest retribution.
    But it is you we weep for,
poor blighted child of Creon,
walking through the gates of death
because you married Jason.   1235
MEDEA. [*In clear, cold tones*]
Now, friends, to complete this mission with dispatch:
to slay my children and hurry from this land.
    I must not dawdle and betray my sons
to much more savage hands than mine to kill.
    There's no way out. They have to die.   1240
    And since they must,
let me be the one to cut them down:
the very one who gave them life!

[*She begins her walk to the door, almost like a sleepwalker, talking to herself*]

    Yes, heart, be steel.
    Why vacillate?
    The act is . . .
necessary as it is cruel and hard.
    Come, reluctant hand,
grip the sword—grip it, Medea:
cross your borderline of lifelong pain.   1245
    Away this flinching!
    Away this longing:
consign to oblivion the love you had for them—
the children of your flesh.
    Even when you kill them they are dear . . .
oh, my sons! . . . I am in despair, despair.   1250

[*Medea, with the Nurse, mutely following in tears, passes into the house*]

SIXTH CHORAL ODE

[*The Chorus of women pray desperately for something to stop the imminent murder*]

STROPHE

Come Earth, come sunshafts of the Sun,
Behold this woman and withhold her
From her laying scarlet fingers
On the children of her blood.

1255 Gold of your gold are they begotten:
Heinous is to spill this holy
Ichor in the blood of mortals.
Curb her, stop her, godborn Light, oh,
Keep this house from murder! Keep it

1260 Never haunted by the Furies.°

ANTISTROPHE

Were those birth pangs wasted bearing:
Children's birth pangs wasted birth?
You, my lady, after sailing
Safe between the dark blue clashing

1265 Gorges, will you hug a rankling
Hatred to your heart, a loathsome
Rage for murder and revenge?
Those that spill the blood of family
Stain themselves with heaven's anger,

1270 Haunt their homes with doom forever.

SEVENTH EPISODE OR DENOUEMENT

[*Cries are heard from inside the house*]

FIRST WOMAN. A shout—listen—a shout from the boys.
FIRST BOY. O-h! What can we do? . . .
   Our mother is on us!
SECOND BOY. Brother, brother! . . . We're going to be
   killed.
SECOND WOMAN. That murderous relentless woman!
THIRD WOMAN. Shall we break in, snatch them from
1275   death?
FIRST BOY. Yes, by heaven . . . save us . . . help!
SECOND BOY. We're trapped, cornered . . . now . . . by
   her sword.

[*As the Chorus beat on the barred doors, there are moans and cries, and presently a trickle of blood oozes from under the doors. The women watch it, fascinated*]

CHORUS. Woman of stone, heart of iron,
1280   Disconsolate woman, ready to kill
   The seed of your hands with the hand that tilled.
   One other only, one have I known
   Murderously handle the fruit of her womb:

Ino the maniac, god-driven one,
Whom Zeus's wife drove out to roam—°
Desperate woman goaded to slaughter   1285
The sons of her flesh, clean against nature.
She pitched from the precipice into the sea,
Fell where her foot fell into the ocean,
Dashing two infants to death with her own.   1290
What ghastlier thing is left to be known?
Women, O women, in love and in pangs,
What ruin you've brought on us human beings!

[*Jason, breathless, his face twisted with hatred, bursts in with a troop of servants*]

JASON. You women standing here outside this house,
   is that she-ravager, Medea, still at home,   1295
   or has she fled?

[*He waits for a reply, but the women cower before the door*]

   Deep down in the earth let that woman hide,
   or wing into the highest alcoves of the sky,
   before she ever saves herself from justice by this
      royal house.
   Does she think that she can kill
   a princess and a country's king
   and vanish with impunity?   1300

[*He strides toward the door*]

   But it is my sons, not her, I fear for.
   She, she shall be repaid
   through her victims.
   I have come to save my children's lives
   from some enormous retribution by the family of
      the dead
   for those enormities their mother did.   1305
LEADER. Jason, you poor optimistic man,
   you still don't know the evils that have come—
   or you would not say what you have said.
JASON. What? Does she mean to kill me too?
LEADER. Your sons are dead: murdered by their
   mother.
JASON. [*Reeling*] What—did—you—say?
   Oh, woman—my own wife—you kill me too.   1310
LEADER. [*As the women form an avenue to the door, and
   Jason sees for the first time the blood beginning to
   trickle down the steps*]
   Yes. Your children.
   You cannot think of them as being alive.

1260**Furies** ministers of the vengeance of the gods, employed in punishing the guilty on earth as well as in the underworld

1284**Ino the maniac . . . out to roam** Ino, a daughter of Cadmus and Harmonia, tried to destroy her two stepchildren so that her own two children might ascend the throne. Pursued, in turn, by their father, her husband Athamas, she leapt into the sea with her two boys. This is Euripides' version.

JASON. [*Limply*]
   Where did she kill them . . . here . . . outside,
   or was it in the house?
LEADER. Force these doors
   and you will see your children in their blood.
JASON. [*Drawing his sword in a frenzy*] Servants, on
     the double,
   break these bolts,
1315   force the hinges: let me see
   the double homicide,
   the murdered dead . . . and the murderess to die.

[*There is a rumbling sound, and out of a cloud above the
house Medea appears in a chariot drawn by dragons. By
her side are the dead bodies of the two Boys*]

MEDEA. [*In triumphant disdain*]
   Why this battering, this beating at the doors?
   Are you looking for their bodies—
   and for me who did this thing?
   Save yourself the trouble.
1320   If there's anything you want, then ask.
   But me you shall not lay a hand upon.
   This chariot, the Sun
   —my father's father—gave me
   to keep me safe against my enemies.
JASON. [*Hissing with revulsion*]
   You miserable, mephitic woman!
   Beyond abhorrence—
   by me, the gods, the rest of men—
1325   you could put your own sons to the sword,
   the sons you bore,
   and kill me too with childlessness . . .
   Yet still look upon the sun, see the earth . . .
   Be damned! . . .
   At last I understand
   what I never understood before,
   when I took you from your foreign home to live
1330   in Greece,
   the sheer wickedness of you,
   the treachery to your father and the land that
     reared you.
   You are possessed
   and the gods have unleashed the fiend in you on *me*,
   on your own brother, too, cut down in his home
1335   before you came aboard the sweet ship *Argo's* hull.
   Your work already had begun.
   You married me, bore my sons,
   and murdered them through jealousy of love.
   No woman in the whole of Hellas
1340   would have dared so much;
   yet you were the one I married,

not a girl from Greece.
   Oh, I married a tigress,
not a woman, not a wife,
and yoked myself to a hater and destroyer:
to a viciousness more fierce than any Tuscan Scylla.°

[*Turning away from the door in a gesture of helplessness*]

   But why go on?
A million accusations would not make you wince:
you are shameless through and through . . .   1345
you—you bloodstained ogress, infanticide . . .
   Hell take you!
   Leave me to mourn my destiny of pain:
my fresh young wedding without joy,
my sons begot and reared and lost—
never to be seen alive again.   1350
MEDEA. [*With acid imperiousness from the chariot*]
   How tediously
I could rebut you point by point!
   Zeus the Father knows
exactly what you got from me
and how you then behaved.
   I would not let you or your royal princess
set our wedded life aside,
make me cheap,
so that you could live in bliss;   1355
or let that match-arranger, Creon,
dismiss me from the land without a fight.
   So, call me a tigress if you like,
or a Scylla haunting the Tyrrhenian shore,
I have done what I ought:
broken your own heart to the core.   1360
JASON. [*Wheeling round to face her*]
   You are in agony too:
   you share my broken life.
MEDEA. It is worth the suffering
     since *you* cannot scoff.
JASON. Poor children, what a monster
     fate gave you for a mother!
MEDEA. Poor sons, what a disaster
     your selfish father was!
JASON. It was not *his* right hand
     that killed and struck them down.   1365
MEDEA. No, it was his pride:
     the lust of his new love.
JASON. You think it right to murder
     just for a thwarted bed.
MEDEA. And do you think that a thwarted bed
     is trifling to a woman?
JASON. A modest woman, yes:
     to you the world's worst crime.

1316Euripides was a past master at theatrical effects. He loved *ex
machina* contrivances.

1343**Tuscan Scylla** a monster that inhabited the straits between
Italy and Sicily and snatched sailors off passing ships and devoured
them

MEDEA. [*Pointing at the dead children*]
    See, they are no more:
1370   I can hurt you too.
JASON. They'll live, I think,
    in your tormented brain.
MEDEA. The gods know who began
    this whole calamity.
JASON. Yes, the gods know well
    your pernicious heart.
MEDEA. Hate then: I spurn
    the wormwood from your lips.
JASON. As I do yours; so let us
1375   be rid of one another.
MEDEA. Yes, but on what terms?
    That's also what *I* want.
JASON. Let me have the boys—
    to mourn and bury them.
MEDEA. Never!
    My own hands shall bury them, they shall be carried
    to the sanctuary of Hera on the Cape,
1380   where no enemy shall ever do them harm
    or violate their sepulchre.
        Here in Corinth, the land of Sisyphus,
    I shall inaugurate a solemn festival°
    with rites in perpetuity
    to exorcise this murder.
        I myself shall go to Athens, land of Erechtheus,
1385   to live with Aegeus, Pandion's son . . .
    you to a paltry death that fits you well:
    your skull smashed by a fragment of the *Argo's*
        hull:
    ironic ending to the saga of your love for me.

THE EXODOS

[*As the Chorus begin to form for the exodos march, the meter changes to anapests and dactyls. Jason strides into the middle of the arena*]

JASON. Murder is punished, and you'll be destroyed
1390   by the avenging phantoms of your children.

MEDEA. What power or divine one is ready to hear
    you:
    perjurer, liar, treacherous guest?
JASON. Vile, vile, murderess of little ones!
MEDEA. Go—go and bury your bride.
JASON. Broken I go: bereft of two sons.   1395
MEDEA. You bemoan too soon: wait till you're old.
JASON. Dearest children!
MEDEA.   Dear to their mother.
JASON. And so she slew them.
MEDEA.   To get at your heart.
JASON. You did! You did! How I long to press
    my little children's lips to mine!   1400
MEDEA. Now you are longing, now you call;
    you utterly turned from them before.
JASON. For the love of the gods, allow me this:
    to stroke my children's tender skin.
MEDEA. No, you shall not: you waste your words.
JASON. [*Flinging out his arms*] Zeus, do you hear
    how I'm at bay,   1405
    Dismissed by this ogress, odious woman,
    Tigress besmirched with the blood of her young?
    So I mourn and call on the gods while I may,
    On the powers to witness how you have slain   1410
    My children, and now prevent my hands
    From touching them, dead, interring their clay.
    I'd rather they'd never been born to me
    Than have lived to see you destroy them this day.

[*Before the end of these words, Medea, with a cold vindictive smile, has moved off in the chariot. Jason staggers out of the arena*]

ENVOI

CHORUS.
    Wide is the range of Zeus on Olympus.   1415
    Wide the surprise which the gods can bring:
    What was expected is never perfected,
    What was not, finds a way opened up . . .
        So ended this terrible thing.

1382**solemn festival** similar ceremonies were still performed at Corinth in Euripides' time

LYSISTRATA

ARISTOPHANES

ARISTOPHANES (C. 440–C. 385 B.C.E.)

Though Epicharmus and Cratinus preceded him in writing comic plays, it is Aristophanes who is generally recognized as the father of comedy in the Western world. Writing when Athens was in decline because of the Peloponnesian War (431–404 B.C.E.), economic turbulence, moral decay, and mounting public cynicism, Aristophanes used the theater to attack satirically those institutions he felt contributed to the demise of his beloved city. The son of a wealthy man, Aristophanes was a knight, a member of the prosperous, conservative class. Indeed, one of the great ironies of *Lysistrata* is that this essentially conservative man mercilessly lampoons Athens's male leadership and makes women the redeemers of the city.

Aristophanes wrote some 40 plays, most of which are classified as Old Comedy (see Spotlight box, Greek Old Comedy, following the play). The 11 extant works demonstrate the range of social, political, and even religious issues that concerned Aristophanes and his peers. When a Mediterranean ruler asked Plato about life in Athens, he suggested that the king read the plays of Aristophanes. In his plays Aristophanes satirized the Athenian educational system (*The Clouds* and the lost *Banqueters*), political structures and corruption (*The Birds* and *The Knights*), war (*Lysistrata, Peace,* and *The Acharnians*), and women's issues (*Thesmophoriazusae* [*Ladies Day*] and *Ecclesiazusae* [*The Congress of Women*]). Aristophanes even burlesqued Greek drama itself; in *The Frogs,* he launched a devastating attack on Euripides, whom he considered an inferior, degenerate playwright. *The Frogs* is not only a hilarious and instructive play, it is among the very first pieces of dramatic criticism.

Though he is a legitimate master of his art, Aristophanes' plays are not performed as frequently as his reputation merits. Because they are satires, much of their bite has been lost to subsequent ages. Modern directors often insert topical material to make the plays relevant to contemporary audiences, though the antiwar sentiment and bawdry of *Lysistrata* are sufficiently universal to insure the play's relevance. (Not surprisingly, it was enormously popular during the Vietnam War for its "make love, not war" message.) Furthermore, Aristophanes was a supreme practitioner of intricate wordplay, puns, and rhythmic verbal patterns. These translate no better from the classical Greek than the linguistic feats of W. S. Gilbert (of Gilbert and Sullivan fame) or Stephen Sondheim translate out of English. Yet Aristophanes' influence on comic drama cannot be disputed, and he has remained a model for generations of satirists and comic artists. The barbs of such diverse entertainments as *Saturday Night Live, Monty Python,* and the *actos* of Luis Valdez reverberate with the voice of Aristophanes.

LYSISTRATA (C. 411 B.C.E.)

For all its raucous comedy, *Lysistrata* was written out of the despair created by the Greek civil war pitting Athens against Sparta for almost thirty years. The Peloponnesian War devastated Athens, depleting the once-great city-state of its treasures and especially its youth. From the carnage emerged two of the greatest antiwar plays known to the Western world: Euripides' *The Trojan Women* (415 B.C.E.) and *Lysistrata*. Inspired by a massacre perpetrated by the Athenian army on the island of Melos, Euripides' play is a powerful polemic against military brutality. It relies on graphic descriptions of the horrors of war and chilling lamentations such as Hecuba's, who saw her children "fall before the spears of Greece."

Unlike Euripides, Aristophanes does not resort to raw pathos to achieve his ends. Children are not thrown from city walls, death is not seen in the play, nor do his women intone somber dirges. What is remarkable about *Lysistrata* is its conspicuous lack of both carnage and lamentations calculated to shock audiences into a revulsion for war. True, Lysistrata (whose name means "disband the army") passionately debates the Athenian Commissioner in the play's *agon*; her eloquent argument that women are the ultimate victims of war is as moving as it is cogent:

> And now, when we ought to enjoy ourselves,
>> making much of our prime and our beauty,
> We are sleeping alone because all the men
>> are away on their soldierly duty.
> But never mind us—when young girls grow old
>> in their bedrooms with no men to share them.

Rather, Aristophanes achieves his ends by subverting the natural order to show the absurdity of a war that had been raging for twenty years when he wrote the play. Comedy commonly relies on an inversion of the norm to induce laughter. Men dress as women and vice versa, fools pretend to be kings, kings become fools, the holy man turns lecherous, the libertine plays the preacher. Many festive celebrations around the world, such as the Carnival of Trinidad, employ this principle of inversion. The laughter it induces signifies the incongruity between the way things are and the way we expect them to be.

In *Lysistrata* the women rule, first by refusing to have sex with their men until the war has ceased, second by seizing the Acropolis and the state treasury to halt the war. In an age of strong leaders such as Margaret Thatcher and Indira Gandhi, the presence of women in power is no longer a source of amusement or curiosity. But to a virtually all male audience at the Theater of Dionysus in 411 B.C.E., the idea of women controlling the country epitomized the ludicrous. Aristophanes' audience no doubt applauded the Commissioner's taunt to Lysistrata in the *agon*: "But never must we let ourselves be overcome by women." Furthermore, he peoples his stage with thoroughly inept males, none more so than the Chorus of Old Men who are pummeled with fruit and vegetables by the women atop the Acropolis. To an Athenian audience, brought up with the memory of Pericles (460–430 B.C.E.), such spectacles were as discomforting as they were hilarious. But these were desperate times and Aristophanes used extreme means to underscore the ultimate Athenian absurdity, the war that was draining the once great polis of its lifeblood. Aristophanes' triumph was that his play not only did not offend his audience, but was actually revived in subsequent festivals, a rare honor. Aristophanes' failure, however, was that the war raged on for seven more years and ceased only when Athens was defeated.

Although Aristophanes' plays are characterized by extraordinary flights of fancy, *Lysistrata* stands unique among his works in that it is the most realistic. Here there is no extraordinary chorus of clouds, wasps, or frogs. No dung beetles descend from the heavens, and Dionysus does not sail through the nether regions in a cosmic boat. Here the two choruses are commoners, old men and women, with a vested interest in human problems. The reactions of the characters are grounded in human psychology. Kalonike's reservation about committing to Lysistrata's "happy idea" ("Anything else you like . . . rather than the prick. Because there's nothing like it") is as honest as it is funny. The woman who tries to escape the female camp by hiding a cooking pot under her dress to feign pregnancy provokes laughter because we recognize her frailty too well. Cinesias (whose name means "agitation") is teased by his wife, Myrrhina ("sweet smelling"), in one of the funniest scenes in dramatic literature, yet the comedy is grounded in elemental human needs. The Spartan and Athenian ambassadors renew their hostilities over the anatomy of the goddess Reconciliation, a grim reminder that we too quickly forget the lessons of war. However hilarious the situations in *Lysistrata*, they are rooted in the reality of human folly.

Though *Lysistrata* is a political and social comedy, it nonetheless retains its religious roots. The names of various gods (including Dionysus himself) are invoked throughout the proceedings as the mortal combatants, much like the Thebans in *Oedipus the King*, seek relief from their plague. Peace breaks out only when the goddess Reconciliation is brought forth, and even she precipitates another conflict. These bits of theology are by-products of a civilization whose belief in the pantheon was diminishing. *Lysistrata* best manifests its spiritual roots in its depiction of the triumph of the life force (as represented by the women's instinct for harmony) over death (the men's obsession with war). The play is a descendant of earlier fertility rites, as the ubiquitous phalluses remind us. The triumphant *komos* in which the men and women unite in dance is a celebratory rite. Onstage, the long winter of the war is over, giving way to the hope of the springtime dance. Alas, for Athens and Aristophanes it was only a theatrical illusion of a more perfect world.

The women of Athens and Sparta plot to halt the war in this contemporary production by the British Arts Council of Aristophanes' comedy.

LYSISTRATA

ARISTOPHANES

Translated by Donald Sutherland

CHARACTERS
LYSISTRATA ⎫
KALONIKE   ⎬ *Athenian women*
MYRRHINA   ⎭
LAMPITO, *a Spartan woman*
CHORUS OF OLD MEN
CHORUS OF WOMEN
ATHENIAN COMMISSIONER
OLD MARKET-WOMEN
CINESIAS, *an Athenian, husband of Myrrhina*
SPARTAN HERALD
SPARTAN AMBASSADORS
ATHENIAN AMBASSADORS

A street in Athens before daylight.

LYSISTRATA.
　　If anyone had asked them to a festival
　　of Aphrodite or of Bacchus or of Pan,
　　you couldn't get through Athens for the tambourines
　　but now there's not one solitary woman here.
　　Except my next-door neighbor. Here she's coming
　　　　out.
　　Hello, Kalonike.
KALONIKE.
　　　　　　　　Hello, Lysistrata.
　　What are you so upset about? Don't scowl so, dear.   5

You're less attractive when you knot your brows and
    glare.
LYSISTRATA.
    I know, Kalonike, but I am smoldering
10   with indignation at the way we women act.
    Men think we are so gifted for all sorts of crime
    that we will stop at nothing—
KALONIKE.
                        Well, we are, by Zeus!
LYSISTRATA.
    —but when it comes to an appointment here with me
    to plot and plan for something really serious
    they lie in bed and do not come.
KALONIKE.
15   They'll come, my dear.
    You know what trouble women have in going out:
    one of us will be wrapped up in her husband still,
    another waking up the maid, or with a child
    to put to sleep, or give its bath, or feed its pap.
LYSISTRATA.
    But they had other more important things to do than
20   those.
KALONIKE.
    What ever is it, dear Lysistrata?
    What have you called us women all together for?
    How much of a thing is it?
LYSISTRATA.
                  Very big.
KALONIKE.
                   And thick?
LYSISTRATA.
    Oh very thick indeed.
KALONIKE.
                Then *how* can we be late?
LYSISTRATA.
25   That's not the way it is. Or we would all be here.
    But it is something I have figured out myself
    and turned and tossed upon for many a sleepless night.
KALONIKE.
    It must be something slick you've turned and tossed
     upon!
LYSISTRATA.
    So slick that the survival of all Greece depends upon the
     women.
KALONIKE.
          On the women? In that case
30   poor Greece has next to nothing to depend upon.
LYSISTRATA.
    Since now it's we who must decide affairs of state:
    either there is to be no Spartan left alive—
KALONIKE.
    A very good thing too, if none were left, by Zeus!
LYSISTRATA.
    —and every living soul in Thebes to be destroyed—

KALONIKE.
    Except the eels! Spare the delicious eels of Thebes!   35
LYSISTRATA.
    —and as for Athens—I can't bring myself to say
    the like of that for us. But just think what I mean!
    Yet if the women meet here as I told them to
    from Sparta, Thebes, and all of their allies,
    and we of Athens, all together we'll save Greece.   40
KALONIKE.
    What reasonable thing could women ever do,
    or glorious, we who sit around all prettied up
    in flowers and scandalous saffron-yellow gowns,
    groomed and draped to the ground in oriental stuffs
    and fancy pumps?
LYSISTRATA.
               And those are just the very things   45
    I count upon to save us—wicked saffron gowns,
    perfumes and pumps and rouge and sheer transparent
     frocks.
KALONIKE.
    But what use can they be?
LYSISTRATA.
              So no man in our time
    will raise a spear against another man again—
KALONIKE.
    I'll get a dress dyed saffron-yellow, come what may!   50
LYSISTRATA.
    —nor touch a shield—
KALONIKE.
              I'll slip into the sheerest gown!
LYSISTRATA.
    —nor so much as a dagger—
KALONIKE.
                I'll buy a pair of pumps!
LYSISTRATA.
    So don't you think the women should be here by now?
KALONIKE.
    I don't. They should have *flown* and got here long
     ago.
LYSISTRATA.
    You'll see, my dear. They will, like good Athenians,   55
    do everything too late. But from the coastal towns
    no woman is here either, nor from Salamis.
KALONIKE.
    I'm certain those from Salamis have crossed the strait:
    they're always straddling *something* at this time of night.
LYSISTRATA.
    Not even those I was expecting would be first   60
    to get here, from Acharnae, from so close to town,
    not even they are here.
KALONIKE.
             But one of them, I know,
    is under way, and three sheets to the wind, by now.
    But look—some women are approaching over there.

LYSISTRATA.
And over here are some, coming this way—
KALONIKE.

65   Phew! Phew!
Where are they from?
LYSISTRATA.
                              Down by the marshes.
KALONIKE.
                                                      Yes, by Zeus!
It smells as if the bottoms had been all churned up!

[*Enter Myrrhina, and others.*]

MYRRHINA.
Hello Lysistrata. Are we a little late?
What's that? Why don't you speak?
LYSISTRATA.
                                        I don't think much of you,
70   Myrrhina, coming to this business only now.
MYRRHINA.
Well, I could hardly find my girdle in the dark.
If it's so urgent, tell us what it is. We're here.
KALONIKE.
Oh no. Let's wait for just a little while until
the delegates from Sparta and from Thebes arrive.
LYSISTRATA.
You show much better judgment.

[*Enter Lampito, and others.*]

75   Here comes Lampito!
LYSISTRATA.
Well, darling Lampito! My dearest Spartan friend!
How very sweet, how beautiful you look! That fresh
complexion! How magnificent your figure is!
Enough to crush a bull!
LAMPITO.
                              Ah shorely think Ah could.
80   Ah take mah exercise. Ah jump and thump mah butt.
KALONIKE.
And really, what a handsome set of tits you have!
LAMPITO.
You feel me ovah lahk a cow fo sacrafahce!
LYSISTRATA.
And this other young thing—where ever is *she* from?
LAMPITO.
She's prominent, Ah sweah, in Thebes—a delegate
ample enough.
LYSISTRATA.
85   By Zeus, she represents Thebes well,
having so trim a ploughland.
KALONIKE.
                              Yes, by Zeus, she does!
There's not a weed of all her field she hasn't plucked.
LYSISTRATA.
And who's the other girl?

LAMPITO.
                              Theah's nothing small, Ah sweah,
or tahght about her folks in Corinth.
KALONIKE.
                                        No, by Zeus!—
to judge by this side of her, nothing small or tight.   90
LAMPITO.
But who has called togethah such a regiment
of all us women?
LYSISTRATA.
                    Here I am. I did.
LAMPITO.
                                        Speak up,
just tell us what you want.
KALONIKE.
                              Oh yes, by Zeus, my dear,
do let us know what the important business is!
LYSISTRATA.
Let me explain it, then. And yet . . . before I do . . .   95
I have one little question
KALONIKE.
                              Anything you like.
LYSISTRATA.
Don't you all miss the fathers of your little ones,
your husbands who have gone away to war? I'm sure
you all have husbands in the armies far from home.
KALONIKE.
Mine's been away five months in Thrace—a
        general's guard,   100
posted to see his general does not desert.
MYRRHINA.
And mine has been away in Pylos seven whole months.
LAMPITO.
And mahn, though he does get back home on leave
        sometahms,
no soonah has he come than he is gone again.
LYSISTRATA.
No lovers either. Not a sign of one is left.   105
For since our eastern allies have deserted us
they haven't sent a single six-inch substitute
to serve as leatherware replacement for our men.
Would you be willing, then, if I thought out a scheme
to join with me to end the war?
KALONIKE.
                                        Indeed I would,   110
even if I had to pawn this very wrap-around
and drink up all the money in one day, I would!
MYRRHINA.
And so would I, even if I had to see myself
split like a flounder, and give half of me away!
LAMPITO.
And so would Ah! Ah'd climb up Mount Taygetos   115
if Ah just had a chance of seeing peace from theah!
LYSISTRATA.
Then I will tell you. I may now divulge my plan.

Women of Greece!—if we intend to force the men
to make a peace, we must abstain . . .
KALONIKE.

From what! Speak out!
LYSISTRATA.
But will you do it?
KALONIKE.

120 We will, though death should be the
price!
LYSISTRATA.
Well then, we must abstain utterly from the prick.
Why do you turn your backs? Where are you off to now?
And you—why pout and make such faces, shake
your heads?
125 Why has your color changed? Why do you shed
those tears?
Will you do it or will you not? Why hesitate?
KALONIKE.
I will not do it. Never. Let the war go on!
MYRRHINA.
Neither will I. By Zeus, no! Let the war go on!
LYSISTRATA.
How can you say so, Madam Flounder, when just now
130 you were declaiming you would split yourself in half?
KALONIKE.
Anything else you like, anything! If I must
I'll gladly walk through fire. That, rather than the prick!
Because there's nothing like it, dear Lysistrata.
LYSISTRATA.
How about you?
MYRRHINA.

I too would gladly walk through fire.
LYSISTRATA.
135 Oh the complete depravity of our whole sex!
It is no wonder tragedies are made of us,
we have such unrelenting unity of mind!
But you, my friend from Sparta, dear, if you alone
stand by me, only you, we still might save the cause.
Vote on my side!
LAMPITO.
140 They'ah hahd conditions, mahty hahd,
to sleep without so much as the fo'skin of one . . .
but all the same . . . well . . . yes. We need peace
just as bad.
LYSISTRATA.
Oh dearest friend!—the one real woman of them all!
KALONIKE.
145 And if we really should abstain from what you say—
which Heaven forbid!—do you suppose on that account
that peace might come to be?
LYSISTRATA.

I'm absolutely sure.
If we should sit around, rouged and with skins
well creamed,
with nothing on but a transparent negligée,

and come up to them with our deltas plucked
quite smooth,
and, once our men get stiff and want to come to grips,   150
we do not yield to them at all but just hold off,
they'll make a truce in no time. There's no doubt of that.
LAMPITO.
We say in Spahta that when Menelaos saw
Helen's ba'e apples he just tossed away his swo'd.
KALONIKE.
And what, please, if our husbands just toss us away?   155
LYSISTRATA.
Well, you have heard the good old saying: Know
Thyself.
KALONIKE.
It isn't worth the candle. I hate cheap substitutes.
But what if they should seize and drag us by brute force
into the bedroom?
LYSISTRATA.

Hang onto the doors!
KALONIKE.

And if—
they beat us?   160
LYSISTRATA.
Then you must give in, but nastily,
and do it badly. There's no fun in it by force.
And then, just keep them straining. They will give it up
in no time—don't you worry. For never will a man
enjoy himself unless the woman coincides.   165
KALONIKE.
If both of you are for this plan, then so are we.
LAMPITO.
And we of Spahta shall pe'suade ouah men to keep
the peace sinceahly and with honah in all ways,
but how could anyone pe'suade the vulgah mob
of Athens not to deviate from discipline?   170
LYSISTRATA.
Don't worry, we'll persuade our men. They'll keep
the peace.
LAMPITO.
They won't, so long as they have battleships afloat
and endless money sto'ed up in the Pahthenon.
LYSISTRATA.
But that too has been carefully provided for:
we shall take over the Acropolis today.   175
The oldest women have their orders to do that:
while we meet here, they go as if to sacrifice
up there, but really seizing the Acropolis.
LAMPITO.
All should go well. What you say theah is very smaht.
LYSISTRATA.
In that case, Lampito, what are we waiting for?   180
Let's take an oath, to bind us indissolubly.
LAMPITO.
Well, just you show us what the oath is. Then
we'll sweah.

LYSISTRATA.
You're right. Where is that lady cop?

[*To the armed Lady Cop looking around for a Lady Cop.*]

What do you think
185   you're looking for? Put down your shield in front of us,
there, on its back, and someone get some scraps of gut.
KALONIKE.
Lysistrata, what in the world do you intend
to make us take an oath on?
LYSISTRATA.
                          What? Why, on a shield,
just as they tell me some insurgents in a play
by Aeschylus once did, with a sheep's blood and guts.
KALONIKE.
190   Oh, *don't*, Lysistrata, don't swear upon a *shield*,
not if the oath has anything to do with peace!
LYSISTRATA.
Well then, what *will* we swear on? Maybe we
   should get
a white horse somewhere, like the Amazons, and cut
some bits of gut from it.
KALONIKE.
                     Where would we get a horse?
LYSISTRATA.
195   But what kind of an oath *is* suitable for us?
KALONIKE.
By Zeus, I'll tell you if you like. First we put down
a big black drinking-cup, face up, and then we let
the neck of a good jug of wine bleed into it,
and take a solemn oath to—add no water in.
LAMPITO.
200   Bah Zeus, Ah jest can't tell you how Ah lahk that oath!
LYSISTRATA.
Someone go get a cup and winejug from inside.

[*Kalonike goes and is back in a flash.*]

KALONIKE.
My dears, my dearest dears—how's *this* for pottery?
You feel good right away, just laying hold of it.
LYSISTRATA.
Well, set it down, and lay your right hand on this pig.
205   O goddess of Persuasion, and O Loving-cup,
accept this victim's blood! Be gracious unto us.
KALONIKE.
It's not anemic, and flows clear. Those are good signs.
LAMPITO.
What an aroma, too! Bah Castah it *is* sweet!
KALONIKE.
My dears, if you don't mind—I'll be the first to swear.
LYSISTRATA.
210   By Aphrodite, no! If you had drawn first place
by lot—but now let all lay hands upon the cup.
Yes, Lampito—and now, let one of you repeat

for all of you what I shall say. You will be sworn
by every word she says, and bound to keep this oath:
No lover and no husband and no man on earth—   215
KALONIKE.
No lover and no husband and no man on earth—
LYSISTRATA.
shall e'er approach me with his penis up. Repeat.
KALONIKE.
shall e'er approach me with his penis up. Oh dear,
my knees are buckling under me, Lysistrata!
LYSISTRATA.
and I shall lead an unlaid life alone at home,   220
KALONIKE.
and I shall lead an unlaid life alone at home,
LYSISTRATA.
wearing a saffron gown and groomed and beautified
KALONIKE.
wearing a saffron gown and groomed and beautified
LYSISTRATA.
so that my husband will be all on fire for me
KALONIKE.
so that my husband will be all on fire for me   225
LYSISTRATA.
but I will never willingly give in to him
KALONIKE.
but I will never willingly give in to him
LYSISTRATA.
and if he tries to force me to against my will
KALONIKE.
and if he tries to force me to against my will
LYSISTRATA.
I'll do it badly and not wiggle in response   230
KALONIKE.
I'll do it badly and not wiggle in response
LYSISTRATA.
nor toward the ceiling will I lift my Persian pumps
KALONIKE.
nor toward the ceiling will I lift my Persian pumps
LYSISTRATA.
nor crouch down as the lions on cheese-graters do
KALONIKE.
nor crouch down as the lions on cheese-graters do   235
LYSISTRATA.
and if I keep my promise, may I drink of this—
KALONIKE.
and if I keep my promise, may I drink of this—
LYSISTRATA.
but if I break it, then may water fill the cup!
KALONIKE.
but if I break it, then may water fill the cup!
LYSISTRATA.
Do you all swear to this with her?
ALL.
                          We do, by Zeus!   240

LYSISTRATA.
I'll consecrate our oath now.
KALONIKE.
Share alike, my dear,
so we'll be friendly to each other from the start.
LAMPITO.
What was that screaming?
LYSISTRATA.
That's what I was telling you:
the women have already seized the Parthenon
245 and the Acropolis. But now, dear Lampito,
return to Sparta and set things in order there—
but leave these friends of yours as hostages with us—
And let *us* join the others in the citadel
and help them bar the gates.
KALONIKE.
But don't you think the men
250 will rally to the rescue of the citadel,
attacking us at once?
LYSISTRATA.
They don't worry me much:
they'll never bring against us threats or fire enough
to force open the gates, except upon our terms.
KALONIKE.
Never by Aphrodite! Or we'd lose our name
255 for being battle-axes and unbearable!

[*Exeunt. The scene changes to the Propylaea of the Acropolis. A Chorus of very old men struggles slowly in, carrying logs and firepots.*]

ONE OLD MAN.
Lead on! O Drakës, step by step, although your
shoulder's aching
and under this green olive log's great weight
your back be breaking!
ANOTHER.
Eh, life is long but always has
more surprises for us!
Now who'd have thought we'd like to hear
this, O Strymodorous?—

260 The wives we fed and looked upon
as helpless liabilities
now dare to occupy the Parthenon
our whole Acropolis, for once they seize
the Propylaea, straightway
265 they lock and bar the gateway.
CHORUS.
Let's rush to the Acropolis with due precipitation
and lay these logs down circlewise, till presently we
turn them
into one mighty pyre to make a general cremation
of all the women up there—eh! with our own hands we'll
burn them,

the leaders and the followers, without discrimination! 270
AN OLD MAN.
They'll never have the laugh on me!
Though I may not look it,
I rescued the Acropolis
when the Spartans took it
about a hundred years ago.
We laid a siege that kept their king
six years unwashed, so when I made him throw 275
his armor off, for all his blustering,
in nothing but his shirt he
looked very very dirty.
CHORUS.
How strictly I besieged the man! These gates were all
invested
with seventeen ranks of armored men all equally
ferocious! 280
Shall women—by Euripides and all the gods detested—
not be restrained—with me on hand—from something
so atrocious?
They shall!—or may our trophies won at Marathon
be bested!
But we must go a long way yet
up that steep and winding road 285
before we reach the fortress where we want to get.
How dare we ever drag this load,
lacking pack-mules, way up there?
I can tell you that my shoulder has caved in
beyond repair!
Yet we must trudge ever higher, 290
ever blowing on the fire,
so its coals will still be glowing when we get
where we are going
Fooh! Fooh!
Whoo! I choke!
What a smoke! 295

Lord Herakles! How fierce it flies
out against me from the pot!
and like a rabid bitch it bites me in the eyes!
It's female fire, or it would not
scratch my poor old eyes like this. 300
Yet undaunted we must onward, up the high
Acropolis
where Athena's temple stands
fallen into hostile hands.
O my comrades! shall we ever have a greater 305
need to save her?
Fooh! Fooh!
Whoo! I choke!
What a smoke!
FIRST OLD MAN.
Well, thank the gods, I see the fire is yet alive
and waking! 310

SECOND OLD MAN.
　Why don't we set our lumber down right here in handy
　　batches,
　then stick a branch of grape-vine in the pot until it
　　catches
THIRD OLD MAN.
　and hurl ourselves against the gate with battering
　　and shaking
FIRST OLD MAN.
　and if the women won't unbar at such an ultimatum
315　we'll set the gate on fire and then the smoke will
　　suffocate 'em.
SECOND OLD MAN.
　Well, let's put down our load. Fooh fooh, what smoke!
　　But blow as needed!
THIRD OLD MAN.
　Your ablest generals *these* days would not carry wood
　　like *we* did.
SECOND OLD MAN.
　At last the lumber ceases grinding my poor back
　　to pieces!
THIRD OLD MAN.
　These are your orders, Colonel Pot: wake up the coals
320　　and bid them
　report here and present to me a torch lit up and flaring.
FIRST OLD MAN.
　O Victory, be with us! If you quell the women's daring
　we'll raise a splendid trophy of how you and we undid
　　them!

[A *Chorus of middle-aged women appears in the offing.*]

A WOMAN.
　I think that I perceive a smoke in which appears a flurry
325　of sparks as of a lighted fire. Women, we'll have to hurry!
CHORUS OF WOMEN.
　　　Oh fleetly fly, oh swiftly flit,
　　　my dears, e'er Kalykë be lit
　　　and with Kritylla swallowed up alive
　　　　in flames which the gales dreadfully drive
330　　　　and deadly old men fiercely inflate!
　　　Yet one thing I'm afraid of: will I not arrive
　　　　too late?
　　　for filling up my water-jug has been no easy
　　　　matter
　　　what with the crowd at the spring in the dusk
　　　　and the clamor and pottery clatter.
　　　　Pushed as I was, jostled by slave-
335　　　　women and sluts marked with a brand
　　　　yet with my jug firmly in hand
　　　　here I have come, hoping to save
　　　　　my burning friends and brave,

　　　　for certain windy, witless, old,
　　　　and wheezy fools, so I was told,
　　　with wood some tons in weight crept up this
340　　　　path,

not having in mind heating a bath
　but uttering threats, vowing they will
consume those nasty women into cinders on grill!
But O Athena! never may I see my friends igniting!
Nay!—let them save all the cities of Greece
　and their　　　　　　　　　　　　　　　　　　　345
　　　people from folly and fighting!
Goddess whose crest flashes with gold,
　they were so bold taking your shine
　only for this—Goddess who hold
Athens—for *this* noble design,　　　　　　　　350
　braving the flames, calling on you
　　to carry water too!

[*One of the old men urinates noisily.*]

CHORUS OF WOMEN.
　Be still! What was that noise? Aha! Oh, wicked
　　and degraded!
　Would any good religious men have ever done what
　　they did?
CHORUS OF MEN.
　Just look! It's a surprise-attack! Oh, dear, we're being
　　raided　　　　　　　　　　　　　　　　　　355
　by swarms of them below us when we've got a swarm
　　above us!
CHORUS OF WOMEN.
　Why panic at the sight of us? This is not many of us.
　We number tens of thousands but you've hardly seen a
　　fraction.
CHORUS OF MEN.
　O Phaidrias, shall they talk so big and we not take some
　　action?
　Oh, should we not be bashing them and splintering our
　　lumber?　　　　　　　　　　　　　　　　360

[*The old men begin to strip for combat.*]

CHORUS OF WOMEN.
　Let us, too, set our pitchers down, so they will not
　　encumber
　our movements if these gentlemen should care to offer
　　battle.
CHORUS OF MEN.
　Oh someone should have clipped their jaws—twice,
　　thrice, until they rattle—
　(as once the poet put it)—then we wouldn't hear their
　　prating.
CHORUS OF WOMEN.
　Well, here's your chance. Won't someone hit me? Here I
　　stand, just waiting!　　　　　　　　　　　365
　No other bitch will ever grab your balls, the way I'll treat
　　you!
CHORUS OF MEN.
　Shut up—or I will drub you so old age will never reach
　　you!

CHORUS OF WOMEN.
  Won't anyone step and lay one finger on Stratyllis?
CHORUS OF MEN.
  And if we pulverize her with our knuckles, will you
    kill us?
CHORUS OF WOMEN.
  No, only chew your lungs out and your innards and
370   your eyes, sir.
CHORUS OF MEN.
  How clever is Euripides! There is no poet wiser: he
    says indeed that women are the worst of living
    creatures.
CHORUS OF WOMEN.
  Now is the time, Rhodippe: let us raise our brimming
    pitchers.
CHORUS OF MEN.
  Why come up here with water, you, the gods' abomina-
    tion?
CHORUS OF WOMEN.
  And why come here with fire, you tomb? To give
    yourself cremation?
CHORUS OF MEN.
375 To set your friends alight upon a pyre erected for them.
CHORUS OF WOMEN.
  And so we brought our water-jugs. Upon your pyre we'll
    pour them.
CHORUS OF MEN.
  You'll put my fire out?
CHORUS OF WOMEN.
                    Any time! You'll see there's nothing to it.
CHORUS OF MEN.
  I think I'll grill you right away, with just this torch to
    do it!
CHORUS OF WOMEN.
  Have you some dusting-powder? Here's your wedding-
    bath all ready.
CHORUS OF MEN.
  You'll bathe me, garbage that you are?
CHORUS OF WOMEN.
380   Yes, bridegroom, just hold steady!
CHORUS OF MEN.
  Friends, you have heard her insolence—
CHORUS OF WOMEN.
                    I'm free-born, not your slave, sir.
CHORUS OF MEN.
  I'll have this noise of yours restrained—
CHORUS OF WOMEN.
                    Court's out—so be less grave, sir.
CHORUS OF MEN.
  Why don't you set her hair on fire?
CHORUS OF WOMEN.
                    Oh, Water, be of service!
CHORUS OF MEN.
  Oh woe is me!
CHORUS OF WOMEN.
                    Was it too hot?

CHORUS OF MEN.
  Oh, stop! What *is* this? Hot? Oh no!   385
CHORUS OF WOMEN.
  I'm watering you to make you grow.
CHORUS OF MEN.
  I'm withered from this chill I got!
CHORUS OF WOMEN.
  You've got a fire, so warm yourself. You're trembling: are
    you nervous?

[*Enter a* Commissioner, *escorted by four Scythian police-
    men with bows and quivers slung on their backs.*]

COMMISSIONER.
  Has the extravagance of women broken out
  into full fury, with their banging tambourines   390
  and constant wailings for their oriental gods,
  and on the rooftops their Adonis festival,
  which I could hear myself from the Assembly once?
  For while Demostratos—that numbskull—had the floor,
  urging an expedition against Sicily,   395
  his wife was dancing and we heard her crying out
  "Weep for Adonis!"—so the expedition failed
  with such an omen. When the same Demostratos
  was urging that we levy troops from our allies
  his wife was on the roof again, a little drunk: 400
  "Weep for Adonis! Beat your breast!" says she. At that,
  he gets more bellicose, that god-Damn-ox-tratos.
  To this has the incontinence of women come!
CHORUS OF MEN.
  You haven't *yet* heard how outrageous they can be!
  With other acts of violence, these women here   405
  have showered us from their jugs, so now we are reduced
  to shaking out our shirts as if we'd pissed in them.
COMMISSIONER.
  Well, by the God of Waters, what do you expect?
  When we ourselves conspire with them in waywardness
  and give them good examples of perversity   410
  such wicked notions naturally sprout in them.
  We go into a shop and say something like this:
  "Goldsmith, about that necklace you repaired: last night
  my wife was dancing, when the peg that bolts the catch
  fell from its hole. I have to sail for Salamis,   415
  but if you have the time, by all means try to come
  towards evening, and put in the peg she needs."
  Another man says to a cobbler who is young
  and has no child's play of a prick, "Cobbler," he says,
  "her sandal-strap is pinching my wife's little toe,   420
  which is quite delicate. So please come by at noon
  and stretch it for her so it has a wider play."
  Such things as that result of course in things like this:
  when I, as a Commissioner, have made a deal
  to fit the fleet with oars and need the money now,   425
  I'm locked out by these women from the very gates.
  But it's no use just standing here. Bring on the bars,
  so I can keep these women in their proper place.

What are *you* gaping at, you poor unfortunate?
430 Where are *you* looking? Only seeing if a bar
is open yet downtown? Come, drive these crowbars in
under the gates on that side, pry away, and I
will pry away on this.

[*Lysistrata comes out.*]

LYSISTRATA.
                    No need to pry at all.
I'm coming out, of my own will. What use are bars?
435 It isn't bolts and bars we need so much as brains.
COMMISSIONER.
Really, you dirty slut? Where is that officer?
Arrest her, and tie both her hands behind her back.
LYSISTRATA.
By Artemis, just let him lift a hand at me
and, public officer or not, you'll hear him howl.
COMMISSIONER.
440 You let her scare you? Grab her round the middle, you.
Then *you* go help him and between you get her tied.

[*Kalonike comes out.*]

KALONIKE.
By Artemis, if you just lay one hand on her
I have a mind to trample the shit out of you.
COMMISSIONER.
It's out already! Look! Now where's the other one?
445 Tie up *that* woman first. She babbles, with it all.

[*Myrrhina comes out.*]

MYRRHINA.
By Hecatë, if you just lay a hand on her
you'll soon ask for a cup—to get your swellings down!

[*The policeman dashes behind the Commissioner and
clings to him for protection.*]

COMMISSIONER.
What happened? Where's that bowman, now? Hold onto
her! [*He moves quickly away downhill.*]
I'll see that none of you can get away through here!
LYSISTRATA.
450 By Artemis, you come near her and I'll bereave
your head of every hair! You'll weep for each one, too.
COMMISSIONER.
What a calamity! This one has failed me too.
But never must we let ourselves be overcome
by women. All together now, O Scythians!—
let's march against them in formation!
LYSISTRATA.
455   You'll find out
that inside there we have four companies
of fighting women perfectly equipped for war.
COMMISSIONER.
Charge! Turn their flanks, O Scythians! and tie their
hands!

LYSISTRATA.
O allies—comrades—women! Sally forth and fight!
O vegetable vendors, O green-grocery- 460
grain-garlic-bread-bean-dealers and inn-keepers all!

[*A group of fierce Old Market-Women, carrying baskets
of vegetables, spindles, etc. emerges. There is a volley of
vegetables. The Scythians are soon routed.*]

Come pull them, push them, smite them, smash them
   into bits!
Rail and abuse them in the strongest words you know!
Halt, Halt! Retire in order! We'll forego the spoils!
COMMISSIONER.
[*Tragically, like say Xerxes.*] Oh what reverses have my
   bowmen undergone! 465
LYSISTRATA.
But what did you imagine? Did you think you came
against a pack of slaves? Perhaps you didn't know
that women can be resolute?
COMMISSIONER.
                    I know they can—
above all when they spot a bar across the way.
CHORUS OF MEN.
Commissioner of Athens, you are spending words
   unduly, 470
to argue with these animals, who only roar the louder,
or don't you know they showered us so coldly and so
   cruelly,
and in our undershirts at that, and furnished us no
   powder?
CHORUS OF WOMEN.
But beating up your neighbor is inevitably bringing
a beating on yourself, sir, with your own eyes black and
   bloody. 475
I'd rather sit securely like a little girl demurely
not stirring up a single straw nor harming anybody,
So long as no one robs my hive and rouses me to
   stinging.
CHORUS OF MEN.
How shall we ever tame these brutes? We cannot
   tolerate
the situation further, so we must investigate 480
   this occurrence and find
   with what purpose in mind
they profane the Acropolis, seize it, and lock
the approach to this huge and prohibited rock,
   to our holiest ground! 485

Cross-examine them! Never believe one word
   they tell you—refute them, confound them!
We must get to the bottom of things like this
   and the circumstances around them.
COMMISSIONER.
Yes indeed! and I want to know first one thing: 490
   just *why* you committed this treason,
barricading the fortress with locks and bars—

I insist on knowing the reason.

LYSISTRATA.

To protect all the money up there from you—
495   you'll have nothing to fight for without it.

COMMISSIONER.

You think it is *money* we're fighting for?

LYSISTRATA.

All the troubles we have are about it.
    It was so Peisander and those in power
        of his kind could embezzle the treasure
500   that they cooked up emergencies all the time.
        Well, let them, if such is their pleasure,
    but they'll never get into this money again,
        though you men should elect them to spend it.

COMMISSIONER.

And just what will *you* do with it?

LYSISTRATA.

                            Can you ask?
505   Of course we shall superintend it.

COMMISSIONER.

You will superintend the treasury, *you!?*

LYSISTRATA.

And why should it strike you so funny?
    when we manage our houses in everything
        and it's we who look after your money.

COMMISSIONER.

But it's not the same thing!

LYSISTRATA.

                Why not?

COMMISSIONER.

510   It's war,
    and *this* money must pay the expenses.

LYSISTRATA.

To begin with, you needn't be waging war.

COMMISSIONER.

      To survive, we don't need our defenses?

LYSISTRATA.

You'll survive: we shall save you.

COMMISSIONER.

              Who? You?

LYSISTRATA.

                      Yes, we.

COMMISSIONER.

515   You absolutely disgust me.

LYSISTRATA.

You may like it or not, but you *shall* be saved.

COMMISSIONER.

    I protest!

LYSISTRATA.

          If you care to, but, trust me,
   this has got to be done all the same.

COMMISSIONER.

                It has?
520   It's illegal, unjust, and outrageous!

LYSISTRATA.

We must save you, sir.

COMMISSIONER.

                 Yes? And if I refuse?

LYSISTRATA.

You will much the more grimly engage us.

COMMISSIONER.

And whence does it happen that war and peace are fit
   matters for women to mention?

LYSISTRATA.

I will gladly explain—

COMMISSIONER.

                 And be quick, or else
   you'll be howling!

LYSISTRATA.

              Now, just pay attention   525
   and keep your hands to yourself, if you can!

COMMISSIONER.

But I can't. You can't think how I suffer
   from holding them back in my anger!

AN OLD WOMAN.

                    Sir—
   if you don't you will have it much rougher.

COMMISSIONER.

You may croak that remark to yourself, you hag?   530
   Will *you* do the explaining?

LYSISTRATA.

              I'll do it.
Heretofore we women in time of war
   have endured very patiently through it,
putting up with whatever you men might do,
   for never a peep would you let us   535
deliver on your unstatesmanly acts
   no matter how much they upset us,
but we knew very well, while we sat at home,
   when you'd handled a big issue poorly,
and we'd ask you then, with a pretty smile   540
   though our heart would be grieving us sorely,
"And what were the terms for a truce, my dear,
   you drew up in assembly this morning?"
"And what's it to you?" says our husband, "Shut up!"
   —so, as ever, at this gentle warning   545
I of course would discreetly shut up.

KALONIKE.

                  Not me!
You can bet I would never be quiet!

COMMISSIONER.

I'll bet, if you weren't, you were beaten up.

LYSISTRATA.

I'd shut up, and I do not deny it,
but when plan after plan was decided on,   550
   so bad we could scarcely believe it,
I would say, "This last is so mindless, dear,
   I cannot think how you achieve it!"
And then he would say, with a dirty look,
   "Just you think what your spindle is for, dear,   555
or your head will be spinning for days on end—
   let the *men* attend to the war, dear."

COMMISSIONER.
By Zeus, *he* had the right idea!

LYSISTRATA.
You fool!

560 Right ideas were quite out of the question,
when your reckless policies failed, and yet
we never could make a suggestion.
And lately we heard you say so yourselves:
in the streets there'd be someone lamenting:
"There's not one man in the country now!"
565 —and we heard many others assenting.
After that, we conferred through our deputies
and agreed, having briefly debated,
to act in common to save all Greece
at once—for why should we have waited?
570 So now, when we women are talking sense,
if you'll only agree to be quiet
and to listen to us as we did to you,
you'll be very much edified by it.

COMMISSIONER.
You will edify *us!* I protest!

LYSISTRATA.
Shut up!

COMMISSIONER.
575 *I'm* to shut up and listen, you scum, you?!
Sooner death! And a veil on your head at that!

LYSISTRATA.
We'll fix that. It may really become you:
do accept this veil as a present from me.
Drape it modestly—so—round your head, do you see?
580 And now—*not* a word more, sir.

KALONIKE.
Do accept this dear little wool-basket, too!
Hitch your girdle and card! Here are beans you may
chew
the way all of the nicest Athenians do—
and the *women* will see to the war, sir!

CHORUS OF WOMEN.
Oh women, set your jugs aside and keep a closer
585 distance:
our friends may need from us as well some resolute
assistance.

Since never shall I weary of the stepping of the
dance
nor will my knees of treading, for these ladies I'll
advance
anywhere they may lead,
and they're daring indeed,
590 they have wit, a fine figure, and boldness of heart,
they are prudent and charming, efficient and smart,
patriotic and brave!

But, O manliest grandmothers, onward now!
595 And you matronly nettles, don't waver!
but continue to bristle and rage, my dears,
for you've still got the wind in your favor!

[*The Chorus of Women and the Old Market-Women
join.*]

LYSISTRATA.
But if only the spirit of tender Love
and the power of sweet Aphrodite
600 were to breathe down over our breasts and thighs
an attraction both melting and mighty,
and infuse a pleasanter rigor in men,
raising only their cudgels of passion,
then I think we'd be known throughout all of Greece
605 as makers of peace and good fashion.

COMMISSIONER.
Having done just what?

LYSISTRATA.
Well, first of all
we shall certainly make it unlawful
to go madly to market in armor.

OLD MARKET-WOMAN.
Yes!
By dear Aphrodite, it's awful!

LYSISTRATA.
610 For now, in the midst of the pottery-stalls
and the greens and the beans and the garlic,
men go charging all over the market-place
in full armor and beetling and warlike.

COMMISSIONER.
They must do as their valor impels them to!

LYSISTRATA.
615 But it makes a man only look funny
to be wearing a shield with a Gorgon's head
and be wanting sardines for less money.

OLD MARKET-WOMEN.
Well, I saw a huge cavalry captain once
on a stallion that scarcely could hold him,
620 pouring into his helmet of bronze a pint
of pea-soup an old woman had sold him,
and a Thracian who, brandishing shield and spear
like some savage Euripides staged once,
when he'd frightened a vendor of figs to death,
625 gobbled up all her ripest and aged ones.

COMMISSIONER.
And how, on the international scale,
can you straighten out the enormous
confusion among all the states of Greece?

LYSISTRATA.
Very easily.

COMMISSIONER.
How? Do inform us.

LYSISTRATA.
630 When our skein's in a tangle we take it thus
on our spindles, or haven't you seen us?
one on this side and one on the other side,
and we work out the tangles between us.
And that is the way we'll undo this war,

635 by exchanging ambassadors, whether
you like it or not, one from either side,
and we'll work out the tangles together.
COMMISSIONER.
Do you really think that with wools and skeins
and just being able to spin you
640 can end these momentous affairs, you fools?
LYSISTRATA.
With any intelligence in you
you statesmen would govern as we work wool,
and in everything Athens would profit.
COMMISSIONER.
How so? Do tell.
LYSISTRATA.
First, you take raw fleece
645 and you wash the beshittedness off it:
just so, you should first lay the city out
on a washboard and beat out the rotters
and pluck out the sharpers like burrs, and when
you find tight knots of schemers and plotters
650 who are out for key offices, card them loose,
but best tear off their heads in addition.
Then into one basket together card
all those of a good disposition
be they citizens, resident aliens, friends,
655 an ally or an absolute stranger,
even people in debt to the commonwealth,
you can mix them in with no danger.
And the cities which Athens has colonized—
by Zeus, you should try to conceive them
660 as so many shreddings and tufts of wool
that are scattered about and not leave them
to lie around loose, but from all of them
draw the threads in here, and collect them
into one big ball and then weave a coat
665 for the people, to warm and protect them.
COMMISSIONER.
Now, isn't this awful? They treat the state
like wool to be beaten and carded,
who have nothing at all to do with war!
LYSISTRATA.
Yes we do, you damnable hard-head!
670 We have none of your honors but we have more
then double your sufferings by it.
First of all, we bear sons whom you send to war.
COMMISSIONER.
Don't bring up our old sorrows! Be quiet!
LYSISTRATA.
And now, when we ought to enjoy ourselves,
675 making much of our prime and our beauty,
we are sleeping alone because all the men
are away on their soldierly duty.
But never mind us—when young girls grow old
in their bedrooms with no men to share them.
COMMISSIONER.
You seem to forget that men, too, grow old.
680

LYSISTRATA.
By Zeus, but you cannot compare them!
When a man gets back, though he be quite gray,
he can wed a young girl in a minute,
but the season of woman is very short:
she must take what she can while she's in it. 685
And you know she must, for when it's past,
although you're not awfully astute, you're
aware that no man will marry her then
and she sits staring into the future.
COMMISSIONER.
But he who can raise an erection still— 690
LYSISTRATA.
Is there some good reason you don't drop dead?
We'll sell you a coffin if you but will.
Here's a string of onions to crown your head
and I'll make a honey-cake large and round
you can feed to Cerberus underground! 695
FIRST OLD MARKET-WOMAN.
Accept these few fillets of leek from me!
SECOND OLD MARKET-WOMAN.
Let me offer you these for your garland, sir!
LYSISTRATA.
What now? Do you want something else you see?
Listen! Charon's calling his passenger—
will you catch the ferry or still delay 700
when his other dead want to sail away?
COMMISSIONER.
Is it not downright monstrous to treat me like this?
By Zeus, I'll go right now to the Commissioners
and show myself in evidence, just as I am!

[He begins to withdraw with dignity and his four Scythian
policemen.]

LYSISTRATA.
Will you accuse us of not giving you a wake? 705
But your departed spirit will receive from us
burnt offerings in due form, two days from now at dawn!

[Lysistrata with the other women goes into the Acropolis.
The Commissioner etc. have left. The male chorus and the
mixed female chorus are alone.]

CHORUS OF MEN.
No man now dare fall to drowsing, if he wishes to stay
free!
Men let's strip and gird ourselves for this eventuality!

To me this all begins to have a smell 710
of bigger things and larger things as well:
most of all I sniff a tyranny afoot. I'm much afraid
certain secret agents of the Spartans may have come,
meeting under cover here, in Cleisthene's home,
instigating those damned women by deceit to make a
raid 715
upon our treasury and that great sum
the city paid my pension from.

Sinister events already!—think of lecturing the state,
women as they are, and prattling on of things like shields
    of bronze,
720 even trying hard to get us reconciled to those we hate—
those of Sparta, to be trusted like a lean wolf when it
    yawns!
All of this is just a pretext, men, for a dictatorship—
but to me they shall not dictate! Watch and ward! A
    sword I'll hide
underneath a branch of myrtle; through the agora I'll
    slip,
725 following Aristogeiton, backing the tyrannicide!

[*The Old Men pair off to imitate the gestures of the famous
group statue of the tryannicides Harmodius and Aristogeiton.*]

Thus I'll take my stand beside him! Now my rage is
    goaded raw
I'm as like as no to clip this damned old woman on the
    jaw!

CHORUS OF WOMEN.
Your own mother will not know you when you come
    home, if you do!
Let us first, though, lay our things down, O my dear old
    friends and true.

730   For now, O fellow-citizens, we would
      consider what will do our city good.
    Well I may, because it bred me up in wealth and
      elegance:
        letting me at seven help with the embroidering
        of Athena's mantle, and at ten with offering
    cakes and flowers. When I was grown and beautiful I
735   had my chance
        to bear her baskets, at my neck a string
        of figs, and proud as anything.

Must I not, then, give my city any good advice I can?
Need you hold the fact against me that I was not born
    a man,
when I offer better methods than the present ones, and
740   when
I've a share in this economy, for I contribute men?
But, you sad old codgers, *yours* is forfeited on many
    scores:
you have drawn upon our treasure dating from the
    Persian wars,
what they call grampatrimony, and you've paid no taxes
    back.
745 Worse, you've run it nearly bankrupt, and the prospect's
    pretty black.
Have you anything to answer? Say you were within the
    law
and I'll take this rawhide boot and clip you one across
    the jaw!

CHORUS OF MEN.

      Greater insolence than ever!—
      that's the method that she calls
      "better"—if you would believe her.   750

But this threat must be prevented! Every man with both
    balls
must make ready—take our shirts off, for a man must reek
    of male
outright—not wrapped up in leafage like an omelet for
    sale!

    Forward and barefoot: we'll do it again
    to the death, just as when we resisted   755
    tyranny out at Leipsydrion, when
    we really existed!

    Now or never we must grow
    young again and, sprouting wings
    over all our bodies, throw   760
    off this heaviness age brings!

For if any of us give them even a just a little hold
nothing will be safe from their tenacious grasp. They are
    so bold
they will soon build ships of war and, with exorbitant
    intent,
send such navies out against us as Queen Artemisia sent. 765
But if they attack with horse, our knights we might as
    well delete:
nothing rides so well as woman, with so marvelous a
    seat,
never slipping at the gallop. Just look at those Amazons
in that picture in the Stoa, from their horses bringing
    bronze
axes down on men. We'd better grab *these* members of
    the sex   770
one and all, arrest them, get some wooden collars on
    their necks!

CHORUS OF WOMEN.

      By the gods, if you chagrin me
      or annoy me, if you dare,
      I'll turn loose the sow that's in me

till you rouse the town to help you with the way I've
    done your hair!   775
Let us too make ready, women, and our garments
    quickly doff
so we'll smell like women angered fit to bite our fingers
    off!

    Now I am ready: let one of the men
    come against me, and *he'll* never hanker

780 after black bean or garlic again:
no woman smells ranker!

Say a single unkind word,
I'll pursue you till you drop,
as the beetle did the bird.
785 My revenge will never stop!

Yet you will not worry me so long as Lampito's alive
and my noble friends in Thebes and other cities still
survive.
You'll not overpower us, even passing seven decrees or
eight,
you, poor brutes, whom everyone and everybody's
neighbors hate.
790 Only yesterday I gave a party, honoring Hecatë,
but when I invited in the neighbor's child to come and
play,
such a pretty thing from Thebes, as nice and quiet as
you please,
just an eel, they said she couldn't, on account of your
decrees.
You'll go on forever passing such decrees without a check
till somebody takes you firmly by the leg and breaks your
795 neck!

[*Lysistrata comes out. The Chorus of Women addresses
her in the manner of tragedy.*]

Oh Queen of this our enterprise and all our hopes,
wherefore in baleful brooding has thou issued forth?
LYSISTRATA.
The deeds of wicked women and the female mind
discourage me and set me pacing up and down.
CHORUS OF WOMEN.
800 What's that? What's that you say?
LYSISTRATA.
The truth, alas, the truth!
CHORUS OF WOMEN.
What is it that's so dreadful? Tell it to your friends.
LYSISTRATA.
A shameful thing to tell and heavy not to tell.
CHORUS OF WOMEN.
Oh, never hide from me misfortune that is ours!
LYSISTRATA.
805 To put it briefly as I can, we are in heat.
CHORUS OF WOMEN.
Oh Zeus!
LYSISTRATA.
Why call on Zeus? This is the way things are.
At least it seems I am no longer capable
of keeping them from men. They are deserting me.
This morning I caught one of them digging away
810 to make a tunnel to Pan's grotto down the slope,

another letting herself down the parapet
with rope and pulley, and another climbing down
its sheerest face, and yesterday was one I found
sitting upon a sparrow with a mind to fly
down to some well-equipped whoremaster's place in
town. 815
Just as she swooped I pulled her backward by the hair.
They think of every far-fetched excuse they can
for going home. And here comes one deserter now.
You there, where are you running?
FIRST WOMAN.
                                        I want to go home,
because I left some fine Milesian wools at home 820
that must be riddled now with moths.
LYSISTRATA.
                                        Oh, damn your moths!
Go back inside.
FIRST WOMAN.
But I shall come back right away,
just time enough to stretch them out upon my bed.
LYSISTRATA.
Stretch nothing out, and don't you go away at all. 825
FIRST WOMAN.
But shall I let my wools be ruined?
LYSISTRATA.
                                        If you must.
SECOND WOMAN.
Oh miserable me! I sorrow for the flax
I left at home unbeaten and unstripped!
LYSISTRATA.
                                        One more—
wanting to leave for stalks of flax she hasn't stripped.
Come back here! 830
SECOND WOMAN.
But, by Artemis, I only want
to strip my flax. Then I'll come right back here again.
LYSISTRATA.
Strip me no strippings! If you start this kind of thing
some other woman soon will want to do the same.
THIRD WOMAN.
O lady Artemis, hold back this birth until 835
I can get safe to some unconsecrated place!
LYSISTRATA.
What is this raving?
THIRD WOMAN.
                                        I'm about to have a child.
LYSISTRATA.
But you weren't pregnant yesterday.
THIRD WOMAN.
                                        I am today.
Oh, send me home this instant, dear Lysistrata,
so I can find a midwife.
LYSISTRATA.
                                        What strange tale is this? 840
What is this hard thing you have here?

THIRD WOMAN.

                             The child is male.

LYSISTRATA.

   By Aphrodite, no! You obviously have
some hollow thing of bronze. I'll find out what it is.
You silly thing!—you have Athena's helmet here—
and claiming to be pregnant!

THIRD WOMAN.

845   So I am, by Zeus!

LYSISTRATA.

   In that case, what's the helmet for?

THIRD WOMAN.

                        So if the pains
came on me while I'm still up here, I might give birth
inside the helmet, as I've seen the pigeons do.

LYSISTRATA.

   What an excuse! The case is obvious. Wait here.
850   I want to show this bouncing baby helmet off.

[*She passes the huge helmet around the Chorus of Women.*]

SECOND WOMAN.

   But I can't even sleep in the Acropolis,
not for an instant since I saw the sacred snake!

FOURTH WOMAN.

   The owls are what are killing *me*. How can I sleep
with their eternal whit-to-whoo-to-whit-to-whoo?

LYSISTRATA.

855   You're crazy! Will you stop this hocus-pocus now?
No doubt you miss your husbands: don't you think that
      they
are missing us as much? I'm sure the nights they pass
are just as hard. But, gallant comrades, do bear up,
and face these gruelling hardships yet a little while.
860   There is an oracle that says we'll win, if we
only will stick together. Here's the oracle.

CHORUS OF WOMEN.

   Oh, read us what it says!

LYSISTRATA.

                Keep silence, then, and hear:

"Now when to one high place are gathered the fluttering
    swallows,
Fleeing the Hawk and the Cock however hotly it
865   *follows,*
Then will their miseries end, and that which is over be
    under:
Thundering Zeus will decide.

A WOMAN.

               Will *we* lie on top now, I wonder?

LYSISTRATA.

   But if the Swallows go fighting each other and springing
    and winging
   Out of the holy and high sanctuary, then people will
    never
   Say there was any more dissolute bitch of a bird
870   *whatsoever.*

A WOMAN.

   The oracle is clear, by Zeus!

LYSISTRATA.

              By *all* the gods!
So let us not renounce the hardships we endure.
But let us go back in. Indeed, my dearest friends,
it would be shameful to betray the oracle.

[*Exeunt into the Acropolis.*]

CHORUS OF MEN.

   Let me tell you a story I heard one day
     when I was a child: 875

   There was once a young fellow Melanion by name
   who refused to get married and ran away
     to the wild.
     To the mountains he came
     and inhabited there
       in a grove
     and hunted the hare   880
     both early and late
     with nets that he wove
     and also a hound
   and he never came home again, such was his hate,
     all women he found   885
     so nasty, and we
     quite wisely agree.

   Let us kiss you, dear old dears!

CHORUS OF WOMEN.

   With no onions, you'll shed tears!

CHORUS OF MEN.

   I mean, lift my leg and *kick*.   890

CHORUS OF WOMEN.

   My, you wear your thicket thick!

CHORUS OF MEN.

   Great Myronides was rough
   at the front and black enough
   in the ass to scare his foes.
     Just ask anyone who knows: 895
     it's with hair that wars are won—
     take for instance Phormion.

CHORUS OF WOMEN.

   Let me tell you a story in answer to
     Melanion's case.
   There is now a man, Timon, who wanders around   900
   in the wilderness, hiding his face from view in a place
     where the brambles abound
     so he looks like a chip
       off a Fury,
     curling his lip.
     Now Timon retired   905
     in hatred and pure
     contempt of all men
   and he cursed them in words that were truly inspired

910   again and again
         but women he found
         delightful and sound.

Would you like your jaw repaired?
CHORUS OF MEN.
  Thank you, no. You've got me scared.
CHORUS OF WOMEN.
  Let me jump and kick it though.
CHORUS OF MEN.
915   You will let your man-sack show.
CHORUS OF WOMEN.
    All the same you wouldn't see,
    old and gray as I may be,
    any superfluity
    of unbarbered hair on me;
920   it is plucked and more, you scamp,
    since I singe it with a lamp!

[Enter Lysistrata on the wall.]

LYSISTRATA.
  Women, O women, come here quickly, here to me!
WOMEN.
  Whatever is it? Tell me! What's the shouting for?
LYSISTRATA.
  I see a man approaching, shaken and possessed,
925   seized and inspired by Aphrodite's power.
  O thou, of Cyprus, Paphos, and Cythera, queen!
  continue straight along this way you have begun!
A WOMAN.
  Whoever he is, where is he?
LYSISTRATA.
                    Near Demeter's shrine.
A WOMAN.
  Why yes, by Zeus, he is. Who ever can he be?
LYSISTRATA.
  Well, look at him. Do any of you know him?
MYRRHINA.
930   Yes.
  I do. He's my own husband, too, Cinesias.
LYSISTRATA.
  Then it's your duty now to turn him on a spit,
  cajole him and make love to him and not make love,
  to offer everything, short of those things of which
  the wine-cup knows.
MYRRHINA.
            I'll do it, don't you fear.
LYSISTRATA.
935   And I
  will help you tantalize him. I will stay up here
  and help you roast him slowly. But now, disappear!

[Enter Cinesias.]

CINESIAS.
  Oh how unfortunate I am, gripped by what spasms,

stretched tight like being tortured on a wheel!
LYSISTRATA.
  Who's there? Who has got this far past the sentries?
CINESIAS.
                         I.   940
LYSISTRATA.
  A man?
CINESIAS.
      A man for sure.
LYSISTRATA.
            Then clear away from here.
CINESIAS.
  Who're you to throw me out?
LYSISTRATA.
                 The lookout for the day.
CINESIAS.
  Then, for the gods' sake, call Myrrhina out for me.
LYSISTRATA.
  You don't say! Call Myrrhina out! And who are you?
CINESIAS.
  Her husband. I'm Cinesias Paionides.   945
LYSISTRATA.
  Well, my dear man, hello! Your name is not unknown
  among us here and not without a certain fame,
  because your wife has it forever on her lips.
  She can't pick up an egg or quince but she must say:
  Cinesias would enjoy it so!
CINESIAS.
           How wonderful!   950
LYSISTRATA.
  By Aphrodite, yes. And if we chance to talk
  of husbands, your wife interrupts and says the rest
  are nothing much compared to her Cinesias.
CINESIAS.
  Go call her.
LYSISTRATA.
      Will you give me something if I do?
CINESIAS.
  Indeed I will, by Zeus, if it is what you want.   955
  I can but offer what I have, and I have this.
LYSISTRATA.
  Wait there. I will go down and call her.
CINESIAS.
                    Hurry up!
  because I find no charm whatever left in life
  since she departed from the house. I get depressed
  whenever I go into it, and everything   960
  seems lonely to me now, and when I eat my food
  I find no taste in it at all—because I'm stiff.
MYRRHINA.
  [Offstage.] I love him, how I love him! But he doesn't
    want
  my love! [on wall] So what's the use of calling me to him?
CINESIAS.
  My sweet little Myrrhina, why do you act like that?   965
  Come down here.

MYRRHINA.

There? By Zeus, I certainly will not.

CINESIAS.

Won't you come down, Myrrhina, when I'm calling you?

MYRRHINA.

Not when you call me without needing anything.

CINESIAS.

Not needing anything? I'm desperate with need.

MYRRHINA.

I'm going now.

CINESIAS.

970   Oh no! No, don't go yet! At least
you'll listen to the baby. Call your mammy, you.

BABY.

Mammy mammy mammy!

CINESIAS.

What's wrong with you? Have you no pity on your child
when it is six days now since he was washed or nursed?

MYRRHINA.

975   Oh, *I* have pity. But his father takes no care
of him.

CINESIAS.

Come down, you flighty creature, for the child.

MYRRHINA.

Oh, what it is to be a mother! I'll come down,
for what else can I do? [*Myrrhina exits to reenter
below.*]

CINESIAS.

It seems to me she's grown
980   much younger, and her eyes have a more tender look.
Even her being angry with me and her scorn
are just the things that pain me with the more
       desire.

MYRRHINA.

Come let me kiss you, dear sweet little baby mine,
with such a horrid father. Mammy loves you, though.

CINESIAS.

985   But why are you so mean? Why do you listen to
those other women, giving me such pain?—And you,
you're suffering yourself.

MYRRHINA.

Take your hands off of me!

CINESIAS.

But everything we have at home, my things and yours,
you're letting go to pieces.

MYRRHINA.

Little do I care!

CINESIAS.

990   Little you care even if your weaving's pecked apart
and carried off by chickens?

MYRRHINA.

[*Bravely.*]

Little I care, by Zeus!

CINESIAS.

You have neglected Aphrodite's rituals
for such a long time now. Won't you come back again?

MYRRHINA.

Not I, unless you men negotiate a truce
and make an end of war.

CINESIAS.

Well, if it's so decreed,   995
we will do even that.

MYRRHINA.

Well, if it's so decreed,
I will come home again. Not now. I've sworn I won't.

CINESIAS.

All right, all right. But now lie down with me once
       more.

MYRRHINA.

No! No!—yet I don't say I'm not in love with you.

CINESIAS.

You love me? Then why not lie down, Myrrhina
       dear?   1000

MYRRHINA.

Don't be ridiculous! Not right before the child!

CINESIAS.

By Zeus, of course not. Manes, carry him back home.
There now. You see the baby isn't in your way.
Won't you lie down?

MYRRHINA.

But, *where*, you rogue, just where
is one to do it?

CINESIAS.

Where? Pan's grotto's a fine place.   1005

MYRRHINA.

But how could I come back to the Acropolis
in proper purity?

CINESIAS.

Well, there's a spring below
the grotto—you can very nicely bathe in that.

[*Ekkyklema or inset-scene with grotto.*]

MYRRHINA.

And then I'm under oath. What if I break my vows?

CINESIAS.

Let me bear all the blame. Don't worry about your oath.   1010

MYRRHINA.

Wait here, and I'll go get a cot for us.

CINESIAS.

No, no,
the ground will do.

MYRRHINA.

No, by Apollo! Though you *are*
so horrid, I can't have you lying on the ground. [*Leaves.*]

CINESIAS.

You know, the woman loves me—that's as plain as day.

MYRRHINA.

There. Get yourself in bed and I'll take off my clothes.   1015
Oh, what a nuisance! I must go and get a mat.

CINESIAS.

What for? I don't need one.

MYRRHINA.

Oh yes, by Artemis!
On the bare cords? How ghastly!

CINESIAS.

Let me kiss you now.

MYRRHINA.

Oh, very well.

CINESIAS.

Wow! Hurry, hurry and come back.

[Myrrhina leaves. A long wait.]

MYRRHINA.

1020   Here is the mat. Lie down now, while I get undressed.
Oh, what a nuisance! You don't have a pillow, dear.

CINESIAS.

But I don't need one, not one bit!

MYRRHINA.

By Zeus, I do!

[Leaves.]

CINESIAS.

Poor prick, the service around here is terrible!

MYRRHINA.

1025   Sit up, my dear, jump up! Now I've got everything.

CINESIAS.

Indeed you have. And now, my golden girl, come here.

MYRRHINA.

I'm just untying my brassiere. Now don't forget:
about that treaty—you won't disappoint me, dear?

CINESIAS.

By Zeus, no! On my life!

MYRRHINA.

You have no blanket, dear.

CINESIAS.

1030   By Zeus, I do not need one. I just want to screw.

MYRRHINA.

Don't worry, dear, you will. I'll be back right away.

[Leaves.]

CINESIAS.

This number, with her bedding, means to murder me.

MYRRHINA.

Now raise yourself upright.

CINESIAS.

But this is upright now!

MYRRHINA.

Wouldn't you like some perfume?

CINESIAS.

By Apollo, no!

MYRRHINA.

1035   By Aphrodite, yes! You must—like it or not.

[Leaves.]

CINESIAS.

Lord Zeus! Just let the perfume spill! That's all I ask!

MYRRHINA.

Hold out your hand. Take some of this and rub it on.

CINESIAS.

This perfume, by Apollo, isn't sweet at all.
It smells a bit of stalling—not of wedding nights!

MYRRHINA.

I brought the *Rhodian* perfume! How absurd of me!   1040

CINESIAS.

It's fine! Let's keep it.

MYRRHINA.

You *will* have your little joke.

[Leaves.]

CINESIAS.

Just let me at the man who first distilled perfumes!

MYRRHINA.

Try this, in the long vial.

CINESIAS.

I've got one like it, dear.
But don't be tedious. Lie down. And please don't bring
anything more.   1045

MYRRHINA.

[*Going*] That's what I'll do, by Artemis!
I'm taking off my shoes. But dearest, don't forget
you're going to vote for peace.

CINESIAS.

I will consider it.
She has destroyed me, murdered me, that woman has!
On top of which she's got me skinned and gone away!   1050
    What shall I do? Oh, whom shall I screw,
    cheated of dear Myrrhina, the first
    beauty of all, a creature divine?
    How shall I tend this infant of mine?
    Find me a pimp: it has to be nursed!   1055

CHORUS OF MEN.

[*In tragic style, as if to Prometheus or Andromeda bound.*]
    In what dire woe, how heavy-hearted
    I see thee languishing, outsmarted!
      I pity thee, alas I do.
    What kidney could endure such pain,
    what spirit could, what balls, what back,   1060
    what loins, what sacroiliac,
    If they came under such a strain
    and never had a morning screw?

CINESIAS.

O Zeus! the twinges! Oh, the twitches!

CHORUS OF MEN.

    And this is what she did to you,   1065
    that vilest, hatefullest of bitches!

CINESIAS.

Oh nay, by Zeus, she's dear and sweet!

CHORUS OF MEN.

    How can she be? She's vile, O Zeus, she's vile!
    Oh treat her, Zeus, like so much wheat—
    O God of Weather, hear my prayer—   1070
    and raise a whirlwind's mighty blast
    to roll her up into a pile
    and carry her into the sky

1075 far up and up and then at last
drop her and land her suddenly
astride that pointed penis there!

[*The ekkyklema turns, closing the inset-scene. Enter, from
opposite sides, a Spartan and an Athenian official.*]

SPARTAN.
Wheah is the Senate-house of the Athenians?
Ah wish to see the chaihman. Ah have news fo him.
ATHENIAN.
And who are you? Are you a Satyr or a man?
SPARTAN.
1080 Ah am a herald, mah young friend, yes, by the gods,
and Ah have come from Sparta to negotiate.
ATHENIAN.
And yet you come here with a spear under your arm?
SPARTAN.
Not Ah, bah Zeus, not Ah!
ATHENIAN.
Why do you turn around?
Why throw your cloak out so in front? Has the long trip
given you a swelling?
SPARTAN.
1085 Ah do think the man is queah!
ATHENIAN.
But you have an erection, oh you reprobate!
SPARTAN.
Bah Zeus, Ah've no sech thing! And don't you fool
around!
ATHENIAN.
And what have you got there?
SPARTAN.
A Spahtan scroll-stick, suh.
ATHENIAN.
Well, if it is, *this* is a Spartan scroll-stick, too.
1090 But look, I know what's up: you can tell *me* the truth.
Just how are things with you in Sparta: tell me that.
SPARTAN.
Theah is uprising in all Spahta. Ouah allies
are all erect as well. We need ouah milkin'-pails.
ATHENIAN.
From where has this great scourge of frenzy fallen on
you?
From Pan?
SPARTAN.
1095 No, Ah think Lampito began it all,
and then, the othah women throughout Spahta joined
togethah, just lahk at a signal fo a race,
and fought theah husbands off and drove them from
theah cunts.
ATHENIAN.
So, how're you getting on?
SPARTAN.
We suffah. Through the town
1100 we walk bent ovah as if we were carrying
lamps in the wind. The women will not let us touch

even theah berries, till we all with one acco'd
have made a peace among the cities of all Greece.
ATHENIAN.
This is an international conspiracy
launched by the women! Now I comprehend it all! 1105
Return at once to Sparta. Tell them they must send
ambassadors fully empowered to make peace.
And our Assembly will elect ambassadors
from our side, when I say so, showing them this prick.
SPARTAN.
Ah'll run! Ah'll flah! Fo all you say is excellent! 1110
CHORUS OF MEN.
No wild beast is more impossible than woman is to fight,
nor is fire, nor has the panther such unbridled appetite!
CHORUS OF WOMEN.
Well you know it, yet you go on warring with me with-
out end,
when you might, you cross-grained creature, have me as
a trusty friend.
CHORUS OF MEN.
Listen: I will never cease from hating women till I die! 1115
CHORUS OF WOMEN.
Any time you like. But meanwhile is there any reason
why
I should let you stand there naked, looking so ridiculous?
I am only coming near you, now, to slip your coat on,
thus.
CHORUS OF MEN.
That was very civil of you, very kind to treat me so,
when in such uncivil rage I took it off a while ago. 1120
CHORUS OF WOMEN.
Now you're looking like a man again, and not ridiculous.
If you hadn't hurt my feelings, I would not have made
a fuss,
I would even have removed that little beast that's in
your eye.
CHORUS OF MEN.
That is what was hurting me! Well, won't you take my
ring to pry
back my eyelid? Rake the beast out. When you have it,
let me see, 1125
for some time now it's been at my eye and irritating me.
CHORUS OF WOMEN.
Very well, I will—though you were *born* an irritable
man.
What a monster of a gnat, by Zeus! Look at it if you can.
Don't you see it? It's a native of great marshes, can't you
tell?
CHORUS OF MEN.
Much obliged, by Zeus! The brute's been digging at me
like a well! 1130
So that now you have removed it, streams of tears come
welling out.
CHORUS OF WOMEN.
I will dry them. You're the meanest man alive, beyond
a doubt,

yet I will, and kiss you, too.
CHORUS OF MEN.

Don't kiss me!
CHORUS OF WOMEN.

If you will or not!
CHORUS OF MEN.

1135 Damn you! Oh, what wheedling flatterers you all are,
born and bred!
That old proverb is quite right and not inelegantly said:
"There's no living *with* the bitches and, without them,
even *less*"—
so I might as well make peace with you, and from now
on, I guess,
I'll do nothing mean to you, and from you, suffer nothing
wrong.
1140 So let's draw our ranks together now and start a little song:

For a change, we're not preparing
any mean remark or daring
aimed at any man in town,
but the very opposite: we plan to do and say
1145 only good to everyone,
when the ills we have already are sufficient anyway.
Any man or woman who
wants a little money, oh
say three minas, maybe two,
1150 kindly let us know.
What we have is right in here.
(Notice we have purses, too!)
And if ever peace appear,
he who takes our loan today
never need repay.

1155 We are having guests for supper,
allies asked in by our upper
classes to improve the town.
There's pea soup, and I had killed a suckling-pig
of mine:
I shall see it is well done,
so you will be tasting something very succulent
1160 and fine.
Come to see us, then, tonight
early, just as soon as you
have a bath and dress up right:
bring your children, too.
1165 Enter boldly, never mind
asking anyone in sight.
Go straight in and you will find
you are quite at home there, but
all the doors are shut.

1170 And here come the Spartan ambassadors,
dragging beards that are really the biggest I
have ever beheld, and around their thighs
they are wearing some sort of a pig-sty.
Oh men of Sparta, let me bid you welcome first,
1175 and then you tell us how you are and why you come.

SPARTAN.
What need is theah to speak to you in many words?
Fo you may see youahself in what a fix we come.
CHORUS OF MEN.
Too bad! Your situation has become
terribly hard and seems to be at fever-pitch.
SPARTAN.
Unutterably so! And what is theah to say? 1180
Let someone bring us peace on any tuhms he will!
CHORUS OF MEN.
And here I see some natives of Athenian soil,
holding their cloaks far off their bellies, like the best
wrestlers, who sicken at the touch of cloth. It seems
that overtraining may bring on this strange disease. 1185
ATHENIAN.
Will someone tell us where to find Lysistrata?
We're men, and here we are, in this capacity.
CHORUS OF MEN.
This symptom and that other one sound much alike.
Toward morning I expect convulsions do occur?
ATHENIAN.
By Zeus, we are exhausted with just doing that, 1190
so, if somebody doesn't reconcile us quick,
there's nothing for it: we'll be screwing Cleisthenes.
CHORUS OF MEN.
Be careful—put your cloaks on, or you might be seen
by some young blade who knocks the phalluses off
herms.
ATHENIAN.
By Zeus, an excellent idea! 1195
SPARTAN.
[*Having overheard.*] Yes, bah the gods!
It altogethah is. Quick, let's put on our cloaks.

[*Both groups cover quick and then recognize each other
with full diplomatic pomp.*]

ATHENIAN.
Greetings, O men of Sparta! [*To his group.*] We have
been disgraced!
SPARTAN.
[*To one of his group.*] Mah dearest fellah, what a dreadful
thing fo *us,*
if these Athenians had seen ouah wo'st defeat! 1200
ATHENIAN.
Come now, O Spartans: one must specify each point.
Why have you come here?
ATHENIAN.

To negotiate a peace.
SPARTAN.
We ah ambassadahs.
ATHENIAN.

Well put. And so are we.
Therefore, why do we not call in Lysistrata,
she who alone might get us to agree on terms? 1205
SPARTAN.
Call her or any man, even a Lysistratus!

CHORUS OF MEN.
But you will have no need, it seems, to call her now,
for here she is. She heard you and is coming out.
CHORUS OF MEN AND CHORUS OF WOMEN.
All hail, O manliest woman of all!
1210   It is time for you now to be turning
into something still better, more dreadful, mean,
    unapproachable, charming, discerning,
for here are the foremost nations of Greece,
    bewitched by your spells like a lover,
1215 who have come to you, bringing you all their claims,
    and to *you* turning everything over.

LYSISTRATA.
The work's not difficult, if one can catch them now
while they're excited and not making passes at
each other. I will soon find out. Where's *Harmony?*

[*A naked maid, perhaps wearing a large ribbon reading
Harmony, appears from inside.*]

1220 Go take the Spartans first, and lead them over here,
not with a rough hand nor an overbearing one,
nor, as our husbands used to do this, clumsily,
but like a woman, in our most familiar style:
If he won't give his hand, then lead him by the prick.
1225 And now, go bring me those Athenians as well,
leading them by whatever they will offer you.
O men of Sparta, stand right here, close by my side,
and *you* stand over there, and listen to my words.
I am a woman, yes, but there is mind in me.
1230 In native judgment I am not so badly off,
and, having heard my father and my elders talk
often enough, I have some cultivation, too.
And so, I want to take and scold you, on both sides,
as you deserve, for though you use a lustral urn
1235 in common at the altars, like blood-relatives,
when at Olympia, Delphi, or Thermopylae—
how many others I might name if I took time!—
yet, with barbarian hords of enemies at hand,
it is Greek men, it is Greek cities, you destroy.
1240 That is one argument so far, and it is done.

ATHENIAN.
My prick is skinned alive—that's what's destroying *me*.

LYSISTRATA.
Now, men of Sparta—for I shall address you first—
do you not know that once one of your kings came here
and as a suppliant of the Athenians
1245 sat by our altars, death-pale in his purple robe,
and begged us for an army? For Messenë then
oppressed you, and an earthquake from the gods as well.
Then Cimon went, taking four thousand infantry,
and saved the whole of Lacedaemon for your state.
1250 That is the way Athenians once treated you;
you ravage their land now, which once received you
    well.

ATHENIAN.
By Zeus, these men are in the wrong, Lysistrata!

SPARTAN.
[*With his eyes on Harmony.*] We'ah wrong . . . What an
unutterably lovely ass!

LYSISTRATA.
Do you suppose I'm letting you Athenians off?   1255
Do you not know that once the Spartans in their turn,
when you were wearing the hide-skirts of slavery,
came with their spears and slew many Thessalians,
many companions and allies of Hippias?
They were the only ones who fought for you that day,   1260
freed you from tyranny and, for the skirt of hide,
gave back your people the wool mantle of free men.

SPARTAN.
Ah nevah saw a woman broadah—in her views.

ATHENIAN.
And I have never seen a lovelier little nook.

LYSISTRATA.
So why, when you have done each other so much good,   1265
go on fighting with no end of malevolence?
Why don't you make a peace? Tell me, what's in your
    way?

SPARTAN.
Whah, *we* ah willin', if *they* will give up to us
that very temptin' cuhve. [*Of Harmony, as hereafter.*]

LYSISTRATA.
                   What curve, my friend?

SPARTAN.
                         The bay
of Pylos, which we've wanted and felt out so long.   1270

ATHENIAN.
No, by Poseidon, you will not get into that!

LYSISTRATA.
Good friend, do let them have it.

ATHENIAN.
                 No! What other town
can we manipulate so well?

LYSISTRATA.
                Ask them for one.

ATHENIAN.
Damn, let me think! Now first suppose you cede to us
that bristling tip of land, Echinos, behind which   1275
the gulf of Malia recedes, and those long walls,
the legs on which Megara reaches to the sea.

SPARTAN.
No, mah deah man, not *everything*, bah Castah, no!

LYSISTRATA.
Oh, give them up. Why quarrel for a pair of legs?

ATHENIAN.
I'd like to strip and get to plowing right away.   1280

SPARTAN.
And *Ah* would lahk to push manuah, still earliah.

LYSISTRATA.
When you have made a peace, then you will do all
    that.
But if you want to do it, first deliberate,
go and inform your allies and consult with them.

ATHENIAN.
1285   Oh, damn our allies, my good woman! We are stiff.
Will all of our allies not stand resolved with us—
namely, to screw?
SPARTAN.
                              And so will ouahs, Ah'll guarantee.
ATHENIAN.
Our mercenaries, even, will agree with us.
LYSISTRATA.
Excellent. Now to get you washed and purified
1290   so you may enter the Acropolis, where we
women will entertain you out of our supplies.
You will exchange your pledges there and vows for
        peace.
And after that each one of you will take his wife,
departing then for home.
ATHENIAN.
                              Let's go in right away.
SPARTAN.
Lead on, ma'am, anywheah you lahk.
ATHENIAN.
1295   Yes, and be quick.

[Exeunt into Acropolis.]

CHORUS OF MEN AND CHORUS OF WOMEN.

          All the rich embroideries, the
          scarves, the gold accessories, the
          trailing gowns, the robes I own
     I begrudge to no man: let him take what things he
          will
     for his children or a grown
1300   daughter who must dress for the procession up
          Athena's hill.
          Freely of my present stocks
          I invite you all to take.
          There are here no seals nor locks
          very hard to break.
1305   Search through every bag and box,
          look—you will find nothing there
          if your eyesight isn't fine—
          sharper far than mine!

1310   Are there any of you needing
          food for all the slaves you're feeding,
          all your little children, too?
     I have wheat in tiny grains for you, the finest sort,
     and I also offer you
     plenty of the handsome strapping grains that slaves
          get by the quart.

          So let any of the poor
1315   visit me with bag or sack
          which my salve will fill with more
          wheat than they can pack,
          giving each his ample share.
          Might I add that at my door

I have watch-dogs?—so beware.   1320
Come too close by day or night,
        you will find they bite.

[Voice of drunken Athenians from inside.]

FIRST ATHENIAN.
Open the door! [Shoves the porter aside.]
                              And will you get out of my way?

[A second drunken Athenian follows. The first sees the chorus.]

What are you sitting there for? Shall I, with this torch,
burn you alive? [Drops character.]
                              How vulgar! Oh, how commonplace!   1325
I can not do it!

[Starts back in. The second Athenian stops him and remonstrates with him in a whisper. The first turns and addresses the audience.]

                              Well, if it really must be done
to please you, we shall face it and go through with it.
CHORUS OF MEN AND CHORUS OF WOMEN.
And we shall face it and go through with it with you.
FIRST ATHENIAN.

[In character again, extravagantly.]

Clear out of here! Or you'll be wailing for your hair!

[Chorus of Women scours away in mock terror.]

Clear out of here! so that the Spartans can come out   1330
and have no trouble leaving, after they have dined.

[Chorus of Men scours away in mock terror.]

SECOND ATHENIAN.
I never saw a drinking-party like this one:
even the Spartans were quite charming, and of course
we make the cleverest company, when in our cups.
FIRST ATHENIAN.
You're right, because when sober we are not quite sane.   1335

If I can only talk the Athenians into it,
we'll always go on any embassy quite drunk,
for now, going to Sparta sober, we're so quick
to look around and see what trouble we can make
that we don't listen to a single word they say—   1340
instead we think we hear them say what they do not—
and none of our reports on anything agree.
But just now everything was pleasant. If a man
got singing words belonging to another song,
we all applauded and swore falsely it was fine!   1345
But here are those same people coming back again
to the same spot! Go and be damned, the pack of you!

[The Chorus, having thrown off their masks, put on other cloaks, and rushed back on stage, stay put.]

SECOND ATHENIAN.
Yes, damn them, Zeus! Just when the party's coming out!

[*The party comes rolling out.*]

SPARTAN.

[*To another.*]

Mah very chahmin friend, will you take youah flutes?
1350   Ah'll dance the dipody and sing a lovely song
of us and the Athenians, of both at once!

FIRST ATHENIAN.

[*As pleasantly as he can.*]

Oh yes, take up your little reeds, by all the gods:
I very much enjoy seeing you people dance.

SPARTAN.

        Memory, come,
1355   come inspiah thah young
        votaries to song,
        come inspiah theah dance!

[*Other Spartans join in.*]

        Bring thah daughtah, bring the sweet
            Muse, fo well she knows
1360   us and the Athenians,
            how at Ahtemisium
        they in godlike onslaught rose
        hahd against the Puhsian fleet,
            drove it to defeat!
1365   Well she knows the Spartan waws,
            how Leonidas
                in the deadly pass
                led us on lahk baws
        whettin' shahp theah tusks, how sweat
1370   on ouah cheeks in thick foam flowahed,
        off ouah legs how thick it showahed,
            fo the Puhsians men were mo'
            than the sands along the sho'.
        Goddess, huntress, Ahtemis,
1375   slayeh of the beasts, descend:
        vuhgin goddess, come to this
        feast of truce to bind us fast
        so ouah peace may nevah end.
        Now let friendship, love, and wealth
1380   come with ouah acco'd at last.
        May we stop ouah villainous
        wahly foxy stealth!
            Come, O huntress, heah to us,
            heah, O vuhgin, neah to us!

LYSISTRATA.

1385   Come, now that all the rest has been so well arranged,
you Spartans take these women home; these others, you.
Let husband stand beside his wife, and let each wife
stand by her husband: then, when we have danced a
        dance
to thank the gods for our good fortune, let's take care
1390   hereafter not to make the same mistakes again.

ATHENIAN.

Bring on the chorus! Invite the three Graces to follow,
and then call on Artemis, call her twin brother,
the leader of choruses, healer Apollo!

CHORUS.

[*Joins.*] Pray for their friendliest favor, the one and the
        other.
Call Dionysus, his tender eyes casting   1395
flame in the midst of his Maenads ecstatic with dancing.
    Call upon Zeus, the resplendent in fire,
    call on his wife, rich in honor and ire,
call on the powers who possess everlasting
memory, call them to aid,   1400
call them to witness the kindly, entrancing
peace Aphrodite has made!
        Alalai!
        Bound, and leap high! Alalai!
        Cry, as for victory, cry   1405
        Alalai!

LYSISTRATA.

Sing us a new song, Spartans, capping our new song.

SPARTANS.

        Leave thah favohed mountain's height,
        Spahtan Muse, come celebrate
        Amyclae's lord with us and great   1410
        Athena housed in bronze;
        praise Tyndareus' paih of sons,
        gods who pass the days in spoht
        wheah the cold Eurotas runs.

[*General dancing.*]

        Now to tread the dance,   1415
        now to tread it light,
        praising Spahta, wheah you find
            love of singing quickened bah the pounding beat of
                dancing feet,
        when ouah guhls lahk foals cavoht
        wheah the cold Eurotas runs,   1420
        when they fleetly bound and prance
            till theah haih unfilleted shakes in the wind,
        as of Maenads brandishin'
        ahvied wands and revelin',
            Leda's daughtah, puah and faiah,   1425
            leads the holy dances theah.

FULL CHORUS.

[*As everyone leaves dancing.*]

        So come bind up youah haih with youah hand,
            with youah feet make a bound
        lahk a deeah; for the chorus clap out
            an encouragin' sound,   1430
        singin' praise of the temple of bronze
            housin' her we adaw:
        sing the praise of Athena: the goddess unvanquished
            in waw!

SPOTLIGHT   GREEK OLD COMEDY

Comedy in the Greco-Roman world evolved in three stages: Old, Middle, and New Comedy. Old Comedy, typified by the plays of Aristophanes, flourished in Athens until the end of the Peloponnesian War (404 B.C.E.), when freedom of speech was severely curtailed. A safer, more neutral comedy focusing on common life and devoid of political humor seems to have thrived until about 336 B.C.E.; *Plutus*, among Aristophanes' last plays, is one of the few extant Middle Comedies. Menander (342–299 B.C.E.) is credited with developing New Comedy, which was subsequently perfected by the twin giants of Roman comic drama, Plautus and Terence. New Comedy, with its emphasis on middle-class people in domestic situations, remains with us today, largely in the guise of television sitcoms. Neil Simon is the master of New Comedy in the contemporary theater; his first play, *Come Blow Your Horn* (1960), resembles Terence's *Brothers*.

Although Old Comedy was characteristically topical and satiric, it retained vestiges of the various fertility and agricultural festivals that preceded the evolution of formal drama in Greece. In addition to political barbs, there is considerable sexual humor, both verbal and physical. Actors frequently wore the *phallus*, a grotesque reproduction of the male sex organ, about the waist, the legacy of ancient fertility rituals. Men played all roles, including female characters, and much of the hilarity stemmed from the "drag show" aspect of the performances. In the spirit of comedy, which exaggerates human folly, the actors also wore heavily padded costumes and relied on broad, physical playing.

Like the tragedies, Old Comedy had a precise structure with which you should be familiar as you read the plays. You already know many of these terms, but they serve particular functions within the comedies. The plays began with a prologue, which not only provided the exposition but established a *happy idea* (i.e., the play's thesis) to be tested. Lysistrata, for instance, suggests that the women of Athens and Sparta unite in a sex strike to curtail the war. The entrance of the chorus, or *parados*, was a spectacular event as they were traditionally dressed in extravagant costumes to suggest clouds, frogs, or birds as appropriate to title of the play or its subject matter; their ensuing song and dance was as colorful and pleasing to the ear as anything the Broadway stage can offer. Like tragedy, the plot was developed through a series of alternating episodes and odes. Customarily, the episodes were a loosely connected series of thematically related sketches that tested the happy idea and satirized the issues of the play. It may help to think of an Old Comedy as an American musical comedy or vaudeville show in which plot was secondary. (*Lysistrata* is, however, more tightly structured than most Old Comedies.) The middle episode traditionally presented the *agon* ("debate") about the merits of the happy idea; the debate between Lysistrata and the Athenian Commissioner is among the most profound agons in Greek comedy. Playwrights were obligated to write agons according to a rigid set of rules concerning the number, length, and meter of the lines, the order of speeches, the role of the *koryphaios* (chorus leader), the climactic moment, and so on. For instance, the first speaker in the agon always lost the debate. In spirit and function the *strophes* were much like production numbers in the modern musical: elaborate songs and dances intended to create mood, comment on the issues of the play, and provide spectacle. One strophe was dedicated to the *parabisis* ("harangue") in which the playwright stopped the action to address topical issues of concern to him and the audiences. In the most famous *parabisis*, Aristophanes inserted a speech into a revival of *The Clouds* that lambasted the judges and his audience for not awarding him a coveted prize for his efforts! Like the agon, the *parabisis* was bound by rigid guidelines; it had to be a hundred lines long and was carefully divided into sections that observed particular moods and meters. Such policies challenged the playwrights' creativity and insured that all entrants were playing by the same rules.

Old Comedy ended with an *exodos* or, more particularly, a *komos* ("joyful celebration") in which the conflicting parties celebrated their newfound unity and the resolution of the happy idea (which, in some plays like *The Clouds*, was rejected). The *komos* in *Lysistrata* bears special mention; technically, it is a *gamos*, or "union of the sexes." The exuberant dance to Aphrodite performed by the women and their newly reformed men represents one of the finest *gamos* in all dramatic literature. In subsequent ages, the spirits of the *komos* and *gamos* manifest themselves in banquets (*The Taming of the Shrew*), weddings (*A Midsummer Night's Dream*), and, of course, more dances. The extraordinary finale of Kenneth Branagh's film version of *Much Ado About Nothing* captures the spirit of Old Comedy's *gamos*.

ROME

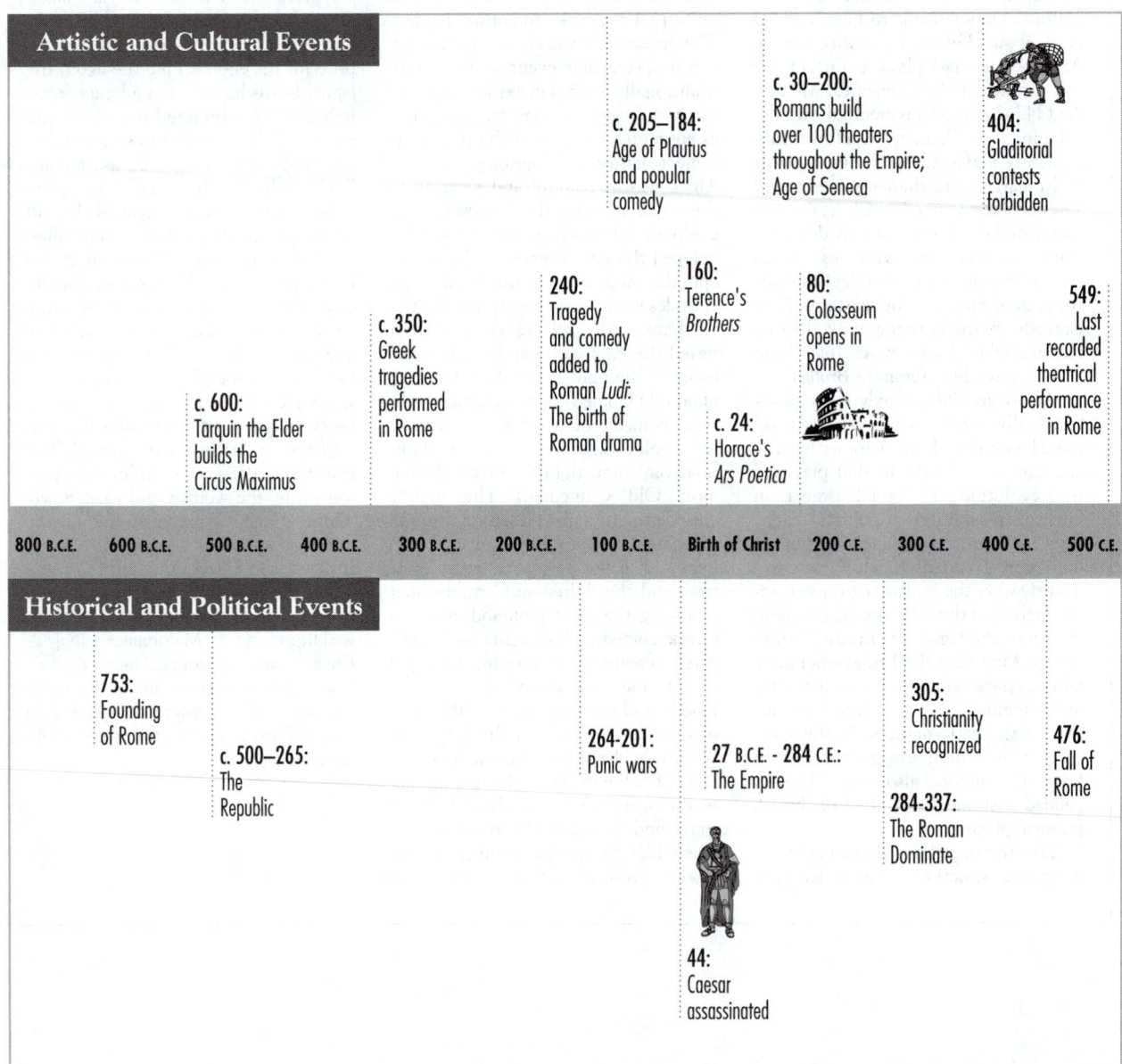

Artistic and Cultural Events

c. 205–184: Age of Plautus and popular comedy

c. 30–200: Romans build over 100 theaters throughout the Empire; Age of Seneca

404: Gladitorial contests forbidden

240: Tragedy and comedy added to Roman *Ludi*: The birth of Roman drama

160: Terence's *Brothers*

80: Colosseum opens in Rome

549: Last recorded theatrical performance in Rome

c. 350: Greek tragedies performed in Rome

c. 600: Tarquin the Elder builds the Circus Maximus

c. 24: Horace's *Ars Poetica*

| 800 B.C.E. | 600 B.C.E. | 500 B.C.E. | 400 B.C.E. | 300 B.C.E. | 200 B.C.E. | 100 B.C.E. | Birth of Christ | 200 C.E. | 300 C.E. | 400 C.E. | 500 C.E. |

Historical and Political Events

753: Founding of Rome

c. 500–265: The Republic

264-201: Punic wars

27 B.C.E. - 284 C.E.: The Empire

305: Christianity recognized

476: Fall of Rome

284-337: The Roman Dominate

44: Caesar assassinated

The Development of Roman Theater

Even as Greece was in decline, Rome was ascending as the supreme Western power. As they conquered the Mediterranean world, Romans assimilated the best features in architecture, literature, and the arts of other cultures. From the Greeks, the Romans borrowed the essential design of the theater space, the tragedies of Euripides, and the comedies of Menander, adding distinctively Roman touches to each.

Prior to their conquest of the Hellenic world, Roman theater had developed from ancient rites (*ludi*) honoring various gods associated with fertility, the planting season, and the harvest. However, Rome did not develop a formal drama until about 240 B.C.E., when the performance of plays was added to the *ludi Romani*, a popular festival that included athletic contests as well as singing, dancing, and clowning. Early Roman actors were called *histriones* ("storytellers"), and we still use the word *histrionic* to describe behavior that is showy or theatrical.

Although the Romans also worshipped a pantheon, neither the early *ludi* nor the subsequent drama evidenced a religious purpose similar to that of the Greeks. Roman religion was less communal, largely because individual families chose particular gods to whom they offered obeisance. The Romans actually referred to their theaters as temples and adorned them with statuary in honor of gods. However, Roman drama never addressed the cosmic and spiritual issues so central to Greek tragedy. For Romans, theater was primarily a diversion.

Playwrights and Popular Entertainments

Though the Romans imitated the Greek tragedians—particularly Euripides who was closest to them in time and temperament—Roman tragedy was decidedly inferior. However, it was the Romans—specifically Seneca (4 B.C.E.–65 C.E.)—who most influenced Renaissance tragedians, particularly in England. The Spanish-born Seneca wrote a number of tragedies, none of which we can be sure was actually performed. His tragedies were probably closet dramas, that is, plays written to be read by aristocratic citizens. Seneca's tragedies are noted for their violent and sensational action, their fascination with villainous characters, and their depiction of ghosts, witches, and the occult. These elements resurfaced in Elizabethan England as *Macbeth's* spirits, as the many dead bodies that cover *Hamlet's* stage, and as the diabolical Iago. As Shakespeare and his contemporaries learned their Latin, they read the plays of Seneca and incorporated many of his characteristics into their plays, which are referred to as "Senecan tragedies."

Seneca was the most eloquent spokesman for Stoicism, one of Rome's dominant philosophies. Despite the wealth generated by their vast empire, Romans saw life as hard and subject to misfortune. Some turned to Hedonism or Epicureanism, with their credos *Carpe diem* ("Seize the day") and "Eat, drink, and be merry, for tomorrow we die." The Stoics resigned themselves to suffer life's tribulations by maintaining a "holy calm" in the face of adversity. Giving in to one's emotions only compounded the problem because passion was an enemy of reason. Stoicism has two implications for drama. First, its philosophy of resignation diminished the possibility of tragedy: tragic heroes do not merely accept adversity, they rise to meet it. Second, the battle between passion and reason became a central concern of Renaissance dramatists who knew Seneca's work.

Roman comedy is more memorable than Roman tragedy, and also had a far more profound influence on Renaissance drama than its Greek counterpart. Roman comedy developed from two strains: folk comedies performed in the provinces of Italy and literate dramas written largely in imitation of the Greek Menander. Indeed, Horace (65–8 B.C.E.), the Roman orator, poet, and literary critic, advised young playwrights to imitate Greek models in his *Ars Poetica*, a document that stands beside Aristotle's *The Poetics* as one of the monuments of classical dramatic theory (see Forum, "The Art of Poetry," following the text of *Brothers*). In the province of Atella, masked and grotesquely padded actors performed short farces about middle-class life. Such comedies produced many of the stock characters we associate with Roman comedy: the braggart warrior, the trickster servant, the Senex (Old Man), and the country bumpkin.

Such types became staples of the literate drama and of the Italian *commedia dell'arte* in the Late Middle Ages and Renaissance.

Rome's finest literary comedies were written by Plautus and Terence, each of whom represents a significantly different approach to the genre. Plautus (254–184 B.C.E.) was the world's first professional playwright because he wrote (and performed) plays as a commercial venture. Such plays as *Amphitryon* and *The Rope* are slight in content yet superbly structured for comic effect. They rely on stock characters to move their improbable, yet entertaining, plots to a satisfying conclusion. A typical Plautine comedy portrays a young man seeking the love of a seemingly unreachable woman. The youth, who often challenges his own father for her affections, is aided by a wise servant who creates mischief and ultimately helps the lad win her. There is little moral purpose to Plautus's plays, as they existed solely to entertain the working-class audiences who filled Rome's public theaters. *The Comedy of Errors*, among Shakespeare's first comedies, was adapted from Plautus's *The Menaechmi*, and the popular Broadway musical *A Funny Thing Happened on the Way to the Forum* (1962, revived 1996) is based on several Plautine scripts.

In contrast to Plautus's comedies are those of Terence (185–159 B.C.E.), a Carthaginian slave (and perhaps Africa's first notable dramatist) who was brought to Rome and educated by Greek teachers. Terence borrowed both techniques and subject matter from the New Comedy of Menander. His comedies, such as *Brothers* (which follows), were written for Roman aristocrats and are more literate and instructive than those of Plautus. A moral strain runs through his works that cannot be found in Plautus; consequently, it was Terence who became the model for medieval and Renaissance playwrights. His comedies were performed in the learning academies of Europe and contributed to the evolution of the *commedia erudita* ("learned comedy") of the Italian Renaissance.

Perhaps Rome's ultimate contribution to world theater was popular entertainment. In addition to the commercially successful works of Plautus, Romans could attend a variety of spectacles catering to the masses. As early as 600 B.C.E., the emperor Tarquin erected the enormous Circus Maximus, the prototype of the modern sports arena, where Romans witnessed chariot races, gladiatorial contests, equestrian events, animal exhibitions and fights (*venationes*), and other entertainments we associate with the modern circus. Romans also produced *naumachiae*, spectacular sea battles staged in flooded arenas; in 46 B.C.E. Julius Caesar constructed a lake for a *naumachia* that featured almost 20,000 combatants. As people were actually killed and wounded in these battles, we might say that Roman spectacles represented some of the most "realistic" theatricals in the history of world theater. When Christian rulers came to power in the fourth century, they pointed to the barbarism of such spectacles and banned theatrical activity.

Theaters and Acting

As the ancient world's supreme architects, the Romans built magnificent theaters to accommodate their entertainments. Using the Greek model of the *theatron*, the *orchestra,* and the *skene*, the Romans built theaters that were noticeably different in one aspect. The typical Roman theater formed a single edifice with no separation of the auditorium (or *cavea*), the orchestra (now a half-circle reflecting the diminished role of the chorus in Roman drama), and the playing space (*pulpitum*), which was backed by the *scaenae*. The *frons scaenae* (facade) contained many alcoves for statues of gods and emperors, and traditionally featured three doors facing the audience. This three-door arrangement is a trademark of Roman comedy, and a large number of Renaissance comedies require "three houses" for their plots. The Romans appear to have used little scenery in their plays, but they did invent the act curtain (*auleum*), which was raised and lowered by telescoping poles from a trough on the forestage. The Roman theater was more intimate than the Greek, allowing for such playwriting devices as the aside (a speech directed to the audience that apparently is not heard by other characters). Asides, especially popular in comedies of intrigue, became one of the most distinctive features of Renaissance comedy. Roman theaters became the models for the great Italian Renaissance theaters such as the Teatro Olympico (1585) and Teatro Farnese (1616).

Tile frescoes found on the walls of Roman ruins tell us much about Roman actors. They wore masks and wigs that were apparently more lifelike than the highly exaggerated masks the Greeks wore in their vast amphitheaters. Unlike Greece, which revered the best actors in the City Dionysia, Rome afforded actors little status. Actors were drawn from the lower classes, even among slaves imported to perform the basest tasks. The lead actor in a Roman company was called the *dominus gregis* ("leader of the sheep"), and his company was the *grex* ("herd"), an indication of the low esteem given actors in Rome. Roscius (c. 126 B.C.E.–62 C.E.) was Rome's best-known actor and perhaps the world's first "star." He is remembered by subsequent generations: Shakespeare refers to him several times in his plays, and the great nineteenth-century American tragedian Edwin Forrest was billed as "the young Roscius."

The Fall of Rome

As Rome fell into decline, its theater also degenerated. Bawdy spectacles and blasphemous parodies of Christian ceremonies offended church fathers who were gaining power in Rome. In 200 C.E., Tertulian wrote "On the Spectacles," in which he attacked actors as a corrupting influence ("The polluted things pollute us"). A hundred years later Constantine became Rome's first Christian emperor, and by the end of the fourth century Christians were forbidden by church edict to attend theater events. The last recorded performance of a theatrical event in Rome occurred in 549 C.E. The long-standing antipathy between some Christian sects and the theater remains another legacy of the late Roman theater.

BROTHERS (ADELPHOE)

TERENCE

TERENCE (PUBLIUS TERENTIUS AFER) (195–159 B.C.E.)

Whereas Plautus was likely the more popular playwright in classical Rome, it was Terence who was favored by intellectuals, and his plays were subsequently the most closely imitated among medieval and early Renaissance playwrights. Like the works of Plautus, Terence's plays were patterned after the New Comedy established by the Greek Menander, but his comedies contain little boisterous farce. They are plotted with greater attention to logic, and they offer pronounced moral messages favored by the Roman intellectual elites for whom he wrote.

Terence was a Carthaginian who was brought to Rome and educated there. In the first half of the second century B.C.E., Roman patricians favored Greek thought and literature. The leaders of this Greek renaissance, the nobles Scipio and Laelius, heard of Terence's writing skills and became his mentors. They promoted his work among Roman intellectuals, among whom Terence enjoyed an enormous popularity with such Greek-inspired plays as *Phormio*, *The Mother-in-Law*, and especially *Brothers*.

Terence contributed two significant developments to Western playwriting. First, he favored the double plot in order to contrast the actions of characters (a device that Shakespeare exploited, particularly in his comedies). In *Brothers*, for instance, we see two approaches to child rearing: the very conservative and the liberal. Terence plotted his plays carefully and logically, largely to make the morals of his comedies more accessible. Thus, he did much to advance the cause of realism in Western theater. And in contrast to many of the playwrights who preceded him, he favored true stage dialogue—as opposed to lengthy monologues—again as a means of making his plays more lifelike and, therefore, more instructive.

Secondly, and as an outgrowth of the double plot, Terence advanced the notion of "the foil" (a specialty of Sophocles in Greece) as he skillfully set one character against another to promote his themes. Again, in *Brothers* we meet two sets of brothers, the fathers (Micio and Demea) and sons (Aeschinus and Ctesipho); through the various contrasts of the brothers we arrive at an understanding of education and raising children. As the brothers learn from their mistakes, and successes, so too does the audience.

Terence's comedies are stoutly moralistic and adhere to the popular Stoic philosophy, which preached restraint and moderation in human action. As Demea says at the end of *Brothers*, "I've discovered . . . that nothing is better for a man than to be easygoing and open-minded." Terence's pleas for temperance appealed to Christian writers in the Middle Ages and to teachers in the learning academies of the Renaissance. Little wonder his plays were often performed as part of Latin lessons—students learned their Latin and morality in a single exercise. The Saxon nun Hrostvitha used the comedies of Terence as models for her novitiates, who wrote plays about Christian saints as part of their instruction.

Not only were Terence's plays filled with "thoughtful laughter," they also relied on sentimental denouements featuring reconciliations between feuding brothers, reunions of long-lost kin, and other devices that perhaps asked audiences to shed a tear amid their laughter. These, too, would become staples of the Renaissance drama and (especially) eighteenth-century sentimental comedies. In our time, the most successful Broadway playwright of the late twentieth century, Neil Simon, owes a debt to Terence; Simon's first play, *Come Blow Your Horn* (1961), is remarkably similar to *Brothers*.

BROTHERS (160 B.C.E.)

Debates about how best to educate one's offspring have raged for centuries. Aristophanes tackled the issue in ancient Greece in *The Clouds*, which attacked the liberal thinking of Socrates. Luis Valdez's short play, *"No saco nada de la escuela"* satirizes an educational system that ignores the needs of minority children. And, as you are well aware, daily headlines and TV talk shows are devoted to "the educational crisis." All of which makes *Brothers* a topical play despite the fact that it was written over two thousand years ago.

Brothers is a *fabula palliata*, a comedy based on Greek models (note the Athenian setting), in which Demea, a conservative farmer, has attempted to raise his son (Ctesipho) conservatively, even rigidly. His city-dwelling brother, Micio, has taken a more liberal approach to raising his son (Aeschinus). As events reveal, the more puritanical upbringing only breeds libertine behavior in Ctesipho and Demea learns that a too-firm hand may be more dangerous than a too-lax hand. "No man has ever calculated up the profits and losses of his life so accurately that circumstances, age, and experience, don't add up to something new." proclaims the prodigal father of his newfound knowledge.

Terence is not necessarily advocating a liberal education: the accusations concerning Aeschinus's "youthful indiscretions" are not unfounded, though Micio's son does eventually prove to be the most level-headed and upright of the four brothers. The trick of the play, however, is the manner in which Terence allows us to think that Aeschinus is little more than a wastrel (and thereby judge the worth of his seemingly indecorous behavior). We are pleasantly surprised at the elder son's redemption at play's end, yet we feel secure in our condemnation of womanizing and other miscreant deeds. Thus Terence allows us to have our moral cake and eat it, too. Such formulas would serve the theater well for hundreds of years (e.g., *She Stoops to Conquer*, see Chapter 6).

Not only does Terence skillfully play the various brothers against one another in order to enhance the instructional value of his comedy, he also uses secondary characters, notably the servants (or more correctly, slaves) to these ends. The wicked procurer, Sannio, is countered by the faithful slaves Geta and Canthara. Syrus, Aeschinus's servant, exhibits something of the duality of his master: he is both conniving trickster (an archetype of Roman comedy) and diligent helper. As Rome relied on slaves and servants for much of its workforce, it is fitting that Terence makes these characters central to his action, however uncomfortable we may feel about slavery.

So, too, are the playwright's depictions of women in Rome. Here we see women—Sostrata and Pamphila—as victims of male aggressions. In this play they are (mostly) accurately portrayed as objects subject to the whims of men, though certainly Aeschinus's conversion implies that some dignity will be afforded Pamphila and her mother. Although the Roman home was matriarchal— the mother (or *domina matrix*) invariably ruled the home in the father's absence—Terence's play shows us the tribulations faced by women in this militaristic culture.

Though Terence's tale of parental and filial errors is relatively simple and needs little elaboration here, a couple of issues invite commentary. First, the prologue to the play is typical of Terence's dramaturgy. Unlike Plautus, and even his Greek models, Terence uses the prologue in a relatively new fashion. Here it is used neither to establish the themes of the play nor provide exposition (as one often finds in Plautus). Rather, Terence's prologue is a scholarly footnote in which he pays tribute to his inspirations and, more important, scolds his critics for their unkind assessment of his works (not unlike Aristophanes did in his *parabises*). Though the prologue is usually the first element cut in contemporary productions, it is a useful example of theater practice in Rome. Clearly the war between playwrights and critics was (as it still is) a heated one.

In the same vein, note that Terence ends his play with an obvious—and very artificial—plea for the audience to applaud. This was the *plaudite*, a request by an actor for the audience's approbation, and it remained a convention in the theater until the nineteenth century. See Puck's final speech in *A Midsummer Night's Dream* for an example of Shakespeare's most famous *plaudite*.

A reading of *Brothers*, then, offers us not only an example of Roman comedy at its finest, but an understanding of Roman private life—and the public life of the theater. How fitting for a play whose central premise is education.

The tricky Syrus, senior slave in Micio's house, leads the conniving Sannio onto the stage in this Roman artist's representation of Brothers.

BROTHERS
(ADELPHOE)

TERENCE

Translation by Charles Mercier*

The Ancient Production Notice

Here begins *Adelphoe (Brothers)* by Terence. The Greek play that Terence translates and adapts is *Adelphoe* by Menander. It was produced at the funeral games for L. Aemilius Paulus which were put on by Q. Fabius Maximus and P. Cornelius Scipio Aemilianus Africanus. The principal actors were L. Hatilius from Praeneste and L. Ambivius Turpio. Flaccus, slave of Claudius, played the accompaniment on the Tyrian double-reeds throughout the production. This was Terences sixth production, produced in the consulship of M. Cornelius Cethegus and L. Anicius Gallus (160 B.C.E.).

CHARACTERS

MICIO (*senex*) is 64, elegant, luxurious, somewhat careless of responsibility. Remarkably for this culture, he is unmarried; he is well-off, has a beautiful city house, and likes his solitary pleasure. He has adopted his brother's teenage son, Aeschinus, some years ago, and has raised him permissively and progressively. Micio has a sententious wit and likes to lecture others, but the action of the piece tests his theories of living.

DEMEA (*senex*) is Micio's brother, tough, frugal, grouchy, espouser of traditional values of thrift, a dweller in the country on his farm. He is a widower and has two sons, the older of which, Aeschinus, he let Micio adopt. Demea is a pain in everyone's neck, but, in his own mind at least, represents old-

fashioned virtue and the responsible child-rearing without which sons are spoiled and corrupted. Micio and Demea clash over this issue.

AESCHINUS (*adulescens*) is the son of Demea adopted by Micio, a teenager, the young lover of the girl next door. He has taken advantage of Micio's permissiveness, but has not lost all of Demea's rigorous sense of responsibility.

CTESIPHO (*adulescens*) is the son of Demea, raised by him on the farm. Another pubescent young lover, he is in love with the slave girl his brother eventually arranges to buy. He adores his older brother, who has opened up for him cultivated city life. Torn about his behavior, he finds it difficult to disobey his father.

SYRUS (*servus*), an older man, senior slave in Micio's household, a tricky slave. Syrus is impudent, sarcastic, an accomplished

*Line numbers were provided by the translator

liar; his deviousness serves his masters well, to whose interests he proves devoted. He is the fixer, the one who successfully drives a hard bargain with a slave dealer.

DROMO (*puer*), slave in Micio's household, a cook.

PARMENO (*servus*), slave in Micio's household.

SANNIO (*leno*), middle-aged man, the nasty, disreputable dealer in slaves, especially young women. He provides a service that is availed of, but is under no illusions about his trade or the contempt in which he is nevertheless held. He is just trying to make a living.

SOSTRATA (*matrona*), an older widow with an unmarried daughter, who lives next door to Micio. She is poor and devoted to the honor and dignity of her family. Her daughter's pregnancy causes her much grief, but is just the challenge to bring out her toughness.

PAMPHILA (*virgo*), Sostrata's daughter, the girl next door, raped and made pregnant by Aeschinus.

GETA (*servus*), an older man, the dutiful senior slave of Sostrata's household. He is serious about doing all he can to uphold the family of Sostrata.

CANTHARA (*anus*), old woman, nurse, slave of Sostrata's family.

HEGIO (*senex*), an older man, a pillar of the community, though of less property than Micio, a serious man who agreed to look out for the family of Sostrata when his friend, her husband, died. He takes this commitment as a sacred obligation.

BACCHIS (*meretrix*), young woman, the prostitute-slave loved and bought by Ctesipho.

PROLOGUE (*Delivery is unaccompanied speech*)

When the playwright realized that his work
was being attacked unfairly and that his enemies
were doing violence to the play we are about to act,
he wanted to submit to trial: *you* will be the judges
whether his work should be praised or blamed.
Synapothneskontes is a comedy by Diphilus.
10 Plautus adapted it as the play *Dying Together*.
In the original Greek, near the beginning, there is a young man
who kidnaps a prostitute from a slave dealer.
Plautus left that scene out entirely, so Terence
translated it word for word and used it in *Brothers*.
We are about to act the play for the first time.
Judge carefully whether you think he stole
or actually rescued a scene that was carelessly cut out.
As for what those evil-minded men are saying,
"he gets help from important Romans,
they practically write his plays for him"
—what they think is a nasty insult he thinks is the highest praise:
he wins the approval of those who win
the approval of all of you, the whole city.
20 Each one of you in time of need has relied upon
their generous service in war, in peace, in industry.
Now don't expect a plot summary.
The two old men who will appear first

will explain the story in part
and the rest will be made clear as the action unfolds.
Make sure your fairness encourages the playwright
to work even harder writing plays!

(*Two houses on a street in a city imagined to be Athens. One, the more opulent, is Micio's; the other, the more humble, is Sostrata's. Two entrances on either side, one from the town, the other from the country.*)

(*Micio enters from his house.*)

MICIO.

(*calling a slave*)
Storax!
Aeschinus never got back last night from his party.
None of the slaves who went to get him either.
Well, I'm sure what they say is true:
if you're gone for a while, or off on your own,
it's better to have happen to you what your wife accuses you of   30
or what she thinks in her heart when she's mad
than what loving parents fear.
Your wife, if you're gone for a while, thinks you're having an affair
or you're out gambling
or you're out drinking and having a good time
off by yourself while she's alone and miserable.
But my son is gone and I know what I'm afraid of.
I'm worried. I hope he's not cold.
I hope he hasn't had an accident. I hope he hasn't broken a bone or something.
Why in the world should a man take it into his head
to make something for himself that is dearer to him
than his own life? He's not my son by birth, you know,   40
but my brother's. Ever since we were children
my brother and I have been totally different.
I've led a charming life here in the city. I like my leisure.
And, what my friends tell me is a blessing, I never married.
My brother's been exactly the opposite.
He lives in the country. Tough. Frugal. He married, had two sons.
I adopted the elder of the two,
and I've brought him up since he was a boy.
I have held him, and loved him, as my own.
He's my greatest joy, the one thing I love.
And I do my best that he should feel the same way about me.   50
I give him money. I let him do what he wants.
I don't think it necessary to exercise my full parental authority.
In fact, other boys keep what they do secret from their fathers
—you know how boys are. But I have trained my son
not to hide anything from me.
If a boy gets used to lying and deceiving his father,
he'll be more likely to lie and deceive others.

I believe that respect and freedom is a better discipline
for freeborn sons than fear.
My brother and I disagree on this, and he's not happy
60   about it.
He's always coming to me and yelling at me,
"What are you doing, Micio?
What's he having these love affairs for?
What's he drinking for? What are you ruining our boy
      for?
Why are you racking up our bills for all this?
You buy him too many clothes! You're a terrible father!"
He's much too harsh, beyond what's the right thing
and the proper thing.
If you want to know my opinion,
it's a terrible mistake to think that authority based on
      force
has more weight and stability
than authority that's joined by friendship.
My theory is this, my philosophy of bringing up children
      is this:
when you use punishment to force your child to obey
      you,
70   he worries only about not getting caught.
If he thinks he can get away with something,
he reverts right back to his natural state.
But when you join your son to you in kindness,
he acts sincerely, he is eager to treat you the same way.
Whether he's with you or far away from you, he behaves
      the same.
That's a real father: training his son
to do what's right on his own,
not out of fear of anyone else.
That's the difference between a father and a slave-owner.
A man who doesn't know the difference
between a father and a slave-owner
should admit he has no idea how to rule his freeborn
      sons.

(*Demea enters from the country.*)

Well, is this the very man I was talking about?
It is the man I was talking about.
I see he's rather angry.
80   I suppose it's time for his usual abuse.

You're looking very well, Demea
DEMEA.
    Well that's just fine. I've been looking for you.
MICIO.
    What's wrong?
DEMEA.
    You're asking me what's wrong.
We've got an Aeschinus on our hands
and you're asking me what's wrong.
MICIO.
    (*aside*) Didn't I tell you?
What's he done?

DEMEA.
    What's he done? A boy who's ashamed of nothing,
who's afraid of no one,
who thinks no law restrains him?
I won't mention what's gone on in the past.
Do you want to know his latest outrage?
MICIO.
    What is it?
DEMEA.
    He broke down a door
and forced his way into a stranger's house.
He beat up the owner and the whole household
almost to death. He abducted a woman he's in love with. 90
It's a disgrace. Everyone's talking about it.
Everyone I run into tells me about it, Micio.
It's on everybody's lips.
I tell you, if he needs an example
why can't he look to his brother, frugal and sober,
who pays attention to his work on the farm?
These two brothers aren't alike at all.
And when I reproach him, Micio, I reproach you:
you've allowed him to be corrupted.
MICIO.
    There's nothing more unjust
than a man without experience of the world;
he thinks nothing right but what he's done himself.
DEMEA.
    And what's that supposed to mean?   100
MICIO.
    That you're misjudging this.
It's not a crime, believe me, for a boy
to fool around a little bit with prostitutes,
to go drinking. It's not.
And breaking down a door isn't a crime either.
If you and I never fooled around, it's because we couldn't
      afford it.
Now you're taking credit for how we behaved
when we just didn't have the money to do anything else?
It's not right. If we had had the opportunity,
we would have done the same thing.
If you were at all a human being,
you'd let that son of yours do this sort of thing now,
while he's young, rather than later,
when at long last he's tossed your corpse out of the house
and behaves that way at a less appropriate age.   110
DEMEA.
    Well, Jupiter! You're the man to drive me insane.
It's not a crime for a boy to do all this?
MICIO.
    Oh, pay attention to me, will you, so you stop
banging my ear again and again and again on this.
You gave me your son to adopt. He's become mine.
If he commits an offense, Demea, he commits it on my
      behalf.
I will take responsibility.

He goes to parties, he drinks, he perfumes himself: it's on
  me.
He's in love, he'll have money from me
as long as it's within reason.
And when it isn't, perhaps then she'll close the door on
  him.
120 So he broke down a door; I'll send a carpenter.
He tore up someone's clothes in a fight; I'll send a tailor.
I have—thank the gods—I have the means to do this,
and so far, it hasn't been a problem.
So, finally, either shut up
or let someone appoint us an arbitrator.
I will prove that you are the one who's at fault, not I.

DEMEA.
Listen to me, learn how to be a father
from one who really knows.

MICIO.
You are his father by nature;
I am his father in the way I brought him up.

DEMEA.
You, in the way you brought him up?

MICIO.
Ah, if you're going to go on, I'm leaving—

DEMEA.
So this is how you're treating me?

MICIO.
And I'm supposed to listen to the same thing
over and over and over . . .

DEMEA.
Well, I'm concerned.

MICIO.
Well, I'm concerned too. But really, Demea,
130 why don't we split the concern:
you take care of your son and I'll take care of mine.
If you're going to try to take care of both,
you might as well demand back the son you gave me to
  adopt.

DEMEA.
Ah, Micio . . .

MICIO.
Well that's the way I see it.

DEMEA.
All right, then. If that's what you want,
let him squander, waste, and be wasted.
What do I care? But if after this I hear one word . . .

MICIO.
Getting angry again, Demea?

DEMEA.
Don't you believe me?
Am I asking for the son I gave you back?
It's sickening. I'm his father.
But if I oppose—oh, all right.
You want me to take care of mine,
I'll take care of mine, and—thank the gods—
he's the kind of son I want.

That son of yours will understand one day.
I won't say anything worse about him.   140

(*Demea exits to the town.*)

MICIO.
There's something to what he says,
but he's not entirely right.
Even if this business is a bit out of hand,
I wasn't going to let him know that I was worried.
He's the sort of man that when I want to calm him down
I've got to find him and scare him off.
Even then he scarcely behaves like a human being.
If I really got him angry or responded to it
I'd immediately become as insane as he is.
It's true Aeschinus has to some degree
offended me in this matter.
What prostitute has he not fallen in love with?
What slave dealer has he not had to pay off?   150
Bored with it all, I guess,
he finally started talking about getting married.
I was hoping his adolescence had cooled down,
and I was pleased. And now look, all over again!
Well, I would like to know exactly what happened
and meet this man. I'll find him in the forum.

(*Micio exits to the town.*)

(*Aeschinus and Parmeno enter from town together leading
Bacchis. Sannio pursues. Delivery changes from unaccompanied speech to canticum.*)

SANNIO.
Help! Help me! I beg you people,
save a wronged and innocent man.
Help me! I need help!

AESCHINUS.
(*to the girl*)
Easy. Stop right here. Don't look back.
There's no danger. As long as I'm here,
he'll never touch you.

SANNIO.
I'll get her all right.

AESCHINUS.
As dirty a criminal as he is,
he won't make the mistake
of getting beaten up twice.

SANNIO.
Aeschinus, listen to me.   160
It's not as if you can say
you didn't know what kind of man I am.
I'm a sex-slave dealer.

AESCHINUS.
I know that.

SANNIO.
But as honest a slave dealer as ever there was.
And as for excusing yourself later,
"I really didn't mean to hurt you,"

you can forget it. Believe me, I'll get my rights in court.
You won't be paying off in words
what you did to me in deeds.
I know the sort of thing you boys say,
"I didn't mean to do it. I'll swear an oath.
You got hurt, but it was unintentional."
Well, I don't deserve this treatment.

AESCHINUS.

Hurry up, open the door.

SANNIO.

So you're going to ignore me?

AESCHINUS.

Get inside now.

SANNIO.

And I won't allow it.

(Scuffle for the girl.)

AESCHINUS.

170   Here, get in front of him, Parmeno.

Yes, that's right. Now don't take your eyes off mine.
If I give the signal, you instantly punch him in the chin.

SANNIO.

I'd like to see him try.

AESCHINUS.

Look out! Let go of the girl.

(Scuffle. Parmeno punches Sannio.)

SANNIO.

It's an outrage! An outrage!

AESCHINUS.

He'll do it again if you're not careful.

(Parmeno again hurts Sannio.)

SANNIO.

Oh, oh . . .

AESCHINUS.

I hadn't given the signal, but true enough,
better to err on the side of violence. Now get inside.

(Parmeno and Bacchis go into Micio's house.)

SANNIO.

So what is this? This is your kingdom, is it?

AESCHINUS.

If I were the king you would be rewarded
according to what you deserve.

SANNIO.

What business do you have with me?

AESCHINUS.

Nothing.

SANNIO.

Do you know the kind of man I am?

AESCHINUS.

I have no desire for that kind of knowledge.

SANNIO.

Have I touched anything of yours?

AESCHINUS.

If you had, you'd be suffering for it.

SANNIO.

What greater right do you have
to possess my girl, whom I paid for? Tell me.

AESCHINUS.

It's better for you not to make a scene here   180
in front of the house. If you continue to bother me
you'll be taken inside and worked over
with the whip until you're dead.

SANNIO.

A whipping for a free man?

AESCHINUS.

Yes, it will happen.

SANNIO.

You scum! And they say that here all men
have equality before the law.

AESCHINUS.

Now if you've raged enough, you slave dealer,
please listen to me.

SANNIO.

Who's the one who's raging, you or me?

AESCHINUS.

Forget that and let's get down to business.

SANNIO.

What business? What am I supposed to get down to?

AESCHINUS.

Are you ready to hear your interest in this?

SANNIO.

Absolutely, as long as it's fair.

AESCHINUS.

Right, a man who buys and sells young women wants a
fair deal.

SANNIO.

I'm a slave dealer, I admit it. I specialize in young women.
I'm the common plague of all young men, a liar, a disease.
All the same, I'm not the origin of this illegality.
Not at all.

AESCHINUS.

My god, so you haven't exhausted your supply of illegality?

SANNIO.

Go back to where you started, Aeschinus.   190

AESCHINUS.

Alright, damn you, you bought that girl for 20 minas.
You'll be paid back that much.

SANNIO.

What? And if I refuse to sell her to you, you'll force me?

AESCHINUS.

Not at all.

SANNIO.

Oh, I was afraid you would.

AESCHINUS.

And I don't think she ought to be sold.
She's a free woman. Yes, I will enter a formal plea
on her behalf to prove her free-born status.

Consider then which of two options you prefer:
take the money or start preparing to litigate.
Think it over till I get back to you, slave dealer.

(*Aeschinus goes into Micio's house.*)

SANNIO.
Good Jupiter in the sky! It's no wonder that
being victimized by crime can drive you insane.
He dragged me from my house, shoved me around,
abducted the girl that belongs to me as I resisted him,
200 beat the crap out of me—a poor little man.
And in exchange for these crimes
he wants me to give her up at cost.
Well then, since he so richly deserves it,
I'll make the deal; he demands his right.
All right, I will do it, just as long as he gives me the
    money.
Wait a minute, though, I see what will happen:
as soon as I agree to the price, he'll produce
some witness on the spot to testify that I sold her to him.
And the money's a dream:
"Soon, soon, I'll pay you tomorrow."
I could still endure that as long as he did pay me the
    money,
whatever the injustice. Really, I have to face the truth:
when you go into my line of business,
you've got to accept and keep quiet about
the violence of young men. Nobody's going to pay me.
None of these considerations mean a damn thing any-
    way.

(*Syrus enters from Micio's house.*)

SYRUS.
(*back inside to Aeschinus*)
Yes, yes, I'll take care of everything myself.
I'll fix it so that he agrees to everything
210 and on top of it says that he's been treated very well.

So what's this I hear, Sannio,
about your having some sort of dispute with my master?
SANNIO.
I never saw a fight that was more unfair
than what we had today. We're both pretty exhausted:
he from beating me up and I from getting beaten up.
SYRUS.
It was your fault.
SANNIO.
What was I supposed to do?
SYRUS.
You should have gratified a young man.
SANNIO.
How could I have gratified him better?
I let him hit me in the mouth.
SYRUS.
Come on, you want to know what I say?
Sometimes forgetting about money at the right moment

is the best way to make a profit.
Look, you fool, you were afraid that if you made
the slightest concession in your rights
and been a little more gratifying to a young man,
that you wouldn't be paid back with interest.
SANNIO.
I do not pay cash for hope.
SYRUS.
You'll never make any money that way.   220
All right, good-bye Sannio,
you just don't know how to bait a trap.
SANNIO.
Look, I'm sure your way is better.
It's just that I have never been far-thinking enough
not to prefer whatever I could get right at the moment.
SYRUS.
Come on, I know what you're like.
As if 20 minas mattered to you
when you could just as easily oblige him.
Besides, I've heard you're about to sail for Cyprus.
SANNIO.
Damn.
SYRUS.
You have a whole line of merchandise to sell there.
You've chartered a boat. I know this must weigh on your
    mind.
When you come back, we can talk about it further.
SANNIO.
I will not budge.
(*to himself*)
Damn it, I'm lost. That was their hope all along
when they started this.

(*Delivery changes to unaccompanied speech.*)

SYRUS.
(*to himself*)
He's scared. I put a stone in his shoe.
SANNIO.
(*to himself*)
Bastards. Look at that, he's hit me
right where I'm vulnerable. I bought a whole shipment   230
of slave women and other goods to export to Cyprus.
And if I don't get there in time for the slave market,
I'll lose the whole investment. But if I let this business
    go
and take it up again when I return, I lose.
The negotiation will be frozen.
"You're coming now, after all this time?
Why did you allow so much time to pass?
Where have you been for so long?"
That's their strategy: it's better for me
just to give her up than to stay here long enough
to get her back or take it up when I return.
SYRUS.
So have you figured out when you think you'll be back?

SANNIO.

This is a tactic worthy of your household, is it?
So that's what Aeschinus is trying to do:
rob me of my girl by violence and illegality?

SYRUS.

(aside) He's wavering.
I have just one thing to say, Sannio, see if you agree.
240   Rather than gambling on getting all or nothing,
take half. He can scrape together 10 minas somewhere or
      other.

SANNIO.

Oh, so a poor man is now in doubt about his principal?
Has he no shame? He's broken all my teeth,
and my whole head is a swollen tumor
because he beat the crap out of me.
On top of that, he's going to cheat me?
Here I draw the line.

SYRUS.

Whatever you say. I'm sure
there's nothing further I can do before I go.

SANNIO.

No, no, Heracles, let me ask you this, Syrus.
Whatever's happened, rather than my going to court,
just let me be repaid what I paid for her.
At cost, Syrus. And I know
250   that up to now you haven't enjoyed my friendship,
but in future you'll have reason to say
that I don't forget a favor.

SYRUS.

I'll do my best.

(Ctesipho enters from the town.)

SYRUS.

Well, here's Ctesipho.
He's thrilled about his girlfriend.

SANNIO.

What about my offer?

SYRUS.

Be patient.

(Sannio hides himself and lurks. Delivery changes to unaccompanied speech.)

CTESIPHO.

There's great joy from someone doing you a favor.
But when the favor comes from the right man . . .
O my brother, my brother, what can I say in your praise?
I'm sure of this: whatever I say
is not magnificent enough to express how wonderful you
      are.
I judge that I have one great advantage over everybody
      else.
There isn't a man whose brother is
such a master of every good quality.

SYRUS.

260   Ctesipho!

CTESIPHO.

Syrus, where's Aeschinus?

SYRUS.

Here at home. He's waiting for you.

CTESIPHO.

Oh!

SYRUS.

What is it?

CTESIPHO.

What is it? Syrus, it's because of him that I'm now alive.
What a sweet guy! He put all of my interests ahead of his.
The fights, the gossip, my trouble, my misdeed,
he took upon himself. Nothing can top this.

The door's opening!

SYRUS.

Wait, wait, it's your brother coming out.

(Aeschinus enters from Micio's house.)

AESCHINUS.

What about that piece of filth now?

SANNIO.

(aside) He means me. He doesn't have anything, does he?
Damn, I can't make it out.

AESCHINUS.

O, glad to see you. I was looking for you.
What's happening, Ctesipho? It's all taken care of.
No more misery for you.

CTESIPHO.

Yes, Heracles, no more misery with a brother like you.
O my Aeschinus, o my true brother.
Oh, if I praise you any more to your face
you'll think it's flattery, not gratitude.   270

AESCHINUS.

Go on, you silly boy, as if you and I
didn't know each other by now, Ctesipho.
I only regret finding out so late
that it was almost beyond the power
of the whole world to help you.

CTESIPHO.

I was ashamed.

AESCHINUS.

That's stupidity, not shame.
A little thing like that and you're ready to leave the
      country?
Terrible. May the gods forbid such a thing.

CTESIPHO.

I made a mistake.

AESCHINUS.

Well, what does our Sannio have to say?

SYRUS.

He's calmed down.

AESCHINUS.

I'm going to the forum to borrow the money to pay him
      off.

You can go in to her now, Ctesipho.

(*Ctesipho goes in Micio's house.*)
(*Sannio emerges.*)

SANNIO.
    Syrus, go ahead.
SYRUS.
    Yes, let's get going, he'll soon be on his way to Cyprus.
SANNIO.
    Not as soon as you think.
    I have plenty of time right now.
SYRUS.
    You'll be paid, don't worry.
SANNIO.
280   But will he pay it all back?
SYRUS.
    He'll pay it all. Just shut up and follow along.
SANNIO.
    All right.
CTESIPHO.
    (*from the door*)
    Hey, hey, Syrus.
SYRUS.
    What?
CTESIPHO.
    I beg you, by Heracles, pay off
    that foul man as soon as possible,
    so that if he gets even madder
    it won't get back to my father somehow
    and I'm ruined for good.
SYRUS.
    It won't happen. Courage! Go on inside
    and enjoy yourself with your girlfriend while we're gone,
    get the couches and everything else ready for dinner.
    As soon as the business is settled,
    I'll be back home with the groceries.
CTESIPHO.
    Do so. Everything's come out so well,
    let's celebrate for the rest of the day.

(*Syrus and Sannio exit towards the town.*)
(*Sostrata and Canthara enter from Sostrata's house.*)

SOSTRATA.
    How is she doing now?
CANTHARA.
    How is she doing? Quite well, I think.

(*We hear Pamphila in labor.*)

    O my poor dear, your labor's just starting.
    (*to Sostrata*) And you're as afraid
290   as if you'd never been present at a childbirth,
    as if you'd never had a child yourself.
SOSTRATA.
    We're in terrible trouble, we have no friends,
    we're alone. And Geta's not here,

and I have no one to send for the midwife
or to bring Aeschinus here.
CANTHARA.
    Oh, he'll soon be here. He always comes,
    he's never missed a day.
SOSTRATA.
    He's been my only support through these troubles.
CANTHARA.
    Consider the circumstances, mistress.
    Things could not have turned out better.
    She may have been raped, but he is a fine man,
    of such character and heart, born of such a fine family.
SOSTRATA.
    Well, by Pollux, I suppose.
    Let's just hope the gods keep him that way.

(*Geta enters from the town.*)

GETA.
    Well, it's down to this: there's nothing
    that all the intelligence in all the world
    can do to figure a way out of our problem.   300
    There's no help for me, for my mistress,
    for my mistress's daughter. O gods!
    Suddenly we're walled in by so many things that there's
        no way out:
    rape, poverty, crime, helplessness, disgrace. What times
        we're living in!
    Injustice! Sacrilege! A shameless man . . . !
SOSTRATA.
    O god, what's Geta so upset about?
GETA.
    . . . whom neither honor, nor oath, nor pity held back or
        restrained, not even when the girl he shamefully and
        violently had his way with
    is on the verge of having his baby . . .
SOSTRATA.
    I can't understand what he's talking about.
CANTHARA.
    Well let's find out, Sostrata.
GETA.
    . . . O, I'm out of my mind I'm so burning with anger.   310
    There's nothing I'd like better
    than having a crack at that whole family
    so I could spill all my anger on them
    while the wound is fresh.
    I wouldn't mind a whipping
    as long as I could get my vengeance on them.
    First I'd strangle the old man himself
    who brought up that criminal son.
    And then that instigator Syrus, O, I'd tear him to shreds.
    I'd get him up by the waist and smash him back to the
        ground
    on his head to spill out his brains on the road.
    I'd pluck out the eyes of the young man
    and then throw him over a cliff.

The others I'll rush and drive and knock
and thrash and trample under my feet.

320 But I'd better stop and inform my mistress immediately.

SOSTRATA.

Let's bring him back! Geta!

GETA.

Let me go, whoever you are.

SOSTRATA.

It's me, Sostrata.

GETA.

Where is she?

You're the one I'm looking for.
I need to talk to you. Perfect timing, mistress.

SOSTRATA.

What's the matter? Why are you shaking?

GETA.

O no . . .

CANTHARA.

What are you running around for? Catch your breath,
Geta.

GETA.

We're absolutely . . .

SOSTRATA.

Absolutely what?

GETA.

Absolutely ruined. It's all over.

SOSTRATA.

Tell me please.

GETA.

Now . . .

SOSTRATA.

What now?

GETA.

Aeschinus . . .

SOSTRATA.

What about Aeschinus?

GETA.

He's separated himself from our family.

SOSTRATA.

What? I can't believe it. Why?

GETA.

He's in love with another girl.

SOSTRATA.

God help us!

GETA.

He makes no secret of it. He carried her off
himself from the sex-slave dealer, all in the open.

SOSTRATA.

Are you sure?

GETA.

I'm sure. I saw it with my own eyes, Sostrata.

SOSTRATA.

330 O, I'm ruined. What can you depend on anymore?
Whom can you trust? Our Aeschinus, the life of us all,

in whom we placed our hopes and dreams?
who swore that he couldn't live a single day with her?
who said he'd put his baby in his father's lap,
and thereby implore his father to let him marry her?

GETA.

Mistress, stop crying and start thinking about what to
do!
Are we just going to let this go by
or are we going to tell someone about it?

CANTHARA.

Man, man, are you in your right mind?
You think this ought to be spread around?

GETA.

I for one don't think so.
In the first place, the facts show
that he is now estranged from us.
If we bring it out in the open now,
he'll deny it, that I know,
and your reputation and your daughter's life will be at
risk.   340
Secondly, even if he admits the whole thing,
it's not in the girl's interest to be married
to a man who's in love with someone else.
Whatever you say, no, we need to keep quiet.

SOSTRATA.

Not for the whole world, I won't.

GETA.

What will you do?

SOSTRATA.

I'll tell.

CANTHARA.

O, Sostrata, do you see what you're doing?

SOSTRATA.

Things can't get worse than they are now.
First, she has no dowry. And then besides that
what was hers in place of a dowry has been lost.
She cannot be married as a virgin. There's one way: on
my side as witness
is the ring he let her have. Since I know well
that I bear no responsibility for my daughter's fault
and that no money has been paid
or any business transacted unworthy of me or my
daughter,
Geta, I will go to court.

GETA.

All right then, your way is better, I admit it.   350

SOSTRATA.

You go immediately to our kinsman Hegio.
He can stand for her in court.
Tell him the whole story from beginning to end.
When my dear husband Simulus was alive,
Hegio was his best friend.
He's always taken care of us.

GETA.

Well, yes, by Heracles, he's the one to turn to.

SOSTRATA.

And you, hurry up, Canthara dear, run,
summon the midwife so she's here the moment she's
      needed.

(*Geta and Canthara exit towards town. Sostrata goes into
her house.*)
(*Enter Demea from town. Delivery changes to unaccompanied speech.*)

DEMEA.

Damn! I have been informed that my son Ctesipho
had a part with Aeschinus in carrying off that girl.
That's the one disaster left to me to suffer,
that it's possible for the son that's still worth something
to be led by the other into debauchery.
Where am I to look for him?
Drawn to some prostitutes' tavern, I presume.
360   The profligate tempted him there, that I know.

(*Syrus with other slaves enters from town with the
groceries.*)

Well, it's Syrus. Now I will find out immediately
where he is. But, Heracles, he's part of that flock.
If he senses I'm looking for him, that coffin meat
will never tell. I won't reveal what I'm after.

SYRUS.

(*sees Demea but doesn't let on; to the other slaves*)
I've just told my master the whole story.
I never saw anyone happier.

DEMEA.

Jupiter almighty, what an idiot!

SYRUS.

He praised his son, and thanked me
for having given him that advice.

DEMEA.

I'm going to burst.

SYRUS.

He counted out the money then and there.
In addition he gave me half a mina for a little dinner
370   party.
That I've spent quite nicely according to his wishes.

DEMEA.

Quite! If you want some dirty business
taken care of properly, ask him.

SYRUS.

Well, Demea, I didn't see you there. What's going on?

DEMEA.

What's going on? I'll never cease being amazed
at how you people live.

SYRUS.

Absolutely, It's incompetent. To be honest, it's absurd.
(*inside to slaves*)
Clean these fish carefully, Dromo.
Except for that nice big conger.

Let him play in the water for a little while.
We won't fillet it till we're ready. Not before.

DEMEA.

This is a scandal.

SYRUS.

I'm not pleased either; I often protest.
Stephanio, make sure those salted fish are nicely soaked.   380

DEMEA.

Gods in heaven, is he doing it on purpose,
or does he think it will be to his credit if he corrupts his
      son?
O me, I can see the day when he will have to run away
in poverty and become a mercenary abroad.

SYRUS.

Ah, Demea, that is wisdom.
To forsee not only what is before your feet
but to forsee what is to come.

DEMEA.

So, is that instrumentalist still in your home?

SYRUS.

Yes, she is.

DEMEA.

He's going to keep her there, is that it?

SYRUS.

I think so. Our household is crazy enough.

DEMEA.

That these things go on!   390

SYRUS.

The father is lenient and permissive.
It's foolish and wicked.

DEMEA.

My brother shames me and angers me.

SYRUS.

That's the difference between you two, Demea,
the enormous difference. And I'm not saying that
just because you're standing here in front of me.
You, every bit of you, is wisdom itself;
he's an insubstantial nothing.
You wouldn't have allowed your son to behave that way.

DEMEA.

Wouldn't have allowed it?
Wouldn't I have smelled it out six whole months
before he started anything?

SYRUS.

No need to tell me how vigilant you are.

DEMEA.

If only he remain as he is now.

SYRUS.

As each of you two wishes his son, so it is.

DEMEA.

What about my son? Have you seen him today?   400

SYRUS.

Your son? (*to himself*) I'll herd him off to the country.
(*to Demea*) I think for a while now
he's been doing something on the farm.

DEMEA.

You're sure he's there?

SYRUS.

I walked out there with him myself.

DEMEA.

Excellent. I was afraid he was hanging around here.

SYRUS.

He was quite angry.

DEMEA.

What about?

SYRUS.

He was taking his brother to task about the girl
right out in the forum.

DEMEA.

Is that so?

SYRUS.

Oh, he didn't mince words.
Just when the money was changing hands,
your son appeared unexpectedly and began to protest:
"Aeschinus, you, disgracing yourself!
you, bringing shame upon our family!"

DEMEA.

Oh, I weep for joy!

SYRUS.

"You're not wasting this money, you're wasting your very
410   life."

DEMEA.

Bless him. He's a chip off the old block.

SYRUS.

(to himself) Whoa!

DEMEA.

Syrus, that son of mine is just full of those moral precepts.

SYRUS.

No wonder. He had someone at home to learn them
    from.

DEMEA.

One does one's best. Careful of every detail.
Constant training. Altogether I tell him
to examine the ways of life of everyone as if in a mirror
and to draw from others an example for himself. "Do
    this."

SYRUS.

Quite right.

DEMEA.

"Don't do that."

SYRUS.

Well done.

DEMEA.

"This does you credit."

SYRUS.

Exactly.

DEMEA.

"This does you shame."

SYRUS.

Very fine.

DEMEA.

And furthermore . . .

SYRUS.

Gods, I don't have time right now to listen to this.   420
I found some really good buys at the fish market
and I have to make sure they're not ruined in the prepa-
    ration.
You know, it's just as much a disgrace for us
not to take care of our things as for you masters
not to take care of the things you just mentioned.
As far as I can, I give moral precepts to my fellow slaves
in the same manner: "Too much salt." "Too well done."
"Not properly cleaned." "That's right. Remember to do it
    that way again."
I do the best I can, given my wisdom.
Altogether, Demea, I tell them to examine
the dishes as if a mirror and I teach them what they must
    do.
I realize these things that we do are silly.   430
As a man is, so must you treat him. Will that be all?

DEMEA.

Get yourself a better mind.

SYRUS.

You'll be going to the country?

DEMEA.

Right away.

SYRUS.

Yes, why spend time in the city
where you can give good moral instruction and nobody
    obeys it.

(Syrus exits into house.)

DEMEA.

Well, of course, I'm off to the country
when my son whom I came to find has gone there already.
He's the only thing I care about. I'm concerned for him.
Just as my brother wishes it. Let him look after the other
    the way he wants.

(Hegio and Geta enter.)

Well, who is this I see? It's Hegio, a man from my home-
    town.
If my eyes don't deceive me it certainly is. Ah, my friend
    from childhood.   440
Good gods, there aren't many citizens of his kind left.
Old-fashioned virtue and honor.
Public affairs are in good hands with him.
I'm happy when I see what's left of his kind still here.
There's still some joy in life.
I'll go up to say hello and talk with him.

HEGIO.

Good gods, it's a shameful crime, Geta.
What are you telling me?

GETA.

It happened.

HEGIO.

It's hard to believe a crime so unbecoming refinement
could have sprung from that family.

450   Aeschinus, you have not taken after your father.

DEMEA.

Obviously he's heard about the music girl.
Even though he's not family
it pains him that the father cares nothing.
O, I wish he were here listening to this!

HEGIO.

If they don't do the right thing,
they won't get away with it.

GETA.

We place all our hopes in you, Hegio.
We have only you. You are her champion,
you are her father. As he lay dying
my old master entrusted us to you.
If you desert us, we are lost.

HEGIO.

Don't even think it. I will not let you down.
I shoulder my responsibilities.

DEMEA.

460   I will go up to him. My fondest greetings, Hegio.

HEGIO.

Ah, hello, Demea, just the one I was looking for.

DEMEA.

Why is that?

HEGIO.

Your elder son Aeschinus,
whom you gave to your brother to adopt,
has not discharged his duty
as an honest man and as a man of refinement.

DEMEA.

And how is that?

HEGIO.

You know our friend and contemporary Simulus?

DEMEA.

Of course.

HEGIO.

Your son has raped his virgin daughter.

DEMEA.

I see.

HEGIO.

Wait, Demea, you have not yet heard the most serious
    charge.

DEMEA.

Can there be anything worse?

HEGIO.

Yes, there is. Part of it can be forgiven.
He was overwhelmed: night, desire, wine, he's a young

470   man.
It's human nature. When he realized what he had done,
on his own he went to the mother of the girl,
in tears, begging, pleading, promising,
swearing that he would marry her.

He was forgiven, the matter was not publicized,
they took his word.
The girl became pregnant from this violation.
She's at the end of her ninth month.
That honest gentleman of ours, please the gods,
has now purchased a music-girl to live with.
He's abandoned the other one.

DEMEA.

Are you quite sure?

HEGIO.

The mother of the girl can testify.
There's the girl. There's the fact that she's pregnant.
And besides that there's Geta here,
who, as slaves go, is rather reliable and energetic.   480
He alone supports and sustains the family.
Take him off, have him tortured and interrogated.

GETA.

Yes, by Heracles, torture me if it's not the truth, Demea.
And Aeschinus won't deny it. Ask him yourself.

DEMEA.

I feel ashamed. I don't know what to do or how to re-
    spond.

PAMPHILA.

(*voice from the house*)

Oh, Oh, the pain, the pain is killing me.
Juno Lucina, help me!
Save me I beg you!

HEGIO.

Well, she's not about to give birth?

GETA.

Yes, she is, Hegio.

HEGIO.

Listen to me, Demea, she's appealing
to the honor of the family.
Please do willingly what honor compels you to do.
I pray the gods that what you do   490
will bring credit to all of you.
But if your intentions are different, Demea,
with the utmost energy I will defend that girl
and the memory of my departed friend.
He was my kinsman, we were brought up together
serving in the army and at home.
We endured together harsh poverty.
Whatever struggle be required now, I will endure it.
I will work hard, I will go to court,
I will even lay down my life before I desert that family.
What do you have to say?

DEMEA.

Hegio, I will speak with my brother.

HEGIO.

Alright, Demea, but have this in mind: 500
the easier your life is, the more powerful you are,
the wealthier, the more well off,
the higher the status you enjoy,

the more you are obligated by what is just and right
to recognize and act upon what is just and right,
if you want a reputation for respectability.

DEMEA.

Return to us. All that is just and right will be done.

HEGIO.

That would be a credit to you. Geta, take me inside to
Sostrata.

(*Hegio and Geta go in Sostrata's house.*)

DEMEA.

This is exactly what I predicted.
I only wish this were the end of it.
This excessive permissiveness will surely
end up in some terrible catastrophe.
I'm going to be sick. I'll go find my brother
510   and vomit this story right out to him.

(*Demea exits towards the town.*)
(*Hegio enters from Sostrata's house.*)

HEGIO.

Don't worry, Sostrata. Do what you can to comfort her.
I will talk to Micio if he's in the forum
and tell him from beginning to end all that's happened.
If it happens that he intends to do his duty,
let him do it.
If he has some other thought in mind on this matter,
let him give me an answer.
I will know what I have to do.

(*Hegio exits towards the town.*)
(*Syrus and Ctesipho enter from Micio's house. Delivery
changes to accompanied speech.*)

CTESIPHO.

So my father has gone to the country?

SYRUS.

Awhile ago.

CTESIPHO.

Please tell me he's gone home.

SYRUS.

He's at your farm. At this very moment
I'm sure he's occupied with some piece of work.

CTESIPHO.

I hope he is. As long as he doesn't hurt himself,
I hope he gets so exhausted that he can't
520   get out of bed for the next three days.

SYRUS.

I hope so too, or for something even better.

CTESIPHO.

Yes, all I want to do is spend
the whole day as I began it, in pleasure.
And what I really hate about that country place
is that it's so near. If it were farther away,

night could overtake him before he had a chance to re-
turn here.
As it is, when he doesn't find me he'll run right back
here,
I'm sure of that. He'll ask me where I've been:
"I haven't seen you all day." What'll I say?

SYRUS.

Nothing comes to mind?

CTESIPHO.

Nothing at all.

SYRUS.

The more fool you are.
Don't you have a client, a friend, a guest friend?

CTESIPHO.

Yes, so . . .

SYRUS.

Can't you say you had business with them?   530

CTESIPHO.

When I didn't? I can't say that.

SYRUS.

Yes you can.

CTESIPHO.

During the day, but what if I spend the night here,
what reasons can I give, Syrus?

SYRUS.

Ah, yes, I've often wished you could get by with
claiming to conduct business with friends at night.
Just relax; I've got the man all figured out.
When he's at his hottest, I can make him as gentle as a
sheep.

CTESIPHO.

How do you do that?

SYRUS.

He loves to hear you being praised.
In front of him, I make you out to be a god.
I tell the virtues.

CTESIPHO.

Mine?

SYRUS.

Yours. Right away, the old man cries like a baby for joy.

(*Syrus sees Demea approaching the house.*)

SYRUS.

Well, there you go.

CTESIPHO.

What?

SYRUS.

The wolf in the story.

CTESIPHO.

It's my father?

SYRUS.

It's your father.

CTESIPHO.

Syrus, what are we going to do?

SYRUS.
Go hide somewhere, I'll take care of it.
CTESIPHO.
If he asks, you never saw me. You hear?
SYRUS.
Can you shut up?

(*Demea enters from the town.*)

DEMEA.
540   I swear, I'm a wretched man.
I can't find my brother anywhere on earth.
Besides that, while I was looking for him,
I saw one of my hired hands from the farm.
He told me my son isn't out on the farm.
I don't know what to do.
CTESIPHO.
Syrus.
SYRUS.
What is it?
CTESIPHO.
Is he looking for me?
SYRUS.
Yes.
CTESIPHO.
On no.
SYRUS.
Just be brave.
DEMEA.
What the hell does this bad luck mean?
I can't figure it out, except I believe
that the reason I was born is to endure pain and
    misery.
I'm the first to hear about our problems,
I'm the first to get wise to everything,
I'm the first to announce the bad news.
When something happens, I'm the only one who trou-
    bles himself.
SYRUS.
Don't make me laugh. He says he's the first to know;
he's the only one who doesn't know.
DEMEA.
Now I return; perhaps my brother is home.
CTESIPHO.
550   Syrus, look, don't let him just rush right inside here.
SYRUS.
Can't you be quiet? I'll take care of it.
CTESIPHO.
Heracles, I will not trust you with that.
I will lock myself up with her in one of the slave rooms.
That's safest.

(*Ctesipho goes in the house.*)

SYRUS.
Alright, I'll get him out of here anyway.
DEMEA.
Well, the scoundrel Syrus.

SYRUS.
I swear to the gods there's nobody who can endure it
if things go on like this.
I would simply like to know how many masters I have.
What a pain this is!
DEMEA.
What's he yapping about? What does he want?
Tell me, my good man, is my brother home?
SYRUS.
Why the hell are you calling me "my good man"? I'm
    finished.
DEMEA.
What's with you?
SYRUS.
You're asking what's with me?
Ctesipho beat me up with his fists
almost to death. And the music girl.
DEMEA.
What are you telling me?
SYRUS.
See, look how he cut my lip.
DEMEA.
Why?   560
SYRUS.
He said that I was the instigator of buying the girl.
DEMEA.
Didn't you tell me that he had left here for the country?
SYRUS.
I did; but he came back here, crazed.
He showed no mercy. Not to feel shame
at beating up an old man!
The boy I used to cradle in my arms
when he was just a little boy.
DEMEA.
Well done, Ctesipho! You take after your father.
Yes, I judge you a man!
SYRUS.
Well done? If he's smart, he'll keep his fists
to himself after this.
DEMEA.
Bravely done!
SYRUS.
Very brave, when he takes advantage of a poor woman
and me, a poor little slave who didn't dare hit back.
Very brave, indeed!
DEMEA.
It couldn't have been better.
He understands what I do—
that you are the root of this problem.
Is my brother home?
SYRUS.
He's not.
DEMEA.
I wonder where I might find him.
SYRUS.
I know where he is, but I will never tell you.   570

DEMEA.

What did you just say to me?

SYRUS.

What I just said to you.

DEMEA.

I'm going to bash your head in.

(*He threatens violence.*)

SYRUS.

Well, I don't know the man's name, but I know the
place.

DEMEA.

Tell me then.

SYRUS.

Do you know the portico down by the meat market?

DEMEA.

Of course.

SYRUS.

Go straight up that street. When you get there,
the Hill is right down in front of you. Down you go.
Then on this side, there's a shrine.
Right next to it is an alley-way.

DEMEA.

Which one?

SYRUS.

Where there's that big wild-fig tree.

DEMEA.

I know it.

SYRUS.

Go that way.

DEMEA.

Wait a minute, that alley's a dead end.

SYRUS.

Yes, yes, you're right. Ah, you must think I'm an idiot.
I made a mistake. Go back to the portico.
580   There's a much faster way and less of a chance
of missing the street. You know the house
of that rich man Cratinus?

DEMEA.

I do.

SYRUS.

When you go past it, go left and straight along the street.
When you get to the sanctuary of Diana, turn right.
Before you come to the city gate, just at the watering
    troughs,
there's a bakery and opposite that there's a workshop.
He's there.

DEMEA.

What's he doing there?

SYRUS.

He's ordering some outdoor couches to be made with
holmoak[1] legs.

[1]**holmoak** ilex (holly)

DEMEA.

For one of your drinking parties, well that's just fine.
I will go find him immediately.

SYRUS.

Go. Please.

(*Demea exits towards the town.*)

SYRUS.

I'll give you today the exercise that you deserve,
you old funeral feast!
Aeschinus is annoyingly late.
Our dinner is spoiling. Ctesipho is totally in love.
Now I'll look out for myself. I will now go off   590
and sample every little tasty morsel
and ladling out one bowl of wine after another
I'll stretch out this day.

(*Syrus exits into Micio's house.*)
(*Enter Micio and Hegio from the town.*)

MICIO.

I see no reason for you
to think especially well of me in this matter, Hegio.
I am doing my duty. I am correcting the wrong we caused.
Surely you didn't think me one of those people
who think that they are being wronged
if you accuse them of the wrong that they have done,
and on top of that accuse you.
You're not thanking me for not behaving that way?

HEGIO.

Not all. It never entered my mind
that you were other than you are. But please,
would you come with me to see the girl's mother,
and tell her exactly what you told me;
what made her suspicious Aeschinus did for his brother,   600
the music girl is his.

MICIO.

If that's the right thing to do,
or you think it's necessary, let's go.

HEGIO.

Good, You'll relieve her. She's been wracked
with pain and anxiety over this.
And you will have performed your duty.
But if you don't think so,
I will tell her myself what you told me.

MICIO.

No, no, on the contrary, I will go.

HEGIO.

Good. Those who aren't quite so well off
are just a little bit—I don't know—more suspicious.
They are ready to take offence at an imagined insult.
They think they're trapped because of their lack of re-
    sources.
To explain yourself in person is therefore the more satis-
    fying course.

MICIO.

Yes, you're quite right.

HEGIO.
Let's go.
MICIO.
By all means.

(*Micio and Hegio go into Sostrata's house.*)
    (*Aeschinus enters from the town. Accompaniment continues. Polymetric song.*)

AESCHINUS.
610   I'm in torture.
Suddenly faced with such a disaster.
I don't know what to do, how to act.
My limbs are weak with fear.
My heart is stunned with terror.
My mind is empty of advice.
Ah, how to get clear of the madness?
I'm under suspicion, a natural one.
Sostrata thinks I bought the music-girl for myself.
That crone made the accusation against me.

(*Polymetric song ends. Accompaniment continues.*)

She had been sent to bring the midwife,
and I ran into her. I was asking how Pamphila was doing,
if she was about to give birth, if she needed the midwife.
620   She screams at me: "Away from me, away,
we want nothing more to do with you, Aeschinus.
You've deceived us long enough.
We've had enough of your broken promises."
I said, "What in the world are you talking about?"
She says, "Good-bye and good riddance.
Have whatever girl you want!"
I immediately understood what they thought I had done,
but I had to hold back. If I said anything about my brother
to that old gossip it would have been all over town.
What should I do now? Say the girl belongs to my
    brother?
That cannot be made public.
But that aside—it's still possible that it won't get out—
they'd never believe what actually happened.
There are so many things that look like the truth
mixed in with the truth. I was the one who carried her
    off;
I was the one who paid off the slave dealer for her;
she was taken into my house.
I admit that what is happening is all my fault.
As bad as the situation was,
I should have told my father about it.
630   I should have gotten his permission to marry her.
I've been slow up to now. Wake up, Aeschinus.
First priority: go to them, clear myself.

I'll go up to the door. I can't.
I always feel so tense when I knock at this door.
Hello. Hello. It's Aeschinus. Open the door, somebody.

Someone's coming out. I'll hide over here.

(*Micio enters from Sostrata's house. Sostrata at the door.*)

MICIO.
All of you do as I have told you, Sostrata.
I will see Aeschinus to let him know
what has been decided.

Where's the person who was knocking at the door?
AESCHINUS.
Gods, it's my father. I'm lost.
MICIO.
Aeschinus!

(*Delivery changes to unaccompanied speech.*)

AESCHINUS.
(*to himself*) What's he doing here?
MICIO.
Was it you who just knocked on this door?
(*to himself*) No answer.
Why shouldn't I have a little fun with him?
He deserves it since he didn't tell me about any of this.   640
(*to Aeschinus*) You have nothing to say to me?
AESCHINUS.
Not about knocking on the door, as far as my knowledge
    goes.
MICIO.
Well, I was wondering what business you could have
    here.
(*to himself*) He's blushing. It will be all right.
AESCHINUS.
Well please tell me, father, what brought you there.
MICIO.
Nothing to do with me. A friend of mine
brought me from the forum to conduct a negotiation for
    him.
AESCHINUS.
What is that?
MICIO.
I will tell you. Some women live next door
who aren't so well off. I don't believe you know them.
I'm sure you don't. They moved here not too long ago.
AESCHINUS.
And . . .
MICIO.
There's an unmarried girl and her mother.   650
AESCHINUS.
Go on.
MICIO.
This girl has been orphaned of her father.
My friend is next of kin, and as you know,
the law requires him to marry her off to someone.
AESCHINUS.
Damn.
MICIO.
What is it?
AESCHINUS.
Nothing, fine, go on.

MICIO.

He's come to take her with him. He lives in Miletus.

AESCHINUS.

I see. He's come to take the girl with him.

MICIO.

That is so.

AESCHINUS.

Across the sea to Miletus?

MICIO.

Yes.

AESCHINUS.

I feel sick. And the women, what do they say?

MICIO.

What do you think? Of course some nonsense.
The mother told a story about a child and some other
    man.
She didn't give his name.
He was first, she said, and her daughter
shouldn't be given to the man from Miletus.

AESCHINUS.

660 What, you don't think these claims are just, do you?

MICIO.

No.

AESCHINUS.

Really, you don't? Then will he take her away, father?

MICIO.

Why shouldn't he?

AESCHINUS.

The matter has been handled by all of you
in a way that's uncivilized and pitiless,
and, not only that, if I must speak more frankly,
in a way that's lacking in generosity of spirit.

MICIO.

In what way?

AESCHINUS.

You're asking me? How in the world do you think
that poor lovesick man is going to feel—
the first man who was intimate with her,
and for all I know still loves her desperately—
when he sees her snatched away from him
right in front of his eyes?
A terrible crime, father.

MICIO.

670 How do you figure? Who betrothed her?
Who gave her in marriage? Who married her?
Who gave her consent and had legal authority to do so?
Why did the man marry another man's wife?

AESCHINUS.

And is an unmarried girl of that age
supposed to sit at home waiting for a kinsman
to arrive from Miletus?
That's what justice demanded you to say, father,
and the position you ought to have defended.

MICIO.

Ridiculous. Was I supposed to argue the case
against the man on whose behalf I had come to court?

Anyway, what business is this of ours, Aeschinus?
What do we have to do with them? Let's go home.

(*Delivery changes to accompanied speech.*)

What's wrong? Why are you crying?

AESCHINUS.

Father, please, listen.

MICIO.

Aeschinus, I heard all about it.   680
I know. I love you.
All the more I care about what you do.

AESCHINUS.

May I always deserve your love,
as long as you live, my father,
as surely as to acknowledge what I have done
pains me deeply and shames me.

MICIO.

Heracles, I believe it.
I know that you are a man born with a generous and free
    spirit.
But I'm afraid you are excessively careless.
Tell me what city you think you're living in.
You have violated a virgin whom it was not lawful for
    you to touch.
Right away that's a serious transgression.
But it's human. It's often happened before,
even with honest men. But after it happened,
tell me, you couldn't have considered
or planned very carefully what you should have done,   690
how you should have done it.
If you were ashamed to tell me yourself,
did you think about how I would find out?
While you were hesitating, nine months went by.
You have betrayed yourself and that poor young woman
and your child, as far as it was in your capacity.
What, did you think that the gods
would do your work for you while you slept?
That without your making arrangements
she would be magically conducted in marriage home to
    your bedroom?
I would not wish to see you as lazy in other affairs
as you have been in this. Don't worry, you'll marry her.

AESCHINUS.

What?

MICIO.

I say don't worry.

AESCHINUS.

Father, please, you're not joking.

MICIO.

Why should I be?

AESCHINUS.

I don't know. It's just that I want this
to be true so badly, I'm all the more afraid.

MICIO.

Go. Pray the god's favor and bring home your wife. Go.

AESCHINUS.
700   What? My wife? Now?

MICIO.
Now.

AESCHINUS.
Now?

MICIO.
Now. As soon as you can.

AESCHINUS.
May the gods curse me if I don't love you more than my
    own eyes.

MICIO.
What? More than her?

AESCHINUS.
Well, just as much.

MICIO.
That's kind of you.

AESCHINUS.
Wait a minute. Where's that Milesian?

MICIO.
He's dead. He's gone. He sailed away on a ship.
What are you waiting for?

AESCHINUS.
You go, father, you pray to the gods.
You are a much better man than I,
and I know for certain
that they're much more likely to listen to you.

MICIO.
Well, we'll make the necessary preparations.
Do what I've told you if you know what's good for you.

(*Micio goes in his house.*)

AESCHINUS.
Can you imagine it?
Is this to be a father or is this to be a son?
If he were my brother or my friend,
could he have done more perfectly what I wanted him to
    do?
Isn't he a man to be loved, just to be hugged.

710   Hmm. Because of his kindness,
I have this great desire not to do carelessly
anything he doesn't want. I will be on guard
not to displease him. But what am I waiting for?
I don't want to be the obstacle to my own wedding.

(*Aeschinus goes into his house.*)
(*Demea enters from town.*)
(*Delivery changes to unaccompanied speech.*)

DEMEA.
I'm exhausted from walking.
Jupiter damn you and your directions, Syrus!
I've crawled over the whole town:
the city gate, the watering troughs, everywhere.
There was no workshop there,

nobody said they had seen my brother.
Now I'm absolutely going to blockade this house until he
    returns.

(*Micio enters from his house.*)

MICIO.
(*speaking inside*)
I will go over and say that we're pretty much ready.

DEMEA.
Well here he is.
I've been looking for you a long time, Micio.   720

MICIO.
What for?

DEMEA.
I bring you other monstrous crimes
committed by that young man of yours.

MICIO.
Oh gods.

DEMEA.
New crimes, capital offenses.

MICIO.
Now wait a minute.

DEMEA.
You don't know the kind of man we're dealing with.

MICIO.
Yes I do.

DEMEA.
Oh, you fool, you're dreaming
that I'm talking about that music girl.
The offense is against a citizen, a virgin.

MICIO.
I know.

DEMEA.
O ho, you know and you let this go on?

MICIO.
Why shouldn't I?

DEMEA.
Don't you ever just start screaming?
Don't you ever just go mad?

MICIO.
No. I might have wished—

DEMEA.
A child has been born.

MICIO.
May the gods bless!

DEMEA.
The girl has nothing.

MICIO.
I've heard.

DEMEA.
And she must be married without a dowry.

MICIO.
Quite.

DEMEA.
What's going to happen?

MICIO.

730   What the situation requires.
     The girl will be moved from that house to this.

DEMEA.

     O Jupiter, is that necessary?

MICIO.

     What more can I do?

DEMEA.

     What more can you do?
     If the situation doesn't cause you genuine pain,
     you can act human and pretend that it does.

MICIO.

     Well, I've already betrothed the girl to him.
     The matter is settled. There will be a wedding.
     I've removed all their cause for apprehension.
     That is even more human.

DEMEA.

     But are you happy with it, Micio?

MICIO.

     No, not if I could change it. But since I can't,
     I'm happy with it. Living our lives is like playing with dice:
740   If the throw you need doesn't fall,
     what is given by chance you can put right with art.

DEMEA.

     Put it right? With your art, as you call it,
     you've wasted 20 minas on the music girl,
     whom you now must sell to I don't know whom,
     if not for a price, then for free.

MICIO.

     She doesn't have to be sold
     and indeed I'm not eager to sell her.

DEMEA.

     What are you going to do then?

MICIO.

     She will remain in my house.

DEMEA.

     Holy gods! A concubine and the mother of the house-
        hold together in one house!

MICIO.

     Why not?

DEMEA.

     Do you really believe that you are in your right mind?

MICIO.

     I think so.

DEMEA.

750   So help me gods, I understand.
     You want to sing again and again to her accompaniment!

MICIO.

     Why not?

DEMEA.

     And the new bride will learn the same songs?

MICIO.

     Quite.

DEMEA.

     And you will dance on a rope between the two?

MICIO.

     Yes.

DEMEA.

     Yes?

MICIO.

     And you will join us if the need arises.

DEMEA.

     Good gods, aren't you ashamed of yourself?

MICIO.

     Alright, alright, Demea. Enough.
     Calm yourself down, and be as pleasant and festive
     as the occasion demands; it's the wedding of your son.
     I'm going to them, then I'll come back.

(Micio goes into the house of Sostrata.)

DEMEA.

     O Jupiter, what a life! What morals! What insanity!
     A wife without a dowry is coming. A music girl lives here.
     A house of wasteful extravagance!   760
     A young man spoiled with luxury!
     A maniac old man!
     Salvation herself could not save this household if she
        wanted to.

(Syrus enters from Micio's house, drunk.)

SYRUS.

     I swear, little Syrus, you've taken care of yourself nicely,
     and discharged the office of slave beautifully.
     OK. Now that I've stuffed myself on everything,
     I think I'd like to take a walk.

DEMEA.

     Look at that! An example of the discipline of the house.

SYRUS.

     Look, here's our old man. What's going on?
     What are you so upset about?

DEMEA.

     Scoundrel!

SYRUS.

     Hey, enough! So, Wisdom herself, you're pouring out
        your sayings.

DEMEA.

     If you belonged to me . . .   770

SYRUS.

     You'd be a rich man, Demea,
     and you would have put your affairs on a strong founda-
        tion.

DEMEA.

     I ought to make an example of you to the whole house-
        hold.

SYRUS.

     For what? What have I done?

DEMEA.

     You're asking me? In the very midst of trouble,

in the very midst of huge disgrace
that has hardly yet been settled,
you're drunk, you scoundrel,
as if celebrating a great achievement.

SYRUS.

Well, I'm sorry I came outside.

DROMO.

(*calling from the door*)
Hey Syrus, Ctesipho wants you.

SYRUS.

Alright.

DEMEA.

What did he say about Ctesipho?

SYRUS.

Nothing.

DEMEA.

Hey, you jail meat, is Ctesipho here?

SYRUS.

He's not.

DEMEA.

Why did he use his name?

SYRUS.

It's somebody else, just some guy who's staying with us.
Do you know him?

DEMEA.

I will soon.

SYRUS.

780   What are you doing? Where are you going?

DEMEA.

Let me go.

SYRUS.

Don't get up, I say.

DEMEA.

I'll whip your hide if you don't let go of me.
Or would you prefer that I knock your brains on the
    pavement?

(*Demea gets free and goes into Micio's house.*)

SYRUS.

Well, he's gone. Not such a welcome guest to the wed-
    ding party,
especially to Ctesipho. What should I do now?
Until the riot calms down,
I think it's best to find some corner
and sleep off this little bit of wine. That's what I'll do.

(*Syrus goes into Micio's house.*)
(*Micio enters from Sostrata's house.*)

MICIO.

(*inside*)
As I've said, everything's ready for you now, Sostrata,
whenever you like.

(*Demea enters from Micio's house.*)

Who's that slamming around my door?

DEMEA.

Great Gods, what am I to do? How am I to act?
What cry, what complaint can I make?
O heaven, o earth, o Neptune's seas!   790

MICIO.

There you have it. He's found out,
that's what he's screaming about. It's all over.
Now we're in trouble. I'd better go to the rescue.

DEMEA.

There he is, the common pimp for both our sons.

MICIO.

Would you please get a hold on your anger
and come back to your senses.

DEMEA.

Alright, I've got a hold, I've come back,
I'll stop the curses. Let's look at the situation.
Was it agreed between us—and the proposal even came
    from you—
that you would not interfere with my raising my son
nor would I interfere with your raising yours? Yes?

MICIO.

That was the agreement, I don't deny it.

DEMEA.

Then why is he now drinking in your house?
Why do you put my son up in your house?   800
Why have you bought him a girlfriend, Micio?
Isn't it fair that I have my rights from you as well as you
have yours from me? I don't interfere with your son,
you don't interfere with mine.

MICIO.

That's not quite right.

DEMEA.

No?

MICIO.

There's an old saying: friends hold all in common.

DEMEA.

Clever! But now's a little late for speeches like that.

MICIO.

Listen to me for a little, Demea, without losing your
    temper.
In the first place, if it's the money
the boys spend that annoys you, think of it this way.
Long ago, you were bringing up your two boys within
    your means,
figuring that your resources would be enough for them
    both.   810
I dare say you also thought that I would marry.
Now stick to that same plan: build up, work, save,
leave them as much as you can for an inheritance.
That's your heritage.
Let them use my resources as an utterly unexpected
    windfall.
Nothing is lost from your capital.
The money that comes from me, count as pure profit.
If you allow yourself to consider this accurately, Demea,

you'll stop being a pain to me and to yourself and to
    them.

DEMEA.

820   I'm not talking about the money,
    it's the way they live their lives.

MICIO.

    Wait, I know, I was coming to that.
    There are many indications in a man
    from which a conclusion can easily be drawn.
    For example, when two people are doing the same thing
    you can often say, "It's dangerous for this one to do
        something,
    but not for the other one."
    Not that the action itself is different,
    but the two doing the action . . .
    Now I see in our two boys indications
    that make me confident they will turn out the way we
        want them to.
    I see that they have sense, understanding,
    inhibition at the right time, love for each other.
    Allow their spirit and character to grow freely,
    and you know that you can bring them back at any time.

830   You may be afraid that nevertheless
    they will be a little too careless in financial matters.
    My dear Demea, in all other matters we grow wiser with
        age.
    This is the only flaw that growing old bestows on a man:
    we all care much too much about money,
    on which point age will make them sharp enough.

DEMEA.

    Just be careful, Micio, that this fine philosophy of yours
    and your permissiveness don't ruin us.

MICIO.

    Quiet, it won't happen. Forget about it.
    Just today, let me tell you what to do.
    Wipe the scowl off your face.

DEMEA.

840   Well, so the occasion requires. I must do it.
    But tomorrow at dawn I will return to the country with
        my son.

MICIO.

    In the middle of the night, I imagine. Just be pleasant
        today.

DEMEA.

    And that music girl I'll drag off with me as well.

MICIO.

    A good strategy. That way you'll bind him to the farm.
    Just make sure *she* doesn't run away.

DEMEA.

    I'll take care of that. I'll have her cooking
    and grinding corn, she'll be full of ash and smoke and
        meal.
    And not only that, I'll have her collecting straw
    under the noonday sun. I'll make her as sunburnt
    and black as a piece of charcoal.

MICIO.

    Good idea. Now I see you have some sense.   850
    And if I were you, I would then force him to sleep with
        her.

DEMEA.

    Are you mocking me? You're lucky to have that disposi-
        tion.
    I take things to heart.

MICIO.

    So you're going to go on?

DEMEA.

    No, no. I'm finished. I'm finished.

MICIO.

    Go ahead into my house then,
    and let us enjoy the day as it ought to be enjoyed.

*(Micio exits into his house. Delivery changes to accompa-
nied speech.)*

DEMEA.

    No man has ever calculated up
    the profits and losses of his life
    so accurately that circumstances,
    age, experience, don't add something new,
    don't teach some new lesson.
    What you thought you knew, you don't know.
    What you thought most important, with experience you
        reject.
    It's happened to me now. The harsh life I've lived up to
        now—
    with life's race almost run—I now renounce. Why?
    I've discovered from this business that nothing is better   860
    for a man than to be easygoing and open-minded.
    Anyone can easily see this looking at my brother and me.
    He's lived his life at leisure, in happy company,
    open-minded, calm, offending no one to his face, a smile
        for everyone.
    He's lived for himself, he spent his money on himself.
    Everyone speaks well of him, everyone loves him.
    I'm from the country, tough, grim,
    thrifty, hot-headed, tenacious, married. What misery!
    Sons were born, more trouble.
    Whoa, in my zeal to provide for them the best I could,
    I ground down the best years of my life in the struggle.
    Now my life completed, the reward I get from them for
        my labors: 870
    everyone hates me. My brother, without working for it,
    enjoys all the pleasures of being a father.
    They love him, they run away from me.
    They confide all their plans to him, they have affection
        for him,
    they both live at his house, I'm left alone.
    They want a long life for him;
    they look forward for me to die, I think.
    To bring them up cost me all my work
    and he has made them his at no expense.

I endure the misery; he enjoys the pleasures.
Alright, now let's try the opposite.
See if I am capable of gracious speech and kindly act.
It's his challenge. I want to be loved and valued by my
    family.
880　If that can happen by my being generous
and giving people what they want
and telling them what they want to hear,
I will play the leading part.
There won't be enough money,
but what do I care? I'm the oldest.

(*Syrus enters from the house. Delivery changes to unaccompanied speech.*)

SYRUS.

Hey, Demea, your brother doesn't want you so far away.

DEMEA.

Who is this? O my good Syrus, hello.
What's going on? How are you doing?

SYRUS.

Well, fine.

DEMEA.

Wonderful!
(*to himself*) Already I've added three unnatural phrases
to my vocabulary: "O my good Syrus,"
"What's going on?" and "How are you doing?"
Even though you're a slave,
you demonstrate some refinement
and I would be happy to do you a favor.

SYRUS.

Well, thank you.

DEMEA.

And Syrus, I really mean it as you will soon find out.

(*Geta enters from Sostrata's house.*)

GETA.

(*inside*) Mistress, I'll go over and find out
890　how soon they'll be receiving the bride.

Hello, Demea. My greetings.

DEMEA.

Hello, ah, what is your name?

GETA.

Geta.

DEMEA.

Geta, I have formed the opinion
that you are a most valuable person.
In my view, the slave that is tried and true
is the one who looks to his master's interest,
and I see that you are such, Geta.
For this reason, should the opportunity arise,
I would be happy to do you a favor.

(*to himself*) I'm practicing being affable,
and it's going very well.

GETA.

You're kind to have such a good opinion of me.

DEMEA.

(*to himself*) For the very first time,
little by little, I'm building a constituency.

(*Aeschinus enters from the house.*)

AESCHINUS.

I'm not going to survive their attention
to every single ritual of a wedding.
They're wasting the day with the preparations.　900

DEMEA.

How's it going, Aeschinus?

AESCHINUS.

Ah, father, you're here.

DEMEA.

Yes, I swear, your father in heart as well as by nature.
A father who loves you more than his own eyes.
But why aren't you bringing your wife on home?

AESCHINUS.

I want to. But there's a delay.
We're waiting for the reed player
and the singers to sing the wedding hymn.

DEMEA.

Listen, will you listen to an old man?

AESCHINUS.

What?

DEMEA.

Forget all that, the wedding hymns, the crowds,
the torches, the reed players.
Just have the garden wall between your two houses
knocked down, immediately. Bring her into your house
    that way.
Make one house of the two. Bring to our house her
    mother　910
and all her family.

AESCHINUS.

Yes, wonderful, my dear father.

DEMEA.

Splendid. I'm called wonderful now.
My brother's house will become a highway.
There will be crowds of people. It will cost lots of money.
What do I care? I'm wonderful. I'm now in favor.
So let that Babylonian spendthrift pay out his twenty
    minas now.
Syrus, why don't you go and do it?

SYRUS.

What am I to do?

DEMEA.

Have the garden wall demolished.

You, go over and bring them around.

GETA.

May the gods bless you, Demea.
I see that you are a sincere benefactor to my household.

DEMEA.

They deserve it. What do you say?

AESCHINUS.

920   I agree.

DEMEA.

That's much better for a woman
who has just given birth and is weak
than to be led through the street.

AESCHINUS.

I've never seen anything better, my father.

DEMEA.

That's my way.
Well, here's Micio coming out the door.

(*Micio enters from his house.*)

MICIO.

My brother ordered this? Where is he?
Demea, you ordered this?

DEMEA.

I did indeed. And in this way and in every other way
I would like us to make one household as best we can:
support, assistance, joining together.

AESCHINUS.

Yes, please, father.

MICIO.

Well, I'm not against it.

DEMEA.

I should think not. It's the only decent thing to do.
Now first, our boy's wife has a mother.

MICIO.

Yes. And . . .

DEMEA.

930   She's honest and reputable.

MICIO.

So they say.

DEMEA.

She's older.

MICIO.

I know that.

DEMEA.

For a while now beyond child-bearing years,
with no one to care for her. She's alone.

MICIO.

(*to himself*) What's he got in mind?

DEMEA.

The right thing to do is that you should marry her,
and you, Aeschinus, should see that it happens.

(*Delivery changes to accompanied speech.*)

MICIO.

I should marry her?

DEMEA.

You should.

MICIO.

I should?

DEMEA.

Yes, you should.

MICIO.

You're crazy.

DEMEA.

If you, Aeschinus, are human, he will do it.

AESCHINUS.

Father.

MICIO.

Why are you listening to him, you fool?

DEMEA.

You're not accomplishing anything. There's no other way.

MICIO.

You're mad.

AESCHINUS.

Let me beg you, father.

MICIO.

You're crazy, get away.

DEMEA.

Come, grant your son's wish.

MICIO.

Are you in your right mind?
I'm finally to become a bridegroom at the age of sixty-
four
and marry a decrepit old woman?
This is what you're trying to persuade me of?

AESCHINUS.

Do it. I promised them.   940

MICIO.

You promised them? Be generous with what's yours to
give, boy.

DEMEA.

Come, what if he had asked for something bigger?

MICIO.

There couldn't be anything bigger.

DEMEA.

Grant his request.

AESCHINUS.

Don't be stubborn.

DEMEA.

Go ahead, promise.

MICIO.

Forget it.

DEMEA.

Not till I get what I want.

MICIO.

This is, this is violence.

DEMEA.

Be generous, Micio.

MICIO.

This seems to me wrong, silly, absurd,
and entirely foreign to my way of life.
But if you want it so much, I agree.

AESCHINUS.

Well done. Thank you.

DEMEA.

You deserve my love. But . . .

MICIO.

What? I'll marry her and that's as much as I'm willing to do.

DEMEA.

There is Hegio to think of, their closest kinsman,
now an inlaw of ours. He is not well off.
The decent thing is to do him a favor.

MICIO.

Do what?

DEMEA.

Outside of town you have a small plot of land
that rents as farm land. Let's give it to him
950   to make some money with.

MICIO.

A small plot you say?

DEMEA.

If it's a large plot, still, we must do it.
He's been a father to her. He's a good man.
He's part of our family now. It's right he should have it.
Let me remind you, Micio, of something you said not too
     long ago:
This is our common flaw, we all care much too much
     about money.
We ought to avoid this stain.
You were right and we ought to realize your meaning.

AESCHINUS.

Please, father.

MICIO.

(unaccompanied)
Alright, the farm will be given to Hegio, since my son
     wishes.

DEMEA.

I'm very happy. Now you're my brother in spirit as well
     as flesh.
(Accompaniment resumes.)
(to himself) I'm cutting his throat with his own sword.

(Syrus enters from Micio's house.)

SYRUS.

I've taken care of what you wanted done, Demea.

DEMEA.

Well, Syrus you're a useful man.
In my opinion at least, I vote that Syrus be made a free
960   man.

MICIO.

Made a free man? Why is that?

DEMEA.

For many reasons.

SYRUS.

O my friend, Demea. I swear you are a good man.
From the time they were boys, I raised your two sons
very carefully. I taught them, counseled them,
always gave them good instruction as far as I could.

DEMEA.

That's obvious. The list goes on:

buying party supplies on credit, procuring them prosti-
     tutes,
preparing dinners in broad daylight.
These are the duties of a distinguished man.

SYRUS.

What a wonderful man!

DEMEA.

And finally, today, he was the facilitator
in buying that music girl. He got the job done.
It's the right thing that he profit from it.
The other slaves will be the better for it.
Besides, your son wants it.

MICIO.

Do you desire it?

AESCHINUS.

Yes, very much.

MICIO.

Of course you want it. Syrus, come here to me.   970
There, be a free man.

SYRUS.

You have done a good thing. Thank you.
I am grateful to all of you, and especially to Demea.

DEMEA.

I'm very happy.

AESCHINUS.

So am I.

SYRUS.

I'm sure you are. If only my joy could now be made com-
     plete.
I wish I could see Phrygia a free woman, together with
     me as my wife.

DEMEA.

Well, she's an excellent woman.

SYRUS.

And hers was the first breast
to nurse your son's son, your grandson.

DEMEA.

In all seriousness, by Heracles,
seeing as how she was the first nurse of my grandson,
there's no doubt that the right thing
is to emancipate her.

MICIO.

For that?

DEMEA.

For that. Here, let me reimburse you for what she's worth.

SYRUS.

May all the gods bestow on you, Demea,
everything that you pray for.

MICIO.

Well, Syrus, you've done very nicely today.

DEMEA.

Only if you do your duty, Micio,
and extend him a little something to live on.   980
I'm sure he will pay it back to you soon.

MICIO.

I won't give him anything.

AESCHINUS.
   He's a good man.
SYRUS.
   I'll pay it back, I swear, if you give me anything.
AESCHINUS.
   Go ahead, father.
MICIO.
   I'll think about it.
DEMEA.
   He'll do it.
SYRUS.
   You're the best of men.
AESCHINUS.
   O my dear father, that's the spirit of the day.
MICIO.
   What is going on here?
   What has caused this sudden change in your behavior?
   What's this urge to give money away?
   What's this generosity that's come over you?
DEMEA.
   I will tell you. I wanted to demonstrate to you
   that what our children think is
   easygoing and generous in you
   doesn't come from sincerity or from what is right and just,

but from telling people what they want to hear,
from indulgence, from wasting money, Micio.
Now Aeschinus, if my life has been hateful to you
because I didn't go along with everything you wanted   990
wholeheartedly, right or wrong, forget it.
Squander, spend, live for whatever is your pleasure.
But if you prefer, in those areas where you lack vision
because of your youth, where your desires
are intense but your consideration is small,
to have someone to point out your fault
and correct you and indulge you at the right time,
here I am to do it for you.
AESCHINUS.
   We'll allow you, father.
   You know better what we need. But what about my
      brother?
DEMEA.
   I'll allow it. Let him keep the girl.
   But let that be the end of that sort of behavior.
MICIO.
   That's right.
ALL.
   Applause!

F O R U M

"The Art of Poetry" (*Ars Poetica*)

HORACE

This tract, written as a letter to a young writer (Piso) in c. 24 B.C.E., is the primary source of dramatic criticism and theory from the Roman Empire. In it, Horace outlines the aesthetic and practical principles a dramatist ought to follow. The most famous passage defines the function of drama: "to either profit or delight." The ideas of Horace served as a model for Renaissance dramatists, especially those who wrote according to the principles of Neoclassicism.

If a painter should wish to unite a horse's neck to a human head, and spread a variety of plumage over limbs [of different

animals] taken from every part [of nature], so that what is a beautiful woman in the upper part terminates unsightly in an ugly fish below—could you, my friends, refrain from laughter, were you admitted to such a sight? Believe, ye Pisos, the book will be perfectly like such a picture, the ideas of which, like a sick man's dreams, are all vain and fictitious: so that neither head nor foot can correspond to any one form. "Poets and painters [you will say] have ever had equal authority for attempting any thing." We are conscious of this, and this privilege we demand and allow in turn: but not to such a degree that the tame should associate with the savage; nor that serpents should be coupled with birds, lambs with tigers.

   In pompous introductions, and such as promise a great deal, it generally happens that one or two verses of purple patchwork, that may make a great show, are tagged on; as when the grove and the altar of Diana and the meandering of a current

From *The Works of Horace Literally Translated into English Prose*, by C. Smart, New York: Harper & Brothers, 1892.

(continued)

hastening through pleasant fields, or the river Rhine, or the rainbow, is described. But here there was no room for these [fine things]: perhaps, too, you know how to draw a cypress: but what is that to the purpose, if he who is painted for the given price, is [to be represented as] swimming hopeless out of a shipwreck? A large vase at first was designed: why, as the wheel revolves, turns out a little pitcher? In a word, be your subject what it will, let it be merely simple and uniform.

The great majority of us as poets—father, and youths worthy such a father—are misled by the appearance of right. I labor to be concise. I become obscure: nerves and spirit fail him that aims at the easy: one, that pretends to be sublime, proves bombastical: he who is too cautious and fearful of the storm, crawls along the ground: he who wants to vary his subject in a marvelous manner, paints the dolphin in the woods, the boar in the sea. The avoiding of an error leads to a fault, if it lack skill. . . .

Ye who write, make choice of a subject suitable to your abilities; and revolve in your thoughts a considerable time what your strength declines, and what it is able to support. Neither elegance of style nor a perspicuous disposition, shall desert the man by whom the subject matter is chosen judiciously.

This, or I am mistaken, will constitute the merit and beauty of arrangement, that the poet just now say what ought just now to be said, put off most of his thoughts, and waive them for the present.

In the choice of his words, too, the author of the projected poem must be delicate and cautious, he must embrace one and reject another: you will express yourself eminently well, if a dexterous combination should give an air of novelty to a well-known word. If it happen to be necessary to explain some abstruse subjects by new-invented terms, it will follow that you must frame words never heard of, by the old-fashioned Cethegi: and the license will be granted, if modestly used: and new and lately-formed words will have authority, if they descend from a Greek source, with a slight deviation. But why should the Romans grant to Plautus and Cæcilius a privilege denied to Vergil and Varius? Why should I be envied, if I have it in my power to acquire a few words, when the language of Cato and Ennius has enriched our native tongue, and produced new names of things? It has been, and ever will be, allowable to coin a word marked with the stamp in present request. As leaves in the woods are changed with the fleeting years; the earliest fall off first: in this manner words perish with old age, and those lately invented flourish and thrive, like men in the time of youth. We and our works are doomed to death: whether Neptune, admitted into the continent, defends our fleet from the north winds, a kingly work; or the lake, for a long time unfertile and fit for oars, now maintains its neighboring cities and feels the heavy plow; or the river, taught to run in a more convenient channel, has changed its course which was so destructive to the fruits. Mortal works must perish: much less can the honor and elegance of language be long-lived. Many words shall revive, which now have fallen off; and many words are now in esteem shall fall off, if it be the will of custom, in which power is the decision and right and standard of language. . . .

If I am incapable and unskillful to observe the distinction described, and the complexions of works [of genius], why am I

accosted by the name of "Poet"? Why, out of false modesty, do I prefer being ignorant to being learned?

A comic subject will not be handled in tragic verse: in like manner, the banquet of Thyestes will not bear to be held in familiar verses, and such as almost suit the sock. Let each peculiar species [of writing] fill with decorum its proper place. Nevertheless sometimes even comedy exalts her voice, and passionate Chremes rails in a tumid strain: and a tragic writer generally expresses grief in a prosaic style. Telephus and Peleus, when they are both in poverty and exile, throw aside their rants and gigantic expressions if they have a mind to move the heart of the spectator with their complaint.

It is not enough, that poems be beautiful; let them be tender and affecting, and bear away the soul of the auditor whithersoever they please. As the human countenance smiles on those that smile, so does it sympathize with those that weep. If you would have me weep you must first express the passion of grief yourself; then, Telephus or Peleus, your misfortunes hurt me: if you pronounce the parts assigned you ill, I shall either fall asleep or laugh.

Pathetic accents suit a melancholy countenance; words full of menace, an angry one; wanton expressions, a sportive look; and serious matter, an austere one. For nature forms us first within to every modification of circumstances; she delights or impels us to anger, or depresses us to the earth and afflicts us with heavy sorrow: then expresses those emotions of the mind by the tongue, its interpreter. If the words be discordant to the station of the speaker, the Roman knights and plebeians will raise an immoderate laugh. It will make a wide difference, whether it be Davus that speaks, or a hero; a man well-stricken in years, or a hot young fellow in his bloom; and a matron of distinction, or an officious nurse; a roaming merchant, or the cultivator of a verdant little farm; a Colchian, or an Assyrian, one educated at Thebes or one at Argos.

You that write, either follow tradition, or invent such fables as are congruous to themselves. If as a poet you have to represent the renowned Achilles; let him be indefatigable, wrathful, inexorable, courageous, let him deny that laws were made for him, let him arrogate everything to force of arms. Let Medea be fierce and untractable, Ino an object of pity, Ixion perfidious, Io wandering, Orestes in distress.

If you offer to the stage anything unattempted, and venture to form a new character, let it be preserved to the last such as it set out at the beginning, and be consistent with itself. It is difficult to write with propriety on subjects to which all writers have a common claim; and you with more prudence will reduce the *Iliad* into acts, than if you first introduce arguments unknown and never treated of before. A public story will become your own property, if you do not dwell upon the whole circle of events, which is paltry and open to every one; nor must you go so faithful a translator, as to take the pains of rendering [the original] word for word; nor by imitating throw yourself into straits, whence either shame or the rules of your work may forbid you to retreat. . . .

As action is either represented on the stage, or, being done elsewhere, is there related. The things which enter by the ear affect the mind more languidly, than such as are submitted to the faithful eyes, and what a spectator presents to himself. You must not, however, bring upon the stage things fit only to be acted behind the scenes: and you must take away from view many actions, which elegant description may soon after deliver in presence [of the spectators]. Let not Medea murder her sons before the people; nor the execrable Atreus openly dress human entrails; nor let Progne be metamorphosed into a bird, Cadmus into a serpent. Whatever you show to me in this manner, not able to give credit to, I detest.

Let a play which would be inquired after, and though seen, represented anew, be neither shorter nor longer than the fifth act. Neither let a god interfere, unless a difficulty worthy a god's unraveling should happen; nor let a fourth person be officious to speak.

Let the chorus sustain the part and manly character of an actor: nor let them sing anything between the acts which is not conducive to, and fitly coherent with, the main design. Let them both patronize the good, and give them friendly advice, and regulate the passionate, and love to appease those who swell [with rage]: let them praise the repast of a short meal, the salutary effects of justice, laws, and peace with her open gates: let them conceal what is told to them in confidence, and supplicate and implore the gods that prosperity may return to the wretched, and abandon the haughty. The flute (not as now, begirt with brass and emulous of the trumpet, but), slender and of simple form, with few stops, was of service to accompany and assist the chorus, and with its tone was sufficient to fill the rows that were not as yet too crowded, where an audience, easily numbered, as being small and sober, chaste and modest, met together. But when the victorious Romans began to extend their territories, and an ampler wall encompassed the city, and their genius was indulged on festivals by drinking wine in the daytime without censure; a greater freedom arose both to the numbers [of poetry], and the measure [of music]. For what taste could an unlettered clown and one just dismissed from labors have, when in company with the polite; the base, with the man of honor? Thus the musician added new movements and a luxuriance to the ancient art, and strutting backward and forward, drew a length of train over the stage: thus likewise new notes were added to the severity of the lyre, and precipitate eloquence produced an unusual language [in the theater]: and the sentiments [of the chorus, then] expert in teaching useful things and prescient of futurity, differ hardly from the oracular Delphi.

The poet who first tried his skill in tragic verse for the paltry [prize of a] goat, soon after exposed to view wild satyrs naked, and attempted raillery with severity, still preserving the gravity [of tragedy]: because the spectator on festivals, when heated with wine and disorderly, was to be amused with captivating shows and agreeable novelty. But it will be expedient so to recommend the bantering, so the rallying satyrs, so to turn earnest into jest that none who shall be exhibited as a god, none who is introduced as a hero lately conspicuous in regal purple and gold, may deviate into the low style of obscure, mechanical shops; or, [on the contrary] while he avoids the ground, affect cloudy mist and empty jargon. Tragedy, disdaining to prate forth trivial verses, like a matron commanded to dance on festival days, will assume an air of modesty, even in the midst of wanton satyrs. As

a writer of satire, ye Pisos, I shall never be fond of unornamented and reigning terms: nor shall I labor to differ so widely from the complexion of tragedy, as to make no distinction, whether Davus be the speaker. And the bold Pythias, who gained a talent by gulling Simo; or Silenus, the guardian and attendant of his pupil-god [Bacchus]. I would so execute a fiction taken from a well-known story, that anybody might entertain hopes of doing the same thing; but, on trial, should sweat and labor in vain. Such power has a just arrangement and connection of the parts: such grace may be added to subjects merely common. In my judgment, the Fauns, that are brought out of the woods, should not be too gamesome with their tender strains, as if they were educated in the city, and almost at the bar; nor, on the other hand, should blunder out their obscene and scandalous speeches. For [at such stuff] all are offended, who have a horse, a father, or an estate: nor will they receive with approbation, nor give the laurel crown, as the purchasers of parched peas and nuts are delighted with. . . .

It is not every judge that discerns inharmonious verses, and an undeserved indulgence is [in this case] granted to the Roman poets. But shall I on this account run riot and write licentiously? Or should not I rather suppose, that all the world are to see my faults; secure, and cautious [never to err] but with hope of being pardoned? Though, perhaps, I have merited no praise, I have escaped censure.

Ye [who are desirous to excel], turn over the Grecian models by night, turn them by day. But our ancestors commended both the numbers of Plautus, and his strokes of unpleasantry; too tamely, I will not say foolishly, admiring each of them; if you and I but know how to distinguish a coarse joke from a smart repartee, and understand the proper cadence, by [using] our fingers and ears.

Thespis is said to have invented a new kind of tragedy, and to have carried his pieces about in carts; which [certain strollers] who had their faces besmeared with lees of wine, sang and acted. After him, Æschylus, the inventor of the vizard mask and decent robe, laid the stage over with boards of a tolerable size, and taught to speak in lofty tone, and strut in the buskin. To these succeeded the old comedy, not without considerable praise: but its personal freedom degenerated into excess and violence, worthy to be regarded by law; a law was made accordingly, and the chorus, the right of abusing being taken away, disgracefully became silent.

Our poets have left no species of the art unattempted; nor have those of them merited the least honor, who dared to forsake the footsteps of the Greeks, and celebrate domestic facts; whether they have instructed us in tragedy, or in comedy. Nor would Italy be raised higher by valor and feats of arms, than by its language, did not the fatigue and tediousness of using the file disgust every one of our poets. Do you, the descendants of Pompilius, reject that poem, which many days and many a blot have not ten times subdued to the most perfect accuracy. Because Democritus believes that genius is more successful than wretched art, and excludes from Helicon all poets who are in their senses, a great number do not care to part with their nails

(continued)

or beard, frequent places of solitude, shun the baths. For he will acquire, [he thinks,] the esteem and title of a poet, if he neither submits his head, which is not to be cured by even three Anticyras, to Licinius the barber. What an unlucky fellow am I, who am purged for the bile in spring-time! Else nobody would compose better poems; but the purchase is not worth the expense. Therefore I will sever instead of a whetstone, which though not able of itself to cut, can make steel sharp: so I, who can write no poetry myself, will teach the duty and business [of an author]; whence he may be stocked with rich materials; what nourishes and forms the poet; what gives grace, what not; what is the tendency of excellence, what that of error.

To have good sense, is the first principle and fountain of writing well. The Socratic papers will direct you in the choice of your subjects; and words will spontaneously accompany the subject, when it is well conceived. He who has learned what he owes to his country, and what to his friends; with what affection a parent, a brother, and a stranger, are to be loved; what is the duty of a senator, what of a judge; what the duties of a general sent out to war; he, [I say,] certainly knows how to give suitable attributes to every character. I should direct the learned imitator to have a regard to the mode of nature and manners, and thence draw his expressions to the life. Sometimes a play, that is showy with common-places, and where the manners are well marked, though of no elegance, without force or art, gives the people much higher delight and more effectually commands their attention, than verse void of matter, and tuneful trifles.

To the Greeks, covetous of nothing but praise, the muse gave genius; to the Greeks the power of expressing themselves in round periods. The Roman youth learn by long computation to subdivided a pound into an hundred parts. Let the son of Albinus tell me, if from five ounces one be subtracted, what remains? He would have said the third of a pound.— Bravely done! you will be able to take care of your own affairs. An ounce is added: what will that be? Half a pound. When this sordid rust and hankering after wealth has once tainted their minds, can we expect that such verses should be made as are worthy of being anointed with the oil of cedar, and kept in the well-polished cypress?

Poets with either to profit or to delight; or to deliver at once both the pleasures and the necessaries of life. Whatever precepts you give, be concise, that docile minds may soon comprehend what is said, and faithfully retain it. All superfluous instructions flow from the too full memory. Let whatever is imagined for the sake of entertainment, have as much likeness to truth as possible; let not your play demand belief for what [absurdities] it is inclinable [to exhibit]: nor take out of a witch's belly a living child, that she had dined upon. The tribes of the seniors rail against everything that is void of edification: the exalted knights disregard poems which are austere. He who joins the instructive with the agreeable, carries off every vote, by delighting and at the same time admonishing the reader. This book gains money for the Sosii; this crosses the sea, and continues to its renowned author a lasting duration.

Yet there are faults, which we should be ready to pardon: for neither does the string [always] form the sound which the hand and conception [of the performer] intends, but very often returns a sharp note when he demands a flat; nor will the bow always hit whatever mark it threatens. But when there is a great majority of beauties in a poem, I will not be offended with a few blemishes, which either inattention has dropped, or human nature has not sufficiently provided against. What therefore [is to be determined in this matter]? As a transcriber, if he still commits the same fault though he has been reproved, is without excuse; and the harper who always blunders on the same string, is sure to be laughed at; so he who is excessively deficient becomes another Chorilus; whom, when I find him tolerable in two or three places, I wonder at with laughter; and at the same time am I grieved whenever honest Homer grows drowsy? But it is allowable, that sleep should steal upon [the progress of] a long work.

As is painting, so is poetry: some pieces will strike you more if you stand near, and some if you are at a greater distance: one who loves the dark; another, which is not afraid of the critic's subtile judgment, chooses to be seen in the light; the one has pleased once; the other will give pleasure if ten times repeated.

O you elder of the youths, though you are framed to a right judgment by your father's instructions, and are wise in yourself, yet take this truth along with you, [and] remember it; that in certain things a medium and tolerable degree of eminence may be admitted: a counselor and pleader at the bar of the middle rate is far removed from the merit of eloquent Messala, nor has so much knowledge of the law as Cassellius Aulus, but yet he is in request; [but] a mediocrity in poets neither gods, nor men, nor [even] the booksellers' shops have endured. As at an agreeable entertainment discordant music, and muddy perfume, and poppies mixed with Sardinian honey give offense, because the supper might have passed without them; so poetry, created and invented for the delight of our souls, if it comes short ever so little of the summit, sinks to the bottom. . . .

It has been made a question, whether good poetry be derived from nature or from art. For my part, I can neither conceive what study can do without a rich natural vein, nor what rude genius can avail of itself: so much does the one require the assistance of the other, and so amicably do they conspire [to produce the same effect]. He who is industrious to reach the wished-for goal, has done and suffered much when a boy; he has sweated, and shivered with cold; he has abstained from love and wine; he who sings the Pythian strains, as first a learner, and in awe of a master. But [in poetry] it is now enough for a man to say to himself: "I make admirable verses: a murrain seize the hindmost: it is scandalous for me to be outstripped, and fairly to acknowledge that I am ignorant of that which I never learned."

Mojin Shoka, *a contemporary Japanese play, was performed in Tokyo in 1973.*

CHAPTER 5

THE THEATER OF INDIA, CHINA, AND JAPAN

Theater in the many countries of Asia also sprang from religious rites, shamanistic ceremonies (especially those devoted to healing), and sacred dances. In India the deity Brahma appeared to the mortal priest Bharata and instructed him in the ways of theater so humans might be enlightened about life in its sublime state. In China the first professional actors may have been priests employed by farmers to perform sacred dances that would insure a bountiful harvest. The Noh theater of Japan evolved from Buddhist temple dances and even today retains a spiritual dimension in its attempt to induce its audience into meditation. Even the more secular Kabuki originated with temple dancers. Today, the Japanese word for "festival," *matsuri* ("to be near a god or sacred thing"), reflects the spiritual roots of such events as the Tanabata Festival (see *Komachi at Sekidera*).

Consider other examples of the spiritual origins of the theater in other Asian locales. As early as the twelfth century B.C.E., Koreans celebrated Yong-go, a religious festival not unlike the Greek Dionysia. During the tenth month of each year, Koreans gathered for singing, dancing, and wine drinking. A short play, *The Welcoming of the Drum*, was central to the Yong-go. By 100 C.E., numerous folk performances in Southeast Asia were associated with animal worship (especially sea creatures in this oceangoing culture). In Indonesia and Malaysia leather figures representing man, gods, and evil spirits were used as shadow puppets to enact the great myths of the people. The puppets were controlled by the *dalang* (an actor-shaman-storyteller) who was thought to be a god. Plays that lasted a full day were performed to depict the progress of a man from youth to spiritual harmony. Such plays were commonplace by 907 C.E. (near the advent of Christian drama in Europe), and they eventually evolved into *khon*, plays about human dilemmas performed by the *dalang* themselves. Similar progressions in the evolution of theater and drama can be found throughout the world.

While there exists a wealth of extraordinary theatrical activity throughout Asia—much of which has influenced contemporary Western performance—the best-known drama comes from India, China, and Japan. Specifically, we will look at the most representative forms of drama from those three cultures:

- The Sanskrit drama of India, which flourished for over a thousand years. You will read the greatest of the Sanskrit plays, a romance called *The Recognition of Śakuntalā*.
- The Chinese theater, which will be considered in two forms:
  - The Classical theater of the Yuan dynasty produced China's greatest literary drama. *Autumn in the Palace of Han* typifies the best of Chinese dramatic literature.
  - The Peking Opera is arguably the most popular theater-form in the world as it is the national drama of the world's most populous country. *The Qing Ding Pearl*, a short melodrama, will allow you to experience the type of play the Chinese have been enjoying for 200 years.

- The *Noh theater* of Japan, which is perhaps most rooted in ritual and ceremony. The short verse play *Komachi at Sekidera* is the work of the Noh theater's finest playwright and theoretician, Zeami.
- The Kabuki, which was developed in the early seventeenth century, and remains Japan's most popular theater form. You will read one of the eighteen treasures of the Kabuki, *Kanjinchō* (*The Subscription List*), a tale of a loyal samurai warrior.
- Contemporary Japanese plays, which are called *shengeki* ("new plays"), and Kobe Abe's *The Man Who Turned into a Stick* represents experimentation in the Japanese theater.

Though these works come from differing cultures and performance traditions, some characteristics are common to most Asian theater:

- There is no pretense of realism in the performance of traditional Asian plays (though that is changing in the contemporary era). The Asian theater has always been presentational and highly theatrical.
- Consequently, there is a high degree of interaction among performers and spectators. While many periods of theater in the West enjoyed such interaction, it remains one of the most distinguishing characteristics of Asian theater. (Ironically, Western artists are rediscovering the appeal of this quality.)
- Dance, mime, and gesture are as important as the verbal aspects of Asian plays.
- Music is integral to the performance. Most Asian plays are sung or, at the very least, accompanied by music as the actors perform.
- Masks and painted faces are essential costume elements. Clothing is richly adorned, usually brightly colored, and rarely realistic as we understand the term.
- Most plays are episodic and reflect the Asian theater's indebtedness to storytelling.
- Though there may be moments of profound insight into human behavior, there is usually little attempt at psychological realism as it has been developed in the West. Characters are more archetypal than specific.
- Actors rarely try to "become" the character they portray. Rather, they "present" the character as a type.
- Though it may be hard for us to ascertain this when reading translations, Asian drama retains its poetic roots, even in nonmusical dialogue or recited passages.

In 1931 a young French actor, Antonin Artaud, saw a performance of the Balinese Barong described in Chapter 1. The experience transformed Artaud and he set out to revitalize the theater by returning it to its roots (see Chapter 9 for a discussion of Artaud's "theater of cruelty"). In his germinal work *The Theater and Its Double*, Artaud compares the theaters of the West and of the East, though his comments reflect a Western bias. He begins by noting that the Balinese theater revealed to him "a physical and non verbal idea of the theatre, in which the theatre is contained within the limits of everything that can happen on a stage, independently of the written text." Western theater, for Artaud, "declared its alliance with the text and finds itself limited by it." His ensuing discussion then contrasts the two worlds of theater:

Balinese (Asian) Theater	Western Theater
Mystical	Realistic
Gesture and Signs	Dialogue and Words
Ritual and Transcendence	Ethics and Morality
Metaphysical States	"The Here and Now"
Does Not Rely on Rational Continuity	Causality
Transcends Reality on Stage	Creates Reality on Stage
Abandons Illusion	Creates Realistic Illusions
Uses Platforms and Spaces	Uses Scenery and Settings
Sounds and Rhythms	Speech

Much contemporary Western theater has conscientiously adopted elements of Asian theater articulated in this analysis of the two cultures. It may prove useful as you read plays throughout this anthology. Conversely, contemporary writers in Asia have shown an increasing interest in Western methods, especially realism, in their works.

Let us begin our study of the theater of Asia by looking at the oldest surviving drama, the Sanskrit from India.

INDIA

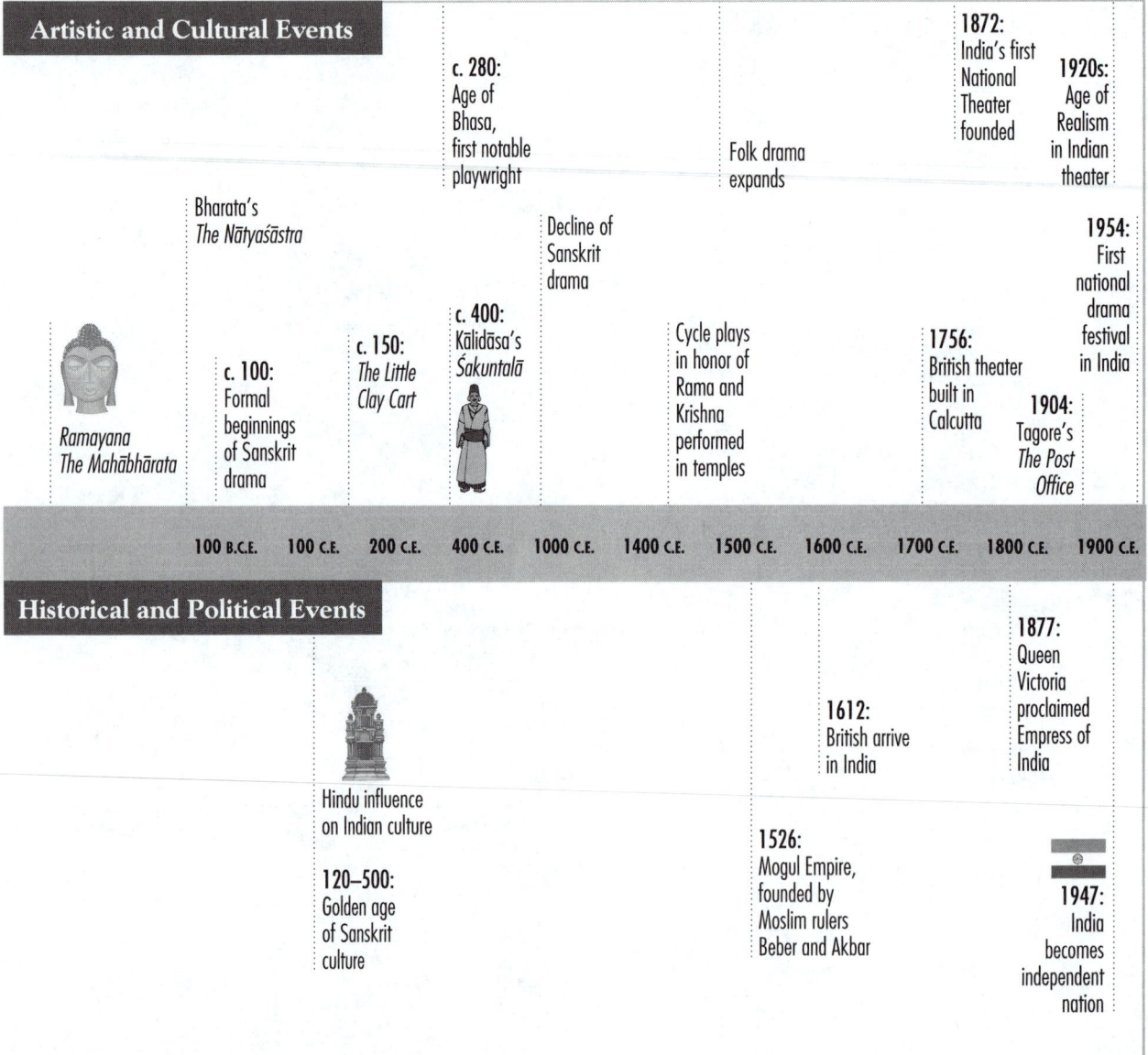

Artistic and Cultural Events

c. 280: Age of Bhasa, first notable playwright

1872: India's first National Theater founded

1920s: Age of Realism in Indian theater

Bharata's *The Nātyaśāstra*

Decline of Sanskrit drama

Folk drama expands

1954: First national drama festival in India

c. 100: Formal beginnings of Sanskrit drama

c. 150: *The Little Clay Cart*

c. 400: Kālidāsa's *Śakuntalā*

Cycle plays in honor of Rama and Krishna performed in temples

1756: British theater built in Calcutta

1904: Tagore's *The Post Office*

Ramayana The Mahābhārata

| 100 B.C.E. | 100 C.E. | 200 C.E. | 400 C.E. | 1000 C.E. | 1400 C.E. | 1500 C.E. | 1600 C.E. | 1700 C.E. | 1800 C.E. | 1900 C.E. |

Historical and Political Events

1877: Queen Victoria proclaimed Empress of India

1612: British arrive in India

Hindu influence on Indian culture

120–500: Golden age of Sanskrit culture

1526: Mogul Empire, founded by Moslim rulers Beber and Akbar

1947: India becomes independent nation

254

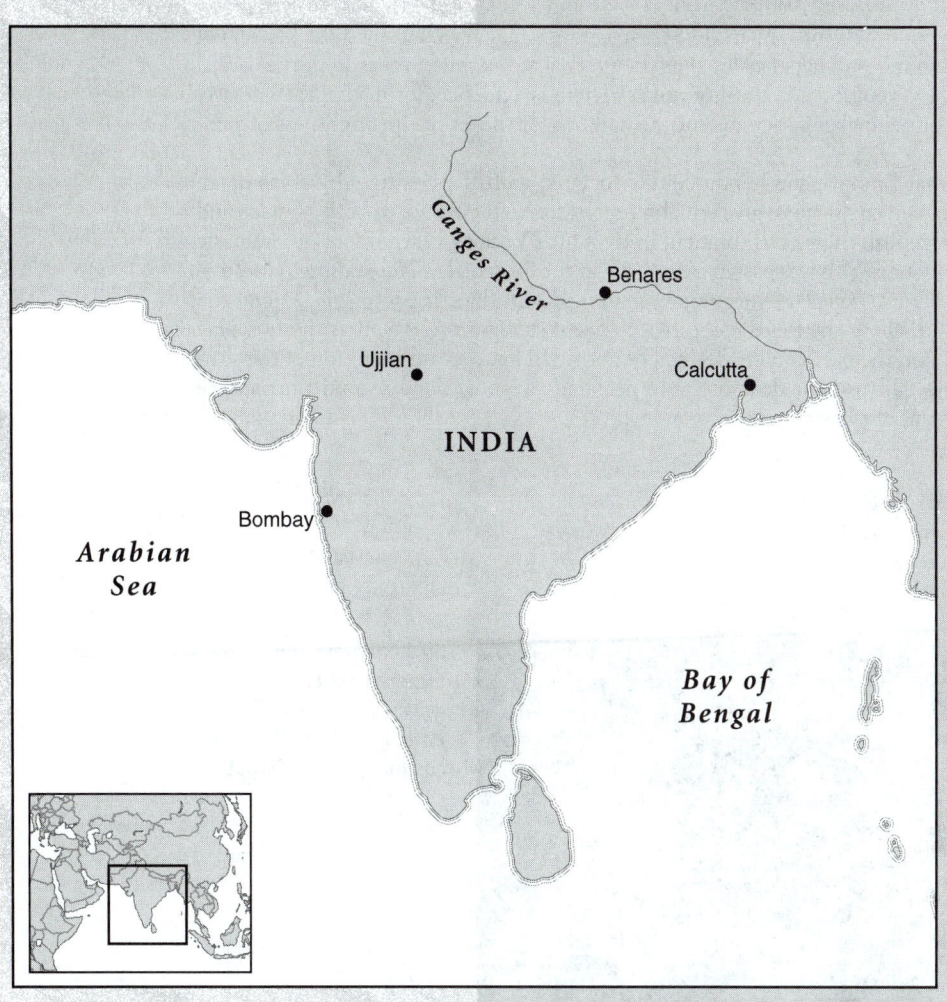

The Origins of Indian Drama

Theater and drama in the vast Asian subcontinent are as varied and ancient as India itself. As religion has permeated most aspects of Indian life, particularly among the Hindus, it is not surprising that the origins of drama can be traced to the sacred scriptures, or Vedas, of India. Like the ancient Greek dithyrambs, Vedic hymns to gods and goddesses in the Hindu pantheon were chanted by a chorus of worshippers. Eventually, priests may have assumed the persona of various gods (*devas*) and prophets (*sadhyas*) as they reenacted cosmic events from the sacred teachings as part of vegetation and fertility rituals. There is evidence, for instance, that early actors wore black or red makeup to represent the darkness of winter or the brightness of summer, respectively.

Legend says that Brahma, the Hindu deity associated with the creative drive (compare with Dionysus), conceived drama to give enlightenment through pleasure to both humans and other gods. To accomplish these ends, Brahma wrote a fifth Veda as a sacred text on dramatic theory and stage practice. This was passed to humans in the form of *The Nātyasāstra* (*The Treatise on Drama*; see Forum, from *The Nātyasāstra*) composed by India's first actor-playwright, the holy sage Bharata, in about the fourth century C.E. *The Nātyasāstra* tells us that the first play performed in India, on the occasion of a festival honoring Indra, was "an imitation of the situation in which the daityas [evil demons] were defeated by gods." The second drama, *The Churning of the Ocean*, was based on a creation myth.

Siva Nataraja, among the most revered Hindu deities, is known as "the Lord of the Dance" and a creator of theater in India.

FORUM

"From *The Nātyaśāstra*"

BHARATA

According to legend, the gods gave the priest Bharata a sacred book of the drama—The Nātyaśāstra—so that humans may reach enlightenment through acts of theater. The book, or Fifth Veda of the Sacred Scriptures, provides a useful explanation of Sanskrit theater practice. In this passage the rasas, or sentiments, of the drama are carefully analyzed. Not only does the discussion proscribe the feelings that drama should engender in the audience, it also suggests something about the acting style of classical India. It is useful to compare what Bharata says about such emotions as fear to Aristotle's comment in The Poetics.

All the great sages, after listening to the rules on the *pūrvaraṅga*, spoke again to Bharata and said: Please answer for us these five questions.

Theorists speak of "*rasas*" in drama—please tell us wherein lies the essence of these *rasas*.

What are *bhāvas* (emotions), and what do they create (*bhāvayanti*)? What really are *saṅgraha*, *kārikā*, and *nirukta*?

When Bharata the sage heard their request, he gave an answer defining *rasa* and *bhāva* . . .

Still I will list the *rasas* and *bhāvas* of drama giving very concisely the subject-matter (*artha*) of the aphoristic definitions (*sūtra*) and their exposition (*grantha*) so that (this list) will allow one to infer (further details) (*anumānaprasādhaka*). . .

Such a list (of the main subjects of dramatic theory includes) *rasas*, *bhāvas*, acting, conventions (or practice), *vrttis*, *pravrttis*, success (of the performance), musical notes (*svara*), as well as instrumental music, singing and stage-craft.

Experts say that in a *kārikā* a subject is briefly (*samāsena*) set down, i.e., in a few words (*alpābhidhānea*), and in the manner of an aphorism (*sūtratah*), (so that it) explains the essential point (*arthapradarśinī*). . . .

O best of Brahmins, I have given briefly the *saṅgraha*. Now I will speak of those topics in more detail and include *nirukta* and *kārikā*.

In a drama there are the following eight *rasas*: erotic (*śrṅgāra*), comic (*hāsya*), compassionate (*karuna*), furious (*raudra*), heroic (*vīra*), terrifying (*bhayānaka*), disgusting (*bībhatsa*) and awesome (*adbhuta*).

For the great Brahmā has declared that these are the eight *rasas*. Now I will list the *bhāvas*—those that are primary (*sthāyi*), those that (only) accompany the primary emotions (and are

thus transitory) (*sañcāri*), and those expression of feeling that stem from a deep-felt emotion (*sattvaja*).

The permanent emotions have been declared to be love (*rati*), amusement (or laughter) (*hāsa*), sorrow (*śoka*), anger (*krodha*), dynamic energy (*utsāha*), fear (*bhaya*), disgust (*jugupsā*) and wonder (*vismaya*). . . .

In drama there are four kinds of dramatic representation (*abhinaya*): that which uses the body (*āngika*), that which uses speech (*vācika*), that which uses costume (*āhārya*), and that which is involuntary (*sāttvika*).

Convention (or practice) (*dharmī*) is divided into two kinds: that which obtains in the real world (*lokadharmī*), and that which is peculiar to the drama (*nātyadharmī*). . . .

There are five kinds of songs, each accompanied by a *dhruvā*: that which is sung on (an actor's) entrance (*praveśa*), that which accompanies the transition from one emotion to another (*ākṣepa*), that which is sung on (an actor's) exit (*niṣkrāma*), that which conveys (the character's) mental mood (*prāsādika*), and that which is sung as the character moves about on the stage (*āntara*). A stage is of three kinds: square, rectangular and triangular. . . .

Among these topics, we will first of all explain what are *rasas*. For without *rasa* no topic (of drama) can appeal (to the mind of the spectator) (*na hi rasād rte kaścid arthah pravartate*—perhaps, "For without *rasa*, there can be no (true) meaning, i.e. no real poetry.") *Rasa* comes from a combination of the *vibhāvas*, the *anubhāvas* and the *vyabhicāribhāvas* (*vibhāvānubhāvavyabhicārisamyogād rasanispattih*).

What is a (good) analogy? Here is one: Just as flavour (*rasa*) comes from a combination of many spices, herbs and other substances (*dravya*), so *rasa* (in a drama) comes from the combination (*upagama*) of many *bhāvas*. For example, in the same way that beverages such as *sādava* (a combination of six flavours) are created (*nirvartyante*) from substances such as molasses, spices (*vyañjana*) and herbs (*osadhi*), the permanent emotions attain the status of *rasa* when they are accompanied (*upagata*) by the various *bhāvas*. At this point someone (might) ask: What is it you call *rasa*? The answer is: (It is called *rasa*) because it can be savored (*āsvādyatvāt*). How is *rasa* savored? As gourmets (*sumanas*) are able to savor the flavour of food prepared with many spices, and attain pleasure etc., so sensitive spectators (*sumanas*) savor the primary emotions suggested (*abhivyañjita*) by the acting out of the various *bhāvas* and presented with the appropriate modulation of the voice, movements of the body and display of involuntary reactions, and attain pleasure, etc. Therefore they are called (*abhivyākhyātāh*) *nātyarasas* (dramatic flavours). On this same subject there are the following two traditional (*ānuvamśya*) verses:

As gourmets (*bhaktavit*) savor food prepared with many tasty ingredients (*dravya*) and many spices.

(continued)

So sensitive people (*budha*) enjoy in their minds the permanent emotions presented with different kinds of the acting out of (transient) emotions (and presentation of their causes). This is why (these primary emotions) are known as *nātyarasas*.

Now one might ask: Do the *bhāvas* come from *rasa*, or does *rasa* come from the *bhāvas*? Some hold that they arise from their relation of mutual dependence, but this is not true. Why? Because we find that *rasas* come from the *bhāvas*, but *bhāvas* do not come from *rasas*. On this point there are the following verses:

Those who stage dramas (*nātyayoktr*) should know that the *bhāvas* are so called because they give rise to (*bhāvayanti*) *rasas* that are related to the various kinds of acting.

As a spicy (flavour) is created from many substances (*dravya*) of different kinds, in the same way the *bhāvas* along with (various kinds of) acting, create *rasas*.

(In literature) there is no *rasa* without *bhāva*, nor any *bhāva* without *rasa*. Their realization in gesture is dependent on their relation of mutual dependence.

As a combination of herbs and spices will bring (*nayet*) food to tastiness (*svādutām*), in the same *bhāvas* and *rasas* create (*bhāvayanti*) each other.

As a tree arises from a seed, and from the tree a flower and fruit, so all the *rasas* are the roots, and on them are founded the *bhāvas*.

Now we will give the origin (*utpatti*), the colors, the presiding deities, and examples (*nidarśana*) of these *rasas*. There are four (major) *rasas* which give rise to the other four. (The original four are): The erotic, the wrathful, the heroic and the disgusting. On this point (there are the following verses):

The comic aesthetic experience comes from the erotic. The compassionate comes from the furious. The awesome aesthetic experience comes from the heroic and the terrifying from the disgusting.

An imitation (*anukrti*) of the erotic is known as the comic. The result (*karma*) of the furious should be known to be an aesthetic experience of compassion.

The result of the heroic (*rasa*) is known as the awesome, and the sight of the disgusting (gives rise to) the terrifying. . . .

Now the presiding deities:

The presiding deity of the erotic *rasa* is Visnu; of the comic it is Pramatha (the attendants of Śiva); for the furious (*rasa*) it is Rudra; Yama is the god of the compassionate; Śiva of the disgusting. The god of time is the presiding deity of the terrifying *rasa*; Indra is the god of the heroic and Brahmā of the awesome.

. . . Now we will explain the definitions and examples (of the *rasas*) with their *anubhāvas*, *vibhāvas* and *vyabhicāribhāvas*. And we will bring (*upaneśyāmah*) the *sthāyibhāvas* to the status of *rasas*.

Of the various *rasas*, the erotic one arises from the *sthāyibhāva* love. Whatever in the ordinary world is bright, pure (*medhya*), shining or beautiful, is associated with love. For example, people say that a man who wears beautiful clothes must be in love. As people are given names according to paternal (*gotra*) and maternal (*kula*) descent and their professions on the basis of a reliable tradition (*āptopadeśasiddha*), so the names of the *rasas*, *bhāvas* and other elements (*artha*) connected with the drama (are given) on the basis of an unbroken tradition according to custom (*ācāra?*). This is why the erotic *rasa*, because it consists

in a charming and beautiful dress is called by a name (namely *śrṅgāra*) which has become established through (conventional) usage. It has for its (*ālambana*)-*vibhāvas* young men and women who are noble-born. It has two major divisions: love in union, and love in separation. To begin with love in union: It arises from (*uddīpāna*)-*vibhāvas* such as a (representation) of the seasons, garlands, ointments, ornaments, people dear to one, objects of the senses, fine homes, love-making (*upabhoga*), going to gardens (and there) experiencing, listening to and seeing, games, sexual play and so forth. It should be acted out by such *anubhāvas* as a skillful (use) of the eyes, frowning, side-glances, flirtatious movements (*lalita*), gentle bodily movements (*aṅgahāra*), and soft speech. The accompanying transitory emotions that do not belong to love are laziness, violence, disgust. As for love in separation, it should be acted out by *anubhāvas* such as world-weariness, physical weakness, anxiety, envy, fatigue, worry, longing, dreaming, awakening, sickness, insanity, apoplexy, lifelessness, and death. Now one might ask: If this erotic, aesthetic experience arises from love, how can its *bhāvas* (i.e., *anubhāvas*) (also) belong to the compassionate? The answer is as follows: We have said above that the erotic (*rasa*) is divided into love in union and love in separation. Writers on erotics (*vaiśikaśāstra*) have explained that love has ten stages. We will give these in the chapter on *sāmānya* acting.

The compassionate (*rasa*), on the other hand, consists in all loss of hope of ever meeting again (*nirapeksabhāva*), and arises from suffering due to a curse (*śāpakleśa*), a fall in status (*vinipatita*) of one's beloved, his imprisonment, his death or the loss of wealth. Love in separation consists in retaining some hope of meeting again (*sāpeksabhāva*) and arises from longing and worry. And so the compassionate (*rasa*) is one thing, and love in separation is another. Thus the erotic (*rasa*) is accompanied by all *bhāvas*. Moreover:

A man who has a young woman, enjoys the seasons, garlands and the like, and is provided with agreeable things, is said to (experience) love (*śṛngāra*). . . .

An aesthetic experience of love arises from listening to music and poems with one's beloved, and from enjoying the seasons, garlands, ornaments, going to gardens and walking.

It should be acted out by showing a pleasant face and eyes, a smile and pleasant words, mental contentment and delight as well as by graceful body movements.

As for the comic (*rasa*), it consists of (or is based on) the primary emotion of laughter. It arises from such *vibhāvas* as wearing clothes and ornaments that belong to someone else or do not fit (*vikrta*), shamelessness (*dhārstya*), greed (*laulya*), tickling certain sensitive parts of the body (*kuhaka*), telling fantastic tales (*asatpralāpa*), seeing some (comic) deformity (*vyanga*), and describing faults (*dosodāhanana*). It should be acted out by puffing out the cheeks, the nose, the lips, widening and contracting one's eyes, sweating, coloring of the face, grabbing one's sides (in laughter) and so forth. The ephemeral emotions (that accompany it) are: dissimulation, laziness, drowsiness (*tandrā*), sleep, dreaming, awakening, envy, etc. It is of two kinds: existing in oneself, and existing in another person. When one laughs on one's own, that laughter is said to be existing in oneself. When one causes another person to laugh, then the laughter is said to be existing in another person. On this subject there are the following two traditional Ārya stanzas:

One laughs because of misplaced ornaments, eccentric behaviour, language and dress, and other peculiar actions (*arthaviśesa?*), and the resulting aesthetic experience is known as the comic (*rasa*).

Because one can make people laugh by eccentric actions, words, and bodily movements and dress, therefore the resulting sentiment (*rasa*) should be known as the comic.

This sentiment is to be found primarily among women and low-class people . . .

And one should know that the aesthetic experience of the comic is two-fold in so far as it arises in oneself or in someone else. Its three stages (*avasthā*) correspond to the three types of characters.

Now (the *rasa*) known as *karuna* arises from the permanent emotion of sorrow. It proceeds from *vibhāvas* such as a curse, affliction (*kleśa*, or "affliction of a curse"), separation from those who are dear, (their) downfall, loss of wealth, death, and imprisonment, or from contact with misfortune (*vyasāna*), destruction (*upaghāta*), and calamity (*vidrava*). It should be acted out by tears, laments, drying up of the mouth, change of color, languour in the limbs, sighs, loss of memory, etc. Its *vyabhicāribhāvas* are: world-weariness, physical weariness, worry, longing, panic, mental aberration (*bhrama*), confusion, weariness, fear, dejection, depression, sickness, lifelessness, insanity, apoplexy, fright, laziness, death, paralysis, trembling, change of color, tears, change of voice and the like. . . .

Now (the *rasa*) called *raudra* has anger for its permanent emotion. Demons, monsters and violent men are its characters. It is caused by battles. It arises (sic) from such *vibhāvas* as anger, provocative actions (*ādharsana*), insult (*adhiksepa*), lies, assault (*upaghāta*), harsh words, oppression (*abhidroha*, or according to A, "murderous intent"), and envy. The appropriate actions that accompany it are: beating, splitting open (*pātana*), crushing, ripping open, breaking, brandishing of weapons (*praharanāharana*), hitting so as to inflict a wound (*samprahāra*), hitting without inflicting a wound (*śastrasampāta*) . . . , drawing of blood, etc. It should be acted out by red eyes, furrowing of the brows, biting one's lips and grinding one's teeth, puffing out the cheeks, wringing the hands, and similar gestures. Its (*vyabhicāri*)-*bhāvas* are: correct perception (*asammoha*), dynamic energy (*utsāha*), panic, resentment, rashness, violence, pride, sweat, trembling, horripilation, stuttering (*gadgada*) and so forth. Now (one might) ask: It was said that *raudrarasa* pertains to demons, monsters, etc. Does this mean that it does not apply to others? The reply is that *raudrarasa* applies equally to others as well. However it is predominant (*adhikāra*) among these particular creatures. For they are by their very nature violent. Why? Because they have many arms, many mouths, their hair is yellow and lies in a wild mess on their heads, their wide-opened eyes are red and their black bodies are terrifying. Whatever they undertake, whether natural actions (i.e. their most casual actions), speech or bodily movements, is terrifying. Generally they even make love in a violent fashion. Men who imitate them give rise to *raudrarasa* (in the spectator) from blows and battles. . . .

Now (the *rasa*) called *vīra* has (only) noble people for its characters and consists in dynamic energy (*utsāha*). It arises from such *vibhāvas* as: correct perception, decisiveness (*adhyavasāya*), political wisdom (*naya*), courtesy (*vinaya*), an army

(*bala*), bravery, skill in battle (*śakti*), might (*pratāpa*), eminence (*prabhāva*), etc. It should be acted out by such *anubhāvas* as firmness, patience, heroism, generosity and shrewdness (*vaiśāradya*). Its (*vyabhicāri*)-*bhāvas* are happiness, attentiveness, pride, panic, violence, resentment, remembrance, and horripilation. . . .

Now (the *rasa*) called *bhayānaka* has fear as its permanent emotion. It arises from such *vibhāvas* as ghastly noises, seeing supernatural beings (ghosts), fear and panic due to the (cries) of owls (or the howling of) jackals, going to an empty house or to a forest, hearing about, speaking about, or seeing the imprisonment or murder of one's relatives. It should be acted out by such actions as trembling of the hands and feet, darting motions of the eyes, the hair standing on end, changing facial color (i.e. going white with fear) or stuttering. Its (*vyabhicāri*)-*bhāvas* are: paralysis, sweating, stuttering, horripilation, trembling, a break in the voice, change of color, anxiety, confusion, depression, panic, rashness, lifelessness, fright, apoplexy, death and so forth. On this subject there are the following Āryā stanzas:

Pretended (*krtaka*) *bhayānaka* results from an offence against a Guru or a king. (*Bhayānaka* also arises) from (hearing) a ghastly noise, seeing a supernatural being, going to battle, to a forest, or to an empty house.

Terror (*bhaya*) (can be acted out?) by violent changes (*bheda*) of the limbs, the face or the eyes, (such as) paralysis of the legs, looking about in panic, collapsing (*sanna*) (on the ground), drying up of the mouth, palpitation of the heart, and horripilation.

The above is genuine (fear). It should be represented as arising from deeply felt emotions (*sattvasamuttha*). Pretended (fear) should be acted out by means of the same *bhāvas* (i.e. *anubhāvas*), only with milder gestures.

Bhayānaka should always be acted out by trembling of the hands and feet, paralysis of the limbs (*gātrastambha?*), fast beating of the heart, and dryness of the lips, palate and throat.

Now (the *rasa*) known as *bībhatsa* has disgust as its permanent emotion. It arises from such *vibhāvas* as discussing, hearing or seeing what is ugly, unpleasant, unclean (*acosya*) and undesired. It should be acted out by contractions of the whole body (*sarvāngasamhāra*), facial contortions (*mukhavikūnana*), vomitting (*ullekhana*), spitting, violent trembling of the body (*udvejana*), and similar gestures. Its (*vyabhicāri*)-*bhāvas* are apoplexy, agitation (*udvega*), panic, confusion, sickness, death and the like.

Now (the *rasa*) called *adbhuta* has for its permanent emotion wonder. It arises from such *vibhāvas* as seeing heavenly beings, gaining one's desired object, going to a temple, a garden (*upavana*) or a meeting place, or (seeing) a flying chariot, a magic show (*māyā*), or a juggler's show. It should be acted out by such *anubhāvas* as opening one's eyes wide, staring, horripilation, sweat, tears, ecstatic delight, cries of "bravo," the donation of gifts, continuous (*prabandha*) cries of "Oh," "Oh," waving the arms, nodding the head (in agreement and admiration), waving one's clothes or one's fingers. Its (*vyabhicāri*)-*bhāvas* are paralysis, tears, sweat, stuttering, horripilation, panic, flurry, lifelessness, fainting, etc. . . .

Thus one should understand the eight *rasas* which I have illustrated with definitions. In what follows I will define the *bhāvas* as well. . . .

In addition to Brahma's invention, Indian mythology claims that Siva brought dance, so indispensable to Indian theater, to the drama. Siva, known as Lord of the Dance, is associated with time and death and thus the length of his dance determines one's longevity. Another deity, Vishnu ("the Preserver") gave Indian drama its characteristic styles. Coincidentally, Vishnu—like Dionysus—was believed to immerse himself in the earth for four months, after which his triumphant resurrection was marked by rituals and theatrical celebrations.

Although stories recounting the divine sources of drama substantiate the sacred dimension of theater in India, we also know that historically theater and subsequently drama developed from a variety of sources. Dance, which remains perhaps Indian drama's dominant distinguishing feature, is one source. Another is the *bhuta* ritual, in which many men wearing massive costumes and armed with swords performed a "demon play" re-creating a cosmic battle between the goddess Kali and the sinister demon Darika. (It may have resembled the Balinese Barong dance described in Chapter 1.) *The Nātyaśāstra* confirms this possible origin in its commentary about the "first play" in Indian drama. Indian theater may also have evolved from the *kuttiyattabm*, a form of shamanistic monologue in which a single shaman-actor created a number of characters while recounting mythic epics. Such narrators were known as a *sútradhara*, or "holder of the strings." The term is ambiguous: it may refer to puppets and their strings (puppetry is especially popular in almost all forms of Asian theater), or it may simply indicate that the storyteller holds the various strands of a story together. *Sútradhara* is a term that is still widely used to denote a playwright or storyteller.

The Types of Indian Drama

Whatever the precise origins of theater in India, several types of theatrical activity have resulted. In practice there is considerable overlap among the various forms. Sanskrit drama, of which *Śakuntalā* is the best-known example, was the formal drama of the court and thrived until the Muslim arrival in India in about 1000 C.E. Sanskrit drama is still regarded as India's premier literary drama. Sanskrit plays fall into two broad categories. *Nátaka* plays, such as *Śakuntalā*, are based on traditional mythology or history, and *prakarana* plays, such as *The Little Clay Cart*, are invented by the playwright and portray less exalted characters. *Nátaka* plays are traditionally five to seven acts in length, while the *prakarana* plays can be as long as ten acts. Both were traditionally performed in court theaters located near the temple, a reminder of the spiritual roots of Indian drama.

The Conventions of Classical Indian Theater

The ultimate goal of performance art in India is to produce *rasa,* or "flavor," an emotional state or mood, in each audience member. Whereas Western audiences concern themselves with the plot and character of a play, Indian audiences judge a production's success by its ability to induce a strong emotional response through the skillful integration of poetry, mime, dance, music, costume, and jewelry. Each play has a dominant *rasa*—for example, the erotic *rasa*—and each act within the larger play produces an individual rasa such as wonder, awe, dread, or love. There is a progression of moods, ultimately leading to serenity or peace. It may be useful to compare an Indian drama to a musical composition. In a symphony each movement exists to create a specific mood, although the entire piece has an identifiable sentiment. Audiences attending an Indian drama are cued to the proper emotional response by a variety of conventions and traditional devices. Words and music are the most obvious, but others include a very elaborate system of hand gestures (*mudras*), dance movements, and body attitudes that take years for the performer to master. A mere reading of a drama such as *Śakuntalā* can only hint at the subtleties of mood so integral to the experience of the Indian theater.

The Nātyaśāstra is very specific about the design and construction of the *natyamandapa,* or playhouse. It was required to be in the shape of a mountain cave, free from gusts of wind "so that the voices of the actors . . . will be resonant." Though the playhouse could be square or even triangular, Bharata suggests that the ideal configuration is a rectangle measuring 96 feet by 48 feet (about the size of a modern basketball court) to encourage an intimacy of playing between the actors and the audiences of some 400. The stage was raised 27 inches off the ground, and, in the days of the great courts, precious jewels were buried beneath the stage. The acting area was backed by a richly adorned curtain with two doors, one for entrances, the other for exits. The curtain was—and remains—an important convention of the Indian theater. It is shaken to create moods and denote emotional states; an actor may be wrapped in its folds to convey him to another locale. Very little scenery and few props were used. Like the Elizabethan theater, the Sanskrit theater relied on language and the poetic imagination to create the many locales of the drama.

As befitting a theater form that evolved in a land where dance is supreme, movement and mimetic gesture were integral to performances; even today Indian actor-dancers spend many years perfecting the *mudras*, gestural grammar, of the Indian theater. *The Nātyaśāstra* carefully catalogues these. In act 6 of *Śakuntalā*, for instance, Madhukarikā, one of the nymphs attending the sacred gardens, "folds her hands together in prayer." Specifically, she would use here a gesture in which the hands form the shape of a dove, a sign of supplication in which the doer's thoughts fly heavenward. Like the Chinese theater, the Indian theater also uses highly stylized movement as part of its conventions of performance. Actors frequently walk in a large circle about the stage to indicate a shift in locale, or enter with a toss of the curtain to suggest a state of agitation. Costuming, hairstyles, and a bold use of color—blue, red, yellow, and black—in masks and makeup further the metaphoric nature of Indian theatre. After Duhsanta has rebuked Śakuntalā, she returns to the stage with her hair in a single braid, a symbol of a woman's grief.

Like so much of the theater of Asia, the Sanskrit drama of classical India celebrates the human imagination. Unfettered by the particulars of realism and the mundane, Indian audiences are free to transport themselves from the limitations of this world to higher realms in which a "oneness" with the universe is possible.

Because India is a tradition-bound country that proudly reveres its past, modern Indian drama still uses many of the conventions of its classical theater, most notably song, dance, and mime. In the nineteenth century the Nawab of Oudh sponsored a national drama festival celebrating the cults of Krishna and Rama. The event, attended by thousands, helped resurrect older theatrical forms and inspired a new generation of Indians to pursue the theater as both a religious and an entertainment enterprise. Contemporary audiences still delight in spectacle that tends to dwarf a more literate drama. The Rajamanickam Company of Madras province is especially popular for its ability to present spectacular dramas based on mythological themes.

Dance and Folk Drama in India

There also exists a vibrant dance theater, which Indians claim is their supreme art form. Kathakali and Chhau are among the best-known forms of dance theater. In the twentieth century dance drama has remained popular, largely because of the work of Uday Shankar, the preeminent teacher of the modern era. Shankar studied in Europe and danced with the great Russian ballerina Irena Pavlova in a classical Indian piece. He used mythological characters such as Krishna and themes of ancient India in his modern works, which frequently combine racy folk dances with the more decorous temple dances. Also, Rabindranath Tagore (see below) composed several important dance dramas, although today he is best remembered as the patriarch of modern drama in India.

A variety of folk plays and entertainments associated with each of India's provinces constitutes the third major form of theatrical activity in this vast country. Often, they are propogandistic and deal with regional, as well as national, problems. For example, *Neel Darpana* (1872) by Dinabandhu Mitra is a Bengali play in the folk style that portrays the ordeals of plantation life in northern India. Because they are so completely indigenous to the provinces from which they spring, few folk plays exist in written form. For a brief overview of India's traditional folk theater, read Jacob Srampickal's informative essay in the Forum at the end of this section.

The Modern Theater of India

Modern theater in India is urban, not rural, and it is created primarily for the middle and upper classes (India yet retains its caste system). Because it was a British colony for several hundred years, Indian theater, like that of Africa (see Chapter 8), owes much of its impetus to European drama, largely because of the Eurocentric education system established at universities in Calcutta, Bombay, and Madras. Drama written in any of the hundreds of Indian languages and performed onstage by Indian actors did not emerge until the last years of the nineteenth century. The success of these native enterprises inspired others to construct public theaters that appealed to the tastes and languages of a variety of castes. Producers with nationalistic tendencies soon employed the theater as a means of propaganda that appealed to a growing concern for self-rule and the eradication of colonialism.

The artist most credited with bridging the gap between the traditional Indian theater and that of the modern era was the Bengali poet and dramatist, Rabindranath Tagore. Some Indian scholars dispute Tagore's influence, arguing that he was too provincial and therefore failed to inspire many twentieth-century Indian dramatists. Nonetheless, it was Tagore who caught the attention of such Western theater artists as William Butler Yeats, who produced his work at Dublin's Abbey Theatre.

It is worth noting that the motion picture dominates Indian entertainment today; no country in the world produces more movies than does India. The popularity of cinema has had an adverse impact on live theater, forcing the closure of some companies. However, a modern Indian theater does exist in commercial, amateur, and educational venues. Calcutta is perhaps the dominant commercial theater center in all of India, and the Star (founded in 1888) is its best-known theater. Because of India's enormous size, and the hundreds of languages spoken by its diverse people, it is difficult to identify major national playwrights. Very few artists can actually make a living writing plays; in Bombay playwrights earn about $8 per performance. Few plays written in Hindi, one of the dominant languages, are translated into other languages, which makes the task of discussing modern Indian theater even more difficult. Ironically, many Western theater artists (Peter Brook and Arianne Mnouchkine are the most prominent) have incorporated elements of the classical Indian theater in their most admired "modern" works.

THE RECOGNITION OF ŚAKUNTALĀ
(ABHIJĀNAŚĀKUNTALAM)
KĀLIDĀSA

KĀLIDĀSA (?373–?415 C.E.)

Little is known about the greatest poet-playwright of classical Sanskrit literature. Legend says that Kālidāsa—which means "the servant of time" or "servant of the creative powers"—was a simple Brahmin orphan possessing extraordinary beauty and grace who was raised by an ox driver. The youth devoted himself to the worship of the goddess Kali (Siva), the Absolute Being whose dance shapes all human life. Kali was taken with the young Brahmin's fidelity and blessed him with infinite knowledge and superior skills in the poetic arts.

Sanskrit scholars have not been able to pinpoint Kālidāsa's dates. He may have written as early as the second century B.C.E., or as late as the fifth century C.E. Popular legend says that Kālidāsa was one of the nine jewels and official poet of the court of the nearly mythical King Vikramaditya, who ruled at Ujjayini (now Ujjain) in the first century B.C.E. Ujjayini was one of the twelve sacred cities of ancient India, the very place where Siva descended into this universe; thus the city has long been a center for the arts, especially theater and dance.

Referred to as "the Master of Poets," Kālidāsa is the greatest innovator among Sanskrit writers. Among the people of India he remains the acknowledged master of the Sanskrit language, imbuing it with a rich variety, subtlety, and musicality; his status in India is comparable to that of Shakespeare in English-speaking countries. Seven of Kālidāsa's works survive: three long poems, an incomplete epic, and three plays, the most prominent of which is *The Recognition of Śakuntalā*, which was itself based on a portion of India's national epic, *The Mahābhārata*.

THE RECOGNITION OF ŚAKUNTALĀ

Though written in India perhaps over 2,000 years ago, *Śakuntalā*—for all its exotic talk of blackbucks, darbha-grass, and the "Path of the Wind Pravaha"—seems strangely familiar to Western audiences. It resonates throughout with the "mythic bells" that are elemental to literature that is truly universal.

Śakuntalā is a romance, a universal genre that was popularized in the West during the Middle Ages. The Arthurian legends set down by Sir Thomas Mallory, Chaucer's *Knight's Tale*, and Shakespeare's last plays, especially *The Tempest*, are among the best-known romances in the Western canon. Like *Śakuntalā*, each is about a respected ruler who makes a grievous error in judgment, suffers the consequences, and is ultimately restored to a newfound knowledge that brings greater prosperity to his kingdom. A virginal heroine, usually wronged and isolated by male arrogance, is inevitably central to the action; her innate goodness and virtue ultimately triumph and traditionally there is a promise of a prosperous future symbolized by a wedding or a child such as we see in Bharata. Romances, it has been said, are tragedies that end happily when the flawed king recognizes his error and reconciles with those whom he has wronged. Indeed, the very act of reconciliation provides the dramatic climax of most romances. Northrop Frye, who has extensively analyzed recurring patterns in romance literature, notes that "the renewing power of the final action [i.e., reconciliation] lifts us to a higher world." That higher world is one that transcends this earth; reconciliation approaches godhead because it promotes harmony and a new order.

Though the play is formally entitled *The Recognition of Śakuntalā*, it may be more apt to call it *Duhsanta's Recognition*, for it is the noble king Duhsanta who undergoes the dramatic journey from ignorance to knowledge. We first see him in his regal glory, hunting the sacred blackbuck, the revered antelope of Indian mythology. Hunting the blackbuck is taboo, akin to killing a great bald eagle in America. The blackbuck leads the king to the sacred hermitage of Kanva, the wise seer so popular in romances (compare with Merlin). There, Duhsanta meets the pure and peerless beauty Śakuntalā, the daughter of an apsara, one of the celestial dancers who guards the pools of water that sustain life. Śakuntalā, whose very name means "she who is protected by the birds," lives in an Edenic "green world," so loved by romanticists. At every turn Kālidāsa reminds us that she is a child of nature:

> If girls bred in a hermitage
>
> can boast of such beauty rare in palaces,
>
> is there any denying woodland vines
>
> far surpass those nurtured in gardens?

But Duhsanta mistakes lust for love—note the erotic poetry that marks the first meeting between the king and Śakuntalā ("with rounded breasts concealed by cloth bark . . . her youthful form enfolded like a flower. . ."). By falsely presenting himself as a "plain visitor," Duhsanta seduces Śakuntalā to satisfy his carnal desires, though he knows that his pleasure is momentary and that he must "wait seeking to know the truth."

Truth, the highest form of knowledge in Hindu theology, comes hard for Duhsanta. As he prepares to take Śakuntalā to his court, Durvāsā, a foul-tempered sage, who is furious that he has been ignored in the courtship, curses the new marriage. Duhsanta returns to the "golden world" of his court, which, despite its many earthly glories, is flawed because its unenlightened inhabitants are corruptible. True to Durvāsā's curse, Duhsanta fails to recognize his bride when she arrives at court. Because she has lost the signet ring he gave her at their betrothal, Duhsanta renounces Śakuntalā. Miraculously, the gods intervene and produce the lost ring, which had been swallowed by a fish. This mystical revelation lifts the veil of doubt from Duhsanta's eyes and he and his bride are joyfully reconciled. To reaffirm his glory, Duhsanta defends his kingdom against invading Titans, for which he is rewarded at the beginning of the final act with a ride through the Hindu cosmos atop Indra's own chariot. This extraordinary stage picture of the renewed king reinforces his greatness and suggests the plenitude all in his kingdom will enjoy.

Śakuntalā, thus, is much more than a secular romance. It is a spiritual journey in which unenlightened humans are led to sacred knowledge by forces greater than they are. Not uncoincidentally, the play is a highly structured religious ritual that mirrors the life cycle itself. As prescribed by *The Nātyaśāstra*, the play opens with a benediction, one of 18 preliminary steps of a Sanskrit performance meant to please the Hindu pantheon. Specifically, the banner of Indra, Lord of Heaven, is raised prior to the benediction in the prologue as a reminder of the spiritual roots of the theater of India. The benediction not only purifies the actors and audience from any evil forces that may be present in the theater, it also elevates the performance to the status of a "special event" distinct from daily life.

Throughout the play there are other reminders that Sanskrit drama evolved from religious rituals marking the cycle of life. For instance, in act 4 Śakuntalā prepares to leave the sacred hermitage by undergoing an ancient purification as she walks "sun wise round the Sacrificial Fires." There is an autumnal quality about the ritual that marks Śakuntalā's leave-taking; one senses the blossom of spring giving way to the dying of the very trees, which were "kin to her during her woodland sojourn." Later, in act 6, King Duhsanta undergoes a symbolic death as he loses consciousness when overcome by sorrow at his cruel treatment of Śakuntalā. Like so many real and fictional kings throughout world literature, he is reborn to lead his country to a new prosperity, a triumph that Kālidāsa equates with the very creation of the universe itself:

As the mountains rear upwards, the land climbs
precipitately down their great peaks, it seems;
trees whose forms were merged within the dense leafage
emerge distinct as their branching shoulders
thrust into view: those fine lines display themselves
as great rivers brimming with water:
see how the Earth looms at my side
as if some mighty hand had flung her up to me.

The play concludes with another benediction in which Mārīca, Indra's royal charioteer, asks "the god of gods" to insure that "both the worlds" [i.e., the heavens and the earth] enjoy glory and plenitude. If we remember that theater in many cultures developed from planting and harvest rituals, prayers for which surely echoed Mārīca's sentiments, Śakuntalā's relationship to the evolution of world theater quickly manifests itself.

We must not, however, ignore the play's distinctly Hindu strains. In addition to its universal appeal, Śakuntalā is very much a product of the fertile Indian imagination that has provided the world with a complex theology. In the final benediction King Duhsanta acknowledges the "Self-Existent Lord who unites in Himself the Dark and the Light." Conflict is central to the dramatic experience and polarities help define conflict. Throughout the play we are constantly aware of the dualities of Śakuntalā's world—the green (natural) world of the hermitage vs. the gilded (cultivated) world of the court, love vs. lust, Duhsanta's royal face vs. his private face, appearances vs. reality, isolation vs. group harmony. Western writers and audiences have a tendency to see the world in terms of its polarities, but the Indian mind sees them as two aspects of a single whole that must be balanced. Life, in the Hindu worldview, is a struggle to reconcile these opposites into a harmonious whole. Thus in the final act, itself a celebration of the harmony of the world's many contradictions, Duhsanta emerges as the complete king, tempered by his errors in judgment, enriched by his sorrow. His failures, as well as his triumphs, thus combine to make the whole person.

Śakuntalā, *the foremost Sanskrit drama of classical India, is still performed regularly by such companies as the Goa Hindu Association of Bombay; this 1985 production honored the tradition of simple staging practices used 1600 years ago at Ujjian.*

THE RECOGNITION OF ŚAKUNTALĀ
(ABHIJĀNAŚĀKUNTALAM)

A Play in Seven Acts

KĀLIDĀSA

Translated by Chandra Rajan

CHARACTERS

Prologue

Chanters of the benediction.
DIRECTOR, *Sūtradharā (one who holds the threads); probably plays the hero.*
ACTRESS, *Natī; wife of the Director; probably plays the heroine.*

Play

KING, *Duhsanta, the hero or nāyaka; monarch of the lunar dynasty of Puru.*
SŪTA, *Royal charioteer.*

ŚAKUNTALĀ, *The heroine or nāyakī; Duhsanta's Queen; adopted daughter of Sage Kanva.*
ANASŪYĀ, PRIYAMVADĀ, *Friends and companions of Śakuntalā.*
MĀDHAVYA, *Jester, the King's friend and constant companion.*
GUARD, *Raivataka, also doorkeeper.*
GENERAL, *Bhadrasena, Senāpati or Commander of the Royal Army.*
GAUTAMĪ, *Matron of Kanva's Hermitage*
HĀRITA, *Hermit boy.*
KANVA, *Head of the Hermitage and foster-father of Śakuntalā.*
ŚĀRNGARAVA, ŚĀRADVATA, *Disciples of Sage Kanva.*

CHAMBERLAIN, *Pārvatāyana, in charge of the Royal Household.*
VETRAVATI, *Doorkeeper of the Royal Apartments.*
SOMARĀTA, *High Priest, the King's preceptor.*
CHIEF OF POLICE
SŪCAKA, JĀNUKA, *Policemen.*
FISHERMAN
MĪŚRAKEŚI, *An apsarā (celestial nymph), friend to Menakā.*
PARABHRTIKĀ (*Little Cuckoo*), MADHUKARIKĀ (*Little Honey-bee*), *Maids tending the pleasure garden adjoining the Royal Apartments.*
CATURIKĀ, *The King's personal attendant.*
MĀTALI, *Indra's charioteer.*
BOY, *Sarva-Damana, later the Emperor Bharata, son of Śakuntalā and the King.*
SUVRATA AND HER COMPANION, *Hermit women in Mārīca's Hermitage.*
MĀRĪCA, *Prajāpāti or Primal Parent and Indra's father.*
ADITL, *Consort of Mārīca and mother of Indra, daughter of Daksa.*

Minor Characters

KARABHAKA, *The Queen Mother's emissary.*
AN ANCHORITE AND HIS DISCIPLE
PUPIL OF KANVA
TWO HERMITS
ROYAL BARDS
ATTENDANT, *Pratihari.*
Male bodyguard of the King, who looked after his weapons and attended him on his hunts.

Characters Off-Stage

DURVĀSĀ, *A sage reputed for his violent temper and quick to curse.*
HAMSAVATĪ, *Duhsanta's junior queen.*
Aerial voices: *Voices of the tree nymphs in Kanva's Hermitage.*
Voice of the cuckoo in the Hermitage.

Persons Mentioned

KAUŚIKA, *The Royal Sage Viśvamitra, real father of Śakuntalā.*
MENAKĀ, *Apsarā (Celestial nymph and dancer at Indra's Court); mother of Śakuntalā.*
INDRA, *King of the Immortals.*
JAYANTA, *Indra's son.*
NĀRADA, *A wandering sage, messenger of the gods.*
VASUMATĪ, *Royal Consort, Duhsanta's Chief Queen.*
MITRĀ-VASU, *The Queen's brother.*
PIŚUNA, *Chief Minister.*
DHANA-VRDDHI, *A wealthy merchant prince, probably head of the guild.*

PROLOGUE

Benediction

That First Creation of the Creator:
That Bearer of oblations offered with Holy Rites:
That one who utters the Holy Chants:
Those two that order Time:

That which extends, World-Pervading,
   in which sound flows impinging on the ear:
That which is proclaimed the Universal Womb of
   Seeds:
That which fills all forms that breathe with the
   Breath of Life.
May the Supreme Lord o the Universe
   who stands revealed in these eight Forms*
   perceptible preserve you.

After the benediction enter the Director.

DIRECTOR (*looking towards the green-room*). Lady! If the preparations in the dressing room are completed, would you be pleased to attend us?

ACTRESS (*entering*). Here I am, my lord; what are your orders regarding this evening's performance?

DIRECTOR (*looks around*). Lady, we have here before us, an august audience that is highly educated and most discerning. This evening we wait upon it with a new play composed by Kalidasa, entitled *The Recognition of Śakuntalā*. Will you see to it that all the actors do their very best?

ACTRESS. With your excellent training and direction, my lord, nothing will be found wanting.

DIRECTOR (*smiling*). The truth of the matter, my lady, is:
   Unless those who know applaud my art,
   I cannot think I know it well;
   even those most expertly schooled
   cannot be wholly self-assured.

ACTRESS. Is that so, my lord? Well, now tell me what is to follow, my lord.

DIRECTOR. Let us treat the audience to something that will delight their ears.

ACTRESS. Which of the seasons shall I sing about?

DIRECTOR. About this very season, I should think—Summer, that set in not so long ago and is enjoyable in so many ways. For at the moment:
   Days draw to a close in quiet beauty;
   plunging in cool waters is delightful;
   sleep drops softly in thick-shaded haunts;
   woodland breezes blow fresh and fragrant
   having consorted with Pātali flowers.

ACTRESS. Very well. (*sings*)
   Exquisite are Śirīsa blossoms—
     see how they sway—
   crested with delicate filaments—
     kissed, lightly, lightly
     by murmurous bees—
      lovely women—
   exulting in their youth—
     place the blossoms
      tenderly—
   as ornaments over their ears—

*The eight forms are in order: Water, Fire, The Priest, Sun and Moon, Space, Earth, Air.

267

DIRECTOR. Beautifully sung, dear lady; aha—just look around you; the audience is still, as if drawn in a picture—spellbound, caught in the web of beauty woven by your singing. Now then, what play shall we put on to honour and entertain them further?

ACTRESS. Why, sir, what you mentioned right at the beginning—the new play entitled *The Recognition of Śakuntalā*.

DIRECTOR. You do well to remind me, dear lady. Indeed, my memory failed me for an instant; because,

I was carried far, far away, lured
by your impassioned song, compelling,

(*looks towards the wings*)

even as the King, Duhsanta here,
was, by the fleet fleeing antelope.

(*Exit.*)

END OF PROLOGUE

ACT ONE

Scene: The forests in the foothills of the Himalayas; later the Hermitage of Kanva, by the river Mālinī.

Enter on a chariot, bow and arrow in hand, in hot pursuit of a deer, the King with his charioteer.

SŪTA (*looking at the King and the deer*). O Long-Lived Majesty!

Casting my eye on the fleeting blackbuck
and on you holding the taut-strung bow,
I seem to see before my very eyes
Pinākī*, the Lord, chasing the deer.

KING. We have come a long, long way, Sūta, drawn by this blackbuck; even now he is seen:

Arching his neck with infinite grace, now and then
he glances back at the speeding chariot,
his form curving fearful of the arrow's fall,
the haunches almost touch his chest.
Panting from fatigue, his jaws gaping wide
spill the half-chewed tender grass to mark his path.
With long leaps bounding high upwards, see how
                                        he soars
flying in the sky, scarce skimming the surface of
                                        the earth.

(*puzzled*) How is it that I can hardly see him, even though we are in such hot pursuit?

SŪTA. Sire, seeing the ground was uneven, I lightly reined in the horses; the chariot's speed slackened. Therefore, the deer was able to put so much distance between himself and us. Now that we are on level ground, you will soon see that he is not beyond your aim.

KING. Slacken the reins.

SŪTA. As His Majesty commands. (*mimes increased speed of the chariot*)

See, see, Sire:

The reins hanging slack,
the horses leap forward,
no, they glide over the track—
bodies out-stretched, ears flung back,
the tips of their plumes motionless;
the very dust whirled up
swiftly advancing cannot outstrip them.

KING (*exulting*). See how they excel even Hari's* bright horses; therefore:

What was minute suddenly looms large;
what's cleft down the middle seems to unite:
the eye sees as straight what's naturally curved;
the chariot rushing along, nothing stays
near or far, even for a moment.

(*A voice off-stage*). Ho there! Stop, hold, O King! This deer belonging to the Hermitage ought not to be struck down . . . aha! . . . do not kill him, O King.

SŪTA (*listens and looks around*). Your Majesty, here are ascetics standing shielding the blackbuck who is now right in your arrow's path.

KING (*urgently*). Quick, rein in the horses.

SŪTA. Yes, Sire. (*stops the chariot*)

Enter an ascetic accompanied by his disciple.

ASCETIC (*holding up his hand*). This deer is of the Hermitage, O King! He should not be killed . . . no . . . no . . . do not strike him down.

How fragile the life of this deer!
How cruel your sharp-pointed arrows, swift-winged!
Never should they fall on his tender frame
like tongues of flame on a heap of flowers.

Quickly withdraw your well-aimed arrow, bound
to protect the distressed, not strike the pure.

KING (*bowing low in respect*). It is withdrawn. (*replaces the arrow in the quiver*)

ASCETIC (*pleased*). This is indeed an act worthy of your Honour, born in Puru's dynasty and the glorious light of kings. May you be blessed with a son who will turn the wheel of empire.

KING (*bowing low*). I accept a Brāhmaṇa's blessings.

ASCETIC. O King! We are on our way to gather wood for the sacrificial Fire. There, clinging to the slopes of the Himālaya, along the banks of the Mālinī is visible the Hermitage of our Guru, the Patriarch Kanva where Śakuntalā dwells like its guardian deity. If other duties do not claim your time, enter and accept the hospitality proffered to a guest. Further:

When you behold the sages rich in holiness
immersed in the tranquil performance of holy rites
free of impediments, you will know how well
your arm scarred by the oft-drawn bowstring protects.

*Siva

*Indra

268

KING. Is the Patriarch at home now?

ASCETIC. Enjoining his daughter Śakuntalā to receive guests with due hospitality, he has gone not long back to Soma-tīrtha, to propitiate the adverse fate threatening her happiness.

KING. I shall pay my respects to her then. She will no doubt inform the great sage of my profound veneration for him.

ASCETIC. We shall then be on our way.

(Exits with his disciple.)

KING. Sūta, urge the horses on and let us purify ourselves with a sight of the holy Hermitage.

SŪTA. As Your Gracious Majesty orders. (mimes increased speed of the chariot)

KING (looking around). Sūta, even without being told, it is plain that we are now at the outskirts of the penance-groves.

SŪTA. How can you tell, my lord?

KING. Do you not see, Sir? Right here:

> Grains of wild rice fallen from tree-hollows
> where parrots nest, lie scattered under the trees;
> those stones there look moist, glossy, from the oil
> of ingudi-nuts split and pounded on them;
> all around, deer browse in their tranquil haunts,
> unafraid of the chariot's approach; yonder,
> drops of water dripping off the edges of bark-garments
> in long lines, trace the paths to pools and streams.

And you see further:

> Rippling beneath a passing breeze, waters flow
> in deep channels to lave the roots of trees;
> smoke drifts up from oblations to the Sacred Fire
> to dim the soft sheen of tender leafbuds;
> free from fear, fawns browse lazily in meadows
> beyond, where darbha-shoots are closely cropped.

SŪTA. Yes, Sire, everything is as you say.

They go some distance.

KING. Sūta, let us not disturb the peace of the Hermitage; stop the chariot right here and I shall get down.

SŪTA. I am holding the reins fast; let His Majesty alight.

KING (alights from the chariot and looks at himself). Hermit-groves should be visited modestly attired. So, here are my jewels and bow. (hands them over to the charioteer) By the time I return from visiting the residents of the Hermitage, see that the horses are watered.

SŪTA. As His Majesty commands.

(Exits.)

KING (turns around and looks). Ah, here is the entrance to the Hermitage; I shall go in. (enters and immediately indicates the presence of a good omen) Ah....

> Tranquil is this hermitage, yet my arm throbs;
> what fulfilment can await me here?
> Yet who knows; coming events find doors
> opening everywhere.

(A voice in the background). This way, this way, dear friends.

KING (listening closely). Aha . . . I hear snatches of conversation to the south of this orchard. (turns and looks around)

I see; here are some hermit-girls coming this way . . . and carrying jars proportionate to their slender frames . . . to water the saplings planted here. O what a charming sight!

> If girls bred in a hermitage
> can boast of such beauty rare in palaces,
> is there any denying woodland vines
> far surpass those nurtured in gardens?

I think I shall wait here in the shade and watch them. (stands observing them)

Enter Śakuntalā with her friends, occupied as described.

FIRST. Listen, dear Śakuntalā; it looks to me as if these trees in the Hermitage are dearer to Father Kanva than even you are; see, he has appointed you who are as delicate as a newly-opened jasmine-flower, to fill these trenches round the roots with water.

ŚAKUNTALĀ. Dear Anasūyā, it is not merely a matter of Father's injunction; I love them like a sister. (she mimes watering the trees)

SECOND. Friend Śakuntalā, the trees of the Hermitage that bloom in summer have all been watered. Shall we now sprinkle those that are past flowering? That would be an act of devotion, not looking for a reward.

ŚAKUNTALĀ. Priyamvadā, my friend, what a lovely thought. (again mimes watering the trees)

KING (to himself). What! Is this Kanva's daughter, Śakuntalā? (surprised) Ah! How utterly lacking in judgement is the venerable Kanva to imprison such beauty in a bark-garment.

> The sage who would inure to harsh penance
> this form ravishing in its artless beauty
> is surely attempting to cut acacia wood
> with the edge of a blue-lotus petal.

Let it be. Hidden behind these trees, I shall watch her undisturbed. (stands concealed)

ŚAKUNTALĀ. Sweet Anasūyā, Priyamvadā has tied my bark-garment so tight that I feel quite uncomfortable; could you loosen it a little?

(Anasūyā loosens it)

PRIYAMVADĀ (laughing merrily). Blame your own budding youth that's making your bosom swell.

KING. She's right in what she says,

> With rounded breasts concealed by cloth of bark
> fastened at the shoulder in a fine knot,
> her youthful form enfolded like a flower
> in its pale leafy sheath unfolds not its glory.

While it is true that bark is not the appropriate dress for her youth, can it be really held that it does not become her like an adornment? Consider,

> Though inlaid in duckweed the lotus glows;
> a dusky spot enhances the moon's radiance;
> this lissom girl is lovelier far dressed in bark!
> What indeed is not an adornment for entrancing
>   forms!

ŚAKUNTALĀ (*looking in front of her*). See, my friends, the mango tree over there fluttering his fingers of tender leaf sprays—as if beckoning to me. I shall go over to him. (*walks over to the tree*)

PRIYAMVADĀ. Dearest Śakuntalā, stand there for a moment.

ŚAKUNTALĀ. What for?

PRIYAMVADĀ. With you beside him, the mango looks as if wedded to a lovely vine.

ŚAKUNTALĀ. You are aptly named—'Sweet-Talker'—aren't you?

KING. Priyamvadā does not speak idly; see how,
> Her lower lip has the rich sheen of young shoots,
> her arms the very grace of tender twining stems;
> her limbs enchanting as a lovely flower
> glow with the radiance of magical youth.

ANASŪYĀ. Look, Śakuntalā, the jasmine that you named *Vana-jyotsni** has chosen the mango as her bridegroom.

Śakuntalā comes close to the vine and looks at it with joy.

ŚAKUNTALĀ. O Anasūyā, what a charming sight, this marriage of vine and tree. See, the jasmine has this very moment entered into her budding youth. And the mango tree is laden with young fruit indicating he is ready for enjoyment. (*she stands gazing at them*)

PRIYAMVADĀ (*smiling archly*). Anasūyā, guess why Śakuntalā is gazing upon *Vana-jyotsni* for so long and with such longing.

ANASŪYĀ. No, I cannot; you tell me.

PRIYAMVADĀ. Well . . . this is what she is thinking: Just as *Vana-jyotsni* has married the tree that is a worthy partner for her, so, may I also find a consort worthy of me.

ŚAKUNTALĀ. That must be your own heart's desire, for sure. (*she pours water from the jar*)

ANASŪYĀ. Hey, Śakuntalā, just look: here is the Mādhavī bush that Father Kanva nurtured with his own hands as he nurtured you. You have forgotten her?

ŚAKUNTALĀ. Then I might as well forget myself. (*comes close to the bush and exclaims in delight*) Look, look, what a surprise! Priyamvadā, listen, I have something to tell that will please you.

PRIYAMVADĀ. Please me? What's that, dear?

ŚAKUNTALĀ. Look, Anasūyā . . . The Mādhavī is covered with buds . . . from the root up; this is not its season for blooming.

BOTH FRIENDS (*come hurrying up*). Really, is it true, Śakuntalā dear?

ŚAKUNTALĀ. Of course it is true—can't you see?

PRIYAMVADĀ (*viewing the blossoming bush with delight*). Well, well, now it is my turn to tell you something which'll please you. You will soon be married.

ŚAKUNTALĀ (*with a show of annoyance*). That must be what you wish for yourself.

PRIYAMVADĀ. No, I am not joking; I swear I heard it from

Father Kanva's own lips that this would signal your wedding.

ANASŪYĀ. Ah! Now we know, don't we, Priyamvadā, why Śakuntalā has been watering Mādhavī so lovingly.

ŚAKUNTALĀ. And why not . . . I love her like a sister. (*waters the Mādhavī*)

KING. I wonder . . . could she be the Patriarch's daughter by a wife not of his own class? Let's be done with doubts:
> It is my firm belief that by the Law
> she can rightly be a warrior's bride,
> for my noble heart yearns deeply for her.
> When in doubt, the truest inner prompting is
> to the virtuous, unassailable authority.

Still, I think I should try and find out the true facts about her.

ŚAKUNTALĀ (*in alarm*). O help, a bee has flown out of the jasmine bush . . . and it is buzzing round my face. (*mimes attempts to ward off the bee*)

KING (*looking longingly at her*).
> Her lovely eyes rove following
> the hovering bee close to her face;
> she knits her brows practising already
> playful glances though not in love—but fear.

(*with a show of vexation*)
> O, you honey-foraging thief! You touch
> ever so often her glancing eyes, tremulous,
> and softly hum, hovering close to her ear
> as if eager to whisper a secret,
> sneaking in to taste her ripe lower lip
> —the quintessence of love's delight—
> even as she piteously flails her hand.
> Blessed indeed are you, while I wait
> seeking to know the truth—undone.

ŚAKUNTALĀ. Friends, friends, help me, protect me from this villain who keeps harassing me.

FRIENDS (*smiling*). Who are we to protect you? Call to mind Duhsanta: the penance-groves are under royal protection.

KING. This is a golden opportunity for me to show myself. O, don't be afraid . . . (*checks himself halfway and speaks to himself*) No, this way, it will be evident that I am the King. Let me think . . . I shall assume the manner of just a plain visitor.

ŚAKUNTALĀ (*rather scared*). This impudent fellow will not leave me alone. I shall go from this place. (*takes a few steps, stops and throws a quick glance behind*) O help! He follows me.

KING (*hastily steps forward*). Ha!
> While the chastiser of the wicked,
> great Puru's scion rules over this rich earth,
> who dares behave in this churlish manner
> to guileless, young girls of the hermitage.

Seeing the King, all three are taken aback.

ANASŪYĀ. O noble Sir, it is nothing very serious; our dear friend here (*pointing to Śakuntalā*) was being bothered by a large bee and became frightened.

*Woodland-Moonglow

KING (*approaching Śakuntalā*). I trust your devotions go well.

Śakuntalā, confused, is silent.

ANASŪYĀ (*addressing the King*). All goes well now, Sir, since we have the honour of waiting on a distinguished guest.

PRIYAMVADĀ. Welcome to you, noble Sir.

ANASŪYĀ. Dear Śakuntalā, go and bring the proper guest-offering and some fruit. The water we have here will serve to wash the guest's feet.

KING. I have already been welcomed by your gracious words; nothing more is needed.

PRIYAMVADĀ. At least, Sir, do sit down under the spreading shade of this Saptaparna tree on this cool seat and rest yourself.

KING. You must all be tired too after performing these pious duties. Do sit down for a while.

PRIYAMVADĀ (*aside*). Śakuntalā, courtesy demands that we keep our guest company. Come, let us all sit down.

They sit down.

ŚAKUNTALĀ (*to herself*). How is it that the sight of this person fills me with emotions out of place in a penance-grove.

KING (*looking at them*). How charming a friendship this of yours, gracious ladies, all of the same age and equally beautiful!

PRIYAMVADĀ (*aside*). Anasūyā, who could he be—mysterious, majestic in manner, yet he speaks with such easy charm and shows such courtesy?

ANASŪYĀ (*aside*). I am curious too; let me sound him. (*aloud*) Noble Sir, encouraged by your gracious words, I would like to ask you this: What great lineage does Your Honour adorn—which land now mourns your absence—and what has brought a delicately nurtured noble like yourself on this wearying journey into our Groves of Righteousness?

ŚAKUNTALĀ (*to herself*). O heart, keep calm; Anasūyā is asking what I wanted to know.

KING (*to himself*). Now what shall I do? Shall I disclose myself—or—shall I conceal my identity? (*reflecting*) Let me do it this way. (*aloud*) Lady, I am one well-versed in the Vedas whom the Paurava monarch has appointed as Minister in Charge of Religious Affairs. In the course of visiting the holy retreats, I chanced to come to these Groves of Righteousness.

ANASŪYĀ. Why then, the followers of the Right Path have now a guardian.

Śakuntalā shows signs of falling in love.

FRIENDS (*noting the demeanour of Śakuntalā and the King, aside*). Śakuntalā, if only Father were here!

ŚAKUNTALĀ (*knitting her brows*). What if he were?

BOTH. He would then make this distinguished guest supremely happy by offering him the sole treasure of his life.

ŚAKUNTALĀ (*pretending to be annoyed*). O be quiet; you two

have some silly notion in your heads and keep prattling; I shan't listen to your nonsense.

KING. We would also like to ask you something about your friend here, if we may.

BOTH. Consider your request a favour done to us.

KING. His Holiness Kanva has been known to observe perpetual celibacy; how then can your friend be a daughter begotten by him.

ANASŪYĀ. Hear what I have to say, Sir. There is a Royal Sage of great renown belonging to the Kuśika clan.

KING. Yes, His Holiness Kauśika.

ANASŪYĀ. He is our friend's real father. Father Kanva is her father by virtue of having reared her when he found her abandoned.

KING. Abandoned! The word greatly rouses my curiosity. Pray let me hear the story from the beginning.

ANASŪYĀ. Once, a long time back, that Royal Sage was immersed in the most formidable austerities for many years. The gods for some reason became nervous and sent the Apsarā Menakā to disturb his singleminded concentration.

KING. O yes, it is well known that the gods often become afraid of the penances of others. Then what happened?

ANASŪYĀ. Spring had just set in; seeing her maddening beauty . . . (*stops halfway in embarrassment*)

KING. What followed is easily understood. So—this lady was born of an Apsarā.

ANASŪYĀ. That's right.

KING. It fits:

How could a form of such matchless beauty
come from the womb of a mortal mother?
The scintillating lightning-flash
does not spring up from the earth.

Śakuntalā, shy, looks down.

KING (*to himself*). O what good fortune! Now my desires find a firm footing.

PRIYAMVADĀ (*turning to the King with a smile*). Your Honour was about to say something?

Śakuntalā raises a warning forefinger.

KING. Gracious lady, you have guessed right. Keen to know more about the lives of the saintly, I *am* eager to ask one further question.

PRIYAMVADĀ. Do not hesitate, Sir; ascetics may be questioned freely.

KING. I wish to ask,

Is it only till she is given in marriage
that your friend is strictly bound by hermit-vows
—an unkind bar that shuts out love—
or must she dwell, alas, for ever
with the gazelles so dear to her
whose lovely eyes mirror her own eyes' dear
                                           loveliness?

PRIYAMVADĀ. Sir, even in the practice of religious duties, she is dependent on another's will. However, it is her father's resolve to give her in marriage to one worthy of her.

KING (*elated, speaks to himself*).

Hold fast, O heart, to your fondest wish:
the troubling doubts are now dispelled.
What you dreaded might be a burning flame,
turns out a glowing item to touch and hold.

ŚAKUNTALĀ (*pretending anger*). Anasūyā, I am leaving.

ANASŪYĀ. For what reason?

ŚAKUNTALĀ. To report to the revered Lady Gautamī that Priyamvadā is talking a lot of nonsense. (*rises to leave*)

ANASŪYĀ. Surely, dear, it is not seemly on the part of residents of a hermitage to leave a distinguished guest in this casual manner before he has received all the rites of hospitality.

Śakuntalā without a word prepares to leave.

KING (*to himself*). How! Is she leaving? (*makes a movement to restrain her, then checks himself*) Strange how a lover's actions mirror his feelings.

Eager to follow the sage's daughter,
vehemently held back by decorum,
no sooner had I left but I returned
it seems, but not stirred from this very spot.

PRIYAMVADĀ (*coming close to Śakuntalā*). Hey, you headstrong girl; you cannot go.

ŚAKUNTALĀ (*knitting her brows*). And why not?

PRIYAMVADĀ. Because you owe me two turns at watering the trees; pay me back, then you may leave. (*forces her back*)

KING. I see that the lady is exhausted from watering the trees; as it is,

Her arms droop, languid, her palms glow
reddened lifting up the watering-jar;
her bosom still heaves as she draws deep breaths.
The Śirīsa blossom adorning her ear,
caught in the sparkling web of beads of sweat,
ceases its delicate play against her cheek.
With one hand she restrains her hair, straying wild,
unruly, released from its knot undone.

Let me release her from her debt to you, if I may. (*offers his ring*)

The friends take it and reading the name on the Signet Ring, look at each other.

KING. O please do not misunderstand; the Ring is a gift from the King.

PRIYAMVADĀ. The more reason then that Your Honour ought not to part with it. Your word is sufficient, Your Honour, to release her from her debt.

ANASŪYĀ. You are free now, friend Śakuntalā—through the magnanimity of this noble gentleman—or—of the great King. Where are you off to, now?

ŚAKUNTALĀ (*to herself*). Were it in my power to leave, I would.

PRIYAMVADĀ. Why don't you leave now?

ŚAKUNTALĀ. Am I still answerable to you? I shall leave when I please.

KING (*watching Śakuntalā closely, to himself*). Could it be that she feels towards me as I feel towards her? In that case, my wishes can find fulfilment. For,

Even though she makes no response to my words
she is all ears whenever I speak;
it is true she faces me not, but then
what other object do her eyes ever seek.

(*A voice off-stage*). Ho there! Ascetics all; get ready to protect the creatures in the vicinity of the penance-groves . . . , King Duhsanta who delights in the chase is in our neighbourhood.

Like swarms of locusts glittering in the sunset glow
the whirling dust threshed by tumultuous hoof-beats
                                                    of horses
falls thick upon the trees in the Hermitage
where wet bark-garments hang from the branches.

KING (*to himself*). Alas! As ill-luck would have it, my armed guards, looking for me are surrounding the penance-groves.

(*Again, the voice off-stage*). Ho there, listen, ascetics all . . . throwing women, children and the aged into wild confusion, here he comes:

Crazed with fear at the sight of a chariot,
scattering terror-stricken antelope-herds,
holding aloft, skewered on one trunk
a branch sliced off a tree by a violent blow,
and in fury dragging along tangled chains
of trailing wild creepers that form fetters round him,
a tusker rampages in our Grove of Righteousness
—the very embodiment of hindrance to penance.

All listen and rise in alarm.

KING. O what a disaster! How gravely have I wronged the ascetics here; I had better go.

FRIENDS. Noble Lord! We are greatly perturbed hearing these warning cries about the elephant; permit us to return to our cottage.

ANASŪYĀ (*addressing Śakuntalā*). Listen Śakuntalā, Lady Gautamī will be racked by anxiety on our account; come quickly; let's all be together.

ŚAKUNTALĀ (*indicating some difficulty in walking*). Ha! a numbness seizes my thighs.

KING. Take care, gentle ladies: go carefully. We too shall take all precautions to prevent damage to the Hermitage.

FRIENDS. Noble Lord! I think we know you well enough to feel that you will forgive us this rude interruption of our welcome; may we request you to visit us once more so that we may make amends for the inadequate hospitality extended to you, Sir.

KING. No, no, that's not true; I am honoured sufficiently by the mere sight of you, gracious ladies.

ŚAKUNTALĀ. See, my foot has been pricked by the needle-like points of fresh blades in Kuśa-grass . . . and my bark-garment is caught in the twigs of this amaranth bush. Wait for me while I free myself.

She follows her friends, gazing at the King all the time.

KING (*sighing deeply*). They are gone; I too should leave. My keenness to return to the Capital has been blunted by meeting Śakuntalā. I shall set up camp with my companions at some distance from the penance-groves; How hard it is for me to tear my thoughts away from Śakuntalā.

> My body moves forward,
> my restless heart rushes back
> like a silken pennon on a chariot's standard
> borne against the wind.

(Exit all.)

END OF ACT ONE
ENTITLED
THE CHASE

ACT TWO

Scene: The Forest

Enter Mādhavya, the Court-jester and companion of the King.

MĀDHAVYA. O, this cruel play of Fate: I am reduced to a state of such misery; and why—because I am the friend and constant companion of the King—he is obsessed with the chase. We rattle along forest trails to the cries of 'here's a deer' and 'there's a boar'; even in the intense heat of the noonday sun in Summer, when there is scarcely any shade to be seen. When we are thirsty, what do we drink—phew—the putrid water of mountain streams, tepid, bitter, with rotting leaves floating in them. And for food—we eat at all odd hours—meat most of the time roasted on spits—wolfing it down flaming hot. O, misery upon misery! The bones in my body are all out of joint, galloping without a break on horseback. How can a man sleep well in this state? On top of it all, at the crack of dawn, the beaters with their pack of hounds—those sons of bitches, all of them are up—getting everybody up for the day's hunt. I am rudely awakened by the ear-splitting cacophony of their halloos. But is that the end of the story—no Sir, no indeed. What do you know—the lump has sprouted a boil. Only yesterday, speeding along, His Majesty left us all far behind and went straight into the Hermitage running after a deer. Then, what happened—as my ill-luck would have it, he chanced upon a beautiful hermit-girl—Śakuntalā is the name. From that moment, Sirs, the very idea of returning to the Capital finds no place in his thoughts. Dawn broke this morning on his sleepless lids, thinking of her alone. Can't do a thing about it. At any rate, I shall see him as soon as he completes his morning rituals. Ah! What do I see . . . here comes His Majesty bow in hand, lost in thoughts of his beloved . . . and wearing garlands of wild flowers. I shall approach him now: (*moves a little towards the King*) no, this is what I shall do: I shall stand right here, drooping, bent down, as if my body were all broken with no strength left in it. May be, may . . . be . . . this will bring me some respite.

(*stands supporting himself on his staff*)

Enter the King as described.

KING (*lost in deep thought, sighs, speaks to himself*). Aah!
> Deeply loved, she is not easy to win;
> but watching her ways, my heart is consoled;
> though love has not found fulfilment yet,
> mutual longing is itself a pleasure.

(*smiling wryly*) Thus indeed does a lover mock himself wishing to believe his beloved's thoughts and feelings reflect his own. However:
> That tender glance—the melting glow in her eyes,
> though she directed them elsewhere—
> her steps languid from the weight of heavy hips,
> that seemed love's response patterned in enticing
>   grace—
> those words she spoke in scorn when her friend held
>   her back,
> saying 'don't go': all this I fancied
> had only me for an object—
> But alas! Love sees only Himself everywhere.

MĀDHAVYA (*stands without moving a step*). My friend, my hands are powerless to extend themselves in greeting; I salute Your Honour with words only. May you be ever-victorious!

KING (*looks at him and smiles*). And what has paralysed your limbs?

MĀDHAVYA. A fine thing to ask; do you hit me in the eye—and then ask why it is watering?

KING. My dear friend, I do not follow; make your meaning clear.

MĀDHAVYA. Now tell me my friend, if the bent reed by the river totters to and fro with the grace of a hunchback's gait, is it from its own force or from the force of the stream's flow?

KING. Why, in the reed's case, the force of the stream's flow is the cause.

MĀDHAVYA. So are you, in mine.

KING. How is that?

MĀDHAVYA (*as if angry*). Go on; you abandon the affairs of the kingdom; you give up those places where one walks without slipping and you stick around here enamoured of the primitive life of foresters, it seems. To tell you the truth, my limbs feel as if they are not my own, so bruised and painful are their joints with galloping daily chasing after wild beasts. Do me a favour please; let us rest at least for one day.

KING (*to himself*). This fellow speaks my own thoughts. My mind is not on the chase either, thinking of Kanva's daughter. For:

> I cannot bear to draw my well-strung bow
> with its perfectly-aimed arrows on these deer
> that dwell always beside my own dear love
> and bestow on her the loveliness of their eyes.

MĀDHAVYA (*looking at the King*). You look as if you are communing with your heart; mine was just a cry in the wilderness then?

KING (*trying to smile*). Thinking that a friend's words ought not to be ignored, I was silent; that was all.

MĀDHAVYA. May you live long. (*prepares to leave*)

KING. No, stay, I haven't finished what I was going to say.

MĀDHAVYA. Command me, my lord.

KING. After you have rested well, Sir, I would like your help in a matter that will not cause you the least bit of exertion.

MĀDHAVYA. Like tasting sweet dumplings perhaps?

KING. I shall let you know.

MĀDHAVYA. I am at your disposal.

KING. Ho there—who is on duty?

Enter the Guard.

GUARD. Your Majesty's command?

KING. Raivataka, let His Lordship, the General, be asked to attend.

RAIVATAKA. As my Royal Master commands.

Goes out and returns with the General.

GENERAL (*looking at the King*). Much abused though the sport of hunting is, in the case of our Royal Master, it has all been to the good. Just see our great lord:

> He carries his magnificent frame
> like a tusker that roams the mountains;
> a frame spare, instinct with energy,
> the sinewy strength hides the loss of rounding flesh;
> he endures the sun's hot rays unharmed,
> not a trace of sweat showing;
> his brawny chest and arms are hard and scored
> by the ceaseless recoil of his twanging bowstring.

RAIVATAKA. Sir, His Majesty is looking fixedly in your direction, as if impatient to give you his commands. Let Your Honour approach.

GENERAL (*approaches the King, bowing low*). Hail, Victory to our Royal Master. The beasts of prey have been tracked down to their lairs deep in the forest. Why then does my lord stay?

KING. Lord Bhadrasena, Mādhavya here has been reviling the chase so bitterly that my ardour for it is cooling off.

GENERAL (*aside*). Mādhavya, be firm in your opposition; in the meantime, I shall follow the bent of my Royal Master's mind. (*aloud*) My Lord, this blockhead doesn't know what he is talking about. Your Royal Highness is a prime example of the benefits of the chase.

> The body light, manly, ready for action,
> trim in the waist, fat melted away; knowledge gained
> of changing responses of woodland creatures seized
> > by fear or anger;
> the archer's elation as arrows hit perfectly the moving
> > mark:
> falsely indeed is the chase cursed as a vice;
> is there another sport so excellent as this?

MĀDHAVYA (*angrily*). Go away; His Majesty is now recovering his true nature; as for you, you may please yourself roaming from one forest to another until like a witless jackal you walk right into the jaws of some old bear.

KING. Bhadrasena, we are in the vicinity of the Hermitage: therefore I cannot really applaud these words of yours. For the present, my good lord:

> Let bisons plunge into forest-pools and revel
> > splashing,
> striking the water repeatedly with their mighty horns;
> let the herds of antelopes clustering in groups
> > in the shade,
> chew the cud undisturbed;
> and let wild boars lining up round puddles
> where the marsh-sedge grows fragrant, root peacefully
> > in the mud:
> and let this my bow with its loose-knotted string
> be allowed to enjoy its well-earned repose.

GENERAL. So please Your Royal Highness, your wish is my command.

KING. Let the beaters hemming in the game be recalled then; and let the soldiers now encamped in the environs of the holy groves encircling them, be ordered to withdraw. Mark you:

> Like sun-crystals cool to the touch
> vomit fiery sparks from deep within
> if struck by another luminous power,
> so, hermits rich in holiness
> in whom Tranquillity presides,
> have hidden deep a blazing energy
> that leaps out to burn when aroused.

MĀDHAVYA. Now, you inciter of strong passions, be off with you and quickly.

GENERAL (*bowing to the King*). As our Royal Master commands.

(*Exits.*)

KING (*to his attendants*). Ladies, you may divest yourselves of your hunting costumes; and you too, Raivataka, resume your duties.

RAIVATAKA. As the Great Lord commands.

(*Exit.*)

MĀDHAVYA (*laughing*). So, now that Your Honour has rid himself of these gadflies, do me a favour; come and sit in comfort in the shade of that tree over there, on that charming stone seat with its canopy of flowering vines, so that I could also sit down and rest.

KING. Lead the way.

MĀDHAVYA. This way, my lord. (*both turn around and sit down*)

KING. Ah! My friend Mādhavya, your eyes have not as yet been richly feasted as they should be; for you have not seen what is truly worth seeing.

MĀDHAVYA. How do you say that? Is Your Honour not right here before my eyes?

KING. Everyone considers the person dear to him as most worth seeing. But, I am referring to her . . . to Śakuntalā, that exquisite ornament of the Hermitage.

MĀDHAVYA (*aside*). I shall not give him room to expatiate on this theme. (*to the King*) Now listen, Your Honour, if she is a hermit-girl beyond your reach, is there any point in seeing her?

KING. O, you blockhead!

> Why do people with upturned faces gaze
> upon the crescent of the new moon with unblinking
>   eyes?

Apart from that, you know that Duhṣanta's mind is never drawn to forbidden things.

MĀDHAVYA. And can you explain that to me?

KING.

> Like a flower of the fragrant white jasmine
> dropped from its parent stalk onto an Arka leaf
> she, sprung from a lovely Apsarā, I hear,
> is the Sage's daughter only found by him, abandoned.

MĀDHAVYA (*laughing*). Oho! So that's how it is, eh! Like one whose palate jaded by enjoying delicate candies made of the sweetest dates hankers after a taste of the sour tamarind, you too, Sir, sated with the pleasure of the Inner Apartments, full of beauties, and each one a gem . . . you are consumed by this passion for a hermit-girl.

KING. It is only because you haven't seen her that you talk like this.

MĀDHAVYA. Why Sir, then she must be a miracle of beauty indeed . . . to arouse such breathless admiration in *you*.

KING. My friend, she needs not many words:

> Contemplating Brahmā's imaging power ineffable,
> and her beauty, she flashes on my eye,
> a jewel among women
> of another order of Creation, extraordinary;
> as if the Mighty Creator gathering
> rarest elements of beauty,
> pictured perfection first,
> then quickened it with the Breath of Life.

MĀDHAVYA. Why then, she must put to shame all other beauties for all time.

KING. And I keep thinking . . . she is:

> A flower whose fragrance none has dared to smell;
> Spring's tenderest shoot no profaning fingers have
>   plucked;
> fresh honey whose taste no lip has relished;
> a gem glowing inviolate. Who can tell
> what sinless mortal Brahmā has named
> the blessed enjoyer of such beauty,

the fruit entire of his holy works in many births.

MĀDHAVYA. For that very reason, go quickly, hurry, Sir, and rescue her before she falls into the hands of some forest-dwelling hermit with greasy head and hair plastered down with *ingudi* oil.

KING. Ah! But the lady is not mistress of herself; and her parent is not in the Hermitage at present.

MĀDHAVYA. Now tell me—what are her feelings towards you? Did her eyes express any hint of love?

KING. You know, my friend, hermit-girls are shy and retiring by nature; Yet:

> When I turned towards her she turned her gaze away:
> her smiles seemed the prologue to some other play;
> with her demeanour thus veiled by modesty,
> Love neither shone radiant nor was it concealed.

MĀDHAVYA (*laughing*). What Sir! Did you then expect her to leap into your arms as soon as she set eyes on Your Honour?

KING. But as she was leaving with her friends, her feelings were amply manifest: How?

> Having gone some steps, she stopped, unforeseen,
>   exclaimed—'Ah! My foot is pricked by a darbha-
>   blade';
> sylph-like she stood, still, turning towards me,
> busy disentangling the bark-garment
> that certainly was not caught on the twigs of any
>   shrub.

MĀDHAVYA. I see it all now; I see it quite clearly. I trust you have laid in a good stock of provisions. For it looks as if you have turned this penance-grove into a pleasure-garden.

KING. My friend, can you not come up with some pretext or other that will gain us entry into the Hermitage once more?

MĀDHAVYA. Hm . . . now . . . let me think; but do not break my concentration with any of your false lamentations. (*as if deep in thought*) Ah! I have it. Why think of some pretext? Are you not the King?

KING. Yes, so what of it?

MĀDHAVYA. Go right in and demand your one-sixth share of wild rice from the hermits.

KING. They pay a tribute far richer than a heap of priceless gems for the protection we provide them; and we cherish that far more. Think:

> Perishable is the fruit of the yield
> raised from the Realm's Four Estates;
> but imperishable is that sixth part
> the hermits give us of their holiness.

(*Voices off-stage*). Good, we have succeeded in our search.

KING (*listening*). From their calm, resonant tones, these must be hermits.

Enter the Guard.

GUARD. Victory to my Royal Lord; here are two young hermits at the entrance.

KING. Usher them in without delay.

GUARD. I shall announce them at once.

Enter two young hermits with the Guard.

GUARD. This way, come this way, honourable sirs.

FIRST HERMIT (*seeing the King*). How admirable! His person radiates such majesty; yet one feels at ease. But that is not surprising in a king who is almost a sage.

> He has embraced the worldly life
> that all must lead to be of use to the world:
> he too practises the Yoga of protection
> and garners for himself each day
> the purest merit of holy rites:
> with all passions under perfect control
> and controlling the world's Righteous Way.
> To him belongs that hallowed praise-word—Sage
> —prefixed merely with the attribute—Royal—
> the praise-word so often chanted
> by pairs of celestial minstrels
> to resound in the Realms of Light.

SECOND HERMIT. Gautama, this is Duhsanta? Friend to Indra, the Destroyer of powerful Vala?

FIRST HERMIT. Who else?

SECOND HERMIT.

> What wonder then that this heroic King
> with arms strong as massive iron beams
> that bar the city's great gates should hold
> single sway over the All-Supporting Earth
> bounded by the dark-blue oceans?
> For the celestials, when the battle lines are drawn
> against the fierce-encountering Titans
> hope for victory only from his taut-drawn bow
> and the clashing thunders of Indra,
> the oft-invoked Lord of the Realms of Light.

HERMITS (*approaching*). Blessing be upon you, Sir. (*offer fruits*)

KING (*rises from his seat with respect*). I welcome you, holy hermits. (*accepts the offering with a deep bow, then sits down*) I am eager to know what has brought you here.

HERMITS. The residents of this Hermitage hearing that you are in the neighbourhood address this request to you.

KING. What are their commands?

HERMITS. In the absence of His Holiness, the Patriarch, demons will begin disturbing the performance of our sacred rites. Therefore they request that you with your charioteer come in and stay for some nights in the Hermitage to guard it.

KING. I am honoured to be asked.

MĀDHAVYA (*aside*). Good Fortune seizes you by the throat, eh?

KING. Raivataka: go, tell the charioteer to bring round the chariot and my bow and quiver.

GUARD. As Your Highness commands. (*goes off*)

HERMITS (*expressing great satisfaction*).

> The Puru monarchs were first and foremost

> consecrated protectors of those in distress;
> as befits your noble descent, O King,
> you now duly follow in their footsteps.

KING. Go first, Holy Sirs; I shall follow close on your heels.

HERMITS. May victory always attend on you.

(*Exit.*)

KING. Mādhavya, are you not eager to see Śakuntalā?

MĀDHAVYA. At first, yes; I was—with eagerness that was brimming over; but—(*looks fearful*) at the mention of the word 'demons', not a drop of it remains.

KING. O, you shouldn't be afraid; you will naturally stay close to me.

MĀDHAVYA. A protector of your chariot wheels then?

Enter the Guard.

GUARD. Your Majesty, the chariot is ready and awaits my lord's triumphal setting out. But—Karabhaka has also arrived—from the Queen's Royal Presence.

KING (*in a reverential tone of voice*). What! From our Royal Mother?

GUARD. Yes, my lord.

KING. He should have been shown in immediately.

GUARD. I shall do so at once, my lord. (*goes out*)

Enter Karabhaka with the doorkeeper.

KARABHAKA (*approaches*). Hail, hail to His Majesty. The Queen Mother's command runs as follows, Sire: 'On the fourth day after today I shall break the fast that I have undertaken, the fast known as "The Safeguarding of the Son's Succession." My long-lived son should be by my side on that solemn occasion without fail.'

KING. Mādhavya, look at me; on the one hand I am bound to honour my commitments to the holy sages; on the other the command of a revered parent is laid on me. Neither obligation may be ignored with impunity. How do we cope with such a situation?

MĀDHAVYA (*laughing*). Hang in between, suspended in mid-air like Triśanku.

KING. I am truly perplexed.

> Required to perform duties in places
> widely separated, I am in two minds,
> like a river that strikes a hill in mid-course,
> and forced back parts into two streams.

(*after reflecting*) Mādhavya, my friend, you have always been accepted as a son by our Mother; so—you could leave now, return to the Capital and acquaint Her Majesty with my deep involvement in the affairs of the Hermitage; you could also take my place at the ceremony and carry out for Her Majesty, all the ritual duties that a son has to perform.

MĀDHAVYA. You don't say that because you think that I am afraid of demons, do you?

KING. O no, O Great Brahmin; you—afraid? That is inconceivable.

MĀDHAVYA. Well then, I shall leave; but I must travel in a manner befitting the younger brother of the King.

KING. Indeed you shall, my friend. I shall have my whole retinue accompany you, so that it will no longer be a disquieting presence in the Holy Groves.

MĀDHAVYA (struts around proudly). Ha, I feel already like the Crown Prince.

KING (to himself). This fellow tends to prattle. He may blurt out something about my interest in Śakuntalā to the ladies in the Royal Apartments. That won't do; I should put a different complexion on the whole matter. (takes the jester by the hand and speaks to him) My friend, listen carefully to me. I am going into the Hermitage solely out of esteem for the sages, to help them. I have no real interest in the hermit-maiden; just a whim, you know. For you can very well see that:

> Between our royal self and that simple girl,
> a stranger to love, bred among gentle fawns
> as one of them, lies a world of difference.
> Do not, my friend,
> take in earnest what was spoken merely in jest.

MĀDHAVYA. Is that all?

(Exit all.)

THUS ENDS ACT TWO
ENTITLED
CONCEALMENT OF THE TELLING

ACT THREE

Prelude

Scene: The Hermitage of Kanva.

Enter one of Kanva's pupils.

PUPIL (with admiration). O what a mighty monarch Duhsanta is. No sooner had he entered our Hermitage than all our sacred rites became completely free of all unexpected disturbances.

> Why tell a long tale of arrows aimed and shot;
> by the mere twang of the bowstring from afar
> as if his bow spoke quivering with rage, he made
> all hindrances flee terrified from the scene.

Now let me gather Kuśa-grass and take it to the Priest to strew on the altar.

Walks around, notices someone and speaks in the air.

Ho there, Priyamvadā, say, for whom are we carrying these lotus leaves on their tender stalks? And the cooling balsam of the fragrant Uśira-root? (as if listening to a reply) What did you say? O, that Śakuntalā has suffered a heatstroke? That these things are to cool her burning frame? Priyamvadā, listen, let her be looked after with the greatest care, for she is the very life-breath of the Patriarch. I

shall also send some hallowed water used for the Sacrifice, with Gautamī; it will soothe Śakuntalā.

(He exits.)

END OF THE PRELUDE

Enter the King deeply in love.

KING (pensive, sighing).

> I know well the Holy Power of penance immense;
> that young girl is dependent on another's will,
> that I know. But like water flowing down,
> my heart is truly powerless to return.

O God who churns men's minds, how is it that your weapons claimed to be flowers, are so sharp? (as if recollecting) O yes, I know why:

> Śiva's fiery wrath must still burn in you
> like Fire smouldering deep in the ocean's depths.
> Were it not so, how can you burn lovers like me,
> when mere ashes is all that is left of you?

Then again, we of the Brotherhood of Love are cruelly deceived by you and the moon—though we put our fullest trust in both. And why do I say this:

> False is the statement to lovers like me
> that flowers are your arrows; that moonbeams are
>   cool;
> the moon's rays pregnant with ice shoot darts of fire,
> and your arrows are tipped with hardest adamant.

On the other hand:

> Even if you drive me to distraction, O dolphin-
>   bannered god!
> With unsleeping anguish, I would still welcome you,
> if only you would assail her too with your darts
> —that lovely girl with long, bewitching eyes.

O blessed god, though reproached bitterly, you show no compassion.

> Wantonly have I made you greatly grow,
>   O Bodiless One!
> nourishing you assiduously with a hundred rites
>   and feelings;
> now, drawing your bow back to your ear,
> it is at me you choose to let your arrow fly.

Now that ascetics, free of impediments, have given me leave to withdraw, where can I find solace for my weary heart? (sighs deeply) What other refuge is there but the beloved's presence. (looking up) At this hour when the noonday sun blazes down with cruel heat, Lady Śakuntalā with her friends usually retires to the Mālini's banks where flowering vines form shady bowers. Well, that's where I shall go. (turns and looks) I can tell that the beautiful girl has just passed through this avenue of young trees. For:

> The cups of flowers she has just plucked
> have not as yet sealed themselves,
> and these tender shoots, broken off,
> are still moist with their milky sap.

(*feeling pleasure at the touch of the breeze*) Aha! How delightful is the breeze blowing here in the woodlands.

> This breeze that wafts the fragrance of lotuses
> with the cool spray of Mālini's rippling stream
> is able to soothe love-fevered limbs,
> enfolding them in a close embrace.

(*noticing something*) Ha! Śakuntalā must be here in this arbour of reeds overhung by flowering vines—it is plain to see,

> At the entrance dusted with pale river sand
> a line of footprints clearly etched, lightly marked
> in front by her toes and indented deeply at the back
> by her heels weighed down by wide heavy hips.

Let me look through these twining stems. (*peers in and exclaims with rapture*) My eyes look upon Paradise; there she is, the beloved of my dreams, reclining on a stone slab strewn with flowers and attended by her friends. Let me hear what they are saying in confidence . . . (*stands watching*)

The scene discovers Śakuntalā with her friends, as described.

FRIENDS (*fanning her*). Dear Śakuntalā, does the breeze of these lotus leaves soothe you somewhat?

ŚAKUNTALĀ (*in deep distress*). What! Are my dear friends fanning me? (*her friends look at each other dismayed*)

KING. Lady Śakuntalā does appear greatly indisposed. (*musing awhile*) I wonder if it is the summer's heat that is the real cause of her distress . . . or, is it what I think it is . . . (*reflecting on it*) O well, have done with doubts:

> With Uśira-balm spread thick over her breasts
> and a single bracelet of tender lotus stalks
> that hangs pale and withered on her wrist,
> my beloved's body though racked with pain . . .
> how exquisite it looks in its pale loveliness:
> Summer's heat can strike as savage as love . . . it's true,
> but . . . to burn young girls into such splendour . . .
> I cannot think *that* lies in Summer's power.

PRIYAMVADĀ (*aside*). Anasūyā, ever since she first saw the King, Śakuntalā has been restless and dejected; there can be no other reason for her sickness.

ANASŪYĀ. I suspected as much myself. Very well, I'll ask her. Śakuntalā dearest, I wish to ask you something . . . see how your limbs are simply burning.

KING. Quite so:

> Those bracelets of plaited lotus-fibre
> bright as moonbeams, now turning brown,
> speak of the fever unendurable
> coursing like fire through her limbs.

ŚAKUNTALĀ (*raising herself*). What did you wish to ask me, dear?

ANASŪYĀ. Listen, dear Śakuntalā, we cannot enter your mind and read your thoughts; but we feel that the state you are in is like that of persons experiencing the pangs of

love as described in romantic tales. So be frank, tell us the cause of your distress. Without knowing the nature of an illness how can a cure be found for it?

KING. Anasūyā thinks the way I do.

ŚAKUNTALĀ. Indeed, I am deeply troubled; but I cannot blurt it out abruptly.

PRIYAMVADĀ. Dearest, Anasūyā is perfectly right; why are you hiding the cause of your distress? You are wasting away day by day; all that is left is the delicate glow of your loveliness—like the lustre of fine pearls.

KING. Priyamvadā is not exaggerating; just see her:

> Wan face with sunken cheeks, breasts no longer firm,
> slender waist grown more slender, shoulders drooping
>   despondent,
> complexion dulled by pallor—O how woebegone she
>   looks,
> limp, struck by maddening love, yet how lovely
> —a Mādhavī, its leaves touched by a scorching wind.

ŚAKUNTALĀ (*sighing*). Whom else can I speak to of my heartache? But it will be a source of anxiety for you both.

BOTH. That's why we insist on knowing; grief shared is easier to bear.

KING.

> Asked by friends who share her joys and sorrows,
> the young girl cannot but speak of the ache
> hid within her heart.
> Although I saw her turn round many a time
> gazing at me with hungering eyes,
> my heart beats now like a coward's
> fearing to hear the answer she makes.

ŚAKUNTALĀ (*shyly*). From the moment that Royal Sage who is the protector of penance-groves came within my sight . . . (*breaks off overcome by shyness*)

BOTH. Go on, tell us, dear.

ŚAKUNTALĀ. From that instant I am pining for love of him.

BOTH. Fortunately, you have set your heart on one truly worthy of you. But then where else would a great river flow except to the ocean!

KING (*ecstatic*). I have heard what I longed to hear.

> Love, the creator of my anguish
> now brings a touch of cooling balm,
> as days dark with clouds at summer's end
> bring relief to the world of living things.

ŚAKUNTALĀ. My friends, if you approve, counsel me as to how I can find favour in the eyes of the Royal Sage; otherwise I shall be just a memory.

KING. Her words remove all doubts.

PRIYAMVADĀ (*aside*). Anasūyā, she is too far gone in love and cannot brook any delay.

ANASŪYĀ. Priyamvadā, what plan can we devise to fulfil our friend's desire secretly and without any delay.

PRIYAMVADĀ. Hm . . . without delay, why that's easy . . . but secretly . . . ah! That bears some thinking.

ANASŪYĀ. And how's that?

PRIYAMVADĀ. Why, the Royal Sage looks at her with so

much tenderness in his eyes; and these days he appears rather wasted . . . as if he spends wakeful nights.

KING. How right she is; such is my state:

> Hot tears welling up of anguish within, as I lie
> night after night, my cheek pillowed on my arm,
> dull the brilliance of gems set in this gold armlet
> that unimpeded by the welt raised by the bowstring,
> slips down as often as I push it up from my wrist.

PRIYAMVADĀ (*after reflecting*). Listen, let Śakuntalā write a love letter; hiding it under some flowers that I shall pretend were part of those offered to the deity, I shall manage to give it to the King.

ANASŪYĀ. My friend, it is a pretty plan, I like it. What does our Śakuntalā have to say about it?

ŚAKUNTALĀ. Can the arrangement be questioned?

PRIYAMVADĀ. Right then, now you think of an elegant song that'll convey your feelings to the King.

ŚAKUNTALĀ. I can think of something, but my heart trembles at the thought of being rebuffed.

KING.

> He from whom you fear a rebuff, O timid girl!
> He stands here, yearning to enfold you in his arms.
> The man who woos Fortune may win her—or he may not,
> but does Fortune ever fail to win the man she woos?

again:

> Longing for your love, the man you assume
> wrongly as one who would spurn that love,
> he, is here, close to you, beautiful girl!
> A gem is sought for, it does not seek.

FRIENDS. O you who belittles her own worth! Who on earth will think of unfurling an umbrella to keep off the cooling autumnal moonlight!

ŚAKUNTALĀ (*smiling*). I am admonished.

KING. My eyes forget to wink while I stand gazing on my beloved; and no wonder;

> With one eyebrow raised, curving deep as a tendril
> as she shapes her feelings into words,
> her face, a blush mantling her cheek, proclaims
> the passionate love she feels for me.

ŚAKUNTALĀ. Dear friends, I have a little song running through my head; but there are no writing materials at hand to set it down.

PRIYAMVADĀ. Why don't you incise the words with your nail on this lotus leaf soft as a parrot's downy breast?

ŚAKUNTALĀ. Now listen to the song and tell me if the words are well-chosen to convey my feelings.

FRIENDS. Go ahead, we are listening.

ŚAKUNTALĀ (*reading*).

> I do not know your heart,
> but my nights and days, O pitiless one!
> Are haunted by Love,
> as every part of me
> yearns to be one with you.

KING (*coming out at once*).

> Love burns you, true, my slender girl!
> But me, He consumes utterly—relentless;
> Day wipes out the moon from view
> but not the water-lily.

FRIENDS (*rising with the greatest joy*). Welcome, welcome to the immediate answer to our inmost wish. (*Śakuntalā tries to get up too*)

KING. Fair lady, no, no, do not exert yourself.

> Your limbs aflame with pain that bite
> into the bed of flowers, fast fading
> your bracelets of lotus-fibre, need not
> bend in the customary courtesies.

ŚAKUNTALĀ (*thrown into confusion, to herself*). O my heart, are you so overcome that you find nothing to say?

ANASŪYĀ. Let His Majesty grace one end of this stone slab.

Śakuntalā moves away a little.

KING (*sitting down*). Priyamvada, I trust your friend's fever is somewhat abated?

PRIYAMVADĀ (*with a smile*). With the right medicine at hand it ought to improve, Sir. Your Majesty, the love you bear to each other is plain to see. But the love I bear my friend prompts me to say something.

KING. Say what is on your mind, gracious lady. What is intended to be said, if left unsaid, becomes a matter of regret later.

PRIYAMVADĀ. Well, I shall say it then, Your Honour. It is the duty of the King to relieve the sufferings of the residents of a hermitage . . .

KING. What higher duty can there be?

PRIYAMVADĀ. The god of love, mighty as he is, has reduced our dear friend here to this state for love of you. You are bound therefore to sustain her life by taking her.

KING. Dear lady, this is a mutual wish and entreaty. I am most highly favoured.

ŚAKUNTALĀ (*with a smile but feigning annoyance*). That's enough, Priyamvadā, do not hold back the good King who must be impatient to return to the Inner Apartments of the Royal Palace.

KING.

> O Lady enshrined in my heart! if you consider my
>   heart
> devoted to none but you, as otherwise, then think
>   of me
> slain once by the arrow of the god who makes men
>   mad,
> as slain once more,
> O lady whose glances pour into me like delicious
>   wine!

ANASŪYĀ. Sire, one hears that kings have many loves. Pray act in such a manner as not to bring sorrow and bitter tears to her kinsfolk.

KING. Gracious Lady! I shall just say this:

> Though many a wife may grace our palace-courts
> none but two shall ever be the glory

and mainstay of our race—the Earth
sea-girdled, and, this lady, your friend.

Śakuntalā is overjoyed.

FRIENDS. We are reassured.

PRIYAMVADĀ (*aside*). Anasūyā, just observe our dear friend;
see how she revives each minute like a pea-hen that feels
the touch of the breeze from fresh rain clouds.

ŚAKUNTALĀ. Listen, friends, beg the Protector of the Earth's
pardon for what might have been spoken among ourselves, that went beyond the bounds of propriety.

FRIENDS (*smiling*). Whoever said something of the sort
should beg his pardon; is anyone else to blame?

ŚAKUNTALĀ. Pray forgive whatever was said in your presence; people say many things behind a person's back.

KING (*smiling*).

I may overlook the offence,
O girl with tapering thighs! If
out of kindness, you offer me a place
on this bed of flowers
sweet from the touch of your limbs,
to allay my weariness.

PRIYAMVADĀ. Would that be sufficient to make her happy?

ŚAKUNTALĀ (*with a show of being peeved*). Stop it, you
naughty girl; how dare you tease me . . . and in the state I
am in.

ANASŪYĀ (*glancing outside*). Priyamvadā, look, this little
fawn is anxiously searching here and there . . . must be
looking for his mother . . . he seems to have lost her; let
me take him to her.

PRIYAMVADĀ. O, this little one . . . he is like quicksilver,
nimble and wayward, my friend; you are no match for
him single-handed. Let me help you.

They prepare to leave.

ŚAKUNTALĀ. Friends, dear friends, do not leave me alone;
let one of you go. I am helpless with no one to turn to.

FRIENDS (*smiling*). He whom the whole world turns to for
help is by your side.

(*They leave.*)

ŚAKUNTALĀ. What, have they gone already . . . and left me
alone?

KING (*looks around*). My love, do not be uneasy. Am I not
near you, your suitor who adores you utterly? Now, tell
me:

Shall I raise cool breezes, waving over you
these broad lotus-leaf fans, moist and refreshing
to relieve your languid weariness?
Shall I place your lotus-pink feet on my lap,
O Lady with beautiful tapering thighs!
And press them tenderly to ease your pain?

ŚAKUNTALĀ. I shall not bring dishonour on those whom I
should honour.

Gets up to leave; the King barring her way addresses her.

KING. Beautiful girl! The day is not cool as yet; look at your
condition:

Leaving your couch of flowers, throwing off
the cool wrap of lotus leaves placed on your breasts,
your delicate body all worn out with pain,
how will you brave this fierce noonday heat?

(*saying this the King forces her to turn around*)

ŚAKUNTALĀ. Let go of me, release me, I am not free to do as
I please. But what can I do when I have only my friends
to help me?

KING. O misery! You make me feel ashamed of myself.

ŚAKUNTALĀ. I don't mean to, Your Majesty; I am just blaming my Fate.

KING. Why do you rail at a fate that is favourable to you?

ŚAKUNTALĀ. And why won't I rail against my Fate that
tempts me when I am not my own mistress, with qualities
not my own.

KING (*to himself*).

It is not Love who torments virgins to gain
                                                                        his ends,
it is they who torment Love, letting the moment
                                                                        slip by;
great though their own eagerness, shrinking
from the advances of the beloved,
and fearful of yielding their bodies
though longing for the pleasure of union.

(*Śakuntalā does leave.*)

KING. What! Shall I not please myself? (*advances and seizes
her by her garment*)

ŚAKUNTALĀ (*with a show of anger*). Paurava!* Act with
decorum; ascetics constantly move about here.

KING. Fair Lady! Such fear of your elders! His Holiness
Kanva is well-versed in the Law; you will not cause him
any distress. Listen,

Many are the daughters of sages,
married by the Gāndharva rite, we hear;
and once married, felicitated
with joyful acceptance by their fathers.

(*looking around*) What! I have walked into the open, have
I? (*lets go of Śakuntalā and retraces his steps*)

ŚAKUNTALĀ (*takes a step forward, turns around; bending*).
Paurava! Even though your wishes remain unfulfilled and
you know me only through conversation, do not forget
me.

KING. My beautiful girl!

However far you may go from me,
you shall never go from my heart,
as the shadow of the tree at evening
never leaves its base on the eastern side.

ŚAKUNTALĀ (*going a little way, to herself*). Alas! What shall I

---

*Ruler of the Puru dynasty.

do? Hearing these words my feet refuse to move forward. Let me hide behind this amaranth hedge and observe how his feelings incline. (*stands still*)

KING. How could you go off like this, my love, without a thought, forsaking me whose unchangeable love is for you and for you only.

> How delicate is your body to be loved most gently!
> And how hard your heart like the stalk of the Śirīsa-
> flower!

ŚAKUNTALĀ. Ah! Hearing this I am powerless to leave.

KING. What'll I do now in this bower, empty of my beloved's presence. (*looking in front*) O, what's this . . . my way is barred.

> This bright bracelet of lotus-stalks fragrant
> with Uśira-balm from her body
> lies here before me, fallen from her wrist
> to become a chain around my heart.

(*he picks it up adoringly*)

ŚAKUNTALĀ (*looking at her arm*). O dear, the bracelet was so loose, it must have slipped off and fallen without my noticing it.

KING (*placing the bracelet on his breast*). O for its touch!

> This charming ornament of yours, my love,
> having left your lovely arm to rest here,
> consoles this unhappy man more than you have,
> though it is only an insentient thing.

ŚAKUNTALĀ. Ha! I cannot hold back any longer. Using this bracelet as a pretext, I shall discover myself. (*approaches the King*)

KING (*seeing her is overjoyed*). Ah! Here is the lady who is my very life; no sooner had I begun to lament my fate than Fate came to my aid to do me a favour.

> Parched with thirst, the bird has only to crave for
> water
> and a shower from a fresh rain-cloud falls into its
> mouth.

ŚAKUNTALĀ (*standing before the King*). Sire, when I was half-way I remembered the bracelet that had slipped off my arm; I have come back for it knowing in my heart that you would have taken it. Let me have it back lest it betray us both to the sages.

KING. Well . . . I'll give it back on one condition.

ŚAKUNTALĀ. And what's that?

KING. That I myself restore it to the place it once occupied.

ŚAKUNTALĀ (*to herself*). There's no way out. (*comes closer to him*)

KING. Let's sit here on this same stone slab.

They both turn around and sit.

KING (*taking hold of Śakuntalā's hand*). O, to feel such a touch!

> Has Fate rained down a shower ambrosial
> to make the tree of love
> once burnt to ashes by Śiva's wrath
> put forth a fresh shoot once more?

ŚAKUNTALĀ (*feeling the touch of his hand*). Quickly, hurry up, my lord.

KING (*filled with happiness, to himself*). How this inspires confidence in me; for she has addressed me by the word used for a husband in speaking. (*aloud*) Oh beautiful girl! The ends of this bracelet of lotus-stalks are not joined very firmly; if you permit me, I'll re-do it.

ŚAKUNTALĀ (*with a smile*). If you wish.

KING (*artfully delays and finally fixes the bracelet*). See, lovely girl!

> Leaving the sky in search of richer beauty,
> the new moon in the form of lotus-stems,
> joining the points of its crescent, has placed itself
> on your arm lovely as a śyama-vine.

ŚAKUNTALĀ. I cannot see very well; the pollen-dust from the lily at my ear shaken by the breeze, has fallen into my eye blurring my sight.

KING (*with a smile*). If you permit me, I can blow it away.

ŚAKUNTALĀ. That would be kind . . . but . . . what if I don't trust you?

KING. Why not? A new servant does not overstep his master's instructions.

ŚAKUNTALĀ. It is just this excess of gallantry that I can't quite trust.

KING (*to himself*). I am certainly not going to pass up an opportunity so pleasant, to minister to her comfort. (*about to raise her face up to his, Śakuntalā resists at first, then gives up*)

KING. O, you with your intoxicating eyes, why don't you stop suspecting me of dishonourable behaviour? (*Śakuntalā glances up at him, then hangs her head*)

KING (*raising her face lightly with two fingers, to himself*).

> My love's lower lip, soft and unbruised,
> trembles with such alluring charm
> as if granting me who thirst for it
> the permission I wait for eagerly.

ŚAKUNTALĀ. My lord is taking his time to do what he promised, it seems.

KING. The lily adorning your ear, sweet lady, was confusing me by its likeness to your eye to which it lies so close. (*blows the pollen dust away*)

ŚAKUNTALĀ. I can now see clearly. But I am sorry, my lord, I have no way of returning the kind favour you have done me.

KING. No matter, there is no need to, beautiful lady!

> To inhale the fragrance of your face
> is itself a favour granted to me;
> is the honey-bee not well-content
> with the mere fragrance of the lotus?

ŚAKUNTALĀ (*with a smile*). But if it were not, what would he* do?

KING (*decisively brings his face close to hers*). This . . . this . . .

---

*The bee stands for the King; the Skt. word is in the masculine.

(*A voice off-stage*): Little bride of the sheldrake, come bid your mate farewell; Night is here.

ŚAKUNTALĀ (*flustered*). My lord! Lady Gautamī is on her way here, to ask after my health, I'm sure. Hide behind this tangle of vines.

KING. Yes. (*goes into a secret place*)

Gautamī enters with a goblet in her hand.

GAUTAMĪ. My child! Here is the sanctified water for you. (*looks at her and helps her up*) A fine state of affairs . . . un-well, and only the gods to keep you company.

ŚAKUNTALĀ. Priyamvadā and Anasūyā went down just this minute to the Mālini.

GAUTAMĪ (*sprinkling Śakuntalā with the holy water*). Dear child, may you live long and in good health. Is your fever somewhat abated now? (*touches her*)

ŚAKUNTALĀ. There is a change for the better, Mother.

GAUTAMĪ. The day is drawing to its close; come, child, let us return to our cottage.

ŚAKUNTALĀ (*rising with difficulty, to herself*). O heart! At first you drew back like a coward, fearing to taste the happi-ness that came knocking at your door. Now to your great regret, the time of parting has come; how bitter is your anguish. O fragrant bower of creepers! Soother of my an-guish! I bid you farewell and take leave of you only to meet again and enjoy your company. (*leaves*)

KING (*returning to his former seat and sighing deeply*). O mis-ery! Many a hindrance lies between desire and its fulfil-ment:

> She turned aside that lovely face
> with beautifully-lashed eyes:
> again and again she guarded with her fingers
> her lower lip, all the more tempting
> for the faltering words of denial
> murmured indistinct:
> after much gentle persuasion
> I raised her face to mine—
> but could not kiss it, alas!

Where, where shall I go now? No, I shall stay right here; here in the bower of creepers where my beloved rested. (*looks round*)

> Here on the stone-slab is the bed of flowers
> crushed by her body; here lies languishing
> her message of love confided to the lotus-leaf;
> an ornament of fine lotus-stalks, banished
> from her hand lies there pathetic, abandoned;
> my eyes cling to each object that I see;
> how can I leave this arbour of reeds
> all of a sudden, deserted though it be.

(*reflecting*) Alas! It was surely a mistake on my part to have delayed and wasted time once I had won my beloved. So now:

> When next I find myself alone with her
> —that girl with a face of chiselled loveliness—
> I'll lose no time: for happiness, as a rule,

is hard to come by: thus my foolish heart,
frustrated by stumbling-blocks, spells it out.
But, in the beloved's presence,
it stands somewhat abashed.

(*A voice in the air*): O, King!

> The evening rituals are in solemn progress;
> flesh-eating demons prowl and press round the
>   altars
> where the Holy Fire blazes.
> Like massed thunder-clouds that reflect the sunset
>   glow,
> their shadowy forms, lurid,
> move around in many ways
> fear-instilling.

KING (*listens, then resolutely speaks*). Ho there, ascetics . . . do not fear . . . here I am . . . I am coming.

(*Leaves.*)

END OF ACT THREE

ENTITLED

LOVE'S FRUITION

ACT FOUR

Prelude

Scene: The Hermitage

Enter Śakuntalā's friends gathering flowers.

ANASŪYĀ. Priyamvadā, although I rejoice greatly knowing that Śakuntalā is happily married to a husband of her own choice who is worthy of her in every respect, I feel rather uneasy about something.

PRIYAMVADĀ. And what may that be?

ANASŪYĀ. The Royal Sage has been given leave to depart by the sages grateful for the successful completion of the Sacrifice; and he has returned to his Capital. Now, in the company of his Queens, will he remember all that hap-pened here in the Hermitage . . . or will he not?

PRIYAMVADĀ. O, surely you should not feel uneasy on that score; such a noble form cannot house a nature so totally at variance with it. But I am anxious about something else; how will Father take it when he hears of all this on his return?

ANASŪYĀ. If you ask me, this marriage will be sealed with Father's approval and blessing.

PRIYAMVADĀ. Why do you think that?

ANASŪYĀ. It is the paramount consideration in the mind of a parent to give a young daughter in marriage to a groom en-dowed with all noble qualities. If the gods themselves send one without any effort on the part of the parent, would he not congratulate himself on being most fortunate?

PRIYAMVADĀ (*looks into the basket*). Anasūyā, don't you think we have picked enough flowers for the worship of the divinities of the home?

ANASŪYĀ. But we also need some flowers for the adoration of Śakuntalā's Goddess of Fortune who watches over her marriage.

PRIYAMVADĀ. Yes, you are right.

They gather more flowers.

(*A voice off-stage rings out*). Ho there, I am here, at your door!

ANASŪYĀ (*listening carefully*). That sounds like a guest announcing himself.

PRIYAMVADĀ. Surely Śakuntalā is not far from the cottage; Ah . . . hm . . . but I'm afraid her heart is far away.

ANASŪYĀ. Then we must go; these flowers will do.

They are about to leave.

(*The same voice off-stage rings out again*). Woe to you, woe, you insolent girl who disregards the honoured guest standing at your door.

> You who do not notice me,
> a hoard of holy merit
> standing at your door,
> because you are lost in thoughts of one
> to the exclusion of all else,
> you shall be lost in his thoughts:
> though you goad his memory hard,
> he shall fail to remember you,
> even as a man drunk remembers not
> thereafter, the tale he told before.

Hearing this, the girls are dismayed.

PRIYAMVADĀ. Alas, alas, the worst has happened. Our darling Śakuntalā, absent-minded, has offended some guest worthy of great reverence.

ANASŪYĀ (*looking ahead*). And it is not just any guest, O cruel Fate! It is the great sage Durvāsā quick to anger. Look where he is going after cursing her so cruelly . . . striding off briskly shaking with passion; it will not be easy to intercept him.

PRIYAMVADĀ. What has the power to burn other than Fire? You must go quickly, Anasūyā; fall at his feet and try to calm him down while I hurry and get water and a guest-offering to welcome him.

ANASŪYĀ. Yes, I am going. (*goes out in haste*)

PRIYAMVADĀ (*takes a few hurried steps, then stumbles*). O, an ill omen! This is what comes of hurrying. The basket has slipped from my hand and the flowers lie all scattered on the ground. I had better pick them up. (*starts picking up the flowers*)

ANASŪYĀ (*entering*). O my friend, anger incarnate that he is, do you think he is one to accept anyone's entreaties? But I managed to squeeze a little compassion out of the old crust.

PRIYAMVADĀ (*smiling*). Even that 'little' is a lot for him; what happened, tell me.

ANASŪYĀ. When he preemptorily refused to turn back, I pleaded with him in these words: 'Most Venerable Holiness, your daughter is unaware of the great power you possess through your austerities; this is also her very first offence; considering these, please, revered Sir, forgive her.'

PRIYAMVADĀ. Then what did he say, go on.

ANASŪYĀ. He said, 'My curse cannot prove false; but its power will cease the moment she presents some ornament as a token of recognition.' With these words he vanished into thin air.

PRIYAMVADĀ. At least we can console ourselves a little with that. There is a token. When the Royal Sage was taking leave of Śakuntalā, he slipped the signet-ring with his name inscribed on it on her finger, as a remembrance. She does have in her possession the means of ensuring recognition.

They turn round and see Śakuntalā at the cottage door.

PRIYAMVADĀ. Look, Anasūyā, do you see our dearest friend there? Still, as if drawn in a picture, her cheek resting on her left hand . . . her mind so totally absorbed in thoughts of her absent lord that she does not seem to be aware of her own self . . . how could she have noticed the presence of a visitor?

ANASŪYĀ. I tell you what; let us keep this matter of the curse between our two selves. Delicate by nature, our dear friend should be spared a shock.

PRIYAMVADĀ. Naturally, who would sprinkle a tender jasmine with boiling water.

(*Both leave.*)

END OF THE PRELUDE

Enter a pupil of Kanva, just got up from sleep.

PUPIL. I have been asked by His Holiness, just returned from his pilgrimage, to look out and see what time it is. Let me go out into the open and ascertain how much of the night remains. (*turns and looks around*) O, it is daybreak already, I see.

> Here, the moon, lord of healing herbs
> sinks behind the western mountain,
> there, on the other, Dawn heralds
> the advance of the rising Sun.
> The rise and setting of the two Lights simultaneous
> regulate the vicissitudes of life on earth.

And further,

> Now that the Moon has set, the pool of moon-lotuses
> delights not my eye—her beauty is but a memory,
> the grief of women let alone when loved ones
> travel far are beyond measure hard to bear.

See how:

> Daybreak's rose-red glow flushes the dew on the
>   jujube trees
> the peacock wakened leaves the cottage roof of
>   darbha-grass;

the blackbuck springs up from the altar's edge, hoof-
                                                           marked,
  stretches his limbs and draws himself up to his noble
                                                           height.
And now:
  The same moon who, stepping on the crown of
                                                           Sumeru,
  Parent of Mountains, dispelled the darkness, and
                                                           traversed
  the middle regions of Visnu's abode,
  now falls down the sky in a pitiful glimmer of light:
  the ascent too high of even the great ends in a fall.

Entering with a toss of the curtain.

ANASŪYĀ (*to herself*). Even one unacquainted with the ways
  of the world cannot help thinking that the King has behaved badly towards our Śakuntalā.
PUPIL. Well, I had better go now and inform our Preceptor
  that it is time for the oblations to the Sacred Fire. (*he de-
  parts*)
ANASŪYĀ. Dawn is breaking. I have woken up early. But
  now that I am awake, what is there for me to do? My
  hands refuse to go about their normal morning duties. Let
  the god of love be now happy since he has brought my
  pure-hearted friend into contact with a perfidious man.
  On the other hand, the Royal Sage may not be to blame.
  Perhaps, Durvāsā's curse is working itself out. Otherwise,
  how is it possible that after all the protestations he made,
  the king has not sent word to her in all this time? (*reflects
  a moment*) Then, shall we send him the Ring he left for
  remembrance? But with whom? Which of these austere
  hermits, serene and devoid of passions can we ask? And
  we can't get our friend into trouble by informing Father
  Kanva that Śakuntalā is married to Duhsanta and now
  bears his child. In such a situation what can we do?
PRIYAMVADĀ. Anasūyā, Anasūyā, come quickly, hurry; the
  festive ceremonies for Śakuntalā's departure are on.
ANASŪYĀ. What? What is all this? (*astonished*)
PRIYAMVADĀ. Listen, just now I went to Śakuntalā's bedside
  to ask if she had slept well.
ANASŪYĀ. Then, then?
PRIYAMVADĀ. What do I see: Father Kanva, embracing
  Śakuntalā whose head was bowed low as if in shame, was
  felicitating her saying: 'Fortunately, my child, even
  though the smoke was blinding the sacrificer's eyes, the
  oblation he made fell right into the Fire. You are like
  knowledge imparted to a good pupil—not to be regretted.
  I shall arrange to send you to your husband this very day
  with an escort of ascetics.'
ANASŪYĀ (*astonished*). But who informed Father Kanva of
  all that had happened during his absence?
PRIYAMVADĀ. As he was entering the Sanctuary of the Mystic Fire, a bodiless voice chanted a verse.
ANASŪYĀ. Repeat it to me.
PRIYAMVADĀ (*speaks in Sanskrit in the metre of the sacred texts*).

As the Holy Tree
  is with the Mystic Fire pregnant,
  so is your daughter;
  know, O great Brāhmana,
  she holds Duhsanta's glowing energy
  pledged for the well-being of the world.
ANASŪYĀ (*embracing Priyamvadā, ecstatically*). O, what great
  news; I am happy, happy beyond all measure; yet, my
  mind is poised between joy and regret; regret that dear
  Śakuntalā will be leaving this very day.
PRIYAMVADĀ. We shall get over our regrets soon enough; let
  the poor girl taste some happiness.
ANASŪYĀ. Of course. It is for such an occasion that I put
  away a garland of Kesara flowers whose fragrance is lasting; there it is, in that casket of palm leaves hanging over
  there from a branch of the mango tree. Will you take it
  down and wrap it in lotus leaves while I go and prepare all
  the auspicious materials for Śakuntalā's adornment: yellow orpiment, holy earth, and Dūrvā sprouts? (*goes out*)

Priyamvadā takes down the casket of Kesara flowers.

(*A voice back-stage*). Gautamī, bid Śārngarava and the other
  hermits get ready to escort Śakuntalā.
PRIYAMVADĀ. Anasūyā, hurry, hurry. They are calling the
  hermits who are to escort Śakuntalā to the Capital.

Anasūyā enters with a tray of toiletries in her hand.

PRIYAMVADĀ (*looks ahead*). Anasūyā, there, do you see
  Śakuntalā, her hair freshly washed at sunrise with hallowed water. She is surrounded by the wives of sages who
  are congratulating her and invoking blessings holding
  grains of wild rice sanctified by prayers in their hands. Let
  us go and join them.

*Śakuntalā is seen seated with Lady Gautamī and wives of
sages.*

ŚAKUNTALĀ. I bow to you all, revered ladies.
GAUTAMĪ. Daughter, may your lord confer on you the title
  of Chief Queen as a mark of his high esteem.
SAGES' WIVES. Child, may you give birth safely to a son who
  will be a hero.

Having blessed her they leave, all except Gautamī.

FRIENDS (*approaching her*). May the Holy Bath shower all
  happiness on you, dear Śakuntalā.
ŚAKUNTALĀ. Welcome, welcome to my dearest friends; sit
  near me, both of you, won't you.
FRIENDS. Now sit still while we apply the auspicious adornments on your person.

*The two friends sit down and pick up the tray containing
the auspicious cosmetics.*

ŚAKUNTALĀ. I value this affectionate service you do me
  today more than I did at any other time. When will I be
  adorned again by my dear friends? (*weeps*)

FRIENDS. Dearest friend, you should not weep on such a happy occasion as this. (*wipe away her tears and begin to apply the decorations on her face*)

PRIYAMVADĀ. These simple adornments are all we have in the Hermitage; they do no justice to your beauty that richly deserves fine jewels and adornments to set it off.

Enter a hermit boy bearing gifts for Śakuntalā.

BOY. Here are rich ornaments to adorn Lady Śakuntalā.

Everybody looks at him in amazement.

GAUTAMĪ. Hārīta, my child, where did you get these?

HĀRĪTA. I found them, Lady, through Father Kanva's favour.

GAUTAMĪ. Created by his mind-power?

HĀRĪTA. No, not quite; he directed me saying: 'Go, bring lovely blossoms from the great forest trees for Śakuntalā's adornment.' So I went:

> A certain tree produced as if by magic
> a garment of silk, pale-bright as moonbeams,
> fitting for this most auspicious occasion;
> another noble tree poured out rich rose-red juice
> to tint beautifully her tender feet;
> in the branches of other stately trees
> woodland nymphs unseen, held out their hands
> rivalling in beauty delicate leaf buds
> unfurling, to offer rich gifts of rare jewels.

PRIYAMVADĀ (*looking at Śakuntalā*). The Queen-bee though born in a tree-hollow deserves nothing less than the honey of the lotus.

GAUTAMĪ. Dear child, the bestowal of such rare gifts augurs well for the great honours that await you in the palace of your lord.

Śakuntalā, bashful, looks down.

HĀRĪTA. I shall go now and inform Father Kanva who went down to the Mālinī for his ablutions, about this homage rendered him by the Lords of the Forest.

ANASŪYĀ. Śakuntalā, my friend, how can we adorn you? We are not used to handling such fine ornaments. (*reflects for a moment*) Drawing from our knowledge of paintings, we shall place these jewels on you as they should be.

ŚAKUNTALĀ (*with a smile*). O, I know how clever you both are.

The two friends begin adorning Śakuntalā with the ornaments. Enter Sage Kanva having finished his ablutions.

KANVA.
> Śakuntalā leaves us today—sobs my heart
> grief-stricken; unshed tears choke my voiceless throat;
> a pale cast of troubled thoughts dims my very sight.
> If affection can make me, a hermit grown old
> in the forest's hard school, so distraught,
> O, how much more bitter must the anguish

> of the first parting from a daughter be
> to fathers who dwell in the heart of home and family.

FRIENDS. Śakuntalā, dear, you are now properly adorned; put on this pair of silk garments that have been blessed by prayer.

Śakuntalā gets up and puts them on.

GAUTAMĪ. Look, dear child, your father is standing there, watching you as if he were embracing you with eyes brimming with happy tears. Greet him with due reverence.

Śakuntalā shyly makes reverential obeisance.

KANVA. My beloved child:
> Be held in high esteem by your lord
> as Śarmisttā was by Yayāti;
> as she bore Puru, may you too bear
> a son to whom the whole world will bow.

GAUTAMĪ. Worshipful Sir, this is a boon, not a blessing.

KANVA. Daughter, come, go round these sacred fires into which oblations have just been offered.

Śakuntalā walks sun-wise round the fires.

KANVA (*chants, using a Vedic metre*).
> May these Sacrificial Fires
> ranged round the Holy Altar
> that blaze fed with sacred wood
> within the circle of strewn darbhā grass,
> whose oblation-fragrant smoke
> billows out chasing away
> all evil, keep you good and pure.

My darling, now start on your journey. (*glancing around*) Where are Śārngarava and his companions?

They enter with—'Holy Sir, here we are.'

KANVA. Śārngarava, show your sister the way.

ŚĀRNGARAVA. This way, come this way, gracious lady.

All walk around.

KANVA. Hear, O hear, all you noble trees of the Holy Grove with indwelling divinities:
> She who never had a drink of water
> before you had all drunk your fill,
> she who never plucked your tender buds
> for love of you, though fond of adorning herself,
> she to whom it was a joyous festival
> when you first burst into bloom; she, Śakuntalā,
> leaves us today for her husband's home:
> All grant her leave to go.

A koel sings.

ŚĀRNGARAVA.
> Kin to her during her woodland sojourn
> the trees now give her leave to go,
> answering your request, Sir, in the Koel's notes.
> Śakuntalā can now bid the grove farewell.

(*Voices in the sky; invisible spirits sing*).
> May her path be safe and gracious,
> as gentle breezes blow,
> pleasant be her way dotted by lakes
> where green lotus-creepers grow;
> may the burning rays of the sun
> filter mellowed through thick shade-trees;
> let the pollen of water-lilies drift
> to lie as softest dust beneath her feet.

All listen in great amazement.

GAUTAMĪ. Dear child, do you hear the divinities of the Holy Grove bidding you farewell in as loving a manner as your own kinsfolk? Bow to them with due reverence.

ŚAKUNTALĀ (*walks around bowing, then speaks aside*). Oh! Priyamvadā, even though my heart yearns to see my lord once more, now that I am deserting the Hermitage, my feet move forward with painful reluctance.

PRIYAMVADĀ. The bitterness of parting is not yours alone; look around and see how the Holy Grove grieves, knowing the hour of parting from you is near:
> The doe tosses out mouthfuls of grass,
> the peacocks dance no more;
> pale leaves flutter down
> as if the vines are shedding their limbs.

ŚAKUNTALĀ (*recollecting*). O Father, I have to say goodbye to Mādhavi, my woodland sister.

KANVA. Yes, my child, I know how much you love her; here she is, to your right.

ŚAKUNTALĀ (*coming close to the jasmine, throws her arms around it*). O, Mādhavi, beloved sister, twine your branching arms round me; from today, I shall be far, far away from you. Dear Father, do care for her as if she were me.

KANVA. My love,
> What I had contemplated from the first for you,
> a worthy husband, by your own merits you have obtained.
> Freed from needful care for you, I shall now make
> the Mango by her side, the loving bridegroom of this vine.

So come this way and start on your journey.

ŚAKUNTALĀ (*approaches her friends*). I leave her in your hands, dearest friends.

FRIENDS. And in whose care are you leaving us, dearest? (*they burst into tears*)

KANVA. O for shame, Anasūyā, Priyamvadā, dry your tears. It is at a time like this that Śakuntalā needs your support to be firm.

All walk around.

ŚAKUNTALĀ. Father, you see that young doe keeping close to the cottage and moving very slowly because she is near her time—when she fawns safely, will you send someone to give me the happy news? You won't forget, dear Father?

KANVA. I shall not forget that, my love.

ŚAKUNTALĀ (*feeling something holding her back*). Hello! Who's this at my heels, tugging again and again at the hem of my garment? (*turns to look*)

KANVA. My darling:
> It is the little fawn, your adopted son,
> whom you fondly reared with handfuls of millet,
> whose mouth you dabbed with healing ingudi oil
> when lacerated by sharp blades of kuśa-grass:
> It is he who will not move out of your path.

ŚAKUNTALĀ (*addressing the fawn*). My fondling, why do you keep following me who abandons her companions? No sooner were you born than your mother died and I brought you up. Now, abandoned by me, it is Father who is left to take care of you. So go back, my little one, go back. (*weeping, she moves on*)

KANVA. O my child, do not weep like this; keep your chin up and see where you are going:
> Brace your will and check this flow of welling tears
> that veil the light of those eyes with up-curving lashes;
> your steps are faltering on the uneven ground
> where your path winds, its ups and downs unnoticed.

ŚĀRNGARAVA. Your Holiness, as you know, a loved one is to be accompanied only up to the water's edge. And this, is the edge of the lake; so give us your instructions and turn back at this point.

KANVA. Well, then, let us withdraw into the shade of this milk-bearing tree. (*they retire into the shade of the fig-tree*) Now . . . what would be a suitable message to send to His Honour Duhsanta? (*reflects deeply for a while*)

ANASŪYĀ. Śakuntalā dearest, have you noticed that there is not one sentient being in the Hermitage that is not sorrowful now at the thought of losing you. See:
> The cakravāka answers not the call of his love
> hidden behind lotus-leaves;
> with lotus-fibre dangling from his beak,
> he gazes only at you.

ŚAKUNTALĀ. Ah! Anasūyā, the cakravākī, not seeing her beloved companion just a lotus-leaf away from her, really shrills in distress . . . (*fearful*) indeed . . . what a hard lot to bear . . .

PRIYAMVADĀ.
> She too spends the night away from her beloved,
> the night stretching out long from sorrow:
> the heart's heavy with the pain of parting,
> but hope's slender thread still supports it.

KANVA. Śārngarava, my son, present Śakuntalā to the good King with these words of mine . . .

ŚĀRNGARAVA. Command me, Your Holiness.

KANVA.
> Consider us, who are rich in self-restraint,
> and consider your own exalted lineage,
> consider well her love, spontaneous,
> that flowed towards you unprompted by her kin.
> Regard her then as worth equal esteem

as your other consorts; more than that rests
on what Fortune has in store for her:
The bride's kin ought not to speak of it.

ŚĀRNGARAVA. I have grasped the message, Your Holiness.

KANVA (*addressing Śakuntalā*). My beloved child, I should now give you some advice. Though I am a forest-dweller, I am conversant with worldly matters.

ŚĀRNGARAVA. No matter is outside the purview of the wise, Your Holiness.

KANVA. My child, you are now leaving for your husband's home; when you enter it:
Serve your elders with diligence; be a friend to your
                                                      co-wives;
even if wronged by your husband do not cross him
                                              through anger;
treat those who serve you with the utmost courtesy;
be not puffed up with pride by wealth and pleasures;
Thus do girls attain the status of mistress of the home;
those who act contrary are the bane of their families.
What does our Gautamī think of this?

GAUTAMĪ. The best advice for a young bride. (*to Śakuntalā*) Dear daughter, keep these precepts always in mind.

KANVA. My beloved child, come, embrace me and your two friends.

ŚAKUNTALĀ. O Father, will my dear friends have to turn back right here?

KANVA. My darling, they also have to be given in marriage. It would not be proper for them to go with you. Gautamī will accompany you.

ŚAKUNTALĀ (*clasping her father in her arms*). Rent from my dear father's lap like a sapling of the sandalwood tree up-rooted from the side of the Malaya mountain, how can I ever survive in an alien soil? (*weeps bitterly*)

KANVA. O my darling, why ever are you so distressed?
Occupying the honoured place of consort
to your nobly-descended lord, you will
each moment be engrossed in great affairs
consequent to his imperial estate
And like the East the bright and holy sun
soon you will give birth to a royal son:
The grief of parting from me will then
count but little with you, my darling.

ŚAKUNTALĀ (*falling at her father's feet*). Father, I bow to you in reverence.

KANVA. My child, may all that I wish for you come true.

ŚAKUNTALĀ (*coming close to her friends*). My dear, dear friends, hold me close, both of you together.

FRIENDS (*embracing her*). Śakuntalā dear, listen, if the good King be at all slow to recognize you, be sure to show him the Ring inscribed with his name.

ŚAKUNTALĀ. You are voicing misgivings that make my heart tremble.

FRIENDS. No, no, don't be afraid; affection always makes one over-anxious.

ŚĀRNGARAVA (*looking up*). The sun has mounted over the tree-tops, Your Holiness, the lady had better hurry.

ŚAKUNTALĀ (*again throwing her arms round her father*). Dear Father, when shall I see this holy Hermitage again?

KANVA.
When you have long been co-wife with this great Earth
extending to the far horizons; and borne
Duhsanta a son, a warrior unrivalled,
who shall bear the yoke of sovereignty,
then you shall set foot in this Hermitage
once more with your lord, seeking tranquillity.

GAUTAMĪ. Daughter, the favourable time for starting your journey is fast going by. Let your father go back. No, she will not let him go for a long while. Your Honour had better turn back.

KANVA. My love, the performance of my holy rites is being interrupted.

ŚAKUNTALĀ. Dear Father, the affairs of the Hermitage will keep you from missing me. But as for me, I am already be-ginning to miss you, Father.

KANVA. O child, child, how could you think I would be so uncaring. (*sighing deeply*)
How can my grief ever leave me,
O my beloved child, when I see
grains of wild rice already scattered by you
sprouting green shoots at the cottage door.
Go, my love, and may your path be blessed.

(*Gautamī, Śārngarava and Śāradvata leave with Śakuntalā.*)

FRIENDS (*following Śakuntalā with their eyes for a long time speak sorrowfully*). Alas, alas, Śakuntalā is now hidden from view by a line of trees.

KANVA. Anasūyā, Priyamvadā, your friend and companion is gone. Check your grief and follow me.

(*All leave.*)

FRIENDS. O Father, we shall be entering the Holy Groves that will be desolate, bereft of Śakuntalā's presence.

KANVA. Your great affection for her makes you feel this way. (*walking about deliberating*) O well, now that I have sent Śakuntalā away to her home, my mind is at peace. Con-sider it:
A daughter is wealth belonging to another;
I have sent her this day to him who took her by the
                                                             hand;
At once, my inner being is calm and clear, as if
I have restored what was left with me in trust.

END OF ACT FOUR
ENTITLED
ŚAKUNTALĀ'S DEPARTURE

ACT FIVE

Prelude

Enter the Royal Chamberlain.

CHAMBERLAIN (*sighing*). Alas, how the years have taken their toll of me.

This ceremonial staff of cane I took
when chosen to head the Royal Household
has with the passage of time become
the support of my faltering steps.

I shall see His Majesty in the Inner Apartments to inform him of some business that he has to attend to himself immediately. (*going a little way*) Yes, but what was it? (*pondering*) Ah! I have it. Some ascetics, pupils of Kanva wish to see him. O, how strange!

Wakeful one moment,
shrouded in darkness the next,
my ageing mind
is like the flame of a dying lamp.

(*turns round and sees the King*) Here is His Majesty,

Wearied caring for his subjects
as if they were his own children,
he now seeks the peace of seclusion
as a lord of elephants who led his herd
to graze all day, burned by the noonday sun
finds at last a quiet, cool spot to rest.

To tell the truth I hesitate to tell His Majesty who has just risen from the seat of judgement that Kanva's pupils are here. But then, where do the protectors of the earth find time to rest. That's how it is,

The Sun yoked his coursers just that once;
the fragrant wind blows night and day;
the Cosmic Serpent ever bears Earth's burden;
And this is the Law that binds him who claims a
    sixth.

Turns around; then enter the King with the jester and retinue in order of rank.

KING (*wearied by the burden of administrative duties*). Every man who gains the object of his desire is happy. Only to kings does the gain itself bring misery. For,

Attainment of sovereignty merely lays to rest
the eager craving of expectancy; guarding
what is gained lays on one a weight of care.
Kingship, like an umbrella held in one's own hand
tires more than it removes tiredness.

(*Voices of two bards, off-stage*). Victory to our lord.
FIRST BARD.

Unmindful of your own ease, you toil
each day for the world's sake—such is your way of
    life;
the tree bares its crown to the blazing heat
while it refreshes those who shelter in its shade.

SECOND BARD.

Grasping the rod of justice, you bring to heel
those who are set on evil paths; you bring calm
where contentions rage; and afford protection.
Where wealth abounds kinsmen come flocking.
But in you, O King, all find kinship's perfect pattern.

KING (*listening*). This is great; hearing these words have revived my spirits worn out by the task of governing the kingdom.

MĀDHAVYA. Tell the bull he is king of the herd and his tiredness disappears.
KING (*with a smile*). Well, let's sit down.

They both sit down while the retinue stands in order of rank; the sound of a lute is heard in the background.

MĀDHAVYA (*listening intently*). Listen carefully to the sounds coming from the Hall of Music, my friend. Do you hear the pure, clear tones of a lovely melody played on the *vina*, keeping perfect rhythm? I think it is Lady Hamsavat practising her singing.
KING (*listening*). Now be quiet, Mādhavya, and let me listen.
CHAMBERLAIN (*watching the King*). Oho! His Majesty seems lost in deep thought. I had better wait for the right moment to approach him. (*he stands on one side*)

(*A voice off-stage, singing*).

O you honey-pilfering bee!
Greedy as ever for fresh honey,
once you lovingly kissed
the mango's fresh spray of flowers—
is she then forgotten so soon?
You are content now merely to stay
within the full-blown lotus.

KING. O, how brimful of passion comes this song borne on the air.
MĀDHAVYA. So . . . you have understood every word of the song?
KING (*smiling*). Yes, once I loved her deeply. She is taunting me now for my neglect of her. Mādhavya, my friend, do go to Queen Hamsavati and tell her that I have taken to heart the reproof that she has conveyed so subtly.
MĀDHAVYA. As Your Honour commands. (*gets up*) Look here, my friend, you are getting someone else to catch a bear by its tail for you. Like a shaven monk still in the grip of passion, I have no hope of release.
KING. Come, come, my friend, speak to her like the cultivated man-about-town that you are.
MĀDHAVYA. I see; there seems to be no way out for me.
    (*He exits.*)
KING (*to himself*). That song I just heard . . . a restless, yearning sadness steals into my heart . . . though I am not separated from someone I love deeply. Or . . . can it be that:

When a sadness ineffable falls
suddenly like a shadow over the heart
—even while one is wrapped in happiness—
the mind trills spontaneous, unknown to itself,
to an intimation from the past
quickened by some fleeting loveliness
or, haunting sounds of exquisite music heard:
lasting impressions of love's remembrance
live on in us from former lives, perhaps,
clinging like fragrance to our migrant soul.

He remains bewildered as if trying to recollect something.

CHAMBERLAIN (*approaching the King*). Victory, victory to His

Majesty. Sire, some hermits who dwell in the forests at the foothills of the Himalayas are here with a message from Kanva; they are accompanied by women. Your orders, Sire.

KING (*surprised*). What—hermits with a message from Kanva and accompanied by women, did you say?

CHAMBERLAIN. Yes, Sire.

KING. Send word to our Preceptor, Somarata, requesting him to welcome the ascetics from the Hermitage with all due Vedic rites and then accompany them to our presence. I shall await their coming in a place suitable for receiving holy guests.

CHAMBERLAIN. Your commands, Sire. (*he leaves*)

KING (*rising*). Vetravatī, lead the way to the sanctuary of the Mystic Fire.

VETRAVATĪ. This way, Your Majesty. (*turns around*) Gracious Sire, here is the terrace of the Fire Sanctuary, newly washed and the cow that gives milk for the holy rites stands close by. Let His Majesty ascend the steps.

KING (*mimes ascent and stands leaning on an attendant*). Vetravatī, I wonder why sage Kanva has sent these sages to our presence.

> Has the penance of sages of strict vows,
> possessed of spiritual energy immense
> been defiled perchance by impediments?
> Or has someone practised evil on creatures
> roaming free in the Groves of Righteousness?
> Or—has some misdeed of my own, alas!
> Stopped the flowering of plants? My mind's
> bewildered
> in the face of so many possible guesses.

VETRAVATĪ. How could this be, in a hermitage free from trouble, defended by your arm? It is my guess that the sages highly pleased with Your Majesty's noble conduct have come to honour you.

Then enter Kanva's pupils accompanied by Gautamī, bringing Śakuntalā; the Chamberlain and the Preceptor are in front leading the way.

CHAMBERLAIN. This way, this way, honoured ones.

ŚĀRNGARAVA. Śāradvata, my friend:

> Granted, this King of unblemished nobleness
> does not swerve from the path of rectitude;
> true, none of his subjects, even those
> in the lowliest walks of life, resort to evil ways;
> even so, my mind enjoying continual solitude,
> prompts me to view this place thronged with people
> as a house encircled by blazing fires.

ŚĀRADVATA. You have become deeply disturbed from the moment we entered the city. It is understandable, for I feel the same:

> As a man freshly bathed views one smeared with oil,
> as one pure the impure, as one wakeful the sleeper,
> as one who can move freely sees one in bondage,
> thus I, freed of the world's will, regard these, bound
>   to the world.

HIGH PRIEST. Therefore persons like you are great.

ŚAKUNTALĀ (*feeling a bad omen*). O you gods! What means this throbbing of my right eye?

GAUTAMĪ. May all evil be averted; and may happiness always attend you.

They walk around.

HIGH PRIEST (*pointing in the King's direction*). O holy sages! *There* is His Honour, the protector of the four estates; risen already from his seat he waits for you. Behold him

ŚĀRNGARAVA. Most commendable, I grant you, O great Brāhmana; even so, we view it all with an equal eye:

> Trees bend down when laden with fruit;
> rain clouds filled with water
> hang low almost to the ground;
> wealth does not make the good haughty;
> this is the true nature
> of those who do good to others.

VETRAVATĪ. From the serene expression on their faces, it is evident that the sages have come on a mission of goodwill.

KING (*looking at Śakuntalā*). That lady?

> Who may she be, standing veiled, I wonder,
> the loveliness of her form, like a bud
> not burst into bloom, is barely-revealed;
> she appears in the midst of ascetics,
> a tender sprout among yellowing leaves.

VETRAVATĪ. Surely she does appear to be very beautiful, worth looking at, Sire.

KING. Enough, it is highly improper to stare at another's wife.

ŚAKUNTALĀ (*laying a hand on her bosom, speaks to herself*). Why are you trembling, O heart? Remembering the love my lord has for me, calm yourself.

HIGH PRIEST (*coming forward*). Good Fortune attend you, Sire; the sages have been honoured with all due rites. They have a message for you from their Preceptor. Will Your Majesty be pleased to hear it?

KING. I am all attention.

SAGES (*approaching the King, they raise their hands in blessing*). May the King be ever victorious!

KING (*with folded hands*). I greet you all.

SAGES. Good Fortune attend you.

KING. Do the penances prosper?

SAGES.

> While you protect the virtuous
> who dares disrupt their pious rites?
> When the bright sun blazes bright
> can darkness show its face?

KING (*to himself*). By this praise, my title of ruler gains its true meaning. (*aloud*) Is Sage Kanva in good health?

ŚĀRNGARAVA. The well-being of those who have attained superhuman powers lies in their own control. He makes kind enquiries of Your Honour's good health and then addresses you thus . . .

KING. What are the commands of His Holiness?

SĀRNGARAVA. You took her, my daughter, in secret, as your wife; pleased, I have assented to the marriage.

> We regard you as foremost among those of high worth,
> and Śakuntalā is Virtue's embodiment,
> having brought together a bride and groom of equal merit,
> the Creator after a long time incurs no reproach.

She bears your child; so take her as your lawful wife and partner in all religious duties.

GAUTAMĪ. Gracious Sir, I wish to say a few words at this point, though it is not my place to speak.

KING. Speak freely, Lady.

> You did not approach the elders in the matter.
> She did not seek advice from her kinsfolk;
> when it was all agreed upon between you two,
> what in the world can one say to either?

ŚAKUNTALĀ (to herself). What will my lord say now?

KING (listens to all this with his mind troubled by doubts). What kind of proposition is this that is being placed before me?

ŚAKUNTALĀ (to herself). Ha! His words are fire in my ears.

SĀRNGARAVA. What means this? This talk of a proposition being placed before you? Your Honour is doubtless quite conversant with the ways of the world.

> The world suspects even the most virtuous woman as otherwise, when with her husband living,
> the parental home becomes her sole resort:
> hence, her kinsfolk wish that she be beside him who took her by the hand as his wife,
> be she dear to him, or be she not.

KING. Are you saying that this lady is already married to me?

ŚAKUNTALĀ (despondent, to herself). O, my heart, your fears are proving true.

SĀRNGARAVA.

> Is this revulsion from a deed done?
> Or disregard for one's own actions?
> Or turning away from one's duty?

KING. This is a case of proceeding on a wrong assumption.

SĀRNGARAVA.

> Such fickleness generally swells
> and comes to a head in those drunk with power.

KING. I am being taken to task too harshly.

GAUTAMĪ. Daughter, lay aside your bashfulness for a while; let me remove your veil. Your lord will not fail to recognize you then.

KING (gazing ardently at Śakuntalā, speaks to himself with astonished admiration).

> This glowing loveliness that is proffered unsought,
> was this held by me once as my own, or not?
> My mind hovers uncertain, like a bee
> circling at daybreak over the jasmine's dew-filled cup.
> I cannot permit myself to possess it;
> nor can I bring myself to relinquish it.

VETRAVATĪ (to herself). O, admirable is His Majesty's regard for right action. Who else would stop to consider right from wrong, when such beauty comes sweetly on its own and offers itself?

SĀRNGARAVA. O King, what means this silence?

KING. O, hermits, rich in holiness, try as I might, I cannot recall to my mind accepting the hand of this lady in marriage at any time. Seeing that she is plainly pregnant, how can I receive her when I have doubts about being the husband?

ŚAKUNTALĀ (aside). Alas, my cruel fate! Even the marriage is now in doubt; where are all those high-mounting hopes of mine?

SĀRNGARAVA. Then don't:

> Assenting gladly to your seizure of his daughter
> the good sage makes you worthy of such a gift,
> as a robber is offered the goods he seized:
> for this he deserves your refusal—does he not?

SĀRADVATA. That is enough Sārngarava; cease expostulating. Śakuntalā, we have said what we had to say; the King has spoken as he has. Now, it is for you to give a fitting reply.

ŚAKUNTALĀ (to herself). What can I say? When such a love has suffered such a change, what use is it reminding him of it now? On the other hand, I should defend myself and clear my name. (aloud) Dear Lord, (stops in the middle) no . . . my right to address you as such has been questioned. Prince of the Purus! In the Hermitage you deceived me, a simple girl, trusting and open by nature; then you made a solemn compact . . . now . . . to disown me with such words . . . is this becoming of you?

KING (stopping his ears). Perish the sinful thought.

> Why are you out to sully your family's honour,
> and to make me fall; you are like a river
> that crumbles its banks to muddy its crystal stream,
> and uproots the tree growing by its edge.

ŚAKUNTALĀ. If you are proceeding in this manner under the impression that I am another man's wife, I can remove your suspicions by showing this highly-prized token.

KING. A proper procedure.

ŚAKUNTALĀ (feeling for the ring). Ha! I am lost. The Ring is missing from my finger.

Looks at Gautamī, shattered.

GAUTAMĪ. The Ring must have slipped off and fallen into the water when you immersed yourself in holy Śaci's Pool next to Indra's Landing.

KING (smiles ironically). A good example of the ready wit that is womankind's gift.

ŚAKUNTALĀ. Alas, Fate shows its inexorable power. But I shall relate something, an incident.

KING. Ah, now we have something that is to be heard.

ŚAKUNTALĀ. You do remember that day in the bower of canes covered by vines—you held a cup of lotus leaves filled with water?

KING. I am listening.

ŚAKUNTALĀ. Just at that moment, the little fawn, my adopted son, whom I had named 'Liquid Long-eyes' came trotting up. Feeling affectionate towards him, you held the cup out saying, 'let him drink first' and coaxed him to drink. But he would not come near, because you were a stranger to him. When I took the cup from you and held it in my hand, he was happy to drink. And you laughed saying 'One trusts one's own kind, you are both creatures of the woods'.

KING (laughs sarcastically). By such honeyed words are pleasure-loving men lured by young women out to gain their own ends.

GAUTAMĪ. Gracious Prince, you should not speak to her like that. Brought up in a sacred grove, this girl is a stranger to guile.

KING. Ascetic matron, listen:

Intuitive cunning is seen even in females
of lower creatures; what then of those
endowed with reason and understanding;
the cuckoo, as we know, has her young reared
by other birds before they take to the air.

ŚAKUNTALĀ (in anger). Ignoble man! You who are like a well covered with grass . . . you judge every one by the measure of your own heart . . . who would stoop to imitate your conduct . . . practising falseness while putting on the mantle of virtue?

KING. The lady's anger is real—the spontaneous outburst of one who lives in the green world.

Her eyes red with anger look straight at me,
her words flung out harsh, not smoothed into a
                                                    drawl;
her lower lip like a ripe bimba-fruit
is all quivering as if struck by an icy blast;
her eyebrows, graceful curves,
knot together in a twisting frown.

Further, her anger fell concentrated on me whose mind is clouded over with uncertainties. Therefore,

When I cruelly denied our secret love
then did she dart flaming glances on me,
fiercely bending the graceful curve of her brow,
it seemed she snapped the bow of Love itself.

(aloud) Gracious lady, Duhsanta's life lies an open book before his subjects; it's there for you to read too.

ŚAKUNTALĀ. O, so,

You are the sole measure, and you, only you know
the firm Rule of Righteousness for the world;
women, who have set aside their modesty,
they understanding nothing—they know nothing, is
    it?

Very well; so be it; putting my trust in the fame of Puru's lineage, I have fallen into the clutches of a man whose mouth is honey, but whose heart is stone . . . and now, I am made out to be a self-willed wanton. (she covers her face with the end of her veil and weeps)

ŚĀRNGARAVA.

Thus does unbridled impulse destroy a person.
Therefore, a marriage, specially one made in secret
should be contracted after careful scrutiny;
affection quickly turns to hate in hearts
that have known each other but slenderly.

KING. O, Sir, you are hurling words of concentrated anger upon me, relying only on the testimony of this lady here.

ŚĀRNGARAVA (disdainfully). O no, that would be quite preposterous, would it not?

The words of one who from birth
has grown up uninstructed in deceit,
should carry no weight; but those who study
the deception of others as an esteemed art,
are infallible speakers of truth.

KING. O, speaker of truth, supposing we are as you say we are, what is gained, do you think, by deceiving her?

ŚĀRNGARAVA. Downfall.

KING. This is incredible; would the Pauravas court their own downfall?

ŚĀRADVATA. O King, why this bandying of words? We have carried out our Preceptor's orders; we shall leave presently.

This then, is your wife, accept her, or abandon her;
a husband's dominion over his wife is absolute.

Gautamī, lead the way.

The sages prepare to leave.

ŚAKUNTALĀ (calling out piteously). What's this; here I am, betrayed by this cheat; are you also abandoning me?

Tries to follow Gautamī.

GAUTAMĪ (stopping). Son, Śārngarava, here is Śakuntalā following us, wailing pitifully. Cruelly repudiated by her husband, what can the poor child do?

ŚĀRNGARAVA (turning back). You forward girl, are you asserting your independence?

Śakuntalā stops, frightened, trembling.

ŚĀRNGARAVA.

If you are what the King says you are,
what will your father have to do with you—
a stain on his family? But, as you know
your own conduct to be pure, even servitude
in your husband's house will be welcome to you.

Stay here; we are leaving.

KING. O ascetic! Why do you give this lady false hopes?

The moon wakes only night-blooming lilies,
the sun day-lotuses only:
the man with mastery over his passions
turns away from the touch of another's wife.

ŚĀRNGARAVA. Assuming that Your Honour has forgotten past events through impressions created by fresh interests, why this fear on your part of losing your virtue?

KING. Very well, I shall ask you this; you tell me, which is the greater and which the lesser evil of the two?

Am I deluded, or, is she false?
this is the question: should I incur
the blame of forsaking my own wife,
or the stain of adultery, alas,
with the wife of another?

HIGH PRIEST (*after some thought*). Supposing we do it this
way.

KING. Instruct me, Your Reverence.

HIGH PRIEST. Let the gracious lady who is with child, stay in
my house till she gives birth. I shall tell you why I suggest
this: the seers have already foretold that your first-born is
destined to be Sovereign of the World. If the sage's
daughter should give birth to a son bearing all the marks
of sovereignty on his person, then, offering her your felicitations, receive her into your Royal Apartments; if it
turns out otherwise then the only thing to do is to take
her back to her father.

KING. As my revered Preceptor deems right.

HIGH PRIEST. Child, follow me.

ŚAKUNTALĀ (*weeping*). O gracious Goddess, Mother Earth,
open wide and take me in.

(*Exit the sages and Śakuntalā with the High Priest.*)

*The King remains musing over Śakuntalā but his memory
is still clouded.*

(*A voice off-stage*). O, a marvel, a marvel has occurred.

KING. What could this be?

The High Priest enters in great astonishment.

HIGH PRIEST. My lord, something quite marvellous has just
occurred.

KING. What is it?

HIGH PRIEST. No sooner had Kanva's disciples left on their
journey back than:
The young girl cursing her stars,
wept aloud, flinging her hands up.

KING. And then?

HIGH PRIEST.
A flash of light in a woman's shape
from Apsarā Pool, snatched her up
and vanished straightaway.

Everyone is amazed.

KING. Reverence, we have already settled this matter and
dismissed it; what is the point of pursuing it further? Your
Honour may go and rest.

HIGH PRIEST. Be victorious.

(*Exits.*)

KING. Vetravatī, I am deeply disturbed; lead the way to my
sleeping-chamber.

VETRAVATĪ. This way, this way, my lord.

KING (*to himself*).
I have spurned the sage's daughter, it is true,
having no recollection of marrying her;
yet, the poignant ache in my heart validates

it seems, the truth of her assertion that I had.

(*All exit.*)

END OF ACT FIVE
ENTITLED
THE REPUDIATION OF ŚAKUNTALĀ

ACT SIX

Prelude

Scene: Duhsanta's Capital.

*Enter the Chief of the City Police with two policemen be-
hind him, leading a man with his hands tied at the back.*

POLICEMEN (*beating the prisoner*). Hey, you thief! Tell us how
you came by this Royal Signet-Ring with a priceless gem
and the King's name engraved round it in the setting.
Come on, tell us.

MAN (*in great fear*). O, please worthy Sirs, please; I am no
thief, indeed I am not.

FIRST POLICEMAN. O, is that so? Did the King then give this
Ring to you as a gift? Because he regarded you highly as
some distinguished Brahmin?

MAN. Please, Sir, listen to me; I am but a poor fisherman
living at Śakrāvatāra.

SECOND POLICEMAN. You foul thief! Did we ask where you
lived or what you lived by?

CHIEF. Sūcaka, let him tell his story in his own way, from the
beginning, in order; and don't interrupt him, either of
you.

POLICEMEN. As Your Honour commands, Sir. Speak, vermin, speak.

MAN. Well, worthy Sirs, I support my family by catching
fish with hooks and nets and other such devices, Sirs.

CHIEF (*laughing*). A most clean and virtuous livelihood, I'm
sure.

MAN. O Master, do not laugh at my trade.
For it's said, a fellow shouldn't give up
the trade he's born to, however low it may be,
the most soft-hearted of butchers engages
in the cruel job of slaughtering animals.

CHIEF. Yes, yes, go on.

MAN. One day as I am cutting up this big carp into pieces,
what do I see lying in its belly—O Sirs, I see this Ring, its
huge gem flashing. Then, Sirs, as I am hawking it around
here, hoping, of course, for a good sale—I am then seized
by these worthy masters. That's all I've to tell you as to how
I got this Ring. Now, either you kill me, or, you set me free.

CHIEF (*sniffing the Ring*). O yes, it's been in a fish's belly alright;
such a stink of raw fish pours out of it. But—how it got into
that damn fish in the first place—that has to be carefully
investigated. So come; to the palace we must go now.

POLICEMEN. Yes, Your Honour. Move, cut-purse, move it,
quick.

They walk around.

CHIEF. Sūcaka, you two look sharp and wait here for me at the tower-gate, while I go in to the Palace and inform the King about finding this Ring and return with his Majesty's orders.

POLICEMEN. Yes, Your Honour. Go in, Your Honour, where royal favour awaits you.

(The Chief goes out.)

SŪCAKA *(after a while)*. His Honour has been away quite a while, it seems, Jānuka.

JĀNUKA. O you know how one has to wait and approach a king at just the right moment.

SŪCAKA. I tell you, my friend, my hands, they just itch to finish off this cut-purse.

FISHERMAN: O Sir, you wouldn't want to kill someone without good reason, would you now?

JĀNUKA *(looking)*. There is our chief coming towards us with a letter in his hand; that must be the Royal Decree. *(to the fisherman)* Hey you, fellow, you will either make your acquaintance soon with the fangs of bloodhounds or become an offering to vultures.

CHIEF *(entering)*. Quickly, make haste, this . . .

FISHERMAN *(cuts in, terrified, before the sentence is completed)*. O misery, misery, I am done for . . .

CHIEF. Hey you, release him, fellows; release the fisherman, I say. It is now quite clear how the Ring came into his hands.

SŪCAKA. As you command, Your Honour. *(unties the bonds)*

JĀNUKA. You might say that this man entered Death's kingdom and returned, mightn't you?

FISHERMAN. O, Master, I owe my life to you. *(falls at his feet)*

CHIEF. Get up, you, and here, take this; the King has graciously ordered that this reward, equal in value to the Ring, be given to you. *(gives him money)*

FISHERMAN *(accepting it with a deep bow)*. Your Honour, I am most highly favoured.

SŪCAKA. Indeed, you might well describe it as a favour. For here is a man who has been taken off the point of an impaling stake and set on the back of an elephant.

JĀNUKA. Your Honour, the princely reward indicates that His Majesty must set great store by this Ring with its priceless gem.

CHIEF. Hm . . . no, I don't think it was the rare gem that mattered so much to his Majesty.

BOTH POLICEMEN. Then what?

CHIEF. Somehow, I got the impression that the Ring made His Majesty remember someone he had loved very much . . . because, as soon as he saw it—for a moment he was much moved—and by nature, His Majesty is very poised and dignified.

SŪCAKA. A great service has then been done to His Majesty by Your Honour.

JĀNUKA. To this enemy of little fishes here, I'd say. *(glares resentfully at the fisherman)*

FISHERMAN *(taking the hint)*. Worshipful Master, let half of this be yours—drink-money, Sirs.

JĀNUKA. Fisherman, as of this very instant, you have become my very best friend. The beginning of such a friendship should be pledged with some good flower-wine. Come, let us to go the tavern.

(All exit.)

END OF PRELUDE

Scene: The Pleasure Gardens attached to the Royal Apartments.

Enter the Apsarā Miśrakeśi flying through the air.

MIŚRAKEŚI. Having completed my spell of duty guarding Apsarā Pool during the season of pilgrimage to its sacred waters by pious devotees, I have a little time now to see with my own eyes how it goes with the Royal Sage. Śakuntalā is like my own flesh and blood because of my great friendship with Menakā; and Menakā had requested me earlier to do this for the sake of her daughter. *(looking around)* How is it that no preparations are seen in the palace-grounds for the commencement of the season's festivities? And today is the day of the Festival? Sure, I have the ability of knowing all that goes on through exercising my powers of mental contemplation; but, out of respect for my friend's high regard for me, I should see it all myself. Therefore, making myself invisible, I shall stay close behind these two girls who seem to be employed to tend the gardens, and learn what has been happening here. *(alights on the ground and waits)*

Enter a female gardener looking at the sprays of mango blossom; another comes behind her.

FIRST GIRL.
O Mango-Blossom, turning from rich copper
to pale-green! O loveliness
breathed by Spring's first fragrant month!
Hail to you! My eyes have been blessed with a
sight of you,
auspicious harbinger of the Festival!

SECOND GIRL *(approaching)*. Hallo there, Parabhrtikā!* What are you muttering to yourself?

PARABHRTIKĀ. Ah, my friend, seeing the spray of mango blossom, the little cuckoo is intoxicated—mad.

SECOND GIRL *(with joy)*. You mean Spring is already here?

FIRST GIRL. Yes, Madhukarikā,† it is now your time to dance with glancing movements and sing your rapturous melodies.

MADHUKARIKĀ. Let me have your support, dear friend, so

---

* Little Cuckoo
† Little Honey-Bee

that I can stand on tiptoe and pluck one little mango blossom and offer it in worship to the God of Love.

PARABHRTIKĀ. Certainly, if half the fruit of the worship is mine.

MADHUKARIKĀ. O my dear friend, do you have to ask in so many words . . . when our hearts are one, though our bodies may divide us? (*leaning on her friend, she plucks a mango flower*) Ah! How exquisite! Even though this bud hasn't opened its eye as yet, the snapping of its stalk releases a divine perfume. (*folds her hands together in prayer*) O Lord Love! O dolphin bannered God! I bow before you.

> O Mango-Blossom, here, I offer you to Love
> who already holds his bow firmly in his hand:
> may this flower be the most potent
> of his five flower-arrows, to aim
> at the young wives of men who travel far.

(*tosses the flower up in the air*)

Enter the Chamberlain, with a toss of the curtain, and very angry.

CHAMBERLAIN. You there, stop, you impudent girl; what do you think you are doing, plucking mango buds when His Majesty has expressly forbidden the celebration of the Spring Festival.

BOTH (*alarmed*). Please, Your Honour, we had not heard about it.

CHAMBERLAIN. Hm . . . so, you have not heard about it, is it? . . . When even the trees that bloom in the Spring, and the birds nesting in them, seem to have . . . and show their respect for His Majesty's decree? Just look around:

> The Mango has long since put out its wealth of buds,
> but the pollen does not gather golden within;
> the amaranth is all set for blossom-time,
> but the buds still linger, tight-folded in their sheaths:
> though winter is past, the melodious koel,
> strangles in his throat his rich burst of song:
> even Love hovers uncertain, withdraws timidly,
> his arrow half-drawn out of the quiver.

MIŚRAKEŚI. Now there is no room for doubt; the Royal Sage possesses great powers.

PARABHRTIKĀ. Honourable Sir, it is only a few days back that Mitra-vasu, the Inspector-General of Police, sent us both to wait on his sister, the Queen; and we have been detailed to perform various duties here in the pleasure-gardens. That's why we had not heard about all this.

CHAMBERLAIN. Very well; let this not happen again.

BOTH. Your Honour, we feel very curious. If it is proper for people like us to know, can you tell us why His Majesty has forbidden the holding of the Spring Festival, please?

MIŚRAKEŚI. Kings are usually fond of festivities; so the reason must be a good one.

CHAMBERLAIN. Seeing as the matter is common knowledge, there is no reason for not telling you. Has the gossip relating to the repudiation of Śakuntalā not reached your ears as yet?

BOTH. It has, Your Honour; we also heard from the King's brother-in-law about the finding of the Ring.

CHAMBERLAIN. Then there is little left to tell. From the moment His Majesty set eyes on the Ring, he remembered that he had married Lady Śakuntalā in secret and then repudiated her through some strange lapse of memory. Since then His Majesty has been struck with bitter remorse.

> He loathes all beautiful things; to his ministers
> he is not free of access as before;
> he passes nights sleepless, tossing in bed;
> to the queens in the Royal Apartments,
> he extends all formal courtesies, but,
> addresses them wrongly, mistaking their names;
> then, he remains long plunged in painful
>   embarrassment.

MIŚRAKEŚI. This pleases me.

CHAMBERLAIN. On account of the King's distraught state of mind, the Festival has been cancelled.

BOTH. A very proper decision, we'd say.

(*A voice off-stage*). The King, the King; come this way, Your Majesty.

CHAMBERLAIN (*listening*). Our Lord is headed this way; now go, attend to your work.

THE GIRLS. Yes, Your Honour.

Both exit; then enter the King costumed to indicate grief, attended by Vetravatī and accompanied by the jester, Mādhavya.

CHAMBERLAIN (*watching the King*). O how handsome our lord looks, notwithstanding his grief. Those blessed with fine looks always present a pleasing appearance, whatever the circumstances.

> Spurning the splendour of dress and adornment
> he wears a single bracelet of gold,
> now slipping down his forearm:
> the lower lip blanched, scorched by his hot breath,
> those eyes shorn of their brilliance
> by unquiet wakefulness; his form,
> glowing with intrinsic lustre, though wasted,
> scarcely seems so, but dazzles the eye
> like some magnificent gem cunningly fined down
> and polished with exquisite art.

MIŚRAKEŚI (*scrutinizing the King*). No wonder our dear Śakuntalā though humiliated by his harsh repudiation of her, still pines for him.

VETRAVATĪ. Let His Majesty walk on.

KING (*pacing slowly in deep thought*).

> Rudely awakened by penitent grief
> this cursed heart, then insensible
> when my doe-eyed beloved tried hard
> to rouse it from sleep, is now painfully awake.

MIŚRAKEŚI. Ah, such is that poor girl's unhappy lot.

MĀDHAVYA (*aside*). There he goes again; the Śakuntalā-fit is upon him. How on earth do we get this sickness of his treated?

CHAMBERLAIN (*approaching*). Hail, Your Majesty. I have inspected the various spots in the pleasure-gardens; Your Majesty can safely resort to any of them as you please.

KING (*to the attendant*). Vetravatī, go, take this message from me to the Chief Minister, the Honourable Piśuna, and say: 'Having spent a long sleepless night, I feel unfit to preside today at the Court in the Hall of Justice. Let those cases of our citizens that Your Honour has personally attended to, be written out and dispatched to me.'

VETRAVATĪ. As His Majesty commands. (*leaves*)

KING. Pārvatāyana, you also attend to your business.

CHAMBERLAIN. As Your Highness commands.

(*He exits.*)

MĀDHAVYA. That has done it; there are no more flies buzzing around. Now you can relax in peace and enjoy the gardens, so pleasant now with the cold weather gone.

KING (*sighing*). Ah, Mādhavya, my friend, is it not a true and tried saying that misfortunes strike a person all at once through chinks in his armour? Look at this:

No sooner is my mind freed from the darkness
that eclipsed the memory of my love
for the daughter of the sage,
than the mind-born God* chooses this moment
to fit the arrow of the mango's flower to his bow,
O my friend—and strikes me down.

And further

With memory restored by the Signet Ring,
of the beloved spurned without real cause,
I weep for her with remorse and longing,
now that the fragrant month† is here with its joys.

MĀDHAVYA. How dare he, just wait; I shall destroy Love's arrow with this stick. (*lifts his stick to knock down the spray of mango blossom*)

KING (*smiling*). Well done; I have witnessed your Brahminic power. Now find me a pleasant spot, my friend, where I can divert my mind watching flowering vines that resemble my beloved a little.

MĀDHAVYA. Did I not hear you instructing your attendant, Caturikā, saying to her, 'I shall pass the hour in the jasmine bower; bring me the drawing-board on which I had painted Lady Śakuntalā's portrait'?

KING. It is the only way I have to console myself. Well, lead the way then to the jasmine-bower.

MĀDHAVYA. This way, this way, Your Honour. (*they turn around, Miśrakeśi follows*)

MĀDHAVYA. See, here is the bower of the spring-creeper with its marble seat, so secluded, it seems to be waiting expectantly for you, extending a silent welcome. Let us enter and sit down. (*they do so*)

MIŚRAKEŚI. I shall stand here hidden behind the vines and take a look at my friend's portrait; then I can let her know of the great love her lord bears her. (*stands still*)

*Kama or Eros
†Spring

KING (*sighing deeply*). Ah! My dear friend, at this moment, all the events relating to my very first meeting with Śakuntalā pass through my mind. You remember I spoke to you about it; however when I disavowed her, you were not there by my side. But even before that you never once mentioned her name. Did you also forget her as I did?

MIŚRAKEŚI. It is for this reason that the lords of the earth should not allow a companion close to their heart, leave their side even for a moment.

MĀDHAVYA. O no, I did not forget. But after telling me all about her, you said at the end that it was all in jest—that there was no truth to it. And I, having a lump of clay for my brains accepted this. Well, when all is said and done, we have to accept that Fate is all-powerful.

MIŚRAKEŚI. How true.

KING (*after brooding for a while*). Help me, my dear friend, help me.

MĀDHAVYA. Hey, hey, what's all this? What has come over you, my dear friend? How can noble men allow themselves to be overcome like this by grief? Mountains stand firm in the fiercest storm.

KING. O my dear friend, when I remember how distraught my love was when she found herself harshly repulsed, I feel totally shorn of all defences. There she was:

Cruelly spurned by me and starting to follow her kin,
but sternly halted by the command—'stay'—
of her father's pupil, like a father to her,
she turned once again her eyes welling with tears
on me, O so pitiless:
How that look burns me like a poisoned dart.

MIŚRAKEŚI. O you gods! Such concern for right conduct!

MĀDHAVYA. An idea just struck me. Do you think some celestial being has carried off the lady?

KING. Who else would dare touch a chaste wife? I learnt from my friends that it was the celestial dancer Menakā who gave birth to her. My heart tells me that one of her mother's companions took her away.

MIŚRAKEŚI. What is surprising is not that he has come out of a state of blank confusion but that he ever got into such a state in the first place.

MĀDHAVYA. Listen, if that's the case, take heart, Sir. You are sure to be reunited with the lady.

KING. What makes you say that?

MĀDHAVYA. Because no mother, or father, can bear to see a daughter separated from her husband for long.

KING. Ah! My friend,

Was it a dream? A magical vision
of loveliness? A hallucination?
Or, the fruit of my good deeds past,
reward in strict measure, and no more?
It is gone, I am quite certain,
never to return: Wishes?—they have fallen,
all, off the edge of a precipice.

MĀDHAVYA. No, no, don't talk like this. The Ring itself proves that reunions that are destined to happen can come about in the most unexpected manner.

KING (*looking at the Ring*). This thing—that fell from a place so hard to gain—it deserves to be pitied.

> The merit of your good deeds, O Ring,
> was as slender as mine, as we see
> from the reward you gained.
> You won a high place on her fingers,
> whose nails are pale-rose like dawn, enchanting—
> then alas, you took such a fall.

MIŚRAKEŚI. If it had been on any other hand, it would have really deserved to be pitied. O, Śakuntalā, dear friend, you are so far and I alone have the happiness of hearing words so sweet to the ear.

MĀDHAVYA. Tell me, my friend, what was the occasion on which you gave this Signet-Ring to the lady?

MIŚRAKEŚI. He is voicing the same curiosity that possesses me.

KING. I'll tell you, my friend, listen; when I was leaving the Holy Grove to return to the Capital, my beloved asked me weeping—'And when will my lord send for me?'

MĀDHAVYA. And then?

KING. Then, putting the Ring on her finger, I said to her:

MĀDHAVYA. What did you say?

KING.

> Count off each day one letter of my name
> on this Ring; and when you come to the last,
> an escort will present himself, my love,
> to lead you to my Royal Apartments.
> But in blank confusion I acted cruelly.

MIŚRAKEŚI. A charming arrangement, no doubt; only Fate stepped in and broke it.

MĀDHAVYA. How on earth did the Ring enter the carp's mouth as if it were a hook?

KING. It slipped off your friend's finger* when she was worshipping the waters at Śacī's Pool.

MĀDHAVYA. Ah! That explains it.

MIŚRAKEŚI. Is that why the Royal Sage, afraid of committing a sin, began to have doubts about his marriage to our unfortunate Śakuntalā? On the other hand, does a love such as this really need a token of recognition? How can that be?

KING. Well; let me scold this Ring.

MĀDHAVYA (*grinning*). I shall also scold this stick; O stick! Why are you so crooked when I myself am so straight?

KING (*as if not hearing him*).

> How could you abandon that hand
> with its delicate curving fingers,
> to drown in the water, O Ring?
> But consider:
> A mindless thing cannot see perfection—
> How could I have brushed aside my sweet love?

MIŚRAKEŚI. Just what I was about to say; he has said it himself.

*Śakuntalā, a formal way of referring to one's wife.

MĀDHAVYA. Look, why am I always left to die of hunger?

KING (*paying no attention to him*). My darling! Pity this man whose heart burns with bitter remorse from having abandoned you without any cause; let him see you again.

Enter Caturikā with a painting.

CATURIKĀ. Your Majesty, here is the portrait of the Queen. (*shows the board*)

KING (*gazing at it*). Aho! What a beautiful subject for a painting. Just look:

> A pair of long expansive eyes, graceful curves of
>   tendril-like eyebrows
> the lower lip bathed in the radiance of smiles bright
>   as moonbeams
> the luscious upper glowing rose-hued with the sheen
>   of jujube-berries:
> *This*, is her face that seems to speak even in a picture,
> a dazzling beauty bursts forth in streaming rays.

MĀDHAVYA (*looks at it*). O, what a lovely painting, so full of feeling; my eyes almost trip over those ups and downs in the landscape. Expecting it to come alive I am eager to start a conversation with it—why say more.

MIŚRAKEŚI. What an accomplished artist the Royal Sage is; I could have sworn that my dear friend stood before me.

KING. My friend,

> Whatever did not come out right was done again;
> yet this painting but hints at her glowing beauty.

MIŚRAKEŚI. Spoken like one whose love has been strengthened by remorse.

KING (*sighing*).

> Once she stood before my eyes and I spurned her,
> now, I adore her painted in a picture.
> Having passed by a full-flowing stream,
> I pant after a mirage, my friend.

MĀDHAVYA. I see three figures here, all beautiful. Which one is Lady Śakuntalā?

MIŚRAKEŚI. O this poor man has not the slightest inkling of my friend's beauty. Of what use is the gift of sight to him, if he has never seen her?

KING. Come on, guess, which one is it?

MĀDHAVYA (*scrutinizing the painting*). This, I think, as she is painted here—standing by the side of the Aśoka tree whose soft young leaves glisten sprayed with water—the hair-knot having become loose, the flowers in her lovely mass of hair falling off—drops of sweat forming on her face—her vine-like arms drooping limp—the knot of her lower garment coming undone—looking rather tired—*this*, is the Lady Śakuntalā. The other two are her companions, I guess.

KING. You are clever, Sir; do you see here the marks of my emotion?

> Her portrait is soiled round the edges
> from marks left by my sweating fingers;
> and on her cheek where I let fall a tear,
> the paint has swelled and blistered.

Caturikā, the landscape is only partly painted in; go, get my paints.

CATURIKĀ. Sir Mādhavya, will you hold this painting while I go and fetch the paints?

KING. I'll hold it myself. (*takes it from her; she leaves*)

MĀDHAVYA. Now tell me, friend, what else remains to be painted in?

MIŚRAKEŚĪ. I guess he wishes to paint each favourite spot that my dear friend loved to haunt.

KING. See, my friend:

Mālini's stream has yet to be drawn where wild-goose
                    pairs rest on sandy banks,
and circling her, the holy foothills of Gaurī's Parent
                    where deer recline;
Then, under a tree where bark-garments are hung out
                    to dry,
I wish to draw a doe rubbing her left eye against
                    a blackbuck's horn.

MĀDHAVYA (*aside*). The way he goes on, I can just see him filling up the board with scores of bent longbeards.

KING. And there is something else I have forgotten that I had planned to put in—Śakuntalā's ornaments.

MĀDHAVYA. Such as?

MIŚRAKEŚĪ. Something appropriate to a sylvan way of life and to her maiden state, no doubt.

KING.

The Sirīsa blossom nestling at her ear,
its filaments hanging down her cheek; lying snug
between her breasts, a necklace of lotus-fibre
soft as autumnal moonbeams: these are not drawn,
                    my friend.

MĀDHAVYA. Why does the lady appear unduly alarmed and covering her face with a hand radiant as a red lotus, if I may ask? (*looks*) O, yes, I see now; there's that bastard, that honey-looter, that rogue of a bee, coveting the lotus of her face.

KING. Then why don't you drive the impertinent fellow off?

MĀDHAVYA. Only you can chastise shameless knaves.

KING. Quite right. Hey you, you welcome guest of flowering-vines! Why do you bother to keep whirling around here?

There on that flower sits Lady Honeybee
waiting, enamoured of you, Your Honour;
though thirsty she will not drink
the sweet honey until you join her.

MIŚRAKEŚĪ. The bee has been most courteously dismissed.

MĀDHAVYA. This sort of creature can turn perverse if driven away.

KING (*getting angry*). Yey! You won't obey my command, is that so? Then hear me now:

If you dare bite my love's lower lip, like a bimba fruit,
and alluring as fresh sprouts of a young tree—that lip
I drank so tenderly celebrating love's raptures,
I'll have you shut up, O Bee, in the heart of a lotus.

MĀDHAVYA. Such a terrible punishment . . . yet the fellow isn't a bit afraid . . . (*laughing, speaks to himself*) He is quite

mad . . . and I, constantly in his company . . . I am also going crazy.

KING. What! He has been driven off . . . yet, he hangs around.

MIŚRAKEŚĪ. Ah! How love can affect the steadiest mind!

MĀDHAVYA (*aloud*). Look, my friend, this is just a picture.

KING. *Just* a picture?

MIŚRAKEŚĪ. He says what I was thinking to myself; but, the King was living in a world of his own.

KING. O, what gratuitous cruelty! How could you do this to me?

With my heart wholly lost in her as if she stood
right here before my eyes, what supreme joy was
                    mine;
waking up my memory you have trans-formed
my beloved into a lifeless image once again.

(*he sheds tears*)

MIŚRAKEŚĪ. His behaviour before and now . . . what a strange pattern they weave of inconsistency.

KING. O, my friend, what unrelenting anguish am I being subjected to:

Denied sleep I cannot dream
she is in my arms; and my tears,
they will not let me gaze on her
even re-presented in a picture.

MIŚRAKEŚĪ. You have completely wiped off Śakuntalā's grief at having been spurned, my friend; I have seen it for myself.

CATURIKĀ (*entering*). Your Majesty! I was on my way here with the box of paints . . .

KING. Yes? What happened?

CATURIKĀ. Her Highness, Queen Vasumatī . . . accompanied by Pingalikā . . . met me and snatched the box out of my hands, saying, 'I shall take this to my noble lord myself.'

MĀDHAVYA. And how did you escape then?

CATURIKĀ. While her maid was freeing the Queen's veil that had got caught on a branch, I slipped away.

(*A voice in the wings*). This way, this way, Your Highness.

MĀDHAVYA (*listening*). Ah! Here comes the tigress of the Royal Apartments ready to pounce on Caturikā and gobble her up as if she were a doe.

KING. Mādhavya, my friend, the Queen is approaching and she is very conscious of the high honour I hold her in. You had better look after this portrait and keep it safe.

MĀDHAVYA. Keep *you* safe you mean—why don't you add that? (*picks up the painting and gets up*) If you manage to get away from the entrapments of the Royal Apartments, shout for me in the Palace of Clouds. And I'll hide this where none but the pigeons can get a look in. (*walks away with quick steps*)

MIŚRAKEŚĪ. Even though his heart belongs to someone else now, the King continues to be considerate to his first love, it seems. He is a man of steady affections.

ATTENDANT (*entering with a letter in her hand*). Victory, victory to our lord.

KING. Vetravatī, did you not meet Queen Vasumatī on your way here?

ATTENDANT. Yes, my lord; but seeing me carrying a document, Her Majesty turned back.

KING. Her Highness is well aware of the proprieties; she would take care not to interrupt me in my work.

ATTENDANT. The Chief Minister begs to make this known to His Majesty: 'The work relating to revenues being very heavy, only one civil case could be reviewed. The papers are sent herewith for His Majesty's consideration.'

KING. Here, show me the document. (*the attendant hands it over*)

KING (*reading*). 'Be it known to his Majesty as follows: A wealthy merchant by name Dhana-Vredhi, who carried on a flourishing trade overseas, is known to have been lost in a shipwreck. He is childless and his wealth runs into millions. As of now it becomes state property. His Majesty's decision is awaited.'

KING (*greatly dejected*). Childlessness is a misery, Vetravatī . . . Since he was so wealthy, he must have had many wives. Let enquiries be therefore made if any one of them is pregnant.

ATTENDANT. We are informed, Sire, that very recently, the daughter of a merchant prince of Śaketa had her Pumsavana rites duly performed.

KING. Then in that case, the child in the womb has the right to the father's property. Go, tell the Chief Minister so.

ATTENDANT. Your commands, Your Majesty. (*prepares to leave*)

KING. No—come here.

ATTENDANT (*returning*). Here, Your Majesty.

KING. On the other hand, what does it matter whether there is an heir or not:

> Proclaim thus to my subjects: Whosoever
> suffers the loss of one dearly loved
> shall find in Duhsanta one to take his place
> in all relations deemed lawful and holy.

ATTENDANT. This proclamation shall be made. (*she leaves, then re-enters*) My lord, your proclamation was received with joy by the leading citizens, like rain at the proper time.

KING (*heaving a deep sigh*). This is how the wealth of families rendered supportless by the break in succession, passes to strangers when the life of the head of the family comes to an end. And this again will be the fate of the fortunes of Puru's lineage when my own end comes.

ATTENDANT. Perish such inauspicious thoughts.

KING. A curse on me for turning my back on Fortune when she came to me.

MIŚRAKEŚI. It is my dear friend alone whom he has in mind when he reproaches himself—I have no doubt.

KING.

> My wife by right, the firm base of my lineage,
> abandoned, though I had implanted myself in her—
> like the rich Earth sown with seed in due season—
>   deserted
> before the promise of the rich harvest came true.

MIŚRAKEŚI. She will not be deserted by you any longer.

CATURIKĀ (*aside*). Lady, our lord is now doubly desolated as a result of the Chief Minister sending him that document. Perhaps you ought to go to the Palace of Clouds and fetch His Honour Mādhavya to console His Majesty.

ATTENDANT. An excellent idea.

(*She leaves.*)

KING. O misery! The shades of Duhsanta's ancestors are beset by mounting doubts, wondering:

> 'After him, who in our line will prepare with
>   ordained rites
> and offer us the oblations of remembrance—'
> My washed tears that I, unblessed with offspring
>   pour out,
> the ancestors, I am certain, drink as their libations.

MIŚRAKEŚI. Though there is light, because it is covered, the good king remains shrouded in darkness.

CATURIKĀ. Sire, do not torture yourself any further. You are in the prime of life and there will be fine sons born to your other queens, who will discharge your debts to the ancestors. (*to herself*) His Majesty pays no heed to my words. But then it is the right medicine that can cure the disease.

KING (*overcome by sorrow*). From earliest times:

> This, the dynasty of Puru, pure from its roots,
> descending in one uninterrupted succession,
> will now have its setting in my life, unfruitful,
> like Sarasvati's stream lost in barbarous sandy
>   wastes.

He loses consciousness.

CATURIKĀ (*alarmed*). Courage, my lord, take heart.

MIŚRAKEŚI. Should I not free him now from his grief? No, I had better not. For I have heard the Mother of Gods speak of this when consoling Śakuntalā—heard from her own lips that the gods themselves in their concern for the continuity of the sacrifices and to secure their own share in them, would see to it that before long, her lord welcomes Śakuntalā as his lawful wedded wife. Well, I should not really linger here any more; let me go and acquaint my dear friend with the happy turn of events. That should cheer her up. (*she ascends into the sky and flies away*)

(*A voice off-stage*). Help! A sacrilege, a sacrilege.

KING (*regaining consciousness*). Hey! What's that; it sounds like Mādhavya's piteous call for help.

CATURIKĀ. Sire, I do hope poor Mādhavya hasn't been caught red-handed by the worthy Madam Pingalikā with the painting in his possession.

KING. Go, Caturikā, go and convey my displeasure to the Queen for not disciplining her servants.

CATURIKĀ. As Your Majesty commands.

(She leaves.)

(The same voice off-stage). Help! A sacrilege, a sacrilege.

KING. The Brahmin's voice sounds truly altered by terror . . . Ho there, who's there?

CHAMBERLAIN *(entering).* Your commands, Majesty.

KING. Go, and find out why our little Mādhavya is crying out so piteously.

CHAMBERLAIN. I shall find out. *(he goes out, then returns in great agitation)*

KING. Pārvatāyana, nothing terrible has happened, I trust?

CHAMBERLAIN. Yes, it has, Sire.

KING. Why are you trembling like this? I see you—

Already trembling from age, your limbs now tremble
even more,
like a pipal tree, shaken by the wind blowing through
it.

CHAMBERLAIN. Let His Majesty come at once and save his friend.

KING. Save him from what?

CHAMBERLAIN. Great danger.

KING. Make your meaning clear, man.

CHAMBERLAIN. The palace known as the Palace of Clouds . . . from where one can see far into the distance, in all directions . . .

KING. Yes, what of it?

CHAMBERLAIN.

From its topmost turret which even the palace-
peacocks
cannot fly up to without frequent pauses,
some being, invisible,
has seized your friend and carried him off.

KING *(getting up at once).* Ah! My own home . . . haunted by evil spirits? But it is known that kingship bears responsibility for many offences.

Each day of our own life we slip and fall into error
through negligence that we are unaware of;
how then can we fully know what paths
the life of each one of our subjects takes?

(A voice in the background). Ho! Protect me, here, protect me, here.

KING *(listening, begins to walk fast).* My friend, don't be afraid, don't be afraid.

(The voice in the background). How can I not be afraid . . . when someone is forcing my head back . . . and trying to break my neck into bits as if it were a piece of sugarcane.

KING *(casting a glance around).* My bow, bring my bow.

Enter a female bodyguard carrying the bow.

BODYGUARD. Sire, here is the bow and arrows and your hand-guard.

The king takes them from her.

(A voice off-stage).

Thirsting for the fresh blood that'll gush from your
throat,
I'll kill you here, as a tiger kills the animal
struggling in its grasp: Let Duhsanta who wields his
bow
to free the distressed of their fear now be your refuge.

KING *(angrily).* How dare he address me thus. Ha! Hold, hold, you foul eater of corpses. From this instant you will cease to live. *(stringing his bow)* Pārvatāyana, lead the way to the staircase.

CHAMBERLAIN. This way, this way, Your Majesty.

All proceed in great haste.

KING *(looking all around).* But this place is completely empty.

(A voice off-stage). Protect me, protect me. I can see you, but alas! You cannot see me . . . like a mouse in a cat's paw, I despair for my life.

KING. Hey! You! You who wax arrogant possessed of the powers of invisibility! Do you imagine that my missile cannot see you either? Just wait. And don't be too confident that you can safely hide behind my friend. I am activating *that* missile—

Which shall strike you who deserves to die and save
him,
the twice-born who deserves to be protected,
just as the swan only takes in the milk
and leaves the water mixed with it behind.

Saying this he aims his weapon; then enter Mātali and Mādhavya with him.

MĀTALI. May you be blessed with long life.
The Titans are your arrows' target
by Indra ordained; on them should you bend your
bow.

The noble direct towards their friends
serene eyes and gentle—not cruel arrows.

KING *(de-activating his missile with alacrity).* Ah! It's you, Mātali, welcome, welcome to the charioteer of the Lord of the Immortals.

MĀDHAVYA. Hm . . . so . . . he was about to slay me as if I were a sacrificial beast . . . and here . . . you welcome him with open arms.

MĀTALI *(smiling).* Gracious lord, now let me tell you why Indra has sent me.

KING. I am all attention.

MĀTALI. There is a race of Titans, the invincible brood of the demon Kālanemi.

KING. I once heard of them from Nārada.

MĀTALI.

Destined for destruction at your hands alone
in the battle's forefront, they are inviolable
before your comrade, the Lord of a Hundred
Powers.*

*Indra

Where the Sun with His spreading beams
cannot spring forth to break Night's massed
                                        darkness,
   the Moon appears and chases it away.
So let Your Honour mount the celestial chariot as you are
with your bow ready and strung and ride forth to victory.

KING. I am indeed highly honoured by this singular mark of
Indra's favour. But tell me, Mātali, why did you act the
way you did towards poor Mādhavya?

MĀTALI. Oh, I shall explain that too. I found you deeply dejected on account of some sorrow or other. Accordingly, I
acted to rouse your anger. For:
   A fire stirred blazes brightly,
   a cobra provoked spreads its hood;
   every form of life possessed of energy
   glows into brilliance invariably, when roused.

KING. My friend, the command of the Lord of Heaven cannot be transgressed. So, go to the Chief Minister, Piśuna,
acquaint him with all that has transpired and give him
this message from me:
   Let your wisdom alone protect the subjects while I am
                                away;
   this drawn bow of mine other duties has to accomplish.

MĀDHAVYA. As Your Honour commands.

                                        (*He leaves.*)

MĀTALI. Let my gracious lord mount the chariot. (*the King
does so*)

                                        (*All exit.*)

END OF ACT SIX
ENTITLED
SEPARATION FROM ŚAKUNTALĀ

ACT SEVEN

Scene: *First the celestial regions; then the Hermitage of Mārica.*

Enter *King Duhsanta and Mātali by the Aerial Path,
mounted on Indra's chariot.*

KING. Mātali, although I have carried out the mission entrusted to me by Indra, the Munificent, I feel that I have
rendered him too slight a service to merit that special
welcome he accorded me.

MĀTALI (*smiling*). It seems neither of you feels truly gratified.
   To you those services you rendered Indra,
   Lord of Mighty Storms, look trifling
   beside the high honours you received;
   which He, marvelling at your glorious deeds
   reckons not high the honours He bestowed.

KING. O no, Mātali, that's not so; the honour He did me at
the time of my leave-taking went far beyond my wildest
expectations. Mark you, in the presence of all the assembled Immortals, He made me share His royal seat. And:
   Glancing up with a smile at Jayanta, his son,

who stood beside him longing inwardly for the same,
Hari* placed round my neck the Mandara-garland,
tinged with golden sandal rubbed off his chest.

MĀTALI. What indeed does Your Honour not deserve that
the Lord of the Immortals can bestow? Just think:
   Once before Paradise was rid of thorns, the Titans,
   by the fierce claws of godhead descended lion-like:
   now, once again it is freed by your smooth stream-
                         lined arrows,
   for Hari to savour His pleasures in peace.

KING. But Mātali, in this case, the glory of the Lord of Hundred Powers alone, is to be celebrated.
   Those delegated to perform momentous deeds,
   know them, O Mātali, to succeed
   only by virtue of the high esteem
   they are held in by their masters:
   could Aruna dispel darkness if the thousand-rayed
                              Sun
   did not place him in the forefront as His charioteer?

MĀTALI. Such words accord with the nobility of your mind,
Sire. (*drives the chariot a little further*) Gracious Prince, can
you see from here how the splendour of your fame spreads
across the high vault of the sky?
   With pigments left from cosmetics blended
   for the lovely women of Paradise,
   celestials inscribe on scrolls
   that hang from the Wish-Granting Vine,
   your deeds of glory that form the themes
   for the well-wrought poems they sing.

KING. Mātali, the other day during our ascent into the ethereal regions, I was burning with such ardour to meet and
do battle with the Titans that I did not pay much attention to the Celestial Path we were traversing. So, tell me,
which of the Paths of the Seven Winds are we on now?

MĀTALI.
   The Path of the Wind Pravaha, hallowed
   by Visnu's wide-stepping second stride,
   and free of all worldly taints:
   its current bears along the Triple-Streamed Gangā
   —her home and resting place the firmament—
   and propels on their circling course
   the luminous orbs of the sky, spraying
   their beams of light evenly around.

KING. No wonder then that my inmost being and my out-
ward-looking senses as well experience such tranquillity.
(*looking down at the wheels*) We have descended into the
Path of the Clouds, I believe, Mātali.

MĀTALI (*smiling*). How do you know that?

KING.
   The rims of the wheels glisten misted with spray;
   cataka birds dart in and out through their spokes;

*Indra

the horses gleam bathed by flickers of lightning;
it is clear that your chariot now rides
over clouds whose bellies are swollen with rain.

MĀTALI. In an instant Your Honour will be landing on the
Earth that you rule over.

KING (*looking down again*). Mātali, see with what rapidity we
are descending; the world of mortals presents a most marvellous sight. Look:

As the mountains rear upwards, the land climbs
precipitately down their great peaks, it seems;
trees whose forms were merged within the dense
leafage
emerge distinct as their branching shoulders
thrust into view; those fine lines display themselves
as great rivers brimming with water:
see how the Earth looms at my side
as if some mighty hand had flung her up to me.

MĀTALI. An acute observation, Sire. (*looking down with profound admiration*) O, what enchanting beauty is this, of
the Earth!

KING. Mātali, what range of mountains is that, glowing with
liquid gold, stretching like a bar of clouds drenched in
sunset colours and plunging deep into the eastern and
western oceans?

MĀTALI. That range of mountains, Your Honour, is known
as Hēma-Kūta, the home of Kimpurusas; it is there that
the highest forms of penance are wrought. And listen further, Gracious Prince:

The Lord of Beings, born of The Light
sprung from the Self-Existent Itself,
He, the revered Parent of Gods and Titans,
leads with his consort, here, a life of penance.

KING (*speaking in reverential tones*). In that case I should pay
my respects to His Supreme Holiness before proceeding
any further; such a rare opportunity for receiving blessings must not be passed by.

MĀTALI. An excellent thought, Sire. (*mimes descent of the
chariot*) There, we have landed.

KING (*in a tone of utmost wonder*). How's this, Mātali!

The wheels glide noiseless; no jolting is felt;
no dust is seen whirling around;
they do not touch the surface of the Earth;
nothing marks the chariot's descent.

MĀTALI. This, needless to say, is the difference, gracious
lord, between the chariot of Indra, Lord of Heroic Fury
and that of Your Honour.

KING. Mātali, whereabouts is the Hermitage of Sage Mārīca
situated?

MĀTALI (*pointing with his hand*). There:

Where stands that sage, still as a tree stump
and faces the disk of the noonday sun,
his form half-buried in an ant hill,
with the slough of a snake a second sacred thread,
his throat squeezed tightly round
by twining tendrils of a dried-up vine;

and wears coiled on his head a tangled mass of matted
hair
where birds build nests and dishevel strands
that fall loose about his shoulders.

KING. I humbly bow to you, O Practiser of Cruel Penance!

MĀTALI (*pulling in the reins*). Now, gracious lord, we are entering the Hermitage of the Lord of Beings, where the
holy Aditi, his consort, tends the young Mandāra trees
herself.

KING. O wondrous! This is a spot far more blissful than Paradise itself, I feel as if I am immersed in the Pool of Nectar.

MĀTALI (*bringing the chariot to a stop*). Dismount, gracious
lord.

KING (*dismounting*). And you, Sir?

MĀTALI. Seeing that the chariot is on level ground and well
secured, I can also get down. (*does so*) Gracious lord,
come this way and look around you; these are the
penance-groves of the Perfected Seers.

KING. I look around at the penance-groves and at the Seers;
and I am filled with wonder.

In groves where trees abound that grant all desires,
air is the sole means of life-support for these Seers;
ablutions for holy rites are performed
in waters that glow with the sheen
of a host of golden lotuses;
meditations are practised in jewelled caves
and restraint in the presence of celestial nymphs.
The Seers here lead lives of penance in this place
that other ascetics seek to win through penances.

MĀTALI. The aims of the truly great soar high. (*he walks
around and speaks in the air*) Venerable Śākalya, how is the
Holy Mārīca occupied now? (*as if listening to a reply*) Ah, I
see; that questioned by Aditi, daughter of Daksa, about
the conduct of a virtuous wife, he is expounding these
truths to her and the wives of other sages? I think we
should wait till the discourse is finished. (*addressing the
King*) Sire, Why don't you stay in the shade of this Aśoka
tree, while I go and wait for the opportune moment to announce your arrival to Indra's Parent.

KING. Yes, whatever you think best.

(*Mātali exits.*)

KING (*indicates feeling a good omen*).
I see no hope for my fondest wish—
yet you throb, O, my arm, all in vain;
Good Fortune once brushed aside
turns to misfortune without fail.

(*Voice offstage*). No, don't do that; don't be so wayward; his
true nature repeatedly breaks out.

KING (*listening*). This is hardly a place for undisciplined behaviour; who is being rebuked, I wonder. (*following in the
direction of the voice, exclaims in astonishment*) And whom
have we here? Just a child . . . he is being held back by
hermit women . . . his strength is certainly not that of a
child.

To amuse himself in play, he pulls
roughly from its mother's half-sucked teat,
a lion's cub; tousling its soft mane
he drags it along by sheer force.

*Enter as described a little boy followed by two hermit
women.*

BOY. Come little lion, come, open wide your jaws; I wish to
count your teeth.

FIRST HERMIT LADY. O you naughty boy, why do you hurt
our animals that we love tenderly like our own children?
Really . . . each day your ways become wilder and more
wayward. The sages have well named you Sarva-Damana.*

KING. Who can this child be for whom I feel an affection as
if he were my own? (*reflecting*) O well, I guess that being
childless, my heart fills with tenderness for him.

SECOND LADY. The lioness over there will spring on you if
you don't let go of her little one, you know?

BOY (*grinning*). O what a shame! I am really scared now.
(*pouts his lower lip*)

KING.

This boy strikes me as the tiny germ
of mighty valour that waits
like a fiery spark for kindling,
before it bursts into a blazing fire.

FIRST LADY. Darling, let go of this little lion cub; I shall give
you something else to play with.

BOY. What is that? Give it to me. (*holds out his right hand*)

KING (*looks in astonishment at the boy's outstretched hand*).
Why, this is incredible, he bears on his palm the mark of
a Sovereign of the World.

With fingers close knit, palms slightly hollowed,
the hand he stretches out in eager expectation
to hold the wished-for plaything, resembles
a single lotus bud, its petals tightly shut,
just prized open by Dawn's first flush of rose.

SECOND LADY. Śuvratā, we cannot fob this child off with
mere promises; so go to my cottage, you will find there a
clay peacock painted in many colours that once belonged
to Mankanaka, the child of one of the hermits. Bring it
and give it to him.

FIRST HERMIT LADY. Very well.

(*She exits.*)

BOY. In the meantime I shall play with this little lion, shan't
I? (*looks at the hermit woman and laughs*)

KING. O how my heart goes out to this wayward little fellow.
(*sighs*)

Blessed are they whose garments get soiled
from the dust of the limbs of their little sons
who clamour in words sweetly indistinct,
to be lifted on to their laps, and for no reason
laugh to reveal glimpses of their budding teeth.

*All-Tamer

HERMIT LADY (*shaking her forefinger at the child*). Very well,
so you won't listen to me. (*turns around to look for help*) Is
any one of the younger hermits around? (*notices the King*)
Gracious Sir, please come and free this little lion cub
from the iron grip of this small boy who takes a childish
pleasure in tormenting it.

KING (*approaches, smiling*). Listen, son of a great sage:
Why do you act in this wanton manner
alien to the life of a hermitage
where the spirit finds its tranquil home?
Why do you flout that rule of gentleness
towards all living things,
like the young of a black serpent that spoils
for other creatures, the pleasant sanctuary
that is the fragrant sandalwood tree?

HERMIT LADY. Gracious Sir, he is not the son of a sage.

KING. His actions that suit his appearance proclaim loudly
that he is not. But meeting him in a place such as this, I
thought he might be. (*doing what was requested of him, the
King feels the touch of the child, and speaks to himself*)
If such pleasure can thrill through my whole body
from a touch of this child—a stranger's offspring—
what bliss must he not then bring to the heart
of the lucky man from whose loins he has sprung?

HERMIT LADY. How extraordinary! O, it is a marvel . . .

KING. What is?

HERMIT LADY. The likeness, Gracious Sir; the likeness of
this boy's appearance to yours, even though you are not
related. It astonishes me. Further, wild as he is, he does
not shy away from you who are a stranger to him; I am
amazed by that.

KING (*fondling the child*). If he is not the son of a hermit, to
which family does he belong?

HERMIT LADY. Puru's family.

KING (*to himself*). The same as mine? That *is* strange. Therefore the noble lady fancies a resemblance between us. It's
true though that the descendants of Puru observe one last
family vow.

As rulers of the earth they wish to pass
in mansions abounding in sensuous delights
their early years: thereafter they make
the roots of trees their home and live
bound by the hermit's single vow.

(*aloud*) But mortals cannot reach these regions on their
own, noble lady.

HERMIT LADY. Yes, Gracious Sir; what you say is true. But
this boy's mother related as she was to an *apsarā*, gave
birth to him here in this Hermitage presided over by the
Father of the Immortals.

KING (*aside*). My hopes are stirred a second time running.
(*aloud*) And the name of the Royal Sage whose wife his
noble mother is, if I may ask?

HERMIT LADY. Who would ever think of even uttering the
name of one who abandoned his lawful wife.

KING (*to himself*). The remark points straight at me, I'm

afraid. If I could only ask the name of the boy's mother. (*reflecting*) No, I shouldn't. It is highly improper to exhibit curiosity about another man's wife.

Enter the other hermit woman with the clay peacock in her hand.

HERMIT LADY. Look, Sarva-Damana, see how pretty the *śakunta** is.

BOY (*looking around*). Mamma, Mamma, where is she?

Both women laugh.

FIRST LADY. So fond is he of his mother that the similarity in sound of the two words has misled him.

SECOND LADY. Darling, she means this clay peacock; she was pointing out to you how pretty the toy is.

KING (*to himself*). So, his mother's name is Śakuntalā; but it is not an uncommon name. Will these events turn out after all to be a mirage that will lead me into further misery?

BOY. Yes, dear Aunt, it is; I like this pretty peacock. (*takes the toy from her*)

HERMIT LADY (*in great alarm*). Look, look, what has happened, great gods; the protective amulet—it is not on his wrist . . .

KING. O, please don't be alarmed, worshipful ladies; here it is. It must have slipped off during his playful scuffle with the lion cub.

Stoops to pick it up.

BOTH LADIES. No, no, don't, don't touch it . . . that is very strange . . . he has picked it up. (*they clasp their hands on their bosoms and stare at each other in amazement*)

KING. Why did you ask me not to touch it?

FIRST LADY. Illustrious monarch, listen: this is an amulet of divine power, made out of a herb of immense virtue, named 'Invincible'; and it was tied on the child's wrist at the time of his natal rites, by His Holiness Mārica. If it falls on the ground, no one except himself or his parents can safely pick it up.

KING. And if someone else does?

FIRST LADY. It is transformed at once into a serpent that bites him.

KING. And have you worthy ladies seen this happen, with your own eyes?

BOTH. Many times.

KING (*overcome with joy*). How can I not rejoice with my whole heart that this moment, my heart's desire has at last found its fulfilment.

He embraces the child.

SECOND LADY. Śuvratā, come, let us go straight to Śakuntalā

who is engaged in the unfailing performance of her ritual vows and inform her of all that has happened.

(*Both exit.*)

BOY. Let me go, let me go; I wish to go to my Mamma.

KING. My little son, we shall both go together to your mother and make her happy, shall we?

BOY. You are not my father; Duhsanta is my father.

KING (*with a smile*). His hot rebuttal is the last bit of proof I need.

Enter Śakuntalā with her hair done in a single braid.

ŚAKUNTALĀ. Even after I was told that Sarva-Damana's amulet did not turn immediately into a serpent, I was afraid to believe that good fortune would greet me again . . . but I do remember Miśrakeśi mentioning something that hinted at just such a possibility.

KING (*sees Śakuntalā*). Ha! Here is Lady Śakuntalā . . . it is she . . .

> Dressed in dusky garments
> her face fined thin from observing strictest vows,
> her hair bound in a single braid; pure, upright,
> she keeps the long vow of cruel separation
> from me who acted so heartless to her.

ŚAKUNTALĀ (*seeing the King pale with remorse*). This does not seem to be my noble lord. Who then is this man? Defiling by his embrace my child who was protected by the sanctified amulet?

BOY (*running to his mother*). Dearest Mamma, here is some stranger who calls me his little son.

KING. My beloved, the cruelty I showed you has come full circle now; it is I who have to plead now to be recognized by you.

ŚAKUNTALĀ (*to herself*). Take courage, O my heart; envious Fate seems to have relented at last; this is indeed my noble lord.

KING. Dear love:

> The light of memory has pierced through
> the sightless night of my dark delusion;
> by Fortune's grace, you now stand before me,
> O Lady of the most gracious face!
> Like Rohini in conjunction with the Moon
> appearing at the end of an eclipse.

ŚAKUNTALĀ. Hail! Vic. . . . (*breaks off in the middle, her voice choked by tears*)

KING.

> Though the greeting of 'victory'
> was strangled by your tears, I have more than won—
> for my eyes have looked upon your face
> with their pale, unadorned, parted lips.

BOY. Who is this, Mamma, who is this?

ŚAKUNTALĀ. Ask your fortunes, my little one. (*weeps bitterly*)

KING.

> Cast off from your heart, O lovely lady,
> the bitter pain of cruel rejection, believe

*A bird

that some strange overpowering blank confusion
took hold of my heart on that fateful day.
Place a wreath on a blind man's brows
and he tears it off, fearing it to be a snake:
It so happens that minds wrought upon by utter
                    darkness
meet the good and beautiful with a perverse response.

With these words, the King falls at her feet.

ŚAKUNTALĀ. O my lord, rise. It must be that I had to reap
the consequences of some wrongdoing on my part in a
former birth; otherwise how could my noble lord, so compassionate by nature, have acted in such an unfeeling
manner towards me.

The King rises.

ŚAKUNTALĀ. How did the memory of this most unhappy
person return to you, my lord?
KING. Once I have plucked this wounding dart of grief from
my heart, I shall tell you all.
    O fair lady! The tear drop that once stood
    trembling on your lower lip
    —and I watched uncaring, lost in delusion—
    while it still clings to your gently-curving lashes,
    I shall now wipe away, my beloved,
    to free myself of remorse.
ŚAKUNTALĀ (*as he wipes away her tears, notices the Ring*). O
my lord, this is the Ring.
KING. Yes, and it was its amazing recovery that restored my
memory.
ŚAKUNTALĀ. Where I failed in convincing my lord, this
thing has succeeded and done just that.
KING. Then let the vine receive once more the blossom that
is the symbol of its union with the springtime.
ŚAKUNTALĀ. No, no, my lord, I don't trust it. Let my lord
wear it himself.

Enter Mātali.

MĀTALI. Indeed, Fortune has blessed you, gracious lord, by
granting you the happiness of meeting again your lawful
wife and of seeing the face of your son.
KING. My cherished desires have more than amply borne
fruit because their fulfilment has been brought about
through the aid of my friend. Mātali, tell me, do you
think that the Destroyer of Darkness* knew this would
happen?
MĀTALI (*with a smile*). What is beyond the knowing of the
Lords of the Universe? Come, Sir, His Holiness Mārīca is
waiting to receive you.
KING. Dearest, hold our child, I wish to present myself before His Holiness with you leading the way.
ŚAKUNTALĀ. I feel that it is indecorous to appear before elders in the company of my husband.

*Indra

KING. It is the proper way of doing things on auspicious occasions; come, my love.

*All turn around. Then Mārīca is seen enthroned with
Aditi by his side.*

MĀRĪCA (*seeing the King*). O Daughter of Daksa!
    Here is the one who is in the forefront of your
                 son's battles
    He, called Duhsanta, is Lord of the Earth; because
               of his bow,
    the myriad-pointed thunderbolt of the Lord of
      Riches*
    giving up its office has become a mere ornament.
ADITI. His mien does proclaim his greatness.
MĀTALI. Lord of the Earth! The Parents of the Universe re-
gard you with eyes that reveal the affection for a son. Ap-
proach them, Your Honour.
KING. Mātali:
    Is this The Twain sprung from Daksa and Marici,
          but one remove from the Creator.
    Whom the seers extol as The Cause of The Efful-
      gence
          that manifests Itself in Twelve Forms,
    Who begat The Protector of the Triple-World and
          Ruler of the gods offered oblations,
    in Whom the World's Self, higher even than the Self-
          Born placed Itself to be born into the world.
MĀTALI. Who else?
KING (*prostrates himself before them*). I, Duhsanta, ever the
servant of Indra, humbly bow before you both.
MĀRĪCA. My son, long may you protect the Earth.
ADITI. Be invincible in battle, my child.

Śakuntalā with her son falls at their feet.

MĀRĪCA. Daughter,
    With a husband the equal of The Breaker of Dark
    Clouds*
    With a son like his son, Jayanta, no other blessing
    fits you but this: Be the equal of Paulomi.
ADITI. My child, may you always be highly esteemed by your
lord; and your little son live long and be the ornament to
both your families. Sit down here.

All sit down.

MĀRĪCA (*pointing to each in turn*).
    Here, Śakuntalā, the virtuous wife,
    here, your fine son and here Your Honour:
    Faith, Promise, Performance—
    The three have happily come together.
KING. Supreme Holiness! This is indeed an unprecedented
favour that you have granted us now—first comes the fulfilment of our wishes, then, the gracious sight of Your Holiness. As a rule, Holiness:

*Indra

The flower appears first, then the fruit,
dense clouds gather followed by rain,
this is the law of cause and effect:
but good fortune has preceded your grace.

MĀTALI. Long-Lived Majesty! This is the way the Parents of the Universe bestow their blessings.

KING. Supreme Holiness! Having married your handmaid here by the rites of mutual love, I cruelly repudiated her because of an unfortunate lapse of memory, when her kinsfolk brought her to me after a period of time; and in so doing, I have gravely wronged your kinsman, His Holiness, Kanva. Subsequently, on seeing this Ring, I realized that I had in fact married her. All this strikes me as most strange:

Just as a man sees an elephant pass by
before his very eyes but doubts its existence,
then, noticing its footprints, ceases to doubt,
such changes has my mind passed through.

MĀRĪCA. You have reproached yourself sufficiently, my son. The delusion you were labouring under was quite natural. Listen to what I have to say.

KING. I am all attention.

MĀRĪCA. The moment Menakā flew in from Apsara Pool and came to Aditi, bearing Śakuntalā grief-stricken on account of her repudiation, I knew from meditating upon it that this unhappy girl, your partner in religious rites, had been repulsed by you under the influence of Durvāsā's curse. And, that the effect of the curse would cease as soon as you saw this Ring.

KING (sighing with relief). Then I am free from blame.

ŚAKUNTALĀ (to herself). Thank my good stars! My lord did not really wish to spurn me. He did so only because he had forgotten all about me . . . But . . . I have no recollection of ever having been cursed. Or . . . is it possible that being absent-minded on account of the separation from my husband, I was oblivious of a curse? I wonder if that was why my friends asked me to be sure and present the Ring to my lord.

MĀRĪCA (addressing Śakuntalā). Dear child, you know all the facts now. Therefore do not harbour any feelings of resentment towards your partner in all religious rites. Remember that:

You were harshly repulsed by your Lord
when the curse clouded darkly his memory;
now that the darkness has lifted,
sovereignty over him is yours.
Tarnished by grime, the mirror's surface
returns no image; polished, its brightness reflects one.

KING. It is as Your Holiness observes.

MĀRĪCA. My son, I trust you have greeted with joy your son born of Śakuntalā; I have myself performed the birth rite and all other sacraments for him.

KING. Supreme Holiness, the enduring glory of my line rests with him.

MĀRĪCA. Yes, that shall be. O King who will live for many years, know this—he will be a Sovereign of the World. Know this too:

Crossing the oceans in a chariot gliding smooth,
he shall conquer and rule unopposed
the rich Earth with her seven continents:
named All-Tamer here, because he subdues all
                                                    creatures
by his strength, the future will see his name
proclaimed Bharata: He who bears the world.

KING. When Your Divine Self has performed all the sacraments for him, all this and more may be expected of him.

ADITI. Divine Lord, should the venerable Sage Kanva not be informed in detail of all the events that has led to the fulfilment of his daughter's hopes and wishes? Menakā, out of love for her daughter, has been living here, attending on us, and knows it all.

ŚAKUNTALĀ. Her Holiness has put in words the longings of my heart.

MĀRĪCA. By the Divine Vision acquired through penance, everything that has happened is present to the eyes of His Reverence Kanva. (on reflection) Even so, it is our obligation to formally acquaint the Sage with the happy turn of events. Ho there, is anyone there?

Enter a disciple.

DISCIPLE. Supreme Holiness! Here I am.

MĀRĪCA. Gālava, my son, go by the Aerial Path at once to His Reverence, Kanva and convey my joyful message to him: that, on the termination of the curse, Śakuntalā with her son has been duly received by Duhsanta, whose memory has been restored.

DISCIPLE. Your command shall be carried out at once, Your Holiness.

(He exits.)

MĀRĪCA (to the King). My son, you too should mount the chariot of Indra, your friend, with your son and wife and return to your Capital.

KING. Your Holiness' command shall be obeyed.

MĀRĪCA.

Honour the gods in full measure
with holy rites and all due offerings;
May the God of gods* in return
bless your people with abundant rains;
Let Time run its round in this pattern
woven of acts of mutual service:
May both the Worlds enjoy Glory and Plenitude
built on such an enduring friendship.

KING. For my part, Divine Holiness, I shall strive to the best of my power to establish this blessed state.

MĀRĪCA. Is there some other blessing that I may bestow on you, my son?

KING (worshipping him with great joy). If His Divine Holi-

---

*Indra

ness wishes to grant me any further favours, let them be
these:

> May kings ever work for the good of their subjects:
> May the utterance of those blessed by the Word
> be ever honoured:
> May the Self-Existent Lord who unites in Himself
> the Dark and the Light,

Whose Infinite Power pervades this Universe
annihilate forever the round of my births.

(Exit all.)

END OF ACT SEVEN
ENTITLED
ŚAKUNTALĀ'S PROSPERITY

THE POST OFFICE
R A B I N D R A N A T H   T A G O R E

RABINDRANATH TAGORE (1861–1941)

As a poet, author, philosopher, essayist, dramatist, and Nobel laureate (1913), Rabindranath Tagore has earned the accolade of India's premiere man of letters in the twentieth century. As the father of the modern Indian theater, Tagore did much to increase international awareness of the drama of India, and indeed of Asia. Deeply committed to the traditions of Indian theater, especially Sanskrit drama (Kālidāsa was his muse), Tagore also brought a new realism inspired by Ibsen and Chekhov to his country's drama even as he wrote his mystic allegories.

Born in Calcutta to a distinguished family who devoted themselves to the arts, Tagore received a classical education and was writing acclaimed poetry by the age of 16. His family lived on a houseboat on the rivers of Bengal, where he learned the "wholeness of life" in the bend of the river, a wedding ceremony under the great trees along the river, and in the marketplaces and temples of the villages. His plays also reflect his love of Indian music, which is at once sad and suddenly happy.

As a young man Tagore traveled extensively in England (where he lived for several years), Ireland, Europe, the United States, Japan, and China. He absorbed much from these international experiences, but he always considered himself foremost an Indian who desired to speak first to his countrymen (coincidentally, he composed India's national anthem). He wrote in his native Bengali tongue and is still recognized as the finest writer in that language; later he translated his work into English.

Although he excelled in a variety of literary arts, particularly lyric poetry, he was a prolific dramatist (over 50 plays) as well as an actor and a director. Most of his plays were performed by his extended family in a large bungalow called Jorasanko House in North Calcutta. He also founded a theater school on his estate, Santiniketan ("the home of peace"). His theater fused Sanskrit methods, Bengal folk opera (*Jatra*), and the experimental theater of Europe to create an eclectic, innovative drama previously unseen in India. Although *The Post Office* is an exception, most of his plays contain much song, mime, and dance that create a mystic aura in such plays as *The King of the Dark Chamber* (1924). They are intended to be performed on a bare stage decorated only with a few well-chosen, symbolic properties. His dialogue melds lyrical poetry and colloquial speech to create a heightened realism. Late in his career, Tagore created almost exclusively dance dramas more typical of the Indian tradition; *Chitrangada* (1936) and *Shyama* (1939) represent the best of these.

Like the ancient philosopher-priest Bharata, Tagore believed drama has been created to instruct contemporary audiences in the moral and spiritual values of India's ancient civilization. His collected short stories (94) and plays frequently expose social tyranny, economic inequities, and the injustices of the caste system (which he satirizes in *The Kingdom of the Cards*). Like Ibsen, whose *A Doll's House* moved him greatly, Tagore was committed to a "purposive art" that would change society, and his writings did much to prepare the way for Mahatma Gandhi and India's liberation movement in 1947. Yet Tagore's social and psychological themes were more than attempts at modernity in his writing; they were the most recent acts in the unfolding drama of the human story.

THE POST OFFICE (1911)

The Post Office belongs to the *Gitanjali* ("Song of Offerings") period of Tagore's literary career, a time in which he meditated on death and a mysterious beckoning from "the far-off." While living on the banks of a Bengal river as a child, Tagore heard the plaintive call of a man to the boatman: "Lead me across to the other side." The line inspired his writing and thinking for decades because he considered it an ideal metaphor for life's great journey. In this symbolic play, the child Amal prepares for just such a journey.

The story is quite simple: Amal, an orphan adopted by Madhav, is dangerously ill and his physician confines him to a room free from the sun and the breezes. The child watches life pass before him, largely in the guise of three colorful characters (one of them the ubiquitous trickster of world theater) who inspire him to pursue the fullness of life despite his solitude. As the provincial government builds a new post office near his home, Amal imagines that the king's postman will bring a letter to him from the king himself.

The letter that Amal has created in his fertile imagination is the key symbol of the play. Because it comes from a distant and mysterious land and it is written by a powerful being whom Amal holds dear, the letter is a bridge between the known world and the unknown, the two spheres of existence that Tagore attempted to reconcile in his writing. To Amal, the postman is a privileged person who establishes a communion between the two worlds of seclusion (Amal's room) and freedom (the distant land about which he can only dream).

When Amal falls into a deep sleep, he dreams that he, too, will become a postman for the king, carrying the message of "the mighty one" from place to place. However, the message is not written with ink on paper. In Tagore's universe of the All (the totality of the cosmos), it comes from "the foot of the mountain [where] the waterfall becomes a stream." The great messenger is Nature itself, where, according to the poet-dramatist, humans are most at home. Trapped in his sunless room, Amal is liberated when his imagination gives over to the healing power of Nature.

Love is the other great healer in Tagore's work, for it is human love that is the prelude to love for the All. At the end of the play little Sudha, the flower girl, brings a bouquet to the sleeping Amal. She leaves the flowers with the play's final words, "Tell him Sudha has not forgotten him." The simple line reverberates with multiple meanings, as does the play itself.

Although *The Post Office* was written early in the twentieth century, Tagore hearkens back to the classical rasas of Sanskrit drama to construct a drama in "the pathetic mode." But the pathetic does not derive from Amal's impending death, for death in this play is a symbolic release from the spiritual bondage of the human soul. Regarded as such, the play is uplifting and joyous. Tagore himself addressed this theme in a letter to his friend, C. F. Andrews:

> Amal represents the man whose soul has received the call of the open road. . . . At last the closed gate [his room] is opened by the King's own physician [the imaginary postman], and that which is 'death' to the world of hoarded wealth and certified creeds brings him awakening in the world of spiritual freedom.

The pathos stems from the realization that humans fail to appreciate the fullness of life until they are trapped in the "sunless rooms" of their existence. It is a theme that Samuel Beckett often explores in such tragicomedies as *Waiting for Godot* and *Rockaby* (see Chapter 7).

Two production notes deserve inclusion here. First, the play was initially performed in an outdoor setting by and for schoolboys at Santiniketan. Tagore intentionally kept its production demands simple and unobtrusive, fitting for a play that asks that we reject the material things of this world in favor of the All. Second, *The Post Office* received its Western premiere at Dublin's Abbey Theatre in 1914; William Butler Yeats, the Irish poet and dramatist, placed it on a bill with one of his Noh-inspired playlets. The Abbey later took the work to London's famed Court Theatre, the birthplace of many of contemporary England's most political dramas. To audiences expecting to see a new, realistic comedy set in an Irish post office, Tagore's play was perhaps too mystifying, especially as it was performed by the Abbey's actors "in the white garments of the East" as the *Globe*'s reviewer described them. While he admitted he found the play "impressive," he ultimately dismissed it as "too tender, too ethereal a thing for the theatre." Judged solely by Western standards, which are often dictated by commercial concerns, *The Post Office* may indeed be "too ethereal." Yet there is a profundity in its simplicity that both intrigues and gives solace. In an age when scores of self-help books advise us to "simplify" and to not "sweat the small stuff, and it's all small stuff," *The Post Office* remains a beacon of essential truths. It remains a standard in the modern repertory of Indian theater.

Dr. Rabindranath Tagore, a Nobel laureate, is recognized as the patriarch of modern literature and drama in India; from a photo taken in the 1920s.

THE POST OFFICE

RABINDRANATH TAGORE

Translated by Devabrata Mukerjea

THE PERSONS OF THE PLAY

MADHAV
AMAL, *his adopted child*
SUDHA, *a little flower girl*
PHYSICIAN
DAIRYMAN

GAFFER
KING'S HERALD
WATCHMAN
VILLAGE HEADMAN, *a bully*
ROYAL PHYSICIAN

ACT I

Scene: Madhav's house.

MADHAV. What a state I am in! Before he came, nothing mattered; I felt so free. But now that he has come, goodness knows from where, my heart is filled with his dear self; and my home will be no home to me when he leaves. Doctor, do you think he—

PHYSICIAN. If there's life in his fate, then he will live long. But what the medical scriptures say, it seems—

MADHAV. Great heavens, what?

PHYSICIAN. The scriptures have it: —'Bile or palsy, cold or gout spring all alike.'

MADHAV. Oh! get along, don't fling your scriptures at me; you only make me more anxious; tell me what I can do.

PHYSICIAN (*taking snuff*). The patient needs the most scrupulous care.

MADHAV. That's true; but tell me how.

PHYSICIAN. I have already mentioned, on no account must he be let out of doors.

MADHAV. Poor child, it is very hard to keep him indoors all day long.

PHYSICIAN. What else can you do? The Autumn sun and the damp are both very bad for the little fellow—for the scriptures have it:—'In wheezing, swooning, or nervous fret, In jaundice or leaden eyes—'

MADHAV. Never mind the scriptures, please. Eh, then we must shut the poor thing up. Is there no other method?

PHYSICIAN. None at all: for 'in the wind and in the sun—'

MADHAV. What will your 'in this and in that' do for me now? Why don't you let them alone and come straight to the point? What's to be done then? Your system is very, very hard for the poor boy; and he is so quiet too with all his pain and sickness. It tears my heart to see him wince, as he takes your medicine.

PHYSICIAN. The more he winces, the surer is the effect. That's why the sage *Chyabana* observes: — 'In medicine as in good advice, the least palatable is the truest.' Ah well! I must be trotting now.

(Exit. Gaffer enters.)

MADHAV. Well, I'm jiggered, there's Gaffer now.

GAFFER. Why, why I won't bite you.

MADHAV. No, but you are a devil to send children off their heads.

GAFFER. But you aren't a child, and you've no child in the house; Why worry then?

MADHAV. Oh, but I have brought a child into the house.

GAFFER. Indeed, how so?

MADHAV. You remember how my wife was dying to adopt a child?

GAFFER. Yes, but that's an old story; you didn't like the idea.

MADHAV. You know, brother, how hard all this getting money in has been. That somebody else's child would sail in and waste all this money earned with so much trouble. Oh, I hated the idea. But this boy clings to my heart in such a queer sort of way—

GAFFER. So that's the trouble; and your money goes all for him and feels jolly lucky it does go at all.

MADHAV. Formerly, earning was a sort of passion with me; I simply couldn't help working for money. Now, I make money and as I know it is all for this dear boy, earning becomes a joy to me.

GAFFER. Ah well, and where did you pick him up?

MADHAV. He is the son of a man who was a brother to my wife by village ties. He has had no mother since infancy; and now the other day he lost his father as well.

GAFFER. Poor thing: and so he needs me all the more.

MADHAV. The doctor says all the organs of his little body are at loggerheads with each other, and there isn't much hope for his life. There is only one way to save him and that is to keep him out of this Autumn wind and sun. But you are such a terror! What with this game of yours at your age, too, to get children out of doors!

GAFFER. God bless my soul! So I'm already as bad as Autumn wind and sun, eh! But, friend, I know something, too, of the game of keeping them indoors. When my day's work is over I am coming in to make friends with this child of yours.

(Exit. Amal enters.)

AMAL. Uncle, I say, uncle!

MADHAV. Hullo! Is that you, Amal?

AMAL. Mayn't I be out of the Courtyard at all?

MADHAV. No, my dear, no.

AMAL. See, there where auntie grinds lentils in the quirn, the squirrel is sitting with his tail up and with his wee hands he's picking up the broken grains of lentils and crunching them. Can't I run up there?

MADHAV. No, my darling, no.

AMAL. Wish I were a squirrel: —it would be lovely. Uncle, why won't you let me go about?

MADHAV. Doctor says it's bad for you to be out.

AMAL. How can the doctor know?

MADHAV. What a thing to say! The doctor can't know and he reads such huge books.

AMAL. Does his book-learning tell him everything?

MADHAV. Of course, don't you know.

AMAL (*with a sigh*). Ah, I am so stupid! I don't read books.

MADHAV. Now, think of it; very, very learned people are all like you; they are never out of doors.

AMAL. Aren't they really?

MADHAV. No, how can they? Early and late they toil and moil at their books, and they've eyes for nothing else. Now my little man you are going to be learned when you grow up; and then you will stay at home and read such big books, and people will notice you and say, he's a wonder.

AMAL. No, no, uncle; I beg of you by your dear feet—I don't want to be learned, I won't.

MADHAV. Dear, dear; it would have been my saving if I could have been learned.

AMAL. No I would rather go about and see everything that there is.

MADHAV. Listen to that! See! What will you see, what is there so much to see?

AMAL. See that far-away hill from our window—I often long to go beyond those hills and right away.

MADHAV. Oh, you silly! As if there's nothing more to be done but just get up to the top of that hill and away! eh! you don't talk sense my boy. Now listen, since that hill stands there upright as a barrier it means, you can't get beyond it. Else, what was the use in heaping up so many large stones to make such a big affair of it, eh!

AMAL. Uncle, do you think it is meant to prevent us crossing over? It seems to me because the earth can't speak it raises its hands into the sky and beckons. And those who live far off and sit alone by their windows can see the signal. But I suppose the learned people—

MADHAV. No, they don't have time for that sort of nonsense. They are not crazy like you.

AMAL. Do you know, yesterday I met someone quite as crazy as I am.

MADHAV. Gracious me, really, how so?

AMAL. He had a bamboo staff on his shoulder with a small bundle at the top, and a brass pot in his left hand, and an old pair of shoes on; he was making for those hills straight across that meadow there.

I called out to him and asked, 'Where are you going?' He answered, 'I don't know, anywhere!'

I asked again, 'Why are you going?' He said, 'I'm going out to seek work.'

Say, uncle, have you to seek work?

MADHAV. Of course I have to. There's many about looking for jobs.

AMAL. How lovely! I'll go about, like them, too, finding things to do.

MADHAV. Suppose you seek and don't find. Then—

AMAL. Wouldn't that be jolly? Then I should go farther! I watched that man slowly walking on with his pair of worn out shoes. And when he got to where the water flows under the fig tree, he stopped and washed his feet in the stream. Then he took out from his bundle some gram-flour, moistened it with water and began to eat. Then he tied up his bundle and shouldered it again; tucked up his cloth above his knees and crossed the stream. I've asked auntie to let me go up to the stream, and eat my gram-flour just like him.

MADHAV. And what did your auntie say to that?

AMAL. Auntie said, 'Get well and then I'll take you over there.' Please, uncle, when shall I get well?

MADHAV. It won't be long, dear.

AMAL. Really, but then I shall go right away the moment I'm well again.

MADHAV. And where will you go?

AMAL. Oh, I will walk on, crossing so many streams, wading through water. Everybody will be asleep with their doors shut in the heat of the day and I will tramp on and on, seeking work far, very far.

MADHAV. I see! I think you had better be getting well first, then—

AMAL. But then you won't want me to be learned, will you, uncle?

MADHAV. What would you rather be then?

AMAL. I can't think of anything just now; but I'll tell you later on.

MADHAV. Very well. But mind you, you aren't to call out and talk to strangers again.

AMAL. But I love to talk to strangers!

MADHAV. Suppose they had kidnapped you?

AMAL. That would have been splendid! But no one ever takes me away. They all want me to stay in here.

MADHAV. I am off to my work—but darling, you won't go out, will you?

AMAL. No, I won't. But uncle, you'll let me be in this room by the roadside.

(*Exit. Madhav goes out.*)

DAIRYMAN. Curds, curds, good nice curds.

AMAL. Curdseller, I say, curdseller.

DAIRYMAN. Why do you call me? Will you buy some curds?

AMAL. How can I buy? I have no money.

DAIRYMAN. What a boy! Why call out then? Ugh! What a waste of time.

AMAL. I would go with you if I could.

DAIRYMAN. With me?

AMAL. Yes, I seem to feel homesick when I hear you call from far down the road.

DAIRYMAN (*lowering his yoke-pole*). Whatever are you doing here, my child?

AMAL. The doctor says I'm not to be out, so I sit here all day long.

DAIRYMAN. My poor child, whatever has happened to you?

AMAL. I can't tell. You see I am not learned, so I don't know what's the matter with me.

Say, Dairyman, where do you come from?

DAIRYMAN. From our village.

AMAL. Your village? Is it very far?

DAIRYMAN. Our village lies on the river Shamli at the foot of the Panch-mura hills.

AMAL. Panch-mura hills! Shamli River! I wonder. I may have seen your village. I can't think when though!

DAIRYMAN. Have you see it? Been to the foot of those hills?

AMAL. Never. But I seem to remember having seen it. Your village is under some very old big trees, just by the side of the red road—isn't that so?

DAIRYMAN. That's right, child.

AMAL. And on the slope of the hill cattle grazing.

DAIRYMAN. How wonderful! Cattle grazing in our village! Indeed, there are!

AMAL. And your women with red sarees fill their pitchers from the river and carry them on their heads.

DAIRYMAN. Good, that's right. Women from our dairy village do come and draw their water from the river; but then it isn't everyone who has a red saree to put on.
But, my dear child, surely you must have been there for a walk some time.

AMAL. Really, Dairyman, never been there at all. But the first day doctor lets me go out, you are going to take me to your village.

DAIRYMAN. I will, my child, with pleasure.

AMAL. And you'll teach me to cry curds and shoulder the yoke like you and walk the long, long road.

DAIRYMAN. Dear, dear, did you ever? Why should you sell curds?
No, you will read big books and be learned.

AMAL. No, I never want to be learned—I'll be like you and take my curds from the village by the red road near the old banyan tree, and I will hawk it from cottage to cottage. Oh, how do you cry—'Curds, curds, fine curds!' Teach me the tune, will you?

DAIRYMAN. Dear, dear, teach you the tune; what a notion!

AMAL. Please do. I love to hear it. I can't tell you how queer I feel when I hear you cry out from the bend of that road, through the line of those trees! Do you know I feel like that when I hear the shrill cry of Kites from almost the end of the sky?

DAIRYMAN. Dear child, will you have some curds? Yes, do.

AMAL. But I have no money.

DAIRYMAN. No, no, no, don't talk of money! You'll make me so happy if you take some curds from me.

AMAL. Say, have I kept you too long?

DAIRYMAN. Not a bit; it has been no loss to me at all. You have taught me how to be happy selling curds.

(Exit.)

AMAL (*intoning*). Curds, curds, good nice curds from the dairy village—from the country of the Panch-mura hill by the Shamli bank. Curds, good curds; in the early morning the women make the cows stand in a row under the trees and milk them, and in the evening they turn the milk into curds. Curds, good curds. Hello, there's the Watchman on his rounds. Watchman, I say, come and have a word with me.

WATCHMAN. What's all this row about. Aren't you afraid of the likes of me?

AMAL. No, why should I be?

WATCHMAN. Suppose I march you off then?

AMAL. Where will you take me to? Is it very far, right beyond the hills?

WATCHMAN. Suppose I march you straight to the King.

AMAL. To the King! Do, will you? But the doctor won't let

me go out. No one can ever take me away. I've got to stay here all day long.

WATCHMAN. Doctor won't let you, poor fellow! So I see! Your face is pale and there are dark rings round your eyes. Your veins stick out from your poor thin hands.

AMAL. Won't you sound the gong, Watchman?

WATCHMAN. Time has not yet come.

AMAL. How curious! Some say time has not come and some say time has gone by! But surely your time will come the moment you strike the gong!

WATCHMAN. That's not possible; I strike up the gong only when it is time.

AMAL. Yes, I love to hear your gong. When it is midday and our meal is over, uncle goes off to his work and auntie falls asleep reading her Ramyana, and in the courtyard under the shadow of the wall our doggie sleeps with his nose in his curled-up tail; then your gong strikes out 'Dong, dong, dong!' Tell me why does your gong sound?

WATCHMAN. My gong sounds to tell the people, Time waits for none, but goes on forever.

AMAL. Where, to what land?

WATCHMAN. That none knows.

AMAL. Then I suppose no one has ever been there! Oh, I do wish to fly with the time to that land of which no one knows anything.

WATCHMAN. All of us have to get there one day, my child.

AMAL. Have I too?

WATCHMAN. Yes, you too!

AMAL. But doctor won't let me out.

WATCHMAN. One day the doctor himself may take you there by the hand.

AMAL. He won't; you don't know him. He only keeps me in.

WATCHMAN. One greater than he comes and lets us free.

AMAL. When will this great doctor come for me? I can't stick in here any more.

WATCHMAN. Shouldn't talk like that, my child.

AMAL. No, I am here where they have left me—I never move a bit. But when your gong goes off, dong, dong, dong, it goes to my heart. Say, Watchman?

WATCHMAN. Yes, my dear.

AMAL. Say, what's going on there in that big house on the other side, where there is a flag flying high up and the people are always going in and out?

WATCHMAN. Oh, there? That's our new Post Office.

AMAL. Post Office! Whose?

WATCHMAN. Whose? Why, the King's surely!

AMAL. Do letters come from the King to his office here?

WATCHMAN. Of course. One fine day there may be a letter for you in there.

AMAL. A letter for me—But I am only a little boy.

WATCHMAN. The King sends tiny notes to little boys.

AMAL. O how splendid! When shall I have my letter? How do you know he'll write to me?

WATCHMAN. Otherwise why should he set his Post Office

here right in front of your open window, with the golden flag flying?

AMAL. But who will fetch me my King's letter when it comes?

WATCHMAN. The King has many postmen—Don't you see them run about with round gilt badges on their chests?

AMAL. Well, where do they go?

WATCHMAN. Oh, from door to door, all through the country.

AMAL. I'll be the King's postman when I grow up.

WATCHMAN. Ha! Ha! Postman, indeed! Rain or shine, rich or poor, from house to house delivering letters—that's a very great work!

AMAL. That's what I'd like best. What makes you smile so? Oh yes, your work is great too. When it is silent everywhere in the heat of the noonday, your gong sounds, dong, dong, dong: —and sometimes when I wake up at night all of a sudden and find our lamp blown out, I can hear through the darkness your gong slowly sounding, Dong, dong, dong!

WATCHMAN. There's the village Headman! I must be off. If he catches me gossiping there'll be a great to do.

AMAL. The Headman? Whereabouts is he?

WATCHMAN. Right down the road there; see that huge palm-leaf umbrella hopping along. That's him!

AMAL. I suppose the King's made him our Headman here.

WATCHMAN. Made him? Oh, no! A fussy busybody! He knows so many ways of making himself unpleasant that everybody is afraid of him. It's just a game for the likes of him, making trouble for everybody.

I must be off now! Mustn't keep work waiting, you know! I'll drop in again to-morrow morning and tell you all the news of the town.

(*Exit.*)

AMAL. It would be splendid to have a letter from the King every day. I'll read them at the window. But, oh! I can't read writing. Who'll read them out to me, I wonder! Auntie reads her Ramyana; she may know the King's writing. If no one will, then I must keep them carefully and read them when I'm grown up. But if the postman can't find me?

Headman, Mr. Headman, may I have a word with you?

HEADMAN. Who is yelling after me on the highway? —Oh, it's you is it, you wretched monkey?

AMAL. You're the Headman. Everybody minds you.

HEADMAN (*looking pleased*). Yes, oh yes, they do! They must!

AMAL. Do the King's postmen listen to you?

HEADMAN. They've got to. By jove, I'd like to see—

AMAL. Will you tell the postman it's Amal who sits by the window here?

HEADMAN. What's the good of that?

AMAL. In case there's a letter for me.

HEADMAN. A letter for you! Whoever's going to write to you?

AMAL. If the King does.

HEADMAN. Ha! Ha! What an uncommon little fellow you are! Ha! Ha! The King indeed, aren't you his bosom friend, eh? You haven't met for a long while and the King is pining for you, I am sure. Wait till to-morrow and you'll have your letter.

AMAL. Say, Headman, why do you speak to me in that tone of voice? Are you cross?

HEADMAN. Upon my word! Cross, indeed! You write to the King!

Madhav is a devilish swell now-a-days. He's made a little pile; and so kings and padishahs are everyday talk with his people. Let me find him once and I'll make him dance. Oh you,—you snipper-snapper! I'll get the King's letter sent to your house—indeed I will!

AMAL. No, no, please don't trouble yourself about it.

HEADMAN. And why not, pray? I'll tell the King about you and he won't be long. One of his footmen will come presently for news of you. Madhav's impudence staggers me. If the King hears of this, that'll take some of his nonsense out of him.   (*Exit.*)

AMAL. Who are you walking there? How your anklets tinkle! Do stop a while, won't you?

(*A girl enters.*)

GIRL. I haven't a moment to spare; it is already late!

AMAL. I see, you don't wish to stop; I don't care to stay on here either.

GIRL. You make me think of some late star of the morning! Whatever's the matter with you?

AMAL. I don't know; the doctor won't let me out.

GIRL. Ah me! Don't go then! Should listen to the doctor. People will be cross with you if you're naughty. I know, always looking out and watching must make you feel tired. Let me close the window a bit for you.

AMAL. No, don't, only this one's open! All the others are shut. But will you tell me who you are? Don't seem to know you.

GIRL. I am Sudha.

AMAL. What Sudha?

SUDHA. Don't you know? Daughter of the flower-seller here.

AMAL. What do *you* do?

SUDHA. I gather flowers in my basket.

AMAL. Oh, flower gathering! That is why your feet seem so glad and your anklets jingle so merrily as you walk. Wish I could be out too. Then I would pick some flowers for you from the very topmost branches right out of sight.

SUDHA. Would you really? Do you know as much about flowers as I?

AMAL. Yes, I *do*, quite as much. I know all about Champa of the fairy tale and his seven brothers. If only they let me, I'll go right into the dense forest where you can't find your way. And where the honey-sipping humming-bird rocks himself on the end of the thinnest branch, I will blossom into a champa. Would you be my sister Parul?

SUDHA. You are silly! How can I be sister Parul when I am Sudha and my mother is Sasi, the flower-seller?

I have to weave so many garlands a day. It would be jolly if I could lounge here like you!

AMAL. What would you do then, all the day long?

SUDHA. I could have great times with my doll Benay the bride and Meni the pussy-cat and—but I say, it is getting late and I mustn't stop, or I won't find a single flower.

AMAL. Oh, wait a little longer; I do like it so!

SUDHA. Ah, well—now don't you be naughty. Be good and sit still, and on my way back home with the flowers I'll come and talk with you.

AMAL. And you'll let me have a flower then?

SUDHA. No, how can I? It has to be paid for.

AMAL. I'll pay when I grow up—before I leave to look for work out on the other side of that stream there.

SUDHA. Very well, then.

AMAL. And you'll come back when you have your flowers?

SUDHA. I will.

AMAL. You will, really?

SUDHA. Yes, I will.

AMAL. You won't forget me? I am Amal, remember that.

SUDHA. I won't forget you, you'll see. (*Exit. A troop of boys enter.*)

AMAL. Say, brothers, where are you all off to? Stop here a little.

A BOY. We're off to play.

AMAL. What will you play at, brothers?

A BOY. We'll play at being ploughmen.

ANOTHER BOY (*showing a stick*). This is our ploughshare.

ANOTHER BOY. We two are the pair of oxen.

AMAL. And you're going to play the whole day?

A BOY. Yes, all day long.

AMAL. And you will come home in the evening by the road along the river bank?

A BOY. Yes.

AMAL. Do you pass our house on your way home?

A BOY. Come out and play with us, yes do.

AMAL. Doctor won't let me out.

A BOY. Doctor! Do you mean to say you mind what the doctor says? Let's be off; it is getting late.

AMAL. Don't go. Play on the road near this window, I could watch you then.

A BOY. What can we play at here?

AMAL. With all these toys of mine that are lying about. Here you are, have them. I can't play alone. They are getting dirty and are of no use to me.

BOYS. How jolly! What fine toys! Look, here's a ship. There's old mother Jatai. Isn't this a gorgeous sepoy? And you'll let us have them all? You don't really mind?

AMAL. No, not a big; have them by all means.

A BOY. You don't want them back?

AMAL. Oh, no, I shan't want them.

A BOY. Say, won't you get a scolding for this?

AMAL. No one will scold me. But will you play with them in front of our door for a while every morning? I'll get you new ones when these are old.

A BOY. Oh, yes, we will. I say, put these sepoys into a line. We'll play at war; where can we get a musket? Oh, look here, this bit of reed will do nicely. Say, but you're off to sleep already.

AMAL. I'm afraid I'm sleepy. I don't know, I feel like it at times. I have been sitting a long while and I'm tired; my back aches.

A BOY. It's hardly mid-day now. How is it you're sleepy? Listen! The gong's sounding the first watch.

AMAL. Yes, dong, dong, dong, it tolls me to sleep.

A BOY. We had better go then. We'll come in again to-morrow morning.

AMAL. I want to ask you something before you go. You are always out—do you know of the King's postmen?

BOYS. Yes, quite well.

AMAL. Who are they? Tell me their names.

A BOY. One's Badal.

ANOTHER BOY. Another's Sarat.

ANOTHER BOY. There's so many of them.

AMAL. Do you think they will know me if there's a letter for me?

A BOY. Surely, if your name's on the letter they will find you out.

AMAL. When you call in to-morrow morning, will you bring one of them along so that he'll know me?

A BOY. Yes, if you like.

ACT II

Scene: Amal in bed.

AMAL. Can't I go near the window to-day, uncle? Would the doctor mind that too?

MADHAV. Yes, darling, you see you've made yourself worse squatting there day after day.

AMAL. Oh, no, I don't know if it's made me more ill, but I always feel well when I'm there.

MADHAV. No, you don't; you squat there and make friends with the whole lot of people round here, old and young, as if they are holding a fair right under my eaves—flesh and blood won't stand that strain. Just see—your face is quite pale.

AMAL. Uncle, I fear my fakir'll pass and not see me by the window.

MADHAV. Your fakir, whoever's that?

AMAL. He comes and chats to me of the many lands where he's been. I love to hear him.

MADHAV. How's that? I don't know of any fakirs.

AMAL. This is about the time he comes in. I beg of you, by your dear feet, ask him in for a moment to talk to me here.

(*Gaffer enters in a Fakir's guise.*)

AMAL. There you are. Come here, Fakir, by my bedside.

MADHAV. Upon my word, but this is—

GAFFER (*winking hard*). I am the Fakir.

MADHAV. It beats my reckoning what you're not.

AMAL. Where have you been this time, Fakir?

FAKIR. To the Isle of Parrots'. I am just back.

MADHAV. The Parrots' Isle!

FAKIR. Is it so very astonishing? I am not like you. A journey doesn't cost a thing. I tramp just where I like.

AMAL (*clapping*). How jolly for you! Remember your promise to take me with you as your follower when I'm well.

FAKIR. Of course, and I'll teach you so many traveller's secrets that nothing in sea or forest or mountain can bar your way.

MADHAV. What's all this rigmarole?

GAFFER. Amal, my dear, I bow to nothing in sea or mountain; but if the doctor joins in with this uncle of yours, then I with all my magic must own myself beaten.

AMAL. No. Uncle won't tell the doctor. And I promise to lie quiet; but the day I am well, off I go with the Fakir, and nothing in sea or mountain or torrent shall stand in my way.

MADHAV. Fie, dear child, don't keep on harping upon going! It makes me so sad to hear you talk so.

AMAL. Tell me, Fakir, what the Parrots' Isle is like.

GAFFER. It's a land of wonders; it's a haunt of birds. No men are there; and they neither speak nor walk, they simply sing and they fly.

AMAL. How glorious! And it's by some sea?

GAFFER. Of course. It's on the sea.

AMAL. And green hills are there?

GAFFER. Indeed, they live among the green hills; and in the time of the sunset where there is a red glow on the hillside, all the birds with their green wings go flocking to their nests.

AMAL. And there are waterfalls!

GAFFER. Dear me, of course; you don't have a hill without its waterfalls. Oh, it's like molten diamonds; and, my dear, what dances they have! Don't they make the pebbles sing as they rush over them to the sea. No devil of a doctor can stop them for a moment. The birds looked upon me as nothing but a man, merely a trifling creature without wings—and they would have nothing to do with me. Were it not so I would build a small cabin for myself among their crowd of nests and pass my days counting the sea waves.

AMAL. How I wish I were a bird! Then—

GAFFER. But that would have been a bit of a job; I hear you've fixed up with the dairyman to be a hawker of curds when you grow up; I'm afraid such business won't flourish among birds; you might land yourself into serious loss.

MADHAV. Really this is too much. Between you two I shall turn crazy. Now, I'm off.

AMAL. Has the dairyman been, Uncle?

MADHAV. And why shouldn't he? He won't bother his head running errands for your pet fakir, in and out among the nests in his Parrots' Isle. But he has left a jar of curds for you saying that he is busy with his niece's wedding in the village, and has to order a band at Kamlipara.

AMAL. But he is going to marry me to his little niece.

GAFFER. Dear me, were in a fix now.

AMAL. He said she would be my lovely little bride with a pair of pearl drops in her ears and dresssed in a lovely red saree; and in the morning, she would milk with her own hands the black cow and feed me with warm milk with foam on it from a brand new earthen cruse; and in the evenings she would carry the lamp round the cow-house, and then come and sit by me to tell me tales of Champa and his six brothers.

GAFFER. How charming! It would even tempt me, a hermit! But never mind, dear, about this wedding. Let it be. I tell you that when you marry there'll be no lack of nieces in his household.

MADHAV. Shut up! This is more than I can stand.   (*Exit.*)

AMAL. Fakir, now that Uncle's off, just tell me, has the King sent me a letter to the Post Office?

GAFFER. I gather that his letter has already started; it is on the way here.

AMAL. On the way? Where is it? Is it on that road winding through the trees which you can follow to the end of the forest when the sky is quite clear after rain?

GAFFER. That is where it is. You know all about it already.

AMAL. I do, everything.

GAFFER. So I see, but how?

AMAL. I can't say; but it's quite clear to me. I fancy I've seen it often in days long gone by. How long ago I can't tell. Do you know when? I can see it all: there, the King's postman coming down the hillside alone, a lantern in his left hand and on his back a bag of letters; climbing down for ever so long, for days and nights, and where at the foot of the mountain the waterfall becomes a stream he takes to the footpath on the bank and walks on through the rye; then comes the sugarcane field and he disappears into the narrow lane cutting through the tall stems of sugarcanes; then he reaches the open meadow where the cricket chirps and where there is not a single man to be seen, only the snipe wagging their tails and poking at the mud with their bills. I can feel him coming nearer and nearer and my heart becomes glad.

GAFFER. My eyes are not young; but you make me see all the same.

AMAL. Say, Fakir, do you know the King who has this Post Office?

GAFFER. I do; I go to him for my alms every day.

AMAL. Good! When I get well, I must have my alms too, from him, mayn't I?

GAFFER. You won't need to ask, my dear, he'll give it to you of his own accord.

AMAL. No, I will go to his gate and cry, 'Victory to thee, O

King!' and dancing to the tabor's sound, ask for alms. Won't it be nice?

GAFFER. It will be splendid, and if you're with me, I shall have my full share. But what will you ask?

AMAL. I shall say, 'Make me your postman, that I may go about, lanterns in hand, delivering your letters from door to door. Don't let me stay at home all day!"

GAFFER. What is there to be sad for, my child, even were you to stay at home?

AMAL. It isn't sad. When they shut me in here first I felt the day was so long. Since the King's Post Office was put there I like and more being indoors, and as I think I shall get a letter one day, I feel quite happy and then I don't mind being quiet and alone. I wonder if I shall make out what'll be in the King's letter?

GAFFER. Even if you didn't, wouldn't it be enough if it just bore your name? (Madav enters.)

MADHAV. Have you any idea of the trouble you've got me into, between you two?

GAFFER. What's the matter?

MADHAV. I hear you've let it get rumoured about that the King has planted his office here to send messages to both of you.

GAFFER. Well, what about it?

MADHAV. Our headman Panchanan has had it told to the King anonymously.

GAFFER. Aren't we aware that everything reaches the King's ears?

MADHAV. Then why don't you look out? Why take the King's name in vain? You'll bring me to ruin if you do.

AMAL. Say, Fakir, will the King be cross?

GAFFER. Cross, nonsense! And with a child like you and a fakir such as I am. Let's see if the King be angry, and then won't I give him a piece of my mind.

AMAL. Say, Fakir, I've been feeling a sort of darkness coming over my eyes since the morning. Everything seems like a dream. I long to be quiet. I don't feel like talking at all. Won't the King's letters come? Suppose this room melts away all on a sudden, suppose—

GAFFER (fanning Amal). The letter's sure to come to-day, my boy. (Physician enters.)

PHYSICIAN. And how do you feel to-day?

AMAL. Feel awfully well to-day, Doctor. All pain seems to have left me.

PHYSICIAN (aside to Madhav). Don't quite like the look of that smile. Bad sign that, his feeling well! Chakradhan has observed—

MADHAV. For goodness sake, Doctor, leave Chakradhan alone. Tell me what's going to happen?

PHYSICIAN. Can't hold him in much longer, I fear! I warned you before—this looks like a fresh exposure.

MADHAV. No, I've used the utmost care, never let him out of doors; and the windows have been shut almost all the time.

PHYSICIAN. There's a peculiar quality in the air to-day. As I came in I found a fearful draught through your front door. That's most hurtful. Better lock it at once. Would it matter if this kept your visitors off for two or three days? If some one happens to call unexpectedly—there's the back door. You had better shut this window as well, it's letting in the sunset rays only to keep the patient awake.

MADHAV. Amal has shut his eyes. I expect he is sleeping. His face tells me—oh, Doctor, I bring in a child who is a stranger and love him as my own, and now I suppose I must lose him!

PHYSICIAN. What's that? There's your headman sailing in!— What a bother! I must be going, brother. You had better stir about and see to the doors being properly fastened. I will send on a strong dose directly I get home. Try it on him—it may save him at last, if he can be saved at all. (Exeunt Madhav and Physician. The Headman enters.)

HEADMAN. Hello, urchin!—

GAFFER (rising hastily). 'Sh, be quiet.

AMAL. No, Fakir, did you think I was asleep? I wasn't. I can hear everything; yes, and voices far away. I feel that mother and father are sitting by my pillow and speaking to me. (Madhav enters.)

HEADMAN. I say, Madhav, I hear you hobnob with bigwigs nowadays.

MADHAV. Spare me your jokes, Headman, we are but common people.

HEADMAN. But your child here is expecting a letter from the King.

MADHAV. Don't you take any notice of him, a mere foolish boy!

HEADMAN. Indeed, why not! It'll beat the King hard to find a better family! Don't you see why the King plans his new Post Office right before your window? Why, there's a letter for you from the King, urchin.

AMAL (starting up). Indeed, really!

HEADMAN. How can it be false? You're the King's chum. Here's your letter (showing a blank slip of paper). Ha, ha, ha! This is the letter.

AMAL. Please don't mock me. Say, Fakir, is it so?

GAFFER. Yes, my dear. I as Fakir tell you it is his letter.

AMAL. How is it I can't see? It all looks so blank to me. What is there in the letter, Mr. Headman?

HEADMAN. The King says, 'I am calling on you shortly; you had better have puffed rice for me.—Palace fare is quite tasteless to me now.' Ha! ha! ha!

MADHAV (with folded palms). I beseech you, Headman, don't you joke about these things—

GAFFER. Joking, indeed! He would not dare.

MADHAV. Are you out of your mind too, Gaffer?

GAFFER. Out of my mind, well then I am; I can read plainly that the King writes he will come himself to see Amal, with the State Physician.

AMAL. Fakir, Fakir, 'sh, his trumpet! Can't you hear?

HEADMAN. Ha! ha! ha! I fear he won't until he's a bit more off his head.

AMAL. Mr. Headman, I thought you were cross with me and didn't love me. I never could have believed you would fetch me the King's letter. Let me wipe the dust off your feet.

HEADMAN. This little child does have an instinct of reverence. Though a little silly, he has a good heart.

AMAL. It's hard on the fourth watch now, I suppose—Hark the gong, 'Dong, dong, ding—Dong, dong, ding.' Is the evening star up? How is it I can't see—

GAFFER. Oh, the windows are all shut, I'll open them. (*A knocking outside.*)

MADHAV. What's that?—Who is it?—What a bother!

VOICE (*from outside*). Open the door.

MADHAV. Headman—I hope they're not robbers.

HEADMAN. Who's there?—It is Panchanan, the headman, who calls.—Aren't you afraid to make that noise? The noise has ceased! Panchanan's voice carries far.—Yes, show me the biggest robbers!—

MADHAV (*peering out of the window*). No wonder the noise has ceased. They've smashed the outer door. (*The King's Herald enters.*)

HERALD. Our Sovereign King comes to-night!

HEADMAN. My God!

AMAL. At what hour of the night, Herald?

HERALD. On the second watch.

AMAL. When my friend the watchman will strike his gong from the city gates, 'Ding dong ding, ding dong ding'—then?

HERALD. Yes, then. The King sends his greatest physician to attend on his young friend. (*Physician enters.*)

PHYSICIAN. What's this? How close it is here! Open wide all the doors and windows. How do you feel, my child?

AMAL. I feel very well, Doctor, very well. All pain is gone. How fresh and open! I can see all the stars now twinkling from the other side of the dark.

PHYSICIAN. Will you feel well enough to leave your bed when the King comes in the middle watches of the night?

AMAL. Of course, I'm dying to be about for ever so long. I'll ask the King to find me the polar star.—I must have seen it often, but I don't know exactly which it is.

PHYSICIAN. He will tell you everything. (*To Madhav.*) Arrange flowers everywhere in the room for the King's visit. (*Indicating the Headman.*) We can't have that person in here.

AMAL. No, let him be, Doctor. He is a friend. It was he who brought me the King's letter.

PHYSICIAN. Very well, my child. He may remain if he is a friend of yours.

MADHAV (*whispering into Amal's ear*). My child, the King loves you. He is coming himself. Beg for a gift from him. You know our humble circumstances.

AMAL. Don't you worry, Uncle.—I've made up my mind about it.

MADHAV. What is it, my child?

AMAL. I shall ask him to make me one of his postmen that I may wander far and wide, delivering his message from door to door.

MADHAV (*slapping his forehead*). Alas, is that all?

AMAL. What'll be our offerings to the King, Uncle, when he comes?

HERALD. He has commanded puffed rice.

AMAL. Puffed rice! Say, Headman, you're right. You said so. You knew all we didn't.

HEADMAN. If you would send word to my house I could manage for the King's advent really nice—

PHYSICIAN. No need at all. Now be quiet all of you. Sleep is coming over him. I'll sit by his pillow; he's dropping asleep. Blow out the oil-lamp. Only let the star-light stream in. Hush, he sleeps.

MADHAV (*addressing Gaffer*). What are you standing there for like a statue, folding your palms?—I am nervous.— Say, are there good omens? Why are they darkening the room? How will star-light help?

GAFFER. Silence, unbeliever. (*Sudha enters.*)

SUDHA. Amal!

PHYSICIAN. He's asleep.

SUDHA. I have some flowers for him. Mayn't I give them into his own hand?

PHYSICIAN. Yes, you may.

SUDHA. When will he be awake?

PHYSICIAN. Directly the King comes and calls him.

SUDHA. Will you whisper a word for me in his ear?

PHYSICIAN. What shall I say?

SUDHA. Tell him Sudha has not forgotten him.

END

FORUM

"The Formal Characteristics of [Indian] Folk Theatre"

JACOB SRAMPICKAL

A contemporary scholar of theater in India, Jacob Srampickal's introduction to popular theater, especially folk dramas, in modern India not only provides a glimpse of theater practice in that country, it also defines the importance of popular theater throughout the world.

On examining the vast area of folk theatre in India, one is struck by the fact that each state or culture has its own form of theatre. A closer examination will show that despite the different names, languages and styles, they have much in common. As Vatsyayan notes:

A mention of the performing arts of India brings to one's mind the single-bodied and many-armed image of Durga or of Shiva in his form as Nataraja, ever destroying, ever creating newer forms of the dance Tandawa. *These symbols in plastic forms suggest at one level the unified equilibrium, the still centre and at the other, the continual display of energy and rhythm in plural forms. The varied art forms like the multiple arms and hands though distinct and separate are all limbs of the same body, the seeming heterogeneity and multiplicity are different modes of the* Tandawa.

Hence, despite a multiplicity of genres, forms, styles and techniques there are a number of common characteristics.

COMMUNITY-BASED, SPONTANEOUS AND VIBRANT

As is well-known, folk performance is normally part of a community celebration. Everyone in the community, from a child in arms to the great grandfather trudging along supported by a stick, takes part in these night-long performances. They have items in them that appeal to everyone in the audience: poor and rich, literate and illiterate, rural and urban, young and old, men and women. Most of the folk performances are held in village squares around which the community lives. Therefore performances can take on an informal and festival note where families, neighbours, relatives and friends gather together in the evening. As the performances run through the whole night as in

a religious worship, it is not surprising that at times some take a nap and wake up to continue watching in rapt attention.

Participating in a folk theatre performance is like attending a fair in one of the busiest streets of India where a person's body acquires an automatic mobility. For in the vast crowd the individual becomes part of a mass of bodies and moves with the crowd to where the action is. In the same way in a folk theatre performance, no one responds to the performance as an individual, but as part of a mass of people.

Folk theatre has evolved in step with the pattern of people's lives and is connected with seasonal changes, the harvests and festival seasons. In these performances there is hardly any distinction between the audience and the actors. Everyone participates spontaneously. Speaking of the participation of the audience in *Ramlila*, Gargi comments:

If an important dialogue or a message or a decisive sentence is spoken by a principal character, it is preceded by a loud ejaculation by the vyasa (stage manager) bol sia pathi Ram Chandra ki jai (shout Ramchandra's victory) and the audience roars in a chorus the last word "jai" of the vyasa.

Sometimes enthusiastic spectators shout slogans in praise of Ram and the rest of the crowd joins in, stopping all other action on the stage. This flow of audience intervention breaks the monotony, enlivens the spectators and acts as a brake on the speech dialogues. In almost all cases the accompanying cheers, laughter, sobbing, wailing and rapt silence of the audience are clear signs of intense participation. It is a common practice for members of the audience to walk onto the stage to offer a prize or a medallion to an actor. At times the audience may be invited onstage and some of them walk up and perform bit parts spontaneously.

The setting of the *Ramlila* of Ramnagar with different acting areas for the performers allows for audience participation. The scenes are performed on multiple stages, each like an island amidst a sea of people. Dialogues, chants and sound-effects come from different locations offering a magnificent vision— easy, intimate, and multi-dimensional. In *yakshagana*, the characters make their entry, not from the green room, but from among the audience. With the accompaniment of drums and torches, the performers proceed through the midst of the audience inviting them to join in. Here is a description of a *Rashdhari Khyal* from Rajastan in the words of Samar, which could broadly be substituted for any other form:

The actors keep on moving all the time in order to be visible to the audience from all sides. Since the acting area is circular and

(continued)

the audience is seated all round, the actors have no particular place for entry. It has to be done at any convenient point by breaking the cordon of spectators. The musical accompaniment does not sit in a conspicuous place. Their usual seat is among the audience. This intermingling of the accompanists with the audience is perhaps necessary for public participation. . . .

A narrow and compact place for its performance is necessary for public participation. Stage decor is deliberately avoided in order to keep the visibility of the play intact and the stage arena comparatively free from physical and visual obstacles. For example, if a throne is required for a king, any person from the audience can be picked up and the actor can use his back as a throne. Any encroachment or forcible participation by the audience is invariably taken in a sporting spirit.

Clearly folk theatre allows spontaneity and improvisation as against the stringent rules of classical theatre. Often the reactions of the audience are as important as the performers' whims in determining the length and intensity of the performance. Certain forms like the *bhand pather* and *khariyala* of Kashmir are entirely improvised. These have a few traditional themes, but an adept artist improvises the whole show on the spot. In *yakshagana*, there is no pre-meditated prose dialogue. While the *bhagavatha* (stage manager) sings a stanza, the actors dance and when he stops singing they interpret the stanza in the form of a dialogue with the audience. As a result, according to the extent of audience participation, each stanza is elaborated by extempore dialogue. In the *bhavai* forms the relevant songs and verses are selected from traditional stock, but the dramatic dialogue in prose is provided by the actors. Such allowances have made these forms extremely flexible enabling a smooth transition from heaven to earth, from the sublime to the absurd. Actors can comment on a contemporary event even while playing a historical or a mythological role without appearing incongruous. If the village audience grows restless, while watching a long, serious scene, a smart actor turns up in a comic role and justifies his presence by clever dialogues. It is an accepted custom that a folk performance varies from day to day depending on the mood of the actors and more so on the demands made by the discerning audience. Thus it takes full advantage of the live nature of theatre.

Although acting in folk theatre incorporates the suggestions of Bharata in the *Natyasastra*, there is a certain amount of non-theatricality associated with these forms. For example, in *Ramlila* the *vyasa* (stage manager) stands close to the actors and openly prompts them. The actors speak in mono-syllabic or even split mono-syllabic speech drawling the words so that they are stretched and made clear. In a *nautanki* performance, when a member of the audience passes a remark at a character, the actor picks it up and makes it a part of his dialogue. All these are taken well by the audience, even while they maintain a spirit of identity with the characters on the stage. Considering the many possibilities offered by folk theatre in audience participation and spontaneity, Habib Tanvir has observed that it is no wonder that Western theatre experimentalists involved in establishing closer interaction between the actors and audience found a goldmine in the Indian folk theatre.

CHINA

Artistic and Cultural Events

Artistic and Cultural Events

1870–1900:
Golden age
of Peking Opera

1200–1297:
Era of Kuan
Han-ch'ing:
Father of
Chinese
drama

1944:
*The White
Haired Girl*,
revolutionary
drama

c.200:
Spectacular court
entertainments
for Han emperors

1790:
Anhui
acting
troupes
introduce
roots of
Peking
(Chinese)
Opera

714:
The children
of the Pear
Garden perform
plays under
Emperor
Ming Huan;
formal
beginnings
of drama

c. 1650:
Era of Li Po,
dramatist
and theorist;
Women
introduced
to the
Chinese
theater

c. 121:
Shadow
puppets
used in
Shamanistic
rituals

1889:
Missionary
colleges
introduce
western
drama

c. 300:
Entertainments
and jesters
at court

300 B.C.E.	200 B.C.E.	0 B.C.E.	300 C.E.	600 C.E.	700 C.E.	900 C.E.	1200 C.E.	1500 C.E.	1700 C.E.	1800 C.E.	1900 C.E.

Historical and Political Events

1911:
Ching
dynasty
falls;
Creation
of modern
China

618–906:
Tang dynasty;
era of the
"Hundred
Entertainments"

1279–1368:
Yuan dynasty:
Golden age of
Chinese theater

214:
Great Wall
completed

906–1279:
Sung dynasty;
beginnings of
popular theater

1949:
Chang Kai-shek
driven from China;
Communist takeover

c. 500:
Prince Lan-ling
wears mask
in battle: the
first "painted
face"

1966–1976:
Cultural Revolution

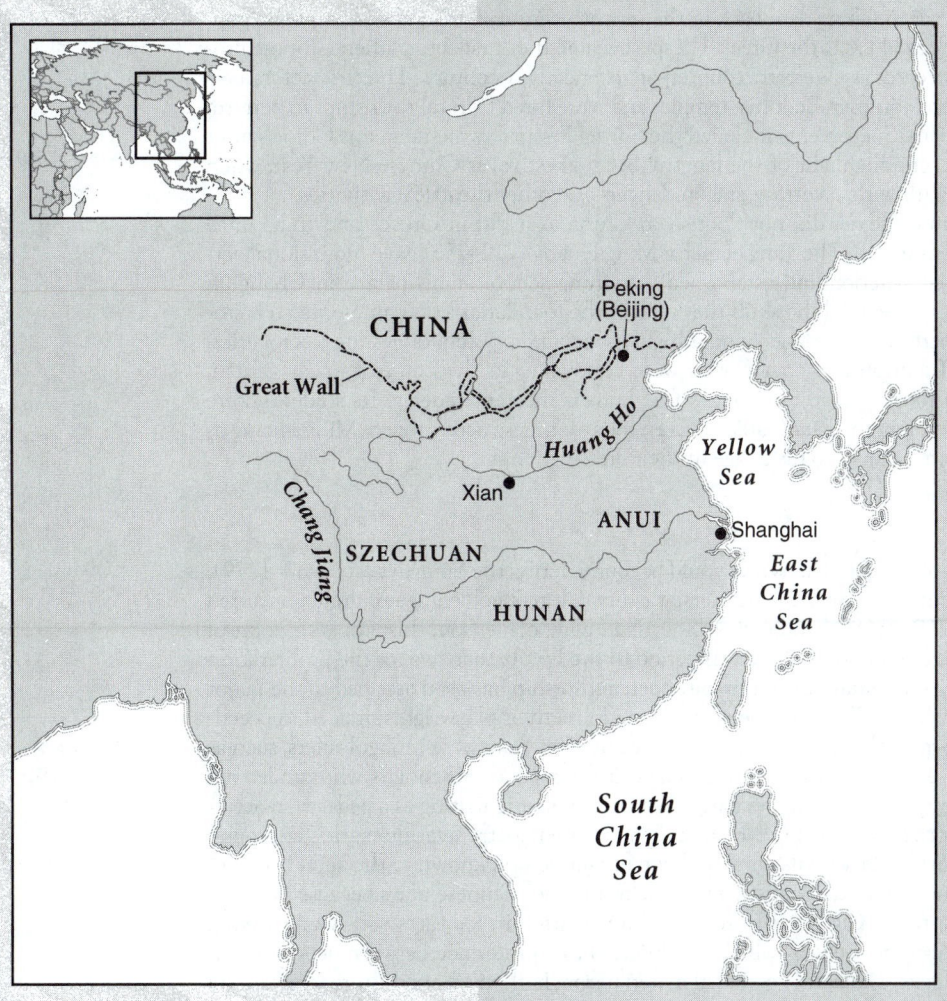

The History of Chinese Theater

Early Theater in China

To such inventions as the printing press and gunpowder, the Chinese can apparently add professional acting on the list of "firsts" emanating from that ancient land. The earliest records that mention an actor in China date back to the seventh century B.C.E.; if we accept the popular notion that in c. 534 B.C.E. the Greek Thespis became the "first actor," then Chinese professional theater predates its Western counterpart by nearly a century. The first actors performed as part of ceremonies in Buddhist temples and were hired by rural townships to perform at agricultural festivals. Such events included the Spring Festival, which remains China's most celebrated holiday. The highlight of the lengthy Spring Festival is Chinese New Year, when the streets of China fill with cavorting dragon dancers and other theatrical activities.

However, literate theater did not flourish in China as it did in Greece and India until about the eighth century C.E. The Tang emperor Ming Huang (712–755) gave professional acting troupes his royal sanction and established a training school at his palace in Chang-an (modern Xian). Actors learned the skills that remain the foundations of Chinese theater: storytelling, musical performance, dance, and a highly specialized system of gestures, acrobatics, and martial arts. Tradition says that classes were conducted in the emperor's pear garden, which became the formal name for China's first known theater academy. Its students were known as "the children of the Pear Garden." Even today Chinese actors revere Ming Huang as their patron and burn incense to his image in their dressing rooms.

Yuan Drama

Although a variety of theatrical activities could be found during the Sung dynasty (960–1279), including the building of permanent theaters at court, China's golden age of drama occurred under the Yuan (1280–1368). China's most cherished plays come from this era. As a point of reference, it may be helpful to compare this period to the Elizabethan age for the proliferation and importance of its literature. Curiously, although authorship has been ascribed to the major plays of the Yuan era, the Chinese are not prone to idolize their playwrights; indeed, succeeding generations are free to adapt the plays as they see fit. The Yuan were Mongol rulers, such as Kublai Khan, whose thirst for theater made playwriting popular by scholars who, under the specter of strict Confucianism, had previously dismissed dramatic writing as a pedestrian activity. Yuan plays (*tsa chu*) were highly lyrical and emphasized poetry over dramatic action and character development. Playwrights employed popular music well known to the audience. Significantly, Yuan dramas are readily distinguishable from other Chinese plays because only the protagonist sings in them. Customarily Yuan drama is written in four acts with many scenes, including the *hsieh-tzu*, or "wedge," which was inserted as an interlude between acts or, occasionally, as the prologue. Dramatists gathered material from both myth and history to create six principal types of Yuan plays:

1. Love stories filled with intrigue;
2. Religious and supernatural tales;
3. Historical and pseudohistorical sagas (see *Autumn in the Palace of Han*);
4. Domestic dramas and comedies;
5. Crime (especially murder) and lawsuit dramas;
6. Bandit-hero plays.

The last, Robin Hood–type stories, were very popular and have been used centuries later by the Communist regime as propaganda pieces. Stock characters were integral to the Yuan dramas, and the varied styles that followed, though there is a remarkable degree of individuation and nuance within these characters. Heroic kings (*K'ung-meng*) and their wise counselors are confronted by the villainous *cao-cao*, while long-suffering wives and servants are tormented by tyrannical stepmothers. Certain features of costume and even voice production became the exclusive properties of such stock types. More famously, the colorful "painted faces" (*hua lien*) became the emblem of Chinese theater. Specific colors were assigned to virtues and vices: white for treachery, black for courage, red for loyalty. Other colors defined status: gods had gold faces, while demon spirits wore green. Colors could be combined on a single face to denote character complexity.

The Yuan elevated drama in China, largely because it was "democratic" in that it consciously appealed to the spectrum of Chinese society. Again, the Elizabethan theater serves as a comparable model to help us understand the popularity of Yuan drama.

Ming Drama

The succeeding Ming dynasty (1368–1644) overthrew the Mongols and returned "pure-blooded" Chinese emperors to the throne. Consequently, the dramas of the Ming dynasty were elitist and highly refined. These dramas, called *ch'uan-ch'i* because they were derived from the south, were written in many acts, and averaged about 40 scenes. Whereas only a single actor sang in Yuan drama, several actors sing in later drama. The instrumentation accompanying them became far more complex and relied heavily on the flute. Though there are a number of quality plays from this era, drama in China gradually lost its vitality under the Ming because it relinquished its contact with the masses.

Ultimately, theater activity during the Ming dynasty is best remembered for the critical writings of Li Yu (1611–1680), who might be called "the Aristotle of China." He was the first to systematically examine the art of playwriting. Ironically, Li Yu urged his fellow playwrights to write for the masses, and his own comedies featured original plots based on observations of daily life. It should also be noted that Li Yu—who had some 40 wives and numerous concubines!—helped legitimize the role of the actress in the Chinese theater.

Peking Opera

The Manchu of northeastern China assumed power in the mid–seventeenth century and established the Qing (Ch'ing) dynasty (1645–1912 C.E.). Qing emperors retained the popular, though less sophisticated, forms of folk drama (*hua pu*), though the older, elitist theater (*ya pu*) continued under courtly scholars. However, little drama of import was written as the Manchu often suppressed new works for political or moral reasons. Happily, the Manchu allowed the *hua pu* drama of the peasants gradually to infiltrate the court drama.

During the reign of Emperor Qian Lung (1736–1795), troupes from the central provinces, especially Anhui, appeared in Peking to celebrate the emperor's seventieth and eightieth birthdays. The provincial troupes remained in the capital, where audiences who enjoyed the simpler stories, the folk music, and especially the acrobatic performances favored them. By 1810 this new style of performance (*ching hsi*) dominated Chinese theater, and it has remained so to this day. Westerners know *ching hsi* by the generic term of Peking Opera, which represents the principal form of Chinese national theater. Like the many regional cuisines for which China is famous, most of China's provinces have retained their unique theatrical forms. For instance, in Hunan province in south central China, one can attend the *hua gu* (or "Flower Drum") opera, whose specialty is folk drama (See Center Stage box, A Night at the Chinese Opera: The *Hua gu* Opera of Hunan).

The term "Chinese Opera" should not evoke images of the grand opera of Western theater. Rather, it combines music, dance, acrobatics, and martial arts to create a spectacular entertainment that is exceptionally theatrical. Today Peking operas are divided into two categories:

- the *wu-hsi* or military plays, which are based on legend and history;
- the *wen-hsi*, which are primarily love stories set amid daily social problems (not unlike the sentimental comedies or bourgeois dramas of eighteenth-century Europe).

Frequently the two styles are incorporated into a single play.

As with Yuan drama, both Peking and regional operas depend on well-known, highly de-

China's Peking Opera, which derived from dance, music, storytelling, and martial arts, is among the most colorful forms of theater in the world.

veloped character types. Chinese actors specialize in a single role and spend their entire careers developing the complex system of hand gestures, physical attitudes, and especially vocal techniques associated with these roles. Audiences, who are familiar with the plots of the plays, attend to see how well the actor interprets the four principal roles in Peking opera: the male (*sheng*), female (*tan*), painted-face (*jing*), and clown (*ch'ou*). It is not uncommon to find a 60-year-old actor still playing the acrobatic *ch'ou* or clown role.

Contemporary Chinese Drama

With the overthrow of the Qing dynasty in 1911, there was an increased assimilation of Western theater methods in China, particularly in Shanghai, the country's most Westernized city. With the rise of communism in the 1940s, drama became more ideological, especially in the works of China's most noted dramatist of the twentieth century, Cao Yu (b. 1910). During the Cultural Revolution (1966–1976), the Maoists resurrected classical drama, particularly those with themes supporting the revolution, as part of their move to purge China of all foreign influences. Mostly, however, theater in Maoist China consisted of spectacular, state-produced song-and-dance extravaganzas that glorified the People and their Great Leader. *The White Haired Girl,* the most famous of these, is a melodrama glorifying the People's Army that liberated rural China from the Japanese; in spirit, it calls to mind the anti-slavery melodrama *Uncle Tom's Cabin* (see Chapter 7). After President Richard Nixon's visit and the ensuing cultural exchange of 1972, the Chinese renewed their interest in Western drama. In 1984 Arthur Miller staged a production of his play *Death of a Salesman* in Beijing (see Chapter 7). Today one can find a variety of theater forms, both classical and decidedly contemporary, performed in China's major cities. In 1988 a Shakespeare festival even enjoyed an eighteen-day run in Beijing and Shanghai. Twenty-two productions of the bard's plays were performed in both the

CENTER STAGE A NIGHT AT THE CHINESE OPERA: THE *HUA-GU* OPERA OF HUNAN

Hunan Province in south central China is famous to Westerners for its spicy food and its status as the birthplace of Chairman Mao Zedong. It also is the home of the *Hua-gu*—or "Flower Drum"—Opera, one of the many provincial styles of theater cultivated outside of Biejing. *Hua-gu* opera has unique conventions, particularly of music and singing, that set it apart from that of China's other many provinces. Still, there are enough similarities between the provincial and Peking operas that a description of several productions by the *Hua-gu* Opera Company will suggest the performance conventions of Chinese opera.

The plays described here were performed in Changsha, the capital of Hunan, in late May 1989. Three short plays were given a private performance held at the company's rehearsal hall, located in a communal housing complex, where all actors, technicians, allied artists, and their families are provided accommodations by the Chinese government. Like most Chinese theater companies, the *Hua-gu* troupe is state

supported and its members live, rehearse, and work together in a spacious facility on Renmen ("The People's") Road near downtown Changsha. Several blocks away is the Hunan Normal School, where Mao taught and articulated his vision for a new China in the 1920s. Later that evening the *Hua-gu* Company performed a fully mounted opera in its vast theater located on Wu-Yi ("May First") Road, Changsha's main thoroughfare. Farther down Wu-Yi Road is the provincial government headquarters, where students from Changsha's many universities had established a tent city in support of the prodemocracy movement in Tiananmen Square in Biejing, 800 miles to the north. Some students passed the time singing songs from Chinese opera.

The afternoon performance, arranged by a director (and principal actor) of the *Hua-gu* Company to honor an American visitor's request to see traditional provincial theater, consisted of three short plays acted on a proscenium stage. Black drapes defined the acting space. In the glow of a light emanating

from behind the stage left proscenium, an orchestra of nine musicians set up their instruments: the traditional two-stringed violin, a couple of woodwinds, and a variety of drums, gongs, cymbals, and wooden clappers. The orchestra, dressed in t-shirts and baggy shorts in deference to the late spring heat, played virtually nonstop throughout the three plays. Every physical action and verbal joke was punctuated by the percussive instruments, especially the cymbals.

The first play, *Picking Turnips,* was a comic romp in which a *ch'ou* (clown) tried to dupe a naive young lady out of her turnip crop. As might be expected, she outwitted the cunning clown, who was left alone at the end to rue his roguery. Though there was dialogue and song in Hunan's distinctive dialect, the action was readily comprehensible because of the physicality of the performance. Exchange the *ch'ou*'s bright blue (to indicate his cunning) costume for a diamond-hued suit, replace his gaily painted face (with traditional white markings on his nose) for a dark mask, and put a slapstick in his hand instead

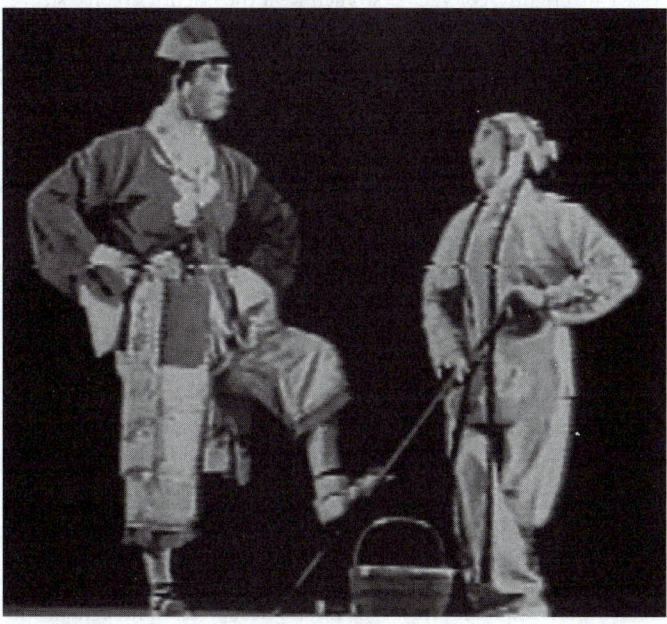

The Hua-gu *Opera of Hunan specializes in folk tales. Here a cunning* ch'ou *(clown) attempts to steal turnips from a* hua tan *(flirtatious woman) in the short play,* Picking Turnips. *(Note that this photograph is reproduced from a video still.)*

(continued)

of a bright orange fan, and a Western audience would immediately think of Arlecchino (Harlequin), the notorious trickster of the *commedia dell'arte*. To punctuate every action, the *ch'ou* struck an exaggerated, comical pose or leapt exuberantly (no easy task for the 57-year-old actor who played him). His gestures were highlighted by brightly colored balls of yarn affixed to his hat and shoe tops. His lines were delivered directly to the audience, even when answering the young woman. The maiden (a *hua-tan*, or "flirt" role) was dressed in a pink jacket and silk trousers, all covered by a festive blue smock with stunning floral embroidery. She sported three knee-length braids of hair and carried a small green basket of imaginary produce. She moved in short, mincing steps, always leading with her heels. Her lines were delivered in the shrill, nasal "singsong" unique to Chinese opera. Her hand movements and facial expressions were so graceful that spectators quickly succumbed to her charms. Certainly the *chou* did. Although he tried to abscond with her harvest, he was quickly duped into pulling her turnips from the soil. His "picking turnips" was done in an exaggerated mime closer to dance than the miming Westerners associate with Marcel Marceau. The play featured several song and dance duets, the most interesting of which was one in which the *chou* unfurled his fan to reveal shimmering feathers while the *hua tan* expertly mimed chopsticks between the third and fourth fingers of her right hand. Given Hunan's importance as one of China's leading agricultural zones, the play's emphasis on harvests and eating was not surprising.

The second playlet was similar in plot, though less rustic in its setting. *The Tuition Fee* told the amusing story of a scheming teacher duped of his income by a quick-witted student. Judging by the reactions of the Chinese audience, wordplay was the source of much of the humor, although the physical comedy compensated for any language barriers. Performed with only the traditional red box and two chairs as scenery, the play featured a comically dressed "professor" (*hsu sheng*) who wore an enormous, drooping mustache and a traditional scholar's hat. His pedantry generated much humor, not unlike that of the "pig Latin" lectures in the Italian *commedia* or, more recently, by the absurdist playwright Eugene Ionesco. The old scholar's delivery was more naturalistic sounding than that of the *chou* in *Turnips*, although one could not mistake the comic intonations. While the particulars of his arguments may have been lost to non-Chinese speakers, the caricature of the teacher and the spirited "sendups" by his student were sufficiently universal that it was still a wonderfully funny play. Most of the action consisted of comic exchanges between student and teacher (with many asides), each of which climaxed with a comic chase and beating. She pursued him about the stage and forced him to leap into the audience, which delighted the children who had gathered near the forestage. Finally, she grabbed his long queue (the traditional hair braid of feudal China) and led him ceremoniously back to his "classroom" (which was always defined by stepping over its threshold). A source of amusement in this and the preceding play was the manner in which a woman outwitted the male. Given the low status China has traditionally afforded its women, such subversion of gender roles seems especially humorous to the Chinese.

The Sister-in-Law concluded the afternoon's bill. It was the most sumptuously mounted of the three works and employed a larger cast, each member of which was dressed in brightly colored silk hand-embroidered in exquisite detail. The story was universal in that it dealt with the impending marriage of a young couple whose love was thwarted by a tyrannical sister-in-law. Of course the play ended happily with a wedding. The termagant sister-in-law (though it is customarily the mother-in-law who plays the comic villain in Chinese opera) was acted hilariously by an older gentleman whose facial features were reminiscent of the great silent film clown Buster Keaton. The actor was noted for his expert rendering of women's roles, and his colleagues in the *Hua-gu* Company affectionately referred to him as Hunan's Mei Lan-Fang, a reference to the most famous actor in the Peking opera. As with the other plays, each actor employed formal hand and body movements to define his or her character. It would take a Westerner considerably more exposure to fathom the nuances of these movements, but even an initial viewing made it apparent that there were distinct differences among the characters in their gestures and singing styles.

The *Hua-gu* Opera House is a large, gray edifice fronted by two columns, over which are hung three enormous gold ideograms that identify the building. The auditorium is spartan and contains wooden chairs for about 1,200 spectators. A velvet green curtain masks the proscenium opening. Unlike the simple folk plays of the afternoon, the evening performance, a tragic tale called *Under the Dragon Stick*, was accompanied by a full orchestra situated in a conventional Western-style pit beneath the forestage. Many children gathered around the orchestra as they tuned their instruments. Entire families attend the opera (at the cost of two or three cents a ticket, which is not inexpensive to laborers who earn about $30 a month). Children are free to roam the auditorium throughout the play, and they especially like to congregate near the stage to watch the actors or amuse themselves with their own games of make-believe. No one seems to mind as there is a festive air about theatergoing. Above all, an evening at the Chinese opera has little sense of the "dressing up" for a social event that one often finds in the West. The audience attends in its blue or green work clothes, and women wear the brightly colored sleeve protectors on their otherwise drab Mao jackets.

As the house lights dimmed, the orchestra played a melodic overture (in contrast to the cacophony of the three folk plays) while the play's title and the names of its author and cast were projected onto the proscenium arch. A series of gongs and cymbals sounded, and *Under the Dragon Stick* began with a spectacular procession in which a large entourage filed into an ancient Chinese court. A huge walled city formed the permanent scenic backdrop for the opera; changes of locale were efficiently handled by placing smaller set units in front of this foreboding backdrop. Ten warriors in classical dress and helmets carried spears to escort the prince consort to the throne room. A retinue of older male citizens followed somberly, each dressed in richly embroidered gowns and headpieces. Throughout the opera, there was an unusually strong emphasis on pictorial composition; at any moment, the stage looked like one of the ancient water colors or wood prints so loved by the Chinese.

Under the Dragon Stick unfolded as a classical tragedy of court intrigue. An old emperor dies and his son inherits the throne. His queen is banished (only to return later as a vengeful ghost), while another warrior-son claims both his younger brother's throne and his wife. A villainous old counselor controls the action, and a beautiful princess adds romantic interest to the complex plot. Ultimately the brothers square off for a death duel, and in the finale the court reconvenes to mourn the loss of its youthful leaders. A new leader is named to inherit the "dragon stick" (i.e., a scepter) which has been cursed for generations. Aeschylus, Shakespeare, or Wagner might have written the script, and there were indeed moments when the heroes might have been called Orestes, Hamlet, or Siegfried.

As interesting as the plot may have been, the play—the equivalent of Western "grand opera"—was most memorable for its visual elements. In addition to the spectacular costumes (even the most lowly extra wore a richly detailed costume of hand-embroidered fabric), the scenery was impressive in its size and design. Settings were both elaborate (a tomb of the dead emperor nearly filled the proscenium opening) and simple (a sumptuously lit bedchamber was defined by glass beads and silk curtains). Legions of attendants, warriors, courtiers, and others added to the stage pictures. A half-dozen ladies-in-waiting attended the princess and performed a graceful dance with the billowing "water sleeves" (*shui hsi*) of their crimson dresses. Ultimately, however, the most captivating visual elements were the beautifully stylized movements of the actors. Many gestures seemed melodramatic in the nineteenth-century sense of the term. When the warrior-son faced separation

from his lover, he held the back of his hand to his forehead, grimaced sadly, and extended his free hand away from his lover who clutched the draperies surrounding her bed and sank to the floor. Later, when he died, he lay on his back, raised his feet (thus exposing the elevated boots that are traditional in serious opera), and slowly lowered his legs to signify his death. Such melodramatic posing might seem comical in the age of realism, but given the size of the character's emotions, the theatricality of the costumes and setting, the florid music, and especially the skill with which the actor performed these long-established conventions, the gesture assumed an aesthetic that was harmonious to the overall tone of the play. The Chinese audience was thoroughly captivated by this ancient tale presented in a centuries-old tradition.

classical Chinese style and in the traditional Western mode. The Chinese retain their affection for the Peking Opera, and in addition to performances in China's many theaters, elaborately mounted Peking operas can be seen daily on Chinese national television. Because Chinese Opera companies are state run, performances are inexpensive and well attended by workers, as well as by students and the emerging middle class.

The Conventions of Chinese Theater

The Chinese theater has never conspicuously attempted to portray life in realistic terms on its stages. It is a symbolic, exquisitely stylized theater that employs a sophisticated system of gestures, poses, stage properties, costumes, and musical accompaniment. The Chinese esteem art that places maximum value on the imagination and symbolic expression. Westerners accustomed to realism may find the Chinese theater noisy and overly "busy," but knowledge of some of its rudimentary conventions offers the potential for a fascinating theater experience. (See Forum, "The World of Chinese Drama," at the end of this section, for an excellent introduction to the subject by a Chinese scholar.)

Though there are specific differences among the many styles of Chinese theater, a knowledge of general conventions may help you understand this venerable theater form. The descriptions below are applicable, in varying degrees, to *Autumn in the Palace of Han* and to *The Qing Ding Pearl*.

Playwriting

Chinese audiences have not lost their fascination with plays that are centuries old, and consequently the repertory comprises a relatively small number of works. In fact, it is not uncommon for Chinese theater troupes to perform a series of acts taken from a variety of famous plays in an evening. Because the plots are well known, playwrights do not need to obey the laws of strict logic. Time and place are manipulated freely for dramatic effect, plays may contain scores of scenes, historical accuracy is not obligatory, and soliloquies, asides, and other presentational modes are commonplace. The plays of Chinese opera represent dramatic storytelling at its most flexible as readers and audiences alike are, according to Harold Acton, "translated into the Kingdom of the Imagination."

Confucianism is inherent in the Chinese culture and its literature. At the risk of oversimplifying a complex issue, Confucianism is a moralistic ideology that teaches correct codes of behavior. A well-defined sense of right and wrong gives rise to the principles of poetic justice. Virtue must be rewarded, particularly that of patience, the paramount virtue of the Confucianists; vice must be punished. Such beliefs are also embodied in the teachings of China's most notable spiritual movements, Buddhism and Taoism. Thus it is not surprising that retribution plays, such as *The Qing Ding Pearl*, should be integral to Chinese drama. There is no well-defined sense of tragedy in the Chinese theater, however, for it was the duty of the playwright to see that the truly good were rewarded and that the transgressors are punished by the final curtain. Liu Wu-chi notes that from the Chinese point of view "it would be a blemish in a literary work not to give its [audience] a sense of satisfaction in the ultimate vindication and triumph of the good and virtuous." Interestingly, contemporary Chinese scholars and theater artists invariably characterize their plays as "melodramas," an apt term because Western melodrama (particularly in the nineteenth century) also emphasized poetic justice.

The Stage

The earliest theaters in China were found in temples and were of simple design, little more than a raised platform with no curtain. Spectators stood on three sides. Variants of this design could be found in court theaters, though they were more elaborate and featured ornate roofs supported by four "posts" that—not unlike the famous posts that supported the roof of Shakespeare's Globe Theater—could be used for a variety of scenic purposes. Frequently there were separate balconies from which women could watch the plays. Such a theater can be found in one of the old court palaces in modern Shanghai. In rural locales, itinerant acting troupes de-

The Guangdong Guild Hall in Tianjin is a traditional Chinese theater with its tea tables and elevated galleries surrounding the stage. The multipurpose red box and two chairs are visible at center stage.

vised temporary theaters of planks, bamboo poles, and roofs made of grass mats, which gives them the generic term "mat-shed" theaters; similar theaters are still found in China and in Hong Kong's New Territories.

Most modern theaters are conventional Western-style proscenium arch theaters. In deference to the raucous musical accompaniment that permeates Chinese opera, lyrics to the songs, cast lists, and "coming attractions" are projected onto the walls of the proscenium so that audiences can read them. Gauzy silk curtains, colored by lights to indicate mood and locale changes, back the stage. Scenery is invariably painted in bright colors in a manner that Western audiences might equate with musical comedy. Even serious scenes are brightly colored and more lightly rendered than one would expect for a comparable scene in Western theater. Even in serious social dramas, there is picturesque idealization of the subject matter.

Staging Devices

Traditionally, the Chinese theater uses a minimum of scenery. Most stories are told with the aid of a couple of wooden chairs and a large box or table either painted red and gold or covered by a bright cloth. These few stage properties are all that is needed to tell even the most complex tales. An actor may sit on a chair, but can also jump from it to suggest a leap from a high place, or leap over it to suggest a suicide (i.e., jumping into a river or into a well). At other times the chair can suggest locale: the slats of the chair back can suggest a prison; tilted sideways it can represent a gate. The box serves as a desk, a throne, or a rock; it may also be a hiding place or a large object such as a wall.

More importantly, actors use movement and gesture to define locale. Perhaps the best known of these is the "threshold" effect (*kua men jian*): when actors want to suggest that they are entering a building, they lift their legs ceremoniously to step over the doorsill, which is customarily about 8 inches high in Chinese houses. If they are moving from one locale to another, actors merely circle the stage; they circle it twice for longer journeys. A rider defines his horse by use of a whip and a ceremoniously lifted leg to suggest mounting the horse. An oar or long pole is sufficient to suggest the entirety of a boat (as in *The Qing Ding Pearl*).

Actors also employ simple, yet highly effective, emblems to further the color and invention of the Chinese theater. Black-clad actors (who are therefore not "seen" by the audience) wave blue silk scarves rhythmically to suggest water. Snowstorms are defined by tossing white confetti, while thunderstorms are created by billowing black cloth. Two yellow flags held horizontally define a chariot or cart; its passengers merely walk between the flags. Ghosts are identified by long strips of white paper affixed to an actor's right ear (and by the cacophony of fireworks set off by stagehands). Gods carry a horsehair switch and enter to the sound of a reverent gong. A yellow cloth over one's face denotes a sick person; the dead wear a red cloth.

A 1925 visitor to an opera in Peking recalls a particularly imaginative illustration of the power of Chinese staging conventions. The play required the slaughter of a pig onstage. An actor with a black cloth over his head mimed the movement of a pig, driven by another actor carrying a swineherd's stick. The actor-pig placed his head on the chair while the butcher mimed the beheading, after which the cloth was removed from the man's head. Now neither actor nor pig, the man simply walked upright offstage to conclude the scene.

Acting Technique

In addition to the many pantomimic gestures employed by actors, Chinese performers are bound by a number of highly refined body movements that denote character. To illustrate, consider hand gestures. Female roles (whether played by a woman or a man) require specialized pointing gestures; never is "she" permitted to expose her thumb, which is hidden by the middle finger. A male juvenile (the *hsiao-sheng*) makes his thumb as inconspicuous as possible, while the *lao-sheng* (a "painted face" depicting a warrior or bandit-hero) sticks his thumb up and extends both middle and index finger before him. A wide variety of walks and foot movements for specific character types must also be mastered. There is even a popular comic character known exclusively by his walk—the mischievous "hobbler" who drags a withered leg about the stage.

In addition to these essentially mimetic techniques, Chinese actors must learn to manipulate costumes and accessories. To cite but a single example, imagine the various uses of the *shui hsui* (or "water sleeves," because their movement suggests rippling water). The sleeves, which adorn traditional costumes, are about two feet long. They denote a variety of symbolic meanings, and they signal the orchestra that the actor will begin singing. Sleeve movements, performed rhythmically to musical accompaniment, suggest a variety of emotional states. For instance, when both arms are used simultaneously, the movement suggests worry. Similar movements apply to hats, fans, and warrior feathers.

Even stranger to non-Chinese audiences than the physical actions, which are usually recognizable to the most naive visitor, are the vocal techniques. There is a specific vocal signature for each major character type. The dignified male roles (*lao sheng*) are softer and more pleasant to listen to, being neither too high-pitched nor too harsh. By contrast, the "young man" (*hsaio sheng*) must have a shrill, high-pitched voice to suggest the unchanged voice of adolescence. The *tan* (women's) roles are divided into a half-dozen types, each with a recognizable vocal quality. The virtuous woman (*jing i*) has a pure, high-pitched voice, while the flirtatious *hua tan* sings in a nasal voice. Because the vocal qualities cannot be put into words, we encourage you to acquire recordings of Chinese operas and listen to the varied vocal techniques.

Because the Chinese language is tonal (i.e., the meaning of a word is determined by the voice inflection), there is an extraordinary musicality in Chinese speech. It is heightened in the theater by the use of meter and rhyme. Actors must learn some 13 different rhyming formulas for their work. Among the most popular is the *shu pan*, a comic tour de force. The *shu pan* is a gigantic tongue twister requiring accelerated speech and body movement. Specialized vocal effects mark entrances and exits. Upon entrance, all principal roles perform the *yin zi*, a two- to four-line poem that is half-sung, half-recited, to introduce a character. *Autumn in the Palace of Han* provides examples of this tradition. Given the rigorous physical and vocal techniques demanded by the traditions of the Chinese theater, actors must spend up to seven years training for their profession.

Music and Sound

Perhaps no aspect of Chinese theater is more daunting to untrained ears than the cacophony of sound produced by the small orchestra (7–9 musicians) that sits in "The Den of the Seven Dragons," a screened area "off left." Banging cymbals and gongs, the sharp retort of drums and percussive sticks (*pan*), and the shrill wail of the two stringed fiddle (*hu qin*) can indeed be overwhelming to the uninitiated. Chinese opera music is not built on Western harmonic scales, but on those introduced by the Mongols in the eleventh century. Music and Chinese theater are inseparable: without music the actors cannot function. Entrances and exits are ceremoniously heralded by music that defines character. The orchestra punctuates every piece of stage business, whether by a simple, reverent gong or a crescendo of all instruments. The musicians, by the way, do not use sheet music: they have memorized the entire repertory of the company, of which they are indispensable members.

AUTUMN IN THE PALACE OF HAN

Ma Chih-yüan

AUTUMN IN THE PALACE OF HAN

Sometimes translated as *The Sorrows of Han* because of its unusually poignant final act, *Autumn in the Palace of Han* is technically not a true Yuan drama. Rather, it slightly predates the Yuan dynasty and is more reflective of the developmental stages of classical Chinese theatre. It is included here because, perhaps more than any drama of this golden age, it is the most thoroughly contemplative and poetic.

Written about 1250 C.E., the play consists largely of poetic arias by the emperor Han. It is not plot oriented and does not contain much of the dramatic action that one finds in more developed stages of Chinese playwriting. It may be useful to compare it to Aeschylus's *Prometheus Bound* because lengthy monologues dominate the action.

Still *Autumn in the Palace of Han* contains many of the elements we associate with classical Chinese theater. It begins with a prologue or *hseih tzu* (the "wedge"). One need not read further than the opening speech to find an example of the traditional *yin tzu*, the couplet, or often pair of couplets, through which principal characters introduce themselves to the audience. Note, too, the lengthy formal speeches of direct address to the audience; there is no "subtext" (to use a modern actors' term) in Chinese plays. Characters speak freely and honestly to the audience in the best storytelling tradition. And in honor of the Yuan era's most venerable traditions only the emperor sings. The principal character types associated with the Chinese theater are manifest: Mao Yen-shou, the wicked counselor (or *t'sao-t'sao*), whose villainy propels the action; the beautiful, pure heroine (or *jing i*), whose presence guarantees pathos; and the powerful *sheng* roles for both the warrior Khan and especially the emperor Han. Given the gravity of the subject matter, there is not a *ch'ou*, or clown, role.

The simple story itself is well known to the Chinese. There are many versions of this famous historical episode in verse and prose, as well as in play form. Indeed, the story is not peculiarly Chinese, but is archetypal in its depiction of thwarted love and the tyranny of time and circumstance. Although there is a *Lear*-like quality to the play—primarily in the melancholy of an older man reflecting on the missed opportunities of his life—the play is reflective and depends on mood to create its effect. As you read *Autumn in the Palace of Han*, do not look for spirited confrontations and high drama. Think of it as a tone poem and open yourself to its many sensory appeals.

Star-crossed lovers, thwarted by the ambition and machinations of others, are certainly the stuff of legend, whatever the country of origin. To such famous lovers as Pyramus and Thisbe, Romeo and Juliet, and their modern counterparts in *West Side Story*, Tony and Maria, can be added the names of the emperor Han and Chao-chün. Their story can be traced back some twelve centuries before Ma Chih-yüan immortalized them in this staple of the classical Chinese repertory. Because of the popularity of this pseudohistorical fairy tale, many versions exist, each with its distinctive twists, particularly in the punishment meted out to the villainous Mao Yen-shou (also known as Wang Chao-chün in its earliest versions).

What is constant about *Autumn in the Palace of Han* is its extraordinary depiction of the sense of loss and loneliness felt by its titular hero. Can anyone who has known loss and despair not identify with the emperor's final sentiments?

> *How can I pass this everlasting night?*
>
> *I loathe the moonlight on the palace steps.*

The emperor identifies himself with the wild goose, who, distraught in his isolation, flies north, not south, as winter approaches. Just as the wicked minister Mao Yen-shou has perverted nature (emblemized by the distorted paintings he commissions of Chao-chün), so is nature perverted in the misguided wanderings of the goose. What should have been a fruitful marriage between the emperor and the simple peasant girl—the idealized union of learned and innate sensibilities—is destroyed by the misuse of worldly powers.

The play also reminds us of the transitory nature of life. Han's lament that

> *My thoughts of her remain, but she is gone,*
>
> *Vanished without a trace, like a mirage,*
>
> *This portrait here is all that I retain*

readily acknowledges the painful truth that beauty, worldly possessions (we should not forget that for all its romantic trappings, Han does own Chao-chün), indeed life itself is fragile and transitory. Images of temporal beauty are as popular in Buddhist stories as in the poetry of Keats and other of the Romantics. Han's cry that his beloved has vanished without a trace echoes a popular Buddhist parable in which a pilgrim visits the exquisite Chu-lin Temple, only to find it has vanished when he momentarily turns his head. Distraught in his grief at Chao-chün's banishment, the emperor does not despair. He chooses to live, albeit in sorrow, content that he can bear his adversity in the best Confucian manner, now armed with the absolute knowledge of life's simplest truth. Things are born to die.

Despite its pervasive melancholy about the transitory nature of life's best offerings, *Autumn in the Palace of Han* is still an affirmation of life. Han himself tells us that Chao-chün

> *. . . is not dead, she lives this day, and yet*
>
> *I truly offer her my veneration.*

After the evil Mao Yen-shou has been destroyed, we learn that a peace treaty is being forged between the formerly warring countries. Fittingly, the peace is celebrated at a banquet, a universal rite of life reminiscent of the *komos* of the Greek theater. More importantly, the desert land where Chao-chün threw herself into the river becomes miraculously green and fruitful. Recall the myth of Osiris of Egypt who brought fertility to the Nile Valley wherever parts of his dismembered corpse had been buried. So, too, Chao-chün, whom Han calls "the Verdant Queen" in the closing couplet of the play, joins a long list of mythological life-givers whose death gives way to life, just as the falling leaves of autumn in the palace of Han, and elsewhere, ultimately give way to the fresh growth of spring.

This woodcut from the early Ming Dynasty suggests the contemplative mood of a drama such as Autumn in the Palace of Han, *as well as traditional Chinese costuming from the classical Yuan era.*

AUTUMN IN THE PALACE OF HAN

MA CHIH-YÜAN

Translated by Donald Keene

PROLOGUE

Hu-han-yeh, the Tartar Khan, and his followers enter.

KHAN (*recites*).
The autumn winds wander in the grass by my tent;
A lonely flute sounds through the moonlit firmament.

A million brave archers acknowledge me their khan,
Yet I affirm allegiance to the House of Han.

I am the Khan Hu-han-yeh. For many years I have lived in the deserts, and I rule the north alone. Hunting is my people's livelihood, and conquest our business. Once Emperor T'ai Wang fled before us to the east, and Wei Chiang, trembling before our might, begged us for peace.

Huns, Tartars, northern savages—each Chinese dynasty has its own abusive name for my people, and the Chinese title for our Tartar Chieftain has changed as often. When China was torn by fighting between the Ch'in and Han, my country was strong and prosperous, and had a million archers and warriors under arms. My ancestor, the Khan Mao-tun, besieged the Han Emperor Kao at Po-teng for seven days. The emperor, adopting the policy proposed by Lou Ching, sued for peace between our two nations, and a Chinese princess was sent in marriage to our khan. This practice has been followed in every generation since the time of the Emperor Hui and the Dowager Empress Lü. In the time of the Emperor Hsüan a dispute among my brothers about the succession weakened the country somewhat, but now the tribes of my people have established me as their khan.

I myself on my mother's side am a member of the house of Han. Now, with my hundred thousand armed warriors, I have moved south and approached the Han borders, intending to declare myself a feudatory of the Han empire. Recently I despatched an envoy to offer tribute and to request that a princess be given me as my bride. As yet I do not know whether or not the Han emperor is willing to renew our treaty of alliance.

Today the heavens are high, the air is clear. Chiefs—would not a round of hunting on the sandy banks be pleasant sport? Truly Tartars own no land, no houses; bows and arrows are our only wealth.   (Exeunt.)

(Enter Mao Yen-shou. He recites.)

I have a hawk's claws, a vulture's beak;
I deceive the great and oppress the weak.
Thanks to flattery and an avaricious bent
I've built a fortune too huge to be spent.

I am no other person than Mao Yen-shou. I now serve the Han court as middle counsellor. I have employed a hundred arts of deceit and steady flattery to dupe that old man, the emperor, and I keep him in sufficiently good spirits. My words are heeded; my plans are followed. Within and without the court, is there a man who does not respect me, does not fear me?

I have been studying a new plan: if I can persuade the emperor to devote as little time as possible to his learned ministers, and to give himself instead to fleshly pleasures, my command over the imperial favor will truly be secure. But while I've been talking, the emperor has arrived.

(Enter the Emperor Han Yüan-ti, with a retinue of eunuchs and women.)

EMPEROR (recites).
Ten reigns since Fiery Liu who founded our line,
China's four hundred counties, the whole world, are mine.

The borders long have been secured by solemn vow;
At night I sleep in peace, no cares afflict me now.

I am Han Yüan-ti. My ancestor, the first Han emperor, arose from among the common people, began his career at Feng-p'ei, crushed the Ch'in dynasty and destroyed Hsiang Yü. It was he who established the imperial authority passed down to me through ten reigns. Ever since I ascended the throne, the country in all its length and breadth has been at peace, not because of my own virtue, but thanks entirely to the civil and military officials on whose support I depend. The palace ladies were all dismissed after my father's death, and now the women's palace is lonely and deserted. What would be best for me to do?

MAO YEN-SHOU. Your majesty, even a country fellow, when he harvests ten more loads of wheat than he had expected, will want to change his wife. Why should your majesty, whose rank is supreme, and whose riches encompass the nation, not enjoy as much? Would it not be wise to send an official throughout the empire to select maidens for the palace? These girls should be chosen without respect to their families' position, the only condition being that they are between fifteen and twenty years of age, and of pleasing features. You should fill the women's palace with the maidens selected. What objection could there be to this plan?

EMPEROR. You have spoken well. I therefore appoint you, in addition to your other duties, commissioner in charge of the selection. When you receive my written edict you will travel over the empire choosing maidens for the palace. You will have a portrait painted of each girl you pick, and send that portrait to me. I shall bestow my favors in accordance with the pictures. When you have returned successful from your mission, I shall reward you as you deserve.

(sings) The world's at peace; no more of swords and horses.
The harvest is rich; war and conquest are ended.
I look to you to choose my palace maids.
I know your search will cost much weariness,
But see that you discover in your quest
A beauty worthy of an emperor.   (Exeunt.)

ACT I

Mao Yen-shou enters.

MAO (recites).
I'll snatch my fill of gold with both my hands,
And fear no seas of blood nor royal commands.
Alive, I only ask for wealth to spare;
When dead, let men spit on me for all I care.

I, Mao Yen-shou, have received a mandate from the emperor directing me to travel far and wide over the country selecting beautiful maidens for the palace. I have already chosen ninety-nine. The family of each of these girls was only too glad to offer me whatever worldly goods it possessed. I have in this manner amassed quite a fortune. Recently, I visited the Tzu-kuei district of Ch'eng-tu, where I chose Chao-chün, the Elder Wang's daughter, a girl of dazzling beauty. She is endowed with every grace and charm, truly without peer in all the world. Unfortunately, her family were originally farmers and have no great wealth. When I asked her father for one hundred ounces of gold to have her name placed at the head of the list, he at first pleaded his poverty, then refused altogether, relying on his daughter's extraordinary beauty to gain her preference. I intend therefore to remove her name from the list.

(*Considers a while, then says*) But would not my removing her name actually prove a kindness? Let me think a moment, some good plan is sure to come. I have it! I'll disfigure the girl's portrait a little, so that when she arrives in the capital she will certainly be relegated to the palace of neglected ladies. I shall make her lead a lifetime of suffering. Truly is it said that a man with little power of hatred is no man at all. Every real man has his venom.   (*Exit.*)

(*Enter Wang Chao-chün with two palace maids. She recites.*)

> One day by royal command I came to this sad place;
> It seems ten years—I've yet to see my sovereign's face.
> This lovely, lonely evening, who will join my song?
> My lute alone has brought me joy the whole night long.

I am Wang Chao-chün. I come from the Tzu-kuei district in Ch'eng-tu. My father, the Elder Wang, has been a farmer all his life. When my mother was about to give me birth, she dreamt that moonlight entered her breast and laid her on the ground. Soon afterwards I was born. When I grew to be eighteen, I was honored by being chosen to enter the women's palace. I did not realize, when I could not give Mao Yen-shou the money he demanded, that he would take his revenge by disfiguring my portrait, so that I could never be seen by His Majesty. Now I have been relegated to this dungeon of neglect.

When I was still in my father's house I was very fond of music, and I learned to play many pieces for the lute. Now, in the lateness and solitude of the night, I shall try to while away the tedium by playing on my lute.

(*She plays. Enter Emperor with eunuchs bearing lanterns.*)

EMPEROR. In all the time that has passed since the selection of maidens for my palace, there are many I have never favored with my affections. How terribly unhappy they must be! Today I have a little respite from my innumerable duties, and the thought came to me to take a walk through the palace grounds. I shall see which lady is destined to meet me.

(*sings*) My carriage wheels crush the fallen flowers,
A girl in the moonlight puts down her flute.
Some palace lady I have never met
Has aged with grief, and white now streaks her hair.
I see the rolled-up blinds, the eyes that stare
Towards Chao-yang Palace,[1] every step a world.
On windless nights they jump at bamboo shadows
And loathe their curtains that only moonbeams touch.
Our carriage moving past midst flutes and strings
Must seem some magic raft, rising to the stars.

(*Chao-chün plays her lute.*)

EMPEROR. Is that a lute being played somewhere?
EUNUCH. It is, your majesty.
EMPEROR (*sings*).
       Who plays in secret plaintive melodies?
EUNUCH. I shall hasten to inform her of your majesty's approach.
EMPEROR. No, do not.

(*sings*) Do not too quickly tell her of my will:
Too sudden favors might upset her so
Her broken notes would startle nesting birds,
And frighten crows atop the palace trees.

Eunuchs, discover what palace lady is playing her lute. Command her to come into my presence, but beware lest you alarm her.

(*Eunuchs go to investigate.*)

EUNUCH. Which of you ladies is playing her lute? The emperor approaches. Prepare at once to meet him. (*Chao-chün comes forward.*)
EMPEROR (*sings*).
       I forgive you, you're guilty of no crime.
       I myself ask you, who lives in these quarters?
       Do not blame me that I've not come before,
       Nor take fright at my sudden visit now.
       I've come to make amends for all the tears
       That have soaked your handkerchiefs of gossamer,
       And to warm your satin slippers chilled by dew.
       Heaven has sent this lovely girl to earth
       That I might offer her my tenderness.
       I'm sure the candle on her silver stand
       Sputtered tonight and left auspicious forms.

(*says*) Eunuchs! See how the candle-flame within the gauze lantern flares brighter! Lift it up that I may see her better!

(*sings*) It strives to shine more brightly than her beauty:

---

[1] The residence of the emperor's consort.

Look—do you see that slender elegance,
Lovely enough to kill a man with joy?

CHAO-CHÜN. Had your humble slave known that your majesty was coming, she would have gone to meet you and not kept you waiting so long. She deserves ten thousand deaths.

EMPEROR (*sings*).

She greets me with the words "your majesty,"
She bows and calls herself my "humble slave."
This surely is no simple peasant girl.

(*says*) What perfection I see in her features! She is truly a lovely girl!

(*sings*) She paints her brows in the palace fashion,
Her face she tints and powders to perfection,
And scented pins and plumes flash in her hair:
A smile from her is worth a captured city.
Had King Kou-chien seen *her* on Soochow Terrace,[2]
He'd have rejected Hsi Shih's wiles and lost
His house and kingdom ten years earlier.

(*says*) Maiden, most beautiful of all, who are you?

CHAO-CHÜN. My name is Wang Chao-chün. I come from the district of Tzu-kuei in Ch'eng-tu, where my father cultivates the fields our ancestors have left us. We are country rustics, and know nothing of court etiquette.

EMPEROR (*sings*).

When I see your brows painted with mascara,
Your hair swept up like piles of ravens' wings,
Your waist as slim as swaying willow boughs,
Your face as lovely as bright-colored clouds,
I wonder which of all my palace halls
Is worthy of you? Who asked if your father
Furrowed the soil to earn his livelihood?
By favor of your lord you'll share his bed:
Heaven that causes the rains and dews to wet
The mulberry and hemp has destined you for me.
If not, in all the breadth of my domains,
Could I have found you in a hut of thatch?

When I see such beauty before me, I wonder why you have never been favored by my visit.

CHAO-CHÜN. At the time of the first selection, the commissioner Mao Yen-shou asked my father for money, but my family was so impoverished that we could raise none. Mao Yen-shou took his revenge by disfiguring the eyes in my portrait. That is why I was sent to the cold palace.

EMPEROR. Eunuch! Bring me her portrait that I may examine it!

(*Eunuch shows Emperor the picture.*)

[2] Apparently an error for King Fu-ch'a of Wu, King Kou-chien of Yüeh sent the beautiful Hsi Shih to Fu-ch'a, hoping to distract him from state business. The plan was successful, and Fu-ch'a lost his kingdom.

(*sings*) One question only have I for the artist—
Why did he fail to give your face its due?
Eyes clear as autumn stream he has made muddy—
Surely the painter's own eyes must be blind!
I doubt that my eight hundred palace maids
Can match this portrait, even with its flaw.

Eunuch! Transmit my order to the imperial guard that Mao Yen-shou be apprehended and decapitated. Report to me his execution.

CHAO-CHÜN. Your majesty, my parents in Ch'eng-tu are commoners. I entreat you in your generosity to show them your favor.

EMPEROR. That is easily done.

(*sings*) Mornings you picked greens, at night watched the melons;
In spring you sowed grain, in summer watered hemp.
You'd like a proclamation on the wall
Exempting all your family from tax:
Lucky that you are married to a prince!
My rank is higher than a village chief,
My palace bigger than a judge's court.
Heaven and earth! Have mercy on this groom!
Who now will dare to mock your father's house?

Approach and hear my command. I appoint you now Princess of the Court.

CHAO-CHÜN. What have I done to deserve your majesty's favor?

EMPEROR (*sings*).

Tonight a while we'll give ourselves to love;
Ask not about tomorrow morning's levee.

CHAO-CHÜN. Your majesty, please come early tomorrow morning. I shall be waiting here for your arrival.

EMPEROR (*sings*).

Tomorrow morning—who knows?—I may lie
In drunken sleep upon my consort's bed.

CHAO-CHÜN. I am a poor and insignificant person. Though I have received your favors, how could I aspire to share your couch?

EMPEROR (*sings*).

Don't take offense: I merely joked with you:
I jested, but you took my words for truth.
My carriage glided smoothly to your door—
Could I again condemn you to neglect?
Tomorrow night wait by the western gate.
You must be silent when you greet my chair:
Your music might awaken other lutes.

(*Exit.*)

CHAO-CHÜN. The emperor has returned. Attendants, shut the gates now. I shall sleep awhile.

ACT II

The Khan enters with his followers.

KHAN. I am the Khan Hu-han-yeh. Recently I sent envoys to offer my allegiance to the Han and to ask in return for a Han princess. The Chinese emperor refused, claiming that the princesses of his palace are still too young for marriage. I am most annoyed. I am sure that the Chinese court holds countless palace ladies, and it would by no means embarrass the emperor to give me one. I shall recall my envoys at once. I intend to raise troops and invade the Han lands to the south. But I fear to destroy the peace of several years' standing. I shall examine conditions and act accordingly.

(*Enter Mao Yen-shou.*)

MAO. I am Mao Yen-shou. When I was charged with selecting maidens for the palace, I demanded money from their families. Later, I defaced the portrait of the beautiful Wang Chao-chün, and she was sent to the cold palace. I never imagined that the emperor would visit her personally and ask how she happened to have been relegated to neglect. I learned that he intended to execute me, but I managed to escape from the Han territories. I have found no refuge as yet. I have with me a portrait of Wang Chao-chün which I intend to present to the khan. I'll induce him to demand this girl. The Chinese court will assuredly yield her.

    I have traveled for days, and now I am here. I can see in the distance an immense number of men and horses. This must be the khan's tent here. (*Shouts to a soldier.*) Chief! Inform his majesty, the khan, that a minister from the Han court has come to see him. (*The soldier reports.*)

KHAN. Ask him to come before me. (*Sees Mao.*) Who are you?

MAO. I am the Middle Counsellor of the Han court, Mao Yen-shou. The women's pavilion of the Han palace holds a lady of surpassing beauty named Wang Chao-chün. When your majesty sent an envoy to ask the Chinese court for a princess, this lady begged to go, but the Han emperor, unable to bear to part with her, refused to release her. I repeatedly remonstrated with the emperor, asking him how he could be so given to lust for a woman as to destroy the friendly relations between our two countries, but the emperor, for an answer, ordered that I be beheaded! I have escaped here, bringing with me a portrait of this beauty for your majesty's approval. If her picture pleases you, your envoy should demand the princess. You will undoubtedly be successful. Here is her likeness.

(*Presents the picture.*)

KHAN. Is it possible that the world contains such a woman? My wishes would all be fulfilled if I could have her for my queen. I shall despatch an official and some retainers with a letter to the Chinese emperor asking for Wang Chao-chün. In exchange for the princess, I shall offer peace between our two nations. If the emperor refuses, I shall invade his domains without delay, and he will not find it easy to defend his rivers and mountains. Meanwhile I and my soldiers will make a foray within the Han borders, pre-

tending it is for a hunt, and when we see our chance, we shall strike.

(*Exit.*)

(*Enter Wang Chao-chün with palace maids.*)

CHAO-CHÜN. A month or more has passed since the emperor first favored me with a visit. His majesty has devoted so much attention to me that he has not held court for a long time. I hear that today he has gone to the Hall of Audience. I shall sit before my dressing stand and touch up my rouge and powder. I want to be ready when he comes. (*She applies cosmetics before a mirror. Enter Emperor.*)

EMPEROR. Ever since I met Chao-chün in the Western Palace I have been inebriated by love for her. It steals my senses away and has kept me from attending court for weeks. Today I went to the Hall of Audience, but could not wait for the levee to end. I had to return to the Western Palace to see her again.

    (*sings*) The rains and dews have fallen in good time;
My country everywhere is prosperous.
My loyal statesmen all are worthy men;
No cares harass my pillow when I sleep.
My love has dazzling teeth and starry eyes;
How could I bear even the daytime without her?
But recently some ailment has assailed me,
One that comes in part from cares of state,
In part from melancholy and from wine.

When with my ministers I try to show
The courtesy that well becomes a king,
But separation from my princess brings
The autumn sorrow Sung Yü once described.
How could I keep from clinging to the sleeves
Of dragon robes scented with her rare perfumes?
Her every feature is adorable,
Her every action matches my desires.
She dissipates all gloom and weariness,
And shares with me my leisure-time delights.
How wonderful to climb with her the terrace
When moonlight lies upon the pear in bloom,
And play at fortunes under gauzy lanterns.
She radiates a warmth and gentleness
That twenty years have polished and perfected.
Ours is a match decreed by destiny
Five hundred years before we even met.
Her face reveals a thousand nameless charms:
I would there were some fit comparison—
She's like the Kwan-yin of Lo-chia Mountain
Although she lacks the sacred willow branch;
A single glance at her adds long years to life.
The love that binds my heart will some day cease,
But only when desire has been sated.

(*Sees her at a distance.*) I must not startle her. I shall watch her secretly awhile.

How deeply once she hated my neglect;
She could not know my dreams would turn to her.
I love her when, as now, her make-up done,
Lovelier than an artist's brush could paint,
She still looks shyly at her mirrored face.

(*Comes up behind Chao-chün.*)

I watch you from behind your dressing-stand;
The goddess of the moon shines from your glass.

(*Chao-chün sees the emperor and gestures in welcome.
Enter the Prime Minister with eunuch.*)

MINISTER.
    A minister should give his mind to affairs of state,
    And to the public good his efforts consecrate,
    But most at banquets their abilities display,
    When have they ever served their lord a single day?

    I am the Prime Minister Wu-lu Ch'ung-tsung and this is the eunuch Shih Hsien. Today, when court was dismissed, a messenger came from the Tartars to ask for the Lady Chao-chün as the condition of making peace. I must report this to the emperor. I have come to the Western Palace and shall now enter. (*Sees Emperor.*) I wish to report to your majesty that the Khan Hu-han-yeh of the northern barbarians has sent an envoy here to say that Mao Yen-shou presented him with a portrait of Lady Chao-chün. The khan demands her in marriage as requisite for making peace and ending hostilities. If his demand is refused, he will march south with great numbers of men, and you will not be able to defend your territories.

EMPEROR. I have maintained my armies for a thousand days just so that I might use them on one occasion. In vain is my court filled with civil and military officials—who of them all will drive back the enemy for me? They all fear the Tartar swords and are anxious to escape the Tartar arrows. How can you let my lady be exiled without lifting a finger to prevent it?

    (*sings*) Success is ever followed by decay,
    And respite from the wars will never come.
    Should not the fate of those who eat my food
    Be mine to order any way I choose?
    In time of peace you boast of your achievements,
    But now that trouble threatens you would send
    The girl I love to lonely banishment.
    Falsely you accept a stipend from our house—
    In what way will you share your sovereign's griefs?
    Brave ministers, afraid to draw your bows!
    Bold counsellors, who fear to lose your lives!

MINISTER. In Tartary they say that your rule is deteriorating because of your majesty's excessive fondness for Wang Chao-chün, and they foresee the ruin of the nation. They declare that if you refuse to surrender Chao-chün to the khan, he will use his troops to enforce his demands. Consider the example of King Chou who, for the love of Ta-chi, destroyed his kingdom and lost his life.

EMPEROR (*sings*).
    I am no evil emperor like Chou
    Who raised a palace to pluck down the stars:
    And why speak only of a wicked king,
    Not of a loyal minister like Yi Yin?
    Once you're dead and reach the underworld,
    If you should meet Chang Liang, the great lieutenant,
    I'm sure you'll feel a shame too great to stifle.
    You sleep beneath thick quilts, rich dishes grace
    Your board, you ride sleek horses, wear soft furs;
    You do not think of Chao-chün's slender waist,
    A willow branch the winds of spring will sway.
    How could you let the shadow of her sash
    Tremble in moonlight by the verdant tomb,[3]
    Or make the echoes of her lute die out
    Beside the autumn-wasted Amur River?

MINISTER. Your majesty, our soldiers are not prepared to fight, and we have no skilled generals to lead them. What would happen if our forces were defeated? Your majesty, I pray you will renounce your attachment to the princess and save the country.

EMPEROR (*sings*).
    Who was it once displayed his bravery
    When he exposed Hsiang Yü's severed head
    As sign the land belonged to fiery Liu?
    All this we owe to Marshal Han's success
    In battles staged before the Nine Mile Mountain—
    Perfected, in one man, the ten great deeds.
    You wear within these halls your golden badges,
    Your purple tassels, hollow marks of glory,
    You love to entertain inside your gates
    Your singing girls with dancing, twisting sleeves;
    Yet if the Tartars break through our defenses,
    You'll ask my wife to intercede for you!
    Like ducks with arrows sticking through your bills,
    Not one of you will even dare to cough!
    It wounds my heart when I recall Chao-chün,
    So young, so bright a vision—and none to save her!
    What harm did Chao-chün ever do to you?
    Did she kill your parents, is that your grievance?
    No, what's the use? My court will soon become
    A swarming den of rogues like Mao Yen-shou.
    Three thousand strong my corps of officers,
    Four hundred the divisions of my land,
    And yet I wait only to cede, to yield.
    Simpler by far to raise a thousand troops
    Than find a single general to lead them.

OFFICIAL. The Tartar emissary is waiting for an audience with your majesty.

EMPEROR. Very well, very well. Let the barbarian approach.

    (*Tartar Eunuch enters.*)

---

[3] Chao-chün's tomb in the desert was celebrated because it remained perpetually green; this remark anticipates the future miracle.

TARTAR EUNUCH. The Khan Hu-han-yeh has sent me to report to the great Han emperor. The northern countries and the southern court have long been united by ties of marriage. The khan has twice sent emissaries to ask for a princess, but without success. Recently Mao Yen-shou presented the khan with a portrait of a beautiful lady. The khan sent me here especially to ask for this lady. He wishes to make Chao-chün his consort. He will then end all hostilities between our two countries. If your majesty does not grant this request, the khan has a million brave soldiers ready to start marching south at a moment's notice to settle the issue. I earnestly implore your majesty not to make an unwise decision.

EMPEROR. Let the emissary rest for a while at his lodgings. (*Exit emissary.*) Deliberate now, my civil and military officers! If you have some plan for driving back the barbarians, present it—anything to save Chao-chün from being delivered over to the Tartars. It must be easy to despise so gentle and good a princess. If the Empress Lü[4] were alive now, who would dare disobey if she uttered a word? In light of this experience, I shall henceforth know better than to trust civil or military officers to settle affairs of state. Beautiful women will be my statesmen.

> (*sings*) Tell me at once, if you have things to tell.
> You need no fear. I have no cauldrons filled
> With boiling oil to punish those I hate.
> I thought you civil ministers would bring
> Our country peace. I thought you generals
> Would settle strife with spear and shield. Alas!
> Your only wisdom, only bravery,
> Consists in trying to be first to cry,
> "Long life, your majesty!"—in posturing,
> And with your scrapings stirring up the dust.
> Oft have you said, "We tremble and we bow,"
> But now you'd have Chao-chün take Yang Kuan
>   Road
> Across the border. Once an empress ruled
> In Wei-yang Palace, inside lowered screens.
> I hardly think, officials, you'd have dared
> Exile the Empress Lü to save the peace.
> It's useless now to hope for martial deeds;
> My only weapons are my palace maids.

CHAO-CHÜN. I have been favored by your majesty's great kindness. Now it is my turn to repay you by my death. I am willing to be married to the barbarian. If, because of my sacrifice, swords are not raised, I shall enjoy a good name in the histories to come. But how can I give up the love I shared with you?

EMPEROR. I cannot let you go.

MINISTER. Your majesty must give up this love, and think instead of your country's good. Send away the princess at once.

EMPEROR (*sings*).

> Today she will be wedded to the khan—
> You must be satisfied, my ministers!
> The Chinese princess has a country still,
> Yet nowhere can she turn. She must go forth
> Where yellow clouds rise not from hills of green.
> Reduced to distant gazing, our eyes will strain
> To sight a lonely goose cross the autumn sky:
> This year, my fate decreed I'd suffer grief,
> And Chao-chün languish too with wasting sorrow.
> Her crown of kingfisher feathers, her sash,
> All her Chinese clothes she must now exchange
> For brocade hoods and beaded robes of fur.

(*says to officials*) Today you will escort the princess to the emissary's residence, and deliver her to him. Tomorrow I myself shall go to Pa-ling Bridge and drink with her a farewell cup of wine.

MINISTER. I am afraid that would not be seemly, your majesty. You will only arouse the contempt of the barbarians.

EMPEROR. I have agreed with everything you have proposed. Why can't you in this one point follow my desires? Come what may, I insist on seeing her off. How I detest that loathsome Mao Yen-shou!

> (*sings*) I only hate that beast who could forget
> My kindnesses and bite his master's hands.
> His portrait could have hung in the Hall of Fame,[5]
> My trusted nobles, the court was in your hands!
> In what did I not share my plans with you,
> In what not follow your memorials?
> How could you cause my first dreams to go astray?
> From now on, instead of Ch'ang-an she will see
> The Dipper hanging in the northern sky:
> Wrenched apart, we'll drift like never meeting stars.

MINISTER. It is not we, your servants, who are forcing the lady to marry the Tartar king. We have no other course; he asked for Chao-chün by name. Many men have lost their kingdoms because of amorous entanglements.

EMPEROR (*sings*).

> For ordinary people like Chao-chün
> There is at least the chance of happiness:
> Who is less obeyed than an emperor?
> How will she ride a massive camel's back?
> She always went by scented palanquins.
> She needs a servant's help to leave her chair,
> And lacks the strength to lift her bamboo blinds.
> Who now will think of her? The empty moon
> Will drop reflections in the flowing water;

---

[4] Wife of the first Han emperor and empress-dowager during the reign of her son the Emperor Hui; a woman known for her strong will.

[5] An anachronistic reference to a gallery hung by command of the Emperor T'ai-tsung of T'ang with portraits of 28 meritorious ministers.

Her lonely, bitter thoughts run on forever.

CHAO-CHÜN: I go now into exile. It is for my country's sake, but I shall never forget your majesty.

EMPEROR (sings).

> I fear that when Chao-chün desires to eat,
> There'll be no food but tasteless salted flesh;
> When thirsty, only clabbered milk and gruel.
> I'll break a sprig of willow as a pledge,
> And drink a parting cup of wine with her.
> I'll watch as long as she remains in sight,
> My heart consumed by grief to see her turn
> Her head to look again, and still again.
> She never more will see our phoenix halls.
> This night, our last, we'll spend by Pa-ling Bridge.

(Exeunt.)

ACT III

Tartar envoy enters escorting Chao-chün. He plays Tartar music.

CHAO-CHÜN. I am Wang Chao-chün. I was selected to serve the Emperor, but my portrait was disfigured by Mao Yen-shou, and I was sent to the cold palace. When at last I began to enjoy his majesty's favors, Mao Yen-shou showed another picture of me to the Tartar khan, and the khan sent an army to demand me. I did not wish to go, but I was afraid that our country would otherwise be lost. I have no choice. I have been sent across the frontier to marry the Tartar khan. The winds and frost are cruel in the northern lands. How shall I endure them? Many tales are told from ancient times of beautiful women who have suffered unhappy fates. But I must not resent the sorrows my beauty has brought on me.

(*Enter Emperor with officials.*)

EMPEROR. Today I am to bid farewell to my princess at Pa-ling Bridge. The time of parting has come so quickly.

> (*sings*) Now she will put aside her Chinese clothes
> And change to robes of fur and coarse brocades.
> I must look at her portrait once again.
> Old pleasures are as short as golden reins;
> New grievances outreach jade-handled whips.
> We who were once a pair of mandarin ducks
> Dwelling in golden chambers, never dreamt
> That we should fly apart on lonely wings.

My civil and military officers, why can you think of no way to repel the Tartar soldiers, and save my princess from marrying a Tartar!

> My ministers, consider what has happened—
> The Tartar envoy will bring rich rewards,
> But leave us to despair, my wife and me.
> The humblest household shakes with grief at parting
> When someone merely takes a little trip.

The willows at Wei-ch'eng increase the gloom;
The flowing water adds its mournful note
At Pa-ling Bridge. Do you alone grieve not?
A world of sadness clings to Chao-chün's lute.

(*Dismounts. Grieves with Chao-chün.*)

Attendants! Sing slowly as you can. I will drink a last cup of wine with the princess.

> Now play that song, "The Parting at Yang Kuan":
> Let it not trip too lightly from the strings.
> A foot from her will seem a world away.
> Slowly, slowly I lift my cup of jade:
> If I could but delay this final hour!
> It does not matter if your lute be tuned,
> As long as you prolong the melody;
> Sing slow and sad a farewell verse for me.

TARTAR ENVOY. I beg the princess to start at once. It is growing late.

EMPEROR (sings).

> Alas, how heavy is this separation!
> I know how anxious you must be to leave.
> My heart will go before her to the north;
> When I return, I'll look for her in dreams.
> Oh, never say that great men soon forget.

CHAO-CHÜN. When shall I see your majesty again? Put away my Chinese clothes.

> (recites) Today I lead a Chinese palace life,
> Tomorrow I shall be a Tartar's wife.
> How could I wear your gifts of former days
> To flaunt my charms and win another's praise?

(*Chao-chün lays aside her robes.*)

EMPEROR (sings).

> Why do you leave behind your dancing robes?
> The wind will blow away their faded scent.
> I truly dread the day my carriage again
> Passes your quarters, overgrown with moss,
> Suddenly to reach the palace of the queen.
> Then I'll remember how you looked when once
> I saw your beauty in a mirror framed,
> That loveliness will brush my heart again.
> Today Chao-chün must leave her native land.
> How long before this banishment will end?

TARTAR ENVOY. I beg the princess again to leave. We have already wasted too much time.

EMPEROR. Very well, very well. Chao-chün, now you must go. Do not hate me for what I have done. (*Leaves her.*) And I am the emperor of the Great Han!

MINISTER. Your majesty must not take these matters too heavily to heart.

EMPEROR (sings).

> She's gone! And none of you is man enough
> To save her! In vain have I maintained my guards
> Along the border. Even you must need
> Someone to serve you—why must I lose my wife?

You wave your swords and spears, but well I know
Your hearts are pounding like a frightened fawn's.
Today you forced the princess to consent:
Is that the way you choose to prove your valor?

MINISTER. Let us return to the palace, your majesty.

EMPEROR (*sings*).

You fear I may refuse to loose the bridle:
It's true—how could I now return triumphant
With cracking whip and jingling golden stirrups?
You are presumed to know the yin and yang,
To hold the reins of court, to calm the nation,
To swell our borders and extend our lands:
Supposing now the emperor had doomed
Your only serving maid to banishment,
Away from native heath, to lie in snow
And sleep in frost—would she not miss your home?
Tell me so; I'll name you Prince Imperial!

MINISTER. Your majesty should not be grieved to leave her.
    Allow her to depart.

EMPEROR (*sings*).

The Tartar king—I can't recall his name—
What right had he to fall in love with her?
How could I bear to look when last she turned,
Or stand to watch the distant storm-whipped flags?
Such doleful drums and horns—they shake the
        mountains!
Before me lie the bleak and ravaged plains,
The grass has yellowed, stricken by the frost,
The mottled coats of dogs grow gray and shaggy.
Men raise their tasseled lances in the chase,
And horses struggle under heavy loads.
Wagons bear provisions for the journey,
And all is ready for the hunt to start.
She, yes, she brokenhearted said good-bye;
I, yes, I took her hand and climbed the bridge.
She and her train ride into the desert;
I in my carriage return now to the palace.
I return now to the palace and pass the wall,
I pass the wall and follow a twisting lane,
A twisting lane that leads close to her room,
Close to her room where the moon grows dusky;
The moon grows dusky and the night turns cold,
The night turns cold and the cicadas weep.
The cicadas weep by green-curtained windows,
By green-curtained windows that feel nothing.
To feel nothing! Only a man of steel
Could feel nothing. No! Even a man of steel
In grief would shed a thousand trickling tears.
Tonight I'll hang her portrait in the palace
And have a service chanted for her there.
Then I'll lift high the sil·er candlestick
And let the light fall on her painted form.

MINISTER. May your majesty return to your palace. The
    princess is already far on her journey.

EMPEROR (*sings*).

I must make some excuse, tell my council

I cannot meet them. They will want to prate
Of state affairs. I cannot bear to talk.
Without her here in flower-like loveliness
What solace do my palace gardens offer?
No doubt she often pauses, paces to and fro,
Irresolute; then suddenly she hears
Caw! Caw! the cries of southward-flying geese:
But all that fills my eyes is sheep and kine,
The sound I heard was but the creaking wheels
Of the felt-covered cart bearing its load
Of sorrow up the slopes of northern hills.   (*Exeunt.*)

(*Enter Tartar Khan with followers leading Chao-chün.*)

KHAN. Today the Han court has shown itself faithful to our
old alliance. The emperor has given me Wang Chao-
chün, and made peace between our two houses. I have
named Chao-chün my consort. She shall live with me in
my chief palace. Now there will be no warfare between
our countries. All has been for the best. Officers! transmit
my command to the ranks that we are to start marching
north. (*They march.*)

CHAO-CHÜN. Where are we now?

ENVOY. This is the Amur River, the boundary between our
territories and those of the Han. The lands to the south
belong to the Han, and those to the north to us.

CHAO-CHÜN. Will your highness gave me a cup of wine that
I may pour a libation facing the south, and take a last
leave of China before my long journey? (*She pours a libation.*) Mighty emperor of the Han! Now is this life ended.
I await you in the next. (*She throws herself into the river.*)

(*The Khan, alarmed, tries to save her, but fails.*)

KHAN (*in tears*). Alas, alas. Chao-chün was so unwilling to
enter my domains that she threw herself into the river
and died. Let her be buried, then, on the bank of this
river at a place we shall call the Green Mound. She
whom I thought to marry is dead. In vain did I create enmity between myself and the Han. It was all schemed by
that knave, Mao Yen-shou. Men! Bring Mao Yen-shou
here, then despatch him under guard to the Han court,
where he will meet his punishment. I shall resume our
traditional alliance with the Emperor of Han, and remain
forever to him as nephew to uncle. All may have proved
for the best.

I see it now: it was because his picture had done an injustice to Chao-chün that Mao Yen-shou betrayed the
Han ruler and secretly absconded. Then he beguiled me
with another portrait of the beauty, and my armies
crossed the border to demand her as a condition of peace.
How could I know that she would throw herself into the
river and die? To no avail was my spirit melted by one
glimpse of her. But such a wicked, treacherous villain will
prove the ruin of my court if I keep him here. It is better
to send him for execution to the Han court. Then, by
virtue of the long-standing courtesy between nephew and
uncle, our two countries will prosper forever.   (*Exit.*)

ACT IV

Emperor enters with officials.

EMPEROR. A hundred days have passed since my princess was sent away to appease the barbarians, but I have been unable to hold court all this time. Tonight is bleak and desolate. I feel unbearably depressed. Perhaps if I hang her portrait on the wall it may dissipate my melancholy a little.

> (*sings*) The palace chills. The night is far advanced,
> And in the women's quarters all is still.
> I face a cold lamp on its silver stand.
> My empty pillow when I go to bed
> Is testimony to my wretched lot.
> I wonder where she rests, my soul, tonight,
> Ten thousand miles from this my dragon hall.

Eunuch! The incense in the stand has burnt out. Put a little more on the stand.

> The royal jar of incense is consumed,
> I place another yellow stick on the stand.
> My thoughts of her remain, but she is gone,
> Vanished without a trace, like a mirage,[6]
> This portrait here is all that I retain.
> She is not dead, she lives this day, and yet
> I truly offer her my veneration.

Of a sudden I feel worn and weary. I shall sleep awhile.

> How sad I cannot dream the dreams I'd choose:
> Oh, dearest, where are you, my dearest one?
> Why do you show no sign of your presence
> But refuse the joys of love, even in a dream?

(*Falls asleep. Enter Chao-chün.*)

CHAO-CHÜN. I was sent to the northern lands to appease the barbarians, but I have secretly escaped and returned. Is that not my lord? Your majesty, I have come.

(*Enter Tartar Soldier.*)

SOLDIER. While I was dozing a while ago, Chao-chün stole away from me and escaped to her own country. I have rushed as quickly as I could to the Han Palace. There she is now! (*Seizes her, and leads her off.*)

(*Emperor wakens.*)

EMPEROR. I thought just now I saw my princess. Why has she vanished so quickly?

> (*sings*) A soldier came here from the Tartar khan
> And called Chao-chün by name, but when I called
> She would not come into the candlelight.

It must have been her portrait, not Chao-chün.
But suddenly I hear a phoenix flute,
Ghost sounds within the Hall of Fairy Music.
Is this the ancient melody of Shun?
By daytime there was none to wait on me,
My griefs denied me sleep, though dawn had come,
And would not grant a single pleasant dream.

(*A wild goose cries.*)

> Listen—a wild goose, calling twice or thrice
> At Chao-chün's empty palace. How could it know
> Another, lonelier than she, waits here?

(*Wild goose cries again.*)

> Probably it is old and strengthless now;
> And must be hungry, bones and feathers light.
> It would turn back, but fears for southern nets;
> It would go forward, but dreads the Tartar bows.
> Its mournful notes are like a voice that tells
> Of Chao-chün's longing for the Lord of Han:
> Sad as the dirges for a fallen hero,
> Heart-rending as the odes of Ch'u at night,
> Doleful as thrice-chanted songs of parting.

(*Wild goose cries again.*)

> That cursed bundle of feathers—its cries make me all
>   the lonelier!
> My thoughts already filled me with despair,
> But now another torturer has come.
> Sometimes you moan in long protracted notes,
> At other times come rapid, nervous cries:
> You harmonize your calls to the watch of night.
> What now? You wheel above the palace roofs
> And all below responds to your lament.
> But surely you mistake the time of year?[7]
> Are you searching for Su Wu, for Li Ling's tomb?
> Is that why you wake me by the candle stand?
> The shadow on the wall stirs bitter grief.
> The Han princess, in that distant land, still lives,
> But sees and hears you not, you bag of feathers!

> Wearisome goose!
> It brings my heart no joy to hear your cries:
> The sound is like the soughing forest wind
> Or icy murmurs of a rocky stream.
> I seem to see an endless mountain range
> And water that reflects a distant sky.
> You surely must have wandered from your way:
> You desolate the twilit Hsiao and Hsiang[8]

---

[7] The goose should be flying south, not north, in autumn.

[8] The rivers Hsiao and Hsiang were famous for their twilight scenery, when wild geese alighted; but this wild goose will not be there for twilight.

[6] Allusion to a Buddhist story of a pilgrim who, after visiting the Chu-lin Temple, turns his head and discovers it has vanished.

And stir again the pangs of separation.
What voices sick with parting do you echo?
How can I pass this everlasting night?
I loathe the moonlight on the palace steps.

EUNUCH. Your majesty, put aside this sorrow and think more
of your august person.

EMPEROR. How can I help but be afflicted?

(*sings*) You must not say my feelings conquer me—
You ministers—how loathsome you seem again!
That bird was not a swallow chattering
On sculptured beams, nor yet the oriole
Singing on a gaily colored tree: it was
The bird of sorrow that Chao-chün of Han
Somewhere, far from home, will hear in misery.

(*Wild goose cries again.*)

Honking, the other geese have flown across
The weed encumbered banks; one lonely bird
Still lingers by the Phoenix Hall of State.
Below the painted eaves the little bells
Tinkle thinly: the palace couch is cold.
The falling leaves are sighing in the wind.
The lamps are dark—her quarters hemmed in silence.

One voice has circled round the palace of Han;
Another goes to Chao-chün at Wei-ch'eng.
My hair has grayed, my body is sick and weak:
My sorrows lie too deep to be assuaged.

MINISTER. Today after the morning council was dismissed,
an envoy came from Tartary with Mao Yen-shou in
chains. The envoy declared that Mao Yen-shou's treachery had caused the rupture in our alliance and all the ensuing calamities. He further reported that Chao-chün is
now dead, and that the khan desires peace between the
two nations. The envoy humbly awaits your word.

EMPEROR. If that be so, execute the traitor and offer his
head to the spirit of the princess. Make preparations in
the Imperial Banqueting Hall for a feast to honor the
envoy before his return.

(*recites*) Leaves fell in the courtyard as the wild goose
cried above,
Bringing to my lonely pillow dreams and thoughts of
love.
Oh lady of the verdant tomb, sign to me where you
are—
I'll put to death the painter who dared your beauty
mar.

THE QING DING PEARL
(THE LUCKY PEARL)

ANONYMOUS

THE QING DING PEARL

This popular play, the plot of which dates back to the Sung dynasty (960–1279 C.E.), is known to the Chinese by a variety of titles. It is best known as *The Qing Ding Pearl* (pronounced "chin deen"), a reference to the engagement pearl that Chinese maidens wear on the crown of their bridal headpieces. In this story the pearl takes on magic powers because it allows the wearer to cross through waters without getting wet. The play is also known as *The Fisherman's Revenge*; *A Fisherman Kills a Family*; or *Collecting the Fishing Tax*, titles which suggest its plot line. It is a *xi-pi* play, which means that it was written to be accompanied by the *xi-pi*, or "Western skins," a reference to the percussive instruments (said to have been invented by the son of the first emperor).

The various titles and traditional instruments suggest that the play is a lively, robust piece loaded with romance, action, and violence. It is. It is also a farcical burlesque in its portrait of corrupt landowners and their bully henchmen. Furthermore, like Romantic melodramas in Western theater, it has characters molded in the Robin Hood tradition of the good-hearted bandits who take on the powerful land baron. To offset the merrymaking and physical humor, there is considerable sentimentality in the relationship of the long-suffering fisherman and his devoted daughter. Little wonder the play has become a favorite of the Peking Opera as well as such regional operas as those from Hubei and Shaanxi provinces.

Perhaps *The Qing Ding Pearl* is best known beyond China because of its association with Mei Lan-fang, unquestionably the greatest performer in the Peking Opera in the twentieth century. Mei Lan-fang was particularly noted for his stunning portraits of women, and it was he who played Kuei-ying when the opera toured both the United States and the Soviet Union in the 1930s. Bertolt Brecht saw Mei Lan-fang's performance and was particularly taken by his masterful pantomime of Kuei-ying's paddling the boat across the river. Brecht cited this moment in his famous comparison between the acting style of the Chinese and that of the Stanislavsky school.

Because this charming play is so dependent on action and a variety of locales which would be challenging to define using conventional scenery, reading provides a good opportunity for you to apply what you have learned about the imaginative staging practices of the Chinese theater. As you read it, try to visualize how skillful actors, trained in dance, mime, and the martial arts, could create the many physical and scenic needs of the play. This is truly a play which must "on your imaginary forces work."

Much of the lasting popularity of *The Qing Ding Pearl* can be ascribed to its theme of the long-suffering "little man" overthrowing his tormentors. Given China's history of oppression under feudalism, the Japanese occupation, and, more recently, communism, one can understand why the Chinese would be drawn to this mostly comic tale. One can also understand why the ruling Communists themselves would sanction the play. The tyrannical landlord Ting could just as easily have been rendered by a Communist propagandist as by the play's creator. Compare Ting to the equally odious Simon Legree in *Uncle Tom's Cabin*; Ting may be less comical than Legree but he is no less grotesque.

In the final analysis, *The Qing Ding Pearl* is a revenge play, a commodity of the Western theater since Aeschylus. Its originality, however, comes from its free mixture of the grossly comical—the battle of the boxers is slapstick in the best Three Stooges tradition—and the deadly serious as the old fisherman, clearly a good and honest man throughout the play, is reduced to a ruthless killer. We are asked to recoil in horror at his bloodlust, just as his daughter does in their final, fateful boat trip down the river. Kuei-ying, of course, overcomes her revulsion—perhaps too quickly?—and the play ends with the violent murders of Ting and his men. All this after a rousing, knockabout farce! The neoclassic rules concerning unity of action and tone are not applicable to the Chinese Opera.

Nor is subtlety of portraiture typically a virtue of the Peking Opera. The characters are servants to the plot and situation, and the playwright makes them only interesting enough to get them from one situation or song to the next. Li Chün, the swashbuckling hero, shows us little more than his derring-do and physical prowess, yet that is enough in the hands of a skilled and acrobatic actor specializing in the *wu sheng* roles. Think of such film actors as John Wayne, Arnold Schwarzenegger, and Chuck Norris: American movie audiences expected little virtuosity in either the playwriting or the acting in the majority of their works.

Motivation, often the obsession of contemporary actors trained in psychological realism, is hardly a concern of actors in the Peking Opera. Very late in the play, Kuei-ying asks her father if he actually intends to murder the tyrant-landlord, a most un-Confucian act. His daughter, horrified by his resolve, declares that she cannot accompany him on his murderous journey. As he turns the boat about in the swift river to return her to their home, she suddenly reconsiders: "I'll go with you, Father. I don't want to return. I could not possibly part with you so!" There is a sentimental reconciliation between father and daughter, they find and quickly kill their prey, and the play ends abruptly (which is a typical feature of Chinese operas: there are no long, drawn-out denouements). A Western actor might well pester her director for clues about Kuei-ying's sudden about face. "What's my motivation? What's happened to her scruples all of a sudden?" she might ask. And while answers such as "Well, in China a child's duty to the parents takes precedence over all else" and "She is duty-bound to show honor to her father" might go a long way to provide her with an objective for her about-face, the answer is much simpler. In the Chinese theater, according to Chinese scholar Huang Shang, the opera artist "may be likened to a connoisseur who has perceived in the vast and colorful and prolific field of life what is primary and what is indispensable and what is secondary and what may be passed by." For in this simple story of the dutiful maiden, the bandit-hero, and the fisherman who learns to say "Enough!", such psychological probing surely may be passed by.

Mei Lan-fang, modern China's foremost actor, specialized in female roles, such as Kuei-ying in The Qing Ding Pearl.

THE QING DING PEARL
(THE LUCKY PEARL)

A N O N Y M O U S

Translated by L. C. Arlington and Harold Acton

PERIOD: *Northern Sung (960–1127 C.E.).*

DRAMATIS PERSONAE

HSIAO ÊN, *a fisherman*	Lao-shêng
KUEI-YING, *his daughter*	Ch'ing-i
LI CHÜN, *a swashbuckler* } NI JUNG, *another* }	Erh-hua-lien
TING LANG, *a servant of the Ting household*	Ch'ou-êrh
TING YÜAN WAI, *a retired official*	Pai-ching
TA CHIAO SHIH, *a champion boxer* } FOUR HSIAO CHIAO SHIH, *assistant boxers* } KUO HSIEN SHÊNG, *secretary to Ting Yüan Wai* }	Ch'ou-êrh

This play is partly a burlesque, holding rapacious officials up to scorn. The victims of oppression are a poor old fisherman and his attractive daughter who, taxed to the limits of endurance, bring retribution on the local bully and his satellites.

The prologue consists of the fisherman and his daughter singing as they cross the stage in a boat. As soon as they row out of sight two swashbucklers appear.

SCENE I

LI CHÜN. I've fought fierce tigers on the southern mountains.

NI JUNG. And I've kicked the scaly dragon that swims the northern seas.

LI CHÜN. My name's Li Chün. I'm known as "the Dragon that confuses the river currents."

NI JUNG. My name is Ni Jung, alias "the Curly-haired Tiger."

LI CHÜN. Since we have leisure to-day, let us take a stroll along the river-bank. (*Sings in hsi-p'i yao-pan*) I can remember when I exterminated the notorious rebel-brigand Fang La in years gone by.

NI JUNG (*also in hsi-p'i yao-pan*). You are truly a hero, Brother!

LI CHÜN (*sings*). I declined to wear the ceremonial robes and belt of jade [*i.e., enter official life*].

NI JUNG. I would rather join the braves of rivers and lakes [*i.e., go about redressing wrongs, in Robin Hood style*]. (*Exeunt.*)

SCENE II

KUEI-YING (*sings behind the curtain in hsi-p'i yao-pan*).
Onward the river rolls, and waves break high. (*Comes on stage and sings in k'uai-pan*) My father and I make our living on the turbulent waters. No painter's brush could depict the beauty of these verdant hills and waves. The home of every fisherman is his bark.

HSIAO ÊN (*enters and sings in hsi-p'i yao-pan*). Father and daughter catch fish in the river: we may be poor, but what do we care if people laugh at us? (*To Kuei-ying*) Hold fast the rudder! I am ready to cast the net. Alas, age is beginning to tell on me: my strength is failing.

KUEI-YING. If you are beginning to feel your age, Father, why not give up fishing?

HSIAO ÊN (*speaks*). If I did that, how could we live?

KUEI-YING (*weeps and sighs*). Alas!

HSIAO ÊN. Don't weep, my dear. The weather is too hot! Let us seek a cool nook under the trees to rest. I have already caught a few fish. Go and put them in the hold ready for sale so that I may procure some wine to cheer me.

Li Chün and Ni Jung appear, singing in hsi-p'i yao-pan.

LI. Idly we saunter by the riverside.

NI. Mightily ever eastwards roll the billows.

LI. I pause to view the prospect far and wide.

NI. I spy a bark beneath a fringe of willows.

LI (*speaking*). Now that I'm nearer I can discern a figure on board that looks remarkably like my old comrade, Brother Hsiao. I'll call out and make sure . . .

KUEI-YING. Father, somebody's calling you from the bank.

HSIAO ÊN. I'll see who it is. (*Stands up and gazes towards the newcomers.*) Why yes, it's Brother Li! Are you coming on board, Brother?

LI AND NI (*in unison*). We were just on our way to see you.

HSIAO ÊN. Wait while your clumsy brother wipes and hands you the oar (*gestures accordingly*) . . . Who is this other

gentleman? I have not yet had the pleasure of his acquaintance.

LI. This is Mr. Ni Jung, the Curly-haired Tiger. Let me introduce you two brethren.

NI JUNG. You are too punctilious, Sir. (*He grasps Hsiao's hand and gives it a tight squeeze.*)

HSIAO ÊN. Why do you grip me so hard, Brother?

NI JUNG. I was only testing your strength.

HSIAO ÊN. I am old and useless. (*Both laugh; Hsiao sings to Kuei-ying*) Come out of the hold and greet your two uncles. (*She obeys. Follows a characteristic specimen of Chinese polite conversation which we print as such rather than for any inherent interest.*)

NI JUNG. Who is this maiden?

HSIAO ÊN. It's my little daughter, Kuei-ying.

LI CHÜN. How old is she?

HSIAO ÊN. Sixteen.

LI CHÜN. Is she engaged to anyone yet?

HSIAO ÊN. Yes, she's already betrothed.

LI CHÜN. To whom, may I ask?

HSIAO ÊN. To Hua P'êng-ch'un, the son of Mr. Hua Jung.

LI CHÜN. I hope the two families are well matched.

Li and Ni turn to take leave.

HSIAO ÊN. Don't go yet! I've caught a few fish to-day; stay and help me to digest them with some wine.

LI AND NI. We fear our visit has put you to a deal of trouble.

HSIAO ÊN. What sort of talk is this among brethren? (*To Kuei-ying*) Bring us the wine, dear. (*They sit down to drink.*) Now, as I live on the produce of the waters, I dread the mention of two words: *kan* and *han* [*i.e., to dry up, either through heavy frost or lack of rain*]. Whoever uses them is to drink three cups as forfeit.

LI CHÜN (*lifts his cup*). "Kan pei!" (*Chinese for "no heeltaps." He is promptly fined three cups*).

KUO (*enters while the party is thus engaged, and sings in hsi-p'i yao-pan*). While idly strolling by the shore, I spy a little boat. (*Speaks*) Hallo! I see there's a pretty wench on board. I'll take a few steps forward and snatch a furtive glance.

LI AND NI. Brother Hsiao, there's a fellow spying on us from the bank.

Hsiao steps on shore and asks him who he is.

KUO. I've only come to ask my way.

HSIAO ÊN. Whither?

KUO. To Mr. Ting's house.

HSIAO ÊN. Do you see that white wall like a figure eight just ahead of you there, with the big black varnished door and the two flag-poles? That's the Ting Mansion. (*Kuo pays no attention: his eyes are riveted on Kuei-ying.*) How now! You are not even listening.

(*Exit Kuo in consternation.*)

HSIAO ÊN (*shouting after him*). Dog's head and brains!* I am sure you're up to no good! (*Returns to boat. Li and Ni inquire who it was and he tells them. Enter Ting Lang, Ting Yüan Wai's servant, calling out for Hsiao Ên: Li Chün draws Hsiao's attention to the fact. Hsiao urges them to drink a little more, but they say they have tippled enough. He then steps on shore again.*) Well, well, if it isn't Ting Lang! And what has brought you hither?

TING LANG. I've come to collect the fishing-tax.

HSIAO ÊN. The river's almost dry for lack of rain and the nets have long been empty. Some other day when I am in funds I'll go along and pay the tax to the Ting family.

TING LANG. Although you offer fair words, I've worn out a pair of shoes on this errand. Who'll give me the money to buy new ones?

Hsiao Ên returns to his boat and tells his friends what Ting had come for.

LI CHÜN. I'll call him back and exchange a few words with him.

HSIAO ÊN. But don't cause a rumpus, whatever you do!

LI CHÜN. I quite understand! (*To Ting Lang*) Ho you, come here!

TING LANG. Oh, there's another of them. Well, I'll turn back.

LI CHÜN. What's your business?

TING LANG. To collect the tax on fishing.

LI CHÜN. Have you the Emperor's permission?

TING LANG. No.

LI CHÜN. Well, where did you get your authority from?

TING LANG. From His Honour the Magistrate.

LI CHÜN. It must be that Lü Tzŭ-ch'iu you refer to?

TING LANG. I refer to His Honour the Magistrate.†

LI CHÜN. Be off with you and tell him to abolish the fishing-tax. If he doesn't, there's a chance that something inconvenient may happen if we meet in the road.

TING LANG. You talk pretty big; what is your name anyway?

LI CHÜN. I'm the Dragon that confuses the Rivers.

TING LANG. You mean you're the stink-bug in a ball of dung.

LI CHÜN. Just wait till I give you a walloping, you eight days' spawn of a turtle! (*Here Hsiao Ên begs them to desist. But Ni Jung joins in the vituperation.*)

NI (*to Ting Lang*). Roll back, and I'll gouge out your eyes and boil them in liquor! I'll flay your hide and mix it with dog-skin to make a plaster for carbuncles.

TING LANG. Stop bragging! What's your name I'd like to know?

NI JUNG. I'm Ni Jung, the Curly-haired Tiger.

TING LANG. What sort of louse in a mongrel's hair are you?

NI JUNG. Look out for a thrashing, you mouldy spawn of a turtle.

TING LANG. Just wait, don't be in such a hurry. I'll first take off my hat and gown . . .

Hsiao Ên attempts to dissuade them from fighting.

TING LANG (*to Hsiao*). You hold him while I run away.

(*Exit.*)

LI AND NI. Why are you so feeble, Brother Hsiao?

HSIAO ÊN. The power and influence of the Ting family are very considerable.

LI AND NI. But they are not princes!

HSIAO ÊN. They have a quantity of retainers.

LI AND NI. But our brethren also are many.

HSIAO ÊN. They have abundance of riches.

LI AND NI. They cannot buy us over, though.

HSIAO ÊN. It's a very ticklish problem.

LI AND NI. You had better retire from this water business.

HSIAO. It's time I did, but then I'd have nothing to live on, I fear. I'd just become a beggar.

LI CHÜN. I'll present you with a hundred ounces of silver.

HSIAO. I'd be too ashamed to accept such a gift.

NI JUNG. And I'll present you with a thousand pounds of rice.

HSIAO. I could not accept, I would really feel ashamed!

LI AND NI. Never mind shame! We'll go and fetch the money and the rice.

Both depart. Hsiao sees them off with expressions of gratitude. Afterwards they discuss the appropriateness of Kuei-ying's engagement "as they are of equal status," and decide to send the wedding presents to her new home. Parallelwise the old fisherman and his daughter admiringly discuss the recent guests and their knight-errantry.

HSIAO ÊN (*sings*). Look yonder, the evening shades are falling fast. (*Speaks*) It is getting late; we had better steer for home. . . . (*Exeunt, after a refrain reminiscent of The Miller of Dee: "I care for nobody, no, not I," etc.*)

SCENE III

Enter Ting Yüan Wai and his secretary Kuo.

YÜAN WAI. I have stored a thousand piculs of grain.

KUO. Yes, all our granaries are full.

TING LANG (*enters*). I've just arrived from the river to report to you, Sir.

YÜAN WAI. Come to the point then. What about the fishing-tax I sent you to collect this morning?

Ting Lang reports his conversation with Hsiao Ên and trouble with the swashbucklers, after which he is told he may go.

---

*Epithet for one whose eyes are continually roving in all directions.
†Li Chün purposely pronounces the magistrate's name, while Ting refers to him as "His Honour," as it is not complimentary to use an official's cognomen.

KUO. This is a trifling affair: let me settle it.

Yüan Wai tells him to proceed with great circumspection.

(*Exit Ting Yüan Wai.*)

KUO (*to himself*). It seems to me that we had better send the boxers along. (*He shouts, and four boxers appear.*) Where is your chief? (*They reply that he is practicing at the back.*) Tell him to come here.

CHIEF BOXER (*appears*). It's good to gorge and good to booze but sleep is better fun. And when there is a fight, I am the very first to run. What's up, my lads?

THE FOUR BOXERS. Mr. Kuo wishes to see you.

Kuo tells them about the fracas with Hsiao Ên, etc., and that they are required to go and enforce payment of the tax and avenge their master's insult.

CHIEF BOXER. We are here to guard the mansion, not to collect taxes.

KUO (*persuasively*). But it's only for this once!

CHIEF BOXER. Well, we'll help you out this time, but mind there's to be no second time. Get the carts ready!

KUO. Are the carts to be used for transporting the money collected?

CHIEF BOXER. No, they're to carry our men, not the silver.

KUO. How ludicrous!   (*Exit laughing.*)

CHIEF BOXER. Are any of you fistical fellows acquainted with this Hsiao Ên?

FOUR BOXERS. Oh yes, we all know him by sight.

CHIEF BOXER. Capital! We'll pick up chicken's feathers as we go along.

FOUR BOXERS. What do you mean by that?

CHIEF BOXER. I mean we'll have more courage if we stick together.

(*Exeunt omnes.*)

SCENE IV

HSIAO ÊN (*enters rather muzzily, singing in hsi-p'i man-pan*). Last night I got tippled and slept in my clothes. Already the cocks are crowing on the rafters. While I was dreaming they woke me up.

My two comrades advised me to have done with fishing. It's high time I did retire, to stay at home and rest. But I'm too poor and can think of no other means of supporting myself in old age. I have woken up early this morning. Is it not crows that I hear?* Hither and thither they fly calling to each other . . . I think I'll go into my grass hut and quench my thirst with tea.

Kuei-ying appears with a tea-tray.

KUEI-YING (*singing in hsi-p'i yao-pan*). How ill-fated am I to have lost my mother in early youth: only poor Father and I are left to fish by the river! (*Speaks*) Here's your tea, Father.

HSIAO ÊN (*takes the cup and drinks, then looking at Kuei-ying's*

*Unlucky omens.

clothes). Didn't I tell you not to wear your fishing-clothes at home?

KUEI-YING. I was born and brought up in a fisherman's family. If you don't want me to dress like this, how am I to dress?

HSIAO ÊN. Not listening to your father's advice shows that you are unfilial.

KUEI-YING. There's no need to be angry, Father. I'll go and change.

HSIAO ÊN. Very well, see that you do so in future.

Here the boxers all strut in and a deal of irrelevant verbiage follows as to whether Hsiao is at home or not, and much dawdling for fear of being attacked by the fisherman's friends. Finally Hsiao opens his cottage door: the chief boxer, true to the universal conventions of farce, slips and stumbles. "Oh, I've slipped on a water-melon peel!" he observes. Pretending not to see Hsiao, one of his myrmidons then inquires: "Has Mr. Hsiao come out?"

CHIEF BOXER. So you are at home, Mr. Hsiao. I wish to see you about something. (*Examining him closely.*) Why he's nothing but a feeble old man!

HSIAO ÊN. Where do you folks come from?

CHIEF BOXER. We're Mr. Ting's fine fistical fellows. *They tell him their mission; he makes the same excuses and says he will pay the tax on some future date at the Ting Mansion.*

CHIEF BOXER. Others have come and heard the same tale. I, the chief boxer, have come to-day to see that you pay up.

HSIAO ÊN. I had nothing for the others, and I have less for you. (*Inflates his chest and strikes a threatening attitude.*)

CHIEF BOXER. He's showing fight! Help me to get out of this quick before I lose any blood. We mustn't show any signs of weakness: we must resist him strength for strength. Have you brought the chains? Shackle him, and drag him away. (*To Hsiao*) Do you know what these things are?

HSIAO ÊN. Yes, they are instruments of Imperial law but what are you applying them to me for?

CHIEF BOXER. These chains are something that will shorten your wretched old life, let me tell you.

HSIAO ÊN. Quite useless! (*He throws them off and tramples on them. The chief boxer, too cowardly to go nearer and pick up the chains, orders his myrmidons to do so.*)

BOXERS (*nervously*). You haven't taught us how to play this sort of trick.

CHIEF BOXER. What a pack of nincompoops! Just look at me! (*To Hsiao*) What ho, Hsiao Ên, have you ever seen a sight so strange as that?

HSIAO ÊN. Strange as what?

CHIEF BOXER. A bird with two polls.

HSIAO ÊN (*looking round*). Where?

CHIEF BOXER. Right here, in my hands: I picked it up while you were looking the other way. (*He begins to fasten the chain round Hsiao's neck.*)

HSIAO ÊN. You sneak-thief, you worthless worm!

CHIEF BOXER. Remove him. If he has the money, well and good: if not, away with him!

An argument ensues as to whether he is to be shackled. Hsiao bursts the chains, throws them over the chief's head and shouts: "Haul him away!" The myrmidons start off with their chief in shackles instead of the fisherman.

CHIEF BOXER. Stop it. Where are you tugging me off to?

ASSISTANTS. Why, we've been heaving the wrong fellow!

CHIEF BOXER. There's not a single eye between the lot of you! This old codger's a wily one. We can't take him by force, better try persuasion. (*To Hsiao*) Your Honour, never mind if you have no cash. Come over the river with us and visit Ting Yüan Wai. Whether you pay or not is up to you; and whether he defers the tax is up to him. It has really nothing to do with us boxers anyway.

HSIAO ÊN. I catch your drift. You want me to cross the river with you to visit Ting Yüan Wai: whether he accepts the money or not rests with him, and not with you. Gentlemen, I have no leisure!

CHIEF BOXER. So you cold-shoulder my advances. You'll neither pay up nor come along with us. If you don't we are many against you . . .

HSIAO ÊN. A set of sucklings. You want a fight, do you? When I was young, I was as keen to fight as a child is to slip on a pair of new shoes on the first of the year: I rejoiced at the very idea. But now I am old and useless in a struggle.

CHIEF BOXER. I'd like to test you.

HSIAO ÊN. In what way?

CHIEF BOXER. Test *you*, you antiquated rat, licking a cat's whiskers right over its nose and waiting for death!

HSIAO ÊN. Are you really so anxious to fight me, baby? (*The dialogue continues in the same strain until the fisherman says*) All right then. Wait until I take off my coat and I'll show you something. (*Sings in hsi-p'i yao-pan*) May I expose the seven apertures of my body to fiery flames if I don't . . .

CHIEF BOXER. I'll go one better and riddle your carcass with eight holes until it smokes!

HSIAO ÊN. Old as I am, I'm in such a boiling rage that I could grind my teeth to powder! (*Starts fighting with the boxers and sings*) I'm the stalwart Hsiao Ên who roams the lakes and rivers.

CHIEF BOXER. And I'm the famous Tso T'ung-chui (Chief Brass-hammer).

HSIAO ÊN. How many battles have you fought, great and small? As for me, I'm the fierce lonely tiger of the mountains.

CHIEF BOXER. We'll see! I'll have a round with you. If you are the tiger, I am the hunter to kill it.

HSIAO ÊN (*sings*). Who's afraid of a mere domestic watchdog?

After further braggadocio, they butt into each other; the four boxers are beaten and quit the stage. The chief begs Hsiao on his knees to let him off.

HSIAO ÊN. It's easy enough to let you off, but first I'll give you three punches to remember me by.

CHIEF BOXER. Three punches! why I'll take three hundred if you let me off and consider myself in luck.

Hsiao continues to belabour him and Kuei-ying joins in with a stick. The chief boxer bolts.

KUEI-YING. I can fight too!

HSIAO ÊN. You can! But this will only bring trouble on us. He is bound to tell the Ting family. Fetch my clothes quick; I'll go to the yamen before him and lodge a complaint.

KUEI-YING. He belongs to an official's household, better not go!

HSIAO ÊN. You are a child: what do you know of such things? You look after the home while I am away.

(*Exit Kuei-ying.*)

HSIAO ÊN (*solo*). Just as I am sitting quietly at home with the door closed, sudden calamity descends from Heaven upon me!

(*Exit.*)

SCENE V

Enter the Boxers and Secretary Kuo.

KUO. So you have returned. Have you brought the money with you?

CHIEF BOXER. No. We were all routed by that old blackguard, Hsiao Ên.

KUO. To-morrow I'll have him taken to the yamen for punishment. That should appease your wrath.

CHIEF BOXER (*to his myrmidons*). Let's go and have our wounds dressed. (*Exeunt omnes.*)

SCENE VI

KUEI-YING (*appears singing in hsi-p'i yao-pan to express her anxiety about her absent father*). Father has been gone a long time, and still no tidings.

The hubbub of a magistrate's yamen is heard from behind the stage. Then voices counting ten, twenty, thirty, forty: Hsiao Ên is getting forty strokes of the bamboo. After which he totters on to the stage.

HSIAO ÊN. Curses on that Lü Tzŭ-ch'iu! He is not an honest and upright official. He had no right to punish me like that. A quiet and peaceful subject like me goes to complain at the yamen and the vicious curs, without a single word, set on me with forty strokes of the heavy bamboo and want me to apologize into the bargain! But there's no help for it. I can only gnash my teeth and hurry home. (*On arriving he sings out*) Kuei-ying, open the door!

KUEI-YING (*opening*). At last you've returned, Father! But why are you in such a dreadful state? (*Hsiao tells her. She bursts into tears*). You have been most barbarously treated!

HSIAO ÊN. I don't mind the pain so much as I resent being ordered to apologize to the Ting family.

KUEI-YING. Are you going to, Father?

HSIAO ÊN. I wish I could grow a pair of wings to fly across and kill the lot of them.

KUEI-YING. Father, you had better not go.

HSIAO ÊN. A mere child like you knows nothing of such matters. Make haste! fetch my coat and cap and the steel sword. (*She fetches them.*) Stay here and look after the place in the meantime.

KUEI-YING. I'll accompany you, Father.

HSIAO ÊN. You are a girl and had better stay at home.

KUEI-YING. But isn't this a fine chance to show my courage?

HSIAO ÊN. All right. Get ready to come along with me.

KUEI-YING. What about our things here?

HSIAO ÊN. We don't need any of them. (*Kuei-ying fears they will be stolen during their absence and bursts into tears.*) Don't cry so. Have you brought that lucky pearl (*Qing Ding Chu*) with you? (*Kuei-ying says yes*). If anything untoward happens, you had better run off to your mother-in-law's, where you'll be safe.

KUEI-YING. What about you, Father?

HSIAO ÊN. Don't worry about me. (*They board the boat.*) My child, sailing by night is not the same as by day: steady the rudder, you must be more cautious than usual. (*Sings in hsi-p'i k'uai-pan*) This affair is none of my seeking. I feel as if I were going through fire. I am crossing the river to-night to slay the whole family. If only I had wings to cross more swiftly! Why have you slackened the ropes, child?

KUEI-YING. Do you really mean to murder them, Father?

HSIAO ÊN. Of course, I am in earnest!

KUEI-YING. In that case I'll not go: I dare not.

HSIAO ÊN. Pah! When I didn't want you to, you insisted on coming: now that we're half-way, you want to turn back! Very well, I'll take you back.

KUEI-YING. I'll go with you, Father. I don't want to return. I could not possibly part with you so!

HSIAO ÊN (*sings and weeps*). Alas, my poor, dear daughter!

SCENE VII

They reach their destination, moor the boat and disembark.

HSIAO ÊN. My child, bear this in mind. Henceforth no matter where we are, if I upbraid, you too upbraid. If I say strike, you strike! We have now arrived at the Ting Mansion. Hey there! Anybody at home? (*The Chief Boxer appears and opens the door.*) I've come to tender my apologies to Ting Yüan Wai. (*The Chief Boxer, after some conventional fooling, goes off to announce him.*)

SCENE VIII

Enter Ting Yüan Wai and his secretary Kuo.

TING. Last night I had a very curious dream.

KUO. So had I! I dreamt that Yen Lo, King of the Underworld, had invited me to drink with him.

CHIEF BOXER. Hsiao Ên has come to offer his apologies.

TING. Show him in. (*Enter Hsiao, whom he addresses*) You impudent old wretch, what made you attack my employees as if they were wild beasts? And what have you to say in defence of such conduct?

HSIAO ÊN. With respect to this fishing-tax, have you the Imperial sanction?

TING. No.

HSIAO ÊN. Have you authority from the Six Boards?

TING. No.

HSIAO ÊN. By whose authority do you levy it, then?

TING. By His Honour the District Magistrate's.

HSIAO ÊN. Can you mean that Lü Tzŭ-ch'iu? (*Sings in hsi-p'i yao-pan*) Lü Tzŭ-ch'iu, you are far too avaricious! By what right did you sentence me to forty strokes of the bamboo? (*To Kuei-ying*) Curse him, denounce him, my dear!

KUEI-YING (*sings in hsi-p'i yao-pan*). The thieving cur and rebel! May Heaven utterly destroy him! He takes advantage of his official status to oppress the innocent. May he die without a clod of earth to cover his wretched carcass!*

TING (*to his servants*). Bring her here!

HSIAO ÊN. Ho, slowly there! We have, in the goodness of our hearts, brought you an offering.

TING. What is it?

HSIAO ÊN. We have come to present you with a pearl which we fished up out of the river.

TING. Let me see it.

HSIAO ÊN. There are too many eyes about.

TING (*to attendants*). Leave the room, all of you. (*Exeunt servants*). Where is it?

HSIAO ÊN. Here! (*Promptly draws his sword and kills Ting Yüan Wai and Kuo. He then says to Kuei-ying*) Daughter, help me to dispose of the rest.

The four assistant boxers come in and are slain. The Chief Boxer follows, and is likewise put to the sword.

(*Exeunt the fisherman and his daughter.*)

FINIS.

*The last is one of the worst maledictions that could blight a Chinese ear.

FORUM

"The World of the Chinese Drama"

TAO-CHING HSU

In this extract from his superb study of Chinese theater, Professor Hsu defines several principal differences between the Western theater—which is essentially based on realism—and the Chinese theater, which goes beyond realism in both its performance style and its subject matter. His comments about the importance of legends are applicable to the mythic dramas of other cultures, from both east and west.

Even if the actors can develop a style of acting suitable for elaborate sets and the audience accept gruesome and exciting details, realistic setting will still be out of place in the Chinese theatre because all the other elements of the stagecraft are unrealistic. Realism grafted to the Chinese theatre would not live. To inject realism into the Chinese theatre successfully it would be necessary to make the rest of the stagecraft consistent with it and that can only be brought about by changing everything of the traditional theatre and making the Chinese theatre disappear altogether. If that happens the aim and achievement of the classical Chinese theatre, to which every feature of it contributes, including the bare stage and the crude property, would be lost, for the artistic effects that it can produce cannot be achieved in the realistic theatre.

The whole Chinese stage is unreal. The characters never look like the audience; they are dressed in clothes which belong to the theatre only and are very different from what the audience wear. They use a stylish language. They do not talk but declaim and sing and they do not walk but strut and stalk and amble and glide. They do not sit, the men lean on the high cushions in the chair and the women perch on the edge of the seat. They do not fight, they clash their weapons, parade across the stage, spin on one leg, turn and jump and walk off the stage. They do not weep, they put their sleeve to the eye and start an aria in *lento*. They do not faint, they fall back into a chair, wipe their eyes with both hands one on each side and start another aria in *adagio*. They do not laugh, they utter sounds like laughing to strict rhythm. They do not get angry, they stamp their feet and then toss their long beards right and left.[1] The costume, the music, the singing, the declamation, the diction, the mime, the make-up and the mask all make the *dramatis personae* a different race of human beings, a race which lived in some bygone ages and of which we now see a few surviving specimens in the theatre. This different race of human beings establishes the world of the Chinese drama.

The Chinese stage becomes an entirely different world not by isolating it with the barrier of the footlights and the curtain but by distinguishing it with the consistently unusual appearance, archaic language and quaint manners of the actors. In the realistic theatre the barrier of the footlights must be guarded religiously because on it depends the assumed identity of the actors. Once they mix with the audience they lose their status of dramatic characters because they can hardly be distinguished from the audience by appearance, and if spectators and stage hands appear on the realistic stage as they do on the Chinese stage, they can be mistaken to be some of the actors. The magic world of the drama, lying behind the proscenium arch which serves as a peep hole, is maintained by sheer physical segregation, and all the things inside the limits of the stage, though they look very much like the things in the world of the audience, belong, by convention, to a different world. Isolation is probably the only possible means of establishing a world of the drama which resembles but is distinct from the world of the audience and the meticulous care with which this separate world is guarded against intrusion and periodically sealed from sight for changes gives some idea of its precarious existence. The Chinese actors, however, are surrounded by spectators on three sides if not four and share the stage with spectators, stage hands and musicians. There is neither curtain nor footlights to serve as boundary for their world. When they are in the front portion of the stage that portion is the domain of the drama but when they require more acting space, the table is pushed back and spectators at the back of the stage make room for them. So far as space is concerned, the world of the drama is in the midst of that of the audience, and yet it is a remote world because its inhabitants are widely different from the audience. It is a world that can remain distinct and intact even though stage hands mix with the actors and the stage and the auditorium almost merge into each other.

The Chinese theatre is legend come to life. Historically, the rise of the Chinese drama was preceded by the formation and propagation of a large body of national legends in Sung dynasty (960–1276) through the agency of various forms of popular entertainment, such as story-telling, shadow play, puppets and ballads, and popular legends have, since then, been the most important raw materials for the Chinese dramas. The legend as subject matter determines the psychology of the Chinese audience: the heroes of the Chinese theatre are national heroes for whom the audience already have, not only sympathy, but admiration and reverence also. The emotional attachment to the dramas far exceeds what is possible in journalistic and sociological themes: there the story and the characters are hypothetical or commonplace, but here they are objects of love and pride; there a good

---

[1] Some conventional stage actions, however, come from the actors' low life, such as dusting the chair with the sleeve and flicking the tears from the fingers.

play thrills the audience and a bad one bores them but here a good play is an act of homage and a bad one is an insult.

In the mind of the Chinese audience, the historical characters in the dramas really looked like their stage versions:

In the reign of Ch'ien Lung (1736–1796) there was an actor called Mi Hsi-Tzu who was famous for the role of Kuan Yü, a warrior in the period of Three Kingdoms (A.D. 220–277). At a private performance for high officials, this actor in his famous part entered, as is customary, with the sleeve in front of his face till he reached the front of the stage and then dropped his arm. The audience, all at once, stood up, thinking that they saw Kuan Yü himself. From then on, for a period of time, the play was banned, because Kuan Yü is a deified hero and realistic representations were felt to be sacrilegious.[2]

Even to-day the character Kuan Yü is treated with religious awe in the theatre: actors about to play the part burn incense in front of his image. The special style of music for his arias and the accompaniment by the Chinese hautboys instead of the usual fiddles add to the weird dignity of this role. The Empress Dowager Tz'u Hsi, in her palace performances, would find an excuse to stand up whenever Kuan Yü appeared on the stage.

Legend, and through it the world of Chinese drama, is the product of collective imagination. The Chinese plays are not, like the modern western dramas, works of individual minds offered to and accepted or rejected by the audience, they are conceived by the whole people and reviewed by them, the real authors, over and over again. Among people who do not understand scientific accuracy, myth and history attract fiction. Around simple stories that excite the imagination of the people, fiction grows and changes according to some obscure law of mass psychology. Legends are parables told by the joint effort of the people; they form the expression of their psyche. The selection of the theme and the embellishments added to them are natural processes which, it may be believed, are dictated by some psychological purpose, but, whatever that psychological purpose may be, logic and historical accuracy do not serve it, nor is it conducive to static products, for legends have a life of their own, sometimes breaking into a multitude of different versions and sometimes transforming themselves through a series of variants. Drama and novel are the two literary forms which the popular entertainment of Sung dynasty produced and the formation and transformation of the legends that became the subjects of the novels and dramas can be partially traced, especially in the later stages.[3] Legends, like rumour, represent the diversity

and even the self-contradiction of the collective mind, hence in the various versions of one story the dramatists can explore its different dramatic possibilities. The Chinese theatre is therefore the testing ground of legends and, in cases where the dramatists break new ground, also their breeding place. The credulity, the naîveté and the simplicity of the popular intellect are all reflected in the legends and the dramas; the ideal and the actual merge into one, there is no sharp distinction between what the public wish the story to be and what they think actually happened. Characters are larger than life-size; both the small and the great are magnified. When the wronged are saved eventually or the innocent suffer till the end, it is only because the audience wish to see them so. The fact that the Chinese audience are still moved by dramatized legends show that the national legends are still a vital part of the Chinese life.

One of the reasons why the new Chinese intelligentsia, educated in the western tradition, cannot appreciate the Chinese theatre, is that they have lost touch with the national legends and another is that they mistake the rules of science and history to be applicable to drama. Truth in art is never empirical truth; the audience come to the theatre for a kind of satisfaction different from what they can derive from the museum. Intelligent people accept the supernatural elements in the dramas not because they are superstitious but because as part of the legend these elements reveal some psychological truth, they no more believe in the doings of the gods than the historical accuracy of the dialogue. Considered in this light, the complaint of inaccuracy in the costume is unnecessarily fastidious, especially as sartorial history is a subject on which few Chinese can hold convinced opinions. The pedagogue can always find something to criticize for historical inaccuracy, he can question whether the diction and idioms are historically correct, or the pronunciation or the manners. When all details of a dramatic performance are historically correct, if that is possible, it is a documentary pageant, not a drama.

Contemporary life is too real for the subject of the theatre, there is always something drab about it and we know it too well to be able to beautify it. It is difficult to make legend out of contemporary life just as it is difficult to deify a contemporary person. The past, however, is to most of the audience happily indefinite, everything is possible in it. What to the historical mind are unchangeable facts to the audience of the theatre are plastic material capable of being moulded into a work of art. This is why the supernatural which is out of place in history is a legitimate element of the legends. Historical events are subject to the influence of a thousand accidents and their pattern is discernible only to experts; drama requires subject matter which has more prominent shape and form. Legends are often inspired by history but they never remain true to it. Only from a scientific point of view are the different versions of a legend contradictory, from the artistic point of view they are mutually complementary. The audience may not be able to explain the appeal of legends in spite of the outraged logic, but they divine their meaning.

The pattern of legend-making in its cruder forms is probably the same all over the world. In the popular theatre in China it

---

[2] Modern Chinese films based on historical themes in which the theatrical costume is used—"tab-sleeve," anachronism and all.

[3] For example, in the case of *Shui Hu Chuan*, the story of the thirty-six robbers in Sung dynasty and the subject of one of the greatest Chinese novels. Modern scholarship has revealed several layers of embellishment in the novel. It is an amazing example of collective literary effort.

(continued)

consists of parading the admirable and the despicable to provide opportunities for exercising envy and contempt, the sharp distinction of the good and the bad and the reward of the kind and punishment of the wicked to exercise the moral judgments of the audience. In the classical theatre, however, dramatic themes are more complicated. There drama becomes a commentary on life but is usually without a moral. The distinction of the good and the bad or the admirable and the contemptible is not always sharp, still less are the good always rewarded and the wicked punished. In the best dramas, a moral problem may be implied but it is left for the audience to solve. The very fact that the end of the story, happy or otherwise, is seldom reached in the classical dramas …

Whether a drama makes one ponder over life depends on one's sensibility; as is said of *Hamlet*, to the simple-minded everything is simple. To the contemplative there is always much to think about life, especially when joy and sorrow are brought back to them by the drama with fresh impact.

JAPAN

Artistic and Cultural Events

c. 600: Records of *gigaku* and *bugaku* dances at court; antecedents of Noh drama

c. 550: Records of erotic dances in honor of sun goddess

c. 1350: Beginnings of Noh drama as Zeami writes *The Kadensho* and *Komachi* plays

c. 1300: Musical story-telling; antecedents of *bunraku* and *kabuki* drama

c. 1490: Kyogen (farce) emerges

1586: Okuni performs dances that become basis for Kabuki theater

1629: Women banned from performing *kabuki*

1617: Young men's kabuki

1749: *The Actors Analects,* major treatise on performace

1642: First *onnagata* Age of Chikumatsu (to 1725); golden age of *kabuki* and *bunraku* puppetry

1881: Modern theater movement begins

c. 1890: New School of Art in Japan; favors western realism

1930s: *Shengeki* theater popularized

1970s: Suzuki Tadeshi forms experimental theater companies

600 B.C.E.	500 C.E.	600 C.E.	1300 C.E.	1400 C.E.	1500 C.E.	1600 C.E.	1700 C.E.	1800 C.E.	1900 C.E.

Historical and Political Events

660: First earthly emperor of Japan: Jimmu Tenno

c. 525: Buddhism appears in Japan

Feudalism weakened

1603–1867: Tokagawa period; last Shogunate rulers

1868: Meiji period

1945: Atomic bombs dropped on Hiroshima and Nagaski

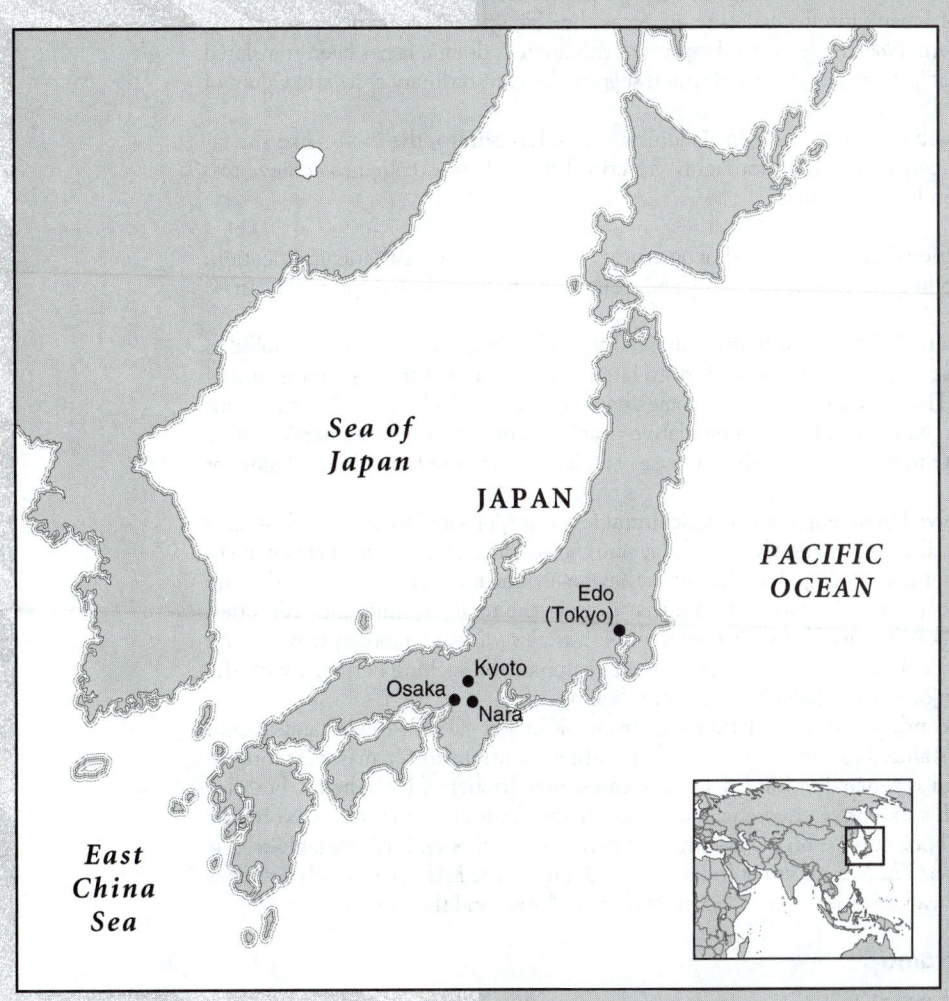

The Noh Theater

The Evolution of Noh Theater

The Noh (also: *Nō*) theater of classical Japan is a fusion of dance, poetry, music, mime, and acting that reflected the ceremonial, meditative life of the ancient aristocracy. Today, it is the drama of choice of Japan's intellectual elite, whereas the Kabuki theater is the drama of the masses. The very term *Noh* implies several aspects of this ancient drama. It has been translated as "accomplishment" or "art play," both of which suggest the extraordinary aesthetic values of the Noh theater.

As an outgrowth of Amida and Zen Buddhism, as well as Shinto, the Noh—like the famous Japanese tea ceremony—is a thoroughly prescribed ritual. It is intended to achieve two virtues important in Japanese culture:

- *yúgen* ("mysterious beauty"), a mood of quietness, meditation, and aesthetic gratification;
- *ran-i* ("the sublime"), a feeling of ecstasy and exaltation produced by exceptional artistry.

From the austere Buddhists, Noh artists derived the belief that suggestion is preferable to overstatement, that small gestures are superior to large, that restraint is the superior means of achieving beauty. Though they may appear somewhat static, even "undramatic," to those unfamiliar with them, Noh dramas are contemplative rituals meant to transport audiences into a transcendental state in harmony with the universe. The Japanese revere *Komachi at Sekedira* for these qualities.

Noh itself evolved from religious and agricultural festivals sponsored by the Buddhist temples at the ancient cities of Nara and Kyoto. Today one can still attend nighttime performances of Noh by firelight at the Kofukuji Temple, just as they have done for over 800 years at this site of Japan's ancient capital. In its earliest forms, that is, from the tenth to thirteenth centuries, Noh evolved from folk dances. Two early names for Noh were *surugaku* ("monkey dance") and *dengaku* ("field dance"), each of which suggests Noh's emphasis on seeking harmony with the natural world, a major tenet of Japan's two major religions.

In the fourteenth century, a father-son team—Kan'ami (1333–1384) and Zeami (1363–1443)—crystallized the diverse strains of the earlier traditions into a major art form in Heian Japan. Zeami is generally regarded as the greatest practitioner of Noh drama, both for his plays and for his extensive theoretical writings on the form and function of Noh. His *Kadensho*, a seven-book treatise on playwriting and performance theory, is comparable to *The Poetics* of Aristotle or *The Nātyaśāstra* of India. An extract from *The Kadensho*, which describes the birth of Noh theater, has been included in the Forum, "Style and the Flower."

Types of Noh Drama

Though well over 2,000 Noh plays have been written—including one based on the conversion of St. Paul—the classical repertory consists of some 240 plays, about half ascribed to Zeami. These are grouped into one of five categories according to subject matter and style:

1. god (*kami* or *waki*) plays celebrating an auspicious religious event;
2. warrior (*shura-mono*) plays in which the protagonist is usually a slain warrior whose ghost returns to relieve human suffering;
3. woman (*kazura*) plays, sometimes referred to as "wig plays" because they are acted by men in wigs (*Komachi at Sekidera* is such a play);
4. "living person pieces" (*genzai*), which often deal with madness, obsessions, and unbridled passion;
5. demon (*kiri*) plays in which the protagonist is a demon, devil, or other supernatural figure, both good and evil.

Because most of the plays in the repertory are short, an evening of Noh theater usually consists of a sample of each of the five types of plays. Short farces (*kyógen*) are performed between the

The renowned Noh actor Sadayo Kita plays a noblewoman who is transformed into a demon to do battle with the warrior-prince Kan Hosh. Demon and god plays are staples of the Noh theater.

lofty dramas, much the way comic satyr plays were performed at the tragic festivals of ancient Athens. The Japanese respect for nature dictates that a play may not be performed out of its appropriate season: when spring comes to Japan the winter plays are put to rest for another year.

The Conventions of Noh Theater

Because its emphasis is not on an unfolding human action and the attendant suspense, Noh theater is not grounded in intricate plotting. Rather, Noh drama exists to create mood, emotion, and a spiritual state. Most Noh plays are dominated by a single, powerful emotion summoned by the harmony of instrumental and vocal music, dance and gesture, and poetry. Whatever their genre, subject matter, or emotional impact, the plots and characters of Noh plays are carefully structured according to ancient formulas. With only a few exceptions (and *Komachi at Sekidera* is an exception), the plays are in two parts. In the first section the central character, called the *shite* ("doer"), appears in disguise, customarily that of a humble person. In the second, the *shite* is transformed into a supernatural being: a god, a demon, or a ghostly specter who, in the tradition of Buddhism, repents past deeds. The *shite* is accompanied by a *tsure*. An objective third party—the *waki*, often a holy person—watches from the "side" and comments on the action. Other roles are often the *kokata*, or child, symbolizing a new order. A servant, or *kyógen* ("clown"), adds irony to the play. While the *kyógen* uses colloquial prose, the *shite* speaks in lofty, poetic language filled with obscure references to Japanese literature and religion. Thus Noh plays virtually defy translation. Imagine a Japanese visitor trying to watch a Western play filled with snippets from the Bible, Shakespeare, Homer, and the Arthurian legends. Still, the themes and emotions elicited by these plays are sufficiently universal that one need not be educated in Buddhist philosophy, classical Japanese literature, or the particulars of sacred gesture and dance.

The Noh theater's aversion to realistic representation is perhaps best manifested by the stage on which these spiritual rituals are enacted. In its earliest days, the Noh stage was perhaps more versatile, particularly as its first performers wandered from temple to temple, court to

FORUM

"Style and the Flower" from *The Kadensho*

Zeami

TRANSLATED BY J. THOMAS RIMER AND YAMAZAKI MASAKAZU

Zeami's lengthy treatise on the art of the Noh theatre is the first principal study of Japanese drama and its aesthetics, and it is comparable in importance and content as Aristotle's The Poetics. *Here the poet-dramatist recounts the evolution of the Noh theatre from early rituals, a pattern that may be found in the development of theater in many cultures. Zeami's history of the Noh reminds us of the spiritual dimension that permeates that drama.*

MATTERS PERTAINING TO THE GODS

The beginnings of *sarugaku* in the age of the gods, it is said, occurred when Amaterasu, the Sun Goddess, concealed herself in the heavenly rocky cave, and the whole earth fell under endless darkness. All the myriad deities gathered at the heavenly Kagu mountain, in order to find a way to calm her. They played sacred music to accompany their comic dances. In the midst of this Ama no Uzume[1] came forward, and, holding a spring of *sakaki* wood and a *shide*,[2] she raised her voice and, in front of a fire that had been lighted, she pounded out the rhythm of her dance with her feet and became possessed by divine inspiration as she sang and danced. The Sun Goddess, hearing the voice of Ama no Uzume, opened the rock door slightly. The land became light, and the faces of the gods could be seen again. It is said that such entertainments marked the beginning of *sarugaku*. There are doubtless other particulars remaining about this in other secret writings.

In the country of the Buddha, a wealthy man named Sudatta had built a Buddhist place of retreat, the Jetavana Monastery.[3] At the dedication ceremonies, the Buddha preached a sermon. Devadatta[4] and a throng of unbelievers cried out and danced wildly, holding branches and bamboo grass in which they had placed *shide*, making it more difficult for the Buddha to carry out the ceremony. The Buddha then signaled his disciple Śāriputra

with his eye; and Śāriputra, through the power of the master, had the idea of arranging for flute and drum music to be played at the rear entrance to the hall. Then three of the disciples—the learned Ānanda, the wise Śāriputra, and the eloquent Pūrṇa[5]—performed sixty-six entertainments. The heretics, listening to the sound of flute and drum, assembled at the rear entrance and fell silent observing the spectacle. During this time, the Buddha was able to continue on with the dedication service. Such were the beginnings of our art in India.

In our own country, during the reign of the Emperor Kimmei [A.D. 509–571], on an occasion when the Hatsuse River in Yamato overflowed its banks, a jar floated down in the current. A high court official picked up the jar near the cedar gate of the Miwa Shrine.[6] Inside was a young child. His face was gentle, and he was like jewel. Because the infant seemed to have descended from heaven, the incident was reported to the emperor at the imperial palace. That very night, the child appeared to the emperor in a dream and said, "I am the reborn spirit of the emperor Shih-huang of the Ch'in Dynasty in China.[7] My destiny has a connection with Japan, and I now appear before you." The emperor, thinking this occurrence a miracle, had the child brought to serve in court. When he grew to manhood, he came to be of surpassing talent and wisdom, and at the age of fifteen, he rose to the rank of Minister. He was given the family name of Chin. Because that Chinese character is pronounced *Hata* in Japanese, he was called Hata no Kōkatsu.

Prince Shōtoku, at a time when there were disturbances in the land, asked this Hata no Kōkatsu to perform sixty-six dramatic pieces, following the precedents set down at the time of the gods and Buddhas, and the prince himself made sixty-six masks for Hata no Kōkatsu's use. Kōkatsu performed these entertainments at the Shishinden Hall at the imperial palace at Tachibana.[8] The country soon became peaceful. Prince Shōtoku then passed this entertainment on for the benefit of later generations. The word *kagura* ["god-given entertainment"] employs [a character which stands for the word "god" and consists of a radical meaning "sacred" and a root which means "to

---

[1] An important heavenly goddess in Shintō legend.

[2] *Sakaki (cleyera ochnacea)* is a type of evergreen tree important in Shintō rites. A *shide* is a specially folded strap of cloth hung as a sacred offering. In later centuries, the use of paper became more common.

[3] Sudatta was a rich man who devoted himself to the Buddha. He constructed the Jetavana monastery for him, where the Buddha remained for more than twenty years.

[4] Devadatta was a cousin of the Buddha who, although at first a follower, later turned against the Buddha and attempted to have him killed.

[5] Three of the "ten great disciples" of Buddha. Śāriputra was the guiding spirit of the early Buddhist monastic order, Ānanda was known for his wisdom, and Pūrṇa for his eloquence.

[6] One of the most sacred Shintō shrines in Japan. The site is approximately eleven miles from the city of Nara.

[7] Emperor Shih-huang (259–210 B.C.) united China under the Ch'in Dynasty. He built the Great Wall and issued the famous edict for the burning of the books.

[8] The site of the present Tachibana Temple, near Nara. The *shishinden* was the main building in the complex.

speak"]. He removed the radical, but left the remainder. As that character is pronounced *saru* and stands for one of the twelve horary signs, he thus gave the name *sarugaku* to this entertainment. Then too, because of the original meaning of the root,[9] "to speak," *sarugaku* also means "to speak of pleasure." This meaning comes about because part of the original character was removed [as described above].

Kōkatsu served a number of emperors, including Kimmei, Bidatsu, Yōmei, and Sushun, as well as Empress Suiko and Prince Shōtoku. He passed his art on to his descendants, and then, as he himself was an apparition and thus could leave no trace of his whereabouts, he set out from Naniwa in the province of Settsu in a boat hollowed out of wood, letting the wind blow him where it would. He landed in the province of Harima, in the bay of Shakushi.[10] The people there, when they pulled the boat on shore, found a being that did not have human shape. This being haunted and cursed many and caused strange things to happen. The people began to worship this being as a god, and their province grew wealthy. They called this god Taikō Dai Myōjin, the Great Raging God. Even now his virtue is still efficacious. His True Body is that of Bishamon Tennō.[11] When Prince Shōtoku put down the rebellion of Moriya of the Mononobe,[12] he used the divine aid of this Kōkatsu in order to defeat his enemy, it is said.

When Kyoto became the capital of our country, during his reign the Emperor Murakami [A.D. 926–967] read what Prince Shōtoku had recorded about the *sarugaku*: first, that the art had originated at the time of the gods and in the land of the Buddha, then that it had come to Japan [from India] through Bactria[13] and China; second, that these "wild words and specious phrases"[14] that constitute this art will serve to praise the Buddha and provide the means to spread his teachings, will chase away evil affinities, and will call forth happiness, so that the country will remain in tranquillity, bringing gentleness and long life to the people. Finding Prince Shōtoku's words efficacious, Emperor Murakami thought that *sarugaku* might serve as a means of supplication for the good of the nation. At this time there was a descendant of Kōkatsu who practiced his art who was named Hata no Ujiyasu. At the emperor's request, he performed sixty-six pieces of *sarugaku* in the Shishinden Hall of the imperial palace.

At that time there was a man of great talent named Ki no Gon no Kami. He was the husband of a younger sister of Hata no Ujiyasu. With him as a partner, Ujiyasu performed *sarugaku*. Later, thinking that it was too difficult to perform all sixty-six items of *sarugaku* in one day, the two decided to select three pieces, *Inatsumi no Okina*, *Yonasumi no Okina*, and *Chichi no Jo*. What is presently referred to as *Shiki samban*[15] doubtless refers to these three plays. These three serve as symbolic representations of the Three Bodies of the Buddha.[16] There are separate secret teachings on this subject.

Komparu Mitsutaro is a descendant of Hata no Ujiyasu in the twenty-ninth generation. He is the head of the Emman-i troupe[17] in the province of Yamato. His family possesses items handed down from Ujiyasu, including a devil's mask carved by Prince Shotoku himself, a portrait of the god of Kasuga Shrine, and bones from the Buddha's own body.

In our present generation [as concerns performances related to religious observances], when the *yuimae* service[18] is performed at the Kōfukuji temple in Nara, the service proper is held in the lecture hall, while *ennen* dances are performed in the dining hall. The dances calm those who do not believe and pacify the devils. During this time, in front of the dining hall, a lecture is given on the *Vimalakīrti sutra*.[19] This practice is based on the ancient example of the Jetavana monastery.

In Yamato province, religious rites of the Kōfukuji Temple and the Kasuga shrines are held on the second and fifth day of the second month. Four *sarugaku* troupes perform at these ceremonies that mark the beginning of the year's religious observances. The performances serve as prayers for the peace of the whole country.

---

[9]Traditionally, the day was divided into twelve parts, each of two hours' duration. *Saru* (monkey) corresponds to the period from 4:00 to 6:00 P.M.

[10]A site to the east of Akō in Okayama Prefecture on the Inland Sea.

[11]The True Body represents the Buddhist identity of a Shintō god. Bishamon (in Sanskrit, Vaísravana), is one of the Four Quarter Kings who protect the various continents. Vaísravana protects the northern part of the world.

[12]Moriya (died 587) was a courtier who attempted to destroy the growing power of Buddhism in Japan. His forces were eventually defeated, and he was killed.

[13]An ancient country of southwestern Asia, now a district of northern Afghanistan.

[14]Thomas J. Harper's translation of the phrase *kyōgen kigo*, an expression derived from the phrase by the Chinese T'ang poet Po Chü-i (A.D. 772–846) in which he expresses the hope that his "wild words and specious phrases" may be transformed into a hymn of praise to the Buddha. The passage is cited in the *Wakanrōeishū* compiled in 1013 by Fujiwara Kintō (A.D. 966–1041), a poetry collection still widely appreciated at Zeami's time.

[15]The titles of these three plays might be tentatively rendered in English as "Old Man of the Harvest," "The Old Man Heir Apparent," and "The Venerable Old Father." *Shiki samban* might be translated as "Three Ceremonial Pieces." The play *Okina* (literally, "Old Man"), which is still performed on ceremonial occasions, doubtless derives from such earlier pieces, now lost.

[16]That is, the Body of Essence, the Body of Bliss, and the Transformation Body. See Wm. Theodore de Bary, ed., *The Buddhist Tradition in India, China, and Japan*, pp. 94–95.

[17]The group later became the Komparu troupe.

[18]A seven-day ceremonial reading of the *Vimalakīrti sutra* (Japanese, *Yuimakyō*) held during October at the Kōfukuji on a regular basis since the ninth century.

[19]This sutra eulogizes Buddha's lay disciple Vimalakīrti, who, while remaining a householder, achieved a greater degree of enlightenment than others who understood monastic discipline.

(continued)

The various companies are as follows:

1. The four troupes that perform at religious functions of the Kasuga Shrine in Yamato: Tobi, Yūzaki, Sakado, Emman-i.[20]
2. The three troupes that perform at religious functions of the Hie Shrine in Ōmi: Yamashina, Shimosaka, and Hie.[21]
3. The two troupes of *shushi* that perform at Ise.
4. The three troupes that perform services at the beginning of the year at the Hossōji temple in Kyoto:[22] the Shinza, the Honza, and the Shuku troupe.[23]

These three troupes also perform for the various ceremonies held at the Kamo Shrines in Kyoto and at the Sumiyoshi Shrine in Settsu.[24]

[20]Tobi is the old name for the present Hōshō troupe. Yūzaki is the former name of the Kanze troupe. Sakado is the old name for the present Kongō troupe. Enman-i is the former name for the Komparu troupe.

[21]The three important troupes of Omi *sarugaku*.

[22]The Hosshōji was an important temple built under the sponsorship of Emperor Shirakawa (1053–1129). Due to natural disasters, it fell into ruin later in the medieval period. The ceremonies mentioned here were held for several days at the beginning of each year as a plea to the Buddha to bring peace and abundant crops.

[23]The Shinza was also known as the Enami troupe. Zeami locates the troupe in Kawachi (an area in present-day Osaka Prefecture). The Honza was resident in Tamba (part of Kyoto Prefecture) and was sometimes referred to as the Yata troupe. The Shuku troupe was located in Settsu, the present-day Hyōgo Prefecture.

[24]The two Kamo shrines in Kyoto held festivals during the sixth month in order to bless the crops grown on their sacred lands. Sacred rice planting ceremonies were held at the Sumiyoshi Shrine, located in what is now a part of Osaka Prefecture.

court, performing their plays. Today, however, the Noh stage has a standard size. The playing space is a 19 feet, 5 inches square; it is always 2 feet, 7 inches high. It projects into the auditorium and is surrounded by the audience on three sides; customarily there is a small moat that separates the forestage from the first row of spectators. The stage is constructed of highly polished wood that reflects the actors and enhances the aesthetics of the production. It is backed by a panel on which is painted an aged pine tree signifying natural beauty and eternity. A roof, supported by four 15-foot pillars, covers the playing space.

The actors enter from the audience's left via the *hashigakari*, a bridge lined by three small trees. Prior to their entrance, the actors sit in the *kagami no ma* ("mirror room") for hours contemplating the polished wooden masks they wear. Only the *shite* and *tsure* wear masks, hewn from a rare wood found in only one area of Japan; they are crafted by a single family that has performed this sacred duty for centuries. The other characters wear masklike makeup; the cho-

The stage of the National Noh Theater of Japan with its traditional posts; the shite pillar is at the upper left. The image of the pine tree is considered sacred and is a fixture of the Noh stage.

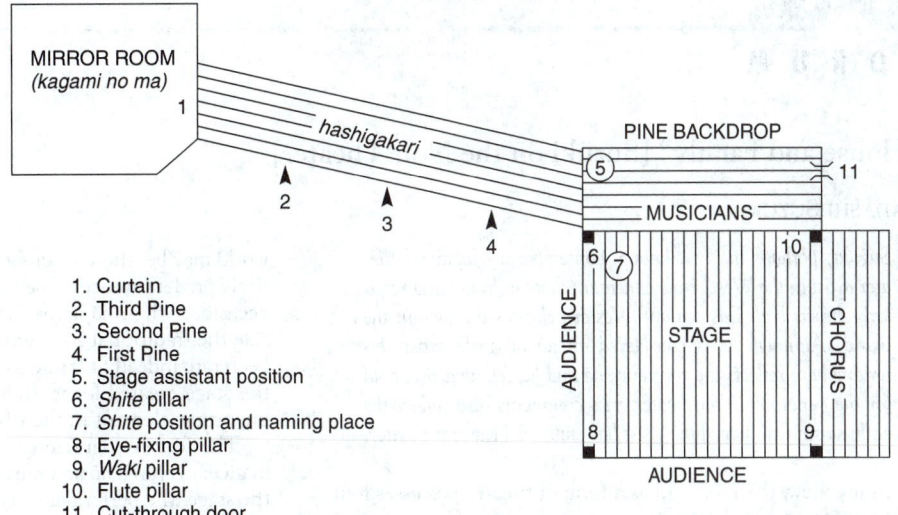

1. Curtain
2. Third Pine
3. Second Pine
4. First Pine
5. Stage assistant position
6. *Shite* pillar
7. *Shite* position and naming place
8. Eye-fixing pillar
9. *Waki* pillar
10. Flute pillar
11. Cut-through door

Diagram of a traditional Noh stage; note especially the bridge (hashikagari) *linking the mirror room with the stage facilities' ceremonial entrances for the principal actors.*

rus and musicians wear none. Four musicians, who play three types of drums and a flute, sit in an alcove upstage, fully visible to the audience. A chorus chants the words of the play while sitting on the right side of the stage. Each of the principal actors, all male, has an assigned area where he sits or performs. The *shite* stands at the place where the *hashigakari* meets the stage, the *waki* at the pillar diagonally opposite the *shite*, and the *kyōgen* at the rear of the stage. The very rigidity of this placement reinforces the ritualistic nature of Noh drama, as well as its presentational style of performance. The costumes are extraordinary works of art in themselves. Little wonder that Noh actors have been a favorite subject for Japanese artists for 600 years.

The performance techniques of Noh drama have been strictly codified in *The Kadensho* and are not subject to variation because the Japanese do not especially embrace innovation in art. According to the principle of *sabi*, they revere the past and judge a work by the exactness of its replication of ancient methods. Thus, each of the five major types of plays employs a particular music that is proper to it alone. A twentieth-century Noh actor must learn and re-create meticulously the gestures, intonations, and dance steps that were perfected in Zeami's age. The gestures and steps are executed with slow precision to enhance the meditative experience of the Noh theater; it is not uncommon for an actor to take many seconds to merely raise an arm. Because of its many conventions and traditions, only the barest elements of Noh performance can be described here. Of the many types of theater described in this text, perhaps none so completely demands a living example as Noh theater because of its stately aestheticism, which words cannot replicate.

The Influence of Noh Drama on the West

Many twentieth-century theater artists in the West have been attracted to the Noh theater, perhaps none more than Irish poet-playwright William Butler Yeats. He especially admired the poetic, antirealistic nature of the Japanese theater and in 1916 began a series of "Plays for Dancers" in which he fused ancient Celtic myth with Noh technique. "I have invented a form of drama, distinguished, indirect, and symbolic . . . an aristocratic form," he announced as he wrote *At the Hawk's Well.* Though more influenced by the Chinese theater, Bertolt Brecht adapted a Noh play in 1930 for his didactic theater, and the noted British composer Sir Ben-

FORUM

"House and Family" [Suzuki on the Noh Theater]

TADASHI SUZUKI

Suzuki, perhaps the best known contemporary Japanese the-ater artist in the West, runs a theater school in Japan and regu-larly directs both Eastern and Western classics throughout the world. Although he is considered an avant-garde artist, his writing here reflects the reverence he and his fellow artists hold for the venerable Noh theater. His comments also reflect the enthusiasm with which the West has embraced Eastern theater.

In my view, the nō [Noh] as a form of theater possesses four characteristics that define its unique existence. The first con-cerns the fact that, from the rehearsal period down to the actual performance, virtually no energy that is not human goes into an artistic creation. Non-human or inert energy is that which is created not by men or by animals but by electricity, oil, even by atomic power. The contemporary theater tends to increase its expressive abilities by the use of such inert energy. Even *kabuki* which, like the nō, is a premodern form of theater, proves no ex-ception. In revolving stage, traps, lighting, even its music, all make some use of inert energy created by modern means. Nō, on the other hand, sustains its performing space with a minimum of electric lighting. The musical accompaniment, the chorus, the masks, the costumes, and the movements of the actors them-selves are all projected through a natural craft. *Kabuki* cannot compare to the nō in terms of the human energy expended on the stage. There is one breed of sociologist who would compare the amount of inert energy used in a nation's manufacturing processes to the amount of physical energy used, so as to judge how advanced the country has become. If you apply that logic to the theater, nō certainly remains a premodern form of art.

The second characteristic is that the nō is non-realistic in its expression. In the established structure of many nō plays, the dream of a priest wandering about the country on a pilgrimage summons up a person long dead, who plays out again a life al-ready lived; the drama makes use of the realm of reverie and consciousness. This world consists of what cannot be seen or heard in everyday life, only what can be felt, absorbed. Such things are conveyed to the audience through a kind of vocal production and gesture that cannot be heard or witnessed in everyday life. The spectacle that unfolds on th stage is no way a realistic portrayal of ordinary human characteristics.

The third point is that the environment in which the whole of the nō exists is altogether fixed. However diverse the real

world may be, there is surely no other form of art which is so en-tirely predetermined. True enough, there have been exceptional occasions when nō actors have performed their repertoire out-side the traditional stage environment. But such moments have been rare indeed; it is safe to say that when nō is enacted, it is on the stage created for it. Indeed, that stage itself constitutes an important element in the whole art.

The fourth characteristic involves the nature of nō perfor-mance: even if a nō actor, in the middle of his role, falls dead on the stage, the performance continues. In the modern theater, or even in *kabuki*, such a thing cannot be imagined. If an actor cannot continue, the curtain is drawn; the manager usually comes out to explain the situation to the audience, apologizing for the interruption. But in the nō, if the *shite*, the main charac-ter, finds himself unable to continue, he is immediately replaced by the *kōken*, the assistant. It is not altogether clear when this practice of substitution started, but the custom has prevailed since the beginning of the Meiji period (1868). Perhaps the ex-planation for the practice lies in some tradition of religious cer-emony, in which the order of the performance must not be dis-turbed whatever happens to the participants; the program must be completed as planned. In any case, the performance of nō today incorporates unique methods. Whatever the logic that gave birth to such a form of theater, the system has long been es-tablished.

I see these four points, then, as characteristics unique to the nō. Tendencies toward the first two of them, however, can be seen in the avant-garde theater developed around the world since the 1960s. The use of human energy has been touted as a means to rehabilitate the actor; some feel that inert energy weakens the actor's effectiveness, drying up the real forces of the drama itself. Grotowski led the movement in this direction. This kind of vision, that seeks a return to fundamentals in the face of a society ever more mechanized, has become less and less a unique property of the nō. For that matter, the theater of an-cient Greece was also performed outdoors and involved only human energy, thus rendering the first characteristic not alto-gether unique to Japan. Still, there are very few forms of theater that break as completely as the nō with the use of such artificial energy.

The question of non-realism, as well, in light of the various techniques that have been developed within the avant-garde theater, cannot be said to belong only to the nō. After all, most forms of avant-garde theater unite in a repudiation of realism. In that regard, these other forms resemble the nō. And although the nō employs an ancient vocabulary, makes use of masks, and incorporates folk elements into its gestures, these elements can-not be said to provide an altogether unique form of theatrical experience either. After all, ancient performance techniques celebrating the repose of the dead with singing and dancing revealed a commonality that transcended individual folk customs and are thus certainly not peculiar to the nō.

Strictly speaking then, the truly unique features of the nō are those third and fourth points I made above: the fact that it is performed in a unique playing space, and the fact that a performance cannot be interrupted even if one of the performers dies. An examination of these two characteristics can reveal a great deal about the relationship of nō to the commonality inherent in the theater. Indeed, it seems to me that the nō does suggest a unique resolution to the issue of commonality that is inevitably confronted when the theater as a communal enterprise, surpassing time and space, attempts to establish its finite existence. In another sense, the third point can be related to the commonality of the actors' physical bodies, while the fourth speaks rather to their spiritual commonality.

The eminent folklorist Yanagita Kunio (1875–1962) has written:

> The Chinese character used to write the word *family* can be pronounced two ways in Japanese, *ie* and *ya*. The history of the word is not altogether clear, but it does seem certain that the meaning of *ie* and *ya* [house; shop] are by no means identical. The idea of a house certainly suggests a covering or shelter, a structure that guards against the rain and the dew. Thus the word *miya* [shrine; literally the honorific *mi* plus *ya*] is certainly intended to represent one such structure. A family, on the other hand, represents something different, a point of inner centrality. As a proof of this, to alter slightly the verbal expressions involved, the *e* of *ie* has sometimes represented "door" and can also signify "oven." This syllable *e* might well be defined as that thing central to the home, the fire that is placed in the middle. The whole idea of an oven may be looked on as a mere commonplace today. But in ancient times, all the family members would gather in the central room and eat together, in the largest available space. The oven or cooking place represented the spot where they gathered, and where they worshipped their gods.

> A house, on the other hand, suggests an opposite connotation. Even a small structure with a roof that can keep off the rain and the dew can easily qualify. In general, "house" in the sense of *ya* suggests part of a larger family, or *ie*; many *ya* may come under that large covering. We tend to get confused because the same Chinese character is used to stand for two different concepts: a single house (*ya*) and a whole group of families (*ie*). The chief reason that these two differing concepts have blended together and are written with one character has to do with technical developments in architectural construction.

(from "The Concept of the Term 'House'")

The point that Yanagita is making, when applied to the nō theater, is a profoundly striking one. In his terms, the House can be explained as the stage that ensures the commonality of the physical performance of the nō actors, while the Family represents a concept which, relying on the logic of blood ties, provides for the establishment of a truly collaborative group represented by the family name. Therefore, according to the double usage of the word "family" as established by Yanagita, the nō is the dramatic form that can bring these special characteristics to life. Indeed, one could argue that it is the idea embodied in the subtitle of the book in which Yanagita's essay appears, "The house one can see and the house one cannot see," that serves to empower the nō, signaling its uniqueness as a form of world theater.

---

jamin Britten wrote the Noh-inspired *Curlew River* (1964) as "a parable for church performance." The minimalist plays of Samuel Beckett summon parallels with the Noh theater in both form and content. The formalist productions of director-*auteurs* such as Robert Wilson suggest a kinship with the stately, static aesthetics of the Noh. Even contemporary Japanese theater artists such as Tadashi Suzuki use the conventions of Noh (and often Kabuki) in their decidedly modern works, including those from the Western canon (see Forum, "House and Family" [Suzuki on the Noh Theater]).

The Kabuki Theater

The Evolution of the Kabuki Theater

The Noh has largely been the theater of sophisticates and intellectuals. In the late sixteenth century Noh was given state sanction when the shogunate government made it the official drama of the court. At the same time Japan was being torn asunder by civil warfare and a dying feudalism. Under the Tokugawa shogunate (1603–1867), the merchant class gained influence, particularly as Portuguese, Spanish, and Dutch explorers opened trade routes between Asia and the West. Merchants sought their entertainment in places other than the court theaters, and they frequented shrines where they were entertained by temple maidens who performed graceful yet lively folk dances called *nembutsu odori*. The *odori* were quite unlike the solemn *mai* dances of the Noh theater.

In 1603 a temple maiden named Okuni brought her company of *odori* dancers to Kyoto's Izumo Shrine, where they performed on a Noh stage. Subsequent performances, curiously, were given in a dry riverbed as the audience sat on the grassy hillside to watch Okuni's troupe. Today the term *shibai* ("grass sitting") still refers to the Kabuki theater and its plays. The *odori* dances were provocative both in their sensual movements and in their clothing. A contemporary woodblock print shows Okuni dressed in Portuguese-style men's pants, wearing a foreign headpiece and a Christian crucifix about her neck. This strange garb offers some clues as to the meaning of the term *kabuki*. Although the three Japanese characters that are used to signify *kabuki* mean "song, dance, skill [in performance]," the word in Okuni's time meant "bizarre" or "avant-garde." Among Okuni's boldest innovations in her avant-garde theater was the placement of actors in the midst of the audience, thereby giving *kabuki* its distinctive actor-audience relationship.

Okuni's fame spread, and in 1607 the shogun at Edo (Tokyo) commanded her to perform at his castle. She enacted short plays, interspersed with her *kabuki* dances, on the same program with the older, more stately Noh dramas. Okuni's dances and plays were as popular with the merchants as they were controversial among the old guard. The plays often featured women dressed as men, men as women, and many of the plots had to do with prostitution; in one play, Okuni appeared as a male customer visiting a teahouse to buy a prostitute. The erotic nature of these early *kabuki* plays caused patrons to quarrel over favorite actresses. Consequently, in 1629 the shogunate forbade the appearance of women on the stage, not because of any moral scruples about prostitution (which thrived among the merchant class) but because any form of disorder—such as fights among *kabuki* spectators—was intolerable in the Japanese culture.

The popular new theater art continued as the Women's Kabuki (*onno*) was replaced by the Young Men's Kabuki (*wakashu*). There had been troupes of young male dancers prior to Okuni's time, but they fell out of favor when the Women's Kabuki became popular. The young males soon adopted the style of Okuni's troupe, and for the next 23 years they were the most popular stage entertainments in Japan. The boys, too, were involved in prostitution and once again quarrels among Kabuki patrons caused the shogunate to outlaw the Young Men's Kabuki. From 1653 only mature males (*yaro*), whose foreheads were shaved to make them less attractive, were allowed to perform Kabuki. The male-only custom continues today (with a few notable exceptions) and one can still see the shaved forelock wigs in many Kabuki costumes. Importantly, the ban on women gave rise to one of present-day Kabuki's most distinguishing features, the *onnagata* role in which a mature man meticulously creates the dress, dance, and manners of the idealized woman.

During the Genrouku period (1673 to 1735) Japanese arts, and consequently Kabuki, expanded and thrived in a manner comparable to that of the Elizabethan age. Power was passing from the feudal warlords to the newly monied class of merchants who fostered the arts. From the Genrouku era came Kabuki's first great actor, Ickikawa Danjúró I [whose descendant created the role of Benkei in *Kanjinchō* (*The Subscription List*)] and its greatest poet-playwright, Chikamatsu Monzaemon (1653–1724), whose stature is comparable to that of Shakespeare. Most of the conventions and form of the Kabuki were fixed during the Genrouku period. The adoption of the curtain and scenery, unthinkable in Noh theater, the emergence of the *hanamichi*, a lengthy ramp through the audience on which actors entered and exited the stage, and the primacy of literary texts were significant developments.

Types of Kabuki Drama

Kabuki plays traditionally comprise five acts, perhaps a remnant of the days in which five separate Noh plays made up a day's program. Traditionally, a Kabuki program lasted about 12 hours, although the length was reduced to 8 in 1868. Audiences are free to come and go as they please, and they often bring food and drink for the day-long event. A Kabuki program is divided into four distinct parts, beginning with an historical play (*jidaimono*) glorifying the samu-

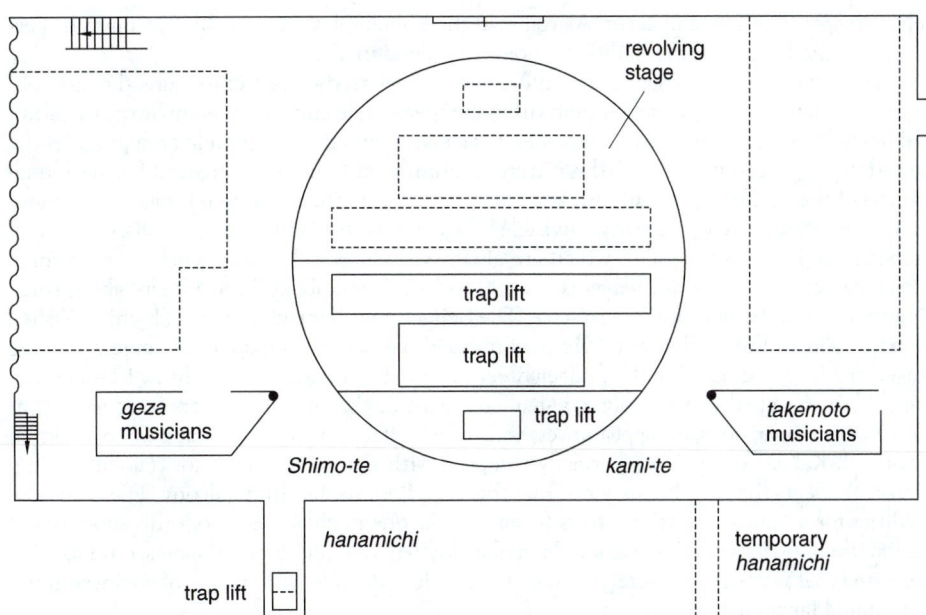

Diagram of a traditional Kabuki stage and its hanamichi *that allows actors to enter and exit through the audience.*

rai code. This is followed by a dance drama intended to be a mood piece. Next, a *sewamono* or domestic drama is presented; it invariably portrays the world of the merchant class that supports Kabuki and is (relatively) more realistic than the *jidaimono* plays. Although Kabuki can never be mistaken for realistic theater, there is an ongoing debate about the degree to which it should be "real." Chikamatsu's celebrated observation that "Art lies in the slender margin between the real and the unreal" suggests Kabuki's attempt to capture genuinely human dilemmas and their emotions in an exquisitely stylized manner. The final portion of a Kabuki program is a one-act dance drama, frequently humorous, like the farcical *kyōgen* of the Noh. Although it is a serious play, *Kanjinchō (The Subscription List)*, which follows later in this section, depends on an essentially comic structure. Today Kabuki programs are much shorter, usually comprised of scenes from longer plays and dances well known to Japanese audiences.

There have been some attempts to alter Kabuki's form and content to accommodate modern sensibilities. For instance, a more realistic format (the *Shin Kabuki*) uses more natural vocal patterns and naturalistic settings in a darkened auditorium. The *Ichikawa* (All-Girl) *Kabuki-za* was formed after World War II. Still, Kabuki remains tradition-bound and resistant to change. One of the liabilities of popular art, of course, is that it is susceptible to changing tastes. Just as the merchants of Kyoto were seduced by Okuni's daring dances in 1603, so, too, have their descendants been enticed by Western film, television, and pop music. At the same time many Western theater artists, such as France's Arianne Mnouchkine, are exploring the theatrical possibilities of Kabuki.

The Conventions of Kabuki

With its roots in middle-class tastes; its techniques drawn from an eclectic mixture of puppetry, song, music, and dance; and its subject matter derived from Japanese myth, folktales, and history, the Kabuki theater is more theatrical than literary. As with the Chinese theater and the older Noh, Kabuki makes no pretense at realism. It is, however, less poetic and abstract than the Noh, and though it uses some techniques similar to Chinese opera (e.g., painted faces), it relies on special effects and decor. As you read the Kabuki play, imagine how it might be performed at the *Kabuki-za*, the traditional home of Kabuki in Tokyo.

The modern Kabuki stage reveals influences of Western theater architecture, the most obvious of which is the large proscenium with a European-style curtain. In many ways, the art of Kabuki is dedicated to creating memorable stage images, and the proscenium arch provides the picture frame necessary to focus the picture. Stunning tableaux are enhanced by the formal parting of the traditional green, rust, and black-striped curtain. The Kabuki stage is enormous as it must house large casts, many "invisible" stage assistants clad in black, a full ensemble of orchestra and chorus (*naugata*), which are always visible, as well as the machinery for ingenious scenic effects. The *Kabuki-za* is over 90 feet wide and about 35 feet deep, about three times the size of the typical Western stage. The Kabuki stage floor, composed of highly polished wood to add to the aesthetics of the performance, has several trapdoors. A large revolving stage, which can be dated to the mid–eighteenth century, enhances scene shifts; in some theaters there are actually two revolves, a smaller one inside the larger. Elevators (used as early as 1736) abet apparitions, disappearances, and other effects, which are referred to as *keren* ("tricks"). Kabuki theaters are normally equipped with flying equipment for *chunori* ("riding the sky") effects that can lift an actor from the stage floor to the third balcony. There are also facilities for a number of water effects (*honmizu*). As one might expect from this small island nation, there exists a whole class of Kabuki plays known as water plays (*mizumono*). It has been suggested that water effects were instituted to provide audiences with images of coolness in the hot, humid Japanese summers.

The Kabuki fosters much interplay between actors and audience. A shallow auditorium (less than 60 feet) puts the audience in close proximity to the actors, who perform almost exclusively on the forestage. As you read *Kanjinchō* note the number of speeches and asides directed to the audience. In the Kabuki it is not uncommon to stop the action and make an announcement (*kojo*) about the accomplishments of an actor.

The most distinctive feature of the Kabuki stage is the *hanamichi* ("the flowery way"), a narrow 65-foot runway that leads from a dressing room behind the audience to the forestage. The actor enters and exits amid the spectators, who frequently shout his name in admiration. An actor does not merely walk the length of the *hanamichi*. He uses an extraordinary walk—part dance, part martial arts—called a *roppo* (or *tobiroppo* for exits). *Roppo* means "six directions," because the actor swings his arms and legs violently up, down, front, back, and side-to-side. The *tobiroppo* often occurs *after* the curtain has been lowered at the conclusion of the action, and the lone actor makes a grandly theatrical exit. For Japanese audiences, this is the true emotional climax of the play. Foreigners unaware of this tradition are occasionally embarrassed as they rise to leave when the curtain closes, only to discover that the Kabuki's grandest moment is yet to come.

While entering, the actor stops at a spot exactly seven-tenths down the *hanamichi* and freezes in an exaggerated pose called the *mie*, which he holds for several seconds. The *mie* allows the audience to study his colorful costume and to assess his psychological state, which is indicated by gestures, makeup, and grimaces. Perhaps you have seen pictures of Kabuki actors with what appear to be crossed eyes, a technique meant to suggest enormous emotional turmoil.

Despite its beginnings in "the Women's Kabuki," the Kabuki today is virtually a male-dominated institution. Among the principal roles, there are three styles of performance for male actors. First, the *aragoto*, or "rough" style, portrays thoroughly masculine virtues, such as power and courage, derived from the ancient *samurai* ("warrior") code. The *aragoto* paints his face in fantastic designs (*kumadori*) to show his manliness, and wears an oversized costume to emphasize his larger-than-life status. Vocally, the *aragoto* uses a high-pitched voice, and often resorts to nonsensical utterances to indicate strong emotion. In *Kanjinchō* Togashi, who guards the gates, is an *aragoto* role; as part of his ruse, Benkei assumes the *aragoto* style to gain Togashi's respect.

In contrast to the "rough" style is the *wagato*, which is much more refined and delicate. The *wagato* is customarily a handsome young lover. Though he is sought after for his looks and grace, he is usually depicted as cowardly and irresponsible. The more virile, harsher tones of the *aragoto* give way to a softer, more melodic vocal pattern in the *wagato*. Prince Yoshitsune (in *Kanjinchō*) is a *wagato*.

Benkei (Danjuro XII) in mie pose as he exits Kanjinchō (The Subscription List); note the hanamichi at the Kabukiza, Japan's foremost theater.

The *onnagata* is perhaps the most famous of the three classical Kabuki styles. In this style a man plays female roles, a convention that grew, of necessity, out of the shogunate's 1629 ban on women in theater. By the eighteenth century the techniques for playing women had been perfected, thanks largely to the efforts of the first great female impersonator of the Kabuki, Yoshizaw Ayame (1673–1729). He advocated that *onnagata* actors live their female roles both on and offstage, but the practice has been abandoned in the twentieth century. Because it is the duty of the *onnagata* to portray an idealized femininity, he must study and master many rigorous poses, gestures, and movements, as well as perfect Japanese ceremonial dances. The *onnagata* always appears in the traditional all-white makeup, and the vocal techniques of the role are much more delicate than that of the *wagato*. Obviously, there is no *onnagata* in *Kanjinchō*.

Kata, a term also used in the Noh theater, are the basic movements and vocal patterns that Kabuki actors must learn. The *mie* is a specialized *kata*, as is the *roppo*. Vocal patterning is intended to create atmosphere through rhythmic, antiphonal patterns of sound. Obviously, *kata* cannot be adequately described and must be seen and heard to be appreciated. The Japanese, who revere the old (*sabi*), expect Kabuki actors to master centuries-old *kata*. Actors are judged not on their originality, but on their ability to raise traditional artistry to new levels and thus achieve *aware*, an appreciation of beauty in the familiar.

There are also scenic *kata*. If the Noh theater is a celebration of the imagination through suggestion, the Kabuki celebrates the ingenuity of its craftsmen to stimulate the senses through an array of sights, colors, and sounds. The Japanese love scenes in which vibrant cherry blossoms fill the stage to denote spring, or in which travelers circling the stage to suggest a long journey (*michiyuki*) are covered with softly falling snow. They also love sensational scenes, transformations, and battles. In one famous Kabuki play a seductive woman is transformed into an enormous spider before the delighted audience. Quick changes, among the Kabuki's supreme artistic accomplishments, are called *hayagawari*. (The transformation of "the Beast" into the handsome prince in the Broadway production of *Beauty and the Beast* is very much in the *hayagawari* tradition.) Unlike the Noh theater, Kabuki actors do not wear masks; in fact, the Kabuki (and, significantly, the women who invented it) placed a new emphasis on the human form in Japanese culture. However, warriors in battle scenes wear special masks which can be "cut open" by samurai swords to suggest a decapitation.

Because the Kabuki evolved from dance, music is as integral to its experience as its visual elements. Indeed, the heart of the Kabuki is the *naguata*, the ensemble of musicians who play the traditional *samisen* (a stringed instrument), flutes, and Noh drums. Kabuki music is livelier than that of the meditative Noh theater. During dance plays, the *nagauta* sit on a raised platform at the rear of the stage; in other plays, they play offstage, though still highly visible in keeping with the theatricality of Kabuki. Two sets of wooden clappers (*ki*) provide the rhythmic accompaniment to the action, especially on entrances and exits. A chorus of eight sings while the actors mime vigorous movements. The *nagauta* music for *Kanjinchō* composed by Kineya Rokusaburo for the play's premiere in 1840, is considered the finest in the Kabuki repertory.

The Contemporary Japanese Theater: *Shingeki*

Although the Noh and Kabuki are the best-known forms of theater outside Japan, there is also a vibrant contemporary theater in Japan, fueled in no small part by a younger generation that has rejected the country's traditional arts in favor of experimentation and current issues. As an alternative to Noh, Kabuki, and Bunraku puppetry, *Shingeki*—"new/other theater"—has evolved since 1868 with the concerted effort on the part of artists who reacted to the inundation of Western influence on Japan. Today the Shingeki thrives alongside the more venerable forms.

In 1873 the Kabuki Reform Movement was formed to "save" traditional Kabuki performances by investing them with Western-style fashions. Though well intentioned, the reforms diminished both the quality and the appeal of Kabuki, and, ironically, only furthered the vogue for Western-style drama. Soon Japanese began to consider Western theater as the model for which modern Japan ought to strive. In 1909 Tsubouchi Shoyo (1859–1935) formed the Literary Arts Society, a school committed to shaping a new theater and drama for Japan as it entered the twentieth century. Tsubouchi considered the Kabuki outmoded, even corrupt, and called for a theater based on such European models as Ibsen and Shakespeare (who is actually one of Japan's most revered playwrights; the Japanese publish more articles about Shakespeare than many English-speaking countries). Tsubouchi's experiments were successful, and Western-style theater became entrenched in Japan.

Japanese theater artists also founded a Free Theater based on Antoine's experiment in Paris. Osani Kaoru (1881–1928), who led this movement, did much to introduce naturalism to the Japanese theater. In particular, he wrote and staged Ibsen-like social dramas that attacked middle-class hypocrisy and corruption. It was Osani who coined the term *Shingeki,* and he pro-

A blend of eastern and western traditions in the contemporary Japanese theater are found in Tadashi Suzuki's 1991 adaptation of Euripides' The Bacchae. *Agave cradles the head of her dead son as Cadmus looks on.*

moted the motto "Ignore tradition" among young theater artists. Though Osani and other innovators called for young Japanese to write plays for Japan, the primary benefit of the Free Theater movement was the importation of popular Western plays by Ibsen, Chekhov, and other new realists from Europe.

By the 1920s Western plays were prominent in Japan, a situation that was as detrimental as it was inspiring. It took almost two decades before Japanese dramatists developed a modern style that was uniquely Japanese. Kishida Kunio (1890–1954), who studied in Paris, emerged as the most respected of the new Shingeki playwrights. In 1947 Morimoto Kaoru wrote *Onna no issho* (*A Woman's Life*), the play generally acknowledged as the work that brought contemporary Japanese playwriting to its maturity. The drama depicts the tragic experiences of a woman who sacrifices herself for her family and captures the angst of a nation devastated by World War II. Although it is decidedly modern, Morimoto's play nonetheless maintains a kinship to the older Noh and Kabuki traditions because it celebrates the inner strength of its central character, who endures the unendurable stoically.

Most Shingeki drama is concerned with a single theme: identity, both personal and national. Because Japan has undergone massive social, economic, and political changes in the wake of World War II, it has in many ways been forced to redefine itself. The tension between traditional virtues and modern values dominates contemporary Japanese literature. Japanese theater and stagecraft exhibit a similar duality. One finds a provocative blend of the naturalistic and the symbolic (a la the Noh theater) in many Japanese plays. Kobo Abe's *The Man Who Turned into a Stick* represents this phenomenon: the acting style is naturalistic, yet its visual imagery is metaphysical, even Noh-like in its classic simplicity.

Tadashi Suzuki's work, well known and much admired in the West, is especially apt at fusing the old and the new. Suzuki has stated that his mission is "to make traditional consciousness compatible with modern habits." In 1974 he staged Euripides' tragic war drama *The Trojan Woman*; it moved freely from the ancient Greek world to modern Japan and employed Noh, Kabuki, and naturalistic theater styles.

Today the Shingeki is truly reflective of contemporary Japan. Having arrived at a point of healthy equilibrium between its own cultural traditions and those of the modern West, it is diverse, and represents a healthy fusion of new and old, Eastern and Western, social and metaphysical concerns.

KOMACHI AT SEKIDERA
(SEKIDERA KOMACHI)

ZEAMI

ZEAMI (1363–1443)

The most celebrated poet of the Japanese theater, Zeami (also, Seami or Zeami Motokiyo) was the son of Kan-ami Kiyotsugo (1333–1384), the illustrious pioneer of Noh drama. Almost one-half of the 240 plays of the traditional Noh repertory are ascribed to Zeami. He also wrote *The Kadensho*, the poetics of Noh theater, which he claims was a compilation of secret ideas and material bequeathed to him as a child by his father; twenty years after his father's death he finally wrote them down.

Zeami was a multitalented artist; in addition to writing plays and treatises on stage practice, he was a musical composer, actor, director, company manager, and acclaimed dancer. His art was imbued with a deep spirituality derived from his practice of Zen Buddhism (he also wrote philosophical and theological tracts). Art, for Zeami, was intended to bring both artist and audience to *yúgen*—an appreciation of beauty that leads to spirituality and inner peace. *Yugen* was realized through *hana* ("flower"), a term with multiple meanings but which generally refers to the aesthetics of Noh acting style. According to Zeami, *hana* is achieved only through many years of rigid training and sacrificing one's life to the practice of one's art: "*Hana* is of the mind, technique is the seed," he wrote in *The Kadensho*. Today Noh actors still train according to the precepts of Zeami's teachings, and his aesthetics and discipline have influenced a number of Western theater artists such as Peter Brook and Jerzy Grotowski.

In addition to *Komachi at Sekidera*, Zeami's best-known plays include *Aoi-no-ue* (a ghost play in which a vengeful spirit torments the mythical Lady Aoi), *Atsu-mori* (a warrior play in which a military man disguises himself as a priest to repent his life of violence) and *Takasago* (the exemplar of god-dance plays in which two pine trees come to life).

KOMACHI AT SEKIDERA

Taken from the third category of Noh plays (i.e., the woman or "wig play"), *Komachi at Sekidera* is considered one of the most difficult plays to perform. Rarely do even the best Noh actors play the *shite* role of the old woman until very late in their careers, much as an actor might wait to play Lear or Mother Courage in the Western repertory. The play also is the exemplar of Zeami's reverence for *yúgen* "obscure beauty," so fitting for a work whose very subject matter is the power of ancient poetry.

Komachi, an actual historical figure, was a beautiful woman gifted with exceptional literary talent who lived at the Heinan court in the ninth century C.E. Her unparalleled beauty and poetry mythologized her among subsequent generations of Japanese. Zeami purposefully sets the play during "the Festival of the Stars," or Tanabata, celebrated on the seventh night of the seventh month to commemorate the annual reunion of the Cowherd with the Weaver-girl, revered mythological lovers comparable to Romeo and Juliet. Traditionally, the young tie love poems to bamboo branches with colored streamers to honor the lovers. (See Center Stage box, *The Tanabata Festival of Japan*, following the text of *Komachi at Sekidera*.) Thus Komachi's faded beauty and melancholy are set ironically against this lovers' holiday, which is itself tinged with sadness because of the short night the ancient lovers may spend together.

Komachi at Sekidera is a death rite. Set amidst the apparent gaiety of the Festival of the Stars in midsummer, an old woman, once beautiful and talented, faces death alone in a simple hut. Her lengthy speech (intoned by the chorus) in the middle of the play captures the melancholy recognition that life is transient, that youth must give way to old age, and that death will eventually overtake life:

> *Oh, how I long for the past!*
>
> *My middle years were spent yearning*
>
> *For the distant glory of my youth.*
>
> *Now even those days of wistful recollection*
>
> *Have become such ancient history*
>
> *I find myself wishing, if not for youth,*
>
> *At least for middle age.*

As the play concludes, Komachi again retreats into her hut (a tomb?) to sit, weep, and await her death. She laments that her former beauty, her material goods ("brocaded quilts / Within a pillowed bridal chamber"), and poetic powers have deserted her and that she must face death alone, impoverished of worldly possessions. In the play's last line, the chorus invites the audience to look on "all that remains of famed Komachi . . . all that is left of Ono no Komachi."

Dramas of the East and West have long acknowledged human mortality and the inevitability of death. Aeschylus's *Agamemnon*, Shakespeare's *Hamlet*, the medieval morality play *Everyman*, and countless other works mark the human passage to death because, as Hamlet says, "the readiness [for death] is all." Komachi knows what "readiness" means, yet there is no sense of the tragic in her demise. It is as natural as when "the dews of spring depart, and autumn frosts appear," it is as expected as the tolling of the temple bell at Sekidera. Because Noh evolved from agricultural and religious rituals that mark the life cycle, it is inevitable that among its greatest plays is one that presents a detached, poetic look at death.

Yet *Komachi at Sekidera* is not a dirge in the manner of Beckett's *Rockaby* (see Chapter 7), which is also about a lonely woman at the point of death. Rather, Zeami celebrates life and all its facets: youth, maturity, extreme old age; pains and pleasures, creation and decay; hope and despair. That Komachi dies while the young celebrate the regenerative power of love is significant; they will surely produce more Komachis. That an eager young priest and would-be poet seeks the wisdom of a venerable old woman is significant; he will pick up her dry pen to write new verses. That a child dances the *gagaku*, a remnant of the ancient dances from which Noh evolved, is significant; the dance of the new dawn inevitably brings "a chorus of morning birdsong." That Komachi herself dances the dream of the butterfly

> *Who dreamed he had spent*
>
> *A hundred years enfolded*
>
> *Within the flowers of a petal*

is the most significant act of all: bodies wither and die while spirits dance forever. Remember that a Noh audience would not view Komachi as an old woman, but as a specter who defies time and space.

Ultimately, however, it is not Komachi's spirit that brings her immortality. It is her poetry. The young priest's questions confirm the eternality of her work. That an audience gathers in a Noh theater in the late twentieth century to witness the tale of a woman who lived a thousand years earlier, and then hears her poetry sung as freshly as if she penned it today, is the consummate testimony to the immortality of the artist. Recall Shakespeare's boast in Sonnet 55: "Not marble, nor the gilded monuments of princes, shall outlive this powerful rhyme." *Komachi at Sekidera*, then, is a monument not only to an illustrious woman in Japan's fabled past, but to the durability of the art that preserves her memory.

Read the play slowly and contemplatively, perhaps with some appropriate mood music in the background. Visualize the various conventions described here. Above all, approach *Komachi at Sekidera* as a meditative ritual. Do not be put off by the allusions to specific Japanese poems. Rather, consider its universal themes of isolation, the seeming futility of human endeavor, the triumph of the creative spirit over our mortality, and consider especially the dance of the child.

The revered poet Ono no Komachi is a favorite subject of the Noh theater; she is played by a man who wears a mask of polished wood.

KOMACHI AT SEKIDERA
(SEKIDERA KOMACHI)

ZEAMI

Translated by Karen Brazell

PERSONS
THE ABBOT OF SEKIDERA (*waki*)
TWO PRIESTS (*wakizure*)
A CHILD (*kokata*)
ONO NO KOMACHI (*shite*)

PLACE: *Sekidera in Ōmi Province*
TIME: *The Beginning of Autumn: The Seventh Day of the Seventh Month*

(*The stage assistants bring forward a simple construction representing a hut with a thatched roof. It is covered with a cloth. The Old Woman is inside.*

As the music begins the Child, the Abbot, and two Priests enter and face each other onstage. The Abbot and the Priests carry rosaries.)

THREE PRIESTS. So long awaited, autumn has come at last,
So long awaited, the lovers' autumn meeting!
Now let us begin the Festival of Stars.[1]

(*The Abbot faces front.*)

ABBOT. I am the chief priest of Sekidera in Ōmi. Today, the seventh day of the seventh month, we come to celebrate the Festival of Stars here in the temple garden. People say that the old woman who has built her hut at the foot of the mountain knows all the secrets of the art of poetry. So, on this festive day dedicated to poetry, I am going to take the young people to hear her stories.

(*He turns to the Child.*)

THREE PRIESTS. Early autumn comes and brings a touch of chill. We feel it in the wind and in our thinning locks.[2]
Soon, soon the Seventh Night will be on us.

(*The Abbot faces front.*)

ABBOT. We bring offerings for the festival today,
The music of flutes and strings,
TWO PRIESTS. And many poems
ABBOT. Composed in our native tongue.[3]

(*He turns to the Child.*)

THREE PRIESTS. Our prayers for skill at poetry are decked
With brightly colored streamers:
Fluttering ribbons, each a token of prayer,
Like silk threads woven into rich brocades
On looms of autumn flowers
And pampas grass pearly with dew.
The winds in the pines

(*The Abbot faces front, takes a few steps, then returns to his former position, indicating he has made a journey.*)

Blend with the strings of the koto
To make music for the offerings tonight,[4]
Our offerings for this festive night.

(*The Abbot and his companions are now at their destination.*)

ABBOT. Here is the hut now. Let us call on the old woman. (*To the Child.*) But first, please sit down.

(*All kneel. A stage assistant removes the cloth around the hut, revealing the Old Woman seated inside. Paper strips inscribed with poems hang from the crossbars of the hut frame. The Old Woman wears the uba mask.*)

OLD WOMAN. Days go by without a single bowl of food:
Whom can I ask for one?
At night my tattered rags fail to cover me,
But there is no way to patch the rents.
Each passing rain
Ages the crimson of the flowers;
The willows are tricked by the wind,
And their green gradually droops.[5]
Man has no second chance at youth;
He grows old. The aged song thrush
Warbles again when spring has come,
But time does not revert to the past.
Oh, how I yearn for the days that are gone!
What would I do to recapture the past!

(*She weeps. The Abbot and the Child rise, and go to kneel before her.*)

ABBOT. Old woman, we have come to speak with you.
OLD WOMAN. Who are you?
ABBOT. I am a priest from Sekidera. These young people are students of poetry. They have heard of your talent, and I have brought them here to question you about poetry and to learn something of your life.
OLD WOMAN. This is an unexpected visit! The log buried in the earth has been so long forgotten you must not expect it will put forth new sprouts.[6] Just remember this: If you will make your heart the seed and your words the blossoms,[7] if you will steep yourself in the fragrance of the art, you will not fail to accomplish true poetry. But how praiseworthy that mere boys should cherish a love of poetry!
ABBOT. May I ask you about a poem everyone knows, "The Harbor of Naniwa?"[8] Do you agree that it should be used as a first guide?
OLD WOMAN. Indeed I do. Poetry goes back to the Age of the Gods, but the meters were then irregular and the

---

[1]The Tanabata Festival, of Chinese origin, is still celebrated in Japan on the seventh day of the seventh month. Bamboo branches are decorated with five-colored streamers and with slips on which poems have been written commemorating the lovers' meeting of the two stars.
[2]From some lines by Po Chü-i included in the *Wakan Rōei Shū*, no. 204: "Who could have arranged things so well? The sighing cool wind and my thinning locks at once announce autumn is here." A parallel is drawn between the coming of autumn in the world and the coming of autumn to the person, evidenced by the thinning locks.
[3]Many poets wrote in Chinese, especially on formal occasions, but the Japanese preferred their own language for their intimate feelings.
[4]The above three lines are based on a poem by the Consort Itsuki-nomiya in the *Shūishū*, no. 451.

[5]Derived from an anonymous poem in Chinese found in a commentary to the history work *Hyakurenshō*.
[6]Quoted, with slight modifications, from the preface to the *Kokinshū*.
[7]Also from the preface to the *Kokinshū*.
[8]This is the "Naniwazu" poem: "In Naniwa Harbor/The flowers have come to the trees;/They slept through the winter,/But now it is the spring—/See how the blossoms have opened!" The preface to the *Kokinshū* characterizes this poem and the one on Asakayama, Mount Asaka, as the "father and mother of poetry." Both poems are given considerable attention in *The Reed Cutter*.

meanings difficult to understand. "The Harbor of Naniwa," however, belongs to the Age of Man. It was composed for the joyous occasion of an emperor's enthronement, and has long been beloved for that reason.[9]

ABBOT. The poem about Mount Asaka, which once soothed the heart of a prince, is also beautifully written.[10]

OLD WOMAN. Truly, you understand the art,
For those two poems are the parents of all poetry.

ABBOT. They serve as models for beginners.

OLD WOMAN. Noblemen and peasantry alike,

ABBOT. City dwellers and country folk,

OLD WOMAN. Even commoners like ourselves

ABBOT. Take pleasure in composing poetry

OLD WOMAN. Following the promptings of our hearts.

CHORUS. Though the sands lapped by the waves
Of the lake in Ōmi should run out,
Though the sands of the shore should melt away,

(*The Abbot and the Child return to kneel with the Priests.*)

The words of poetry will never fail.[11]
They are enduring as evergreen boughs of pine,
Continuous as trailing branches of willow;
For poetry, whose source and seed is found
In the human heart, is everlasting.
Though ages pass and all things vanish,
As long as words of poetry remain,
Poems will leave their marks behind,
And the traces of poetry will never disappear.

ABBOT. Thank you for your words of explanation. It is true that countless poems survive from the past, but they are rarely by women. Few women know as much as you about poetry. Tell me—the poem
"I know my lover
is coming tonight—
See how the spider
Spins her web:
That is a sure sign!"[12]
Was that not by a woman?

OLD WOMAN. Yes, that poem was written long ago by Princess Sotōri, the consort of Emperor Ingyō. I tried, if only in form, to master her style.

ABBOT. Ah! You have studied the style of Princess Sotōri? I

have heard that Ono no Komachi, who's so much talked of these days, wrote in that style.[13]
"Wretched that I am—
A floating water weed,
Broken from its roots—
If a stream should beckon,
I would follow it, I think."
That poem is by Komachi.

OLD WOMAN. Yes, once my husband, Ōe no Koreaki, took up with another woman, and I grieved at the fickleness of the world. Then, Funya no Yasuhide[14] invited me to accompany him to Mikawa, where he was to be the governor. I wrote that poem in response to his urging and to his promises that life in the country would bring solace.
Alas, memories of the past!
So long forgotten, they rise up again
Before me as I talk to you.
Tears well up from my suffering heart.

(*She weeps.*)

ABBOT. Strange! This old woman says she wrote the poem "Wretched that I am." And she says she wrote in the Sotōri style, just as Komachi did. She must be nearly a hundred years old, and if Komachi were still alive today. . . . And is there any reason why she couldn't be? It must be so! (*To the Old Woman.*) You are what is left of Ono no Komachi. Do not deny it.

OLD WOMAN. Ah, I burn with shame to be called Komachi, I who wrote
"With no outward sign

CHORUS. It withers—
The flower in the human heart."[15]
How ashamed I am to be seen!
"Wretched that I am—
A floating water weed,
Broken from its roots—
If a stream should beckon,
I would follow it, I think."
How ashamed I am!

(*She weeps.*)

"Hide them though I may,
The tears keep flowing,
Too many for my sleeves to hold—
A rain of tears dissolving
Everything except the past."[16]
Now that my life has reached its end,
Like a withered flower,
Why should there still be tears?

---

[9]The poem was traditionally supposed to have been composed to encourage the future Emperor Nintoku, who reigned in the fourth century C.E., to accept the throne.

[10]The poem runs, literally: "Mount Asaka—/Its reflection appears In the mountain spring/That is not shallow, and of you/My thoughts are not shallow either." The Prince of Kazuraki was sent to the distant province of Mutsu where he was badly received by the governor. He was so angry that he refused to eat, but the governor's daughter cheered him by offering saké and reciting this poem.

[11]Based on lines from the *Kokinshū* preface: "Though you count up my love you could never come to the end, not even if you could count every grain of sand on the shore of the wild sea."

[12]An anonymous poem, no. 1110 in the *Kokinshū.*

[13]So stated in the preface to the *Kokinshū.*

[14]An early Heian poet, one of the "Six Immortals of Poetry." The explanation of the "Wretched that I am" poem was traditional.

[15]From poem no. 757 in the *Kokinshū,* by Komachi.

[16]A poem by Abe no Kiyoyuki, no. 556 in the *Kokinshū.*

OLD WOMAN. "Longing for him,
  I fell asleep,
  Then he appeared before me . . ."[17]
CHORUS. The joy I felt when I composed those lines
  Is gone forever, but still my life goes on,
  Attending the months and years as they come and go.
  The dews of spring depart, and autumn frosts appear,
  The leaves and grasses turn, and insect voices fade.
OLD WOMAN. My life is over, and now I see
CHORUS. It was like a rose of Sharon that knows
  Only a single day of glory.[18]
    "The living go on dying,
    The dead increase in number;
    Left in this world, ah—
    How long must I go on
    Lamenting for the dead?"[19]
  And how long must I, who wrote that poem,
  Live on, like flowers fallen, like leaves scattered,
  With nothing left but life—dewlike, they always said.
  Oh, how I long for the past!
  My middle years were spent in yearning
  For the distant glory of my youth.
  Now even those days of wistful recollection
  Have become such ancient history
  I find myself wishing, if not for youth,
  At least for middle age.
  Long ago, wherever I spent a single night
  My room would be bright with tortoise shell,
  Golden flowers hung from the walls,
  And in the door were strings of crystal beads.[20]
  Brilliant as the Emperor's chair in grand procession
  The jewellike gowns I wore, a hundred colors.
  I lay on bright brocaded quilts
  Within a pillowed bridal chamber.
  Look at it now, my mud-daubed hut!
  Can this be my resplendent room?
OLD WOMAN. The temple bell of Sekidera
CHORUS. Tolls the vanity of all creation—
  To ancient ears a needless lesson.
  A mountain wind blows down Ōsaka's slope
  To moan the certainty of death;
  Its message still eludes me.
  Yet, when blossoms scatter and leaves fall,
  Still in this hut I find my pleasure:
  Grinding ink, I dip my brush and write.

My words are all dry, like seaweed on the shore.
Touching, they once said, but lacking strength[21]—
My poems lacked strength because they were a woman's.
Now when I have grown decrepit
My poems are weaker still. Their life is spent.
How wretched it is to be old!

(*She weeps. The Child turns to the Abbot.*)

CHILD. I'm afraid we'll be late for the Festival of Stars. Let's ask the old lady to come with us.

(*The Abbot kneels before the Old Woman.*)

ABBOT. Please join us on this Seventh Night, the Festival of Stars.
OLD WOMAN. Alas! An old woman should not intrude on such an occasion. I cannot go.

(*She takes down the paper poem cards.*)

ABBOT. What harm could come of it? Please come with us.

(*He goes to the hut and helps the Old Woman to stand.*)

CHORUS. The Seventh Night—
  How many years since first I offered the gods
  Bamboo tied with colored streamers?
  How long has shriveled old Komachi lived?

(*Assisted by the Abbot and leaning on a staff, the Old Woman leaves the hut.*)

Has Ono no Komachi reached a hundred years?
Or even more?
I who used to watch the Festival of Stars,
Familiar of the noblest lords and ladies,

(*She kneels beside the shite-pillar. The Abbot goes back beside the others.*)

Now stand in shameful hempen rags!
A sight too painful for eyes to bear!

(*The Abbot weeps.*)

Still, tonight we hold the Festival of Stars,

(*The Child stands and mimes serving wine to the Old Woman.*)

Tonight we celebrate the Seventh Night
With multitudes of offerings for the stars.
Prayer streamers hang from bamboo,

(*While the following lines are being sung the Child goes to the gazing-pillar, moves clockwise around the stage, then stands at the center preparatory to beginning his dance.*)

---

[17]The first part of a poem by *Komachi*, no. 552 in the *Kokinshū*. The last two lines run: "If I had known it was a dream/I should never have wakened."
[18]These lines are based on verses by Po Chü-i, no. 291 in the *Wakan Rōei Shū*.
[19]A poem by Komachi, no. 850 in the *Shinkokinshū*.
[20]This description is based on a passage in the *Tamatsukuri Komachi Sōsuisho*, a work in Chinese, apparently by a Buddhist priest of the Heian period, describing Komachi's decline and her eventual salvation.

[21]The appraisal of Komachi's poetry given in the preface to the *Kokinshū*.

Music plays and cups of wine go round.
The young dancer—look how gracefully
He twirls his sleeves, like snow
Swirling in the moonlight.

(*The Old Woman, still seated, watches the Child dance.*)

We celebrate the Festival of Stars,
Streamers flutter from the bamboos. . . .
OLD WOMAN. May it be celebrated through ages as many
As the joints of the bamboo!

(*The Old Woman, hardly aware of what she does, taps the rhythm with her fan.*)

CHORUS. We pray for eternal prosperity;
We dance the "Ten Thousand Years."[22]

(*The Child completes his dance, then sits as before.*)

OLD WOMAN. How gracefully that boy has danced! I remember how, long ago in the Palace, the Goeschi dancing girls swirled their sleeves five times at the Harvest Festival. They say that if a madman runs, even the sane will run after him. But tonight the proverb is reversed! Enticed by the boy's floating sleeves, see how a madwoman prances!

(*She stands with the aid of her staff and begins her dance.*)

One hundred years—
The dance of the butterfly
Who dreamt he had spent
A hundred years enfolded
Within a flower petal.[23]

CHORUS. How sad it is! It breaks my heart!
A flowering branch on a withered tree!
OLD WOMAN. I have forgotten how to move my hands.
CHORUS. Unsteady feet, uncertain wave of sleeves,
OLD WOMAN. Billow after billow, floating wave on wave.
CHORUS. My dancing sleeves rise up.
But sleeves cannot wave back the past.

(*She goes before the hut.*)

OLD WOMAN. I miss those vanished days!

(*She kneels and weeps.*)

CHORUS. But as I dance the early autumn night,
The short night, gives way to dawn.
The temple bell of Sekidera tolls.
OLD WOMAN. A chorus of morning birdsong heralds
CHORUS. The coming dawn, the day's approaching light,
The dawn's fresh light that reveals my shame!
OLD WOMAN. Where is the forest of Hazukashi?[24]

(*She stands, propping herself on her staff.*)

CHORUS. Where is the forest of Hazukashi?
There is no forest here to hide my shame.
Farewell, I take my leave.
Now, leaning heavily on her stick,
She slowly returns to her straw hut.

(*She enters the hut, sits and weeps.*)

The hundred-year-old woman you have spoken to
Is all the remains of famed Komachi,
Is all that is left of Ono no Komachi.

---

[22]The name of a *gagaku* dance, *Manzairaku*.

[23]A reference to a poem by Ōe no Masafusa in the collection *Horikawa-in Ontoki Hyakushu Waka*: "This world where I have dwelt a hundred years lodged in a flower is the dream of a butterfly." The poem in turn refers to a famous passage in Chuang Tzu. See *The Complete Works of Chuang Tzu* (New York, 1968), translated by Burton Watson, p. 49.

[24]Hazukashi, the name of a wood near Kyoto, also has the meaning "ashamed."

CENTER STAGE   THE TANABATA FESTIVAL OF JAPAN

Among the most prevalent archetypes in myth and literature is that of star-crossed lovers, a phrase taken from the most famous play about lovers who are forbidden to see each other, *Romeo and Juliet*. *A Midsummer Night's Dream*—perhaps written the same year as *Romeo and Juliet*—also portrays young lovers (Hermia and Lysander, Pyramis and Thisbe) who are separated by tyrannical fathers. The Chinese drama *Autumn in the Palace of Han* depicts the emperor's pain when he is forced to relinquish his favorite concubine. And think of the scores of pop ballads in which a singer laments that the world is cruel because he or she cannot be with a lover.

Life slows in Japan on July 7 as people, especially children, pause to remember the plight of Orihime (or Shokujo), a beautiful weaving girl, and her lover, the cowherd Hikoboshi (or Kengyu). Their story of frustrated love (appropriated from an ancient Chinese fairy tale) is set against the backdrop of the universe itself on this "Festival of the Stars." Legend says that when they

fell in love and married eons ago, Orihime's father, a celestial king, was angered because she neglected her weaving and he his herd. He separated them on opposite sides of the Milky Way as the stars Vega and Altair and decreed that they might meet only one night a year. Customarily, the stars are aligned on the evening of July 7 (though the cities of Daito and Sendai actually celebrate Tanabata on August 6). Of course, the lovers may be reunited only on a clear night; if it is overcast or raining, they must wait another year for their night of love.

Tanabata is a major civic occasion, especially in Sendai, the city most closely associated with this festival (over 2 million people visit Sendai during the Tanabata). Children and young lovers write *haiku* and *tanka* poems, as well as wishes, on brightly colored paper (*tanzaku*). These are affixed to bamboo poles that have been placed in gardens. Shopping centers are decorated with the same enthusiasm Westerners see at Christmas. Offerings of

food, especially corn and eggplant, are left for the lovers. Girls pray that their handiwork might be as beautiful as Orihime's. After they have been displayed, the *tanzaku* are burned so that the wishes may rise with the smoke into the heavens where Orihime and Hikobashi can read them. The lucky and the faithful have their wishes granted.

The highlight of the evening is a spectacular parade in which children, dressed in traditional Japanese costumes, march through town beating drums as they sing

Ten Ten Ten Ten,
Tentekoten-no-tanabatasan
Tanabatsan-o-okuwa.

The translation—"we are off to see the god Tanabata"—cannot capture the rhythmic joy of the song. The parade is climaxed by a fireworks show that lights the sky so that the lovers might find each other.

There is certainly great charm in this age-old story. In it we see yet another attempt by humans to explain

An audience watches young dancers at a Tanabata Festival in Sendai; the colorful banners display love poems in honor of the star-crossed lovers of Japanese mythology.

natural phenomenon through myth (i.e., the presence of stars), to reconcile life's bitter disappointments, and to control events through a ritual or—in this case—a ceremonial festival. Although the story that inspired the Tanabata is founded on an unhappy situation, the festival is predicated upon hope that lovers will be reunited, that wishes will be granted. The theatrical embellishments (costumes, decorations, parades, songs, and fireworks) elevate the festivities to something beyond ordinary life.

That Zeami should set his Noh drama *Komachi at Sekidira* against the background of the Tanabata is not surprising. The beautiful and talented Komachi was a great poet who, like Orihime and Hikoboshi, inspired generations of lovers.

Ayumi Kazama and Sayaka Sudo
Texas A&M University

KANJINCHŌ
(THE SUBSCRIPTION LIST)
Namiki Gohei III

Namiki Gohei III (1789–1855)

Little is known about Namiki Gohei III, one of four playwrights bearing that name. In Japan it is customary for artists—both writers and actors—to adopt the name of a renowned predecessor even though one is not related to another. Of the four writers named Namiki Gohei, only the first (1747–1808) was prolific enough to merit scholarly attention.

Namiki Gohei III (nee Shindo Soruku) was a disciple of Namiki Gohei II (1768–1819, nee Shinodo Kinji), a critic and author of a dance drama. Namiki Gohei III was the father of Namiki Gohei IV (1829–1901), and thus they are the only blood relatives among the four artists bearing that name.

Although Namiki Gohei III is a minor figure in the annals of Japanese theater, *Kanjinchō* assures that he will be remembered as the author of one of the most celebrated plays in the Kabuki repertory.

Kanjinchō (1841)

Kanjinchō is the last of the *juhachiban,* or "Eighteen Favorite Plays" of the Kabuki theater. The music of this play is considered the finest in the entire Kabuki repertory, and in terms of its stature, it is the equivalent of a work such as Verdi's *Otello* in its fusion of dramatic literature and music for the theater. Like Verdi's opera, *Kanjinchō* was adopted from an older and revered tradition, in this case the Noh theater. In 1841 Namiki refashioned the venerable Noh drama *Ataka* for the Kabuki; specifically, it was created for the premiere actor of the mid–nineteenth century, Ichikawa Danjūrō VII, who played the role of Benkei, a popular character who appears in other Noh and Kabuki plays. The warrior-monk is a prized challenge for an actor because he portrays a broad range of emotions, as well as engaging in a clever battle of wits with a worthy opponent in Togashi, the protector of the bridge at Kaga. Though all principal Kabuki roles demand great physical and vocal virtuosity, Benkei is among the most difficult because of the extraordinary dance and martial arts movements. His exit down the *hanamichi* after the play is regarded as the most famous *roppo* in all of Kabuki.

The Noh roots of *Kanjinchō* are readily apparent. Based on an actual event from the twelfth century, the play is composed in three movements, as were Noh plays: Benkei's cunning deception, which frees Prince Yoshitsune from Togashi's trap; the melancholy account of the prince's fall from power; and finally the "dance of longevity" Benkei performs to celebrate his triumph. Each of the three principal roles is aligned with a traditional Noh character: Benkei is the *shite* who is the focal point of the story; Togashi is the *waki*, or antagonist to the *shite*, and Prince Yoshitsune is the *kokata*, or child's role, here played as a young adult in the *wogata* style. Because it is derived from the sacred Noh theater, *Kanjinchō* is more dignified, less melodramatic, and certainly less spectacular than most Kabuki plays. Today it is performed, Noh-like, against a simple backdrop of the sacred pine tree. The drama's appeal derives from the skillful balance of its intellectual and emotional elements. In fact, the play's earliest audiences rejected it as being too lofty, and the play only became a classic as actors revived it in their eagerness to portray Benkei.

To audiences unfamiliar with Japanese thought and the nuances of the Kabuki, *Kanjinchō* might seem a comedy. Its central premise, in which a cunning underling disguises himself to dupe an adversary, is about as archetypal a comic situation as one can imagine. Add to this a drinking scene (which is intended to amuse) and the scene in which a servant beats his master, who cannot protest, and you have the stuff of a thousand comedies from around the world. But culture and context make *Kanjinchō* a dignified, even profound, play about duty and human feeling.

The plot of *Kanjinchō* is reminiscent of classical Roman comedy. A young man has an overpowering desire: Prince Yoshitsune wishes to escape from his brother's tyranny. He turns to a resourceful, cunning retainer for help: Benkei. Seemingly insurmountable barriers confront the schemers—Togashi's intelligence and suspicion, his guards, and especially the barrier that blocks the escape route. The serving man devises a brilliant, if deceitful, stratagem that not only thwarts the resistance but draws sympathy and cooperation from their opponents. The conflict is resolved by a disturbing breech of decorum: Benkei beats his master and even threatens him with death. The denouement features a union of the adversaries sharing food and drink.

Benkei appears every bit as Machiavellian as the servants of Roman and Renaissance Italian comedy. His lie about the subscription list—"he who contributes even a trifling amount shall live in ease in this world and shall sit among thousands of lotus in the next"—seems blasphemous. However, Namiki ennobles both Benkei and his adversary, Togashi. Benkei is not operating out of self-interest. He is no parasite, but one who is obligated, according to the *samurai* code, to protect his master at all costs. The Japanese ideogram for *samurai* is translated as "he who serves" and loyalty to one's master was the preeminent virtue expected of the servant-warrior. (Loyalty was a Confucian concept imported from China and fused with Shintoism and Zen Buddhism.) To ensure his master's safety, Benkei lies because of his reverence for *giri* ("obligation"). He has no choice because he and his small band of retainers are outnumbered by Togashi's superior forces, and while the *samurai* would willingly fight to the death, combat is not an option because it would surely lead to Yoshitsune's death.

Benkei's beating of the prince actually represents the play's most dramatic moment, that is, the moment of greatest conflict. The conflict is internal, as Benkei must suppress his natural feelings of affection and unqualified respect for his prince. He thrashes him only to make the ruse succeed when one of the guards recognizes Yoshitsune. In true *samurai* fashion, he suppresses his *ninjo* (human feelings or sympathy) and performs an odious task. His remorse is clearly manifested in the last movement of the play: "I have struck my own dear Lord. The heavenly reprisals are frightening to contemplate!" And he weeps bitterly, perhaps even contemplating *seppuku*, the ritual suicide expected of the *samurai* who errs. But Benkei knows he has triumphed on a higher level by performing *giri*, and thus his "dance of the winding stream" becomes a celebration of duty over personal feelings.

Namiki explores the problem from another perspective as Togashi also faces the conflict between *giri* and *ninjo*. It is his obligation to protect the barrier at Kaga, which he states unequivocally in his opening speech. He, too, is a the superb *samurai* who is loyal and unswerving in his duty to his lord, Prince Yoritomo. But he is equally loyal to his other lord, the Buddha. Benkei's arguments are cloaked in the authority of Buddhist teaching. The section concerning Buddhist orthodoxy was added by Danjūrō (the actor who first played Benkei) after he heard a famous storyteller recite the exchange. Benkei's loyalty to his master is so compelling that Togashi—who has recognized Yoshitsune—has no choice but to let his *ninjo* supersede his *giri*. In the Japanese mind Togashi is not duped; rather, he emerges as an honorable warrior with a good heart, just as Benkei emerges as an honorable man with a warrior's heart. And therein lies the lesson of the play: there are times when obligation takes precedence over sentiment, just as there are times when sympathy is more honorable than duty. The two resolutions need not be contradictory. Indeed, they are complementary, just as the *yin* (the feminine force, represented here by *ninjo*) and the *yang* (the masculine force, represented by *giri* and the *samurai* code) unite to complete the great circle that embraces all that comes to be in this world of paradoxes.

Benkei (center) and his retinue protect their prince (right) in a Grand Kabuki Theater production of Kanjinchō; the chorus and musicians, as well as the Noh pine trees, form a traditional background.

KANJINCHŌ
(THE SUBSCRIPTION LIST)

A Kabuki Play

NAMIKI GOHEI III

Adapted by James R. Brandon and Tamako Niwa

As we enter the theater the traditional Kabuki curtain of broad green, rust, and black stripes is closed; the house lights are partially dimmed. In a few moments two sharp claps are heard from backstage, wood against wood, as the stage manager signals the start of the performance with his Hyoshigi sticks. From off-stage right comes the cry "Hoo-yoo!", and the three musicians in the off-stage music cage (Geza) take up the opening music of Kanjinchō: first, the quavering, high pitched notes of flute, then the measured beating of drums. The sounds drift clearly through the light silk curtain. The audience settles down. Then two more claps of the stage manager's sticks signal that the cast is in place. The

drumming rapidly increases in tempo and a stage assistant (Kyogen Kata), kneeling beside the left proscenium arch, begins to beat out a furious tatoo with two wood clappers on a board in front of him. Just as the crescendo of sound reaches its peak another stage assistant, robed and hooded in black, runs swiftly across the stage pushing the curtain before him.

Before us is revealed the sweeping expanse of the ninety-foot wide Kabuki stage, its full area suffused with light and reflecting warmly on the polished surface of the cypress dance floor. The setting is simple and stylized, representing as it does the Noh stage. On a backpiece and two side pieces is painted a background of light tan wooden planking, and a single gnarled pine tree flanked by bamboos. The series of slits in the scenery stage right show the location of the off-stage musicians' cage. Except for a small area upstage left, where a small group of hand properties is placed, partially covered by a purple silk cloth, the entire area of the stage is available for the action of the play. There are three entrances. A colorfully striped curtain (Kirimaku) covers the large entrance stage right. On the opposite side of the stage is a small door (Kirido-guchi), used by the stage assistants who are stationed on the left of the stage and by actors for less important exits. The main entrance, however, is the "flower way" or Hanamichi, a raised platform which leads from the rear of the auditorium, through the audience, to the right side of the stage, and which serves as an extension of the stage proper into the audience.

A "long-song," or Nagauta, orchestra of twenty-two men can be seen formally seated at the rear of the stage, singers and Samisen (a three stringed instrument) players in the top row, and the musicians who play the small hand-drums (Tsuzumi and Kotsuzumi), the larger stand drums (Taiko), and the flute (Yokobue) in the bottom row. They wear identical black kimonos and wide-shouldered outer garments of deep blue marked with the crest of the Ichikawa family, the famous Kabuki acting family that originally produced Kanjinchō.

There is a moment of silence as the off-stage music stops. Then slowly the "long-song" flutist lifts his instrument to his lips, a drummer deliberately raises his sticks and they begin to play. The curtain stage right flies open and Togashi, three soldiers, and a sword bearer enter in stately procession. They move slowly, deliberately, using the sliding step of Noh dance. The foot never leaves the floor. This style of movement is used by all the characters in Kanjinchō. Each controlled movement blends into the next, so that the character appears to glide, rather than walk.

When Togashi reaches center stage he stops, pivots slowly, and faces the audience. It is obvious that he is a Samurai, for he wears the sumptuous ceremonial dress of nobility. His outer kimono is a voluminous affair of pale blue brocade figured with white and silver cranes. Its sleeves almost touch the floor. His legs are encased in the long trousers of court dress (Nagabakama), which trail away a full four feet behind him. He carries a fan in his right hand. His face and hands are pure white except for black lip and eye markings. Togashi addresses the audience directly, in a stately, half-changing style of speech.

TOGASHI. I stand before you here at the Kaga barrier gate! I, Togashi-Zaemon! Our Lord Yoritomo has commanded barriers to be raised throughout the realm to apprehend his younger brother Yoshitsune now reported fleeing northward toward Michinoku. The rift between the brothers is deep and Yoshitsune is said to have disguised himself as a priest in order to escape. We are strictly ordered by Our Lord Yoritomo to stop and investigate every passing priest. In faithful duty I guard this barrier for Our Lord! I command you all to be of this same mind. (No

flicker of expression has crossed Togashi's face, composure being one of the highest virtues of the Samurai code.)

FIRST SOLDIER. (Replying strongly, but also without any visible expression.) Already the heads of three doubtful priests hang from the trees!

SECOND SOLDIER. As you command, every priest shall be brought before you!

THIRD SOLDIER. Captured! Bound on the spot!

FIRST SOLDIER. We are alert . . .

ALL THREE SOLDIERS. . . . ever on guard!

TOGASHI. Well spoken! Seize each and every priest who attempts to pass! We shall put at ease the mind of Our Lord of Kamakura.[1] Now, all of you to your posts!

ALL THREE SOLDIERS. As you command, sir!

(There is a shrill cry from the flute, followed by metallic beats on the Tsuzumi drum. Togashi turns and slowly leads his small procession across the stage, this movement symbolizing their arriving at the barrier. The soldiers kneel in a row upstage. The sword bearer kneels directly behind Togashi, holding the sword before him in readiness. From under the purple property cloth Togashi's personal stage assistant [Koken] brings out a black lacquered cask ornamented with gold. Togashi seats himself on it. Another stage assistant arranges the folds of his costume.)

FULL CHORUS. (To flute and drum accompaniment the eight singers seated at the rear of the stage tell the tale of Yoshitsune's wanderings.)

Their travel garments are those of a priest . . .
Their travel garments are those of a wandering priest,
  with sleeves wet by dew and tears.
The time is the tenth night of the second moon.
  The tenth night of the second moon.
And so having left the capital on a moonlit night . . .

CHORUS LEADER. (The lead singer continues the story of the past.)

Passed is the Mountain of Osaka,
  Before whom those coming and going part,
  Where friends and strangers meet.
Beautiful the hills,
  Shrouded by the mists of spring.

(The curtain at the rear of the Hanamichi flies up and Yoshitsune enters. Using quick sliding steps he moves down the Hanamichi toward the stage, then sees Togashi and the soldiers at the barrier. He stops and turns back toward the audience. For a moment he poses, a subdued tragic figure. He wears a dark purple kimono and pale green trousers. His long hair is gathered together and falls down his back. His face, hands, and dancing socks [tabi] are pure white. As

---

[1]Yoshitsune's brother Yoritomo had several titles. He was the Shogun, or supreme military ruler of Japan. He was also the Lord of Kamakura, for he ruled from the city of Kamakura.

part of his disguise he carries a large coolie's hat and a pil-grim's staff. The blue oi box strapped to his back supposedly contains Benkei's sutras and other religious objects; actually it contains Yoshitsune's armor. Next, Yoshitsune's four re-tainers stride purposefully down the Hanamichi one by one. They pass their master and form a line between him and the stage. They wear priests' vestments and carry Buddhist rosaries. Each has a short sword at his waist.)

FULL CHORUS. *(Continuing the story of their journey.)*
  By furtive ship,
    Through distant paths of waves,
  Arriving, now at last,
    At Kaizu Bay.

(At this point Benkei moves quickly down the Hanamichi. He wears a priest's pill-box hat and vestments. He is an im-posing figure dressed entirely in black brocade silk figured with gold. As Yoshitsune turns to him, the retainers kneel.)

YOSHITSUNE. So, Benkei. The roads ahead are blocked as you say. And this was our last hope. I know now I shall never see the North. For myself I have decided: rather than suf-fer an ignoble death at the hand of some nameless soldier I shall take my own life first. But I must consider your wishes, too, as I did in disguising myself a common porter. At this crucial moment have you any suggestions?

FIRST RETAINER. My Lord, why do we carry these swords? When shall they be painted with blood? Now is the cru-cial moment of My Lord's life.

SECOND RETAINER. Let us resolve! Cut the soldiers down! We shall fight our way through this barrier!

THIRD RETAINER. The years of obligation to Our Lord shall be repaid today! We must pass through, My Lord!

FIRST, SECOND, AND THIRD RETAINERS. *(They rise, hands on the hilts of their swords.)* We shall pass through! *(They turn to go, but the Fourth Retainer, an older man, blocks their path with an imperative gesture and Benkei speaks.)*

BENKEI. Stop! Wait a moment! *(Reluctantly the three retainers return to their kneeling positions.)* A crisis is no time for rash action. If we fight now, even though we succeed, the news will travel ahead making it all the more difficult to pass further barriers. *(Very respectfully to Yoshitsune.)* It was with this in mind that My Lord was asked to remove his priest's vestments and assume the role of a mountain porter when first My Lord put this matter in my charge. And now, My Lord, I beg you, pull your hat low over your eyes and make a pretense of being exhausted. If you will but follow behind us, far in our rear, surely no one will suspect who My Lordship is.

YOSHITSUNE. You plan well, Benkei. *(To the chaffing retain-ers.)* We shall do exactly as Benkei says.

THE FOUR RETAINERS. *(Bowing slightly.)* As Our Lord com-mands.

BENKEI. Then pass peacefully on.

THE FOUR RETAINERS. We obey.

(Benkei passes Yoshitsune and moves onto the stage to the accompaniment of samisen music. The retainers follow closely behind.)

FULL CHORUS.
  And so the travelers,
    Bent upon passing through,
    Drew near the barrier gate.

(There are irregular metallic taps from the tsuzumi drum. Still on the Hanamichi, Yoshitsune ties his hat low over his eyes, then moves slowly onto the stage, taking a position between Benkei, who is almost center stage, and the re-tainers who are kneeling in a row upstage right. His per-sonal stage assistant places a small stool for him to sit on, and arranges his costume. Yoshitsune poses with his head low, clasping the pilgrim's staff over his shoulder. Though he remains motionless in this position throughout most of the play, his noble bearing is such that we are always aware of his presence.)

BENKEI. *(Faces front and speaks in a dignified manner befitting a priest.)* Ho there! We are priests who wish to pass!

TOGASHI. What's that? Priests, you say? *(In all his dignity he rises, strides forward, and addresses Benkei in measured tones.)* Now my friends, know that this is a barrier!

BENKEI. *(Facing Togashi, but feigning deference.)* I know, sir. Throughout the country priests are now soliciting contri-butions for the rebuilding of the Todai Temple in the Southern Capital. It is our honored mission to be dis-patched to the Northern Provinces.

TOGASHI. A praiseworthy project, indeed. However, the very purpose of this barrier is to stop priests like your-selves. You shall find it very difficult to pass.

BENKEI. This is hard to understand. What can it mean?

TOGASHI. Relations between Our Lord Yoritomo and the Hogan[2] having become strained, three years ago Yoshit-sune left his brother's service. Now he flees to the north, disguised as a priest, to seek the aid of his friend Hidehira. Hearing this the Lord of Kamakura has caused these bar-riers to be raised. *(He draws himself up and speaks deliber-ately.)* Know you that I am in command of this barrier!

FIRST SOLDIER. We stand guard with orders to detain all priests!

SECOND SOLDIER. And now before us, behold, many priests!

THIRD SOLDIER. We shall not allow . . .

THE THREE SOLDIERS. . . . even one to pass!

BENKEI. Your orders are to stop all those *disguised* as priests, are they not? They surely say nothing of stopping real priests.

FIRST SOLDIER. *(Not sharing Togashi's lofty politeness, he speaks roughly and to the point.)* Say what you will. Yester-day we killed three priests!

---

[2]Another name for Yoshitsune.

SECOND SOLDIER. So your saying you are real priests will not excuse you!

THIRD SOLDIER. And if you try to pass by force . . .

FIRST, SECOND, AND THIRD SOLDIER. (*In unison.*) . . . not one of you will survive!

BENKEI. (*Reacting with mock horror.*) And these priests you beheaded . . . Was one Yoshitsune?

TOGASHI. Who can say? (*Speaks commandingly.*) It is useless for you to argue. No priest . . .

THE THREE SOLDIERS. (*With great force.*) . . . shall pass this barrier!

(*Togashi imperiously turns his back on Benkei, kicking the long trailing ends of his trousers as he does so. He strides back to his former position stage left and resumes his seat.*)

BENKEI. Monstrous horror! (*Turning to the retainers, but speaking loudly for Togashi's benefit.*) Why should such misfortune be ours? Human strength is powerless against such unforeseen fate! But at least we shall be killed with honor. Come, draw near. Let us perform our last rites!

THE FOUR RETAINERS. We shall, sir.

BENKEI. (*Gravely.*) This is our final rite! (*So saying he moves majestically up right where two stage assistants tie back the long sleeves of his kimono and hand him a scarlet Buddhist rosary. Meanwhile the retainers form a square center stage; they kneel, their hands folded in an attitude of meditation. With a quick glance at Togashi to see how he is taking all this, Benkei moves swiftly into the square, and as the chorus sings, dances a prayer to the gods.*)

FULL CHORUS. (*To full orchestra accompaniment.*)

To detain here Yamabushi priests,
Who are versed in the austere teaching of *En no Ubazoku,*
Whose bodies and spirit are one and the same with the Lord Buddha . . .
(*Benkei raises his arms in supplication to the heavens.*)
Surely the Gods will look with disfavor upon this impious act,
The wrath of God
Yuya Gongen shall strike this spot!
(*In simulated anger Benkei leaps high in the air and stamps loudly upon the floor.*)
"On A Bi Ra Un Ken" . . .
So chanting they rubbed the beads of their rosaries in prayer.

(*Benkei rises to his full height and with a sweeping upward motion begins to rub the beads of his rosary. The others follow suit. The beads of the rosaries buzz and chatter. Then the retainers turn their backs to Benkei, clap their hands in unison, and kneel, hands still folded in prayer. The tableau thus formed is similar to a statue grouping seen in many temples, that of Buddha, protected on the four sides by his kneeling guardian angels, thus implying their closeness to Buddha. Fade music no. 5.*)

TOGASHI. (*Suspicious, he determines to test Benkei's story.*) A noble decision, to die. However, you mentioned a mission of soliciting for the Todai Temple. If this is so surely you cannot be without a list of contributors. (*An order.*) Bring out this *Kanjinchō*! I demand to hear it!

BENKEI. What? (*Momentarily stunned.*) You . . . you say read the *kanjinchō* list?

TOGASHI. Read it I say!

BENKEI. (*His confident voice betrays nothing.*) It shall be done. (*He moves up stage right, where a stage assistant hands him a scroll.*)

CHORUS LEADER.
Ah, were there but a *kanjinchō*!
Instead, from the *oi* box he draws a single unused letter scroll,
And calling it the *kanjinchō*,
He boldly reads aloud.

BENKEI. (*Moving back to center stage, he unrolls the scroll and, holding it so Togashi cannot see it, pretends to read the dedicatory passage. As Benkei is a priest, he has a considerable knowledge of Buddhist ritual and is able to make up a plausible passage.*) Even Buddha, like the autumn moon, has taken refuge in the dark clouds of death. (*Togashi rises and stealthily begins edging toward Benkei.*) Who then, in this world, should be surprised that life is but a long night's dream! (*Suddenly Benkei senses Togashi's presence, and he whirls to face him. The two pose for a moment, glaring angrily at each other. Then Togashi, his suspicions confirmed, strides back to his position stage left and regally resumes his seat. Uncertain whether he has been found out or not, Benkei determines to brazen it out. With a flourish he unrolls the scroll once more and in even louder tones than before continues to "read" from the* kanjinchō.) In the Middle Ages, there once lived an Emperor whose name was Shomu! Having lost his beloved wife, his grief became too much for him to bear. The tears flowed from his eyes in a continuous chain; his cheeks were never dry. To aid her advance as a Bodhisattva, he then built in her memory the great Rushana Buddha, the same that burned to the ground in the era of Juei. I, the priest Chogen, lamenting the loss of this place of worship, have received the Imperial Order to solicit throughout the provinces to rebuild this holy temple. I appeal to priests, high and low, and to laymen alike. He who contributes even a trifling amount shall live in ease in this world and shall sit among thousands of lotus in the next. I address you most reverently!

CHORUS LEADER. He reads as if challenging the heavens to reverberate!

(*Benkei rolls up the scroll with utter composure and is about to turn away.*)

TOGASHI. (*There is little doubt in Togashi's mind that this is Yoshitsune's party, yet he is impressed by Benkei's bold improvisation. Rising, he decides to test Benkei further.*) I see. I have heard the *kanjinchō* now, and should have no further doubts. Nevertheless, let me put a few questions to you. In this world Buddha has many kinds of followers. There are some who show a warlike appearance, and who, it is difficult to believe, are true disciples of the religious austerities. Is there an explanation for this?

BENKEI. (*Without hesitation he fabricates a plausible answer.*) There is indeed a simple explanation. It is the stern prescript of the Shungen Order, in which the principles of Buddha and Shinto combine, that its followers should wander through the precipitous mountains, there to undergo hardship and pain, subduing wild beasts and poisonous reptiles which are harmful to the world, and showing compassion toward their fellow men. Thus do they accumulate meritorious works as was our Lord Buddha's command. Thus do they save evil and lost souls and show them the way toward Nirvana. They pray for purity; they pray for the brightness of the sun and moon and for the everlasting peace of the world. In this way, within themselves they nurture the twin virtues of stoicism and benevolence, while outwardly they conquer evil and subdue heretical doctrines in a warlike manner. All is Shinto and Buddha . . . the one-hundred-eight beads of the rosary representing the multitudinous blessings of the Gods!

TOGASHI. (*Pressing another question without pause.*) You appear to be followers of Buddha, wearing a priest's *kesa* vestment. Why then do you wear a pilgrim's *tokin* hat at the same time?

BENKEI. The *tokin* hat and the *suzukake* vestments are like the warrior's helmet and armor. With the sharp sword of Amida Buddha at his side, and breaking a path with the Kongo staff, the pilgrim crosses the highest mountains and the most dangerous places.

TOGASHI. I know that priests carry the Shakujo scepter, with its soft sounding bells. But how does carrying a Kongo staff protect a pilgrim's body and limbs?

BENKEI. A foolish question! The Kongo staff has been famous as the pilgrim's staff since first used by the Holy Arara, the divine being who lived in the Dantaloka Mountains in India, and under whose guidance our Buddha first accumulated meritorious deeds. It was this seer who gave to our Buddha the new name of Shofubiku in recognition of his pupil's great faith and strength of purpose. The spirit of Buddha dwells within the staff! As a child grows in his mother's womb, so the spirit of Buddha grows within us all!

TOGASHI. How has this tradition been handed down?

BENKEI. Our predecessors carried it as the holy staff of Our Lord Buddha when traveling in the mountains and valleys and this has become the practice down through the ages!

TOGASHI. Though a priest, you wear a sword. Is this merely a symbol of defense, or is it used to do physical harm?

BENKEI. Like the bow of the scarecrow, it serves to frighten our enemies. At the same time we do not hesitate to strike down those evil beasts and poisonous snakes, and human beings as well, that violate Buddha's law or the Princely Way. For with one death many lives may be saved!

TOGASHI. One can, of course, cut down a solid object, that obstructs the eye, but what of those formless evils that may obstruct Buddha's law or the Princely Way? With what would you cut them down?

BENKEI. What difficulty is there in destroying formless evils? One would dispel them with the nine-word Shingon prayer!

TOGASHI. (*Moving in toward Benkei, he presses another series of questions without pause.*) Now tell me, what is the significance of your dress?

BENKEI. It is patterned in the likeness of the ferocious deity Fudo!

TOGASHI. What is the meaning of your *tokin* hat?

BENKEI. It is the headdress of the five wisdoms, its twelve folds symbolizing the affinity of cause and retribution!

TOGASHI. (*Moves in another step.*) And the *kesa* vestment you wear about your neck?

BENKEI. (*He moves in toward Togashi.*) It is a *suzukake* of persimmon in color, signifying the nine stages of Buddha's paradise!

TOGASHI. Why the bindings about your legs?

BENKEI. They are the black leggings of the Shingon Sect!

TOGASHI. And your eight-knobbed straw sandals?

BENKEI. In the spirit of treading on the eight-petaled lotus!

TOGASHI. (*Almost spitting it out.*) And the air you breathe?

BENKEI. (*They are face to face, just a few feet apart. Benkei controls himself, but he is trembling with anger. For a moment they glare at each other in tableau.*) In the holy sutras, the beginning and the end, the two reverend sounds—"A and UN"!

TOGASHI. (*Still pressing.*) And now one final question. What is the meaning of the nine-word Shingon prayer! (*For a moment Benkei cannot reply. Togashi senses the lapse he has been waiting for. He draws back a pace, and raises his fan in a commanding gesture. He speaks imperiously.*) Come, come! What do you say!

BENKEI. (*The question is far beyond Benkei's knowledge of Buddhism. He is furious with Togashi and being by nature an impetuous and proud man, he is sorely tempted to abandon his pose. Benkei is renowned as a warrior; he knows he could easily defeat Togashi. Nevertheless, he controls himself and launches into a brilliant improvisation of Buddhist jargon.*) This nine-word prayer is a precious secret of the Shingon faith and its meaning is most difficult to explain. But to still your doubt I shall undertake to do so. The nine words are: *Rin Byoh Toh Sha Kai Chin Retsu Zai Zen!* Before you draw your sword, first, you must strike your teeth thirty-six times with hands folded in supplication. Then, with the thumb of your right hand, you draw four lines from earth to sky and five lines from horizon to horizon. Simultaneously, you rapidly incant the blessing "*kyuu kyuu nyo ritsu ryoo."* So doing, all evil—the evil of worldly passions and the devil of heresy—will disappear like frost before the vapors of steam. Sharp and shining, the prayer cuts through to the very heart of the world's darkness. In this it is beyond compare, even to the miraculous sword of Bakuya, and the warrior who utters it cannot fail to defeat his enemy! Now . . . have you any further questions regarding our religious practices? I shall reply to them all in full, that you may share in the power of their virtue, which is all-embracing and infinite! engrave these words on your heart, but reveal their secrets to no one! Oh, Gods and Bodhisattvas of Japan, I call upon you to witness the words I most reverently speak! I bow before you! (*He does, then turns to Togashi.*) I speak to you with utmost respect.

FULL CHORUS. (*To samisen music.*)
　　The barrier guard seems impressed.

(*Benkei dances a few steps expressive of his success, then he and Togashi pose in tableau: Benkei with the scroll held high as in triumph, and Togashi with his fan held over his head. This is a high point of the play. From the audience come loud cries of "Well done!", "We've waited for this!", "Like your father before you!"*)

TOGASHI. (*Togashi is certain they are Benkei and Yoshitsune, yet Benkei has not faltered in his defense of his master. Impressed, Togashi decides to let them pass.*) That I should have doubted such honorable priests even for a moment. I should like to be added to your list of contributors. Guards, bring gifts for the priests!

THE THREE SOLDIERS. Yes, sir.

(*The mood relaxes perceptibly. Quiet samisen music underlies the following actions. Togashi returns to his seat stage left. Benkei gives the scroll to his stage assistant up right and receives a rosary. At the same time, The Three Soldiers pick up gift trays which have just been brought in through the small door stage left by Togashi's stage assistant. The soldiers place the trays center stage and return to their kneeling positions up stage of Togashi.*)

FULL CHORUS.
　　On wide stands, brought forth by the guards,
　　　　A ceremonial skirt of pure white silk,
　　　　Many rolls of Kaga silk,
　　　　A mirror and golden coins.

TOGASHI. Though the gifts are small it would be accredited as a meritorious deed for me should you accept them on behalf of the priests of Todaiji. Respectfully, I beg you accept them.

BENKEI. (*Standing before the gifts, ready to receive them, he speaks impressively.*) You are indeed a benevolent Lord. There can be no doubt of ; our peaceful, happy existence in this world and the next. (*He rubs his rosary over the gifts in blessing.*) One thing more. We will be traveling through the neighboring provinces, not returning to the capital until the middle of the fourth moon. I beg you to keep the larger articles for us until then. (*He kneels before the gifts. When he rises he takes only the two bags of money from the center tray. These he gives to two of the retainers.*) Now, pass through!

THE FOUR RETAINERS. Yes, sir!

BENKEI. (*He take out his fan, flips it open, and holds it in front of him. His actions appear unconcerned, but his voice betrays his anxiety over their delicate situation.*) Go! Go now! Hurry!

THE FOUR RETAINERS. We go, sir!

CHORUS LEADER.
　　Rejoicing within
　　　　The warrior-priests
　　　　Quietly rise and move away.

(*Benkei moves swiftly down the Hanamichi followed by the four retainers. Yoshitsune rises and, with head bent low, slowly begins to leave the stage. Suddenly one of the soldiers crosses to Togashi's side and whispers in his ear.*)

TOGASHI. (*Rises abruptly.*) What? That porter? (*With the help of his stage assistant, Togashi slips the kimono from his right shoulder, freeing his arm for action. Receiving his sword from the bearer, he takes two deliberate paces forward, and stops, hand poised on the hilt of his sword in a threatening gesture.*) Stop! Stop, I say! (*The action now is very rapid, Yoshitsune stops, and then as if pulled by invisible strings, he backs toward Togashi. He kneels again in the same position he was in previously, head low and staff held against one shoulder. At the same time, Benkei turns and rushes past the retainers toward the stage but before he can reach Yoshitsune, the retainers also turn and start toward the stage. They have their hands on their swords ready to draw, thinking their master is discovered. But with viciously twirling rosary and outstretched arms Benkei succeeds in blocking their headlong rush at the very end of the Hanamichi.*)

BENKEI. No! Rashness will lose it all!

FULL CHORUS.
　　"Our Lord is suspected!
　　　　Now is the moment
　　　　Between sinking and floating!"
　　These are their thoughts as they turn.

BENKEI. (*In feigned rage, shakes his head violently and stamps loudly on the floor. He twirls the rosary about his head in a sweeping arc, and crosses in swiftly to Yoshitsune, attempting to shield him from Togashi's searching gaze.*) You! Strong One! why haven't you passed through?

TOGASHI. (*In a fearsome voice.*) Because I have detained him!

BENKEI. Detained him? What for?

TOGASHI. There are those who say he resembles . . . a certain person. That is why I have detained him.

BENKEI. Well? What's strange about that? One person often resembles another! (*Brazening it out.*) Who do you think he resembles?

TOGASHI. My soldiers say the Hogan, Yoshitsune. He is to be held for questioning.

BENKEI. The Hogan? The Strong One resembles the *Hogan*, you say? (*Turning on Yoshitsune in feigned fury.*) This is something to remember a lifetime! Ohhhh! It's unendurable! We'd planned to reach Noto by sundown and now, just because of this lagging porter . . . *this* has happened! If people begin suspecting you of being the Hogan on the slightest provocation, you'll be the cause of the failure of our mission! (*Grinds his teeth as if in uncontrollable rage.*) The more I think of it the more despicable you become! (*He growls through clenched teeth; he leaps in the air and stamps on the floor.*) You are hateful I say! Hateful! Hateful!!

FULL CHORUS. (*To rapid and excited samisen music.*)
  Snatching up the Kongo staff,
  He strikes right . . .

(*Restraining the tears, Benkei raises the staff high, then strikes his master on the right shoulder. His whole body jerks as if he himself had been struck. Once again he raises the staff, hesitates, his face contorted with grief, then strikes his master on the left shoulder.*)

He strikes left!

BENKEI. Now, move on, I tell you!

CHORUS LEADER.
  He berates him soundly,
  Ordering him to pass through!

(*Shielding his face, Yoshitsune rises and quickly crosses up stage right and kneels with his back to the audience, in effect, removing himself from the scene which follows.*)

TOGASHI. No matter how you plead his case, he shall not . . .

THE THREE SOLDIERS. . . . pass through! (*The soldiers stand in a resolute row with their hands on their sword hilts. Yoshitsune's retainers reach for their swords and are about to attack. Still trying to avert a conflict, Benkei makes an excuse for the retainers' actions.*)

BENKEI. For you to eye the *oi* box as you do, you're not guards at all. You must be thieves! (*He strikes the staff loudly on the floor and poses with it threateningly. The retainers surge forward. Benkei quickly uses the staff to block their path.*) Here! Here!

(*Benkei forces the retainers back once, but they press forward again. He pushes them back a second time, holding them with the staff until they are calmed. Benkei now turns to face Togashi, holding the staff before him in both hands. The sight of Benkei striking his own master has come as a physical shock to Togashi. Impressed with Benkei's daring, momentarily he cannot bring himself to act. But now he dismisses such thoughts and resolves to attack.*)

FULL CHORUS. (*Accompanied by full orchestra.*)
  "How cowardly it is!
    To draw swords

    Against a lowly porter!"
  With such seeming thoughts,
    And god-frightening looks,
    The priests prepared for battle.

(*Slowly the two opposing groups move toward each other until they meet center stage. On each side the men press against their leader. Benkei and Togashi glare fiercely at each other. Then Togashi and the soldiers begin to advance. Slowly, deliberately, using the sliding dance step of Noh, they take one, two, three slow-motion strides forward. In unison, Benkei and the retainers take one, two, three strides backward. The two masses of men pivot and surge as one, bound together by their fierce antagonism. Now Benkei summons his last resources and halts Togashi. Holding the staff before him, he begins to push Togashi back. The soldiers and the retainers stand aside as Benkei forces Togashi back step by step to his original position. The implication is that Togashi can no longer bring himself to attack in the face of Benkei's great display of courage on behalf of Yoshitsune. Benkei has succeeded in preventing first his own men and now Togashi from launching an attack. The victory is his. Defiantly he faces Togashi. Twirling the rosary, he swings the staff about his head, and strikes it on the floor. He raises the staff over his head and poses. Togashi poses with his legs spread wide apart and his hand on the hilt of his sword. They hold their tableau for a moment.*)

BENKEI. If you still think this miserable creature is the Hogan, then hold him along with the gifts until our return! Investigate him any way you wish. Or would you rather I kill him with this now? (*He strikes the staff on the floor and brandishes it threateningly.*)

TOGASHI. You are too harsh!

BENKEI. Then why do you still doubt us?

TOGASHI. There is the complaint of my soldiers.

BENKEI. (*With grim determination.*) Then I shall kill him before your own eyes! Will that convince you?

TOGASHI. (*Togashi visibly recoils at the thought. He is caught up in conflicting emotions. He is aghast to think that Benkei would actually raise his hand against his own master, an unheard of act in feudal Japan. At the same time he recognizes this as an act of supreme devotion on Benkei's part and is overwhelmed with admiration. In Benkei he recognizes his moral superior. He makes his decision.*) Stop! Do not be hasty! Because of the baseless suspicions of my soldiers you have already severely beaten this person who . . . is not the Hogan. My doubts are now dispelled. (*Speaking brusquely to cover his emotions.*) Quickly now, pass through the barrier!

BENKEI. (*Continuing the pretense to the end.*) Were it not for the words of the Great Lord here, I should have killed you on the spot! You laggard, you've been lucky this time! Don't tempt the Gods again!

TOGASHI. From now on, it is my duty to maintain even stricter guard! (*His stage assistant fixes the sleeve of his kimono.*) Come with me, men!

THE THREE SOLDIERS. Yes, My Lord.

(*Benkei and Togashi face each other once more in tableau. The air fairly crackles with emotion. Benkei has succeeded; he knows this, yet cannot show it. For Togashi's part, he knows full well who Benkei and Yoshitsune are, yet he cannot show this. Further, there is the implication that, having failed his own master Yoritomo, the honorable course for him now would be to take his own life. He averts his face so the soldiers cannot see his struggle to maintain composure. Just as he is about to give way to tears, he shakes his head, dismissing the thought of death from his mind. He draws himself up to his full height, pivots regally about, kicking out the long trailing ends of his trousers, and strides off the stage.*)

FULL CHORUS.

Taking his soldiers with him,
The barrier guard enters within the gate.

(*Togashi and the soldiers exit through the small door stage left. Benkei looks after them. The music now becomes plaintive and halting in tempo. Yoshitsune's hat and oi box have been taken by his stage assistant and now he moves to left center stage where he kneels. Benkei slowly moves to center stage right. He kneels facing Yoshitsune, his head bent in grief. The retainers kneel in a line up stage between the two. They have symbolically passed through the barrier and are now stopping some distance beyond it.*)

YOSHITSUNE. (*He speaks quietly. In spite of their success he seems subdued and melancholy.*) Benkei, you acted with great presence of mind. Indeed no one but you could have succeeded with such a daring plan. Without hesitation you struck me as recklessly as though I were a lowly servant and so saved me. I stand in awe, for having received the divine protection of our patron, Sho Hachiman, the God of War.

FIRST RETAINER. The barrier guard stopped us and we all felt, "Now is the moment to fight for Our Lord's safety!"

SECOND RETAINER. It is a sign that Sho Hachiman is protecting Our Lord. Our trip from here on to Michinoku should be a swift one.

THIRD RETAINER. Yet without the quick thinking of our Priest of Musashi here, it would have been hard to escape.

FIRST RETAINER. We were . . .

ALL FOUR RETAINERS. . . . truly amazed!

BENKEI. (*Benkei's head is bent to the floor. He can scarcely speak for remorse.*) The seers have preached that the end of the world is soon at hand. Yet the sun and the moon have not yet fallen from their places in the heavens. Fate has been kind to Yoshitsune also. How grateful we all are. You speak of strategy, but the fact is I have *struck* my own dear Lord. The heavenly reprisals are frightening to con-

template. These two arms which can lift a thousand *kin* are as though benumbed. How wrong I have been! How wrong!

CHORUS LEADER.

How noble, now,
Even Benkei,
Who has never given way before,
Finally sheds the tears of a lifetime.

(*His whole body shaking with grief, Benkei bows his head and holds his hand before his eyes in the symbolic gesture of weeping.*)

FULL CHORUS. The Hogan then took his hand.

(*Rising to one knee, Yoshitsune extends his right hand to Benkei in token of forgiveness. Benkei starts forward as if to accept his master's gesture, then is overcome with the enormity of his crime. He pulls back sharply, flings down his fan, and bows his head once more to the floor in remorse.*)

YOSHITSUNE. (*To see the rock-like Benkei reduced to tears on his behalf, brings home to Yoshitsune the full misery and the hopelessness of their position. He too raises his hand to his eyes to cover his tears.*) Why should it be? Why should Yoshitsune, nobly born, his whole life spent in devoted service to his brother, end his life as a corpse sinking unheralded beneath the waves of the Western Sea?

BENKEI. (*Picking up his fan, he holds it before him formally and begins to tell the story of Yoshitsune's wanderings.*)

Midst mountain places,
And rock-bound coasts,
Awake and asleep,
The warrior spends his lonely existence.

FULL CHORUS. (*As the chorus takes up the story, Benkei dances its meaning to the accompaniment of a plaintive melody played by the full orchestra. The pace is slow, the mood softly melancholy.*)

The warrior,
With armor and sleeve-pillow
As sole companions . . .

(*Benkei mimes sleeping, his head cradled on his kimono sleeve.*)

Sometimes,
Adrift at sea,
At the mercy of wind and tide . . .

(*He sculls a boat; his open fan flutters overhead as in the wind.*)

Sometimes,
In mountain fastnesses,
Where no hoofprint breaks the white snow . . .

(*The upside-down fan becomes a mountain.*)

While he endures it all,
From small evening waves of the sea,
Come whispers of disgrace and banishment.

(*To emphasize the strength of the thought, Benkei draws the string of an imaginary bow. Then he gestures the throwing of a stone, indicating that Yoshitsune's fortunes are being dashed to earth in the same way. For a moment he holds a powerful pose, right hand extended, left hand over his head. Then he slowly crosses his eyes, executing a "mie," the most expressive type of pose in Kabuki. Two sharp claps of the stage manager's hyoshigi sticks empha- size the emotional tension of the moment.)*

> For three long years past,
>> Like the *oniazami* thistle,
>> Which has begun to wither and die,
>> Covered only by the frost and dew.
> How pitiful it is!

(Benkei indicates Yoshitsune with his closed fan. Then he and the four retainers bow low. Straightening up, they cover their eyes to hide their tears.)

THE FOUR RETAINERS. Quickly now, My Lord, let us with- draw!

FULL CHORUS.
>> Pulling on each other's sleeves,
>> They seem anxious to be on their way.

(But Benkei does not move. The fan falls from his nerve- less fingers, his head sinks to his chest.)

TOGASHI. *(Off stage.)* Wait. Wait a moment! *(As Benkei rises instantly, prepared to meet whatever new challenge may come, Yoshitsune retires up stage right where he is covered from view by the four retainers. Togashi and the soldiers enter through the main entrance stage right and cross immediately to their original positions stage left.)* Forgive my abruptness, but I have brought some *sake*, and though it is nothing much, I hope you will drink with me. *(A small cup is placed on a tray before Togashi by one of the soldiers, and filled. As is the custom, Togashi, the host, drinks first. Then the cup on the tray is ceremoniously placed before Benkei, who accepts it center stage, kneeling facing the audience. The cup is filled and Benkei looks at it with undisguised pleasure.)*

BENKEI. My kind Lord, I shall drink with you with pleasure!

CHORUS LEADER. *(Accompanied by a single samisen.)*
>> Truly, truly, Benkei understands this gesture.
>>> How can he ever forget,
>>> Having received this cup of human sympathy?

(Benkei tosses off the drink in one swallow. In an expan- sive mood, now that the crisis is past, he laughingly ges- tures for the lid of the big lacquered cask stage left to be brought to him and filled with wine. Two soldiers do so, then watch in open-mouthed amazement as Benkei buries his face in the lid and downs an enormous draught. Benkei comes up for air, smacks his lips, and then with a sly chuckle points straight to the audience. The soldiers lean forward, straining to see what is out there, and as they do so, Benkei pushes them off balance and they tumble to the floor. Benkei roars with good-natured laughter.)

And now for tales of the past . . .

(As a kind of counterpoint to Benkei's actions, the chorus leader tells of an early love affair Benkei once had as a priest, obliquely comparing the difficulties he faced then to the crossing of the barrier now.)

> What embarrassment
>> my heart
>> once met.
> Once met
>> a woman
>> and confusion.
> Along the road of confusion,
>> this barrier
>> once was crossed.
> Being crossed,
>> yet another now,
>> with difficulty passed.
> Ah, to pass the barrier
>> of people's eyes
>> is difficult to bear.
> It is a transient world!
>> We never know enlightenment!

(Benkei empties the lid, then gestures for it to be filled once more. The soldiers hesitate, afraid of the consequences, but a menacing glare and a roar of mock anger quickly convince them which is the lesser of the two evils. They fill the lid at once. His eyes gleaming with delight, Benkei raises the lid to his lips and drains the entire contents in a single, breathtaking swallow. The soldiers stand amazed. Now slightly tipsy, Benkei puts the lid on his head, and then as a stage assistant raises the lid, he rises unsteadily to his feet to dance, beating time with the closed fan. Now the fan is flicked open and it becomes a sake cup; it sails in a graceful arc across the stage and it is a sake cup floating down a mountain stream.)

FULL CHORUS.
>> How amusing,
>>> Floating the wine cup
>>> Down the mountain stream.
>> The swirling water,
>>> In eddies and currents,
>> Splashes the sleeves
>>> Covering the reaching hand.

(Benkei dances his unsteady way along the "river bank" after his "sake cup." He trips, stumbles, almost falls, then at the last moment recovers his balance. Then, the dance over, and his tipsiness gone, he retrieves the fan, folds it, and formally turns to face Togashi.)

>> Now, let us perform a dance!

BENKEI. In gratitude, I come to offer you wine! *(He holds out the open fan to Togashi, thus symbolizing an offering of drink.)*

TOGASHI. Come, dance for us.

BENKEI. (*Benkei turns to the audience and kneels. When he speaks, it is with great emotion. The implied meaning is that he, Benkei, recognizes what Togashi has done for them, and that he wishes to express his gratitude. At the same time, it is implied that Togashi recognizes the true meaning of Benkei's words.*)

> Live myriad long years!
> As the turtle dwells
> On the rocks!
> *Aryu dondo!*

(*As further expression of his gratitude, Benkei now rises and performs a dance taken from the Noh drama. In the first section of the dance, he circles the stage twice with closed fan and three times with fan open, as the drums and flute play a lively rhythmic passage. This is a standard Noh dance pattern with no particular meaning. In the second section, the tempo becomes much slower, and a samisen joins the drums and flute. Benkei crosses the stage in a triangular figure. His foot movements remain the simple sliding steps they were in the first section, but his arm movements and gestures with the open fan become increasingly complicated. In the third and final section of the dance, the tempo quickens again and Benkei's dancing takes on an infectious, rhythmic quality. In a gold and red arc the open fan flashes through the air. Benkei leaps high and stamps loudly on the floor. With outstretched arms he twirls the long red rosary. The dance is concluded as he kneels and ceremoniously closes the fan.*)

FULL CHORUS.

> Originally Benkei was the Wandering Priest of Santo.
> As a youth he danced the Ennen dance.

(*Benkei now performs a short ennen dance, a dance of longevity, traditionally performed by priests. Inasmuch as Benkei was famous in his youth for his skill in this dance, and inasmuch as Togashi would be expected to know this, to dance it now is a daring and subtle way for Benkei to express his gratitude. The complex web of recognition is now complete: both Benkei and Togashi know that the other knows, yet neither can acknowledge the fact directly. At the conclusion of the dance Benkei kneels again. Once more playing the role, he comments politely on the beauty of the scene where they have stopped.*)

BENKEI.

> The sound of the falling mountain stream,
> Reverberates on the rocks below.
> > (*A piercing note is heard from the flute.*)
> That which roars is the waterfall!
> That which roars is the waterfall!

FULL CHORUS. (*With full orchestra accompaniment.*)

> The waterfall will roar,
> The sun will shine
> Let us take our leave
> Of the barrier guards!

(*As the music reaches a crescendo, Benkei rises and signals the party to leave with a single, sudden gesture of the fan. Yoshitsune and the retainers move swiftly down the Hanamichi and exit at the rear of the auditorium.*)

> So saying, Benkei
> Shouldered the oi box.

(*Two stage assistants help Benkei into the oi box harness. Then as he moves quickly toward the Hanamichi, Togashi rises, following his progress with an intent gaze. At the Hanamichi, Benkei pauses, and stands with legs spread wide apart, the staff held over his head in both hands. Togashi steps forward a pace, twirls the long sleeve of his kimono over his left arm, and raises his closed fan high in the air. This climactic pose is held for a moment.*)

> Feeling as though,
> They had trod on the tail of a tiger,
> And slipped through the jaws of a dragon,
> They departed for the Province of Michinoku.

(*Benkei moves quickly onto the Hanamichi, and the curtain is run closed behind him. Again Benkei pauses; all is silence. He cannot but think of the great sacrifice Togashi has made on their behalf. His eyes are drawn back toward the place where Togashi was a moment ago. Then his thoughts abruptly return to the many difficulties still lying ahead. He resolutely faces front. He twirls the staff round his head, and poses again, eyes crossed in a "mie." Now he begins his famous "flying roppo," or "moving-in-six-directions-at-once," exit. He remains poised for a long instant on one leg, bending and flexing it. Then he makes a powerful leap forward onto the other leg. Bending and flexing again, he prepares for the next leap. With a twirl of the staff he makes another bound, landing on the opposite leg. Again the bending and flexing, then another leap, and another, and another. Faster and faster he goes, arms and legs flashing in all directions. By the time he reaches the end of the sixty-foot Hanamichi he is moving at full speed, in prodigious leaps and bounds, a brilliant and theatrical projection of masculine strength. As Benkei disappears from sight through the agemaku curtain, the music and clapping of the sticks reach a crescendo, then quickly taper off. The play ends as it began, with a few minutes of quiet drum and flute music played by the musicians off stage right.*)

THE MAN WHO TURNED INTO A STICK

KOBO ABE

KOBO ABE (1924–1993)

Among the most versatile artists in contemporary Japan, Kobo Abe was a novelist, short-story writer, poet, and dramatist. In the West he is best known for his novel *The Woman in the Dunes* (1964), which was transformed into an award-winning film by Hiroshi Teshigahara, a leading avant-garde filmmaker. Abe later adapted his novel into a stage play. In 1971 he opened the Abe Studio, an enterprise dedicated to actor training and experimental theater. It is recognized as among the most innovative sources of contemporary Japanese theater and literature. *The Man Who Turned into a Stick* was conceived as an acting exercise at Abe's studio.

Although he was born in Tokyo, whose urbanization has inspired much of his artistic work, Abe was raised in Mukden, Manchuria, where his father, a doctor, served at the Manchurian School of Medicine. Mukden, a desolate desert outpost whose barren landscape haunted Abe, provided the most notable theme in his work: the solitary figure suspended in space. As a Japanese living in a Chinese colony that was often violent and inhospitable, Abe also understood alienation and loneliness, another theme that permeates his work. Of his childhood experience, he told Donald Keene, the principal translator of his works into English, "Living in Manchuria I began to be accustomed to doubting what it means for a person to belong to a nation called Japan or even belong to a certain society."

Abe intended to follow his father into the medical profession, and—like his inspiration, Chekhov—he wrote short stories and other literary pieces while in medical school. Gradually, his creative urge led him to abandon medicine and devote his energy to writing, the profession of his novelist mother. He did, however, continue to draw on the sciences for inspiration; mathematics in particular informs his writing and his stagecraft. His favorite Western writer, coincidentally, was Lewis Carroll, also a mathematician turned writer. From mathematics and Carroll, Abe learned to look at the world from unconventional vantage points:

> When I was a child, I liked geometrical proofs. The trick in solving problems in geometry is to break away from the preconceived idea related to a particular form and to discover an unexpected additional line. Flexible thinking and a leap in imagination are necessary.

He likens his theater pieces, both as they evolve in the studio and as they are performed for an audience, to algebraic equations that must be solved. (Costumes and scenery in Abe productions frequently bear mathematical symbols.) His central character in *The Woman in the Dunes* asks a question central to Abe's work: "Where in God's name should he start on this equation filled with unknowns?" In his plays and other works, there are no ready solutions for the questions he raises; indeed, there may be no answer at all. Thus Abe's plays and productions (he does not distinguish between his written work and his stagework) demand an active participation from his audiences to solve the problem.

Abe is primarily a metaphysical dramatist whose works transcend topicality and politics. He was at one time a member of the Communist Party of Japan, which grew out of the ruin of World War II, but resigned when the Russians invaded Hungary in 1956. (Actually, the Party refused his resignation and expelled him.) His work is social and political only in that it decries the debasement of individuals by urbanization, automation, and rigid thinking, themes inherent in *The Man Who Turned into a Stick*. Abe died in January 1993, leaving a legacy of some of the most innovative literary and theatrical experiments in contemporary Japan. Among his best theater works are *Friends* (1974), *Fake Fish* (1973), and *Green Stockings* (1974). Nancy Shields's *Fake Fish: The Theater of Kobo Abe* (1996) provides a fascinating look at the process behind Abe's work.

THE MAN WHO TURNED INTO A STICK (1976)

Perhaps no aspect of Abe's dramaturgy is as compelling as his notion that his starting place in the creation of a new work is "to deal with an object as object itself." By this Abe means:

> The important thing is to think into an object, allow an object to be an obstacle to the mind and not, as most people do, allow it to pass easily through the mind. Once one thinks into an object, one gets a kind of surprise. My function as a writer is to see between these two extremes. I always try to start not from a concept but . . . to start from a concrete object that is visible, that can be touched.

Such is the seed from which *The Man Who Turned into a Stick* grew. Abe conceived the piece as a studio exercise for his company's most junior members. He had an image of a man, standing atop a rooftop in Tokyo, who suddenly turned into a stick and fell to the ground. The challenge was for the actor playing the stick—and for those who react to him—to make the experience believable and meaningful. (In a companion piece, Abe asked an actor to play a suitcase.) His actors experimented with the concept. Originally the "plot"—Abe's plays are distinctly nonlinear, often formless—centered on the trial, conducted by a student and her teacher, of the "stick man," who is accused of rigidity and conformity. In another version that suggests a possible meaning for this perplexing work, a man and a woman actually refuse to pass judgment on the stick because the percentage of men turning into sticks is common: "98.4 percent of all those who die . . . turn into sticks." In light of this line we see that the play suggests that contemporary life, which can reduce people to rigid-thinking automatons, turns people into sticks, something more dead than alive. Certainly the presence of the Man and Woman from Hell lends a morality-play aura to this modern fable about the dangers of conformity, especially at the conclusion when the Man from Hell points to the audience and says, "Look—there's a whole forest of sticks around you."

For all its modernity, Abe's play yet retains its kinship to Japan's traditional theaters, the Noh and the Kabuki. Transformations and mutations (favorite Abe themes, as the title of this play suggests) were commonplace in both. (The Kabuki, in fact, had a whole category of stage tricks—the *hayagawari*—devoted to transformations.) Traditional Japanese thought, shaped by Shinto and Zen Buddhism, sees life as an ongoing transformation throughout eternity. Nothing is permanent, and objects and people continually mutate into other beings, which gives creation a unified wholeness. Abe's play adds contemporary social commentary to this centuries-old recognition of the mutability of existence.

Among the aesthetic values the Japanese cherish are *aware*, which allows the beholder to find beauty in ordinary objects (such as a stick), and *okashi*, the ability to find amusement in those things that are ponderous. Out of these come *yūgen*, the ideal to which Zeami aspired as he wrote his Noh plays 600 years ago. *Yūgen* is the ability to find truth in the simple and the beautiful. Abe's short play asks its audience to look at a stick as if for the first time and to find sad humor in the circumstances in which the "stick man" finds himself. Ultimately the play leads to a moment of clarity about the human condition in the last decades of the twentieth century. Though the message is disturbing, there is an inherent beauty in the simplicity and imagination that calls it forth.

The two hippies in the play, by the way, are more than a nod from Abe to topicality in the mid-1970s. They are emblems of the dispossessed who reject the limitations of modern urban life. In 1957 Abe traveled to Europe and spent time in a Czechoslovakian Gypsy village, where he witnessed, ironically, the second-class citizenship the Communist government afforded Gypsies. But he also found himself inspired by the spirit of the Gypsies, who knew no geographical boundaries; for Abe, the Gypsies became a symbol of "the complexities of the relationship between society and consciousness." In Abe's world, Gypsies do not turn into sticks.

The late Kobe Abe, a novelist turned playwright and stage director, was one of contemporary Japan's leading literary figures; the events of his own life inspired The Man Who Turned into a Stick.

THE MAN WHO TURNED INTO A STICK

KOBO ABE

Translated by Donald Keene

CAST OF CHARACTERS
MAN FROM HELL (a supervisor)
WOMAN FROM HELL (recently appointed to the Earth Duty Squad)
THE MAN WHO TURNED INTO A STICK
HIPPIE BOY
HIPPIE GIRL
VOICE FROM HELL

A hot, sticky Sunday afternoon in June. A main thoroughfare with the Terminal Department Store in the background. Crowds of people passing back and forth. (It is best not to attempt to represent this realistically.) A young man and a young woman sit on the sidewalk curb at stage center front about three yards apart. They are hippies. They stare vacantly ahead, completely indifferent to their surroundings, with withdrawn expressions. (If desired they can be shown sniffing glue.)

All of a sudden a stick comes hurtling down from the sky. A very ordinary stick, about four feet long. (It can be manipulated, perhaps in the manner of Grand Guignol, by the actor playing the part of the man before he turned into a stick.)

The stick rolls over and over, first striking against the edge of the sidewalk, then bouncing back with a clatter, and finally coming to rest horizontally in the gutter near the curbstone, less than a yard from the two hippies. Reflex action makes them look at where the stick has fallen, then upwards, frowning, to see where it came from. But, considering the danger to which they have been exposed, their reactions are somewhat lacking in urgency.

Man from Hell enters from stage-left, and Woman from Hell from stage-right. Both are spot-lighted.

HIPPIE BOY. (*Still looking up.*) God-damned dangerous.
MAN FROM HELL. In the twilight a white crescent moon,
    A fruit knife peeling the skin of fate.

WOMAN FROM HELL. Today, once again, a man
   Has changed his shape and become a stick.
HIPPIE BOY. (*Turns his gaze back to the stick and picks it up.*)
   Just a couple of feet closer and it would have finished me.
HIPPIE GIRL. (*Looks at the stick and touches it.*) Which do you
   suppose is the accident—when something hits you or
   when it misses?
HIPPIE BOY. How should I know? (*Bangs the stick on the pave-
   ment, making a rhythm.*)
MAN FROM HELL. The Moon, the color of dirty
   chromium plate,
   Looks down and the streets
   are swirling.
WOMAN FROM HELL. Today, once again, a man
   Turned into a stick and vanished.
HIPPIE GIRL. Hey, what's that rhythm you're tapping?
HIPPIE BOY. Try and guess.
HIPPIE GIRL (*Glancing up.*) Look! I'm sure that kid was the
   culprit!
HIPPIE BOY. (*Intrigued, looks up.*)
HIPPIE GIRL. Isn't he cute? I'll bet he's still in grade school.
   He must've been playing on the roof.
HIPPIE BOY. (*Looks into the distance, as before.*) Damned
   brats. I hate them all.
HIPPIE GIRL. Ohh—it's dangerous, the way he's leaning over
   the edge. . . . I'm sure he's ashamed now he threw it. . . .
   He seems to be trying to say something, but I can't hear
   him.
HIPPIE BOY. He's probably disappointed nobody got hurt, so
   now he's cursing us instead.
STICK. (*To himself.*) No, that's not so. He's calling me. The
   child saw me fall.
HIPPIE GIRL. (*Abruptly changing the subject.*) I know what it
   is, that rhythm. This is the song, isn't it? (*She hums some
   tune or other.*)
HIPPIE BOY. Hmmm.
HIPPIE GIRL. Was I wrong?
HIPPIE BOY. It's always been my principle to respect other
   people's tastes.
HIPPIE GIRL. (*Unfazed by this, she wiggles her body to the
   rhythm, and goes on humming.*)
   (*In the meantime, The Man Who Turned into a Stick is coor-
   dinating the movements of his body with those of the stick in
   Hippie Boy's hand, all the while keeping his eyes fastened on a
   point somewhere in the sky.*)
MAN FROM HELL. (*Walks slowly towards stage center.*)
   The moon is forgotten
   In a sky the color of cement,
   And the stick lies forgotten
   Down in the gutter.
WOMAN FROM HELL (*Also walks in the same deliberate fashion
   towards stage-center.*)
   The stick lies forgotten in the gutter,
   The streets from above form a whirlpool.

A boy is searching for his vanished father.
(*Man and Woman from Hell meet at stage-center, several feet
behind Hippie Boy and Girl, just as they finish this recitation.*)
MAN FROM HELL. (*In extremely matter-of-fact tones.*) You
   know, it wouldn't surprise me if this time we happened to
   have arrived exactly where we intended.
WOMAN FROM HELL. (*Opens a large notebook.*) The time is
   precisely twenty-two minutes and ten seconds before—
MAN FROM HELL. (*Looks at his wristwatch.*) On the button
   . . .
WOMAN FROM HELL. (*Suddenly notices the stick in Hippie Boy's
   hand.*) I wonder, could that be the stick?
MAN FROM HELL. (*Rather perplexed.*) If it is, we've got a most
   peculiar obstacle in our path . . . (*Walks up to Hippie Boy
   and addresses him from behind, over his shoulder.*) Say, pal,
   where did you get that stick?
HIPPIE BOY. (*Throws him a sharp glance, but does not answer.*)
WOMAN FROM HELL. Lying in the gutter, wasn't it?
HIPPIE GIRL. It fell from the roof. We had a hairbreadth es-
   cape.
WOMAN FROM HELL. (*Delighted to have her theory confirmed.*)
   I knew it! (*To Man from Hell.*) Sir, it was this stick, as I
   suspected.
MAN FROM HELL. (*To Hippie Boy.*) Sorry to bother you, but
   would you mind handing me that stick?
WOMAN FROM HELL. I'm sure you don't need it especially.
HIPPIE BOY. I don't know about that. . . .
MAN FROM HELL. We're making a survey. A little investiga-
   tion.
HIPPIE GIRL. You from the police?
WOMAN FROM HELL. No, not exactly . . .
MAN FROM HELL. (*Interrupting.*) But you're not too far off . . .
HIPPIE BOY. Liars! You're the ones who threw the stick at us.
   And now you're trying to suppress the evidence. You
   think I'm going to play your game? Fat chance! (*Beating
   out a rhythm with the stick, he starts to hum the melody Hip-
   pie Girl was singing.*)
MAN FROM HELL. (*In mollifying tones.*) If you really suspect
   us, I'd be glad to go with you to the police station.
HIPPIE BOY. Don't try to wheedle your way around me.
HIPPIE GIRL. (*Looks up.*) You know, I think it was that kid
   we saw awhile ago . . . He's not there any more.
HIPPIE BOY. You shut up.
WOMAN FROM HELL. (*Animatedly.*) That's right, there was a
   child watching everything, wasn't there? From the railing
   up there on the roof . . . And didn't you hear him calling
   his father? In a frightened, numb little voice . . .
HIPPIE GIRL. (*Trying not to annoy Hippie Boy.*) How could I
   possibly hear him? The average noise level in this part of
   town is supposed to be over 120 decibels, on an average.
   (*Shaking her body to a go-go rhythm.*)
WOMAN FROM HELL. (*To Man from Hell.*) Sir, shall I verify
   the circumstances at the scene?

MAN FROM HELL. Yes, I suppose so. (*Hesitates a second.*) . . . But don't waste too much time over it.

(*Woman from Hell hurries off to stage-left.*)

STICK. (*To himself. His voice is filled with anguish.*) There's no need for it . . . I can hear everything . . . In the grimy little office behind the staircase marked "For store employees only" . . . my son, scared to death, surrounded by scabby-looking, mean security guards . . .

MAN FROM HELL. (*To Hippie Boy.*) It's kind of hard to explain, but the fact is, we have been entrusted, for the time being, with the custodianship of that stick . . . I wish you'd try somehow to understand.

HIPPIE BOY. I don't understanding nothing.

HIPPIE GIRL. (*With a wise look.*) This is the age of the generation gap. We're alienated.

STICK. (*To himself. In tones of unshakeable grief.*) The child is lodging a complaint . . . He says I turned into a stick and dropped from the roof . . .

MAN FROM HELL. (*To Hippie Boy.*) Well, let me ask you a simple question. What do you intend to use the stick for? I'm sure you haven't any particular aim in mind.

HIPPIE BOY. I'm not interested in aims.

HIPPIE GIRL. That's right. Aims are out of date.

MAN FROM HELL. Exactly. Aims don't amount to a hill of beans. So why can't you let me have it? It isn't doing you any good. All it is is a stick of wood. But, as far as we're concerned, it is a valuable item of evidence relating to a certain person . . .

HIPPIE GIRL. (*Dreamily.*) But one should have a few. People don't have enough . . .

MAN FROM HELL. Enough what?

HIPPIE GIRL. Aims!

MAN FROM HELL. You're making too much of nothing. It's bad for your health to want something that doesn't really exist. The uncertainty you feel at the thought you haven't got any aims, your mental anguish at the thought you have lost track of whatever aims you once had—they're a lot better proof that you are there, in that particular spot, than any aim I can think of. That's true, isn't it?

HIPPIE GIRL. (*To Hippie Boy.*) How about a kiss, huh?

HIPPIE BOY. (*Gives her a cold sidewise glance.*) I don't feel like it.

HIPPIE GIRL. You don't have to put on such airs with me.

HIPPIE BOY. I don't want to.

HIPPIE GIRL. Come on!

HIPPIE BOY. I told you, lay off the euphoria.

HIPPIE GIRL. Then, scratch my back.

HIPPIE BOY. Your back?

(*Hippie Girl bends over in Hippie Boy's direction, and lifts the back of her collar. Hippie Boy, with an air of great reluctance, thrusts the stick down into her collar and moves the stick around inside her dress, scratching her back.*)

HIPPIE GIRL. More to the left. . . . That's right, there. . . .

HIPPIE BOY. (*Pulls out the stick and hands it to Hippie Girl.*) Now you scratch me. (*Bends over towards Hippie Girl.*)

HIPPIE GIRL. You don't mean it from the heart . . . (*All the same, she immediately gives way and thrusts the stick down the back of Hippie Boy's collar.*) Is this the place?

HIPPIE BOY. Yes, there. And everywhere else.

HIPPIE GIRL. Everywhere?

HIPPIE BOY. (*Twisting his body and emitting strange noises.*) Uhhh . . . uhhh . . . uhhh. . . . It feels like I haven't had a bath in quite some time . . .

HIPPIE GIRL. (*Throwing down the stick.*) You egoist!

(*Man From Hell nimbly jumps between the two of them and attempts to grab the stick. But Hippie Boy brushes his hand away and picks up the stick again.*)

MAN FROM HELL. Look, my friend. I'm willing to make a deal with you. How much will you charge for letting me have this stick?

HIPPIE GIRL. (*Instantly full of life.*) One dollar.

MAN FROM HELL. A dollar? For a stick of wood like this?

HIPPIE BOY. Forget it. Not even for two dollars.

HIPPIE GIRL. (*To Hippie Boy in a low voice, reproachfully.*) You can find any number of sticks just like this one, if you really want it.

MAN FROM HELL. A dollar will keep you in cigarettes for a while.

HIPPIE BOY. Me and this stick, we understand each other . . . Don't know why . . . (*Strikes a pose, holding the end of the stick in his hand.*)

HIPPIE GIRL. (*With scorn in her voice.*) You look alike. A remarkable resemblance.

HIPPIE BOY. (*Staring at the stick.*) So we look alike, do we? Me and this stick? (*Reflects a while, then suddenly turns to Hippie Girl.*) You got any brothers and sisters?

HIPPIE GIRL. A younger sister.

HIPPIE BOY. What was her name for you? (*Hippie Girl hesitates.*) You must have been known as *something*. A nickname, maybe.

HIPPIE GIRL. You mean, the way she called me.

HIPPIE BOY. Precisely.

HIPPIE GIRL. Gaa-gaa.

HIPPIE BOY. Gaa-gaa?

HIPPIE GIRL. No, that's what my brother called me. My sister was different. She called me Mosquito.

HIPPIE BOY. What does Gaa-gaa mean?

HIPPIE GIRL. Mosquito—that's what my sister called me.

HIPPIE BOY. I'm asking what Gaa-gaa is.

HIPPIE GIRL. You don't know what Gaa-gaa is?

HIPPIE BOY. Has it got something to do with mosquitoes?

HIPPIE GIRL. Yes, but it's very complicated to explain.

MAN FROM HELL. Excuse me, but would you . . .

HIPPIE BOY. Yesterday there was a funeral at that haberdashery across the street.

HIPPIE GIRL. (*Looking around at the crowd.*) But it had nothing to do with any of these people, had it?

HIPPIE BOY. But what about Gaa-gaa and Mosquito?

MAN FROM HELL. Wasn't it Gar-gar rather than Gaa-gaa?

HIPPIE GIRL. She died.

MAN FROM HELL. Who died?

HIPPIE GIRL. My sister.

MAN FROM HELL. What happened to her?

HIPPIE BOY. She became a corpse, naturally.

MAN FROM HELL. Of course. That's not surprising.

HIPPIE GIRL. That's why I don't understand anything anymore. Everything is wrapped in riddles.

HIPPIE BOY. What, for instance?

HIPPIE GIRL. Was it Gaa-gaa or Gar-gar?

HIPPIE BOY. You're just plain stupid.

MAN FROM HELL. By the way, in reference to that stick—she says you look like it. Let's suppose for the moment you do look like the stick—the meaning is not what you think it is.

HIPPIE GIRL. Tomorrow people will be calling tomorrow today.

MAN FROM HELL. To begin with, your conceptual framework with respect to the stick is basically—

HIPPIE BOY. I see. Once a human hand grabs something there's no telling what it can do.

HIPPIE GIRL. I missed grabbing it. It's too awful to think that the day after tomorrow will always be tomorrow even hundreds of years from now.

(*Woman from Hell returns, walking quickly.*)

WOMAN FROM HELL. (*She stops at some distance from the others.*) Sir . . .

MAN FROM HELL. (*Goes up to Woman.*) Well, what happened?

WOMAN FROM HELL. We've got to hurry . . .

MAN FROM HELL. (*Turns towards Hippies.*) This crazy bunch—I offered them a dollar for the stick, but they refuse to part with it.

WOMAN FROM HELL. The child is coming.

MAN FROM HELL. What for?

WOMAN FROM HELL. Just as I got into the department store I heard them making an announcement about a lost child. The child was apparently raising quite a rumpus. He claimed he saw his father turn into a stick and fall off the roof. But nobody seemed to believe him.

MAN FROM HELL. Of course not.

WOMAN FROM HELL. Then the child gave the matron the slip and ran out of the store, looking for his father.

(*Man and Woman from Hell look uneasily off to stage-left.*)

STICK. (*Talking brokenly to himself.*) The child saw it. I know he did. I was leaning against the railing at the time, the one that runs between the air ducts and the staircase, on a lower level. I was looking down at the crowds below,

with nothing particular on my mind. A whirlpool . . . Look—it's just like one big whirlpool . . .

(*Actual noises of city traffic gradually swell in volume, sounding something like a monster howling into a tunnel. Suddenly Hippie Boy lets the stick drop in alarm.*)

HIPPIE GIRL. What happened?

STICK. (*Continuing his monologue.*) I stood there, feeling dizzy, as if the noises of the city were a waterfall roaring over me, clutching tightly to the railing, when my boy called me. He was pestering me for a dime, so he could look through the telescope for three minutes . . . And that second my body sailed out into mid-air . . . I had not the least intention of running away from the child or anything like that . . . But I turned into a stick . . . Why did it happen? Why should such a thing have happened to me?

HIPPIE GIRL. What's the matter, anyway?

HIPPIE BOY. (*Stares at the stick lying at his feet with a bewildered expression.*) It twitched, like a dying fish . . .

HIPPIE GIRL. It couldn't have . . . You're imagining things.

WOMAN FROM HELL. (*Stands on tiptoes and stares off into the distance at stage-left.*) Look! Sir, look! Do you see that child? The little boy with the short neck, prowling around, looking with his big glasses over the ground?

MAN FROM HELL. He seems to be gradually coming closer.

STICK. (*To himself.*) I can hear the child's footsteps . . . bouncing like a little rubber ball, the sound threading its way through the rumblings of the earth shaking under the weight of a million people . . .

HIPPIE GIRL. (*Steals a glance in the direction of the Man and Woman from Hell.*) Somehow those guys give me the creeps . . . Why don't you make some sort of deal with him?

(*Hippie Boy, who has kept his eyes glued on the stick at his feet, snaps out of his daze and stands up. Girl also stands.*)

HIPPIE BOY. (*With irritation.*) I can't figure it out, but I don't like it. That stick looks too much like me.

HIPPIE GIRL. (*Her expression is consoling.*) It doesn't really look all that much like you. Just a little.

HIPPIE BOY. (*Calls to Man from Hell, who has just that moment turned towards him, as if anticipating something.*) Five dollars. What do you say? (*He keeps his foot on the stick.*)

MAN FROM HELL. Five dollars?

STICK. (*To himself.*) He doesn't have to stand on me . . . I'm soaked from lying in the gutter . . . I'll be lucky if I don't catch a cold.

HIPPIE BOY. I'm not going to force you, if you don't want it.

WOMAN FROM HELL. (*Nervously glancing off to stage-left.*) Sir, he's almost here.

(*The Man Who Turned into a Stick shows a subtle, complex reaction, a mixture of hope and rejection.*)

HIPPIE BOY. I'm selling it because I don't want to sell it.

That's a contradiction of circumstances. Do you follow me?

HIPPIE GIRL. That's right. He's selling it because he doesn't want to.

Can you understand that?

MAN FROM HELL. (*Annoyed.*) All right, guess . . . (*He pulls some bills from his pocket and selects from them a five-dollar bill.*) Here you are . . . But I'll tell you one thing, my friend, you may imagine you've struck a clever bargain, but one of these days you'll find out. It wasn't just a stick you sold, but yourself.

(*But Hippie Boy, without waiting for Man to finish his words, snatches away the five-dollar bill and quickly exits to stage-right. Hippie Girl follows after him, smiling innocently. She waves her hand.*)

HIPPIE GIRL. It's the generation gap. (*She exits with these words.*)

(*Man and Woman from Hell, leaping into action, rush to the gutter where the stick is lying. Just then the sun suddenly goes behind a cloud, and the street noises gradually fade. At the very end, for just a second, a burst of rivetting is heard from a construction site somewhere off in the distance.*)

MAN FROM HELL. (*Gingerly picks up the dirty stick with his fingertips. With his other hand he takes the newspaper that can be seen protruding from his pocket, spreads it open, and uses it to wipe the stick.*) Well, that was a close one . . .

WOMAN FROM HELL. Earth duty isn't easy, is it?

MAN FROM HELL. It was a good experience on your first day of on-the-job training.

WOMAN FROM HELL. I was on tenterhooks, I can tell you.

(*The Man Who Turned into a Stick suddenly exhibits a strong reaction to something. Man and Woman from Hell alertly respond to his reaction.*)

WOMAN FROM HELL. There's the child!

(*Man from Hell, greatly alarmed, at once hides the stick behind his back. On a sudden thought, he pushes the stick under his jacket, and finally down into his trousers. He stands ramrod stiff for several seconds. Then, all at once, the excitement melts from the face of the Man Who Turned into a Stick. Man and Woman from Hell, relieved, also relax their postures.*)

STICK. (*To himself.*) It doesn't matter . . . There was nothing I could have done anyway, was there?

MAN FROM HELL. (*Pulling out the stick.*) Wow! That was a close shave . . .

WOMAN FROM HELL. But you know, I kind of feel sorry for him.

MAN FROM HELL. Sympathy has no place in our profession. Well, let's get cracking. (*Holds out the stick.*) That crazy interruption has certainly played havoc with our schedule.

WOMAN FROM HELL. (*Accepts the stick and holds it in both hands, as if to make a ceremonial offering.*) I didn't realize how light it was.

MAN FROM HELL. It couldn't be better for a first tryout. Now, make your report, in exactly the order you learned . . .

WOMAN FROM HELL. Yes, sir. (*Examines the stick from every angle, with the earnestness of a young interne.*) The first thing I notice is that a distinction may be observed between the top and bottom of this stick. The top is fairly deeply incrusted with dirt and grease from human hands. Note, on the other hand, how rubbed and scraped the bottom is . . . I interpret this as meaning that the stick has not always been lying in a ditch, without performing any useful function, but that during its lifetime it was employed by people for some particular purpose.

STICK. (*To himself. Angrily.*) That's obvious, isn't it? It's true of everybody.

WOMAN FROM HELL. But it seems to have suffered rather harsh treatment. The poor thing has scars all over it . . .

MAN FROM HELL. (*Laughs.*) Excellent! But what do you mean by calling it a poor thing? I'm afraid you've been somewhat infected by human ideas.

WOMAN FROM HELL. Infected by human ideas?

MAN FROM HELL. We in Hell have a different approach. To our way of thinking, this stick, which has put up with every kind of abuse, until its whole body is covered with scars, never running away and never being discarded, should be called a capable and faithful stick.

WOMAN FROM HELL. Still, it's only a stick. Even a monkey can make a stick do what he wants. A human being with the same qualities would be simple-minded.

MAN FROM HELL. (*Emphatically.*) That's precisely what I meant when I said it was capable and faithful. A stick can lead a blind man, and it can also train a dog. As a lever it can move heavy objects, and it can be used to thrash an enemy. In short, the stick is the root and source of all tools.

WOMAN FROM HELL. But with the same stick you can beat me and I can beat you back.

MAN FROM HELL. Isn't that what faithfulness means? A stick remains a stick, no matter how it is used. You might almost say that the etymology of the word faithful is a stick.

WOMAN FROM HELL. (*Unconvinced.*) But what you're saying is too—miserable.

MAN FROM HELL. All it boils down to is, a living stick has turned into a dead stick—right? Sentimentality is forbidden to Earth Duty personnel. Well, continue with your analysis. (*Woman remains silent.*) What's the matter now? I want the main points of your report!

WOMAN FROM HELL. (*Pulling herself together.*) Yes, sir. Next I will telephone headquarters and inform them of the exact time and place of the disappearance of the person in question, and verify the certification number. Then I decide the punishment and register the variety and the disposition.

MAN FROM HELL. And what decision have you made on the punishment? (*Woman does not reply.*) Surely there can be no doubt in your mind. A simple case like this . . .

WOMAN FROM HELL. You know, I rather enjoy wandering around the specimen room, but I just don't seem to recall any specimens of a stick. (*Shakes her head dubiously.*)

MAN FROM HELL. There aren't any, of course.

WOMAN FROM HELL. (*Relieved.*) So it *is* a special case, isn't it?

MAN FROM HELL. Now calm yourself, and just think . . . I realize this is your first taste of on-the-job training, but it's disturbing to hear anything quite so wide off the mark . . . The fact that something isn't in the specimen room doesn't necessarily mean it's so rare. On the contrary . . .

WOMAN FROM HELL. (*Catching on at last.*) You mean, it's because sticks are so common!

MAN FROM HELL. Exactly. During the last twenty or thirty years the percentage of sticks has steadily gone up. Why, I understand that in extreme cases, 98.4 percent of all those who die in a given month turn into sticks.

WOMAN FROM HELL. Yes, I remember now . . . Probably it'll be all right if I leave the stick as it was during its lifetime, without any special punishment.

MAN FROM HELL. Now you're on the right track!

WOMAN FROM HELL. The only thing I have to do is verify the certification number. It won't be necessary to register the punishment.

MAN FROM HELL. Do you remember what it says in our textbook? "They who came up for judgment, but were not judged, have turned into sticks and filled the earth. The Master has departed and the earth has become a grave of rotten sticks . . ." That's why the shortage of help in Hell has never become especially acute.

WOMAN FROM HELL. (*Takes out a walkie-talkie.*) Shall I call headquarters?

MAN FROM HELL. (*Takes the walkie-talkie from her.*) I'll show you how it's done, just the first time. (*Switches it on.*) Hello, headquarters? This is MC training squad on earth duty.

VOICE FROM HELL. Roger. Headquarters here.

MAN FROM HELL. Request verification of a certification number. MC 621 . . . I repeat, MC 621 . . .

VOICE FROM HELL. MC 621. Roger.

MAN FROM HELL. The time was 22 minutes ten seconds before the hour . . . The place was Ward B, 32 stroke 4 on the grid. Stick fell from the roof of Terminal Department Store. . . .

VOICE FROM HELL. Roger. Go ahead.

MAN FROM HELL. No punishment. Registration unnecessary. Over.

VOICE FROM HELL. Roger. Registration unnecessary.

MAN FROM HELL. Request information on next assignment.

VOICE FROM HELL. Six minutes twenty-four seconds from now, in Ward B, 32 stroke 8 on the grid. Over.

WOMAN FROM HELL. (*Opens her notebook and jots down a memo.*) That would make it somewhere behind the station . . .

MAN FROM HELL. Roger. Thirty-two stroke eight.

VOICE FROM HELL. Good luck on your mission. Over.

MAN FROM HELL. Roger. Thanks a lot. (*Suddenly changing his tone.*) I'm sorry to bother you, but if my wife comes over, would you mind telling her I forgot to leave the key to my locker?

VOICE FROM HELL. (*With a click of the tongue.*) You're hopeless. Well, this is the last time. Over.

MAN FROM HELL. (*Laughs.*) Roger. (*Turns off walkie-talkie.*) That, in general, is how to do it.

WOMAN FROM HELL. Thank you. I think I understand now.

MAN FROM HELL. What's the matter? You look kind of down in the mouth. (*Returns walkie-talkie to Woman.*)

WOMAN FROM HELL. (*Barely manages a smile.*) It's nothing, really . . .

MAN FROM HELL. Well, shall we say good-bye to our stick somewhere around here?

WOMAN FROM HELL. You mean you're going to throw it away, just like that?

MAN FROM HELL. Of course. That's the regulation. (*Looks around, discovers a hole in the gutter, and stands the stick in it.*) If I leave it standing this way it'll attract attention and somebody is sure to pick it up before long. (*Takes a step back and examines it again.*) It's a handy size and, as sticks go, it's a pretty good specimen. It could be used for the handle of a placard . . .

(*Woman suddenly takes hold of the stick and pulls it from the hole.*)

MAN FROM HELL. What do you think you're doing?

WOMAN FROM HELL. It's too cruel!

MAN FROM HELL. Cruel? (*He is too dumbfounded to continue.*)

WOMAN FROM HELL. We should give it to the child. Don't you think that's the least we can do? As long as we're going to get rid of it anyway . . .

MAN FROM HELL. Don't talk nonsense. A stick is nothing more than a stick, no matter who has it.

WOMAN FROM HELL. But it's something special to that child.

MAN FROM HELL. Why?

WOMAN FROM HELL. At least it ought to serve as a kind of mirror. He can examine himself and make sure he won't become a stick like his father.

MAN FROM HELL. (*Bursts out laughing.*) Examine himself! Why should anyone who's satisfied with himself do that?

WOMAN FROM HELL. Was this stick satisfied with himself?

MAN FROM HELL. Don't you see, it was precisely because he was so satisfied that he turned into a stick?

WOMAN FROM HELL. (*Stares at stick. A short pause.*) Just supposing this stick could hear what we have been saying . . .

STICK. (*To himself. Weakly.*) Of course I can hear. Every last word.

MAN FROM HELL. I have no specific information myself,

since it's quite outside my own speciality, but scholars in the field have advanced the theory that they can in fact hear what we are saying.

WOMAN FROM HELL. How do you suppose he feels to hear us talk this way?

MAN FROM HELL. Exactly as a stick would feel, naturally. Assuming, of course, that sticks have feelings . . .

WOMAN FROM HELL. Satisfied?

MAN FROM HELL. (*With emphasis.*) There's no room for arguments. A stick is a stick. That simple fact takes precedence over problems of logic. Come now, put the stick back where it was. Our next assignment is waiting for us.

(*Woman from Hell, with a compassionate expression, gently returns Stick to the hole in the gutter. The Man Who Turned into a Stick up until this point has been registering various shades of reaction to the conversation of Man and Woman, but from now on his emotions are petrified into any immobile state between fury and despair.*)

STICK. (*To himself.*) Satisfied . . .

WOMAN FROM HELL. But why must we go through the motions of whipping a dead man this way?

MAN FROM HELL. We are not particularly concerned with the dead. Our job is to record their lives accurately. (*Lowering his voice.*) To tell the truth, it is extremely dubious whether or not we in fact exist.

WOMAN FROM HELL. What do you mean by that?

MAN FROM HELL. There is a theory that we are no more than the dreams that people have when they are on the point of death.

WOMAN FROM HELL. If those are dreams, they are horrible nightmares.

MAN FROM HELL. That's right.

WOMAN FROM HELL. Then there's no likelihood that they're satisfied. To have nightmares even though you're satisfied—that's a terrible contradiction, isn't it?

MAN FROM HELL. Perhaps it might be described as the moment of doubt that follows satisfaction. In any case, what's done is done . . . (*In tones meant to cheer Woman.*) We'll have to hurry. We have exactly three minutes. If we're late there'll be all hell to pay later on . . . (*Starts walking, leading the way.*) Don't worry. You'll get used to it, before you know it. I was the same way myself. Sometimes you get confused by the false fronts people put on. But once you realize that a stick was a stick, even while it was alive . . .

WOMAN FROM HELL. (*Still turns to look back at Stick, but somewhat more cheerful now.*) Is the next person going to be a stick too?

MAN FROM HELL. Mmm. It would be nice if we got something more unusual this time.

WOMAN FROM HELL. What do you suppose those kids who tried to keep us from getting the stick will turn into?

MAN FROM HELL. Those hippies?

WOMAN FROM HELL. They didn't seem much like sticks, did they?

MAN FROM HELL. If they don't turn into sticks maybe they'll become rubber hoses.

(*Man and Woman from Hell exit to stage-right.*)

STICK. (*To himself.*) Satisfied? Me? Stupid fools. Would a satisfied man run away from his own child and jump off a roof?

(*In another section of the stage Man and Woman from Hell reappear as silhouettes.*)

MAN FROM HELL. The sky is the color of a swamp, cloudy with disinfectant.
On the cold, wet ground.
Another man has changed into a stick.

WOMAN FROM HELL. He has been verified but not registered.
He is shut up inside the shape of a stick.
He is not unlucky, so he must be happy.

STICK. (*To himself.*) I've never once felt satisfied But I wonder what it would be better to turn into, rather than a stick. The one thing somebody in the world is sure to pick up is a stick.

MAN FROM HELL. He has been verified but not registered. The man's been shut up inside the shape of a stick. He can't so much as budge anymore, and that's a problem.

WOMAN FROM HELL. Supposing he begins to itch somewhere—
What'll he do? How will he fare?

MAN FROM HELL. I'm afraid a stick would probably lack
The talent needed to scratch his own back.

WOMAN FROM HELL. But anyway, you mustn't mind,
You're not the only one of your kind.

MAN FROM HELL. (*Steps forward and points his finger around the audience.*) Look—there's a whole forest of sticks around you. All those innocent people, each one determined to turn into a stick slightly different from everybody else, but nobody once thinking of turning into anything besides a stick . . . All those sticks. You may never be judged, but at least you don't have to worry about being punished. (*Abruptly changes his tone and leans farther out towards the audience.*) You know, I wouldn't want to think I'm saying these things just to annoy you. Surely, you don't suppose I would be capable of such rudeness . . . Heaven forbid . . . (*Forces a smile.*) It's just the simple truth, the truth as I see it . . .

WOMAN FROM HELL. (*Goes up to The Man Who Turned into a Stick and speaks in pleading, rather jerky phrases.*) Yes, that's right. You're not alone. You've lots of friends . . . men who turned into sticks.

CURTAIN

*A 1772 oil painting by Marco Marcola captures the energy and color of a
street performance by a commedia dell'arte company; it also suggests that
the middle class has emerged as a powerful force in theater.*

CHAPTER 6

THE EARLY MODERN THEATER

It may seem strange to note that the "modern" theater began in the Middle Ages, but the designation exists for two reasons:

- Modern, as it is used here, merely distinguishes those plays written after the ancient—or classical—ages of Greece and Rome. After the fall of Rome, little formal drama existed until the Middle Ages, although considerable theatrical activity took place in the guise of rituals, folk customs, and especially in the work of itinerant actors, troubadours, minstrels, and others who kept the art of performance alive.
- We can actually trace the evolution of the modern theater to the plays of medieval writers as well as those of the Renaissance and subsequent eras. Collectively they portrayed the dilemmas of individuals faced with the challenges of living in this world and thus increased the secularization of a drama that culminates in the great social dramas of the modern era. Though Greek and Roman plays also focused on individuals within a social setting, the modern theater has been more influenced by—and developed in an unbroken line from—the drama of the Middle Ages.

THE MIDDLE AGES

Artistic and Cultural Events

c. 1480:
Master Pierre Pathelin
written in France

c. 965:
Earliest
extant
playscript

Golden
age of
liturgical
drama

c. 1495:
Everyman,
Dutch/English
morality play

Mystery play
(Adam)
performed
outside
churches

Processions
and street
pageants
popular

1283:
French
Robin Hood
folk play

Itinerant
actors and
performers

c. 925:
Oldest
Easter
trope

c. 970:
Hrotsvitha
writes
short
plays

c. 1425:
*Castle of
Perseverance,*
English
morality play

800 C.E.	900 C.E.	1000 C.E.	1100 C.E.	1200 C.E.	1300 C.E.	1400 C.E.

Historical and Political Events

1264:
Church
establishes
Feast of
Corpus Christi

Charlemagne
and the Holy
Roman Empire

1066:
Norman conquest
of England

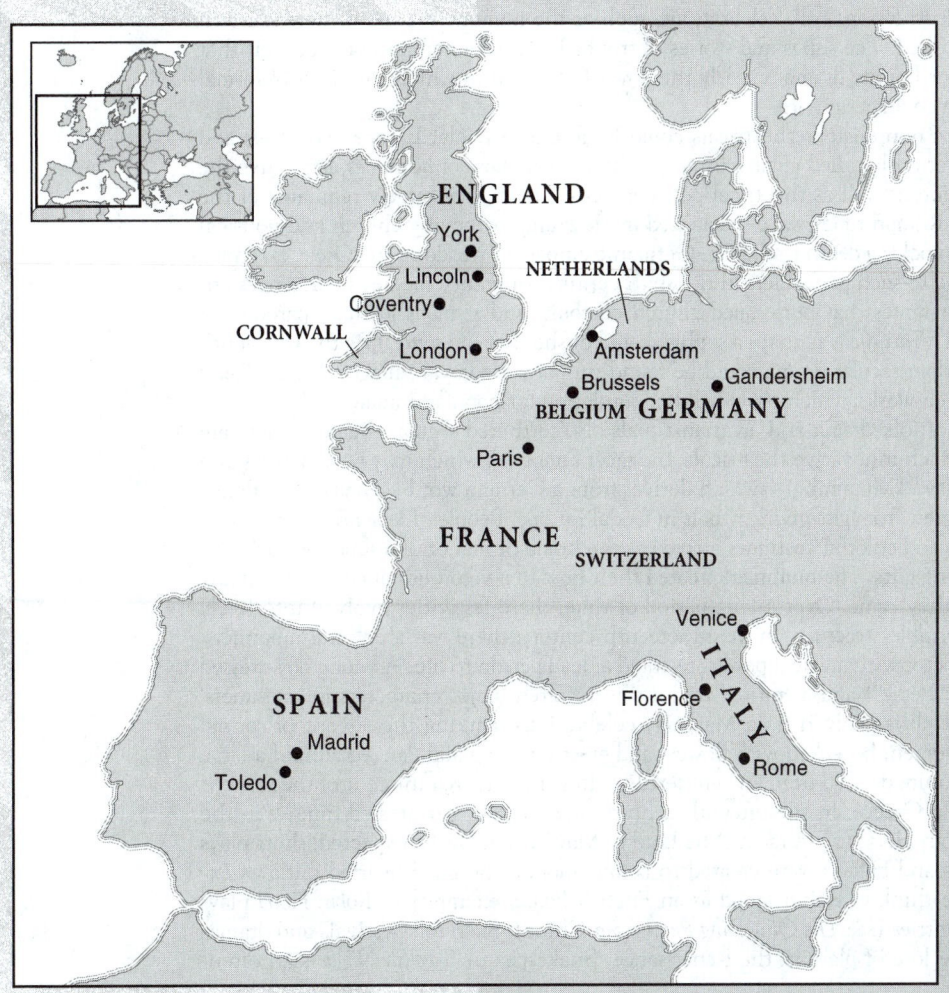

Rites and Folk Drama

Though there was little written drama after the fall of Rome, the spirit of theater was kept alive in pagan rites, many of which were subsumed into Christian ceremonies and holy days. Ironically, the Christians, who had curtailed theater in Roman times, used many attributes we associate with the theater: costumes (vestments), antiphonal song, storytelling, the re-creation of past events, and instruction. Folk celebrations, such as the mummers' plays of northwestern Europe, also flourished. The songs and stories of troubadours sustained an oral tradition that inspired subsequent literate drama. Clearly there was fertile soil in which the seeds of formal theater and drama could germinate.

Two strains of nonreligious theatricals could be found in feudal Europe. Minstrels and traveling actors, variously called *mimi, scurrae, joculatores, jongleurs,* or *histriones,* kept alive the storytelling tradition as well as theatrical performances. These were largely remnants of the antique mimes of Roman times, who specialized in clowning, parodying church and political figures, and even mocking death itself. The Germanic emperor Theodoric the Great extended his royal patronage to such performers in the sixth century. In France medieval audiences enjoyed *sotties,* short farces that burlesqued church customs, and *sermons joyeaux,* parodies of liturgical homilies. (*Tartuffe* is perhaps a sophisticated offshoot of the *sottie.*) By the thirteenth century mature urban secular drama could be found in many medieval villages. *Master Pierre Pathelin* typifies such works, which provided the foundation for popular drama.

A rich body of folk drama and agrarian rituals also furthered secular theater. There are many varieties of such innovative theatricals, the most famous of which may be *mummery* and the *Robin Hood* plays. "Mumming"—which derives from a German word (*mumme*) for silence or "closed lips"—grew from gift-giving rituals in feudal Europe. People of lesser social rank disguised with masks and colorful costumes arrived at the home or manor of a superior, such as a king or lord, bearing gifts. The mummers treated their host to a vigorous dance before departing as silently as they came. Over a long period of time, these festivities evolved into lively plays with a discernible structure. In the nineteenth century, there was a colorful mummers' play in which a doctor with magical powers restored a dead person to life. A young boy dressed as a woman (the "Betsy") and a spirited trickster were often major characters in mummers' plays. *Robin Hood* plays evolved from May Day celebrations marking the advent of spring. Young men and women, bedecked with flowers and greenery, sang and danced around a large pole (its phallic nature derived from ancient fertility rites) in a rite reminiscent of the ancient Dionysian revels in Greece. In the fifteenth century one such reveler dressed himself as the heroic outlaw Robin Hood to preside as "the Lord of May." As might be expected, short plays based on folktales and ballads were created to commemorate the good-hearted outlaw's exploits. Though we think of Robin Hood as an English figure, examples of *Robin Hood* plays exist in many countries (see *The Qing Ding Pearl* from China). Such folk festivals and dramas contributed to the lore of plays in the Renaissance. Shakespeare's *Twelfth Night* is an often-cited example.

Religious Drama

The most memorable drama (if only because we have better records) and that which first reflected uniquely medieval values was created in the great churches that dominated the medieval landscape. Whereas the Greeks sang dithyrambs honoring Dionysus, medieval Christians sang *tropes,* short biblical passages set to music, as part of their liturgy. The most famous of these is the *Quem Quaeritis* trope, a reenactment of the visit of the three Marys to the tomb of Christ on Easter morning. About 965 C.E. this trope was performed when a deacon played the attending angel who asked the women, "Whom do you seek (i.e., *Quem quaeritis?*) in the tomb, O Christian women?" Three subalterns answered, "We seek Jesus who has died," to which the deacon-angel responded: "He is not here, he has risen." This short exchange is generally recognized as among the first formal dramas in the post-Roman Western world. Like its Greek antecedent, it derived from communal celebrations observing the resurrection of a slain god-king. It was held in the early spring, and it too used mimicry, costumes (or priestly vestments), simple spectacle, and storytelling to impart sacred tenets to the congregation. Other stories from the Bible were enacted in various locations (*sedes*) throughout the church.

Another form of biblically inspired drama soon emerged as a complement to such simple church dramas as the *Quem Quaeritis* trope. These were vernacular plays—as opposed to the Latin plays in the church—that were performed in town squares or open fields, usually in conjunction with the Feast of Corpus Christi, which Pope Urban VI established in 1264. In fact, they are often referred to as the Corpus Christi cycles because they portrayed the cycle of biblical events from the Creation to the Day of Judgment. As the plays grew in size and scope, trade and craft guilds were given the responsibility of performing individual stories from the great biblical epic. The individual plays are often called mystery plays because they were performed by the *maestri* (skilled) guilds. Individual towns, such as York, England, soon became known for their great cycle dramas, which included as many as 42 individual mystery plays. The cycles thrived between 1350 and 1550, though records also document much later performances. Though the cycles were similar in many respects, significant and often colorful differences indicate the contributions of various towns and guilds. *Abraham and Isaac* suggests the kind of play performed in the great cycles, though there are several variants on this famous story.

In addition to the biblical epics, anonymous Christian dramatists also portrayed the dilemmas of ordinary men and women tempted by the world, the flesh, and, of course, the devil. These allegorical works, called *morality plays*, instructed the faithful in correct behavior and featured allegorical characters symbolizing virtues (Strength, Beauty, Goodness) and vices (Greed, Lust, Rumor). *Mankind* and *The Apple Tree* are included here as examples of comical morality plays.

These liturgical dramas, however sacred their stories and messages, were also significant social and political events in medieval towns. Indeed a curious mixture of the heavenly and the earthly became a hallmark of medieval religious plays. In one famous example, *The Second Shepherd's Play*, a medieval version of the "trickster" steals a sheep on Christmas Eve. When angry shepherds invade his home to reclaim the lost lamb, the thief and his wife wrap it in swaddling clothes and lay it in a manger to pass it off as their newborn child. This parody of Christ's birth was not intended to be sacrilegious; rather, it was a reminder to medieval audiences that Christ entered the world to redeem sinners like the sheep thief.

The actual presentation of the plays enhanced this humanization of the great religious tales. The plays were customarily performed by common laborers; not until the fifteenth century did professional actors take over the presentation of the cycle plays, and then only in some areas of Europe. Actors wore contemporary clothing, used colloquial speech, and performed workaday tasks instantly recognized by the audiences who gathered in squares or fields. To the medieval mind, history was cyclical, and all humans, whatever their place in time, were subject to the same errors and tribulations while on their pilgrimage to heaven. This notion of *historification* had two implications for the drama. First, the plays themselves were prefigurations of subsequent events, that is, a story from the Old Testament foreshadowed one from the New (see the discussion of *Abraham and Isaac* preceding the play). Both the Old and New Testament stories had immediate implications for a contemporary audience. Second, because one's place in history was relative, there was no need for historical accuracy in costuming, stage business, or even storytelling. Noah was properly dressed in a medieval leather apron and jerkin, and it was entirely natural that he should use medieval tools to build his ark. One might say that the medieval performers invented "modern dress" theater, but not in ignorance; rather, it was a forthright attempt to make the stories of the Bible immediate and accessible to the people who watched them. Well-educated writers in the Renaissance, including Shakespeare, retained such anachronisms in their plays.

Performance Conventions

Medieval artists relied heavily on visual stimuli because few people could read or write. Thus *illuminations* were cultivated to make concrete—in purely visual terms—those things that

A mansion (or "little house") was one of the primary scenic backdrops for medieval liturgical plays; from the 1547 Valenciennes Passion Play.

seemed abstract. Prominent examples of illuminations can still be found in the enormous cathedrals that dominated medieval towns. Their walls were adorned with brilliant stained-glass illustrations of the events of the Bible, while the great rosette windows at either end of the church were visual metaphors of "God's eye" watching human deeds. Manuscripts were illustrated with vividly colored pictures to illuminate the texts. The mystery and morality plays themselves were, in essence, living illuminations that made Christian lore and doctrine concrete and accessible.

Consequently, medieval plays were presented with an extraordinary attention to the visual. In addition to the simple stages (*mansions*) found in the churches, the outdoor dramas were performed on several types of stages that varied from town to town, century to century. The *booth stage* was a raised platform (*platea*) on trestles (or perhaps ale kegs) backed by a colorful curtain. *Pageant wagons*, perhaps the most famous of the medieval stages, were ambulatory stages using carts or farm wagons, the beds of which served as the stage. The *simultaneous stage*, such as that employed in Valenciennes, France, was actually a single enormous stage containing a number of *mansions* representing locales such as Jerusalem, the Temple, God's throne, and, of course, hell. *Rounds* were found largely in southwestern England, where Caesar's legions had encampments. They consisted of a large circle (based on the ancient orchestra?) that contained seating for the audience and, at perhaps a half-dozen places on the perimeter, mansions representing heaven, Abraham's house, and hell itself.

Skilled craftsmen, who spent much of the year in preparation for the cycle, presented the plays. Accordingly, the ingenuity and complexity of the scenery was remarkable. We know there were imaginative flying devices and other technical wizardry, called *secrets* because they created an aura of mystery. An especially noteworthy scenic device was the Hellmouth, a huge

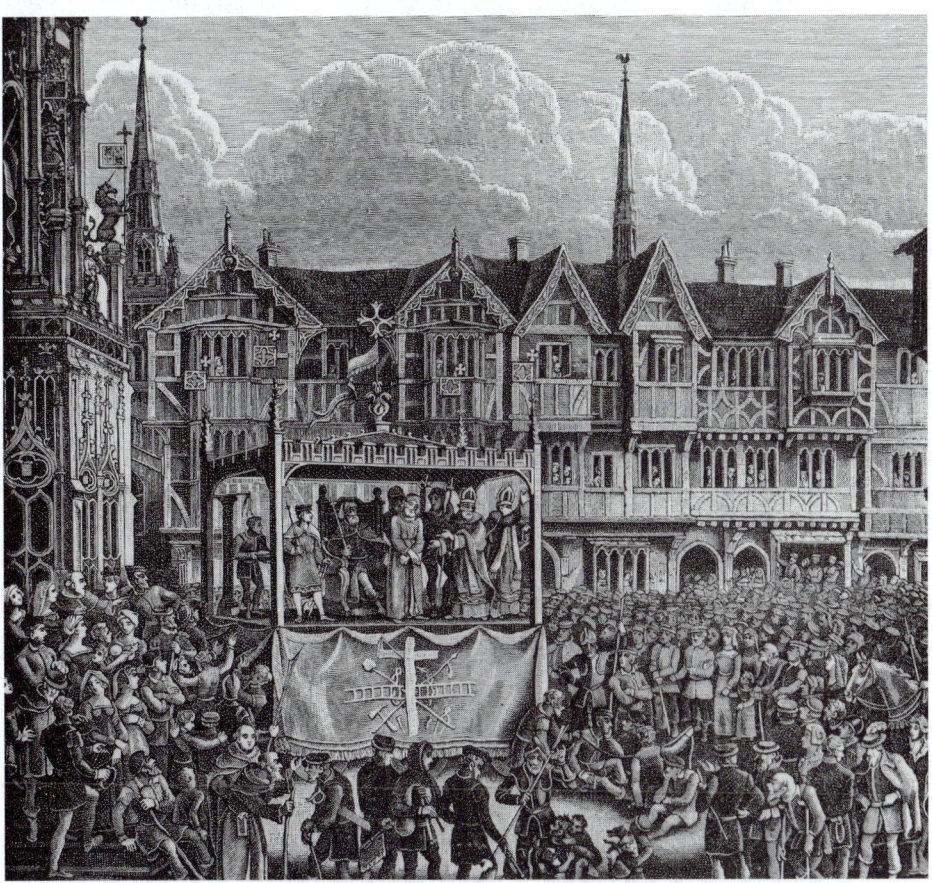

Pageant wagons, the forerunners of parade floats, were perhaps the most versatile scenic devices used in the Middle Ages; they are also referred to as "ambulatory stages."

structure representing the grotesque face of a devil. Sinners were dragged through the jaws of the Hellmouth by cavorting devils; often smoke and ashes billowed from the jaws to suggest the horrors of hell. One French Hellmouth was so elaborate that it required 17 men to operate its various pulleys, winches, and bellows.

Devils were among the most carefully costumed characters in the medieval plays; animal skins and grotesque masks were intended to frighten medieval audiences. Yet the devils were comedic as well as frightening, and often provided much of the comic relief with their tricks and jests, as Titivillus does in *Mankind,* one of the three mortality plays that follows. The devils were yet another variation on the trickster found in entertainments around the world. Arlecchino in the *commedia dell'arte* is akin to the medieval devil; he usually wore a black, grotesque mask. Devils, by the way, often "passed the hat" among audiences to collect money to underwrite the performance of the plays.

The medieval cycle plays, then, were as much a celebration of medieval life and community as they were a religious experience. Virtually all members of society participated in the plays as audience, craftsman, or performer. They were sources of civic pride, and they instilled in the people an appetite for theater. As Europe became more secularized, its drama become more human-centered. The medieval religious and secular plays—simultaneously simple and sophisticated, sublime and grotesque—provided a solid foundation on which the great humanist dramas of the Renaissance were built.

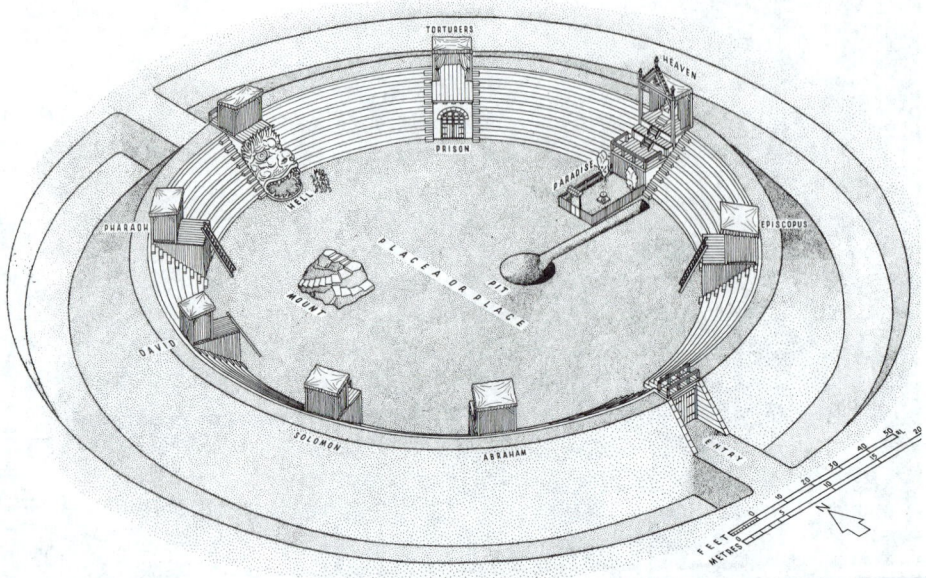

"Rounds" may have derived from ancient Roman theaters, especially those found near Cornwall in southwestern England.

The booth stage, a raised platform backed by a curtain, may have been the model for the stage in Elizabethan theaters such as Shakespeare's Globe.

THE BROME PLAY OF ABRAHAM AND ISAAC

Anonymous

Abraham and Isaac (c. 1300–1400)

Abraham and Isaac is an anonymous medieval play of the genre commonly known as mystery plays, short dramas based on events from the Bible. While the subject matter may well concern the "mysteries" of the Judeo-Christian heritage, the term actually derives from a Middle English term, *maestri*, which referred to the trade and craft guilds—or "masters"—who were assigned the performance of various plays within the lengthy, multiplay cycles. This text of *Abraham and Isaac* has not been attributed to a particular cycle (although each had its version) but was preserved in a fifteenth-century manuscript at Brome Manor in England. It is a superb example of the universality of the mystery plays; though it is based on Jewish characters and told through Christian eyes, it is ultimately about human feelings.

Despite its doggerel verse—the pronounced meter and rhyme were memory aids for illiterate actors—the play is emotionally powerful because of the humanity rendered by the unknown playwright (or playwrights—these plays were frequently developed over a number of years). The biblical account (Gen. 22:1–19) of the testing of Abraham's fidelity to God is, frankly, rather sterile, matter-of-fact, and undramatic. There is no conflict between God and Abraham. Nowhere is there a sense of the patriarch's agony (". . . this child's words wound my heart"); unlike Prometheus, he does not "dare" challenge his Lord. In particular, there is no hint of Isaac's heart-wrenching reactions, which are simultaneously human and heroic. The two requests that he makes of his father in the play—first, that Abraham spare Sarah any anguish over the ordeal (tell not my mother of God's request, say that I am gone to a far country) and second, that the sacrifice happen quickly and painlessly—are so profoundly touching that they eclipse the original biblical passage.

The common denominator among the many surviving mystery plays is their extraordinary humanity. Consider two examples from other plays. There were several versions of the Great Flood that destroyed the world; while the particulars may vary, virtually all include comic portraits of Noah and his wife. Noah is pictured as a harried, somewhat henpecked husband weary of his shrewish wife's nagging. In some of the plays she is rendered as a drunkard who has to be forcibly carried onto the ark by her sons. Noah's news that the Lord has commanded him to make an ark in preparation for a great deluge provokes a raucous argument which disintegrates into a Punch-and-Judy show, as the following lines suggest:

WIFE.   But in a little while,
        What with game and guile,
        I shall smite and smile
        And pay him [Noah] back instead.
NOAH.   Hush! hold thy tongue, ramshit, or I shall thee still.
WIFE.   As I thrive, if thou smite, I shall pay thee back with skill.

And the fight is on. Certainly the medieval playwrights intended no disrespect for their subject matter; these were, after all, church-sanctioned events. Rather, the comic portraiture, the colloquial language, and the physical humor were intended to entertain the commoners for whom

415

the plays were intended. Having engaged the audience on one level, the lessons of the Bible stories could be more successfully imparted. Also, the actor playing Noah was most likely a common workingman, perhaps a shipwright (who better to perform the story of the Flood?). Suppose the week before the play, given in conjunction with the Corpus Christi holy days in spring, the townspeople overheard that shipwright arguing with his wife; imagine the effect when he plays the biblical character and fights with his stage wife. Life meets Art, and the reality of the biblical message is comically and truthfully manifested.

More seriously, in a play from the York cycle called *The Crucifixion*, Christ is a relatively minor character. The focus is on the executioners who fall into petty arguments about the most efficient manner to fulfill their gory task. They argue about measurements, body weights, how tight the ropes should be stretched, and the like. Each soldier becomes more petty and sadistic than the others, and in the process, the audience appreciates both the agony of Christ's death and the reasons why he returned to die for sinners. The play chillingly exposes human cruelty and self-centeredness in the realistic characterizations of the executioners.

In each of the plays described here the actors would have dressed in contemporary clothing, that is, the apparel of the workingman. In many ways, both the texts and performance of medieval plays contributed to the growth of realism in Western theater. The actor playing God in *Noah* and the angel who liberates Isaac may have worn clerical robes because biblical patriarchs and other elevated figures often wore the clothes of church officials to reinforce the stature of clerics in the Christian community. Contemporary, rather than biblical, dress was purposeful rather than a result of ignorance. To the medieval mind, all people were pilgrims on a journey to eternity. It mattered little where a person was placed on the great continuum of existence, so it was plausible for a medieval audience to accept Noah dressed as a shipwright or Isaac in the jerkin and hose worn by young men in medieval England. Such anachronisms continue into the secular dramas of the Renaissance, which is why we find clocks chiming in Shakespeare's *Julius Caesar*.

Anachronisms actually provide an understanding of biblical literature in whatever form it was rendered. *Prefiguration*—that is, one incident in the Bible foreshadowing another—was a central tenet of Christian teaching. The story of Abraham and Isaac prefigures that of Christ and the Father, who allowed his son to be slain for a greater good. The story of the flood prefigures the Day of Judgment, when the world will be destroyed and humans will be judged worthy or unworthy of salvation. Thus the theatrical anachronisms were reminders that the events of the Bible were relevant to contemporary life because they would likely happen again. This spirit of the past informing the present shaped the great history plays, or chronicles, of Elizabethan England. In our time, Brecht "historicizes" contemporary social problems by setting them in parallel situations of the past. Indeed, it is a function of drama to depict human stories, regardless of the particulars of time and place, so that others may apply them to their own needs.

A medieval illumination from a Jewish manuscript depicts the sacrifice of Isaac by his father Abraham; the biblical tale inspired many artists and dramatists.

THE BROME PLAY OF ABRAHAM AND ISAAC

A N O N Y M O U S

CHARACTERS
ABRAHAM
ISAAC, *his son*
DEUS
THE ANGEL
THE DOCTOR

   [Enter Abraham and Isaac.]

ABRAHAM *[Kneeling]*. Father of Heaven, omnipotent,
   With all my heart to thee I call.
   Thou hast given me both land and rent;

And my livelihood thou hast me sent;
I thank thee highly evermore of all.
First of the earth thou madest Adam,
And Eve also to be his wife;
All other creatures of them two came.
And now thou hast granted to me, Abraham,
Here in this land to lead my life.

In my age thou hast granted me this,
That this young child with me shall wone.
I love nothing so much, ywis,
Except thine own self, dear Father of bliss,

As Isaac here, my own sweet son.

I have divers children mo,
The which I love not half so well.
This fair sweet child, he cheers me so
In every place where that I go,
That no disease may me befall.

And therefore, Father of Heaven, I thee pray
For his health and also for his grace.
Now, Lord, keep him both night and day,
That never disease nor terror may
Come to my child in no place.

          [Rises.]

Now come on, Isaac, my own sweet child;
Go we home and take our rest.
ISAAC. Abraham, mine own father so mild,
To follow you I am full pressed,
Both early and late.
ABRAHAM. Come on, sweet child; I love thee best
Of all the children that ever I begot.
DEUS [*Speaks from above*]. Mine angel, fast hie thee thy way,
And on to middle-earth anon thou go;
Abraham's heart now will I assay,
Whether that he be steadfast or no.

Say I commanded him for to take
Isaac, his young son, that he loves so well,
And with his blood sacrifice he make,
If any of my friendship he will fell.

Show him the way on to the hill
Where that his sacrifice shall be.
I shall assay now his good will,
Whether he loveth better his child or me.
All men shall take example by him
My commandments how they shall keep.
ABRAHAM [*Kneeling*]. Now, Father of Heaven, that formed
    all thing,
My prayers to thee I make again,
For this day my tender-offering
Here must I give to thee, certain.
Ah! Lord God, Almighty King,
What manner best will make thee most fain?
If I had thereof true knowing,
It should be done with all my main,
Full soon anon.
To do thy pleasing on a hill,
Verily, it is my will,
Dear Father, God in Trinity.

THE ANGEL. Abraham! Abraham! will thou rest!
Our Lord commandeth thee for to take
Isaac, thy young son, that thou loveth best,
And with his blood sacrifice that thou make.

Into the Land of Vision thou go,

And offer thy child unto thy Lord;
I shall thee lead and show also.
Unto God's behest, Abraham, accord,

And follow me upon this green.
ABRAHAM. Welcome to me be my Lord's command,
And his behest I will not withstand.
Yet Isaac, my young son in land,
A full dear child to me hath been.

I had rather, if God had been pleased,
For to a for-bore all the goods that I have,
Than Isaac my son should be diseased,
So God in Heaven my soul may save!

I loved no thing so much on earth,
And now I must the child go kill.
Ah, Lord God, my conscience is strongly stirred!
And yet, my dear Lord, I am sore afraid
To begrudge anything against your will.
I love my child as my life,
But yet I love my God much more.
For though my heart would make any strife,
Yet will I not spare for child nor wife,
But do after my Lord's lore.

Though I love my son never so well,
Yet smite off his head soon I shall.
Ah! Father of Heaven, to thee I kneel;
A hard death my son shall feel,
For to honor thee, Lord, withal!

THE ANGEL. Abraham! Abraham! This is well said,
And all these commandments look that thou keep.
But in thy heart be nothing dismayed.
ABRAHAM. Nay, nay, forsooth, I hold me well paid
To please my God the best that I have.

For though my heart be heavily set
To see the blood of my own dear son,
Yet for all this I will not let,
But Isaac, my son, I will go get,
And come as fast as ever we can.

Now, Isaac, my own son dear,
Where art thou, child? Speak to me.
ISAAC. My father, sweet father, I am here,
And make my prayers to the Trinity.

ABRAHAM. Rise up, my child, and fast come hither,
My gentle bairn that art so wise,
For we two, child, must go together
And unto my Lord make sacrifice.

ISAAC. I am full ready, my father. Lo!
Given at your hands, I stand right here,
And whatsoever ye bid me do,
It shall be done with glad cheer,

Full well and fine.

ABRAHAM. Ah! Isaac, my own son so dear,
God's blessing I give thee, and mine.

Hold this faggot upon thy back,
And here myself fire shall bring.
ISAAC. Father, all this here will I pack,
I am full fain to do your bidding.
ABRAHAM [Aside]. Ah! Lord of Heaven, my hands I wring,
This child's words all do wound my heart.

Now, Isaac, son, go we our way
Unto yon mount with all our main.
ISAAC. Go we, my dear father, as fast as I may;
To follow you I am full fain,
Although I be slender.
ABRAHAM [Aside]. Ah! Lord, my heart breaketh in twain,
This child's words, they be so tender.

[They arrive at the Mount.]

Ah, Isaac, son, anon lay it down,
No longer upon thy back it hold,
For I must make ready full soon
To honor my Lord God as I should.

ISAAC. Lo, my dear father, where it is.

To cheer you always I draw me near.
But, father, I marvel sore of this,
Why that ye make this heavy cheer;

And also, father, evermore dread I:
Where is your quick beast that ye should kill?
Both fire and wood we have ready,
But quick beast have we none on this hill.

A quick beast, I wot well, must be dead
Your sacrifice for to make.
ABRAHAM. Dread thee naught, my child, I thee red,
Our Lord will send me one to this stead
Some manner of beast for to take
Through his sweet sond.
ISAAC. Yea, father, but my heart beginneth to quake
To see that sharp sword in your hand.

Why bear ye your sword drawn so?
Of your countenance I have much wonder.
ABRAHAM. Ah! Father of Heaven, so I am woe!
This child here breaks my heart asunder.

ISAAC. Tell me, my dear father, ere that ye cease,
Bear ye your sword drawn for me?
ABRAHAM. Ah, Isaac, sweet son, peace, peace!
For ywis thou breakest my heart in three.
ISAAC. Now truly, somewhat, father, ye think,
That ye mourn thus more and more.
ABRAHAM [Aside]. Ah! Lord of Heaven, thy grace let sink,
For my heart was never half so sore.

ISAAC. I pray you, father, that ye will let me that wit,
Whether shall I have any harm or no.
ABRAHAM. Ywis, sweet son, I may not tell thee yet,
My heart is now so full of woe.

ISAAC. Dear father, I pray you, hide it not from me,
But some of your thought that ye tell me.
ABRAHAM. Ah! Isaac, Isaac, I must kill thee!
ISAAC. Kill me, father? Alas! what have I done?
If I have trespassed against you ought,
With a rod ye may make me full mild;
And with your sharp sword kill me nought,
For ywis, father, I am but a child.

ABRAHAM. I am full sorry, son, thy blood for to spill,
But truly, my child, I may not choose.
ISAAC. Now I would to God my mother were here on this hill!
She would kneel for me on both her knees
To save my life.
And since that my mother is not here,
I pray you, father, change your cheer,
And kill me not with your knife.

ABRAHAM. Forsooth, son, unless I thee kill,
I should grieve God right sore, I dread.
It is his commandment and also his will,
That I should do this same deed.

He commanded me, son, for certain,
To make my sacrifice with thy blood.
ISAAC. And is it God's will that I should be slain?
ABRAHAM. Yea, truly, Isaac, my son so good,
And therefore my hands I wring.

ISAAC. Now, father, against my Lord's will
I will never grudge, loud nor still.
He might have sent me a better destiny
If it had been his pleasure.

ABRAHAM. Forsooth, son, but if I did this deed,
Grievously displeased our Lord will be.
ISAAC. Nay, nay, father, God forbid
That ever ye should grieve him for me.
Ye have other children, one or two,
The which ye should love well by kind.
I pray you, father, make ye no woe;
For, be I once dead, and from you go,
I shall be soon out of your mind.
Therefore do our Lord's bidding,
And when I am dead, then pray for me.
But, good father, tell ye my mother nothing;
Say that I am in another country dwelling.
ABRAHAM. Ah, Isaac, Isaac, blessèd may thou be!

My heart beginneth strongly to rise,
To see the blood of thy blessèd body.

ISAAC. Father, since it may be no other wise,
    Let it pass over, as well as I.
    But, father, ere I go unto my death,
    I pray you bless me with your hand.
ABRAHAM. Now, Isaac, with all my breath
    My blessing I give thee upon this land,
    And God's also thereto, ywis.
    Isaac, Isaac, son, up thou stand,
    Thy fair sweet mouth that I may kiss.

ISAAC. Now farewell, my own father so fine;
    And greet well my mother on earth.
    But I pray you, father, to hide my eyne,
    That I see not the stroke of your sharp sword,
    That my flesh shall defile.
ABRAHAM. Son, thy words make me to weep full sore;
    Now, my dear son Isaac, speak no more.

ISAAC. Ah! my own dear father, wherefore?
    We shall speak together her but a while.

    And since that I must needs be dead,
    Yet, my dear father, to you I pray,
    Smite but few strokes at my head,
    And make an end as soon as ye may,
    And tarry not too long.
ABRAHAM. Thy meek words, child, make me afraid;
    So "Welaway!" may be my song,
    Except alone God's will.
    Ah! Isaac, my own sweet child,
    Yet kiss me again upon this hill!
    In all this world is none so mild.
ISAAC. Now truly, father, all this tarrying
    It doth my heart but harm;
    I pray you, father, make an ending.
ABRAHAM. Come up, sweet son, into my arm.
    I must bind thy hands two,
    Although thou be never so mild.
ISAAC. Ah! mercy, father! Why should ye do so?
ABRAHAM. That thou should'st not hinder me, my child.

ISAAC. Nay, ywis, father, I will not hinder you.
    Do on, for me, your will;
    And on the purpose that ye have set you,
    For God's love, keep it for thee still.

    I am full sorry this day to die,
    But yet I want not my God to grieve.
    Do on your list for me hardily;
    My fair sweet father, I give you leave.

    But father, I pray you evermore,
    Tell my mother never a bit;
    If she wist it, she would weep full sore,
    For ywis, father, she loveth me full well.
    God's blessing may she have!

    Now farewell, my mother so sweet!
    We two be like no more to meet.
ABRAHAM. Ah, Isaac, Isaac, son, thou makest me weep,
    And with thy words thou distemperest me.

ISAAC. Ywis, sweet father, I am sorry to grieve you.
    I cry you mercy of that I have done.
    And of all tresspass that ever I did move you;
    Now, dear father, forgive me that I have done.
    God of Heaven be with me!

ABRAHAM. Ah! dear child, leave off thy moans;
    In all thy life thou grieved me never once.
    Now blessèd be thou, body and bones,
    That ever thou wert bred and born!
    Thou hast been to me child full good.
    But ywis, child, though I mourn never so fast,
    Yet must I needs here at the last
    In this place shed all thy blood.
    Therefore, my dear son, here shall thou lie.
    Unto my work I must me stead.
    I wish, I had as lief myself to die,
    If God will be pleased with my deed,
    And mine own body for to offer.
ISAAC. Ah, mercy, father, mourn ye no more!
    Your weeping maketh my heart sore,
    As my own death that I shall suffer.

    Your kerchief, father, about my eyes ye wind.
ABRAHAM. So I shall, my sweetest child on earth.
ISAAC. Now yet, good father, have this in mind,
    And smite me not often with your sharp sword,
    But hastily that it be sped.

Here Abraham laid a cloth on Isaac's face, thus saying:

ABRAHAM. Now farewell, my child so full of grace.
ISAAC. Ah!! father, father, turn downward my face,
    For of your sharp sword I am ever adread.
ABRAHAM [*Aside*]. To do this deed I am full sorry,
    But, Lord, thy behest I will not withstand.
ISAAC. Ah! Father of Heaven, to thee I cry;
    Lord, receive me into thy hand.

ABRAHAM. Lo! now is the time come, certain,
    That my sword in his neck shall bite.
    Ah, Lord, my heart resisteth thee again;
    I may not find it in my heart to smite;
    My heart will not now thereto.
    Yet fain I would work my Lord's will,
    But this young innocent lieth so still,
    I may not find it in my heart him to kill.
    Oh! Father of heaven, what shall I do?

ISAAC. Ah, mercy, father, why tarry ye so,
    And let me lie thus long on this heath?
    Now I would to God the stroke were do!

Father, I pray you heartily, shorten me of my woe,
And let me not look thus after my death.

ABRAHAM. Now, heart, why would'st not thou break in
  three?
Yet shall thou not make me to my God unmild.
I will no longer hold back for thee,
For that my God aggrieved would be.
Now hold the stroke, my own dear child.

Here Abraham drew his stroke, and the Angel took the
sword in his hand suddenly.

THE ANGEL. I am an angel, thou mayest see blithe,
  That from heaven to thee is sent.
  Our Lord thanks thee an hundred sythe
  For the keeping of his commandment.
  He knoweth thy will, and also thy heart,
  That thou dreadest him above all things;
  And some of thy heaviness for to depart
  A fair ram yonder I did bring.

  He standeth tied, lo, among the briars.
  Now, Abraham, amend thy mood,
  For Isaac, thy young son that here is,
  This day shall not shed his blood.

  Go, make thy sacrifice with yonder ram.
  Now farewell, blessèd Abraham,
  For unto heaven I go now home;
  The way is full straight.
  Take up thy son so free.

ABRAHAM. Ah! Lord, I thank thee of thy great grace,
  Now am I eased in divers wise.
  Arise up, Isaac, my dear son, arise;
  Arise up, sweet child, and come to me.

ISAAC. Ah! mercy, father, why smite ye not?
  Ah! smite on, father, once with your knife.
ABRAHAM. Peace, my sweet son, and take no thought,
  For our Lord of Heaven hath granted thy life
  By his angel now,

  That thou shalt not die this day, son, truly.
ISAAC. Ah, father, full glad then were I;
  I wish—father—I say—I wish
  If this tale were true!
ABRAHAM. An hundred times, my son fair of hue,
  For joy thy mouth now will I kiss.

ISAAC. Ah! my dear father, Abraham,
  Will not God be wroth that we do thus?
ABRAHAM. No, no, hardily, my sweet son,
  For yon same ram he hath us sent
  Hither down to us.

  Yon beast shall die here in thy stead,
  In the worship of our Lord alone.

Go, fetch him hither, my child, indeed.
ISAAC. Father, I will go seize him by the head,
  And bring yon beast with me anon.
  Ah, sheep, sheep, blessèd may thou be,
  That ever thou were sent down hither!
  Thou shall this day die for me
  In the worship of the Holy Trinity.
  Now come fast and go we together
  To my Father of Heaven.
  Though thou be never so gentle and good,
  Yet had I liefer thou sheddest thy blood
  I wish, sheep, than I.
  Lo, father, I have brought here full smart
  This gentle sheep, and him to you I give.
  But, Lord God, I thank thee with all my heart,
  For I am glad that I shall live,
  And kiss once my dear mother.
ABRAHAM. Now be right merry, my sweet child,
  For this quick beast, that is so mild,
  Here I shall present before all other.

ISAAC. And I will fast begin to blow;
  This fire shall burn a full good speed.
  But father, while I stoop down low,
  Ye will not kill me with your sword, I trow?
ABRAHAM. No, hardily, sweet son; have no dread;
  My mourning is past.
ISAAC. Yea! but I would that sword were in a gled,
  For, ywis, father, it makes me full ill aghast.

Here Abraham made his offering, kneeling and saying
thus:

ABRAHAM. Now, Lord God of Heaven in Trinity,
  Almighty God omnipotent,
  My offering I make in the worship of thee,
  And with this quick beast I thee present.
  Lord, receive thou mine intent,
  As [thou] art God and ground of our grace.

DEUS. Abraham, Abraham, well may thou speed,
  And Isaac, thy young son, thee by!
  Truly, Abraham, for this deed
  I shall multiply both your seed,
  As thick as stars be in the sky,
  Both more and less.
  And as thick as gravel in the sea,
  So thick multiplied your seed shall be.
  This grant I you for your goodness.

  Of you shall come fruits great [won],
  And ever be in bliss without end,
  For ye dread me as God alone
  And keep my commandments every one;
  My blessing I give, wheresoever ye wend.
ABRAHAM. Lo Isaac, my son, how think ye

Of this work that we have wrought?
Full glad and blithe we may be,
Against the will of God that we grudged naught,
Upon this fair heath.

ISAAC. Ah! father, I thank our Lord in every deal,
That my wit served me so well
For to dread God more than my death.

ABRAHAM. Why, dear worthy son, wert thou adread?
Heartily, child, tell me thy lore.

ISAAC. Yea, by my faith, father, now have I red,
I was never so afraid before
As I have been on yon hill.
But, by my faith, father, I swear
I will nevermore come there
But it be against my will.

ABRAHAM. Yea! come on with me, my own sweet son,
And homeward fast now let us go.

ISAAC. By my faith, father, thereto I grant;
I had never so good will to go home,
And to speak with my dear mother.

ABRAHAM. Ah! Lord of Heaven, I thank thee.
For now may I lead home with me
Isaac, my young son so free,
The gentlest child above all other,
This may I well avow.

Now go we forth, my blessèd son.

ISAAC. I grant, father, and let us go;
For, by my troth, were I at home,
I would never go out again so.
I pray God give us grace evermore,
And all those that we be beholden to.

[Exeunt.]

[Enter Doctor.]

DOCTOR. Lo, sovereigns and sirs, now have we showed
This solemn story to great and small.
It is a good lesson to be learnèd and lewd
And to the wisest of us all,
Without any barring.
For this story showeth you [here]
How we should keep, to our power,
God's commandments without grudging.

Think ye, sirs, and God sent an angel
And commanded you your child be slain,
By your troth, is there any of you
That either would grudge or strive there again?
How think ye now, sirs, thereby?

I think there be three or four or more.
And these women, that weep so sorrowfully
When that their children die them fro,
As nature will and kind,
It is but folly, I may well avow,
To grudge against God or to grieve you;
For ye shall never see him mischiefed, well I know,
By land nor water, bear this in mind.

And grudge not against our Lord God
In wealth or woe, whether that he you send,
Though ye be never so hard bestead;
For when he will, he may it amend,
His commandments truly if ye keep with good heart,
As this story hath now showed you before;
And faithfully serve him while ye be quart,
That ye may please God both even and morn.
Now Jesu, that wore the crown of thorn,
Bring us all to heaven's bliss!

FINIS.

THREE MORALITY PLAYS: EVERYMAN, MANKIND, AND THE APPLE TREE

A N O N Y M O U S

In addition to mystery plays, two other forms of Christian drama developed in the Middle Ages: the *miracle play* and the *morality play*. The former dealt with the saints and martyrs of the Roman Catholic Church and are thus referred to as *saints plays*. We may think of these venerated souls as the equivalents of Greek heroes for they, too, were admired for their courage and virtue. But in the Christian schema, classical tragedy was impossible. The tragedy in Christendom was to lose one's soul in the next life. In this world the Christian was expected to bear "the slings and arrows of outrageous fortune" silently. Though serene acceptance of misfortune may bolster one's chances for eternal salvation, it is decidedly undramatic. The most memorable Saints plays were those that fused popular legend and folk works to create a hybrid drama. For instance, the English *St. George Play* mixed sword dancing, popular folk plays, and Christian lore to create a popular entertainment that has lasted a thousand years.

It is the morality play, however, that retains the most lasting influence on subsequent Western drama. Whereas mystery and miracle plays dealt with specific biblical or historical figures, the moralities were about common people and as such helped lay a foundation for subsequent secular drama.

EVERYMAN (C. 1495)

The most famous morality play was simply called *Everyman*, a work that might have been derived from a fifteenth-century Dutch drama called *Elkerlyc*. The title indicates that the play's protagonist represented each person who watched it. Moralities dramatized the battle between good and evil for the soul of an ordinary person on life's pilgrimage towards eternity. Abstractions of virtues and vices were personified as allegorical characters such as Beauty, Strength, Wantonness, Rumor, and Greed. Because he was omnipresent in medieval life in the form of wars and plagues, the character of Death (*Mors*) hovered over the action, grim and indifferent to the battle between good angels and those three great tempters of humans, "the World, the Flesh, and the Devil." Death tells Everyman:

> . . . the tide abideth no man,
>
> And in the world each living creature
>
> For Adam's sin must die of nature.

"Adam's sin" is a reference to the Fall in the Garden of Eden, the Christian version of the tragic paradigm. In Christian plays, the Fall becomes the equivalent of Fate in the ancient world because it accounts for human weaknesses and their consequences. Although the protagonist is usually saved by the heavenly virtues, in some moralities he is lost and a horde of devils, alternately frightening and comical, drags the soul of the unrepentant sinner into eternal hell fire, often depicted as a Hellmouth. Thus we see an attempt to induce pity and fear in medieval au-

¶Here begynneth a treatyse how the hye fader of heuen sendeth dethe to somon euery creature to come and gyue a counte of theyr lyues in this worlde and is in maner of a morall playe.

Eueryman.

Medievals saw Death, who might appear at any moment, as a very real presence in their lives; thus he was a leading actor in their serious and comic morality plays, as well as in their art.

diences. Though there may be little subtlety in the message of these didactic plays, we do find remarkably well drawn characters and truthful insights into the human personality in many of the allegorical characters. This emphasis on the plight of the individual establishes a foundation for the human-centered dramas of the Renaissance and thereafter. Martin Stevens argues that, in fact, medieval drama "can be seen as the birth of bourgeois literature—the beginning, not the ending, of something important—as an expression of a time of transition."

Many of the most highly regarded Renaissance plays show discernible elements of the morality play, Christopher Marlowe's *Doctor Faustus* (1588) being the most prominent example. A malcontented scholar sells his soul to Mephistopheles in exchange for 24 years of worldly delights. In one memorable scene Faustus is confronted by a "good" and a "bad" angel; elsewhere he is entertained by visions of the Seven Deadly Sins in a dazzling theatrical coup. Alvin Kernan has argued that Shakespeare's chronicle plays are political moralities in which England is an "every-country" tempted by good and evil forces (represented by rebels). Sir John Falstaff is referred to as an "old reverend Vice," an unmistakable allusion to a prominent morality character. Later, Restoration and Georgian comedies, such as *The School for Scandal*, presented characters such as Sir Benjamin Backbite and Lady Sneerwell, descendants of Rumor and Gossip, two of the most vicious characters in the moralities. In the twentieth century, the plays of Bernard Shaw and Bertolt Brecht, often characterized as didactic, contain elements drawn from the morality play tradition.

MANKIND (C. 1475)

Unlike the solemn *Everyman, Mankind* (or, "A Morality Portraying the Life of Ne'er-Do-Wells in Late Plantagenet and Early Tudor Times") is a ribald, rollicking play that may shock you with its scatological language and bawdy songs. The respected medieval scholar Hardin Craig labels it "a play of the utmost ignorance and crudity." Yet Sister Phillipa Coogan, in a dissertation published at Catholic University (1946), defends the lewd comedy as an effective means of illustrating the lessons taught in Mercy's opening sermon.

On one hand, *Mankind* is a traditional morality. The universal hero is sorely tempted by three vices: New Guise (or "fashion"), Now-a-days (who embodies the hedonistic command to "live for today"), and Nought (*no* rules, *no* cares, *no* scruples for him!). The "Three N's" (the alliteration is purposeful) are themselves provoked by Mischief, among the most common of the morality Vices; in other plays and cultures he might be referred to as the Lord of Misrule or the Trickster. He represents the spirit of chaos and anarchy that creates human woes. When the Vices are foiled by Mankind's resolution to follow Mercy's ways, the diabolical Titivillus appears, "dressed devilwise," to con Mankind into forsaking the path of virtue. Note that Titivillus uses a dream to trick the sleeping hero; the dream conceit is noteworthy because it is an attempt by the playwright (possibly a monk named Hyngham) to invest Mankind with psychological complexity. Keep the "dream trick" in mind as you read about Puck's mischief in *A Midsummer Night's Dream*; his kinship to the Vices of medieval moralities has been the subject of much scholarly writing.

What sets *Mankind* apart from most moralities is its reliance on low humor to advance its plot and to preach its gospel that "the world is but a vanity, and Mankind is wretched." There are comic beatings with a spade in the best Three Stooges tradition; there are comic disguises; and most of all there are numerous verbal jokes and songs that can only be described as bathroom humor. The bawdy round "It Is Written with a Coal" was likely a popular song used to further audience identification with the reality of the issues the play depicts. Most scholars argue that the play was actually written for uneducated rural audiences (or "rustics," to use a popular term). But Larry Clopper argues, quite rightly, that the number of untranslated Latin passages (many of which are moral epigrams) suggests that the play was also intended for well-educated people. *Mankind*, like the great secular plays that followed it, no doubt appealed to the spectrum of medieval society. It may have contributed to the manner in which later Tudor and Elizabethan plays were conspicuously designed to appeal to a multiclass audience.

Most importantly, *Mankind*, even more than most moralities, actively engages the audience. It is imperative that you consider the audience (including yourself) a character in this play. The play begins with a lengthy sermon directed at the audience, which is immediately followed by Mischief's mock sermon. The sermons not only establish the dialectics of the play, but also make the audience choose sides between the combatants. The audience becomes the object of a favorite device of medieval playwrights, *psychomachia*, in which virtues and vices buzz in the ear of the protagonist to win favor. Each character takes his case directly to the audience; and the bawdy round sung by the Three N's encouraged an audience "sing-a-long." Titivillus's plea for money upon his entrance was no doubt carried into the audience itself (perhaps to enhance the acting company's coffers?). It was this free commingling of life on the stage and life in the street that made the morality plays, especially *Mankind*, potent teaching devices. And it is both a theme (i.e., life is a play) and a performance device that later flourished in the Elizabethan and Jacobean theaters. Accordingly, *Mankind* serves as both a record of medieval performance conditions and a harbinger of things to come.

THE APPLE TREE (C. 1500)

The Apple Tree originated in the Low Countries, specifically the Netherlands, where drama flourished in the Late Middle Ages. We must not forget that liturgical drama was widespread across Europe, although most of the more accessible plays have been preserved in English manuscripts. The play is a comical variant on the morality play in which we find traditional allegorical figures—Open Heart, his faithful wife Steadfast Faith, Insatiable, et al. As was customary, Death is a central character and motivator. But in the best comic tradition, this inventive play subverts the norm. Open Heart, our Everyman, becomes the tempter and outwits the Vices (Insatiable, Reckless Living, and Lusty Youth), Death, and eventually the Devil himself. God makes a cameo appearance to provide both dignity and a moral—a steadfast faith in his benevolence will reap bounty. That Open Heart and his wife manage to accumulate more than a few bits of material wealth for their efforts is of small consequence; how much better to give the Vices, Death, and the Devil their comeuppance. Like *Mankind*, *The Apple Tree* suggests the spirit of the New Secularism in Europe in the sixteenth century. Its high spirits and jocularity supersede the more solemn theological message of the play. Reckless Living says in the *plaudite* (the salute to the audience that ends the play), "And for our part, To serve our art is to serve you all." If we take the command literally, it would suggest that playmaking was moving away from its church-sanctioned didacticism to an aesthetic enterprise for its own sake.

The roots of *The Apple Tree* run deep into the rich soil of non-Christian theatrical forms. The mummers' play, for instance, was a popular Christmas (i.e., winter) play in which villagers disguised themselves to perform a comic drama in which a dead character was, with the aid of a mysterious doctor, brought back to life to dance a vigorous jig. Like the Dutch morality, mummery tricked death and life triumphed. (Philadelphia, by the way, still celebrates the New Year with a huge mummers' parade in which colorfully costumed revelers dance down Broad Street, impervious to winter's icy blasts.) Open Heart is a medieval rendition of the Trickster, the conniving underling who outwits his betters. He thrived in the ancient Roman farces of Atella, where he was known as Macchus, then in the more formal Roman plays of Plautus, who called him Pseudolus. Early French farceurs named him Pierre Pathelin, and the Italian street comedians, who were already thriving in the squares of such towns as Venice, immortalized him as Arlecchino (or Harlequin). Finally, *The Apple Tree*, for all its morality play heritage, shows kinship to a new species of play appearing at European courts and manor houses: the *interlude*, a short, often comical play (*ludi*) usually performed by professional actors between courses of a banquet. Interludes eventually became full-blown theatrical forms in theater's new golden age, the Renaissance.

EVERYMAN

──A N O N Y M O U S──

CHARACTERS
GOD
MESSENGER
DEATH
EVERYMAN
FELLOWSHIP
KINDRED
COUSIN
GOODS
GOOD DEEDS
KNOWLEDGE
CONFESSION
BEAUTY
STRENGTH
DISCRETION
FIVE WITS
ANGEL
DOCTOR

Here Beginneth a Treatise how the High Father of Heaven Sendeth Death to Summon Every Creature to Come and Give Account of their Lives in this World, and is in Manner of a Moral Play.

[*Enter Messenger as a Prologue.*]

MESSENGER.
 I pray you all give your audience,
 And hear this matter with reverence,
 By figure° a moral play.
 The *Summoning of Everyman* called it is,
5 That of our lives and ending shows
 How transitory we be all day.
 This matter is wondrous precious,
 But the intent° of it is more gracious,
 And sweet to bear away.
10 The story saith: Man, in the beginning
 Look well, and take good heed to the ending,
 Be you never so gay!
 Ye think sin in the beginning full sweet,
 Which in the end causeth the soul to weep,
15 When the body lieth in clay.
 Here shall you see how Fellowship and Jollity,

Both Strength, Pleasure, and Beauty,
Will fade from thee as flower in May;
For ye shall hear how our Heaven King
Calleth Everyman to a general reckoning. 20
Give audience, and hear what he doth say.

            [*Exit.*]

God speaketh.

GOD.
 I perceive, here in my majesty,
 How that all creatures be to me unkind,°
 Living without dread in worldly prosperity.
 Of ghostly sight° the people be so blind, 25
 Drowned in sin, they know me not for their God.
 In worldly riches is all their mind;
 They fear not my rightwiseness,° the sharp rod.
 My law that I showed, when I for them died,
 They forget clean, and shedding of my blood red; 30
 I hanged between two, it cannot be denied;
 To get them life I suffered° to be dead;
 I healed their feet, with thorns hurt was my head.
 I could do no more than I did, truly;
 And now I see the people do clean forsake me. 35
 They use the seven deadly sins° damnable,
 As pride, covetise, wrath, and lechery
 Now in the world be made commendable;
 And thus they leave of angels, the heavenly company.
 Every man liveth so after his own pleasure, 40
 And yet of their life they be nothing sure.
 I see the more that I them forbear
 The worse they be from year to year.
 All that liveth appaireth° fast;
 Therefore I will, in all the haste, 45
 Have a reckoning of every man's person;
 For, and° I leave the people thus alone
 In their life and wicked tempests,
 Verily they will become much worse than beasts;
 For now one would by envy another up eat; 50
 Charity° they do all clean forget.
 I hoped well that every man
 In my glory should make his mansion,

2–3 matter . . . figure the *matter* is the story and the moral doctrine; the *figure* is the literary form, in this case a play **8 intent** meaning

22 unkind (1) unnatural (2) ungrateful **25 ghostly sight** spiritual insight **28 rightwiseness** righteousness **32 suffered** allowed **36 seven deadly sins** four are named in the next line; the other three are envy, gluttony, and sloth **44 appaireth** becomes worse **47 and** if **51 Charity** love (of God and of one's fellows)

And thereto I had them all elect.
55 But now I see, like traitors deject,
They thank me not for the pleasure that I to them meant,
Nor yet for their being that I them have lent.
I proffered the people great multitude of mercy,
And few there be that asketh it heartily.
60 They be so cumbered with worldly riches
That needs on them I must do justice,
On every man living, without fear.
Where art thou, Death, thou mighty messenger?

[Enter Death.]

DEATH.
Almighty God, I am here at your will,
65 Your commandment to fulfill.
GOD.
Go thou to Everyman,
And show him, in my name,
A pilgrimage he must on him take,
Which he in no wise may escape;
70 And that he bring with him a sure reckoning
Without delay or any tarrying.

[Exit God.]

DEATH.
Lord, I will in the world go run overall,°
And cruelly outsearch both great and small.
Every man will I beset that liveth beastly
75 Out of God's laws, and dreadeth not folly.
He that loveth riches I will strike with my dart,
His sight to blind, and from heaven to depart°—
Except that alms be his good friend—
In hell for to dwell, world without end.
80 Lo, yonder I see Everyman walking.
Full little he thinketh on my coming;
His mind is on fleshly lusts and his treasure,
And great pain it shall cause him to endure
Before the Lord, Heaven King.

[Enter Everyman.]

85 Everyman, stand still! Whither art thou going
Thus gaily? Hast thou thy Maker forget?
EVERYMAN.
Why askest thou?
Wouldest thou wit?°
DEATH.
Yea, sir; I will show you:
90 In great haste I am sent to thee
From God out of his majesty.
EVERYMAN.
What, sent to me?
DEATH.
Yea, certainly.

Though thou have forget him here,
He thinketh on thee in the heavenly sphere, 95
As, ere we depart, thou shalt know.
EVERYMAN.
What desireth God of me?
DEATH.
That shall I show thee:
A reckoning he will needs have
Without any longer respite. 100
EVERYMAN.
To give a reckoning longer leisure I crave;
This blind° matter troubleth my wit.
DEATH.
On thee thou must take a long journey;
Therefore thy book of count° with thee thou bring,
For turn again° thou cannot by no way. 105
And look thou be sure of thy reckoning,
For before God thou shalt answer, and show
Thy many bad deeds, and good but a few;
How thou hast spent thy life, and in what wise,
Before the chief Lord of paradise. 110
Have ado that we were in that way,°
For, wit thou well, thou shalt make none attorney.°
EVERYMAN.
Full unready I am such reckoning to give.
I know thee not. What messenger art thou?
DEATH.
I am Death, that no man dreadeth,° 115
For every man I rest,° and no man spareth;
For it is God's commandment
That all to me shall be obedient.
EVERYMAN.
O Death, thou comest when I had thee least in mind!
In thy power it lieth me to save; 120
Yet of my good° will I give thee, if thou will be kind;
Yea, a thousand pound shalt thou have,
And defer this matter till another day.
DEATH.
Everyman, it may not be, by no way.
I set not by gold, silver, nor riches, 125
Ne° by pope, emperor, king, duke, ne princes;
For, and I would receive gifts great,
All the world I might get;
But my custom is clean contrary.
I give thee no respite. Come hence, and not tarry. 130
EVERYMAN.
Alas, shall I have no longer respite?
I may say Death giveth no warning!
To think on thee, it maketh my heart sick,

---

102 blind obscure **104 book of count** account book **105 turn again** return **111 Have . . . way** Get ready that we may be on that road **112 make none attorney** have no attorney **115 no man dreadeth** dreads no man **116 rest** arrest **121 good** wealth **126 Ne** Nor

---

72 overall everywhere **77 depart** sunder **88 wit** know

For all unready is my book of reckoning.
135 But twelve year and I might have abiding,
My counting-book I would make so clear
That my reckoning I should not need to fear.
Wherefore, Death, I pray thee, for God's mercy,
Spare me till I be provided of remedy.

DEATH.
140 Thee availeth not to cry, weep, and pray;
But haste thee lightly° that thou were gone that journey,
And prove thy friends, if thou can;
For, wit thou well, the tide° abideth no man,
And in the world each living creature
145 For Adam's sin must die of nature.°

EVERYMAN.
Death, if I should this pilgrimage take,
And my reckoning surely make,
Show me, for° Saint Charity,
Should I not come again shortly?

DEATH.
150 No, Everyman; and thou be once there,
Thou mayst never more come here,
Trust me verily.

EVERYMAN.
O gracious God in the high seat celestial,
Have mercy on me in this most need!
155 Shall I have no company from this vale terrestrial
Of mine acquaintance, that way me to lead?

DEATH.
Yea, if any be so hardy
That would go with thee and bear thee company.
Hie° thee that thou were gone to God's magnificence,
160 Thy reckoning to give before his presence.
What, weenest° thou thy life is given thee,
And thy worldly goods also?

EVERYMAN.
I had wend° so, verily.

DEATH.
Nay, nay; it was but lent thee;
165 For as soon as thou art go,
Another a while shall have it, and then go therefro,°
Even as thou hast done.
Everyman, thou art mad! Thou hast thy wits five,
And here on earth will not amend thy life;
170 For suddenly I do come.

EVERYMAN.
O wretched caitiff,° whither shall I flee,
That I might scape this endless sorrow?
Now, gentle Death, spare me till tomorrow,
That I may amend me
175 With good advisement.°

DEATH.
Nay, thereto I will not consent,
Nor no man will I respite;
But to the heart suddenly I shall smite
Without any advisement.
And now out of thy sight I will me hie.   180
See thou make thee ready shortly,
For thou mayst say this is the day
That no man living may scape away.

[Exit Death.]

EVERYMAN.
Alas, I may well weep with sighs deep!
Now have I no manner of company   185
To help me in my journey, and me to keep;
And also my writing is full unready.
How shall I do now for to excuse me?
I would to God I had never be get!°
To my soul a full great profit it had be;   190
For now I fear pains huge and great.
The time passeth. Lord, help, that all wrought!
For though I mourn it availeth nought.
The day passeth, and is almost ago.°
I wot° not well what for to do.   195
To whom were I best my complaint to make?
What and I to Fellowship thereof spake,
And showed him of this sudden chance?
For in him is all mine affiance;°
We have in the world so many a day   200
Be good friends in sport and play.
I see him yonder certainly.
I trust that he will bear me company;
Therefore to him will I speak to ease my sorrow.
Well met, good Fellowship, and good morrow!   205

[Fellowship speaketh.]

FELLOWSHIP.
Everyman, good morrow, by this day!
Sir, why lookest thou so piteously?
If any thing be amiss, I pray thee me say,
That I may help to remedy.

EVERYMAN.
Yea, good Fellowship, yea;   210
I am in great jeopardy.

FELLOWSHIP.
My true friend, show to me your mind;
I will not forsake thee to my life's end
In the way of good company.

EVERYMAN.
That was well spoken, and lovingly.   215

FELLOWSHIP.
Sir, I must needs know your heaviness;°

141 **lightly** quickly   143 **tide** time   145 **of nature** as a natural thing   148 **for** in the name of   159 **Hie** Hurry   161 **weenest** think   163 **wend** thought   166 **therefro** from it   171 **wretched caitiff** captive wretch   175 **good advisement** proper reflection

189 **be get** been born   194 **ago** gone by   195 **wot** know   199 **affiance** trust   216 **heaviness** sorrow

I have pity to see you in any distress.
If any have you wronged, ye shall revenged be,
Though I on the ground be slain for thee,
220 Though that I know before that I should die.
EVERYMAN.
　Verily, Fellowship, gramercy.°
FELLOWSHIP.
　Tush! by thy thanks I set not a straw.
　Show me your grief, and say no more.
EVERYMAN.
　If I my heart should to you break,°
225 And then you to turn your mind from me,
　And would not me comfort when ye hear me speak,
　Then should I ten times sorrier be.
FELLOWSHIP.
　Sir, I say as I will do, indeed.
EVERYMAN.
　Then be you a good friend at need!
230 I have found you true here before.
FELLOWSHIP.
　And so ye shall evermore;
　For, in faith, and thou go to hell,
　I will not forsake thee by the way.
EVERYMAN.
　Ye speak like a good friend; I believe you well.
235 I shall deserve it, and I may.
FELLOWSHIP.
　I speak of no deserving, by this day!
　For he that will say, and nothing do,
　Is not worthy with good company to go;
　Therefore show me the grief of your mind,
240 As to your friend most loving and kind.
EVERYMAN.
　I shall show you how it is:
　Commanded I am to go a journey—
　A long way, hard and dangerous—
　And give a strait count, without delay,
245 Before the high Judge, Adonai.°
　Wherefore, I pray you, bear me company,
　As ye have promised, in this journey.
FELLOWSHIP.
　That is matter indeed. Promise is duty;
　But, and I should take such a voyage on me,
250 I know it well, it should be to my pain.
　Also it maketh me afeard, certain.
　But let us take counsel here as well as we can,
　For your words would fear° a strong man.
EVERYMAN.
　Why, ye said if I had need
255 Ye would me never forsake, quick° ne dead,
　Though it were to hell, truly.

FELLOWSHIP.
　So I said, certainly,
　But such pleasures be set aside, the sooth° to say.
　And also, if we took such a journey,
　When should we come again? 260
EVERYMAN.
　Nay, never again, till the day of doom.
FELLOWSHIP.
　In faith, then will not I come there!
　Who hath you these tidings brought?
EVERYMAN.
　Indeed, Death was with me here.
FELLOWSHIP.
　Now, by God that all hath bought,° 265
　If Death were the messenger,
　For no man that is living today
　I will not go that loath journey—
　Not for the father that begat me!
EVERYMAN.
　Ye promised otherwise, pardie.° 270
FELLOWSHIP.
　I wot well I said so, truly.
　And yet if thou wilt eat, and drink, and make good
　　cheer,
　Or haunt to women the lusty company,°
　I would not forsake you while the day is clear,
　Trust me verily. 275
EVERYMAN.
　Yea, thereto ye would be ready!
　To go to mirth, solace, and play,
　Your mind will sooner apply,
　Than to bear me company in my long journey.
FELLOWSHIP.
　Now, in good faith, I will not that way. 280
　But and thou will murder, or any man kill,
　In that I will help thee with a good will.
EVERYMAN.
　O, that is a simple advice, indeed.
　Gentle fellow, help me in my necessity!
　We have loved long, and now I need; 285
　And now, gentle Fellowship, remember me.
FELLOWSHIP.
　Whether ye have loved me or no,
　By Saint John, I will not with thee go.
EVERYMAN.
　Yet, I pray thee, take the labor, and do so much for me
　To bring me forward,° for Saint Charity, 290
　And comfort me till I come without the town.
FELLOWSHIP.
　Nay, and thou would give me a new gown,

---

221 **gramercy** thanks　224 **break** open　245 **Adonai** a Hebrew
name for God; in Christian liturgy, Christ　253 **fear** frighten
255 **quick** alive

258 **sooth** truth　265 **bought** redeemed　270 **pardie** by God
273 **haunt ... company** frequent the delightful company of
women　290 **bring me forward** accompany me

I will not a foot with thee go;
But, and thou had tarried, I would not have left thee so.
295   And as now God speed thee in thy journey,
For from thee I will depart as fast as I may.
EVERYMAN.
  Whither away, Fellowship? Will you forsake me?
FELLOWSHIP.
  Yea, by my fay!° To God I betake° thee.
EVERYMAN.
  Farewell, good Fellowship; for thee my heart is sore.°
300   Adieu for ever! I shall see thee no more.
FELLOWSHIP.
  In faith, Everyman, farewell now at the end,
For you I will remember that parting is mourning.
                                   [Exit Fellowship.]
EVERYMAN.
  Alack! shall we thus depart° indeed—
  Ah, Lady, help!—without any more comfort?
305   Lo, Fellowship forsaketh me in my most need.
For help in this world whither shall I resort?
Fellowship here before with me would merry make,
And now little sorrow for me doth he take.
It is said, "In prosperity men friends may find,
310   Which in adversity be full unkind."
Now whither for succor shall I flee,
Sith that° Fellowship hath forsaken me?
To my kinsmen I will, truly,
Praying them to help me in my necessity.
315   I believe that they will do so,
For kind° will creep where it may not go.
I will go say,° for yonder I see them go.
Where be ye now, my friends and kinsmen?

[Enter Kindred and Cousin.]

KINDRED.
  Here be we now at your commandment.
320   Cousin, I pray you show us your intent
In any wise, and do not spare.°
COUSIN.
  Yea, Everyman, and to us declare
If ye be disposed to go any whither;
For, wit you well, we will live and die together.
KINDRED.
325   In wealth and woe we will with you hold,
For over his kin a man may be bold.°
EVERYMAN.
  Gramercy, my friends and kinsmen kind.
Now shall I show you the grief of my mind:
I was commanded by a messenger,
330   That is a high king's chief officer;

He bade me go a pilgrimage, to my pain,
And I know well I shall never come again;
Also I must give a reckoning strait,
For I have a great enemy° that hath me in wait,
Which intendeth me for to hinder.   335
KINDRED.
  What account is that which ye must render?
That would I know.
EVERYMAN.
  Of all my works I must show
How I have lived and my days spent;
Also of ill deeds that I have used°   340
In my time sith life was me lent;
And of all virtues that I have refused.
Therefore, I pray you, go thither with me
To help to make mine account, for Saint Charity.
COUSIN.
  What, to go thither? Is that the matter?   345
Nay, Everyman, I had leifer fast° bread and water
All this five year and more.
EVERYMAN.
  Alas, that ever I was bore!°
For now shall I never be merry,
If that you forsake me.   350
KINDRED.
  Ah, sir, what, ye be a merry man!
Take good heart to you, and make no moan.
But one thing I warn you, by Saint Anne—
As for me, ye shall go alone.
EVERYMAN.
  My Cousin, will you not with me go?   355
COUSIN.
  No, by Our Lady! I have the cramp in my toe.
Trust not to me, for, so God me speed.°
I will deceive you in your most need.
KINDRED.
  It availeth not us to tice.°
Ye shall have my maid with all my heart;   360
She loveth to go to feasts, there to be nice,°
And to dance, and abroad to start.°
I will give her leave to help you in that journey,
If that you and she may agree.
EVERYMAN.
  Now show me the very effect of your mind: 365
Will you go with me, or abide behind?
KINDRED.
  Abide behind? Yea, that will I, and I may!
Therefore farewell till another day.
                                  [Exit Kindred.]

---

298 fay faith **betake** commend   **303 depart** separate   **312 Sith that** Since   **316 kind** kinship, family (the idea is that blood ties will find a way)   **317 say** try, essay   **321 spare** hold back   **326 over his kin . . . bold** a man may command his kinsmen

334 enemy that is, the Devil   **340 used** practiced   **346 leifer fast** would rather have nothing but   **348 bore** born   **357 so God me speed** so may God cause me to prosper   **359 tice** entice   **361 nice** wanton   **362 abroad to start** go gadding about

EVERYMAN.
How should I be merry or glad?
370   For fair promises men to me make,
But when I have most need they me forsake.
I am deceived; that maketh me sad.
COUSIN.
Cousin Everyman, farewell now,
For verily I will not go with you.
375   Also of mine own an unready reckoning
I have to account; therefore I make tarrying.
Now God keep thee, for now I go.   [Exit Cousin.]
EVERYMAN.
Ah, Jesus, is all come hereto?°
Lo, fair words maketh fools fain;°
380   They promise, and nothing will do certain.
My kinsmen promised me faithfully
For to abide with me steadfastly;
And now fast away do they flee.
Even so Fellowship promised me.
385   What friend were best me of to provide?°
I lose my time here longer to abide.
Yet in my mind a thing there is;
All my life I have loved riches;
If that my Good° now help me might,
390   He would make my heart full light.
I will speak to him in this distress.
Where art thou, my Goods and riches?
GOODS.
[Within.] Who calleth me? Everyman? What! hast thou
haste?
I lie here in corners, trussed and piled so high,
395   And in chests I am locked so fast,
Also sacked in bags. Thou mayst see with thine eye
I cannot stir; in packs low I lie.
What would ye have? Lightly me say.
EVERYMAN.
Come hither, Good, in all the haste thou may,
400   For of counsel I must desire thee.
[Enter Goods.]
GOODS.
Sir, and ye in the world have sorrow or adversity,
That can I help you to remedy shortly.
EVERYMAN.
It is another disease that grieveth me;
In this world it is not, I tell thee so.
405   I am sent for another way to go,
To give a strait count general
Before the highest Jupiter of all;
And all my life I have had joy and pleasure in thee,
Therefore, I pray thee, go with me;
410   For, peradventure, thou mayst before God Almighty

My reckoning help to clean and purify;
For it is said ever among°
That "money maketh all right that is wrong."
GOODS.
Nay, Everyman, I sing another song.
I follow no man in such voyages;   415
For, and I went with thee,
Thou shouldst fare much the worse for me;
For because on me thou did set thy mind,
Thy reckoning I have made blotted and blind,
That thine account thou cannot make truly—   420
And that hast thou for the love of me.
EVERYMAN.
That would grieve me full sore,
When I should come to that fearful answer.
Up, let us go thither together.
GOODS.
Nay, not so! I am too brittle, I may not endure.   425
I will follow no man one foot, be ye sure.
EVERYMAN.
Alas, I have thee loved, and had great pleasure
All my life-days on good and treasure.
GOODS.
That is to thy damnation, without lesing,°
For my love is contrary to the love everlasting.   430
But if thou had me loved moderately during,
As to the poor to give part of me,
Then shouldst thou not in this dolor be,
Nor in this great sorrow and care.
EVERYMAN.
Lo, now was I deceived ere I was ware,   435
And all I may wite° misspending of time.
GOODS.
What, weenest thou that I am thine?
EVERYMAN.
I had wend so.
GOODS.
Nay, Everyman, I say no.
As for a while I was lent thee;   440
A season thou hast had me in prosperity.
My condition is man's soul to kill;
If I save one, a thousand I do spill.°
Weenest thou that I will follow thee?
Nay, not from this world, verily.   445
EVERYMAN.
I had wend otherwise.
GOODS.
Therefore to thy soul Good is a thief;
For when thou art dead, this is my guise°—
Another to deceive in this same wise
As I have done thee, and all to his soul's reprief.°   450

378 **hereto** to this   379 **fain** glad   385 **me of to provide** to provide me with   389 **Good** wealth

412 **ever among** every now and then   429 **lesing** lying   436 **wite** blame on   443 **spill** destroy   448 **guise** custom, practice   450 **reprief** reproof

EVERYMAN.
O false Good, cursed may thou be,
Thou traitor to God, that hast deceived me
And caught me in thy snare!
GOODS.
Mary!° thou brought thyself in care,
455 Whereof I am right glad;
I must needs laugh, I cannot be sad.
EVERYMAN.
Ah, Good, thou hast had long my heartly° love;
I gave thee that which should be the Lord's above.
But wilt thou not go with me indeed?
460 I pray thee truth to say.
GOODS.
No, so God me speed!
Therefore farewell, and have good day.   [Exit Goods.]
EVERYMAN.
O, to whom shall I make my moan
For to go with me in that heavy journey?
465 First Fellowship said he would with me gone—
His words were very pleasant and gay,
But afterward he left me alone.
Then spake I to my kinsmen, all in despair,
And also they gave me words fair—
470 They lacked no fair speaking,
But all forsook me in the ending.
Then went I to my Goods, that I loved best,
In hope to have comfort, but there had I least;
For my Goods sharply did me tell
475 That he bringeth many into hell.
Then of myself I was ashamed,
And so I am worthy to be blamed.
Thus may I well myself hate.
Of whom shall I now counsel take?
480 I think that I shall never speed
Till that I go to my Good Deed.
But, alas, she is so weak
That she can neither go° nor speak.
Yet will I venture on her now.
485 My Good Deeds, where be you?

[Good Deeds speaks from the ground.]

GOOD DEEDS.
Here I lie, cold in the ground.
Thy sins hath me sore bound,
That I cannot stir.
EVERYMAN.
O Good Deeds, I stand in fear!
490 I must you pray of counsel,
For help now should come right well.
GOOD DEEDS.
Everyman, I have understanding

454 Mary By Mary (an expletive) 457 heartly hearty 483 go walk

That ye be summoned account to make
Before Messias, of Jerusalem King;
And you do by me,° that journey with you will I take.   495
EVERYMAN.
Therefore I come to you, my moan to make.
I pray you that ye will go with me.
GOOD DEEDS.
I would full fain, but I cannot stand, verily.
EVERYMAN.
Why, is there anything on you fall?
GOOD DEEDS.
Yea, sir, I may thank you of° all;   500
If ye had perfectly cheered me,
Your book of count full ready had be.
Look, the books of your works and deeds eke!°
Behold how they lie under the feet
To your soul's heaviness.   505
EVERYMAN.
Our Lord Jesus help me!
For one letter here I cannot see.
GOOD DEEDS.
There is a blind reckoning in time of distress.
EVERYMAN.
Good Deeds, I pray you help me in this need,
Or else I am for ever damned indeed;   510
Therefore help me to make reckoning
Before the Redeemer of all thing,
That King is, and was, and ever shall.
GOOD DEEDS.
Everyman, I am sorry of your fall,
And fain would I help you, and I were able.   515
EVERYMAN.
Good Deeds, your counsel I pray you give me.
GOOD DEEDS.
That shall I do verily;
Though that on my feet I may not go,
I have a sister that shall with you also,
Called Knowledge,° which shall with you abide,   520
To help you to make that dreadful reckoning.

[Enter Knowledge.]

KNOWLEDGE.
Everyman, I will go with thee, and be thy guide,
In thy most need to go by thy side.
EVERYMAN.
In good condition I am now in every thing,
And am wholly content with this good thing,   525
Thanked be God my creator.

495 And you do by me If you do as I advise 500 of for 503 eke also 520 Knowledge acknowledgement of sin, the first step to contrition (Knowledge is not scientific knowledge, but is knowledge of Christianity—the knowledge that tells us we are dependent on God's grace)

GOOD DEEDS.
　　And when she hath brought you there
　　Where thou shalt heal thee of thy smart,°
　　Then go you with your reckoning and your Good Deeds
　　together,
530　For to make you joyful at heart
　　Before the Blessed Trinity.
EVERYMAN.
　　My Good Deeds, gramercy!
　　I am well content, certainly,
　　With your words sweet.
KNOWLEDGE.
535　Now go we together lovingly
　　To Confession, that cleansing river.
EVERYMAN.
　　For joy I weep; I would we were there!
　　But, I pray you give me cognition
　　Where dwelleth that holy man, Confession?
KNOWLEDGE.
540　In the House of Salvation:
　　We shall find him in that place,
　　That shall us comfort, by God's grace.

[Knowledge leads Everyman to Confession.]

　　Lo, this is Confession. Kneel down and ask mercy,
　　For he is in good conceit° with God Almighty.
EVERYMAN.
545　O glorious fountain, that all uncleanness doth clarify,
　　Wash from me the spots of vice unclean,
　　That on me no sin may be seen.
　　I come with Knowledge for my redemption,
　　Redempt with heart and full contrition;
550　For I am commanded a pilgrimage to take,
　　And great accounts before God to make.
　　Now I pray you, Shrift,° mother of Salvation,
　　Help my Good Deeds for my piteous exclamation.
CONFESSION.
　　I know your sorrow well, Everyman.
555　Because with Knowledge ye come to me,
　　I will you comfort as well as I can,
　　And a precious jewel I will give thee,
　　Called penance, voider of adversity;
　　Therewith shall your body chastised be,
560　With abstinence and perseverance in God's service.
　　Here shall you receive that scourge of me,
　　Which is penance strong that ye must endure,
　　To remember thy Savior was scourged for thee
　　With sharp scourges, and suffered it patiently;
565　So must thou, ere thou scape that painful pilgrimage.
　　Knowledge, keep him in this voyage,
　　And by that time Good Deeds will be with thee.

But in any wise be siker° of mercy,
For your time draweth fast; and° ye will saved be,
Ask God mercy, and he will grant truly.　　　　　570
When with the scourge of penance man doth him° bind,
The oil of forgiveness then shall he find.
EVERYMAN.
　　Thanked be God for his gracious work!
　　For now I will my penance begin;
　　This hath rejoiced and lighted my heart,　　　　575
　　Though the knots be painful and hard within.
KNOWLEDGE.
　　Everyman, look your penance that ye fulfill,
　　What pain that ever it to you be;
　　And Knowledge shall give you counsel at will
　　How your account ye shall make clearly.　　　　580
EVERYMAN.
　　O eternal God, O heavenly figure,
　　O way of rightwiseness, O goodly vision,
　　Which descended down in a virgin pure
　　Because he would every man redeem,
　　Which Adam forfeited by his disobedience,　　　585
　　O blessed Godhead, elect and high divine,
　　Forgive my grievous offense;
　　Here I cry thee mercy in this presence.
　　O ghostly treasure, O ransomer and redeemer,
　　Of all the world hope and conductor,°　　　　590
　　Mirror of joy, and founder of mercy,
　　Which enlumineth heaven and earth thereby,
　　Hear my clamorous complaint, though it late be;
　　Receive my prayers, unworthy of thy benignity.
　　Though I be a sinner most abominable,　　　　595
　　Yet let my name be written in Moses' table.
　　O Mary, pray to the Maker of all thing,
　　Me for to help at my ending,
　　And save me from the power of my enemy,
　　For Death assaileth me strongly.　　　　　600
　　And, Lady, that I may by mean of thy prayer
　　Of your Son's glory to be partner,
　　By the means of his passion, I it crave.
　　I beseech you help my soul to save.
　　Knowledge, give me the scourge of penance;　　605
　　My flesh therewith shall give acquittance.°
　　I will now begin, if God give me grace.
KNOWLEDGE.
　　Everyman, God give you time and space!
　　Thus I bequeath you in the hands of our Savior.
　　Now may you make your reckoning sure.　　　610
EVERYMAN.
　　In the name of the Holy Trinity,
　　My body sore punished shall be.
　　Take this, body, for the sin of the flesh! *[Scourges himself.]*

---

528 smart pain　**544 good conceit** high esteem　**552 Shrift** Confession

568 siker certain　**569 and** if　**571 him** himself　**590 conductor** guide　**606 acquittance** atonement

Also thou delightest to go gay and fresh,
615 And in the way of damnation thou did me bring;
Therefore suffer now strokes of punishing.
Now of penance I will wade the water clear,
To save me from purgatory, that sharp fire.

[Good Deeds rises from the floor.]

GOOD DEEDS.
I thank God, now I can walk and go,
620 And am delivered of my sickness and woe.
Therefore with Everyman I will go, and not spare;
His good works I will help him to declare.
KNOWLEDGE.
Now, Everyman, be merry and glad!
Your Good Deeds cometh now; ye may not be sad.
625 Now is your Good Deeds whole and sound,
Going upright upon the ground.
EVERYMAN.
My heart is light, and shall be evermore;
Now will I smite faster than I did before.
GOOD DEEDS.
Everyman, pilgrim, my special friend,
630 Blessed be thou without end;
For thee is prepare° the eternal glory.
Ye have me made whole and sound,
Therefore I will bide by thee in every stound.°
EVERYMAN.
Welcome, my Good Deeds! Now I hear thy voice,
635 I weep for very sweetness of love.
KNOWLEDGE.
Be no more sad, but ever rejoice;
God seeth thy living in his throne above.
Put on this garment to thy behove,°
Which is wet with your tears,
640 Or else before God you may it miss,
When ye to your journey's end come shall.
EVERYMAN.
Gentle Knowledge, what do ye it call?
KNOWLEDGE.
It is a garment of sorrow;
From pain it will you borrow;°
645 Contrition it is,
That getteth forgiveness;
It pleaseth God passing well.
GOOD DEEDS.
Everyman, will you wear it for your heal?
EVERYMAN.
Now blessed be Jesu, Mary's Son,
650 For now have I on true contrition.
And let us go now without tarrying.
Good Deeds, have we clear our reckoning?

GOOD DEEDS.
Yea, indeed, I have here.
EVERYMAN.
Then I trust we need not fear.
Now, friends, let us not part in twain. 655
KNOWLEDGE.
Nay, Everyman, that will we not, certain.
GOOD DEEDS.
Yet must thou lead with thee
Three persons of great might.
EVERYMAN.
Who should they be?
GOOD DEEDS.
Discretion and Strength they hight,° 660
And thy Beauty may not abide behind.
KNOWLEDGE.
Also ye must call to mind
Your Five Wits° as for your counselors.
GOOD DEEDS.
You must have them ready at all hours.
EVERYMAN.
How shall I get them hither? 665
KNOWLEDGE.
You must call them all together,
And they will hear you incontinent.°
EVERYMAN.
My friends, come hither and be present,
Discretion, Strength, my Five Wits, and Beauty.

[Enter Beauty, Strength, Discretion, and Five Wits.]

BEAUTY.
Here at your will we be all ready. 670
What will ye that we should do?
GOOD DEEDS.
That ye would with Everyman go,
And help him in his pilgrimage.
Advise you, will ye with him or not in that voyage?
STRENGTH.
We will bring him all thither, 675
To his help and comfort, ye may believe me.
DISCRETION.
So will we go with him all together.
EVERYMAN.
Almighty God, loved may thou be!
I give thee laud that I have hither brought
Strength, Discretion, Beauty, and Five Wits. Lack I
nought. 680
And my Good Deeds, with Knowledge clear,
All be in my company at my will here.
I desire no more to° my business.

631 **preparate** prepared   633 **stound** moment (i.e., in every fierce attack)   638 **behove** benefit   644 **borrow** redeem

660 **hight** are called   663 **Five Wits** five physical senses (they are Everyman's "counselors" because they provide him with sensory data on which Discretion, that is, reason, operates)   667 **incontinent** immediately   683 **to** for

STRENGTH.
 And I, Strength, will by you stand in distress,
685 Though thou would in battle fight on the ground.
FIVE WITS.
 And though it were through the world round,
 We will not depart for sweet ne sour.
BEAUTY.
 No more will I unto death's hour,
 Whatsoever thereof befall.
DISCRETION.
690 Everyman, advise you° first of all;
 Go with a good advisement and deliberation.
 We all give you virtuous monition°
 That all shall be well.
EVERYMAN.
 My friends, harken what I will tell:
695 I pray God reward you in his heavenly sphere.
 Now harken, all that be here,
 For I will make my testament
 Here before you all present:
 In alms half my good I will give with my hands twain
700 In the way of charity with good intent,
 And the other half still shall remain
 In queth,° to be returned there° it ought to be.
 This I do in despite of the fiend of hell,
 To go quite out of his peril
705 Ever after and this day.
KNOWLEDGE.
 Everyman, harken what I say:
 Go to Priesthood, I you advise,
 And receive of him in any wise
 The holy sacrament and ointment together.
710 Then shortly see ye turn again hither;
 We will all abide you here.
FIVE WITS.
 Yea, Everyman, hie you that ye ready were.
 There is no emperor, king, duke, ne baron,
 That of God hath commission
715 As hath the least priest in the world being;°
 For of the blessed sacraments pure and benign
 He bareth the keys, and thereof hath the cure°
 For man's redemption—it is ever sure—
 Which God for our soul's medicine
720 Gave us out of his heart with great pain
 Here in this transitory life, for thee and me.
 The blessed sacraments seven there be:
 Baptism, confirmation, with priesthood good,
 And the sacrament of God's precious flesh and blood,
725 Marriage, the holy extreme unction, and penance.

These seven be good to have in remembrance,
Gracious sacraments of high divinity.
EVERYMAN.
 Fain would I receive that holy body,
 And meekly to my ghostly° father I will go.
FIVE WITS.
 Everyman, that is the best that ye can do. 730
 God will you to salvation bring,
 For priesthood exceedeth all other thing:
 To us Holy Scripture they do teach,
 And converteth man from sin heaven to reach;
 God hath to them more power given 735
 Than to any angel that is in heaven.
 With five words° he may consecrate,
 God's body in flesh and blood to make,
 And handleth his Maker between his hands.
 The priest bindeth and unbindeth all bands, 740
 Both in earth and in heaven.
 Thou ministers° all the sacraments seven;
 Though we kissed thy feet, thou were worthy;
 Thou art surgeon that cureth sin deadly;
 No remedy we find under God 745
 But all only° priesthood.
 Everyman, God gave priests that dignity,
 And setteth them in his stead among us to be.
 Thus be they above angels in degree.
  [Exit Everyman to receive the last sacraments from the
               priest.]

KNOWLEDGE.
 If priests be good, it is so,° surely. 750
 But when Jesus hanged on the cross with great smart,
 There he gave out of his blessed heart
 The same sacrament in great torment.
 He sold them not to us, that Lord omnipotent.
 Therefore Saint Peter the apostle doth say 755
 That Jesu's curse hath all they
 Which God their Savior do buy or sell,
 Or they for any money do take or tell.°
 Sinful priests giveth the sinners example bad;
 Their children sitteth by other men's fires, I have heard; 760
 And some haunteth women's company
 With unclean life, as lusts of lechery:
 These be with sin made blind.
FIVE WITS.
 I trust to God no such may we find.
 Therefore let us priesthood honor, 765
 And follow their doctrine for our souls' succor.
 We be their sheep, and they shepherds be,
 By whom we all be kept in surety.

690 **advise you** consider the matter **692 monition** admonition
702 queth bequest **there** where **715 being** living **717 cure**
charge, spiritual responsibility (with a pun on medical healing, indicated in 719)

729 **ghostly** spiritual **737 five words** *Hoc est enim corpus meum*
(For this is my body), from the sacrament of the Eucharist **742**
ministers administers **746 only** except **750 it is so** that is,
"above angels in degree" **758 tell** count

Peace, for yonder I see Everyman come,
770   Which hath made true satisfaction.
GOOD DEEDS.
   Methink it is he indeed.

[Re-enter Everyman.]

EVERYMAN.
   Now Jesu be your alder speed!°
   I have received the sacrament for my redemption,
   And then mine extreme unction.°
775   Blessed be all they that counseled me to take it!
   And now, friends, let us go without longer respite;
   I thank God that ye have tarried so long.
   Now set each of you on this rod° your hand,
   And shortly follow me.
780   I go before there° I would be; God be our guide!
STRENGTH.
   Everyman, we will not from you go
   Till ye have done this voyage long.
DISCRETION.
   I, Discretion, will bide by you also.
KNOWLEDGE.
   And though this pilgrimage be never so strong,°
785   I will never part you fro.
STRENGTH.
   Everyman, I will be as sure by thee
   As ever I did by Judas Maccabee.°

[They go together to the grave.]

EVERYMAN.
   Alas, I am so faint I may not stand;
   My limbs under me doth fold.
790   Friends, let us not turn again to this land,
   Not for all the world's gold;
   For into this cave must I creep
   And turn to earth, and there to sleep.
BEAUTY.
   What, into this grave? Alas!
EVERYMAN.
795   Yea, there shall ye consume, more and less.°
BEAUTY.
   And what, should I smother here?
EVERYMAN.
   Yea, by my faith, and never more appear.
   In this world live no more we shall,
   But in heaven before the highest Lord of all.
BEAUTY.
800   I cross out all this! Adieu, by Saint John!
   I take my cap in my lap, and am gone.

EVERYMAN.
   What, Beauty, whither will ye?
BEAUTY.
   Peace, I am deaf; I look not behind me,
   Not and thou wouldest give me all the gold in thy chest.
                                 [Exit Beauty.]
EVERYMAN.
   Alas, whereto may I trust?   805
   Beauty goeth fast away from me;
   She promised with me to live and die.
STRENGTH.
   Everyman, I will thee also forsake and deny;
   Thy game liketh° me not at all.
EVERYMAN.
   Why, then, ye will forsake me all?   810
   Sweet Strength, tarry a little space.
STRENGTH.
   Nay, sir, by the rood of grace!
   I will hie me from thee fast,
   Though thou weep till thy heart to-brast.°
EVERYMAN.
   Ye would ever bide by me, ye said.   815
STRENGTH.
   Yea, I have you far enough conveyed.
   Ye be old enough, I understand,
   Your pilgrimage to take on hand;
   I repent me that I hither came.
EVERYMAN.
   Strength, you to displease I am to blame;   820
   Yet promise is debt, this ye well wot.
STRENGTH.
   In faith, I care not.
   Thou are but a fool to complain;
   You spend your speech and waste your brain.
   Go, thrust thee into the ground!   825
                              [Exit Strength.]
EVERYMAN.
   I had wend surer I should you have found.
   He that trusteth in his Strength
   She him deceiveth at the length.
   Both Strength and Beauty forsaketh me;
   Yet they promised me fair and lovingly.   830
DISCRETION.
   Everyman, I will after Strength be gone;
   As for me, I will leave you alone.
EVERYMAN.
   Why, Discretion, will ye forsake me?
DISCRETION.
   Yea, in faith, I will go from thee,
   For when Strength goeth before   835
   I follow after evermore.

---

772 Now Jesu . . . speed Now may Jesus let you all prosper   **778 rod** cross   **780 there** where   **784 strong** hard   **787 Judas Maccabee** Judas Maccabeus, ancient Jewish leader noted for his military exploits   **795 more and less** high and low, that is, people of all ranks

809 liketh pleases   **814 to-brast** burst to pieces

EVERYMAN.
Yet, I pray thee, for the love of the Trinity,
Look in my grave once piteously.
DISCRETION.
Nay, so nigh will I not come;
840   Farewell, everyone!

                     [Exit Discretion.]
EVERYMAN.
O, all thing faileth, save God alone—
Beauty, Strength, and Discretion;
For when Death bloweth his blast,
They all run from me full fast.
FIVE WITS.
845   Everyman, my leave now of thee I take;
I will follow the other, for here I thee forsake.
EVERYMAN.
Alas, then may I wail and weep,
For I took you for my best friend.
FIVE WITS.
I will no longer thee keep;
850   Now farewell, and there an end.

                     [Exit Five Wits.]
EVERYMAN.
O Jesu, help! All hath forsaken me.
GOOD DEEDS.
Nay, Everyman; I will bide with thee.
I will not forsake thee indeed;
Thou shalt find me a good friend at need.
EVERYMAN.
855   Gramercy, Good Deeds! Now may I true friends see.
They have forsaken me, every one;
I loved them better than my Good Deeds alone.
Knowledge, will ye forsake me also?
KNOWLEDGE.
Yea, Everyman, when ye to Death shall go;
860   But not yet, for no manner of danger.
EVERYMAN.
Gramercy, Knowledge, with all my heart.
KNOWLEDGE.
Nay, yet I will not from hence depart
Till I see where ye shall be come.
EVERYMAN.
Methink, alas, that I must be gone
865   To make my reckoning and my debts pay,
For I see my time is nigh spent away.
Take example, all ye that this do hear or see,
How they that I loved best do forsake me,
Except my Good Deeds that bideth truly.
GOOD DEEDS.
870   All earthly things is but vanity:
Beauty, Strength, and Discretion do man forsake,
Foolish friends, and kinsmen, that fair spake—
All fleeth save Good Deeds, and that am I.
EVERYMAN.
Have mercy on me, God most mighty;

And stand by me, thou mother and maid, Holy Mary.   875
GOOD DEEDS.
Fear not; I will speak for thee.
EVERYMAN.
Here I cry God mercy.
GOOD DEEDS.
Short° our end, and minish° our pain;
Let us go and never come again.
EVERYMAN.
Into thy hands, Lord, my soul I commend;   880
Receive it, Lord, that it be not lost.
As thou me boughtest, so me defend,
And save me from the fiend's boast,
That I may appear with that blessed host
That shall be saved at the day of doom.   885
In manus tuas, of might's most
For ever, *commendo spiritum meum.*°
       [Everyman and Good Deeds descend into the grave.]
KNOWLEDGE.
Now hath he suffered that we all shall endure;
The Good Deeds shall make all sure.
Now hath he made ending.   890
Methinketh that I hear angels sing,
And make great joy and melody
Where Everyman's soul received shall be.

[Enter Angel.]

ANGEL.
Come, excellent elect spouse, to Jesu!
Here above thou shalt go   895
Because of thy singular virtue.
Now the soul is taken the body fro,
Thy reckoning is crystal clear.
Now shalt thou in to the heavenly sphere,
Unto the which all ye shall come   900
That liveth well before the day of doom.
                    [Exit Knowledge.]

[Enter Doctor of Theology.]

DOCTOR.
This moral men may have in mind.
Ye hearers, take it of worth,° old and young,
And forsake Pride, for he deceiveth you in the end;
And remember Beauty, Five Wits, Strength, and Discretion,
tion,   905
They all at the last do every man forsake,
Save° his Good Deeds there doth he take.
But beware, and they be small
Before God, he hath no help at all;

878 **Short** Shorten **minish** diminish   886–87 **In manus ... meum** "Into thy hands I commit my spirit"; Christ's last words, according to Luke 23.46   903 **take it of worth** value it   907 **Save** Only

910 None excuse may be there for every man.
Alas, how shall he do then?
For after death amends may no man make,
For then mercy and pity doth him forsake.
If his reckoning be not clear when he doth come,
915 God will say: "*Ite, maledicti, in ignem eternum.*"°
And he that hath his account whole and sound,
High in heaven he shall be crowned;

Unto which place God bring us all thither,
That we may live body and soul together.
Thereto help the Trinity!   920
Amen, say ye, for Saint Charity.

[Exit Doctor.]

THUS ENDETH THIS MORAL PLAY OF EVERYMAN.

915 Ite . . . eternum "Depart from me, ye cursed, into everlasting fire" (Christ's words in Matthew 25.41)

MANKIND

A N O N Y M O U S

THE CHARACTERS

MERCY	NEW GUISE
MANKIND	NOUGHT
MISCHIEF	NOW-A-DAYS
TITIVILLUS	

[Enter Mercy.]

MERCY. The very Founder and Beginner of our first
    creation,
  Among us sinful wretches He oweth to be magnified;
  That, for our disobedience, He had none indignation
  To send His own Son to be torn and crucified.
  Our obsequious service to Him should be applied:
  Where He was Lord of all, and made all thing of nought,
  For the sinful sinner, to have him revived,
  And, for his redemption, set His own Son at nought.
  That may be said and verified: Mankind was dear bought;
  By the piteous death of Jesu he had his remedy;
  He was purged of his default—that wretchedly had
    wrought—
  By His glorious passion, that blessed lavatory.
  O sovereigns! I beseech you your conditions to rectify;
  And, with humility and reverence, to have a remotion
  To this blessed Prince, that our nature doth glorify;
  That ye may be participable of His retribution.
  I have be[en] the very mean for your restituion:
  Mercy is my name, that mourneth for your offence.
  Divert not yourself in time of temptation,
  That ye may be acceptable to God at your going hence;
  The great mercy of God, that is of most preeminence,
  By meditation of our Lady, that is ever abundant
  To the sinful creature that will repent his negligence;
  I pray God, at your most need, that Mercy be your
    defendant.
  In good works I advise you, sovereigns! to be perseverant;
  To purify your souls that they be not corrupt;
  For your ghostly enemy will make his avaunt,
  Your good conditions if he may interrupt.
  O! ye sovereigns that sit, and ye brothern that stand right
    up,
  Pryke not your felicities in things transitory!
  Behold not the earth, but lift your eye up!
  See how the head the members daily do magnify.
  Who is the head? forsooth! I shall you certify:
  I mean our Saviour that was likened to a lamb;
  And His saints be the members, that daily He doth satisfy

With the precious river that runneth from His womb.
  There is none such food by water, nor by land;
  So precious, so glorious, so needful to our intent;
  For it hath dissolved Mankind from the bitter bond
  Of the mortal enemy, that venomous serpent:
  From the which, God preserve you all at the last judgment!
  For, sikerly, there shall be a strerat examination:
  The corn shall be saved; the chaff shall be brent—
  I beseech you heartily have this premeditation.

[Enter Mischief.]

MISCHIEF. I beseech you heartily leave your calculation!
  Leave your chaff! leave your corn! leave your dalliation!
  Your wit is little; your head is mickle; ye are full of predi-
    cation!
  But, sir! I pray [you] this question to clarify:
  Driff, draff! mish, mash!
  Some was corn, and some was chaff;
  My dame said my name was Raff.
  Unshut your lock and take an halfpenny!
MER. Why come ye hither, brother? ye were not desired.
MIS. For a winter corn thresher, sir! I have hired.
  And he said: the corn should be saved and the chaff
    should be fired;
  And he proveth nay, as it showeth by this verse;
  Corn serveth breadibus, chaff horsibus, straw firibusque.
  This is as much to say, to your lewd understanding,
  As: the corn shall serve to bread at the next baking;
    chaff horsibus, et reliqu[i]d,
  The chaff to horse shall be good produce;
  When a man is for-cold the straw may be brent;
  And so forth, etc.
MER. Avoid, good brother! ye been culpable
  To interrupt thus my talking delectable.
MIS. Sir! I have nother horse nor saddle;
  Therefore, I may not ride.
MER. Hie you forth on foot, brother! in God's name!
MIS. I say, sir! I am come hither to make you game;
  Yet, bade ye me not go out in the devil's name,
  And I will abide.

*[A leaf of the manuscript has probably been lost at this point.
  It commences again by the entry of New Guise, Nought,
  and Now-a-days with a band of minstrels.]*

NEW GUISE. And ho, minstrels! play the common trace;
  Lay on with thy bales till his belly brest!
NOUGHT. I put case: I break my neck—how than?
NEW G. I have no force, by saint Anne!
NOW-A-DAYS. Leap about lively! thou art a white man;
  Let us be merry while we be here!
NOUGHT. Shall I break my neck to show you sport?
NOW. Therefore, ever beware of thy report!
NOUGHT. I beshrew you all! here is a shrewd sort;
  Have there at them, with a merry cheer!
  [Here they dance. Mercy saith,]
MER. Do way! do way this revel, sirs! do way!
NOW. Do way, good Adam! do way!
  This is no part of thy play.
NOUGHT. Yes, marry! I pray you; for I love not this
    revelling;
  Come forth, good father! I you pray;
  By a little ye may assay.
  Anon, off with your clothes! if ye will pray.
  Go to! I have had a pretty scottling.
MER. Nay, brother! I will not dance;
NEW G. If ye will, sir! my brother will make you to prance.
NOW. With all my heart, sir! if I may you avance;
  Ye may assay by a little trance.
NOUGHT. Yea, sir! will ye do well?
  Trace not with them, by my counsel!
  For I have traced somewhat to fell;
  I tell [you] it is a narrow space.
  But, sir! I trow, of us three I heard you speak.
NEW G. Christ's curse have ye, therefore! for I was in sleep.
NOW. A[nd] I had the cup in my hand, ready to go to
    meat—
  Therefore, sir! curtly, greet you well!
MER. Few words! few, and well set!
NEW G. Sir! it is the new guise and the new jet.
  Many words and shortly set—
  This is the new guise every deal.
MER. Lady, help! how wretches delight in their simple
    ways!
NOW. Say no[ugh]t again the new guise now-[a-days!
  Thou shall find us sh[r]ews at all assays:
  Beware! ye may soon lick a buffet.
MER. He was well occupied that brought you hither!
NOUGHT. I heard you call New Guise, Now-a-days,
  Nought: all these three together.
  If he say that I lie, I shall make you to slither:
  Lo, take you here a trepitt!
MER. Say me your names! I know you not.
NEW G. [Now. and Nought. in turn.] New Guise, I! Now-a-
  days, [I]! I, Nought!
MER. By Jesu Christ! that me dear bought;
  Ye betray many men.
NEW G. Betray? nay, nay, sir! nay, nay!
  We make them both fresh and gay.

But, of your name, sir, I you pray!
  That we may you ken.
MER. Mercy is my name and my denomination.
  I conceive ye have but a little force in my communication.
NEW G. Ay, ay! your body is full of English Latin.
NOW. I pray you heartily, worshipful clerk!
  I have eaten a dishful of curds,
  And I have shitten your mouth full of turds.
  Now, open your satchel with Latin words,
  And say me this, in clerical manner:
  Also, I have a wife; her name is Rachael;
  Betwixt her and me was a great battle;
  And fain, of you, I would hear tell
  Who was the most master.
NOUGHT. Thy wife, Rachel, I dare lay twenty lice!
NOW. Who spake to thee? fool! thou art not wise;
  Go and do that longeth to thine office:
  Osculare fundamentum!
NOUGHT. Lo, master! here is a pardon by limit;
  It is granted of Pope Pockett:
  If ye will put your nose in his wife's socket,
  Ye shall have forty days of pardon.
MER. This idle language ye shall repent;
  Out of this place I would ye went.
NEW G. Go we hence, all three, with one assent;
  My father is irk of our eloquence;
  Therefore, I will no longer tarry.
  God bring you, master, and blessed Mary!
  To the number of the demonical frayry—
NOW. Come wind: come rain!
  Though I come never again;
  The devil put out both your eyne!
  Fellows! go we hence tight!
NOUGHT. Go we hence, a devil way!
  Here is the door; here is the way!
  Farewell, gentle Geoffrey!
  I pray God give you good night!   Exeunt.
MER. Thanked be God! we have a fair deliverance.
  Of these three unthrifty guests:
  They know full little what is their ordinance.
  I preve by reason they be worse than beasts:
  A beast doth after his natural institution;
  Ye may conceive, by their disport and behaviour,
  Their joy and delight is in derision.
  Of their own Christ, to His dishonour.
  This condition of living, it is prejudicial;
  Beware thereof! it is worse than any felony or treason.
  How may it be excused before the justice of all
  When, for every idle word, we must yield a reason?
  They have great ease; therefore, they will take no thought;
  But how then, when the angel of heaven shall blow the
    trump,
  And say to the transgressors that wickedly have wrought:
  "Come forth unto your Judge, and yield your account!"

Then shall I, Mercy begin sore to weep;
Nother comfort nor counsel, there shall none be had;
But, such as they have sown, such shall they reap;
They be wanton now; but, then, shall they be sad.
The good new guise, now-a-days, I will not disallow;
I discommend the vicious guise—I pray have me excused—
I need not to speak of it; your reason will tell it you:
Take that is to be taken, and leave that is to be refused!

[Enter Mankind.]

MANKIND. Of the earth and of the clay we have our propagation;
By the providence of God thus we be derived:
To whose mercy I recommend this whole congregation.
I hope unto His bliss ye be all predestinate:
Every man, for his degree, I trust shall be participate;
If he will mortify our carnal condition,
And our voluntary desires that ever be pervertionate—
To renounce these and yield us under God's provision.
My name is Mankind; I have my composition
Of a body and of a soul, of condition contrary.
Betwixt the twain of a great division:
He that should be s[u]bject, now he hath the victory.
This is to me a lamentable story:
To see my flesh, of my soul to have governance;
Where the good wife is master, the goodman may be sorry.
Alas! what was thy fortune and thy chance
To be associate with my flesh, that stinking dunghill?
Lady, help! Sovereigns! it doth my soul much ill
To see the flesh prosperous, and the soul trodden under foot.
I shall go to yonder man; and assay him I will;
I trust of ghostly solace he will be my boot.

[Mankind approaches Mercy.]

All hail, seemly father! ye be welcome to this house;
Of the very wisdom ye have participation.
My body with my soul is ever querulous;
I pray you, for Saint Charity! of your supportation.
I beseech you, heartily, of your ghostly comfort;
I am unsteadfast in living; my name is Mankind;
My ghostly enemy, the devil, will have a great disporte
In sinful guiding, if he may see me end.
MER. Christ send you good comfort! ye be welcome, my friend!
Stand up on your feet! I pray you, arise!
My name is Mercy; ye be to me full hend:
To eschew vice I will you advise.
MAN. O, Mercy! of all grace and virtue ye are the well:
I have heard tell, of right-worshipful clerks,
Ye be approximate to God and near of His counsel;
He hath institute you above all His works—
Oh! your lovely works to my soul are sweeter than honey.
MER. The temptation of the flesh ye must resist, like a man;
For, there is ever a battle betwixt and soul and the body:

Vita hominis est milicia super terram.
Oppress your ghostly enemy, and be Christ's own knight;
Be never a coward again your adversary;
If ye will be crowned, ye must needs fight!
Intend well; and God will be you[r] adjutory!
Remember, my friend! the time of continuance;
So, help me God! it is but a chery-time.
Spend it well! serve God with heart's affiance!
Distemper not your brain with good ale, nor with wine!
Measure is treasure; I forbid you not the use;
Measure yourself! ever beware of excess!
The superfluous guise, I will that ye refuse:
When nature is sufficed, anon that ye cease.
If a man have an horse, and keep him not too high,
He may then rule him at his own desire;
If he be fed over well he will disobey;
And in hap, cast his master in the mire.
NEW G. Ye say true, sir! ye are no faitour;
I have fed my wife so well till she is my master.
I have a great wound on my head; lo! and thereon layeth a plaster;
And another—there! I piss my peson.
And my wife were your horse, she would you all to-samne.
Ye feed your horse in measure: ye are a wise man!
I trow and ye were the king's palfry-man,
A good horse should be gesumme.
MAN. Where speaks this fellow? will he not come near?
MER. All too soon, my brother! I fear me for you.
He was here right now—by Him that bought me dear! —
With other of his fellows; they can much sorrow,
They will be here right soon, if I out depart.
Think on my doctrine! that shall be your defence;
Learn while I am here! set my words in heart!
Within a short space I must needs hence.

[Now-a-days and Nought return.]

NOW. The sooner the liever; and that be even anon!
I trow your name is Do-little—ye be so long from home;
If ye would go hence we shall come, everyone,
Mo than a good sort!
Ye have liever, I dare well say!
To them ye will go forth your way—
Men have little dainty of your play
Because ye make no sport.
NOUGHT. Your pottage shall be for-cold, sir! when will ye go dine?
I have seen a man lost twenty nobles in as little time;
Yet it was not I, by saint Quintin!
For I was never worth a potful a' worts sithen I was born.
My name is Nought; I love well to make merry;
I have be sithen with the common tapster of Bury.
I played so long the fool that I am even very weary:
Yet shall I be there again, to-morrow.   *Exeunt.*
MER. I have much care for you, my own friend!
Your enemies will be here anon; they make their avaunt.

Think well in your heart—your name is Mankind—
Be not unkind to God, I pray you! be His servant!
Be steadfast in condition! see ye be not variant!
Lose not, through folly, that is bought so dear.
God will prove you soon; and, if that ye be constant,
Of His bliss perpetual ye shall be partner.
Ye may not have your intent at your first desire;
See the great impatience of Job in tribulation:
Like as the smith trieth iron in the fire,
So was he tried by God's visitation.
He was of your nature, and of your fragility:
Follow the steps of him, my own sweet son!
And say, as he said, in your trouble and adversity:
Dominus dedit, Dominus abstulit, sicut sibi placuit; sit
   nomen Domini benedictum!
Moreover, in special, I give you in charge:
Beware of New Guise, Now-a-days and Nought!
Nice in their array, in language they be large;
To pervert your conditions all their means shall be sought.
Good son! intermise yourself not in their company!
They heard not a mass thi[s] twelvemonth, I dare well say;
Give them none audience! they will tell you many a lie;
Do truly your labour, and keep your holyday!
Beware of Titivillus—for he leseth no way—
That goeth invisible and will not be seen;
He will rond in your ear, and cast a net before your eyne;
He is worst of all: God let him never thene!
If ye displease God, ask mercy anon;
Else Mischief will be ready to brace you in his bridle.
Kiss me now, my dear darling! God shie[l]d you from
   your fone!
Do truly your labour, and be never idle!
The blessing of God be with you, and with all these
   worshipful men!
MAN. Amen! for saint Charity, Amen!
Now, blessed be Jesu! my soul is well satiate
With the mellifluous doctrine of this worshipful man.
The rebellion of my flesh, now it is superate.
Thanking be [to] God, of the cunning that I can.
Here will I sit, and tittle in this paper
The incomparable estate of my promotion.
Worshipful Sovereigns! I have written here
The glorious remembrance of my noble condition,
To have remo[r]se and memory of myself: thus written it is
To defend me from all superstitious charms:
Memento, homo, quod cinis es, et in cinerem reverteris.
Lo! I bear on my breast the badge of mine arms.

[New Guise enters, but remains in the background.]

NEW G. The weather is cold; God send us good fires!
Cum sancto sanctus eris, et cum perverso, per verteris.
Ecce quam bonum et quam jocundum, quod the devil to
  the friars,
Habitare fratres in unum.
MAN. I hear a fellow speak; with him I will not mell.

This earth with my space I shall assay to delve;
To eschew idleness I do that mine own self;
I pray God send it His fusion!

[Enter Now-a-days and Nought.]

NOW. Make room, sirs, for we have be long!
   We will come give you a Christmas song.
NOUGHT. Now, I pray all the yemandry, that is here,
   To sing with us with a merry cheer:

                           [Nought sings.]
   It is written with a coal, it is written with a coal—
NEW G. AND NOW. *It is written with a coal, it is written, etc.*
NOUGHT. *He that shitteth with his hole, he that shitteth with his*
   hole—
NEW G. [AND] NOW. *He that shitteth with his hole, etc.*
NOUGHT. *But he wipe his arse clean, but he, etc. —*
NEW G. [AND] NOW. *But he wipe his arse clean, but he, etc.*
NOUGHT. *On his breech it shall be seen, on his breech, etc.—*
NEW G.[AND] NOW. *On his breech it shall be seen, on his*
   breech, etc.
   Cantant omnes. Hoylyke, holyke, holyke! holyke, holyke,
   holyke!
NEW G. Hey, Mankind! God speed you with your spade!
   I shall tell you of a marriage:
   I would your mouth and his arse, that is made,
   Were married junctly together!
MAN. Hie you hence, fellows! with breeding;
   Leave our derision and your japing!
   I must needs labour; it is my living.
NOW. What, sir! we came but late hither—
   Shall all this corn grow here
   That he shall have the next year?
   If it be so, corn had need be dear;
   Else ye shall have a poor life.
NOUGHT. Alas, good father! this labour fretteth you to the
   bone;
   But, for your crop I take great moan;
   Ye shall never spend it alone—
   I shall assay to get you a wife.
   How many acres suppose ye here, by estimation?
NEW G. Hey! how ye turn the earth up and down!
   I have be, in my days, in many good town,
   Yet saw I never such another tilling!
MAN. Why stand ye idle? it is pity that ye were born!
NOW. We shall bargain with you; and nother mock nor
   scorn—
   Take a good cart in harvest, and load it with your corn,
   And what shall we give you for the leaving?
NOUGHT. He is a good, stark labourer; he would fain do
   well—
   He hath met with the good man, Mercy, in a shroud cell:
   For all this, he may have many a hungry meal.
   Yet, well ye see, he is politic:
   Here shall be good corn; he may not miss it;
   If he will have rain, he may overpiss it;

And if he will have compos[t] he may overbliss it
A little, with his arse like.
MAN. Go, and do your labour! God let you never thee!
Or, with my spade, I shall you ding, by the holy Trinity!
Have ye none other man to mock, but ever me?
Ye would have me of your set?
Hie you forth, lively! for hence I will you driffe!

[Mankind belabours them with his spade.]

NEW G. Alas, my jewels! I shall be shent of my wife!
NOW. Alas! and I am like never for to thrive;
I have such a buffet!
MAN. Hence, I say, New Guise, Now-a days, and Nought!
It was said beforn: all the means shall be sought
To pervert my conditions and bring me to nought—
Hence, thieves! ye have made many a leasing!
NOUGHT. Marred I was for cold, but now am I warm!
Ye are evil advised, sir! for ye have done harm.
By Cock's body sacred! I have such a pain in my arm
I may not change a man a farthing!
MAN. Now, I thank God, kneeling on my knee!
Blessed be His name! He is of high degree.
By the aid of His grace, that He hath sent me,
Three of mine enemies I have put to flight;
                                        [Shows his spade.]
Yet this instrument, sovereigns! is not made to defend—
David saith: *Nec in hasta, nec in gladio, saluat Dominus.*
NOUGHT. No, marry! I beshew you! it is in spadibus!
Therefore, Christ's curse come on your headibus,
To send you less might!
                                        [They go out.]
MAN. I promit you, these fellows will no more come here;
For some of them, certainly, were somewhat too near!
My father, Mercy, advised me to be of a good cheer,
And again my enemies manly for to fight.
I shall convict them, I hope, every one—
Yet I say amiss; I do it not alone—
With the help of the grace of God I resist my fone
And their malicious heart.
With my spade I will depart, my worship[f]ul sovereigns!
And live ever with labour, to correct my insolence.
I shall go fet corn for my land; I pray you of patience;
Right soon I shall revert.   [Exit.]

[Enter Mischief.]

MIS. Alas, alas! that ever I was wrought!
Alas! the while I [am] worse than nought!
Sithen I was here, by Him that me bought!
I am utterly undone!
I, Mischief, was here, at the beginning of the game,
And argued with Mercy; God gave him shame!
He hath taught Mankind, while I have be vane,
To fight manly again his fone;
For, with his spade—that was his weapon—

New Guise, Now-a-days, Nought hath [he] all to-beaten:
I have great pity to see them weeping.
Will ye list? I hear them cry!

[New Guise, Now-a-days, and Nought enter.]

Alas, alas! come hither! I shall be your borrow.
Alack; alack! *veni, veni!* Come hither, with sorrow!
Peace, fair babies! ye shall have a napple to-morrow:
Why greet you so, why?
NEW G. Alas, master! alas my privity!

[Commences to untruss.]

MIS. A! where? alack! fair babe, ba me!
Abide! too soon I shall it see!
NOW. Here, here! see my head, good master!
MIS. Lady, help! silly darling! *veni, veni!*
I shall help the of thy pain;
I shall smite off thy head, and set it on again.
NOUGHT. By our Lady, sir! a fair plaster!
Will ye off with his head? it is a shrewd charm!
As for me I have none harm;
I were loth to forbear mine arm.
Ye play: *in nomine Patris,* chop!
NEW G. Ye shall not chop my jewels, and I may!
NOW. Yea, Christ's cross! will ye smite my head away?
There! we're on anon; out! ye shall not assay—
I might well be called a fop!
MIS. I can chop it off, and make it again.
NEW G. I had a shrewd recumbentibus, but I feel no pain.
NOW. And my head is all safe and whole again.
Now, touching the matter of Mankind,
Let us have an interlection sithen ye be come hither;
It were good to have an end.
MIS. Ho, ho! a minstrel! know ye any aught?
NOUGHT. I can pipe on a Walsingham whistle, I, Nought,
Nought.
MIS. Blow apace! thou shall bring him in with a flowte.

[Titivillus roars from outside.]

TITIVILLUS. I come with my legs under me!
MIS. Ho! New Guise, Now-a-days, hark! or I go:
When our heads were together I spake of "Si didero."
NEW G. So! go thy way! we shall gather money unto;
Else there shall no man him see.
Now, ghostly to our purpose, worshipful sovereigns!
We intend to gather money, if it please your negligence,
For a man with a head that [is] of great omnipotence—
NOW. Keep your tail! in goodness, I pray you, good
brother! —
He is a worshipful man, sirs, saving your reverence!
He loveth no groats, nor pence, nor two pence;
Give us red royals if ye will see his abominable presence!
NEW G. Not so! ye that mow not pay the tone, pay the
tother—
At the good man of this house first we will assay!

God bless you, master! ye say us ill, yet ye will not say nay.
Let us go by and by, and do them pay!
Ye pay all alike? well mu[s]t ye fare!

NOUGHT. I say, New Guise, Now-a-days!
Estis vos pecuniatus?
I have cried a fair while, I beshrew your patus!

NOW. *Ita vere magister;* come forth now, your gatus!
He is a goodly man, sirs! make space and beware!

[Enter Titivillus dressed devilwise, net in hand.]

TITI. *Ego sum dominantium nominus,* and my name is
Titivillus!
Ye that have good horse, to you I say *Caveatis.*
Here is an able fellowship to trise him out at your gates.

[Loquitur ad New Guise.]

Ego probo sic: sir New Guise, lend me a penny!

NEW G. I have a great purse, sir! but I have no money:
By the mass! I fail two farthings of an half-penny;
Yet had I ten pounds this night that was.

[Loquitur ad Now-a-days.]

TITI. What is in thy purse? thou art a stout fellow!

NOW. The devil have [thee]! while I am a clean gentleman
I pray God I be never worse stored than I am!
It shall be otherwise, I hope, or this night pass.

[Loquitur ad Nought.]

TITI. Hark now, I say! thou hast many a penny?

NOUGHT. No[n] *nobis, Domine, non nobis:* by saint Denis!
The devil may dance in my purse for any penny;
It is as clean as a bird's arse.

TITI. Now I say, yet again, *Caveatis!*
Here is an able fellowship to trise them out of your gates.
Now, I say, New Guise, Now-a-days, and Nought,
Go and search the country, anon, that be sought!
Some here, some there—what if ye may catch aught—
If ye fail of horse, take what ye may else!

NEW G. Then speak to Mankind for the recumbentibus of
my jewels!

NOW. Remember my broken head in the worship of the
five vowels!

NOUGHT. Yea, good sir! and the sitica in my arm—

TITI. I know full well what Mankind did to you;
Mischief hat[h] informed [me] of all the matter through;
I shall venge your quarrel, I make God a vow!
Forth! and espy where ye may do harm!
Take W[illiam] Fide if ye will have any mo—
I say, New Guise! whither art thou advised to go?

NEW G. First, I shall begin at m[aster] Huntington of
Sanston;
From thence I shall go to William Thurlay of Hanston,
And so, forth to Pichard of Trumpington:
I will keep me to these three.

NOW. I shall go to William Baker of Walton;

To Richard Bollman of Gayton;
I shall spare Master Wood of Fulbourn:
He is a *noli-me-tangere!*

NOUGHT. I shall go to William Patrick of Massingham;
I shall spare Master Allington of Bottisham,
And Hammond of Swaftham,
For dread of *In manus tuas queck.*
Fellows, come forth! and go we hence together!

NEW G. Sith we shall go, let us see well where and whither;
If we may be take, we come no more hither;
Let us con well our neck-verse that we have not a check.

TITI. Go your way—a devil way—go your way, all!
I bless you with my left hand: foul you befall!
Come again, I warn, as soon as I you call,
A[nd] bring your advantage into this place!

[They go out and leave Titivillus.]

To speak with Mankind I will tarry here this tide,
And assay his good purpose for to set aside;
The good man, Mercy, shall no longer be his guide:
I shall make him to dance another trace!
Ever I go invisible—it is my jet—
And before his eye, thus, I will hang my net
To blench his sight; I hope to have his foot met.
To irk him of his labour I shall make a frame:
This board shall be hid under the earth, privily;
His space shall enter, I hope, unreadily.
By then he hath assayed he shall be very angry,
And lost his patience, pain of shame!
I shall menge his corn with drawk and with dranel;
It shall not be like to sow nor to sell—
Yonder he cometh: I pray of counsell;
He shall ween grace were wane.

[Enter Mankind.]

MAN. Now, God, of His mercy, send us of His sonde!
I have brought seed here to sow with my lond;
While I over-delve it, here it shall stond.
In nomine Patris, et Filii, et Spiritus sancti! now I will begin.
This land is so hard, it maketh unlusty and irk;
I shall sow my corn at winter, and let God work.
Alas! my corn is lost; here is a foul work!
I see well, by tilling, little shall I win;
Here I give up my spade, for now and for ever.

[Here Titivillus goes out with the spade.]

To occupy my body, I will not put me in dever;
I will hear my evensong here or I dissever.
This place I assign as for my kirk;
Here, in my kirk, I kneel on my knees:
Pater noster, qui es in celis—

[Enter Titivillus.]

TITI. I promise you I have no lead on my heels;
I am here again to make this fellow irk.

Whist! peace! I shall go to his ear and tittle therein—

[Goes to Mankind.]

A short prayer thirleth heaven—of thy prayer blin!
Thou art holier than ever was any of thy kin:
Arise, and avent thee! nature compels!
MAN. I will into thi[s] yard, sovereigns! and come again
    soon;
For dread of the colic, and eke of the stone,
I will go do that needs must be done;
My beads shall be here for whosomever will come.

[Mankind goes out.]

TITI. Mankind was busy in his prayer, yet I did him arise;
He is conveyed, by Christ! from his divine service.
Whither is he? trow ye? I-wis, I am wonder-wise:
I have sent him forth to shit lesings.
If ye have any silver, in hap pure brass,
Take a little pow[d]er of Paris and cast over his face;
And even in the owl-flight let him pass—
Titivillus can learn you many pretty things!
I trow Mankind will come again soon,
Or else, I fear me, evensong will be done:
His beades shall be triced aside, and that anon.
Ye shall [see] a good sport if ye will abide—
Mankind cometh again; well fare he!
I shall answer him ad omnia quare.
There shall he set abroach a clerical maller;
I hope of his purpose to set him aside.

[Re-enter Mankind.]

MAN. Evensong hath be in the saying, I trow, a fair while;
I am irk of it; it is too long by one mile.
Do way! I will no more, so oft, on the church
Be as it may, I shall do another.
Of labour and prayer, I am near irk of both; stile;
I will no more of it though Mercy be wroth.
My head is very heavy; I tell you, forsooth!
I shall sleep, full my belly and he were my brother.

[Mankind sleeps and snores.]

TITI. And ever ye did, for me keep now your silence!
Not a word! I charge you, pain of forty pence!
A praty game shall be showed you or ye go hence.
Ye may hear him snore; he is sad a-sleep.
Whist! peace! the devil is dead! I shall go rond in his ear:
Alas, Mankind, alas! Mercy [has] stolen a mare;
He is run away from his master, there wot no man where;
Moreover, he stale both a horse and a neat.
But yet, I heard say, he brake his neck as he rode in France;
But I think he rideth over the gallows, to learn for to dance,
Because of his theft: that is his governance.
Trust no more on him; he is a marred man!
Mickle sorrow with thy spade beforn thou hast wrought;

Arise, and ask mercy of New Guise, Now-a-days, and
    Nought!
They come! Advise thee for the best; let their good will
    be sought;
And thy own wife brethel, and take thee a leman!
Farewell, everyone! for I have done my game;
For I have brought Mankind to mischief and to shame.

[Titivillus goes out.]

MAN. Whoop! ho! Mercy hath broken his neckercher, a
    vows!
Or he hangeth by the neck high up on the gallows.
Adieu, fair master! I will haste me to the ale-house,
And speak with New Guise, Now-a-days, and Nought;
A[nd] get me a leman with a smattering face.

[Enter New Guise.]

NEW G. Make space! for Cock's body sacred, make space!
Aha! well on run! God gave him evil grace!
We were near saint Patrick's way, by Him that me bought!
I was twitched by the neck; the game was begun;
A grace was; the halter brast asunder—Ecce signum—
The half is about my neck: we had a near run!
"Beware!" quod the good wife when she smote off her
    husband's head—"beware!"
Mischief is a convict, for he could his neck-verse—
My body gave a swing when I hung upon the casse.
Alas! who will hang such a likely man, and a fierce,
For stealing of an horse? I pray God give him care!
Do way this halter! what [the] devil doth Mankind here?
    with sorrow! —
Alas, how my neck is sore, I make avow!
M[AN]. Ye be welcome, New Guise! Sir! what cheer with
    you?
NEW G. Well, sir! I have no cause to mourn.
M[AN]. What was there about your neck? so God you
    amend!
NEW G. In faith! saint Audrey's holy bend;
I have a little dishele, as it please God to send,
With a running ringworm.

[Enter Now-a-days.]

NOW. Stand, aroom! I pray thee, brother mine!
I have laboured all this night; when shall we go dine?
A church, here beside, shall pay for ale, bread, and wine;
Lo! here is stuff will serve.
NEW G. Now, by the holy Mary! thou art better merchant
    than I!

[Enter Nought.]

NOUGHT. Avaunt, knaves! let me go by!
I can not geet, and I should starve.

[Enter Mischief.]

MIS. Here cometh a man of arms; why stand ye so still?

Of murder and manslaughter I have my belly fill.
NOW. What, Mischief! have ye been in prison? and it be
    your will,
    Meseemeth ye have sco[u]red a pair of fetters.
MIS. I was chained by the arms; lo! I have them here.
    The chains I brast asunder and killed the jailor;
    Yea, and his fair wife halsed in a corner:
    A! how sweetly I kissed that sweet mouth of hers!
    When I had do, I was mine own bottler;
    I brought away with me both dish and doubler.
    Here is enou' for me: be of good cheer!
    Yet, well fare the new che[vi]sance!
MAN. I ask mercy of New Guise, Now-a-days, and Nought;
    Once, with my spade, I remember that I fought;
    I will make you amends if I hurt you aught,
    Or did any grievance.
NEW G. What a devil liketh thee to be of this disposition?
MAN. I dreamt Mercy was hang[ed]; this was my vision;
    And that, to you three, I should have recourse and remo-
    tion.
    Now, I pray you, heartily, of your good will;
    I cry you mercy of all that I did amiss!
NOW. [Aside.] I say, New Guise, Nought! Titivillus made all
    this;
    As siker as God is in heaven, so it is!
NOUGHT. Stand up on your feet! why stand ye so still?
NEW G. Master Mischief! we will you exhort,
    Mankind's name, in your book for to report.
MIS. I will not so! I will set a court—
    Ah! do it [in] forma juris d'hasard!

[Now-a-days make[th] proclamation.]

NOW. Oyez! oyez! oyez!
    All manner of men, and common women,
    To the Court of Mischief either come or send;
    Mankind shall return, he is one of our men!
MIS. Nought! come forth! thou shall be steward.
NEW G. Master Mischief! his side-gown may be sold;
    He may have a jacket thereof, and money told.
MAN. I will do for the best, so I have no cold.
    Hold! I pray you, and take it with you,
NOUGHT (scri[bit]). And let me have it again in any wise.
NEW G. I promise you a fresh jacket after the new guise.
MAN. Go! and do that longeth to your office;
    A[nd] spare that ye may!

[New Guise goeth out.]

NOUGHT. Hold, Master Mischief, and read this!
MIS. Here is blottibus in blottis,
    Blottorum blottibus istis:
    I beshrew your ears! a fair hand!
NOW. Yea! it is a good running fist;
    Such an hand may not be missed!   [Goes out.]
NOUGHT. I should have done better, had I wits.
MIS. Take heed, sirs, it stand you on hand!

Curia tenta generalis,
In a place—there good ale is!—
Anno regni regitalis.
Edwardi millatene,
On yestern-day in Febru'ry—the year passeth fully—
As Nought hath written—here is our Tulli,
Anno regni regis nulli.
NOW. What ho, New Guise! thou makest much [tarrying];
    That jacket shall not be worth a farthing.

[Re-enter New Guise.]

NEW G. Out of my way, sirs! for dread of fighting!
    Lo! here is a feat tail, light to leap about!
NOUGHT. It is not shapen worth a morsel of bread;
    There is too much cloth; it weighs as any lead.
    I shall go and mend it; else I will lose my head—
    Make space, sirs! let me go out!

[Nought goes out.]

MIS. Mankind, come hither! God send you the gout!
    Ye shall go to all the good fellows in the country about;
    Unto the good-wife when the good-man is out—
    "I will," say ye!
MAN. I will, sir!
NEW G. There arn'[t] but six deadly sins; lechery is none;
    As it may be verified by us brethels everyone.
    Ye shall go rob, steal, and kill, as fast as ye may gone—
    "I will," say ye!
MAN. I will, sir!
NOW. On Sundays, on the morrow, early betime,
    Ye shall with us to the ale-house early, to go dine;
    A[nd] forbear mass and matins, hours and prime—
    "I will," say ye!
M[AN]. I will, sir!
MIS. Ye must have by your side for a long da pacem,
    As true men ride by the way, for to unbrace them;
    Take their money, cut their throats; thus over face them—
    "I will," say ye!
MAN. I will, sir!

[Re-enter Nought.]

NOUGHT. Here is a jolly jacket—how say ye?
NEW G. It is a good jake of fence for a man's body—
    Hi, dog! hi! whoop, ho! go your way lightly!
    Ye are well made for to ren!
MIS. Tidings! tidings! I have espied one!
    Hence with your stuff! fast we were gone!
    I beshrew the last shall come to his home!
    Amen!

[Dicant omnes.]
[Enter Mercy.]

MER. What ho, Mankind! flee that fellowship, I you pray!
MAN. I shall speak with [thee] another time; to-morn or
    the next day.

[To the others.]

We shall go forth together to keep my father's year-day;
A tapster! a tapster! stow, statt, stow!

MIS. A mischief go with [thee]! here I have a foul fall.
Hence! away from me! or I shall beshit you all!

NEW G. What ho, ostler! lend us a foot-ball!
Whoop! ho! anow, anow, anow!

[They go out.]

MER. My mind is dispersed; my body tir-trimmeleth as the
aspen leaf;
The tears should trickle down by my cheeks, were not
your reverence!
It were to me solace, the cruel visitation of death!
Without rude behaviour, I can[not] express this inconve-
nience:
Weeping, sighing, and sobbing, were my sufficiance;
All natural nutriment, to me, as carene, is odible;
My inward affliction yieldeth me tedious unto your pres-
ence;
I cannot bear it evenly that Mankind is so flexible.
Man unkind, wherever thou be! for all this world was
not apprehensible
To discharge thine original offence, thraldom and captivity,
Till God's own well-beloved son was obedient and passible:
Every drop of His blood was shed to purge thine iniquity.
I discommend and disallow this often mutability!
To every creature thou art dispectuous and odible—
Why art thou so uncurtess, so inconsiderate? alas, woe is
me!
As the vane that turneth with the wind, so thou art con-
vertible!
In trust is treason: thy promise is not credible;
Thy perversious ingratitude I cannot rehearse;
To go over, to all the holy court of heaven thou art dis-
pectable,
As a noble versifier maketh mention in his verse:
"*Lex et natura, Christus en omnia jura*
Damnant ingratum; lugetur eum fore natum."
O, good Lady, and Mother of Mercy! have pity and com-
passion
Of the wretchedness of Mankind, that is so wanton and
so frail!
Let mercy exceed justice, dear Mother! admit this sup-
plication!
Equity to be laid over part[l]y, and mercy to prevail!
Too sensual living is reprovable, that is now-a-days,
As by the comprehence of this matter, it may be specified.
New Guise, Now-a-days, Nought, with their allectuous
ways.
They have perverted Mankind, my sweet son, I have
well espied.
A! with these cursed caitiffs, and I may, he shall not long
endure;
I, Mercy, his father ghostly, will proceed forth and do my
property.

Lady, help! this manner of living is a detestable pleasure;
Vanitas vanitatum: all is but a vanity!
Mercy shall never be convict of his uncurtess condition;
With weeping tears, by night and by day, I will go and
never cease.
Shall I not find him? Yes, I hope; now, God be my pro-
tection!
My predelict son! where be ye? Mankind! *Ubi es?*

[Mischief re-enters with his companions.]

MIS. My prepotent father! when ye sup, sup out your mess!
Ye are all to-gloried in your terms; ye make many a lesse.
Will ye hear? he cryeth over Mankind, *Ubi es?*

NEW G. Hic, hic, hic! hic, hic, hic! hic, hic!

That is to say: here! here! here! nigh dead in the crick.
If he will have him, go and seek, seek, seek!
Seek not over long, for losing of your mind!

NOW. If ye will have Mankind—ho, *domine, domine
domine* —
Ye must speak to the shrive for a *cepe coppus*;
Else ye must be fain to return with *non est inventus*.
How say ye, sir? my bolt is shot!

NOUGHT. I am doing of my needings; beware how ye shoot!
Fie, fie, fie! I have foul arrayed my foot!
Be wise for shooting with your tackles, for, God wot!
My foot is foully over-shit.

MIS. A parlement! a parlement! come forth, Nought,
behind!
A counsel, belive! I am afeared Mercy will him find.
How say ye? and what say ye? how shall we do with
Mankind?

NEW G. Tush, a fly's wing! will ye do well?
He weeneth Mercy were hung for stealing of a mare.
Mischief! go say to him that Mercy seeketh everywhere;
He will hang himself, I undertake, for fear.

MIS. I assent thereto; it is wittily said, and well.

NOW. I whip it in thy coat! anon it were done!
Now, saint Gabriel's mother save the clothes of thy shoon!
All the books in the world, if they had be undone,
Could not a counselled us bet.

*Hic exit Mischief [apparently meeting Mankind as he is
going out, and salutes him].*

MIS. Ho, Mankind! Come and speak with Mercy; he is
here, fast-by!

MAN. A rope! a rope! a rope! I am not worthy.

MIS. Anon, anon, anon! I have it here ready;
With a tree also that I have get.
Hold the tree, Now-a-days! Nought! take heed and be wise!

NEW G. Lo, Mankind! do as I do! this is thy new guise;
Give the rope just to thy neck: this is mine advice.

MIS. Help thyself, Nought! lo, Mercy is here!
He scareth us with a bales; we may no longer tarry.

NEW G. Queck, queck, queck! alas, my throat! I beshrew
you, marry!

A, Mercy! Christ's copped curse go with you, and saint
Davy!

Alas, my weasand! ye were somewhat too near!

[All but Mercy and Mankind go out.]

MER. Arise, my precious redempt son! ye be to me full dear.

He is so timorous; meseemeth his vital spirit doth expi[re].

MAN. Alas! I have to be bestially disposed; I dare not
appear;

To see your solicitous face, I am not worthy to desire.

MER. Your criminous complaint woundeth my heart as a
lance.

Dispose yourself meekly to ask mercy, and I will assent.

Yield me neither gold nor treasure, but your humble
obeisance,

The voluntary subjection of your heart, and I am content.

MAN. What! ask mercy yet once again? alas! it were a wild
petition.

Ever to offend, and ever to ask mercy—that is a puerility.

It is so abominable to rehearse my worst transgression;

I am not worth to have mercy, by no possibility.

MER. O, Mankind! my sing'ler solace! this is a lamentable
excuse!

The dolorous fears of my heart, how they begin to amount!

O, blessed Jesu! help thou this sinful sinner to redeem!

*Nam hæc est mutatio, dexteræ Excelsi; vertit Impios, et non
sunt.*

Arise! and ask mercy, Mankind! and be associated to me.

Thy death shall be my heaviness; alas! 'tis pity it should
be thus.

Thy obstinacy will exclude [thee] from the glorious per-
petuity.

Yet, for my love, ope thy lips and say, *Miserere me, Deus!*

MAN. The egal justice of God will not permit such a sinful
wretch

To be revived and restored again: it were impossible.

MER. The justice of God will, as I will, as Himself doth
precise:

Nolo mortem peccatoris, inquit, and if he will [be] reducible.

MAN. Then, mercy, good Mercy! what is a man without
mercy?

Little is our part of paradise were mercy ne where.

Good Mercy! excuse the inevitable objection of my
ghostly enemy;

The proverb saith: the truth tryeth thyself. Alas! I have
much care!

MER. God will not make you privy unto His last judgment:

Justice and equity shall be fortified, I will not deny;

Truth may not so cruelly proceed in his straight argument

But that mercy shall rule the matter, without controversy.

Arise now, and go with me in this deambulatory.

Incline your capacity; my doctrine is convenient.

Sin not in hope of mercy; that is a crime notory;

To trust overmuch in a prince, it is not expedient.

In hope, when we sin, ye think to have mercy—beware
of that adventure!

The good Lord said to the lecherous woman of Canaan—

The holy gospel is the authority, as we read in Scripture—

"Vade! et jam amplius noli peccare!"

Christ preserved this sinful woman taken in advoutry;

He said to her these words: "Go, and sin no more!"

So to you; Go, and sin no more! Beware of vain confidence of mercy!

Offend not a prince on trust of his favour! as I said before.

If ye feel yourself trapped in the snare of your ghostly
enemy,

Ask mercy anon: beware of the continuance!

While a wound is fresh it is proved curable by surgery;

That, if it proceed over long, it is cause of great grievance.

MAN. To ask mercy and to have—this is a liberal possession:

Shall this expeditious petition ever be allowed, as ye
have in sight?

MER. In this present life mercy is plenty, till death maketh
his division;

But when ye be go, *usque ad minimum quadranteum*—ye
sha[ll] reckon this right.

Ask mercy and have, while the body with the sou[l] hath
his annexion;

If ye tarry till your decease, ye may hap of your desire to
miss;

Be repentant here; trust not the hour of death; think on
this lesson:

Ecce nunc tempus acceptabile! ecce nunc dies salutis!

All the virtue in the wor[l]d, if ye might comprehend,

Your merits were not premiable to the bliss above;

Not to the lowli'st joy of heaven, of your proper effort to
ascend;

With Mercy ye may: I tell ye no fable—Scripture doth
prove.

MAN. O, Mercy! my suavious solace and singular recre-
atory!

My predelict special! ye are worthy to have my love;

For, without desert and means supplicatory,

Ye be compatient to my inexcusable reproof.

A! it swimmeth my heart to think how unwisely I have
wrought!

Titivily, that goeth invisible, hung his net before my eye;

And, by his fantastical visions, sedulously sought,

By New Guise, Now-a-days, Nought, caused me to obey.

MER. Mankind! ye were oblivious of my doctrine manitory;

I said before: Titivily would assay you a bront.

Before from henceforth of his fables delusory!

The proverb saith: *Jacula prefata minus ledunt.*

Ye have three adversaries—he is master of them all—

That is to say, the devil, the world, the flesh, and the fell;

The New Guise, Now-a-days, and Nought, the world we
may them call;

And, prope[r]ly, Titivilly signifies the fiend of hell;
The flesh, that is the unclean concupiscence of your body.
These be your three ghostly enemies in whom ye have
    put your confidence;
They brought you to Mischief to conclude your temporal
    glory:
As it hath be showed before this worship[f]ul audience.
Remember how ready I was to help you; from such I was
    not dangerous;
Wherefore, good son! abstain from sin evermore after this!
Ye may both save and spoil your soul, that is so precious:
Libere velle, libere velle! God may not deny, I wis.
Beware of Titivilly with his net, and of all his envious will;
Of your sinful delectation that grieveth your ghostly sub-
    stance:
Your body is your enemy: let him not have his will.
Take your leave when ye will; God send you good perse-
    verance!
[MAN]. Sith I shall depart, bless me, father! hence then I
    go—
    God send us all plenty of His great mercy!
MER. *Dominus custodi[a]t te ab omni malo!*
    In nomine Patris, et Filii, et Spiritus Sancti. Amen!
    -                               *Hic exit Mankind.*

EPILOGUE.

Worship[f]ul sovereigns! I have do my property;
Mankind is delivered by my several patrociny.
God preserve him from all wicked captivity;
And send him grace, his sensual conditions to mortify!
Now for His love, that for us received His humanity,
Search your conditions with due examination!
Think and remember: the world is but a vanity,
As it is proved daily by d[i]verse transmutation,
Mankind is wretched; he hath sufficient proof;
Therefore, God [keep] you all *per suam misericordiam,*
That ye may be pleyseris with the angels above,
And have to you portion *vitam eternam.*
Amen!

FINIS.

*O liber, si quis cui constas forte queretur, Hyngham, quem
monacho dices, super omnia consta[s].*

THE APPLE TREE
(ESBATEMENT VANDEN APPELBOOM)

A N O N Y M O U S

English translation by John Cartwright

C H A R A C T E R S
OPEN HEART, a peasant
STEADFAST FAITH, his wife
GOD
INSATIABLE, a pedlar
RECKLESS LIVING, a young man
LUSTY YOUTH, a young woman
DEATH
THE DEVIL

(*Enter Open Heart*)

OPEN HEART.
    Hey, Steadfast Faith!
STEADFAST FAITH.
                What is it, Open Heart?
OPEN HEART.
    Come out, I've never been so depressed.
STEADFAST FAITH.
    Don't be upset, I'm coming, dear.
OPEN HEART.
    Oh, Steadfast Faith!

(*Enter Steadfast Faith*)

STEADFAST FAITH.
             All right, let's hear.
OPEN HEART.
    God gives us nothing but troubles, I fear.
STEADFAST FAITH.
    What is it, husband?
OPEN HEART.
             It'll soon appear.
STEADFAST FAITH.
    What's that?
OPEN HEART.
        I've never been so depressed.
STEADFAST FAITH.
    But what's your problem, dear?
OPEN HEART.
               All my best
Turns into worst, and all my gaining
Turns into loss, but it's no use complaining.
My spirit is beaten into the ground.
STEADFAST FAITH.
    For God's sake, why?

OPEN HEART.
             Our goat is drowned,
Dear wife, that's why you heard me groan.
STEADFAST FAITH.
    Drowned?
OPEN HEART.
          Yes, drowned in a ditch, my own—
In the ditch in the field, and our calf as well.
STEADFAST FAITH.
    Then the balm of our life is gone, I can tell.
    Oh, you won't find anything sweeter
    Than the milk our little goat gave by the litre.
OPEN HEART.
    Ah, little goat, your milk was famous.
    Everyone will mourn you.
STEADFAST FAITH.
            And who can blame us?
OPEN HEART.
    And Lulu the lamb, with her little bell,
    Has been eaten by the wolf, I'm sorry to tell.
STEADFAST FAITH.
    Our Lulu?
OPEN HEART.
        That's right.
STEADFAST FAITH.
           My heart is breaking—
    I've never heard of such a taking.
OPEN HEART.
    That's true—and our goosey stuck his head
    In the barrel of bran, and choked himself dead.
    And now my wits are starting to go.
STEADFAST FAITH.
    Oh, God bless us! That's a hard blow.
    Is Popsy smothered? I'm knocked in a heap.
    And Lulu eaten? Now I must weep
    That all our beasts have lost their life.
    Oh, oh!
OPEN HEART.
        Oh, dearest wife,
    We're born to bad luck, that's clear as day.
STEADFAST FAITH.
    We must be patient.
OPEN HEART.
          That's easy to say,

But everything's gone, and we must go
Begging from door to door.
STEADFAST FAITH.

                      Not so—
We still have plenty of all we need.
OPEN HEART.
  We've had it.
STEADFAST FAITH.

            Be quiet, you wretch. Indeed
God will never forget his own.
OPEN HEART.
  Our children are starving—hear them moan!
Lulu, who gave sweet milk, is dead,
So what will they eat?
STEADFAST FAITH.

                 Come, use your head.
If God makes a mouth, he makes good bread,
And if he makes bread, he'll find us cheese.
If you think of that, you'll find heart's ease.
OPEN HEART.
  I'm Open Heart.
STEADFAST FAITH.

             Steadfast Faith is my name.
Though evil fate tries to make you tame,
Steadfast Faith will keep you from hurt—
God will save all, you can bet your shirt.
We still have our beautiful apple-tree,
With the finest fruit you ever could see,
Loads of them.
OPEN HEART.

           I know that's so.
Anyone seeing those apples grow
Lusts after them, that lovely tree.
STEADFAST FAITH.
  Don't worry dear. Wait and see—
Our tree will repay us all our sweat,
All who see it long to get
Its apples, they're so sweet and tasty.
It'll make us rich, dear.
OPEN HEART.

             Not so hasty—
There's one thing bothers me still, my sweet,
That is, our tree hangs over the street,
And people who come along, walking past,
When they see the apples hanging, fast
They're up in the tree and then, quite shameless,
They pick all our fruit.
STEADFAST FAITH.

            That's far from blameless.
OPEN HEART.
  They break down the fence, like any vandal,
And shake the apple-tree.
STEADFAST FAITH.

             What a scandal!
OPEN HEART.
  Then all the pigs come crashing in

And gobble the fruit up. We can't win—
The children will then have nothing to eat.
STEADFAST FAITH.
  Patience, Open Heart.
OPEN HEART.

            Oh yes, it's a treat
To suffer, Steadfast Faith.
STEADFAST FAITH.

             You'll have enough.
Trust in God's word.
OPEN HEART.

           Trust huff, trust puff!
How will that help me to get them back,
Those apples they're stealing by the pack?
The other day some rascal climbed the tree
And stuffed his bag full, all for free.
He was still up there when I came striding
To see what was up, and to give him a hiding.
When he saw me coming, he was so afraid
He fell out of the tree, and his wife, dismayed
Out of her wits, shrieked, "My man is dead!"
I was so embarrassed I lost my head
And crept away, leaving them the fruit.
Are you surprised that I don't give a hoot
For your chat? All that we ever get
Is bad luck.
STEADFAST FAITH.

          Patience now, my pet.
keep on in faith, and banish fear.
OPEN HEART.
  Oh apple-tree, oh apple-tree.
STEADFAST FAITH.

            The Lord is here
And everywhere—He showers His grace on men.
If you lose one apple, he'll give you ten.
Just have faith.
OPEN HEART.

        Ten apples for one?
STEADFAST FAITH.
  Yes, Open Heart.
OPEN HEART.

          His will be done
If He can manage a trick like that.
STEADFAST FAITH.
  Of course He can, you can bet your hat.
Now just suppose that our tree was bending
With loads of apples, never-ending
Through summer and winter, what would you say?
OPEN HEART.
  If that could happen, what a joyful day
I'd say it was.
STEADFAST FAITH.

         Get ready to cheer—
You'll eat apples in winter and summer right here.
OPEN HEART.
  Winter and summer?

STEADFAST FAITH.

      Yes, I guarantee,
If we have faith, God hears our plea,
For He's almighty.

OPEN HEART.

     If He's so smart
That summer and winter, through His art,
He can make apples grow, I'd say
That's true enough.

STEADFAST FAITH.

     That's just by the way:
Out of two grubby mittens, through his great forces,
He could make two young gentlemen riding horses;
And out of a milk-dish cracked in two
A girl driving a wagon, smiling at you.
He could make apple-tarts come raining down
Wherever we go.

OPEN HEART.

     God bless this town!
If God's so great He can do such things,
He can see that summer and winter brings
Fruit to our apple-tree, through His grace.

STEADFAST FAITH.

  That's quite true.

OPEN HEART.

     Oh, Steadfast Faith.
You make my heart leap up in my chest.

STEADFAST FAITH.

  Wait, Open Heart, that's not the best—
If we long for God truly, He won't refuse
To come to us now.

OPEN HEART.

     That's good news.
And what if we ask for God to appear
In His physical form?

STEADFAST FAITH.

     He'll be right here—
We are His children He'll come to see.

OPEN HEART.

  Let Him come then speedily.
I'll put out a chair for Him to sit.

STEADFAST FAITH.

  Do, Open Heart.

OPEN HEART.

     Let's hurry with it—
I'll put a cushion on it too.

STEADFAST FAITH.

  God wants no cushion.

OPEN HEART.

     I'm telling you,
Put out a cushion right away.
No cushion for God? That'll be the day!
He deserves all the honour we can give.

STEADFAST FAITH.

  He's where the saints in blessedness live,
And he's here below with beasts and men.

We might well love him.

OPEN HEART.

     From one apple to ten?
Then I'd certainly owe Him love.

(*Enter God*)

GOD.

  Well, my children?

OPEN HEART.

     Welcome, Lord from above,
All our worship to you is vowed.

STEADFAST FAITH.

  Merciful God.

OPEN HEART.

     Lord, you're not proud,
You're kind and loving, as all can see.

STEADFAST FAITH.

  You don't despise those in poverty,
Who often suffer hardship and pain.

OPEN HEART.

  He chose to be poor Himself, that's plain,
To find out what it's like down here.

STEADFAST FAITH.

  O gracious God.

OPEN HEART.

     Oh refuge dear,
Show us your mercy now, we pray.

STEADFAST FAITH.

  Look on us kindly, don't turn us away.

OPEN HEART.

  We ask you a prayer, on bended knee.

GOD.

  Ask what you like, it will come to be.

OPEN HEART.

  Great God almighty, we thank your grace.
I pray you lovingly in this place
That I through your mercy may be granted
That our fine tree that you see here planted
May be loaded with apples all year long,
And that anyone who climbs up to do me wrong
Will stay there sitting in the tree
Till I say the word.

GOD.

     Yes, I agree
For your steadfast faith, so be happy both.

STEADFAST FAITH.

  Praise the Lord's grace.

OPEN HEART.

     I'll take my oath
All joy and blessing is coming our way.

STEADFAST FAITH.

  Where is our Lord?

OPEN HEART.

     He's gone away
Without a greeting. Isn't that odd?

STEADFAST FAITH.

    That was badly done—we didn't offer God
    Even a mug of some good drink.

OPEN HEART.

    That's true, I think.
    He had such a nice familiar face;
    Next time we'll do better, in any case,
    Than this wasted chance.

STEADFAST FAITH.

                  I hope so, we'll see.

OPEN HEART.

    Let them come now to my apple-tree
    To pinch the fruit. Till I say the word,
    They'll never come down, but sit like a bird,
    No matter what tricks they think they'll try.

STEADFAST FAITH.

    It's our tree for sure.

OPEN HEART.

              We're rich till we die.
    Let's eat and drink and celebrate,
    Start while it's early, and feast till it's late.

(*Exeunt. Enter Insatiable, dressed like a pedlar, carrying a pack.*)

INSATIABLE.

    Oh Lord, how tired I am of drudging,
    From village to village always trudging.
    I'd rather be washing my dusty throttle,
    But what have I got? Kicks and blows, no bottle,
    No rest from my load. All I'm getting
    Is trouble. Phew! What a sweat I'm sweating!
    This pack feels like a ton of bricks.
    Oh Lord, apples! What apples! My heart pricks
    Me to climb at any price up this tree
    And quench my thirst with these apples for free.
    I'll leave my pack here, and without stopping
    Climb up and stuff my belly to popping,
    For I bet these apples are fine and tasty.

    (*Enter Open Heart and Steadfast Faith*)

OPEN HEART.

    So—you needn't plan to be hasty
    Getting down from there till you've paid for your meal.

STEADFAST FAITH.

    That'll teach him to grab and steal.
    Let's get back to our food and drink.

OPEN HEART.

    We've got him in clink!
    I'll take his pack to pay for our loss.

INSATIABLE.

    What beautiful fruit! Thanks, Lord on the cross.
    I'm slurping them fit to bust my jaw—
    That's fifty at least I've stuffed in my craw
    Of these fine apples. Oh, my rumbling gut!
    And my shirt's packed so full it will hardly shut.
    Time for me to be on my way.

    Hey! I can't get off. What can I say?
    Here I sit, trapped like a clod—
    What, am I nailed to this tree, my God?
    I think so, and my money gone too, more's the pity.

OPEN HEART.

    Don't you think he's sitting pretty?
    I bet he'll be singing another song
    Before he gets down, and that may be long.

(*Exeunt Open Heart and Steadfast Faith*)
(*Enter Reckless Living and Lusty Youth*)

RECKLESS LIVING.

    Oh Lusty Youth.

LUSTY YOUTH.

              Oh Reckless Living.

RECKLESS LIVING.

    Just look what beautiful apples are here.

LUSTY YOUTH.

    Oh Lord, are those apples there for the giving?

RECKLESS LIVING.

    Oh Lusty Youth.

LUSTY YOUTH.

           Yes, Reckless Living?

RECKLESS LIVING.

    No better apples.

LUSTY YOUTH.

           My heart's misgiving—
    I must have those lovely apples, I fear.

RECKLESS LIVING.

    Oh Lusty Youth.

LUSTY YOUTH.

           Yes, Reckless Living?

RECKLESS LIVING.

    Just look what beautiful apples are here.

LUSTY YOUTH.

    We have to have some.

RECKLESS LIVING.

             That's quite clear.
    We have to eat from this apple-tree.

LUSTY YOUTH.

    But there's a pedlar sitting there, see!
    He's gobbling as if the world's going to end.

RECKLESS LIVING.

    Ahoy, pedlar, hoy!

LUSTY YOUTH.

           Hey there, friend—
    Are you going to eat this tree quite bare?

RECKLESS LIVING.

    Leave some for us.

INSATIABLE.

           Climb up and share—
    Come and eat apples without a worry.

RECKLESS LIVING.

    I'll leave my jacket.

LUSTY YOUTH.
                    And my cloak. Come, hurry—
I have to eat apples now or burst.
RECKLESS LIVING.
   Climb up the ladder.
LUSTY YOUTH.
                    No, you go first—
I'll be right behind at your feet.
RECKLESS LIVING.
   What beautiful apples.
LUSTY YOUTH.
                    They're so sweet,
Better than Fancy Mac's, I'd say.
RECKLESS LIVING.
   Yes, or Granny Smiths, by a long way.
   I've never tasted such juicy sap.
LUSTY YOUTH.
   Tuck in, tuck in.
RECKLESS LIVING.
                    Shut your trap.
They're like sweet medicine to my heart.

(*Enter Open Heart and Steadfast Faith*)

OPEN HEART.
   Tuck in, go on, but I'll have my part.
   This cloak and jacket can pay your fine.
RECKLESS LIVING.
   Eat up, dear.
LUSTY YOUTH.
                    No, I resign—
I think my belly's going to explode.
OPEN HEART.
   Hey there, friends, shall I take what you owed
For wiping out all the apples I've got?
STEADFAST FAITH.
   Ai, apple-thieves!
OPEN HEART.
                    It's a criminal plot,
But you'll be sorry before you go.
LUSTY YOUTH.
   Oh no, help! This is a blow—
Here's the man who owns the tree.
Let's run away.
RECKLESS LIVING.
                    I can't budge, just see.
I must be bewitched, take my word.
LUSTY YOUTH.
   It's as if I'm tied to the tree, it's absurd—
I'm fixed to the spot like with sticking plaster.
RECKLESS LIVING.
   We'll have to stay here.
LUSTY YOUTH.
                    What a disaster!
We have to stay trapped on this tree.

INSATIABLE.
   I'd be sorry if they did better than me—
I can't move an arm or a leg, it's true.
RECKLESS LIVING.
   We've all landed in the same stew.
   Only he who's in it can feel it this way.
INSATIABLE.
   That's true, I'd say.
   I needn't ask, for I can feel it.
   Sharing trouble helps to heal it.
   But we're in it now, we must suffer the pain—
   After sunshine comes the rain

(*Enter Open Heart*)

OPEN HEART.
   Ai, what sickness! Oh God, show your grace!
   My limbs fail, my heart is quaking.
   My joy turns to sorrow before my face.
   Ai, what sickness! Oh God, show your grace!
   I'm quite bewildered, of hope there's no trace
   If now my thread of life is breaking.
   Ai, what sickness! Oh God, show your grace!
   My limbs fail, my heart is quaking.
   My body grows feeble, weak and shaking.
   I'm fading away, whatever I try.

(*Enter Death*)

DEATH.
   Prepare yourself. Open Heart, you must die.
OPEN HEART.
   Die? Oh Lord, fear makes me numb.
DEATH.
   Yes, die, for your time has come.
   Hasten now, and fear my blow.
OPEN HEART.
   Spare me, dear Death.
DEATH.
                    I may not, no.
You must pay your debts on earth right now.
OPEN HEART.
   For God's sake, then, will you allow
   One last wish? will you go to that tree
   And pick me an apple?
DEATH.
                    Because I see
   How you are suffering, I'll do that gladly.
OPEN HEART.
   If you don't, my death will go badly.
   Won't you hurry? Get it with haste.
DEATH. (*to the others*)
   I'll join these people and have a taste.
   Don't worry—no need to hold your breath.
INSATIABLE.
   Who's that coming?

LUSTY YOUTH.
>   My God, it's death!
May the Lord's power protect us all.
RECKLESS LIVING.
I'm dying of fright, I'm ready to bawl,
I see myself sitting in Beelzebub's lair.
LUSTY YOUTH.
What can we do?
RECKLESS LIVING.
>   I don't know, I declare.
My heart shrinks like a snail in its shell.
LUSTY YOUTH.
My pulse is beating like a bell,
making my eyes pop out of my head.
DEATH.
Now I have the apple as the man said,
I'll return to him as quick as I may.
Hey, what's all this? I can't get away.
I've been tricked—this is rare!
OPEN HEART.
Caught fish is best fish, you stay right there.
It won't help to struggle and fuss.
DEATH.
What a fraud!
OPEN HEART.
>   It's wasted on us.
You're subject to us now, be assured.
STEADFAST FAITH.
Stay there, apple thief.
OPEN HEART.
>   I'm quite cured
Of being hauled away by Death.
DEATH.
Please let me down!
STEADFAST FAITH.
>   Save your breath.
You won't get away from us, no matter how.
OPEN HEART.
There'll be no-one you'll bring to death from now.
From now on we're going to live for ever.
DEATH.
Let me down in God's name!
OPEN HEART.
>   Never.
You stay on that tree, it suits you fine.
We're off to make merry and wine and dine.

(*Exeunt Open Heart and Steadfast Faith*)
(*Enter the Devil*)

DEVIL.
Borra! Where has Death gone to?
I long to see him, whatever he's onto.
Have goblins eaten him up, I wonder,
Or has he crept in a mouse-hole, six feet under,
That there's no-one dying in the world?

But Lucifer's fury will be hurled
On all foolish creatures, wherever they hide.
So I must seek Death on every side.
Where shall I find him? Help, Lucifer's sweat!
I search around for what I can get.
But Modecax' dream is all that I see.
Hey! What's that in the apple-tree?
It's Death himself, that's quite clear.
O Death, what the devil are you doing there?
Not learning apple-farming, I hope?
DEATH.
Leave me in peace.
DEVIL.
>   How will you cope
With bringing death now and misery?
DEATH.
I can't find a way down from this tree.
DEVIL.
I'll get you down—I know the tricks.
And these creatures' necks I'll break like sticks.
DEATH.
Accursed spirit, that's not so easy.
INSATIABLE.
I'm terrified.
RECKLESS LIVING.
>   Fear makes me queasy.
I see we must die—that makes me numb.
LUSTY YOUTH.
O God, save us.
INSATIABLE.
>   O, the Devil has come.
I'm gong crazy—did you hear how he rants?
RECKLESS LIVING.
Veni Creator.
LUSTY YOUTH.
>   I'll piss in my pants.
Fear is drowning me like a tide.
INSATIABLE.
My heart is cracking.
RECKLESS LIVING.
>   I'm petrified.
Ave, credo, salus, I shake like a jelly.
My heart's going to fall right down through my belly.
I've never suffered worse than this hour.
DEVIL.
The life of Death depends on my power.
I'll get you down, whatever the cost.
Hey! By Modecax' sweat, my power is lost-
I can't skip or walk a yard
From this tree.
DEATH.
>   I too found it hard,
And no force can save us, o devil from Hell.

(*Enter Open Heart*)

OPEN HEART.
    Oh Steadfast Faith.

STEADFAST FAITH (*off*).
                   Yes, Open Heart?

OPEN HEART.
                          Look out, look well,
In our trap there, there's another rat.

STEADFAST FAITH.
    Is it worth anything?

OPEN HEART.
                  No doubt of that—
It's the Devil, come, it's quite a sight.

(*Enter Steadfast Faith*)

STEADFAST FAITH.
    Oh, I'm afraid.

OPEN HEART.
              Make a cross right
In front of you, and you're protected.

STEADFAST FAITH.
    Hellish spirit, this is unexpected.
What have you lost upon our tree
That you dare to climb it?

DEVIL.
                 Have pity on me,
Noble lord, let me go with speed.

DEATH.
    Let me down in God's name.

OPEN HEART.
                   That's a joke indeed.
You, Death, how long will you spare me here
Living on earth?

DEATH.
             Friend, without fear
You can go on living forty years free
If you'll let me down.

OPEN HEART.
              And you, accursed one, let's see.
What's your bribe? What's your defence?

DEVIL.
    I'll never tempt you to sin or offence.
Just let me fly back on my road.

OPEN HEART.
    And you, pedlar?

INSATIABLE.
             You can have my load
With pleasure, if you'll let me out of this trouble.

RECKLESS LIVING.
    You can have my jacket.

LUSTY YOUTH.
             And my cloak, at the double.
Dear noble lord, give me leave to go—
I'm nearly half-dead.

RECKLESS LIVING.
          I'm shaking also.

I've never been in such a state.

ALL.
    Let us down, dear friend!

OPEN HEART.
             No hurry, wait—
If you go, will you keep your promises duly
That you've promised here?

ALL.
             Yes sir, truly.

INSATIABLE.
    Dear noble lord, show us your grace.

OPEN HEART.
    I give you permission to leave this place
For any other that you desire,
But keep your promise.

DEVIL.
             Thanks, noble sire.
Borra, hach, hach, ha, just watch me go.

                                 (*Exit*)

DEATH.
    I thank God. He's arranged it so
That I've got down from that tree at last.

                                 (*Exit*)

LUSTY YOUTH.
    I may be scared, shaken and aghast,
But I'm alive, so I hardly mind.
But still, my cloak will stay behind.
Damn the apple-tree!

RECKLESS LIVING.
             Amen to that.
He took my jacket while I sat,
As a bonus—it makes me want to yell.

INSATIABLE.
    I've forfeited my pack as well.

LUSTY YOUTH.
    The foolish person, sad to tell,
Lives thoughtlessly, and ends in tears.

RECKLESS LIVING.
    Though things may sometimes start with cheers,
They end in groans and recrimination.

INSATIABLE.
    We earned our loss and our frustration
It's a clear example for you, my friends.

LUSTY YOUTH.
    If anyone climbs such a tree, and intends
To steal the fruit, by night or day,
They'll be on the watch, it'll happen this way.
But as for me, I'm sorry now.

INSATIABLE.
    Shared pain is half pain.

RECKLESS LIVING.
             We'll take a bow,
And hope you're happy with what you've seen.

Anonymous

LUSTY YOUTH.
   Take it with thanks if you've grasped what we mean.
   Accept the efforts we've made for the art
   We love and serve.
RECKLESS LIVING.
               And for our part,
   To serve our art is to serve you all.
LUSTY YOUTH.
   Our powers are weak.

RECKLESS LIVING.
                   But, great or small,
   The spirit is joyful, not mean or base.
INSATIABLE.
   Take it with thanks.
LUSTY YOUTH.
              May God of His grace
Watch over you, that the Devil not hurt you,
And grant you bliss, good health, and virtue.

THE EUROPEAN RENAISSANCE

Artistic and Cultural Events

c. 1315–1500:
Plays modeled on Roman dramas and comedies written in Latin in Italy

1486:
Vetruvius's *De Architectura* advances scene design

1504:
Michaelangelo completes *David*

1521:
Ariosto's *The Casket,* the first vernacular drama in Italy

1539:
Dutch adaptation of *Everyman*

1545:
Serlio's treatise on architecture and scene painting

1561:
Hans Sachs' comedies in Germany

1585:
Teatro Olympico opens in Italy

1597:
Peri's *Dafne,* first opera

1611:
Scala publishes *commedia dell'arte* scenarios

1618:
Teatro Farnese opens in Italy; first proscenium arch theater in Europe

1633:
Oberammergau passion play begins

| 1300 C.E. | 1400 C.E. | 1500 C.E. | 1600 C.E. |

Historical and Political Events

Beginnings of Italian Renaissance

1450:
Gutenberg's printing press

1453:
Constantinople falls to Turks

1478:
Medici family controls Florence

1492:
Columbus's expeditions

1517:
Martin Luther begins Protestant reformation

1519:
Magellan circumnavigates the globe

1545:
Council of Trent

1588:
England defeats the Spanish Armada

1642:
Galileo dies

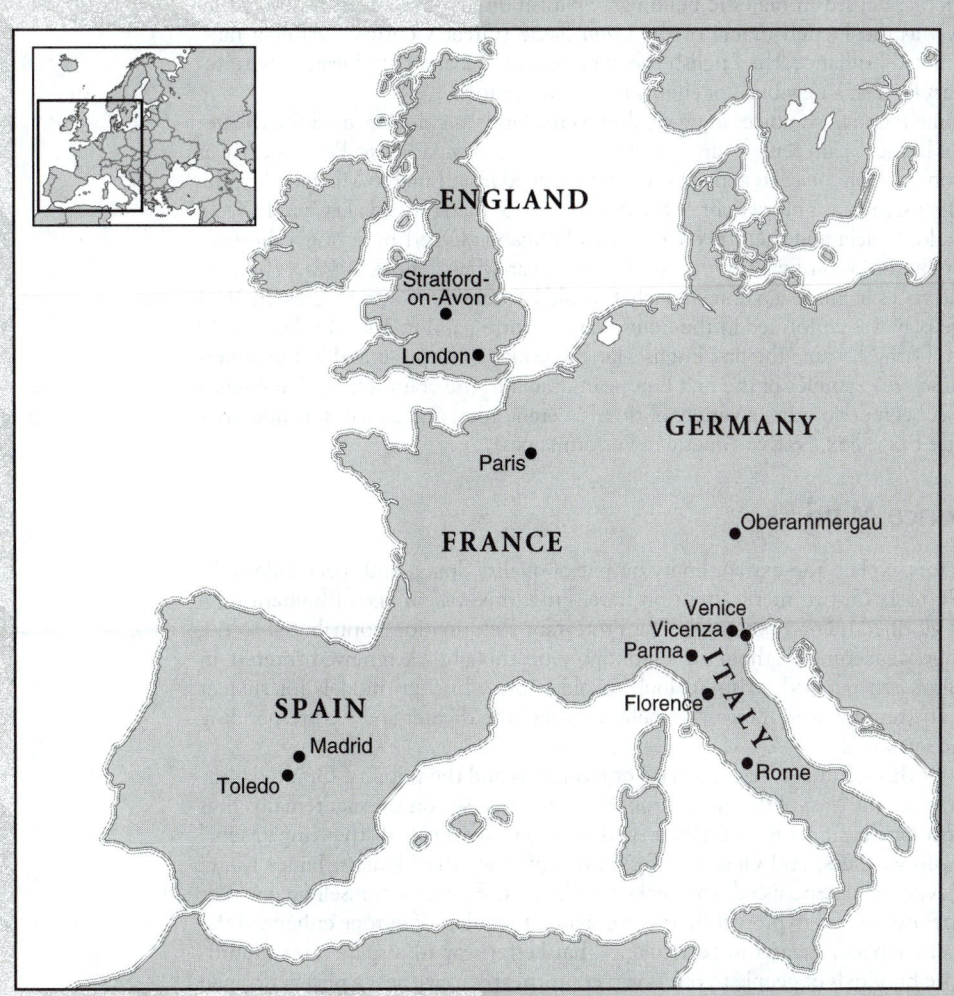

In a roughly hundred-year span—from 1576, when the first public theater was erected in England, to 1675, when France and Spain were enjoying their finest dramas—Western theater achieved perhaps its greatest artistry on all levels. This was the age of exceptional playwrights, as well as the heyday of the Italian street comedy (see Center Stage box, *Commedia dell'arte*). Scenic splendor and stage machinery emerged as a principal reason to attend the theater as drama moved indoors, housed in majestic buildings. Spanish drama reveled in its *Siglo d'Oro* (Golden Century), as did French drama of the *Gran Siècle* (Great Century). After a half-century of unparalleled brilliance, the English theaters were closed amid civil war, only to re-open eighteen years later in a new burst of energy in the Restoration.

European drama found fresh voices in newly discovered lands as colonists used the theater to remind them of home. Spain sent its first professional acting companies to Peru as early as the 1520s, and soon Spanish *comedias* and *autos* were performed from Lima to Mexico City, the birthplace of the first significant playwright of the Americas, Sor Juana Inés de la Cruz. In 1598 Spanish conquistadors celebrated their trek across the Chihuahua Desert by acting a short *comedia*, written for the occasion by Farfan de los Gobos, near what is now El Paso, Texas—among the first instances of European drama in what would become the United States. In 1604 a French-language play was performed in the Louisiana territories, and in 1665 *Ye Bare and Ye Cubbe*, by William Darby, became the first English-language play to be presented in the American colonies. These are examples of the first European drama in the colonies; Native Americans had, of course, been performing a variety of rituals, ceremonies, and dances for thousands of years (see Center Stage box, Native American Performances).

The Renaissance Mind

Though many factors explain the extraordinary output of quality drama and spectacular production from 1576 to 1675, two merit attention here. First, this was an age of humanism, a time when artists glorified human potential. The Protestant Reformation contributed to the humanist revival by weakening Catholicism's monopoly on thought. A renewed interest in Greco-Roman culture encouraged artists to look to older, pre-Christian models for subject matter and style. The result was an increased secularization of the theater and a corresponding emphasis on life in *this* world.

Second, theater thrived under the patronage of monarchs and the nobility. Granted, self-aggrandizement was not the least of the motivations for royal largesse. Yet the fact remains that Shakespeare and Molière each wrote—and flourished in—companies called "the King's Men." Sebastiano Serlio, Inigo Jones, and Giacomo Torelli designed for the Medicis, James I, and Louis XIV, respectively, while Spanish drama peaked under King Felipe IV, himself an amateur actor. To glorify themselves and to protect their power bases, the rulers of Europe enhanced the quality of the arts in general, theater in particular. What better way to display one's munificence than to invite hundreds of people to one's own court theater to witness a play performed by the country's finest actors amid the grandest spectacle one could imagine? In the ducal palaces of Italy, at Whitehall in London, at Louis XIV's retreat at Versailles, and at Felipe IV's Palacio Buen Retiro in Madrid, theater flourished (see Center Stage box, The Masque).

Although the powerful contributed to the growth of the theater, we must also remember that this was the age in which capitalism and the free market system were born. Shakespeare's company might indeed have been the King's Men, but it had to compete with other companies vying for audiences on the South Bank of London. Much of the dynamic in Renaissance drama was generated by a need to serve two masters simultaneously—royalty and the emerging middle-class theater patron.

Like the society it mirrored, Renaissance theater represented a synthesis of religion, the new humanism, royal politics, and changing economic structures. The worldview—one of several competing philosophies that shaped Renaissance thought—is perhaps best understood within the context of *The Great Chain of Being*. Originally a medieval concept, it was adapted for more secular uses during the Renaissance to sustain political hierarchies. The Chain of Being depicted the totality of creation as an interlinked chain with the Divinity at the highest end and nonliving matter (i.e., a grain of sand) at the other. Below God on this vertical chain

CENTER STAGE   *COMMEDIA DELL'ARTE*

Although the *commedia dell'arte* cannot be counted among the great literary movements in the history of theater, it is among the most influential and colorful. From Watteau to Picasso, commedia actors have long been among the favorite subjects of artists; no prephotographic period in Western theater history is as well documented in artwork as is the *commedia*. (The Kabuki theater enjoys a similar status in Japan.) The improvised antics of wandering street players of Renaissance Italy have given us many words that are commonplace in our daily lives: *harlequin, domino, zany,* and, most notably, *slapstick*. The writings of Molière, Lope de Vega, and Shakespeare show the discernible influence of the Italian comedians. Modern actors and directors such as Stanislavsky, Chaplin, Reinhardt, and Brook admit indebtedness to the improvisational style of the *commedia*.

The various names associated with Italian street theater suggest its salient features:

- *commedia dell'arte* ("comedy of the guild or by professionals in the art"; art here means not only "artistry" but "savoir faire")
- *commedia improvisa* ("improvised comedy")
- *commedia non scrita* ("unscripted comedy")
- *commedia a mascera* ("masked comedy")
- *commedia dell'arte all'improviso* ("professional improvised comedy")

Commedia may thus be defined as a form of comedy which, unlike the formal, scripted, aristocratic comedies of the Italian courts and learning academies, was performed by professional comedians in the streets of Renaissance Italy. Such artists were professionals in that they depended on the generosity of their audiences for their livelihood. But textbook definitions cannot begin to capture the essence of these street performances, which remain among the West's most significant examples of populist theater.

Despite scholarly debate as to its origins, the resemblance between the street comedy of sixteenth-century Italy and that of the ancient world are undeniable. Roving bands of comedians entertained ancient Greeks with improvised performances, and even Thespis—the so-called first tragic actor—traveled from town to town, like Sustarion before him, with a wagonload of white-faced vagabonds who performed comedy with music. The *hilarodi* of ancient Greece were famed for their ability to improvise farcical bits of comedy from loosely constructed scenarios, as were the Roman *lenones* (or "flatfeet," so named because they did not wear the

Pantalone's Serenade depicts old Pantalone attempting to impress an attractive young inamorata while Arlecchino—in his traditional diamond suit—laughs at his folly.

(continued)

tragic buskins). The Italian province of Atella was renowned for its farces, frequently performed at harvest time, which bear a resemblance to the subsequent *commedia* plays. Two centuries before Christ, Plautus, the father of popular entertainment in the West, wrote comedies for Roman workingmen containing situations and character types found throughout the *commedia*. The *commedia* as we know it took root in late-fifteenth-century Italy, and blossomed in the sixteenth and seventeenth centuries (Molière shared a theater with an Italian company in Paris in the mid–seventeenth century), and slowly decayed into little more than obscene, predictable street performances when Carlo Goldoni (1707–1792) and Carlo Gozzi (1720–1806) attempted to rescue it by the mid–eighteenth century.

A typical *commedia* company consisted of some twelve to fifteen *maschere* ("maskers"), each of whom played well-honed roles befitting their age, talent, and physical type. Two elderly men (the lecherous, greedy Pantalone and the pedantic Doctor), two servants (the witty Arlecchino, or Harlequin, and the wicked Brighella), a sassy maidservant (Columbina or Smeraldina), a bragging military man (the Capitano), and at least two pair of *inamorati* (lovers) formed the nucleus of the company. These were augmented by various *zanni* (clowns, musicians, acrobats) who played minor roles and occasionally took center stage when the imaginations of the traditional characters flagged.

The company arrived in a town square towing their properties in wooden carts; they announced their presence with song, dances, and comical physical feats to attract crowds. The players set up a makeshift theater on a mountebank stage: a raised platform with a curtained backdrop. The properties of these itinerant companies were necessarily few and purely functional: a bench, a chair, a trunk, musical instruments, perhaps a monkey, and a chest of brightly colored drapes.

The artistic success of the company—not to mention its livelihood—depended almost entirely on the acting rather than the scenarios or stage effects. The Italian comedians developed a unique spirit of camaraderie in their playing, not unlike a vaudeville act like Abbott and Costello, which produced an impressive ensemble. *Commedia* actors had to meet demands rarely encountered in more conventional theater forms. They were obliged to be acrobats, dancers, orators—men and women of extraordinary imagination grounded in a thorough knowledge of human nature. Their stage movement was spirited, often violent, and acrobatic; their verbal ingenuity was uncanny.

Though they relied on their imaginations to improvise a witty speech, the comedians were guided by a *scenario*, a brief outline of each scene and of what each actor was expected to do in it. Gozzi tells us that such *scenari* were "written entirely on a small slip of paper and posted under a little light in the wings for greater convenience of the troupe." Prior to the performance, the company manager (*il guido maestro*), who usually composed the scenario, read the outline to the company. The plots were familiar to actors and audiences alike: young lovers, frustrated by imposing parents or guardians, are aided in their love quest by conniving servants.

Each actor kept a *zibbaldoni*, or "commonplace book," which contained hundreds of phrases, jokes, and set speeches that could be readily adapted to virtually any comic situation. These comic speeches, collectively known as *concetti*, were described by a seventeenth-century actor, Niccolo Barbieri, who noted that each actor was "stored with phrases, declarations of love, reproaches, deliriums, and despairs." According to the type of role he played, an actor's *zibbaldoni* also contained boasts, obscene jokes, angry tirades, streams of wild oaths, and occasionally gibberish. For instance, the Doctor specialized in riddling couplets, gnomic aphorisms, and burlesque prescriptions, and punctuated by nonsensical Latin. The young lovers excelled in mythological tirades and classical quotations.

Of all the trappings of the *commedia dell'arte*, perhaps the *lazzi*—physical stage business—are the most intriguing. These hilarious stage antics have been preserved in the performances of circus clowns, vaudevillians, and silent film comedians. Because it depended on visual humor, *lazzi* became the foundation of a *commedia* performance. According to tradition, the word *lazzi* was derived from a Lombard pronunciation of the Tuscan "*lacci*," which meant "ribbon" or "laces." It may also mean "knots" because the stage business "tied" the plot strands together. In addition to producing laughter, *lazzi* fulfilled several functions in the telling of a *commedia* tale: an actor would resort to *lazzi* whenever a scene began to lag or his eloquence gave out. *Zanni* kept the audience amused with their *lazzi* as the ever-active troupe caught its collective breath.

Other cultures have also produced *commedia*-like theatrics, a testimony to the universality of clowning and comic theater. The Cherokee of North America, for instance, developed the Booger Dance, an example of clowning that predates European contact. Later, it was altered to make the European invaders the objects of satire. Masked "boogers," or non–Native Americans, invaded an all-night dance party, playfully hitting spectators, grabbing women, breaking wind, acting deranged. Asked their identity, they broke wind and gave nonsensical, obscene answers. Hopi clowns were especially noted for their parodies of fertility rites in the pueblos, as were the Chapayekas described in the Yaqui Easter ceremony. The skeleton dancers of Mexico's *Día de los Muertos* attempt to laugh death away with their improvised clowning in the cemeteries (see Chapter 9). Devil figures in the medieval cycle plays were more often comic than fearsome. The Chinese folk play *Picking Turnips* (described in the Center Stage box, A Night at the Chinese Opera), features a traditional clown, known as a *ch'ou*, whom sixteenth-century Italians would instantly recognize as Arlecchino's Asian cousin. Most cultures, in fact, offer a variant on this wily underling, or trickster. The Germans call him Hanswurst or Peter Pickleherring; the French know him as Scapin; and to the British he is Punch. He is also prevalent in folktales from myriad cultures: the Coyote stories of Native Americans, the Monkey King of the Far East, and B'rer Rabbit in the American South. The Italian *commedia dell'arte*, however, remains as the theater's most noteworthy example of improvised clowning and comic chaos.

CENTER STAGE   NATIVE AMERICAN PERFORMANCE

Through film and television portrayals—which are not necessarily accurate—you are familiar with some types of performance by Native Americans, many of which are rooted in communal celebrations and ancient rituals of cosmic significance. Because the indigenous peoples of North America belonged to literally hundreds of nations, each with its own language and customs, performances by Native Americans are diverse and cannot be neatly categorized. They are as rich and varied as the culture itself.

Among the best-known performance rituals of Native Americans (though similar examples may be found in other cultures) is the so-called rain dance, in which dancers imitate the action of falling rain in the hope that nature itself will imitate them and send rain. Among the oldest forms of performance impulse known to humans, this is called *sympathetic* (or *homeopathic*)

magic. Other dances, such as the Hopi Corn Dance or the Sioux Buffalo Dance, also are rooted in sympathetic magic. Healing and curative dances and songs were also common; a shaman or other healer attempted to drive impurities from a sick body through the performance of dances, chants, and prayer. After the massacre of Native Americans at Wounded Knee (Christmas Day, 1890), an Indian seer named Black Elk had a vision in which native peoples would reclaim their land. And, it must be stressed, Black Elk did not merely tell his people of his vision; he performed it through a dance that is still repeated by Native Americans. The Ghost Dance is, in essence, a communal healing dance. Again, we see that cleansing and catharsis are integral elements of ritual and the drama that evolved from it.

Storytelling, either as highly polished one-person dramas or improvisa-

tions by shamans, is also central to Native American performances. The Navajo of the southwest United States developed *chantways*, 100-hour performances involving entire communities that carefully planned every aspect of this storytelling ritual. The Pawnee of the northern Plains danced the Hako, a three-day ceremony performed for Mother Corn under the direction of a single person (the *kurahus*) entrusted with the "memory" of the ceremony. The dance gave promise of children and longevity and established a social bond among the various elements within the nation. The Hako was performed by one group—collectively known as the Father—for the benefit of another, the Son. The structure of the Hako was not unlike that of the medieval cycle plays because it comprised many rituals, each complete unto itself. Yet each unit was related to a controlling idea, and the combined rituals formed an unbroken

Native Americans used clowning, as well as solemn dances, in their ceremonies. These costumes, worn by the Hopi tribe of the western United States, bear a striking similarity to the traditional motley of clowns throughout the world.

(continued)

465

sequence that, in the mind of the Pawnee, formed a cosmic whole.

While we often think of Native American dances, rituals, and ceremonies as austere and solemn occasions, they often contained comedic elements. The Cherokee Booger Dance typifies clowning dances found among Native Americans. Though its roots can be traced to pre-Columbian times, the dance changed with the arrival of white settlers who were made the objects of satire. A company of masked men—the "boogers," representing non-Indians—invaded a dance party in a raucous display of stumbling, striking spectators, grabbing women, acting insane, and laughing. Asked to identify themselves, the dancers farted and gave nonsensical names such as Black Buttocks and Big Testicles, or they imitated the guttural sounds of the white invaders. They also abducted women and carried them away from the performance site. The dancers often wore gourds about their loins, reminiscent of the *phalli* of the classical theater of Greece. Elders, who proclaimed they were peaceable and nonviolent, drove off the boogers and restored order to the Pawnee nation.

Today a Native American theater does exist, though its development was seriously curtailed by a long history of anti-Indian policies. As early as 1646 the Massachusetts Bay Colony prohibited curing ceremonies among the indigenous peoples, and in 1865 the Office of Indian Affairs issued a proclamation outlawing "any (religious) dance . . . and frequent or prolonged periods of celebration . . . any disorderly or plainly excessive performance that promotes superstitious cruelty, licentiousness, idleness, danger to health, and shiftless indifference to family welfare." While such ignorant legislation has been eradicated, barriers that inhibit the development of a truly Native American theater remain, most notably the confinement of many Indians to reservations.

There have been admirable attempts to foster both traditional and contemporary theater and drama by Native Americans. In 1972 Hanay Geiogamah founded the Native American Theatre Ensemble to develop traditional myths and plays that would restore ethnic pride in Indian audiences; today Geiogamah heads the American Indian Dance Theatre, which regularly performs work from an intertribal repertory. In 1975 three women of the Cuna/Rappahannock nation formed the Spiderwoman Theatre, a combination of Native American and feminist theater. Spiderwoman is the Hopi goddess of creation noted for her weaving, and thus this innovative company weaves traditional stories into performance pieces that fuse indigenous rites with Western practice. One of Spiderwoman's most noted pieces was *Lysistrata Numbah*, an updating of the Aristophanic comedy. The company also creates works such as *Winnetou's Snake-Oil Show from Wigwam City*, a caustic satire that exposes the treatment of Native Americans in general, and women in particular.

were angels, below them humanity, followed by the animal kingdom, plants, and so on. Smaller chains extended horizontally from each link: ranked categories of angels, for example, formed hierarchies. The chain called *humanitas* had its series of links, with the king or queen in superior positions, followed by other nobles, an upper class, a middle class, common laborers, and ultimately beggars at the lower extreme. Shakespeare had some fun with this precept in *Hamlet* (4.2): The prince tells Claudius that "a man may fish with the worm that hath eat of a king, and eat of the fish that hath fed of that worm," all of which shows "how a king may go a progress through the guts of a beggar." Hamlet, like so many Renaissance artists, was keenly aware that Death was the sole being truly indifferent to one's place on the chain.

King Lear speaks of the "little world of man" (3.1.10), yet another reference to an integral aspect of Renaissance thought. Each person, king or beggar, was a microcosm of the larger world, and thus all people were monarchs unto themselves and thus charged with the responsibility of ruling wisely. Just as a hierarchy existed in the greater cosmos, so, too, one's body had a hierarchical structure. The intellect, which elevated humans above beasts, was preeminent, with the passions and biological drives subservient to the mind. Thus when passion rules—as it does for Sigismund in *Life's a Dream*—chaos follows.

The Need for Order

Renaissance artists were acutely aware of the presence of chaos in their ostensibly ideal world. The chain of being suggested order and harmony for all of creation, and thus it was used to validate the so-called divine right of kings. But human greed, jealousy, and ambition often provoked lesser beings to climb upward. The majority of the era's plays explore the turmoil that results from "vaulting ambition." In one of Shakespeare's lesser-known plays, *Troilus and Cressida* (1607), Ulysses, commander of the Greek army, argues that the Trojan War has thrown the

CENTER STAGE   THE MASQUE

If one of its key elements is spectacle, then the theater certainly reached its height in purely visual terms during the Renaissance, with the Italian *intermezzi* and the English court masques. No expense was spared to ensure that the masquers and their audiences reveled in opulent splendor. In addition to their entertainment value, masques became a primary means by which monarchs and nobles displayed their wealth and power through the politics of conspicuous consumption. The court masque contributed in no small way to the English civil war: it was cited by commoners and Puritans as examples of royal decadence and fiscal irresponsibility.

On the evening of January 6, 1512, Henry VIII and nine courtly companions celebrated Twelfth Night, the official end of the Christmas season, by dressing themselves in elaborate costumes to "invade" the English court, where they shocked the ladies by asking them to dance. The women demurely refused the masked gentlemen's requests because they had heard scandalous stories about licentious wit at the Italian

courts, where courtiers participated in spectacular entertainments (*intermezzi*) performed between courses of a banquet. Historian Edward Hall, who described the events in Henry's court, wrote that this "maske" was "a thyne not seen afore in England." Actually, masquelike activities appeared in England as early as 1377, when 130 Londoners donned the costumes of devils, knights, and clerical figures such as priests, bishops, and even the pope himself. These maskers gamboled to Prince Richard's retreat at Kennington, where they entertained the future king, who was so charmed by their merrymaking that he joined their revelry. In 1501 Prince Arthur's marriage to Catherine of Aragon was celebrated with dances and pageants, and the great hall at Westminster was adorned with spectacular scenery, including a castle housing eight maidens and a sailing ship carrying eight knights. Whether the English masque can be dated from Kennington, Westminster, or Henry's court is of less importance than recognizing that royal entertainments played an integral part in shaping the history of Eng-

lish theater.

Originally, interludes (England), *intermezzi* (Italy), *entreméses* (Spain), and *entremets* (France) were brief skits or dialogues, often allegorical, devised to entertain royalty and the wealthy between courses at lengthy banquets (which might last eight to ten hours). Songs and dances, frequently derived from rustic agricultural festivals, were added to the playlets. In fifteenth-century Italian courts *intermezzi* were performed as part of pastoral plays about shepherds and woodland nymphs. Eventually these expanded into extravaganzas portraying classical themes with lavish scenery, costumes, and lighting effects. The country's finest composers and musicians were hired to orchestrate these spectacles, and poets, actors, and dancers added their artistry. Thus *intermezzi* evolved into a full-blown theater genre unto itself.

Consider a famous example of an *intermezzo*. To celebrate the marriage of Lucrezia Borgia to the son of the Duke of Ferrara, the Pope himself hosted a banquet at which an allegorical drama about the alliance between Ferrara and Rome

Bernardo Buontalenti's design for The Harmony of the Spheres *(1589) illustrates the grand spectacle that epitomized the* intermezzi *and masques at Renaissance courts.*

(continued)

was presented. Royal couples participated in masked dancing, led by no less than the powerful Cesare Borgia. The duke returned the Pope's favor (to best him?) by arranging an entertainment for the newlyweds in Ferrara. It included a dance of savages around the figure of a beautiful woman who was saved by the triumphant arrival of the god of love, accompanied by a full orchestra of musicians. As Eros set the maiden free, a large model of the globe split in half to reveal twelve Swiss guards performing a military dance with full weaponry.

Word of such extravaganzas soon reached England, where the vainglorious Henry determined to dazzle his court with comparable entertainments. When Hall described the masque at Henry's court, he dutifully noted that all was done "after the manner of Italie." Masques—to use the French spelling, which did not come into vogue until the early seventeenth century—continued throughout the reigns of Henry VIII and his daughter, Elizabeth I, who enjoyed expensive court entertainments despite her reputation for frugality. In particular, Elizabeth enjoyed masques that portrayed various trades such as fishmongers, farmers, and mariners. In 1591 the gentlemen of Gray's Inn presented a masque at Elizabeth's court entitled *Proteus and the Adamantine Rock*, which became the prototype of subsequent court entertainments.

One might compare the unfolding of a masque to the unwrapping of an exotic gift in which many layers are exposed one at a time, each more colorful and elaborate than the previous one. Masques were customarily "one-shot" affairs, often consuming a full year's resources of time, money, and labor; hence, there was a sense of a ritual unfolding in these meticulously planned spectacles. They traditionally began with an introductory song and, beginning with Elizabeth's reign, a "presenter" (or master of ceremonies), whose poetic speech set the tone and theme of the events to follow. This was followed by the entry of the masquers, a magnificent procession in resplendent costumes. A series of dances, derived from popular social dances of the day, alternated with stories drawn from classical mythology. Not surprisingly, they emphasized the restorative powers of the reigning mon-

archs, who were compared to the deities of antiquity. After a final song, dance, and perhaps a bit of dialogue, the masquers were carried away, often via cloud machines that hoisted them into the heavens. Professional actors were hired to recite the dialogue, but the dances and nonspeaking roles were usually played by courtiers and, on occasion, the royalty. Queen Anne, wife of James I, was a frequent participant, as were Charles I, his wife Henrietta Maria, and their children. There is evidence that the actor who played Ariel in Shakespeare's last play, *The Tempest* (1612), wore a costume designed specifically for James's son, the duke of York, who had appeared in a masque at Whitehall.

The masque was elevated as an artistic enterprise when poet-playwright Ben Jonson assumed the status of royal masquer for James in 1603. The scholarly Jonson believed the masque should be a dramatic poem based on classical learning. He devised a unified piece in which poet, designer, and musicians collaborated to achieve a single vision. Jonson's intentions were undermined, however, when he feuded with Inigo Jones, who designed scenery and costumes for the Stuart court. Jones, who argued for the supremacy of the visual elements, turned Charles and Henrietta Maria against Jonson, who lost his position as court poet, a development that marked the beginning of the decline of the masque in England.

In addition to his unparalleled poetry, perhaps Jonson's greatest contribution to the masque was the development of the so-called antimasque. In 1609, at Queen Anne's request, Jonson wrote *The Masque of Queens Celebrated from the House of Fame*, in which he sought to bring novelty to the performance by inserting a grotesque parody of the traditional masque. Every manner of fiendish character (witches, monsters, and devils) cavorted to the delight of the audience in this antimasque, which became a staple of future court revels.

Under Charles and Henrietta Maria the masques degenerated into flimsy excuses for ingenious displays of scenography and a variety of dances that had little relationship to one another. For those outside the palace walls, the masques became a loathed symbol of court decadence. Ironically, the final masque at the

court of Charles I, *Salmacida Spolia* (1640), depicted a violent storm in which a Fury challenged evil spirits to "bring discord throughout England."

At their height, the masques were a powerful tool for reinforcing the authority of the monarchy. They asserted the divine right of kings by equating royalty with the gods themselves. The god-kings were invariably idealized as beneficent, protective beings who brought prosperity and harmony to their subjects. As people became more critical of the monarchy, the masques only enforced the notion that kingship was about artifice and false shows of power and glory.

Masques are more than a curiosity from the royal theater of the Renaissance. They influenced much of the high-quality literature of the era. Many romances, such as Beaumont and Fletcher's *The Faithful Shepardess*, and Shakespeare's later plays, *The Winter's Tale* and *The Tempest*, contain masques within their dramatic construction. In *The Tempest*, Prospero calls up the goddesses of fertility (Juno, Iris, Ceres) to bless the wedding of Miranda and Ferdinand; elsewhere the miscreants who would overthrow Prospero are tormented and chased by strange, frightening beings in what Shakespeare intended to be an antimasque. A number of the Jacobean tragedies used antimasques, most notably Webster's *The Duchess of Malfi*, which features a horrific scene in which the Duchess is tormented by the criminally insane.

Not only did the masque affect the structure of late Renaissance drama, but to some degree grand opera, the operetta, and even the modern musical theater retain an element of the Renaissance masques in their scenic splendor. For example, *Cats* has an essentially masquelike construction: it is a series of colorful dances performed by mythological cats against spectacular scenery. It even ends with Deuteronomy, King of Cats, escorting Grizabella into the heavens atop a floating tire—a modern variant on the cloud machine. Charity balls, presidential inaugurals, coronations, and other major civic events often use theatrical embellishments we associate with masques. Though monarchs may not preside over them (beauty queens aside), they give us some sense of the spirit of the Renaissance masque.

Mediterranean world into disarray. He cites an example from nature to illustrate his point; the phrase that is not italicized is a variant on the chain-of-being metaphor:

> *The heavens themselves, the planets, and this centre*
>
> *Observe degree, priority, and place*
>
> . . . .
>
> *. . . But when the planets*
>
> *In evil mixture to disorder wander,*
>
> *What plagues, and what portents, what mutiny,*
>
> *What raging of the sea, shaking of the earth,*
>
> *Commotion of the winds, frights, changes, horrors,*
>
> *Divert and crack, rend and deracinate*
>
> *The unity and married calm of states*
>
> *Quite from their future? O, when degree is shaked,*
>
> Which *is the ladder of all high designs,*
>
> *The enterprise is sick. . . .*
>
> *Take but degree away, untune the string,*
>
> *And hark what discord follows.*
>
> (1.3.75 ff.)

Hierarchies Onstage and Off

As might be expected, Renaissance-era plays feature protagonists who are royalty (Hamlet), who are of high birth (the Duchess of Malfi), or who have acquired power (Othello). Even the comedies—which traditionally center on middle-class life—feature the specter of royalty controlling events. Note that it is the King's Officer who intervenes to save Orgon and his family in *Tartuffe*, less a contrived ending than a nod to the beneficence of Louis XIV. Playwrights portrayed the dilemmas of the royal and upper classes because they were (as they remain today) a source of fascination for audiences and because the fall of the mighty served as a powerful lesson for lesser mortals. Witnessing the catastrophes of kings and queens reinforced the belief that each man and woman was a "little kingdom" that must be ruled with wisdom and temperance. As Sigismund says at the conclusion of *Life's a Dream*, a play about the proper uses of public and personal kingship:

> *Since I would be a conqueror*
>
> *I see I must first*
>
> *Make a conquest of myself.*

Quickly scan the Cast of Characters prefacing each Renaissance play, especially the tragedies. You will note that the characters are listed not in order of dramatic importance, nor in order of appearance. In this age, playwrights customarily listed characters in a strict hierarchical order that reflected the society in which they lived. Women are listed separately from—and only after—the male roles, a reflection of the patriarchal societies depicted in the plays.

Another manifestation of the hierarchical nature of the drama can be found in the final speech of each play. Note that invariably it is the highest-ranking person onstage who, quite literally, gets the last word. In Shakespeare's tragedies, it is the new sovereign who speaks, a symbol of the new order that will emerge from the chaos. Hence, Fortinbras speaks last in *Hamlet*. Such formality carries into comedy as well. In *A Midsummer Night's Dream* Shakespeare gives each of the reigning powers—Duke Theseus and King Oberon—a final speech. We can, however, note a subtle shift in *Tartuffe* and Aphra Behn's *The Rover*, in which members of the middle class deliver the final speeches. Commoners, enriched by world exploration and new economic opportunities, were clearly emerging as a power in society and in the theater, onstage and off.

The Role of Tragedy

The exploration of the Americas and the Far East was an important by-product of the strong monarchies that dominated Europe. Royalty, who sought to enrich their coffers, kingdoms, and egos, financed the expeditions of Columbus and those who followed him. Whatever deleterious effects these conquerors may have had on indigenous cultures, their exploits fueled the imaginations of their nations. Correspondingly, the dramas of the age reflect this same sense of discovery and optimism. The great paradox of the Renaissance rests on this simultaneous recognition of humanity's dual nature: superhuman accomplishments in art, exploration, and statecraft were offset by human weakness, folly, and—of course—death. A. C. Bradley's assessment of the Shakespearean tragic hero is no less applicable to those created by Marlowe, Corneille, Racine, Lope de Vega, or Calderón:

> The center of the tragic impression . . . is the impression of waste. "What a piece of work is man!" we cry, "so much more terrible than we knew! Why should he be so if this beauty and greatness only tortures itself and throws itself away?" . . . Everywhere from the crushed rocks beneath our feet to the soul of man, we see power, intelligence, life and glory, which astound us and seem to call for our worship. And everywhere we see them perishing, devouring one another and destroying themselves, often with dreadful pain, as though they came into being for no other end.
>
> A. C. Bradley, SHAKESPEAREAN TRAGEDY, 1904

As we saw with the Greek dramas, the characters, all "overreachers," speak in a language that transcends the ordinary. With few exceptions, Renaissance plays were written in verse, or "heightened language." There are no small issues nor ordinary men and women here, and they require extraordinary language—"the mighty line" of English verse and the lofty Alexandrines of the French—to express themselves.

Playhouses and Scenery

The very playhouses in which Renaissance dramas (and others into the eighteenth century) were performed reinforced social stratification. Then, as now, people with more power, prestige, and money sat in preferred seats, while the middle class sat in the next best seats and the commoners, when they were permitted to attend the theater, stood or sat in the farthest reaches of the auditorium. In Elizabethan England, however, "groundlings" stood in front of the great thrust stage.

Interestingly, it was a major development in scenic design that affected the architecture and seating practices of this era. In 1545 Sebastiano Serlio, a painter and historian, published a treatise on perspective, the technique of rendering three-dimensional space on flat surfaces by making objects in the distance seem smaller than those in the foreground. Perspective was actually an outgrowth of science, especially geometry and its study of planes and a "vanishing point." Serlio applied his theories of scenic design at the court theaters in Italy, rendering examples of comical, tragic, and pastoral scenes. As marvelous, even life like, as these perspective drawings were, there were two liabilities. Actors could not venture upstage and act amid the drawings without grossly distorting the illusion. And the perspective was perfectly accurate from but a single seat in the auditorium—the so-called duke's seat placed on a straight line directly in front of the vanishing point. The farther one sat to the right or left of this point, the more distorted the perspective. When permanent theater spaces were built, as they were in Vicenza and Versailles, they retained the royal box and the elongated auditorium from which royal retinues could better view the scenic spectacle.

Though Elizabethan public theaters were more democratic, they too reflected the society that attended them. There were clearly defined areas for the working class (the "pit" or yard where they stood), the middle class (any one of three galleries), and the gentry ("the lords' room"). After the Puritans seized power in 1642, courtiers fled to France and Italy, where they attended plays in newly designed playhouses. When drama returned to the English stage in 1660, new theaters were built in imitation of the Continental playhouses, right down to the "king's box" where Charles II and his consorts sat. More thorough accounts of the structures and conventions of the English, French, and Spanish theaters are appended to representative plays from these countries.

Acting

European theaters may have been smaller and more intimate than the enormous Greek spaces, but actors still had to measure up to their characters and the language of the plays. The acting style of the period demanded size and stature, particularly in France and Italy, where actors portrayed an idealized version of their heroes. Consequently, they employed formal gestures and poses to manifest their characters. Again, reigning monarchs may have contributed to this stylization. King Louis XIV prided himself on his balletic skills. Eager to please their king, French courtiers quickly adopted the formal, self-conscious poses of ballet dancers, and soon actors mirrored these customs in their performances. The English theater seems to have undergone a transition from the blustering style of an Edward Alleyn in the 1580s to a more moderate technique, typified by Richard Burbage, as the theater moved into the new century. Unfortunately, little is known about the acting style of the Spanish, though Lope de Vega wrote about the need for a more naturalistic performance mode. We must remember that his advice to the players, like Shakespeare's in act 3 of *Hamlet*, must be taken within the context of his time.

Playwriting: The Neoclassicists Versus the Romantics

Renaissance plays may be divided into two general categories:

- Those that followed the strict rules of Neoclassicism; patterned after Greek and Roman dramas, these plays respected the rules of time, place, and action; used few characters; and did not mix comic with serious material.
- Those that disregarded the unities of time, place, and action; freely mixed genres, plots, and subplots; and incorporated the full spectrum of society in their tales.

The former were found largely in Italy and France, the bastions of Neoclassicism, while the latter flourished in England and Spain, whose drama later inspired the Romantics.

Despite its beginnings in Italy in the mid–sixteenth century, by 1630 Neoclassicism found its true home in France, where it remained firmly entrenched until Victor Hugo led an artistic revolution with the production of *Hernani* in 1830 (See Chapter 7). Because France became the artistic and cultural center of Europe by the late seventeenth century, Neoclassic drama influenced the development of drama throughout Europe and America.

In 1561 the Italian theorist Julius Caesar Scaliger's "Seven Books of the Poetics" was published in Paris, and soon the French offered their observations on Aristotle's "rules." In particular, Jean de La Taille (c. 1540–1608) insisted on observing the unities of time, place, and action in his "On the Art of Tragedy," published in 1572. The dictates of Scaliger, La Taille, and others provided Neoclassic drama with its most distinctive characteristic: a nearly idolatrous adherence to the rules.

Neoclassicism embraced more than the laws of the unities, the segregation of the tragic and comic impulses, and the simplicity of form and language. It sought *vraisemblance* ("appearance of Truth"), which was an idealized truth, that is, the way the world *ought* to be. Dramas had to be plausible and could not offend anyone's sense of day-to-day reality. The doctrine rested on the impulse, equal parts Christian dogma and classical humanism, to use the theater to teach moral lessons through three critical elements:

- *Morality* assumed that the universe is organized and just. Playwrights were duty bound to show that the good were rewarded and the wicked punished—which is, of course, the doctrine of "poetic justice," on which melodrama thrived.
- *Generality* dictated that what was shown on the stage must be applicable to all humanity.
- *Decorum* divided humanity into well-defined categories according to social status, sex, age, and so on. Playwrights—and actors—were compelled to show individual behavior that was in accordance with society's expectations. A king must speak with the dignity of a king and servants must provide wise counsel to their betters.

The Neoclassic rules were severely tested in 1637 in one of the most famous controversies in theater history. Pierre Corneille (1606–1684) wrote *Le Cid*, an undeniably entertaining play based on a Spanish mythic hero. Conscious of Neoclassic dictates, Corneille compressed the events of many years and locales into a five-act play, dutifully observing the unity of time by limiting the action to a single day. Despite the play's popularity, critics complained that the play violated a number of principles. Cardinal Richelieu, chief counselor to Louis XIV and an avid theater patron himself, submitted the play to the French Academy, which he founded to promote French arts and sciences. The merits and weaknesses of the play were passionately debated. Its sternest critics cited a number of irregularities that violated the principles of *vraisemblance*:

- it contained too many events for a single day;
- the play's heroine failed to mourn properly the death of her father;
- she received her lover in her private chambers, an unthinkable breach of decorum in the eyes of French Christians who expected much more of a noblewoman;
- it provided a happy resolution to an otherwise serious play.

The playwright argued that audiences enjoyed the play despite these lapses. He pointed to the ancients, who themselves violated virtue and poetic justice in plays such as Euripides' *Medea*. Ultimately, Corneille was mildly censured for his "irregularities"—and he indignantly retired from the stage for three years. Significantly, the controversy established the inviolability of the Neoclassic rules. Thus "living classicism"—sought by a public that wanted pleasure from its drama—suffered at the hands of "theoretical classicism"—which dictated codes of writing in the name of reason and morality. The Academy's proclamation that "any pleasure outside the rules cannot bring quality" influenced French writing for almost two hundred years. Of the subsequent French tragedians, only Jean Racine had the genius to use the rules to his advantage.

Such controversies did not affect English or Spanish playwriting. Shakespeare and Calderón, and their talented peers, wrote sprawling dramas with multiple plots that contained both comic and serious elements. They portrayed kings and commoners with equal enthusiasm; and they conjured locales that defied the unities of time and place. The most memorable and lasting drama of the Renaissance (save Molière's work) was produced in the Elizabethan public theaters and the Spanish *corrales*. The English theater, in particular, became a more commercial enterprise that could not afford to be bound by rules and tradition. The middle class, which sought entertainment, became the arbiter of taste. As the commercial theater expanded elsewhere, English plays provided a model for the theatrical free market. Middle-class tastes influenced the drama as much, perhaps more, than did monarchs and wealthy patrons.

ENGLAND

Artistic and Cultural Events

1550:
Ralph Roister-Doister, Nicholas Udall advances popular theater

1520:
The Four PP, farce by John Heywood, first major secular drama

1564:
Shakespeare born in Stratford-upon-Avon

1572:
Acting profession legalized

1576:
James Burbage builds *The Theatre,* first public theater in London

1588:
Doctor Faustus, Christopher Marlowe; bridges medieval and Renaissance tragedy

1599:
Globe Theater opens

1611:
King James Bible

1613:
Globe Theatre burns

1623:
Shakespeare's actors publish Folio edition of his plays

1400 C.E.   **1500 C.E.**   **1600 C.E.**

Historical and Political Events

1487:
War of the Roses ends and Tudor line established

1507–1558:
Henry VIII

1558–1603:
Elizabeth I

1592–1594:
Plague years in London

1588:
England defeats the Spanish Armada

1601:
Earl of Essex disgraced; England disillusioned

1603–1625:
King James I

1605:
Gunpowder plot against monarchy

1625–1642:
King Charles I

1642–1660:
Civil War; Puritans close public theaters

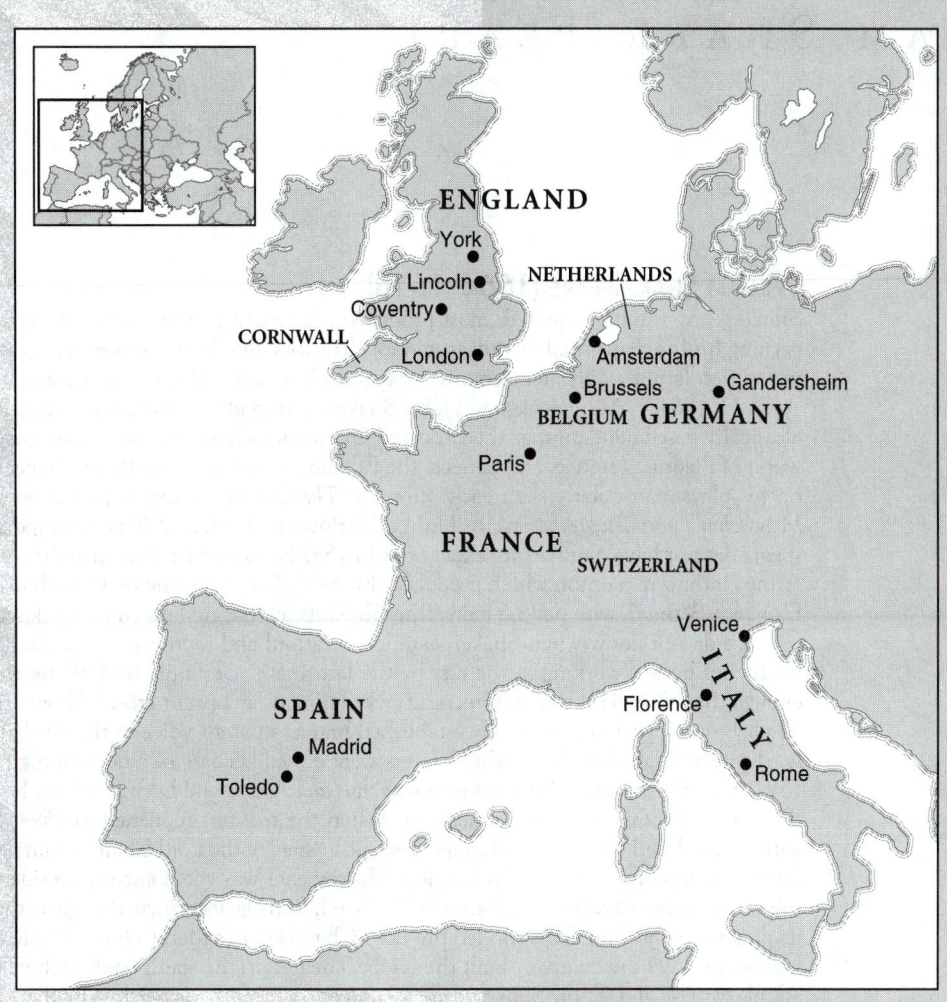

A MIDSUMMER NIGHT'S DREAM

WILLIAM SHAKESPEARE

WILLIAM SHAKESPEARE (1564–1616)

Shakespeare, the most quoted, most produced playwright in the world, left us few facts concerning his life. Baptismal records from Holy Trinity Church in Stratford-upon-Avon, located in the rich farming and sheep country of central England, indicate that he was likely born on April 23, 1564, to Mary Arden and John Shakespeare, a glover and civic leader. He received a classically based education at the Stratford Grammar School, where he first encountered the works of Plautus, Terence, and Seneca, the Roman playwrights who show a traceable influence on his plays, particularly such early efforts as *The Comedy of Errors* (based on Plautus's *The Menaechmi*) and *Titus Andronicus*. Unlike Marlowe and other of his contemporaries, Shakespeare did not have a university education. In 1582 he married a woman eight years his senior, Anne Hathaway, a union which produced three children, only one of whom had a child, Lady Elizabeth Bernard, who had no heirs; thus Shakespeare has no known direct descendants.

We do not know when Shakespeare left Stratford and journeyed to London, though it is likely that he was working in the city by the late 1580s. Certainly by 1592 he was prominent enough that playwright Robert Greene attacked him as "an upstart crow." About 1590 his *Henry VI* plays had appeared and quickly established him as a potent voice in the newly thriving public theaters of London. While the theaters were closed because of a devastating plague in late 1592, Shakespeare wrote his great poems, *Venus and Adonis* and *Lucrece*, which he dedicated to the Earl of Southampton, his benefactor. When the theaters reopened in 1594, Shakespeare, with Richard Burbage and Will Kempe, became a "star" of the Lord Chamberlain's Men, a newly formed professional company in London. Shakespeare was the company's resident playwright (although it also acted plays by Jonson and others), Burbage its principal tragic actor, and Kempe its premiere comedian. This trio led the Lord Chamberlain's Men to both artistic and financial success; by 1599 the company built the Globe Theater on the south bank of the Thames River. As playwright and actor, Shakespeare was given one-tenth ownership in the Globe. When James I became king in 1603, the Chamberlain's Men were given the title of the King's Men, a testimony to their prestige in England's cultural life. Shakespeare, however, retired from the theater and London life in 1612 to return to Stratford, where he lived at New Place, the stately home he had purchased in 1597. He died on April 23 (his traditional birthday) in 1616 and was buried in the sanctuary of Holy Trinity Church. A plaque celebrating his artistry was erected over the grave, but his most enduring monument was the collection of his plays, the so-called *First Folio*, published in 1623 by the actors for whom he wrote. His colleague and rival, Ben Jonson, wrote his epitaph, proclaiming that Shakespeare wrote "not for an age, but for all time."

Shakespeare is credited with 37 plays and had a hand in several others, as joint authorship was a common practice of the age. The canon embraces virtually all of the genres popular in the English Renaissance, and he employs a remarkable variety of literary styles in his work. From vulgar prose to exquisite verse, from rhetorical bombast to lyrical poetry, from patriotic speeches to intensely personal soliloquies, Shakespeare created the fullest spectrum of human discourse ever written by a single person. (See Spotlight box, Making Shakespeare's Language User-Friendly, preceding *A Midsummer Night's Dream*).

After some initial experimentation with style and form, Shakespeare wrote sequences of plays that generally can be grouped by period and genre. "The chronicle plays" were based on medieval English history and served as a warning to his countrymen that rebellion is ruinous; although the plays are about such monarchs as Richard II, Henry IV (two parts), Henry V, Henry VI (three parts), and Richard III, England herself is the protagonist of the chronicles as her very soul is warred over by Vices (rebel factions) and Virtues (legitimate kings, culminating with Henry VII, who began the Tudor dynasty). These plays were Shakespeare's primary endeavor until the mid–1590s, when he turned his attention to romantic comedies (*Two Gentlemen of Verona, The Merchant of Venice, A Midsummer Night's Dream, As You Like It, The Merry Wives of Windsor, Much Ado About Nothing,* and *Twelfth Night*) and the tragic *Romeo and Juliet*; the plays are bound by an exploration of the various facets of love and are marked by a benevolent treatment of human folly. From 1600 to about 1607 Shakespeare produced his great tragedies (*Julius Caesar, Hamlet, Othello, Macbeth, King Lear, Coriolanus,* and *Antony and Cleopatra*), in which he explored deeper questions of mortality and human failure. At this time he also wrote a group of plays, neither fully comedic nor tragic, known as "the problem plays" (*Measure for Measure, All's Well That Ends Well, Troilus and Cressida,* and *Timon of Athens*), which reflect the uncertainty and cynicism of the first years of the reign of James I (1603–1625). Shakespeare spent the last four years of his playwriting career writing the great romances (*Pericles, Cymbeline, The Winter's Tale,* and *The Tempest*), which fuse the sweep of the chronicles, the mystery of the tragedies, and the optimistic resolution of the comedies. These plays portray the fullest range of human types and behaviors, explore the broadest range of public and private issues, and embrace the most complete emotional palette created by the mind of a single artist in human history.

Shakespeare is truly the world's playwright. Today more than 250 theater companies throughout the world are dedicated to the production of his plays (over 120 in the United States alone). In 1988 China held a Shakespeare festival in which 22 plays were performed in an 18-day span in Beijing and Shanghai. The Japanese publish more Shakespearean articles and books than are generated in many English-speaking countries. More is written about Shakespeare and his works than about any other nonreligious being, and only the Judeo-Christian Bible is more frequently quoted than Shakespeare's lines, a fact that more than validates the prophecy of the opening of his Sonnet 55:

> *Not marble, nor the gilded monuments*
> *Of princes shall outlive this pow'rful rhyme.*

A MIDSUMMER NIGHT'S DREAM (C. 1595)

Forget that *A Midsummer Night's Dream* was written by William Shakespeare, and forget especially that it is "a classic" of great literature. Consider the play as (a) an example of first-rate theatrical entertainment; (b) a practical illustration of Aristotle's six elements of the drama; and (c) a remnant of some of the rituals discussed in the first chapter (see Center Stage box, The Midsummer Festivals of Europe, following the text of the play).

The *Dream*, as it is called in theatrical shorthand, is a veritable casebook of those elements people want in their entertainments. It is a romantic tale; no less than four love stories unravel simultaneously, five if you count the ill-fated Pyramus and Thisbe. Its five acts offer lovely ladies and handsome young men, mistaken identities, comic chases through a mysterious, magical forest, damsels in distress, petty jealousies, lovers' quarrels, love triangles, powerful passions, kings and queens, fools and clowns, spirits and sprites, practical jokes and pratfalls, death threats, a duel, tearful reunions, low comedy, high comedy, satire, hilarious amateur theatricals, songs, dances, playful language, stirring poetry, "campy" poetry, crude jokes, lewd jokes, men in drag, kinky sex, lofty ideals, perceptive ideas, a meddling father, generational battles, battles between the sexes, a pompous know-it-all who gets his comeuppance, weddings galore, courtly grandeur, apparitions, disappearances, men transformed into animals, and, quite predictably, a happy ending. Little wonder the *Dream* has been played on virtually every continent by professional and amateur actors for hundreds of years, for it is about as failproof a piece of theater as can be found.

It is also a sophisticated piece of playwriting.

Plots? There are three here—that of the courtly lovers, that of the fairy kingdom (King Oberon and Queen Titania are in a "custody battle" over a child from India), and that of a group of workingmen who prepare a short play of "tragical mirth" for the duke's wedding. The three strands intertwine effortlessly and become a harmonious whole in the final act: the amateur actors perform for the newlyweds while the fairies look on. Think about the philosophical implications of this final image: the fairies watch the lovers watch the actors as we, the audience, watch them. Who, then, is watching us?

The plots are also linked by theme because Shakespeare uses subplots as a prism through which an idea is examined from different perspectives. Each plot explores the nature of love and the "madness" that often accompanies it. Midsummer's Eve was traditionally a night when rationality took a holiday and madness reigned. The *Dream* also examines the nature of illusion and reality. Its play-within-a-play reminds us that illusions can teach us much about reality. It makes us ask questions about what is real: Is Demetrius really in love with Hermia? Does Bottom truly need that donkey's head to make him an ass? Is the silliness of the workers' play any sillier than the actions of the lovers in the forest? The destructiveness of power struggles is considered: Theseus versus Hippolyta, Egeus versus Hermia, Lysander versus Demetrius, Oberon versus Titania, Quince versus Bottom. Ultimately the play asks us to celebrate the triumph of harmony over chaos: the lovers are reunited, the fairy kingdom is restored to order, the workers perform their play.

Shakespeare borrows the most popular stock characters from Renaissance comedy and weaves them into his tri-plot. They are not as subtly etched as in his more mature comedies, but they need not be: they exist to move the intricate plot forward at a brisk pace. The lovers are the stock *inamorati* of comedy, likeable yet flawed and human. The Theseus-Hippolyta relationship is troubling: she is a prisoner of war whose melancholy must be overcome if their pending marriage is to be fruitful. Demetrius is callow and self-serving, Lysander too full of grand sentiments, Hermia a bit too precious. Of the lovers only Helena emerges as thoughtful and truly sympathetic; she is fidelity idealized. Egeus is the disagreeable old man of Roman comedy, and his threats to his daughter in act 1 hint at tragedy, but he gradually accepts the natural order of things. Oberon is a majestic and poetic fairy king—but there is a disturbing side to him. Like Othello, he is jealous and vengeful as he punishes Titania by making her love "some vile thing." Titania is radiant and queenly, but she can be petty and possessive. Puck (aka Robin Goodfellow) is the most archetypal of the characters—the ubiquitous trickster or spirit of misrule. He is also an ironist who judges the folly of human action: "What fools these mortals be!" Yet he, too, is flawed, which is his most human characteristic. He puts the magic flower drops into the wrong eyes in act 2 and increases the chaos in Athens's mysterious woods. Nick Bottom, the would-be actor and warrior, is the play's most memorable character, an amalgam of two stock characters in comic plays throughout the world. First, he is the braggart warrior, both in his egotistical pronouncements about his acting prowess and in his hammy overacting of Pyramus. His great monologue in act 5 parodies traditional braggart warrior speeches. Bottom is also the ancient *bomolochos*, the comic buffoon whose every word and deed induces laughter at his gross stupidity. But however flawed and foibled the characters may be, they are not figures of scorn. This is a benevolent or "festive" comedy, as opposed to the scathingly satiric comedies of Ben Jonson and Molière. If we laugh at the characters it is because they are not grotesqueries like Tartuffe; they are much like we, well intentioned but error-prone and entirely human. When Puck asks the audience's forgiveness in his final speech ("If you pardon, we will mend"), we willingly oblige because we have watched the characters move from ignorance and selfishness to knowledge and self-discovery. In the speeches that end act 4, scene 1, each character proclaims his or her newfound awareness. Demetrius then speaks for all when he proclaims, "Why, then we are awake."

Diction in the *Dream* runs the gamut from the sublime ("I know a bank where the wild thyme grows . . .") to the ridiculous:

> *Thus die I, thus, thus, thus.*
>> *Now am I dead,*
>> *Now am I fled;*
> *My soul is in the sky.*
>> *Tongue, lose thy light;*
>> *Moon, take thy flight.*
>> *Now die, die, die, die, die.*

There is inventive wordplay and punning, as in Demetrius's exhortation to Helena in act 2; note how words like *not*, *slay*, and *wood* enjoy multiple meanings:

> *I love thee not; therefore pursue me not.*
> *Where is Lysander and fair Hermia?*
> *The one I'll slay; the other slayeth me.*
> *Though toldst me they were stol'n unto this wood;*
> *And here am I, and wood within this wood*
> *Because I cannot meet my Hermia.*
> *Hence, get thee gone, and follow me no more.*

Bottom is master of the malaprop ("We will meet that we may rehearse most obscenely"), the oxymoron ("I will speak in a monstrous little voice"), and in the misguided metaphor ("The eye of man hath not heard, the ear of man hath not seen . . ."). While these linguistic flights are enjoyable in themselves, they, like good theater language, serve a dramatic purpose. Foremost, they define character: Oberon is superhuman and his language transcends that of mere mortals. Demetrius is a courtier, well educated and witty: his puns and wordplay are a sign of his intelligence and sex appeal. Bottom is an ignorant ass, both with and without that donkey's head.

Music, songs, and dance permeate *A Midsummer Night's Dream*, which has inspired several ballets, operas, and at least one Broadway musical (*Babes in the Woods*, 1950). The fairies sing Titania to sleep and dance a roundel in act 2, the workers conclude their play with a Bergomask dance, and—most importantly—Titania and Oberon lead the fairies in song as they bless the newlyweds. While these musical moments are aesthetically pleasing, they also reinforce key themes. The Bergomask dance is a remnant of the ancient *komos*, a celebration of harmony among mortals. So, too, is the final fairy dance: Oberon and Titania dance and sing together—as they did in their reconciliation in act 4—in marked contrast to their tempestuous meeting in act 2. Out of the discord of the earlier acts comes a perfect concord among all the parties at play's end.

The *Dream* was written for an essentially bare stage that required little if any scenery. Nevertheless, spectacle is an integral part of the play. In a play that celebrates the power of the human imagination and the ability of the poet to give "to airy nothing a local habitation and a name," the script itself paints vivid word pictures to set his scenes, as when Titania describes the troubled fairy knoll:

> *Therefore the winds, piping to us in vain,*
> *As in revenge, have sucked up from the sea*
> *Contagious fogs . . .*

Little wonder the Elizabethan actors could perform on an unadorned stage.

The play abounds with memorable stage pictures: the frightened young Hermia surrounded by a male-dominated court in the opening scene; the lovers stumbling their way through the woods, taunted by sprites they cannot see; the transformation of Bottom into an ass and the ensuing comic chase that scares off his coworkers; Bottom and Titania attended by Mustardseed and the other fairies; the comical costumes hastily gotten together by the fledgling actors in act 5; and the stately fairy dance that concludes the action.

In addition to its extraordinary fusion of entertainment, dramatic, and theatrical elements, *A Midsummer Night's Dream* remains a staple of world theater for reasons that transcend its literary values. At its heart, the play is akin to the rituals and ceremonies described earlier. Fundamentally, it is a springtime ritual in which a virginal heroine goes into a wood. Think of fairytales and children's stories that begin with this archetypal situation: Snow White, Sleeping Beauty, Little Red Riding Hood. In the woods the heroine is threatened by supernatural forces, awakens from a deep sleep to find her love, and reemerges from her perilous journey a happy bride-to-be. The play is an initiation rite of passage to adulthood common in many cultures. Initiation rites in ancient Greece consisted of three parts: the *pompei* (leave-taking), the *agon* (suffering), and the *komos* (joyful return). The new generation, provoked by a stern and uncompromising elder, leaves the community, is tested by the forces of nature in a "green world," symbolically "dies" (the lovers fall asleep in act 4), and finally is reborn. They return to the community wiser for their experiences. Old and young alike unite to celebrate the homecoming to the "golden world" with dances, feasting, and finally a wedding that promises a new life for the community. The rite is performed under the watchful eye of divine forces who sanction the endeavor:

> To the best bride-bed will we,
>
> Which by us shall blessèd be;
>
> And the issue there create
>
> Ever shall be fortunate.

A Midsummer Night's Dream is also a ritual of atonement and reconciliation. Until act 4 characters notoriously abuse one another: Theseus has captured Hippolyta in war; Egeus is tyrannical toward his daughter; Demetrius disdains the faithful Helena; Lysander cruelly rejects Hermia; Hermia and Helena quarrel; Titania taunts Oberon with the changeling; in retaliation, Oberon causes Titania to make love to an ass. Note this is all done in the darkness of night, but comes the dawn, the miscreants repent their transgressions. Oberon says that he pities Titania's plight and will "undo this hateful imperfection from her eyes." Demetrius, the most boorish of the four earthly lovers, awakens to recant his treatment of Helena, whom he compares to a rich feast to be savored.

The most significant act of contrition comes from Puck, whose very mission is mischief. After the play is completed and blessings have been bestowed upon the house, the actor playing Puck steps forward to beg the audience's forgiveness for any transgressions the characters and, importantly, the actors may have committed:

> If we shadows have offended,
>
> Think but this, and all is mended,

Puck's speech is derived from the ancient Roman *plaudite*, a request for applause that formally ended Roman plays. It was also the moment when the actors "dropped" their characters and became themselves again, the final transformation in an art that is based on illusion. The *plaudite*, like the modern curtain call, is an integral rite within the theater experience. Shakespeare uses it to conclude the *Dream*, although he does not use it in many of his plays. Why did he use it here? In a play that emphasizes ritual atonement, he gives the audience an uncommonly active role in the process of reconciliation. At play's end, actors, characters, and audience, transgressors all in the great dream of life, join together "in new amity."

Can we—in 1595 or today—enjoy *A Midsummer Night's Dream* without an intimate knowledge of its ritualistic roots? Of course we can. However, our enjoyment of the *Dream* may also be attributed to our subliminal response to this ancient rite that addresses our innate desire for harmony.

SPOTLIGHT | MAKING SHAKESPEARE'S LANGUAGE USER-FRIENDLY

Shakespeare's language need not be a source of anxiety if you understand a few simple precepts. First of all, it is not "Old English" but is among the first uses of Modern English. The history of the English language can be divided into three phases. Old English derived from various Germanic tribes and lasted until the Norman Conquest (1066 C.E.); *Beowulf* is the best-known literary work composed in Old English, which is very much a foreign language. After the French conquered Britain, there was an infusion of Latin-based language, mostly in the form of French, which became the official language of the English court. This blend of Old English and French produced Middle English, which flourished from about 1200 to 1500. Chaucer's famous *Canterbury Tales* is a masterpiece of Middle English. After the Wars of the Roses and the establishment of the Tudor line under King Henry VII, there was a move to purge English of its French influence. Though this attempt largely failed, the linguistic phenomenon known as "the great vowel shift" in the late fifteenth and early sixteenth centuries precipitated an essentially new language: Modern English. Shakespeare was among its pioneers and is estimated to have contributed over 8,000 words to our vocabulary. If there is anything foreign about Shakespeare's language, it is the exceptional ingenuity with which he used it. Shakespeare and his contemporaries were experimenting with the possibilities of their new language to discover its potential. You, too, should read the plays in that same spirit of discovery and playfulness.

You are probably aware that most of Shakespeare's plays are written in *iambic pentameter*, a term that indicates the number of stressed syllables—or beats—in a line. The typical line of Shakespearean blank (unrhymed) verse does indeed consist of 10 syllables, half of them stressed, the other half unstressed, in a pattern like this:

u [unstressed] / [stressed] **u / u / u / u /**

Or to borrow a line from Sonnet 29, you might say:

that THEN i SCORN to CHANGE my STATE with KINGS.

Shakespeare used this metric form to approximate natural speech in English drama, which had inherited the verse forms of the medievals who relied heavily on the symmetrical four-beat line:

And now I wax old,
Sick, sorry, and cold;
As muck upon cold
I wither away.

(from "Noah and His Sons," *The Wakefield Pageant*, modern version by John Gassner)

Some early Tudor tragedies used the unwieldy "fourteener," a 14-syllable, 7-beat line:

Do well or ill, I do dare avouch, some evil on me will speak.
No, truly, yet I do not mean the King's precepts to break;
To place I mean for to return my duty to fulfill.

(Thomas Preston, *Cambises*, 1569)

Read each set of lines aloud and you quickly hear the artificiality of the lines; imagine listening to this for a couple of hours! By using the five-beat line, Shakespeare and his contemporaries approximated the normal rhythms of English speech. The iambic pattern—puh-POM, puh-POM, puh-POM—has been likened to the sound of the heartbeat. We can say that iambic pentameter, then, is as natural as life itself.

If Shakespeare wrote every line in strict iambic pentameter, the verse would become monotonous and predictable. Shakespeare breaks the pattern to achieve variety and, more importantly, to provide his actors with subtle stage directions about how to interpret a line. Shakespeare did not, like so many modern playwrights, write detailed stage directions, but they are there in the lines. A basic understanding of his "code" can make reading his plays easier—and more enjoyable.

Shakespeare gets his effects by setting up iambic pentameter as the norm for dramatic speech, and then—signifi-

(continued)

cantly—he breaks the pattern to highlight key moments. Look at this short passage from act 2, scene 2 of *Macbeth*, in which Macbeth has just returned from killing King Duncan:

MACBETH. I have done the deed.
   Didst thou not hear a noise?
LADY MACBETH. I heard the owl
   screech and the crickets cry.
   Did not you speak?
MACBETH.   When?
LADY MACBETH.   Now.
MACBETH.   As
        I descended?
LADY MACBETH. Ay.
MACBETH. Hark!
   Who lies i'the second chamber?
LADY MACBETH.   Don-
        albain.
MACBETH. This is a sorry sight.
LADY MACBETH. A foolish thought
   to say a sorry sight.

Don't be dismayed by the way the words are written on the page; it is all part of the code and there is nothing terribly mysterious about it. Here the language, and the way it is constructed, *is* the dramatic action.

Macbeth's first line contains an abnormal number of stresses to show that his mind is troubled by the horrible murder he has just committed: "I have DONE the DEED. DIDST thou NOT HEAR a NOISE?" Note also that the repeated "d" and "t" sounds echo Macbeth's own heartbeat, which surely must be pounding frantically. Lady Macbeth

responds with a more regular line: "I HEARD the OWL SCREAM and the CRICKets CRY." It is a five-beat line, but just irregular enough to suggest Lady Macbeth's anxiety. Nature is rebelling at the act ("owl scream") and she, too, is a bit unnerved. Notice that Shakespeare plants a couple of interesting sound effects to heighten the scene. The phrases "owl scream" and "crickets cry" are onomatopoetic; that is, they imitate the very sounds they describe to create atmosphere.

The next four lines are "shared lines"—combined they make up a single line of blank verse. Shakespeare is telling his actors to "pick up the pace," to speak quickly without pausing between lines. The Macbeths are jumping at shadows and their hurried speech reflects this. The dialogue here is as naturalistic and clipped as any modern passage. Lady Macbeth's response ("Ay") is a line unto itself; in contrast to the quickly paced lines before it, Shakespeare is scripting a lengthy pause as the Macbeths pause to regain their composure. Macbeth's "Hark!" also denotes a long pause. "Hark," of course, means "Listen!" and the pause is there to allow time for them to listen.

After another shared line to establish that King Duncan's son (and potential heir) sleeps in the adjoining chamber, Shakespeare concludes this sequence with two very telling lines. Macbeth's line ("THIS is a SORry SIGHT") is short and irregular in its rhythm to reflect his anxiety. The pause implied by the short line suggests that

Lady Macbeth takes a moment to compose herself (and to assess Macbeth's panic?). She then responds with a line of perfect iambic pentameter: "a FOOL-ish THOUGHT to SAY a SORry SIGHT." She is in complete control (or wishes to suggest she is), and her line has a calming effect on Macbeth. Note the dominance of the "s" (or sibilant) sounds in Lady Macbeth's line; they, too, are a stage direction to the actor to "Shhhh" Macbeth. As the play progresses, by the way, Lady Macbeth's speech becomes more irregular to reflect her growing madness; by contrast, Macbeth's speech becomes more composed as he adjusts to his status as murderer-king. Shakespeare's language invariably mirrors its character's personality, or as actor Ben Kingsley says: "In Shakespeare, language *is* the character."

Did Shakespeare sit down and consciously plan each line for these effects? Perhaps a couple, but most of it came instinctively. It was his genius, just as Beethoven's genius was to hear music in his head.

Shakespeare and his contemporaries used other forms of writing in their plays: rhymed verse, couplets, occasionally doggerel verse, and prose. For now, remember that Shakespeare's language, in addition to its vivid word pictures and emotional power, is an integral part of the dramatic action. Not only does it define character and situation, its very structure helps actors—and you—read the plays.

Peter Brook staged A Midsummer Night's Dream *in a white box at the Royal Shakespeare Company (1970). Hippolyta's line "it must be in your imagination" was the inspiration for this inventive production.*

A MIDSUMMER NIGHT'S DREAM

WILLIAM SHAKESPEARE

[DRAMATIS PERSONAE
THESEUS, *Duke of Athens*
HIPPOLYTA, *Queen of the Amazons, betrothed to Theseus*
PHILOSTRATE, *Master of the Revels*
EGEUS, *father of Hermia*
HERMIA, *daughter of Egeus, in love with Lysander*
LYSANDER, *in love with Hermia*
DEMETRIUS, *in love with Hermia and favored by Egeus*
HELENA, *in love with Demetrius*
OBERON, *King of the Fairies*
TITANIA, *Queen of the Fairies*
PUCK, or ROBIN GOODFELLOW
PEASEBLOSSOM
COBWEB,   } *fairies attending*
MOTE,   *Titania*
MUSTARDSEED,
Other *Fairies* attending
PETER QUINCE, *a carpenter,*   *Prologue*
NICK BOTTOM, *a weaver,*   *Pyramus*

FRANCIS FLUTE, *a bellows*   *representing*
  mender,   *Thisbe*
TOM SNOUT, *a tinker,*   *Wall*
SNUG, *a joiner,*   *Lion*
ROBIN STARVELING, *a tailor,*   *Moonshine*
LORDS AND ATTENDANTS ON THESEUS AND HIPPOLYTA

SCENE: Athens, and a wood near it]

1.1   *Enter Theseus, Hippolyta, [and Philostrate,] with others.*°

THESEUS.
  Now, fair Hippolyta, our nuptial hour
  Draws on apace. Four happy days bring in
  Another moon; but, O, methinks, how slow

1.1 Location: Athens: Theseus' court.

483

This old moon wanes! She lingers° my desires,
5   Like to a stepdame° or a dowager°
     Long withering out° a young man's revenue.
HIPPOLYTA.
     Four days will quickly steep themselves° in night;
     Four nights will quickly dream away the time;
     And then the moon, like a silver bow
10   New bent in heaven, shall behold the night
     Of our solemnities°
THESEUS.
                    Go, Philostrate,
     Stir up the Athenian youth to merriments.
     Awake the pert and nimble spirit of mirth.
     Turn melancholy forth to funerals;
15   The pale companion° is not for our pomp.°
                                    [*Exit Philostrate.*]
     Hippolyta, I wooed thee with my sword°
     And won thy love doing thee injuries;
     But I will wed thee in another key,
     With pomp, with triumph,° and with reveling.

*Enter Egeus and his daugher Hermia, and Lysander, and
Demetrius.*

EGEUS.
20   Happy be Theseus, our renownèd duke!
THESEUS.
     Thanks, good Egeus. What's the news with thee?
EGEUS.
     Full of vexation come I, with complaint
     Against my child, my daughter Hermia.—
     Stand forth, Demetrius.—My noble lord,
25   This man hath my consent to marry her.—
     Stand forth, Lysander.—And, my gracious Duke,
     This man hath bewitched the bosom of my child.
     Thou, thou Lysander, thou hast given her rhymes
     And interchanged love tokens with my child.
30   Thou hast by moonlight at her window sung
     With feigning voice verses of feigning° love,
     And stol'n the impression of her fantasy°
     With bracelets of thy hair, rings, gauds,° conceits,°
     Knacks,° trifles, nosegays, sweetmeats—messengers

Of strong prevailment in° unhardened youth.   35
With cunning hast thou filched my daughter's heart,
Turned her obedience, which is due to me,
To stubborn harshness. And, my gracious Duke,
Be it so° she will not here before Your Grace
Consent to marry with Demetrius,   40
I beg the ancient privilege of Athens:
As she is mine, I may dispose of her,
Which shall be either to this gentleman
Or to her death, according to our law
Immediately° provided in that case.   45
THESEUS.
     What say you, Hermia? Be advised, fair maid.
     To you your father should be as a god—
     One that composed your beauties, yea, and one
     To whom you are but as a form in wax
     By him imprinted, and within his power   50
     To leave° the figure or disfigure° it.
     Demetrius is a worthy gentleman.
HERMIA.
     So is Lysander.
THESEUS.
                    In himself he is;
     But in this kind,° wanting° your father's voice,°
     The other must be held the worthier.   55
HERMIA.
     I would my father looked but with my eyes.
THESEUS.
     Rather your eyes must with his judgment look.
HERMIA.
     I do entreat Your Grace to pardon me.
     I know not by what power I am made bold,
     Nor how it may concern° my modesty   60
     In such a presence here to plead my thoughts;
     But I beseech Your Grace that I may know
     The worst that may befall me in this case
     If I refuse to wed Demetrius.
THESEUS.
     Either to die the death° or to abjure   65
     Forever the society of men.
     Therefore, fair Hermia, question your desires,
     Know of your youth, examine well your blood,°
     Whether, if you yield not to your father's choice,
     You can endure the livery° of a nun,   70
     For aye° to be in shady cloister mewed,°
     To live a barren sister all your life,
     Chanting faint hymns to the cold fruitless moon.

---

4 lingers postpones, delays the fulfillment of   **5 stepdame** stepmother. **a dowager** i.e., a widow (whose right of inheritance from
her dead husband is eating into her son's estate)   **6 withering out**
causing to dwindle   **7 steep themselves** saturate themselves, be absorbed in   **11 solemnities** festive ceremonies of marriage   **15
companion** fellow. **pomp** ceremonial magnificence   **16 with my
sword** i.e., in a military engagement against the Amazons, when
Hippolyta was taken captive   **19 triumph** public festivity   **31
feigning** (1) counterfeiting (2) faining, desirous   **32 And . . . fantasy** and made her fall in love with you (imprinting your image on
her imagination) by stealthy and dishonest means   **33 gauds** play-
things. **conceits** fanciful trifles   **34 Knacks** knickknacks

35 prevailment in influence on   **39 Be it so** if   **45 Immediately**
directly, with nothing intevening   **51 leave** i.e., leave unaltered.
disfigure obliterate   **54 kind** respect. **wanting** lacking. **voice** approval   **60 concern** befit   **65 die the death** be executed by legal
process   **68 blood** passions   **70 livery** habit, costume   **71 aye**
ever. **mewed** shut in. (Said of a hawk, poultry, etc.)

Thrice blessèd they that master so their blood
75 To undergo such maiden pilgrimage;
But earthlier happy° is the rose distilled°
Than that which, withering on the virgin thorn,
Grows, lives, and dies in single blessedness.

HERMIA.
So will I grow, so live, so die, my lord,
80 Ere I will yield my virgin patent° up
Unto his lordship, whose unwishèd yoke
My soul consents not to give sovereignty.

THESEUS.
Take time to pause, and by the next new moon—
The sealing day betwixt my love and me
85 For everlasting bond of fellowship—
Upon that day either prepare to die
For disobedience to your father's will,
Or° else to wed Demetrius, as he would,
Or on Diana's altar to protest°
90 For aye austerity and single life.

DEMETRIUS.
Relent, sweet Hermia, and, Lysander, yield
Thy crazèd° title to my certain right.

LYSANDER.
You have her father's love, Demetrius;
Let me have Hermia's. Do you marry him.

EGEUS.
95 Scornful Lysander! True, he hath my love,
And what is mine my love shall render him.
And she is mine, and all my right of her
I do estate unto° Demetrius.

LYSANDER.
I am, my lord, as well derived° as he,
100 As well possessed;° my love is more than his;
My fortunes every way as fairly° ranked,
If not with vantage,° as Demetrius';
And, which is more than all these boasts can be,
I am beloved of beauteous Hermia.
105 Why should not I then prosecute my right?
Demetrius, I'll avouch it to his head,°
Made love to Nedar's daughter, Helena,
And won her soul; and she, sweet lady, dotes,
Devoutly dotes, dotes in idolatry
110 Upon this spotted° and inconstant man.

THESEUS.
I must confess that I have heard so much,
And with Demetrius thought to have spoke thereof;

But, being overfull of self-affairs,°
My mind did lose it. But, Demetrius, come,
And come, Egeus, you shall go with me;   115
I have some private schooling° for you both.
For you, fair Hermia, look you arm° yourself
To fit your fancies° to your father's will,
Or else the law of Athens yields you up—
Which by no means we may extenuate°—   120
To death or to a vow of single life.
Come, my Hippolyta. What cheer, my love?
Demetrius and Egeus, go° along,
I must employ you in some business
Against° our nuptial, and confer with you   125
Of something nearly that° concerns yourselves.

EGEUS.
With duty and desire we follow you.

Exeunt [all but Lysander and Hermia].

LYSANDER.
How now, my love, why is your cheek so pale?
How chance the roses there do fade so fast?

HERMIA.
Belike° for want of rain, which I could well,   130
Beteem° them from the tempest of my eyes.

LYSANDER.
Ay me! For aught that I could ever read,
Could ever hear by tale or history,
The course of true love never did run smooth;
But either it was different in blood°—   135

HERMIA.
O cross!° Too high to be enthralled to low.

LYSANDER.
Or else misgrafted° in respect of years—

HERMIA.
O spite! Too old to be engaged to young.

LYSANDER.
Or else it stood upon the choice of friends°—

HERMIA.
O hell, to choose love by another's eyes!   140

LYSANDER.
Or if there were a sympathy° in choice,
War, death, or sickness did lay siege to it,
Making it momentany° as a sound,
Swift as a shadow, short as any dream,
Brief as the lightning in the collied° night   145

That in a spleen° unfolds° both heaven and earth,
And ere a man hath power to say "Behold!"
The jaws of darkness do devour it up.
So quick° bright things come to confusion.°

HERMIA.
150   If then true lovers have been ever crossed,°
It stands as an edict in destiny.
Then let us teach our trial patience,°
Because it is a customary cross,
As due to love as thoughts, and dreams, and sighs,
155   Wishes, and tears, poor fancy's° followers.

LYSANDER.
A good persuasion.° Therefore, hear me, Hermia:
I have a widow aunt, a dowager
Of great revenue, and she hath no child.
From Athens is her house remote seven leagues;
160   And she respects° me as her only son.
There, gentle Hermia, may I marry thee,
And to that place the sharp Athenian law
Cannot pursue us. If thou lovest me, then,
Steal forth thy father's house tomorrow night;
165   And in the wood, a league without° the town,
Where I did meet thee once with Helena
To do° observance to a morn of May,
There will I stay for thee.

HERMIA.
                                    My good Lysander!
I swear to thee, by Cupid's strongest bow,
170   By his best arrow° with the golden head,
By the simplicity° of Venus' doves,°
By that which knitteth souls and prospers loves,
And by that fire which burned the Carthage queen°
When the false Trojan° under sail was seen,
175   By all the vows that ever men have broke,
In number more than ever women spoke,
In that same place thou hast appointed me
Tomorrow truly will I meet with thee.

LYSANDER.
Keep promise, love. Look, here comes Helena.

Enter Helena.

HERMIA.
Good speed, fair° Helena! Whither away?   180

HELENA.
Call you me fair? That "fair" again unsay.
Demetrius loves your fair.° O happy fair!°
Your eyes are lodestars,° and your tongue's sweet air°
More tunable° than lark to shepherd's ear
When wheat is green, when hawthorn buds appear.   185
Sickness is catching. O, where favor° so,
Yours would I catch, fair Hermia, ere I go;
My ear should catch your voice, my eye your eye,
My tongue should catch your tongue's sweet melody.
Were the world mine, Demetrius being bated,°   190
The rest I'd give to be to you translated.°
O, teach me how you look and with what art
You sway° the motion° of Demetrius' heart.

HERMIA.
I frown upon him, yet he loves me still.

HELENA.
O, that your frowns would teach my smiles such
      skill!   195

HERMIA.
I give him curses, yet he gives me love.

HELENA.
O, that my prayers could such affection° move!°

HERMIA.
The more I hate, the more he follows me.

HELENA.
The more I love, the more he hateth me.

HERMIA.
His folly, Helena, is no fault of mine.   200

HELENA.
None, but your beauty. Would that fault were mine!

HERMIA.
Take comfort. He no more shall see my face.
Lysander and myself will fly this place.
Before the time I did Lysander see
Seemed Athens as a paradise to me.°   205
O, then, what graces in my love do dwell,
That he hath turned a heaven unto a hell?

LYSANDER.
Helena, to you our minds we will unfold.
Tomorrow night, when Phoebe° doth behold

146 in a spleen in a swift impulse, in a violent flash. **enfolds** reveals **149 quick** quickly; also, living, alive. **confusion** ruin   **150 ever crossed** always thwarted   **152 teach . . . patience** i.e., teach ourselves patience in this trial   **155 fancy's** amorous passion's   **156 persuasion** doctrine   **160 respects** regards   **165 without** outside **167 do . . . May** perform the ceremonies of May Day   **170 best arrow** (Cupid's best gold-pointed arrows were supposed to induce love; his blunt leaden arrows, aversion.)   **171 simplicity** innocence. **doves** i.e., those that drew Venus' chariot   **173, 174 Carthage queen, false Trojan** (Dido, Queen of Carthage, immolated herself on a funeral pyre after having been deserted by the Trojan hero Aeneas.)

180 fair fair-complexioned (generally regarded by the Elizabethans as more beautiful than a dark complexion)   **182 your fair** your beauty (even though Hermia is dark complexioned) **happy fair** lucky fair one   **183 lodestars** guiding stars. **air** music   **184 tunable** tuneful, melodious   **186 favor** appearance, looks   **190 bated** excepted   **191 translated** transformed   **193 sway** control. **motion** impulse   **197 affection** passion. **move** arouse   **204–205 Before . . . to me** (Hermia seemingly means that love has led to complications and jealousies, making Athens hell for her.)   **209 Phoebe** Diana, the moon

210 Her silver visage in the watery glass,°
    Decking with liquid pearl the bladed grass,
    A time that lovers' flights doth still° conceal,
    Through Athens' gates have we devised to steal.
HERMIA.
    And in the wood, where often you and I
215 Upon faint° primrose beds were wont to lie,
    Emptying our bosoms of their counsel° sweet,
    There my Lysander and myself shall meet,
    And thence from Athens turn away our eyes
    To seek new friends and stranger companies.°
220 Farewell, sweet playfellow. Pray thou for us,
    And good luck grant thee thy Demetrius!
    Keep word, Lysander. We must starve our sight
    From lovers' food till morrow deep midnight.
LYSANDER.
    I will, my Hermia. (*Exit Hermia.*) Helena, adieu.
225 As you on him, Demetrius dote on you!

                                        Exit Lysander.
HELENA.
    How happy some o'er other some can be!°
    Through Athens I am thought as fair as she.
    But what of that? Demetrius thinks not so;
    He will not know what all but he do know.
230 And as he errs, doting on Hermia's eyes,
    So I, admiring of° his qualities.
    Things base and vile, holding no quantity,°
    Love can transpose to form and dignity.
    Love looks not with the eyes, but with the mind,
235 And therefore is winged Cupid painted blind.
    Nor hath Love's mind of any judgment taste;°
    Wings and no eyes figure° unheedy haste.
    And therefore is Love said to be a child,
    Because in choice° he is oft beguiled.°
240 As waggish° boys in game° themselves forswear,
    So the boy Love is perjured everywhere.
    For ere Demetrius looked on Hermia's eyne,°
    He hailed down oaths that he was only mine;
    And when this hail some heat from Hermia felt,
245 So he dissolved, and showers of oaths did melt.
    I will go tell him of fair Hermia's flight.
    Then to the wood will he tomorrow night

Pursue her; and for this intelligence°
If I have thanks, it is a dear expense.°
But herein mean I to enrich my pain,   250
To have his sight thither and back again.

                                        Exit.

1.2 °   *Enter Quince the carpenter, and Snug the joiner, and*
         Bottom the weaver, and Flute the bellows mender,
         and Snout the tinker, and Starveling the tailor.

QUINCE. Is all our company here?
BOTTOM. You were best to call all them generally,° man by
    man, according to the scrip.°
QUINCE. Here is the scroll of every man's name which is
    thought fit, through all Athens, to play in our interlude°   5
    before the Duke and the Duchess on his wedding day at
    night.
BOTTOM. First, good Peter Quince, say what the play treats
    on, then read the names of the actors, and so grow to° a
    point.   10
QUINCE. Marry,° our play is "The most lamentable comedy
    and most cruel death of Pyramus and Thisbe."
BOTTOM. A very good piece of work, I assure you, and a
    merry. Now, good Peter Quince, call forth your actors by
    the scroll. Masters, spread yourselves.   15
QUINCE. Answer as I call you. Nick Bottom,° the weaver.
BOTTOM. Ready. Name what part I am for, and proceed.
QUINCE. You, Nick Bottom, are set down for Pyramus.
BOTTOM. What is Pyramus? A lover or a tyrant?
QUINCE. A lover, that kills himself most gallant for love.   20
BOTTOM. That will ask some tears in the true performing of
    it. If I do it, let the audience look to their eyes. I will
    move storms; I will condole° in some measure. To the
    rest—yet my chief humor° is for a tyrant. I could play Er-
    cles° rarely, or a part to tear a cat° in, to make all split.° 25
       "The raging rocks
       And shivering shocks
       Shall break the locks
          Of prison gates;

248 intelligence information   **249 a dear expense** i.e., a trouble
worth taking on my part, or a begrudging effort on his part. **dear**
costly
1.2 Location: Athens.
2 generally (Bottom's blunder for "individually.")   **3 scrip** scrap.
(Bottom's error for "script.")   **5 interlude** play   **9 grow to** come
to   **11 Marry** (A mild oath; originally the name of the Virgin
Mary.)   **16 Bottom** (As a weaver's term, a *bottom* was an object
around which thread was wound.)   **23 condole** lament, arouse pity
24 humor inclination, whim   **25 Ercles** Hercules. (The tradition
of ranting came from Seneca's *Hercules Furens.*) **tear a cat** i.e., rant.
make all split i.e., cause a stir, bring the house down

210 glass mirror   **212 still** always   **215 faint** pale   **216 counsel**
secret thought   **219 stranger companies** the company of strangers
226 o'er . . . can be can be in comparison to some others   **231 ad-**
miring of wondering at   **232 holding no quantity** i.e., unsubstan-
tial, unshapely   **236 Nor . . . taste** i.e., nor has Love, which dwells
in the fancy or imagination, any *taste* or least bit of judgment or reason   **237 figure** are a symbol of   **239 in choice** in choosing. **be-**
guiled self-deluded, making unaccountable choices   **240 waggish**
playful, mischievous. **game** sport, jest   **242 eyne** eyes. (Old form of
plural.)

30   And Phibbus' car°
        Shall shine from far
        And make and mar
            The foolish Fates."
        This was lofty! Now name the rest of the players. This is
35   Ercles' vein, a tyrant's vein. A lover is more condoling.
        QUINCE. Francis Flute, the bellows mender.
        FLUTE. Here, Peter Quince.
        QUINCE. Flute, you must take Thisbe on you.
        FLUTE. What is Thisbe? A wandering knight?
40   QUINCE. It is the lady that Pyramus must love.
        FLUTE. Nay, faith, let not me play a woman. I have a
            beard coming.
        QUINCE. That's all one.° You shall play it in a mask, and you
            may speak as small° as you will.
45   BOTTOM. An° I may hide my face, let me play Thisbe too.
            I'll speak in a monstrous little voice: "Thisne, Thisne!"
            "Ah, Pyramus, my lover dear! Thy Thisbe dear, and lady
            dear!"
        QUINCE. No, no, you must play Pyramus, and Flute, you
50   Thisbe.
        BOTTOM. Well, proceed.
        QUINCE. Robin Starveling, the tailor.
        STARVELING. Here, Peter Quince.
        QUINCE. Robin Starveling, you must play Thisbe's mother.
55   Tom Snout, the tinker.
        SNOUT. Here, Peter Quince.
        QUINCE. You, Pyramus' father; myself, Thisbe's father; Snug,
            the joiner, you, the lion's part; and I hope here is a play
            fitted.
60   SNUG. Have you the lion's part written? Pray you, if it be,
            give it me, for I am slow of study.
        QUINCE. You may do it extempore, for it is nothing but
            roaring.
        BOTTOM. Let me play the lion too. I will roar that I will do
65   any man's heart good to hear me. I will roar that I will
            make the Duke say, "Let him roar again, let him roar
            again."
        QUINCE. An you should do it too terribly, you would fright
            the Duchess and the ladies, that they would shriek; and
70   that were enough to hang us all.
        ALL. That would hang us, every mother's son.
        BOTTOM. I grant you, friends, if you should fright the ladies
            out of their wits, they would have no more discretion but
            to hang us; but I will aggravate° my voice so that I will
75   roar you° as gently as any sucking dove;° I will roar you an
            'twere° any nightingale.

QUINCE. You can play no part but Pyramus; for Pyramus is a
    sweet-faced man, a proper° man as one shall see in a sum-
    mer's day, a most lovely gentlemanlike man. Therefore
    you must needs play Pyramus.   80
BOTTOM. Well, I will undertake it. What beard were I best
    to play it in?
QUINCE. Why, what you will.
BOTTOM. I will discharge° it in either your° straw-color
    beard, your orange-tawny beard, your purple-in-grain°   85
    beard, or your French-crown-color° beard, your perfect
    yellow.
QUINCE. Some of your French crowns° have no hair at all,
    and then you will play barefaced. But, masters, here are
    your parts. [He distributes parts.] And I am to entreat you,   90
    request you, and desire you to con° them by tomorrow
    night, and meet me in the palace wood, a mile without
    the town, by moonlight. There will we rehearse; for if we
    meet in the city, we shall be dogged with company, and
    our devices° known. In the meantime I will draw a bill° of   95
    properties, such as our play wants. I pray you, fail me not.
BOTTOM. We will meet, and there we may rehearse most ob-
    scenely° and courageously. Take pains, be perfect.° Adieu.
QUINCE. At the Duke's oak we meet.
BOTTOM. Enough. Hold, or cut bowstrings.°   100

                                                    Exeunt.

2.1 °   Enter a Fairy at one door, and Robin Goodfellow
        [Puck] at another.
PUCK.
    How now, spirit, whither wander you?
FAIRY.
        Over hill, over dale,
            Thorough bush, thorough° brier,
        Over park, over pale,°
            Thorough flood, thorough fire,   5
        I do wander everywhere,
        Swifter than the moon's sphere;°
        And I serve the Fairy Queen,
        To dew° her orbs° upon the green.

---

78 proper handsome   **84 discharge** perform. **your** i.e., you know
the kind I mean   **85 purple-in-grain** dyed a very deep red. (From
grain, the name applied to the dried insect used to make the dye.)
86 French-crown-color i.e., color of a French crown, a gold coin
88 crowns heads bald from syphilis, the "French disease"   **91 con**
learn by heart   **95 devices** plans. **draw a bill** draw up a list   **98
obscenely** (An unintentionally funny blunder, whatever Bottom
meant to say.) **perfect** i.e., letter-perfect in memorizing your parts
100 Hold . . . bowstrings (An archers' expression, not definitely
explained, but probably meaning here "keep your promises, or give
up the play.")
2.1 Location: A wood near Athens.
3 Thorough through   **4 pale** enclosure   **7 sphere** orbit   **9 dew**
sprinkle with dew. **orbs** circles, i.e., fairy rings (circular bands of grass,
darker than the surrounding area, caused by fungi enriching the soil)

---

30 Phibbus' car Phoebus', the sun god's, chariot   **43 That's all
one** it makes no difference   **44 small** high-pitched   **45 An** if
(Also at line 68.)   **74 aggravate** (Bottom's blunder for "moderate.")   **75 roar you** i.e., roar for you. **sucking dove** (Bottom con-
flates *sitting dove* and *sucking lamb*, two proverbial images of innocence.)   **76 an 'twere** as if it were

10   The cowslips tall her pensioners° be.
        In their gold coats spots you see;
        Those be rubies, fairy favors;°
        In those freckles live their savors.°
        I must go seek some dewdrops here
15   And hang a pearl in every cowslip's ear.
        Farewell, thou lob° of spirits; I'll be gone.
        Our Queen and all her elves come here anon.°
PUCK.
        The King doth keep his revels here tonight.
        Take heed the Queen come not within his sight.
20   For Oberon is passing fell° and wrath,°
        Because that she as her attendant hath
        A lovely boy, stolen from an Indian king;
        She never had so sweet a changeling.°
        And jealous Oberon would have the child
25   Knight of his train, to trace° the forests wild.
        But she perforce° withholds the lovèd boy,
        Crowns him with flowers, and makes him all her joy.
        And now they never meet in grove or green,
        By fountain° clear, or spangled starlight sheen,°
30   But they do square,° that all their elves for fear
        Creep into acorn cups and hide them there.
FAIRY.
        Either I mistake your shape and making quite,
        Or else you are that shrewd° and knavish sprite°
        Called Robin Goodfellow. Are not you he
35   That frights the maidens of the villagery,°
        Skim milk,° and sometimes labor in the quern,°
        And bootless° make the breathless huswife° churn,
        And sometimes make the drink to bear no barm,°
        Mislead night wanderers,° laughing at their harm?
40   Those that "Hobgoblin" call you, and "Sweet Puck,"°
        You do their work, and they shall have good luck.
        Are you not he?
PUCK.
                Thou speakest aright;
        I am that merry wanderer of the night.

I jest to Oberon and make him smile
When I a fat and bean-fed° horse beguile,   45
Neighing in likeness of a filly foal;
And sometimes lurk I in a gossip's° bowl
In very likeness of a roasted crab,°
And when she drinks, against her lips I bob
And on her withered dewlap° pour the ale.   50
The wisest aunt,° telling the saddest° tale,
Sometimes for three-foot stool mistaketh me;
Then slip I from her bum, down topples she,
And "Tailor"° cries, and falls into a cough;
And then the whole choir° hold their hips and laugh,   55
And waxen° in their mirth, and neeze,° and swear
A merrier hour was never wasted° there.
But, room,° fairy! Here comes Oberon.
FAIRY.
        And here my mistress. Would that he were gone!

*Enter [Oberon] the King of Fairies at one door, with his
train, and [Titania] the Queen at another, with hers.*

OBERON.
        Ill met by moonlight, proud Titania.   60
TITANIA.
        What, jealous Oberon? Fairies, skip hence.
        I have forsworn his bed and company.
OBERON.
        Tarry, rash wanton.° Am not I thy lord?
TITANIA.
        Then I must be thy lady; but I know
        When thou hast stolen away from Fairyland   65
        And in the shape of Corin° sat all day,
        Playing on pipes of corn° and versing love
        To amorous Phillida. Why art thou here
        Come from the farthest step° of India,
        But that, forsooth, the bouncing Amazon,   70
        Your buskined° mistress and your warrior love,
        To Theseus must be wedded, and you come
        To give their bed joy and prosperity.
OBERON.
        How canst thou thus for shame, Titania,
        Glance at my credit with Hippolyta,°   75

---

10 pensioners retainers, members of the royal bodyguard   **12 favors** love tokens   **13 savors** sweet smells   **16 lob** country bumpkin   **17 anon** at once   **20 passing fell** exceedingly angry. **wrath** wrathful   **23 changeling** child exchanged for another by the fairies   **25 trace** range through   **26 perforce** forcibly   **29 fountain** spring. **starlight sheen** shining starlight   **30 square** quarrel   **33 shrewd** mischievous. **sprite** spirit   **35 villagery** village population   **36 Skim milk** i.e., steal the cream. **quern** hand mill (where Puck presumably hampers the grinding of grain)   **37 bootless** in vain. (Puck prevents the cream from turning to butter.) **huswife** housewife   **38 barm** head on the ale. (Puck prevents the barm or yeast from producing fermentation.)   **39 Mislead night wanderers** i.e., mislead with false fire those who walk abroad at night (hence earning Puck his other names of Jack o' Lantern and Will o' the Wisp)   **40 Those . . . Puck** i.e., those who call you by the names you favor rather than those denoting the mischief you do

45 bean-fed well fed on field beans   **47 gossip's** old woman's   **48 crab** crab apple   **50 dewlap** loose skin on neck   **51 aunt** old woman. **saddest** most serious   **54 Tailor** (possibly because she ends up sitting cross-legged on the floor, looking like a tailor, or else referring to the *tail* or buttocks)   **55 choir** company   **56 waxen** increase. **neeze** sneeze   **57 wasted** spent   **58 room** stand aside, make room   **63 wanton** headstrong creature   **66, 68 Corin, Phillida** (Conventional names of pastoral lovers.)   **67 corn** (Here, oat stalks.)   **69 step** farthest limit of travel, or, perhaps, *steep*, "mountain range"   **71 buskined** wearing half-boots called buskins   **75 Glance . . . Hippolyta** make insinuations about my favored relationship with Hippolyta

Knowing I know thy love to Theseus?
Didst not though lead him through the glimmering night
From Perigenia,° whom he ravishèd?
And make him with fair Aegles° break his faith,
80   With Ariadne° and Antiopa?°
TITANIA.
These are the forgeries of jealousy;
And never, since the middle summer's spring,°
Met we on hill, in dale, forest, or mead,°
By pavèd° fountain or by rushy° brook,
85   Or in° the beachèd margent° of the sea,
To dance our ringlets° to° the whistling wind,
But with thy brawls thou hast disturbed our sport.
Therefore the winds, piping to us in vain,
As in revenge, have sucked up from the sea
90   Contagious° fogs which, falling in the land,
Hath every pelting° river made so proud
That they have overborne their continents.°
The ox hath therefore stretched his yoke° in vain,
The plowman lost his sweat, and the green corn°
95   Hath rotted ere his youth attained a beard;
The fold° stands empty in the drownèd field,
And crows are fatted with the murrain° flock;
The nine-men's morris° is filled up with mud,
And the quaint mazes° in the wanton° green
100   For lack of tread are undistinguishable.
The human mortals want° their winter° here;
No night is now with hymn or carol blessed.
Therefore° the moon, the governess of floods,
Pale in her anger, washes° all the air,

That rheumatic diseases° do abound.   105
And thorough this distemperature° we see
The seasons alter: hoary-headed frosts
Fall in the fresh lap of the crimson rose,
And on old Hiems'° thin and ice crown
An odorous chaplet of sweet summer buds   110
Is, as in mockery, set. The spring, the summer,
The childing° autumn, angry winter, change
Their wonted liveries,° and the mazèd° world
By their increase° now knows not which is which.
And this same progeny of evils comes   115
From our debate,° from our dissension.
We are their parents and original.°
OBERON.
Do you amend it, then. It lies in you.
Why should Titania cross her Oberon?
I do but beg a little changeling boy   120
To be my henchman.°
TITANIA.
                    Set your heart at rest.
The fairy land buys not the child of me.
His mother was a vot'ress of my order,°
And in the spicèd Indian air by night
Full often hath she gossiped by my side   125
And sat with me on Neptune's yellow sands,
Marking th' embarkèd traders° on the flood,°
When we have laughed to see the sails conceive
And grow big-bellied with the wanton° wind;
Which she, with pretty and with swimming° gait,   130
Following—her womb then rich with my young
        squire—
Would imitate, and sail upon the land
To fetch me trifles, and return again
As from a voyage, rich merchandise.
But she, being mortal, of that boy did die;   135
And for her sake do I rear up her boy,
And for her sake I will not part with him.
OBERON.
How long within this wood intend you stay?
TITANIA.
Perchance till after Theseus' wedding day.
If you will patiently dance in our round°   140
And see our moonlight revels, go with us;
If not, shun me, and I will spare° your haunts.

78 Perigenia i.e., Perigouna, one of Theseus' conquests. (This and the following women are named in Thomas North's translation of Plutarch's "Life of Theseus.") **79 Aegles** i.e., Aegle, for whom Theseus deserted Ariadne according to some accounts **80 Ariadne** the daugher of Minos, King of Crete, who helped Theseus to escape the labyrinth after killing the Minotaur; later she was abandoned by Theseus. **Antiopa** Queen of the Amazons and wife of Theseus; elsewhere identified with Hippolyta, but here thought of as a separate woman **82 middle summer's spring** beginning of midsummer **83 mead** meadow **84 pavèd** with pebbled bottom. **rushy** bordered with rushes **85 in** on. **margent** edge, border **86 ringlets** dances in a ring. (See *orbs* in line 9.) **to** to the sound of **90 Contagious** noxious **91 pelting** paltry **92 continents** banks that contain them **93 stretched his yoke** i.e., pulled at his yoke in plowing **94 corn** grain of any kind **96 fold** pen for sheep or cattle **97 murrain** having died of the plague **98 nine-men's morris** i.e., portion of the village green marked out in a square for a game played with nine pebbles or pegs **99 quaint mazes** i.e., intricate paths marked out on the village green to be followed rapidly on foot as a kind of contest. **wanton** luxuriant **101 want** lack. **winter** i.e., regular winter season; or, proper observances of winter, such as the *hymn* or *carol* in the next line (?) **103 Therefore** i.e., as a result of our quarrel **104 washes** saturates with moisture

105 rheumatic diseases colds, flu, and other respiratory infections **106 distemperature** disturbance in nature **109 Hiems'** the winter god's **112 childing** fruitful, pregnant **113 wonted liveries** usual apparel. **mazèd** bewildered **114 their increase** their yield, what they produce **116 debate** quarrel **117 original** origin **121 henchman** attendant, page **123 was . . . order** had taken a vow to serve me **127 traders** trading vessels. **flood** flood tide **129 wanton** (1) playful (2) amorous **130 swimming** smooth, gliding **140 round** circular dance **142 spare** shun

OBERON.
    Give me that boy, and I will go with thee.
TITANIA.
    Not for thy fairy kingdom. Fairies, away!
145   We shall chide downright, if I longer stay.
                       Exeunt [Titania with her train].
OBERON.
    Well, to thy way. Thou shalt not from° this grove
    Till I torment thee for this injury.
    My gentle Puck, come hither. Thou rememb'rest
    Since° once I saw upon a promontory,
150   And heard a mermaid on a dolphin's back
    Uttering such dulcet° and harmonious breath°
    That the rude° sea grew civil at her song,
    And certain stars shot madly from their spheres
    To hear the sea-maid's music?
PUCK.
                       I remember.
155 OBERON.
    That very time I saw, but thou couldst not,
    Flying between the cold moon and the earth
    Cupid, all° armed. A certain° aim he took
    At a fair vestal° thronèd by° the west,
    And loosed° his love shaft smartly from his bow
160   As° it should pierce a hundred thousand hearts;
    But I might° see young Cupid's fiery shaft
    Quenched in the chaste beams of the watery moon,
    And the imperial vot'ress passèd on,
    In maiden meditation, fancy-free.°
165   Yet marked I where the bolt° of Cupid fell:
    It fell upon a little western flower,
    Before milk-white, now purple with love's wound,
    And maidens call it love-in-idleness.°
    Fetch me that flower; the herb I showed thee once.
170   The juice of it on sleeping eyelids laid
    Will make or man or° woman madly dote
    Upon the next live creature that it sees.
    Fetch me this herb, and be thou here again
    Ere the leviathan° can swim a league.
PUCK.
175   I'll put a girdle round about the earth
    In forty° minutes.
                        [Exit.]
OBERON.
          Having once this juice,
    I'll watch Titania when she is asleep

146 **from** go from   149 **Since** when   151 **dulcet** sweet. **breath** voice, song   152 **rude** rough   157 **all** fully. **certain** sure   158 **vestal** vestal virgin. (Contains a complimentary allusion to Queen Elizabeth as a votaress of Diana and probably refers to an actual entertainment in her honor at Elvetham in 1591.) **by** in the region of   159 **loosed** released   160 **As** as if   161 **might** could   164 **fancy-free** free of love's spell   165 **bolt** arrow   168 **love-in-idleness** pansy, heartsease   171 **or . . . or** either . . . or   174 **leviathan** sea monster, whale   176 **forty** (Used indefinitely.)

And drop the liquor of it in her eyes.
The next thing then she waking looks upon,
Be it on lion, bear, or wolf, or bull,   180
On meddling monkey, or on busy ape,
She shall pursue it with the soul of love.
And ere I take this charm from off her sight,
As I can take it with another herb,
I'll make her render up her page to me.   185
But who comes here? I am invisible,
And I will overhear their conference.

Enter Demetrius, Helena following him.

DEMETRIUS.
    I love thee not; therefore pursue me not.
    Where is Lysander and fair Hermia?
    The one I'll slay; the other slayeth me.   190
    Thou toldst me they were stol'n unto this wood;
    And here am I, and wood° within this wood
    Because I cannot meet my Hermia.
    Hence, get thee gone, and follow me no more.
HELENA.
    You draw me, you hardhearted adamant!°   195
    But yet you draw not iron, for my heart
    Is true as steel. Leave you° your power to draw,
    And I shall have no power to follow you.
DEMETRIUS.
    Do I entice you? Do I speak you fair?°
    Or rather do I not in plainest truth   200
    Tell you I do not nor I cannot love you?
HELENA.
    And even for that do I love you the more.
    I am your spaniel; and, Demetrius,
    The more you beat me I will fawn on you.
    Use me but as your spaniel, spurn me, strike me,   205
    Neglect me, lose me; only give me leave,
    Unworthy as I am, to follow you.
    What worser place can I beg in your love—
    And yet a place of high respect with me—
    Than to be usèd as you use your dog?   210
DEMETRIUS.
    Tempt not too much the hatred of my spirit,
    For I am sick when I do look on thee.
HELENA.
    And I am sick when I look not on you.
DEMETRIUS.
    You do impeach° your modesty too much
    To leave° the city and commit yourself   215

192 **and wood** and mad, frantic (with an obvious wordplay on *wood*, meaning "woods")   195 **adamant** lodestone, magnet (with pun on *hardhearted*, since adamant was also thought to be the hardest of all stones and was confused with the diamond)   197 **Leave you** give up   199 **speak you fair** speak courteously to you   214 **impeach** call into question   215 **To leave** by leaving

Into the hands of one that loves you not,
To trust the opportunity of night
And the ill counsel of a desert° place
With the rich worth of your virginity.

HELENA.
220   Your virtue° is my privilege.° For that°
It is not night when I do see your face,
Therefore I think I am not in the night;
Nor doth this wood lack worlds of company,
For you, in my respect,° are all the world.
225   Then how can it be said I am alone
When all the world is here to look on me?

DEMETRIUS.
I'll run from thee and hide me in the brakes,°
And leave thee to the mercy of wild beasts.

HELENA.
The wildest hath not such a heart as you.
230   Run when you will. The story shall be changed:
Apollo flies and Daphne holds the chase,°
The dove pursues the griffin,° the mild hind°
Makes speed to catch the tiger—bootless° speed,
When cowardice pursues and valor flies!

DEMETRIUS.
235   I will not stay° thy questions.° Let me go!
Or if thou follow me, do not believe
But I shall do thee mischief in the wood.

HELENA.
Ay, in the temple, in the town, the field,
You do me mischief. Fie, Demetrius!
240   Your wrongs do set a scandal on my sex.°
We cannot fight for love, as men may do;
We should be wooed and were not made to woo.

                 [Exit Demetrius.]

I'll follow thee and make a heaven of hell,
To die upon° the hand I love so well.

                 [Exit.]

OBERON.
245   Fare thee well, nymph. Ere he do leave this grove
Thou shalt fly him, and he shall seek thy love.

Enter Puck.

Hast thou the flower there? Welcome, wanderer.

PUCK.
Ay, there it is.   *[He offers the flower.]*

OBERON.
         I pray thee, give it me.
I know a bank where the wild thyme blows,°
Where oxlips° and the nodding violet grows,   250
Quite overcanopied with luscious woodbine,°
With sweet muskroses° and with eglantine.°
There sleeps Titania sometime° of the night,
Lulled in these flowers with dances and delight;
And there the snake throws° her enameled skin,   255
Weed° wide enough to wrap a fairy in.
And with the juice of this I'll streak° her eyes
And make her full of hateful fantasies.
Take thou some of it, and seek through this grove.

           [He gives some love juice.]

A sweet Athenian lady is in love   260
With a disdainful youth. Anoint his eyes,
But do it when the next thing he espies
May be the lady. Thou shalt know the man
By the Athenian garments he hath on.
Effect it with some care, that he may prove   265
More fond on° her than she upon her love;
And look thou meet me ere the first cock crow.

PUCK.
Fear not, my lord, your servant shall do so.

                Exeunt [separately].

2 . 2 °   *Enter Titania, Queen of Fairies, with her train.*

TITANIA.
Come, now a roundel° and a fairy song;
Then, for the third part of a minute,° hence—
Some to kill cankers° in the muskrose buds,
Some war with reremice° for their leathern wings
To make my small elves coats, and some keep back   5
The clamorous owl, that nightly hoots and wonders
At our quaint° spirits. Sing me now asleep.
Then to your offices, and let me rest.

Fairies sing.

FIRST FAIRY.
You spotted snakes with double° tongue,

---

218 desert deserted   **220 virtue** goodness or power to attract.
privilege safeguard, warrant. **For that** because   **224 in my respect**
as far as I am concerned, in my esteem   **227 brakes** thickets   **231
Apollo . . . chase** (In the ancient myth, Daphne fled from Apollo
and was saved from rape by being transformed into a laurel tree;
here it is the female who *holds the chase*, or pursues, instead of the
male.)   **232 griffin** a fabulous monster with the head and wings of
an eagle and the body of a lion. **hind** female deer   **233 bootless**
fruitless   **235 stay** wait for, put up with. **questions** talk or argument   **240 Your . . . sex** i.e., the wrongs that you do me cause me
to act in a manner that disgraces my sex   **244 upon** by

249 blows blooms   **250 oxlips** flowers resembling cowslip and
primrose   **251 woodbine** honeysuckle   **252 muskroses** a kind of
large, sweet-scented rose. **eglantine** sweetbrier, another kind of rose
253 sometime of for part of   **255 throws** sloughs off, sheds   **256
Weed** garment   **257 streak** anoint, touch gently   **266 fond on**
doing on
2.2 Location: The wood.
1 roundel dance in a ring   **2 the third . . . minute** (Indicative of
the fairies' quickness.)   **3 cankers** cankerworms (i.e., caterpillars
or grubs)   **4 reremice** bats   **7 quaint** dainty   **9 double** forked

10   Thorny hedgehogs, be not seen;
          Newts° and blindworms, do no wrong;
          Come not near our Fairy Queen.

CHORUS [*dancing*].
          Philomel°, with melody
          Sing in our sweet lullaby;
15   Lulla, lulla, lullaby, lulla, lulla, lullaby.
          Never harm
          Nor spell nor charm
          Come our lovely lady nigh.
          So good night, with lullaby.

FIRST FAIRY.
20   Weaving spiders, come not here;
          Hence, you long-legged spinners, hence!
          Beetles black, approach not near;
          Worm nor snail, do no offense.°

CHORUS [*dancing*].
          Philomel, with melody
25   Sing in our sweet lullaby;
    Lulla, lulla, lullaby, lulla, lulla, lullaby.
          Never harm
          Nor spell nor charm
          Come our lovely lady nigh.
30   So good night, with lullaby.

                           [*Titania sleeps.*]

SECOND FAIRY.
    Hence, away! Now all is well.
    One aloof stand sentinel.°

          [*Exeunt Fairies, leaving one sentinel.*]

*Enter Oberon [and squeezes the flower on Titania's
eyelids].*

OBERON.
    What thou seest when thou dost wake,
    Do it for true love take;
35   Love and anguish for his sake.
    Be it ounce,° or cat, or bear,
    Pard,° or boar with bristled hair,
    In thy eye that shall appear
    When thou wak'st, it is thy dear.
40   Wake when some vile thing is near.

                          [*Exit.*]

Enter Lysander and Hermia.

LYSANDER.
    Fair love, you faint with wandering in the wood;

And to speak truth, I have forgot our way.
    We'll rest us, Hermia, if you think it good,
    And tarry for the comfort of the day.

HERMIA.
    Be it so, Lysander. Find you out a bed,   45
    For I upon this bank will rest my head.

LYSANDER.
    One turf shall serve as pillow for us both;
    One heart, one bed, two bosoms, and one troth.°

HERMIA.
    Nay, good Lysander, for my sake, my dear.
    Lie further off yet. Do not lie so near.   50

LYSANDER.
    O, take the sense, sweet, of my innocence!°
    Love takes the meaning in love's conference.°
    I mean that my heart unto yours is knit,
    So that but one heart we can make of it;
    Two bosoms interchainèd with an oath—   55
    So then two bosoms and a single troth.
    Then by your side no bed-room me deny,
    For lying so, Hermia, I do not lie.°

HERMIA.
    Lysander riddles very prettily.
    Now much beshrew° my manners and my pride 60
    If Hermia meant to say Lysander lied.
    But, gentle friend, for love and courtesy
    Lie further off, in human° modesty.
    Such separation as may well be said
    Becomes a virtuous bachelor and a maid,   65
    So far be distant; and, good night, sweet friend.
    Thy love ne'er alter till thy sweet life end!

LYSANDER.
    Amen, amen, to that fair prayer, say I,
    And then end life when I end loyalty!
    Here is my bed. Sleep give thee all his rest!   70

HERMIA.
    With half that wish the wisher's eyes be pressed!°
          [*They sleep, separated by a short distance.*]

Enter Puck.

PUCK.
    Through the forest have I gone,
    But Athenian found I none
    On whose eyes I might approve°

---

11 Newts water lizards (considered poisonous, as were *blindworms*—small snakes with tiny eyes—and spiders) **13 Philomel** the nightingale. (Philomela, daughter of King Pandion, was transformed into a nightingale, according to Ovid's *Metamorphoses* 6, after she had been raped by her sister Procne's husband, Tereus.) **23 offense** harm **32 sentinel** (Presumably Oberon is able to outwit or intimidate this guard.) **36 ounce** lynx **37 Pard** leopard

48 troth faith, trothplight **51 take . . . innocence** i.e., interpret my intention as innocent **52 Love . . . conference** i.e., when lovers confer, love teaches each lover to interpret the other's meaning lovingly **58 lie** tell a falsehood (with a riddling pun on *lie*, "recline") **60 beshrew** curse. (But mildly meant.) **63 human** courteous (and perhaps suggesting "humane," the Quarto spelling) **71 With . . . pressed** i.e., may we share your wish, so that your eyes too are *pressed*, closed, in sleep **74 approve** test

75   This flower's force in stirring love.
      Night and silence.—Who is here?
      Weeds of Athens he doth wear.
      This is he, my master said,
      Despisèd the Athenian maid;
80   And here the maiden, sleeping sound,
      On the dank and dirty ground.
      Pretty soul, she durst not lie
      Near this lack-love, this kill-courtesy.
      Churl, upon thy eyes I throw
85   All the power this charm doth owe.°
                              [*He applies the love juice.*]
      When thou wak'st, let love forbid
      Sleep his seat on thy eyelid.
      So awake when I am gone,
      For I must now to Oberon.   *Exit.*

      Enter Demetrius and Helena, running.

HELENA.
90   Stay, though thou kill me, sweet Demetrius!
DEMETRIUS.
      I charge thee, hence, and do not haunt me thus.
HELENA.
      O, wilt though darkling° leave me? Do not so.
DEMETRIUS.
      Stay, on thy peril!° I alone will go.   [*Exit.*]
HELENA.
      O, I am out of breath in this fond° chase!
95   The more my prayer, the lesser is my grace.°
      Happy is Hermia, wheresoe'er she lies,°
      For she hath blessèd and attractive eyes.
      How came her eyes so bright? Not with salt tears;
      If so, my eyes are oftener washed than hers.
100   No, no, I am as ugly as a bear,
      For beasts that meet me run away for fear.
      Therefore no marvel though Demetrius
      Do, as a monster, fly my presence thus.°
      What wicked and dissembling glass of mine
105   Made me compare° with Hermia's sphery eyne?°
      But who is here? Lysander, on the ground?
      Dead, or asleep? I see no blood, no wound.
      Lysander, if you live, good sir, awake.
LYSANDER [*awaking*].
      And run through fire I will for thy sweet sake.
110   Transparent° Helena! Nature shows art,°

      That through thy bosom makes me see thy heart.
      Where is Demetrius? O, how fit a word
      Is that vile name to perish on my sword!
HELENA.
      Do not say so, Lysander; say not so.
      What though he love your Hermia? Lord, what
        though?   115
      Yet Hermia still loves you. Then be content.
LYSANDER.
      Content with Hermia? No! I do repent
      The tedious minutes I with her have spent.
      Not Hermia but Helena I love.
      Who will not change a raven for a dove?   120
      The will° of man is by his reason swayed,
      And reason says you are the worthier maid.
      Things growing are not ripe until their season;
      So I, being young, till now ripe not° to reason.
      And, touching° now the point° of human skill,°   125
      Reason becomes the marshal to my will
      And leads me to your eyes, where I o'erlook°
      Love's stories written in love's richest book.
HELENA.
      Wherefore° was I to this keen mockery born?
      When at our hands did I deserve this scorn?   130
      Is 't not enough is 't not enough, young man,
      That I did never—no, nor never can—
      Deserve a sweet look from Demetrius' eye,
      But you must flout my insufficiency?
      Good troth,° you do me wrong, good sooth,° you do, 135
      In such disdainful manner me to woo.
      But fare you well. Perforce I must confess
      I thought you lord of° more true gentleness.°
      O, that a lady, of° one man refused,
      Should of another therefore be abused!°
                                          Exit.   140
LYSANDER.
      She sees not Hermia. Hermia, sleep thou there,
      And never mayst thou come Lysander near!
      For as a surfeit of the sweetest things
      The deepest loathing to the stomach brings,
      Or as the heresies that men do leave
      Are hated most of those they did deceive,°   145
      So though, my surfeit and my heresy,
      Of all be hated, but the most of° me!
      And, all my powers, address° your love and might
      To honor Helen and to be her knight!
                                          Exit.   150

---

85 **owe** own   92 **darkling** in the dark   93 **on thy peril** i.e., on pain of danger to you if you don't obey me and stay   94 **fond** doting   95 **my grace** the favor I obtain   96 **lies** dwells   102–103 **no marvel . . . thus** i.e., no wonder that Demetrius flies from me as from a monster   105 **compare** vie. **sphery eyne** eyes as bright as stars in their spheres   110 **Transparent** (1) radiant (2) able to be seen through, lacking in deceit. **art** skill, magic power

121 **will** desire   124 **ripe not** (am) not ripened   125 **touching** reaching. **point** summit. **skill** judgment   127 **o'erlook** read   129 **Wherefore** why   135 **Good troth, good sooth** i.e., indeed, truly   138 **lord of** i.e., possessor of. **gentleness** courtesy   139 **of** by   140 **abused** ill treated   145–146 **as . . . deceive** as renounced heresies are hated most by those persons who formerly were deceived by them   148 **Of . . . of** by . . . by   149 **address** direct, apply

HERMIA [*awaking*].
      Help me, Lysander, help me! Do thy best
      To pluck this crawling serpent from my breast!
      Ay me, for pity! What a dream was here!
      Lysander, look how I do quake with fear.
155   Methought a serpent ate my heart away,
      And you sat smiling at his cruel prey.°
      Lysander! What, removed? Lysander! Lord!
      What, out of hearing? Gone? No sound, no word?
      Alack, where are you? Speak, an° if you hear;
160   Speak, of all loves!° I swoon almost with fear.
      No? Then I well perceive you are not nigh.
      Either death, or you, I'll find immediately.
                        Exit. [*The sleeping Titania remains.*]

3.1°   *Enter the clowns*° [*Quince, Snug, Bottom, Flute,
        Snout, and Starveling*].
BOTTOM. Are we all met?
QUINCE. Pat,° pat; and here's a marvelous convenient place
    for our rehearsal. This green plot shall be our stage, this
    hawthorn brake° our tiring-house,° and we will do it in
5   action as we will do it before the Duke.
BOTTOM. Peter Quince?
QUINCE. What sayest thou, bully° Bottom?
BOTTOM. There are things in this comedy of Pyramus and
    Thisbe that will never please. First, Pyramus must draw a
10 sword to kill himself, which the ladies cannot abide. How
    answer you that?
SNOUT. By 'r lakin,° a parlous° fear.
STARVELING. I believe we must leave the killing out, when
    all is done.°
15 BOTTOM. Not a whit. I have a device to make all well. Write
    me° a prologue, and let the prologue seem to say, we will
    do no harm with our swords, and that Pyramus is not
    killed indeed; and for the more better assurance, tell
    them that I, Pyramus, am not Pyramus but Bottom the
20 weaver. This will put them out of fear.
QUINCE. Well, we will have such a prologue, and it shall be
    written in eight and six.°
BOTTOM. No, make it two more: let it be written in eight
    and eight.
25 SNOUT. Will not the ladies be afeard of the lion?
STARVELING. I fear it, I promise you.

BOTTOM. Masters, you ought to consider with yourself, to
    bring in—God shield us!—a lion among ladies° is a most
    dreadful thing. For there is not a more fearful° wildfowl
    than your lion living, and we ought to look to 't.   30
SNOUT. Therefore another prologue must tell he is not a
    lion.
BOTTOM. Nay, you must name his name, and half his face
    must be seen through the lion's neck, and he himself must
    speak through, saying thus or to the same defect:°   35
    "Ladies," or "Fair ladies, I would wish you," or "I would re-
    quest you," or "I would entreat you, not to fear, not to
    tremble; my life for yours.° If you think I come hither as a
    lion, it were pity of my life.° No, I am no such thing; I am
    a man as other men are." And there indeed let him name   40
    his name, and tell them plainly he is Snug the joiner.
QUINCE. Well, it shall be so. But there is two hard things:
    that is, to bring the moonlight into a chamber; for, you
    know, Pyramus and Thisbe meet by moonlight.
SNOUT. Doth the moon shine that night we play our play?   45
BOTTOM. A calendar, a calendar! Look in the almanac. Find
    out moonshine, find out moonshine.
                            [*They consult an almanac.*]
QUINCE. Yes, it doth shine that night.
BOTTOM. Why then may you leave a casement of the great
    chamber window where we play open, and the moon may   50
    shine in at the casement.
QUINCE. Ay; or else one must come in with a bush of
    thorns° and a lantern and say he comes to disfigure,° or to
    present,° the person of Moonshine. Then there is another
    thing: we must have a wall in the great chamber; for Pyra- 55
    mus and Thisbe, says the story, did talk through the chink
    of a wall.
SNOUT. You can never bring in a wall. What say you, Bot-
    tom?
BOTTOM. Some man or other must present Wall. And let   60
    him have some plaster, or some loam, or some roughcast°
    about him, to signify wall; or let him hold his fingers thus,
    and through that cranny shall Pyramus and Thisbe whis-
    per.
QUINCE. If that may be, then all is well. Come, sit down,   65

<hr/>

3.1 Location: The action is continuous.
s.d. clowns rustics   **2 Pat** on the dot, punctually   **4 brake**
thicket. **tiring-house** attiring area, hence backstage   **7 bully** i.e.,
worthy, jolly, fine fellow   **12 By 'r lakin** by our ladykin, i.e., the
Virgin Mary. **parlous** perilous, alarming   **14 when all is done** i.e.,
when all is said and done   **16 Write me** i.e., write at my suggestion. (*Me* is used colloquially.)   **22 eight and six** alternate lines of
eight and six syllables, a common ballad measure

28 lion among ladies (A contemporary pamphlet tells how, at the
christening in 1594 of Prince Henry, eldest son of King James VI of
Scotland, later James I of England, a "blackamoor" instead of a lion
drew the triumphal chariot, since the lion's presence might have
"brought some fear to the nearest.")   **29 fearful** fear-inspiring
35 defect (Bottom's blunder for "effect.")   **38 my life for yours**
i.e., I pledge my life to make your lives safe   **39 it were . . . life**
i.e., I should be sorry, by my life; or, my life would be endangered
52–53 bush of thorns bundle of thornbush fagots (part of the accoutrements of the man in the moon, according to the popular notions of the time, along with his lantern and his dog)   **53 disfigure** (Quince's blunder for "figure.")   **54 present** represent   **61
roughcast** a mixture of lime and gravel used to plaster the outside
of buildings

every mother's son, and rehearse your parts. Pyramus, you
begin. When you have spoken your speech, enter into
that brake, and so everyone according to his cue.

Enter Robin [Puck].

PUCK *[aside].*
      What hempen homespuns° have we swaggering here
70 So near the cradle° of the Fairy Queen?
      What, a play toward?° I'll be an auditor,
      An actor, too, perhaps, if I see cause.
QUINCE. Speak, Pyramus. Thisbe, stand forth.
BOTTOM *[as Pyramus].*
      "Thisbe, the flowers of odious savors sweet—"
75 QUINCE. Odors, odors.
BOTTOM "—Odors savors sweet;
      So hath thy breath, my dearest Thisbe dear.
      But hark, a voice! Stay thou but here awhile,
      And by and by I will to thee appear."
                                                            Exit.
PUCK.
80 A stranger Pyramus than e'er played here.°
                                                        [Exit.]
FLUTE. Must I speak now?
QUINCE. Ay, marry, must you; for you must understand he
      goes but to see a noise that he heard, and is to come
      again.
FLUTE *[as Thisbe].*
85 "Most radiant Pyramus, most lily-white of hue,
      Of color like the red rose on triumphant° brier,
      Most briskly juvenal° and eke° most lovely Jew,°
      As true as truest horse that yet would never tire.
      I'll meet thee, Pyramus, at Ninny's tomb."
90 QUINCE. "Ninus'° tomb," man. Why, you must not speak
      that yet. Then you answer to Pyramus. You speak all your
      part° at once, cues and all. Pyramus, enter. Your cue is
      past; it is "never tire."
FLUTE.
      O—"As true as truest horse, that yet would never tire."

[Enter Puck, and Bottom as Pyramus with the ass head.°]

BOTTOM.
      "If I were fair,° Thisbe, I were° only thine."   95
QUINCE. O, monstrous! O, strange! We are haunted. Pray,
      masters! Fly, masters! Help!
            [Exeunt Quince, Snug, Flute, Snout, and Starveling.]
PUCK.
      I'll follow you, I'll lead you about a round,°
            Thorough bog, thorough bush, thorough brake,
                  thorough brier.
      Sometimes a horse I'll be, sometimes a hound,   100
      A hog, a headless bear, sometimes a fire;°
      And neigh, and bark, and grunt, and roar, and burn,
      Like horse, hound, hog, bear, fire, at every turn.
                                                            Exit.
BOTTOM. Why do they run away? This is a knavery of them
      to make me afeard.   105

Enter Snout.

SNOUT. O Bottom, thou art changed! What do I see on
      thee?
BOTTOM. What do you see? You see an ass head of your own,
      do you?   *[Exit Snout.]*

Enter Quince.

QUINCE. Bless thee, Bottom, bless thee! Thou art trans-   110
      lated.°
                                                            Exit.
BOTTOM. I see their knavery. This is to make an ass of me, to
      fright me, if they could. But I will not stir from this place,
      do what they can. I will walk up and down here, and will
      sing, that they shall hear I am not afraid.   115
                                                        [He sings.]
            The ouzel cock° so black of hue,
                  With orange-tawny bill,
            The throstle° with his note so true,
                  The wren with little quill°—
TITANIA *[awaking].*
      What angel wakes me from my flowery bed?   120
BOTTOM *[sings].*
            The finch, the sparrow, and the lark,
                  The plainsong° cuckoo gray,
            Whose note full many a man doth mark,
                  And dares not answer nay°—
      For indeed, who would set his wit to° so foolish a bird? Who 125
      would give a bird the lie,° though he cry "cuckoo" never
      so?°

---

69 hempen homespuns i.e., rustics dressed in clothes woven of
coarse, homespun fabric made from hemp   **70 cradle** i.e., Titania's
bower   **71 toward** about to take place   **80 A stranger . . . here**
(Either Puck refers to an earlier dramatic version played in the same
theater, or he has conceived of a plan to present a "stranger" Pyramus than ever seen before.)   **86 triumphant** magnificent   **87
brisky juvenal** lively youth. **eke** also. **Jew** (An absurd repetition of
the first syllable of *juvenal* and an indication of how desperately
Quince searches for his rhymes.)   **90 Ninus** mythical founder of
Nineveh (whose wife, Semiramis, was supposed to have built the
walls of Babylon where the story of Pyramus and Thisbe takes place)
93 part (An actor's *part* was a script consisting only of his speeches
and their cues.)   **95 s.d. with the ass head** (This stage direction,
taken from the Folio, presumably refers to a standard stage property.)

95 fair handsome. **were** would be   **98 about a round** roundabout
101 fire will-o'-the-wisp   **110–111 translated** transformed   **116
ouzel cock** male blackbird   **118 throstle** song thrush   **119 quill**
(Literally, a reed pipe; hence, the bird's piping song.)   **122 plain-
song** singing a melody without variations   **124 dares . . . nay** i.e.,
cannot deny that he is a cuckold   **125 set his wit** to employ his intelligence to answer   **126 give . . . lie** call the bird a liar   **127
never so** ever so much

TITANIA.

    I pray thee, gentle mortal, sing again.

    Mine ear is much enamored of thy note;

130   So is mine eye enthrallèd to thy shape;

    And thy fair virtue's force° perforce doth move me

    On the first view to say, to swear, I love thee.

BOTTOM. Methinks, mistress, you should have little reason

    for that. And yet, to say the truth, reason and love keep

135   little company together nowadays—the more the pity

    that some honest neighbors will not make them friends.

    Nay, I can gleek° upon occasion.

TITANIA.

    Thou art as wise as thou art beautiful.

BOTTOM. Not so, neither. But if I had wit enough to get out

140   of this wood, I have enough to serve mine own turn.°

TITANIA.

    Out of this wood do not desire to go.

    Thou shalt remain here, whether thou wilt or no.

    I am a spirit of no common rate.°

    The summer still doth tend upon my state,°

145   And I do love thee. Therefore, go with me.

    I'll give thee fairies to attend on thee,

    And they shall fetch thee jewels from the deep,

    And sing while thou on pressèd flowers dost sleep.

    And I will purge thy mortal grossness° so

150   That thou shalt like an airy spirit go.

    Peaseblossom, Cobweb, Mote,° and Mustardseed!

    Enter four Fairies [Peaseblossom, Cobweb, Mote, and
    Mustardseed].

PEASEBLOSSOM. Ready.

COBWEB.

    And I.

MOTE. And I.

MUSTARDSEED. And I.

ALL.   Where shall we go?

TITANIA.

    Be kind and courteous to this gentleman.

155   Hop in his walks and gambol in his eyes;°

    Feed him with apricots and dewberries,°

    With purple grapes, green figs, and mulberries;

    The honey bags steal from the humble-bees,

    And for night tapers crop their waxen thighs

160   And light them at the fiery glowworms' eyes,

    To have my love to bed and to arise;

And pluck the wings from painted butterflies

To fan the moonbeams from his sleeping eyes.

Nod to him, elves, and do him courtesies.

PEASEBLOSSOM. Hail, mortal!   165

COBWEB. Hail!

MOTE. Hail!

MUSTARDSEED. Hail!

BOTTOM. I cry your worships mercy,° heartily. I beseech your

    worship's name.   170

COBWEB. Cobweb.

BOTTOM. I shall desire you of more acquaintance,° good

    Master Cobweb. If I cut my finger, I shall make bold with

    you.°—Your name, honest gentleman?

PEASEBLOSSOM. Peaseblossom.   175

BOTTOM. I pray you, commend me to Mistress Squash,° your

    mother, and to Master Peascod,° your father. Good Mas-

    ter Peaseblossom, I shall desire you of more acquaintance

    too.—Your name, I beseech you, sir?

MUSTARDSEED. Mustardseed.   180

BOTTOM. Good Master Mustardseed, I know your patience°

    well. That same cowardly, giantlike ox-beef hath de-

    voured many a gentleman of your house. I promise you,

    your kindred hath made my eyes water° ere now. I desire

    you of more acquaintance, good Master Mustardseed.   185

TITANIA.

    Come wait upon him; lead him to my bower.

    The moon methinks looks with a watery eye;

    And when she weeps,° weeps every little flower,

    Lamenting some enforcèd° chastity.

    Tie up my lover's tongue;° bring him silently.   190

                                      Exeunt.

3.2 °   *Enter [Oberon,] King of Fairies.*

OBERON.

    I wonder if Titania be awaked;

    Then, what it was that next came in her eye,

    Which she must dote on in extremity.

    [Enter] Robin Goodfellow [Puck].

    Here comes my messenger. How now, mad spirit?

    What night-rule° now about this haunted° grove?   5

---

169 **I cry . . . mercy** I beg pardon on your worships (for presuming to ask a question)   172 **I . . . acquaintance** I crave to be better acquainted with you   173–174 **If . . . you** (Cobwebs were used to stanch bleeding.)   176 **Squash** unripe pea pod   177 **Peascod** ripe pea pod   181 **your patience** what you have endured. (Mustard is eaten with beef.)   184 **water** (1) weep for sympathy (2) smart, sting   188 **she weeps** i.e., she causes dew   189 **enforcèd** forced, violated; or, possibly, constrained (since Titania at this moment is hardly concerned about chastity)   190 **Tie . . . tongue** (Presumably Bottom is braying like an ass.)

3.2 Location: The wood.

5 night-rule diversion or misrule for the night. **haunted** much frequented

---

131 **thy . . . force** the power of your unblemished excellence   137 **gleek** jest   140 **serve . . . turn** answer my purpose   143 **rate** rank, value   144 **still . . . state** always waits upon me as a part of my royal retinue   149 **mortal grossness** materiality (i.e., the corporal nature of a mortal being)   151 **Mote** i.e., speck. (The two words *moth* and *mote* were pronounced alike, and both meanings may be present.)   155 **in his eyes** in his sight (i.e., before him)   156 **dewberries** blackberries

PUCK.
My mistress with a monster is in love.
Near to her close° and consecrated bower,
While she was in her dull° and sleeping hour,
A crew of patches,° rude mechanicals,°
10 That work for bread upon Athenian stalls,°
Were met together to rehearse a play
Intended for great Theseus' nuptial day.
The shallowest thickskin of that barren sort,°
Who Pyramus presented,° in their sport
15 Forsook his scene° and entered in a brake.
When I did him at this advantage take,
An ass's noll° I fixèd on his head.
Anon his Thisbe must be answerèd,
And forth my mimic° comes. When they him spy,
20 As wild geese that the creeping fowler° eye,
Or russet-pated choughs,° many in sort,°
Rising and cawing at the gun's report,
Sever° themselves and madly sweep the sky,
So, at his sight, away his fellows fly;
25 And, at our stamp, here o'er and o'er one falls;
He "Murder!" cries and help from Athens calls.
Their sense thus weak, lost with their fears thus strong,
Made senseless things begin to do them wrong,
For briers and thorns at their apparel snatch;
Some, sleeves—some, hats; from yielders all things
30   catch.°
I led them on in this distracted fear
And left sweet Pyramus translated there,
When in that moment, so it came to pass,
Titania waked and straightway loved an ass.
OBERON.
35 This falls out better than I could devise.
But hast thou yet latched° the Athenian's eyes
With the love juice, as I did bid thee do?
PUCK.
I took him sleeping—that is finished too—
And the Athenian woman by his side,
40 That, when he waked, of force° she must be eyed.

Enter Demetrius and Hermia.

OBERON.
Stand close. This is the same Athenian.
PUCK.
This is the woman, but not this the man.

[*They stand aside.*]

DEMETRIUS.
O, why rebuke you him that loves you so?
Lay breath so bitter on your bitter foe.
HERMIA.
Now I but chide; but I should use thee worse,   45
For thou, I fear, hast given me cause to curse.
If thou hast slain Lysander in his sleep,
Being o'er shoes° in blood, plunge in the deep,
And kill me too.
The sun was not so true unto the day   50
As he to me. Would he have stolen away
From sleeping Hermia? I'll believe as soon
This whole° earth may be bored, and that the moon
May through the center creep, and so displease
Her brother's° noontide with th' Antipodes.°   55
It cannot be but thou hast murdered him;
So should a murderer look, so dead,° so grim.
DEMETRIUS.
So should the murdered look, and so should I,
Pierced through the heart with your stern cruelty.
Yet you, the murderer, look as bright, as clear   60
As yonder Venus in her glimmering sphere.
HERMIA.
What's this to° my Lysander? Where is he?
Ah, good Demetrius, wilt thou give him me?
DEMETRIUS.
I had rather give his carcass to my hounds.
HERMIA.
Out, dog! Out, cur! Thou driv'st me past the bounds   65
Of maiden's patience. Hast thou slain him, then?
Henceforth be never numbered among men.
O, once° tell true, tell true, even for my sake:
Durst thou have looked upon him being awake?
And hast thou killed him sleeping? O brave touch!°   70
Could not a worm,° an adder, do so much?
An adder did it; for with doubler° tongue
Than thine, thou serpent, never adder stung.
DEMETRIUS.
You spend your passion° on a misprised mood.°
I am not guilty of Lysander's blood,   75
Nor is he dead, for aught that I can tell.
HERMIA.
I pray thee, tell me then that he is well.
DEMETRIUS.
And if I could, what should I get therefor?°

---

7 **close** secret, private   8 **dull** drowsy   9 **patches** clowns, fools.
rude mechanicals ignorant artisans   10 **stalls** market booths   13
barren sort stupid company or crew   14 **presented** acted   15
scene playing area   17 **noll** noddle, head   19 **mimic** burlesque
actor   20 **fowler** hunter of game birds   21 **russet-pated choughs**
reddish brown or gray-headed jackdaws. **in sort** in a flock   23
Sever i.e., scatter   29-30 **from . . . catch** i.e., everything preys on
those who yield to fear   36 **latched** fastened, snared   40 **of force**
perforce

48 **Being o'er shoes** having waded in so far   53 **whole** solid   55
Her brother's i.e., the sun's. **th' Antipodes** the people on the opposite side of the earth (where the moon is imagined bringing night to
noontime)   57 **dead** deadly, or deathly pale   62 **to** to do with
68 **once** once and for all   70 **brave touch!** fine stroke! (Said ironically.)   71 **worm** serpent   72 **doubler** (1) more forked (2) more
deceitful.   74 **passion** violent feelings. **misprised mood** anger
based on misconception   78 **therefor** in return for that

HERMIA.
      A privilege never to see me more.
80   And from thy hated presence part I so.
      See me no more, whether he be dead or no.

                                                          Exit.

DEMETRIUS.
      There is no following her in this fierce vein.
      Here therefore for a while I will remain.
      So sorrow's heaviness doth heavier° grow
85   For debt that bankrupt° sleep doth sorrow owe,
      Which now in some slight measure it will pay,
      If for his tender here I make some stay.°

                                    [*He*] *lie*[*s*] *down* [*and sleeps*].

OBERON.
      What has thou done? Thou hast mistaken quite
      And laid the love juice on some true love's sight.
90   Of thy misprision° must perforce ensue
      Some true love turned, and not a false turned true.
PUCK.
      Then fate o'errules, that, one man holding troth,°
      A million fail, confounding oath on oath.°
OBERON.
      About the wood go swifter than the wind,
95   And Helena of Athens look° thou find.
      All fancy-sick° she is and pale of cheer°
      With sighs of love, that cost the fresh blood° dear.
      By some illusion see thou bring her here.
      I'll charm his eyes against° she do appear.
PUCK.
100   I go, I go, look how I go,
      Swifter than arrow from the Tartar's bow.°

                                                          [*Exit.*]

OBERON [*applying love juice to Demetrius' eyes*].
      Flower of this purple due,
      Hit with Cupid's archery,
      Sink in apple° of his eye.
105   When his love he doth espy,
      Let her shine as gloriously
      As the Venus of the sky.
      When thou wak'st, if she be by,
      Beg of her for remedy.

      Enter Puck.

PUCK.
      Captain of our fairy band,   110
      Helena is here at hand,
      And the youth, mistook by me,
      Pleading for a lover's fee.°
      Shall we their fond pageant° see?
      Lord, what fools these mortals be!   115
OBERON.
      Stand aside. The noise they make
      Will cause Demetrius to awake.
PUCK.
      Then will two at once woo one;
      That must needs be sport alone.°
      And those things do best please me   120
      That befall preposterously.°

                                         [*They stand aside.*]

      Enter Lysander and Helena.

LYSANDER.
      Why should you think that I should woo in scorn?
         Scorn and derision never come in tears.
      Look when° I vow, I weep; and vows so born,
         In their nativity all truth appears.°   125
      How can these things in me seem scorn to you,
      Bearing the badge° of faith to prove them true?
HELENA.
      You do advance° your cunning more and more.
         When truth kills truth,° O, devilish-holy fray!
      These vows are Hermia's. Will you give her o'er?   130
         Weigh oath with oath, and you will nothing weigh.
      Your vows to her and me, put in two scales,
      Will even weigh, and both as light as tales.°
LYSANDER.
      I had no judgment when to her I swore.
HELENA.
      Nor none, in my mind, now you give her o'er.   135
LYSANDER.
      Demetrius loves her, and he loves not you.
DEMETRIUS [*awaking*].
      O Helen, goddess, nymph, perfect, divine!
      To what, my love, shall I compare thine eyne?
      Crystal is muddy. O, how ripe in show°
      Thy lips, those kissing cherries, tempting grow!   140
      That pure congealèd white, high Taurus'° snow,
      Fanned with the eastern wind, turns to a crow°

84 heavier (1) harder to bear (2) more drowsy   **85 bankrupt**
(Demetrius is saying that his sleepiness adds to his weariness caused
by sorrow.)   **86–87 Which . . . stay** i.e., to a small extent, I will be
able to "pay back" and hence find some relief from sorrow, if I pause
here awhile (*make some stay*) while sleep "tenders" or offers itself by
way of paying the debt owed to sorrow   **90 misprision** mistake
92 that . . . troth in that, for each man keeping true faith in love
93 confounding . . . oath i.e., breaking oath after oath   **95 look**
i.e., be sure   **96 fancy-sick** lovesick. **cheer** face   **97 sighs . . .
blood** (An allusion to the physiological theory that each sigh costs
the heart a drop of blood.)   **99 against . . . appear** in anticipation
of her coming.   **101 Tartar's bow** (Tartars were famed for their
skill with the bow.)   **104 apple** pupil

113 fee privilege, reward   **114 fond pageant** foolish spectacle
119 alone unequaled   **121 preposterously** out of the natural
order   **124 Look when** whenever   **124–125 vows . . . appears**
i.e., vows made by one who is weeping give evidence thereby of
their sincerity   **127 badge** identifying device such as that worn on
servants' livery (here, his tears)   **128 advance** carry forward, display   **129 truth kills truth** i.e., one of Lysander's vows must inval-
idate the other   **133 tales** lies   **139 show** appearance   **141
Taurus** a lofty mountain range in Asia Minor   **142 turns to a
crow** i.e., seems black by contrast

When thou hold'st up thy hand. O, let me kiss
This princess of pure white, this seal° of bliss!

HELENA.
145 O spite! O hell! I see you all are bent
To set against° me for your merriment.
If you were civil and knew courtesy,
You would not do me thus much injury.
Can you not hate me, as I know you do,
150 But you must join in souls° to mock me too?
If you were men, as men you are in show,
You would not use a gentle lady so—
To vow, and swear, and superpraise° my parts,°
When I am sure you hate me with your hearts.
155 You both are rivals, and love Hermia,
And now both rivals to mock Helena.
A trim° exploit, a manly enterprise,
To conjure tears up in a poor maid's eyes
With your derision! None of noble sort°
160 Would so offend a virgin and extort°
A poor soul's patience, all to make you sport.

LYSANDER.
You are unkind, Demetrius. Be not so.
For you love Hermia; this you know I know.
And here, with all good will, with all my heart,
165 In Hermia's love I yield you up my part;
And yours of Helena to me bequeath,
Whom I do love, and will do till my death.

HELENA.
Never did mockers waste more idle breath.

DEMETRIUS.
Lysander, keep thy Hermia; I will none.°
170 If e'er I loved her, all that love is gone.
My heart to her but as guestwise sojourned,°
And now to Helen is it home returned,
There to remain.

LYSANDER.
                    Helen, it is not so.

DEMETRIUS.
Disparage not the faith thou dost not know,
175 Lest, to thy peril, thou aby° it dear.
Look where thy love comes; yonder is thy dear.

Enter Hermia.

HERMIA.
Dark night, that from the eye his° function takes,
The ear more quick of apprehension makes;
Wherein it doth impair the seeing sense,

It pays the hearing double recompense.   180
Thou art not by mine eye, Lysander, found;
Mine ear, I thank it, brought me to thy sound.
But why unkindly didst thou leave me so?

LYSANDER.
Why should he stay, whom love doth press to go?

HERMIA.
What love could press Lysander from my side?   185

LYSANDER.
Lysander's love, that would not let him bide—
Fair Helena, who more engilds° the night
Than all yon fiery oes° and eyes of light.
Why seek'st thou me? Could not this make thee
    know
The hate I bear thee made me leave thee so?   190

HERMIA.
You speak not as you think. It cannot be.

HELENA.
Lo, she is one of this confederacy!
Now I perceive they have conjoined all three
To fashion this false sport, in spite of me.°
Injurious Hermia, most ungrateful maid!   195
Have you conspired, have you with these contrived°
To bait° me with this foul derision?
Is all the counsel° that we two have shared—
The sisters' vows, the hours that we have spent
When we have chid the hasty-footed time   200
For parting us—O, is all forgot?
All schooldays' friendship, childhood innocence?
We, Hermia, like two artificial° gods
Have with our needles created both one flower,
Both on one sampler, sitting on one cushion,   205
Both warbling of one song, both in one key,
As if our hands, our sides, voices, and minds
Had been incorporate.° So we grew together,
Like to a double cherry, seeming parted,
But yet an union in partition,   210
Two lovely° berries molded on one stem;
So, with two seeming bodies but one heart,
Two of the first, like coats in heraldry,
Due but to one and crownèd with one crest.°
And will you rend our ancient love asunder,   215
To join with men in scorning your poor friend?
It is not friendly, 'tis not maidenly.
Our sex, as well as I, may chide you for it,
Though I alone do feel the injury.

---

187 **engilds** gilds, brightens with a golden light   188 **oes** spangles (here, stars)   194 **in spite of me** to vex me   196 **contrived** plotted   197 **bait** torment, as one sets on dogs to bait a bear   198 **counsel** confidential talk   203 **artificial** skilled in art or creation   208 **incorporate** of one body   211 **lovely** loving   213–214 **Two . . . crest** i.e., we have two separate bodies, just as a coat of arms in heraldry can be represented twice on a shield but surmounted by a single crest

---

144 **seal** pledge   146 **set against** attack   150 **in souls** i.e., heart and soul   153 **superpraise** overpraise. **parts** qualities   157 **trim** pretty, fine. (Said ironically.)   159 **sort** character, quality   160 **extort** twist, torture   169 **will none** i.e., want no part of her   171 **to . . . sojourned** only visited with her   175 **aby** pay for   177 **his** its

HERMIA.

220   I am amazèd at your passionate words.

    I scorn you not. It seems that you scorn me.

HELENA.

    Have you not set Lysander, as in scorn,

    To follow me and praise my eyes and face?

    And made your other love, Demetrius,

225   Who even but now did spurn me with his foot,

    To call me goddess, nymph, divine, and rare,

    Precious, celestial? Wherefore speaks he this

    To her he hates? And wherefore doth Lysander

    Deny your love, so rich within his soul,

230   And tender° me, forsooth, affection,

    But by your setting on, by your consent?

    What though I be not so in grace° as you,

    So hung upon with love, so fortunate,

    But miserable most, to love unloved?

235   This you should pity rather than despise.

HERMIA.

    I understand not what you mean by this.

HELENA.

    Ay, do! Persever, counterfeit sad° looks,

    Make mouths° upon° me when I turn my back,

    Wink at each other, hold the sweet jest up.°

240   This sport, well carried,° shall be chronicled.

    If you have any pity, grace, or manners,

    You would not make me such an argument.°

    But fare ye well. 'Tis partly my own fault,

    Which death, or absence, soon shall remedy.

LYSANDER.

245   Stay, gentle Helena; hear my excuse,

    My love, my life, my soul, fair Helena!

HELENA.

    O excellent!

HERMIA [to Lysander].   Sweet, do not scorn her so.

DEMETRIUS [to Lysander].

    If she cannot entreat,° I can compel.

LYSANDER.

    Thou canst compel no more than she entreat.

250   Thy threats have no more strength than her weak prayers.

    Helen, I love thee, by my life, I do!

    I swear by that which I will lose for thee,

    To prove him false that says I love thee not.

DEMETRIUS [to Helena].

    I say I love thee more than he can do.

LYSANDER.

255   If thou say so, withdraw, and prove it too.°

DEMETRIUS.

    Quick, come!

HERMIA.   Lysander, whereto tends all this?

LYSANDER.

    Away, you Ethiope!°

                     [*He tries to break away from Hermia.*]

DEMETRIUS.   No, no; he'll

    Seem to break loose; take on° as you would follow,

    But yet come not. You are a tame man. Go!

LYSANDER [to Hermia].

    Hang off,° thou cat, thou burr! Vile thing, let loose,   260

    Or I will shake thee from me like a serpent!

HERMIA.

    Why are you grown so rude? What change is this,

    Sweet love?

LYSANDER.   Thy love? Out, tawny Tartar, out!

    Out, loathèd med'cine!° O hated potion, hence!

HERMIA.

    Do you not jest?

HELENA.   Yes, sooth,° and so do you.   265

LYSANDER.

    Demetrius, I will keep my word with thee.

DEMETRIUS.

    I would I had your bond, for I perceive

    A weak bond° holds you. I'll not trust your word.

LYSANDER.

    What, should I hurt her, strike her, kill her dead?

    Although I hate her, I'll not harm her so.   270

HERMIA.

    What, can you do me greater harm than hate?

    Hate me? Wherefore? O me, what news,° my love?

    Am not I Hermia? Are not you Lysander?

    I am as fair now as I was erewhile.°

    Since night you love me; yet since night you left

        me.   275

    Why, then you left me—O, the gods forbid!—

    In earnest, shall I say?

LYSANDER.

                  Ay, by my life!

    And never did desire to see thee more.

    Therefore be out of hope, of question, of doubt;

    Be certain, nothing truer. 'Tis no jest   280

    That I do hate thee and love Helena.

HERMIA [to Helena].

    O me! You juggler! You are cankerblossom!°

    You thief of love! What, have you come by night

---

230 tender offer   **232 grace** favor   **237 sad** grave, serious   **238 mouths** i.e., mows, faces, grimaces. **upon** at   **239 hold . . . up** keep up the joke   **240 carried** managed   **242 argument** subject for a jest   **248 entreat** i.e., succeed by entreaty   **255 withdraw . . . too** i.e., withdraw with me and prove your claim in a duel. (The two gentlemen are armed.)

257 Ethiope (Referring to Hermia's relatively dark hair and complexion; see also *tawny Tartar* six lines later.)   **258 take on as** act as if, make a fuss as if   **260 Hang off** let go   **264 med'cine** i.e., poison   **265 sooth** truly   **268 weak bond** i.e., Hermia's arm (with a pun on *bond*, "oath," in the previous line)   **272 what news** what is the matter   **274 erewhile** just now   **282 cankerblossom** worm that destroys the flower bud, or wild rose

And stol'n my love's heart from him?

HELENA.   Fine, i' faith!

285 Have you no modesty, no maiden shame,
     No touch of bashfulness? What, will you tear
     Impatient answers from my gentle tongue?
     Fie, fie! You are counterfeit, you puppet,° you!

HERMIA.

     "Puppet"? Why, so!° Ay, that way goes the game.
290 Now I perceive that she hath made compare
     Between our statures; she hath urged her height,
     And with her personage, her tall personage,
     Her height, forsooth, she hath prevailed with him.
     And are you grown so high in his esteem
295 Because I am so dwarfish and so low?
     How low am I, thou painted maypole? Speak!
     How low am I? I am not yet so low
     But that my nails can reach unto thine eyes.

                    [She flails at Helena but is restrained.]

HELENA.

     I pray you, though you mock me, gentlemen,
300 Let her not hurt me. I was never curst;°
     I have no gift at all in shrewishness;
     I am a right° maid for my cowardice.
     Let her not strike me. You perhaps may think,
     Because she is something° lower than myself,
     That I can match her.

HERMIA.

                         Lower? Hark, again!
305
HELENA.

     Good Hermia, do not be so bitter with me.
     I evermore did love you, Hermia,
     Did ever keep your counsels, never wronged you,
     Save that, in love unto Demetrius,
310 I told him of your stealth° unto this wood.
     He followed you; for love I followed him.
     But he hath chid me° hence and threatened me
     To strike me, spurn me, nay, to kill me too.
     And now, so° you will let me quiet go,
315 To Athens will I bear my folly back
     And follow you no further. Let me go.
     You see how simple and how fond° I am.

HERMIA.

     Why, get you gone. Who is 't that hinders you?

HELENA.

     A foolish heart, that I leave here behind.

HERMIA.

     What, with Lysander?

HELENA.   With Demetrius.   320

LYSANDER.

     Be not afraid; she shall not harm thee, Helena.

DEMETRIUS.

     No, sir, she shall not, though you take her part.

HELENA.

     O, when she is angry, she is keen° and shrewd.°
     She was a vixen when she went to school;
     And though she be but little, she is fierce.   325

HERMIA.

     "Little" again? Nothing, but "low" and "little"?
     Why will you suffer her to flout me thus?
     Let me come to her.

LYSANDER.   Get you gone, you dwarf!
     You minimus,° of hindering knotgrass° made!
     You bead, you acorn!

DEMETRIUS.   You are too officious   330
     In her behalf that scorns your services.
     Let her alone. Speak not of Helena;
     Take not her part. For, if thou dost intend°
     Never so little show of love to her,
     Thou shalt aby° it.

LYSANDER.   Now she holds me now.   335
     Now follow if thou dar'st, to try whose right,
     Of thine or mine, is most in Helena.   [Exit.]

DEMETRIUS.

     Follow? Nay, I'll go with thee, cheek by jowl.°

                              [Exit, following Lysander.]

HERMIA.

     You, mistress, all this coil° is 'long of° you.
     Nay, go not back.°

HELENA.   I will not trust you, I,   340
     Nor longer stay in your curst company.
     Your hands than mine are quicker for a fray;
     My legs are longer, though, to run away.   [Exit.]

HERMIA.

     I am amazed and know not what to say.   Exit.

[Oberon and Puck come forward.]

OBERON.

     This is thy negligence. Still thou mistak'st,   345
     Or else committ'st thy knaveries willfully.

PUCK.

     Believe me, king of shadows, I mistook.
     Did not you tell me I should know the man
     By the Athenian garments he had on?
     And so far blameless proves my enterprise   350

---

288 **puppet** (1) counterfeit (2) dwarfish woman (in reference to Hermia's smaller stature)   289 **Why, so** i.e., Oh, so that's how it is   300 **curst** shrewish   302 **right** true   304 **something** somewhat   310 **stealth** stealing away   312 **chid me hence** drive me away with his scolding   314 **so** if only   317 **fond** foolish

323 **keen** fierce, cruel. **shrewd** shrewish   329 **minimus** diminutive creature. **knotgrass** a weed, an infusion of which was thought to stunt the growth   333 **intend** give sign of   335 **aby** pay for   338 **cheek by jowl** i.e., side by side   339 **coil** turmoil, dissension. **'long of** on account of   340 **go not back** i.e., don't retreat. (Hermia is again proposing a fight.)

That I have 'nointed an Athenian's eyes;
And so far° am I glad it so did sort,°
As° this their jangling I esteem a sport.
OBERON.
    Thou seest these lovers seek a place to fight.
355   Hie° therefore, Robin, overcast the night;
    The starry welkin° cover thou anon
    With drooping fog as black as Acheron,°
    And lead these testy rivals so astray
    As° one come not within another's way.
360   Like to Lysander sometimes frame thy tongue,
    Then stir Demetrius up with bitter wrong;°
    And sometimes rail thou like Demetrius.
    And from each other look thou lead them thus,
    Till o'er their brows death-counterfeiting sleep
365   With leaden legs and batty° wings doth creep.
    Then crush this herb° into Lysander's eye,

                                   [giving herb]

    Whose liquor hath this virtuous° property,
    To take from thence all error with his° might
    And make his eyeballs roll with wonted° sight.
370   When they next wake, all this derision°
    Shall seem a dream and fruitless vision,
    And back to Athens shall the lovers wend
    With league whose date° till death shall never end.
    Whiles I in this affair do thee employ,
375   I'll to my queen and beg her Indian boy;
    And then I will her charmèd eye release
    From monster's view, and all things shall be peace.
PUCK.
    My fairy lord, this must be done with haste,
    For night's swift dragons° cut the clouds full fast,
380   And yonder shines Aurora's° harbinger,
    At whose approach ghosts, wand'ring here and
        there,
    Troop home to churchyards. Damnèd spirits all,
    That in crossways and floods have burial,°
    Already to their wormy beds are gone.
385   For fear lest day should look their shames upon,
    They willfully themselves exile from light

And must for aye° consort with black-browed night.
OBERON.
    But we are spirits of another sort.
    I with the Morning's love° have oft made sport,
    And, like a forester,° the groves may tread   390
    Even till the eastern gate, all fiery red,
    Opening on Neptune with fair blessèd beams,
    Turns into yellow gold his salt green streams.
    But notwithstanding, haste, make no delay.
    We may effect this business yet ere day.   395

                                    [Exit.]

PUCK.
    Up and down, up and down,
    I will lead them up and down.
    I am feared in field and town.
    Goblin,° lead them up and down.
    Here comes one.   400

    Enter Lysander.

LYSANDER.
    Where art thou, proud Demetrius? Speak thou now.
PUCK [*mimicking Demetrius*].
    Here, villain, drawn° and ready. Where art thou?
LYSANDER.
    I will be with thee straight.°
PUCK   Follow me, then,
    To plainer° ground.
        [Lysander wanders about,° following the voice.]

    Enter Demetrius.

DEMETRIUS.   Lysander! Speak again!
    Thou runaway, thou coward, art thou fled?   405
    Speak! In some bush? Where dost thou hide thy
        head?
PUCK [*mimicking Lysander*].
    Thou coward, art thou bragging to the stars,
    Telling the bushes that thou look'st for wars,
    And wilt not come? Come, recreant;° come, thou
        child,
    I'll whip thee with a rod. He is defiled   410
    That draws a sword on thee.
DEMETRIUS.   Yea, art thou there?
PUCK.
    Follow my voice. We'll try° no manhood here.

                                  Exeunt.

---

352 so far at least to this extent. **sort** turn out   **353 As** in that **355 Hie** hasten   **356 welkin** sky   **357 Acheron** river of Hades (here representing Hades itself)   **359 As** that   **361 wrong** insults   **365 batty** batlike   **366 this herb** i.e., the antidote (mentioned in 2.1.184) to love-in-idleness   **367 virtuous** efficacious **368 his** its   **369 wonted** accustomed   **370 derision** laughable business   **373 date** term of existence   **379 dragons** (Supposed by Shakespeare to be yoked to the car of the goddess of night or the moon.)   **380 Aurora's harbinger** the morning star, precursor of dawn   **383 crossways . . . burial** (Those who had committed suicide were buried at crossways, with a stake driven through them; those who intentionally or accidentally drowned (in *floods* or deep water) would be condemned to wander disconsolately for lack of burial rites.)

387 for aye forever   **389 the Morning's love** Cephalus, a beautiful youth beloved by Aurora; or perhaps the goddess of the dawn herself   **390 forester** keeper of a royal forest   **399 Goblin** Hobgoblin. (Puck refers to himself.)   **402 drawn** with drawn sword **403 straight** immediately   **404 plainer** more open. **s.d. Lysander wanders about** (Lysander may exit here, but perhaps not; neither exit nor reentrance is indicated in the early texts.)   **409 recreant** cowardly wretch   **412 try** test

[*Lysander returns.*]

LYSANDER.
  He goes before me and still dares me on.
  When I come where he calls, then he is gone.
415 The villain is much lighter-heeled than I.
  I followed fast, but faster he did fly,
  That fallen am I in dark uneven way,
  And here will rest me. [*He lies down.*] Come, thou
    gentle day!
  For if but once thou show me thy gray light,
420 I'll find Demetrius and revenge this spite.
                                    [*He sleeps.*]

[*Enter*] Robin [*Puck*] *and Demetrius.*

PUCK.
  Ho, ho, ho! Coward, why com'st thou not?
DEMETRIUS.
  Abide° me, if thou dar'st; for well I wot°
  Thou runn'st before me, shifting every place,
  And dar'st not stand nor look me in the face.
  Where art thou now?
425 PUCK.   Come hither. I am here.
DEMETRIUS.
  Nay, then, thou mock'st me. Thou shalt buy° this
    dear,°
  If ever I thy face by daylight see.
  Now go thy way. Faintness constraineth me
  To measure out my length on this cold bed.
430 By day's approach look to be visited.
                        [*He lies down and sleeps.*]

Enter Helena.

HELENA.
  O weary night, O long and tedious night,
    Abate° thy hours! Shine comforts from the east,
  That I may back to Athens by daylight
    From these that my poor company detest;
435 And sleep, that sometimes shuts up sorrow's eye,
  Steal me awhile from mine own company.
                    [*She lies down and*] sleep[*s*].

PUCK.
  Yet but three? Come one more;
  Two of both kinds makes up four.
  Here she comes, curst° and sad.
440 Cupid is a knavish lad,
  Thus to make poor females mad.

[*Enter Hermia.*]

HERMIA.
  Never so weary, never so in woe,

  Bedabbled with the dew and torn with briers,
  I can no further crawl, no further go;
    My legs can keep no pace with my desires.   445
  Here will I rest me till the break of day.
  Heavens shield Lysander, if they mean a fray!
                    [*She lies down and sleeps.*]

PUCK.
      On the ground
      Sleep sound.
      I'll apply   450
      To your eye,
      Gentle lover, remedy.
              [*He squeezes the juice on Lysander's eyes.*]
        When thou wak'st,
        Thou tak'st
        True delight   455
        In the sight
      Of thy former lady's eye;
      And the country proverb known,
      That every man should take his own,
      In your waking shall be shown: 460
        Jack shall have Jill;°
        Naught shall go ill;
      The man shall have his mare again, and all shall be
      well.   [*Exit. The four sleeping lovers remain.*]

4.1°   *Enter* [*Titania,*] *Queen of Fairies, and* [*Bottom the*]
        clown, and Fairies; and [*Oberon,*] *the King, behind*
        them.

TITANIA.
  Come, sit thee down upon this flowery bed,
    While I thy amiable° cheeks do coy,
  And stick muskroses in thy sleek smooth head,
    And kiss thy fair large ears, my gentle joy.
                                    [*They recline.*]

BOTTOM. Where's Peaseblossom?   5
PEASEBLOSSOM. Ready.
BOTTOM. Scratch my head, Peaseblossom. Where's Monsieur Cobweb?
COBWEB. Ready.
BOTTOM. Monsieur Cobweb, good monsieur, get you your 10
  weapons in your hand, and kill me a red-hipped humble-
  bee on the top of a thistle; and, good monsieur, bring me
  the honey bag. Do not fret yourself too much in the action, monsieur; and, good monsieur, have a care the
  honey bag break not. I would be loath to have you over- 15
  flown with a honey bag, signor. [*Exit Cobweb.*] Where's
  Monsieur Mustardseed?

461 **Jack shall have Jill** (Proverbial for "boy gets girl.")
4.1 Location: The action is continuous. The four lovers are still
asleep onstage. (Compare with the Folio stage direction: "They
sleep all the act.")
2 **amiable** lovely. **coy** caress

422 **Abide** confront, face. **wot** know   426 **buy** aby, pay for. **dear**
dearly   432 **Abate** lessen, shorten   439 **curst** ill-tempered

MUSTARDSEED. Ready.

BOTTOM. Give me your neaf,° Monsieur Mustardseed. Pray
20   you, leave your courtesy,° good monsieur.

MUSTARDSEED. What's your will?

BOTTOM. Nothing, good monsieur, but to help Cavalery°
      Cobweb° to scratch. I must to the barber's, monsieur, for
      methinks I am marvelous hairy about the face; and I am
25   such a tender ass, if my hair do but tickle me I must
      scratch.

TITANIA.
      What, wilt thou hear some music, my sweet love?

BOTTOM. I have a reasonable good ear in music. Let's have
      the tongs and the bones.°

                              [Music: tongs, rural music.]°

TITANIA.
30   Or say, sweet love, what thou desirest to eat.

BOTTOM. Truly, a peck of provender.° I could munch your
      good dry oats. Methinks I have a great desire to a bottle°
      of hay. Good hay, sweet hay, hath no fellow.°

TITANIA.
      I have a venturous fairy that shall seek
35   The squirrel's hoard, and fetch thee new nuts.

BOTTOM. I had rather have a handful or two of dried peas.
      But, I pray you, let none of your people stir° me. I have an
      exposition of° sleep come upon me.

TITANIA.
      Sleep thou, and I will wind thee in my arms.
40   Fairies, begone, and be all ways° away.

                              [Exeunt Fairies.]

      So doth the woodbine° the sweet honeysuckle
      Gently entwist; the female ivy so
      Enrings the barky fingers of the elm.
      O, how I love thee! How I dote on thee!

                              [They sleep.]

Enter Robin Goodfellow [Puck].

OBERON [coming forward].
45   Welcome, good Robin. Seest thou this sweet sight?
      Her dotage now I do begin to pity.
      For, meeting her of late behind the wood
      Seeking sweet favors° for this hateful fool,

I did upbraid her and fall out with her.
For she his hairy temples then had rounded   50
With coronet of fresh and fragrant flowers;
And that same dew, which sometime° on the buds
Was wont to swell like round and orient pearls,°
Stood now within the pretty flowerets' eyes
Like tears that did their own disgrace bewail.   55
When I had at my pleasure taunted her,
And she in mild terms begged my patience,
I then did ask of her her changeling child,
Which straight she gave me, and her fairy sent
To bear him to my bower in Fairyland.   60
And, now I have the boy, I will undo
This hateful imperfection of her eyes.
And, gentle Puck, take this transformèd scalp
From off the head of this Athenian swain,
That he, awaking when the other° do,   65
May all to Athens back again repair,°
And think no more of this night's accidents
But as the fierce vexation of a dream.
But first I will release the Fairy Queen.

                    [He squeezes an herb on her eyes.]

      Be as thou wast wont to be;   70
      See as thou wast wont to see.
      Dian's bud° o'er Cupid's flower
      Hath such force and blessèd power.
Now, my Titania, wake you, my sweet queen.

TITANIA [awaking].
      My Oberon! What visions have I seen!   75
      Methought I was enamored of an ass.

OBERON.
      There lies your love.

TITANIA.   How came these things to pass?
      O, how mine eyes do loathe his visage now!

OBERON.
      Silence awhile. Robin, take off this head.
      Titania, music call, and strike more dead   80
      Than common sleep of all these five° the sense.

TITANIA.
      Music, ho! Music, such as charmeth° sleep!   [Music.]

PUCK [removing the ass head].
      Now, when thou wak'st, with thine own fool's eyes
        peep.

OBERON.
      Sound, music! Come, my queen, take hands with me,
      And rock the ground whereon these sleepers be.   85

19 neaf fist   20 leave your courtesy i.e., stop bowing, or put on
your hat   22–23 Cavalery cavalier. (Form of address for a gentleman.)   23 Cobweb (Seemingly an error, since Cobweb has been
sent to bring honey, while Peaseblossom has been asked to scratch.)
29 tongs . . . bones instruments for rustic music. (The tongs were
played like a triangle, whereas the bones were held between the fingers and used as clappers.)   s.d. Music . . . music (This stage direction is added from the Folio.)   31 peck of provender one-
quarter bushel of grain   32 bottle bundle   33 fellow equal   37
stir disturb   38 exposition of (Bottom's phrase for "disposition
to.")   40 all ways in all directions   41 woodbine bindweed, a
climbing plant that twines in the opposite direction from that of
honeysuckle   48 favors i.e., gifts of flowers

52 sometime formerly   53 orient pearls i.e., the most beautiful of
all pearls, those coming from the Orient   65 other others   66 repair return   72 Dian's bud (Perhaps the flower of the agnus castus
or chaste-tree, supposed to preserve chastity; or perhaps referring
simply to Oberon's herb by which he can undo the effects of
"Cupid's flower," the love-in-idleness of 2.1.166–168.)   81 these
five i.e., the four lovers and Bottom   82 charmeth brings about, as
though by a charm

[They dance.]

Now thou and I are new in amity,
And will tomorrow midnight solemnly°
Dance in Duke Theseus' house triumphantly,
And bless it to all fair prosperity.
90   There shall the pairs of faithful lovers be
Wedded, with Theseus, all in jollity.

PUCK.
      Fairy King, attend, and mark:
      I do hear the morning lark.

OBERON.
      Then, my queen, in silence sad,°
95   Trip we after night's shade.
      We the globe can compass soon,
      Swifter than the wandering moon.

TITANIA.
      Come, my lord, and in our flight
      Tell me how it came this night
100   That I sleeping here was found
      With these mortals on the ground.

                    Exeunt [*Oberon, Titania, and Puck*].
                    Wind horn [*within*].

Enter Theseus and all his train; [*Hippolyta, Egeus*].

THESEUS.
      Go, one of you, find out the forester,
      For now our observation° is performed;
      And since we have the vaward° of the day,
105   My love shall hear the music of my hounds.
      Uncouple° in the western valley; let them go.
      Dispatch, I say, and find the forester.

                              [Exit an Attendant.]

      We will, fair queen, up to the mountain's top
      And mark the musical confusion
110   Of hounds and echo in conjunction.

HIPPOLYTA.
      I was with Hercules and Cadmus° once
      When in a wood of Crete they bayed° the bear
      With hounds of Sparta.° Never did I hear
      Such gallant chiding;° for, besides the groves,
115   The skies, the fountains, every region near
      Seemed all one mutual cry. I never heard
      So musical a discord, such sweet thunder.

THESEUS.
      My hounds are bred out of the Spartan kind,°

So flewed,° so sanded;° and their heads are hung
With ears that sweep away the morning dew;   120
Crook-kneed, and dewlapped° like Thessalian bulls;
Slow in pursuit, but matched in mouth like bells,
Each under each.° A cry° more tunable°
Was never holloed to nor cheered° with horn
In Crete, in Sparta, nor in Thessaly.   125
Judge when you hear. [*He sees the sleepers.*] But soft!°
      What nymphs are these?

EGEUS.
      My lord, this is my daughter here asleep,
      And this Lysander; this Demetrius is;
      This Helena, old Nedar's Helana.
      I wonder° of their being here together.   130

THESEUS.
      No doubt they rose up early to observe
      The rite of May, and hearing our intent,
      Came here in grace of our solemnity.°
      But speak, Egeus. Is not this the day
      That Hermia should give answer of her choice? 135

EGEUS. It is, my lord.

THESEUS.
      Go bid the huntsmen wake them with their horns.

                              [Exit an Attendant.]

Shout within. Wind horns. They all start up.

      Good morrow, friends. Saint Valentine° is past.
      Begin these woodbirds but to couple now?

LYSANDER.
      Pardon, my lord.   *[They kneel.]*

THESEUS.   I pray you all, stand up.   140

                              [They stand.]

      I know you two are rival enemies;
      How comes this gentle concord in the world,
      That hatred is so far from jealousy°
      To sleep by hate and fear no enmity?

LYSANDER.
      My lord, I shall reply amazedly,   145
      Half sleep, half waking; but as yet, I swear,
      I cannot truly say how I came here.
      But, as I think—for truly would I speak,
      And now I do bethink me, so it is—
      I came with Hermia hither. Our intent   150

87 **solemnly** ceremoniously   94 **sad** sober   103 **observation** i.e.,
observance to a morn of May (1.1.167).   104 **vaward** vanguard,
i.e., earliest past   106 **Uncouple** set free for the hunt   111 **Cadmus** mythical founder of Thebes. (This story about him is unknown.)   112 **bayed** brought to bay   113 **hounds of Sparta** (A
breed famous in antiquity for their hunting skill.)   114 **chiding**
i.e., yelping   118 **kind** strain, breed

119 **So flewed** similarly having large hanging chaps or fleshy covering of the jaw. **sanded** of sandy color   121 **dewlapped** having pen-
dulous folds of skin under the neck   122–123 **matched . . . each**
i.e., harmoniously matched in their various cries like a set of bells,
from treble down to bass   123 **cry** pack of hounds. **tunable** well
tuned, melodious   124 **cheered** encouraged   126 **soft** i.e., gently,
wait a minute   130 **wonder of** wonder at   133 **in . . . solemnity**
in honor of our wedding ceremony   138 **Saint Valentine** (Birds
were supposed to choose their mates on Saint Valentine's Day.)
143 **jealousy** suspicion

Was to be gone from Athens, where° we might,
Without° the peril of the Athenian law—
EGEUS.
  Enough, enough, my lord; you have enough.
  I beg the law, the law, upon his head.
  They would have stol'n away; they would,
155   Demetrius,
  Thereby to have defeated° you and me,
  You of your wife and me of my consent,
  Of my consent that she should be your wife.
DEMETRIUS.
  My lord, fair Helen told me of their stealth,
160 Of this their purpose hither° to this wood,
  And I in fury hither followed them,
  Fair Helena in fancy° following me.
  But, my good lord, I wot not by what power—
  But by some power it is—my love to Hermia,
165 Melted as the snow, seems to me now
  As the remembrance of an idle gaud°
  Which in my childhood I did dote upon;
  And all the faith, the virtue of my heart,
  The object and the pleasure of mine eye,
170 Is only Helena. To her, my lord,
  Was I betrothed ere I saw Hermia,
  But like a sickness did I loathe this food;
  But, as in health, come to my natural taste,
  Now I do wish it, love it, long for it,
175 And will forevermore be true to it.
THESEUS.
  Fair lovers, you are fortunately met.
  Of this discourse we more will hear anon.
  Egeus, I will overbear your will;
  For in the temple, by and by, with us
180 These couples shall eternally be knit.
  And, for° the morning now is something° worn,
  Our purposed hunting shall be set aside.
  Away with us to Athens. Three and three,
  We'll hold a feast in great solemnity.°
185 Come, Hippolyta.
          [Exeunt Theseus, Hippolyta, Egeus, and train.]
DEMETRIUS.
  These things seem small and undistinguishable,
  Like far-off mountains turnèd into clouds.
HERMIA.
  Methinks I see these things with parted° eye,
  When everything seems double.
HELENA.   So methinks;

And I have found Demetrius like a jewel,   190
Mine own, and not mine own.°
DEMETRIUS.   Are you sure
  That we are awake? It seems to me
  That yet we sleep, we dream. Do not you think
  The Duke was here, and bid us follow him?
HERMIA.
  Yea, and my father.
HELENA.   And Hippolyta.   195
LYSANDER.
  And he did bid us follow to the temple.
DEMETRIUS.
  Why, then, we are awake. Let's follow him,
  And by the way let us recount our dreams.
                              [Exeunt the lovers.]
BOTTOM [awaking]. When my cue comes, call me, and I will
  answer. My next is "Most fair Pyramus." Heigh-ho! Peter 200
  Quince! Flute, the bellows mender! Snout, the tinker!
  Starveling! God's° my life, stolen hence and left me
  asleep! I have had a most rare vision. I have had a dream,
  past the wit of man to say what dream it was. Man is but
  an ass if he go about° to expound this dream. Methought   205
  I was—there is no man can tell what. Methought I was—
  and methought I had—but man is but a patched° fool if
  he will offer° to say what methought I had. The eye of
  man hath not heard, the ear of man hath not seen, man's
  hand is not able to taste, his tongue to conceive, nor his 210
  heart to report, what my dream was. I will get Peter
  Quince to write a ballad° of this dream. It shall be called
  "Bottom's Dream," because it hath no bottom;° and I will
  sing it in the latter end of a play, before the Duke. Peradventure, to make it the more gracious, I shall sing it at   215
  her° death.
                                          [Exit.]

4 . 2 °   Enter Quince, Flute, [Snout, and Starveling].

QUINCE. Have you sent to Bottom's house? Is he come home
  yet?
STARVELING. He cannot be heard of. Out of doubt he is
  transported.°
FLUTE. If he come not, then the play is marred. It goes not 5
  forward. Doth it?

---

151 **where** wherever; or, to where   152 **Without** outside of, beyond   156 **defeated** defrauded   160 **hither** in coming hither
162 **in fancy** driven by love   166 **idle gaud** worthless trinket
181 **for** since. **something** somewhat   184 **in great solemnity** with
great ceremony   188 **parted** i.e., improperly focused

190–191 **like . . . mine own** i.e., like a jewel that one finds by
chance and therefore possesses but cannot certainly consider one's
own property   202 **God's** may God save   205 **go about** attempt
207-08 **patched** wearing motley, i.e., a dress of various colors. **offer**
venture   209–211 **The eye . . . report** (Bottom garbles the terms
of 1 Corinthians 2:9.)   212 **ballad** (The proper medium for relating sensational stories and preposterous events.)   213 **hath no
bottom** is unfathomable   216 **her** Thisbe's (?)
4.2 Location: Athens.
4 **transported** carried off by fairies; or, possibly, transformed

QUINCE. It is not possible. You have not a man in all Athens
  able to discharge° Pyramus but he.
FLUTE. No, he hath simply the best wit° of any handicraft
10 man in Athens.
QUINCE. Yea, and the best person° too, and he is a very
  paramour for a sweet voice.
FLUTE. You must say "paragon." A paramour is, God bless us,
  a thing of naught.°

Enter Snug the joiner.

15 SNUG. Masters, the Duke is coming from the temple, and
  there is two or three lords and ladies more married. If our
  sport had gone forward, we had all been made men.°
FLUTE. O sweet bully Bottom! Thus hath he lost sixpence a
  day° during his life; he could not have scaped sixpence a
20 day. An the Duke had not given him sixpence a day for
  playing Pyramus, I'll be hanged. He would have deserved
  it. Sixpence a day in Pyramus, or nothing.

Enter Bottom.

BOTTOM. Where are these lads? Where are these hearts?°
QUINCE. Bottom! O most courageous day! O most happy
25 hour!
BOTTOM. Masters, I am to discourse wonders.° But ask me
  not what, for if I tell you, I am no true Athenian. I will
  tell you everything, right as it fell out.
QUINCE. Let us hear, sweet Bottom.
30 BOTTOM. Not a word of° me. All that I will tell you is that
  the Duke hath dined. Get your apparel together, good
  strings° to your beards, new ribbons to your pumps;° meet
  presently° at the palace; every man look o'er his part; for
  the short and the long is, our play is preferred.° In any
35 case, let Thisbe have clean linen; and let not him that
  plays the lion pare his nails, for they shall hang out for
  the lion's claws. And, most dear actors, eat no onions nor
  garlic, for we are to utter sweet breath; and I do not doubt
  but to hear them say it is a sweet comedy. No more words.
40 Away! Go, away!

[*Exeunt.*]

5 . 1 °   *Enter Theseus, Hippolyta, and Philostrate, [lords,*
  and attendants].

HIPPOLYTA.
  'Tis strange, my Theseus, that° these lovers speak of.

THESEUS.
  More strange than true. I never may° believe
  These antique° fables nor these fairy toys.°
  Lovers and madmen have such seething brains
  Such shaping fantasies,° that apprehend°   5
  More than cool reason ever comprehends.°
  The lunatic, the lover, and the poet
  Are of imagination all compact.°
  One sees more devils than vast hell can hold;
  That is the madman. The lover, all as frantic,   10
  Sees Helen's° beauty in a brow of Egypt.°
  The poet's eye, in a fine frenzy rolling,
  Doth glance from heaven to earth, from earth to
    heaven;
  And as imagination bodies forth
  The forms of things unknown, the poet's pen   15
  Turns them to shapes and gives to airy nothing
  A local habitation and a name.
  Such tricks hath strong imagination
  That, if it would but apprehend some joy,
  It comprehends some bringer° of that joy;   20
  Or in the night, imagining some fear,°
  How easy is a bush supposed a bear!

HIPPOLYTA.
  But all the story of the night told over,
  And all their minds transfigured so together,
  More witnesseth than fancy's images°   25
  And grows to something of great constancy;°
  But, howsoever,° strange and admirable.°

Enter lovers: Lysander, Demetrius, Hermia, and Helena.

THESEUS.
  Here come the lovers, full of joy and mirth.
  Joy, gentle friends! Joy and fresh days of love
  Accompany your hearts!
LYSANDER.   More than to us   30
  Wait in your royal walks, your board, your bed!
THESEUS.
  Come now, what masques,° what dances shall we
    have,
  To wear away this long age of three hours
  Between our after-supper and bedtime?
  Where is our usual manager of mirth?   35
  What revels are in hand? Is there no play

---

8 **discharge** perform **9 wit** intellect **11 person** appearance
14 a . . . naught a shameful thing **17 we . . . men** i.e., we would
have had our fortunes made **18–19 sixpence a day** i.e., as a royal
pension **23 hearts** good fellows **26 am . . . wonders** have wonders to relate **30 of** out of **32 strings** (to attach the beards).
pumps light shoes or slippers **33 presently** immediately **34 preferred** selected for consideration
5.1 Location: Athens. The palace of Theseus.
1 that that which

2 **may** can **3 antique** old-fashioned (punning, too, on *antic*,
"strange," "grotesque"). **fairy toys** trifling stories about fairies **5
fantasies** imaginations. **apprehend** conceive, imagine **6 comprehends** understands **8 compact** formed, composed **11 Helen's**
i.e., of Helen of Troy, pattern of beauty. **brow of Egypt** i.e., face of a
gypsy **20 bringer** i.e., source **21 fear** object of fear **25 More
. . . images** testifies to something more substantial than mere imaginings **26 constancy** certainty **27 howsoever** in any case. **admirable** a source of wonder **32 masques** courtly entertainments

To ease the anguish of a torturing hour?
Call Philostrate.
PHILOSTRATE.　　　　　Here, mighty Theseus.
THESEUS.
Say, what abridgment° have you for this evening?
40　What masque? What music? How shall we beguile
The lazy time, if not with some delight?
PHILOSTRATE [*giving him a paper*].
There is a brief° how many sports are ripe.
Make choice of which Your Highness will see first.
THESEUS [*reads*].
"The battle with the Centaurs,° to be sung
45　By an Athenian eunuch to the harp"?
We'll none of that. That have I told my love,
In glory of my kinsman° Hercules.
[*He reads.*] "The riot of the tipsy Bacchanals,
Tearing the Thracian singer in their rage"?°
50　That is an old device;° and it was played
When I from Thebes came last a conqueror.
[*He reads.*] "The thrice three Muses mourning for the
　　death
Of Learning, late deceased in beggary"?°
That is some satire, keen and critical,
55　Not sorting with° a nuptial ceremony.
[*He reads.*] "A tedious brief scene of young Pyramus
And his love Thisbe; very tragical mirth"?
Merry and tragical? Tedious and brief?
That is, hot ice and wondrous strange° snow.
60　How shall we find the concord of this discord?
PHILOSTRATE.
A play there is, my lord, some ten words long,
Which is as brief as I have known a play;
But by ten words, my lord, it is too long,
Which makes it tedious. For in all the play
65　There is not one word apt, one player fitted.
And tragical, my noble lord, it is,
For Pyramus therein doth kill himself.
Which, when I saw rehearsed, I must confess,

Made mine eyes water; but more merry tears
The passion of loud laughter never shed.　　　　　　70
THESEUS.　What are they that do play it?
PHILOSTRATE.
Hardhanded men that work in Athens here,
Which never labored in their minds till now,
And now have toiled° their unbreathed memories
With this same play, against° your nuptial.　　　　　75
THESEUS.
And we will hear it.
PHILOSTRATE.　　　　　No, my noble lord,
It is not for you. I have heard it over,
And it is nothing, nothing in the world;
Unless you can find sport in their intents,
Extremely stretched° and conned with cruel pain　　80
To do you service.
THESEUS.　　　　　I will hear that play;
For never anything can be amiss
When simpleness° and duty tender it.
Go, bring them in; and take your places, ladies.
　　　　　　　[*Philostrate goes to summon the players.*]
HIPPOLYTA.
I love not to see wretchedness o'ercharged,°　　　　85
And duty in his service° perishing.
THESEUS.
Why, gentle sweet, you shall see no such thing.
HIPPOLYTA.
He says they can do nothing in this kind.°
THESEUS.
The kinder we, to give them thanks for nothing.
Our sport shall be to take what they mistake;　　　90
And what poor duty cannot do, noble respect°
Takes it in might, not merit.°
Where I have come, great clerks° have purposèd
To greet me with premeditated welcomes;
Where I have seen them shiver and look pale,　　　95
Make periods in the midst of sentences,
Throttle their practiced accent° in their fears,
And in conclusion dumbly have broken off,
Not paying me a welcome. Trust me, sweet,
Out of this silence yet I picked a welcome;　　　100
And in the modesty of fearful duty
I read as much as from the rattling tongue
Of saucy and audacious eloquence.
Love, therefore, and tongue-tied simplicity

---

39 abridgment pastime (to abridge or shorten the evening)　**42 brief** short written statement, summary　**44 battle . . . Centaurs** (Probably refers to the battle of the Centaurs and the Lapithae, when the Centaurs attempted to carry off Hippodamia, bride of Theseus' friend Pirothous. The story is told in Ovid's *Metamorphoses* 12.)　**47 kinsman** (Plutarch's "Life of Theseus" states that Hercules and Theseus were near kinsmen. Theseus is referring to a version of the battle of the Centaurs in which Hercules was said to be present.)　**48–49 The riot . . . rage** (This was the story of the death of Orpheus, as told in *Metamorphoses* 11.)　**50 device** show, performance　**52–53 The thrice . . . beggary** (Possibly an allusion to Spenser's *Teares of the Muses*, 1591, though "satires" deploring the neglect of learning and the creative arts were commonplace.)　**55 sorting with** befitting　**59 strange** (Sometimes emended to an adjective that would contrast with *snow*, just as *hot* contrasts with *ice*.)

74 toiled taxed. **unbreathed** unexercised　**75 against** in preparation for　**80 stretched** strained. **conned** memorized　**83 simpleness** simplicity　**85 wretchedness o'ercharged** social or intellectual inferiors overburdened　**86 his service** its attempt to serve　**88 kind** kind of thing　**91 respect** evaluation, consideration　**92 Takes . . . merit** values it for the effort made rather than for the excellence achieved.　**93 clerks** learned men　**97 practiced accent** i.e., rehearsed speech; or, usual way of speaking

105 　In least° speak most, to my capacity.°

　　　　[*Philostrate returns.*]

PHILOSTRATE.
　So please Your Grace, the Prologue° is addressed.°
THESEUS.　Let him approach.　　　　[*A flourish of trumpets.*]

　　　Enter the Prologue [*Quince*].

PROLOGUE.
　If we offend, it is with our good will.
　　That you should think, we come not to offend,
110 　But with good will. To show our simple skill,
　　That is the true beginning of our end.
　Consider, then, we come but in despite.
　　We do not come, as minding° to content you,
　Our true intent is. All for your delight
115 　　We are not here. That you should here repent you,
　The actors are at hand; and, by their show,
　You shall know all that you are like to know.
THESEUS.　This fellow doth not stand upon points.°
LYSANDER.　He hath rid° his prologue like a rough° colt; he
120 　knows not the stop.° A good moral, my lord: it is not
　enough to speak, but to speak true.
HIPPOLYTA.　Indeed, he hath played on his prologue like a
　child on a recorder:° a sound, but not in government.°
THESEUS.　His speech was like a tangled chain: nothing° im-
125 　paired, but all disordered. Who is next?

　　　Enter Pyramus [*Bottom*], *and Thisbe* [*Flute*], *and Wall*
　　　[*Snout*], *and Moonshine* [*Starveling*], *and Lion* [*Snug*].

PROLOGUE.
　Gentles, perchance you wonder at this show;
　　But wonder on, till truth make all things plain.
　This man is Pyramus, if you would know;
　　This beauteous lady Thisbe is, certain.
130 　This man with lime and roughcast doth present
　　Wall, that vile wall which did these lovers sunder;
　And through Wall's chink, poor souls, they are content
　　To whisper. At the which let no man wonder.
　This man, with lantern, dog, and bush of thorn,
135 　　Presenteth Moonshine; for, if you will know,
　By moonshine did these lovers think no scorn°
　　To meet at Ninus' tomb, there, there to woo.
　This grisly beast, which Lion hight° by name,

The trusty Thisbe coming first by night
Did scare away, or rather did affright;　　　　　140
　And as she fled, her mantle she did fall,°
　Which Lion vile with bloody mouth did stain.
Anon comes Pyramus, sweet youth and tall,°
　And finds his trusty Thisbe's mangle slain;
Whereat, with blade, with bloody, blameful blade,　145
　He bravely broached° his boiling bloody breast.
And Thisbe, tarrying in mulberry shade,
　His dagger drew, and died. For all the rest,
Let Lion, Moonshine, Wall, and lovers twain
At large° discourse, while here they do remain.　150
　　　　　Exeunt Lion, Thisbe, and Moonshine.
THESEUS.　I wonder if the lion be to speak.
DEMETRIUS.　No wonder, my lord. One lion may, when many
　asses do.
WALL.
　In this same interlude° it doth befall
　That I, one Snout by name, present a wall;　　　155
　And such a wall as I would have you think
　That had in it a crannied hole or chink,
　Through which the lovers, Pyramus and Thisbe,
　Did whisper often, very secretly.
　This loam, this roughcast, and this stone doth show　160
　That I am that same wall; the truth is so.
　And this the cranny is, right and sinister,°
　Through which the fearful lovers are to whisper.
THESEUS.　Would you desire lime and hair to speak better?
DEMETRIUS.　It is the wittiest partition° that ever I heard dis-　165
　course, my lord.

　　　[*Pyramus comes forward.*]

THESEUS.　Pyramus draws near the wall. Silence!
PYRAMUS.
　O grim-looked° night! O night with hue so black!
　　O night, which ever art when day is not!
　O night, O night! Alack, alack, alack,　　　　170
　　I fear my Thisbe's promise is forgot.
　And thou, O wall, O sweet, O lovely wall,
　　That stand'st between her father's ground and mine,
　Thou wall, O wall, O sweet and lovely wall,
　　Show me thy chink, to blink through with mine eyne.　175
　　　　　[*Wall makes a chink with his fingers.*]
　Thanks, courteous wall. Jove shield thee well for this.
　　But what see I? No Thisbe do I see.
　O wicked wall, through whom I see no bliss!
　　Cursed be thy stones for thus deceiving me!

---

105 least i.e., saying least. **to my capacity** in my judgment and un-derstanding　**106 Prologue** speaker of the prologue. **addressed** ready　**113 minding** intending　**118 stand upon points** (1) heed niceties or small points (2) pay attention to punctuation in his read-ing. (The humor of Quince's speech is in the blunders of its punctu-ation.)　**119 rid** ridden. **rough** unbroken　**120 stop** (1) stopping of a colt by reining it in (2) punctuation mark　**123 recorder** wind instrument like a flute. **government** control　**124 nothing** not at all　**136 think no scorn** think it no disgraceful matter　**138 hight** is called

141 fall let fall　**143 tall** courageous　**146 broached** stabbed **150 At large** in full, at length　**154 interlude** play　**162 right and sinister** i.e., the right side of it and the left; or, running from right to left, horizontally　**166 partition** (1) wall (2) section of a learned treatise or oration　**168 grim-looked** grim-looking

180 THESEUS. The wall, methinks, being sensible,° should curse
         again.°
     PYRAMUS. No, in truth, sir, he should not. "Deceiving me" is
         Thisbe's cue: she is to enter now, and I am to spy her
         through the wall. You shall see, it will fall pat° as I told
185   you. Yonder she comes.

         Enter Thisbe.

     THISBE.
         O wall, full often hast thou heard my moans
             For parting my fair Pyramus and me.
         My cherry lips have often kissed thy stones,
             Thy stones with lime and hair knit up in thee.
190 PYRAMUS.
         I see a voice. Now will I to the chink,
             To spy an° I can hear my Thisbe's face.
         Thisbe!
     THISBE.   My love! Thou art my love, I think.
     PYRAMUS.
             Think what thou wilt, I am thy lover's grace,°
         And like Limander° am I trusty still.
     THISBE.
195   And I like Helen,° till the Fates me kill.
     PYRAMUS.
         Not Shafalus to Procrus° was so true.
     THISBE.
         As Shafalus to Procrus, I to you.
     PYRAMUS.
         O, kiss me through the hole of this vile wall!
     THISBE.
         I kiss the wall's hole, not your lips at all.
     PYRAMUS.
200   Wilt thou at Ninny's tomb meet me straightway?
     THISBE.
         'Tide° life, 'tide death, I come without delay.
                                 [*Exeunt Pyramus and Thisbe.*]
     WALL.
         Thus have I, Wall, my part dischargèd so;
         And, being done, thus Wall away doth go.   [*Exit.*]
     THESEUS. Now is the mural down between the two neigh-
205   bors.
     DEMETRIUS. No remedy, my lord, when walls are so willful°
         to hear without warning.°
     HIPPOLYTA. This is the silliest stuff that ever I heard.
     THESEUS. The best in this kind° are but shadows;° and the
210   worst are no worse, if imagination amend them.

180 **sensible** capable of feeling   181 **again** in return   184 **pat** exactly   191 **an** if   193 **lover's grace** i.e., gracious lover   194,
195 **Limander, Helen** (Blunders for "Leander" and "Hero.")   196
Shafalus, Procrus (Blunders for "Cephalus" and "Procris," also famous lovers.)   201 **'Tide** betide, come   206–207 **willful** willing.
without warning i.e., without warning the parents. (Demetrius
makes a joke on the proverb "Walls have ears.")   209 **in this kind**
of this sort. **shadows** likenesses, representations

HIPPOLYTA. It must be your imagination then, and not theirs.
THESEUS. If we imagine no worse of them than they of
     themselves, they may pass for excellent men. Here come
     two noble beasts in, a man and a lion.

     Enter Lion and Moonshine.

LION.
     You, ladies, you, whose gentle hearts do fear   215
         The smallest monstrous mouse that creeps on floor,
     May now perchance both quake and tremble here,
         When lion rough in wildest rage doth roar.
     Then know that I, as Snug the joiner, am
     A lion fell,° nor else no lion's dam;   220
     For, if I should as lion come in strife
     Into this place, 'twere pity on my life.
THESEUS. A very gentle beast, and of a good conscience.
DEMETRIUS. The very best at a beast, my lord, that e'er I saw.
LYSANDER. This lion is a very fox for his valor.°   225
THESEUS. True; and a goose for his discretion.°
DEMETRIUS. Not so, my lord, for his valor cannot carry his
     discretion, and the fox carries the goose.
THESEUS. His discretion, I am sure, cannot carry his valor;
     for the goose carries not the fox. It is well. Leave it to his 230
     discretion, and let us listen to the moon.
MOON.
     This lanthorn° doth the hornèd moon present—
DEMETRIUS. He should have worn the horns on his head.°
THESEUS. He is no crescent,° and his horns are invisible
     within the circumference.   235
MOON.
     This lanthorn doth the hornèd moon present;
     Myself the man i' the moon do seem to be.
THESEUS. This is the greatest error of all the rest. The man
     should be put into the lanthorn. How is it else the man i'
     the moon?   240
DEMETRIUS. He dares not come there for the candle, for°
     you see it is already in snuff.°
HIPPOLYTA. I am aweary of this moon. Would he would
     change!
THESEUS. It appears, by his small light of discretion, that he
     is in the wane; but yet, in courtesy, in all reason, we must 245
     stay the time.
LYSANDER. Proceed, Moon.

220 **lion fell** fierce lion (with a play on the idea of "lion skin")
225 **is . . . valor** i.e., his valor consists of craftiness and discretion
226 **a goose . . . discretion** i.e., as discreet as a goose, that is, more
foolish than discreet   232 **lanthorn** (This original spelling, *lanthorn*, may suggest a play on the *horn* of which lanterns were made
and also on a cuckold's horns; however, the spelling *lanthorn* is not
used consistently for comic effect in this play or elsewhere. At
5.1.134, for example, the word *lantern* in the original.)   233 **on his
head** (as a sign of cuckoldry)   234 **crescent** a waxing moon   241
for because of, for fear of   242 **in snuff** (1) offended (2) in need of
snuffing or trimming

MOON. All that I have to say is to tell you that the lanthorn
is the moon, I, the man i' the moon, this thornbush my
250   thornbush, and this dog my dog.
DEMETRIUS. Why, all these should be in the lanthorn, for all
these are in the moon. But silence! Here comes Thisbe.

Enter Thisbe.

THISBE.
This is old Ninny's tomb. Where is my love?
LION [*roaring*]. O!
255 DEMETRIUS. Well roared, Lion.
                                        [*Thisbe runs off, dropping her mantle.*]
THESEUS. Well run, Thisbe.
HIPPOLYTA. Well shone, Moon. Truly the moon shines with
a good grace.
                                        [*The Lion worries Thisbe's mantle.*]
THESEUS. Well moused,° Lion.

[*Enter Pyramus; exit Lion.*]

260 DEMETRIUS. And then came Pyramus.
LYSANDER. And so the lion vanished.
PYRAMUS.
Sweet Moon, I thank thee for thy sunny beams;
I thank thee, Moon, for shining now so bright;
For, by thy gracious, golden, glittering gleams,
265   I trust to take of truest Thisbe sight.
But stay, O spite!
But mark, poor knight,
What dreadful dole° is here?
Eyes, do you see?
270   How can it be?
O dainty duck! O dear!
Thy mantle good,
What, stained with blood?
Approach, ye Furies° fell!°
275   O Fates,° come, come,
Cut thread and thrum;°
Quail,° crush, conclude, and quell!°
THESEUS. This passion, and the death of a dear friend,
would go near to make a man look sad.°
280 HIPPOLYTA. Beshrew my heart, but I pity the man.
PYRAMUS.
O, wherefore, Nature, didst thou lions frame?

Since lion vile hath here deflowered my dear,
Which is—no, no, which was—the fairest dame
That lived, that loved, that liked, that looked with
cheer.°
Come, tears, confound,   285
Out, sword, and wound
The pap of Pyramus;
Ay, that left pap,°
Where heart doth hop.
[*He stabs himself.*]
Thus die I, thus, thus, thus.   290
Now am I dead,
Now am I fled;
My soul is in the sky.
Tongue, lose thy light;
Moon, take thy flight.   [*Exit Moonshine.*]   295
Now die, die, die, die, die.   [*Pyramus dies.*]
DEMETRIUS. No die, but an ace,° for him; for he is but one.°
LYSANDER. Less than an ace, man; for he is dead, he is noth-
ing.
THESUS. With the help of a surgeon he might yet recover,   300
and yet prove an ass.°
HIPPOLYTA. How chance Moonshine is gone before Thisbe
comes back and finds her lover?
THESEUS. She will find him by starlight.

[*Enter Thisbe.*]

Here she comes; and her passion ends the play.   305
HIPPOLYTA. Methinks she should not use a long one for such
a Pyramus. I hope she will be brief.
DEMETRIUS. A mote° will turn the balance, which Pyramus,
which° Thisbe, is the better: he for a man, God warrant
us; she for a woman, God bless us.   310
LYSANDER. She hath spied him already with those sweet
eyes.
DEMETRIUS. And thus she means,° videlicet:°
THISBE.
Asleep, my love?
What, dead, my dove?   315
O Pyramus, arise!
Speak, speak. Quite dumb?
Dead, dead? A tomb
Must cover thy sweet eyes.
These lily lips,
This cherry nose,   320

---

259 moused shaken, torn, bitten   **268 dole** grievous event   **274
Furies** avenging goddesses of Greek myth. **fell** fierce   **275 Fates**
the three goddesses (Clotho, Lachesis, Atropos) of Greek myth who
spun, drew, and cut the thread of human life   **276 thread and
thrum** i.e., everything—the good and bad alike; literally, the warp
in weaving and the loose end of the warp   **277 Quail** overpower.
quell kill, destroy   **278–279 This . . . sad** i.e., if one had other
reason to grieve, one might be sad, but not from this absurd portrayal of passion

284 cheer countenance   **288 pap** breast   **297 ace** the side of the
die featuring the single pip, or spot. (The pun is on *die* as a singular
of *dice*; Bottom's performance is not worth a whole *die* but rather
one single face of it, one small portion.) **one** (1) an individual person (2) unique   **301 ass** (with a pun on ace)   **308 mote** small
particle   **308–309 which . . . which** whether . . . or   **313 means**
moans, laments (with a pun on the meaning, "lodge a formal complaint"). **videlicet** to wit

These yellow cowslip cheeks,
　　Are gone, are gone!
　　Lovers, make moan.
His eyes were green as leeks.
325　　O Sisters Three,°
　　Come, come to me,
With hands as pale as milk;
　　Lay them in gore,
330　　Since you have shore°
With shears his thread of silk.
　　Tongue, not a word.
　　Come, trusty sword,
Come, blade, my breast imbrue!°

　　　　　　　　　　　　　　[She stabs herself.]

335　　And farewell, friends.
　　Thus Thisbe ends.
　　Adieu, adieu, adieu.

　　　　　　　　　　　　　　　　　[She dies.]

THESEUS. Moonshine and Lion are left to bury the dead.
DEMETRIUS. Ay, and Wall too.
340 BOTTOM [starting up, as Flute does also]. No, I assure you, the
　　wall is down that parted their fathers. Will it please you
　　to see the epilogue, or to hear a Bergomask dance° be-
　　tween two of our company?

　　[The other players enter.]

THESEUS. No epilogue, I pray you; for your play needs no ex-
345　cuse. Never excuse; for when the players are all dead,
　　there need none to be blamed. Marry, if he that writ it
　　had played Pyramus and hanged himself in Thisbe's
　　garter, it would have been a fine tragedy; and so it is,
　　truly, and very notably discharged. But, come, your
350　Bergomask. Let your epilogue alone. [A dance.]
　　The iron tongue° of midnight hath told° twelve.
　　Lovers, to bed, 'tis almost fairy time.
　　I fear we shall outsleep the coming morn
　　As much as we this night have overwatched.°
355　This palpable-gross° play hath well beguiled
　　The heavy° gait of night. Sweet friends, to bed.
　　A fortnight hold we this solemnity,
　　In nightly revels and new jollity.

　　　　　　　　　　　　　　　　　Exeunt.

Enter Puck [carrying a broom].

PUCK.
　　Now the hungry lion roars,
360　　And the wolf behowls the moon,

Whilst the heavy° plowman snores,
　　All with weary task fordone.°
Now the wasted brands° do glow,
　　Whilst the screech owl, screeching loud,
Puts the wretch that lies in woe   365
　　In remembrance of a shroud.
Now it is the time of night
　　That the graves, all gaping wide,
Every one lets forth his sprite,°
　　In the church-way paths to glide.   370
And we fairies, that do run
　　By the triple Hecate's° team.
From the presence of the sun,
　　Following darkness like a dream,
Now are frolic.° Not a mouse   375
　　Shall disturb this hallowed house.
I am sent with broom before,
To sweep the dust behind° the door.

Enter [Oberon and Titania,] King and Queen of Fairies,
with all their train.

OBERON.
　　Through the house give glimmering light,
　　　By the dead and drowsy fire;   380
　　Every elf and fairy sprite
　　　Hop as light as bird from brier;
　　And this ditty, after me,
　　Sing, and dance it trippingly.
TITANIA.
　　First, rehearse° your song by rote,   385
　　To each word a warbling note.
　　Hand in hand, with fairy grace,
　　Will we sing, and bless this place.

　　　　　　　　　　　　　　　[Song and dance.]

OBERON.
　　Now, until the break of day,
　　Through this house each fairy stray.   390
　　To the best bride-bed will we,
　　Which by us shall blessèd be;
　　And the issue there create°
　　Ever shall be fortunate.
　　So shall all the couples three   395
　　Ever true in loving be;
　　And the blots of Nature's hand
　　Shall not in their issue stand;

326 Sisters Three the Fates   330 shore shorn   334 imbrue
stain with blood   342 Bergomask dance a rustic dance named
from Bergamo, a province in the state of Venice   351 iron tongue
i.e., of a bell. told counted, struck ("tolled")   354 overwatched
stayed up too late   355 palpable-gross palpably gross, obviously
crude   356 heavy drowsy, dull

361 heavy tired   362 fordone exhausted   363 wasted brands
burned-out logs   369 Every . . . sprite every grave lets forth its
ghost   372 triple Hecate's (Hecate ruled in three capacities: as
Luna or Cynthia in heaven, as Diana on earth, and as Proserpina in
hell.)   375 frolic merry   378 behind from behind, or else like
sweeping the dirt under the carpet. (Robin Goodfellow was a household spirit who helped good housemaids and punished lazy ones, but
he could, of course, be mischievous.)   385 rehearse recite   393
create created

Never mole, harelip, nor scar,
400   Nor mark prodigious,° such as are
Despisèd in nativity,
Shall upon their children be.
With this field dew consecrate,°
Every fairy take his gait,°
405   And each several° chamber bless,
Through this palace, with sweet peace;
And the owner of it blest
Ever shall in safety rest.
Trip away; make no stay;
410   Meet me all by break of day.
                Exeunt [Oberon, Titania, and train].
PUCK [*to the audience*].
  If we shadows have offended,

Think but this, and all is mended,
That you have but slumbered here°
While these visions did appear.
And this weak and idle theme,   415
No more yielding but° a dream,
Gentles, do not reprehend.
If you pardon, we will mend.°
And, as I am an honest Puck,
If we have unearnèd luck   420
Now to scape the serpent's tongue,°
We will make amends ere long;
Else the Puck a liar call.
So, good night unto you all.
Give me your hands,° if we be friends,   425
And Robin shall restore amends.°   [*Exit.*]

413 **That . . . here** i.e., that it is a "midsummer night's dream"
416 **No . . . but** yielding no more than   **418 mend** improve   **421**
serpent's tongue i.e., hissing   **425 Give . . . hands** applaud   **426**
restore amends give satisfaction in return

400 **prodigious** monstrous, unnatural   **403 consecrate** consecrated   **404 take his gait** go his way   **405 several** separate

---

CENTER STAGE   THE MIDSUMMER FESTIVALS OF EUROPE

It is no accident that Shakespeare chose Midsummer's Eve as the setting for his play about mad lovers and mischievous spirits, or that Swedish playwright August Strindberg begins *Miss Julie* with the line, "The Countess Julie is mad tonight." "Tonight" refers to Midsummer's Eve, a time of revelry in the colder climes of northern Europe. It occurs at the summer solstice in mid-June and marks the longest day of the year. It is a time of nocturnal merrymaking that celebrates the procreative spirit and the passionate side of humanity. The festival is associated with madness or "lunacy"—i.e., being "moonstruck," with all its implications of love, lust, and wooing. Today the festival is an entertaining diversion that people eagerly anticipate because it celebrates youth and enchantment, much like Shakespeare's famous comedy.

Europeans mark Midsummer in different ways, yet there are common elements, such as flowers and greenery (symbols of youth, fertility, and life giving), bonfires and fireflies (light in the

Midsummer festivals, such as this in Rättvik, Sweden, are still celebrated throughout northern Europe; the dancers and the pole adorned with greenery remind us that older fertility rites spawned such fêtes.

darkness), and maypoles (totems about which young men and women dance in modern fertility rituals). In France, bonfires are built on every hillside while peasants in holiday dress dance throughout the night to a shepherd's horn. Superstition says that a maiden who dances around nine fires before midnight will be married within the year. In Czechoslovakia brightly dressed women and children search for herbs with mystical healing powers, while a comically dressed farmer leads singing as the herbs are plucked. Russians have a similar custom in which girls search for the blood-red flowers of a fern that blooms only on *Ivana Kupala* (St. John's

Eve). Those who find the flowers are granted their most private wishes.

The Russians also enjoy a short play that demonstrates the dangers of the quest for the ferns. A maiden in peasant dress sets out to find the cherished flowers, but she is hindered by *roussalki*, water nymphs who lure girls entering the forbidden forest into a dangerous water pool. They circle her in a threatening dance, but she repels them by making the sign of the cross. Witches (*vedmi*) with loose hair and long nails shriek and threaten the maiden with broomsticks. The girl fends them off with a crucifix. Thunder rumbles and lightning flashes as a gnomish man

beckons her from behind a tree. He is a *leshji* in bark costume who enchants young girls and then tickles them to death. He, too, is driven away by the sacred relic, and—as the village church bells chime—the girl discovers the red blossoms. Her face is bathed in radiance and her handsome young lover appears from the trees. The play ends with dances around the bonfire, while children cavort with fireflies. The community is renewed by this universal love story, assured that the malevolent forces have been checked for yet another year.

CENTER STAGE A MIDSUMMER NIGHT'S DREAM AT THE GLOBE THEATRE

Old Cade pauses to catch his breath; the long climb up four flights of wooden steps tires him. As he looks across the thatched roof, he can see London rising gloriously on the north bank of the Thames. Both the river and city flourish with activity on this warm June morning. Huge sailing ships, fresh from the Low Countries, the Mediterranean, and especially from the Indies, compete for space with small boats. Cade watches men and animals, carts and carriages, all bustling in the shadows of St. Paul's, the great cathedral that dominates the London skyline. To the east, just beyond London Bridge, stands Tower Hill, where men are hanged even as Londoners picnic on the green near the dreaded Tower of London. To the west, upriver, Parliament and Whitehall beckon proudly as England still basks in the glory of its victory over the Spanish Armada only ten years ago.

Cade savors the view, and then turns to the flagpole to affix a white banner to its ropes. He tugs on the weathered line, and the flag unfurls to reveal the

image of Hercules bearing the weight of the world on his shoulders. He lights the fuse on the old cannon, waits a second, and watches as it flashes, listens as it booms its message to the tradesmen across the river: "Today, a play at the Globe!" Cade douses some smoldering straw on the roof with a bucket of water. "S'blood, that cannon shall burn this theatre to the ground one day," he grumbles as he hurries down the stairs to place props for the play.

By 1:30 the river is awash with boats ferrying people to the South Bank, as many more stream across the bridge, stopping to buy sweetmeats and baked goods from the merchants whose stalls line the bridge. The workday, which began at four, is done and London's citizens, nobility and commoner, rich and poor, are coming to the Globe to see the Lord Chamberlain's Men revive a popular work, A *Midsummer Night's Dream*. Rumor, which constantly races through London's crowded streets, has proclaimed the *Dream* a delight. A coachman saw it at the Worcester estate last

week when it was performed for the earl's daughter's wedding. "By my two thumbs, 'tis a most excellent and mirthful comedy," he told his mates at an Eastcheap tavern. As the Londoners walk along Bankside—amid the ale houses, the stews (where prostitutes beckon), the bear-baiting rings, the cockpits—they talk of fairies and goblins, of deeds wondrous and strange, and of the young dramatist who has caught their imagination with such plays as *Henry V*, *Romeo and Juliet*, and *The Taming of the Shrew*. Over 2,000 spectators file into the theater through a small door, the commoners paying a penny to stand shoulder to shoulder on the ground around the great stage of the Globe. The wealthy offer an additional penny to sit in one of the three tiers of galleries that overlook the stage. Young girls wriggle their way through the crowd to sell oranges, oysters, and nuts to the carpenters, weavers, joiners, bellows menders, and tinkers.

Backstage two dozen members of the Lord Chamberlain's Men are

(continued)

ROBIN
GOOD-FELLOW,
HIS MAD PRANKES AND MERRY IESTS.

Full of honeſt Mirth, and is a fit Medicine for Melancholy.

Printed at *London* by *Thomas Cotes,* and are to be ſold by *Franſis Grove,* at his ſhop on Snow-hill, neere the Sarazens-head. 1639.

This 1639 drawing of Robin Goodfellow suggests that Shakespeare's audience likely viewed Puck as a sinister figure. Note the Dionysian imagery (goat horns and hair, vine leaves, and phallus) in Puck's costume.

dressing. Some wear clothing much like that of the workers in the pit; others attire themselves in handsome doublets and gowns bequeathed to them by nobles who brag that their garments can be seen at the Globe. George Bryan, the acrobatic comedian, is bare chested; he plops a crown of ivy and wildflowers on his head, smears a paste of wheat flour on his face, turns and yells across the room, "D'ye think I look like a proper hobgoblin, Henry Condell?" "Aye, as proper a Puck as any man in England," Condell laughs. In another corner sits tall, portly Richard Burbage, the company's finest actor and son of the carpenter who built London's first public theater over twenty years ago. Burbage reviews Oberon's lines with young Richard Sharpe, who will play the Fairie Queen. Near them, several boy apprentices softly rehearse a song, "You spotted snakes with double tongue. . . ."

Cade enters and taps the hard wooden floor three times with his staff. The actors grow quiet, and 31-year-old Will Shakespeare gathers the company about him. "Speak your speeches as I told you; but if you mouth them I'll soon get the town crier to speak them. And you, Will Kempe, speak no more than is set down for you. Bottom's part is written excellent well and needs not your saucy jests. You showed a most pitiful ambition at the earl's last week. Reform it well, Will. Use all gently, my masters, and o'erstep not the modesty of nature. Now go make yourselves ready."

At precisely two o'clock the musicians play the opening sennet from a small gallery on the third floor. Their trumpets quiet the boisterous crowd, and a doorway at stage right opens for a boy carrying a large placard announcing the name of the play—"Midfommer Nights Dreame" [sic]. Another youth enters from the stage left door with a sign proclaiming "The Courte of Theseus, Duke of Athens," as Cade settles onto a stool on the side stage, script in hand, ready to prompt any actor whose memory falters. Behind him, upstage, a multicolored curtain, used only for comic plays, opens to reveal a large throne and a handsome young boy dressed as a Tudor noblewoman—indeed, he looks like Elizabeth herself! On the throne sits William Ostler—"the Sole King of Actors"—looking more like the renowned Sir Francis Drake in his doublet, hose, and ruff than an Athenian duke. Ostler speaks the play's first lines, "Now, fair Hippolyta, our nuptial hour draws on apace . . . ," and the audience is transported to another kingdom years removed from the London of 1599.

The musicians play softly as Theseus and Hippolyta discuss their impending marriage. Their scene is interrupted when Egeus, played by Shakespeare himself, bursts through the door, leading his daughter Hermia, impersonated by a boy of 14 who has recently been hired from the Children of the Queen's Revels. Demetrius and Lysander follow, and the company groups itself on the forestage. Although the platform is almost 30 feet deep, the actors prefer to play close to the audience, especially in these first scenes. In the open-air theater, the huge audience, still settling in for the afternoon's performance, can better hear these first crucial lines that

set up the story. The Chamberlain's Men are noted for their more natural, less bombastic acting, and the Globe's intimate stage allows them to speak more quietly to the audience. Gradually the stage empties, leaving only young Robert Gough, playing the lanky Helena, to address the audience in a soliloquy about her unhappy state. The mostly male audience laughs—perhaps a bit uncomfortably—at the jests about man's fickle nature.

As Gough exits through one door to the strains of a popular ballad, a half-dozen of the company's funniest actors—led by the irrepressible Kempe—emerge through the other. Their scene is acted broadly, and they openly court the approval of the groundlings. Despite Shakespeare's warning, Kempe improvises a few jokes and tosses in a little dance to illustrate that he—Bottom—can best play Thisbe. The men in the pit laugh heartily, and even the nobles in the upper galleries are amused by Kempe's antics. The comedians exit to loud applause and excited chatter until eerie music stills the theater and hushes the crowd.

Another signboard informs the audience that the scene is shifting to "Athens's Wood." Bryan appears, magically, behind the sign (though many in the audience surmise that he crept onstage via the trapdoor cut into the floor). During his brief scene with the Fairy—a boy dressed in hose and greenery—Bryan leaps athletically about the stage. He punctuates the line "then slip I from her bum, down topples she" with a comical pratfall, much to the delight of the audience. He is indeed "that merry wanderer of the night." The playwright's words transform the bare Globe stage into nature's wonderland:

The cowslips tall her pensioners be:
In their gold coats spots you see;
Those be rubies, fairy favours,
In those freckles live their savours.

The byplay between Fairy and Puck halts abruptly when a flash of gunpowder suggests lightning and fog. A cannonball rolled across one of the upper floors of the tiring house sounds like thunder as Oberon and Titania appear. Oberon stands on the balcony above the inner stage, towering some 15 feet above the floor. The audience gasps as Titania is lowered onto the stage from an opening in the roof covering the back half of the playing space. Backstage, two workers skillfully work the ropes that allow the Fairy Queen to descend slowly from the machines room over the stage, the underside of its ceiling painted with astrological signs to signify "the Heavens." As Titania scolds Oberon, she points to the painted moon on the ceiling when she says, " . . . the moon, the governess of floods, pale in her anger, washes all the air."

The play moves swiftly, one set of actors entering even as another exits. Yet, the spectators have no difficulty following the action despite the lack of scenery, lighting, or act curtains. They need only listen and let their minds create the details of each scene. Of course, the architecture of the Globe helps define locale. The two wooden posts that support the Heavens double, when necessary, as trees for Oberon to hide behind. At one point Bryan slithers up a post to indicate that Puck is flying above the forest. Hermia falls asleep under one of these "great oaks," and later Quince and his players refer to them as a "hawthorne-brake," a marvelous, convenient place for their rehearsal of the Pyramus and Thisbe play.

Without a break in the action, Shakespeare knows he must provide a bit of theatrical razzle-dazzle at the midpoint to please the groundlings. Sure enough, in the third act Puck lures Bottom offstage to transform him into a donkey. Kempe, assisted by two apprentices, puts on a huge, hairy mask shaped like an ass's head. As he straps it into place, the actor remembers his father telling him that his great-grandfather had worn a similar head in one of the biblical plays over a century before. Kempe reenters to howls of laughter and a comical chase about the Globe's great stage ensues. "Bottom—thou art translated," shouts Quince as he scurries through a side stage door.

The merriment continues as Titania, who has been sleeping in her "bower" behind the upstage curtain, awakens to discover Bottom-the-Ass. Four boys, whose cavorting, more than their costumes, suggests their elfishness, escort Bottom and his "bride" to the bower as the musicians play a spritely march. As the inner curtain closes, Hermia and Demetrius enter from one

doorway and are soon joined by Helena, who has been chased through the other door by Lysander. The scene in which the lovers quarrel amuses, both for its wordplay and its physical humor. The boys playing the women have great fun with the jokes about the height differences between Hermia and Helena, while the actors playing Demetrius and Lysander demonstrate their swordsmanship in a mock duel. The audience enjoys the comic fighting and recalls the superb fights between these same two actors as Mercutio and Tybalt in *Romeo and Juliet* last year. Being so close to the swirling blades only adds to their excitement.

After these raucous scenes, Shakespeare slows the action in preparation for the final act. Puck maneuvers the feuding lovers to either side of the wooden posts and comically, magically induces sleep. Burbage, who has been watching these events from the balcony, lowers himself to the stage floor and awakens the sleeping Titania. The musicians accommodate Titania's request for "music, such as charmeth sleep," and Oberon and his queen disappear into the darkness upstage. As the fairies leave, Theseus and Hippolyta appear in their place, carrying hunting bows. The lovers awaken, the music swells as they are reunited, and they exit happily anticipating their wedding. Shakespeare provides them time to change for the final act's nuptials by scripting a short scene in which Bottom, too, is reunited with the workingmen.

Again the inner curtain opens to reveal Theseus and Hippolyta, who have added pieces to their costume to indicate wedding regalia. They and the young lovers gather around the inner stage to watch the "tedious brief scene of Pyramus and Thisbe" acted in all its "tragical mirth" by Quince's amateur actors. The court, like the audience in the pit and galleries, enjoys the comic performance, partly for the witty costumes the Lord Chamberlain's Men have devised for Moonshine, Wall, and Lion, partly for the clowning of the actor playing Thisbe. Though the audience is used to seeing young men act women's roles—and very well, too—they enjoy the broad, comic playing of this mature actor, especially when he

speaks in a monstrous little voice.

Mostly, however, the audience enjoys the play-within-the-play because it is a wicked satire on other plays performed in London's theater. Many in the audience have been to the Fortune Theatre (a mile north of the City walls), where the Lord Admiral's Men specialize in gory melodramas, such as Kyd's *The Spanish Tragedy* and Marlowe's *Tamburlaine*. The audience at the Globe is aware of the fierce rivalry among the two companies, especially between its leading actors, the Admiral's Edward Alleyn and the Chamberlain's Burbage. Pyramus's bravado speeches—"Approach, ye Furies fell! O fates, come, come"—allow Kempe to burlesque the robustious, periwig-pated Alleyn tearing a passion to tatters. Not even Shakespeare, onstage as Egeus, or Burbage (as Oberon, lurking in the shadows of the balcony) can suppress a smile at Kempe's hilarious mockery of Alleyn.

The comedians finish their play with a rousing Bergomask, a stomping dance inherited from Italian comedians. Soon, the audience is hushed by the sweet tolling of a bell from within the tiring house. As the shadows lengthen over the Globe's stage, the courtly lovers disappear dreamily into the upstage recess of the discovery space. In the dusk, Oberon, standing close to the audience, blesses all present—onstage and off—then dances a stately pavane with Titania as the fairies sing. Alone onstage, Puck delivers the plaudite—"Give us your hands if we be friends." As the audience erupts into loud applause, the Chamberlain's Men again fill the stage to acknowledge their audience and treat them to a final song and dance—in this case, "Thumpkin and His Crying Mum."

As the audience leaves the theater, happily talking about sprites and lovers, the donkey's head, and the lively music, they are greeted by criers in the street who announce that on Wednesday next, they can return to the Globe for a revival of the popular history play *Richard II*, which raised royal eyebrows earlier that spring. Atop the Globe, old Cade lowers the flag and chuckles to himself as he hears Shakespeare's voice echo through the theater, "Mister Kempe, I must see you, now!"

FORUMS

"A *Midsummer Night's Dream* in 1853: A Review from *The Times* of London"

The following review appeared in The Times *of London on October 10, 1853 and describes Samuel Phelps's production of* A Midsummer Night's Dream *at the Sadler's Wells Theatre. The anonymous reviewer also provides a history of the play on the London stage; we learn that theater artists were revising Shakespeare's plays within a century of his death. Note that the review refers to Madame Vestris's production at Covent Garden in 1840; Madame Vestris played the role of Oberon—not Titania—in that production.*

SADLER'S WELLS THEATRE

Until Madame Vestris revived Shakespeare's *Midsummer Night's Dream* during her brilliant management of the Coventgarden [sic] Theatre, that celebrated play scarcely had a theatrical existence. In 1816 Mr. [Frederick] Reynolds, the dramatist, brought out a three-act version, enlivened by several interpolated songs. Fifty years had elapsed since it had been seen on the stage, and even the version which, *longo intervallo*, had preceded his own, was so much modified by [David] Garrick, and, perhaps, [George] Coleman, that the original was terribly marred, one of the alterations being the omission of nearly the whole of the mock tragedy. Between these two versions—namely, in the year 1777, a short piece, entitled a *Fairy Tale* was made out of a few scenes of *Midsummer Night's Dream*, but this was too insignificant to be styled a reproduction of the play. We have never seen this *Fairy Tale*, and we cannot conceive what it was about. The only *dramatis personae* seem to have been the clowns and the fairies, and yet not only the burlesque tragedy, but also the incident of the ass's head was left out.

In 1840, when Madame Vestris revised the play at Coventgarden [sic], even Reynold's version was forgotten, having passed into obscurity, together with various other Shakespearean plays which the same dramatist had similarly reduced to the form of operas, or, as we should now rather say, "plays with songs," and which owed their popularity for the times being partly to the music of Sir H. R. Bishop, partly to the interpolations of that music by Miss Stephens and Miss M. Tree. Madame Vestris revived the play in its integrity, still retaining some of the music, to which her heartfelt voice could do ample justice, and found it, we believe, one of the most successful productions of her management. It was done *"a grande spectacle"* and was illustrated by several scenic effects of a novel kind, of which the judicious employment of a sloped green sward in the background of a landscape was the most remarkable. But after the retirement of Madame Vestris from Coventgarden [sic], *Midsummer Night's Dream* was again forgotten as an acting play, and it was not until last Saturday, when Mr. [Samuel] Phelps brought

it out at Sadler's Wells Theatre that it recovered a theatrical position.

Midsummer Night's Dream is not one of those plays which, while they are seldom brought upon the stage, are little read in the closet, save by the profound Shakespeare student. On the contrary, while a whole generation of playgoers have never witnessed it, there are a few works of Shakespeare more familiar to the general reader, more pregnant with topics of allusion, and more influential on popular literature. Everybody knows that Oberon and Titania are the king and queen of the fairies, but had not Shakespeare written his *Midsummer Night's Dream* this fairy-fact would possibly have been no more diffused among the multitude, than precise information about the functions of the Valkyren or of Odin's ravens. As a poetical illustration of early female friendship, the first passage which occurs to every one's mind is the speech of Helena to Hermia:—

"We, Hermia, like two artificial gods, etc.—

and certainly if there is one quotation in the whole language that has become common place for all ranks and conditions of men, and women, too, it is the aphorism uttered by Lysander—

"The course of true love never did run smooth."

The tendency of managers to shun *Midsummer Night's Dream* must not, therefore, be sought in a want of sympathy between the poet and his readers, as, for instance, in the case of *Titus Andronicus*, which is usually voted "disagreeable." *Midsummer Night's Dream* is a play that requires a large company of actors, and, with the exception of one or two leading comic parts (we may almost say one), gives little opportunity for the display of histrionic talent. We can admire in Theseus the courtly high-breeding of a princely patron of the arts, but the words in which it is expressed gain little from oral utterance. Theseus, as well as Hippolyta, is a theatrical nonentity, and so are Oberon and Titania. The four lovers, whose embarrassment arises in the first instance from a state of things similar to that described in the 33d ode of Horace, and are afterwards doubled by the mistake of Puck, are rather figures in an idyll than in a play; and though their language is sometimes vituperative to a rare degree, it would not be hard to work them up into theatrical importance. They are not strong individuals, and we rather remember what they *say* than what they *are*.

But there are two reasons that render this play, with all those difficulties which managers have naturally felt, excellently suited to the stage at Sadler's Wells. In the first place, decoration is an all important matter at that establishment, where it is a principle to bring out every season one work at least which, while it belongs to the highest dramatic literature of our country, shall also stand as a specimen of scenic art. *Midsummer Night's Dream*, as a spectacle is inferior to none that have already been produced at Sadler's Wells. While the palace of Theseus is elaborately "set," and the places in which the fairy action takes place are represented by a beautiful series of landscapes, we may especially mention a new, but simple expedient, of giving an aerial appearance to the lightsome creatures of the poet's brain. The front of the stage is, according to custom, covered with green cloth; a greenish hue is cast upon the scene by *media* placed before the lights; the lustre of the chandeliers in the *salle* is subdued or extinguished; and the fairies, merely being dressed in garments of a blueish or greenish tint, so completely blend with the general hue of the scene, that they have all the approach to semi-invisibility, which is rarely obtained by the grosser expedient of gauze, and the effect is singularly beautiful.

In the second place, Mr. Phelps takes the character of Bottom as one of that series of comic studies which he has, from time to time, especially of late years, presented to the public. Those studies belong, after the decorations, to the most remarkable features of his management, and their announcement always awakens a certain amount of curiosity. We know that Mr. Phelps is not a comedian who will interpret a part according to received comic traditions, but a tragedian, who when he acts comedy, does so from some new theory of interpretation. His interpretation of Bottom the Weaver is certainly a most singular performance, reminding us, occasionally, of the last person in the world we should be apt to connect with that most British of Athenians, Bottom—namely, the Robert Macaire of M. Frederic Lemaitre [the leading Romantic actor of France, noted for his attention to physical detail]. It is a character of eccentric gesticulation, such as Retzsch might devise in a highly fantastic mood, and evidently corresponds to some subtle idea in the mind of the actor, which is not so easy to detect. Those strange gestures in which Bottom seems to be practicing for some athletic exhibition—what do they portend? We would suggest that Mr. Phelps's notion of Bottom in the earlier scenes is that of a low, dogmatic man in a state of habitual "muzziness," who, without having a perception of where his emphasis should be laid, has got a habit of emphasis in general, which we often find in persons who grow eloquent in a "state of beer." That this is his notion we only conjecture, but the latter portion of the character we can praise with certain knowledge. The dreamy state of a naturally stupid mind, to devine what has actually taken place, when the ass's head has been put on and taken off again, was admirably represented, the movement of the hands to ascertain whether the objectionable skull was on the human shoulders or not being natural in the highest degree. He clutched at the long ears, which were gone, and his whole aspect was that of a man with a foot in dreamland and the other on *terra firma*. The performance of Bottom in the mock tragedy was profoundly conceived as an ideal of bad acting, the tendency to violent gesticulation coming into perpetual contrast with the hard prosaic tone in which the lines were uttered. This mock tragedy, it should be observed, was a "roar" throughout, and shows that those early managers who omitted it made an egregious blunder. The ass's head was also a great source of merriment, for it opened its mouth and moved its ears, so as to signify diverse gallantries; and Mr. Phelp's contrivance to work the directing strings, while keeping his hands in a tolerably natural position may be mentioned as a striking evidence of technical skill.

Mr. Phelps has made a bolder experiment with *Midsummer Night's Dream* than any of his predecessors, all of whom—even an early reviewer in 1692—gave something of an operatic tone to the play. He indeed allows his band to play Mendelssohn's overture and occasional music, and retains Shakespeare's choruses, but all introduced songs he sedulously thrusts out, like a conscientious "legitimist," as he is, and the piece stands essentially as Shakespeare wrote it. The loud applause which he received, the beauty of his decorations, and the very remarkable manner in which he plays the chief character, leads us to hope that on this occasion his unwearying exertions to preserve a veneration for the national romantic drama of England will prove as successful as heretofore.

"A Review of *A Midsummer Night's Dream*: Royal Shakespeare Company, 1970"
Robert Speight

Perhaps the most admired production of A Midsummer Night's Dream in the twentieth century was that by the Royal Shakespeare Company directed by Peter Brook in August 1970. It was so popular it stayed in the Royal Shakespeare Company repertory for five years and had a world tour. The following review was written for Shakespeare Quarterly *by Robert Speight, a former actor and director. Speight saw numerous productions of Shakespeare's plays during his distinguished career as an actor, director, and critic.*

From Robert Speight, "Shakespeare in Britain," SQ 21.4, 1970. Reprinted by permission of *Shakespeare Quarterly*.

A Midsummer Night's Dream used to come to us through many thicknesses of muslin and Mendelssohn until [Harley] Graville-Barker [who directed the play at London's Savoy Theatre in 1912], who didn't, I think, hold very much with fairies, turned these ones into gilded sprites, and called in Cecil Sharp to make the whole thing more folksy. Norman Wilkinson put the lovers in doublet and hose, and Bridges-Adams sent them to bed in any Jacobean mansion that came to mind. The Stratford

(continued)

stage has seen nothing lovelier than that sextet in white. Peter Hall [founder of the RSC] . . . did not read the play very differently, and it seemed as if the only way you could give a new look to the *Dream* was to turn it into a nightmare. The paradoxical Professor [Jan] Kott [author of *Shakespeare, Our Contemporary,* 1964] had already worked this transformation with his customary disregard of any evidence to the contrary; and since the admiration of Peter Brook and Professor Kott for one another was mutual and declared, I awaited Mr. Brook's interpretation of the play with curiosity not unmixed with apprehension.

It was eight years since Mr. Brook had directed a play at Stratford, and one assumed that he would not have directed the *Dream* unless he had something very particular to say about it. In fact, he forced one to forget—not, let me emphasize, the play itself—but anything one had seen done with it, or imagined being done with it, in the theatre. He swept the mind of the spectator as clear as he has swept his stage, allowing the text of the play, beautifully and deliberately spoken, to play upon you with the freshness of words seen for the first time on the printed page. He persuaded you to forget a century of theatrical tradition, with its conventions and its cliches; and commanded you into a frame of mind where the very notion of magic, of supernatural agency, had to be created afresh. You could, if you chose, harbor a reminiscence of *Alice in Wonderland,* but of nothing else. The French have a phrase which communicates the peculiar, the explosively original, quality of this production. They speak of a *mystere en pleine lumiere,* and this suggests the brilliant white light that Mr. Brook threw upon his staring white stage, with only Titania's bright red feather bed to relieve it.

One saw nothing remotely resembling a tree—only coils of wire played out from a fishing rod over the iron railings which encircled the decor from above. One saw nothing remotely resembling a fairy—but then we were not supposed to have been brought up on fairies. Puck, who was also Philostrate, might have reminded you a little of Pierrot; Theseus dreamt himself into Oberon, and Titania dreamt herself into Hippolyta. There was much play with steel ladders and spinning tops; and if you asked yourself how Mr. Brook was getting away with it all, you might have answered: "Marry, how *trapsically*"—because Oberon and Puck descended from the skies on swings with an acrobatic agility. Indeed the virtuosities of the circus gave one a clue to Mr. Brook's translation of midsummer magic into surrealism. Yes, one might object, but how can a play spun out of

cobwebs and gossamer, and drenched in morning dew, stand up to a treatment so metallic and so apparently defiant of mystery? The answer is that the mystery was all the deeper because it was seen so clearly—as clearly, no doubt, as it was once seen on the bare platform of the Globe. Because the words had no visual counterpart, they seized the imagination more surely. The play was recognized as timeless, because it was neither brought up, nor brought back, to date. Mr. Brook's audacious originality compelled respect, because he himself, in his creation of a play about which everything had seemed to be said, had allowed it, in the last analysis, to stand gravely and lyrically, and also very amusingly, on its own feet. Utterly novel, it was still endearingly familiar. The laughs came at the right place, and when the poetry soared you caught your breath. This production was no brilliant exercise in cerebration; the pit of the stomach responded to it. Of course it would have been intolerable if the text had not been treated like the Ark of the Covenant, but here I can imagine Mr. Brook saying—"'Night's swift dragons cut the clouds asunder', don't ask me to assist a line like *that* with stage lighting."

The humours of the play were safe—and indeed traditionally secure—with Mr. [David] Waller as Bottom principally in charge of them. No one I have seen since Ralph Richardson has played the part as well—and that was nearly forty years ago. Mr. Locke's Quince was exquisitely muted to a kind of saintly (and no doubt celibate) simplicity, although why he should have doubled the part with Aegeus I could not quite understand. Miss [Sara] Kestelman's Titania was as easy to look at as to listen to. But the production was ruled, as it should be, by its Oberon and its Puck. Mr. [John] Kane salted his mischief with a Gallic wit, which I found a welcome relief from the conventional caperings, and spoke his verse as well as I have ever heard it spoken. Mr. Alan Howard combined a patrician charm with an effortless authority, and justified his doubling of the part with Theseus, for alone in this play Theseus and Oberon are rulers. Each untangles the knot which others have tied. Mr. Howard's luminously clear handling of the verse was never so labored that it disturbed the melodic line. At a time when black magic is the only magic that most people any longer believe in, there was much excuse for a production of the *Dream* where the magic was as white as Arctic snows or the swan's down on the Avon; and there was never a moment's doubt after the opening performance that this one had taken its place in history.

"Moonbeams and Menaces:
A Brilliantly Idiosyncratic *Dream* at Minneapolis' Guthrie"

BY WILLIAM A. HENRY III

For most of the nearly four centuries since it was written, *A Midsummer Night's Dream* was regarded as one of William Shake-

speare's slighter works, an "airy nothing" in the play's own words, of no more substance than a trick that moonlight might play on the eye. But since Peter Brook's landmark rediscovery of the play's darker essence in his 1970 production with the Royal Shakespeare Company, scholars and theatergoers alike have recognized that *Dream* is much more than a slapstick farce of lovers tangling in a green glade. Its narrative blends wars of the sexes, of social classes, of generations, even a war between the everyday and the supernatural. The play has become a summit that virtually every world-class director seeks to scale.

Rumanian-born Liviu Ciulei, 62, is the epitome of a world-class director: he has staged films, operas and plays in some five languages and ten countries. Since 1981 he has been artistic director of the Guthrie Theater in Minneapolis and has burnished the company's reputation for accommodating mainstream audiences to unconventional, often fiercely intellectual interpretations of the classics. Ciulei will leave next year to move to New York City and will become a free-lance director. For his final Guthrie season, he has restored the company's tradition of rotating repertory. Among the current offerings: *Cyrano de Bergerac* and an adaptation of Dickens' *Great Expectations*. The highlight of the season, however, is Ciulei's final production as artistic director, an idiosyncratic and brilliant *Dream* that is probably the best since Brook's.

Ciulei's vision, which downplays romance and sees courtship and marriage as raw struggles for power, owes much to Brook. But the insights into the characters, the reasoned resistance to happy endings and especially the mesmeric visual imagery are Ciulei's own. From the first moment, this *Dream* shows itself to be more about grim realities and revelatory nightmares. The captive Amazon Queen Hippolyta (Lorraine Toussaint), garbed as a soldier and coiffed with a Grace Jones–style Mohawk, stands mute yet defiant as the guards of Duke Theseus (Gary Reineke) surround her. They tear off her uniform and toss it onto a fire, revealing her torso clad in a confining, seductive undergarment: she is being turned from a woman into a girl. Throughout the play, Hippolyta's fury abates but never completely dies. Ciulei, ever attentive to nuances in the text, points up her poignant reminiscence about lost freedom on the very morning of her wedding.

The production finds the same raw ambivalence in the quartet of lovers. The rivals Demetrius and Lysander come into the forest armed with flick knives. Later, under the influence of a love poison, they are ready to fight and die for the love of He-lena, whom hours before they both had ignored, and are almost willing to kill Hermia, to whom they both had sworn undying devotion. Even after a restorative drug has returned them to orderly pairings, all four eye one another uneasily: they have lost the sweet certainty of first love. At the curtain call, the pairs come out again mismatched. Only as they start to bow do they exchange partners.

Ciulei perceives class bitterness in passages that are usually taken as innocuously comic. When the sprite Puck is sent off on an errand, he pledges to "put a girdle round about the earth in forty minutes." The actress playing the part, Lynn Chausow, does not hurry as she speaks, but pauses, then skulks off. When Nick Bottom (Jay Patterson) and his craftsmen offer to dance as a postlude to their fractured production of *Pyramus and Thisby*, the Duke accepts. Then he and his guests, who have hooted at the ineptitude of these "rude mechanicals," hear the clock strike and head off to bed. The group bursts in, singing and stamping, to find no one there.

The most biting scenes involve Oberon (Peter Francis-James) and Titania (Harriet Harris). This Fairy King and Queen are not lithe spirits but a married couple stung with jealousy engendered by their "open" relationship. After Oberon has contrived to have Bottom turned into a jackass, with whom a drugged Titania will fall in love, he rages at the very infidelity he has brought into being. When Titania wakens from her interlude, she shrieks at her humiliation.

The play's underlying tensions are mimed in a wordless dream sequence that Ciulei has interpolated. As the quartet of lovers crash through the forest, they become enmeshed in gauzy strips of fabric that spin them to and fro, then swaddle them for sleep. During their slumber, their dream selves arise and re-enact the night's confrontations beneath a web of the same gauze. Then the dream form of another nearby sleeping lover, Titania, rises and cavorts with an image of Bottom. He lifts off his ass's head and reveals himself to be Oberon; Titania recoils in horror. Thus the prank with Bottom, the trademark joke of the play, becomes the symbol of all the self-destructive cruelties committed in the name of love . . .

"Shakespeare as Carnival in Amazonean 'Dream'"

Mel Gussow

With its spells and incantations, *A Midsummer Night's Dream* freely lends itself to directorial invention, as amply demonstrated in the Brazilian production of the play that opened last night at the Delacorte Theater in [New York's] Central Park. As adapted and staged by Caca Rosset, this is a lithe and fanciful *Dream*. Through graceful use of nudity, the production underlines the natural primitivism of the story.

The members of Mr. Rosset's *Teatro do Ornitorrinco* perform in Portuguese and there is no simultaneous translation. For an English-speaking audience, the Shakespearean language certainly is missed, but the action is easy to follow and there is something to be said for hearing familiar words spoken in a lilting, unfamiliar language. Fortunately, the dialogue is communicated through actors who are vocally and physically expressive.

There have been more magical, metaphorical productions (beginning with Peter Brook's version [1970]). Mr. Rosset takes a lighter, less ambitious approach. Clearly he is interested in the

(continued)

comedy as a springboard for entertainment and performance art with a distinct Brazilian tang. The actors are acrobats, jugglers, mimes, and even fire-eaters. This robust troupe of variety performers might be equally at home in a circus, but they have a forthright feeling for Shakespeare and for the imagery evoked by the director.

A dance of half-naked nymphs looks like an animated Cézanne. Performed in soft moonlight, the scene casts a glow across the Delacorte. The open-air New York Shakespeare Festival Theatre has seldom seemed more ethereal than at this moment. There are revels and parades with colorful streamers, music (by Villa-Lobos and Mendelssohn and a Brazilian rap song for Puck), played by an onstage band. Late in the evening there is a scene of aerialist daring as elves swing, precariously from perch to perch.

It is certainly an unusual *Dream* when the outstanding performances are given by the fairies (female) and elves (male), and in which cameo roles are added for a strongman and a belly dancer. With its expanded population, the forest kingdom is in fact the dominant element in the production.

The evening is less secure in court, though some of this reaction may be a result of hearing scenes with extended exposition in a foreign language. José Rubens Chacha and Christiane Tricerri, doubling in the regal roles, are more persuasive as Oberon and Titania than as Theseus and Hippolyta. Augusto Pompeo is a particularly saucy Puck.

The clowns are led by Tacito Rocha's amusingly instructive Peter Quince. Mr. Rosset himself appears as Bottom, a role he plays with the buffoonery of an American vaudevillian. In an act of modesty, Bottom's love scene with Titania seems to have been shortened, one of a number of reductions in the text. Later there is an episode that can be taken as self-criticism. When the clowns offer to present an epilogue to their mildly funny version of "Pyramus and Thisby," the members of the court rise in unison and shout a loud "no."

While the spirit of the show is never less than playful, there is a covert, unexplored social message. Perhaps taking a cue from the fact that Titania is the queen of the Amazons, the play is staged in an Amazonian rain forest, but one that has been defoliated by an unspecified calamity. The scenery is spare and there is only a small pool at the center of the stage to indicate an aspect of an oasis.

Except for the setting, the darker elements of the play do not fall under the director's scrutiny. He is content to present a frolicsome Brazilian carnival, what could be called Bottom's *Dream*, and it is most welcome in its outdoor environment.

HAMLET, PRINCE OF DENMARK

WILLIAM SHAKESPEARE

HAMLET (C.1601)

No play in the history of the theater has generated more commentary than *Hamlet*. In 1964 the Polish critic Jan Kott observed that a *bibliography* of the books and essays written about the play would equal the size of the Warsaw telephone directory—imagine how that volume has grown since then! And with the possible exceptions of *A Midsummer Night's Dream* and *Richard III*, no play has been produced more often than Shakespeare's tragedy of the prince of Denmark. The greatest actors in Western theater have played the role, from Richard Burbage (who created the role) to Kenneth Branagh (whose four-hour-and-twenty-minute 1996 film presented the text in its entirety). For four centuries actors have been judged by how well they play Hamlet. There are at least a score of film versions of the play, including one starring Mel Gibson, who portrayed the "delicate and tender prince" as a "lethal weapon." The role has also attracted actors throughout Asia, Africa, and Latin America. Many women have played the role, including the great French actor Sarah Bernhardt and Dame Judith Anderson (who was 72 when she played Hamlet). And in Denver an enterprising gambler won a hundred-dollar bet in 1874 when he memorized the complete text in three days!

What, then, may be said of *Hamlet* that has not already been said, either in essays or in performance? Not much, though we frequently use *Hamlet* throughout this text to illustrate points about dramaturgy, performance, and tragedy. The more pertinent question may be "Why has this play proven irresistible to actors, audiences, and critics since Shakespeare wrote it in (probably) 1601?" We might add psychologists to this list of *Hamlet* devotees. Numerous case studies have been written about the prince—all for a man whom Shakespeare would call "a fiction, a dream of passion" (2.2.552).

This is precisely Hamlet's attraction: he seems genuinely real to us, partly because he is among the most essential archetypes created by humanity, partly because he is so recognizably human in his many contradictions. As he is a part of the "collective unconscious" described by Jung, he is the universal portrait of the essentially decent person confronted by an onerous task. At the same time he emerges as a particular individual, who—like each of us—is a mass of contradictions defying categorization.

Shakespeare did not "invent" Hamlet. His roots may be found as far back as Aeschylus's Orestes, the prince of Argos who was compelled to avenge the death of his father, Agamemnon. To accomplish this he had to kill his mother (Clytemnestra) and his morally reprehensible stepfather (Aegisthus). In contrast to Hamlet, Orestes goes mad *after* he murders them. Furthermore, psychologist Ernest Jones, among others, has argued that Hamlet may also be aligned with Oedipus, partly because he too must discover who he is, largely because of his preoccupation with his mother's sex life. The Oedipal implications of the Hamlet-Gertrude relationship were prominent in both the 1948 Laurence Olivier film and in Franco Zeffirelli's 1992 version with Gibson and Glenn Close.

Though Shakespeare never mentions the Greek legends of either Orestes or Oedipus in his writings, we cannot conclude that he was unaware of them. In any case, the story of "the put-upon prince" is so ingrained in the human psyche that he found in it the Norse myth of Amlothi. This Viking warrior, whose name means "desperate in battle," feigned madness to conquer his enemies. The story worked its way into the Elizabethan world through Saxo Grammaticus's thirteenth-century *History of the Danish People* and in a 1576 French text by Belleforêst, with significant changes, just as Shakespeare made alterations for his needs. Also, the anonymous *Ur-Hamlet* may have preceded Shakespeare's play or been influenced by it; both contain the Ghost, the play-within-the-play, and the climactic duel between the prince and his young rival. Clearly Shakespeare saw material for a rich theater tale in these early sources.

Actually, the playwright need have looked no further for inspiration than his rival theaters on London's South Bank. A bloody melodrama called *The Spanish Tragedy* was among the most popular plays in the 1590s. It was written by Thomas Kyd, a mediocre playwright who might be forgotten had not *Hamlet* made him the most famous footnote to Elizabethan drama. (To be fair, Kyd's play is still performed with some regularity, though largely as a curiosity.) *The Spanish Tragedy* heightened the vogue for the revenge tragedy in England; though the British did not invent the genre (the Roman Seneca is often credited with this feat), they made it a mainstay of their dramatic tradition. Contrary to the Shakespearean *Hamlet*, Kyd's play portrays a crazed father (Hieronimo) who avenges the death of his son (Horatio) by performing in a play that reconstructs the son's death. However, in this "play within the play" two guilty individuals are actually killed by Hieronimo, who, to avoid confessing, bites out his own tongue before killing himself. Such gory goings-on packed them in at the Rose and other theaters, where it was revived regularly. Shakespeare the theater owner no doubt urged Shakespeare the playwright to devise a script that would make Londoners forget Kyd. Shakespeare the actor is believed to have played Old Hamlet's Ghost at the Globe and later at the Blackfriars. (See Spotlight box, Shakespeare's Two Theaters, following the text of *Hamlet*.)

As he did throughout his career, Shakespeare took these several well-known tales and fashioned a fresh work that surpasses the originals as a story, as a portrait of people in action (or even inaction), and as a statement about the human condition. First, he added a subplot in which two other sons (Fortinbras and Laertes) must also avenge the murder of their fathers. Each follows a different path to revenge. Laertes is the man of passion who comes "hot-blooded" from France and will not be deterred from his mission. He dies "a victim of mine own treachery." Hamlet, in his own words, thinks "too precisely on th'event," and is (seemingly) paralyzed into inaction. He is the new Renaissance man who weighs things carefully before acting. He also dies. It is the third son, Fortinbras, the Norwegian prince, who achieves his end and—significantly to Shakespeare's audience—gains the crown. Fortinbras balances reason and passion, and thereby triumphs in this morality about the right uses of our intellects and emotions. (It is worth noting that the Fortinbras subplot is often cut because of the play's length, which unfortunately diminishes the multiple perspectives inherent in Shakespeare's design.)

But if *Hamlet* were merely a cautionary tale about the battle between our reason and our emotions, it would not enjoy its status as the world's most scrutinized play. Rather, the play's fascination comes from the ambiguity of its central character. Even if you have neither read nor seen the play, you probably have heard that Hamlet's problem is that he procrastinates, that he is the man of inaction in a world demanding action. But does a procrastinator follow the "most horrible" spirit of his father despite the warnings of his friends, whom he threatens to kill if they stop him? Can a man of inaction ruthlessly kill the counselor to the king without a moment's hesitation? Can he concoct a scheme to get some traveling actors to play "something like the murder of his father," and even compose with lightning speed "some dozen or sixteen lines" to insert in their play? Does a paralyzed man leap into the grave of his dead lover to fight her brother to prove that "forty thousand brothers / Could not with their quantity equal his love?" This was, by the way, the same woman to whom he said, "I loved you not."

Consider also other common perceptions of Hamlet:

- He has been called the consummate rationalist, yet throughout much of the play we can never be sure if he is feigning madness or if he has indeed slipped into madness.

- He is "a delicate and tender prince" who is repulsed by the thought of having to murder, yet he coldly dispatches his schoolmates (Rosencrantz and Guildenstern) to brutal deaths. They are, he says, "not near my conscience."
- He is, we are told, consumed by melancholy and spends much of the play meditating on death, yet he emerges as Shakespeare's only tragic hero with an enviable sense of humor. He speaks some of Shakespeare's most comical lines as he mocks both those around him and himself.
- Ophelia tells us he is "the scholar's eye, the expectancy and rose of the fair state" (i.e., the ideal gentleman), yet he abuses her and his mother with some of the most vile language uttered by any Shakespearean character.
- He will not kill himself because he fears that "the Almighty hath set his canon 'gainst self-slaughter," yet he has no qualms about playing god himself. In 3.4, he deliberately refuses to kill his uncle, who, he knows with certainty, is the murderer of his father. He chooses to wait until he is certain that death will dispatch Claudius to eternal damnation. This is his fatal "error in judgment"; it precipitates his tragic ending as well as those of Polonius, Ophelia, Laertes, Rosencrantz, Guildenstern, Gertrude, and—only finally—Claudius.

Hamlet himself is awed by his contradictory nature. His many soliloquies—no Shakespearean character is alone onstage more than Hamlet—are his attempts to resolve his many ambiguities. That he entrusts the audience with the privilege of sharing his innermost doubts and fears further endears him to us.

In the final analysis, Hamlet seems not the creation of a playwright—yet he assuredly is. This playwright has created a human portrait of such complexity and contradiction that we cannot help but think of him as one of us. Or, as Coleridge said, "I have a smack of Hamlet." Surely each of us has a smack of Hamlet as we, too, stand before a world that makes impossible demands on us, armed only with the myriad contradictions that make us human.

Hamlet is perhaps the world's best-known play: Roger Rees played the prince at Stratford-on-Avon in 1984, and the Korean Drama Center produced the tragedy in Seoul in 1977.

HAMLET, PRINCE OF DENMARK

WILLIAM SHAKESPEARE

[DRAMATIS PERSONAE
GHOST of Hamlet, *the former King of Denmark*
CLAUDIUS, *King of Denmark, the former King's brother*
GERTRUDE, *Queen of Denmark, widow of the former King and now wife of Claudius*
HAMLET, *Prince of Denmark, son of the late King and of Gertrude*
POLONIUS, *councillor to the King*
LAERTES, *his son*
OPHELIA, *his daughter*
REYNALDO, *his servant*
HORATIO, *Hamlet's friend and fellow student*
VOLTIMAND,
CORNELIUS,
ROSENCRANTZ,
GUILDENSTERN, } *members of the Danish court*
OSRIC,
A GENTLEMAN,
A LORD,
BERNARDO,
FRANCISCO, } *officers and soldiers on watch*
MARCELLUS,
FORTINBRAS, *Prince of Norway*

CAPTAIN *in his army*
Three or Four Players, taking the roles of PROLOGUE, PLAYER KING, PLAYER QUEEN, *and* LUCIANUS
Two MESSENGERS
FIRST SAILOR
Two CLOWNS, *a gravedigger and his companion*
PRIEST
FIRST AMBASSADOR *from England*
Lords, Soldiers, Attendants, Guards, other Players, Followers of Laertes, other Sailors, another Ambassador or Ambassadors from England
SCENE: *Denmark*]

1.1° *Enter Bernardo and Francisco, two sentinels, [meeting].*

BERNARDO. Who's there?
FRANCISCO.
Nay, answer me.° Stand and unfold yourself.°
BERNARDO. Long live the King!

1.1. Location: Elsinore castle. A guard platform.
2 me (Francisco emphasizes that *he* is the sentry currently on watch.) **unfold yourself** reveal your identity

FRANCISCO. Bernardo?

5 BERNARDO. He.

FRANCISCO.
You come most carefully upon your hour.

BERNARDO.
'Tis now struck twelve. Get thee to bed, Francisco.

FRANCISCO.
For this relief much thanks. 'Tis bitter cold,
And I am sick at heart.

10 BERNARDO. Have you had quiet guard?

FRANCISCO. Not a mouse stirring.

BERNARDO. Well, good night.
If you do meet Horatio and Marcellus,
The rivals° of my watch, bid them make haste.

Enter Horatio and Marcellus.

FRANCISCO.
15 I think I hear them.—Stand, ho! Who is there?

HORATIO. Friends to this ground.°

MARCELLUS. And liegemen to the Dane.°

FRANCISCO. Give° you good night.

MARCELLUS.
O, farewell, honest soldier. Who hath relieved you?

FRANCISCO.
20 Bernardo hath my place. Give you good night.

Exit Francisco.

MARCELLUS. Holla! Bernardo!

BERNARDO. Say, what, is Horatio there?

HORATIO. A piece of him.

BERNARDO.
Welcome, Horatio. Welcome, good Marcellus.

HORATIO.
25 What, has this thing appeared again tonight?

BERNARDO. I have seen nothing.

MARCELLUS.
Horatio says 'tis but our fantasy,°
And will not let belief take hold of him
Touching this dreaded sight twice seen of us.
30 Therefore I have entreated him along°
With us to watch° the minutes of this night,
That if again this apparition come
He may approve° our eyes and speak to it.

HORATIO.
Tush, tush, 'twill not appear.

BERNARDO.
Sit down awhile,
35 And let us once again assail your ears,
That are so fortified against our story,
What° we have two nights seen.

HORATIO.   Well, sit we down,
And let us hear Bernardo speak of this.

BERNARDO. Last night of all,°
When yond same star that's westward from the pole°   40
Had made his° course t' illume° that part of heaven
Where now it burns, Marcellus and myself,
The bell then beating one—

Enter Ghost.

MARCELLUS.
Peace, break thee off! Look where it comes again!

BERNARDO.
In the same figure like the King that's dead.   45

MARCELLUS.
Thou art a scholar.° Speak to it, Horatio.

BERNARDO.
Looks 'a° not like the King? Mark it, Horatio.

HORATIO.
Most like. It harrows me with fear and wonder.

BERNARDO.
It would be spoke to.°

MARCELLUS.   Speak to it, Horatio.

HORATIO.
What art thou that usurp'st° this time of night,   50
Together with that fair and warlike form
In which the majesty of buried Denmark°
Did sometime° march? By heaven, I charge thee,
   speak!

MARCELLUS.
It is offended.

BERNARDO.   See, it stalks away.

HORATIO.
Stay! Speak, speak! I charge thee, speak!   55

Exit Ghost.

MARCELLUS. 'Tis gone and will not answer.

BERNARDO.
How now, Horatio? You tremble and look pale.
Is not this something more than fantasy?
What think you on 't?°

HORATIO.
Before my God, I might not this believe   60
Without the sensible° and true avouch°
Of mine own eyes.

MARCELLUS.   Is it not like the King?

HORATIO. As thou art to thyself.
Such was the very armor he had on

---

14 rivals partners   **16 ground** country, land   **17 liegemen to the Dane** men sworn to serve the Danish king   **18 Give** i.e., may God give   **27 fantasy** imagination   **30 along** to come along   **31 watch** keep watch during   **33 approve** corroborate   **37 What** with what

39 Last . . . all i.e., this very last night. (Emphatic.)   **40 pole** polestar, north star   **41 his** its. **illume** illuminate   **46 scholar** one learned enough to know how to question a ghost properly   **47 'a** he   **49 It . . . to** (It was commonly believed that a ghost could not speak until spoken to.)   **50 usurp'st** wrongfully takes over   **52 buried Denmark** the buried King of Denmark   **53 sometime** formerly   **59 on 't** of it   **61 sensible** confirmed by the senses. **avouch** warrant, evidence

65 When he had the ambitious Norway° combated.
    So frowned he once when, in an angry parle,°
    He smote the sledded° Polacks° on the ice.
    'Tis strange.
    MARCELLUS.
       Thus twice before, and jump° at this dead hour,
70   With martial stalk° hath he gone by our watch.
    HORATIO.
       In what particular thought to work° I know not,
       But in the gross and scope° of mine opinion
       This bodes some strange eruption to our state.
    MARCELLUS.
       Good now,° sit down, and tell me, he that knows,
75   Why this same strict and most observant watch
       So nightly toils° the subject° of the land,
       And why such daily cast° of brazen cannon
       And foreign mart° for implements of war,
       Why such impress° of shipwrights, whose sore task
80   Does not divide the Sunday from the week.
       What might be toward,° that this sweaty haste
       Doth make the night joint-laborer with the day?
       Who is 't that can inform me?
    HORATIO.   That can I;
       At least, the whisper goes so. Our last king,
85   Whose image even but now appeared to us,
       Was, as you know, by Fortinbras of Norway,
       Thereto pricked on° by a most emulate° pride,°
       Dared to the combat; in which our valiant Hamlet—
       For so this side of our known world° esteemed him—
90   Did slay this Fortinbras; who by a sealed° compact
       Well ratified by law and heraldry
       Did forfeit, with his life, all those his lands
       Which he stood seized° of, to the conqueror;
       Against the° which a moiety competent°
95   Was gagèd° by our king, which had returned°
       To the inheritance° of Fortinbras,
       Had he been vanquisher, as, by the same cov'nant°
       And carriage of the article designed,°
       His fell to Hamlet. Now, sir, young Fortinbras,

Of unimprovèd mettle° hot and full,   100
Hath in the skirts° of Norway here and there
Sharked up° a list° of lawless resolutes°
For food and diet° to some enterprise
That hath a stomach° in 't, which is no other—
As it doth well appear unto our state—   105
But to recover of us, by strong hand
And terms compulsatory, those foresaid lands
So by his father lost. And this, I take it,
Is the main motive of our preparations,
The source of this our watch, and the chief head°   110
Of this posthaste and rummage° in the land.
    BERNARDO.
       I think it be no other but e'en so.
       Well may it sort° that this portentous figure
       Comes armèd through our watch so like the King
       That was and is the question° of these wars.   115
    HORATIO.
       A mote° it is to trouble the mind's eye.
       In the most high and palmy° state of Rome,
       A little ere the mightiest Julius fell,
       The graves stood tenantless, and the sheeted° dead
       Did squeak and gibber in the Roman streets;   120
       As° stars with trains° of fire and dews of blood,
       Disasters° in the sun; and the moist star°
       Upon whose influence Neptune's° empire stands°
       Was sick almost to doomsday° with eclipse.
       And even the like precurse° of feared events,   125
       As harbingers° preceding still° the fates
       And prologue to the omen° coming on,
       Have heaven and earth together demonstrated
       Unto our climatures° and countrymen.

       Enter Ghost.

       But soft,° behold! Lo, where it comes again!   130
       I'll cross° it, though it blast° me. (*It spread his° arms.*)
          Stay, illusion!

100 **unimprovèd mettle** untried, undisciplined spirits   101 **skirts** outlying regions, outskirts   102 **Sharked up** gathered up, as a shark takes fish. **list** i.e., troop. **resolutes** desperadoes   103 **For food and diet** i.e., they are to serve as *food,* or "means," *to some enterprise;* also they serve in return for the rations they get   104 **stomach** (1) a spirit of daring (2) an appetite that is fed by the *lawless resolutes*   110 **head** source   111 **rummage** bustle, commotion   113 **sort** suit   115 **question** focus of contention   116 **mote** speck of dust   117 **palmy** flourishing   119 **sheeted** shrouded   121 **As** (This abrupt transition suggests that matter is possibly omitted between lines 120 and 121.) **trains** trails   122 **Disasters** unfavorable signs or aspects. **moist star** i.e., moon, governing tides   123 **Neptune** god of the sea. **stands** depends   124 **sick . . . doomsday** (See Matthew 24:29 and Revelation 6:12.)   125 **precurse** heralding, foreshadowing   126 **harbingers** forerunners. **still** continually   127 **omen** calamitous event   129 **climatures** regions   130 **soft** i.e., enough, break off   131 **cross** stand in its path, confront. **blast** wither, strike with a curse. **s.d. his** its

65 **Norway** King of Norway   66 **parle** parley   67 **sledded** traveling on sleds. **Polacks** Poles   69 **jump** exactly   70 **stalk** stride   71 **to work** i.e., to collect my thoughts and try to understand this   72 **gross and scope** general drift   74 **Good now** (An expression denoting entreaty or expostulation.)   76 **toils** causes to toil. **subject** subjects   77 **cast** casting   78 **mart** buying and selling   79 **impress** impressment, conscription   81 **toward** in preparation   87 **Thereto . . . pride** (Refers to old Fortinbras, not the Danish King.) **pricked on** incited. **emulate** emulous, ambitious   89 **this . . . world** i.e., all Europe, the Western world   90 **sealed** certified, confirmed   93 **seized** possessed   94 **Against the** in return for. **moiety competent** corresponding portion   95 **gagèd** engaged, pledged. **had returned** would have passed   96 **inheritance** possession   97 **cov'nant** i.e., the *sealed compact* of line 90   98 **carriage . . . designed** carrying out of the article or clause drawn up to cover the point

If thou hast any sound or use of voice,
Speak to me!
If there be any good thing to be done
135 That may to thee do ease and grace to me,
Speak to me!
If thou art privy to° thy country's fate,
Which, happily,° foreknowing may avoid,
O, speak!
140 Or if thou hast uphoarded in thy life
Extorted treasure in the womb of earth,
For which, they say, you spirits oft walk in death,
Speak of it! (*The cock crows.*) Stay and speak!—
   Stop it, Marcellus.

MARCELLUS.
   Shall I strike at it with my partisan?°
145 HORATIO. Do, if it will not stand.   [*They strike at it.*]
BERNARDO. 'Tis here!
HORATIO. 'Tis here!   [*Exit Ghost.*]
MARCELLUS. 'Tis gone.
   We do it wrong, being so majestical,
150 To offer it the show of violence,
For it is as the air invulnerable,
And our vain blows malicious mockery.

BERNARDO.
   It was about to speak when the cock crew.

HORATIO.
   And then it started like a guilty thing
155 Upon a fearful summons. I have heard
The cock, that is the trumpet° to the morn,
Doth with his lofty and shrill-sounding throat
Awake the god of day, and at his warning,
Whether in sea or fire, in earth or air,
160 Th' extravagant and erring° spirit hies°
To his confine; and of the truth herein
This present object made probation.°

MARCELLUS.
   It faded on the crowing of the cock.
Some say that ever 'gainst° that season comes
165 Wherein our Savior's birth is celebrated,
This bird of dawning singeth all night long,
And then, they say, no spirit dare stir abroad;
The nights are wholesome, then no planets strike,°
No fairy takes,° nor witch hath power to charm,
170 So hallowed and so gracious° is that time.

HORATIO.
   So have I heard and do in part believe it.
But, look, the morn in russet mantle clad

Walks o'er the dew of yon high eastward hill.
Break we our watch up, and by my advice
Let us impart what we have seen tonight   175
Unto young Hamlet; for upon my life,
This spirit, dumb to us, will speak to him.
Do you consent we shall acquaint him with it,
As needful in our loves, fitting our duty?

MARCELLUS.
   Let's do 't, I pray, and I this morning know   180
Where we shall find him most conveniently.

                           Exeunt.

1 . 2 °   *Flourish. Enter Claudius, King of Denmark,*
          Gertrude the Queen, [the] Council, as° Polonius
          and his son Laertes, Hamlet, cum aliis° [including
          Voltimand and Cornelius].

KING.
   Though yet of Hamlet our° dear brother's death
The memory be green, and that it us befitted
To bear our hearts in grief and our whole kingdom
To be contracted in one brow of woe,
Yet so far hath discretion fought with nature   5
That we with wisest sorrow think on him
Together with remembrance of ourselves.
Therefore our sometime° sister, now our queen,
Th' imperial jointress° to this warlike state,
Have we, as 'twere with a defeated joy—   10
With an auspicious and a dropping eye,°
With mirth in funeral and with dirge in marriage,
In equal scale weighing delight and dole°—
Taken to wife. Nor have we herein barred
Your better wisdoms, which have freely gone   15
With this affair along. For all, our thanks.
Now follows that you know° young Fortinbras,
Holding a weak supposal° of our worth,
Or thinking by our late dear brother's death
Our state to be disjoint and out of frame,   20
Co-leaguèd with° this dream of his advantage,°
He hath not failed to pester us with message
Importing° the surrender of those lands
Lost by his father, with all bonds° of law,
To our most valiant brother. So much for him.   25

---

137 **privy to** in on the secret of   138 **happily** haply, perchance
144 **partisan** long-handled spear   156 **trumpet** trumpeter   160
extravagant and erring wandering beyond bounds. (The words
have similar meaning.) **hies** hastens   162 **probation** proof   164
'gainst just before   168 **strike** destroy by evil influence   169
takes bewitches   170 **gracious** full of grace

1.2. Location: The castle.
s.d. as i.e., such as including. **cum aliis** with others   **1 our** my.
(The royal "we"; also in the following lines.)   **8 sometime** former
9 jointress woman possessing property with her husband   **11 With
. . . eye** with one eye smiling and the other weeping   **13 dole** grief
17 that you know what you know already, that; or, that you be informed as follows   **18 weak supposal** low estimate   **21 Co-
leaguèd with** jointed to, allied with. **dream . . . advantage** illusory
hope of having the advantage. (His only ally is this hope.)   **23 importing** pertaining to   **24 bonds** contracts

Now for ourself and for this time of meeting.
Thus much the business is: we have here writ
To Norway, uncle of young Fortinbras—
Who, impotent° and bed-rid, scarcely hears
30 Of this his nephew's purpose—to suppress
His° further gait° herein, in that the levies,
The lists, and full proportions are all made
Out of his subject;° and we here dispatch
You, good Cornelius, and you, Voltimand,
35 For bearers of this greeting to old Norway,
Giving to you no further personal power
To business with the King more than the scope
Of these dilated° articles allow.   [*He gives a paper.*]
Farewell, and let your haste command your duty.°

CORNELIUS, VOLTIMAND.
40 In that, and all things, will we show our duty.

KING.
We doubt it nothing.° Heartily farewell.
          [*Exeunt Voltimand and Cornelius.*]
And now, Laertes, what's the news with you?
You told us of some suit; what is 't, Laertes?
You cannot speak of reason to the Dane°
And lose your voice.° What wouldst thou beg,
45   Laertes,
That shall not be my offer, not thy asking?
The head is not more native° to the heart,
The hand more instrumental° to the mouth,
Than is the throne of Denmark to thy father.
What wouldst thou have, Laertes?

50 LAERTES.   My dread lord,
Your leave and favor° to return to France,
From whence though willingly I came to Denmark
To show my duty in your coronation,
Yet now I must confess, that duty done,
55 My thoughts and wishes bend again toward France
And bow them to your gracious leave and pardon.°

KING.
Have you your father's leave? What says Polonius?

POLONIUS.
H'ath,° my lord, wrung from me my slow leave
By laborsome petition, and at last
60 Upon his will I sealed° my hard° consent.
I do beseech you, give him leave to go.

KING.
Take thy fair hour,° Laertes. Time be thine,
And thy best graces spend it at thy will!°
But now, my cousin° Hamlet, and my son—

HAMLET.
A little more than kin, and less than kind.°   65

KING.
How is it that the clouds still hang on you?

HAMLET.
Not so, my lord. I am too much in the sun.°

QUEEN.
Good Hamlet, cast thy nighted color° off,
And let thine eye look like a friend on Denmark.°
Do not forever with thy vailèd lids°   70
Seek for thy noble father in the dust.
Thou know'st 'tis common,° all that lives must die,
Passing through nature to eternity.

HAMLET.
Ay, madam, it is common.

QUEEN.   If it be,
Why seems it so particular° with thee?   75

HAMLET.
Seems, madam? Nay, it is. I know not "seems."
'Tis not alone my inky cloak, good Mother,
Nor customary° suits of solemn black,
Nor windy suspiration° of forced breath,
No, nor the fruitful° river in the eye,   80
Nor the dejected havior° of the visage,
Together with all forms, moods,° shapes of grief,
That can denote me truly. These indeed seem,
For they are actions that a man might play.
But I have that within which passes show;   85
These but the trappings and the suits of woe.

KING.
'Tis sweet and commendable in your nature, Hamlet,
To give these mourning duties to your father.
But you must know your father lost a father,
That father lost, lost his, and the survivor bound   90

---

29 **impotent** helpless   31 **His** i.e., Fortinbras'. **gait** proceeding   31–33 **in that . . . subject** since the levying of troops and supplies is drawn entirely from the King of Norway's own subjects   38 **dilated** set out at length   39 **let . . . duty** let your swift obeying of orders, rather than mere words, express your dutifulness   41 **nothing** not at all   44 **the Dane** the Danish king   45 **lose your voice** waste your speech   47 **native** closely connected, related   48 **instrumental** serviceable   51 **leave and favor** kind permission   56 **bow . . . pardon** entreatingly make a deep bow, asking your permission to depart   58 **H'ath** he has   60 **sealed** (as if sealing a legal document). **hard** reluctant

62 **Take thy fair hour** enjoy your time of youth   63 **And . . . will** and may your finest qualities guide the way you choose to spend your time   64 **cousin** any kin not of the immediate family   65 **A little . . . kind** i.e., closer than an ordinary nephew (since I am stepson), and yet more separated in natural feeling (with pun on *kind* meaning "affectionate" and "natural," "lawful." This line is often read as an aside, but it need not be. The King chooses perhaps not to respond to Hamlet's cryptic and bitter remark.)   67 **the sun** i.e., the sunshine of the King's royal favor (with pun on *son*)   68 **nighted color** (1) mourning garments of black (2) dark melancholy   69 **Denmark** the King of Denmark   70 **vailèd lids** lowered eyes   72 **common** of universal occurrence. (But Hamlet plays on the sense of "vulgar" in line 74.)   75 **particular** personal   78 **customary** (1) socially conventional (2) habitual with me   79 **suspiration** sighing   80 **fruitful** abundant   81 **havior** expression   82 **moods** outward expression of feeling

In filial obligation for some term
To do obsequious° sorrow. But to persever°
In obstinate condolement° is a course
Of impious stubbornness. 'Tis unmanly grief.
95   It shows a will more incorrect to heaven,
A heart unfortified,° a mind impatient,
An understanding simple° and unschooled.
For what we know must be and is as common
As any the most vulgar thing to sense,°
100 Why should we in our peevish opposition
Take it to heart? Fie, 'tis a fault to heaven,
A fault against the dead, a fault to nature,
To reason most absurd, whose common theme
Is death of fathers, and who still° hath cried,
105 From the first corpse° till he that died today,
"This must be so." We pray you, throw to earth
This unprevailing° woe and think of us,
As of a father; for let the world take note,
You are the most immediate° to our throne,
110 And with no less nobility of love
Than that which dearest father bears his son
Do I impart toward° you. For° your intent
In going back to school° in Wittenberg,°
It is most retrograde° to our desire,
115 And we beseech you bend you° to remain
Here in the cheer and comfort of our eye,
Our chiefest courtier, cousin, and our son.

QUEEN.
Let not thy mother lose her prayers, Hamlet.
I pray thee, stay with us, go not to Wittenberg.

HAMLET.
120 I shall in all my best° obey you, madam.

KING.
Why, 'tis a loving and a fair reply.
Be as ourself in Denmark. Madam, come.
This gentle and unforced accord of Hamlet
Sits smiling to° my heart, in grace° whereof
125 No jocund° health that Denmark drinks today
But the great cannon to the clouds shall tell,
And the King's rouse° the heaven shall bruit° again,
Respeaking earthly thunder°. Come away.

Flourish. Exeunt all but Hamlet.

HAMLET.
O, that this too too sullied° flesh would melt,
Thaw, and resolve itself into a dew!   130
Or that the Everlasting had not fixed
His canon° 'gainst self-slaughter! O God, God,
How weary, stale, flat, and unprofitable
Seem to me all the uses° of this world!
Fie on 't, ah fie! 'Tis an unweeded garden   135
That grows to seed. Things rank and gross in nature
Possess it merely°. That it should come to this!
But two months dead—nay, not so much, not two.
So excellent a king, that was to° this
Hyperion° to a satyr°, so loving to my mother   140
That he might not beteem° the winds of heaven
Visit her face too roughly. Heaven and earth,
Must I remember? Why, she would hang on him
As if increase of appetite had grown
By what it fed on, and yet within a month—   145
Let me not think on 't; frailty, thy name is
    woman!—
A little month, or ere° those shoes were old
With which she followed my poor father's body,
Like Niobe°, all tears, why she, even she—
O God, a beast, that wants discourse of reason,°   150
Would have mourned long—married with my
    uncle,
My father's brother, but no more like my father
Than I to Hercules. Within a month,
Ere yet the salt of most unrighteous tears
Had left the flushing in her gallèd° eyes,   155
She married. O, most wicked speed, to post°
With such dexterity to incestuous° sheets!
It is not, nor it cannot come to good.
But break, my heart, for I must hold my tongue.

Enter Horatio, Marcellus, and Bernardo.

HORATIO.
Hail to your lordship!

HAMLET.   I am glad to see you well.   160
Horatio!—or I do forget myself.

---

92 **obsequious** suited to obsequies or funerals. **persever** persevere
93 **condolement** sorrowing   96 **unfortified** i.e., against adversity
97 **simple** ignorant   99 **As . . . sense** as the most ordinary experience   104 **still** always   105 **the first corpse** (Abel's)   107 **un-**
prevailing unavailing, useless   109 **most immediate** next in succession   112 **impart toward** i.e., bestow my affection on. **For** as for
113 **to school** i.e., to your studies. **Wittenberg** famous German university founded in 1502   114 **retrograde** contrary   115 **bend you**
incline yourself   120 **in all my best** to the best of my ability   124
to i.e., at. **grace** thanksgiving   125 **jocund** merry   127 **rouse**
drinking of a draft of liquor. **bruit again** loudly echo   128 **thunder**
i.e., of trumpet and kettledrum, sounded when the King drinks; see
1.4.8–12

129 **sullied** defiled. (The early quartos read *sallied;* the Folio, *solid.*)
132 **canon** law   134 **all the uses** the whole routine   137 **merely**
completely   139 **to** in comparison to   140 **Hyperion** Titan sun-
god, father of Helios. **satyr** a lecherous creature of classical mythology, half-human but with a goat's legs, tail, ears, and horns   141 **be-**
teem allow   147 **or ere** even before   149 **Niobe** Tantalus'
daughter, Queen of Thebes, who boasted that she had more sons and
daughters than Leto; for this, Apollo and Artemis, children of Leto,
slew her fourteen children. She was turned by Zeus into a stone that
continually dropped tears.   150 **wants . . . reason** lacks the faculty
of reason   155 **gallèd** irritated, inflamed   156 **post** hasten   157
incestuous (In Shakespeare's days, the marriage of a man like
Claudius to his deceased brother's wife was considered incestuous.)

HORATIO.
  The same, my lord, and your poor servant ever.
HAMLET.
  Sir, my good friend; I'll change that name° with you.
  And what make you from° Wittenberg, Horatio?
165 Marcellus.
MARCELLUS. My good lord.
HAMLET.
  I am very glad to see you. [*To Bernardo.*] Good even,
    sir.—
  But what in faith make you from Wittenberg?
HORATIO.
  A truant disposition, good my lord.
HAMLET.
170 I would not hear your enemy say so,
  Nor shall you do my ear that violence
  To make it truster of your own report
  Against yourself. I know you are no truant.
  But what is your affair in Elsinore?
175 We'll teach you to drink deep ere you depart.
HORATIO.
  My lord, I came to see your father's funeral.
HAMLET.
  I prithee, do not mock me, fellow student;
  I think it was to see my mother's wedding.
HORATIO.
  Indeed, my lord, it followed hard° upon.
HAMLET.
180 Thrift, thrift, Horatio! The funeral baked meats°
  Did coldly° furnish forth the marriage tables.
  Would I had met my dearest° foe in heaven
  Or ever° I had seen that day, Horatio!
  My father!—Methinks I see my father.
HORATIO.
  Where, my lord?
185 HAMLET.   In my mind's eye, Horatio.
HORATIO.
  I saw him once. 'A° was a goodly king.
HAMLET.
  'A was a man. Take him for all in all,
  I shall not look upon his like again.
HORATIO.
  My lord, I think I saw him yesternight.
190 HAMLET. Saw? Who?
HORATIO. My lord, the King your father.
HAMLET. The King my father?
HORATIO.
  Season your admiration° for a while

With an attent° ear till I may deliver,
Upon the witness of these gentlemen,   195
This marvel to you.
HAMLET.   For God's love, let me hear!
HORATIO.
  Two nights together had these gentlemen,
  Marcellus and Bernardo, on their watch,
  In the dead waste° and middle of the night,
  Been thus encountered. A figure like your father,   200
  Armèd at point° exactly, cap-à-pie,°
  Appears before them, and with solemn march
  Goes slow and stately by them. Thrice he walked
  By their oppressed and fear-surprisèd eyes
  Within his truncheon's° length, whilst they, distilled°   205
  Almost to jelly with the act° of fear,
  Stand dumb and speak not to him. This to me
  In dreadful° secrecy impart they did,
  And I with them the third night kept the watch,
  Where, as they had delivered, both in time,   210
  Form of the thing, each word made true and good,
  The apparition comes. I knew your father;
  These hands are not more like.
HAMLET.   But where was this?
MARCELLUS.
  My lord, upon the platform where we watch.
HAMLET.
  Did you speak to it?
HORATIO.   My lord, I did,   215
  But answer made it none. Yet once methought
  It lifted up its head and did address
  Itself to motion, like as it would speak;°
  But even then° the morning cock crew loud,
  And at the sound it shrunk in haste away   220
  And vanished from our sight.
HAMLET.   'Tis very strange.
HORATIO.
  As I do live, my honored lord, 'tis true,
  And we did think it writ down in our duty
  To let you know of it.
HAMLET.
  Indeed, indeed, sirs. But this troubles me.   225
  Hold you the watch tonight?
ALL.   We do, my lord.
HAMLET. Armed, say you?
ALL. Armed, my lord.
HAMLET. From top to toe?
ALL. My lord, from head to foot.   230

---

163 **change that name** i.e., give and receive reciprocally the name of "friend" (rather than talk of "servant") 164 **make you from** are you doing away from 179 **hard** close 180 **baked meats** meat pies 181 **coldly** i.e., as cold leftovers 182 **dearest** closest (and therefore deadliest) 183 **Or ever** before 186 **'A** he 193 **Season your admiration** restrain your astonishment

194 **attent** attentive 199 **dead waste** desolate stillness 201 **at point** correctly in every detail. **cap-à-pie** from head to foot 205 **truncheon** officer's staff. **distilled** dissolved 206 **act** action, operation 208 **dreadful** full of dread 217–218 **did . . . speak** began to move as though it were about to speak 219 **even then** at that very instant

HAMLET. Then saw you not his face?
HORATIO.
   O, yes, my lord, he wore his beaver° up.
HAMLET. What° looked he, frowningly?
HORATIO.
   A countenance more in sorrow than in anger.
235 HAMLET. Pale or red?
HORATIO. Nay, very pale.
HAMLET. And fixed his eyes upon you?
HORATIO. Most constantly.
HAMLET. I would I had been there.
240 HORATIO. It would have much amazed you.
HAMLET. Very like, very like. Stayed it long?
HORATIO.
   While one with moderate haste might tell° a hundred.
MARCELLUS, BERNARDO. Longer, longer.
HORATIO. Not when I saw 't.
245 HAMLET. His beard was grizzled°—no?
HORATIO.
   It was, as I have seen it in his life,
   A sable silvered.°
HAMLET.   I will watch tonight.
   Perchance 'twill walk again.
HORATIO.   I warrant° it will.
HAMLET.
   If it assume my noble father's person,
250 I'll speak to it though hell itself should gape
   And bid me hold my peace. I pray you all,
   If you have hitherto concealed this sight,
   Let it be tenable° in your silence still,
   And whatsoever else shall hap tonight,
255 Give it an understanding but no tongue.
   I will requite your loves. So, fare you well.
   Upon the platform twixt eleven and twelve
   I'll visit you.
ALL.   Our duty to your honor.
HAMLET.
   Your loves, as mine to you. Farewell.

                           Exeunt [all but Hamlet].
260 My father's spirit in arms! All is not well.
   I doubt° some foul play. Would the night were come!
   Till then sit still, my soul. Foul deeds will rise,
   Though all the earth o'erwhelm them, to men's eyes.

                                  Exit.

1 . 3 °   *Enter Laertes and Ophelia, his sister.*

LAERTES.
   My necessaries are embarked. Farewell.

And, sister, as the winds give benefit
And convoy is assistant,° do not sleep
But let me hear from you.
OPHELIA.   Do you doubt that?
LAERTES.
   For Hamlet, and the trifling of his favor,   5
   Hold it a fashion and a toy in blood,°
   A violet in the youth of primy° nature,
   Forward,° not permanent, sweet, not lasting,
   The perfume and suppliance° of a minute—
   No more.
OPHELIA.   No more but so?
LAERTES.   Think it no more.   10
   For nature crescent° does not grow alone
   In thews° and bulk, but as this temple° waxes
   The inward service of the mind and soul
   Grows wide withal.° Perhaps he loves you now,
   And now no soil° nor cautel° doth besmirch   15
   The virtue of his will;° but you must fear,
   His greatness weighed,° his will is not his own.
   For he himself is subject to his birth.
   He may not, as unvalued persons do,
   Carve° for himself, for on his choice depends   20
   The safety and health of this whole state,
   And therefore must his choice be circumscribed
   Unto the voice and yielding° of that body
   Whereof he is the head. Then if he says he
      loves you,
   It fits your wisdom so far to believe it   25
   As he in his particular act and place°
   May give his saying deed, which is no further
   Than the main voice° of Denmark goes withal.°
   Then weigh what loss your honor may sustain
   If with too credent° ear you list° his songs,   30
   Or lose your heart, or your chaste treasure open
   To his unmastered importunity.
   Fear it, Ophelia, fear it, my dear sister,
   And keep you in the rear or your affection,°
   Out of the shot and danger of desire.   35
   The chariest° maid is prodigal enough
   If she unmask° her beauty to the moon.°

---

232 **beaver** visor on the helmet   233 **What** how   242 **tell** count
245 **grizzled** gray   247 **sable silvered** black mixed with white
248 **warrant** assure you   253 **tenable** held   261 **doubt** suspect
1.3. Location: Polonius' chambers.

3 **convey is assistant** means of conveyance are available   6 **toy in blood** passing amorous fancy   7 **primy** in its prime, springtime   8 **Forward** precocious   9 **suppliance** supply, filler   11 **crescent** growing, waxing   12 **thews** bodily strength. **temple** i.e., body   14 **Grows wide withal** grows along with it   15 **soil** blemish. **cautel** deceit   16 **will** desire   17 **His greatness weighed** if you take into account his high position   20 **Carve** i.e., choose   23 **voice and yielding** assent, approval   26 **in . . . place** in his particular restricted circumstances   28 **main voice** general assent. **withal** along with   30 **credent** credulous. **list** listen to   34 **keep . . . affection** don't advance as far as your affection might lead you. (A military metaphor.)   36 **chariest** most scrupulously modest   37 **If she unmask** if she does no more than show her beauty. **moon** (Symbol of chastity.)

Virtue itself scapes not calumnious strokes.
The canker galls° the infants of the spring
40 Too oft before their buttons° be disclosed,°
And in the morn and liquid dew° of youth
Contagious blastments° are most imminent.
Be wary then; best safety lies in fear.
Youth to itself rebels,° though none else near.

OPHELIA.
45 I shall the effect of this good lesson keep
As watchman to my heart. But, good my brother,
Do not, as some ungracious° pastors do,
Show me the steep and thorny way to heaven,
Whiles like a puffed° and reckless libertine
50 Himself the primrose path of dalliance treads,
And recks° not his own rede.°

     Enter Polonius.

LAERTES.   O, fear me not.°
I stay too long. But here my father comes.
A double blessing is a double° grace;
Occasion smiles upon a second leave.°

POLONIUS.
55 Yet here, Laertes? Aboard, aboard, for shame!
The wind sits in the shoulder of your sail,
And you are stayed for. There—my blessing with
    thee!
And these few precepts in thy memory
Look° thou character.° Give thy thoughts no tongue,
60 Nor any unproportioned° thought his° act.
Be thou familiar,° but by no means vulgar.°
Those friends thou hast, and their adoption tried,°
Grapple them unto thy soul with hoops of steel,
But do not dull thy palm° with entertainment
65 Of each new-hatched, unfledged courage.° Beware
Of entrance to a quarrel, but being in,
Bear 't that° th' opposèd may beware of thee.
Give every man thy ear, but few thy voice;
Take each man's censure,° but reserve thy judgment.

Costly thy habit° as thy purse can buy,   70
But not expressed in fancy°; rich, not gaudy,
For the apparel oft proclaims the man,
And they in France of the best rank and station
Are of a most select and generous chief in that.°
Neither a borrower nor a lender be,   75
For loan oft loses both itself and friend,
And borrowing dulleth edge of husbandry.°
This above all: to thine own self be true,
And it must follow, as the night the day,
Thou canst not then be false to any man.   80
Farewell. My blessing season° this in thee!

LAERTES.
Most humbly do I take my leave, my lord.

POLONIUS.
The time invests° you. Go, your servants tend.°

LAERTES.
Farewell, Ophelia, and remember well
What I have said to you.   85

OPHELIA.   'Tis in my memory locked,
And you yourself shall keep the key of it.

LAERTES   Farewell.   *Exit Laertes.*

POLONIUS.
What is 't, Ophelia, he hath said to you?

OPHELIA.
So please you, something touching the Lord Hamlet.   90

POLONIUS.   Marry,° well bethought.
'Tis told me he hath very oft of late
Given private time to you, and you yourself
Have of your audience been most free and bounteous.
If it be so—as so 'tis put on° me,   95
And that in way of caution—I must tell you
You do not understand yourself so clearly
As it behooves° my daughter and your honor.
What is between you? Give me up the truth.

OPHELIA.
He hath, my lord, of late made many tenders°   100
Of his affection to me.

POLONIUS.
Affection? Pooh! You speak like a green girl,
Unsifted° in such perilous circumstance.
Do you believe his tenders, as you call them?

OPHELIA.
I do not know, my lord, what I should think.   105

POLONIUS.
Marry, I will teach you. Think yourself a baby
That you have ta'en these tenders for true pay

---

39 canker galls cankerworm destroys   **40 buttons** buds. **disclosed** opened   **41 liquid dew** i.e., time when dew is fresh and bright   **42 blastments** blights   **44 Youth ... rebels** youth is inherently rebellious   **47 ungracious** ungodly   **49 puffed** bloated, or swollen with pride   **51 recks** heeds. **rede** counsel. **fear me not** don't worry on my account   **53 double** (Laertes has already bid his father good-bye.)   **54 Occasion ... leave** happy is the circumstance that provides a second leave-taking. (The goddess Occasion, or Opportunity, smiles.)   **59 Look** be sure that. **character** inscribe   **60 unproportioned** badly calculated, intemperate. **his** its   **61 familiar** sociable. **vulgar** common   **62 and their adoption tried** and also their suitability for adoption as friends having been tested   **64 dull thy palm** i.e., shake hands so often as to make the gesture meaningless   **65 courage** young man of spirit   **67 Bear 't that** manage it so that   **69 censure** opinion, judgment

70 habit clothing   **71 fancy** excessive ornament, decadent fashion   **74 Are ... that** are of a most refined and well-bred preeminence in choosing what to wear   **77 husbandry** thrift   **81 season** mature   **83 invests** besieges, presses upon. **tend** attend, wait   **91 Marry** i.e., by the Virgin Mary. (A mild oath.)   **95 put on** impressed on, told to   **98 behooves** befits   **100 tenders** offers   **103 Unsifted** i.e., untried

Which are not sterling.° Tender° yourself more dearly,
Or—not to crack the wind° of the poor phrase,
110 Running it thus—you'll tender me a fool.°
OPHELIA.
My lord, he hath importuned me with love
In honorable fashion.
POLONIUS.
Ay, fashion° you may call it. Go to,° go to.
OPHELIA.
And hath given countenance° to his speech, my lord,
115 With almost all the holy vows of heaven.
POLONIUS.
Ay, springes° to catch woodcocks.° I do know,
When the blood burns, how prodigal° the soul
Lends the tongue vows. These blazes, daughter,
Giving more light than heat, extinct in both
120 Even in their promise as it° is a-making,
You must not take for fire. From this time
Be something° scanter of your maiden presence.
Set your entreatments° at a higher rate
Than a command to parle.° For Lord Hamlet,
125 Believe so much in him° that he is young,
And with a larger tether may he walk
Than may be given you. In few,° Ophelia,
Do not believe his vows, for they are brokers°,
Not of that dye° which their investments° show,
130 But mere implorators° of unholy suits,
Breathing° like sanctified and pious bawds,
The better to beguile. This is for all:°
I would not, in plain terms, from this time forth
Have you so slander° any moment° leisure
135 As to give words or talk with the Lord Hamlet.
Look to 't, I charge you. Come your ways.°
OPHELIA.
I shall obey, my lord.   *Exeunt.*

---

108 **sterling** legal currency. **Tender** hold, look after, offer   109
crack the wind i.e., run it until it is broken-winded   110 **tender
me a fool** (1) show yourself to me as a fool (2) show me up as a fool
(3) present me with a grandchild. (*Fool* was a term of endearment
for a child.)   113 **fashion** mere form, pretense. **Go to** (An expression of impatience.)   114 **countenance** credit, confirmation
116 **springes** snares. **woodcocks** birds easily caught; here used to
connote gullibility   117 **prodigal** prodigally   120 **it** i.e., the
promise   122 **something** somewhat   123 **entreatments** negotiations for surrender. (A military term.)   124 **parle** discuss terms
with the enemy. (Polonius urges his daughter, in the metaphor of
military language, not to meet with Hamlet and consider giving in
to him merely because he requests an interview.)   125 **so . . . him**
this much concerning him   127 **in few** briefly   128 **brokers** go-
betweens, procurers   129 **dye** color or sort. **investments** clothes.
(The vows are not what they seem.)   130 **mere implorators** out
and out solicitors   131 **Breathing** speaking   132 **for all** once for
all, in sum   134 **slander** abuse, misuse. **moment** moment's   136
Come your ways come along

---

1 . 4 °   *Enter Hamlet, Horatio, and Marcellus.*

HAMLET.
The air bites shrewdly;° it is very cold.
HORATIO.
It is a nipping and an eager° air.
HAMLET.
What hour now?
HORATIO.   I think it lacks of° twelve.
MARCELLUS.
No, it is struck.
HORATIO.   Indeed? I heard it not.
It then draws near the season°   5
Wherein the spirit held his wont° to walk.
    A flourish of trumpets, and two pieces° go off
    [*within*].
What does this mean, my lord?
HAMLET.
The King doth wake° tonight and takes his rouse°,
Keeps wassail,° and the swaggering upspring° reels;°
And as he drains his drafts of Rhenish° down,   10
The kettledrum and trumpet thus bray out
The triumph of his pledge.°
HORATIO.   Is it a custom?
HAMLET. Ay, marry, is 't,
But to my mind, though I am native here
And to the manner° born, it is a custom   15
More honored in the breach than the observance.°
This heavy-headed revel east and west°
Makes us traduced and taxed of° other nations.
They clepe° us drunkards, and with swinish phrase°
Soil our addition;° and indeed it takes   20
From our achievements, though performed at height,°
The pith and marrow of our attribute.°
So, oft it chances in particular men,
That for° some vicious mole of nature° in them,
As in their birth—wherein they are not guilty,   25
Since nature cannot choose his° origin—
By their o'ergrowth of some complexion,°

1.4. Location: The guard platform.
1 **shrewdly** keenly, sharply   2 **eager** biting   3 **lacks of** is just
short of   5 **season** time   6 **held his wont** was accustomed. **s.d.
pieces** i.e., of ordnance, cannon   8 **wake** stay awake and hold
revel. **takes his rouse** carouses   9 **wassail** carousal. **upspring** wild
German dance. **reels** dances   10 **Rhenish** Rhine wine   12 **The
triumph . . . pledge** i.e., his feat in draining the wine in a single
draft   15 **manner** custom (of drinking)   16 **More . . . observances** better neglected than followed   17 **east and west** i.e.,
everywhere   18 **taxed of** censured by   19 **clepe** call. **with swinish phrase** i.e., by calling us swine   20 **addition** reputation   21 **at
height** outstandingly   22 **The pith . . . attribute** the essence of
the reputation that others attribute to us   24 **for** on account of.
mole of nature natural blemish in one's constitution   26 **his** its
27 **their o'ergrowth . . . complexion** the excessive growth in individuals of some natural trait

Oft breaking down the pales° and forts of reason,
Or by some habit that too much o'erleavens°
30 The form of plausive° manners, that these men,
Carrying, I say, the stamp of one defect,
Being nature's livery° or fortune's star,°
His virtues else,° be they as pure as grace,
As infinite as man may undergo,°
35 Shall in the general censure° take corruption
From that particular fault. The dram of evil
Doth all the noble substance often dout
To his own scandal.°

Enter Ghost.

HORATIO.   Look, my lord, it comes!
HAMLET.
    Angels and ministers of grace° defend us!
40 Be thou° a spirit of health° or goblin damned,
Bring° with thee airs from heaven or blasts from hell,
Be thy intents° wicked or charitable,
Thou com'st in such a questionable° shape
That I will speak to thee. I'll call thee Hamlet,
45 King, father, royal Dane. O, answer me!
Let me not burst in ignorance, but tell
Why thy canonized° bones, hearsèd° in death,
Have burst their cerements;° why the sepulcher
Wherein we saw thee quietly inurned°
50 Hath oped his ponderous and marble jaws
To cast thee up again. What may this mean,
That thou, dead corpse, again in complete steel,°
Revisits thus the glimpses of the moon,°
Making night hideous, and we fools of nature°
55 So horridly to shake our disposition°
With thoughts beyond the reaches of our souls?
Say, why is this? Wherefore? What should we do?
                    [*The Ghost*] *beckons* [*Hamlet*].

HORATIO.
    It beckons you to go away with it,
As if it some impartment° did desire
To you alone.
MARCELLUS.   Look with what courteous action   60
It wafts you to a more removèd ground.
But do not go with it.
HORATIO.   No, by no means.
HAMLET.
    It will not speak. Then I will follow it.
HORATIO.
    Do not, my lord!
HAMLET.   Why, what should be the fear?
I do not set my life at a pin's fee,°   65
And for my soul, what can it do to that,
Being a thing immortal as itself?
It waves me forth again. I'll follow it.
HORATIO.
    What if it tempt you toward the flood,° my lord,
Or to the dreadful summit of the cliff   70
That beetles o'er° his° base into the sea,
And there assume some other horrible form
Which might deprive your sovereignty of reason°
And draw you into madness? Think of it.
The very place puts toys of desperation,°   75
Without more motive, into every brain
That looks so many fathoms to the sea
And hears it roar beneath.
HAMLET.
    It wafts me still.—Go on, I'll follow thee.
MARCELLUS.
    You shall not go, my lord.   [*They try to stop him.*]
HAMLET.   Hold off your hands!   80
HORATIO.
    Be ruled. You shall not go.
HAMLET.   My fate cries out,°
And makes each petty° artery° in this body
As hardy as the Nemean lion's° nerve.°
Still am I called. Unhand me, gentlemen.
By heaven, I'll make a ghost of him that lets° me!   85
I say, away!—Go on, I'll follow thee.
                    Exeunt Ghost and Hamlet.
HORATIO.
    He waxes desperate with imagination.

28 **pales** palings, fences (as of a fortification)   29 **o'erleavens** induces a change throughout (as yeast works in dough)   30 **plausive**
pleasing   32 **nature's livery** sign of one's servitude to nature. **fortune's star** the destiny that chance brings   33 **His virtues else** i.e.,
the other qualities of *these men* (line 30)   34 **may undergo** can sustain   35 **general censure** general opinion that people have of him
36–38 **The dram . . . scandal** i.e., the small drop of evil blots out or
works against the noble substance of the whole and brings it into
disrepute. To *dout* is to blot out. (A famous crux.)   39 **ministers of
grace** messengers of God   40 **Be thou** whether you are. **spirit of
health** good angel   41 **Bring** whether you bring   42 **Be thy intents** whether your intentions are   43 **questionable** inviting question   47 **canonized** buried according to the canons of the church.
hearsèd coffined   48 **cerements** grave clothes   49 **inurned** en-
tombed   52 **complete steel** full armor   53 **glimpses of the moon**
pale and uncertain moonlight   54 **fools of nature** mere men, limited to natural knowledge and subject to nature   55 **So . . . disposition** to distress our mental composure so violently

59 **impartment** communication   65 **fee** value   69 **flood** sea   71
beetles o'er overhangs threateningly (like bushy eyebrows). **his** its
73 **deprive . . . reason** take away the rule of reason over your mind
75 **toys of desperation** fancies of desperate acts, i.e., suicide   81
My fate cries out my destiny summons me   82 **petty** weak. **artery**
(through which the vital spirits were thought to have been conveyed)   83 **Nemean lion** one of the monsters slain by Hercules in
his twelve labors. **nerve** sinew   85 **lets** hinders

MARCELLUS.
    Let's follow. 'Tis not fit thus to obey him.
HORATIO.
    Have after.° To what issue° will this come?
MARCELLUS.
90   Something is rotten in the state of Denmark.
HORATIO.
    Heaven will direct it.°
MARCELLUS.   Nay, let's follow him.

                                                                        Exeunt.

1 . 5 °   *Enter Ghost and Hamlet.*

HAMLET.
    Whither will thou lead me? Speak. I'll go no further.
GHOST.
    Mark me.
HAMLET.   I will.
GHOST.   My hour is almost come,
    When I to sulfurous and tormenting flames
    Must render up myself.
HAMLET.   Alas, poor ghost!
GHOST.
5   Pity me not, but lend thy serious hearing
    To what I shall unfold.
HAMLET. Speak. I am bound° to hear.
GHOST.
    So art thou to revenge, when thou shalt hear.
HAMLET. What?
GHOST.
10   I am thy father's spirit,
    Doomed for a certain term to walk the night,
    And for the day confined to fast° in fires,
    Till the foul crimes° done in my days of nature°
    Are burnt and purged away. But that° I am forbid
15   To tell the secrets of my prison house,
    I could a tale unfold whose lightest word
    Would harrow up° thy soul, freeze thy young blood,
    Make thy two eyes like stars start from their spheres,°
    Thy knotted and combinèd locks° to part,
20   And each particular hair to stand on end
    Like quills upon the fretful porcupine.

    But this eternal blazon° must not be
    To ears of flesh and blood. List, list, O, list!
    If thou didst ever thy dear father love—
HAMLET. O God!   25
GHOST.
    Revenge his foul and most unnatural murder.
HAMLET. Murder?
GHOST.
    Murder most foul, as in the best° it is,
    But this most foul, strange, and unnatural.
HAMLET.
    Haste me to know 't, that I, with wings as swift   30
    As meditation or the thoughts of love,
    May sweep to my revenge.
GHOST.   I find thee apt;
    And duller shouldst thou be° than the fat° weed
    That roots itself in ease on Lethe° wharf,
    Wouldst thou not stir in this. Now, Hamlet, hear.   35
    'Tis given out that, sleeping in my orchard,°
    A serpent stung me. So the whole ear of Denmark
    Is by a forgèd process° of my death
    Rankly abused.° But know, thou noble youth,
    The serpent that did sting thy father's life   40
    Now wears his crown.
HAMLET. O, my prophetic soul! My uncle!
GHOST.
    Ay, that incestuous, that adulterate° beast,
    With witchcraft of his wit, with traitorous gifts°—
    O wicked wit and gifts, that have the power   45
    So to seduce!—won to his shameful lust
    The will of my most seeming-virtuous queen.
    O Hamlet, what a falling off was there!
    From me, whose love was of that dignity
    That it went hand in hand even with the vow°   50
    I made to her in marriage, and to decline
    Upon a wretch whose natural gifts were poor
    To° those of mine!
    But virtue,° as it never will be moved,
    Though lewdness court it in a shape of heaven,°   55
    So lust, though to a radiant angel linked,
    Will sate itself in a celestial bed°
    And prey on garbage.
    But soft, methinks I scent the morning air.
    Brief let me be. Sleeping within my orchard,   60

89 Have after let's go after him. **issue** outcome   **91 it** i.e., the outcome
1.5. Location: The battlements of the castle.
7 bound (1) ready (2) obligated by duty and fate. (The Ghost, in line 8, answers in the second sense.)   **12 fast** do penance by fasting   **13 crimes** sins. **of nature** as a mortal   **14 But that** were it not that   **17 harrow up** lacerate, tear   **18 spheres** i.e., eye-sockets, here compared to the orbits or transparent revolving spheres in which, according to Ptolemaic astronomy, the heavenly bodies were fixed   **19 knotted . . . locks** hair neatly arranged and confined

22 eternal blazon revelation of the secrets of eternity   **28 in the best** even at best   **33 shouldst thou be** you would have to be. **fat** torpid, lethargic   **34 Lethe** the river of forgetfulness in Hades   **36 orchard** garden   **38 forgèd process** falsified account   **39 abused** deceived   **43 adulterate** adulterous   **44 gifts** (1) talents (2) presents   **50 even with the vow** with the very vow   **53 To** compared to   **54 virtue, as it** as virtue   **55 shape of heaven** heavenly form   **57 sate . . . bed** cease to find sexual pleasure in a virtuously lawful marriage

My custom always of the afternoon,
Upon my secure° hour thy uncle stole,
With juice of cursèd hebona° in a vial,
And in the porches of my ears° did pour
65 The leprous distillment,° whose effect
Holds such an enmity with blood of man
That swift as quicksilver it courses through
The natural gates and alleys of the body,
And with a sudden vigor it doth posset°
70 And curd, like eager° droppings into milk,
The thin and wholesome blood. So did it mine,
And a most instant tetter° barked° about,
Most lazar-like°, with vile and loathsome crust,
All my smooth body.
75 Thus was I, sleeping, by a brother's hand
Of life, of crown, of queen at once dispatched,°
Cut off even in the blossoms of my sin,
Unhouseled,° disappointed,° unaneled,°
No reckoning° made, but sent to my account
80 With all the imperfections on my head.
O, horrible! O, horrible, most horrible!
If thou hast nature° in thee, bear it not.
Let not the royal bed of Denmark be
A couch for luxury° and damnèd incest.
85 But, howsoever thou pursues this act,
Taint not thy mind nor let thy soul contrive
Against thy mother aught. Leave her to heaven
And to those thorns that in her bosom lodge,
To prick and sting her. Fare thee well at once.
90 The glowworm shows the matin° to be near,
And 'gins to pale his° uneffectual fire.
Adieu, adieu, adieu! Remember me.   [Exit.]
HAMLET.
O all you host of heaven! O earth! What else?
And shall I couple° hell? O, fie! Hold, hold,° my heart,
95 And you, my sinews, grow not instant° old,
But bear me stiffly up. Remember thee?
Ay, thou poor ghost, whiles memory holds a seat
In this distracted globe.° Remember thee?
Yea, from the table° of my memory

I'll wipe away all trivial fond° records,   100
All saws° of books, all forms,° all pressures° past
That youth and observation copied there,
And thy commandment all alone shall live
Within the book and volume of my brain,
Unmixed with baser matter. Yes, by heaven!   105
O most pernicious woman!
O villain, villain, smiling, damnèd villain!
My tables°—meet it is° I set it down
That one may smile, and smile, and be a villain.
At least I am sure it may be so in Denmark.   110

                                        [Writing.]

So, uncle, there you are.° Now to my word:
It is "Adieu, adieu! Remember me."
I have sworn 't.

            Enter Horatio and Marcellus.

HORATIO. My lord, my lord!
MARCELLUS. Lord Hamlet!   115
HORATIO. Heavens secure him!°
HAMLET. So be it.
MARCELLUS. Hilo, ho, ho, my lord!
HAMLET. Hillo, ho, ho, boy! Come, bird, come.°
MARCELLUS. How is 't, my noble lord?   120
HORATIO. What news, my lord?
HAMLET. O, wonderful!
HORATIO. Good my lord, tell it.
HAMLET. No, you will reveal it.
HORATIO. Not I, my lord, by heaven.   125
MARCELLUS. Nor I, my lord.
HAMLET.
How say you, then, would heart of man once° think
    it?
But you'll be secret?
HORATIO, MARCELLUS. Ay, by heaven, my lord.
HAMLET.
There's never a villain dwelling in all Denmark
But he's an arrant° knave.   130
HORATIO.
There needs no ghost, my lord, come from the grave
To tell us this.
HAMLET.   Why, right, you are in the right.
And so, without more circumstance° at all,
O hold it fit that we shake hands and part,
You as your business and desire shall point you—   135
For every man hath business and desire,

62 **secure** confident, unsuspicious   63 **hebona** a poison. (The word seems to be a form of *ebony*, though it is thought perhaps to be related to *henbane*, a poison, or to *ebenus*, "yew.")   64 **porches of my ears** ears as a porch or entrance of the body   65 **leprous distillment** distillation causing leprosylike disfigurement   69 **posset** coagulate, curdle   70 **eager** sour, acid   72 **tetter** eruption of scabs. **barked** covered with a rough covering, like bark on a tree   73 **lazar-like** leperlike   76 **dispatched** suddenly deprived   78 **Unhouseled** without having received the Sacrament. **disappointed** unready (spiritually) for the last journey. **unaneled** without having received extreme unction   79 **reckoning** settling of accounts   82 **nature** i.e., the promptings of a son   84 **luxury** lechery   90 **matin** morning   91 **his** its   94 **couple** add. **Hold** hold together   95 **instant** instantly   98 **globe** (1) head (2) world   99 **table** tablet, slate

100 **fond** foolish   101 **saws** wise sayings. **forms** shapes or images copied onto the slate; general ideas. **pressures** impressions stamped   108 **tables** writing tablets. **meet it is** it is fitting   111 **there you are** i.e., there, I've written that down against you   116 **secure him** keep him safe   119 **Hillo . . . come** (A falconer's call to a hawk in air. Hamlet mocks the hallooing as though it were a part of hawking.)   127 **once** ever   130 **arrant** thoroughgoing   133 **circumstance** ceremony, elaboration

Such as it is—and for my own poor part,
Look you, I'll go pray.
HORATIO.
These are but wild and whirling words, my lord.
HAMLET.

140 I am sorry they offend you, heartily;
Yes, faith, heartily.
HORATIO.   There's no offense, my lord.
HAMLET.
Yes, by Saint Patrick,° but there is, Horatio,
And much offense° too. Touching this vision here,
It is an honest ghost,° that let me tell you.

145 For your desire to know what is between us,
O'ermaster 't as you may. And now, good friends,
As you are friends, scholars, and soldiers,
Give me one poor request.
HORATIO. What is 't, my lord? We will.
HAMLET.

150 Never make known what you have seen tonight.
HORATIO, MARCELLUS. My lord, we will not.
HAMLET. Nay, but swear 't.
HORATIO. In faith, my lord, not I.°
MARCELLUS. Nor I, my lord, in faith.

155 HAMLET. Upon my sword.°   [He holds out his sword.]
MARCELLUS. We have sworn, my lord, already.°
HAMLET. Indeed, upon my sword, indeed.
GHOST (cries under the stage). Swear.
HAMLET.
Ha, ha, boy, sayst thou so? Are thou there,
     truepenny?°

160 Come on, you hear this fellow in the cellarage.
Consent to swear.
HORATIO.   Propose the oath, my lord.
HAMLET.
Never to speak of this that you have seen,
Swear by my sword.
GHOST [beneath]. Swear.   [They swear.]°
HAMLET.

165 Hic et ubique° Then we'll shift our ground.
                              [He moves to another spot.]
Come hither, gentlemen,

And lay your hands again upon my sword.
Swear by my sword
Never to speak of this that you have heard.
GHOST [beneath]. Swear by his sword.   [They swear.] 170
HAMLET.
Well said, old mole. Canst work i' th' earth so fast?
A worthy pioner!°—Once more remove, good friends.
                              [He moves again.]
HORATIO.
O day and night, but this is wondrous strange!
HAMLET.
And therefore as a stranger° give it welcome,
There are more things in heaven and earth, Horatio,   175
Than are dreamt of in your philosophy.°
But come;
Here, as before, never, so help you mercy,°
How strange or odd soe'er I bear myself—
As I perchance hereafter shall think meet   180
To put an antic° disposition on—
That you, at such times seeing me, never shall,
With arms encumbered° thus, or this headshake,
Or by pronouncing of some doubtful phrase
As "Well, we know," or "We could, an if° we
     would,"   185
Or "If we list° to speak," or "There be, an if they
     might,"°
Or such ambiguous giving out,° to note°
That you know aught° of me—this not to do:
So grace and mercy at your most need help you: Swear.
GHOST [beneath]. Swear.   [They swear.] 190
HAMLET.
Rest, rest, perturbèd spirit! So, gentlemen,
With all my love I do commend me to you;°
And what so poor a man as Hamlet is
May do t' express his love and friending° to you,
God willing, shall not lack.° Let us go in together, 195
And still° your fingers on your lips, I pray.
The time° is out of joint. O cursèd spite°
That ever I was born to set it right!
                              [They wait for him to leave first.]
Nay, come, let's go together.°   Exeunt.

---

142 **Saint Patrick** (The keeper of Purgatory and patron saint of all blunders and confusion.) 143 **offense** (Hamlet deliberately changes Horatio's "no offense taken" to "an offense against all decency.") 144 **an honest ghost** i.e., a real ghost and not an evil spirit 153 **In faith . . . I** i.e., I swear not to tell what I have seen. (Horatio is not refusing to swear.) 155 **sword** i.e., the hilt in the form of a cross 156 **We . . . already** i.e., we swore *in faith* 159 **truepenny** honest old fellow 164 **s.d. They swear** (Seemingly they swear here, and at lines 170 and 190, as they lay their hands on Hamlet's sword. Triple oaths would have particular force; these three oaths deal with what they have seen, what they have heard, and what they promise about Hamlet's *antic disposition*.) 165 **Hic et ubique** here and everywhere. (Latin.)

172 **pioner** foot soldier assigned to dig tunnels and excavations 174 **as a stranger** i.e., needing your hospitality 176 **your philosophy** this subject called "natural philosophy" or "science" that people talk about 178 **so help you mercy** as you hope for God's mercy when you are judged 181 **antic** fantastic 183 **encumbered** folded 185 **an if** if 186 **list** wished. **There . . . might** i.e., there are people here (we, in fact) who could tell news if we were at liberty to do so 187 **giving out** intimation. **note** draw attention to the fact 188 **aught** i.e., something secret 192 **do . . . you** entrust myself to you 194 **friending** friendliness 195 **lack** be lacking 196 **still** always 197 **The time** the state of affairs. **spite** i.e., the spite of Fortune 199 **let's go together** (Probably they wait for him to leave first, but he refuses this ceremoniousness.)

2 . 1 °   *Enter old Polonius with his man [Reynaldo].*

POLONIUS.
  Give him this money and these notes, Reynaldo.
                     [He gives money and papers.]
REYNALDO. I will, my lord.
POLONIUS.
  You shall do marvelous° wisely, good Reynaldo,
  Before you visit him, to make inquire°
  Of his behavior.
5 REYNALDO.   My lord, I did intend it.
POLONIUS.
  Marry, well said, very well said. Look you, sir,
  Inquire me first what Danskers° are in Paris,
  And how, and who, what means,° and where they
    keep°,
  What company, at what expense; and finding
10 By this encompassment° and drift° of question
  That they do know my son, come you more nearer
  Than your particular demands will touch it.°
  Take you,° as 'twere, some distant knowledge of him,
  As thus, "I know his father and his friends,
15 And in part him." Do you mark this, Reynaldo?
REYNALDO. Ay, very well, my lord.
POLONIUS.
  "And in part him, but," you may say, "not well.
  But if 't be he I mean, he's very wild.
  Addicted so and so," and there put on° him
20 What forgeries° you please—marry, none so rank°
  As may dishonor him, take heed of that,
  But, sir, such wanton,° wild, and usual slips
  As are companions noted and most known
  To youth and liberty.
25 REYNALDO. As gaming, my lord.
POLONIUS. Ay, or drinking, fencing, swearing,
  Quarreling, drabbing°—you may go so far.
REYNALDO. My lord, that would dishonor him.
POLONIUS.
  Faith, no, as you may season° it in the charge.
30 You must not put another scandal on him
  That he is open to incontinency;°
  That's not my meaning. But breathe his faults so quaintly°
  That they may seem the taints of liberty,°
  The flash and outbreak of a fiery mind,

  A savageness in unreclaimèd blood,   35
  Of general assault.°
REYNALDO. But, my good lord—
POLONIUS.
  Wherefore should you do this?
REYNALDO. Ay, my lord, I would know that.
POLONIUS. Marry, sir, here's my drift,   40
  And I believe it is a fetch of warrant.°
  You laying these slight sullies on my son,
  As 'twere a thing a little soiled wi' the working,°
  Mark you,
  Your party in converse,° him you would sound,°   45
  Having ever° seen in the prenominate crimes°
  The youth you breathe° of guilty, be assured
  He closes with you in this consequence:°
  "Good sir," or so, or "friend," or "gentleman,"
  According to the phrase or the addition°   50
  Of man and country.
REYNALDO.   Very good, my lord.
POLONIUS. And then, sir, does 'a this—'a does—what was
  I about to say? By the Mass, I was about to say
  something. Where did I leave?
REYNALDO. At "closes in the consequence."   55
POLONIUS.
  At "closes in the consequence," ay, marry.
  He closes thus: "I know the gentleman,
  I saw him yesterday," or "th' other day,"
  Or then, or then, with such or such, "and as you
    say,
  There was 'a gaming," "there o'ertook in 's rouse,"°   60
  "There falling out° at tennis," or perchance
  "I saw him enter such a house of sale,"
  Videlicet° a brothel, or so forth. See you now,
  Your bait of falsehood takes this carp° of truth;
  And thus do we of wisdom and of reach,°   65
  With windlasses° and with assays of bias,°
  By indirections find directions° out.
  So by my former lecture and advice
  Shall you my son. You have me, have° you not?

2.1. Location: Polonius' chambers.
3 marvelous marvelously **4 inquire** inquiry **7 Danskers** Danes
8 what means what wealth (they have). **keep** dwell **10 encompass-ment** roundabout talking. **drift** gradual approach or course **11–12 come . . . it** you will find out more this way than by asking pointed questions (*particular demands*) **13 Take you** assume, pretend **19 put on** impute to **20 forgeries** invented tales. **rank** gross **22 wan-ton** sportive, unrestrained **27 drabbing** whoring **29 season** tem-per, soften **31 incontinency** habitual sexual excess **32 quaintly** artfully, subtly **33 taints of liberty** faults resulting from free living

35–36 A savageness . . . assault a wildness in untamed youth that assails all indiscriminately **41 fetch of warrant** legitimate trick **43 soiled wi' the working** soiled by handling while it is being made, i.e., by involvement in the ways of the world. **45 converse** conversation. **sound** i.e., sound out **46 Having ever** if he has ever. **prenominate crimes** before-mentioned offenses **47 breathe** speak **48 closes . . . consequence** takes you into his confidence in some fashion, as follows **50 addition** title **60 o'ertook in 's rouse** overcome by drink **61 falling out** quarreling **63 Videlicet** namely **64 carp** a fish **65 reach** capacity, ability **66 wind-lasses** i.e., circuitous paths. (Literally, circuits made to head off the game in hunting.) **assays of bias** attempts through indirection (like the curving path of the bowling ball, which is biased or weighted to one side) **67 directions** i.e., the way things really are **69 have** understand

REYNALDO.

    My lord, I have.

70 POLONIUS.   God b' wi'° ye; fare ye well.

REYNALDO. Good my lord.

POLONIUS.

    Observe his inclination in yourself.°

REYNALDO. I shall, my lord.

POLONIUS. And let him ply his music.

75 REYNALDO. Well, my lord.

POLONIUS.

    Farewell.   *Exit Reynaldo.*

      Enter Ophelia.

        How now, Ophelia, what's the matter?

OPHELIA.

    O my lord, my lord, I have been so affrighted!

POLONIUS. With what, i' the name of God?

OPHELIA.

    My lord, as I was sewing in my closet,°

80   Lord Hamlet, with his doublet° all unbraced,°

    No hat upon his head, his stockings fouled,

    Ungartered, and down-gyvèd° to his ankle,

    Pale as his shirt, his knees knocking each other,

    And with a look so piteous in purport°

85   As if he had been loosèd out of hell

    To speak of horrors—he comes before me.

POLONIUS.

    Mad for thy love?

OPHELIA.   My lord, I do not know,

    But truly I do fear it.

POLONIUS.   What said he?

OPHELIA.

    He took me by the wrist and held me hard.

90   Then goes he to the length of all his arm.

    And, with his other hand thus o'er his brow

    He falls to such perusal of my face

    As° 'a would draw it. Long stayed he so.

    At last, a little shaking of mine arm

95   And thrice his head thus waving up and down,

    He raised a sigh so piteous and profound

    As it did seem to shatter all his bulk°

    And end his being. That done, he lets me go,

    And with his head over his shoulder turned

100   He seemed to find his way without his eyes,

    For out o' doors he went without their helps,

    And to the last bended their light on me.

POLONIUS.

    Come, go with me. I will go seek the King.

This is the very ecstasy° of love,

Whose violent property° fordoes° itself   105

And leads the will to desperate undertakings

As oft as any passion under heaven

That does afflict our natures. I am sorry.

What, have you given him any hard words of late?

OPHELIA.

    No, my good lord, but as you did command   110

    I did repel his letters and denied

    His access to me.

POLONIUS.   That hath made him mad.

    I am sorry that with better heed and judgment

    I had not quoted° him. I feared he did but trifle

    And meant to wrack° thee. But beshrew my jealousy!° 115

    By heaven, it is as proper to our age°

    To cast beyond° ourselves in our opinions

    As it is common for the younger sort

    To lack discretion. Come, go we to the King.

    This must be known,° which, being kept close,° might

        move   120

    More grief to hide than hate to utter love.°

    Come.   *Exeunt.*

2.2°   *Flourish. Enter King and Queen, Rosencrantz, and*
        Guildenstern [with others].

KING.

    Welcome dear Rosencrantz and Guildenstern.

    Moreover that° we much did long to see you,

    The need we have to use you did provoke

    Our hasty sending. Something have you heard

    Of Hamlet's transformation—so call it,   5

    Sith nor° th' exterior nor the inward man

    Resembles that° it was. What it should be,

    More than his father's death, that thus hath put him

    So much from th' understanding of himself,

    I cannot dream of. I entreat you both   10

    That, being of so young days° brought up with him,

    And sith so neighbored to° his youth and havior,°

---

104 ecstasy madness   **105 property** nature. **fordoes** destroys
114 quoted observed   **115 wrack** ruin, seduce. **beshrew my jealousy** a plague upon my suspicious nature   **116 proper . . . age**
charateristic of us (old) men   **117 cast beyond** overshoot, miscal-
culate. (A metaphor from hunting.)   **120 known** made known (to
the King). **close** secret   **120–121 might . . . love** i.e., might cause
more grief (because of what Hamlet might do) by hiding the knowledge of Hamlet's strange behavior to Ophelia than unpleasantness
by telling it
2.2. Location: The castle.
2 Moreover that besides the fact that   **6 Sith nor** since neither
7 that what   **11 of . . . days** from such early youth   **12 And sith
so neighbored to** and since you are (or, and since that time you are)
intimately acquainted with. **havior** demeanor

---

be with   **72 in yourself** in your own person (as well as by
asking questions)   **79 closet** private chamber   **80 doublet** close-
fitting jacket. **unbraced** unfastened   **82 down-gyvèd** fallen to the
ankles (like gyves or fetters)   **84 in purport** in what it expressed
93 As as if (also in line 97)   **97 bulk** body

That you vouchsafe your rest° here in our court
Some little time, so by your companies
15 To draw him on to pleasures, and to gather
So much as from occasion° you may glean,
Whether aught to us unknown afflicts him thus
That, opened,° lies within our remedy.

QUEEN.
Good gentlemen, he hath much talked of you,
20 And sure I am two men there is not living
To whom he more adheres. If it will please you
To show us so much gentry° and good will
As to expend your time with us awhile
For the supply and profit of our hope,°
25 Your visitation shall receive such thanks
As fits a king's remembrance.°

ROSENCRANTZ.   Both Your Majesties
Might, by the sovereign power you have of° us,
Put your dread° pleasures more into command
Than to entreaty.

GUILDENSTERN.   But we both obey,
30 And here give up ourselves in the full bent°
To lay our service freely at your feet,
To be commanded.

KING.
Thanks, Rosencrantz and gentle Guildenstern.

QUEEN.
Thanks, Guildenstern and gentle Rosencrantz.
35 And I beseech you instantly to visit
My too much changèd son. Go, some of you,
And bring these gentlemen where Hamlet is.

GUILDENSTERN.
Heavens make our presence and our practices°
Pleasant and helpful to him!

QUEEN.   Ay, amen!

        Exeunt Rosencrantz and Guildenstern [with some
                                        attendants].

        Enter Polonius.

POLONIUS.
40 Th' ambassadors from Norway, my good lord,
Are joyfully returned.

KING.
Thou still° hast been the father of good news.

POLONIUS.
Have I, my lord? I assure my good liege
I hold° my duty, as° I hold my soul,

Both to my God and to my gracious king;   45
And I do think, or else this brain of mine
Hunts not the trail of policy° so sure
As it hath used to do, that I have found
The very cause of Hamlet's lunacy.

KING.
O, speak of that! That do I long to hear.   50

POLONIUS.
Give first admittance to th' ambassadors.
My news shall be the fruit° to that great feast.

KING.
Thyself do grace° to them and bring them in.
                                        [Exit Polonius.]
He tells me, my dear Gertrude, he hath found
The head and source of all your son's distemper.   55

QUEEN.
I doubt° it is no other but the main,°
His father's death and our o'erhasty marriage.

        Enter Ambassadors [Voltimand and Cornelius, with
        Polonius].

KING.
Well, we shall sift him.°—Welcome, my good
    friends!
Say, Voltimand, what from our brother° Norway?

VOLTIMAND.
Most fair return of greetings and desires.°   60
Upon our first°, he sent out to suppress
His nephew's levies, which to him appeared
To be a preparation 'gainst the Polack,
But, better looked into, he truly found
It was against Your Highness. Whereat grieved   65
That so his sickness, age, and impotence°
Was falsely borne in hand,° sends out arrests°
On Fortinbras, which he, in brief, obeys,
Receives rebuke from Norway, and in fine°
Makes vow before his uncle never more   70
To give th' assay° of arms against Your Majesty.
Whereon old Norway, overcome with joy,
Gives him three thousand crowns in annual fee
And his commission to employ those soldiers,
So levied as before, against the Polack,   75
With an entreaty, herein further shown,
                                        [giving a paper]
That it might please you to give quiet pass
Through your dominions for this enterprise

---

13 **vouchsafe your rest** please to stay   16 **occasion** opportunity
18 **opened** being revealed   22 **gentry** courtesy   24 **supply . . .
hope** aid and furtherance of what we hope for   26 **As fits . . . remembrance** as would be a fitting gift of a king who rewards true service   27 **of** over   28 **dread** inspiring awe   30 **in . . . bent** to the
utmost degree of our capacity. (An archery metaphor.)   38 **practices** doings   42 **still** always   44 **hold** maintain. **as** as firmly as

47 **policy** sagacity   52 **fruit** dessert   53 **grace** honor (punning on
grace said before a *feast*, line 52)   56 **doubt** fear, suspect. **main**
chief point, principal concern   58 **sift him** question Polonius
closely   59 **brother** fellow king   60 **desires** good wishes   61
Upon our first at our first words on the business   66 **impotence**
helplessness   67 **borne in hand** deluded, taken advantage of. **ar-
rests** orders to desist   69 **in fine** in conclusion   71 **give th' assay**
make trial of strength, challenge

On such regards of safety and allowance°
As therein are set down.

80 KING.   It likes° us well,
And at our more considered° time we'll read,
Answer, and think upon this business.
Meantime we thank you for your well-took labor.
Go to your rest; at night we'll feast together.
Most welcome home!   *Exeunt Ambassadors.*

85 POLONIUS.   This business is well ended.
My liege, and madam, to expostulate°
What majesty should be, what duty is,
Why day is day, night night, and time is time,
Were nothing but to waste night, day, and time.
90 Therefore, since brevity is the soul of wit,°
And tediousness the limbs and outward flourishes,
I will be brief. Your noble son is mad.
Mad call I it, for, to define true madness,
What is 't but to be nothing else but mad?
But let that go.
95 QUEEN.   More matter, with less art.
POLONIUS.
Madame, I swear I use no art at all.
That he's mad, 'tis true; 'tis true 'tis pity,
And pity 'tis 'tis true—a foolish figure,°
But farewell it, for I will use no art.
100 Mad let us grant him, then, and now remains
That we find out the cause of this effect,
Or rather say, the cause of this defect,
For this effect defective comes by cause.°
Thus it remains, and the remainder thus.
105 Perpend.°
I have a daughter—have while she is mine—
Who, in her duty and obedience, mark,
Hath given me this. Now gather and surmise.°
[*He reads the letter.*] "To the celestial and my soul's
110   idol, the most beautified Ophelia"—
That's an ill phrase, a vile phrase; "beautified" is a
    vile phrase. But you shall hear. Thus: [*He reads.*]
"In her excellent white bosom,° these,° etc."
QUEEN. Came this from Hamlet to her?
POLONIUS.
115 Good madam, stay° awhile, I will be faithful.°
                                                        [*He reads.*]

"Doubt thou the stars are fire,
    Doubt that the sun doth move,

Doubt° truth to be a liar,
    But never doubt I love.
O dear Ophilia, I am ill at these numbers.° I have not art   120
to reckon° my groans. But that I love thee best, O most
best, believe it. Adieu.
            Thine evermore, most dear lady, whilst this
                    machine° is to him, Hamlet."
This in obedience hath my daughter shown me,   125
And, more above,° hath his solicitings,
As they fell out° by time, by° means, and place,
All given to mine ear.°
KING.   But how hath she
Received his love?
POLONIUS.   What do you think of me?
KING.
As a man faithful and honorable.   130
POLONIUS.
I would fain° prove so. But what might you think,
When I had seen this hot love on the wing—
As I perceived it, I must tell you that,
Before my daughter told me—what might you,
Or my dear Majesty your queen here, think,   135
If I had played the desk or table book,°
Or given my heart a winking,° mute and dumb,
Or looked upon this love with idle° sight?
What might you think? No, I went round° to work,
And my young mistress thus I did bespeak:°   140
"Lord Hamlet is a prince out of thy star;°
This must not be." And then I prescripts° gave her,
That she should lock herself from his resort,°
Admit no messengers, receive no tokens.
Which done, she took the fruits of my advice;   145
And he, repellèd—a short tale to make—
Fell into a sadness, then into a fast,
Thence to a watch,° thence into a weakness,
Thence to a lightness,° and by this declension°
Into the madness wherein now he raves,   150
And all we mourn for.°
KING [*to the Queen*].   Do you think 'tis this?
QUEEN. It may be, very like.

---

79 On . . . allowance i.e., with such considerations for the safety of Denmark and permission for Fortinbras 80 likes pleases 81 considered suitable for deliberation 86 expostulate expound, inquire into 90 wit sense or judgment 98 figure figure of speech 103 For . . . cause i.e., for this defective behavior, this madness, has a cause 105 Perpend consider 108 gather and surmise draw your own conclusions 113 In . . . bosom (The letter is poetically addressed to her heart.) these i.e., the letter 115 stay wait. faithful i.e., in reading the letter accurately

118 Doubt suspect 120 ill . . . numbers unskilled at writing verses 121 reckon (1) count (2) number metrically, scan 124 machine i.e., body 126 more above moreover 127 fell out occurred. by according to 128 given . . . ear i.e., told me about 131 fain gladly 136 played . . . table book i.e., remained shut up, concealing the information 137 given . . . winking closed the eyes of my heart to this 138 with idle sight complacently or incomprehendingly 139 round roundly, plainly 140 bespeak address 141 out of thy star above your sphere, position 142 prescripts orders 143 his resort his visits 148 watch state of sleeplessness 149 lightness lightheadedness. declension decline, deterioration (with a pun on the grammatical sense) 151 all we all of us, or, into everything that we

POLONIUS.
Hath there been such a time—I would fain know
   that—
That I have positively said "'Tis so,"
When it proved otherwise?

155 KING.   Not that I know.

POLONIUS.
Take this from this,° if this be otherwise.
If circumstances lead me, I will find
Where truth is hid, though it were hid indeed
Within the center.°

KING.   How may we try° it further?

POLONIUS.

160 You know sometimes he walks four hours together
Here in the lobby.

QUEEN.   So he does indeed.

POLONIUS.
At such a time I'll loose° my daughter to him.
Be you and I behind an arras° then.
Mark the encounter. If he love her not

165 And be not from his reason fall'n thereon,°
Le me be no assistant for a state,
But keep a farm and carters.°

KING.   We will try it.

Enter Hamlet [reading on a book].

QUEEN.
But look where sadly° the poor wretch comes reading.

POLONIUS.
Away, I do beseech you both, away.

170 I'll board° him presently.° O, give me leave.°
      Exeunt King and Queen [with attendants].
How does my good Lord Hamlet?

HAMLET. Well, God-a-mercy.°

POLONIUS. Do you know me, my lord?

HAMLET. Excellent well. You are a fishmonger.°

175 POLONIUS. Not I, my lord.

HAMLET. Then I would you were so honest a man.

POLONIUS. Honest, my lord?

HAMLET. Ay, sir. To be honest, as this world goes, is to be
one picked out of ten thousand.

180 POLONIUS. That's very true, my lord.

HAMLET. For if the sun breed maggots in a dead dog, being a
good kissing carrion°—Have you a daughter?

POLONIUS. I have, my lord.

HAMLET. Let her not walk i' the sun.° Conception° is a
blessing, but as your daughter may conceive, friend, look   185
to 't.

POLONIUS [*aside*]. How say you by that? Still harping on my
daughter. Yet he knew me not at first; 'a° said I was a fishmonger. 'A is far gone. And truly in my youth I suffered
much extremity for love, very near this. I'll speak to him   190
again—What do you read, my lord?

HAMLET. Words, words, words.

POLONIUS. What is the matter,° my lord?

HAMLET. Between who?

POLONIUS. I mean, the matter that you read, my lord.   195

HAMLET. Slanders, sir; for the satirical rogue says here that
old men have gray beards, that their faces are wrinkled,
their eyes purging° thick amber° and plum-tree gum, and
that they have a plentiful lack of wit,° together with most
weak hams. All which, sir, though I most powerfully and   200
potently believe, yet I hold it not honesty° to have it thus
set down, for yourself, sir, shall grow old° as I am, if like a
crab you could go backward.

POLONIUS [*aside*]. Though this be madness, yet there is
method in 't.—Will you walk out of the air,° my lord?   205

HAMLET. Into my grave.

POLONIUS. Indeed, that's out of the air. [*Aside.*] How preg-
nant° sometimes his replies are! A happiness° that often
madness hits on, which reason and sanity could not so
prosperously° be delivered of. I will leave him and sud-   210
denly° contrive the means of meeting between him and
my daughter.—My honorable lord, I will most humbly
take my leave of you.

HAMLET. You cannot, sir, take from me anything that I will
more willing part withal°—except my life, except my life,   215
except my life.

Enter Guildenstern and Rosencrantz.

POLONIUS. Fare you well, my lord.

HAMLET. These tedious old fools!°

POLONIUS. You go to seek the Lord Hamlet. There he is.

---

156 **Take this from this** (The actor probably gestures, indicating that he means his head from his shoulders, or his staff of office or chain from his hands or neck, or something similar.) 159 **center** middle point of the earth (which is also the center of the Ptolemaic universe). **try** test, judge 162 **loose** (as one might release an animal that is being mated) 163 **arras** hanging, tapestry 165 **thereon** on that account 167 **carters** wagon drivers 168 **sadly** seriously 170 **board** accost. **presently** at once. **give me leave** i.e., excuse me, leave me alone. (Said to those he hurries offstage, including the King and Queen.) 172 **God-a-mercy** God have mercy, i.e., thank you 174 **fishmonger** fish merchant

182 **a good kissing carrion** i.e., a good piece of flesh for kissing, or for the sun to kiss 184 **i' the sun** in public (with additional implication of the sunshine of princely favors). **Conception** (1) understanding (2) pregnancy 188 **'a** he 193 **matter** substance. (But Hamlet plays on the sense of "basis for a dispute.") 198 **purging** discharging. **amber** i.e., resin, like the resinous *plum-tree gum* 199 **wit** understanding 201 **honesty** decency, decorum 202 **old** as old 205 **out of the air** (The open air was considered dangerous for sick people.) 208 **pregnant** quick-witted, full of meaning. **happiness** felicity of expression 210 **prosperously** successfully 211 **suddenly** immediately 215 **withal** with 218 **old fools** i.e., old men like Polonius

220 ROSENCRANTZ [*to Polonius*]. God save you, sir!

[*Exit Polonius.*]

GUILDENSTERN. My honored lord!

ROSENCRANTZ. My most dear lord!

HAMLET. My excellent good friends! How dost thou, Guildenstern? Ah, Rosencrantz! Good lads, how do you both?

225 ROSENCRANTZ. As the indifferent° children of the earth.

GUILDENSTERN.

Happy in that we are not overhappy.

On Fortune's cap we are not the very button.

HAMLET. Nor the soles of her shoe?

230 ROSENCRANTZ. Neither, my lord.

HAMLET. Then you live about her waist, or in the middle of her favors?°

GUILDENSTERN. Faith, her privates we.°

HAMLET. In the secret parts of Fortune? O, most true, she is a strumpet.° What news?

235

ROSENCRANTZ. None, my lord, but the world's grown honest.

HAMLET. Then is doomsday near. But your news is not true. Let me question more in particular. What have you, my good friends, deserved at the hands of Fortune that she sends you to prison hither?

240

GUILDENSTERN. Prison, my lord?

HAMLET. Denmark's a prison.

ROSENCRANTZ. Then is the world one.

HAMLET. A goodly one, in which there are many confines,° wards,° and dungeons, Denmark being one o' the worst.

245

ROSENCRANTZ. We think not so, my lord.

HAMLET. Why then 'tis none to you, for there is nothing either good or bad but thinking makes it so. To me it is a prison.

250

ROSENCRANTZ. Why then, your ambition makes it one. 'Tis too narrow for your mind.

HAMLET. O God, I could be bounded in a nutshell and count myself a king of infinite space, were it not that I have bad dreams.

255

GUILDENSTERN. Which dreams indeed are ambition, for the very substance of the ambitious° is merely the shadow of a dream.

260 HAMLET. A dream itself is but a shadow.

ROSENCRANTZ. Truly, and I hold ambition of so airy and light a quality that it is but a shadow's shadow.

HAMLET. Then are our beggars bodies,° and our monarchs

and outstretched° heroes the beggars' shadows. Shall we to the court? For, by my fay,° I cannot reason.   265

ROSENCRANTZ, GUILDENSTERN. We'll wait upon° you.

HAMLET. No such matter. I will not sort° with you with the rest of my servants, for, to speak to you like an honest man, I am most dreadfully attended.° But, in the beaten way° of friendship, what make° you at Elsinore?   270

ROSENCRANTZ. To visit you, my lord, no other occasion.

HAMLET. Beggar that I am, I am even poor in thanks; but I thank you, and sure, dear friends, my thanks are too dear a halfpenny.° Were you not sent for? Is it your own inclining? Is it a free° visitation? Come, come, deal justly   275 with me. Come, come. Nay, speak.

GUILDENSTERN. What should we say, my lord?

HAMLET. Anything but to the purpose.° You were sent for, and there is a kind of confession in your looks which your modesties° have not craft enough to color. I know the   280 good King and Queen have sent for you.

ROSENCRANTZ. To what end, my lord?

HAMLET. That you must teach me. But let me conjure° you, by the rights of our fellowship, by the consonancy of our youth,° by the obligation of our ever-preserved love, and   285 by what more dear a better° proposer could charge° you withal, be even° and direct with me whether you were sent for or no.

ROSENCRANTZ [*aside to Guildenstern*]. What say you?

HAMLET [*aside*]. Nay, then, I have an eye of° you.—If you   290 love me, hold not off.°

GUILDENSTERN. My lord, we were sent for.

HAMLET. I will tell you why; so shall my anticipation prevent your discovery,° and your secrecy to the King and Queen molt no feather.° I have of late—but wherefore I   295 know not—lost all my mirth, forgone all custom of exercises; and indeed it goes so heavily with my disposition that this goodly frame, the earth, seems to me a sterile promontory; this most excellent canopy, the air, look you, this brave° o'erhanging firmament, this majestical roof   300 fretted° with golden fire, why, it appeareth nothing to me

---

226 **indifferent** ordinary, at neither extreme of fortune or misfortune   232 **favors** i.e., sexual favors   233 **her privates we** i.e., (1) we are sexually intimate with Fortune, the fickle goddess who bestows her favors indiscriminately (2) we are her private citizens   235 **strumpet** prostitute. (A common epithet for indiscriminate Fortune; see line 493.)   246 **confines** places of confinement. **wards** cells   258 **the very . . . ambitious** that seemingly very substantial thing that the ambitious pursue   263 **bodies** i.e., solid substances rather than shadows (since beggars are not ambitious)

264 **outstretched** (1) far-reaching in their ambition (2) elongated as shadows   265 **fay** faith   266 **wait upon** accompany, attend. (But Hamlet uses the phrase in the sense of providing menial service.)   267 **sort** class, categorize   269 **dreadfully attended** waited upon in slovenly fashion   270 **beaten way** familiar path, tried-and-true course. **make** do   274 **too dear a halfpenny** (1) too expensive at even a halfpenny, i.e., of little worth (2) too expensive *by* a halfpenny in return for worthless kindness   275 **free** voluntary   278 **Anything but to the purpose** anything except a straightforward answer. (Said ironically.)   280 **modesties** sense of shame. **color** disguise   283 **conjure** adjure, entreat   284–285 **the consonancy of our youth** our closeness in our younger days   286 **better** more skillful   286–287 **charge** urge. **even** straight, honest   290 **of** on   291 **hold not off** don't hold back   293–294 **so . . . discovery** in that way my saying it first will spare you from revealing the truth   295 **molt no feather** i.e., not diminish in the least   300 **brave** splendid   301 **fretted** adorned (with fretwork, as in a vaulted ceiling)

but a foul and pestilent congregation° of vapors. What a
piece of work° is a man! How noble in reason, how infinite in faculties, in form and moving how express° and
305 admirable, in action how like an angel, in apprehension°
how like a god! The beauty of the world, the paragon of
animals! And yet, to me, what is this quintessence° of
dust? Man delights not me—no, nor woman neither,
though by your smiling you seem to say so.
310 ROSENCRANTZ. My lord, there was no such stuff in my
thoughts.
HAMLET. Why did you laugh, then, when I said man delights not me?
ROSENCRANTZ. To think, my lord, if you delight not in man,
315 what Lenten entertainment° the players shall receive
from you. We coted° them on the way, and hither are
they coming to offer you service.
HAMLET. He that plays the king shall be welcome; His
Majesty shall have tribute° of° me. The adventurous
320 knight shall use his foil and target,° the lover shall not
sign gratis,° the humorous man° shall end his part in
peace,° the clown shall make those laugh whose lungs are
tickle o' the sear,° and the lady shall say her mind freely,
or the blank verse shall halt° for 't. What players are
325 they?
ROSENCRANTZ. Even those you were wont to take such delight in, the tragedians° of the city.
HAMLET. How chances it they travel? Their residence°,
both in reputation and profit, was better both ways.
330 ROSENCRANTZ. I think their inhibition° comes by the
means of the late° innovation.°
HAMLET. Do they hold the same estimation they did when I
was in the city? Are they so followed?
ROSENCRANTZ. No, indeed are they not.
335 HAMLET. How comes it? Do they grow rusty?

ROSENCRANTZ. Nay, their endeavor keeps° in the wonted°
pace. But there is, sir, an aerie° of children, little eyases,°
that cry out on the top of question° and are most tyranni-
cally° clapped for 't. These are now the fashion, and so
berattle° the common stages°—so they call them—that 340
many wearing rapiers° are afraid of goose quills° and dare
scarce come thither.
HAMLET. What, are they children? Who maintains 'em?
How are they escoted?° Will they pursue the quality° no
longer than they can sing?° Will they not say afterwards, 345
if they should grow themselves to common° players—as it
is most like°, if their means are no better°—their writers
do them wrong to make them exclaim against their own
succession?°
ROSENCRANTZ. Faith, there has been much to-do° on both 350
sides, and the nation holds it no sin to tar° them to controversy. There was for a while no money bid for argument unless the poet and the player went to cuffs in the
question.°
HAMLET. Is 't possible? 355
GUILDENSTERN. O, there has been much throwing about of
brains.
HAMLET. Do the boys carry it away?°
ROSENCRANTZ. Ay, that they do, my lord—Hercules and his
load° too. 360
HAMLET. It is not very strange; for my uncle is King of Denmark, and those that would make mouths° at him while
my father lived give twenty, forty, fifty, a hundred ducats°
apiece for his picture in little.° 'Sblood,° there is something in this more than natural, if philosophy° could find 365
it out.

A flourish [of trumpets within].

GUILDENSTERN. There are the players.
HAMLET. Gentlemen, you are welcome to Elsinore. Your

302–303 **congregation** mass. **piece of work** masterpiece   304 **express** well-framed, exact, expressive   305 **apprehension** power of
comprehending   307 **quintessence** the fifth essence of ancient
philosophy, beyond earth, water, air, and fire, supposed to be the
substance of the heavenly bodies and to be latent in all things
315 **Lenten entertainment** meager reception (appropriate to Lent)
316 **coted** overtook and passed by   319 **tribute** (1) applause (2)
homage paid in money. **of** from   320 **foil and target** sword and
shield   321 **gratis** for nothing. **humorous man** eccentric character, dominated by one trait or "humor"   321–322 **in peace** i.e.,
with full license   323 **tickle o' the sear** easy on the trigger, ready
to laugh easily. (A *sear* is part of a gunlock.)   324 **halt** limp   327
tragedians actors   328 **residence** remaining in their usual place,
i.e., in the city   330 **inhibition** formal prohibition (from acting
plays in the city)   331 **late** recent. **innovation** i.e., the new fashion in satirical plays performed by boy actors in the "private" theaters; or possibly a political uprising; or the strict limitations set on
the theaters in London in 1600   335–360 **How . . . load too** (The
passage, omitted from the early quartos, alludes to the so-called War
of the Theaters, 1599–1602, the rivalry between the children's
companies and the adult actors.)

336 **keeps** continues. **wonted** usual   337 **aerie** nest. **eyases** young
hawks   338 **cry . . . question** speak shrilly, dominating the controversy (in decrying the public theaters)   338–339 **tyrannically**
outrageously   340 **berattle** berate, clamor against. **common stages**
public theaters   341 **many wearing rapiers** i.e., many men of fashion, afraid to patronize the common players for fear of being satirized by the poets writing for the boy actors. **goose quills** i.e., pens of
satirists   344 **escoted** maintained. **quality** (acting) profession
344–345 **no longer . . . sing** i.e., only until their voices change
346 **common** regular, adult   347 **like** likely. **if . . . better** if they
find no better way to support themselves   349 **succession** i.e., future careers   350 **to-do** ado   351 **tar** set on (as dogs)   352–354
There . . . question i.e., for a while, no money was offered by the
acting companies to playwrights for the plot to a play unless the
satirical poets who wrote for the boys and the adult actors came to
blows in the play itself   358 **carry it away** i.e., win the day
359–360 **Hercules . . . load** (Thought to be an allusion to the sign
of the Globe Theatre, which was Hercules bearing the world on his
shoulders.)   362 **mouths** faces   363 **ducats** gold coins   364 **in
little** in miniature. **'Sblood** by God's (Christ's) blood   365 **philosophy** i.e., scientific inquiry

hands, come then. Th' appurtenance° of welcome is
370 fashion and ceremony. Let me comply° with you in this
garb,° lest my extent° to the players, which, I tell you,
must show fairly outwards,° should more appear like
entertainment° than yours. You are welcome. But my
uncle-father and aunt-mother are deceived.
375 GUILDENSTERN. In what, my dear lord?
HAMLET. I am but mad north-north-west.° When the wind
is southerly I know a hawk from a handsaw.°

Enter Polonius.

POLONIUS. Well be with you, gentlemen!
HAMLET. Hark you, Guildenstern, and you too; at each ear a
380 hearer. That great baby you see there is not yet out of his
swaddling clouts.°
ROSENCRANTZ. Haply° he is the second time come to them,
for they say an old man is twice a child.
HAMLET. I will prophesy he comes to tell me of the players.
385 Mark it.—You say right, sir, o' Monday morning, 'twas
then indeed.
POLONIUS. My lord, I have news to tell you.
HAMLET. My lord, I have news to tell you. When Roscius°
was an actor in Rome—
390 POLONIUS. The actors are come hither, my lord.
HAMLET. Buzz, buzz!°
POLONIUS. Upon my honor—
HAMLET. Then came each actor on his ass.
POLONIUS. The best actors in the world, either for tragedy,
395 comedy, history, pastoral, pastoral-comical, historical-
pastoral, tragical-historical, tragical-comical-historical-
pastoral, scene individable,° or poem unlimited.°
Seneca° cannot be too heavy, nor Plautus° too light.
For the law of writ and the liberty,° these are the only
400 men.
HAMLET. O Jephthah, judge of Israel,° what a treasure hadst
thou!

POLONIUS. What a treasure had he, my lord?
HAMLET. Why,
"One fair daughter, and no more,   405
The which he lovèd passing° well."
POLONIUS [*aside*]. Still on my daughter.
HAMLET. Am I not i' the right, old Jephthah?
POLONIUS. If you call me Jephthah, my lord, I have a daugh-
ter that I love passing well.   410
HAMLET. Nay, that follows not.
POLONIUS. What follows then, my lord?
HAMLET. Why,
"As by lot,° God wot,"°
and then, you know,   415
"It came to pass, as most like° it was"—
the first row° of the pious chanson° will show you
more,
for look where my abridgement° comes.

Enter the Players.

You are welcome, masters; welcome, all. I am glad to see   420
thee well. Welcome, good friends. O, old friend! Why,
thy face is valanced° since I saw thee last. Com'st thou
to beard° me in Denmark? What, my young lady° and
mistress! By 'r Lady,° your ladyship is nearer to heaven
than when I saw you last, by the altitude of a chopine.°   425
Pray God your voice, like a piece of uncurrent° gold, be
not cracked within the ring.° Masters, you are all
welcome. We'll e'en to 't° like French falconers, fly at
anything we see. We'll have a speech straight.° Come,
give us a taste of your quality.° Come, a passionate   430
speech.
FIRST PLAYER. What speech, my good lord?
HAMLET. I heard thee speak me a speech once, but it was
never acted, or if it was, not above once, for the play, I remember, pleased not the million; 'twas caviar to the gen-   435
eral.° But it was—as I received it, and others, whose judgments in such matters cried in the top of° mine—an
excellent play, well digested° in the scenes, set down with
as much modesty° as cunning.° I remember one said there

---

369 **appurtenance** proper accompaniment   370 **comply** observe
the formalities of courtesy   371 **garb** i.e., manner. **my extent** that
which I extend, i.e., my polite behavior   372 **show fairly outwards** show every evidence of cordiality   373 **entertainment** a
(warm) reception   376 **north-north-west** just off true north, only
partly   377 **hawk, handsaw** i.e., two very different things, though
also perhaps meaning a mattock (or *hack*) and a carpenter's cutting
tool, respectively; also birds, with a play on *hernshaw*, or heron
381 **swaddling clouts** cloths in which to wrap a newborn baby
382 **Haply** perhaps   388 **Roscius** a famous Roman actor who died
in 62 B.C.   391 **Buzz** (An interjection used to denote stale news.)
397 **scene individable** a play observing the unity of place; or perhaps one that is unclassifiable, or performed without intermission
397–398 **poem unlimited** a play disregarding the unities of time
and place; one that is all-inclusive   398 **Seneca** writer of Latin
tragedies. **Plautus** writer of Latin comedy   399 **law ... liberty**
dramatic composition both according to the rules and disregarding
the rules. **these** i.e., the actors   401 **Jephthah ... Israel** (Jephthah had to sacrifice his daughter; see Judges 11. Hamlet goes on to
quote from a ballad on the theme.)

406 **passing** surpassingly   414 **lot** chance. **wot** knows   416 **like**
likely, probable   417 **row** stanza. **chanson** ballad, song   419 **my
abridgment** something that cuts short my conversation; also, a diversion   422 **valanced** fringed (with a beard)   423 **beard** confront, challenge (with obvious pun). **young lady** i.e., boy playing
women's parts   424 **By 'r Lady** by Our Lady   426 **chopine** thick-
soled shoe of Italian fashion   426–427 **uncurrent** not passable as
lawful coinage   427 **cracked ... ring** i.e., changed from adolescent to male voice, no longer suitable for women's roles. (Coins featured rings enclosing the sovereign's head; if the coin was cracked
within this ring, it was unfit for currency.)   428 **e'en to 't** go at it
429 **straight** at once   430 **quality** professional skill   435–436
caviar to the general caviar to the multitude, i.e., a choice dish too
elegant for coarse tastes   437–438 **cried in the top of** i.e., spoke
with greater authority than   438 **digested** arranged, ordered
439 **modesty** moderation, restraint. **cunning** skill

440 were no sallets° in the lines to make the matter savory,
nor no matter in the phrase that might indict° the author
of affectation, but called it an honest method, as wholesome as sweet, and by very much more handsome° than
fine.° One speech in 't I chiefly loved: 'twas Aeneas' tale
445 to Dido, and thereabout of it especially when he speaks of
Priam's slaughter.° If it live in your memory, begin at this
line: let me see, let me see—

    "The rugged Pyrrhus,° like th' Hyrcanian beast"°—
'Tis not so. It begins with Pyrrhus:

450   "The rugged° Pyrrhus, he whose sable° arms,
    Black as his purpose, did the night resemble
    When he lay couchèd° in the ominous horse,°
    Hath now this dread and black complexion
    smeared
455   With heraldry more dismal.° Head to foot
    Now is he total gules,° horridly tricked°
    With blood of fathers, mothers, daughters, sons,
    Baked and impasted° with the parching streets,°
    That lend a tyrannous° and a damnèd light
460   To their lord's° murder. Roasted in wrath and fire,
    And thus o'ersizèd° with coagulate gore,
    With eyes like carbuncles,° the hellish Pyrrhus
    Old grandsire Priam seeks."
So proceed you.

465 POLONIUS. 'Fore God, my lord, well spoken, with good accent and good discretion.

FIRST PLAYER.   "Anon he finds him
    Striking too short at Greeks. His antique° sword,
    Rebellious to his arm, lies where it falls,
    Repugnant° to command. Unequal matched,
470   Pyrrhus at Priam drives, in rage strikes wide,
    But with the whiff and wind of his fell° sword

    Th' unnervèd° father falls. Then senseless Ilium,°
    Seeming to feel this blow, with flaming top
    Stoops to his° base, and with a hideous crash
    Takes prisoner Pyrrhus' ear. For, lo! His sword,   475
    Which was declining° on the milky° head
    Of reverend Priam, seemed i' th' air to stick.
    So as a painted° tyrant Pyrrhus stood,
    And, like a neutral to his will and matter,°
    Did nothing.   480
    But as we often see against° some storm
    A silence in the heavens, the rack° stand still,
    The bold winds speechless, and the orb° below
    As hush as death, anon the dreadful thunder
    Doth rend the region,° so, after Pyrrhus' pause,   485
    A rousèd vengeance sets him new a-work,
    And never did the Cyclops'° hammers fall
    On Mars's armor forged for proof eterne°
    With less remorse° than Pyrrhus' bleeding sword
    Now falls on Priam.   490
    Out, out, thou strumpet Fortune! All you gods
    In general synod° take away her power!
    Break all the spokes and fellies° from her wheel,
    And bowl the round nave° down the hill of heaven°
    As low as to the fiends!"   495

POLONIUS. This is too long.

HAMLET. It shall to the barber's with your beard.—Prithee,
say on. He's for a jig° or a tale of bawdry, or he sleeps. Say
on; come to Hecuba.°

FIRST PLAYER. "But who, ah woe! had° seen the moblèd°   500
    queen"—

HAMLET. "The moblèd queen?"

POLONIUS. That's good. "Moblèd queen" is good.

FIRST PLAYER.
    "Run barefoot up and down, threat'ning the flames°
    With bisson rheum,° a clout° upon that head.   505
    Where late° the diadem stood, and, for a robe,
    About her lank and all o'erteemèd° loins
    A blanket, in the alarm of fear caught up—
    Who this had seen, with tongue in venom steeped,

440 **sallets** i.e., something savory, spicy improprieties **441 indict**
convict **443 handsome** well-proportioned **444 fine** elaborately
ornamented, showy **446 Priam's slaughter** the slaying of the ruler
of Troy, when the Greeks finally took the city **448 Pyrrhus** a
Greek hero in the Trojan War, also known as Neoptolemus, son of
Achilles—another avenging son. **Hyrcanian beast** i.e., tiger. (On
the death of Priam, see Virgil, *Aeneid*, 2.506 ff.; compare the whole
speech with Marlow's *Dido Queen of Carthage*, 2.1.214 ff. On the
Hyrcanian tiger, see *Aeneid*, 4.366–367. Hyrcania is on the Caspian
Sea.) **450 rugged** shaggy, savage. **sable** black (for reasons of camouflage during the episode of he Trojan horse) **452 couchèd** concealed. **ominous horse** fateful Trojan horse, by which the Greeks
gained access to Troy **455 dismal** ill-omened **456 total gules**
entirely red. (A heraldic term.) **tricked** spotted and smeared.
(Heraldic.) **458 impasted** crusted, like a thick paste. **with . . .
streets** by the parching heat of the streets (because of the fires
everywehre) **459 tyrannous** cruel **460 their lord's** i.e., Priam's
461 o'ersizèd covered as with size or glue **462 carbuncles** large
fiery-red precious stones thought to emit their own light **467 antique** ancient, long-used **469 Repugnant** disobedient, resistant
471 fell cruel

472 unnervèd strengthless. **senseless Ilium** inanimate citadel of
Troy **474 his** its **476 declining** descending. **milky** white-haired
478 painted i.e., painted in a picture **479 like . . . matter** i.e., as
though suspended between his intention and its fulfillment **481
against** just before **482 rack** mass of clouds **483 orb** globe,
earth **485 region** sky **487 Cyclops** giant armor makers in the
smithy of Vulcan **488 proof eterne** eternal resistance to assault
489 remorse pity **492 synod** assembly **493 fellies** pieces of
wood forming the rim of a wheel **494 nave** hub. **hill of heaven**
Mount Olympus **498 jig** comic song and dance often given at the
end of a play **499 Hecuba** wife of Priam **500 who . . . had** anyone who had (also in line 509). **moblèd** muffled **504 threat'ning
the flames** i.e., weeping hard enough to dampen the flames **505
bisson rheum** blinding tears. **clout** cloth **506 late** lately **507
all o'erteemèd** utterly worn out with bearing children

'Gainst Fortune's state° would treason have
510   pronounced.°
But if the gods themselves did see her then
When she saw Pyrrhus make malicious sport
In mincing with his sword her husband's limbs,
The instant burst of clamor that she made,
515 Unless things mortal move them not at all,
Would have made milch° the burning eyes of heaven,°
And passion° in the gods."

POLONIUS. Look whe'er° he has not turned his color and has
tears in 's eyes. Prithee, no more.

520 HAMLET. 'Tis well; I'll have thee speak out the rest of this
soon.—Good my lord, will you see the players well bestowed?° Do you hear, let them be well used, for they are
the abstract° and brief chronicles of the time. After your
death you were better have a bad epitaph than their ill
525 report while you live.

POLONIUS. My lord, I will use them according to their
desert.

HAMLET. God's bodikin,° man, much better. Use every man
after° his desert, and who shall scape whipping? Use them
530 after your own honor and dignity. The less they deserve,
the more merit is in your bounty. Take them in.

POLONIUS. Come, sirs.   [Exit.]

HAMLET. Follow him, friends. We'll hear a play tomorrow.
[As they start to leave, Hamlet detains the First Player.] Dost
535 thou hear me, old friend? Can you play The Murder of
Gonzago?

FIRST PLAYER. Ay, my lord.

HAMLET. We'll ha 't° tomorrow night. You could, for a need,
study° a speech of some dozen or sixteen lines which I
540 would set down and insert in 't, could you not?

FIRST PLAYER. Ay, my lord.

HAMLET. Very well. Follow that lord, and look you mock
him not. (Exeunt Players.) My good friends, I'll leave you
till night. You are welcome to Elsinore.

545 ROSENCRANTZ. Good my lord!
                            Exeunt [Rosencrantz and Guildenstern].

HAMLET.
Ay, so, goodbye to you.—Now I am alone.
O, what a rogue and peasant slave am I!
Is it not monstrous that this player here,
But° in a fiction, in a dream of passion,
550 Could force his soul so to his own conceit°

That from her working° all his visage wanned,°
Tears in his eyes, distraction in his aspect,°
A broken voice, and his whole function suiting
With forms to his conceit?° And all for nothing!
For Hecuba!   555
What's Hecuba to him, or he to Hecuba,
That he should weep for her? What would he do
Had he the motive and the cue for passion
That I have? He would drown the stage with tears
And cleave the general ear° with horrid° speech,   560
Make mad the guilty and appall° the free,°
Confound the ignorant,° and amaze° indeed
The very faculties of eyes and ears. Yet I,
A dull and muddy-mettled° rascal, peak°
Like John-a-dreams°, unpregnant of° my cause,   565
And can say nothing—no, not for a king
Upon whose property° and most dear life
A damned defeat° was made. Am I a coward?
Who calls me villain? Breaks my pate° across?
Plucks off my beard and blows it in my face?   570
Tweaks me by the nose? Gives me the lie i' the throat°
As deep as to the lungs? Who does me this?
Ha, 'swounds,° I should take it; for it cannot be
But I am pigeon-livered° and lack gall
To make oppression bitter,° or ere this   575
I should ha' fatted all the region kites°
With this slave's offal.° Blood, bawdy villain!
Remorseless,° treacherous, lecherous, kindless° villain!
O, vengeance!
Why, what an ass am I! This is most brave,°   580
That I, the son of a dear father murdered,
Prompted to my revenge by heaven and hell,
Must like a whore unpack my heart with words
And fall a-cursing, like a very drab,°
A scullion!° Fie upon 't, foh! About,° my brains!   585
Hum, I have heard

---

510 state rule, managing. pronounced proclaimed 516 milch
milky, moist with tears. burning eyes of heaven i.e., heavenly bodies
517 passion overpowering emotion 518 whe'er whether 522
bestowed lodged 523 abstract summary account 528 God's
bodikin by God's (Christ's) little body, bodykin. (Not to be confused
with bodkin, "dagger.") 529 after according to 538 ha 't have it
539 study memorize 549 But merely 550 force . . . conceit
bring his innermost being so entirely into accord with his conception (of the role)

551 from her working as a result of, or in response to, his soul's activity. wanned grew pale 552 aspect look, glance 553–554 his
whole . . . conceit all his bodily powers responding with actions to
suit his thought 560 the general ear everyone's ear. horrid horrible 561 appall (Literally, make pale.) free innocent 562 Confound the ignorant i.e., dumbfound those who know nothing of the
crime that has been committed. amaze stun 564 muddy-mettled
dull-spirited. peak mope, pine 565 John-a-dreams a sleepy,
dreaming idler. unpregnant of not quickened by 567 property
i.e., the crown; also character, quality 568 damned defeat
damnable act of destruction 569 pate head 571 Gives . . .
throat calls me an out-and-out liar 573 'swounds by his
(Christ's) wounds 574 pigeon-livered (The pigeon or dove was
popularly supposed to be mild because it secreted no gall.) 575
bitter i.e., bitter to me 576 region kites kites (birds of prey) of
the air 577 offal entrails 578 Remorseless pitiless. kindless
unnatural 580 brave fine, admirable. (Said ironically.) 584
drab whore 585 scullion menial kitchen servant (apt to be foul-
mouthed). About about it, to work

That guilty creatures sitting at a play
Have by the very cunning° of the scene°
Been struck so to the soul that presently°
590 They have proclaimed their malefactions;
For murder, though it have no tongue, will speak
With most miraculous organ. I'll have these players
Play something like the murder of my father
Before mine uncle. I'll observe his looks;
595 I'll tent° him to the quick.° If 'a do blench,°
I know my course. The spirit that I have seen
May be the devil, and the devil hath power
T' assume a pleasing shape; yea, and perhaps,
Out of my weakness and my melancholy,
600 As he is very potent with such spirits,°
Abuses° me to damn me. I'll have grounds
More relative° than this. The play's the thing
Wherein I'll catch the conscience of the King.   *Exit.*

3.1°   *Enter King, Queen, Polonius, Ophelia,*
         Rosencrantz, Guildenstern, lords.

KING.
   And can you by no drift of conference°
   Get from him why he puts on this confusion,
   Grating so harshly all his days of quiet
   With turbulent and dangerous lunacy?
ROSENCRANTZ.
   He does confess he feels himself distracted,
   But from what cause 'a will by no means speak.
GUILDENSTERN.
5 Nor do we find him forward° to be sounded,°
   But with a crafty madness keeps aloof
   When we would bring him on to some confession
   Of his true state.
QUEEN.   Did he receive you well?
ROSENCRANTZ. Most like a gentleman.
GUILDENSTERN.
10 But with much forcing of his disposition.°
ROSENCRANTZ.
   Niggard° of question,° but of our demands
   Most free in his reply.
QUEEN.   Did you assay° him
   To any pastime?
ROSENCRANTZ.
   Madam, it so fell out that certain players
15

We o'erraught° on the way. Of these we told him,
And there did seem in him a kind of joy
To hear of it. They are here about the court.
And, as I think, they have already order   20
This night to play before him.
POLONIUS.   'Tis most true,
   And he beseeched me to entreat Your Majesties
   To hear and see the matter.
KING.
   With all my heart, and it doth much content me
   To hear him so inclined.   25
   Good gentlemen, give him a further edge°
   And drive his purpose into these delights.
ROSENCRANTZ.
   We shall, my lord.
                    Exeunt Rosencrantz and Guildenstern.
KING.   Sweet Gertrude, leave us too,
   For we have closely° sent for Hamlet hither,
   That he, as 'twere by accident, may here   30
   Affront° Ophelia.
   Her father and myself, lawful espials,°
   Will so bestow ourselves that seeing, unseen,
   We may of their encounter frankly judge,
   And gather by him, as he is behaved,   35
   If 't be th' affliction of his love or no
   That thus he suffers for.
QUEEN.   I shall obey you.
   And for your part, Ophelia, I do wish
   That your good beauties be the happy cause
   Of Hamlet's wildness. So shall I hope your virtues 40
   Will bring him to his wonted° way again,
   To both your honors.
OPHELIA.   Madam, I wish it may.
                                        [*Exit Queen.*]
POLONIUS.
   Ophelia, walk you here.—Gracious,° so please you,
   We will bestow° ourselves. [*To Ophelia.*] Read on this
      book,   [*giving her a book*]
   That show of such an exercise° may color°   45
   Your loneliness.° We are oft to blame in this—
   'Tis too much proved°—that with devotion's visage
   And pious action we do sugar o'er
   The devil himself.
KING [*aside*]. O, 'tis too true!   50
   How smart a lash that speech doth give my conscience!
   The harlot's cheek, beautied with plastering art,

---

588 cunning art, skill. **scene** dramatic presentation   **589 presently**
at once   **595 tent** probe. **the quick** the tender part of a wound, the
core. **blench** quail, flinch   **600 spirits** humors (of melancholy)
601 Abuses deludes   **602 relative** cogent, pertinent
3.1. Location: The castle.
1 drift of conference directing of conversation   **7 forward** willing.
sounded questioned   **12 disposition** inclination   **13 Niggard**
stingy. **question** conversation   **14 assay** try to win

17 o'erraught overtook   **26 edge** incitement   **29 closely** privately   **31 Affront** confront, meet   **32 espials** spies   **41 wonted**
accustomed   **43 Gracious** Your Grace (i.e., the King)   **44 bestow**
conceal   **45 exercise** religious exercise. (The book she reads is one
of devotion.) **color** give a plausible appearance to   **46 loneliness**
being alone   **47 too much proved** too often shown to be true, too
often practiced

Is not more ugly to° the thing° that helps it
Than is my deed to my most painted word.
55   O heavy burden!
POLONIUS.
    I hear him coming. Let's withdraw, my lord.
               [The King and Polonius withdraw.]°

    Enter Hamlet. [Ophelia pretends to read a book.]

HAMLET.
    To be, or not to be, that is the question:
    Whether 'tis nobler in the mind to suffer
    The slings° and arrows of outrageous fortune,
60   Or to take arms against a sea of troubles
    And by opposing end them. To die, to sleep—
    No more—and by a sleep to say we end
    The heartache and the thousand natural shocks
    That flesh is heir to. 'Tis a consummation
65   Devoutly to be wished. To die, to sleep;
    To sleep, perchance to dream. Ay, there's the rub,°
    For in that sleep of death what dreams may come,
    When we have shuffled° off this mortal coil,
    Must give us pause. There's the respect°
70   That makes calamity of so long life.°
    For who would bear the whips and scorns of time,
    Th' oppressor's wrong, the proud man's contumely,°
    The pangs of disprized° love, the law's delay,
    The insolence of office,° and the spurns°
75   That patient merit of th' unworthy takes,°
    When he himself might his quietus° make
    With a bare bodkin?° Who would fardels° bear,
    To grunt and sweat under a weary life,
    But that the dread of something after death,
80   The undiscovered country from whose bourn°
    No traveler returns, puzzles the will,
    And makes us rather bear those ills we have
    Than fly to others that we know not of?
    Thus conscience does make cowards of us all;
85   And thus the native hue° of resolution
    Is sicklied o'er with the pale cast° of thought,
    And enterprises of great pitch° and moment°

With this regard° their currents° turn awry
And lose the name of action.—Soft you° now,
The fair Ophelia. Nymph, in thy orisons°   90
Be all my sins remembered.
OPHELIA.   Good my lord,
    How does your honor for this many a day?
HAMLET.
    I humbly thank you; well, well, well.
OPHELIA.
    My lord, I have remembrances of yours,
    That I have longèd long to redeliver.   95
    I pray you, now receive them.   *[She offers tokens.]*
HAMLET.
    No, not I, I never gave you aught.
OPHELIA.
    My honored lord, you know right well you did,
    And with them words of so sweet breath composed
    As made the things more rich. Their perfume lost,   100
    Take these again, for to the noble mind
    Rich gifts wax poor when givers prove unkind.
    There, my lord.   *[She gives tokens.]*
HAMLET. Ha, ha! Are you honest?°
OPHELIA. My lord?   105
HAMLET. Are you fair?°
OPHELIA. What means your lordship?
HAMLET. That if you be honest and fair, your honesty°
    should admit no discourse to° your beauty.
OPHELIA. Could beauty, my lord, have better commerce° 110
    than with honesty?
HAMLET. Ay, truly, for the power of beauty will sooner trans-
    form honesty from what it is to a bawd than the force of
    honesty can translate beauty into his° likeness. This was
    sometime° a paradox,° but now the time° gives it proof. I 115
    did love you once.
OPHELIA. Indeed, my lord, you made me believe so.
HAMLET. You should not have believed me, for virtue can-
    not so inoculate° our old stock but we shall relish of it.° I
    loved you not.   120
OPHELIA. I was the more deceived.
HAMLET. Get thee to a nunnery.° Why wouldst thou be a
    breeder of sinners? I am myself indifferent honest,° but
    yet I could accuse me of such things that it were better my
    mother had not borne me: I am very proud, revengeful, 125

---

53 to compared to. **the thing** i.e., the cosmetic   **56 s.d. withdraw** (The King and Polonius may retire behind an arras. The stage directions specify that they "enter" again near the end of the scene.) **59 slings** missiles   **66 rub** (Literally, an obstacle in the game of bowls). **68 shuffled** sloughed, cast. **coil** turmoil   **69 respect** consideration   **70 of . . . life** so long-lived, something we willingly endure for so long (also suggesting that long life is itself a calamity). **72 contumely** insolent abuse   **73 disprized** unvalued   **74 office** officialdom. **spurns** insults   **75 of . . . takes** receives from unworthy persons   **76 quietus** acquaintance; here, death   **77 a bare bodkin** a mere dagger, unsheathed. **fardels** burdens   **80 bourn** frontier, boundary   **85 native hue** natural color, complexion   **86 cast** tinge, shade of color   **87 pitch** height (as of a falcon's flight). **moment** importance

88 regard respect, consideration. **currents** courses   **89 Soft you** i.e., wait a minute, gently   **90 orisons** prayers   **104 honest** (1) truthful (2) chaste   **106 fair** (1) beautiful (2) just, honorable   **108 your honesty** your chastity   **109 discourse to** familiar dealings with   **110–111 commerce** dealings, intercourse   **114 his** its   **115 sometime** formerly. **a paradox** a view opposite to commonly held opinion. **the time** the present age   **119 inoculate** graft, be engrafted to   **119–120 but . . . it** that we do not still have about us a taste of the old stock, i.e., retain our sinfulness   **122 nunnery** convent (with possibly an awareness that the word was also used derisively to denote a brothel)   **123 indifferent honest** reasonably virtuous

ambitious, with more offenses at my beck° than I have thoughts to put them in, imagination to give them shape, or time to act them in. What should such fellows as I do crawling between earth and heaven? We are arrant
130 knaves all; believe none of us. Go thy ways to a nunnery. Where's your father?

OPHELIA. At home, my lord.

HAMLET. Let the doors be shut upon him, that he may play the fool nowhere but in 's own house. Farewell.

135 OPHELIA. O, help him, you sweet heavens!

HAMLET. If thou dost marry, I'll give thee this plague for thy dowry: be thou as chaste as ice, as pure as snow, thou shalt not escape calumny. Get thee to a nunnery, farewell. Or, if thou wilt needs marry, marry a fool, for wise men know
140 well enough what monsters° you° make of them. To a nunnery, go, and quickly too. Farewell.

OPHELIA. Heavenly powers, restore him!

HAMLET. I have heard of your paintings too, well enough. God hath given you one face, and you make yourselves
145 another. You jig,° you amble,° and you lisp, you nickname God's creatures,° and make your wantonness your ignorance.° Go to, I'll no more on 't°; it hath made me mad. I say we will have no more marriage. Those that are married already—all but one—shall live. The rest shall keep
150 as they are. To a nunnery, go.   *Exit.*

OPHELIA.
    O, what a noble mind is here o'erthrown!
    The courtier's, soldier's, scholar's, eye, tongue, sword,
    Th' expectancy° and rose° of the fair state,
    The glass of fashion and the mold of form,°
155 Th' observed of all observers,° quite, quite down!
    And I, of ladies most deject and wretched,
    That sucked the honey of his music° vows,
    Now see that noble and most sovereign reason
    Like sweet bells jangled out of tune and harsh,
160 That unmatched form and feature of blown° youth
    Blasted° with ecstasy.° O, woe is me,
    T' have seen what I have seen, see what I see!

            Enter King and Polonius.

KING.
    Love? His affections° do not that way tend;

Nor what he spake, though it lacked form a little,
Was not like madness. There's something in his soul   165
O'er which his melancholy sits on brood,°
And I no doubt° the hatch and the disclose°
Will be some danger; which for to prevent,
I have in quick determination
Thus set it down:° he shall with speed to England   170
For the demand of° our neglected tribute.
Haply the seas and countries different
With variable objects° shall expel
This something-settled matter in his heart,°
Whereon his brains still° beating puts him thus   175
From fashion of himself.° What think you on 't?

POLONIUS.
    It shall do well. But yet do I believe
    The origin and commencement of his grief
    Sprung from neglected love.—How now, Ophelia?
    You need not tell us what Lord Hamlet said;   180
    We heard it all.—My lord, do as you please,
    But, if you hold it fit, after the play
    Let his queen-mother° all alone entreat him
    To show his grief. Let her be round° with him;
    And I'll be placed, so please you, in the ear   185
    Of all their conference. If she find him not,°
    To England send him, or confine him where
    Your wisdom best shall think.

KING.   It shall be so.
    Madness in great ones must not unwatched go.

                                                Exeunt.

3.2°   *Enter Hamlet and three of the Players.*

HAMLET. Speak the speech, I pray you, as I pronounced it to you, trippingly on the tongue. But if you mouth it, as many of our players° do, I had as lief° the town crier spoke my lines. Nor do not saw the air too much with your hand, thus, but use all gently; for in the very torrent,   5
tempest, and, as I may say, whirlwind of your passion, you must acquire and beget a temperance that may give it smoothness. O, it offends me to the soul to hear a robustious° periwig-pated° fellow tear a passion to tatters, to

---

126 **beck** command   140 **monsters** (An illusion to the horns of a cuckold.) **you** i.e., you women   145 **jig** dance. **amble** move coyly
145–146 **you nickname . . . creatures** i.e., you give trendy names to things in place of their God-given names   146–147 **make . . . ignorance** i.e., excuse your affectation on the grounds of pretended ignorance   147 **on 't** of it   153 **expectancy** hope. **rose** ornament
154 **The glass . . . form** the mirror of true self-fashioning and the pattern of courtly behavior   155 **Th' observed . . . observers** i.e., the center of attention and honor in the court   157 **music** musical, sweetly uttered   160 **blown** blooming   161 **Blasted** withered. **ecstasy** madness   163 **affections** emotions, feelings

166 **sits on brood** sits like a bird on a nest, about to *hatch* mischief (line 167)   167 **doubt** fear. **disclose** disclosure, hatching   170 **set it down** resolved   171 **For . . . of** to demand   173 **variable objects** various sights and surroundings to divert him   174 **This something . . . heart** the strange matter settled in his heart   175 **still** continually   176 **From . . . himself** out of his natural manner
183 **queen-mother** queen and mother   184 **round** blunt   186 **find him not** fails to discover what is troubling him
3.2. Location: The castle.
3 **our players** players nowadays. **I had as lief** I would just as soon
8–9 **robustious** violent, boisterous. **periwig-pated** wearing a wig

10 very rags, to split the ears of the groundlings°, who for the most part are capable of° nothing but inexplicable dumb shows° and noise. I would have such a fellow whipped for o'erdoing Termagant.° It out-Herods Herod.° Pray you, avoid it.

15 FIRST PLAYER. I warrant your honor.

HAMLET. Be not too tame neither, but let our own discretion be your tutor. Suit the action to the word, the word to the action, with this special observance, that you o'erstep not the modesty° of nature. For anything so o'erdone is from°
20 the purpose of playing, whose end, both at the first and now, was and is to hold as 't were the mirror up to nature, to show virtue her feature, scorn° her own image, and the very age and body of the time° his° form and pressure.° Now this overdone or come tardy off,° though it makes
25 the unskillful° laugh, cannot but make the judicious grieve, the censure of the which one° must in your al-lowance° o'erweigh a whole theater of others. O, there be players that I have seen play, and heard others praise, and that highly, not to speak it profanely,° that, neither hav-
30 ing th' accent of Christians° nor the gait of Christian, pagan, nor man,° have so strutted and bellowed that I have thought some of nature's journeymen° had made men and not made them well, they imitated humanity so abominably.°

35 FIRST PLAYER. I hope we have reformed that indifferently° with us, sir.

HAMLET. O, reform it altogether. And let those that play your clowns speak no more than is set down for them; for there be of them° that will themselves laugh, to set on
40 some quantity of barren° spectators to laugh too, though in the meantime some necessary question of the play be then to be considered. That's villainous, and shows a

most pitiful ambition in the fool that uses it. Go make you ready.

[*Exeunt Players.*]

Enter Polonius, Guildenstern, and Rosencrantz.

How now, my lord, will the King hear this piece of work? 45
POLONIUS. And the Queen too, and that presently.°
HAMLET. Bid the players make haste.   [*Exit Polonius.*]
Will you two help to hasten them?
ROSENCRANTZ.
Ay, my lord.   *Exeunt they two.*
HAMLET.   What ho, Horatio!

Enter Horatio.

HORATIO. Here, sweet lord, at your service.   50
HAMLET.
Horatio, thou art e'en as just a man
As e'er my conversation coped withal.°
HORATIO.
O, my dear lord—
HAMLET.   Nay, do not think I flatter,
For what advancement may I hope from thee
That no revenue hast but thy good spirits   55
To feed and clothe thee? Why should the poor be
    flattered?
No, let the candied° tongue lick absurd pomp,
And crook the pregnant° hinges of the knee
Where thrift° may follow fawning. Dost thou hear?
Since my dear soul was mistress of her choice   60
And could of men distinguish her election,°
Sh' hath sealed thee° for herself, for thou hast been
As one, in suffering all, that suffers nothing,
A man that Fortune's buffets and rewards
Hast ta'en with equal thanks; and blest are those   65
Whose blood° and judgment are so well commeddled°
That they are not a pipe for Fortune's finger
To sound what stop° she please. Give me that man
That is not passion's slave, and I will wear him
In my heart's core, ay, in my heart of heart,   70
As I do thee.—Something too much of this.—
There is a play tonight before the King.
One scene of it comes near the circumstance
Which I have told thee of my father's death.
I prithee, when thou seest that act afoot,   75
Even with the very comment of thy soul°

10 **groundlings** spectators who paid least and stood in the yard of the theater   11 **capable of** able to understand   11–12 **dumb shows** mimed performances, often used before Shakespeare's time to precede a play or each act   13 **Termagant** a supposed deity of the Mohammedans, not found in any English medieval play but elsewhere portrayed as violent and blustering. **Herod** Herod of Jewry. (A character in *The Slaughter of the Innocents* and other cycle plays. The part was played with great noise and fury.)   19 **modesty** restraint, moderation. **from** contrary to   22 **scorn** i.e., something foolish and deserving of scorn   22–23 **the very . . . time** i.e., the present state of affairs   23 **his** its. **pressure** stamp, impressed char-acter   24 **come tardy off** inadequately done   25 **the unskillful** those lacking in judgment   26 **the censure . . . one** the judgment of even one of whom   26–27 **your allowance** your scale of values   29 **not . . . profanely** (Hamlet anticipates his idea in lines 33–34 that some men were not made by God at all.)   30 **Christians** i.e., ordinary decent folk   31 **nor man** i.e., nor any human being at all   32 **journeymen** laborers who are not yet masters in their trade   34 **abominably** (Shakespeare's usual spelling, *abhominably*, suggests a literal though etymologically incorrect meaning, "removed from human nature.")   35 **indifferently** tolerably   39 **of them** some among them   40 **barren** i.e., of wit

46 **presently** at once   52 **my . . . withal** my dealings encountered   57 **candied** sugared, flattering   58 **pregnant** compliant   59 **thrift** profit   61 **could . . . election** could make distinguishing choices among persons   62 **sealed thee** (Literally, as one would seal a legal document to mark possession.)   66 **blood** passion. **commeddled** commingled   68 **stop** hole in a wind instrument for controlling the sound   76 **very . . . soul** your most penetrating observation and consideration

Observe my uncle. If his occulted° guilt
Do not itself unkennel° in one speech,
It is a damnèd° ghost that we have seen,
80 And my imaginations are as foul
As Vulcan's stithy.° Give him heedful note,
For I mine eyes will rivet to his face,
And after we will both our judgments join
In censure of his seeming.°

HORATIO.   Well, my lord.
85 If 'a steal aught° the whilst this play is playing
And scape detecting, I will pay the theft.

> [*Flourish.*] *Enter trumpets and kettledrums, King,*
> *Queen, Polonius, Ophelia, [Rosencrantz, Guilden-*
> *stern, and other lords, with guards carrying torches].*

HAMLET. They are coming to the play. I must be idle.°
Get you a place. [*The King, Queen, and courtiers sit.*]
KING. How fares our cousin° Hamlet?
90 HAMLET. Excellent, i' faith, of the chameleon's dish:° I eat
the air, promise-crammed. You cannot feed capons° so.
KING. I have nothing with° this answer, Hamlet. These
words are not mine.°
HAMLET. No, nor mine now.° [*To Polonius.*] My lord, you
95 played once i' th' university, you say?
POLONIUS. That did I, my lord, and was accounted a good
actor.
HAMLET. What did you enact?
POLONIUS. I did enact Julius Caesar. I was killed i' the Capi-
100 tol; Brutus killed me.
HAMLET. It was a brute° part° of him to kill so capital a
calf° there.—Be the players ready?
ROSENCRANTZ. Ay, my lord. They stay upon° your
patience.
105 QUEEN. Come hither, my dear Hamlet, sit by me.
HAMLET. No, good Mother, here's metal° more attractive.
POLONIUS [*to the King*]. O, ho, do you mark that?
HAMLET. Lady, shall I lie in your lap?

> [*Lying down at Ophelia's feet.*]

OPHELIA. No, my lord.
HAMLET. I mean, my head upon your lap?   110
OPHELIA. Ay, my lord.
HAMLET. Do you think I meant country matters?°
OPHELIA. I think nothing, my lord.
HAMLET. That's a fair thought to lie between maids'
legs.   115
OPHELIA. What is, my lord?
HAMLET. Nothing.°
OPHELIA. You are merry, my lord.
HAMLET. Who, I?
OPHELIA. Ay, my lord.   120
HAMLET. O God, your only jig maker.° What should a man
do but be merry? For look you how cheerfully my mother
looks, and my father died within 's° two hours.
OPHELIA. Nay, 'tis twice two months, my lord.
HAMLET. So long? Nay then, let the devil wear black, for I'll   125
have a suit of sables.° O heavens! Die two months ago,
and not forgotten yet? Then there's hope a great man's
memory may outlive his life half a year. But, by 'r Lady, 'a
must build churches, then, or else shall 'a suffer not
thinking on,° with the hobbyhorse, whose epitaph is "For   130
O, for O, the hobbyhorse is forgot."°

> *The trumpets sound. Dumb show follows.*

> *Enter a King and a Queen [very lovingly]; the*
> *Queen embracing him, and he her. [She kneels,*
> *and makes show of protestation unto him.] He*
> *takes her up, and declines his head upon her neck.*
> *He lies him down upon a bank of flowers. She,*
> *seeing him asleep, leaves him. Anon comes in*
> *another man, takes off his crown, kisses it, pours*
> *poison in the sleeper's ears, and leaves him. The*
> *Queen returns, finds the King dead, makes*
> *passionate action. The Poisoner with some three or*
> *four come in again, seem to condole with her. The*
> *dead body is carried away. The Poisoner woos the*
> *Queen with gifts; she seems harsh awhile, but in*
> *the end accepts love.*

---

77 occulted hidden   **78 unkennel** (As one would say of a fox driven from its lair.)   **79 damnèd** in league with Satan   **81 stithy**
smithy, place of stiths (anvils)   **84 censure of his seeming** judgment of his appearance or behavior   **85 If 'a steal aught** if he gets
away with anything   **87 idle** (1) unoccupied (2) mad   **89 cousin**
i.e., close relative   **90 chameleon's dish** (Chameleons were supposed to feed on air. Hamlet deliberately misinterprets the King's
fares as "feeds." By his phrase *eat the air* he also plays on the idea of
feeding himself with the promise of succession, of being the *heir*.)
91 capons roosters castrated and *crammed* with feed to make them
succulent   **92 have . . . with** make nothing of, or gain nothing
from   **93 are not mine** do not respond to what I asked   **94 nor
mine now** (Once spoken, words are proverbially no longer the
speaker's own—and hence should be uttered warily.)   **101 brute**
(The Latin meaning of *brutus,* "stupid," was often used punningly
with the name Brutus.)   **part** (1) deed (2) role   **102 calf** fool   **103
stay upon** await   **106 metal** substance that is *attractive,* i.e., mag-
netic, but with suggestion also of *mettle,* "disposition"

112 country matters sexual intercourse (making a bawdy pun on
the first syllable of *country*)   **117 Nothing** the figure zero or
naught, suggesting the female sexual anatomy. (*Thing* not infrequently has a bawdy connotation of male or female anatomy, and
the reference here could be male.)   **121 only jig maker** very best
composer of jigs, i.e., pointless merriment. (Hamlet replies sardonically to Ophelia's observation that he is merry by saying, "If you're
looking for someone who is really merry, you've come to the right
person.")   **123 within 's** within this (i.e., these)   **126 suit of
sables** garments trimmed with the fur of the sable and hence suited
for a wealthy person, not a mourner (but with a pun on *sable,*
"black," ironically suggesting mourning once again)   **130 suffer
. . . on** undergo oblivion   **131 For . . . forgot** (Verse of a song occurring also in *Love's Labor's Lost,* 3.1.27–28. The hobbyhorse was a
character made up to resemble a horse and rider, appearing in the
morris dance and such May-game sports. This song laments the disappearance of such customs under pressure from the Puritans.)

[*Exeunt players.*]

OPHELIA. What means this, my lord?

HAMLET. Marry, this' miching mallico;° it means mischief.

135 OPHELIA. Belike° this show imports the argument° of the play.

Enter Prologue.

HAMLET. We shall know by this fellow. The players cannot keep counsel;° they'll tell all.

OPHELIA. Will 'a tell us what this show meant?

140 HAMLET. Ay, or any show that you will show him. Be not you° ashamed to show, he'll not shame to tell you what it means.

OPHELIA. You are naught, you are naught.° I'll mark the play.

PROLOGUE.

145   For us, and for our tragedy,
         Here stooping° to your clemency,
         We beg your hearing patiently.   [*Exit.*]

HAMLET. Is this a prologue, or the posy of a ring?°

OPHELIA. 'Tis brief, my lord.

150 HAMLET. As woman's love.

Enter [two Players as] King and Queen.

PLAYER KING.

         Full thirty times hath Phoebus' cart° gone round
         Neptune's salt wash° and Tellus'° orbèd ground,
         And thirty dozen moons with borrowed° sheen
         About the world have times twelve thirties been,
155   Since love our hearts and Hymen° did our hands
         Unite commutual° in most sacred bands.°

PLAYER QUEEN.

         So many journeys may the sun and moon
         Make us again count o'er ere love be done!
         But, woe is me, you are so sick of late,
160   So far from cheer and from your former state,
         That I distrust you. Yet, though I distrust,°
         Discomfort° you, my lord, it nothing° must.
         For women's fear and love hold quantity;°
         In neither aught, or in extremity.°

         Now, what my love is, proof° hath made you know,   165
         And as my love is sized,° my fear is so.
         Where love is great, the littlest doubts are fear;
         Where little fears grow great, great loves grows there.

PLAYER KING.

         Faith, I must leave thee, love, and shortly too;
         My operant powers° their functions leave to do.°   170
         And thou shalt live in this fair world behind,°
         Honored, beloved; and haply one as kind
         For husband shalt thou—

PLAYER QUEEN.   O, confound the rest!
         Such love must needs be treason in my breast.
         In second husband let me be accurst!   175
         None° wed the second but who° killed the first.

HAMLET. Wormwood, wormwood.°

PLAYER QUEEN.

         The instances° that second marriage move°
         Are base respects of thrift,° but none of love.
         A second time I kill my husband dead   180
         When second husband kisses me in bed.

PLAYER KING.

         I do believe you think what now you speak,
         But what we do determine oft we break.
         Purpose is but the slave to memory,°
         Of violent birth, but poor validity,°   185
         Which° now, like fruit unripe, sticks on the tree,
         But fall unshaken when they mellow be.
         Most necessary 'tis that we forget
         To pay ourselves what to ourselves is debt.°
         What to ourselves in passion we propose,   190
         The passion ending, doth the purpose lose.
         The violence of either grief or joy
         Their own enactures° with themselves destroy.
         Where joy most revels, grief doth most lament;
         Grief joys, joy grieves, on slender accident.°   195
         This world is not for aye,° nor 'tis not strange
         That even our loves should with our fortunes change;
         For 'tis a question left us yet to prove,
         Whether love lead fortune, or else fortune love.
         The great man down,° you mark his favorite flies;   200

133 **this' miching mallico** this is sneaking mischeif   135 **Belike**
probably. **argument** plot   138 **counsel** secret   140–141 **Be not
you** provided you are not   143 **naught** indecent. (Ophelia is reacting to Hamlet's pointed remarks about not being ashamed to
show all.)   146 **stooping** bowing   148 **posy . . . ring** brief motto
in verse inscribed in a ring   151 **Phoebus' cart** the sun-god's chariot, making its yearly cycle   152 **salt wash** the sea. **Tellus** goddess
of the earth, of the *orbèd ground*   153 **borrowed** i.e., reflected
155 **Hymen** god of matrimony   156 **commutual** mutually. **bands**
bonds   161 **distrust** am anxious about   162 **Discomfort** distress.
nothing not at all   163 **hold quantity** keep proportion with one
another   164 **In . . . extremity** i.e., women fear and love either
too little or too much, but the two, fear and love, are equal in either
case

165 **proof** experience   166 **sized** in size   170 **operant powers**
vital functions. **leave to do** cease to perform   171 **behind** after I
have gone   176 **None** i.e., let no woman. **but who** except the one
who   177 **Wormwood** i.e., how bitter. (Literally, a bitter-tasting
plant.)   178 **instances** motives. **move** motivate   179 **base . . .
thrift** ignoble considerations of material prosperity   184 **Purpose
. . . memory** our good intentions are subject to forgetfulness   185
validity strength, durability   186 **Which** i.e., purpose   188–189
Most . . . debt it's inevitable that in time we forget the obligations
we have imposed on ourselves   193 **enactures** fulfillments
194–195 **Where . . . accident** the capacity for extreme joy and
grief go together, and often one extreme is instantly changed into
its opposite on the slightest provocation   196 **aye** ever   200
down fallen in fortune

555

The poor advanced makes friends of enemies.°
And hitherto° doth love on fortune tend;°
For who not needs° shall never lack a friend,
And who in want° a hollow friend doth try°
205 Directly seasons him° his enemy.
But, orderly to end where I begun,
Our wills and fates do so contrary run°
That our devices still° are overthrown;
Our thoughts are ours, their ends° none of our own.
210 So think thou wilt no second husband wed,
But die thy thoughts when thy first lord is dead.
PLAYER QUEEN.
Nor° earth to me give food, nor heaven light,
Sport and repose lock from me day and night,°
To desperation turn my trust and hope,
215 An anchor's cheer° in prison be my scope!°
Each opposite that blanks° the face of joy
Meet what I would have well and it destroy!°
Both here and hence° pursue me lasting strife
If, once a widow, ever I be wife!
220 HAMLET. If she should break it now!
PLAYER KING.
'Tis deeply sworn. Sweet, leave me here awhile;
My spirits° grow dull, and fain I would beguile
The tedious day with sleep.
PLAYER QUEEN.   Sleep rock thy brain,
And never come mischance between us twain!
        [He sleeps.] Exit [Player Queen].
225 HAMLET. Madam, how like you this play?
QUEEN. The lady doth protest too much,° methinks.
HAMLET. O, but she'll keep her word.
KING. Have you heard the argument?° Is there no offense
in 't?
230 HAMLET. No, no, they do but jest, poison in jest.° No of-
fense i' the world.
KING. What do you call the play?
HAMLET. The Mousetrap. Marry, how? Tropically.° This

play is the image of a murder done in Vienna. Gonzago
is the Duke's° name, his wife, Baptista. You shall   235
see anon. 'Tis a knavish piece of work, but what of
that? Your Majesty, and we that free° souls, it touches
us not. Let the galled jade° wince, our withers° are
unwrung.°

        Enter Lucianus.

This is one Lucianus, nephew to the King.   240
OPHELIA. You are as good as a chorus,° my lord.
HAMLET. I could interpret° between you and your love, if I
could see the puppets dallying.°
OPHELIA. You are keen, my lord, you are keen.°
HAMLET. It would cost you a groaning to take off mine   245
edge.
OPHELIA. Still better, and worse.°
HAMLET. So° you mis-take° your husbands. Begin, murderer;
leave thy damnable faces and begin. Come, the croaking
raven doth bellow for revenge.   250
LUCIANUS.
Thoughts black, hands apt, drugs fit, and time agree-
ing,
Confederate season,° else° no creature seeing,°
Thou mixture rank, of midnight weeds collected,
With Hecate's ban° thrice blasted, thrice infected,
Thy natural magic and dire property°   255
On wholesome life usurp immediately.
        [He pours the poison into the sleeper's ear.]
HAMLET. 'A poisons him i' the garden for his estate.° His
name's Gonzago. The story is extant, and written in very
choice Italian. You shall see anon how the murderer gets
the love of Gonzago's wife.   260
        [Claudius rises.]
OPHELIA. The King rises.
HAMLET. What, frighted with false fire?°

---

201 The poor . . . enemies when one of humble station is promoted,
you see his enemies suddenly becoming his friends   202 hitherto up
to this point in the argument, or, to this extent. tend attend   203
who not needs he who is not in need (of wealth)   204 who in want
he who, being in need. try test (his generosity)   205 seasons him
ripens him into   207 Our . . . run what we want and what we get
go so contrarily   208 devices still intentions continually   209
ends results   212 Nor let neither   213 Sport . . . night may day
deny me its pastimes and night its repose   215 anchor's cheer anchorite's or hermit's fate. my scope the extent of my happiness
216–217 Each . . . destroy may every adverse thing that causes the
face of joy to turn pale meet and destroy everything that I desire to
see prosper. blanks causes to blanch or grow pale   218 hence in the
life hereafter   222 spirits vital spirits   226 doth . . . much makes
too many promises and protestations   228 argument plot
229–231 offense . . . offense cause for objections . . . actual injury,
crime   230 jest make belief   233 Tropically figuratively. (The
First Quarto reading, trapically, suggests a pun on trap in Mousetrap.)

235 Duke's i.e., King's. (A slip that may be due to Shakespeare's
possible source, the alleged murder of the Duke of Urbino by Luigi
Gonzaga in 1538.)   237 free guiltless   238 galled jade horse
whose hide is rubbed by saddle or harness. withers the part between
the horse's shoulder blades   239 unwrung not rubbed sore   241
chorus (In many Elizabethan plays, the forthcoming action was explained by an actor known as the "chorus"; at a puppet show, the
actor who spoke the dialogue was known as an "interpreter," as indicated by the lines following.)   242 interpret (1) ventriloquize
the dialogue, as in pupet show (2) act as pander   243 puppets dallying (With suggestions of sexual play, continued in keen, "sexually
aroused," groaning, "moaning in pregnancy" and edge, "sexual desire" or "impetuosity.")   244 keen sharp, bitter   247 Still . . .
worse more keen, always bettering what other people say with witty
wordplay, but at the same time more offensive   248 So even thus
(in marriage). mis-take take falseheartedly and cheat on. (The marriage vows say "for better, for worse.")   252 Confederate season
the time and occasion conspiring (to assist the murderer). else otherwise. seeing seeing me   254 Hecate's ban the curse of Hecate,
the goddess of witchcraft   255 dire property baleful quality   257
estate i.e., the kingship. His i.e., the King's   262 false fire the
blank discharge of a gun loaded with powder but no shot

QUEEN. How fares my lord?

POLONIUS. Give o'er the play.

265 KING. Give me some light. Away!

POLONIUS. Lights, lights, lights!

Exeunt all but Hamlet and Horatio.

HAMLET.
　　"Why, let the strucken deer go weep,
　　　　The hart ungallèd° play.
　　For some must watch°, while some must sleep;
270　　　　Thus runs the world away."°
　　Would not this,° sir, and a forest of feathers°—if the rest
　　of my fortunes turn Turk with° me—with two Provincial
　　roses° on my razed° shoes, get me a fellowship in a cry° of
　　players?°

275 HORATIO. Half a share.

HAMLET. A whole one, I.
　　"For thou dost know, O Damon° dear,
　　　　This realm dismantled° was
　　Of Jove himself, and now reigns here
280　　　　A very very—pajock."°

HORATIO. You might have rhymed.

HAMLET. O good Horatio, I'll take the ghost's word for a
　　thousand pound. Didst perceive?

HORATIO. Very well, my lord.

285 HAMLET. Upon the talk of the poisoning?

HORATIO. I did very well note him.

Enter Rosencrantz and Guildenstern.

HAMLET. Aha! Come, some music! Come, the record-
　　ers.°
　　"For if the King like not the comedy,
290　　Why then, belike, he likes it not, perdy."°
　　Come, some music.

GUILDENSTERN. Good my lord, vouchsafe me a word with
　　you.

HAMLET. Sir, a whole history.

295 GUILDENSTERN. The King, sir—

HAMLET. Ay, sir, what of him?

GUILDENSTERN. Is in his retirement° marvelous distem-
　　pered.°

HAMLET. With drink, sir?

300 GUILDENSTERN. No, my lord, with choler.°

HAMLET. Your wisdom should show itself more richer to
　　signify this to the doctor, for for me to put him to his
　　purgation° would perhaps plunge him into more
　　choler.

305 GUILDENSTERN. Good my lord, put our discourse into some
　　frame° and start° not so wildly from my affair.

HAMLET. I am tame, sir. Pronounce.

GUILDENSTERN. The Queen, your mother, in most great af-
　　fliction of spirit, hath sent me to you.

310 HAMLET. You are welcome.

GUILDENSTERN. Nay, good my lord, this courtesy is not of
　　the right breed.° If it shall please you to make me a
　　wholesome answer, I will do your mother's command-
　　ment; if not, your pardon° and my return shall be the end
315　　of my business.

HAMLET. Sir, I cannot.

ROSENCRANTZ. What, my lord?

HAMLET. Make you a wholesome answer; my wit's diseased.
　　But, sir, such answer as I can make, you shall command,
320　　or rather, as you say, my mother. Therefore no more, but
　　to the matter. My mother, you say—

ROSENCRANTZ. Then thus she says: your behavior hath
　　struck her into amazement and admiration.°

HAMLET. O wonderful son, that can so stonish a mother!
325　　But is there no sequel at the heels of this mother's admi-
　　ration? Impart.

ROSENCRANTZ. She desires to speak with you in her closet°
　　ere you go to bed.

HAMLET. We shall obey, were she ten times our mother.
330　　Have you any further trade with us?

ROSENCRANTZ. My lord, you once did love me.

HAMLET. And do still, by these pickers and stealers.°

ROSENCRANTZ. Good my lord, what is your cause of distem-
　　per? You do surely bar the door upon your own liberty° if
335　　you deny° your griefs to your friend.

HAMLET. Sir, I lack advancement.

267–270 **Why . . . away** (Probably from an old ballad, with allusion to the popular belief that a wounded deer retires to weep and
die; compare with *As You Like It*, 2.1.33–66.) 268 **ungallèd** unaf-
flicted 269 **watch** remain awake 270 **Thus . . . away** thus the
world goes 271 **this** i.e., the play. **feathers** (Allusion to the
plumes that Elizabethan actors were fond of wearing.) 272 **turn
Turk with** turn renegade against, go back on 273 **Provincial
roses** rosettes of ribbon, named for roses grown in a part of France.
razed with ornamental slashing 273–274 **fellowship . . . players**
partnership in a theatrical company 274 **cry** pack (of hounds)
277 **Damon** the friend of Pythias, as Horatio is friend of Hamlet; or,
a traditional pastoral name 279–280 **This realm . . . pajock** i.e.,
Jove, representing divine authority and justice, has abandoned this
realm to its own devices, leaving in his stead only a peacock or vain
pretender to virtue (though the rhyme-word expected in place of
pajock or "peacock" suggests that the realm is now ruled over by an
"ass"). 278 **dismantled** stripped, divested 287–288 **recorders**
wind instruments of the flute kind 290 **perdy** (A corruption of
the French *par dieu*, "by God.")

297 **retirement** withdrawal to his chambers 297–298 **distem-
pered** out of humor. (But Hamlet deliberately plays on the wider application to any illness of mind or body, as in lines 333–334, especially to drunkenness.) 300 **choler** anger. (But Hamlet takes the
word in its more basic humoral sense of "bilious disorder.")
302–303 **purgation** (Hamlet hints at something going beyond
medical treatment to blood-letting and the extraction of confession.) 306 **frame** order. **start** shy or jump away (like a horse; the
opposite of *tame* in line 307) 312 **breed** (1) kind (2) breeding,
manners 314 **pardon** permission to depart 323 **admiration** bewilderment 327 **closet** private chamber 332 **pickers and stealers** i.e., hands. (So called from the catechism, "to keep my hands
from picking and stealing.") 335 **liberty** i.e., being freed from *distemper*, line 334; but perhaps with a veiled threat as well. **deny**
refuse to share

ROSENCRANTZ. How can that be, when you have the voice
  of the King himself for our succession in Denmark?
HAMLET. Ay, sir, but "While the grass grows"°—the proverb
340   is something° musty.

          Enter the Players° *with recorders.*

  O, the recorders. Let me see one. [*He takes a recorder.*]
  To withdraw° with you: why do you go about to recover
  the wind° of me, as if you would drive me into a toil?°
GUILDENSTERN. O, my lord, if my duty be too bold, my love
345   is too unmannerly.°
HAMLET. I do not well understand that.° Will you play upon
  this pipe?
GUILDENSTERN. My lord, I cannot.
HAMLET. I pray you.
350 GUILDENSTERN. Believe me, I cannot.
HAMLET. I do beseech you.
GUILDENSTERN. I know no touch of it, my lord.
HAMLET. It is as easy as lying. Govern these ventages° with
  your fingers and thumb, give it breath with your mouth,
355   and it will discourse most eloquent music. Look you,
  these are the stops.
GUILDENSTERN. But these cannot I command to any utterance of harmony. I have not the skill.
HAMLET. Why, look you now, how unworthy a thing you
360   make of me! You would play upon me, you would seem to
  know my stops, you would pluck out the heart of my mystery, you would sound° me from my lowest note to the top
  of my compass,° and there is much music, excellent
  voice, in this little organ,° yet cannot you make it speak.
365   'Sblood, do you think I am easier to be played on than a
  pipe? Call me what instrument you will, though you can
  fret° me, you cannot play upon me.

          Enter Polonius.

  God bless you, sir!
POLONIUS. My lord, the Queen would speak with you, and
370   presently.°
HAMLET. Do you see yonder cloud that's almost in shape of a
  camel?
POLONIUS. By the Mass and 'tis, like a camel indeed.

HAMLET. Methinks it is like a weasel.
POLONIUS. It is backed like a weasel.   375
HAMLET. Or like a whale.
POLONIUS. Very like a whale.
HAMLET. Then I will come to my mother by and by.°
  [*Aside.*] They fool me° to the top of my bent.°—I will
  come by and by.   380
POLONIUS. I will say so.   [*Exit.*]
HAMLET. "By and by" is easily said. Leave me, friends.
                              [*Exeunt all but Hamlet.*]
  'Tis now the very witching time° of night,
  When churchyards yawn and hell itself breathes out
  Contagion to this world. Now could I drink hot blood   385
  And do such bitter business as the day
  Would quake to look on. Soft, now to my mother.
  O heart, lose not thy nature!° Let not ever
  The soul of Nero° enter this firm bosom.
  Let me be cruel, not unnatural;   390
  I will speak daggers to her, but use none.
  My tongue and soul in this be hypocrites:
  How in my words soever° she be shent,°
  To give them seals° never my soul consent!   *Exit.*

3.3 °   *Enter King, Rosencrantz, and Guildenstern.*

KING.
  I like him not,° nor stands it safe with us
  To let his madness range. Therefore prepare you.
  I your commission will forthwith dispatch,°
  And he to England shall along with you.
  The terms of our estate° may not endure
  Hazard so near 's as doth hourly grow   5
  Out of his brows.°
GUILDENSTERN.   We will ourselves provide.
  Most holy and religious fear° it is
  To keep those many many bodies safe
  That live and feed upon Your Majesty.
ROSENCRANTZ.   10
  The single and peculiar° life is bound
  With all the strength and armor of the mind
  To keep itself from noyance,° but much more

---

339 While . . . grows (The rest of the proverb is "the silly horse
starves"; Hamlet may not live long enough to succeed to the kingdom.)   **340 something** somewhat. **s.d. Players** actors   **342 withdrawn** speak privately   **342–343 recover the wind** get to the
windward side (thus driving the game into the *toil,* or "net")   **344
toil** snare   **344–345 if . . . unmannerly** if I am using an unmannerly boldness, it is my love that occasions it   **346 I . . . that** i.e., I
don't understand how genuine love can be unmannerly   **353 ven-
tages** finger-holes or *stops* (line 357) of the recorder   **362 sound**
(1) fathom (2) produce sound in   **363 compass** range (of voice)
364 organ musical instrument   **367 fret** irritate (with a quibble
on *fret,* meaning the piece of wood, gut, or metal that regulates the
fingering on an instrument)   **370 presently** at once

378 by and by quite soon   **379 fool me** trifle with me, humor my
fooling. **top of my bent** limit of my ability or endurance. (Literally,
the extent to which a bow may be bent.)   **383 witching time** time
when spells are cast and evil is abroad   **388 nature** natural feeling
389 Nero murderer of his mother, Agrippina   **393 How . . . soever** however much by my words. **shent** rebuked   **394 give them
seals** i.e., confirm them with deeds
3.3. Location: The castle.
1 him i.e., his behavior   **3 dispatch** prepare, cause to be drawn up
5 terms of our estate circumstances of my royal position   **7 Out of
his brows** i.e., from his brain, in the form of plots and threats   **8
religious fear** sacred concern   **11 single and peculiar** individual
and private   **13 noyance** harm

That spirit upon whose weal depends and rests
15   The lives of many. The cess° of majesty
Dies not alone, but like a gulf° doth draw
What's near it with it; or it is a massy° wheel
Fixed on the summit of the highest mount,
To whose huge spokes ten thousand lesser things
20   Are mortised° and adjoined, which, when it falls,
Each small annexment, petty consequence,°
Attends° the boisterous ruin. Never alone
Did the King sigh, but with a general groan.

KING.
Arm° you, I pray you, to this speedy voyage,
25   For we will fetters put about this fear,
Which now goes too free-footed.

ROSENCRANTZ.   We will haste us.

Exeunt gentlemen [Rosencrantz and Guildenstern].

Enter Polonius.

POLONIUS.
My lord, he's going to his mother's closet.
Behind the arras° I'll convey myself
To hear the process.° I'll warrant she's tax him home,°
30   And, as you said—and wisely was it said—
'Tis meet° that some more audience than a mother,
Since nature makes them partial, should o'erhear
The speech, of vantage.° Fare you well, my liege.
I'll call upon you ere you go to bed.
And tell you what I know.

35   KING.   Thanks, dear my lord.

Exit [Polonius]

O, my offense is rank! It smells to heaven.
It hath the primal eldest curse° upon 't,
A brother's murder. Pray can I not,
Though inclination be as sharp as will;°
40   My stronger guilt defeats my strong intent,
And like a man to double business bound°
I stand in pause where I shall first begin,
And both neglect. What if this cursèd hand
Were thicker than itself with brother's blood,
45   Is there not rain enough in the sweet heavens

To wash it white as snow? Whereto serves mercy
But to confront the visage of offense?°
And what's in prayer but this twofold force,
To be forestallèd° ere we come to fall,
Or pardoned being down? Then I'll look up.   50
My fault is past. But O, what form of prayer
Can serve my turn? "Forgive me my foul murder"?
That cannot be, since I am still possessed
Of those effects for which I did the murder:
My crown, mine own ambition, and my queen.   55
May one be pardoned and retain th' offense?°
In the corrupted currents° of this world
Offense's gilded hand° may shove by° justice,
And oft 'tis seen the wicked prize° itself
Buys out the law. But 'tis not so above.   60
There° is no shuffling,° there the action lies°
In his° true nature, and we ourselves compelled,
Even to the teeth and forehead° of our faults,
To give in° evidence. What then? What rests?°
Try what repentance can. What can it not?   65
Yet what can it, when one cannot repent?
O wretched state, O bosom black as death,
O limèd °soul that, struggling to be free,
Art more engaged! Help, angels! Make assay.°
Bow, stubborn knees, and heart with strings of steel,   70
Be soft as sinews of the newborn babe!
All may be well.   [*He kneels.*]

Enter Hamlet.

HAMLET.
Now might I do it pat,° now 'a is a-praying;
And now I'll do 't. [*He draws his sword.*] And so 'a goes
    to heaven,
And so am I revenged. That would be scanned:°   75
A villain kills my father, and for that,
I, his sole son, do this same villain send
To heaven.
Why, this is hire and salary, not revenge.
'A took my father grossly, full of bread,°   80
With all his crimes broad blown,° as flush° as May;

---

15 cess decease, cessation   **16 gulf** whirlpool   **17 massy** massive
20 mortised fastened (as with a fitted joint). **when it falls** i.e.,
when it descends, like the wheel of Fortune, bringing a king down
with it   **21 Each . . . consequence** i.e., every hanger-on and unimportant person or thing connected with the King   **22 Attends** participates in   **24 Arm** prepare   **28 arras** screen of tapestry placed
around the walls of household apartments. (On the Elizabethan
stage, the arras was presumably over a door or discovery space in the
tiring-house facade.)   **29 process** proceedings. **tax him home** reprove him severely   **31 meet** fitting   **33 of vantage** from an advantageous place, or, in addition   **37 the primal eldest curse** the
curse of Cain, the first murderer; he killed his brother Abel   **39
Through . . . will** though my desire is as strong as my determination
41 bound (1) destined (2) obliged. (The King wants to repent and
still enjoy what he has gained.)

46–47 Whereto . . . offense what function does mercy serve other
than to meet sin face to face?   **49 forestallèd** prevented (from sin-
ning)   **56 th' offense** the thing for which one offended   **57 currents** courses   **58 gilded hand** hand offering gold as a bribe. **shove
by** thrust aside   **59 wicked prize** prize won by wickedness   **61
There** i.e., in heaven. **shuffling** escape by trickery. **the action lies**
the accusation is made manifest. (A legal metaphor.)   **62 his** its
63 to the teeth and forehead face to face, concealing nothing   **64
give in** provide. **rests** remains   **68 limèd** caught as with birdlime, a
sticky substance used to ensnare birds   **69 engaged** entangled.
assay trial. (Said to himself.)   **73 pat** opportunely   **75 would be
scanned** needs to be looked into, or, would be interpreted as follows
80 grossly, full of bread i.e., enjoying his worldly pleasures rather
than fasting. (See Ezekiel 16:49.)   **81 crimes broad blown** sins in
full bloom. **flush** vigorous

And how his audit° stands who knows save° heaven?
But in our circumstance and course of thought°
'Tis heavy with him. And am I then revenged,
85   To take him in the purging of his soul,
When he is fit and seasoned° for his passage?
No!
Up, sword, and know thou a more horrid hent.°
                              [*He puts up his sword.*]
When he is drunk asleep, or in his rage°
90   Or in th' incestuous pleasure of his bed,
At game,° a-swearing, or about some act
That has no relish° of salvation in 't —
Then trip him, that his heels may kick at heaven,
And that his soul may be as damned and black
95   As hell, whereto it goes. My mother stays.°
This physic° but prolongs thy sickly days.   *Exit.*
KING.
My words fly up, my thoughts remain below.
Words without thoughts never to heaven go.   *Exit.*

3 . 4 °   *Enter [Queen] Gertrude and Polonius.*

POLONIUS.
'A will come straight. Look you lay home° to him.
Tell him his pranks have been too broad° to bear with,
And that Your Grace screened and stood between
Much heat° and him. I'll shroud° me even here.
5   Pray you, be round° with him.
HAMLET (*within*). Mother, Mother, Mother!
QUEEN. I'll warrant you, fear me not.
Withdraw, I hear him coming.
                    [*Polonius hides behind the arras.*]

        Enter Hamlet.

HAMLET. Now, Mother, what's the matter?
QUEEN.
10   Hamlet, thou hast thy father° much offended.
HAMLET.
Mother, you have my father much offended.
QUEEN.
Come, come, you answer with an idle° tongue.

HAMLET.
Go, go, you question with a wicked tongue.
QUEEN.
Why, how now, Hamlet?
HAMLET.   What's the matter now?
QUEEN.
Have you forgot me?°
HAMLET.   No, by the rood,° not so: 15
You are the Queen, your husband's brother's wife,
And—would it were not so!—you are my mother.
QUEEN.
Nay, then, I'll set those to you that can speak.°
HAMLET.
Come, come, and sit you down; you shall not budge.
You go not till I set you up a glass   20
Where you may see the inmost part of you.
QUEEN.
What will thou do? Thou wilt not murder me?
Help, ho!
POLONIUS [*behind the arras*]. What ho! Help!
HAMLET [*drawing*].
How now? A rat? Dead for a ducat, dead!°   25

        [*He thrusts his rapier through the arras.*]

POLONIUS [*behind the arras*].
O, I am slain!   [*He falls and dies.*]
QUEEN.   O me, what hast thou done?
HAMLET. Nay, I know not. Is it the King?
QUEEN.
O, what a rash and bloody deed is this!
HAMLET.
A bloody deed—almost as bad, good Mother,
As kill a king, and marry with his brother.   30
QUEEN.
As kill a king!
HAMLET.   Ay, lady, it was my word.
            [*He parts the arras and discovers Polonius.*]
Thou wretched, rash, intruding fool, farewell!
I took thee for thy better. Take thy fortune.
Thou find'st to be too busy° is some danger.—
Leave wringing of your hands. Peace, sit you down,   35
And let me wring your heart, for so I shall,
If it be made of penetrable stuff,
If damnèd custom° have not brazed° it so
That it be proof° and bulwark against sense.°
QUEEN.
What have I done, that thou dar'st wag thy tongue   40
In noise so rude against me?
HAMLET.   Such an act

82 audit account. **save** except for   **83 in . . . thought** as we see it
from our mortal perspective   **86 seasoned** matured, readied   **88
know . . . hent** await to be grasped by me on a more horrid occasion. **hent** act of seizing   **89 drunk . . . rage** dead drunk, or in a fit
of sexual passion   **91 game** gambling   **92 relish** trace, savor   **95
stays** awaits (me)   **96 physic** purging (by prayer), or, Hamlet's
postponement of the killing
3.4. Location: The Queen's private chamber.
1 lay home thrust to the heart, reprove him soundly   **2 broad** unrestrained   **4 Much heat** i.e., the King's anger. **shroud** conceal
(with ironic fitness to Polonius' imminent death. The word is only
in the First Quarto; the Second Quarto and the Folio read "silence.")   **5 round** blunt   **10 thy father** i.e., your stepfather,
Claudius   **12 idle** foolish

15 forgot me i.e., forgotten that I am your mother. **rood** cross of
Christ   **18 speak** i.e., to someone so rude   **25 Dead for a ducat**
i.e., I bet a ducat he's dead; or, a ducat is his life's fee   **34 busy**
nosey   **38 damnèd custom** habitual wickedness. **brazed** brazened,
hardened   **39 proof** armor. **sense** feeling

That blurs the grace and blush of modesty,
Calls virtue hypocrite, takes off the rose
From the fair forehead of an innocent love
45 And sets a blister° there, makes marriage vows
As false as dicers' oaths. O, such a deed
As from the body of contraction° plucks
The very soul, and sweet religion makes°
A rhapsody° of words. Heaven's face does glow
50 O'er this solidity and compound mass
With tristful visage, as against the doom,
Is thought-sick at the act.°
QUEEN.   Ay me, what act,
That roars so loud and thunders in the index?°
HAMLET [*showing her two likenesses*].
Look here upon this picture, and on this,
55 The counterfeit presentment° of two brothers.
See what a grace was seated on this brow:
Hyperion's° curls, the front° of Jove himself,
An eye like Mars° to threaten and command,
A station° like the herald Mercury°
60 New-lighted° on a heaven-kissing hill—
A combination and a form indeed
Where every god did seem to set his seal°
To give the world assurance of a man.
This was your husband. Look you now what follows:
65 Here is your husband, like a mildewed ear,°
Blasting° his wholesome brother. Have you eyes?
Could you on this fair mountain leave° to feed
And batten° on this moor? Ha, have you eyes?
You cannot call it love, for at your age
70 The heyday° in the blood° is tame, it's humble,
And waits upon the judgment, and what judgment
Would step from this to this? Sense,° sure, you have
Else could you not have motion, but sure that sense
Is apoplexed,° for madness would not err,°

Nor sense to ecstasy was ne'er so thralled,   75
But° it reserved some quantity of choice
To serve in such a difference.° What devil was 't
That thus hath cozened° you at hoodman-blind?°
Eyes without feeling, feeling without sight,
Ears without hands or eyes, smelling sans° all,   80
Or but a sickly part of one true sense
Could not so mope.° O shame, where is thy blush?
Rebellious hell,
If thou canst mutine° in a matron's bones,
To flaming youth let virtue be as wax   85
And melt in her own fire.° Proclaim no shame
When the compulsive ardor gives the charge,
Since frost itself as actively doth burn,
And reason panders will.°
QUEEN. O Hamlet, speak no more!   90
Thou turn'st mine eyes into my very soul,
And there I see such black and grainèd° spots
As will not leave their tinct.°
HAMLET.   Nay, but to live
In the rank sweat of an enseamèd° bed,
Stewed° in corruption, honeying and making love   95
Over the nasty sty!
QUEEN. O, speak to me no more!
These words like daggers enter in my ears.
No more, sweet Hamlet!
HAMLET.   A murderer and a villain,
A slave that is not twentieth part the tithe°   100
Of your precedent lord,° a vice of kings,
A cutpurse of the empire and the rule,
That from a shelf the precious diadem stole
And put it in his pocket!
QUEEN. No more!   105

Enter Ghost [in his nightgown].

HAMLET. A king of shreds and patches°—
Save me, and hover o'er me with your wings,

---

45 sets a blister i.e., brands as a harlot **47 contraction** the marriage contract **48 sweet religion makes** i.e., makes marriage vows **49 rhapsody** senseless string **49–52 Heaven's . . . act** heaven's face blushes at this solid world compounded of the various elements, with sorrowful face as though the day of doom were near, and is sick with horror at the deed (i.e., Gertrude's marriage) **53 index** table of contents, prelude or preface **55 counterfeit presentment** portrayed representation **57 Hyperion's** the sun-god's. **front** brow **58 Mars** god of war **59 station** manner of standing. **Mercury** winged messenger of the gods **60 New-lighted** newly alighted **62 set his seal** i.e., affix his approval **65 ear** i.e., of grain **66 Blasting** blighting **67 leave** cease **68 batten** gorge. **moor** barren or marshy ground (suggesting also "dark-skinned") **70 heyday** state of excitement. **blood** passion **72 Sense** perception through the five senses (the function of the middle or sensible soul) **74 apoplexed** paralyzed. (Hamlet goes on to explain that, without such a paralysis of will, mere madness would not so err, nor would the five senses so enthrall themselves to *ecstacy* or lunacy; even such deranged states of mind would be able to make the obvious choice between Hamlet Senior and Claudius.) **err** so err

76 But but that **77 To . . . difference** to help in making a choice between two such men **78 cozened** cheated. **hoodman-blind** blindman's buff. (In this game, says Hamlet, the devil must have pushed Claudius toward Gertrude while she was blindfolded.) **80 sans** without **82 mope** be dazed, act aimlessly **84 mutine** incite mutiny **85–86 be as wax . . . fire** melt like a candle or stick of sealing wax held over the candle flame **86–89 Proclaim . . . will** call it no shameful business when the compelling ardor of youth delivers the attack, i.e., commits lechery, since the *frost* of advanced age burns with as active a fire of lust and reason perverts itself by fomenting lust rather than restraining it. **92 grainèd** dyed in grain, indelible **93 leave their tinct** surrender their color **94 enseamèd** saturated in the grease and filth of passionate lovemaking **95 Stewed** soaked, bathed (with a suggestion of "stew," brothel) **100 tithe** tenth part **101 precedent lord** former husband. **vice** buffoon. (A reference to the Vice of the morality plays.) **106 shreds and patches** i.e., motley, the traditional costume of the clown or fool

You heavenly guards! What would your gracious figure?
QUEEN. Alas, he's mad!
HAMLET.
110 Do you not come your tardy son to chide,
That, lapsed° in time and passion, lets go by
Th' important° acting of your dread command?
O, say!
GHOST.
Do not forget. This visitation
115 Is but to whet thy almost blunted purpose.
But look, amazement° on thy mother sits.
O, step between her and her fighting soul!
Conceit° in weakest bodies strongest works.
Speak to her, Hamlet.
HAMLET.   How is it with you, lady?
120 QUEEN. Alas, how is 't with you,
That you do bend your eye on vacancy,
And with th' incorporal° air do hold discourse?
Forth at your eyes your spirits wildly peep,
And, as the sleeping soldiers in th' alarm,°
125 Your bedded° hair, like life in excrements,°
Start up and stand on end. O gentle son,
Upon the heat and flame of thy distemper°
Sprinkle cool patience. Whereon do you look?
HAMLET.
On him, on him! Look you how pale he glares!
130 His form and cause conjoined,° preaching to stones,
Would make them capable.°—Do not look upon me,
Lest with this piteous action you convert
My stern effects.° Then what I have to do
Will want true color—tears perchance for blood.°
135 QUEEN. To whom do you speak this?
HAMLET. Do you see nothing there?
QUEEN.
Nothing at all, yet all that is I see.
HAMLET. Nor did you nothing hear?
QUEEN. No, nothing but ourselves.
HAMLET.
140 Why, look you there, look how it steals away!
My father, in his habit° as° he lived!
Look where he goes even now out at the portal!

                                        Exit Ghost.

QUEEN.
This is the very° coinage of your brain.
This bodiless creation ecstasy
Is very cunning in.°   145
HAMLET. Ecstasy?
My pulse as yours doth temperately keep time,
And makes as healthful music. It is not madness
That I have uttered. Bring me to the test,
And I the matter will reword,° which madness   150
Would gambol° from. Mother, for love of grace,
Lay not that flattering unction° to your soul
That not your trespass but my madness speaks.
It will but skin° and film the ulcerous place,
Whiles rank corruption, mining° all within,   155
Infects unseen. Confess yourself to heaven,
Repent what's past, avoid what is to come,
And do not spread the compost° on the weeds
To make them ranker. Forgive me this my virtue;°
For in the fatness° of these pursy° times   160
Virtue itself of vice must pardon beg,
Yea, curb° and woo for leave° to do him good.
QUEEN.
O Hamlet, thou hast cleft my heart in twain.
HAMLET.
O, throw away the worser part of it,
And live the purer with the other half.   165
Good night. But go not to my uncle's bed;
Assume a virtue, if you have it not.
That monster, custom, who will sense doth eat,°
Of habits devil,° is angel yet in this,
That to the use of actions fair and good   170
He likewise gives a frock or livery°
That aptly° is put on. Refrain tonight,
And that shall lend a kind of easiness
To the next abstinence; the next more easy;
For use° almost can change the stamp of nature,°   175
And either° . . . the devil, or throw him out
With wondrous potency. Once more, good night;
And when you are desirous to be blest,

---

111 **lapsed** delaying   112 **important** importunate, urgent   116 **amazement** distraction   118 **Conceit** imagination   122 **incorporal** immaterial   124 **as . . . alarm** like soldiers called out of sleep by an alarum   125 **bedded** laid flat. **like life in excrements** i.e., as though hair, an outgrowth of the body, had a life of its own. (Hair was thought to be lifeless because it lacks sensation, and so its standing on end would be unnatural and ominous.)   127 **distemper** disorder   130 **His . . . conjoined** his appearance joined to his cause for speaking   131 **capable** receptive   132–133 **convert . . . effects** divert me from my stern duty   134 **want . . . blood** lack plausibility so that (with a play on the normal sense of *color*) I shall shed colorless tears instead of blood   141 **habit** clothes. **as** as when

143 **very** mere   144–145 **This . . . in** madness is skillful in creating this kind of hallucination   150 **reword** repeat word for word   151 **gambol** skip away   152 **unction** ointment   154 **skin** grow a skin for   155 **mining** working under the surface   158 **compost** manure   159 **this my virtue** my virtuous talk in reproving you   160 **fatness** grossness. **pursy** flabby, out of shape   162 **curb** bow, bend the knee. **leave** permission   168 **who . . . eat** which consumes all proper or natural feeling, all sensibility   169 **Of habits devil** devil-like in prompting evil habits   171 **livery** an outer appearance, a customary garb (and hence a predisposition easily assumed in time of stress)   172 **aptly** readily   175 **use** habit. **the stamps of nature** our inborn traits   176 **And either** (A defective line, usually emended by inserting the word *master* after *either*, following the Fourth Quarto and early editors.)

I'll blessing beg of you.° For this same lord,

[pointing to Polonius]

180   I do repent; but heaven hath pleased it so
To punish me with this, and this with me,
That I must be their scourge and minister.°
I will bestow° him, and will answer° well
The death I gave him. So, again, good night.

185   I must be cruel only to be kind.
This° bad begins, and worse remains behind.°
One word more, good lady.

QUEEN.   What shall I do?

HAMLET.

Not this by no means that I bid you do:
Let the bloat° king tempt you again to bed,

190   Pinch wanton° on your cheek, call you his mouse,
And let him, for a pair of reechy kisses,
Or paddling° in your neck with his damned fingers,
Make you to ravel all this matter out°
That I essentially am not in madness,

195   But mad in craft.° 'Twere good° you let him know,
For who that's but a queen, fair, sober, wise,
Would from a paddock,° from a bat, a gib,°
Such dear concernings° hide? Who would do so?
No, in despite of sense and secrecy,°

200   Unpeg the basket° on the house's top,
Let the birds fly, and like the famous ape,°
To try conclusions,° in the basket creep
And break your own neck down.°

QUEEN.

Be thou assured, if words be made of breath,

205   And breath of life, I have no life to breathe
What thou hast said to me.

HAMLET.

I must to England. You know that?

QUEEN.   Alack,
I had forgot. 'Tis so concluded on.

HAMLET.

There's letters sealed, and my two schoolfellows,
Who I will trust as I will adders fanged,   210
They bear the mandate; they must sweep my way
And marshall me to knavery.° Let it work.°
For 'tis the sport to have the enginer°
Hoist with° his own petard,° and 't shall go hard
But I will° delve one yard below their mines°   215
And blow them at the moon. O, 'tis most sweet
When in one line° two crafts° directly meet.
This man shall set me packing.°
I'll lug the guts into the neighbor room.
Mother, good night indeed. This counselor   220
Is now most still, most secret, and most grave,
Who was in life a foolish prating knave.—
Come, sir, to draw toward an end° with you.—
Good night, Mother.

Exeunt [separately, Hamlet dragging in Polonius].

4.1°   Enter King and Queen,° with Rosencrantz and
        Guildenstern.

KING.

There's matter° in these sighs, these profound heaves.°
You must translate; 'tis fit we understand them.
Where is your son?

QUEEN.

Bestow this place on us a little while.

[Exeunt Rosencrantz and Guildenstern.]
Ah, mine own lord, what have I seen tonight!   5

KING.

What, Gertrude? How does Hamlet?

QUEEN.

Mad as the sea and wind when both contend
Which is the mightier. In his lawless fit,

178–179 when . . . you i.e., when you are ready to be penitent and seek God's blessing, I will ask your blessing as a dutiful son should 182 their scourge and minister i.e., agent of heavenly retribution. (By scourge, Hamlet also suggests that he himself will eventually suffer punishment in the process of fulfilling heaven's will.) 183 bestow stow, dispose of. answer account or pay for. 186 This i.e., the killing of Polonius. behind to come 189 bloat bloated 190 Pinch wanton i.e., leave his love pinches on your cheeks, branding you as wanton 191 reechy dirty, filthy 192 paddling fingering amorously 193 ravel . . . out unravel, disclose 195 in craft by cunning. good (Said sarcastically; also the following eight lines.) 197 paddock toad. gib tomcat 198 dear concernings important affairs 199 sense and secrecy secrecy that common sense requires 200 Unpeg the basket open the cage, i.e., let out the secret 201 famous ape (In a story now lost.) 202 try conclusions test the outcome (in which the ape apparently enters a cage from which birds have been released and then tries to fly out of the cage as they have done, falling to its death) 203 down in the fall; utterly

211–212 sweep . . . knavery sweep a path before me and conduct me to some knavery or treachery prepared for me 212 work proceed 213 enginer maker of military contrivances 214 Hoist with blown up by. petard an explosive used to blow in a door or make a breach 214–215 't shal . . . will unless luck is against me, I will 215 mines tunnels used in warfare to undermine the enemy's emplacements; Hamlet will countermine by going under their mines 217 in one line i.e., mines and countermines on a collision course, or the countermines directly below the mines. crafts acts of guile, plots 218 set me packing set me to making schemes, and set me to lugging (him), and, also, send me off in a hurry 223 draw . . . end finish up (with a pun on draw, "pull") 4.1. Location: The castle. s.d. Enter . . . Queen (Some editors argue that Gertrude never exits in 3.4 and that the scene is continuous here, as suggested in the Folio, but the Second Quarto marks an entrance for her and at line 35 Claudius speaks of Gertrude's closet as though it were elsewhere. A short time has elapsed, during which the King has become aware of her highly wrought emotional state.) 1 matter significance. heaves heavy sighs

Behind the arras hearing something stir,
10   Whips out his rapier, cries, "A rat, a rat!"
And in this brainish apprehension° kills
The unseen good old man.
KING.
                                    O heavy° deed!
It had been so with us,° had we been there.
His liberty is full of threats to all—
15   To you yourself, to us, to everyone.
Alas, how shall this bloody deed be answered?°
It will be laid to us, whose providence°
Should have kept short,° restrained, and out of haunt°
This mad young man. But so much was our love,
20   We would not understand what was most fit,
But, like the owner of a foul disease,
To keep it from divulging,° let it feed
Even on the pith of life. Where is he gone?
QUEEN.
To draw apart the body he hath killed,
25   O'er whom his very madness, like some ore°
Among a mineral° of metals base,
Shows itself pure: 'a weeps for what is done.
KING. O Gertrude, come away!
The sun no sooner shall the mountains touch
30   But we will ship him hence, and this vile deed
We must with all our majesty and skill
Both countenance° and excuse.—Ho, Guildenstern!

Enter Rosencrantz and Guildenstern.

Friends both, go join you with some further aid.
Hamlet in madness hath Polonius slain,
35   And from his mother's closet hath he dragged him.
Go seek him out, speak fair, and bring the body
Into the chapel. I pray you, haste in this.
                    [*Exeunt Rosencrantz and Guildenstern.*]
Come, Gertrude, we'll call up our wisest friends
And let them know both what we mean to do
40   And what's ultimately done° . . . .
Whose whisper o'er the world's diameter,°
As level° as the cannon to his blank,°
Transports his poisoned shot, may miss our name
And hit the woundless° air. O, come away!
45   My soul is full of discord and dismay.   *Exeunt.*

---

4 . 2 °   *Enter Hamlet.*

HAMLET. Safely stowed.
ROSENCRANTZ, GUILDENSTERN (*within*). Hamlet! Lord
    Hamlet!
HAMLET. But soft, what noise? Who calls on Hamlet? O,
    here they come.   5

Enter Rosencrantz and Guildenstern.

ROSENCRANTZ.
    What have you done, my lord, with the dead body?
HAMLET.
    Compounded it with dust, whereto 'tis kin.
ROSENCRANTZ.
    Tell us where 'tis, that we may take it thence
    And bear it to the chapel.
HAMLET. Do not believe it.   10
ROSENCRANTZ. Believe what?
HAMLET. That I can keep your counsel and not mine own.°
    Besides, to be demanded of° a sponge, what replication°
    should be made by the son of a king?
ROSENCRANTZ. Take you me for a sponge, my lord?   15
HAMLET. Ay, sir, that soaks up the King's countenance,° his
    rewards, his authorities.° But such officers do the King
    best service in the end. He keeps them, like an ape, an
    apple, in the corner of his jaw, first mouthed to be last
    swallowed. When he needs what you have gleaned, it is   20
    but squeezing you, and, sponge, you shall be dry again.
ROSENCRANTZ. I understand you not, my lord.
HAMLET. I am glad of it. A knavish speech sleeps° in a fool-
    ish ear.
ROSENCRANTZ. My lord, you must tell us where the body is 25
    and go with us to the King.
HAMLET. The body is with the King, but the King is not
    with the body.° The King is a thing—
GUILDENSTERN. A thing, my lord?
HAMLET. Of nothing.° Bring me to him. Hide fox, and all   30
    after!°   *Exeunt* [*running*].

4.2. Location: The castle.
12 That . . . own i.e., that I can follow your advice (by telling where the body is) and still keep my own secret   **13 demanded of** questioned by   **13 replication** reply   **16 countenance** favor   **17 authorities** delegated power, influence   **23 sleeps in** has no meaning to   **27–28 The . . . body** (Perhaps alludes to the legal commonplace of "the king's two bodies," which drew a distinction between the sacred office of kingship and the particular mortal who possessed it at any given time. Hence, although Claudius' body is necessarily a part of him, true kingship is not contained in it. Similarly, Claudius will have Polonius' body when it is found, but there is no kingship in this business either.)   **30 Of nothing** (1) of no account (2) lacking the essence of kingship, as in lines 28–29 and note   **30–31 Hide . . . after** (An old signal cry in the game of hide-and-seek, suggesting that Hamlet now runs away from them.)

---

11 brainish apprehension headstrong conception   **12 heavy** grievous   **13 us** i.e., me. (The royal "we"; also in line 15.)   **16 answered** explained   **17 providence** foresight   **18 short** i.e., on a short tether. **out of haunt** secluded   **22 divulging** becoming evident   **25 ore** vein of gold   **26 mineral** mine   **32 countenance** put the best face on   **40 And . . . done** (A defective line; conjectures as to the missing words include *So, haply, slander* [Capell and others]; *For, haply, slander* [Theobald and others]; and *So envious slander* [Jenkins].)   **41 diameter** extent from side to side.   **42 As level** with as direct aim. **his blank** its target at point-blank range.   **44 woundless** invulnerable

4 . 3 °   *Enter King, and two or three.*

KING.
I have sent to seek him, and to find the body.
How dangerous is it that this man goes loose!
Yet must not we put the strong law on him.
He's loved of° the distracted° multitude,
5 Who like not in their judgment, but their eyes,°
And where 'tis so, th' offender's scourge° is weighed,°
But never the offense. To bear all smooth and even,°
This sudden sending him away must seem
Deliberate pause.° Diseases desperate grown
10 By desperate appliance° are relieved,
Or not at all.

     Enter Rosencrantz, [Guildenstern,]
     and all the rest.

        How now, what hath befall'n?
ROSENCRANTZ.
Where the dead body is bestowed, my lord,
We cannot get from him.
KING.   But where is he?
ROSENCRANTZ.
Without, my lord; guarded, to know your pleasure.
KING.
Bring him before us.
15 ROSENCRANTZ.   Ho! Bring in the lord.

   They enter [with Hamlet].

KING. Now, Hamlet, where's Polonius?
HAMLET. At supper.
KING. At supper? Where?
HAMLET. Not where he eats, but where 'a is eaten. A certain
20   convocation of politic worms° are e'en° at him. Your
   worm° is your only emperor for diet.° We fat all creatures
   else to fat us, and we fat ourselves for maggots. Your fat
   king and your lean beggar is but variable service°—two
   dishes, but to one table. That's the end.
25 KING. Alas, alas!
HAMLET. A man may fish with the worm that hath eat° of a
   king, and eat of the fish that hath fed of that worm.

KING. What dost thou mean by this?
HAMLET. Nothing but to show you how a king may go a
   progress° through the guts of a beggar.   30
KING. Where is Polonius?
HAMLET. In heaven. Send thither to see. If your messenger
   find him not there, seek him i' th' other place yourself.
   But if indeed you find him not within this month, you
   shall nose him as you go up the stairs into the lobby.   35
KING [*to some attendants*]. Go seek him there.
HAMLET. 'A will stay till you come.   [*Exeunt attendants.*]
KING.
Hamlet this deed, for thine especial safety—
Which we do tender,° as we dearly° grieve
For that which thou has done—must send thee hence   40
With fiery quickness. Therefore prepare thyself.
The bark° is ready, and the wind at help,
Th' associates tend,° and everything is bent°
For England
HAMLET. For England!   45
KING. Ay, Hamlet.
HAMLET. Good.
KING.
So is it, if thou knew'st our purposes.
HAMLET. I see a cherub° that sees them. But come, for Eng-
   land! Farewell, dear mother.   50
KING. Thy loving father, Hamlet.
HAMLET. My mother. Father and mother is man and wife,
   man and wife is one flesh, and so, my mother. Come, for
   England.   *Exit.*
KING. Follow him at foot;° tempt him with speed abroad.   55
Delay it not. I'll have him hence tonight.
Away! For everything is sealed and done
That else leans on° th' affair. Pray you, make haste.
                    [*Exeunt all but the King.*]
And, England,° if my love thou hold'st at aught°—
As my great power thereof may give thee sense,°   60
Since yet thy cicatrice° looks raw and red
After the Danish sword, and thy free awe°
Pays homage to us—thou mayst not coldly set°
Our sovereign process,° which imports at full,°
By letters congruing° to that effect,   65
The present° death of Hamlet. Do it, England,
For like the hectic° in my blood he rages,

4.3. Location: The castle.
4 of by. **distracted** fickle, unstable   **5 Who . . . eyes** who choose
not by judgment but by appearance   **6 scourge** punishment. (Literally, blow with a whip.) **weighed** sympathetically considered   **7
To . . . even** to manage the business in an unprovocative way   **9
Deliberate pause** carefully considered action   **10 appliance** remedies   **20 politic worms** crafty worms (suited to a master spy like
Polonius). **e'en** even now   **21 Your worm** your average worm.
Compare *your fat king and your lean beggar* in line 23.) **diet** food, eating (with a punning reference to the Diet of Worms, a famous *convocation* held in 1521)   **23 variable service** different courses of a
single meal   **26 eat** eaten. (pronounced *et*.)

30 progress royal journey of state   **39 tender** regard, hold dear.
dearly intensely   **42 bark** sailing vessel   **43 tend** wait. **bent** in
readiness   **49 cherub** (Cherubim are angles of knowledge. Hamlet
hints that both he and heaven are onto Claudius' tricks.)   **55 at
foot** close behind, at heel   **58 leans on** bears upon, is related to
59 England i.e., King of England. **at aught** at any value   **60 As
. . . sense** for so my great power may give you a just appreciation of
the importance of valuing my love   **61 cicatrice** scar   **62 free
awe** voluntary show of respect   **63 coldly set** regard with indifference   **64 process** command. **imports at full** conveys specific directions for   **65 congruing** agreeing   **66 present** immediate   **67
hectic** persistent fever

And thou must cure me. Till I know 'tis done,
Howe'er my haps,° my joys were ne'er begun.   *Exit.*

4 . 4 °   *Enter Fortinbras with his army over the stage.*

FORTINBRAS.
    Go, Captain, from me greet the Danish king.
    Tell him that by his license° Fortinbras
    Craves the conveyance of° a promised march
    Over his kingdom. You know the rendezvous.
5   If that His Majesty would aught with us,
    We shall express our duty° in his eye;°
    And let him know so.
CAPTAIN. I will do 't, my lord.
FORTINBRAS. Go softly° on.   *[Exeunt all but the Captain.]*

    Enter Hamlet, Rosencrantz, [Guildenstern,] etc.

10 HAMLET. Good sir, whose powers° are these?
CAPTAIN. They are of Norway, sir.
HAMLET. How purposed, sir, I pray you?
CAPTAIN. Against some part of Poland.
HAMLET. Who commands them, sir?
CAPTAIN.
15   The nephew to old Norway, Fortinbras.
HAMLET.
    Goes it against the main° of Poland, sir,
    Or for some frontier?
CAPTAIN.
    Truly to speak, and with no addition,°
    We go to gain a little patch of ground
20   That hath in it no profit but the name.
    To pay° five ducats, five, I would not farm it;°
    Nor will it yield to Norway or the Pole
    A ranker° rate, should it be sold in fee.°
HAMLET.
    Why, then the Polack never will defend it.
CAPTAIN.
25   Yes, it is already garrisoned.
HAMLET.
    Two thousand souls and twenty thousand ducats
    Will not debate the question of this straw.°
    This is th' impostume° of much wealth and peace,
    That inward breaks, and shows no cause without
30   Why the man dies. I humbly thank you, sir.
CAPTAIN.
    God b' wi' you, sir.   *[Exit.]*

69 **haps** fortunes
4.4. Location: The coast of Denmark.
2 **license** permission   3 **the conveyance of** escort during   6 **duty**
respect. **eye** presence   9 **softly** slowly, circumspectly   10 **powers**
forces   16 **main** main part   18 **addition** exaggeration   21 **To
pay** i.e., for a yearly rental of. **farm it** take a lease of it   23 **ranker**
higher. **in fee** fee simple, outright   27 **debate . . . straw** settle this
trifling matter   28 **impostume** abscess

ROSENCRANTZ.
    Will 't please you go, my lord?
HAMLET.
    I'll be with you straight. Go a little before.
        [Exeunt all except Hamlet.]
    How all occasions do inform against° me
    And spur my dull revenge! What is a man,
    If his chief good and market of° his time   35
    Be but to sleep and feed? A beast, no more.
    Sure he that made us with such large discourse,°
    Looking before and after°, gave us not
    That capability and godlike reason
    To fust° in us unused. Now, whether it be   40
    Bestial oblivion,° or some craven° scruple
    Of thinking too precisely° on th' event°—
    A thought which, quartered, hath but one part wisdom
    And ever three parts coward—I do not know
    Why yet I live to say "This thing's to do,"   45
    Sith° I have cause, and will, and strength, and means
    To do 't. Examples gross° as earth exhort me:
    Witness this army of such mass and charge,°
    Led by a delicate and tender° prince,
    Whose spirit with divine ambition puffed   50
    Makes mouths° at the invisible event,°
    Exposing what is mortal and unsure
    To all that fortune, death, and danger dare,°
    Even for an eggshell. Rightly to be great
    Is not to stir without great argument   55
    But greatly to find quarrel in a straw
    When honor's at the stake.° How stand I, then,
    That have a father killed, a mother stained,
    Excitements of° my reason and my blood,
    And let all sleep, while to my shame I see   60
    The imminent death of twenty thousand men
    That for a fantasy° and trick° of fame
    Go to their graves like beds, fight for a plot°
    Whereon the numbers cannot try the cause,°
    Which is not tomb enough and continent°   65

33 **inform against** denounce, betray; take shape against   35 **market of** profit of, compensation for   37 **discourse** power of reasoning   38 **looking before and after** able to review past events and anticipate the future   40 **fust** grow moldy   41 **oblivion** forgetfulness. **craven** cowardly   42 **precisely** scrupulously. **event** outcome   46 **Sith** since   47 **gross** obvious   48 **charge** expense   49 **delicate and tender** of fine and youthful qualities   51 **Makes mouths** makes scornful faces. **invisible event** unforeseeable outcome   53 **dare** could do (to him)   54–57 **Rightly . . . stake** true greatness does not normally consist of rushing into action over some trivial provocation; however, when one's honor is involved, even a trifling insult requires that one respond greatly (?) **at the stake** (A metaphor from gambling or bear-baiting.)   59 **Excitements of** promptings by   62 **fantasy** fanciful caprice, illusion. **trick** trifle, deceit   63 **plot** plot of ground   64 **Whereon . . . cause** on which there is insufficient room for the soldiers needed to engage in a military contest   65 **continent** receptacle, container

To hide the slain? O, from this time forth
My thoughts be bloody or be nothing worth!   *Exit.*

4.5°   *Enter Horatio, [Queen] Gertrude, and a*
                 Gentleman.

QUEEN.
   I will not speak with her.
GENTLEMAN.   She is importunate,
   Indeed distract.° Her mood will needs be pitied.
QUEEN. What would she have?
GENTLEMAN.
   She speaks much of her father, says she hears
   There's tricks° i' the world, and hems,° and beats her
5   heart,°
   Spurns enviously at straws,° speaks things in doubt°
   That carry but half sense. Her speech is nothing,
   Yet the unshapèd use° of it doth move
   The hearers to collection;° they yawn° at it,
10   And botch° the words up fit to their own thoughts,
   Which,° as her winks and nods and gestures yield°
      them,
   Indeed would make one think there might be thought,°
   Though nothing sure, yet much unhappily.°
HORATIO.
   'Twere good she were spoken with, for she may strew
15   Dangerous conjectures in ill-breeding° minds.
QUEEN. Let her come in.   *[Exit Gentleman.]*
   [Aside.] To my sick soul, as sin's true nature is,
   Each toy° seems prologue to some great amiss.°
   So full of artless jealousy is guilt,
20   It spills itself in fearing to be spilt.°

            Enter Ophelia° *[distracted].*

OPHELIA.
   Where is the beauteous majesty of Denmark?
QUEEN. How now, Ophelia?
OPHELIA *(she sings).*
      "How should I your true love know
         From another one?

By his cockle hat° and staff,   25
   And his sandal shoon."°
QUEEN. Alas, sweet lady, what imports this song?
OPHELIA. Say you? Nay, pray you, mark.
      "He is dead and gone, Lady,   *(Song.)*
         He is dead and gone;   30
      At his head a grass-green turf,
         At his heels a stone."
   O, ho!
QUEEN. Nay, but Ophelia—
OPHELIA. Pray you, mark.   35
   [Sings.] "White his shroud as the mountain snow"—

      Enter King.

QUEEN. Alas, look here, my lord.
OPHELIA.
      "Larded° with sweet flowers;   *(Song.)*
      Which bewept to the ground did not go
         With true-love showers."°   40
KING. How do you, pretty lady?
OPHELIA. Well, God 'ild° you! They say the owl° was a
   baker's daughter. Lord, we know what we are, but know
   not what we may be. God be at your table!
KING. Conceit° upon her father.   45
OPHELIA. Pray let's have no words of this; but when they
   ask you what it means, say you this:
      "Tomorrow is Saint Valentine's day,   *(Song.)*
         All in the morning betime,°
      And I a maid at your window,   50
         To be your Valentine.
      Then up he rose, and donned his clothes,
         And dupped° the chamber door,
      Let in the maid, that out a maid
         Never departed more."   55
KING. Pretty Ophelia—
OPHELIA. Indeed, la, without an oath, I'll make an end
   on 't:
      [Sings.] "By Gis° and by Saint Charity,
         Alack, and fie for shame!   60
      Young men will do 't, if they come to 't;
         By Cock,° they are to blame.
      Quoth she, 'Before you tumbled me,
         You promised me to wed.' "
   He answers: 65
      " 'So would I ha' done, by yonder sun,
         An° thou hadst not come to my bed.' "

4.5. Location: The castle.
2 distract distracted   **5 tricks** deceptions. **hems** makes "hmm" sounds. **heart** i.e., breast   **6 Spurns . . . straws** kicks spitefully, takes offense at trifles. **in doubt** obscurely   **8 unshapèd use** incoherent manner   **9 collection** inference, a guess at some sort of meaning. **yawn** gape, wonder; grasp. (The Folio reading, *aim*, is possible.)   **10 botch** patch   **11 Which** which words. **yield** deliver, represent   **12 thought** intended   **13 unhappily** unpleasantly near the truth, shrewdly   **15 ill-breeding** prone to suspect the worst and to make mischief   **18 toy** trifle. **amiss** calamity   **19–20 So . . . spilt** guilt is so full of suspicion that it unskillfully betrays itself in fearing betrayal   **20 s.d. Enter Ophelia** (In the First Quarto, Ophelia enters "playing on a lute, and her hair down, singing.")

25 cockle hat hat with cockleshell stuck in it as a sign that the wearer had been a pilgrim to the shrine of Saint James of Compostella in Spain.   **26 shoon** shoes   **38 Larded** decorated   **40 showers** i.e., tears   **42 God 'ild** God yield or reward. **owl** (Refers to a legend about a baker's daughter who was turned into an owl for being ungenerous when Jesus begged a loaf of bread.)   **45 Conceit** brooding   **49 betime** early   **53 dupped** did up, opened   **59 Gis** Jesus   **62 Cock** (A perversion of "God" in oaths; here also with a quibble on the slang word for penis.)   **67 An** if

KING. How long hath she been thus?

OPHELIA. I hope all will be well. We must be patient, but I
70   cannot choose but weep to think they would lay him i'
the cold ground. My brother shall know of it. And so I
thank you for your good counsel. Come, my coach! Good
night, ladies, good night, sweet ladies, good night, good
night.   [Exit.]

KING [to Horatio].
75   Follow her close. Give her good watch, I pray you.
[Exit Horatio.]

O, this is the poison of deep grief; it springs
All from her father's death—and now behold!
O Gertrude, Gertrude,
When sorrows come, they come not single spies,°
80   But in battalions. First, her father slain;
Next, your son gone, and he most violent author
Of his own just remove;° the people muddied,°
Thick and unwholesome in their thoughts and whispers
For good Polonius' death—and we have done but
greenly,°
85   In hugger-mugger° to inter him; poor Ophelia
Divided from herself and her fair judgment.
Without the which we are pictures or mere beasts;
Last, and as much containing° as all these,
Her brother is in secret come from France,
90   Feeds on this wonder, keeps himself in clouds,°
And wants° not buzzers° to infect his ear
With pestilent speeches of his father's death,
Wherein necessity,° of matter beggared,°
Will nothing stick our person to arraign
95   In ear and ear.° O my dear Gertrude, this,
Like to a murdering piece,° in many places
Gives me superfluous death.°   A noise within.

QUEEN. Alack, what noise is this?

KING. Attend!°
100   Where is my Switzers?° Let them guard the door.

Enter a Messenger.

What is the matter?

MESSENGER.   Save yourself, my lord!
The ocean, overpeering of his list,°

Eats not the flats° with more impetuous° haste
Than young Laertes, in a riotous head,°
O'erbears your officers. The rabble call him lord,   105
And, as° the world were now but to begin,
Antiquity forgot, custom not known,
The ratifiers and props of every word,°
They cry, "Choose we! Laertes shall be king!"
Caps,° hands, and tongues applaud it to the clouds,   110
"Laertes shall be king, Laertes king!"

QUEEN.
How cheerfully on the false trail they cry! A noise within.
O, this is counter,° you false Danish dogs!

Enter Laertes with others.

KING. The doors are broke.

LAERTES.
Where is this King?—Sirs, stand you all without.   115

ALL. No, let's come in.

LAERTES. I pray you, give me leave.

ALL. We will, we will.

LAERTES.
I thank you. Keep the door. [Exeunt followers.] O thou
vile king,
Give me my father!

QUEEN [restraining him]. Calmly, good Laertes.   120

LAERTES.
That drop of blood that's calm proclaims me bastard,
Cries cuckold to my father, brands the harlot
Even here, between° the chaste unsmirchèd brow
Of my true mother.

KING.   What is the cause, Laertes,
That thy rebellion looks so giantlike?   125
Let him go, Gertrude. Do not fear our° person.
There's such divinity doth hedge° a king
That treason can but peep to what it would,°
Acts little of his will°. Tell me, Laertes,
Why thou art thus incensed. Let him go, Gertrude.   130
Speak, man.

LAERTES.   Where is my father?

KING.   Dead.

QUEEN.
But not by him.

KING.   Let him demand his fill.

79 spies scouts sent in advance of the main force   82 remove removal. muddied stirred up, confused   84 greenly in an inexperienced way, foolishly   85 hugger-mugger secret haste   88 as much containing as full of serious matter   90 Feeds . . . clouds feeds his resentment or shocked grievance, holds himself inscrutable and aloof amid all this rumor   91 wants lacks. buzzers gossipers, informers   93 necessity i.e., the need to invent some plausible explanation. of matter beggared unprovided with facts   94–95 Will . . . ear will not hesitate to accuse my (royal) person in everybody's ears   96 murdering piece cannon loaded so as to scatter its shot   97 Gives . . . death kills me over and over   99 Attend i.e., guard me   100 Switzers Swiss guards, mercenaries   102 overpeering of his list overflowing its shore, boundary

103 flats i.e., flatlands near shore. impetuous violent (perhaps also with the meaning of impiteous [impitious, Q2], "pitiless")   104 head insurrection   106 as as if   108 The ratifiers . . . word i.e., antiquity (or tradition) and custom ought to confirm (ratify) and underprop our every word or promise   110 Caps (The caps are thrown in the air.)   113 counter (A hunting term, meaning to follow the trail in a direction opposite to that which the game has taken.)   123 between in the middle of   126 fear our fear for my   127 hedge protect, as with a surrounding barrier   128 can . . . would can only peep furtively, as through a barrier, at what it would intend   129 Acts . . . will (but) performs little of what it intends

LAERTES.

How came he dead? I'll not be juggled with.°
To hell, allegiance! Vows, to the blackest devil!
135   Conscience and grace, to the profoundest pit!
I dare damnation. To this point I stand,°
That both the worlds I give to negligence,°
Let come what comes, only I'll be revenged
Most throughly° for my father.

140   KING. Who shall stay you?

LAERTES. My will, not all the world's.°
And for my means, I'll husband them so well
They shall go far with little.

KING.   Good Laertes,
If you desire to know the certainty
145   Of your dear father, is 't writ in your revenge
That, swoopstake,° you will draw both friend and foe,
Winner and loser?

LAERTES. None but his enemies.

KING. Will you know them, then?

LAERTES.

150   To his good friends thus wide I'll ope my arms,
And like the kind life-rendering pelican°
Repast° them with my blood.

KING.

                                    Why, now you speak
Like a good child and a true gentleman.
That I am guiltless of your father's death,
155   And am most sensibly° in grief for it,
It shall as level° to your judgment 'pear
As day does to your eye.   A noise within.

LAERTES.

How now, what noise is that?

            Enter Ophelia.

KING.   Let her come in.

LAERTES.

O heat, dry up my brains! Tears seven times salt
160   Burn out the sense and virtue° of mine eye!
By heaven, thy madness shall be paid with weight°
Till our scale turn the beam.° O rose of May!
Dear maid, kind sister, sweet Ophelia!
O heavens, is 't possible a young maid's wits

Should be as mortal as an old man's life?   165
Nature is fine in° love, and where 'tis fine
It sends some precious instance° of itself
After the thing it loves.°

OPHELIA.

"They bore him barefaced on the bier,   (Song.)
Hey non nonny, nonny, hey nonny,   170
And in his grave rained many a tear—"

Fare you well, my dove!

LAERTES.

Hadst thou thy wits and didst persuade° revenge,
It could not move thus.

OPHELIA. You must sing "A-down a-down," and you "call   175
him a-down-a.°" O, how the wheel° becomes it! It is the
false steward that stole his master's daughter.

LAERTES. This nothing's more than matter.°

OPHELIA. There's rosemary,° that's for remembrance; pray
you, love, remember. And there is pansies;° that's for   180
thoughts.

LAERTES. A document° in madness, thoughts and remembrance fitted.

OPHELIA. There's fennel° for you, and columbines.° There's
rue° for you, and here's some for me; we may call it herb   185
of grace o' Sundays. You must wear your rue with a difference.° There's a daisy.° I would give you some violets,°
but they withered all when my father died. They say 'a
made a good end—
[Sings.] "For bonny sweet Robin is all my joy."   190

LAERTES.

Thought° and affliction, passion,° hell itself,
She turns to favor° and to prettiness.

OPHELIA.

"And will 'a not come again?   (Song.)
And will 'a not come again?

---

133 **juggled with** cheated, deceived   136 **To . . . stand** I am resolved in this   137 **both . . . negligence** i.e., both this world and
the next are of no consequence to me   139 **throughly** thoroughly
141 **My will . . . world's** I'll stop (stay) when my will is accomplished, not for anyone else's.   142 **for** as for   146 **swoopstake**
i.e., indiscriminately. (Literally, taking all stakes on the gambling
table at once. *Draw* is also a gambling term, meaning "take from.")
151 **pelican** (Refers to the belief that the female pelican fed its
young with its own blood.)   152 **Repast** feed   155 **sensibly** feelingly   156 **level** plain   160 **virtue** faculty, power   161 **paid
with weight** repaid, avenged equally or more   162 **beam** crossbar
of a balance

166 **fine in** refined by   167 **instance** token   168 **After . . . loves**
i.e., into the grave, along with Polonius   173 **persuade** argue cogently for   175–176 **You . . . a-down-a** (Ophelia assigns the
singing of refrains, like her own "Hey non nonny," to others present.)   176 **wheel** spinning wheel as accompaniment to the song,
or refrain   188 **false steward** (The story is unknown.)   178 **This
. . . matter** this seeming nonsense is more eloquent than sane utterance   179 **rosemary** (Used as a symbol of remembrance both at
weddings and at funerals.)   180 **pansies** (Emblem of love and
courtship; perhaps from French *pensées*, "thoughts.")   182 **document** instruction, lesson   184 **fennel** (Emblem of flattery.)
columbines (Emblems of unchastity or ingratitude.)   185 **rue**
(Emblem of repentance—a signification that is evident in its popular name, *herb of grace*.)   187 **with a difference** (A device used in
heraldry to distinguish one family from another on the coat of arms,
here suggesting that Ophelia and the others have different causes of
sorrow and repentance, perhaps with a play on *rue* in the sense of
"ruth," "pity.")   **daisy** (Emblem of dissembling, faithlessness.)   **violets**
(Emblems of faithfulness.)   191 **Thought** melancholy. **passion**
suffering   192 **favor** grace, beauty

195   No, no, he is dead.
                 Go to thy deathbed,
                 He never will come again.

                 "His beard was as white as snow,
                 All flaxen was his poll.°
200   He is gone, he is gone,
                 And we cast away moan.
                 God ha' mercy on his soul!"
                 And of all Christian souls, I pray God. God b' wi' you.
                                 [*Exit, followed by Gertrude.*]
         LAERTES. Do you see this, O God?
         KING.
205   Laertes, I must commune with your grief,
                 Or you deny me right. Go but apart,
                 Make choice of whom° your wisest friends you will,
                 And they shall hear and judge twixt you and me.
                 If by direct or by collateral hand°
210   They find us touched,° we will our kingdom give,
                 Our crown, our life, and all that we call ours
                 To you in satisfaction; but if not,
                 Be you content to lend your patience to us,
                 And we shall jointly labor with your soul
                 To give it due content.
215   LAERTES.   Let this be so.
                 His means of death, his obscure funeral—
                 No trophy,° sword, nor hatchment° o'er his bones,
                 No noble rite, nor formal ostentation°—
                 Cry to be heard, as 'twere from heaven to earth,
                 That° I must call 't in question.°
220   KING.   So you shall,
                 And where th' offense is, let the great ax fall.
                 I pray you, go with me.   *Exeunt.*

4 . 6 °   *Enter Horatio and others.*

HORATIO. What are they that would speak with me?
GENTLEMAN. Seafaring men, sir. They say they have letters
     for you.
HORATIO. Let them come in.   [*Exit Gentleman.*]
5   I do not know from what part of the world
         I should be greeted, if not from Lord Hamlet.

                 Enter Sailors.

FIRST SAILOR. God bless you, sir.
HORATIO. Let him bless thee too.
FIRST SAILOR. 'A shall, sir, an 't° please him. There's a letter

for you, sir—it came from th' ambassador° that was bound   10
for England—if your name be Horatio, as I am let to
know it is.   [*He gives a letter.*]
HORATIO [*reads*]. "Horatio, when thou shalt have over-
looked° this, give these fellows some means° to the King;
they have letters for him. Ere we were two days old at sea,   15
a pirate of very warlike appointment° gave us chase. Finding ourselves too slow of sail, we put on a compelled
valor, and in the grapple I boarded them. On the instant
they got clear of our ship, so I alone became their prisoner. They have dealt with me like thieves of mercy,° but   20
they knew what they did: I am to do a good turn for them.
Let the King have the letters I have sent, and repair° thou
to me with as much speed as thou wouldest fly death. I
have words to speak in thine ear will make thee dumb,
yet are they much too light for the bore° of the matter.   25
These good fellows will bring thee where I am. Rosencrantz and Guildenstern hold their course for England. Of
them I have much to tell thee. Farewell.
                     He that thou knowest thine, Hamlet."
Come, I will give you way° for these your letters,   30
And do 't the speedier that you may direct me
To him from whom you brought them.   *Exeunt.*

4 . 7 °   *Enter King and Laertes.*

KING.
         Now must your conscience my acquittance seal,°
         And you must put me in your heart for friend,
         Sith° you have heard, and with a knowing ear,
         That he which hath your noble father slain
         Pursued my life.
LAERTES.   It well appears. But tell me   5
         Why you proceeded not against these feats°
         So crimeful and so capital° in nature,
         As by your safety, greatness, wisdom, all things else,
         You mainly° were stirred up.
KING. O, for two special reasons,   10
         Which may to you perhaps seem much unsinewed,°
         But yet to me they're strong. The Queen his mother
         Lives almost by his looks, and for myself—
         My virtue or my plague, be it either which—
         She is so conjunctive° to my life and soul   15

---

10 th' ambassador (Evidently Hamlet. The sailor is being circum-
spect.)   13–14 overlooked looked over   14 means means of access   16 appointment equipage   20 thieves of mercy merciful
thieves   22 repair come   25 bore caliber, i.e., importance   30
way means of access
4.7. Location: The castle.
1 my acquittance seal confirm or acknowledge my innocence
3 Sith since   6 feats acts   7 capital punishable by death
9 mainly greatly   11 unsinewed weak   15 conjunctive closely
united. (An astronomical metaphor.)

199 poll head   207 whom whichever of   209 collateral hand
indirect agency   210 us touched me implicated   217 trophy
memorial. hatchment tablet displaying the armorial bearings of a
deceased person   218 ostentation ceremony   220 That so that.
call 't in question demand an explanation
4.6. Location: The castle.
9 an 't if it

That, as the star moves not but in his° sphere,°
I could not but by her. The other motive
Why to a public count° I might not go
Is the great love the general gender° bear him,
20   Who, dipping all his faults in their affection,
Work° like the spring° that turneth wood to stone,
Convert his gyves° to graces, so that my arrows,
Too slightly timbered° for so loud° a wind,
Would have reverted° to my bow again
25   But not where I had aimed them.

LAERTES.
And so I have a noble father lost,
A sister driven into desperate terms,°
Whose worth, if praises may go back° again,
Stood challenger on mount° of all the age
30   For her perfections. But my revenge will come.

KING.
Break not your sleeps for that. You must not think
That we are made of stuff so flat and dull
That we can let our beard be shook with danger
And think it pastime. You shortly shall hear more.
35   I loved your father, and we love ourself;
And that, I hope, will teach you to imagine—

Enter a Messenger with letters.

How now? What news?
MESSENGER.   Letters, my lord, from Hamlet:
This is Your Majesty, this to the Queen.
                                              [*He gives letters.*]
KING. From Hamlet? Who brought them?
MESSENGER.
40   Sailors, my lord, they say. I saw them not.
They were given me by Claudio. He received them
Of him that brought them.
KING.   Laertes, you shall hear them.—
Leave us.   [*Exit Messenger.*]
[*He reads.*] "High and might, you shall know I am set
45   naked° on your kingdom. Tomorrow shall I beg leave to
see your kingly eyes, when I shall, first asking your par-
don,° thereunto recount the occasion of my sudden and
more strange return.   Hamlet."
What should this mean? Are all the rest come back?
50   Or is it some abuse,° and no such thing?°

LAERTES.
Know you the hand?
KING.   'Tis Hamlet's character.° "Naked!"
And in a postscript here he says "alone."
Can you devise° me?
LAERTES.
I am lost in it, my lord. But let him come.
It warms the very sickness in my heart   55
That I shall live and tell him to this teeth,
"Thus didst thou."°
KING.   If it be so, Laertes—
As how should it be so? How otherwise?°—
Will you be ruled by me?
LAERTES.   Ay, my lord,
So° you will not o'errule me to a peace.   60
KING.
To thine own peace. If he be now returned,
As checking° at his voyage, and that° he means
No more to undertake it, I will work him
To an exploit, now ripe in my device,°
Under the which he shall not choose but fall;   65
And for his death no wind of blame shall breathe,
But even his mother shall uncharge the practice°
And call it accident.
LAERTES.   My lord, I will be ruled,
The rather if you could devise it so
That I might be the organ.°
KING.   It falls right.   70
You have been talked of since your travel much,
And that in Hamlet's hearing, for a quality
Wherein they say you shine. Your sum of parts°
Did not together pluck such envy from him
As did that one, and that, in my regard,   75
Of the unworthiest siege.°
LAERTES. What part is that, my lord?
KING.
A very ribbon in the cap of youth,
Yet needful too, for youth no less becomes°
The light and careless livery that it wears   80
Than settled age his sables and his weeds°
Importing health and graveness.° Two months since
Here was a gentleman of Normandy.

---

16 his its. **sphere** one of the hollow spheres in which, according to Ptolemaic astronomy, the planets were supposed to move **18 count** account, reckoning, indictment **19 general gender** common people **21 Work** operate, act. **spring** i.e., a spring with such a concentration of lime that it coats a piece of wood with limestone, in effect, gilding and petrifying it **22 gyves** fetters (which, gilded by the people's praise, would look like badges of honor) **23 slightly timbered** light. **loud** (suggesting public outcry on Hamlet's behalf) **24 reverted** returned **27 terms** state, condition **28 go back** i.e., recall what she was **29 on mount** set up on high **45 naked** destitute, unarmed, without following **46–47 pardon** permission **50 abuse** deceit. **no such thing** not what it appears

51 character handwriting **53 devise** explain to **57 Thus didst thou** i.e., here's for what you did to my father **58 As . . . otherwise** how can this (Hamlet's return) be true? Yet how otherwise than true (since we have the evidence of his letter)? **60 So** provided that **62 checking at** i.e., turning aside from (like a falcon leaving the quarry to fly at a chance bird). **that** if **64 device** devising, invention **67 uncharge the practice** acquit the stratagem of being a plot **70 organ** agent, instrument **73 Your . . . parts** i.e., all your other virtues **76 unworthiest siege** least important rank **79 no less becomes** is no less suited by **81 his sables** its rich robes furred with sable. **weeds** garments **82 Importing . . . graveness** signifying a concern for health and dignified prosperity; also, giving an impression of comfortable prosperity

I have seen myself, and served against, the French,
85 And they can well° on horseback, but this gallant
Had witchchraft in 't; he grew unto his seat,
And to such wondrous doing brought his horse
As had he been incorpsed and demi-natured°
With the brave beast. So far he topped° my thought
90 That I in forgery° of shapes and tricks
Come short of what he did.

LAERTES.   A Norman was 't?
KING. A Norman.
LAERTES.
Upon my life, Lamord.
KING.   The very same.
LAERTES.
I know him well. He is the brooch° indeed
95 And gem of all the nation.
KING. He made confession° of you,
And gave you such a masterly report
For art and exercise in your defense,°
And for your rapier most especial,
100 That he cried out 'twould be a sight indeed
If one could match you. Th' escrimers° of their nation,
He swore, had neither motion, guard, nor eye
If you opposed them. Sir, this report of his
Did Hamlet so envenom with his envy
105 That he could nothing do but wish and beg
Your sudden° coming o'er, to play° with you.
Now, out of this—
LAERTES.   What out of this, my lord?
KING.
Laertes, was your father dear to you?
Or are you like the painting of a sorrow,
A face without a heart?
110 LAERTES.   Why ask you this?
KING.
Not that I think you did not love your father,
But that I know love is begun by time,°
And that I see, in passages of proof,°
Time qualifies° the spark and fire of it.
115 There lives within the very flame of love
A kind of wick or snuff° that will abate it,
And nothing is at a like goodness still,°

For goodness, growing to a pleurisy,°
Dies in his own too much.° That° we would do,
We should do when we would; for this "would" changes   120
And hath abatements° and delays as many
As there are tongues, are hands, are accidents,°
And then this "should" is like a spendthrift sigh,°
That hurts by easing.° But, to the quick o' th' ulcer:°
Hamlet comes back. What would you undertake   125
To show yourself in deed your father's son
More than in words?
LAERTES.   To cut his throat i' the church.
KING.
No place, indeed, should murder sanctuarize;°
Revenge should have no bounds. But good Laertes,
Will you do this,° keep close within your chamber.   130
Hamlet returned shall know you are come home.
We'll put on those shall° praise your excellence
And set a double varnish on the fame
The Frenchman gave you, bring you in fine° together,
And wager on your heads. He, being remiss,°   135
Most generous°, and free from all contriving,
Will not peruse the foils, so that with ease,
Or with a little shuffling, you may choose
A sword unbated,° and in a pass of practice°
Requite him for your father.
LAERTES.   I will do 't,   140
And for that purpose I'll anoint my sword.
I bought an unction° of a mountebank°
So mortal that, but dip a knife in it,
Where it draws blood no cataplasm° so rare,
Collected from all simples° that have virtue°   145
Under the moon,° can save the thing from death
That is but scratched withal. I'll touch my point
With this contagion, that if I gall° him slightly,
It may be death.

118 **pleurisy** excess, plethora. (Literally, a chest inflammation.) 119 **in . . . much** of its own excess. **That** that which   121 **abatements** diminutions   122 **As . . . accidents** as there are tongues to dissuade, hands to prevent, and chance events to intervene   123 **spendthrift sigh** (An allusion to the belief that sighs draw blood from heart.)   124 **hurts by easing** i.e., costs the heart blood and wastes precious opportunity even while it affords emotional relief. **quick o' th' ulcer** i.e., heart of the matter   128 **sanctuarize** protect from punishment. (Alludes to the right of sanctuary with which certain religious places were invested.)   130 **Will you do this** if you wish to do this   132 **put on those shall** arrange for some to   134 **in fine** finally   135 **remiss** negligently unsuspicious   136 **generous** noble-minded   139 **unbated** not blunted, having no button. **pass of practice** treacherous thrust   142 **unction** ointment. **mountebank** quack doctor   144 **cataplasm** plaster or poultice   145 **simples** herbs. **virtue** potency   146 **Under the moon** i.e., anywhere (with reference perhaps to the belief that herbs gathered at night had a special power)   148 **gall** graze, wound

85 **can well** are skilled   88 **As . . . demi-natured** as if he had been of one body and nearly of one nature (like the centaur)   89 **topped** surpassed   90 **forgery** imagining   94 **brooch** ornament   96 **confession** testimonial, admission of superiority   98 **For . . . defense** with respect to your skill and practice with your weapon   101 **escrimers** fencers   106 **sudden** immediate. **play** fence   112 **begun by time** i.e., created by the right circumstance and hence subject to change   113 **passages of proof** actual instances that prove it   114 **qualifies** weakens, moderates   116 **snuff** the charred part of a candlewick   117 **nothing . . . still** nothing remains at a constant level of perfection

KING.   Let's further think of this,
150   Weigh what convenience both of time and means
       May fit us to our shape.° If this should fail,
       And that our drift look through our bad performance,°
       'Twere better not assayed. Therefore this project
       Should have a back or second, that might hold
155   If this did blast in proof.° Soft, let me see.
       We'll make a solemn wager on your cunnings°—
       I ha 't!
       When in your motion you are hot and dry—
       As° make your bouts more violent to that end—
160   And that he calls for drink, I'll have prepared him
       A chalice for the nonce,° whereon but sipping,
       If he by chance escape your venomed stuck,°
       Our purpose may hold there. [A cry within.] But stay,
           what noise?

           Enter Queen.

QUEEN.
       One woe doth tread upon another's heel,
165   So fast they follow. Your sister's drowned, Laertes.
LAERTES.   Drowned! O, where?
QUEEN.
       There is a willow grows askant° the brook,
       That shows his hoar leaves° in the glassy stream;
       Therewith fantastic garlands did she make
170   Of crowflowers, nettles, daisies, and long purples,°
       That liberal° shepherds give a grosser name,°
       But our cold° maids do dead men's fingers call them.
       There on the pendent° boughs her crownet° weeds
       Clamb'ring to hang, an envious sliver° broke,
175   When down her weedy° trophies and herself
       Fell in the weeping brook. Her clothes spread wide,
       And mermaidlike awhile they bore her up,
       Which time she chanted snatches of old lauds,°
       As one incapable of° her own distress,
180   Or like a creature native and endued°
       Unto that element. But long it could not be
       Till that her garments, heavy with their drink,
       Pulled the poor wretch from her melodious lay

To muddy death.
LAERTES.   Alas, then she is drowned?
QUEEN.   Drowned, drowned.   185
LAERTES.
       Too much of water hast thou, poor Ophelia,
       And therefore I forbid my tears. But yet
       It is our trick;° nature her custom holds,
       Let shame say what it will. [He weeps.] When these
           are gone,
       The woman will be out.° Adieu, my lord.   190
       I have a speech of fire that fain would blaze,
       But that this folly douts° it.   Exit.
KING.   Let's follow, Gertrude.
       How much I had to do to calm his rage!
       Now fear I this will give it start again;
       Therefore let's follow.   Exeunt.

5 . 1 °   Enter two Clowns° [with spades and mattocks].

FIRST CLOWN.   Is she to be buried in Christian burial, when
       she willfully seeks her own salvation?°
SECOND CLOWN.   I tell thee she is; therefore make her grave
       straight.° The crowner° hath sat on her,° and finds it°
       Christian burial.   5
FIRST CLOWN.   How can that be, unless she drowned herself
       in her own defense?
SECOND CLOWN.   Why, 'tis found so.°
FIRST CLOWN.   It must be se offendendo,° it cannot be else.
       For here lies the point: if I drown myself wittingly, it ar-   10
       gues an act, and an act hath three branches—it is to act,
       to do, and to perform. Argal,° she drowned herself wit-
       tingly.
SECOND CLOWN.   Nay, but hear you, goodman° delver—
FIRST CLOWN.   Give me leave. Here lies the water; good.   15
       Here stands the man; good. If the man go to this water
       and drown himself, it is, will he, nill he,° he goes, mark

---

151 **shape** part we propose to act   152 **drift . . . performance** intention should be made visible by our bungling   155 **blast in
proof** burst in the test (like a cannon)   156 **cunnings** respective
skills   159 **As** i.e., and you should   161 **nonce** occasion   162
stuck thrust. (From *stoccado,* a fencing term.)   167 **askant** aslant
168 **hoar leaves** white or gray undersides of the leaves   170 **long
purples** early purple orchids   171 **liberal** free-spoken. **a grosser
name** (The testicle-resembling tubers of the orchid, which also in
some cases resemble *dead men's fingers,* have earned various slang
names like "dogstones" and "cullions.")   172 **cold** chaste   173
pendent overhanging. **crownet** made into a chaplet or coronet
174 **envious sliver** malicious branch   175 **weedy** i.e., of plants
178 **lauds** hymns   179 **incapable of** lacking capacity to apprehend
180 **endued** adapted by nature

188 **It is our trick** i.e., weeping is our natural way (when sad)
189–190 **When . . . out** when my tears are all shed, the woman in
me will be expended, satisfied   192 **douts** extinguishes. (The Second Quarto reads "drowns.")
5.1. Location: A churchyard.
s.d. **Clowns** rustics   2 **salvation** (A blunder for "damnation," or
perhaps a suggestion that Ophelia was taking her own shortcut to
heaven.)   4 **straight** straightaway, immediately. (But with a pun on
strait, "narrow.")   **crowner** coroner. **sat on her** conducted an inquest
on her case. **finds it** gives his official verdict that her means of
death was consistent with   8 **found so** determined so in the coroner's verdict   9 **se offendendo** (A comic mistake for *se defendendo,*
a term used in verdicts of justifiable homicide.)   12 **Argal** (Corruption of *ergo,* "therefore.")   14 **goodman** (An honorific title
often used with the name of a profession or craft.)   17 **will he, nill
he** whether he will or not, willy-nilly

you that. But if the water come to him and drown him, he
drowns not himself. Argal, he that is not guilty of his own
20   death shortens not his own life.

SECOND CLOWN. But is this law?

FIRST CLOWN. Ay, marry, is 't —crowner's quest° law.

SECOND CLOWN. Will you ha' the truth on 't? If this had not
been a gentlewoman, she should have been buried out o'
25   Christian burial.

FIRST CLOWN. Why, there thou sayst.° And the more pity
that great folk should have countenance° in this world to
drown or hang themselves, more than their even-
Christian.° Come, my spade. There is no ancient° gentle-
30   man but gardeners, ditchers, and grave makers. They hold
up° Adam's profession.

SECOND CLOWN. Was he a gentleman?

FIRST CLOWN. 'A was the first that ever bore arms.°

SECOND CLOWN. Why, he had none.

35   FIRST CLOWN. What, art a heathen? How dost thou understand the Scripture? The Scripture says Adam digged.
Could he dig without arms?° I'll put another question to
thee. If thou answerest me not to the purpose, confess
thyself°—

40   SECOND CLOWN. Go to.

FIRST CLOWN. What is he that builds stronger than either
the mason, the shipwright, or the carpenter?

SECOND CLOWN. The gallows maker, for that frame° out-
lives a thousand tenants.

45   FIRST CLOWN. I like thy wit well, in good faith. The gallows
does well. But how does it well? It does well° to those that
do ill. Now thou dost ill to say the gallows is built
stronger than the church. Argal, the gallows may do well
to thee. To 't again, come.

50   SECOND CLOWN. "Who builds stronger than a mason, a
shipwright, or a carpenter?"

FIRST CLOWN. Ay, tell me that, and unyoke.°

SECOND CLOWN. Marry, now I can tell.

FIRST CLOWN. To 't.

55   SECOND CLOWN. Mass,° I cannot tell.

Enter Hamlet and Horatio [at a distance].

FIRST CLOWN. Cudgel thy brains no more about it, for your
dull ass will not mend his pace with beating; and when
you are asked this question next, say "a grave maker." The

houses he makes last till doomsday. Go get thee in and
fetch me a stoup° of liquor.   60

[Exit Second Clown. First Clown digs.]
Song.

"In youth, when I did love, did love,°
    Methought it was very sweet,
To contract—O—the time for—a—my behove,°
    O, methought there—a—was nothing—a—
        meet."°

HAMLET. Has this fellow no feeling of his business, 'a° sings   65
in grave-making?

HORATIO. Custom hath made it in him a property of easiness.°

HAMLET. 'Tis e'en so. The hand of little employment hath
the daintier sense.°   70

FIRST CLOWN.

                                                              Song.

"But age with his stealing steps
    Hath clawed me in his clutch,
And hath shipped me into the land,°
    As if I had never been such."

[He throws up a skull.]

HAMLET. That skull had a tongue in it and could sing once.   75
How the knave jowls° it to the ground, as if 'twere Cain's
jawbone, that did the first murder! This might be the pate
of a politician,° which this ass now o'erreaches,° one that
would circumvent God, might it not?

HORATIO. It might, my lord.   80

HAMLET. Or of a courtier, which could say, "Good morrow, sweet lord! How dost thou, sweet lord?" This
might be my Lord Such-a-one, that praised my Lord
Such-a-one's horse when 'a meant to beg it, might it
not?   85

HORATIO. Ay, my lord.

HAMLET. Why, e'en so, and now my Lady Worm's, chapless,° and knocked about the mazard° with a sexton's
spade. Here's fine revolution,° an° we had the trick to
see° 't. Did these bones cost no more the breeding but° to   90

---

60 stoup two-quart measure   **61 In . . . love** (This and the two following stanzas with nonsensical variations, are from a poem attributed to Lord Vaux and printed in *Tottel's Miscellany*, 1557. The *O*
and *a* [for "ah"] seemingly are the grunts of the digger.)   **63 To contract . . . behove** i.e., to shorten the time for my own advantage.
(Perhaps he means to *prolong* it.)   **64 meet** suitable, i.e., more suitable   **65 'a** that he   **67–68 property of easiness** something he
can do easily and indifferently   **70 daintier sense** more delicate
sense of feeling   **73 into the land** i.e., toward my grave (?) (But
note the lack of rhyme in *steps, land.*)   **76 jowls** dashes (with a pun
on *jowl*, "jawbone")   **78 politician** schemer, plotter.   **o'erreaches**
circumvents, gets the better of (with a quibble on the literal sense)
87–88 chapless having no lower jaw.   **mazard** i.e., head. (Literally, a
drinking vessel.)   **89 revolution** turn of Fortune's wheel, change.
an if   **89–90 trick to see** knack of seeing.   **cost . . . but** involve so
little expense and care in upbringing that we may

---

22 quest inquest   **26 there thou sayst** i.e., that's right   **27 countenance** privilege   **28–29 even-Christian** fellow Christians. **ancient** going back to ancient times   **31 hold up** maintain   **33 bore
arms** (To be entitled to bear a coat of arms would make Adam a gentleman, but as one who bore a spade, our common ancestor was an
ordinary delver in the earth.)   **37 arms** i.e., the arms of the body
38–39 confess thyself (The saying continues, "and be hanged.")
43 frame (1) gallows (2) structure   **46 does well** (1) is an apt answer (2) does a good turn   **52 unyoke** i.e., after this great effort, you
may unharness the team of your wits   **55 Mass** by the Mass

play at loggets° with them? Mine ache to think on 't.

FIRST CLOWN.   *Song.*

   "A picksax and a spade, a spade,
     For and° a shrouding sheet;
   O, a pit of clay for to be made
95   For such a guest is meet."

                      [*He throws up another skull.*]

HAMLET. There's another. Why may not that be the skull of
a lawyer? Where be his quiddities° now, his quillities,° his
cases, his tenures,° and his tricks? Why does he suffer this
mad knave now to knock him about the sconce° with a
100 dirty shovel, and will not tell him of his action of battery?° Hum, this fellow might be in 's time a great buyer of
land, with his statutes, his recognizances,° his fines, his
double° vouchers,° his recoveries.° Is this the fine of his
fines and the recovery of his recoveries, to have his fine
105 pate full of fine dirt?° Will his vouchers vouch him no
more of his purchases, and double ones too, than the
length and breadth of a pair of indentures?° The very
conveyances° of his lands will scarcely lie in this box,°
and must th' inheritor° himself have no more, ha?

110 HORATIO. Not a jot more, my lord.

HAMLET. Is not parchment made of sheepskins?

HORATIO. Ay, my lord, and of calves' skins too.

HAMLET. They are sheep and calves which seek out assurance in that.° I will speak to this fellow.—Whose grave's
115 this, sirrah?°

FIRST CLOWN. Mine, sir.

   [*Sings.*] "O, pit of clay for to be made
    For such a guest is meet."

HAMLET. I think it be thine, indeed, for thou liest in 't.

120 FIRST CLOWN. You lie out on 't, sir, and therefore 'tis not
yours. For my part, I do not lie in t', yet it is mine.

HAMLET. Thou dost lie in 't, to be in 't and say it is thine.
'Tis for the dead, not for the quick;° therefore thou liest.

FIRST CLOWN. 'Tis a quick lie, sir; 'twill away again from me
to you.   125

HAMLET. What man dost thou dig it for?

FIRST CLOWN. For no man, sir.

HAMLET. What woman, then?

FIRST CLOWN. For none, neither.

HAMLET. Who is to be buried in 't?   130

FIRST CLOWN. One that was a woman, sir, but, rest her soul,
she's dead.

HAMLET. How absolute° the knave is! We must speak by the
card°, or equivocation° will undo us. By the Lord, Horatio, this three years I have took° note of it: the age is   135
grown so picked° that the toe of the peasant comes so
near the heel of the courtier, he galls his kibe.°—How
long hast thou been grave maker?

FIRST CLOWN. Of all the days i' the year, I came to 't that
day that our last king Hamlet overcame Fortinbras.   140

HAMLET. How long is that since?

FIRST CLOWN. Cannot you tell that? Every fool can tell that.
It was that very day that young Hamlet was born—he
that is mad and sent into England.

HAMLET. Ay, marry, why was he sent into England?   145

FIRST CLOWN. Why, because 'a was mad. 'A shall recover his
wits there, or if 'a do not, 'tis no great matter there.

HAMLET. Why?

FIRST CLOWN. 'Twill not be seen in him there. There the
men are as mad as he.   150

HAMLET. How came he mad?

FIRST CLOWN. Very strangely, they say.

HAMLET. How strangely?

FIRST CLOWN. Faith, e'en with losing his wits.

HAMLET. Upon what ground?°   155

FIRST CLOWN. Why, here in Denmark. I have been sexton
here, man and boy, thirty years.

HAMLET. How long will a man lie i' th' earth ere he rot?

FIRST CLOWN. Faith, if 'a be not rotten before 'a die—as we
have many pocky° corpses nowadays, that will scarce   160
hold the laying in°—'a will last you° some eight year or
nine year. A tanner will last you nine year.

HAMLET. Why he more than another?

FIRST CLOWN. Why, sir, his hide is so tanned with his trade
that 'a will keep out water a great while, and your water is a 165
sore° decayer of your whoreson° dead body. [*He picks up a*

---

91 **loggets** a game in which pieces of hard wood shaped like Indian
clubs or bowling pins are thrown to lie as near as possible to a stake
93 **For and** and moreover   97 **quiddities** subtleties, quibbles.
(From Latin *quid,* "a thing.") **quillities** verbal niceties, subtle distinctions. (Variation of *quiddities.*)   98 **tenures** the holding of a piece of
property or office, or the conditions or period of such holding   99
sconce head   100–101 **action of battery** lawsuit about physical assault   102 **statutes, recognizances** legal documents guaranteeing a
debt by attaching land and property   103 **fines . . . recoveries** ways
of converting entailed estates into "fee simple" or freehold. **double**
signed by two signatories. **vouchers** guarantees of the legality of a
title to real estate   104–105 **fine of his fines . . . fine pate . . . fine
dirt** end of his legal maneuvers . . . elegant head . . . minutely sifted
dirt   107 **pair of indentures** legal document drawn up in duplicate
on a single sheet and then cut apart on a zigzag line so that each pair
was uniquely matched. (Hamlet may refer to two rows of teeth or
dentures.)   108 **conveyances** deeds. **box** (1) deed box (2) coffin.
("Skull" has been suggested.)   109 **inheritor** possessor, owner
113–114 **assurance in that** safety in legal parchments   115 **sirrah**
(A term of address to inferiors.)   123 **quick** living

133 **absolute** strict, precise   133–134 **by the card** i.e., with precision. (Literally, by the mariner's compass-card, on which the points of
the compass were marked.) **equivocation** ambiguity in the use of terms
135 **took** taken   136 **picked** refined, fastidious   137 **galls his kibe**
chafes the courtier's chilblain   155 **ground** cause. (But, in the next
line, the gravedigger takes the word in the sense of "land," "country.")
160 **pocky** rotten, diseased. (Literally, with the pox, or syphilis.)
161 **hold the laying in** hold together long enough to be interred. **last
you** last. (*You* is used colloquially here and in the following lines.)
167 **sore** i.e., terrible, great. **whoreson** i.e., vile, scurvy

skull.] Here's a skull now hath lien you° i' th' earth three-
and-twenty years.

170 HAMLET. Whose was it?

FIRST CLOWN. A whoreson mad fellow's it was. Whose do
you think it was?

HAMLET. Nay, I know not.

FIRST CLOWN. A pestilence on him for a mad rogue! 'A
175 poured a flagon of Rhenish° on my head once. This same
skull, sir, was, sir, Yorick's skull, the King's jester.

HAMLET. This?

FIRST CLOWN. E'en that.

HAMLET. Let me see. [*He takes the skull.*] Alas, poor Yorick! I
180 knew him, Horatio, a fellow of infinite jest, of most excellent fancy. He hath bore° me on his back a thousand
times, and now how abhorred in my imagination it is! My
gorge rises° at it. Here hung those lips that I have kissed I
know not how oft. Where be your gibes now? Your gam-
185 bols, your songs, your flashes of merriment that were
wont° to set the table on a roar? Not one now, to mock
your own grinning?° Quite chopfallen?° Now get you to
my lady's chamber and tell her, let her paint an inch
thick, to this favor° she must come. Make her laugh at
190 that. Prithee, Horatio, tell me one thing.

HORATIO. What's that, my lord?

HAMLET. Dost thou think Alexander looked o' this fashion
i' th' earth?

HORATIO. E'en so.

195 HAMLET. And smelt so? Pah! [*He throws down the skull.*]

HORATIO. E'en so, my lord.

HAMLET. To what base uses we may return, Horatio! Why
may not imagination trace the noble dust of Alexander
till 'a find it stopping a bunghole?°

200 HORATIO. 'Twere to consider too curiously° to consider so.

HAMLET. No, faith, not a jot, but to follow him thither with
modesty° enough, and likelihood to lead it. As thus:
Alexander died, Alexander was buried, Alexander retur-
neth to dust, the dust is earth, of earth we make loam,°
205 and why of that loam whereto he was converted might
they not stop a beer barrel?

Imperious° Caesar, dead and turned to clay,
Might stop a hole to keep the wind away.
O, that that earth which kept the world in awe
210 Should patch a wall t' expel the winter's flaw!°

Enter King, Queen, Laertes, and the corpse [*of
Ophelia, in procession, with Priest, lords, etc.*].

But soft, but soft° awhile! Here comes the King,
The Queen, the courtiers. Who is this they follow?
And with such maimèd° rites? This doth betoken
The corpse they follow did with desperate hand
Fordo° its own life. 'Twas of some estate.°   215
Couch we° awhile and mark.

[*He and Horatio conceal themselves.
Ophelia's body is taken to the grave.*]

LAERTES. What ceremony else?

HAMLET [*to Horatio*].
That is Laertes, a very noble youth. Mark.

LAERTES. What ceremony else?

PRIEST.
Her obsequies have been as far enlarged   220
As we have warranty.° Here death was doubtful,
And but that great command o'ersways the order°
She should in ground unsanctified been lodged°
Till the last trumpet. For° charitable prayers,
Shards,° flints, and pebbles should be thrown on her. 225
Yet here she is allowed her virgin crants,°
Her maiden strewments, and the bringing home
Of bell and burial.°

LAERTES.
Must there no more be done?

PRIEST.   No more be done.
We should profane the service of the dead   230
To sing a requiem and such rest° to her
As to peace-parted souls.°

LAERTES.   Lay her i' th' earth,
And from her fair and unpolluted flesh
May violets° spring! I tell thee, churlish priest,
A ministering angel shall my sister be   235
When thou liest howling.°

HAMLET [*to Horatio*].   What, the fair Ophelia!

QUEEN [*scattering flowers*]. Sweets to the sweet! Farewell.
I hoped thou shouldst have been my Hamlet's wife.
I thought thy bride-bed to have decked, sweet maid,
And not t' have strewed thy grave.

LAERTES.   O, treble woe   240

---

168 **lien you** lain. (See the note at line 163.)   175 **Rhenish** Rhine
wine   181 **bore** borne   183 **My gorge rises** i.e., I feel nauseated
185–186 **were wont** used   186–187 **mock your own grinning**
mock at the way your skull seems to be grinning (just as you used to
mock at yourself and those who grinned at you)   187 **chopfallen**
(1) lacking the lower jaw (2) dejected   189 **favor** aspect, appearance   199 **bunghole** hole for filling or emptying a cask   200 **curiously** minutely   202 **modesty** plausible moderation   204 **loam**
mortar consisting chiefly of moistened clay and straw   207 **Imperious** imperial   210 **flaw** gust of wind

211 **soft** i.e., wait, be careful   213 **maimèd** mutilated, incomplete
215 **Fordo** destroy. **estate** rank   216 **Couch we** let's hide, lie low
221 **warranty** i.e., ecclesiastical authority   222 **great . . . order**
orders from on high overrule the prescribed procedures   223 **She
should . . . lodged** she should have been buried in unsanctified
ground   224 **For** in place of   225 **Shards** broken bits of pottery
226 **crants** garlands betokening maidenhood   227 **strewments**
flowers strewn on a coffin   227–228 **bringing . . . burial** laying
the body to rest, to the sound of the bell   231 **such rest** i.e., to
pray for such rest   232 **peace-parted souls** those who have died at
peace with God   234 **violets** (See 4.5.187 and note.)   236 **howling** i.e., in hell

Fall ten times treble on that cursèd head
Whose wicked deed thy most ingenious sense°
Deprived thee of! Hold off the earth awhile,
Till I have caught her once more in mine arms.
          [*He leaps into the grave and embraces Ophelia.*]
245   Now pile your dust upon the quick and dead,
Till of this flat a mountain you have made
T' o'ertop old Pelion or the skyish head
Of blue Olympus.°
HAMLET [*coming forward*]. What is he whose grief
Bears such an emphasis,° whose phrase of sorrow
250   Conjures the wandering stars° and makes them stand
Like wonder-wounded° hearers? This is I,
Hamlet the Dane.°
LAERTES [*grappling with him*]. The devil take thy soul!
HAMLET. Thou pray'st not well.
255   I prithee, take thy fingers from my throat,
For though I am not splenitive° and rash,
Yet have I in me something dangerous,
Which let thy wisdom fear. Hold off thy hand.
KING. Pluck them asunder.
260   QUEEN. Hamlet, Hamlet!
ALL. Gentlemen!
HORATIO. Good my lord, be quiet.
                    [*Hamlet and Laertes are parted.*]
HAMLET.
Why, I will fight with him upon this theme
Until my eyelids will no longer wag.°
265   QUEEN. O my son, what theme?
HAMLET.
I loved Ophelia. Forty thousand brothers
Could not with all their quantity of love
Make up my sum. What wilt thou do for her?
KING. O, he is mad, Laertes.
270   QUEEN. For love of God, forbear him.°
HAMLET.
'Swounds°, show me what thou'lt do.

Woo't° weep? Woo't fight? Woo't fast? Woo't tear thyself?
Woo't drink up° eisel?° Eat a crocodile?°
I'll do 't. Dost come here to whine?
To outface me with leaping in her grave?   275
Be buried quick° with her, and so will I.
And if thou prate of mountains, let them throw
Millions of acres on us, till our ground,
Singeing his pate° against the burning zone,°
Make Ossa° like a wart! Nay, an° thou'lt mouth,°   280
I'll rant as well as thou.
QUEEN.   This is mere° madness,
And thus awhile the fit will work on him;
Anon, as patient as the female dove
When that her golden couplets° are disclosed,°
His silence will sit drooping.
HAMLET.   Hear you, sir.   285
What is the reason that you use me thus?
I loved you ever. But it is no matter.
Let Hercules himself do what he may,
The cat will mew, and dog will have his day.°
                    Exit Hamlet.
KING.
I pray thee, good Horatio, wait upon him.   290
                    [*Exit*] *Horatio.*
[*To Laertes.*] Strengthen your patience in° our last night's
    speech;
We'll put the matter to the present push.°—
Good Gertrude, set some watch over your son.—
This grave shall have a living° monument.
An hour of quiet° shortly shall we see;   295
Till then, in patience our proceeding be.   *Exeunt.*

5.2 °   *Enter Hamlet and Horatio.*

HAMLET.
So much for this, sir; now shall you see the other.°

---

242 **ingenious sense** a mind that is quick, alert, of fine qualities
247–248 Pelion, Olympus sacred mountains in the north of Thessaly; see also *Ossa*, below, at line 281   **249 emphasis** i.e., rhetorical and florid emphasis. (*Phrase* has a similar rhetorical connotation.)   **250 wandering stars** planets   **251 wonder-wounded** struck with amazement   **252 the Dane** (This title normally signifies the King; see 1.1.17 and note.)   **253 s.d. grappling with him** The testimony of the First Quarto that "*Hamlet leaps in after Laertes*" and the "Elegy on Burbage" ("Oft have I seen him leap into the grave") seem to indicate one way in which this fight was staged; however, the difficulty of fitting two contenders and Ophelia's body into a confined space (probably the trapdoor) suggests to many editors the alternative, that Laertes jumps out of the grave to attack Hamlet.)   **256 splenitive** quick-tempered   **264 wag** move. (A fluttering eyelid is a conventional sign that life has not yet gone.)   **270 forbear him** leave him alone   **271 'Swounds** by His (Christ's) wounds

272 **Woo't** wilt thou   273 **drink up** drink deeply. **eisel** vinegar. **crocodile** (Crocodiles were tough and dangerous, and were supposed to shed hypocritical tears.)   276 **quick** alive   279 **his pate** its head, i.e., top. **burning zone** zone in the celestial sphere containing the sun's orbit, between the tropics of Cancer and Capricorn   280 **Ossa** another mountain in Thessaly. (In their war against the Olympian gods, the giants attempted to heap Ossa on Pelion to scale Olympus.)   **an** if. **mouth** i.e., rant   281 **mere** utter   284 **golden couplets** two baby pigeons, covered with yellow down. **disclosed** hatched   288–289 **Let . . . day** i.e., (1) even Hercules couldn't stop Laertes' theatrical rant (2) I, too, will have my turn; i.e., despite any blustering attempts at interference, every person will sooner or later do what he or she must do   291 **in** i.e., by recalling   292 **present push** immediate test   294 **living** lasting. (For Laertes' private understanding, Claudius also hints that Hamlet's death will serve as such a monument.)   **295 hour of quiet** time free of conflict
5.2. Location. The castle.
1 **see the other** hear the other news

You do remember all the circumstance?
HORATIO. Remember it, my lord!
HAMLET.
   Sir, in my heart there was a kind of fighting
5   That would not let me sleep. Methought I lay
   Worse than the mutines° in the bilboes.° Rashly,°
   And praised be rashness for it—let us know°
   Our indiscretion °sometimes serves as well
   When our deep plots do pall,° and that should
     learn° us
10   There's a divinity that shapes our ends,
   Rough-hew° them how we will—
HORATIO.   That is most certain.
HAMLET. Up from my cabin,
   My sea-gown° scarfed° about me, in the dark
   Groped I to find out them,° had my desire,
15   Fingered° their packet, and in fine° withdrew
   To mine own room again, making so bold,
   My fears forgetting manners, to unseal
   Their grand commission; where I found, Horatio—
   Ah, royal knavery!—an exact command,
20   Larded° with many several° sorts of reasons
   Importing° Denmark's health and England's too,
   With, ho! such bugs° and goblins in my life,°
   That on the supervise,° no leisure bated,°
   No, not to stay° the grinding of the ax,
   My head should be struck off.
25 HORATIO.   Is 't possible?
HAMLET [*giving a document*].
   Here's the commission. Read it at more leisure.
   But will thou hear now how I did proceed?
HORATIO. I beseech you.
HAMLET.
   Being thus benetted round with villainies—
30   Ere I could make a prologue to my brains,
   They had begun the play°—I sat me down,
   Devised a new commission, wrote it fair.°
   I once did hold it, as our statists° do,
   A baseness° to write fair, and labored much
35   How to forget that learning, but, sir, now

It did me yeoman's° service. Wilt thou know
   Th' effect° of what I wrote?
HORATIO.   Ay, good my lord.
HAMLET.
   An earnest conjuration° from the King,
   As England was his faithful tributary,
   As love between them like the palm° might flourish,   40
   As peace should still° her wheaten garland° wear
   And stand a comma° 'tween their amities,
   And many suchlike "as"es° of great charge,°
   That on the view and knowing of these contents,
   Without debatement further more or less,   45
   He should those bearers put to sudden death,
   Not shriving time° allowed.
HORATIO.   How was this sealed?
HAMLET.
   Why, even in that was heaven ordinant.°
   I had my father's signet° in my purse,
   Which was the model° of that Danish seal;   50
   Folded the writ° up in the form of th' other,
   Subscribed° it, gave 't th' impression,° placed it safely,
   The changeling° never known. Now, the next day
   Was our sea fight, and what to this was sequent°
   Thou knowest already.   55
HORATIO.
   So Guildenstern and Rosencrantz go to 't.
HAMLET.
   Why, man, they did make love to this employment.
   They are not near my conscience. Their defeat°
   Does by their own insinuation° grow.
   'Tis dangerous when the baser° nature comes   60
   Between the pass° and fell° incensèd points
   Of mighty opposites.°
HORATIO.   Why, what a king is this!
HAMLET.
   Does it not, think thee, stand me now° upon—
   He that hath killed my king and whored my mother,
   Popped in between th' election° and my hopes,   65

---

36 yeoman's i.e., substantial, faithful, loyal **37 effect** purport
38 conjuration entreaty **40 palm** (An image of health; see Psalm
92:12.) **41 still** always. **wheaten** garland (Symbolic of fruitful
agriculture, of peace and plenty.) **42 comma** (Indicating continuity, link.) **43 "as"es** (1) the "where-ases" of a formal document
(2) asses. **charge** (1) important (2) burden (appropriate to asses)
47 shriving time time for confession and absolution **48 ordinant**
directing **49 signet** small seal **50 model** replica **51 writ** writing **52 Subscribed** signed (with forged signature). **impression** i.e.,
with a wax seal **53 changeling** i.e., substituted letter. (Literally, a
fairy child substituted for a human one.) **54 was sequent** followed
58 defeat destruction **59 insinuation** intrusive intervention,
sticking their noses in my business **60 baser** of lower social station **61 pass** thrust. **fell** fierce **62 opposites** antagonists **63
stand me now upon** become incumbent on me now **65 election**
(The Danish monarch was "elected" by a small number of high-
ranking electors.)

---

6 mutines mutineers. **bilboes** shackles. **Rashly** on impulse. (This
adverb goes with lines 12 ff.) **7 know** acknowledge **8 indiscretion** lack of foresight and judgment (not an indiscreet act) **9 pall**
fail, falter, go stale. **learn** teach **11 Rough-hew** shape roughly
13 sea-gown seaman's coat. **scarfed** loosely wrapped **14 them** i.e.,
Rosencrantz and Guildenstern **15 Fingered** pilfered, pinched. **in
fine** finally, in conclusion **20 Larded** garnished. **several** different
21 Importing relating to **22 bugs** bugbears, hobgloblins. **in my
life** i.e., to be feared if I were allowed to live **23 supervise** reading. **leisure bated** delay allowed **24 stay** await **30–31 Ere . . .
play** before I could consciously turn my brain to the matter, it had
started working on a plan **32 fair** in a clear hand **33 statists**
statesmen **34 baseness** i.e., lower-class trait

Thrown out his angle° for my proper° life,
And with such cozenage°—is 't not perfect conscience
To quit° him with this arm? And is 't not to be damned
To let this canker° of our nature come
70 In° further evil?

HORATIO.
It must be shortly known to him from England
What is the issue of the business there.

HAMLET.
It will be short. The interim is mine,
And a man's life's no more than to say "one."°
75 But I am very sorry, good Horatio,
That to Laertes I forgot myself,
For by the image of my cause I see
The portraiture of his. I'll court his favors.
But, sure, the bravery° of his grief did put me
Into a tow'ring passion.

80 HORATIO.   Peace, who comes here?

        Enter a Courtier [Osric].

OSRIC. Your lordship is right welcome back to Denmark.
HAMLET. I humbly thank you, sir. [*To Horatio.*] Dost know
    this water fly?
HORATIO. No, my good lord.
85 HAMLET. Thy state is the more gracious, for 'tis a vice to
    know him. He hath much land, and fertile. Let a beast be
    lord of beasts, and his crib° shall stand at the King's
    mess.° 'Tis a chuff,° but, as I say, spacious in the posses-
    sion of dirt.
90 OSRIC. Sweet lord, if your lordship were at leisure, I should
    impart a thing to you from His Majesty.
HAMLET. I will receive it, sir, with all diligence of spirit. Put
    your bonnet° to his right use; 'tis for the head.
OSRIC. I thank your lordship, it is very hot.
95 HAMLET. No, believe me, 'tis very cold. The wind is
    northerly.
OSRIC. It is indifferent° cold, my lord, indeed.
HAMLET. But yet methinks it is very sultry and hot for my
    complexion.°
100 OSRIC. Exceedingly, my lord. It is very sultry as 'twere —I
    cannot tell how. My lord, His Majesty bade me signify to
    you that 'a has laid a great wager on your head. Sir, this is
    the matter—
HAMLET. I beseech you, remember.
        [*Hamlet moves him to put on his hat.*]

OSRIC. Nay, good my lord; for my ease,° in good faith. Sir, 105
    here is newly come to court Laertes—believe me, an ab-
    solute° gentleman, full of most excellent differences,° of
    very soft society° and great showing.° Indeed, to speak
    feelingly° of him, he is the card° or calendar° of gentry,°
    for you shall find in him the continent of what part a gen- 110
    tleman would see.°
HAMLET. Sir, his definement° suffers no perdition° in
    you,° though I know to divide him inventorially°
    would dozy° th' arithmetic of memory, and yet but yaw°
    neither° in respect of° his quick sail. But, in the verity 115
    of extolment,° I take him to be a soul of great article,°
    and his infusion° of such dearth and rareness° as, to
    make true diction° of him, his semblable° is his mirror
    and who else would trace° him his umbrage,° nothing
    more.   120
OSRIC. Your lordship speaks most infallibly of him.
HAMLET. The concernancy,° sir? Why do we wrap the gen-
    tleman in our more rawer breath?°
OSRIC. Sir?
HORATIO. Is 't not possible to understand in another 125
    tongue?° You will do 't,° sir, really.
HAMLET. What imports the nomination° of this gentle-
    man?
OSRIC. Of Laertes?
HORATIO [*to Hamlet*]. His purse is empty already; all 's 130
    golden words are spent.
HAMLET. Of him, sir.
OSRIC. I know you are not ignorant—
HAMLET. I would you did, sir. Yet in faith if you did, it would
    not much approve° me. Well, sir?   135

66 **angle** fishhook. **proper** very   67 **cozenage** trickery   68 **quit**
requite, pay back   69 **canker** ulcer   69–70 **come in** grow into
74 **a man's . . . "one"** one's whole life occupies such a short time,
only as long as it takes to count to 1   79 **bravery** bravado   86–88
Let . . . mess i.e., if a man, no matter how beastlike, is as rich in
livestock and possessions as Osric, he may eat at the King's table
87 **crib** manger   88 **chuff** boor, churl. (The Second Quarto
spelling, *chough,* is a variant spelling that also suggests the meaning
here of "chattering jackdaw.")   93 **bonnet** any kind of cap or hat.
his its   97 **indifferent** somewhat   99 **complexion** temperament

105 **for my ease** (A conventional reply declining the invitation to
put his hat back on.)   106–107 **absolute** perfect   107 **differences** special qualities   108 **soft society** agreeable manners. **great
showing** distinguished appearance   109 **feelingly** with just perception. **card** chart, map. **calendar** guide   110 **gentry** good breeding   110–111 **the continent . . . see** one who contains in him all
the qualities a gentleman would like to see. (A *continent* is that
which contains.)   112 **definement** definition. (Hamlet proceeds
to mock Osric by throwing his lofty diction back at him.) **perdition**
loss, diminution   113 **you** your description. **divide him inventori-
ally** enumerate his graces   114 **dozy** dizzy. **yaw** swing unsteadily
off course. (Said of a ship.)   115 **neither** for all that. **in respect of**
in comparison with   115–116 **in . . . extolment** in true praise (of
him)   116 **of great article** one with many articles in his inventory
117 **infusion** essence, character infused into him by nature. **dearth
and rareness** rarity   117–118 **make true diction** speak truly
118 **semblable** only true likeness   119 **who . . . trace** any other
person who would wish to follow. **umbrage** shadow   122 **concernancy** import, relevance   123 **rawer breath** unrefined speech that
can only come short in praising him   125–126 **to understand . . .
tongue** i.e., for you, Osric, to understand when someone else speaks
your language. (Horatio twits Osric for not being able to understand
the kind of flowery speech he himself uses, when Hamlet speaks in
such a vein. Alternatively, all this could be said to Hamlet.)   126
You will do 't i.e., you can if you try, or, you may well have to try (to
speak plainly)   127 **nomination** naming   135 **approve** commend

OSRIC. You are not ignorant of what excellence Laertes
is—

HAMLET. I dare not confess that, lest I should compare with
him in excellence. But to know a man well were to know
140   himself.°

OSRIC. I mean, sir, for° his weapon; but in the imputation
laid on him by them,° in his meed° he's unfellowed.°

HAMLET. What's his weapon?

OSRIC. Rapier and dagger.

145 HAMLET. That's two of his weapons—but well.°

OSRIC. The King, sir, hath wagered with him six Barbary
horses, against the which he° has impawned,° as I take
it, six French rapiers and poniards,° with their assigns,°
as girdle, hangers,° and so.° Three of the carriages,° in
150   faith, are very dear to fancy,° very responsive° to the
hilts, most delicate° carriages, and of very liberal conceit.°

HAMLET. What call you the carriages?

HORATIO [to Hamlet]. I knew you must be edified by the
155   margent° ere you had done.

OSRIC. The carriages, sir, are the hangers.

HAMLET. The phrase would be more germane to the matter
if we could carry a cannon by our sides; I would it might
be hangers till then. But, on: six Barbary horses against
160   six French swords, their assigns, and three liberal-con-
ceited carriages; that's the French bet against the Danish.
Why is this impawned, as you call it?

OSRIC. The King, sir, hath laid,° sir, that in a dozen passes°
between yourself and him, he shall not exceed you three
165   hits. He hath laid on twelve for nine, and it would come
to immediate trial, if your lordship would vouchsafe the
answer.°

HAMLET. How if I answer no?

OSRIC. I mean, my lord, the opposition of your person in
170   trial.

HAMLET. Sir, I will walk here in the hall. If it please His
Majesty, it is the breathing time° of day with me. Let° the
foils be brought, the gentlemen willing, and the King
hold his purpose, I will win for him an I can; if not, I will
gain nothing but my shame and the odd hits.   175

OSRIC. Shall I deliver you° so?

HAMLET. To this effect, sir—after what flourish your nature
will.

OSRIC. I commend° my duty to your lordship.

HAMLET. Yours, yours. [Exit Osric.] 'A does well to commend   180
it himself; there are no tongues else for 's turn.°

HORATIO. This lapwing° runs away with the shell on his
head.

HAMLET. 'A did comply with his dug° before 'a sucked it.
Thus has he—and many more of the same breed that I   185
know the drossy° age dotes on—only got the tune° of the
time and, out of an habit of encounter,° a kind of yeasty°
collection,° which carries them through and through the
most fanned and winnowed opinions;° and do° but blow
them to their trial, the bubbles are out.°   190

Enter a Lord.

LORD. My lord, His Majesty commended him to you by
young Osric, who brings back to him that you attend him
in the hall. He sends to know if your pleasure hold to play
with Laertes, or that° you will take longer time.

HAMLET. I am constant to my purposes; they follow the   195
King's pleasure. If his fitness speaks, mine is ready;° now
or whensoever, provided I be so able as now.

LORD. The King and Queen and all are coming down.

HAMLET. In happy time.°

138–140 I dare . . . himself I dare not boast of knowing Laertes'
excellence lest I seem to imply a comparable excellence in myself.
Certainly, to know another person well, one must know oneself.
141 for i.e., with   141–142 imputation . . . them reputation
given him by others   142 meed merit. unfellowed unmatched
145 but well but never mind   147 he i.e., Laertes. impawned
staked, wagered   148 poniards daggers. assigns appurtenances
149 hangers straps on the sword belt (*girdle*), from which the sword
hung. and so and so on. carriages (An affected way of saying *hangers*; literally, gun carriages.)   150 dear to fancy delightful to the
fancy. responsive corresponding closely, matching or well adjusted
151 delicate (i.e., in workmanship)   151–152 liberal conceit
elaborate design   155 margent margin of a book, place for explanatory notes   163 laid wagered. passes bouts. (The odds of the
betting are hard to explain. Possibly the King bets that Hamlet will
win at least five out of twelve, at which point Laertes raises the odds
against himself by betting he will nine.)   166–167 vouchsafe the
answer be so good as to accept the challenge. (Hamlet deliberately
takes the phase in its literal sense of replying.)

172 breathing time exercise period. Let i.e., if   176 deliver you
report what you say   179 commend commit to your favor. (A conventional salutation, but Hamlet wryly uses a more literal meaning,
"recommend," "praise," in line 180.)   181 for 's turn for his
purposes, i.e., to do it for him   182 lapwing (A proverbial type of
youthful forwardness. Also, a bird that draws intruders away from its
nest and was thought to run about with its head in the shell when
newly hatched; a seeming reference to Osric's hat.)   184 comply
. . . dug observe ceremonious formality toward his nurse's or
mother's teat   186 drossy laden with scum and impurities, frivolous. tune temper, mood, manner of speech   187 an habit of encounter a demeanor in conversing (with courtiers of his own kind)
yeasty frothy   188 collection i.e., of current phrases   188–189
carries . . . opinions sustains them right through the scrutiny of
persons whose opinions are select and refined. (Literally, like grain
separated from its chaff. Osric is both the chaff and the bubbly froth
on the surface of the liquor that is soon blown away.)   189 and do
yet do   189–190 blow . . . out test them by merely blowing on
them, and their bubbles burst   194 that if   196 If . . . ready if he
declares his readiness, my convenience waits on his   199 In happy
time (A phrase of courtesy indicating that the time is convenient.)

200 LORD. The Queen desires you to use some gentle entertain-
      ment° to Laertes before you fall to play.
    HAMLET. She well instructs me.   [*Exit Lord.*]
    HORATIO. You will lose, my lord.
    HAMLET. I do not think so. Since he went into France, I
205   have been in continual practice; I shall win at the odds.
      But thou wouldst not think how ill all's here about my
      heart; but it is no matter.
    HORATIO. Nay, good my lord—
    HAMLET. It is but foolery, but it is such a kind of gaingiving°
210   as would perhaps trouble a woman.
    HORATIO. If your mind dislike anything, obey it. I will fore-
      stall their repair° hither and say you are not fit.
    HAMLET. Not a whit, we defy augury. There is special provi-
      dence in the fall of a sparrow. If it be now, 'tis not to
215   come; if it be not to come, it will be now; if it be not now;
      yet it will come. The readiness is all. Since no man of
      aught he leaves knows, what is 't to leave betimes? Let
      be.°

          A table prepared. [Enter] trumpets, drums, and offi-
          cers with cushions; King, Queen, [Osric,] and all the
          state; foils, daggers, [and wine borne in;] and
          Laertes.

    KING.
      Come, Hamlet, come and take this hand from me.
                    [*The King puts Laertes' hand into Hamlet's.*]
    HAMLET [*to Laertes*].
220   Give me your pardon, sir. I have done you wrong,
      But pardon 't as you are a gentleman.
      This presence° knows,
      And you must needs have heard, how I am punished°
      With a sore distraction. What I have done
225   That might your nature, honor, and exception°
      Roughly awake, I here proclaim was madness.
      Was 't Hamlet wronged Laertes? Never Hamlet.
      If Hamlet from himself be ta'en away,
      And when he's not himself does wrong Laertes,
230   Then Hamlet does it not, Hamlet denies it.
      Who does it, then? His madness. If 't be so,
      Hamlet is of the faction° that is wronged;
      His madness is poor Hamlet's enemy.
      Sir, in this audience
235   Let my disclaiming from a purposed evil

      Free me so far in your most generous thoughts
      That I have° shot my arrow o'er the house
      And hurt my brother.
    LAERTES.   I am satisfied in nature,°
      Whose motive° in this case should stir me most
      To my revenge. But in my terms of honor   240
      I stand aloof, and will no reconcilement
      Till by some elder masters of known honor
      I have a voice° and precedent of peace°
      To keep my name ungored.° But till that time
      I do receive your offered love like love,   245
      And will not wrong it.
    HAMLET.   I embrace it freely,
      And will this brothers' wager frankly° play.—
      Give us the foils. Come on.
    LAERTES.   Come, one for me.
    HAMLET.
      I'll be your foil,° Laertes. In mine ignorance
      Your skill shall, like a star i' in the darkest night, 250
      Stick fiery off° indeed.
    LAERTES.   You mock me, sir.
    HAMLET. No, by this hand.
    KING.
      Give them the foils, young Osric. Cousin Hamlet,
      You know the wager?
    HAMLET.   Very well, my lord.
      Your Grace has laid the odds o'° the weaker side. 255
    KING.
      I do not fear it; I have seen you both.
      But since he is bettered,° we have therefore odds.
    LAERTES.
      This is too heavy. Let me see another.
                    [*He exchanges his foil for another.*]
    HAMLET.
      This likes me° well. These foils have all a length?
                    [*They prepare to play.*]
    OSRIC. Ay, my good lord.   260
    KING.
      Set me the stoups of wine upon that table.
      If Hamlet give the first or second hit,
      Or quit in answer of the third exchange,°

      ---

      237 That I have as if I had   **238 in nature** i.e., as to my personal
      feelings   **239 motive** prompting   **243 voice** authoritative pro-
      nouncement. **of peace** for reconciliation   **244 name ungored** rep-
      utation unwounded   **247 frankly** without ill feeling or the burden
      of rancor   **249 foil** thin metal background which sets a jewel off
      (with pun on the blunted rapier for fencing)   **251 Stick fiery off**
      stand out brilliantly   **255 laid the odds o'** bet on, backed   **257 is
      bettered** has improved; is the odds-on favorite. (Laertes' handicap is
      the "three hits" specified in line 164.)   **259 likes me** pleases me
      263 Or . . . exchange i.e., or requites Laertes in the third bout for
      having won the first two

200–201 **entertainment** greeting   209 **gaingiving** misgiving
212 **repair** coming   216–218 **Since . . . Let be** since no one has
knowledge of what he is leaving behind, what does an early death
matter after all? Enough; don't struggle against it.   222 **presence**
royal assembly   223 **punished** afflicted   225 **exception** disapproval   232 **faction** party

Let all the battlements their ordnance fire.
265 The King shall drink to Hamlet's better breath,°
And in the cup an union° shall he throw
Richer than that which four successive kings
In Denmark's crown have worn. Give me the cups,
And let the kettle° to the trumpet speak,
270 The trumpet to the cannoneer without,
The cannons to the heavens, the heaven to earth,
"Now the King drinks to Hamlet." Come, begin.
                                        Trumpets the while.
And you, the judges, bear a wary eye.
HAMLET. Come on, sir.
275 LAERTES. Come, my lord. [*The play. Hamlet scores a hit.*]
HAMLET. One.
LAERTES. No.
HAMLET. Judgment.
OSRIC.   A hit, a very palpable hit.
                        Drum, trumpets, and shot. Flourish.
                                        A piece goes off.
LAERTES. Well, again.
KING.
280   Stay, give me drink. Hamlet, this pearl is thine.
                        [*He drinks, and throws a pearl in*
                                        Hamlet's cup.]
Here's to thy health. Give him the cup.
HAMLET.
I'll play this bout first. Set it by awhile.
Come. [*They play.*] Another hit; what say you?
LAERTES. A touch, a touch, I do confess 't.
KING.
Our son shall win.
285 QUEEN.   He's fat° and scant of breath.
Here, Hamlet, take my napkin,° rub thy brows.
The Queen carouses° to thy fortune, Hamlet.
HAMLET. Good madam!
KING. Gertrude, do not drink.
QUEEN.
290   I will, my lord, I pray you pardon me.   [*She drinks.*]
KING [*aside*].
It is the poisoned cup. It is too late.
HAMLET.
I dare not drink yet, madam; by and by
QUEEN. Come, let me wipe thy face.
LAERTES [*to King*].
My lord, I'll hit him now.
KING.   I do not think 't.

LAERTES [*aside*].
And yet it is almost against my conscience.   295
HAMLET.
Come, for the third, Laertes. You do but dally.
I pray you, pass° with your best violence;
I am afeard you make a wanton of me.°
LAERTES. Say you so? Come on.   [*They play.*]
OSRIC. Nothing neither way.   300
LAERTES.
Have at you now!
        [*Laertes wounds Hamlet; then, in scuffling, they change
                        rapiers°, and Hamlet wounds Laertes.*]
KING.   Part them! They are incensed.
HAMLET.
Nay, come, again.   [*The Queen falls.*]
OSRIC.   Look to the Queen there, ho!
HORATIO.
They bleed on both sides. How is it, my lord?
OSRIC. How is 't, Laertes?
LAERTES.
Why, as a woodcock° to mine own springes, Osric;   305
I am justly killed with mine own treachery.
HAMLET.
How does the Queen?
KING.   She swoons to see them bleed.
QUEEN.
No, no, the drink, the drink—O my dear Hamlet—
The drink, the drink! I am poisoned.   [*She dies.*]
HAMLET.
O villainy! Ho, let the door be locked!   310
Treachery! Seek it out.   [*Laertes falls. Exit Osric.*]
LAERTES.
It is here, Hamlet. Hamlet, thou art slain.
No med'cine in the world can do thee good;
In thee there is not half an hour's life.
The treacherous instrument is in thy hand,   315
Unbated° and envenomed. The foul practice°
Hath turned itself on me. Lo, here I lie,
Never to rise again. Thy mother's poisoned.
I can no more. The King, the King's to blame.
HAMLET.
The point envenomed too? Then, venom, to thy work.   320
                                        [*He stabs the King.*]

---

297 pass thrust   **298 make . . . me** i.e., treat me like a spoiled child, trifle with me   **301 s.d. in scuffling,** they change rapiers (This stage direction occurs in the Folio. According to a widespread stage tradition, Hamlet receives a scratch, realizes that Laertes' sword is unbated, and accordingly forces an exchange.)   **305 woodcock** a bird, a type of stupidity or as a decoy. **springe** trap, snare   **316 Unbated** not blunted with a button. **practice** plot

265 better breath improved vigor   **266 union** pearl. (So called, according to Pliny's *Natural History*, 9, because pearls are *unique*, never identical.)   **269 kettle** kettledrum   **285 fat** not physically fit, out of training   **286 napkin** handkerchief   **287 carouses** drinks a toast

ALL. Treason! Treason!

KING.
  O, yet defend me, friends! I am but hurt.

HAMLET [*forcing the King to drink*]. Here, thou incestuous,
  murderous, damnèd Dane,
325   Drink off this potion. Is thy union° here?
  Follow my mother.   [*The King dies.*]

LAERTES.   He is justly served.
  It is a poison tempered° by himself.
  Exchange forgiveness with me, noble Hamlet.
  Mine and my father's death come not upon thee,
330   Nor thine on me!   [*He dies.*]

HAMLET.
  Heaven make thee free of it! I follow thee.
  I am dead, Horatio. Wretched Queen, adieu!
  You that look pale and tremble at this chance,°
  That are but mutes° or audience to this act,
335   Had I but time—as this fell° sergeant,° Death,
  Is strict° in his arrest°—O, I could tell you—
  But let it be. Horatio, I am dead;
  Thou livest. Report me and my cause aright
  To the unsatisfied.

HORATIO.   Never believe it.
340   I am more an antique Roman° than a Dane.
  Here's yet some liquor left.
           [*He attempts to drink from the poisoned cup.
               Hamlet prevents him.*]

HAMLET.   As thou'rt a man.
  Give me the cup! Let go! By heaven, I'll ha 't.
  O God, Horatio, what a wounded name,
  Things standing thus unknown, shall I leave
      behind me!
345   If thou didst ever hold me in thy heart,
  Absent thee from felicity awhile,
  And in this harsh world draw thy breath in pain
  To tell my story.   A *march afar off* [*and a volley within*].
     What warlike noise is this?

           Enter Osric.

OSRIC.
350   Young Fortinbras, with conquest come from Poland,
  To th' ambassadors of England gives
  This warlike volley.

HAMLET.   O, I die, Horatio!

The potent poison quite o'ercrows° my spirit.
  I cannot live to hear the news from England,
  But I do prophesy th' election lights   355
  On Fortinbras. He has my dying voice.°
  So tell him, with th' occurrents° more and less
  Which have solicited°—the rest is silence.   [*He dies.*]

HORATIO.
  Now cracks a noble heart. Good night, sweet prince,
  And flights of angels sing thee to thy rest!   360
                          [*March within.*]
  Why does the drum come hither?

      *Enter Fortinbras, with the [English] Ambassadors
      [with drum, colors, and attendants].*

FORTINBRAS.
  Where is this sight?

HORATIO.   What is it you would see?
  If aught of woe or wonder, cease your search.

FORTINBRAS.
  This quarry° cries on havoc.° O proud Death,
  What feast° is toward° in thine eternal cell,   365
  That thou so many princes at a shot
  So bloodily hast struck?

FIRST AMBASSADOR.   The sight is dismal,
  And our affairs from England come too late.
  The ears are senseless that should give us hearing,
  To tell him his commandment is fulfilled,   370
  That Rosencrantz and Guildenstern are dead.
  Where should we have our thanks?

HORATIO.   Not from his° mouth,
  Had it th' ability of life to thank you.
  He never gave commandment for their death.
  But since, so jump° upon this bloody question,°   375
  You from the Polack wars, and you from England,
  Are here arrived, give order that these bodies
  High on a stage° be placèd to the view,
  And let me speak to th' yet unknowing world
  How these things came about. So shall you hear   380
  Of carnal, bloody, and unnatural acts,
  Of accidental judgments,° casual° slaughters,
  Of deaths put on° by cunning and forced cause,°

---

325 **union** pearl. (See line 266; with grim puns on the word's other meanings: marriage, shared death.)   327 **tempered** mixed   333 **chance** mischance   334 **mutes** silent observers. (Literally, actors with nonspeaking parts.)   335 **fell** cruel. **sergeant** sheriff's officer   336 **strict** (1) severely just (2) unavoidable. **arrest** (1) taking into custody (2) stopping my speech   340 **Roman** (Suicide was an honorable choice for many Romans as an alternative to a dishonorable life.)

353 **o'ercrows** triumphs over (like the winner in a cockfight)   356 **voice** vote   357 **occurrents** events, incidents   358 **solicited** moved, urged. (Hamlet doesn't finish saying what the events have prompted—presumably, his acts of vengeance, or his reporting of those events to Fortinbras.)   364 **quarry** heap of dead. **cries on havoc** proclaims a general slaughter   365 **feast** i.e., Death feasting on those who have fallen. **toward** in preparation   372 **his** i.e., Claudius'   375 **jump** precisely, immediately. **question** dispute, affair   378 **stage** platform   382 **judgments** retributions. **casual** occurring by chance.   383 **put on** instigated. **forced cause** contrivance

And, in this upshot, purposes mistook
385 Fall'n on th' inventors' heads. All this can I
Truly deliver.
FORTINBRAS.　　　Let us haste to hear it,
And call the noblest to the audience.
For me, with sorrow I embrace my fortune.
I have some rights of memory° in this kingdom,
390 Which now to claim my vantage° doth invite me.
HORATIO.
Of that I shall have also cause to speak,
And from his mouth whose voice will draw on more.°
But let this same be presently° performed,
Even while men's minds are wild, lest more mischance

On° plots and errors happen.
FORTINBRAS.　　　Let four captains　　　395
Bear Hamlet, like a soldier, to the stage,
For he was likely, had he been put on,°
To have proved most royal; and for his passage,°
The soldiers' music and the rite of war
Speak° loudly for him.　　　400
Take up the bodies. Such a sight as this
Becomes the field,° but here shows much amiss.
Go bid the soldiers shoot.
　　　Exeunt [*marching, bearing off the dead bodies;*
　　　　　a peal of ordnance is shot off].

---

389 of memory traditional, remembered, unforgotten　**390 vantage** favorable opportunity　**392 voice . . . more** vote will influence still others　**393 presently** immediately

395 On on the basis of; on top of　**397 put on** i.e., invested in royal office and so put to the test　**398 passage** i.e., from life to death　**400 Speak** (let them) speak　**402 Becomes the field** suits the field of battle

---

SPOTLIGHT　　SHAKESPEARE'S TWO THEATERS

Because it is the most famous theater in the world, there is a tendency to think of the Globe Theatre as the primary type of playhouse in Shakespeare's England. However, by 1600 English drama was in full blossom and London, a large capital city of about 150,000, had developed a variety of performance spaces for the many acting companies drawing enthusiastic crowds.

For simplicity's sake, Elizabethan public and private theaters can be divided into two categories, the indoor and the outdoor, that is, those with at least a portion of the roof open to the elements. There were four types of indoor theaters, all private:

1. Academic playhouses, such as the Middle Temple, which were affixed to schools and used for student performances.
2. Nonscenic court playhouses, such as the great banqueting hall at Hampton Court, where plays were produced on an ad hoc basis and the playing space was adapted for the occasion.
3. Scenic court playhouses, such as the Great Hall at Whitechapel, where plays and masques were regularly performed in a space created to house scenery and other accoutrements of performance.
4. Private playhouses, which were fully functional theater spaces, usually within the city limits, where children's and professional acting companies performed for an exclusive clientele. There were four major private theaters: St. Paul's Boys Playhouse; the First Blackfriars; the Second Blackfriars; and the Whitefriars.

Two types of public outdoor theaters were used by professional adult acting companies:

1. Makeshift playhouses (e.g., the Boar's Head) which were adapted as permanent theaters from pre-existing spaces such as innyards, or animal baiting rings.
2. Permanent public playhouses specifically constructed, usually beyond London's city limits, for the presentation of plays. The Globe Theatre is the best known of these, but there were six others: the Theatre; the Curtain; the Rose; the Swan; the Fortune; and the Red Bull. Of these, the Swan is most noteworthy because a Dutch traveler, Johannes de Witt, sketched its interior in his diary in 1596. De Witt's drawing was lost, but a copy by Arend van Buchell remains the only extant contemporary illustration of an Elizabethan public theater.

Shakespeare was a shareholder of both a public playhouse, the Globe, and a private theater, the Second Blackfriars. The original Blackfriars was converted from a monastery whose dining hall became a playing space for a boys' company that performed regularly for the queen. James Burbage constructed the Second Blackfriars in 1596, twenty years after he built London's first public theater, the Theatre. Burbage was the father of Shakespeare's principal actor, Richard Burbage; when the elder Burbage died in 1597, he willed the Blackfriars to his son, who leased it to a popular children's company. By 1608 the King's Men were performing at the Blackfriars from October through May, returning to the Globe only in the summer months. The company preferred the interior space for financial, artistic, and climatic reasons; its revenues more than doubled at the Blackfriars, which catered to a wealthier audience.

You have some familiarity with the Globe and its trappings (recall the reconstruction of an early performance of *A Midsummer Night's Dream*). The Blackfriars had some elements in common with the Globe: trapdoors in the stage floor; suspension gear for flying effects; an upper station for action above the stage level; and a "discovery space" located upstage center that was curtained off to reveal interior scenes. But each theatre had distinctive features:

Public Theaters (The Globe, the Swan)	**Private Theaters** (Blackfriars)
Location	
Bankside; outside London's city limits.	Within the city limits; occasionally they were housed in private mansions.
Design and Configuration	
Open air; sunlit and exposed to the elements; daytime performances.	Enclosed and roofed; heated and lit by artificial means; evening performances.
Round or polygonal	Rectangular or oblong
Thrust stage	Modified thrust stage with a modified proscenium arch.
Backed by a "tiring house" with (most likely) two entrance doors.	Classical three-door arrangement
Dimensions and Capacity	
stage: c. 27' × 42'	18.5' × 29'
capacity: c. 2,500 spectators	c. 700 spectators
Audience-Actor Relationship	
Some spectators stood in the pit on three sides of the stage; galleries on three sides of stage with seating.	All audiences members seated, either on benches on the floor or in galleries; all seating in front of the stage.

The public theaters drew their audiences from the full spectrum of English society, while the private playhouses catered largely to a well-educated, aristocratic, socially homogenous clientele. Hence, the plays written for the private theaters are discernibly more literary. Because the private theaters were better equipped for scenic effects, plays in which environment and spectacle are important found their way into spaces like the Blackfriars. Shakespeare devoted his last years as a playwright to composing romances, such as *The Tempest*, partly because of the availability of a new type of theater and its technology. Still, whether public or private, indoor or out, the English theater relied principally on the evocative power of the word for impact.

SPAIN AND THE AMERICAS

Artistic and Cultural Events

Tlatzaque act in religious celebrations; *Popul Vuh; Rabinal Achí*

c. 1490: First Spanish secular drama (*La Celestina*)

1492: Spanish observe *areítos* (rites)

1509: Maria de Toledo uses *elogas* to educate indigenous people in Santo Domingo

c. 1525: Professional acting troupes in Lima, Peru

1567: Comedies performed at Spanish mission in Florida

1579: Corral de la Cruz, first permanent theater in Spain

1598: Spanish soldiers perform *comedias* near El Paso, Texas

c. 1630: Lope de Vega dominates Spanish theater

1605: *Don Quixote*

1627: Coliseo Theatre built in Mexico City

1690: Sor Juana Inés de la Cruz' *The Divine Narcissus*

1755: First Cuban play, The *Gardener Prince and Imagined Cloidano* (Santiago Pita y Borroto)

| 250 C.E. - 900 C.E. | 1200 C.E. | 1500 C.E. | 1600 C.E. | 1700 C.E. |

Historical and Political Events

Classic Maya Civilization

1200-1276: Christian war with Moors; Aztec civilization

1478: Inquisition begins

1519: King Carlos V becomes emperor of Holy Roman Empire

1521: Cortéz conquers Mexico; begins Spanish conquest

1492: Ferdinand and Isabella sponsor new world explorations

1588: Defeat of Spanish Armada

1607: Jamestown colony founded in Virginia

1609: Moors expelled from Spain

1621: Philip IV becomes king

ATLANTIC
OCEAN

SPAIN
Barcelona
Madrid
Toledo
Granada

MEXICO

CUBA
HAITI
DOMINICAN REPUBLIC
PUERTO RICO

Mexico City

GUATEMALA

TRINIDAD & TOBAGO

COLOMBIA
Bogotá

PERU
Lima

ATLANTIC
OCEAN

PACIFIC
OCEAN

ARGENTINA
Buenos Aires

Aztec territory

Mayan territory

LIFE'S A DREAM
(LA VIDA ES SUEÑO)

PEDRO CALDERÓN DE LA BARCA

PEDRO CALDERÓN DE LA BARCA (1600–1681)

As Shakespeare is to the English and Molière to the French, Calderón is recognized as Spain's greatest dramatist. Fittingly, Calderón succeeded Lope de Vega as the official court poet in 1635, but the variety and profundity of his work eclipse those of his chief rival. Calderón wrote more than 200 full-length plays (over 100 are extant) and a number of short works, and he invented the *zarzuela*, the Spanish form of musical comedy. When he died at age 81 in Madrid, he is said to have been working on a new play at his writing table. Typical of gentlemen of his era, Calderón was not merely a writer but was actively involved in Spanish life, both secular (as an army officer and court diplomat) and religious (he became a Jesuit priest in 1651).

Calderón was the son of the secretary of the king's royal treasury and, as boy and man, he spent much of his life in service to the court. He received a rigorous Jesuit education, which provided the stylistic and thematic foundation for his writing. Of the principal Spanish dramatists, Calderón is most closely associated with the allegorical *autos sacramentales*, theological plays that explored church teachings. His first literary efforts, poetry, attracted the attention of Lope de Vega, who judged a poetry competition that Calderón entered while a student. In 1623 he began writing plays with considerable success, and by the time he was appointed to succeed Lope as director of the court theater, he had written almost 70 plays. His dramatic talents earned him a knighthood in 1637.

During the decade of the 1640s Calderón suffered numerous hardships: a painful stint in the army, the closing of the theaters in Spain, the loss of two brothers and a mistress. After his ordination as a priest in 1651 (thus fulfilling his father's deathbed wish: see below), Calderón resumed his writing career and produced over 50 plays in a two-year span. Most of these were *autos* reflecting his new religious career. He also rewrote earlier works (including *Life's a Dream*) to explore metaphysical and theological issues. His later plays are noted for their symbolism and allegory, and for their blend of classical and biblical subject matter. Although they are rooted in the teachings of the Catholic Church, Calderón's best works transcend his Catholicism. Calderón was particularly fascinated by the theater as a metaphor for life, which is merely a "rehearsal" for eternity. In *The Great Theater of the World* (1649) a character says, "All men dream the lives they lead. Act well, for God is God." Calderón thus anticipates the twentieth-century plays of Pirandello, Beckett, Genet, and Stoppard, who also see life as a script that we, as characters assigned to roles we do not always fathom, must improvise. (See Spotlight box, The Spanish Theater: *The Corrales,* following the text of *Life's a Dream.*)

LIFE'S A DREAM (1673)

Calderón wrote two versions of *Life's a Dream*. The second, written in 1673, very late in his long life, represents a synthesis of his personal, theatrical, and philosophical growth. He used the world of classic myth, setting his action in distant but still very Catholic Poland, and the play reverberates with echoes of the Prometheus and Oedipus legends. Like Shakespeare, he uses the romance device of the wronged woman who must disguise herself as a man to survive in a disordered masculine world. By fusing the purely religious, with its emphasis on dogma and theology, with a more secular subject matter grounded in myth, the romance, and the traditional Spanish *comedias* of honor, Calderón crafted a more universal drama that is at once spiritual, humanist, political, moralistic, and more entertaining than his earlier work. Written about 1635, the earlier *Dream* was purely allegorical in the medieval sense. It opens with the four elements of Fire, Earth, Water, and Air each claiming supremacy and shows how God created order out of chaos, a favorite theme of Calderón. James Maraniss states that "Calderón's theatre is a sober celebration of order triumphant—the order of the universe; of the state; of the family; of the human personality; and, not the least, of language and thought."

To understand the implications of *Life's a Dream*, it is helpful to consider the central event of Calderón's life: his personal crisis of faith, which was precipitated by his father's deathbed wish that young Pedro become a priest. For thirty-five years Calderón rebelled against his father's will—which he equated with God's will—and suffered profound guilt as a consequence. The majority of Calderón's plays were an attempt by a tortured artist to reconcile his personal passions with the demands of duty and honor. Calderón felt he was hounded by the will of heaven as he fled through a labyrinthian world: for him, the labyrinth was like a carnival funhouse, filled with mirrors, or as Sigismund states in act 2:

> *In this strange world to live's a kind of dreaming,*
>
> *And each of us must dream the thing he is*
>
> *Till he awakes. . . .*
>
> *. . . . So what's this life? A fraud, a frenzy,*
>
> *A trick, a tale, a shadow, an illusion.*
>
> *And all our life is nothing but a dream.*

To make this incomprehensible world comprehensible, Calderón posits three principles—a trinity—upon which his philosophy and dramaturgy are based. First, one must accept the order of the universe, nature, political systems, and, especially for Calderón, the individual. One disturbs this order only at great peril to self and society, as King Basilio, Clotaldo, Astolfo, and Sigismund learn. Significantly, the play begins amid chaos and darkness. Rosaura, the woman who dresses as a man to combat the disorder of her world, speaks to her runaway horse:

> *I'm lost . . .*
>
> *Somewhere in the mountains.*
>
> *I'm a stranger.*
>
> *I am tired from riding,*
>
> *The sun is going down . . .*

Calderón's second principle tells us that human passions must be controlled if they conflict with the order established by the cosmos, nature, and society. "My soul cries for vengeance," says Sigismund very late in the play, "but I see my victory must be my own surrender." The third principle derives from the first two: self-denial—or to put it more positively, the freedom to choose to restrain one's worldly desires. Self-denial is predicated on another trinity sacred to the playwright: humility (i.e., the recognition of a higher authority); submission (the acceptance of authority); and obedience (the fulfillment of the law). Acceptance of this triad allows Sigismund to proclaim that he aims "at the highest triumph, that over myself." Basilio notes that Sigismund has attained wisdom through his self-denial (i.e., his choice to accept the order of the world), echoing the message of classic dramatists since Aeschylus.

Specifically, Calderón's beliefs, and his theater methodology, are derived from Augustine's theory of illumination, which states that a "divine impulse" invests humans with self-knowledge and virtuous conduct. The former embraces two extremes—which fits nicely into Calderón's theater of dualities—humanity's nothingness and its greatness. Understanding lets humans comprehend their nothingness, the state in which we find Sigismund in act 1. Clad in animal skins and chained in a mountain dungeon, Sigismund lives in a dark ("non-illuminated") world as "a monster in a labyrinth." Rosaura's essential goodness, Basilio's recantation of his past errors, and Sigismund's determination to restore Rosaura's lost honor lead him to his greatness. It is this conflict between understanding and ignorance, free will and self-indulgence, that provide the dramatic tension in Calderón's work.

At first Sigismund, representative of all humans who must make similar choices, resists his submission to the natural order. Basilio, who has turned over the reins of kingship to his son, scolds Sigismund in act 2: "See how the stars have kept their promises. See, see how cruel and arrogant he is." In the final act Sigismund leads a successful rebellion against his tyrant father and reconciles with the older man; Sigismund "chooses," godlike, to forgive his father's past transgressions, to which the old and now wiser king responds:

> My son, my own son,
>
> By this act I am reborn inside you.
>
> You have overcome yourself.
>
> You have overcome the stars.
>
> You have won yourself a crown.

Sigismund's rebirth marks a moment of *desengaño*, a Spanish concept that is most easily translated as "disillusionment." Here the word is not to be taken in the negative sense of being disenchanted, but as the positive act of stripping away all illusions about earthly power; that is, Sigismund's free will has awakened him from the illusory dream his life has been. For Calderón the theater itself provided the perfect vehicle for examining worldly illusions.

But Sigismund's dilemma is only part of the play's equation. If Sigismund is an Everyman whom experience teaches the need for restraint, then Basilio is an "Every-God" who acquires hard-won knowledge about the nature of humanity. Calderón implies that God must respond to the will of humanity just as humans must submit to the order of God. The playwright goes to great lengths to establish the godlike nature of Basilio. In act 1, he is given an arialike speech that defines him as "Basilio the Learned," "Basilio the Great," and allows him to boast that "I want to test [the stars], test out heaven."

A 1984 production of *Life's a Dream*, staged by the Royal Shakespeare Company, for which this translation was commissioned, effected this godliness in Basilio's costume: a cloak, literally covering the stage, that was embroidered with stars and other heavenly bodies. He looked like a walking universe, his wizened gray head peering from the constellatory cloak. More than his words, Basilio's actions make him godlike: he manipulates Sigismund, first turning him into a captive beast. Basilio, like God before the Flood, laments what his creation has wrought: "I knew . . . that his wildness would debauch the Kingdom into a foul academy of chaos." Experience also teaches Basilio that wrath and oppression only embitter humans and incite rebellion. Basilio recants his harsh treatment of Sigismund, realizing that by depriving his son of his "rights by laws both divine and human," he has acted intemperately. Basilio recognizes that he must act in consort with Sigismund, rather than tyrannically, and thus he becomes a more benevolent man, father, and king. He permits Sigismund to rise to his birth-ordained greatness and share in the governance of Poland. After considerable trial and error, Sigismund matures into "the mirror of Christian kings" when he performs the consummate godlike act: he forgives Basilio. The final moment of the play depicts a reconciliation between father and son, that most archetypal of images, in which a covenant of forgiveness and mutual respect is forged to make parent and progeny, God and Man, partners in the ordering of the world.

One wonders if perhaps Calderón, himself an old man when he penned these concluding lines in 1673, was not thinking of his own circumstances and his own father on his deathbed over six decades earlier.

Anne Bogart merged Spain's classical tradition (Calderón's play) and its modern sensibilities (a Salvador Dali landscape) in Life's a Dream *at the American Repertory Company in Cambridge (1989).*

LIFE'S A DREAM

—— PEDRO CALDERÓN DE LA BARCA ——

Adapted by Adrian Mitchell and John Barton

CHARACTERS
ROSAURA, *a confused woman*
CLARION, *a foolish servant*
SIGISMUND, *Prince of Poland*
CLOTALDO, *his keeper*
ASTOLFO, *Duke of Muscovy*
ESTRELLA, *Princess of Poland*
BASILIO, *King of Poland*
SOLDIERS
COURTIERS
SERVANTS

ACT ONE

SCENE ONE

(A stage. Enter Rosaura dressed as a man. She mounts a hobby horse and rides gently. Drums and trumpets sound suddenly and the horse neighs and goes wild. She tries to control it but it careens around the stage. She falls off.)

ROSAURA. You're not a horse,
   You're a hippogriff.
   Why have you thrown me?
   Coward, you shied and bucked
   At a shadow, a nothing.   5
   Flash without flame!
   Fish without scales!
   Bird without feathers!
   You threw me on these rocks.
   Stay in the mountains then: 10
   Make friends with the wolves.
   But what about me?
   I'm lost . . .
   Somewhere in Poland.
   Somewhere in the mountains.   15
   I'm a stranger.
   I am tired from riding,

The sun is going down
And I've nobody for company
20 But Clarion the Clown.

(Enter Clarion.)

CLARION. So this is Poland. What a place.
About as friendly as outer space.
Up there black crags, down there a gloomy
lake.
I'm hungry and thirsty and my shoulders
ache.
25 ROSAURA. Trouble breeds trouble. We must endure it.
CLARION. A hogshead of wine is the best way to cure it.
Why did we leave our Muscovite nest
To trudge round Europe on some crazy quest?
ROSAURA. You know very well
30 Why we've come to Poland:
To find my lost father
And win back my honour.
CLARION (sings).
I never had a father
But if I had have done
35 I'm sure he would have told me:
"Be a man of honour, son."

So I rose up one morning
And hurried to the fair,
For I had heard the rumour
40 That the folk sold honour there.

As I walked through the fairground
My heart was struck by fear.
I heard a giant shouting
"Come and buy your honour here."

45 I asked him for some honour.
He laughed and turned away,
Said: "Honour is expensive
Son, are you prepared to pay?

"You pay your legs, your eyesight,
50 Your land, your house, your wife,
Your sanity, your children
And your money and your life."

I told him: "Keep your honour:
I don't want to be dead."
55 So I went and found a tavern
And I bought some wine instead.
ROSAURA. Clarion, look there;
Look . . . do you see?
A tower hewn out of massive blocks
60 Lies at the centre of a maze of rocks
Like a chunk hewn out of solid midnight,
Or a great mill for grinding sunlight:
A tower darker than darkness.
(Sound of chains.)

CLARION. Rosaura. Listen. Clanking.
ROSAURA. I can't move. I'm freezing.   65
I can't move. I'm burning.
SIGISMUND (cries out within).
I am unhappy.
CLARION. Let us leave this tower.
ROSAURA. Look. A flickering. A gleam
In the blackness. Shifting, shimmering.   70
There's a man, a wild man,
In a tomb there or a dungeon.
Let's hear what he has to say.
(Sigismund comes forward, chained. He is carrying a
picture-book.)
SIGISMUND. What have I done that I should suffer so?
What crime have I committed? Tell me, stars.   75
I have been born. Is that a crime in men?
Were other men not born as I was born?
Yet they are blessed and I have here no
blessings.
(Turns over the pages of the book.)
A bird is born, a swallow,
Little and damp and shaken,   80
It grows so bright and dark and feathery,
A spray of flowers on the wing.
It slices through the air so speedily
That it outflies imagining
And leaves its nest forsaken.   85
Then why can't I
Be like a swallow flying free?
(He turns the page to a picture of a salmon.)
A fish is born, a salmon.
Child of the waterfall's rock and sprays.
Its rainbow armour fitting perfectly,   90
It cuts the oceans like a knife,
Charting and measuring the sea
And all the million forms of life
In the vast cold waterways.
Then why can't I   95
Be like a salmon swimming free?
(He turns the page to a picture of a waterfall.)
A spring is born, a stream,
Welling up among grass to go
As serpents travel, swift and windingly.
The river sings its silver thanks   100
And joys in its mobility
To flowers and beasts along its banks
As they watch its dazzling flow.
Then why can't I
Be like a river, flowing free?   105
(He turns to a picture of a leopard.)
A beast is born, a leopard,
Delicate as a hyacinth.
Its shaven hide is dappled cunningly
With paintbrush marks of black and gold.
But the grown leopard shows a cruelty   110

That's natural, so we are told,
A monster in a labyrinth.
Then why, why, can't I
Be like a leopard running free?

115 Born out of rage,
Eaten with rage,
I'm a volcano. Watch me bleed.
Give me a knife—I'll show you surgery
And wrench out, raggedy and raw
120 Bits of my heart. Captivity!
So is there some reason or some law
Denies me the one thing I need,
Which God gave swallows and salmon too,
And beasts and leopards: to be free?
125 ROSAURA. What a sad story.
SIGISMUND. Who's that? I can't see.
  Clotaldo, is it you?
CLARION. Go on, say it is,
  But don't mention me.
130 ROSAURA. We are travellers
  Lost in this ravine
  We heard your sorrow.
SIGISMUND. So you know I'm weak?
  Then you must die.
135 CLARION. Would you repeat that? I didn't quite hear.
  I'm a little bit deaf in my right ear.
SIGISMUND. I'll tear you both in pieces.
ROSAURA. I kneel. If you are human
  I know that you will spare us.
140 We are humble creatures.
SIGISMUND. Your voice is gentle. When I look on you
  I find that I grow soft. You trouble me.
  Who are you? O I know the world so little,
  For I have spent my whole life in this prison.
145 If how I am is living. Since my birth
  I have known nothing but this wilderness
  Where I have lived alone, a living dead thing.
  Till now I never spoke to anyone
  But one old man who listens to my sorrows
  And teaches me rare words and how to
150   name things,
  And tells me tales about the earth and sky.
  But till today no one has calmed my anger,
  O you have eased my eyes and charmed my
    ears,
  For you refresh me and you make me wonder.
155 ROSAURA. I do not know how I should answer you.
  I'm full of wonder too . . .
  What shall I say? Did Heaven lead me here
  To see someone unhappier than myself?
  I cannot tell and yet I think it must be.
  There was a wise man once who lived on
160   herbs:
  "Can there be anyone," he asked himself,

"More poor and sad than I?" And then he saw
Another wise man picking up the leaves
That he had thrown away. He found his
  answer.
And so have I, for I have been complaining   165
Of this bad world, and you have answered me.
For what I think of as unhappiness
You would call joy, as if you picked my
  leaves up.
Then if you can find comfort from my sorrows
Take them and let me tell you who I am.   170

(*Enter Clotaldo. He fires a shot.*)

CLOTALDO. Guards! Soporific cowards!
  There are intruders in the tower.
CLARION. More trouble.
SIGISMUND. That's Clotaldo. He's my jailer.
CLOTALDO. Place them under strict arrest   175
  And cut them down if they resist.

(*Enter Guards with masked faces.*)

CLARION. I'm a completely lovable clown.
  I'll be very cut up if you cut me down.
CLOTALDO. The King of Poland has decreed
  This a forbidden place   180
  And that the penalty is death
  To see this monster's face.
  Surrender to the guard
  Of the tower by the lake
  Or my pistol will tear out your throats   185
  Like a sudden snake.
SIGISMUND. Do not harm them, master.
  You'll all die if you do,
  For with my nails and teeth
  I will fight with you.   190
CLOTALDO. Sigismund, remember your own fate
  When you threaten homicide,
  Heaven has decreed
  When you were born, you died.
  Remember this prison   195
  Is a curb upon your pride.
  Lock the tower door
  And take him back inside.
SIGISMUND. Yes, heavens, you are right to steal my
    freedom.
  If I was free I'd rise up like a giant   200
  And pile up stones and make a staircase
    mountain
  And batter down the windows of the sun.
CLOTALDO. Perhaps your present sufferings are meant
  To stop you doing just that. Away with him.

(*Guards take Sigismund out.*)

205 Surrender to the guards.
ROSAURA. Here is my sword.
    I surrender it to you.
    I will not yield it
    Into less noble hands.
210 CLARION. My sword's a bit bent
    And blunt at the end.
    It's a prize for a booby:
    Here you are, friend.

(Clarion gives the sword to a Guard.
Clotaldo takes Rosaura's. Guard takes
Clarion out.)

ROSAURA. If I must die, sir,
215 Please guard it well.
    It holds some great secret:
    It is a legacy
    From my lost father.
CLOTALDO. And who was he?
220 ROSAURA. I never knew him,
    But I trust his sword,
    And so I came to Poland,
    For revenge on a man
    Who has wronged my honour.
CLOTALDO (takes his mask off. Aside).
225 What is this, heavens?
    I am flabbergasted.
    All my own confusions,
    My shame and my sorrows
    Swamp my heart and mind.
230 Who gave it to you?
ROSAURA. My mother.
CLOTALDO.   Her name?
ROSAURA. I cannot tell you that.
CLOTALDO (aside).
    Heaven help me! Can this be
    Illusion or reality?
235 This is the sword I gave to my sweet love
    When I was living still in Muscovy.
    I swore that whosoever wore that sword
    Would find me kind as if he was my son.
    I am bewildered. Stranger, do not think
240 You are alone in your misfortunes here.
    You must go in but I will use you gently.
                                    (Exit Rosaura.)
    He has her eyes, as hot as shooting stars.
    Now am I like a man locked in a room
    Who hears a sound in the street and runs to
        the window.
245 My heart flies out of my eyes to stare at him.
    I'm weeping. He's my son. What shall I do?
    Let's work it out. One, he has offered me
    My own good sword to win favour. Two,

By coming here he's brought his death day
    with him.
What must I do? O heavens, what must I do?   250
Take him before the King? That's certain
    death.
Hide him? I cannot, I should break my oath.
Now is it with me as in some old tale:
On one side, love, on one side, loyalty.
I'm torn. But why? I should not hesitate.   255
For loyalty to Kings is more than life
And more than honour. I believe that's true,
So do not mock me. What was it he said?
He came here to avenge some injury.
To leave an insult unavenged is shameful.   260
That is our code. Honour's so delicate,
A little breath, a puff of wind can smear it.
He is my son, my blood is in his veins:
What shall I do? I'll seek some middle way.
In this bad world that's best. I'll tell the King   265
This boy is mine. My loyalty may move him.
Then I can help him to avenge his honour.
But if the King is cruel, my son must die.
What's the worst fate the gods can give?
Some say to die, but others say . . . to live.   270

SCENE TWO

(Dawn. Drums and trumpets. Enter on one side Astolfo,
Duke of Muscovy, attended, and on the other side
Princess Estrella, also attended.)

ASTOLFO. Estrella! Star-girl! Princess! Empress! Queen!
    Your eyes are bright as comets. Drums and
        trumpets
    Greet you and mix their homage with sweet
        nature.
    Look how the birds and fountains blend
        their music
    And all things wonder that behold your face.   5
    Trumpets made of feathers, birds of brass
    And the rough cannons hail you as their queen.
    The birds cry out, "Look, that is bright
        Aurora,"
    The trumpets, that Athene's here, the flowers
    That you are Flora. O you mock the day   10
    Even as the bright day mocks the banished
        night.
    You are the dawn, Aurora, as you shine,
    Athene as you war, in peace sweet Flora,
    And all in all you are my proud heart's queen.
ESTRELLA. If deeds prove words, you will be proved a liar.   15
    You do me wrong to flatter me, Astolfo.
    Your courteous, amorous vocabulary

And your display of military might do not
    quite blend.
    Your silver tongue talks love
20   But in your mind you dream of iron power.
ASTOLFO. No, you are wrong to doubt my faith, Estrella.
    Fair cousin, hear me out. Basilio
    Is King of Poland and a widower.
    He is old now (Time mocks us all with age)
25   And more inclined to study than to women.
    He has no child, so we both claim the throne . . .
ESTRELLA. I am the daughter of his eldest sister.
ASTOLFO. It's true I am the youngest sister's son,
    For I was born to her in Muscovy,
30   Yet, being a man, I must take precedence.
    This has been argued with our uncle King
    Who says he means to reconcile us both,
    And he has fixed this day and place to do it.
    And that is why I've come from Muscovy.
35   Not to make war, though you make war on me
    With all the weapons of your loveliness,
    But to make love and win you, my Estrella.
    If we two marry, Poland will be strong.
ESTRELLA. My heart thanks yours for your kind courtesy.
40   Yet I am only partly satisfied:
    There is a picture hanging round your neck
    Which rather gives the lie to what you say.
    Do not confuse your longings for the throne
    With other nicer longings of your own.
45 ASTOLFO. I'll satisfy you fully as to that . . .
    (*Drums and trumpets sound.*)
    But may not do so now. The king is coming.

(*Enter King Basilio, attended.*)

    O most wise King . . .
ESTRELLA.   O learned King . . .
ASTOLFO.   Who rules
    Among the stars . . .
ESTRELLA.   The galaxies . . .
ASTOLFO.   The heavens . . .
ESTRELLA. You plot the star-paths . . .
ASTOLFO.   Trace their fiery footsteps.
ESTRELLA. You hear their music . . .
50 ASTOLFO.   And you read their meaning . . .
ESTRELLA. O let me kneel before your royal feet.
ASTOLFO. O let me press my lips upon your hand.
BASILIO. Dutiful nephew, loving niece, embrace me.
    You come in love and hope. However high
55   Your wishes soar you shall be satisfied.
    So clear your minds of that, and all be silent.
    Brave peers of Poland, vassals, kinsmen,
      friends.
    You know already that for my deep wisdom
    I am surnamed the Learned by the world,
60   And in defiance of Time's dusty heel

Painters and sculptors all around the globe
Create star-glowing images of me,
Which will outlive by tens of centuries
This fading face, these failing bones, this
    flesh:
Basilio the Learned. And the Great.   65
You know the science that I love the most:
The mathematics, by the means of which
I make a fool of Fate and cheat old Time,
Whose function is to unfold fate itself.
I am the canny duellist who so far   70
Has always made the winning thrust. Poor
    Time,
His every stroke and counter-stroke is marked
Upon my charts ahead of him. I read him.
There are star mountains and I climb their
    peaks.
There are star forests and I know their paths,   75
And there are swamps and whirlpools made
    of stars.
Circles of snow, bright canopies of glass,
Cut by the moon, illumined by the sun,
These crystalline, concentric necklaces
These specks, these beads, these spirals,
    whirling tear-drops: 80
These are my life, my study and my passion,
These are my books, their diamond lettering
Printed upon bright sapphire-paper pages
By the great golden printing-press of Heaven.
I turn one blue page of the Universe   85
And, cruel or kind, there is our human future,
Easy to read as a child's alphabet.
And yet I wish, before I'd understood
The universe's simplest syllable,
The stars had poured their poison-fire on me.   90
A learned man's the victim of his learning.
For he who has foreknowledge of his fate
Murders himself and plays the suicide
In his own story. So perhaps with me.
Be silent still and hear me out with wonder.   95

I'm old now, but when I was young and fresh
I had a secret and unhappy son
At whose sad birth there was high rage in
    heaven.
Before the warm grave of his mother's womb
Transmitted him into the yellow daylight   100
(For birth and death are very much alike)
His mother dreamed a child monstrosity
Smeared with her life's blood, burst out of
    her entrails,
Took life and was her death. And when the day
Came for his birth, this omen was proved true: 105
In my experience, omens always are.

The sun was red as blood and fought the moon.
They took our planet as their wrestling-ground;
Silver and gold grappled and interlocked.
110 It was the greatest and most terrible
Of all the eclipses that the sun has suffered
Since it wept blood, mourning the death of
    Christ.
There was no star-fire in the firmament.
Palaces shook. And Sigismund was born.
115 He tore his mother's life out and so showed
His nature to the world as if to say,
"I repay good with evil. I'm a man."

I knew then he would grow up to be vicious.
A cruel prince and a despotic King;
120 That Poland would be torn by civil war
And that his wildness would debauch the
    Kingdom
Into a foul academy of chaos.
I knew he'd strike me down and use my beard
As if it were a carpet for his boots.
125 Who'd not believe such omens? I decided
That I must cage the beast and find out
    whether
One cunning King could overcome the stars.
I gave out that my son had died at birth.
I built a tower among night-black boulders
130 In a ravine beyond the reach of daylight,
And that is where he lives. The penalty
For trespassers is death without a trial.
He sees and talks with no one but Clotaldo
Who tutors him in science and religion
135 And is the only witness of his woes.

Three things must now be thought on. Pray
    you, mark me.
One, I love Poland and I won't allow her to
    be oppressed or crushed by tyranny.
Two, Christian charity: what right have I
To keep my son from that prerogative
140 Which by divine and human law is his?
Shall I turn criminal because of crimes
Which he has not committed, though he may?
Three, what if I have been too credulous?
What if he's gentle? The most cruel star
145 Can influence the will but cannot force it
Because a man's will is a gift from God.

I've wavered and I've weighed this, and I have
Devised a remedy which will amaze you.
I mean to set my son upon my throne
150 And to invest him with my royal power,
And you must all obey him as your King.
This stratagem can lead us to three outcomes
Which complement the three points I have
    made.

One, if he's prudent, wise and kind and gentle
And gives the lie to what is prophesied, 155
Then you shall have him as your own true
    King.
Two, if he proves reckless and cruel and wild
My moral obligation's at an end,
And it will seem in me a kind of mercy
To reimprison him, not punishment 160
But justice. Three, if that should be the
    outcome
I will ensure the Polish throne shall be
By you two occupied illustriously.
This, as I am your King, I now command
And, as I am his father, I require 165
And, as I am a wise man, I advise it,
And, as I'm told, I tell you blunt and plain.
And last, if Kings be slaves to their own
    kingdoms,
I, as your humble slave, beseech you all.
ASTOLFO. Justice herself could form no plan more fair. 170
ESTRELLA. God save the Prince and let him be your heir.
ASTOLFO. Long live Basilio.
ESTRELLA. God save the King.
ALL. Long live Basilio.
                  God save the King.

(*Music. Exit all but Basilio.*)

BASILIO. I thank you for listening. 175
    We shall learn tomorrow
    Whether my son shall be a King
    Or whether he'll bring sorrow.

(*Enter Clotaldo with Rosaura and Clarion
chained and blindfolded*).

CLOTALDO. A word, sire.
BASILIO. Clotaldo. You are always welcome. 180
    What's wrong?
CLOTALDO. My lord, a grievous thing has happened,
    Though in a sense it is a joyful thing . . .
BASILIO. Go on.
CLOTALDO. These two young men have seen the Prince. 185
    They got into the tower . . .
BASILIO.   Don't fret, Clotaldo.
Since I have publicly proclaimed the truth,
Discovering the secret is no crime.
Attend me in an hour. I've much to tell you,
And you will have a busy day tomorrow, 190
For you must help me with the strangest act
The planet earth has seen. As for your
    prisoners,
I will forgive you for your negligence.
Unbind their arms and eyes. You are all
    pardoned.   (*Exit.*) 195
CLOTALDO. God save the King
    And may he live forever! Heaven is kind.

I thought it would be hard but it was easy.
(*Aside.*) I will not tell him that he is my son.
200 I did his mother wrong, and if he knew me
I fear he'd hate me. Strangers, you are free.
ROSAURA. I kiss your feet, Your Grace.
CLARION. I'll kiss you any place.
ROSAURA. You saved my life.
CLARION.   I'll be your slave forever.
205 CLOTALDO. Get up, both of you.
(*To Clarion.*) Don't try to be clever.
CLARION. I'm trying to be foolish.
CLOTALDO.   You've succeeded.
CLARION. Why, then I'll be outside if I am needed.
CLOTALDO. If needed I'll give you a clarion call.
210 CLARION. Sir, you could be the biggest fool of them all.
                                    (*Exit Clarion.*)

ROSAURA. You saved my life . . .
CLOTALDO. You have no life. You say you have been
wronged,
But noble men have neither life nor honour
Until they are avenged. (*Aside.*) I see that I
Must educate the boy. Sure, this will move
215 him.
ROSAURA. I am not ashamed. I have done nothing wrong.
CLOTALDO. Honour's not what you do
But what is done to you.
You can wash your face
220 If it's splashed with mud
But honour can only
Be washed with blood.
A man without honour's a mongrel pup
Snapping at fleas. (*Aside.*) That should stir
225 him up.
ROSAURA. I will avenge my honour
And so win life.
CLOTALDO.   Well said.
Take back your sword.
Vow vengeance on your enemy.
230 That sword was mine
(I mean it was, just now)
It will serve you well:
Use it like a man.
ROSAURA. Then in your name
235 I gird it on again
And swear as I am man
To be revenged on him
Who has wronged my honour.
CLOTALDO. And I will likewise swear on oath to help you.
240 ROSAURA. You would not say so if you knew his name.
CLOTALDO. Have I not sworn it? Is it some great man?
ROSAURA. So great, I dare not tell you who he is.
I fear to lose your favour.
CLOTALDO.   No, you'd win it
If you would trust me.
ROSAURA.   No, I dare not tell you.

CLOTALDO. If only I could find out who he is.   245
Tell me his name. I am your friend. You
need me.
ROSAURA. I trust you. You shall know my enemy
Is great Astolfo, Duke of Muscovy.
CLARION (*aside*).
Why, this is worse than I thought possible.
I must learn more of this. Let us examine   250
This carefully. You are a Muscovite.
Therefore Astolfo is your natural lord.
And therefore he cannot have wronged your
honour.
Quench this mad ardour.
ROSAURA.   Though he is my prince,
He's wronged me.
CLOTALDO.   No, a prince can do no wrong,   255
Not even if he struck you in the face.
ROSAURA. My wrong was worse than that.
CLOTALDO.   Then tell it to me.
ROSAURA. I am not what I seem,
This is show, disguise, a costume.
My name is Rosaura.   260
(*Lets down her hair.*)
I had a noble mother
In the court of Muscovy.
A deceiver wooed and won her.
I do not know his name
For she would never tell me,   265
But I think he was valiant
Because I sometimes feel
His courage in myself.
He told her the old story:
He'd be true to her,   270
He would marry her.
But one day he left her:
She was too low-born
For his nobility.
From this loose knot   275
I came into the world,
And so in time her tale
Was told again in me.
Astolfo is the man
Who despoiled my honour.   280
He swore he'd marry me
And for a little while
I thought I was happy.
Suddenly he left.
He came here to Poland   285
To marry his Estrella.
As a star first joined us
So a star destroyed us.
I wept within.
I was mocked,   290
I was angry,
I was mad,

I was dead,
I was . . . me . . .
295 Babel . . . Muddle . . . Hell.
Pain is felt, not words.
But my mother understood.
When you know the person
To whom you tell your weakness
300 Has been weak herself,
It's as if you are both lost
In the same strange country.
That is a comfort.
She said, "Go to Poland,
305 Either make him marry you
Or kill him. Kill him with
Your father's sword."
I swore that.

She dressed me as a man
310 And said, "Show this sword
To the noblemen in Poland,
One of them will know it
And be kind to you
Because you are his child."

315 I want to meet my father
And tell him how I hate him.
It is because of him
That my Astolfo left me.
He said he could not marry
320 A girl who had no father
And did not know his name.
Hate is a clear thing.
Though I am in the darkness
I am clear about my father.
CLOTALDO (aside).
325 O what a maze. I don't know what to do.
My honour's gored. Astolfo's powerful.
He is my overlord, she just a woman.
She must not know yet that I am her father,
For then she would compel me to avenge her.
330 That is our code. Besides she loves me now.
That's sweet to me. Best leave it as it is.
I don't know what to do or what to say,
Best to say nothing till I find my way.
ROSAURA. Why do I feel such trust and fondness for you?
335 I think it is because you are kind and gentle.
Why are you silent?
CLOTALDO.   You have sworn two oaths;
One of revenge and blood and one to win
Your love Astolfo. These oaths are at odds.
I think that is because you do not know
Whether you love or hate him.
ROSAURA.   Both.
340 CLOTALDO.   That's common.
But I believe your oaths are dreams, Rosaura.

You cannot marry one of such high blood.
You must accept that.
ROSAURA.   I have tried to do so.
I locked my rage within but it will out.
Damn his fine phrases, damn his gentle
    smiling.   345
Damn his sweet kisses, his fumblings and
    his fondlings.
I'll cut his lying throat. How dare he leave me?
CLOTALDO. You are violent because you have been hurt,
But Time will mend that. For the good of
    Poland
The Duke must wed Estrella. He must do it.   350
ROSAURA. I will prevent him.
CLOTALDO.   How?
ROSAURA.   I do not know.
CLOTALDO. Do you still hope to win his love again?
ROSAURA. I cannot tell.
CLOTALDO.   Well, you will never win him
Unless you put a dress on.
ROSAURA.   I'll not do that.
CLOTALDO. You must. As you are now you are immodest,   355
Unnatural, and, which is worst, unreal.
You are very fair.
ROSAURA.   My hair is foul and matted.
CLOTALDO. There, you are a woman.
ROSAURA.   I will put a dress on
But I will keep my oath.
CLOTALDO.   I don't believe you.
ROSAURA. The only man I'll marry is Astolfo.   360
CLOTALDO. We will speak further. For the present time
Since you are unhappy it's not good for you
To be alone. Therefore I will contrive
That you shall serve Estrella.
ROSAURA.   I can't do that.
CLOTALDO. We often think we cannot when we can,   365
And what we think we can we often cannot.
ROSAURA. You must not make me break my oath
Or go against my honour.
CLOTALDO.   We'll speak further.
I must attend the King on some great purpose.
Go in Rosaura, and put on a dress.   370
            (Exit Clotaldo. Rosaura takes off the
            rest of her disguise. As she does so she sings.)
ROSAURA. Dreamed I was the lover
Of a beautiful thief
But when I woke up
I was a shipwreck on a reef.
Dreamed that I was happy   375
Or so it seemed to seem.
My lover smiled
Just like a clown in a dream.

A clown in a dream,
A clown in a dream   380

I had a dream
I was a clown in a dream.
A clown in a dream
Falling upside down,
385 And when I woke up,
I was a dream in a clown.

(Exit Rosaura.)

END OF ACT ONE

ACT TWO

SCENE ONE

(Enter King Basilio and Clotaldo.)

CLOTALDO. Your orders, sire, have all been carried out.
BASILIO. Tell me, Clotaldo.
CLOTALDO.   I went back to the tower
    And had a pleasant sleeping draft prepared;
    A blend of certain rare and powerful herbs,
    Whose secret strength lays waste the human
5   mind
    So that the victim becomes numb to pain,
    And at the last is like a living corpse.
BASILIO. Sweet medicine is so full of Nature's secrets
    That there's no plant nor animal nor stone
10 That does not have rare powers or properties.
    For if the matchless malice of mankind
    Can find a thousand poisons, is it strange
    That violent drugs, if they be checked and
        tempered,
    Can bring us sleep, unto death? It's
15 palpable.
CLOTALDO. I took this drink down to the Prince's cell
    And talked a little with him of the arts
    And sciences, which he had learned from birds,
    From beasts and fishes, mountains and clouds
        and me.
20 To raise his spirits to your enterprise
    I made him watch a fiery-feathered eagle,
    Flying through tree-tall flames of gold and
        white,
    Winging beyond the clouded, lower skies,
    Soaring up high into the land of the sun.
25 Until he turned into a shooting star,
    A feathered ray of streaming gilded light.
    I praised that bright adventurer and said,
    "The eagle is the King of all the birds,
    The undisputed lord." This image spurred him
30 To speak of sovereignty. Ambitiously
    And proudly too his heart began to stir
    Heroically. He said: "It is amazing

Within the airy Kingdom of the birds
One bird holds sway. So many citizens
And yet they all seem happy to obey.   35
But I'm a subject through some fault of birth,
And, were I free, I never could become
Subject to any man on earth."
BASILIO. So, he was roused.
CLOTALDO.   And so I thought it good
    To offer him the potion, and he took it.   40
    No sooner had it trickled down his throat
    Than he turned grey as lead. If I'd not known
    The drug's effects I'd have supposed him dead.
    We brought him to your room, to your own
        bed.
    When he awakes they'll clothe him in your
        robes   45
    And serve him as they'd serve Your Majesty.
BASILIO. You have done well, Clotaldo. Now all is ready.
CLOTALDO. Your Highness, if my long obedient years
    Have earned, forgive me, any kind of pay,
    Will you explain why you have had the Prince 50
    Brought to the palace in this curious way?
BASILIO. Your curiosity is just, Clotaldo.
    The stars, it is the stars above that threaten
    Innumerable tragedies of blood.
    I want to test them, yes, test out heaven.   55
    I must discover if his destiny
    (However scientifically correct)
    May not in fact be slightly mitigated
    Or even conquered. I believe a man
    Is master of his stars. I wish to try him.   60
    I mean to tell him that he is my son
    That I may know his nature. You'll ask why
    He was brought here asleep. I'll answer that.
    If he should learn today that he's my son
    And if he then proves cruel and so tomorrow   65
    Awakes in prison, will he not despair?
    Therefore I have contrived a kind of ease.
    I'll make him think that it is all a dream.
    Thus I'll discover his true character,
    For he will act by instinct when he wakes.   70
    And, if he fails he'll have some consolation;
    For if one day he's worshipped as a King,
    The next flung back into his dungeon den,
    He will be able to believe he dreamed it.
    And that's a useful, realistic creed: 75
    To live life is a dream indeed.
CLOTALDO. I believe you are mistaken, sire,
    To embark on this experiment.
    But as the subject is awake
    There's no time now for argument.   80
BASILIO. I will withdraw. Stay here: you are his tutor.
    Tell him the truth. Don't let him be
        bewildered
    But help him clear his mind.

CLOTALDO.   Am I to tell him
   Everything?
85 BASILIO. Yes, for if he knows the truth
   He may succeed and pass the test I've set
      him.
   I'll send the Duke and Princess to him also,
   So all the court shall shortly test my son.
   A danger known is often not a danger,
90   And so it will be with Sigismund.

                                          (*Exit Basilio.*)

(*Enter Clarion in court livery.*)

CLARION. I've come to see King Basil's play.
   To get in his theatre I've had to pay:
   One glass of beer to a growling guard,
   Two chops to the dogs in the Palace yard,
   Three rings to a chambermaid—real
95   imitation—
   In exchange for some curious information.
   Four tots of rum and a barrel of beer
   To a royal red-nosed halberdier.
   Five silk gowns, ornate and oriental
100 To a lady-in-waiting who's sentimental.
   That's what I paid, but what have I bought?
   An under-flunkey's position at court,
   Where I am guaranteed a ringside view
   Of the Royal Circus of How D'Ye Do,
   With performing Princesses, Kings who eat
105   fire,
   And a Prince walking along the High Wire.
CLOTALDO. Good morning, Clarion,
   What is the news?
   New clothes I see,
110 But rather strange shoes.
CLARION. Now you've agreed
   To avenge her offences,
   My mistress Rosaura
   Has come to her senses.
115 You've done so much
   To relieve her distress
   That she's even put on
   A beautiful dress.
CLOTALDO. I'm glad. Those clothes
120 Put her sex to shame.
CLARION. On top of all that
   She's changed her name
   To the lady Astraea.
   She says she's your niece,
125 And she's landed a job,
   Wonders never cease,
   As a lady-in-waiting
   To Princess Estrella,
   (Which she couldn't have done
130 If she'd stayed as a feller).

CLOTALDO. And how does your life
   As a court clown feel?
CLARION. I'm desperate, sir,
   I long for a meal.
   A six-course dinner   135
   Is what I deserve
   But nobody feeds me.
   I've no one to serve.
CLOTALDO. Then be my servant.
   Though the fare is frugal.   140
CLARION. I am your slave, sir.
CLOTALDO. Then don't blow that bugle.
CLARION. I'm full of joy
   And I'll learn to diet.
CLOTALDO. But first you must learn   145
   To try to be quiet.
   (*Music.*)
   Ah, here he comes in princely splendour.
CLARION.   Who?
CLOTALDO. Prince Sigismund, and his royal retinue.

(*Sigismund enters, carried on a litter by Servants. He
wakes up. They help to dress him as he speaks.*)

SIGISMUND. Stars above . . . what's all this brightness?
   Stars above . . . am I in a vision?   150
   Sigismund, waking in an amazing bed,
   Flowing with softnesses and shining . . .
   Sigismund, clothed in robes as light
   As sunset clouds and shining . . .
   Sigismund, carried down sunny corridors   155
   By silent servants, eyes and faces shining . . .
   This isn't a dream. I know I am awake.
   It doesn't make sense, but it's joy.
   I am as I thought I never would be:
   My chains are gone. Today I'm free.   160
1ST SERVANT. How sad he is.
2ND SERVANT.   And wouldn't you be sad
   If you were him?
CLARION.   I wouldn't be.
2ND SERVANT.   What, him?
CLARION. No, sad.
2ND SERVANT. And yet who would change places with him?
CLARION. Me, for a start.
2ND SERVANT.   We'd better speak to him.   165
1ST SERVANT. Will you be pleased to hear the Palace choir?
SIGISMUND. No singing. No.
2ND SERVANT.   For your delight we planned
   Some songs.
SIGISMUND. (*Fanfare.*) I want a military band.
   This sound is wondrous to my ears: 170
   Now I throw off all doubts and fears.
CLOTALDO. Your highness, my dear lord,
   I kiss your hand and say
   I'm proud that I may humbly

175   Pay homage thus today.

SIGISMUND. It is Clotaldo. What's his mind, his meaning?
    In prison he tormented me but now
    He treats me with respect. What's happening?

CLOTALDO. I understand your wonderment.

180   In a world where all is strange,
    Your mind is full of doubts and fears
    Because of this sudden change.
    But I can soothe away all doubts
    And beat all terrors down.

185   I'm charged to tell you that you are
    Heir to the Polish Crown.
    You have been kept away from men
    Because astrology
    Predicted that your rule as King

190   Would prove a tyranny.
    You have been brought here to defy
    What the stars relate,
    For the man who is magnanimous
    Can triumph over fate.

195   While you were unconscious
    You were brought here to this place.
    The King, your father, will tell you the rest
    Of your story, face to face.

SIGISMUND. Traitor: one who betrays.

200   Traitor, you are my traitor.
    Now I know who I am,
    I am full of pride.
    Because of what I am,
    I am full of power.

205   Traitor to Poland, traitor,
    Hiding me away
    Like a dirty secret
    Traitor to me, Sigismund,
    Your prisoner, your prince . . .

210 CLOTALDO. My lord.

SIGISMUND. Savage to me and servile to the King.
    Therefore the law, the King and I condemn
       you
    To death. I'll execute you with these hands.

1ST SERVANT. My lord . . .

2ND SERVANT.   Your highness . . .

3RD SERVANT.   Sir . . .

CLOTALDO.   My lord . . .

215 SIGISMUND. Out of my way. Nobody stops me, no one.
    Out of my way, by God, or I will throw you
    Out of that window down into the lake.

CLARION. It's a dark lake.

1ST SERVANT.   Go, sir.

2ND SERVANT.   You'd better go.

CLOTALDO. I pity you. How powerful you seem

220   But you may find you're acting in a dream.

                            (*Exit Clotaldo.*)

2ND SERVANT. Consider, sir . . .

SIGISMUND.   Get out of here.

2ND SERVANT. He only obeyed his King.

SIGISMUND. He should have refused. I was his Prince.
    To lock me away was an unjust thing.

2ND SERVANT. It wasn't for him but the King to decide   225
    Right from wrong and white from black.

SIGISMUND. You must dislike yourself very much
    To risk answering me back.

CLARION. The Prince is right and you are wrong.

2ND SERVANT. And who asked you to say?   230

CLARION. Poland's a free country, isn't it?

1ST SERVANT. Who are you, anyway?

CLARION. I'm the world champion busy-body.
    I've a finger in every pie.
    I could kill you two birds   235
    With one bush if I liked
    But I've bigger fish to fry.

SIGISMUND. I know you. You're Clarion the Clown.

CLARION. Local vodka. Chuck it down.

(*Clarion passes Sigismund the bottle.*)

SIGISMUND (*drinks*).
    I like you,   240
    Clarion the Clown.
    You please me,
    You're the only one
    I like out of all these.

CLARION. Where pleasing's to be done,   245
    It pleases me to please.

(*Enter Astolfo. He leaves his hat on.*)

ASTOLFO. This is a happy day, most noble prince:
    This is the day when you, the sun of Poland,
    Must rise and fill the sky and shed your
       brightness
    On our horizons like the blushful dawn,   250
    For you have risen like the sunrise does
    Above the darkness of the dusky mountains.
    O may the lovely laurels on your brow,
    These late adornments, flourish long upon
       you
    And never wither.

SIGISMUND.   God be with you, sir.   255

ASTOLFO. Sir, I forgive you that you do not know me
    And do not give me honour when it's due.
    I am Astolfo, Duke of Muscovy,
    And we are cousins. You and I are equals.

1ST SERVANT. Remember, your grace, his highness was
       brought   260
    Up in the mountains, not in the court.

2ND SERVANT. The Duke, my lord, is an aristocrat.

SIGISMUND. He bores me. And he won't take off his hat.

1ST SERVANT. His rank allows that.

2ND SERVANT.   More respect is due.

SIGISMUND. To me, not him. I'm getting tired of you.   265

(*Enter Estrella.*)

ESTRELLA. Sir, welcome to the throne which longs for
    you
    And gratefully receives you. May you reign,
    Confounding fate, and live a thousand
       years.
SIGISMUND. Clarion, who is she? Who is this human
    goddess?
1ST SERVANT. Princess Estrella, sir.
270 2ND SERVANT.   She is your cousin.
SIGISMUND. Estrella? That's a star, but I should say
    She is the sun. I thank you for your kindness.
    Queen of the skies, you are the waking
      daylight.
    You could add brightness to the morning star
    And light the heavens. When you rise at
275   morning
    There's nothing left for the dull sun to do.
    O let me kiss your hand, that snow-pure cap
    From which the gentle breeze drinks
      whiteness up.
ESTRELLA. Eloquent Prince, I did not mean . . .
ASTOLFO. He must not touch her.
280 2ND SERVANT.   I'll intervene.
1ST SERVANT. Astolfo's angry.
2ND SERVANT.   Sir, is not your greeting
    Too ardent and too rough for a first meeting?
SIGISMUND. Didn't I say keep out of my way?
    Didn't I say keep out of my sight?
285   The coach is coming. Keep off the highway.
2ND SERVANT. You have just said that rulers must
    Always cleave to what is just.
SIGISMUND. I also said, for Jesus' sake,
    That I would throw you in the lake.
290 2ND SERVANT. You couldn't, sire, a man of my standing . . .
SIGISMUND. O couldn't I?
ESTRELLA.   Stop him!
SIGISMUND.   Happy landings!

(*Lifts him in his arms and rushes out.*)

ASTOLFO. Sweet, fetch the King.
ESTRELLA.   I'll ask him to hurry.
CLARION. Tell him I'm here and not to worry.

(*Exit Estrella. Re-enter Sigismund.*)

SIGISMUND. Your standing notwithstanding, slave.
295   Rest your bones in that chilly grave.
ASTOLFO. Restrain yourself, my lord: the difference
    Between a beast and man should be as great
    As that between a mountain and a palace.
SIGISMUND. Astolfo, if you carry on
300   Giving advice like that,
    You'll find you have no stupid head
    On which to put your stupid hat.

(*Exit Astolfo. Enter King Basilio.*)

BASILIO. What have you done?
SIGISMUND. Nothing much. I taught a
    Slave a lesson. Dropped him in the water.   305

(*Pause.*)

    Are you my father?
BASILIO. I am and love you . . .
SIGISMUND.   No, you've done me wrong.
BASILIO. You have done wrong, my son. What, take
    a life
    The very first day that you taste your
      freedom?
SIGISMUND. He said I couldn't do it, so I did.   310
BASILIO. This grieves me, Prince. Be more intelligent.
    I hoped to find a new, wise, prudent man
    Triumphing over destiny and the stars.
    Instead I find a brutal murderer.
    How can I give you love? How can I open   315
    My arms to yours? They are a killer's arms.
    I thought to embrace you with a father's
      love.
    But now you'll understand if I prefer
    To avoid the arms of a murderer.
SIGISMUND. I do not want your love or your embraces.   320
    You are a cruel father. You have kept me
    Away from you and reared me like a beast.
    You have denied my human dignity,
    So I feel nothing for you, father. Nothing.
BASILIO. I gave you life. I wish I never had.   325
SIGISMUND. And if you hadn't, I'd have no complaints.
    You gave me life and then wrenched it away.
    To give is blessed but give and take away
    Is twisted work.
BASILIO.   Is that the thanks I get
    For making a poor prisoner a Prince?   330
SIGISMUND. What have you given me that was not mine?
    You took my free will, chained it to the wall,
    And now you are an old, weak dying King,
    And you must leave me everything. It's mine.
    Poland is mine. There's nothing that I owe
      you.   335
    You owe me life and happiness and freedom.
    You should be thanking me I do not force
      you
    To pay your debt.
BASILIO.   Look on him, everyone:
    See how the stars have kept their promises.
    See, see how cruel and arrogant he is.   340
    My son, I warn you, be more kind, more
      gentle,
    More humble. That is good advice to take:
    Perhaps you only dream that you're awake.
SIGISMUND. Is this a dream? I feel, I hear, I touch.
    I know what I have been and what I am.   345
    You may regret it but you can't undo it.
    For I am what I am. What's done is done.

I am half-man, half-beast. I'm not your son.

(*All exit. Enter Rosaura dressed in white.*)

ROSAURA. Now Sigismund's a prince and I a lady.
350   O it is sweet to wear a dress again.
          I'm full of joy. Astolfo loves me still.
          I saw him come to visit his Estrella
          And he still wears my picture. He'd not do
              that
          Unless he loved me. I will work on him.
355   There's time enough to think upon revenge.
          Am I not fair? Am I not painted fine?
          As I am now I'm fit to wed a King.
          A Duke is easy, I will woo and win him.
          Clotaldo says I must not speak to him.
360   I owe him much and therefore should obey.
          And yet I will not. I am strong today
          Because I find I'm fairer than Estrella.
          What jewel's best to wear? Or this? Or this?
          I'll find out ways to make myself more fine.
365   When I was man my heart was torn by strife.
          But now I'm woman I may yet be wife.
          (*She puts on various jewels.*)

(*Enter Sigismund.*)

SIGISMUND. The world is all as I thought it would be.
          Through books and pictures I foresaw it all.
          But if I had to wonder at one thing
370   In this new world, I'd wonder at a woman
          And at her beauty. Once in some old book
          I read that of all things in God's creation
          Man was God's loveliest and noblest work
          Because a man is like a little world.
375   But I believe that woman is the noblest,
          For she's a little heaven and more lovely . . .
          And far more so, if she's the one I look on.
ROSAURA (*sees Sigismund*).
          It is the prince. I'll leave him.
SIGISMUND. Wait, woman, listen. Tell me who you are.
380 ROSAURA. I think, but am not sure, that I have seen you.
SIGISMUND. I think I've seen your beauty once before.
ROSAURA. I've seen your rage and sorrow in your prison.
SIGISMUND. Who are you? You are fair. I've found my
              life.
ROSAURA. I'm a poor lady in Estrella's train.
385 SIGISMUND. No, do not say that. Say you are the sun
          And that Estrella is a petty star
          Who gets her splendour from your borrowed
              flame.
          O I have seen the kingdom of the flowers
          Where every odour is and every hue,
390   And where the rose is goddess o'er the rest
          And queen because she is most beautiful.
          And I have seen a world of precious gems
          Deep in the dark academy of the mines,

And how the rest all hail the diamond
And call it emperor for its radiance.   395
And I have seen up in the courts of heaven,
High in the lovely empire of the stars,
The morning star in royal pre-eminence.
And I have seen how in the very spheres
The sun, that is the oracle of day,   400
Calls up the planets to his parliament
And plays the speaker. If among all these,
The flowers, the mines, the firmament, the
    planets,
The fairest is exalted, how can I
Serve one who is less beautiful than you,   405
Who are for loveliness and excellence
The peer of roses, diamonds, sun and stars?

(*Enter Clotaldo, unseen.*)

CLOTALDO (*aside*). I educated him. It's up to me
          To advise the boy. But first I'll wait and see.
ROSAURA. My lord, I'm honoured by your eloquence.   410
          But I'm lost for words. My reply is silence.
SIGISMUND. Your body speaks and everything about you.
          You shine. O do not leave me in the dark.
ROSAURA. I beg your leave to go . . .
SIGISMUND.   Stay where you are.
          You do not beg my leave, you simply take it.   415
ROSAURA. If you won't give it I am bound to take it.
SIGISMUND. Well then, you'll see the dark side of my
              passion,
          The Beast-man. Say, why are you dressed
              so fine
          Unless you mean to set a man on fire?
ROSAURA. I did not dress to please you.
SIGISMUND.   But you do.   420
          You've made yourself a lure and flame to
              men.
ROSAURA. I have not . . .
SIGISMUND.   Come, resistance poisons patience.
          I've seen you thus, and seen you as a man.
          Now I will see you as you truly are.
ROSAURA. You would not dare. You will respect my
              honour.   425
SIGISMUND. We'll see. You'll make me try it, though
              I am
          Afraid of you because you are so fair.
          I must know whether I can love or not.
          I want to conquer the impossible.
          Today I threw a man over that balcony   430
          Down into the black lake. I did it, lady,
          Because he said I couldn't. Now I'll throw
          Your chastity out of the window after.
          (*He throws her on the bed and starts to tear
          her clothes off.*)

CLOTALDO (*aside*). It is not good that he should thus divest
              him,

And yet the King has said that we must test
435   him.
ROSAURA. The stars were right. They spoke the truth.
      I see
      You'll be a tyrant. You will fill up Poland
      With riot, slaughter, treachery and crime.
      What else can be expected of a creature
440   As barbarous, inhuman and relentless,
      As is a beast that is brought up with beasts?
CLOTALDO (*aside*).
      I've waited long enough and I have seen
      What he intends. I'd better intervene.
SIGISMUND. I've tried to speak to you with gentleness
445   Because I hoped you would be kind to me,
      But since you are so sure I am a beast,
      I'll prove I am one.
CLOTALDO.   Pardon me, my lord . . .
SIGISMUND. How did you get in here?
CLOTALDO.   I . . .
SIGISMUND.   Go away.
ROSAURA. I'm lost. Wait, listen . . .
SIGISMUND.   No, I am a tyrant.
450   I am the Beast-man.
CLOTALDO. Wait, my lord. Be careful.
SIGISMUND. Doddering old fool, how dare you interrupt?
CLOTALDO. I heard your voice raised angrily
      And wanted, Prince, to say:
455   Try to be mild and humble
      And show gentleness today,
      Or you may wake to find your power
      Has melted, like a dream away.
SIGISMUND. Now I will kill you. We'll soon see
460   If this is a dream or reality.
CLOTALDO (*kneels and grabs hold of Sigismund*).
      I mean to live.
SIGISMUND.   Let go.
CLOTALDO.   I'll not let go.
      I know you mean to throw me in the lake.
ROSAURA. For God's sake help.
SIGISMUND.   Old fool, I say, let go.
      Or I will crush you in my arms to death.
ROSAURA. Quickly, come quickly! Clotaldo's being
465   murdered.

      (*Exit Rosaura. Enter Astolfo.*)

ASTOLFO. Stay, noble prince.
      What, stain an old man's blood? You will
          not do that.
SIGISMUND. If blood is in his dusty veins, I will.
ASTOLFO. I'll answer for his life.
SIGISMUND.   You'll answer, will you?
470   You have insulted me. Now I shall kill you.
ASTOLFO. Then I will draw in self-defence, my lord,
      And that's no treason.
      (*They fight.*)

CLOTALDO (*to Astolfo*). Do not hurt him, sire.

      (*Enter Basilio, Estrella, Servants, and Clarion.*)

BASILIO. What, swords?
ESTRELLA.   Astolfo, hold.
BASILIO.   Hold, both of you.
      What is it?
ASTOLFO.   Nothing. You are here: it's over.   475
      (*Astolfo sheathes his sword.*)

      No man will draw his sword before his King.
SIGISMUND. You should have said you drew against your
      King.
CLOTALDO. Humour him, sire. Do it all gently.
BASILIO. What was the cause? Explain it, pray.
SIGISMUND. I wanted to make love to a lady   480
      But those old bones appeared.
      I wanted to kill that old fool
      But the Cossack interfered.
BASILIO. What, do you not respect a lady's honour?
      Don't you respect this good old man's grey
      hair?   485
CLOTALDO. Her honour's untarnished. So is my grey hair.
SIGISMUND. I was brought up with horror and grey air.
      I'm getting ready for the day
      When I'll squash your Royal honour
      Under my boots and use your silver beard   490
      As a mat to wipe my feet on.
BASILIO. Wild, monstrous, rash. O you are barbarous.
SIGISMUND. You brought me up like a rat in a box
      But I'll be revenged on you, Grizzly-locks.
BASILIO. Now I am sure the cruel stars spoke true.   495
      All of you, mark him, mark his insolence.
      You have all heard him. He would be
          revenged.
      No, Sigismund, my son, before that happens,
      You'll sleep again where you slept
          yesterday.

      (*Basilio signals to the Servants. They seize Sigismund and
      Clarion. Basilio pours a potion into Sigismund's mouth.
      He falls asleep.*)

      Now you shall think that everything which
          passed   500
      Here in the palace on your happy day,
      Like all good things on earth, was so much
          dreaming.
      Clotaldo, take him back into the mountains.
      Estrella and the Duke shall reign in Poland.

                                        (*Exeunt.*)

      (*Enter Astolfo and Estrella.*)

ASTOLFO. I see, Estrella, that the stars spoke true: 505
      Take Sigismund and myself, for we were
          born
      Under two signs. For him there was foretold

A life of crime and it has come to pass;
But for my part, when I first saw your eyes
They were as stars, my stars, for then they
510   spoke
To me of bliss and fame and great
          possessions.
Is it not so? Or are the fickle stars
True only when they tell of evil things?
ESTRELLA. I do not doubt that these fine words of yours
515   Are finely meant, but are they meant for me?
What of the woman whose bewitching
          picture
You wore about your neck when we first
          met?
I think it must be so. These compliments
Belong to her, so go and take them to her,
520   And she'll reward you for your gentleness.
Kind words and courtesies to other women
Are scarcely current in the Court of Love.
ASTOLFO. I never wear that portrait now. It chokes me.
I have made room for you and for your
          beauty.
525   For where Estrella is there are no shadows,
As there are no stars by the noonday sun.
I'll fetch the picture, madam.
                              (Exit Estrella.)
                    Fair Rosaura,
Forgive me now. I know too well that I
Do ill in this, but when a man or woman
530   Is separated from the one they love,
They rarely keep their faiths. And so with me.
I'll get the portrait.
                              (Exit Astolfo.)

(Re-enter Estrella.)

ESTRELLA. O how we act and do not show our minds.
I know he does not love me but he woos
535   In policy. And I in likewise act
And now seem cold. That's likewise policy,
For I believe that is the way to win him.

(Enter Rosaura, demurely dressed.)

ROSAURA (aside).
I changed my dress because I thought it safer.
ESTRELLA. Astraea . . .
ROSAURA.   Yes, my lady?
ESTRELLA.   I am glad
540   That you have come. I have a secret for you.
ROSAURA. You honour me and I obey you, madam.
ESTRELLA. I have not known you long and yet I trust you.
I want to share my inmost mind with you.
ROSAURA. I am your slave.
ESTRELLA.   Then as you know, Astolfo,
545   Who is my cousin, means to marry me,

Which it is hoped, will cancel much
          misfortune
With one great joy. But though I dote on him
I dare not show it. Something troubles me.
When he arrived in Poland he was wearing
A portrait of a lady round his neck.   550
I asked him if he loved her. He denied it.
He's gone to fetch it but I'd be embarrassed
To take it from him. You stay here instead,
And when he comes ask him to give it to you.
                              (Exit Estrella.)
ROSAURA. What woman is there wise and calm enough   555
To know what she should do if she was I?
When I was man, I wished I was a woman,
But now I am I wish I was a man.
O what a pickle and a maze I'm in:
I curse the hour that I was born feminine.   560
I'm sworn to serve Estrella and to get
My picture back. I'm sworn to obey Clotaldo
Who saved my life. He said I must not woo
Astolfo, yet I'm sworn to or to kill him.
Nor am I now suited to please the man.   565
I fear that I am ugly, dull and nasty.
I am the fool of love. What shall I do?
I can't pretend, I. When Astolfo comes,
However much I plan and I prepare
I'll do . . . O God, I don't know what I'll do.   570

(Enter Astolfo.)

ASTOLFO. Here is the portrait, madam . . .
Good God!
ROSAURA.   What troubles you?
Why do you stare at my face?
ASTOLFO. To see you in this place.
Rosaura . . .
ROSAURA.   I am sorry, sir,   575
You're very much mistaken,
I am called Astraea.
I'm a lady-in-waiting.
I am not the noble lady you seek,
If I may judge by the way you speak.   580
ASTOLFO. Do not pretend, Rosaura,
What if you're called Astraea,
I love you as Rosaura . . .
ROSAURA. I do not understand one word you utter.
So please, your highness, all that I can say   585
Is that Estrella (who may be the star
Of love itself, since that's Estrella's
          meaning)
Told me to wait for you and in her place
To take a picture which you'd bring for her.
The lady wants it and I must obey her.   590
ASTOLFO. Inform your eyes, they contradict your voice.
If you uttered lies with perfect control
I'd look through your eyes and see your soul.

ROSAURA. I want the picture. That is why I'm here.
595 ASTOLFO. Then, if you want to lie like you do,
    Go to the princess and say this, Astraea:
    She asked me for a picture but I prize her
    Too much to send her such a petty gift.
    Instead of that, in love and in devotion,
600   I send her now the sweet original.
    Go, take it to her. You are bound to take it
    Wherever you may go.
ROSAURA.   If I return
    With the original and not the copy
    I shall have failed my duty to my mistress.
605   I came for the portrait.
    Give me the portrait.
    I must have the portrait.
ASTOLFO. I will not give it
    And you cannot take it.
610 ROSAURA. I'll tear it from you.
    You devil. Let go.
    (*She tries to seize it.*)

ASTOLFO. What use is that?
ROSAURA.   By God,
    I will not let it fall
    Into another woman's hands.
615 ASTOLFO. You admit you're Rosaura.
    You said that you'd give it
    Back to your mistress.
ROSAURA. I do not care what I said.
ASTOLFO. You're angry.
ROSAURA.   You're base.
620 ASTOLFO. That's enough. You are mine.
ROSAURA. I am not, you lie.
    You bully, you liar.
    (*She grabs the picture again.*)

    (*Enter Estrella.*)

ESTRELLA. Astraea. Astolfo.
    What is this?
ASTOLFO.   Estrella.
ROSAURA (*aside*).
625   Love, grant me all your cunning
    So I can get the picture.
    My lady, I'll explain.
ASTOLFO. Now what's her plan?
ROSAURA. Madam, you told me to wait
630   For Astolfo to bring a portrait.
    I was day-dreaming:
    You know the way. I remembered
    A portrait of my own.
    I opened it but dropped it.
635   Then Astolfo came.
    He would not give me his
    But picked up mind instead
    And would not give it back.

    I pleaded but he held on,
    So I tried to take it from him. 640
    There it is, in his hand.
    It's mine. It looks like mine.
ESTRELLA. Astolfo, give it to me.
ASTOLFO. Madam . . .
ESTRELLA.   It flatters you:
    There is a calm about it. 645
ROSAURA. Yes, it's my portrait.
ESTRELLA. I do not doubt it.
ROSAURA. Then you should order him
    To give you the other one.
ESTRELLA. Take your own and go. 650
ROSAURA (*aside*).
    Now I've got mine back
    I'll watch and see what happens.
ASTOLFO. Madam, I can explain . . .
ESTRELLA. Give me the picture which you promised me.
    Although I hope that I shall never see you 655
    Or speak to you again, I do not want it
    To stay in your hands. I see I was foolish
    To ask for it. So give it back again.
ASTOLFO. Lovely Estrella, I do not know how
    I can return the portrait.
ESTRELLA.   Do not try. 660
    Flirt with my servant: so much for your love.
    I don't want your picture. Whatever you do
    It would only remind me I begged it of you.
               (*Exit Estrella.*)

ASTOLFO. Estrella, listen!
    Damn you, Rosaura. Everything was fine 665
    Till you arrived in Poland. You'll destroy
      me.
    My hopes hang on this marriage. If it fails
    I'll tear Rosaura's eyes out with my nails.
ROSAURA (*comes forward*).
    Then tear them out. I will be glad of it.
ASTOLFO. Rosaura, you have done much mischief to me. 670
ROSAURA. Astolfo, you have done much mischief to me.
ASTOLFO. That's past. What you've just done will
      undo Poland.
    You see how Sigismund's unfit to reign.
ROSAURA. You're not fit either. You have broke your
      oath.
ASTOLFO. Yes, I did as the world does.
ROSAURA.   Then you're base 675
    As mean men are.
ASTOLFO.   I could not marry you
    (I see that I must spell it out again)
    Because you do not know who was your
      father.
    You know that is our law, our code,
      our custom.
    I will not, cannot go against my honour. 680
ROSAURA. You went against it when you mangled mine.

ASTOLFO. It's true I did you wrong . . .

ROSAURA.   Why then,

ASTOLFO. No, listen.

685   You do wrong now to make so much of it.
Love does not last. It fades. To cling to it
When it is done is tedious and foolish.
I know that you love to torment yourself:
You hug your woes just as your mother did.
That's why you serve Estrella and that's why
690   You tried to get me to give up your picture.

ROSAURA. You're full of reasons but what's in your
         heart?
Tell me one thing.

ASTOLFO.   What?

ROSAURA.   Do you love Estrella?

ASTOLFO. I will not tell you. If I said I did
You'd plague yourself, and if I said I did not
You'd go on clinging to your hopes and
695   dreams.

ROSAURA. To live in doubt's a plague.

ASTOLFO.   That's how you are.
You twist and turn all that I say to you.
That is your woman's nature.

ROSAURA.   You are so vile.
You twist and turn, not I. That's your man's
         nature.
You broke your oath but I will not break
700   mine.

ASTOLFO. What have you sworn?

ROSAURA.   Either to marry you
Or kill you. Why do you laugh?

ASTOLFO.   You can do neither.

ROSAURA. Let time tell that.

ASTOLFO.   No, let time tell it now.
I challenge you. Here is my dagger. Use it.

705   ROSAURA. I will not kill you with a mean man's weapon.
I am sworn to slay you with my father's
         sword.

ASTOLFO. Well, keep your oath.

ROSAURA.   I do not have it with me.

ASTOLFO. Fetch it and I will wait. Why, it's apparent
You cannot do it. Now I know that I
710   did right when I forsook you, for I see
You are not of noble blood. Do not reproach
         me
That I'm forsworn, for you are now as I am.
Therefore have done, go home to Muscovy,
Forget what's past and get yourself a husband,
And talk no more of vengeance, oaths and
715   honour.
(Aside.) Some men might say that was quite
         a close call.
But I know about love. There was no risk
         at all.

(Exit Astolfo.)

ROSAURA. Alas. I'm worse off than I was before.
O what a fool I was. Alone with him:
I should have wooed him or I should have
         killed him.   720
All that he said is true. I have no honour.
I am forsworn. I do torment myself.
I am a mingle, I am full of voices
That war in me and buzz inside my head.
I cannot help it. I am as I am.   725
It cannot be but that I have bad stars.
What shall I do? How shall I find a clearness?
An oath is clear, and I will keep mine yet.
Then, stars, be kind and help me find a way
To kill Astolfo. There's no more to say.   730

(Exit Rosaura.)

SCENE TWO

(Clotaldo and Guards carry in Sigismund and Clarion.
They leave Sigismund on the floor and chain him.)

CLOTALDO. He has had his day.

1ST GUARD. Here's his old rusty chain.

CLOTALDO. His pride has led him back
Into black night again.

(Exit Clotaldo and Guards.)

CLARION. Somnolent, somniferous.
When the arms of Morpheus   5
Give you back to consciousness
You will find your luck
Has drowned in the black lake.
All your pomp is muck:
It was all a fake.   10
Your life is a game,
A little shadow-play
Lit by death's candle-flame
For one brief day.
                                                        15
(Re-enter Guards and Clotaldo with a candle.)

CLOTALDO. You talk too much.
Go, chain him in a cell.

CLARION. Why me?

CLOTALDO.   You know too much.
You're a noisy Clarion.

CLARION. What have I done?   20
I ask you? Have I ever tried
To kill my father or something worse?
Or tried to rape a Princess?
Never! Quite the reverse.
Do I throw servants in the lake?   25
Do I get reborn, for God's sake?
Do I dream? Do I sleep? I do not. So
Why lock me up?

CLOTALDO.   Because of what you know.

CLARION. At least make sure

30   I'm properly fed
    With plenty to drink.
CLOTALDO (*to Guards*).
    You heard what he said.

(*Guards take Clarion out. Enter King Basilio, cloaked
and masked.*)

BASILIO. Clotaldo.
CLOTALDO.   Sire, why have you come disguised?
BASILIO. It was perhaps unwise but I am curious
35   To see what happens now to Sigismund.
CLOTALDO. Well, there he lies as he did formerly.
BASILIO. Unlucky Prince. Tragic nativity.
CLOTALDO. He's restless. He is talking in his sleep.
BASILIO. What does he dream of now? We'll listen
    to him.
SIGISMUND (*in his sleep*).
    Princes show mercy when they murder
40   tyrants.
    I'll crush Clotaldo. He'll be old dead meat.
    Where is my father? Let him kiss my feet.
CLOTALDO. He threatens me with death.
BASILIO. And me with shame.
SIGISMUND (*in his sleep*).
    I will be brave, my cue is blood and
45   vengenance.
    I'll be revenged upon the King, my father,
    And trample him in dust on this great stage,
    The theatre of the world . . .
    (*Wakes.*)   O where am I?
    Light . . . darkness . . . Fetters again?
50   A slave? What things I've dreamed of . . .
CLOTALDO (*aside*).
    I will delude the Prince.
    Time to wake up. Have you slept all day
        long?
    We talked last night of eagles, and I think
    You've slept since then.
SIGISMUND.   I've slept since then . . .
CLOTALDO.   I've tracked
55   An eagle in the air while you were sleeping.
SIGISMUND. I think that I am still asleep, Clotaldo.
    It must be so, for if the things I saw
    When I was dreaming were so clear and
        bright,
    What I see now must be unreal and
        shadows.
CLOTALDO. Tell me your dream.
60 SIGISMUND.   If it had been a dream
    I would not tell it. What I saw, Clotaldo,
    I saw indeed, and it was real I saw.
    I woke. And then I saw myself, in bed
    Soft comforting, the cover sweetly woven

    Like springtime meadows in our mountain
65   lands,

    Cornflower, wild strawberry and lady's
        slipper.
    Courtiers knelt and hailed me as their Prince,
    And then you told me I was Prince of
        Poland.
CLOTALDO. And when I told you that, how did you thank
    me?
SIGISMUND. Not well. I think I tried to kill you twice.   70
    Yes, I was angry and I called you traitor.
CLOTALDO. Were you so cruel?
SIGISMUND.   I thought I saw my father
    And hated him. For I was all men's master
    And wanted my revenge upon them all,
    Except one woman whom I know I loved.   75
    The rest have vanished, but her picture is
    Branded upon my mind. She must be real.

                (*Exit Basilio.*)

CLOTALDO (*aside*).
    The King has gone. He's moved.
    Because we talked a while last night of
        eagles
    You dreamed of empires when you went to
        bed.   80
    But you would do well, even in your dreams,
    To honour those who care for you each day.
    Kindness is never wasted, even in dreams,
    And gentleness is never thrown away.

                (*Exit Clotaldo.*)

SIGISMUND. Perhaps that's true. Perhaps I should snuff
    out   85
    This flame of rage, this blaze of red ambition.
    The time may come when we shall dream
        again.
    In this strange world to live's a kind of
        dreaming,
    And each of us must dream the thing he is
    Till he awakes. The King dreams he's a
        King,   90
    Lives, orders, governs in a royal illusion,
    Because his fame is written in the wind.
    For every King that rules men in his
        King-dream
    Must wake at last in the cold sleep of death.
    The rich man dreams his riches which are
        cares,   95
    The poor man dreams his penury and pain,
    The man who prospers dreams, the man
        who strives,
    The man who hurts men, and the man who's
        hurt,
    All dream. So what's this life? A fraud, a
        frenzy,
    A trick, a tale, a shadow, an illusion.   100
    And all our life is nothing but a dream.
    And what are dreams? They are no more
    than dreamstuff.

And what is real is nothing, and a man
Is nothing neither.

(*Snuffs out the candle.*)

105   It is all a dream.

                              (*Exit Sigismund.*)

END OF ACT TWO

ACT THREE

SCENE ONE

(*Enter Clarion.*)

CLARION (*sings*).
      Lord, I am a drinking man
      With nothing left to lose.
      My quest is for oblivion,
      My weapon is the booze.
5   My enemy's reality—
      I dodge her when I can.
      God bless the drinking man . . .

      Lord, I am a drinking man.
      I'm drinking to forget
10   Something I remembered
      When my memory was wet.
      O brandy sun, shine down on me
      And give me tippler's tan.
      God bless the drinking man . . .

15   Though they've locked me in a cell
      Like Cervantes in the clink,
      I shall manage very well,
      If I have enough to drink.
      I'll swig it from a goblet,
20   I'll sip it from a can,
      God bless the drinking man . . .

      Lord, I am a drinking man
      And when I die of thirst,
      Place me in a champagne vat,
25   Totally immersed.
      An after-life of stupor
      Is my religious plan.
      God bless the drinking man . . .

(*Drums. Clamour and banging outside. Enter Soldiers.*)

1ST SOLDIER. This is the tower. Where is the prisoner?
30 CLARION. It must be me that they are looking for.
2ND SOLDIER. He's here.
CLARION.   No, he's not here.
1ST SOLDIER.   Your Majesty.
CLARION. You must be drunk.
1ST SOLDIER.   You are our rightful prince.
2ND SOLDIER. We want our natural lord.
3RD SOLDIER.   No Muscovite.

2ND SOLDIER. No foreign prince for us. Break off his chains.
CLARION. It's real. They are not joking. They want me.   35
   It must be a custom in this curious kingdom
   To make someone a prince here for a day
   And then to throw him back in jail again.
   And now it's my turn.
3RD SOLDIER. We kiss your feet, sire.
1ST SOLDIER.   Sir, give us your feet.   40
CLARION. I can't. I need them. Princes need their feet.
2ND SOLDIER. What is your will, my lord?
CLARION.   What is my will?
   Now I am Prince of Poland
   I'll free all drunks and debtors.
   I'll put the politicians   45
   Respectfully in fetters.

   I promise to my subjects
   Steaks shall grow on trees
   And a cathedral shall be carved
   From Gorgonzola cheese.   50

   My kingdom's cows shall give us
   Vodka instead of milk.
   Harlots will pay their clients
   And beggars sleep in silk.

   My policy for Poland   55
   Is: set the people free.
   And when I say the people,
   I mean people like me.
1ST SOLDIER. We've told the King
   We want no other prince but you to rule us.   60
CLARION. Did you not treat my father with respect?
2ND SOLDIER. We spoke out of our loyalty to you.
CLARION. If you were being loyal then I forgive you.
1ST SOLDIER. Prince Sigismund, come forth and rule your
      kingdom.
CLARION. That seems to be the name they give to all   65
   Their player princes.
SOLDIERS.   Long live Sigismund.

(*Enter Sigismund.*)

SIGISMUND. Who calls on Sigismund?
1ST SOLDIER.   Who is this man?
CLARION. That is the true prince. I am just a player.
   I abdicate.
1ST SOLDIER. Which one of you is the prince?   70
SIGISMUND. I have been told that I am.
2ND SOLDIER.   Little fool,
   Why did you say you were?
CLARION.   I didn't, you did.
   You Sigismunded me. You are the fool,
   Not I.
                              (*Exit Clarion.*)
1ST SOLDIER. Enough of this, Prince Sigismund.   75
   Your father is a clever, cunning man
   But he believes the world's run by the stars.
   He is afraid of prophecies which say

He will kneel at your feet. Therefore he wants
80 To lock you up, deprive you of your rights
And give them to the Duke of Muscovy.
And to that end he called a parliament
And so awoke the people. We know now
That we already have a native heir
85 And do not want a foreigner to rule us,
Especially a Muscovite. So come with us.
We all know how to fight. The mountain's
    swarming
With soldiers, outlaws, peasants, prisoners,
Who hail you as their King. Then come away
And seize the crown and sceptre from the
90   tyrant.
    (*Drums and trumpets.*)

SOLDIERS. Long live King Sigismund.
SIGISMUND.   It sounds again.
What do you want with me this time, you
    stars?
Another bubble? Another shadow-play?
And will it once more vanish in the dark?
95 No, not again. No dreaming. I'll not do it.
Ghosts, go away. You all seem to have bodies
And voices, but you have none. You are
    shadows.
You are like me: you are asleep. You're
    dream-men.
I will not be the plaything of the stars.
100 I will not be like some rash almond tree
Which buds too soon so that its pink and
    white
Shatters like glass in the first ruthless frost
And all its loveliness and light is lost.
1ST SOLDIER. If you believe that we are lying to you,
Look at the mountainside: all those men are
105   with us.
2ND SOLDIER. They await your orders.
SIGISMUND.   Yes, I see them clearly.
I see you clearly too. But once before
I saw as clearly as that but I was dreaming.
1ST SOLDIER. My lord, they say before a great event
There's some great sign. Your king-dreaming
110   was an omen
To make you ready.
2ND SOLDIER.   This event is real.
SIGISMUND. What are your names?
1ST SOLDIER.   We don't have names, my lord.
2ND SOLDIER. We leave our names at home.
3RD SOLDIER.   It's dangerous
To use real names.
SIGISMUND.   How many of you are there?
1ST SOLDIER. We're numberless.
2ND SOLDIER.   As stars are.
115 3RD SOLDIER.   You could say
That we go on forever.

SIGISMUND.   I believe
You speak the truth and my dream was an
    omen.
Let us suppose that. But what then? Life's
    brief,
So let us dream. And yet I know my nature.
Therefore I must remember as I dream   120
I must be politic. Let's all remember
That we must wake up when we least expect it.
Since we know that and know that we must
    suffer
We'll suffer less because we know we shall.

I will go on. I thank your loyalty.   125
I'll free you all from foreign rule in Poland.
I'll prove the stars spoke true and make my
    father
Grovel before me . . . if I don't wake up . . .
SOLDIERS. King Sigismund!

    (*Drums. Enter Clotaldo.*)

CLOTALDO. Guards! Where are the guards!
SIGISMUND.   It is Clotaldo.   130
CLOTALDO. I kiss your feet. I know that I must die.
SIGISMUND. No. You must be the North Star in my sky.
Stand up, Clotaldo, do not be afraid.
You must still be my guide and counsellor.
CLOTALDO. What do you mean?
SIGISMUND.   I mean that I am dreaming.   135
But I would like to act well in my dream.
CLOTALDO. If doing good is now your game
Do not be surprised
If I want to do the same.
You do not know these men.   140
If you'll wage war against your father
How can I be your adviser?
He is my King. All I can do
Is offer up my life to you.
SIGISMUND. I am your King. You are a traitor to me.   145
1ST SOLDIER. Your fine words are a mockery, Clotaldo.
CLOTALDO. You are all traitors. Where's your loyalty?
2ND SOLDIER. We are the loyal ones and you are the traitor.
CLOTALDO. Rebellion is damnation in a subject.
3RD SOLDIER. To be a subject is a true damnation.   150
CLOTALDO. You twist my words.
1ST SOLDIER.   You twist reality.
SIGISMUND. Enough of this.
CLOTALDO.   My lord . . .
SIGISMUND.   Clotaldo, listen:
If that is how you feel, go to the King.
Don't try to tell me what is good or bad,
I think that each man's honour is his own,   155
Farewell. We'll meet in a battle.
CLOTALDO. You're generous, but if you hope to reign,
You must remember things may change
    again.

(Exit Clotaldo.)

SIGISMUND. Now to the Palace. Drums and trumpets,
160   sound.

(Drums and trumpets.)

Come Zodiac, we go to reign.
I am as my stars make me.
If this is real don't let me sleep.
If I'm asleep, don't wake me.
165   What matters is to try
To do what is right.
Then if it is real
Right justifies itself,
And if it is unreal
170   It does no harm to have
Some credit up in heaven.
It may be useful on the day
That we awake and end the play.

(They go out of the prison.)

SCENE TWO

(Enter Estrella and Rosaura.)

ESTRELLA. He picked it up? You did not give it to him?
ROSAURA. No, madam.
ESTRELLA.   Swear it, girl.
ROSAURA.   I swear I did not
Give him my picture, no, not yesterday.
ESTRELLA. I'm satisfied. Forgive me my jealousy.
ROSAURA. I understand it.
5   ESTRELLA.   Then you know it is
A monster that preys most where love is
    greatest.
ROSAURA. I know.
ESTRELLA. Then help me.
ROSAURA.   I will do your will.
ESTRELLA. I am on fire. Astolfo treats me cruelly
But I love him the more. I burn for him,
I ache for him, Astraea. Yet I've sworn
10   That I will never speak to him again.
How may I then undo what I have said?
ROSAURA. I think you cannot.
ESTRELLA.   No, I think I can.
Because our marriage is a thing of state
I've never spoken with the Duke in private.
15   I long to do so and to know his nature
To judge if he is fit to marry me.
ROSAURA. Indeed?
ESTRELLA.   I have a bower in my garden
That's walled around, a pleasant secret place.
Give him this key and bid him enter in.
20   Say I'll be there tonight but do not tell him
I gave it to you but rather say you are

His friend, not mine. Take it, Astraea. Take it.
ROSAURA. And when he comes, what then?
ESTRELLA.   I do not know.
Time must try that. Now I am wild with love
And I must have my will. I long for night   25
And for Astolfo. Heaven do me right.

(Exit Estrella.)

ROSAURA. I'll get a copy of this garden key:
Then when he comes, God knows who he
    will see.

(Exit Rosaura. Enter King Basilio and Astolfo.)

BASILIO. But who can stop a bolting horse, Astolfo?
Or stop a river roaring to the sea?   30
Such is the pride and anger of the people:
Some shout "Astolfo," others "Sigismund."
My realm is turned into a stage for Fate
To play out monstrous tragedies of blood.
ASTOLFO. I see I must forget my love awhile.   35
Now war must serve. This is no time for
    wooing.
If Poland now resists me as her heir
It is because I have not proved myself,
And yet one day I'll sit upon her throne.
I'll take a horse. I'm proud and I am angry.   40
I'll strike those rebels like a thunderstone.

(Exit Astolfo.)

BASILIO. O it is dangerous, foreseeing danger.
I ran away and ran to what I ran from.
I hid a thing, and hiding it I found it,
And so I have destroyed my own dear land.   45

(Enter Estrella.)

ESTRELLA. Your Majesty, you must go now in person
And curb the turmoil raging in the streets,
For everything is havoc and confusion.
They clamour that you should release your
    son.

(Enter Clotaldo.)

CLOTALDO. Thank God you're safe, sire.
BASILIO.   Where is Sigismund? 50
CLOTALDO. The rebels found the tower and freed the
    Prince.
BASILIO. Basil the Learned. What's my learning won?
Basil the Great. What has my greatness done?
This is the ruin of my lovely land.
The winds have died. The stars, the sun have
    gone.   55
The houses and the farms stand now like
    tombs.
Each soldier is a walking skeleton.
I see this nightmare with my eyes wide open;
Before me stands an enormous hill
Of men and horses, red and broken,   60

And the whole hill cries out and will not be
    still.
CLOTALDO. There's some organ in man
    That seems to need death
    As the heart needs blood,
65   As the lungs need breath.
ESTRELLA. What I would do
    Cannot now be done.
    And yet there's a battle
    Still to be won.
70 BASILIO. Yes, I'll ride out
    To meet my son.

                  (Exit King Basilio and Estrella.)

CLOTALDO. Why did he tell his son he was his father?
    That has bred chaos. That was his mistake.
    I'll never tell my daughter who I am
75   For fear lest Fortune throws me in the lake.

(Enter Rosaura with her father's sword and a skull.)

ROSAURA. The Duke must die.
CLOTALDO.   What would you now, Rosaura?
    What is this show? What is this skull of death?
ROSAURA. It is myself. For when Astolfo left me
    I died. So he must die.
CLOTALDO.   No.
ROSAURA.   Hear me out.
80   Tonight he meets Estrella in a garden.
    You told me that he woo'd in policy
    But now I see it's lust. Then take this key
    And this your sword and there cut down
      Astolfo.
    Uphold my honour. Give me my revenge.
85 CLOTALDO. Skulls, garden keys . . . Why this is fantasy.
    The Duke has gone to fight Prince Sigismund.
ROSAURA. Then you must follow him.
CLOTALDO.   I cannot do that.
ROSAURA. You swore to help me
    And you must keep your oath.
90 CLOTALDO. I did plan for your honour's sake
    To kill him if I could,
    A tumble into the lake
    Or a garrotte in the wood.
    But then the young prince tried
95   To crush me murderously
    And I surely would have died
    But Astolfo rescued me.
    I owe him my life, so how
    Can I kill him now?
100   I'm bound to him and you:
    So what am I to do?
ROSAURA. You are a man.
    You know the code.
    Giving is noble
105   But receiving's base.
    You gave me life

So I ennoble you.
    You received life from him
    So you owe him nothing.
    Do you accept that?   110
CLOTALDO. Yes, in principle.
    Yet though giving shows nobility
    The generous must condemn
    All those who react ungratefully
    To those who succour them.   115
    My reputation is unmarred
    And I find meanness hateful.
    My good name would be scarred
    Were I to prove ungrateful.
    I respect in my liberality   120
    Giving and receiving equally.
ROSAURA. You said to me that life
    Without honour is no life,
    So the life you gave me
    Is no life at all.   125
    And if being generous
    Comes before being grateful
    (As you seem to say),
    I'm waiting for my life:
    I haven't got it yet.   130
CLOTALDO. You have convinced me.
    But what can we do?
    We must find you sanctuary.
    I will give you all my wealth.
    You shall live in a nunnery.   135
    The advantages are three:
    One, no civil feud;
    Two, I deal generously;
    Three, I show my gratitude.
    There, I don't believe   140
    I could hatch a better plot.
    If I was your father;
    I'm sure I could not.
ROSAURA. If you were my father
    I'd take the insult: 145
    Since you're not, I will not.
    Money and a nunnery!
CLOTALDO. Were I your father . . .
ROSAURA. I would spit at you.
CLOTALDO. You are forsworn   150
    Because you swore to kill him.
    Do not reproach me
    If I am forsworn too.
ROSAURA. Then I'll kill the Duke myself.
CLOTALDO. I don't believe you.   155
ROSAURA. I swear I will do it.
CLOTALDO. You are a woman
    And you have such courage?
ROSAURA. Yes.
CLOTALDO.   What inspires you?
ROSAURA.   My good name.

CLOTALDO.   Astolfo
Is going to be . . .
ROSAURA.   My honour.
160 CLOTALDO.   Both your King
And your Estrella's husband.
ROSAURA.   I'll prevent him.
By God, I swear it.
CLOTALDO.   This is madness.
ROSAURA.   Yes.
CLOTALDO. Then stop it.
ROSAURA.   I cannot.
CLOTALDO.   Then you will lose . . .
ROSAURA. I know I will.
CLOTALDO.   Your honour and your life.
ROSAURA. I well believe it.
CLOTALDO.   What do you gain?
165 ROSAURA.   My death?
CLOTALDO. This is mere spite.
ROSAURA.   It's honour.
CLOTALDO.   No, it's madness.
ROSAURA. It's courage.
CLOTALDO.   No, it's frenzy.
ROSAURA.   No, it's rage:
I call it rage.
CLOTALDO.   No, it is jealousy.
You're jealous of your mistress.
170 ROSAURA. I do not care if it's jealousy
Or spite or rage or madness
I have so many passions
I don't know which is greatest.
I will do it alone.
                          (Exit Rosaura.)
175 CLOTALDO. Stars, show us all some shrewd way out of this,
If you know one. O there is such confusion.
Above the omens of the skies are bad.
Below, it's worse. I fear the whole world's
mad.
                          (Exit Clotaldo.)

SCENE THREE

(Trumpets and drums. Enter Sigismund, armed, with his Soldiers.)

SIGISMUND. I wish that Rome could see me here today,
Rome in her heyday, in her golden age.
Would not her legions laugh and whoop for joy
To see a wild beast marching at the head
5   Of such an army, great and proud enough
To conquer heaven? No, that's not the way
To mock illusion. Let's return to earth.
Before the gold sun sinks in the dark green sea
We will unthrone the King.

(Enter Astolfo, followed by Rosaura on horseback.)

CLARION. Here comes a horse, a tumultuous steed   10
(Pardon me, but I feel the need
To make a vivid, poetical speech)
Its mouth foams round the bit like a
    sea-beach,
Its breath pounds like the hurricano,
Its heart pulses like a ripe volcano.   15
A horse of fire and water, earth and air:
Rosaura rides him. She is fair.
ROSAURA. Honour: I wish to speak to you of honour.
Be generous, Sigismund. Your fame has sprung
From night's dim shadows into royal day,   20
And as the sun leaps from the arms of dawn
And bathes the hills and paints the shining
    sea-foam,
So may you now, that are the sun of Poland,
Shine upon me, a poor unhappy woman.
Three times we've met.   25
Three times you haven't known me.
First, I was a man
When you lay in prison
And your story eased me.
Second, I was a woman   30
When you were a King,
A dream King, a shadow.
Now I am whole,
I am both man and woman.
I had a love in Muscovy.   35
He is the Duke Astolfo.
He swore to marry me
But he broke his oath:
I seek revenge on him
As you seek it today   40
Against your royal father.

I wear both silk and steel.
Both of us wish to destroy this marriage.
I, that the man who is my lawful husband
May not be married to another woman;   45
You, to prevent Poland and Muscovy
Joining in one. Then as I am a woman,
Help me to win my honour. As I am man,
I say, go on and seize on Poland's crown;
Destroy Astolfo, do not let him have it.   50
Yet as I am a woman, I beseech your pity
And pray you will be gentle now and kind.
Yet as I'm man, I offer you my sword.
But if you touch me as I am woman,
Then as I am a living breathing man,   55
I will defend my honour like a man
And I will kill you. In this war of love
I am a woman in my woe and fury,
But as I am a man, I'm strong for honour.
SIGISMUND. What is the truth of this? I do not know.   60
If I have only dreamed my former greatness,

How can this woman speak of how she saw
    me?
Now counterfeits ring true and truth sounds
    hollow.
What does the shadow of a shadow look like?
What happens when two mirrors face each
65   other?
If we cannot distinguish fact from fiction
Or what is real from what is an illusion,
Let's take the dream and use it to the limits
While we still can. Rosaura's in my power,
70 My heart shakes as her beauty shines on me.
What if she kneels? This is a dream. Enjoy it.
Regret it later. No, no. Work it out.
It is vainglory. All the good that's past
Is dreaming. We are born to disillusion.
75 Then if our pleasures are a little flame
Which the sharp wind will turn to ash and dust,
I'll hold to what is lasting and divine.
She tempts me but I'll turn from this
    temptation.
Sound the attack!

(*Alarum.*)

80 ROSAURA. Sir, look at me.
Look at me, my lord,
Doesn't my honesty
Deserve a single word?
SIGISMUND. I look away because it's necessary.
85 Rosaura, if I am to save your honour
I must be cruel both to you and me.
I will not answer you but I will act.
Don't look at me, Rosaura, or my duty
Will be exterminated by your beauty.
90 I'll do you good if we thrive today
And save your honour. Soldiers, march away.

(*Drums. Exit Sigismund and Soldiers.*)

ROSAURA. What do these riddles mean? He's clear and
    strong
And will destroy a kingdom for revenge.
He is awake,
95 But I am . . . I am I.

(*Sings.*)

Dreamed the world was simple
Sweet and gentle-eyed.
But when I woke up
There was a monster at my side.
100 Dreamed that I had thought of
A cunning clever scheme.
Then I began to laugh,
Like a clown in a dream.

(*Alarums. Enter Clarion.*)

CLARION. With banners flowing and trumpets thrilling
The King is going to do some killing.   105
ROSAURA. I'll throw myself with joy into this chaos.
I'll ride and fight beside Prince Sigismund,
The scandal and the wonder of the world.

    (*Exit Rosaura. Alarums.*)

CLARION. Battle rages, let the hero
Hack his way into the middle.   110
I will play the role of Nero
At a distance on the fiddle.
If I want to feel compassion
I'll feel sorry for myself.
Watch the guns and sabres flashing,   115
Unmolested on my shelf.
(*Climbs up. Music continues.*)
From up here I'll watch the show,
Safely from this perch of mine.
Death won't find me up here, so
I can give him the old sign.   120
(*Clarion hides above.*)

(*Alarums. Enter Astolfo.*)

ASTOLFO. A sword has cut my vein:
I bleed to death.
Is there nobody by
To bind my wound?
Is no one here among   125
These cruel rocks?
I faint. Help. Help me now.

(*Enter Rosaura on horseback.*)

ROSAURA. My name is Death.
ASTOLFO.   Lo, here's another furore.
ROSAURA. I am your death.
ASTOLFO.   Those are words, Rosaura.
I know you well from when we both were
    wooing:
You're good at talking but less good at doing.   130
You love to act but this is not a stage.
This blood is real. So is your father's sword.
Then keep your oath, Rosaura, if you can.
(*She unhorses and binds his wounds.*)
I like you best when silent.   135

(*Alarums. Enter Basilio, Estrella and Clotaldo in
retreat.*)

BASILIO. I need a new name. Basilio the broken-hearted.
ESTRELLA. The traitors triumph.
CLOTALDO.   Your army has deserted.
BASILIO. All meanings change when a battle's done.
Traitors are patriots if they've won.
ESTRELLA. Now we must hide from your tyrannous son.   140

(*Shot within. Clarion falls wounded from his hiding-place.*)

CLARION. Heaven and Hell! I think I'm done.
ASTOLFO. Who is this fellow?
CLOTALDO.   Somebody's son.
CLARION. Got any brandy? Hurts where I fell down.
ASTOLFO. Who are you, man?
CLARION.   I'm just a bloody clown.

145 Hey! Can I give you
One bit of advice?
If you want to survive,
You ought to pick
The part where the battle
150 Is really thick,
Where the corpses pile up
In a rough pyramid.
It's a damn sight safer
Than hiding like I did.
155 You can't escape Fate,
The stars do not lie.
When God wants it
We have to die.
Hey friend, pass the cup.
(*Clotaldo gives him a drink.*)
160 Strange, it feels
Like I'm waking up.
(*Sings.*)
A clown in a dream
Falling upside down
And when I woke up
165 I was a dream in a clown.
(*Dies.*)
BASILIO. When God wants it we have to die:
That truth is written in the sky.
CLOTALDO. Yet it's not Christianity to state
There's no defence against men's fate.

(*Takes up Clarion's jacket and cap.*)

170 Disguise yourself, and hide and wait.
ESTRELLA. A horse is over here: he is swift and fleet.
ASTOLFO. Ride off. We'll cover your retreat.
BASILIO. No, I'll await death in this place:
I want to look him in the face.
(*Alarum. Clotaldo disguises Basilio in
Clarion's clothes.*)
ASTOLFO. Take it and fly.
175 CLOTALDO.   And we will guard the way.
ESTRELLA. Make haste, my lord.
ASTOLFO.   Escape while you still may.

(*Alarum. Enter Soldiers. They find Basilio's robe.*)

1ST SOLDIER. The King's in hiding here.
2ND SOLDIER. Seek him out. And Astolfo.
1ST SOLDIER. Search every cave and rock.
180 CLOTALDO. O fly, my lord.
BASILIO. Clotaldo, stand aside.

(*Enter Sigismund, horsed. Basilio steps forward.*)

Your hunt is over,
Prince, I am here.
Now make your carpet
Of my grizzled hair.   185
I am your prisoner.
Do what you must do:
Let the predictions
Of the stars come true.
SIGISMUND (*to audience*).
You who have witnessed these high words
and deeds,   190
Listen to me. Attend your lawful Prince.
(*He dismounts.*)
Those star words, written by God
On the blue tablet of the sky,
Those books with diamond letters
Printed on sapphire pages,   195
They never cheat or lie.
The one who lies and cheats
Is the man who claims
He understands the stars.
My father to protect himself   200
Made me a beast-man.
I could have been gentle,
But raised in a monster's den
Of course I grew up
A monstrosity.   205

If it was prophesied that you would be
Killed by a beast, would it be sensible
For you to seek out sleeping beasts or
beast-men
And wake them up? If you were warned,
"the sword
You wear will be your death," would it be
sense   210
To carry that same sword between your teeth?
If someone said, "A green and silver mass
Of salty water will be your sad grave,"
Would it be sense to sail forth on the sea-waves
When they hurl up their curling, snow-topped
peaks?   215
With all your wisdom this is what you did.

Look at this man. He tried to rule the stars
Yet now he kneels before me and is humble.
How can I quell the hate he's bred in me?
What shall I do. What is my way? My answer? 220
What's right for me to do at this brief moment?
My soul cries out for vengeance but I see
My victory must be my own surrender.
Sir, now that heaven has proved you wrong,
I kneel
And offer you my neck to tread upon.   225
BASILIO. My son, my own son,

By this act I am reborn inside you.
You have overcome yourself.
You have overcome the stars.
230   You have won yourself a crown.
        (*Basilio crowns and robes Sigismund.*
        Drums and trumpets.)
ALL. King Sigismund.
SIGISMUND. Then all of you mark well
        How I mean to rule in Poland.
        Since I would be a conqueror
235   I see that I must first
        Make a conquest of myself.
        Astolfo, you have a debt
        To pay from long ago.
        Take Rosaura by the hand
240   And pay the debt you owe.
ASTOLFO. It's true there's a debt and obligation,
        But think: she does not even know her name.
        It would be base to wed . . .
CLOTALDO.   No, say no more.
        Rosaura is as noble as yourself:
245   She is my daughter.
        You loved me well, girl, when you were my
                niece;
        Then will you hate me now I am your father?
ROSAURA. I cannot tell.
ASTOLFO. What, is this true?
CLOTALDO.   I did not wish it known
250   Until I saw her honourably married.
        She is my daughter.
ASTOLFO.   Then since this is so,
        And I have no hope to rule in Poland
        I'll keep my word. Give me your hand,
                Rosaura,
        We're both forsworn.
SIGISMUND (*to Rosaura*). Come, take what you
255   have dreamed of.
        Clotaldo, you were loyal both to me
        And to my father. Ask me anything
        And I will grant it you.

CLOTALDO.   Then ask my daughter
        To forgive me.
SIGISMUND. So I do. Embrace your father.   260
        Now for Estrella. She must not be left
        Unhappy by the loss of such a prince.
        Lady, I'll find you out another husband
        Who is, I think, as good in birth and fortune.
        Give me your hand. You shall be Poland's
                Queen.   265
ESTRELLA. I am content. It is good policy,
        And so I trust I may in time be happy.
1ST SOLDIER. What about us? Clotaldo fought against you
        And yet you honour him. We made you King,
        Rescued you from the tower and fought beside
                you: 270
        What's our reward?
SIGISMUND.   The tower. Chains. No daylight.
        There is no need of traitors
        When the work of treason's done.
ASTOLFO. How changed he is.
ROSAURA.   How wise.
BASILIO. How like a king.   275
SIGISMUND. Do I surprise you? Do not be amazed.
        Is it a wonder if a dream has taught me
        A little wisdom, I should fear to wake
        And find myself once more a prisoner?
        (*To audience.*)
        Yet even if that time never arrives,   280
        I believe now that all human lives
        Are just like dreams. They come, they go.
        Perfection is impossible, we know.
        Then noble hearts, show mercy, thus,
        And for our worst faults, gently pardon us.   285
        Remember as you each pass on your way,
        Our actors, our musicians and our play.

SPOTLIGHT THE SPANISH THEATER: *THE CORRALES*

The Spanish developed a theater space quite unlike that found in Italy and France, although it shares some similarities with the English public theater, perhaps because both may have evolved from innyards. Spanish public theaters, as opposed to those of the court, were called *corrales* and were administered by charitable societies (*cofradías*), not by actors as was the English custom. This association with charities benefited the actors who consequently enjoyed a greater degree of social acceptance than some of their European and English counterparts.

The earliest *corrales* were makeshift affairs, but in 1579 the Corral de la Cruz, the first permanent theater in Spain, was opened in Madrid. Four years later the famous Corral del Príncipe—the Madrid equivalent of the Globe—opened. Like the English public theater, the design of the Spanish *corrales* varied, but there were some common features. Most were square or rectangular because they were adapted from existing courtyards, which were unroofed. The central courtyard, or *patio*, was occupied by standing spectators, much as the groundlings occupied Shakespeare's theatre; preening *mosqueteros* strutted about the *patio*, wanting to be seen, as much as wanting to see the plays. Elevated seating (*gradas*)

lined two sides of the courtyard; at the back of the theater was a tavern and a *cazuela*, a segregated gallery for women (perhaps as much an influence of the Moorish occupation as a response to Christian scruples about women attending the theater). Above the tavern and *cazuela* were raised galleries or boxes (*aposentos*), complete with balconies, from which gentry could watch the plays performed on a raised stage equipped with trap doors and other stage machinery. Actors dressed and awaited entrances in the *vestuario*, which backed the playing area. The *corrales* could accommodate a total of about 2,000 spectators. Spanish audiences were quite vocal, shouting "Victor, Victor" when they approved of performances and playwrights, jangling keys or other noisemakers when they dissapproved.

Touring professional acting companies were performing in the *corrales* of Madrid by 1560. These *garnachas*, led by an *autore* (actor-manager), consisted of five or six men, a woman who played the major female character, and a boy who played other women's roles. The standard repertory of such a company was four *comedias* (which could be serious or comic), three *autos sacramentales* (allegorical dramas), and numerous *entremeses* (short comedies, usually on topical

matters). The *garnachas* customarily remained in a city or village for eight days. They shared accommodations, often sleeping four to a bed. Their costumes, properties, and personal belongings were transported by four-pack mules. The women rode the mules, while the men took turns riding for a quarter-league and walking. Larger companies (*farándulas* and *compañías*) employed carts and drivers for their properties. These companies could afford better meals and better quarters, and generally enjoyed more prestige than the *garnachas*. A contemporary wrote of these professionals, "Their labor is excessive because of the continuous amount of study, the continuous rehearsals." When Spanish explorers ventured into the Americas in the early sixteenth century, professional acting companies followed. There were *compañías* in Peru and in Mexico City in the 1520s.

Unfortunately, little is known about Spanish acting styles. The plays themselves and the *corrales* suggest a formal style emphasizing voice and gesture. However, Lope de Vega, a theorist as well as a superb playwright, wrote essays praising the naturalistic style used by his actors. But, as is always the case, such terms as "realistic" and "naturalistic" must be considered within the context of the time.

CENTER STAGE THEATER IN MESOAMERICA

The complex glyph writings, calendars, and buildings in the Central American jungles of Yucatan, Chiapas, and Guatemala verify the exceptional artistry of the Mayans, among the most intellectual peoples of Mesoamerica. Curiously, however, the Mayans had no word for "art" in their vocabulary be-

cause "art" was not an entity separate from other religious or social activities. Mayan art—including theatrical activity—was a functional tool that maintained order and harmony between individuals, within society, and especially between the world and the cosmos. Though enjoyed for its craftsmanship,

Mayan art was not merely an object of aesthetic pleasure but a spiritual and social necessity.

Archaeologists have traced the origins of the Mayan culture to about 2000 B.C.E.; by the first century C.E., the Mayans had developed a variety of rituals performed by the principal social

(continued)

A drawing of Huitzilopotli, the god of storms and war, and his temple (with sacred maguey cacti at top right) illustrate a history of the Aztecs written by Spanish conquerors in the sixteenth century. Occident and America worship Huitzilopotli in The Divine Narcissus.

classes: peasants, priests, and nobles. They were bound by a common mythology set forth in the *Popol Vuh* (People's Book), a sacred tome that has been called the Old Testament of the Maya because it details the cosmogony, traditions, and history of the race. It was refined and passed from generation to generation orally or through the sacred glyphs. A version was preserved in the Quiche dialect of the Mayan language in the mid–sixteenth century C.E. Though this text was lost, Francisco Ximenez, a seventeenth century priest working in Guatemala, transcribed the material when he borrowed a worn copy from one of his parishioners. The *Popol Vuh* is too complex to summarize here, but it glorifies the solar deity worshipped by the people of this warm-weather climate.

The Mayans were an agricultural people who valued harmony between the material and spiritual worlds. The majority of peasants worked as farmers who often achieved a degree of prosperity. Indeed, a recognizable middle class emerged, infusing the Mayan culture with a love of artistry and leisure time. Many Mayan peasants became prolific craftsmen, particularly in the arts, as painters, potters, sculptors, musicians, and *tlaquetzque* (entertainers). The combination of artistry and religious ceremonies in honor of the sun deity—and other Mayan gods—spawned dances, popular entertainment, and rituals inspired by various intoxicants (recall that the Greeks drank wine in their homage to Dionysus). Through documents passed down by the Spanish conquistadors, we know the indigenous peoples had a repertoire of more than a thousand choreographed dances. Likewise, peasant-actors wore spectacular costumes and masks to perform mythical stories to the accompaniment of drums and musical instruments. Just as goats and deer were imitated in other cultures, the *tlaquetzque* dressed themselves as creatures of this jungle kingdom: ocelots, sacred snakes, and colorful birds.

The principal Mayan dramatic rituals were performed in mid-June when the sun is at its zenith. A fragment from a sixteenth-century Nahua manuscript recounts the invention of music at the command of the Tezcatlipoca, the god of heaven and the four quarters of the sky:

Wind the earth is sick from silence.
Though we possess light and color and fruit,
Yet we have no music.
We must bestow music on all creation.
. . . life should be all music!

The wind dutifully carries out the god's bidding and

Thus music was born on the bosom of the earth.
Thus did all things learn to sing:
the awakening dawn,
the dreaming man,
the awaiting mother,
the passing water and the flying bird.
Life was all music from then on.

Thus intertwined through the arts, the material world and the spiritual world are rendered inseparable in this great myth.

As evidenced by the glyphs, these rituals—in which the priests were both celebrants and mediators between the people and the orderly, often harsh, universe—were highly theatrical. Notable were the formalized costumes, masks, and especially the stylized physicality of the performers. Furthermore, sacrifices of both animals and humans were central events in the rituals. The Mayan theater space was a pyramid, its stage a stone altar, its people the audience, and the sacrificial offering itself was the sacred performance. To the Mayans, sacrifice was not a barbaric act, but a sacred duty that induced harmony between man and nature, manifestation of the belief that life naturally extended into death and vice versa. "Life," according to the Mexican scholar and writer Octavio Paz, "had no higher function than to flow into death."

Like the dramas of classical Greece, Mayan rituals also assumed a social, as well as spiritual, dimension. The Mayans were a hierarchical society, and the nobles enjoyed privilege, depending upon familial lineage. Again, as evidenced by sculptural works of art, vases, and jade plaques, we see an elaborate pageantry among Mayan nobles who used art as a propagandistic vehicle to explain their social standing within the cosmos. Thus dance rituals, as well as storytelling performances, were common means of asserting one's status. In the fourteenth century a Mayan court, for instance, could easily comprise more than a hundred artists whose sole purpose was to provide music, storytelling, and dance to aggrandize the aristocrat who presided over it. There was spirited competition among the nobles to produce the best artistic work. The artifacts of the so-called Late Classic period (*Chichen Itza*, c. 1250–1400 C.E.) attest to the superiority of Mayan artistry. We may assume that performance also became as sophisticated as other artistry, but theater, alas, is temporal. Performance records are difficult to maintain, and we have virtually no "scripts" and little empirical evidence of Mayan drama. The *Rabinal Achí* remains the single drama from the ancient Mayans.

The Rabinal Achí
The *Rabinal Achí* is a pre-Spanish conquest drama-cum-dance of Aeschylean

proportions; it was first transcribed in Guatemala in 1859 from a performance by Indians in a remote village. Like Aeschylus's *Prometheus Bound*, this pageant has to do with bondage, sacrifice, and transgressions by mythical characters chronicled in the *Popol Vuh*. Like so many tragedies, it dramatizes the conflict between fierce pride and the personal responsibility associated with political power. In short, the unknown storyteller of the *Rabinal Achí* matches Aeschylus in intellectual scope, but he goes beyond Aristotelian dramaturgy to create a mythic, magical world of tragic ecstasy.

Structured like the earliest Greek plays, the *Rabinal Achí* is composed of a series of alternating monologues, which clarify the character's actions, and choric dance sequences, which comment on the action. Its episodic plot dramatizes the religious, philosophical, and idealistic reasons why the Warrior Chief of the Quiche must meet his doom at the sacrificial altar. He has made choices that have affected his people and his captors. For this he must die. Unlike our own Greco-Roman dramatic tradition, which attaches guilt to our "errors in judgment," the Mayan hero's misjudgment displaced a cosmic schema much too difficult to decipher. Thus sacrificial death—and not merely mutilation as in *Oedipus*—was the only way to restore tranquility to the world.

Lamentably, we know little about the performance of the *Rabinal Achi* in the preconquest era. We can only imagine that it was majestic, colorful, and epic in nature. Given the Mayan emphasis on communion with their environment, it could only be satisfactorily played in the outdoors against a backdrop of the universe itself. Its cast was large and splendidly dressed. In addition to the three great warriors (Quiché, Rabinal, and Fifth Rain), the cast consisted of twin choruses of twelve Yellow Eagles and twelve Yellow Jaguars, as well as assorted soldiers, peasants, barons, and priests. Only portions of the text remain, but a sample suggests its majesty. In the epic's final scene, the Quiché Warrior prepares for his sacrificial death by divesting himself of his worldly possessions:

O my gold and silver, my bow and shield, my Toltec mace, my Yaqui axe! You are all that will remain of me! Even my sandals will be left! For here is what our lord and master will be saying by now: "It is far too long since my valor and courage went hunting the game we like to see upon our table." Our lord and master will be saying that, but he will never guess that I am only waiting my doom here between Heaven and Earth! Alas! . . . If I must die here, oh let me change places with that squirrel or with that bird! They die upon the branches or on the tender grass where they find all their needs.

Mesoamerican theatrical activity was subsumed by European dramaturgy. Spanish priests, for example, used liturgical dramas to convert native peoples, which is perhaps why the Yaqui Easter (see Center Stage box, The Yaqui Easter of the Southwest United States on page 629), contains both preconquest and European dramatic elements. Its spirit is kept alive, however, in the late twentieth century by a number of socially conscious, politically active Hispanic-American theater companies. Luis Valdez' *Teatro Campesino* is particularly active in this tradition. In 1974 Valdez's company performed *El baile de los gigantes* (*The Dance of the Giants*) in Mexico City. Based on material taken from the *Popol Vuh*, it depicts Mayan gods before the first dawn and the creation of humans. Valdez, who narrated the play, intoned a contemporary version of a Mayan hymn to begin the performance:

Dear god of the sky, we came to this place so that you can concentrate all your energy on this town. We came in the name of justice, in the name of love, in the name of unity, in homage to the Solar Deity.

It is a hymn—like the reenactment of creation that followed it—that would not seem strange to the Greek Thespis or to the Japanese Zeami. It, like the Dionysian dithyramb or Noh chant, speaks to those elemental human concerns that are often realized through acts of theater.

THE DIVINE NARCISSUS
(EL DIVINO NARCISSO)

SOR JUANA INÉS DE LA CRUZ

SOR JUANA INÉS DE LA CRUZ (1648–1695)

Although she has been called "the ornament of her century" and is now recognized as the first significant playwright of the Americas, little was known about Sor Juana Inés de la Cruz until 1947. Guillermo Ramírez España discovered an extraordinary document, a public testimony written by Isabel Ramírez, the mother of Sor Juana. In her testimony, Isabel confirmed that on November 12, 1648, in the village of San Miguel Nepantla, she gave birth to Juana de Asbaje y Ramírez de Santillana. According to Isabel, Juana was the youngest of three daughters born out of wedlock; thus Juana was registered as illegitimate, or as "a daughter of the church." The father was captain Pedro Manuel de Asbaje. Isabel's testament was extraordinary because she openly proclaimed "I am a single woman and I have given birth to my natural children . . . [including] the nun Juana de la Cruz." For a single woman to make such a proclamation in this fiercely Catholic world was a courageous act, but Isabel Ramírez was a courageous and extraordinary woman. When her father died in 1669 Isabel took over the family estate, no easy task on a frontier outpost. Sor Juana was truly her mother's daughter in that she, too, broke new ground in seventeenth-century Spanish America.

Juana was a precocious child who entered school at the age of three. A popular legend says that at the age of six she begged to be sent to the university dressed as a man (women were denied access to the university). She learned Latin at the home of a relative in Mexico City; she is reputed to have mastered the language in a mere 20 lessons. At the age of 17 she became a lady-in-waiting to the Marqueza de Mancera at the palace in Mexico City, but left two years later (1667) to enter the Convento of San José de Carmelitas Descalzas. The Marqueza attended the ceremony at which Sor Juana took her sacred vows. Within three months, however, the young nun became gravely ill and left the Carmelites. She later joined the Convento de San Jerónimo, where, among other duties, she was the bookkeeper. At San Jerónimo she began amassing what would become one of the largest personal libraries in the New World; it contained over 4,000 volumes of prose, histories, and scientific works.

Sor Juana became a nun partly because of her devout religious beliefs and—in no small part—because the religious life permitted her to pursue a literary career. Women, especially in post-Inquisition Spain, were not encouraged to write or involve themselves in the arts, but nuns were afforded both the education and the opportunity to write. Though Sor Juana wrote in a variety of dramatic genres, including imitations of the popular *comedias* and *sainetes* (interludes), she always maintained that the writer had an obligation to "study divine knowledge" or risk becoming "a slave to human [i.e., secular] writing." Furthermore, she claimed that a woman had a sacred duty to write for "the greater honor and glory" of her husband, Jesus Christ.

And write she did. As poet and dramatist she produced over 45,000 lines of material. At the age of 15 she wrote a dozen *villancicos* (brief compositions based on sacred writings) which were performed in Puebla and Oaxaca. Combined, they totaled some 5,500 lines of verse, some written in Nahuatl, an indigenous language of Mexico. Her mature work, as typified by *The Divine Narcissus*, reflects this early love of poetry, music, and indigenous material.

Her first dramatic work was *Los empeños de una casa* (*The Zeal of a House*, 1683), which was performed in a private home for the benefit of visiting viceroys. The play was a variant of popular *capa y espada* plays from Spain. Originally "saints plays," the *capa y espada* ("cloak and dagger") evolved into comedies of intrigue. Sor Juana looked to the works of Pedro Calderón de la Barca. Several years later she wrote *Amor es más laberinto* (*Love Is a Great Labyrinth*), which fuses secular and mythological themes. Her interest in mythology can also be seen in *The Divine Narcissus*. While the performance of her plays was limited to gentry in private homes, that in itself is remarkable. Imagine the irony of Spanish noblemen, steeped in a chauvinistic tradition, being entertained by the works of a woman!

In addition to a prolific writing career, Sor Juana performed scientific experiments, yet another manifestation of her curious mind. Unfortunately, by 1691 Mexico was besieged by mutinies, pestilence, and hunger, and Sor Juana abandoned her literary career to care for the dying and the needy. She sold her entire library, a collection of musical instruments, and other personal possessions to buy food and supplies for the suffering. Malnourished and overworked in service of the poor, Sor Juana died in April 1695.

THE DIVINE NARCISSUS (1690)

Sor Juana's short play represents two literary types. Generically, it is composed as an *auto sacramental*, that is, an allegorical drama developed in medieval Spain. Originally *autos* concerned purely theological topics, but they were secularized by Calderón. Historically, the play is the first notable example of "conquest literature," that is, literary material about the conquest of the Americas by the Spanish and other European colonialists. The tension between these two impulses—to convert and to conquer—makes the play remarkable.

On its simplest level, *The Divine Narcissus* recounts the story of the conversion of the indigenous Mexican people, allegorically represented by Occident ("the West") and his wife, America. When we first meet them, Occident and America are worshipping Huitzilopoxtli (HWEE-tlo-POX-lee), the Aztec god of war. Their hymns contain references to human sacrifice to appease the god who "sustains our kingdom and our harvest," a reminder that the theater is linked to ancient rituals. Sor Juana, who apparently learned of these rites from the Spanish conquistadors, is ambivalent about the bloodletting. On one hand, she seems to respect the passion of the indigenous peoples; on the other, her Christian background causes her to recoil at "the cruel sacrifice of humanity."

Her ambivalence is no less pronounced when the "heroes" of the story enter. Religion immediately condemns Zealot, who conquers "with arrogant blindness" and thereby brings disgrace. Throughout the play, Zealot is portrayed as a ruthless, but necessary, accomplice in the forced conversion of America. To achieve his ends Zealot eagerly employs the very tactics he and Religion condemn in the Aztecs: killing. As Religion and Zealot attempt to convert America, Sor Juana skillfully injects fragments of ancient songs to suggest that there is a true zealotry about the indigenous rites that makes that of the Christians pale by comparison. Similar tensions and ironies permeate the play, elevating it above the level of mere polemic.

Though Occident and America ultimately succumb to Religion's arguments (which Sor Juana sanctions by incorporating the words from Paul's epistles), we remain skeptical of the conversion. This may be due to the 400-year perspective we bring to the play. Disease, exploitation, poverty, and the loss of a people's essential identity were lamentable by-products of Spain's conquest of the indigenous peoples. Yet Sor Juana raised many of these issues even as Spain was entrenching itself on Mexican soil. America's accusation to Religion that "your blindness prevents you from understanding the tranquility which lives within us" becomes an unfortunate prophecy of subsequent events. Accordingly, *The Divine Narcissus* emerges as the first testament of Latin American identity. On one hand, Sor Juana accepts the reality of the conquest, but she also laments that the cultural roots of a great civilization were lost in the quest to "enlighten this hemisphere."

Such issues would be raised again 300 years later, largely in the work of Luis Valdez and his *Teatro Campesino* (see Chapter 9). As the Chicano theater movement evolved from purely political issues, it again brought the god Huitzilopoxtli and his brothers to the stage. Near Mexico City in 1974, the *Teatro Campesino* performed a ritual drama called *El baile de los gigantes* (*The Dance of the Giants*). It recalled the creation—and, sadly, the defeat—of the nation of the Tenochcas (i.e., Aztecs), the soul of *"la raza."* How fitting that the play was performed on the very land that prompted Sor Juana to write *The Divine Narcissus*. (See Center Stage box, The Yaqui Easter of the Southwest United States, following the text of *The Divine Narcissus*.)

A 1651 portrait of the
poet and playwright Sor
Juana Inés de la Cruz, the
first notable dramatist of
the New World.

THE DIVINE NARCISSUS

SOR JUANA INÉS DE LA CRUZ

Translated and Adapted by Roberto D. Pomo

PERSONAGES
OCCIDENT
AMERICA
ZEALOT
RELIGION
MUSICIAN
SOLDIERS/AZTEC INDIANS
CHORUS AND DANCERS

SCENE I

*(Enter Occident, a stunning and gallant Indian wearing a
type of Aztec headpiece with America by his side who is
also dressed in splendorous garb. They stare into the audience for a few seconds, then slowly face one another. At
the count of five, Occident and America break into a stylized dance. A chorus of male and female Indian dancers*

623

enter the stage. As the chorus joins in the frantic dance,
Occident and America sit on their stone-like thrones.
They observe as the chorus continues to dance. The char-
acter of Music enters. Slowly he crosses downstage,
singing to the audience. Note: the dance should continue
as Music sings to the audience.

MUSIC.
  Noble Mexicans,
  whose ancient lineage
  created the bright rays
  of the sun,
5 today we are blessed and
  consecrate our lives
  with devotion as we
  celebrate the power of
  the God of Seeds, the mighty
10 Huitzilopoxtli, the God of War!
  To him we owe our abundance.
  He who has sowed our fertile
  provinces,
  we stand devout, we are thankful
15 for the offerings of our first fruits.
  To him we offer our pure blood,
  and through this sacrifice and during
  this great feast, we honor
  Huitzilopoxtli!
OCCIDENT.
20 But, in our fair city,
  amongst so many gods,
  who have witnessed the cruel
  sacrifices of humanity,
  more than two thousand of them;
25 the shedding of blood,
  the pulsated entrails,
  the throbbing heart touching the cold ground;
  I repeat again, among so many gods,
  my attention embodies
30 Huitzilopoxtli.
AMERICA.
  And with due reason,
  for he sustains our kingdom
  and our harvest.
  Our hopes
35 are due to him—
  he who preserves our lives.
  What matters if America is replete
  with gold, if our lands are sterile?
  His protection spreads beyond
40 our corporal sustenance and
  purifies our souls.
  Therefore, let us all
  repeat:
  (*accompanied by music and a choral interlude*)

In this splendorous feast, we praise
Huitzilopoxtli!   45

SCENE II

RELIGION.
  Zealot,
  you
  who suffer the wrath
  of Christianity
  with arrogant blindness,   5
  celebrating idolatry
  and superstitious cults.
  Why bring disgrace to our
  Christian Religion?
ZEALOT.
  Religion, do not   10
  be so swift
  in judging my neglect,
  nor lament my caresses!
  For I shall raise my arm
  and my sword will avenge you!   15
  Stand aside as I
  avenge your
  injuries!
MUSIC.
  In this splendorous feast, we praise
  Huitzilopoxtli!   20
ZEALOT.
  I have arrived!
  All of you may leave!
RELIGION.
  No!
  I wish to speak
  in the hope that my mercy   25
  will bring peace
  before your wrath
  is upon them.
ZEALOT.
  Their bawdy rituals
  becomes them!   30
MUSIC.
  In this splendorous feast we praise
  Huitzilopoxtli!
RELIGION.
  Mighty and all-powerful
  Occident,
  Rich and beautiful America,   35
  you who live in misery bathed
  in your own riches,
  leave your profane cults
  which the evil spirits have
  bestowed upon you!   40

Open your eyes to the
truth!
Feel the warmth of my
love!
OCCIDENT.
45   My eyes do not recognize
you.
AMERICA.
What nations would dare
oppose the laws of our
ancient dominion?
OCCIDENT.
50   You, most beautiful
foreigner . . .
most appealing traveling
maiden . . .
who are you to disrupt
55   our pleasures?
RELIGION.
I am the Christian Religion!
Your domain shall be ours!
OCCIDENT.
Your determination has
charm . . .
AMERICA.
60   And your feigned insanity as well.
OCCIDENT.
A most eloquent trick, indeed!
AMERICA.
Without a doubt, she is insane.
Leave us now! Let us proceed
with our daily affairs.
MUSIC.
65   In this splendorous feast, we praise
Huitzilopoxtli!
ZEALOT.
Barbarous Occident,
in your blind, idolatrous
path,
70   how dare you reject
Religion, My sweet spouse?
Look deep at your iniquities!
Our God can no longer permit your
transgressions!
75   Punishment is His! I am His sword!
OCCIDENT.
Do you think your
countenance intimidates me?
ZEALOT.
I am a Zealot!
And since your excesses
80   lead you to forswear
Religion,
I shall punish your audacity

as His Servant; having seen
the limits of your tyrannical ways
for so very long.   85
His punishment is at hand!
We are His army
amidst steel flashes of lightning!
We are the ministers of His wrath,
the instruments of His rage!   90
OCCIDENT.
What god?
What excesses?
What turpitude
are you hinting at?
I do not know who you are!   95
Nor do I understand your vague
reasoning,
or your bold
assumptions
in not allowing my people   100
to say:
MUSIC.
In this splendorous feast, we praise
Huitzilopoxtli!
AMERICA.
You are a barbarian—
insane!   105
Your blindness prevents
you
from understanding
the tranquillity which
lives   110
within us.
If you refuse
you will be reduced to ashes!
Not even the wind will know of
your   115
whereabouts!
And you, my husband,
together with
your
vassals,   120

(to Occident)

ignore his words
and fantasies.
Let us proceed!
MUSIC.
In this splendorous feast, we praise
Huitzilopoxtli!   125
ZEALOT.
Since our first proposal
was rejected in arrogance,
our second one—war—
you shall heed.

130 TAKE UP ARMS!
THIS IS WAR!!

(*Loud electronic sounds denoting trumpets, the clashing of steel swords, distorted cries and shouts*)

OCCIDENT.
  Why is heaven against me?
  What arms are these
  that my eyes
135 have never witnessed?
  GUARDS!
  PREPARE YOUR ARROWS!
  SHOOT!!

(*The playing space dims to total darkness. The electronic sound becomes almost intolerable in its intensity. From behind the rear scrim, silhouettes in stylized movement denote physical combat. This stylized movement should be choreographed in a ritualistic dance pattern. After a few seconds, total darkness again, followed by a shower of lightning effects.*)

AMERICA.
  Why is this lightning persecuting me?
140 These leaded pellets?
  These monstrous centaurs running against my people?
  WAR! WAR!
  LONG LIVE THE KING!
  LONG LIVE SPAIN!
145 FOR EVER AND EVER!

(*Low intensity lighting from behind the scrim. The Indians retreat followed by the Spanish army.*)

SCENE III

RELIGION.
  Yield! Give up!
OCCIDENT.
  Your brute strength, not your reason
  compels me to do so.
ZEALOT.
  Die, insolent America!
RELIGION.
5 Wait! She's needed alive!
ZEALOT.
  Why defend her now
  when she was so offensive?
RELIGION.
  Your valor defeated her,
  but my mercy
10 will preserve her life.
  You win in strength; I
  with reason and gentle
  persuasion.

ZEALOT.
  But you abhor her
  wantonness?   15
  Is it not best that they
  should perish?
RELIGION.
  Halt your sense of
  justice!
  I do not wish for them   20
  to die, but only to be reformed
  in eternal life.
AMERICA.
  If you do not wish
  for me to perish—
  in your compassionate   25
  guise—
  then
  will you try to defeat me
  corporally
  as well as   30
  intellectually?
  No, you're mistaken!
  Even though I lament
  my
  freedom,   35
  my
  free will,
  I shall always
  worship
  my deities!   40
OCCIDENT.
  I am obliged to render
  to your brute force,
  but,
  even in captivity, you will
  never prevent me from   45
  expressing,
  that in here, (*pointing to his heart*)
  I will always
  praise,
  honor, and   50
  adore
  Huitzilopoxtli!

SCENE IV

RELIGION.
  What is this god that you honor so?
OCCIDENT.
  A god of abundance,
  a god who enriches our soil,
  a god who gives us nourishment and fruits.
  Even mother wind obeys our god—   5

he who cleanses our souls of sin.
Our god is everything!
I have said enough.
RELIGION.
   (*as an aside*)
   Bless me, my dear God!
10   What is this description?
   This imitation?
   This figure
   who is not Thee?
   What are these lies?
15   Oh, you foul serpent,
   whose seven mouths spill
   venom!
   My dear God, allow me
   to speak in Your
20   Truth!
   AMERICA.
   What is this uncertainty
   you imagine?
   Have you ever met a god
   who can confirm his
25   so-called deeds?
RELIGION.
   It is with the doctrine of
   Paul that I will speak
   the truth—
   just as he spoke to the
30   Athenians when
   he warned them
   against the worship of new gods.
   It was Paul who uttered:
   "It is not a new deity you are
35   seeking, but rather a voice
   you have not yet heard."
   And this is my quest!
   Occident, hear me,
   and hear me well!
40   My message will lead you
   to eternal happiness!
   These miracles you speak of—
   these marvels you indicate—
   these pretenses clouded
45   by a shield of superstition—
   they are nothing but illusion.
   If the ground is fertile
   and the earth fruitful,
   if the fields are sown
50   and the rain plentiful,
   it is God
   who provides!
   For it matters not
   the arms that till—
55   or the drops of rain
   that fertilize—

or the warmth that
livens vegetation.
Without God and
His providence,   60
we are alone.
AMERICA.
   If this is the case,
   tell me:
   would my hands
   be able to touch   65
   this
   Deity?
RELIGION.
   Although
   His Divine Being is
   immense and invisible,   70
   He remains near to
   our human nature, and only through
   the unworthy hands of a priest
   may He be touched.
AMERICA.
   I agree with   75
   your words. For no one
   but the priests that serve
   him
   may touch our God nor enter
   His temple.   80
ZEALOT.
   Oh, how
   you pretend
   to know the
   truth!
OCCIDENT.
   In your burst of eloquence,   85
   tell me.
   Will this God of
   rare substance
   keep you,
   sustain you—as   90
   Huitzilopoxtli?
RELIGION.
   I have warned you
   that His incorporeal and infinite Majesty,
   His blessed Being,
   is always present within us   95
   in the offering of the mass.
   In the altar of the cross,
   His pure and innocent blood
   redeems our world.
AMERICA.
   If I were to believe these   100
   marvelous things;
   is this loving Deity
   capable of nourishing
   our needs?

RELIGION.
105   Yes.
      Infinite wisdom among men
      is His ultimate plan.
AMERICA.
      I wish to see this
      Deity! Then, I
110   will believe!
OCCIDENT.
      So that once and for all
      you may abandon your
      beliefs.
RELIGION.
      Yes. And
115   you will be
      cleansed by the pure
      waters of
      baptism.
OCCIDENT.
120   For I know
      that before I kneel at
      His communion table,
      I must cleanse myself.
      This has been our ancient custom.
ZEALOT.
      Your deeds
125   do not need to be cleansed in
      that manner!
OCCIDENT.
      How then?
RELIGION.
      Only the sacrament
      of baptism will
130   wash away your sins!
AMERICA.
      As I hear your words,
      I am still lost, but
      my spirit is moved by some
      divine inspiration.
OCCIDENT.
135   I am moved as well! For
      I know that through
      His life and death—
      can knowledge be gained.
RELIGION.
      Let us go then.
140   I know your beliefs
      are metaphorical, coated
      in colorful rhetoric.
      But knowing that you seek
      tangible evidence more than
145   faith, your eyes must believe.
OCCIDENT.
      Yes. More than words,
      I must see it before my eyes.

SCENE V

RELIGION.
      Let us go, then.
ZEALOT.
      Tell me, Religion,
      how will you prove
      all this?
RELIGION.
      Through an allegorical play,   5
      these things will be shown
      to America and Occident
      so that they may believe.
ZEALOT.
      And what is the title
      of this allegorical play?   10
RELIGION.
      The Divine Narcissus,
      because this unhappy being
      had an idol that he worshipped—
      who pretended to partake
      of the sacrament of the Holy   15
      Communion. A being who
      impressed the gentiles
      with false signs.
ZEALOT.
      And where will you stage this play?
RELIGION.
      In the great seat of Madrid—   20
      the center of faith.
      Where the Catholic Kings
      imparted light and truth
      to the Indians and the Occident.
ZEALOT.
      Do you not think it   25
      inappropriate that
      a play written in Mexico
      be staged in Madrid?
RELIGION.
      It must be done to
      accomplish what   30
      is needed.
      It does not matter if the
      play is coarse and without
      polish, as long as it
      serves the purpose.   35
ZEALOT.
      Then tell me, Religion,
      how may you
      overcome the beliefs
      of these Indians?
      How can you take them to   40
      Madrid?
RELIGION.
      They will see

personages in the abstract,
whose words will be
45 heard.
And they will not recant,
not even if they are taken
to Madrid!
No form of intelligence,
50 or the giant seas
will prevent the truth
from being heard!
ZEALOT.
Knowing now the meaning
of the truth, both worlds must
55 kneel and implore forgiveness!
RELIGION.
And His divine enlightenment—
AMERICA.
whose supreme ground
caresses the humble Indian—
ZEALOT.
whose final counsel—
RELIGION.
60 enlightens this hemisphere—
AMERICA.
In all humbleness

we ask to be forgiven
for wanting a sign to be the Truth.
OCCIDENT.
Let us depart!
In my own agony, I   65
wish to know the Lord
who will give me
nourishment!

(*America, Occident and Zealot sing the following lines*)

Now that our indigenous pasts
have acquired faith in   70
the God of Seeds—
with joy, soft tears,
and festive voices—
we proclaim:

(*All*)

Blessed be the day   75
when we found
our Lord!

(*All exit in song and dance.*)

CENTER STAGE   THE YAQUI EASTER OF THE SOUTHWEST UNITED STATES

The rites of Native Americans merge with those of European Christians in the southwestern United States each Easter, a religious feast day that marks the triumph of life over death in the commemoration of the Resurrection of Christ. This Easter rite of the Yaqui Indians of southern Arizona is nearer than most ceremonies of Native Americans to formal theater and drama, perhaps because it is akin to medieval Passion plays about Christ's death. Jesuit priests who came to the region in 1617 at the invitation of the Yaqui not only brought religion to the indigenous peoples, but evidence suggests they also brought their knowledge of popular theater such as the Italian *commedia dell'arte*. The

clowning *Chapayekas*, wearing grotesque masks as they mock Christian rites, are central players in the Yaqui Easter drama; their antics are similar in spirit and technique to the *zannis* of the *commedia*. These are contrasted with the sacred *Matachinis* ("the little angels"), whose mimetic dances attempt to drive away the *Fariseos*, the hypocritical Pharisees of the Bible. Thus the Yaqui Easter ritual is both a cosmic and a religious battle between virtues and vices, not unlike the medieval morality plays or the dance dramas of Asia. It is also comparable to *The Divine Narcissus*, Sor Juana's play about the conflict between indigenous and European rituals and theology.

The most compelling figure in this drama is the ancient, pagan Deer, which is danced by the most privileged of the Yaqui men. His dance, a blend of Spanish and indigenous steps, heightens the aesthetic and spiritual nature of the ceremony, held in the plaza of the Pueblo Pasqua near Tucson. As the sacrilegious *Chapayekas* worship an effigy of Judas in front of the church, the Deer dancer mysteriously appears: he is a slender young man wearing only a painted blanket about his waist. He carries sacred rattles, and a white kerchief and a stuffed deer's head with black, shining eyes cover his head. (The Japanese also have a deer dance in which the dancer is similarly cos-

(*continued*)

Yaqui Indians dressed as the clowning Chapayekas *prepare to perform their Easter drama near Tucson, Arizona.*

tumed.) His dance consists of foot movements that imitate those of a deer's forelegs; there is minimal arm motion. His head moves gracefully as he glances carefully over his shoulder looking for possible danger. Although these movements may seem real, there is nothing naturalistic in the dance, as each move is calculated for symbolic effect. The dancer is transformed as the dance takes possession of his body. Intimidated by his artistry, the *Chapayekas* disperse.

The dance is repeated with varia-tions throughout Holy Week, and the climax of the drama occurs on Good Friday. Women reenacting the pilgrim-age of Christ to Calvary carry a statue of the mourning Virgin at the head of a procession even as the *Chapayekas* per-form the Way of the Cross in the wrong direction to mock the sacred dance of the *Matachinis*. A solitary figure re-moves a bouquet of flowers from the sa-cred bier of the dead Christ and carries it ceremoniously into the church, and thus the *Chapayekas* are robbed of their triumph. Their artifacts—masks, rat-tles, swords, and sandals—are burned on a pyre while the effigy of Judas is led from town on a burro. The Deer dancer repeats his hypnotic movements as the audience celebrates a communal tri-umph with food and drink. On Easter Sunday, the Deer dancer leads the priest and his congregation into the church, where he dances atop the Christian altar. The Yaqui Easter ends with a Friendship Circle in which all partici-pants, actors and audience alike, ac-knowledge their contact with chaos and the triumph of good over treachery.

FRANCE

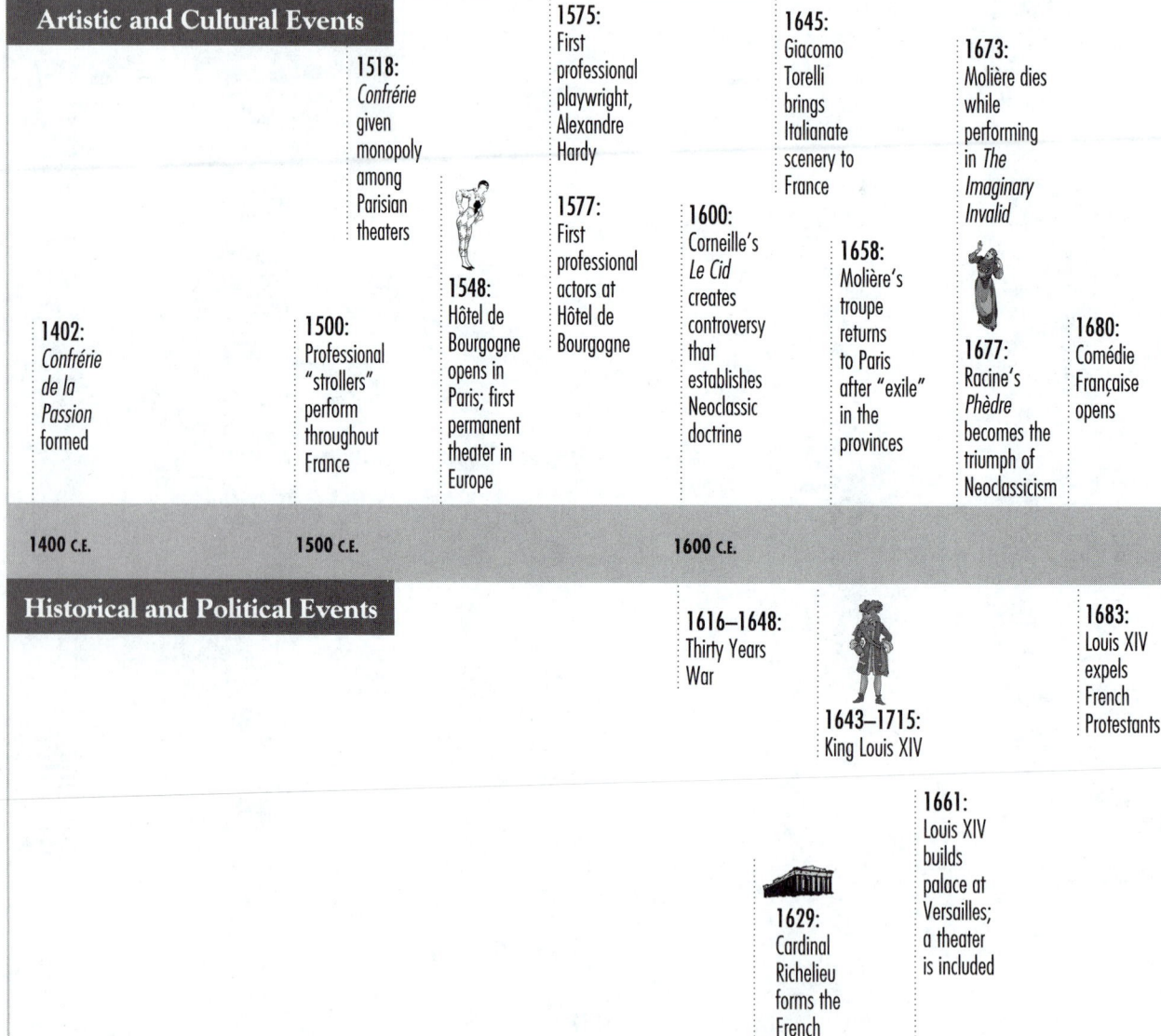

Artistic and Cultural Events

1402:
Confrérie de la Passion formed

1500:
Professional "strollers" perform throughout France

1518:
Confrérie given monopoly among Parisian theaters

1548:
Hôtel de Bourgogne opens in Paris; first permanent theater in Europe

1575:
First professional playwright, Alexandre Hardy

1577:
First professional actors at Hôtel de Bourgogne

1600:
Corneille's *Le Cid* creates controversy that establishes Neoclassic doctrine

1645:
Giacomo Torelli brings Italianate scenery to France

1658:
Molière's troupe returns to Paris after "exile" in the provinces

1673:
Molière dies while performing in *The Imaginary Invalid*

1677:
Racine's *Phèdre* becomes the triumph of Neoclassicism

1680:
Comédie Française opens

1400 C.E.   1500 C.E.   1600 C.E.

Historical and Political Events

1616–1648:
Thirty Years War

1643–1715:
King Louis XIV

1683:
Louis XIV expels French Protestants

1629:
Cardinal Richelieu forms the French Academy

1661:
Louis XIV builds palace at Versailles; a theater is included

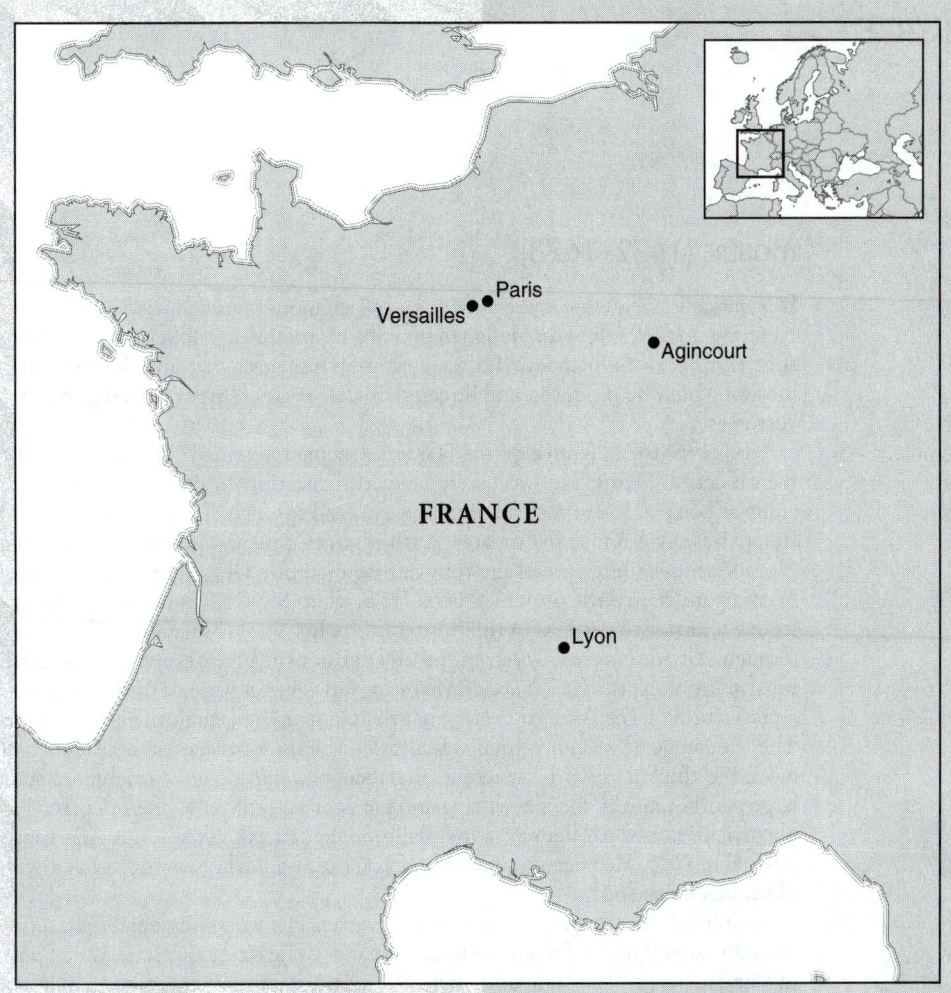

TARTUFFE

MOLIÈRE

MOLIÈRE (1622–1673)

It is difficult to imagine a playwright of any age more involved with his theater than Molière. Here was an actor, director, designer, playwright, producer, publicist and company manager—a theatrical jack-of-all-trades who was, against type, master of all. He wrote at least 33 plays, most of which he produced and directed as well as acted in, even designing their scenery and costumes.

Born in 1622, Jean-Baptiste Poquelin seemed destined for life as a courtier in seventeenth-century Paris. He was given a superb education to prepare him for a position in the court of Louis XIV, but instead of taking the road to Versailles, this son of a prosperous upholsterer chose a path into the theater. At the age of 21 he and nine comrades formed the *Théâtre Illustre*, whose failure earned the young artist a stint in debtors' prison. Undaunted, the youthful company toured the provinces until 1658, when Molière (as he then called himself) and his troupe returned to perform in the theater of the *Roi Soleil* (Sun King). The success of their performance of *The Lovesick Doctor* in the Guard Room at Vieux Louvre brought the company the royal grant of the title of *Troupe de Monsieur*. However, it was not until the next year, thanks to a production of *The Affected Ladies*, that the company's place in theatrical history was assured. The Troupe de Monsieur, which was allowed the use of the Petit Bourbon until it was razed, moved to the Palais Royal, where its members became the most celebrated actors in Paris, in large part because of the playwriting and performing skills of Molière. By 1663 his success as a playwright earned Molière an annual allowance of 1,000 livres, a stipend that was increased six-fold in 1665. He became a favorite of Louis himself, who served as godfather and namesake of Molière's first son.

Molière's lot was not an easy one, however. His work—especially *Tartuffe*—came under constant attack on moral and aesthetic grounds. The strenuous schedule of writing, performing, and managing the company, coupled with the deaths of two infant children and his failing health, exacted their toll. He was taken violently ill during a performance (ironically, *The Imaginary Invalid*) in February 1673 and died the same day.

Although Molière authored a number of farces patterned after the *commedia dell'arte* (*The Tricks of Scapin*), many comedic ballets for court performances (*The Forced Marriage*), and spectacular "machine plays" (*Amphitryon*), we think first of his satiric comedies: *Tartuffe, The Misanthrope, The Miser,* and *The Imaginary Invalid*. Characterized by intricate plots, archetypal characters, and social criticism, these works are invariably set in contemporary upper-class French society. Their action usually revolves around the archetypal pattern of young lovers who are separated by an older man—a blocking force—and often employ a *deus ex machina* to resolve the conflict.

While much of his subject matter is borrowed from Roman comedy and scenarios of the *commedia dell'arte* (his company shared a theater with a commedia troupe in the 1640s), his characters have a quality unique to Molière. Molière focuses most often not on traditional lovers, but on the blocking force, an older man, typically the father of one of the lovers who represents a conservative lifestyle and who is guided by a distinctive character flaw. In *Tartuffe,*

Orgon is gullible; in *The Miser*, Harpagon is greedy; in *The Imaginary Invalid*, Argan is the victim of his imagination and weak state of mind. These characters' names are variations of the French word *ogre*, a monster who devours children. The Molièrian father indeed devours his children, as you shall see in *Tartuffe*.

Unlike most other comic writers, Molière chooses not to have his aberrant characters rejoin the other, more sensible characters at the play's conclusion. With few exceptions, his miscreants do not overcome their deviant behavior and are not incorporated into the new society. And although Molière writes in his preface to *Tartuffe* that "the duty of comedy is to correct men by entertaining them," it seems Molière believed that the rehabilitation of his misfits is mostly impossible. Rather than trying to reclaim them he seems content in the belief that, as the eighteenth-century critic Gotthold Lessing observed, "it is enough for comedy that, if it cannot cure an incurable disease, it can confirm the healthy in their health."

TARTUFFE (1669)

The French philosopher Voltaire speaks for generations of *Tartuffe* admirers when he says that "as long as there are hypocrites and people who enjoy great art, *Tartuffe* will remain a masterpiece." What is it about this play that makes it a masterpiece? It appears, on first glance, to be a judicious comedy in which Molière gives us a plot that is easily followed, archetypal characters who are readily identifiable, and an obviously satiric theme. *Tartuffe* tells the story of a gullible man who is hoodwinked by a crafty hypocrite into sacrificing not only his daughter, his son, and his wife, but his good name and all that he owns. In addition to the fool (Orgon) and the charlatan (Tartuffe) are obligatory young lovers (Mariane and Valère), a dutiful son (Damis), a loyal wife (Elmire), a saucy maid (Dorine), an imposing mother-in-law (Pernelle), and a voice of reason (Cléante). These rather conventional characters provide a scathing criticism of pretense and hypocrisy in a seventeenth-century bourgeois household. Indeed, the play's title is derived from *truffe* ("deception"), and *tartuffe* was a common epithet for schemers, connivers, and con men. So, if the play is so conventional, what makes it "a masterpiece"?

In this deceptively simple comedy, we see the nearly perfect interweaving of content and form—a dramatic criticism of pretense in the form of theatrical pretense. What Molière has given us is a plot, characters, and theme so expertly interwoven that at first reading we are not aware that such a tapestry exists. In addition, he has incorporated a metatheatrical (theater within theater) motif into his fabric and employed the comic mechanisms of jeopardy, fancy footwork, and exposure as the threads that bind it together. All of this leads to a conclusion that only "pretends" to be a *deus ex machina*.

The entire play is based on pretense—pretending to be something one is not or pretending that something is so when it is not. In its simplest form the audience is asked to observe a solo performance by a pretender (i.e., Tartuffe) who watches not only his own performance but its effect on his onstage audience and his audience's reaction as well. In its more complicated form the motif presents an ensemble performance, often scripted by the pretender, which involves other characters not only as performers but as audience.

Obviously, without Tartuffe's pretense of piety we have no play. But Molière is not content with a single pretense. Many other characters also resort to pretense. In act 2, Dorine pretends to agree with Orgon and encourages Mariane to marry Tartuffe. Shortly thereafter, Mariane and Valère, in the midst of their lovers' quarrel, pretend nonchalance as they try to convince each other of their ambivalence. In act 4, Elmire, with Tartuffe as her scene partner and Orgon as her audience, pretends to be genuinely interested in Tartuffe. In each case the pretense is prompted by personal gain. Tartuffe wants all he can get, Mariane and Valère want each other, and Elmire wants to rid her household of the imposter. Orgon, of course, wants to prove Elmire wrong so he will not be seen as a fool.

As is often the case, pretense precipitates comic action. First, the pretenders find themselves in jeopardy—the threat of exposure or physical violence. To avoid exposure, they each engage in fancy footwork—the literal or figurative evasion of danger—to rationalize their pretense. Such comic mechanisms are interrelated; their interplay propels the comic situation.

Throughout the play, Tartuffe is in jeopardy. When he is exposed by Damis at the end of act 3, he employs some figurative footwork to convince Orgon of his piety. In act 4, Elmire finds herself in jeopardy as her pretense of affection is called into question by Tartuffe's demands for proof and Orgon's inability to play his role as audience. Jeopardized, she must verbally placate Tartuffe while she physically avoids his advances in some of the play's fanciest footwork.

By act 5, it appears that Molière's various pretenses have created such an intricately complicated entanglement that the only way to untie the knot is through some outside help—a *deus ex machina*. When all appears lost, the Prince, in the form of the Officer, appears to expose Tartuffe's pretense and restore Orgon's property, thus insuring the Mariane-Valère marriage. And all live happily ever after—except Tartuffe. On closer examination, however, it may be that Molière's metatheatrical design extends beyond the dramatic world of the play, and that the *deus ex machina* is more than a convenient device for ending the play. Without question, the Prince represents Louis XIV, and given the Renaissance belief in the divine right of kings, it is logical that a "good" Prince, as God's emissary on earth, would be aware of evil in his realm and move to exorcise it. Given that Molière was indebted to his king for granting him permission to perform *Tartuffe*, it is also logical that he compliment Louis for his munificence. And since the purpose of a Neoclassic play was to teach proper moral (i.e., Christian) behavior, Molière presented "poetic justice" while reinforcing the omnipotence of God's emissary in France.

But Molière does not stop here. Clever playwright that he is, he takes his metatheatrics a step further. While he pretends to give us a vision of a righteous king watching the work of a hypocrite and then intervening to restore truth and goodness, what Molière actually presents is the portrait of a king who, as the ultimate censor, has allowed a noble citizen to suffer unduly at the hands of a scoundrel before rescuing him. Given the ending of the play, we can only believe that the Prince has not only been aware of everything that has transpired, but has been amused by the "play" he has been watching. What other explanation can there be for his delay in unmasking Tartuffe's pretense? It also appears that Molière may have been only pretending to pay a compliment to the king while he was, in fact, pointing out the pretentiousness of censorship. Remember, Louis waited nearly five years before granting Molière permission to produce the play. It may be that, by allowing the Prince to dawdle in his exposure of Tartuffe, Molière was indicting Louis for his delay. Although Molière states in his preface to *Tartuffe* that the play "in nowise tends to make sport for things that we must revere," he further notes that his work is "nothing other than a skillful poem which, by agreeable lessons, reprimands men's defects." Including those of the king?

Molière himself performed in the famous table scene in Tartuffe; *a contemporary engraving suggests what his Parisian audience viewed in 1669.*

TARTUFFE

──MOLIÈRE──

Translated by Richard Wilbur

CHARACTERS
MADAME PERNELLE, *Orgon's mother*
ORGON, *Elmire's husband*
ELMIRE, *Orgon's wife*

DAMIS, *Orgon's son, Elmire's stepson*
MARIANE, *Orgon's daughter, Elmire's stepdaughter,*
in love with Valère
VALÈRE, *in love with Mariane*

CLÉANTE, *Orgon's brother-in-law*
TARTUFFE, *a hypocrite*
DORINE, *Mariane's lady's-maid*
M. LOYAL, *a bailiff*
A POLICE OFFICER
FLIPOTE, *Mme Pernelle's maid*

THE SCENE THROUGHOUT: *Orgon's house in Paris*

ACT ONE

SCENE ONE

*Madame Pernelle and Flipote, her maid, Elmire,
Mariane, Dorine, Damis, Cléante*

MADAME PERNELLE.
Come, come, Flipote; it's time I left this place.
ELMIRE.
I can't keep up, you walk at such a pace.
MADAME PERNELLE.
Don't trouble, child; no need to show me out.
It's not your manners I'm concerned about.
ELMIRE.
5   We merely pay you the respect we owe.
But, Mother, why this hurry? Must you go?
MADAME PERNELLE.
I must. This house appals me. No one in it
Will pay attention for a single minute.
Children, I take my leave much vexed in spirit.
10 I offer good advice, but you won't hear it.
You all break in and chatter on and on.
It's like a madhouse with the keeper gone.
DORINE.
If . . .
MADAME PERNELLE.
      Girl, you talk too much, and I'm afraid
You're far too saucy for a lady's-maid.
15 You push in everywhere and have your say.
DAMIS.
But . . .
MADAME PERNELLE.
      You, boy, grow more foolish every day.
To think my grandson should be such a dunce!
I've said a hundred times, if I've said it once,
That if you keep the course on which you've started,
20 You'll leave your worthy father broken-hearted.
MARIANE.
I think . . .
MADAME PERNELLE.
      And you, his sister, seem so pure,

So shy, so innocent, and so demure.
But you know what they say about still waters.
I pity parents with secretive daughters.
ELMIRE.
Now, Mother . . .
MADAME PERNELLE.
      And as for you, child, let me add   25
That your behavior is extremely bad,
And a poor example for these children, too.
Their dear, dead mother did far better than you.
You're much too free with money, and I'm distressed
To see you so elaborately dressed.   30
When it's one's husband that one aims to please,
One has no need of costly fripperies.
CLÉANTE.
Oh, Madam, really . . .
MADAME PERNELLE.
      You are her brother, Sir,
And I respect and love you; yet if I were
My son, this lady's good and pious spouse,   35
I wouldn't make you welcome in my house.
You're full of worldly counsels which, I fear,
Aren't suitable for decent folk to hear.
I've spoken bluntly, Sir; but it behooves us
Not to mince words when righteous fervor moves us.   40
DAMIS.
Your man Tartuffe is full of holy speeches . . .
MADAME PERNELLE.
And practises precisely what he preaches.
He's a fine man, and should be listened to.
I will not hear him mocked by fools like you.
DAMIS.
Good God! Do you expect me to submit   45
To the tyranny of that carping hypocrite?
Must we forgo all joys and satisfactions
Because that bigot censures all our actions?
DORINE.
To hear him talk—and he talks all the time—
There's nothing one can do that's not a crime.   50
He rails at everything, your dear Tartuffe.
MADAME PERNELLE.
Whatever he reproves deserves reproof.
He's out to save your souls, and all of you
Must love him, as my son would have you do.
DAMIS.
Ah no, Grandmother, I could never take   55
To such a rascal, even for my father's sake.
That's how I feel, and I shall not dissemble.
His every action makes me seethe and tremble
With helpless anger, and I have no doubt
That he and I will shortly have it out.   60
DORINE.
Surely it is a shame and a disgrace
To see this man usurp the master's place—
To see this beggar who, when first he came,

Had not a shoe or shoestring to his name
65 So far forget himself that he behaves
As if the house were his, and we his slaves.

MADAME PERNELLE.

Well, mark my words, your souls would fare far better
If you obeyed his precepts to the letter.

DORINE.

You see him as a saint. I'm far less awed;
70 In fact, I see right through him. He's a fraud.

MADAME PERNELLE.

Nonsense!

DORINE.

              His man Laurent's the same, or worse;
I'd not trust either with a penny purse.

MADAME PERNELLE.

I can't say what his servant's morals may be;
His own great goodness I can guarantee.
75 You all regard him with distaste and fear
Because he tells you what you're loath to hear,
Condemns your sins, points out your moral flaws,
And humbly strives to further Heaven's cause.

DORINE.

If sin is all that bothers him, why is it
80 He's so upset when folk drop in to visit?
Is Heaven so outraged by a social call
That he must prophesy against us all?
I'll tell you what I think: if you ask me,
He's jealous of my mistress' company.

MADAME PERNELLE.

Rubbish! (*To Elmire:*) He's not alone, child, in com-
85   plaining
Of all your promiscuous entertaining.
Why, the whole neighborhood's upset, I know,
By all these carriages that come and go,
With crowds of guests parading in and out
90 And noisy servants loitering about.
In all of this, I'm sure there's nothing vicious;
But why give people cause to be suspicious?

CLÉANTE.

They need no cause; they'll talk in any case.
Madam, this world would be a joyless place
95 If, fearing what malicious tongues might say,
We locked our doors and turned our friends away.
And even if one did so dreary a thing,
D'you think those tongues would cease their chattering?
One can't fight slander; it's a losing battle;
100 Let us instead ignore their tittle-tattle.
Let's strive to live by conscience' clear decrees,
And let the gossips gossip as they please.

DORINE.

If there is talk against us, I know the source:
It's Daphne and her little husband, of course.
105 Those who have greatest cause for guilt and shame
Are quickest to besmirch a neighbor's name.
When there's a chance for libel, they never miss it;

When something can be made to seem illicit
They're off at once to spread the joyous news,
Adding to fact what fantasies they choose.   110
By talking up their neighbor's indiscretions
They seek to camouflage their own transgressions,
Hoping that others' innocent affairs
Will lend a hue of innocence to theirs,
Or that their own black guilt will come to seem   115
Part of a general shady color-scheme.

MADAME PERNELLE.

All that is quite irrelevant. I doubt
That anyone's more virtuous and devout
Than dear Orante; and I'm informed that she
Condemns your mode of life most vehemently.   120

DORINE.

Oh, yes, she's strict, devout, and has no taint
Of worldliness; in short, she seems a saint.
But it was time which taught her that disguise;
She's thus because she can't be otherwise.
So long as her attractions could enthrall,   125
She flounced and flirted and enjoyed it all,
But now that they're no longer what they were
She quits a world which fast is quitting her,
And wears a veil of virtue to conceal
Her bankrupt beauty and her lost appeal.   130
That's what becomes of old coquettes today:
Distressed when all their lovers fall away,
They see no recourse but to play the prude,
And so confer a style on solitude.
Thereafter, they're severe with everyone,   135
Condemning all our actions, pardoning none,
And claiming to be pure, austere and zealous
When, if the truth were known, they're merely jealous,
And cannot bear to see another know
The pleasures time has forced them to forgo.   140

MADAME PERNELLE (*Initially to Elmire:*).

That sort of talk is what you like to hear;
Therefore you'd have us all keep still, my dear,
While Madam rattles on the livelong day.
Nevertheless, I mean to have my say.
I tell you that you're blest to have Tartuffe   145
Dwelling, as my son's guest, beneath this roof;
That Heaven has sent him to forestall its wrath
By leading you, once more, to the true path;
That all he reprehends is reprehensible,
And that you'd better heed him, and be sensible.   150
These visits, balls, and parties in which you revel
Are nothing but inventions of the Devil.
One never hears a word that's edifying:
Nothing but chaff and foolishness and lying,
As well as vicious gossip in which one's neighbor   155
Is cut to bits with epee, foil, and saber.
People of sense are driven half-insane
At such affairs, where noise and folly reign
And reputations perish thick and fast.

160 As a wise preacher said on Sunday last,
Parties are Towers of Babylon, because
The guests all babble on with never a pause;
And then he told a story, which, I think . . .
(*To Cléante:*)
I heard that laugh, Sir, and I saw that wink!
165 Go find your silly friends and laugh some more!
Enough; I'm going; don't show me to the door.
I leave this household much dismayed and vexed;
I cannot say when I shall see you next.
(*Slapping Flipote:*)
Wake up, don't stand there gaping into space!
170 I'll slap some sense into that stupid face.
Move, move, you slut.

SCENE TWO

Cléante, Dorine

CLÉANTE.
                              I think I'll stay behind;
I want no further pieces of her mind.
How that old lady . . .
DORINE.
                              Oh, what wouldn't she say
If she could hear you speak of her that way!
175 She'd thank you for the *lady*, but I'm sure
She'd find the *old* a little premature.
CLÉANTE.
My, what a scene she made, and what a din!
And how this man Tartuffe has taken her in!
DORINE.
Yes, but her son is even worse deceived;
180 His folly must be seen to be believed.
In the late troubles, he played an able part
And served his king with wise and loyal heart,
But he's quite lost his senses since he fell
Beneath Tartuffe's infatuating spell.
185 He calls him brother, and loves him as his life,
Preferring him to mother, child, or wife.
In him and him alone will he confide;
He's made him his confessor and his guide;
He pets and pampers him with love more tender
190 Than any pretty mistress could engender,
Gives him the place of honor when they dine,
Delights to see him gorging like a swine,
Stuffs him with dainties till his guts distend,
And when he belches, cries "God bless you, friend!"
195 In short, he's mad; he worships him; he dotes;
His deeds he marvels at, his words he quotes,
Thinking each act a miracle, each word
Oracular as those that Moses heard.
Tartuffe, much pleased to find so easy a victim,

Has in a hundred ways beguiled and tricked him,   200
Milked him of money, and with his permission
Established here a sort of Inquisition.
Even Laurent, his lackey, dares to give
Us arrogant advice on how to live;
He sermonizes us in thundering tones   205
And confiscates our ribbons and colognes.
Last week he tore a kerchief into pieces
Because he found it pressed in a *Life of Jesus*:
He said it was a sin to juxtapose
Unholy vanities and holy prose.   210

SCENE THREE

Elmire, Mariane, Damis, Cléante, Dorine

ELMIRE (*To Cléante:*).
You did well not to follow; she stood in the door
And said *verbatim* all she'd said before.
I saw my husband coming. I think I'd best
Go upstairs now, and take a little rest.
CLÉANTE.
I'll wait and greet him here; then I must go.   215
I've really only time to say hello.
DAMIS.
Sound him about my sister's wedding, please.
I think Tartuffe's against it, and that he's
Been urging Father to withdraw his blessing.
As you well know, I'd find that most distressing. 220
Unless my sister and Valère can marry,
My hopes to wed *his* sister will miscarry,
And I'm determined . . .
DORINE.
                              He's coming.

SCENE FOUR

Orgon, Cléante, Dorine

ORGON.
                              Ah, Brother, good-day.
CLÉANTE.
Well, welcome back. I'm sorry I can't stay.
How was the country? Blooming, I trust, and green? 225
ORGON.
Excuse me, Brother; just one moment.
(*To Dorine:*)
                              Dorine . . .

(*To Cléante:*)
To put my mind at rest, I always learn
The household news the moment I return.
(*To Dorine:*)

Has all been well, these two days I've been gone?
230 How are the family? What's been going on?
DORINE.
    Your wife, two days ago, had a bad fever,
    And a fierce headache which refused to leave her.
ORGON.
    Ah. And Tartuffe?
DORINE.
                        Tartuffe? Why, he's round and red,
    Bursting with health, and excellently fed.
ORGON.
    Poor fellow!
DORINE.
235   That night, the mistress was unable
    To take a single bite at the dinner-table.
    Her headache-pains, she said, were simply hellish.
ORGON.
    Ah. And Tartuffe?
DORINE.
                        He ate his meal with relish,
    And zealously devoured in her presence
240 A leg of mutton and a brace of pheasants.
ORGON.
    Poor fellow!
DORINE.
                Well, the pains continued strong.
    And so she tossed and tossed the whole night long,
    Now icy-cold, now burning like a flame.
    We sat beside her bed till morning came.
ORGON.
    Ah. And Tartuffe?
DORINE.
245   Why, having eaten, he rose
    And sought his room, already in a doze,
    Got into his warm bed, and snored away
    In perfect peace until the break of day.
ORGON.
    Poor fellow!
DORINE.
            After much ado, we talked her
250 Into dispatching someone for the doctor.
    He bled her, and the fever quickly fell.
ORGON.
    Ah. And Tartuffe?
DORINE.
                    He bore it very well.
    To keep his cheerfulness at any cost,
    And make up for the blood *Madame* had lost,
255 He drank, at lunch, four beakers full of port.
ORGON.
    Poor fellow!
DORINE.
            Both are doing well, in short.
    I'll go and tell *Madame* that you've expressed
    Keen sympathy and anxious interest.

SCENE FIVE

Orgon, Cléante

CLÉANTE.
    That girl was laughing in your face, and though
    I've no wish to offend you, even so   260
    I'm bound to say that she had some excuse.
    How can you possibly be such a goose?
    Are you so dazed by this man's hocus-pocus
    That all the world, save him, is out of focus?
    You've given him clothing, shelter, food, and care;   265
    Why must you also . . .
ORGON.
                        Brother, stop right there.
    You do not know the man of whom you speak.
CLÉANTE.
    I grant you that. But my judgment's not so weak
    That I can't tell, by his effect on others . . .
ORGON.
    Ah, when you meet him, you two will be like
        brothers!   270
    There's been no loftier soul since time began.
    He is a man who . . . a man who . . . an excellent man.
    To keep his precepts is to be reborn,
    And view this dunghill of a world with scorn.
    Yes, thanks to him I'm a changed man indeed.   275
    Under his tutelage my soul's been freed
    From earthly loves, and every human tie:
    My mother, children, brother, and wife could die,
    And I'd not feel a single moment's pain.
CLÉANTE.
    That's a fine sentiment, Brother; most humane.   280
ORGON.
    Oh, had you seen Tartuffe as I first knew him,
    Your heart, like mine, would have surrendered to him.
    He used to come into our church each day
    And humbly kneel nearby, and start to pray.
    He'd draw the eyes of everybody there   285
    By the deep fervor of his heartfelt prayer;
    He'd sigh and weep, and sometimes with a sound
    Of rapture he would bend and kiss the ground;
    And when I rose to go, he'd run before
    To offer me holy-water at the door.   290
    His serving-man, no less devout than he,
    Informed me of his master's poverty;
    I gave him gifts, but in his humbleness
    He'd beg me every time to give him less.
    "Oh, that's too much," he'd cry, "too much by twice!   295
    I don't deserve it. The half, Sir, would suffice."
    And when I wouldn't take it back, he'd share
    Half of it with the poor, right then and there.
    At length, Heaven prompted me to take him in
    To dwell with us, and free our souls from sin.   300
    He guides our lives, and to protect my honor

Stays by my wife, and keeps an eye upon her;
He tells me whom she sees, and all she does,
And seems more jealous than I ever was!
305 And how austere he is! Why, he can detect
A mortal sin where you would least suspect;
In smallest trifles, he's extremely strict.
Last week, his conscience was severely pricked
Because, while praying, he had caught a flea
310 And killed it, so he felt, too wrathfully.

CLÉANTE.
Good God, man! Have you lost your common sense—
Or is this all some joke at my expense?
How can you stand there and in all sobriety . . .

ORGON.
Brother, your language savors of impiety.
315 Too much free-thinking's made your faith unsteady,
And as I've warned you many times already,
'Twill get you into trouble before you're through.

CLÉANTE.
So I've been told before by dupes like you:
Being blind, you'd have all others blind as well;
320 The clear-eyed man you call an infidel,
And he who sees through humbug and pretense
Is charged, by you, with want of reverence.
Spare me your warnings, Brother; I have no fear
Of speaking out, for you and Heaven to hear,
325 Against affected zeal and pious knavery.
There's true and false in piety, as in bravery,
And just as those whose courage shines the most
In battle, are the least inclined to boast,
So those who hearts are truly pure and lowly
330 Don't make a flashy show of being holy.
There's a vast difference, so it seems to me,
Between true piety and hypocrisy:
How do you fail to see it, may I ask?
Is not a face quite different from a mask?
335 Cannot sincerity and cunning art,
Reality and semblance, be told apart?
Are scarecrows just like men, and do you hold
That a false coin is just as good as gold?
Ah, Brother, man's a strangely fashioned creature
340 Who seldom is content to follow Nature,
But recklessly pursues his inclination
Beyond the narrow bounds of moderation,
And often, by transgressing Reason's laws,
Perverts a lofty aim or noble cause.
345 A passing observation, but it applies.

ORGON.
I see, dear Brother, that you're profoundly wise;
You harbor all the insight of the age.
You are our one clear mind, our only sage,
The era's oracle, its Cato too,
350 And all mankind are fools compared to you.

CLÉANTE.
Brother, I don't pretend to be a sage,

Nor have I all the wisdom of the age.
There's just one insight I would dare to claim:
I know that true and false are not the same;
And just as there is nothing I more revere   355
Than a soul whose faith is steadfast and sincere,
Nothing that I more cherish and admire
Than honest zeal and true religious fire,
So there is nothing that I find more base
Than specious piety's dishonest face—   360
Than these bold mountebanks, these histrios
Whose impious mummeries and hollow shows
Exploit our love of Heaven, and make a jest
Of all that men think holiest and best;
These calculating souls who offer prayers   365
Not to their Maker, but as public wares,
And seek to buy respect and reputation
With lifted eyes and sighs of exaltation;
These charlatans, I say, whose pilgrim souls
Proceed, by way of Heaven, toward earthly goals,   370
Who weep and pray and swindle and extort,
Who preach the monkish life, but haunt the court,
Who make their zeal the partner of their vice—
Such men are vengeful, sly, and cold as ice,
And when there is an enemy to defame   375
They cloak their spite in fair religion's name,
Their private spleen and malice being made
To seem a high and virtuous crusade,
Until, to mankind's reverent applause,
They crucify their foe in Heaven's cause.   380
Such knaves are all too common; yet, for the wise,
True piety isn't hard to recognize,
And, happily, these present times provide us
With bright examples to instruct and guide us.
Consider Ariston and Périandre;   385
Look at Oronte, Alcidamas, Clitandre;
Their virtue is acknowledged; who could doubt it?
But you won't hear them beat the drum about it.
They're never ostentatious, never vain,
And their religion's moderate and humane;   390
It's not their way to criticize and chide:
They think censoriousness a mark of pride,
And therefore, letting others preach and rave,
They show, by deeds, how Christians should behave.
They think no evil of their fellow man,   395
But judge of him as kindly as they can.
They don't intrigue and wangle and conspire;
To lead a good life is their one desire;
The sinner wakes no rancorous hate in them;
It is the sin alone which they condemn;   400
Nor do they try to show a fiercer zeal
For Heaven's cause than Heaven itself could feel.
These men I honor, these men I advocate
As models for us all to emulate.
Your man is not their sort at all, I fear: 405
And, while your praise of him is quite sincere,

I think that you've been dreadfully deluded.

ORGON.
　　Now then, dear Brother, is your speech concluded?

CLÉANTE.
　　Why, yes.

ORGON.
　　　　　　Your servant, Sir. (*He turns to go.*)

CLÉANTE.
　　　　　　　　No, Brother; wait.
410　There's one more matter. You agreed of late
That young Valère might have your daughter's hand.

ORGON.
　　I did.

CLÉANTE.
　　　　And set the date, I understand.

ORGON.
　　Quite so.

CLÉANTE.
　　　　You've now postponed it; is that true?

ORGON.
　　No doubt.

CLÉANTE.
　　　　The match no longer pleases you?

ORGON.
　　Who knows?

CLÉANTE.
415　　　　D'you mean to go back on your word?

ORGON.
　　I won't say that.

CLÉANTE.
　　　　　　Has anything occurred
Which might entitle you to break your pledge?

ORGON.
　　Perhaps.

CLÉANTE.
　　　　Why must you hem, and haw, and hedge?
The boy asked me to sound you in this affair . . .

ORGON.
　　It's been a pleasure.

CLÉANTE.
420　　　　　But what shall I tell Valère?

ORGON.
　　Whatever you like.

CLÉANTE.
　　　　　　But what have you decided?
What are your plans?

ORGON.
　　　　　　I plan, Sir, to be guided
By Heaven's will.

CLÉANTE.
　　　　　Come, Brother, don't talk rot.
You've given Valère your word; will you keep it, or
　　not?

ORGON.
　　Good day.

CLÉANTE.
　　　　This looks like poor Valère's undoing;　　425
I'll go and warn him that there's trouble brewing.

ACT TWO

SCENE ONE

Orgon, Mariane

ORGON.
　　Mariane.

MARIANE.
　　　　　Yes, Father?

ORGON.
　　A word with you; come here.

MARIANE.
　　What are you looking for?

ORGON (*Peering into a small closet:*).
　　　　　　　　Eavesdroppers, dear.
I'm making sure we shan't be overheard.
Someone in there could catch our every word.
Ah, good, we're safe. Now, Mariane, my child,　　5
You're a sweet girl who's tractable and mild,
Whom I hold dear, and think most highly of.

MARIANE.
　　I'm deeply grateful, Father, for your love.

ORGON.
　　That's well said, Daughter; and you can repay me
If, in all things, you'll cheerfully obey me.　　10

MARIANE.
　　To please you, Sir, is what delights me best.

ORGON.
　　Good, good. Now, what d'you think of Tartuffe, our
　　guest?

MARIANE.
　　I, Sir?

ORGON.
　　Yes. Weigh your answer; think it through.

MARIANE.
　　Oh, dear. I'll say whatever you wish me to.

ORGON.
　　That's wisely said, my Daughter. Say of him, then,　　15
That he's the very worthiest of men,
And that you're fond of him, and would rejoice
In being his wife, if that should be my choice.
Well?

MARIANE.
　　What?

ORGON.
　　　　What's that?

MARIANE.
　　　　　　I . . .

ORGON.

                Well?

MARIANE.

                       Forgive me, pray.

ORGON.

    Did you not hear me?

MARIANE.

20   Of *whom*, Sir, must I say
    That I am fond of him, and would rejoice
    In being his wife, if that should be your choice?

ORGON.

    Why, of Tartuffe.

MARIANE.

             But, Father, that's false, you know.
    Why would you have me say what isn't so?

ORGON.

25   Because I am resolved it shall be true.
    That it's my wish should be enough for you.

MARIANE.

    You can't mean, Father . . .

ORGON.

                   Yes, Tartuffe shall be
    Allied by marriage to this family,
    And he's to be your husband, is that clear?
    It's a father's privilege . . .

SCENE TWO

Dorine, Orgon, Mariane

ORGON (*To Dorine:*).

30   What are you doing in here?
    Is curiosity so fierce a passion
    With you, that you must eavesdrop in this fashion?

DORINE.

    There's lately been a rumor going about—
    Based on some hunch or chance remark, no doubt—
35   That you mean Mariane to wed Tartuffe.
    I've laughed it off, of course, as just a spoof.

ORGON.

    You find it so incredible?

DORINE.

             Yes, I do.
    I won't accept that story, even from you.

ORGON.

    Well, you'll believe it when the thing is done.

DORINE.

40   Yes, yes, of course. Go on and have your fun.

ORGON.

    I've never been more serious in my life.

DORINE.

    Ha!

ORGON.

    Daughter, I mean it; you're to be his wife.

DORINE.

    No, don't believe your father; it's all a hoax.

ORGON.

    See here, young woman . . .

DORINE.

             Come, Sir, no more jokes;
    You can't fool us.

ORGON.

           How dare you talk that way?   45

DORINE.

    All right, then: we believe you, sad to say.
    But how a man like you, who looks so wise
    And wears a moustache of such splendid size,
    Can be so foolish as to . . .

ORGON.

             Silence, please!
    My girl, you take too many liberties.   50
    I'm master here, as you must not forget.

DORINE.

    Do let's discuss this calmly; don't be upset.
    You can't be serious, Sir, about this plan.
    What should that bigot want with Mariane?
    Praying and fasting ought to keep him busy.   55
    And then, in terms of wealth and rank, what is he?
    Why should a man of property like you
    Pick out a beggar son-in-law?

ORGON.

                That will do.
    Speak of his poverty with reverence.
    His is a pure and saintly indigence.   60
    Which far transcends all worldly pride and pelf.
    He lost his fortune, as he says himself,
    Because he cared for Heaven alone, and so
    Was careless of his interests here below.
    I mean to get him out of his present straits   65
    And help him to recover his estates—
    Which, in his part of the world, have no small fame.
    Poor though he is, he's a gentleman just the same.

DORINE.

    Yes, so he tells us; and, Sir, it seems to me
    Such pride goes very ill with piety.   70
    A man whose spirit spurns this dungy earth
    Ought not to brag of lands and noble birth;
    Such worldly arrogance will hardly square
    With meek devotion and the life of prayer.
    . . . But this approach, I see, has drawn a blank;   75
    Let's speak, then, of his person, not his rank.
    Doesn't it seem to you a trifle grim
    To give a girl like her to a man like him?
    When two are so ill-suited, can't you see
    What the sad consequence is bound to be?   80
    A young girl's virtue is imperilled, Sir,
    When such a marriage is imposed on her;

For if one's bridegroom isn't to one's taste,
It's hardly an inducement to be chaste,
85   And many a man with horns upon his brow
Has made his wife the thing that she is now.
It's hard to be a faithful wife, in short,
To certain husbands of a certain sort,
And he who gives his daughter to a man she hates
90   Must answer for her sins at Heaven's gates.
Think, Sir, before you play so risky a role.

ORGON.
This servant-girl presumes to save my soul!

DORINE.
You would do well to ponder what I've said.

ORGON.
Daughter, we'll disregard this dunderhead.
95   Just trust your father's judgment. Oh, I'm aware
That I once promised you to young Valère;
But now I hear he gambles, which greatly shocks me;
What's more, I've doubts about his orthodoxy.
His visits to church, I note, are very few.

DORINE.
100   Would you have him go at the same hours as you,
And kneel nearby, to be sure of being seen?

ORGON.
I can dispense with such remarks, Dorine.
(To Mariane:)
Tartuffe, however, is sure of Heaven's blessing,
And that's the only treasure worth possessing.
105   This match will bring you joys beyond all measure;
Your cup will overflow with every pleasure;
You two will interchange your faithful loves
Like two sweet cherubs, or two turtle-doves.
No harsh word shall be heard, no frown be seen,
110   And he shall make you happy as a queen.

DORINE.
And she'll make him a cuckold, just wait and see.

ORGON.
What language!

DORINE.
Oh, he's a man of destiny;
He's *made* for horns, and what the stars demand
Your daughter's virtue surely can't withstand.

ORGON.
115   Don't interrupt me further. Why can't you learn
That certain things are none of your concern?

DORINE.
It's for your own sake that I interfere.

(She repeatedly interrupts Orgon just as he is turning
to speak to his daughter:)

ORGON.
Most kind of you. Now, hold your tongue, d'you hear?

DORINE.
If I didn't love you . . .

ORGON.
                 Spare me your affection.

DORINE.
I'll love you, Sir, in spite of your objection.   120

ORGON.
Blast!

DORINE.
        I can't bear, Sir, for your honor's sake,
To let you make this ludicrous mistake.

ORGON.
You mean to go on talking?

DORINE.
               If I didn't protest
This sinful marriage, my conscience couldn't rest.

ORGON.
If you don't hold your tongue, you little shrew . . .   125

DORINE.
What, lost your temper? A pious man like you?

ORGON.
Yes! Yes! You talk and talk. I'm maddened by it.
Once and for all, I tell you to be quiet.

DORINE.
Well, I'll be quiet. But I'll be thinking hard.

ORGON.
Think all you like, but you had better guard   130
That saucy tongue of yours, or I'll . . .

(Turning back to Mariane:)

                     Now, child,
I've weighed this matter fully.

DORINE (Aside:).
               It drives me wild
That I can't speak.

(Orgon turns his head, and she is silent.)

ORGON.
              Tartuffe is no young dandy,
But, still, his person . . .

DORINE (Aside:).
              Is as sweet as candy.

ORGON.
Is such that, even if you shouldn't care   135
For his other merits . . .

(He turns and stands facing Dorine, arms crossed.)

DORINE (Aside:).
             They'll make a lovely pair.
If I were she, no man would marry me
Against my inclination, and go scot-free.
He'd learn, before the wedding-day was over,
How readily a wife can find a lover.   140

ORGON (To Dorine:).
It seems you treat my orders as a joke.

DORINE.
Why, what's the matter? 'Twas not to you I spoke.

ORGON.
    What *were* you doing?
DORINE.
                    Talking to myself, that's all.
ORGON.
    Ah! (*Aside:*) One more bit of impudence and gall,
145   And I shall give her a good slap in the face.

    (*He puts himself in position to slap her; Dorine, whenever
    he glances at her, stands immobile and silent:*)

    Daughter, you shall accept, and with good grace,
    The husband I've selected . . . Your wedding-day . . .
    (*To Dorine:*)
    Why don't you talk to yourself?
DORINE.
                            I've nothing to say.
ORGON.
    Come, just one word.
DORINE.
                    No, thank you, Sir. I pass.
ORGON.
    Come, speak; I'm waiting.
DORINE.
150   I'd not be such an ass.
ORGON (*Turning to Mariane:*).
    In short, dear Daughter, I mean to be obeyed,
    And you must bow to the sound choice I've made.
DORINE (*Moving away:*).
    I'd not wed such a monster, even in jest.

    (*Orgon attempts to slap her, but misses.*)

ORGON.
    Daughter, that maid of yours is a thorough pest;
155   She makes me sinfully annoyed and nettled.
    I can't speak further; my nerves are too unsettled.
    She's so upset me by her insolent talk,
    I'll calm myself by going for a walk.

SCENE THREE

Dorine, Mariane

DORINE (*Returning:*).
    Well, have you lost your tongue, girl? Must I play
160   Your part, and say the lines you ought to say?
    Faced with a fate so hideous and absurd,
    Can you not utter one dissenting word?
MARIANE.
    What good would it do? A father's power is great.
DORINE.
    Resist him now, or it will be too late.
MARIANE.
    But . . .

DORINE.
                    Tell him one cannot love at a father's whim;   165
    That you shall marry for yourself, not him;
    That since it's you who are to be the bride,
    It's you, not he, who must be satisfied;
    And that if his Tartuffe is so sublime,
    He's free to marry him at any time.   170
MARIANE.
    I've bowed so long to Father's strict control,
    I couldn't oppose him now, to save my soul.
DORINE.
    Come, come, Mariane. Do listen to reason, won't you?
    Valère has asked your hand. Do you love him, or don't
        you?
MARIANE.
    Oh, how unjust of you! What can you mean   175
    By asking such a question, dear Dorine?
    You know the depth of my affection for him;
    I've told you a hundred times how I adore him.
DORINE.
    I don't believe in everything I hear;
    Who knows if your professions were sincere?   180
MARIANE.
    They were, Dorine, and you do me wrong to doubt it;
    Heaven knows that I've been all too frank about it.
DORINE.
    You love him, then?
MARIANE.
                        Oh, more than I can express.
DORINE.
    And he, I take it, cares for you no less?
MARIANE.
    I think so.
DORINE.
                    And you both, with equal fire,   185
    Burn to be married?
MARIANE.
                        That is our one desire.
DORINE.
    What of Tartuffe, then? What of your father's plan?
MARIANE.
    I'll kill myself, if I'm forced to wed that man.
DORINE.
    I hadn't thought of that recourse. How splendid!
    Just die, and all your troubles will be ended!   190
    A fine solution. Oh, it maddens me
    To hear you talk in that self-pitying key.
MARIANE.
    Dorine, how harsh you are! It's most unfair.
    You have no sympathy for my despair.
DORINE.
    I've none at all for people who talk drivel   195
    And, faced with difficulties, whine and snivel.
MARIANE.
    No doubt I'm timid, but it would be wrong . . .

DORINE.
  True love requires a heart that's firm and strong.
MARIANE.
  I'm strong in my affection for Valère,
200 But coping with my father is his affair.
DORINE.
  But if your father's brain has grown so cracked
  Over his dear Tartuffe that he can retract
  His blessing, though your wedding-day was named,
  It's surely not Valère who's to be blamed.
MARIANE.
205 If I defied my father, as you suggest,
  Would it not seem unmaidenly, at best?
  Shall I defend my love at the expense
  Of brazenness and disobedience?
  Shall I parade my heart's desires, and flaunt . . .
DORINE.
210 No, I ask nothing of you. Clearly you want
  To be Madame Tartuffe, and I feel bound
  Not to oppose a wish so very sound.
  What right have I to criticize the match?
  Indeed, my dear, the man's a brilliant catch.
215 Monsieur Tartuffe! Now, there's a man of weight!
  Yes, yes, Monsieur Tartuffe, I'm bound to state,
  Is quite a person; that's not to be denied;
  'Twill be no little thing to be his bride.
  The world already rings with his renown;
220 He's a great noble—in his native town;
  His ears are red, he has a pink complexion,
  And all in all, he'll suit you to perfection.
MARIANE.
  Dear God!
DORINE.
                Oh, how triumphant you will feel
  At having caught a husband so ideal!
MARIANE.
225 Oh, do stop teasing, and use your cleverness
  To get me out of this appalling mess.
  Advise me, and I'll do whatever you say.
DORINE.
  Ah no, a dutiful daughter must obey
  Her father, even if he weds her to an ape.
230 You've a bright future; why struggle to escape?
  Tartuffe will take you back where his family lives,
  To a small town as warm with relatives—
  Uncles and cousins whom you'll be charmed to
      meet.
  You'll be received at once by the elite,
235 Calling upon the bailiff's wife, no less—
  Even, perhaps, upon the mayoress,
  Who'll sit you down in the *best* kitchen chair.
  Then, once a year, you'll dance at the village fair
  To the drone of bagpipes—two of them, in fact—
240 And see a puppet-show, or an animal act.
  Your husband . . .

MARIANE.
                    Oh, you turn my blood to ice!
  Stop torturing me, and give me your advice.
DORINE (*threatening to go:*).
  Your servant, Madam.
MARIANE.
                      Dorine, I beg of you . . .
DORINE.
  No, you deserve it; this marriage must go through.
MARIANE.
  Dorine!
DORINE.
          No.
MARIANE.
              Not Tartuffe! You know I think him . . .   245
DORINE.
  Tartuffe's your cup of tea, and you shall drink him.
MARIANE.
  I've always told you everything, and relied . . .
DORINE.
  No. You deserve to be tartuffified.
MARIANE.
  Well, since you mock me and refuse to care,
  I'll henceforth seek my solace in despair: 250
  Despair shall be my counsellor and friend,
  And help me bring my sorrows to an end.

(*She starts to leave.*)

DORINE.
  There now, come back; my anger has subsided.
  You do deserve some pity, I've decided.
MARIANE.
  Dorine, if Father makes me undergo   255
  This dreadful martyrdom, I'll die, I know.
DORINE.
  Don't fret; it won't be difficult to discover
  Some plan of action . . . But here's Valère, your lover.

SCENE FOUR

Valère, Mariane, Dorine

VALÈRE.
  Madam, I've just received some wondrous news
  Regarding which I'd like to hear your views.   260
MARIANE.
  What news?
VALÈRE.
              You're marrying Tartuffe.
MARIANE.
                                        I find
  That Father does have such a match in mind.

VALÈRE.
Your father, Madam . . .
MARIANE.
         . . . has just this minute said
That it's Tartuffe he wishes me to wed.
VALÈRE.
Can he be serious?
MARIANE.
265   Oh, indeed he can;
He's clearly set his heart upon the plan.
VALÈRE.
And what position do you propose to take,
Madam?
MARIANE.
        Why—I don't know.
VALÈRE.
              For heaven's sake—
You don't know?
MARIANE.
      No.
VALÈRE.
        Well, well!
MARIANE.
           Advise me, do.
VALÈRE.
270   Marry the man. That's my advice to you.
MARIANE.
That's your advice?
VALÈRE.
       Yes.
MARIANE.
       Truly?
VALÈRE.
          Oh, absolutely.
You couldn't choose more wisely, more astutely.
MARIANE.
Thanks for this counsel; I'll follow it, of course.
VALÈRE.
Do, do; I'm sure 'twill cost you no remorse.
MARIANE.
275   To give it didn't cause your heart to break.
VALÈRE.
I gave it, Madam, only for your sake.
MARIANE.
And it's for your sake that I take it, Sir.
DORINE (*Withdrawing to the rear of the stage:*).
Let's see which fool will prove the stubborner.
VALÈRE.
So! I am nothing to you, and it was flat
Deception when you . . .
MARIANE.
          Please, enough of that.
280   You've told me plainly that I should agree
To wed the man my father's chosen for me,

And since you've deigned to counsel me so wisely,
I promise, Sir, to do as you advise me.
VALÈRE.
Ah, no, 'twas not by me that you were swayed.   285
No, your decision was already made;
Though now, to save appearances, you protest
That you're betraying me at my behest.
MARIANE.
Just as you say.
VALÈRE.
         Quite so. And I now see
That you were never truly in love with me.   290
MARIANE.
Alas, you're free to think so if you choose.
VALÈRE.
I choose to think so, and here's a bit of news:
You've spurned my hand, but I know where to turn
For kinder treatment, as you shall quickly learn.
MARIANE.
I'm sure you do. Your noble qualities   295
Inspire affection . . .
VALÈRE.
          Forget my qualities, please.
They don't inspire you overmuch, I find.
But there's another lady I have in mind
Whose sweet and generous nature will not scorn
To compensate me for the loss I've borne.   300
MARIANE.
I'm no great loss, and I'm sure that you'll transfer
Your heart quite painlessly from me to her.
VALÈRE.
I'll do my best to take it in my stride.
The pain I feel at being cast aside
Time and forgetfulness may put an end to.   305
Or if I can't forget, I shall pretend to.
No self-respecting person is expected
To go on loving once he's been rejected.
MARIANE.
Now, that's a fine, high-minded sentiment.
VALÈRE.
One to which any sane man would assent.   310
Would you prefer it if I pined away
In hopeless passion till my dying day?
Am I to yield you to a rival's arms
And not console myself with other charms?
MARIANE.
Go then: console yourself; don't hesitate.   315
I wish you to; indeed, I cannot wait.
VALÈRE.
You wish me to?
MARIANE.
         Yes.
VALÈRE.
        That's the final straw.

Madam, farewell. Your wish shall be my law.

(*He starts to leave, and then returns: this repeatedly:*)

MARIANE.
 Splendid.
VALÈRE (*Coming back again:*).
                    This breach, remember, is of your making;
320   It's you who've driven me to the step I'm taking.
MARIANE.
 Of course.
VALÈRE (*Coming back again:*).
                    Remember, too, that I am merely
 Following your example.
MARIANE.
                        I see that clearly.
VALÈRE.
 Enough. I'll go and do your bidding, then.
MARIANE.
 Good.
VALÈRE (*Coming back again:*).
                    You shall never see my face again.
MARIANE.
 Excellent.
VALÈRE (*Walking to the door, then turning about:*).
                        Yes?
MARIANE.
                    What?
VALÈRE.
325   What's that? What did you say?
MARIANE.
 Nothing. You're dreaming.
VALÈRE.
                        Ah. Well, I'm on my way.
 Farewell, *Madame*.

(*He moves slowly away.*)

MARIANE.
                    Farewell.
DORINE (*To Mariane:*).
                        If you ask me,
 Both of you are as mad as mad can be.
 Do stop this nonsense, now. I've only let you
330   Squabble so long to see where it would get you.
 Whoa there, Monsieur Valère!

(*She goes and seizes Valère by the arm; he makes a great show of resistance.*)

VALÈRE.
                        What's this, Dorine?
DORINE.
 Come here.
VALÈRE.
                    No, no, my heart's too full of spleen.
 Don't hold me back; her wish must be obeyed.

DORINE.
 Stop!
VALÈRE.
                It's too late now; my decision's made.
DORINE.
 Oh, pooh!
MARIANE (*Aside:*).
                    He hates the sight of me, that's plain.   335
 I'll go, and so deliver him from pain.
DORINE (*Leaving Valère, running after Mariane:*).
 And now *you* run away! Come back.
MARIANE.
                                No, no.
 Nothing you say will keep me here. Let go!
VALÈRE (*Aside:*).
 She cannot bear my presence, I perceive.
 To spare her further torment, I shall leave.   340
DORINE (*Leaving Mariane, running after Valère:*).
 Again! You'll not escape, Sir; don't you try it.
 Come here, you two. Stop fussing, and be quiet.
 (*She takes Valère by the hand, then Mariane, and draws them together.*)
VALÈRE (*To Dorine:*).
 What do you want of me?
MARIANE (*To Dorine:*).
                        What is the point of this?
DORINE.
 We're going to have a little armistice.
 (*To Valère:*).
 Now, weren't you silly to get so overheated?   345
VALÈRE.
 Didn't you see how badly I was treated?
DORINE (*To Mariane:*).
 Aren't you a simpleton, to have lost your head?
MARIANE.
 Didn't you hear the hateful things he said?
DORINE (*To Valère:*).
 You're both great fools. Her sole desire, Valère,
 Is to be yours in marriage. To that I'll swear.   350
 (*To Mariane:*).
 He loves you only, and he wants no wife
 But you, Mariane. On that I'll stake my life.
MARIANE (*To Valère:*).
 Then why you advised me so, I cannot see.
VALÈRE (*To Mariane:*).
 On such a question, why ask advice of *me*?
DORINE.
 Oh, you're impossible. Give me your hands, you two.   355
 (*To Valère:*).
 Yours first.
VALÈRE (*Giving Dorine his hand:*).
                    But why?
DORINE (*To Mariane:*).
                        And now a hand from you.

MARIANE (*Also giving Dorine her hand:*).
　　What are you doing?
DORINE.
　　　　　　　　　　There: a perfect fit.
　　You suit each other better than you'll admit.

　　(*Valère and Mariane hold hands for some time without
　　looking at each other.*)

VALÈRE (*Turning toward Mariane:*).
　　Ah, come, don't be so haughty. Give a man
360　A look of kindness, won't you, Mariane?

　　(*Mariane turns toward Valère and smiles.*)

DORINE.
　　I tell you, lovers are completely mad!
VALÈRE (*To Mariane:*).
　　Now come, confess that you were very bad
　　To hurt my feelings as you did just now.
　　I have a just complaint, you must allow.
MARIANE.
365　*You* must allow that you were most unpleasant . . .
DORINE.
　　Let's table that discussion for the present;
　　Your father has a plan which must be stopped.
MARIANE.
　　Advise us, then; what means must we adopt?
DORINE.
　　We'll use all manner of means, and all at once.
　　(*To Mariane:*).
370　Your father's addled; he's acting like a dunce.
　　Therefore you'd better humor the old fossil.
　　Pretend to yield to him, be sweet and docile,
　　And then postpone, as often as necessary,
　　The day on which you have agreed to marry.
375　You'll thus gain time, and time will turn the trick.
　　Sometimes, for instance, you'll be taken sick,
　　And that will seem good reason for delay;
　　Or some bad omen will make you change the day—
　　You'll dream of muddy water, or you'll pass
380　A dead man's hearse, or break a looking-glass.
　　If all else fails, no man can marry you
　　Unless you take his ring and say "I do."
　　But now, let's separate. If they should find
　　Us talking here, our plot might be divined.
　　(*To Valère:*).
385　Go to your friends, and tell them what's occurred,
　　And have them urge her father to keep his word.
　　Meanwhile, we'll stir her brother into action,
　　And get Elmire, as well, to join our faction.
　　Good-bye.
VALÈRE (*To Mariane:*).
　　　　　　　Though each of us will do his best,
390　It's your true heart on which my hopes shall rest.
MARIANE (*To Valère:*).
　　Regardless of what Father may decide,
　　None but Valère shall claim me as his bride.

VALÈRE.
　　Oh, how those words content me! Come what will . . .
DORINE.
　　Oh, lovers, lovers! Their tongues are never still.
　　Be off, now.
VALÈRE (*Turning to go, then turning back:*).
　　　　　　　One last word . . .
DORINE.
　　　　　　　　　　　　　No time to chat:
　　You leave by this door; and *you* leave by that.　　395

　　(*Dorine pushes them, by the shoulders, toward
　　opposing doors.*)

ACT THREE

SCENE ONE

Damis, Dorine

DAMIS.
　　May lightning strike me even as I speak,
　　May all men call me cowardly and weak,
　　If any fear or scruple holds me back
　　From settling things, at once, with that great quack!
DORINE.
　　Now, don't give way to violent emotion.
　　Your father's merely talked about this notion,　　5
　　And words and deeds are far from being one.
　　Much that is talked about is left undone.
DAMIS.
　　No, I must stop that scoundrel's machinations;
　　I'll go and tell him off; I'm out of patience.
DORINE.
　　Do calm down and be practical. I had rather　　10
　　My mistress dealt with him—and with your father.
　　She has some influence with Tartuffe, I've noted.
　　He hangs upon her words, seems most devoted,
　　And may, indeed, be smitten by her charm.
　　Pray Heaven it's true! 'Twould do our cause no harm.　　15
　　She sent for him, just now, to sound him out
　　On this affair you're so incensed about;
　　She'll find out where he stands, and tell him, too,
　　What dreadful strife and trouble will ensue
　　If he lends countenance to your father's plan.　　20
　　I couldn't get in to see him, but his man
　　Says that he's almost finished with his prayers.
　　Go, now. I'll catch him when he comes downstairs.
DAMIS.
　　I want to hear this conference, and I will.
DORINE.
　　No, they must be alone.　　25
DAMIS.
　　　　　　　　Oh, I'll keep still.

DORINE.
>Not you. I know your temper. You'd start a brawl,
>And shout and stamp your foot and spoil it all.
>Go on.

DAMIS.
>   I won't; I have a perfect right . . .

DORINE.
>Lord, you're a nuisance! He's coming; get out of sight.

(*Damis conceals himself in a closet at the rear of
the stage.*)

30

SCENE TWO

Tartuffe, Dorine

TARTUFFE (*Observing Dorine, and calling to his manservant offstage:*).
>Hang up my hair-shirt, put my scourge in place,
>And pray, Laurent, for Heaven's perpetual grace.
>I'm going to the prison now, to share
>My last few coins with the poor wretches there.

DORINE (*Aside:*).
>Dear God, what affectation! What a fake!

TARTUFFE.
35
>You wished to see me?

DORINE.
>   Yes . . .

TARTUFFE (*Taking a handkerchief from his pocket:*).
>   For mercy's sake,
>Please take this handkerchief, before you speak.

DORINE.
>What?

TARTUFFE.
>   Cover that bosom, girl. The flesh is weak,
>And unclean thoughts are difficult to control.
>Such sights as that can undermine the soul.

DORINE.
40
>Your soul, it seems, has very poor defenses,
>And flesh makes quite an impact on your senses.
>It's strange that you're so easily excited;
>My own desires are not so soon ignited,
>And if I saw you naked as a beast,
>Not all your hide would tempt me in the least.

TARTUFFE.
45
>Girl, speak more modestly; unless you do,
>I shall be forced to take my leave of you.

DORINE.
>Oh, no, it's I who must be on my way;
>I've just one little message to convey.
>*Madame* is coming down, and begs you, Sir,
50
>To wait and have a word or two with her.

TARTUFFE.
>Gladly.

DORINE (*Aside:*).
>   *That* had a softening effect!
>I think my guess about him was correct.

TARTUFFE.
>Will she be long?

DORINE.
>   No: that's her step I hear.

Ah, here she is, and I shall disappear.

55

SCENE THREE

Elmire, Tartuffe

TARTUFFE.
>May Heaven, whose infinite goodness we adore,
>Preserve your body and soul forevermore,
>And bless your days, and answer thus the plea
>Of one who is its humblest votary.

ELMIRE.
>I thank you for that pious wish. But please,
60
>Do take a chair and let's be more at ease.

(*They sit down.*)

TARTUFFE.
>I trust that you are once more well and strong?

ELMIRE.
>Oh, yes: the fever didn't last for long.

TARTUFFE.
>My prayers are too unworthy, I am sure,
>To have gained from Heaven this most gracious cure;
>But lately, Madam, my every supplication
65
>Has had for objects your recuperation.

ELMIRE.
>You shouldn't have troubled so. I don't deserve it.

TARTUFFE.
>Your health is priceless, Madam, and to preserve it
>I'd gladly give my own, in all sincerity.

ELMIRE.
70
>Sir, you outdo us all in Christian charity.
>You've been most kind. I count myself your debtor.

TARTUFFE.
>'Twas nothing, Madam. I long to serve you better.

ELMIRE.
>There's a private matter I'm anxious to discuss.
>I'm glad there's no one here to hinder us.

TARTUFFE.
75
>I too am glad; it floods my heart with bliss
>To find myself alone with you like this.
>For just this chance I've prayed with all my power—
>But prayed in vain, until this happy hour.

ELMIRE.
>This won't take long, Sir, and I hope you'll be
80
>Entirely frank and unconstrained with me.

TARTUFFE.

    Indeed, there's nothing I had rather do
    Than bare my inmost heart and soul to you.
85   First, let me say that what remarks I've made
    About the constant visits you are paid
    Were prompted not by any mean emotion,
    But rather by a pure and deep devotion,
    A fervent zeal . . .

ELMIRE.

                No need for explanation.
90   Your sole concern, I'm sure, was my salvation.

TARTUFFE (*Taking Elmire's hand and pressing her
    fingertips:*).

    Quite so; and such great fervor do I feel . . .

ELMIRE.

    Ooh! Please! You're pinching!

TARTUFFE.

                   'Twas from excess of zeal.
    I never meant to cause you pain, I swear.
    I'd rather . . .

(*He places his hand on Elmire's knee.*)

ELMIRE.

           What can your hand be doing there?

TARTUFFE.

95   Feeling your gown, what soft, fine-woven stuff.

ELMIRE.

    Please, I'm extremely ticklish. That's enough.

(*She draws her chair away; Tartuffe pulls his after her.*)

TARTUFFE. (*Fondling the lace collar of her gown:*).

    My, my, what lovely lacework on your dress!
    The workmanship's miraculous, no less.
    I've not seen anything to equal it.

ELMIRE.

100   Yes, quite. But let's talk business for a bit.
    You say my husband means to break his word
    And give his daughter to you, Sir. Had you heard?

TARTUFFE.

    He did once mention it. But I confess
    I dream of quite a different happiness.
105   It's elsewhere, Madam, that my eyes discern
    The promise of that bliss for which I yearn.

ELMIRE.

    I see: you care for nothing here below.

TARTUFFE.

    Ah, well—my heart's not made of stone, you know.

ELMIRE.

    All your desires mount heavenward, I'm sure,
110   In scorn of all that's earthly and impure.

TARTUFFE.

    A love of heavenly beauty does not preclude
    A proper love for earthly pulchritude;
    Our senses are quite rightly captivated
    By perfect works our Maker has created.

Some glory clings to all that Heaven has made;   115
In you, all Heaven's marvels are displayed.
On that fair face, such beauties have been lavished,
The eyes are dazzled and the heart is ravished;
How could I look on you, O flawless creature,
And not adore the Author of all Nature,   120
Feeling a love both passionate and pure
For you, his triumph of self-portraiture?
At first, I trembled lest that love should be
A subtle snare that Hell had laid for me;
I vowed to flee the sight of you, eschewing   125
A rapture that might prove my soul's undoing;
But soon, fair being, I became aware
That my deep passion could be made to square
With rectitude, and with my bounden duty.
I thereupon surrendered to your beauty.   130
It is, I know, presumptuous on my part
To bring you this poor offering of my heart,
And it is not my merit, Heaven knows,
But your compassion on which my hopes repose.
You are my peace, my solace, my salvation;   135
On you depends my bliss—or desolation;
I bide your judgment and, as you think best,
I shall be either miserable or blest.

ELMIRE.

Your declaration is most gallant, Sir,
But don't you think it's out of character?   140
You'd have done better to restrain your passion
And think before you spoke in such a fashion.
It ill becomes a pious man like you . . .

TARTUFFE.

I may be pious, but I'm human too:
With your celestial charms before his eyes,   145
A man has not the power to be wise,
I know such words sound strangely, coming from me,
But I'm no angel, nor was meant to be,
And if you blame my passion, you must needs
Reproach as well the charms on which it feeds.   150
Your loveliness I had no sooner seen
Than you became my soul's unrivalled queen;
Before your seraph glance, divinely sweet,
My heart's defenses crumbled in defeat,
And nothing fasting, prayer, or tears might do   155
Could stay my spirit from adoring you.
My eyes, my sighs have told you in the past
What now my lips make bold to say at last,
And if, in your great goodness, you will deign
To look upon your slave, and ease his pain,—   160
If, in compassion for my soul's distress,
You'll stoop to comfort my unworthiness,
I'll raise to you, in thanks for that sweet manna,
An endless hymn, an infinite hosanna.
With me, of course, there need be no anxiety,   165
No fear of scandal or of notoriety.
These young court gallants, whom all the ladies fancy,

Are vain in speech, in action rash and chancy;
When they succeed in love, the world soon knows it;
170 No favor's granted them but they disclose it
And by the looseness of their tongues profane
The very altar where their hearts have lain.
Men of my sort, however, love discreetly,
And one may trust our reticence completely.
175 My keen concern for my good name insures
The absolute security of yours;
In short, I offer you, my dear Elmire,
Love without scandal, pleasure without fear.

ELMIRE.
I've heard your well-turned speeches to the end,
180 And what you urge I clearly comprehend.
Aren't you afraid that I may take a notion
To tell my husband of your warm devotion,
And that, supposing he were duly told,
His feelings toward you might grow rather cold?

TARTUFFE.
185 I know, dear lady, that your exceeding charity
Will lead your heart to pardon my temerity;
That you'll excuse my violent affection
As human weakness, human imperfection;
And that—O fairest!—you will bear in mind
190 That I'm but flesh and blood, and am not blind.

ELMIRE.
Some women might do otherwise, perhaps,
But I shall be discreet about your lapse;
I'll tell my husband nothing of what's occurred
If, in return, you'll give your solemn word
195 To advocate as forcefully as you can
The marriage of Valère and Mariane,
Renouncing all desire to dispossess
Another of his rightful happiness,
And . . .

SCENE FOUR

Damis, Elmire, Tartuffe

DAMIS (*Emerging from the closet where he has been hiding:*).
                    No! We'll not hush up this vile affair;
200 I heard it all inside that closet there,
Where Heaven, in order to confound the pride
Of this great rascal, prompted me to hide.
Ah, now I have my long-awaited chance
To punish his deceit and arrogance,
205 And give my father clear and shocking proof
Of the black character of his dear Tartuffe.

ELMIRE.
Ah no, Damis; I'll be content if he
Will study to deserve my leniency.
I've promised silence—don't make me break my word;

To make a scandal would be too absurd.   210
Good wives laugh off such trifles, and forget them;
Why should they tell their husbands, and upset them?

DAMIS.
You have your reasons for taking such a course,
And I have reasons, too, of equal force.
To spare him now would be insanely wrong.   215
I've swallowed my just wrath for far too long
And watched this insolent bigot bringing strife
And bitterness into our family life.
Too long he's meddled in my father's affairs,
Thwarting my marriage-hopes, and poor Valère's. 220
It's high time that my father was undeceived,
And now I've proof that can't be disbelieved—
Proof that was furnished me by Heaven above.
It's too good not to take advantage of.
This is my chance, and I deserve to lose it   225
If, for one moment, I hesitate to use it.

ELMIRE.
Damis . . .

DAMIS.
                    No, I must do what I think right
Madam, my heart is bursting with delight,
And, say whatever you will, I'll not consent
To lose the sweet revenge on which I'm bent.   230
I'll settle matters without more ado;
And here, most opportunely, is my cue.

SCENE FIVE

Orgon, Damis, Tartuffe, Elmire

DAMIS.
Father, I'm glad you've joined us. Let us advise you
Of some fresh news which doubtless will surprise you.
You've just now been repaid with interest   235
For all your loving-kindness to our guest.
He's proved his warm and grateful feelings toward you;
It's with a pair of horns he would reward you.
Yes, I surprised him with your wife, and heard
His whole adulterous offer, every word.   240
She, with her all too gentle disposition,
Would not have told you of his proposition;
But I shall not make terms with brazen lechery,
And feel that not to tell you would be treachery.

ELMIRE.
And I hold that one's husband's peace of mind   245
Should not be spoilt by tattle of this kind.
One's honor doesn't require it: to be proficient
In keeping men at bay is quite sufficient.
These are my sentiments, and I wish, Damis,
That you had heeded me and held your peace.   250

SCENE SIX

Orgon, Damis, Tartuffe

ORGON.
Can it be true, this dreadful thing I hear?
TARTUFFE.
Yes, Brother, I'm a wicked man, I fear:
A wretched sinner, all depraved and twisted,
The greatest villain that has ever existed.
My life's one heap of crimes, which grows each
255 minute;
There's naught but foulness and corruption in it;
And I perceive that Heaven, outraged by me,
Has chosen this occasion to mortify me.
Charge me with any deed you wish to name;
260 I'll not defend myself, but take the blame.
Believe what you are told, and drive Tartuffe
Like some base criminal from beneath your roof;
Yes, drive me hence, and with a parting curse:
I shan't protest, for I deserve far worse.
ORGON (*To Damis:*).
265 Ah, you deceitful boy, how dare you try
To stain his purity with so foul a lie?
DAMIS.
What! Are you taken in by such a bluff?
Did you not hear . . . ?
ORGON.
     Enough, you rogue, enough!
TARTUFFE.
Ah, Brother, let him speak: you're being unjust.
270 Believe his story; the boy deserves your trust.
Why, after all, should you have faith in me?
How can you know what I might do, or be?
Is it on my good actions that you base
Your favor? Do you trust my pious face?
275 Ah, no, don't be deceived by hollow shows;
I'm far, alas, from being what men suppose;
Though the world takes me for a man of worth,
I'm truly the most worthless man on earth.
(*To Damis:*)
Yes, my dear son, speak out now: call me the chief
280 Of sinners, a wretch, a murderer, a thief;
Load me with all the names men most abhor;
I'll not complain; I've earned them all, and more;
I'll kneel here while you pour them on my head
As a just punishment for the life I've led.
ORGON (*To Tartuffe:*).
This is too much, dear Brother.
(*To Damis:*)
      Have you no heart?
285
DAMIS.
Are you so hoodwinked by this rascal's art . . . ?
ORGON.
Be still, you monster.

(*To Tartuffe:*)
     Brother, I pray you, rise.
(*To Damis:*)
Villain!
DAMIS.
   But . . .
ORGON.
     Silence!
DAMIS.
     Can't you realize . . . ?
ORGON.
Just one word more, and I'll tear you limb from limb.
TARTUFFE.
In God's name, Brother, don't be harsh with him. 290
I'd rather far be tortured at the stake
Than see him bear one scratch for my poor sake.
ORGON (*To Damis:*).
Ingrate!
TARTUFFE.
   If I must beg you, on bended knee,
To pardon him . . .
ORGON (*Falling to his knees, addressing Tartuffe:*).
     Such goodness cannot be!
(*To Damis:*)
Now, *there's* true charity!
DAMIS.
     What, you . . . ?
ORGON.
      Villain, be still! 295
I know your motives; I know you wish him ill:
Yes, all of you—wife, children, servants, all—
Conspire against him and desire his fall,
Employing every shameful trick you can
To alienate me from this saintly man. 300
Ah, but the more you seek to drive him away,
The more I'll do to keep him. Without delay,
I'll spite this household and confound its pride
By giving him my daughter as his bride.
DAMIS.
You're going to force her to accept his hand? 305
ORGON.
Yes, and this very night, d'you understand?
I shall defy you all, and make it clear
That I'm the one who gives the orders here.
Come, wretch, kneel down and clasp his blessed feet,
And ask his pardon for your black deceit. 310
DAMIS.
I ask that swindler's pardon? Why, I'd rather . . .
ORGON.
So! You insult him, and defy your father!
A stick! A stick! (*To Tartuffe:*) No, no—release me, do.
(*To Damis:*)
Out of my house this minute! Be off with you,
And never dare set foot in it again. 315
DAMIS.
Well, I shall go, but . . .

ORGON.

                         Well, go quickly, then.
I disinherit you; an empty purse
Is all you'll get from me—except my curse!

SCENE SEVEN

Orgon, Tartuffe

ORGON.
    How he blasphemed your goodness! What a son!
TARTUFFE.
320   Forgive him, Lord, as I've already done.
    (To Orgon:)
    You can't know how it hurts when someone tries
    To blacken me in my dear Brother's eyes.
ORGON.
    Ahh!
TARTUFFE.
            The mere thought of such ingratitude
    Plunges my soul into so dark a mood . . .
325   Such horror grips my heart . . . I gasp for breath,
    And cannot speak, and feel myself near death.
ORGON.

    *(He runs, in tears, to the door through which he
    has just driven his son.)*

    You blackguard! Why did I spare you? Why did I not
    Break you in little pieces on the spot?
    Compose yourself, and don't be hurt, dear friend.
TARTUFFE.
330   These scenes, these dreadful quarrels, have got to end.
    I've much upset your household, and I perceive
    That the best thing will be for me to leave.
ORGON.
    What are you saying!
TARTUFFE.
               They're all against me here:
    They'd have you think me false and insincere.
ORGON.
335   Ah, what of that? Have I ceased believing in you?
TARTUFFE.
    Their adverse talk will certainly continue,
    And charges which you now repudiate
    You may find credible at a later date.
ORGON.
    No, Brother, never.
TARTUFFE.
              Brother, a wife can sway
    Her husband's mind in many a subtle way.
ORGON.
    No, no.
TARTUFFE.
         To leave at once is the solution;

Thus only can I end their persecution.   340
ORGON.
    No, no, I'll not allow it; you shall remain.
TARTUFFE.
    Ah, well; 'twill mean much martyrdom and pain,
    But if you wish it . . .
ORGON.
              Ah!
TARTUFFE.
                  Enough; so be it.   345
    But one thing must be settled, as I see it.
    For your dear honor, and for our friendship's sake,
    There's one precaution I feel bound to take.
    I shall avoid your wife, and keep away . . .
ORGON.
    No, you shall not, whatever they may say.   350
    It pleases me to vex them, and for spite
    I'd have them see you with her day and night.
    What's more, I'm going to drive them to despair
    By making you my only son and heir;
    This very day, I'll give to you alone   355
    Clear deed and title to everything I own.
    A dear, good friend and son-in-law-to-be
    Is more than wife, or child, or kin to me.
    Will you accept my offer, dearest son?
TARTUFFE.
    In all things, let the will of Heaven be done.   360
ORGON.
    Poor fellow! Come, we'll go draw up the deed,
    Then let them burst with disappointed greed!

ACT FOUR

SCENE ONE

Cléante, Tartuffe

CLÉANTE.
    Yes, all the town's discussing it, and truly,
    Their comments do not flatter you unduly.
    I'm glad we've met, Sir, and I'll give my view
    Of this sad matter in a word or two.
    As for who's guilty, that I shan't discuss;   5
    Let's say it was Damis who caused the fuss;
    Assuming, then, that you have been ill-used
    By young Damis, and groundlessly accused,
    Ought not a Christian to forgive, and ought
    He not to stifle every vengeful thought?   10
    Should you stand by and watch a father make
    His only son an exile for your sake?
    Again I tell you frankly, be advised:
    The whole town, high and low, is scandalized;
    This quarrel must be mended, and my advice is   15
    Not to push matters to a further crisis.
    No, sacrifice your wrath to God above,

And help Damis regain his father's love.
TARTUFFE.
20 Alas, for my part I should take great joy
In doing so. I've nothing against the boy.
I pardon all, I harbor no resentment;
To serve him would afford me much contentment.
But Heaven's interest will not have it so:
If he comes back, then I shall have to go.
25 After his conduct—so extreme, so vicious—
Our further intercourse would look suspicious.
God knows what people would think! Why, they'd
  describe
My goodness to him as a sort of bribe;
They'd say that out of guilt I made pretense
30 Of loving-kindness and benevolence—
That, fearing my accuser's tongue, I strove
To buy his silence with a show of love.
CLÉANTE.
Your reasoning is badly warped and stretched,
And these excuses, Sir, are most far-fetched.
35 Why put yourself in charge of Heaven's cause?
Does Heaven need our help to enforce its laws?
Leave vengeance to the Lord, Sir; while we live,
Our duty's not to punish, but forgive;
And what the Lord commands, we should obey
40 Without regard to what the world may say.
What! Shall the fear of being misunderstood
Prevent our doing what is right and good?
No, no; let's simply do what Heaven ordains,
And let no other thoughts perplex our brains.
TARTUFFE.
45 Again, Sir, let me say that I've forgiven
Damis, and thus obeyed the laws of Heaven;
But I am not commanded by the Bible
To live with one who smears my name with libel.
CLÉANTE.
Were you commanded, Sir, to indulge the whim
50 Of poor Orgon, and to encourage him
In suddenly transferring to your name
A large estate to which you have no claim?
TARTUFFE.
'Twould never occur to those who know me best
To think I acted from self-interest.
55 The treasures of this world I quite despise;
Their specious glitter does not charm my eyes;
And if I have resigned myself to taking
The gift which my dear Brother insists on making,
I do so only, as he well understands,
60 Lest so much wealth fall into wicked hands,
Lest those to whom it might descend in time
Turn it to purposes of sin and crime,
And not, as I shall do, make use of it
For Heaven's glory and mankind's benefit.
CLÉANTE.
65 Forget these trumped-up fears. Your argument
Is one the rightful heir might well resent;

It *is* a moral burden to inherit
Such wealth, but give Damis a chance to bear it.
And would it not be worse to be accused
Of swindling, than to see that wealth misused? 70
I'm shocked that you allowed Orgon to broach
This matter, and that you feel no self-reproach;
Does true religion teach that lawful heirs
May freely be deprived of what is theirs?
And if the Lord has told you in your heart 75
That you and young Damis must dwell apart,
Would it not be the decent thing to beat
A generous and honorable retreat,
Rather than let the son of the house be sent,
For your convenience, into banishment? 80
Sir, if you wish to prove the honesty
Of your intentions . . .
TARTUFFE.
      Sir, it is half-past three.
I've certain pious duties to attend to,
And hope my prompt departure won't offend you.
CLÉANTE (*Alone:*).
Damn.

SCENE TWO

Elmire, Mariane, Cléante, Dorine

DORINE.
    Stay, Sir, and help Mariane, for Heaven's sake! 85
She's suffering so, I fear her heart will break.
Her father's plan to marry her off tonight
Has put the poor child in a desperate plight.
I hear him coming. Let's stand together, now,
And see if we can't change his mind, somehow, 90
About this match we all deplore and fear.

SCENE THREE

Orgon, Elmire, Mariane, Cléante, Dorine

ORGON.
Hah! Glad to find you all assembled here.
(*To Mariane:*)
This contract, child, contains your happiness,
And what it says I think your heart can guess.
MARIANE (*Falling to her knees:*).
Sir, by that Heaven which sees me here distressed, 95
And by whatever else can move your breast,
Do not employ a father's power, I pray you,
To crush my heart and force it to obey you,
Nor by your harsh commands oppress me so
That I'll begrudge the duty which I owe— 100
And do not so embitter and enslave me
That I shall hate the very life you gave me.
If my sweet hopes must perish, if you refuse
To give me to the one I've dared to choose,

105 Spare me at least—I beg you, I implore—
The pain of wedding one whom I abhor;
And do not, by a heartless use of force,
Drive me to contemplate some desperate course.
ORGON (*Feeling himself touched by her:*).
Be firm, my soul. No human weakness, now.
MARIANE.
110 I don't resent your love for him. Allow
Your heart free rein, Sir; give him your property,
And if that's not enough, take mine from me;
He's welcome to my money; take it, do,
But don't, I pray, include my person too.
115 Spare me, I beg you; and let me end the tale
Of my sad days behind a convent veil.
ORGON.
A convent! Hah! When crossed in their amours,
All lovesick girls have the same thought as yours.
Get up! The more you loathe the man, and dread him,
120 The more ennobling it will be to wed him.
Marry Tartuffe, and mortify your flesh!
Enough; don't start that whimpering afresh.
DORINE.
But why . . . ?
ORGON.
Be still, there. Speak when you're spoken to.
Not one more bit of impudence out of you.
CLÉANTE.
125 If I may offer a word of counsel here . . .
ORGON.
Brother, in counseling you have no peer;
All your advice is forceful, sound, and clever;
I don't propose to follow it, however.
ELMIRE (*To Orgon:*).
I am amazed, and don't know what to say;
130 Your blindness simply takes my breath away.
You are indeed bewitched, to take no warning
From our account of what occurred this morning.
ORGON.
Madam, I know a few plain facts, and one
Is that you're partial to my rascal son;
135 Hence, when he sought to make Tartuffe the victim
Of a base lie, you dared not contradict him.
Ah, but you underplayed your part, my pet;
You should have looked more angry, more upset.
ELMIRE.
When men make overtures, must we reply
140 With righteous anger and a battle-cry?
Must we turn back their amorous advances
With sharp reproaches and with fiery glances?
Myself, I find such offers merely amusing,
And make no scenes and fusses in refusing;
145 My taste is for good-natured rectitude,
And I dislike the savage sort of prude
Who guards her virtue with her teeth and claws,
And tears men's eyes out for the slightest cause:
The Lord preserve me from such honor as that,

Which bites and scratches like an alley-cat!   150
I've found that a polite and cool rebuff
Discourages a lover quite enough.
ORGON.
I know the facts, and I shall not be shaken.
ELMIRE.
I marvel at your power to be mistaken.
Would it, I wonder, carry weight with you   155
If I could *show* you that our tale was true?
ORGON.
Show me?
ELMIRE.
Yes.
ORGON.
Rot.
ELMIRE.
Come, what if I found a way
To make you see the facts as plain as day?
ORGON.
Nonsense.
ELMIRE.
Do answer me; don't be absurd.
I'm not now asking you to trust our word.   160
Suppose that from some hiding-place in here
You learned the whole sad truth by eye and ear—
What would you say of your good friend, after that?
ORGON.
Why, I'd say . . . nothing, by Jehoshaphat!
It can't be true.
ELMIRE.
You've been too long deceived,   165
And I'm quite tired of being disbelieved.
Come now: let's put my statements to the test,
And you shall see the truth made manifest.
ORGON.
I'll take that challenge. Now do your uttermost.
We'll see how you make good your empty boast.   170
ELMIRE (*To Dorine:*).
Send him to me.
DORINE.
He's crafty; it may be hard
To catch the cunning scoundrel off his guard.
ELMIRE.
No, amorous men are gullible. Their conceit
So blinds them that they're never hard to cheat.
Have him come down. (*To Cléante & Mariane:*) Please
leave us, for a bit.   175

SCENE FOUR

Elmire, Orgon

ELMIRE.
Pull up this table, and get under it.
ORGON.
What?

ELMIRE.
        It's essential that you be well-hidden.
ORGON.
    Why there?
ELMIRE.
            Oh, Heaven's! Just do as you are bidden.
    I have my plans; we'll soon see how they fare.
180 Under the table, now; and once you're there,
    Take care that you are neither seen nor heard.
ORGON.
    Well, I'll indulge you, since I gave my word
    To see you through this infantile charade.
ELMIRE.
    Once it is over, you'll be glad we played.
    (*To her husband, who is now under the table:*)
185 I'm going to act quite strangely, now, and you
    Must not be shocked at anything I do.
    Whatever I may say, you must excuse
    As part of that deceit I'm forced to use.
    I shall employ sweet speeches in the task
190 Of making that imposter drop his mask;
    I'll give encouragement to his bold desires,
    And furnish fuel to his amorous fires.
    Since it's for your sake, and for his destruction,
    That I shall seem to yield to his seduction,
195 I'll gladly stop whenever you decide
    That all your doubts are fully satisfied.
    I'll count on you, as soon as you have seen
    What sort of man he is, to intervene,
    And not expose me to his odious lust
200 One moment longer than you feel you must.
    Remember: you're to save me from my plight
    Whenever . . . He's coming! Hush! Keep out of sight!

SCENE FIVE

Tartuffe, Elmire, Orgon

TARTUFFE.
    You wish to have a word with me, I'm told.
ELMIRE.
    Yes. I've a little secret to unfold.
205 Before I speak, however, it would be wise
    To close that door, and look about for spies.
    (*Tartuffe goes to the door, closes it, and returns.*)
    The very last thing that must happen now
    Is a repetition of this morning's row.
    I've never been so badly caught off guard.
210 Oh, how I feared for you! You saw how hard
    I tried to make that troublesome Damis
    Control his dreadful temper, and hold his peace.
    In my confusion, I didn't have the sense
    Simply to contradict his evidence;
215 But as it happened, that was for the best,
    And all has worked out in our interest.
    This storm has only bettered your position;

My husband doesn't have the least suspicion,
And now, in mockery of those who do,
He bids me be continually with you.   220
And that is why, quite fearless of reproof,
I now can be alone with my Tartuffe,
And why my heart—perhaps too quick to yield—
Feels free to let its passion be revealed.
TARTUFFE.
    Madam, your words confuse me. Not long ago,   225
    You spoke in quite a different style, you know.
ELMIRE.
    Ah, Sir, if that refusal made you smart,
    It's little that you know of woman's heart,
    Or what that heart is trying to convey
    When it resists in such a feeble way!   230
    Always, at first, our modesty prevents
    The frank avowal of tender sentiments;
    However high the passion which inflames us,
    Still, to confess its power somehow shames us.
    Thus we reluct, at first, yet in a tone   235
    Which tells you that our heart is overthrown,
    That what our lips deny, our pulse confesses,
    And that, in time, all noes will turn to yesses.
    I fear my words are all too frank and free,
    And a poor proof of woman's modesty;   240
    But since I'm started, tell me, if you will—
    Would I have tried to make Damis be still,
    Would I have listened, calm and unoffended,
    Until your lengthy offer of love was ended,
    And been so very mild in my reaction,   245
    Had your sweet words not given me satisfaction?
    And when I tried to force you to undo
    The marriage-plans my husband has in view,
    What did my urgent pleading signify
    If not that I admired you, and that I   250
    Deplored the thought that someone else might own
    Part of a heart I wished for mine alone?
TARTUFFE.
    Madam, no happiness is so complete
    As when, from lips we love, come words so sweet;
    Their nectar floods my every sense, and drains   255
    In honeyed rivulets through all my veins.
    To please you is my joy, my only goal;
    Your love is the restorer of my soul;
    And yet I must beg leave, now, to confess
    Some lingering doubts as to my happiness.   260
    Might this not be a trick? Might not the catch
    Be that you wish me to break off the match
    With Mariane, and so have feigned to love me?
    I shan't quite trust your fond opinion of me
    Until the feelings you've expressed so sweetly   265
    Are demonstrated somewhat more concretely,
    And you have shown, by certain kind concessions,
    That I may put my faith in your professions.
ELMIRE (*She coughs, to warn her husband*).
    Why be in such a hurry? Must my heart

270   Exhaust its bounty at the very start?
      To make that sweet admission cost me dear,
      But you'll not be content, it would appear,
      Unless my store of favors is disbursed
      To the last farthing, and at the very first.
TARTUFFE.
275   The less we merit, the less we dare to hope,
      And with our doubts, mere words can never cope.
      We trust no promised bliss till we receive it;
      Not till a joy is ours can we believe it.
      I, who so little merit your esteem,
280   Can't credit this fulfillment of my dream,
      And shan't believe it, Madam, until I savor
      Some palpable assurance of your favor.
ELMIRE.
      My, how tyrannical your love can be,
      And how it flusters and perplexes me!
285   How furiously you take one's heart in hand,
      And make your every wish a fierce command!
      Come, must you hound and harry me to death?
      Will you not give me time to catch my breath?
      Can it be right to press me with such force,
290   Give me no quarter, show me no remorse,
      And take advantage, by your stern insistence,
      Of the fond feelings which weaken my resistance?
TARTUFFE.
      Well, if you look with favor upon my love,
      Why, then, begrudge me some clear proof thereof?
ELMIRE.
295   But how can I consent without offense
      To Heaven, toward which you feel such reverence?
TARTUFFE.
      If Heaven is all that holds you back, don't worry.
      I can remove that hindrance in a hurry.
      Nothing of that sort need obstruct our path.
ELMIRE.
300   Must one not be afraid of Heaven's wrath?
TARTUFFE.
      Madam, forget such fears, and be my pupil,
      And I shall teach you how to conquer scruple.
      Some joys, it's true, are wrong in Heaven's eyes;
      Yet Heaven is not averse to compromise;
305   There is a science, lately formulated,
      Whereby one's conscience may be liberated,
      And any wrongful act you care to mention
      May be redeemed by purity of intention.
      I'll teach you, Madam, the secrets of that science;
310   Meanwhile, just place on me your full reliance.
      Assuage my keen desires, and feel no dread:
      The sin, if any, shall be on my head.
      (*Elmire coughs, this time more loudly.*)
      You've a bad cough.
ELMIRE.
                    Yes, yes. It's bad indeed.
TARTUFFE (*Producing a little brown bag:*).
      A bit of licorice may be what you need.

ELMIRE.
      No, I've a stubborn cold, it seems. I'm sure it   315
      Will take much more than licorice to cure it.
TARTUFFE.
      How aggravating.
ELMIRE.
                    Oh, more than I can say.
TARTUFFE.
      If you're still troubled, think of things this way:
      No one shall know our joys, save us alone,
      And there's no evil till the act is known;   320
      It's scandal, Madam, which makes it an offense,
      And it's no sin to sin in confidence.
ELMIRE (*Having coughed once more:*).
      Well, clearly I must do as you require,
      And yield to your importunate desire.
      It is apparent, now, that nothing less   325
      Will satisfy you, and so I acquiesce.
      To go so far is much against my will;
      I'm vexed that it should come to this; but still,
      Since you are so determined on it, since you
      Will not allow mere language to convince you,   330
      And since you ask for concrete evidence, I
      See nothing for it, now, but to comply.
      If this is sinful, if I'm wrong to do it,
      So much the worse for him who drove me to it.
      The fault can surely not be charged to me.   335
TARTUFFE.
      Madam, the fault is mine, if fault there be,
      And . . .
ELMIRE.
                Open the door a little, and peek out;
      I wouldn't want my husband poking about.
TARTUFFE.
      Why worry about the man? Each day he grows
      More gullible; one can lead him by the nose.   340
      To find us here would fill him with delight,
      And if he saw the worst, he'd doubt his sight.
ELMIRE.
      Nevertheless, do step out for a minute
      Into the hall, and see that no one's in it.

SCENE SIX

Orgon, Elmire

ORGON (*Coming out from under the table:*).
      That man's a perfect monster, I must admit!   345
      I'm simply stunned. I can't get over it.
ELMIRE.
      What, coming out so soon? How premature!
      Get back in hiding, and wait until you're sure.
      Stay till the end, and be convinced completely;
      We mustn't stop till things are proved concretely.   350
ORGON.
      Hell never harbored anything so vicious!

ELMIRE.
Tut, don't be hasty. Try to be judicious.
Wait, and be certain that there's no mistake.
No jumping to conclusions, for Heaven's sake!
(*She places Orgon behind her, as Tartuffe re-enters.*)

SCENE SEVEN

Tartuffe, Elmire, Orgon

TARTUFFE (*Not seeing Orgon:*).
355   Madam, all things have worked out to perfection;
I've given the neighboring rooms a full inspection;
No one's about; and now I may at last . . .
ORGON (*Intercepting him:*).
Hold on, my passionate fellow, not so fast!
I should advise a little more restraint.
360   Well, so you thought you'd fool me, my dear saint!
How soon you wearied of the saintly life—
Wedding my daughter, and coveting my wife!
I've long suspected you and had a feeling
That soon I'd catch you at your double-dealing.
365   Just now, you've given me evidence galore;
It's quite enough; I have no wish for more.
ELMIRE (*To Tartuffe:*).
I'm sorry to have treated you so slyly,
But circumstances forced me to be wily.
TARTUFFE.
Brother, you can't think . . .
ORGON.
                                        No more talk from you;
370   Just leave this household, without more ado.
TARTUFFE.
What I intended . . .
ORGON.
                                   That seems fairly clear.
Spare me your falsehoods and get out of here.
TARTUFFE.
No, I'm the master, and you're the one to go!
This house belongs to me, I'll have you know,
375   And I shall show you that you can't hurt *me*
By this contemptible conspiracy,
That those who cross me know not what they do,
And that I've means to expose and punish you,
Avenge offended Heaven, and make you grieve
380   That ever you dared order me to leave.

SCENE EIGHT

Elmire, Orgon

ELMIRE.
What was the point of all that angry chatter?

ORGON.
Dear God, I'm worried. This is no laughing matter.
ELMIRE.
How so?
ORGON.
                            I fear I understood his drift.
I'm much disturbed about that deed of gift.
ELMIRE.
You gave him . . . ?
ORGON.
                            Yes, it's all been drawn and signed.   385
But one thing more is weighing on my mind.
ELMIRE.
What's that?
ORGON.
                            I'll tell you; but first let's see if there's
A certain strong-box in his room upstairs.

ACT FIVE

SCENE ONE

Orgon, Cléante

CLÉANTE.
Where are you going so fast?
ORGON.
                                        God knows!
CLÉANTE.
                            Then wait;
Let's have a conference, and deliberate
On how this situation's to be met.
ORGON.
That strong-box has me utterly upset;
This is the worst of many, many shocks.   5
CLÉANTE.
Is there some fearful mystery in that box?
ORGON.
My poor friend Argas brought that box to me
With his own hands, in utmost secrecy;
'Twas on the very morning of his flight.
It's full of papers which, if they came to light,   10
Would ruin him—or such is my impression.
CLÉANTE.
Then why did you let it out of your possession?
ORGON.
Those papers vexed my conscience, and it seemed best
To ask the counsel of my pious guest.
The cunning scoundrel got me to agree   15
To leave the strong-box in his custody,
So that, in case of an investigation,
I could employ a slight equivocation
And swear I didn't have it, and thereby,
At no expense to conscience, tell a lie.   20

CLÉANTE.
It looks to me as if you're out on a limb.
Trusting him with that box, and offering him
That deed of gift, were actions of a kind
25 Which scarcely indicate a prudent mind.
With two such weapons, he has the upper hand,
And since you're vulnerable, as matters stand,
You erred once more in bringing him to bay.
You should have acted in some subtler way.

ORGON.
Just think of it: behind that fervent face,
30 A heart so wicked, and a soul so base!
I took him in, a hungry beggar, and then . . .
Enough, by God! I'm through with pious men:
Henceforth I'll hate the whole false brotherhood,
And persecute them worse than Satan could.

CLÉANTE.
35 Ah, there you go—extravagant as ever!
Why can you not be rational? You never
Manage to take the middle course, it seems,
But jump, instead, between absurd extremes.
You've recognized your recent grave mistake
40 In falling victim to a pious fake;
Now, to correct that error, must you embrace
An even greater error in its place,
And judge our worthy neighbors as a whole
By what you've learned of one corrupted soul?
45 Come, just because one rascal made you swallow
A show of zeal which turned out to be hollow,
Shall you conclude that all men are deceivers,
And that, today, there are no true believers?
Let atheists make that foolish inference;
50 Learn to distinguish virtue from pretense,
Be cautious in bestowing admiration,
And cultivate a sober moderation.
Don't humor fraud, but also don't asperse
True piety; the latter fault is worse,
55 And it is best to err, if err one must,
As you have done, upon the side of trust.

SCENE TWO

Damis, Orgon, Cléante

DAMIS.
Father, I hear that scoundrel's uttered threats
Against you; that he pridefully forgets
How, in his need, he was befriended by you,
60 And means to use your gifts to crucify you.

ORGON.
It's true, my boy. I'm too distressed for tears.

DAMIS.
Leave it to me, Sir; let me trim his ears.
Faced with such insolence, we must not waver.

I shall rejoice in doing you the favor
Of cutting short his life, and your distress.   65

CLÉANTE.
What a display of young hotheadedness!
Do learn to moderate your fits of rage.
In this just kingdom, this enlightened age,
One does not settle things by violence.

SCENE THREE

Madame Pernelle, Mariane, Elmire, Dorine, Damis,
Orgon, Cléante

MADAME PERNELLE.
I hear strange tales of very strange events.   70

ORGON.
Yes, strange events which these two eyes beheld.
The man's ingratitude is unparalleled.
I save a wretched pauper from starvation,
House him, and treat him like a blood relation,
Shower him every day with my largesse,   75
Give him my daughter, and all that I possess;
And meanwhile the unconscionable knave
Tries to induce my wife to misbehave;
And not content with such extreme rascality,
Now threatens me with my own liberality,   80
And aims, by taking base advantage of
The gifts I gave him out of Christian love,
To drive me from my house, a ruined man,
And make me end a pauper, as he began.

DORINE.
Poor fellow!

MADAME PERNELLE.
                    No, my son, I'll never bring   85
Myself to think him guilty of such a thing.

ORGON.
How's that?

MADAME PERNELLE.
                    The righteous always were maligned.

ORGON.
Speak clearly, Mother. Say what's on your mind.

MADAME PERNELLE.
I mean that I can smell a rat, my dear.
You know how everybody hates him, here.   90

ORGON.
That has no bearing on the case at all.

MADAME PERNELLE.
I told you a hundred times, when you were small,
That virtue in this world is hated ever;
Malicious men may die, but malice never.

ORGON.
No doubt that's true, but how does it apply?   95

MADAME PERNELLE.
They've turned you against him by a clever lie.

ORGON.
> I've told you, I was there and saw it done.

MADAME PERNELLE.
> Ah, slanderers will stop at nothing, Son.

ORGON.
> Mother, I'll lose my temper . . . For the last time,
> I tell you I was witness to the crime.

MADAME PERNELLE.
> The tongues of spite are busy night and noon,
> And to their venom no man is immune.

ORGON.
> You're talking nonsense. Can't you realize
> I saw it; saw it; saw it with my eyes?
> Saw, do you understand me? Must I shout it
> Into your ears before you'll cease to doubt it?

MADAME PERNELLE.
> Appearances can deceive, my son. Dear me,
> We cannot always judge by what we see.

ORGON.
> Drat! Drat!

MADAME PERNELLE.
>   One often interprets things awry;
> Good can seem evil to a suspicious eye.

ORGON.
> Was I to see his pawing at Elmire
> As an act of charity?

MADAME PERNELLE.
>   Till his guilt is clear,
> A man deserves the benefits of the doubt.
> You should have waited, to see how things turned out.

ORGON.
> Great God in Heaven, what more proof did I need?
> Was I to sit there, watching, until he'd . . .
> You drive me to the brink of impropriety.

MADAME PERNELLE.
> No, no, a man of such surpassing piety
> Could not do such a thing. You cannot shake me.
> I don't believe it, and you shall not make me.

ORGON.
> You vex me so that, if you weren't my mother,
> I'd say to you . . . some dreadful thing or other.

DORINE.
> It's your turn now, Sir, not to be listened to;
> You'd not trust us, and now she won't trust you.

CLÉANTE.
> My friends, we're wasting time which should be
>   spent
> In facing up to our predicament.
> I fear that scoundrel's threats weren't made in sport.

DAMIS.
> Do you think he'd have the nerve to go to court?

ELMIRE.
> I'm sure he won't: they'd find it all too crude
> A case of swindling and ingratitude.

CLÉANTE.
> Don't be too sure. He won't be at a loss

> To give his claims a high and righteous gloss;
> And clever rogues with far less valid cause
> Have trapped their victims in a web of laws.
> I say again that to antagonize
> A man so strongly armed was most unwise.

ORGON.
> I know it; but the man's appalling cheek
> Outraged me so, I couldn't control my pique.

CLÉANTE.
> I wish to Heaven that we could devise
> Some truce between you, or some compromise.

ELMIRE.
> If I had known what cards he held, I'd not
> Have roused his anger by my little plot.

ORGON (*To Dorine, as M. Loyal enters:*).
> What is that fellow looking for? Who is he?
> Go talk to him—and tell him that I'm busy.

SCENE FOUR

*Monsieur Loyal, Madame Pernelle, Orgon, Damis,
Mariane, Dorine, Elmire, Cléante*

MONSIEUR LOYAL.
> Good day, dear sister. Kindly let me see
> Your master.

DORINE.
>   He's involved with company,
> And cannot be disturbed just now, I fear.

MONSIEUR LOYAL.
> I hate to intrude; but what has brought me here
> Will not disturb your master, in any event.
> Indeed, my news will make him most content.

DORINE.
> Your name?

MONSIEUR LOYAL.
>   Just say that I bring greetings from
> Monsieur Tartuffe, on whose behalf I've come.

DORINE (*To Orgon:*).
> Sir, he's a very gracious man, and bears
> A message from Tartuffe, which, he declares,
> Will make you most content.

CLÉANTE.
>   Upon my word,
> I think this man had best be seen, and heard.

ORGON.
> Perhaps he has some settlement to suggest.
> How shall I treat him? What manner would be best?

CLÉANTE.
> Control your anger, and if he should mention
> Some fair adjustment, give him your full attention.

MONSIEUR LOYAL.
> Good health to you, good Sir. May Heaven confound
> Your enemies, and may your joys abound.

ORGON (*Aside, to Cléante:*).
> A gentle salutation: it confirms

My guess that he is here to offer terms.
MONSIEUR LOYAL.
165   I've always held your family most dear;
       I served your father, Sir, for many a year.
ORGON.
       Sir, I must ask your pardon; to my shame,
       I cannot now recall your face or name.
MONSIEUR LOYAL.
       Loyal's my name; I come from Normandy,
170   And I'm a bailiff, in all modesty.
       For forty years, praise God, it's been my boast
       To serve with honor in that vital post,
       And I am here, Sir, if you will permit
       The liberty, to serve you with this writ . . .
ORGON.
       To—*what?*
MONSIEUR LOYAL.
175   Now, please, Sir, let us have no friction:
       It's nothing but an order of eviction.
       You are to move your goods and family out
       And make way for new occupants, without
       Deferment or delay, and give the keys . . .
ORGON.
       I? Leave this house?
MONSIEUR LOYAL.
180   Why yes, Sir, if you please.
       This house, Sir, from the cellar to the roof,
       Belongs now to the good Monsieur Tartuffe,
       And he is lord and master of your estate
       By virtue of a deed of present date,
185   Drawn in due form, with clearest legal phrasing . . .
DAMIS.
       Your insolence is utterly amazing!
MONSIEUR LOYAL.
       Young man, my business here is not with you,
       But with your wise and temperate father, who,
       Like every worthy citizen, stands in awe
190   Of justice, and would never obstruct the law.
ORGON.
       But . . .
MONSIEUR LOYAL.
               Not for a million, Sir, would you rebel
       Against authority; I know that well.
       You'll not make trouble, Sir, or interfere
       With the execution of my duties here.
DAMIS.
195   Someone may execute a smart tattoo
       On that black jacket of yours, before you're through.
MONSIEUR LOYAL.
       Sir, bid your son be silent. I'd much regret
       Having to mention such a nasty threat
       Of violence, in writing my report.
DORINE (*Aside:*).
200   This man Loyal's a most disloyal sort!
MONSIEUR LOYAL.
       I love all men of upright character,

And when I agreed to serve these papers, Sir,
It was your feelings that I had in mind.
It couldn't bear to see the case assigned
To someone else, who might esteem you less   205
And so subject you to unpleasantness.
ORGON.
What's more unpleasant than telling a man to
       leave
His house and home?
MONSIEUR LOYAL.
                    You'd like a short reprieve?
If you desire it, Sir, I shall not press you,
But wait until tomorrow to dispossess you.   210
Splendid. I'll come and spend the night here, then,
Most quietly, with half a score of men.
For form's sake, you might bring me, just before
You go to bed, the keys to the front door.
My men, I promise, will be on their best   215
Behavior, and will not disturb your rest.
But bright and early, Sir, you must be quick
And move out all your furniture, every stick:
The men I've chosen are both young and strong,
And with their help it shouldn't take you long.   220
In short, I'll make things pleasant and convenient,
And since I'm being so extremely lenient,
Please show me, Sir, a like consideration,
And give me your entire cooperation.
ORGON (*Aside:*).
I may be all but bankrupt, but I vow   225
I'd give a hundred louis, here and now,
Just for the pleasure of landing one good clout
Right on the end of that complacent snout.
CLÉANTE.
Careful; don't make things worse.
DAMIS.
                              My bootsole itches
To give that beggar a good kick in the breeches.   230
DORINE.
Monsieur Loyal, I'd love to hear the whack
Of a stout stick across your fine broad back.
MONSIEUR LOYAL.
Take care: a woman too may go to jail if
She uses threatening language to a bailiff.
CLÉANTE.
Enough, enough, Sir. This must not go on.   235
Give me that paper, please, and then begone.
MONSIEUR LOYAL.
Well, *au revoir.* God give you all good cheer!
ORGON.
May God confound you, and him who sent you here!

SCENE FIVE

Orgon, Cléante, Mariane, Elmire, Madame Pernelle,
Dorine, Damis

ORGON.
    Now, Mother, was I right or not? This writ
240 Should change your notion of Tartuffe a bit.
    Do you perceive his villainy at last?
MADAME PERNELLE.
    I'm thunderstruck. I'm utterly aghast.
DORINE.
    Oh, come, be fair. You mustn't take offense
    At this new proof of his benevolence.
245 He's acting out of selfless love, I know.
    Material things enslave the soul, and so
    He kindly has arranged your liberation
    From all that might endanger your salvation.
ORGON.
    Will you not ever hold your tongue, you dunce?
CLÉANTE.
250 Come, you must take some action, and at once.
ELMIRE.
    Go tell the world of the low trick he's tried.
    The deed of gift is surely nullified
    By such behavior, and public rage will not
    Permit the wretch to carry out his plot.

SCENE SIX

Valère, Orgon, Cléante, Elmire, Mariane,
Madame Pernelle, Damis, Dorine

VALÈRE.
255 Sir, though I hate to bring you more bad news,
    Such is the danger that I cannot choose.
    A friend who is extremely close to me
    And knows my interest in your family
    Has, for my sake, presumed to violate
260 The secrecy that's due to things of state,
    And sends me word that you are in a plight
    From which your one salvation lies in flight.
    That scoundrel who's imposed upon you so
    Denounced you to the King an hour ago
265 And, as supporting evidence, displayed
    The strong-box of a certain renegade
    Whose secret papers, so he testified,
    You had disloyally agreed to hide.
    I don't know just what charges may be pressed,
270 But there's a warrant out for your arrest;
    Tartuffe has been instructed, furthermore,
    To guide the arresting officer to your door.
CLÉANTE.
    He's clearly done this to facilitate
    His seizure of your house and your estate.
ORGON.
275 That man, I must say, is a vicious beast!
VALÈRE.
    Quick, Sir; you mustn't tarry in the least.

    My carriage is outside, to take you hence;
    This thousand louis should cover all expense.
    Let's lose no time, or you shall be undone;
    The sole defense, in this case, is to run. 280
    I shall go with you all the way, and place you
    In a safe refuge to which they'll never trace you.
ORGON.
    Alas, dear boy, I wish that I could show you
    My gratitude for everything I owe you.
    But now is not the time; I pray the Lord 285
    That I may live to give you your reward.
    Farewell, my dears; be careful . . .
CLÉANTE.
                       Brother, hurry.
    We shall take care of things; you needn't worry.

SCENE SEVEN

The Officer, Tartuffe, Valère, Orgon, Elmire,
Mariane, Madame Pernelle, Dorine, Cléante, Damis

TARTUFFE.
    Gently, Sir, gently; stay right where you are.
    No need for haste; your lodging isn't far. 290
    You're off to prison, by order of the Prince.
ORGON.
    This is the crowning blow, you wretch; and since
    It means my total ruin and defeat,
    Your villainy is now at last complete.
TARTUFFE.
    You needn't try to provoke me; it's no use. 295
    Those who serve Heaven must expect abuse.
CLÉANTE.
    You are indeed most patient, sweet, and blameless.
DORINE.
    How he exploits the name of Heaven! It's shameless.
TARTUFFE.
    Your taunts and mockeries are all for naught;
    To do my duty is my only thought. 300
MARIANE.
    Your love of duty is most meritorious,
    And what you've done is little short of glorious.
TARTUFFE.
    All deeds are glorious, Madam, which obey
    The sovereign prince who sent me here today.
ORGON.
    I rescued you when you were destitute; 305
    Have you forgotten that, you thankless brute?
TARTUFFE.
    No, no, I well remember everything;
    But my first duty is to serve my King.
    That obligation is so paramount

310 That other claims, beside it, do not count;
And for it I would sacrifice my wife,
My family, my friend, or my own life.
ELMIRE.
   Hypocrite!
DORINE.
            All that we most revere, he uses
To cloak his plots and camouflage his ruses.
CLÉANTE.
315 If it is true that you are animated
By pure and loyal zeal, as you have stated,
Why was this zeal not roused until you'd sought
To make Orgon a cuckold, and been caught?
Why weren't you moved to give your evidence
320 Until your outraged host had driven you hence?
I shan't say that the gift of all his treasure
Ought to have damped your zeal in any measure;
But if he is a traitor, as you declare,
How could you condescend to be his heir?
TARTUFFE (*To the Officer:*).
325 Sir, spare me all this clamor; it's growing shrill.
Please carry out your orders, if you will.
OFFICER.
   Yes, I've delayed too long, Sir. Thank you kindly.
You're just the proper person to remind me.
Come, you are off to join the other boarders
330 In the King's prison, according to his orders.
TARTUFFE.
   Who? I, Sir?
OFFICER.
            Yes.
TARTUFFE.
            To prison? This can't be true!
OFFICER.
   I owe an explanation, but not to you.
(*To Orgon:*).
   Sir, all is well; rest easy, and be grateful.
   We serve a Prince to whom all sham is hateful,
335 A Prince who sees into our inmost hearts,
And can't be fooled by any trickster's arts.
His royal soul, though generous and human,
Views all things with discernment and acumen;
His sovereign reason is not lightly swayed,
340 And all his judgments are discreetly weighed.
He honors righteous men of every kind,
And yet his zeal for virtue is not blind,
Nor does his love of piety numb his wits
And make him tolerant of hypocrites.
345 'Twas hardly likely that this man could cozen
A King who's foiled such liars by the dozen.
With one keen glance, the King perceived the whole
Perverseness and corruption of his soul,

And thus high Heaven's justice was displayed:
Betraying you, the rogue stood self-betrayed. 350
The King soon recognized Tartuffe as one
Notorious by another name, who'd done
So many vicious crimes that one could fill
Ten volumes with them, and be writing still.
But to be brief: our sovereign was appalled 355
By this man's treachery toward you, which he called
The last, worst villainy of a vile career,
And bade me follow the impostor here
To see how gross his impudence could be,
And force him to restore your property. 360
Your private papers, by the King's command,
I hereby seize and give into your hand.
The King, by royal order, invalidates
The deed which gave this rascal your estates,
And pardons, furthermore, your grave offense 365
In harboring an exile's documents.
By these decrees, our Prince rewards you for
Your loyal deeds in the late civil war,
And shows how heartfelt is his satisfaction
In recompensing any worthy action, 370
How much he prizes merit, and how he makes
More of men's virtues than of their mistakes.
DORINE.
   Heaven be praised!
MADAME PERNELLE.
            I breathe again, at last.
ELMIRE.
   We're safe.
MARIANE.
            I can't believe the danger's past.
ORGON (*To Tartuffe:*).
   Well, traitor, now you see . . .
CLÉANTE.
            Ah, Brother, please 375
Let's not descend to such indignities.
Leave the poor wretch to his unhappy fate,
And don't say anything to aggravate
His present woes; but rather hope that he
Will soon embrace an honest piety, 380
And mend his ways, and by a true repentance
Move our just King to moderate his sentence.
Meanwhile, go kneel before your sovereign's throne
And thank him for the mercies he has shown.
ORGON.
   Well said: let's go at once and, gladly kneeling, 385
Express the gratitude which all are feeling.
Then, when that first great duty has been done,
We'll turn with pleasure to a second one,
And give Valère, whose love has proven so true,
The wedded happiness which is his due. 390

SPOTLIGHT · THE FRENCH THEATER

Curiously, former playgrounds of the wealthy provided France with its distinctively shaped theaters. *Jeu des paumes*, or tennis courts, were converted into theaters. In 1634 the acclaimed French actor Montdory built such a theater in the Marais district of Paris; Richelieu frequently patronized the Thèâtre du Marais, which became the prototype for subsequent French theaters. Montdory placed a stage at one end of the long rectangle of the tennis court and used existing galleries that surrounded the courts for seating. Eventually, other spectators, primarily preening young men, sat on benches or stood on the floor (*parterre*) in front of the stage; some actually sat on the stage itself, the better to be seen. These theaters were about 100 feet long, and about 55 feet wide. The auditorium comprised roughly two-thirds of the theater, the stage-backstage area the remaining third. This configuration, which fully separates the actors from the audience, further increased the development of the proscenium stage and became the dominant archi-

tectural model throughout Europe and America until the twentieth century.

Play scripts and playhouses affected French acting styles, especially in tragedy. The philosophical ideal the French called *vraisemblance*, which sought to portray "idealized" life onstage, caused actors to adopt a heightened acting style. By today's standards it excessively emphasizes declaration and posing, but those were the means by which French actors signaled the heroic nature of the characters they portrayed. It is perhaps useful to think of the performance of a French tragedy in the seventeenth century as a recital in which the actors stood in a semicircle on the forestage and declaimed their lines. Characters also recited lengthy passionate speeches, which the French called *tirades*. (Today we still refer to a lengthy, angry outburst as a tirade, another example of how we appropriate the language of theater in our daily lives.) The *tirades* are as integral to French plays as the soliloquy is to Elizabethan drama. Like their English counterparts, the French enjoyed lengthy

speeches because it was a means of celebrating the glory of the French language. John Dryden, the Restoration playwright and critic, complained that French actors spoke "by the hour-glass, as our parsons do; nay, they account it the grace of their parts, and think themselves disparaged by the poet, if they may not twice or thrice in a play entertain the audience with a speech of an hundred or two hundred lines." Such speeches naturally invited the more formal, grandiose acting style we associate with French Neoclassicism.

To heighten the heroic impact even more, French actors wore costumes that suggested Roman antiquity—the *habit à la romaine*—which were among the first attempts at historical costuming. Again we must remember that even this historical costuming was idealized and not an attempt at realism in costuming. Rather, realism made huge strides in the comic plays, such as Molière's, which reflect a conscious attempt to dress, behave, and talk like the actual people who watched the plays.

CENTER STAGE · THE (THIRD) OPENING NIGHT OF *TARTUFFE*

For the third time we await an "opening" of Molière's *Tartuffe*. Two previous presentations of the play have resulted in its being banned. The first, on May 12, 1664, concluded a two-week celebration entitled "The Pleasures of the Enchanted Island," which Louis XIV hosted for his court at Versailles. We heard that although the king enjoyed the performance, others did not, especially the queen mother, the archbishop of Paris, and the secret Company of the Holy Sacrament. This "cabal of the

pious," as it is contemptuously known, wields great power and applied sufficient political pressure to draw a royal ban on the play. In their eyes *Tartuffe* was "absolutely harmful to religion and capable of producing very dangerous effects." Luckily for us, Monsieur Molière has no time for these hypocrites. Undaunted, he has continued to present the play in private readings and performances at various country estates of Parisian society. Ironically, the ban has only increased interest in the play. Fol-

lowing three years of such performances, Molière mounted the play publicly under a new title, *The Impostor*. Once more the censors prevailed; not only did the constabulary ban the play, the archbishop decreed excommunication for any who saw or read the "vile work." However, the valiant Monsieur Molière would not knuckle under to censorship and drafted a petition to the king pleading that he "need not think of writing comedies if the Tartuffes are triumphant." It is our good fortune that

Antony Sher (interviewed in the Spotlight box on page 670) played the hypocritical Tartuffe at the Royal Shakespeare Company in 1983.

the king finally made public his private sentiments and authorized tonight's public performances of *Tartuffe*.

It is February 9, 1669, and we are in the Palais Royal. Soon we will be treated to our first glimpse of what will surely become the most celebrated comedy in all Europe. The Palais Royal provides a regal atmosphere, but attending plays here is always a peculiar experience. Built by Cardinal Richelieu in 1641 for elaborate spectacles like Molière's *Amphitryon*, the theater is not suited for the "daily life" comedies of the King's Troupe. Although the stage is well-equipped, it is too large—nearly 60 feet deep and over 45 feet wide—for intimate plays like *Tartuffe*. Also, the very low proscenium arch frames scenes of unpleasing proportions.

The theater holds about 1,000 spectators, most of whom sit in a stepped amphitheater. On the main floor, or *parterre*, other spectators stand to watch the play, though some sit on a few benches very near the stage. Surrounding us are three tiers of ornate boxes, above which is an open gallery. Unlike many of the contemporary Italian theaters, the tiers form a ∨ as they extend away from the proscenium, thus creating improved sightlines for those of us seated in the boxes. Though the view is good, the narrow amphitheater makes the boxes cramped.

The goings-on on the *parterre* are even more distracting than our uncomfortable seats. While it has been many years since Cyrano de Bergerac banished the fat, old Monfleury from the stage at the Hôtel de Bourgogne, much of our audience in the public theater is still rowdy. The jostling and camaraderie of the riff-raff on the *parterre*, coupled with the loud barking of the food and liquor vendors hawking their goods, often ruins a performance. Only slightly less irritating than these buffoons are the would-be courtiers who occupy the benches near the stage. Often they actually seat themselves on the stage itself so they can vie with the actors for the audience's attention. Fortunately Molière's entertaining comedies are so absorbing that distracting behaviors are kept to a minimum and we are able to enjoy his satires on Parisian life.

As the beginning of the show draws near, the sunlight that had earlier flooded through the windows that line the walls of the theater begins to fade and the great candelabra is lighted and raised into position over the auditorium and the stage. From offstage we hear the rhythmic banging of the stage manager's staff, and the theater falls silent as the curtain rises to reveal Orgon's unhappy family complaining about Tartuffe's hold on them.

We are soon rewarded for our five-year wait, as *Tartuffe* proves as wickedly funny as we have heard. Under the economical direction of Molière himself, the troupe succeeds in holding our attention by creating the ludicrous—yet believable—world of Orgon's household. The *Comédiens du Roi* are dressed in the high fashion of the day, and each intones in a beautiful voice the rich Alexandrines of Molière's verse. Their

(continued)

sense of language is inspiring, and their comic timing impeccable. They assume an exaggerated physical style that achieves a proper balance between the real and the ridiculous. Monsieur Molière, no doubt the greatest comic actor of our time, is amusingly gullible as Orgon. His work is nicely complemented by the women of the company, namely Madeleine Béjart as Dorine, Mlle. Hervé as Mariane, and his beautiful young wife, Armande Béjart, as Elmire. We are particularly amused by the bickering between Orgon and Elmire, as we have heard that Molière and Armande have a troubled marriage themselves.

While we enjoy the ready banter among the various characters, we most enjoy the scene in which Orgon hides under a small table to observe Tartuffe's despicable behavior toward Elmire. It is surely the funniest scene we have ever seen performed by Molière's troupe. And just when we think our favorite playwright cannot possibly top this scene, the old master triumphs with his marvelous ending. An officer of the prince, dressed in a shimmering costume so bright that it looks as if it has been lit by the sun itself, appears mysteriously to save Orgon's household and lead the hypocrite Tartuffe to the Bastille. His speech about his magnani-

mous prince fills us with pride because we know that Molière is praising our beloved King Louis. The king himself is obviously moved and rises from his seat at the center of the theater to lead the applause as Molière's company acknowledges our cheers.

As we leave the Palais Royal and step into the frigid night air, we are warmed by our thoughts of the comedy. We hope it will be performed again soon and often. (It was—it ran for a record-breaking thirty-three performances!—Eds.)

CENTER STAGE   TARTUFFE AT THE *THÉÂTRE DU SOLEIL*, 1995

Parisian director Arianne Mnouchkine undertook Molière's *Tartuffe* as the Théâtre du Soleil's artistic response to encroachments on citizens' rights throughout the world, terrorist violence, and the excesses of religious fundamentalism. The production played in Vienna in June 1995, at the Festival d'Avignon in July, and at the Théâtre du Soleil's Paris home, the Cartoucherie, throughout the fall. The Soleil's powerfully dark production exemplifies the company's stated goal of creating "a theatre taken directly from social reality, one which is not a simple account, but an encouragement to change the conditions in which we live. We want to recount our History to move it forward."

In August 1995 Mnouchkine and other French artists protested the inaction of the French government and the United Nations in Bosnia-Herzegovina with a hunger strike; similarly, the Soleil's *Tartuffe* depicted metaphorically what happens when the Western world, in Mnouchkine's words, "by a mixture of cowardice and alleged political lucidity, continues to discuss and negotiate with [the extremists]. . . . Like Orgon, the Occident is complicitous, and us with them. Every ten or fifteen

years this play dips back into our history due to current events which confirms its importance and insight" (Festival d'Avignon Program).

Mnouchkine set the play in the summer heat of an indeterminate Mediterranean locale. Blooming bougainvillea atop towering wrought-iron gates surrounded Orgon's bourgeois courtyard, itself bedecked with a stunning array of Byzantine doors and Middle Eastern carpets. Glass carafes of water, bowls of pistachios, bright oranges and green apples, and rows of well-worn leather slippers underneath two Indian cots rounded out the details of Orgon's spacious oasis. In light of France's complex sociopolitical relationship with its former North African colony Algeria, the Soleil's *Tartuffe* immediately called to mind modern-day Algiers and the terror that reigns there under the banner of Islamic fundamentalism. However, because Mnouchkine considers *Tartuffe* a timeless metaphor for societies in crisis, the overall setting was suggestive of diverse locations and political movements cross borders of time and place.

Molière's characters were also not clearly delineated as belonging to a specific time period, country, or religion;

rather, they existed as metaphors open to interpretation depending on the spectator's frame of reference. Madame Pernell conjured up "a mixture of a Mother Superior and a Muslim," as Mnouchkine characterized her in rehearsal. Orgon and Cléante, with their full goatees and mustaches, collarless white shirts, immaculate vests, and flowing black coats, suggested a Turkish-Mediterranean-European blend at the turn of various centuries. Tartuffe and his faithful followers wore long, sweeping black coats, skullcaps and full beards inspired by (among other sources) seventeenth-century Islamic apparel to conjure images of a range of fundamentalist figures, of whatever century, who resort to violence in order to impose their philosophies on society.

In the opening scene, the family's fresh white linens sat in crisp, neat piles or hung along the gateposts of the courtyard; they suggested innocence in Orgon's warm, idyllic haven. It was a festive occasion at which Mariane and her lover, Valère, danced together to the undulating rhythms of *rai* music; they were goaded on by a graceful Cléante. The women of the house, Elmire and Dorine, watched in amusement while young Damis buried his

Tartuffe was transported to the modern Middle East in Arianne Mnouchkine's 1995 production for the Théâtre du Soleil.

head in a book he purchased from a local merchant peddling his wares from a colorful cart outside the gates. Madame Pernelle's servants, Flippe and Pote (formerly Flipote), were adorned from head to foot in black religious garments covered with white work aprons. They sneaked away from the house to purchase a record of forbidden music from the merchant. Madame Pernelle's emergence from the house was the first intrusion into this otherwise pleasant and protected world. Upon seeing the irreverent goings-on, her jaw dropped and she blew a silver whistle that hung about her neck to call the courtyard to order. She tossed Damis's book aside, chastised the servants as she flung their record—like a frisbee—into the wings, and sent Valère scampering over the gates. According to Mnouchkine, the material objects in this Eden "maintain an important role, and the family's treasures—the traces of paradise—transform themselves into hell." Madame Pernelle's vehement rejection and ceaseless criticism of free thought were not surprising (however annoying) to the assembled family who tried to placate her. However, it was her blind faith in the houseguest, Tartuffe, that re-

mained disquieting and suggested impending danger. Outnumbered and ignored, a frustrated Madame Pernelle collected herself and bopped the servants on their heads with her handbag to wake them from a catnap.

Wearing a fez, Orgon returned to his home to find the family worried about Tartuffe's encroachment upon their world. This threat took physical form as Tartuffe finally streamed onstage amid a thunderous roar of demonstrators and the strains of triumphant military music; he was flanked by four cohorts wearing pointed, black Ku Klux Klan–like hoods. Whereas Tartuffe is a convincing player "who forbids others to do what he himself is in the process of doing" (Mnouchkine), he is most dangerous when he is most sincere. By contrast, Orgon was prone to flare into physical bursts of anger when he was not obeyed. His instability and desperation were simultaneously droll and terrifying as he erupted into hysterics or smashed apples against his forehead in moments of crisis. For example, when Damis revealed that Tartuffe tried to seduce Elmire, Orgon commanded Tartuffe's men to drag the boy away on his heels; Damis cried out to his father who was busily

consoling a "wounded" Tartuffe. Later in act 4, Orgon brought in a team of notaries and their guards to sign away his daughter to Tartuffe forever. Only after Mariane pulled a knife and threatened to commit suicide did an embarrassed and shaken Orgon order them away. The issues surrounding a daughter's sacrifice as a tool to maintain the patriarchal order recalled images of the Soleil's recent production of Aeschylus's *Oresteia* in which Agamemnon sacrifices his daughter Iphigenia.

However, *Tartuffe* is a comedy, and the resistors inside Orgon's family would not let the patriarch get away with murder. Together, the clever Dorine-Elmire team mounted their defense despite the obvious risks involved. Both women (played by Nirupama Nitanyanden and Juliana Carnerio de Cunha) are consummate actors who strategically employ different tactics to undermine Orgon and Tartuffe. Throughout the production, the wise, witty, well-seasoned Dorine was the cement holding the family together as she gave courage to the children, and support to Elmire as she confronted Tartuffe. In contrast to her humor and high spirits, the gravity of the situation

(continued)

was heightened as Dorine broke down and cried when Tartuffe threatened to take Orgon's estate in act 5. As night fell and shadows flickered in the light of the candle that Elmire lit on the table while awaiting Tartuffe, the personal peril she was willing to face to prove his deceit was evident. Her forced enclosure in this unwanted nightmare was further underlined when an eager, smiling Tartuffe seductively, yet comically, set the scene by pulling down the linen

that lined the gates. He then rhythmically disrobed by tossing pieces of his clothing around the stage as he attempted to turn the entire courtyard into a bedroom.

The Soleil's reading of Molière's brilliantly wrought comedy offered a trenchant view of contemporary French society and its many contradictions by trusting the playwright's text "*au pied de la lattre*" ("to the word"). It revived the interplay of socially inscribed roles and

the incisive and potent political critique that initially caused the play to be banned in 1664 and again in 1667. The dexterity of the actors enabled Molière's characters—and the production as a whole—to dance along the narrow precipice between comedy and its chilly underside. The Théâtre du Soleil reinforced *Tartuffe's* relevance in 1995.

Lisa Jo Epstein
The University of Texas

SPOTLIGHT

THE SECRET LIFE OF A CON MAN: ANTONY SHER ON PLAYING TARTUFFE

(The following is an interview with Antony Sher, an actor with The Royal Shakespeare Company.

"A man, or rather a demon disguised as a man, and the most notorious blasphemer and libertine who ever lived . . . He deserves to be tortured and burnt for this sacrilegious outrage," thundered a contemporary cleric at Molière after the one and only performance of *Tartuffe* in 1664. A modern audience seeing Molière's comedy about the unmasking of a religious hypocrite might well wonder what the uproar was about. To illuminate the furor surrounding *Tartuffe*, which opens at the Barbican this Thursday, the RSC has paired it with Bulgakov's *Molière*, about Molière's conflict with the Church over what has become the most performed French classical play.

The controversy centered on the character of Tartuffe, who impersonates a holy man and so bewitches a wealthy businessman, Orgon, that he has to catch Tartuffe *in flagrante* with his wife Elmire before realizing he has been duped. The French clergy were incensed, and *Tartuffe* was banned for five years until Molière did extensive rewriting.

In Bulgakov's not entirely factual account, Molière is persecuted by the Church both for *Tartuffe* and for his

marriage to a woman suspected of being his daughter. Although Louis XIV initially supports Molière against his clerical enemies, he arbitrarily withdraws his patronage and bans *Tartuffe*, a final blow which causes Molière to suffer a heart attack on stage.

Bulgakov's play is also a clever pastiche of Molière's plots. As in *Tartuffe*, sons are disinherited, old men deceived, and Molière's double-act with his servant Bouton mirrors the Master/Servant relationship of Orgon and Dorine.

Antony Sher, 34, plays both title roles, adding Tartuffe and his creator to a distinguished list of predatory manipulators (*The History Man*) and farcical anti-heroes (the Arab in *Goosepimples*; Clive in *Cloud 9*). "The great joy of doing the plays together is that *Tartuffe* is mentioned throughout *Molière* so that one approaches *Tartuffe* with all that background knowledge," says Sher. "Seeing *Molière* informs people about the religious issues behind *Tartuffe*: you see *Tartuffe* and then understand what the fuss is about in *Molière*."

Bulgakov's play exaggerates Molière's persecution by the Church and caricatures his sycophantic relationship with Louis. "Bulgakov hasn't written a biography," says Sher, "he has used the character of Molière and twisted the facts of his life to write a play about the artist in a repressive society."

Pairing *Tartuffe* and *Molière* sets up all sorts of political resonances. Molière was as dependent on Louis' support as Bulgakov was on Stalin's, and both plays were banned, ironically. *Tartuffe* ends with Louis saving Orgon, and Bulgakov's play with the King destroying Molière.

But Sher stresses that although links exist, "it could be about South Africa now, [where Sher was born] or any totalitarian society." Bulgakov charts the state's destruction of the individual because he's not fitting in. It becomes Kafkaesque: he's a man in a nightmare where everyone is after him.

"But it's a difficulty in the part that Bulgakov makes Molière much more neurotic than he probably was, a man who panics, who is desperate with fear and grief. Bulgakov puts him where the entire force of Church and state comes down on him, and then makes him behave like you or me rather than some super-hero."

Tartuffe, however, thrives on adversity, "a great improviser who thinks on his feet." But he is hardly a subtle portrait of a religious importer. He doesn't come on stage until Act 3, giving the other characters two acts to run him down. "Because of the objections that people wouldn't realize Tartuffe was a hypocrite, Molière had to do so much nudge-nudge, wink-wink to the audience that Tartuffe was a fraud that I think he came close to ruining the play," says Sher.

Molière explicitly made Tartuffe a scoundrel who says or does nothing that does not reveal his evil nature. Making Tartuffe one-dimensional may have partially appeased Molière's enemies, but it also makes the role difficult to play.

Sher explains; "There is actually no such man as Tartuffe; he's a criminal with a long record, and Tartuffe is just a role that he's playing. For rehearsal purposes, we have invented the real man, whom we call 'Eric.' 'Eric' is a con-man, who has done a lot of different cons, and this one happens to be a religious man called Tartuffe.

"And because it's a role he's playing, it doesn't have to be too fixed; he's a chameleon, constantly changing, he can go from full Rasputic powers to a lost little boy. He's got to have the ability to change and swop and surprise people at a rate of knots."

"Richard III is similar to Tartuffe. They're both manipulators, and very clever actors: they play whatever scene people want them to play. But the difference is that with Richard you do see the man himself, in soliloquy. Because Molière hasn't given Tartuffe one bit of 'Eric' to do, it's frustrating; you can't investigate him at all as a human being." Even when Tartuffe is unmasked at the end, Molière has him "dragged off without a grace note or a final line. It's moments like that when you know there has been a lot of re-writing."

To counter-balance the odds Molière was obliged to stack against Tartuffe to get the play on, Sher's original idea was to fight tradition and go for "as pure an image as possible, young, Christ-like, and angelic." He discovered, however, that playing so much against the text didn't work.

"You can with Shakespeare: I think we have to some extent with Lear [Sher played the Fool as a double-act with Michael Gambon's King], but what Molière has written is very clear and clean ... and it simply will not take such a drastic re-interpretation. Now I'm going towards something that is a bit creepier, more in keeping with the servant Dorine's comment that Tartuffe looks like a gargoyle off the side of Notre Dame. One must always remember that Molière started with commedia dell'arte stock characters. And although he greatly improved on them that stock element must be there, though that doesn't mean they need to be cartoon people."

Sher points out that doing Molière's plays like pantomime is an exclusively English tradition. "Bill Alexander [who has directed both Tartuffe and Molière] and I went to Paris to see the Comèdie Française do L'Avare ("The Miser"), and it was a real eye-opener, because they do Molière terribly seriously. In England the plays become so thin they're like confections, but when you actually see them done with great seriousness, the comedy takes care of itself and the plays become rather rich and fascinating exposes of human weakness. I think that's especially true of Tartuffe because it's unsettling and quite frightening what's going on in Orgon's house. It's a black comedy."

"The Secret Life of a Con Man: Antony Sher on Playing Tartuffe" by Francesca Simon. The Sunday Times, 24 July 1983. Reprinted by permission of Antony Sher.

THE LATE-SEVENTEENTH AND EIGHTEENTH CENTURIES

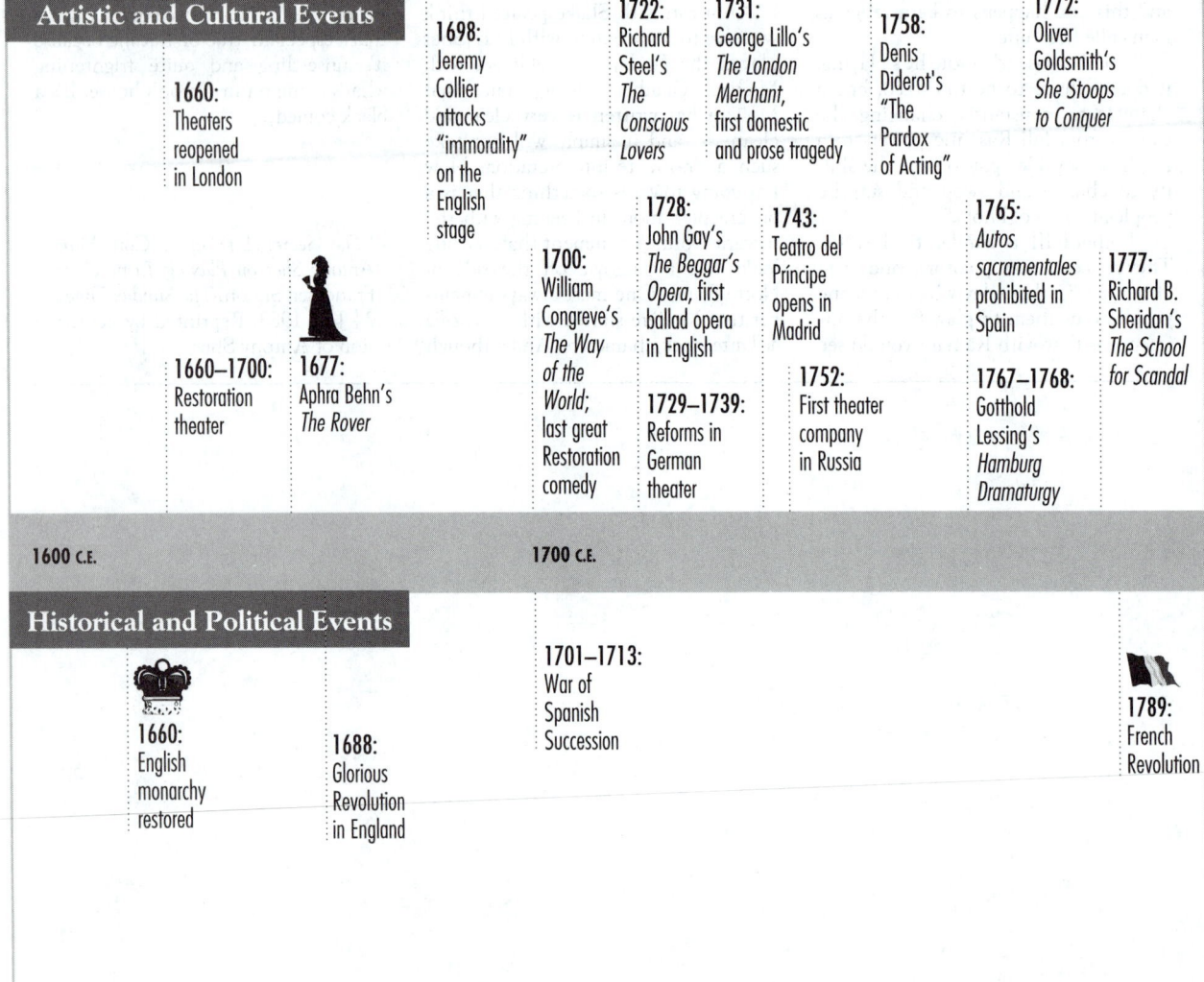

Artistic and Cultural Events

1660:
Theaters
reopened
in London

1660–1700:
Restoration
theater

1677:
Aphra Behn's
The Rover

1698:
Jeremy
Collier
attacks
"immorality"
on the
English
stage

1700:
William
Congreve's
*The Way
of the
World*;
last great
Restoration
comedy

1722:
Richard
Steel's
*The
Conscious
Lovers*

1728:
John Gay's
*The Beggar's
Opera*, first
ballad opera
in English

1729–1739:
Reforms in
German
theater

1731:
George Lillo's
*The London
Merchant*,
first domestic
and prose tragedy

1743:
Teatro del
Príncipe
opens in
Madrid

1752:
First theater
company
in Russia

1758:
Denis
Diderot's
"The
Pardox
of Acting"

1765:
*Autos
sacramentales*
prohibited in
Spain

1767–1768:
Gotthold
Lessing's
*Hamburg
Dramaturgy*

1772:
Oliver
Goldsmith's
*She Stoops
to Conquer*

1777:
Richard B.
Sheridan's
*The School
for Scandal*

1600 C.E.

1700 C.E.

Historical and Political Events

1660:
English
monarchy
restored

1688:
Glorious
Revolution
in England

1701–1713:
War of
Spanish
Succession

1789:
French
Revolution

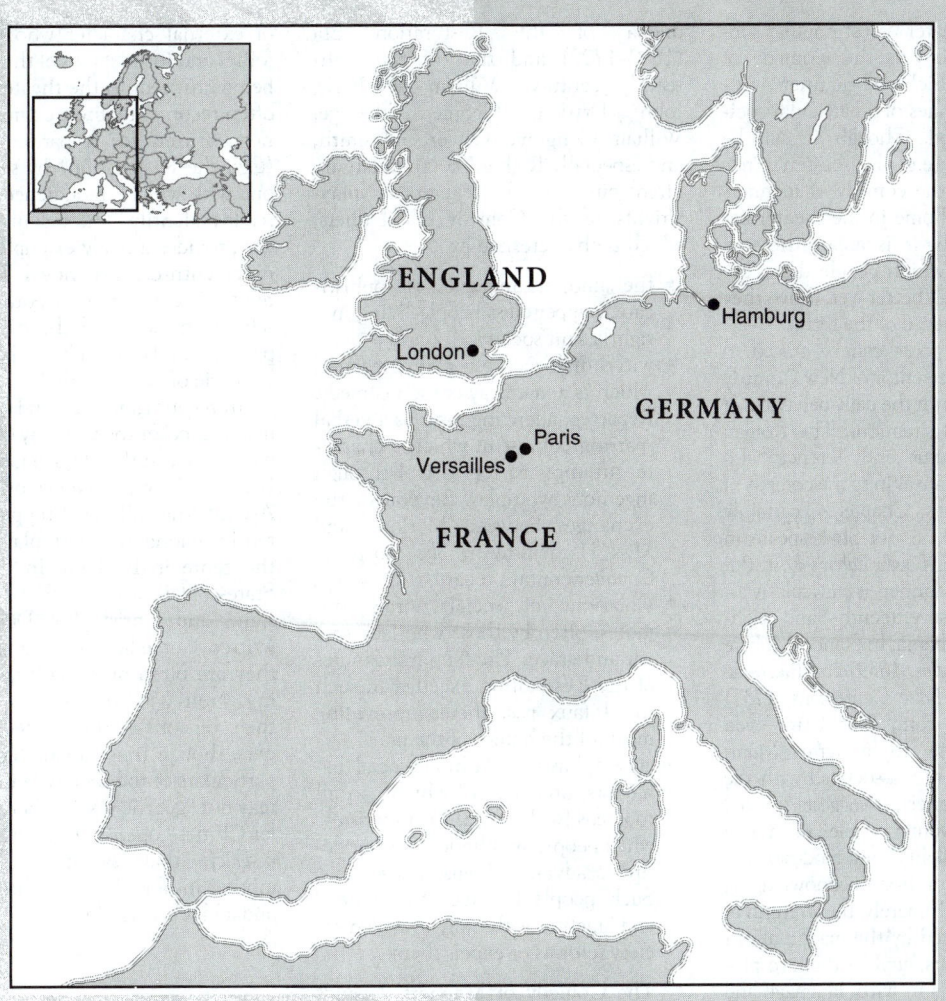

Among the theater's most popular sub-genres of comedy is the Comedy of Manners, in which the manners, customs, and attitudes of a particular society are satirized. Though it can be found in novels (e.g. Jane Austen's *Pride and Prejudice*), the comedy of manners is especially at home in the theater because frequently it is about the way ("manner") in which people dress, behave, and talk—better yet, how they "act," in every sense of the term.

Its Western roots can be traced to Menander, the inventor of New Comedy and its emphasis on the daily behaviors of people in social situations. The Roman comedians, Plautus and Terence, also wrote plays that are akin to the comedy of manners (*Brothers*, Chapter 4, certainly fits the criteria), as did Shakespeare in such comedies as *Love's Labor's Lost*. But the Comedy of Manners is particularly associated with seventeenth- and eighteenth-century drama. In France, Molière (*The Learned Ladies*, 1659) and Pierre de Marivaux (*The False Confessions*, 1737) excelled in the form. The latter even lends his name to a term—*Maravaudage*—frequently associated with the Comedy of Manners; it suggests spirited plays in which young people fall in love (often at first sight), but modesty and pride keep them from acknowledging their feelings. Ultimately, the strength of their love, abetted by the machinations of skillful servants, enables them to profess their feelings in witty language and win their heart's desires.

However, we most closely associate the Comedy of Manners with English drama of the Restoration Era (1660–1700) and that of the eighteenth century. William Wycherly, John Dryden, George Etherege, William Congreve, Oliver Goldsmith, and especially Richard B. Sheridan are often cited as the exemplary playwrights of the Comedy of Manners, which is characterized by

- the amorous intrigues of sophisticated, upper-class people living in a tightly knit society.
- witty dialogue, especially *repartée*, which is a mainstay of such comedy. Repartee, a fencing term, is a verbal sparring contest in which a character attempts to top a rival through ingenious wordplay. Several of the exchanges between Marlowe and Miss Hardcastle in *She Stoops to Conquer* contain repartée.
- violations of social norms and mores, often by those who lack true wit and grace. The fops and dandies of the Restoration excelled in such social faux pas, thereby providing much of the humor of the play.
- an emphasis on fashion, social behaviors, and speech, which can all too easily become "mannerisms" when people are blinded by their desire to advance themselves socially. Such people become "living lies," and laughter is the way in which society reforms or expels them.

The Comedy of Manners depends on an audience knowledgeable about the particulars of the society in question. Thus the audience becomes a kind of external character who judges the follies and social lapses of the characters being satirized. In the theater, directors often recontextualize a comedy of manners written for a particular society (e.g., the Restoration) by setting it in one with which an audience may more readily identify. The recent film *Clueless* provides a ready example; Austen's nineteenth-century novel *Emma* was reset in a contemporary American high school and satirized the dress, speech patterns, and especially the behaviors of a coterie of "valley girls."

In recent times England has continued to excel at the Comedy of Manners, particularly in the plays of Oscar Wilde, Bernard Shaw, and Noel Coward. Allen Ayckbourne and Tom Stoppard are currently among the best playwrights of the genre in England. In the United States, Neil Simon, Wendy Wasserstein, and Christopher Durang have written Comedies of Manners, though they are often quite dark and disturbing. Non-Western cultures also have their versions of the Comedy of Manners, though those unfamiliar with the particulars of the society being satirized may not "get the joke." There is a popular Chinese opera, *The Perfumed Handkerchief*, that satirizes a would-be mother-in-law, her daughter's suitor, and a blabbering old auntie.

In 1642 the Puritans, led by Oliver Cromwell, seized power in England and immediately closed the public theaters, which they had long considered "the devil's workshop." The supporters of King Charles I, who was executed on the steps of Parliament in 1649, fled England. Many went to the American colonies (the Carolinas were named for King Charles), where they eventually established theaters in Williamsburg, Jamestown, and Charleston. Others fled to Italy, where they were introduced to spectacular scenic effects and to the opera. But most royalists found refuge in France, where they attended the Parisian and court theaters, quite unlike those they left in London. They were enamored of the intimate, indoor French theaters, and they enjoyed the Neoclassic dramas of Corneille and the topical comedies of Molière. When the monarchists returned to England after the Interregnum (1642–1660), they demanded plays and playing conditions in keeping with the French fashion. And having seen women perform in France and Italy, they also made it possible for women to act in English theaters.

From 1660, when Charles II returned to the throne taken from his father, until 1700, the English theater presented heroic tragedies, such as Thomas Otway's *Venice Preserv'd*, and spectacles employing the new (to the English) Italian scenery. But the most popular plays were comedies portraying the affairs (sexual and otherwise) of the well-to-do who sought favor at Charles's court. (Charles II attended the theater regularly and enjoyed a private box where he entertained his mistresses, one of whom was the popular actress Nell Gywnn.) Courtiers wrote these plays about courtiers and for courtiers. (See Spotlight box, The Comedy of Manners.) At no other time in the history of the English theater has playwriting and performance been controlled by such a small, yet powerful, coterie. However, Restoration comedies retain a lasting appeal because of their wit and the brilliance of their satirical portraits of the manners and social customs of the society they mirrored. William Wycherly's *The Country Wife* (1675), Sir George Etherege's *The Man of Mode* (1676), and William Congreve's *The Way of the World* (1700) remain among the most popular Restoration comedies. Mrs. Aphra Behn, the first woman to achieve success as a professional playwright, wrote *The Rover*, which has enjoyed major revivals in the twentieth century.

After eighteen years of Puritanism, England's moral pendulum swung wildly in an opposite direction. Charles II and his courtiers (and would-be courtiers) were obsessed with the pursuit of material goods and sexual pleasure. Consequently, Restoration comedies are notoriously bawdy and amoral. Furthermore, they espouse one of the dominant philosophies of the age, as set forth in Thomas Hobbes's social tract *The Leviathan* (1651): "[Men] are in that condition which is called war; and such a war, as is of every man against every man." In the Restoration the battlefield became the boudoir, and those who survived were those who conquered through cunning, wit, deception, and charm. The hero of the Restoration play—"the rake"—is the antithesis of the conventional hero of serious drama. Whereas the latter idealistically pursues his goals (love and dignity) through honor and duty, the rake cynically pursues his (lust and self-indulgence) through deceit and sexual conquest. For the rake, it was a badge of honor to cuckold an enemy, a triumph to seduce a virtuous woman.

Within the comedies, the antithesis of the rake was the fop, one who lacks true wit and charm and who is excessive in dress and mannerisms. The grotesquely comical fop invariably steals the show in a Restoration comedy. Rakes especially enjoyed duping middle-class merchants and the nouveau riche. Whomever they attacked, rakes invariably bested because they were skillful at the most prized Restoration-era virtue: using one's wit (and therefore language) well.

Restoration comedies celebrate the game of love, and "the chase" is all in their plots. Those who play well—though not necessarily fairly—win; those who lack wit and invention, lose. In Restoration England, fidelity was not necessarily a virtue onstage or off. John Dryden, a fine playwright and a superb dramatic critic, captures such attitudes in the preface to his witty play, *Marriage à la Mode* (1672):

> *Why should a foolish marriage vow*
>
> *Which long ago was made*
>
> *Oblige us to each other now*
>
> *When passion is decayed?*
>
> *But our marriage is dead*
>
> *When the pleasure is fled. . . .*

Lest we be too shocked at such celebrations of adultery, we must remember that marriages, particularly among the nobility, were prearranged, usually for political and economic gain. Love was rarely the prime motivator for marriage. As audiences grew weary of the decadence exhibited in Restoration plays, and especially as the middle class (and its traditional morality) assumed greater economic and political power, there was a discernable shift in the attitudes ex-

SPOTLIGHT   THE CONVENTIONS OF THE RESTORATION THEATER

Because the Restoration theater was virtually the property of England's privileged class, it has peculiarities of style and performance. Reading a play from this era can be more entertaining if you imagine how *The Rover* might have been staged at the Dorset Garden Theater in March 1677, when King Charles II saw it performed.

Intimacy perhaps best characterizes Restoration plays in performance. Not only were the comedies about intimate relationships (i.e., sexual conquests), they were performed in an intimate space by actors who often had personal knowledge of the lives of their audience (and vice versa). In gossip-ridden London, courtiers and the wealthy seemingly had little to do but indulge themselves in intrigues when not attending the theater, which was itself among the most popular public meetingplaces of the time. Playhouses were a favorite rendezvous for assignations because ladies customarily wore vizards (masks) to protect their identities. Not surprisingly, the actions onstage often mirrored the offstage high jinks of the Dorset Garden's clientele—and everyone knew it. Except perhaps poor Lord So-and-So who was being cuckolded by Lady So-and-So and Sir You Know Who; Lord So-and-So was thereby the offstage butt of onstage jokes.

About 600 people could fill the new theaters being erected in London during the Restoration. The audience sat on benches on the floor (the "pit"), in elegant boxes located above the stage (the better to be seen at the play), or in galleries above the pit. No one was farther than about 35 feet from the stage, which itself was only about 12 feet deep (excluding the upstage scenic area). This meant that actors and audience, who were lit by a common candelabra, were very close to each other. Such intimacy encouraged frequent use of the aside, perhaps the most prominent convention of the Restoration theater. An aside occurs when a character speaks a short line directly to the audience (apparently) without the other characters

hearing him or her. Although asides are not the exclusive property of Restoration comedy, they are used with greater frequency and effectiveness there than elsewhere (save perhaps the old-fashioned melodrama, where the villain's "Curses, foiled again" emerged as the most famous aside in Western theater). Asides actively involved the audience in the onstage intrigues. In Restoration comedies the audience is always "in" on the joke. Additionally, asides brought the reality of the onstage escapades into the auditorium, where the playgoers understood too well the implications of the plot. Consider two asides taken from act 4 of *The Rover*. Imagine the effect if the actor playing Willmore shares his exit line with a dandy in the pit who himself lives by a similar credo:

> I'm glad on this release. Now for my gipsy [sic]:
> For though to worse we change, yet still we find
> New joys, new charms, in a new miss that's kind.

Imagine how the fun is doubled if he says it to a friend with whom he has been out wenching. Consider the possibilities if he says it to an attractive young woman seated in a box above the stage as a flirtation. Or suppose he says it directly to the king, whom the entire audience knows to be interested in "a new miss that's kind." Now, look at Helena's simple aside, "So, now is he [Willmore] for another woman." Again, consider the impact—not to mention the fun—if the line is shared with a lady in the audience whose own husband is "for another woman." What if she takes her case directly to the king? Or suppose she directs it to a notorious libertine in the third row? Such were the dynamics of a Restoration comedy in performance; when reading such plays, you can more easily enter into the spirit of the plays if you think of the asides as more than mere throwaways to the audience.

Not only did actors directly address the audience, but it was the practice of

the time that some in the audience could actually rise and speak to the actors and others in the audience. The plays themselves, which are invariably filled with commentary about theatergoing and behavior, evidence this. In William Wycherly's *The Country Wife* (1675) the doltish fop, Sparkish, brags that he and his fellow dandies go to a play as if they were going to a picnic:

> I carry my own wine to one, and my own wit to t'other, or else I am sure I would not be merry at either; and the reason why we are so often louder than the players is because we think we speak more wit, and so become the [playwright's] rivals in the audience. For to tell you the truth, we hate the silly rogues; nay, so much that we find fault even with their bawdy upon the stage, whilst we talk nothing else in the pit as loud.

Actors no doubt had to be as quick-thinking and inventive to parry the thrusts of wits in the audience as modern standup comics working a room full of hecklers. To further add to the color of the event, wenches circulated throughout the audience selling oranges and other favors to the spectators. Clearly there was as much theater in the boxes, the pit, and the gallery as on the stage.

Perhaps you are familiar with the dress and wigs, physical posturing, and the use of such accoutrements as walking sticks, snuff boxes, and fans during this period in European history. They influenced the performance style required of Restoration comedy actors. In the late seventeenth century such things as "making a leg" or talking in "the language of the fan" were not the performance conventions they are today; rather, they were part of the social world the plays mirrored. A young man extended his ribbon-bedecked leg as a means of preening; such behavior was considered "sexy" and was part of a mating ritual. When a young woman demurely lowered her fan to reveal her eyes, it was not only a signal that she enjoyed a dandy's flirtations but an encouragement for him to continue. Should she place the fan over her lips, it meant that he was treading on thin ice and had better choose his words carefully. If she snapped it shut, it meant "end of conversation—now!" Though few of these societal conventions are scripted, actors must know when to use them to build their characters and enhance the interplay with other actors. When reading Restoration plays, it is easy to forget that such behaviors are as integral as any dialogue the playwright supplies. Aphra Behn alludes to those who carry social gestures to the point of mere affectation (a not uncommon occurrence of the time) in her epilogue to *The Rover*.

Both prologues and epilogues were *de rigueur* in the Restoration theater. Customarily, the prologue was delivered by the leading actor, and the epilogue by the favored actress. Like the aside, these lengthy, witty speeches heightened the interplay between stage and auditorium. Also, they were often topical and depended upon a sophisticated audience that understood the satirical barbs. Principal actors customarily bowed to the audience on their first entrances and only then assumed their characters. Orchestral music was played before the play, between its acts, and often as underscoring during the action. Thus, virtually every aspect of the Restoration theater was calculated to heighten the theatrical atmosphere of the event. Little wonder that *The Rover*, like the majority of plays of its time, employs the artifice of theater and disguisings as a central component of its plot. Keep these things in mind as you read Mrs. Behn's wickedly funny play to enter more fully the world she envisioned as she wrote it.

---

pressed in Restoration plays. *The Way of the World* is generally considered the last true Restoration play; its hero and heroine ultimately reject the wicked ways of the world and commit themselves to a new society. (See Spotlight box, The Conventions of the Restoration Theater.)

Sentimental Comedy

The licentiousness of Restoration comedies gave way to sentimental or "weeping" comedies popular among the new merchant class in the early eighteenth century. The new drama was shaped by the doctrine of benevolence, an outgrowth of the optimism engendered by the prosperity that accompanied colonialism. This philosophy claimed that God planted within humans the natural instinct to love others, and each person therefore had a moral responsibility to demonstrate this innate goodwill (i.e., benevolence) through acts of charity. Moral acts incited strong, positive feelings of virtue in both the doer and the observer, thereby engendering more acts of kindness. The theater became a temple where virtuous people congregated to learn about virtue and sentiment. Richard Steele (1672–1729), who wrote England's most popular sentimental comedies, declared that "there is no human institution so aptly calculated for the forming of a free-born people as that of the theater." Steele wrote plays calculated to reward virtue and correct (as opposed to punishing) vices.

Consider a speech from Steele's *The Conscious Lovers*, the hit of the 1722 theater season in London. Here, the preeminently virtuous heroine, Indiana, describes the misfortunes of her infancy and childhood to her benefactor, a kindly old merchant named Sealand:

> What have I to do but sigh, and weep, to rave, run wild, a lunatic in chains, or, hid in darkness, mutter in distracted starts and broken accents my strange, strange story! . . . All my comfort must be to expostulate in madness, to relieve with my frenzy and despair, and, shrieking, to demand of fate why—why was I born to such a variety of sorrows? . . . 'Twas heaven's high will I should be plundered in my cradle! Tossed on seas! And even there, an infant captive! To lose my mother, hear but of my father! To be adopted! To lose my adopter! Then plunged again in worse calamities!

But all is not lost for Indiana, who remained virtuous and true despite these severe tests. "Heaven's high will" rewards her by reuniting her with her lost and newly wealthy father, Sealand, whose real name is Danforth. (For good measure, kindly old Isabella, who has taken Indiana under her wing, is revealed as Sealand's long-lost sister!)

We may find such contrived playwriting laughable by our standards, but such plays dominated the English, French, and—quite significantly—early American stages because their sim-

FORUM

"A Comparison Between Sentimental and Laughing Comedy"

OLIVER GOLDSMITH

Sentimental (or "weeping") comedies dominated the British stage throughout much of the eighteenth century. Oliver Goldsmith (1728–1774), an Irish immigrant, sought to restore the theater to the traditional "laughing comedy" of Plautus, Terence, and Shakespeare by writing She Stoops to Conquer: or The Mistakes of a Night. *To prepare audiences for the opening of his comedy at the Covent Garden Theatre, Goldsmith wrote the following essay, which was published anonymously in* Westminster *magazine. It did much to restore common sense to the English theater and it helped prepare the way for Sheridan's great comedies.*

The theatre, like all other amusements, has its fashions and its prejudices; and when satiated with its excellence, mankind begin to mistake change for improvement. For some years tragedy was the reigning entertainment; but of late it has entirely given way to comedy, and our best efforts are now exerted in these lighter kinds of composition. The pompous train, the swelling phrase, and the unnatural rant, are displaced for that natural portrait of human folly and frailty, of which all are judges, because all have sat for the picture.

But as in describing nature it is presented with a double face, either of mirth or sadness, our modern writers find themselves at a loss which chiefly to copy from; and it is now debated, whether the exhibition of human distress is likely to afford the mind more entertainment than that of human absurdity?

Comedy is defined by Aristotle to be a picture of the frailties of the lower part of mankind, to distinguish it from tragedy, which is an exhibition of the misfortunes of the great. When comedy therefore ascends to produce the characters of princes or generals upon the stage, it is out of its walk, since low life and middle life are entirely its object. The principal question therefore is, whether in describing low or middle life, an exhibition of its follies be not preferable to a detail of its calamities? Or, in other words, which deserves the preference—the weeping sentimental comedy, so much in fashion at present, or the laughing and even low comedy, which seems to have been last exhibited by Vanbrugh and Cibber?

If we apply to authorities, all the great masters in the dramatic art have but one opinion. Their rule is, that as tragedy displays the calamities of the great, so comedy should excite our laughter, by ridiculously exhibiting the follies of the lower part of mankind. Boileau, one of the best modern critics, asserts, that comedy will not admit of tragic distress:

> Le comique, ennemi des soupirs et des pleurs,
> N'admet point dans ses vers de tragiques douleurs.[1]

---

[1] "The comic muse, averse to tears and sighs, / From tragic sorrows with abhorrence flies" [Goldsmith's note].

Nor is this rule without the strongest foundation in nature, as the distresses of the mean by no means affect us so strongly as the calamities of the great. When tragedy exhibits to us some great man fallen from his height, and struggling with want and adversity, we feel his situation in the same manner as we suppose he himself must feel, and our pity is increased in proportion to the height from which he fell. On the contrary, we do not so strongly sympathize with one born in humbler circumstances, and encountering accidental distress: so that while we melt for Belisarius, we scarcely give halfpence to the beggar who accosts us in the street. The one has our pity; the other our contempt. Distress, therefore, is the proper object of tragedy, since the great excite our pity by their fall; but not equally so of comedy, since the actors employed in it are originally so mean, that they sink but little by their fall.

Since the first origin of the stage, tragedy and comedy have run in distinct channels, and never till of late encroached upon the provinces of each other. Terence, who seems to have made the nearest approaches, always judiciously stops short before he comes to the downright pathetic; and yet he is even reproached by Caesar for wanting the *vis comica*. All other comic writers of antiquity aim only at rendering folly or vice ridiculous, but never exalt their characters into buskin pomp, or make what Voltaire humorously calls "a tradesman's tragedy."

Yet notwithstanding this weight of authority, and the universal practice of former ages, a new species of dramatic composition has been introduced under the name of *sentimental comedy*, in which the virtues of private life are exhibited, rather than the vices exposed; and the distresses rather than the faults of mankind make our interest in the piece. These comedies have had of late great success, perhaps from their novelty, and also from their flattering every man in his favourite foible. In these plays almost all the characters are good, and exceedingly generous; they are lavish enough of their tin money on the stage; and though they want humour, have abundance of sentiment and feeling. If they happen to have faults or foibles, the spectator is taught not only to pardon, but to applaud them, in consideration of the goodness of their hearts; so that folly, instead of being ridiculed, is commended, and the comedy aims at touching our passions, without the power of being truly pathetic. In this manner we are likely to lose one great source of entertainment on the stage; for while the comic poet is invading the province of the tragic muse, he leaves her lovely sister quite neglected. Of this, however, he is no way solicitous, as he measures his fame by his profits.

But it will be said, that the theatre is formed to amuse mankind, and that it matters little, if this end be answered, by what means it is obtained. If mankind find delight in weeping at comedy, it would be cruel to abridge them in that or any other innocent pleasure. If those pieces are denied the name of comedies, yet call them by any other name, and if they are delightful, they are good. Their success, it will be said, is a mark of their merit, and it is only abridging our happiness to deny us an inlet to amusement.

These objections, however, are rather specious than solid. It is true, that amusement is a great object at a theatre; and it will be allowed, that these sentimental pieces do often amuse us; but the question is, whether the true comedy would not amuse us more? The question is, whether a character supported throughout a piece, with its ridicule still attending, would not give us more delight than this species of bastard tragedy, which only is applauded because it is new.

A friend of mine who was sitting unmoved at one of the sentimental pieces, was asked how he could be so indifferent? "Why truly," says he, "as the hero is but a tradesman, it is indifferent to me whether he be turned out of his counting-house on Fishstreet Hill, since he will still have enough left to open shop in St. Giles's."

The other objection is as ill-grounded; for though we should give these pieces another name, it will not mend their efficacy. It will continue a kind of mulish production, with all the defects of its opposite parents, and marked with sterility. If we are permitted to make comedy weep, we have an equal right to make tragedy laugh, and to set down in blank verse the jests and repartees of all the attendants in a funeral procession.

But there is one argument in favor of sentimental comedy which will keep it on the stage, in spite of all that can be said against it. It is of all others the most easily written. Those abilities that can hammer out a novel, are fully sufficient for the production of a sentimental comedy. It is only sufficient to raise the characters a little; to deck out the hero with a riband, or give the heroine a title; then to put an insipid dialogue, without character or humour, into their mouths, give them mighty good hearts, very fine clothes, furnish a new set of scenes, make a pathetic scene or two, with a sprinkling of tender melancholy conversation through the whole, and there is no doubt but all the ladies will cry, and all the gentlemen applaud.

Humour at present seems to be departing from the stage; and it will soon happen that our comic players will have nothing left for it but a fine coat and a song. It depends upon the audience, whether they will actually drive those poor merry creatures from the stage, or sit at a play as gloomy as at the tabernacle. It is not easy to recover an art when once lost; and it will be but a just punishment, that when, by our being too fastidious, we have banished humour from the stage, we should ourselves be deprived of the art of laughing.

---

ple lessons reflected middle-class morality. Two elements of sentimental comedy in particular influenced subsequent theater. First, drama turned its full attention to the daily problems of its middle-class audiences. Second, it provided the underpinnings of the full-fledged melodrama, which emerged by the end of the century.

Laughing Comedy

In 1772 Oliver Goldsmith exposed the artificiality of "weeping comedies," which (in Steele's words) existed only "to introduce a joy too exquisite for laughter." He called for a return of "laughing comedy" to the stage (see Forum, "A Comparison Between Sentimental and Laughing Comedy"). He wrote *She Stoops to Conquer* to satirize sentimentality and reestablish traditional comedy in the theater. Its success inspired Richard Brinsley Sheridan's *The School for Scandal*, which triumphed at London's Drury Lane Theater in 1777. These plays (with Sheridan's *The Rivals*) remain the preeminent examples of the eighteenth-century Comedy of Manners.

The American theater, which emerged at precisely the time when sentimental comedies enjoyed their greatest popularity, has always had a pronounced strain of sentimentality running through it. Little Eva's famous deathbed speech in *Uncle Tom's Cabin* is a remarkable example of sentimentality fused with abolitionist propaganda. In our century Lorraine Hansberry's civil rights drama *A Raisin in the Sun* (1959) depends on sentimentality, although its issues are quite serious. Television sitcoms, especially in the 1950s, are sentimentalist at heart; *Father Knows Best* epitomized the genre. One of the most popular films in the history of American cinema, Stephen Spielberg's *E.T.*, is a thoroughly sentimental comedy. Recall the moment when Eliot revives E.T. by uttering the battle cry of the sentimentalists, "Love."

Bourgeois Tragedy

Though we remember the comedies of the late seventeenth and eighteenth centuries, we must not forget that there was a corresponding growth of serious plays depicting middle-class problems. "Domestic tragedy," "*le drame*," and "*genre sérieux*" are terms variously used to describe such plays. In 1731 George Lillo (c. 1696–1739) wrote the first prose tragedy in English. Based on an actual murder, *The London Merchant* depicted the fall of a young man who murders his employer, the merchant, to get money for his lover, Mrs. Marwood. Lillo's preface to the play reveals much about the intent of bourgeois dramas. He claimed that his "private tale of woe" was an attempt to "accommodate tragedy to the circumstances of the generality of mankind" because all humans are prey to misfortune. (See Forum, "Dedication to *The London Merchant*.")

In the bourgeois tragedies of Europe, we see the precursors of the social realist drama that would emerge in the modern theater, but—like the sentimental comedies—these works were contrived, sensational, and too eager to preach moral lessons. Furthermore, purely external forces most often created the misfortune. Heroes were more victims than truly tragic beings. Nonetheless, the domestic tragedies placed common people at center stage and infused the theater with a concern for topical problems that would become the hallmark of the nineteenth century and ultimately the modern theater.

FORUM

"Dedication to *The London Merchant*"

GEORGE LILLO

In 1731 George Lillo (1693–1739) wrote The London Merchant, *the first prose tragedy in English and among the first attempts to place an ordinary citizen at the center of a tragedy. Although the play is, by our standards, a simplistic melodrama, Lillo's prologue is still among the most eloquent arguments for the dignity of the common man and woman in serious drama. Compare Lillo's comments with those of Arthur Miller (see Chapter 7), whose* Death of a Salesman *culminates the tradition of the bourgeois tragedy begun in 1731. Note especially Lillo's praise for the merchant class, whom he considered Europe's new "heroes."*

If Tragic Poetry be, as Mr. Dryden has somewhere said, the most excellent and most useful kind of writing, the more extensively useful the moral of any tragedy is, the more excellent that piece must be of its kind.

I hope I shall not be thought to insinuate that this, to which I have presumed to prefix your name, is such; that depends on its fitness to answer the end of tragedy, the exciting of the passions, in order to the correcting such of them as are criminal, either in their nature, or through their excess. Whether the following scenes do this in any tolerable degree, is, with the deference that becomes one who would not be thought vain, submitted to your candid and impartial judgment.

What I would infer is this, I think, evident truth; that tragedy is so far from losing its dignity, by being accommodated to the circumstances of the generality of mankind, that it is more truly august in proportion to the extent of its influence, and the numbers that are properly affected by it. As it is more truly great to be the instrument of good to many, who stand in need of our assistance, than to a very small part of that number.

If Princes, etc. were alone liable to misfortunes, arising from vice, or weakness in themselves, or others, there would be good reason for confining the characters in tragedy to those of superior rank; but, since the contrary is evident, nothing can be more reasonable than to proportion the remedy to the disease.

I am far from denying that tragedies, founded on any instructive and extraordinary events in History, or well-invented Fable, where the persons introduced are of the highest rank, are without their use, even to the bulk of the audience. The strong contrast between a Tamerlane and a Bajazet, may have its weight with an unsteady people, and contribute to the fixing of them in the interest of a Prince of the character of the former, when, through their own levity, or the arts of designing men, they are rendered factious and uneasy, though they have the highest reason to be satisfied. The sentiments and example of a Cato, may inspire his spectators with a just sense of the value of liberty, when they see that honest patriot prefer death to an obligation from a tyrant, who would sacrifice the constitution of his country, and the liberties of mankind, to his ambition or revenge. I have attempted, indeed, to enlarge the province of the graver kind of poetry, and should be glad to see it carried on by some abler hand. Plays, founded on moral tales in private life, may be of admirable use, by carrying conviction to the mind, with such irresistible force, as to engage all the faculties and powers of the soul in the cause of virtue, by stifling vice in its first principles. They who imagine this too much to be attributed to Tragedy, must be strangers to the energy of that noble species of poetry. Shakespeare, who has given such amazing proofs of his genius, in that as well as in Comedy, in his Hamlet, has the following lines:

Had he the motive and the cue for passion
That I have; he would drown the stage with tears

And cleave the general ear with horrid speech;
Make mad the guilty, and appal the free,
Confound the ignorant; and amaze indeed
The very faculties of eyes and ears.

And farther, in the same speech,

. . . . .I have heard,
. . . . .That guilty creatures sitting at a play,
Have, by the very cunning of the scene,
Been struck so to the soul, that presently
They have proclaim'd their malefactions.

Prodigious! yet strictly just. But I shall not take up your valuable time with my remarks; only give me leave just to observe, that he seems so firmly persuaded of the power of a well wrote piece to produce the effect here ascribed to it, as to make Hamlet ven-ture his soul on the event, and rather trust that, than a messenger from the other world, though it assumed, as he expresses it, his noble father's form, and assured him, that it was his spirit. I'll have, says Hamlet, grounds more relative,

. . . . .The Play's the thing,
Wherein I'll catch the conscience of the king.

Such Plays are the best answers to them who deny the lawfulness of the stage.

Considering the novelty of this attempt, I thought it would be expected from me to say something in its excuse; and I was unwilling to lose the opportunity of saying something of the usefulness of Tragedy in general, and what may be reasonably expected from the farther improvement of this excellent kind of poetry.

THE ROVER; OR, THE BANISHED CAVALIERS

APHRA BEHN

MRS. APHRA BEHN (C. 1640–1689)

In a profession historically dominated by males, Aphra Behn is significant in that she was the first woman to write professionally for the theater. Other women had written plays prior to Mrs. Behn, most notably Hrotswitha of Gandersheim, a tenth-century German nun who wrote short saints plays to instruct the novices in her convent. The sixteenth-century *autos* of Sor Juana Inés de la Cruz were among the first plays written in the New World. We are only now discovering "closet dramas"—plays intended to be read in private circles—written by noble women in England; for instance, Elizabeth Carey (Lady Falkland) wrote *The Tragedy of Miriam* in 1613. But it is Aphra Behn who is regarded as the matriarch of women playwrights in Western theater.

Unfortunately, because of biases against women during the seventeenth and eighteenth centuries, the specifics of Behn's life are sketchy. We are not sure of her birth date, and there is no record of her maiden name. About 1664 she married a merchant named Behn, who died in 1665. She began her theatrical career in 1670 by writing *The Forced Marriage*, a title which suggests a recurring theme of her works, the "forced marriage" of women in order to preserve property rights and increase financial gain of men. She wrote poetry, novellas, and 17 plays, such as *The Unfortunate Bride* and *The Unfortunate Happy Lady*, further testimonies to the plight of women sold into marriage for economic expediency. Her most important novel was *Oronooko* (1688), a sympathetic portrait of a black man who is compromised by the white society in which he lives. After her death in April 1689, Behn was buried in Poets' Corner in Westminster Abbey, among the highest honors England bestows upon its literati.

More than a theatrical pioneer, Behn advanced the status of women in seventeenth-century society. She was among the first white women to venture into South America; she lived in Surinam (Dutch Guiana), sometime between 1655 and 1660, an experience that provided material for *Oronooko*. In England, she was active at the court of Charles II, who sent her to Belgium and the Netherlands as a spy in July 1666. Her loyalty to the restored monarchy advanced her writing career as she was in constant contact with the leading wits of the court. Her candid observations about English politics created enemies, and she was once arrested by the king's men for sedition. She was equally outspoken about literary trends, as evidenced by her attack on Neoclassicism in her epilogue to *The Rover*:

> With canting rule you would the stage refine,
>
> And to dull method all our sense confine.

Her harshest criticisms were reserved for the society in which she lived. Like her male colleagues such as Wycherly, Etheredge, and Congreve, she satirized the pretentiousness of English gentility, and she did so in a manner no less bawdy than that found in plays written by men. Yet she added a new voice to Restoration comedy in her condemnation of customs that rendered women as chattel in the marriage game.

Among Behn's most remembered plays are the tragedy *Abdelazer* (1675), *The Amorous Prince* (1671), and *The Dutch Lover* (1673), a Comedy of Manners. *The Rover* remains her masterpiece and enjoys frequent production. When the Royal Shakespeare Company opened the Swan Theatre at Stratford in 1987, *The Rover* was the first non-Shakespearean work produced there.

THE ROVER; OR, THE BANISHED CAVALIERS (1677)

The Rover combines older theater traditions with a newer sensibility that was emerging in European theater in the late seventeenth century. Its characters are drawn from stock types popular since Plautus in ancient Rome, and it is set against the merrymaking of Italy at carnival time. Its three plots are part Comedy of Manners, part farce, and part comedy of intrigue, a form popularized in the Spanish *capa y espalda* (cape and dagger) plays. Politically, the play shows evidence of the continuing animosities between the English and the Spanish, whose navies had fought so fiercely 90 years before Behn wrote the play. Despite these elements from a bygone world, the play suggests a new order emerging in Europe, especially in its depiction of the merchant class and the growing independence of women.

In a tradition perfected by Shakespeare, Behn contrasts several sets of lovers to portray amorous adventures in her society. At one end of the spectrum stands Blunt, a country gentleman, whose theatrical ancestry can be traced to Rome. Blunt is a variant of the Braggart Warrior; the silly lies he tells in act 5 are clearly reminiscent of Sir John Falstaff's untruths about his exploits in *Henry IV, Part 1*. Blunt is also the classic *agroikos*, the country bumpkin who is duped by con artists in the big city. As England was moving from an agrarian to an urban society, such figures became the source of amusement. Furthermore, Blunt typifies the most popular of the Restoration stage fools—the fop, an overdressed dandy who too eagerly displays his wit. Blunt's name does not mean he is candid and outspoken; here it means dull and slow-witted. Thus the only time Blunt does not lie to others (or himself) is when he says "I am a dull believing English country fop." His foray into the game of love involves only self-gratification and lust. When he is gulled by that "jilting wench," Lucetta, he gets exactly his due, notably a trip through the sewers of Naples, clad only in his Dutch drawers and nightshirt. His nakedness, as symbolic as it is hilarious, strips him of his pretensions.

At the other extreme is the true wit, Willmore, who epitomizes the Restoration rake whose guile abets his pursuit of pleasure. Such types, true "rovers" all, preserve their status through the conquest of women and their rivals. Their lineage is traceable to the notorious Don Juan Tenorio, created by Tirso de Molina in *The Trickster of Seville* (1630). Marriage is anathema to the rake because it "is as certain a bane to love as lending money is to friendship." The Willmores of the world scorn virtuous women, whom they consider "ill-natured creatures that take pride to torment a lover." Rather, they, "like cheerful birds, sing in all groves, and perch on every bough." At least until they meet a Hellena, *The Rover*'s most refreshing character. She represents the new woman whose innate wit surpasses Willmore's and thereby forces the rake to reform his libertine ways. Hellena, an antidote to the too-loose woman (Angellica Bianca, Lucetta) and the too-conventional woman (Florinda), is—in Willmore's estimation— "a mad mistress," who is filled with honesty in a corrupt world. Hellena's chosen costume, a gypsy, symbolizes her free spirit; she too is a "rover" in search of the ideal mate. The Willmore-Hellena relationship evolves from a process of natural selection in which a vital young woman seeks, finds, and reforms an equally vital young man. Behn suggests that the world is best served by such marriages, though her argument is hardly unique. Shakespeare conjured such a couple (Beatrice and Benedick) in *Much Ado About Nothing*, while William Congreve made such a pair (Mirabel and Millimant) the centerpiece of *The Way of the World* (1700). Much of Bernard Shaw's canon is devoted to coupling superior people who rise above the conventionality of the world; Jack Tanner and Anne Whitfield in *Man and Superman* (1904) epitomize the Shavian dream couple. The witty, and politely erotic, exchange between Willmore and Hellena at the end of act 5 is not only the best written scene in *The Rover*, it typifies Restoration humor at its very best.

Standing between the extremes of the foolish Blunt and the truly witty *joie de vivre* of Willmore and Hellena are the conventional romantic lovers so typical of Renaissance drama: young Belvile and Florinda. Like Romeo and Juliet, they are victims of an old order that seeks to keep them apart. Florinda's brother, Don Pedro, has promised her to the viceroy's son, Don Antonio. Such forced marriages explain why infidelities were commonplace. Marriage had precious little to do with love, and the marriage partners felt guiltless in their pursuit of lust in other quarters. But Belvile and Florinda are ever faithful, and quite frankly ever dull in their conventional approach to love. While there is admirable virtue in their unflinching devotion to each other, they are the least interesting of the trio of love pairs. Their story is the stuff of tragedy, or at least melodrama, and they will resurface in 1830 when Victor Hugo recasts them in *Hernani* (see Chapter 7). The Frederick-Valeria relationship seems something of an afterthought by Behn, and is the least satisfying of the love plots.

The Spaniards, Pedro and Antonio, are also conventional characters, but in quite another way. They are a throwback to the Elizabethan Spanish villain (e.g., Iago). When Blunt says "I'll show her [Lucetta's] husband a Spanish trick," he is echoing the English contempt for Spaniards, who were considered untrustworthy. Behn extends this sentiment into a joke: in the final scene Blunt loses his clothes to Lucetta's trickery and appears dressed in "a Spanish habit with a vengeance," a sight that would have filled the Dorset Garden with howls of disdainful laughter.

Angellica Bianca is the elegant courtesan who is quite used to having her way with men until she runs into the rover. Behn did not invent "the whore with the heart of gold" or "the woman scorned," but she melds the two types to render one of the most memorable portraits in *The Rover*. Angellica is precisely the kind of woman who attracts rakes such as Willmore—independent, sexually liberal, wealthy, and beautiful. She succumbs to his charms and, against the code of the courtesan, falls in love with him. When he rejects her in favor of Hellena, Angellica is furious and seeks the ultimate revenge on Willmore: death. Though the resolution of the Angellica plot is not satisfying, it represents a bold experiment by the playwright. Although Behn elicits unexpected sympathy for Angellica, the violent solution takes the play into darker areas than we expect of comedy.

The Rover attests to Behn's dramatic and theatrical savoir faire. She freely borrowed the plot from Thomas Killegrew's closet drama *Thomaso*, a sprawling play of over 70 scenes filled with lengthy, meandering speeches. Behn unifies Killegrew's original plot by using the device of Florinda's lost ring to tie the Belvile and Blunt stories together, and she creates Belvile and Hellena to enhance her themes. Belvile provides a constancy that Willmore lacks, and Hellena provides not only a witty heroine, but a model of the new woman in this male-dominated world. She marries *only* on her terms ("'Tis but getting my consent [to marry], then the business is soon done"). She will not be "bought," and on the battlefield of love, she will prove her mettle as well as any man. Note how the love (lust) affairs are discussed by the men in either economic or military terms. The rhetoric of war peppers the dialogue of Restoration comedies, which themselves echo Thomas Hobbes's *The Leviathan*.

Finally, Behn enlivens *The Rover* with an unerring sense of theatricality. From the huge painting of Angellica Bianca to the ingenious bed trick played on Blunt, the play is filled with one coup de theatre after another. She uses the new scenography of sliding panels (wing and groove scenery) to quickly transform scenes in an almost cinematic manner. The many masquerades, the colorful costumes of carnival (derived from medieval mummery) provide *The Rover* with its finest theatrical flair. Virtually every entrance finds characters attired "in antic different dresses from what they were in before." Not only does this perpetual costume parade provide color and charm, it reinforces a principal theme of this and other Restoration plays: people are poseurs who present false fronts to the world. It is appropriate that vizards and masks are integral to Behn's play, as they are the ideal symbol of the era. Almost. Actually, the perfect emblem of the Restoration was the "beauty mark," the decorative patch worn by both men and women to enhance their attractiveness—and, of course, to cover pox marks on their skin.

Aphra Behn, author of The Rover, *was the first woman to succeed as a commercial playwright; her own adventurous life provided material for her plays of intrigue.*

APHRA BEHN
THE ROVER; OR, THE BANISHED CAVALIERS*

PROLOGUE

Wits, like physicians, never can agree
When of a different society.
And Rabel's drops[1] were never more cried down
By all the learned doctors of the town,
Than a new play whose author is unknown.
Nor can those doctors with more malice sue
(And powerful purses) the dissenting few,
Than those, with an insulting pride, do rail
At all who are not of their own cabal.[2]
  If a young poet hit your humor[3] right,
You judge him then out of revenge and spite.
So amongst men there are ridiculous elves,
Who monkeys hate for being too like themselves.
So that the reason of the grand debate
Why wit so oft is damned when good plays take,
Is that you censure as you love, or hate.
  Thus like a learned conclave poets sit,

---

*Cavaliers supporters of the English monarchy during the English civil war. After the execution of Charles I in 1649, many cavaliers left England.   [1]Rabel's drops a patent medicine

[2]cabal secret group   [3]hit your humor accurately portray your characteristics

Catholic judges[4] both of sense and wit,
And damn or save as they themselves think fit.
Yet those who to others' faults are so severe,
Are not so perfect but themselves may err.
Some write correct, indeed, but then the whole
(Bating[5] their own dull stuff i'th' play) is stole:
As bees do suck from flowers their honeydew,
So they rob others striving to please you.
　　Some write their characters genteel and fine,
But then they do so toil for every line,
That what to you does easy seem, and plain,
Is the hard issue of their laboring brain.
And some th' effects of all their pains, we see,
Is but to mimic good extempore.[6]
Others, by long converse about the town,
Have wit enough to write a lewd lampoon,
But their chief skill lies in a bawdy song.
In short, the only wit that's now in fashion,
Is but the gleanings of good conversation.
As for the author of this coming play,
I asked him[7] what he thought fit I should say
In thanks for your good company today:
He called me fool, and said it was well known
You came not here for our sakes, but your own.
New plays are stuffed with wits, and with deboches,[8]
That crowd and sweat like cits[9] in May-Day coaches.[10]

> Written by a Person of Quality

THE ACTORS' NAMES

[Men]

DON ANTONIO, *the Viceroy's son*
DON PEDRO, *a noble Spaniard, his friend*
BELVILE, *an English colonel in love with Florinda*
WILLMORE, *the Rover*[11]
FREDERICK, *an English genleman, and friend to Belvile and Blunt*
BLUNT, *an English country gentleman*
STEPHANO, *servant to Don Pedro*
PHILIPPO, *Lucetta's gallant*
SANCHO, *pimp to Lucetta*
BISKEY AND SEBASTIAN, *two Bravos*[12] *to Angellica*
OFFICER AND SOLDIERS
[DIEGO,] *Page to Don Antonio*

---

[4]**Catholic judges** broadminded judges [5]**Bating** excepting [6]**extempore** that is, a performance given without adequate preparation [7]**him** the play was published anonymously, and the writer of the prologue speaks of the author as a male. [8]**deboches** dissipations [9]**cits** tradesman and their families (a mildly contemptuous term) [10]**May-Day coaches** on May 1, pretentious "cits" customarily took a carriage ride through Hyde Park. [11]**Rover** wanderer (also pirate) [12]**Bravos** hired ruffians

[Women]

FLORINDA, *sister to Don Pedro*
HELLENA, *a gay young woman designed for a nun, and sister to Florinda*
VALERIA, *a kinswoman to Florinda*
ANGELLICA BIANCA, *a famous courtesan*
MORETTA, *her woman*
CALLIS, *governess to Florinda and Hellena*
LUCETTA, *a jilting wench*
SERVANTS, *other* MASQUERADERS, MEN *and* WOMEN

THE SCENE: *Naples, in Carnival time.*

ACT 1

SCENE 1

(*A Chamber. Enter Florinda and Hellena.*)

FLORINDA. What an impertinent thing is a young girl bred in a nunnery! How full of questions! Prithee no more, Hellena; I have told thee more than thou understand'st already.

HELLENA. The more's my grief. I would fain[13] know as much as you which makes me so inquisitive; nor is't enough I know you're a lover, unless you tell me too who 'tis you sigh for.

FLORINDA. When you're a lover I'll think you fit for a secret of that nature.

HELLENA. 'Tis true, I never was a lover yet, but I begin to have a shrewd guess what 'tis to be so, and fancy it very pretty to sign, and sing, and blush, and wish, and dream and wish, and long and wish to see the man, and when I do, look pale and tremble, just as you did when my brother brought home the fine English colonel to see you. What do you call him? Don Belvile?

FLORINDA. Fie, Hellena.

HELLENA. That blush betrays you. I am sure 'tis so. Or is it Don Antonio the Viceroy's son? Or perhaps the rich old Don Vincentio, whom my father designs you for a husband? Why do you blush again?

FLORINDA. With indignation; and how near soever my father thinks I am to marrying that hated object, I shall let him see I understand better what's my due to my beauty, birth, and fortune, and more to my soul, than to obey those unjust commands.

HELLENA. Now hang me, if I don't love thee for that dear disobedience. I love mischief strangely, as most of our sex do who are come to love nothing else. But tell me, dear Florinda, don't you love that fine *Anglese?*[14] For I vow, next to loving him myself, 'twill please me most that you do so, for he is so gay and so handsome.

---

[13]**fain** gladly   [14]***Anglese*** Englishman, that is, Belvile

FLORINDA. Hellena, a maid designed for a nun ought not to be so curious in a discourse of love.

HELLENA. And dost thou think that ever I'll be a nun? Or at least till I'm so old I'm fit for nothing else? Faith no, sister; and that which makes me long to know whether you love Belvile, is because I hope he has some mad companion or other that will spoil my devotion. Nay, I'm resolved to provide myself this Carnival, if there be e'er a handsome proper fellow of my humor[15] above ground, though I ask first.

FLORINDA. Prithee be not so wild.

HELLENA. Now you have provided yourself of a man you take no care of poor me. Prithee tell me, what dost thou see about me that is unfit for love? Have I not a world of youth? A humor gay? A beauty passable? A vigor desirable? Well shaped? Clean limbed? Sweet breathed? And sense enough to know how all these ought to be employed to the best advantage? Yes, I do and will; therefore lay aside your hopes of my fortune by my being a devote,[16] and tell me how you came acquainted with this Belvile. For I perceive you knew him before he came to Naples.

FLORINDA. Yes. I knew him at the siege of Pamplona;[17] he was then a colonel of French horse,[18] who when the town was ransacked, nobly treated my brother and myself, preserving us from all insolences. And I must own, besides great obligations, I have I know not what that pleads kindly for him about my heart, and will suffer no other to enter. But see, my brother.

(*Enter Don Pedro, Stephano with a masking habit,[19] and Callis.*)

PEDRO. Good morrow, sister. Pray when saw you your lover Don Vincentio?

FLORINDA. I know not, sir. Callis, when was he here? For I consider it so little I know not when it was.

PEDRO. I have a command from my father here to tell you you ought not to despise hm, a man of so vast a fortune, and such a passion for you—Stephano, my things.

(*Puts on his masking habit.*)

FLORINDA. A passion for me? 'Tis more than e'er I saw, or he had a desire should be known. I hate Vincentio, sir, and I would not have a man so dear to me as my brother follow the ill customs of our country and make a slave of his sister. And, sir, my father's will I'm sure you may divert.

PEDRO. I know not how dear I am to you, but I wish only to be ranked in your esteem equal with the English colonel Belvile. Why do you frown and blush? Is there any guilt belongs to the name of that cavalier?

FLORINDA. I'll not deny I value Belvile. When I was exposed to such dangers as the licensed lust of common soldiers threatened when rage and conquest flew through the city, then Belvile, this criminal for my sake, threw himself into all dangers to save my honor. And will you not allow him my esteem?

PEDRO. Yes, pay him what you will in honor, but you must consider Don Vincentio's fortune, and the jointure[20] he'll make you.

FLORINDA. Let him consider my youth, beauty, and fortune, which ought not to be thrown away on his age and jointure.

PEDRO. 'Tis true, he's not so strong and fine a gentleman as that Belvile. But what jewels will that cavalier present you with? Those of his eyes and heart?

HELLENA. And are not those better than any Don Vincentio has brought from the Indies?

PEDRO. Why, how now! Has your nunnery breeding taught you to understand the value of hearts and eyes?

HELLENA. Better than to believe Vincentio's deserve value from any woman. He may perhaps increase her bags, but not her family.[21]

PEDRO. This is fine! Go! Up to your devotion! You are not designed for the conversation of lovers.

HELLENA (*aside*). Nor saints yet a while, I hope.—Is't not enough you make a nun of me, but you must cast my sister away too, exposing her to a worse confinement than a religious life?

PEDRO. The girl's mad! It is a confinement to be carried into the country to an ancient villa belonging to the family of the Vincentios these five hundred years, and have no other prospect than that pleasing one of seeing all her own that meets her eyes: a fair air, large fields, and gardens where she may walk and gather flowers?

HELLENA. When, by moonlight? For I am sure she dares not encounter with the heat of the sun; that were a task only for Don Vincentio and his Indian breeding, who loves it in the dog days.[22] And if these be her daily divertissements,[23] what are those of the night? To lie in a wide moth-eaten bedchamber with furniture in fashion in the reign of King Sancho the First; the bed, that which his forefathers lived and died in.

PEDRO. Very well.

HELLENA. This apartment, new furbrushed[24] and fitted out for the young wife, he out of freedom makes his dressing room; and being a frugal and a jealous coxcomb,[25] instead of a valet to uncase[26] his feeble carcass, he desires you to do that office. Signs of favor, I'll assure you, and such as you must not hope for unless your woman be out of the way.

---

[15]**humor** mood [16]**devote** nun [17]**Pamplona** town in northern Spain [16]**of French horse** in the French cavalry [19]**masking habit** masquerade costume for the Carnival

[20]**jointure** a marriage settlement, providing for the wife's support after her husband's death [21]**increase . . . family** that is, he may make her rich but he is too old to make her pregnant [22]**dog days** hot summer days [23]**divertissements** diversions [24]**new furbrushed** refurbished [25]**coxcomb** conceited fop [26]**uncase** undress

PEDRO. Have you done yet?

HELLENA. That honor being past, the giant stretches itself, yawns and sighs a belch or two loud as a musket, throws himself into bed, and expects you in his foul sheets; and ere you can get yourself undressed, calls you with a snore or two. And are not these fine blessings to a young lady?

PEDRO. Have you done yet?

HELLENA. And this means you must kiss, nay you must kiss none but him too, and nuzzle through his beard to find his lips. And this you must submit to for threescore years, and all for a jointure.

PEDRO. For all your character of Don Vincentio, she is as like to marry him as she was before.

HELLENA. Marry Don Vincentio! Hang me, such a wedlock would be worse than adultery with another man. I had rather see her in the *Hostel de Dieu,*[27] to waste her youth there in vows, and be a handmaid to lazars[28] and cripples, than to lose it in such a marriage.

PEDRO. You have considered, sister, that Belvile has no fortune to bring you to; banished his country, despised at home, and pitied abroad.

HELLENA. What then? The Viceroy's son is better than that old Sir Fifty. Don Vincentio! Don Indian! He thinks he's trading to Gambo[29] still, and would barter himself—that bell and bauble—for your youth and fortune.

PEDRO. Callis, take her hence and lock her up all this Carnival, and at Lent she shall begin her everlasting penance in a monastery.

HELLENA. I care not; I had rather be a nun than be obliged to marry as you would have me if I were designed for't.

PEDRO. Do not fear the blessing of that choice. You shall be a nun.

HELLENA (*aside*). Shall I so? You may chance to be mistaken in my way of devotion. A nun! Yes, I am like to make a fine nun! I have an excellent humor for a grate![30] No, I'll have a saint of my own to pray to shortly, if I like any that dares venture on me.

PEDRO. Callis, make it your business to watch this wildcat.—As for you, Florinda, I've only tried you all this while and urged my father's will; but mine is that you would love Antonio: He is brave and young, and all that can complete the happiness of a gallant maid. This absence of my father will give us opportunity to free you from Vincentio by marrying here, which you must do tomorrow.

FLORINDA. Tomorrow!

PEDRO. Tomorrow, or 'twill be too late. 'Tis not my friendship to Antonio which makes me urge this, but love to thee and hatred to Vincentio; therefore resolve upon tomorrow.

FLORINDA. Sir, I shall strive to do as shall become your sister.

PEDRO. I'll both believe and trust you. Adieu.

(*Exeunt*[31] *Pedro and Stephano.*)

HELLENA. As becomes his sister! That is to be as resolved your way as he is his.

(*Hellena goes to Callis.*)

FLORINDA.

I ne'er till now perceived my ruin near.
I've no defense against Antonio's love,
For he has all the advantages of nature,
The moving arguments of youth and fortune.

HELLENA. But hark you, Callis, you will not be so cruel to lock me up indeed, will you?

CALLIS. I must obey the commands I have. Besides, do you consider what a life you are going to lead?

HELLENA. Yes, Callis, that of a nun; and till then I'll be indebted a world of prayers to you if you'll let me now see what I never did, the divertissements of a Carnival.

CALLIS. What, go in masquerade? 'Twill be a fine farewell to the world, I take it. Pray what would you do there?

HELLENA. That which all the world does, as I am told: Be as mad as the rest and take all innocent freedoms. Sister, you'll go too, will you not? Come, prithee be not sad. We'll outwit twenty brothers if you'll be ruled by me. Come, put off this dull humor with your clothes, and assume one as gay and as fantastic as the dress my cousin Valeria and I have provided, and let's ramble.

FLORINDA. Callis, will you give us leave to go?

CALLIS (*aside*). I have a youthful itch of going myself.— Madam, if I thought your brother might not know it, and I might wait on you; for by my troth I'll not trust young girls alone.

FLORINDA. Thou seest my brother's gone already, and thou shalt attend and watch us.

(*Enter Stephano.*)

STEPHANO. Madame, the habits[32] are come, and your cousin Valeria is dressed and stays for you.

FLORINDA (*aside*). 'Tis well. I'll write a note, and if I chance to see Belvile and want an opportunity to speak to him, that shall let him know what I've resolved in favor of him.

HELLENA. Come, let's in and dress us.

(*Exeunt.*)

SCENE 2

(*A long street. Enter Belvile, melancholy; Blunt and Frederick.*)

FREDERICK. Why, what the devil ails the colonel, in a time when all the world is gay to look like mere Lent thus? Hadst thou been long enough in Naples to have been in

---

[27]**Hostel de Dieu** hospital run by nuns [28]**lazars** lepers [29]**Gambo** Gambia, in West Africa [30]**grate** a grille covering a convent window (i.e., the convent)

[31]***Exeunt*** they go out (Latin) [32]**habits** costumes (of a religious order)

love, I should have sworn such judgment had befallen thee.

BELVILE. No, I have made no new amours since I came to Naples.

FREDERICK. You have left none behind you in Paris?

BELVILE. Neither.

FREDERICK. I cannot divine the cause then, unless the old cause, the want of money.

BLUNT. And another old cause, the want of a wench. Would not that revive you?

BELVILE. You are mistaken, Ned.

BLUNT. Nay, 'adsheartlikins,[33] then thou'rt past cure.

FREDERICK. I have found it out: Thou has renewed thy acquaintance with the lady that cost thee so many sighs at the siege of Pamplona—pox on't, what d'ye call her—her brother's a noble Spaniard, nephew to the dead general. Florinda. Ay, Florinda. And will nothing serve thy turn but that damned virtuous woman, whom on my conscience thou lov'st in spite too, because thou seest little or no possibility of gaining her.

BELVILE. Thou art mistaken; I have int'rest enough in that lovely virgin's heart to make me proud and vain, were it not abated by the severity of a brother, who, perceiving my happiness—

FREDERICK. Has civilly forbid thee the house?

BELVILE. 'Tis so, to make way for a powerful rival, the Viceroy's son, who has the advantage of me in being a man of fortune, a Spaniard, and her brother's friend; which gives him liberty to make his court, whilst I have recourse only to letters and distant looks from her window, which are as soft and kind as those which heaven sends down on penitents.

BLUNT. Heyday! 'Adsheartlikins, simile! By this light the man is quite spoiled. Fred, what the devil are we made of that we cannot be thus concerned for a wench? 'Adsheartlikins, our Cupids are like the cooks of the camp: They can roast or boil a woman, but they have none of the fine tricks to set 'em off; no hogoes[34] to make the sauce pleasant and the stomach sharp.

FREDERICK. I dare swear I have had a hundred as young, kind, and handsome as this Florinda; and dogs eat me if they were not as troublesome to me i'th' morning as they were welcome o'er night.

BLUNT. And yet I warrant he would not touch another woman if he might have her for nothing.

BELVILE. That's thy joy, a cheap whore.

BLUNT. Why, 'adheartlikins, I love a frank soul. When did you ever hear of an honest woman that took a man's money? I warrant 'em good ones. But gentlemen, you may be free; you have been kept so poor with parliaments and protectors[35] that the little stock you have is not worth

preserving. But I thank my stars I had more grace than to forfeit my estate by cavaliering.

BELVILE. Me thinks only following the court should be sufficient to entitle 'em to that.

BLUNT. 'Adsheartlikins, they know I follow it to do it no good, unless they pick a hole in my coat for lending you money now and then, which is a greater crime to my conscience, gentlemen, than to the Commonwealth.[36]

(*Enter Willmore.*)

WILLMORE. Ha! Dear Belvile! Noble colonel!

BELVILE. Willmore! Welcome ashore, my dear rover! What happy wind blew us this good fortune?

WILLMORE. Let me salute my dear Fred, and then command me.—How is't, honest lad?

FREDERICK. Fair, sir, the old compliment, infinitely the better to see my dear mad Willmore again. Prithee, why camest thou ashore? And where's the Prince?[37]

WILLMORE. He's well, and reigns still lord of the wat'ry element. I must aboard again within a day or two, and my business ashore was only to enjoy myself a little this Carnival.

BELVILE. Pray know our new friend, sir; he's but bashful, a raw traveler, but honest, stout, and one of us. (*Embraces Blunt.*)

WILLMORE. That you esteem him gives him an int'rest[38] here.

BLUNT. Your servant, sir.

WILLMORE. But well, faith, I'm glad to meet you again in a warm climate, where the kind sun has its godlike power still over the wine and women. Love and mirth are my business in Naples, and if I mistake not the place, here's an excellent market for chapmen[39] of my humor.

BELVILE. See, here be those kind merchants of love you look for.

(*Enter several men in masking habits, some playing on music, others dancing after; women dressed like courtesans, with papers pinned on their breasts, and baskets of flowers in their hands.*)

BLUNT. 'Adsheartlikins, what have we here?

FREDERICK. Now the game begins.

WILLMORE. Fine pretty creatures! May a stranger have leave to look and love? What's here? "Roses for every month"? (*Reads the papers.*)

BLUNT. Roses for every month? What means that?

BELVILE. They are, or would have you think they're courtesans, who here in Naples are to be hired by the month.

WILLMORE. Kind and obliging to inform us, pray where do these roses grow? I would fain plant some of 'em in bed of mine.

---

[33]**'adsheartlikins** God's little heart (a mild oath)   [34]**hogoes** relishes
[35]**protectors** Oliver Cromwell used this title

[36]**Commonwealth** the republican government of England, 1649–53, replaced by the Protectorate.   [37]**Prince** Charles II, who was in exile on the Continent during Cromwell's reign in England
[38]**int'rest** recommendation   [39]**chapmen** merchants (of love)

WOMAN. Beware such roses, sir.

WILLMORE. A pox of fear:[40] I'll be baked with thee between a pair of sheets, and that's thy proper still;[41] so I might but strew such roses over me and under me. Fair one, would you would give me leave to gather at your bush this idle month; I would go near to make somebody smell of it all the year after.

BELVILE. And thou hast need of such a remedy, for thou stink'st of tar and ropes' ends like a dock or pesthouse.

(*The Woman puts herself into the hands of a man and exeunt.*)

WILLMORE. Nay, nay, you shall not leave me so.

BELVILE. By all means use no violence here.

WILLMORE. Death! Just as I was going to be damnably in love, to have her led off! I could pluck that rose out of his hand, and even kiss the bed the bush grew in.

FREDERICK. No friend to love like a long voyage at sea.

BLUNT. Except a nunnery, Fred.

WILLMORE. Death! But will they not be kind? Quickly be kind? Thou know'st I'm no tame sigher, but a rampant lion of the forest.

(*Advances from the farther end of the scenes two men dressed all over with horns[42] of several sorts, making grimaces at one another, with papers pinned on their backs.*)

BELVILE. Oh the fantastical rogues, how they're dressed! 'Tis a satire against the whole sex.

WILLMORE. Is this a fruit that grows in this warm country?

BELVILE. Yes, 'tis pretty to see these Italians start, swell, and stab at the word cuckold, and yet stumble at horns on every threshold.

WILLMORE. See what's on their back. (*Reads.*) "Flowers of every night." Ah, rogue! And more sweet than roses of every month! This is a gardener of Adam's own breeding.

(*They dance.*)

BELVILE. What think you of these grave people? Is a wake[43] in Essex half so mad or extravagant?

WILLMORE. I like their sober grave way; 'tis a kind of legal authorized fornication, where the men are not chid[44] for't, nor the women despised, as amongst our dull English. Even the monsieurs[45] want[46] that part of good manners.

BELVILE. But here in Italy, a monsieur is the humblest best-bred gentleman: Duels are so baffled by bravos that an age shows not one but between a French man and a hang-man, who is as much too hard for him on the Piazza as they are for a Dutchman on the New Bridge.[47] But see, another crew.

(*Enter Florinda, Hellena, and Valeria, dressed like gypsies; Callis and Stephano, Lucetta, Philippo, and Sancho in masquerade.*)

HELLENA. Sister, there's your Englishman, and with him a handsome proper fellow. I'll to him, and instead of telling him his fortune, try my own.

WILLMORE. Gypsies, on my life. Sure these will prattle if a man cross their hands.[48] (*Goes to Hellena.*)—Dear, pretty, and, I hope, young devil, will you tell an amorous stranger what luck he's like to have?

HELLENA. Have a care how you venture with me, sir, lest I pick your pocket, which will more vex your English humor than an Italian fortune will please you.

WILLMORE. How the devil cam'st thou to know my country and humor?

HELLENA. The first I guess by a certain forward impudence, which does not displease me at this time; and the loss of your money will vex you because I hope you have but very little to lose.

WILLMORE. Egad, child, thou'rt i'th' right; it is so little I dare not offer it thee for a kindness. But cannot you divine what other things of more value I have about me that would more willingly part with?

HELLENA. Indeed no, that's the business of a witch, and I am but a gypsy yet. Yet without looking in your hand, I have a parlous guess[49] 'tis some foolish heart you mean, an inconstant English heart, as little worth stealing as your purse.

WILLMORE. Nay, then thou dost deal with the devil, that's certain. Thou hast guessed as right as if thou hadst been one of that number it has languished for. I find you'll be better acquainted with it, nor can you take it in a better time; for I am come from sea, child, and Venus not being propitious to me in her own element,[50] I have a world of love in store. Would you would be good-natured and take some on't[51] off my hands.

HELLENA. Why, I could be inclined that way, but for a foolish vow I am going to make to die a maid.

WILLMORE. Then thou art damned without redemption, and as I am a good Christian, I ought in charity to divert so wicked a design. Therefore prithee, dear creature, let me know quickly when and where I shall begin to set a helping hand to so good a work.

HELLENA. If you should prevail with my tender heart, as I

---

[40]**pox of fear** a curse on fear [41]**baked ... still** a bawdy joke comparing women to roses, which are distilled to make rose water; the bawdiness continues in *bush*, that is, pubic hair. [42]**horns** allusion to the old belief that a cuckolded husband sprouted horns on his forehead that could be seen by everyone but himself [43]**wake** vigil over a corpse [44]**chid** chided [45]**monsieurs** Frenchmen [46]**want** lack

[47]**Dutchman ... Bridge** a reference to recent French military successes in Flanders [48]**prattle ... hands** tell his fortune if he gives them silver [49]**a parlous guess** a hunch [50]**Venus ... element** Venus, the goddess of love, was born from sea foam [51]**on't** of it

begin to fear you will, for you have horrible loving eyes, there will be difficulty in't that you'll hardly undergo for my sake.

WILLMORE. Faith, child, I have been bred in dangers, and wear a sword that has been employed in a worse cause than for a handsome kind woman. Name the danger; let it be anything but a long siege, and I'll undertake it.

HELLENA. Can you storm?[52]

WILLMORE. Oh, most furiously.

HELLENA. What think you of a nunnery wall? For he that wins me must gain that first.

WILLMORE. A nun! Oh, now I love thee for't! There's no sinner like a young saint. Nay, now there's no denying me; the old law had no curse to a woman like dying a maid: Witness Jeptha's daughter.[53]

HELLENA. A very good text this, if well handled; and I perceive, Father Captain, you would impose no severe penance on her who were inclined to console herself before she took orders.[54]

WILLMORE. If she be young and handsome.

HELLENA. Ay, there's it. But if she be not—

WILLMORE. By this hand, child, I have an implicit faith, and dare venture on thee with all faults. Besides, 'tis more meritorious to leave the world when thou hast tasted and proved the pleasure on't. Then 'twill be a virtue in thee, which now will be pure ignorance.

HELLENA. I perceive, good Father Captain, you design only to make me fit for heaven. But if, on the contrary, you should quite divert me from it, and bring me back to the world again, I should have a new man to seek, I find. And what a grief that will be; for when I begin, I fancy I shall love like anything; I never tried yet.

WILLMORE. Egad, and that's kind! Prithee, dear creature, give me credit for a heart, for faith, I'm a very honest fellow. Oh, I long to come first to the banquet of love! And such a swinging appetite I bring. Oh, I'm impatient. Thy lodging, sweetheart, thy lodging, or I'm a dead man!

HELLENA. Why must we be either guilty of fornication or murder if we converse with you men? And is there no difference between leave to love me, and leave to lie with me?

WILLMORE. Faith, child, they were made to go together.

LUCETTA (pointing to Blunt). Are you sure this is the man?

SANCHO. When did I mistake your game?

LUCETTA. This is a stranger, I know by his gazing; if he be brisk he'll venture to follow me, and then, if I understand my trade, he's mine. He's English, too, and they say that's a sort of good-natured loving people, and have generally so kind an opinion of themselves that a woman with any wit may flatter 'em into any sort of fool she pleases.

(She often passes by Blunt and gazes on him; he struts and cocks, and walks and gazes on her.)

BLUNT. 'Tis so, she is taken; I have beauties which my false glass[55] at home did not discover.[56]

FLORINDA (aside). This woman watches me so, I shall get no opportunity to discover myself to him, and so miss the intent of my coming.—[To Belvile.] But as I was saying, sir, by this line you should be a lover.

(Looking in his hand.)

BELVILE. I thought how right you guessed: All men are in love, or pretend to be so. Come, let me go; I'm weary of this fooling.

(Walks away.)

FLORINDA. I will not, sir, till you have confessed whether the passion that you have vowed Florinda be true or false.

(She holds him; he strives to get from her.)

BELVILE. Florinda!   (Turns quick toward her.)

FLORINDA. Softly.

BELVILE. Thou hast nam'd one will fix me here forever.

FLORINDA. She'll be disappointed then, who expects you this night at the garden gate. And if you fail not, as—(Looks on Callis, who observes 'em.) Let me see the other hand—you will go near to do, she vows to die or make you happy.

BELVILE. What canst thou mean?

FLORINDA. That which I say. Farewell.

(Offers to go.)

BELVILE. O charming sibyl,[57] stay; complete that joy which as it is will turn into distraction! Where must I be? At the garden gate? I know it. At night, you say? I'll sooner forfeit heaven than disobey.

(Enter Don Pedro and other maskers, and pass over the stage.)

CALLIS. Madam, your brother's here.

FLORINDA. Take this to instruct you farther.

(Gives him a letter, and goes off.)

FREDERICK. Have a care, sir, what you promise; this may be a trap laid by her brother to ruin you.

BELVILE. Do not disturb my happiness with doubts.

(Opens the letter.)

WILLMORE. My dear pretty creature, a thousand blessings on thee! Still in this habit, you say? And after dinner at this place?

HELLENA. Yes, if you will swear to keep your heart and not bestow it between this and that.

WILLMORE. By all the little gods of love, I swear; I'll leave it with you, and if you run away with it, those deities of justice[58] will revenge me.

---

[52]**storm** attack   [53]**Jeptha's daughter** the virgin daughter of a Hebrew judge who rashly sacrificed her. See Judges 11:39–40.   [54]**took orders** entered a convent

[55]**false glass** lying mirror   [56]**discover** reveal   [57]**sybil** prophetess, here a fortuneteller   [58]**deities of justice** in Greek mythology, the Erynys, avenging spirits

(*Exeunt all the women [except Lucetta].*)

FREDERICK. Do you know the hand?

BELVILE. 'Tis Florinda's.

All blessings fall upon the virtuous maid.

FREDERICK. Nay, no idolatry; a sober sacrifice I'll allow you.

BELVILE. Oh friends, the welcom'st news! The softest letter! Nay, you shall all see it. And could you now be serious, I might be made the happiest man the sun shines on!

WILLMORE. The reason of this mighty joy?

BELVILE. See how kindly she invites me to deliver her from the threatened violence of her brother. Will you not assist me?

WILLMORE. I know not what thou mean'st, but I'll make one at any mischief where a woman's concerned. But she'll be grateful to us for the favor, will she not?

BELVILE. How mean you?

WILLMORE. How should I mean? Thou know'st there's but one way for a woman to oblige me.

BELVILE. Do not profane; the maid is nicely virtuous.

WILLMORE. Who, pox,[59] then she's fit for nothing but a husband. Let her e'en go, colonel.

FREDERICK. Peace, she's the colonel's mistress, sir.

WILLMORE. Let her be the devil; if she be thy mistress, I'll serve her. Name the way.

BELVILE. Read here this postscript.

(*Gives him a letter.*)

WILLMORE (*reads*). "At ten at night, at the garden gate, of which, if I cannot get the key, I will contrive a way over the wall. Come attended with a friend or two."—Kind heart, if we three cannot weave a string to let her down a garden wall, 'twere pity but the hangman wove one for us all.

FREDERICK. Let her alone for that; your woman's wit, your fair kind woman, will outtrick a broker or a Jew, and contrive like a Jesuit[60] in chains. But see, Ned Blunt is stolen out after the lure of a damsel.

(*Exeunt Blunt and Lucetta.*)

BELVILE. So, he'll scarce find his way home again unless we get him cried by the bellman[61] in the market place. And 'twould sound prettily: "A lost English boy of thirty."

FREDERICK. I hope 'tis some common crafty sinner, one that will fit him. It may be she'll sell him for Peru:[62] The rogue's sturdy, and would work well in a mine. At least I hope she'll dress him for our mirth, cheat him of all, then have him well-favoredly banged, and turned out at midnight.

WILLMORE. Prithee what humor is he of, that you wish him so well?

BELVILE. Why, of an English elder brother's humor: educated in a nursery, with a maid to tend him till fifteen, and lies with his grandmother till he's of age; one that knows no pleasure beyond riding to the next fair, or going up to London with his right worshipful father in parliament time, wearing gay clothes, or making honorable love to his lady mother's laundry maid; gets drunk at a hunting match, and ten to one then gives some proofs of his prowess. A pox upon him, he's our banker, and has all our cash about him; and if he fail, we are all broke.

FREDERICK. Oh, let him alone for that matter; he's of a damned stingy quality that will secure our stock. I know not in what danger it were indeed if the jilt[63] should pretend she's in love with him, for 'tis a kind believing coxcomb; otherwise, if he part with more than a piece of eight,[64] geld him—for which offer he may chance to be beaten if she be a whore of the first rank.

BELVILE. Nay, the rogue will not be easily beaten; he's stout enough. Perhaps if they talk beyond his capacity he may chance to exercise his courage upon some of them, else I'm sure they'll find it as difficult to beat as to please him.

WILLMORE. 'Tis a lucky devil to light upon so kind a wench!

FREDERICK. Thou hadst a great deal of talk with thy little gypsy; couldst thou do no good upon her? For mine was hardhearted.

WILLMORE. Hang her, she was some damned honest person of quality, I'm sure, she was so very free and witty. If her face be but answerable to her wit and humor, I would be bound to constancy this month to gain her. In the meantime, have you made no kind acquaintance since you came to town? You do not use to be honest[65] so long, gentlemen.

FREDERICK. Faith, love has kept us honest: We have been all fir'd with a beauty newly come to town, the famous Paduana[66] Angellica Bianca.

WILLMORE. What, the mistress of the dead Spanish general?

BELVILE. Yes, she's now the only ador'd beauty of all the youth in Naples, who put on all their charms to appear lovely in her sight: Their coaches, liveries, and themselves all gay as on a monarch's birthday to attract the eyes of this fair charmer, while she has the pleasure to behold all languish for her that see her.

FREDERICK. 'Tis pretty to see with how much love the men regard her, and how much envy the women.

WILLMORE. What gallant has she?

BELVILE. None; she's exposed to sale, and four days in the week she's yours, for so much a month

WILLMORE. The very thought of it quenches all manner of fire in me. Yet prithee, let's see her.

BELVILE. Let's first to dinner, and after that we'll pass the day as you please. But at night ye must all be at my devotion.

WILLMORE. I will not fail you.

[*Exeunt.*]

---

[59]**pox** damn [60]**Jew . . . Jesuit** Jews and Jesuits were widely distrusted and feared in this period [61]**the bellman** town crier [62]**sell . . . Peru** sell him as a slave to Peru

[63]**jilt** whore [64]**piece of eight** obsolete Spanish coin [65]**honest** chaste [66]**Paduana** Angellica comes from Padua

ACT 2

SCENE 1

(The long street. Enter Belvile and Frederick in masking habits, and Willmore in his own clothes, with a vizard[67] in his hand.)

WILLMORE. But why thus disguised and muzzled?

BELVILE. Because whatever extravagances we commit in these faces, our own may not be obliged to answer 'em.

WILLMORE. I should have changed my eternal buff,[68] too; but no matter, my little gypsy would not have found me out then. For if she should change hers, it is impossible I should know her unless I should hear her prattle. A pox on't, I cannot get her out of my head. Pray heaven, if ever I do see her again, she prove damnably ugly, that I may fortify myself against her tongue.

BELVILE. Have a care of love, for o' my conscience she was not of a quality to give thee any hopes.

WILLMORE. Pox on 'em, why do they draw a man in then? She has played with my heart so, that 'twill never lie still till I have met with some kind wench that will play the game out with me. Oh, for my arms full of soft, white, kind woman—such as I fancy Angellica.

BELVILE. This is her house, if you were but in stock to get admittance. They have not dined yet; I perceive the picture is not out.[69]

(Enter Blunt.)

WILLMORE. I long to see the shadow of the fair substance; a man may gaze on that for nothing.

BLUNT. Colonel, thy hand. And thine, Fred. I have been an ass, a deluded fool, a very coxcomb from my birth till this hour, and heartily repent my little faith.

BELVILE. What the devil's the matter with thee, Ned?

BLUNT. Oh, such a mistress, Fred! Such a girl!

WILLMORE. Ha! Where?

FREDERICK. Ay, where?

BLUNT. So fond, so amorous, so toying, and so fine! And all for sheer love, ye rogue! Oh, how she looked and kissed! And soothed my heart from my bosom! I cannot think I was awake, and yet methinks I see and feel her charms still. Fred, try if she have not left the taste of her balmy kisses upon my lips.

(Kisses him.)

BELVILE. Ha! Ha! Ha!

WILLMORE. Death, man, where is she?

BLUNT. What a dog was I to stay in dull England so long!

How have I laughed at the colonel when he sighed for love! But now the little archer[70] has revenged him! And by this one dart I can guess at all his joys, which then I took for fancies, mere dreams and fables. Well, I'm resolved to sell all in Essex and plant here forever.

BELVILE. What a blessing 'tis, thou hast a mistress thou dar'st boast of; for I know thy humor is rather to have a proclaimed clap[71] than a secret amour.

WILLMORE. Dost know her name?

BLUNT. Her name? No, 'adsheartlikins. What care I for names? She's fair, young, brisk and kind, even to ravishment! And what a pox care I for knowing her by any other title?

WILLMORE. Didst give her anything?

BLUNT. Give her? Ha! Ha! Ha! Why, she's a person of quality. That's a good one! Give her? 'Adsheartlikins, dost think such creatures are to be bought? Or are we provided for such a purchase? Give her, quoth ye? Why, she presented me with this bracelet for the toy of a diamond I used to wear. No, gentlemen, Ned Blunt is not everybody. She expects me again tonight.

WILLMORE. Egad, that's well; we'll all go.

BLUNT. Not a soul! No, gentlemen, you are wits; I am a dull country rogue, I.

FREDERICK. Well, sir, for all your person of quality, I shall be very glad to understand your purse be secure; 'tis our whole estate at present, which we are loath to hazard in one bottom.[72] Come sir, unlade.

BLUNT. Take the necessary trifle useless now to me, that am beloved by such a gentlewoman. 'Adsheartlikins, money! Here, take mine too.

FREDERICK. No, keep that to be cozened,[73] that we may laugh.

WILLMORE. Cozened? Death! Would I could meet with one that would cozen me of all the love I could spare tonight.

FREDERICK. Pox, 'tis some common whore, upon my life.

BLUNT. A whore? Yes, with such clothes, such jewels, such a house, such furniture, and so attended! A whore!

BELVILE. Why yes, sir, they are whores, though they'll neither entertain you with drinking, swearing, or bawdry; are whores in all those gay clothes and right[74] jewels; are whores with those great houses richly furnished with velvet beds, store of plate,[75] handsome attendance, and fine coaches; are whores, and errant[76] ones.

WILLMORE. Pox on't, where do these fine whores live?

BELVILE. Where no rogues in office, ycleped[77] constables, dare give 'em laws, nor the wine-inspired bullies of the town break their windows; yet they are whores though this Essex calf[78] believe 'em persons of quality.

---

[67]**vizard** mask   [68]**buff** leather military coat   [69]**the picture . . . out** when Angellica's picture is hung, she is open for business; see stage direction line later in the scene, referring to a great picture of Angellica

[70]**the little archer** Cupid   [71]**proclaimed clap** sexual disease that everyone knows of   [72]**loath . . . bottom** reluctant to risk cargo in one ship   [73]**cozened** cheated   [74]**right** real   [75]**plate** silverware   [76]**errant** arrant, unmitigated   [77]**ycleped** called   [78]**Essex calf** fool from Essex (Blunt's county in England)

BLUNT. 'Adsheartlikins, y'are all fools. These are things about this Essex calf that shall take with the ladies, beyond all your wit and parts. This shape and size, gentlemen, are not to be despised; my waist, too, tolerably long, with other inviting signs that shall be nameless.

WILLMORE. Egad, I believe he may have met with some person of quality that may be kind to him.

BELVILE. Dost thou perceive any such tempting things about him that should make a fine woman, and of quality, pick him out from all mankind to throw away her youth and beauty upon; nay, and her dear heart, too. No, no, Angellica has raised the price too high.

WILLMORE. May she languish for mankind till she die, and be damned for that one sin alone.

(*Enter two Bravos and hang up a great picture of Angellica's against the balcony, and two little ones at each side of the door.*)

BELVILE. See there the fair sign to the inn where a man may lodge that's fool enough to give her price.

(*Willmore gazes on the picture.*)

BLUNT. 'Adsheartlikins, gentlemen, what's this?

BELVILE. A famous courtesan, that's to be sold.

BLUNT. How? To be sold? Nay, then I have nothing to say to her. Sold? What impudence is practiced in this country; with what order and decency whoring's established here by virtue of the Inquisition![79] Come, let's be gone; I'm sure we're no chapmen[80] for this commodity.

FREDERICK. Thou art none, I'm sure, unless thou couldst have her in thy bed at a price of a coach in the street.

WILLMORE. How wondrous fair she is! A thousand crowns a month? By heaven, as many kingdoms were too little! A plague of this poverty, of which I ne'er complain but when it hinders my approach to beauty which virtue ne'er could purchase.

(*Turns from the picture.*)

BLUNT. What's this? (*Reads.*) "A thousand crowns a month"! 'Adsheartlikins, here's a sum! Sure 'tis a mistake.—[*To one of the Bravos.*] Hark you, friend, does she take or give so much by the month?

FREDERICK. A thousand crowns! Why, 'tis a portion for the Infanta.[81]

BLUNT. Hark ye, friends, won't she trust?[82]

BRAVO. This is a trade, sir, that cannot live by credit.

(*Enter Don Pedro in masquerade, followed by Stephano.*)

BELVILE. See, here's more company; let's walk off a while.

(*Exeunt English,[83] Pedro reads.*)

PEDRO. Fetch me a thousand crowns; I never wished to buy this beauty at an easier rate.

(*Passes off.*)

(*Enter Angellica and Moretta in the balcony, and draw a silk curtain.*)

ANGELLICA. Prithee, what said those fellows to thee?

BRAVO. Madam, the first were admirers of beauty only, but no purchasers; they were merry with your price and picture, laughed at the sum, and so passed off.

ANGELLICA. No matter, I'm not displeased with their rallying; their wonder feeds my vanity, and he that wishes but to buy gives me more pride than he that gives my price can make my pleasure.

BRAVO. Madam, the last I knew through all his disguises to be Don Pedro, nephew to the general, and who was with him in Pamplona.

ANGELLICA. Don Pedro? My old gallant's nephew? When his uncle died he left him a vast sum of money; it is he who was so in love with me at Padua, and who used to make the general so jealous.

MORETTA. Is this he that used to practice before our window, and take such care to show himself an amorous ass? If I am not mistaken, he is the likeliest man to give your price.

ANGELLICA. The man is brave and generous, but of a humor so uneasy and inconstant that the victory over his heart is as soon lost as won; a slave that can add little to the triumph of the conqueror. But inconstancy's the sin of all mankind, therefore I'm resolved that nothing but gold shall charm my heart.

MORETTA. I'm glad on't; 'tis only interest that women of our profession ought to consider, though I wonder what has kept you from that general disease of our sex so long; I mean, that of being in love.

ANGELLICA. A kind but sullen star under which I had the happiness to be born. Yet I have had no time for love; the bravest and noblest of mankind have purchased my favors at so dear a rate, as if no coin but gold were current with our trade. But here's Don Pedro again; fetch me my lute, for 'tis for him or Don Antonio the Viceroy's son that I have spread my nets.

(*Enter at one door Don Pedro, Stephano; Don Antonio and Diego [his page] at the other door, with people following him in masquerade, antically attired, some with music. They both go up to the picture.*)

ANTONIO. A thousand crowns! Had not the painter flattered her, I should not think it dear.[84]

PEDRO. Flattered her? By heaven, he cannot. I have seen the original, nor is there one charm here more than adorns

---

[79]**Inquisition** prostitutes forced out of Spain by the Spanish Inquisition came to Italy   [80]**chapmen** merchants   [81]**portion . . . Infanta** dowry for the Spanish princess   [82]**trust** extend credit   [83]**English** all the Englishmen

[84]**dear** expensive

her face and eyes; all this soft and sweet, with a certain languishing air that no artist can represent.

ANTONIO. What I heard of her beauty before had fired my soul, but this confirmation of it has blown it to a flame.

PEDRO. Ha!

PAGE. Sir, I have known you throw away a thousand crowns on a worse face, and though y'are near your marriage, you may venture a little love here; Florinda will not miss it.

PEDRO (aside). Ha! Florinda! Sure 'tis Antonio.

ANTONIO. Florinda! Name not those distant joys; there's not one thought of her will check my passion here.

PEDRO [aside]. Florinda scorned! (A noise of a lute above.) And all my hopes defeated of the possession of Angellica! (Antonio gazes up.) Her injuries, by heaven, he shall not boast of!

(Song to a lute above.)

SONG

[I]

When Damon first began to love
He languished in a soft desire,
And knew not how the gods to move,
To lessen or increase his fire.
For Caelia in her charming eyes
Wore all love's sweets, and all his cruelties.

II

But as beneath a shade he lay,
Weaving of flowers for Caelia's hair,
She chanced to lead her flock that way,
And saw the am'rous shepherd there.
She gazed around upon the place,
And saw the grove, resembling night,
To all the joys of love invite,
Whilst guilty smiles and blushes dressed her face.
At this the bashful youth all transport grew,
And with kind force he taught the virgin how
To yield what all his sighs could never do.

(Angellica throws open the curtains and bows to Antonio, who pulls off his vizard and bows and blows up kisses. Pedro, unseen, looks in's face. [The curtains close.])

ANTONIO. By heaven, she's charming fair!

PEDRO (aside). 'Tis he, the false Antonio!

ANTONIO (to the Bravo[85]).
  Friend; where must I pay my off'ring of love?
  My thousand crowns I mean.

PEDRO.
  That off'ring I have designed to make,
  And yours will come too late.

ANTONIO.
  Prithee begone; I shall grow angry else,
  And then thou art not safe.

PEDRO.
  My anger may be fatal, sir, as yours,
  And he that enters here may prove this truth.

ANTONIO. I know not who thou art, but I am sure thou'rt worth my killing, for aiming at Angellica.

(They draw and fight.)

(Enter Willmore and Blunt, who draw and part 'em.)

BLUNT. 'Adsheartlikins, here's fine doings.

WILLMORE. Tilting[86] for the wench, I'm sure. Nay, gad, if that would win her I have as good a sword as the best of ye. Put up, put up, and take another time and place, for this is designed for lovers only.   (They all put up.)

PEDRO.
  We are prevented; dare you meet me tomorrow on the Molo?[87]
  For I've a title to a better quarrel,
  That of Florinda, in whose credulous heart
  Thou'st made an int'rest, and destroyed my hopes.

ANTONIO. Dare!
  I'll meet thee there as early as the day.

PEDRO. We will come thus disguised, that whosoever chance to get the better, he may escape unknown.

ANTONIO. It shall be so.

(Exeunt Pedro and Stephano.)

—Who should this rival be? Unless the English colonel, of whom I've often heard Don Pedro speak. It must be he, and time he were removed who lays a claim to all my happiness.

(Willmore, having gazed all this while on the picture[s], pulls down a little one.)

WILLMORE. This posture's loose and negligent;
  The sight on't would beget a warm desire
  In souls whom impotence and age had chilled.
  This must along with me.

BRAVO. What means this rudeness, sir? Restore the picture.

ANTONIO. Ha! Rudeness committed to the fair Angellica!—Restore the picture, sir.

WILLMORE. Indeed I will not, sir.

ANTONIO. By heaven, but you shall.

WILLMORE. Nay, do not show your sword; if you do, by this dear beauty, I will show mine too.

ANTONIO. What right can you pretend to't?

WILLMORE. That of possession, which I will maintain. You, perhaps, have a thousand crowns to give for the original.

ANTONIO. No matter, sir, you shall restore the picture.

([The curtains open.] Angellica and Moretta above.)

ANGELLICA. Oh, Moretta, what's the matter?

---

[85]**Bravo** ruffian

[86]**Tilting** fighting (normally charging on horseback, with a lance)
[87]**Molo** stone pier

ANTONIO. Or leave your life behind.

WILLMORE. Death! You lie; I will do neither.

([Willmore and Antonio] fight. The Spaniards join with Antonio, Blunt [joins with Willmore,] laying on like mad.)

ANGELLICA. Hold, I command you, if for me you fight.

(They leave off and bow.)

WILLMORE [aside]. How heavenly fair she is! Ah, plague of her price.

ANGELLICA. You sir, in buff, you that appear a soldier, that first began this insolence—

WILLMORE. 'Tis true, I did so, if you call it insolence for a man to preserve himself. I saw your charming picture and was wounded; quite through my soul each pointed beauty ran; and wanting a thousand crowns to procure my remedy, I laid this little picture to my bosom, which, if you cannot allow me, I'll resign.

ANGELLICA. No, you may keep the trifle.

ANTONIO. You shall first ask me leave, and this.

(Fight again as before.)

(Enter Belvile and Frederick, who join with the English.)

ANGELLICA. Hold! Will you ruin me?—Biskey! Sebastian! Part 'em.

(The Spaniards are beaten off.)

MORETTA. Oh, madam, we're undone. A pox upon that rude fellow; he's set on to ruin us. We shall never see good days again till all these fighting poor rogues are sent to the galleys.

(Enter Belvile, Blunt, Frederick, and Willmore with's shirt bloody.)

BLUNT. 'Adsheartlikins, beat me at this sport and I'll ne'er wear sword more.

BELVILE (to Willmore). The devil's in thee for a mad fellow; thou art always one at an unlucky adventure. Come, let's be gone whilst we're safe, and remember these are Spaniards, a sort of people that know how to revenge an affront.

FREDERICK. You bleed! I hope you are not wounded.

WILLMORE. Not much. A plague on your dons; if they fight no better they'll ne'er recover Flanders.[88] What the devil was't to them that I took down the picture?

BLUNT. Took it! 'Adsheartlikins, we'll have the great one too; 'tis ours by conquest. Prithee help me up and I'll pull it down.

ANGELLICA [to Willmore]. Stay, sir, and ere you affront me farther let me know how you durst commit this outrage. To you I speak, sir, for you appear a gentleman.

WILLMORE. To me, madam?—Gentlemen, your servant.

(Belvile stays him.)

BELVILE. Is the devil in thee? Dost know the danger of ent'ring the house of an incensed courtesan?

WILLMORE. I thank you for your care, but there are other matters in hand, there are, though we have no great temptation. Death! Let me go!

FREDERICK. Yes, to your lodging if you will, but not in here. Damn these gay harlots; by this hand I'll have as sound and handsome a whore for a patacoon.[89] Death, man, she'll murder thee!

WILLMORE. Oh, fear me not. Shall I not venture where a beauty calls? A lovely charming beauty! For fear of danger? When, by heaven, there's none so great as to long for her whilst I want money to purchase her.

FREDERICK. Therefore 'tis loss of time unless you had the thousand crowns to pay.

WILLMORE. It may be she may give a favor; at least I shall have the pleasure of saluting her when I enter and when I depart.

BELVILE. Pox, she'll as soon lie with thee as kiss thee, and sooner stab than do either. You shall not go.

ANGELLICA. Fear not, sir, all I have to wound with is my eyes.

BLUNT. Let him go. 'Adsheartlikins, I believe the gentlewoman means well.

BELVILE. Well, take thy fortune; we'll expect you in the next street. Farewell, fool, farewell.

WILLMORE. 'Bye, colonel.

(Goes in.)

FREDERICK. The rogue's stark mad for a wench.

(Exeunt.)

SCENE 2

(A fine chamber. Enter Willmore, Angellica, and Moretta.)

ANGELLICA. Insolent sir, how durst you pull down my picture?

WILLMORE. Rather, how durst you set it up to tempt poor am'rous mortals with so much excellence, which I find you have but too well consulted by the unmerciful price you set upon't. Is all this heaven of beauty shown to move despair in those that cannot buy? And can you think th'effects of that despair should be less extravagant than I have shown?

ANGELLICA. I sent for you to ask my pardon, sir, not to aggravate your crime. I thought I should have seen you at my feet imploring it.

WILLMORE. You are deceived. I came to rail at you, and rail such truths too, as shall let you see the vanity of that price which taught you how to set such price on sin.

---

[88]**Flanders** in 1659 Spain ceded the Netherlands to France

[89]**patacoon** Spanish coin

For such it is whilst that which is love's due
Is meanly bartered for.

ANGELLICA. Ha! Ha! Ha! Alas, good captain, what pity 'tis your edifying doctrine will do no good upon me. Moretta, fetch the gentleman a glass,[90] and let him survey himself to see what charms he has.—(*Aside, in a soft tone.*) And guess my business.

MORETTA. He knows himself of old: I believe those breeches and he have been acquainted ever since he was beaten at Worcester.[91]

ANGELLICA. Nay, do not abuse the poor creature.

MORETTA. Good weather-beaten corporal, will you march off? We have no need of your doctrine, though you have of our charity. But at present we have no scraps; we can afford no kindness for God's sake. In fine, sirrah, the price is too high i'th' mouth[92] for you, therefore the troop, I say.

WILLMORE. Here, good forewoman of the shop, serve me and I'll be gone.

MORETTA. Keep it to pay your laundress; your linen stinks of the gun room. For here's no selling by retail.

WILLMORE. Thou hast sold plenty of thy stale ware at a cheap rate.

MORETTA. Ay, the more silly kind heart I, but this is an age wherein beauty is at higher rates. In fine, you know the price of this.

WILLMORE. I grant you 'tis here set down, a thousand crowns a month. Pray, how much may come to my share for a pistole? Bawd, take your black lead[93] and sum it up, that I may have a pistole's worth[94] of this vain gay thing, and I'll trouble you no more.

MORETTA. Pox on him, he'll fret me to death! Abominable fellow, I tell thee we only sell by the whole piece.

WILLMORE. 'Tis very hard, the whole cargo or nothing. Faith, madam, my stock will not reach it; I cannot be your chapman. Yet I have countrymen in town, merchants of love like me; I'll see if they'll put in for a share. We cannot lose much by it, and what we have no use for, we'll sell upon the Friday's mart at "Who gives more?"—I am studying, madam, how to purchase you, though at present I am unprovided of money.

ANGELLICA (*aside*). Sure this from any other man would anger me; nor shall he know the conquest he has made.— Poor angry man, how I despite this railing.

WILLMORE.
Yes, I am poor. But I'm a gentleman,
And one that scorns this baseness which you practice.
Poor as I am I would not sell myself,
No, not to gain your charming high-prized person.
Though I admire you strangely for your beauty,

Yes I contemn your mind.
And yet I would at any rate enjoy you;
At your own rate; but cannot. See here
The only sum I can command on earth:
I know not where to eat when this is gone.
Yet such a slave I am to love and beauty
This last reserve I'll sacrifice to enjoy you.
Nay, do not frown, I know you're to be bought,
And would be bought by me. By me.
For a meaning trifling sum, if I could pay it down.
Which happy knowledge I will still repeat,
And lay it to my heart: It has a virtue in't,
And soon will cure those wounds your eyes have made.
And yet, there's something so divinely powerful there—
Nay, I will gaze, to let you see my strength.

(*Holds her, looks on her, and pauses and sighs.*)

By heav'n, bright creature, I would not for the world
Thy fame were half so fair as is thy face.
						(*Turns her away from him.*)

ANGELLICA (*aside*).
His words go through me to the very soul.—
If you have nothing else to say to me—

WILLMORE.
Yes, you shall hear how infamous you are—
For which I do not hate thee—
But that secures my heart, and all the flames it feels
Are but so many lusts:
I know it by their sudden bold intrusion.
The fire's impatient and betrays; 'tis false.
For had it been the purer flame of love,
I should have pined and languished at your feet,
Ere found the impudence to have discovered it.
I now dare stand your scorn and your denial.

MORETTA. Sure she's bewitched, that she can stand thus tamely and hear his saucy railing.—Sirrah, will you be gone?

ANGELLICA (*to Moretta*). How dare you take this liberty! Withdraw!—Pray tell me, sir, are not you guilty of the same mercenary crime? When a lady is proposed to you for a wife, you never ask how fair, discreet, or virtuous she is, but what's her fortune; which, if but small, you cry "She will not do my business," and barely leave her, though she languish for you. Say, is not this as poor?

WILLMORE. It is a barbarous custom, which I will scorn to defend in our sex, and do despise in yours.

ANGELLICA.
Thou'rt a brave fellow! Put up thy gold, and know,
That were thy fortune as large as is thy soul,
Thou shouldst not buy my love
Couldst thou forget those mean effects of vanity
Which set me out to sale,
And as a lover prize my yielding joys.
Canst thou believe they'll be entirely thine,
Without considering they were mercenary?

[90]**glass** mirror   [91]**Worcester** Cromwell defeated Charles II at Worcester and forced him into exile   [92]**high i'th' mouth** expensive   [93]**black lead** pencil   [94]**a pistole's worth** as much as a Spanish gold coin will buy

WILLMORE.

I cannot tell, I must bethink me first.

(*Aside.*) Ha! Death, I'm going to believe her.

ANGELLICA.

Prithee confirm that faith, or if thou canst not,

Flatter me a little. 'Twill please me from thy mouth.

WILLMORE (*aside*).

Curse on thy charming tongue! Dost thou return

My feigned contempt with so much subtlety?—

Thou'st found the easiest way into my heart,

Though I yet know that all thou say'st is false.

(*Turning from her in rage.*)

ANGELLICA.

By all that's good, 'tis real;

I never loved before, though oft a mistress.

Shall my first vows be slighted?

WILLMORE (*aside*).

What can she mean?

ANGELLICA (*in an angry tone*).

I find you cannot credit me.

WILLMORE.

I know you take me for an errant ass,

An ass that may be soothed into belief,

And then be used at pleasure;

But, madam, I have been so often cheated

By perjured, soft, deluding hypocrites,

That I've no faith left for the cozening sex,

Especially for women of your trade.

ANGELLICA.

The low esteem you have of me perhaps

May bring my heart again:

For I have pride that yet surmounts my love.

(*She turns with pride; he holds her.*)

WILLMORE.

Throw off this pride, this enemy to bliss,

And show the power of love: 'Tis with those arms

I can be only vanquished, made a slave.

ANGELLICA.

Is all my mighty expectation vanished?

No, I will not hear thee talk; thou hast a charm

In every word that draws my heart away,

And all the thousand trophies I designed

Thou hast undone. Why are thou soft?

Thy looks are bravely rough, and meant for war.

Couldst thou not storm on still?

I then perhaps had been as free as thou.

WILLMORE (*aside*).

Death, how she throws her fire about my soul!—

Take heed, fair creature, how you raise my hopes,

Which once assumed pretends to all dominion:

There's not a joy thou hast in store

I shall not then command.

For which I'll pay you back my soul, my life!

Come, let's begin th'account this happy minute!

ANGELLICA.

And will you pay me then the price I ask?

WILLMORE.

Oh, why dost thou draw me from an awful worship,

By showing thou art no divinity.

Conceal the fiend, and show me all the angel!

Keep me but ignorant, and I'll be devout

And pay my vows forever at this shrine.

(*Kneels and kisses her hand.*)

ANGELLICA.

The pay I mean is but thy love for mine.

Can you give that?

WILLMORE. Entirely. Come, let's withdraw where I'll renew my vows, and breathe 'em with such ardor thou shalt not doubt my zeal.

ANGELLICA. Thou hast a power too strong to be resisted.

MORETTA. Now my curse go with you! Is all our project fallen to this? To love the only enemy to our trade? Nay, to love such a shameroon;[95] a very beggar; nay, a pirate beggar, whose business is to rifle and be gone; a no-purchase, no-pay tatterdemalion, and English picaroon;[96] a rogue that fights for daily drink, and takes a pride in being loyally lousy? Oh, I could curse now, if I durst. This is the fate of most whores.

Trophies, which from believing fops we win,

Are spoils to those who cozen us again.

[*Exit.*]

ACT 3

SCENE 1

(*A street. Enter Florinda, Valeria, Hellena, in antic*[97] *different dresses from what they were in before; Callis attending.*)

FLORINDA. I wonder what should make my brother in so ill a humor? I hope he has not found out our ramble this morning.

HELLENA. No, if he had, we should have heard on't at both ears, and have been mew'd up[98] this afternoon, which I would not for the world should have happened. Hey ho, I'm as sad as a lover's lute.

VALERIA. Well, methinks we have learnt this trade of gypsies as readily as if we had been bred upon the road to Loretto, and yet I did so fumble when I told the stranger his fortune that I was afraid I should have told my own

---

[95]**shameroon** deceiver [96]**picaroon** rogue [97]**antic** grotesque
[98]**mew'd up** confined

and yours by mistake. But methinks Hellena has been very serious ever since.

FLORINDA. I would give my garters she were in love, to be revenged upon her for abusing me. How is't, Hellena?

HELLENA. Ah, would I had never seen my mad monsieur. And yet, for all your laughing, I am not in love. And yet this small acquaintance, o' my conscience, will never out of my head.

VALERIA. Ha! Ha! Ha! I laugh to think how thou art fitted with a lover, a fellow that I warrant loves every new face he sees.

HELLENA. Hum, he has not kept his word with me here, and may be taken up. That thought is not very pleasant to me. What the deuce should this be now that I feel?

VALERIA. What is't like?

HELLENA. Nay, the Lord knows, but if I should be hanged I cannot choose but be angry and afraid when I think that mad fellow should be in love with anybody but me. What to think of myself I know not: Would I could meet with some true damned gypsy, that I might know my fortune.

VALERIA. Know it! Why there's nothing so easy: Thou wilt love this wand'ring inconstant till thou find'st thyself hanged about his neck, and then be as mad to get free again.

FLORINDA. Yes, Valeria, we shall see her bestride his baggage horse and follow him to the campaign.

HELLENA. So, so, now you are provided for there's no care taken of poor me. But since you have set my heart a-wishing, I am resolved to know for what; I will not die of the pip,[99] so I will not.

FLORINDA. Art thou mad to talk so? Who will like thee well enough to have thee, that hears what a mad wench thou art?

HELLENA. Like me? I don't intend every he that likes me shall have me, but he that I like. I should have stayed in the nunnery still if I had liked my lady abbess as well as she liked me. No, I came thence not, as my wise brother imagines, to take an eternal farewell of the world, but to love and to be beloved; and I will be beloved, or I'll get one of your men, so I will.

VALERIA. Am I put into[100] the number of lovers?

HELLENA. You? Why, coz, I know thou'rt too good-natured to leave us in any design; thou wouldst venture a cast[101] though thou comest off a loser, especially with such a gamester. I observed your man, and your willing ear incline that way; and if you are not a lover, 'tis an art soon learnt—that I find.   (Sighs.)

FLORINDA. I wonder how you learnt to love so easily. I had a thousand charms to meet my eyes and ears ere I could yield, and 'twas the knowledge of Belvile's merit, not the surprising person, took my soul. Thou art too rash, to give a heart at first sight.

HELLENA. Hang your considering lover! I never thought beyond the fancy that 'twas a very pretty, idle, silly kind of pleasure to pass one's time with: to write little soft nonsensical billets,[102] and with great difficulty and danger receive answers in which I shall have my beauty praised, my wit admired, though little or none, and have the vanity and power to know I am desirable. Then I have the more inclination that way because I am to be a nun, and so shall not be suspected to have any such earthly thoughts about me; but when I walk thus—and sigh thus—they'll think my mind's upon my monastery, and cry, "How happy 'tis she's so resolved." But not a word of man.

FLORINDA. What a mad creature's this!

HELLENA. I'll warrant, if my brother hears either of you sigh, he cries gravely, "I fear you have the indiscretion to be in love, but take heed of the honor of our house, and your own unspotted fame"; and so he conjures on till he has laid the soft winged god in your hearts, or broke the bird's nest.[103] But see, here comes your lover, but where's my inconstant? Let's step aside, and we may learn something.
                                    (Go aside.)

(Enter Belvile, Frederick, and Blunt.)

BELVILE. What means this! The picture's taken in.

BLUNT. It may be the wench is good-natured, and will be kind gratis.[104] Your friend's a proper handsome fellow.

BELVILE. I rather think she has cut his throat and is fled; I am mad he should throw himself into dangers. Pox on't, I shall want him, too, at night. Let's knock and ask for him.

HELLENA. My heart goes a-pit, a-pat, for fear 'tis my man they talk of.

(Knock; Moretta above.)

MORETTA. What would you have?

BELVILE. Tell the stranger that entered here about two hours ago that his friends stay here for him.

MORETTA. A curse upon him for Moretta: Would he were at the devil! But he's coming to you.

(Enter Willmore.)

HELLENA. Ay, ay 'tis he. Oh, how this vexes me!

BELVILE. And how and how, dear lad, has fortune smiled? Are we to break her windows, or raise up altars to her, hah?

WILLMORE. Does not my fortune sit triumphant on my brow? Dost not see the little wanton god there all gay and smiling? Have I not an air about my face and eyes that distinguish me from the crowd of common lovers? By heaven, Cupid's quiver has not half so many darts as her eyes! Oh, such a bona roba![105] To sleep in her arms is lying in fresco,[106] all perfumed air about me.

---

[99]**die of the pip** die of some minor ailment   [100]**into** among   [101]**venture a cast** throw dice

[102]**billets** love notes   [103]**laid . . . bird's nest** stimulated your love, or destroyed the place where love dwells (bird = Cupid)   [104]**gratis** freely   [105]**bona roba** courtesan   [106]**in fresco** outdoors

HELLENA (*aside*). Here's fine encouragement for me to fool on!

WILLMORE. Hark'ee, where didst thou purchase that rich Canary[107] we drank today? Tell me, that I may adore the spigot and sacrifice to the butt.[108] The juice was divine; into which I must dip my rosary, and then bless all things that I would have bold or fortunate.

BELVILE. Well, sir, let's go take a bottle and hear the story of your success.

FREDERICK. Would not French wine do better?

WILLMORE. Damn the hungry balderdash![109] Cheerful sack[110] has a generous virtue in't inspiring a successful confidence, gives eloquence to the tongue and vigor to the soul, and has in a few hours completed all my hopes and wishes! There's nothing left to raise a new desire in me. Come, let's be gay and wanton. And, gentlemen, study; study what you want, for here are friends that will supply gentlemen. [*Jingles gold coins.*] Hark what a charming sound they make! 'Tis he and she gold whilst here, and shall beget new pleasures every moment.

BLUNT. But hark'ee, sir, you are not married, are you?

WILLMORE. All the honey of matrimony but none of the sting, friend.

BLUNT. 'Adsheartlikins, thou'rt a fortunate rogue!

WILLMORE. I am so, sir: let these inform you! Ha, how sweetly they chime! Pox of poverty: It makes a man a slave, makes wit and honor sneak. My soul grew lean and rusty for want of credit.

BLUNT. 'Adsheartlikins, this I like well; it looks like my lucky bargain! Oh, how I long for the approach of my squire, that is to conduct me to her house again. Why, here's two provided for!

FREDERICK. By this light, y'are happy men.

BLUNT. Fortune is pleased to smile on us, gentlemen, to smile on us.

(*Enter Sancho and pulls down Blunt by the sleeve; they go aside.*)

SANCHO. Sir, may lady expects you. She has removed all that might oppose your will and pleasure, and is impatient till you come.

BLUNT. Sir, I'll attend you.—Oh the happiest rogue! I'll take no leave, lest they either dog me or stay me.

(*Exit with Sancho.*)

BELVILE. But then the little gypsy is forgot?

WILLMORE. A mischief on thee for putting her into my thoughts! I had quite forgot her else, and this night's debauch had drunk her quite down.

HELLENA. Had it so, good captain!

(*Claps him on the back.*)

WILLMORE (*aside*). Ha! I hope she did not hear me!

HELLENA. What, afraid of such a champion?

WILLMORE. Oh, you're a fine lady of your word, are you not? To make a man languish a whole day—

HELLENA. In tedious search of me.

WILLMORE. Egad, child, thou'rt in the right. Hadst thou seen what a melancholy dog I have been ever since I was a lover, how I have walked the streets like a Capuchin,[111] with my hands in my sleeves—faith, sweetheart, thou wouldst pity me.

HELLENA [*aside*]. Now if I should be hanged I can't be angry with him, he dissembles so heartily.—Alas, good captain, what pains you have taken; now were I ungrateful not to reward so true a servant.

WILLMORE. Poor soul, that's kindly said; I see thou barest a conscience. Come then, for a beginning show me thy dear face.

HELLENA. I'm afraid, my small acquaintance, you have been staying that swinging stomach you boasted of this morning. I then remember my little collation[112] would have gone down with you without the sauce of a handsome face. Is your stomach so queasy now?

WILLMORE. Faith, long fasting, child, spoils a man's appetite. Yet if you durst treat, I could so lay about me still—

HELLENA. And would you fall to before a priest says grace?

WILLMORE. O fie, fie, what an old out-of-fashioned thing hast thou named? Thou couldst not dash me more out of countenance shouldst thou show me an ugly face.

(*Whilst he is seemingly courting Hellena, enter Angellica, Moretta, Biskey, and Sebastian, all in masquerade. Angellica sees Willmore and stares.*)

ANGELLICA. Heavens, 'tis he! And passionately fond to see another woman!

MORETTA. What could you less expect from such a swaggerer?

ANGELLICA.
Expect? As much as I paid him: a heart entire,
Which I had pride enough to think when'er I gave,
It would have raised the man above the vulgar,
Made him all soul, and that all soft and constant.

HELLENA. You see, captain, how willing I am to be friends with you, till time and ill luck make us lovers; and ask you the question first rather than put your modesty to the blush by asking me. For alas, I know you captains are such strict men, and such severe observers of your vows to chastity, that 'twill be hard to prevail with your tender conscience to marry a young willing maid.

WILLMORE. Do not abuse me, for fear I should take thee at thy word and marry thee indeed, which I'm sure will be revenge sufficient.

[107]**Canary** sweet wine, from the Canary Islands   [108]**butt** large cask   [109]**hungry balderdash** cheap mixture of liquor   [110]**sack** dry wine from Spain

[111]**Capuchin** monk   [112]**collation** light meal

HELLENA. O' my conscience, that will be our destiny, because we are both of one humor: I am as inconstant as you, for I have considered, captain, that a handsome woman has a great deal to do whilst her face is good. For then is our harvest-time to gather friends, and should I in these days of my youth catch a fit of foolish constancy, I were undone: 'tis loitering by daylight in our great journey. Therefore, I declare I'll allow but one year for love, one year for indifference, and one year for hate; and then go hang yourself, for I profess myself the gay, the kind, and the inconstant. The devil's in't if this won't please you!

WILLMORE. Oh, most damnably. I have a heart with a hole quite through it too; no prison mine, to keep a mistress in.

ANGELLICA (aside). Perjured man! How I believe thee now!

HELLENA. Well, I see our business as well as humors are alike: yours to cozen as many maids as will trust you, and I as many men as have faith. See if I have not as desperate a lying look as you can have for the heart of you. (Pulls off her vizard; he starts.) How do you like it, captain?

WILLMORE. Like it! By heaven, I never saw so much beauty! Oh, the charms of those sprightly black eyes! That strangely fair face, full of smiles and dimples! Those soft round melting cherry lips and small even white teeth! Not to be expressed, but silently adored! [She replaces her mask.] Oh, one look more, and strike me dumb, or I shall repeat nothing else till I'm mad.

(He seems to court her to pull off her vizard; she refuses.)

ANGELLICA. I can endure no more. Nor is it fit to interrupt him, for if I do, my jealousy has so destroyed my reason I shall undo him. Therefore I'll retire, and you, Sebastian (to one of her Bravos), follow that woman and learn who 'tis; while you (to the other Bravo) tell the fugitive I would speak to him instantly.

(Exit.)

(This while Florinda is talking to Belvile, who stands sullenly: Frederick courting Valeria.)

VALERIA [to Belvile]. Prithee, dear stranger, be not so sullen, for though you have lost your love you see my friend frankly offers you hers to play with in the meantime.

BELVILE. Faith, madam, I am sorry I can't play at her game.

FREDERICK [to Valeria]. Pray leave your intercession and mind your own affair. They'll better agree apart: He's a modest sigher in company, but alone no woman 'scapes him.

FLORINDA [aside]. Sure he does but rally. Yet, if it should be true? I'll tempt him farther.—Believe me, noble stranger, I'm no common mistress. And for a little proof on't, wear this jewel. Nay, take it, sir, 'tis right, and bills of exchange may sometimes miscarry.

BELVILE. Madam, why am I chose out of all mankind to be the object of your bounty?

VALERIA. There's another civil question asked.

FREDERICK [aside]. Pox of's modesty; it spoils his own markets and hinders mine.

FLORINDA. Sir, from my window I have often seen you, and women of my quality have so few opportunities for love that we ought to lose none.

FREDERICK [to Valeria]. Ay, this is something! Here's a woman! When shall I be blest with so much kindness from your fair mouth?—(Aside to Belvile.) Take the jewel, fool!

BELVILE. You tempt me strangely, madam, every way—

FLORINDA (aside). So, if I find him false, my whole repose is gone.

BELVILE. And but for a vow I've made to a very fair lady, this goodness had subdued me.

FREDERICK [aside to Belvile]. Pox on't, be kind, in pity to me be kind. For I am to thrive here but as you treat her friend.

HELLENA. Tell me what you did in yonder house, and I'll unmask.

WILLMORE. Yonder house? Oh, I went to a—to—why, there's a friend of mine lives there.

HELLENA. What, a she or a he friend?

WILLMORE. A man, upon honor, a man. A she friend? No, no, madam, you have done my business, I thank you.

HELLENA. And was't your man friend that had more darts in's eyes than Cupid carries in's whole budget[113] of arrows?

WILLMORE. So—

HELLENA. "Ah, such a *bona roba!* To be in her arms is lying *in fresco,* all perfumed air about me." Was this poor man friend too?

WILLMORE. So—

HELLENA. That gave you the he and the she gold, that begets young pleasures?

WILLMORE. Well, well, madam, then you can see there are ladies in the world that will not be cruel. There are, madam, there are.

HELLENA. And there be men, too, as fine, wild, inconstant fellows as yourself. There be, captain, there be, if you go to that now. Therefore, I'm resolved—

WILLMORE. Oh!

HELLENA. To see your face no more—

WILLMORE. Oh!

HELLENA. Till tomorrow.

WILLMORE. Egad, you frighted me.

HELLENA. Nor then neither, unless you'll swear never to see that lady more.

WILLMORE. See her! Why, never to think of womankind again.

HELLENA. Kneel and swear.

(Kneels; she gives him her hand.)

---

[113]**budget** bag, quiver

WILLMORE. I do, never to think, to see, to love, nor lie with any but thyself.

HELLENA. Kiss the book.

WILLMORE. Oh, most religiously.

(*Kisses her hand.*)

HELLENA. Now what a wicked creature am I, to damn a proper fellow.

CALLIS (*to Florinda*). Madam, I'll stay no longer: 'tis e'en dark.

FLORINDA [*to Belvile*]. However, sir, I'll leave this with you, that when I'm gone you may repent the opportunity you have lost by your modesty.

(*Gives him the jewel, which is her picture, and exits. He gazes after her.*)

WILLMORE [*to Hellena*]. 'Twill be an age till tomorrow, and till then I will most impatiently expect you. Adieu, my dear pretty angel.

(*Exeunt all the women.*)

BELVILE. Ha! Florinda's picture! 'Twas she herself. What a dull dog was I! I would have given the world for one minute's discourse with her.

FREDERICK. This comes of your modesty. Ah, pox o' your vow; 'twas ten to one but we had lost the jewel by't.

BELVILE. Willmore, the blessed'st opportunity lost! Florinda, friends, Florinda!

WILLMORE. Ah, rogue! Such black eyes! Such a face! Such a mouth! Such teeth! And so much wit!

BELVILE. All, all, and a thousand charms besides.

WILLMORE. Why, dost thou know her?

BELVILE. Know her! Ay, ay, and a pox take me with all my heart for being so modest.

WILLMORE. But hark'ee, friend of mine, are you my rival? And have I been only beating the bush all this while?

BELVILE. I understand thee not. I'm mad! See here—

(*Shows the picture.*)

WILLMORE. Ha! Whose picture's this? 'Tis a fine wench!

FREDERICK. The colonel's mistress, sir.

WILLMORE. Oh, oh, here. (*Gives the picture back.*) I thought't had been another prize. Come, come, a bottle will set thee right again.

BELVILE. I am content to try, and by that time 'twill be late enough for our design.

WILLMORE. Agreed.

Love does all day the soul's great empire keep,
But wine at night lulls the soft god asleep.

(*Exeunt.*)

SCENE 2

(*Lucetta's house. Enter Blunt and Lucetta with a light.*)

LUCETTA. Now we are safe and free: no fears of the coming home of my old jealous husband, which made me a little thoughtful when you came in first. But now love is all the business of my soul.

BLUNT. I am transported!—(*Aside.*) Pox on't, that I had but some fine things to say to her, such as lovers use. I was a fool not to learn of Fred a little by heart before I came. Something I must say.—'Adsheartlikins, sweet soul, I am not used to compliment, but I'm an honest gentleman, and thy humble servant.

LUCETTA. I have nothing to pay for so great a favor, but such a love as cannot but be great, since at first sight of that sweet face and shape it made me your absolute captive.

BLUNT (*aside*). Kind heart, how prettily she talks! Egad, I'll show her husband a Spanish trick: Send him out of the world and marry her; she's damnably in love with me, and will ne'er mind settlements,[114] and so there's that saved.

LUCETTA. Well, sir, I'll go and undress me, and be with you instantly.

BLUNT. Make haste then, for 'adsheartlikins, dear soul, thou canst not guess at the pain of a longing lover when his joys are drawn within the compass of a few minutes.

LUCETTA. You speak my sense, and I'll make haste to prove it.

(*Exit.*)

BLUNT. 'Tis a rare girl, and this one night's enjoyment with her will be worth all the days I ever passed in Essex. Would she would go with me into England, though to say truth, there's plenty of whores already. Put a pox on 'em, they are such mercenary prodigal whores that they want such a one as this, that's free and generous, to give 'em good examples. Why, what a house she has, how rich and fine!

(*Enter Sancho.*)

SANCHO. Sir, my lady has sent me to conduct you to her chamber.

BLUNT. Sir, I shall be proud to follow.—(*Aside.*) Here's one of her servants too; 'adsheartlikins, by this garb and gravity he might be a justice of peace in Essex, and is but a pimp here.

(*Exeunt.*)

SCENE 3

(*The scene changes to a chamber with an alcove bed in't, a table, etc.; Lucetta in bed. Enter Sancho and Blunt, who takes the candle of Sancho at the door.*)

SANCHO. Sir, my commission reaches no farther.

BLUNT. Sir, I'll excuse your compliment.

[*Exit Sancho.*]

—What, in bed, my sweet mistress?

[114]**settlements** prenuptial agreement setting property on a wife

LUCETTA. You see, I still outdo you in kindness.

BLUNT. And thou shalt see what haste I'll make to quit scores. Oh, the luckiest rogue!

(*He undresses himself.*)

LUCETTA. Should you be false or cruel now—

BLUNT. False! 'Adsheartlikins, what dost thou take me for, a Jew? An insensible heathen? A pox of thy old jealous husband! An[115] he were dead, egad,[116] sweet soul, it should be none of my fault if I did not marry thee.

LUCETTA. It never should be mine.

BLUNT. Good soul! I'm the fortunatest dog!

LUCETTA. Are you not undressed yet?

BLUNT. As much as my impatience will permit.

(*Goes toward the bed in his shirt, drawers, etc.*)

LUCETTA. Hold, sir, put out the light; it may betray us else.

BLUNT. Anything; I need no other light but that of thine eyes.—(*Aside.*) 'Adsheartlikins, there I think I had it.

(*Puts out the candle; the bed descends; he gropes about to find it.*)

Why, why, where am I got? What, not yet? Where are you, sweetest?—Ah, the rogue's silent now. A pretty lovetrick this; how she'll laugh at me anon!—You need not, my dear rogue, you need not! I'm all on fire already; come, come, now call me, in pity.—Sure I'm enchanted! I have been round the chamber, and can find neither woman nor bed. I locked the door; I'm sure she cannot go that way, or if she could, the bed could not.—Enough, enough, my pretty wanton; do not carry the jest too far! (*Lights on a trap, and is let down.*) —Ha! Betrayed! Dogs. Rogues! Pimps! Help! Help!

(*Enter Lucetta, Philippo, and Sancho with a light.*)

PHILIPPO. Ha! Ha! Ha! He's dispatched finely.

LUCETTA. Now sir, had I been coy, we had missed of this booty.

PHILIPPO. Nay, when I saw 'twas a substantial fool, I was mollified. But when you dote upon a serenading coxcomb, upon a face, fine clothes, and a lute, it makes me rage.

LUCETTA. You know I was never guilty of that folly, my dear Philippo, but with yourself. But come, let's see what we have got by this.

PHILIPPO. A rich coat; sword and hat; these breeches, too, are well lined! See here, a gold watch! A purse—Ha! Gold! At least two hundred pistoles! A bunch of diamond rings, and one with the family arms! A gold box, with a medal of his king, and his lady mother's picture! These were sacred relics, believe me. See, the waistband of his breeches have a mine of gold—old queen Bess's![117]

We have a quarrel to her even since eighty-eight,[118] and may therefore justify the theft: The Inquisition might have committed it.

LUCETTA. See, a bracelet of bowed[119] gold! These his sisters tied about his arm at parting. But well, for all this, I fear his being a stranger may make a noise and hinder our trade with them hereafter.

PHILIPPO. That's our security: He is not only a stranger to us, but to the county too. The common shore[120] into which he is descended, thou know'st, conducts him into another street, which this light will hinder him from ever finding again. He knows neither your name, nor that of the street where your house is; nay, nor the way to his own lodgings.

LUCETTA. And art thou not an unmerciful rogue, not to afford him one night for all this? I should not have been such a Jew.

PHILIPPO. Blame me not, Lucetta, to keep as much of thee as I can to myself. Come, that thought makes me wanton; let's to bed.—Sancho, lock up these.

This is the fleece which fools do bear,
Designed for witty men to shear.

(*Exeunt.*)

SCENE 4

(*The scene changes, and discovers Blunt creeping out of a common shore; his face, etc., all dirty.*)

BLUNT (*climbing up*). Oh, Lord, I am got out at last, and, which is a miracle, without a clue. And now to damning and cursing! But if that would ease me, where shall I begin? With my fortune, myself, or the quean[121] that cozened me! What a dog was I to believe in woman! Oh, coxcomb! Ignorant conceited coxcomb! To fancy she could be enamored with my person! At first sight enamored! Oh, I'm a cursed puppy! 'Tis plain, fool was writ upon my forehead! She perceived it; saw the Essex calf there. For what allurements could there be in this countenance, which I can endure because I'm acquainted with it. Oh dull, silly dog, to be thus soothed into a cozening! Had I been drunk, I might fondly have credited the young queen; but as I was in my right wits to be thus cheated, confirms it: I am a dull believing English country fop. But my comrades! Death and the devil, there's the worst of all! Then a ballad will be sung tomorrow on the Prado,[122] to a lousy tune of the enchanted squire and the annihilated damsel. But Fred—that rogue—and the colonel will abuse me beyond all Christian patience. Had she left me my clothes, I have a bill of exchange at home would have

---

[115]**An** if   [116]**egad** a mild oath   [117]**old queen Bess** Queen Elizabeth I (reigned 1558–1603)

[117]**eighty-eight** 1588, the year the English defeated the Spanish   [119]**bowed** curved(?) braided(?)   [120]**common shore** sewer   [121]**quean** harlot   [122]**Prado** promenade

saved my credit. But now all hope is taken from me. Well, I'll home, if I can find the way, with this consolation: that I am not the first kind believing coxcomb; but there are, gallants, many such good natures amongst ye.

> And though you've better arts to hid your follies,
> 'Adsheartlikins, y'are all as errant cullies.[123]

(Exit.)

SCENE 5

(Scene: the garden in the night. Enter Florinda in an undress,[124] with a key and a little box.)

FLORINDA. Well, thus far I'm in my way to happiness. I have got myself free from Callis; my brother too, I find by yonder light, is got into his cabinet,[125] and thinks not of me; I have by good fortune got the key of the garden back door. I'll open it to prevent Belvile's knocking: A little noise will now alarm my brother. Now am I as fearful as a young thief. *(Unlocks the door.)* Hark! What noise is that? Oh, 'twas the wind that played amongst the boughs. Belvile stays long, methinks; it's time. Stay, for fear of a surprise, I'll hide these jewels in yonder jasmine.

(She goes to lay down the box.)

(Enter Willmore, drunk.)

WILLMORE. What the devil is become of these fellows Belvile and Frederick? They promised to stay at the next corner for me, but who the devil knows the corner of a full moon? Now, whereabouts am I? Ha, what have we here? A garden! A very convenient place to sleep in. Ha! What has God sent us here? A female! By this light, a woman! I'm a dog if it be not a very wench!

FLORINDA. He's come! Ha! Who's there?

WILLMORE. Sweet soul, let me salute thy shoestring.

FLORINDA [*aside*]. 'Tis not my Belvile. Good heavens, I know him not!—Who are you, and from whence come you?

WILLMORE. Prithee, prithee, child, not so many hard questions! Let it suffice I am here, child. Come, come kiss me.

FLORINDA. Good gods! What luck is mine?

WILLMORE. Only good luck, child, parlous[126] good luck. Come hither.—'Tis a delicate shining wench. By this hand, she's perfumed, and smells like any nosegay.— Prithee, dear soul, let's not play the fool and lose time— precious time. For as God shall save me, I'm as honest a fellow as breathes, though I'm a little disguised[127] at present. Come, I say. Why, thou mayest be free with me: I'll

be very secret. I'll not boast who 'twas obliged me, not I; for hang me if I know thy name.

FLORINDA. Heavens! What a filthy beast is this!

WILLMORE. I am so, and thou ought'st the sooner to lie with me for that reason. For look you, child, there will be no sin in't, because 'twas neither designed nor premeditated: 'Tis pure accident on both sides. That's a certain thing now. Indeed, should I make love to you, and you vow fidelity, and swear and lie till you believed and yielded— that were to make it willful fornication, the crying sin of the nation. Thou art, therefore, as thou art a good Christian, obliged in conscience to deny me nothing. Now, come be kind without any more idle prating.

FLORINDA. Oh, I am ruined! Wicked man, unhand me!

WILLMORE. Wicked? Egad, child, a judge, were he young and vigorous, and saw those eyes of thine, would know 'twas they gave the first blow, the first provocation. Come, prithee let's lose no time, I say. This is a fine convenient place.

FLORINDA. Sir, let me go, I conjure[128] you, or I'll call out.

WILLMORE. Ay, ay, you were best to call witness to see how finely you treat me. Do!

FLORINDA. I'll cry murder, rape, or anything, if you do not instantly let me go!

WILLMORE. A rape? Come, come, you lie, you baggage, you lie. What! I'll warrant you would fain have the world believe now that you are not so forward as I. No, not you. Why at this time of night was your cobweb door set open, dear spider, but to catch flies? Ha! Come, or I shall be damnably angry. Why, what a coil[129] is here!

FLORINDA. Sir, can you think—

WILLMORE. That you would do't for nothing? Oh, oh, I find what you would be at. Look here, here's a pistole[130] for you. Here's a work indeed! Here, take it, I say!

FLORINDA. For heaven's sake, sir, as you're a gentleman—

WILLMORE. So now, now, she would be wheedling me for more! What, you will not take it then? You are resolved you will not? Come, come, take it or I'll put it up again, for look ye, I never give more. Why, how now, mistress, are you so high i'th' mouth[131] a pistole won't down with you? Ha! Why, what a work's here! In good time! Come, no struggling to be gone. But an y'are good at a dumb wrestle, I'm for ye. Look ye. I'm for ye.

(She struggles with him.)

(Enter Belvile and Frederick.)

BELVILE. The door is open. A pox of this mad fellow! I'm angry that we've lost him; I durst have sworn he had followed us.

FREDERICK. But you were so hasty, colonel, to be gone.

FLORINDA. Help! Help! Murder! Help! Oh, I am ruined!

---

[123]**errant cullies** arrant fools   [124]**undress** informal clothing   [125]**cabinet** private room   [126]**parlous** excessively, with pun on perilous   [127]**disguised** drunk

[128]**conjure** implore   [129]**coil** disturbance   [130]**pistole** gold coin   [131]**high i'th' mouth** stuck up

BELVILE. Ha! Sure that's Florinda's voice. (*Comes up to them.*) A man!—Villain, let go that lady!

(*A noise; Willmore turns and draws: Frederick interposes.*)

FLORINDA. Belvile! Heavens! My brother too is coming, and 'twill be impossible to escape. Belvile, I conjure you to walk under my chamber window, from whence I'll give you some instructions what to do. This rude man has undone us. (*Exit.*)

WILLMORE. Belvile!

(*Enter Pedro, Stephano, and other servants, with lights.*)

PEDRO. I'm betrayed! Run, Stephano, and see if Florinda be safe.

(*Exit Stephano.*)

(*They fight, and Pedro's party beats 'em out.*)

—So, whoe'er they be, all is not well. I'll to Florinda's chamber.

(*Going out, meets Stephano.*)

STEPHANO. You need not, sir: The poor lady's fast asleep, and thinks no harm. I would not awake her, sir, for fear of frighting her with your danger.

PEDRO. I'm glad she's there.—Rascals, how came the garden door open?

STEPHANO. That question comes too late, sir. Some of my fellow servants masquerading, I'll warrant.

PEDRO. Masquerading! A lewd custom to debauch our youth! There's something more in this than I imagine.

(*Exeunt.*)

SCENE 6

(*Scene changes to the street. Enter Belvile in rage, Frederick holding him, Willmore melancholy.*)

WILLMORE. Why, how the devil should I know Florinda?

BELVILE. Ah, plague of your ignorance! If it had not been Florinda, must you be a beast? A brute? A senseless swine?

WILLMORE. Well, sir, you see I am endued[132] with patience: I can bear. Though egad, y'are very free with me, methink. I was in good hopes the quarrel would have been on my side, for so uncivilly interrupting me.

BEVILE. Peace, brute, whilst thou'rt safe. Oh, I'm distracted!

WILLMORE. Nay, nay, I'm an unlucky dog, that's certain.

BELVILE. Ah, curse upon the star that ruled my birth, or whatsoever other influence that makes me still so wretched.

WILLMORE. Thou break'st my heart with these complaints.

There is no star in fault, no influence but sack, the cursed sack I drunk.

FREDERICK. Why, how the devil came you so drunk?

WILLMORE. Why, how the devil came you so sober?

BELVILE. A curse upon his thin skull, he was always beforehand that way.

FREDERICK. Prithee, dear colonel, forgive him; he's sorry for his fault.

BELVILE. He's always so after he has done a mischief. A plague on all such brutes!

WILLMORE. By this light, I took her for an errant harlot.

BELVILE. Damn your debauched opinion! Tell me, sot, hadst thou so much sense and light about thee to distinguish her woman, and couldst not see something about her face and person to strike an awful reverence into thy soul?

WILLMORE. Faith no, I considered her as mere a woman as I could wish.

BELVILE. 'Sdeath, I have no patience. Draw, or I'll kill you!

WILLMORE. Let that alone till tomorrow, and if I set not all right again, use your pleasure.

BELVILE. Tomorrow! Damn it.
The spiteful light will lead me to no happiness.
Tomorrow is Antonio's, and perhaps
Guides him to my undoing. Oh, that I could meet
This rival, this powerful fortunate!

WILLMORE. What then?

BELVILE. Let thy own reason, or my rage, instruct thee.

WILLMORE. I shall be finely informed then, no doubt. Hear me, colonel, hear me; show me the man and I'll do his business.

BELVILE. I know him no more than thou, or if I did I should not need thy aid.

WILLMORE. This you say is Angellica's house; I promised the kind baggage to lie with her tonight.

(*Offers to go in.*)

(*Enter Antonio and his Page. Antonio knocks on the hilt of's sword.*)

ANTONIO. You paid the thousand crowns I directed?

PAGE. To the lady's old woman, sir, I did.

WILLMORE. Who the devil have we here?

BELVILE. I'll now plant myself under Florinda's window, and if I find no comfort there, I'll die.

(*Exeunt Belvile and Frederick.*)

(*Enter Moretta.*)

MORETTA. Page?

PAGE. Here's my lord.

WILLMORE. How is this? A picaroon[133] going to board my frigate?—Here's one chase gun for you!

(*Drawing his sword, justles Antonio, who turns and draws. They fight; Antonio falls.*)

---

[132]**endued** endowed

[133]**picaroon** pirate

MORETTA. Oh, bless us! We're all undone!

(*Runs in and shuts the door.*)

PAGE. Help! Murder!

(*Belvile returns at the noise of fighting.*)

BELVILE. Ha! The mad rogue's engaged in some unlucky adventure again.

(*Enter two or three Masqueraders.*)

MASQUERADER. Ha! A man killed!

WILLMORE. How, a man killed? Then I'll go home to sleep.

(*Puts up and reels out. Exeunt Masqueraders another way.*)

BELVILE. Who should it be? Pray heaven the rogue is safe, for all my quarrel to him.

(*As Belvile is groping about, enter an Officer and six Soldiers.*)

SOLDIER. Who's there?

OFFICER. So, here's one dispatched. Secure the murderer.

BELVILE. Do not mistake my charity for murder! I came to his assistance!

(*Soldiers seize on Belvile.*)

OFFICER. That shall be tried, sir. St. Jago! Swords drawn in the Carnival time!

(*Goes to Antonio.*)

ANTONIO. Thy hand, prithee.

OFFICER. Ha! Don Antonio! Look well to the villain there.—How is it, sir?

ANTONIO. I'm hurt.

BELVILE. Has my humanity made me a criminal?

OFFICER. Away with him!

BELVILE. What a curst chance is this!

(*Exeunt soldiers with Belvile.*)

ANTONIO [*aside*]. This is the man that has set upon me twice.—(*To the officer.*) Carry him to my apartment till you have further orders from me.

(*Exit Antonio, led.*)

ACT 4

SCENE 1

(*A fine room. Discovers Belvile as by dark alone.*)

BELVILE. When shall I be weary of railing on fortune, who is resolved never to turn with smiles upon me? Two such defeats in one night none but the devil and that mad rogue could have contrived to have plagued me with. I am here a prisoner. But where, heaven knows. And if there be murder done, I can soon decide the fate of a stranger in a nation without mercy. Yet this is nothing to the torture my soul bows with when I think of losing my fair, my dear Florinda. Hark, my door opens. A light! A man, and seems of quality. Armed, too! Now shall I die like a dog, without defense.

(*Enter Antonio in a nightgown, with a light; his arm in a scarf, and a sword under his arm. He sets the candle on the table.*)

ANTONIO. Sir, I come to know what injuries I have done you, that could provoke you to so mean an action as to attack me basely without allowing time for my defense?

BELVILE. Sir, for a man in my circumstances to plead innocence would look like fear. But view me well, and you will find no marks of coward on me, nor anything that betrays that brutality you accuse me with.

ANTONIO. In vain, sir, you impose upon my sense. You are not only he who drew on me last night, but yesterday before the same house, that of Angellica. Yet there is something in your face and mien[134] that makes me wish I were mistaken.

BELVILE. I own I fought today in the defense of a friend of mine with whom you, if you're the same, and your party were first engaged. Perhaps you think this crime enough to kill me; but if you do, I cannot fear you'll do it basely.

ANTONIO. No sir, I'll make you fit for a defense with this. (*Gives him the sword.*)

BELVILE. This gallantry surprises me, nor know I how to use this present, sir, against a man so brave.

ANTONIO. You shall not need. For know, I come to snatch you from a danger that is decreed against you: perhaps your life, or long imprisonment. And 'twas with so much courage you offended, I cannot see you punished.

BELVILE. How shall I pay this generosity?

ANTONIO. It had been safer to have killed another than have attempted me. To show your danger, sir, I'll let you know my quality:[135] And 'tis the Viceroy's son whom you have wounded.

BELVILE. The Viceroy's son!—(*Aside.*) Death and confusion! Was this plague reserved to complete all the rest? Obliged by[136] him, the man of all the world I would destroy!

ANTONIO. You seem disordered, sir.

BELVILE. Yes, trust me, I am, and 'tis with pain that man receives such bounties who wants the power to pay 'em back again.

ANTONIO. To gallant spirits 'tis indeed uneasy, but you may quickly overpay me, sir.

BELVILE (*aside*). Then I am well. Kind heaven, but set us even, that I may fight with him and keep my honor safe.—Oh, I'm impatient, sir, to be discounting the mighty debt I owe you. Command me quickly.

---

[134]**mien** manner   [135]**quality** rank   [136]**Obliged by** favored by

ANTONIO. I have a quarrel with a rival, sir, about the maid we love.

BELVILE (*aside*). Death 'tis Florinda he means! That thought destroys my reason, and I shall kill him.

ANTONIO. My rival, sir, is one has all the virtues man can boast of—

BELVILE (*aside*). Death, who should this be?

ANTONIO. He challenged me to meet him on the Molo[137] as soon as day appeared, but last night's quarrel has made my arm unfit to guide a sword.

BELVILE. I apprehend you, sir. You'd have to kill the man that lays a claim to the maid you speak of. I'll do't. I'll fly to do't!

ANTONIO. Sir, do you know her?

BELVILE. No, sir, but 'tis enough she is admired by you.

ANTONIO. Sir, I shall rob you of the glory on't, for you must fight under my name and dress.

BELVILE. That opinion must be strangely obliging that makes you think I can personate the brave Antonio, whom I can but strive to imitate.

ANTONIO. You say too much to my advantage. Come, sir, the day appears that calls you forth. Within, sir, is the habit.[138]

(*Exit Antonio.*)

BELVILE. Fantastic fortune, thou deceitful light,
That cheats the wearied traveler by night,
Though on a precipice each step you tread,
I am resolved to follow where you lead.

(*Exit.*)

SCENE 2

(*The Molo. Enter Florinda and Callis in masks, with Stephano.*)

FLORINDA (*aside*). I'm dying with my fears: Belvile's not coming as I expected under my window makes me believe that all those fears are true.—Canst thou not tell with whom my brother fights?

STEPHANO. No, madam, they were both in masquerade. I was by when they challenged one another, and they had decided the quarrel then, but were prevented by some cavaliers; which made 'em put it off till now. But I am sure 'tis about you they fight.

FLORINDA (*aside*). Nay, then, 'tis with Belvile, for what other lover have I that dares fight for me except Antonio, and he is too much in favor with my brother. If it be he, for whom shall I direct my prayers to heaven?

STEPHANO. Madam, I must leave you, for if my master see me, I shall be hanged for being your conductor. I escaped

narrowly for the excuse I made for you last night i'th' garden.

FLORINDA. I'll reward thee for't. Prithee, no more.

(*Exit Stephano.*)

(*Enter Don Pedro in his masking habit.*)

PEDRO. Antonio's late today; the place will fill, and we may be prevented.[139]

(*Walks about.*)

FLORINDA (*aside*). Antonio? Sure I heard amiss.

PEDRO.
But who will not excuse a happy lover
When soft fair arms confine the yielding neck.
And the kind whisper languishingly breathes
"Must you be gone so soon?"
Sure I had dwelt forever on her bosom—
But stay, he's here.

(*Enter Belvile dressed in Antonio's clothes.*)

FLORINDA (*aside*). 'Tis not Belvile; half my fears are vanished.

PEDRO. Antonio!

BELVILE (*aside*). This must be he.—You're early, sir; I do not use to be outdone this way.

PEDRO. The wretched, sir, are watchful, and 'tis enough You're the advantage of me in Angellica.

BELVILE (*aside*). Angellica! Or[140] I've mistook my man, or else Antonio! Can he forget his interest in Florinda And fight for common prize?

PEDRO.
Come, sir, you know our terms.

BELVILE (*aside*).
By heaven, not I.
No talking; I am ready, sir.

(*Offers to fight; Florinda runs in.*)

FLORINDA (*to Belvile*).
Oh, hold! Whoe'er you be, I do conjure you hold!
If you strike here, I die!

PEDRO. Florinda!

BELVILE. Florinda imploring for my rival!

PEDRO.
Away; this kindness is unseasonable.

(*Puts her by; they fight; she runs in just as Belvile disarms Pedro.*)

FLORINDA.
Who are you, sir, that dares deny my prayers?

BELVILE.
Thy prayers destroy him; if thou wouldst preserve him,
Do that thou'rt unacquainted with, and curse him.

(*She holds him.*)

---

[137]**Molo** wharf　　　[138]**habit** Antonio's clothing　　　[139]**we may be prevented** we may be too late　　　[140]**Or** either

FLORINDA.
By all you hold most dear, by her you love,
I do conjure you, touch him not.
BELVILE.
By her I love?
See, I obey, and at your feet resign
The useless trophy of my victory.

(*Lays his sword at her feet.*)

PEDRO. Antonio, you've done enough to prove you love Florinda.
BELVILE. Love Florinda! Does heaven love adoration, prayer, or penitence? Love her? Here, sir, your sword again.

(*Snatches up the sword and gives it to him.*)

Upon this truth I'll fight my life away.
PEDRO. No, you've redeemed my sister, and my friendship.

(*He gives him Florinda, and pulls off his vizard to show his face, and puts it on again.*)

BELVILE. Don Pedro!
PEDRO.
Can you resign your claims to other women,
And give your heart entirely to Florinda?
BELVILE.
Entire, as dying saints' confessions are!
I can delay my happiness no longer:
This minute let me make Florinda mine.
PEDRO.
This minute let it be. No time so proper:
This night my father will arrive from Rome,
And possibly may hinder what we purpose.
FLORINDA. O, heavens! This minute?

(*Enter Masqueraders and pass over.*)

BELVILE. Oh, do not ruin me!
PEDRO. The place begins to fill, and that we may not be observed, do you walk off to St. Peter's church, where I will meet you and conclude your happiness.
BELVILE. I'll meet you there.—(*Aside.*) If there be no more saints' churches in Naples.
FLORINDA.
Oh, stay, sir, and recall your hasty doom!
Alas, I have not yet prepared my heart
To entertain so strange a guest.
PEDRO.
Away; this silly modesty is assumed too late.
BELVILE.
Heaven, madam, what do you do?
FLORINDA.
Do? Despise the man that lays a tyrant's claim
To what he ought to conquer by submission.
BELVILE.
You do not know me. Move a little this way.

(*Draws her aside.*)

FLORINDA.
Yes, you may force me even to the altar,
But not the holy man that offers there
Shall force me to be thine.

(*Pedro talks to Callis this while.*)

BELVILE.
Oh, do not lose so blest an opportunity!

(*Pulls off his vizard.*)

See, 'tis your Belvile, not Antonio,
Whom your mistaken scorn and anger ruins.
FLORINDA. Belvile!
Where was my soul it could not meet thy voice,
And take this knowledge in.

(*As they are talking, enter Willmore, finely dressed, and Frederick.*)

WILLMORE. No intelligence? No news of Belvile yet? Well, I am the most unlucky rascal in nature. Ha! Am I deceived, or is it he? Look, Fred! 'Tis he, my dear Belvile!

(*Runs and embraces him; Belvile's vizard falls out on's hand.*)

BELVILE. Hell and confusion seize thee!
PEDRO. Ha! Belvile! I beg your pardon, sir.

(*Takes Florinda from him.*)

BELVILE.
Nay, touch her not. She's mine by conquest, sir;
I won her by my sword.
WILLMORE.
Didst thou so? And egad, child, we'll keep her by the sword.

(*Draws on Pedro; Belvile goes between.*)

BELVILE. Stand off!
Thou'rt so profanely lewd, so curst by heaven,
All quarrels thou espousest must be fatal.
WILLMORE.
Nay, an you be so hot, my valor's coy,
And shall be courted when you want it next.

(*Puts up his sword.*)

BELVILE (*to Pedro*).
You know I ought to claim a victor's right,
But you're the brother to divine Florinda,
To whom I'm such a slave. To purchase her
I durst not hurt the man she holds so dear.
PEDRO.
Twas by Antonio's, not by Belvile's sword
This question should have been decided, sir.
I must confess much to your bravery's due,
Both now and when I met you last in arms;
But I am nicely punctual in my word,
As men of honor ought, and beg your pardon:
For this mistake another time shall clear.

(*Aside to Florinda as they are going out.*)

—This was some plot between you and Belvile,
But I'll prevent you.

> [*Exeunt Pedro and Florinda.*]

(*Belvile looks after her and begins to walk up and down in rage.*)

WILLMORE. Do not be modest now and lose the woman. But if we shall fetch her back so—

BELVILE. Do not speak to me!

WILLMORE. Not speak to you? Egad, I'll speak to you, and will be answered, too.

BELVILE. Will you, sir?

WILLMORE. I know I've done some mischief, but I'm so dull a puppy that I'm the son of a whore if I know how or where. Prithee inform my understanding.

BELVILE. Leave me, I say, and leave me instantly!

WILLMORE. I will not leave you in this humor, nor till I know my crime.

BELVILE. Death, I'll tell you, sir—

(*Draws and runs at Willmore; he runs out, Belvile after him; Frederick interposes.*)
(*Enter Angellica, Moretta, and Sebastian.*)

ANGELLICA. Ha! Sebastian, is that not Willmore? Haste! haste and bring him back.

> [*Exit Sebastian.*]

FREDERICK [*aside*]. The colonel's mad: I never saw him thus before. I'll after 'em lest he do some mischief, for I am sure Willmore will not draw on him.

> (*Exit.*)

ANGELLICA.
I am all rage! My first desires defeated!
For one for aught he knows that no
Other merit than her quality,
Her being Don Pedro's sister. He loves her!
I know 'tis so. Dull, dull, insensible,
He will not see me now, though oft invited,
And broke his word last night. False perjured man!
He that but yesterday fought for my favors,
And would have made his life a sacrifice
To've gained one night with me,
Must now be hired and courted to my arms.

MORETTA. I told you what would come on't, but Moretta's an old doting fool. Why did you give him five hundred crowns, but to set himself out for other lovers? You should have kept him poor if you had meant to have had any good from him.

ANGELLICA.
Oh, name not such mean trifles! Had I given
Him all my youth has earned from sin,
I had not lost a thought nor sign upon't.
But I have given him my eternal rest,
My whole repose, my future joys, my heart!
My virgin heart, Moretta! Oh, 'tis gone!

MORETTA.
Curse on him, here he comes. How fine she has made him, too.

(*Enter Willmore and Sebastian; Angellica turns and walks away.*)

WILLMORE.
How now, turned shadow?
Fly when I pursue, and follow when I fly? (*Sings.*)
      Stay, gentle shadow of my dove,
            And tell me ere I go,
      Whether the substance may not prove
            A fleeting thing like you.

(*As she turns she looks on him.*)

There's a soft kind look remaining yet.

ANGELLICA. Well, sir, you may be gay: All happiness, all joys pursue you still. Fortune's your slave, and gives you every hour choice of new hearts and beauties, till you are cloyed[141] with the repeated bliss which others vainly languish for. But know, false man, that I shall be revenged.

> (*Turns away in rage.*)

WILLMORE. So, gad, there are of those faint-hearted lovers, whom such a sharp lesson next their hearts would make as impotent as fourscore.[142] Pox o' this whining; my business is to laugh and love. A pox on't, I hate your sullen lover: A man shall lose as much time to put you in humor now as would serve to gain a new woman.

ANGELLICA.
I scorn to cool that fire I cannot raise.
Or do the drudgery of your virtuous mistress.

WILLMORE. A virtuous mistress? Death, what a thing thou has found out for me! Why, what the devil should I do with a virtuous woman, a sort of ill-natured creatures that take a pride to torment a lover. Virtue is but an infirmity in woman, a disease that renders even the handsome ungrateful; whilst the ill-favored, for want of solicitations and address, only fancy themselves so. I have lain with a woman of quality who has all the while been railing at whores.

ANGELLICA.
I will not answer for your mistress's virtue,
Though she be young enough to know no guilt;
And I could wish you would persuade my heart
'Twas the two hundred thousand crowns you courted.

WILLMORE. Two hundred thousand crowns! What story's this? What trick? What woman, ha?

ANGELLICA. How strange you make it. Have you forgot the creature you entertained on the Piazzo last night?

WILLMORE (*aside*). Ha! My gypsy worth two hundred thou-

---

[141]**cloyed** sickened   [142]**as fourscore** as an eighty-year old

sand crowns! Oh, how I long to be with her! Pox, I knew she was of quality.

ANGELLICA.

False man! I see my ruin in thy face.
How many vows you breathed upon my bosom
Never to be unjust. Have you forgot so soon?

WILLMORE. Faith, no; I was just coming to repeat 'em. But here's a humor indeed would make a man a saint.— (*Aside.*) Would she would be angry enough to leave me, and command me not to wait on her.

(*Enter Hellena dressed in man's clothes.*)

HELLENA. This must be Angellica: I know it by her mumping[143] matron here. Ay, ay, 'tis she. My mad captain's with her, too, for all his swearing. How this unconstant humor makes me love them!—Pray, good grave gentlewoman, is not this Angellica?

MORETTA. My too young sir, it is.—[*Aside.*] I hope 'tis one from Don Antonio.   (*Goes to Angellica.*)

HELLENA (*aside*). Well, something I'll do to vex him for this.

ANGELLICA. I will not speak with him. Am I in humor to receive a lover?

WILLMORE. Not speak with him? Why, I'll be gone, and wait your idler minutes. Can I show less obedience to the thing I love so fondly?

(*Offers to go.*)

ANGELLICA.

A fine excuse this! Stay—

WILLMORE.

And hinder your advantage? Should I repay your bounties so ungratefully?

ANGELLICA [*to Hellena*].

Come hither, boy.—[*To Willmore.*] That I may let you see
How much above the advantages you name
I prize one minute's joy with you.

WILLMORE (*impatient to be gone*). Oh, you destroy me with this endearment.—[*Aside.*] Death, how shall I get away?—Madam, 'twill not be fit I should be seen with you. Besides, it will not be convenient. And I've a friend—that's dangerously sick.

ANGELLICA. I see you're impatient. Yet you shall stay.

WILLMORE (*aside*). And miss my assignation with my gypsy. (*Walks about impatiently; Moretta brings Hellena, who addresses herself to Angellica.*)

HELLENA. Madam.

You'll hardly pardon my intrusion
When you shall know my business,
And I'm too young to tell my tale with art;
But there must be a wondrous store of goodness
Where so much beauty dwells.

ANGELLICA.

A pretty advocate, whoever sent thee.

Prithee proceed. (*To Willmore, who is stealing off.*)—Nay, sir, you shall not go.

WILLMORE (*aside*). Then I shall lose my dear gypsy forever. Pox on't, she stays me out of spite.

HELLENA.

I am related to a lady, madam.
Young, rich, and nobly born, but has the fate
To be in love with a young English gentleman.
Strangely she loves him, at first sight she loved him,
But did adore him when she heard him speak;
For he, she said, had charms in every word
That failed not to surprise, to wound and conquer.

WILLMORE (*aside*). Ha! Egad, I hope this concerns me.

ANGELLICA (*aside*).

'Tis my false man he means. Would he were gone:
This praise will raise his pride, and ruine me. (*To Willmore.*)—Well,
Since you are so impatient to be gone,
I will release you, sir.

WILLMORE (*aside*). Nay, then I'm sure 'twas me he spoke of: This cannot be the effects of kindness in her.—No, Madam, I've considered better on't, and will not give you cause of jealousy.

ANGELLICA. But sir, I've business that—

WILLMORE. This shall not do; I know 'tis but to try me.

ANGELLICA. Well, to your story, boy.—(*Aside*). Though 'twill undo me.

HELLENA.

With this addition to his other beauties
He won her unresisting tender heart.
He vowed, and sighed, and swore he loved her dearly;
And she believed the cunning flatterer,
And thought herself the happiest maid alive.
Today was the appointed time by both
To consummate their bliss:
The virgin, altar, and the priest were dressed;
And whilst she languished for th'expected bridegroom,
She heard he paid his broken vows to you.

WILLMORE (*aside*). So, this is some dear rogue that's in love with me, and this way lets me know it. Or, if it be not me, he means someone whose place I may supply.

ANGELLICA. Now I perceive
The cause of thy impatience to be gone,
And all the business of this glorious dress.

WILLMORE. Damn the young prater; I know not what he means.

HELLENA. Madam,
In your fair eyes I read too much concern
To tell my further business.

ANGELLICA.

Prithee, sweet youth, talk on: Thou mayst perhaps
Raise here a storm that may undo my passion,
And then I'll grant thee anything.

HELLENA.

Madam, 'tis to entreat you (oh unreasonable)

---

[143]**mumping** moping

You would not see this stranger.
For if you do, she vows you are undone;
Though nature never made a man so excellent,
And sure he 'ad been a god, but for inconstancy.

WILLMORE (*aside*). Ah, rogue, how finely he's instructed! 'Tis plain, some woman that has seen me *en passant*.[144]

ANGELLICA. Oh, I shall burst with jealousy! Do you know the man you speak of?

HELLENA. Yes, madam, he used to be in buff and scarlet.

ANGELLICA (*to Willmore*). Thou false as hell, what canst thou say to this?

WILLMORE. By heaven—

ANGELLICA. Hold, do not damn thyself—

HELLENA. Nor hope to be believed.

(*He walks about; they follow.*)

ANGELLICA. Oh purjured man!
Is't thus you pay my generous passion back?

HELLENA. Why would you, sir, abuse my lady's faith?

ANGELLICA. And use me so unhumanely.

HELLENA. A maid so young, so innocent—

WILLMORE. Ah, young devil!

ANGELLICA. Dost thou not know thy life is in my power?

HELLENA. Or think my lady cannot be revenged?

WILLMORE (*aside*). So, so, the storm comes finely on.

ANGELLICA.
Now thou art silent: Guilt has struck thee dumb.
Oh, hadst thou still been so, I'd lived in safety.
                              (*She turns away and weeps.*)

WILLMORE (*aside to Hellena*). Sweetheart, the lady's name and house—quickly! I'm impatient to be with her.

(*Looks toward Angellica to watch her turning, and as she comes towards them he meets her.*)

HELLENA (*aside*). So, now is he for another woman.

WILLMORE.
The impudent'st young thing in nature:
I cannot persuade him out of his error, madam.

ANGELLICA.
I know he's in the right; yet thou'st a tongue
That would persuade him to deny his faith.
                              (*In rage walks away.*)

WILLMORE (*said softly to Hellena*). Her name, her name, dear boy!

HELLENA. Have you forgot it, sir?

WILLMORE (*aside*). Oh, I perceive it's not to know I am a stranger to his lady.—Yes, yes, I do know, but I have forgot the—

(*Angellica turns.*)

By heaven, such early confidence I never saw.

ANGELLICA.
Did I not charge you with this mistress, sir?

Which you denied, though I beheld your perjury.
This little generosity of thine has rendered back my heart.   (*Walks away.*)

WILLMORE (*to Hellena*). So, you have made sweet work here, my little mischief. Look your lady be kind and good-natured now, or I shall have but a cursed bargain on't.

(*Angellica turns toward them.*)

—The rogue's bred up to mischief;
Art thou so great a fool to credit him?

ANGELLICA.
Yes, I do, and you in vain impose upon me.
Come hither, boy. Is not this he you spake of?

HELLENA. I think it is. I cannot swear, but I vow he has just such another lying lover's look.

(*Hellena looks in his face; he gazes on her.*)

WILLMORE (*aside*).
Ha! Do I not know that face?
By heaven, my little gypsy! What a dull dog was I:
Had I but looked that way I'd known her.
Are all my hopes of a new woman banished?—
Egad, if I do not fit thee for this, hang me.—
[*To Angellica.*] Madam, I have found out the plot.

HELLENA [*aside*]. Oh lord, what does he say? Am I discovered now?

WILLMORE. Do you see this young spark here?

HELLENA [*aside*]. He'll tell her who I am.

WILLMORE. Who do you think this is?

HELLENA [*aside*]. Ay, ay, he does know me.—
Nay, dear captain, I am undone if you discover me.

WILLMORE. Nay, nay, no cogging;[145] she shall know what a precious mistress I have.

HELLENA. Will you be such a devil?

WILLMORE. Nay, nay, I'll teach you to spoil sport you will not make.—This small ambassador comes not from a person of quality, as you imagine and he says, but from a very errant gypsy: the talking'st, prating'st, canting'st little animal thou ever saw'st.

ANGELLICA. What news you tell me, that's the thing I mean.

HELLENA (*aside*). Would I were well off the place! If ever I go a-captain-hunting again—

WILLMORE. Mean that thing? That gypsy thing? Thou mayst as well be jealous of thy monkey or parrot as of her. A German motion[146] were worth a dozen of her, and a dream were a better enjoyment—a creature of a constitution fitter for heaven than man.

HELLENA (*aside*). Though I'm sure he lies, yet this vexes me.

ANGELLICA. You are mistaken: she's a Spanish woman made up of no such dull materials.

WILLMORE. Materials? Egad, and she be made of any that will either dispense or admit of love, I'll be bound to continence.

---

[144]**en passant** in passing

[145]**cogging** fawning   [146]**motion** puppet show

HELLENA (*aside to him*). Unreasonable man, do you think so?

WILLMORE. You may return, my little brazen head, and tell your lady, that till she be handsome enough to be beloved, or I dull enough to be religious, there will be small hopes of me.

ANGELLICA. Did you not promise, then, to marry her?

WILLMORE. Not I, by heaven.

ANGELLICA. You cannot undeceive my fears and torments, till you have vowed you will not marry her.

HELLENA (*aside*). If he swears that, he'll be revenged on me indeed for all my rogueries.

ANGELLICA. I know what arguments you'll bring against me: fortune and honor.

WILLMORE. Honor! I tell you, I hate it in your sex; and those that fancy themselves possessed of that foppery are the most impertinently troublesome of all womankind, and will transgress nine commandments to keep one. And to satisfy your jealousy, I swear—

HELLENA (*aside to him*). Oh, no swearing, dear captain.

WILLMORE. If it were possible, I should ever be inclined to marry, it should be some kind young sinner: one that has generosity enough to give a favor handsomely to one that can ask it discreetly, one that has wit enough to manage an intrigue of love. Oh, how civil such a wench is to a man that does her the honor to marry her.

ANGELLICA. By heaven, there's no faith in anything he says.

(*Enter Sebastian.*)

SEBASTIAN. Madam, Don Antonio—

ANGELLICA. Come hither.

HELLENA [*aside*]. Ha! Antonio! He may be coming hither, and he'll certainly discover me. I'll therefore retire without a ceremony.

(*Exit Hellena.*)

ANGELLICA. I'll see him. Get my coach ready.

SEBASTIAN. It waits you, madam.

WILLMORE [*aside*]. This is lucky.—What, madam, now I may be gone and leave you to the enjoyment of my rival?

ANGELLICA.
Dull man, that canst not see how ill, how poor,
That false dissimulation looks. Be gone,
And never let me see thy cozening face again,
Lest I relapse and kill thee.

WILLMORE. Yes, you can spare me now. Farewell, till you're in better humor.—[*Aside.*] I'm glad of this release.
Now for my gypsy:
For through to worse we change, yet still we find
New joys, new charms, in a new miss that's kind.
(*Exit Willmore.*)

ANGELLICA.
He's gone, and in this ague[147] of my soul
The shivering fit returns.
Oh, with what willing haste he took his leave,

As if the longed-for minute were arrived
Of some blest assignation.
In vain I have consulted all my charms,
In vain this beauty prized, in vain believed
My eyes could kindle any lasting fires;
I had forgot my name, my infamy,
And the reproach that honor lays on those
That dare pretend a sober passion here.
Nice[148] reputation, though it leave behind
More virtues than inhabit where that dwells,
Yet that once gone, those virtues shine no more.
Then since I am not fit to be beloved,
I am resolved to think on a revenge
On him that soothed[149] me thus to my undoing.
(*Exeunt.*)

SCENE 3

(*A street. Enter Florinda and Valeria in habits different from what they have been seen in.*)

FLORINDA. We're happily escaped, and yet I tremble still.

VALERIA. A lover, and fear? Why, I am but half an one, and yet I have courage for any attempt. Would Hellena were here: I would fain have had her as deep in this mischief as we; she'll fare but ill else, I doubt.

FLORINDA. She pretended a visit to the Augustine nuns; but I believe some other design carried her out; pray heaven we light on her. Prithee, what didst do with Callis?

VALERIA. When I saw no reason would do good on her, I followed her into the wardrobe, and as she was looking for something in a great chest, I topped her in by the heels, snatched the key of the apartment where you were confined, locked her in, and left her bawling for help.

FLORINDA. 'Tis well you resolve to follow my fortunes, for thou darest never appear at home again after such an action.

VALERIA. That's according as the young stranger and I shall agree. But to our business. I delivered your note to Belvile when I got out under pretense of going to mass. I found him at his lodging, and believe me it came seasonably, for never was man in so desperate a condition. I told him of your resolution of making your escape today if your brother would be absent long enough to permit you; if not, to die rather than be Antonio's.

FLORINDA. Thou should'st have told him I was confined to my chamber upon my brother's suspicion that the business on the Molo was a plot laid between him and I.

VALERIA. I said all this, and told him your brother was now gone to his devotion; and he resolves to visit every church till he find him, and not only undeceive him in

[147]**ague** fever

[148]**nice** scrupulous   [149]**soothed** flattered

that, but caress him so as shall delay his return home.

FLORINDA. Oh heavens! He's here, and Belvile with him, too.

(*They put on their vizards.*)

(*Enter Don Pedro, Belvile, Willmore; Belvile and Don Pedro seeming in serious discourse.*)

VALERIA. Walk boldy by them, and I'll come at a distance, lest he suspect us.

(*She walks by them and looks back on them.*)

WILLMORE. Ha! A woman, and of excellent mien!

PEDRO. She throws a kind look back on you.

WILLMORE. Death, 'tis a likely wench, and that kind look shall not be cast away. I'll follow her.

BELVILE. Prithee do not.

WILLMORE. Do not? By heavens, to the antipodies,[150] with such an invitation.

(*She goes out, and Willmore follows her.*)

BELVILE. 'Tis a mad fellow for a wench.

(*Enter Frederick.*)

FREDERICK. Oh, colonel, such news!

BELVILE. Prithee what?

FREDERICK. News that will make you laugh in spite of fortune.

BELVILE. What, Blunt has had some damned trick put upon him? Cheated, banged, or clapped?[151]

FREDERICK. Cheated, sir, rarely cheated of all but his shirt and drawers; the unconscionable whore too turned him out before consummation, so that, traversing the streets at midnight, the watch found him in this *fresco* and conducted him home. By heaven, 'tis such a sight, and yet I durst as well been hanged as laughed at him or pity him: He beats all that do but ask him a question, and is in such an humor.

PEDRO. Who is't has met with this ill usage, sir?

BELVILE. A friend of ours whom you must see for mirth's sake.—(*Aside.*) I'll employ him to give Florinda time for an escape.

PEDRO. What is he?

BELVILE. A young countryman of ours, one that has been educated at so plentiful a rate he yet ne'er knew the want of money; and 'twill be a great jest to see how simply he'll look without it. For my part, I'll lend him none: And the rogue know not how to put on a borrowing face and ask first, I'll let him see how good 'tis to play our parts whilst I play his. Prithee, Fred, do you go home and keep him in that posture till we come.

(*Exeunt.*)

(*Enter Florinda from the farther end of the scene, looking behind her.*)

FLORINDA. I am followed still. Ha! My brother too advancing this way! Good heavens defend me from being seen by him! (*She goes off.*)

(*Enter Willmore, and after him Valeria, at a little distance.*)

WILLMORE. Ah, there she sails! She looks back as she were willing to be boarded; I'll warrant her prize.[152]

(*He goes out, Valeria following.*)

(*Enter Hellena, just as he goes out, with a page.*)

HELLENA. Ha, is not that my captain that has a woman in chase? 'Tis not Angellica.—Boy, follow those people at a distance, and bring me an account where they go in. (*Exit Page.*) —I'll find his haunts, and plague him everywhere. Ha! My brother!

(*Belvile, Willmore, Pedro cross the stage; Hellena runs off.*)

SCENE 4

(*Scene changes to another street. Enter Florinda.*)

FLORINDA.
What shall I do? My brother now pursues me.
Will no kind power protect me from his tyranny?
Ha! Here's a door open; I'll venture in, since nothing can be worse than to fall into his hands. My life and honor are at stake, and my necessity has no choice.

(*She goes in.*)

(*Enter Valeria, Hellena's Page peeping after Florinda.*)

PAGE. Here she went in; I shall remember this house.

(*Exit Boy.*)

VALERIA. This is Belvile's lodging; she's gone in as readily as if she knew it. Ha! Here's that mad fellow again; I dare not venture in. I'll watch my opportunity.

(*Goes aside.*)

(*Enter Willmore, gazing about him.*)

WILLMORE. I have lost her hereabouts. Pox on't, she must not 'scape me so.

(*Goes out.*)

SCENE 5

(*Scene changes to Blunt's chamber, discovers him sitting on a couch in his shirt and drawers, reading.*)

BLUNT. So, now my mind's a little at peace, since I have resolved revenge. A pox on this tailor, though, for not

---

[150]**antipodies** Antopodes, on the opposite side of the earth
[151]**clapped** (1) beaten; or (2) infected with a venereal disease

[152]**warrant her prize** consider her worthy of pursuing

bringing home the clothes I bespoke. And a pox of all poor cavaliers: A man can never keep a spare suit for 'em, and I shall have these rogues come in and find me naked, and then I'm undone. But I'm resolved to arm myself: The rascals shall not insult over me too much. (*Puts on an old rusty sword and buff belt.*) Now, how like a morris dancer[153] I am equipped! A fine ladylike whore to cheat me thus without affording me a kindness for my money! A pox light on her, I shall never be reconciled to the sex more; she has made me as faithless as a physician, as uncharitable as a churchman, and as ill-natured as a poet. Oh, how I'll use all womankind hereafter! What would I give to have one of 'em within my reach now! Any mortal thing in petticoats, kind fortune, send me, and I'll forgive thy last night's malice.—Here's a cursed book, too—a warning to all young travelers—that can instruct me how to prevent such mischiefs now 'tis too late. Well, 'tis a rare convenient thing to read a little now and then, as well as hawk and hunt.

(*Sits down again and reads.*)

(*Enter to him Florinda.*)

FLORINDA. This house is haunted, sure: 'Tis well furnished, and no living thing inhabits it. Ha! A man! Heavens, how he's attired! Sure 'tis some rope dancer, or fencing master. I tremble now for fear, and yet I must venture now to speak to him.—Sir, if I may not interrupt your meditations—

(*He starts up and gazes.*)

BLUNT. Ha. What's here? Are my wishes granted? And is not that a she creature? 'Adsheartlikins, 'tis.—What wretched thing art thou, ha?

FLORINDA. Charitable sir, you've told yourself already what I am: a very wretched maid, forced by a strange unlucky accident to seek a safety here, and must be ruined if you do not grant it.

BLUNT. Ruined! Is there any ruin so inevitable as that which now threatens thee? Dost thou know, miserable woman, into what den of mischiefs thou art fallen; what abyss of confusion, ha? Dost not see something in my looks that frights thy guilty soul, and makes thee wish to change that shape of woman for any humble animal, or devil? For those were safer for thee, and less mischievous.

FLORINDA. Alas, what mean you, sir? I must confess, your looks have something in 'em makes me fear, but I beseech you, as you seem a gentleman, pity a harmless virgin that takes your house for sanctuary.

BLUNT. Talk on, talk on; and weep, too, till my faith return. Do, flatter me out of my senses again. A harmless virgin with a pox; as much one as t'other, 'adsheartlikins. Why, what the devil, can I not be safe in my house for you, not in my chamber? Nay, not even being naked too cannot

secure me? This is an impudence greater than has invaded me yet. Come, no resistance.

(*Pulls her rudely.*)

FLORINDA. Dare you be so cruel?

BLUNT. Cruel? 'Adsheartlikins, as a galley slave, or a Spanish whore. Cruel? Yes, I will kiss and beat thee all over, kiss and see thee all over; thou shalt lie with me too, not that I care for the enjoyment, but to let thee see I have ta'en deliberated malice to thee, and will be revenged on one whore for the sins of another. I will smile and deceive thee; flatter thee, and beat thee; embrace thee and rob thee, as she did me; fawn on thee, and strip thee stark naked; then hang thee out at my window by the heels, with a paper of scurvy verses fastened to thy breast in praise of damnable women. Come, come, along.

FLORINDA. Alas, sir, must I be sacrificed for the crimes of the most infamous of my sex? I never understood the sins you name.

BLUNT. Do, persuade the fool you love him, or that one of you can be just or honest; tell me I was not an easy coxcomb, or any strange impossible tale: It will be believed sooner than thy false showers or protestations. A generation of damned hypocrites! To flatter my very clothes from my back! Dissembling witches! Are these the returns you make an honest gentleman that trusts, believes, and loves you? But if I be not even with you—Come along, or I shall—

(*Pulls her again.*)

(*Enter Frederick.*)

FREDERICK. Ha, what's here to do?

BLUNT. 'Adsheartlikins, Fred, I am glad thou art come, to be a witness of my dire revenge.

FREDERICK. What's this, a person of quality too, who is upon the ramble[154] to supply the defects of some grave impotent husband?

BLUNT. No, this has another pretense: Some very unfortunate accident brought her hither, to save a life pursued by I know not who or why, and forced to take sanctuary here at fool's haven. 'Adsheartlikins, to me of all mankind for protection? Is the ass to be cajoled again, think ye? No, young one, no prayers or tears shall mitigate my rage; therefore prepare for both my pleasures of enjoyment and revenge. For I am resolved to make up my loss here on thy body: I'll take it out in kindness and in beating.

FREDERICK. Now, mistress of mind, what do you think of this?

FLORINDA. I think he will not, dares not be so barbarous.

FREDERICK. Have a care, Blunt, she fetched a deep sigh; she is enamored with thy shirt and drawers. She'll strip thee even of that; there are of her calling such unconscionable baggages and such dexterous thieves, they'll flea[155] a man

---

[153]**morris dancer** fantastically attired dancer

[154]**upon the ramble** wandering   [155]**flea** flay

and he shall ne'er miss his skin till he feels the cold. There was a countryman of ours robbed of a row of teeth whilst he was a-sleeping, which the jilt made him buy again when he waked. You see, lady, how little reason we have to trust you.

BLUNT. 'Adsheartlikins, why this is most abominable!

FLORINDA. Some such devils there may be, but by all that's holy, I am none such. I entered here to save a life in danger.

BLUNT. For no goodness, I'll warrant her.

FREDERICK. Faith, damsel, you had e'en confessed the plain truth, for we are fellows not to be caught twice in the same trap. Look on that wreck: a tight vessel when he set out of haven, well trimmed and laden. And see how a female picaroon of this island of rogues has shattered him, and canst thou hope for any mercy?

BLUNT. No, no, gentlewoman, come along; 'adsheartlikins, we must be better acquainted.—We'll both lie with her, and then let me along to bang her.

FREDERICK. I'm ready to serve you in matters of revenge that has a double pleasure in't.

BLUNT. Well said.—You hear, little one, how you are condemned by public vote to the bed within; there's no resisting your destiny, sweetheart.

(Pulls her.)

FLORINDA. Stay, sir. I have seen you with Belvile, an English cavalier. For his sake, use me kindly. You know him, sir.

BLUNT. Belvile? Why yes, sweeting, we do know Belvile, and wish he were with us now. He's a cormorant at whore and bacon:[156] He'd have a limb or two of thee, my virgin pullet. But 'tis no matter; we'll leave him the bones to pick.

FLORINDA. Sir, if you have any esteem for that Belvile, I conjure you to treat me with more gentleness; he'll thank you for the justice.

FREDERICK. Hark'ee, Blunt, I doubt we are mistaken in this matter.

FLORINDA. Sir, if you find me not worth Belvile's care, use me as you please. And that you may think I merit better treatment than you threaten, pray take this present.

(Gives him a ring; he looks at it.)

BLUNT. Hum, a diamond! Why, 'tis a wonderful virtue now that lies in this ring, a mollifying virtue. 'Adsheartlikins, there's more persuasive rhetoric in't than all her sex can utter.

FREDERICK. I begin to suspect something, and 'twould anger us vilely to be trussed up for a rape upon a maid of quality, when we only believe we ruffle a harlot.

BLUNT. Thou art a credulous fellow, but 'adsheartlikins, I have no faith yet. Why, my saint prattled as parlously as this does, she gave me a bracelet, too, a devil on her! But I sent my man to sell it today for necessaries, and it proved as counterfeit as her vows of love.

---

[156]**cormorant . . . bacon** glutton for sex

FREDERICK. However, let it reprieve her till we see Belvile.

BLUNT. That's hard, yet I will grant it.

(Enter a Servant.)

SERVANT. Oh, sir, the colonel is just come in with his new friend and a Spaniard of quality, and talks of having you to dinner with 'em.

BLUNT. 'Adsheartlikins, I'm undone! I would not see 'em for the world. Hark'ee, Fred, lock up the wench in your chamber.

FREDERICK. Fear nothing, madam: Whate'er he threatens, you are safe whilst in my hands.

(Exeunt Frederick and Florinda.)

BLUNT. And sirrah, upon your life, say I am not at home, or that I'm asleep, or—or—anything. Away; I'll prevent their coming this way.

(Locks the door, and exeunt.)

ACT 5

(Blunt's chamber. After a great knocking as at his chamber door, enter Blunt softly crossing the stage, in his shirt and drawers as before.)

[VOICES] *(call within)*. Ned! Ned Blunt! Ned Blunt!

BLUNT. The rogues are up in arms. 'Adsheartlikins, this villainous Frederick has betrayed me: They have heard of my blessed fortune.

[VOICES] *(and knocking within)*. Ned Blunt! Ned! Ned!

BELVILE [*within*]. Why, he's dead, sir, without dispute dead; he has not been seen today. Let's break open the door. Here, boy—

BLUNT. Ha, break open the door? 'Adsheartlikins, that mad fellow will be as good as his word.

BELVILE [*within*]. Boy, bring something to force the door.

(A great noise within, at the door again.)

BLUNT. So, now must I speak in my own defense; I'll try what rhetoric will do.—Hold, hold! What do you mean, gentlemen, what do you mean?

BELVILE *(within)*. Oh, rogue, art alive? Prithee open the door and convince us.

BLUNT. Yes, I am alive, gentlemen, but at present a little busy.

BELVILE *(within)*. How, Blunt grown a man of business? Come, come, open and let's see this miracle.

BLUNT. No, no, no, no, gentlemen, 'tis no great business. But—I am—at—my devotion. 'Adsheartlikins, will you not allow a man time to pray?

BELVILE *(within)*. Turned religious? A greater wonder than the first! Therefore open quickly, or we shall unhinge, we shall.

BLUNT [*aside*]. This won't do.—Why hark'ee, colonel, to tell you the truth, I am about a necessary affair of life: I have a wench with me. You apprehend me?—The devil's in't if they be so uncivil as to disturb me now.

WILLMORE [*within*]. How, a wench? Nay then, we must enter and partake. No resistance. Unless it be your lady of quality, and then we'll keep our distance.

BLUNT. So, the business is out.

WILLMORE [*within*]. Come, come, lend's more hands to the door. Now heave, all together. (*Breaks open the door.*) So, well done, my boys.

(*Enter Belvile [and his Page], Willmore, Frederick, and Pedro. Blunt looks simply,*[157] *they all laugh at him; he lays his hand on his sword, and comes up to Willmore.*)

BLUNT. Hark'ee, sir, laugh out your laugh quickly, d'ye hear, and be gone. I shall spoil your sport else, 'adsheartlikins, sir. I shall. The jest has been carried on too long.— (*Aside.*) A plague upon my tailor!

WILLMORE. 'Sdeath, how the whore has dressed him! Faith, sir, I'm sorry.

BLUNT. Are you so, sir? Keep't to yourself then, sir, I advise you, d'ye hear, for I can as little endure your pity as his mirth.

(*Lays his hand on's sword.*)

BELVILE. Indeed, Willmore, thou wert a little too rough with Ned Blunt's mistress. Call a person of quality whore, and one so young, so handsome, and so eloquent? Ha, ha, he.

BLUNT. Hark'ee, sir, you know me, and know I can be angry. Have a care, for 'adsheartlikins, I can fight too, I can, sir. Do you mark me? No more.

BELVILE. Why so peevish, good Ned? Some disappointments, I'll warrant. What, did the jealous count, her husband, return just in the nick?

BLUNT. Or the devil, sir. (*They laugh.*) D'ye laugh? Look ye settle me a good sober countenance, and that quickly, too, or you shall know Ned Blunt is not—

BELVILE. Not everybody, we know that.

BLUNT. Not an ass to be laughed at, sir.

WILLMORE. Unconscionable sinner! To bring a lover so near his happiness—a vigorous passionate lover—and then not only cheat him of his movables, but his very desires, too.

BELVILE. Ah, sir, a mistress is a trifle with Blunt; he'll have a dozen the next time he looks abroad. His eyes have charms not to be resisted; there needs no more than to expose that taking person to the view of the fair, and he leads 'em all in triumph.

PEDRO. Sir, though I'm a stranger to you, I am ashamed at the rudeness of my nation; and could you learn who did it, would assist you to make an example of 'em.

BLUNT. Why ay, there's one speaks sense now, and handsomely. And let me tell you, gentlemen, I should not have showed myself like a jack pudding[158] thus to have made you mirth, but that I have revenge within my power. For know, I have got into my possession a female, who had better have fallen under any curse than the ruin I design her. 'Adsheartlikins, she assaulted me here in my own lodgings, and had doubtless committed a rape upon me, had not this sword defended me.

FREDERICK. I know not that, but o' my conscience thou had ravished her, had she not redeemed herself with a ring. Let's see't, Blunt.

(*Blunt shows the ring.*)

BELVILE [*aside*]. Ha! The ring I gave Florinda when we exchanged our vows!—Hark'ee, Blunt—
                                    (*Goes to whisper to him.*)

WILLMORE. No whispering, good colonel, there's a woman in the case. No whispering.

BELVILE [*aside to Blunt*]. Hark'ee, fool, be advised, and conceal both the ring and the story for your reputation's sake. Do not let people know what despised cullies[159] we English are; to be cheated and abused by one whore, and another rather bribe thee than be kind to thee, is an infamy to our nation.

WILLMORE. Come, come, where's the wench? We'll see her; let her be what she will, we'll see her.

PEDRO. Ay, ay, let us see her. I can soon discover whether she be of quality, or for your diversion.

BLUNT. She's in Fred's custody.

WILLMORE. Come, come, the key—
                    (*To Frederick, who gives him the key; they are going.*)

BELVILE [*aside*]. Death, what shall I do?—Stay, gentlemen.— [*Aside.*] Yet if I hinder 'em, I shall discover all.—Hold, let's go one at once.[160] Give me the key.

WILLMORE. Nay, hold there, colonel, I'll go first.

FREDERICK. Nay, no dispute, Ned and I have the property of her.

WILLMORE. Damn propriety! Then we'll draw cuts. (*Belvile goes to whisper [to] Willmore.*) Nay, no corruption, good colonel. Come, the longest sword carries her.

(*They all draw, forgetting Don Pedro, being a Spaniard, had the longest.*)

BLUNT. I yield up my interest to you, gentleman, and that will be revenge sufficient.

WILLMORE (*to Pedro*). The wench is yours.—[*Aside.*] Pox of his Toledo.[161] I had forgot that.

FREDERICK. Come, sir, I'll conduct you to the lady.
                                    (*Exeunt Frederick and Pedro.*)

BELVILE (*aside*). To hinder him will certainly discover her.— Dost know, dull beast, what mischief thou hast done?

---

[157]**simply** foolishly

[158]**jack pudding** clown   [159]**cullies** dupes   [160]**one at once** one after the other   [161]**Toledo** sword made in Toledo

(*Willmore, walking up and down, out of humor.*)

WILLMORE. Ay, ay, to trust our fortune to lots! A devil on't, 'twas madness, that's the truth on't.

BELVILE. Oh, intolerable sot—

(*Enter Florinda running, masked, Pedro after her; Willmore gazing round her.*)

FLORINDA (*aside*). Good heaven defend me from discovery!

PEDRO. 'Tis but in vain to fly me; you've fallen to my lot.

BELVILE [*aside*]. Sure she's undiscovered yet, but now I fear there is no way to bring her off.

WILLMORE [*aside*]. Why, what a pox, is not this my woman, the same I followed but now?

(*Pedro talking to Florinda, who walks up and down.*)

PEDRO. As if I did not know ye, and your business here.

FLORINDA (*aside*). Good heaven. I fear he does indeed!

PEDRO. Come, pray be kind; I know you meant to be so when you entered here, for these are proper gentlemen.

WILLMORE. But sir, perhaps the lady will not be imposed upon: She'll choose her man.

PEDRO. I am better bred than not to leave her choice free.

(*Enter Valeria, and is surprised at sight of Don Pedro.*)

VALERIA (*aside*). Don Pedro here! There's no avoiding him.

FLORINDA (*aside*). Valeria! Then I'm undone.

VALERIA (*to Pedro, running to him*). Oh, I have found you, sir! The strangest accident—if I had breath—to tell it.

PEDRO. Speak! Is Florinda safe? Hellena well?

VALERIA. Ay, ay, sir. Florinda is safe.—[*Aside.*] From any fears of you.

PEDRO. Why, where's Florinda? Speak!

VALERIA. Ay, where indeed, sir; I wish I could inform you. But to hold you no longer in doubt—

FLORINDA (*aside*). Oh, what will she say?

VALERIA. She's fled away in the habit—of one of her pages, sir. But Callis thinks you may retrieve her yet, if you make haste away. She'll tell you, sir, the rest.—(*Aside.*) If you can find her out.

PEDRO. Dishonorable girl, she has undone my aim.—[*To Belvile.*] Sir, you see my necessity of leaving you, and I hope you'll pardon it. My sister, I know, will make her flight to you; and if she do, I shall expect she should be rendered back.

BELVILE. I shall consult my love and honor, sir.

(*Exit Pedro.*)

FLORINDA (*to Valeria*). My dear preserver, let me embrace thee.

WILLMORE. What the devil's all this?

BLUNT. Mystery, by this light.

VALERIA. Come, come, make haste and get yourselves married quickly, for your brother will return again.

BELVILE. I'm so surprised with fears and joys, so amazed to find you here in safety, I can scarce persuade my heart into a faith of what I see.

WILLMORE. Hark'ee, colonel, is this that mistress who has cost you so many signs, and me so many quarrels with you?

BELVILE. It is.—[*To Florinda.*] Pray give him the honor of your hand.

WILLMORE. Thus it must be received, then. (*Kneels and kisses her hand.*) And with it give your pardon, too.

FLORINDA. The friend to Belvile may command me anything.

WILLMORE (*aside*). Death, would I might; 'tis a surprising beauty.

BELVILE. Boy, run and fetch a father[162] instantly.

(*Exit Boy.*)

FREDERICK. So, now do I stand like a dog, and have not a syllable to plead my own cause with. By this hand, madam, I was never thoroughly confounded before, nor shall I ever more dare look up with confidence, till you are pleased to pardon me.

FLORINDA. Sir, I'll be reconciled to you on one condition: that you'll follow the example of your friend in marrying a maid that does not hate you, and whose fortune, I believe, will not be unwelcome to you.

FREDERICK. Madam, had I no inclinations that way, I should obey your kind commands.

BELVILE. Who, Fred marry? He has so few inclinations for womankind that had he been possessed of paradise he might have continued there to this day, if no crime but love could have disinherited him.

FREDERICK. Oh, I do not use to boast of my intrigues.

BELVILE. Boast! Why, thou dost nothing but boast. And I dare swear, wert thou as innocent from the sin of the grape as thou art from the apple, thou might'st yet claim that right in Eden which our first parents lost by too much loving.

FREDERICK. I wish this lady would think me so modest a man.

VALERIA. She would be sorry then, and not like you half so well. And I should be loath to break my word with you, which was, that if your friend and mine agreed, it should be a match between you and I. (*She gives him her hand.*)

FREDERICK. Bear witness, colonel, 'tis a bargain.

(*Kisses her hand.*)

BLUNT (*to Florinda*). I have a pardon to beg, too; but 'adsheartlikins, I am so out of countenance that I'm a dog if I can say anything to purpose.

FLORINDA. Sir, I heartily forgive you all.

BLUNT. That's nobly said, sweet lady.—Belvile, prithee present her her ring again, for I find I have not courage to approach her myself.

(*Gives him the ring; he gives it to Florinda.*)

(*Enter Boy.*)

BOY. Sir, I have brought the father that you sent for.

[*Exit Boy.*]

---

[162]**father** priest

BELVILE. 'Tis well. And now, my dear Florinda, let's fly to complete that mighty joy we have so long wished and signed for.—Come, Fred, you'll follow?

FREDERICK. Your example, sir, 'twas ever my ambition in war, and must be so in love.

WILLMORE. And must not I see this juggling[163] knot tied?

BELVILE. No, thou shalt do us better service and be our guard, lest Don Pedro's sudden return interrupt the ceremony.

WILLMORE. Content; I'll secure this pass.

(*Exeunt Belvile, Florinda, Frederick, and Valeria.*)

(*Enter Boy.*)

BOY (*to Willmore*). Sir, there's a lady without would speak to you.

WILLMORE. Conduct her in; I dare not quit my post.

BOY [*to Blunt*]. And sir, your tailor waits you in your chamber.

BLUNT. Some comfort yet: I shall not dance naked at the wedding.

(*Exeunt Blunt and Boy.*)

(*Enter again the Boy, conducting in Angellica in a masking habit and a vizard. Willmore runs to her.*)

WILLMORE [*aside*]. This can be none but my pretty gypsy.— Oh, I see you can follow as well as fly. Come, confess thyself the most malicious devil in nature; you think you have done my business with Angellica—

ANGELLICA. Stand off, base villain!

(*She draws a pistol and holds it to his breast.*)

WILLMORE. Ha, 'tis not she! Who art thou, and what's thy business?

ANGELLICA. One thou hast injured, and who comes to kill thee for't.

WILLMORE. What the devil canst thou mean?

ANGELLICA. By all my hopes to kill thee—

(*Holds still the pistol to his breast; he going back, she following still.*)

WILLMORE. Prithee, on what acquaintance? For I know thee not.

ANGELLICA.
Behold this face so lost to thy remembrance.
                              (*Pulls off her vizard.*)
And then call all thy sins about thy soul,
And let 'em die with thee.

WILLMORE. Angellica!

ANGELLICA. Yes, traitor!
Does not thy guilty blood run shivering through thy veins?
Hast thou no horror at this sight, that tells thee

Thou hast not long to boast thy shameful conquest?

WILLMORE. Faith, no, child. My blood keeps its old ebbs and flows still, and that usual heat too, that could oblige thee with a kindness, had I but opportunity.

ANGELLICA. Devil! Dost wanton with my pain? Have at thy heart!

WILLMORE. Hold, dear virago![164] Hold thy hand a little; I am not now at leisure to be killed. Hold and hear me.— (*Aside.*) Death, I think she's in earnest.

ANGELLICA (*aside, turning from him*).
Oh, if I take not heed,
My coward heart will leave me to his mercy.—
What have you, sir, to say?—But should I hear thee,
Thoud'st talk away all that is brave about me.
And I have vowed thy death by all that's sacred.
                              (*Follows him with the pistol to his breast.*)

WILLMORE.
Why then, there's an end of a proper handsome fellow.
That might 'a lived to have done good service yet.
That's all I can say to't.

ANGELLICA (*pausingly*).
Yet—I would give thee time for—penitence.

WILLMORE.
Faith, child, I thank God I have ever took
Care to lead a good, sober, hopeful life, and am of a religion
That teaches me to believe I shall depart in peace.

ANGELLICA.
So will the devil! Tell me,
How many poor believing fools thou hast undone?
How many hearts thou hast betrayed to ruin?
Yet these are little mischiefs to the ills
Thou'st taught mine to commit: Thou'st taught it love.

WILLMORE.
Egad, 'twas shrewdly hurt the while.

ANGELLICA.
Love, that has robbed it of its unconcern,
Of all that pride that taught me how to value it.
And in its room
A mean submissive passion was conveyed,
That made me humbly bow, which I ne'er did
To anything but heaven.
Thou, perjured man, didst this; and with thy oaths,
Which on thy knees thou didst devoutly make,
Softened my yielding heart, and then I was a slave.
Yet still had been content to've worn my chains,
Worn 'em with vanity and joy forever,
Hadst thou not broke those vows that put them on.
'Twas then I was undone.
                              (*All this while follows him with the pistol to his breast.*)

WILLMORE. Broke my vows? Why, where hast thou lived?

---

[163]**juggling** deceptive

[164]**virago** dominating woman

Amongst the gods? For I never heard of mortal man that has not broke a thousand vows.

ANGELLICA. Oh, impudence!

WILLMORE. Angellica, that beauty has been too long tempting, not to have made a thousand lovers languish; who, in the amorous fever, no doubt have sworn like me. Did they all die in that faith, still adoring? I do not think they did.

ANGELLICA. No, faithless man; had I repaid their vows, as I did thine, I would have killed the ingrateful that had abandoned me.

WILLMORE. This old general has quite spoiled thee: Nothing makes a woman so vain as being flattered. Your old lover ever supplies the defects of age with intolerable dotage, vast charge, and that which you call constancy; and attributing all this to your own merits, you domineer, and throw your favors in's teeth, upbraiding him still with the defects of age, and cuckold him as often as he deceives your expectations. But the gay, young, brisk lover, that brings his equal fires, and can give you dart for dart, you'll find will be as nice as you sometimes.

ANGELLICA.

All this thou'st made me know, for which I hate thee.
Had I remained in innocent security,
I should have thought all men were born my slaves,
And worn my power like lightning in my eyes,
To have destroyed at pleasure when offended.
But when love held the mirror, the undeceiving glass
Reflected all the weakness of my soul, and made me know
My richest treasure being lost, my honor,
All the remaining spoil could not be worth
The conqueror's care or value.
Oh, how I feel, like a long-worshiped idol,
Discovering all the cheat.
Would not the incense and rich sacrifice
Which blind devotion offered at my altars
Have fallen to thee?
Why wouldst thou then destroy my fancied power?

WILLMORE.

By heaven, thou'rt brave, and I admire thee strangely.
I wish I were that dull, that constant thing
Which thou wouldst have, and nature never meant me.
I must, like cheerful birds, sing in all groves,
And perch on every bough,
Billing the next kind she that flies to meet me;
Yet, after all, could build my nest with thee,
Thither repairing when I'd loved my round,
And still reserve a tributary flame.
To gain your credit, I'll pay you back your charity,
And be obliged for nothing but for love.

(Offers her a purse of gold.)

ANGELLICA.

Oh, that thou wert in earnest!
So mean a thought of me
Would turn my rage to scorn, and I should pity thee,
And give thee leave to live;

Which for the public safety of our sex,
And my own private injuries, I dare not do.
Prepare—(Follows still, as before.)
I will no more be tempted with replies.

WILLMORE. Sure—

ANGELLICA. Another word will damn thee! I've heard thee talk too long.

(She follows him with the pistol ready to shoot; he retires, still amazed. Enter Don Antonio, his arm in a scarf, and lays hold on the pistol.)

ANTONIO. Ha! Angellica!

ANGELLICA. Antonio! What devil brought thee hither?

ANTONIO.

Love and curiosity, seeing your coach at door.
Let me disarm you of this unbecoming instrument of death.

(Takes away the pistol.)

Amongst the number of your slaves was there not one
worthy the honor to have fought your quarrel?—
[To Willmore.] Who are you, sir, that are so very wretched
To merit death from her?

WILLMORE. One, sir, that could have made a better end of an amorous quarrel without you, than with you.

ANTONIO. Sure 'tis some rival. Ha! The very man took down her picture yesterday; the very same that set on me last night! Blessed opportunity—

(Offers to shoot him.)

ANGELLICA. Hold, you're mistaken, sir.

ANTONIO. By heaven, the very same!—Sir, what pretensions have you to this lady?

WILLMORE. Sir, I do not use to be examined, and am ill at all disputes but this—

(Draws; Antonio offers to shoot.)

ANGELLICA (to Willmore).

Oh, hold! You see he's armed with certain death.
—And you, Antonio, I command you hold,
By all the passion you've so lately vowed me.

(Enter Don Pedro, sees Antonio, and stays.)

PEDRO (aside). Ha! Antonio! And Angellica!

ANTONIO.

When I refuse obedience to your will,
May you destroy me with your mortal hate.
By all that's holy, I adore you so,
That even my rival, who has charms enough
To make him fall a victim to my jealousy,
Shall live; nay, and have leave to love on still.

PEDRO (aside). What's this I hear?

ANGELLICA (pointing to Willmore).

Ah thus, 'twas thus he talked, and I believed.
Antonio, yesterday
I'd not have sold my interest in his heart
For all the sword has won and lost in battle.

—But now, to show my utmost of contempt,
I give thee life; which, if thou wouldst preserve,
Live where my eyes may never see thee more.
Live to undo someone whose soul may prove
So bravely constant to revenge my love.

(*Goes out. Antonio follows, but Pedro pulls him back.*)

PEDRO. Antonio, stay.

ANTONIO. Don Pedro!

PEDRO.
What coward fear was that prevented thee
From meeting me this morning on the Molo?

ANTONIO. Meet thee?

PEDRO. Yes, me; I was the man that dated thee to't.

ANTONIO.
Hast thou so often seen me fight in war,
To find no better cause to excuse my absence?
I sent my sword and one to do thee right,
Finding myself uncapable to use a sword.

PEDRO.
But 'twas Florinda's quarrel that we fought,
And you, to show how little you esteemed her,
Sent me your rival, giving him your interest.
But I have found the cause of this affront,
And when I meet you fit for the dispute,
I'll tell you my resentment.

ANTONIO.
I shall be ready, sir, ere long, to do you reason.

(*Exit Antonio.*)

PEDRO. If I could find Florinda, now whilst my anger's high,
I think I should be kind, and give her to Belvile in revenge.

WILLMORE. Faith, sir, I know not what you would do, but I
believe the priest within has been so kind.

PEDRO. How? My sister married?

WILLMORE. I hope by this time he is, and bedded too, or he
has not my longings about him.

PEDRO. Dares he do this? Does he not fear my power?

WILLMORE. Faith, not at all; if you will go in and thank him
for the favor he has done your sister, so; if not, sir, my
power's greater in this house than yours: I have a damned
surly crew here that will keep you till the next tide, and
then clap you on board for prize. My ship lies but a league
off the Molo, and we shall show your donship a damned
Tramontana[165] rover's trick.

(*Enter Belvile.*)

BELVILE. This rogue's in some new mischief. Ha! Pedro returned!

PEDRO. Colonel Belvile, I hear you have married my sister.

BELVILE. You have heard truth then, sir.

PEDRO. Have I so? Then, sir, I wish you joy.

BELVILE. How?

PEDRO. By this embrace I do, and I am glad on't.

BELVILE. Are you in earnest?

PEDRO.
By our long friendship and my obligations to thee, I am;
The sudden change I'll give you reasons for anon.
Come, lead me to my sister,
That she may know I now approve her choice.

(*Exit Belvile with Pedro.*)

(*Willmore goes to follow them. Enter Hellena, as before in
boy's clothes, and pulls him back.*)

WILLMORE. Ha! My gypsy! Now a thousand blessings on
thee for this kindness. Egad, child, I was e'en in despair of
ever seeing thee again; my friends are all provided for
within, each man his kind woman.

HELLENA. Ha! I thought they had served me some such
trick!

WILLMORE. And I was e'en resolved to go aboard, and condemn myself to my lone cabin, and the thoughts of thee.

HELLENA. And could you have left me behind? Would you
have been so ill natured?

WILLMORE. Why, 'twould have broke my heart, child. But
since we are met again I defy foul weather to part us.

HELLENA. And would you be a faithful friend now, if a maid
should trust you?

WILLMORE. For a friend I cannot promise: Thou art of a
form so excellent, a face and humor too good for cold dull
friendship. I am parlously afraid of being in love, child;
and you have not forgotten how severely you have used
me?

HELLENA. That's all one; such usage you must still look for:
to find out all your haunts, to rail at you to all that love
you, till I have made you love only me in your own defense, because nobody else will love you.

WILLMORE. But hast thou no better quality to recommend
thyself by?

HELLENA. Faith, none, captain. Why, 'twill be the greater
charity to take me for thy mistress. I am a lone child, a
kind of orphan lover; and why I should die a maid, and in
a captain's hands too, I do not understand.

WILLMORE. Egad, I was never clawed away with broadsides
from any female before. Thou hast one virtue I adore—
good nature. I hate a coy demure mistress, she's as troublesome as a colt; I'll break none. No, give me a mad mistress when mewed, and in flying, one I dare trust upon the
wing, that whilst she's kind will come to the lure.[166]

HELLENA. Nay, as kind as you will, good captain, whilst it
lasts. But let's lose no time.

WILLMORE. My time's as precious to me as thine can be.
Therefore, dear creature, since we are so well agreed, let's
retire to my chamber; and if ever thou wert treated with
such savory love! Come, my bed's prepared for such a
guest all clean and sweet as thy fair self. I love to steal a

---

[165]**Tramontana** in Northen Italy (literally: beyond the mountains)

[166]**whilst . . . lure** will follow her nature and will do what she
should(?); while she is happy with him she will be faithful(?)

dish and a bottle with a friend, and hate long graces. Come, let's retire and fall to.

HELLENA. 'Tis but getting my consent, and the business is soon done. Let but old gaffer Hymen[167] and his priest say amen to't, and I dare lay my mother's daughter by as proper a fellow as your father's son, without fear or blushing.

WILLMORE. Hold, hold, no bug words,[168] child. Priest and Hymen? Prithee add a hangman to 'em to make up the consort. No, no, we'll have no vows but love, child, nor witness but the lover: The kind deity enjoins naught but love and enjoy. Hymen and priest wait still upon portion and jointure; love and beauty have their own ceremonies. Marriage is as certain a bane to love as lending money is to friendship. I'll neither ask nor give a vow, though I could be content to turn gypsy and become a left-handed bridegroom to have the pleasure of working that great miracle of making a maid a mother, if you durst venture. 'Tis upse gypsy[169] that, and if I miss I'll lose my labor.

HELLENA. And if you do not lose, what shall I get? A cradle full of noise and mischief, with a pack of repentance at my back? Can you teach me to weave incle[170] to pass my time with? 'Tis upse gypsy that, too.

WILLMORE. I can teach thee to weave a true love's knot better.

HELLENNA. So can my dog.

WILLMORE. Well, I see we are both upon our guards, and see there's no way to conquer good nature but by yielding. Here, give me thy hand: One kiss, and I am thine.

HELLENA. One kiss! How like my page he speaks! I am resolved you shall have none, for asking such a sneaking sum. He that will be satisfied with one kiss will never die of that longing. Good friend single-kiss, is all your talking come to this? A kiss, a caudle![171] Farewell, captain single-kiss.

(Going out; he stays her.)

WILLMORE. Nay, if we part so, let me die like a bird upon a bough at the sheriff's charge. By heaven, both the Indies shall not buy thee from me. I adore thy humor and will marry thee, and we are so of one humor it must be a bargain. Give me thy hand. (Kisses her hand.) And now let the blind ones, love and fortune, do their worst.

HELLENA. Why, god-a-mercy, captain!

WILLMORE. But hark'ee: the bargain is now made, but is it not fit we should know each other's names, that when we have reason to curse one another hereafter, and people ask me who 'tis I give to the devil, I may at least be able to tell what family you came of?

HELLENA. Good reason, captain; and where I have cause, as

I doubt not but I shall have plentiful, that I may know at whom to throw my—blessings, I beseech ye your name.

WILLMORE. I am called Robert the Constant.

HELLENA. A very fine name! Pray was it your faulkner[172] or butler that christened you? Do they not use to whistle when they call you?

WILLMORE. I hope you have a better, that a man may name without crossing himself—you are so merry with mine.

HELLENA. I am called Hellena the Inconstant.

(Enter Pedro, Belvile, Florinda, Frederick, Valeria.)

PEDRO. Ha! Hellena!

FLORINDA. Hellena!

HELLENA. The very same. Ha! My brother! Now, captain, show your love and courage; stand to your arms and defend me bravely, or I am lost forever.

PEDRO. What's this I hear? False girl, how came you hither, and what's your business? Speak!

(Goes roughly to her.)

WILLMORE. Hold off, sir; you have leave to parley[173] only.

(Puts himself between.)

HELLENA. I had e'en as good tell it, as you guess it. Faith, brother, my business is the same with all living creatures of my age: to love and be beloved—and here's the man.

PEDRO. Perfidious maid, hast thou deceived me too; deceived thyself and heaven?

HELLENA.
'Tis time enough to make my peace with that;
Be you but kind, let me alone with heaven.

PEDRO. Belvile, I did not expect this false play from you. Was't not enough you'd gain Florinda, which I pardoned, but your lewd friends too must be enriched with the spoils of a noble family?

BELVILE. Faith, sir, I am as much surprised at this as you can be. Yet, sir, my friends are gentlemen, and ought to be esteemed for their misfortunes, since they have the glory to suffer with the best of men and kings. 'Tis true, he's a rover of fortune, yet a prince aboard his little wooden world.

PEDRO. What's this to the maintenance of a woman of her birth and quality?

WILLMORE. Faith, sir, I can boast of nothing but a sword which does me right where'er I come, and has defended a worse cause than a woman's; and since I loved her before I either knew her birth or name, I must pursue my resolution and marry her.

PEDRO. And is all your holy intent of becoming a nun debauched into a desire of man?

HELLENA. Why, I have considered the matter, brother, and find the three hundred thousand crowns my uncle left me, and you cannot keep from me, will be better laid out in love than in religion, and turn to as good an account. Let most voices carry it: for heaven or the captain?

---

[167]**gaffer Hymen** old Hymen, God of Marriage   [168]**bug words** frightening words, threats   [169]**upse gypsy** like a gypsy   [170]**incle** linen tape   [171]**caudle** warm drink given to the sick

[172]**faulkner** falconer, a trainer of falcons   [173]**parley** speak

ALL CRY. A captain! A captain!

HELLENA. Look ye, sir, 'tis a clear case.

PEDRO. Oh, I am mad!—(*Aside.*) If I refuse, my life's in danger.—Come, there's one motive induces me. Take her; I shall now be free from fears of her honor. Guard it you now, if you can; I have been a slave to't long enough.

(*Gives her to him.*)

WILLMORE. Faith, sir, I am of a nation that are of opinion a woman's honor is not worth guarding when she has a mind to part with it.

HELLENA. Well said, captain.

PEDRO (*to Valeria*). This was your plot, mistress, but I hope you have married one that will revenge my quarrel to you.

VALERIA. There's no altering destiny, sir.

PEDRO. Sooner than a woman's will; therefore I forgive you all, and wish you may get my father's pardon as easily, which I fear.

(*Enter Blunt dressed in a Spanish habit, looking very ridiculous; his Man adjusting his band.*[174])

MAN. 'Tis very well, sir.

BLUNT. Well, sir! 'Adsheartlikins, I tell you 'tis damnable ill, sir. A Spanish habit! Good Lord! Could the devil and my tailor devise no other punishment for me but the mode of a nation I abominate?

BELVILE. What's the matter, Ned?

BLUNT. Pray view me round, and judge.

(*Turns round.*)

BELVILE. I must confess thou art a kind of an odd figure.

BLUNT. In a Spanish habit with a vengeance! I had rather be in the Inquisition for Judaism[175] than in this doublet and breeches; a pillory were an easy collar to this, three handfuls high; and these shoes, too, are worse than the stocks, with the sole an inch shorter than my foot. In fine, gentlemen, methinks I look like a bag of bays[176] stuffed full of fool's flesh.

BELVILE. Methinks 'tis well, and makes thee look e'en cavalier. Come, sir, settle your face and salute our friends. Lady—

BLUNT (*to Hellena*). Ha! Sayst thou so, my little rover? Lady, if you be one, give me leave to kiss your hand, and tell you, 'adsheartlikins, for all I look so, I am your humble servant. A pox of my Spanish habit!

(*Music is heard to play.*)

WILLMORE. Hark! What's this?

(*Enter Boy.*)

BOY. Sir, as the custom is, the gay people in masquerade, who make every man's house their own, are coming up.

(*Enter several men and women in masking habits, with music; they put themselves in order and dance.*)

BLUNT. 'Adsheartlikins, would 'twere lawful to pull off their false faces, that I might see if my doxy[177] were not amongst 'em.

BELVILE (*to the maskers*). Ladies and gentlemen, since you are come so *a propos*,[178] you must take a small collation with us.

WILLMORE (*to Hellena*). Whilst we'll to the good man within, who stays to give us a cast of his office.[179] Have you no trembling at the near approach?

HELLENA. No more than you have in an engagement or a tempest.

WILLMORE. Egad, thou'rt a brave girl, and I admire thy love and courage.

Lead on; no other dangers they can dread,
Who venture in the storms o'th' marriage bed.

(*Exeunt.*)

EPILOGUE

The banished cavaliers! A roving blade!
A popish carnival! A masquerade!
The devil's in't if this will please the nation
In these our blessed times of reformation,
When conventickling[180] is so much in fashion.
And yet—
That mutinous tribe[181] less factions do beget,
Than your continual differing in wit.
Your judgment's, as your passion's, a disease:
Nor muse nor miss your appetite can please;
You've grown as nice as queasy consciences,
Whose each convulsion, when the spirit moves,
Damns everything that maggot[182] disapproves.
    With canting[183] rule you would the stage refine,
And to dull method all our sense confine.
With th'insolence of commonwealths you rule,
Where each gay fop and politic grave fool
On monarch wit impose, without control.
As for the last, who seldom sees a play,
Unless it be the old Blackfriars[184] way;
Shaking his empty noddle[185] o'er bamboo,[186]
He cries, "Good faith, these plays will never do!

---

[174]**band** neckband   [175]**Inquisition for Judaism** the Spanish Inquisition persecuted Jews as well as heretics   [176]**bag of bays** bag of spices used in cooking

[177]**doxy** prostitute   [178]*a propos* opportunely   [179]**cast of office** sample of his work (in marrying people)   [180]**conventickling** attending conventicles, that is, participating in secret meets of religious dissenters (with a pun on *tickling*)   [181]**mutinous tribe** dissenters   [182]**maggot** the inner light (the *spirit* of the preceding line) that guides dissenters   [183]**canting** hypocritical   [184]**Blackfriars** a London theater, closed in 1642   [185]**noddle** head   [186]**bamboo** a cane, that is, an infirm man is shaking his head

Ah, sir, in my young days, what lofty wit,
What high-strained scenes of fighting there were writ.
These are slight airy toys. But tell me, pray,
What has the House of Commons done today?"
Then shows his politics, to let you see
Of state affairs he'll judge as notably
As he can do of wit and poetry.
The younger sparks, who higher do resort,
Cry,
"Pox o' your genteel things! Give us more sport!
Dame me, I'm sure 'twill never please the court."

Such fops are never pleased, unless the play
Be stuffed with fools as brisk and dull as they.
Such might the half-crown[187] spare, and in a glass
At home behold a more accomplished ass.
Where they may set their cravats, wigs, and faces,
And practice all their buffoonry grimaces:
See how this huff becomes, this damny,[188] stare,
Which they at home may act because they dare,
But must with prudent caution do elsewhere.
Oh that our Nokes, or Tony Lee,[189] could show
A fop but half so much to th' life as you.

POSTSCRIPT

This play had been sooner in print, but for a report about the town (made by some either very malicious or very ignorant) that 'twas Thomaso[190] altered; which made the booksellers fear some trouble from the proprietor of that admirable play, which indeed has wit enough to stock a poet, and is not to be pieced or mended by any but the excellent author himself. That I have stolen some hints from it, may be a proof that I valued it more than to pretend to alter it, had I the dexterity of some poets, who are not more expert in stealing than in the art of concealing, and who even that way outdo the Spartan boys.[191] I might have appropriated all to myself; but I, vainly proud of my judgment, hang out the sign of Angellica (the only stolen object) to give notice where a great part of the wit dwelt; though if the Play of the Novella[192] were as well worth remembering as Thomaso, they might (bating[193] the name) have as well said I took it from thence. I will only say the plot and business (not to boast on't) is my own; as for the words and characters, I leave the reader to judge and compare 'em with Thomaso, to whom I recommend the great entertainment of reading it. Though had this succeeded ill, I should have had no need of imploring that justice from the critics, who are naturally so kind to any that pretend to usurp their dominion, especially of our sex: They would doubtless have given me the whole honor on't. Therefore I will only say in English what the famous Vergil does in Latin: I make verses, and others have the fame.

---

[187]**half-crown** coin   [188]**damny** damn me   [189]**Nokes ... Lee** James Nokes and Anthony Leigh, two comedians of the period

[190]**Thomaso** play by Thomas Killigrew, *Thomaso; or The Wanderer* (1654)   [191]**Spartan boys** soldiers who hid in the Trojan horse   [192]**Play of the Novella** Richard Brome's *The Novella* (1632)   [193]**bating** excepting

SHE STOOPS TO CONQUER: OR THE MISTAKES OF A NIGHT

OLIVER GOLDSMITH

OLIVER GOLDSMITH (1728–1774)

Like his countrymen Richard Brinsley Sheridan and Bernard Shaw, Oliver Goldsmith was a transplanted Irishman who achieved success in the British literary world. And like Sheridan and Shaw, his status as an outsider living in London allowed him to satirize the manners and mores of English society. As an essayist, poet, novelist, and dramatist, Goldsmith remains among the most popular and influential figures in eighteenth-century literature.

Although he was born the son of a clergyman in Pallas, Ireland, Goldsmith lived a rakish life; it has been suggested that the spirited portrait of Tony Lumpkin in *She Stoops to Conquer* is something of a self-portrait. A mediocre student, Goldsmith received a degree from Dublin's prestigious Trinity University in 1745. To pay his tuition, Goldsmith became a "sizar"—one who waited on tables and performed other menial tasks at the college. Perhaps we may better appreciate his sympathy for Kate's predicament in *She Stoops to Conquer* as Goldsmith knew well the humiliation of being an underling in a world populated by self-serving gentility.

Thanks to the financial support of a kindly uncle, Contarine, Goldsmith pursued careers in law and medicine in Scotland before embarking on a "grand tour" (his words) of Europe in 1755. His travels provided him with background for his writing, which included essays ("An Enquiry into the Present State of Polite Learning in Europe"), a history of Greece, a biography of Voltaire, and poetry ("The Traveller"). Penniless, Goldsmith returned to London in 1756, where he worked as a writer and proofreader for Samuel Richardson (who wrote what is widely considered the first English novel, *Pamela*). He lived on Grub Street, a locale notorious for hack writers who churned out cheap, sentimental novels and plays—which Goldsmith attacked in his own writings.

Fortunately, Goldsmith's talent was recognized by some of London's leading artists, especially Dr. Samuel Johnson, the patriarch of English literati (and to whom Goldsmith dedicated *She Stoops to Conquer*). Johnson introduced Goldsmith into "the Club," a group of famous and brilliant men that included the painter Sir Joshua Reynolds, the political theorist Edmund Burke, and David Garrick, the greatest actor of eighteenth-century England. Members of the Club amused themselves by writing witty epitaphs for one another. Garrick, for instance, wrote that Goldsmith "wrote like an angel." The last lines Goldsmith ever penned were for a mock epitaph for Reynolds in April 1774.

Despite a prodigious output in virtually every literary genre popular in eighteenth-century England, Goldsmith is most remembered for three works. His novel *The Vicar of Wakefield* (1766) sets the Job story from the Bible in a contemporary village and remains among the finest portraits of town life in England. His essay "A Comparison Between Sentimental and Laughing Comedy" (see Forum, page 678) changed the course of English (and by extension, American) playwriting. *She Stoops to Conquer* is recognized as one of the three most important dramas written in England in the eighteenth century. Of it, Dr. Johnson wrote: "I know of no comedy that has so much exhilarated an audience; that answered so well the great end of comedy, making the audience merry."

SHE STOOPS TO CONQUER: OR THE MISTAKES OF A NIGHT (1773)

There is a misconception that *She Stoops to Conquer* is a Restoration comedy. Certainly it borrows its characters from the world of Wycherly and Congreve. There is the obligatory rakish hero (Young Marlow), a witty maiden (Kate Hardcastle) to reform him, a shallow gossip and hypocrite (Mrs. Hardcastle), a pair of virtuous lovers (Hastings and Miss Neville), a befuddled old squire (Hardcastle), and a young hellion (Tony Lumpkin).

But Goldsmith's comedy is assuredly not a Restoration play. It was written three-quarters of a century after Congreve's *The Way of the World* (1700), the last of the great Restoration comedies. It is not nearly as licentious nor as cynical as Restoration plays, but neither is it a sentimental comedy, which dominated English stages throughout most of the eighteenth century. True, *She Stoops to Conquer* borrows several key ingredients found in sentimentality's moral dramas and novels (the likes of which Miss Neville constantly reads). We meet the rake who is reformed by the love of a pure woman, we experience the reconciliation of husband and wife after an indiscretion, and we see faithful servants who represent commoners at their most noble. Kate's disguise as a kitchen maid epitomizes the new spirit of democracy that was about to sweep Europe and America. Furthermore, the play borrows the pithy morality of sentimentality as heard in Marlow's apology for his boorish behavior towards Miss Hardcastle:

> Your beauty at first caught my eye; for who could see that without emotion. But every moment that I converse with you, steals in some new grace, heightens the picture, and gives it stronger expression. What at first seemed rustic plainness, now appears refined simplicity. What seem'd forward assurance, now strikes me as the result of courageous innocence and conscious virtue.

"Love conquers all" was more than an aphorism of the sentimental age; it was the very foundation of its philosophy.

Neither a Restoration nor a sentimental comedy, *She Stoops to Conquer* synthesizes the two earlier forms and emerges as a new strain of British comedy. Unlike Shakespeare, whose mature comedies are set in exotic locales, Goldsmith sets his play in a world very much like that of his audience. The manners, dress, and especially the language faithfully replicated those of the audience who frequented the Covent Garden, one of London's finest theaters, in 1773. Unlike Molière and the Restoration playwrights, Goldsmith is not as cynical in his exposure of vice and hypocrisy. The play's ending celebrates reconciliation and looks forward to a world in which, as Hardcastle tells us, "the Mistakes of a Night shall be crown'd with a merry morning."

Despite his upbeat ending, Goldsmith goes beyond the simple moralizing and cheaply gained emotions of the sentimental comedies. He provides his audiences with sufficient emotional distance so that they may judge the follies of Marlow's inexcusable behavior towards Kate the Kitchen Maid, Mrs. Hardcastle's superficial concerns about her reputation, the sentimental shallowness of the Hastings-Constance affair, and especially Tony Lumpkin's dissolute behavior. Indeed, the riotous Tony turns out to be the "hero" (an unheard-of development in the old sentimental comedies) when he exposes his mother's hypocrisy in the garden. At the same time, Goldsmith keeps his characters, who are rarely caricatures, familiar enough that they always seem human and worthy of our sympathy and forgiveness. Unlike Tartuffe—whom we are relieved to see prison bound—we feel that both Marlow and Mrs. Hardcastle are sufficiently punished by their humiliating exposures. Better yet, we feel they will be reformed and henceforth live as upstanding citizens of the new society promised in the play's final speech. Goldsmith's "laughing comedy" is satirical without being mean-spirited.

Though the play is, generically speaking, a Comedy of Manners because it satirizes the manners, customs, dress, and speech of a particular society, it is also a universal morality tale. Young Marlow, duped by Tony Lumpkin at the Three Pigeons tavern in act 1 (Goldsmith was similarly tricked in his youth), does not know where he is throughout most of the play. More importantly, he does not know *who* he is. He assumes he cannot speak to a highborn woman. Ironically, he is thus the very antithesis of the Restoration rake, noted for his ability to speak well in all situations. His encounter with the crafty Kate—among the most independent and resourceful women in eighteenth-century drama—ultimately allows him to discover his natural self. By act 5, he makes the double discovery of where he is and who he is. Like Oedipus, his has been a journey of self-discovery, perhaps the most elemental impulse behind the world's finest dramas.

Parkinson's 1773 painting of the act 5 garden scene in She Stoops to Conquer *captures the spirit of Goldsmith's play as it was performed at London's Covent Garden Theater.*

SHE STOOPS TO CONQUER: OR THE MISTAKES OF A NIGHT

OLIVER GOLDSMITH

CHARACTERS
SIR CHARLES MARLOW
YOUNG MARLOW (*his son*)
HARDCASTLE
HASTINGS
TONY LUMPKIN
DIGGORY
MRS. HARDCASTLE
MISS HARDCASTLE
MISS NEVILLE
MAID

PROLOGUE

by David Garrick, Esq.

Enter Mr. Woodward, dressed in black, and holding a handkerchief to his eyes.

Excuse me, sirs, I pray—I can't yet speak—
I'm crying now—and have been all the week!
'Tis not alone this mourning suit, good masters;
I've that within—for which there are no plasters!
Pray would you know the reason why I'm crying?
The Comic muse, long sick, is now a-dying!
And if she goes, my tears will never stop:
For as a play'r, I can't squeeze out one drop:
I am undone, that's all—shall lose my bread—
I'd rather, but that's nothing—lose my head.
When the sweet maid is laid upon the bier,
Shuter[1] and I shall be chief mourners here.
To *her* a mawkish drab of spurious breed,
Who deals in *sentimentals* will succeed!
Poor *Ned* and *I* are dead to all intents,
We can as soon speak *Greek* as *sentiments!*
Both nervous grown, to keep our spirits up,
We now and then take down a hearty cup.
What shall we do?—If Comedy forsake us!

[1]**Shuter** Ned Shuter, the actor who played Hardcastle in the 1772 production

They'll turn us out, and no one else will take us,
But why can't I be moral?—Let me try—
My heart thus pressing—fix'd my face and eye—
With a sententious look, that nothing means
(Faces are blocks, in sentimental scenes),
Thus I begin—All is not gold that glitters,
Pleasure seems sweet, but proves a glass of bitters.
When ign'rance enters, folly is at hand;
Learning is better far than house and land.
Let not your virtue trip, who trips may stumble,
And virtue is not virtue, if she tumble.

    I give it up—morals won't do for me;
To make you laugh I must play tragedy.
One hope remains—hearing the maid was ill,
A *doctor* comes this night to show his skill.
To cheer her heart, and give your muscles motion,
He in *five draughts* prepar'd, presents a potion:
A kind of magic charm—for be assur'd,
If you will *swallow* it, the maid is cur'd.
But desperate the Doctor, and her case is,
If you reject the dose, and make wry faces!
This truth he boasts, will boast it while he lives,
No *pois'nous drugs* are mix'd in what he gives;
Should he succeed, you'll give him his degree;
If not, within he will receive no fee!
The college *you*, must his pretentions back,
Pronounce him *regular*, or dub him *quack*.

ACT ONE

SCENE I: A CHAMBER IN AN OLD-FASHIONED HOUSE

Enter Mrs. Hardcastle and Mr. Hardcastle.

MRS. HARDCASTLE. I vow, Mr. Hardcastle, you're very particular. Is there a creature in the whole country, but ourselves, that does not take a trip to town now and then, to rub off the rust a little? There's the two Miss Hoggs, and our neighbour, Mrs. Grigsby, go to take a month's polishing every winter.

HARDCASTLE. Ay, and bring back vanity and affectation to last them the whole year. I wonder why London cannot keep its own fools at home. In my time, the follies of the town crept slowly among us, but now they travel faster than a stage-coach. Its fopperies come down, not only as inside passengers, but in the very basket.

MRS. HARDCASTLE. Ay, *your* times were fine times, indeed; you have been telling us of them for many a long year. Here we live in an old rumbling mansion, that looks for all the world like an inn, but that we never see company. Our best visitors are old Mrs. Oddfish, the curate's wife, and little Cripplegate, the lame dancing-master, and all

our entertainment your old stories of Prince Eugene[2] and the Duke of Marlborough. I hate such old-fashioned trumpery.

HARDCASTLE. And I love it. I love everything that's old: old friends, old times, old manners, old books, old wine; and, I believe, Dorothy [*taking her hand*], you'll own I have been pretty fond of an old wife.

MRS. HARDCASTLE. Lord, Mr. Hardcastle, you're for ever at your Dorothys and your old wifes. You may be a Darby, but I'll be no Joan, I promise you. I'm not so old as you'd make me, by more than one good year. Add twenty to twenty, and make money of that.

HARDCASTLE. Let me see; twenty added to twenty, makes just fifty and seven!

MRS. HARDCASTLE. It's false, Mr. Hardcastle: I was but twenty when I was brought to bed of Tony, that I had by Mr. Lumpkin, my first husband; and he's not come to years of discretion yet.

HARDCASTLE. Nor ever will, I dare answer for him. Ay, have taught *him* finely!

MRS. HARDCASTLE. No matter, Tony Lumpkin has a good fortune. My son is not to live by his learning. I don't think a boy wants much learning to spend fifteen hundred a year.

HARDCASTLE. Learning, quotha! A mere composition of tricks and mischief!

MRS. HARDCASTLE. Humour, my dear: nothing but humour. Come, Mr. Hardcastle, you must allow the boy a little humour.

HARDCASTLE. I'd sooner allow him a horse-pond! If burning the footmen's shoes, frightening the maids, and worrying the kittens, be humour, he has it. It was but yesterday he fastened my wig to the back of my chair, and when I went to make a bow, I popt my bald head in Mrs. Frizzle's face!

MRS. HARDCASTLE. And am I to blame! The poor boy was always too sickly to do any good. A school would be his death. When he comes to be a little stronger, who knows what a year or two's Latin may do for him?

HARDCASTLE. Latin for him! A cat and fiddle! No, no, the ale-house and the stable are the only schools he'll ever go to!

MRS. HARDCASTLE. Well, we must not snub the poor boy now, for I believe we shan't have him long among us. Anybody that looks in his face may see he's consumptive.

HARDCASTLE. Ay, if growing too fat be one of the symptoms.

MRS. HARDCASTLE. He coughs sometimes.

HARDCASTLE. Yes, when his liquor goes the wrong way.

MRS. HARDCASTLE. I'm actually afraid of his lungs.

HARDCASTLE. And truly, so am I; for he sometimes whoops like a speaking-trumpet [*Tony hallooing behind the scenes*] O, there he goes.—A very consumptive figure, truly!

Enter Tony, crossing the stage.

[2]**Prince Eugene** hero in the War of Spanish Succession

MRS. HARDCASTLE. Tony, where are you going, my charmer? Won't you give papa and I a little of your company, lovey?

TONY. I'm in haste, mother, I cannot stay.

MRS. HARDCASTLE. You shan't venture out this raw evening, my dear. You look most shockingly.

TONY. I can't stay, I tell you. The "Three Pigeons" expects me down every moment. There's some fun going forward.

HARDCASTLE. Ay; the ale-house, the old place. I thought so.

MRS. HARDCASTLE. A low, paltry set of fellows.

TONY. Not so low, neither. There's Dick Muggins the exciseman, Jack Slang the horse doctor, Little Aminadab that grinds the music-box, and Tom Twist that spins the pewter platter.

MRS. HARDCASTLE. Pray, my dear, disappoint them for one night, at least.

TONY. As for disappointing *them*, I should not much mind; but I can't abide to disappoint *myself!*

MRS. HARDCASTLE. [Detaining him] You shan't go.

TONY. I will, I tell you.

MRS. HARDCASTLE. I say you shan't.

TONY. We'll see which is strongest, you or I.

[Exit hauling her out.]

HARDCASTLE. [Alone] Ay, there goes a pair that only spoil each other. But is not the whole age in a combination to drive sense and discretion out of doors? There's my pretty darling Kate; the fashions of the times have almost infected her too. By living a year or two in town, she is as fond of gauze, and French frippery, as the best of them.

Enter Miss Hardcastle.

HARDCASTLE. Blessings on my pretty innocence! Dressed out as usual, my Kate! Goodness! What a quantity of superfluous silk hast thou got about thee, girl! I could never teach the fools of this age, that the indigent world could be clothed out of the trimmings of the vain.

MISS HARDCASTLE. You know our agreement, sir. You allow me the morning to receive and pay visits, and to dress in my own manner; and in the evening, I put on my housewife's dress, to please you.

HARDCASTLE. Well, remember, I insist on the terms of our agreement; and, by-the-bye, I believe I shall have occasion to try your obedience this very evening.

MISS HARDCASTLE. I protest, sir, I don't comprehend your meaning.

HARDCASTLE. Then to be plain with you, Kate, I expect the young gentleman I have chosen to be your husband from town this very day. I have his father's letter, in which he informs me his son is set out, and that he intends to follow himself shortly after.

MISS HARDCASTLE. Indeed! I wish I had known something of this before. Bless me, how shall I behave? It's a thousand to one I shan't like him; our meeting will be so formal, and so like a thing of business, that I shall find no room for friendship or esteem.

HARDCASTLE. Depend upon it, child, I'll never control your choice; but Mr. Marlow, whom I have pitched upon, is the son of my old friend, Sir Charles Marlow, of whom you have heard me talk so often. The young gentleman has been bred a scholar, and is designed for an employment in the service of his country. I am told he's a man of an excellent understanding.

MISS HARDCASTLE. Is he?

HARDCASTLE. Very generous.

MISS HARDCASTLE. I believe I shall like him.

HARDCASTLE. Young and brave.

MISS HARDCASTLE. I'm sure I shall like him.

HARDCASTLE. And very handsome.

MISS HARDCASTLE. My dear papa, say no more [kissing his hand], he's mine, I'll have him!

HARDCASTLE. And, to crown all, Kate, he's one of the most bashful and reserved young fellows in all the world.

MISS HARDCASTLE. Eh! you have frozen me to death again. That word reserved has undone all the rest of his accomplishments. A reserved lover, it is said, always makes a suspicious husband.

HARDCASTLE. On the contrary, modesty seldom resides in a breast that is not enriched with nobler virtues. It was the very feature in his character that first struck me.

MISS HARDCASTLE. He must have more striking features to catch me, I promise you. However, if he be so young, so handsome, and so everything, as you mention, I believe he'll do still. I think I'll have him.

HARDCASTLE. Ay, Kate, but there is still an obstacle. It is more than an even wager, he may not have *you.*

MISS HARDCASTLE. My dear papa, why will you mortify one so?—Well, if he refuses, instead of breaking my heart at his indifference, I'll only break my glass for its flattery, set my cap to some newer fashion, and look out for some less difficult admirer.

HARDCASTLE. Bravely resolved! In the meantime I'll go prepare the servants for his reception; as we seldom see company, they want as much training as a company of recruits the first day's muster.

[Exit.]

MISS HARDCASTLE. [Alone] Lud, this news of papa's puts me all in a flutter. Young, handsome; these he put last; but I put them foremost. Sensible, good-natur'd; I like all that. But then reserved, and sheepish, that's much against him. Yet can't he be cured of his timidity, by being taught to be proud of his wife? Yes, and can't I—But I vow I'm disposing of the husband before I have secured the lover!

Enter Miss Neville.

MISS HARDCASTLE. I'm glad you're come, Neville, my dear. Tell me, Constance, how do I look this evening? Is there anything whimsical about me? Is it one of my well-looking days, child? Am I in face to-day?[3]

MISS NEVILLE. Perfectly, my dear. Yet, now I look again—bless me!—sure no accident has happened among the ca-

[3]**Am . . . face?** "Am I looking good today?"

nary birds or the goldfishes? Has your brother or the cat been meddling? Or has the last novel been too moving?

MISS HARDCASTLE. No; nothing of all this. I have been threatened—I can scarce get it out—I have been threatened with a lover!

MISS NEVILLE. And his name—

MISS HARDCASTLE. Is Marlow.

MISS NEVILLE. Indeed!

MISS HARDCASTLE. The son of Sir Charles Marlow.

MISS NEVILLE. As I live, the most intimate friend of Mr. Hastings, *my* admirer. They are never asunder. I believe you must have seen him when we lived in town.

MISS HARDCASTLE. Never.

MISS NEVILLE. He's a very singular character, I assure you. Among women of reputation and virtue, he is the modestest man alive: but his acquaintance give him a very different character among creatures of another stamp: you understand me?

MISS HARDCASTLE. An odd character, indeed! I shall never be able to manage him. What shall I do? Pshaw, think no more of him, but trust to occurrences for success. But how goes on your own affair, my dear? Has my mother been courting you for my brother Tony, as usual?

MISS NEVILLE. I have just come from one of our agreeable *tête-à-têtes*. She has been saying a hundred tender things, and setting off her pretty monster as the very pink of perfection.

MISS HARDCASTLE. And her partiality is such that she actually thinks him so. A fortune like yours is no small temptation. Besides, as she has the sole management of it, I'm not surprised to see her unwilling to let it go out of the family.

MISS NEVILLE. A fortune like mine, which chiefly consists in jewels, is no such mighty temptation. But, at any rate, if my dear Hastings be but constant, I make no doubt to be too hard for her at last. However, I let her suppose that I am in love with her son, and she never once dreams that my affections are fixed upon another.

MISS HARDCASTLE. My good brother holds out stoutly. I could almost love him for hating you so.

MISS NEVILLE. It is a good-natur'd creature at bottom, and I'm sure would wish to see me married to anybody but himself. But my aunt's bell rings for our afternoon's walk through the improvements. *Allons*. Courage is necessary, as our affairs are critical.

MISS HARDCASTLE. Would it were bed-time and all were well.

[*Exeunt.*]

SCENE II: AN ALE-HOUSE ROOM

Several shabby fellows, with punch and tobacco. Tony at the head of the table, a little higher than the rest: a mallet in his hand.

OMNES. Hurrea, hurrea, hurrea, bravo!

FIRST FELLOW. Now, gentlemen, silence for a song. The 'Squire is going to knock himself down for a song.

OMNES. Ay, a song, a song.

TONY. Then I'll sing you, gentlemen, a song I made upon this ale-house, the Three Pigeons.

SONG

Let school-masters puzzle their brain,
  With grammar, and nonsense, and learning;
Good liquor, I stoutly maintain,
  Gives genus[4] a better discerning,
Let them brag of their Heathenish Gods,
  Their Lethes, their Styxes, and Stygians;
Their Quis, and their Quæs, and their Quods,
  They're all but a parcel of Pigeons.
  Toroddle, toroddle, toroll!

When Methodist preachers come down,
  A-preaching that drinking is sinful,
I'll wager the rascals a crown,
  They always preach best with a skinful.
But when you come down with your pence,
  For a slice of their scurvy religion,
I'll leave it to all men of sense,
  But you, my good friend, are the pigeon.
  Toroddle, toroddle, toroll!

Then come, put the jorum[5] about,
  And let us be merry and clever,
Our hearts and our liquors are stout,
  Here's the Three Jolly Pigeons for ever.
Let some cry up woodcock or hare,
  Your bustards, your ducks, and your widgeons:[6]
But of all the birds in the air,
  Here's a health to the Three Jolly Pigeons.
  Toroddle, toroddle, toroll!

OMNES. Bravo, bravo!

FIRST FELLOW. The 'Squire has got spunk in him.

SECOND FELLOW. I loves to hear him sing, bekeays he never gives us nothing that's *low*.

THIRD FELLOW. O damn anything that's *low*, I cannot bear it!

FOURTH FELLOW. The genteel thing is the genteel thing at any time. If so be that a gentleman bees in a concatenation[7] accordingly.

THIRD FELLOW. I like the maxum of it, Master Muggins. What, though I am obligated to dance a bear, a man may be a gentleman for all that. May this be my poison if my

---

[4]**Genus** genius [5]**jorum** large container for ail, spirits and other drinks [6]**widgeons** pigeons [7]**concatenation** appropriate, the man is trying to impress or outdo the others

bear ever dances but to the very genteelest of tunes, *Water Parted*, or the minuet in *Ariadne*.[8]

SECOND FELLOW. What a pity it is the 'Squire is not come to his own. It would be well for all the publicans within ten miles round of him.

TONY. Ecod, and so it would, Master Slang. I'd then show what it was to keep choice of company.

SECOND FELLOW. O, he takes after his own father for that. To be sure, old 'Squire Lumpkin was the finest gentleman I ever set my eyes on. For winding the straight horn, or beating a thicket for a hare, or a wench, he never had his fellow. It was a saying in the place that he kept the best horses, dogs, and girls in the whole country.

TONY. Ecod, and when I'm of age I'll be no bastard, I promise you. I have been thinking of Bet Bouncer and the miller's grey mare to begin with. But come, my boys, drink about and be merry, for you pay no reckoning. Well, Stingo, what's the matter?

Enter Landlord.

LANDLORD. There be two gentlemen in a post-chaise at the door. They have lost their way upo' the forest; and they are talking something about Mr. Hardcastle.

TONY. As sure as can be, one of them must be the gentleman that's coming down to court my sister. Do they seem to be Londoners?

LANDLORD. I believe they may. They look woundily like Frenchmen.

TONY. Then desire them to step this way, and I'll set them right in a twinkling. [*Exit Landlord*] Gentlemen, as they mayn't be good enough company for you, step down for a moment, and I'll be with you in the squeezing of a lemon.
[*Exeunt Mob.*]

TONY. [*Alone*] Father-in-law[9] has been calling me whelp, and hound, this half year. Now, if I pleased, I could be so revenged upon the old grumbletonian. But then I'm afraid—afraid of what? I shall soon be worth fifteen hundred a year, and let him frighten me out of *that* if he can!

Enter Landlord, conducting Marlow and Hastings.

MARLOW. What a tedious uncomfortable day have we had of it! We were told it was but forty miles across the country, and we have come above threescore!

HASTINGS. And all, Marlow from that unaccountable reserve of yours, that would not let us enquire more frequently on the way.

MARLOW. I own, Hastings, I am unwilling to lay myself under an obligation to every one I meet, and often stand the chance of an unmannerly answer.

HASTINGS. At present, however, we are not likely to receive any answer.

TONY. No offence, gentlemen. But I'm told you have been enquiring for one Mr. Hardcastle, in these parts. Do you know what part of the country you are in?

HASTINGS. Not in the least, sir, but should thank you for information.

TONY. Nor the way you came?

HASTINGS. No, sir, but if you can inform us—

TONY. Why, gentlemen, if you know neither the road you are going, nor where you are, nor the road you came, the first thing I have to inform is, that—you have lost your way.

MARLOW. We wanted no ghost to tell us that.

TONY. Pray, gentlemen, may I be so bold as to ask the place from whence you came?

MARLOW. That's not necessary towards directing us where we are to go.

TONY. No offence; but question for question is all fair, you know. Pray, gentlemen, is not this same Hardcastle a cross-grained, old-fashioned, whimsical fellow with an ugly face; a daughter, and a pretty son?

HASTINGS. We have not seen the gentleman, but he has the family you mention.

TONY. The daughter, a tall, trapesing, trolloping, talkative maypole— The son, a pretty, well-bred, agreeable youth, that everybody is fond of!

MARLOW. Our information differs in this. The daughter is said to be well-bred and beautiful; the son an awkward booby, reared up and spoiled at his mother's apron-string.

TONY. He-he-hem—then, gentlemen, all I have to tell you is, that you won't reach Mr. Hardcastle's house this night, I believe.

HASTINGS. Unfortunate!

TONY. It's a damned long, dark, boggy, dirty, dangerous way. Stingo, tell the gentlemen the way to Mr. Hardcastle's [*winking upon the Landlord*]; Mr. Hardcastle's of Quagmire Marsh, you understand me.

LANDLORD. Master Hardcastle's! Lack-a-daisy, my masters, you're come a deadly deal wrong! When you came to the bottom of the hill, you should have crossed down Squash Lane.

MARLOW. Cross down Squash Lane!

LANDLORD. Then you were to keep straight forward, until you came to four roads.

MARLOW. Come to where four roads meet!

TONY. Ay, but you must be sure to take only one of them.

MARLOW. O, sir, you're facetious!

TONY. Then, keeping to the right, you are to go sideways till you come upon Crack-skull common; there you must look sharp for the track of the wheel, and go forward, till you come to farmer Murrain's barn. Coming to the farmer's barn, you are to turn to the right, and then to the left, and then to the right about again, till you find out the old mill—

MARLOW. Zounds, man! we could as soon find out the longitude!

HASTINGS. What's to be done, Marlow?

[8]**Water . . . Ariadne** popular songs from contemporary operas
[9]**Father-in-law** Tony is referring to Hardcastle and he really means stepfather

MARLOW. This house promises but a poor reception, though, perhaps, the landlord can accommodate us.

LANDLORD. Alack, master, we have but one spare bed in the whole house.

TONY. And to my knowledge, that's taken up by three lodgers already. [*After a pause, in which the rest seem disconcerted*] I have hit it. Don't you think, Stingo, our landlady could accommodate the gentlemen by the fire-side with—three chairs and a bolster?

HASTINGS. I hate sleeping by the fire-side.

MARLOW. And I detest your three chairs and a bolster.

TONY. You do, do you?—then let me see—what—if you go on a mile further, to the Buck's Head; the old Buck's Head on the hill, one of the best inns in the whole country?

HASTINGS. Oh, oh! so we have escaped an adventure for this night, however.

LANDLORD. [*Apart to Tony*] Sure, you ben't sending them to your father's as an inn, be you?

TONY. Mum, you fool, you. Let *them* find that out. [*To them*] You have only to keep on straight forward, till you come to a large old house by the roadside. You'll see a pair of large horns over the door. That's the sign. Drive up the yard, and call stoutly about you.

HASTINGS. Sir, we are obliged to you. The servants can't miss the way?

TONY. No, no. But I tell you though, the landlord is rich, and going to leave off business; so he wants to be thought a gentleman, saving your presence, he! he! he! He'll be for giving you his company, and, ecod, if you mind him, he'll persuade you that his mother was an alderman, and his aunt a justice of the peace!

LANDLORD. A troublesome old blade, to be sure; but 'a keeps as good wines and beds as any in the whole country.

MARLOW. Well, if he supplies us with these, we shall want no further connection. We are to turn to the right, did you say?

TONY. No, no; straight forward. I'll just step myself, and show you a piece of the way. [*To the Landlord*] Mum.

LANDLORD. Ah, bless your heart, for a sweet, pleasant— damned mischievous son.

[*Exeunt.*]

ACT TWO

SCENE I: AN OLD-FASHIONED HOUSE

Enter Hardcastle, followed by three or four awkward Servants.

HARDCASTLE. Well, I hope you're perfect in the table exercise I have been teaching you these three days. You all know your posts and your places, and can show that you have been used to good company, without ever stirring from home.

OMNES. Ay, ay.

HARDCASTLE. When company comes, you are not to pop out and stare, and then run in again, like frightened rabbits in a warren.

OMNES. No, no.

HARDCASTLE. You, Diggory, whom I have taken from the barn are to make a show at the side-table; and you, Roger, whom I have advanced from the plough, are to place yourself behind *my* chair. But you're not to stand so, with your hands in your pockets. Take your hands from your pockets, Roger; and from your head, you blockhead, you. See how Diggory carries his hands. They're a little too stiff, indeed, but that's no great matter.

DIGGORY. Ay, mind how I hold them. I learned to hold my hands this way, when I was upon drill for the militia. And so being upon drill—

HARDCASTLE. You must not be so talkative, Diggory. You must be all attention to the guests. You must hear us talk, and not think of talking; you must see us drink and not think of drinking; you must see us eat and not think of eating.

DIGGORY. By the laws, your worship, that's parfectly unpossible. Whenever Diggory sees yeating going forward, ecod, he's always wishing for a mouthful himself.

HARDCASTLE. Blockhead! Is not a bellyful in the kitchen as good as a bellyful in the parlour? Stay your stomach with that reflection.

DIGGORY. Ecod, I thank your worship, I'll make a shift to stay my stomach with a slice of cold beef in the pantry.

HARDCASTLE. Diggory, you are too talkative. Then, if I happen to say a good thing, or tell a good story at table, you must not all burst out a-laughing, as if you made part of the company.

DIGGORY. Then, ecod, your worship must not tell the story of Ould Grouse in the gun-room: I can't help laughing at that—he! he! he!—for the soul of me! We have laughed at that these twenty years—ha! ha! ha!

HARDCASTLE. Ha! ha! ha! The story is a good one. Well, honest Diggory, you may laugh at that—but still remember to be attentive. Suppose one of the company should call for a glass of wine, how will you behave? A glass of wine, sir, if you please [*To Diggory*]—Eh, why don't you move?

DIGGORY. Ecod, your worship, I never have courage till I see the eatables and drinkables brought upo' the table, and then I'm as bauld as a lion.

HARDCASTLE. What, will nobody move?

FIRST SERVANT. I'm not to leave this pleace.

SECOND SERVANT. I'm sure it's no pleace of mine.

THIRD SERVANT. Nor mine for sartain.

DIGGORY. Wauns,[10] and I'm sure it canna be mine.

HARDCASTLE. You numskulls! and so while, like your betters, you are quarrelling for places, the guests must be starved. O, you dunces! I find I must begin all over again.—But don't I hear a coach drive into the yard? To

---

[10] **wauns** by "God's wounds," an oath

your posts, you blockheads! I'll go in the meantime and give my old friend's son a hearty reception at the gate.

[*Exit Hardcastle.*]

DIGGORY. By the elevens, my pleace is gone quite out of my head!

ROGER. I know that my pleace is to be everywhere!

FIRST SERVANT. Where the devil is mine?

SECOND SERVANT. My pleace is to be nowhere at all; and so I'ze go about my business!

[*Exeunt Servants, running about as if frighted, different ways.*]

Enter Servants with candles, showing in Marlow and Hastings.

SERVANT. Welcome, gentlemen, very welcome. This way.

HASTINGS. After the disappointments of the day, welcome once more, Charles, to the comforts of a clean room and a good fire. Upon my word, a very well-looking house; antique but creditable.

MARLOW. The usual fate of a large mansion. Having first ruined the master by good housekeeping, it at last comes to levy contributions as an inn.

HASTINGS. As you say, we passengers are to be taxed to pay all these fineries. I have often seen a good sideboard, or a marble chimney-piece, though not actually put in the bill, inflame a reckoning confoundedly.

MARLOW. Travellers, George, must pay in all places. The only difference is that in good inns you pay dearly for luxuries; in bad inns you are fleeced and starved.

HASTINGS. You have lived pretty much among them. In truth, I have been often surprised that you who have seen so much of the world, with your natural good sense, and your many opportunities, could never yet acquire a requisite share of assurance.

MARLOW. The Englishman's malady. But tell me, George, where could I have learned that assurance you talk of? My life has been chiefly spent in a college, or an inn, in seclusion from that lovely part of the creation that chiefly teach men confidence. I don't know that I was ever familiarly acquainted with a single modest woman—except my mother—but among females of another class, you know—

HASTINGS. Ay, among them you are impudent enough of all conscience!

MARLOW. They are of *us*, you know.

HASTINGS. But in the company of women of reputation I never saw such an idiot, such a trembler; you look for all the world as if you wanted an opportunity of stealing out of the room.

MARLOW. Why, man, that's because I *do* want to steal out of the room. Faith, I have often formed a resolution to break the ice, and rattle away at any rate. But I don't know how, a single glance from a pair of fine eyes has totally overset my resolution. An impudent fellow may counterfeit modesty, but I'll be hanged if a modest man can ever counterfeit impudence.

HASTINGS. If you could but say half the fine things to them that I have heard you lavish upon the barmaid of an inn, or even a college bedmaker—

MARLOW. Why, George, I can't say fine things to them. They freeze, they petrify me. They may talk of a comet, or a burning mountain, or some such bagatelle;[11] but to me a modest woman, dressed out in all her finery, is the most tremendous object of the whole creation.

HASTINGS. Ha! ha! ha! At this rate, man, how can you ever expect to marry!

MARLOW. Never; unless, as among kings and princes, my bride were to be courted by proxy. If, indeed, like an Eastern bridegroom, one were to be introduced to a wife he never saw before, it might be endured. But to go through all the terrors of a formal courtship, together with the episode of aunts, grandmothers, and cousins, and at last to blurt out the broad staring question of, "Madam, will you marry me?" No, no, that's a strain much above me, I assure you!

HASTINGS. I pity you. But how do you intend behaving to the lady you are come down to visit at the request of your father?

MARLOW. As I behave to all other ladies. Bow very low; answer yes, or no, to all her demands. But for the rest, I don't think I shall venture to look in her face till I see my father's again.

HASTINGS. I'm surprised that one who is so warm a friend can be so cool a lover.

MARLOW. To be explicit, my dear Hastings, my chief inducement down was to be instrumental in forwarding your happiness, not my own. Miss Neville loves you; the family don't know you. As my friend you are sure of a reception, and let honour do the rest.

HASTINGS. My dear Marlow! But I'll suppress the emotion. Were I a wretch, meanly seeking to carry off a fortune, you should be the last man in the world I would apply to for assistance. But Miss Neville's person is all I ask, and that is mine, both from her deceased father's consent and her own inclination.

MARLOW. Happy man! You have talents and art to captivate any woman. I'm doomed to adore the sex, and yet to converse with the only part of it I despise. This stammer in my address, and this awkward prepossessing visage of mine, can never permit me to soar above the reach of a milliner's apprentice, or one of the duchesses of Drury Lane. Pshaw! this fellow here to interrupt us.

Enter Hardcastle.

HARDCASTLE. Gentlemen, once more you are heartily welcome. Which is Mr. Marlow? Sir, you're heartily welcome. It's not my way, you see, to receive my friends with

---

[11]**bagatelle** trivial thing

my back to the fire. I like to give them a hearty reception in the old style at my gate. I like to see their horses and trunks taken care of.

MARLOW. [*Aside*] He has got our names from the servants already. [*To him*] We approve your caution and hospitality, sir. [*To Hastings*] I have been thinking, George, of changing our travelling dresses in the morning. I am grown confoundedly ashamed of mine.

HARDCASTLE. I beg, Mr. Marlow, you'll use no ceremony in this house.

HASTINGS. I fancy, George, you're right. The first blow is half the battle. I intend opening the campaign with the white and gold.

HARDCASTLE. Mr. Marlow—Mr. Hastings—gentlemen—pray be under no constraint in this house. This is Liberty Hall, gentlemen. You may do just as you please here.

MARLOW. Yet, George, if we open the campaign too fiercely at first, we may want ammunition before it is over. I think to reserve the embroidery to secure a retreat.

HARDCASTLE. Your talking of a retreat, Mr. Marlow, puts me in mind of the Duke of Marlborough, when we went to besiege Denain. He first summoned the garrison—

MARLOW. Don't you think the *ventre d'or*[12] waistcoat will do with the plain brown?

HARDCASTLE. He first summoned the garrison, which might consist of about five thousand men—

HASTINGS. I think not: brown and yellow mix but very poorly.

HARDCASTLE. I say, gentlemen, as I was telling you, he summoned the garrison, which might consist of about five thousand men—

MARLOW. The girls like finery.

HARDCASTLE. Which might consist of about five thousand men, well appointed with stores, ammunition, and other implements of war. "Now," says the Duke of Marlborough to George Brooks, that stood next to him—you must have heard of George Brooks; "I'll pawn my Dukedom," says he, "but I take that garrison without spilling a drop of blood!" So—

MARLOW. What, my good friend, if you gave us a glass of punch in the meantime, it would help us to carry on the siege with vigour.

HARDCASTLE. Punch, sir! [*Aside*] This is the most unaccountable kind of modesty I ever met with!

MARLOW. Yes, sir, punch! A glass of warm punch, after our journey, will be comfortable. This is Liberty Hall, you know.

HARDCASTLE. Here's cup, sir.

MARLOW. [*Aside*] So this fellow, in his Liberty Hall, will only let us have just what he pleases.

HARDCASTLE. [*Taking the cup*] I hope you'll find it to your mind. I have prepared it with my own hands, and I be-

lieve you'll own the ingredients are tolerable. Will you be so good as to pledge me, sir? Here, Mr. Marlow, here is our better acquaintance!

[*Drinks.*]

MARLOW. [*Aside*] A very impudent fellow this! but he's a character, and I'll humour him a little. Sir, my service to you.

[*Drinks.*]

HASTINGS. [*Aside*] I see this fellow wants to give us his company, and forgets that he's an innkeeper, before he has learned to be a gentleman.

MARLOW. From the excellence of your cup, my old friend, I suppose you have a good deal of business in this part of the country. Warm work, now and then, at elections, I suppose?

HARDCASTLE. No, sir, I have long given that work over. Since our betters have hit upon the expedient of electing each other, there's no business "for us that sell ale."[13]

HASTINGS. So, then you have no turn for politics, I find.

HARDCASTLE. Not in the least. There was a time, indeed, I fretted myself about the mistakes of government, like other people; but finding myself every day grow more angry, and the government growing no better, I left it to mend itself. Since that, I no more trouble my head about Heyder Ally, Ally Cawn, than about Ally Croker.[14] Sir, my service to you.

HASTINGS. So that, with eating above stairs, and drinking below, with receiving your friends within, and amusing them without, you lead a good pleasant bustling life of it.

HARDCASTLE. I do stir about a great deal, that's certain. Half the differences of the parish are adjusted in this very parlour.

MARLOW. [*After drinking*] And you have an argument in your cup, old gentleman, better than any in Westminster Hall.

HARDCASTLE. Ay, young gentleman, that, and a little philosophy.

MARLOW. [*Aside*] Well, this is the first time I ever heard of an innkeeper's philosophy.

HASTINGS. So then, like an experienced general, you attack them on every quarter. If you find their reason manageable, you attack it with your philosophy; if you find they have no reason, you attack them with this. Here's your health, my philosopher.

[*Drinks.*]

HARDCASTLE. Good, very good, thank you; ha! ha! Your generalship puts me in mind of Prince Eugene, when he fought the Turks at the battle of Belgrade. You shall hear.

---

[13]**for . . . ale** Hardcastle is trying to joke with Marlowe and Hastings but they take him literally   [14]**Heyder . . . Croker** Hardcastle's mispronunciations of the Haider Ali and Ali Kahn, who were Indian leaders. Ally Croker is a character from a popular contemporary song.

---

[12]***ventre d'or*** gold trim.

MARLOW. Instead of the battle of Belgrade, I believe it's almost time to talk about supper. What has your philosophy got in the house for supper?

HARDCASTLE. For supper, sir! [*Aside*] Was ever such a request to a man in his own house!

MARLOW. Yes, sir, supper, sir; I begin to feel an appetite. I shall make devilish work to-night in the larder, I promise you.

HARDCASTLE. [*Aside*] Such a brazen dog sure never my eyes beheld. [*To him*] Why, really, sir, as for supper I can't well tell. My Dorothy, and the cook maid, settle these things between them. I leave these kind of things entirely to them.

MARLOW. You do, do you?

HARDCASTLE. Entirely. By-the-bye, I believe they are in actual consultation upon what's for supper this moment in the kitchen.

MARLOW. Then I beg they'll admit *me* as one of their privy council. It's a way I have got. When I travel, I always choose to regulate my own supper. Let the cook be called. No offence, I hope, sir.

HARDCASTLE. O, no, sir, none in the least; yet, I don't know how. Our Bridget, the cook maid, is not very communicative upon these occasions. Should we send for her, she might scold us all out of the house.

HASTINGS. Let's see your list of the larder, then. I ask it as a favour. I always match my appetite to my bill of fare.

MARLOW. [*To Hardcastle, who looks at them with surprise*] Sir, he's very right, and it's my way, too.

HARDCASTLE. Sir, you have a right to command here. Here, Roger, bring us the bill of fare for to-night's supper. I believe it's drawn out. Your manner, Mr. Hastings, puts me in mind of my uncle, Colonel Wallop. It was a saying of his, that no man was sure of his supper till he had eaten it.

HASTINGS. [*Aside*] All upon the high ropes! His uncle a colonel! We shall soon hear of his mother being a justice of peace. But let's hear the bill of fare.

MARLOW. [*Perusing*] What's here? For the first course; for the second course; for the desert. The devil, sir, do you think we have brought down the whole Joiners' Company, or the Corporation of Bedford, to eat up such a supper? Two or three little things, clean and comfortable, will do.

HASTINGS. But let's hear it.

MARLOW. [*Reading*] For the first course at the top, a pig, and prune sauce.

HASTINGS. Damn your pig, I say!

MARLOW. And damn your prune sauce, say I!

HARDCASTLE. And yet, gentlemen, to men that are hungry, pig, with prune sauce, is very good eating.

MARLOW. At the bottom, a calf's tongue and brains.

HASTINGS. Let your brains be knocked out, my good sir; I don't like them.

MARLOW. Or you may clap them on a plate by themselves. I do.

HARDCASTLE. [*Aside*] Their impudence confounds me. [*To them*] Gentlemen, you are my guests, make what alterations you please. Is there anything else you wish to retrench or alter, gentlemen?

MARLOW. Item. A pork pie, a boiled rabbit and sausages, a florentine,[15] a shaking pudding, and a dish of tiff—taff—taffety cream!

HASTINGS. Confound your made dishes, I shall be as much at a loss in this house as at a green and yellow dinner at the French ambassador's table. I'm for plain eating.

HARDCASTLE. I'm sorry, gentlemen, that I have nothing you like, but if there be anything you have a particular fancy to—

MARLOW. Why, really, sir, your bill of fare is so exquisite, that any one part of it is full as good as another. Send us what you please. So much for supper. And now to see that our beds are aired, and properly taken care of.

HARDCASTLE. I entreat you'll leave all that to me. You shall not stir a step.

MARLOW. Leave that to you! I protest, sir, you must excuse me, I always look to these things myself.

HARDCASTLE. I must insist, sir, you'll make yourself easy on that head.

MARLOW. You see I'm resolved on it. [*Aside*] A very troublesome fellow this, as ever I met with.

HARDCASTLE. Well, sir, I'm resolved at least to attend you. [*Aside*] This may be modern modesty, but I never saw anything look so like old-fashioned impudence.

[*Exeunt Marlow and Hardcastle.*]

HASTINGS. [*Alone*] So I find this fellow's civilities begin to grow troublesome. But who can be angry at those assiduities which are meant to please him! Miss Neville, by all that's happy!

Enter Miss Neville.

MISS NEVILLE. My dear Hastings! To what unexpected good fortune? to what accident am I to ascribe this happy meeting?

HASTINGS. Rather let me ask the same question, as I could never have hoped to meet my dearest Constance at an inn.

MISS NEVILLE. An inn! sure you mistake! my aunt, my guardian, lives here. What could induce you to think this house an inn?

HASTINGS. My friend, Mr. Marlow, with whom I came down, and I, have been sent here as to an inn, I assure you. A young fellow whom we accidentally met at a house hard by directed us hither.

MISS NEVILLE. Certainly it must be one of my hopeful cousin's tricks, of whom you have heard me talk so often; ha! ha! ha! ha!

[15]**Florentine** a popular dish

HASTINGS. He whom your aunt intends for you? He of whom I have such just apprehensions?

MISS NEVILLE. You have nothing to fear from him, I assure you. You'd adore him if you knew how heartily he despises me. My aunt knows it too, and has undertaken to court me for him, and actually begins to think she has made a conquest.

HASTINGS. Thou dear dissembler! You must know, my Constance, I have just seized this happy opportunity of my friend's visit here to get admittance into the family. The horses that carried us down are now fatigued with their journey, but they'll soon be refreshed; and then if my dearest girl will trust in her faithful Hastings, we shall soon be landed in France, where even among slaves the laws of marriage are respected.

MISS NEVILLE. I have often told you that though ready to obey you, I yet should leave my little fortune behind with reluctance. The greatest part of it was left to me by my uncle, the India Director, and chiefly consists in jewels. I have been for some time persuading my aunt to let me wear them. I fancy I'm very near succeeding. The instant they are put into my possession you shall find me ready to make them and myself yours.

HASTINGS. Perish the baubles! Your person is all I desire. In the meantime, my friend Marlow must not be let into his mistake. I know the strange reserve of his temper is such that if abruptly informed of it, he would instantly quit the house before our plan was ripe for execution.

MISS NEVILLE. But how shall we keep him in the deception? Miss Hardcastle is just returned from walking; what if we still continue to deceive him?—This, this way—

[*They confer.*]

Enter Marlow.

MARLOW. The assiduities of these good people tease me beyond bearing. My host seems to think it ill manners to leave me alone, and so he claps not only himself, but his old-fashioned wife on my back. They talk of coming to sup with us, too; and then, I suppose, we are to run the gauntlet through all the rest of the family.—What have we got here?—

HASTINGS. My dear Charles! Let me congratulate you!— The most fortunate accident!—Who do you think is just alighted?

MARLOW. Cannot guess.

HASTINGS. Our mistresses, boy, Miss Hardcastle and Miss Neville. Give me leave to introduce Miss Constance Neville to your acquaintance. Happening to dine in the neighbourhood, they called, on their return, to take fresh horses, here. Miss Hardcastle has just stept into the next room, and will be back in an instant. Wasn't it lucky? eh!

MARLOW. [*Aside*] I have just been mortified enough of all conscience, and here comes something to complete my embarrassment.

HASTINGS. Well! but wasn't it the most fortunate thing in the world?

MARLOW. Oh! yes. Very fortunate—a most joyful encounter— But our dresses, George, you know, are in disorder— What if we should postpone the happiness till tomorrow— To-morrow at her own house—It will be every bit as convenient— And rather more respectful— To-morrow let it be.   [*Offering to go.*]

MISS NEVILLE. By no means, sir. Your ceremony will displease her. The disorder of your dress will shew the ardour of your impatience. Besides, she knows you are in the house, and will permit you to see her.

MARLOW. O! the devil! how shall I support it? Hem! hem! Hastings, you must not go. You are to assist me, you know. I shall be confoundly ridiculous. Yet, hang it! I'll take courage. Hem!

HASTINGS. Pshaw, man! it's but the first plunge, and all's over. She's but a woman, you know.

MARLOW. And of all women, she that I dread most to encounter!

Enter Miss Hardcastle, as returned from walking, a bonnet, etc.

HASTINGS. [*Introducing them*] Miss Hardcastle, Mr. Marlow, I'm proud of bringing two persons of such merit together, that only want to know, to esteem each other.

MISS HARDCASTLE. [*Aside*] Now for meeting my modest gentleman with a demure face, and quite in his own manner. [*After a pause, in which he appears very uneasy and disconcerted*] I'm glad of your safe arrival, sir—I'm told you had some accidents by the way.

MARLOW. Only a few, madam. Yes, we had some. Yes, madam, a good many, accidents, but should be sorry— madam—or rather glad of any accidents—that are so agreeably concluded. Hem!

HASTINGS. [*To him*] You never spoke better in your whole life. Keep it up, and I'll insure you the victory.

MISS HARDCASTLE. I'm afraid you flatter, sir. You that have seen so much of the finest company can find little entertainment in an obscure corner of the country.

MARLOW. [*Gathering courage*] I have lived, indeed, in the world, madam; but I have kept very little company. I have been but an observer upon life, madam, while others were enjoying it.

MISS NEVILLE. But that, I am told, is the way to enjoy it at last.

HASTINGS. [*To him*] Cicero never spoke better. Once more, and you are confirmed in assurance for ever.

MARLOW. [*To him*] Hem! Stand by me, then, and when I'm down, throw in a word or two to set me up again.

MISS HARDCASTLE. An observer, like you, upon life were, I fear, disagreeably employed, since you must have had much more to censure than to approve.

MARLOW. Pardon me, madam. I was always willing to be

amused. The folly of most people is rather an object of mirth than uneasiness.

HASTINGS. [*To him*] Bravo, bravo. Never spoke so well in your whole life. Well, Miss Hardcastle, I see that you and Mr. Marlow are going to be very good company. I believe our being here will but embarrass the interview.

MARLOW. Not in the least, Mr. Hastings. We like your company of all things. [*To him*] Zounds! George, sure you won't go? How can you leave us?

HASTINGS. Our presence will but spoil conversation, so we'll retire to the next room. [*To him*] You don't consider, man, that we are to manage a little *tête-à-tête* of our own.

[*Exeunt.*]

MISS HARDCASTLE. [*After a pause*] But you have not been wholly an observer, I presume, sir. The ladies, I should hope, have employed some part of your addresses.

MARLOW. [*Relapsing into timidity*] Pardon me, madam, I—I—I—as yet have studied—only—to—deserve them.

MISS HARDCASTLE. And that some say is the very worst way to obtain them.

MARLOW. Perhaps so, madam. But I love to converse only with the more grave and sensible part of the sex.—But I'm afraid I grow tiresome.

MISS HARDCASTLE. Not at all sir; there is nothing I like so much as grave conversation myself. I could hear it for ever. Indeed, I have often been surprised how a man of *sentiment* could ever admire those light airy pleasures, where nothing reaches the heart.

MARLOW. It's—a disease—of the mind, madam. In the variety of tastes there must be some who, wanting a relish for—un-a-um.

MISS HARDCASTLE. I understand you, sir. There must be some, who, wanting a relish for refined pleasures, pretend to despise what they are incapable of tasting.

MARLOW. My meaning, madam, but infinitely better expressed. And I can't help observing—a—

MISS HARDCASTLE. [*Aside*] Who could ever suppose this fellow impudent upon some occasions. [*To him*] You were going to observe, sir—

MARLOW. I was observing, madam—I protest, madam, I forget what I was going to observe.

MISS HARDCASTLE. [*Aside*] I vow and so do I. [*To him*] You were observing, sir, that in this age of hypocrisy—something about hypocrisy, sir.

MARLOW. Yes, madam. In this age of hypocrisy, there are few who up on strict enquiry do not—a—a—a—

MISS HARDCASTLE. I understand you perfectly, sir.

MARLOW. [*Aside*] Egad! and that's more than I do myself!

MISS HARDCASTLE. You mean that in this hypocritical age there are few that do not condemn in public what they practise in private, and think they pay every debt to virtue when they praise it.

MARLOW. True, madam; those who have most virtue in their mouths, have least of it in their bosoms. But I'm sure I tire you, madam.

MISS HARDCASTLE. Not in the least, sir; there's something so agreeable and spirited in your manner, such life and force—pray, sir, go on.

MARLOW. Yes, madam. I was saying—that there are some occasions—when a total want of courage, madam, destroys all the—and puts us—upon a—a—a—

MISS HARDCASTLE. I agree with you entirely, a want of courage upon some occasions assumes the appearance of ignorance, and betrays us when we most want to excel. I beg you'll proceed.

MARLOW. Yes, madam. Morally speaking, madam—but I see Miss Neville expecting us in the next room. I would not intrude for the world.

MISS HARDCASTLE. I protest, sir, I never was more agreeably entertained in all my life. Pray go on.

MARLOW. Yes, madam. I was—But she beckons us to join her. Madam, shall I do myself the honour to attend you?

MISS HARDCASTLE. Well then, I'll follow.

MARLOW. [*Aside*] This pretty smooth dialogue has done for me.

[*Exit.*]

MISS HARDCASTLE. [*Alone*] Ha! ha! ha! Was there ever such a sober sentimental interview? I'm certain he scarce looked in my face the whole time. Yet the fellow, but for his unaccountable bashfulness, is pretty well, too. He has good sense, but then so buried in his fears that it fatigues one more than ignorance. If I could teach him a little confidence, it would be doing somebody that I know of a piece of service. But who is that somebody?—that, faith, is a question I can scarce answer.

[*Exit.*]

Enter Tony and Miss Neville, followed by Mrs. Hardcastle and Hastings.

TONY. What do you follow me for, cousin Con? I wonder you're not ashamed to be so very engaging.

MISS NEVILLE. I hope, cousin, one may speak to one's own relations, and not be to blame.

TONY. Ay, but I know what sort of a relation you want to make me, though; but it won't do. I tell you, cousin Con, it won't do, so I beg you'll keep your distance, I want no nearer relationship.

[*She follows coquetting him to the back scene.*]

MRS. HARDCASTLE. Well! I vow, Mr. Hastings, you are very entertaining. There's nothing in the world I love to talk of so much as London, and the fashions, though I was never there myself.

HASTINGS. Never there! You amaze me! From your air and manner, I concluded you had been bred all your life either at Ranelagh, St. James's, or Tower Wharf.[16]

[16]**Ranelagh . . . Wharf** all were popular recreational areas or parks; Ranelagh and St. James Parks were frequented by the upper class, while Tower Wharf was frequented by the lower classes

MRS. HARDCASTLE. O! sir, you're only pleased to say so. We country persons can have no manner at all. I'm in love with the town, and that serves to raise me above some of our neighbouring rustics; but who can have a manner, that has never seen the Pantheon, the Grotto Gardens, the Borough,[17] and such places where the nobility chiefly resort? All I can do is to enjoy London at second-hand. I take care to know every *tête-à-tête* from the *Scandalous Magazine*, and have all the fashions as they come out, in a letter from the two Miss Rickets of Crooked Lane. Pray how do you like this head, Mr. Hastings?

HASTINGS. Extremely elegant and *degagé*,[18] upon my word, madam. Your friseur[19] is a Frenchman, I suppose?

MRS. HARDCASTLE. I protest, I dressed it myself from a print in the *Ladies' Memorandum-book* for the last year.

HASTINGS. Indeed. Such a head in a side-box, at the play-house, would draw as many gazers as my Lady Mayoress at a City Ball.

MRS. HARDCASTLE. I vow, since inoculation[20] began, there is no such thing to be seen as a plain woman; so one must dress a little particular or one may escape in the crowd.

HASTINGS. But that can never be your case, madam, in any dress!

[*Bowing.*]

MRS. HARDCASTLE. Yet, what signifies *my* dressing when I have such a piece of antiquity by my side as Mr. Hardcastle? All I can say will never argue down a single button from his clothes. I have often wanted him to throw off his great flaxen wig, and where he was bald, to plaster it over like my Lord Pately, with powder.

HASTINGS. You are right, madam; for, as among the ladies there are none ugly, so among the men there are none old.

MRS. HARDCASTLE. But what do you think his answer was? Why, with his usual Gothic[21] vivacity, he said I only wanted him to throw off his wig to convert it into a *tête* for my own wearing!

HASTINGS. Intolerable! At your age you may wear what you please, and it must become you.

MRS. HARDCASTLE. Pray, Mr. Hastings, what do you take to be the most fashionable age about town?

HASTINGS. Some time ago forty was all the mode; but I'm told the ladies intend to ring up fifty for the ensuing winter.

MRS. HARDCASTLE. Seriously? Then I shall be too young for the fashion!

HASTINGS. No lady begins now to put on jewels till she's past forty. For instance, Miss there, in a polite circle, would be considered as a child, as a mere maker of samplers.

MRS. HARDCASTLE. And yet Mrs. Niece thinks herself as much a woman, and is as fond of jewels as the oldest of us all.

HASTINGS. Your niece, is she? And that young gentleman, a brother of yours, I should presume?

MRS. HARDCASTLE. My son, sir. They are contracted to each other. Observe their little sports. They fall in and out ten times a day, as if they were man and wife already. [*To them*] Well, Tony, child, what soft things are you saying to your cousin Constance, this evening?

TONY. I have been saying no soft things; but that it's very hard to be followed about so. Ecod! I've not a place in the house now that's left to myself but the stable.

MRS. HARDCASTLE. Never mind him, Con, my dear. He's in another story behind your back.

MISS NEVILLE. There's something generous in my cousin's manner. He falls out before faces to be forgiven in private.

TONY. That's a damned confounded—crack.

MRS. HARDCASTLE. Ah! he's a sly one. Don't you think they're like each other about the mouth, Mr. Hastings? The Blenkinsop mouth to a T. They're of a size, too. Back to back, my pretties, that Mr. Hastings may see you. Come, Tony.

TONY. You had as good not make me, I tell you. [*Measuring.*]

MISS NEVILLE. O lud! he has almost cracked my head.

MRS. HARDCASTLE. O, the monster! For shame, Tony. You a man, and behave so!

TONY. If I'm a man, let me have my fortin. Ecod! I'll not be made a fool of no longer.

MRS. HARDCASTLE. Is this, ungrateful boy, all that I'm to get for the pains I have taken in your education? I that have rocked you in your cradle, and fed that pretty mouth with a spoon! Did not I work that waistcoat to make you genteel! Did not I prescribe for you every day, and weep while the receipt was operating?

TONY. Ecod! you had reason to weep, for you have been dosing me ever since I was born. I have gone through every receipt in the *Complete Housewife* ten times over; and you have thoughts of coursing me through *Quincy*[22] next spring. But, ecod! I tell you, I'll not be made a fool of no longer.

MRS. HARDCASTLE. Wasn't it all for your good, viper? Wasn't it all for your good?

TONY. I wish you'd let me and my good alone, then. Snubbing this way when I'm in spirits! If I'm to have any good, let it come of itself; not to keep dinging it, dinging it into one so.

MRS. HARDCASTLE. That's false; I never see you when you're in spirits. No, Tony, you then go to the ale-house or ken-

---

[17]**Pantheon . . . Borough** Mrs. Hardcastle is trying to impress Hastings but mistakenly names recreation areas or parks that would have been frequented by the lower classes.	[18]**degagé** unpretentious	[19]**friseur** hairdresser	[20]**inoculation** a shot to prevent small-pox, a disease which inflicted numerous scars	[21]**Gothic** barbarous

[22]**Quincy** John Quincy's *Complete English Dispensatory* (medical text)

nel. I'm never to be delighted with your agreeable, wild notes, unfeeling monster!

TONY. Ecod! Mamma, your own notes are the wildest of the two.

MRS. HARDCASTLE. Was ever the like? But I see he wants to break my heart; I see he does.

HASTINGS. Dear madam, permit me to lecture the young gentleman a little. I'm certain I can persuade him to his duty.

MRS. HARDCASTLE. Well! I must retire. Come, Constance, my love. You see, Mr. Hastings, the wretchedness of my situation. Was ever poor woman so plagued with a dear, sweet, pretty, provoking, undutiful boy?

[*Exeunt Mrs. Hardcastle and Miss Neville.*]

Hastings, Tony.

TONY. [*Singing*] *There was a young man riding by, and fain would have his will. Rang do didlo dee.*—Don't mind her. Let her cry. It's the comfort of her heart. I have seen her and sister cry over a book for an hour together, and they said, they liked the book the better the more it made them cry.

HASTINGS. Then you're no friend to the ladies, I find, my pretty young gentleman?

TONY. That's as I find 'um.

HASTINGS. Not to her of your mother's choosing, I dare answer! And yet she appears to me a pretty, well-tempered girl.

TONY. That's because you don't know her as well as I. Ecod! I know every inch about her; and there's not a more bitter cantankerous toad in all Christendom!

HASTINGS. [*Aside*] Pretty encouragement, this, for a lover.

TONY. I have seen her since the height of that. She has as many tricks as a hare in a thicket, or a colt the first day's breaking.

HASTINGS. To me she appears sensible and silent!

TONY. Ay, before company. But when she's with her play-mates she's as loud as a hog in a gate.

HASTINGS. But there is a meek modesty about her that charms me.

TONY. Yes, but curb her never so little, she kicks up, and you're flung in a ditch.

HASTINGS. Well, but you must allow her a little beauty.— Yes, you must allow her some beauty.

TONY. Bandbox! She's all a made-up thing, mun. Ah! could you but see Bet Bouncer of these parts, you might then talk of beauty. Ecod, she has two eyes as black as sloes, and cheeks as broad and red as a pulpit cushion. She'd make two of she.

HASTINGS. Well, what say you to a friend that would take this bitter bargain off your hands?

TONY. Anon!

HASTINGS. Would you thank him that would take Miss Neville, and leave you to happiness and your dear Betsy?

TONY. Ah; but where is there such a friend, for who would take *her?*

HASTINGS. I am he. If you but assist me, I'll engage to whip her off to France, and you shall never hear more of her.

TONY. Assist you! Ecod, I will, to the last drop of my blood. I'll clap a pair of horses to your chaise that shall trundle you off in a twinkling, and may be get you a part of her fortin besides, in jewels, that you little dream of.

HASTINGS. My dear 'Squire, this looks like a lad of spirit.

TONY. Come along then, and you shall see more of my spirit before you have done with me.

[*Singing.*]

We are the boys
That fears no noise
Where the thundering cannons roar.

[*Exeunt.*]

ACT THREE

SCENE I: THE HOUSE

Enter Hardcastle.

HARDCASTLE. What could my old friend Sir Charles mean by recommending his son as the modestest young man in town? To me he appears the most impudent piece of brass that ever spoke with a tongue. He has taken possession of the easy chair by the fireside already. He took off his boots in the parlour, and desired me to see them taken care of. I'm desirous to know how his impudence affects my daughter.—She will certainly be shocked at it.

Enter Miss Hardcastle, plainly dressed.

HARDCASTLE. Well, my Kate, I see you have changed your dress as I bid you; and yet, I believe, there was no great occasion.

MISS HARDCASTLE. I find such a pleasure, sir, in obeying your commands, that I take care to observe them without ever debating their propriety.

HARDCASTLE. And yet, Kate, I sometimes give you some cause, particularly when I recommended my *modest* gentleman to you as a lover to-day.

MISS HARDCASTLE. You taught me to expect something extraordinary, and I find the original exceeds the description!

HARDCASTLE. I was never so surprised in my life! He has quite confounded all my faculties!

MISS HARDCASTLE. I never saw anything like it: And a man of the world, too!

HARDCASTLE. Ay, he learned it all abroad. What a fool was I, to think a young man could learn modesty by travelling. He might as soon learn wit at a masquerade.

MISS HARDCASTLE. It seems all natural to him.

HARDCASTLE. A good deal assisted by bad company and a French dancing-master.

MISS HARDCASTLE. Sure, you mistake, papa! a French dancing-master could never have taught him that timid look,—that awkward address,—that bashful manner—

HARDCASTLE. Whose look? whose manner? child!

MISS HARDCASTLE. Mr. Marlow's: his *mauvaise honte*,[23] his timidity struck me at the first sight.

HARDCASTLE. Then your first sight deceived you; for I think him one of the most brazen first sights that ever astonished my senses!

MISS HARDCASTLE. Sure, sir, you rally![24] I never saw anyone so modest.

HARDCASTLE. And can you be serious! I never saw such a bouncing swaggering puppy since I was born. Bully Dawson was but a fool to him.

MISS HARDCASTLE. Surprising! He met me with a respectful bow, a stammering voice, and a look fixed on the ground.

HARDCASTLE. He met me with a loud voice, a lordly air, and a familiarity that made my blood freeze again.

MISS HARDCASTLE. He treated me with diffidence and respect; censured the manners of the age; admired the prudence of girls that never laughed; tired me with apologies for being tiresome; then left the room with a bow, and, "Madam, I would not for the world detain you."

HARDCASTLE. He spoke to me as if he knew me all his life before; asked twenty questions, and never waited for an answer; interrupted my best remarks with some silly pun, and when I was in my best story of the Duke of Marlborough and Prince Eugene, he asked if I had not a good hand at making punch. Yes, Kate, he asked your father if he was a maker of punch!

MISS HARDCASTLE. One of us must certainly be mistaken.

HARDCASTLE. If he be what he has shown himself, I'm determined he shall never have my consent.

MISS HARDCASTLE. And if he be the sullen thing I take him, he shall never have mine.

HARDCASTLE. In one thing then we are agreed—to reject him.

MISS HARDCASTLE. Yes. But upon conditions. For if you should find him less impudent, and I more presuming; if you find him more respectful, and I more importunate—I don't know—the fellow is well enough for a man—Certainly we don't meet many such at a horse race in the country.

HARDCASTLE. If we should find him so—But that's impossible. The first appearance has done my business. I'm seldom deceived in that.

MISS HARDCASTLE. And yet there may be many good qualities under that first appearance.

HARDCASTLE. Ay, when a girl finds a fellow's outside to her taste, she then sets about guessing the rest of his furniture. With her, a smooth face stands for good sense, and a genteel figure for every virtue.

MISS HARDCASTLE. I hope, sir, a conversation begun with a compliment to my good sense won't end with a sneer at my understanding!

HARDCASTLE. Pardon me, Kate. But if young Mr. Brazen can find the art of reconciling contradictions, he may please us both, perhaps.

MISS HARDCASTLE. And as one of us must be mistaken, what if we go to make further discoveries?

HARDCASTLE. Agreed. But depend on't I'm in the right.

MISS HARDCASTLE. And depend on't I'm not much in the wrong.

[*Exeunt.*]

Enter Tony running in with a casket.

TONY. Ecod! I have got them. Here they are. My Cousin Con's necklaces, bobs and all. My mother shan't cheat the poor souls out of their fortin neither. O! my genus, is that you?

Enter Hastings.

HASTINGS. My dear friend, how have you managed with your mother? I hope you have amused her with pretending love for your cousin, and that you are willing to be reconciled at last? Our horses will be refreshed in a short time, and we shall soon be ready to set off.

TONY. And here's something to bear your charges by the way. [*Giving the casket*] Your sweetheart's jewels. Keep them, and hang those, I say, that would rob you of one of them!

HASTINGS. But how have you procured them from your mother?

TONY. Ask me no questions, and I'll tell you no fibs. I procured them by the rule of thumb. If I had not a key to every drawer in mother's bureau, how could I go to the alehouse so often as I do? An honest man may rob himself of his own at any time.

HASTINGS. Thousands do it every day. But to be plain with you, Miss Neville is endeavouring to procure them from her aunt this very instant. If she succeeds, it will be the most delicate way at least of obtaining them.

TONY. Well, keep them, till you know how it will be. But I know how it will be well enough. She'd as soon part with the only sound tooth in her head!

HASTINGS. But I dread the effects of her resentment, when she finds she has lost them.

TONY. Never you mind her resentment. Leave *me* to manage that. I don't value her resentment the bounce of a cracker. Zounds! here they are! Morrice![25] Prance!

[*Exit Hastings.*]

---

[23] ***mauvaise honte*** timidity [24] **you rally** you're jesting/joking

[25] **Morrice** Morris Dance, meaning here "Let's get out of here!"

Tony, Mrs. Hardcastle, Miss Neville.

MRS. HARDCASTLE. Indeed, Constance, you amaze me. Such a girl as you want jewels? It will be time enough for jewels, my dear, twenty years hence, when your beauty begins to want repairs.

MISS NEVILLE. But what will repair beauty at forty will certainly improve it at twenty, madam.

MRS. HARDCASTLE. Yours, my dear, can admit of none. That natural blush is beyond a thousand ornaments. Besides, child, jewels are quite out at present. Don't you see half the ladies of our acquaintance, my Lady Killdaylight, and Mrs. Crump, and the rest of them, carry their jewels to town, and bring nothing but paste and marcasites back?

MISS NEVILLE. But who knows, madam, but somebody that shall be nameless would like me best with all my little finery about me?

MRS. HARDCASTLE. Consult your glass, my dear, and then see if, with such a pair of eyes, you want any better sparklers. What do you think, Tony, my dear? Does your cousin Con want any jewels, in your eyes, to set off her beauty?

TONY. That's as thereafter may be.

MISS NEVILLE. My dear aunt, if you knew how it would oblige me.

MRS. HARDCASTLE. A parcel of old-fashioned rose and table-cut things.[26] They would make you look like the court of King Solomon at a puppet-show. Besides, I believe I can't readily come at them. They may be missing, for aught I know to the contrary.

TONY. [*Apart to Mrs. Hardcastle*] Then why don't you tell her so at once, as she's so longing for them. Tell her they're lost. It's the only way to quiet her. Say they're lost, and call me to bear witness.

MRS. HARDCASTLE. [*Apart to Tony*] You know, my dear, I'm only keeping them for you. So if I say they're gone, you'll bear me witness, will you? He! he! he!

TONY. Never fear me. Ecod! I'll say I saw them taken out with my own eyes.

MISS NEVILLE. I desire them but for a day, madam, just to be permitted to show them as relics, and then they may be locked up again.

MRS. HARDCASTLE. To be plain with you, my dear Constance, if I could find them, you should have them. They're missing, I assure you. Lost, for aught I know; but we must have patience wherever they are.

MISS NEVILLE. I'll not believe it; this is but a shallow pretence to deny me. I know they're too valuable to be so slightly kept, and as you are to answer for the loss—

MRS. HARDCASTLE. Don't be alarmed, Constance. If they be lost, I must restore an equivalent. But my son knows they are missing, and not to be found.

TONY. That I can bear witness to. They are missing, and not to be found, I'll take my oath on't!

MRS. HARDCASTLE. You must learn resignation, my dear; for though we lose our fortune, yet we should not lose our patience. See me, how calm I am!

MISS NEVILLE. Ay, people are generally calm at the misfortunes of others.

MRS. HARDCASTLE. Now, I wonder a girl of your good sense should waste a thought upon such trumpery. We shall soon find them; and, in the meantime, you shall make use of my garnets till your jewels be found.

MISS NEVILLE. I detest garnets!

MRS. HARDCASTLE. The most becoming things in the world to set off a clear complexion. You have often seen how well they look upon me. You shall have them.

[*Exit.*]

MISS NEVILLE. I dislike them of all things. You shan't stir.— Was ever anything so provoking—to mislay my own jewels, and force me to wear her trumpery?

TONY. Don't be a fool. If she gives you the garnets, take what you can get. The jewels are your own already. I have stolen them out of her bureau, and she does not know it. Fly to your spark, he'll tell you more of the matter. Leave me to manage *her*.

MISS NEVILLE. My dear cousin!

TONY. Vanish. She's here, and has missed them already. Zounds! how she fidgets and spits about like a Catharine wheel.[27]   [*Exit Miss Neville.*]

Enter Mrs. Hardcastle.

MRS. HARDCASTLE. Confusion! thieves! robbers! We are cheated, plundered, broke open, undone!

TONY. What's the matter, what's the matter, mamma? I hope nothing has happened to any of the good family!

MRS. HARDCASTLE. We are robbed. My bureau has been broke open, the jewels taken out, and I'm undone!

TONY. Oh! is that all? Ha! ha! ha! By the laws, I never saw it better acted in my life. Ecod, I thought you was ruined in earnest, ha, ha, ha!

MRS. HARDCASTLE. Why, boy, I *am* ruined in earnest. My bureau has been broke open, and all taken away.

TONY. Stick to that; ha, ha, ha! stick to that. I'll bear witness, you know, call me to bear witness.

MRS. HARDCASTLE. I tell you, Tony, by all that's precious, the jewels are gone, and I shall be ruined for ever.

TONY. Sure I know they're gone, and I am to say so.

MRS. HARDCASTLE. My dearest Tony, but hear me. They're gone, I say.

TONY. By the laws, mamma, you make me for to laugh, ha! ha! I know who took them well enough, ha! ha! ha!

MRS. HARDCASTLE. Was there ever such a blockhead, that can't tell the difference between jest and earnest. I tell you I'm not in jest, booby!

TONY. That's right, that's right. You must be in a bitter passion, and then nobody will suspect either of us. I'll bear witness that they are gone.

---

[26]**table-cut things** crudely cut gem stones

[27]**Catharine wheel** fireworks display

MRS. HARDCASTLE. Was there ever such a cross-grained brute, that won't hear me! Can you bear witness that you're no better than a fool? Was ever poor woman so beset with fools on one hand, and thieves on the other?

TONY. I can bear witness to that.

MRS. HARDCASTLE. Bear witness again, you blockhead, you, and I'll turn you out of the room directly. My poor niece, what will become of *her*? Do you laugh, you unfeeling brute, as if you enjoyed my distress?

TONY. I can bear witness to that.

MRS. HARDCASTLE. Do you insult me, monster? I'll teach you to vex your mother, I will!

TONY. I can bear witness to that.

[*He runs off, she follows him.*]

Enter Miss Hardcastle and Maid.

MISS HARDCASTLE. What an unaccountable creature is that brother of mine, to send them to the house as an inn, ha! ha! I don't wonder at his impudence.

MAID. But what is more, madam, the young gentleman as you passed by in your present dress, asked me if you were the barmaid. He mistook you for the barmaid, madam!

MISS HARDCASTLE. Did he? Then as I live I'm resolved to keep up the delusion. Tell me, Pimple, how do you like my present dress? Don't you think I look something like Cherry in the *Beaux' Stratagem*?[28]

MAID. It's the dress, madam, that every lady wears in the country, but when she visits or receives company.

MISS HARDCASTLE. And are you sure he does not remember my face or person?

MAID. Certain of it!

MISS HARDCASTLE. I vow, I thought so; for though we spoke for some time together, yet his fears were such that he never once looked up during the interview. Indeed, if he had, my bonnet would have kept him from seeing me.

MAID. But what do you hope from keeping him in his mistake?

MISS HARDCASTLE. In the first place, I shall be *seen*, and that is no small advantage to a girl who brings her face to market. Then I shall perhaps make an acquaintance, and that's no small victory gained over one who never addresses any but the wildest of her sex. But my chief aim is to take my gentleman off his guard and, like an invisible champion of romance, examine the giant's force before I offer to combat.

MAID. But you are sure you can act your part, and disguise your voice so that he may mistake that, as he has already mistaken your person?

MISS HARDCASTLE. Never fear me. I think I have got the true bar cant.—Did your honour call?—Attend the Lion there.—Pipes and tobacco for the Angel.—The Lamb[29] has been outrageous this half hour!

[28]**Cherry . . . Stratagem** the heroine in George Farquhar's 1707 comedy *The Beaux' Srategem* [29]**Lion . . . Angel . . . Lamb** fictitious names for rooms in a fictitious inn

MAID. It will do, madam. But he's here.

[*Exit Maid.*]

Enter Marlow.

MARLOW. What a bawling in every part of the house! I have scarce a moment's repose. If I go to the best room, there I find my host and his story. If I fly to the gallery, there we have my hostess with her curtsey down to the ground. I have at last got a moment to myself, and now for recollection. [*Walks and muses.*]

MISS HARDCASTLE. Did you call, sir? did your honour call?

MARLOW. [*Musing*] As for Miss Hardcastle, she's too grave and sentimental for me.

MISS HARDCASTLE. Did your honour call?

[*She still places herself before him, he turning away.*]

MARLOW. No, child! [*Musing*] Besides, from the glimpse I had of her I think she squints.

MISS HARDCASTLE. I'm sure, sir, I heard the bell ring.

MARLOW. No! no! [*Musing*] I have pleased my father, however, by coming down, and I'll to-morrow please myself by returning. [*Taking out his tablets, and perusing.*]

MISS HARDCASTLE. Perhaps the other gentleman called, sir?

MARLOW. I tell you, no.

MISS HARDCASTLE. I should be glad to know, sir. We have such a parcel of servants.

MARLOW. No, no, I tell you. [*Looks full in her face*] Yes, child, I think I did call. I wanted— I wanted—I vow, child, you are vastly handsome!

MISS HARDCASTLE. O la, sir, you'll make one ashamed.

MARLOW. Never saw a more sprightly malicious eye. Yes, yes, my dear, I did call. Have you got any of your—a— what d'ye call it in the house?

MISS HARDCASTLE. No, sir, we have been out of that these ten days.

MARLOW. One may call in this house, I find, to very little purpose. Suppose I should call for a taste, just by way of trial, of the nectar of your lips; perhaps I might be disappointed in that, too!

MISS HARDCASTLE. Nectar! nectar! that's a liquor there's no call for in these parts. French, I suppose. We keep no French wines here, sir.

MARLOW. Of true English growth, I assure you.

MISS HARDCASTLE. Then it's odd I should not know it. We brew all sorts of wines in this house, and I have lived here these eighteen years.

MARLOW. Eighteen years! Why one would think, child, you kept the bar before you were born. How old are you?

MISS HARDCASTLE. O! sir, I must not tell my age. They say women and music should never be dated.

MARLOW. To guess at this distance, you can't be much above forty. [*Approaching*] Yet nearer I don't think so much. [*Approaching*] By coming close to some women they look younger still; but when we come very close indeed—[*Attempting to kiss her.*]

MISS HARDCASTLE. Pray, sir, keep your distance. One would

think you wanted to know one's age as they do horses, by mark of mouth.

MARLOW. I protest, child, you use me extremely ill. If you keep me at this distance, how is it possible you and I can be ever acquainted?

MISS HARDCASTLE. And who wants to be acquainted with you? I want no such acquaintance, not I. I'm sure you did not treat Miss Hardcastle that was here awhile ago in this obstropalous manner. I'll warrant me, before her you looked dashed, and kept bowing to the ground, and talked, for all the world, as if you was before a justice of peace.

MARLOW. [Aside] Egad! she has hit it, sure enough. [To her] In awe of her, child? Ha! ha! ha! A mere awkward, squinting thing! No, no! I find you don't know me. I laughed, and rallied her a little; but I was unwilling to be too severe. No, I could not be too severe, curse me!

MISS HARDCASTLE. O! then, sir, you are a favourite, I find, among the ladies?

MARLOW. Yes, my dear, a great favourite. And yet, hang me, I don't see what they find in me to follow. At the Ladies' Club in town I'm called their agreeable Rattle. Rattle, child, is not my real name, but one I'm known by. My name is Solomons. Mr. Solomons, my dear, at your service. [Offering to salute her.]

MISS HARDCASTLE. Hold, sir; you were introducing me to your club, not to yourself. And you're so great a favourite there you say?

MARLOW. Yes, my dear. There's Mrs. Mantrap, Lady Betty Blackleg, the Countess of Sligo, Mrs. Longhorns, old Miss Biddy, Buckskin, and your humble servant keep up the spirit of the place.

MISS HARDCASTLE. Then it's a very merry place, I suppose.

MARLOW. Yes, as merry as cards, suppers, wine, and old women can make us.

MISS HARDCASTLE. And their agreeable Rattle, ha! ha! ha!

MARLOW. [Aside] Egad! I don't quite like this chit. She looks knowing, methinks. You laugh, child!

MISS HARDCASTLE. I can't but laugh to think what time they all have for minding their work or their family.

MARLOW. [Aside] All's well, she don't laugh at me. [To her] Do you ever work, child?

MISS HARDCASTLE. Ay, sure. There's not a screen or a quilt in the whole house but what can bear witness to that.

MARLOW. Odso! Then you must show me your embroidery. I embroider and draw patterns myself a little. If you want a judge of your work you must apply to me. [Seizing her hand.]

MISS HARDCASTLE. Ay, but the colours don't look well by candle light. You shall see all in the morning. [Struggling.]

MARLOW. And why not now, my angel? Such beauty fires beyond the power of resistance.—Pshaw! the father here! My old luck. I never nicked seven that I did not throw ames-ace three times following.

[Exit Marlow.]

Enter Hardcastle, who stands in surprise.

HARDCASTLE. So, madam! So I find this is your modest lover. This is your humble admirer that kept his eyes fixed on the ground, and only adored at humble distance. Kate, Kate, art thou not ashamed to deceive your father so?

MISS HARDCASTLE. Never trust me, dear papa, but he's still the modest man I first took him for. You'll be convinced of it as well as I.

HARDCASTLE. By the hand of my body, I believe his impudence is infectious! Didn't I see him seize your hand? Didn't I see him haul you about like a milk maid? And now you talk of his respect and his modesty, forsooth!

MISS HARDCASTLE. But if I shortly convince you of his modesty—that he has only the faults that will pass off with time, and the virtues that will improve with age—I hope you'll forgive him.

HARDCASTLE. The girl would actually make one run mad! I tell you I'll not be convinced. I am convinced. He has scarcely been three hours in the house, and he has already encroached on all my prerogatives. You may like his impudence, and call it modesty. But my son-in-law, madam, must have very different qualifications.

MISS HARDCASTLE. Sir, I ask but this night to convince you.

HARDCASTLE. You shall not have half the time, for I have thoughts of turning him out this very hour.

MISS HARDCASTLE. Give me that hour then, and I hope to satisfy you.

HARDCASTLE. Well, an hour let it be then. But I'll have no trifling with your father. All fair and open; do you mind me?

MISS HARDCASTLE. I hope, sir, you have ever found that I considered your commands as my pride; for your kindness is such that my duty as yet has been inclination.

[Exeunt.]

ACT FOUR

SCENE I: THE HOUSE

Enter Hastings and Miss Neville.

HASTINGS. You surprise me! Sir Charles Marlow expected here this night? Where have you had your information?

MISS NEVILLE. You may depend upon it. I just saw his letter to Mr. Hardcastle, in which he tells him he intends setting out a few hours after his son.

HASTINGS. Then, my Constance, all must be completed before he arrives. He knows me, and should he find me here, would discover my name, and perhaps my designs, to the rest of the family.

MISS NEVILLE. The jewels, I hope, are safe.

HASTINGS. Yes, yes. I have sent them to Marlow, who keeps the keys of our baggage. In the meantime, I'll go to prepare matters for our elopement. I have had the 'Squire's promise of a fresh pair of horses; and, if I should not see him again, will write him further directions.

[*Exit.*]

MISS NEVILLE. Well! success attend you. In the meantime, I'll go amuse my aunt with the old pretence of a violent passion for my cousin.

[*Exit.*]

Enter Marlow, followed by a Servant.

MARLOW. I wonder what Hastings could mean by sending me so valuable a thing as a casket to keep for him, when he knows the only place I have is the seat of a post-coach at an inn door. Have you deposited the casket with the landlady, as I ordered you? Have you put it into her own hands?

SERVANT. Yes, your honour.

MARLOW. She said she'd keep it safe, did she?

SERVANT. Yes, she said she'd keep it safe enough. She asked me how I came by it and she said she had a great mind to make me give an account of myself.

[*Exit Servant.*]

MARLOW. Ha! ha! ha! They're safe, however. What an unaccountable set of beings have we got amongst! This little barmaid though runs in my head most strangely, and drives out the absurdities of all the rest of the family. She's mine, she must be mine, or I'm greatly mistaken.

Enter Hastings.

HASTINGS. Bless me! I quite forgot to tell her that I intended to prepare at the bottom of the garden. Marlow here, and in spirits too.

MARLOW. Give me joy, George! Crown me, shadow me with laurels! Well, George, after all, we modest fellows don't want for success among the women.

HASTINGS. Some women, you mean. But what success has your honour's modesty been crowned with now, that it grows so insolent upon us?

MARLOW. Didn't you see the tempting, brisk, lovely little thing that runs about the house with a bunch of keys to its girdle?

HASTINGS. Well! and what then?

HARLOW. She's mine, you rogue, you. Such fire, such motion, such eyes, such lips—but egad! she would not let me kiss them though.

HASTINGS. But are you sure, so very sure of her?

MARLOW. Why, man, she talked of showing me her work above-stairs, and I am to improve the pattern.

HASTINGS. But how can *you*, Charles, go about to rob a woman of her honour?

MARLOW. Pshaw! pshaw! we all know the honour of the barmaid of an inn. I don't intend to *rob* her, take my word

for it; there's nothing in this house, I shan't honestly *pay* for!

HASTINGS. I believe the girl has virtue.

MARLOW. And if she has, I should be the last man in the world that would attempt to corrupt it.

HASTINGS. You have taken care, I hope, of the casket I sent you to lock up? It's in safety?

MARLOW. Yes, yes. It's safe enough. I have taken care of it. But how could you think the seat of a post-coach at an inn door a place of safety? Ah! numbskull! I have taken better precautions for you than you did for yourself.—I have—

HASTINGS. What!

MARLOW. I have sent it to the landlady to keep for you.

HASTINGS. To the landlady!

MARLOW. The landlady.

HASTINGS. You did!

MARLOW. I did. She's to be answerable for its forthcoming, you know.

HASTINGS. Yes, she'll bring it forth with a witness.

MARLOW. Wasn't I right? I believe you'll allow that I acted prudently upon this occasion?

HASTINGS. [*Aside*] He must not see my uneasiness.

MARLOW. You seem a little disconcerted, though, methinks. Sure nothing has happened?

HASTINGS. No, nothing. Never was I in better spirits in all my life. And so you left it with the landlady, who, no doubt, very readily undertook the charge?

MARLOW. Rather too readily. For she not only kept the casket, but, through her great precaution, was going to keep the messenger too. Ha! ha! ha!

HASTINGS. He! he! he! They're safe, however.

MARLOW. As a guinea in a miser's purse.

HASTINGS. [*Aside*] So now all hopes of fortune are at an end, and we must set off without it. [*To him*] Well, Charles, I'll leave you to your meditations on the pretty barmaid, and, he! he! he! may you be as successful for yourself as you have been for me.

[*Exit.*]

MARLOW. Thank ye, George! I ask no more. Ha! ha! ha!

Enter Hardcastle.

HARDCASTLE. I no longer know my own house. It's turned all topsy-turvy. His servants have got drunk already. I'll bear it no longer; and yet, from my respect for his father, I'll be calm. [*To him*] Mr. Marlow, your servant. I'm your very humble servant.

[*Bowing low.*]

MARLOW. Sir, your humble servant. [*Aside*] What's to be the wonder now?

HARDCASTLE. I believe, sir, you must be sensible, sir, that no man alive ought to be more welcome than your father's son, sir. I hope you think so?

MARLOW. I do, from my soul, sir. I don't want much entreaty. I generally make my father's son welcome wherever he goes.

HARDCASTLE. I believe you do, from my soul, sir. But though I say nothing to your own conduct, that of your servants is insufferable. Their manner of drinking is setting a very bad example in this house, I assure you.

MARLOW. I protest, my very good sir, that's no fault of mine. If they don't drink as they ought *they* are to blame. I ordered them not to spare the cellar; I did, I assure you. [*To the side scene*] Here, let one of my servants come up. [*To him*] My positive directions were, that as I did not drink myself, they should make up for my deficiencies below.

HARDCASTLE. Then they had your orders for what they do! I'm satisfied!

MARLOW. They had, I assure you. You shall hear from one of themselves.

Enter Servant, drunk.

MARLOW. You, Jeremy! Come forward, sirrah! What were my orders? Were you not told to drink freely, and call for what you thought fit, for the good of the house?

HARDCASTLE. [*Aside*] I begin to lose my patience.

JEREMY. Please your honour, liberty and Fleet Street for ever! Though I'm but a servant, I'm as good as another man. I'll drink for no man before supper, sir, dammy! Good liquor will sit upon a good supper, but a good supper will not sit upon—hiccup—upon my conscience, sir.

MARLOW. You see, my old friend, the fellow is as drunk as he can possibly be. I don't know what you'd have more, unless you'd have the poor devil soused in a beer-barrel.

HARDCASTLE. Zounds![30] He'll drive me distracted if I contain myself any longer. Mr. Marlow. Sir; I have submitted to your insolence for more than four hours, and I see no likelihood of its coming to an end. I'm now resolved to be master here, sir, and I desire that you and your drunken pack may leave my house directly.

MARLOW. Leave your house!— Sure, you jest, my good friend! What, when I'm doing what I can to please you!

HARDCASTLE. I tell you sir, you don't please me; so I desire you'll leave my house.

MARLOW. Sure, you cannot be serious! At this time of night, and such a night! You only mean to banter me!

HARDCASTLE. I tell you, sir, I'm serious; and, now that my passions are roused, I say this house is mine, sir; this house is mine, and I command you to leave it directly.

MARLOW. Ha! ha! ha! A puddle in a storm. I shan't stir a step, I assure you. [*In a serious tone*] This your house, fellow! It's my house. This is my house. Mine, while I choose to stay. What right have you to bid me leave this house, sir? I never met with such impudence, curse me, never in my whole life before!

HARDCASTLE. Nor I, confound me if ever I did! To come to my house, to call for what he likes, to turn me out of my own chair, to insult the family, to order his servants to get drunk, and then to tell me "This house is mine, sir!" By all that's impudent, it makes me laugh. Ha! ha! ha! Pray, sir, [*bantering*] as you take the house, what think you of taking the rest of the furniture? There's a pair of silver candlesticks, and there's a fire-screen, and here's a pair of brazen-nosed bellows; perhaps you may take a fancy to them?

MARLOW. Bring me your bill, sir; bring me your bill, and let's make no more words about it.

HARDCASTLE. There are a set of prints, too. What think you of the *Rake's Progress*[31] for your own apartment?

MARLOW. Bring me your bill, I say; and I'll leave you and your infernal house directly.

HARDCASTLE. Then there's a mahogany table, that you may see your own face in.

MARLOW. My bill, I say.

HARDCASTLE. I had forgot the great chair, for your own particular slumbers, after a hearty meal.

MARLOW. Zounds! bring me your bill, I say, and let's hear no more on't.

HARDCASTLE. Young man, young man, from your father's letter to me, I was taught to expect a well-bred modest man, as a visitor here, but now I find him no better than a coxcomb and a bully. But he will be down here presently, and shall hear more of it.

[*Exit.*]

MARLOW. How's this? Sure, I have not mistaken the house? Everything looks like an inn. The servants cry "coming." The attendance is awkward; the barmaid, too, to attend us. But she's here, and will further inform me. Whither so fast, child? A word with you.

Enter Miss Hardcastle.

MISS HARDCASTLE. Let it be short, then. I'm in a hurry. [*Aside*] I believe he begins to find out his mistake, but it's too soon quite to undeceive him.

MARLOW. Pray, child, answer me one question. What are you, and what may your business in this house be?

MISS HARDCASTLE. A relation of the family, sir.

MARLOW. What? A poor relation?

MISS HARDCASTLE. Yes, sir. A poor relation appointed to keep the keys, and to see that the guests want nothing in my power to give them.

MARLOW. That is, you act as the barmaid of this inn.

MISS HARDCASTLE. Inn! O law!—What brought that in your head? One of the best families in the county keep an inn! Ha, ha, ha, old Mr. Hardcastle's house an inn!

MARLOW. Mr. Hardcastle's house! Is this house Mr. Hardcastle's house, child?

---

[30]**Zounds** an oath; a euphemistic abbreviation for "by God's (Jesus's) wounds"

[31]**Rake's Progress** satirist William Hogarth's collected drawings that depicted London

MISS HARDCASTLE. Ay, sure. Whose else should it be?

MARLOW. So then all's out, and I have been damnably imposed on. O, confound my stupid head, I shall be laughed at over the whole town. I shall be stuck up in caricature in all the print-shops. The *Dullissimo Macaroni.*[32] To mistake this house, of all others, for an inn, and my father's old friend for an inn-keeper! What a swaggering puppy must he take me for. What a silly puppy do I find myself. There again, may I be hanged, my dear, but I mistook you for the barmaid!

MISS HARDCASTLE. Dear me! dear me! I'm sure there's nothing in my *behaviour* to put me upon a level with one of that stamp.

MARLOW. Nothing, my dear, nothing. But I was in for a list of blunders, and could not help making you a subscriber. My stupidity saw everything the wrong way. I mistook your assiduity for assurance, and your simplicity for allurement. But it's over—this house I no more show *my* face in!

MISS HARDCASTLE. I hope, sir, I have done nothing to disoblige you. I'm sure I should be sorry to affront any gentleman who has been so polite, and said so many civil things to me. I'm sure I should be sorry [*pretending to cry*] if he left the family upon my account. I'm sure I should be sorry people said anything amiss, since I have no fortune but my character.

MARLOW. [*Aside*] By heaven, she weeps. This is the first mark of tenderness I ever had from a modest woman, and it touches me. [*To her*] Excuse me, my lovely girl, you are the only part of the family I leave with reluctance. But to be plain with you, the difference of our birth, fortune, and education make an honourable connexion impossible; and I can never harbour a thought of seducing simplicity that trusted in my honour, or bringing ruin upon one whose only fault was being too lovely.

MISS HARDCASTLE. [*Aside*] Generous man! I now begin to admire him. [*To him*] But I'm sure my family is as good as Miss Hardcastle's, and though I'm poor, that's no great misfortune to a contented mind, and, until this moment, I never thought that it was bad to want fortune.

MARLOW. And why now, my pretty simplicity?

MISS HARDCASTLE. Because, it puts me at a distance from one, that if I had a thousand pound I would give it all to.

MARLOW. [*Aside*] This simplicity bewitches me, so that if I stay I'm undone. I must make one bold effort, and leave her. [*To her*] Your partiality in my favour, my dear, touches me most sensibly, and were I to live for myself alone, I could easily fix my choice. But I owe too much to the opinion of the world, too much to the authority of a father, so that—I can scarcely speak it—it affects me. Farewell.

[*Exit.*]

MISS HARDCASTLE. I never knew half his merit till now. He shall not go, if I have power or art to detain him. I'll still preserve the character in which I *stooped to conquer,* but will undeceive my papa, who, perhaps, may laugh him out of his resolution.

[*Exit.*]

Enter Tony, Miss Neville.

TONY. Ay, you may steal for yourselves the next time. I have done my duty. She has got the jewels again, that's a sure thing; but she believes it was all a mistake of the servants.

MISS NEVILLE. But, my dear cousin, sure you won't forsake us in this distress? If she in the least suspects that I am going off, I shall certainly be locked up, or sent to my aunt Pedigree's, which is ten times worse.

TONY. To be sure, aunts of all kinds are damned bad things. But what can I do? I have got you a pair of horses that will fly like Whistlejacket,[33] and I'm sure you can't say but I have courted you nicely before her face. Here she comes. We must court a bit or two more, for fear she should suspect us.

[*They retire, and seem to fondle.*]

Enter Mrs. Hardcastle.

MRS. HARDCASTLE. Well, I was greatly fluttered, to be sure. But my son tells me it was all a mistake of the servants. I shan't be easy, however, till they are fairly married, and then let her keep her own fortune. But what do I see! Fondling together, as I'm alive! I never saw Tony so sprightly before. Ah! have I caught you, my pretty doves! What, billing, exchanging stolen glances, and broken murmurs! Ah!

TONY. As for murmurs, mother, we grumble a little now and then, to be sure. But there's no love lost between us.

MRS. HARDCASTLE. A mere sprinkling, Tony, upon the flame, only to make it burn brighter.

MISS NEVILLE. Cousin Tony promises to give us more of his company at home. Indeed, he shan't leave us any more. It won't leave us, cousin Tony, will it?

TONY. O! it's a pretty creature. No, I'd sooner leave my horse in a pound, than leave you when you smile upon one so. Your laugh makes you so becoming.

MISS NEVILLE. Agreeable cousin! Who can help admiring that natural humour, that pleasant, broad, red, thoughtless, [*patting his cheek*] ah! it's a bold face.

MRS. HARDCASTLE. Pretty innocence!

TONY. I'm sure I always loved cousin Con's hazel eyes, and her pretty, long fingers, that she twists this way and that, over the haspicholls,[34] like a parcel of bobbins.

MRS. HARDCASTLE. Ah, he would charm the bird from the tree. I was never so happy before. My boy takes after his

---

[32]**Dullissimo Macaroni** a derisive term for fops who imitated foreign dress and customs

[33]**Whistlejacket** a racehorse   [34]**haspicholls** harpsichord, a forerunner of the modern piano

father, poor Mr. Lumpkin, exactly. The jewels, my dear Con, shall be yours incontinently. You shall have them. Isn't he a sweet boy, my dear? You shall be married to-morrow, and we'll put off the rest of his education, like Dr. Drowsy's sermons to a fitter opportunity.

Enter Diggory.

DIGGORY. Where's the 'Squire? I have got a letter for your worship.

TONY. Give it to my mamma. She reads all my letters first.

DIGGORY. I had orders to deliver it into your own hands.

TONY. Who does it come from?

DIGGORY. Your worship mun ask that of the letter itself.

TONY. I could wish to know, though.

[*Turning the letter, and gazing on it.*]

MISS NEVILLE. [*Aside*] Undone, undone! A letter to him from Hastings. I know the hand. If my aunt sees it we are ruined for ever. I'll keep her employed a little if I can. [*To Mrs. Hardcastle*] But I have not told you, madam, of my cousin's smart answer just now to Mr. Marlow. We so laughed—you must know, madam—this way a little, for he must not hear us.

[*They confer.*]

TONY. [*Still gazing*] A damned cramp piece of penmanship, as ever I saw in my life. I can read your printhand very well. But here there are such handles, and shanks, and dashes, that one can scarce tell the head from the tail. *To Anthony Lumpkin, Esquire.* It's very odd, I can read the outside of my letters, where my own name is, well enough. But when I come to open it, it's all—buzz. That's hard, very hard; for the inside of the letter is always the cream of the correspondence.

MRS. HARDCASTLE. Ha! ha! ha! Very well, very well. And so my son was too hard for the philosopher!

MISS NEVILLE. Yes, madam; but you must hear the rest, madam. A little more this way, or he may hear us. You'll hear how he puzzled him again.

MRS. HARDCASTLE. He seems strangely puzzled now himself, methinks.

TONY. [*Still gazing*] A damned up and down hand, as if it was disguised in liquor. [*Reading*] *Dear Sir.* Ay, that's that. Then there's an M, and a T, and an S, but whether the next be an *izzard* or an R, confound me, I cannot tell!

MRS. HARDCASTLE. What's that, my dear? Can I give you any assistance?

MISS NEVILLE. Pray, aunt, let me read it. Nobody reads a cramp hand better than I. [*Twitching the letter from her*] Do you know who it is from?

TONY. Can't tell, except from Dick Ginger the feeder.

MISS NEVILLE. Ay, so it is. [*Pretending to read*] Dear 'Squire, Hoping that you're in health, as I am at this present. The gentlemen of the Shakebag Club has cut the gentlemen of Goose-green quite out of feather. The odds—um—odd battle—um—long fighting—um, here, here, it's all about

cocks, and fighting; it's of no consequence, here, put it up, put it up.

[*Thrusting the crumpled letter upon him.*]

TONY. But I tell you, miss, it's of all the consequence in the world! I would not lose the rest of it for a guinea! Here, mother, do you make it out? Of no consequence!

[*Giving Mrs. Hardcastle the letter.*]

MRS. HARDCASTLE. How's this! [*Reads*] *Dear 'Squire, I'm now waiting for Miss Neville, with a post-chaise and pair, at the bottom of the garden, but I find my horses yet unable to perform the journey. I expect you'll assist us with a pair of fresh horses, as you promised. Dispatch is necessary, as the hag (ay, the hag), your mother, will otherwise suspect us. Yours, Hastings.* Grant me patience. I shall run distracted! My rage chokes me.

MISS NEVILLE. I hope, madam, you'll suspend your resentment for a few moments, and not impute to me any impertinence or sinister design that belongs to another.

MRS. HARDCASTLE. [*Curtseying very low*] Fine spoken, madam. You are most miraculously polite and engaging, and quite the very pink of courtesy and circumspection, madam. [*Changing her tone*] And you, you great ill-fashioned oaf, with scarce sense enough to keep your mouth shut. Were you, too, joined against me? But I'll defeat all your plots in a moment. As for you, madam, since you have got a pair of fresh horses ready, it would be cruel to disappoint them. So, if you please, instead of running away with your spark, prepare, this very moment, to run off with *me.* Your old aunt Pedigree will keep you secure, I'll warrant me. You too, sir, may mount your horse, and guard us upon the way. Here, Thomas, Roger, Diggory, I'll show you that I wish you better than you do yourselves.

[*Exit.*]

MISS NEVILLE. So now I'm completely ruined.

TONY. Ay, that's a sure thing.

MISS NEVILLE. What better could be expected from being connected with such a stupid fool, and after all the nods and signs I made him.

TONY. By the laws, miss, it was your own cleverness, and not my stupidity, that did your business. You were so nice and so busy with your Shakebags and Goose-greens, that I thought you could never be making believe.

Enter Hastings.

HASTINGS. So, sir, I find by my servant, that you have shown my letter, and betrayed us. Was this well done, young gentleman?

TONY. Here's another. Ask miss there who betrayed you. Ecod, it was her doing, not mine.

Enter Marlow.

MARLOW. So I have been finely used here among you—rendered contemptible, driven into ill manners, despised, insulted, laughed at.

TONY. Here's another. We shall have old Bedlam[35] broke loose presently.

MISS NEVILLE. And there, sir, is the gentleman to whom we all owe every obligation.

MARLOW. What can I say to him, a mere boy, an idiot, whose ignorance and age are a protection.

HASTINGS. A poor contemptible booby, that would but disgrace correction.

MISS NEVILLE. Yet with cunning and malice enough to make himself merry with all our embarrassments.

HASTINGS. An insensible cub.

MARLOW. Replete with tricks and mischief.

TONY. Baw! damme, but I'll fight you both one after the other,—with baskets.

MARLOW. As for him, he's below resentment. But your conduct, Mr. Hastings, requires an explanation. You knew of my mistakes, yet would not undeceive me.

HASTINGS. Tortured as I am with my own disappointments, is this a time for explanations? It is not friendly, Mr. Marlow.

MARLOW. But, sir—

MISS NEVILLE. Mr. Marlow, we never kept on your mistake, till it was too late to undeceive you. Be pacified.

Enter Servant.

SERVANT. My mistress desires you'll get ready immediately, madam. The horses are putting to. Your hat and things are in the next room. We are to go thirty miles before morning.

[*Exit Servant.*]

MISS NEVILLE. Well, well, I'll come presently.

MARLOW. [*To Hastings*] Was it well done, sir, to assist in rendering me ridiculous. To hang me out for the scorn of all my acquaintance? Depend upon it, sir, I shall expect an explanation.

HASTINGS. Was it well done, sir, if you're upon that subject, to deliver what I entrusted to yourself, to the care of another, sir?

MISS NEVILLE. Mr. Hastings. Mr. Marlow. Why will you increase my distress by this groundless dispute? I implore, I entreat you—

Enter Servant.

SERVANT. Your cloak, madam. My mistress is impatient.

MISS NEVILLE. I come. Pray be pacified. If I leave you thus, I shall die with apprehension!

Enter Servant.

SERVANT. Your fan, muff, and gloves, madam. The horses are waiting.

---

[35]**Bedlam** a hospital for the insane

MISS NEVILLE. O, Mr. Marlow! if you knew what a scene of constraint and ill-nature lies before me, I'm sure it would convert your resentment into pity.

MARLOW. I'm so distracted with a variety of passions, that I don't know what I do. Forgive me, madam. George, forgive me. You know my hasty temper, and should not exasperate it.

HASTINGS. The torture of my situation is my only excuse.

MISS NEVILLE. Well, my dear Hastings, if you have that esteem for me that I think, that I am sure you have, your constancy for three years will but increase the happiness of our future connection. If—

MRS. HARDCASTLE. [*Within*] Miss Neville. Constance, why, Constance, I say.

MISS NEVILLE. I'm coming. Well, constancy. Remember, constancy is the word.

[*Exit.*]

HASTINGS. My heart! How can I support this! To be so near happiness, and such happiness!

MARLOW. [*To Tony*] You see now, young gentleman, the effects of your folly. What might be amusement to you, is here disappointment, and even distress.

TONY. [*From a reverie*] Ecod, I have hit it. It's here. Your hands. Yours and yours, my poor Sulky. My boots there, ho! Meet me two hours hence at the bottom of the garden; and if you don't find Tony Lumpkin a more goodnatur'd fellow than you thought for, I'll give you leave to take my best horse, and Bet Bouncer into the bargain! Come along. My boots, ho!

[*Exeunt.*]

ACT FIVE

SCENE I: THE HOUSE

Enter Hastings and Servant.

HASTINGS. You saw the old lady and Miss Neville drive off, you say?

SERVANT. Yes, your honour. They went off in a post-coach, and the young 'Squire went on horseback. They're thirty miles off by this time.

HASTINGS. Then all my hopes are over.

SERVANT. Yes, sir. Old Sir Charles is arrived. He and the old gentleman of the house have been laughing at Mr. Marlow's mistake this half hour. They are coming this way.

HASTINGS. Then I must not be seen. So now to my fruitless appointment at the bottom of the garden. This is about the time.

[*Exit.*]

Enter Sir Charles and Hardcastle.

HARDCASTLE. Ha! ha! ha! The peremptory tone in which he sent forth his sublime commands.

SIR CHARLES. And the reserve with which I suppose he treated all your advances.

HARDCASTLE. And yet he might have seen something in me above a common innkeeper, too.

SIR CHARLES. Yes, Dick, but he mistook you for an uncommon inkeeper, ha! ha! ha!

HARDCASTLE. Well, I'm in too good spirits to think of anything but joy. Yes, my dear friend, this union of our families will make our personal friendships hereditary, and though my daughter's fortune is but small—

SIR CHARLES. Why, Dick, will you talk of fortune to *me*? My son is possessed of more than a competence already, and can want nothing but a good and virtuous girl to share his happiness and increase it. If they like each other, as you say they do—

HARDCASTLE. *If*, man! I tell you they *do* like each other. My daughter as good as told me so.

SIR CHARLES. But girls are apt to flatter themselves, you know.

HARDCASTLE. I saw him grasp her hand in the warmest manner myself; and here he comes to put you out of your *ifs*, I warrant him.

Enter Marlow.

MARLOW. I come, sir, once more, to ask pardon for my strange conduct. I can scarce reflect on my insolence without confusion.

HARDCASTLE. Tut, boy, a trifle. You take it too gravely. An hour or two's laughing with my daughter will set all to rights again. She'll never like you the worse for it.

MARLOW. Sir, I shall be always proud of her approbation.

HARDCASTLE. Approbation is but a cold word, Mr. Marlow; if I am not deceived, you have something more than approbation thereabouts. You take me.

MARLOW. Really, sir, I have not that happiness.

HARDCASTLE. Come, boy, I'm an old fellow, and know what's what, as well as you that are younger. I know what has past between you; but mum.

MARLOW. Sure, sir, nothing has past between us but the most profound respect on my side, and the most distant reserve on hers. You don't think, sir, that my impudence has been past upon all the rest of the family.

HARDCASTLE. Impudence! No, I don't say that—not quite impudence—though girls like to be played with, and rumpled a little too, sometimes. But she has told no tales, I assure you.

MARLOW. I never gave her the slightest cause.

HARDCASTLE. Well, well, I like modesty in its place well enough. But this is over-acting, young gentleman. You may be open. Your father and I will like you the better for it.

MARLOW. May I die, sir, if I ever—

HARDCASTLE. I tell you, she don't dislike you; and as I'm sure you like her—

MARLOW. Dear sir—I protest, sir—

HARDCASTLE. I see no reason why you should not be joined as fast as the parson can tie you.

MARLOW. But hear me, sir—

HARDCASTLE. Your father approves the match, I admire it, ever moment's delay will be doing mischief, so—

MARLOW. But why won't you hear me? By all that's just and true, I never gave Miss Hardcastle the slightest mark of my attachment, or even the most distant hint to suspect me of affection. We had but one interview, and that was formal, modest, and uninteresting.

HARDCASTLE. [*Aside*] This fellow's formal modest impudence is beyond bearing.

SIR CHARLES. And you never grasped her hand, or made any protestations!

MARLOW. As heaven is my witness, I came down in obedience to your commands. I saw the lady without emotion, and parted without reluctance. I hope you'll exact no further proofs of my duty, nor prevent me from leaving a house in which I suffer so many mortifications.

[*Exit.*]

SIR CHARLES. I'm astonished at the air of sincerity with which he parted.

HARDCASTLE. And I'm astonished at the deliberate intrepidity of his assurance.

SIR CHARLES. I dare pledge my life and honour upon his truth.

HARDCASTLE. Here comes my daughter, and I would stake my happiness upon her veracity.

Enter Miss Hardcastle.

HARDCASTLE. Kate, come hither, child. Answer us sincerely, and without reserve; has Mr. Marlow made you any professions of love and affection?

MISS HARDCASTLE. The question is very abrupt, sir! But since you require unreserved sincerity, I think he has.

HARDCASTLE. [*To Sir Charles*] You see.

SIR CHARLES. And pray, madam, have you and my son had more than one interview?

MISS HARDCASTLE. Yes, sir, several.

HARDCASTLE. [*To Sir Charles*] You see.

SIR CHARLES. But did he profess any attachment?

MISS HARDCASTLE. A lasting one.

SIR CHARLES. Did he talk of love?

MISS HARDCASTLE. Much, sir.

SIR CHARLES. Amazing! And all this formally?

MISS HARDCASTLE. Formally.

HARDCASTLE. Now, my friend, I hope you are satisfied.

SIR CHARLES. And how did he behave, madam?

MISS HARDCASTLE. As most professed admirers do. Said some civil things of my face, talked much of his want of merit, and the greatness of mine; mentioned his heart, gave a short tragedy speech, and ended with pretended rapture.

SIR CHARLES. Now I'm perfectly convinced, indeed. I know his conversation among women to be modest and submissive. This forward, canting, ranting manner by no means describes him, and I am confident he never sat for the picture.

MISS HARDCASTLE. Then what, sir, if I should convince you to your face of my sincerity? If you and my papa, in about half-an-hour, will place yourselves behind that screen, you shall hear him declare his passion to me in person.

SIR CHARLES. Agreed. And if I find him what you describe, all my happiness in him must have an end.

[*Exit.*]

MISS HARDCASTLE. And if you don't find him what I describe—I fear my happiness must never have a beginning.

[*Exeunt.*]

SCENE II: THE BACK OF THE GARDEN

Enter Hastings.

HASTINGS. What an idiot am I, to wait here for a fellow, who probably takes a delight in mortifying me. He never intended to be punctual, and I'll wait no longer. What do I see? It is he, and perhaps with news of my Constance.

Enter Tony, booted and spattered.

HASTINGS. My honest 'Squire! I now find you a man of your word. This looks like friendship.

TONY. Ay, I'm your friend, and the best friend you have in the world, if you knew but all. This riding by night, by-the-bye, is cursedly tiresome. It has shook me worse than the basket of a stage-coach.

HASTINGS. But how? Where did you leave your fellow-travellers? Are they in safety? Are they housed?

TONY. Five and twenty miles in two hours and a half is no such bad driving. The poor beasts have smoked for it. Rabbit me, but I'd rather ride forty miles after a fox, than ten with such *varmint*.

HASTINGS. Well, but where have you left the ladies? I die with impatience.

TONY. Left them? Why, where should I leave them, but where I found them?

HASTINGS. This is a riddle.

TONY. Riddle me this, then. What's that goes round the house, and round the house, and never touches the house?

HASTINGS. I'm still astray.

TONY. Why, that's it, mon. I have led them astray. By jingo, there's not a pond or slough within five miles of the place but they can tell the taste of.

HASTINGS. Ha, ha, ha, I understand; you took them in a round, while they supposed themselves going forward. And so you have at last brought them home again.

TONY. You shall hear. I first took them down Feather-bed-lane, where we stuck fast in the mud. I then rattled them crack over the stones of Up-and-down Hill. I then introduced them to the gibbet on Heavytree Heath, and from that, with a circumbendibus, I fairly lodged them in the horsepond at the bottom of the garden.

HASTINGS. But no accident, I hope.

TONY. No, no. Only mother is confoundedly frightened. She thinks herself forty miles off. She's sick of the journey, and the cattle can scarce crawl. So, if your own horses be ready, you may whip off with cousin, and I'll be bound that no soul here can budge a foot to follow you.

HASTINGS. My dear friend, how can I be grateful?

TONY. Ay, now it's dear friend, noble 'Squire. Just now, it was all idiot, cub, and run me through the guts. Damn *your* way of fighting, I say. After we take a knock in this part of the country, we kiss and be friends. But if you had run me through the guts, then I should be dead, and you might go kiss the hangman.

HASTINGS. The rebuke is just. But I must hasten to relieve Miss Neville; if you keep the old lady employed, I promise to take care of the young one.

[*Exit Hastings.*]

TONY. Never fear me. Here she comes. Vanish. She's got from the pond, and draggled up to the waist like a mermaid.

Enter Mrs. Hardcastle.

MRS. HARDCASTLE. Oh, Tony, I'm killed. Shook. Battered to death. I shall never survive it. That last jolt that laid us against the quickset hedge[36] has done my business.

TONY. Alack, mamma, it was all your own fault. You would be for running away by night, without knowing one inch of the way.

MRS. HARDCASTLE. I wish we were at home again. I never met so many accidents in so short a journey. Drenched in the mud, overturned in a ditch, stuck fast in a slough, jolted to a jelly, and at last to lose our way! Whereabouts do you think we are, Tony?

TONY. By my guess we should be upon Crackskull Common, about forty miles from home.

MRS. HARDCASTLE. O lud! O lud! the most notorious spot in all the country. We only want a robbery to make a complete night on't.

TONY. Don't be afraid, mamma, don't be afraid. Two of the five that kept here are hanged, and the other three may not find us. Don't be afraid. Is that a man that's galloping behind us? No; it's only a tree. Don't be afraid.

MRS. HARDCASTLE. The fright will certainly kill me.

[36]**quickset hedge** bushes

TONY. Do you see anything like a black hat moving behind the thicket?

MRS. HARDCASTLE. O death!

TONY. No, it's only a cow. Don't be afraid, mamma, don't be afraid.

MRS. HARDCASTLE. As I'm alive, Tony, I see a man coming towards us. Ah! I'm sure on't. If he perceives us, we are undone.

TONY. [Aside] Father-in-law, by all that's unlucky, come to take one of his night walks. [To her] Ah, it's a highwayman, with pistols as long as my arm. A damned ill-looking fellow.

MRS. HARDCASTLE. Good heaven defend us! He approaches.

TONY. Do you hide yourself in that thicket, and leave me to manage him. If there be any danger I'll cough and cry hem. When I cough be sure to keep close.

[Mrs. Hardcastle hides behind a tree in the back scene.]

Enter Hardcastle.

HARDCASTLE. I'm mistaken, or I heard voices of people in want of help. Oh, Tony, is that you? I did not expect you so soon back. Are your mother and her charge in safety?

TONY. Very safe, sir, at my aunt Pedigree's. Hem.

MRS. HARDCASTLE. [From behind] Ah! I find there's danger.

HARDCASTLE. Forty miles in three hours; sure, that's too much, my youngster.

TONY. Stout horses and willing minds make short journeys, as they say. Hem.

MRS. HARDCASTLE. [From behind] Sure he'll do the dear boy no harm.

HARDCASTLE. But I heard a voice here; I should be glad to know from whence it came.

TONY. It was I, sir, talking to myself, sir. I was saying that forty miles in four hours was very good going. Hem. As to be sure it was. Hem. I have got a sort of cold by being out in the air. We'll go in if you please. Hem.

HARDCASTLE. But if you talked to yourself, you did not answer yourself. I am certain I heard two voices, and am resolved [raising his voice] to find the other out.

MRS. HARDCASTLE. [From behind] Oh! he's coming to find me out. Oh!

TONY. What need you go, sir, if I tell you? Hem. I'll lay down my life for the truth—hem—I'll tell you all, sir.

[Detaining him.]

HARDCASTLE. I tell you I will not be detained. I insist on seeing. It's in vain to expect I'll believe you.

MRS. HARDCASTLE. [Running forward from behind] O lud, he'll murder my poor boy, my darling. Here, good gentleman, whet your rage upon me. Take my money, my life, but spare that young gentleman; spare my child, if you have any mercy.

HARDCASTLE. My wife! as I'm a Christian. From whence can she come, or what does she mean?

MRS. HARDCASTLE. [Kneeling] Take compassion on us, good Mr. Highwayman. Take our money, our watches, all we have, but spare our lives. We will never bring you to justice, indeed we won't, good Mr. Highwayman.

HARDCASTLE. I believe the woman's out of her senses. What, Dorothy, don't you know me?

MRS. HARDCASTLE. Mr. Hardcastle, as I'm alive! My fears blinded me. But who, my dear, could have expected to meet you here, in this frightful place, so far from home. What has brought you to follow us?

HARDCASTLE. Sure, Dorothy, you have not lost your wits! So far from home, when you are within forty yards of your own door! [To him] This is one of your old tricks, you graceless rogue, you! [To her] Don't you know the gate, and the mulberry-tree; and don't you remember the horsepond, my dear?

MRS. HARDCASTLE. Yes, I shall remember the horsepond as long as I live; I have caught my death in it. [To Tony] And is it to you, you graceless varlet, I owe all this? I'll teach you to abuse your mother, I will.

TONY. Ecod, mother, all the parish says you have spoiled me, and so you may take the fruits on't.

MRS. HARDCASTLE. I'll spoil you, I will.

[Follows him off the stage. Exit.]

HARDCASTLE. There's morality, however, in his reply.

[Exit.]

Enter Hastings and Miss Neville.

HASTINGS. My dear Constance, why will you deliberate thus? If we delay a moment, all is lost for ever. Pluck up a little resolution, and we shall soon be out of the reach of her malignity.

MISS NEVILLE. I find it impossible. My spirits are so sunk with the agitations I have suffered that I am unable to face any new danger. Two or three years' patience will at last crown us with happiness.

HASTINGS. Such a tedious delay is worse than inconstancy. Let us fly, my charmer. Let us date our happiness from this very moment. Perish fortune. Love and content will increase what we possess beyond a monarch's revenue. Let me prevail.

MISS NEVILLE. No, Mr. Hastings, no. Prudence once more comes to my relief, and I will obey its dictates. In the moment of passion, fortune may be despised, but it ever produces a lasting repentance. I'm resolved to apply to Mr. Hardcastle's compassion and justice for redress.

HASTINGS. But though he had the will, he has not the power to relieve you.

MISS NEVILLE. But he has influence, and upon that I am resolved to rely.

HASTINGS. I have no hopes. But since you persist, I must reluctantly obey you.

[Exeunt.]

SCENE III: THE HOUSE

Enter Sir Charles and Miss Hardcastle.

SIR CHARLES. What a situation am I in! If what you say appears, I shall then find a guilty son. If what he says be true, I shall then lose one that, of all others, I most wished for a daughter.

MISS HARDCASTLE. I am proud of your approbation; and, to show I merit it, if you place yourselves as I directed, you shall hear his explicit declaration. But he comes.

SIR CHARLES. I'll to your father, and keep him to the appointment.

[*Exit Sir Charles.*]

Enter Marlow.

MARLOW. Though prepared for setting out, I come once more to take leave, nor did I, till this moment, know the pain I feel in the separation.

MISS HARDCASTLE. [*In her own natural manner*] I believe these sufferings cannot be very great, sir, which you can so easily remove. A day or two longer, perhaps, might lessen your uneasiness by showing the little value of what you think proper to regret.

MARLOW. [*Aside*] This girl every moment improves upon me. [*To her*] It must not be, madam. I have already trifled too long with my heart. My very pride begins to submit to my passion. The disparity of education and fortune, the anger of a parent, and the contempt of my equals, begin to lose their weight; and nothing can restore me to myself but this painful effort of resolution.

MISS HARDCASTLE. Then go, sir. I'll urge nothing more to detain you. Though my family be as good as hers you came down to visit, and my education, I hope, not inferior, what are these advantages without equal affluence? I must remain contented with the slight approbation of imputed merit; I must have only the mockery of your addresses, while all your serious aims are fixed on fortune.

Enter Hardcastle and Sir Charles from behind.

SIR CHARLES. Here, behind this screen.

HARDCASTLE. Ay, ay, make no noise. I'll engage my Kate covers him with confusion at last.

MARLOW. By heavens, madam, fortune was ever my smallest consideration. Your beauty at first caught my eye; for who could see that without emotion? But every moment that I converse with you, steals in some new grace, heightens the picture, and gives it stronger expression. What at first seemed rustic plainness, now appears refined simplicity. What seemed forward assurance, now strikes me as the result of courageous innocence, and conscious virtue.

SIR CHARLES. What can it mean? He amazes me!

HARDCASTLE. I told you how it would be. Hush!

MARLOW. I am now determined to stay, madam, and I have too good an opinion of my father's discernment, when he sees you, to doubt his approbation.

MISS HARDCASTLE. No, Mr. Marlow, I will not, cannot detain you. Do you think I could suffer a connexion, in which there is the smallest room for repentance? Do you think I would take the mean advantage of a transient passion, to load you with confusion? Do you think I could ever relish that happiness which was acquired by lessening yours?

MARLOW. By all that's good, I can have no happiness but what's in your power to grant me. Nor shall I ever feel repentance, but in not having seen your merits before. I will stay, even contrary to your wishes; and though you should persist to shun me, I will make my respectful assiduities atone for the levity of my past conduct.

MISS HARDCASTLE. Sir, I must entreat you'll desist. As our acquaintance began, so let it end, in indifference. I might have given an hour or two to levity; but, seriously, Mr. Marlow, do you think I could ever submit to a connexion, where I must appear mercenary, and you imprudent? Do you think I could ever catch at the confident addresses of a secure admirer?

MARLOW. [*Kneeling*] Does this look like security? Does this look like confidence? No, madam, every moment that shows me your merit only serves to increase my diffidence and confusion. Here let me continue—

SIR CHARLES. I can hold it no longer. Charles, Charles, how hast thou deceived me! Is this your indifference, your uninteresting conversation!

HARDCASTLE. Your cold contempt! your formal interview! What have you to say now?

MARLOW. That I'm all amazement! What can it mean?

HARDCASTLE. It means that you can say and unsay things at pleasure. That you can address a lady in private, and deny it in public; that you have one story for us, and another for my daughter!

MARLOW. Daughter!—this lady your daughter!

HARDCASTLE. Yes, sir, my only daughter. My Kate, whose else should she be?

MARLOW. Oh, the devil.

MISS HARDCASTLE. Yes, sir, that very identical tall, squinting lady you were pleased to take me for. [*Curtseying*] She that you addressed as the mild, modest, sentimental man of gravity, and the bold, forward, agreeable Rattle of the Ladies' Club: ha, ha, ha!

MARLOW. Zounds, there's no bearing this; it's worse than death!

MISS HARDCASTLE. In which of your characters, sir, will you give us leave to address you? As the faltering gentleman, with looks on the ground, that speaks just to be heard, and hates hypocrisy; or the loud confident creature, that keeps it up with Mrs. Mantrap, and old Miss Biddy Buckskin, till three in the morning? Ha, ha, ha!

MARLOW. Oh, curse on my noisy head. I never attempted to be impudent yet, that I was not taken down. I must be gone.

HARDCASTLE. By the hand of my body, but you shall not. I see it was all a mistake, and I am rejoiced to find it. You shall not, sir, I tell you. I know she'll forgive you. Won't you forgive him, Kate? We'll all forgive you. Take courage, man.

> [*They retire, she tormenting him, to the back scene.*]

Enter Mrs. Hardcastle, Tony.

MRS. HARDCASTLE. So, so, they're gone off. Let them go, I care not.

HARDCASTLE. Who gone?

MRS. HARDCASTLE. My dutiful niece and her gentleman, Mr. Hastings, from town. He who came down with our modest visitor, here.

SIR CHARLES. Who, my honest George Hastings? As worthy a fellow as lives, and the girl could not have made a more prudent choice.

HARDCASTLE. Then, by the hand of my body, I'm proud of the connexion.

MRS. HARDCASTLE. Well, if he has taken away the lady, he has not taken her fortune. That remains in this family to console us for her loss.

HARDCASTLE. Sure, Dorothy, you would not be so mercenary?

MRS. HARDCASTLE. Ay, that's my affair, not yours. But you know, if your son, when of age, refuses to marry his cousin, her whole fortune is then at her own disposal.

HARDCASTLE. Ay, but he's not of age, and she has not thought proper to wait for his refusal.

Enter Hastings and Miss Neville.

MRS. HARDCASTLE. [*Aside*] What! returned so soon! I begin not to like it.

HASTINGS. [*To Hardcastle*] For my late attempt to fly off with your niece, let my present confusion be my punishment. We are now come back, to appeal from your justice to your humanity. By her father's consent, I first paid her my addresses, and our passions were first founded in duty.

MISS NEVILLE. Since his death, I have been obliged to stoop to dissimulation to avoid oppression. In an hour of levity, I was ready even to give up my fortune to secure my choice. But I'm now recovered from the delusion, and hope from your tenderness what is denied me from a nearer connexion.

MRS. HARDCASTLE. Pshaw, pshaw! this is all but the whining end of a modern novel.

HARDCASTLE. Be it what it will, I'm glad they're come back to reclaim their due. Come hither, Tony, boy. Do you refuse this lady's hand whom I now offer you?

TONY. What signifies my refusing? You know I can't refuse her till I'm of age, father.

HARDCASTLE. While I thought concealing your age, boy, was likely to conduce to your improvement, I concurred with your mother's desire to keep it secret. But since I find she turns it to a wrong use, I must now declare, you have been of age these three months.

TONY. Of age! Am I of age, father?

HARDCASTLE. Above three months.

TONY. Then you'll see the first use I'll make of my liberty. [*Taking Miss Neville's hand*] Witness all men by these presents, that I, Anthony Lumpkin, Esquire of BLANK place, refuse you, Constantia Neville, spinster, of no place at all, for my true and lawful wife. So Constance Neville may marry whom she pleases, and Tony Lumpkin is his own man again!

SIR CHARLES. O brave 'Squire!

HASTINGS. My worthy friend!

MRS. HARDCASTLE. My undutiful offspring!

MARLOW. Joy, my dear George, I give you joy sincerely. And could I prevail upon my little tyrant here to be less arbitrary, I should be the happiest man alive, if you would return me the favour.

HASTINGS. [*To Miss Hardcastle*] Come, madam, you are now driven to the very last scene of all your contrivances. I know you like him, I'm sure he loves you, and you must and shall have him.

HARDCASTLE. [*Joining their hands*] And I say so, too. And, Mr. Marlow, if she makes as good a wife as she has a daughter, I don't believe you'll ever repent your bargain. So now to supper; to-morrow we shall gather all the poor of the parish about us, and the Mistakes of the Night shall be crowned with a merry morning; so boy, take her; as you have been mistaken in the mistress, my wish is, that you may never be mistaken in the wife.

EPILOGUE

By Dr. Goldsmith.

To be spoken by Mrs. Bulkley as Kate.

Well, having stoop'd to conquer with success,
And gain'd a husband without aid from dress,
Still as a Barmaid, I could wish it too,
As I have conquered him to conquer you:
And let me say, for all your resolution,
That pretty Barmaids have done execution.
Our life is all a play, compos'd to please,
"We have our exits and our entrances."
The first act shows the simple country maid,
Harmless and young, of ev'rything afraid;
Blushes when hir'd, and with unmeaning action,
I hopes as how to give you satisfaction.
Her second act displays a livelier scene,—

Th' unblushing Barmaid of a country inn,
Who whisks about the house, at market caters,
Talks loud, coquets the guests, and scolds the waiters.
Next the scene shifts to town, and there she soars,
The chop-house toast of ogling connoisseurs.
On 'Squires and Cits she there displays her arts,
And on the gridiron broils her lovers' hearts—
And as she smiles, her triumphs to complete,
Even Common Councilmen forget to eat.
The fourth act shows her wedded to the 'Squire,
And Madam now begins to hold it higher;
Pretends to taste, at Operas cries *caro*,
And quits her *Nancy Dawson*, for *Che Faro*.[37]
Doats upon dancing, and in all her pride,
Swims round the room, the *Heinel*[38] of Cheapside:
Ogles and leers with artificial skill,
Till having lost in age the power to kill,
She sits all night at cards, and ogles at spadille.[39]
Such, thro' our lives, the eventful history—
The fifth and last act still remains for me.
The Barmaid now for your protection prays,
Turns female Barrister, and pleads for Bayes.[40]

EPILOGUE

By J. Cradock Esq.

To be spoken in the character of Tony Lumpkin.

Well—now all's ended—and my comrades gone,
Pray what becomes of *Mother's nonly son?*
A hopeful blade—in town I'll fix my station,
And try to make a bluster in the nation.
As for my cousin Neville, I renounce her,
Off—in a crack—I'll carry big Bet Bouncer.
Why should not I in the great world appear?
I soon shall have a thousand pounds a year;
No matter what a man may here inherit,
In London—'gad, they've some regard for spirit.
I see the horses prancing up the streets,
And big Bet Bouncer bobs to all she meets;
Then hoikes to jiggs and pastimes ev'ry night—
Not to the plays—they say it a'n't polite,
To Sadler's-Wells[41] perhaps, or Operas go,
And once by chance, to the roratorio.[42]
Thus here and there, for ever up and down,
We'll set the fashions too, to half the town;
And then at auctions—money ne'er regard,
Buy pictures like the great, ten pounds a yard:
Zounds, we shall make these London gentry say,
We know what's damned genteel, as well as they.

---

[37]**Nancy . . . Faro** popular contemporary songs　[38]**Heinel** [Madame] a popular contemporary German dancer　[39]**spadille** ace of spades, the highest of playing cards　[40]**Bayes** character in George Villiers' *The Rehearsal*

[41]**Sadler's-Wells** a popular theater　[42]**roratorio** Tony "invents" this term to suggest an "oratorio"

Samuel Beckett's tragicomedy Waiting for Godot *is among the most important plays in the modern theater; South African actors Winston Ntshona and John Kani performed it at the Long Wharf Theater in 1981.*

CHAPTER 7

THE MODERN THEATER

A cursory examination of most anthologies of Western drama suggests that very little theatrical activity occurred from the time of Molière and the Restoration to the emergence of Ibsen in the late-nineteenth century. Relatively few plays from this nearly 200-year span are performed today (save the comedies of Goldsmith and Sheridan); nonetheless, major cultural changes during this time laid the foundation for the work of the early realists. In Asia, a similar upheaval was taking place as the Japanese Kabuki and the Peking Opera emerged, partly in response to middle-class calls for new entertainment. In more recent times, the theaters of Asia and Africa have also turned toward the social drama, sometimes portraying life in realistic terms and sometimes using the theatrical traditions that have served them well for centuries as they confront modern problems.

The Romantic melodramas of the early nineteenth century paved the way for the realistic dramas of Ibsen, Chekhov, and their successors. The novelist and playwright Émile Zola acknowledged this debt when he wrote, "Romanticism is the first step toward realism." In addition to realism (and its extension, naturalism), such theatrical styles as Expressionism, the epic theater of Brecht, and the theater of the absurd also evolved in the modern era. These various styles shared a common impulse: the desire to examine humans as social beings trapped in outmoded political, economic, and philosophical systems. While the spirit of Romanticism may be found, if darkly, in modern plays, its idealism has generally been supplanted by cynicism or—more accurately—a more "realistic" assessment of the human dilemma in a rapidly changing world.

ROMANTICISM

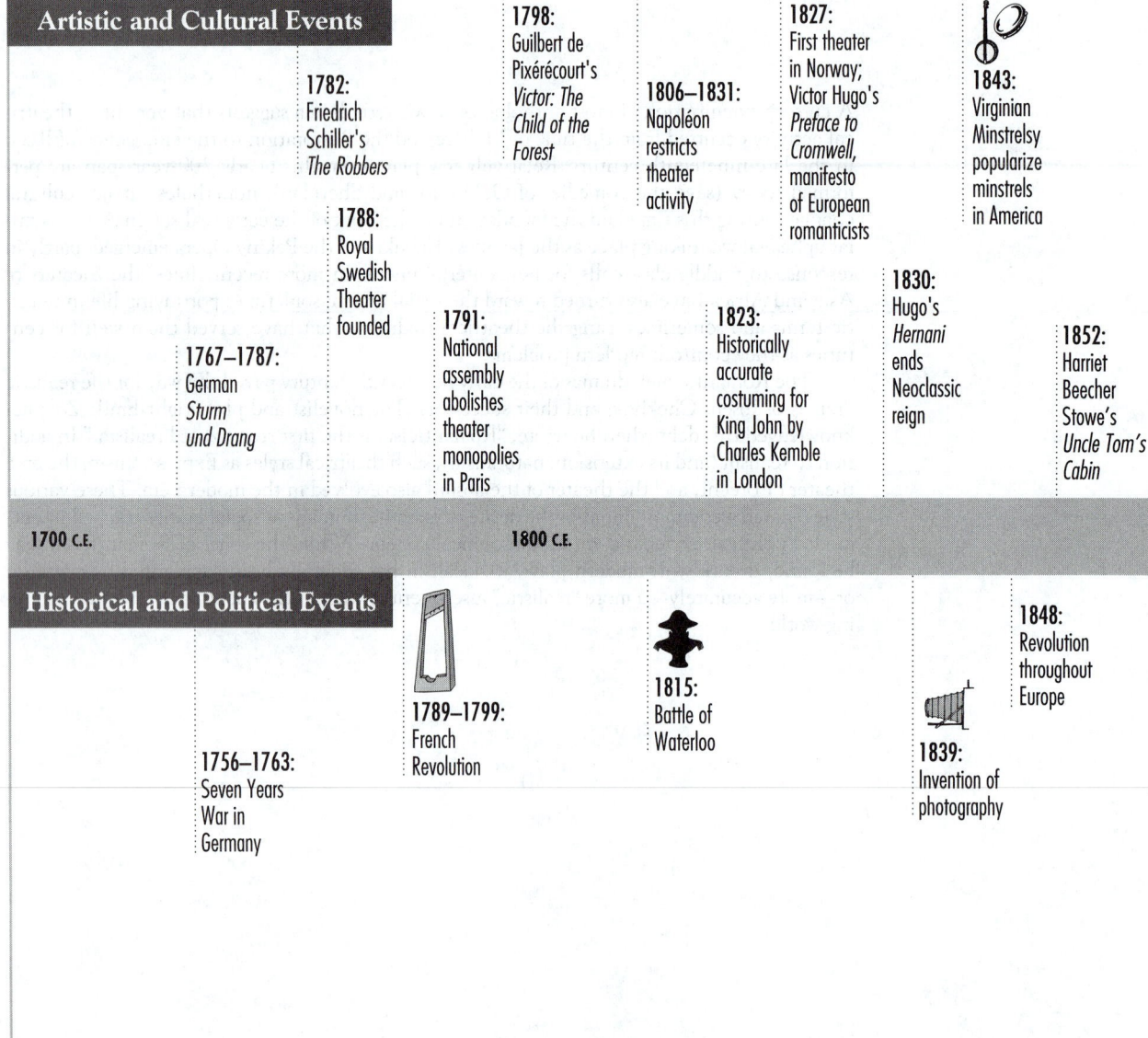

Artistic and Cultural Events

1782:
Friedrich
Schiller's
The Robbers

1788:
Royal
Swedish
Theater
founded

1767–1787:
German
*Sturm
und Drang*

1791:
National
assembly
abolishes
theater
monopolies
in Paris

1798:
Guilbert de
Pixérécourt's
*Victor: The
Child of the
Forest*

1806–1831:
Napoléon
restricts
theater
activity

1823:
Historically
accurate
costuming for
King John by
Charles Kemble
in London

1827:
First theater
in Norway;
Victor Hugo's
*Preface to
Cromwell*,
manifesto
of European
romanticists

1830:
Hugo's
Hernani
ends
Neoclassic
reign

1843:
Virginian
Minstrelsy
popularize
minstrels
in America

1852:
Harriet
Beecher
Stowe's
*Uncle Tom's
Cabin*

1700 C.E.   1800 C.E.

Historical and Political Events

1756–1763:
Seven Years
War in
Germany

1789–1799:
French
Revolution

1815:
Battle of
Waterloo

1839:
Invention of
photography

1848:
Revolution
throughout
Europe

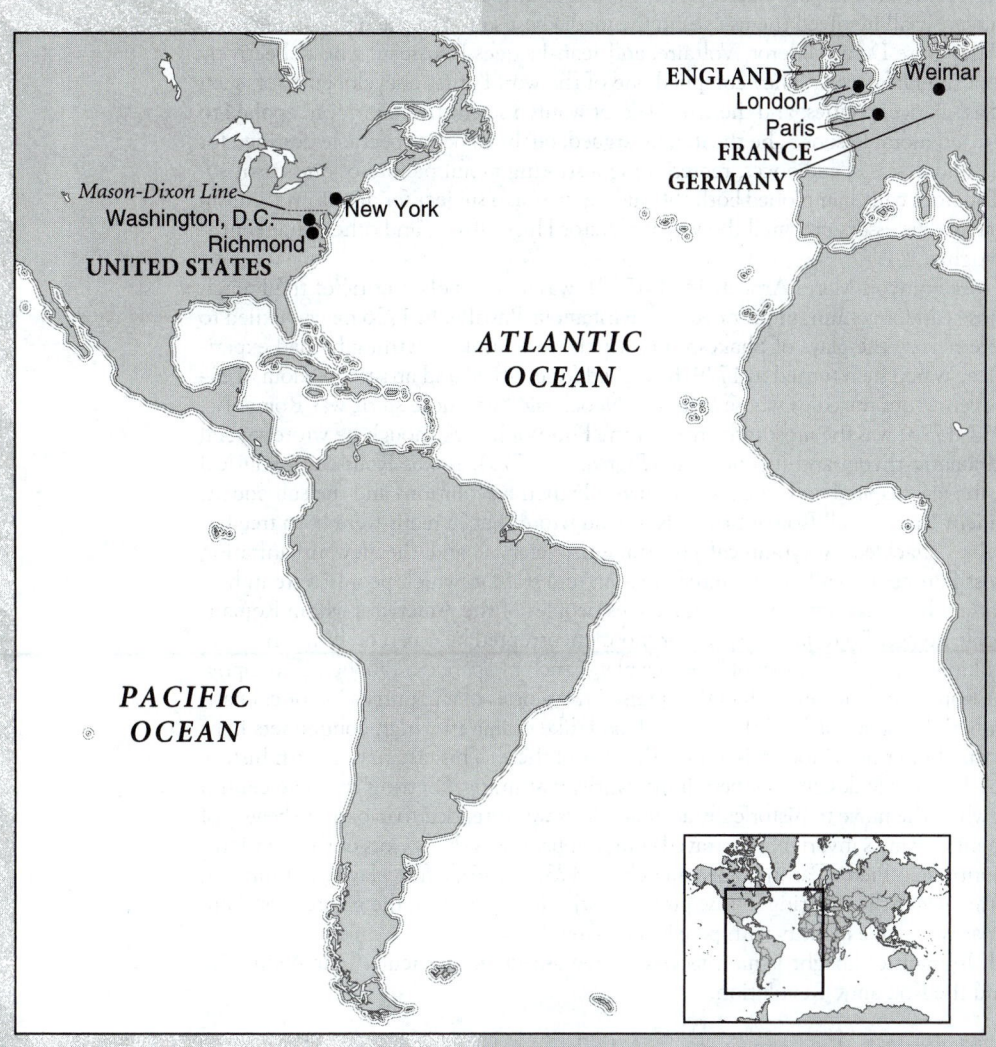

Romanticism was both an outgrowth of and a reaction to the Enlightenment, the eighteenth-century philosophical movement that extolled free thought, rationality, and scientific inquiry. The Enlightenment actually began in northwestern Europe in the mid–seventeenth century and spread to England, but its sanction came from France, the beacon of European culture and thought. Three Frenchmen in particular exerted enormous influence on the new intellectualism, and significantly all involved themselves in the media best suited to reach mass audiences: the theater. They were Denis Diderot, Voltaire, and Jean-Jacques Rousseau, who collectively bore the title of the *Philosophes*. They compiled one of the world's first encyclopedias on such diverse topics as science, politics, and the arts. Diderot wanted scientific empiricism applied to the drama to teach moral lessons. The theater, he argued, ought to be "a spectacle destined for bourgeois [i.e., middle-class] audiences, representing a striking moral picture of one's own social milieu." Diderot's call championed both the middle-class as a subject for drama and realism as its artistic style. His essays prepared the way for Victor Hugo, Ibsen, and other nineteenth-century playwrights.

Voltaire (*nee* François-Marie Arouet, 1694–1778), was an outspoken critic of the French monarchy whose candor got him imprisoned in the infamous Bastille. In 1726 he was exiled to England, where he saw the plays of Shakespeare, which were unlike anything he had experienced in France. When he returned in 1729, he argued for political and artistic freedom of expression and even wrote tragedies whose style was Neoclassic but whose spirit was Romantic. Rousseau (1712–1778) was the most influential of the Philosophes. Although he wrote several treatises on dramatic theory and a short play (*Pygmalion*, 1775), it was Rousseau's political writings that, in part, inspired both the American and French Revolutions and the subsequent artistic movement that we call Romanticism. Rousseau wrote that humans were born free but found themselves shackled by tyrannical governments, science, and the new urbanization spreading across Europe. He called for a return to a natural state in which people were in harmony with nature. Rousseau admired the indigenous peoples of the Americas, whom Romantics called "noble savages," a term of respect for those uncorrupted by urban civilization.

Such thinking inspired a number of "antique plays" such as *Spartacus* (about a slave uprising in ancient Rome) and medieval plays that praised the glories of a country's historical past. Friedrich Schiller's *William Tell* (1804), a Robin Hood–like drama in which commoners fight tyranny from the shelter of the forest, is among the best of these. This fascination with history manifested itself in scenic design and, very importantly, costuming. "Setting" became central to the drama, while the move to historically accurate dress was intended to evoke the beauty of the past. Romantic dramas invariably portrayed common people as the saviors of their nations. Rousseau's countryman Pierre Caron de Beaumarchais (1732–1799), a fine playwright himself, argued that "the nearer the suffering [of the protagonist] is to my station, the greater his claim upon my sympathy. . . . We identify with people, not kings."

Although Romantic thought is multifaceted, three aspects in particular help define the impulse behind the Romantic Revolution:

- "Freedom" became the battle cry of the new thinkers of the mid–eighteenth century— freedom from political oppression, freedom to think for oneself, freedom to create art independent of stultifying rules and traditions.
- The heroes of the Romantic Revolution were the common man and woman. This was after all the age when Thomas Jefferson wrote that "all men are created equal" and French workers stormed the Bastille with the cry of "Liberty, Equality, Fraternity."
- Passion and feeling supplanted what the Romantics perceived to be the cold, analytical thought of the Enlightenment.

The Melodrama

Consequently, melodrama and its ringing passions became the theatrical embodiment of Romantic idealism. Melodrama is as old as Euripides, and Shakespeare wrote it, as did Lope de Vega in Spain. But melodrama as a full-fledged genre evolved in Europe in the late-eighteenth century. By 1830 it was the dominant theatrical form in Europe and America. Though it is associated with the French theater during the years immediately after the 1789 Revolution, there was a significant German movement, the *Sturm und Drang* ("storm and stress"). In 1776 Friedrich Klinger wrote a drama expressing many of the same political sentiments that sparked the political revolutions in the American colonies and in France. Klinger called his play *Der Wirrwarr* (*The Hurly-Burly*), but retitled it *Sturm und Drang* because it reflected the "storm and stress" Germany was experiencing. The play's title was soon applied to a brigade of young intellectuals who wrote tumultuous dramas that rebelled against political, economic, and artistic tyranny. Their plays celebrated ordinary people in natural—even primitive—settings; they depicted heroic peasants overthrowing villainous land barons and tyrannical princes. Using the language of the common man and woman, the plays contained sensational action and elemental conflicts between the forces of good and evil. Schiller's *The Robbers* (1782) established the plot and character prototypes for the melodrama: the damsel in distress, the falsely accused hero, and the ruthless villain whose castle is filled with dungeons, secret passageways, and trap doors.

Historically, however, true melodrama was born on the boulevards of Paris after the Revolution. At this time, Parisian theaters were of two kinds: "restricted theaters" that were licensed to perform classical drama, and playhouses in working-class neighborhoods where laborers gathered to watch popular entertainments such as animal acts, prizefighting, and variety acts. Among the favorite diversions at these "boulevard theaters" were *pantomimes*, which appealed to a largely nonliterate audience. Pantomimes evolved into *tableaux vivants* ("living pictures") depicting spectacular scenes of violence and suspense (a hero dangling from a cliff) as well as historical events (the storming of the Bastille.) The finale of *Uncle Tom's Cabin* offers a stunning *tableau vivant.*

A young writer named Guilbert de Pixérécourt (1773–1844) frequented such theaters and began writing full-length plays that incorporated spectacles and violence, or at least dangerous situations. In 1796 he wrote *Victor, or The Child of the Forest*, generally regarded as the play that defines melodrama as an art form. Pixérécourt's melodramas gained international popularity as they championed justice and liberty. In Germany, August Iffland (1759–1814) wrote *Familienstücke*, middle-class dramas dealing with families in crisis (e.g., foreclosure on the old homestead by a heartless banker). August Kotzebue (1761–1819), the most popular playwright in the Western world by 1810, wrote melodramas that appealed to middle-class morality. William Dunlap, the "father of the American theater," imported many of Kotzebue's dramas and thus began America's long-standing fascination with the melodrama, the most popular of which was *Uncle Tom's Cabin.*

Because melodramas emphasized plot over character development, the sensational over the profound, simple morality over complex issues, the quality of the playwriting diminished. "I write for those who cannot read," Pixérécourt once said. As a result, the scene designer, the technical wizard, and the costume designer became forces as powerful as the actor and the playwright. Scenery drew people into the theater because middle-class audiences were eager to escape into the magical illusions created by designers. The death-defying situations melodramatists imposed on their heroes and heroines necessitated the invention of new stage machinery—and vice versa. Dioramas, panoramas, treadmills, trapdoors, elevators for moving scenery on- and offstage, and flying devices were developed to stage train wrecks, horse races, apparitions, and disappearances. Playwrights and theater managers often incorporated special effects into the plays simply because the machinery existed. *Uncle Tom's Cabin*—which depicts a shipwreck, Eliza trapped on the ice floes of the Ohio River, and a concluding *tableau*—illustrates the kinds of effects audiences clamored to see in 1852, just as modern audiences thrill to the sinking of the great ship in *Titanic.*

The Romantic Revolution and *Hernani*

On February 25, 1830, Victor Hugo's *Hernani* premiered at Paris's Comédie Française in one of the most famous opening nights in the history of the theater. It was a defining moment for Western drama, as it incorporated true Romantic drama into the popular theater.

In 1827 actors from London's Covent Garden performed Shakespeare's plays in Paris, the bastion of Neoclassicism. Playgoers at the Odeon Theater were enthralled by the romantic drama of Shakespeare, who freely mixed comedy with tragedy while defying the classical unities in his sprawling epics. The English actors sparked the imaginations of young intellectuals, most notably the 25-year-old Victor Hugo (1802–1885), who hurriedly wrote a play, *Cromwell*, in the manner of Shakespearean drama. Though a flawed work, Hugo's preface to the play became the manifesto for a new generation of playwrights, and his next play, *Hernani*, became the most celebrated and controversial French drama since Corneille's *Le Cid*. The avant-garde clashed openly with traditionalists, brawls ensued, and the papers were filled with essays about the merits of Hugo's bold experiment. Audiences voted with their pocketbooks, and the phenomenal success of *Hernani* finally released the Neoclassic stranglehold on European drama and promoted experimentation with form and content. Furthermore, it represented the triumph of populism in the French theater, thus making the common voice a respectable, as well as an economically powerful, influence on subsequent drama. More will be said about *Hernani*, but note that Hugo remains "good box office" even today. *Les Misérables* (1989), among the most successful musical dramas in the world, was adapted from his 1862 novel.

HERNANI

VICTOR HUGO

VICTOR HUGO (1802–1885)

Victor Hugo was the most influential and admired literary figure in nineteenth-century France. Fittingly, his personal life was as lively, controversial, and romantic as the characters he created in his dramas, novels, and poems. The premiere of his play *Hernani* on February 25, 1830, is acknowledged as the most important date in the history of nineteenth-century European theater, and his novel *Les Misérables* (1862) remains among the century's finest. Not only was he the leader of the French literati, he was a force in the country's political life at a time when France underwent radical change. His literary and political status earned him seats in both the French Academy of Arts and Sciences and the French Senate. When he died of lung congestion at 83, his body lay in state beneath the Arc de Triomphe as France observed a national day of mourning, and he was buried in the Panthéon, reserved for France's greatest figures. All this from a man who as a child had written a poem with the prophetic line, "Fame, to you I aspire."

Hugo was educated in Spain, where he stayed in the village of Ernani, which provided him with the title of his most memorable drama. He became acquainted with Spanish literature, and as a 10-year-old child wrote melodramas (e.g., *The Devil's Castle*) in imitation of the *punto de honor* ("point of honor") plays so loved by Spaniards. *Hernani* is not only set in the Spain of Hugo's youth, but also relies on the point of honor to further its action (he considered titling the play *Spanish Honor*). After graduating from a Parisian boarding school, he was given a generous allowance by his father (a general in the army of Napoléon) to attend law school. Instead, Hugo and his brother invested the money in a magazine, *Le Conservateur Littéraire*, which discussed French cultural life, including the theater. Here we see the first stirrings of the Romantic Revolution in French literature.

In 1822 Hugo married Adèle Foucher, a union that produced five children, although he was hardly an ideal husband and father. By his own count, he had affairs with 84 women, including prominent French actresses such as Léonie d'Aunet and the internationally famous Sarah Bernhardt. His affair with d'Aunet created a national scandal and led to a sensational trial. Though Hugo was set free, his lover was sent to prison and subsequently to a convent. (Ironically, Hugo resigned from the French Assembly in 1871 to protest that body's failure to abolish the death penalty and to establish women's rights in France.)

From 1827 to 1843 Hugo devoted himself almost exclusively to the writing of plays. Inspired by a visit by English Shakespearean actors to Paris, *Cromwell* (1827) was given a public showing and introduced Romantic drama to the French. The play is forgettable, but his "Preface to *Cromwell*" remains the manifesto of the Romantics in France. In 1830 *Hernani* premiered at the Comédie Française and forever changed French drama. Of Hugo's two dozen other dramas, perhaps the most significant is *Le Roi s'amuse* (*The King Amuses Himself*, 1832), which inspired Verdi's opera, *Rigoleto*.

The Romantic spirit Hugo expressed in his plays and novels extended to France's political life. Once a staunch monarchist, he became as fervent an anti-emperorist and in 1851 wrote a series of pamphlets attacking Louis-Napoléon. His rhetoric sparked an uprising in which over 400 people were killed, and Hugo fled to the isle of Guernsey, where he lived in exile for almost 20 years, writing novels, criticism, political essays, and some drama. *Les Misérables* was written during this exile. (Significantly, his son, François-Victor, translated all of Shakespeare's dramas into French during the exile. His translations remain the standard acting editions in France today.)

In 1870 France's Second Empire collapsed when Bismarck attacked. On September 3 Hugo returned triumphantly to Paris, where he was greeted by thousands at the train station. For the next 15 years he enjoyed prominence as a leader of French cultural and political life. He retained his lifelong passion for writing, and, at the age of 80, Hugo completed his final play, *Torqeumada*, again turning to Spain for his subject matter.

HERNANI (1830)

Perhaps more than any play in this collection, it is important that you read *Hernani* with a sense of its history. Through 20th-century eyes, the play seems a creaky melodrama, filled with purple passages, contrivances, and other debris from the nineteenth-century theater. In our age of self-serving antiheroes, the play's depiction of honor seems improbable, perhaps even laughable. (Curiously, *Les Misérables* enjoys tremendous success in our time, but its grand and Romantic sentiments are cloaked in almost operatic music.)

As the most revolutionary play of its time, *Hernani* both stirred and shocked the audience at the Comédie Française in February 1830. An examination of the play's novelties provides a review of Neoclassical dramatic theory and an introduction to Romantic literature. Furthermore, there are hints of realism in *Hernani* that would be realized by the end of the century.

Some of Hugo's most striking innovations cannot be readily apprehended by reading the play. The translation here is in contemporary English prose, though Hugo wrote in French verse. He made stunning changes in the metrical form that had dominated French tragic playwriting since Racine. Additionally, many of Hugo's most celebrated inventions were found in the staging of the play, both in the movement of the actors and in the extraordinary scenery demanded by the script.

Hugo, who wrote the play in 28 days in August 1829, spent weeks rehearsing his actors, who were forced to change their performance style. The company at the Comédie Française was grounded in the classical style, which meant that they were accustomed to standing on the forestage and declaiming their lines, full front, to the audience. Indeed, some actors strongly objected to both Hugo's writing and staging—it was rumored that Michelot, the famed tragedian who played Don Carlos, intended to sabotage the play because he so resented Hugo's anticlassical style. Fortunately, he didn't. In a realistic innovation for its time, Hugo devised natural movement patterns to encourage his actors to move freely *within* the setting rather than merely in front of it. Actors sat on or leaned against the scenery, something unheard of in classical tragic plays, as it was considered indecorous for tragic figures to assume such mundane poses because it diminished their heroic stature. When Doña Sol died in the final moments, the actress playing her writhed in her death throes, a distinct (and indecorous) departure from the artificially dignified death scenes to which French audiences were accustomed. In short, Hugo imposed a more lifelike acting style on his production because he wanted life on his stage to reflect that of the common people who filled the Comédie Française to support his dramatic revolt.

Instead of the declamatory delivery customary for French actors, Hugo asked his company to speak in more natural cadences. Note the dialogue between Doña Josefa and Don Carlos in the opening lines: it comprises short speeches—often one-word exchanges—a style that approximates realistic speech more than the lofty Alexandrines that marked French drama for 300 years. The play's first line signaled that *Hernani* was breaking new ground. Doña Josefa's speech "ran over," that is, it exceeded the 12 syllables of the traditional Alexandrine line, and it was not "end stopped." According to people who attended the opening night performance, there was an audible ripple of shock (both delighted and incensed) throughout the auditorium when Doña Josefa finished the irregular line. Hugo continued his assault on traditions by including stichomythic dialogue throughout the script. He used images and metaphors that were considered unbecoming of kings and heroic figures. In act 5 Doña Sol tells Don Ruy Gomez that he "would do better to tear their young from the tigers than the one I love from me." While the comparison with a jungle creature was judged undignified by the old guard, it was audacious and thrilling to the new. Don Carlos, the Spanish king, involves himself in mundane conversations about the time of day and hides in a closet (both of which provoked laughter from the audience).

In another supreme act of defiance against Neoclassicism, Hugo appropriated that most distinctive convention of Shakespeare's theater, the soliloquy. Though lengthy, passionate speeches (tirades) were common in classical French drama, characters alone onstage could not speak their thoughts aloud because it violated verisimilitude ("likeness to truth"), which gave plays their moral authority. Hugo not only concludes his first act with a soliloquy by Hernani (note its antimonarchist sentiments), but makes Don Carlos's soliloquy in act 4 the moral centerpiece of the play. Set in the crypt of Charlemagne, who symbolizes the mythic past the Romantics revered, the scene depicts the reformation of the truant King Carlos, who is inspired by the medieval emperor's nobility of purpose. Like Sigismund in *Life's a Dream*, Carlos concludes that "clemency" is the ultimate manifestation of a monarch's godliness. Albert Bermel, an authority on French literature, considers Carlos's soliloquy "apart from one or two passages in *The Song of Roland*, the finest monologue in the French language."

The settings throughout the play also represent a major departure for European drama, especially those of Charlemagne's tomb and the portrait gallery in the Silva castle. With *Hernani* locale becomes an indispensable character within the drama. The portrait scene in act 3, in which Don Ruy hides Hernani to protect him from the king, cannot be performed without the scenic effects Hugo scripts. Also, the portraits of the Silva ancestry are thematic devices, reminding Don Ruy of his noble duties—first to protect the guest in his castle, second to exact revenge. Charlemagne's tomb is also indispensable, although one might argue the power of Don Carlos's words evokes the memory of the great emperor and the soliloquy could be played on a bare stage. But the dramatic point is that Carlos is dwarfed by the monument and vows to reform so that he might achieve Charlemagne's greatness. The expansive setting, which stunned the audience in its magnificence, created the right ambience to make Carlos's words necessary. In terms of Western theater history, such scenes created not only the possibility, but the necessity, for humans to perform *in* an environment instead of in front of one; even more importantly, characters are influenced by their environment. These are necessary steps on the road to realism.

On occasion Hugo's actors literally step into their environments, as when Don Carlos hides in the secret closet in act 1. Here the playwright is borrowing situations from the world of comedy and especially farce. (In fact, one of the populist vaudevilles on the boulevard got wind of such devices in *Hernani* and actually performed a burlesque of the play *before* it opened.) Hugo, who decried the rigidity of Classicism's separation of genres in his "Preface to *Cromwell*," sought a "harmony of contraries." The nearly farcical comings-and-goings (often in elaborate disguises), the joyous wedding scene in the final act, the lyrical passages between Hernani and Doña Sol are borrowed from the world of comedy. The titanic struggles between Hernani and the king, the political uprising among the Alsatian mountaineers, and the trio of suicides that concludes the play are from tragic and historical drama. Yet Hugo freely moves from what he calls the "grotesque" to the "sublime" in a manner quite unseen in Continental drama prior to *Hernani*. He cited examples from *The Iliad* to justify his boldness.

Hugo patterned his play on the Elizabethan and episodic models that preceded him, and he disdained the unities of time and place that had limited French drama. We see five distinct locales housing a story line that covers many days in the telling. Hugo replaced "solemn narration" of offstage events with a rapid series of events and spectacular theater moments that carried him into the world of melodrama, despite his intention to write a tragedy in the Shakespearean manner. The play falls short of tragedy for reasons other than its melodramatic excesses. Though Hernani and his lover die, and however much we regret their passing, they are nonetheless victims of external forces—Don Ruy's treachery, a code of honor they have inherited, even the playwright's contrivances. Hernani does not contain the seeds of his own destruction, and nowhere is there the discovery of one's own contribution to one's death. Though the ending of *Hernani* may be excellent theater (it received thunderous ovations at the Comédie Française), it fails to achieve true tragic dignity. Nonetheless, *Hernani* succeeded on so many other levels that it remains among the most important plays of the prerealist era.

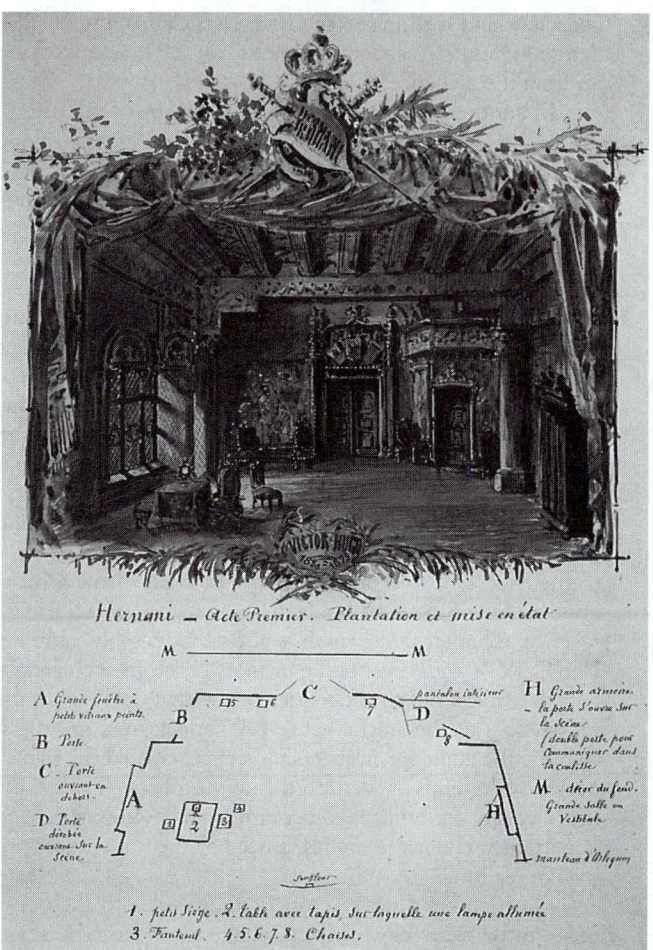

A French artist sketched a scene from Victor Hugo's romantic melodrama, Hernani, which premiered at the Comédie Française in 1830.

HERNANI

─VICTOR HUGO─

Translated from the French by Linda Asher

CHARACTERS
HERNANI
DON CARLOS
DON RUY GOMEZ DE SILVA
DOÑA SOL DE SILVA
DUKE OF BAVARIA
DUKE OF GOTHA
DUKE OF LUTZELBURG
DON SANCHO SANCHEZ DE ZUÑIGA

DON MATIAS CENTURION
DON RICARDO DE ROXAS
DON GARCI SUAREZ DE CARBAJAL
DON FRANCISCO DE SOTOMAYOR
DON JUAN DE HARO
DON GIL TELLEZ GIRON
FIRST CONSPIRATOR
A HIGHLANDER
IAQUEZ

Doña Josefa Duarte
A Lady
Other Conspirators, Highlanders, Lords, Soldiers, Pages, Townsfolk, and so on.

Spain, 1519.

ACT I: THE KING

(*Saragossa: a bedchamber. It is night. A lamp on the table.*)

SCENE 1

(*Doña Josefa Duarte, an old woman in black, with the bodice of her gown ornamented in jet, in the style of Isabella the Catholic; she draws the crimson window drapes and arranges a few chairs. There is a knock at a small hidden door on the right. She listens; there is a second knock.*)

Doña Josefa. Is he here already? (*Another knock.*) It is from the secret stairway, no doubt of that. (*A fourth knock.*) Quick, then—I must open it. (*She opens the covered door. Don Carlos enters, his cloak across his lower face, and his hat low over his eyes.*) Good evening to you, sir. (*She leads him in. He opens his cloak and reveals a rich outfit of velvet and silk, in the fashion of Castile in 1519. She looks at him more closely, and draws back, astonished.*) What? Señor Hernani—but it is not you! Help! Guards!

Don Carlos (*gripping her arm*). Two or more words out of you, old woman, and you die! (*He stares hard at her; she subsides into terrified silence.*) Is this the apartment of Doña Sol? Who's promised to her uncle, the old duke . . . a good nobleman—decrepit, distinguished, and very jealous? They say this beauty loves a beardless youth, and every night—despite the general envy—she welcomes this young lover with no beard or mustache beneath the very nose of the old man. Is this all true? (*She is silent; he shakes her arm.*) Well? Will you answer me?

Doña Josefa. You forbade me to speak even two words, my lord.

Don Carlos. I want just one—a yes or no. Doña Sol de Silva is your mistress? Speak.

Doña Josefa. Yes. why?

Don Carlos. No matter. And her old betrothed, the duke—he is out at present?

Doña Josefa. Yes.

Don Carlos. She must be awaiting her young man, then?

Doña Josefa. Yes.

Don Carlos. Oh, let me die!

Doña Josefa. Yes.

Don Carlos. Duenna—is this where they meet?

Doña Josefa. Yes.

Don Carlos. Hide me here somehow!

Doña Josefa. Hide you!

Don Carlos. Yes.

Doña Josefa. But why?

Don Carlos. No matter why.

Doña Josefa. You're asking me to hide you?

Don Carlos. Yes—somewhere here.

Doña Josefa. Never!

Don Carlos (*drawing a knife and a purse at once from his sash*). Madame, do me the honor of choosing—this purse or else this blade.

Doña Josefa (*taking the purse*). So you're the devil, then?

Don Carlos. Yes, duenna.

Doña Josefa (*opening a narrow closet in the wall*). Come in here.

Don Carlos (*looking in*). This box?

Doña Josefa (*closing it*). If it does not suit you, leave.

Don Carlos (*opening it again*). It will do perfectly. (*Examining it again:*) Could this be the stable where you keep your broomstick between rides? (*He cramps himself into it with difficulty.*) Ouff!

Doña Josefa (*clasping her hands in horror*). A man—here in this room!

Don Carlos (*from the still-open closet*). Oh, then your lady was expecting a woman?

Doña Josefa. Good heavens—I hear her coming now—please, my lord, close the door, quickly! (*She pushes the door shut.*)

Don Carlos (*from inside*). Remember, duenna—say one word, and you die.

Doña Josefa (*alone*). Who is this man? Good Jesus! Shall I call for help? But whom can I call? Except my lady and myself, all the palace is asleep. Well, the other one will be arriving soon, and this is his business—he has a good sword. May the Lord save us from perdition! (*Weighs the purse in her hand.*) After all, this is no burglar.

(*Doña Sol enters, in white; Doña Josefa hides the purse.*)

SCENE 2

Doña Sol. Josefa!

Doña Josefa. My lady?

Doña Sol. I am afraid—Hernani should be here by now! (*Sound of steps at the small door.*) Listen—I hear him on the stair. Open before he knocks—and be quick—hurry!

(*Josefa opens the small door. Hernani enters, in a great cloak and broad hat. Underneath he is dressed as an*

Aragonese highlander, in gray with a leather jerkin; a sword, a dagger, and a horn are at his waist.)

DOÑA SOL (*running to him*). Hernani!

HERNANI. Doña Sol! Ah, it's you I see at last, and the voice I hear is your voice! Ah, why must fate set my path so far from yours? I need you so to help me forget the rest!

DOÑA SOL. Your cloak is drenched! Is the rain so heavy?

HERNANI. I do not know.

DOÑA SOL. You must be chilled.

HERNANI. It is nothing.

DOÑA SOL. Take off that cloak.

HERNANI. Doña sol, my beloved, tell me this: when you fall to rest at night, all calm, and innocent and pure—when a happy sleep half-opens your fresh lips, and when its finger closes your dark eyes—does some angel come and tell you how dear a thing you are to me, a man deserted and re-buffed by all the world?

DOÑA SOL. You are so late, my lord! But tell me, are you cold?

HERNANI. Beside you I only burn! When a fierce love rages in my head, when my heart swells with its own swirling storms—then how can it matter what storms and light-ning nature hurls on us?

DOÑA SOL (*unfastening his cloak*). Come, now! give me your cape. And your sword too.

HERNANI. No—this is another friend, as innocent and loyal as you. Doña Sol, the old duke, your uncle, your promised husband—is he away?

DOÑA SOL. Yes, this hour belongs to us.

HERNANI. This hour, and nothing more! No more than just an hour for our love! And afterwards, I must forget, or die. My angel, one hour with you when I want all of life and all eternity.

DOÑA SOL. My Hernani!

HERNANI (*bitterly*). How fortunate I am, that the duke has left the palace! Like a miserable thief I force the door—I creep within and see you, and rob the old fellow of an hour of your sweet song and gaze. And I am lucky, and others envy me for stealing an hour from him, while he takes my whole life.

DOÑA SOL. Please, Hernani. (*Handing the cloak to the old woman.*) Josefa, dry his cloak. (*Josefa goes out. Doña Sol sits down, and gestures to Hernani to come closer.*) Come here by me.

HERNANI (*not hearing her*). So the duke is away from the cas-tle . . . .

DOÑA SOL (*smilingly*). How tall you are!

HERNANI. He is gone awhile—

DOÑA SOL. Dear Hernani, let us not think about the duke.

HERNANI. But we must think about him! That old man loves you, and will marry you. . . . Did he not take a kiss from you the other day? Not think about him!

DOÑA SOL (*laughing*). Is that what's thrown you into such despair? An uncle's kiss—and on the brow besides! Al-most a father's kiss . . .

HERNANI. No; a lover's kiss, a husband's—a jealous man's. Oh, my lady, you will soon belong to him! Do you realize that? The mad, stooped old man, he needs a wife to end his journey and complete his day—and so the chilly specter takes himself a young girl! The mad old man! Does he not see that while he marries you with one hand, death weds him by the other? He comes and flings him-self into our love without a fear! Old man! go get yourself measured by the gravedigger instead! Doña Sol, who made this match? You were forced to it, I hope?

DOÑA SOL. The king desires it, they say.

HERNANI. The king! the king! My father died upon the gal-lows, condemned by him! And though we have grown older since that day, my hatred is still fresh toward the old king's ghost, his widow, and his son—toward all his flesh. He is dead, he counts no more; but when I was a child I made a vow to avenge my father on his son. Carlos, king of the Castiles—I have sought you everywhere! For the loathing between our houses does not die! Our fathers battled without pity or remorse for thirty years; that they died means nothing, for their enmity lives on. They have no peace, for their sons still stand, and still pursue the duel. So it is you, Carlos, who made this hateful match! So much the better. I sought for you, and here you are astride my path.

DOÑA SOL. You frighten me.

HERNANI. Commanded to carry out a curse, I must frighten even myself. Listen. The man they have betrothed you to, Don Ruy de Silva, is duke of Pastraña; he is a nobleman of Aragon, a count and grandee of Castile. He cannot give you youth, my sweet young girl; but in its place he of-fers you such gold, such jewels and gems that your brow will shine among the glittering crowns of royalty. His duchess will hold power and pride, splendor and wealth, that many a queen could envy her. Such is the duke. While I—I am poor; as a child I had nothing but the forests where I roamed barefoot. I too may have some glowing coat of arms, hid now by clotted blood; I too may have rights, which now are cloaked in the folds and shad-ows of a black gallowscloth; unless my waiting be in vain, one day those rights will emerge from this sheath again with my sword. Meanwhile, a jealous heaven has granted me nothing but air, and light, and water—no more than the dowry it offers every man. Let me free you now from one of us, the duke or me. You must choose between us: marry him, or come with me.

DOÑA SOL. I shall go with you.

HERNANI. To live among my rough companions? They are outlaws, whose names the hangman already knows, men whose blades never grow blunt, nor their hearts tender—each of them with some blood vengeance that whips him on. Would you come and be the queen of such a band? For you do not know—a bandit is what I am! When I was hunted throughout the land of Spain, only old Catalonia welcomed me like a mother into her forests, her harsh mountains, her rough rocks where none but the soaring eagle peers. Among her highlanders, her solemn, poor, free men, I grew to manhood; and tomorrow if I sound this horn, three thousand of them will come. . . . You shiver—think again. Would you follow me into the trees, over the hills, along the river's edge? To the land of men who look like the devils in your dreams? And live suspecting everything—eyes, voices, footfalls, rustlings; and sleep on the bare grass, and drink from the stream; and as you nurse some waking child at night, hear musket balls go hissing by your ear? Would you be an outlawed wanderer with me, and if need be, follow me to where I shall follow my father—onto the scaffold?

DOÑA SOL. I will follow you.

HERNANI. The duke is rich, powerful, prosperous. The duke has no stain on his old family name. The duke can do what he will. The duke offers you not just his hand, but treasure, titles, and contentment.

DOÑA SOL. We will leave tomorrow. Hernani, do not condemn me for my new boldness. Are you my demon or my angel? I cannot tell—but I am your slave. Listen, wherever you go I will go. Stay, or depart—I belong to you. Why? I cannot say. I need to see you, and see you more, and see you all the time. When the sound of your step fades, then I think my heart has stopped its beating; I miss you, and I am missing from myself. But no sooner does that beloved footfall finally strike my ear again, than I remember I'm alive, and feel my soul return!

HERNANI (taking her in his arms). My love!

DOÑA SOL. At midnight, then, tomorrow. Bring your men to my window, and clap your hands three times. You will see—I will be strong and brave.

HERNANI. Do you realize now who I am?

DOÑA SOL. My lord, what does it matter? I am going with you.

HERNANI. No—since you want to follow me, impulsive woman, you must learn what name, what rank, what soul, what destiny is hidden in this rough Hernani. You would take a brigand; but would you take a banished man?

DON CARLOS (clattering the cupboard door open). Will you never finish telling her your tale? Do you suppose it's pleasant, cramped into this closet?

(Hernani starts back, astonished. Doña Sol cries out and flies into his arms, staring fearfully at Don Carlos.)

HERNANI (his hand on his sword hilt). Who is this man?

DOÑA SOL. Great heavens! Help! Help, guards!

HERNANI. Quiet, Doña Sol! You'll waken angry eyes! When I am with you, please, whatever comes, never call for any hand but mine to aid you. (To Don Carlos.) What were you doing there?

DON CARLOS. Well, by the looks of it, I can hardly claim I was out for a gallop through the woods.

HERNANI. When a man banters after he offends, his heir is likely to enjoy the joke as well.

DON CARLOS. One good line deserves another. Sir, let us speak frankly. You love this lady and her dark eyes; you come to watch yours in hers each night: very good. I love

her too, and want to know who it is I have seen so often entering by the window while I stand waiting at the door.

HERNANI. I swear you shall leave the way I enter, sir.

DON CARLOS. We shall see. So then, I offer my lady my love too. Let us share her, shall we? I've seen such love, such goodness and tender feeling in her soul, that I should think she had enough for two lovers. And so, tonight, I thought to bring my plans to fruit. Passing for you, I slipped in by surprise; I hid, I listened—you see how frank I am—but in this slot I was hearing very badly and suffocating very well. Besides, my French vest was crumpling. I am coming out.

HERNANI. My dagger is uneasy in its hiding place too, and eager to come out.

DON CARLOS (acknowledging the challenge). As you like, sir.

HERNANI (drawing his sword). En garde!

(Don Carlos draws his own.)

DOÑA SOL (throwing herself between them). Hernani! No!

DON CARLOS. Peace, señora.

HERNANI. Tell me your name.

DON CARLOS. Tell me your own!

HERNANI. I am keeping it a deadly secret for another man— one day he will lie beneath my conquering knee and feel my name in his ear, and my knife at his heart.

DON CARLOS. Then what is that man's name?

HERNANI. What can it matter to you? En garde! Defend yourself!

(They cross swords. Doña Sol falls trembling onto a chair. Knocking at the main door.)

DOÑA SOL (rising in alarm). Someone is at the door! (The duel stops. Josefa enters through the small door, highly agitated.)

HERNANI (to Josefa). Who is knocking there?

DOÑA JOSEFA (to Doña Sol). My lady, a terrible thing! The duke has just returned!

DOÑA SOL (wringing her hands). The duke! All is lost! Woe is me!

DOÑA JOSEFA (glancing about her). Gracious Lord—the stranger, and swords—they're battling! This is a fine affair!

(The two adversaries slip their swords back into the sheaths. Don Carlos wraps himself in his cloak and pulls his hat down over his eyes. The knock is heard again.)

HERNANI. What shall we do?

(Another knock.)

A VOICE OUTSIDE. Doña Sol, open this door to me!

(Doña Josefa takes a step toward the door, but Hernani stops her.)

HERNANI. No.

DOÑA JOSEFA (*fingering her rosary*). Good Saint James, help us!

(*More knocking.*)

HERNANI. We must hide. (*He points to the closet.*)

DON CARLOS. In that closet again?

HERNANI (*opening its door*). Go on in, yes; it will hold the two of us.

DON CARLOS. No thanks, it's far too large.

HERNANI. Let us leave then, through the small door.

DON CARLOS. Good night. I shall stay here.

HERNANI. The devil! You will pay for this! (*To Doña Sol.*) Can I barricade the door?

DON CARLOS (*to Josefa*). Open it.

HERNANI. What is he saying?

DON CARLOS. Open it, I say! (*Josefa is standing transfixed. The knocking is repeated. Doña Josefa goes trembling to answer it.*)

DOÑA SOL. I am done for!

SCENE 3

DON RUY GOMEZ DE SILVA (*white-haired, white-bearded, dressed in black*). Men at this hour in my niece's room! Guards, come closer—this calls for brighter light! (*To Doña Sol.*) By Saint John of Avila, there are three of us here—two more than should be, madam! (*To the young men.*) You young cavaliers, what business have you here? When the Cid lived, and in Bernardo's day, those two giants of Spain and of the world moved through the Castiles doing honor to the aged and granting women the safeguard of their shields. Those were powerful men—their iron and their steel rode lighter on their shoulders than your velvet does on yours. Those men respected a gray beard; they brought their love to consecration in the church and betrayed no man, and their reason was that they must keep the honor of their line. When they desired a wife, they took her unsullied and in full daylight before the eyes of all, and with their sword, or halberd, or lance firmly in hand.

But these criminals who skulk by dark, trusting only the night with their shameful deeds, who steal a woman's honor behind her husband's back—I tell you that the Cid, the ancestor of us all, would have called them vile and forced them to their knees, and to strip them of their usurped nobility, would have defaced their coats of arms with a slap of his sword.

Ah, how bitterly I think of it—how those men of other times would deal with the men of today! Why are you here? To tell me I am just an old man the young will laugh at? Laugh at me, who fought at Zamora? When I pass by, white-headed, will they laugh? Not you—no, you at least will not be there to laugh!

HERNANI. Duke—

DON RUY. Silence! . . . You have your swords, your rings, your lances; you have hunting, and banquets, festivals, and falcons; songs to sing at evening under a balcony, plumes in your hats, and cloaks of silk, and balls and tournaments, and youth, and joy—and yet you children weary of all that! You must have a new plaything; you cast about and pick an old man for it—and now, you have smashed the toy! But God willing, the pieces will spring up whole again and burst in your very teeth! Come out with me!

HERNANI. My lord duke—

DON RUY. Come out with me! Draw your swords! Gentlemen, was this just a prank? Was it? There is a treasure in my house—a young girl's honor, the honor of a woman and of a whole family. I love this girl; she is my niece, and soon she will exchange her ring for mine. I believe her to be chaste and pure, and sacred to all men. I must needs leave the house an hour, and I, Ruy Gomez de Silva, cannot do so but a thief slips in to steal my honor. Back! and wash your hands, you soulless men—for by a mere touch you taint our women. Or better—have I still something more for you? (*He pulls off his gold collar of knighthood.*) Here, take and trample this, my Golden Fleece! (*Throws off his hat.*) Wrench out my hair, treat it as vile, and tomorrow go and boast throughout the town that never in their shameless games have scoundrels defiled a nobler head, nor whiter hairs.

DOÑA SOL. My lord—

DON RUY (*to his attendants*). Squires! Squires! Come stand by me! My hatchet, and my knife, and my Toledo blade. (*To the young rivals.*) And you two, come out with me now!

DON CARLOS (*stepping forward*). Duke, there is more pressing business first. I came to tell you of Maximilian, emperor of Germany: he is dead. (*He throws off his cloak, and uncovers his face.*)

DON RUY. You joke? . . . God, it is the king!

DOÑA SOL. The king!

HERNANI (*his eyes flaring*). The king of Spain!

DON CARLOS. Yes, Carlos of Spain. My lord duke, then, do you understand? My grandsire the emperor has died; I heard this only now, and hastened here in person to tell you the news, as a loyal and beloved subject. I came by dark, and incognito, to ask your guidance—all quite simple, and yet see what confusion you arouse!

(*Don Ruy sends his servants away with a sign. He draws closer to Don Carlos, whom Doña Sol watches in fear and surprise. Hernani looks on attentively, from his corner.*)

DON RUY GOMEZ. But why that long delay before the door was opened?

DON CARLOS. For good reason—you come with a whole escort. When a state secret brings me to your house, am I expected to confide in all your men?

DON RUY. Highness, forgive me! Appearances—

DON CARLOS. Good father, I named you governor of the Figueras castle. Now who will govern you?

DON RUY. Forgive me—

DON CARLOS. Enough. We'll talk no more of it, my lord. Well. The emperor is dead.

DON RUY. Your highness' grandfather—he is dead?

DON CARLOS. I stand before you heavy with grief.

DON RUY. Who will succeed him?

DON CARLOS. A Saxon duke, perhaps; or Francis the First of France, who is one of the contenders.

DON RUY. Where will the electors meet?

DON CARLOS. At Aix-la-Chapelle, I think, or Speyer or Frankfurt.

DON RUY. And our own Spanish king, whose days God guard—has he never considered the throne of empire for himself?

DON CARLOS. Incessantly.

DON RUY. It goes to you by right.

DON CARLOS. I know it.

DON RUY. Your father was archduke of Austria; and I hope the electors will bear in mind that the man who has just fallen from the imperial purple to the shroud was your ancestor.

DON CARLOS. Besides, I am a citizen of Ghent.

DON RUY. I saw your grandfather once when I was young— alas, I am the last survivor of a whole century; all else has died now. He was a superb, a mighty emperor.

DON CARLOS. Rome is on my side.

DON RUY. Valiant, firm—and yet no tyrant that head well suited the old Germanic body! (*He bends to kiss the king's hands.*) I pity you, so young and plunged into so terrible a grief.

DON CARLOS. The Pope wants Sicily back, and it belongs to me. An emperor cannot own Sicily; so he makes me emperor, and I, the docile son, give Naples over to him. Let us first win the eagle and then we'll see whether I let its wings be clipped!

DON RUY. What joy that old ruler would feel to see your already broad brow assume his crown. My lord, we weep with you for that very great and good and Christian emperor!

DON CARLOS. The Holy Father is nimble. What is Sicily, after all: an island dangling from my realm; an island, a ragged tag, a shred that barely clings to Spain and trails along beside her. He will say this: "What use have you, my son, for that ungainly island stitched by a thread to the imperial world? Your empire is misshapen. Quick, here, the shears, and let us cut it off."

Most Holy Father, thanks! For if fortune is good to me, I shall expect to stitch a couple of those pieces back again onto the Holy empire; and if some few strips are missing here and there, I'll patch my estates together again with duchies and with islands!

DON RUY. May you find consolation. There is an empire of just men where the dead go on, still holier and grander than they were in life.

DON CARLOS. This King Francis the First is an ambitious man. No sooner does the emperor die than he ogles the throne! He already has his France—a fine piece of Christian land, and well worth holding to. My grandfather the emperor used to say to King Louis, "If I were God the Father, and I had two sons, I should make the elder God, and the other king of France." (*To the duke.*) Do you suppose that Francis has a chance?

DON RUY. He has a habit of success.

DON CARLOS. Everything would have to be amended. The Golden Bull forbids a foreigner to reign.

DON RUY. But as to that, Your Highness, you *are* king of Spain.

DON CARLOS. But I am a citizen of Ghent.

DON RUY. His latest campaign has made King Francis very strong.

DON CARLOS. The eagle who may hatch upon my crest can spread his wings wide too.

DON RUY. Does Your Highness know Latin?

DON CARLOS. Only poorly.

DON RUY. That is a pity. The German nobles like to be addressed in Latin.

DON CARLOS. They will be satisfied with a noble Spanish. For mark my words, it makes small difference what tongue a voice may speak, if it speaks loud enough. I am setting out for Flanders. Your king, dear Silva, must return to you as emperor. The king of France will do all that he can to win his way; I must overtake him. I shall go shortly.

DON RUY. Will you leave us, sire, with Aragon still unpurged of these new bandits who raise their brazen heads throughout our mountainland?

DON CARLOS. I shall leave orders with the Duke of Arcos to wipe them out.

DON RUY. And will you also order their leader to let that happen?

DON CARLOS. Who is their leader—his name?

DON RUY. I do not know it. But he is said to be a formidable man.

DON CARLOS. Nonsense. I know that just now he is hidden in Galicia, and I will put him down with a few militia troops.

DON RUY. Then the rumors are wrong that say he is nearby?

DON CARLOS. Completely wrong. . . . You will give me a bed for the night.

DON RUY (*bowing to the floor*). Thank you, sire. (*Calling his servants.*) All of you, do honor to the king, my guest.

(*The servants bring torches, and the duke forms them into two rows to the door in rear. Meanwhile Doña Sol draws imperceptibly closer to Hernani; the king watches the pair of them.*)

DOÑA SOL (*low to Hernani*). Tomorrow at midnight, beneath my window—do not fail. And clap three times.

HERNANI (*softly*). Tomorrow night . . .

DON CARLOS (*to himself*). Tomorrow! (*And aloud to Doña Sol, toward whom he moves with courtly gesture.*) Allow me to escort you. (*He leads her to the door; she exits.*)

HERNANI (*his hand inside his breast, on the pommel of his dagger*). My faithful blade! . . .

DON CARLOS (*returning; aside*). Our friend has the look of a man who is trapped. (*He draws Hernani aside.*) I did you the honor, sir, of touching your sword. I could mistrust you for a hundred different reasons—but King Carlos has no taste for betrayals. Go. I deign still to protect your escape.

DON RUY (*coming closer and indicating Hernani*). Who is this gentleman?

DON CARLOS. One of my followers. He is leaving now.

(*They go out with the servants and the torches, the duke ahead of the king, with a candle in his hand.*)

SCENE 4

HERNANI (*alone*). One of your followers—yes, King! Your follower, true! Night and day, and step by step, I follow you. A knife in my fist I go, my eye fixed on your trail—my race in me pursues your race in you. And now besides, you are become my rival. For a moment I hung hesitant between love and hatred; my heart was not large enough to hold both you and her. In loving her I forgot the hatred for you that weighs on me; but since you wish it, since you yourself come to remind me, good! I remember! My love tips the undecided scales, and falls now wholly to the side of hatred. Yes, I am one of your followers. No courtier dancing in your accursed halls, no noble lord kissing your shadow, no steward denying his own man's heart to serve yours, no palace dogs trained to the king's heel, will dog your step more diligently than I! All that those Castilian grandees want of you is some pointless title, some shiny trinket, some golden sheep to hang about their throats; I'm not so foolish as to yearn so small! What I want from you is no vain favor—it is your body's soul, your vein's blood; I want what a fuming, conquering knife can dredge out from a heart's dark root. Lead on! I follow you. My vengeance is alert, it moves with me and speaks into my ear. Lead! I am here, I watch and I listen; my step seeks yours soundlessly, pursues it, and draws close. By day, my king, you'll never turn your head but you shall find me motionless and dark amid your celebration. By night you shall not turn your eyes, my king, but you shall see my burning eyes glow hot behind you. (*He goes out the small door.*)

ACT II: THE BANDIT

(*Saragossa. A patio in the Silva palace. At left, the palace's high walls, with a balconied window. Beneath the window is a small door. At right and rear are houses and streets. It is night. Here and there in the buildings a few windows are still showing light.*)

SCENE 1

(*Don Carlos; Don Sancho Sanchez de Zuñiga, Count of Monterey; Don Matias Centurion, Marquis of Almuñan; Don Ricardo de Roxas, Lord of Casapalma. All four arrive onstage, with Don Carlos at their head. Their hats are pulled low and they are enveloped in long cloaks whose hems are lifted by their sword-tips.*)

DON CARLOS (*surveying the balcony*). There is the balcony, and the door, just as she said. . . . My blood is boiling hot. (*Pointing to the unlit window.*) No light there yet! (*His eyes rove over the other lighted casements.*) Lights everywhere that are no use to me, and none where I would see one!

DON SANCHO. That traitor, my lord—you simply let him leave?

DON CARLOS. Yes.

DON MATIAS. And he may have been the bandit chief!

DON CARLOS. He might have been their chief or their drummer boy, but no sceptered king ever bore himself more nobly.

DON SANCHO. What was his name, my lord?

DON CARLOS (*his eyes on the casement window*). Muñoz—. . . Fernan— . . . (*He suddenly remembers something.*) A name that ends in *i*.

DON SANCHO. Hernani, possibly?

DON CARLOS. Yes.

DON MATIAS. Hernani? Then it *was* the chief!

DON SANCHO (*to the king*). Do you remember anything of what he said?

DON CARLOS (*who has not taken his eyes from the window*). I could not hear a thing in their damned closet.

DON SANCHO. But why let him go when he was in your hands?

DON CARLOS (*turning slowly and staring at him*). Count of Monterey, do you question me? (*The two lords draw back and are silent.*) Besides, that is not what concerns me now. I want his mistress, not his head. I want her black eyes, friends! The loveliest in the world! Two mirrors! Two black beams of light, two dark torches! I heard nothing of their babble but these few words: "Tomorrow, come at midnight"—but they are the important ones. A perfect arrangement, no?: while this winsome bandit dallies at some murder or other, or digging someone's grave, I come at my ease and make off with his dove.

DON RICARDO. Your Highness, to finish the matter, better to take the dove by killing off the vulture.

DON CARLOS (*to Don Ricardo*). A valuable suggestion, Count! Your hand is quick!

DON RICARDO (*bowing deeply*). By what title does the king please to name me Count?

DON SANCHO (*angrily*). That was an error!

DON RICARDO (*to Don Sancho*). The king called me Count.

DON CARLOS. That's enough. (*To Don Ricardo.*) I dropped that title. Pick it up.

DON RICARDO (*bowing again*). Thank you, Highness.

DON SANCHO (*to Don Matias*). A fine count—a count by accident!

(*The king walks about stage rear, looking at the lighted windows impatiently. The three noblemen converse in the foreground.*)

DON MATIAS (*to Don Sancho*). But what will the king do once he has the woman?

DON SANCHO (*watching Ricardo out of the corner of his eye*). Make her a countess, and then a lady in waiting; then, if he has a son by her, it will be king.

DON MATIAS. Oh, come now. A bastard? Count, even a king can't get a king out of a countess.

DON SANCHO. He'll make her a marquise then, my dear marquis.

DON MATIAS. Bastards are kept to be viceroys of conquered countries—that is what they are used for.

(*Don Carlos comes back.*)

DON CARLOS (*looking about at all the lighted windows*). They are watching us like dozens of jealous eyes. . . . Well, finally—two have just gone out. Now for the rest of them! Gentlemen, how long these waiting minutes are! Who can make the time move faster?

DON SANCHO. We often wonder that in Your Highness' court.

DON CARLOS. And meanwhile my people are saying it of you. (*The last bright window dims.*) The last of them is out! (*He turns toward the balcony of Doña Sol's room; it is still dark.*) You damned glass, when will you turn light? This night is very dark. Doña Sol, come shine like a star in all this blackness! (*To Don Ricardo.*) What time is it?

DON RICARDO. Nearly midnight.

DON CARLOS. This business must be done with soon—the other one may come at any moment! (*Doña Sol's window brightens. Her shadow is visible on the lighted panes.*) Friends! a torch! her shadow at the window! No dawn was ever more beautiful to me than this one. I must be quick: give the signal she is waiting for, and clap my hands three times. In an instant, friends, you'll see her! . . . But our number will frighten her, perhaps—go, the three of you, into the shadow there, and watch for him. We'll share the loving pair among us—I take the lady, and you three the brigand.

DON RICARDO. A thousand thanks.

DON CARLOS. If he comes, get to him quickly, and stun him with your swords. Then, while he is still unconscious, I'll go off with the girl; we shall meet later. But be careful not to kill him. He is a valiant man, and a man's death is a serious thing.

(*The three noblemen bow and leave. Don Carlos waits till they disappear, then claps the signal twice. At the second, the window opens, and Doña Sol appears on the balcony.*)

SCENE 2

DOÑA SOL (*from the balcony*). Is it you, Hernani?

DON CARLOS (*to himself*). I must not speak! (*He claps his hands once more.*)

DOÑA SOL. I shall come down.

(*She closes the window, and the light goes out. A moment later, the small door opens and she emerges, a lantern in her hand and a cloak over her shoulders.*)

DOÑA SOL. Hernani! (*Don Carlos pulls his hat low over his face, and hurries to her.*) That is not his step! (*She turns to go back. Don Carlos runs to her and holds her by the arm.*)

DON CARLOS. Doña Sol!

DOÑA SOL. And not his voice!

DON CARLOS. What more adoring voice could you desire? It is still a lover's voice, and a royal lover's besides.

DOÑA SOL. The king!

DON CARLOS. Wish or command—a kingdom is yours to have! For the man whose gentle grasp you would break is the king your lord, Carlos your slave!

DOÑA SOL (*struggling to free herself*). Hernani, help me!

DON CARLOS. You fear the wrong man—this is not your bandit holding you; it is the king.

DOÑA SOL. No. *You* are the bandit! Do you feel no shame! I blush for you. Are these the exploits for a king to boast? To come by night and take a woman by force? My bandit is worth a thousand of you! King, I declare that if a man's birth matched his nobility—if God gave rank according to men's hearts—then he would be the king, and you the criminal!

DON CARLOS (*trying to draw her to him*). Madame—

DOÑA SOL. Have you forgotten that my father was a count?

DON CARLOS. I shall make you a duchess.

DOÑA SOL (*pushing him away*). Shame! (*She draws back a few steps.*) There can be nothing between us, Don Carlos. My aged father poured out his blood for you. I am a noblewoman, I come from that proud blood—too haughty for a concubine, and too lowly for a bride.

DON CARLOS. Princess!

DOÑA SOL. Go offer your love games to common girls, King Carlos; else, if you dare to treat me in such disgraceful manner, I can show you quite clearly that I am a lady and a woman both.

DON CARLOS. Well then, come share my throne and my name too. Come—you shall be queen, and empress!

DOÑA SOL. No. That is a ruse. Besides, Your Highness, I must speak honestly—no matter who you were, I would rather wander with Hernani, my own king; rather live outside the world, and the law, in hunger and thirst, forever hunted and in flight; rather share his sorry destiny from day to day, share his solitude, his battles and his exile, his grief, his poverty, his fear—I would rather all that than be empress to any emperor.

DON CARLOS. How fortunate he is!

DOÑA SOL. What! He is a pitiful exile!

DON CARLOS. But fortunate even so, for he is loved. I am alone, and an angel walks with him. Do you loathe me?

DOÑA SOL. I do not love you.

DON CARLOS (*seizing her violently*). Well, whether you love me or not, it makes no difference! You will come! My hand is stronger than yours—you will come! I want you! We shall soon see if I am king of Spain and of the Indies for nothing.

DOÑA SOL (*struggling*). Have pity on me, my lord! You are king! You are royal! You have but to select a duchess, a marquise, or a countess. The ladies of the court always have a love ready for yours. But my exiled beloved—what did the miserly heavens ever grant to him? You have Castile, Aragon, and Navarre; and Murcia and Leon; ten other realms, and Flanders; you have India with all its golden mines! You own an empire vast beyond any other king's, a domain so wide it never sees a setting sun! And with all of this, could you—you, the king!—take a poor girl from him who has nothing else? (*She throws herself to her knees. He tries to draw her along.*)

DON CARLOS. Come! I will not listen. Come, and if you do, I give you any four of my Spains. Which will you have? Choose! (*She struggles in his arms.*)

DOÑA SOL. For my honor's sake, I want nothing of you but this dagger, sir! (*She wrenches the knife from his belt. He releases her and falls back.*) Come forward now! Take a single step!

DON CARLOS. So that is how she plays! I no longer wonder that she should love a rebel! (*He moves to take a step; she raises the dagger.*)

DOÑA SOL. One step and I kill you and myself. (*He draws back again. She turns away and cries loudly.*) Hernani! Hernani!

DON CARLOS. Quiet!

DOÑA SOL (*the knife ready*). One step, and all is over!

DON CARLOS. Madam! Now you have gone too far; I can be gentle no longer. I have three men here to force you . . .

HERNANI (*springing from behind him*). There is one you did not count!

(*The king turns and sees Hernani poised behind him in the shadows, his arms crossed under his long cloak, and the broad border of his hat raised. Doña Sol cries out, runs to Hernani, and throws her arms around him.*)

SCENE 3

HERNANI (*motionless, his arms still crossed and his glittering eyes set on the king*). As God is my witness, I did not want to confront you now, nor here.

DOÑA SOL. Hernani, save me from him!

HERNANI. Be calm, my love.

DON CARLOS. What are my men doing in the town to have let this gypsy chieftain pass? Monterey! (*He calls.*)

HERNANI. Your men are in the hands of mine—no use to cry out for their powerless swords. For any three that came to your call, sixty would run to mine. Sixty, and every one of them worth four of yours. So . . . we shall settle our quarrel between the two of us. You raised your hand against this girl! It was an unwise move, my lord king of Castile; a coward's act.

DON CARLOS (*smiling disdainfully*). My lord bandit, let there be no reproach from you to me.

HERNANI. He laughs! I am no king; but when a king insults me, and then scoffs, my rage springs up and lifts me to his height. Beware, for when I am offended, men fear my angry brow more than any kingly crest! You are mad if you have some illusion of hope. (*He seizes the king.*) Do you know whose hand grips you now? Listen. Your father caused mine to die. For that I hate you. You took my title and my estate. For that I hate you. We love the same woman, both of us. For that I hate you, I hate you for everything—I hate you from my soul!

DON CARLOS. Very well.

HERNANI. And yet this evening my hatred seemed far away. I felt only one desire, one passion, one need—Doña Sol! I hastened here, full of love—and I find you in this vile attempt on her! I had forgotten you, but you are set across my path! You are mad, Don Carlos! You are caught in your own snare without help, or hope of escape. I have you in my hand! You are alone, surrounded by furious enemies. What will you do?

DON CARLOS (*proudly*). Come now! You dare to question me!

HERNANI. No, no, I will not have you struck down by some strange hand—my vengeance must not elude me now. No one but I shall touch you; defend yourself. (*He draws his sword.*)

DON CARLOS. I am the king, your master. Strike; but I will not duel with you.

HERNANI. If you recall, only yesterday you crossed your blade with mine.

DON CARLOS. Yesterday it still could be. I did not know your name, nor you my rank. Today you know who I am and I know you.

HERNANI. Perhaps.

DON CARLOS. No duel, then. Assassinate me.

HERNANI. Do you suppose that kings are sacred to me? Draw your sword!

DON CARLOS. You must murder me. (*Hernani draws back. Don Carlos sets his eagle eyes on him.*) Do you believe your bandit gangs can roam through our towns at will? Striped with gore and stained with murder as you are, do you believe that you can still strut and pose as gracious men, and expect that we should dignify your knives by striking ours against them? Are we such gullible victims? No, crime holds you in its grip; it trails you where you go. And we— are we to duel with you? Never. Murder me.

HERNANI (*brooding and thoughtful, stands for a few seconds gripping and releasing the hilt of his sword; then he turns abruptly back to the king, and snaps the swordblade against the flagstones*). Then leave here. (*The king half turns back toward him, and stares haughtily at him.*) Go.

DON CARLOS. Very well, sir. In a few hours I shall return. My first concern will be to call for the prosecutor. Is there a price already set upon your head?

HERNANI. Yes.

DON CARLOS. From this day forward you shall be considered a traitor and a rebel. I warn you of this; I shall pursue you everywhere. I hereby ban you from the kingdom.

HERNANI. I am already banned.

DON CARLOS. Good.

HERNANI. But France is close by Spain; it will be a haven.

DON CARLOS. I shall be emperor. I ban you from the whole empire.

HERNANI. As you will. I have the rest of the world to defy you from. There are other asylums where your power does not reach.

DON CARLOS. And when I have the world?

HERNANI. Then I shall have the grave.

DON CARLOS. I will put an end to your insolent activities.

HERNANI. Revenge is lame; it comes with halting steps— but it does come.

DON CARLOS (*half laughing, disdainful*). That I should touch the woman this outlaw loves!

HERNANI (*his eyes blazing again*). Have you forgotten you are still within my grasp? You would-be Roman Caesar, do not remind me that you lie frail and small in the hollow of my hand; that if I were to clench this too-honorable fist, I would crush the imperial eagle in the egg!

DON CARLOS. Then do it.

HERNANI. Go! Go! (*He takes off his mantle and throws it over the king's shoulders.*) Flee, and take my cloak; without it you could not pass alive among my men. (*The king wraps himself in the cloak.*) You may leave in safety now. My thirsting rage makes your head sacrosanct against any hand but mine.

DON CARLOS. Remember how you spoke to me tonight, and ask no mercy of me when we meet again. (*He goes out.*)

SCENE 4

DOÑA SOL (*seizing Hernani's hand*). Let us go now quickly!

HERNANI (*holding her away, with gentle gravity*). My love, you have determined to join more firmly in my misery each day; to hold to it always, and to share my days without reserve until they end. Your scheme is a noble one, one worthy of so steadfast a heart. But Lord God, you can see it is too late now to accept so much of her, and heedlessly to carry off to my lair this beauteous gem a king wants for

his own; to have my Doña Sol follow me and belong to me, to take her life and wed it to my own, to lead her off with no shame or remorse—there is no time! The scaffold looms too near!

DOÑA SOL. What are you saying?

HERNANI. I defied the king to his face, and he will punish me for having dared to free him. He is gone; perhaps already in his palace, gathering his men, his soldiers, and his noblemen; calling his executioners . . .

DOÑA SOL. Hernani! I am frightened! Then hurry—we must leave now together!

HERNANI. Together . . . no. No. The time for that is past. Doña Sol, when first you revealed yourself to me, so good, and kind enough to love me with a willing love, I dared to offer you everything I have: my mountain, my woods, my stream. Your sympathy emboldened me; I offered you my outlaw's bread, and half the green and tufted bed the forest gives me. But to offer you half my gallows—oh no, my Doña Sol—the gallows is mine alone!

DOÑA SOL. Yet you promised to share everything.

HERNANI (*falling to his knees*). My saint! At this moment when death perhaps is near, when my dark destiny draws to a dark close, I must tell you this: banished, and burdened by a solemn mission born in a bloody cradle; and as black as is the grief that shades my life—I am a happy man, and call upon all men to envy me! For you have loved me! for you have told me so! for you have leaned and blessed my cursed brow!

DOÑA SOL (*bending over him*). Hernani!

HERNANI. How kind is the fate that set this flower at the chasm's edge for me! (*He rises.*) And I speak not for your sake; I speak for the listening heavens, and for God.

DOÑA SOL. Let me go with you.

HERNANI. It would be a crime to wrench out the flower as I fall into the abyss! No, I have breathed its perfume, and that is enough. Go link the life I've troubled to another man's. Marry the old duke. I myself unbind you. I return into my night. And you—be happy, and forget!

DOÑA SOL. No, I shall come with you. I want my share of your shroud! I shall go where you go!

HERNANI (*grasping her in his arms*). Ah, let me go alone! (*He turns from her with a convulsive movement.*)

DOÑA SOL (*mournfully, and clasping her hands*). Hernani, you would go from me! So, foolish woman, to have given your life and see yourself rejected; and after so much love and so much pain, not even have the joy of dying by his side.

HERNANI. I am a banished man! I am outlawed! I bring misfortune!

DOÑA SOL. You are ungrateful!

HERNANI (*turning back to her*). Then no! no, I shall stay. You desire it—then I am here. Come . . . oh, come into my arms! I shall stay, and for as long as you shall want me. Let us forget the others. We shall stay here. (*He seats her on a bench.*) Sit here on this stone. (*He settles at her feet.*) Flames from your eyes wash over my lids; sing me some song as you used to sing at evening, with tears in your dark eyes. Let us be happy! And drink, for the cup is filled, for this hour is ours, and all the rest is madness. Speak to me, sing, and say: Is it not sweet to love and to know you are adored? To be two? To be alone? And is it not sweet to speak our love at night, when all's at rest? . . . Oh let me sleep and dream upon your breast. Doña Sol! My love, my beauty!

(*Sound of alarm bells in the distance.*)

DOÑA SOL (*rising, frightened*). The alarm! Do you hear it? The alarm!

HERNANI (*still on his knees*). No . . . they are tolling our wedding! (*The sound of bells grows louder. There are cries, torches, and lights at all the windows, on all the roofs, in every street.*)

DOÑA SOL. Hernani, flee! Almighty God! All Saragossa is alight!

HERNANI (*half-rising*). Our wedding shall be lit by torches!

DOÑA SOL. A wedding of the dead! A wedding of the tomb!

(*Sound of swords and cries.*)

HERNANI (*reclining again on the stone bench*). Come lie here in my arms!

(*A Highlander runs in, his sword in hand.*)

HIGHLANDER. My lord, long columns of militia and police are entering the square! Be quick, my lord! (*Hernani rises.*)

DOÑA SOL (*pale*). Ah, you were right!

HIGHLANDER. Men—to the rescue!

HERNANI (*to the Highlander*). I am ready. All is well. (*Cries offstage:* "Death to the bandit!") Your sword. (*To Doña Sol.*) Then farewell!

DOÑA SOL. You are lost through my doing! Where will you go? (*Pointing to the small door.*) Come this way! We can leave by that open door.

HERNANI. Abandon my comrades? What are you saying?

DOÑA SOL. This clamor stabs my heart. (*She holds Hernani.*) Remember that if you die, I die!

HERNANI (*holding her close*). One kiss!

DOÑA SOL. My husband! My Hernani! Oh, my master!

HERNANI (*kissing her brow*). Alas—it is our first.

DOÑA SOL. It is perhaps our last.

(*He leaves. She falls to the bench.*)

ACT III: THE OLD MAN

(*The Silva Castle, in the mountains of Aragon. The portrait gallery of the Silva family: a large hall in which the portraits form the decor, in rich frames with ducal coronets and golden blazons. In rear, a tall gothic door. Between every two portraits stands a full panoply of armor, a suit representing each of the different centuries.*)

SCENE 1

(*Doña Sol, pale, standing by a table; Don Ruy Gomez de Silva, seated in his great ducal chair of oak.*)

DON RUY GOMEZ. At last! Today, within an hour, you shall be my duchess, and I no longer an uncle. And you will embrace me! But have you forgiven me? I was wrong, I know; I made your forehead flush, I made your cheek turn pale. My doubts surged up too soon; I should not have condemned you thus before I heard you. How false appearances can be—how unjust we are! Two fine young men were there indeed with you; still, I should not have believed my eyes. But what can you expect, my poor child, from an old man like me?

DOÑA SOL (*motionless and grave*). You still return to that. Who has blamed you for it?

DON RUY GOMEZ. I myself! I was wrong. I should have known that a Doña Sol would allow no lovers courting—not such a woman as you, nor one whose heart is flushed with good Spanish blood.

DOÑA SOL. It is good and pure blood indeed, my lord; perhaps it will soon be seen.

DON RUY GOMEZ (*rising and going toward her*). Understand, a man is not master over himself when he loves as I love you, and when he is old. Why might a man be jealous, and even cruel? Because he is old. Because grace and fairness, youth in another man, all make for fear, all threaten him. Because he is envious of others, and ashamed of himself. What a mockery is this limping love—it brings a drunken fire back to the heart, it makes the soul young again, but it forgets the body! Often when some young shepherd goes by—ah yes, it's come to that—as we pass, he singing and I musing, he to his green pasture, I to my dark halls, often I murmur low beneath my breath "How gladly I would give my battlements, my ancient ducal keep; and I would give my fields and forestlands, and the vast herds that browse upon my hills, my ancient name, my title, and all my ruins, and all my old forbears who soon will welcome me among them—I would give it all for his new-thatched cottage and for his youthful brow!" His hair is black, his eye gleams like your own; you might see him and say "A young man!" and then think of me who am old. I know this. I bear the Silva name, but it is no longer enough. And my mind is ever running on this theme. You see how great a love I bear you. I would give all I have to be young and fair as you. But what am I dreaming of, I young and fair? I who must go so long before you to the grave!

DOÑA SOL. Who can tell?

DON RUY GOMEZ. But believe me, Doña Sol; such gay gallants as those can give no love more lasting than fine phrases. Let a girl love and give her faith to such a youngster, she may die of it and he will laugh. All those young cockerels, with their bright wings and with their languid song—their love molts like their plumage. The aged ones, whose tone and tints are muted by the years, have a more trusty wing and they are better, though less fair to see. We love well. Our steps may be heavy, our eyes dull, perhaps, and our brows deep-lined, but the heart does not show the crease of age. Alas! When an old man loves, one must treat him gently; the heart is still young, and it still can bleed. My love is no crystal toy that gleams and trembles; it is a stern and solid love—deep, sure, paternal, friendly, carved of the same oak as my ducal throne. See then how I love you—and I love you too a hundred other ways, as one loves the dawn, as one loves flowers, and as one loves the skies. To know that I shall see you every day—you with your graceful step and your pure brow, the rich fire in your proud eye—I laugh, and in my soul I feel an endless joy.

DOÑA SOL. Alas!

DON RUY GOMEZ. And then, you know, when a man is waning limb by limb, when he stumbles against the marble of the tomb, the world thinks well of the woman watching over him; an innocent dove, an angel sheltering him and suffering a useless antique that's only good for dying. It is a sacred labor, and they are right to praise it, when a devoted heart performs this crowning good—consoling a dying man until he ends his day—and perhaps without love, has all the look of love.

Ah, you shall be my woman-hearted angel, who still sweetens the soul of a pitiful old man, and helps to bear the weight of his last years—a daughter in respect, a sister in compassion.

DOÑA SOL. Far from preceding me, you may well follow, my lord. Being young is not reason enough for living. Often the old ones linger, the younger go before; suddenly their eyelids drop like an open tomb whose stone falls back to place.

DON RUY GOMEZ. What mournful talk! I must scold you, my child—a day like this is holy and joyful. But the hour is late; how is it you are not ready for the chapel? Hurry then, and dress yourself. I shall count every second. Put on your wedding gown!

DOÑA SOL. There will be time enough.

DON RUY GOMEZ. Not much of it. (A page enters.) What does Iaquez want of us?

PAGE. My lord, a man—a pilgrim or a beggar—is at the door and asks you for asylum.

DON RUY GOMEZ. Whatever he may be, good fortune enters with the stranger who's made welcome. Let him come. Has there been any report from the outside? What do they say of the treacherous bandit who fills our forests with his rebel acts?

PAGE. Hernani is done for; the mountain lion is finished.

DOÑA SOL (aside). Oh God!

DON RUY GOMEZ. What?

PAGE. The band has been destroyed. They say the king himself set after them. Hernani's head is worth a thousand crowns; but I have heard he is dead.

DOÑA SOL (aside). Without me, Hernani!

DON RUY GOMEZ. Thanks be to heaven! the rebel's dead! Now, my dear, we can truly rejoice. Go and prepare yourself, my love, my pride! Today's a double holiday!

DOÑA SOL (aside). . . . A wedding dress for widow's weeds! . . . (She goes out.)

DON RUY GOMEZ (to the page). Send her the jewel case I prepared for her. (He sits down again in his armchair.) I want to see her adorned like a madonna; I want her gentle eyes and all my jewels to make her so beautiful a pilgrim would fall upon his knees at sight of her. Oh—and the one who has begged shelter of us, tell him to enter, and ask his pardon. Hurry. (The page salutes and goes out.) Leaving a guest to linger at the door! A shameful thing.

(The rear door opens. Hernani appears, disguised as a pilgrim. The duke rises and goes toward him.)

SCENE 2

HERNANI (stopping on the threshold). My lord, peace and happiness!

DON RUY GOMEZ (saluting him with a gesture). Peace and happiness to you, my guest! (Hernani enters. The duke sits again.) You are a pilgrim?

HERNANI. Yes. (He bows.)

DON RUY GOMEZ. You probably come from Armillas?

HERNANI. No. I took another road. There was fighting there.

DON RUY GOMEZ. The outlaw's men?

HERNANI. I do not know.

DON RUY GOMEZ. And Hernani, their leader—what of him? Do you know?

HERNANI. Who is this man, my lord?

DON RUY GOMEZ. You do not know him? A pity, then you shall not win the bounty for him. Hernani is a rebel who has gone too long unpunished. If you go to Madrid, you still may see him hang.

HERNANI. I am not going there.

DON RUY GOMEZ. The reward goes to whatever man can take him.

HERNANI (aside). Let them come!

DON RUY GOMEZ. Where are you bound for, good pilgrim?

HERNANI. My lord, I go to Saragossa.

DON RUY GOMEZ. For a vow made to some saint? to Our Lady?

HERNANI. Yes, Duke, to Our Lady.

DON RUY GOMEZ. Of Pilar?

HERNANI. Of Pilar.

DON RUY GOMEZ. It would be an empty soul that failed to carry out the vows made to saints. But when you have accomplished yours, have you no further plans? To see Pilar is all you want?

HERNANI. Yes, I want to see the torches and the candles burn; to see Our Lady glowing in her brilliant shrine, with all her golden vestments, and then turn home again.

DON RUY GOMEZ. Very good, Your name, my brother? I am Ruy de Silva.

HERNANI (*hesitating*). My name . . . ?

DON RUY GOMEZ. You need not tell it, if you so choose. None has the right to know it here. Have you not come to ask asylum?

HERNANI. Yes, Duke.

DON RUY GOMEZ. Thank you. Be welcome; stay here, my friend, and want for nothing. As for your name, you are called my guest. Whoever you be, it is well. I'd welcome Satan himself with peace of mind, if God sent him to me.

(*The double door at rear opens. Doña Sol enters, dressed in Castilian wedding costume of the period. Behind her are pages and attendants; two women carry upon a velvet cushion a chiseled silver box which they place upon a table. It holds a rich array of jewels: a duchess' coronet, bracelets, collars, necklaces, pearls, and diamonds in a tumbled heap. Hernani, breathless and startled, his eyes burning, stares at Doña Sol without listening to the duke.*)

SCENE 3

DON RUY GOMEZ (*continuing*). Here is my own holy lady. A prayer to her will bring you good fortune. (*He goes to offer his hand to Doña Sol, who is still pale and grave.*) My lovely bride, come forward. What? You wear no ring, and still no coronet?

HERNANI (*in a thunderous voice*). Who here would earn a thousand crowns? (*All turn toward him, astonished. He rips off his pilgrim's robe, throws it to the door, and appears in his mountaineer's outfit.*) I am Hernani.

DOÑA SOL (*aside, joyfully*). He is alive!

HERNANI (*to the valets*). I am the man they seek. (*To the duke.*) You asked if I were called—what, Perez, or Diego? No, I am named Hernani. It is a name much greater, an exile's name, an outlaw's name! You see this head? It is worth enough to pay for your whole feast! (*To the attendants.*) I offer it to all of you. You will be well rewarded! Take it! Tie my hands, and bind my feet—bind them! No, that is needless; there is a chain that holds me and that I shall never break!

DOÑA SOL (*apart*). Ah, woe!

DON RUY GOMEZ. Madness—my guest is a madman!

HERNANI. Your guest is a bandit.

DOÑA SOL. Do not listen to him!

HERNANI. I have said what I have said.

DON RUY GOMEZ. A thousand golden crowns! Sir, the sum is a high one, and I cannot be sure of all my men.

HERNANI. What does it matter? So much the better if there is one among them who will do it. (*To the attendants.*) Give me up! Sell me!

DON RUY GOMEZ (*trying to quiet him*). Be still! Someone may take you at your word.

HERNANI. My friends, it is a matchless opportunity! I tell you I am the criminal, the rebel—I am Hernani!

DON RUY GOMEZ. Quiet!

HERNANI. Hernani!

DOÑA SOL (*her voice muffled, in his ear*). Oh be still, my love!

HERNANI (*half turning toward her*). There is a wedding here! And I shall share in it! My bride awaits me too. (*To the duke.*) She is less lovely than your own, my lord, but no less faithful. Her name is Death. (*To the servants.*) Not one of you steps forward?

DOÑA SOL (*low*). Have pity on me!

HERNANI (*to the servants*). Hernani! A thousand crowns in gold!

DON RUY GOMEZ. It is the devil himself!

HERNANI (*to the young servant*). Come, you there! you can win the bounty; you shall be rich, and from a servant become a man again. (*To the other unmoving men.*) And you, you tremble too! Oh, have I not misery enough!

DON RUY GOMEZ. Brother, in touching your head they risk their own. Were you Hernani, were you a thousand times worse; if the reward for your head were more than gold, were it a whole empire, I still must protect you in this house, against the king himself, for as my guest you are here by God's will. May I die if a single hair falls from your brow. (*To Doña Sol.*) My niece, within the hour you shall be my wife. Go to your rooms. I must order the castle armed, and bar the door. (*He goes out, and the servants follow him.*)

HERNANI (*glancing despairingly at his weaponless sash*). Not even a knife! (*When the duke has gone, Doña Sol starts to follow her ladies off, then stops. When they have disappeared, she comes anxiously back to Hernani.*)

SCENE 4

(*Hernani gazes coldly at the nuptial jewel casket on the table, and seems almost unaware of her. Then he raises his head abruptly, and his eyes flare.*)

HERNANI. I congratulate you! More than I can say, your jewelry enchants, delights me—I stand in admiration! (*He moves to the casket.*) The ring is most tasteful; I like the coronet; the necklace is lovely work, the bracelet quite rare—but a hundred, a hundred times less so than the woman who can hide such perfidy behind so pure a brow! (*He examines the box again.*) And what have you paid for all of this? A little of your love? Why, excellent! That is nothing at all. Good God! To so betray, to feel no shame, and still live on! (*Looking through the jewel box.*) But perhaps, after all, these are only painted pearls, and copper that seems gold, and glass and lead; unreal diamonds, false sapphires, false gems, false brilliants, false stones! If that is so, then your heart is false as well, Duchess—false as these ornaments, and you are only gilt! (*He goes back to the case.*) But no. No. It is all real, all good, and every piece is fine. He would not dare to cheat, so near the grave. There is nothing lacking. (*He takes one piece after another from the case.*) Necklets, brilliants, ear pendants . . . a ducal coronet, a ring of gold—marvelous! A fitting thanks to steadfast, true, and deepest love! the precious jewel case!

DOÑA SOL (*going to the casket; she reaches beneath the jewels, and draws out a dagger*). You have not reached deep enough. (*Hernani utters a cry and falls prostrate at her feet.*) Here is the knife I took from King Carlos with my holy Lady's help, when he was offering me a throne; and I refused, for you who vilify me.

HERNANI (*still kneeling*). Oh—I beg you, on my knees let me wipe those bitter beloved tears out from your sorrowing eyes. Take my blood for your tears!

DOÑA SOL (*softened*). Hernani! I love you and forgive you. I feel only love for you.

HERNANI. She has forgiven me, and loves me! But how can I forgive and love myself again, after what I have said? My heavenly angel, show me where you have walked, and let me kiss the pavement where it was.

DOÑA SOL. My love!

HERNANI. No, I cannot be but hateful to my eyes! Listen, tell me: "I love you!" Assure a doubtful heart, and tell me. Often a woman's lips have healed much pain with those few words.

DOÑA SOL (*absorbed, unhearing*). How could he think my love so short of memory? That lusterless men could shrink a heart where his name has entered down to the size of other loves, however noble the world might think them!

HERNANI. I have blasphemed! Doña Sol, if I were in your stead, I should have had enough; I should be weary of this wild fool, of this brooding, senseless man who cannot kiss till after he has wounded. I should tell him "Go." Turn me away, you must! And I shall only bless you, for you were good, and kind; for you have borne me far too long already, for I am evil—I would darken your days with my black nights.

It is too much—your spirit is high and good and pure; if I am bad, why should you suffer for it? Wed the old duke, he is a good man, and noble; he owns Olmedo from his mother, Alcala from his father. Once more I bid you, be rich with him; be happy! Do you know what splendid gifts my own generous hand can offer you? A dowry of sorrow. A choice between blood and tears. Exile, chains, death, the constant fear around me—there is your golden necklace, and your handsome crown, and never has proud husband offered his bride a richer treasure chest of misery and mourning! Marry the old man, I tell you. He deserves you. Who would ever match my doomed head with your clear brow? Who ever, seeing the two of us—you calm and fair, me violent and perilous, you tranquil and blossoming like a shaded flower, me storm-tossed against a thousand different reefs—who would think to say our fates are joined by the same law? No. God, who determines good things, did not make you

for me. I have no heaven-sent right to you. I am resigned. I have your heart, but I have it by theft. I hand it to another, worthier man. Heaven has never consented to our love. When I told you it was your destiny, I lied. And in any case, farewell to all revenge and love! My day is done. I'll go then, futile, with my double dream, ashamed that I could neither punish nor beguile. I should have been built to hate, but I could only love! Forgive me, and flee! These prayers are all I ask; do not refuse them, for they are my last. You live, and I am dead. You must not wall yourself into my tomb with me.

DOÑA SOL. Ungrateful!

HERNANI. Mountains of Aragon! Galicia, Estremadura! I bring misfortune to all who join with me. I have taken your best sons to serve my claims; relentless, I have sent them into battle, and they are dead of it. They were the most valiant in all of valiant Spain. And they are dead. They have fallen in the mountains, all of them upon their backs as brave men do, before God; if they were to open their eyes again, they would see the blue heavens. And this is what I do to all who join me. Is this a destiny that you should want to share? Doña Sol, take the duke, take hell itself, take the ring! Anyone is better! There is not one friend left to remember me; everything deserts me, and now finally your turn has come, for I must live alone. Flee my contamination; do not make a religion of love. Oh, have mercy on yourself, and flee! . . . Perhaps you think me a man like all the rest, a rational thing who first dreams of his goal and then moves straight toward it. Do not be fooled. I am a restless energy!—the blind, deaf agent of doleful mysteries, a soul of sorrows shaped with shadows! Where am I bound? I cannot say. But yet I feel myself hurled on by some impulsive gale, some wild determination. I fall, and fall, and never do I rest. . . . If once, gasping for breath, I dare to turn my head, a voice commands "Go on!"; and the chasm is a deep one, and the depth of it is red with blood or flame! And meanwhile, along my headlong course, all things are crushed, or die. Woe to him who comes close to me! Oh, flee! Turn from my fated path. Against my will I'll do you injury!

DOÑA SOL. Oh God!

HERNANI. My devil is a fearsome one. The single miracle he cannot work is my happiness. And you are happiness! So you are not meant for me; seek out another man. Heaven has rejected me; if ever it should smile upon my fate, do not believe in it! It would only be in irony. Marry the duke.

DOÑA SOL. So it still was not enough—you tore my heart and now you crush it. Ah, you no longer love me.

HERNANI. You are my heart, my soul! The glowing hearth that warms me by its flames is you! Do not hate me that I flee, my love.

DOÑA SOL. I do not hate you. But I shall die of it.

HERNANI. Die? For whom? For me? Could you die for so little?

DOÑA SOL (*letting her tears come*). It is everything!

HERNANI (*sitting beside her*). You weep, and once more through my doing. And who will punish me? For you, I know, will pardon me again. Can you ever know what pain I feel when even a single tear drowns the radiance in your eyes? For their brightness is my joy. Oh, my friends are dead! I am a fool. Forgive me. I want to love, but I do not know the way—and yet I love so deeply! Weep no more—let's die instead! Would that I had a world—I would give it to you. What misery this is!

DOÑA SOL (*throwing herself at his neck*). Oh my proud, my noble lion! I love you.

HERNANI. How supreme a blessing love would be, if one could die of loving too well!

DOÑA SOL. I love you, my lord! I love you and I am wholly yours!

HERNANI (*dropping his head onto her shoulder*). How sweet a dagger blow would be from you. . . .

DOÑA SOL (*imploring*). Have you no fear that God will punish you for words like those?

HERNANI (*still leaning on her breast*). Let him unite us then! . . . You wish it—let it be! I have fought against it!

(*They gaze ecstatically at one another in an embrace, hearing nothing, seeing nothing else, and totally absorbed in their own gaze. Don Ruy Gomez enters by the door at rear. He sees them and stops frozen on the doorsill.*)

SCENE 5

DON RUY GOMEZ (*motionless, his arms crossed, on the threshold*). Then this is hospitality's reward!

DOÑA SOL. It is the duke! (*The two turn as if shocked awake.*)

DON RUY GOMEZ (*still unmoving*). Are these my wages, guest? Run, my lord host, and see if the wall is high enough, if the gate is strongly barred and the archer in his tower; go look once, and once again, about your castle for our sake. Look through your arsenal for armor that will fit—try on your battle trappings again at sixty years! And here's our kind of loyalty in payment for your good faith. You do that for us; we do this for you. Saints in heaven! I have lived more than sixty years, and seen a hundred wild-spirited bandits; often, as I drew my dagger from its sheath, I have flushed the hangman's quarry where I walked. I have seen murderers, forgers, traitors and faithless grooms serve poison to their masters. I have seen men die without the cross, and without prayer. I saw Sforza, and Borgia, I see Luther now—but never have I seen depravity so great it did not fear a thunderbolt for betrayal of a host! I come from other times. So black a treason petrifies an old man on the threshold of his home and gives the aging master, before he dies, the aura of a statue carved for his own tomb. Moors and Castilians! Tell me, what is this man? (*He raises his eyes and runs them over the portraits that circle the hall.*) Oh all ye Silvas who hear me now, forgive me if I say this to you—forgive me if my wrath pronounces hospitality a poor adviser!

HERNANI (*rising*). Duke—

DON RUY. Silence! (*He takes three or four slow steps into the hall, and again looks about him at the Silva portraits on the walls.*) Sacred departed ones! My ancestors! Men of iron! You who see all that comes from heaven and hell—tell me, my lords, tell me—what is this man? He is not Hernani, no; his name is Judas! Oh strain to speak, and tell me who he is! (*Crossing his arms.*) Have you ever in your times seen such a thing? No!

HERNANI. My lord duke—

DON RUY GOMEZ (*still to the portraits*). Do you see this? The villain wants to speak! But you can read better in his soul than I. Oh do not hear him, he is a knave! He predicts that my own hand will drench my house with blood; that my heart may be brewing some revenge amid its storm, akin to the feast of the Seven Heads. He will say he is outlawed, he'll say the name of Silva will ring with all the horror of the Lara name. He will say he is my guest, and thus yours. . . . My fathers, oh my lords, say, am I to blame? Judge between the two of us!

HERNANI. Ruy Gomez de Silva, if ever a noble brow was raised to heaven, if ever there was fine heart, or lofty soul, they are yours, my lord! I who speak to you am guilty; I have nothing more to say than that I am most surely damned. Yes, I desired to take your bride from you; I did wish to soil your marriage bed, and that is infamous. I have life and blood in me. You have the right to spill it, then wipe your sword and think no more of it.

DOÑA SOL. My lord, the fault is mine, not his! Strike me instead!

HERNANI. Be silent, Doña Sol. This moment is supreme; this time belongs to me, and it is all I own. Then let me talk to the duke. Sir, believe these last words from my lips: I swear that I am guilty, but be at peace, for she is innocent. That is the whole tale—I guilty and she pure. Your good faith must go to her, and the thrust of a sword or knife to me. Then toss the body away and wash the floor if you wish; it matters not.

DOÑA SOL. No! I alone have done it all! Because I love him. (*Don Ruy starts at this word, and turns a terrible gaze on Doña Sol. She throws herself to her knees.*) Yes, forgive me. I love him, my lord.

DON RUY GOMEZ. You love him! (*To Hernani.*) Then tremble! (*A blare of trumpets outside. The page enters. To the page.*) What is that sound?

PAGE. It is the king himself, my lord, with a troop of archers, and his herald.

DOÑA SOL. The king! A final stab of fate!

PAGE (*to the duke*). He demands to know the reason why the gate is closed, and wants it opened.

DON RUY GOMEZ. Open to the king. (*The page bows and leaves.*)

DOÑA SOL. He is lost!

(*Don Ruy goes to one of the paintings, which is his own portrait, the last on the left; he touches a spring, the portrait turns out like a door, and shows a hiding place in the wall. He turns to Hernani.*)

DON RUY GOMEZ. Step in here, sir.

HERNANI. My life belongs to you. Surrender it, my lord; I hold it ready. I am your prisoner.

(*He steps into the hiding place. Don Ruy touches the spring again, and the painting moves back into place.*)

PAGE (*returning*). His Highness the King. (*Doña Sol quickly lowers her veil. The double door opens. Don Carlos enters outfitted for war, followed by a crowd of gentlemen armed as he is, and halberdiers, arquebusiers, and crossbowmen.*)

SCENE 6

(*Don Carlos advances slowly, his left hand on the hilt of his sword, his right inside his bosom, and stares at the duke in anger. The duke steps before the king and bows deeply. Silence. Suspense and fear in the atmosphere. Finally the king, reaching the duke, lifts his own head abruptly.*)

DON CARLOS. How is it that today, my cousin, your gate is so firmly locked? By the very saints, I had thought your blade more rusty by now! I should not have imagined it would be so quick to flash in your fist again when we should come to see you. (*Don Ruy Gomez attempts to speak, but the king continues, with an imperious gesture.*) It is a little late to play the young man! Do we wear a turban? Are we named Boabdil, or Mohammed, and not Carlos—answer!—that you should lower the portcullis or raise the bridge before us?

DON RUY GOMEZ (*bowing*). Highness—

DON CARLOS (*to his men*). Take the keys and seize the gates. (*Two officers go out. Several others arrange the soldiers into triple file in the hall, from the king to the main door. Don Carlos turns again toward the duke.*) So, you yearn to wake dead mutinies: God in heaven!—if you dukes assume such airs with me, the king will act the king! I shall go among the mountains and crush their lordships in their battlemented nests with my own warring hands!

DON RUY GOMEZ (*straightening*). Highness, the Silvas are loyal—

DON CARLOS (*interrupting him*). Answer me without guile, Duke, or I shall have your eleven towers razed to earth. A spark still glows from the extinguished blaze; of all the slaughtered bandits, their chief survives. Who is concealing him? You! This Hernani, this vicious rebel—you are hiding him here within your castle!

DON RUY GOMEZ. My lord, it is true.

DON CARLOS. Very well. I want his head—or else your own, you understand, my cousin?

DON RUY GOMEZ (*bowing*). Of course! You shall be satisfied. (*Doña Sol hides her face in her hands and falls into a chair.*)

DON CARLOS (*softening*). Ah, you mend your ways. Go get me my prisoner.

(*The duke crosses his arms, lowers his head, and remains thoughtful for a few moments. The king and Doña Sol watch him in silence, and with contrary emotions. Finally the duke raises his head, goes to the king, takes his hand, and leads him slowly up to the oldest of the portraits, the one starting the row at the spectator's right.*)

DON RUY GOMEZ (*showing the portrait to the king*). This is the oldest of the Silvas, the forefather, the ancestor, the great man! Don Silvius, who three times was Roman consul. (*Moving to the next portrait.*) Here is Don Galcerán de Silva, the other Cid. At Toro, near Valladolid, there is a golden case that holds his remains, and a thousand candles burn around the shrine. He liberated the city of Leon from the tribute of the hundred virgins. (*He passes to another.*) Don Blas, who by his own decision and his conscience went into exile, for having given the king poor counsel. (*At another.*) Christovál. At the battle of the Escalona, the king Don Sancho was fleeing on foot, and the furious blows fell hard around his royal white plume. He cried out "Christovál!" Christovál took on the plume and gave the king his horse. (*At the next.*) Don Jorge, who paid the ransom for Ramirez, king of Aragon.

DON CARLOS (*crossing his arms and looking at Don Ruy from head to toe*). Don Ruy, by God, I wonder at you! I want my prisoner now!

DON RUY (*moving to another portrait*). This is Ruy Gomez de Silva; he was named Grand Master of Saint James and of Calatrava. His giant armor would far surpass our size. He took three hundred flags, won thirty battles; he conquered Motril for the king, and Antequera, Suez and Nijar, and died a pauper. Highness, salute them. (*He himself bows and uncovers his head, then goes on to another. The king listens to him with growing impatience and anger.*) Beside him, Gil his son, beloved by noble hearts. His hand upon an oath was worth a king's. (*At another.*) Don Gaspard, the glory of Mendoza and of Silva! Every noble house has some alliance with the Silvas, Highness. The house of Sandoval dreads and weds us in alternation; Manrico's line is envious, the Laras jealous, and Alencastro hates us. Our feet touch all the dukes at once, and our foreheads all the kings.

DON CARLOS (*annoyed*). Do you make sport of us?

DON RUY (*going to other portraits*). Here is Don Vasquez, called the Wise; and Don Jaime, called the Strong. One day as he went by he stopped Zamet and a hundred Moors alone. I shall pass over others, some better still! (*As the king makes an angry gesture, he moves past a great many of the paintings, and stops at the last three portraits at the specta-*

tor's left.) My noble grandfather. He lived for sixty years, keeping his promised word even to Jews. (At the next-to-last.) This old man, this holy face—this is my father. He was a great man, although he came the last. The Moors at Granada had taken prisoner Count Alvar Giron, his friend. But my father gathered six hundred soldiers to find and free him. He had a Count Alvar Giron carved out in stone, and carried the statue with him, swearing by his patron saint that never would he turn back until the stony count itself should turn and seek retreat. He battled, reached the count, and saved him.

DON CARLOS. My prisoner, Duke!

DON RUY GOMEZ. He was a Gomez de Silva. This is what one says on seeing all these heroes in this house. . . .

DON CARLOS. My prisoner, and instantly!

(Don Ruy Gomez bows deeply before the king, takes his hand and leads him to the last portrait, the one behind which he has hidden Hernani. Doña Sol watches him anxiously, and the others are silent and attentive.)

DON RUY GOMEZ. This portrait is my own. And I thank you, King Carlos; for what you ask is that on seeing it, all men should say "This last one, the son of such heroic race: he was a traitor that sold his guest away."

(Joy on Doña Sol's face; a murmur of astonishment among the others present. The king, disconcerted, moves off in fury, and keeps silence for several moments, his lips trembling and eyes blazing.)

DON CARLOS. Duke, your castle is in my way, and I shall throw it down!

DON RUY GOMEZ. For you would indeed pay me for his head, Your Highness, would you not?

DON CARLOS. For such defiance, I shall level all its towers, and order nettles sown where once it stood.

DON RUY GOMEZ. Better that nettles grow where my towers rose, than that a stain should mark the Silva name. (To the portraits.) Is that not so, my fathers?

DON CARLOS. Duke, his head is ours, and you had promised me.

DON RUY GOMEZ. I promised one head or the other. (To the portraits.) Is that not so, my sires? (Touching his own head; to the king.) I give you this one. Take it.

DON CARLOS. I thank you, Duke, but I lose by this arrangement. The head I need is young; once severed, it must be lifted by the hair before the people. But yours! What use have I for it? The headsman would seek in vain to grasp its hair. You have not even enough to fill the hand!

DON RUY GOMEZ. Highness, do not insult me! My head is still a good one, and easily worth a rebel's, I think. You disdain a Silva head?

DON CARLOS. Give us Hernani!

DON RUY GOMEZ. My lord, I have spoken.

DON CARLOS (to his men). Search everywhere! In every wing, in every cellar and tower—

DON RUY GOMEZ. My dungeon is as faithful as myself. Alone it knows the secret that I know, and both of us will guard it well.

DON CARLOS. I am the king!

DON RUY GOMEZ. Short of demolishing the castle, stone by stone, and murdering its master, they will find nothing.

DON CARLOS. Pleas and threats are all in vain! Give me the bandit, Duke, or I will destroy the head and castle both!

DON RUY GOMEZ. I have spoken.

DON CARLOS. Well then, instead of one, I shall take two heads. (To the Duke of Alcala.) Jorge, arrest the duke.

DOÑA SOL (tearing off her veil and throwing herself between the duke and the guards). Carlos, King Don Carlos, you are an evil king!

DON CARLOS. Good Lord, what is this? Doña Sol!

DOÑA SOL. Highness, you have not a Spaniard's heart!

DON CARLOS (disturbed and hesitant). Madam, you are too harsh toward the king. (He approaches Doña Sol, and speaks low to her.) You yourself have put this fury in my heart. A man turns saint or monster by your touch. How quickly one grows evil when one is loathed! I was already great; if you had wished it, perhaps I might have been the lion of Castile! You have made me its tiger with your rage. And now that tiger roars. Be silent, then. (Doña Sol looks at him. He bows.) However, I'll obey. (He turns back to the duke.) My cousin, I respect you. Your scruples after all have something worthy in them. Be loyal to your guest, and disloyal to your king. Very well, I pardon you and am the better man. I shall only take your niece with me as hostage.

DON RUY GOMEZ. Only!

DOÑA SOL (shocked and frightened). Take me, my lord?

DON CARLOS. Yes, you!

DON RUY GOMEZ. So you exact no more than that of me? Oh, what splendid clemency! Oh, generous victor, to spare the head and torture the heart instead! Fine mercy, this!

DON CARLOS. Make your choice—Doña Sol or the traitor. I must have one of them.

DON RUY GOMEZ. Ah, you are the master!

(Don Carlos approaches Doña Sol to take her away. She retreats toward Don Ruy Gomez.)

DOÑA SOL. Save me, my lord! (She stops; then, to herself.) But I must! My uncle's head or his—no, sooner myself. (To the king.) I go with you.

DON CARLOS (aside). By all the saints! What an excellent idea this was! You shall have to soften finally, my girl! (Doña Sol moves with deliberate step toward the box that holds the jewels; she opens it and takes the dagger out, hiding it in her bosom. Don Carlos comes up beside her and offers her his hand.) What have you there?

DOÑA SOL. Nothing.

DON CARLOS. Some precious jewel?

DOÑA SOL. Yes.

DON CARLOS (*smiling*). Let us see it.

DOÑA SOL. Later you shall. (*She gives him her hand and prepares to go with him. Don Ruy Gomez, who has remained motionless and deeply absorbed in thought, turns and takes a few steps, shouting.*)

DON RUY GOMEZ. Doña Sol! Heaven and earth. Doña Sol! . . . Since this man has no heart in him, help me, my bastions and walls! Crumble! (*He runs to the king.*) Leave me my child! I have nothing but her, my king!

DON CARLOS (*dropping Doña Sol's hand*). My prisoner, then!

(*The duke bends his head, and seems caught by a tortured hesitation; then he raises his eyes and gazes at the portraits, clasping and stretching his hands toward them imploringly.*)

DON RUY GOMEZ. Have pity on me, my fathers! (*He takes a step toward the hiding place; Doña Sol's eyes follow him in anguish. He turns back toward the portraits; to them.*) Oh, cover your eyes—your gaze will hold me back! (*He advances falteringly as far as his own portrait, then turns back to the king again.*) It is your will?

DON CARLOS. Yes.

(*The duke raises his trembling hand toward the spring.*)

DOÑA SOL. God in heaven!

DON RUY GOMEZ (*shoving at the wall with his foot*). No! (*He throws himself at the king's feet*). Have pity, take my head!

DON CARLOS. Your niece!

DON RUY GOMEZ (*rising*). Then take her! And leave me my honor!

DON CARLOS (*seizing Doña Sol's trembling hand*). Farewell, Duke.

DON RUY GOMEZ. Until we meet again. (*His eyes follow the king, who moves slowly off with Doña Sol; then he puts his hand to his dagger.*) God protect you, Highness! (*He comes forward again, and stands motionless, hearing and seeing nothing; his gaze is fixed, his arms crossed on his chest, which rises and falls in a convulsive rhythm. Meanwhile, the king goes out with Doña Sol, and all the courtiers go gravely after him, two by two, in order of rank. They speak low among themselves.*)

DON RUY (*to himself*). King, as you leave my home rejoicing, my ancient loyalty leaves my weeping heart. (*He raises his eyes, looks about him, and sees that he is alone. He dashes to the wall, takes down two swords from a display there, compares and examines them, and sets them on a table. This done, he goes to the portrait, pushes the spring, and opens the secret door.*)

SCENE 7

DON RUY. Come out. (*Hernani appears at the doorway of the hiding place. Don Ruy points to the two swords on the table.*) Choose one of them. Don Carlos has left my house; now you must settle with me. Choose, and do it swiftly. . . . Come now! Your hand is trembling!

HERNANI. A duel! Old man, we cannot fight one another.

DON RUY GOMEZ. And why not? Are you afraid? Or is it that you are not a nobleman? Damnation! Noble or not, any man who injures me is gentleman enough to cross his sword with mine!

HERNANI. Old man—

DON RUY GOMEZ. Kill me, or die yourself.

HERNANI. Die—yes. You have saved me against my will, and so my life is yours to take.

DON RUY GOMEZ. That is your wish? (*To the portraits.*) You see he wishes it. (*To Hernani.*) Very well; then say your prayer.

HERNANI. I make my last to you, my lord.

DON RUY GOMEZ. Address the other Lord.

HERNANI. No—no, to you! Old man, strike me down. Anything will do, dagger, sword, or knife! But grant me this last joy, in pity's name, Duke—before I die, let me see her!

DON RUY GOMEZ. See her!

HERNANI. Or at least let me hear her voice once more— only one last time!

DON RUY GOMEZ. Hear her voice!

HERNANI. My lord, I understand your jealousy; but death already clutches at my young life, forgive me. Tell me that I may hear her voice again, even if it must be without the sight of her. And I shall die tonight. Only to hear her! Fill my last longing—how contented I should breathe out my life, if you would let my soul look into hers again, into her eyes, before I fly to heaven! I shall not speak to her—you will be there, my father. And take me afterwards!

DON RUY GOMEZ (*looking amazed at the open door of the cupboard*). Can that closet be so deep, so tightly sealed, that he heard nothing?

HERNANI. I heard nothing at all.

DON RUY GOMEZ. I was forced to yield him Doña Sol, or you.

HERNANI. Yield her to whom?

DON RUY GOMEZ. The king.

HERNANI. You old fool! He loves her!

DON RUY GOMEZ. Loves her!

HERNANI. He has stolen her from us! He is our rival!

DON RUY GOMEZ. My God! . . . Men! To your horses, your horses! We must go after the abductor!

HERNANI. Listen. Sure-footed vengeance makes less noise as it comes. I belong to you; you have the right to kill me. But why not use me first, to avenge your niece and her honor? Let me share in your revenge! Ah, grant me that, and if I must kiss your feet, I kiss them! Let us pursue the king together! Come, I shall be your striking arm—I shall avenge you, Duke. And you can slay me afterwards.

DON RUY GOMEZ. And then, just as today, you will let that be?

HERNANI. Yes, Duke.

DON RUY GOMEZ. How do you swear it?

HERNANI. Upon my father's head.

DON RUY GOMEZ. And will you swear to recall the vow yourself?

HERNANI (*handing him the horn he takes from his belt*). Take this horn. Whatever may happen, whenever you wish, lord, and wherever, if it crosses your mind that it is time I die, then sound this trumpet, nothing more. It shall be done.

DON RUY GOMEZ (*offering his hand*). Your hand. (*They clasp hands. Then, to the portraits.*) And you, my fathers—you all are witness to it!

ACT IV: THE TOMB

(*Aix-la-Chapelle: the underground crypt that holds the tomb of Charlemagne. The great vaults of Lombard architecture, arches, massive low pillars, their capitals carved with birds and flowers. To the right, Charlemagne's tomb with a small bronze door, low and arched. A single lamp hung from the height of a vault picks out its inscription: Carolus Magnus. It is dark. The far end of the cavern cannot be seen; it is lost among the arcades, the stairs and pillars that merge and disappear into the dimness.*)

SCENE 1

(*Don Carlos and Don Ricardo de Roxas, with a lantern in his hand. Full cloaks, hatbrims pulled low.*)

DON RICARDO (*his hat in his hand*). This is the place.

DON CARLOS. This is the place the conspirators will meet—and I shall have them all in the hollow of my hand! My Lord Elector of Trier, this is the place and you have lent it to them. . . . It is an admirable choice; a black plot flourishes in the air of catacombs, and tombstones are good for sharpening stilettos. And yet the game is crucial—a life is at stake, my lords assassins. We shall see. Well, they are wise indeed to choose a sepulcher for such a conference; they will have less distance to go. (*To Don Ricardo.*) Do these caverns stretch far beneath the ground?

DON RICARDO. Down to the castle-fort.

DON CARLOS. More space than I shall need.

DON RICARDO. Others on this side go as far as the monastery at Altenheim. . . .

DON CARLOS. Where Rudolph killed Lothair. Good—now once again, Count, recite me all the names and grievances: where, why, and how.

DON RICARDO. Gotha—

DON CARLOS. I know why that good duke would plot with them: he wants a German emperor for Germany.

DON RICARDO. Hohenburg—

DON CARLOS. Hohenburg, I think, would prefer hell with Francis to heaven itself with me.

DON RICARDO. Don Gil Tellez Giron—

DON CARLOS. Saint Mary and Castile! So he is in revolt against his king! The traitor!

DON RICARDO. They say he found you with Lady Giron, the night you'd made him baron. He would avenge the honor of his sweet wife.

DON CARLOS. And thus turns rebel against Spain? . . . Who else is there?

DON RICARDO. The Reverend Vasquez, the bishop of Avila, is said to be among them.

DON CARLOS. Is that to avenge his wife's dishonor too?

DON RICARDO. Then Guzman de Lara is discontent; he wants the collar of your knighthood.

DON CARLOS. Ah! Guzman de Lara—if a collar's all he wants, he'll have one.

DON RICARDO. The duke of Lutzelburg. As for his intentions—

DON CARLOS. The duke of Lutzelburg stands just a head too tall.

DON RICARDO. And Juan de Haro, who wants Astorga.

DON CARLOS. Those Haros have always earned the headsman twice his wages.

DON RICARDO. That is the list.

DON CARLOS. You have named only seven, Count, and I had been warned of more.

DON RICARDO. There are some bandits besides, in the pay of Trier, or France. . . .

DON CARLOS. Men without a true allegiance, whose ever-ready knives turn toward the fattest purse like compass needles toward the pole.

DON RICARDO. I did make out two more conspirators, though, both of them newly arrived. One young, one old.

DON CARLOS. Their names? (*Don Ricardo shrugs his shoulders; he does not know.*) Their ages then?

DON RICARDO. The younger one seems twenty.

DON CARLOS. What a pity!

DON RICARDO. The elder, sixty at least.

DON CARLOS. The one is too young, the other too old. Too bad; I shall take care of them. The headsman can count upon my help when it is needed. My sword will not be kind to treachery, and I shall lend it when his ax grows dull; and if the gallows-cloth should prove too small, I shall stitch my imperial purple onto it. But shall I indeed be emperor?

DON RICARDO. The college of electors is gathered now to vote.

DON CARLOS. I cannot tell—they will name Francis the First, or else their Saxon, their Frederick the Wise. Ah, Luther is right, Europe is in bad times! Fine men to choose a sacred majesty—the only reasons they accept are reasons in gold! A Saxon heretic! An imbecilic count palatine, and a primate of Trier who is a libertine! The Bohemian king will vote for me. But Hessian princes even smaller than their fiefs—young idiots and debauched old men. Oh, crowns—there are many crowns, but heads? only try to find one! Dwarfs all of them, that laughable council, whom I could carry off like Hercules draped in my lionskin. Without their purple mantles, they would none of them have a skull as large as Triboulet's! . . .

I lack three voices, Ricardo! And lacking them, I shall lack everything! Oh, I would give Toledo, Ghent, and Salamanca or any three cities they could wish, for three more votes! For those three voices, mark thee, Count, I would give up three cities in Castile or in Flanders! For I could take them back another time. (*Don Ricardo bows deeply to the king, and puts his hat on his head.*) You cover your head before me?

DON RICARDO. My lord, you called me "thou" (*he bows again*); that makes me a grandee.

DON CARLOS (*aside*). Ah, you pitiful thing, so ambitious for a pittance! A self-seeking breed of animals! How they follow their single-minded purpose right through our own concerns! This shabby barnyard where they beg shamelessly of the king, and he dispenses scraps of greatness to all these famished beasts. (*Reflectively.*) Only God and the emperor are great—and the Holy Father. The rest, the kings and dukes—what are they?

DON RICARDO. Indeed, I hope they will select Your Highness for the throne.

DON CARLOS (*aside*). Highness! Am I still only Highness? Misfortune in everything! If I should remain only king . . .

DON RICARDO (*aside*). Enough! Emperor or not, I am now a grandee of Spain.

DON CARLOS. How will they announce his name when they elect the German emperor?

DON RICARDO. If it is the duke of Saxony, a single cannon shot. Two for the king of France, and three if it is Your Highness.

DON CARLOS. And then that Doña Sol! Everything has joined to irritate and wound me! Count, if fortune falls my way and makes me emperor, quickly bring her here. Perhaps she will find a Caesar more to her taste.

DON RICARDO (*smiling*). Your Highness is most generous.

DON CARLOS (*interrupting him haughtily*). Silence, upon that subject! I have not yet said what I wish opinion to be. When will we know the council's choice?

DON RICARDO. Within the hour at latest, I think.

DON CARLOS. Three voices! Only three . . . But first we must crush this plotting rabble here, and afterwards see who will have the empire. (*He counts on his fingers and stamps his foot.*) Still three votes too few! The others have it! Yet that Cornelius Agrippa predicted them—he saw thirteen stars in the celestial sea come sailing swiftly toward my northern one. I'll have the empire then! . . . But on the other hand, they say that Abbé Jean Trithème prophesied for Francis. I should have helped the auguries along by military means, for then my fate would be clear! Predictions by the sharpest sorcerer come best to birth and better outcome when a good army—with cannon and pikes, with

foot- and horse-soldiers, trumpets and bands, prepared to point wavering fate in the right direction—serves as midwife and brings them to bed. Which of the two is better, Cornelius Agrippa or Jean Trithème? The one with regiments behind his words; the one who makes his points with iron lance, who underlines them with troops and mercenaries; their swords can set imperfect fortune straight, and mold the event according to the prophet.

They are poor fools who aim to have the empire of the world, who with proud eye and brow declare "It is my right!" They have a thousand cannon stretched in rows, whose hot breath could melt cities; they've vassals, soldiers, horses, and one assumes that they will march to their goal over the conquered peoples. . . . But no! When they have reached the great crossroads of human destiny, where more paths lead to the pit than to the throne, they hardly take three steps but stop in indecision; wondering, they try in vain to read the book of fate; they hesitate, uncertain of themselves; and, caught by doubt, go running to the neighboring necromancer, to ask their way!

(*To Don Ricardo.*) Leave me now; the plotters will soon be here. Oh—and the key to the tomb?

DON RICARDO (*handing it to him*). My lord, you will remember the Count of Limburg, the guardian here? He gave me the key, and he does all he can to please you.

DON CARLOS (*dismissing him*). Do everything I said! Everything!

DON RICARDO (*bowing*). I go at once, Your Highness.

DON CARLOS. I need three cannon shots, you said?

(*Don Ricardo bows and leaves. Don Carlos, left alone, falls into a deep reverie. His arms cross, his head falls to his chest; then he lifts it and turns toward the tomb.*)

SCENE 2

DON CARLOS. Charlemagne, forgive me! These silent vaults should not reverberate with any but solemn words. You must be indignant at hearing our ambition hum about your monument. . . . Charlemagne is here! You somber sepulcher, how can you hold so great a spirit and yet not burst? Are you truly there, giant creator of a world? And can you stretch your length within those walls? . . . It is a spectacle to astound the mind, Europe as it was before he came, and as he later left it! A vast structure with two men at its top, elected lords to whom each king is subject. Each state and duchy, military fief, kingdom, and march—almost all are hereditary reigns; yet the people sometimes have their pope or Caesar. The mechanism works, and one chance corrects another; so equilibrium comes, and order triumphs. Electors in cloth of gold, and scarlet cardinals—the sacred double senate that stirs the earth—are but display, and God will have His will. An idea may rise one day born of the times; it grows, and burns, and spreads, and mingles with all things; takes human form, grips hearts, and carves a furrow; many a king will trample it underfoot, or gag its voice. But if one day it penetrates the Diet, or the papal conclave, then suddenly the kings will see the once-enslaved idea loom up, with orb in hand or tiara on its brow, and bow their royal heads beneath its feet.

The pope and emperor are everything. Nothing is on earth but for or by them. A sublime mystery dwells in them; and heaven, from which they hold their privilege, endows them with a feast of peoples and of kings; heaven keeps them underneath its thunderous canopy of cloud, seated alone at table where God serves them up the world. Side by side, they sit to rule and sentence, arranging the universe as a reaper does his field. All that is occurs between those two. The kings stand at the door, breathing the savory steam of dishes carried past, staring through the window, watchful, agitated, and rising on their toes to see. Beneath them the world falls into ranks and groups. They do and they undo. One disentangles, the other cuts. The one is truth, the other might. Their purpose is contained within them; they are because they are. When they emerge from the sanctuary, both equal, the one in purple, the other in his white soutane, the dazzled universe in terror regards these two halves of God, the pope and the emperor.

Emperor! Emperor! To be emperor—oh fury, not to be!—and to feel one's heart filled with courage! How fortunate was he who sleeps within this tomb; how great was he! And it was still finer in his time. The pope and the emperor: they were no longer just two men, Peter and Caesar—in themselves coupling the two Romes, each fertilizing the other in mystic marriage, giving new form and soul to human kind; melding peoples and kingdoms pell-mell, into a new Europe, the two of them with their own hands refilling the mold with the bronze remnants from the old Roman world! Ah, what a destiny! And yet, this tomb is his. Is all so trivial then, that this is where it ends? To have been prince, and king, and emperor—to have been the sword and been the law . . . a giant, with Germany for his pedestal, with Caesar for his title, and Charlemagne for name! To have been greater than Hannibal, or than Attila, as great as all the world—and this is where it ends!

Then scheme for empire, and see the dust an emperor leaves! Cover the earth entire with fanfare and with tumult; raise and build your endless empire; slash and carve out an enormous edifice—do you know what will remain one day? Ah, lunacy—this stone! And of the title and the triumphal name? A few letters, that serve to teach a child his spelling! However high the goal your pride envisions, here is the last limit! Oh empire! I do not care—I touch at it, and it to my liking. Something tells me: "You shall have it." It shall be mine . . . ah, that it should be!

Oh, heaven, to be what is beginning! Alone, upright, atop the enormous spiral; to be the keystone in the arch of all the states arranged one on the other, to see beneath one all the many kings, and wipe one's sandals on them. To see below the kings the feudal houses, margraves and cardinals, doges, and dukes with floral seals; then bishops, abbots, heads of clans, great barons! Then priests and soldiers next; then in the shadow, far below the peak whereon we stand—deep within the chasm—are men!

Men—a mass, a sea, a great clamor, tears and cries, sometimes a bitter laugh—a whole lament that wakes the startled earth, and through a hundred thousand echoes reaches us as a skirl of trumpets! Men! . . . Cities, towers, a vast swarm of high church belfries to ring their gongs! (*Musingly.*) A base of human nations, bearing on their shoulders the enormous pyramid that leans on the two poles; living waves that grasp it always in their hollows, and float it pitching on their vast swells; waves that shift everything about, and at its upper reaches topple thrones like footstools, so that all kings cease their vain disputes and raise their eyes to heaven.

Kings! Look down beneath you! Ah, the people— that ocean—that never-resting wave, where nought can be cast in but stirs the whole! A swell that may crush a throne or gently rock a tomb! Mirror wherein a king will rarely find a handsome image of himself. If he should sometimes gaze into that dark swell, he'd see at bottom numberless empires, great shipwrecked vessels swaying in its ebb and flow, empires that had disturbed the ocean's stream and now exist no more!

To think of ruling over all of that! To mount up to that pinnacle if the electors call—to climb there, conscious that one is but a man! To see the chasm below! If only I do not at that same moment grow dazed with vertigo—oh, shifting pyramid of kings and countries, your summit is so narrow! Woe to the fearful foot! By whom should I hold steady? Suppose I stumble at feeling the world shudder beneath my feet! At feeling the earth live, and surge, and pulse! Or when I have that globe between my hands, what then? Shall I be capable of carrying it? What is there in me? Emperor, my God! being king was hard enough! Surely the man is rare whose soul can stretch with fortune. But I—who will make me great? Who will be my guest and give me counsel!

(*He falls to his knees before the tomb.*) Charlemagne— you will! Since God, before whom all obstacles fall back, has taken our two majesties and set them face to face, then from the depths of this your grave imbue my heart with something sublime! Ah, show me all things from their every aspect, show me that the world is small, for I dare not lay my hand on it. Show me that within this tower of Babel, rising from shepherd to Caesar to the skies, each man at his own rank is self-satisfied, admires himself, observes the man beneath him and stifles a laugh. Teach me your secrets of conquest and of rule, and tell me that it is better to punish than forgive—is this not so? If it is true that sometimes the world's clatter wakes a great shadow in his lonely resting place; if it is true his wide bright tomb can open suddenly, and throw the world a flare in its dark night—if these things are true, emperor of Germany, then tell me, what can a man do after Charlemagne?

Speak! Though it mean your sovereign breath by speaking must crack this bronze door across my brow! Or rather, let me enter alone within your sanctuary, and see your face in death—do not repulse me by an icy breath, but raise yourself upon your bed of stone, and let us talk. Yes, even though you should tell me, in your fateful voice, of things that darken the eye and pale the brow! Speak, and do not blind your fearful son, for your tomb must be so full with light! Or else, if you will say nothing, let me study that deeply peaceful head, as if it were a world; let me measure you carefully, oh giant, for nothing here below is great as is thy dust! Let the ashes guide me if the spirit would not.

(*He puts the key to the lock.*) We shall go in. (*He draws back.*) But what if he should speak to me indeed? If he is there, awake and upright, walking with slow steps! And I should reappear with my hair white! Still—I shall enter. (*Sound of footsteps.*) Someone is approaching. Who but I could dare to come here at this hour, and rouse the home of such a corpse? Who is it? (*The noise is closer.*) Ah, I had forgotten—it is my murderers. Let us go in then.

(*He opens the door to the tomb and closes it behind him. Several men come on with muffled steps, hidden in their cloaks and hats.*)

SCENE 3

(*The Conspirators; they move about among themselves, clasping hands and exchanging a few words in low voices.*)

FIRST CONSPIRATOR (*who alone carries a lighted torch*). Ad augusta.
SECOND CONSPIRATOR. *Per angusta.*
THIRD. May the dead serve us.
FIRST. God keep us.

(*Sound of steps in the darkness.*)

SECOND. Who goes there?
VOICE. *Ad augusta.*
SECOND. *Per angusta.*

(*Other Conspirators appear. Sound of footsteps again.*)

FIRST CONSPIRATOR (*to the Third*). Look there, another's coming.
THIRD. Who goes there?
VOICE IN SHADOWS. *Ad augusta.*
THIRD. *Per angusta.*

(*Still others appear, with signs of greeting.*)

FIRST. Good, we are all here. Gotha, give us your report. My friends, the dark awaits the light.

(*All the Conspirators seat themselves on tombs in a half circle. The First Conspirator passes among them, and from his torch each lights a candle and holds it in his hand. Then the First Conspirator takes a seat silently upon a tomb at the center of the circle and higher than the others.*)

DUKE OF GOTHA (*rising*). Friends, this Charles of Spain, a foreigner through his mother, lays claim to the Holy Empire.
FIRST CONSPIRATOR. He shall have the grave instead.
GOTHA (*throwing his torch to the ground and grinding it out with his foot*). May his skull be as this flame!
ALL. May it be!
FIRST. Death to him!
GOTHA. May he die!
ALL. May he be slain!
DON JUAN DE HARO. His father was a German.
DUKE OF LUTZELBURG. His mother was Spanish.
GOTHA. He is Spanish no longer, and not a German. Death!
ONE OF THE CONSPIRATORS. What if the electors are naming him emperor at this moment?
FIRST. They? Name him? Never!
DON GIL TELLEZ GIRON. What does that matter, friends! We strike the head, and the crown dies with it!
FIRST. Whatever he may be, if he wins the Holy Empire, he becomes mighty and august, and only God can touch him.
GOTHA. The surest way is to act before he gains that state.
FIRST. He shall not be elected.
ALL. He shall not have the Empire!
FIRST. How many hands are needed to wind him in his shroud?
ALL. Only one.
FIRST. How many strokes to the heart?
ALL. Only one!
FIRST. Who will do it?
ALL. All of us!
FIRST. Our victim is a traitor. They are making an emperor; let us make a high priest. We shall draw lots.

(*All the Conspirators write their name on their tablets, tear off the sheet, roll it up, and go one after the other to drop it into an urn on one of the tombs.*)

FIRST CONSPIRATOR. Let us pray. (*They all kneel. The First rises.*) May the chosen one put his faith in God, strike like a Roman, and die like a Hebrew! May he brave the wheel and pincers, sing at the rack and laugh at the fiery brand; may he do everything to kill and die with resignation! (*He draws one of the parchment sheets from the urn.*)
ALL. What name is it?
FIRST (*loudly*). Hernani.
HERNANI (*emerging from the group*). I've won! Ah, revenge, I have you now, you whom I have pursued so long!

DON RUY GOMEZ (*moving through the crowd and taking Hernani aside*). Let me take your place!

HERNANI. No, upon my life! My lord, do not grudge me my fortune! It is the first time luck has come to me!

DON RUY. You have nothing. Then listen—I give you my fiefs, my castles, and my vassalages—a hundred thousand peasants in my three hundred villages—I give them all to you, my friend, for the right to strike that blow!

HERNANI. No!

GOTHA. Your weaker arm would strike with less effect, old man.

DON RUY GOMEZ. Silence! If not the arm, I have the spirit for it! Do not judge the blade by the rust that coats its scabbard. (*To Hernani.*) You belong to me.

HERNANI. My life is yours, yes, but his belongs to me!

DON RUY GOMEZ (*drawing the horn from his waist*). Listen, my friend: I give you back this horn.

HERNANI (*shaken*). What? My life? Ah, what does it mean to me? My vengeance is at hand! God is with me in this. I have my father to avenge, and more perhaps! . . . And her—do you give her back to me?

DON RUY GOMEZ. Never! But I yield up this horn!

HERNANI. No.

DON RUY GOMEZ. Reflect upon it, boy!

HERNANI. Duke, leave me my prey.

DON RUY. Then be accursed for denying me that joy. (*He replaces the horn in his belt.*)

FIRST CONSPIRATOR (*to Hernani*). Brother! Before they can elect him, it would be well to watch for Carlos on this very night—

HERNANI. Fear not! I know how to put a man into his grave.

FIRST CONSPIRATOR. May any treason fall back upon the traitor, and God be with you! And if he should fall without having slain, then, counts and barons, we shall go on! Let us swear to strike, each of us in turn, without evasion—for Carlos must die.

ALL. We swear it!

GOTHA (*to the First Conspirator*). Upon what, my brother?

DON RUY GOMEZ (*upending his sword, taking it by the tip and raising it over his head*). Let us swear upon this cross!

ALL (*raising their swords*). May he die unrepentant.

(*A far-off cannon shot is heard. They all stop, silent. The door to the tomb opens slightly; Don Carlos appears on the threshold. Pale, he listens. A second shot. A third. He opens the door wide, but without stepping forward; he stands motionless on the doorsill.*)

SCENE 4

DON CARLOS. Go on, my lords! The emperor is listening. (*All the torches go out at once. Deep silence. He moves a step in the shadows, so dark that the mute and motionless Conspirators are scarcely visible.*) Silence and darkness! the swarm emerges from the black, and now returns there. Do you believe somehow that all of this will seem a dream, and that because you have put out your flares, I shall take you all for stone figures seated on their tombs? But a moment since, my statues, your voices were still loud! Come now! raise up your lowered heads, for Charles the Fifth is here! Strike me now—take even a step. Let us see it, do you dare? No, you dare not. Your torches flamed like blood beneath these vaults; and my breath alone sufficed to put them out. But look, more. (*He strikes the iron key on the bronze door of the tomb; at the sound, the depths of the cavern fill with soldiers bearing torches and halberds. At their head are the Duke of Alcala and the Marquis of Almuñan.*) Come here, my falcons! I have the nest, and I have the prey! (*To the Conspirators.*) Now I bring light in my turn. Look, the sepulcher's aflame. (*To the Soldiers.*) Come forward, all of you; this is a flagrant crime.

HERNANI (*looking at the Soldiers*). That is better now. Alone, he seemed too large. At first I thought that it was Charlemagne; it is only Charles the Fifth.

DON CARLOS (*to the Duke of Alcala*). Constable of Spain! (*To the Marquis of Almuñan.*) Admiral of Castile, come forward! Disarm them all. (*The plotters are surrounded and disarmed.*)

DON RICARDO (*running up and bowing to the ground*). Majesty!

DON CARLOS. I name thee alcalde of the palace.

DON RICARDO (*bowing again*). Two electors are come to congratulate Your Sacred Majesty, in the name of the Golden Chamber.

DON CARLOS. Let them come in. (*Low, to Ricardo.*) Doña Sol.

RICARDO. Oh—(*Salutes and leaves. The King of Bohemia and the Duke of Bavaria enter with torches and trumpet flourishes; both are clothed in their gold-embroidered mantles, with crowns on their heads. A large cortège follows them, made up of German Lords carrying the imperial banner—the two-headed eagle with the Spanish shield at its center. The Soldiers form an aisle to the emperor for the two electors. They salute him deeply and he returns it by raising his hat.*)

DUKE OF BAVARIA. Charles, King of the Romans, Most Sacred Majesty, Emperor! The world is now within your hands, for the Empire is yours. Yours, the throne that every monarch covets! Frederick, Duke of Saxony, was first elected; but he judged you more worthy of it, and declined. Come then, receive this crown and take the globe. The Holy Empire, King, invests you with its purple robe; it arms you with its sword, and you are very great.

DON CARLOS. I shall thank the council on my return. Go now, my lords. Thank you, my brother Bohemia, and my cousin Bavaria. Go now—and I myself must leave.

KING OF BOHEMIA. Charles, our ancestors were friends; my father loved your father, and their sires too loved each other. Charles, you are so young a man to face disturbing fortunes—tell me, would you wish me to be your brother among brothers? I knew you as a child, and I cannot forget—

DON CARLOS (*interrupting him*). King of Bohemia, you are most familiar! (*He presents his hand for the King to kiss, and to the Duke of Bavaria, then dismisses the two electors, who bow deeply.*) Go now. (*They leave with their suites.*)

CROWD. Long live the emperor!

DON CARLOS (*aside*). I am emperor! And everything has made way for me. Emperor! through the refusal, though, of Frederick the Wise!

(*Doña Sol enters, led by Ricardo.*)

DOÑA SOL. Soldiers! and the emperor—oh God, I did not expect this! Hernani!

HERNANI. Doña Sol!

DON RUY (*beside Hernani, to himself*). She does not even see me!

(*Doña Sol runs to Hernani; his mistrustful stare stops her.*)

HERNANI. My lady!

DOÑA SOL (*drawing the knife from her bodice*). I have his dagger still.

HERNANI. My beloved!

DON CARLOS. Silence, all of you. (*To the plotters.*) Have you recovered your determination? It is fitting that I show the world a lesson here. Lara the Castilian, and Saxon Gotha—all of you—what did you come here to do? Speak!

HERNANI (*stepping forward*). Sire, it is a simple thing, and we can tell you of it: we were writing the sentence upon Balthazar's wall. (*He draws his knife and brandishes it.*) We render unto Caesar what is Caesar's.

DON CARLOS. I see. (*To Don Ruy Gomez.*) And you, Silva—a traitor!

DON RUY GOMEZ. Which of us two is traitor, sire?

HERNANI (*turning to the other Conspirators*). He has what he desires—our heads and the empire both! (*To the Emperor.*) A king's blue robe could hamper your steps. This purple suits you better; it does not show blood.

DON CARLOS (*to Don Ruy Gomez*). My cousin Silva—this is crime enough to strike your barony from your coat of arms. It is high treason, Don Ruy; consider that well.

DON RUY GOMEZ. Count Julians are made by King Rodrigos.

DON CARLOS (*to the Duke of Alcala*). Take only the dukes or counts. The rest—

(*Don Ruy Gomez, the Duke of Lutzelburg, the Duke of Gotha, Don Juan de Haro, Don Guzman de Lara, Don Gil Tellez Giron, and the Baron of Hohenburg step out of the group; Hernani remains with it. The Duke of Alcala surrounds the Lord with guards.*)

DOÑA SOL (*aside*). He is safe!

HERNANI (*stepping forward*). I claim my place among these others! (*To Don Carlos.*) Since this is a matter of the ax;

since Hernani the humble peasant would slip beneath your feet unpunished; since his brow is no longer worthy of your sword; since one must be a nobleman to die, I rise. God who awards the scepter and who gave it you, god made me Duke of Segorbia and Cardona, the Marquis of Monroy, Count Albatera and Viscount of Gor—and lord of lands whose number or whose names I cannot count. I am Juan of Aragon, grand master of Avis, born in exile—the banished son of a father slaughtered by your father's word, King Carlos of Castile! Murder is a family affair between us. You have the scaffold; we have the knife. Thus, heaven made me a duke, and exile a highlander. I have whetted my sword against the hills and tempered it in rushing streams; but since all my preparation must come to nothing—(*he puts on his hat, and says to the other Conspirators*)—cover your heads, all you grandees of Spain! (*All the Nobles do so. To Don Carlos.*) Yes, King—our heads have the right to fall before you covered! (*To the Prisoners.*) Silva, Haro, Lara—men of title and of race—open your ranks to Juan of Aragon! Dukes and counts, give me my place! (*To the Courtiers and Guards.*) I am Juan of Aragon, king, headsmen and grooms. And if your scaffolds are too small, fix them! (*He joins the group of captured Lords.*)

DOÑA SOL. Great heavens!

DON CARLOS. True, I had forgotten that whole story.

HERNANI. The man whose flesh has bled remembers better. The wrong forgotten by the offender lives on still active in the injured heart.

DON CARLOS. Then I am the son of men who felled your fathers' heads—that is title enough for me.

DOÑA SOL (*throwing herself to her knees before the Emperor*). Sire, pardon! Pity, sire be merciful! Or else then kill us both by the same stroke, for he is my beloved, my husband! I live in him alone. Oh, I tremble, sire; find the compassion to kill the two of us together! Majesty, I cling to your sainted feet! I love him! He is mine, as the empire is yours! Oh mercy! (*Don Carlos watches her, impassive.*) What dark idea absorbs you now?

DON CARLOS. Rise, Duchess of Segorbia, Countess Albatera, Marquise of Monroy . . . . (*To Hernani.*) What are your other names, Don Juan?

HERNANI. Who is it says these things? The king?

DON CARLOS. No, the emperor.

DOÑA SOL (*rising*). Great heavens!

DON CARLOS (*indicating her to Hernani*). Duke, here is your wife.

HERNANI (*his eyes raised to heaven, and Doña Sol in his arms*). God of justice!

DON CARLOS (*to Don Ruy Gomez*). Cousin, you are jealous for your noble rank, I know. But an Aragon may wed a Silva.

DON RUY GOMEZ (*darkly*). It is not for my noble rank.

HERNANI (*gazing lovingly at Doña Sol, and holding her close*).

Ah, I feel my hatred vanishing. . . . (*He throws down his dagger.*)

DON RUY GOMEZ (*watching the pair*). Shall my rage burst from me? Ah no—senseless love, and senseless grief. . . . They would pity your old Spanish head. Burn flameless, old man—love and suffer secretly. Let your heart be consumed, but not a cry, for they would laugh.

DOÑA SOL (*still in Hernani's arms*). My duke!

HERNANI. I have nothing left in my heart but love.

DOÑA SOL. What happiness! . . .

DON CARLOS (*aside, his hand upon his breast*). Quiet, my young and flaming heart! Now let rule the mind, which for too long you have flouted. Henceforward all your loves, and alas, your only mistresses are Germany and Flanders and old Spain. (*He eyes his banner.*) The emperor is like the eagle, his companion: in the heart's stead he has only an escutcheon.

HERNANI. Ah, you are truly Caesar!

DON CARLOS (*to Hernani*). Your heart is worthy of your noble line, Don Juan. (*Indicating Doña Sol.*) And worthy too of her. On your knees, Duke! (*Hernani kneels. Don Carlos takes off the collar of the Golden Fleece, and sets it around Hernani's neck.*) Receive this collar. (*Don Carlos draws his sword and taps him three times upon the shoulder.*) Be faithful. In the name of Saint Stephen, Duke, I name thee knight. (*He raises and embraces him.*) But you have the best and sweetest collar yet, one I have not, and one that even the highest rank can lack: the arms of a beloved woman loving you. Ah, you shall be happy; and I—I am emperor. . . . (*To the Conspirators.*) I know your names no more, sirs. Hatred and anger—I would forget them all. Go then; I pardon you. This is the lesson I must give the world. It shall not be in vain that the emperor Charles the Fifth succeeds to Charles the First, the king; nor that, before a mourning, orphaned Europe, a law should change a Catholic highness into a sacred majesty.

(*The plotters fall to their knees.*)

CONSPIRATORS. Glory to Carlos! Hail!

DON RUY GOMEZ (*to Don Carlos*). And so I alone remain condemned to suffering.

DON CARLOS. And I.

DON RUY (*aside*). But unlike him, I have not forgiven!

HERNANI. Who is it has changed us all?

ALL (*Soldiers, Conspirators, Nobles*). Long live Germany and Charles the Fifth!

DON CARLOS (*turning toward the tomb*). Honor to Charlemagne! Leave the two of us together now. (*All exeunt.*)

SCENE 5

DON CARLOS (*alone; he bows before the tomb*). Are you content with me? Have I stripped away the pettiness of kings, Charlemagne, and am I indeed become another man?

May I join my helmet to the Roman miter? Have I the right to bend the fortunes of the world? Have I a firm and steady foot, one that may walk upon this path, all strewn with vandal's ruins, that you have beaten out for us with your broad sandals? Have I caught your flame to kindle my own torch? And understood the voice that speaks within your tomb? Ah, I was alone and lost before an empire, a whole howling, plotting, threatening world—there is the Dane to punish, the Holy Father to pay, Venice and Suleiman, Luther, Francis the First—a thousand jealous blades already gleaming in the dark, snares and hidden reefs, and enemies unnumbered; twenty peoples, and each of them enough to frighten twenty kings—all hurrying and urgent, all to do at once. And I cried out to you: "How shall I start?" And you replied: "My son, by clemency!"

ACT V: THE WEDDING

(*Saragossa. A terrace of the palace of Aragon. At stage rear, a flight of stairs down into the garden. At right and left, two doors opening onto the terrace, which is enclosed by a balustrade topped by two rows of Moorish arcades; above and through them are visible the palace gardens, fountains in the shade, clumps of trees with lights moving among them, and beyond it all the Gothic and Arab lines of the brightly lit palace. It is night. Faraway band music. Persons in masks and dominoes, single or in groups, cross over the terrace here and there. In the foreground, a group of young lords, their masks in hand, are laughing and chattering noisily.*)

SCENE 1

DON GARCI. Well, here's to joy, and long live the lovely bride!

DON MATIAS (*watching the balcony*). All Saragossa is hanging out of its windows tonight.

DON GARCI. And so it should! There has never been a wedding with gayer lights, nor a gentler night, nor for a handsomer pair!

DON MATIAS. The emperor is good!

DON SANCHO. Marquis, I remember a dusky night when we went out with him to try our chance. Who could have told that it would end this way?

DON RICARDO (*interrupting him*). I was there too. (*To the others.*) Listen to this tale. Three lovers—one a bandit destined for the block, and a duke, and then a king—all three lay siege to a single woman's heart. When the battle clears, who holds it? It is the bandit.

DON FRANCISCO. But nothing is astonishing in that. In Spain as everywhere, love and luck turn on a play of loaded dice. The thief will always win!

DON RICARDO. And I, I've made my fortune by watching

lovemaking. First count, then grandee, and now alcalde of the court; I have put my time to good use, with no one suspecting.

DON SANCHO. Your secret is to hang about the king's path . . .

DON RICARDO. And turn my rights and actions to advantage.

DON GARCI. You profited by his preoccupation.

DON MATIAS. What is the old duke doing now? Having his coffin built?

DON SANCHO. Marquis, do not scoff. He is a valiant man. And he loved Doña Sol. Sixty years had turned his hair to gray; a single day turned it white.

DON GARCI. He has not appeared again in Saragossa, they say.

DON SANCHO. Would you have this celebration send him sooner to the grave?

DON FRANCISCO. And the emperor? how is he?

DON SANCHO. The emperor is sad today; Luther distresses him.

DON RICARDO. That Luther is fine cause for worry and alarm! With three or four armed men I'd make quick work of him!

DON MATIAS. He is disturbed by Suleiman as well.

DON GARCI. Oh, Luther, Suleiman, Neptune, the devil, Jupiter—what are they all to me? The women are pretty, the masquerade's a good one, and I've talked nonsense all evening long!

DON SANCHO. Those are the things that count.

DON RICARDO. Garci is right—on holidays I am no longer myself, and think when I pull on a mask I change completely! I do!

DON SANCHO (low to Don Matias). If only every day were a holiday!

DON FRANCISCO (pointing to the door at right). My lords, is that not the bridal apartment?

DON GARCI (nodding). They will appear in just a moment.

DON FRANCISCO. Do you think so?

DON GARCI. I am sure of it!

DON FRANCISCO. Good! The bride is so very beautiful.

DON RICARDO. How generous the emperor is! To think this rebel Hernani should have the Golden Fleece—and be wed—and pardoned too! If he had taken my advice, the emperor would have given the outlaw a bed of stone, and the lady one of down.

DON SANCHO (low to Don Matias). Ah, how my blade would love to slit his throat—that false, tinsel lord, all patched together with string! A count's doublet stuffed with a steward's soul!

DON RICARDO (drawing near). What are you saying?

DON MATIAS (low to Don Sancho). Count, let's have no quarrels here! (Aloud to Don Ricardo.) He was singing me one of Petrarch's sonnets to his love.

DON GARCI. Gentlemen, among the flowers and the women, and all these brightly colored costumes, have you noticed that specter leaning at the parapet and dimming the feast with his black domino?

DON RICARDO. I have indeed!

DON GARCI. Who is it?

DON RICARDO. Well, from his height, his manner . . . it must be Don Prancasio, the admiral.

DON FRANCISCO. No.

DON GARCI. He has not taken off his mask.

DON FRANCISCO. He has been cautious not to. It is the duke of Soma, who wants to draw attention—nothing more.

DON RICARDO. No, the duke spoke to me.

DON GARCI. Who is he then? Look now, there he goes.

(A black domino slowly crosses the terrace at the rear. All turn to watch him, without his seeming to notice.)

DON SANCHO. If the dead walk, that is their step.

DON GARCI (approaching the dark figure). Good sir! . . . (The figure turns and stops; Don Garci draws back.) Gentlemen, I swear, a flame gleams in his eyes!

DON SANCHO. If he is the devil, he has found the man to talk to. (He goes to the black domino, who stands motionless.) Evil one! Have you come to us from hell?

MASKED FIGURE. I do not come; I go there. (He continues his progress and disappears by the flight of stairs. All watch him go with a kind of horror.)

DON MATIAS. His voice comes from the grave!

DON GARCI. Enough now! what's frightening otherwise is only amusing at a ball!

DON SANCHO. It is some sorry joke!

DON GARCI. Or if it's Lucifer who's come to watch us dance on his way to hell, then let us dance!

DON SANCHO. It is certainly some game.

DON MATIAS. We shall find out tomorrow.

DON SANCHO (to Don Matias). Look below, I beg you. Where is he now?

DON MATIAS (leaning over the balustrade). He has gone down the staircase. I see no more of him.

DON SANCHO. A droll trick . . . (musingly) it is curious. . . .

DON GARCI (to a lady passing by). Marquise, shall we have this dance? (He bows and presents his hand.)

LADY. My dear sir, you know my husband counts the ones we dance together.

DON GARCI. Only the more reason. If that amuses him, so be it. He shall count, and we shall dance, you and I. (The Lady gives him her hand, and they go out.)

DON SANCHO (thoughtfully). It is curious, indeed.

DON MATIAS. Here is the bridal pair! Silence!

(Enter Hernani and Doña Sol hand in hand. Doña Sol wears a magnificent bridal costume; Hernani is all in black velvet, the Golden Fleece about his neck. Behind them, a crowd of masked figures, ladies and lords forming a retinue. Two halberdiers in rich livery follow them, and four pages precede them. All present separate and bow as they pass. Fanfare.)

SCENE 2

HERNANI (*saluting*). My dear friends!

DON RICARDO (*going up to him and bowing*). Your happiness is ours, Excellency!

DON FRANCISCO (*gazing at Doña Sol*). Holy Saint James! It's Venus on his arm!

DON MATIAS. On such a day as this, a happy night's to come!

DON FRANCISCO (*pointing to the window of the marriage chamber*). What glorious things will happen there! To be invisible, and see it all—lights out, doors closed, would that not be fine?

DON SANCHO (*to Don Matias*). It is late. Shall we go now?

(*All of them move forward to salute the pair and then leave, some through the door, others by the stairway in rear.*)

HERNANI (*moving with them*). God keep you all!

DON SANCHO (*the last to go, grips his hand*). I wish you joy. (*He leaves.*)

(*Hernani and Doña Sol remain alone. The sound of footsteps and voices fades and disappears completely. Throughout the beginning of the following scene, the faraway trumpets and the lights dim gradually, and darkness and silence return.*)

SCENE 3

DOÑA SOL. They all have gone, at last.

HERNANI (*attempting to draw her into his arms*). My dearest love!

DOÑA SOL (*blushing and drawing back*). It—it is late, I think.

HERNANI. My angel, it is always late for us to come together!

DOÑA SOL. All the activity was tiring me. Do you not find, my dear lord, that so much gaiety turns happiness numb?

HERNANI. It is true. Happiness, beloved, is a thing of gravity. It seeks out hearts of bronze, and carves itself there slowly; pleasure startles it off by tossing flowers to it. Joy's smile is less like laughter than like tears.

DOÑA SOL. In your eyes, that smile is daybreak. (*Hernani tries to lead her toward the door. She flushes.*) Soon.

HERNANI. I am your slave—yes, linger, linger! Do what you will, I ask you nothing. You know what you do; whatever you do is good! I shall laugh if you desire it, or sing. My soul burns. Ah, tell the volcano to smother its flame—the volcano will close its gaping chasms, and only clothe its slopes with flowers and green grass. For the giant is taken captive, Vesuvius is enslaved! What does its lava-boiling heart matter to you? It is flowers you want? Very well! Then the spitting volcano must do its best to burst with blossom before your eyes!

DOÑA SOL. How kind you are to a poor woman, Hernani of my heart!

HERNANI. What name is that, my lady? Ah, never call me by that name again, I beg of you! You remind me then of all I have forgotten. I know that once upon a time, in some dream, there lived a Hernani, whose eye glinted like a sword—a man of night and of the mountains, an outlaw who wore the word "revenge" scrawled everywhere upon him, a miserable man who trailed a curse behind him! But I do not know this Hernani. I am a man who loves meadows, and flowers, and woods, and the nightingale's soft song; I am Juan of Aragon, and wed to Doña Sol! I am a happy man!

DOÑA SOL. I too am happy!

HERNANI. What do I care for the rags I left behind me at the door? Here I am returned to my grieving palace; an angel of the Lord awaits me on the stair. I enter, and set upright the shattered columns; I light the fire, I open wide the casements, and tear the growth from between the flagstones in the court—I am nothing now but joy, enchantment, love.

Let them return my towers, my cellars and bastilles, my crest and seat within the council of the Castiles; give me my Doña Sol, all flushed, and her brow bent low—let the two of us be left alone, and the rest is past, forgotten. I have seen nothing, said and done nothing. I begin anew, wipe everything away, forget! Be it wisdom or madness, I have you, I love you, and you are all my joy!

DOÑA SOL (*examining his collar*). How handsome this collar is against the velvet black!

HERNANI. You saw the king dressed thus before myself.

DOÑA SOL. I did not notice it. What is another man to me? And then besides, is it the velvet, or the satin anyhow? No, my duke, it is your throat that suits the gold so well. You are noble and proud, my lord. (*He urges her indoors again.*) Soon! A moment yet! Look at me, do you see? This is joy, and I am weeping with it! Come look upon the lovely night! (*She goes to the balustrade.*) Only a moment, my duke! Only for long enough to breathe and gaze. All is dimmed now, the flares and festive tunes. Only the night and us. Perfect delight. . . . Say then, do you not feel that dreaming nature still half-watches over us with love? There is not a cloud. All is at rest, as we are. Come, breathe the rose-perfumed air with me. No torches, not a sound. All is still. A while ago the moon climbed up from the horizon, and as you spoke your voice and its trembling light both pierced my heart together. I felt joyful and calm, oh my beloved; I should have liked to die then.

HERNANI. Who'd not forget all things at that celestial voice? Your tones are a song with nothing human left in it. And like a traveler carried on a stream, who glides over the waters on a summer night, and sees a thousand flowery fields slip past him, my bewitched spirit goes wandering in your reveries. . . .

DOÑA SOL. This silence is too dark, this peace is too profound. Would you not set a star there in the sky? Or hear a night voice sing out suddenly, all tender and sweet? . . .

HERNANI (*smiling*). Capricious girl—only a moment since, you yearned for the light and singing to be done!

DOÑA SOL. The celebration, yes! But a bird who would sing above the meadow, a single nightingale amid the moss and shadow, or else a distant flute. . . . Such music is sweet; it brings its harmony into the soul, and sets a thousand voices singing in the heart like heavenly choirs! Oh, how lovely it would be! (*The distant sound of a horn is heard.*) God! My prayer is answered!

HERNANI (*starting; aside*). Ah no! It cannot be!

DOÑA SOL. An angel heard my thought—your guardian angel!

HERNANI (*bitterly*). Yes, my guardian angel! (*The horn is heard again. Aside.*) Again!

DOÑA SOL (*smilingly*). Don Juan, I recognize the sound of your own horn!

HERNANI. Yes.

DOÑA SOL. Have you then some part in this serenade?

HERNANI. Some part . . . yes.

DOÑA SOL. Dreary wedding feast—how much more I love the horn deep in the wood. And then besides, it is your horn, and so like your own voice.

(*Sound of the horn again.*)

HERNANI (*aside*). The tiger is below, and howling for his prey!

DOÑA SOL. Its music fills my heart with delight, Don Juan.

HERNANI (*rising, in terrible fury*). Call me Hernani! Hernani! For I have not yet done with that terrible name!

DOÑA SOL (*trembling*). What is wrong?

HERNANI. The old man!

DOÑA SOL. My God! What horror in your eyes! What is it?

HERNANI. The old man, laughing in the dark! Can you not see him?

DOÑA SOL. What wildness is this? What old man?

HERNANI. The old man!

DOÑA SOL (*falling to her knees*). I beg you from my knees, tell me, what secret tears at you? What is it?

HERNANI. I gave my oath!

DOÑA SOL. Your oath? (*She watches all his movements anxiously. He stops suddenly and wipes his hand over his brow.*)

HERNANI (*aside*). What did I nearly tell? I must spare her. (*Aloud.*) Nothing, nothing. What did I say to you?

DOÑA SOL. You said—

HERNANI. No . . . no. I was distressed. I am a little ill, it is nothing . . . Do not be frightened.

DOÑA SOL. Is there something you need? Tell me, I am your servant!

(*The horn begins again.*)

HERNANI (*aside*). He demands it, and he has my vow! (*He feels at his waist, but finds no sword, no dagger.*) Nothing there! It should be done by now!

DOÑA SOL. Do you suffer such pain?

HERNANI. An old wound, one I thought had healed. It has reopened. (*Aside.*) She must be sent away. (*Aloud.*) Doña Sol, beloved, listen. The box I carried with me always in less happy days—

DOÑA SOL. I know the one you mean—what do you want of it?

HERNANI. There is a vial inside; it holds a remedy to end the pain I feel. Go!

DOÑA SOL. I go, my lord. (*She leaves by the door to the marriage chamber.*)

SCENE 4

HERNANI (*alone*). So this is what he would do to my happiness! This is the fateful finger that gleams upon the wall! Oh, how sardonically fate laughs at me! (*He falls into a deep, convulsive reverie; then turns abruptly.*) Well? . . . But all is still. . . . I hear nothing approach. . . . Could I have been mistaken?

(*The masked figure in its black domino appears at the head of the stairs. Hernani stops, frozen.*)

SCENE 5

MASK. "Whatever may happen, whenever you wish it, and wherever—when you feel that it is time for me to die, then sound this trumpet, nothing more. It shall be done." The dead were witness to that pact. Well now, and is it done?

HERNANI (*his voice low*). It is he!

MASK. I come now to your home, and tell you it is time. Now is the hour I choose. I find you late.

HERNANI. Very well. What is your will? What would you do with me? Speak.

MASK. You may choose the knife or poison. I have brought both. We shall go together.

HERNANI. So be it.

MASK. Shall we pray?

HERNANI. What does it matter?

MASK. Which will you take?

HERNANI. The poison.

MASK. Very well. Give me your hand. (*He gives a small flask to Hernani, who takes it, paling.*) Now drink—and let me finish it.

HERNANI. Oh, Duke, have pity! Tomorrow! Ah, if you have still a heart, or even a soul—if you are not a specter from the flames, one of the damned dead, a phantom or a demon till eternity, if God has not yet set the hideous mark of "Never" on your brow, if you have known this highest joy—to love, to be twenty, and to marry your beloved—if ever a cherished woman has trembled in your arms, then wait until tomorrow! Tomorrow come for me!

MASK. What a fool you are to say this! Tomorrow! Tomorrow! You must be mocking me! The bells you rang this morning tolled your end! What would become of me, this night? I should die of it, and who would come and take you afterwards? Shall I go alone to death? Young man, you must come with me!

HERNANI. No! No, you devil, I free myself from you—I shall not obey!

MASK. I suspected you would not. Very well, For after all, how did you swear this vow? On nothing so important, after all—only your father's head. That can be overlooked. Youth's vows are frivolous.

HERNANI. My father! Father! Oh, I shall go mad!

MASK. No, it is only perjury and treason.

HERNANI. Duke!

MASK. Since the sons of Spanish houses play so lightly now with pledges and denials, farewell! (*He makes as if to go.*)

HERNANI. Stay!

MASK. Well then—

HERNANI. Cruel old man! (*He raises the vial.*) I turn about and trace my steps back to heaven's door!

(*Doña Sol returns, but does not see the masked figure, who stands at the rear.*)

SCENE 6

DOÑA SOL. I could not find your box—

HERNANI (*aside*). She has returned! And at so terrible a moment!

DOÑA SOL. I startle him, he shudders at my voice.... What have you in your hand? No!—What have you in your hand? Answer me! (*The domino approaches and unmasks. She cries out as she recognizes Don Ruy.*) It is poison!

HERNANI. Great heaven!

DOÑA SOL (*to Hernani*). What have I done to you? What hellish mystery! You meant to betray me, Don Juan!

HERNANI. I should have hid it from you. When the duke saved me I promised him that I would die at his command. Aragon must pay its debt to Silva.

DOÑA SOL. You belong to me, and not to him. What do I care for any other of your vows? (*To Don Ruy Gomez.*) Duke, love makes me strong. I shall defend him, against you and all the world.

DON RUY GOMEZ (*immobile*). Defend him if you can against a sworn vow.

DOÑA SOL. What vow?

HERNANI. I did swear it.

DOÑA SOL. No, no—nothing shall bind you! It cannot be! It is a crime! Murder! Madness!

DON RUY GOMEZ. Duke, let us proceed.

(*Hernani makes as if to obey. Doña Sol tries to draw him away.*)

HERNANI. No, Doña Sol; I must. The Duke has my word, and my father is watching from above.

DOÑA SOL (*to Don Ruy Gomez*). You would do better to tear their young from the tigers than the one I love from me! Do you know this Doña Sol? For a long while, compassion for your age and for your sixty years made me the docile daughter, all innocent and mild and timid. But now do you see my eyes wet with tears of rage? (*She draws a dagger from her bodice.*) And do you see this dagger? Ah, you mad old man, do you not fear the knife, when the eye has already sent its threat? Take care, Don Ruy, my uncle; I am of your line! Listen to me. Were I your very daughter, woe to you if you should lift your hand against my husband! (*She throws down the knife and falls to her knees before the Duke.*) Ah, I fall at your feet. Have pity on us! Grace! Alas! My lord, I am only a woman! I am weak, my strength stops short within my soul. I break too easily. I fall to your feet! Ah, I implore you, have pity on us!

DON RUY GOMEZ. Doña Sol!

DOÑA SOL. Forgive! We Spaniards speak our pain in hasty words, you know that. You were not cruel before! Pity! Uncle, you kill me in wounding him! Pity—I love him so!

DON RUY GOMEZ (*darkly*). You love him too well!

HERNANI (*to Doña Sol*). You weep!

DOÑA SOL. No, no, my love you must not die! No, I will not let you! (*To Don Ruy.*) Be merciful today! I shall love you as well!

DON RUY GOMEZ. After him! Do you think to appease the thirst that harrows me with such leavings of love—of friendship—no, even less than that! (*Pointing to Hernani.*) He is the only one. He is everything. But I, fine pity! What can I do with your affection? Oh, fury! He, he would have your heart, your love, the throne, and he would offer me the alms of a kind glance from you! And if a word were needed to calm my wild desires, he would tell you "Say this, and nothing more," cursing below his breath the avid beggar who gets the dregs in the empty cup. Shame! and mockery! No. It must be ended. Drink!

HERNANI. He has my word, and I must keep it.

DON RUY GOMEZ. Drink!

(*Hernani brings the vial to his lips. Doña Sol throws herself upon his arm.*)

DOÑA SOL. Not yet! Both of you, ah, hear me!

DON RUY GOMEZ. The grave is open, and I cannot wait.

DOÑA SOL. A moment! My lord, and my Don Juan! Ah, both of you, you are so harsh! What do I ask of them? An instant only, I ask no more! A moment to let this sorry women speak what is in her heart! Oh let me speak!

DON RUY GOMEZ (*to Hernani*). I cannot wait.

DOÑA SOL. My lords, you make me tremble! What have I done to you?

HERNANI. Her cry undoes me!

DOÑA SOL (*still clutching his arm*). You see I have a thousand things to say!

DON RUY GOMEZ (*to Hernani*). Death is waiting.

DOÑA SOL (*still hanging from Hernani's arm*). Don Juan, when I have spoken, you shall do what you will. (*She snatches the vial from him.*) I have it now! (*She raises the vial to the gaze of Hernani and the astonished old man.*)

DON RUY GOMEZ. Since I must deal here with two women, Don Juan, I shall go elsewhere to seek souls. You make fine vows upon the blood you spring from; I shall go now among the dead and speak of it to your father. Farewell. (*He takes a few steps away. Hernani holds him back.*)

HERNANI. Duke, stop! (*To Doña Sol.*) Alas, I implore you, would you have me be a man of false word, a felon, a perjurer? Would you have me go about the world with treason written on my brow? For pity's sake, give me back that poison! By our love, by our immortal souls! . . .

DOÑA SOL (*somberly*). You want it? (*She drinks.*) Here, take it now.

DON RUY GOMEZ (*aside*). Then it was meant for her!

DOÑA SOL (*handing Hernani the half-empty vial*). Take it, I tell you!

HERNANI (*to Don Ruy*). You see this, vile old man!

DOÑA SOL. Do not be angry with me; I saved your share for you.

HERNANI (*taking the vial*). Lord God!

DOÑA SOL. You would not have left me mine. You! You have not the heart a Christian wife has. You cannot love as a Silva loves. But I have drunk first and am at peace. Go on! Drink if you wish!

HERNANI. Alas, what have you done, my wretched love!

DOÑA SOL. It is you who forced me to it.

HERNANI. It is a hideous death!

DOÑA SOL. No, why should it be?

HERNANI. This potion takes us to the grave!

DOÑA SOL. Were we not to sleep together tonight? Does it matter in what bed?

HERNANI. My father, you have your revenge on me, for I forgot you! (*He puts the vial to his lips.*)

DOÑA SOL (*throwing herself upon him*). Ah heaven! What unearthly agony! Ah, throw that flask far from you! My reason's wandering. Stop! Alas, my Don Juan, this poison is a living thing! It opens out a hundred-toothed hydra in the heart that gnaws and then devours! Ah, I did not know one could feel such hideous pain! What is that thing? Pure fire! Do not drink it! You would suffer too horribly!

HERNANI (*to Don Ruy*). Ah, your soul is wicked! Could you not choose a different way for her? (*He drinks, and throws down the vial.*)

DOÑA SOL. What are you doing?

HERNANI. What have you done?

DOÑA SOL. Come, oh my young lover, come to my arms. (*They sit by one another.*) Is it not a terrible pain?

HERNANI. No.

DOÑA SOL. So now begins our wedding night! Am I not strangely pale for a young bride?

HERNANI. Ah!

DON RUY GOMEZ. Now destiny is done.

HERNANI. What torment! That Doña Sol should suffer, and I watch!

DOÑA SOL. Be calm. It is better now. Soon we shall open our wings together, and move toward some new brightness. Let us fly side by side toward a better world. . . . A kiss, though; a kiss! (*They embrace.*)

DON RUY GOMEZ. Oh, what pain to see them. . . .

HERNANI (*his voice weakening*). Oh, blessed be heaven; it gave me a life hemmed in by chasms and haunted by shades; but when I wearied of so hard a road, it let me drop to sleep with my lips pressed to your hand!

DON RUY GOMEZ. They are happy!

HERNANI (*his voice weaker and weaker*). Come, come . . . Doña Sol . . . it is dark. Are you in pain?

DOÑA SOL (*her voice as faint*). Nothing, nothing now. . . .

HERNANI. Do you see flames within the shade?

DOÑA SOL. Not yet.

HERNANI (*with a sigh*). Here . . . (*He falls.*)

DON RUY GOMEZ (*raising his head, then dropping it*). Dead!

DOÑA SOL (*disheveled, half rising from her bench*). Dead! No, not dead! We are asleep. He sleeps. You see, he is my husband. We love one another. We are abed here. This is our bridal night. (*Her voice failing.*) Do not wake him, lord Duke Mendoza. He is weary. (*She turns Hernani's head.*) Turn your face to me, my love. Nearer . . . nearer still. . . . (*She falls back.*)

DON RUY GOMEZ. Dead! Oh, I am damned! (*He kills himself.*)

THE END

UNCLE TOM'S CABIN

GEORGE AIKEN (ADAPTED FROM THE NOVEL BY HARRIET BEECHER STOWE)

HARRIET BEECHER STOWE (1811–1896)

Although Stowe is remembered for her novel of the Old South, her best work was devoted to local-color tales of life in her native New England. Her collected stories (e.g., *Oldtown Folks*, 1869) represent one of the first concentrated efforts by an American writer to render successfully the speech and daily habits of a region. However, Stowe does not romanticize her subjects, most of whom are descendents of the Puritans. Rather, she depicts them in a harsh, realistic light to expose their self-righteousness and emotional sterility.

Stowe's severity may be attributed to her stern Calvinist upbringing. Her father, Lyman Beecher, was one of New England's most renowned clergymen and the principal spokesman for Calvinist thought in the nineteenth century. Her brother, Henry Ward Beecher, was a fervent evangelist and reformer. Harriet Beecher was no less ardent than her father and brother, and consequently she—constrained by the limited status of women—turned to writing to spread her gospel of abolition and moral fervor. As one might expect, the social novels of Charles Dickens served as models for her work, as did the Romantic fiction of James Fenimore Cooper, Walter Scott, and Daniel Defoe.

She was educated at a female seminary where she was immersed in Calvinist theology and New England history. When she was 21 she moved to Cincinnati, where her father assumed the presidency of a seminary. Because that city was a terminus for the "underground railway," which funneled slaves from the South to freedom in northern states such as Ohio, Stowe learned about slavery firsthand from newly emancipated refugees. She also visited plantations across the river in rural Kentucky.

In 1835 she married Calvin Stowe, a college professor and minister, who encouraged her literary career, arguing that "God has written it in His book that you must be a literary woman, and who are we that we should contend against God?" In 1850 Mr. Stowe was appointed to a teaching position at Bowdoin College in Brunswick, Maine, and thus Stowe returned to New England, where she wrote her finest work. In 1850, while seated at the communion table of the Brunswick Congregational Church, Stowe was inspired to write *Uncle Tom's Cabin*, which she ultimately wrote at her kitchen table "under the direction of God."

The novel was an immediate success (in its first year it sold a phenomenal 300,000 copies), and she wrote a second antislavery novel, *Dread: A Tale of the Great Dismal Swamp*, which explored the effects of slavery on owners and traders. She adamantly refused requests to dramatize *Uncle Tom's Cabin* because she believed the theater to be a sinful place that would tempt Christians. (Aiken's adaptation was unauthorized.) With the unparalleled success of the G. C. Howard production, Stowe reluctantly accepted the invitation of a friend to attend the play. She was given a private viewing from the manager's box. The friend wrote that she "never saw such delight upon a human face as [Stowe] displayed when she first comprehended the full power of Mrs. Howard's Topsy."

Though Stowe's collected works total 16 volumes, none so altered her nation's history as *Uncle Tom's Cabin*.

George Aiken (1830–1876)

Little is known about the man who, at age 22, authored the most successful adaptation of Stowe's novel for the stage. He might have been a speculator (not unlike Gumption Cute in the play), but it is certain that he achieved some fame as a writer of "dime novels," popular mid-nineteenth-century adventure books that mythologized such heroes as Buffalo Bill Cody. Aiken's apprenticeship as a writer of pulp fiction served him well as he learned what would sell to the American mainstream. Indeed, the commercial success of *Uncle Tom's Cabin* is attributable as much to Aiken's skillful dramatization (especially the "curtain moments" that end each act) as to Stowe's message.

In addition to his literary skills, Aiken was an actor who created the role (in blackface) of George Harris in the Howard Company production of *Uncle Tom's Cabin*. Aiken, by the way, was G. C. Howard's cousin. Howard commissioned Aiken to devise a role for his 14-year-old daughter, Cordelia, and the dramatist invented Little Eva, whose deathbed speech became one of the most potent propaganda tools of the abolitionists. Howard was so grateful for his cousin's invention that he gave him an extra week's pay and a gold watch. Despite the enormous success of *Uncle Tom's Cabin*, Aiken wrote no other works for the stage.

Uncle Tom's Cabin

When President Abraham Lincoln met Harriet Beecher Stowe (1811–1896), whose novel *Uncle Tom's Cabin* (*UTC*) was published in March 1852, he is reported to have said to her, "So, you are the little lady who caused this big war," referring to the American Civil War (1861–1865). With due respect for Lincoln's assessment of her influence on the war (which was considerable), it might be more accurate to say that George Aiken's script for the Boston-based Howard Company caused the big war, for many more people saw *UTC* onstage than read the novel. It has been estimated that for every person who read Stowe's book, 50 became acquainted with its abolitionist message in the theater. Aiken's was not the first American version of the play: that honor goes to C. W. Taylor. But it was Aiken, a Boston writer of cheap novels, who created the most successful and dramatically satisfying version of the play's many adaptations.

Transforming any novel to the stage is no easy task, and Stowe's work was a particular challenge because of its several plots, sprawling locales, and numerous characters. Aiken's first attempt included only those portions of the novel up to Little Eva's death (now in act 3). Later he added the killing of Tom, the reformation of Topsy, and the death of Legree. In the novel Legree is not punished for his crimes (in fact, he does not kill St. Clare), but the laws of melodrama demanded the triumph of poetic justice on which to ring down the curtain. The scene in which Eliza Harris and Little Harry are trapped on the ice floes of the Ohio is relatively minor in Stowe's novel (it merits two brief paragraphs and there are no bloodhounds). Realizing its theatrical potential—especially in an age of stage machinery—Aiken transformed the scene into what is arguably the most famous scene in the American theater. Most importantly, Aiken made the death of Uncle Tom the climax of the play (it is less dramatic in the novel), giving him a deathbed speech guaranteed to raise audience sympathies. Tom's dying words to his evil nemesis—"my troubles will be over soon, but if you don't repent, yours will never end"—are typical of the sentimental reform dramas of the era. Aiken also added a stunning tableau with Little Eva, now an angel, descending to bless the play's martyrs, Tom and St. Clare. It was far more effective propaganda for the abolitionist cause than Stowe's lengthy antislavery debates because of its emotional impact. However, though the tableau made a potent ending, there is something disturbing about Aiken's message that divine justice for slaves is perhaps more desirable than earthly justice.

The Howard version opened in Troy, New York, on September 27, 1852 at the Museum (a common euphemism for theaters in the Puritan North, where antitheater sentiment existed). It ran for 57 performances, easily the longest run of a play in a small town (c. 30,000) in the theater's history. In July 1853 it began a lengthy run at the National Theater in New York, and the rest, as they say, is history.

And what a history! The popularity of the play is unparalleled. Not only did it thrive throughout the Civil War, it was even more successful after the war and the abolition of slavery. For instance, in 1879 the New York *Dramatic Mirror* listed 49 companies touring America with various versions of *UTC*; within a decade that number swelled tenfold as almost 500 companies criss-crossed America "tomming" in cities and towns. (The ultimate insult for actors was to be accused of "Tomming the tanks," which implied that the actors were so bad they could perform *UTC* in only the tiniest towns.) The play was so popular with actors as well as audiences that it was not uncommon to have "double shows" in which two actors played the same role. Lawyer Marks, Simon Legree, Uncle Tom, and especially Topsy were often played by two actors in the same show. The Tom Shows grew in size and soon rivaled circuses as major attractions; in fact, P. T. Barnum mounted a "Tom Show" that was equal parts theater and circus. By the time Stowe died in 1896, there had been, by a conservative estimate, some 250,000 performances of *UTC*. Ironically, she received no royalties because copyright laws had not been instituted.

Among the best accounts of the stage history of *UTC* is Harry Birdoff's *The World's Greatest Hit* (1947). (See Forum, "Prologue to *The World's Greatest Hit: Uncle Tom's Cabin*," following the text of *Uncle Tom's Cabin*.) The title is no exaggeration, as adaptations of Stowe's anti-slavery novel were also an unequaled international success. We think of the play as an American entity, but there were no less than eight productions of *UTC* playing in London by the end of 1852, including puppet and "panto"—i.e., Christmas show—versions. The most prominent English *UTC* opened at the Olympic Theater in September (less than a month after the American premiere); it was subtitled *Negro Life in America*, as opposed to the traditional *Life Among the Lowly*. The Olympic version was rewritten to include a scene in which the slaves were freed (over a decade before Lincoln's Emancipation Proclamation!). British reviewers, conveniently forgetting that it was English traders who introduced slavery to the colonies, scolded Americans, saying that they hoped the play would "make America ashamed of herself for suffering such an anomaly in her institutions."

Versions of *UTC* could be found in German (*Onkle Tom's Hutte*), French (*La Cabine de l'Oncle Tom*), Spanish (*La Cabaña de Tom, o La Esclavitud de los Negros*), Polish (*Chata Wuja Tomasza*), Swedish (*Onkel Tom's Stuga*), Russian (*Khiszhina dyadi Toma*), Italian (*La Cappanna dello Zio Tommaso*), and even Finnish (*Seta Tumon Tupa*). In 1853 an actor was accidentally killed onstage in a gun misfire in a Bade, Switzerland, production of the play. Gold miners in California were entertained by Charles R. Thorne's troupe, which was actually on its way to Australia.

The popularity of the play continued well into the twentieth century. It was made into a silent film in 1903 by Thomas Edison's company, and again in 1916 (with Lillian Gish). A very young Spencer Tracy played St. Clare in a hometown production in Grand Rapids, Michigan. Child stars Shirley Temple and Judy Garland played Eva and Topsy, respectively, in musical films featuring scenes from *UTC*. Rodgers and Hammerstein included a Siamese setting for "The Small House of Uncle Thomas" in their Broadway musical *The King and I*.

UTC is rarely performed in the post–civil rights era. However much we may sympathize with its antislavery message, we cannot deny its plotting is contrived, its language artificial, its characters stereotypical and too neatly divided into good and evil, and its propaganda blatant. And despite the best intentions of Stowe and Aiken, its portrait of non-whites is understandably offensive. The Negro dialect, while a then-honest attempt at realistic speech patterns, is crude and demeaning. Of greater concern are the stereotypical portraits of the slaves, especially Topsy, whose presence was intended as comic relief (and no doubt embellished by actors going for the cheap laugh). Although Topsy is an ironist whose comments actually reveal a strong sense of self-worth ("My name isn't Charcoal, it's Topsy" she declares to Cute in act 5), nineteenth-century audiences saw her as the stereotype of the uneducated, eye-rolling slave. The several songs she sings were derived from the minstrel show (see Spotlight box, The Minstrel Show, following the text of *Uncle Tom's Cabin*) and contributed to the stereotype. Much has been made of the character of Uncle Tom, who seems too much the faithful servant who willingly accepts the status quo. Only George Harris, who flees with wife (Eliza) and child (Harry) to Canada, emerges as an individual who takes his fate into his own hands. (Remember, George and Eliza are of mixed race, which made them more sympathetic to white audiences, especially when George kills his pursuers.)

For all its imperfections, as literature and especially as social tract, *Uncle Tom's Cabin* remains the most important play in the history of the American theater. As a piece of mass entertainment, no play offers a better sense of audience predilections in the nineteenth century. Of more importance, as a historical document, no other play better reflects the country's attitudes—both positively and negatively—about slavery, about race relations, and about its destiny at a turning point in its development.

The most famous scene in the American theater: Eliza and her baby cross the ice floes of the Ohio River to escape slave trackers in the 1901 production of Uncle Tom's Cabin.

UNCLE TOM'S CABIN

GEORGE AIKEN

THE CAST

UNCLE TOM	MARKS
GEORGE HARRIS	SAMBO
GEORGE SHELBY	QUIMBO
ST. CLARE	DOCTOR
PHINEAS FLETCHER	WAITER
GUMPTION CUTE	HARRY, A CHILD
MR. WILSON	EVA
DEACON PERRY	ELIZA
SHELBY	CASSY
HALEY	MARIE
LEGREE	ORPHELIA
TOM LOKER	CHLOE
	TOPSY

ACT I

SCENE I

Plain Chamber. Enter Eliza, meeting George.

ELIZA. Ah! George, is it you? Well, I am so glad you've come. (*George regards her mournfully.*) Why don't you smile, and ask after Harry?

GEORGE. (*Bitterly.*) I wish he'd never been born! I wish I'd never been born myself!

ELIZA. (*Sinking her head upon his breast and weeping.*) Oh George!

GEORGE. There now, Eliza, it's too bad for me to make you feel so. Oh! how I wish you had never seen me—you might have been happy!

ELIZA. George! George! how can you talk so? What dreadful thing has happened, or is going to happen? I'm sure we've been very happy till lately.

GEORGE. So we have, dear. But oh! I wish I'd never seen you, nor you me.

ELIZA. Oh, George! how can you?

GEORGE. Yes, Eliza, it's all misery! misery! The very life is burning out of me! I'm a poor, miserable, forlorn drudge! I shall only drag you down with me, that's all! What's the use of our trying to do anything—trying to know anything—trying to be anything? I wish I was dead!

ELIZA. Oh! now, dear George, that is really wicked. I know how you feel about losing your place in the factory, and you have a hard master; but pray be patient—

GEORGE. Patient! Haven't I been patient? Did I say a word when he came and took me away—for no earthly reason—from the place where everybody was kind to me? I'd paid him truly every cent of my earnings, and they all say I worked well.

ELIZA. Well, it is dreadful; but, after all, he is your master, you know.

GEORGE. My master! And who made him my master? That's what I think of. What right has he to me? I'm as much a man as he is. What right has he to make a dray-horse of me?—to take me from things I can do better than he can, and put me to work that any horse can do? He tries to do it; he says he'll bring me down and humble me, and he puts me to just the hardest, meanest and dirtiest work, on purpose.

ELIZA. Oh, George! George! you frighten me. Why, I never heard you talk so. I'm afraid you'll do something dreadful. I don't wonder at your feelings at all; but oh! do be careful—for my sake, for Harry's.

GEORGE. I have been careful, and I have been patient, but it's growing worse and worse—flesh and blood can't bear it any longer. Every chance he can get to insult and torment me he takes. He says that though I don't say anything, he sees that I've got the devil in me, and he means to bring it out; and one of these days it will come out, in a way that he won't like, or I'm mistaken.

ELIZA. Well, I always thought that I must obey my master and mistress, or I couldn't be a Christian.

GEORGE. There is some sense in it in your case. They have brought you up like a child—fed you, clothed you and taught you, so that you have a good education—that is some reason why they should claim you. But I have been kicked and cuffed and sworn at, and what do I owe? I've paid for all my keeping a hundred times over. I won't bear it!—no, I *won't*! Master will find out that I'm one whipping won't tame. My day will come yet, if he don't look out!

ELIZA. What are you going to do? Oh! George, don't do anything wicked; if you only trust in heaven and try to do right, it will deliver you.

GEORGE. Eliza, my heart's full of bitterness. I can't trust in heaven. Why does it let things be so?

ELIZA. Oh, George! we must all have faith. Mistress says that when all things go wrong to us, we must believe that heaven is doing the very best.

GEORGE. That's easy for people to say who are sitting on their sofas and riding in their carriages; but let them be where I am—I guess it would come some harder. I wish I could be good; but my heart burns and can't be reconciled. You couldn't, in my place, you can't now, if I tell you all I've got to say; you don't know the whole yet.

ELIZA. What do you mean?

GEORGE. Well, lately my master has been saying that he was a fool to let me marry off the place—that he hates Mr. Shelby and all his tribe—and he says he won't let me come here any more, and that I shall take a wife and settle down on his place.

ELIZA. But you were married to *me* by the minister, as much as if you had been a white man.

GEORGE. Don't you know I can't hold you for my wife if he chooses to part us? That is why I wish I'd never seen you—it would have been better for us both—it would have been better for our poor child if he had never been born.

ELIZA. Oh! but my master is so kind.

GEORGE. Yes, but who knows?—he may die, and then Harry may be sold to nobody knows who. What pleasure is it that he is handsome and smart and bright? I tell you, Eliza, that a sword will pierce your soul for every good and pleasant thing your child is or has. It will make him worth too much for you to keep.

ELIZA. Heaven forbid!

GEORGE. So, Eliza, my girl, bear up now, and good by, for I'm going.

ELIZA. Going, George! Going where?

GEORGE. To Canada; and when I'm there I'll buy you—that's all the hope that's left us. You have a kind master, that won't refuse to sell you. I'll buy you and the boy—heaven helping me, I will!

ELIZA. Oh, dreadful! If you should be taken?

GEORGE. I won't be taken, Eliza—I'll die first! I'll be free, or I'll die.

ELIZA. You will not kill yourself?

GEORGE. No need of that; they will kill me, fast enough. I will never go down the river alive.

ELIZA. Oh, George! for my sake, do be careful. Don't lay hands on yourself, or anybody else. You are tempted too much, but don't. Go, if you must, but go carefully, prudently, and pray heaven to help you!

GEORGE. Well, then Eliza, hear my plan. I'm going home quite resigned, you understand, as if all was over. I've got some preparations made, and there are those that will help me; and in the course of a few days I shall be among the missing. Well, now, good by.

ELIZA. A moment—our boy.

GEORGE. (*Choked with emotion.*) True, I had forgotten him; one last look, and then farewell!

ELIZA. And heaven grant it be not forever! (*Exeunt.*)

SCENE II

A dining room. Table and chairs..Dessert, wine, etc., on table. Shelby and Haley discovered at table.

SHELBY. That is the way I should arrange the matter.

HALEY. I can't make trade that way—I positively can't, Mr. Shelby. (*Drinks.*)

SHELBY. Why, the fact is, Haley, Tom is an uncommon fellow! He is certainly worth that sum anywhere—steady, honest, capable, manages my whole farm like a clock!

HALEY. You mean honest, as niggers go. (*Fills glass.*)

SHELBY. No; I mean, really, Tom is a good, steady, sensible, pious fellow. He got religion at a camp-meeting, four years ago, and I believe he really did get it. I've trusted him since then, with everything I have—money, house, horses, and let him come and go round the country, and I always found him true and square in everything.

HALEY. Some folks don't believe there is pious niggers, Shelby, but *I* do. I had a fellow, now, in this yer last lot I took to Orleans—'twas as good as a meetin' now, really, to hear that critter pray; and he was quite gentle and quiet like. He fetched me a good sum, too, for I bought him cheap of a man that was 'bliged to sell out, so I realized six hundred on him. Yes, I consider religion a valeyable thing in a nigger, when it's the genuine article and no mistake.

SHELBY. Well, Tom's got the real article, if ever a fellow had. Why last fall I let him go to Cincinnati alone, to do business for me and bring home five hundred dollars. "Tom," says I to him, "I trust you, because I think you are a Christian—I know you wouldn't cheat." Tom comes back sure enough, I knew he would. Some low fellows, they say, said to him—"Tom, why don't you make tracks for Canada?" "Ah, master trusted me, and I couldn't," was his answer. They told me all about it. I am sorry to part with Tom, I must say. You ought to let him cover the whole balance of the debt and you would, Haley, if you had any conscience.

HALEY. Well, I've got just as much conscience as any man in business can afford to keep, just a little, you know, to swear by, as twere; and then I'm ready to do anything in reason to 'blige friends, but this yer, you see, is a leetle too hard on a fellow—a leetle too hard! (*Fills glass again.*)

SHELBY. Well, then, Haley, how will you trade?

HALEY. Well, haven't you a boy or a girl that you could throw in with Tom?

SHELBY. Hum! none that I could well spare; to tell the truth, it's only hard necessity makes me willing to sell at all. I don't like parting with any of my hands, that's a fact. (*Harry runs in.*) Hulloa! Jim Crow! (*Throws a bunch of raisins towards him.*) Pick that up now! (*Harry does so.*)

HALEY. Bravo, little 'un! (*Throws an orange, which Harry catches. He sings and dances around the stage.*) Hurrah! Bravo! What a young 'un! That chap's a case, I'll promise. Tell you what, Shelby, fling in that chap, and I'll settle the business. Come, now, if that ain't doing the thing up about the rightest!

(*Eliza enters. Starts on beholding Haley, and gazes fearfully at Harry, who runs and clings to her dress, showing the orange, etc.*)

SHELBY. Well, Eliza?

ELIZA. I was looking for Harry, please, sir.

SHELBY. Well, take him away, then.

(*Eliza grasps the child eagerly in her arms, and casting another glance of apprehension at Haley, exits hastily.*)

HALEY. By Jupiter! there's an article, now. You might make your fortune on that ar gal in Orleans any day. I've seen over a thousand in my day, paid down for gals not a bit handsomer.

SHELBY. I don't want to make my fortune on her. Another glass of wine. (*Fills the glasses.*)

HALEY. (*Drinks and smacks his lips.*) Capital wine—first chop. Come, how will you trade about the gal? What shall I say for her? What'll you take?

SHELBY. Mr. Haley, she is not to be sold. My wife wouldn't part with her for her weight in gold.

HALEY. Ay, ay! women always say such things, 'cause they hain't no sort of calculation. Just show 'em how many watches, feathers and trinkets one's weight in gold would buy, and that alters the case, I reckon.

SHELBY. I tell you, Haley, this must not be spoken of—I say no, and I mean no.

HALEY. Well, you'll let me have the boy tho'; you must own that I have come down pretty handsomely for him.

SHELBY. What on earth can you want with the child?

HALEY. Why, I've got a friend that's going into this yer branch of the business—wants to buy up handsome boys to raise for the market. Well, what do you say?

SHELBY. I'll think the matter over and talk with my wife.

HALEY. Oh, certainly, by all means; but I'm in a devil of a

hurry and shall want to know as soon as possible, what I may depend on.

(Rises and puts on his overcoat, which hangs on a chair. Takes hats and whip.)

SHELBY. Well, call up this evening, between six and seven, and you shall have my answer.

HALEY. All right. Take care of yourself, old boy! (*Exit.*)

SHELBY. If anybody had ever told me that I should sell Tom to those rascally traders, I should never have believed it. Now it must come for aught I see, and Eliza's child too. So much for being in debt, heigho! The fellow sees his advantage and means to push it. (*Exit.*)

SCENE III

Snowy landscape. Uncle Tom's Cabin. Snow on roof. Practicable door and window. Dark stage. Music. Enter Eliza hastily, with Harry in her arms.

ELIZA. My poor boy! they have sold you, but your mother will save you yet!

(Goes to Cabin and taps on window. Aunt Chloe appears at window with a large white night-cap on.)

CHLOE. Good Lord! what's that? My sakes alive if it ain't Lizy! Get on your clothes, old man, quick! I'm gwine to open the door.

(The door opens and Chloe enters followed by Uncle Tom in his shirt sleeves holding a tallow candle.)

TOM. (*Holding the light towards Eliza.*) Lord bless you! I'm skeered to look at ye, Lizy! Are ye tuck sick, or what's come over ye?

ELIZA. I'm running away, Uncle Tom and Aunt Chloe, carrying off my child! Master sold him!

TOM & CHLOE. Sold him!

ELIZA. Yes, sold him! I crept into the closet by mistress' door tonight and heard master tell mistress that he had sold my Harry and you, Uncle Tom, both, to a trader, and that the man was to take possession to-morrow.

CHLOE. The good lord have pity on us! Oh, it don't seem as if it was true. What has he done that master should sell *him?*

ELIZA. He hasn't done anything—it isn't for that. Master don't want to sell, and mistress—she's always good. I heard her plead and beg for us, but he told her 'twas no use—that he was in this man's debt, and he had got the power over him, and that if he did not pay him off clear, it would end in his having to sell the place and all the people and move off.

CHLOE. Well, old man, why don't you run away, too? Will you wait to be toted down the river, where they kill nig-gers with hard work and starving? I'd a heap rather die than go there, any day! There's time for ye, be off with Lizy—you've got a pass to come and go any time. Come, bustle up, and I'll get your things together.

TOM. No, no—I ain't going. Let Eliza go—it's her right. I wouldn't be the one to say no—'taint in natur' for her to say; but you heard what she said? If I must be sold, or all the people on the place, and everything go to rack, why, let me be sold. I s'pose I can bar it as well as any one. Mas'r always found me on the spot—he always will. I never have broken trust, nor used my pass no ways contrary to my word, and I never will. It's better for me to go alone, than to break up the place and sell all. Mas'r ain't to blame, and he'll take care of you and the poor little 'uns! (*Overcome.*)

CHLOE. Now, old man, what is you gwine to cry for? Does you want to break this old woman's heart? (*Crying.*)

ELIZA. I saw my husband only this afternoon, and I little knew then what was to come. He told me he was going to run away. Do try, if you can, to get word to him. Tell him how I went and why I went, and tell him I'm going to try and find Canada. You must give my love to him, and tell him if I never see him again on earth, I trust we shall meet in heaven!

TOM. Dat is right, Lizy, trust in the Lord—he is our best friend—our own comforter.

ELIZA. You won't go with me, Uncle Tom?

TOM. No; time was when I would, but the Lord's given me a work among these yer poor souls, and I'll stay with 'em and bear my cross with 'em till the end. It's different with you—it's more'n you could stand, and you'd better go if you can.

ELIZA. Uncle Tom, I'll try it!

TOM. Amen! The lord help ye!

(Exit Eliza and Harry.)

CHLOE. What is you gwine to do, old man! What's to become of you?

TOM: (*Solemnly.*). Him that saved Daniel in the den of lions—that saved the children in the fiery furnace—Him that walked on the sea and bade the winds be still—He's alive yet! and I've faith to believe he can deliver me.

CHLOE. You is right, old man.

TOM. The Lord is good unto all that trust him, Chloe. (*Exeunt into cabin.*)

SCENE IV

Room in Tavern by the river side. A large window in flat, through which the river is seen, filled with floating ice. Moon light. Table and chairs brought on. Enter Phineas.

PHINEAS. Chaw me up into tobaccy ends! how in the name of all that's onpossible am I to get across that yer pesky river? It's a reg'lar blockade of ice! I promised Ruth to meet her to-night, and she'll be into my har if I don't come. (*Goes to window.*) That's a conglomerated prospect for a loveyer! What in creation's to be done? That thar river looks like a permiscuous ice-cream shop come to an awful state of friz. If I war on the adjacent bank, I wouldn't care a teetotal atom. Rile up, you old varmit, and shake the ice off your back!

(*Enter Eliza and Harry.*)

ELIZA. Courage, my boy—we have reached the river. Let it but roll between us and our pursuers, and we are safe! (*Goes to window.*) Gracious powers! the river is choked with cakes of ice!

PHINEAS. Holla, gal!—what's the matter? You look kind of streaked.

ELIZA. Is there any ferry or boat that takes people over now?

PHINEAS. Well, I guess not; the boats have stopped running.

ELIZA. (*In dismay.*) Stopped running?

PHINEAS. Maybe you're wanting to get over—anybody sick? Ye seem mighty anxious.

ELIZA. I—I—I've got a child that's very dangerous. I never heard of it till last night, and I've walked quite a distance to-day, in hopes to get to the ferry.

PHINEAS. Well, now, that's onlucky; I'm re'lly consarned for ye. Thar's a man, a piece down here, that's going over with some truck this evening, if he duss to; he'll be in here to supper to-night, so you'd better set down and wait. That's a smart little chap. Say, young'un, have a chaw tobacky? (*Takes out a large plug and a bowie-knife.*)

ELIZA. No, no! not any for him.

PHINEAS. Oh! he don't use it, eh? Hain't come to it yet? Well, I have. (*Cuts off a large piece, and returns the plug and knife to pocket.*) What's the matter with the young 'un? He looks kind of white in the gills!

ELIZA. Poor fellow! he is not used to walking, and I've hurried him on so.

PHINEAS. Tuckered, eh? Well, there's a little room there, with a fire in it. Take the baby in there, make yourself comfortable till that thar ferryman shows his countenance—I'll stand the damage.

ELIZA. How shall I thank you for such kindness to a stranger?

PHINEAS. Well, if you don't know how, why, don't try; that's the teetotal. Come, vamose! (*Exit, Eliza and Harry.*) Chaw me into sassage meat, if that ain't a perpendicular fine gal! She's a reg'lar A No. 1 sort of female! How'n thunder am I to get across this refrigerated stream of water? I can't wait for that ferryman. (*Enter Marks.*) Halloa! what sort of a critter's this? (*Advances.*) Say, stranger, will you have something to drink?

MARKS. You are excessively kind: I don't care if I do.

PHINEAS. Ah! he's a human. Holloa, thar! bring us a jug of whisky instantaneously, or expect to be teetotally chawed up! Squat yourself, stranger, and go in for enjoyment. (*They sit at table.*) Who are you, and what's your name?

MARKS. I am a lawyer, and my name is Marks.

PHINEAS. A land shark, eh? Well, I don't think no worse on you for that. The law is a kind of necessary evil; and it breeds lawyers just as an old stump does fungus. Ah! here's the whiskey. (*Enter Waiter, with jug and tumblers. Places them on table.*) Here, you—take that shin-plaster. (*Gives bill.*) I don't want any change—thar's a gal stopping in that room—the balance will pay for her—d'ye hear? —vamose! (*Exit Waiter. Fills glass.*) Take hold, neighbor Marks—don't shirk the critter. Here's hoping your path of true love may never have an ice-choked river to cross! (*They drink.*)

MARKS. Want to cross the river, eh?

PHINEAS. Well, I do, stranger. Fact is, I'm in love with the teetotalist pretty girl, over on the Ohio side, that ever wore a Quaker bonnet. Take another swig, neighbor. (*Fills glasses, and they drink.*)

MARKS. A Quaker, eh?

PHINEAS. Yes—kind of strange, ain't it? The way of it was this:—I used to own a grist of niggers—had 'em to work on my plantation, just below here. Well, stranger, do you know I fell in with that gal—of course I was considerably smashed—knocked into a pretty conglomerated heap— and I told her so. She said she wouldn't hear a word from me so long as I owned a nigger!

MARKS. You sold them, I suppose?

PHINEAS. You're teetotally wrong, neighbor. I gave them all their freedom, and told 'em to vamose!

MARKS. Ah! yes—very noble, I dare say, but rather expensive. This act won you your lady-love, eh?

PHINEAS. You're off the track again, neighbor. She felt kind of pleased about it, and smiled, and all that; but she said she could never be mine unless I turned Quaker! Thunder and earth! what do you think of that? You're a lawyer—come, now, what's your opinion? Don't you call it a knotty point?

MARKS. Most decidedly. Of course you refused.

PHINEAS. Teetotally; but she told me to think better of it, and come to-night and give her my final conclusion. Chaw me into mince meat, if I haven't made up my mind to do it!

MARKS. You astonish me!

PHINEAS. Well, you see, I can't get along without that gal;— she's sort of fixed my flint, and I'm sure to hang fire without her. I know I shall make a queer sort of Quaker, because you see, neighbor, I ain't precisely the kind of material to make a Quaker out of.

MARKS. No, not exactly.

PHINEAS. Well, I can't stop no longer. I must try to get across that candaverous river some way. It's getting late—take care of yourself, neighbor lawyer. I'm a teetotal victim to a pair of black eyes. Chaw me up to feed hogs, if I'm not in a reinatious state! (*Exit.*)

MARKS. Queer genius, that, very! (*Enter Tom Loker.*) So you've come at last.

LOKER. Yes. (*Looks into jug.*) Empty! Waiter! more whisky!

(*Waiter enters, with jug, and removes the empty one. Enter Haley.*)

HALEY. By the land! if this yer ain't the nearest, now, to what I've heard people call Providence! Why, Loker, how are ye?

LOKER. The devil! What brought you here, Haley?

HALEY. (*Sitting at table.*) I say, Tom, this yer's the luckiest thing in the world. I'm in a devil of a hobble, and you must help me out!

LOKER. Ugh! aw! like enough. A body may be pretty sure of that when you're glad to see 'em, or can make something off of 'em. What's the blow now?

HALEY. You've got a friend here—partner, perhaps?

LOKER. Yes, I have. Here, Marks—here's that ar fellow that I was with in Natchez.

MARKS. (*Grasping Haley's hand.*) Shall be pleased with his acquaintance. Mr. Haley, I believe?

HALEY. The same, sir. The fact is, gentlemen, this morning I bought a young 'un of Shelby up above here. His mother got wind of it, and what does she do but cut her lucky with him; and I'm afraid by this time that she has crossed the river, for I tracked her to this very place.

MARKS. So, then, ye're fairly sewed up, ain't ye? He! he! he! it's nearly done, too.

HALEY. This young 'un business makes lots of trouble in the trade.

MARKS. Now, Mr. Haley, what is it? Do you want us to undertake to catch this gal?

HALEY. The gal's no matter of mine—she's Shelby's—it's only the boy. I was a fool for buying the monkey.

LOKER. You're generally a fool!

MARKS. Come now, Loker, none of your huffs; you see, Mr. Haley's a-puttin' us in a way of a good job. I reckon: just hold still—these yer arrangements are my forte. This yer gal, Mr. Haley—how is she? what is she?

(*Eliza appears, with Harry, listening.*)

HALEY. Well, white and handsome—well brought up. I'd have given Shelby eight hundred or a thousand, and then made well on her.

MARKS. White and handsome—well brought up! Look here now, Loker, a beautiful opening. We'll do a business here on our own account. We does the catchin'; the boy, of course, goes to Mr. Haley—we takes the gal to Orleans to speculate on. Ain't it beautiful? (*They confer together.*)

ELIZA. Powers of mercy, protect me! How shall I escape these human bloodhounds? Ah! the window—the river of ice! That dark stream lies between me and liberty! Surely the ice will bear my trifling weight. It is my only chance of escape—better sink beneath the cold waters, with my child locked in my arms, then have him torn from me and sold into bondage. He sleeps upon my breast—Heaven, I put my trust in thee! (*Gets out of window.*)

MARKS. Well, Tom Loker, what do you say?

LOKER. It'll do.

(*Strikes his hand violently on the table. Eliza screams. They all start to their feet. Eliza disappears. Music, chord.*)

HALEY. By the land, there she is now! (*They all rush to the window.*)

MARKS. She's making for the river!

LOKER. Let's after her!

(*Music: They all leap through the window. Change.*)

SCENE V

Snow. Landscape. Music. Enter Eliza, with Harry, hurriedly.

ELIZA. They press upon my footsteps—the river is my only hope. Heaven grant me strength to reach it, ere they overtake me! Courage, my child!—we will be free—or perish! (*Rushes off. Music continued.*)

(*Enter Loker, Haley and Marks.*)

HALEY. We'll catch her yet; the river will stop her!

MARKS. No, it won't, for look! she has jumped upon the ice! She's a brave gal, anyhow!

LOKER. She'll be drowned!

HALEY. Curse that young 'un! I shall lose him, after all.

LOKER. Come on, Marks, to the ferry!

HALEY. Aye, to the ferry!—a hundred dollars for a boat!

(*Music. They rush off.*)

SCENE VI

The entire depth of stage, representing the Ohio River filled with Floating Ice. Set bank on right and in front. Eliza appears, with Harry, on a cake of ice, and floats slowly across to left. Haley, Loker, and Marks, on bank right, observing. Phineas on opposite shore.

END OF ACT I

ACT II

SCENE I

A Handsome Parlor. Marie discovered reclining on a sofa.

MARIE. (*Looking at a note.*) What can possibly detain St. Clare? According to this note he should have been here a fortnight ago. (*Noise of carriage without.*) I do believe he has come at last.

(*Eva runs in.*)

EVA. Mamma! (*Throws her arms around Marie's neck, and kisses her.*)

MARIE. That will do—take care, child—don't you make my head ache! (*Kisses her languidly.*)

(*Enter St. Clare, Ophelia, and Tom, nicely dressed.*)

ST. CLARE. Well, my dear Marie, here we are at last. The wanderers have arrived, you see. Allow me to present my cousin, Miss Ophelia, who is about to undertake the office of our housekeeper.

MARIE. (*Rising to a sitting posture.*) I am delighted to see you. How do you like the appearance of our city?

EVA. (*Running to Ophelia.*) Oh! is it not beautiful? My own darling home!—is it not beautiful?

OPHELIA. Yes, it is a pretty place, though it looks rather old and heathenish to me.

ST. CLARE. Tom, my boy, this seems to suit you?

TOM. Yes, mas'r, it looks about the right thing.

ST. CLARE. See here, Marie, I've brought you a coachman, at last, to order. I tell you, he is a regular hearse for blackness and sobriety, and will drive you like a funeral, if you wish. Open your eyes, now, and look at him. Now, don't say I never think about you when I'm gone.

MARIE. I know he'll get drunk.

ST. CLARE. Oh! no he won't. He's warranted a pious and sober article.

MARIE. Well, I hope he may turn out well; it's more than I expect, though.

ST. CLARE. Have you no curiosity to learn how and where I picked up Tom?

EVA. *Uncle* Tom, papa; that's his name.

ST. CLARE. Right, my little sunbeam!

TOM. Please, mas'r, that ain't no 'casion to say nothing bout me.

ST. CLARE. You are too modest, my modern Hannibal. Do you know, Marie, that our little Eva took a fancy to Uncle Tom—whom we met on board the steamboat—and persuaded me to buy him.

MARIE. Ah! she is so odd.

ST. CLARE. As we approached the landing, a sudden rush of the passengers precipitated Eva into the water—

MARIE. Gracious heavens!

ST. CLARE. A man leaped into the river, and, as she rose to the surface of the water, grasped her in his arms, and held her up until she could be drawn on the boat again. Who was that man, Eva?

EVA. Uncle Tom! (*Runs to him. He lifts her in his arms. She kisses him.*)

TOM. The dear soul!

OPHELIA. (*Astonished.*) How shiftless!

ST. CLARE. (*Overhearing her.*) What's the matter now, pray?

OPHELIA. Well, I want to be kind to everybody, and I wouldn't have anything hurt, but as to kissing—

ST. CLARE. Niggers! that you're not up to, hey?

OPHELIA. Yes, that's it—how can she?

ST. CLARE. Oh! bless you, it's nothing when you are used to it!

OPHELIA. I could never be so shiftless!

EVA. Come with me, Uncle Tom, and I will show you about the house. (*Crosses with Tom.*)

TOM. Can I go mas'r?

ST. CLARE. Yes, Tom; she is your little mistress—your only duty will be to attend to her! (*Tom bows and exits.*)

MARIE. Eva, my dear!

EVA. Well, mamma?

MARIE. Do not exert yourself too much!

EVA. No, mamma! (*Runs out.*)

OPHELIA. (*Lifting up her hands.*) How shiftless!

(*St. Clare sits next to Marie on sofa. Ophelia next to St. Clare.*)

ST. CLARE. Well, what do you think of Uncle Tom, Marie?

MARIE. He is a perfect behemoth!

ST. CLARE. Come, now, Marie, be gracious, and say something pretty to a fellow!

MARIE. You've been gone a fortnight beyond the time!

ST. CLARE. Well, you know I wrote you the reason.

MARIE. Such a short, cold letter!

ST. CLARE. Dear me! the mail was just going, and it had to be that or nothing.

MARIE. That's just the way; always something to make your journeys long and letters short!

ST. CLARE. Look at this. (*Takes an elegant velvet case from his pocket.*) Here's a present I got for you in New York—a Daguerreotype of Eva and myself.

MARIE. (*Looks at it with a dissatisfied air.*) What made you sit in such an awkward position?

ST. CLARE. Well, the position may be a matter of opinion, but what do you think of the likeness?

MARIE. (*Closing the case snappishly.*) If you don't think anything of my opinion in one case, I suppose you wouldn't in another.

OPHELIA. (*Sententiously, aside.*) How shiftless!

ST. CLARE. Hang the woman! Come, Marie, what do you think of the likeness? Don't be nonsensical now.

MARIE. It's very inconsiderate of you, St. Clare, to insist on my talking and looking at things. You know I've been lying all the day with the sick headache, and there's been such a tumult made ever since you came, I'm half dead!

OPHELIA. You're subject to the sick headache, ma'am?

MARIE. Yes, I'm a perfect martyr to it!

OPHELIA. Juniper-berry tea is good for sick head-ache; at least, Molly, Deacon Abraham Perry's wife, used to say so; and she was a great nurse.

ST. CLARE. I'll have the first juniper-berries that get ripe in our garden by the lake brought in for that especial purpose. Come, cousin, let us take a stroll in the garden. Will you join us, Marie?

MARIE. I wonder how you can ask such a question, when you know how fragile I am. I shall retire to my chamber, and repose till dinner time. (*Exit.*)

OPHELIA. (*Looking after her.*) How shiftless!

ST. CLARE. Come, cousin! (*As he goes out.*) Look out for the babies! If I step upon anybody, let them mention it.

OPHELIA. Babies under foot! How shiftless!

(*Exeunt.*)

SCENE II

A Garden. Tom discovered, seated on a bank, with Eva on his knee—his buttonholes are filled with flowers, and Eva is hanging a wreath around his neck. Music at opening of scene. Enter St. Clare and Ophelia, observing.

EVA. Oh, Tom! you look so funny.

TOM. (*Sees St. Clare and puts Eva down.*) I begs pardon, mas'r, but the young missis would do it. Look yer, I'm like the ox, mentioned in the good book, dressed for the sacrifice.

ST. CLARE. I say, what do you think, Pussy? Which do you like the best—to live as they do at your uncle's, up in Vermont, or to have a house-full of servants, as we do?

EVA. Oh! of course our way is the pleasantest.

ST. CLARE. (*Patting her head.*) Why so?

EVA. Because it makes so many more round you to love, you know.

OPHELIA. Now, that's just like Eva—just one of her odd speeches.

EVA. Is it an odd speech, papa?

ST. CLARE. Rather, as this world goes, Pussy. But where has my little Eva been?

EVA. Oh! I've been up in Tom's room, hearing him sing.

ST. CLARE. Hearing Tom sing, hey?

EVA. Oh, yes! he sings such beautiful things, about the new Jerusalem, and bright angels, and the land of Canaan.

ST. CLARE. I dare say; it's better than the opera, isn't it?

EVA. Yes; and he's going to teach them to me.

ST. CLARE. Singing lessons, hey? You are coming on.

EVA. Yes, he sings for me, and I read to him in my Bible, and he explains what it means. Come, Tom. (*She takes his hand and they exit.*)

ST. CLARE. (*Aside.*) Oh, Evangeline! Rightly named; hath not heaven made thee an evangel to me?

OPHELIA. How shiftless! How can you let her?

ST. CLARE. Why not?

OPHELIA. Why, I don't know: it seems so dreadful.

ST. CLARE. You would think no harm in a child's caressing a large dog even if he was black; but a creature that can think, reason and feel, and is immortal, you shudder at. Confess it, cousin. I know the feeling among some of you Northerners well enough. Not that there is a particle of virtue in our not having it, but custom with us does what Christianity ought to do: obliterates the feelings of personal prejudice. You loathe them as you would a snake or a toad, yet you are indignant at their wrongs. You would not have them abused but you don't want to have anything to do with them yourselves. Isn't that it?

OPHELIA. Well, cousin, there may be some truth in this.

ST. CLARE. What would the poor and lowly do without children? Your little child is your own true democrat. Tom, now, is a hero to Eva; his stories are wonders in her eyes: his songs and Methodist hymns are better than an opera, and the traps and little bits of trash in his pockets a mine of jewels, and he the most wonderful Tom that ever wore a black skin. This is one of the roses of Eden that the Lord has dropped down expressly for the poor and lowly, who get few enough of any other kind.

OPHELIA. It's strange, cousin: one might almost think you was a *professor*, to hear you talk.

ST. CLARE. A professor?

OPHELIA. Yes, a professor of religion.

ST. CLARE. Not at all; not a professor as you town folks have it, and, what is worse, I'm afraid, not a *practicer*, either.

OPHELIA. What makes you talk so, then?

ST. CLARE. Nothing is easier than talking. My forte lies in talking, and yours, cousin, lies in doing. And speaking of that puts me in mind that I have made a purchase for your department. There's the article now. Here, Topsy! (*Whistles.*)

(*Topsy runs on.*)

OPHELIA. Good gracious! what a heathenish, shiftless looking object! St. Clare, what in the world have you brought that thing here for?

ST. CLARE. For you to educate, to be sure, and train in the way she should go. I thought she was rather a funny specimen in the Jim Crow line. Here, Topsy, give us a song, and show us some of your dancing. (*Topsy sings a verse and dances a breakdown.*)

OPHELIA. (*Paralyzed.*) Well, of all things! If I ever saw the like!

ST. CLARE. (*Smothering a laugh.*) Topsy, this is your new mistress—I'm going to give you up to her. See now that you behave yourself.

TOPSY. Yes, Mas'r.

ST. CLARE. You're going to be good, Topsy, you understand?

TOPSY. Oh, yes, mas'r.

OPHELIA. Now, St. Clare, what upon earth is this for? Your house is so full of these plagues now, that a body can't set down their foot without treading on 'em. I get up in the morning and find one asleep behind the door, and see one black head poking out from under the table—one lying on the door mat, and they are moping and mowing and grinning between all the railings, and tumbling over the kitchen floor! What on earth did you want to bring this one for?

ST. CLARE. For you to educate—didn't I tell you? You're always preaching about educating, I thought I would make you a present of a fresh caught specimen, and let you try your hand on her and bring her up in the way she should go.

OPHELIA. I don't want her, I am sure; I have more to do with 'em now than I want to.

ST. CLARE. That's you Christians, all over. You'll get up a society, and get some poor missionary to spend all his days among just such heathen; but let me see one of you that would take one into your house with you, and take the labor of their conversion upon yourselves.

OPHELIA. Well, I didn't think of it in that light. It might be a real missionary work. Well, I'll do what I can. (*Advances to Topsy.*) She's dreadful dirty and shiftless! How old are you, Topsy?

TOPSY. Dunno, missis.

OPHELIA. How shiftless! Don't know how old you are? Didn't anybody ever tell you? Who was your mother?

TOPSY. (*Grinning.*) Never had none.

OPHELIA. Never had any mother? What do you mean? Where was you born?

TOPSY. Never was born.

OPHELIA. You musn't answer me in that way. I'm not playing with you. Tell me where you was born, and who your father and mother were?

TOPSY. Never was born, tell you; never had no father, nor mother, nor nothin'; I war raised by a speculator, with lots of others. Old Aunt Sue used to take car on us.

ST. CLARE. She speaks the truth, cousin. Speculators buy them up cheap, when they are little, and get them raised for the market.

OPHELIA. How long have you lived with your master and mistress?

TOPSY. Dunno, missis.

OPHELIA. How shiftless! Is it a year, or more, or less?

TOPSY. Dunno, missis.

ST. CLARE. She does not know what a year is; she don't even know her own age.

OPHELIA. Have you ever heard anything about heaven, Topsy? (*Topsy looks bewildered and grins.*) Do you know who made you?

TOPSY. Nobody, as I knows on, he, he, he! I spect I growed. Don't think nobody ever made me.

OPHELIA. The shiftless heathen! What can you do? What did you do for your master and mistress?

TOPSY. Fetch water—and wash dishes—and rub knives—and wait on folks—and dance breakdowns.

OPHELIA. I shall break down, I'm afraid, in trying to make anything of you, you shiftless mortal!

ST. CLARE. You find virgin soil there, cousin; put in your own ideas—you won't find many to pull up. (*Exit, laughing.*)

OPHELIA. (*Takes out her handkerchief. A pair of gloves falls. Topsy picks them up slyly and puts them in her sleeve.*) Follow me, you benighted innocent!

TOPSY. Yes, missis.

(*As Ophelia turns her back to her, she seizes the end of the ribbon she wears around her waist, and twitches it off. Ophelia turns and sees her as she is putting it in her other sleeve. Ophelia takes ribbon from her.*)

OPHELIA. What's this? You naughty, wicked girl, you've been stealing this?

TOPSY. Laws! why, that ar's missis' ribbon, a'nt it? How could it got caught in my sleeve?

OPHELIA. Topsy, you naughty girl, don't you tell me a lie—you stole that ribbon!

TOPSY. Missis, I declare for't, I didn't—never seed it till dis yer blessed minnit.

OPHELIA. Topsy, don't you know it's wicked to tell lies?

TOPSY. I never tells no lies, missis; it's just de truth I've been telling now and nothing else.

OPHELIA. Topsy, I shall have to whip you, if you tell lies so.

TOPSY. Laws missis, if you's to whip all day, couldn't say no other way. I never seed dat ar—it must a got caught in my sleeve. (*Blubbers.*)

OPHELIA. (*Seizes her by the shoulders.*) Don't you tell me that again, you barefaced fibber! (*Shakes her. The gloves fall on stage.*) There you, my gloves too—you outrageous young heathen! (*Picks them up.*) Will you tell me, now, you didn't steal the ribbon?

TOPSY. No, missis; stole de gloves, but didn't steal de ribbon. It was permiskus.

OPHELIA. Why, you young reprobate!

TOPSY. Yes—I's knows I's wicked!

OPHELIA. Then you know you ought to be punished. (*Boxes her ears.*) What do you think of that?

TOPSY. He, he, he! De Lord, missus; dat wouldn't kill a 'skeeter. (*Runs off laughing, Ophelia follows indignantly*).

SCENE III

The Tavern by the River. Table and chairs. Jug and glasses on table. On flat is a printed placard, headed: "Four Hundred Dollars Reward—Runaway—George Harris!" Phineas is discovered, seated at table.

PHINEAS. So yer I am; and a pretty business I've undertook to do. Find the husband of the gal that crossed the river on the ice two or three days ago. Ruth said I must do it, and I'll be teetotally chawed up if I don't do it. I see they've offered a reward for him, dead or alive. How in creation am I to find the varmint? He isn't likely to go round looking natural, with a full description of his hide and figure staring him in the face. (*Enter Mr. Wilson.*) I say, stranger, how are ye? (*Rises and comes forward.*)

WILSON. Well, I reckon.

PHINEAS. Any news? (*Takes out plug and knife.*)

WILSON. Not that I know of.

PHINEAS. (*Cutting a piece of tobacco and offering it.*) Chaw?

WILSON. No, thank ye—it don't agree with me.

PHINEAS. Don't, eh! (*Putting it in his own mouth.*) I never felt any the worse for it.

WILSON. (*Sees placard.*) What's that?

PHINEAS. Nigger advertised. (*Advances towards it and spits on it.*) There's my mind upon that.

WILSON. Why, now, stranger, what's that for?

PHINEAS. I'd do it all the same to the writer of that ar paper, if he was here. Any man that owns a boy like that, and can't find any better way of treating him, than branding him on the hand with the letter H, as that paper states, deserves to lose him. Such papers as this ar' a shame to old Kaintuck! that's my mind right out, if anybody wants to know.

WILSON. Well, now, that's a fact.

PHINEAS. I used to have a gang of boys, sir—that was before I fell in love—and I just told em:—"Boys," says I, "run now! Dig! put! just when you want to. I never shall come to look after you!" That's the way I kept mine. Let 'em know they are free to run any time, and it jest stops their wanting to. It stands to reason it should. Treat 'em like men, and you'll have men's work.

WILSON. I think you are altogether right, friend, and this man described here is a fine fellow—no mistake about that. He worked for me some half dozen years in my bagging factory, and he was my best hand, sir. He is an ingenious fellow, too; he invented a machine for the cleaning of hemp—a really valuable affair; it's gone into use in several factories. His master holds the patent of it.

PHINEAS. I'll warrant ye; holds it, and makes money out of it, and then turns round and brands the boy in his right hand! If I had a fair chance, I'd mark him, I reckon, so that he'd carry it *one* while!

(*Enter George Harris, disguised.*)

GEORGE. (*Speaking as he enters.*) Jim, see to the trunks. (*Sees Wilson.*) Ah! Mr. Wilson here?

WILSON. Bless my soul, can it be?

GEORGE. (*Advances and grasps his hand.*) Mr. Wilson, I see you remember me Mr. Butler, of Oaklands, Shelby county.

WILSON. Ye—yes—yes—sir.

PHINEAS. Holloa! there's a screw loose here somewhere. That old gentleman seems to be struck into a pretty con-

siderable heap of astonishment. May I be teetotally chawed up! if I don't believe that's the identical man I'm after. (*Crosses to George.*) How are ye, George Harris?

GEORGE. (*Starting back and thrusting his hands into his breast.*) You know me?

PHINEAS. Ha, ha, ha! I rather conclude I do; but don't get riled, I an't a bloodhound in disguise.

GEORGE. How did you discover me?

PHINEAS. By a teetotal smart guess. You're the very man I want to see. Do you know I was sent after you?

GEORGE. Ah! by my master?

PHINEAS. No; by your wife.

GEORGE. My wife! Where is she?

PHINEAS. She's stopping with a Quaker family over on the Ohio side.

GEORGE. Then she is safe?

PHINEAS. Teetotally!

GEORGE. Conduct me to her.

PHINEAS. Just wait a brace of shakes and I'll do it. I've got to go and get the boat ready. 'Twon't take me but a minute—make yourself comfortable till I get back. Chaw me up! but this is what I call doing things in short order. (*Exit.*)

WILSON. George!

GEORGE. Yes, George!

WILSON. I couldn't have thought it!

GEORGE. I am pretty well disguised, I fancy; you see I don't answer to the advertisement at all.

WILSON. George, this is a dangerous game you are playing; I could not have advised you to it.

GEORGE. I can do it on my own responsibility.

WILSON. Well, George, I suppose you're running away—leaving your lawful master, George, (I don't wonder at it) at the same time, I'm sorry, George, yes, decidedly. I think I must say that it's my duty to tell you so.

GEORGE. Why are you sorry, sir?

WILSON. Why to see you, as it were, setting yourself in opposition to the laws of your country.

GEORGE. My country! What country have I, but the grave? And I would to heaven that I was laid ther!

WILSON. George, you've got a hard master, in fact he is—well, he conducts himself reprehensibly—I can't pretend to defend him. I'm sorry for you, now; it's a bad case—very bad; but we must all submit to the indications of providence. George, don't you see?

GEORGE. I wonder, Mr. Wilson, if the Indians should come and take you a prisoner away from your wife and children, and want to keep you all your life hoeing corn for them, if you'd think it your duty to abide in the condition in which you were called? I rather imagine that you'd think the first stray horse you could find an indication of providence, shouldn't you?

WILSON. Really, George, putting the case in that somewhat peculiar light—I don't know—under those circumstances—but what I might. But it seems to me you are running an awful risk. You can't hope to carry it out. If you're taken it will be worse with you than ever; they'll only abuse you, and half kill you, and sell you down river.

GEORGE. Mr. Wilson, I know all this. I *do* run a risk, but— (*Throws open coat and shows pistols and knife in his belt.*) There! I'm ready for them. Down South I never *will* go! no, if it comes to that, I can earn myself at least six feet of free soil—the first and last I shall ever own in Kentucky!

WILSON. Why, George, this state of mind is awful—it's getting really desperate. I'm concerned. Going to break the laws of your country?

GEORGE. My country again! Sir, I haven't any country any more than I have any father. I don't want anything of *your* country except to be left alone—to go peaceably out of it; but if any man tries to stop me, let him take care, for I am desperate. I'll fight for my liberty, to the last breath I breathe! You say your fathers did it, if it was right for them, it is right for me!

WILSON. (*Walking up and down and fanning his face with a large yellow silk handkerchief.*) Blast 'em all! Haven't I always said so—the infernal old cusses! Bless me! I hope I an't swearing now! Well, go ahead, George, go ahead. But be careful, my boy; don't shoot anybody, unless—well, you'd *better* not shoot—at least I wouldn't *hit* anybody, you know.

GEORGE. Only in self-defense.

WILSON. Well, well. (*Fumbling in his pocket.*) I suppose, perhaps, I an't following my judgment—hang it, I won't follow my judgment. So here, George. (*Takes out a pocketbook and offers George a roll of bills.*)

GEORGE. No, my kind, good sir, you've done a great deal for me, and this might get you into trouble. I have money enough, I hope, to take me as far as I need it.

WILSON. No; but you must, George. Money is a great help everywhere, can't have too much, if you get it honestly. Take it, *do* take it, *now* do, my boy!

GEORGE. (*Taking the money.*) On condition, sir, that I may repay it at some future time, I will.

WILSON. And now, George, how long are you going to travel in this way? Not long or far I hope? It's well carried on, but too bold.

GEORGE. Mr. Wilson, it is so *bold*, and this tavern is so near, that they will never think of it; they will look for me on ahead, and you yourself wouldn't know me.

WILSON. But the mark on your hand?

GEORGE. (*Draws off his glove and shows scar.*) That is a parting mark of Mr. Harris' regard. Looks interesting, doesn't it? (*Puts on glove again.*)

WILSON. I declare, my very blood runs cold when I think of it—your condition and your risks.

GEORGE. Mine has run cold a good many years; at present, it's about up to the boiling point.

WILSON. George, something has brought you out wonderfully. You hold up your head, and move and speak like another man.

GEORGE. (*Proudly.*) Because I'm a *freeman!* Yes, sir; I've said "master" for the last time to any man. *I'm free!*

WILSON. Take care! You are not sure; you may be taken.

GEORGE. All men are free and equal *in the grave*, if it comes to that, Mr. Wilson.

(*Enter Phineas.*)

PHINEAS. Them's my sentiment, to a teetotal atom, and I don't care who knows it! Neighbor, the boat is ready, and the sooner we make tracks the better. I've seen some mysterious strangers lurking about these diggings, so we'd better put.

GEORGE. Farewell, Mr. Wilson, and heaven reward you for the many kindnesses you have shown the poor fugitive!

WILSON. (*Grasping his hand.*) You're a brave fellow, George. I wish in my heart you were safe through, though—that's what I do.

PHINEAS. And ain't I the man of all creation to put him through, stranger? Chaw me up if I don't take him to his dear little wife, in the smallest possible quantity of time. Come, neighbor, let's vamose.

GEORGE. Farewell, Mr. Wilson.

WILSON. My best wishes go with you, George. (*Exit.*)

PHINEAS. You're a trump, old Slow-and-Easy.

GEORGE. (*Looking off.*) Look! look!

PHINEAS. Consarn their picters, here they come! We can't get out of the house without their seeing us. We're teetotally treed!

GEORGE. Let us fight our way through them!

PHINEAS. No, that won't do; there are too many of them for a fair fight—we should be chawed up in no time. (*Looks round and sees trap door.*) Holloa! here's a cellar door. Just you step down here a few minutes, while I parley with them. (*Lifts trap.*)

GEORGE. I am resolved to perish sooner than surrender! (*Goes down trap.*)

PHINEAS. That's your sort! (*Closes trap and stands on it.*) Here they are!

(*Enter Haley, Marks, Loker and three Men.*)

HALEY. Say, stranger, you haven't seen a runaway darkey about these parts, eh?

PHINEAS. What kind of a darkey?

HALEY. A mulatto chap, almost as light-complexioned as a white man.

PHINEAS. Was he a pretty good-looking chap?

HALEY. Yes.

PHINEAS. Kind of tall?

HALEY. Yes.

PHINEAS. With brown hair?

HALEY. Yes.

PHINEAS. And dark eyes?

HALEY. Yes.

PHINEAS. Pretty well-dressed?

HALEY. Yes.

PHINEAS. Scar on his right hand?

HALEY. Yes, yes.

PHINEAS. Well, I ain't seen him.

HALEY. Oh, bother! Come, boys, let's search the house. (*Exeunt.*)

PHINEAS. (*Raises trap.*) Now, then, neighbor George. (*George enters up trap.*) Now's the time to cut your lucky.

GEORGE. Follow me, Phineas. (*Exit.*)

PHINEAS. In a brace of shakes. (*Is closing trap as Haley, Marks, Loker, etc., reenter.*)

HALEY. Ah! he's down in the cellar. Follow me, boys! (*Thrusts Phineas aside, and rushes down trap, followed by the others. Phineas closes trap and stands on it.*)

PHINEAS. Chaw me up! but I've got 'em in a trap. (*Knocking below.*) Be quiet, you perky varmints! (*Knocking.*) They're getting mighty uneasy. (*Knocking.*) Will you be quiet, you savagerous critters! (*The trap is forced open. Haley and Marks appear. Phineas seizes a chair and stands over trap— picture.*) Down with you or I'll smash you into apple-fritters! (*Tableau—closed in.*)

SCENE IV

A Plain chamber.

TOPSY. (*Without.*) You go 'long. No more nigger dan you be! (*Enters, shouts and laughter without—looks off.*) You seem to think yourself white folks. You ain't nerry one—black nor white. I'd like to be one or turrer. Law! you niggers, does you know you's all sinners? Well, you is—everybody is. White folks is sinners too—Miss Freely says so—but I 'spects niggers is the biggest ones. But Lor! ye ain't any on ye up to me. I's so awful wicked there can't nobody do nothin' with me. I used to keep old missis a-swarin' at me ha' de time. I 'spects I's de wickedest critter in de world. (*Song and dance introduced. Enter Eva.*)

EVA. Oh, Topsy! Topsy! you have been very wrong again.

TOPSY. Well, I 'spects I have.

EVA. What makes you do so?

TOPSY. I dunno; I 'spects it's cause I's so wicked.

EVA. Why did you spoil Jane's earrings?

TOPSY. 'Cause she's so proud. She called me a little black imp, and turned up her pretty nose at me 'cause she is whiter than I am. I was gwine by her room, and I seed her coral earrings lying on de table, so I threw dem on de floor, and put my foot on 'em, and scrunches 'em all to little bits—he! he! he! I's so wicked.

EVA. Don't you know that was very wrong?

TOPSY. I don't car'! I despises dem what sets up for fine ladies, when dey ain't nothing but cream-colored niggers! Dere's Miss Rosa—she gives me lots of pertinent remarks. T'other night she was gwine to a ball. She put on a beau'-ful dress dat missis gave her—wid her har curled, all nice and pretty. She hab to go down de back stairs—dem am dark—and I puts a pail of hot water on dem, and she put her foot into it, and den she go tumbling to de bottom of the stairs, and de water go all ober her, and spile her dress, and scald her dreadful bad! He! he! he! I's so wicked!

EVA. Oh! how could you!

TOPSY. Don't dey despise me cause I don't know nothing? Don't dey laugh at me 'cause I'm brack, and dey ain't?

EVA. But you shouldn't mind them.

TOPSY. Well, I don't mind dem; but when dey are passing under my winder, I trows dirty water on 'em and dat spiles der complexions.

EVA. What does make you so bad, Topsy? Why won't you try and be good? Don't you love anybody, Topsy?

TOPSY. Can't recommember.

EVA. But you love your father and mother?

TOPSY. Never had none, ye know, I telled ye that, Miss Eva.

EVA. Oh! I know; but hadn't you any brother, or sister, or aunt, or—

TOPSY. No, none on 'em —never had nothing nor nobody. I's brack—no one loves me!

EVA. Oh! Topsy, I love you! (*Laying her hand on Topsy's shoulder.*) I love you because you haven't had any father, or mother, or friends. I love you, I want you to be good. I wish you would try to be good for my sake. (*Topsy looks astonished for a moment, and then bursts into tears.*) Only think of it, Topsy—you can be one of those spirits bright Uncle Tom sings about!

TOPSY. Oh! dear Miss Eva—dear Miss Eva! It will try—I will try. I never did care nothin' about it before.

EVA. If you try, you will succeed. Come with me. (*Crosses and takes Topsy's hand.*)

TOPSY. I will try; but den, I's so wicked! (*Exit Eva followed by Topsy, crying.*)

SCENE V

Chamber. Enter George, Eliza and Harry.

GEORGE. At length, Eliza, after many wanderings, we are united.

ELIZA. Thanks to these generous Quakers, who have so kindly sheltered us.

GEORGE. Not forgetting our friend Phineas.

ELIZA. I do indeed owe him much. 'Twas he I met upon the icy river's bank, after that fearful, but successful attempt, when I fled from the slave-trader with my child in my arms.

GEORGE. It seems almost incredible that you could have crossed the river on the ice.

ELIZA. Yes, I did. Heaven helping me, I crossed on the ice, for they were behind me—right behind—and there was no other way.

GEORGE. But the ice was all in broken-up blocks, swinging and heaving up and down in the water.

ELIZA. I know it was—I know it; I did not think I should get over, but I did not care—I could but die if I did not! I leaped on the ice, but how I got across I don't know; the first I remember, a man was helping me up the bank—that man was Phineas.

GEORGE. My brave girl! you deserve your freedom—you have richly earned it!

ELIZA. And when we get to Canada I can help you to work, and between us we can find something to live on.

GEORGE. Yes, Eliza, so long as we have each other, and our boy. Oh, Eliza, if these people only knew what a blessing it is for a man to feel that his wife and child belong to him! I've often wondered to see men that could call their wives and children *their own,* fretting and worrying about anything else. Why, I feel rich and strong, though we have nothing but our bare hands. If they will only let me alone now, I will be satisfied—thankful!

ELIZA. But we are not quite out of danger; we are not yet in Canada.

GEORGE. True, but it seems as if I smelt free air, and it makes me strong!

(*Enter Phineas, dressed as a Quaker.*)

PHINEAS. (*With a snuffle.*) Verily, friends, how is it with thee? —hum!

GEORGE. Why, Phineas, what means this metamorphosis?

PHINEAS. I've become a Quaker, that's the meaning on't.

GEORGE. What—you?

PHINEAS. Teetotally! I was driven to it by a strong argument, composed of a pair of sparkling eyes, rosy cheeks, and pouting lips. Them lips would persuade a man to assassinate his grandmother! (*Assumes the Quaker tone again.*) Verily, George, I have discovered something of importance to the interests of thee and thy party, and it were well for thee to hear it.

GEORGE. Keep us not in suspense!

PHINEAS. Well, after I left you on the road, I stopped at a little, lone tavern, just below here. Well, I was tired with hard driving, and after my supper I stretched myself down on a pile of bags in the corner, and pulled a buffalo hide over me—and what does I do but get fast asleep.

GEORGE. With one ear open, Phineas?

PHINEAS. No, I slept ears and all for an hour or two, for I was pretty well tired; but when I came to myself a little, I found that there were some men in the room, sitting round a table, drinking and talking; and I thought, before I made much muster, I'd just see what they were up to, especially as I heard them say something about the Quakers. Then I listened with both ears and found they were talking about you. So I kept quiet, and heard them lay off all their plans. They've got a right notion of the track we are going to-night, and they'll be down after us, six or eight strong. So, now, what's to be done?

ELIZA. What *shall* we do, George?

GEORGE. I know what I shall do! (*Takes out pistols.*)

PHINEAS. Ay-ay, thou seest, Eliza, how it will work—pistols—phitz—poppers!

ELIZA. I see; but I pray it come not to that!

GEORGE. I don't want to involve any one with or for me. If you will lend me your vehicle, and direct me, I will drive alone to the next stand.

PHINEAS. Ah! well, friend, but thee'll need a driver for all that. Thee's quite welcome to do all the fighting thee knows; but I know a thing or two about the road that thee doesn't.

GEORGE. But I don't want to involve you.

PHINEAS. Involve me! Why, chaw me—that is to say—when thee does involve me, please to let me know.

ELIZA. Phineas is a wise and skillful man. You will do well, George, to abide by his judgment. And, oh! George, be not hasty with these—young blood is hot! (*Laying her hand on pistols.*)

GEORGE. I will attack no man. All I ask of this country is to be left alone, and I will go out peaceably. But I'll fight to the last breath before they shall take from me my wife and son! Can you blame me?

PHINEAS. Mortal men cannot blame thee, neighbor George! Flesh and blood could not do otherwise. Woe unto the world because of offenses, but woe unto them through whom the offense cometh! That's gospel, teetotally!

GEORGE. Would not even you, sir, do the same, in my place?

PHINEAS. I pray that I be not tried; the flesh is weak—but I think my flesh would be pretty tolerably strong in such a case; I ain't sure, friend George, that I shouldn't hold a fellow for thee, if thee had any accounts to settle with him.

ELIZA. Heaven grant we be not tempted.

PHINEAS. But if we are tempted too much, why, consarn 'em! let them look out, that's all.

GEORGE. It's quite plain you was not born for a Quaker. The old nature has its way in you pretty strong yet.

PHINEAS. Well, I reckon you are pretty teetotally right.

GEORGE. Had we not better hasten our flight?

PHINEAS. Well, I rather conclude we had; we're full two hours ahead of them, if they start at the time they planned; so let's vamose.

(*Exeunt.*)

SCENE VI

A Rocky Pass in the Hills. Large set rock and platform.

PHINEAS. (*Without.*) Out with you in a twinkling, every one, and up into these rocks with me! run now, if you ever did run! (*Music. Phineas enters, with Harry in his arms. George supporting Eliza.*) Come up here; this is one of our old hunting dens. Come up. (*They ascend the rock.*) Well, here we are. Let 'em get us if they can. Whoever comes here has to walk single file between those two rocks, in fair range of your pistols—d'ye see?

GEORGE. I do see. And now, as this affair is mine, let me take all the risk, and do all the fighting.

PHINEAS. Thee's quite welcome to do the fighting, George; but I may have the fun of looking on, I suppose. But see, these fellows are kind of debating down there, and looking up, like hens when they are going to fly up onto the roost. Hadn't thee better give 'em a word of advice, before they come up, just to tell 'em handsomely they'll be shot if they do.

(*Loker, Marks, and three Men enter.*)

MARKS. Well, Tom, your coons are fairly treed.

LOKER. Yes, I see 'em go up right here; and here's a path—I'm for going right up. They can't jump down in a hurry, and it won't take long to ferret 'em out.

MARKS. But, Tom, they might fire at us from behind the rocks. That would be ugly, you know.

LOKER. Ugh! always for saving your skin, Marks. No danger, niggers are too plaguy scared!

MARKS. I don't know why I shouldn't save my skin, it's the best I've got; and niggers do fight like the devil sometimes.

GEORGE. (*Rising on the rock.*) Gentlemen, who are you down there and what do you want?

LOKER. We want a party of runaway niggers. One George and Eliza Harris, and their son. We've got the officers here, and a warrant to take 'em too. D'ye hear? An't you George Harris, that belong to Mr. Harris, of Shelby country, Kentucky?

GEORGE. I am George Harris. A Mr. Harris of Kentucky did call me his property. But now I'm a freeman, standing on heaven's free soil! My wife and child I claim as mine. We have arms to defend ourselves and we mean to do it. You can come up if you like but the first one that comes within range of our bullets is a dead man!

MARKS. Oh, come—come, young man, this ar no kind of talk at all for you. You see we're officers of justice. We've got the law on our side, and the power and so forth; so you'd better give up peaceably, you see—for you'll certainly have to give up at last.

GEORGE. I know very well that you've got the law on your side, and the power; but you haven't got us. We are standing here as free as you are, and by the great power that made us, we'll fight for our liberty till we die! (*During this, Mark draws a pistol, and when he concludes fires at him. Eliza screams.*) It's nothing, Eliza; I am unhurt.

PHINEAS. (*Drawing George down.*) Thee'd better keep out of sight with thy speechifying; they're teetotal mean scamps.

LOKER. What did you do that for, Marks?

MARKS. You see, you get jist as much for him dead as alive in Kentucky.

GEORGE. Now, Phineas, the first man that advances I fire at; you take the second and so on. It won't do to waste two shots on one.

PHINEAS. But what if you don't hit?

GEORGE. I'll try my best.

PHINEAS. Creation! chaw me up if there a'nt stuff in you!

MARKS. I think I must have hit some on'em. I heard a squeal.

LOKER. I'm going right up for one. I never was afraid of niggers, and I an't a going to be now. Who goes after me?

(*Music. Loker dashes up the rock. George fires. He staggers for a moment, then springs to the top. Phineas seizes him. A struggle.*)

PHINEAS. Friend, thee is not wanted here! (*Throws Loker over the rock.*)

MARKS. (*Retreating.*) Lord help us—they're perfect devils!

(*Music. Marks and Party run off. George and Eliza kneel in an attitude of thanksgiving, with the Child between them. Phineas stands over them exulting. Tableau.*)

END OF ACT II

ACT III

SCENE I

Chamber. Enter St. Clare, followed by Tom.

ST. CLARE. (*Giving money and papers to Tom.*) There, Tom, are the bills, and the money to liquidate them.

TOM. Yes, mas'r.

ST. CLARE. Well, Tom, what are you waiting for? Isn't all right there?

TOM. I'm 'fraid not, mas'r.

ST. CLARE. Why, Tom, what's the matter? You look as solemn as a judge.

TOM. I feel very bad, mas'r. I allays have thought that mas'r would be good to everybody.

ST. CLARE. Well, Tom, haven't I been? Come, now, what do you want? There's something you haven't got, I suppose, and this is the preface.

TOM. Mas'r allays been good to me. I haven't nothing to complain of on that head; but ther is one that mas'r isn't good to.

ST. CLARE. Why, Tom, what's got into you? Speak out—what do you mean?

TOM. Last night, between one and two, I thought so. I studied upon the matter then—mas'r isn't good to *himself*.

ST. CLARE. Ah! now I understand; you allude to the state in which I came home last night. Well, to tell the truth, I *was* slightly elevated—a little more champagne on board than I could comfortably carry. That's all, isn't it?

TOM. (*Deeply affected—clasping his hands and weeping.*) All! Oh! my dear young mas'r, I'm 'fraid it will be *loss of all—all*, body and soul. The good book says "it biteth like a serpent and stingeth like an adder," my dear mas'r.

ST. CLARE. You poor, silly fool! I'm not worth crying over.

TOM. Oh, mas'r! I implore you to think of it before it gets too late.

ST. CLARE. Well, I won't go to any more of their cursed nonsense, Tom—on my honor, I won't. I don't know why I haven't stopped long ago; I've always despised it, and myself for it. So now, Tom, wipe up your eyes and go about your errands.

TOM. Bless you, mas'r. I feel much better now. You have taken a load from poor Tom's heart. Bless you!

ST. CLARE. Come, come, no blessings; I'm not so wonderfully good, now. There, I'll pledge my honor to you, Tom, you don't see me so again. (*Exit Tom.*) I'll keep my faith with him, too.

OPHELIA. (*Without.*) Come along, you shiftless mortal!

ST. CLARE. What new witchcraft has Topsy been brewing? That commotion is of her raising, I'll be bound.

(*Enter Ophelia, dragging in Topsy.*)

OPHELIA. Come here now; I will tell your master.

ST. CLARE. What's the matter now?

OPHELIA. The matter is that I cannot be plagued with this girl any longer. It's past all bearing; flesh and blood cannot endure it. Here I locked her up and gave her a hymn to study; and what does she do but spy out where I put my key, and has gone to my bureau, and got a bonnet-trimming and cut it all to pieces to make dolls' jackets! I never saw anything like it in my life!

ST. CLARE. What have you done to her?

OPHELIA. What have I done? What haven't I done? Your wife says I ought to have her whipped till she couldn't stand.

ST. CLARE. I don't doubt it. Tell me of the lovely rule of woman. I never saw above a dozen women that wouldn't half kill a horse or servant, either, if they had their own way with them—let alone a man.

OPHELIA. I am sure, St. Clare, I don't know what to do. I've taught and taught—I've talked till I'm tired; I've whipped her, I've punished her in every way I could think of, and still she's just what she was at first.

ST. CLARE. Come here, Tops, you monkey! (*Topsy crosses to St. Clare, grinning.*) What makes you behave so?

TOPSY. 'Spects it's my wicked heart—Miss Feely says so.

ST. CLARE. Don't you see how much Miss Ophelia has done for you? She says she has done everything she can think of.

TOPSY. Lord, yes, mas'r! old missis used to say so, too. She whipped me a heap harder, and used to pull my ha'r, and knock my head agin the door; but it didn't do me no good. I 'spects if they's to pull every spear of ha'r out o' my head, it wouldn't do no good neither—I's so wicked! Laws! I's nothin' but a nigger, no ways! (*Goes up.*)

OPHELIA. Well, I shall have to give her up; I can't have that trouble any longer.

ST. CLARE. I'd like to ask you one question.

OPHELIA. What is it?

ST. CLARE. Why, if your doctrine is not strong enough to save one heathen child, that you can have at home here, all to yourself, what's the use of sending one or two poor missionaries off with it among thousands of just such? I suppose this girl is a fair sample of what thousands of your heathen are.

OPHELIA. I'm sure I don't know; I never saw such a girl as this.

ST. CLARE. What makes you so bad, Tops? Why won't you try and be good? Don't you love any one, Topsy?

TOPSY. (*Comes down.*) Dunno nothing 'bout love; I loves candy and sich, that's all.

OPHELIA. But, Topsy, if you'd only try to be good, you might.

TOPSY. Couldn't never be nothing but a nigger, if I was ever so good. If I could be skinned and come white, I'd try then.

ST. CLARE. People can love you, if you are black, Topsy. Miss Ophelia would love you, if you were good. (*Topsy laughs.*) Don't you think so?

TOPSY. No, she can't b'ar me, 'cause I'm a nigger—she'd soon have a toad touch her. There can't nobody love niggers, and niggers can't do nothin'! I don't car'! (*Whistles.*)

ST. CLARE. Silence, incorrigible imp, and begone!

TOPSY. He! he! he! didn't get much out of dis chile! (*Exit.*)

OPHELIA. I've always had a prejudice against negroes, and it's a fact—I never could bear to have that child touch me, but I didn't think she knew it.

ST. CLARE. Trust any child to find that out, there's no keeping it from them, but I believe all the trying in the world to benefit a child, and all the substantial favors you can do them, will never excite one emotion of gratitude, while that feeling of repugnance remains in the heart. It's a queer kind of a fact, but so it is.

OPHELIA. I don't know how I can help it—they are disagreeable to me, this girl in particular. How can I help feeling so?

ST. CLARE. Eva does, it seems.

OPHELIA. Well, she's so loving. I wish I was like her. She might teach me a lesson.

ST. CLARE. It would not be the first time a little child had been used to instruct an old discipline, if it were so. Come, let us seek Eva, in her favorite bower by the lake.

OPHELIA. Why, the dew is falling, she mustn't be out there. She is unwell, I know.

ST. CLARE. Don't be croaking, cousin—I hate it.

OPHELIA. But she has that cough.

ST. CLARE. Oh, nonsense, of that cough—it is not anything. She has taken a little cold, perhaps.

OPHELIA. Well, that was just the way Eliza Jane was taken—and Ellen—

ST. CLARE. Oh, stop these hobgoblin, nurse legends. You old hands get so wise, that a child cannot cough or sneeze,

but you see desperation and ruin at hand. Only take care
of the child, keep her from the night air, and don't let her
play too hard, and she'll do well enough.

(*Exeunt.*)

SCENE II

*The flat represents the lake. The rays of the setting sun
tinge the waters with gold. A large tree. Beneath this a
grassy bank, on which Eva and Tom are seated side by
side. Eva has a Bible open on her lap. Music.*

TOM. Read dat passage again, please, Miss Eva?

EVA. (*Reading.*) "And I saw a sea of glass, mingled with fire."
(*Stopping suddenly and pointing to lake.*) Tom, there it is!

TOM. What, Miss Eva?

EVA. Don't you see there? There's a "sea of glass mingled
with fire."

TOM. True enough, Miss Eva. (*Sings.*)

Oh, had I the wings of the morning,
I'd fly away to Canaan's shore;
Bright angels should convey me home,
To the New Jerusalem.

EVA. Where do you suppose New Jerusalem is, Uncle Tom?

TOM. Oh, up in the clouds, Miss Eva.

EVA. Then I think I see it. Look in those clouds, they look
like great gates of pearl; and you can see beyond them—
far, far off—it's all gold! Tom, sing about 'spirits bright.'

TOM. (*Sings.*)

I see a band of spirits bright,
That taste the glories there;
They are all robed in spotless white,
And conquering palms they bear.

EVA. Uncle Tom, I've seen *them*.

TOM. To be sure you have; you are one of them yourself. You
are the brightest spirit I ever saw.

EVA. They come to me sometimes in my sleep—those spirits bright—

They are all robed in spotless white,
And conquering palms they bear.
Uncle Tom, I'm going there.

TOM. Where, Miss Eva?

EVA. (*Pointing to the sky.*) I'm going there, to the spirits
bright, Tom; I'm going before long.

TOM. It's jest no use tryin' to keep Miss Eva here; I've allays
said so. She's got the Lord's mark in her forehead. She
wasn't never like a child that's to live—there was always
something deep in her eyes. (*Rises and comes forward. Eva
also comes forward, leaving Bible on bank.*)

(*Enter St. Clare.*)

ST. CLARE. Ah! my little pussy, you look as blooming as a
rose! You are better now-a-days, are you not?

EVA. Papa, I've had things I wanted to say to you a great
while. I want to say them now, before I get weaker.

ST. CLARE. Nay, this is an idle fear, Eva; you know you grow
stronger every day.

EVA. It's all no use, papa, to keep it to myself any longer.
The time is coming that I am going to leave you, I am
going, and never to come back.

ST. CLARE. Oh, now, my dear little Eva! you've got nervous
and low spirited; you mustn't indulge such gloomy
thoughts.

EVA. No, papa, don't deceive yourself, I am *not* any better; I
know it perfectly well, and I am going before long. I am
not nervous—I am not low spirited. If it were not for you,
papa, and my friends, I should be perfectly happy. I want
to go—I long to go!

ST. CLARE. Why, dear child, what has made your poor little
heart so sad? You have everything to make you happy that
could be given you.

EVA. I had rather be in heaven! There are a great many
things here that make me sad—that seem dreadful to me;
I had rather be there; but I don't want to leave you—it almost breaks my heart!

ST. CLARE. What makes you sad, and what seems dreadful,
Eva?

EVA. I feel sad for our poor people; they love me dearly, and
they are all good and kind to me. I wish, papa, they were
all *free*!

ST. CLARE. Why, Eva, child, don't you think they are well
enough off now?

EVA. (*Not heeding the question.*) Papa, isn't there a way to
have slaves made free? When I am dead, papa, then you
will think of me and do it for my sake?

ST. CLARE. When you are dead, Eva? Oh, child, don't talk to
me so. You are all I have on earth!

EVA. Papa, these poor creatures love their children as much
as you do me. Tom loves his children. Oh, do something
for them!

ST. CLARE. There, there, darling; only don't distress yourself,
and don't talk of dying, and I will do anything you wish.

EVA. And promise me, dear father, that Tom shall have his
freedom as soon as—(*Hesitating.*) —I am gone!

ST. CLARE. Yes, dear, I will do anything in the world—anything you could ask me to. There, Tom, take her to her
chamber, this evening air is too chill for her. (*Music.
Kisses her. Tom takes Eva in his arms, and exits. Gazing
mournfully after Eva.*) Has there ever been a child like
Eva? Yes, there has been; but their names are always on
grave-stones, and their sweet smiles, their heavenly eyes,
their singular words and ways, are among the buried treasures of yearning hearts. It is as if heaven had an especial
band of angels, whose office it is to sojourn for a season
here, and endear to them the wayward human heart, that
they might bear it upward with them in their homeward
flight. When you see that deep, spiritual light in the eye

when the little soul reveals itself in words sweeter and wiser than the ordinary words of children, hope not to retain that child; for the seal of heaven is on it, and the light of immortality looks out from its eyes! (*Music. Exit.*)

SCENE III

A corridor. Proscenium doors on. Music. Enter Tom, he listens at door and then lies down. Enter Ophelia, with candle.

OPHELIA. Uncle Tom, what alive have you taken to sleeping anywhere and everywhere, like a dog, for? I thought you were one of the orderly sort, that liked to lie in bed in a Christian way.

TOM. (*Rises. Mysteriously.*) I do, Miss Feely, I do, but now—

OPHELIA. Well, what now?

TOM. We mustn't speak loud; Mas'r St. Clare won't hear on't; but Miss Feely, you know there must be somebody watchin' for the bridegroom.

OPHELIA. What do you mean, Tom?

TOM. You know it says in Scripture, "At midnight there was a great cry made, behold, the bridegroom cometh!" That's what I'm spectin' now, every night, Miss Feely, and I couldn't sleep out of hearing, noways.

OPHELIA. Why, Uncle Tom, what makes you think so?

TOM. Miss Eva, she talks to me. The Lord, he sends his messenger in the soul. I must be thar, Miss Feely; for when that ar blessed child goes into the kingdom, they'll open the door so wide, we'll all get a look at the glory!

OPHELIA. Uncle Tom, did Miss Eva say she felt more unwell than usual tonight?

TOM. No; but she told me she was coming nearer—thar's them that tells it to the child, Miss Feely. It's the angels—it's the trumpet sound afore the break o' day!

OPHELIA. Heaven grant your fears be vain! Come in, Tom.
(*Exeunt.*)

SCENE IV

Eva's Chamber. Eva discovered on a couch. A table stands near the couch with a lamp on it. The light shines upon Eva's face, which is very pale. Scene half dark. Uncle Tom is kneeling near the foot of the couch, Ophelia stands at the head, St. Clare at back. Scene opens to plaintive music. After a strain enter Marie, hastily.

MARIE. St. Clare! Cousin! Oh! what is the matter now?

ST. CLARE. (*Hoarsely.*) Hush! she is dying!

MARIE. (*Sinking on her knees, beside Tom.*) Dying!

ST. CLARE. Oh! if she would only wake and speak once more. (*Bending over Eva.*) Eva, darling! (*Eva uncloses her eyes, smiles, raises her head and tries to speak.*) Do you know me, Eva?

EVA. (*Throwing her arms feebly about his neck.*) Dear papa. (*Her arms drop and she sinks back.*)

ST. CLARE. Oh heaven! this is dreadful! Oh! Tom, my boy, it is killing me!

TOM. Look at her, mas'r. (*Points to Eva.*)

ST. CLARE. (*A pause.*) She does not hear. Oh Eva! tell us what you see. What is it?

EVA. (*Feebly smiling.*) Oh! love! joy! peace! (*Dies.*)

TOM. Oh, bless the Lord! it's over, dear mas'r, it's over.

ST. CLARE. (*Sinking on his knees.*) Farewell, beloved child! the bright eternal doors have closed after thee. We shall see thy sweet face no more. Oh! woe for them who watched thy entrance into heaven when they shall wake and find only the cold, gray sky of daily life and thou gone forever. (*Solemn music, slow curtain.*)

END OF ACT III

ACT IV

SCENE I

A street in New Orleans. Enter Gumption Cute, meeting Marks.

CUTE. How do ye dew?

MARKS. How are you?

CUTE. Well, now, squire, it's a fact that I am dead broke and busted up.

MARKS. You have been speculating, I suppose!

CUTE. That's just it and nothing shorter.

MARKS. You have had poor success, you say?

CUTE. Tarnation bad, now I tell you. You see I came to this part of the country to make my fortune.

MARKS. And you did not do it?

CUTE. Scarcely. The first thing I tried my hand at was keeping school. I opened an academy for the instruction of youth in the various branches of orthography, geography, and other graphies.

MARKS. Did you succeed in getting any pupils?

CUTE. Oh, lots of 'em! and a pretty set of dunces they were too. After the first quarter, I called on the respectable parents of the juveniles, and requested them to fork over. To which they politely answered—don't you wish you may get it?

MARKS. What did you do then?

CUTE. Well, I kind of pulled up stakes and left those diggins. Well then I went into Spiritual Rappings for a living. That paid pretty well for a short time, till I met with an accident.

MARKS. An accident?

CUTE. Yes; a tall Yahoo called on me one day, and wanted me to summon the spirit of his mother—which, of course, I did. He asked me about a dozen questions which I answered to his satisfaction. At last he wanted to know what she died of—I said, Cholera. You never did see a critter so riled as he was. 'Look yere, stranger,' said he, 'it's my opinion that you're a pesky humbug! for my mother was blown up in a *Steamboat!*' with that he left the premises. The next day the people furnished me with a conveyance, and I rode out of town.

MARKS. Rode out of town?

CUTE. Yes; on a rail!

MARKS. I suppose you gave up the spirits, after that?

CUTE. Well, I reckon I did; it had such an effect on my spirits.

MARKS. It's a wonder they didn't tar and feather you.

CUTE. There was some mention made of that, but when they said *feathers*, I felt as if I had wings and flew away.

MARKS. You cut and run?

CUTE. Yes; I didn't like their company and I cut it. Well, after that I let myself out as an overseer on a cotton plantation. I made a pretty good thing of that, though it was dreadful trying to my feelings to flog the darkies; but I got used to it after a while, and then I used to lather 'em like Jehu. Well, the proprietor got the fever and ague and shook himself out of town. The place and all the fixings were sold at auction and I found myself adrift once more.

MARKS. What are you doing at present?

CUTE. I'm in search of a rich relation of mine.

MARKS. A rich relation?

CUTE. Yes, a Miss Ophelia St. Clare. You see, a niece of hers married one of my second cousins—that's how I came to be a relation of hers. She came on here from Vermont to be housekeeper to a cousin of hers, of the same name.

MARKS. I know him well.

CUTE. The deuce you do!—well, that's lucky.

MARKS. Yes, he lives in this city.

CUTE. Say, you just point out the locality, and I'll give him a call.

MARKS. Stop a bit. Suppose you shouldn't be able to raise the wind in that quarter, what have you thought of doing?

CUTE. Well, nothing particular.

MARKS. How should you like to enter into a nice, profitable business—one that pays well?

CUTE. That's just about my measure—it would suit me to a hair. What is it?

MARKS. Nigger catching.

CUTE. Catching niggers! What on earth do you mean?

MARKS. Why, when there's a large reward offered for a runaway darkey, we goes after him, catches him, and gets the reward.

CUTE. Yes, that's all right so far—but s'pose there ain't no reward offered?

MARKS. Why, then we catches the darkey on our own account, sells him, and pockets the proceeds.

CUTE. By chowder, that ain't a bad speculation!

MARKS. What do you say? I want a partner. You see, I lost my partner last year, up in Ohio—he was a powerful fellow.

CUTE. Lost him! How did you lose him?

MARKS. Well, you see, Tom and I—his name was Tom Loker—Tom and I were after a mulatto chap, called George Harris, that run away from Kentucky. We traced him through the greater part of Ohio, and came up with him near the Pennsylvania line. He took refuge among some rocks, and showed fight.

CUTE. Oh! then runaway darkies show fight, do they?

MARKS. Sometimes. Well, Tom—like a headstrong fool as he was—rushed up the rocks, and a Quaker chap, who was helping this George Harris, threw him over the cliff.

CUTE. Was he killed?

MARKS. Well, I didn't stop to find out. Seeing that the darkies were stronger than I thought, I made tracks for a safe place.

CUTE. And what became of this George Harris?

MARKS. Oh! he and his wife and child got away safe into Canada. You see they will get away sometimes though it isn't very often. Now what do you say? You are just the figure for a fighting partner. Is it a bargain?

CUTE. Well, I rather calculate our teams won't hitch, no how. By chowder, I hain't no idea of setting myself up as a target for darkies to fire at—that's a speculation that don't suit my constitution.

MARKS. You're afraid, then?

CUTE. No, I ain't, it's against my principles.

MARKS. Your principles—how so?

CUTE. Because my principles are to keep a sharp lookout for No. 1. I shouldn't feel wholesome if a darkie was to throw me over that cliff to look after Tom Loker. (*Exeunt arm-in-arm.*)

SCENE II

Gothic Chamber. Slow music. St. Clare discovered, seated on sofa. Tom at left.

ST. CLARE. Oh! Tom, my boy, the whole world is as empty as an egg shell.

TOM. I know it, mas'r, I know it. But oh! if mas'r could look up—up where our dear Miss Eva is—

ST. CLARE. Ah, Tom! I do look up; but the trouble is, I don't see anything when I do. I wish I could. It seems to be given to children and poor, honest fellows like you, to see what we cannot. How comes it?

TOM. Thou hast hid from the wise and prudent, and revealed unto babies; even so, Father, for so it seemed good in thy sight.

ST. CLARE. Tom, I don't believe—I've got the habit of doubting—I want to believe and I cannot.

TOM. Dear mas'r, pray to the good Lord: "Lord, I believe; help thou my unbelief."

ST. CLARE. Who knows anything about anything? Was all that beautiful love and faith only one of the ever-shifting phases of human feeling, having nothing real to rest on, passing away with the little breath? And is there no more Eva—nothing?

TOM. Oh! dear mas'r, there is. I know it; I'm sure of it. Do, do, dear mas'r, believe it!

ST. CLARE. How do you know there is, Tom? You never saw the Lord.

TOM. Felt Him in my soul, mas'r—feel Him now! Oh, mas'r! when I was sold away from my old woman and the children, I was jest a'most broken up—I felt as if there warn't nothing left—and then the Lord stood by me, and He says, "Fear not, Tom," and He brings light and joy into a poor fellow's soul—makes all peace; and I's so happy, and loves everybody, and feels willin' to be jest where the Lord wants to put me. I know it couldn't come from me, 'cause I's a poor, complaining creature—it comes from above, and I know He's willin' to do for mas'r.

ST. CLARE. (Grasping Tom's hand.) Tom, you love me!

TOM. I's willin' to lay down my life this blessed day for you.

ST. CLARE. (Sadly.) Poor, foolish fellow! I'm not worth the love of one good, honest heart like yours.

TOM. Oh, mas'r! there's more than me loves you—the blessed Saviour loves you.

ST. CLARE. How do you know that, Tom?

TOM. The love of the Saviour passeth knowledge.

ST. CLARE. (Turns away.) Singular! that the story of a man who lived and died eighteen hundred years ago can affect people so yet. But He was no man. (Rises.) No man ever had such long and living power. Oh! that I could believe what my mother taught me, and pray as I did when I was a boy! But, Tom, all this time I have forgotten why I sent for you. I'm going to make a freeman of you. Go have your trunk packed, and get ready to set out for Kentucky.

TOM. (Joyfully.) Bless the Lord!

ST. CLARE. (Dryly.) You haven't had such very bad times here, that you need be in such a rapture, Tom.

TOM. No, no, mas'r, 'tain't that; it's being a *freeman*—that's what I'm joyin' for.

ST. CLARE. Why, Tom, don't you think, for your own part, you've been better off than to be free?

TOM. No, *indeed*, Mas'r St. Clare—no, indeed!

ST. CLARE. Why, Tom, you couldn't possibly have earned, by your work, such clothes and such living as I have given you.

TOM. I know all that, Mas'r St. Clare—mas'r's been too good; but I'd rather have poor clothes, poor house, poor everything, and have 'em *mine*, than have the best, if they belong to somebody else. I had *so*, mas'r; I think it's natur', mas'r.

ST. CLARE. I suppose so, Tom; and you'll be going off and leaving me in a month or so—though why you shouldn't no mortal knows.

TOM. Not while mas'r is in trouble. I'll stay with mas'r as long as he wants me, so as I can be any use.

ST. CLARE. (Sadly.) Not while I'm in trouble, Tom? And when will my trouble be over?

TOM. When you are a believer.

ST. CLARE. And you really mean to stay by me till that day comes? (Smiling and laying his hand on Tom's shoulder.) Ah, Tom! I won't keep you till that day. Go home to your wife and children, and give my love to all.

TOM. I's faith to think that day will come—the Lord has a work for mas'r.

ST. CLARE. A work, hey? Well, now, Tom, give me your views on what sort of a work it is—let's hear.

TOM. Why, even a poor fellow like me has a work; and Mas'r St. Clare, that has larnin', and riches, and friends, how much he might do for the Lord.

ST. CLARE. Tom, you seem to think the Lord needs a great deal done for him.

TOM. We does for him when we does for his creatures.

ST. CLARE. Good theology, Tom. Thank you, my boy; I like to hear you talk. But go now, Tom, and leave me alone. (Exit Tom.) That faithful fellow's words have excited a train of thoughts that almost bear me, on the strong tide of faith and feeling, to the gates of that heaven I so vividly conceive. They seem to bring me nearer to Eva.

OPHELIA. (Outside.) What are you doing there, you limb of Satan? You've been stealing something, I'll be bound.

(Ophelia drags in Topsy.)

TOPSY. You go 'long, Miss Feely, 'tain't none o' your business.

ST. CLARE. Heyday! what is all this commotion?

OPHELIA. She's been stealing.

TOPSY. (Sobbing.) I hain't neither.

OPHELIA. What have you got in your bosom?

TOPSY. I've got my hand dar.

OPHELIA. But what have you got in your hand?

TOPSY. Nuffin'.

OPHELIA. That's a fib, Topsy.

TOPSY. Well, I 'spects it is.

OPHELIA. Give it to me, whatever it is.

TOPSY. It's mine—I hope I may die this bressed minute, if it don't belong to me.

OPHELIA. Topsy, I order you to give me that article; don't let me have to ask you again. (Topsy reluctantly takes the foot of an old stocking from her bosom and hands it to Ophelia.) Sakes alive! what is all this? (Takes from it a lock of hair, and a small book, with a bit of crape twisted around it.)

TOPSY. Dat's a lock of ha'r dat Miss Eva give me—she cut it from her own beau'ful head herself.

ST. CLARE. (Takes book.) Why did you wrap this (Pointing to crape) around the book?

TOPSY. 'Cause—'cause—'cause 'twas Miss Eva's. Oh! don't take 'em away, please! (Sits down on stage, and, putting her apron over her head, begins to sob vehemently.)

OPHELIA. Come, come, don't cry; you shall have them.

TOPSY. (*Jumps up joyfully and takes them.*) I wants to keep 'em, 'cause dey makes me good; I ain't half so wicked as I used to was. (*Runs off.*)

ST. CLARE. I really think you can make something of that girl. Any mind that is capable of a *real sorrow* is capable of good. You must try and do something with her.

OPHELIA. The child has improved very much; I have great hopes of her.

ST. CLARE. I believe I'll go down the street, a few moments, and hear the news.

OPHELIA. Shall I call Tom to attend you?

ST. CLARE. No, I shall be back in an hour. (*Exit.*)

OPHELIA. He's got an excellent heart, but then he's so dreadful shiftless! (*Exit.*)

SCENE III

Front Chamber, Enter Topsy.

TOPSY. Dar's somethin' de matter wid me—I isn't a bit like myself. I haven't done anything wrong since poor Miss Eva went up in de skies and left us. When I's gwine to do anything wicked, I tinks of her, and somehow I can't do it. I's getting to be good, dat's a fact. I 'spects when I's dead I shall be turned into a little brack angel.

(*Enter Ophelia.*)

OPHELIA. Topsy, I've been looking for you; I've got something very particular to say to you.

TOPSY. Does you want me to say the catechism?

OPHELIA. No, not now.

TOPSY. (*Aside.*) Golly! dat's one comfort.

OPHELIA. Now, Topsy, I want you to try and understand what I am going to say to you.

TOPSY. Yes, missis, I'll open my ears dreful wide.

OPHELIA. Mr. St. Clare has given you to me, Topsy.

TOPSY. Den I b'longs to you, don't I? Golly! I thought I always belong to you.

OPHELIA. Not till to-day have I received any authority to call you my property.

TOPSY. I's your property, am I? Well, if you say so, I 'spects I am.

OPHELIA. Topsy, I can give you your liberty.

TOPSY. My liberty?

OPHELIA. Yes, Topsy.

TOPSY. Has you got 'um with you?

OPHELIA. I have, Topsy.

TOPSY. Is it clothes or wittles?

OPHELIA. How shiftless! Don't you know what your liberty is, Topsy?

TOPSY. How should I know when I never seed 'um?

OPHELIA. Topsy, I am going to leave this place; I am going many miles away—to my home in Vermont.

TOPSY. Den what's to become of dis chile?

OPHELIA. If you wish to go, I will take you with me.

TOPSY. Miss Feely, I doesn't want to leave you no how, I loves you I does.

OPHELIA. Then you shall share my home for the rest of your days. Come, Topsy.

TOPSY. Stop, Miss Feely does dey hab any oberseers in Varmount?

OPHELIA. No, Topsy.

TOPSY. Nor cotton plantations, nor sugar factories, nor darkies, nor whipping nor nothing?

OPHELIA. No, Topsy.

TOPSY. By Golly! de quicker you is gwine de better den.

(*Enter Tom, hastily.*)

TOM. Oh, Miss Feely! Miss Feely!

OPHELIA. Gracious me, Tom! what's the matter?

TOM. Oh, Mas'r St. Clare! Mas'r St. Clare!

OPHELIA. Well, Tom, well?

TOM. They've just brought him home and I do believe he's killed.

OPHELIA. Killed?

TOPSY. Oh, dear! what's to become of de poor darkies now?

TOM. He's dreadful weak. It's just as much as he can do to speak. He wanted me to call you.

OPHELIA. My poor cousin! Who would have thought of it? Don't say a word to his wife, Tom; the danger may not be so great as you think; it would only distress her. Come with me; you may be able to afford some assistance.

(*Exeunt.*)

SCENE IV

Handsome Chamber. St. Clare discovered seated on sofa. Ophelia, Tom and Topsy are clustered around him. Doctor back of sofa feeling his pulse. Scene opens to slow music.

ST. CLARE. (*Raising himself feebly.*) Tom—poor fellow!

TOM. Well, mas'r?

ST. CLARE. I have received my death wound.

TOM. Oh, no, no, mas'r!

ST. CLARE. I feel that I am dying—Tom, pray!

TOM. (*Sinking on his knees.*) I do, pray, mas'r! I do pray!

ST. CLARE. (*After a pause.*) Tom, one thing preys upon my mind—I have forgotten to sign your freedom papers. What will become of you when I am gone?

TOM. Don't think of that, mas'r.

ST. CLARE. I was wrong, Tom, very wrong, to neglect it. I may be the cause of much suffering to you hereafter. Marie, my wife—she—oh!—

OPHELIA. His mind is wandering.

ST. CLARE. (*Energetically.*) No! it is coming home at last! (*Sinks back.*) At last! at last! Eva, I come! (*Dies. Music— slow curtain.*)

END OF ACT IV

ACT V

SCENE I

An Auction Mart. Uncle Tom and Emmeline at back. Adolf, Skeggs, Marks, Mann, and various spectators discovered. Marks and Mann come forward.

MARKS. Hulloa, Alf! what brings you here?

MANN. Well, I was wanting a valet, and I heard that St. Clare's valet was going. I thought I'd just look at them.

MARKS. Catch me ever buying any of St. Clare's people. Spoiled niggers every one—impudent as the devil.

MANN. Never fear that; if I get 'em, I'll soon have their airs out of them—they'll soon find that they've another kind of master to deal with than St. Clare. 'Pon my word, I'll buy that fellow—I like the shape of him. (*Pointing to Adolf.*)

MARKS. You'll find it'll take all you've got to keep him—he's deucedly extravagant.

MANN. Yes, but my lord will find that he can't be extravagant with me. Just let him be sent to the calaboose a few times, and thoroughly dressed down, I'll tell you if it don't bring him to a sense of his ways. Oh! I'll reform him, up hill and down, you'll see. I'll buy him; that's flat.

(Enter Legree, he goes up and looks at Adolf, whose boots are nicely blacked.)

LEGREE. A nigger with his boots blacked—bah! (*Spits on them.*) Holloa, you! (*To Tom.*) Let's see your teeth. (*Seizes Tom by the jaw and opens his mouth.*) Strip up your sleeve and show your muscle. (*Tom does so.*) Where was you raised?

TOM. In Kintuck, mas'r.

LEGREE. What have you done?

TOM. Had care of mas'r's farm.

LEGREE. That's a likely story. (*Turns to Emmeline.*) You're a nice-looking girl enough. How old are you? (*Grasps her arm.*)

EMMELINE. (*Shrieking.*) Ah! you hurt me.

SKEGGS. Stop that, you minx! No whimpering here. The sale is going to begin. (*Mounts the rostrum.*) Gentlemen, the next article I shall offer you to-day is Adolf, late valet to Mr. St. Clare. How much am I offered? (*Various bids are made. Adolf is knocked down to Mann for eight hundred dollars.*) Gentlemen, I now offer a prime article—the quadroon girl, Emmeline, only fifteen years of age, warranted in every respect. (*Business as before. Emmeline is sold to Legree for one thousand dollars.*) Now, I shall close to-day's sale by offering you the valuable article known as Uncle Tom, the most useful nigger ever raised. Gentlemen in want of an overseer, now is the time to bid.

(Business as before. Tom is sold to Legree for twelve hundred dollars.)

LEGREE. Now look here, you two belong to me. (*Tom and Emmeline sink on their knees.*)

TOM. Heaven help us, then!

(Music. Legree stands over them exulting. Picture—closed in.)

SCENE II

The Garden of Miss Ophelia's House in Vermont. Enter Ophelia and Deacon Perry.

DEACON. Miss Ophelia, allow me to offer you my congratulations upon your safe arrival in your native place. I hope it is your intention to pass the remainder of your days with us?

OPHELIA. Well, Deacon, I have come here with that express purpose.

DEACON. I presume you were not over-pleased with the South?

OPHELIA. Well, to tell you the truth, Deacon, I wasn't; I liked the country very well, but the people there are so dreadful shiftless.

DEACON. The result, I presume, of living in a warm climate.

OPHELIA. Well, Deacon, what is the news among you all here?

DEACON. Well, we live on in the same even jog-trot pace. Nothing of any consequence has happened—Oh! I forgot. (*Takes out handkerchief.*) I've lost my wife; my Molly has left me. (*Wipes his eyes.*)

OPHELIA. Poor soul! I pity you, Deacon.

DEACON. Thank you. You perceive I bear my loss with resignation.

OPHELIA. How you must miss her tongue!

DEACON. Molly certainly was fond of talking. She always would have the last word—heigho!

OPHELIA. What was her complaint, Deacon?

DEACON. A mild and soothing one, Miss Ophelia: she had a severe attack of the lockjaw.

OPHELIA. Dreadful!

DEACON. Wasn't it? When she found she couldn't use her tongue, she took it so much to heart that it struck to her stomach and killed her. Poor dear! Excuse my handkerchief; she's been dead only eighteen months.

OPHELIA. Why, Deacon, by this time you ought to be setting your cap for another wife.

DEACON. Do you think so, Miss Ophelia?

OPHELIA. I don't see why you shouldn't—you are still a good-looking man, Deacon.

DEACON. Ah! well, I think I do wear well—in fact, I may say remarkably well. It has been observed to me before.

OPHELIA. And you are not much over fifty?

DEACON. Just turned of forty, I assure you.

OPHELIA. Hale and hearty?

DEACON. Health excellent—look at my eye! Strong as a lion—look at my arm!! A No. 1 constitution—look at my leg!!!

OPHELIA. Have you no thoughts of choosing another partner?

DEACON. Well, to tell you the truth, I have.

OPHELIA. Who is she?

DEACON. She is not far distant. (*Looks at Ophelia in an anguishing manner.*) I have her in my eye at this present moment.

OPHELIA. (*Aside.*) Really, I believe he's going to pop. Why, surely, Deacon, you don't mean to—

DEACON. Yes, Miss Ophelia, I do mean; and believe me, when I say—(*Looking off.*) The Lord be good to us, but I believe there is the devil coming!

(*Topsy runs on, with bouquet. She is now dressed very neatly.*)

TOPSY. Miss Feely, here is some flowers dat I hab been gathering for you. (*Gives bouquet.*)

OPHELIA. That's a good child.

DEACON. Miss Ophelia, who is this young person?

OPHELIA. She is my daughter.

DEACON. (*Aside.*) Her daughter! Then she must have married a colored man off South. I was not aware that you had been married, Miss Ophelia.

OPHELIA. Married! Sakes alive! what made you think I had been married?

DEACON. Good gracious, I'm getting confused. Didn't I understand you to say that this—somewhat tanned—young lady was your daughter?

OPHELIA. Only by adoption. She is my adopted daughter.

DEACON. O—oh! (*Aside.*) I breathe again.

TOPSY. By Golly! dat old man's eyes stick out of 'um head dre'ful. Guess he never seed anything like me afore.

OPHELIA. Deacon, won't you step into the house and refresh yourself after your walk?

DEACON. I accept your polite invitation. (*Offers his arm.*) Allow me.

OPHELIA. As gallant as ever, Deacon. I declare, you grow younger every day.

DEACON. You can never grow old, madam.

OPHELIA. Ah, you flatterer! (*Exeunt.*)

TOPSY. Dar dey go, like an old goose and gander. Guess dat ole gemblemun feels kindof confectionary—rather sweet on my old missis. By Golly! she's been dre'ful kind to me ever since I come away from de South; and I loves her, I does, 'cause she takes such car' on me and gives me dese fine clothes. I tries to be good too, and I's getting 'long 'mazin' fast. I's not so wicked as I used to was. (*Looks out.*) Holloa! dar's some one comin' here. I wonder what he wants now. (*Retires, observing.*)

(*Enter Gumption Cute, very shabby, a small bundle, on a stick, over his shoulder.*)

CUTE. By chowder, here I am again. Phew, it's a pretty considerable tall piece of walking between here and New Orleans, not to mention the wear of shoe-leather. I guess I'm about done up. If this streak of bad luck lasts much longer, I'll borrow sixpence to buy a rope, and hang myself right straight up! When I went to call on Miss Ophelia, I swow if I didn't find out that she had left for Vermont; so I kind of concluded to make tracks in that direction myself and as I didn't have any money left, why I had to foot it, and here I am in old Varmount once more. They told me Miss Ophelia lived up here. I wonder if she will remember the relationship. (*Sees Topsy.*) By chowder, there's a darkey. Look here, Charcoal!

TOPSY. (*Comes forward.*) My name isn't Charcoal—it's Topsy.

CUTE. Oh! your name is Topsy, is it, you juvenile specimen of Day & Martin?

TOPSY. Tell you I don't know nothin' 'bout Day & Martin. I's Topsy and I belong to Miss Feely St. Clare.

CUTE. I'm much obleeged to you, you small extract of Japan, for your information. So Miss Ophelia lives up there in the white house, does she?

TOPSY. Well, she don't do nothin' else.

CUTE. Well, then, just locomote your pins.

TOPSY. What—what's dat?

CUTE. Walk your chalks!

TOPSY. By Golly! dere ain't no chalk 'bout me.

CUTE. Move your trotters.

TOPSY. How you does spoke! What you mean by trotters?

CUTE. Why, your feet, Stove Polish.

TOPSY. What does you want me to move my feet for?

CUTE. To tell your mistress, you ebony angel, that a gentleman wishes to see her.

TOPSY. Does you call yourself a gentleman! By Golly! You look more like a scar'crow.

CUTE. Now look here, you Charcoal, don't you be sassy. I'm a gentleman in distress; a done-up speculator; one that has seen better days—long time ago—and better clothes too, by chowder! My creditors are like my boots—they've no soles. I'm a victim to circumstances. I've been through much and survived it. I've taken walking exercise for the benefit of my health; but as I was trying to live on air at the same time, it was a losing speculation, 'cause it gave me such a dreadful appetite.

TOPSY. Golly! you look as if you could eat an ox, horns and all.

CUTE. Well, I calculate I could, if he was roasted—it's a speculation I should like to engage in. I have returned like the fellow that run away in Scripture; and if anybody's got a fatted calf they want to kill, all they got to do is to fetch him along. Do you know, Charcoal, that your mistress is a relation of mine?

TOPSY. Is she your uncle?

CUTE. No, no, not quite so near as that. My second cousin married her niece.

TOPSY. And does you want to see Miss Feely?

CUTE. I do. I have come to seek a home beneath her roof, and take care of all the spare change she don't want to use.

TOPSY. Den just you follow me, mas'r.

CUTE. Stop! By chowder, I've got a great idea. Say, you Day & Martin, how should you like to enter into a speculation?

TOPSY. Golly! I don't know what a spec—spec—cu—what-do-you-call-'um am.

CUTE. Well, now, I calculate I've hit upon the right thing. Why should I degrade the manly dignity of the Cutes by becoming a beggar—expose myself to the chance of receiving the cold shoulder as a poor relation? By chowder, my blood biles as I think of it! Topsy, you can make my fortune, and your own, too. I've an idee in my head that is worth a million of dollars.

TOPSY. Golly! is your head worth dat? Guess you wouldn't bring dat out South for de whole of you.

CUTE. Don't you be too severe, now, Charcoal; I'm a man of genius. Did you ever hear of Barnum?

TOPSY. Barnum! Barnum! Does he live out South?

CUTE. No, he lives in New York. Do you know how he made his fortin?

TOPSY. What is him fortin, hey? Is it something he wears?

CUTE. Chowder, how green you are!

TOPSY. (Indignantly.) Sar, I hab you to know I's not green; I's brack.

CUTE. To be sure you are, Day & Martin. I calculate, when a person says another has a fortune, he means he's got plento of money, Charcoal.

TOPSY. And did he make the money?

CUTE. Sartin sure, and no mistake.

TOPSY. Golly! now I thought money always growed.

CUTE. Oh, git out! You are too cute—you are cuterer than I am—and I'm Cute by name and cute by nature. Well, as I was saying, Barnum made his money by exhibiting a *woolly* horse; now wouldn't it be an all-fired speculation to show you as the woolly gal?

TOPSY. You want to make a sight of me?

CUTE. I'll give you half the receipts, by chowder!

TOPSY. Should I have to leave Miss Feely?

CUTE. To be sure you would.

TOPSY. Den you hab to get a woolly gal somewhere else, Mas'r Cute. (Runs off.)

CUTE. There's another speculation gone to smash, by chowder! (Exit.)

SCENE III

A Rude Chamber. Tom is discovered, in old clothes, seated on a stool. He holds in his hand a paper containing a curl of Eva's hair. The scene opens to the symphony of "Old Folks at Home."

TOM. I have come to de dark places; I's going through de vale of shadows. My heart sinks at times and feels just like a big lump of lead. Den it gits up in my throat and chokes me till de tears roll out of my eyes; den I take out dis curl of little Miss Eva's hair, and the sight of it brings calm to my mind and I feels strong again. (*Kisses the curl and puts it in his breast—takes out a silver dollar, which is suspended around his neck by a string.*) Dere's de bright silver dollar dat Mas'r George Shelby gave me the day I was sold away from old Kentuck, and I've kept it ever since. Mas'r George must have grown to be a man by this time. I wonder if I shall see him again.

(*Song. "Old Folks at Home." Enter Legree, Emmeline, Sambo and Quimbo.*)

LEGREE. Shut up, you black cuss! Did you think I wanted any of your infernal howling? (*Turns to Emmeline.*) We're home. (*Emmeline shrinks from him. He takes hold of her ear.*) You didn't ever wear earrings?

EMMELINE. (*Trembling.*) No, master.

LEGREE. Well, I'll give you a pair, if you're a good girl. You needn't be so frightened. I don't mean to make you work very hard. You'll have fine times with me and live like a lady; only be a good girl.

EMMELINE. My soul sickens as his eyes gaze upon me. His touch makes my very flesh creep.

LEGREE. (*Turns to Tom, and points to Sambo and Quimbo.*) Ye see what ye'd get if ye'd try to run off. These yer boys have been raised to track niggers and they'd just as soon chaw one on ye up as eat their suppers; so mind yourself. (*To Emmeline.*) Come, mistress, you go in here with me. (*Taking Emmeline's hand, and leading her off.*)

EMMELINE. (*Withdrawing her hand, and shrinking back.*) No, no! let me work in the fields; I don't want to be a lady.

LEGREE. Oh! you're going to be contrary, are you? I'll soon take all that out of you.

EMMELINE. Kill me, if you will.

LEGREE. Oh! you want to be killed, do you? Now come here, you Tom, you see I told you I didn't buy you jest for the common work; I mean to promote you and make a driver of you, and to-night ye may jest as well begin to get yer hand in. Now ye jest take this yer gal, and flog her; ye've seen enough on't to know how.

TOM. I beg mas'r's pardon—hopes mas'r won't set me at that. It's what I a'nt used to—never did—and can't do—no way possible.

LEGREE. Ye'll larn a pretty smart chance of things ye never did know before I've done with ye! (*Strikes Tom with whip, three blows. Music chord each blow.*) There! now will ye tell me ye can't do it?

TOM. Yes, mas'r! I'm willing to work night and day, and work while there's life and breath in me; but this yer thing I can't feel it right to do, and, mas'r, I never shall do it, *never!*

LEGREE. What! ye black beast! tell *me* ye don't think it right to do what I tell ye! What have any of you cussed cattle to do with thinking what's right? I'll put a stop to it. Why, what do ye think ye are? May be ye think yer a gentleman, master Tom, to be telling your master what's right and what a'nt! So you pretend it's wrong to flog the gal?

TOM. I think so, mas'r: 'twould be downright cruel, and it's what I never will do, mas'r. If you mean to kill me, kill me; but as to raising my hand agin any one here, I never shall—I'll die first!

LEGREE. Well, here's a pious dog at last, let down among us sinners—powerful holy critter he must be. Here, you rascal! you make believe to be so pious, didn't you never read out of your Bible, "Servants, obey your masters"? An't I your master? Didn't I pay twelve hundred dollars, cash, for all there is inside your cussed old black shell? An't you mine, body and soul?

TOM. No, no! My soul a'nt yours, mas'r; you haven't bought it—ye can't buy it; it's been bought and paid for by one that is able to keep it, and you can't harm it!

LEGREE. I can't? we'll see, we'll see! Here, Sambo! Quimbo! give this dog such a breaking in as he won't get over this month!

EMMELINE. Oh, no! you will not be so cruel—have some mercy! (*Clings to Tom.*)

LEGREE. Mercy? you won't find any in this shop! Away with the black cuss! Flog him within an inch of his life!

(*Music, Sambo and Quimbo seize Tom and drag him up stage. Legree seizes Emmeline, and throws her round. She falls on her knees, with her hands lifted in supplication. Legree raises his whip, as if to strike Tom. Picture closed in.*)

SCENE IV

Plain Chamber. Enter Ophelia, followed by Topsy.

OPHELIA. A person inquiring for me, did you say, Topsy?

TOPSY. Yes, missis.

OPHELIA. What kind of a looking man is he?

TOPSY. By golly! he's very queer looking man, anyway; and den he talks so dre'ful funny. What does you think?—yah! yah! he wanted to 'zibite me as de woolly gal! yah! yah!

OPHELIA. Oh! I understand. Some cute Yankee, who wants to purchase you, to make a show of—the heartless wretch!

TOPSY. Dat's just him, missis; dat's just his name. He tole me dat it was Cute—Mr. Cute Speculashum—dat's him.

OPHELIA. What did you say to him, Topsy?

TOPSY. Well, I didn't say much, it was brief and to the point—I tole him I wouldn't leave you, Miss Feely, no how.

OPHELIA. That's right, Topsy; you know you are very comfortable here—you wouldn't fare quite so well if you went away among strangers.

TOPSY. By golly! I know dat; you takes care on me, and makes me good. I don't steal any now, and I don't swar,

and I don't dance breakdowns. Oh! I isn't so wicked as I used to was.

OPHELIA. That's right, Topsy; now show the gentleman, or whatever he is, up.

TOPSY. By golly! I guess he won't make much out of Miss Freely. (*Crosses and exits.*)

OPHELIA. I wonder who this person can be? Perhaps it is some old acquaintance, who has heard of my arrival, and who comes on a social visit.

(*Enter Cute.*)

CUTE. Aunt, how do ye do? Well, I swan, the sight of you is good for weak eyes. (*Offers his hand.*)

OPHELIA. (*Coldly drawing back.*) Really, sir, I can't say that I ever had the pleasure of seeing you before.

CUTE. Well, it's a fact that you never did. You see I never happened to be in your neighborhood afore now. Of course you've heard of me? I'm one of the Cutes—Gumption Cute, the first and only son of Josiah and Maria Cute, of Oniontown, on the Onion river in the north part of this ere State of Varmount.

OPHELIA. Can't say I ever heard the name before.

CUTE. Well then, I calculate your memory must be a little ricketty. I'm a relation of yours.

OPHELIA. A relation of mine! Why, I never heard of any Cutes in our family.

CUTE. Well, I shouldn't wonder if you never did. Don't you remember your niece, Mary?

OPHELIA. Of course I do. What a shiftless question!

CUTES. Well, you see my second cousin, Abijah Blake, married her. So you see that makes me a relation of yours.

OPHELIA. Rather a distant one, I should say.

CUTE. By chowder! I'm *near* enough, just at present.

OPHELIA. Well, you certainly are a sort of connection of mine.

CUTE. Yes, kind of sort of.

OPHELIA. And of course you are welcome to my house, as long as you wish to make it your home.

CUTE. By chowder! I'm booked for the next six months— this isn't a bad speculation.

OPHELIA. I hope you left all your folks well at home?

CUTE. Well, yes, they're pretty comfortably disposed of. Father and mother's dead, and Uncle Josh has gone to California. I am the only representative of the Cutes left.

OPHELIA. There doesn't seem to be a great deal of *you* left. I declare, you are positively in rags.

CUTE. Well, you see, the fact is, I've been speculating—trying to get banknotes—specie-rags, as they say—but I calculate I've turned out rags of another sort.

OPHELIA. I'm sorry for your ill luck, but I am afraid you have been shiftless.

CUTE. By chowder! I've done all that a fellow could do. You see, somehow, everything I take hold of kind of bursts up.

OPHELIA. Well, well, perhaps you'll do better for the future; make yourself at home. I have got to see to some household matters; so excuse me for a short time. (*Aside.*) Impudent and shiftless. (*Exit.*)

CUTE. By chowder! I rather guess that this speculation will hitch. She's a good-natured old critter; I reckon I'll be a son to her while she lives, and take care of her valuables arter she's a defunct departed. I wonder if they keep the vittles in this ere room? Guess not. I've got extensive accommodations for all sorts of eatables. I'm a regular vacuum, throughout—pockets and all. I'm chuck full of emptiness. (*Looks out.*) Holloa! who's this elderly individual coming up stairs? He looks like a compound essence of starch and dignity. I wonder if he isn't another relation of mine. I should like a rich old fellow now for an uncle.

(*Enter Deacon Perry.*)

DEACON. Ha! a stranger here!

CUTE. How d'ye do?

DEACON. You are a friend to Miss Ophelia, I presume?

CUTE. Well, I rather calculate that I am a leetle more than a friend.

DEACON. (*Aside.*) Bless me! what can he mean by those mysterious words? Can he be her—no I don't think he can. She said she wasn't—well, at all events, it's very suspicious.

CUTE. The old fellow seems kind of stuck up.

DEACON. You are a particular friend to Miss Ophelia, you say?

CUTE. Well, I calculate I am.

DEACON. Bound to her by tender tie?

CUTE. It's something more than a tie—it's a regular double-twisted knot.

DEACON. Ah! just as I expected. (*Aside.*) Might I inquire the nature of that tie?

CUTE. Well, it's the natural tie of relationship.

DEACON. A relation—what relation?

CUTE. Why, you see, my second cousin, Abijah Blake, married her niece, Mary.

DEACON. Oh! is that all?

CUTE. By chowder, ain't that enough?

DEACON. Then you are not her husband?

CUTE. To be sure I ain't. What put that ere idee into your cranium?

DEACON. (*Shaking him vigorously by the hand.*) My dear sir, I'm delighted to see you.

CUTE. Holloa! you ain't going slightly insane, are you?

DEACON. No, no fear of that; I'm only happy, that's all.

CUTE. I wonder if he's been taking a nipper?

DEACON. As you are a relation of Miss Ophelia's, I think it proper that I should make you my confidant; in fact, let you into a little scheme that I have lately conceived.

CUTE. Is it a speculation?

DEACON. Well, it is, just at present; but I trust before many hours to make it a surety.

CUTE. By chowder! I hope it won't serve you the way my speculations have served me. But fire away, old boy, and give us the prospectus.

DEACON. Well, then, my young friend, I have been thinking, ever since Miss Ophelia returned to Vermont, that she was just the person to fill the place of my lamented Molly.

CUTE. Say, you, you couldn't tell us who your lamented Molly was, could you?

DEACON. Why, the late Mrs. Perry, to be sure.

CUTE. Oh! then the lamented Molly was your wife?

DEACON. She was.

CUTE. And now you wish to marry Miss Ophelia?

DEACON. Exactly.

CUTE. (*Aside.*) Consarn this old porpoise! if I let him do that he'll Jew me out of my living. By chowder! I'll put a spoke in his wheel.

DEACON. Well, what do you say? will you intercede for me with your aunt?

CUTE. No! bust me up if I do!

DEACON. No?

CUTE. No, I tell you. I forbid the bans. Now, ain't you a purty individual, to talk about getting married, you old superannuated Methuselah specimen of humanity! Why, you've got one foot in eternity already, and t'other ain't fit to stand on. Go home and go to bed! have your head shaved, and send for a lawyer to make your will, leave your property to your heirs—if you hain't got any, why leave it to me—I'll take care of it, and charge nothing for the trouble.

DEACON. Really, sir, this language to one of my standing, is highly indecorous—it's more, sir, than I feel willing to endure, sir. I shall expect an explanation, sir.

CUTE. Now, you see, old gouty toes, you're losing your temper.

DEACON. Sir, I'm a deacon; I never lost my temper in all my life, sir.

CUTE. Now, you see, you're getting excited; you had better go; we can't have a disturbance here!

DEACON. No, sir! I shall not go, sir! I shall not go until I have seen Miss Ophelia. I wish to know if she will countenance this insult.

CUTE. Now keep cool, old stick-in-the-mud! Draw it mild, old timber-toes!

DEACON. Damn it all, sir, what—

CUTE. Oh! only think, now, what would people say to hear a deacon swearing like a trooper?

DEACON. Sir—I—you—this is too much, sir.

CUTE. Well, now, I calculate that's just about my opinion, so we'll have no more of it. Get out of this! start your boots, or by chowder! I'll pitch you from one end of the stairs to the other.

(*Enter Ophelia.*)

OPHELIA. Hoity toity! What's the meaning of all these loud words?

CUTE. (*Together.*) Well, you see, Aunt—

DEACON. Miss Ophelia, I beg—

CUTE. Now, look here, you just hush your yap! How can I fix up matters if you keep jabbering?

OPHELIA. Silence! for shame, Mr. Cute. Is that the way you speak to the deacon?

CUTE. Darn the deacon!

OPHELIA. Deacon Perry, what is all this?

DEACON. Madam, a few words will explain everything. Hearing from this person that he was your nephew, I ventured to tell him that I cherished hopes of making you my wife, whereupon he flew into a violent passion, and ordered me out of the house.

OPHELIA. Does this house belong to you or me, Mr. Cute?

CUTE. Well, to you, I reckon.

OPHELIA. Then how dare you give orders in it?

CUTE. Well, I calculated that you wouldn't care about marrying old half a century there.

OPHELIA. That's enough; I will marry him; and as for you, (*Points*) get out.

CUTE. Get out?

OPHELIA. Yes; the sooner the better.

CUTE. Darned if I don't serve him out first though.

(*Music. Cute makes a dash at Deacon, who gets behind Ophelia. Topsy enters, with a broom and beats Cute around stage. Ophelia faints in Deacon's arms. Cute falls, and Topsy butts him kneeling over him. Quick drop.*)

ACT VI

SCENE I

Dark landscape. An old, roofless shed. Tom is discovered in shed, lying on some old cotton bagging. Cassy kneels by his side, holding a cup to his lips.

CASSY. Drink all ye want. I knew how it would be. It isn't the first time I've been out in the night, carrying water to such as you.

TOM. (*Returning cup.*) Thank you, missis.

CASSY. Don't call me missis. I'm a miserable slave like yourself—a lower one than you can ever be! It's no use, my poor fellow, this you've been trying to do. You were a brave fellow. You had the right on your side; but it's all in vain for you to struggle. You are in the Devil's hands; he is the strongest, and you must give up.

TOM. Oh! how can I give up?

CASSY. You see *you* don't know anything about it; I do. Here you are, on a lone plantation, ten miles from any other, in the swamps; not a white person here who could testify, if you were buried alive. There's no law here that can do you, or any of us, the least good; and this man! there's no earthly thing that he is not bad enough to do. I could make one's hair rise, and their teeth chatter, if I should only tell what I've seen and been knowing to here; and it's no use resisting! Did I *want* to live with him? Wasn't I

a woman delicately bred? and he!—Father in Heaven! what was he and is he? And yet I've lived with him these five years, and cursed every moment of my life, night and day.

TOM. Oh heaven! have you quite forgot us poor critters?

CASSY. And what are these miserable low dogs you work with, that you should suffer on their account? Every one of them would turn against you the first time they get a chance. They are all of them as low and cruel to each other as they can be; there's no use in your suffering to keep from hurting them?

TOM. What made 'em cruel? If I give out I shall get used to it and grow, little by little, just like 'em. No, no, Missis, I've lost everything, wife, and children, and home, and a kind master, and he would have set me free if he'd only lived a day longer—I've lost everything in *this* world, and now I can't lose heaven, too: no I can't get to be wicked besides all.

CASSY. But it can't be that He will lay sin to our account; he won't charge it to us when we are forced to it; he'll charge it to them that drove us to it. Can I do anything more for you? Shall I give you some more water?

TOM. Oh missis! I wish you'd go to Him who can give you living waters!

CASSY. Go to him! Where is he? Who is he?

TOM. Our Heavenly Father!

CASSY. I used to see the picture of him, over the altar, when I was a girl but *he isn't here*! there's nothing here but sin, and long, long despair! There, there, don't talk any more, my poor fellow. Try to sleep, if you can. I must hasten back, lest my absence be noted. Think of me when I am gone, Uncle Tom, and pray, pray for me.

(*Music. Exit Cassy. Tom sinks back to sleep.*)

SCENE II

Street in New Orleans. Enter George Shelby.

GEORGE. At length my mission of mercy is nearly finished. I have reached my journey's end. I have now but to find the house of Mr. St. Clare, re-purchase old Uncle Tom, and convey him back to his wife and children, in old Kentucky. Some one approaches; he may, perhaps, be able to give me the information I require. I will accost him. (*Enter Marks.*) Pray, sir can you tell me where Mr. St. Clare dwells?

MARKS. Where I don't *think* you'll be in a hurry to seek him.

GEORGE. And where is that?

MARKS. In the grave!

GEORGE. Stay, sir! you may be able to give some information concerning Mr. St. Clare.

MARKS. I beg pardon, sir, I am a lawyer; I can't afford to *give* anything.

GEORGE. But you would have no objections to selling it?

MARKS. Not the slightest.

GEORGE. What do you value it at?

MARKS. Well, say five dollars, that's reasonable.

GEORGE. There they are. (*Gives money.*) Now answer me to the best of your ability. Has the death of St. Clare caused his slaves to be sold?

MARKS. It has.

GEORGE. How were they sold?

MARKS. At auction—they went dirt cheap.

GEORGE. How were they bought—all in one lot?

MARKS. No, they went to different bidders.

GEORGE. Was you present at the sale?

MARKS. I was.

GEORGE. Do you remember seeing a negro among them called Tom?

MARKS. What, Uncle Tom?

GEORGE. The same—who bought him?

MARKS. A Mr. Legree.

GEORGE. Where is his plantation?

MARKS. Up in Louisiana, on the Red River; but a man never could find it, unless he had been there before.

GEORGE. Who could I get to direct me there?

MARKS. Well, stranger, I don't know of any one just at present 'cept myself, could find it for you; it's such an out-of-the-way sort of hole; and if you are a mind to come down handsomely, why, I'll do it.

GEORGE. The reward shall be ample.

MARKS. Enough said, stranger; let's take the steamboat at once. (*Exeunt.*)

SCENE III

A Rough Chamber. Enter Legree. Sits.

LEGREE. Plague on that Sambo, to kick up this yer row between Tom and the new hands. (*Cassy steals on and stands behind him.*) The fellow won't be fit to work for a week now, right in the press of the season.

CASSY. Yes, just like you.

LEGREE. Hah! you she-devil! you've come back, have you? (*Rises.*)

CASSY. Yes, I have; come to have my own way, too.

LEGREE. You lie, you jade! I'll be up to my word. Either behave yourself or stay down in the quarters and fare and work with the rest.

CASSY. I'd rather, ten thousand times, live in the dirtiest hole at the quarters, than be under your hoof!

LEGREE. But you are under my hoof, for all that, that's one comfort; so sit down here and listen to reason. (*Grasps her wrist.*)

CASSY. Simon Legree, take care! (*Legree lets go his hold.*) You're afraid of me, Simon, and you've reason to be; for I've got the Devil in me!

LEGREE. I believe to my soul you have. After all, Cassy, why can't you be friends with me, as you used to?

CASSY. (*Bitterly.*) Used to!

LEGREE. I wish, Cassy, you'd behave yourself decently.

CASSY. *You* talk about behaving decently! and what have you been doing? You haven't even sense enough to keep from spoiling one of your best hands, right in the most pressing season, just for your devilish temper.

LEGREE. I was a fool, it's fact, to let any such brangle come up. Now when Tom set up his will he had to be broke in.

CASSY. You'll never break *him* in.

LEGREE. Won't I? I'd like to know if I won't! He'd be the first nigger that ever come it round me! I'll break every bone in his body but he shall give up. (*Enter Sambo, with a paper in his hand, stands bowing.*) What's that, you dog?

SAMBO. It's a witch thing, mas'r.

LEGREE. A what?

SAMBO. Something that niggers gits from witches. Keep 'em from feeling when they's flogged. He had it tied round his neck with a black string.

(Legree takes the paper and opens it. A silver dollar drops on the stage, and a long curl of light hair twines around his finger.)

LEGREE. Damnation. (*Stamping and writhing as if the hair burned him.*) Where did this come from? Take it off! burn it up! burn it up! (*Throws the curl away.*) What did you bring it to me for?

SAMBO. (*Trembling.*) I beg pardon, mas'r; I thought you would like to see um.

LEGREE. Don't you bring me any more of your devilish things. (*Shakes his fist at Sambo, who runs off. Legree kicks the dollar after him.*) Blast it! where did he get that? If it didn't look just like—whoo! I thought I'd forget that. Curse me if I think there's any such thing as forgetting anything, any how.

CASSY. What is the matter with you, Legree? What is there in a simple curl of fair hair to appall a man like you—you are familiar with every form of cruelty.

LEGREE. Cassy, to-night the past has been recalled to me—the past that I have so long and vainly striven to forget.

CASSY. Has aught on this earth power to move a soul like thine?

LEGREE. Yes, for hard and reprobate as I now seem, there has been a time when I have been rocked on the bosom of a mother, cradled with prayers and pious hymns, my now seared brow bedewed with the waters of holy baptism.

CASSY. (*Aside.*) What sweet memories of childhood can thus soften down that heart of iron?

LEGREE. In early childhood a fair-haired woman has led me, at the sound of Sabbath bells, to worship and to pray. Born of a hard-tempered sire, on whom that gentle woman had wasted a world of unvalued love, I followed in the steps of my father. Boisterous, unruly and tyrannical, I despised all her counsel, and would have none of her reproof, and, at an early age, broke from her to seek my fortunes on the sea. I never came home but once after that; and then my mother, with the yearning of a heart that must love something, and had nothing else to love, clung to me, and sought with passionate prayers and entreaties to win me from a life of sin.

CASSY. That was your day of grace, Legree; then good angels called you, and mercy held you by the hand.

LEGREE. My heart inly relented; there was a conflict, but sin got the victory, and I set all the force of my rough nature against the conviction of my conscience. I drank and swore, was wilder and more brutal than ever. And one night, when my mother, in the last agony of her despair, knelt at my feet, I spurned her from me, threw her senseless on the floor, and with brutal curses fled to my ship.

CASSY. Then the fiend took thee for his own.

LEGREE. The next I heard of my mother was one night while I was carousing among drunken companions. A letter was put in my hands. I opened it, and a lock of long, curling hair fell from it, and twined about my fingers, even as that lock twined but now. The letter told me that my mother was dead, and that dying she blest and forgave me! (*Buries his face in his hands.*)

CASSY. Why did you not even then renounce your evil ways?

LEGREE. There is a dread, unhallowed necromancy of evil, that turns things sweetest and holiest to phantoms of horror and affright. That pale, loving mother,—her dying prayers, her forgiving love,—wrought in my demoniac heart of sin only as a damning sentence, bringing with it a fearful looking for of judgment and fiery indignation.

CASSY. And yet you would not strive to avert the doom that threatened you.

LEGREE. I burned the lock of hair and I burned the letter; and when I saw them hissing and crackling in the flame, inly shuddered as I thought of everlasting fires! I tried to drink and revel, and swear away the memory; but often in the deep night, whose solemn stillness arraigns the soul in forced communion with itself, I have seen that pale mother rising by my bed-side, and felt the soft twining of that hair around my fingers, 'till the cold sweat would roll down my face, and I would spring from my bed in horror—horror! (*Falls in chair—After a pause.*) What the devil ails me? Large drops of sweat stand on my forehead, and my heart beats heavy and thick with fear. I thought I saw something white rising and glimmering in the gloom before me, and it seemed to bear my mother's face! I know one thing; I'll let that fellow Tom alone, after this. What did I want with his cussed paper? I believe I am bewitched sure enough! I've been shivering and sweating ever since! Where did he get that hair? It couldn't have been that! I *burn'd* that up, I know I did! It would be a joke if hair could rise from the dead! I'll have Sambo and Quimbo up here to sing and dance one of their dances,

and keep off these horrid notions. Here, Sambo! Quimbo! (*Exit.*)

CASSY. Yes, Legree, that golden tress was charmed; each hair had in it a spell of terror and remorse for thee, and was used by a mightier power to bind thy cruel hands from inflicting uttermost evil on the helpless! (*Exit.*)

SCENE IV

Street. Enter Marks meeting Cute, who enters dressed in an old faded uniform.

MARKS. By the land, stranger, but it strikes me that I've seen you somewhere before.

CUTE. By chowder! do you know how, that's just what I was a going to say?

MARKS. Isn't your name Cute?

CUTE. You're right, I calculate. Yours is Marks, I reckon.

MARKS. Just so.

CUTE. Well, I swow, I'm glad to see you. (*They shake hands.*) How's your wholesome?

MARKS. Hearty as ever. Well, who would have thought of ever seeing you again. Why, I thought you was in Vermont?

CUTE. Well, so I was. You see I went there after that rich relation of mine—but the speculation didn't turn out well.

MARKS. How so?

CUTE. Why, you see, she took a shine to an old fellow—Deacon Abraham Perry—and married him.

MARKS. Oh, that rather put your nose out of joint in that quarter.

CUTE. Busted me right up, I tell you. The Deacon did the hand-some thing though, he said if I would leave the neighborhood and go out South again, he'd stand the damage. I calculate I didn't give him much time to change his mind, and so, you see, here I am again.

MARKS. What are you doing in that soldier rig?

CUTE. Oh, this is my sign.

MARKS. Your sign?

CUTE. Yes; you see, I'm engaged just at present in an all-fired good speculation, I'm a Fillibusterow.

MARKS. A what?

CUTE. A Fillubusterow! Don't you know what that is? It's Spanish for Cuban Volunteer; and means a chap that goes the whole perker for glory and all that ere sort of thing.

MARKS. Oh! you've joined the order of the Lone Star!

CUTE. You've hit it. You see I bought this uniform at a second hand clothing store, I puts it on and goes to a benevolent individual and I says to him,—appealing to his feelings,—I'm one of the fellows that went to Cuba and got massacred by the bloody Spaniards. I'm in a destitute condition—give me a trifle to pay for passage back, so I can whop the tyrannical cusses and avenge my brave fellow soger what got slewed there.

MARKS. How pathetic!

CUTE. I tell you it works up the feelings of benevolent individuals dreadfully. It draws tears from their eyes and money from their pockets. By chowder! one old chap gave me a hundred dollars to help on the cause.

MARKS. I admire a genius like yours.

CUTE. But I say, what are you up to?

MARKS. I am the traveling companion of a young gentleman by the name of Shelby, who is going to the plantation of a Mr. Legree of the Red River, to buy an old darkey who used to belong to his father.

CUTE. Legree—Legree? Well, now, I calculate I've heard that ere name afore.

MARKS. Do you remember that man who drew a bowie knife on you in New Orleans?

CUTE. By chowder! I remember the circumstances just as well as if it was yesterday; but I can't say that I recollect much about the man, for you see I was in something of a hurry about that time and didn't stop to take a good look at him.

MARKS. Well, that man was this same Mr. Legree.

CUTE. Do you know, now, I should like to pay that critter off!

MARKS. Then I'll give you an opportunity.

CUTE. Chowder! how will you do that?

MARKS. Do you remember the gentleman that interfered between you and Legree?

CUTE. Yes—well?

MARKS. He received the blow that was intended for you, and died from the effects of it. So, you see, Legree is a murderer, and we are the only witnesses of the deed. His life is in our hands.

CUTE. Let's have him right up and make him dance on nothing to the tune of Yankee Doodle!

MARKS. Stop a bit. Don't you see a chance for a profitable speculation?

CUTE. A speculation! Fire away, don't be bashful, I'm the man for a speculation.

MARKS. I have made a deposition to the Governor of the state on all the particulars of that affair at Orleans.

CUTE. What did you do that for?

MARKS. To get a warrant for his arrest.

CUTE. Oh! and have you got it?

MARKS. Yes; here it is. (Takes out paper.)

CUTE. Well, now, I don't see how you are going to make anything by that bit of paper.

MARKS. But I do. I shall say to Legree, I have a warrant against you for murder; my friend, Mr. Cute, and myself are the only witnesses who can appear against you. Give us a thousand dollars, and we will tear the warrant and be silent.

CUTE. Then Mr. Legree forks over a thousand dollars, and your friend Cute pockets five hundred of it, is that the calculation?

MARKS. If you will join me in the undertaking.

CUTE. I'll do it, by chowder!

MARKS. Your hand to bind the bargain.

CUTE. I'll stick by you thro' thick and thin.

MARKS. Enough said.

CUTE. Then shake. (They shake hands.)

MARKS. But I say, Cute, he may be contrary and show fight.

CUTE. Never mind, we've got the law on our side, and we're bound to stir him up. If he don't come down handsomely we'll present him with a neck-tie made of hemp!

MARKS. I declare you're getting spunky.

CUTE. Well, I reckon, I am. Let's go and have something to drink. Tell you what, Marks, if we don't get him, we'll have his hide, by chowder! (Exeunt, arm in arm.)

SCENE V

Rough Chamber. Enter Legree, followed by Sambo.

LEGREE. Go and send Cassy to me.

SAMBO. Yes, mas'r. (Exit.)

LEGREE. Curse the woman! she's got a temper worse than the devil; I shall do her an injury one of these days, if she isn't careful. (Re-enter Sambo, frightened.) What's the matter with you, you black scoundrel?

SAMBO. S'help me, mas'r, she isn't dere.

LEGREE. I suppose she's about the house somewhere?

SAMBO. No, she isn't, mas'r; I's been all over de house and I can't find nothing of her nor Emmeline.

LEGREE. Bolted, by the Lord! Call out the dogs! saddle my horse. Stop! are you sure they really have gone?

SAMBO. Yes, mas'r; I's been in every room 'cept the haunted garret and dey wouldn't go dere.

LEGREE. I have it! Now, Sambo, you jest go and walk that Tom up here, right away! (Exit Sambo.) The old cuss is at the bottom of this yer whole matter; and I'll have it out of his infernal black hide, or I'll know the reason why! I hate him—I hate him! And isn't he mine? Can't I do what I like with him? Who's to hinder, I wonder? (Tom is dragged on by Sambo and Quimbo, Legree grimly confronting Tom.) Well, Tom, do you know I've made up my mind to kill you?

TOM. It's very likely, Mas'r.

LEGREE. I—have—done—just—that—thing, Tom, unless you'll tell me what do you know about these yer gals? (Tom is silent.) D'ye year? Speak!

TOM. I han't got anything to tell, mas'r.

LEGREE. Do you dare to tell me, you old black rascal, you don't know? Speak! Do you know anything?

TOM. I know, mas'r; but I can't tell anything. I can die!

LEGREE. Hark ye, Tom! ye think 'cause I have let you off before, I don't mean what I say; but, this time, I have made up my mind, and counted the cost. You've always stood it out agin me; now, I'll conquer ye or kill ye! one or t'other. I'll count every drop of blood there is in you, and take 'em, one by one, 'till ye give up!

TOM. Mas'r, if you was sick, or in trouble, or dying, and I

could save you, I'd *give* you my heart's blood; and, if taking every drop of blood in this poor old body would save your precious soul, I'd give 'em freely. Do the worst you can, my troubles will be over soon; but if you don't repent yours won't ever end.

(*Legree strikes Tom down with the butt of his whip.*)

LEGREE. How do you like that?

SAMBO. He's most gone, mas'r!

TOM. (*Rises feebly on his hands.*) There an't no more you can do. I forgive you with all my soul. (*Sinks back, and is carried off by Sambo and Quimbo.*)

LEGREE. I believe he's done for finally. Well, his mouth is shut up at last—that's one comfort. (*Enter George Shelby, Marks and Cute.*) Strangers! Well what do you want?

GEORGE. I understand that you bought in New Orleans a negro named Tom.

LEGREE. Yes, I did buy such a fellow, and a devil of a bargain I had of it, too! I believe he's trying to die, but I don't know as he'll make it out.

GEORGE. Where is he? Let me see him!

SAMBO. Dere he is. (*Points to Tom.*)

LEGREE. How dare you speak? (*Drives Sambo and Quimbo off. George exits.*)

CUTE. Now's the time to nab him.

MARKS. How are you, Mr. Legree?

LEGREE. What the devil brought you here?

MARKS. This little bit of paper. I arrest you for the murder of Mr. St. Clare. What do you say to that?

LEGREE. This is my answer! (*Makes a blow at Marks, who dodges, and Cute receives the blow—he cries out and runs off, Marks fires at Legree, and follows Cute.*) I am hit!—the game's up! (*Falls dead. Quimbo and Sambo return and carry him off laughing.*)

(*George Shelby enters, supporting Tom. Music. They advance to front and Tom falls.*)

GEORGE. Oh! dear Uncle Tom! do wake—do speak once more! look up! Here's Master George—your own little Master George. Don't you know me?

TOM. (*Opening his eyes and speaking in a feeble tone.*) Mas'r George! Bless de Lord! it's all I wanted! They hav'n't forgot me! It warms my soul; it does my old heart good! Now I shall die content!

GEORGE. You shan't die! you mustn't die, nor think of it. I have come to buy you, and take you home.

TOM. Oh, Mas'r George, you're too late. The Lord has bought me, and is going to take me home.

GEORGE. Oh! don't die. It will kill me—it will break my heart to think what you *have* suffered, poor, poor fellow!

TOM. Don't call me, poor fellow! I have been poor fellow; but that's all past and gone now. I'm right in the door, going into glory! Oh, Mas'r George! *Heaven has come!* I've got the victory, the Lord has given it to me! Glory be to His name! (*Dies.*)

(*Solemn music. George covers Uncle Tom with his cloak, and kneels over him. Clouds work on and conceal them, and then work off.*)

SCENE VI

Gorgeous clouds, tinted with sunlight. Eva, robed in white, is discovered on the back of a milk-white dove, with expanded wings, as if just soaring upward. Her hands are extended in benediction over St. Clare and Uncle Tom who are kneeling and gazing up to her. Expressive music. Slow curtain.

END

SPOTLIGHT   THE MINSTREL SHOW

It has been said that the minstrel show is the unique contribution of the United States to world theater. Because of its sociological implications and its influence on the most popular theater piece in nineteenth-century America, *Uncle Tom's Cabin*, it is worth considering here.

The minstrel show evolved, almost by accident, out of a curious custom of nineteenth-century theater practice. To give their audiences a full evening's entertainment, theater managers regularly scheduled *entr'actes* and "after-pieces" on their bills. Between each act of a play, often a song or a dance was performed while scenery was changed; after the regular play was concluded, a short play, often a farce, was presented to showcase the actors' versatility and to send the audience home on an upbeat note. Thus, it was not unusual for an audience to spend five or more hours in the theater. *Uncle Tom's Cabin*, by the way, was the first major American stage play to be performed without an after-piece because of its length.

In 1827 a middling actor named Thomas D. Rice was walking to a theater in Louisville, Kentucky, when he heard an intriguing melody. He followed the sound to a stable where he saw a slave grooming a horse while singing a catchy little song that went:

You wheel about and turn about and do just so,

You wheel about and turn about and jump Jim Crow.

To accompany his singing, the stable hand danced a little shuffle step. Rice saw the potential of this song for an entr'acte piece and paid the man to teach him the song and the dance. Rice hurried to the theater, where he applied bootblack to his face and performed his "Jim Crow" number. Audiences loved Rice's innovation, and soon scores of imitators were presenting their own "blackface" acts, usually within the context of a formal theater piece. In 1843 the first complete evening of blackface acts was performed in New York by the Virginia Minstrels, who took their name from a popular variety act from Austria, the Tyrolean Minstrels. Thus "minstrels" (or "minstrelsy") became the generic term for this form of entertainment. Historically, the more significant term was "Jim Crow"—which became a generic term applied to Africans brought to America as slaves. So-called Jim Crow laws, written to deny people of African descent their rights, were common until the mid–twentieth century, when the civil rights movement finally forced their repeal.

The typical American minstrel show was divided into parts, three if the short comedy or farce performed as an afterpiece is counted. The first section was the actual minstrel show, in which about nine performers sat in a semicircle of chairs onstage. In the middle chair was the emcee for the show, Mr. Interlocutor, who introduced the various acts and asked the right questions of the two comic "sidemen" who sat at either end of the row: Mr. Tambo played a tambourine while Mr. Bones shook a percussive instrument. Tambo and Bones provided most of the humor, most of it racist stereotyping of the worst kind. The other performers played musical instruments as they sang and danced. Much of the music was derived from songs of the plantation slaves, though sentimentalized and filtered for white audience tastes. Stephen Foster, who wrote such songs as "Camp Town Races" and "My Old Kentucky Home," was the foremost composer of minstrel music. The minstrel shows purported to show audiences slices of plantation life, but the portrait was skewed and only preserved the myth of the "happy slave." The first half of the minstrel show concluded with the "walk around," in which the individual performers displayed their specialty for a final time. The second half was called the olio, named after the colorful painted backdrops that provided visual interest for what was essentially a conventional vaudeville show. It was not performed entirely in blackface.

In *Uncle Tom's Cabin* the character of Topsy, the comic relief, is derived from the minstrel show. As you read the play, note the songs she sings, most of which have nothing to do with the plot but were inserted to please audiences.

It should be noted that the popularity of minstrelsy also promoted the formation of African American troupes who also "blacked up" (the common term for applying makeup) to conform to audience expectations. Callender's Georgia Minstrels (and its superstar Billy Kersands) and Haverly's Colored Minstrels were among the most popular of these; there was even an all-female troupe of minstrels performing with Sam T. Jack's Creoles. Ironically, the minstrel show, despite its racist elements, provided employment for many black entertainers.

However entertaining and popular the minstrel shows may have been— and they were phenomenally popular, even into the twentieth century—they perpetuated racist stereotypes. Minstrel shows withered away in the early twentieth century, largely because of protests led by W. E. B. Du Bois, among the earliest and most influential civil rights leaders. Even after minstrel shows disappeared, their influence could still be detected. For instance, the popular Christmas film *Holiday Inn* (1944) features Bing Crosby and Fred Astaire in a blackface number. Few popular entertainments in the history of world theater have so influenced the social fabric of a country as did the minstrel show.

FORUMS

"A Critique of *Uncle Tom's Cabin*"

JAMES GORDON BENNETT

This review appeared in the New York Herald *on September 3, 1852; it was written in response to the C. W. Taylor adaptation of Stowe's novel. Aiken's version, produced by the Howard Company did not open until November in Troy, New York. The reviewer was James Gordon Bennett, whose name did not appear.*

Mrs. Harriet Beecher Stowe's novel of *Uncle Tom's Cabin* has been dramatized at the National Theatre, and, being something of a novelty, it draws crowded houses nightly.

The practice of dramatizing a popular novel, as soon as it takes a run, has become very common. In many instances, and particularly with regard to the highly dramatic and graphic novels of Dickens, these new plays have been very successful, giving pleasure and satisfaction to the public, and putting money into the pockets of the chuckling manager. But in the presentation of *Uncle Tom's Cabin* upon the boards of a popular theatre, we apprehend the manager has committed a serious mischievous blunder, the tendencies of which he did not comprehend, or did not care to consider, but in relation to which we have a word or two of friendly counsel to submit.

The novel of *Uncle Tom's Cabin* is at present our nine days' literary wonder. It has sold by thousands, and tens and hundreds of thousands—not, however, on account of any surpassing or wonderful literary merits which it may be supposed to possess, but because of the widely extended sympathy, in all the North, with the pernicious abolition sympathies and "higher law" moral of this ingenious and cunningly devised abolition fable. The *furore* which it has thus created, has brought out quite a number of catchpenny imitators, *pro* and *con*, desirous of filling their sails while yet the breeze is blowing, though it does appear to us to be the meanest kind of stealing of a lady's thunder. This is, indeed, a new epoch and a new field of abolition authorship—a new field of fiction, humbug and deception, for a more extended agitation of the slavery question—than any that has heretofore imperiled the peace and safety of the Union.

The success of *Uncle Tom's Cabin* as a novel, has naturally suggested its success upon the stage; but the fact has been overlooked, that any such representation must be an insult to the South—an exaggerated mockery of Southern institutions—and calculated, more than any other expedient of agitation, to poison the minds of our youth with the pestilent principles of abolitionism. The play, as performed at the National, is a crude and aggravated affair, following the general plot of the story, except in the closing scene, where, instead of allowing Tom to die under the cruel treatment of his new master in Louisiana, he is brought back to a reunion with Wilmot and his wife—returned runaways—all of whom, with Uncle Tom and Aunt Chloe, are set free, with the privilege of remaining upon the old plantation. The incidents of the piece are thus set forth in the "small bill:—

PROGRAMME

ACT 1—Exterior of Uncle Tom's Cabin on Shelbey's Planation; Negro Celebration. Chorus, "Nigga in de Cornfield;" Kentucky Breakdown Dance; Innocence Protected; Slave Dealers on hand. Chorus, "Come then to the Feast;" the Mother's Appeal; Capture of Morna [Eliza]; Interior of Uncle Tom's Cabin; Midnight Escape; Tom driven from his Cabin; Search of the Traders; Miraculous Escape of Morna and her Child. Offering Prayer; the Negro's Hope; Affecting Tableau.

ACT 2—Family Excitement; Dark Threatenings; Ohio River Frozen over; Snow Storm; Flight of Morna and her Child; Pursuit of the Traders; Desperate Resolve and Escape of Morna on Flowing Ice; Mountain Torrent and Ravine; Cave of Crazy Mag; Chase of Edward; Maniac's Protection; Desperate Encounter of Edward and Traders on the Bridge; Fall of Springer down the Roaring Torrent; Negro Chorus, "We Darkies Hoe the Corn;" Meeting of Edward and Morna; Escape over Mountain Rocks.

ACT 3—Roadside Inn; Advertisement Extraordinary; the Slave Auctioneer; Rencontre between Edward and Slave Dealers; Interposition of Crazy Mag; Arrival from the West Indies; Singular Discovery, Mountain Dell; Recognition of the Lost Mother; Repentance and Remorse; Return of Tom; the Log Cabin in its Pride; Freedom of Edward and Morna &c.

In the progress of these varied scenes, we have the most extravagant exhibition of the imaginary horrors of Southern slavery. The negro traders, with their long whips, cut and slash their poor slaves about the stage for mere pastime, and a gang of poor wretches, handcuffed to a chain which holds them all in marching order, two by two, are thrashed like cattle to quicken their pace. Uncle Tom is scourged by the trader, who has bought him, for "whining" at his bad luck. A reward is posted up, offering four hundred dollars for the runaway, Edward Wilmot, (who, as well as his wife, is nearly white,) the reward to be paid upon "his recovery, or upon proof that he has been killed." But Wilmot shoots down his pursuers in real Christian style, as fast as they come, and after many marvellous escapes, and many fine ranting abolition speeches, (generally preceding his dead shots,) he is liberated as we have described.

This play, and these scenes, are nightly received at one of our most popular theatres with repeated rounds of applause. True, the audience appears to be pleased with the novelty, without being troubled about the moral of the story, which is mischievous in the extreme.

The institution of Southern slavery is recognized and protected by the federal constitution, upon which this Union was established, and which holds it together. But for the compro-

(continued)

mises on the slavery question, we should have no constitution and no Union—and would, perhaps, have been at this day, in the condition of the South American republics, divided into several military despotisms, constantly warring with each other, and each within itself. The Fugitive Slave law only carries out one of the plain provisions of the constitution. When a Southern slave escapes to us, we are in honor bound to return him to his master. And yet, here in this city—which owes its wealth, population, power, and prosperity, to the Union and the constitution, and this institution of slavery, to a greater degree than any other city in the Union—here we have highly represented, at a popular theatre, the most exaggerated enormities of Southern slavery, playing directly into the hands of the abolitionists and abolition kidnappers of slaves, and doing their work for them. What will our Southern friends think of all our profes-sions of respect for their delicate social institution of slavery, when they find that even our amusements are overdrawn carica-tures exhibiting our hatred against it and against them? Is this consistent with good faith, or honor, or the every day obliga-tions of hospitality? No, it is not. It is a sad blunder; for when our stage shall become the deliberate agent in the cause of abo-litionism, with the sanction of the public, and their approba-tion, the peace and harmony of this Union will soon be ended.

We would, from all these considerations, advise all con-cerned to drop the play of *Uncle Tom's Cabin* at once and for ever. The thing is in bad taste—is not according to good faith to the constitution, or consistent with either of the two Baltimore platforms; and is calculated, if persisted in, to become a fire-brand of the most dangerous character to the peace of the whole country.

"'The Prologue' from *The World's Greatest Hit: Uncle Tom's Cabin*"

HARRY BIRDOFF

The following description of a "Tom Show" as performed in a small American town toward the end of the nineteenth century was written by Harry Birdoff as the "Prologue" to his superb study of the stage history of Uncle Tom's Cabin. *It is reprinted here because it captures the sense of event that "Tommers" brought to the common people.*

I've been a good boy to my dear mamma;
    I never tried to deceive her;
So I think she orter give me a quarter
    To see Uncle Thomas and Eva.

                  —*Air*

With the coming of spring they blossomed forth—covering barns and fences, and in flaming colors overrunning stone walls; the "three sheet" lithographs could not be read from a distance, but there wasn't a boy who didn't recognize immediately the fa-miliar figures: Little Eva ensconced in old Tom's lap, Eliza pur-sued across the ice by the hounds, Lawyer Marks striking that grandiloquent posture, and Topsy doing a breakdown! Never, never was a traveling Tom show known to curtail its lavish posters, for they outdid the circus. Only the elements and mali-cious boys might destroy them.

A week before the arrival, the countryside was plastered with:

REWARD!!!

GEORGE HARRIS, *Absconded from My Plantation, Is Reported Headed for Canada.*
Reward for His Return. SIMON LEGREE (*owner*).

With the crack o' dawn came the little caravan, wagons with gilded gingerbread, the sides depicting draperies of scrollwork—

and a legend in red and gold letters. Proclaiming its massive scenic allegories, one was embellished with the Apocalypse scene, Eva surrounded by chubby cupids and overflowing cornu-copias; another, the tableau that unfolded as the greatest Amer-ican drama reached its terrifying climax: Legree whipping Tom in a sulphurous red light! More wagons, with golden sunburst wheels, for the baggage, for the Tommers' living quarters, and for the accessory menagerie.

The grand, gala free street parade was advertised for 11:45 A.M., but it never really got started before the noon hour. Agile boys shinnied onto the roof of the grocery sidewalk shed, and had the best view, gazing enthralled at the long cer-emonial procession. Two uniformed bands came in the stri-dent wake—one white, one colored, often supplemented by a Ladies' Drum Corps; a strutting figure in scarlet twirled a drum-major's baton. They played "slave melodies," and also "There'll Be a Hot Time in the Old Town, To-night," with plenty of ginger in it.

A carriage drawn by spirited white horses, decked in span-gled nosegays, carried a famous trio: Old Tom sandwiched in be-tween Mr. St. Claire and Simon Legree, the raiser and purchaser both looking proud and self-satisfied as if they had calved him between them. Often an open barouche held golden-haired Eva, at her father's side, facing Topsy, whose topsails shivered in the wind, and strait-laced Aunt Ophelia, who kept calling folks, "Shiftless!" Sometimes Little Eva rode her beplumed Shetland pony; or she appeared in an "Apocalypse" on wheels, in virginal white, with a papier-maché halo, in all the moving splendor of a gilded float, from which vantage point she worked havoc in the hearts of her youthful admirers.

An avalanche of hisses and catcalls greeted that old terror, Legree. Gargantuan in his small mule cart, with slouch hat at a rakish angle—(S-s-s-s!), he glowered (S-s-s-s!), snarling half-muffled oaths at the would-be upholders of virtue and truth (S-s-s-s!), cracking a great blacksnake whip at them (S-s-s-s-s!), and he made it work overtime on their invisible hides. It only wanted somebody to say the word to the youthful lovers of humanity on the sidewalk, and they would have lynched the infernal slavemonger. Surprisingly, his fellow actors vouched, "Hard though he is, even he was once rocked on the bosom of a mother!" It was difficult to believe *that,* and although the Mayor of the town was enlightened, other officials argued, "It doesn't matter—he must be wicked to be able to play such a character!"

In Legree's cart rode Eliza, displaying her charms. And if she were put up on the auction block, there wasn't a citizen who willingly wouldn't have put in a bid toward her purchase.

Lawyer Marks, with his famous umbrella, sat astride a docile, mouse-colored donkey, dragging his white-legginged feet on Main Street, offering everyone his card from an accordion-pleated wallet. The crowd echoed, "Yea-a—a, verilie!" when Phineas Fletcher, the Quaker, greeted his host of imitators. He placed the ends of his fingers together, pausing to rise slowly on his toes, with a teetotally this and a teetotally that. Gumption Cute, hard by, chawed tobacco, whittling away on half a tree with his Barlow knife.

Most climactic of all were *"The genuine bloodhounds: 12—Count Em—12."* As pale green programmes of long ago put it, they supported the rest of the cast as "the full strength of the Company." Boys in faded, oversized overcoats led them in the parade and excited the envy of other boys, who traded apples, marbles and candy for the privilege of holding the leash.

A feature in the parade was a log cabin on wheels, real smoke issuing from the chimney, and Aunt Chloe washed clothes on the doorstep, while Uncle Tom gidapped the horses. Then on a belching calliope, the old steam fiddle, chanted Foster melodies, but chronically afflicted with the croup, frightened the horses on Main Street.

The Tommers later waylaid the innocent bystanders. On the sidewalk Simon Legree cracked a whip fearsomely, thundering out, "I'm looking for a likely-looking yaller gal named Eliza. . . . She belongs t'me, an' I want her. . . . I want t'find Uncle Tom, tew. . . . They tell me they're both with this hyer show that's at the—(here naming the local theatre), an' I wish ye'd tell me whar that is." A shabby-genteel figure rubbered into windows, entered stores to wander aimlessly about, and buttonholed passerby to ask, "Can you tell me, please, where the Theatre is? I understand that they're showing there a great play called *Uncle Tom's Cabin,* and as I, myself, am Marks, the lawyer, I'd like right well to see it."

One caught a glimpse of the classic features of St. Clair in a lithograph in a saloon window, close to the stodgy goat of the brewery advertisement. The soda fountains in town hung up signs: "Try our Topsy Tipple," "Try our Uncle Tom Special," "Taste the little Eva Sundae," and "Special—with Eliza Icing." At the schoolhouse gates, an individual in ante-bellum dress offered the pupils, with magnanimity, "This Ticket and Ten Cents" pasteboards.

Blazing away, the Tom band's concert before the theatre, at one o'clock, drew a throng. Then it entered, and became the orchestra; when the plantation scene went on, the same musicians donned "slave" clothes, as Jubilee singers.

From the rise of the curtain until the final tableau, anything might happen. Invariably the mechanical equipment was crude, the drops neither dropped nor lifted, but caught in some of the other scenery, and refused to be extricated. A curtain came down on a horse (that drew the barouche) amidships, as she turned her hind quarters squarely upon the spectators. On the creaking pulleys, Eva was drawn up to Heaven feet first, or got stuck en route; while the red fire in the Ascension wouldn't burn, and if it did, made everyone in the audience cough. In the whipping scene Legree would catch hold of Tom by the slack of his blue shirt, pulling it out of his belt and exposing a wide spanse of white skin. "The street in New Orleans" fluttered in every backstage breeze, yet worked its own illusion. A stock curtain of Leutze's famous painting of Washington Crossing the Delaware might rise on Eliza and the "prop" floes. She often outran the hounds, had to wait for them, urge them on, and they chased the wrong people; she lost her balance, as the hounds bounded up, sympathetically licking her face. Critics made much of these mishaps.

The play was never like Mrs. Stowe's novel, but native as a patchwork quilt. Bits of "business" from generations of Tommers had developed the "sure-fire" stuff, the ad libbing making permanent the bristling lines. Some characters were built up into flesh and blood and sinew, others cut down to the grim essentials, or jettisoned. The original connecting passages were altogether cut and lost, but the scenes beat forcibly upon the heart and brain. Like Topsy, it "just grow'd"—giving us the true folk play.

With the traditional text lost sight of, any number of Tom companies claimed they were giving the "only original." A verbal form was handed down. Stock companies failed when they put on the piece—no, what kept the play alive wasn't in any printed script: It was stuff that came down by word-of-mouth from generations of Uncle Toms, Markses, Topsies, Legrees.

The intense rivalry among Tom troupes, playing with gusto in their brassiest days, exacted a fierce vitality. Often a performance lasted five hours, embracing six acts, fifty scenes and eight tableaux, an elaborate chorus of two hundred Jubilee singers, a mother-of-pearl Apotheosis, and an "ice-gorged river"—Nature herself imported! It brought a decade of "Double Mammoth Productions," all the characters in pairs—as if one mammoth was not sufficient!

They traveled along every tank-water line and gave it at every whistle-stop, stepping from the wagon flap onto the platform, before flaring acetylene torches. They were born in the show-wagon, named after the early parts they were to play—"Harry" or "Eva," and when only a few months old Eliza carried them across the ice as gurgling infantile "properety." Little Evas grew to Topsies, Maries, Elizas, and then to Aunt Chloes. Gangling boys attempted the irrepressible Topsies, went on to Markses, then to Legrees, and in old age achieved the epitome—Uncle Toms. If some were arrested in their dramatic growth, they at least attained some degree of perfection in a given part. Steeped in the lore, they spent their lives as Tommers, and finally shuffled offstage without ever having appeared in any other play. You did not find their names in the Who's Who on the Stage. The newspapers found it economical in space to refer to them merely as "U.T.C." companies, but to the actors themselves they were Tom shows, or Tommers.

The American cross-roads expected the play, with its touching morality, at least once a year, and it did appear with the regularity of an almanac. Their sole contact with the "the-ayter," the hinterlanders came in wagons from miles around to mingle their tears with Little Eva and the old colored gentleman. There were, also, the semi-annual and monthly arrivals, called "ragtime Tom shows," because the tents were worn to rags.

REALISM AND NATURALISM

1852:
Alexandre
Dumas'
fils, *The
Lady of the
Camellias,*
first "thesis"
play

1879:
Emile Zola's
*Naturalism
in the
Theater*

1898:
Moscow
Art Theater
founded

1909:
Constantin
Stanislavsky
outlines
his "System"
for acting

1931–1941:
The Group
Theatre

1840s:
Eugène
Scribe's
well-made
plays

1874–1890:
Meiningen
players tour
Europe;
advent of
the stage
director

1887:
Théâtre-
Libre
founded
in Paris by
Antoine

1900:
Freud's
*Interpretation
of Dreams*

1904:
Abbey
Theatre
founded
in Dublin

1915:
Provincetown
Players
founded
in New York

1947:
Actors
Studio
founded
in New
York

1956:
English
Stage
Company
founded

1800 C.E.   1900 C.E.

1830:
Birth of
sociology

1859:
Charles
Darwin's *The
Origin of
Species*

1867:
Karl Marx's
Das Kapital

1905:
Russian
Revolution

1914–1918:
World War I

1939–1945:
World War II

1951-1953:
McCarthy
hearings:
theater
and film
artists
blacklisted

1929:
The
Great
Depression
begins

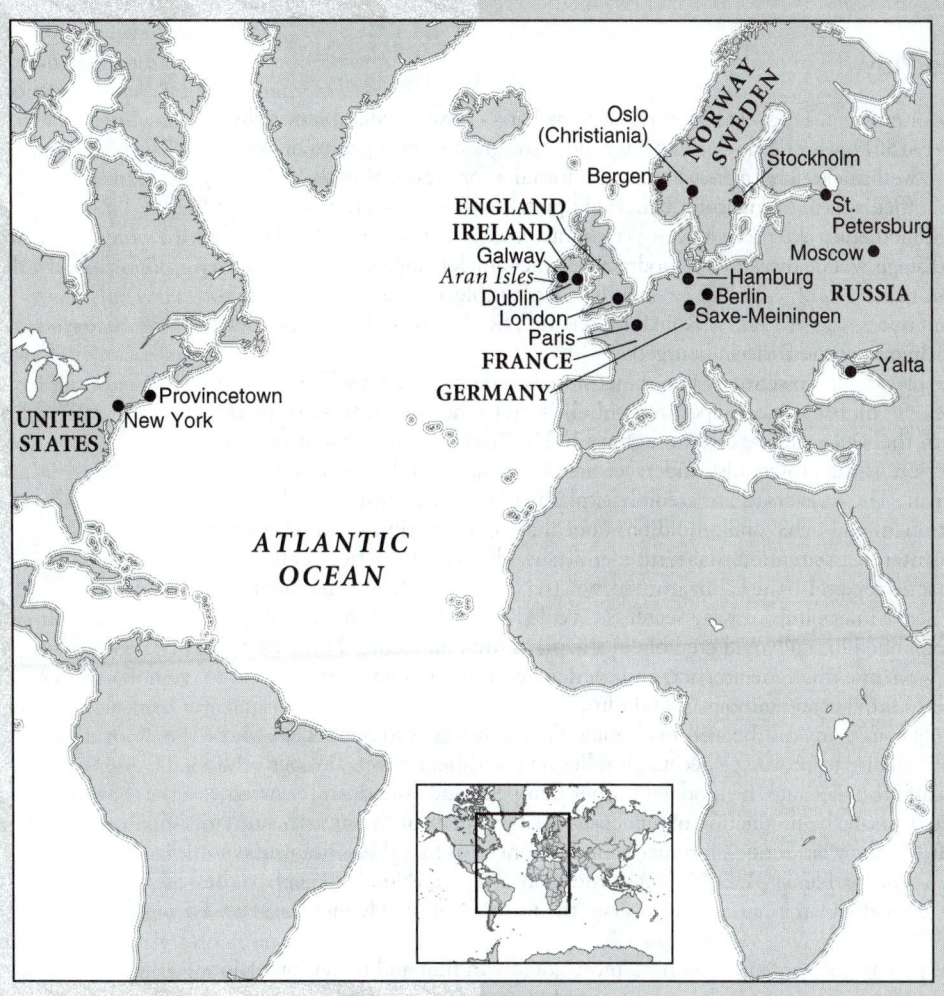

The Romantic spirit swept Europe and America amid the continuation of the scientific revolution fostered by the Enlightenment. It was spurred by empiricism, which placed a primary value on observation and experience. Consequently, this phenomenon inspired a new approach to playwriting that created a central component in the fully developed social drama: the well-made play.

The Well-Made Play

Despite the success of *Hernani*, Hugo was soon replaced as Paris's most popular playwright by Eugène Scribe (1791–1861), whom Eric Bentley has called "the greatest non-genius of drama." Scribe perfected the well-made play (*pièce bien faite*), a formula for playwriting that virtually guaranteed the box office appeal of intricate, believable plots in which suspense, action, and brilliantly theatrical moments take precedence over characterization and theme. Scribe, who composed over 400 stage works, disdained melodrama's penchant for improbable events and applied the scientific principles of "causality" to make them plausible, or—as he said—to make "the accidental seem necessary." Instead of Romantic settings, Scribe favored domestic scenes in his gently satiric dramas of the Parisian bourgeois.

The well-made play depicts essentially two-dimensional characters that are lively enough to engage audiences. Its plots are based upon a withheld secret (thereby creating suspense), which is hinted at in the well-crafted exposition of act 1. The Aristotelian principle of reversal advances the action as the protagonist undergoes a series of ups and downs in a battle of wits with an archrival. These reversals are credibly explained by letters, mistaken identities, carefully timed entrances and exits, and a quid pro quo, that is, a situation in which two or more characters misinterpret a situation that further enmeshes them in the action. Late in the play there is a climactic reversal—the "obligatory scene" (or *scène à faire*). This moment usually represents the hero's low point until the secret is revealed to vindicate him and vanquish the villain. All is explained logically and credibly in the play's final moments. This pattern is repeated in subtler ways in each scene and act, and each act ends on a moment of reversal to ensure suspense and to provide an ominous "curtain line."

Scribe did not, of course, invent the well-made play. That honor goes to Sophocles, whose *Oedipus the King* still remains its prototype because it relies on a withheld secret. But Scribe did perfect the formula and thus became the model for other European and American playwrights at midcentury. Ibsen oversaw the production of numerous Scribean plays at the state theater he managed in Norway. He drew on Scribe's formula as he fashioned his first thesis dramas to attack contemporary social problems. *A Doll's House* turns on a secret (Nora's forgery of the banknote) and the letter from Krogstad, which reverses the fortunes of the Helmer household forever.

The well-made play is still very much with us, most notably in film and television scriptwriting. Bound by well-defined time blocks and the need to stop the action for commercial messages (the equivalent of the nineteenth-century "curtain line"), TV writers necessarily adhere to the Scribean formula as they, too, write for mass audiences.

Influences on Realism

The new empiricism transformed society into a laboratory for sciences unknown to Galileo: sociology, economics, and especially psychology. Out of these would grow prescriptions for reordering human behavior, as the century's most provocative thinkers attempted to redress injustices spawned by outmoded beliefs about class, gender, and workers' rights. During the Industrial Revolution cities expanded to house factories and provide jobs for those who had previously tilled the soil. Some prospered, largely by exploiting workers, especially women and children, but many others were condemned to lives of poverty in teeming slums that bred disease and crime. Just as serfs rebelled against feudal lords and plebians toppled monarchs, so too would workers eventually rise against the captains of industry.

Predictably, a cultural revolution occurred in which the arts addressed social problems. The theater became a meetingplace in which audiences observed contemporary ills, live and close-up, considered arguments for their solution, and (in theory) returned to their communities to improve the world for all. Theater became a "here and now" enterprise, and no longer viewed the human situation through the Romantic past. A concern for social problems is hardly a new phenomenon emanating from Western stages. Because it is a communal activity, the theater has an innate social dimension. What made the social voice of the late nineteenth century so distinctive was its insistence on being heard in uncompromising and realistic terms.

While Romantic philosophers and literary artists laid much of the foundation for the socially conscious dramas, other important contributors also changed the theater, though they were not themselves artists. Six are noteworthy because they represent significant new disciplines that changed Western drama:

- **Auguste Comte** (1798–1857), often called the father of sociology, was a mathematician and philosopher who defined "the science of society." Comte and his disciples employed the empirical methodology of the hard sciences to social problems. Applying Comte's methods to the stage, artists saw the theater as a "bell jar" in which the precise conditions of a social problem (e.g., poverty) were re-created. The audience observed them with the detachment and rationality of a laboratory scientist as the problem was dissected and a cure was suggested.
- **Charles Darwin** (1809–1892) wrote *The Origin of Species* in 1859 and radically altered human thought. His studies of plant and animal life caused Darwin to conclude that beings (including humans) are products of their heredity and environment, and that life involves a perpetual battle in which only the "fittest" (i.e., those who adapt favorably) survive. Darwin's controversial theories, articulated by Herbert Spencer in his writings about "social Darwinism," had a number of implications for the theater. His emphasis on environment provoked theater artists to create, as faithfully as possible, the environment that created social problems. Whether it be the stultifying propriety of the Helmer household in Ibsen's *A Doll's House* or the dismal squalor of Maxim Gorky's Russian "flophouse" in *The Lower Depths*, playwrights, directors, and scene designers labored to create absolute worlds in which characters acted as their heredity and environments dictated.
- **Friedrich Nietzsche** (1844–1900), a German philosopher and theater critic, proclaimed "God is dead" in 1885. Because heredity and environment were viewed as determinants of human behavior, the role of divine providence was significantly reduced in dramatic literature. Miraculous endings and the *deus ex machina* disappeared. Tragic resolutions, which implied a kind of cosmic justice, gave way to the unhappy ending. Villainy diminished as moral absolutism was replaced by situational ethnics because playwrights argued that miscreants were victims of forces beyond their control.
- **Karl Marx** (1818–1883) advanced socialism, a term that existed long before he wrote his famous manifesto, *Das Kapital,* in 1867. Like Darwin, Marx argued that change was inevitable and that workers could change their social and economic institutions by banding together to overthrow their oppressors. For Marx, art was the property of the bourgeois (which had usurped the monarchy) and must reflect the plight of the proletariat, which he esteemed as rulers in a classless society. Many early realistic plays, such as Gerhart Hauptmann's *The Weavers* (1892), reflected Marx's attitude in their focus on the economic conditions that repressed them. Dramatists, such as George Bernard Shaw in England and Eugene O'Neill in the United States, reflected many of the social concerns espoused by Europe's socialist reformers. Today Marxist and cultural materialist literary criticism considers art in terms of its class and economic issues.
- **Sigmund Freud** (1856–1939) and **Carl Jung** (1875–1961) studied the workings of the mind and popularized psychology. Though their approaches differed, both were concerned with motivations of human behavior. To Freud, actions were the result of a subconscious battle among the id (the agent of pleasure in the psyche), the ego (the ethical agent), and the superego (the "reality" or "parent" agent). Freud drew on classical mythology for his vocabulary. An ancient Greek might have argued that the id was the Dionysian force

pulsing through a human, while the ego was the Apollonian. To Jung, the struggle was between one's conscious and the unconscious. While the ideas of these early psychologists are too complex to summarize here, their influence on drama and performance was enormous. Playwrights often dealt with abnormal states of mind, as in Strindberg's *Miss Julie* and O'Neill's *The Hairy Ape*. Formerly taboo (a Freudian term) subjects, such as sexual frustration, became commonplace. Deviant behavior was no longer condemned, for behavior was now considered a product of a mental state over which one had little control. Most importantly, the old Aristotelian element of character usurped the primacy of plot in dramatic structure. Modern playwrights were—and still are—more concerned with the complexities of the human mind than with telling intricate stories. For actors, the psychologist's concern for the reasons behind human behavior was translated into a new acting style in which concepts like "subtext," "intentions," and "motivations" are paramount.

The Problem Play

Sociologists, evolutionists, philosophers, socialists, and psychologists created an atmosphere that precipitated radical changes in the drama in the late nineteenth century. But, as is often the case, an earlier dramatist anticipated such changes. In 1849 Alexander Dumas *fils* (1824–1895) wrote *La Dame aux Camellias*, often regarded as the first *pièce à thèse* ("thesis" or "discussion" play). In it, he attempted to defend the dignity of the "fallen woman" as he portrayed a love affair between a respectable young man (Armande) and a courtesan (Marguerite). Though this much-imitated play, known as *Camille*, is a melodrama, Dumas' *fils* was an attempt to break new ground. He stated his intentions in a letter to a friend; the italicized portions here most directly reflect the spirit of the drama that followed:

> I realize the prime requisites of a play are laughter, tears, passion, emotion, interest, curiosity: to leave life at the cloak room. But I maintain that if, by means of all these ingredients and without minimizing one of them, I can exercise some influence over society; if, instead of treating effects, I can treat causes; if, for example, while I satirize and dramatize adultery, *I can find means to force people to discuss the problems* and the lawmakers to revise the law, I shall have done more than my part as a poet, I shall have done my duty as a man. . . . We need invent nothing, we have only to observe, remember, feel, coordinate, restore. *As for the basis, the real*; as for the facts, what is possible; as for means, what is ingenious: that is all that can be asked of us. [Emphasis added]

The decade of the 1870s was especially important in the Western theater's march toward realism. Although Ibsen wrote *The Pillars of Society* in 1877 and *A Doll's House* two years later—the works most often cited as the first genuine "problem plays"—events in Germany and France helped create the cultural atmosphere for Ibsen's daring new works. (See Forum, "The Sociology of Modern Drama.")

The Rise of the Director

In 1874 Berlin hosted a provincial theater company, the Meiningen Players, who arrived in the capital for a four-week engagement. However, they extended their run by six weeks to satisfy audiences clamoring for the new "realism" they brought to the stage. The company derived its name from the small duchy of Saxe-Meiningen, where Duke Georg II indulged his passion for theater by mounting extraordinary productions in which all of the elements of scenery, custom, music, acting, and stage pictures were coordinated by a single vision: the duke's. Working with Ludwig Chronegk, his stage manager, the duke meticulously created realistic worlds for such plays as Shakespeare's *Julius Caesar* and Schiller's *William Tell*. He invented appropriate stage business for even the most faceless "extra," and grouped his crowds in aesthetically ap-

FORUM

"The Sociology of Modern Drama"

George Lukács

George Lukács was a Hungarian critic who, in 1909, was among the first to examine Europe's "new" drama, largely from the perspective of a Marxist. He noted that the unheroic protagonists of modern drama are too often passive and victimized by their society. Through Lukács we may experience how contemporaries regarded the new realistic and social dramas, even as Europe was on the verge of war and social revolution.

Modern drama is the drama of the bourgeoisie; modern drama is bourgeois drama. By the end of our discussion, we believe, a real and specific content will have filled out this abstract formulation. . . .

The drama has now taken on new social dimensions. This development became necessary, and necessary at this particular time, because of the specific social situation of the bourgeoisie. For bourgeois drama is the first to grow out of conscious class confrontation; the first with the set intention of expressing the patterns of thought and emotion, as well as the relations with other classes, of a class struggling for power and freedom. . . . Although in Elizabethan drama the representatives of several classes appear, the true human beings, the dramatic characters, are derived on the whole from a single class. Infrequently, we find a figure that represents the petty nobility, as in *Arden of Feversham*. The lower classes merely take part in comic episodes, or they are on hand simply so their inferiority will highlight the refinements of the heroes. For this reason, class is not decisive in structuring the character and action of these plays. . . .

A new determinant is joined to the new drama: value judgment. In the new drama not merely passions are in conflict, but ideologies, *Weltanschauungen*, as well. Because men collide who come from differing situations, value judgments must necessarily function as importantly, at least, as purely individual characteristics. . . . The moral outlooks of Hamlet and Claudius, and even of Richard and Richmond, are at bottom identical. Each man is resolute, and feels contemptible if he acts contrary to this moral view. Claudius knows the murder of his brother to be a sin; he is even incapable of seeking motives that might justify his action, and it is inconceivable that he would attempt a relativist justification (as Hebbel's Herodes will, following the murder of Aristobulus). Also the "skeptical" and "philosophical" Hamlet never for a moment doubts that he is impelled as though by categorical imperative to seek blood revenge. So long as he remains incapable of acting as he knows he must, he feels

From "The Sociology of Modern Drama" by George Lukács. Translated by Lee Baxandall. *Tulane Drama Review* 9, (T28):146–170. Reprinted by permission of the *Tulane Drama Review*.

sinful and blameworthy. Hegel is therefore correct when he says the deeds of Shakespeare's heroes are not "morally justified." For the ethical value judgment of that epoch rested upon such solid metaphysical foundations, showed such little tolerance for any kind of relativity, and gained universality from such mystic, nonanalyzable emotions, that no person violating it—for whatever reasons and motive—could justify his act even subjectively. His deed could be explained by his soul's condition, but no amount of reasoning could provide absolution. . . .

The conflict of generations as a theme is but the most striking and extreme instance of a phenomenon new to drama, but born of general emotion. For the stage has turned into the point of intersection for pairs of worlds distinct in time; the realm of drama is one where "past" and "future," "no longer" and "not yet," come together in a single moment. What we usually call "the present" in drama is the occasion of self-appraisal; from the past is born the future, which struggles free of the old and of all that stands in opposition. The end of each tragedy sees the collapse of an entire world. The new drama brings what in fact is new, and what follows the collapse differs qualitatively from the old; whereas in Shakespeare the difference was merely quantitative. Looked at from an ethical perspective: the bad is replaced by the good, or by something better than the old, and at any rate decidedly different in kind. In *Götz von Berlichingen* Goethe depicts the collapse of a world; a tragedy is possible in this case only because Götz was born at the particular time. A century or perhaps even a generation earlier, and he would have become a hero of legend, perhaps rather like a tragicomic Don Quixote; and a scant generation later as well, this might have been the result. . . .

. . . The heroes of the new drama—in comparison to the old—are more passive than active; they are acted upon more than they act for themselves; they defend rather than attack; their heroism is mostly a heroism of anguish, of despair, not one of bold aggressiveness. Since so much of the inner man has fallen prey to destiny, the last battle is to be enacted within. We can best summarize by saying that the more the vital motivating center is displaced outward (i.e., the greater the determining force of external factors), the more the center of tragic conflict is drawn inward; it becomes internalized, more exclusively a conflict in the spirit. For up to a certain limit, the inner powers of resistance upon which the spirit can depend become greater and more intense in direct proportion to the greatness and intensity of the outwardly opposing forces. And since the hero now is confronted not only with many more external factors than formerly, but also by actions which have become not his own and turn against him, the struggle in which he engages will be heightened into anguish. He must engage in the struggle: something drives him into it which he cannot resist; it is not his to decide whether he even wishes to resist.

(continued)

This is the dramatic conflict: man as merely the intersection point of great forces, and his deeds not even his own. Instead something independent of him mixes in, a hostile system which he senses as forever indifferent to him, thus shattering his will. And the why of his acts is likewise never wholly his own, and what he senses as his inner motivating energy also partakes of an aspect of great complex which directs him toward his fall. The dialectical force comes to reside more exclusively in the idea, in the abstract. Men are but pawns, their will is but their possible moves, and it is what remains forever alien to them (the *abstractum*) which moves them. Man's significance consists only of this, that the game cannot be played without him, that men are the only possible hieroglyphs with which mysterious inscription may be composed. . . .

The new drama is nevertheless the drama of individualism, and that with a force, an intensity and an exclusiveness no other drama ever had. Indeed, one can well conceive an historical perspective on the drama which would see in this the most profound distinction between the old and new drama; such an outlook would place the beginnings of new drama at the point where individualism commences to become dramatic. . . . We said previously that new drama is bourgeois and historicist; we add now that it is a drama of individualism. And in fact these three formulas express a single point of demarcation; they merely view the parting of ways from distinct vantage points. The first perspective is the question of sociological basis, the foundation on which the other two are based and from which they grow. It states simply that the social and economic forms which the bourgeoisie opposed to remaining vestiges of the feudal order became, from the eighteenth century onward, the prevailing forms. Also, that life proceeds within this framework, and in the tempo and rhythm it dictates, and thus the problems this fact provokes are precisely the problems of life; in a word, that culture today is bourgeois culture. . . . Both historicism and individualism have their roots in the soil of this one culture, and though it may seem from several points of view that they would be sharply conflicting, mutually exclusive opposites, we must nevertheless ask how much this opposition really amounts to an antagonism. . . .

In the course of German Romanticism the historicist sense grew to consciousness together with and parallel to Romantic Individualism, and the two were never felt to exclude one another. We must regard as no accident the way both of these sensibilities rose to consciousness coincidentally and closely associated with the first great event of bourgeois culture, and perhaps its most decisive, the French Revolution, and all that happened around and because of it. . . .

If we examine even the superficial externals of modern life, we are struck by the degree to which it has grown uniform, though it theoretically has engendered a most extreme individualism. Our clothing has grown uniform, as has the communications system; the various forms of employment, from the employee's viewpoint, have grown ever more similar (bureaucracy, mechanized industrial labor); education and the experiences of childhood are more and more alike (the effect and increasing influence of big-city life); and so on. Parallel to this is the ongoing *rationalizing* of our life. Perhaps the essence of the modern division of labor, as seen by the individual, is that ways are

sought to make work independent of the worker's capacities, which, always irrational, are but qualitatively determinable; to this end, work is organized according to production outlooks which are objective, super-personal and independent of the employee's character. This is the characteristic tendency of the economics of capitalism. Production is rendered more objective, and freed from the personality of the productive agent. An objective abstraction, capital, becomes the true productive agent in capitalist economy, and it scarcely has an organic relation with the personality of its accidental owner; indeed, personality may often become superfluous, as in corporations.

Also, scientific methodologies gradually cease to be bound up with personality. In medieval science a single individual personally would command an entire sphere of knowledge (e.g., chemistry, astrology), and masters passed on their knowledge or "secret" to the pupils. The same situation was true in the medieval trades and commerce. But the modern specialized methodologies become continually more objective and impersonal. The relation between work and its performers grows more loose; less and less does the work engage the employee's personality, and conversely, the work is related ever less to the workers' personal qualities. Thus work assumes an oddly objective existence, detached from the particularities of individual men, and they must seek means of self-expression outside their work. The relations between men grow more impersonal as well. Possibly the chief characteristic of the feudal order was the way men's dependencies and relations were brought into unity; by contrast, the bourgeois order rationalizes them. The same tendency to depersonalize, with the substitution of quantitative for qualitative categories, is manifested in the overall state organization (electoral system, bureaucracy, military organization, etc.). Together with all this, man too develops a view of life and the world which is inclined toward wholly objective standards, free of any dependency upon human factors.

The style of the new individualism, especially the aspect of importance to us, is defined by this displacement in the relations of liberty and constraint. The transformation can be briefly formulated; previously, life itself was individualistic, now men, or rather their convictions and their outlooks on life, are. Early ideology emphasized constraint, because man felt his place within a binding order to be natural and consistent with the world system; and yet, all occasions of concrete living offered him the opportunity to inject his personality into the order of things by means of his deeds. Hence a spontaneous and continuous individualism of this sort was feasible, whereas today it has grown conscious and problematic as a result of the transformation we have sketched. Previously it was—in Schiller's sense—naïve, and today sentimental. The formulation is this, applied to drama: the old drama, by which we mean here primarily that of the Renaissance, was drama of great individuals, today's is that of individualism. In other words, the realization of personality, its per se expression in life, could in no wise become a theme of earlier drama, since personality was not yet problematic. It is, in the drama of today, the chief and most central problem. Though it is true that in most tragedies the action consisted of the clash at some point of someone's maximum attainment with what lay outside him, and the existing order of things refused to let a figure rise to the peak of his possibilities without destroying him, yet this was never associated, consciously at least, with the blunt concept of maximized attainment. The arrangement of the situation was never such that the tragedy had necessarily to result, as it were, from the bare fact of willing, the mere realization of personality. In summary: where the tragedy was previously brought on by the particular *direction* taken by the will, the mere *act* of willing suffices to induce it in the new tragedy. Once again Hebbel offers the most precise definition. He stated that it did not matter for the purposes of drama whether the hero's fall was caused by good or bad actions.

The realization and maintenance of personality has become on the one hand a conscious problem of living; the longing to make the personality prevail grows increasingly pressing and urgent. On the other hand, external circumstances, which rule out this possibility from the first, gain ever greater weight. It is in this way that survival as an individual, the integrity of individuality, becomes the vital center of drama. Indeed the bare fact of Being begins to turn tragic. In view of the augmented force of external circumstance, the least disturbance or incapacity to adjust is enough to induce dissonances which cannot be resolved. Just so, the esthetic of Romanticism regarded tragedy—with a metaphysical rationale and explanation, to be sure—as a consequence of mere being, and the necessary inevitable consequence and natural correlate of individuation. Thus, the contention of these mutually opposed forces is emphasized with increasing sharpness. The sense of being constrained grows, as does its dramatic expression; likewise the longing grows for a man to shatter the bonds which bind men, even though the price he pays is his downfall. . . .

Thus we can say that the drama of individualism (and historicism) is as well the drama of milieu. For only this much-heightened sense of the significance of milieu enables it to function as a dramatic element; only this could render individualism truly problematic, and so engender the drama of individualism. This drama signals the collapse of eighteenth-century doctrinaire individualism. What then was treated as a formal contention between ideologies and life, now becomes a portion of content, an integral part of the historicist drama. Modern life liberates man from many old constraints and it causes him to feel each bond between men (since there are no longer organic) as a bondage. But in turn, man comes to be enclasped by an entire chain of abstract bondages, which are yet more complicated. He feels, whether or not he is conscious of it, that every bond whatsoever is bad and so every bond between men must be resisted as an imposition upon human dignity. In every case, however, the bondage will prove stronger than the resistance. In this perspective Schiller's first play is one typical commencement of the new drama, just as Goethe's play was in another perspective. . . .

In sum, life as the subject of poetry has grown more epic, or to be precise, more novelistic than ever (we refer, of course, to the psychological rather than the primitive form of the novel). The transposition of life into the drama is achieved only by the symptomatic rendering of the life data. For the significance of life's external particulars has declined, if we regard them with the task in mind of rendering man dramatic. Thus, the threat to

personality becomes almost of necessity the subject of theoretical discussion. Only if the problem is presented abstractly, dialectically, can we succeed in turning the particular event, which is the basic stuff of drama, into an event touching upon, and expressive of, dramatic man's inner essence. The personage must be consciously aware that in the given case directly involving him, the perpetuation of his personality is at stake. The new drama is on this account the drama of individualism: a drama of demands upon personality made conscious. For this reason men's convictions, their ideologies, are of the highest artistic importance, for they alone can lend a symptomatic significance to the naked data. Only they can bring the vital centers of drama and of character into adjustment. However, this adjustment will always remain problematic; it will never be more than a "solution," an almost miraculous coherence of mutually antagonistic forces, for the ideology threatens in turn to reduce character to a "contrapuntal necessity." . . .

The only ideology which men will not feel to be an ideology is one which prevails absolutely and tolerates no opposition or doubt; only such a one ceases to be abstract and intellectual and is entirely transformed into feeling, so that it is received emotionally just as though no problem of value-judgment were ever involved (e.g., the medieval ideology of Revenge as still found in Shakespeare, or the dictates of Honor among the Spanish). Until the ideologies motivating men became relativized, a man was right or he was wrong. If right, he recognized no relative justification of his opponents whatsoever; nothing might justify them since they were wrong. Were one to suppose that demonic passions drove them to transgress norms which otherwise were absolutely binding, then the nature of the motivating forces was itself enough to forbid sympathy for the others' state of mind, specially with opponents. The final implication of a struggle between persons was such that one could scarcely see in the opponent anyone less than a mortal enemy, and this is precisely because the struggle was irrational. How different are conflicts where the individual is taken for the mere proxy of something external to him, something objective, conflicts where the pairing of particular opponents is virtually accidental, the result of intersected necessities. This is why the man of Shakespeare's time, ripping and tearing his opponent in the wild grip of unbridled passions, could hardly be thought to conceive a sense of community with those whom he destroyed and who destroyed him. . . .

In the main, this explains why intrigue has become superfluous and even disruptive. When ever action can be "understood," man's wickedness (though its forms remain unchanged) can no longer be regarded as the ultimate cause of events (as, e.g., Shakespeare's Iago still was). The Count in Lessing's *Emilia Galotti* represents the first stage of this development; and, after the wild excesses of his initial dramas, Schiller comes to this point almost against his will, in the opinion of Philipp. Again it is Hebbel who grasps the situation in its theoretical purity, when he declares that a dramatist's worth is in inverse ratio to the number of scoundrels he requires. . . .

The new life lacks a mythology; what this means is that the thematic material of tragedies must be distanced from life artifi-

(continued)

cially. For the esthetic significance of mythology is twofold. In the first place it projects, in the concrete symbols of concrete fables, man's vital emotions concerning the most profound problems of his life. These fables are not so rigid that they cannot incorporate displacements of the general sensibility, should these occur. Should it happen, however, the retained elements will always outweigh the added elements; the perceptible event will amount to more than the new way of valuing it. The second aspect, and possibly the more important, is that the tragic situation so expressed is held at a constant natural distance from the public—a constant distance, since the event is projected into vast dark distances of time. A natural distance, since subject and content, and indeed form, have been molded in the public's midst as something their own life partakes of, something passed along from their ancestors and without which life itself could scarcely be imagined. Whatever can be made into myth is by its nature poetic. This means, in the always paradoxical fashion of every poetic work, that it is both distant and near to life, and bears in itself, without conscious stylization, the real and irreal, the naïve and all-signifying, the spontaneous and symbolic, adornment and simple pathos. At its origins, or in the process of turning the past into myth (as for instance, Shakespeare with the War of the Roses), everything that is accidental or superfluous or derives from the individual will, or depends for its effect upon the willfulness of individual taste—everything which, despite its "interestingness," renders the profound trivial—is torn from the subjects of poetry. . . .

The bourgeois drama is by nature problematic, as theory and practice both agree, and countless circumstantial and formal signs indicate. Apart from the general stylistic problems of any new drama, drama becomes problematic at its base as soon as its subject is a bourgeois destiny enacted among bourgeois personages. The thematic material of bourgeois drama is trivial, because it is all too near to us; the natural pathos of its living men is nondramatic and its most subtle values are lost when heightened into drama; the fable is willfully invented and so cannot retain the natural and poetic resonance of an ancient tradition. In consequence, most modern dramas are historical, whether they are set in a definite epoch or the timeless past, and, in view of the foregoing, their historicity gains new meaning. History is meant as a substitute for mythology, creating artificial distances, producing monumentality, clearing away trivia and injecting a new pathos. However, the distance to be gained by projecting back in history is more conscious than formerly, and it is for this reason less spirited and forced to appeal more to the facts,

forced, because more timid, to cling more strongly to empirical data. The essence of historical distancing is that it substitutes what happened long ago for what happens today. But always, one event takes the place of another; never does a symbol replace a reality. (Naturally I am not concerned here with trivial "historical truth." A modern fantasy drama is historical; it is less free of the facts than are Shakespeare's historical dramas.) . . .

When a mythology is absent—which explains why this case is perhaps more striking than others—the basis on which everything must be justified is character. When the motivations are wholly based upon character, however, the wholly inward origin of this destiny will drive the character relentlessly to the limits of pathology. The nonpathological Orestes of Aeschylus was driven from without by what drives Goethe's from within; what once was destiny, becomes character for the modern poets. When we find a pathological trait in one or another personage of the ancient poets (Heracles, Ajax, Lear, Ophelia, etc.), then it is the destiny of that personage to so become and his tragedy is that this is what becomes of him; but this tragedy does not originate in his being so. Even where the tragedy is built upon a pathological situation, as in *Phaedra*, it is still projected entirely from without: the gods have inflicted it. Perhaps this seems only a technical problem; it may appear to matter little whether Orestes is pursued by the Furies or his own heated imagination, whether it is the witches' enticing words which bring Macbeth's stormy hunger for power to ripeness, or whether Holophernes seeks his own run. In practice, however, we will see that what comes from without, what is sent upon man by the gods, is universal; it is destiny. In the same way, to the same degree, it might happen to anyone, and in the final analysis it becomes a destiny without reference to the composition of the particular character—or at any rate, not solely with reference to it. But when all has become an inner event and can follow only from the character—if, indeed, all is not so infinitely far from the nature of the concerned that they become incapable of dramatic action (as Oswald, Rank) —its intensity must be heightened into an illness if it is to be seen and heard. In pathology and in it alone lies the possibility of rendering undramatic men dramatic. Nothing else is capable of lending them that concentration of action, that intensity of the senses, which will make the act and the situation symbolic and raise the figures above the ordinary, above the everyday. Says Kerr, "in disease we find the permitted poetry of naturalism. . . . The figure is lent infinitely more dimensions and yet can be justified in reality." . . .

---

pealing compositions. The star system, which dominated Western theater in the nineteenth century, was replaced by an ensemble approach to performance. By 1880 the Meiningen Players were the most admired theatrical troupe in the Western world. They toured throughout Europe, Scandinavia, and eventually Russia, where the young Konstantin Stanislavsky saw them and was inspired to liberate the Russian theater from its ponderous acting techniques. The Duke of Saxe-Meiningen is often referred to as the progenitor of the modern stage director because he transformed the theater by encouraging visual realism and ensemble performance.

Naturalism

Meanwhile, in France, Emile Zola (1840–1902), who had applied Comte's theories to the novel, turned the theater into a social laboratory where audiences could observe humans in the squalid environments that shaped their aberrant behaviors. Zola declared that he was "antiart" because art—especially in the French theater, now dominated by tawdry melodramas and farces—was too contrived to be effective. He wanted a theater that depicted random, mundane events: "One simply takes from life the history of a being, or a group of beings, whose acts one faithfully records." Zola referred to such actions, and the all-important environment in which they take place, as "*la tranche à vie*" ("slice of life"), a key term in the evolution of realistic drama.

Actually, Zola, like his countryman Henri Becque (1837–1899), and the Swedish playwright August Strindberg (1849–1912), was advancing an extreme form of realism: *naturalism*. The term defines both a philosophy and a theatrical style:

- Naturalism is a philosophy of determinism (derived from Darwin and Spencer) contending that humans are products of their heredity and their environment. Naturalistic plays are characterized by gloominess and pessimism because their characters are trapped in a world from which there is no escape.
- Naturalism, as a theatrical style, places a premium on actualistic details in scenery, costumes, and lighting, and it demands an acting style that is thoroughly lifelike. Naturalism is familiar, largely in the form of modern films about the "mean streets." Actors such as Al Pacino, Denzel Washington, Meryl Streep, and Edward James Olmos specialize in naturalistic films. Film accommodates naturalism especially well because the camera takes us into actual locations and captures their details with photographic precision.

At the risk of oversimplifying complex issues, one might say that naturalism places realism under a microscope in its quest to portray life onstage. Or as one wag put it, "Realism shows life as it is, while Naturalism shows life as it is—only worse."

Concerns with heredity and environment have lasted well into this century. The 1957 Broadway musical *West Side Story* illustrates these points in one of the play's most provocative songs, "Gee, Officer Krupke." The Jets, a street gang, satirize their frequent encounters with police officers, social workers, psychologists, and penologists. At one point they rationalize their delinquency with these lines:

> *Our mothers all are junkies,*
>
> *Our fathers all are drunks,*
>
> *Golly Moses, naturally we're punks.*

We might refer to this defense as the "hereditary principle." Later in the song, one of the Jets asserts that "I'm depraved on accounta I'm deprived." This is the other half of the equation, which we might call "the environmental principle." Although lyricist Stephen Sondheim and composer Leonard Bernstein are satirizing social problems in the 1950s, they echo the concerns of the early realists of the previous century.

While Zola was a visionary, he was more successful as a novelist than as a playwright because he found it difficult to reduce the random details of this novels on the stage. Despite his calls for reform, his plays, such as *Thérèse Raquin* (1873), retained an essentially melodramatic quality in which sensationalism supersedes logic. Zola's "Preface to *Thérèse Raquin*," a manifesto for the naturalists, is more important than the play. Zola's dreams of a "history of a group of beings" were realized by Anton Chekhov and his successors. His call for a theater language that replicates "spoken conversation . . . free from declamation, big words, and grand sentiments" manifests itself in the writings of such contemporaries as David Mamet and Marsha Norman. The triumph of Zola's ideal may be found in Norman's Pulitzer Prize–winning play, 'Night Mother, which probes a woman's suicide in one lengthy act.

The Fathers of Realism: Ibsen, Strindberg, and Chekhov

Ironically, true realism in the modern theater sprang from the least likely places—Scandinavia and Russia. The geographical and cultural remoteness of Norway, Sweden, and czarist Russia allowed the Scandinavians Henrik Ibsen and August Strindberg and the Russians Anton Chekhov and Konstantin Stanislavsky the freedom to experiment with new forms, unfettered by the weight of long-standing dramatic traditions.

Ibsen's most famous works were shaped in no small part by popular Continental dramas, particularly Scribe's well-made plays. From Scribe he learned how to engage an audience through a well-structured play that builds to a satisfying climax. Ibsen's genius, as Bernard Shaw points out in his seminal essay "The Quintessence of Ibsenism" (1913), was the manner in which he inserted pointed discussions about social issues between the crisis and climax of the old Scribean formula. Shaw's analysis remains among the best explications of Ibsen's method:

> Formerly you had what was called a well-made play: an exposition in the first act, a situation in the second, an unraveling in the third. Now you have exposition, situation, and discussion; and the discussion is the test of the playwright. The critics protest in vain. They declare that discussions are not dramatic, and that art should not be didactic. Neither the playwrights nor the public take the smallest notice of them. The discussion conquered Europe in Ibsen's *A Doll's House* and now the serious playwright recognizes in the discussion not only the main test of his highest powers, but also the real center of the play's interest.

Ibsen's provocative dramas stuck a chord as he outraged the old establishment, who considered him dangerous; he left Norway and wrote the majority of his works in Germany and Italy. The new generation saw in Ibsen's works a defiant voice that spoke for them: Hauptmann in Germany, Shaw in England, and James A. Herne in America. Women also emerged as important voices, both as characters in plays and, gradually, as writers. Susan Glaspell, instrumental in the emergence of a new American drama, wrote Ibsen-like plays as early as 1915. American actresses such as Minnie Maddern Fiske built their reputations, in part, by playing Ibsen's well-etched heroines.

In Sweden, Strindberg was also writing the new drama, though his plays are less concerned with the social implications of their protagonists' dilemmas. Strindberg, who suffered periods of mental illness, was drawn more to the inner workings of his characters' minds. If Ibsen was the most influential in portraying social dilemmas, Strindberg inspired modernists with his intense psychological portraits. In particular, the Swedish playwright had a profound effect on the style and thematic concerns of Eugene O'Neill, whose autobiographical play *Long Day's Journey into Night* is more aligned with Strindberg's dramaturgy than that of Ibsen's.

With the benefit of a hundred years of hindsight, we can now say that it was the Russian Anton Chekhov (1860–1904) who most fully portrayed realism onstage. Although Ibsen claimed that he wished "to produce the illusion of reality," his plays retain elements associated with nineteenth-century melodrama. Chekhov, however, devised a drama of what has been called "the action of inaction." In a letter to a friend, Chekhov defined his theatrical purpose:

> Let the things that happen on stage be just as complex and yet as simple as they are in real life. For instance, people are having a meal at a table, just having a meal, but at the same time their happiness is being created or their lives are being smashed up.

Here Chekhov suggests one of the primary characteristics of his dramaturgy: the action most often occurs offstage, and his protagonists are most often unaware of the changes in their lives. Hence, Chekhovian plays are frequently considered "anticlimactic" because they do not build to a traditional climax and a resolution of the conflict. As so often happens in life, characters go on in ignorance, trapped by their own inertia. Sadly, they remain static in a world that is changing rapidly.

The typical Chekhov play consists primarily of a series of seemingly inconsequential conversations among a variety of characters. Rather than place an audience's emotional investment in a single character, Chekhov diffuses the sympathetic response to distance audiences from the dramatic action so they can see the folly (a comic response) of the frustrated, nearly tragic lives of his characters. For this reason, Chekhov's plays are customarily designated as tragicomedies. With its lack of discernible action, absence of theatrical climaxes, focus on the mundane, and refusal to resolve conflicts in either the traditional comedic or tragic ways, Chekhov invented a drama that is, in Francis Ferguson's estimation, "the closest to the reality of the human situation." Both realists (e.g., Tennessee Williams) and nonrealists (e.g., Samuel Beckett) have acknowledged their indebtedness to Chekhov's style.

Intimate Theaters

The new realism necessitated changes in theatrical architecture. Nineteenth-century playhouses across Europe and in America were cavernous because they were designed to house the elaborate scenery required by melodrama and to ensure enough seats to generate revenues to pay for the spectacles. These enormous spaces forced actors to enlarge gestures, to speak in thundering tones, and, in general, to portray characters in large-than-life dimensions. (You can still see this style in many of the early silent movies that used actors trained in the older methods.) New theater spaces provided intimacy so actors could sit and talk in the natural tones necessi-

Anton Chekhov reads one of his plays for Stanislavsky and the members of the Moscow Art Theatre.

tated by the scripts. Furthermore, the controversial nature of the new works meant smaller audiences and the threat of censorship. Consequently, a number of intimate theaters sprang up
that placed audiences, now numbering perhaps a hundred, closer to the actors, who could
speak naturally and who no longer needed grand gestures and grimaces. Strindberg's own theater in Stockholm was aptly named the Intimate Theatre.

Among the most important of the new theaters was the *Théâtre-Libre* (Free Theatre),
founded in Paris and in May 1887 by André Antoine (1858–1941), a French civil servant
whose interest in the new social dramas led him to transform performance modes. Antoine
named his enterprise after Victor Hugo's Romantic essay "A Theatre Set Free." Like Hugo,
Antoine wanted to free the theater from its old constraints by creating a new art for the commoner who could see plays addressing relevant social problems. To finance his venue, he sold
season subscriptions to his "theater club," where he produced the new works of such dramatists
as Zola, Ibsen, Strindberg, Tolstoy, and Hauptmann. Not only were the new scripts daring, the
style in which they were presented was also innovative. Antoine insisted on new three-dimensional scenery for each production, and he advocated the use of natural light sources. He often
brought "the real thing" onstage (he used actual beef carcasses in Fernand Icre's *The Butchers*).
His actors stood with their backs to the audience and spoke in conversational tones. Everything about an Antoine production was calculated to suggest that the audience was watching
real life through an invisible fourth wall.

The integrity and success of the Théâtre-Libre inspired imitators across Europe and, eventually, the United States and Latin America. In Germany, Otto Brahm created the *Frei Buhne*
(Free Theatre) in 1889. In London, J. T. Grien opened the Independent Theater in March
1891 with a production of Ibsen's *Ghosts*. He soon persuaded one of London's most thoughtful
critics and social thinkers, Bernard Shaw, to write plays for his avant-garde enterprise. In 1904
the Abbey Theatre opened in Dublin to encourage native voices, speaking in purely Irish accents. The poet-playwright William Butler Yeats, Lady Augusta Gregory (herself an excellent
dramatist), and John Millington Synge founded the Abbey, which still flourishes today. The
"little theater" movement arrived in the United States in 1915 when George Cram Cook and
his wife, Susan Glaspell, founded the Provincetown Players on Cape Cod. In New York City,
Cook and his company converted a stable on Macdougal Street into the Playwright's Theatre.
In 1918 it became the Provincetown Playhouse, the site generally recognized as the birthplace
of the modern American theater. Closer to our time, the Market Theatre in Johannesburg,
South Africa, has captured the spirit of the independent theater; you may read about its inception and purpose in Chapter 8.

Whether in Paris, Berlin, Stockholm, Dublin, or Greenwich Village, the new independent theaters had common goals. All were committed to new works concerned with contemporary society. All were drawn to the new production style that sought to give the illusion of
real life onstage (though they also experimented with Expressionism and symbolist drama).
Perhaps most importantly, all disdained the commercial theater.

The Second Generation of Realists

Realism and naturalism have flourished in the West throughout much of the twentieth century, particularly in the United States, where the Group Theater and Actors Studio fostered
actors and playwrights who were especially adept at realism. The period from 1930 through the
1950s might be considered the golden age of realistic drama. Playwrights such as O'Neill, Lillian Hellman, Clifford Odets, Tennessee Williams, and Arthur Miller were at the height of
their powers. In turn, they influenced a new generation of American playwrights, including
Lorraine Hansberry, Edward Albee, David Mamet, and even commercial playwrights such as
Neil Simon.

As might be expected, a vibrant African American theater has emerged in response to
problems created by segregation and racism. Most of these dramas tend toward the tradition of

the social realists, though they have been attempts to incorporate traditional African theater modes in the writing and performance of the plays. Because so much African-American theater is a product of the African diaspora, which uprooted people from their homeland, important plays by Lorraine Hansberry, Amiri Baraka, and August Wilson may be found in the following chapter, which is dedicated to the theater of Africa and the diaspora.

England, too, produced a number of significant realists, none more important than John Osborne (1929–1995), whose scathing social drama *Look Back in Anger* (1956) reinvigorated the British theater and yielded a new generation of angry young men and women such as John Arden, Edward Bond, Sheilah Delaney, and Caryl Churchill. Like their predecessor in social drama, Bernard Shaw, they questioned those institutions and social conventions that limited an individual's freedom and growth. (See Forum, "The Theatre of Revolt.")

However, by midcentury social drama frequently was driven by a cynicism and hopelessness that was prompted by the cold war and atomic weapons, and that transcended the earlier realism of Ibsen, Shaw, and Odets. Compare two speeches by leading realists. In Odets's *Awake and Sing* (1936), a Depression-era youth vows to fight for a better world:

> Get teams [of workers] together all over. Spit on your hands and get to work. And with enough teams together maybe we'll get steam in the warehouse so our fingers don't freeze off. Maybe we'll fix it so life won't be printed on dollar bills.

In Osborne's drama, written only 20 years later, a spokesman for the postwar generation of disaffected youth laments that

> there aren't any good, brave causes left. If the big bang does come, and we all get killed off, it won't be in aid of the old-fashioned grand design. It'll just be for the Brave New-nothing-very-much-thank-you. About as pointless and inglorious as stepping in front of a bus.

As you read the varied social dramas herein, note those in which change seems possible and those in which the protagonists feel trapped by time and circumstance.

Social Drama in Asia and Latin America

By contrast, Asia has remained conspicuously nonrealistic in its drama, though the plays of India's Rabindranath Tagore (1861–1941) echo much of the social criticism, usually in a satirical mode, emanating from the West. Japan and China have seen the emergence of some realistic dramas, but for the most part contemporary social problems are addressed in more traditional, or at least nonrealistic, terms. In Japan, for example, Shigure Hasegawa has used the forms of Kabuki theater in such plays as *Wavering Traces* to address the problems of being a woman in contemporary Japan. In China, the Maoist government sponsored spectacular operas, such as *The White-Haired Girl*, to validate the Communist regime and to attack the feudal system that precipitated the revolution.

In Latin America playwrights, especially Mexico's Rudolfo Usigli (1905–1979), often combine fantasy and psychological realism to their advantage as they probe the social dilemmas of nations emerging from colonialism to independence. *Paper Flowers* (Chapter 9), by Chile's Egon Wolff (1926–), works on two levels—as psychological realism and as grotesque fantasy—in its symbolic depiction of the revolt against the old monied order by the oppressed. In one relevant speech, a impoverished young man tells a wealthy woman that "I only know I am what I seem and not that I am what I don't seem. In other words, you have your fantasy and I have only reality, which is much poorer, much sadder, much more disillusioning."

FORUM

"The Theatre of Revolt"

ROBERT BRUSTEIN

Robert Brustein is both an academic and a practicing theater artist. He served as Artistic Director of the American Repertory Theatre (ART) in Cambridge, Massachusetts while teaching at Harvard; formerly he was head of the Yale School of Drama. The Theatre of Revolt (1965) remains among the finest studies of modern drama and its thematic concerns.

Let us begin with a pair of images.

First, imagine an open temple of classical proportions, surrounded by rising tiers. Gathered on separate levels are artisans, citizens, nobility—divided into classes but forming a unified congregation of spectators. In front of the temple is an altar before which stands a high priest in hieratic robes. Beyond the temple is a city; beyond the city, the celestial spheres, moving steadily in their orbits. The priest conducts a ritual ceremony by miming a myth of heroism and violence. The congregation is startled by the growing frenzy of the action; the atmosphere grows taut and strained. The high priest concludes his service with a ritual sacrifice, and blood pours from the alter. The congregation screams as if it were the victim. Some spectators fall from their seats; the temple cracks; the city begins to crumble; the spheres start wildly form their course. At the point when total dissolution seems imminent, the scene freezes. The spectators file out, their anxiety mingled with an ethereal calm.

Now, imagine a perfectly level plain in a desolate land. In the foreground, an uneasy crowd of citizens huddle together on the ruins of an ancient temple. Beyond them, a broken altar, bristling with artifacts. Beyond that, empty space. An emaciated priest in disreputable garments stands before the ruined altar, level with the crowd, glancing into a distorting mirror. He cavorts grotesquely before it, inspecting his own image in several outlandish positions. The crowd mutters ominously and partially disperses. The priest turns the mirror on those who remain to reflect them sitting stupidly on rubble. They gaze at their images for a moment, painfully transfixed; then, horrorstruck, they run away, hurling stones at the altar and angry imprecations at the priest. The priest, shaking with anger, futility, and irony, turns the mirror on the void. He is alone in the void.

The first is an image for the theatre of communion; the second for the theatre of revolt.

By theatre of communion, I mean the theatre of the past, dominated by Sophocles, Shakespeare, and Racine, where traditional myths were enacted before an audience of believers against the background of a shifting but still coherent universe. By theatre of revolt, I mean the theatre of the great insurgent modern dramatists, where myths of rebellion are enacted before a dwindling number of spectators in a flux of vacancy, bafflement, and accident. I have described these two theatres

metaphorically in order to make two points rapidly: (1) that the traditional and the modern theatres are clearly distinguishable from each other in regard to the function of their dramatists, the engagement of their audiences, and the nature of the worlds they imply and evoke, and (2) that the playwrights of the modern theatre form a movement just as distinctive as the various schools of the past. Ibsen, Strindberg, Chekhov, Shaw, Brecht, Pirandello, O'Neill, and Genet—to name the dramatists discussed at length in this book—are all highly individualistic artists. Yet they share one thing in common which separates them from their predecessors and links them to each other. This is their attitude of revolt, an attitude which is the product of an essentially Romantic inheritance....

While the theatre of revolt has immediate roots in nineteenth-century Romanticism, it is, in a large sense, the inevitable consequence of a long preparatory process which begins in the Middle Ages. The ruins in the second image are the remains of the proud monuments of the first. It is atop the broken hierarchies, discredited values, and collapsed institutions of traditional culture that the modern dramatist meditates his revolt.

The theatre of communion, in fact, reaches its historical climax with a premonitory glimpse into the disintegration of the traditional world order. The drama of the Western world, like the drama of the Greeks, describes a trajectory which arches from belief to uncertainty to unbelief, always developing in the direction of greater skepticism toward temporal and spiritual laws. Greek tragedy, for example, moves from the religious piety of Aeschylus to the tragic ambivalence of Sophocles to the angry agnosticism of Menander and New Comedy. And Western drama develops from the religious certainty of the medieval playwrights to the doubts and hesitations of the Stuart dramatists, where the characters of Webster and Middleton look up to empty heavens and Shakespeare's tragic heroes peer into a vast abyss. A growing sense of futility and despair infects both Hellenistic culture and the culture of late Renaissance Europe, which is reflected in certain Naturalistic philosophies, calling everything in doubt....

The modern drama, in short, rides in on the second wave of Romanticism—not the cheerful optimism of Rousseau, with his emphasis on institutional reform, but rather the dark fury of Nietzsche, with his radical demands for a total transformation of man's spiritual life. And Nietzsche remains the most seminal philosophical influence on the theatre of revolt, the intellect against which almost every modern dramatist must measure his own. When Nietzsche declared the death of God, he declared the death of all traditional values as well. Man could create new values only by becoming God: the only alternative to nihilism lay in revolt. Nietzsche's arrogant *I will* was a desperate response to an absurd universe. And all modern revolt, as Albert Camus writes in his monumental study *The Rebel* (*L'Homme Révolté*), is "born of the spectacle of irrationality, confronted with an unjust and incomprehensible condition." Confronted with the same metaphysical absurdity, the modern dramatist takes up Neitzsche's challenge, assuming an attitude of refusal which puts him in conflict with the laws of modern necessity. Rejecting God, church, community, and family—vindicating the rights of the individual against the claims of government, morality, conventions, and rules—he adopts the posture of the rebel, chafing against restraints, determined to make all barriers crack. . . .

The modern dramatist is essentially a metaphysical rebel, not a practical revolutionary; whatever his personal political convictions, his art is the expression of a spiritual condition. For he is a militant of the ideal, an anarchic individualist, concerned with the impossible rather than the possible; and his discontent extends to the very roots of existence. The work of art itself becomes a subversive gesture—a more imaginative reconstruction of a chaotic, disordered world. . . .

The theatre of revolt, in other words, is extremely self-conscious and self-involved, as befits a Romantic movement. And like the other Romantics, the dramatist begins to enter his work to a hitherto unprecedented degree. Strindberg and O'Neill are almost indistinguishable from their heroes; Ibsen and Shaw identify themselves with their heroes to a large extent; Brecht hides his experiences in his plays, but speaks out directly through the figure of a third-person narrator; Pirandello and Genet shape their works to an almost solipsistic concept; and even Chekhov hovers about his plays as a moral presence. Whether involved as an idea or a character, the modern dramatist is continually exploring the possibilities of his own personality—not only representing but exhorting, not only dramatizing the others but examining the self. This self-examination, common enough to the other Romantic arts, does not with them constitute such a radical break with tradition. The material of the lyric poet has always been largely personal, and even the autobiographic element in Proust or Joyce does not violate the conventions of a form which, even since Homer, has permitted the author his part in the narrative. The subjectivity of the rebel dramatist, on the other hand, is unique, since the drama has traditionally been a form of imitation—impersonal, objective, detached—with the author excluded from the work.

Still, the theatre of revolt is only partially subjective; the rebel dramatist continues to observe the requirements of his form. A play proceeds by dialogue, and dialogue implies debate and conflict. Without debate, the drama is propaganda; without conflict, mere fantasizing. The rebel dramatist may desire to live out his revolt in his art, but this desire is disciplined by his objective consciousness. Personal fantasies and abstract ideas enter the modern drama, but concrete action and imitation remain— the self shares the stage with the others. . . . The rebel who wishes to transform the world is also an artist who must accurately represent it; the Romantic who would destroy all boundaries is also a Classicist, accepting limitations in life and art. This ambivalence makes the rebel dramatist vacillate between negation and affirmation, between rebellion and reality. Unable to master his contradictions, he dramatizes them in his plays, grateful for a form in which tensions do not have to be resolved.

The theatre of revolt, then, is the temple of a priest without a God, without an orthodoxy, without even much of a congregation, who conducts his service within the hideous architecture of the absurd. A missionary of discord, he spreads a gospel of insurrection, trying to substitute his inspired vision for traditional values, trying to improvise a ritual out of anguish and frustration. Instead of myths of communion, he offers myths of dispersal; instead of consoling sermons, painful demands; instead of a liturgy of acceptance, a liturgy of complaint. He is an apostate priest, and one who secretly would be God. Taking as his motto Lucifer's *Non serviam*, he emerges as the spirit of denial, the man who says No, pursuing his Yes down the countless avenues of revolt.

To chart these avenues is the purpose of this book. The process is difficult and complicated, since their direction varies with each dramatist. But, in general, we can distinguish three main highways into which the avenues run. The first is extremely broad, the second more narrow, and the third a one-way street, for the modern drama grows progressively more confined as the exigencies of the time begin to limit the possibilities of revolt. I have called these categories of revolt *messianic, social, existential*. These terms will be more fully elaborated, but I can define them quickly through reference to my initial images. *Messianic revolt* occurs when the dramatist rebels against God and tries to take His place—the priest examines his image in the mirror. *Social revolt* occurs when the dramatist rebels against the conventions, morals, and values of the social organism—the priest turns the mirror on the audience. *Existential revolt* occurs when the dramatist rebels against the conditions of his existence—the priest turns the mirror on the void. Each of the eight dramatists considered in this book—in fact, most of the dramatists in the modern theatre—can be classified as messianic, social, or existential rebels; some fall into one category, some into two, some into all three. To demonstrate this, it is necessary to examine the background, nature, and style of each aspect of dramatic revolt.

Messianic revolt is the initial stage of the modern drama, and the most unashamedly Romantic. It can be found in Ibsen, Strindberg, Shaw, and O'Neill . . . it revolves around the thought and actions of a new Messiah, who thinks himself destined to replace the old God and change the life of man. Messianic revolt is the most subjective, grandiose, and egotistical of all dramatic rebellion—and so persistent in the drama that one is forced to say it is with Ibsen's early messianic epics, and not with his later "modern" plays, that the modern drama properly begins. For it is messianism which detonates the theatre of revolt. And though the explosion is loudest at the beginning of the movement, when the dramatist is bursting with a turbulent Romanticism and everything seems possible, its reverberations can be felt throughout the entire modern theatre.

Messianic drama is a medium of absolute liberation, unrestrained by dramatic rules or human limitations, through which the rebel dramatist indulges his insatiable appetite for the infinite. Conceiving the universe to be a projection of his own personality, which can be altered or manipulated through superhuman will, he imagines himself a Creator superior to God, and destined to transform life into something more ordered than the meaningless botch he sees around him. . . .

(continued)

The messianic play, in short, is a dramatization of the Romantic quest for faith; as such, it is the most personal mode in the theatre of revolt, and functions as the dramatist's religious testament. This is not to say the material is autobiographical (though it sometimes is), but rather that the messianic dramatist always has strong affinities with his protagonist. The messianic hero, in one way or another, is an extension of the playwright, who thus provides himself with superhuman faculties: the hero is the imaginative realization of the playwright's dreams, the vicarious acting out of his moral imagination. . . .

As a literary genre, the messianic drama falls into the category of myth or romance, for its central figure conforms to the definitions supplied by Northrop Frye, in *The Anatomy of Criticism,* of the mythic hero ("superior in *kind* both to other men and to the environment of other men") and of the Romantic hero ("superior in *degree* to other men and to his environment"). His actions are the marvelous doings of a superhuman figure—sometimes a god, sometimes a great hero, sometimes an inspired visionary. Still, his superiority lies not so much in noble birth, physical prowess, or miraculous deeds as in certain lofty oral and spiritual qualities which raise him above the common run of men. Ibsen looked forward to an "aristocracy of character, of will, of mind"—Nietzsche to a "new nobility . . . which shall be the adversary of all populace and potentate rule"—that is the class to which the messianic hero belongs. For, despite the touch of divinity about him, he is still mortal. (Shaw's Ancients live to be over three hundred, and Genet's Chief of Police will reign for two thousand years, but most messianic heroes ultimately face death and disillusionment.)

Finally, the language of messianic drama is lofty and elevated. Some plays are written in verse, some in a heightened prose—but messianic diction is invariably oracular, if not bombastic. For the messianic drama is informed by a powerful prophetic quality. It is the newest testament of the author, who functions as an inspired seer, handing his enlightened revelation to a benighted world.

The second stage of the modern theatre, *social revolt,* is much less ambitious, though much more familiar to modern audiences: it characterizes the best-known plays of the contemporary stage. Social revolt dominates Ibsen's "modern" plays, Strindberg's "Naturalist" dramas, Chekhov's inner actions, most of Shaw, a large part of Brecht, and some of Pirandello. . . . Social revolt, of course, is usually an aspect of messianic drama, but there it is subordinate to other matters; when it dominates a play, it is a relatively modest manifestation. The emphasis of the drama shifts from radical cures to careful diagnoses, with the patient taking the stage and the physician withdrawing behind the scenes. Instead of examining the relationship between man and God, the social dramatist concentrates on man in society, in conflict with community, government, academy, church, or family.

There is a corresponding change in dramatic form. The episodic play gives way to the three- and four-act structure; the drama loses its untidy flamboyance and becomes tight, compact, well-made. Social drama is Classical in the sense of Edmund Wilson's definition of Classicism: "In the domain of politics and morals, a preoccupation with society as a whole; and in art, an ideal of objectivity." Though the social drama is occasionally Expressionistic, it is more frequently written in the realistic or Naturalist style, through which the objective ideal is best maintained. Messianic voluptuousness and exuberance are replaced by more controlled and modulated feelings, as the playwright absents himself from the proceedings and permits the action to speak for itself. Social, political, moral, and economic questions are aired in an atmosphere of impartiality; sociological and psychological insights grow common; scientific ideas begin to influence the dramatist, particularly Darwin's theory of heredity and environment. Ibsen, Strindberg, Shaw, and Brecht all begin to think of themselves as literary scientists under the influence of Darwin, Lamarck, or Marx, while Chekhov, who claims no intellectual influences, adheres to an ideal of juridical detachment.

As for characters, the social drama puts contemporary society on the stage and draws its *dramatist personae* from the middle class. The protagonist is subject to the same laws as the rest of us, shares the same ambitions (or lack of them), performs the same domestic duties, speaks the same unlovely prose. Human stature shrinks to average height, and man's surroundings close in. . . .

Social drama, in short, represents modern life for the purpose of whipping and scourging it—it is an imitation for essentially satiric purposes. Such revolt, however, is negative. The dramatist may still be trying to kill God (if only through His earthly institutions and delegated figures of authority), but he is no longer much occupied with building a Church: the social rebel rarely suggests any clear-cut alternatives to the things he would like to destroy. It is true that propaganda plays and problem dramas are offshoots of social revolt, but I am excluding such works from this study. When Sean O'Casey writes about a Communist revolution bringing sensuality to Puritan Ireland, or when Arthur Miller evokes our sympathy for the plight of the common man, we are confronted less with works of art than with political acts or social gestures, and it is by utilitarian rather than literary criteria that such acts and gestures should be judged. As for Shaw and Brecht, these writers may also be political revolutionaries, but insofar as a positive ideology informs their work, their work is compromised. And as a matter of fact, Shaw's Socialism, discussed at length in prefaces and tracts, remains outside his plays, while Brecht's Communism is a matter of implication in all but his explicit agitprop dramas. The major social rebels are philosophical anarchists, whatever their political affiliations, for they display a profound distaste for every form of human organization, if not for humankind itself. . . .

The drama of social revolt is usually written in what Frye calls the "low mimetic mode," the style of most realistic fiction: "The hero is one of us; we respond to a sense of his common humanity, and demand from the poet the same canons of probability that we find in our experience." This hero is "superior neither to other men nor to his environment"—as Frye proceeds to observe, in fact, the word "hero" no longer retains its full meaning. This degeneration of the hero is evident, in the social drama, in a moral, structural, and sexual sense. The central character disappears from Chekhov's dramas altogether, and the group takes the stage; in Brecht, the protagonist is retained, but is now significant less for heroism than for cowardice and rapacity; in most social dramas, women begin to assume central roles.

The setting of the social play is usually contemporary; its structure is compact, and organized towards climaxes of feeling; its language is the prose vernacular of everyday life. In social revolt, the rebel dramatist has suppressed his will to power in order to examine and protest against the institutionalized life of man.

In the last stage of the modern drama, *existential revolt*, the dramatist examines the metaphysical life of man and protests against it; existence itself becomes the source of his rebellion.[1] The drama of existential revolt is a mode of the utmost restriction, a cry of anguish over the insufferable state of being human.

This form of revolt is identical with what Camus calls "metaphysical rebellion . . . the movement by which man protests against his condition and against the whole of creation." Such a definition could be applied, with equal accuracy, to messianic revolt, and, indeed, existential drama embodies the same kind of discontent with the basic structure of life. On the other hand, while messianic revolt is potent and positive, existential revolt is impotent and despairing. The messianic dramatist makes his characters superhuman; the existential dramatist makes them subhuman. The one exaggerates the extent of human freedom; the other, of human bondage. It is significant that the existential drama begins to appear with increasing frequency in our own age—an age of totalitarianism. The Gods and supermen of messianic drama have turned into animals and prisoners; the world is a vast concentration camp where social intercourse is strictly forbidden. Alone in a terrifying emptiness, the central figure of existential drama is doomed, as it were, to a life of solitary confinement.

Existential revolt, in short, occurs during the old age of the modern drama, though chronologically it may sometimes appear much earlier. It is the revolt of the fatigued and the hopeless, reflecting—after the disintegration of idealist energies—exhaustion and disillusionment. This explains its close relationship to messianic revolt, for it is actually an inverted development of the messianic impulse. . . .

Existential revolt represents Romanticism turned in on itself and beginning to rot. Extremely contemptuous of messianic ideals, disbelieving totally in messianic individualism, the existential rebel, nevertheless, shows vestiges of the old radical demands. He is a Neo-Romantic, raging against existence, ashamed of being human, revolted by the body itself. One of the strongest identifying marks of the existential drama is its attitude towards the flesh, which is usually described in images of muck, mud, ashes, and fecal matter, in a state of decomposition and decay. . . .

. . . [Existential drama] *is, in tone and atmosphere,* the most tragic of the modern genres. The messianic rebel may project himself into the heroic exploits of his dramatic characters, but the existential dramatist projects himself into their melancholy and complaint, and often manages to transcend his disgust with genuine feelings of compassion. "Humankind is pitiable," Strindberg's Daughter of Indra intones repeatedly, while the author, recoiling from the abyss of absurdity, forces himself to accept the painful riddles and contradictions of life. Strindberg's stoicism is rather typical of existential drama, which frequently subsides into a kind of resignation—an acceptance of waiting, patience, and ordeals. O'Neill's derelicts wait for death; Beckett's tramps wait for Godot; Gelber's junkies wait for their connection—even Brecht, the most relentless of the existential writer, eventually works his way through to a state of Confucian calm and serenity. Thus, if the existential drama is tragic, it is tragic in its perceptions. It lacks a tragic hero, but it evokes a tragic sense of life, that mood one often finds in Sophocles:

> Never to have lived is best, ancient writers say;
> Never to have drawn the breath of life, never to have
>   looked into the light of day;
> The second best's a gay goodnight an quickly turn away.

Here, as translated by Yeats, in the third stasimon of another drama of old age, *Oedipus at Colonus*, one finds the underlying theme of existential rebellion, a theme restated almost as beautifully in Beckett's *Godot:* "They give birth astride a grave, the light gleams an instant, then it's night once more."

"And a man's life's no more than to say 'One.'" muses Hamlet, while Beckett's Pozzo, three hundred years later, makes the same observations on the awful brevity of life: "One day we were born, one day we shall die, the same day, the same second." But if the gravedigger puts on the forceps, it takes him an eternity—time's winged chariot rushes by a scene of intense boredom and ennui. This sense of double time, alternatively swift and tedious, is implicit in most existential drama,[2] and becomes the lament of the existential rebel. Hating the present, fearing the future, he withdraws into the past, and writes his plays on the theme of time and memory. Williams's *Glass Menagerie*, for example, is an existential exploration of memory; O'Neill in *A Long Day's Journey* moves forward in time and backwards in memory simultaneously; and time is the central subject of Pirandello, who, agonized by the formless flux, conceives of characters escaping into the immobility of history or the timelessness of art. Bergson's philosophical theories, especially his theory of duration, strongly influence the existential drama—from him, the existential dramatist borrows the concept of subjective, as opposed to clock, time. This emphasis on time suggests the reflective,

---

[1]Unfortunately, the adjective *existential* has recently been monopolized by a fashionable French philosophy, but I am using this late seventeenth-century word in its original, more neutral sense. As the *Oxford English Dictionary* defines "existential," it means simply: "of and pertaining to existence." Existentialism is a highly self-conscious movement; existential revolt is not. And though Sartre and Camus may be existential rebels on occasion, very few existential rebels are formal Existentialists.

[2]It is also implicit in Chekhov. In *The Cherry Orchard*, old Firs concludes a play about apathy and tedium with the remark, "Life has slipped by as though I'd never lived"; and in *The Three Sisters*, Chekhov shows his characters aging while seeming to stand stock-still. Like the existential dramatists, Chekhov often writes of regret for a wasted life, and of paralysis and inertia—but he lacks their rage and disgust. The existential dramatist is in revolt against life; Chekhov seems to be more in revolt against his characters.

(continued)

nostalgic quality of this drama; its central figure is a man whose life is spent mournfully meditating on his past. The antihero is no longer a Cartesian *chose qui pense*—he is now the Bergsonian *chose qui dure*.

This melancholy resignation, however, is accompanied by a continuous protest, occasionally expressed through violent outbursts, almost always through a mordant, biting style. If all the more vigorous forms of revolt have now become futile, the rebel can still express his outrage verbally. To the nothingness of life, he responds with the dry mock, even though this irony is sometimes expended on himself. Even in the act of accepting the absurd, in short, he is still caught in an act of negation. And the best personification of this ambivalent mood is Strindberg's Poet, in *A Dream Play*, one who bathes in mud while he continues to scan the heavens:

> POET, ecstatically. *Out of the clay the God Ptah fashioned man on a potter's wheel, a lathe*, mockingly, *or some other damned thing. . . .* Ecstatically. *Out of clay the sculptor fashioned his more or less immortal masterpieces*, mockingly, *which are usually only rubbish. . . .* Ecstatically. *Such is clay! When clay is fluid, it is called mud.*

O'Neill's characters alternate in the same manner between yea- and nay-saying, between ecstasy and mockery; and hope and despair, of course, are the vacillating moods of Beckett's tramps. Pirandello also breaks his compassionate mood with loud, mocking laughter; and Brecht's scorching irony is one of the most famous marks of this style.

Irony, in fact, is the mark of the entire existential drama, which is written in what Frye calls the "ironic mode." In the ironic mode, the word "hero" has lost its meaning entirely—the central figure is "inferior in power and intelligence to ourselves, so that we have a sense of looking down on a scene of bondage, frustration, or absurdity." This is the scene of the antihero—usually a tramp, a proletarian, a criminal, an old man, a prisoner, confined in body and spirit, and deteriorating in his confinement. Strindberg imprisons his characters in a nightmare, and

Beckett in an undefined world (probably the future) of bareness and infertility. But even when the setting is relatively realistic—as in the plays of Pirandello, Brecht, and O'Neill—the claustrophobic atmosphere is just as oppressive. For in existential drama, nature, society, man no longer exist. In this final phase of the modern drama—in these nightmares, chimeras, hallucinations, and feverish fables—revolt finds its most pessimistic, contracted, and exhausted form.

Existential revolt is the final phase—but it is not the conclusion of the modern drama, even though so many recent plays are permeated by it. For in the radical theory of the French writer Antonin Artaud, the theatre of revolt again begins to develop messianic ambitions, and in the plays of Jean Genet, these ambitions are now being imaginatively realized. Could it be that the drama is about to repeat its cycle? According to Giovanni Battista Vico, civilization itself has a cyclical form, proceeding from divine to heroic to human manifestations—after which a clap of thunder signals the repetition of the process. This theory certainly describes the development of Greece and the West, and the concomitant development of the theatre of communion. Does it describe the development of the theatre of revolt as well? Since Vico, an eighteenth-century philosopher, could not imagine a cycle of civilization lower than the human, or a form of life baser than civic man, his *Science Nuova* omits an important stage of the modern experience. But Vico's prophecy is otherwise fulfilling itself in the theatre of revolt, and that clap of thunder is especially ominous. The new messianic writers are consciously striving to re-create the conditions of traditional theatre. Artaud wishes to restore to the drama its primitive function, and Genet's work takes the form of hieroglyphic ritual. But these very efforts become acts of revolt. With Artaud and Genet, the modern theatre turns apocalyptic once again, and once again Romanticism is in full flower. If the modern theatre is an Eternal Recurrence, and Gods and Heroes are again to take the stage, then the obvious place to start this study is where the theatre of revolt began—in the magnificent messianic mind of Henrik Ibsen.

A DOLL'S HOUSE

Henrik Ibsen

Henrik Ibsen (1828–1906)

Ibsen, often called the "Father of Modern Drama," was born in the small village of Skien in southeastern Norway. The son of a prosperous merchant, he was raised in the relative comfort of a large mansion until 1836, when his father declared bankruptcy. The move to less plush environs and ostracism from the local community left a permanent mark on Ibsen. His bitterness is reflected in many of his early poems, his 1881 unfinished autobiography, and particularly in the thematic concerns of his great social dramas.

Working as an apprentice to an apothecary, the young Ibsen dreamed of becoming a doctor. When the qualifying exams proved too difficult for him, he immersed himself in the theater as both a scholar and manager. While he was a successful scholar, theater management was not his forte. At the age of 23 he accepted the position of stage manager at the new theater in Bergen, and six years later he was named artistic director of the Christiania [Oslo] Norway Theater. Neither venue proved successful, and when the Christiania Theater was closed in 1862, Ibsen began a self-imposed exile. He spent most of the remainder of his life in Italy and Germany, sharpening his critical vision of late-nineteenth-century Europe and honing his craft as a playwright. In 1891 he returned to his homeland, where, after being incapacitated by paralyzing strokes, he died in 1906.

His dramatic works may be divided into five distinct literary styles. His earliest works, completed between 1850 and 1865, consist of verse dramas such as *Cataline* (1850)—his first attempt at drama—and *The Pretenders* (1864), which dealt with Scandinavian history. Out of this period grew a series of dramatic poems, also based on his native history. They are epic tales of individual struggles, like *Brand* (1866) and *Peer Gynt* (1867). His next plays, usually called "social protest plays," include *The Pillars of Society* (1877), *A Doll's House* (1879), *Ghosts* (1881), and *An Enemy of the People* (1882). They deal with the social and economic inequities he observed throughout Europe. As he continued to mature, he moved to psychological dramas about interpersonal relationships: *The Wild Duck* (1885), *Rosmersholm* (1887), and *Hedda Gabler* (1890) typify these plays. He concluded his career deeply immersed in plays that were symbolist—*The Master Builder* (1892), *John Gabriel Borkman* (1896), and *When We Dead Awaken* (1900).

Bernard Shaw, his chief defender in England, saw Ibsen as an innovator who placed discussion at the heart of modern drama and as a courageous leader who tackled social injustice no matter how unpopular or offensive the subject matter. Indeed, it was not uncommon for critics to declare him vulgar and coarse. Witness a brief sampling of critical commentary that greeted *Ghosts*, which deals with venereal disease, in 1881:

> Ibsen's positively abominable play entitled *Ghosts* [is a] disgusting representation. . . . An open drain; a loathsome sore unbandaged; a dirty act done publicly. . . . Absolutely loathsome and fetid . . . a mass of vulgarity, egotism, coarseness, and absurdity.

> As foul and filthy a concoction as has ever been allowed to disgrace the boards of an English theatre. . . . Dull and disgusting. . . . Nastiness and malodorousness laid on thickly as with a trowel.

> [A] Morbid, unhealthy, unwholesome and disgusting story.

In spite of this reception, Ibsen's work survives.

While his poetic dramas are marked by episodic plots, his social and psychological plays, generally considered to be his most important works, are essentially realistic. Their climactic plots grow from a gradual illumination of past transgressions, the discovery of which leads to the major reversal in the play. In *A Doll's House* the revelation of Nora's loan precipitates the climax of the play. In crafting these works, Ibsen employs the components of the well-made play: the withheld secret and the obligatory scene. Rather than using them as a springboard to move the action swiftly to its resolution, however, he suspends the action for an in-depth discussion of the play's social issues. Thus, his plays move from the realm of entertainment, sentimentality, and melodrama to genuine social commentary.

The conflicts between one's duty to self and one's duty to society, between social and moral restrictions and one's quest for personal sovereignty are Ibsen's primary thematic concerns. His leading characters, whether in pursuit of personal or political goals, invariably end up unfulfilled because they either sacrifice their own integrity or achieve success at the expense of others on whom they trample. *Brand* and *Peer Gynt* are excellent illustrations of this concept. Brand, uncompromising in his dedication to his ideal of what religion should be, sacrifices everything dear to him only to be destroyed by an avalanche that thunders, "God is love!" Peer follows a life of hedonism and compromise, only to find himself facing death with no sense of integrity, purpose, or accomplishment.

A DOLL'S HOUSE (1879)

Like many realistic plays, *A Doll's House* is based on an actual occurrence. A young mother named Laura Kieler illegally signed a large banknote to finance treatment for her tubercular husband. Trying to cash a forged check, she was apprehended, charged as an unfit mother by her husband, and committed to an asylum. Similarly, *A Doll's House* tells the simple story of a young wife, Nora Helmer, who appears to be the perfect model of a nineteenth-century homemaker. She is totally devoted to husband and children, but she unknowingly creates a potentially explosive situation. In borrowing money to finance a lifesaving trip for her sick husband, Torvald, Nora forges her father's name and thus violates both social customs and public statutes. After her husband's recovery, the Helmers are "one happy little family" until the loan's originator, Nils Krogstad, attempts to blackmail Nora. Assuming that Torvald will appreciate her lifesaving initiative when her secret is revealed, Nora is shattered when her husband castigates her as "a hypocrite, a liar—worse, worse—a criminal!" with "no religion, no morals, no sense of duty!" Horrified, Nora refuses to continue playing the "doll's role" and tells Torvald that she is leaving. When he reminds her that should she leave she would be neglecting her "most sacred duties"—her duties toward her husband and her children, she reveals that she must follow "another duty which is equally sacred. . . . My duty towards myself." As Nora exited, the reverberation of the heavy door closing was heard throughout the Western theatrical world.

The ending of the play was so shocking that many producers refused to stage the play and demanded that the ending be changed. (A leading actress of the day turned down the role of Nora for fear that her admirers might see her as one who supported Nora's "unwomanly" action.) To secure venues for his work, Ibsen wrote an alternate ending to the play in which Nora remains with Torvald, an outcome much more palatable to his conservative, Victorian audience.

Both the content and form of the play shocked nineteenth-century audiences. Accustomed to sentimental comedies, well-made plays, and melodramas wherein traditional values always triumphed, the original audiences of *A Doll's House* were taken aback by the effrontery of a woman who asserts her individuality at the expense of her family. As the climax of the play approached, they no doubt anticipated a contrite Nora who would win forgiveness from a benevolent Torvald, thereby ensuring a happy ending.

The dramatic form in which Ibsen's ideas were expressed was equally foreign to audiences in 1879. They were accustomed to plays in which the emotional intensity grew gradually from the exposition to the climax; Ibsen halted the action in midcrisis to discuss the reasons behind

Nora's forgery and for her leaving. The audience was thus forced to hold its emotions in check and confront the social implications of her actions.

Beyond its revolutionary style, two problems arise when analyzing the play. First, Ibsen's basic premise was misunderstood. Original audiences mistakenly assumed, "much to Ibsen's chagrin," as theater historian Oscar Brockett has noted, that he was promoting a "feminist" point of view. True, the play served as a rallying point for early advocates of feminism who demanded suffrage and more legal rights. While considering this interpretation, we must remember that fundamentally the play advocates the sovereignty of the individual and is not a piece of feminist propaganda. Michael Meyer, among Ibsen's most respected biographers, argues that the play stresses "that the primary duty of anyone was to find out who he or she really was and to become that person." Indeed, Ibsen himself, in an address to the Norwegian Women's Rights League, stated that he "must disclaim the honor of having consciously worked for the women's rights movement. I am not even quite clear what this women's rights movement really is. To me it has seemed a problem of humanity in general."

Second, what we regard as a glaring error in Ibsen's craftsmanship went essentially unnoticed during early productions of the play. While those who debated the appropriateness of Nora's departure focused on her action, the most disconcerting aspect from the point of view of the play's construction is that in the discussion scene Nora, heretofore a rather sheltered "plaything" or "doll," suddenly metamorphoses into an articulate social advocate. She launches into an exquisite discourse on the new morality, which champions the rights of the individual over the expectations of society. Her sudden transformation seems an abrupt departure from the logic of the action which governed the play to that point.

Furthermore, the 1879 audience may have overlooked another innovative aspect of Ibsen's style: his use of the setting as an analogy for theme. Even contemporary audiences, predisposed to adopt a feminist reading of the play, might also overlook the significance of the setting so carefully described by Ibsen. While Neoclassic writers confined the action to a single location, and Romantic writers, who disdained the unity of place, presented their action as sprawling across a continent, Ibsen confined the action to a single setting to *enhance* his theme rather than to observe or oppose any "rules." In *A Doll's House,* Ibsen gives us the literal and figurative creation of Torvald's "doll house."

It is no accident that the play transpires in what Victorians called the "parlor" (literally, a room for talk or discussion). Today we might call it a "living room." The first words of the text describe it as "A comfortably and tastefully . . . furnished room," with all the amenities of the day—"a piano . . . a stove lined with porcelain . . . armchairs and a rocking chair"—a cozy home for a "twittering skylark," a safe habitat for a "rustling squirrel." In the opening scenes it is an ideal "doll's house." But before we are 20 minutes into the play, it is clear that this comfortable "living room" becomes an uncomfortable "dying room" in which Nora is incarcerated. She has been sentenced by Torvald and society to spend her life shuffling between the other important rooms—the bedroom, the kitchen, and the children's room—to carry out the traditional roles of the Victorian woman. Nora is confronted with the choice of accepting this fate or exerting her individuality.

Should she remain confined in this room where there is security without liberty? Or, should she liberate herself at the expense of security? While she initially accepts her imprisonment because she believes in the possibility of what Torvald calls "the miracle of miracles" happening in their marriage, her optimism is destroyed by Torvald's reaction to her secret. His selfishness, his preoccupation with his public reputation, and his attacks on her fitness as wife and mother expose him as a self-centered manipulator, not as a loving husband. Ironically, the living room eventually becomes not only a "liberating room" for Nora but a prison for Torvald, its former warden.

The original production of A Doll's House *(1879) and a recent version of Ibsen's famous play as performed in India by actor-director Rudra Prasad Sen Gupta and his wife Swatilekha Sen Gupta.*

A DOLL'S HOUSE

HENRIK IBSEN

Translated by Michael Meyer

LIST OF CHARACTERS

TORVALD HELMER, *a lawyer*
NORA, *his wife*
DR. RANK
MRS. LINDE
NILS KROGSTAD, *also a lawyer*
The Helmers' three small children
ANNE-MARIE, *their nurse*
HELEN, *the maid*
A PORTER

SCENE: *The action takes place in the Helmers' apartment.*

ACT 1

A comfortably and tastefully, but not expensively furnished room. Backstage right a door leads out to the hall; backstage left, another door to Helmer's study. Between these two doors stands a piano. In the middle of the left-hand wall is a door, with a window downstage of it. Near the window, a round table with armchairs and a small sofa. In the right-hand wall, slightly upstage, is a door, downstage of this, against the same wall, a stove lined with porcelain tiles, with a couple of armchairs and a rocking-chair in front of it. Between the stove and the side door is a small table. Engravings on the wall. A what-not with china and other bric-a-brac; a small bookcase with leather-bound books. A carpet on the floor; a fire in the stove. A winter day.

A bell rings in the hall outside. After a moment, we hear the front door being opened. Nora enters the room, humming contentedly to herself. She is wearing outdoor clothes and carrying a lot of parcels, which she puts down on the table right. She leaves the door to the hall open; through it, we can see a Porter carrying a Christmas tree and a basket. He gives these to the Maid, who has opened the door for them.

NORA. Hide that Christmas tree away, Helen. The children mustn't see it before I've decorated it this evening. (*To the porter, taking out her purse.*) How much—?

PORTER. A shilling.

NORA. Here's half a crown. No, keep it.

The Porter touches his cap and goes. Nora closes the door. She continues to laugh happily to herself as she removes her coat, etc. She takes from her pocket a bag containing macaroons and eats a couple. Then, she tiptoes across and listens at her husband's door.

NORA. Yes, he's here. (*Starts humming again as she goes over to the table, right.*)

HELMER (*from his room*). Is that my skylark twittering out there?

NORA (*opening some of the parcels*). It is!

HELMER. Is that my squirrel rustling?

NORA. Yes!

HELMER. When did my squirrel come home?

NORA. Just now. (*Pops the bag of macaroons in her pocket and wipes her mouth.*) Come out here, Torvald, and see what I've bought.

HELMER. You mustn't disturb me! (*Short pause; then he opens the door and looks in, his pen in his hand.*) Bought, did you say? All that? Has my little squanderbird been overspending again?

NORA. Oh, Torvald, surely we can let ourselves go a little this year! It's the first Christmas we don't have to scrape.

HELMER. Well, you know, we can't afford to be extravagant.

NORA. Oh yes, Torvald, we can be a little extravagant now. Can't we? Just a tiny bit? You've got a big salary now, and you're going to make lots and lots of money.

HELMER. Next year, yes. But my new salary doesn't start till April.

NORA. Pooh; we can borrow till then.

HELMER. Nora! (*Goes over to her and takes her playfully by the ear.*) What a little spendthrift you are! Suppose I were to borrow fifty pounds today, and you spent it all over Christmas, and then on New Year's Eve a tile fell off a roof onto my head—

NORA (*puts her hand over his mouth*). Oh, Torvald! Don't say such dreadful things!

HELMER. Yes, but suppose something like that did happen? What then?

NORA. If anything as frightful as that happened, it wouldn't make much difference whether I was in debt or not.

HELMER. But what about the people I'd borrowed from?

NORA. Them? Who cares about them? They're strangers.

HELMER. Oh, Nora, Nora, how like a woman! No, but seriously, Nora, you know how I feel about this. No debts! Never borrow! A home that is founded on debts can never be a place of freedom and beauty. We two have stuck it out bravely up to now; and we shall continue to do so for the short time we still have to.

NORA (*goes over towards the stove*). Very well, Torvald. As you say.

HELMER (*follows her*). Now, now! My little songbird mustn't droop her wings. What's this? Is little squirrel sulking? (*Takes out his purse.*) Nora; guess what I've got here!

NORA (*turns quickly*). Money!

HELMER. Look. (*Hands her some banknotes.*) I know how these small expenses crop up at Christmas.

NORA (*counts them*). One—two—three—four. Oh, thank you, Torvald, thank you! I should be able to manage with this.

HELMER. You'll have to.

NORA. Yes, yes, of course I will. But come over here, I want to show you everything I've bought. And so cheaply! Look, here are new clothes for Ivar—and a sword. And a horse and a trumpet for Bob. And a doll and a cradle for Emmy—they're nothing much, but she'll pull them apart in a few days. And some bits of material and handkerchiefs for the maids. Old Anne-Marie ought to have had something better, really.

HELMER. And what's in that parcel?

NORA (*cries*). No, Torvald, you mustn't see that before this evening!

HELMER. Very well. But now, tell me, you little spendthrift, what do you want for Christmas?

NORA. Me? Oh, pooh, I don't want anything.

HELMER. Oh, yes, you do. Now tell me, what, within reason, would you most like?

NORA. No, I really don't know. Oh, yes—Torvald—!

HELMER. Well?

NORA (*plays with his coat-buttons; not looking at him*). If you really want to give me something, you could—you could—

HELMER. Come on, out with it.

NORA (*quickly*). You could give me money, Torvald. Only as much as you feel you can afford; then later I'll buy something with it.

HELMER. But, Nora—

NORA. Oh yes, Torvald dear, please! Please! Then I'll wrap up the notes in pretty gold paper and hang them on the Christmas tree. Wouldn't that be fun?

HELMER. What's the name of that little bird that can never keep any money?

NORA. Yes, yes, squanderbird; I know. But let's do as I say, Torvald; then I'll have time to think about what I need most. Isn't that the best way? Mm?

HELMER (*smiles*). To be sure it would be, if you could keep what I give you and really buy yourself something with it. But you'll spend it on all sorts of useless things for the house, and then I'll have to put my hand in my pocket again.

NORA. Oh, but Torvald—

HELMER. You can't deny it, Nora dear. (*Puts his arm round her waist.*) The squanderbird's a pretty little creature, but she gets through an awful lot of money. It's incredible what an expensive pet she is for a man to keep.

NORA. For shame! How can you say such a thing? I save every penny I can.

HELMER (*laughs*). That's quite true. Every penny you can. But you can't.

NORA (*hums and smiles, quietly gleeful*). Hm. If you only knew how many expenses we larks and squirrels have, Torvald.

HELMER. You're a funny little creature. Just like your father used to be. Always on the look-out for some way to get money, but as soon as you have any it just runs through your fingers, and you never know where it's gone. Well, I suppose I must take you as you are. It's in your blood. Yes, yes, yes, these things are hereditary, Nora.

NORA. Oh, I wish I'd inherited more of Papa's qualities.

HELMER. And I wouldn't wish my darling little songbird to be any different from what she is. By the way, that reminds me. You look awfully—how shall I put it?—awfully guilty today.

NORA. Do I?

HELMER. Yes, you do. Look me in the eyes.

NORA (*looks at him*). Well?

HELMER (*wags his finger*). Has my little sweet-tooth been indulging herself in town today, by any chance?

NORA. No, how can you think such a thing?

HELMER. Not a tiny little digression into a pastry shop?

NORA. No, Torvald, I promise—

HELMER. Not just a wee jam tart?

NORA. Certainly not.

HELMER. Not a little nibble at a macaroon?

NORA. No, Torvald—I promise you, honestly—

HELMER. There, there. I was only joking.

NORA (*goes over to the table, right*). You know I could never act against your wishes.

HELMER. Of course not. And you've given me your word—(*Goes over to her.*) Well, my beloved Nora, you keep your little Christmas secrets to yourself. They'll be revealed this evening, I've no doubt, once the Christmas tree has been lit.

NORA. Have you remembered to invite Dr. Rank?

HELMER. No. But there's no need; he knows he'll be dining with us. Anyway, I'll ask him when he comes this morning. I've ordered some good wine. Oh Nora, you can't imagine how I'm looking forward to this evening.

NORA. So am I. And, Torvald, how the children will love it!

HELMER. Yes, it's a wonderful thing to know that one's position is assured and that one has an ample income. Don't you agree? It's good to know that, isn't it?

NORA. Yes, it's almost like a miracle.

HELMER. Do you remember last Christmas? For three whole weeks you shut yourself away every evening to make flowers for the Christmas tree, and all those other things you were going to surprise us with. Ugh, it was the most boring time I've ever had in my life.

NORA. I didn't find it boring.

HELMER (*smiles*). But it all came to nothing in the end, didn't it?

NORA. Oh, are you going to bring that up again? How could I help the cat getting in and tearing everything to bits?

HELMER. No, my poor little Nora, of course you couldn't. You simply wanted to make us happy, and that's all that matters. But it's good that those hard times are past.

NORA. Yes, it's wonderful.

HELMER. I don't have to sit by myself and be bored. And you don't have to tire your pretty eyes and your delicate little hands—

NORA (*claps her hands*). No, Torvald, that's true, isn't it—I don't have to any longer? Oh, it's really all just like a miracle. (*Takes his arm.*) Now, I'm going to tell you what I thought we might do, Torvald. As soon as Christmas is over—(*A bell rings in the hall.*) Oh, there's the doorbell. (*Tidies up one or two things in the room.*) Someone's coming. What a bore.

HELMER. I'm not at home to any visitors. Remember!

MAID (*in the doorway*). A lady's called, madam. A stranger.

NORA. Well, ask her to come in.

MAID. And the doctor's here too, sir.

HELMER. Has he gone to my room?

MAID. Yes, sir.

Helmer goes into his room. The Maid shows in Mrs. Linde, who is dressed in traveling clothes, and closes the door.

MRS. LINDE (*shyly and a little hesitantly*). Good evening, Nora.

NORA (*uncertainly*). Good evening—

MRS. LINDE. I don't suppose you recognize me.

NORA. No, I'm afraid I—Yes, wait a minute—surely—(*Exclaims.*) Why, Christine! Is it really you?

MRS. LINDE. Yes, it's me.

NORA. Christine! And I didn't recognize you! But how could I—? (*More quietly.*) How you've changed, Christine!

MRS. LINDE. Yes, I know. It's been nine years—nearly ten—

NORA. Is it so long? Yes, it must be. Oh, these last eight years have been such a happy time for me! So you've come to town? All that way in winter! How brave of you!

MRS. LINDE. I arrived by the steamer this morning.

NORA. Yes, of course—to enjoy yourself over Christmas. Oh, how splendid! We'll have to celebrate! But take off your coat. You're not cold, are you? (*Helps her off with it.*) There! Now let's sit down here by the stove and be comfortable. No, you take the armchair. I'll sit here in the rocking-chair. (*Clasps Mrs. Linde's hands.*) Yes, now you look like your old self. It was just at first that—you've got a little paler, though, Christine. And perhaps a bit thinner.

MRS. LINDE. And older, Nora. Much, much older.

NORA. Yes, perhaps a little older. Just a tiny bit. Not much. (*Checks herself suddenly and says earnestly.*) Oh, but how thoughtless of me to sit here and chatter away like this! Dear, sweet Christine, can you forgive me?

MRS. LINDE. What do you mean, Nora?

NORA (*quietly*). Poor Christine, you've become a widow.

MRS. LINDE. Yes. Three years ago.

NORA. I know, I know—I read it in the papers. Oh, Christine, I meant to write to you so often, honestly. But I always put it off, and something else always cropped up.

MRS. LINDE. I understand, Nora dear.

NORA. No, Christine, it was beastly of me. Oh, my poor darling, what you've gone through! And he didn't leave you anything?

MRS. LINDE. No.

NORA. No children, either?

MRS. LINDE. No.

NORA. Nothing at all, then?

MRS. LINDE. Not even a feeling of loss or sorrow.

NORA (*looks incredulously at her*). But, Christine, how is that possible?

MRS. LINDE (*smiles sadly and strokes Nora's hair*). Oh, these things happen, Nora.

NORA. All alone. How dreadful that must be for you. I've three lovely children. I'm afraid you can't see them now, because they're out with nanny. But you must tell me everything—

MRS. LINDE. No, no, no. I want to hear about you.

NORA. No, you start. I'm not going to be selfish today, I'm just going to think about you. Oh, but there's one thing I *must* tell you. Have you heard of the wonderful luck we've just had?

MRS. LINDE. No. What?

NORA. Would you believe it—my husband's just been made manager of the bank!

MRS. LINDE. Your husband? Oh, how lucky—!

NORA. Yes, isn't it? Being a lawyer is so uncertain, you know, especially if one isn't prepared to touch any case that isn't—well—quite nice. And of course Torvald's been very firm about that—and I'm absolutely with him. Oh, you can imagine how happy we are! He's joining the bank in the New Year, and he'll be getting a big salary, and lots of percentages too. From now on we'll be able to live quite differently—we'll be able to do whatever we want. Oh, Christine, it's such a relief! I feel so happy! Well, I mean, it's lovely to have heaps of money and not to have to worry about anything. Don't you think?

MRS. LINDE. It must be lovely to have enough to cover one's needs, anyway.

NORA. Not just our needs! We're going to have heaps and heaps of money!

MRS. LINDE (*smiles*). Nora, Nora, haven't you grown up yet? When we were at school you were a terrible little spendthrift.

NORA (*laughs quietly*). Yes, Torvald still says that. (*Wags her finger.*) But "Nora, Nora" isn't as silly as you think. Oh, we've been in no position for me to waste money. We've both had to work.

MRS. LINDE. You too?

NORA. Yes, little things—fancy work, crocheting, embroidery and so forth. (*Casually.*) And other things too. I suppose you know Torvald left the Ministry when we got married? There were no prospects of promotion in his department, and of course he needed more money. But the first year he overworked himself quite dreadfully. He had to take on all sorts of extra jobs, and worked day and night. But it was too much for him, and he became frightfully ill. The doctors said he'd have to go to a warmer climate.

MRS. LINDE. Yes, you spent a whole year in Italy, didn't you?

NORA. Yes. It wasn't easy for me to get away, you know. I'd just had Ivar. But of course we had to do it. Oh, it was a marvelous trip! And it saved Torvald's life. But it cost an awful lot of money, Christine.

MRS. LINDE. I can imagine.

NORA. Two hundred and fifty pounds. That's a lot of money, you know.

MRS. LINDE. How lucky you had it.

NORA. Well, actually, we got it from my father.

MRS. LINDE. Oh, I see. Didn't he die just about that time?

NORA. Yes, Christine, just about then. Wasn't it dreadful, I couldn't go and look after him. I was expecting little Ivar any day. And then I had my poor Torvald to care for—we really didn't think he'd live. Dear, kind Papa! I never saw him again, Christine. Oh, it's the saddest thing that's happened to me since I got married.

MRS. LINDE. I know you were very fond of him. But you went to Italy—?

NORA. Yes. Well, we had the money, you see, and the doctors said we mustn't delay. So we went the month after Papa died.

MRS. LINDE. And your husband came back completely cured?

NORA. Fit as a fiddle!

MRS. LINDE. But—the doctor?

NORA. How do you mean?

MRS. LINDE. I thought the maid said that the gentleman who arrived with me was the doctor.

NORA. Oh yes, that's Doctor Rank, but he doesn't come because anyone's ill. He's our best friend, and he looks us up at least once every day. No, Torvald hasn't had a moment's illness since we went away. And the children are fit and healthy and so am I. (*Jumps up and claps her hands.*) Oh God, oh God, Christine, isn't it a wonderful thing to be alive and happy! Oh, but how beastly of me! I'm only talking about myself. (*Sits on a footstool and rests her arms on Mrs. Linde's knee.*) Oh, please don't be angry with me! Tell me, is it really true you didn't love your husband? Why did you marry him, then?

MRS. LINDE. Well, my mother was still alive; and she was helpless and bedridden. And I had my two little brothers to take care of. I didn't feel I could say no.

NORA. Yes, well, perhaps you're right. He was rich then, was he?

MRS. LINDE. Quite comfortably off, I believe. But his business was unsound, you see, Nora. When he died it went bankrupt, and there was nothing left.

NORA. What did you do?

MRS. LINDE. Well, I had to try to make ends meet somehow, so I started a little shop, and a little school, and anything else I could turn my hand to. These last three years have been just one endless slog for me, without a moment's rest. But now it's over, Nora. My poor dear mother doesn't need me any more; she's passed away. And the boys don't need me either; they've got jobs now and can look after themselves.

NORA. How relieved you must feel—

MRS. LINDE. No, Nora. Just unspeakably empty. No one to live for any more. (*Gets up restlessly.*) That's why I couldn't bear to stay out there any longer, cut off from the world. I thought it'd be easier to find some work here that will exercise and occupy my mind. If only I could get a regular job—office work of some kind—

NORA. Oh, but Christine, that's dreadfully exhausting; and you look practically finished already. It'd be much better for you if you could go away somewhere.

MRS. LINDE (*goes over to the window*). I have no Papa to pay for my holidays, Nora.

NORA (*gets up*). Oh, please don't be angry with me.

MRS. LINDE. My dear Nora, it's I who should ask you not to be angry. That's the worst thing about this kind of situation—it makes one so bitter. One has no one to work for; and yet one has to be continually sponging for jobs. One has to live; and so one becomes completely egocentric. When you told me about this luck you've just had with Torvald's new job—can you imagine?—I was happy not so much on your account, as on my own.

NORA. How do you mean? Oh, I understand. You mean Torvald might be able to do something for you?

MRS. LINDE. Yes, I was thinking that.

NORA. He will too, Christine. Just you leave it to me. I'll lead up to it so delicately, so delicately; I'll get him in the right mood. Oh, Christine, I do so want to help you.

MRS. LINDE. It's sweet of you to bother so much about me, Nora. Especially since you know so little of the worries and hardships of life.

NORA. I? You say I know little of—?

MRS. LINDE (*smiles*). Well, good heavens—those bits of fancy work of yours—well, really—! You're a child, Nora.

NORA (*tosses her head and walks across the room*). You shouldn't say that so patronizingly.

MRS. LINDE. Oh?

NORA. You're like the rest. You all think I'm incapable of getting down to anything serious—

MRS. LINDE. My dear—

NORA. You think I've never had any worries like the rest of you.

MRS. LINDE. Nora dear, you've just told me about all your difficulties—

NORA. Pooh—that! (*Quietly.*) I haven't told you about the big thing.

MRS. LINDE. What big thing? What do you mean?

NORA. You patronize me, Christine; but you shouldn't. You're proud that you've worked so long and so hard for your mother.

MRS. LINDE. I don't patronize anyone, Nora. But you're right—I am both proud and happy that I was able to make my mother's last months on earth comparatively easy.

NORA. And you're also proud of what you've done for your brothers.

MRS. LINDE. I think I have a right to be.

NORA. I think so too. But let me tell you something, Christine. I too have done something to be proud and happy about.

MRS. LINDE. I don't doubt it. But—how do you mean?

NORA. Speak quietly! Suppose Torvald should hear! He mustn't, at any price—no one must know, Christine—no one but you.

MRS. LINDE. But what is this?

NORA. Come over here. (*Pulls her down on to the sofa beside her.*) Yes, Christine—I too have done something to be happy and proud about. It was I who saved Torvald's life.

MRS. LINDE. Saved his—? How did you save it?

NORA. I told you about our trip to Italy. Torvald couldn't have lived if he hadn't managed to get down there—

MRS. LINDE. Yes, well—your father provided the money—

NORA (*smiles*). So Torvald and everyone else thinks. But—

MRS. LINDE. Yes?

NORA. Papa didn't give us a penny. It was I who found the money.

MRS. LINDE. You? All of it?

NORA. Two hundred and fifty pounds. What do you say to that?

MRS. LINDE. But Nora, how could you? Did you win a lottery or something?

NORA (*scornfully*). Lottery? (*Sniffs.*) What would there be to be proud of in that?

MRS. LINDE. But where did you get it from, then?

NORA (*hums and smiles secretively*). Hm; tra-la-la-la.

MRS. LINDE. You couldn't have borrowed it.

NORA. Oh? Why not?

MRS. LINDE. Well, a wife can't borrow money without her husband's consent.

NORA (*tosses her head*). Ah, but when a wife has a little business sense, and knows how to be clever—

MRS. LINDE. But Nora, I simply don't understand—

NORA. You don't have to. No one has said I borrowed the money. I could have got it in some other way. (*Throws herself back on the sofa.*) I could have got it from an admirer. When a girl's as pretty as I am—

MRS. LINDE. Nora, you're crazy!

NORA. You're dying of curiosity now, aren't you, Christine?

MRS. LINDE. Nora dear, you haven't done anything foolish?

NORA (*sits up again*). Is it foolish to save one's husband's life?

MRS. LINDE. I think it's foolish if without his knowledge, you—

NORA. But the whole point was that he mustn't know! Great heavens, don't you see? He hadn't to know how dangerously ill he was. I was the one they told that his life was in danger and that only going to a warm climate could save him. Do you suppose I didn't try to think of other ways of getting him down there? I told him how wonderful it would be for me to go abroad like other young wives; I cried and prayed; I asked him to remember my condition, and said he ought to be nice and tender to me; and then I suggested he might quite easily borrow the money. But then he got almost angry with me, Christine. He said I was frivolous, and that it was his duty as a husband not to pander to my moods and caprices—I think that's what he called them. Well, well, I thought, you've got to be saved somehow. And then I thought of a way—

MRS. LINDE. But didn't your husband find out from your father that the money hadn't come from him?

NORA. No, never. Papa died just then. I'd thought of letting him into the plot and asking him not to tell. But since he was so ill—! And as things turned out, it didn't become necessary.

MRS. LINDE. And you've never told your husband about this?

NORA. For heaven's sake, no! What an idea! He's frightfully strict about such matters. And besides—he's so proud of being a *man*—it'd be so painful and humiliating for him to know that he owed anything to me. It'd completely wreck our relationship. This life we have built together would no longer exist.

MRS. LINDE. Will you never tell him?

NORA (*thoughtfully, half-smiling*). Yes—some time, perhaps. Years from now, when I'm no longer pretty. You mustn't laugh! I mean of course, when Torvald no longer loves me as he does now; when it no longer amuses him to see me dance and dress up and play the fool for him. Then it might be useful to have something up my sleeve. (*Breaks off.*) Stupid, stupid, stupid! That time will never come. Well, what do you think of my big secret, Christine? I'm not completely useless, am I? Mind you, all this has caused me a frightful lot of worry. It hasn't been easy for me to meet my obligations punctually. In case you don't know, in the world of business there are things called quarterly installments and interest, and they're a terrible problem to cope with. So I've had to scrape a little here and save a little there as best I can. I haven't been able to save much on the housekeeping money, because Torvald likes to live well; and I couldn't let the children go short of clothes—I couldn't take anything out of what he gives me for them. The poor little angels!

MRS. LINDE. So you've had to stint yourself, my poor Nora?

NORA. Of course. Well, after all, it was my problem. Whenever Torvald gave me money to buy myself new clothes, I never used more than half of it; and I always bought what was cheapest and plainest. Thank heaven anything suits me, so that Torvald's never noticed. But it made me a bit sad sometimes, because it's lovely to wear pretty clothes. Don't you think?

MRS. LINDE. Indeed it is.

NORA. And then I've found one or two other sources of income. Last winter I managed to get a lot of copying to do. So I shut myself away and wrote every evening, late into the night. Oh, I often got so tired, so tired. But it was great fun, though, sitting there working and earning money. It was almost like being a man.

MRS. LINDE. But how much have you managed to pay off like this?

NORA. Well, I can't say exactly. It's awfully difficult to keep an exact check on these kind of transactions. I only know I've paid everything I've managed to scrape together. Sometimes I really didn't know where to turn. (*Smiles.*) Then I'd sit here and imagine some rich old gentleman had fallen in love with me—

MRS. LINDE. What! What gentleman?

NORA. Silly! And that now he'd died and when they opened his will it said in big letters: "Everything I possess is to be paid forthwith to my beloved Mrs. Nora Helmer in cash."

MRS. LINDE. But, Nora dear, who was this gentleman?

NORA. Great heavens, don't you understand? There wasn't any old gentleman, he was just something I used to dream up as I sat here evening after evening wondering how on earth I could raise some money. But what does it matter? The old bore can stay imaginary as far as I'm concerned, because now I don't have to worry any longer! (*Jumps up.*) Oh, Christine, isn't it wonderful! I don't have to worry any more! No more troubles! I can play all day with the children, I can fill the house with pretty things, just the way Torvald likes. And, Christine, it will soon be spring, and the air will be fresh and the skies blue—and then perhaps we'll be able to take a little trip somewhere. I shall be able to see the sea again. Oh, yes, yes, it's a wonderful thing to be alive and happy!

The bell rings in the hall.

MRS. LINDE (*gets up*). You've a visitor. Perhaps I'd better go.

NORA. No stay. It won't be for me. It's someone for Torvald—

MAID (*in the doorway*). Excuse me, madam, a gentleman's called who says he wants to speak to the master. But I didn't know—seeing as the doctor's with him—

NORA. Who is this gentleman?

KROGSTAD (*in the doorway*). It's me, Mrs. Helmer.

Mrs. Linde starts, composes herself; and turns away to the window.

NORA (*takes a step toward him and whispers tensely*). You? What is it? What do you want to talk to my husband about?

KROGSTAD. Business—you might call it. I hold a minor post in the bank, and I hear your husband is to become our new chief—

NORA. Oh—then it isn't—?

KROGSTAD. Pure business, Mrs. Helmer. Nothing more.

NORA. Well, you'll find him in his study.

Nods indifferently as she closes the hall door behind him. Then she walks across the room and sees to the stove.

MRS. LINDE. Nora, who was that man?

NORA. A lawyer called Krogstad.

MRS. LINDE. It was him, then.

NORA. Do you know that man?

MRS. LINDE. I used to know him—some years ago. He was a solicitor's clerk in our town, for a while.

NORA. Yes, of course, so he was.

MRS. LINDE. How he's changed!

NORA. He was very unhappily married, I believe.

MRS. LINDE. Is he a widower now?

NORA. Yes, with a lot of children. Ah, now it's alight.

She closes the door of the stove and moves the rocking-chair a little to one side.

MRS. LINDE. He does—various things now, I hear?

NORA. Does he? It's quite possible—I really don't know. But don't let's talk about business. It's so boring.

Dr. Rank enters from Helmer's study.

RANK (*still in the doorway*). No, no, my dear chap, don't see me out. I'll go and have a word with your wife. (*Closes the door and notices Mrs. Linde.*) Oh, I beg your pardon. I seem to be de trop here too.

NORA. Not in the least. (*Introduces them.*) Dr. Rank. Mrs. Linde.

RANK. Ah! A name I have often heard in this house. I believe I passed you on the stairs as I came up.

MRS. LINDE. Yes. Stairs tire me; I have to take them slowly.

RANK. Oh, have you hurt yourself?

MRS. LINDE. No, I'm just a little run down.

RANK. Ah, is that all? Then I take it you've come to town to cure yourself by a round of parties?

MRS. LINDE. I have come here to find work.

RANK. Is that an approved remedy for being run down?

MRS. LINDE. One has to live, Doctor.

RANK. Yes, people do seem to regard it as a necessity.

NORA. Oh, really, Dr. Rank. I bet you want to stay alive.

RANK. You bet I do. However miserable I sometimes feel, I still want to go on being tortured for as long as possible. It's the same with all my patients; and with people who are morally sick, too. There's a moral cripple in with Helmer at this very moment—

MRS. LINDE (*softly*). Oh!

NORA. Whom do you mean?

RANK. Oh, a lawyer fellow called Krogstad—you wouldn't know him. He's crippled all right; morally twisted. But

even he started off by announcing, as though it were a matter of enormous importance, that he had to live.

NORA. Oh? What did he want to talk to Torvald about?

RANK. I haven't the faintest idea. All I heard was something about the bank.

NORA. I didn't know that Krog—that this man Krogstad had any connection with the bank.

RANK. Yes, he's got some kind of job down there. (*To Mrs. Linde.*) I wonder if in your part of the world you too have a species of human being that spends its time fussing around trying to smell out moral corruption? And when they find a case they give him some nice, comfortable position so that they can keep a good watch on him. The healthy ones just have to lump it.

MRS. LINDE. But surely it's the sick who need care most?

RANK (*shrugs his shoulders*). Well, there we have it. It's that attitude that's turning human society into a hospital.

Nora, lost in her own thoughts, laughs half to herself and claps her hands.

RANK. Why are you laughing? Do you really know what society is?

NORA. What do I care about society? I think it's a bore. I was laughing at something else—something frightfully funny. Tell me, Dr. Rank—will everyone who works at the bank come under Torvald now?

RANK. Do you find that particularly funny?

NORA (*smiles and hums*). Never you mind! Never you mind! (*Walks around the room.*) Yes, I find it very amusing to think that we—I mean, Torvald—has obtained so much influence over so many people. (*Takes the paper bag from her pocket.*) Dr. Rank, would you like a small macaroon?

RANK. Macaroons! I say! I thought they were forbidden here.

NORA. Yes, well, these are some Christine gave me.

MRS. LINDE. What? I—?

NORA. All right, all right, don't get frightened. You weren't to know Torvald had forbidden them. He's afraid they'll ruin my teeth. But, dash it—for once—! Don't you agree, Dr. Rank? Here! (*Pops a macaroon into his mouth.*) You too, Christine. And I'll have one too. Just a little one. Two at the most. (*Begins to walk round again.*) Yes, now I feel really, really happy. Now there's just one thing in the world I'd really love to do.

RANK. Oh? And what is that?

NORA. Just something I'd love to say to Torvald.

RANK. Well, why don't you say it?

NORA. No, I daren't. It's too dreadful.

MRS. LINDE. Dreadful?

RANK. Well, then, you'd better not. But you can say it to us. What is it you'd so love to say to Torvald?

NORA. I've the most extraordinary longing to say: "Bloody hell!"

RANK. Are you mad?

MRS. LINDE. My dear Nora—!

RANK. Say it. Here he is.

NORA (*hiding the bag of macaroons*). Ssh! Ssh!

Helmer, with his overcoat on his arm and his hat in his hand, enters from his study.

NORA (*goes to meet him*). Well, Torvald dear, did you get rid of him?

HELMER. Yes, he's just gone.

NORA. May I introduce you—? This is Christine. She's just arrived in town.

HELMER. Christine—? Forgive me, but I don't think—

NORA. Mrs. Linde, Torvald dear. Christine Linde.

HELMER. Ah. A childhood friend of my wife's, I presume?

MRS. LINDE. Yes, we knew each other in earlier days.

NORA. And imagine, now she's traveled all this way to talk to you.

HELMER. Oh?

MRS. LINDE. Well, I didn't really—

NORA. You see, Christine's frightfully good at office work, and she's mad to come under some really clever man who can teach her even more than she knows already—

HELMER. Very sensible, madam.

NORA. So when she heard you'd become head of the bank—it was in her local paper—she came here as quickly as she could and—Torvald, you will, won't you? Do a little something to help Christine? For my sake?

HELMER. Well, that shouldn't be impossible. You are a widow, I take it, Mrs. Linde?

MRS. LINDE. Yes.

HELMER. And you have experience of office work?

MRS. LINDE. Yes, quite a bit.

HELMER. Well then, it's quite likely I may be able to find some job for you—

NORA (*claps her hands*). You see, you see!

HELMER. You've come at a lucky moment, Mrs. Linde.

MRS. LINDE. Oh, how can I ever thank you—?

HELMER. There's absolutely no need. (*Puts on his overcoat.*) But now I'm afraid I must ask you to excuse me—

RANK. Wait. I'll come with you.

He gets his fur coat from the hall and warms it at the stove.

NORA. Don't be long, Torvald dear.

HELMER. I'll only be an hour.

NORA. Are you going too, Christine?

MRS. LINDE (*puts on her outdoor clothes*). Yes, I must start to look round for a room.

HELMER. Then perhaps we can walk part of the way together.

NORA (*helps her*). It's such a nuisance we're so cramped here—I'm afraid we can't offer to—

MRS. LINDE. Oh, I wouldn't dream of it. Goodbye, Nora dear, and thanks for everything.

NORA. *Au revoir.* You'll be coming back this evening, of course. And, you too, Dr. Rank. What? If you're well enough? Of course you'll be well enough. Wrap up warmly, though.

They go out, talking, into the hall. Children's voices are heard from the stairs.

NORA. Here they are! Here they are!

She runs out and opens the door. Anne-Marie, the nurse, enters with the children.

NORA. Come in, come in! (*Stoops down and kisses them.*) Oh, my sweet darlings—! Look at them, Christine! Aren't they beautiful?

RANK. Don't stand here chattering in this draught!

HELMER. Come, Mrs. Linde. This is for mothers only.

Dr. Rank, Helmer, and Mrs. Linde go down the stairs. The Nurse brings the children into the room. Nora follows, and closes the door to the hall.

NORA. How well you look! What red cheeks you've got! Like apples and roses! (*The children answer her inaudibly as she talks to them.*) Have you had fun? That's splendid. You gave Emmy and Bob a ride on the sledge? What, both together? I say! What a clever boy you are, Ivar! Oh, let me hold her for a moment, Anne-Marie! My sweet little baby doll! (*Takes the smallest child from the nurse and dances with her.*) Yes, yes, Mummy will dance with Bob too. What? Have you been throwing snowballs? Oh, I wish I'd been there! No, don't—I'll undress them myself, Anne-Marie. No, please let me; it's such fun. Go inside and warm yourself; you look frozen. There's some hot coffee on the stove. (*The nurse goes into the room on the left. Nora takes off the children's outdoor clothes and throws them anywhere while they all chatter simultaneously.*) What? A big dog ran after you? But he didn't bite you? No, dogs don't bite lovely little baby dolls. Leave those parcels alone, Ivar. What's in them? Ah, wouldn't you like to know! No, no; it's nothing nice. Come on, let's play a game. What shall we play? Hide and seek. Yes, let's play hide and seek. Bob shall hide first. You want me to? All right, let me hide first.

Nora and the children play around the room, and in the adjacent room to the left, laughing and shouting. At length Nora hides under the table. The children rush in, look, but cannot find her. Then they hear her half-stifled laughter, run to the table, lift up the cloth, and see her. Great excitement. She crawls out as though to frighten them. Further excitement. Meanwhile, there has been a knock on the door leading from the hall, but no one has noticed it. Now the door is half-opened and Krogstad enters. He waits for a moment; the game continues.

KROGSTAD. Excuse me, Mrs. Helmer—

NORA (*turns with a stifled cry and half jumps up*). Oh! What do you want?

KROGSTAD. I beg your pardon; the front door was ajar. Someone must have forgotten to close it.

NORA (*gets up*). My husband is not at home, Mr. Krogstad.

KROGSTAD. I know.

NORA. Well, what do want here, then?

KROGSTAD. A word with you.

NORA. With—? (*To the children, quietly.*) Go inside to Anne-Marie. What? No, the strange gentleman won't do anything to hurt Mummy. When he's gone we'll start playing again.

She takes the children into the room on the left and closes the door behind them.

NORA (*uneasy, tense*). You want to speak to me?

KROGSTAD. Yes.

NORA. Today? But it's not the first of the month yet.

KROGSTAD. No, it is Christmas Eve. Whether or not you have a merry Christmas depends on you.

NORA. What do you want? I can't give you anything today—

KROGSTAD. We won't talk about that for the present. There's something else. You have a moment to spare?

NORA. Oh, yes. Yes, I suppose so; though—

KROGSTAD. Good. I was sitting in the café down below and I saw your husband cross the street—

NORA. Yes.

KROGSTAD. With a lady.

NORA. Well?

KROGSTAD. Might I be so bold as to ask: was not that lady a Mrs. Linde?

NORA. Yes.

KROGSTAD. Recently arrived in town?

NORA. Yes, today.

KROGSTAD. She is a good friend of yours, is she not?

NORA. Yes, she is. But I don't see—

KROGSTAD. I used to know her too once.

NORA. I know.

KROGSTAD. Oh? You've discovered that. Yes, I thought you would. Well then, may I ask you a straight question: is Mrs. Linde to be employed at the bank?

NORA. How dare you presume to cross-examine me, Mr. Krogstad? You, one of my husband's employees? But since you ask, you shall have an answer. Yes, Mrs. Linde is to be employed by the bank. And I arranged it, Mr. Krogstad. Now you know.

KROGSTAD. I guessed right, then.

NORA (*walks up and down the room*). Oh, one has a little influence, you know. Just because one's a woman it doesn't necessarily mean that—When one is in a humble position, Mr. Krogstad, one should think twice before offending someone who—hm—

KROGSTAD. —who has influence?

NORA. Precisely.

KROGSTAD (*changes his tone*). Mrs. Helmer, will you have the kindness to use your influence on my behalf?

NORA. What? What do you mean?

KROGSTAD. Will you be so good as to see that I keep my humble position at the bank?

NORA. What do you mean? Who is thinking of removing you from your position?

KROGSTAD. Oh, you don't need to play innocent with me. I realize it can't be very pleasant for your friend to risk bumping into me; and now I also realize whom I have to thank for being hounded out like this.

NORA. But I assure you—

KROGSTAD. Look, let's not beat about the bush. There's still time, and I'd advise you to use your influence to stop it.

NORA. But, Mr. Krogstad, I have no influence—

KROGSTAD. Oh? I thought you just said—

NORA. But I didn't mean it like that! I? How on earth could you imagine that I would have any influence over my husband?

KROGSTAD. Oh, I've known your husband since we were students together. I imagine he has his weaknesses like other married men.

NORA. If you speak impertinently of my husband, I shall show you the door.

KROGSTAD. You're a bold woman, Mrs. Helmer.

NORA. I'm not afraid of you any longer. Once the New Year is in, I'll soon be rid of you.

KROGSTAD (*more controlled*). Now listen to me, Mrs. Helmer. If I'm forced to, I shall fight for my little job at the bank as I would fight for my life.

NORA. So it sounds.

KROGSTAD. It isn't just the money; that's the last thing I care about. There's something else—well, you might as well know. It's like this, you see. You know of course, as every one else does, that some years ago I committed an indiscretion.

NORA. I think I did hear something—

KROGSTAD. It never came into court; but from that day, every opening was barred to me. So I turned my hand to the kind of business you know about. I had to do something; and I don't think I was one of the worst. But now I want to give up all that. My sons are growing up; for their sake, I must try to regain what respectability I can. This job in the bank was the first step on the ladder. And now your husband wants to kick me off that ladder back into the dirt.

NORA. But my dear Mr. Krogstad, it simply isn't in my power to help you.

KROGSTAD. You say that because you don't want to help me. But I have the means to make you.

NORA. You don't mean you'd tell my husband that I owe you money?

KROGSTAD. And if I did?

NORA. That'd be a filthy trick! (*Almost in tears.*) This secret that is my pride and my joy—that he should hear about it in such a filthy, beastly way—hear about it from you! It'd involve me in the most dreadful unpleasantness—

KROGSTAD. Only—unpleasantness?

NORA (*vehemently*). All right, do it! You'll be the one who'll suffer. It'll show my husband the kind of man you are, and then you'll never keep your job.

KROGSTAD. I asked you whether it was merely domestic unpleasantness you were afraid of.

NORA. If my husband hears about it, he will of course immediately pay you whatever is owing. And then we shall have nothing more to do with you.

KROGSTAD (*takes a step closer*). Listen, Mrs. Helmer. Either you've a bad memory or else you know very little about financial transactions. I had better enlighten you.

NORA. What do you mean?

KROGSTAD. When your husband was ill, you came to me to borrow two hundred and fifty pounds.

NORA. I didn't know anyone else.

KROGSTAD. I promised to find that sum for you—

NORA. And you did find it.

KROGSTAD. I promised to find that sum for you on certain conditions. You were so worried about your husband's illness and so keen to get the money to take him abroad that I don't think you bothered much about the details. So it won't be out of place if I refresh your memory. Well—I promised to get you the money in exchange for an I.O.U., which I drew up.

NORA. Yes, and which I signed.

KROGSTAD. Exactly. But then I added a few lines naming your father as security for the debt. This paragraph was to be signed by your father.

NORA. Was to be? He did sign it.

KROGSTAD. I left the date blank for your father to fill in when he signed this paper. You remember, Mrs. Helmer?

NORA. Yes, I think so—

KROGSTAD. Then I gave you back this I.O.U. for you to post to your father. Is that not correct?

NORA. Yes.

KROGSTAD. And of course you posted it at once; for within five or six days you brought it along to me with your father's signature on it. Whereupon I handed you the money.

NORA. Yes, well. Haven't I repaid the installments as agreed?

KROGSTAD. Mm—yes, more or less. But to return to what we were speaking about—that was a difficult time for you just then, wasn't it, Mrs. Helmer?

NORA. Yes, it was.

KROGSTAD. And your father was very ill, if I am not mistaken.

NORA. He was dying.

KROGSTAD. He did in fact die shortly afterwards?

NORA. Yes.

KROGSTAD. Tell me, Mrs. Helmer, do you by any chance remember the date of your father's death? The day of the month, I mean.

NORA. Papa died on the twenty-ninth of September.

KROGSTAD. Quite correct; I took the trouble to confirm it. And that leaves me with a curious little problem—(*Takes out a paper.*)—which I simply cannot solve.

NORA. Problem? I don't see—

KROGSTAD. The problem, Mrs. Helmer, is that your father signed this paper three days after his death.

NORA. What? I don't understand—

KROGSTAD. Your father died on the twenty-ninth of September. But look at this. Here your father has dated his signature the second of October. Isn't that a curious little problem, Mrs. Helmer? (*Nora is silent.*) Can you suggest any explanation? (*She remains silent.*) And there's another curious thing. The words "second of October" and the year are written in a hand which is not your father's, but which I seem to know. Well, there's a simple explanation to that. Your father could have forgotten to write in the date when he signed, and someone else could have added it before the news came of his death. There's nothing criminal about that. It's the signature itself I'm wondering about. It is genuine, I suppose, Mrs. Helmer? It was your father who wrote his name here?

NORA (*after a short silence, throws back her head and looks defiantly at him*). No, it was not. It was I who wrote Papa's name there.

KROGSTAD. Look, Mrs. Helmer, do you realize this is a dangerous admission?

NORA. Why? You'll get your money.

KROGSTAD. May I ask you a question? Why didn't you send this paper to your father?

NORA. I couldn't. Papa was very ill. If I'd asked him to sign this, I'd have had to tell him what the money was for. But I couldn't have told him in his condition that my husband's life was in danger. I couldn't have done that!

KROGSTAD. Then you would have been wiser to have given up your idea of a holiday.

NORA. But I couldn't! It was to save my husband's life. I couldn't put it off.

KROGSTAD. But didn't it occur to you that you were being dishonest towards me?

NORA. I couldn't bother about that. I didn't care about you. I hated you because of all the beastly difficulties you'd put in my way when you knew how dangerously ill my husband was.

KROGSTAD. Mrs. Helmer, you evidently don't appreciate exactly what you have done. But I can assure you that it is no bigger nor worse a crime than the one I once committed, and thereby ruined my whole social position.

NORA. You? Do you expect me to believe that you would have taken a risk like that to save your wife's life?

KROGSTAD. The law does not concern itself with motives.

NORA. Then the law must be very stupid.

KROGSTAD. Stupid or not, if I show this paper to the police, you will be judged according to it.

NORA. I don't believe that. Hasn't a daughter the right to shield her father from worry and anxiety when he's old and dying? Hasn't a wife the right to save her husband's life? I don't know much about the law but there must be something somewhere that says that such things are allowed. You ought to know about that, you're meant to be a lawyer, aren't you? You can't be a very good lawyer, Mr. Krogstad.

KROGSTAD. Possibly not. But business, the kind of business we two have been transacting—I think you'll admit I understand something about that? Good. Do as you please. But I tell you this. If I get thrown into the gutter for a second time, I shall take you with me.

He bows and goes out through the hall.

NORA (*stands for a moment in thought, then tosses her head*). What nonsense! He's trying to frighten me! I'm not that stupid. (*Busies herself gathering together the children's clothes; then she suddenly stops.*) But—? No, it's impossible. I did it for love, didn't I?

CHILDREN (*in the doorway, left*). Mummy, the strange gentleman's gone out into the street.

NORA. Yes, yes, I know. But don't talk to anyone about the strange gentleman. You hear? Not even to Daddy.

CHILDREN. No, Mummy. Will you play with us again now?

NORA. No, no. Not now.

CHILDREN. Oh but, Mummy, you promised!

NORA. I know, but I can't just now. Go back to the nursery. I've a lot to do. Go away, my darlings, go away. (*She pushes them gently into the other room and closes the door behind them. She sits on the sofa, takes up her embroidery, stitches for a few moments, but soon stops.*) No! (*Throws the embroidery aside, gets up, goes to the door leading to the hall, and calls.*) Helen! Bring in the Christmas tree! (*She goes to the table on the left and opens the drawer in it; then pauses again.*) No, but it's utterly impossible!

MAID (*enters with the tree*). Where shall I put it, madam?

NORA. There, in the middle of the room.

MAID. Will you be wanting anything else?

NORA. No, thank you, I have everything I need.

The Maid puts down the tree and goes out.

NORA (*busy decorating the tree*). Now—candles here—and flowers here. That loathsome man! Nonsense, nonsense, there's nothing to be frightened about. The Christmas tree must be beautiful. I'll do everything that you like. Torvald. I'll sing for you, dance for you—

Helmer, with a bundle of papers under his arm, enters.

NORA. Oh—are you back already?

HELMER. Yes. Has anyone been here?

NORA. Here? No.

HELMER. That's strange. I saw Krogstad come out of the front door.

NORA. Did you? Oh yes, that's quite right—Krogstad was here for a few minutes.

HELMER. Nora, I can tell from your face, he's been here and asked you to put in a good word for him.

NORA. Yes.

HELMER. And you were to pretend you were doing it of your own accord? You weren't going to tell me he'd been here? He asked you to do that too, didn't he?

NORA. Yes, Torvald. But—

HELMER. Nora, Nora! And you were ready to enter into such a conspiracy? Talking to a man like that, and making him promises—and then, on top of it all, to tell me an untruth!

NORA. An untruth?

HELMER. Didn't you say no one had been here? (*Wags his finger.*) My little songbird must never do that again. A songbird must have a clean beak to sing with; otherwise she'll start twittering out of tune. (*Puts his arm round her waist.*) Isn't that the way we want things? Yes, of course it is. (*Lets go of her.*) So let's hear no more about that. (*Sits down in front of the stove.*) Ah, how cozy and peaceful it is here. (*Glances for a few moments at his papers.*)

NORA (*busy with the tree; after a short silence*). Torvald.

HELMER. Yes.

NORA. I'm terribly looking forward to that fancy dress ball at the Stenborgs on Boxing Day.

HELMER. And I'm terribly curious to see what you're going to surprise me with.

NORA. Oh, it's so maddening.

HELMER. What is?

NORA. I can't think of anything to wear. It all seems so stupid and meaningless.

HELMER. So my little Nora's come to that conclusion, has she?

NORA (*behind his chair, resting her arms on its back*). Are you very busy, Torvald?

HELMER. Oh—

NORA. What are those papers?

HELMER. Just something to do with the bank.

NORA. Already?

HELMER. I persuaded the trustees to give me authority to make certain immediate changes in the staff and organization. I want to have everything straight by the New Year.

NORA. Then that's why this poor man Krogstad—

HELMER. Hm.

NORA (*still leaning over his chair, slowly strokes the back of his head*). If you hadn't been so busy, I was going to ask you an enormous favor, Torvald.

HELMER. Well, tell me. What was it to be?

NORA. You know I trust your taste more than anyone's. I'm so anxious to look really beautiful at the fancy dress ball. Torvald, couldn't you help me to decide what I shall go as, and what kind of costume I ought to wear?

HELMER. Aha! So little Miss Independent's in trouble and needs a man to rescue her, does she?

NORA. Yes, Torvald. I can't get anywhere without your help.

HELMER. Well, well, I'll give the matter thought. We'll find something.

NORA. Oh, how kind of you! (*Goes back to the tree. Pause.*)

How pretty these red flowers look! But, tell me, is it so dreadful, this thing that Krogstad's done?

HELMER. He forged someone else's name. Have you any idea what that means?

NORA. Mightn't he have been forced to do it by some emergency?

HELMER. He probably just didn't think—that's what usually happens. I'm not so heartless as to condemn a man for an isolated action.

NORA. No, Torvald, of course not!

HELMER. Men often succeed in re-establishing themselves if they admit their crime and take their punishment.

NORA. Punishment?

HELMER. But Krogstad didn't do that. He chose to try and trick his way out of it; and that's what has morally destroyed him.

NORA. You think that would—?

HELMER. Just think how a man with that load on his conscience must always be lying and cheating and dissembling; how he must wear a mask even in the presence of those who are dearest to him, even his own wife and children! Yes, the children. That's the worst danger, Nora.

NORA. Why?

HELMER. Because an atmosphere of lies contaminates and poisons every corner of the home. Every breath that the children draw in such a house contains the germs of evil.

NORA (comes closer behind him). Do you really believe that?

HELMER. Oh, my dear, I've come across it so often in my work at the bar. Nearly all young criminals are the children of mothers who are constitutional liars.

NORA. Why do you say mothers?

HELMER. It's usually the mother; though of course the father can have the same influence. Every lawyer knows that only too well. And yet this fellow Krogstad has been sitting at home all these years poisoning his children with his lies and pretenses. That's why I say that, morally speaking, he is dead. (Stretches out his hands towards her.) So my pretty little Nora must promise me not to plead his case. Your hand on it. Come, come, what's this? Give me your hand. There. That's settled, now. I assure you it'd be quite impossible for me to work in the same building as him. I literally feel physically ill in the presence of a man like that.

NORA (draws her hand from his and goes over to the other side of the Christmas tree). How hot it is in here! And I've so much to do.

HELMER (gets up and gathers his papers). Yes, and I must try to get some of this read before dinner. I'll think about your costume too. And I may even have something up my sleeve to hang in gold paper on the Christmas tree. (Lays his hand on her head.) My precious little songbird!

He goes into his study and closes the door.

NORA (softly, after a pause). It's nonsense. It must be. It's impossible. It must be impossible!

NURSE (in the doorway, left). The children are asking if they can come in to Mummy.

NORA. No, no, no; don't let them in! You stay with them, Anne-Marie.

NURSE. Very good, madam. (Closes the door.)

NORA (pale with fear). Corrupt my little children—! Poison my home! (Short pause. She throws back her head.) It isn't true! It couldn't be true!

ACT 2

The same room. In the corner by the piano the Christmas tree stands, stripped and disheveled, its candles burned to their sockets. Nora's outdoor clothes lie on the sofa. She is alone in the room, walking restlessly to and fro. At length she stops by the sofa and picks up her coat.

NORA (drops the coat again). There's someone coming! (Goes to the door and listens.) No, it's no one. Of course—no one'll come today, it's Christmas Day. Nor tomorrow. But perhaps—! (Opens the door and looks out.) No. Nothing in the letter-box. Quite empty. (Walks across the room.) Silly, silly. Of course he won't do anything. It couldn't happen. It isn't possible. Why, I've three small children.

The Nurse, carrying a large cardboard box, enters from the room on the left.

NURSE. I found those fancy dress clothes at last, madam.

NORA. Thank you. Put them on the table.

NURSE (does so). They're all rumpled up.

NORA. Oh, I wish I could tear them into a million pieces!

NURSE. Why, madam! They'll be all right. Just a little patience.

NORA. Yes, of course. I'll go and get Mrs. Linde to help me.

NURSE. What, out again? In this dreadful weather? You'll catch a chill, madam.

NORA. Well, that wouldn't be the worst. How are the children?

NURSE. Playing with their Christmas presents, poor little dears. But—

NORA. Are they still asking to see me?

NURSE. They're so used to having their Mummy with them.

NORA. Yes, but, Anne-Marie, from now on I shan't be able to spend so much time with them.

NURSE. Well, children get used to anything in time.

NORA. Do you think so? Do you think they'd forget their mother if she went away from them—for ever?

NURSE. Mercy's sake, madam! For ever!

NORA. Tell me, Anne-Marie—I've so often wondered. How could you bear to give your child away—to strangers?

NURSE. But I had to when I came to nurse my little Miss Nora.

NORA. Do you mean you wanted to?

NURSE. When I had the chance of such a good job? A poor girl what's got into trouble can't afford to pick and choose. That good-for-nothing didn't lift a finger.

NORA. But your daughter must have completely forgotten you.

NURSE. Oh no, indeed she hasn't. She's written to me twice, once when she got confirmed and then again when she got married.

NORA (*hugs her*). Dear old Anne-Marie, you were a good mother to me.

NURSE. Poor little Miss Nora, you never had any mother but me.

NORA. And if my little ones had no one else, I know you would—no, silly, silly, silly! (*Opens the cardboard box.*) Go back to them, Anne-Marie. Now I must—Tomorrow you'll see how pretty I shall look.

NURSE. Why, there'll be no one at the ball as beautiful as my Miss Nora.

She goes into the room, left.

NORA (*begins to unpack the clothes from the box, but soon throws them down again*). Oh, if only I dared to go out! If I could be sure no one would come, and nothing would happen while I was away! Stupid, stupid! No one will come. I just mustn't think about it. Brush this muff. Pretty gloves, pretty gloves! Don't think about it, don't think about it! One, two, three, four, five, six—(*Cries.*) Ah—they're coming—!

She begins to run toward the door, but stops uncertainly. Mrs. Linde enters from the hall, where she has been taking off her outdoor clothes.

NORA. Oh, it's you, Christine. There's no one else out there, is there? Oh, I'm so glad you've come.

MRS. LINDE. I hear you were at my room asking for me.

NORA. Yes, I just happened to be passing. I want to ask you to help me with something. Let's sit down here on the sofa. Look at this. There's going to be a fancy dress ball tomorrow night upstairs at Consul Stenborg's, and Torvald wants me to go as a Neapolitan fisher-girl and dance the tarantella. I learned it on Capri.

MRS. LINDE. I say, are you going to give a performance?

NORA. Yes, Torvald says I should. Look, here's the dress. Torvald had it made for me in Italy; but now it's all so torn, I don't know—

MRS. LINDE. Oh, we'll soon put that right; the stitching's just come away. Needle and thread? Ah, here we are.

NORA. You're being awfully sweet.

MRS. LINDE (*sews*). So you're going to dress up tomorrow, Nora? I must pop over for a moment to see how you look. Oh, but I've completely forgotten to thank you for that nice evening yesterday.

NORA (*gets up and walks across the room*). Oh, I didn't think it was as nice as usual. You ought to have come to town a little earlier, Christine. . . . Yes, Torvald understands how to make a home look attractive.

MRS. LINDE. I'm sure you do, too. You're not your father's daughter for nothing. But, tell me. Is Dr. Rank always in such low spirits as he was yesterday?

NORA. No, last night it was very noticeable. But he's got a terrible disease; he's got spinal tuberculosis, poor man. His father was a frightful creature who kept mistresses and so on. As a result Dr. Rank has been sickly ever since he was a child—you understand—

MRS. LINDE (*puts down her sewing*). But, my dear Nora, how on earth did you get to know about such things?

NORA (*walks about the room*). Oh, don't be silly, Christine—when one has three children, one comes into contact with women who—well, who know about medical matters, and they tell one a thing or two.

MRS. LINDE (*sews again; a short silence*). Does Dr. Rank visit you every day?

NORA. Yes, every day. He's Torvald's oldest friend, and a good friend to me too. Dr. Rank's almost one of the family.

MRS. LINDE. But, tell me—is he quite sincere? I mean, doesn't he rather say the sort of thing he thinks people want to hear?

NORA. No, quite the contrary. What gave you that idea?

MRS. LINDE. When you introduced me to him yesterday, he said he'd often heard my name mentioned here. But later I noticed your husband had no idea who I was. So how could Dr. Rank—?

NORA. Yes, that's quite right, Christine. You see, Torvald's so hopelessly in love with me that he wants to have me all to himself—those were his very words. When we were first married, he got quite jealous if I as much as mentioned any of my old friends back home. So naturally, I stopped talking about them. But I often chat with Dr. Rank about that kind of thing. He enjoys it, you see.

MRS. LINDE. Now listen, Nora. In many ways you're still a child; I'm a bit older than you and have a little more experience of the world. There's something I want to say to you. You ought to give up this business with Dr. Rank.

NORA. What business?

MRS. LINDE. Well, everything. Last night you were speaking about this rich admirer of yours who was going to give you money—

NORA. Yes, and who doesn't exist—unfortunately. But what's that got to do with—?

MRS. LINDE. Is Dr. Rank rich?

NORA. Yes.

MRS. LINDE. And he has no dependents?

NORA. No, no one. But—

MRS. LINDE. And he comes here to see you every day?

NORA. Yes, I've told you.

MRS. LINDE. But how dare a man of his education be so forward?

NORA. What on earth are you talking about?

MRS. LINDE. Oh, stop pretending, Nora. Do you think I haven't guessed who it was who lent you that two hundred pounds?

NORA. Are you out of your mind? How could you imagine

such a thing? A friend, someone who comes here every day! Why, that'd be an impossible situation!

MRS. LINDE. Then it really wasn't him?

NORA. No, of course not. I've never for a moment dreamed of—anyway, he hadn't any money to lend then. He didn't come into that till later.

MRS. LINDE. Well, I think that was a lucky thing for you, Nora dear.

NORA. No, I could never have dreamed of asking Dr. Rank—Though I'm sure that if I ever did ask him—

MRS. LINDE. But of course you won't.

NORA. Of course not. I can't imagine that it should ever become necessary. But I'm perfectly sure that if I did speak to Dr. Rank—

MRS. LINDE. Behind your husband's back?

NORA. I've got to get out of this other business; and *that's* been going on behind his back. I've *got* to get out of it.

MRS. LINDE. Yes, well, that's what I told you yesterday. But—

NORA (*walking up and down*). It's much easier for a man to arrange these things than a woman—

MRS. LINDE. One's own husband, yes.

NORA. Oh, bosh. (*Stops walking.*) When you've completely repaid a debt, you get your I.O.U. back, don't you?

MRS. LINDE. Yes, of course.

NORA. And you can tear it into a thousand pieces and burn the filthy, beastly thing!

MRS. LINDE (*looks hard at her, puts down her sewing, and gets up slowly*). Nora, you're hiding something from me.

NORA. Can you see that?

MRS. LINDE. Something has happened since yesterday morning. Nora, what is it?

NORA (*goes toward her*). Christine! (*Listens.*) Ssh! There's Torvald. Would you mind going into the nursery for a few minutes? Torvald can't bear to see sewing around. Anne-Marie'll help you.

MRS. LINDE (*gathers some of her things together*). Very well. But I shan't leave this house until we've talked this matter out.

She goes into the nursery, left. As she does so, Helmer enters from the hall.

NORA (*runs to meet him*). Oh, Torvald dear, I've been so longing for you to come back!

HELMER. Was that the dressmaker?

NORA. No, it was Christine. She's helping me mend my costume. I'm going to look rather splendid in that.

HELMER. Yes, that was quite a bright idea of mine, wasn't it?

NORA. Wonderful! But wasn't it nice of me to give in to you?

HELMER (*takes her chin in his hand*). Nice—to give in to your husband? All right, little silly, I know you didn't mean it like that. But I won't disturb you. I expect you'll be wanting to try it on.

NORA. Are you going to work now?

HELMER. Yes. (*Shows her a bundle of papers.*) Look at these. I've been down to the bank—(*Turns to go into his study.*)

NORA. Torvald.

HELMER (*stops*). Yes.

NORA. If little squirrel asked you really prettily to grant her a wish—

HELMER. Well?

NORA. Would you grant it to her?

HELMER. First I should naturally have to know what it was.

NORA. Squirrel would do lots of pretty tricks for you if you granted her wish.

HELMER. Out with it, then.

NORA. Your little skylark would sing in every room—

HELMER. My little skylark does that already.

NORA. I'd turn myself into a little fairy and dance for you in the moonlight, Torvald.

HELMER. Nora, it isn't that business you were talking about this morning?

NORA (*comes closer*). Yes, Torvald—oh, please! I beg of you!

HELMER. Have you really the nerve to bring that up again?

NORA. Yes, Torvald, yes, you must do as I ask! You must let Krogstad keep his place at the bank!

HELMER. My dear Nora, his is the job I'm giving to Mrs. Linde.

NORA. Yes, that's terribly sweet of you. But you can get rid of one of the other clerks instead of Krogstad.

HELMER. Really, you're being incredibly obstinate. Just because you thoughtlessly promised to put in a word for him, you expect me to—

NORA. No, it isn't that, Helmer. It's for your own sake. That man writes for the most beastly newspapers—you said so yourself. He could do you tremendous harm. I'm so dreadfully frightened of him—

HELMER. Oh, I understand. Memories of the past. That's what's frightening you.

NORA. What do you mean?

HELMER. You're thinking of your father, aren't you?

NORA. Yes, yes. Of course. Just think what those dreadful men wrote in the papers about Papa! The most frightful slanders. I really believe it would have lost him his job if the Ministry hadn't sent you down to investigate, and you hadn't been so kind and helpful to him.

HELMER. But my dear little Nora, there's a considerable difference between your father and me. Your father was not a man of unassailable reputation. But I am; and I hope to remain so all my life.

NORA. But no one knows what spiteful people may not dig up. We could be so peaceful and happy now, Torvald—we could be free from every worry—you and I and the children. Oh, please, Torvald, please—!

HELMER. The very fact of your pleading his cause makes it impossible for me to keep him. Everyone at the bank already knows that I intend to dismiss Krogstad. If the rumor got about that the new manager had allowed his wife to persuade him to change his mind—

NORA. Well, what then?

HELMER. Oh, nothing, nothing. As long as my little Miss Obstinate gets her way—Do you expect me to make a laughing-stock of myself before my entire staff—give people the idea that I am open to outside influence? Believe me, I'd soon feel the consequences! Besides—there's something else that makes it impossible for Krogstad to remain in the bank while I am its manager.

NORA. What is that?

HELMER. I might conceivably have allowed myself to ignore his moral obloquies—

NORA. Yes, Torvald, surely?

HELMER. And I hear he's quite efficient at his job. But we—well, we were school friends. It was one of those friendships that one enters into over hastily and so often comes to regret later in life. I might as well confess the truth. We—well, we're on Christian name terms. And the tactless idiot makes no attempt to conceal it when other people are present. On the contrary, he thinks it gives him the right to be familiar with me. He shows off the whole time, with "Torvald this," and "Torvald that." I can tell you, I find it damned annoying. If he stayed, he'd make my position intolerable.

NORA. Torvald, you can't mean this seriously.

HELMER. Oh? And why not?

NORA. But it's so petty.

HELMER. What did you say? Petty? You think *I* am petty?

NORA. No, Torvald dear, of course you're not. That's just why—

HELMER. Don't quibble! You call my motives petty. Then I must be petty too. Petty! I see. Well, I've had enough of this. (*Goes to the door and calls into the hall.*) Helen!

NORA. What are you going to do?

HELMER. (*searching among his papers*). I'm going to settle this matter once and for all. (*The Maid enters.*) Take this letter downstairs at once. Find a messenger and see that he delivers it. Immediately! The address is on the envelope. Here's the money.

MAID. Very good, sir. (*Goes out with the letter.*)

HELMER. (*putting his papers in order*). There now, little Miss Obstinate.

NORA. (*tensely*). Torvald—what was in that letter?

HELMER. Krogstad's dismissal.

NORA. Call her back, Torvald! There's still time. Oh, Torvald, call her back! Do it for my sake—for your own sake—for the children! Do you hear me, Torvald? Please do it! You don't realize what this may do to us all!

HELMER. Too late.

NORA. Yes. Too late.

HELMER. My dear Nora, I forgive you this anxiety. Though it is a bit of an insult to me. Oh, but it is! Isn't it an insult to imply that I should be frightened by the vindictiveness of a depraved hack journalist? But I forgive you, because it so charmingly testifies to the love you bear me. (*Takes her in his arms.*) Which is as it should be, my own dearest Nora. Let what will happen, happen. When the real crisis comes, you will not find me lacking in strength or courage. I am man enough to bear the burden for us both.

NORA. (*fearfully*). What do you mean?

HELMER. The whole burden, I say—

NORA. (*calmly*). I shall never let you do that.

HELMER. Very well. We shall share it, Nora—as man and wife. And that is as it should be. (*Caresses her.*) Are you happy now? There, there, there; don't look at me with those frightened little eyes. You're simply imagining things. You go ahead now and do your tarantella, and get some practice on that tambourine. I'll sit in my study and close the door. Then I won't hear anything, and you can make all the noise you want. (*Turns in the doorway.*) When Dr. Rank comes, tell him where to find me. (*He nods to her, goes into his room with his papers, and closes the door.*)

NORA. (*desperate with anxiety, stands as though transfixed, and whispers*). He said he'd do it. He will do it. He will do it, and nothing'll stop him. No, never that. I'd rather anything. There must be some escape—Some way out—! (*The bell rings in the hall.*) Dr. Rank—! Anything but that! Anything, I don't care—!

She passes her hand across her face, composes herself, walks across, and opens the door to the hall. Dr. Rank is standing there, hanging up his fur coat. During the following scene, it begins to grow dark.

NORA. Good evening, Dr. Rank. I recognized your ring. But you mustn't go to Torvald yet. I think he's busy.

RANK. And—you?

NORA. (*as he enters the room and she closes the door behind him*). Oh, you know very well I've always time to talk to you.

RANK. Thank you. I shall avail myself of that privilege as long as I can.

NORA. What do you mean by that? As long as you *can*?

RANK. Yes. Does that frighten you?

NORA. Well, it's rather a curious expression. Is something going to happen?

RANK. Something I've been expecting to happen for a long time. But I didn't think it would happen quite so soon.

NORA. (*seizes his arm*). What is it? Dr. Rank, you must tell me!

RANK. (*sits down by the stove*). I'm on the way out. And there's nothing to be done about it.

NORA. (*sighs with relief*). Oh, it's you—?

RANK. Who else? No, it's no good lying to oneself. I am the most wretched of all my patients, Mrs. Helmer. These last few days I've been going through the books of this poor body of mine, and I find I am bankrupt. Within a month I may be rotting up there in the churchyard.

NORA. Ugh, what a nasty way to talk!

RANK. The facts aren't exactly nice. But the worst is that there's so much else that's nasty to come first. I've only one more test to make. When that's done I'll have a pretty accurate idea of when the final disintegration is likely to begin. I want to ask you a favour. Helmer's a sensitive chap, and I know how he hates anything ugly. I don't want him to visit me when I'm in hospital—

NORA. Oh but, Dr. Rank—

RANK. I don't want him there. On any pretext. I shan't have him allowed in. As soon as I know the worst, I'll send you my visiting card with a black cross on it, and then you'll know that the final filthy process has begun.

NORA. Really, you're being quite impossible this evening. And I did hope you'd be in a good mood.

RANK. With death on my hands? And all this to atone for someone else's sin? Is there justice in that? And in every single family, in one way or another, the same merciless law of retribution is at work—

NORA (*holds her hands to her ears*). Nonsense! Cheer up! Laugh!

RANK. Yes, you're right. Laughter's all the damned thing's fit for. My poor innocent spine must pay for the fun my father had as a gay young lieutenant.

NORA (*at the table, left*). You mean he was too fond of asparagus and *foie gras*?

RANK. Yes, and truffles too.

NORA. Yes, of course, truffles, yes. And oysters too, I suppose?

RANK. Yes, oysters, oysters. Of course.

NORA. And all that port and champagne to wash them down. It's too sad that all those lovely things should affect one's spine.

RANK. Especially a poor spine that never got any pleasure out of them.

NORA. Oh yes, that's the saddest thing of all.

RANK (*looks searchingly at her*). Hm—

NORA (*after a moment*). Why did you smile?

RANK. No, it was you who laughed.

NORA. No, it was you who smiled, Dr. Rank!

RANK (*gets up*). You're a worse little rogue than I thought.

NORA. Oh, I'm full of stupid tricks today.

RANK. So it seems.

NORA (*puts both her hands on his shoulders*). Dear, dear Dr. Rank, you mustn't die and leave Torvald and me.

RANK. Oh, you'll soon get over it. Once one is gone, one is soon forgotten.

NORA (*looks at him anxiously*). Do you believe that?

RANK. One finds replacements, and then—

NORA. Who will find a replacement?

RANK. You and Helmer both will, when I am gone. You seem to have made a start already, haven't you? What was this Mrs. Linde doing here yesterday evening?

NORA. Aha! But surely you can't be jealous of poor Christine?

RANK. Indeed I am. She will be my successor in this house. When I have moved on, this lady will—

NORA. Ssh—don't speak so loud! She's in there!

RANK. Today again? You see!

NORA. She's only come to mend my dress. Good heavens, how unreasonable you are! (*Sits on the sofa.*) Be nice now, Dr. Rank. Tomorrow you'll see how beautifully I shall dance; and you must imagine that I'm doing it just for

you. And for Torvald of course; obviously. (*Takes some things out of the box.*) Dr. Rank, sit down here and I'll show you something.

RANK (*sits*). What's this?

NORA. Look here! Look!

RANK. Silk stockings!

NORA. Flesh-colored. Aren't they beautiful? It's very dark in here now, of course, but tomorrow—No, no, no; only the soles. Oh well, I suppose you can look a bit higher if you want to.

RANK. Hm—

NORA. Why are you looking so critical? Don't you think they'll fit me?

RANK. I can't really give you a qualified opinion on that.

NORA (*looks at him for a moment*). Shame on you! (*Flicks him on the ear with the stockings.*) Take that. (*Puts them back in the box.*)

RANK. What other wonders are to be revealed to me?

NORA. I shan't show you anything else. You're being naughty.

She hums a little and looks among the things in the box.

RANK (*after a short silence*). When I sit here like this being so intimate with you, I can't think—I cannot imagine what would have become of me if I had never entered this house.

NORA (*smiles*). Yes, I think you enjoy being with us, don't you?

RANK (*more quietly, looking into the middle distance*). And now to have to leave it all—

NORA. Nonsense. You're not leaving us.

RANK (*as before*). And not to be able to leave even the most wretched token of gratitude behind; hardly even a passing sense of loss; only an empty place, to be filled by the next comer.

NORA. Suppose I were to ask you to—? No—

RANK. To do what?

NORA. To give me proof of your friendship—

RANK. Yes, yes?

NORA. No, I mean—to do me a very great service—

RANK. Would you really for once grant me that happiness?

NORA. But you've no idea what it is.

RANK. Very well, tell me, then.

NORA. No, but, Dr. Rank, I can't. It's far too much—I want your help and advice, and I want you to do something for me.

RANK. The more the better. I've no idea what it can be. But tell me. You do trust me, don't you?

NORA. Oh, yes, more than anyone. You're my best and truest friend. Otherwise I couldn't tell you. Well then, Dr. Rank—there's something you must help me to prevent. You know how much Torvald loves me—he'd never hesitate for an instant to lay down his life for me—

RANK (*leans over towards her*). Nora—do you think he is the only one—?

NORA (*with a slight start*). What do you mean?

RANK. Who would gladly lay down his life for you?

NORA (*sadly*). Oh, I see.

RANK. I swore to myself I would let you know that before I go. I shall never have a better opportunity.... Well, Nora, now you know that. And now you also know that you can trust me as you can trust nobody else.

NORA (*rises; calmly and quietly*). Let me pass, please.

RANK (*makes room for her but remains seated*). Nora—

NORA (*in the doorway to the hall*). Helen, bring the lamp. (*Goes over to the stove.*) Oh, dear Dr. Rank, this was really horrid of you.

RANK (*gets up*). That I have loved you as deeply as anyone else has? Was that horrid of me?

NORA. No—but that you should go and tell me. That was quite unnecessary—

RANK. What do you mean? Did you know, then—?

The Maid enters with the lamp, puts it on the table, and goes out.

RANK. Nora—Mrs. Helmer—I am asking you, did you know this?

NORA. Oh, what do I know, what did I know, what didn't I know—I really can't say. How could you be so stupid, Dr. Rank? Everything was so nice.

RANK. Well, at any rate now you know that I am ready to serve you, body and soul. So—please continue.

NORA (*looks at him*). After this?

RANK. Please tell me what it is.

NORA. I can't possibly tell you now.

RANK. Yes, yes! You mustn't punish me like this. Let me be allowed to do what I can for you.

NORA. You can't do anything for me now. Anyway; I don't need any help. It was only my imagination—you'll see. Yes, really. Honestly. (*Sits in the rocking-chair, looks at him, and smiles.*) Well, upon my word you *are* a fine gentleman, Dr. Rank. Aren't you ashamed of yourself, now that the lamp's been lit?

RANK. Frankly, no. But perhaps I ought to say—*adieu*?

NORA. Of course not. You will naturally continue to visit us as before. You know quite well how Torvald depends on your company.

RANK. Yes, but you?

NORA. Oh, I always think it's enormous fun having you here.

RANK. That was what misled me. You're a riddle to me, you know. I'd often felt you'd just as soon be with me as with Helmer.

NORA. Well, you see, there are some people whom one loves, and others whom it's almost more fun to be with.

RANK. Oh yes, there's some truth in that.

NORA. When I was at home, of course I loved Papa best. But I always used to think it was terribly amusing to go down and talk to the servants; because they never told me what I ought to do; and they were such fun to listen to.

RANK. I see. So I've taken their place?

NORA (*jumps up and runs over to him*). Oh, dear, sweet Dr. Rank, I didn't mean that at all. But I'm sure you understand—I feel the same about Torvald as I did about Papa.

MAID (*enters from the hall*). Excuse me, madam. (*Whispers to her and hands her a visiting card.*)

NORA (*glances at the card*). Oh! (*Puts it quickly in her pocket.*)

RANK. Anything wrong?

NORA. No, no, nothing at all. It's just something that—it's my new dress.

RANK. What? But your costume is lying over there.

NORA. Oh—that, yes—but there's another—I ordered it specially—Torvald mustn't know—

RANK. Ah, so that's your big secret?

NORA. Yes, yes. Go in and talk to him—he's in his study—keep him talking for a bit—

RANK. Don't worry. He won't get away from me. (*Goes into Helmer's study.*)

NORA (*to the Maid*). Is he waiting in the kitchen?

MAID. Yes, madam, he came up the back way—

NORA. But didn't you tell him I had a visitor?

MAID. Yes, but he wouldn't go.

NORA. Wouldn't go?

MAID. No, madam, not until he'd spoken with you.

NORA. Very well, show him in; but quietly. Helen, you mustn't tell anyone about this. It's a surprise for my husband.

MAID. Very good, madam. I understand. (*Goes.*)

NORA. It's happening. It's happening after all. No, no, no, it can't happen, it mustn't happen.

She walks across and bolts the door of Helmer's study. The Maid opens the door from the hall to admit Krogstad, and closes it behind him. He is wearing an overcoat, heavy boots, and a fur cap.

NORA (*goes towards him*). Speak quietly. My husband's at home.

KROGSTAD. Let him hear.

NORA. What do you want from me?

KROGSTAD. Information.

NORA. Hurry up, then. What is it?

KROGSTAD. I suppose you know I've been given the sack.

NORA. I couldn't stop it, Mr. Krogstad. I did my best for you, but it didn't help.

KROGSTAD. Does your husband love you so little? He knows what I can do to you, and yet he dares to—

NORA. Surely you don't imagine I told him?

KROGSTAD. No. I didn't really think you had. It wouldn't have been like my old friend Torvald Helmer to show that much courage—

NORA. Mr. Krogstad, I'll trouble you to speak respectfully of my husband.

KROGSTAD. Don't worry, I'll show him all the respect he deserves. But since you're so anxious to keep this matter hushed up, I presume you're better informed than you were yesterday of the gravity of what you've done?

NORA. I've learned more than you could ever teach me.

KROGSTAD. Yes, a bad lawyer like me—

NORA. What do you want from me?

KROGSTAD. I just wanted to see how things were with you, Mrs. Helmer. I've been thinking about you all day. Even duns and hack journalists have hearts, you know.

NORA. Show some heart, then. Think of my little children.

KROGSTAD. Have you and your husband thought of mine? Well, let's forget that. I just wanted to tell you, you don't need to take this business too seriously. I'm not going to take any action, for the present.

NORA. Oh, no—you won't, will you? I knew it.

KROGSTAD. It can all be settled quite amicably. There's no need for it to become public. We'll keep it among the three of us.

NORA. My husband must never know about this.

KROGSTAD. How can you stop him? Can you pay the balance of what you owe me?

NORA. Not immediately.

KROGSTAD. Have you any means of raising the money during the next few days?

NORA. None that I would care to use.

KROGSTAD. Well, it wouldn't have helped anyway. However much money you offered me now I wouldn't give you back that paper.

NORA. What are you going to do with it?

KROGSTAD. Just keep it. No one else need ever hear about it. So in case you were thinking of doing anything desperate—

NORA. I am.

KROGSTAD. Such as running away—

NORA. I am.

KROGSTAD. Or anything more desperate—

NORA. How did you know?

KROGSTAD. —just give up the idea.

NORA. How did you know?

KROGSTAD. Most of us think of that at first. I did. But I hadn't the courage—

NORA (dully). Neither have I.

KROGSTAD (relieved). It's true, isn't it? You haven't the courage either?

NORA. No. I haven't. I haven't.

KROGSTAD. It'd be a stupid thing to do anyway. Once the first little domestic explosion is over. . . . I've got a letter in my pocket here addressed to your husband—

NORA. Telling him everything?

KROGSTAD. As delicately as possible.

NORA (quickly). He must never see that letter. Tear it up. I'll find the money somehow—

KROGSTAD. I'm sorry, Mrs. Helmer, I thought I'd explained—

NORA. Oh, I don't mean the money I owe you. Let me know how much you want from my husband, and I'll find it for you.

KROGSTAD. I'm not asking your husband for money.

NORA. What do you want, then?

KROGSTAD. I'll tell you. I want to get on my feet again, Mrs. Helmer. I want to get to the top. And your husband's going to help me. For eighteen months now my record's been clean. I've been in hard straits all that time; I was content to fight my way back inch by inch. Now I've been chucked back into the mud, and I'm not going to be satisfied with just getting back my job. I'm going to get to the top, I tell you. I'm going to get back into the bank, and it's going to be higher up. Your husband's going to create a new job for me—

NORA. He'll never do that!

KROGSTAD. Oh, yes he will. I know him. He won't dare to risk a scandal. And once I'm in there with him, you'll see! Within a year I'll be his right-hand man. It'll be Nils Krogstad who'll be running that bank, not Torvald Helmer!

NORA. That will never happen.

KROGSTAD. Are you thinking of—?

NORA. Now I *have* the courage.

KROGSTAD. Oh, you can't frighten me. A pampered little pretty like you—

NORA. You'll see! You'll see!

KROGSTAD. Under the ice? Down in the cold, black water? And then, in the spring, to float up again, ugly, unrecognizable, hairless—?

NORA. You can't frighten me.

KROGSTAD. And you can't frighten me. People don't do such things, Mrs. Helmer. And anyway, what'd be the use? I've got him in my pocket.

NORA. But afterwards? When I'm no longer—?

KROGSTAD. Have you forgotten that then your reputation will be in my hands? (*She looks at him speechlessly.*) Well, I've warned you. Don't do anything silly. When Helmer's read my letter, he'll get in touch with me. And remember, it's your husband who's forced me to act like this. And for that I'll never forgive him. Goodbye, Mrs. Helmer. (*He goes out through the hall.*)

NORA (*runs to the hall door, opens it a few inches, and listens*). He's going. He's not going to give him the letter. Oh, no, no, it couldn't possibly happen. (*Opens the door a little wider.*) What's he doing? Standing outside the front door. He's not going downstairs. Is he changing his mind? Yes, he—!

A letter falls into the letter-box. Krogstad's footsteps die away down the stairs.

NORA (*with a stifled cry runs across the room towards the table by the sofa. A pause*). In the letter-box. (*Steals timidly over towards the hall door.*) There it is! Oh, Torvald, Torvald! Now we're lost!

MRS. LINDE (*enters from the nursery with Nora's costume*). Well, I've done the best I can. Shall we see how it looks—?

NORA (*whispers hoarsely*). Christine, come here.

MRS. LINDE (*throws the dress on the sofa*). What's wrong with you? You look as though you'd seen a ghost!

NORA. Come here. Do you see that letter? There—look—through the glass of the letter-box.

MRS. LINDE. Yes, yes, I see it.

NORA. That letter's from Krogstad—

MRS. LINDE. Nora! It was Krogstad who lent you the money!

NORA. Yes. And now Torvald's going to discover everything.

MRS. LINDE. Oh, believe me, Nora, it'll be best for you both.

NORA. You don't know what's happened. I've committed a forgery—

MRS. LINDE. But, for heaven's sake—!

NORA. Christine, all I want is for you to be my witness.

MRS. LINDE. What do you mean? Witness what?

NORA. If I should go out of my mind—and it might easily happen—

MRS. LINDE. Nora!

NORA. Or if anything else should happen to me—so that I wasn't here any longer—

MRS. LINDE. Nora, Nora, you don't know what you're saying!

NORA. If anyone should try to take the blame, and say it was all his fault—you understand—?

MRS. LINDE. Yes, yes—but how can you think?

NORA. Then you must testify that it isn't true, Christine. I'm not mad—I know exactly what I'm saying—and I'm telling you, no one else knows anything about this. I did it entirely on my own. Remember that.

MRS. LINDE. All right. But I simply don't understand—

NORA. Oh, how could you understand? A—miracle—is about to happen.

MRS. LINDE. Miracle?

NORA. Yes. A miracle. But it's so frightening. Christine. It *mustn't* happen, not for anything in the world.

MRS. LINDE. I'll go over and talk to Krogstad.

NORA. Don't go near him. He'll only do something to hurt you.

MRS. LINDE. Once upon a time he'd have done anything for my sake.

NORA. He?

MRS. LINDE. Where does he live?

NORA. Oh, how should I know—? Oh, yes, wait a moment—! (*Feels in her pocket.*) Here's his card. But the letter, the letter—!

HELMER (*from his study, knocks on the door*). Nora!

NORA (*cries in alarm*). What is it?

HELMER. Now, now, don't get alarmed. We're not coming in; you've closed the door. Are you trying on your costume?

NORA. Yes, yes—I'm trying on my costume. I'm going to look so pretty for you, Torvald.

MRS. LINDE (*who has been reading the card*). Why, he lives just around the corner.

NORA. Yes; but it's no use. There's nothing to be done now. The letter's lying there in the box.

MRS. LINDE. And your husband has the key?

NORA. Yes, he always keeps it.

MRS. LINDE. Krogstad must ask him to send the letter back unread. He must find some excuse—

NORA. But Torvald always opens the box at just about this time—

MRS. LINDE. You must stop him. Go in and keep him talking. I'll be back as quickly as I can.

She hurries out through the hall.

NORA (*goes over to Helmer's door, opens it and peeps in*). Torvald!

HELMER (*offstage*). Well, may a man enter his own drawing-room again? Come on, Rank, now we'll see what—(*In the doorway.*) But what's this?

NORA. What, Torvald dear?

HELMER. Rank's been preparing me for some great transformation scene.

RANK (*in the doorway*). So I understood. But I seem to have been mistaken.

NORA. Yes, no one's to be allowed to see me before tomorrow night.

HELMER. But, my dear Nora, you look quite worn out. Have you been practicing too hard?

NORA. No, I haven't practiced at all yet.

HELMER. Well, you must.

NORA. Yes, Torvald, I must, I know. But I can't get anywhere without your help. I've completely forgotten everything.

HELMER. Oh, we'll soon put that to rights.

NORA. Yes, help me, Torvald. Promise me you will? Oh, I'm so nervous. All those people—! You must forget everything except me this evening. You mustn't think of business—I won't even let you touch a pen. Promise me, Torvald?

HELMER. I promise. This evening I shall think of nothing but you—my poor, helpless little darling. Oh, there's just one thing I must see to—(*Goes towards the hall door.*)

NORA. What do you want out there?

HELMER. I'm only going to see if any letters have come.

NORA. No, Torvald, no!

HELMER. Why, what's the matter?

NORA. Torvald, I beg you. There's nothing there.

HELMER. Well, I'll just make sure.

He moves towards the door. Nora runs to the piano and plays the first bars of the tarantella.

HELMER (*at the door, turns*). Aha!

NORA. I can't dance tomorrow if I don't practice with you now.

HELMER (*goes over to her*). Are you really so frightened, Nora dear?

NORA. Yes, terribly frightened. Let me start practicing now, at once—we've still time before dinner. Oh, do sit down and play for me, Torvald dear. Correct me, lead me, the way you always do.

HELMER. Very well, my dear, if you wish it.

He sits down at the piano. Nora seizes the tambourine and a long multi-colored shawl from the cardboard box, wraps the latter hastily around her, then takes a quick leap into the center of the room.

NORA. Play for me! I want to dance!

Helmer plays and Nora dances. Dr. Rank stands behind Helmer at the piano and watches her.

HELMER (*as he plays*). Slower, slower!

NORA. I can't!

HELMER. Not so violently, Nora.

NORA. I must!

HELMER (*stops playing*). No, no, this won't do at all.

NORA (*laughs and swings her tambourine*). Isn't that what I told you?

RANK. Let me play for her.

HELMER (*gets up*). Yes, would you? Then it'll be easier for me to show her.

Rank sits down at the piano and plays. Nora dances more and more wildly. Helmer has stationed himself by the stove and tries repeatedly to correct her, but she seems not to hear him. Her hair works loose and falls over her shoulders; she ignores it and continues to dance. Mrs. Linde enters.

MRS. LINDE (*stands in the doorway as though tongue-tied*). Ah—!

NORA (*as she dances*). Oh, Christine, we're having such fun!

HELMER. But, Nora darling, you're dancing as if your life depended on it.

NORA. It does.

HELMER. Rank, stop it! This is sheer lunacy. Stop it, I say!

Rank ceases playing. Nora suddenly stops dancing.

HELMER (*goes over to her*). I'd never have believed it. You've forgotten everything I taught you.

NORA (*throws away the tambourine*). You see!

HELMER. I'll have to show you every step.

NORA. You see how much I need you! You must show me every step of the way. Right to the end of the dance. Promise me you will, Torvald?

HELMER. Never fear. I will.

NORA. You mustn't think about anything but me—today or tomorrow. Don't open any letters—don't even open the letter-box—

HELMER. Aha, you're still worried about that fellow—

NORA. Oh, yes, yes, him too.

HELMER. Nora, I can tell from the way you're behaving, there's a letter from him already lying there.

NORA. I don't know. I think so. But you mustn't read it now. I don't want anything ugly to come between us till it's all over.

RANK (*quietly, to Helmer*). Better give her her way.

HELMER (*puts his arm round her*). My child shall have her way. But tomorrow night, when your dance is over—

NORA. Then you will be free.

MAID (*appears in the doorway, right*). Dinner is served, madam.

NORA. Put out some champagne, Helen.

MAID. Very good, madam. (*Goes.*)

HELMER. I say! What's this, a banquet?

NORA. We'll drink champagne until dawn! (*Calls.*) And, Helen! Put out some macaroons! Lots of macaroons—for once!

HELMER (*takes her hands in his*). Now, now, now. Don't get so excited. Where's my little songbird, the one I know?

NORA. All right. Go and sit down—and you too, Dr. Rank. I'll be with you in a minute. Christine, you must help me put my hair up.

RANK (*quietly, as they go*). There's nothing wrong, is there? I mean, she isn't—er—expecting—?

HELMER Good heavens no, my dear chap. She just gets scared like a child sometimes—I told you before—

They go out right.

NORA. Well?

MRS. LINDE. He's left town.

NORA. I saw it from your face.

MRS. LINDE. He'll be back tomorrow evening. I left a note for him.

NORA. You needn't have bothered. You can't stop anything now. Anyway, it's wonderful really, in a way—sitting here and waiting for the miracle to happen.

MRS. LINDE. Waiting for what?

NORA. Oh, you wouldn't understand. Go in and join them. I'll be with you in a moment.

Mrs. Linde goes into the dining-room.

NORA (*stands for a moment as though collecting herself. Then she looks at her watch*). Five o'clock. Seven hours till midnight. Then another twenty-four hours till midnight tomorrow. And then the tarantella will be finished. Twenty-four and seven? Thirty-one hours to live.

HELMER (*appears in the doorway, right*). What's happened to my little songbird?

NORA (*runs to him with her arms wide*). Your songbird is here!

ACT 3

The same room. The table which was formerly by the sofa has been moved into the center of the room; the chairs surround it as before. The door to the hall stands open. Dance music can be heard from the floor above. Mrs. Linde is seated at the table, absent-mindedly glancing through a book. She is trying to read, but seems unable to keep her mind on it. More than once she turns and listens anxiously towards the front door.

MRS. LINDE (*looks at her watch*). Not here yet. There's not much time left. Please God he hasn't—! (*Listens again.*) Ah, here he is. (*Goes out into the hall and cautiously opens the front door. Footsteps can be heard softly ascending the stairs. She whispers.*) Come in. There's no one here.

KROGSTAD (*in the doorway*). I found a note from you at my lodgings. What does this mean?

MRS. LINDE. I must speak with you.

KROGSTAD. Oh? And must our conversation take place in this house?

MRS. LINDE. We couldn't meet at my place; my room has no separate entrance. Come in. We're quite alone. The maid's asleep, and the Helmers are at the dance upstairs.

KROGSTAD (*comes into the room*). Well, well! So the Helmers are dancing this evening? Are they indeed?

MRS. LINDE. Yes, why not?

KROGSTAD. True enough. Why not?

MRS. LINDE. Well, Krogstad. You and I must have a talk together.

KROGSTAD. Have we two anything further to discuss?

MRS. LINDE. We have a great deal to discuss.

KROGSTAD. I wasn't aware of it.

MRS. LINDE. That's because you've never really understood me.

KROGSTAD. Was there anything to understand? It's the old story, isn't it—a woman chucking a man because something better turns up?

MRS. LINDE. Do you really think I'm so utterly heartless? You think it was easy for me to give you up?

KROGSTAD. Wasn't it?

MRS. LINDE. Oh, Nils, did you really believe that?

KROGSTAD. Then why did you write to me the way you did?

MRS. LINDE. I had to. Since I had to break with you, I thought it my duty to destroy all the feelings you had for me.

KROGSTAD (*clenches his fists*). So that was it. And you did this for money!

MRS. LINDE. You mustn't forget I had a helpless mother to take care of, and two little brothers. We couldn't wait for you, Nils. It would have been so long before you'd had enough to support us.

KROGSTAD. Maybe. But you had no right to cast me off for someone else.

MRS. LINDE. Perhaps not. I've often asked myself that.

KROGSTAD (*more quietly*). When I lost you, it was just as though all solid ground had been swept from under my feet. Look at me. Now I am a shipwrecked man, clinging to a spar.

MRS. LINDE. Help may be near at hand.

KROGSTAD. It was near. But then you came, and stood between it and me.

MRS. LINDE. I didn't know, Nils. No one told me till today that this job I'd found was yours.

KROGSTAD. I believe you, since you say so. But now you know, won't you give it up?

MRS. LINDE. No—because it wouldn't help you even if I did.

KROGSTAD. Wouldn't it? I'd do it all the same.

MRS. LINDE. I've learned to look at things practically. Life and poverty have taught me that.

KROGSTAD. And life has taught me to distrust fine words.

MRS. LINDE. Then it's taught you a useful lesson. But surely you still believe in actions?

KROGSTAD. What do you mean?

MRS. LINDE. You said you were like a shipwrecked man clinging to a spar.

KROGSTAD. I have good reason to say it.

MRS. LINDE. I'm in the same position as you. No one to care about, no one to care for.

KROGSTAD. You made your own choice.

MRS. LINDE. I had no choice—then.

KROGSTAD. Well?

MRS. LINDE. Nils, suppose we two shipwrecked souls could join hands?

KROGSTAD. What are you saying?

MRS. LINDE. Castaways have a better chance of survival together than on their own.

KROGSTAD. Christine!

MRS. LINDE. Why do you suppose I came to this town?

KROGSTAD. You mean—you came because of me?

MRS. LINDE. I must work if I'm to find life worth living. I've always worked, for as long as I can remember; it's been the greatest joy of my life—my only joy. But now I'm alone in the world, and I feel so dreadfully lost and empty. There's no joy in working just for oneself. Oh, Nils, give me something—someone—to work for.

KROGSTAD. I don't believe all that. You're just being hysterical and romantic. You want to find an excuse for self-sacrifice.

MRS. LINDE. Have you ever known me to be hysterical?

KROGSTAD. You mean you really—? Is it possible? Tell me—you know all about my past?

MRS. LINDE. Yes.

KROGSTAD. And you know what people think of me here?

MRS. LINDE. You said just now that with me you might have become a different person.

KROGSTAD. I know I could have.

MRS. LINDE. Couldn't it still happen?

KROGSTAD. Christine—do you really mean this? Yes—you do—I see it in your face. Have you really the courage—?

MRS. LINDE. I need someone to be a mother to; and your children need a mother. And you and I need each other. I believe in you, Nils. I am afraid of nothing—with you.

KROGSTAD (*clasps her hands*). Thank you, Christine—thank you! Now I shall make the world believe in me as you do! Oh—but I'd forgotten—

MRS. LINDE (*listens*). Ssh! The tarantella! Go quickly, go!

KROGSTAD. Why? What is it?

MRS. LINDE. You hear that dance? As soon as it's finished, they'll be coming down.

KROGSTAD. All right, I'll go. It's no good, Christine. I'd forgotten—you don't know what I've just done to the Helmers.

MRS. LINDE. Yes, Nils. I know.

KROGSTAD. And yet you'd still have the courage to—?

MRS. LINDE. I know what despair can drive a man like you to.

KROGSTAD. Oh, if only I could undo this!

MRS. LINDE. You can. Your letter is still lying in the box.

KROGSTAD. Are you sure?

MRS. LINDE. Quite sure. But—

KROGSTAD (*looks searchingly at her*). Is that why you're doing this? You want to save your friend at any price? Tell me the truth. Is that the reason?

MRS. LINDE. Nils, a woman who has sold herself once for the sake of others doesn't make the same mistake again.

KROGSTAD. I shall demand my letter back.

MRS. LINDE. No, no.

KROGSTAD. Of course I shall. I shall stay here till Helmer comes down. I'll tell him he must give me back my letter—I'll say it was only to do with my dismissal, and that I don't want him to read it—

MRS. LINDE. No, Nils, you mustn't ask for that letter back.

KROGSTAD. But—tell me—wasn't that the real reason you asked me to come here?

MRS. LINDE. Yes—at first, when I was frightened. But a day has passed since then, and in that time I've seen incredible things happen in this house. Helmer must know the truth. This unhappy secret of Nora's must be revealed. They must come to a full understanding; there must be an end of all these shiftings and evasions.

KROGSTAD. Very well. If you're prepared to risk it. But one thing I can do—and at once—

MRS. LINDE (*listens*). Hurry! Go, go! The dance is over. We aren't safe here another moment.

KROGSTAD. I'll wait for you downstairs.

MRS. LINDE. Yes, do. You can see me home.

KROGSTAD. I've never been so happy in my life before!

He goes out through the front door. The door leading from the room into the hall remains open.

MRS. LINDE (*tidies the room a little and gets her hat and coat*). What a change! Oh, what a change! Someone to work for—to live for! A home to bring joy into! I won't let this chance of happiness slip through my fingers. Oh, why don't they come? (*Listens.*) Ah, here they are. I must get my coat on.

She takes her hat and coat. Helmer's and Nora's voices become audible outside. A key is turned in the lock and Helmer leads Nora almost forcibly into the hall. She is dressed in an Italian costume with a large black shawl. He is in evening dress, with a black cloak.

NORA (*still in the doorway, resisting him*). No, no, no—not in here! I want to go back upstairs. I don't want to leave so early.

HELMER. But my dearest Nora—

NORA. Oh, please, Torvald, please! Just another hour!

HELMER. Not another minute, Nora, my sweet. You know what we agreed. Come along, now. Into the drawing-room. You'll catch cold if you stay out here.

He leads her, despite her efforts to resist him, gently into the room.

MRS. LINDE. Good evening.

NORA. Christine!

HELMER. Oh, hullo, Mrs. Linde. You still here?

MRS. LINDE. Please forgive me. I did so want to see Nora in her costume.

NORA. Have you been sitting here waiting for me?

MRS. LINDE. Yes. I got here too late, I'm afraid. You'd already gone up. And I felt I really couldn't go back home without seeing you.

HELMER (*takes off Nora's shawl*). Well, take a good look at her. She's worth looking at, don't you think? Isn't she beautiful, Mrs. Linde?

MRS. LINDE. Oh, yes, indeed—

HELMER. Isn't she unbelievably beautiful? Everyone at the party said so. But dreadfully stubborn she is, bless her pretty little heart. What's to be done about that? Would you believe it, I practically had to use force to get her away!

NORA. Oh, Torvald, you're going to regret not letting me stay—just half an hour longer.

HELMER. Hear that, Mrs. Linde? She dances her tarantella—makes a roaring success—and very well deserved—though possibly a trifle too realistic—more so than was aesthetically necessary, strictly speaking. But never mind that. Main thing is—she had a success—roaring success. Was I going to let her stay on after that and spoil the impression? No, thank you. I took my beautiful little Capri signorina—my capricious little Capricienne, what?—under my arm—a swift round of the ballroom, a curtsey to the company, and, as they say in novels, the beautiful apparition disappeared! An exit should always be dramatic, Mrs. Linde. But unfortunately that's just what I can't get Nora to realize. I say, it's hot in here. (*Throws his cloak on a chair and opens the door to his study.*) What's this? It's dark in here. Ah, yes, of course—excuse me. (*Goes in and lights a couple of candles.*)

NORA (*whispers swiftly, breathlessly*). Well?

MRS. LINDE (*quietly*). I've spoken to him.

NORA. Yes?

MRS. LINDE. Nora—you must tell your husband everything.

NORA (*dully*). I knew it.

MRS. LINDE. You've nothing to fear from Krogstad. But you must tell him.

NORA. I shan't tell him anything.

MRS. LINDE. Then the letter will.

NORA. Thank you, Christine. Now I know what I must do. Ssh!

HELMER (*returns*). Well, Mrs. Linde, finished admiring her?

MRS. LINDE. Yes. Now I must say good night.

HELMER. Oh, already? Does this knitting belong to you?

MRS. LINDE (*takes it*). Thank you, yes. I nearly forgot it.

HELMER. You knit, then?

MRS. LINDE. Why, yes.

HELMER. Know what? You ought to take up embroidery.

MRS. LINDE. Oh? Why?

HELMER. It's much prettier. Watch me, now. You hold the embroidery in your left hand, like this, and then you take the needle in your right hand and go in and out in a slow, easy movement—like this. I am right, aren't I?

MRS. LINDE. Yes, I'm sure—

HELMER. But knitting, now—that's an ugly business—can't help it. Look—arms all huddled up—great clumsy needles going up and down—makes you look like a damned Chinaman. I say, that really was a magnificent champagne they served us.

MRS. LINDE. Well, good night, Nora. And stop being stubborn. Remember!

HELMER. Quite right, Mrs. Linde!

MRS. LINDE. Good night, Mr. Helmer.

HELMER (*accompanies her to the door*). Good night, good night! I hope you'll manage to get home all right? I'd gladly—but you haven't far to go, have you? Good night, good night. (*She goes. He closes the door behind her and returns.*) Well, we've got rid of her at last. Dreadful bore that woman is!

NORA. Aren't you very tired, Torvald?

HELMER. No, not in the least.

NORA. Aren't you sleepy?

HELMER. Not a bit. On the contrary, I feel extraordinarily exhilarated. But what about you? Yes, you look very sleepy and tired.

NORA. Yes, I am very tired. Soon I shall sleep.

HELMER. You see, you see! How right I was not to let you stay longer!

NORA. Oh, you're always right, whatever you do.

HELMER (*kisses her on the forehead*). Now my little songbird's talking just like a real big human being. I say, did you notice how cheerful Rank was this evening?

NORA. Oh? Was he? I didn't have a chance to speak with him.

HELMER. I hardly did. But I haven't seen him in such a jolly mood for ages. (*Looks at her for a moment, then comes closer.*) I say, it's nice to get back to one's home again, and be all alone with you. Upon my word, you're a distractingly beautiful young woman.

NORA. Don't look at me like that, Torvald!

HELMER. What, not look at my most treasured possession? At all this wonderful beauty that's mine, mine alone, all mine.

NORA (*goes round to the other side of the table*). You mustn't talk to me like that tonight.

HELMER (*follows her*). You've still the tarantella in your

blood, I see. And that makes you even more desirable. Listen! Now the other guests are beginning to go. (*More quietly.*) Nora—soon the whole house will be absolutely quiet.

NORA. Yes, I hope so.

HELMER. Yes, my beloved Nora, of course you do! Do you know—when I'm out with you among other people like we were tonight, do you know why I say so little to you, why I keep so aloof from you, and just throw you an occasional glance? Do you know why I do that? It's because I pretend to myself that you're my secret mistress, my clandestine little sweetheart, and that nobody knows there's anything at all between us.

NORA. Oh, yes, yes, yes—I know you never think of anything but me.

HELMER. And then when we're about to go, and I wrap the shawl round your lovely young shoulders, over this wonderful curve of your neck—then I pretend to myself that you are my young bride, that we've just come from the wedding, that I'm taking you to my house for the first time—that, for the first time, I am alone with you—quite alone with you, as you stand there young and trembling and beautiful. All evening I've had no eyes for anyone but you. When I saw you dance the tarantella, like a huntress, a temptress, my blood grew hot, I couldn't stand it any longer! That was why I seized you and dragged you down here with me—

NORA. Leave me, Torvald! Get away from me! I don't want all this.

HELMER. What? Now, Nora, you're joking with me. Don't want, don't want—? Aren't I your husband—?

There is a knock on the front door.

NORA (*starts*). What was that?

HELMER (*goes towards the hall*). Who is it?

RANK (*outside*). It's me. May I come in for a moment?

HELMER (*quietly, annoyed*). Oh, what does he want now? (*Calls.*) Wait a moment. (*Walks over and opens the door.*) Well! Nice of you not to go by without looking in.

RANK. I thought I heard your voice, so I felt I had to say goodbye. (*His eyes travel swiftly around the room.*) Ah, yes—these dear rooms, how well I know them. What a happy, peaceful home you two have.

HELMER. You seemed to be having a pretty happy time yourself upstairs.

RANK. Indeed I did. Why not? Why shouldn't one make the most of this world? As much as one can, and for as long as one can. The wine was excellent—

HELMER. Especially the champagne.

RANK. You noticed that too? It's almost incredible how much I managed to get down.

NORA. Torvald drank a lot of champagne too, this evening.

RANK. Oh?

NORA. Yes. It always makes him merry afterwards.

RANK. Well, why shouldn't a man have a merry evening after a well-spent day?

HELMER. Well-spent? Oh, I don't know that I can claim that.

RANK (*slaps him across the back*). I can though, my dear fellow!

NORA. Yes, of course, Dr. Rank—you've been carrying out a scientific experiment today, haven't you?

RANK. Exactly.

HELMER. Scientific experiment! Those are big words for my little Nora to use!

NORA. And may I congratulate you on the finding?

RANK. You may indeed.

NORA. It was good, then?

RANK. The best possible finding—both for the doctor and the patient. Certainty.

NORA (*quickly*). Certainty?

RANK. Absolute certainty. So aren't I entitled to have a merry evening after that?

NORA. Yes, Dr. Rank. You were quite right to.

HELMER. I agree. Provided you don't have to regret it tomorrow.

RANK. Well, you never get anything in this life without paying for it.

NORA. Dr. Rank—you like masquerades, don't you?

RANK. Yes, if the disguises are sufficiently amusing.

NORA. Tell me. What shall we two wear at the next masquerade?

HELMER. You little gadabout! Are you thinking about the next one already?

RANK. We two? Yes, I'll tell you. You must go as the Spirit of Happiness—

HELMER. You try to think of a costume that'll convey that.

RANK. Your wife need only appear as her normal, everyday self—

HELMER. Quite right! Well said! But what are you going to be? Have you decided that?

RANK. Yes, my dear friend. I have decided that.

HELMER. Well?

RANK. At the next masquerade, I shall be invisible.

HELMER. Well, that's a funny idea.

RANK. There's a big, black hat—haven't you heard of the invisible hat? Once it's over your head, no one can see you any more.

HELMER (*represses a smile*). Ah yes, of course.

RANK. But I'm forgetting what I came for. Helmer, give me a cigar. One of your black Havanas.

HELMER. With the greatest pleasure. (*Offers him the box.*)

RANK (*takes one and cuts off the tip*). Thank you.

NORA (*strikes a match*). Let me give you a light.

RANK. Thank you. (*She holds out the match for him. He lights his cigar.*) And now—goodbye.

HELMER. Goodbye, my dear chap, goodbye.

NORA. Sleep well, Dr. Rank.

RANK. Thank you for that kind wish.

NORA. Wish me the same.

RANK. You? Very well—since you ask. Sleep well. And thank you for the light. (*He nods to them both and goes.*)

HELMER (*quietly*). He's been drinking too much.

NORA (*abstractedly*). Perhaps.

Helmer takes his bunch of keys from his pocket and goes out into the hall.

NORA. Torvald, what do you want out there?

HELMER. I must empty the letter-box. It's absolutely full. There'll be no room for the newspapers in the morning.

NORA. Are you going to work tonight?

HELMER. You know very well I'm not. Hullo, what's this? Someone's been at the lock.

NORA. At the lock—?

HELMER. Yes, I'm sure of it. Who on earth—? Surely not one of the maids? Here's a broken hairpin. Nora, it's yours—

NORA (*quickly*). Then it must have been the children.

HELMER. Well, you'll have to break them of that habit. Hm, hm. Ah, that's done it. (*Takes out the contents of the box and calls into the kitchen.*) Helen! Put out the light on the staircase. (*Comes back into the drawing-room with the letters in his hand and closes the door to the hall.*) Look at this! You see how they've piled up? (*Glances through them.*) What on earth's this?

NORA (*at the window*). The letter! Oh, no, Torvald, no!

HELMER. Two visiting cards—from Rank.

NORA. From Dr. Rank?

HELMER (*looks at them*). Peter Rank, M.D. They were on top. He must have dropped them in as he left.

NORA. Has he written anything on them?

HELMER. There's a black cross above his name. Look. Rather gruesome, isn't it? It looks just as though he was announcing his death.

NORA. He is.

HELMER. What? Do you know something? Has he told you anything?

NORA. Yes. When these cards come, it means he's said goodbye to us. He wants to shut himself up in his house and die.

HELMER. Ah, poor fellow. I knew I wouldn't be seeing him for much longer. But so soon—! And now he's going to slink away and hide like a wounded beast.

NORA. When the time comes, it's best to go silently. Don't you think so, Torvald?

HELMER (*walks up and down*). He was so much a part of our life. I can't realize that he's gone. His suffering and loneliness seemed to provide a kind of dark background to the happy sunlight of our marriage. Well, perhaps it's best this way. For him, anyway. (*Stops walking.*) And perhaps for us too, Nora. Now we have only each other. (*Embraces her.*) Oh, my beloved wife—I feel as though I could never hold you close enough. Do you know, Nora, often I wish some terrible danger might threaten you, so that I could offer my life and my blood, everything, for your sake.

NORA (*tears herself loose and says in a clear, firm voice*). Read your letters now, Torvald.

HELMER. No, no. Not tonight. Tonight I want to be with you, my darling wife—

NORA. When your friend is about to die—?

HELMER. You're right. This news has upset us both. An ugliness has come between us; thoughts of death and dissolution. We must try to forget them. Until then—you go to your room; I shall go to mine.

NORA (*throws her arms around his neck*). Good night, Torvald! Good night!

HELMER (*kisses her on the forehead*). Good night, my darling little songbird. Sleep well, Nora. I'll go and read my letters.

He goes into the study with the letters in his hand, and closes the door.

NORA (*wild-eyed, fumbles around, seizes Helmer's cloak, throws it round herself and whispers quickly, hoarsely*). Never see him again. Never. Never. Never. (*Throws the shawl over her head.*) Never see the children again. Them too. Never. Never. Oh—the icy black water! Oh—that bottomless—that—! Oh, if only it were all over! Now he's got it—he's reading it. Oh, no, no! Not yet! Goodbye, Torvald! Goodbye, my darlings!

She turns to run into the hall. As she does so, Helmer throws open his door and stands there with an open letter in his hand.

HELMER. Nora!

NORA (*shrieks*). Ah—!

HELMER. What is this? Do you know what is in this letter?

NORA. Yes, I know. Let me go! Let me go!

HELMER (*holds her back*). Go? Where?

NORA (*tries to tear herself loose*). You mustn't try to save me, Torvald!

HELMER (*staggers back*). Is it true? Is it true, what he writes? Oh, my God! No, no—it's impossible, it can't be true!

NORA. It *is* true. I've loved you more than anything else in the world.

HELMER. Oh, don't try to make silly excuses.

NORA (*takes a step towards him*). Torvald—

HELMER. Wretched woman! What have you done?

NORA. Let me go! You're not going to suffer for my sake. I won't let you!

HELMER. Stop being theatrical. (*Locks the front door.*) You're going to stay here and explain yourself. Do you understand what you've done? Answer me! Do you understand?

NORA (*looks unflinchingly at him and, her expression growing colder, says*). Yes. Now I am beginning to understand.

HELMER (*walking around the room*). Oh, what a dreadful awakening! For eight whole years—she who was my joy and my pride—a hypocrite, a liar—worse, worse—a criminal! Oh, the hideousness of it! Shame on you, shame!

Nora is silent and stares unblinkingly at him.

HELMER (*stops in front of her*). I ought to have guessed that something of this sort would happen. I should have foreseen it. All your father's recklessness and instability—be quiet!—I repeat, all your father's recklessness and instability he has handed on to you. No religion, no morals, no sense of duty! Oh, how I have been punished for closing my eyes to his faults! I did it for your sake. And now you reward me like this.

NORA. Yes. Like this.

HELMER. Now you have destroyed all my happiness. You have ruined my whole future. Oh, it's too dreadful to contemplate! I am in the power of a man who is completely without scruples. He can do what he likes with me, demand what he pleases, order me to do anything—I dare not disobey him. I am condemned to humiliation and ruin simply for the weakness of a woman.

NORA. When I am gone from this world, you will be free.

HELMER. Oh, don't be melodramatic. Your father was always ready with that kind of remark. How would it help me if you were "gone from this world," as you put it? It wouldn't assist me in the slightest. He can still make all the facts public; and if he does, I may quite easily be suspected of having been an accomplice in your crime. People may think that I was behind it—that it was I who encouraged you! And for all this I have to thank you, you whom I have carried on my hands through all the years of our marriage! Now do you realize what you've done to me?

NORA (*coldly calm*). Yes.

HELMER. It's so unbelievable I can hardly credit it. But we must try to find some way out. Take off that shawl. Take it off, I say! I must try to buy him off somehow. This thing must be hushed up at any price. As regards our relationship—we must appear to be living together just as before. Only *appear*, of course. You will therefore continue to reside here. That is understood. But the children shall be taken out of your hands. I dare no longer entrust them to you. Oh, to have to say this to the woman I once loved so dearly—and whom I still—! Well, all that must be finished. Henceforth there can be no question of happiness; we must merely strive to save what shreds and tatters— (*The front door bell rings. Helmer starts.*) What can that be? At this hour? Surely not—? He wouldn't—? Hide yourself, Nora. Say you're ill.

Nora does not move. Helmer goes to the door of the room and opens it. The Maid is standing half-dressed in the hall.

MAID. A letter for madam.

HELMER. Give it to me. (*Seizes the letter and shuts the door.*) Yes, it's from him. You're not having it. I'll read this myself.

NORA. Read it.

HELMER (*by the lamp*). I hardly dare to. This may mean the end for us both. No, I must know. (*Tears open the letter hastily; reads a few lines; looks at a piece of paper which is enclosed with it; utters a cry of joy.*) Nora! (*She looks at him questioningly.*) Nora! No—I must read it once more. Yes, yes, it's true! I am saved! Nora, I am saved!

NORA. What about me?

HELMER. You too, of course. We're both saved, you and I. Look! He's returning your I.O.U. He writes that he is sorry for what has happened—a happy accident has changed his life—oh, what does it matter what he writes? We are saved, Nora! No one can harm you now. Oh, Nora, Nora—no, first let me destroy this filthy thing. Let me see—! (*Glances at the I.O.U.*) No, I don't want to look at it. I shall merely regard the whole business as a dream. (*He tears the I.O.U. and both letters into pieces, throws them into the stove, and watches them burn.*) There. Now they're destroyed. He wrote that ever since Christmas Eve you've been—oh, these must have been three dreadful days for you, Nora.

NORA. Yes. It's been a hard fight.

HELMER. It must have been terrible—seeing no way out except—no, we'll forget the whole sordid business. We'll just be happy and go on telling ourselves over and over again: "It's over! It's over!" Listen to me, Nora. You don't seem to realize. It's over! Why are you looking so pale? Ah, my poor little Nora, I understand. You can't believe that I have forgiven you. But I have, Nora. I swear it to you. I have forgiven you everything. I know that what you did you did for your love of me.

NORA. That is true.

HELMER. You have loved me as a wife should love her husband. It was simply that in your inexperience you chose the wrong means. But do you think I love you any the less because you don't know how to act on your own initiative? No, no. Just lean on me. I shall counsel you. I shall guide you. I would not be a true man if your feminine helplessness did not make you doubly attractive in my eyes. You mustn't mind the hard words I said to you in those first dreadful moments when my whole world seemed to be tumbling about my ears. I have forgiven you, Nora. I swear it to you; I have forgiven you.

NORA. Thank you for your forgiveness.

She goes out through the door, right.

HELMER. No, don't go—(*Looks in.*) What are you doing there?

NORA (*offstage*). Taking off my fancy dress.

HELMER (*by the open door*). Yes, do that. Try to calm yourself and get your balance again, my frightened little songbird. Don't be afraid. I have broad wings to shield you. (*Begins to walk around near the door.*) How lovely and peaceful this little home of ours is, Nora. You are safe here; I shall watch over you like a hunted dove which I have snatched unharmed from the claws of the falcon. Your wildly beating little heart shall find peace with me. It will happen, Nora; it will take time, but it will happen, believe me. Tomorrow all this will seem quite different. Soon everything will be as it was before. I shall no longer need to remind you that I have forgiven you; your own heart will tell you that it is true. Do you really think I could ever bring myself to disown you, or even to reproach you? Ah, Nora, you don't understand what goes on in a husband's heart. There is something indescribably wonderful and satisfying for a husband in knowing that he has forgiven his wife—forgiven her unreservedly, from the bottom of his heart. It means that she has become his property in a double sense; he has, as it were, brought her into the world anew; she is now not only his wife but also his child. From now on that is what you shall be to me, my poor, helpless, bewildered little creature. Never be frightened of anything again, Nora. Just open your heart to me. I shall be both your will and your conscience. What's this? Not in bed? Have you changed?

NORA (*in her everyday dress*). Yes, Torvald. I've changed.

HELMER. But why now—so late—?

NORA. I shall not sleep tonight.

HELMER. But, my dear Nora—

NORA (*looks at her watch*). It isn't that late. Sit down here, Torvald. You and I have a lot to talk about.

She sits down on one side of the table.

HELMER. Nora, what does this mean? You look quite drawn—

NORA. Sit down. It's going to take a long time. I've a lot to say to you.

HELMER (*sits down on the other side of the table*). You alarm me, Nora. I don't understand you.

NORA. No, that's just it. You don't understand me. And I've never understood you—until this evening. No, don't interrupt me. Just listen to what I have to say. You and I have got to face facts, Torvald.

HELMER. What do you mean by that?

NORA (*after a short silence*). Doesn't anything strike you about the way we're sitting here?

HELMER. What?

NORA. We've been married for eight years. Does it occur to you that this is the first time that we two, you and I, man and wife, have ever had a serious talk together?

HELMER. Serious? What do you mean, serious?

NORA. In eight whole years—no, longer—ever since we first met—we have never exchanged a serious word on a serious subject.

HELMER. Did you expect me to drag you into all my worries—worries you couldn't possibly have helped me with?

NORA. I'm not talking about worries. I'm simply saying that we have never sat down seriously to try to get to the bottom of anything.

HELMER. But, my dear Nora, what on earth has that got to do with you?

NORA. That's just the point. You have never understood me. A great wrong has been done to me, Torvald. First by Papa, and then by you.

HELMER. What? But we two have loved you more than anyone in the world!

NORA (*shakes her head*). You have never loved me. You just thought it was fun to be in love with me.

HELMER. Nora, what kind of a way is this to talk?

NORA. It's the truth, Torvald. When I lived with Papa, he used to tell me what he thought about everything, so that I never had any opinions but his. And if I did have any of my own, I kept them quiet, because he wouldn't have liked them. He called me his little doll, and he played with me just the way I played with my dolls. Then I came here to live in your house—

HELMER. What kind of a way is that to describe our marriage?

NORA (*undisturbed*). I mean, then I passed from Papa's hands into yours. You arranged everything the way you wanted it, so that I simply took over your taste in everything—or pretended I did—I don't really know—I think it was a little of both—first one and then the other. Now I look back on it, it's as if I've been living here like a pauper, from hand to mouth. I performed tricks for you, and you gave me food and drink. But that was how you wanted it. You and Papa have done me a great wrong. It's your fault that I have done nothing with my life.

HELMER. Nora, how can you be so unreasonable and ungrateful? Haven't you been happy here?

NORA. No; never. I used to think I was; but I haven't ever been happy.

HELMER. Not—not happy?

NORA. No. I've just had fun. You've always been very kind to me. But our home has never been anything but a playroom. I've been your doll-wife, just as I used to be Papa's doll-child. And the children have been my dolls. I used to think it was fun when you came in and played with me, just as they think it's fun when I go in and play games with them. That's all our marriage has been, Torvald.

HELMER. There may be a little truth in what you say, though you exaggerate and romanticize. But from now on it'll be different. Playtime is over. Now the time has come for education.

NORA. Whose education? Mine or the children's?

HELMER. Both yours and the children's, my dearest Nora.

NORA. Oh, Torvald, you're not the man to educate me into being the right wife for you.

HELMER. How can you say that?

NORA. And what about me? Am I fit to educate the children?

HELMER. Nora!

NORA. Didn't you say yourself a few minutes ago that you dare not leave them in my charge?

HELMER. In a moment of excitement. Surely you don't think I meant it seriously?

NORA. Yes. You were perfectly right. I'm not fitted to educate them. There's something else I must do first. I must educate myself. And you can't help me with that. It's something I must do by myself. That's why I'm leaving you.

HELMER (*jumps up*). What did you say?

NORA. I must stand on my own feet if I am to find out the truth about myself and about life. So I can't go on living here with you any longer.

HELMER. Nora, Nora!

NORA. I'm leaving you now, at once. Christine will put me up for tonight—

HELMER. You're out of your mind! You can't do this! I forbid you!

NORA. It's no use your trying to forbid me any more. I shall take with me nothing but what is mine. I don't want anything from you, now or ever.

HELMER. What kind of madness is this?

NORA. Tomorrow I shall go home—I mean, to where I was born. It'll be easiest for me to find some kind of a job there.

HELMER. But you're blind! You've no experience of the world—

NORA. I must try to get some, Torvald.

HELMER. But to leave your home, your husband, your children! Have you thought what people will say?

NORA. I can't help that. I only know that I must do this.

HELMER. But this is monstrous! Can you neglect your most sacred duties?

NORA. What do you call my most sacred duties?

HELMER. Do I have to tell you? Your duties towards your husband, and your children.

NORA. I have another duty which is equally sacred.

HELMER. You have not. What on earth could that be?

NORA. My duty towards myself.

HELMER. First and foremost you are a wife and a mother.

NORA. I don't believe that any longer. I believe that I am first and foremost a human being, like you—or anyway, that I must try to become one. I know most people think as you do, Torvald, and I know there's something of the sort to be found in books. But I'm no longer prepared to accept what people say and what's written in books. I must think things out for myself, and try to find my own answer.

HELMER. Do you need to ask where your duty lies in your own home? Haven't you an infallible guide in such matters—your religion?

NORA. Oh, Torvald, I don't really know what religion means.

HELMER. What are you saying?

NORA. I only know what Pastor Hansen told me when I went to confirmation. He explained that religion meant this and that. When I get away from all this and can think things out on my own, that's one of the questions I want to look into. I want to find out whether what Pastor Hansen said was right—or anyway, whether it is right for me.

HELMER. But it's unheard of for so young a woman to behave

like this! If religion cannot guide you, let me at least appeal to your conscience. I presume you have some moral feelings left? Or—perhaps you haven't? Well, answer me.

NORA. Oh, Torvald, that isn't an easy question to answer. I simply don't know. I don't know where I am in these matters. I only know that these things mean something quite different to me from what they do to you. I've learned now that certain laws are different from what I'd imagined them to be; but I can't accept that such laws can be right. Has a woman really not the right to spare her dying father pain, or save her husband's life? I can't believe that.

HELMER. You're talking like a child. You don't understand how society works.

NORA. No, I don't. But now I intend to learn. I must try to satisfy myself which is right, society or I.

HELMER. Nora, you're ill; you're feverish. I almost believe you're out of your mind.

NORA. I've never felt so sane and sure in my life.

HELMER. You feel sure that it is right to leave your husband and your children?

NORA. Yes. I do.

HELMER. Then there is only one possible explanation.

NORA. What?

HELMER. That you don't love me any longer.

NORA. No, that's exactly it.

HELMER. Nora! How can you say this to me?

NORA. Oh, Torvald, it hurts me terribly to have to say it, because you've always been so kind to me. But I can't help it. I don't love you any longer.

HELMER (*controlling his emotions with difficulty*). And you feel quite sure about this too?

NORA. Yes, absolutely sure. That's why I can't go on living here any longer.

HELMER. Can you also explain why I have lost your love?

NORA. Yes, I can. It happened this evening, when the miracle failed to happen. It was then that I realized you weren't the man I'd thought you to be.

HELMER. Explain more clearly. I don't understand you.

NORA. I've waited so patiently, for eight whole years—well, good heavens, I'm not such a fool as to suppose that miracles occur every day. Then this dreadful thing happened to me, and then I *knew*: "Now the miracle will take place!" When Krogstad's letter was lying out there, it never occurred to me for a moment that you would let that man trample over you. I *knew* that you would say to him: "Publish the facts to the world." And when he had done this—

HELMER. Yes, what then? When I'd exposed my wife's name to shame and scandal—

NORA. Then I was certain that you would step forward and take all the blame on yourself, and say: "I am the one who is guilty!"

HELMER. Nora!

NORA. You're thinking I wouldn't have accepted such a sacrifice from you? No, of course I wouldn't! But what would my word have counted for against yours? That was the miracle I was hoping for, and dreading. And it was to prevent it happening that I wanted to end my life.

HELMER. Nora, I would gladly work for you night and day, and endure sorrow and hardship for your sake. But no man can be expected to sacrifice his honor, even for the person he loves.

NORA. Millions of women have done it.

HELMER. Oh, you think and talk like a stupid child.

NORA. That may be. But you neither think nor talk like the man I could share my life with. Once you'd got over your fright—and you weren't frightened of what might threaten me, but only of what threatened you—once the danger was past, then as far as you were concerned it was exactly as though nothing had happened. I was your little songbird just as before—your doll whom henceforth you would take particular care to protect from the world because she was so weak and fragile. (*Gets up.*) Torvald, in that moment I realized that for eight years I had been living here with a complete stranger, and had borne him three children—! Oh, I can't bear to think of it! I could tear myself to pieces!

HELMER (*sadly*). I see it, I see it. A gulf has indeed opened between us. Oh, but Nora—couldn't it be bridged?

NORA. As I am now, I am no wife for you.

HELMER. I have the strength to change.

NORA. Perhaps—if your doll is taken from you.

HELMER. But to be parted—to be parted from you! No, no, Nora, I can't conceive of it happening!

NORA (*goes into the room, right*). All the more necessary that it should happen.

She comes back with her outdoor things and a small traveling-bag, which she puts down on a chair by the table.

HELMER. Nora, Nora, not now! Wait till tomorrow!

NORA (*puts on her coat*). I can't spend the night in a strange man's house.

HELMER. But can't we live here as brother and sister, then—?

NORA (*fastens her hat*). You know quite well it wouldn't last. (*Puts on her shawl.*) Goodbye, Torvald. I don't want to see the children. I know they're in better hands than mine. As I am now, I can be nothing to them.

HELMER. But some time, Nora—some time—?

NORA. How can I tell? I've no idea what will happen to me.

HELMER. But you are my wife, both as you are and as you will be.

NORA. Listen, Torvald. When a wife leaves her husband's house, as I'm doing now, I'm told that according to the law he is freed of any obligations towards her. In any case, I release you from any such obligations. You mustn't feel bound to me in any way, however small, just as I shall not feel bound to you. We must both be quite free. Here is your ring back. Give me mine.

HELMER. That too?

NORA. That too.

HELMER. Here it is.

NORA. Good. Well, now it's over. I'll leave the keys here. The servants know about everything to do with the house—much better than I do. Tomorrow, when I have left town, Christine will come to pack the things I brought here from home. I'll have them sent on after me.

HELMER. This is the end then! Nora, will you never think of me any more?

NORA. Yes, of course. I shall often think of you and the children and this house.

HELMER. May I write to you, Nora?

NORA. No, never. You mustn't do that.

HELMER. But at least you must let me send you—

NORA. Nothing. Nothing.

HELMER. But if you should need help?—

NORA. I tell you, no. I don't accept things from strangers.

HELMER. Nora—can I never be anything but a stranger to you?

NORA (picks up her bag). Oh, Torvald! Then the miracle of miracles would have to happen.

HELMER. The miracle of miracles?

NORA. You and I would both have to change so much that—oh, Torvald, I don't believe in miracles any longer.

HELMER. But I want to believe in them. Tell me. We should have to change so much that—?

NORA. That life together between us two could become a marriage. Goodbye.

She goes out through the hall.

HELMER (sinks down on a chair by the door and buries his face in his hands). Nora! Nora! (Looks round and gets up.) Empty! She's gone! (A hope strikes him.) The miracle of miracles—?

The street door is slammed shut downstairs.

HEDDA GABLER

H E N R I K   I B S E N

HEDDA GABLER (1890)

Until the middle of the nineteenth century critics and playwrights continued to accept Aristotle's theory of the primacy of plot; however, with the advent of realism some have argued that character supersedes plot as the most important element of drama. Ibsen's plays in general, and *Hedda Gabler* in particular, reflect this momentous shift in the focus of the drama.

Recall, if you will, the opening chapters of this book and the description of the football game as a ritual reflecting American culture and the discussion of Aristotle's qualitative elements of drama, particularly plot and character. Let us examine Ibsen's *Hedda Gabler* using a football analogy as we contemplate the structure and character of this play. There is a popular trick play in football called the "draw play" in which a player feigns throwing a forward pass while his teammates appear to block the opposing defenders. In reality they allow the defensive players to push them aside as they charge at full speed toward the quarterback, who cleverly hands the ball off to one of his teammates, who then finds himself in a relatively open playing field as the defenders rush by him. In essence, the defenders are tricked into expecting one thing and receive something quite different.

With this trick play in mind, let us return to Aristotle's commentary on dramatic structure. Aristotle argued forcefully that, among the elements of drama, plot is most important. However, the great Spanish playwright Lope de Vega, perhaps the most prolific dramatist in Western theater, advised the playwright to surprise the audience, to "always trick expectancy." Lope was referring to the structure of plot, but the admonition is equally helpful when developing character and something Ibsen accomplished admirably in such dramas as *Hedda Gabler*.

The male character we meet first is George. From his initial "Auntie Juju! Dear Auntie Juju!," through his continual "By Jove! Fancy that!," to his naïvéte regarding Hedda's disdain for him, we are led to believe that here is a man who in contemporary society might be referred to as a "nerd" or "dweeb." On the surface he appears to be a combination of the absent-minded professor and spineless bookworm type. At first glance he seems to be putty in the hands of all of those around him. He jumps at every opportunity to please Auntie Juju, Thea, Hedda, and even Bertha, as well as Lœvborg and Judge Brack. Indeed, our initial response to George is that he is destined for unhappiness and failure. However, Ibsen has tricked us. As we near the end of the play George Tesman has, much to our amazement, accomplished nearly everything he set out to do. He has married the most sought-after woman in the community and obtained the home of his dreams. With the death of Lœvborg, he is assured of the professorship that guarantees his financial well-being, and he ends the play deeply engaged in his "specialty"—putting other people's papers in order. Though he has lost Hedda, it can be argued, given his myopia and self-absorption, that her death will be overshadowed by his "specialty." Remember, this is a man who was more excited by the possibility of using the nursery for a library than he was about his incipient fatherhood.

The "down and out" Eilert Lœvborg seems a loser who (with the help of Thea Elvsted) has for the moment turned his life around. However, after having been goaded by Hedda into attending Judge Brack's bachelor party, it appears that he is merely another reclaimed degenerate who has once again "fallen off the wagon." And when we see him leave, gun in hand, with no apparent sense of purpose, we are convinced that, just like the manuscript he claims to have scattered across the fjord, he will surely "lose" himself. When we hear that he is dead we, not unlike Hedda, jump to the conclusion that he has purposely ended his life. But once again Ibsen has trapped us. When Judge Brack informs us of what has actually happened, it is clear that Lœvborg was, indeed, a man of strength and commitment, drive and determination. Like a tragic hero (note that Ibsen aligns him with Dionysus, who also wore "vine leaves" in his hair), Lœvborg is struck down as he struggles to reclaim what is his; in the form of his book, he will speak his mind about the human condition.

As we consider Judge Brack, we anticipate Ibsen's next attempt to "trick expectancy." Our first impressions of Brack leads us to believe that he is a sleazy, self-serving opportunist. From his entrance via the "back door," to his first allusions to the establishment of "the triangle" and his celebration of Eilert's demise, to his blackmailing of Hedda, he appears to be a man of no character. As George's friend, he has made all the arrangements for the Tesmans' new home while they honeymooned, but before they have spent so much as a day there, he is on the scene suggesting the development of a sexual liaison with Hedda. After his party, Brack takes a perverse joy in Lœvborg's apparent fall as he relishes the prospect that "every respectable house will once again be closed to Eilert Lœvborg." And after Eilert's death, he uses his knowledge of Hedda's pistols and his relationship with George to complete the arrangement of his "triangle." To George's invitation that he spend some time with Hedda while he is busy restoring Loevborg's manuscript, Brack responds, "I'll be delighted, Mrs. Tesman. I'll be here every evening. We'll have great fun together, you and I." With this character, however, Ibsen compounds his trickery. Having set us up with his deceptive creation of Eilert and George, we look for Brack's redemption only to be hoodwinked once again. At the play's conclusion, Brack, unlike George and Eilert, is exactly what he first appeared to be—a sleazy, self-serving opportunist who quite fittingly gets the last word.

What then can we expect from Ibsen as we examine the principal women of this drama, Thea Elvsted and Hedda Gabler? When we first meet Thea, we are confronted by a "delicately built woman . . . with a frightened, questioning expression," a woman "nervously trying to control herself." By the end of act 1 we are certain that Thea is a weak, worried, and insecure woman. This impression is reinforced in subsequent scenes as she is battered verbally by both Hedda and Eilert and physically at the end of the act 2 when Hedda "drags [her] almost forcibly toward the open doorway." By act 3, having heard that Eilert has destroyed their "child" (the manuscript), she appears to be a thoroughly defeated woman who "can't see anything except—darkness." By the final moments of the play she is the outward picture of dejection. Thus, our initial impression of her is one who might be described in modern terms as "mousy"— or even the stereotypical "dumb blond." (Note that Ibsen describes her as having "light blue, large, and somewhat prominent" eyes and "hair [that] is extremely fair, almost flaxen, and . . . extremely wavy and abundant.") But, of course, there is more to Thea than meets the eye.

As we examine Thea more carefully, we realize that Ibsen has tricked us again. In her Ibsen has created a woman of almost undetectable strength and character who is true to herself and committed to the development of the "child." During the late nineteenth century it was almost unheard-of for a woman to leave her husband; should she do so, she was surely destined for a life as a domestic servant or prostitute. In either case she was a woman without power, influence, or social position. By having the courage to leave her husband, Thea becomes a major player in the reclamation of Eilert and his life's work. Above all she becomes a woman who possesses what Hedda only dreams about—"the power to shape a man's destiny." She has certainly been a driving force in Eilert's life, and as coauthor of Tesman's version of Eilert's book, Thea has tremendous influence on Tesman's success as a professor.

As for Hedda, Ibsen begins by describing her as "distinguished" and "aristocratic," with steel gray eyes and "an expression of cold, calm serenity." Into the mouths of every other character he places an acknowledgement of her beauty, power, and control. From the opening scene when Auntie Juju congratulates Tesman for having "won Hedda Gabler! The beautiful Hedda Gabler!" everyone is in awe of Hedda Gabler. They seem to be mesmerized by her and seek to gain her approval. In short, she appears to be the picture of the intelligent, self-assured woman who, through careful planning, controls all things from her husband and the furnishing of her new home to her former "pal," Eilert, whom she goads into an evening of carousing. Ibsen even equips her with the quintessential props that exude power and control—the pistols.

But as we have come to expect of our trickster playwright, beneath this superficial portrait of strength, Ibsen has created not a mature, thoughtful woman worthy of awe, but a childishly impulsive, selfish, and, above all, lonely individual. She is the sum of her many contradictions (and thereby a plum role for actresses since 1890). Her capricious marriage, her shooting at Judge Brack, her giving Eilert the pistol, and her burning of the manuscript are the manifestations of a destructive impulsiveness. Her rudeness to Auntie Juju, her condescending attitude toward Thea, her manipulation of Eilert, her flirtations with Judge Brack, and her exploitation of Tesman are vivid manifestations of her selfishness. Her aberrant behavior produces an utter loneliness that we witness when, near the end of the play, she desperately asks, "Can't I be of use to you two in any way?" To which, of course, the answer is "No." This forces her to the ultimate act of impulsiveness, selfishness, and loneliness—her suicide, an action that Ibsen presents to us unexpectedly. It is the playwright's ultimate trick on his audience, and it produced one of the most memorable denouements in dramatic literature.

Thematically, such tricks are Ibsen's way of instructing us that things are rarely what they seem, that the human mind is infinitely more complex than most dramatists had imagined for centuries. Through his oblique, yet unfailingly realistic creation of character, he reminds us that the social fabric of his society, and our own, is the product of a collection of multifaceted individuals, very few of whom are what they appear to be.

A determined Hedda takes aim at the manipulative Judge Brack in the opening scene of act 2 in this production of Hedda Gabler staged by Roger Schultz at the University of Minnesota, Duluth, in 1972.

HEDDA GABLER

HENRIK IBSEN

Translated by Michael Meyer

CHARACTERS

GEORGE TESMAN   *research graduate in cultural history*
HEDDA   *his wife*
MISS JULIANA TESMAN   *his aunt*
JUDGE BRACK
EILERT LŒVBORG
BERTHA   *a maid*
MRS. ELVSTED

The action takes place in Tesman's villa in the fashionable quarter of town.

ACT ONE

A large drawing-room, handsomely and tastefully furnished, decorated in dark colours. In the rear wall is a broad open doorway, with curtains drawn back to either side. It leads to a smaller room, decorated in the same style as the drawing-room. In the right-hand wall of the drawing-room a folding door leads out to the hall. The opposite wall, on the left, contains french windows, also with curtains drawn back on either side. Through the glass we can see part of a veranda, and trees in autumn colours. Down-

*stage stands an oval table covered by a cloth and sur-
rounded by chairs. Downstage right, against the wall, is a
broad stove tiled with dark porcelain; in front of it stand a
high-backed armchair, a cushioned footrest and two footstools. Upstage right, in an alcove, is a corner sofa, with a
small, round table. Downstage left, a little away from the
wall, is another sofa. Upstage of the french windows, a
piano. On either side of the open doorway in the rear wall
stand what-nots holding ornaments of terra-cotta and ma-
jolica. Against the rear wall of the smaller room can be seen
a sofa, a table and a couple of chairs. Above this sofa hangs
the portrait of a handsome old man in general's uniform.
Above the table a lamp hangs from the ceiling, with a shade
of opalescent, milky glass. All round the drawing-room
bunches of flowers stand in vases and glasses. More
bunches lie on the tables. The floors of both rooms are covered with thick carpets. Morning light. The sun shines in
through the french windows.*

*Miss Juliana Tesman, wearing a hat and carrying a
parasol, enters from the hall, followed by Bertha, who is
carrying a bunch of flowers wrapped in paper. Miss Tesman is about sixty-five, of pleasant and kindly appearance.
She is neatly but simply dressed in grey outdoor clothes.
Bertha, the maid, is rather simple and rustic-looking. She is
getting on in years.*

MISS TESMAN (*stops just inside the door, listens, and says in a
hushed voice*). Well, fancy that! They're not up yet!

BERTHA (*also in hushed tones*). What did I tell you, miss? The
boat didn't get in till midnight. And when they did turn
up—Jesus, miss, you should have seen all the things
madam made me unpack before she'd go to bed!

MISS TESMAN. Ah, well. Let them have a good lie in. But
let's have some nice fresh air waiting for them when they
do come down. (*Goes to the french windows and throws
them wide open.*)

BERTHA (*bewildered at the table, the bunch of flowers in her
hand*). I'm blessed if there's a square inch left to put anything. I'll have to let it lie here, miss. (*Puts it on the piano.*)

MISS TESMAN. Well, Bertha dear, so now you have a new
mistress. Heaven knows it nearly broke my heart to have
to part with you.

BERTHA (*snivels*). What about me, Miss Juju? How do you
suppose I felt? After all the happy years I've spent with
you and Miss Rena?

MISS TESMAN. We must accept it bravely, Bertha. It was the
only way. George needs you to take care of him. He could
never manage without you. You've looked after him ever
since he was a tiny boy.

BERTHA. Oh, but, Miss Juju, I can't help thinking about
Miss Rena, lying there all helpless, poor dear. And that
new girl! She'll never learn the proper way to handle an
invalid.

MISS TESMAN. Oh, I'll manage to train her. I'll do most of

the work myself, you know. You needn't worry about my
poor sister, Bertha dear.

BERTHA. But, Miss Juju, there's another thing. I'm frightened madam may not find me suitable.

MISS TESMAN. Oh, nonsense, Bertha. There may be one or
two little things to begin with—

BERTHA. She's a real lady. Wants everything just so.

MISS TESMAN. But of course she does! General Gabler's
daughter! Think of what she was accustomed to when the
general was alive. You remember how we used to see her
out riding with her father? In that long black skirt? With
the feather in her hat?

BERTHA. Oh, yes, miss. As if I could forget! But, Lord! I
never dreamed I'd live to see a match between her and
Master Georgie.

MISS TESMAN. Neither did I. By the way, Bertha, from now
on you must stop calling him Master Georgie. You must
say Dr. Tesman.

BERTHA. Yes, madam said something about that too. Last
night—the moment they'd set foot inside the door. Is it
true, then, miss?

MISS TESMAN. Indeed it is. Just fancy, Bertha, some foreigners have made him a doctor. It happened while they were
away. I had no idea till he told me when they got off the
boat.

BERTHA. Well, I suppose there's no limit to what he won't
become. He's that clever. I never thought he'd go in for
hospital work, though.

MISS TESMAN. No, he's not that kind of doctor. (*Nods impressively.*) In any case, you may soon have to address him
by an even grander title.

BERTHA. You don't say! What might that be, miss?

MISS TESMAN (*smiles*). Ah, If you only knew! (*Moved.*)
Dear God, if only poor Joachim could rise out of his grave
and see what his little son has grown into! (*Looks round.*)
But, Bertha, why have you done this? Taken the chintz
covers off all the furniture!

BERTHA. Madam said I was to. Can't stand chintz covers on
chairs, she said.

MISS TESMAN. But surely they're not going to use this room
as a parlour.

BERTHA. So I gathered, miss. From what madam said. He
didn't say anything. The Doctor.

*George Tesman comes into the rear room from the right,
humming, with an open, empty travelling-bag in his hand.
He is about thirty-three, of medium height and youthful
appearance, rather plump, with an open, round, contented
face, and fair hair and beard. He wears spectacles, and is
dressed in comfortable indoor clothes.*

MISS TESMAN. Good morning! Good morning, George!

TESMAN (*in open doorway*). Auntie Juju! Dear Auntie Juju!
(*Comes forward and shakes her hand.*) You've come all the
way out here! And so early! What?

MISS TESMAN. Well, I had to make sure you'd settled in comfortably.
TESMAN. But you can't have had a proper night's sleep.
MISS TESMAN. Oh, never mind that.
TESMAN. But you got home safely?
MISS TESMAN. Oh, yes. Judge Brack kindly saw me home.
TESMAN. We were so sorry we couldn't give you a lift. But you saw how it was—Hedda had so much luggage—and she insisted on having it all with her.
MISS TESMAN. Yes, I've never seen so much luggage.
BERTHA (to Tesman). Shall I go and ask madam if there's anything I can lend her a hand with?
TESMAN. Er—thank you, Bertha, no, you needn't bother. She says if she wants you for anything she'll ring.
BERTHA (over to right). Oh. Very good.
TESMAN. Oh, Bertha—take this bag, will you?
BERTHA (takes it). I'll put it in the attic.

She goes out into the hall.

TESMAN. Just fancy, Auntie Juju, I filled that whole bag with notes for my book. You know, it's really incredible what I've managed to find rooting through those archives. By Jove! Wonderful old things no one even knew existed—
MISS TESMAN. I'm sure you didn't waste a single moment of your honeymoon, George dear.
TESMAN. No, I think I can truthfully claim that. But, Auntie Juju, do take your hat off. Here. Let me untie it for you. What?
MISS TESMAN (as he does so). Oh, dear, oh dear! It's just as if you were still living at home with us.
TESMAN (turns the hat in his hand and looks at it). I say! What a splendid new hat!
MISS TESMAN. I bought it for Hedda's sake.
TESMAN. For Hedda's sake? What?
MISS TESMAN. So that Hedda needn't be ashamed of me, in case we ever go for a walk together.
TESMAN (pats her cheek). You still think of everything, don't you, Auntie Juju? (Puts the hat down on a chair by the table.) Come on, let's sit down here on the sofa. And have a little chat while we wait for Hedda?

They sit. She puts her parasol in the corner of the sofa.

MISS TESMAN (clasps both his hands and looks at him). Oh, George, it's so wonderful to have you back, and be able to see you with my own eyes again! Poor dear Joachim's own son!
TESMAN. What about me? It's wonderful for me to see you again, Auntie Juju. You've been a mother to me. And a father, too.
MISS TESMAN. You'll always keep a soft spot in your heart for your old aunties, won't you, George dear?
TESMAN. I suppose Auntie Rena's no better? What?
MISS TESMAN. Alas, no. I'm afraid she'll never get better, poor dear. She's lying there just as she has for all these years. Please God I may be allowed to keep her for a little longer. If I lost her I don't know what I'd do. Especially now I haven't you to look after.
TESMAN (pats her on the back). There, there, there!
MISS TESMAN (with a sudden change of mood). Oh, but, George, fancy you being a married man! And to think it's you who've won Hedda Gabler! The beautiful Hedda Gabler! Fancy! She was always so surrounded by admirers.
TESMAN (hums a little and smiles contentedly). Yes, I suppose there are quite a few people in this town who wouldn't mind being in my shoes. What?
MISS TESMAN. And what a honeymoon! Five months! Nearly six.
TESMAN. Well, I've done a lot of work. All those archives to go through. And I've had to read lots of books.
MISS TESMAN. Yes, dear, of course. (Lowers her voice confidentially.) But tell me, George—haven't you any—any extra little piece of news to give me?
TESMAN. You mean, arising out of the honeymoon?
MISS TESMAN. Yes.
TESMAN. No, I don't think there's anything I didn't tell you in my letters. My doctorate, of course—but I told you about that last night, didn't I?
MISS TESMAN. Yes, yes, I didn't mean that kind of thing. I was just wondering—are you—are you expecting—?
TESMAN. Expecting what?
MISS TESMAN. Oh, come on, George, I'm your old aunt!
TESMAN. Well, actually—yes, I am expecting something.
MISS TESMAN. I knew it!
TESMAN. You'll be happy to learn that before very long I expect to become a—professor.
MISS TESMAN. Professor?
TESMAN. I think I may say that the matter has been decided. But, Auntie Juju, you know about this.
MISS TESMAN (gives a little laugh). Yes, of course, I'd forgotten. (Changes her tone.) But we were talking about your honeymoon. It must have cost a dreadful amount of money, George?
TESMAN. Oh well, you know, that big research grant I got helped a good deal.
MISS TESMAN. But how on earth did you manage to make it do for two?
TESMAN. Well, to tell the truth it was a bit tricky. What?
MISS TESMAN. Especially when one's travelling with a lady. A little bird tells me that makes things very much more expensive.
TESMAN. Well, yes, of course it does make things a little more expensive. But Hedda has to do things in style, Auntie Juju. I mean, she has to. Anything less grand wouldn't have suited her.
MISS TESMAN. No, no, I suppose not. A honeymoon abroad seems to be the vogue nowadays. But tell me, have you had time to look round the house?
TESMAN. You bet. I've been up since the crack of dawn.
MISS TESMAN. Well, what do you think of it?

TESMAN. Splendid. Absolutely splendid. I'm only wondering what we're going to do with those two empty rooms between that little one and Hedda's bedroom.

MISS TESMAN (*laughs slyly*). Ah: George dear, I'm sure you'll manage to find some use for them—in time.

TESMAN. Yes, of course, Auntie Juju, how stupid of me. You're thinking of my books? What?

MISS TESMAN. Yes, yes, dear boy. I was thinking of your books.

TESMAN. You know, I'm so happy for Hedda's sake that we've managed to get this house. Before we became engaged she often used to say this was the only house in town she felt she could really bear to live in. It used to belong to Mrs. Falk—you know, the Prime Minister's widow.

MISS TESMAN. Fancy that! And what a stroke of luck it happened to come into the market. Just as you'd left on your honeymoon.

TESMAN. Yes, Auntie Juju, we've certainly had all the luck with us. What?

MISS TESMAN. But, George dear, the expense! It's going to make a dreadful hole in your pocket, all this.

TESMAN (*a little downcast*). Yes, I—I suppose it will, won't it?

MISS TESMAN. Oh, George, really!

TESMAN. How much do you think it'll cost? Roughly, I mean? What?

MISS TESMAN. I can't possibly say till I see the bills.

TESMAN. Well, luckily Judge Brack's managed to get it on very favourable terms. He wrote and told Hedda so.

MISS TESMAN. Don't you worry, George dear. Anyway, I've stood security for all the furniture and carpets.

TESMAN. Security? But dear, sweet Auntie Juju, how could you possibly stand security?

MISS TESMAN. I've arranged a mortgage on our annuity.

TESMAN (*jumps up*). What? On your annuity? And—Auntie Rena's?

MISS TESMAN. Yes. Well, I couldn't think of any other way.

TESMAN (*stands in front of her*). Auntie Juju, have you gone completely out of your mind? That annuity's all you and Auntie Rena have.

MISS TESMAN. All right, there's no need to get so excited about it. It's a pure formality, you know. Judge Brack told me so. He was so kind as to arrange it all for me. A pure formality; those were his very words.

TESMAN. I dare say. All the same—

MISS TESMAN. Anyway, you'll have a salary of your own now. And, good heavens, even if we did have to fork out a little—tighten our belts for a week or two—why, we'd be happy to do so for your sake.

TESMAN. Oh, Auntie Juju! Will you never stop sacrificing yourself for me?

MISS TESMAN (*gets up and puts her hands on his sholders*). What else have I to live for but to smooth your road a little, my dear boy? You've never had any mother or father to turn to. And now at last we've achieved our goal. I won't deny we've had our little differences now and then.

But now, thank the good Lord, George dear, all your worries are past.

TESMAN. Yes, it's wonderful really how everything's gone just right for me.

MISS TESMAN. Yes! And the enemies who tried to bar your way have been struck down. They have been made to bite the dust. The man who was your most dangerous rival has had the mightiest fall. And now he's lying there in the pit he dug for himself, poor misguided creature.

TESMAN. Have you heard any news of Eilert? Since I went away?

MISS TESMAN. Only that he's said to have published a new book.

TESMAN. What! Eilert Lœvborg? You mean—just recently? What?

MISS TESMAN. So they say. I don't imagine it can be of any value, do you? When your new book comes out, that'll be another story. What's it going to be about?

TESMAN. The domestic industries of Brabant in the Middle Ages.

MISS TESMAN. Oh, George! The things you know about!

TESMAN. Mind you, it may be some time before I actually get down to writing it. I've made these very extensive notes, and I've got to file and index them first.

MISS TESMAN. Ah, yes! Making notes; filing and indexing; you've always been wonderful at that. Poor dear Joachim was just the same.

TESMAN. I'm looking forward so much to getting down to that. Especially now I've a home of my own to work in.

MISS TESMAN. And above all, now that you have the girl you set your heart on, George dear.

TESMAN (*embraces her*). Oh, yes, Auntie Juju, yes! Hedda's the loveliest thing of all! (*Looks towards the doorway.*) I think I hear her coming. What?

Hedda enters the rear room from the left, and comes into the drawing-room. She is a woman of twenty-nine. Distinguished, aristocratic face and figure. Her complexion is pale and opalescent. Her eyes are steel-grey, with an expression of cold, calm serenity. Her hair is of a handsome auburn colour, but is not especially abundant. She is dressed in an elegant, somewhat loose-fitting morning gown.

MISS TESMAN (*goes to greet her*). Good morning, Hedda dear! Good morning!

HEDDA (*holds out her hand*). Good morning, dear Miss Tesman. What an early hour to call. So kind of you.

MISS TESMAN (*seems somewhat embarrassed*). And has the young bride slept well in her new home?

HEDDA. Oh—thank you, yes. Passably well.

TESMAN (*laughs*). Passably? I say. Hedda, that's good! When I jumped out of bed, you were sleeping like a top.

HEDDA. Yes. Fortunately. One has to accustom oneself to anything new, Miss Tesman. It takes time. (*Looks left.*)

Oh, that maid's left the french windows open. This room's flooded with sun.

MISS TESMAN (*goes towards the windows*). Oh—let me close them.

HEDDA. No, no, don't do that. Tesman dear, draw the curtains. This light's blinding me.

TESMAN (*at the windows*). Yes, yes, dear. There, Hedda, now you've got shade and fresh air.

HEDDA. This room needs fresh air. All of these flowers—! But my dear Miss Tesman, won't you take a seat?

MISS TESMAN. No, really not, thank you. I just wanted to make sure you have everything you need. I must see about getting back home. My poor dear sister will be waiting for me.

TESMAN. Be sure to give her my love, won't you? Tell her I'll run over and see her later today.

MISS TESMAN. Oh yes, I'll tell her that. Oh, George—(*Fumbles in the pocket of her skirt.*) I almost forgot. I've brought something for you.

TESMAN. What's that, Auntie Juju? What?

MISS TESMAN (*pulls out a flat package wrapped in newspaper and gives it to him*). Open and see, dear boy.

TESMAN (*opens the package*). Good heavens! Auntie Juju, you've kept them! Hedda, this is really very touching. What?

HEDDA (*by the what-nots, on the right*). What is it, Tesman?

TESMAN. My old shoes! My slippers, Hedda!

HEDDA. Oh, them. I remember you kept talking about them on our honeymoon.

TESMAN. Yes, I missed them dreadfully. (*Goes over to her.*) Here, Hedda, take a look.

HEDDA (*goes away towards the stove*). Thanks, I won't bother.

TESMAN (*follows her*). Fancy, Hedda, Auntie Rena's embroidered them for me. Despite her being so ill. Oh, you can't imagine what memories they have for me.

HEDDA (*by the table*). Not for me.

MISS TESMAN. No, Hedda's right there, George.

TESMAN. Yes, but I thought since she's one of the family now—

HEDDA (*interrupts*). Tesman, we really can't go on keeping this maid.

MISS TESMAN. Not keep Bertha?

TESMAN. What makes you say that, dear? What?

HEDDA (*points*). Look at that! She's left her old hat lying on the chair.

TESMAN (*appalled, drops his slippers on the floor*). But, Hedda—!

HEDDA. Suppose someone came in and saw it?

TESMAN. But, Hedda—that's Auntie Juju's hat.

HEDDA. Oh?

MISS TESMAN (*picks up the hat*). Indeed it's mine. And it doesn't happen to be old, Hedda dear.

HEDDA. I didn't look at it very closely, Miss Tesman.

MISS TESMAN (*tying on the hat*). As a matter of fact, it's the first time I've worn it. As the good Lord is my witness.

TESMAN. It's very pretty, too. Really smart.

MISS TESMAN. Oh, I'm afraid it's nothing much really. (*Looks round.*) My parasol. Ah, there it is. (*Takes it.*) This is mine, too. (*Murmurs*) Not Bertha's.

TESMAN. A new hat and a new parasol! I say, Hedda, fancy that!

HEDDA. Very pretty and charming.

TESMAN. Yes, isn't it? What? But, Auntie Juju, take a good look at Hedda before you go. Isn't she pretty and charming?

MISS TESMAN. Dear boy, there's nothing new in that. Hedda's been a beauty ever since the day she was born. (*Nods and goes right.*)

TESMAN (*follows her*). Yes, but have you noticed how strong and healthy she's looking? And how she's filled out since we went away?

MISS TESMAN (*stops and turns*). Filled out?

HEDDA (*walks across the room*). Oh, can't we forget it?

TESMAN. Yes, Auntie Juju—you can't see it so clear with that dress on. But I've good reason to know—

HEDDA (*by the french windows, impatiently*). You haven't good reason to know anything.

TESMAN. It must have been the mountain air up there in the Tyrol—

HEDDA (*curtly, interrupts him*). I'm exactly the same as when I went away.

TESMAN. You keep on saying so. But you're not. I'm right, aren't I, Auntie Juju?

MISS TESMAN (*has folded her hands and is gazing at her*). She's beautiful—beautiful Hedda is beautiful. (*Goes over to Hedda, takes her head between her hands, draws it down and kisses her hair.*) God bless and keep you, Hedda Tesman. For George's sake.

HEDDA (*frees herself politely*). Oh—let me go, please.

MISS TESMAN (*quietly, emotionally*). I shall come and see you both every day.

TESMAN. Yes, Auntie Juju, please do. What?

MISS TESMAN. Good-bye! Good-bye!

She goes out into the hall. Tesman follows her. The door remains open. Tesman is heard sending his love to Aunt Rena and thanking Miss Tesman for his slippers. Meanwhile Hedda walks up and down the room, raising her arms and clenching her fists as though in desperation. Then she throws aside the curtains from the french windows and stands there, looking out. A few moments later Tesman returns and closes the door behind him.

TESMAN (*picks up his slippers from the floor*). What are you looking at Hedda?

HEDDA (*calm and controlled again*). Only the leaves. They're so golden and withered.

TESMAN (*wraps up the slippers and lays them on the table*). Well, we're in September now.

HEDDA (*restless again*). Yes. We're already into September.

TESMAN. Auntie Juju was behaving rather oddly, I thought,

didn't you? Almost as though she was in church or something. I wonder what came over her. Any idea?

HEDDA. I hardly know her. Does she often act like that?

TESMAN. Not to the extent she did today.

HEDDA (*goes away from the french windows*). Do you think she was hurt by what I said about the hat?

TESMAN. Oh, I don't think so. A little at first, perhaps—

HEDDA. But what a thing to do, throw her hat down in someone's drawing-room. People don't do such things.

TESMAN. I'm sure Auntie Juju doesn't do it very often.

HEDDA. Oh, well, I'll make it up with her.

TESMAN. Oh Hedda, would you?

HEDDA. When you see them this afternoon invite her to come out here this evening.

TESMAN. You bet I will! I say, there's another thing which would please her enormously.

HEDDA. Oh?

TESMAN. If you could bring yourself to call her Auntie Juju. For my sake, Hedda? What?

HEDDA. Oh, no, really, Tesman, you mustn't ask me to do that. I've told you so once before. I'll try to call her Aunt Juliana. That's as far as I'll go.

YESMAN (*after a moment*). I say, Hedda, is anything wrong? What?

HEDDA. I'm just looking at my old piano. It doesn't really go with all this.

TESMAN. As soon as I start getting my salary we'll see about changing it.

HEDDA. No, no, don't let's change it. I don't want to part with it. We can move it into that little room and get another one to put in here.

TESMAN (*a little downcast*). Yes, we—might do that.

HEDDA (*picks up the bunch of flowers from the piano*). These flowers weren't here when we arrived last night.

TESMAN. I expect Auntie Juju brought them.

HEDDA. Here's a card. (*Takes it out and reads.*) 'Will come back later today.' Guess who it's from?

TESMAN. No idea. Who? What?

HEDDA. It says: 'Mrs. Elvsted.'

TESMAN. No, really? Mrs. Elvsted. She used to be Miss Rysing, didn't she?

HEDDA. Yes. She was the one with that irritating hair she was always showing off. I hear she used to be an old flame of yours.

TESMAN (*laughs*). That didn't last long. Anyway, that was before I got to know you, Hedda. By Jove, fancy her being in town?

HEDDA. Strange she should call. I only knew her at school.

TESMAN. Yes. I haven't seen her for—oh, heavens knows how long. I don't know how she manages to stick it out up there in the north. What?

HEDDA (*thinks for a moment, then says suddenly*). Tell me, Tesman, doesn't he live somewhere up in those parts? You know—Eilert Lœvborg?

TESMAN. Yes, that's right. So he does.

Bertha *enters from the hall.*

BERTHA. She's here again, madam. The lady who came and left the flowers (*Points.*) The ones you're holding.

HEDDA. Oh, is she? Well, show her in.

Bertha opens the door for Mrs. Elvsted and goes out. Mrs. Elvsted is a delicately built woman with gentle, attractive features. Her eyes are light blue, large, and somewhat prominent, with a frightened, questioning expression. Her hair is extremely fair, almost flaxen, and is exceptionally wavy and abundant. She is two or three years younger than Hedda. She is wearing a dark visiting dress, in good taste but not quite in the latest fashion.

HEDDA (*goes cordially to greet her*). Dear Mrs. Elvsted, good morning! How delightful to see you again after all this time!

MRS. ELVSTED (*nervously, trying to control herself*). Yes, it's many years since we met.

TESMAN. And since *we* met. What?

HEDDA. Thank you for your lovely flowers.

MRS. ELVSTED. I wanted to come yesterday afternoon. But they told me you were away—

TESMAN. You've only just arrived in town, then? What?

MRS. ELVSTED. I got here yesterday, around midday. Oh, I became almost desperate when I heard you weren't here.

HEDDA. Desperate? Why?

TESMAN. My dear Mrs. Rysing—Elvsted—

HEDDA. There's nothing wrong, I hope?

MRS. ELVSTED. Yes, there is. And I don't know anyone else here whom I can turn to.

HEDDA (*puts the flowers down on the table*). Come and sit with me on the sofa—

MRS. ELVSTED. Oh, I feel too restless to sit down.

HEDDA. You must. Come along, now.

She pulls Mrs. Elvsted down on to the sofa and sits beside her.

TESMAN. Well? Tell us. Mrs.—er—

HEDDA. Has something happened at home?

MRS. ELVSTED. Yes—that is, yes and no. Oh, I do hope you won't misunderstand me—

HEDDA. Then you'd better tell us the whole story, Mrs. Elvsted.

TESMAN. That's why you've come. What?

MRS. ELVSTED. Yes—yes, it is. Well, then—in case you don't already know—Eilert Lœvborg is in town.

HEDDA. Lœvborg here?

TESMAN. Eilert back in town? Fancy, Hedda, did you hear that?

HEDDA. Yes, of course I heard.

MRS. ELVSTED. He's been here a week. A whole week! In this city. Alone. With all those dreadful people—

HEDDA. But, my dear Mrs. Elvsted, what concern is he of yours?

MRS. ELVSTED (*gives her a frightened look and says quickly*). He's been tutoring the children.

HEDDA. Your children?

MRS. ELVSTED. My husband's. I have none.

HEDDA. Oh, you mean your stepchildren.

MRS. ELVSTED. Yes.

TESMAN (*gropingly*). But was he sufficiently—I don't know how to put it—sufficiently regular in his habits to be suited to such a post? What?

MRS. ELVSTED. For the past two to three years he has been living irreproachably.

TESMAN. You don't say! Hedda, do you hear that?

HEDDA. I hear.

MRS. ELVSTED. Quite irreproachably, I assure you. In every respect. All the same—in this big city—with money in his pockets—I'm so dreadfully frightened something may happen to him.

TESMAN. But why didn't he stay up there with you and your husband?

MRS. ELVSTED. Once his book had come out, he became restless.

TESMAN. Oh, yes—Auntie Juju said he's brought out a new book.

MRS. ELVSTED. Yes, a big new book about the history of civilization. A kind of general survey. It came out a fortnight ago. Everyone's been buying it and reading it—it's created a tremendous stir—

TESMAN. Has it really? It must be something he's dug up, then.

MRS. ELVSTED. You mean from the old days?

TESMAN. Yes.

MRS. ELVSTED. No, he's written it all since he came to live with us.

TESMAN. Well, that's splendid news, Hedda. Fancy that!

MRS. ELVSTED. Oh, yes! If only he can go on like this!

HEDDA. Have you met him since you came here?

MRS. ELVSTED. No, not yet. I had such dreadful difficulty finding his address. But this morning I managed to track him down at last.

HEDDA (*looks searchingly at her*). I must say I find it a little strange that your husband—hm—

MRS. ELVSTED (*starts nervously*). My husband! What do you mean?

HEDDA. That he should send you all the way here on an errand of this kind. I'm surprised he didn't come himself to keep an eye on his friend.

MRS. ELVSTED. Oh, no, no—my husband hasn't the time. Besides, I—er—wanted to do some shopping here.

HEDDA (*with a slight smile*). Ah. Well, that's different.

MRS. ELVSTED (*gets up quickly, restlessly*). Please, Mr. Tesman, I beg you—be kind to Eilert Lœvborg if he comes here. I'm sure he will. I mean, you used to be such good friends in the old days. And you're both studying the same subject, as far as I can understand. You're in the same field, aren't you?

TESMAN. Well, we used to be, anyway.

MRS. ELVSTED. Yes—so I beg you earnestly, do please, please, keep an eye on him. Oh, Mr. Tesman, do promise me you will.

TESMAN. I shall be only too happy to do so, Mrs. Rysing.

HEDDA. Elvsted.

TESMAN. I'll do everything for Eilert that lies in my power. You can rely on that.

MRS. ELVSTED. Oh, how good and kind you are! (*Presses his hands.*) Thank you, thank you, thank you. (*Frightened.*) My husband's so fond of him, you see.

HEDDA (*gets up*). You'd better send him a note, Tesman. He may not come to you of his own accord.

TESMAN. Yes, that'd probably be the best plan, Hedda. What?

HEDDA. The sooner the better. Why not do it now?

MRS. ELVSED (*pleadingly*). Oh yes, if only you would!

TESMAN. I'll do it this very moment. Do you have his address, Mrs.—er—Elvsted?

MRS. ELVSTED. Yes. (*Takes a small piece of paper from her pocket and gives it to him.*)

TESMAN. Good, good. Right, well, I'll go inside and—(*Looks round.*) Where are my slippers? Oh yes, here. (*Picks up the package and is about to go.*)

HEDDA. Try to sound friendly. Make it a nice long letter.

TESMAN. Right, I will.

MRS. ELVSTED. Please don't say anything about my having seen you.

TESMAN. Good heavens, no, of course not. What?

He goes out through the rear room to the right.

HEDDA (*goes over to Mrs. Elvsted, smiles, and says softly*). Well! Now we've killed two birds with one stone.

MRS. ELVSTED. What do you mean?

HEDDA. Didn't you realize I wanted to get him out of the room?

MRS. ELVSTED. So that he could write the letter?

HEDDA. And so that I could talk to you alone.

MRS. ELVSTED (*confused*). About this?

HEDDA. Yes, about this.

MRS. ELVSTED (*in alarm*). But there's nothing more to tell, Mrs. Tesman. Really there is isn't.

HEDDA. Oh, yes, there is. There's a lot more. I can see that. Come along, let's sit down and have a little chat.

She pushes Mrs. Elvsted down into the armchair by the stove and seats herself on one of the footstools.

MRS. ELVSTED (*looks anxiously at her watch*). Really, Mrs. Tesman, I think I ought to be going now.

HEDDA. There's no hurry. Well? How are things at home?

MRS. ELVSTED. I'd rather not speak about that.

HEDDA. But, my dear, you can tell me. Good heavens, we were at school together.

MRS. ELVSTED. Yes, but you were a year senior to me. Oh, I used to be terribly frightened of you in those days.

HEDDA. Frightened of me?

MRS. ELVSTED. Yes, terribly frightened. Whenever you met me on the staircase you used to pull my hair.

HEDDA. No, did I?

MRS. ELVSTED. Yes. And once you said you'd burn it all off.

HEDDA. Oh, that was only in fun.

MRS. ELVSTED. Yes, but I was so silly in those days. And then afterwards—I mean, we've drifted so far apart. Our backgrounds were so different.

HEDDA. Well, now we must try to drift together again. Now listen. When we were at school we used to call each other by our Christian names—

MRS. ELVSTED. No, I'm sure you're mistaken.

HEDDA. I'm sure I'm not. I remember it quite clearly. Let's tell each other our secrets, as we used to in the old days. (*Moves closer on her footstool.*) There, now. (*Kisses her on the cheek.*) You must call me Hedda.

MRS. ELVSTED (*squeezes her hands and pats them*). Oh, you're so kind. I'm not used to people being so nice to me.

HEDDA. Now, now, now. And I shall call you Tora, the way I used to.

MRS. ELVSTED. My name is Thea.

HEDDA. Yes, of course. Of course. I meant Thea. (*Looks at her sympathetically.*) So you're not used to kindness, Thea? In your own home?

MRS. ELVSTED. Oh, if only I had a home! But I haven't. I've never had one.

HEDDA (*looks at her for a moment*). I thought that was it.

MRS. ELVSTED (*stares blankly and helplessly*). Yes—yes—yes.

HEDDA. I can't remember exactly, but didn't you first go to Mr. Elvsted as a housekeeper?

MRS. ELVSTED. Governess, actually. But his wife—at the time, I mean—she was an invalid, and had to spend most of her time in bed. So I had to look after the house, too.

HEDDA. But in the end, you became mistress of the house.

MRS. ELVSTED (*sadly*). Yes, I did.

HEDDA. Let me see. Roughly how long ago was that?

MRS. ELVSTED. When I got married, you mean?

HEDDA. Yes.

MRS. ELVSTED. About five years.

HEDDA. Yes, it must be about that.

MRS. ELVSTED. Oh, those five years! Especially the last two or three. Oh, Mrs. Tesman, if you only knew—!

HEDDA (*slaps her hand gently*). Mrs. Tesman? Oh, Thea!

MRS. ELVSTED. I'm sorry, I'll try to remember. Yes—if you had any idea—

HEDDA (*casually*). Eilert Lœvborg's been up there, too, for about three years, hasn't he?

MRS. ELVSTED (*looks at her uncertainly*). Eilert Lœvborg? Yes, he has.

HEDDA. Did you know him before? When you were here?

MRS. ELVSTED. No, not really. That is—I knew him by name, of course.

HEDDA. But up there, he used to visit you?

MRS. ELVSTED. Yes, he used to come and see us every day. To

give the children lessons. I found I couldn't do that as well as manage the house.

HEDDA. I'm sure you couldn't. And your husband—? I suppose being a magistrate he has to be away from home a good deal?

MRS. ELVSTED. Yes. You see, Mrs.—you see, Hedda, he has to cover the whole district.

HEDDA (*leans against the arm of Mrs. Elvsted's chair*). Poor, pretty little Thea! Now you must tell me the whole story. From beginning to end.

MRS. ELVSTED. Well—what do you want to know?

HEDDA. What kind of man is your husband, Thea? I mean, as a person. Is he kind to you?

MRS. ELVSTED (*evasively*). I'm sure he does his best to be.

HEDDA. I only wonder if he isn't too old for you. There's more than twenty years between you, isn't there?

MRS. ELVSTED (*irritably*). Yes, there's that, too. Oh, there are so many things. We're different in every way. We've nothing in common. Nothing whatever.

HEDDA. But he loves you, surely? In his own way?

MRS. ELVSTED. Oh, I don't know. I think he just finds me useful. And then I don't cost much to keep. I'm cheap.

HEDDA. Now you're being stupid.

MRS. ELVSTED (*shakes her head*). It can't be any different. With him. He doesn't love anyone except himself. And perhaps the children—a little.

HEDDA. He must be fond of Eilert Lœvborg, Thea.

MRS. ELVSTED (*looks at her*). Eilert Lœvborg? What makes you think that?

HEDDA. Well, if he sends you all the way down here to look for him—(*Smiles almost imperceptibly.*) Besides, you said so yourself to Tesman.

MRS. ELVSTED (*with a nervous twitch*). Did I? Oh yes, I suppose I did. (*Impulsively, but keeping her voice low.*) Well, I might as well tell you the whole story. It's bound to come out sooner or later.

HEDDA. But, my dear Thea—?

MRS. ELVSTED. My husband had no idea I was coming here.

HEDDA. What? Your husband didn't know?

MRS. ELVSTED. No, of course not. As a matter of fact, he wasn't even there. He was away at the assizes. Oh, I couldn't stand it any longer, Hedda! I just couldn't. I'd be so dreadfully lonely up there now.

HEDDA. Go on.

MRS. ELVSTED. So I packed a few things. Secretly. And went.

HEDDA. Without telling anyone?

MRS. ELVSTED. Yes. I caught the train and came straight here.

HEDDA. But, my dear Thea! How brave of you!

MRS. ELVSTED (*gets up and walks across the room*). Well, what else could I do?

HEDDA. But what do you suppose your husband will say when you get back?

MRS. ELVSTED (*by the table, looks at her*). Back there? To him?

HEDDA. Yes. Surely—?

MRS. ELVSTED. I shall never go back to him.

HEDDA (*gets up and goes closer*). You mean you've left your home for good?

MRS. ELVSED. Yes. I didn't see what else I could do.

HEDDA. But to do it so openly!

MRS. ELVSTED. Oh, it's no use trying to keep a thing like that secret.

HEDDA. But what do you suppose people will say?

MRS. ELVSTED. They can say what they like. (*Sits sadly, wearily on the sofa.*) I had to do it.

HEDDA (*after a short silence*). What do you intend to do now? How are you going to live?

MRS. ELVSTED. I don't know. I only know that I must live wherever Eilert Lœvborg is. If I am to go on living.

HEDDA (*moves a chair from the table, sits on it near Mrs. Elvsted and strokes her hands*). Tell me, Thea, how did this—friendship between you and Eilert Lœvborg begin?

MRS. ELVSTED. Oh, it came about gradually. I developed a kind of—power over him.

HEDDA. Oh?

MRS. ELVSTED. He gave up his old habits. Not because I asked him to. I'd never have dared to do that. I suppose he just noticed that I didn't like that kind of thing. So he gave it up.

HEDDA (*hides a smile*). So you've made a new man of him! Clever little Thea!

MRS. ELVSTED. Yes—anyway, he says I have. And he's made a—sort of—real person of me. Taught me to think—and to understand all kinds of things.

HEDDA. Did he give you lessons, too?

MRS. ELVSTED. Not exactly lessons. But he talked to me. About—oh, you've no idea—so many things! And then he let me work with him. Oh, it was wonderful. I was so happy to be allowed to help him.

HEDDA. Did he allow you to help him?

MRS. ELVSTED. Yes. Whenever he wrote anything we always—did it together.

HEDDA. Like good friends?

MRS. ELVSTED (*eagerly*). Friends! Yes—why, Hedda that's exactly the word he used! Oh, I ought to feel so happy. But I can't. I don't know if it will last.

HEDDA. You don't seem very sure of him.

MRS. ELVSTED (*sadly*). Something stands between Eilert Lœvborg and me. The shadow of another woman.

HEDDA. Who can that be?

MRS. ELVSTED. I don't know. Someone he used to be friendly with in—in the old days. Someone he's never been able to forget.

HEDDA. What has he told you about her?

MRS. ELVSTED. Oh, he only mentioned her once, casually.

HEDDA. Well! What did he say?

MRS. ELVSTED. He said when he left her she tried to shoot him with a pistol.

HEDDA (*cold, controlled*). What nonsense. People don't do such things. The kind of people we know.

MRS. ELVSTED. No. I think it must have been that red-haired singer he used to—

HEDDA. Ah yes, very probably.

MRS. ELVSTED. I remember they used to say she always carried a loaded pistol.

HEDDA. Well then, it must be her.

MRS. ELVSTED. But, Hedda, I hear she's come back, and is living here. Oh, I'm so desperate—!

HEDDA (*glances toward the rear room*). Ssh! Tesman's coming. (*Gets up and whispers.*) Thea, we mustn't breathe a word about this to anyone.

MRS. ELVSTED (*jumps up*). Oh, no, no! Please don't!

George Tesman appears from the right in the rear room with a letter in his hand, and comes into the drawing-room.

TESMAN. Well, here's my little epistle all signed and sealed.

HEDDA. Good. I think Mrs. Elvsted wants to go now. Wait a moment—I'll see you as far as the garden gate.

TESMAN. Er—Hedda, do you think Bertha could deal with this?

HEDDA (*takes the letter*). I'll give her instructions.

Bertha enters from the hall.

BERTHA. Judge Brack is here and asks if he may pay his respects to madam and the Doctor.

HEDDA. Yes, ask him to be so good as to come in. And— wait a moment—drop this letter in the post box.

BERTHA (*takes the letter*). Very good, madam.

She opens the door for Judge Brack, and goes out. Judge Brack is forty-five; rather short, but well built, and elastic in his movements. He has a roundish face with an aristocratic profile. His hair, cut short, is still almost black, and is carefully barbered. Eyes lively and humorous. Thick eyebrows. His moustache is also thick, and is trimmed square at the ends. He is wearing outdoor clothes which are elegant but a little too youthful for him. He has a monocle in one eye; now and then he lets it drop.

BRACK (*hat in hand, bows*). May one presume to call so early?

HEDDA. One may presume.

TESMAN (*shakes his hand*). You're welcome here any time. Judge Brack—Mrs. Rysing.

Hedda sighs.

BRACK (*bows*). Ah—charmed—

HEDDA (*looks at him and laughs*). What fun to be able to see you by daylight for once, Judge.

BRACK. Do I look—different?

HEDDA. Yes. A little younger, I think.

BRACK. Too kind.

TESMAN. Well, what do you think of Hedda? What? Doesn't she look well? Hasn't she filled out—?

HEDDA. Oh, do stop it. You ought to be thanking Judge Brack for all the inconvenience he's put himself to—

BRACK. Nonsense, it was a pleasure—

HEDDA. You're a loyal friend. But my other friend is pining to get away. *Au revoir*, Judge. I won't be a minute.

Mutual salutations. Mrs. Elvsted and Hedda go out through the hall.

BRACK. Well, is your wife satisfied with everything?

TESMAN. Yes, we can't thank you enough. That is—we may have to shift one or two things around, she tells me. And we're short of one or two little items we'll have to purchase.

BRACK. Oh? Really?

TESMAN. But you mustn't worry your head about that. Hedda says she'll get what's needed. I say, why don't we sit down? What?

BRACK. Thanks, just for a moment. (*Sits at the table.*) There's something I'd like to talk to you about, my dear Tesman.

TESMAN. Oh? Ah yes, of course. (*Sits.*) After the feast comes the reckoning. What?

BRACK. Oh, never mind about the financial side—there's no hurry about that. Though I could wish we'd arranged things a little less palatially.

TESMAN. Good heavens, that'd never have done. Think of Hedda, my dear chap. You know her. I couldn't possibly ask her to live like a petty bourgeois.

BRACK. No, no—that's just the problem.

TESMAN. Anyway, it can't be long now before my nomination comes through.

BRACK. Well, you know, these things often take time.

TESMAN. Have you heard any more news? What?

BRACK. Nothing definite. (*Changing the subject*). Oh, by the way, I have one piece of news for you.

TESMAN. What?

BRACK. Your old friend Eilert Lœvborg is back in town.

TESMAN. I know that already.

BRACK. Oh? How did you hear that?

TESMAN. She told me. That lady who went out with Hedda.

BRACK. I see. What was her name? I didn't catch it.

TESMAN. Mrs. Elvsted.

BRACK. Oh, the magistrate's wife. Yes, Lœvborg's been living up near them, hasn't he?

TESMAN. I'm delighted to hear he's become a decent human being again.

BRACK. Yes, so they say.

TESMAN. I gather he's published a new book, too. What?

BRACK. Indeed he has.

TESMAN. I hear it's created rather a stir.

BRACK. Quite an unusual stir.

TESMAN. I say, isn't that splendid news! He's such a gifted chap—and I was afraid he'd gone to the dogs for good.

BRACK. Most people thought he had.

TESMAN. But I can't think what he'll do now. How on earth will he manage to make ends meet? What?

As he speaks his last words Hedda enters from the hall.

HEDDA (*to Brack, laughs slightly scornfully*). Tesman is always worrying about making ends meet.

TESMAN. We were talking about poor Eilert Lœvborg, Hedda dear.

HEDDA (*gives him a quick look*). Oh, were you? (*Sits in the armchair by the stove and asks casually.*) Is he in trouble?

TESMAN. Well, he must have run through his inheritance long ago by now. And he can't write a new book every year. What? So I'm wondering what's going to become of him.

BRACK. I may be able to enlighten you there.

TESMAN. Oh?

BRACK. You mustn't forget he has relatives who wield a good deal of influence.

TESMAN. Relatives? Oh, they've quite washed their hands of him, I'm afraid.

BRACK. They used to regard him as the hope of the family.

TESMAN. Used to, yes. But he's put an end to that.

HEDDA. Who knows? (*With a little smile.*) I hear the Elvsteds have made a new man of him.

BRACK. And then this book he's just published—

TESMAN. Well, let's hope they find something for him. I've just written him a note. Oh, by the way, Hedda, I asked him to come over and see us this evening.

BRACK. But, my dear chap, you're coming to me this evening. My bachelor party. You promised me last night when I met you at the boat.

HEDDA. Had you forgotten, Tesman?

TESMAN. Good heavens, yes, I'd quite forgotten.

BRACK. Anyway, you can be quite sure he won't turn up here.

TESMAN. Why do you think that? What?

BRACK (*a little unwillingly, gets up and rests his hand on the back of his chair*). My dear Tesman—and you, too, Mrs. Tesman—there's something I feel you ought to know.

TESMAN. Concerning Eilert?

BRACK. Concerning him and you.

TESMAN. Well, my dear Judge, tell us please!

BRACK. You must be prepared for your nomination not to come through quite as quickly as you hope and expect.

TESMAN (*jumps up uneasily*). Is anything wrong? What?

BRACK. There's a possibility that the appointment may be decided by competition—

TESMAN. Competition! Hedda, fancy that!

HEDDA (*leans further back in her chair*). Ah! How interesting!

TESMAN. But who else—? I say, you don't mean—?

BRACK. Exactly. By competition with Eilert Lœvborg.

TESMAN (*clasps his hands in alarm*). No, no, but this is inconceivable? It's absolutely impossible! What?

BRACK. Hm. We may find it'll happen, all the same.

TESMAN. No, but—Judge Brack, they couldn't be so inconsiderate towards me! (*Waves his arms.*) I mean, by Jove, I—I'm a married man! It was on the strength of this that Hedda and I got married! We've run up some pretty hefty debts. And borrowed money from Auntie Juju! I mean, good heavens, they practically promised me the appointment. What?

BRACK. Well, well, I'm sure you'll get it. But you'll have to go through a competition.

HEDDA (*motionless in her armchair*): How exciting, Tesman. It'll be a kind of duel, by Jove.

TESMAN. My dear Hedda, how can you take it so lightly?

HEDDA (*as before*). I'm not. I can't wait to see who's going to win.

BRACK. In any case, Mrs. Tesman, it's best you should know how things stand. I mean before you commit yourself to these little items I hear you're threatening to purchase.

HEDDA. I can't allow this to alter my plans.

BRACK. Indeed? Well, that's your business. Good-bye. (*To Tesman*) I'll come and collect you on the way home from my afternoon walk.

TESMAN. Oh, yes, yes. I'm sorry. I'm all upside down just now.

HEDDA (*lying in her chair, holds out her hand*). Good-bye, Judge. See you this afternoon.

BRACK. Thank you. Good-bye, good-bye.

TESMAN (*sees him to the door*). Good-bye, my dear Judge. You will excuse me, won't you?

Judge Brack goes out through the hall.

TESMAN (*pacing up and down*). Oh, Hedda! One oughtn't to go plunging off on wild adventures. What?

HEDDA (*looks at him and smiles*). Like you're doing?

TESMAN. Yes. I mean, there's no denying it, it was a pretty big adventure to go off and get married and set up house merely on expectation.

HEDDA. Perhaps you're right.

TESMAN. Well, anyway, we have our home, Hedda. My word, yes! The home we dreamed of. And set our hearts on. What?

HEDDA (*gets up slowly, wearily*). You agreed that we should enter society. And keep open house. That was the bargain.

TESMAN. Yes. Good heavens, I was looking forward to it all so much. To seeing you play hostess to a select circle! By Jove! What? Ah, well, for the time being we shall have to make do with each other's company, Hedda. Perhaps have Auntie Juju in now and then. Oh dear, this wasn't at all what you had in mind—

HEDDA. I won't be able to have a liveried footman. For a start.

TESMAN. Oh no, we couldn't possibly afford a footman.

HEDDA. And the bay mare you promised me—

TESMAN (*fearfully*). Bay mare!

HEDDA. I mustn't even think of that now.

TESMAN. Heaven forbid!

HEDDA (*walks across the room*). Ah, well. I still have one thing left to amuse myself with.

TESMAN (*joyfully*). Thank goodness for that. What's that, Hedda? What?

HEDDA (*in the open doorway, looks at him with concealed scorn*). My pistols, George darling.

TESMAN (*alarmed*). Pistols!

HEDDA (*her eyes cold*). General Gabler's pistols.

She goes into the rear room and disappears.

TESMAN (*runs to the doorway and calls after her*). For heaven's sake, Hedda dear, don't touch those things. They're dangerous. Hedda—please—for my sake! What?

ACT TWO

The same as in Act One, except that the piano has been removed and an elegant little writing-table, with a bookcase, stands in its place. By the sofa on the left a smaller table has been placed. Most of the flowers have been removed. Mrs. Elvsted's bouquet stands on the larger table, downstage. It is afternoon.

Hedda, dressed to receive callers, is alone in the room. She is standing by the open french windows, loading a revolver. The pair to it is lying in an open pistol-case on the writing-table.

HEDDA (*looks down into the garden and calls*). Good afternoon, Judge.

BRACK (*in the distance, below*). Afternoon, Mrs. Tesman.

HEDDA (*raises the pistol and takes aim*). I'm going to shoot you, Judge Brack.

BRACK (*shouts from below*). No, no, no! Don't aim that thing at me!

HEDDA. This'll teach you to enter houses by the back door.

She fires.

BRACK (*below*). Have you gone completely out of your mind?

HEDDA. Oh dear! Did I hit you?

BRACK (*still outside*). Stop playing these silly tricks.

HEDDA. All right, Judge. Come along in.

Judge Brack, dressed for a bachelor party, enters through the french windows. He has a light overcoat on his arm.

BRACK. For God's sake, haven't you stopped fooling around with those things yet? What are you thing to hit?

HEDDA. Oh, I was just shooting at the sky.

BRACK (*takes the pistol gently from her hand*). By your leave, ma'am. (*Looks at it.*) Ah, yes—I know this old friend well. (*Looks around.*) Where's the case? Oh, yes. (*Puts the pistol in the case and closes it.*) That's enough of that little game for today.

HEDDA. Well, what on earth *am* I to do?

BRACK. You haven't had any visitors?

HEDDA (*closes the french windows*). Not one. I suppose the best people are all still in the country.

BRACK. Your husband isn't home yet?

HEDDA (*locks the pistol-case away in a drawer of the writing-table*). No. The moment he'd finished eating he ran off to his aunties. He wasn't expecting you so early.

BRACK. Ah, why didn't I think of that? How stupid of me.

HEDDA (*turns her head and looks at him*). Why stupid?

BRACK. I'd have come a little sooner.

HEDDA (*walks across the room*). There'd have been no one to receive you. I've been in my room since lunch, dressing.

BRACK. You haven't a tiny crack in the door through which we might have negotiated?

HEDDA. You forgot to arrange one.

BRACK. Another stupidity.

HEDDA. Well, we'll have to sit down here. And wait. Tesman won't be back for some time.

BRACK. Sad. Well, I'll be patient.

Hedda sits on the corner of the sofa. Brack puts his coat over the back of the nearest chair and seats himself, keeping his hat in his hand. Short pause. They look at each other.

HEDDA. Well?

BRACK (*in the same tone of voice*). Well?

HEDDA. I asked first.

BRACK (*leans forward slightly*). Yes, well, now we can enjoy a nice, cosy little chat—Mrs. Hedda.

HEDDA (*leans further back in her chair*). It seems ages since we had a talk. I don't count last night or this morning.

BRACK. You mean: *à deux*?

HEDDA. Mm—yes. That's roughly what I meant.

BRACK. I've been longing so much for you to come home.

HEDDA. So have I.

BRACK. You? Really, Mrs. Hedda? And I thought you were having such a wonderful honeymoon.

HEDDA. Oh, yes. Wonderful!

BRACK. But your husband wrote such ecstatic letters.

HEDDA. He! Oh, yes! He thinks life has nothing better to offer than rooting around in libraries and copying old pieces of parchment, or whatever it is he does.

BRACK (*a little maliciously*). Well, that *is* his life. Most of it, anyway.

HEDDA. Yes, I know. Well, it's all right for him. But for me! Oh no, my dear Judge. I've been bored to death.

BRACK (*sympathetically*). Do you mean that? Seriously?

HEDDA. Yes. Can you imagine? Six whole months without ever meeting a single person who was one of us, and to whom I could talk about the kind of things we talk about.

BRACK. Yes, I can understand. I'd miss that, too.

HEDDA. That wasn't the worst, though.

BRACK. What was?

HEDDA. Having to spend every minute of one's life with—with the same person.

BRACK (*nods*). Yes. What a thought! Morning; noon; *and*—

HEDDA (*coldly*). As I said: every minute of one's life.

BRACK. I stand corrected. But dear Tesman is such a clever fellow, I should have thought one ought to be able—

HEDDA. Tesman is only interested in one thing, my dear Judge. His special subject.

BRACK. True.

HEDDA. And people who are only interested in one thing don't make the most amusing company. Not for long, anyway.

BRACK. Not even when they happen to be the person one loves?

HEDDA. Oh, don't use that sickly, stupid word.

BRACK (*starts*). But, Mrs. Hedda—!

HEDDA (*half laughing, half annoyed*). You must try it, Judge. Listening to the history of cvilization, morning, noon and—

BRACK (*corrects her*). Every minute of one's life.

HEDDA. All right. Oh, and those domestic industries of Brabant in the Middle Ages! That really is beyond the limit.

BRACK (*looks at her searchingly*). But, tell me—if you feel like this why on earth did you—? Hm—

HEDDA. Why on earth did I marry George Tesman?

BRACK. If you like to put it that way.

HEDDA. Do you think it so very strange?

BRACK. Yes—and no, Mrs. Hedda.

HEDDA. I'd danced myself tired, Judge. I felt my time was up—(*Gives a slight shudder.*) No, I mustn't say that. Or even think it.

BRACK. You've no rational cause to think it.

HEDDA. Oh—cause, cause—(*Looks searchingly at him.*) After all, George Tesman—well, I mean, he's a very respectable man.

BRACK. Very respectable, sound as a rock. No denying that.

HEDDA. And there's nothing exactly ridiculous about him. Is there?

BRACK. Ridiculous? N-no, I wouldn't say that.

HEDDA. Mm. He's very clever at collecting material and all that, isn't he? I mean, he may go quite far in time.

BRACK (*looks at her a little uncertainly*). I thought you believed, like everyone else, that he would become a very prominent man.

HEDDA (*looks tired*). Yes, I did. And when he came and begged me on his bended knees to be allowed to love and to cherish me, I didn't see why I shouldn't let him.

BRACK. No, well—if one looks at it like that—

HEDDA. It was more than my other admirers were prepared to do, Judge dear.

BRACK (*laughs*). Well, I can't answer for the others. As far as I myself am concerned, you know I've always had a considerable respect for the institution of marriage. As an institution.

HEDDA (*lightly*). Oh, I've never entertained any hopes of you.

BRACK. All I want is to have a circle of friends whom I can trust, whom I can help with advice or—or by any other means, and into whose houses I may come and go as a—trusted friend.

HEDDA. Of the husband?

BRACK (*bows*). Preferably, to be frank, of the wife. And of the husband too, of course. Yes, you know, this kind of triangle is a delightful arrangement for all parties concerned.

HEDDA. Yes, I often longed for a third person while I was

away. Oh, those hours we spent alone in railway compartments—

BRACK. Fortunately your honeymoon is now over.

HEDDA (*shakes her head*). There's a long, long way still to go.
I've only reached a stop on the line.

BRACK. Why not jump out and stretch your legs a little,
Mrs. Hedda?

HEDDA. I'm not the jumping sort.

BRACK. Aren't you?

HEDDA. No. There's always someone around who—

BRACK (*laughs*). Who looks at one's legs?

HEDDA. Yes. Exactly.

BRACK. Well, but surely—

HEDDA (*with a gesture of rejection*). I don't like it. I'd rather
stay where I am. Sitting in the compartment. *À deux.*

BRACK. But suppose a third person were to step into the
compartment?

HEDDA. That would be different.

BRACK. A trusted friend—someone who understood—

HEDDA. And was lively and amusing—

BRACK. And interested in—more subjects than one—

HEDDA (*sighs audibly*). Yes, that'd be a relief.

BRACK (*hears the front door open and shut*). The triangle is
completed.

HEDDA (*half under her breath*). And the train goes on.

*George Tesman, in grey walking dress with a soft felt hat,
enters from the hall. He has a number of paper-covered
books under his arm and in his pockets.*

TESMAN (*goes over to the table by the corner sofa*). Phew! It's
too hot to be lugging all this around. (*Puts the books
down.*) I'm positively sweating, Hedda. Why, hullo,
hullo! You here already, Judge? What? Bertha didn't tell
me.

BRACK (*gets up*). I came in through the garden.

HEDDA. What are all those books you've got there?

TESMAN (*stands glancing through them*). Oh, some new publications dealing with my special subject. I had to buy them.

HEDDA. Your special subject?

BRACK. His special subject, Mrs. Tesman.

Brack and Hedda exchange a smile.

HEDDA. Haven't you collected enough material on your special subject?

TESMAN. My dear Hedda, one can never have too much.
One must keep abreast of what other people are writing.

HEDDA. Yes. Of course.

TESMAN (*rooting among the books*). Look—I bought a copy of
Eilert Lœvborg's new book, too. (*Holds it out to her.*) Perhaps you'd like to have a look at it, Hedda? What?

HEDDA. No, thank you. Er—yes, perhaps I will, later.

TESMAN. I glanced through it on my way home.

BRACK. What's your opinion—as a specialist on the subject?

TESMAN. I'm amazed how sound and balanced it is. He

never used to write like that. (*Gathers his books together.*)
Well, I must get down to these at once. I can hardly wait
to cut the pages. Oh, I've got to change, too. (*To Brack*)
We don't have to be off just yet, do we? What?

BRACK. Heavens, no. We've plenty of time yet.

TESMAN. Good, I needn't hurry, then. (*Goes with his books,
but stops and turns in the doorway.*) Oh, by the way, Hedda,
Auntie Juju won't be coming to see you this evening.

HEDDA. Won't she? Oh—the hat, I suppose.

TESMAN. Good heavens, no. How could you think such a
thing of Auntie Juju? Fancy—! No, Auntie Rena's very
ill.

HEDDA. She always is.

TESMAN. Yes, but today she's been taken really bad.

HEDDA. Oh, then it's quite understandable that the other
one should want to stay with her. Well, I shall have to
swallow my disappointment.

TESMAN. You can't imagine how happy Auntie Juju was in
spite of everything. At your looking so well after the
honeymoon!

HEDDA (*half beneath her breath, as she rises*). Oh, these everlasting aunts!

TESMAN. What?

HEDDA (*goes over to the french windows*). Nothing.

TESMAN. Oh. All right. (*Goes into the rear room and out of
sight.*)

BRACK. What was that about the hat?

HEDDA. Oh, something that happened with Miss Tesman
this morning. She'd put her hat down on a chair. (*Looks
at him and smiles.*) And I pretended to think it was the
servant's.

BRACK (*shakes his head*). But, my dear Mrs. Hedda, how
could you do such a thing? To that poor old lady?

HEDDA (*nervously, walking across the room*). Sometimes a
mood like that hits me. And I can't stop myself. (*Throws
herself down in the armchair by the stove.*) Oh, I don't know
how to explain it.

BRACK (*behind her chair*). You're not really happy. That's the
answer.

HEDDA (*stares ahead of her*). Why on earth should I be
happy? Can you give me a reason?

BRACK. Yes. For one thing you've got the home you always
wanted.

HEDDA (*looks at him*). You really believe that story?

BRACK. You mean it isn't true?

HEDDA. Oh, yes, it's partly true.

BRACK. Well?

HEDDA. It's true I got Tesman to see me home from parties
last summer—

BRACK. It was a pity my home lay in another direction.

HEDDA. Yes. Your interests lay in another direction, too.

BRACK (*laughs*). That's naughty of you, Mrs. Hedda. But to
return to you and George—

HEDDA. Well, we walked past this house one evening. And

poor Tesman was fidgeting in his boots trying to find something to talk about. I felt sorry for the great scholar—

BRACK (*smiles incredulously*). Did you? Hm.

HEDDA. Yes, honestly I did. Well, to help him out of his misery, I happened to say quite frivolously how much I'd love to live in this house.

BRACK. Was that all?

HEDDA. That evening, yes.

BRACK. But—afterwards?

HEDDA. Yes. My little frivolity had its consequences, my dear Judge.

BRACK. Our little frivolities do. Much too often, unfortunately.

HEDDA. Thank you. Well, it was our mutual admiration for the late Prime Minister's house that brought George Tesman and me together on common ground. So we got engaged, and we got married, and we went on our honeymoon, and—Ah well, Judge, I've—made my bed and I must lie in it, I was about to say.

BRACK. How utterly fantastic! And you didn't really care in the least about the house?

HEDDA. God knows I didn't.

BRACK. Yes, but now that we've furnished it so beautifully for you?

HEDDA. Ugh—all the rooms smell of lavender and dried roses. But perhaps Auntie Juju brought that in.

BRACK (*laughs*). More likely the Prime Minister's widow, rest her soul.

HEDDA. Yes, it's got the odour of death about it. It reminds me of the flowers one has worn at a ball—the morning after. (*Clasps her hands behind her neck, leans back in the chair and looks up at him.*) Oh, my dear Judge, you've no idea how hideously bored I'm going to be out here.

BRACK. Couldn't you find some—occupation, Mrs. Hedda? Like your husband?

HEDDA. Occupation? That'd interest me?

BRACK. Well—preferably.

HEDDA. God knows what. I've often thought—(*Breaks off.*) No, that wouldn't work either.

BRACK. Who knows? Tell me about it.

HEDDA. I was thinking—if I could persuade Tesman to go into politics, for example.

BRACK (*laughs*). Tesman! No, honestly, I don't think he's quite cut out to be a politician.

HEDDA. Perhaps not. But if I could persuade him to have a go at it?

BRACK. What satisfaction would that give you? If he turned out to be no good? Why do you want to make him do that?

HEDDA. Because I'm bored. (*After a moment.*) You feel there's absolutely no possibility of Tesman becoming Prime Minister, then?

BRACK. Well, you know, Mrs. Hedda, for one thing he'd have to be pretty well off before he could become that.

HEDDA (*gets up impatiently*). There you are! (*Walks across the room.*) It's this wretched poverty that makes life so hateful. And ludicrous. Well, it is!

BRACK. I don't think that's the real cause.

HEDDA. What is, then?

BRACK. Nothing really exciting has ever happened to you.

HEDDA. Nothing serious, you mean?

BRACK. Call if that if you like. But now perhaps it may.

HEDDA (*tosses her head*). Oh, you're thinking of this competition for that wretched professorship? That's Tesman's affair. I'm not going to waste my time worrying about that.

BRACK. Very well, let's forget about that, then. But suppose you were to find yourself faced with what people call—to use the conventional phrase—the most solemn of human responsibilities? (*Smiles.*) A new responsibility, little Mrs. Hedda.

HEDDA (*angrily*). Be quiet! Nothing like that's going to happen.

BRACK (*warily*). We'll talk about it again in a year's time. If not earlier.

HEDDA (*curtly*). I've no leanings in that direction, Judge. I don't want any—responsibilities.

BRACK. But surely you must feel some inclination to make use of that—natural talent which every woman—

HEDDA (*over by the french windows*). Oh, be quiet, I say! I often think there's only one thing for which I have any natural talent.

BRACK (*goes closer*). And what is that, if I may be so bold as to ask?

HEDDA (*stands looking out*). For boring myself to death. Now you know. (*Turns, looks towards the rear room and laughs.*) Talking of boring, here comes the professor.

BRACK (*quietly, warningly*). Now, now, now, Mrs. Hedda!

George Tesman, in evening dress, with gloves and hat in his hand, enters through the rear room from the right.

TESMAN. Hedda, hasn't any message come from Eilert? What?

HEDDA. No.

TESMAN. Ah, then we'll have him here presently. You wait and see.

BRACK. You really think he'll come?

TESMAN. Yes, I'm almost sure he will. What you were saying about him this morning is just gossip.

BRACK. Oh?

TESMAN. Yes, Auntie Juju said she didn't believe he'd ever dare to stand in my way again. Fancy that!

BRACK. Then everything in the garden's lovely.

TESMAN (*puts his hat, with his gloves in it, on a chair, right*). Yes, but you really must let me wait for him as long as possible.

BRACK. We've plenty of time. No one'll be turning up at my place before seven or half past.

TESMAN. Ah, then we can keep Hedda company a little longer. And see if he turns up. What?

HEDDA (*picks up Brack's* coat *and* hat *and carries them over to the corner sofa*). And if the worst comes to the worst, Mr. Lœvborg can sit here and talk to me.

BRACK (*offering to take his things from her*). No, please. What do you mean by 'if the worst comes to the worst'?

HEDDA. If he doesn't want to go with you and Tesman.

TESMAN (*looks doubtfully at her*). I say, Hedda, do you think it'll be all right for him to stay here with you? What? Remember Auntie Juju isn't coming.

HEDDA. Yes, but Mrs. Elvsted is. The three of us can have a cup of tea together.

TESMAN. Ah, that'll be all right.

BRACK (*smiles*). It's probably the safest solution as far as he's concerned.

HEDDA. Why?

BRACK. My dear Mrs. Tesman, you always say of my little bachelor parties that they should only be attended by men of the strongest principles.

HEDDA. But Mr. Lœvborg is a man of principle now. You know what they say about a reformed sinner—

Bertha enters from the hall.

BERTHA. Madam, there's a gentleman here who wants to see you—

HEDDA. Ask him to come in.

TESMAN (*quietly*). I'm sure it's him. By Jove. Fancy that!

Eilert Lœvborg enters from the hall. He is slim and lean, of the same age as Tesman, but looks older and somewhat haggard. His hair and beard are of a blackish-brown; his face is long and pale, but with a couple of reddish patches on his cheekbones. He is dressed in an elegant and fairly new black suit, and carries black gloves and a top-hat in his hand. He stops just inside the door and bows abruptly. He seems somewhat embarrassed.

TESMAN (*goes over and shakes his hand*). My dear Eilert! How grand to see you again after all these years!

EILERT LŒVBORG: (*speaks softly*). It was good of you to write, George. (*Goes near to Hedda.*) May I shake hands with you, too, Mrs. Tesman?

HEDDA (*accepts his hand*). Delighted to see you, Mr. Lœvborg. (*With a gesture.*) I don't know if you two gentlemen—

LŒVBORG (*bows slightly*). Judge Brack, I believe.

BRACK (*also with a slight bow*). Correct. We—met some years ago—

TESMAN (*puts his hands on Lœvborg's shoulders*). Now, you're to treat this house just as though it were your own home, Eilert. Isn't that right, Hedda? I hear you've decided to settle here again. What?

LŒVBORG. Yes, I have.

TESMAN. Quite understandable. Oh, by the by—I've just bought your new book. Though to tell the truth I haven't found time to read it yet.

LŒVBORG. You needn't bother.

TESMAN. Oh? Why?

LŒVBORG. There's nothing much in it.

TESMAN. By Jove, fancy hearing that from you!

BRACK. But everyone's praising it.

LŒVBORG. That was exactly what I wanted to happen. So I only wrote what I knew everyone would agree with.

BRACK. Very sensible.

TESMAN. Yes, but my dear Eilert—

LŒVBORG. I want to try to re-establish myself. To begin again—from the beginning.

TESMAN (*a little embarrassed*). Yes, I—er—suppose you do. What?

LŒVBORG (*smiles, puts down his hat and takes a package wrapped in paper from his coat pocket*). But when this gets pubished—George Tesman—read it. This is my real book. The one in which I have spoken with my own voice.

TESMAN. Oh, really? What's it about?

LŒVBORG. It's the sequel.

TESMAN. Sequel? To what?

LŒVBORG. To the other book.

TESMAN. The one that's just come out?

LŒVBORG. Yes.

TESMAN. But my dear Eilert, that covers the subject right to the present day.

LŒVBORG. It does. But this about the future.

TESMAN. The future! But, I say, we don't know anything about that.

LŒVBORG. No. But there are one or two things that need to be said about it. (*Opens the package.*) Here, have a look.

TESMAN. Surely that's not your handwriting?

LŒVBORG. I dictated it. (*Turns the pages.*) It's in two parts. The first deals with the forces that will shape our civilization. (*Turns further on towards the end.*) And the second indicates the direction in which that civilization may develop.

TESMAN. Amazing! I'd never think of writing about anything like that.

HEDDA (*by the french windows, drumming on the pane*). No. You wouldn't.

LŒVBORG (*puts the pages back into their cover and lays the package on the table*). I brought it because I thought I might possibly read you a few pages this evening.

TESMAN. I say, what a kind idea! Oh, but this evening—? (*Glances at Brack.*) I'm not quite sure whether—

LŒVBORG. Well, some other time, then. There's no hurry.

BRACK. The truth is, Mr. Lœvborg, I'm giving a little dinner this evening. In Tesman's honour, you know.

LŒVBORG (*looks round for his hat*). Oh—then I mustn't—

BRACK. No, wait a minute. Won't you do me the honour of joining us?

LŒVBORG (*curtly, with decision*). No, I can't. Thank you so much.

BRACK. Oh, nonsense. Do—please. There'll only be a few of us. And I can promise you we shall have some good sport, as Hed—Mrs. Tesman puts it.

LŒVBORG. I've no doubt. Nevertheless—

BRACK. You could bring your manuscript along and read it to Tesman at my place. I could lend you a room.

TESMAN. Well, yes, that's an idea. What?

HEDDA (*interposes*). But, Tesman, Mr. Lœvborg doesn't want to go. I'm sure Mr. Lœvborg would much rather sit here and have supper with me.

LŒVBORG (*looks at her*). With you, Mrs. Tesman?

HEDDA. And Mrs. Elvsted.

LŒVBORG. Oh. (*Casually.*) I ran into her this afternoon.

HEDDA. Did you? Well, she's coming here this evening. So you really must stay, Mr. Lœvborg. Otherwise she'll have no one to see her home.

LŒVBORG. That's true. Well—thank you, Mrs. Tesman, I'll stay then.

HEDDA. I'll just tell the servant.

She goes to the door which leads into the hall, and rings. Bertha enters. Hedda talks softly to her and points toward the rear room. Bertha nods and goes out.

TESMAN (*to Lœvborg as Hedda does this*). I say, Eilert. This new subject of yours—the—er—future—is that the one you're going to lecture about?

LŒVBORG. Yes.

TESMAN. They told me down at the bookshop that you're going to hold a series of lectures here during the autumn.

LŒVBORG. Yes, I am. I —hope you don't mind, Tesman.

TESMAN. Good heavens, not! But—?

LŒVBORG. I can quite understand it might queer your pitch a little.

TESMAN (*dejectedly*). Oh well, I can't expect you to put them off for my sake.

LŒVBORG. I'll wait till your appointment's been announced.

TESMAN. You'll wait! But—but—aren't you going to compete with me for the post? What?

LŒVBORG. No. I only want to defeat you in the eyes of the world.

TESMAN. Good heavens! Then Auntie Juju was right after all! Oh, I knew it, I knew it! Hear that, Hedda? Fancy! Eilert *doesn't* want to stand in our way.

HEDDA (*curtly*). Our? Leave me out of it, please.

She goes towards the rear room, where Bertha is setting a tray with decanters and glasses on the table. Hedda nods approval, and comes back into the drawing-room. Bertha goes out.

TESMAN (*while this is happening*). Judge Brack, what do you think about all this? What?

BRACK. Oh, I think honour and victory can be very splendid things—

TESMAN. Of course they can. Still—

HEDDA (*looks at Tesman, with a cold smile*). You look as if you'd been hit by a thunderbolt.

TESMAN. Yes, I feel rather like it.

BRACK. There was a black cloud looming up, Mrs. Tesman. But it seems to have passed over.

HEDDA (*points towards the rear room*). Well, gentlemen, won't you go in and take a glass of cold punch?

BRACK (*glances at his watch*). One for the road. Yes, why not?

TESMAN. An admirable suggestion, Hedda. Admirable! Oh, I feel so relieved!

HEDDA. Won't you have one, too, Mr. Lœvborg?

LŒVBORG. No, thank you. I'd rather not.

BRACK. Great heavens, man, cold punch isn't poison. Take my word for it.

LŒVBORG. Not for everyone, perhaps.

HEDDA. I'll keep Mr. Lœvborg company while you drink.

TESMAN. Yes, Hedda dear, would you?

He and Brack go into the rear room, sit down, drink punch, smoke cigarettes and talk cheerfully during the following scene. Eilert Lœvborg remains standing by the stove. Hedda goes to the writing-table.

HEDDA (*raising her voice slightly*). I've some photographs I'd like to show you, if you'd care to see them. Tesman and I visited the Tyrol on our way home.

She comes back with an album, places it on the table by the sofa and sits in the upstage corner of the sofa. Eilert Lœvborg comes towards her, stops, and looks at her. Then he takes a chair and sits down on her left, with his back towards the rear room.

HEDDA (*opens the album*). You see these mountains, Mr. Lœvborg? That's the Ortler group. Tesman has written the name underneath. You see: 'The Ortler Group near Meran.'

LŒVBORG (*has not taken his eyes from her; says softly, slowly*). Hedda—Gabler!

HEDDA (*gives him a quick glance*). Ssh!

LŒVBORG (*repeats softly*). Hedda Gabler!

HEDDA (*looks at the album*). Yes, that used to be my name. When we first knew each other.

LŒVBORG. And from now on—for the rest of my life—I must teach myself never to say: Hedda Gabler.

HEDDA (*still turning the pages*). Yes, you must. You'd better start getting into practice. The sooner the better.

LŒVBORG (*bitterly*). Hedda Gabler married? And to George Tesman!

HEDDA. Yes. Well—that's life.

LŒVBORG. Oh, Hedda, Hedda! How could you throw yourself away like that?

HEDDA (*looks sharply at him*). Stop it.

LŒVBORG. What do you mean?

Tesman comes in and goes toward the sofa.

HEDDA (*hears him coming and says casually*). And this, Mr. Lœvborg, is the view from the Ampezzo valley. Look at those mountains. (*Glances affectionately up at* Tesman.) What did you say those curious mountains were called, dear?

TESMAN. Let me have a look. Oh, those are the Dolomites.

HEDDA. Of course. Those are the Dolomites, Mr. Lœvborg.

TESMAN. Hedda, I just wanted to ask you, can't we bring some punch in here? A glass for you, anyway. What?

HEDDA. Thank you, yes. And a biscuit or two, perhaps.

TESMAN. You wouldn't like a cigarette?

HEDDA. No.

TESMAN. Right.

He goes into the rear room and over to the right. Brack is seated there, glancing occasionally at Hedda and Lœvborg.

LŒVBORG (*softly, as before*). Answer me, Hedda. How could you do it?

HEDDA (*apparently absorbed in the album*). If you go on calling me Hedda I won't talk to you any more.

LŒVBORG. Mayn't I even when we're alone?

HEDDA. No. You can think it. But you mustn't say it.

LŒVBORG. Oh, I see. Because you love George Tesman.

HEDDA (*glances at him and smiles*). Love? Don't be funny.

LŒVBORG. You don't love him?

HEDDA. I don't intend to be unfaithful to him. That's not what I want.

LŒVBORG. Hedda—just tell me one thing—

HEDDA. Ssh!

Tesman enters from the rear room, carrying a tray.

TESMAN. Here we are! Here come the refreshments.

He puts the tray down on the table.

HEDDA. Why didn't you ask the servant to bring it in?

TESMAN (*fills the glasses*). I like waiting on you, Hedda.

HEDDA. But you've filled both glasses. Mr. Lœvborg doesn't want to drink.

TESMAN. Yes, but Mrs. Elvsted'll be here soon.

HEDDA. Oh yes, that's true. Mrs. Elvsted—

TESMAN. Had you forgotten her? What?

HEDDA. We're so absorbed with these photographs. (*Shows him one.*) You remember this little village?

TESMAN. Oh, that one down by the Brenner Pass. We spent a night there—

HEDDA. Yes, and met all those amusing people.

TESMAN. Oh yes, it was there, wasn't it? By Jove, if only we could have had you with us, Eilert! Ah, well.

He goes back into the other room and sits down with Brack.

LŒVBORG. Tell me one thing, Hedda.

HEDDA. Yes?

LŒVBORG. Didn't you love me either? Not—just a little?

HEDDA. Well now, I wonder? No, I think we were just good friends. (*Smiles.*) You certainly poured your heart out to me.

LŒVBORG. You begged me to.

HEDDA. Looking back on it, there was something beautiful and fascinating—and brave—about the way we told each other everything. That secret friendship no one else knew about.

LŒVBORG. Yes, Hedda, yes! Do you remember? How I used to come up to your father's house in the afternoon—and the General sat by the window and read his newspapers—with his back toward us—

HEDDA. And we sat on the sofa in the corner—

LŒVBORG. Always reading the same illustrated magazine—

HEDDA. We hadn't any photograph album.

LŒVBORG. Yes, Hedda. I regarded you as a kind of confessor. Told you things about myself which no one else knew about—then. Those days and nights of drinking and—oh, Hedda, what power did you have to make me confess such things?

HEDDA. Power? You think I had some power over you?

LŒVBORG. Yes—I don't know how else to explain it. And all those—oblique questions you asked me—

HEDDA. You knew what they meant.

LŒVBORG. But that you could sit there and ask me such questions! So unashamedly—

HEDDA. I thought you said they were oblique.

LŒVBORG. Yes, but you asked them so unashamedly. That you could question me about—about that kind of thing!

HEDDA. You answered willingly enough.

LŒVBORG. Yes—that's what I can't understand—looking back on it. But tell me, Hedda—what you felt for me—wasn't that—love? When you asked me those questions and made me confess my sins to you, wasn't it because you wanted to wash me clean?

HEDDA. No, not exactly.

LŒVBORG. Why did you do it, then?

HEDDA. Do you find it so incredible that a young girl, given the chance in secret, should want to be allowed a glimpse into a forbidden world of whose existence she is supposed to be ignorant?

LŒVBORG. So that was it?

HEDDA. One reason. One reason—I think.

LŒVBORG. You didn't love me, then. You just wanted—knowledge. But if that was so, why did you break it off?

HEDDA. That was your fault.

LŒVBORG. It was you who put an end to it.

HEDDA. Yes, when I realized that our friendship was threatening to develop into something—something else. Shame on you, Eilert Lœvborg! How could you abuse the trust of your dearest friend?

LŒVBORG (*clenches his fist*). Oh, why didn't you do it? Why didn't you shoot me dead? As you threatened to!

HEDDA. I was afraid. Of the scandal.

LŒVBORG. Yes, Hedda. You're a coward at heart.

HEDDA. A dreadful coward. (*Changes her tone.*) Luckily
for you. Well, now you've found consolation with the
Elvsteds.

LŒVBORG. I know what Thea's been telling you.

HEDDA. I dare say you told her about us.

LŒVBORG. Not a word. She's too silly to understand that
kind of thing.

HEDDA. Silly?

LŒVBORG. She's silly about that kind of thing.

HEDDA. And I'm a coward. (*Leans closer to him, without looking him in the eyes, and says quietly*) But let me tell you
something. Something you don't know.

LŒVBORG (*tensely*). Yes?

HEDDA. My failure to shoot you wasn't my worst act of cowardice that evening.

LŒVBORG (*looks at her for a moment, realizes her meaning, and
whispers passionately*). Oh, Hedda! Hedda Gabler! Now I
see what was behind those questions. Yes! It wasn't
knowledge you wanted! It was life!

HEDDA (*flashes a look at him and says quietly*). Take care!
Don't you delude yourself!

*It has begun to grow dark. Bertha, from outside, opens the
door leading into the hall.*

HEDDA (*closes the album with a snap and cries, smiling*). Ah, at
last! Come in, Thea dear!

*Mrs. Elvsted enters from the hall, in evening dress. The
door is closed behind her.*

HEDDA (*on the sofa, stretches out her arms towards her*). Thea
darling, I thought you were never coming!

*Mrs. Elvsted makes a slight bow to the gentlemen in the
rear room as she passes the open doorway, and they to her.
Then she goes to the table and holds out her hand to
Hedda. Eilert Lœvborg has risen from his chair. He and
Mrs. Elvsted nod silently to each other.*

MRS. ELVSTED. Perhaps I ought to go in and say a few words
to your husband?

HEDDA. Oh, there's no need. They're happy by themselves.
They'll be going soon.

MRS. ELVSTED. Going?

HEDDA. Yes, they're off on a spree this evening.

MRS. ELVSTED (*quickly, to Lœvborg*). You're not going with
them?

LŒVBORG. No.

HEDDA. Mr. Lœvborg is staying here with us.

MRS. ELVSTED (*takes a chair and is about to sit down beside
him*). Oh, how nice it is to be here!

HEDDA. No, Thea darling, not there. Come over here and
sit beside me. I want to be in the middle.

MRS. ELVSTED. Yes, just as you wish.

*She goes round the table and sits on the sofa, on Hedda's
right. Lœvborg sits down again in his chair.*

LŒVBORG (*after a short pause, to* Hedda). Isn't she lovely to
look at?

HEDDA (*strokes her hair gently*). Only to look at?

LŒVBORG. Yes. We're just good friends. We trust each other
implicitly. We can talk to each other quite unashamedly.

HEDDA. No need to be oblique?

MRS. ELVSTED (*nestles close to Hedda and says quietly*). Oh,
Hedda, I'm so happy. Imagine—he says I've inspired him!

HEDDA (*looks at her with a smile*). Dear Thea! Does he really?

LŒVBORG. She has the courage of her convictions, Mrs.
Tesman.

MRS. ELVSTED. I? Courage?

LŒVBORG. Absolute courage. Where friendship is concerned.

HEDDA. Yes. Courage. Yes. If only one had that—

LŒVBORG. Yes?

HEDDA. One might be able to live. In spite of everything.
(*Changes her tone suddenly.*) Well, Thea darling now
you're going to drink a nice glass of cold punch.

MRS. ELVSTED. No thank you. I never drink anything like
that.

HEDDA. Oh. You, Mr. Lœvborg?

LŒVBORG. Thank you, I don't either.

MRS. ELVSTED. No, he doesn't, either.

HEDDA (*looks into his eyes*). But if I want you to.

LŒVBORG. That doesn't make any difference.

HEDDA (*laughs*). Have I no power over you at all? Poor me!

LŒVBORG. Not where this is concerned?

HEDDA. Seriously, I think you should. For your own sake.

MRS. ELVSTED. Hedda!

LŒVBORG. Why?

HEDDA. Or perhaps I should say for other people's sake.

LŒVBORG. What do you mean?

HEDDA. People might think you didn't feel absolutely and
unashamedly sure of yourself. In your heart of hearts.

MRS. ELVSTED (*quietly*). Oh, Hedda, no!

LŒVBORG. People can think what they like. For the present.

MRS. ELVSTED (*happily*). Yes, that's true.

HEDDA. I saw it so clearly in Judge Brack a few minutes ago.

LŒVBORG. Oh. What did you see?

HEDDA. He smiled so scornfully when he saw you were
afraid to go in there and drink with them.

LŒVBORG. Afraid! I wanted to say here and talk to you.

MRS. ELVSTED. That was only natural, Hedda.

HEDDA. But the Judge wasn't to know that. I saw him wink
at Tesman when you showed you didn't dare to join their
wretched little party.

LŒVBORG. Didn't dare! Are you saying I didn't dare?

HEDDA. I'm not saying so. But that was what Judge Brack
thought.

LŒVBORG. Well, let him.

HEDDA. You're not going, then?

LŒVBORG. I'm staying with you and Thea.

MRS. ELVSTED. Yes, Hedda, of course he is.

HEDDA (*smiles, and nods approvingly to Lœvborg*). Firm as a rock! A man of principle! That's how a man should be! (*Turns to Mrs. Elvsted and strokes her cheek.*) Didn't I tell you so this morning when you came here in such a panic—?

LŒVBORG (*starts*). Panic?

MRS. ELVSTED (*frightened*). Hedda! But—Hedda!

HEDDA. Well, now you can see for yourself. There's no earthly need for you to get scared to death just because— (*Stops.*) Well! Let's all three cheer up and enjoy ourselves.

LŒVBORG. Mrs. Tesman, would you mind explaining to me what this is all about?

MRS. ELVSTED. Oh, my God, my God, Hedda, what are you saying? What are you doing?

HEDDA. Keep calm. That horrid Judge has his eye on you.

LŒVBORG. Scared to death, were you? For my sake?

MRS. ELVSTED (*quietly, trembling*). Oh, Hedda! You've made me so unhappy!

LŒVBORG (*looks coldly at her for a moment. His face is distorted*). So that was how much you trusted me.

MRS. ELVSTED. Eilert dear, please listen to me—

LŒVBORG (*takes one of the glasses of punch, raises it and says quietly, hoarsely*). Skoal, Thea!

He empties the glass, puts it down and picks up one of the others.

MRS. ELVSTED (*quietly*). Hedda, Hedda! Why did you want this to happen?

HEDDA. I—want it? Are you mad?

LŒVBORG. Skoal to you, too, Mrs. Tesman. Thanks for telling me the truth. Here's to the truth!

He empties his glass and refills it.

HEDDA (*puts her hand on his arm*). Steady. That's enough for now. Don't forget the party.

MRS. ELVSTED. No, no, no!

HEDDA. Ssh! They're looking at you.

LŒVBORG (*puts down his glass*). Thea, tell me the truth—

MRS. ELVSTED. Yes!

LŒVBORG. Did your husband know you were following me?

MRS. ELVSTED. Oh, Hedda!

LŒVBORG. Did you and he have an agreement that you should come here and keep an eye on me? Perhaps he gave you the idea? After all, he's a magistrate. I suppose he needed me back in his office. Or did he miss my companionship at the card-table?

MRS. ELVSTED (*quietly, sobbing*). Eilert, Eilert!

LŒVBORG (*seizes a glass and is about to fill it*). Let's drink to him, too.

HEDDA. No more now. Remember you're going to read your book to Tesman.

LŒVBORG (*calm again, puts down his glass*). That was silly of me, Thea. To take it like that, I mean. Don't be angry

with me, my dear. You'll see—yes, and they'll see, too— that though I fell, I—I have raised myself up again. With your help, Thea.

Mrs. Elvsed (*happily*). Oh, thank God!

Brack has meanwhile glanced at his watch. He and Tesman get up and come into the drawing-room.

BRACK (*takes his hat and overcoat*). Well, Mrs. Tesman, it's time for us to go.

HEDDA. Yes, I suppose it must be.

LŒVBORG (*gets up*). Time for me, too, Judge.

MRS. ELVSTED (*quietly, pleadingly*). Eilert, please don't!

HEDDA (*pinches her arm*). They can hear you.

MRS. ELVSTED (*gives a little cry*). Oh!

LŒVBORG (*to Brack*). You were kind enough to ask me to join you.

BRACK. Are you coming?

LŒVBORG. If I may.

BRACK. Delighted.

LŒVBORG (*puts the paper package in his pocket and says to Tesman*). I'd like to show you one or two things before I send it off to the printer.

TESMAN. I say, that'll be fun. Fancy—! Oh, but, Hedda, how'll Mrs. Elvsted get home? What?

HEDDA. Oh, we'll manage somehow.

LŒVBORG (*glances over towards the ladies*). Mrs. Elvsted? I shall come back and collect her, naturally. (*Goes closer.*) About ten o'clock, Mrs. Tesman? Will that suit you?

HEDDA. Yes. That'll suit me admirably.

TESMAN. Good, that's settled. But you mustn't expect me back so early, Hedda.

HEDDA. Stay as long as you c—as long as you like, dear.

MRS. ELVSTED (*trying to hide her anxiety*). Well then, Mr. Lœvborg, I'll wait here till you come.

LŒVBORG (*his hat in his hand*). Pray do, Mrs. Elvsted.

BRACK. Well gentlemen, now the party begins. I trust that, in the words of a certain fair lady, we shall enjoy good sport.

HEDDA. What a pity the fair lady can't be there, invisible.

BRACK. Why invisible?

HEDDA. So as to be able to hear some of your uncensored witticisms, your honour.

BRACK (*laughs*). Oh, I shouldn't advise the fair lady to do that.

TESMAN (*laughs, too*). I say, Hedda, that's good. What!

BRACK. Well, good night, ladies, good night!

LŒVBORG (*bows farewell*). About ten o'clock then.

Brack, Lœvborg and Tesman go out through the hall. As they do so, Bertha enters from the rear room with a lighted lamp. She puts it on the drawing-room table, then goes out the way she came.

MRS. ELVSTED (*has got up and is walking uneasily to and fro*). Oh, Hedda, Hedda! How is all this going to end?

HEDDA. At ten o'clock, then. He'll be here. I can see him.

With a crown of vine leaves in his hair. Burning and unashamed!

MRS. ELVSTED. Oh, I do hope so!

HEDDA. Can't you see? Then he'll be himself again! He'll be a free man for the rest of his days!

MRS. ELVSTED. Please God you're right.

HEDDA. That's how he'll come! (*Gets up and goes closer.*) You can doubt him as much as you like. I believe in him! Now we'll see which of us—

MRS. ELVSTED. You're after something, Hedda.

HEDDA. Yes, I am. For once in my life I want to have the power to shape a man's destiny.

MRS. ELVSTED. Haven't you that power already?

HEDDA. No, I haven't. I've never had it.

MRS. ELVSTED. What about your husband?

HEDDA. Him! Oh, if you could only understand how poor I am. And you're allowed to be so rich, so rich! (*Clasps her passionately.*) I think I'll burn your hair off after all!

MRS. ELVSTED. Let me go! Let me go! You frighten me, Hedda!

BERTHA (*in the open doorway*). I've laid tea in the dining-room, madam.

HEDDA. Good, we're coming.

MRS. ELVSTED. No, no, no! I'd rather go home alone! Now—at once!

HEDDA. Rubbish! First you're going to have some tea, you little idiot. And then—at ten o'clock—Eilert Lœvborg will come. With a crown of vine leaves in his hair!

She drags Mrs. Elvsted almost forcibly towards the open doorway.

ACT THREE

The same. The curtains are drawn across the open doorway, and also across the french windows. The lamp, half turned down, with a shade over it, is burning on the table. In the stove, the door of which is open, a fire has been burning, but it is now almost out. Mrs. Elvsted, wrapped in a large shawl and with her feet resting on a footstool, is sitting near the stove, huddled in the armchair. Hedda is lying asleep on the sofa, fully dressed, with a blanket over her.

MRS. ELVSTED (*after a pause, suddenly sits up in her chair and listens tensely. Then she sinks wearily back again and sighs.*). Not back yet! Oh, God! Oh, God! Not back yet!

Bertha tiptoes cautiously in from the hall. She has a letter in her hand.

MRS. ELVSTED (*turns and whispers*). What is it? Has someone come?

BERTHA (*quietly*). Yes, a servant's just called with this letter.

MRS. ELVSTED (*quickly, holding out her hand*). A letter! Give it to me!

BERTHA. But it's for the Doctor, madam.

MRS. ELVSTED. Oh, I see.

BERTHA. Miss Tesman's maid brought it. I'll leave it here on the table.

MRS. ELVSTED. Yes, do.

BERTHA (*puts down the letter*). I'd better put the lamp out. It's starting to smoke.

MRS. ELVSTED. Yes, put it out. It'll soon be daylight.

BERTHA (*puts out the lamp*). It's daylight already, madam.

MRS. ELVSTED. Yes. Broad day. And not home yet.

BERTHA. Oh dear, I was afraid this would happen.

MRS. ELVSTED. Were you?

BERTHA. Yes. When I heard that a certain gentleman had returned to town, and saw him go off with them. I've heard all about him.

MRS. ELVSTED. Don't talk so loud. You'll wake your mistress.

BERTHA (*looks at the sofa and sighs*). Yes. Let her go on sleeping, poor dear. Shall I put some more wood on the fire?

MRS. ELVSTED. Thank you, don't bother on my account.

BERTHA. Very good.

She goes quietly out through the hall.

HEDDA (*wakes as the door closes and looks up*). What's that?

MRS. ELVSTED. It was only the maid.

HEDDA (*looks round*). What am I doing here? Oh, now I remember. (*Sits up on the sofa, stretches herself and rubs her eyes.*) What time is it, Thea?

MRS. ELVSTED. It's gone seven.

HEDDA. When did Tesman get back?

MRS. ELVSTED. He's not back yet.

HEDDA. Not home yet?

MRS. ELVSTED (*gets up*). No one's come.

HEDDA. And we sat up waiting for them till four o'clock.

MRS. ELVSTED. God! How I waited for him!

HEDDA (*yawns and says with her hand in front of her mouth*). Oh, dear. We might have saved ourselves the trouble.

MRS. ELVSTED. Did you manage to sleep?

HEDDA. Oh, yes. Quite well, I think. Didn't you get any?

MRS. ELVSTED. Not a wink. I couldn't, Hedda. I just couldn't.

HEDDA (*gets up and comes over to her*). Now, now, now. There's nothing to worry about. I know what's happened.

MRS. ELVSTED. What? Please tell me.

HEDDA. Well, obviously the party went on very late—

MRS. ELVSTED. Oh dear, I suppose it must have. But—

HEDDA. And Tesman didn't want to come home and wake us all up in the middle of the night. (*Laughs.*) Probably wasn't too keen to show his face either, after a spree like that.

MRS. ELVSTED. But where could he have gone?

HEDDA. I should think he's probably slept at his aunts'. They keep his old room for him.

MRS. ELVSTED. No, he can't be with them. A letter came for him just now from Miss Tesman. It's over there.

HEDDA. Oh? (*Looks at the envelope.*) Yes, it's Auntie Juju's handwriting. Well, he must still be at Judge Brack's, then. And Eilert Lœvborg is sitting there, reading to him. With a crown of vine leaves in his hair.

MRS. ELVSTED. Hedda, you're only saying that. You don't believe it.

HEDDA. Thea, you really are a little fool.

MRS. ELVSTED. Perhaps I am.

HEDDA. You look tired to death.

MRS. ELVSTED. Yes. I am tired to death.

HEDDA. Go to my room and lie down for a little. Do as I say, now; don't argue.

MRS. ELVSTED. No, no. I couldn't possibly sleep.

HEDDA. Of course you can.

MRS. ELVSTED. But your husband'll be home soon. And I must know at once—

HEDDA. I'll tell you when he comes.

MRS. ELVSTED. Promise me, Hedda?

HEDDA. Yes, don't worry. Go and get some sleep.

MRS. ELVSTED. Thank you. All right, I'll try.

She goes out through the rear room. Hedda goes to the french windows and draws the curtains. Broad daylight floods into the room. She goes to the writing-table, takes a small hand-mirror from it and arranges her hair. Then she goes to the door leading into the hall and presses the bell. After a few moments, Bertha enters.

BERTHA. Did you want anything, madam?

HEDDA. Yes, put some more wood on the fire. I'm freezing.

BERTHA. Bless you, I'll soon have this room warmed up. (*She rakes the embers together and puts a fresh piece of wood on them. Suddenly she stops and listens.*) There's someone at the front door, madam.

HEDDA. Well, go and open it. I'll see to the fire.

BERTHA. It'll burn up in a moment.

She goes out through the hall. Hedda kneels on the footstool and puts more wood in the stove. After a few seconds, George Tesman enters from the hall. He looks tired, and rather worried. He tiptoes towards the open doorway and is about to slip through the curtains.

HEDDA (*at the stove, without looking up*). Good morning.

TESMAN (*turns*). Hedda! (*Comes nearer.*) Good heavens, are you up already? What?

HEDDA. Yes, I got up very early this morning.

TESMAN. I was sure you'd still be sleeping. Fancy that!

HEDDA. Don't talk so loud. Mrs. Elvsted's asleep in my room.

TESMAN. Mrs. Elvsted? Has she stayed the night here?

HEDDA. Yes. No one came to escort her home.

TESMAN. Oh. No, I suppose not.

HEDDA (*closes the door of the stove and gets up*). Well. Was it fun?

TESMAN. Have you been anxious about me? What?

HEDDA. Not in the least. I asked if you'd had fun.

TESMAN. Oh yes, rather! Well, I thought, for once in a while—! The first part was the best; when Eilert read his book to me. We arrived over an hour too early—what about that, eh? Fancy—! Brack had a lot of things to see to, so Eilert read to me.

HEDDA (*sits at the right-hand side of the table*). Well? Tell me about it.

TESMAN (*sits on a footstool by the stove*). Honestly, Hedda, you've no idea what a book that's going to be. It's really one of the most remarkable things that's ever been written. By Jove!

HEDDA. Oh, never mind about the book—

TESMAN. I'm going to make a confession to you, Hedda. When he'd finished reading a sort of beastly feeling came over me.

HEDDA. Beastly feeling?

TESMAN. I found myself envying Eilert for being able to write like that. Imagine that, Hedda!

HEDDA. Yes. I can imagine.

TESMAN. What a tragedy that with all those gifts he should be so incorrigible.

HEDDA. You mean he's less afraid of life than most men?

TESMAN. Good heavens, no. He just doesn't know the meaning of the word moderation.

HEDDA. What happened afterwards?

TESMAN. Well, looking back on it, I suppose you might almost call it an orgy, Hedda.

HEDDA. Had he vine leaves in his hair?

TESMAN. Vine leaves? No, I didn't see any of them. He made a long, rambling oration in honour of the woman who'd inspired him to write this book. Yes, those were the words he used.

HEDDA. Did he name her?

TESMAN. No. But I suppose it must be Mrs. Elvsted. You wait and see!

HEDDA. Where did you leave him?

TESMAN. On the way home. We left in a bunch—the last of us, that is—and Brack came with us to get a little fresh air. Well, then, you see, we agreed we ought to see Eilert home. He'd had a drop too much.

HEDDA. You don't say?

TESMAN. But now comes the funny part, Hedda. Or I should really say the tragic part. Oh, I'm almost ashamed to tell you. For Eilert's sake, I mean—

HEDDA. Why, what happened?

TESMAN. Well, you see, as we were walking towards town I happened to drop behind for a minute. Only for a minute—er—you understand—

HEDDA. Yes, yes—?

TESMAN. Well then, when I ran on to catch them up, what do you think I found by the roadside. What?

HEDDA. How on earth should I know?

TESMAN. You mustn't tell anyone, Hedda. What? Promise me that—for Eilert's sake. (*Takes a package wrapped in paper from his coat pocket.*) Just fancy! I found this.

HEDDA. Isn't this the one he brought here yesterday?

TESMAN. Yes! The whole of that precious, irreplaceable manuscript! And he went and lost it! Didn't even notice! What about that? Tragic.

HEDDA. But why didn't you give it back to him?

TESMAN. I didn't dare to, in the state he was in.

HEDDA. Didn't you tell any of the others?

TESMAN. Good heavens, no. I didn't want to do that. For Eilert's sake, you understand.

HEDDA. Then no one else knows you have his manuscript?

TESMAN. No. And no one must be allowed to know.

HEDDA. Didn't it come up in the conversation later?

TESMAN. I didn't get a chance to talk to him any more. As soon as we got into the outskirts of town, he and one or two of the others gave us the slip. Disappeared, by Jove!

HEDDA. Oh? I suppose they took him home.

TESMAN. Yes, I imagine that was the idea. Brack left us, too.

HEDDA. And what have you been up to since then?

TESMAN. Well, I and one or two of the others—awfully jolly chaps, they were—went back to where one of them lived and had a cup of morning coffee. Morning-after-coffee—what? Ah, well. I'll just lie down for a bit and give Eilert time to sleep it off, poor chap, then I'll run over and give this back to him.

HEDDA (*holds out her hand for the package*). No, don't do that. Not just yet. Let me read it first.

TESMAN. Oh no, really, Hedda dear, honestly, I daren't do that.

HEDDA. Daren't?

TESMAN. No—imagine how desperate he'll be when he wakes up and finds his manuscript's missing. He hasn't any copy, you see. He told me so himself.

HEDDA. Can't a thing like that be rewritten?

TESMAN. Oh no, not possibly, I shouldn't think. I mean, the inspiration, you know—

HEDDA. Oh, yes, I'd forgotten that. (*Casually.*) By the way, there's a letter for you.

TESMAN. Is there? Fancy that!

HEDDA (*holds it out to him*). It came early this morning.

TESMAN. I say, it's from Auntie Juju! What on earth can it be? (*Puts the package on the other footstool, opens the letter, reads it and jumps up.*) Oh, Hedda! She says poor Auntie Rena's dying.

HEDDA. Well, we've been expecting that.

TESMAN. She says if I want to see her I must go quickly. I'll run over at once.

HEDDA (*hides a smile*). Run?

TESMAN. Hedda dear, I suppose you wouldn't want to come with me? What about that, eh?

HEDDA (*gets up and says wearily and with repulsion*). No, no,

don't ask me to do anything like that. I can't bear illness or death. I loathe anything ugly.

TESMAN. Yes, yes. Of course. (*In a dither.*) My hat? My overcoat? Oh yes, in the hall. I do hope I won't get there too late, Hedda! What?

HEDDA. You'll be all right if you run.

Bertha enters from the hall.

BERTHA. Judge Brack's outside and wants to know if he can come in.

TESMAN. At this hour? No, I can't possibly receive him now.

HEDDA. I can. (*To Bertha*) Ask his honour to come in.

Bertha goes.

HEDDA (*whispers quickly*). The manuscript, Tesman.

She snatches it from the footstool.

TESMAN. Yes, give it to me.

HEDDA. No, I'll look after it for now.

She goes over to the writing-table and puts it in the bookcase. Tesman stands dithering, unable to get his gloves on. Judge Brack enters from the hall.

HEDDA (*nods to him*). Well, you're an early bird.

BRACK. Yes, aren't I? (*To Tesman*) Are you up and about, too?

TESMAN. Yes, I've got to go and see my aunts. Poor Auntie Rena's dying.

BRACK. Oh dear, is she? Then you mustn't let me detain you. At so tragic a—

TESMAN. Yes, I really must run. Good-bye! Good-bye!

He runs out through the hall.

HEDDA (*goes nearer*). You seem to have had excellent sport last night—Judge.

BRACK. Indeed yes, Mrs. Hedda. I haven't even had time to take my clothes off.

HEDDA. *You* haven't either?

BRACK. As you see. What's Tesman told you about last night's escapades?

HEDDA. Oh, only some boring story about having gone and drunk coffee somewhere.

BRACK. Yes, I've heard about that coffee-party. Eilert Lœvborg wasn't with them, I gather?

HEDDA. No, they took him home first.

BRACK. Did Tesman go with him?

HEDDA. No, one or two of the others, he said.

BRACK (*smiles*). George Tesman is a credulous man, Mrs. Hedda.

HEDDA. God knows. But—has something happened?

BRACK. Well, yes, I'm afraid it has.

HEDDA. I see. Sit down and tell me.

She sits on the left of the table, Brack at the long side of it, near her.

HEDDA. Well?

BRACK. I had a special reason for keeping track of my guests last night. Or perhaps I should say some of my guests.

HEDDA. Including Eilert Lœvborg?

BRACK. I must confess—yes.

HEDDA. You're beginning to make me curious.

BRACK. Do you know where he and some of my other guests spent the latter half of last night, Mrs. Hedda?

HEDDA. Tell me. If it won't shock me.

BRACK. Oh, I don't think it'll shock you. they found themselves participating in an exceedingly animated *soirée*.

HEDDA. Of a sporting character?

BRACK. Of a highly sporting character.

HEDDA. Tell me more.

BRACK. Lœvborg had received an invitation in advance—as had the others. I knew all about that. But he had refused. As you know, he's become a new man.

HEDDA. Up at the Elvsteds', yes. But he went?

BRACK. Well, you see, Mrs. Hedda, last night at my house, unhappily, the spirit moved him.

HEDDA. Yes, I hear he became inspired.

BRACK. Somewhat violently inspired. And as a result, I suppose, his thoughts strayed. We men, alas, don't always stick to our principles as firmly as we should.

HEDDA. I'm sure you're an exception, Judge Brack. But go on about Lœvborg.

BRACK. Well, to cut a long story short, he ended up in the establishment of a certain Mademoiselle Danielle.

HEDDA. Mademoiselle Danielle?

BRACK. She was holding the *soirée*. For a selected circle of friends and admirers.

HEDDA. Has she got red hair?

BRACK. She has.

HEDDA. A singer of some kind?

BRACK. Yes—among other accomplishments. She's also a celebrated huntress—of men, Mrs. Hedda. I'm sure you've heard about her. Eilert Lœvborg used to be one of her most ardent patrons. In his salad days.

HEDDA. And how did all this end?

BRACK. Not entirely amicably, from all accounts. Mademoiselle Danielle began by receiving him with the utmost tenderness and ended by resorting to her fists.

HEDDA. Against Lœvborg?

BRACK. Yes. He accused her, or her friends, of having robbed him. He claimed his pocket-book had been stolen. Among other things. In short, he seems to have made a blood-thirsty scene.

HEDDA. And what did this lead to?

BRACK. It led to a general free-for-all, in which both sexes participated. Fortunately, in the end the police arrived.

HEDDA. The police, too?

BRACK. Yes. I'm afraid it may turn out to be rather an expensive joke for Master Eilert. Crazy fool!

HEDDA. Oh?

BRACK. Apparently he put up a very violent resistance. Hit one of the constables on the ear and tore his uniform. He had to accompany them to the police station.

HEDDA. Where did you learn all this?

BRACK. From the police.

HEDDA (*to herself*). So that's what happened. He didn't have a crown of vine leaves in his hair.

BRACK. Vine leaves, Mrs. Hedda?

HEDDA (*in her normal voice again*). But, tell me, Judge, why do you take such a close interest in Eilert Lœvborg?

BRACK. For one thing it'll hardly be a matter of complete indifference to me if it's revealed in court that he came there straight from my house.

HEDDA. Will it come to court?

BRACK. Of course. Well, I don't regard that as particularly serious. Still, I thought it my duty, as a friend of the family, to give you and your husband a full account of his nocturnal adventures.

HEDDA. Why?

BRACK. Because I've a shrewd suspicion that he's hoping to use you as a kind of screen.

HEDDA. What makes you think that?

BRACK. Oh, for heaven's sake, Mrs. Hedda, we're not blind. You wait and see. This Mrs. Elvsted won't be going back to her husband just yet.

HEDDA. Well, if there were anything between these two there are plenty of other places where they could meet.

BRACK. Not in anyone's home. From now on every respectable house will once again be closed to Eilert Lœvborg.

HEDDA. And mine should be, too, you mean?

BRACK. Yes. I confess I should find it more than irksome if this gentleman were to be granted unrestricted access to this house. If he were superfluously to intrude into—

HEDDA. The triangle?

BRACK. Precisely. For me it would be like losing a home.

HEDDA (*looks at him and smiles*). I see. You want to be the cock of the walk.

BRACK (*nods slowly and lowers his voice*). Yes, that is my aim. And I shall fight for it with—every weapon at my disposal.

HEDDA (*as her smile fades*). You're a dangerous man, aren't you? When you really want something.

BRACK. You think so?

HEDDA. Yes, I'm beginning to think so. I'm deeply thankful that you haven't any kind of hold over me.

BRACK (*laughs equivocally*). Well, well, Mrs. Hedda—perhaps you're right. If I had, who knows what I might not think up?

HEDDA. Come, Judge Brack. That sounds almost like a threat.

BRACK (*gets up*). Heaven forbid! In the creation of a triangle—and its continuance—the question of compulsion should never arise.

HEDDA. Exactly what I was thinking.

BRACK. Well, I've said what I came to say. I must be getting back. Good-bye, Mrs. Hedda. (*Goes towards the french windows.*)

HEDDA (*gets up*). Are you going out through the garden?

BRACK. Yes, it's shorter.

HEDDA. Yes. And it's the back door, isn't it?

BRACK. I've nothing against back doors. They can be quite intriguing—sometimes.

HEDDA. When people fire pistols out of them, for example?

BRACK (*in the doorway, laughs*). Oh, people don't shoot tame cocks.

HEDDA (*laughs too*). I suppose not. When they've only got one.

They nod good-bye, laughing. He goes. She closes the french windows behind him, and stands for a moment, looking out pensively. Then she walks across the room and glances through the curtains in the open doorway. Goes to the writing-table, takes Lœvborg's package from the bookcase and is about to turn through the pages when Bertha is heard remonstrating loudly in the hall. Hedda turns and listens. She hastily puts the package back in the drawer, locks it and puts the key on the inkstand. Eilert Lœvborg, with his overcoat on and his hat in his hand, throws the door open. He looks somewhat confused and excited.

LŒVBORG (*shouts as he enters*). I must come in, I tell you! Let me pass!

He closes the door, turns, sees Hedda, controls himself immediately and bows.

HEDDA (*at the writing table*). Well, Mr. Lœvborg, this is rather a late hour to be collecting Thea.

LŒVBORG. And an early hour to call on you. Please forgive me.

HEDDA. How do you know she's still here?

LŒVBORG. They told me at her lodgings that she has been out all night.

HEDDA (*goes to the table*). Did you notice anything about their behaviour when they told you?

LŒVBORG (*looks at her, puzzled*). Notice anything?

HEDDA. Did they sound as if they thought it—strange?

LŒVBORG (*suddenly understands*). Oh, I see what you mean. I'm dragging her down with me. No, as a matter of fact I didn't notice anything. I suppose Tesman isn't up yet?

HEDDA. No, I don't think so.

LŒVBORG. When did he get home?

HEDDA. Very late.

LŒVBORG. Did he tell you anything?

HEDDA. Yes. I gather you had a merry party at Judge Brack's last night.

LŒVBORG. He didn't tell you anything else?

HEDDA. I don't think so. I was so terribly sleepy—

Mrs. Elvsted comes through the curtains in the open doorway.

MRS. ELVSTED (*runs towards him*). Oh, Eilert! At last!

LŒVBORG. Yes—at last. And too late.

MRS. ELVSTED. What is too late?

LŒVBORG. Everything—now. I'm finished, Thea.

MRS. ELVSTED. Oh, no, no! Don't say that!

LŒVBORG. You'll say it yourself, when you've heard what I—

MRS. ELVSTED. I don't want to hear anything!

HEDDA. Perhaps you'd rather speak to her alone? I'd better go.

LŒVBORG. No, stay.

MRS. ELVSTED. But I don't want to hear anything, I tell you!

LŒVBORG. It's not about last night.

MRS. ELVSTED. Then what—?

LŒVBORG. I want to tell you that from now on we must stop seeing each other.

MRS. ELVSTED. Stop seeing each other!

HEDDA (*involuntarily*). I knew it!

LŒVBORG. I have no further use for you, Thea.

MRS. ELVSTED. You can stand there and say that! No further use for me! Surely I can go on helping you? We'll go on working together, won't we?

LŒVBORG. I don't intend to do any more work from now on.

MRS. ELVSTED (*desperately*). Then what use have I for my life?

LŒVBORG. You must try to live as if you had never known me.

MRS. ELVSTED. But I can't!

LŒVBORG. Try to, Thea. Go back home—

MRS. ELVSTED. Never! I want to be wherever you are! I won't let myself be driven away like this! I want to stay here—and be with you when the book comes out.

HEDDA (*whispers*). Ah, yes! The book!

LŒVBORG (*looks at her*). Our book; Thea's and mine. It belongs to both of us.

MRS. ELVSTED. Oh, yes! I feel that, too! And I've a right to be with you when it comes into the world. I want to see the people respect and honour you again. And the joy! The joy! I want to share it with you!

LŒVBORG. Thea—our book will never come into the world.

HEDDA. Ah!

MRS. ELVSTED. Not—?

LŒVBORG. It cannot. Ever.

MRS. ELVSTED. Eilert—what have you done with the manuscript?

HEDDA. Yes—the manuscript?

MRS. ELVSTED. Where is it?

LŒVBORG. Oh, Thea, please don't ask me that!

MRS. ELVSTED. Yes, yes—I must know. I've a right to know. Now!

LŒVBORG. The manuscript. Yes. I've torn it up.

MRS. ELVSTED (*screams*). No, no!

HEDDA (*involuntarily*). But that's not—!

LŒVBORG (*looks at her*). Not true, you think.

HEDDA (*controls herself*). Why—yes, of course it is, if you say so. It sounded so incredible—

LŒVBORG. It's true, nevertheless.

MRS. ELVSTED. Oh, my God, my God, Hedda—he's destroyed his own book!

LŒVBORG. I have destroyed my life. Why not my life's work, too?

MRS. ELVSTED. And you—did this last night?

LŒVBORG. Yes, Thea. I tore it into a thousand pieces. And scattered them out across the fjord. It's good, clean, salt water. Let it carry them away; let them drift in the current and the wind. And in a little while, they will sing. Deeper and deeper. As I shall, Thea.

MRS. ELVSTED. Do you know, Eilert—this book—all my life I shall feel as though you'd killed a little child.

LŒVBORG. You're right. It is like killing a child.

MRS. ELVSTED. But how could you? It was my child, too!

HEDDA (*almost inaudibly*). Oh—the child—!

MRS. ELVSTED (*breathes heavily*). It's all over, then. Well—I'll go now, Hedda.

HEDDA. You're not leaving town?

MRS. ELVSTED. I don't know what I'm going to do. I can't see anything except—darkness.

She goes out through the hall.

HEDDA (*waits a moment*). Aren't you going to escort her home, Mr. Lœvborg?

LŒVBORG. I? Through the streets? Do you want me to let people see her with me?

HEDDA. Of course, I don't know what else may have happened last night. But is it so utterly beyond redress?

LŒVBORG. It isn't just last night. It'll go on happening. I know it. But the curse of it is, I don't want to live that kind of life. I don't want to start all that again. She's broken my courage. I can't spit in the eyes of the world any longer.

HEDDA (*as though to herself*). That pretty little fool's been trying to shape a man's destiny. (*Looks at him.*) But how could you be so heartless towards her?

LŒVBORG. Don't call me heartless!

HEDDA. To go and destroy the one thing that's made her life worth living? You don't call that heartless?

LŒVBORG. Do you want to know the truth, Hedda?

HEDDA. The truth?

LŒVBORG. Promise me first—give me your word—that you'll never let Thea know about this.

HEDDA. I give you my word.

LŒVBORG. Good. Well; What I told her just now was a lie.

HEDDA. About the manuscript?

LŒVBORG. Yes, I didn't tear it up. Or throw it in the fjord.

HEDDA. You didn't? But where is it, then?

LŒVBORG. I destroyed it, all the same. I destroyed it, Hedda!

HEDDA. I don't understand.

LŒVBORG. Thea said that what I had done was like killing a child.

HEDDA. Yes. That's what she said.

LŒVBORG. But to kill a child isn't the worst thing a father can do to it.

HEDDA. What could be worse than that?

LŒVBORG. Hedda—suppose a man came home one morning, after a night of debauchery, and said to the mother of his child: 'Look here. I've been wandering round all night. I've been to—such-and-such a place and such-and-such a place. And I had our child with me. I took him to—these places. And I've lost him. Just—lost him. God knows where he is or whose hands he's fallen into.'

HEDDA. I see. But when all's said and done, this was only a book—

LŒVBORG. Thea's heart and soul were in that book. It was her whole life.

HEDDA. Yes, I understand.

LŒVBORG. Well, then you must also understand that she and I cannot possibly ever see each other again.

HEDDA. Where will you go?

LŒVBORG. Nowhere. I just want to put an end to it all. As soon as possible.

HEDDA (*takes a step towards him*). Eilert Lœvborg, listen to me. Do it—beautifully!

LŒVBORG. Beautifully? (*Smiles.*) With a crown of vine leaves in my hair? The way you used to dream of me—in the old days?

HEDDA. No. I don't believe in that crown any longer. But—do it beautifully, all the same. Just this once. Goodbye. You must go now. And don't come back.

LŒVBORG. *Adieu*, madame. Give my love to George Tesman. (*Turns to go.*)

HEDDA. Wait. I want to give you a souvenir to take with you.

She goes over to the writing-table, opens the drawer and the pistol-case, and comes back to Lœvborg with one of the pistols.

LŒVBORG (*looks at her*). This? Is this the souvenir?

HEDDA (*nods slowly*). You recognize it? You looked down its barrel once.

LŒVBORG. You should have used it then.

HEDDA. Here! Use it now!

LŒVBORG (*puts the pistol in his breast pocket*). Thank you.

HEDDA. Do it beautifully, Eilsert Lœvborg. Only promise me that!

LŒVBORG. Good-bye, Hedda Gabler.

He goes through the hall. Hedda stands by the door for a moment, listening. Then she goes over to the writing-table, takes out the package containing the manuscript, glances inside it, pulls some of the pages half out and looks at them. Then she takes it to the armchair by the stove and sits down with the package in her lap. After a moment, she opens the door of the stove; then she opens the packet.

HEDDA (*throws one of the pages into the stove and whispers to herself*). I'm burning your child, Thea! You with your beautiful, wavy hair! (*She throws a few more pages into the stove.*) The child Eilert Lœvborg gave you. (*Throws the rest of the manuscript in.*) I'm burning it! I'm burning your child!

ACT FOUR

The same. It is evening. The drawing-room is in darkness. The small room is illuminated by the hanging lamp over the table. The curtains are drawn across the french windows. Hedda, dressed in black, is walking up and down in the darkened room. Then she goes into the small room and crosses to the left. A few chords are heard from the piano. She comes back into the drawing-room.

Bertha comes through the small room from the right with a lighted lamp, which she places on the table in front of the corner sofa in the drawing-room. Her eyes are red with crying, and she has black ribbons on her cap. She goes quietly out, right. Hedda goes over to the french windows, draws the curtains slightly to one side and looks out into the darkness.

A few moments later, Miss Tesman enters from the hall. She is dressed in mourning, with a black hat and veil. Hedda goes to meet her and holds out her hand.

MISS TESMAN. Well, Hedda, here I am in the weeds of sorrow. My poor sister has ended her struggles at last.

HEDDA. I've already heard. Tesman sent me a card.

MISS TESMAN. Yes, he promised me he would. But I thought, no, I must go and break the news of death to Hedda myself—here, in the house of life.

HEDDA. It's very kind of you.

MISS TESMAN. Ah, Rena shouldn't have chosen a time like this to pass away. This is no moment for Hedda's house to be a place of mourning.

HEDDA (*changing the subject*). She died peacefully, Miss Tesman?

MISS TESMAN. Oh, it was quite beautiful! The end came so calmly. And she was so happy at being able to see George once again. And say good-bye to him. Hasn't he come home yet?

HEDDA. No. He wrote that I mustn't expect him too soon. But please sit down.

MISS TESMAN. No, thank you, Hedda dear—bless you. I'd like to. But I've so little time. I must dress her and lay her out as well as I can. She shall go to her grave looking really beautiful.

HEDDA. Can't I help with anything?

MISS TESMAN. Why, you mustn't think of such a thing! Hedda Tesman mustn't let her hands be soiled by contact with death. Or her thoughts. Not at this time.

HEDDA. One can't always control one's thoughts.

MISS TESMAN (*continues*). Ah, well, that's life. Now we must start to sew poor Rena's shroud. There'll be sewing to be done in this house, too, before long. I shouldn't wonder. But not for a shroud, praise God.

George Tesman enters from the hall.

HEDDA. You've come at last! Thank heavens!

TESMAN. Are you here, Auntie Juju? With Hedda? Fancy that!

MISS TESMAN. I was just on the point of leaving, dear boy. Well, have you done everything you promised me?

TESMAN. No, I'm afraid I forgot half of it. I'll have to run over again tomorrow. My head's in a complete whirl today. I can't collect my thoughts.

MISS TESMAN. But, George dear, you mustn't take it like this.

TESMAN. Oh? Well—er—how should I?

MISS TESMAN. You must be happy in your grief. Happy for what's happened. As I am.

TESMAN. Oh, yes, yes. You're thinking of Aunt Rena.

HEDDA. It'll be lonely for you now, Miss Tesman.

MISS TESMAN. For the first few days, yes. But it won't last long, I hope. Poor dear Rena's little room isn't going to stay empty.

TESMAN. Oh? Whom are you going to move in there? What?

MISS TESMAN. Oh, there's always some poor invalid who needs care or attention.

HEDDA. Do you really want another cross like that to bear?

MISS TESMAN. Cross! God forgive you, child. It's been no cross for me.

HEDDA. But now—if a complete stranger comes to live with you—?

MISS TESMAN. Oh, one soon makes friends with invalids. And I need so much to have someone to live for. Like you, my dear. Well, I expect there'll soon be work in this house too for an old aunt, praise God!

HEDDA. Oh—please!

TESMAN. My word, yes! What a splendid time the three of us could have together if—

HEDDA. If?

TESMAN (*uneasily*). Oh, never mind. It'll all work out. Let's hope so—what?

MISS TESMAN. Yes, yes. Well, I'm sure you two would like to be alone. (*Smiles.*) Perhaps Hedda may have something to tell you, George. Good-bye. I must go home to Rena. (*Turns to the door.*) Dear God, how strange! Now Rena is with me and with poor dear Joachim.

TESMAN. Yes, yes, Auntie Juju! What?

Miss Tesman goes out through the hall.

HEDDA (*follows Tesman coldly and searchingly with her eyes*). I really believe this death distresses you more than it does her.

TESMAN. Oh, it isn't just Auntie Rena. It's Eilert I'm so worried about.

HEDDA (*quickly*). Is there any news of him?

TESMAN. I ran over to see him this afternoon. I wanted to tell him his manuscript was in safe hands.

HEDDA. Oh? You didn't find him?

TESMAN. No. He wasn't at home. But later I met Mrs. Elvsted and she told me he'd been here early this morning.

HEDDA. Yes, just after you'd left.

TESMAN. It seems he said he'd torn the manuscript up. What?

HEDDA. Yes, he claimed to have done so.

TESMAN. You told him we had it, of course?

HEDDA. No. (*Quickly.*) Did you tell Mrs. Elvsted?

TESMAN. No. I didn't like to. But you ought to have told him. Think if he should go home and do something desperate! Give me the manuscript, Hedda. I'll run over to him with it right away. Where did you put it?

HEDDA (*cold and motionless, leaning against the armchair*). I haven't got it any longer.

TESMAN. Haven't got it? What on earth do you mean?

HEDDA. I've burned it.

TESMAN (*starts, terrified*). Burned it! Burned Eilert's manuscript!

HEDDA. Don't shout. The servant will hear you.

TESMAN. Burned it! But in heaven's name—! Oh, no, no, no! This is impossible!

HEDDA. Well, it's true.

TESMAN. But, Hedda, do you realize what you've done? That's appropriating lost property! It's against the law! By God! You ask Judge Brack and see if I'm not right.

HEDDA. You'd be well advised not to talk about it to Judge Brack or anyone else.

TESMAN. But how could you go and do such a dreadful thing? What on earth put the idea into your head? What came over you? Answer me! What?

HEDDA (*represses an almost imperceptible smile*). I did it for your sake, George.

TESMAN. For my sake?

HEDDA. When you came home this morning and described how he'd read this book to you—

TESMAN. Yes, yes?

HEDDA. You admitted you were jealous of him.

TESMAN. But, good heavens, I didn't mean it literally!

HEDDA. No matter. I couldn't bear the thought that anyone else should push you into the background.

TESMAN (*torn between doubt and joy*). Hedda—is this true? But—but—but I never realized you loved me like that! Fancy that!

HEDDA. Well, I suppose you'd better know. I'm going to have—(*Breaks off and says violently*) No, no—you better ask your Auntie Juju. She'll tell you.

TESMAN. Hedda! I think I understand what you mean. (*Clasps his hands.*) Good heavens, can it really be true? What?

HEDDA. Don't shout. The servant will hear you.

TESMAN (*laughing with joy*). The servant! I say, that's good! The servant! Why, that's Bertha! I'll run out and tell her at once!

HEDDA (*clenches her hands in despair*). Oh, it's destroying me, all this—it's destroying me!

TESMAN. I say, Hedda, what's up? What?

HEDDA (*cold, controlled*). Oh, it's all so—absurd—George.

TESMAN. Absurd? That I'm so happy? But surely—? Ah, well—perhaps I won't say anything to Bertha.

HEDDA. No, do. She might as well know, too.

TESMAN. No, no, I won't tell her yet. But Auntie Juju—I must let her know! And you—you called me George! For the first time! Fancy that! Oh, it'll make Auntie Juju so happy, all this! So very happy!

HEDDA. Will she be happy when she hears I've burned Eilert Lœvborg's manuscript—for your sake?

TESMAN. No, I'd forgotten about that. Of course, no one must be allowed to know about the manuscript. But that you're burning with love for me, Hedda, I must certainly let Auntie Juju know that. I say, I wonder if young wives often feel like that towards their husbands? What?

HEDDA. You might ask Auntie Juju about that, too.

TESMA. I will, as soon as I get the chance. (*Looks uneasy and thoughtful again.*) But I say, you know, that manuscript. Dreadful business. Poor Eilert!

Mrs. Elvsted, dressed as on her first visit, with hat and overcoat, enters from the hall.

MRS. ELVSTED (*greets them hastily and tremulously*). Oh, Hedda dear, do please forgive me for coming here again.

HEDDA. Why, Thea, what's happened?

TESMAN. Is it anything to do with Eilert Lœvbog? What?

MRS. ELVSTED. Yes—I'm so dreadfully afraid he may have met with an accident.

HEDDA (*grips her arm*). You think so?

TESMAN. But, good heavens, Mrs. Elvsted, what makes you think that?

MRS. ELVSTED. I head them talking about him at the boarding-house, as I went in. Oh, there are the most terrible rumours being spread about him in town today.

TESMAN. Er—yes, I heard about them, too. But I can testify that he went striaght home to bed. Fancy—!

HEDDA. Well—what did they say in the boarding-house?

MRS. ELVSTED. Oh, I couldn't find out anything. Either they didn't know, or else—They stopped talking when they saw me. And I didn't dare to ask.

TESMAN (*fidgets uneasily*). We must hope—we must hope you misheard them, Mrs. Elvsted.

MRS. ELVSTED. No, no, I'm sure it was him they were talking about. I heard them say something about a hospital—

TESMAN. Hospital!

HEDDA. Oh no, surely that's impossible.

MRS. ELVSTED. Oh, I became so afraid. So I went up to his rooms and asked to see him.

HEDDA. Do you think that was wise, Thea?

MRS. ELVSTED. Well, what else could I do? I couldn't bear the uncertainty any longer.

TESMAN. But *you* didn't manage to find him either? What?

MRS. ELVSTED. No. And they had no idea where he was. They said he hadn't been home since yesterday afternoon.

TESMAN. Since yesterday? Fancy that!

MRS. ELVSTED. I'm sure he must have met with an accident.

TESMAN. Hedda, I wonder if I ought to go to town and make one or two enquiries?

HEDDA. No, no, don't you get mixed up in this.

Judge Brack enters from the hall, hat in hand. Bertha, who has opened the door for him, closes it. He looks serious and greets them silently.

TESMAN. Hullo, my dear Judge. Fancy seeing you!

BRACK. I had to come and talk to you.

TESMAN. I can see Auntie Juju's told you the news.

BRACK. Yes, I've heard about that, too.

TESMAN. Tragic, isn't it?

BRACK. Well, my dear chap, that depends on how you look at it.

TESMAN (*looks uncertainly at him*). Has something else happened?

BRACK. Yes.

HEDDA. Another tragedy?

BRACK. That also depends on how you look at it, Mrs. Tesman.

MRS. ELVSTED. Oh, it's something to do with Eilert Lœvborg!

BRACK (*looks at her for a moment*). How did you guess? Perhaps you've heard already—?

MRS. ELVSTED (*confused*). No, no, not at all—I—

TESMAN. For heaven's sake, tell us!

BRACK (*shrugs his shoulders*). Well, I'm afraid they've taken him to the hospital. He's dying.

MRS. ELVSTED (*screams*). Oh God, God!

TESMAN. The hospital! Dying!

HEDDA (*involuntarily*). So quickly!

MRS. ELVSTED (*weeping*). Oh, Hedda! And we parted enemies!

HEDDA (*whispers*). Thea—Thea!

MRS. ELVSTED (*ignoring her*). I must see him! I must see him before he dies!

BRACK. It's no use, Mrs. Elvsted. No one's allowed to see him now.

MRS. ELVSTED. But what's happened to him? You must tell me!

TESMAN. He hasn't tried to do anything to himself? What?

HEDDA. Yes, he has. I'm sure of it.

TESMAN. Hedda, how can you—?

BRACK (*who has not taken his eyes from her*). I'm afraid you've guessed correctly, Mrs. Tesman.

MRS. ELVSTED. How dreadful!

TESMAN. Attempted suicide! Fancy that!

HEDDA. Shot himself!

BRACK. Right again, Mrs. Tesman.

MRS. ELVSTED (*tries to compose herself*). When did this happen, Judge Brack?

BRACK. This afternoon. Between three and four.

TESMAN. But, good heavens—where? What?

BRACK (*a little hesitantly*). Where? Why, my dear chap, in his rooms, of course.

MRS. ELVSTED. No, that's impossible. I was there soon after six.

BRACK. Well, it must have been somewhere else, then. I don't know exactly. I only know that they found him. He's shot himself—through the breast.

MRS. ELVSTED. Oh, how horrible! That he should end like that!

HEDDA (*to Brack*). Through the breast, you said?

BRACK. That is what I said.

HEDDA. Not through the head?

BRACK. Through the breast, Mrs. Tesman.

HEDDA: The breast. Yes; yes. That's good, too.

BRACK. Why, Mrs. Tesman?

HEDDA. Oh—no, I didn't mean anything.

TESMAN. And the wound's dangerous, you say? What?

BRACK. Mortal. He's probably already dead.

MRS. ELVSTED. Yes, yes—I feel it! It's all over. All over. Oh, Hedda—!

TESMAN. But, tell me, how did you manage to learn all this?

BRACK (*curtly*). From the police. I spoke to one of them.

HEDDA (*loudly, clearly*). Thank God! At last!

TESMAN (*appalled*). For God's sake, Hedda, what are you saying?

HEDDA. I am saying there's beauty in what he has done.

BRACK. Hm—Mrs. Tesman—

TESMAN. Beauty! Oh, but I say!

MRS. ELVSTED. Hedda, how can you talk of beauty in connexion with a thing like this?

HEDDA. Eilert Lœvborg has settled his account with life. He's had the courage to do what—what he had to do.

MRS. ELVSTED. No, that's not why it happened. He did it because he was mad.

TESMAN. He did it because he was desperate.

HEDDA. You're wrong! I know!

MRS. ELVSTED. He must have been mad. The same as when he tore up the manuscript.

BRACK (*starts*). Manuscript? Did he tear it up?

MRS. ELVSTED. Yes. Last night.

TESMAN (*whispers*). Oh, Hedda, we shall never be able to escape from this.

BRACK. Hm. Strange.

TESMAN (*wanders round the room*). To think of Eilert dying like that. And not leaving behind him the thing that would have made his name endure.

MRS. ELVSTED. If only it could be pieced together again!

TESMAN. Yes, yes, yes! If only it could! I'd give anything—

MRS. ELVSTED. Perhaps it can, Mr. Tesman.

TESMAN. What do you mean?

MRS. ELVSTED (*searches in the pocket of her dress*). Look, I kept the notes he dictated it from.

HEDDA (*takes a step nearer*). Ah!

TESMAN. You kept them, Mrs. Elvsted! What?

MRS. ELVSTED. Yes, here they are. I brought them with me when I left home. They've been in my pocket ever since.

TESMAN. Let me have a look.

MRS. ELVSTED (*hands him a wad of small sheets of paper*). They're in a terrible muddle. All mixed up.

TESMAN. I say, just fancy if we could sort them out! Perhaps if we work on them together—?

MRS. ELVSTED. Oh, yes! Let's try, anyway!

TESMAN. We'll manage it. We must! I shall dedicate my life to this.

HEDDA. *You*, George? Your life?

TESMAN. Yes—well, all the time I can spare. My book'll have to wait. Hedda, you do understand? What? I owe it to Eilert's memory.

HEDDA. Perhaps.

TESMAN. Well, my dear Mrs. Elvsted, you and I'll have to pool our brains. No use crying over spilt milk, what? We must try to approach this matter calmly.

MRS. ELVSTED. Yes, yes, Mr. Tesman. I'll do my best.

TESMAN. Well, come over here and let's start looking at these notes right away. Where shall we sit? Here? No, the other room. You'll excuse us, won't you, Judge? Come along with me, Mrs. Elvsted.

MRS. ELVSTED. Oh, God! If only we can manage to do it!

Tesman and Mrs. Elvsted go into the rear room. He takes off his hat and overcoat. They sit at the table beneath the hanging lamp and absorb themselves in the notes. Hedda walks across to the stove and sits in the armchair. After a moment, Brack goes over to her.

HEDDA (*half aloud*). Oh, Judge! This act of Eilert Lœvborg's—doesn't it give one a sense of release!

BRACK. Release, Mrs. Hedda? Well, it's a release for him, of course—

HEDDA. Oh, I don't mean him—I mean me! The release of knowing that someone can do something really brave! Something beautiful!

BRACK (*smiles*). Hm—my dear Mrs. Hedda—

HEDDA. Oh, I know what you're going to say. You're a *bourgeois* at heart, too, just like—ah, well!

BRACK (*looks at her*). Eilert Lœvborg has meant more to you than you're willing to admit to yourself. Or am I wrong?

HEDDA. I'm not answering questions like that from you. I only know that Eilert Lœvborg has had the courage to live according to his own principles. And now, at last, he's done something big! Something beautiful! To have the courage and the will to rise from the feast of life so early!

BRACK. It distresses me deeply, Mrs. Hedda, but I'm afraid I must rob you of that charming illusion.

HEDDA. Illusion?

BRACK. You wouldn't have been allowed to keep it for long, anyway.

HEDDA. What do you mean?

BRACK. He didn't shoot himself on purpose.

HEDDA. Not on purpose?

BRACK. No. It didn't happen quite the way I told you.

HEDDA. Have you been hiding something? What is it?

BRACK. In order to spare poor Mrs. Elvsted's feelings, I permitted myself one or two small—equivocations.

HEDDA. What?

BRACK. To begin with, he is already dead.

HEDDA. He died at the hospital?

BRACK. Yes. Without regaining consciousness.

HEDDA. What else haven't you told us?

BRACK. The incident didn't take place at his lodgings.

HEDDA. Well, that's utterly unimportant.

BRACK. Not utterly. The fact is, you see, that Eilert Lœvborg was found shot in Mademoiselle Danielle's boudoir.

HEDDA (*almost jumps up, but instead sinks back in her chair*). That's impossible. He can't have been there today.

BRACK. He was there this afternoon. He went to ask for something he claimed they'd taken from him. Talked some crazy nonsense about a child which had got lost—

HEDDA. Oh! So that was the reason!

BRACK. I thought at first he might have been referring to his manuscript. But I hear he destroyed that himself. So he must have meant his pocket-book—I suppose.

HEDDA. Yes, I suppose so. So they found him there?

BRACK. Yes, there. With a discharged pistol in his breast pocket. The shot had wounded him mortally.

HEDDA. Yes. In the breast.

BRACK. No. In the—stomach. The—lower part—

HEDDA (*looks at him with an expression of repulsion*). That, too! Oh, why does everything I touch become mean and ludicrous? It's like a curse!

BRACK. There's something else, Mrs. Hedda. It's rather disagreeable, too.

HEDDA. What?

BRACK. The pistol he had on him—

HEDDA. Yes? What about it?

BRACK. He must have stolen it.

HEDDA (*jumps up*). Stolen it! That isn't true! He didn't!

BRACK. It's the only explanation. He must have stolen it. Ssh!

Tesman and Mrs. Elvsted have got up from the table in the rear room and come into the drawing-room.

TESMAN (*his hands full of papers*). Hedda, I can't see properly under that lamp. Do you think—?

HEDDA. I am thinking.

TESMAN. Do you think we could possibly use your writing-table for a little? What?

HEDDA. Yes, of course. (*Quickly.*) No, wait! Let me tidy it up first.

TESMAN. Oh, don't you trouble with that. There's plenty of room.

HEDDA. No, no, let me tidy up first, I say. I'll take these in and put them on the piano. Here.

She pulls an object, covered with sheets of music, out from under the bookcase, puts some more sheets on top and carries it all into the rear room and away to the left. Tesman puts his papers on the writing-table and moves the lamp over from the corner table. He and Mrs. Elvsted sit down and begin working again. Hedda comes back.

HEDDA (*behind Mrs. Elvsted's chair, ruffles her hair gently*). Well, my pretty Thea. And how is work progressing on Eilert Lœvborg's memorial?

MRS. ELVSTED (*looks up at her, dejectedly*). Oh, it's going to be terribly difficult to get these into any order.

TESMAN. We've got to do it. We must! After all, putting other people's papers into order is rather my speciality, what?

Hedda goes over to the stove and sits on one of the footstools. Brack stands over her, leaning against the armchair.

HEDDA (*whispers*). What was that you were saying about the pistol?

BRACK (*softly*). I said he must have stolen it.

HEDDA. Why do you think that?

BRACK. Because any other explanation is unthinkable, Mrs. Hedda. Or ought to be.

HEDDA. I see.

BRACK (*looks at her for a moment*). Eilert Lœvborg was here this morning. Wasn't he?

HEDDA. Yes.

BRACK. Were you alone with him?

HEDDA. For a few moments.

BRACK. You didn't leave the room while he was here?

HEDDA. No.

BRACK. Think again. Are you sure you didn't go out for a moment?

HEDDA. Oh—yes, I might have gone into the hall. Just for a few seconds.

BRACK. And where was your pistol-case during this time?

HEDDA. I'd locked it in that—

BRACK. Er—Mrs. Hedda?

HEDDA. It was lying over there on my writing-table.

BRACK. Have you looked to see if both the pistols are still there?

HEDDA. No.

BRACK. You needn't bother. I saw the pistol Lœvborg had when they found him. I recognized it at once. From yesterday. And other occasions.

HEDDA. Have you got it?

BRACK. No. The police have it.

HEDDA. What will the police do with this pistol?

BRACK. Try to trace the owner.

HEDDA. Do you think they'll succeed?

BRACK (*leans down and whispers*). No, Hedda Gabler. Not as long as I hold my tongue.

HEDDA (*looks nervously at him*). And if you don't?

BRACK (*shrugs his shoulders*). You could always say he'd stolen it.

HEDDA. I'd rather die!

BRACK (*smiles*). People say that. They never do it.

HEDDA (*not replying*). And suppose the pistol wasn't stolen? And they trace the owner? What then?

BRACK. There'll be a scandal, Hedda.

HEDDA. A scandal!

BRACK. Yes, a scandal. The thing you're so frightened of. You'll have to appear in court together with Mademoiselle Danielle. She'll have to explain how it all happened. Was it an accident, or was it—homicide? Was he about to take the pistol from his pocket to threaten her? And did it go off? Or did she snatch the pistol from his hand, shoot him and then put it back in his pocket? She might quite easily have done it. She's a resourceful lady, is Mademoiselle Danielle.

HEDDA. But I have nothing to do with this repulsive business.

BRACK. No. But you'll have to answer one question. Why did you give Eilert Lœvborg this pistol? And what conclusions will people draw when it is proved you did give it to him?

HEDDA (*bows her head*). That's true. I hadn't thought of that.

BRACK. Well, luckily there's no danger as long as I hold my tongue.

HEDDA (*looks up at him*). In other words, I'm in your power, Judge. From now on, you've got your hold over me.

BRACK (*whispers, more slowly*). Hedda, my dearest—believe me—I will not abuse my position.

HEDDA. Nevertheless, I'm in your power. Dependent on your will, and your demands. Not free. Still not free! (*Rises passionately.*) No. I couldn't bear that. No.

BRACK (*looks half-derisively at her*). Most people resign themselves to the inevitable, sooner or later.

HEDDA (*returns his gaze*). Possibly they do.

She goes across to the writing-table.

HEDDA (*represses an involuntary smile and says in* Tesman's *voice*). Well, George. Think you'll be able to manage? What?

TESMAN. Heaven knows, dear. This is going to take months and months.

HEDDA (*in the same tone as before*). Fancy that, by Jove! (*Runs her hands gently through Mrs. Elvsted's hair.*) Doesn't it feel strange, Thea? Here you are working away with Tesman just the way you used to work with Eilert Lœvborg.

MRS. ELVSTED. Oh—if only I can inspire your husband, too!

HEDDA. Oh, it'll come. In time.

TESMAN. Yes—do you know, Hedda, I really think I'm beginning to feel a bit—well—that way. But you go back and talk to Judge Brack.

HEDDA. Can't I be of use to you two in any way?

TESMAN. No, none at all. (*Turns his head.*) You'll have to keep Hedda company from now on, Judge, and see she doesn't get bored. If you don't mind.

BRACK (*glances at Hedda*). It'll be a pleasure.

HEDDA. Thank you. But I'm tired this evening. I think I'll lie down on the sofa in there for a little while.

TESMAN. Yes, dear—do. What?

Hedda goes into the rear room and draws the curtains behind her. Short pause. Suddenly she begins to play a frenzied dance melody on the piano.

MRS. ELVSTED (*starts up from her chair*). Oh, what's that?

TESMAN (*runs to the doorway*). Hedda dear, please! Don't play dance music tonight! Think of Auntie Rena. And Eilert.

HEDDA (*puts her head through the curtains*). And Auntie Juju. And all the rest of them. From now on I'll be quiet.

She closes the curtains behind her.

TESMAN (*at the writing-table*). It distresses her to watch us doing this. I say, Mrs. Elvsted, I've an idea. Why don't you move in with Auntie Juju? I'll run over each evening, and we can sit and work there. What?

MRS. ELVSTED. Yes, that might be the best plan.

HEDDA (*from the rear room*). I can hear what you're saying, Tesman. But how shall I spend the evenings out here?

TESMAN (*looking through his papers*). Oh, I'm sure Judge Brack'll be kind enough to come over and keep you company. You won't mind my not being here, Judge?

BRACK (*in the armchair, calls gaily*). I'll be delighted, Mrs. Tesman. I'll be here every evening. We'll have great fun together, you and I.

HEDDA (*loud and clear*). Yes, that'll suit you, won't it, Judge? The only cock on the dunghill—

A shot is heard from the rear room. Tesman, Mrs. Elvsted and Judge Brack start from their chairs.

TESMAN. Oh, she's playing with those pistols again.

He pulls the curtains aside and runs in. Mrs. Elvsted follows him. Hedda is lying dead on the sofa. Confusion and shouting. Bertha enters in alarm from the right.

TESMAN (*screams to Brack*). She's shot herself! Shot herself in the head! Fancy that!

BRACK (*half paralysed in the armchair*). But, good God! People don't do such things!

MISS JULIE
AUGUST STRINDBERG

AUGUST STRINDBERG (1849–1912)

Strindberg's plays, particularly those described as naturalistic, are noted for their violent confrontations, especially between men and women. Considering the circumstances of his childhood and three painful marriages, all of which failed, the violence and contentiousness is understandable. Born in Stockholm out of wedlock to a tyrannical father and a weak-willed mother, Strindberg was one of a dozen children. His family lived in the kind of cramped quarters and squalor often depicted by late-nineteenth century naturalists. His mother died when he was 13, but his family life only worsened when his father remarried. Consequently, Strindberg was a melancholy, irritable youth who quarreled with his teachers and subsequently lost his scholarship to Uppsala University.

He found work as a teacher and journalist, and eventually he attracted some fame with the publication of a small novel, *The Red Room* (1879). Strindberg traveled extensively and chose to live abroad because of his discontent with Swedish puritanism (he was once censured for "unseemly" material in his short stories). From 1882 through 1897 he lived in Switzerland, Germany, Austria, Denmark, and primarily France. In 1892 his plays were produced by Antoine at the *Théâtre-Libre*. In 1907 Strindberg founded the Intimate Theatre in Stockholm, among the most important "little theaters" that proliferated in Europe and America in the new century.

Strindberg was a multitalented figure. In addition to his literary accomplishments, he excelled as a painter, a photographer (who did much to raise the medium to an art form), and a noted amateur chemist. He is, however, remembered for his plays and some fine novels, especially *The Inferno* (1897), written from the depths of a mental illness that institutionalized him for several years. Of the early modernists, Strindberg was the boldest experimenter with form and subject matter. Not only did he write naturalistic plays, of which *The Father* (1886) and *Miss Julie* (1888) are the finest, but he also wrote 20 chronicle plays based on Nordic history and several "chamber plays," intimate symbolist dramas popularized in France and northwestern Europe. His Expressionist dramas, such as *The Road to Damascus* (1901) and *The Dream Play* (1906), legitimized the style and exerted a profound influence on Eugene O'Neill, Elmer Rice, and the German Expressionists.

With Emile Zola, Strindberg is credited with advancing naturalism, both as a theatrical style and as a philosophy. Despite the intensely real settings, situations, dialogue, and especially the psychological portraiture of his naturalistic plays, Strindberg was still too much the poet not to incorporate symbolism and ritual into his work. The lasting appeal of *Miss Julie* can be attributed to his skillful blend of naturalism with an older, more poetic strain.

Even the briefest survey of Strindberg's life must address his alleged misogyny. It is tempting to believe that Strindberg loathed women, especially given his tempestuous marriages. Lines culled from his plays only reinforce the notion that he hated women and that women hated him. Miss Julie tells Jean that her mother taught her "to distrust and hate all men— you've heard how she hated men—and I swore never to be slave to any man." Still, Strindberg is too complicated to be reduced to a single psychological state (interestingly, his life has in-

917

spired several case studies by psychologists). Like so many of his characters, notably Julie herself, he vacillated wildly in his feelings, especially where the sexes were concerned. The cliché pointing out the fine line between love and hate is particularly applicable to Strindberg and the lost souls of his dramas. The most tormented of contemporary American dramatists, O'Neill said of the man who inspired his works: "Strindberg was the precursor of all modernity in the modern theater . . . the greatest interpreter of the characteristic spiritual conflicts which constitute drama—the blood—of our lives today."

MISS JULIE (1888)

We have trod *Miss Julie*'s path before in this anthology. Like Shakespeare's comedy, the play covers a single night in which a couple, caught in the revelry of the madness of Midsummer's Eve, make love, quarrel, and succumb to every manner of "lunacy." As with the Egeus-Hermia relationship, the specter of a tyrant-father hovers over the action, symbolized by the omnipresence of the "high riding boots with spurs." When we first hear about her, the Countess Julie is frolicking in an enchanted forest, not unlike the various maidens described in the survey of midsummer festivals throughout Northern Europe. Strindberg is placing us on familiar ground as we begin the play.

But by its end we are in bold, new territory, watching in horror as Julie receives her "gift" from Jean and exits to her death, among the cruelest and most disturbing in all of dramatic literature. From its festive opening to its tragic conclusion, *Miss Julie* unfolds rapidly and with all the frightening inevitability of Greek tragedy. In itself, the spectacle of the highborn plummeting to tragic depths is not new. Nor are violent, destructive confrontations between warring lovers new subject matter; even Strindberg is hard-pressed to top Euripides' savage depiction of Jason and Medea. What makes *Miss Julie* a watershed in Western theater is its fusion of the tragic impulse with naturalism, social drama, and modern psychology, all the while retaining the poetic and ritual elements that are germane to theater.

In earlier eras, tragedy was most often ascribed to fate, karma, or some similar abstraction that accounted for human misery. But Heredity and Environment became the nineteenth-century equivalents of the *Moira*, the three sisters of Greek myth who spun out human destiny. Miss Julie is what she is because she is very much her mother's daughter. Strindberg is explicit about the genetic roots of Julie's destructiveness. In his preface to the play he states, "I have motivated the tragic fate of Miss Julie with an abundance of circumstances: her mother's base instincts, her father's improper bringing-up, her own inborn nature . . . " There is evidence throughout the text: Jean tells her that he has "read the whole history of your family. . . . Do you know who the founder [of your family] was? He was miller who let the king sleep with his wife one night . . . " Elsewhere we learn that Julie's mother was an arsonist. Her pedigree dooms her to her tragic failure.

Julie's environment also contributes to her fall. On an external level, we are told in the play's preface that she is caught up in the Dionysian revelry—"the Festive atmosphere of Midsummer's Eve . . . the erotic excitement of the dance, the long summer twilight, the highly aphrodisiac influence of the flowers." Much of the play's conflict stems from tension between the pagan abandon of the festival and the oppressive religious and class strictures of late-nineteenth-century Sweden. Strindberg purposely sets the play's action in the serving quarters of the estate—the large kitchen where menials work, and, just offstage, the sleeping quarters. It is into this environment that Julie enters. We must view the play through the eyes of Strindberg's original audience, who realized the taboo nature of Julie's visit. For the daughter of the estate owner to fraternize with servants in their quarters was unquestionably scandalous, no matter how innocent her intentions. Here Strindberg fuses social issues with older dramatic traditions: class war intersects forbidden love. We have seen ill-fated love in earlier dramas (*A Midsummer Night's Dream*, *Hernani*), but the lovers therein are invariably social equals. However, with the breakdown of class distinctions in the nineteenth century, affairs between the highborn and the commoner became subjects and symbols for avant-garde artists. Julie deliberately chooses a social inferior as a lover because doing so is strictly taboo within the context of her society. It was Strindberg's most effective way of illustrating the self-destructiveness of her actions.

Because most of her words are subtextual, Julie rarely articulates her sense of the social taboos she so willfully violates. But Jean does. He has an aristocrat's mind trapped in a valet's body. In the initial stages of their flirtation, Jean tells Julie that his father worked as a menial on the estate next to hers; despite their proximity "you didn't notice me," he says, thereby suggesting the resentment he has harbored for her class. Later Julie and Jean exchange accounts of recurring dreams. She describes the horror of falling from a high pillar, a classic image of the tragic hero, as well as a dream rife with Freudian implications. He dreams of climbing "a high tree in a dark forest . . . to look out over the bright landscape where the sun is shining," a none-too-subtle symbol of his desire to overcome his social limitations. In purely social or Marxist terms, one can argue that the misalliance between mistress and servant and its violent consequences are manifestations of class conflict. Jean enters into the seduction to get back at those who have subjugated him; he tells Julie to kill herself to attain the ultimate revenge on the class he despises.

If *Miss Julie* were merely a social tract, however, it would be relegated to the status of Hauptmann's *The Weavers* (1892), an important naturalistic work that has had little life in the theater. Strindberg transcends class conflict in the depth of his psychological portraiture. In his preface, the playwright contends that he has created "characterless" persons for his drama. "Character," for him, was a "fixed [being] who was always one and the same, always drunk, always joking, always moving, and who needed to be characterized only by some physical defect." Strindberg envisioned characters that mirrored his time ("a transitional era more hectic and hysterical than the previous one") and were therefore "more unstable, as torn and divided, a mixture of the old and new." Like Ibsen's Hedda Gabbler (whom she resembles), Julie epitomizes the modern stage character—contradictory, vacillating, full of opposite impulses. At one moment she seeks to dominate, at another she craves domination. She is fierce and proud, every inch the aristocrat, yet she is filled with self-loathing and demeans herself. On one page she can tell Jean that "You give me strength. . . . Tell me you love me," and only a few pages later she screams that "I'd like to see your blood and your brains on a chopping block." These violent swings of emotion and motivation, often seemingly inexplicable, make Julie fascinating for audiences—and, of course, for the century's worth of superb actors who have played her. Julie's character is the sum total of her contradictions. As much as any character created for the theater, she embodies Aristotle's precept about being "consistently inconsistent."

Fittingly, Strindberg uses many of the devices that would become *de rigueur* among the new generation of playwrights committed to psychological realism: the expression of dreams, subtext, and even stream of consciousness. Examine Julie's lengthy monologue to Christine about traveling through Europe, and note how it deteriorates into a strange "word association" game that reveals much about Julie's inner turmoil.

For all the modernity of its social themes and naturalistic techniques, there remains something primordial about the play. The midsummer revels account for much of the play's antique feel. When Jean tells Julie that they ought to sleep on nine midsummer flowers so their dreams will come true he evokes ancient superstitions and magical rites. Strindberg's ingenious use of the chorus of festival dancers to mark the time lapse between the first and second halves of the play returns theater to its original impulses, especially when we regard the ballet as a fertility dance. Even Strindberg's use of symbols conjures primitive images. Julie carries a riding crop, which is as much a symbol of power and domination as her father's omnipresent boots and spurs. Jean's razor, which is handed to Julie in the climactic moment of the play, is both a sacrificial knife and a phallic symbol of male dominance. When Jean savagely kills the canary, a ritual act that anticipates Julie's death, we are reminded that ancient rites often included animal sacrifice. Julie's subsequent death also has a ceremonial significance. Strindberg's preface aligns her with the "old warrior nobility" who must commit a ritual suicide "because of that inherited or acquired sense of honor that has been transmitted to the upper classes from . . . the age of barbarism, from chivalry, from the Middle Ages."

In the final analysis, however, it is not Strindberg's masterful fusion of old rites with newer social concerns that gives *Miss Julie* its primordial edge. Rather, it is the depiction of an uncompromising and thoroughly destructive passion that cannot be explained by psychologists or sociologists. Julie's passion and death are as terrifying as they are fascinating.

PREFACE TO MISS JULIE

Translated by Harry G. Carlson

The theatre has long seemed to me to be, like art in general, a *Biblia pauperum*, a Bible in pictures for those who can't read what is written or printed, and the playwright a lay preacher hawking the ideas of the day in popular form, so popular that the middle classes, the theatre's primary audience, can understand the basic questions without too much effort. And so the theatre has always been a public school for the young, the half-educated, and women, who still possess that primitive capacity for deceiving themselves or letting themselves be deceived, that is to say, are receptive to the illusion, to the playwright's power of suggestion. It seems to me, therefore, in our time, when rudimentary, undeveloped, and fanciful ways of thinking seem to be evolving toward reflection, investigation, and analysis, that the theatre, like religion, is dying out, a form for whose enjoyment we lack the necessary preconditions. Supporting this assertion is the serious theatre crisis now prevailing throughout Europe, especially in those bastions of culture that produced the greatest thinkers of the age, England and Germany, where the art of drama, like most of the other fine arts, is dead.

In other countries people have believed it possible to create a new drama by filling old forms with new contents. For a number of reasons, however, this has failed: in part because there has not been sufficient time to popularize the new ideas, so that the public does not understand the basic questions: in part because partisan politics has stirred up emotions, making dispassionate enjoyment impossible—how can people be objective when their innermost beliefs are offended or when they are subjected in the confines of a theatre to the public pressure of an applauding or hissing audience?; and in part because new forms have not been found for the new contents, so that the new wine has burst the old bottles.

In the following play, instead of trying to do anything new—which is impossible—I have simply modernized the form in accordance with demands I think contemporary audiences make upon this art. Toward this end, I have chosen, or let myself be moved by, a theme that can be said to lie outside partisan politics since the problem of social climbing or falling, or higher or lower, better or worse, man or woman, are, have been, and will be of lasting interest. When I took this theme from a true story I heard told some years ago, which made a strong impression on me, I found it appropriate for tragedy, for it still seems tragic to see someone favored by fortune go under, much more to see a family die out. Perhaps the time will come when we will be so advanced, so enlightened, that we can witness with indifferences what now seem the coarse, cynical, heartless dramas life has to offer, when we have closed down those lower, unreliable mechanisms of thought called feelings, because better developed organs or judgment will have found them superfluous and harmful. The fact that the heroine arouses compassion is because we are too weak to resist the fear that the same fate could overtake us. A hypersensitive spectator may not be satisfied with compassion alone, while a man with faith in the future may demand some positive proposals to remedy the evil, in other words, a program of some kind. But for one thing there is no absolute evil. The fall of one family can mean a chance for another family to rise, and the alternation of rising and falling fortunes is one of life's greatest delights since happiness lies only in comparison. And to the man who wants a program to remedy the unpleasant fact that the bird of prey eats the dove and the louse eats the bird of prey I ask: why should it be remedied? Life is not so idiotically mathematical that only the great eat the small; it is just as common for a bee to kill a lion or at least drive it mad.

If my tragedy depresses many people, it is their own fault. When we become as strong as the first French revolutionaries, it will afford nothing but pleasure and relief to witness the thinning out in royal parks of overage, decaying trees that have long stood in the way of others equally entitled to their time in the sun, the kind of relief we feel when we see someone incurably ill die!

Recently, my tragedy *The Father* was criticized for being too sad, as if one should expect cheerful tragedies. People clamor pretentiously for "the joy of life," and theatre managers call for farces, as if the joy of life lay in being silly and depicting people as if they were all afflicted with St. Vitus's dance or imbecility. I find the joy of life in its cruel and powerful struggles, and my enjoyment comes from being able to know something, being able to learn something. That is why I have chosen an unusual case, but one from which we can learn much—in a word an exception, but an important exception which proves the rule—though this will probably offend those who love the conventional and predictable. What will next shock simple minds is that I have not motivated the action in a simple way, nor is there a singe point of view. Every event in life—and this is a rather new discovery! is ordinarily the result of a whole series of more or less deep-lying motives. The spectator, however, usually singles out the one that is either easiest for him to understand or is most advantageous to him personally. Take the case of a suicide. "Financial problems," says a businessman. "Unrequited love," says a woman. "Physical illness," says an invalid. "Dashed hopes," says a shipwrecked man. It might be that all or none of these were motives and that the deceased concealed the real motive by advancing a totally different one that would bring the most credit to his memory!

I have motivated Miss Julie's tragic fate by a great number of circumstances: her mother's primary instincts, her father raising her incorrectly, her own nature, and the influence of her fiancé on her weak and degenerate brain. Also, more particularly: the festive atmosphere of midsummer night, her father's absence, her monthly indisposition, her preoccupation with animals, the provocative effect of the dancing, the magical midsummer twilight, the powerfully aphrodisiac influence of flowers, and, finally, the chance that drives the couples together into a room alone—plus the boldness of the aroused man.

My treatment of the subject is thus neither one-sidedly physiological nor exclusively psychological. I have not put the entire blame on what she inherited from her mother, nor on her monthly indisposition, nor on immortality. I have not even preached morality—this I left to the cook in the absence of a minister.

This multiplicity of motives, it pleases me to assert, is in keeping with the times. And if others have done it before me, then it pleases me that I have not been alone in my "paradoxes," as all discoveries are called.

As for characterization, I have made my people rather "characterless" for the following reasons:

The word *character* has come to mean many things over the course of time. Originally, it must have meant the dominant trait in the soul-complex and was confused with temperament. Later it became the middle-class expression for the automaton, one whose disposition was fixed once and for all or had adapted himself to a particular role in life. In a word, someone who had stopped growing was called a character. In contrast the person who continued to develop, the skillful navigator on the river of life, sailing not with sheets belayed, but veering before the wind to luff again, was called characterless—in a derogatory sense, of course—because he was so difficult to understand, classify, and keep track of. This bourgeois concept of the immobility of the soul was transferred to the stage, which the bourgeoisie has always dominated. There a character became a man who was ready-made; whenever he appeared, he was drunk or comical or sad. The only thing necessary to characterize him was to give him a physical defect—a clubfoot, a wooden leg, a red nose—or have him repeat an expression, such as "that was splendid" or "Barkis is willin'." This simplified view of human character still survives in the great Molière. Harpagon is nothing but a miser although he could have been not only a miser but an excellent financier, or splendid father and good citizen. What is worse is that his "defect" is very advantageous to his son-in-law and daughter, who are his heirs and therefore should not criticize him, even if they have to wait a bit before climbing into bed together. Therefore, I do not believe in simple theatrical characters. And an author's summary judgments of people—this one is stupid, that one brutal, this one jealous, that one stingy—should be challenged by naturalists, who know how rich the soul-complex is and realize that "vice" has a reverse side closely resembling virtue.

As modern characters living in an age of transition more compulsively hysterical than the one that preceded it at least, I have depicted my people as more vacillating and disintegrating than their predecessors, a mixture of the old and the new. If the valet belches something modern from the depths of his ancient slave's soul, it is because I think it not improbable that through newspapers and conversations modern ideas filter down even to the level a servant lives on. There are those who find it wrong in modern drama for characters to speak Darwinism. At the same time they hold up Shakespeare as a model. I would like to remind these critics that the gravedigger in *Hamlet* speaks the fashionable philosophy of the day—Giordana Bruno's (Bacon's) —which is more improbable since there were fewer means then for the spread of ideas than there are now. Besides, "Darwinism" has existed in every age, ever since the description in Genesis of the steps in creation from lower animals to man. It is just that only now have we discovered and formulated it.

My souls (characters) are conglomerates of past and present cultural phases, bits from books and newspapers, scraps of humanity, pieces torn from fine clothes and become rags, patched together as is the human soul. I have also added a little evolutionary history by having the weaker mind steal and repeat words from the stronger. Ideas are induced through the power of suggestion: from other people, from the surroundings (the blood of the greenfinch), and from attributes (the straight razor); and I have inanimate objects (the Count's boots, the bell) serve as agents for *Gedankenübertragung* ["thought transference."]. Finally, I have used "open suggestion," a variation of sleeplike hypnosis, which is now so well known and popularized that it cannot arouse the kind of ridicule or skepticism it would have done in Mesmer's time.

Miss Julie is a modern character. Not that the man-hating half-woman has not existed in all ages but because now that she has been discovered, she has come out in the open to make herself heard. The half-woman is a type who pushes her way ahead, selling herself nowadays for power, decorations, honors, and diplomas, as formerly she used to do for money. The type implies a retrogressive step in evolution, an inferior species who cannot endure. Unfortunately, they are able to pass on their wretchedness; degenerate men seem unconsciously to choose their mates from among them. And so they breed, producing an indeterminate sex for whom life is a torture. Fortunately, the offspring go under either because they are out of harmony with reality or because their repressed instincts break out uncontrollably or because their hopes of achieving equality with men are crushed. The type is tragic, revealing the drama of a desperate struggle against Nature, tragic as the romantic heritage now being dissipated by naturalism, which has a contrary aim: happiness, and happiness belongs only to the strong and skillful species.

But Miss Julie is also: a relic of the old warrior nobility now giving way to a new nobility of nerve and intellect, a victim of her own flawed constitution, a victim of the discord caused in a family by a mother's "crime," a victim of the delusions and conditions of her age—and together these are the equivalent of the concept of Destiny, or Universal Law, of antiquity. Guilt has been abolished by the naturalist, along with God, but the consequences of an action—punishment, imprisonment or the fear of it—that he cannot erase, for the simple reason that they remain, whether he pronounces acquittal or not. Those who have been injured are not as kind and understanding as an unscathed outsider can afford to be. Even if her father felt constrained not to seek revenge, his daughter would wreak vengeance upon herself, as she does here, out of an innate or acquired sense of honor, which the upper classes inherit—from where? From barbarism, from the ancient Aryan home of the race, from medieval chivalry. It is a beautiful thing, but nowadays a hindrance to the survival of the race. It is the nobleman's harikari, which compels him to slit open his own stomach when someone insults him and which survives in a modified form in the duel, that privilege of the nobility. That is why Jean, the servant, lives, while Miss Julie cannot live without honor. The slave's advantage over the nobleman is that he lacks this fatal preoccupation with honor. But in all of us Aryans there is something of the nobleman, or a Don Quixote. And so we sympathize with the suicide, whose act means a loss of honor. We are noblemen enough to be pained when we see the mighty fallen and as superfluous as a corpse, yes, even if the fallen should rise again and make amends through an honorable act. The servant Jean is a race-founder, someone in whom the process of differentiation can be detected. Born the son of a tenant farmer, he has educated himself in the things a gentleman should know. He has been quick to learn, has finely developed senses (smell, taste, sight) and a feeling for what is beautiful. He is already moving up in the world and is not embarrassed about using other people's help. He is alienated from his fellow servants, despising them as parts of a past he has already put behind him. He fears and flees them because they know his secrets, pry into his intentions, envy his rise, and look forward eagerly to his fall. Hence his dual, indecisive nature, vacillating between sympathy for people in high social positions and hatred for those who currently occupy those positions. He is an aristocrat, as he himself says, has learned the secrets of good society, is polished on the surface but coarse beneath, wears a frock coat tastefully but without any guarantee that his body is clean.

He has respect for Miss Julie, but is afraid of Kristine because she knows his dangerous secrets. He is sufficiently callous not to let the night's events disturb his plans for the future. With both a slave's brutality and a master's lack of squeamishness, he can see blood without fainting and shake off misfortune easily. Consequently, he comes through the struggle unscathed and will probably end up an innkeeper. And even if *he* does not become a Rumanian count, his son will become a university student and possibly a county police commissioner.

In any case he has important things to say about the lower classes' view of life—when he is telling the truth, that is, which he often does not do, for he is more interested in saying what is favorable to himself than in telling the truth. When Miss Julie says she assumes the lower classes feel oppressed from above, Jean naturally agrees since it is his intention to win sympathy, but he quickly changes his attitude when he realizes that it is more to his advantage to distance himself from the "rabble."

Apart from the fact that Jean is rising in the world, he is superior to Miss Julie because he is a man. Sexually, he is an aristocrat because of his masculine strength, his more keenly developed senses, and his capacity for taking the initiative. His sense of inferiority is mostly due to the social circumstances in which he happens to be living, and he can probably shed it along with his valet's jacket.

His slave mentality expresses itself in the tearful respect he has for the Count (the boots) and his religious superstition; but he respects the Count mainly as the occupant of the kind of high position to which he himself aspires; and the respect remains even after he has conquered the daughter of the house and seen how empty the lovely shell was.

I do not believe that love in any "higher" sense can exist between two people of such different natures, and so I have Miss Julie's love as something she fabricates in order to protect and excuse herself; and I have Jean suppose himself capable of loving her under other social circumstances. I think it is the same with love as with the hyacinth, which must take root in darkness *before* it can produce a sturdy flower. Here a flower shoots up, blooms, and goes to seed all at once, and that is why it dies so quickly.

Kristine, finally, is a female slave. Years standing over the stove have made her conventional and lethargic; instinctively hypocritical, she uses morality and religion as cloaks and scapegoats. A strong person would not need these because he can either bear his guilt or reason it away. Kristine goes to church as a quick and easy way to unload her household thefts on Jesus and to take on a new charge of innocence. Furthermore, she is a minor character, and I purposely simply sketched her in, as I did the minister and the doctor in *The Father*, because I wanted ordinary people, as country ministers and provincial doctors usually are. If my minor characters seem abstract to some people, it is because ordinary people are abstract to some extent in their occupations. As they carry out their duties, they lose their individuality, showing only one side of themselves, and as long as the spectator has no need to see them from several sides, my abstract depiction of them is probably correct.

As for the dialogue, I have broken with tradition somewhat by not making my characters catechists who ask stupid questions in order to elicit clever replies. I have avoided the symmetrical, mathematical, constructed dialogue of French drama and let characters' minds function irregularly, as they do in a real-life conversation, where no topic of discussion is exhausted entirely and one mind by chance finds a cog in another mind in which to engage. Consequently, the dialogue also wanders, presenting material in the opening scenes that is later taken up, reworked, repeated, expanded, and developed, like the theme in a musical composition.

The plot is serviceable enough, and since it really concerns only two people, I have concentrated on them, including only one minor character, the cook, and having the father's unhappy spirit hover over and behind the action. I have done this because I believe that people of today are most interested in the psychological process. Our inquisitive souls are not satisfied just to see something happen; we want to know how it happened. We want to see the strings, the machinery, examine the double-bottomed box, feel for the seam in the magic ring, look at the cards to see how they are marked.

In this regard I have kept in mind the monographic novels of the brothers Goncourt, which I find more appealing than anything else in contemporary literature.

As for the technical aspects of composition, I have experimented with eliminating act divisions. The reason is that I believe our dwindling capacity for accepting illusion is possibly further disturbed by intermissions, during which the spectator has time to reflect and thereby escape the suggestive influence of the author-hypnotist. My play will probably run an hour and a half, and since people can listen to a lecture, sermon, or conference discussion for just as long or longer, I imagine that a ninety-minute theatre piece will not be too tiring. I tested this concentrated form in 1872 in one of my first plays, *The Outlaw*, although with little success. The first draft was in five acts, and when I noticed the disjointed, restless effect it produced, I burned it. From the ashes rose a single, long, coherent act of fifty pages in print, with a playing time of one hour. And so the form is not new, and I seem to have a feel for it; changing tastes may make it timely. My hope for the future is to so educate audiences that they can sit through a one-act play that lasts an entire evening. But this will require experimentation. Meanwhile, in order to relax tension for the audience and the actors, without breaking the illusion for the audience, I have used three art forms traditionally associated with drama: monologue, mime, and ballet. The original association was with the tragedy of antiquity, monody having become monologue, and chorus, ballet.

Our realists today condemn the monologue as implausible, but if I motivate it, I can make it plausible and use it to advantage. It is perfectly plausible for an orator to pace the floor alone and practice his speech aloud, plausible for an actor to rehearse his lines aloud, for a servant girl to talk to her cat, a mother babble to her baby, an old maid jabber to her parrot, a sleeper talk in his sleep. And in order to give the actor a chance, for once, to work independently, free for a moment of the author's authority, I have sketched in the monologues rather than worked them out in detail. Since it is irrelevant what someone says in his sleep or to a parrot or to a cat, for this has no influence on the action, a talented actor, absorbed in the mood and the situation, perhaps can improvise the monologue more effectively than the author, who cannot determine in advance how much may be spoken, and for how long, before an audience senses that the illusion is broken.

As we know, some Italian theatres have returned to improvisation, producing actors who are creative in their own right, although in accordance with the author's intentions. This could be the beginning of a fertile new art form, something worthy of the name *creative*.

In places where a monologue would be implausible, I have resorted to mime, and here I leave the actor even greater freedom to be creative—and to win independent acclaim. But in order not to try the audience beyond its limits, I have let music—coming from the midsummer dance, and thus believably motivated—exercise its illusion-evoking power during the sections of dumb show. I beg the music director to consider carefully his choice of pieces; the wrong mood may be produced if there are familiar selections from popular dances or operettas, or unusual folk melodies, no matter how ethnographically correct.

The ballet I have indicated cannot be replaced by a so-called "crowd scene" because crowd scenes are always badly acted, with a mob of grimacing idiots trying to use the occasion to appear clever and so disturb the illusion. And since uneducated people do not improvise when they wish to poke fun maliciously but use ready-made material that can take on a double meaning, I did not compose the taunting song they sing. Instead, I used a little-known dance song I discovered myself in the Stockholm area. The words are only approximately appropriate, but this is intentional, for the slyness (weakness) of the slave does not permit him to make a direct attack. And so the seriousness of the action forbids clowning; there must be no coarse sneering in a situation which closes the lid on a family coffin.

As for the scenery, I have borrowed from impressionist painting the device of making a setting appear cut off and asymmetrical, thus strengthening the illusion. When we see only part of a room and a portion of the furniture, we are left to conjecture, that is to say, our imagination goes to work and complements what is seen. I have also profited by doing away with those tiresome exits through doors because scenery doors, made of canvas, wobble at the slightest touch; they cannot even allow a father to express his anger after a bad dinner by going out and slamming the door behind him "so that the whole house shakes." (In the theatre it wobbles.) I have also confined the action to one setting, both to allow the characters more time to interact with their environment and to break with the tradition of expensive scenery. With only one setting we should be able to demand that it be realistic, but nothing is more difficult than to get a room on stage to look like a room, however easily the scene painter can produce flaming volcanoes and waterfalls. Even if the walls must be of canvas, it is surely time to stop painting shelves and kitchen utensils on them. We have so many other stage conventions in which we are asked to believe, we should not have to strain ourselves trying to believe in painted pots and pans.

I have placed the upstage wall and the table diagonally so that the actors can play facing the audience or in half-profile when they sit opposite each other at the table. I saw a diagonal backdrop in a production of Aïda; it led the eye out into unknown vistas and did not look simply like a defiant reaction to the boredom of straight lines.

Another perhaps necessary innovation is the removal of footlights. The purpose of this lighting from below is said to be to make the actors' faces fatter, but I ask: why must all actors have fat faces? Does not this lighting obliterate many subtleties in the lower part of the face, especially the jaws, distort the shape of the nose, and cast shadows up over the eyes? Even if this were not so, one thing is certain: actors find it so painful for their eyes that they are unable to use them with full expressiveness. Footlights strike the retina in places usually protected (except in the case of seamen, who have to look at the sun's reflection in the water), and so we seldom see anything but a crude rolling of the eyes, either to the side or up toward the balconies, exposing the whites. Perhaps this also accounts for the tedious habit, especially common among actresses, of blinking eyelashes. And when anyone on stage wants to speak with his eyes, he must resort to staring straight out, thus breaking the wall of the curtain line and coming into direct contact with the audience. Justly or unjustly, this unfortunate practice is called "greeting your friends."

Would not sufficiently strong side lighting (using parabolic reflectors, for example) provide the actor with a new advantage: the strengthening of mime effects through the most expressive asset in his face—the play of his eyes?

I have no illusions about getting the actor to play for the audience rather than with it, although this would be desirable. I cannot hope to see an actor play with his back to the audience throughout an entire important scene, though I wish very much that crucial scenes were staged, not next to the prompter's box, like duets intended to invoke applause, but in places more appropriate to the action. In other words, I call for no revolution, just small modifications, for to really transform the stage into a room where the fourth wall is removed, and consequently a portion of the furniture faces away from the audience, would probably, for the present, produce a disturbing effect.

When it comes to makeup, I dare not hope to be listened to by the ladies, who would rather be beautiful than believable. But the actor might consider whether it is really to his advantage when putting on makeup to fix an abstract character, like a mask on his face. Picture an actor who has put the sharp, charcoal lines of anger of an old man between his eyes and then, with that incensed look, has to smile in response to someone else's line. What a terrible grimace there would be as a result! And how would the false forehead attached to his wig, bald as a billiard ball, wrinkle when the old man got angry?

In a modern psychological drama, where the subtlest movements of the soul must be revealed more through the face than through gesture and sound, it would probably be best to experiment with strong side lighting on a small stage, and with actors wearing no makeup, or at least a minimum of it.

If, in addition, we could avoid having the orchestra visible, its lights disturbing, and the musicians' faces turned toward the audience; if the seating in the auditorium were raised so that eye level for the spectator was higher than the hollow of the actor's knee; if we could get rid of stage boxes (behind bull's-eye openings), with their grinning late arrivals from dinners and supper parties; if we could have complete darkness during performances; and, finally, and most importantly, a *small* stage and a *small* auditorium, then perhaps we might see a new drama arise, or at the very least a theatre that was once again a place of entertainment for educated people. While waiting for this theatre, we will just have to go on writing, preparing the repertoire that will one day be needed.

Here is an attempt! If it fails, there is surely time enough for another!

The eroticism and danger inherent in Miss Julie *were explored in London's Roundabout Theater production of Strindberg's psychological drama.*

MISS JULIE

AUGUST STRINDBERG

Translated by Harry G. Carlson

CHARACTERS

MISS JULIE, *25 years old*
JEAN, *her father's valet, 30 years old*
KRISTINE, *her father's cook, 35 years old*

(*The action takes place in the Count's kitchen on midsummer eve.*)

SETTING: (*A large kitchen, the ceiling and side walls of which are hidden by draperies. The rear wall runs diagonally from down left to up right. On the wall down left are two shelves with copper, iron, and pewter utensils; the shelves are lined with scalloped paper. Visible to the right is most of a set of large, arched glass doors, through which can be seen a fountain with a statue of Cupid, lilac bushes in bloom, and the tops of some Lombardy poplars. At down left is the corner of a large tiled stove; a portion of its hood is showing. At right, one end of the servants' white pine dining table juts out; several chairs stand around it. The stove is decorated with birch branches; juniper twigs are strewn on the floor. On the end of the table stands a large Japanese spice jar, filled with lilac blossoms. An ice box, a sink, and a washstand. Above the door is an old-fashioned bell on a spring; to the left of the door, the mouthpiece of a speaking tube is visible.)*

(Kristine is frying something on the stove. She is wearing a light-colored cotton dress and an apron. Jean enters. He is wearing livery and carries a pair of high riding boots with spurs, which he puts down on the floor where they can be seen by the audience.)

JEAN. Miss Julie's crazy again tonight; absolutely crazy!

KRISTINE. So you finally came back?

JEAN. I took the Count to the station and when I returned past the barn I stopped in for a dance. Who do I see but Miss Julie leading off the dance with the gamekeeper! But as soon as she saw me she rushed over to ask me for the next waltz. And she's been waltzing ever since—I've never seen anything like it. She's crazy!

KRISTINE. She always has been, but never as bad as the last two weeks since her engagement was broken off.

JEAN. Yes, I wonder what the real story was there. He was a gentleman, even if he wasn't rich. Ah! These people have such romantic ideas. *(Sits at the end of the table.)* Still, it's strange, isn't it? I mean that she'd rather stay home with the servants on midsummer eve instead of going with her father to visit relatives?

KRISTINE. She's probably embarrassed after that row with her fiancé.

JEAN. Probably! He gave a good account of himself, though. Do you know how it happened, Kristine? I saw it, you know, though I didn't let on I had.

KRISTINE. No! You saw it?

JEAN. Yes, I did.———That evening they were out near the stable, and she was "training" him—as she called it. Do you know what she did? She made him jump over her riding crop, the way you'd teach a dog to jump. He jumped twice and she hit him each time. But the third time he grabbed the crop out of her hand, hit her with it across the cheek, and broke it in pieces. Then he left.

KRISTINE. So, that's what happened! I can't believe it!

JEAN. Yes, that's the way it went!———What have you got for me that's tasty, Kristine?

KRISTINE *(serving him from the pan)*. Oh, it's only a piece of kidney I cut from the veal roast.

JEAN *(smelling the food)*. Beautiful! That's my favorite délice.[1] *(Feeling the plate.)* But you could have warmed the plate!

KRISTINE. You're fussier than the Count himself, once you start! *(She pulls his hair affectionately.)*

JEAN *(angry)*. Stop it, leave my hair alone! You know I'm touchy about that.

KRISTINE. Now, now, it's only love, you know that. *(Jean eats. Kristine opens a bottle of beer.)*

JEAN. Beer? On midsummer eve? No thank you. I can do better than that. *(Opens a drawer in the table and takes out a bottle of red wine with yellow sealing wax.)* See that? Yellow seal! Give me a glass! A wine glass! I'm drinking this pur.[2]

KRISTINE *(returns to the stove and puts on a small saucepan)*. God help the woman who gets you for a husband! What a fussbudget.

JEAN. Nonsense! You'd be damned lucky to get a man like me. It certainly hasn't done you any harm to have people call me your sweetheart. *(Tastes the wine.)* Good! Very good! Just needs a little warming. *(Warms the glass between his hands.)* We bought this in Dijon. Four francs a liter, not counting the cost of the bottle, or the customs duty.———What are you cooking now? It stinks like hell!

KRISTINE. Oh, some slop Miss Julie wants to give Diana.

JEAN. Watch your language, Kristine. But why should you have to cook for that damn mutt on midsummer eve? Is she sick?

KRISTINE. Yes, she's sick! She sneaked out with the gatekeeper's dog—and now there's hell to pay. Miss Julie won't have it!

JEAN. Miss Julie has too much pride about some things and not enough about others, just like her mother was. The Countess was most at home in the kitchen and the cowsheds, but a one-horse carriage wasn't elegant enough for her. The cuffs of her blouse were dirty, but she had to have her coat of arms on her cufflinks.———And Miss Julie won't take proper care of herself either. If you ask me, she just isn't refined. Just now, when she was dancing in the barn, she pulled the gamekeeper away from Anna and made him dance with her. *We* wouldn't behave like that, but that's what happens when aristocrats pretend they're common people—they get *common!*———But she is quite a woman! Magnificent! What shoulders, and what—et cetera!

KRISTINE. Oh, don't overdo it! I've heard what Clara says, and she dresses her.

JEAN. Ha, Clara! You're all jealous of each other! I've been out riding with her. . . . And the way she dances!

KRISTINE. Listen, Jean! You're going to dance with me, when I'm finished here, aren't you?

JEAN. Of course I will.

KRISTINE. Promise?

JEAN. Promise? When I say I'll do something, I do it! By the way, the kidney was very good. *(Corks the bottle.)*

[1] *délice* delight

[2] *pur* pure; the first drink from the bottle

JULIE (*in the doorway to someone outside*). I'll be right back! You go ahead for now! (*Jean sneaks the bottle back into the table drawer and gets up respectfully. Miss Julie enters and crosses to Kristine by the stove.*) Well? Is it ready? (*Kristine indicates that Jean is present.*)

JEAN (*gallantly*). Are you ladies up to something secret?

JULIE (*flicking her handkerchief in his face*). None of your business!

JEAN. Hmm! I like the smell of violets!

JULIE (*coquettishly*). Shame on you! So you know about perfumes, too? You certainly know how to dance. Ah, ah! No peeking! Go away.

JEAN (*boldly but respectfully*). Are you brewing up a magic potion for midsummer eve? Something to prophesy by under a lucky star, so you'll catch a glimpse of your future husband!

JULIE (*caustically*). You'd need sharp eyes to see him! (*To Kristine.*) Pour out half a bottle and cork it well.——— Come and dance a schottische[3] with me, Jean . . .

JEAN (*hesitating*). I don't want to be impolite to anyone, and I've already promised this dance to Kristine . . .

JULIE. Oh, she can have another one—can't you, Kristine? Won't you lend me Jean?

KRISTINE. It's not up to me, ma'am. (*To Jean.*) If the mistress is so generous, it wouldn't do for you to say no. Go on, Jean, and thank her for the honor.

JEAN. To be honest, and no offense intended, I wonder whether it's wise for you to dance twice running with the same partner, especially since these people are quick to jump to conclusions . . .

JULIE (*flaring up*). What's that? What sort of conclusions? What do you mean?

JEAN (*submissively*). If you don't understand, ma'am, I must speak more plainly. It doesn't look good to play favorites with your servants. . . .

JULIE. Play favorites! What an idea! I'm astonished! As mistress of the house, I honor your dance with my presence. And when I dance, I want to dance with someone who can lead, so I won't look ridiculous.

JEAN. As you order, ma'am! I'm at your service!

JULIE (*gently*). Don't take it as an order! On a night like this we're all just ordinary people having fun, so we'll forget about rank. Now, take my arm!———Don't worry, Kristine! I won't steal your sweetheart! (*Jean offers his arm and leads Miss Julie out.*)

MIME

(*The following should be played as if the actress playing Kristine were really alone. When she has to, she turns her back to the audience. She does not look toward them, nor does she hurry as if she were afraid they would grow impatient. Schottische music played on a fiddle sounds in the distance. Kristine hums along with the music. She clears the tables, washes the dishes, dries them, and puts them away. She takes off her apron. From a table drawer she removes a small mirror and leans it against the bowl of lilacs on the table. She lights a candle, heats a hairpin over the flame, and uses it to set a curl on her forehead. She crosses to the door and listens, then returns to the table. She finds the handkerchief Miss Julie left behind, picks it up, and smells it. Then, preoccupied, she spreads it out, stretches it, smoothes out the wrinkles, and folds it into quarters, and so forth.*)

JEAN (*enters alone*). God, she really is crazy! What a way to dance! Everybody's laughing at her behind her back. What do you make of it, Kristine?

KRISTINE. Ah! It's that time of the month for her, and she always gets peculiar like that. Are you going to dance with me now?

JEAN. You're not mad at me, are you, for leaving . . . ?

KRISTINE. Of course not!—Why should I be, for a little thing like that? Besides, I know my place . . .

JEAN (*puts his arm around her waist*). You're a sensible girl, Kristine, and you'd make a good wife . . .

JULIE (*entering, uncomfortably surprised; with forced good humor*). What a charming escort—running away from his partner.

JEAN. On the contrary, Miss Julie. Don't you see how I rushed back to the partner I abandoned!

JULIE (*changing her tone*). You know, you're a superb dancer!———But why are you wearing livery on a holiday? Take it off at once!

JEAN. Then I must ask you to go outside for a moment. You see, my black coat is hanging over here . . . (*Gestures and crosses right.*)

JULIE. Are you embarrassed about changing your coat in front of me? Well, go in your room then. Either that or stay and I'll turn my back.

JEAN. With your permission, ma'am! (*He crosses right. His arm is visible as he changes his jacket.*)

JULIE (*to Kristine*). Tell me, Kristine—you two are so close —. Is Jean your fiancé?

KRISTINE. Fiancé? Yes, if you wish. We can call him that.

JULIE. What do you mean?

KRISTINE. You had a fiancé yourself, didn't you? So . . .

JULIE. Well, we were properly engaged . . .

KRISTINE. But nothing came of it, did it? (*Jean returns dressed in a frock coat and bowler hat.*)

JULIE. *Très gentil, Monsieur Jean! Très gentil!*

JEAN. *Vous voulez plaisanter, madame!*

JULIE. *Et vous voulez parler français!*[4] Where did you learn that?

---

[3]**schottische** a Scottish round dance resembling a polka

[4]**Très gentil . . . français!** Very pleasing, Mr. Jean! Very pleasing. You would trifle with me, madam! And you want to speak French!

JEAN. In Switzerland, when I was wine steward in one of the biggest hotels in Lucerne!

JULIE. You look like a real gentleman in that coat! Charmant![5] (*Sits at the table.*)

JEAN. Oh, you're flattering me!

JULIE (*offended*). Flattering you?

JEAN. My natural modesty forbids me to believe that you would really compliment someone like me, and so I took the liberty of assuming that you were exaggerating, which polite people call flattering.

JULIE. Where did you learn to talk like that? You must have been to the theater often.

JEAN. Of course. And I've done a lot of traveling.

JULIE. But you come from here, don't you?

JEAN. My father was a farmhand on the district attorney's estate nearby. I used to see you when you were little, but you never noticed me.

JULIE. No! Really?

JEAN. Sure. I remember one time especially . . . but I can't talk about that.

JULIE. Oh, come now! Why not? Just this once!

JEAN. No, I really couldn't, not now. Some other time, perhaps.

JULIE. Why some other time? What's so dangerous about now?

JEAN. It's not dangerous, but there are obstacles.———Her, for example. (*Indicating Kristine, who has fallen asleep in a chair by the stove.*)

JULIE. What a pleasant wife she'll make! She probably snores, too.

JEAN. No, she doesn't, but she talks in her sleep.

JULIE (*cynically*). How do you know?

JEAN (*audaciously*). I've heard her! (*Pause, during which they stare at each other.*)

JULIE. Why don't you sit down?

JEAN. I couldn't do that in your presence.

JULIE. But if I order you to?

JEAN. Then I'd obey.

JULIE. Sit down, then.———No, wait. Can you get me something to drink first?

JEAN. I don't know what we have in the ice box. I think there's only beer.

JULIE. Why do you say "only"? My tastes are so simple I prefer beer to wine. (*Jean takes a bottle of beer from the ice box and opens it. He looks for a glass and a plate in the cupboard and serves her.*)

JEAN. Here you are, ma'am.

JULIE. Thank you. Won't you have something yourself?

JEAN. I'm not partial to beer, but if it's an order . . .

JULIE. An order?———Surely a gentleman can keep his lady company.

JEAN. You're right, of course. (*Opens a bottle and gets a glass.*)

JULIE. Now, drink to my health! (*He hesitates.*) What? A man of the world—and shy?

JEAN (*in mock romantic fashion, he kneels and raises his glass*). Skål to my mistress!

JULIE. Bravo!———Now kiss my shoe, to finish it properly. (*Jean hesitates, then boldly seizes her foot and kisses it lightly.*) Perfect! You should have been an actor.

JEAN (*rising*). That's enough now, Miss Julie! Someone might come in and see us.

JULIE. What of it?

JEAN. People talk, that's what? If you knew how their tongues were wagging just now at the dance, you'd . . .

JULIE. What were they saying? Tell me!———Sit down!

JEAN (*sits*). I don't want to hurt you, but they were saying things———suggestive things, that, that . . . well, you can figure it out for yourself! You're not a child. If a woman is seen drinking alone with a man—let alone a servant—at night—then . . .

JULIE. Then what? Besides, we're not alone. Kristine is here.

JEAN. Asleep!

JULIE. Then I'll wake her up. (*Rising.*) Kristine! Are you asleep? (*Kristine mumbles in her sleep.*)

JULIE. Kristine!———She certainly can sleep!

KRISTINE (*in her sleep*). The Count's boots are brushed—put the coffee on—right away, right away—uh, huh,—oh!

JULIE (*grabbing Kristine's nose*). Will you wake up!

JEAN (*severely*). Leave her alone—let her sleep!

JULIE (*sharply*). What?

JEAN. Someone who's been standing over a stove all day has a right to be tired by now. Sleep should be respected . . .

JULIE (*changing her tone*). What a considerate thought—it does you credit—thank you! (*Offering her hand.*) Come outside and pick some lilacs for me! (*During the following, Kristine awakens and shambles sleepily off right to bed.*)

JEAN. Go with you?

JULIE. With me!

JEAN. We couldn't do that! Absolutely not!

JULIE. I don't understand. Surely you don't imagine . . .

JEAN. No, I don't, but the others might.

JULIE. What? That I've fallen in love with a servant?

JEAN. I'm not a conceited man, but such things happen—and for these people, nothing is sacred.

JULIE. I do believe you're an aristocrat!

JEAN. Yes, I am.

JULIE. And I'm stepping down . . .

JEAN. Don't step down, Miss Julie, take my advice. No one'll believe you stepped down voluntarily. People will always say you fell.

JULIE. I have a higher opinion of people than you. Come and see!———Come! (*She stares at him broodingly.*)

JEAN. You're very strange, do you know that?

JULIE. Perhaps! But so are you!———for that matter, everything is strange. Life, people everything. Like floating scum, drifting on and on across the water, until it sinks down and down! That reminds me of a dream I have now

---

[5]**Charmant** charming

and then. I've climbed up on top of a pillar. I sit there and see no way of getting down. I get dizzy when I look down, and I must get down, but I don't have the courage to jump. I can't hold on firmly, and I long to be able to fall, but I don't fall. And yet I'll have no peace until I get down, no rest unless I get down, down on the ground! And if I did get down to the ground, I'd want to be under the earth . . . Have you ever felt anything like that?

JEAN. No. I dream that I'm lying under a high tree in a dark forest. I want to get up, up on top, and look out over the bright landscape, where the sun is shining, and plunder the bird's nest up there, where the golden eggs lie. And I climb and climb, but the trunk's so thick and smooth, and it's so far to the first branch. But I know if I just reached that first branch, I'd go right to the top, like up a ladder. I haven't reached it yet, but I will, even if it's only in a dream!

JULIE. Here I am chattering with you about dreams. Come, let's go out! Just into the park! (*She offers him her arm, and they start to leave.*)

JEAN. We'll have to sleep on nine midsummer flowers, Miss Julie, to make our dreams come true! (*They turn at the door. Jean puts his hand to his eye.*)

JULIE. Did you get something in your eye?

JEAN. It's nothing—just a speck—it'll be gone in a minute.

JULIE. My sleeve must have brushed against you. Sit down and let me help you. (*She takes him by the arm and seats him. She tilts his head back and with the tip of a handkerchief tries to remove the speck.*) Sit still, absolutely still! (*She slaps his hand.*) Didn't you hear me?————Why, you're trembling; the big, strong man is trembling! (*Feels his biceps.*) What muscles you have!

JEAN (*warning*). Miss Julie!

JULIE. Yes, monsieur Jean.

JEAN. *Attention! Je ne suis qu'un homme!*[6]

JULIE. Will you sit still!—There! Now it's gone! Kiss my hand and thank me.

JEAN (*rising*). Miss Julie, listen to me!————Kristine has gone to bed!————Will you listen to me!

JULIE. Kiss my hand first!

JEAN. Listen to me!

JULIE. Kiss my hand first!

JEAN. All right, but you've only yourself to blame!

JULIE. For what?

JEAN. For what? Are you still a child at twenty-five? Don't you know that it's dangerous to play with fire?

JULIE. Not for me. I'm insured.

JEAN (*boldly*). No, you're not! But even if you were, there's combustible material close by.

JULIE. Meaning you?

JEAN. Yes! Not because it's me, but because I'm young————

JULIE. And handsome—what incredible conceit! A Don Juan perhaps! Or a Joseph![7] Yes, that's it, I do believe you're a Joseph!

JEAN. Do you?

JULIE. I'm almost afraid so. (*Jean boldly tries to put his arm around her waist and kiss her. She slaps his face.*) How dare you?

JEAN. Are you serious or joking?

JULIE. Serious.

JEAN. Then so was what just happened. You play games too seriously, and that's dangerous. Well, I'm tired of games. You'll excuse me if I get back to work. I haven't done the count's boots yet and it's long past midnight.

JULIE. Put the boots down!

JEAN. No! It's the work I have to do. I never agreed to be your playmate, and never will. It's beneath me.

JULIE. You're proud.

JEAN. In certain ways, but not in others.

JULIE. Have you ever been in love?

JEAN. We don't use that word, but I've been fond of many girls, and once I was sick because I couldn't have the one I wanted. That's right, sick, like those princes in the Arabian Nights—who couldn't eat or drink because of love.

JULIE. Who was she? (*Jean is silent.*) Who was she?

JEAN. You can't force me to tell you that.

JULIE. But if I ask you as an equal, as a—friend! Who was she?

JEAN. You!

JULIE (*sits*). How amusing . . .

JEAN. Yes, if you like! It was ridiculous!————You see, that was the story I didn't want to tell you earlier. Maybe I will now. Do you know how the world looks from down below?————Of course you don't. Neither do hawks and falcons, whose backs we can't see because they're usually soaring up there above us. I grew up in a shack with seven brothers and sisters and a pig, in the middle of a wasteland, where there wasn't a single tree. But from our window I could see the tops of apple trees above the wall of your father's garden. That was the Garden of Eden, guarded by angry angels with flaming swords. All the same, the other boys and I managed to find our way to the Tree of Life.————Now you think I'm contemptible, I suppose.

JULIE. Oh, all boys steal apples.

JEAN. You say that, but you think I'm contemptible anyway. Oh well! One day I went into the Garden of Eden with my mother, to weed the onion beds. Near the vegetable garden was a small Turkish pavilion in the shadow of jasmine bushes and overgrown with honeysuckle. I had no idea what it was used for, but I'd never seen such a beautiful building. People went in and came out again, and one day the door was left open. I sneaked close and saw walls

---

[6] **Attention! Je ne suis qu'un homme!** Watch out! I am only a man!

[7] **Don Juan . . . Joseph** Don Juan in Spanish legend is a seducer of women; in Genesis, Joseph resists the advances of Potiphar's wife.

covered with pictures of kings and emperors, and red curtains with fringes at the windows———now you know the place I mean. I———(*Breaks off a sprig of lilac and holds it in front of Miss Julie's nose.*)—I'd never been inside the manor house, never seen anything except the church—but this was more beautiful. From then on, no matter where my thoughts wandered, they returned—there. And gradually I got a longing to experience, just once, the full pleasure of—*enfin*,[8] I sneaked in, saw, and marveled! But then I heard someone coming! There was only one exit for ladies and gentlemen, but for me there was another, and I had no choice but to take it! (*Miss Julie, who has taken the lilac sprig, lets it fall on the table.*) Afterwards, I started running. I crashed through a raspberry bush, flew over a strawberry patch, and came up onto the rose terrace. There I caught sight of a pink dress and a pair of white stockings—it was you. I crawled under a pile of weeds, and I mean under—under thistles that pricked me and wet dirt that stank. And I looked at you as you walked among the roses, and I thought: If it's true that a thief can enter heaven and be with the angels, then why can't a farmhand's son here on God's earth enter the manor house garden and play with the Count's daughter?

JULIE (*romantically*). Do you think all poor children would have thought the way you did?

JEAN (*at first hesitant, then with conviction*). If *all* poor—yes,—of course. Of course!

JULIE. It must be terrible to be poor!

JEAN (*with exaggerated suffering*). Oh, Miss Julie! Oh!———A dog can lie on the Countess's sofa, a horse can have his nose patted by a young lady's hand, but a servant—(*Changing his tone.*)———oh, I know—now and then you find one with enough stuff in him to get ahead in the world, but how often?———Anyhow, do you know what I did then?———I jumped in the millstream with my clothes on, was pulled out, and got a beating. But the following Sunday, when my father and all the others went to my grandmother's, I arranged to stay home. I scrubbed myself with soap and water, put on my best clothes, and went to church so that I could see you! I saw you and returned home, determined to die. But I wanted to die beautifully and pleasantly, without pain. And then I remembered that it was dangerous to sleep under an elder bush. We had a big one, and it was in full flower. I plundered its treasures and bedded down under them in the oat bin. Have you ever noticed how smooth oats are?—and soft to the touch, like human skin . . . ! Well, I shut the lid and closed my eyes. I fell asleep and woke up feeling very sick. But I didn't die, as you can see. What was I after?———I don't know. There was no hope of winning you, of course.———You were a symbol of the hopelessness of ever rising out of the class in which I was born.

JULIE. You're a charming storyteller. Did you ever go to school?

JEAN. A bit, but I've read lots of novels and been to the theater often. And then I've listened to people like you talk—that's where I learned most.

JULIE. Do you listen to what we say?

JEAN. Naturally! And I've heard plenty, too, driving the carriage or rowing the boat. Once I heard you and a friend . . .

JULIE. Oh?———What did you hear?

JEAN. I'd better not say. But I was surprised little. I couldn't imagine where you learned such words. Maybe at bottom there isn't such a great difference between people as we think.

JULIE. Shame on you! We don't act like you when we're engaged.

JEAN (*staring at her*). Is that true?———You don't have to play innocent with me, Miss . . .

JULIE. The man I gave my love to was a swine.

JEAN. That's what you all say—afterwards.

JULIE. All?

JEAN. I think so. I know I've heard that phrase before, on similar occasions.

JULIE. What occasions?

JEAN. Like the one I'm talking about. The last time . . .

JULIE (*rising*). Quiet! I don't want to hear any more!

JEAN. That's interesting—that's what *she* said, too. Well, if you'll excuse me, I'm going to bed.

JULIE (*gently*). To bed? On midsummer eve?

JEAN. Yes! Dancing with the rabble out there doesn't amuse me much.

JULIE. Get the key to the boat and row me out on the lake. I want to see the sun come up.

JEAN. Is that wise?

JULIE. Are you worried about your reputation?

JEAN. Why not? Why should I risk looking ridiculous and getting fired without a reference, just when I'm trying to establish myself. Besides, I think I owe something to Kristine.

JULIE. So, now it's Kristine . . .

JEAN. Yes, but you, too.———Take my advice, go up and go to bed!

JULIE. Am I to obey you?

JEAN. Just this once—for your own good! Please! It's very late. Drowsiness makes people giddy and liable to lose their heads! Go to bed! Besides—unless I'm mistaken—I hear the others coming to look for me. And if they find us together, you'll be lost!

(*The Chorus approaches, singing.*)

The swineherd found his true love
a pretty girl so fair,
The swineherd found his true love
but let the girl beware.

For then he saw the princess
the princess on the golden hill,

[8]**enfin** finally

but then saw the princess,
so much fairer still.

So the swineherd and the princess
they danced the whole night through,
and he forgot his first love,
to her he was untrue.

And when the long night ended,
and in the light of day, of day,
the dancing too was ended,
and the princess could not stay.

Then the swineherd lost his true love,
and the princess grieves him still,
and never more she'll wander
from atop the golden hill.

JULIE. I know all these people and I love them, just as they love me. Let them come in and you'll see.

JEAN. No, Miss Julie, they don't love you. They take your food, but they spit on it! Believe me! Listen to them, listen to what they're singing!———No, don't listen to them!

JULIE (*listening*). What are they singing?

JEAN. It's a dirty song! About you and me!

JULIE. Disgusting! Oh! How deceitful!———

JEAN. The rabble is always cowardly! And in a battle like this, you don't fight; you can only run away!

JULIE. Run away? But where? We can't go out—or into Kristine's room.

JEAN. True. But there's my room. Necessity knows no rules. Besides, you can trust me. I'm your friend and I respect you.

JULIE. But suppose—suppose they look for you in there?

JEAN. I'll bolt the door, and if anyone tries to break in, I'll shoot!—Come! (*On his knees.*) Come!

JULIE (*urgently*). Promise me . . . ?

JEAN. I swear! (*Miss Julie runs off right. Jean hastens after her.*)

BALLET

(*Led by a fiddler, the servants and farm people enter, dressed festively, with flowers in their hats. On the table they place a small barrel of beer and a keg of schnapps, both garlanded. Glasses are brought out, and the drinking starts. A dance circle is formed and "The Swineherd and the Princess" is sung. When the dance is finished, everyone leaves, singing.*)

(*Miss Julie enters alone. She notices the mess in the kitchen, wrings her hands, then takes out her powder puff and powders her nose.*)

JEAN (*enters, agitated*). There, you see? And you heard them. We can't possibly stay here now, you know that.

JULIE. Yes, I know. But what can we do?

JEAN. Leave, travel, far away from here.

JULIE. Travel? Yes, but where?

JEAN. To Switzerland, to the Italian lakes. Have you ever been there?

JULIE. No. Is it beautiful?

JEAN. Oh, an eternal summer—oranges growing everywhere, laurel trees, always green . . .

JULIE. But what'll we do there?

JEAN. I'll open a hotel—with first-class service for first-class people.

JULIE. Hotel?

JEAN. That's the life, you know. Always new faces, new languages. No time to worry or be nervous. No hunting for something to do—there's always work to be done: bells ringing night and day, train whistles blowing, carriages coming and going, and all the while gold rolling into the till! That's the life!

JULIE. Yes, it sounds wonderful. But what'll I do?

JEAN. You'll be mistress of the house: the jewel in our crown! With your looks . . . and your manner—oh, success is guaranteed! It'll be wonderful! You'll sit in your office like a queen and push an electric button to set your slaves in motion. The guests will file past your throne and timidly lay their treasures before you.———You have no idea how people tremble when they get their bill.——— I'll salt the bills[9] and you'll sweeten them with your prettiest smile.———Let's get away from here———(*Takes a timetable out of his pocket.*)———Right away, on the next train!———We'll be in Malmö six-thirty tomorrow morning, Hamburg at eight-forty; from Frankfort to Basel will take a day, then on to Como by way of the St. Gotthard Tunnel, in, let's see, three days. Three days!

JULIE. That's all very well! But Jean—you must give me courage!———Tell me you love me! Put your arms around me!

JEAN (*hesitating*). I want to—but I don't dare. Not in this house, not again. I love you—never doubt that—you don't doubt it, do you, Miss Julie?

JULIE (*shy, very feminine*). "Miss!"———Call me Julie! There are no barriers between us anymore. Call me Julie!

JEAN (*tormented*). I can't. There'll always be barriers between us as long as we stay in this house.———There's the past and there's the Count. I've never met anyone I had such respect for.———When I see his gloves lying on a chair, I feel small.———When I hear that bell up there ring, I jump like a skittish horse.———And when I look at his boots standing there to stiff and proud, I feel like bowing! (*Kicking the boots.*) Superstitions and prejudices we learned as children—but they can easily be forgotten. If I can just get to another country, a republic, people will bow and scrape when they see my livery—*they'll bow* and scrape, you hear, not me! I wasn't born to cringe. I've got

---

[9]**salt the bills** inflate or pad the bills

stuff in me, I've got character, and if I can only grab onto that first branch, you watch me climb! I'm a servant today, but next year I'll own my own hotel. In ten years I'll have enough to retire. Then I'll go to Rumania and be decorated. I could—mind you I said *could*—end up a count!

JULIE. Wonderful, wonderful!

JEAN. Ah, in Rumania you just buy your title, and so you'll be a countess after all. My countess!

JULIE. But I don't care about that—that's what I'm putting behind me! Show me you love me, otherwise—otherwise, what am I?

JEAN. I'll show you a thousand times—afterwards! Not here! And whatever you do, no emotional outbursts, or we'll both be lost! We must think this through coolly, like sensible people. (*He takes out a cigar, snips the end, and lights it.*) You sit there, and I'll sit here. We'll talk as if nothing happened.

JULIE (*desperately*). Oh, my God! Have you no feelings?

JEAN. Me? No one has more feeling than I do, but I know how to control them.

JULIE. A little while ago you could kiss my shoe—and now!

JEAN (*harshly*). Yes, but that was before. Now we have other things to think about.

JULIE. Don't speak harshly to me!

JEAN. I'm not—just sensibly! We've already done one foolish thing, let's not have any more. The Count could return any minute, and by then we've got to decide what to do with our lives. What do you think of my plans for the future? Do you approve?

JULIE. They sound reasonable enough. I have only one question: For such a big undertaking you need capital—do you have it?

JEAN (*chewing on the cigar*). Me? Certainly! I have my professional expertise, my wide experience, and my knowledge of languages. That's capital enough, I should think!

JULIE. But that that won't even buy a train ticket.

JEAN. That's true. That's why I'm looking for a partner to advance me the money.

JULIE. Where will you find one quickly enough?

JEAN. That's up to you, if you want to come with me.

JULIE. But I can't; I have no money of my own. (*Pause.*)

JEAN. Then it's all off . . .

JULIE. And . . .

JEAN. Things stay as they are.

JULIE. Do you think I'm going to stay in this house as your lover? With all the servants pointing their fingers at me? Do you imagine I can face my father after this? No! Take me away from here, away from shame and dishonor———Oh, what have I done! My God, my God! (*She cries.*)

JEAN. Now, don't start that old song!———What have you done? The same as many others before you.

JULIE (*Screaming convulsively*). And now you think I'm contemptible!———I'm falling, I'm falling!

JEAN. Fall down to my level and I'll lift you up again.

JULIE. What terrible power drew me to you? The attraction of the weak to the strong? The falling to the rising? Or was it love? Was this love? Do you know what love is?

JEAN. Me? What do you take me for? You don't think this was my first time, do you?

JULIE. The things you say, the thoughts you think?

JEAN. That's the way I was taught, and that's the way I am! Now don't get excited and don't play the grand lady, because we're in the same boat now!———Come on, Julie, I'll pour you a glass of something special! (*He opens a drawer in the table, takes out a wine bottle, and fills two glasses already used.*)

JULIE. Where did you get that wine?

JEAN. From the cellar.

JULIE. My father's burgundy!

JEAN. That'll do for his son-in-law, won't it?

JULIE. And I drink beer! Beer!

JEAN. That only shows I have better taste.

JULIE. Thief!

JEAN. Planning to tell?

JULIE. Oh, oh! Accomplice of a common thief! Was I drunk? Have I been walking in a dream the whole evening? Midsummer eve! A time of innocent fun!

JEAN. Innocent, eh?

JULIE (*pacing back and forth*). Is there anyone on earth more miserable than I am at this moment?

JEAN. Why should you be? After such a conquest? Think of Kristine in there. Don't you think she has feelings, too?

JULIE. I thought so awhile ago, but not any more. No, a servant is a servant . . .

JEAN. And a whore is a whore!

JULIE (*on her knees, her hands clasped*). Oh, God in heaven, end my wretched life! Take me away from the filth I'm sinking into! Save me! Save me!

JEAN. I can't deny I feel sorry for you. When I lay in that onion bed and saw you in the rose garden, well . . . I'll be frank . . . I had the same dirty thoughts all boys have.

JULIE. And you wanted to die for me!

JEAN. In the oat bin? That was just talk.

JULIE. A lie, in other words!

JEAN (*beginning to feel sleepy*). More or less! I got the idea from a newspaper story about a chimney sweep who curled up in a firewood bin full of lilacs because he got a summons for not supporting his illegitimate child . . .

JULIE. So, that's what you're like . . .

JEAN. I had to think of something. And that's the kind of story women always go for.

JULIE. Swine!

JEAN. *Merde!*

JULIE. And now you've seen the hawk's back . . .

JEAN. Not exactly its *back* . . .

JULIE. And I was to be the first branch . . .

JEAN. But the branch was rotten . . .

JULIE. I was to be the sign on the hotel . . .

JEAN. And I the hotel . . .

JULIE. Sit at your desk, entice your customers, pad their bills . . .

JEAN. That I'd do myself . . .

JULIE. How can anyone be so thoroughly filthy?

JEAN. Better clean up then!

JULIE. You lackey, you menial, stand up, when I speak to you!

JEAN. Menial's strumpet, lackey's whore, shut up and get out of here! Who are you to lecture me on coarseness? None of my kind is ever as coarse as you were tonight. Do you think one of your maids would throw herself at a man the way you did? Have you ever seen any girl of my class offer herself like that? I've only seen it among animals and streetwalkers.

JULIE (crushed). You're right. Hit me, trample on me. I don't deserve any better. I'm worthless. But help me! If you see any way out of this, help me, Jean, please!

JEAN (more gently). I'd be lying if I didn't admit to a sense of triumph in all this, but do you think that a person like me would have dared even to look at someone like you if you hadn't invited it? I'm still amazed . . .

JULIE. And proud . . .

JEAN. Why not? Though I must say it was too easy to be really exciting.

JULIE. Go on, hit me, hit me harder!

JEAN (rising). No! Forgive me for what I've said! I don't hit a man when he's down, let alone a woman. I can't deny though, that I'm pleased to find out that what looked so dazzling to us from below was only tinsel, that the hawk's back was only gray, after all, that the lovely complexion was only powder, that those polished fingernails had black edges, and that a dirty handkerchief is still dirty, even if it smells of perfume . . . ! On the other hand, it hurts me to find out that what I was striving for wasn't finer, more substantial. It hurts me to see you sunk so low that you're inferior to your own cook. It hurts like watching flowers beaten down by autumn rains and turned into mud.

JULIE. You talk as if you were already above me.

JEAN. I am. You see, I could make you a countess, but you could never make me a count.

JULIE. But I'm the child of a count—something you could never be!

JEAN. That's true. But I could be the father of counts—if . . .

JULIE. But you're a thief. I'm not.

JEAN. There are worse things than being a thief! Besides, when I'm working in a house, I consider myself sort of a member of the family, like one of the children. And you don't call it stealing when a child snatches a berry off a full bush. (His passion is aroused again.) Miss Julie, you're a glorious woman, much too good for someone like me! You were drinking and you lost your head. Now you want to cover up your mistake by telling yourself that you love me! You don't. Maybe there was a physical attraction—but then your love is no better than mine.———I could never be satisfied to be no more than an animal to you, and I could never arouse real love in you.

JULIE. Are you sure of that?

JEAN. You're suggesting it's possible———Oh, I could fall in love with you, no doubt about it. You're beautiful, you're refined———(approaching and taking her hand)———cultured, lovable when you want to be, and once you start a fire in a man, it never goes out. (Putting his arm around her waist.) You're like hot, spicy wine, and one kiss from you . . . (He tries to lead her out, but she slowly frees herself.)

JULIE. Let me go?———You'll never win me like that.

JEAN. How then?———Not like that? Not with caresses and pretty speeches. Not with plans about the future or rescue from disgrace! How then?

JULIE. How? How? I don't know!—I have no idea!—I detest you as I detest rats, but I can't escape from you.

JEAN. Escape with me!

JULIE (pulling herself together). Escape? Yes, we must escape!———But I'm so tired. Give me a glass of wine? (Jeans pours the wine. She looks at her watch.) But we must talk first. We still have a little time. (She drains the glass, then holds it out for more.)

JEAN. Don't drink so fast. It'll go to your head.

JULIE. What does it matter?

JEAN. What does it matter? It's vulgar to get drunk! What did you want to tell me?

JULIE. We must escape! But first we must talk, I mean I must talk. You've done all the talking up to now. You told about your life, now I want to tell about mine, so we'll know all about each other before we go off together.

JEAN. Just a minute! Forgive me! If you don't want to regret it afterwards, you'd better think twice before revealing any secrets about yourself.

JULIE. Aren't you my friend?

JEAN. Yes, sometimes! But don't rely on me.

JULIE. You're only saying that.———Besides, everyone already knows my secrets.———You see, my mother was a commoner—very humble background. She was brought up believing in social equality, women's rights, and all that. The idea of marriage repelled her. So, when my father proposed, she replied that she would never become his wife, but he could be her lover. He insisted that he didn't want the woman he loved to be less respected than he. But his passion ruled him, and when she explained that the world's respect meant nothing to her, he accepted her conditions.

But now his friends avoided him and his life was restricted to taking care of the estate, which couldn't satisfy him. I came into the world—against my mother's wishes, as far as I can understand. She wanted to bring me up as a child of nature, and, what's more, to learn everything a boy had to learn, so that I might be an example of how a woman can be as good as a man. I had to wear boy's clothes and learn to take care of horses, but I was never allowed in the cowshed. I had to groom and harness the horses and go hunting—and even had to watch them slaughter animals—that was disgusting! On the estate men were put on women's jobs and women on men's jobs—with the result that the property became run down and we became the laughingstock of the district. Finally, my father must have awakened from his trance because he rebelled and changed everything his way. My parents were then married quietly. Mother became ill—I don't know what illness it was—but she often had convulsions, hid in the attic and in the garden, and sometimes stayed out all night. Then came the great fire, which you've heard about. The house, the stables, and the cowshed all burned down, under very curious circumstances, suggesting arson, because the accident happened the day after the insurance had expired. The quarterly premium my father sent in was delayed because of a messenger's carelessness and didn't arrive in time. (*She fills her glass and drinks.*)

JEAN. Don't drink any more!

JULIE. Oh, what does it matter.———We were left penniless and had to sleep in the carriages. My father had no idea where to find money to rebuild the house because he had so slighted his old friends that they had forgotten him. Then my mother suggested that he borrow from a childhood friend of hers, a brick manufacturer who lived nearby. Father got the loan without having to pay interest, which surprised him. And that's how the estate was rebuilt.———(*Drinks again.*) Do you know who started the fire?

JEAN. The Countess, your mother.

JULIE. Do you know who the brick manufacturer was?

JEAN. Your mother's lover?

JULIE. Do you know whose money it was?

JEAN. Wait a moment—no, I don't.

JULIE. It was my mother's.

JEAN. You mean the Count's, unless they didn't sign an agreement when they were married.

JULIE. They didn't.—My mother had a small inheritance which she didn't want under my father's control, so she entrusted it to her—friend.

JEAN. Who stole it!

JULIE. Exactly! He kept it.———All this my father found out, but he couldn't bring it to court, couldn't repay his wife's lover, couldn't prove it was his wife's money! It was my mother's revenge for being forced into marriage against her will. It nearly drove him to suicide—there was a rumor that he tried with a pistol, but failed. So, he managed to live through it and my mother had to suffer for what she'd done. You can imagine that those were a terrible five years for me. I loved my father, but I sided with my mother because I didn't know the circumstances. I learned from her to hate men—you've heard how she hated the whole male sex—and I swore to her I'd never be a slave to any man.

JEAN. But you got engaged to that lawyer.

JULIE. In order to make him my slave.

JEAN. And he wasn't willing?

JULIE. He was willing, all right, but I wouldn't let him. I got tired of him.

JEAN. I saw it—out near the stable.

JULIE. What did you see?

JEAN. I saw—how he broke off the engagement.

JULIE. That's a lie! I was the one who broke it off. Has he said that he did? That swine . . .

JEAN. He was no swine, I'm sure. So, you hate men, Miss Julie?

JULIE. Yes!———Most of the time! But sometimes—when the weakness comes, when passion burns! Oh, God, will the fire never die out?

JEAN. Do you hate me, too?

JULIE. Immeasurably! I'd like to have you put to death, like an animal . . .

JEAN. I see—the penalty for bestiality—the woman gets two years at hard labor and the animal is put to death. Right?

JULIE. Exactly!

JEAN. But there's no prosecutor here—and no animal. So, what'll we do?

JULIE. Go away!

JEAN. To torment each other to death?

JULIE. No! To be happy for—two days, a week, as long as we can be happy, and then—die . . .

JEAN. Die? That's stupid! It's better to open a hotel!

JULIE (*without listening*). ———on the shore of Lake Como, where the sun always shines, where the laurels are green at Christmas and the oranges glow.

JEAN. Lake Como is a rainy hole, and I never saw any oranges outside the stores. But tourists are attracted there because there are plenty of villas to be rented out to lovers, and that's a profitable business.———Do you know why? Because they sign a lease for six months—and then leave after three weeks!

JULIE (*naively*). Why after three weeks?

JEAN. They quarrel, of course! But they still have to pay the rent in full! And so you rent the villas out again. And that's the way it goes, time after time. There's never a shortage of love—even if it doesn't last long!

JULIE. You don't want to die with me?

JEAN. I don't want to die at all! For one thing, I like living, and for another, I think suicide is a crime against the Providence which gave us life.

JULIE. You believe in God? *You?*

JEAN. Of course I do. And I go to church every other Sunday.———To be honest, I'm tired of all this, and I'm going to bed.

JULIE. Are you? And do you think I can let it go at that? A man owes something to the woman he's shamed.

JEAN (*taking out his purse and throwing a silver coin on the table*). Here! I don't like owing anything to anybody.

JULIE (*pretending not to notice the insult*). Do you know what the law states . . .

JEAN. Unfortunately the law doesn't state any punishment for the woman who seduces a man!

JULIE (*as before*). Do you see any way out but to leave, get married, and then separate?

JEAN. Suppose I refuse such a *mésalliance*?[10]

JULIE. *Mésalliance* . . .

JEAN. Yes, for me! You see, I come from better stock than you. There's no arsonist in my family.

JULIE. How do you know?

JEAN. You can't prove otherwise. We don't keep charts on our ancestors—there's just the police records! But I've read about your family. Do you know who the founder was? He was a miller who let the king sleep with his wife one night during the Danish War. I don't have any noble ancestors like that. I don't have any noble ancestors at all, but I could become one myself.

JULIE. This is what I get for opening my heart to someone unworthy, for giving my family's honor . . .

JEAN. Dishonor!———Well, I told you so: When people drink, they talk, and talk is dangerous!

JULIE. Oh, how I regret it!———How I regret it!———If you at least loved me.

JEAN. For the last time———what do you want? Shall I cry; shall I jump over your riding crop? Shall I kiss you and lure you off to Lake Como for three weeks, and then God knows what . . . ? What shall I do? What do you want? This is getting painfully embarrassing! But that's what happens when you stick your nose in women's business. Miss Julie! I see that you're unhappy. I know you're suffering, but I can't understand you. We don't have such romantic ideas; there's not this kind of hate between us. Love is a game we play when we get time off from work, but we don't have all day and night, like you. I think you're sick, really sick. Your mother was crazy, and her ideas have poisoned your life.

JULIE. Be kind to me. At least now you're talking like a human being.

JEAN. Be human yourself, then. You spit on me, and you won't let me wipe myself off———

JULIE. Help me! Help me! Just tell me what to do, where to go!

JEAN. In God's name, if I only knew myself!

JULIE. I've been crazy, out of my mind, but isn't there any way out?

JEAN. Stay here and keep calm! No one knows anything!

JULIE. Impossible! The others know and Kristine knows.

JEAN. No, they don't, and they'd never believe a thing like that!

JULIE (*hesitantly*). But—it could happen again!

JEAN. That's true!

JULIE. And then?

JEAN (*frightened*). Then?———Why didn't I think about that? Yes, there is only one thing to do—get away from here! Right away! I can't come with you, then we'd be finished, so you'll have to go alone—away—anywhere!

JULIE. Alone?———Where?———I can't do that!

JEAN. You must! And before the Count gets back! If you stay, you know what'll happen. Once you make a mistake like this, you want to continue because the damage has already been done. . . . Then you get bolder and bolder—until finally you're caught! So leave! Later you can write to the Count and confess everything—except that it was me! He'll never guess who it was, and he's not going to be eager to find out, anyway.

JULIE. I'll go if you come with me.

JEAN. Are you out of your head? Miss Julie runs away with her servant! In two days it would be in the newspapers, and that's something your father would never live through.

JULIE. I can't go and I can't stay! Help me! I'm so tired, so terribly tired.—Order me! Set me in motion—I can't think or act on my own . . .

JEAN. What miserable creatures you people are! You strut around with your noses in the air as if you were the lords of creation. All right, I'll order you. Go upstairs and get dressed! Get some money for the trip, and then come back down!

JULIE (*in a half-whisper*). Come up with me!

JEAN. To your room?———Now you're crazy again! (*Hesitates for a moment.*) No! Go, at once! (*Takes her hand to lead her out.*)

JULIE: (*as she leaves*). Speak kindly to me, Jean!

JEAN. An order always sounds unkind—now you know how it feels. (*Jean, alone, sighs with relief. He sits at the table, takes out a notebook and pencil, and begins adding up figures, counting aloud as he works. He continues in dumb show until Kristine enters, dressed for church. She is carrying a white tie and shirt front.*)

KRISTINE. Lord Jesus, what a mess! What have you been up to?

JEAN. Oh, Miss Julie dragged everybody in here. You mean you didn't hear anything? You must have been sleeping soundly.

KRISTINE. Like a log.

JEAN. And dressed for church already?

KRISTINE. Of course! You remember you promised to come with me to communion today!

JEAN. Oh, yes, that's right.———And you brought my things. Come on, then! (*He sits down. Kristine starts to put on his shirt front and tie. Pause. Jean begins sleepily.*) What's the gospel text for today?

KRISTINE. On St. John's Day?—the beheading of John the Baptist, I should think!

JEAN. Ah, that'll be a long one, for sure.———Hey, you're choking me!———Oh, I'm sleepy, so sleepy!

KRISTINE. Yes, what have you been doing, up all night? Your face is absolutely green.

JEAN. I've been sitting here gabbing with Miss Julie.

---

[10]**mésalliance** misalliance or mismatch, especially regarding relative social status

KRISTINE. She has no idea what's proper, that one! (*Pause.*)

JEAN. You know, Kristine . . .

KRISTINE. What?

JEAN. It's really strange when you think about it.———Her!

KRISTINE. What's so strange?

JEAN. Everything! (*Pause.*)

KRISTINE (*looking at the half-empty glasses standing on the table*). Have you been drinking together, too?

JEAN. Yes.

KRISTINE. Shame on you!———Look me in the eye!

JEAN. Well?

KRISTINE. Is it possible? Is it possible?

JEAN (*thinking it over for a moment*). Yes, it is.

KRISTINE. Ugh! I never would have believed it! No, shame on you, shame!

JEAN. You're not jealous of her, are you?

KRISTINE. No, not of her! If it had been Clara or Sofie I'd have scratched your eyes out!———I don't know why, but that's the way I feel.———Oh, it's disgusting!

JEAN. Are you angry at her, then?

KRISTINE. No, at you! That was an awful thing to do, awful! Poor girl!———No, I don't care who knows it—I won't stay in a house where we can't respect the people we work for.

JEAN. Why should we respect them?

KRISTINE. You're so clever, you tell me! Do you want to wait on people who can't behave decently? Do you? You disgrace yourself that way, if you ask me.

JEAN. But it's a comfort to know they aren't any better than us.

KRISTINE. Not for me. If they're no better, what do we have to strive for to better ourselves.———And think of the Count! Think of him! As if he hasn't had enough misery in his life! Lord Jesus! No, I won't stay in this house any longer!———And it had to be with someone like you! If it had been that lawyer, if it had been a real gentleman . . .

JEAN. What do you mean?

KRISTINE. Oh, you're all right for what you are, but there are men and gentlemen, after all!—No, this business with Miss Julie I can never forget. She was so proud, so arrogant with men, you wouldn't have believed she could just go and give herself—and to someone like you. And she was going to have poor Diana shot for running after the gatekeepers' mutt———Yes, I'm giving my notice, I mean it—I won't stay here any longer. On the twenty-fourth of October, I leave!

JEAN. And then?

KRISTINE. Well, since the subject has come up, it's about time you looked around for something since we're going to get married, in any case.

JEAN. Where am I going to look? I couldn't find a job like this if I was married.

KRISTINE. No, that's true. But you can find work as a porter or as a caretaker in some government office. The state doesn't pay much, I know, but it's secure, and there's a pension for the wife and children . . .

JEAN (*grimacing*). That's all very well, but it's a bit early for me to think about dying for a wife and children. My ambitions are a little higher than that.

KRISTINE. Your ambitions, yes! Well, you have obligations, too! Think about them!

JEAN. Don't start nagging me about obligations. I know what I have to do! (*Listening for something outside.*) Besides, this is something we have plenty of time to think over. Go and get ready for church.

KRISTINE. Who's that walking around up there?

JEAN. I don't know, unless it's Clara.

KRISTINE (*going*). You don't suppose it's the Count, who came home without us hearing him?

JEAN (*frightened*). The Count? No, I don't think so. He'd have rung.

KRISTINE (*going*). Well, God help us! I've never seen anything like this before. (*The sun has risen and shines through the treetops in the park. The light shifts gradually until it slants in through the windows. Jean goes to the door and signals. Miss Julie enters, dressed in travel clothes and carrying a small bird cage, covered with a cloth, which she places on a chair.*)

JULIE. I'm ready now.

JEAN. Shh! Kristine is awake.

JULIE (*very nervous during the following*). Does she suspect something?

JEAN. She doesn't know anything. But my God, you look awful!

JULIE. Why? How do I look?

JEAN. You're pale as a ghost and—excuse me, but your face is dirty.

JULIE. Let me wash up then.—(*She goes to the basin and washes her hands and face.*) Give me a towel!—Oh—the sun's coming up.

JEAN. Then the goblins will disappear.

JULIE. Yes, there must have been goblins out last night!———Jean, listen, come with me! I have some money now.

JEAN (*hesitantly*). Enough?

JULIE. Enough to start with. Come with me! I just can't travel alone on a day like this—midsummer day on a stuffy train—jammed in among crowds of people staring at me. Eternal delays at every station, while I'd wish I had wings. No, I can't, I can't! And then there'll be memories, memories of midsummer days when I was little. The church—decorated with birch leaves and lilacs; dinner at the big table with relatives and friends, the afternoons in the park, dancing, music, flowers, and games. Oh, no matter how far we travel, the memories will follow in the baggage car, with remorse and guilt!

JEAN. I'll go with you—but right away, before it's too late. Right this minute!

JULIE. Get dressed, then! (*Picking up the bird cage.*)

JEAN. But no baggage! It would give us away!

JULIE. No, nothing! Only what we can have in the compartment with us.

JEAN (*has taken his hat*). What've you got there? What is it?

JULIE. It's only my greenfinch. I couldn't leave her behind.

JEAN. What? Bring a bird cage with us? You're out of your head! Put it down!

JULIE. It's the only thing I'm taking from my home—the only living being that loves me, since Diana was unfaithful! Don't be cruel! Let me take her!

JEAN. Put the cage down, I said!———And don't talk so loudly—Kristine will hear us!

JULIE. No, I won't leave her in the hands of strangers! I'd rather you killed her.

JEAN. Bring the thing here, then, I'll cut its head off!

JULIE. Oh! But don't hurt her! Don't . . . no, I can't.

JEAN. Bring it here! I can!

JULIE (*taking the bird out of the cage and kissing it*). Oh, my little Serena, must you die and leave your mistress?

JEAN. Please don't make a scene! Your whole future is at stake! Hurry up! (*He snatches the bird from her, carries it over to the chopping block, and picks up a meat cleaver. Miss Julie turns away.*) You should have learned how to slaughter chickens instead of how to fire pistols. (*He chops off the bird's head.*) Then you wouldn't feel faint at the sight of blood.

JULIE (*screaming*). Kill me, too! Kill me! You, who can slaughter an innocent animal without blinking an eye! Oh, how I hate, how I detest you! There's blood between us now! I curse the moment I set eyes on you! I curse the moment I was conceived in my mother's womb!

JEAN. What good does cursing do? Let's go!

JULIE (*approaching the chopping block, as if drawn against her will*). No, I don't want to go yet. I can't . . . until I see . . . Shh! I hear a carriage———(*She listens, but her eyes never leave the cleaver and the chopping block.*) Do you think I can't stand the sight of blood? You think I'm so weak . . . Oh—I'd like to see your blood and see your brains on a chopping block!———I'd like to see your whole sex swimming in a sea of blood, like my little bird . . . I think I could drink from your skull! I'd like to bathe my feet in your open chest and eat your heart roasted whole!——— You think I'm weak. You think I love you because my womb craved your seed. You think I want to carry your spawn under my heart and nourish it with my blood— bear your child and take your name! By the way, what is your family name? I've never heard it.—Do you have one? I was to be Mrs. Bootblack—or Madame Pigsty.———You dog, who wears my collar, you lackey, who bears my coat of arms on your buttons—do I have to share you with my cook, compete with my own servant? Oh! Oh! Oh!——— You think I'm a coward who wants to run away! No, now I'm staying—and let the storm break! My father will come home . . . to find his desk broken open . . . and his money gone! Then he'll ring—that bell . . . twice for his valet—and then he'll send for the police . . . and then I'll tell everything! Everything! Oh, what a relief it'll be to have it all end—if only it will end!———And then he'll have a stroke and die . . . That'll be the end of all of us— and there'll be peace . . . quiet . . . eternal rest!———And then our coat of arms will be broken against his coffin—

the family title extinct—but the valet's line will go on in an orphanage . . . win laurels in the gutter, and end in jail!

JEAN. There's the blue blood talking! Very good, Miss Julie! Just don't let that miller out of the closet! (*Kristine enters, dressed for church, with a psalmbook in her hand.*)

JULIE (*rushing to Kristine and falling into her arms, as if seeking protection*). Help me, Kristine! Help me against this man!

KRISTINE (*unmoved and cold*). What a fine way to behave on a Sunday morning! (*Sees the chopping block.*) And look at this mess!———What does all this mean? Why all this screaming and carrying on?

JULIE. Kristine! You're a woman and my friend! Beware of this swine!

JEAN (*uncomfortable*). While you ladies discuss this, I'll go in and shave. (*Slips off right.*)

JULIE. You must listen to me so you'll understand!

KRISTINE. No, I could never understand such disgusting behavior! Where are you off to in your traveling clothes?——— —And he had his hat on.———Well?———Well?———

JULIE. Listen to me, Kristine! Listen, and I'll tell you everything———

KRISTINE. I don't want to hear it . . .

JULIE. But you must listen to me . . .

KRISTINE. What about? If it's about this silliness with Jean, I'm not interested, because it's none of my business. But if you're thinking of tricking him into running out, we'll soon put a stop to that!

JULIE (*extremely nervous*). Try to be calm now, Kristine, and listen to me! I can't stay here, and neither can Jean—so we must go away . . .

KRISTINE. Hm, hm!

JULIE (*brightening*). You see, I just had an idea———What if all three of us go—abroad—to Switzerland and start a hotel together?———I have money, you see—and Jean and I could run it—and I thought you, you could take care of the kitchen . . . Wouldn't that be wonderful? ———Say yes! And come with us, and then everything will be settled!———Oh, do say yes! (*Embracing Kristine and patting her warmly.*)

KRISTINE (*coolly, thoughtfully*). Hm, Hm!

JULIE (*presto tempo*).[11] You've never traveled, Kristine.——— You must get out and see the world. You can't imagine how much fun it is to travel by train—always new faces—new countries.———And when we get to Hamburg, we'll stop off at the zoo—you'll like that.———and then we'll go to the theater and the opera—and when we get to Munich, dear, there we have museums, with Rubens and Raphael, the great painters, as you know.———You've heard of Munich, where King Ludwig lived—the king who went mad.———And then we'll see his castles—they're still there and they're like castles in fairy tales.———And from there it isn't far to Switzerland—and the Alps.———Imagine—the Alps have snow on them even in the middle of

---

[11]**presto tempo** at a rapid pace

summer!————And oranges grow there and laurel trees that are green all year round————(*Jean can be seen in the wings right, sharpening his razor on a strop which he holds with his teeth and his left hand. He listen to the conversation with satisfaction, nodding now and then in approval. Miss Julie continues tempo prestissimo.*)[12] And then we'll start a hotel—and I'll be at the desk, while Jean greets the guests . . . does the shopping . . . writes letters.————You have no idea what a life it'll be—the train whistles blowing and the carriages arriving and the bells ringing in the rooms and down in the restaurant.————And I'll make out the bills—and I know how to salt them! . . . You'll never believe how timid travelers are when they have to pay their bills!————And you— you'll be in charge of the kitchen.————Naturally, you won't have to stand over the stove yourself.————And since you're going to be seen by people, you'll have to wear beautiful clothes.—And you, with your looks—no, I'm not flattering you—one fine day you'll grab yourself a husband!————You'll see!————A rich Englishman— they're so easy to————(*Slowing down.*)————catch—and then we'll get rich—and build ourselves a villa on Lake Como.————It's true it rains there a little now and then, but————(*Dully.*)————the sun has to shine sometimes— although it looks dark—and then . . . of course we could always come back home again————(Pause.)————here— or somewhere else————

KRISTINE. Listen, Miss Julie, do you believe all this?

JULIE (*crushed*). Do I believe it?

KRISTINE. Yes!

JULIE (*wearily*). I don't know. I don't believe in anything anymore. (*She sinks down on the bench and cradles her head in her arms on the table.*) Nothing! Nothing at all!

KRISTINE (*turning right to where Jean is standing*). So, you thought you'd run out!

JEAN (*embarrassed; puts the razor on the table*). Run out? That's no way to put it. You hear Miss Julie's plan, and even if she is tired after being up all night, it's still a practical plan.

KRISTINE. Now you listen to me! Did you think I'd work as a cook for that . . .

JEAN (*sharply*). You watch what you say in front of your mistress! Do you understand?

KRISTINE. Mistress!

JEAN. Yes!

KRISTINE. Listen to him! Listen to him!

JEAN. Yes, you listen! It'd do you good to listen more and talk less! Miss Julie is your mistress. If you despise her, you have to despise yourself for the same reason!

KRISTINE. I've always had enough self-respect————

JEAN. ————to be able to despise other people!

KRISTINE. ————to stop me from doing anything that's beneath me. You can't say that the Count's cook has been up to something with the groom or the swineherd! Can you?

JEAN. No, you were lucky enough to get hold of a gentleman!

KRISTINE. Yes, a gentleman who sells the Count's oats from the stable.

JEAN. You should talk—taking a commission from the grocer and bribes from the butcher.

KRISTINE. What?

JEAN. And you say you can't respect your employers any longer. You, you, you!

KRISTINE. Are you coming to church with me, now? You could use a good sermon after your fine deed!

JEAN. No, I'm not going to church today. You'll have to go alone and confess what you've been up to.

KRISTINE. Yes, I'll do that, and I'll bring back enough forgiveness for you, too. The Savior suffered and died on the Cross for all our sins, and if we go to Him with faith and a penitent heart, He takes all our sins on Himself.

JEAN. Even grocery sins?

JULIE. And do you believe that, Kristine?

KRISTINE. It's my living faith, as sure as I stand here. It's the faith I learned as a child, Miss Julie, and kept ever since. "Where sin abounded, grace did much more abound!"

JULIE. Oh, if I only had your faith. If only . . .

KRISTINE. Well, you see, we can't have it without God's special grace, and that isn't given to everyone————

JULIE. Who is it given to then?

KRISTINE. That's the great secret of the workings of grace, Miss Julie, and God is no respecter of persons, for the last shall be the first . . .

JULIE. Then He does respect the last.

KRISTINE (*continuing*). . . . and it is easier for a camel to go through the eye of a needle, than for a rich man to enter the Kingdom of God. That's how it is, Miss Julie! Anyhow, I'm going now—alone, and on the way I'm going to tell the groom not to let any horses out, in case anyone wants to leave before the Count gets back!————Goodbye! (*Leaves.*)

JEAN. What a witch!————And all this because of a greenfinch!————

JULIE (*dully*). Never mind the greenfinch!————Can you see any way out of this? Any end to it?

JEAN (*thinking*). No!

JULIE. What would you do in my place?

JEAN. In your place? Let's see—as a person of position, as a woman who had—fallen. I don't know—wait, now I know.

JULIE (*taking the razor and making a gesture*). You mean like this?

JEAN. Yes! But—understand—I wouldn't do it! That's the difference between us!

[12]*tempo prestissimo* at a very rapid pace

JULIE. Because you're a man and I'm a woman! What sort of difference is that?

JEAN. The usual difference—between a man and a woman.

JULIE (*with the razor in her hand*). I want to, but I can't——— My father couldn't either, the time he should have done it.

JEAN. No, he shouldn't have! He had to revenge himself first.

JULIE. And now my mother is revenged again, through me.

JEAN. Didn't you ever love your father, Miss Julie?

JULIE. Oh yes, deeply, but I've hated him, too. I must have done so without realizing it! It was he who brought me up to despise my own sex, making me half woman, half man. Whose fault is what's happened? My father's, my mother's, my own? My own? I don't have anything that's my own. I don't have a single thought that I didn't get from my father, not an emotion that I didn't get from my mother, and this last idea—that all people are equal—I got that from my fiancé.———That's why I called him a swine! How can it be my fault? Shall I let Jesus take on the blame, the way Kristine does?———No, I'm too proud to do that and too sensible—thanks to my father's teachings.———And as for someone rich not going to heaven, that's a lie. But Kristine won't get in—how will she explain the money she has in the savings bank? Whose fault is it?———What does it matter whose fault it is? I'm still the one who has to bear the blame, face the consequences . . .

JEAN. Yes, but . . . (*The bell rings sharply twice. Miss Julie jumps up. Jean changes his coat.*) The Count is back! Do you suppose Kristine—(*He goes to the speaking tube, taps the lid, and listens.*)

JULIE. He's been to his desk!

JEAN. It's Jean, sir! (*Listening; the audience cannot hear the Count's voice.*) Yes, sir! (*Listening.*) Yes, sir! Right away! (*Listening.*) At once, sir! (*Listening.*) I see, in half an hour!

JULIE (*desperately frightened*). What did he say? Dear Lord, what did he say?

JEAN. He wants his boots and his coffee in half an hour.

JULIE. So, in half an hour! Oh, I'm so tired. I'm not able to do anything. I can't repent, can't run away, can't stay, can't live—can't die! Help me now! Order me, and I'll obey like a dog! Do me this last service, save my honor, save his name! You know what I *should* do, but don't have the will to . . . You will it, you order me to do it!

JEAN. I don't know why———but now I can't either——— I don't understand.———It's as if this coat made it impossible for me to order you to do anything.———And

now, since the Count spoke to me—I—I can't really explain it—but—ah, it's the damn lackey in me!———I think if the count came down here now—and ordered me to cut my throat, I'd do it on the spot.

JULIE. Then pretend you're he, and I'm you!———You gave such a good performance before when you knelt at my feet.—You were a real nobleman.———Or—have you ever seen a hypnotist in the theater? (*Jean nods.*) He says to his subject: "Take the broom," and he takes it. He says: "Sweep," and he sweeps———

JEAN. But the subject has to be asleep.

JULIE (*ecstatically*). I'm already asleep.———The whole room is like smoke around me . . . and you look like an iron stove . . . shaped like a man in black, with a tall hat—and your eyes glow like coals when the fire is dying—and your face is a white patch, like ashes——— (*The sunlight has reached the floor and now shines on Jean.*)—it's so warm and good———(*She rubs her hands as if warming them before a fire.*)———and bright—and so peaceful!

JEAN (*taking the razor and putting it in her hand*). Here's the broom! Go now while it's bright—out to the barn—and . . . (*Whispers in her ear.*)

JULIE (*awake*). Thank you. I'm going now to rest! But just tell me—that those who are first can also receive the gift of grace. Say it, even if you don't believe it.

JEAN. The first? No, I can't———But wait—Miss Julie— now I know! You're no longer among the first—you're now among—the last!

JULIE. That's true.———I'm among the very last. I'm the last one of all! Oh!———But now I can't go!———Tell me once more to go!

JEAN. No, now I can't either! I can't!

JULIE. And the first shall be the last!

JEAN. Don't think, don't think! You're taking all my strength from me, making me a coward.———What was that? I thought the bell moved!———No! Shall we stuff paper in it?———To be so afraid of a bell!———But it isn't just a bell.———There's someone behind it—a hand sets it in motion—and something else sets the hand in motion.———Maybe if you cover your ears—cover your ears! But then it rings even louder! rings until someone answers.———And then it's too late! And then the police come—and—then———(*The bell rings twice loudly. Jean flinches, then straightens up.*) It's horrible! But there's no other way!———Go! (*Miss Julie walks firmly out through the door.*)

THE CHERRY ORCHARD

ANTON CHEKHOV

ANTON CHEKHOV (1860–1904)

Few other playwrights have achieved such an exalted reputation on the basis of so few plays. Other than a number of short plays and farces (e.g., *The Marriage Proposal* and *The Boor*), Chekhov's place in the pantheon of the world's finest dramatists rests on four principal works: *The Seagull* (1895), *Uncle Vanya* (1899), *The Three Sisters* (1901), and *The Cherry Orchard* (1903). Perhaps more than his contemporaries in realism, Ibsen and Strindberg, Chekhov has inspired subsequent generations of writers who attempt to capture the ease with which he captures the day-to-day drama of life in all its simplicity. Tennessee Williams, William Inge, Samuel Beckett, and Wendy Wasserstein, to name but a few, are among the many playwrights who have acknowledged Chekhov as their mentor. Even Bernard Shaw attempted to write "a fantasia in the Russian manner" (*Heartbreak House*, 1918) and produced the kind of play Chekhov might have written were he Ibsen.

The son of a despotic storekeeper from the seaport village of Taganrog, Chekhov wrote to support himself while studying medicine at the University of Moscow. He wrote superb short stories and "vaudevilles," many based on his observations as a doctor. His daily rounds permitted him to see firsthand the rhythms of life: birth, death, recovery, lingering illness, despair, joy, uncertainty, and faith. These became the subjects of his stories and particularly his dramatic masterpieces. His own life was marked by many of these universal difficulties. His first attempts at serious drama were rejected, largely because they were misunderstood. He was chronically ill and spent his last years in the warm-weather city of Yalta, struggling against the tuberculosis that eventually killed him in 1904. (He did not see his plays performed successfully until Stanislavsky and the Moscow Art Theater toured the Crimea in 1900.) And like many of his characters, he was victimized by unrequited love. In 1890 he trekked to the Sakhalin gulag to study penal conditions, motivated in part by his immense humanitarianism and in part to forget the woman who spurned him. In 1901 he married a leading actress of the MAT, Olga Knipper, only to die three years later. Despite the disappointments that plagued him, he remained a lover of humanity, however imperfect. In *The Seagull*, Nina perhaps comes closer than any of his characters to articulating Chekhov's credo: "What matters most for us, whether we're writers or actors, isn't fame or glamour, or any of the things I used to dream of. What matters most is knowing how to endure, knowing how to bear your cross and still have faith. I have faith now and I can stand my suffering. . . I am not afraid of life."

Chekhov's distinctive techniques have been discussed in conjunction with the rise of realistic drama. His use of the anticlimax, his focus on a number of individuals rather than a central protagonist, and his depiction of trivial actions and seemingly inconsequential exchanges among his characters are trademarks of his dramaturgy. Perhaps the most innovative aspect of the four great seriocomic dramas, however, is the use of the parallel monologue. His subtle plots are structured around a series of shared monologues in which characters voice their innermost desires, fears, and delusions. In this sense he is among the foremost psychological realists. But in these ongoing monologues, which are interspersed with those of the other characters, there is a failure to communicate. Chekhov depicts individuals trapped in an isolated universe in a manner that anticipates the work of the absurdists in the mid–twentieth century.

Unfortunately, Chekhov's plays are misinterpreted, and even a source of embarrassment among the Russian people. Too often they are presented as exercises in gloomy melancholy, largely because the monologues are rendered as angst-ridden laments by actors who take Chekhov's description of his plays as showing too literally "all the grayness of everyday life." Chekhov and Stanislavsky clashed over the MAT's overly somber treatment of his plays, which the writer believed turned his characters into pathetic whiners. For Chekhov, the plays were comedies, albeit serious ones, in which his characters (among whom there are no villains) are like so many people in life: destined to fail, partly because of the inexorable march of time, mostly because of the folly of their misguided aspirations.

Prior to Chekhov, the theater had faced neither characters such as these nor the unflinching realism in which their predicaments were handled. Fortunately, his friend and literary colleague Count Leo Tolstoy, Russia's leading novelist, accurately predicted his legacy: "It is possible that in the future, perhaps a hundred years hence, people will be amazed at what they find in Chekhov about the inner workings of the human soul."

THE CHERRY ORCHARD (1904)

The Breaking String (Maurice Valency, 1966) remains among the finest studies of Chekhov's dramaturgy. The title is taken from a stage direction found in act 2 of *The Cherry Orchard:*

> All sit lost in thought. The silence is broken only by the subdued muttering of Firs. Suddenly a distant sound is heard, as if from the sky, like the sound of a snapped string mournfully dying away.

It is fitting that Valency selects this moment because it crystallizes the whole of Chekhov's drama. Here we see a cluster of people on a remote Russian estate, so typical of the "ensemble pathos" that typifies Chekhov's style. Though they sit together, each is very much alone, "lost in thought." In the distance we see telegraph poles (the new technology), and beyond them the skyline of a growing city. Clearly the landscape of Mother Russia is changing, for it, too, is "mournfully dying away." Note that the play premiered in the year of the first of two great revolutions that transformed Russia between 1903 and 1917. Significantly, old Firs is a link to the 1862 revolution that overthrew feudalism. Though Chekhov was not a political writer in the manner of Ibsen or Shaw, *The Cherry Orchard* resonates with the social tensions of its time. The orchard itself, which is being chopped down as the final curtain falls, is emblematic of the outmoded aristocratic order.

Whatever its social relevance in 1904, the play, like each of Chekhov's major works, transcends the particulars of time and place and remains a universal study of the human dilemma, even a century after its composition. *The Cherry Orchard* is a four-act study of frustrated human aspirations, the dominant theme in each of the playwright's four masterpieces. His characters consistently demonstrate an uncanny ability to desire most that which they are least likely to obtain, and they do little to help themselves realize their dreams. Lopakhin is perhaps the most notable exception to this Chekhovian law. While he does indeed attain the estate and the revered orchard upon which his ancestors had toiled, he never quite gets around to marrying Varya, the object of his affection.

As detached observers, we see the absurdity of his characters' futile quests for the unachievable. Unlike the similarly delusional Don Quixote, who also chased impossible dreams, Chekhov's characters are trapped by their own inertia (and folly) as much as any external force. Thus Chekhov's plays are simultaneously amusing and pathetic, even nearly tragic. Real lives are "being smashed up" (to use Chekhov's own phrase), but there is invariably something oddly absurd, even silly, about the characters' dilemmas. Evidence of such folly abounds throughout *The Cherry Orchard:*

- Madame Ranevskaya desperately wants to retain her estate, but she fritters away her money, most notably by throwing a lavish ball even as the estate is being sold to the very man (Lopakhin) who has provided sound business advice that would permit her to salvage the cherry orchard. Of her mother's profligacy, Anya says, "Dear Mother, the same as ever. Hasn't changed a bit. If you let her, she'd give everything away."

- Gayev, her silly, sentimental brother, clings to the past while refusing to adjust to the present. He is too settled into a way of life in which "I keep thinking, racking my brains, I have many remedies, a great many, and that means, in effect, I have none."
- In contrast to Gayev, Trofimov expounds loftily about his visions for the future, but his credibility is undermined as we learn that he is little more than a professional student who will not venture out into the "real" world.
- Madame Ranevskaya's daughters, Anya and Varya, are ineffectual in their pursuit of love—the former too eager to involve herself in irresponsible relationships, the latter too bound by her work to feel genuine emotions.
- Even the parlormaid, Dunyasha, falls in love with the one person least likely to return her love: the self-absorbed valet, Yasha.
- And there is Yepikhodov, the bumbling bookkeeper whose very nickname epitomizes Chekhovian pathos: "Two-and-twenty Troubles."

It is perhaps natural for us to assign blame for the various predicaments of Chekhov's characters. In the tradition of melodrama, in which the family estate is lost, Lopakhin, the newly rich landowner, might be something of a villain. But here we are actually pleased that he gains the estate because it affirms his family's progress from serfdom to respectability. In Chekhov's world, however, there is truly only one villain: time. In the world of Sophocles or Ibsen, time abets change, reveals truths, and ultimately liberates (and frequently vindicates) protagonists from their ordeals. In time, Oedipus learns his identity and is thus liberated from the lie of his past; and in time, Nora Helmer (of *A Doll's House*) realizes that "I must stand on my own feet if I am to find out the truth about myself and my life." But in Chekhov's world, time only further entraps the characters because past, present, and future are virtually interchangeable. Note that Lopakhin opens the play with the question "What time is it"? And throughout the action, such as there is in this drama of "inaction," each character dwells on the inexorable passage of time, most notably in Uncle Gayev's famed speech to the bookcase in act 1. But perhaps the most telling reference to time is found in the play's finale. As the family leaves the estate for the last time, and as Firs settles onto the sofa for a nap—or death?—we again hear the sound of the breaking string, backed by the metronomic thud of an ax on the cherry trees, like the ticking of a cosmic clock.

Samuel Beckett (perhaps the dramatist most often aligned with Chekhov by modern critics), also meditates on the villainy of time in plays such as *Rockaby*. Perhaps Beckett best captured the essential Chekhovian dilemma in his masterpiece, *Waiting for Godot*, when one of the characters explodes in a tirade against time: "Time! Time! Will you not stop tormenting me with your cursed Time? One day we are born, one day we die . . . that's how it is on this bitch of an earth." (Compare the exchange about death between Trofimov and Gayev near the end of act 2.) The inexorable march of time invests Chekhov's plays with their characteristic melancholy, far more than any of the lamentations of the characters. And it is here that Chekhov emerges as the most unflinchingly realistic of dramatists.

Andrei Serban's 1977 production of The Cherry Orchard *at Lincoln Center is considered among the finest interpretations of Chekhov's comedy; the director and designers intentionally poeticized this customarily realistic play.*

THE CHERRY ORCHARD

ANTON CHEKHOV

Translated by Ann Dunnigan

CHARACTERS

RANEVSKAYA, LYUBOV ANDREYEVNA, *a landowner*
ANYA, *her daughter, seventeen years old*
VARYA, *her adopted daughter, twenty-four years old*
GAYEV, LEONID ANDREYEVICH, *Madame Ranevskaya's brother*
LOPAKHIN, YERMOLAI ALEKSEYEVICH, *a merchant*
TROFIMOV, PYOTR SERGEYEVICH, *a student*
SEMYONOV-PISHCHIK, BORIS BORISOVICH, *a landowner*
CHARLOTTA IVANOVNA, *a governess*
YEPIKHODOV, SEMYON PANTELEYEVICH, *a clerk*
DUNYASHA, *a maid*
FIRS, *an old valet, eighty-seven years old*
YASHA, *a young footman*
A STRANGER
THE STATIONMASTER
A POST OFFICE CLERK
GUESTS, SERVANTS

The action takes place on Madame Ranevskaya's estate.

ACT I

(*A room that is still called the nursery. One of the doors leads into Anya's room. Dawn; the sun will soon rise. It is May, the cherry trees are in bloom, but it is cold in the orchard; there is a morning frost. The windows in the room are closed. Enter Dunyasha with a candle, and Lopakhin with a book in his hand.*)

LOPAKHIN. The train is in, thank God. What time is it?

DUNYASHA. Nearly two. (*Blows out the candle.*) It's already light.

LOPAKHIN. How late is the train, anyway? A couple of hours at least. (*Yawns and stretches.*) I'm a fine one! What a fool I've made of myself! Came here on purpose to meet them at the station, and then overslept. . . . Fell asleep in the chair. It's annoying. . . . You might have waked me.

DUNYASHA. I thought you had gone. (*Listens.*) They're coming now, I think!

LOPAKHIN. (*listens*). No . . . they've got to get the luggage and one thing and another. (*Pause.*) Lyubov Andreyevna has lived abroad for five years, I don't know what she's like now. . . . She's a fine person. Sweet-tempered, simple. I remember when I was a boy of fifteen, my late father—he had a shop in the village then—gave me a punch in the face and made my nose bleed. . . . We had come into the yard here for some reason or other, and he'd had a drop too much. Lyubov Andreyevna—I remember as if it were yesterday—still young, and so slender, led me to the washstand in this very room, the nursery. "Don't cry, little peasant," she said, "it will heal in time for your wedding. . . ." (*Pause.*) Little peasant . . . my father was a peasant, it's true, and here I am in a white waistcoat and tan shoes. Like a pig in a pastry shop. . . . I may be rich, I've made a lot of money, but if you think about it, analyze it, I'm a peasant through and through. (*Turning pages of the book.*) Here I've been reading this book, and I didn't understand a thing. Fell asleep over it. (*Pause.*)

DUNYASHA. The dogs didn't sleep all night: They can tell that their masters are coming.

LOPAKHIN. What's the matter with you, Dunyasha, you're so . . .

DUNYASHA. My hands are trembling. I'm going to faint.

LOPAKHIN. You're much too delicate, Dunyasha. You dress like a lady, and do your hair like one, too. It's not right. You should know your place.

(*Enter Yepikhodov with a bouquet; he wears a jacket and highly polished boots that squeak loudly. He drops the flowers as he comes in.*)

YEPIKHODOV (*picking up the flowers*). Here, the gardener sent these. He says you're to put them in the dining room. (*Hands the bouquet to Dunyasha.*)

LOPAKHIN. And bring me some kvas.[1]

DUNYASHA. Yes, sir. (*Goes out.*)

YEPIKHODOV. There's a frost this morning—three degrees—and the cherry trees are in bloom. I cannot approve of our climate. (*Sighs.*) I cannot. Our climate is not exactly conducive. And now, Yermolai Alekseyevich, permit me to append: The day before yesterday I bought myself a pair of boots, which, I venture to assure you, squeak so that it's quite infeasible. What should I grease them with?

LOPAKHIN. Leave me alone. You make me tired.

YEPIKHODOV. Every day some misfortune happens to me. But I don't complain, I'm used to it, I even smile.

[1]**kvas** beer

(*Dunyasha enters, serves Lopakhin the kvas.*)

YEPIKHODOV. I'm going. (*Stumbles over a chair and upsets it.*) There! (*As if in triumph.*) Now you see, excuse the expression . . . the sort of circumstances, incidentally. . . . It's really quite remarkable! (*Goes out.*)

DUNYASHA. You know, Yermolai Alekseyich, I have to confess that Yepikhodov has proposed to me.

LOPAKHIN. Ah!

DUNYASHA. And I simply don't know. . . . He's a quiet man, but sometimes, when he starts talking, you can't understand a thing he says. It's nice, and full of feeling, only it doesn't make sense. I sort of like him. He's madly in love with me. But he's an unlucky fellow: Every day something happens to him. They tease him about it around here; they call him Two-and-twenty Troubles.

LOPAKHIN (*listening*). I think I hear them coming . . .

DUNYASHA. They're coming! What's the matter with me? I'm cold all over.

LOPAKHIN. They're really coming. Let's go and meet them. Will she recognize me? It's five years since we've seen each other.

DUNYASHA (*agitated*). I'll faint this very minute . . . oh, I'm going to faint!

(*Two carriages are heard driving up to the house. Lopakhin and Dunyasha go out quickly. The stage is empty. There is a hubbub in the adjoining rooms. Firs hurriedly crosses the stage leaning on a stick. He has been to meet Lyubov Andreyevna and wears old-fashioned livery and a high hat. He mutters something to himself, not a word of which can be understood. The noise offstage grows louder and louder. A voice: "Let's go through here. . . ." Enter Lyubov Andreyevna, Anya, Charlotta Ivanovna with a little dog on a chain, all in traveling dress; Varya wearing a coat and kerchief; Gayev, Semyonov-Pishchik, Lopakhin, Dunyasha with a bundle and parasol; servants with luggage—all walk through the room.*)

ANYA. Let's go this way. Do you remember, Mama, what room this is?

LYUBOV ANDREYEVNA (*joyfully, through tears*). The nursery!

VARYA. How cold it is! My hands are numb. (*To Lyubov Andreyevna.*) Your rooms, both the white one and the violet one, are just as you left them, Mama.

LYUBOV ANDREYEVNA. The nursery . . . my dear, lovely nursery. . . . I used to sleep here when I was little. . . . (*Weeps.*) And now, like a child, I . . . (*Kisses her brother, Varya, then her brother again.*) Varya hasn't changed; she still looks like a nun. And I recognized Dunyasha. . . . (*Kisses Dunyasha.*)

GAYEV. The train was two hours late. How's that? What kind of management is that?

CHARLOTTA (*to Pishchik*). My dog even eats nuts.

PISHCHIK (*amazed*). Think of that now!

(*They all go out except Anya and Dunyasha.*)

DUNYASHA. We've been waiting and waiting for you.... (*Take off Anya's coat and hat.*)

ANYA. I didn't sleep for four nights on the road ... now I feel cold.

DUNYASHA. It was Lent when you went away, there was snow and frost then, but now? My darling! (*Laughs and kisses her.*) I've waited so long for you, my joy, my precious ... I must tell you at once, I can't wait another minute....

ANYA (*listlessly*). What now?

DUNYASHA. The clerk, Yepikhodov, proposed to me just after Easter.

ANYA. You always talk about the same thing.... (*Straightening her hair.*) I've lost all my hairpins.... (*She is so exhausted she can hardly stand.*)

DUNYASHA. I really don't know what to think. He loves me—he loves me so!

ANYA (*looking through the door into her room, tenderly*). My room, my windows ... it's just as though I'd never been away. I am home! Tomorrow morning I'll get up and run into the orchard.... Oh, if I could only sleep! I didn't sleep during the entire journey, I was so tormented by anxiety.

DUNYASHA. Pyotr Sergeich arrived the day before yesterday.

ANYA (*joyfully*). Petya!

DUNYASHA. He's asleep in the bathhouse, he's staying there. "I'm afraid of being in the way," he said. (*Looks at her pocket watch.*) I ought to wake him up, but Varvara Mikhailovna told me not to. "Don't you wake him," she said.

(*Enter Varya with a bunch of keys at her waist.*)

VARYA. Dunyasha, coffee, quickly ... Mama's asking for coffee.

DUNYASHA. This very minute. (*Goes out.*)

VARYA. Thank God, you've come! You're home again. (*Caressing her.*) My little darling has come back! My pretty one is here!

ANYA. I've been through so much.

VARYA. I can imagine!

ANYA. I left in Holy Week, it was cold then. Charlotta never stopped talking and doing her conjuring tricks the entire journey. Why did you saddle me with Charlotta?

VARYA. You couldn't have traveled alone, darling. At seventeen!

ANYA. When we arrived in Paris, it was cold, snowing. My French is awful.... Mama was living on the fifth floor, and when I got there, she had all sorts of Frenchmen and ladies with her, and an old priest with a little book, and it was full of smoke, dismal. Suddenly I felt sorry for Mama, so sorry. I took her head in my arms and held her close and couldn't let her go. Afterward she kept hugging me and crying....

VARYA. (*through her tears*). Don't talk about it, don't talk about it....

ANYA. She had already sold her villa near Mentone, and she had nothing left, nothing. And I hadn't so much as a kopeck left, we barely managed to get there. But Mama doesn't understand! When we had dinner in a station restaurant, she always ordered the most expensive dishes and tipped each of the waiters a ruble. Charlotta is the same. And Yasha also ordered a dinner, it was simply awful. You know, Yasha is Mama's footman; we brought him with us.

VARYA. I saw the rogue.

ANYA. Well, how are things? Have you paid the interest?

VARYA. How could we?

ANYA. Oh, my God, my God!

VARYA. In August the estate will be put up for sale.

ANYA. My God!

(*Lopakhin peeps in at the door and moos like a cow.*)

LOPAKHIN. Moo-o-o! (*Disappears.*)

VARYA. (*through her tears*). What I couldn't do to him! (*Shakes her fist.*)

ANYA. (*embracing Varya, softly*). Varya, has he proposed to you? (*Varya shakes her head.*) But he loves you.... Why don't you come to an understanding, what are you waiting for?

VARYA. I don't think anything will ever come of it. He's too busy, he has no time for me ... he doesn't even notice me. I've washed my hands of him, it makes me miserable to see him.... Everyone talks of our wedding, they all congratulate me, and actually there's nothing to it—it's like a dream.... (*In a different tone.*) You have a brooch like a bee.

ANYA. (*sadly*). Mama bought it. (*Goes into her own room; speaks gaily, like a child.*) In Paris I went up in a balloon!

VARYA. My darling is home! My pretty one has come back!

(*Dunyasha has come in with the coffeepot and prepares coffee.*)

VARYA (*stands at the door of Anya's room*). You know, darling, all day long I'm busy looking after the house, but I keep dreaming. If we could marry you to a rich man I'd be at peace. I could go into a hermitage, then to Kiev, to Moscow, and from one holy place to another.... I'd go on and on. What a blessing!

ANYA. The birds are singing in the orchard. What time is it?

VARYA. It must be after two. Time you were asleep, darling. (*Goes into Anya's room.*) What a blessing!

(*Yasha enters with a lap robe and a traveling bag.*)

YASHA (*crosses the stage mincingly*). May one go through here?

DUNYASHA. A person would hardly recognize you, Yasha. Your stay abroad has done wonders for you.

YASHA. Hm.... And who are you?

DUNYASHA. When you left here I was only that high—(*indi-*

cating with her hand). I'm Dunyasha, Fyodor Kozoyedov's daughter. You don't remember?

YASHA. Hm.... A little cucumber! (*Looks around, then embraces her; she cries out and drops a saucer. He quickly goes out.*)

VARYA (*in a tone of annoyance, from the doorway*). What's going on here?

DUNYASHA (*tearfully*). I broke a saucer.

VARYA. That's good luck.

ANYA. We ought to prepare Mama: Petya is here....

VARYA. I gave orders not to wake him.

ANYA (*pensively*). Six years ago Father died, and a month later brother Grisha drowned in the river . . . a pretty little seven-year-old boy. Mama couldn't bear it and went away . . . went without looking back.... (*Shudders.*) How I understand her, if she only knew! (*Pause.*) And Petya Trofimov was Grisha's tutor, he may remind her....

(*Enter Firs wearing a jacket and a white waistcoat.*)

FIRS (*goes to the coffeepot, anxiously*). The mistress will have her coffee here. (*Puts on white gloves.*) Is the coffee ready? (*To Dunyasha, sternly.*) You! Where's the cream?

DUNYASHA. Oh, my goodness! (*Quickly goes out.*)

FIRS (*fussing over the coffeepot*). Ah, what an addlepate! (*Mutters to himself.*) They've come back from Paris.... The master used to go to Paris ... by carriage.... (*Laughs.*)

VARYA. What is it, Firs?

FIRS. If you please? (*Joyfully.*) My mistress has come home! At last! Now I can die.... (*Weeps with joy.*)

(*Enter Lyubov Andreyevna, Gayev, and Semyonov-Pishchik, the last wearing a sleeveless peasant coat of fine cloth and full trousers. Gayev, as he comes in, goes through the motions of playing billiards.*)

LYUBOV ANDREYEVNA. How does it go? Let's see if I can remember . . . cue ball into the corner! Double the rail to center table.

GAYEV. Cut shot into the corner! There was a time, sister, when you and I used to sleep here in this very room, and now I'm fifty-one, strange as it may seem....

LOPAKHIN. Yes, time passes.

GAYEV. How's that?

LOPAKHIN. Time I say, passes.

GAYEV. It smells of patchouli here.

ANYA. I'm going to bed. Good night, Mama. (*Kisses her mother.*)

LYUBOV ANDREYEVNA. My precious child. (*Kisses her hands.*) Are you glad to be home? I still feel dazed.

ANYA. Good night, Uncle.

GAYEV (*kisses her face and hands*). God bless you. How like your mother you are! (*To his sister.*) At her age you were exactly like her, Lyuba.

(*Anya shakes hands with Lopakhin and Pishchik and goes out, closing the door after her.*)

LYUBOV ANDREYEVNA. She's exhausted.

PISHCHIK. Must have been a long journey.

VARYA. Well, gentlemen? It's after two, high time you were going.

LYUBOV ANDREYEVNA (*laughs*). You haven't changed, Varya. (*Draws Varya to her and kisses her.*) I'll just drink my coffee and then we'll all go. (*Firs places a cushion under her feet.*) Thank you, my dear. I've got used to coffee. I drink it day and night. Thanks, dear old man. (*Kisses him.*)

VARYA. I'd better see if all the luggage has been brought in.

LYUBOV ANDREYEVNA. Is this really me sitting here? (*Laughs.*) I feel like jumping about and waving my arms. (*Buries her face in her hands.*) What if it's only a dream! God knows I love my country, love it dearly. I couldn't look out the train window, I was crying so! (*Through tears.*) But I must drink my coffee. Thank you, Firs, thank you, my dear old friend. I'm so glad you're still alive.

FIRS. The day before yesterday.

GAYEV. He's hard of hearing.

LOPAKHIN. I must go now, I'm leaving for Kharkov about five o'clock. It's so annoying! I wanted to have a good look at you, and have a talk. You're as splendid as ever.

PISHCHIK. (*breathing heavily*). Even more beautiful.... Dressed like a Parisienne.... There goes my wagon, all four wheels!

LOPAKHIN. Your brother here, Leonid Andreyevich, says I'm a boor, a moneygrubber, but I don't mind. Let him talk. All I want is that you should trust me as you used to, and that your wonderful, touching eyes should look at me as they did then. Merciful God! My father was one of your father's serfs, and your grandfather's, but you yourself did so much for me once, that I've forgotten all that and love you as if you were my own kin—more than my kin.

LYUBOV ANDREYEVNA. I can't sit still, I simply cannot.

(*Jumps up and walks about the room in great excitement.*) I cannot bear this joy.... Laugh at me, I'm silly.... My dear little bookcase . . . (*kisses bookcase*) my little table . . .

GAYEV. Nurse died while you were away.

LYUBOV ANDREYEVNA (*sits down and drinks coffee*). Yes, God rest her soul. They wrote me.

GAYEV. And Anastasy is dead. Petrushka Kosoi left me and is now with the police inspector in town. (*Takes a box of hard candies from his pocket and begins to suck one.*)

PISHCHIK. My daughter, Dashenka . . . sends her regards . . .

LOPAKHIN. I wish I could tell you something very pleasant and cheering. (*Glances at his watch.*) I must go directly, there's no time to talk, but . . . well, I'll say it in a couple of words. As you know, the cherry orchard is to be sold to pay your debts. The auction is set for August twenty-second, but you need not worry, my dear, you can sleep in peace, there is a way out. This is my plan. Now, please listen! Your estate is only twenty versts[2] from town, the rail-way runs close by, and if the cherry orchard and the land along the river were cut up into lots and leased for summer cottages, you'd have, at the very least, an income of twenty-five thousand a year.

GAYEV. Excuse me, what nonsense!

LYUBOV ANDREYEVNA. I don't quite understand you, Yermolai Alekseyevich.

LOPAKHIN. You will get, at the very least, twenty-five rubles a year for a two-and-half-acre lot, and if you advertise now, I guarantee you won't have a single plot of ground left by autumn, everything will be snapped up. In short, I congratulate you, you are saved. The site is splendid, the river is deep. Only, of course, the ground must be cleared . . . you must tear down all the old outbuildings, for instance, and this house, which is worthless, cut down the old cherry orchard—

LYUBOV ANDREYEVNA. Cut it down? Forgive me, my dear, but you don't know what you are talking about. If there is one thing in the whole province that is interesting, not to say remarkable, it's our cherry orchard.

LOPAKHIN. The only remarkable thing about this orchard is that it is very big. There's a crop of cherries every other year, and then you can't get rid of them, nobody buys them.

GAYEV. This orchard is even mentioned in the *Encyclopedia*.

LOPAKHIN. (*glancing at his watch*). If we don't think of something and come to a decision, on the twenty-second of August the cherry orchard, and the entire estate, will be sold at auction. Make up your minds! There is no other way out, I swear to you. None whatsoever.

FIRS. In the old days, forty or fifty years ago, the cherries were dried, soaked, marinated, and made into jam, and they used to—

GAYEV. Be quiet, Firs.

FIRS. And they used to send cartloads of dried cherries to Moscow and Kharkov. And that brought in money! The dried cherries were soft and juicy in those days, sweet, fragrant. . . . They had a method then . . .

LYUBOV ANDREYEVNA. And what has become of that method now?

FIRS. Forgotten. Nobody remembers. . . .

PISHCHIK. How was it in Paris? What's it like there? Did you eat frogs?

LYUBOV ANDREYEVNA. I ate crocodiles.

PISHCHIK. Think of that now!

LOPAKHIN. There used to be only the gentry and the peasants living in the country, but now these summer people have appeared. All the towns, even the smallest ones, are surrounded by summer cottages. And it is safe to say that in another twenty years these people will multiply enor-

mously. Now the summer resident only drinks tea on his porch, but it may well be that he'll take to cultivating his acre, and then your cherry orchard will be a happy, rich, luxuriant—

GAYEV. (*indignantly*). What nonsense!

(*Enter Varya and Yasha.*)

VARYA. There are two telegrams for you, Mama. (*Picks out a key and with a jingling sound opens an old-fashioned bookcase.*) Here they are.

LYUBOV ANDREYEVNA. From Paris. (*Tears up the telegrams without reading them.*) That's all over. . . .

GAYEV. Do you know, Lyuba, how old this bookcase is? A week ago I pulled out the bottom drawer, and what do I see? Some figures burnt into it. The bookcase was made exactly a hundred years ago. What do you think of that? Eh? We could have celebrated its jubilee. It's an inanimate object, but nevertheless, for all that, it's a bookcase.

PISHCHIK. A hundred years . . . think of that now!

GAYEV. Yes . . . that is something. . . . (*Feeling the bookcase.*) Dear, honored bookcase. I salute thy existence, which for over one hundred years has served the glorious ideals of goodness and justice; thy silent appeal to fruitful endeavor, unflagging in the course of a hundred years, tearfully sustaining through generations of our family, courage and faith in a better future, and fostering in us ideals of goodness and social consciousness. . . .

(*A pause.*)

LOPAKHIN. Yes . . .

LYUBOV ANDREYEVNA. You are the same as ever, Lyonya.

GAYEV. (*somewhat embarrassed*). Carom into the corner, cut shot to center table.

LOPAKHIN (*looks at his watch*). Well, time for me to go.

YASHA (*hands medicine to Lyubov Andreyevna*). Perhaps you will take your pills now.

PISHCHIK. Don't take medicaments, dearest lady, they do neither harm nor good. Let me have them, honored lady. (*Takes the pillbox, shakes the pills into his hand, blows on them, puts them into his mouth, and washes them down with kvas.*) There!

LYUBOV ANDREYEVNA (*alarmed*). Why, you must be mad!

PISHCHIK. I've taken all the pills.

LOPAKHIN. What a glutton!

(*Everyone laughs.*)

FIRS. The gentleman stayed with us during Holy Week . . . ate half a bucket of pickles. . . . (*Mumbles.*)

LYUBOV ANDREYEVNA. What is he saying?

VARYA. He's been muttering like that for three years now. We've grown used to it.

YASHA. He's in his dotage.

(*Charlotta Ivanovna, very thin, tightly laced, in a white dress with a lorgnette at her belt, crosses the stage.*)

---

[2]**versts** A verst is a little more than half a mile.

LOPAKHIN. Forgive me, Charlotta Ivanovna, I haven't had a chance to say how do you do to you. (*Tries to kiss her hand.*)

CHARLOTTA (*pulls her hand away*). If I permit you to kiss my hand you'll be wanting to kiss my elbow next, then my shoulder.

LOPAKHIN. I have no luck today. (*Everyone laughs.*) Charlotta Ivanovna, show us a trick!

LYUBOV ANDREYEVNA. Charlotta, show us a trick!

CHARLOTTA. No. I want to sleep. (*Goes out.*)

LOPAKHIN. In three weeks we'll meet again. (*Kisses Lyubov Andreyevna's hand.*) Good-bye till then. Time to go. (*To Gayev.*) Good-bye. (*Kisses Pishchik.*) Good-bye. (*Shakes hands with Varya, then with Firs and Yasha.*) I don't feel like going. (*To Lyubov Andreyevna.*) If you make up your mind about the summer cottages and come to a decision, let me know; I'll get you a loan of fifty thousand or so. Think it over seriously.

VARYA (*angrily*). Oh, why don't you go!

LOPAKHIN. I'm going, I'm going. (*Goes out.*)

GAYEV. Boor. Oh, pardon. Varya's going to marry him, he's Varya's young man.

VARYA. Uncle dear, you talk too much.

LYUBOV ANDREYEVNA. Well, Varya, I shall be very glad. He's a good man.

PISHCHIK. A man, I must truly say . . . most worthy. . . . And my Dashenka . . . says, too, that . . . says all sorts of things. (*Snores but wakes up at once.*) In any case, honored lady, oblige me . . . a loan of two hundred and forty rubles . . . tomorrow the interest on my mortgage is due. . . .

VARYA (*in alarm*). We have nothing, nothing at all!

LYUBOV ANDREYEVNA. I really haven't any money.

PISHCHIK. It'll turn up. (*Laughs.*) I never lose hope. Just when I thought everything was lost, that I was done for, lo and behold—the railway line ran through my land . . . and they paid me for it. And before you know it, something else will turn up, if not today—tomorrow. . . . Dashenka will win two hundred thousand . . . she's got a lottery ticket.

LYUBOV ANDREYEVNA. The coffee is finished, we can go to bed.

FIRS (*brushing Gayev's clothes, admonishingly*). You've put on the wrong trousers again. What am I to do with you?

VARYA (*softly*). Anya's asleep. (*Quietly opens the window.*) The sun has risen, it's no longer cold. Look, Mama dear, what wonderful trees! Oh, Lord, the air! The starlings are singing!

GAYEV (*opens another window*). The orchard is all white. You haven't forgotten, Lyuba? That long avenue there that runs straight—straight as a stretched-out strap; it gleams on moonlight nights. Remember? You've not forgotten?

LYUBOV ANDREYEVNA (*looking out the window at the orchard*). Oh, my childhood, my innocence! I used to sleep in this nursery, I looked out from here into the orchard, happi-

ness awoke with me each morning, it was just as it is now, nothing has changed. (*Laughing with joy.*) All, all white! Oh, my orchard! After the dark, rainy autumn and the cold winter, you are young again, full of happiness, the heavenly angels have not forsaken you. . . . If I could cast off this heavy stone weighing on my breast and shoulders, if I could forget my past!

GAYEV. Yes, and the orchard will be sold for our debts, strange as it may seem. . . .

LYUBOV ANDREYEVNA. Look, our dead mother walks in the orchard . . . in a white dress! (*Laughs with joy.*) It is she!

GAYEV. Where?

VARYA. God be with you, Mama dear.

LYUBOV ANDREYEVNA. There's no one there, I just imagined it. To the right, as you turn to the summerhouse, a slender white sapling is bent over . . . it looks like a woman.

(*Enter Trofimov wearing a shabby student's uniform and spectacles.*)

LYUBOV ANDREYEVNA. What a wonderful orchard! The white masses of blossoms, the blue sky—

TROFIMOV. Lyubov Andreyevna! (*She looks around at him.*) I only want to pay my respects, then I'll go at once. (*Kisses her hand ardently.*) I was told to wait until morning, but I hadn't the patience.

(*Lyubov Andreyevna looks at him, puzzled.*)

VARYA (*through tears*). This is Petya Trofimov.

TROFIMOV. Petya Trofimov, I was Grisha's tutor. . . . Can I have changed so much?

(*Lyubov Andreyevna embraces him, quietly weeping.*)

GAYEV (*embarrassed*). There, there, Lyuba.

VARYA (*crying*): Didn't I tell you, Petya, to wait till tomorrow?

LYUBOV ANDREYEVNA. My Grisha . . . my little boy . . . Grisha . . . my son. . . .

VARYA. What can we do, Mama dear? It's God's will.

TROFIMOV (*gently, through tears*). Don't, don't. . . .

LYUBOV ANDREYEVNA (*quietly weeping*). My little boy dead, drowned. . . . Why? Why, my friend? (*In a lower voice.*) Anya is sleeping in there, and I'm talking loudly . . . making all this noise. . . . But Petya, why do you look so bad? Why have you grown so old?

TROFIMOV. A peasant woman in the train called me a mangy gentleman.

LYUBOV ANDREYEVNA. You were just a boy then, a charming little student, and now your hair is thin—and spectacles! Is it possible you are still a student? (*Goes toward the door.*)

TROFIMOV. I shall probably be an eternal student.

LYUBOV ANDREYEVNA (*kisses her brother, then Varya*). Now, go to bed. . . . You've grown older too, Leonid.

PISHCHIK (*follows her*). Well, seems to be time to sleep. . . . Oh, my gout! I'm staying the night. Lyubov Andreyevna, my soul, tomorrow morning . . . two hundred and forty rubles. . . .

GAYEV. He keeps at it.

PISHCHIK. Two hundred and forty rubles . . . to pay the interest on my mortgage.

LYUBOV ANDREYEVNA. I have no money, my friend.

PISHCHIK. My dear, I'll pay it back. . . . It's a trifling sum.

LYUBOV ANDREYEVNA. Well, all right, Leonid will give it to you. . . . Give it to him, Leonid.

GAYEV. Me give it to him! . . . Hold out your pocket!

LYUBOV ANDREYEVNA. It can't be helped, give it to him. . . . He needs it. . . . He'll pay it back.

(*Lyubov Andreyevna, Trofimov, Pishchik, and Firs go out. Gayev, Varya, and Yasha remain.*)

GAYEV. My sister hasn't yet lost her habit of squandering money. (*To Yasha.*) Go away, my good fellow, you smell of the henhouse.

YASHA (*with a smirk*). And you, Leonid Andreyevich, are just the same as ever.

GAYEV. How's that? (*To Varya.*) What did he say?

VARYA. Your mother has come from the village; she's been sitting in the servants' room since yesterday, waiting to see you. . . .

YASHA. Let her wait, for God's sake!

VARYA. Aren't you ashamed?

YASHA. A lot I need her! She could have come tomorrow. (*Goes out.*)

VARYA. Mama's the same as ever, she hasn't changed a bit. She'd give away everything, if she could.

GAYEV. Yes. . . . (*A pause.*) If a great many remedies are suggested for a disease, it means that the disease is incurable. I keep thinking, racking my brains, I have many remedies, a great many, and that means, in effect, that I have none. It would be good to receive a legacy from someone, good to marry our Anya to a very rich man, good to go to Yaroslav and try our luck with our aunt, the Countess. She is very, very rich, you know.

VARYA (*crying*). If only God would help us!

GAYEV. Stop bawling. Auntie's very rich, but she doesn't like us. In the first place, sister married a lawyer, not a nobleman . . . (*Anya appears in the doorway.*) She married beneath her, and it cannot be said that she has conducted herself very virtuously. She is good, kind, charming, and I love her dearly, but no matter how much you allow for extenuating circumstances, you must admit she leads a sinful life. You feel it in her slightest movement.

VARYA (*in a whisper*). Anya is standing in the doorway.

GAYEV. What? (*Pause.*) Funny, something got into my right eye . . . I can't see very well. And Thursday, when I was in the district court . . .

(*Anya enters.*)

VARYA. Why aren't you asleep, Anya?

ANYA. I can't get to sleep. I just can't.

GAYEV. My little one! (*Kisses Anya's face and hands.*) My child. . . . (*Through tears.*) You are not my niece, you are my angel, you are everything to me. Believe me, believe . . .

ANYA. I believe you, Uncle. Everyone loves you and respects you, but, Uncle dear, you must keep quiet, just keep quiet. What were you saying just now about my mother, about your own sister? What made you say that?

GAYEV. Yes, yes. . . . (*Covers his face with her hand.*) Really, it's awful! My God! God help me! And today I made a speech to the bookcase . . . so stupid! And it was only when I had finished that I realized it was stupid.

VARYA. It's true, Uncle dear, you ought to keep quiet. Just don't talk, that's all.

ANYA. If you could keep from talking, it would make things easier for you, too.

GAYEV. I'll be quiet. (*Kisses Anya's and Varya's hands.*) I'll be quiet. Only this is about business. On Thursday I was in the district court, well, a group of us gathered together and began talking about one thing and another, this and that, and it seems it might be possible to arrange a loan on a promissory note to pay the interest at the bank.

VARYA. If only God would help us!

GAYEV. On Tuesday I'll go and talk it over again. (*To Varya.*) Stop bawling. (*To Anya.*) Your mama will talk to Lopakhin; he, of course, will not refuse her. . . . And as soon as you've rested, you will go to Yaroslav to the Countess, your great-aunt. In that way we shall be working from three directions—and our business is in the hat. We'll pay the interest, I'm certain of it. . . . (*Puts a candy in his mouth.*) On my honor, I'll swear by anything you like, the estate shall not be sold. (*Excitedly.*) By my happiness, I swear it! Here's my hand on it, call me a worthless, dishonorable man if I let it come to auction! I swear by my whole being!

ANYA (*a calm mood returns to her, she is happy*). How good you are, Uncle, how clever! (*Embraces him.*) Now I am at peace! I'm at peace! I'm happy!

(*Enter Firs.*)

FIRS (*reproachfully*). Leonid Andreyevich, have you no fear of God? When are you going to bed?

GAYEV. Presently, presently. Go away, Firs. I'll . . . all right, I'll undress myself. Well, children, bye-bye. . . . Details tomorrow, and now go to sleep. (*Kisses Anya and Varya.*) I am a man of the eighties. . . . They don't think much of that period today, nevertheless, I can say that in the course of my life I have suffered not a little for my convictions. It is not for nothing that the peasant loves me. You have to know the peasant! You have to know from what—

ANYA. There you go again, Uncle!

VARYA. Uncle dear, do be quiet.

FIRS (*angrily*). Leonid Andreyevich!

GAYEV. I'm coming, I'm coming. . . . Go to bed. A clean

double rail shot to center table.... (*Goes out; Firs hobbles after him.*)

ANYA. I'm at peace now. I would rather not go to Yaroslav, I don't like my great-aunt, but still, I'm at peace, thanks to Uncle. (*She sits down.*)

VARYA. We must get some sleep. I'm going now. Oh, something unpleasant happened while you were away. In the old servants' quarters, as you know, there are only the old people: Yefimushka, Polya, Yevstignei, and, of course, Karp. They began letting in all sorts of rogues to spend the night—I didn't say anything. But then I heard they'd been spreading a rumor that I'd given an order for them to be fed nothing but dried peas. Out of stinginess, you see.... It was all Yevstignei's doing.... Very well, I think, if that's how it is, you just wait. I send for Yevstignei ... (*yawning*) he comes.... "How is it, Yevstignei," I say, "that you could be such a fool...." (*Looks at Anya.*) She's fallen asleep. (*Takes her by the arm.*) Come to your little bed.... Come along. (*Leading her.*) My little darling fell asleep. Come.... (*They go.*)

(*In the distance, beyond the orchard, a shepherd is playing on a reed pipe. Trofimov crosses the stage and, seeing Varya and Anya, stops.*)

VARYA. Sh! She's asleep ... asleep.... Come along, darling.

ANYA (*softly, half-asleep*). I'm so tired.... Those bells ... Uncle ... dear ... Mama and Uncle ...

VARYA. Come, darling, come along. (*They go into Anya's room.*)

TROFIMOV (*deeply moved*). My sunshine! My spring!

ACT II

(*A meadow. An old, lopsided, long-abandoned little chapel; near it a well, large stones that apparently were once tombstones, and an old bench. A road to the Gayev manor house can be seen. On one side, where the cherry orchard begins, tall poplars loom. In the distance a row of telegraph poles, and far, far away, on the horizon, the faint outline of a large town, which is visible only in very fine, clear weather. The sun will soon set. Charlotta, Yasha, and Dunyasha are sitting on the bench; Yepikhodov stands near playing something sad on the guitar. They are all lost in thought. Charlotta wears an old forage cap; she has taken a gun from her shoulder and is addressing the buckle on the sling.*)

CHARLOTTA (*reflectively*). I haven't got a real passport, I don't know how old I am, but it always seems to me that I'm quite young. When I was a little girl, my father and mother used to travel from one fair to another giving performances—very good ones. And I did the *salto mortale*

and all sorts of tricks. Then when Papa and Mama died, a German lady took me to live with her and began teaching me. Good. I grew up and became a governess. But where I come from and who I am—I do not know.... Who my parents were—perhaps they weren't even married—I don't know. (*Takes a cucumber out of her pocket and eats it.*) I don't know anything. (*Pause.*) One wants so much to talk, but there isn't anyone to talk to ... I have no one.

YEPIKHODOV (*plays the guitar and sings*). "What care I for the clamorous world, what's friend or foe to me?" ... How pleasant it is to play a mandolin!

DUNYASHA. That's a guitar, not a mandolin. (*Looks at herself in a hand mirror and powders her face.*)

YEPIKHODOV. To a madman, in love, it is a mandolin.... (*Sings.*) "Would that the heart were warmed by the flame of required love ... "

(*Yasha joins in.*)

CHARLOTTA. How horribly these people sing? ... Pfui! Like jackals!

DUNYASHA (*to Yasha*). Really, how fortunate to have been abroad!

YASHA. Yes, to be sure. I cannot but agree with you there. (*Yawns, then lights a cigar.*)

YEPIKHODOV. It stands to reason. Abroad everything has long since been fully constituted.

YASHA. Obviously.

YEPIKHODOV. I am a cultivated man, I read all sorts of remarkable books, but I am in no way able to make out my own inclinations, what it is I really want, whether, strictly speaking, to live or to shoot myself; nevertheless, I always carry a revolver on me. Here it is. (*Shows revolver.*)

CHARLOTTA. Finished. Now I'm going. (*Slings the gun over her shoulder.*) You're a very clever man, Yepikhodov, and quite terrifying; women must be mad about you. Brrr! (*Starts to go.*) These clever people are all so stupid, there's no one for me to talk to.... Alone, always alone, I have no one ... and who I am, and why I am, nobody knows.... (*Goes out unhurriedly.*)

YEPIKHODOV. Strictly speaking, all else aside, I must state regarding myself, that fate treats me unmercifully, as a storm does a small ship. If, let us assume, I am mistaken, then why, to mention a single instance, do I wake up this morning, and there on my chest see a spider of terrifying magnitude? ... Like that. (*Indicates with both hands.*) And likewise, I take up some kvas to quench my thirst, and there see something in the highest degree unseemly, like a cockroach. (*Pause.*) Have you read Buckle?[3] (*Pause.*) If I may trouble you, Avdotya Fedorovna, I should like to have a word or two with you.

DUNYASHA. Go ahead.

[3]**Buckle** Thomas Henry Buckle (1821–1862) an historian; he formulated a scientific basis for history emphasizing the interrelationship of climate, food production, population, and wealth.

YEPIKHODOV. I prefer to speak with you alone. . . . (*Sighs.*)

DUNYASHA (*embarrassed*). Very well . . . only first bring me my little cape . . . you'll find it by the cupboard. . . . It's rather damp here. . . .

YEPIKHODOV. Certainly, ma'am . . . I'll fetch it, ma'am. . . . Now I know what to do with my revolver. . . . (*Takes the guitar and goes off playing it.*)

YASHA. Two-and-twenty Troubles! Between ourselves, a stupid fellow. (*Yawns.*)

DUNYASHA. God forbid that he should shoot himself. (*Pause.*) I've grown so anxious, I'm always worried. I was only a little girl when I was taken into the master's house, and now I'm quite unused to the simple life, and my hands are white as can be, just like a lady's. I've become so delicate, so tender and ladylike, I'm afraid of everything. . . . Frightfully so. And, Yasha, if you deceive me, I just don't know what will become of my nerves.

YASHA (*kisses her*). You little cucumber! Of course, a girl should never forget herself. What I dislike above everything is when a girl doesn't conduct herself properly.

DUNYASHA. I'm passionately in love with you, you're educated, you can discuss anything. (*Pause.*)

YASHA (*yawns*). Yes. . . . As I see it, it's like this: If a girl loves somebody, that means she's immoral. (*Pause.*) Very pleasant smoking a cigar in the open air. . . . (*Listens.*) Someone's coming this way. . . . It's the masters. (*Dunyasha impulsively embraces him.*) You go home, as if you'd been to the river to bathe; take that path, otherwise they'll see you and suspect me of having a rendezvous with you. I can't endure that sort of thing.

DUNYASHA (*with a little cough*). My head is beginning to ache from your cigar. . . . (*Goes out.*)

(*Yasha remains, sitting near the chapel. Lyubov Andreyevna, Gayev, and Lopakhin enter.*)

LOPAKHIN. You must make up your mind once and for all—time won't stand still. The question, after all, is quite simple. Do you agree to lease the land for summer cottages or not? Answer in one word: Yes or no? Only one word!

LYUBOV ANDREYEVNA. Who is it that smokes those disgusting cigars out here? (*Sits down.*)

GAYEV. Now that the railway line is so near, it's made things convenient. (*Sits down.*) We went to town and had lunch . . . cue ball to the center! I feel like going to the house first and playing a game.

LYUBOV ANDREYEVNA. Later.

LOPAKHIN. Just one word! (*Imploringly.*) Do give me an answer.

GAYEV (*yawning*). How's that?

LYUBOV ANDREYEVNA (*looks into her purse*). Yesterday I had a lot of money, and today there's hardly any left. My poor Varya tries to economize by feeding everyone milk soup, and in the kitchen the old people get nothing but dried peas, while I squander money foolishly. . . . (*Drops the purse, scattering gold coins.*) There they go. . . . (*Vexed.*)

YASHA. Allow me, I'll pick them up in an instant. (*Picks up the money.*)

LYUBOV ANDREYEVNA. Please do, Yasha. And why did I go to town for lunch? . . . That miserable restaurant of yours with its music, and tablecloths smelling of soap. . . . Why drink so much, Lyonya? Why eat so much? Why talk so much? Today in the restaurant again you talked too much, and it was all so pointless. About the seventies, about the decadents. And to whom? Talking to waiters about the decadents!

LOPAKHIN. Yes.

GAYEV (*waving his hand*). I'm incorrigible, that's evident. . . . (*Irritably to Yasha.*) Why do you keep twirling about in front of me?

YASHA (*laughs*). I can't help laughing when I hear your voice.

GAYEV (*to his sister*). Either he or I—

LYUBOV ANDREYEVNA. Go away, Yasha, run along.

YASHA (*hands Lyubov Andreyevna her purse*): I'm going, right away. (*Hardly able to contain his laughter.*) This very instant. . . . (*Goes out.*)

LOPAKHIN. That rich man, Deriganov, is prepared to buy the estate. They say he's coming to the auction himself.

LYUBOV ANDREYEVNA. Where did you hear that?

LOPAKHIN. That's what they're saying in town.

LYUBOV ANDREYEVNA. Our aunt in Yaroslav promised to send us something, but when and how much, no one knows.

LOPAKHIN. How much do you think she'll send? A hundred thousand? Two hundred?

LYUBOV ANDREYEVNA. Oh . . . ten or fifteen thousand, and we'll be thankful for that.

LOPAKHIN. Forgive me, but I have never seen such frivolous, such queer, unbusinesslike people as you, my friends. You are told in plain language that your estate is to be sold, and it's as though you don't understand it.

LYUBOV ANDREYEVNA. But what are we to do? Tell us what to do.

LOPAKHIN. I tell you every day. Every day I say the same thing. Both the cherry orchard and the land must be leased for summer cottages, and it must be done now, as quickly as possible—the auction is close at hand. Try to understand! Once you definitely decide on the cottages, you can raise as much money as you like, and then you are saved.

LYUBOV ANDREYEVNA. Cottages, summer people—forgive me, but it's so vulgar.

GAYEV. I agree with you, absolutely.

LOPAKHIN. I'll either burst into tears, start shouting, or fall into a faint! I can't stand it! You've worn me out! (*To Gayev.*) You're an old woman!

GAYEV. How's that?

LOPAKHIN. An old woman! (*Starts to go.*)

LYUBOV ANDREYEVNA (*alarmed*). No, don't go, stay, my dear. I beg you. Perhaps we'll think of something!

LOPAKHIN. What is there to think of?

LYUBOV ANDREYEVNA. Don't go away, please. With you here it's more cheerful somehow. . . . (*Pause.*) I keep expecting something to happen, like the house caving in on us.

GAYEV (*in deep thought*). Double rail shot into the corner. . . . Cross table to the center. . . .

LYUBOV ANDREYEVNA. We have sinned so much. . . .

LOPAKHIN. What sins could you have—

GAYEV (*puts a candy into his mouth*). They say I've eaten up my entire fortune in candies. . . . (*Laughs.*)

LYUBOV ANDREYEVNA. Oh, my sins. . . . I've always squandered money recklessly, like a madwoman, and I married a man who did nothing but amass debts. My husband died from champagne—he drank terribly—then, to my sorrow, I fell in love with another man, lived with him, and just at that time—that was my first punishment, a blow on the head—my little boy was drowned . . . here in the river. And I went abroad, went away for good, never to return, never to see this river. . . . I closed my eyes and ran, beside myself, and *he* after me . . . callously, without pity. I bought a villa near Mentone, because he fell ill there, and for three years I had no rest, day or night. The sick man wore me out, my soul dried up. Then last year, when the villa was sold to pay my debts, I went to Paris, and there he stripped me of everything, and left me for another woman; I tried to poison myself. . . . So stupid, so shameful. . . . And suddenly I felt a longing for Russia, for my own country, for my little girl. . . . (*Wipes away her tears.*) Lord, Lord, be merciful, forgive my sins! Don't punish me anymore! (*Takes a telegram out of her pocket.*) This came today from Paris. . . . He asks my forgiveness, begs me to return. . . . (*Tears up telegram.*) Do I hear music? (*Listens.*)

GAYEV. That's our famous Jewish band. You remember, four violins, a flute, and double bass.

LYUBOV ANDREYEVNA. It's still in existence? We ought to send for them sometime and give a party.

LOPAKHIN (*listens*). I don't hear anything. . . . (*Sings softly.*) "The Germans, for pay, will turn Russians into Frenchmen, they say." (*Laughs.*) What a play I saw yesterday at the theater—very funny!

LYUBOV ANDREYEVNA. There was probably nothing funny about it. Instead of going to see plays you ought to look at yourselves a little more often. How drab your lives are, how full of futile talk!

LOPAKHIN. That's true. I must say, this life of ours is stupid. . . . (*Pause.*) My father was a peasant, an idiot; he understood nothing, taught me nothing; all he did was beat me when he was drunk, and always with a stick. As a matter of fact, I'm as big a blockhead and idiot as he was. I never learned anything, my handwriting's disgusting, I write like a pig—I'm ashamed to have people see it.

LYUBOV ANDREYEVNA. You ought to get married, my friend.

LOPAKHIN. Yes . . . that's true.

LYUBOV ANDREYEVNA. To our Varya. She's a nice girl.

LOPAKHIN. Yes.

LYUBOV ANDREYEVNA. She's a girl who comes from simple people, works all day long, but the main thing is she loves you. Besides, you've liked her for a long time now.

LOPAKHIN. Well? I've nothing against it. . . . She's a good girl. (*Pause.*)

GAYEV. I've been offered a place in the bank. Six thousand a year. . . . Have you heard?

LYUBOV ANDREYEVNA. How could you! You stay where you are. . . .

(*Firs enters carrying an overcoat.*)

FIRS (*to Gayev*). If you please, sir, put this on, it's damp.

GAYEV (*puts on the overcoat*). You're a pest, old man.

FIRS. Never mind. . . . You went off this morning without telling me. (*Looks him over.*)

LYUBOV ANDREYEVNA. How you have aged, Firs!

FIRS. What do you wish, madam?

LOPAKHIN. She says you've grown very old!

FIRS. I've lived a long time. They were arranging a marriage for me before your papa was born. . . . (*Laughs.*) I was already head footman when the emancipation came. At that time I wouldn't consent to my freedom, I stayed with the masters. . . . (*Pause.*) I remember, everyone was happy, but what they were happy about, they themselves didn't know.

LOPAKHIN. It was better in the old days. At least they flogged them.

FIRS (*not hearing*). Of course. The peasants kept to the masters, the masters kept to the peasants; but now they have all gone their own ways, you can't tell about anything.

GAYEV. Be quiet, Firs. Tomorrow I must go to town. I've been promised an introduction to a certain general who might let us have a loan.

LOPAKHIN. Nothing will come of it. And you can rest assured, you won't even pay the interest.

LYUBOV ANDREYEVNA. He's raving. There is no such general.

(*Enter Trofimov, Anya, and Varya.*)

GAYEV. Here come our young people.

ANYA. There's Mama.

LYUBOV ANDREYEVNA (*tenderly*). Come, come along, my darlings. (*Embraces Anya and Varya.*) If you only knew how I love you both! Sit here beside me—there, like that.

(*They all sit down.*)

LOPAKHIN. Our eternal student is always with the young ladies.

TROFIMOV. That's none of your business.

LOPAKHIN. He'll soon be fifty, but he's still a student.

TROFIMOV. Drop your stupid jokes.

LOPAKHIN. What are you so angry about, you queer fellow?

TROFIMOV. Just leave me alone.

LOPAKHIN (*laughs*). Let me ask you something: What do you make of me?

TROFIMOV. My idea of you, Yermolai Alekseyevich, is this:

You're a rich man, you will soon be a millionaire. Just as the beast of prey, which devours everything that crosses its path, is necessary in the metabolic process, so are you necessary.

(*Everybody laughs.*)

VARYA. Petya, you'd better tell us something about the planets.

LYUBOV ANDREYEVNA. No, let's go on with yesterday's conversation.

TROFIMOV. What was it about?

GAYEV. About the proud man.

TROFIMOV. We talked a long time yesterday, but we didn't get anywhere. In the proud man, in your sense of the word, there's something mystical. And you may be right from your point of view, but if you look at it simply, without being abstruse, why even talk about pride? Is there any sense in it if, physiologically, man is poorly constructed, if, in the vast majority of cases, he is coarse, ignorant, and profoundly unhappy? We should stop admiring ourselves. We should just work, and that's all.

GAYEV. You die, anyway.

TROFIMOV. Who knows? And what does it mean—to die? It may be that man has a hundred senses, and at his death only the five that are known to us perish, and the other ninety-five go on living.

LYUBOV ANDREYEVNA. How clever you are, Petya!

LOPAKHIN (*ironically*). Terribly clever!

TROFIMOV. Mankind goes forward, perfecting its powers. Everything that is now unattainable will some day be comprehensible and within our grasp, only we must work, and help with all our might those who are seeking the truth. So far, among us here in Russia, only a very few work. The great majority of the intelligentsia that I know seek nothing, do nothing, and as yet are incapable of work. They call themselves the intelligentsia, yet they belittle their servants, treat the peasants like animals, are wretched students, never read anything serious, and do absolutely nothing; they only talk about science and know very little about art. They all look serious, have grim expressions, speak of weighty matters, and philosophize; and meanwhile anyone can see that the workers eat abominably, sleep without pillows, thirty or forty to a room, and everywhere there are bedbugs, stench, dampness, and immorality. . . . It's obvious that all our fine talk is merely to delude ourselves and others. Show me the day nurseries they are always talking about—and where are the reading rooms? They only write about them in novels, but in reality they don't exist. There is nothing but filth, vulgarity, asiaticism.[4] . . . I'm afraid of those very serious countenances, I don't like them, I'm afraid of serious conversations. We'd do better to remain silent.

LOPAKHIN. You know, I get up before five in the morning, and I work from morning to night; now, I'm always handling money, my own and other people's, and I see what people around me are like. You have only to start doing something to find out how few honest, decent people there are. Sometimes, when I can't sleep, I think: "Lord, Thou gavest us vast forests, boundless fields, broad horizons, and living in their midst we ourselves ought truly to be giants. . . ."

LYUBOV ANDREYEVNA. Now you want giants! They're good only in fairy tales, otherwise they're frightening.

(*Yepikhodov crosses at the rear of the stage, playing the guitar.*)

LYUBOV ANDREYEVNA (*pensively*). There goes Yepikhodov . . .

ANYA (*pensively*). There goes Yepikhodov . . .

GAYEV. The sun has set, ladies and gentlemen.

TROFIMOV. Yes.

GAYEV (*in a low voice, as though reciting*). Oh, Nature, wondrous Nature, you shine with eternal radiance, beautiful and indifferent; you, whom we call mother, unite within yourself both life and death, giving life and taking it away. . . .

VARYA (*beseechingly*). Uncle dear!

ANYA. Uncle, you're doing it again!

TROFIMOV. You'd better cue ball into the center.

GAYEV. I'll be silent, silent.

(*All sit lost in thought. The silence is broken only by the subdued muttering of Firs. Suddenly a distant sound is heard, as if from the sky, like the sound of a snapped string mournfully dying away.*)

LYUBOV ANDREYEVNA. What was that?

LOPAKHIN. I don't know. Somewhere far off in a mine shaft a bucket's broken loose. But somewhere very far away.

GAYEV. It might be a bird of some sort . . . like a heron.

TROFIMOV. Or an owl . . .

LYUBOV ANDREYEVNA (*shudders*). It's unpleasant somehow. . . . (*Pause.*)

FIRS. The same thing happened before the troubles: An owl hooted and the samovar hissed continually.

GAYEV. Before what troubles?

FIRS. Before the emancipation.

LYUBOV ANDREYEVNA. Come along, my friends, let us go, evening is falling. (*To Anya.*) There are tears in your eyes—what is it, my little one? (*Embraces her.*)

ANYA. It's all right, Mama. It's nothing.

TROFIMOV. Someone is coming.

(*A Stranger appears wearing a shabby white forage cap and an overcoat. He is slightly drunk.*)

---

[4]**asiaticism** Trofimov is referring to Asian apathy; a common Russian prejudice of the time.

STRANGER. Permit me to inquire, can I go straight through here to the station?

GAYEV. You can follow the road.

STRANGER. I am deeply grateful to you. (*Coughs.*) Splendid weather.... (*Reciting.*) "My brother, my suffering brother ... come to the Volga, whose groans" ... (*To Varya.*) Mademoiselle, will you oblige a hungry Russian with thirty kopecks?

(*Varya, frightened, cries out.*)

LOPAKHIN (*angrily*). There's a limit to everything.

LYUBOV ANDREYEVNA (*panic-stricken*). Here you are—take this ... (*Fumbles in her purse.*) I have no silver.... Never mind, here's a gold piece for you....

STRANGER. I am deeply grateful to you. (*Goes off.*)

(*Laughter.*)

VARYA (*frightened*). I'm leaving ... I'm leaving.... Oh, Mama, dear, there's nothing in the house for the servants to eat, and you give him a gold piece!

LYUBOV ANDREYEVNA. What's to be done with such a silly creature? When we get home I'll give you all I've got. Yermolai Alekseyevich, you'll lend me some more!

LOPAKHIN. At your service.

LYUBOV ANDREYEVNA. Come, my friends, it's time to go. Oh, Varya, we have definitely made a match for you. Congratulations!

VARYA (*through tears*). Mama, that's not something to joke about.

LOPAKHIN. "Aurelia, get thee to a nunnery ... "[5]

GAYEV. Look, my hands are trembling: It's a long time since I've played a game of billiards.

LOPAKHIN. "Aurelia, O Nymph, in thy orisons, be all my sins remember'd!"

LYUBOV ANDREYEVNA. Let us go, my friends, it will soon be suppertime.

VARYA. He frightened me. My heart is simply pounding.

LOPAKHIN. Let me remind you, ladies and gentlemen: On the twenty-second of August the cherry orchard is to be sold. Think about that!—Think!

(*All go out except Trofimov and Anya.*)

ANYA (*laughs*). My thanks to the stranger for frightening Varya, now we are alone.

TROFIMOV. Varya is so afraid we might suddenly fall in love with each other that she hasn't left us alone for days. With her narrow mind she can't understand that we are above love. To avoid the petty and the illusory, which prevent our being free and happy—that is the aim and meaning of life. Forward! We are moving irresistibly toward the bright star that burns in the distance! Forward! Do not fall behind, friends!

ANYA (*clasping her hands*). How well you talk! (*Pause.*) It's marvelous here today!

TROFIMOV. Yes, the weather is wonderful.

ANYA. What have you done to me, Petya, that I no longer love the cherry orchard as I used to? I loved it so tenderly, it seemed to me there was no better place on earth than our orchard.

TROFIMOV. All Russia is our orchard. It is a great and beautiful land, and there are many wonderful places in it. (*Pause.*) Just think, Anya: Your grandfather, your great-grandfather, and all your ancestors were serf-owners, possessors of living souls. Don't you see that from every cherry tree, from every leaf and trunk, human beings are peering out at you? Don't you hear their voices? To possess living souls—that has corrupted all of you, those who lived before and you who are living now, so that your mother, you, your uncle, no longer perceive that you are living in debt, at someone else's expense, at the expense of those whom you wouldn't allow to cross your threshold.... We are at least two hundred years behind the times, we have as yet absolutely nothing, we have no definite attitude toward the past, we only philosophize, complain of boredom, or drink vodka. Yet it's quite clear that to begin to live we must first atone for the past, be done with it, and we can atone for it only by suffering, only by extraordinary, unceasing labor. Understand this, Anya.

ANYA. The house we live in hasn't really been ours for a long time, and I shall leave it, I give you my word.

TROFIMOV. If you have the keys of the household, throw them into the well and go. Be as free as the wind.

ANYA (*ecstasy*). How well you put that!

TROFIMOV. Believe me, Anya, believe me! I am not yet thirty, I am young, still a student, but I have already been through so much! As soon as winter comes, I am hungry, sick, worried, poor as a beggar, and—where has not fate driven me! Where have I not been? And yet always, every minute of the day and night, my soul was filled with inexplicable premonitions. I have a premonition of happiness, Anya, I can see it ...

ANYA. The moon is rising.

(*Yepikhodov is heard playing the same melancholy song on the guitar. The moon rises. Somewhere near the poplars Varya is looking for Anya and calling: "Anya, where are you?"*)

TROFIMOV. Yes, the moon is rising. (*Pause.*) There it is—happiness ... it's coming, nearer and nearer, I can hear its footsteps. And if we do not see it, if we do not recognize it, what does it matter? Others will see it.

VARYA'S VOICE. Anya! Where are you?

TROFIMOV. That Varya again! (*Angrily.*) It's revolting!

ANYA. Well? Let's go down to the river. It's lovely there.

TROFIMOV. Come on. (*They go.*)

VARYA'S VOICE. Anya! Anya!

---

[5]**"Aurelia ... nunnery"** Lopakhin misquotes Hamlet's famous line rejecting Ophelia. His next line is also from *Hamlet*).

ACT III

(The drawing room, separated by an arch from the ball-room. The chandelier is lighted. The Jewish band that was mentioned in act II is heard playing in the hall. It is evening. In the ballroom they are dancing a grand rond. The voice of Semyonov-Pishchik: "Promenade à une paire!"[6] They all enter the drawing room: Pishchik and Charlotta Ivanovna are the first couple, Trofimov and Lyubov Andreyevna the second, Anya and the Post-Office Clerk the third, Varya and the Stationmaster the fourth, etc. Varya, quietly weeping, dries her tears as she dances. Dunyasha is in the last couple. As they cross the drawing room Pishchik calls: "Grand rond, balancez!" and "Les cavaliers à genoux et remercier vos dames!"[7] Firs, wearing a dress coat, brings in a tray with seltzer water. Pishchik and Trofimov come into the drawing room.)

PISHCHIK. I'm a full-blooded man, I've already had two strokes, and dancing's hard work for me, but as they say, "If you run with the pack, you can bark or not, but at least wag your tail." At that, I'm as strong as a horse. My late father—quite a joker he was, God rest his soul—used to say, talking about our origins, that the ancient line of Semyonov-Pishchik was descended from the very horse that Caligula had seated in the Senate.[8] . . . *(Sits down.)* But the trouble is—no money! A hungry dog believes in nothing but meat. . . . *(Snores but wakes up at once.)* It's the same with me—I can think of nothing but money. . . .

TROFIMOV. You know, there really is something equine about your figure.

PISHCHIK. Well, a horse is a fine animal. . . . You can sell a horse.

(There is the sound of a billiard game in the next room. Varya appears in the archway.)

TROFIMOV *(teasing her)*: Madame Lopakhina! Madame Lopakhina!

VARYA *(angrily)*. Mangy gentleman!

TROFIMOV. Yes, I am a mangy gentleman, and proud of it!

VARYA *(reflecting bitterly)*. Here we've hired musicians, and what are we going to pay them with? *(Goes out.)*

TROFIMOV *(to Pishchik)*. If the energy you have expended in the course of your life trying to find money to pay interest had gone into something else, ultimately, you might very well have turned the world upside down.

PISHCHIK. Nietzsche . . . the philosopher . . . the greatest, most renowned . . . a man of tremendous intellect . . . says in his works that it is possible to forge banknotes.

TROFIMOV. And have you read Nietzsche?

PISHCHIK. Well . . . Dashenka told me. I'm in such a state now that I'm just about ready for forging. . . . The day after tomorrow I have to pay three hundred and ten rubles . . . I've got a hundred and thirty. . . . *(Feels in his pocket, grows alarmed.)* The money is gone! I've lost the money! *(Tearfully.)* Where is my money? *(Joyfully.)* Here it is, inside the lining. . . . I'm all in a sweat. . . .

(Lyubov Andreyevna and Charlotta Ivanovna come in.)

LYUBOV ANDREYEVNA *(humming a Lezginka)*.[9] Why does Leonid take so long? What is he doing in town? *(To Dunyasha.)* Dunyasha, offer the musicians some tea.

TROFIMOV. In all probability, the auction didn't take place.

LYUBOV ANDREYEVNA. It was the wrong time to have the musicians, the wrong time to give a dance. . . . Well, never mind. . . . *(Sits down and hums softly.)*

CHARLOTTA *(gives Pishchik a deck of cards)*. Here's a deck of cards for you. Think of a card.

PISHCHIK. I've thought of one.

CHARLOTTA. Now shuffle the pack. Very good. And now, my dear Mr. Pishchik, hand it to me. *Ein, zwei, drei!* Now look for it—it's in your side pocket.

PISHCHIK. *(takes the card out of his side pocket)*. The eight of spades—absolutely right! *(Amazed.)* Think of that, now!

CHARLOTTA. *(holding the deck of cards in the palm of her hand, to Trofimov)*. Quickly, tell me, which card is on top?

TROFIMOV. What? Well, the queen of spades.

CHARLOTTA. Right! *(To Pishchik.)* Now which card is on top?

PISHCHIK. The ace of hearts.

CHARLOTTA. Right! *(Claps her hands and the deck of cards disappears.)* What lovely weather we're having today! *(A mysterious feminine voice, which seems to come from under the floor, answers her: "Oh, yes, splendid weather, madam.")* You are so nice, you're my ideal. . . . *(The voice: "And I'm very fond of you, too, madam.")*

STATIONMASTER *(applauding)*. Bravo, Madame Ventriloquist!

PISHCHIK *(amazed)*. Think of that, now! Most enchanting Charlotta Ivanovna . . . I am simply in love with you. . . .

CHARLOTTA. In love? *(Shrugs her shoulders.)* Is it possible that you can love? *Guter Mensch, aber schlechter Musikant.*[10]

TROFIMOV *(claps Pishchik on the shoulder)*. You old horse, you!

CHARLOTTA. Attention, please! One more trick. *(Takes a lap robe from a chair.)* Here's a very fine lap robe; I should like to sell it. *(Shakes it out.)* Doesn't anyone want to buy it?

---

[6]*"Promenade à une paire!"* promenade in pairs.
[7]*"Grand rond . . . dames!"* "Large circle!" and "Gentlemen, kneel down and thank our ladies!"
[8]*Caligula . . . Senate:* Caligula (A.D. 12–41), a Roman cavalry soldier; Roman emperor (A.D. 37–41) said to have appointed a horse to the Senate.

[9]*Lezginka* a lively Russian tune for a dance
[10]*Guter Mensch, aber schlechter Musikant:* "Good man, but poor musician"

PISHCHIK (*amazed*). Think of that, now!

CHARLOTTA. *Ein, zwei, drei!* (*Quickly raises the lap robe; behind it stands Anya, who curtsies, runs to her mother, embraces her, and runs back into the ballroom amid the general enthusiasm.*)

LYUBOV ANDREYEVNA (*applauding*). Bravo, bravo!

CHARLOTTA. Once again! *Ein, zwei, drei.* (*Raises the lap robe; behind it stands Varya, who bows.*)

PISHCHIK. (*amazed*). Think of that, now!

CHARLOTTA. The end! (*Throws the robe at Pishchik, makes a curtsy, and runs out of the room.*)

PISHCHIK (*hurries after her*). The minx! . . . What a woman! What a woman! (*Goes out.*)

LYUBOV ANDREYEVNA. And Leonid still not here. What he is doing in town so long, I do not understand! It must be all over by now. Either the estate is sold, or the auction didn't take place—but why keep us in suspense so long!

VARYA (*trying to comfort her*). Uncle has bought it, I am certain of that.

TROFIMOV (*mockingly*). Yes.

VARYA. Great-aunt sent him power of attorney to buy it in her name and transfer the debt. She's doing it for Anya's sake. And I am sure, with God's help, Uncle will buy it.

LYUBOV ANDREYEVNA. Our great-aunt in Yaroslav sent fifteen thousand to buy the estate in her name—she doesn't trust us—but that's not even enough to pay the interest. (*Covers her face with her hands.*) Today my fate will be decided, my fate . . .

TROFIMOV (*teasing Varya*). Madame Lopakhina!

VARYA (*angrily*). Eternal student! Twice already you've been expelled from the university.

LYUBOV ANDREYEVNA. Why are you so cross, Varya? If he teases you about Lopakhin, what of it? Go ahead and marry Lopakhin if you want to. He's a nice man, he's interesting. And if you don't want to, don't. Nobody's forcing you, my pet.

VARYA. To be frank, Mama dear, I regard this matter seriously. He is a good man, I like him.

LYUBOV ANDREYEVNA. Then marry him. I don't know what you're waiting for!

VARYA. Mama, I can't propose to him myself. For the last two years everyone's been talking to me about him; everyone talks, but he is either silent or he jokes. I understand. He's getting rich, he's absorbed in business, he has no time for me. If I had some money, no matter how little, if it were only a hundred rubles, I'd drop everything and go far away. I'd go into a nunnery.

TROFIMOV. A blessing!

VARYA (*to Trofimov*). A student ought to be intelligent! (*In a gentle tone, tearfully.*) How homely you have grown, Petya, how old! (*To Lyubov Andreyevna, no longer crying.*) It's just that I cannot live without work, Mama. I must be doing something every minute.

(*Yasha enters.*)

YASHA (*barely able to suppress his laughter.*) Yepikhodov has broken a billiard cue! (*Goes out.*)

VARYA. But why is Yepikhodov here? Who gave him permission to play billiards? I don't understand these people. . . . (*Goes out.*)

LYUBOV ANDREYEVNA. Don't tease her, Petya. You can see she's unhappy enough without that.

TROFIMOV. She's much too zealous, always meddling in other people's affairs. All summer long she's given Anya and me no peace—afraid a romance might develop. What business is it of hers? Besides, I've given no occasion for it, I am far removed from such banality. We are above love!

LYUBOV ANDREYEVNA. And I suppose I am beneath love. (*In great agitation.*) Why isn't Leonid here? If only I knew whether the estate had been sold or not! The disaster seems to me so incredible that I don't even know what to think, I'm lost. . . . I could scream this very instant . . . I could do something foolish. Save me, Petya. Talk to me, say something. . . .

TROFIMOV. Whether or not the estate is sold today—does it really matter? That's all done with long ago; there's no turning back, the path is overgrown. Be calm, my dear. One must not deceive oneself; at least once in one's life one ought to look the truth straight in the eye.

LYUBOV ANDREYEVNA. What truth? You can see where there is truth and where there isn't, but I seem to have lost my sight, I see nothing. You boldly settle all the important problems, but tell me, my dear boy, isn't it because you are young and have not yet had to suffer for a single one of your problems? You boldly look ahead, but isn't it because you neither see nor expect anything dreadful, since life is still hidden from your young eyes? You're bolder, more honest, deeper than we are, but think about it, be just a little bit magnanimous, and spare me. You see, I was born here, my mother and father lived here, and my grandfather. I love this house, without the cherry orchard my life has no meaning for me, and if it must be sold, then sell me with the orchard. . . . (*Embraces Trofimov and kisses him on the forehead.*) And my son was drowned here. . . . (*Weeps.*) Have pity on me, you good, kind man.

TROFIMOV. You know I feel for you with all my heart.

LYUBOV ANDREYEVNA. But that should have been said differently, quite differently. . . . (*Takes out her handkerchief and a telegram falls to the floor.*) My heart is heavy today, you can't imagine. It's so noisy here, my soul quivers at every sound, I tremble all over, and yet I can't go to my room. When I am alone the silence frightens me. Don't condemn me, Petya . . . I love you as if you were my own. I would gladly let you marry Anya, I swear it, only you must study, my dear, you must get your degree. You do nothing, fate simply tosses you from place to place—it's so strange. . . . Isn't that true? Isn't it? And you must do something about your beard, to make it grow somehow. . . . (*Laughs.*) You're so funny!

TROFIMOV (*picks up the telegram*). I have no desire to be an Adonis.

LYUBOV ANDREYEVNA. That's a telegram from Paris. I get them every day. One yesterday, one today. That wild man has fallen ill again, he's in trouble again. . . . He begs my forgiveness, implores me to come, and really, I ought to go to Paris to be near him. Your face is stern, Petya, but what can one do, my dear? What am I to do? He is ill, he's alone and unhappy, and who will look after him there, who will keep him from making mistakes, who will give him his medicine on time? And why hide it or keep silent, I love him, that's clear. I love him, love him. . . . It's a millstone round my neck, I'm sinking to the bottom with it, but I love that stone, I cannot live without it. (*Presses Trofimov's hand.*) Don't think badly of me, Petya, and don't say anything to me, don't say anything. . . .

TROFIMOV (*through tears*). For Gods sake, forgive my frankness: You know that he robbed you!

LYUBOV ANDREYEVNA. No, no, no, you mustn't say such things! (*Covers her ears.*)

TROFIMOV. But he's a scoundrel! You're the only one who doesn't know it! He's a petty scoundrel, a nonentity—

LYUBOV ANDREYEVNA (*angry, but controlling herself*). You are twenty-six or twenty-seven years old, but you're still a schoolboy!

TROFIMOV. That may be!

LYUBOV ANDREYEVNA. You should be a man, at your age you ought to understand those who love. And you ought to be in love yourself. (*Angrily.*) Yes, yes! It's not purity with you, it's simply prudery, you're a ridiculous crank, a freak—

TROFIMOV (*horrified*). What is she saying!

LYUBOV ANDREYEVNA. "I am above love!" You're not above love, you're just an addlepate, as Firs would say. Not to have a mistress at your age!

TROFIMOV (*in horror*). This is awful! What is the saying! . . . (*Goes quickly toward the ballroom.*) This is awful . . . I can't . . . I won't stay here. . . . (*Goes out, but immediately returns.*) All is over between us! (*Goes out to the hall.*)

LYUBOV ANDREYEVNA (*calls after him*). Petya, wait! You absurd creature, I was joking! Petya!

(*In the hall there is the sound of someone running quickly downstairs and suddenly falling with a crash. Anya and Varya scream, but a moment later laughter is heard.*)

LYUBOV ANDREYEVNA. What was that?

(*Anya runs in.*)

ANYA (*laughing*). Petya fell down the stairs! (*Runs out.*)

LYUBOV ANDREYEVNA. What a funny boy that Petya is!

(*The Stationmaster stands in the middle of the ballrrom and recites A. Tolstoy's[11] "The Sinner." Everyone listens*

[11] **A. Tolstoy** Aleksey Konstantinovich Tolstoy (1817–1875), Russian novelist, dramatist, and poet

to him, but he has no sooner spoken a few lines than the sound of a waltz is heard from the hall and the recitation is broken off. They all dance. Trofimov, Anya, Varya, and Lyubov Andreyevna come in from the hall.*)

LYUBOV ANDREYEVNA. Come, Petya . . . come, you pure soul . . . please, forgive me. . . . Let's dance. . . . (*They dance.*)

(*Anya and Varya dance. Firs comes in, puts his stick by the side door. Yasha also comes into the drawing room and watches the dancers.*)

YASHA. What is it, grandpa?

FIRS. I don't feel well. In the old days, we used to have generals, barons, admirals, dancing at our balls, but now we send for the post office clerk and the stationmaster, and even they are none too eager to come. Somehow I've grown weak. The late master, their grandfather, dosed everyone with sealing wax, no matter what ailed them. I've been taking sealing wax every day for twenty years or more; maybe that's what's kept me alive.

YASHA. You bore me, grandpa. (*Yawns.*) High time you croaked.

FIRS. Ah, you . . . addlepate! (*Mumbles.*)

(*Trofimov and Lyubov Andreyevna dance from the ballroom into the drawing room.*)

LYUBOV ANDREYEVNA. *Merci.* I'll sit down a while. (*Sits.*) I'm tired.

(*Anya comes in.*)

ANYA (*excitedly*). There was a man in the kitchen just now saying that the cherry orchard was sold today.

LYUBOV ANDREYEVNA. Sold to whom?

ANYA. He didn't say. He's gone. (*Dances with Trofimov; they go into the ballroom.*)

YASHA. That was just some old man babbling. A stranger.

FIRS. Leonid Andreyevich is not back yet, still hasn't come. And he's wearing the light, between-seasons overcoat; like enough he'll catch cold. Ah, when they're young they're green.

LYUBOV ANDREYEVNA. This is killing me. Yasha, go and find out who it was sold to.

YASHA. But that old man left long ago. (*Laughs.*)

LYUBOV ANDREYEVNA (*slightly annoyed*). Well, what are you laughing at? What are you so happy about?

YASHA. That Yepikhodov is very funny! Hopeless! Two-and-twenty Troubles.

LYUBOV ANDREYEVNA. Firs, if the estate is sold, where will you go?

FIRS. Wherever you tell me to go, I'll go.

LYUBOV ANDREYEVNA. Why do you look like that? Aren't you well? You ought to go to bed.

FIRS. Yes. . . . (*With a smirk.*) Go to bed, and without me who will serve, who will see to things? I'm the only one in the whole house.

YASHA (*to Lyubov Andreyevna*). Lyubov Andreyevna! Permit me to make a request, be so kind! If you go back to Paris again, do me the favor of taking me with you. It is positively impossible for me to stay here. (*Looking around, then in a low voice.*) There's no need to say it, you can see for yourself, it's an uncivilized country, the people have no morals, and the boredom! The food they give us in the kitchen is unmentionable, and besides, there's this Firs who keeps walking about mumbling all sorts of inappropriate things. Take me with you, be so kind!

(*Enter Pishchik.*)

PISHCHIK. May I have the pleasure of a waltz with you, fairest lady? (*Lyubov Andreyevna goes with him.*) I really must borrow a hundred and eighty rubles from you, my charmer . . . I really must. . . . (*Dancing.*) Just a hundred and eighty rubles. . . . (*They pass into the ballroom.*)

YASHA (*softly sings*). "Wilt thou know my soul's unrest . . . "

(*In the ballroom a figure in a gray top hat and checked trousers is jumping about, waving its arms; there are shouts of "Bravo, Charlotta Ivanovna!"*)

DUNYASHA (*stopping to powder her face*). The young mistress told me to dance—there are lots of gentlemen and not enough ladies—but dancing makes me dizzy, and my heart begins to thump. Firs Nikolayevich, the post office clerk just said something to me that took my breath away.

(*The music grows more subdued.*)

FIRS. What did he say to you?

DUNYASHA. "You," he said, "are like a flower."

YASHA (*yawns*). What ignorance. . . . (*Goes out.*)

DUNYASHA. Like a flower. . . . I'm such a delicate girl, I just adore tender words.

FIRS. You'll get your head turned.

(*Enter Yepikhodov.*)

YEPIKHODOV. Avdotya Fyodorovna, you are not desirous of seeing me. . . . I might also be some sort of insect. (*Sighs.*) Ah, life!

DUNYASHA. What is you want?

YEPIKHODOV. Indubitably, you may be right. (*Sighs.*) But, of course, if one looks at it from a point of view, then, if I may so express myself, and you will forgive my frankness, you have completely reduced me to a state of mind. I know my fate, every day some misfortune befalls me, but I have long since grown accustomed to that; I look upon my fate with a smile. But you gave me your word, and although I—

DUNYASHA. Please, we'll talk about it later, but leave me in peace now. Just now I'm dreaming. . . . (*Plays with her fan.*)

YEPIKHODOV. Every day, a misfortune, and yet, if I may so express myself, I merely smile, I even laugh.

(*Varya enters from the ballroom.*)

VARYA. Are you still here, Semyon? What a disrespectful man you are, really! (*To Dunyasha.*) Run along, Dunyasha. (*To Yepikhodov.*) First you play billiards and break a cue, then you wander about the drawing room as though you were a guest.

YEPIKHODOV. You cannot, if I may so express myself, penalize me.

VARYA. I am not penalizing you, I'm telling you. You do nothing but wander from one place to another, and you don't do your work. We keep a clerk, but for what, I don't know.

YEPIKHODOV (*offended*). Whether I work, or wander about, or eat, or play billiards, these are matters to be discussed only by persons of discernment, and my elders.

VARYA. You dare say that to me! (*Flaring up.*) You dare? You mean to say I have no discernment? Get out of here! This instant!

YEPIKHODOV (*intimidated*). I beg you to express yourself in a more delicate manner.

VARYA (*beside herself*). Get out, this very instant! Get out! (*He goes to the door, she follows him.*) Two-and-twenty Troubles! Don't let me set eyes on you again!

YEPIKHODOV (*goes out, his voice is heard behind the door*). I shall lodge a complaint against you!

VARYA. Oh, you're coming back? (*Seizes the stick left near the door by Firs.*) Come, come on. . . . Come, I'll show you. . . . Ah, so you're coming, are you? Then take that— (*Swings the stick just as Lopakhin enters.*)

LOPAKHIN. Thank you kindly.

VARYA (*angrily and mockingly*). I beg your pardon.

LOPAKHIN. Not at all. I humbly thank you for your charming reception.

VARYA. Don't mention it. (*Walks away, then looks back and gently asks.*) I didn't hurt you, did I?

LOPAKHIN. No, it's nothing. A huge bump coming up, that's all.

(*Voices in the ballroom: "Lopakhin has come! Yermolai Alekseyevich!" Pishchik enters.*)

PISHCHIK. As I live and breathe! (*Kisses Lopakhin.*) There is a whiff of cognac about you, dear soul. And we've been making merry here, too.

(*Enter Lyubov Andreyevna.*)

LYUBOV ANDREYEVNA. Is that you, Yermolai Alekseyevich? What kept you so long? Where's Leonid?

LOPAKHIN. Leonid Andreyevich arrived with me, he's coming . . .

LYUBOV ANDREYEVNA (*agitated*). Well, what happened? Did the sale take place? Tell me!

LOPAKHIN (*embarrassed, fearing to reveal his joy*). The auction was over by four o'clock. . . . We missed the train, had to wait till half past nine. (*Sighing heavily.*) Ugh! My head is swimming. . . .

(*Enter Gayev; he carries his purchases in one hand and wipes away his tears with the other.*)

LYUBOV ANDREYEVNA. Lyonya, what happened? Well, Lyonya? (*Impatiently, through tears.*) Be quick, for God's sake!

GAYEV (*not answering her, simply waves his hand. To Firs, weeping*). Here, take these. . . . There's anchovies, Kerch herrings. . . . I haven't eaten anything all day. . . . What I have been through! (*The click of billiard balls is heard through the open door to the billiard room, and Yasha's voice: "Seven and eighteen!" Gayev's expression changes, he is no longer weeping.*) I'm terribly tired. Firs, help me change. (*Goes through the ballroom to his own room, followed by Firs.*)

PISHCHIK. What happened at the auction? Come on, tell us!

LYUBOV ANDREYEVNA. Is the cherry orchard sold?

LOPAKHIN. It's sold.

LYUBOV ANDREYEVNA. Who bought it?

LOPAKHIN. I bought it. (*Pause.*)

(*Lyubov Andreyevna is overcome; she would fall to the floor if it were not for the chair and table near which she stands. Varya takes the keys from her belt and throws them on the floor in the middle of the drawing room and goes out.*)

LOPAKHIN. I bought it! Kindly wait a moment, ladies and gentlemen, my head is swimming. I can't talk. . . . (*Laughs.*) We arrived at the auction, Deriganov was already there. Leonid Andreyevich had only fifteen thousand, and straight off Deriganov bid thirty thousand over and above the mortgage. I saw how the land lay, so I got into the fight and bid forty. He bid forty-five. I bid fifty-five. In other words, he kept raising it by five thousand, and I by ten. Well, it finally came to an end. I bid ninety thousand above the mortgage, and it was knocked down to me. The cherry orchard is now mine! Mine! (*Laughs uproariously.*) Lord! God in heaven! The cherry orchard is mine! Tell me I'm drunk, out of my mind, that I imagine it. . . . (*Stamps his feet.*) Don't laugh at me! If my father and my grandfather could only rise from their graves and see all that has happened, how their Yermolai, their beaten, half-literate Yermolai, who used to run about barefoot in winter, how that same Yermolai has bought an estate, the most beautiful estate in the whole world! I bought the estate where my father and grandfather were slaves, where they weren't even allowed in the kitchen. I'm asleep, this is just some dream of mine, it only seems to be. . . . It's the fruit of your imagination, hidden in the darkness of uncertainty. . . . (*Picks up the keys, smiling tenderly.*) She threw down the keys, wants to show that she's not mistress here anymore. . . . (*Jingles the keys.*) Well, no matter. (*The orchestra is heard tuning up.*) Hey, musicians, play, I want to hear you! Come on, everybody, and see how Yermolai Lopakhin will lay the ax to the cherry orchard, how the trees will fall to the ground! We're going to build summer cottages and our grandsons and great-grandsons will see a new life here. . . . Music! Strike up!

(*The orchestra plays. Lyubov Andreyevna sinks into a chair and weeps bitterly.*)

LOPAKHIN (*reproachfully*). Why didn't you listen to me, why? My poor friend, there's no turning back now. (*With tears.*) Oh, if only all this could be over quickly, if somehow our discordant, unhappy life could be changed!

PISHCHIK (*takes him by the arm; speaks in an undertone*). She's crying. Let's go into the ballroom, let her be alone. . . . Come on. . . . (*Leads him into the ballroom.*)

LOPAKHIN. What's happened? Musicians, play so I can hear you! Let everything be as I want it! (*Ironically.*) Here comes the new master, owner of the cherry orchard! (*Accidentally bumps into a little table, almost upsetting the candelabrum.*) I can pay for everything! (*Goes out with Pishchik.*)

(*There is no one left in either the drawing room or the ballroom except Lyubov Andreyevna, who sits huddled up and weeping bitterly. The music plays softly. Anya and Trofimov enter hurriedly. Anya goes to her mother and kneels before her. Trofimov remains in the doorway of the ballroom.*)

ANYA. Mama! . . . Mama, you're crying! Dear, kind, good Mama, my beautiful one, I love you . . . I bless you. The cherry orchard is sold, it's gone, that's true, true, but don't cry, Mama, life is still before you, you still have your good, pure soul. . . . Come with me, come, darling, we'll go away from here! . . . We'll plant a new orchard, more luxuriant than this one. You will see it and understand; and joy, quiet, deep joy, will sink into your soul, like the evening sun, and you will smile, Mama! Come, darling, let us go. . . .

ACT IV

(*The scene is the same as act I. There are neither curtains on the windows nor pictures on the walls, and only a little furniture piled up in one corner, as if for sale. There is a sense of emptiness. Near the outer door, at the rear of the stage, suitcases, traveling bags, etc., are piled up. Through the open door on the left the voices of Varya and Anya can be heard. Lopakhin stands waiting. Yasha is holding a tray with little glasses of champagne. In the hall, Yepikhodov is tying up a box. Offstage, at the rear, there is a hum of voices. It is the peasants who have come to say good-bye. Gayev's voice: "Thanks, brothers, thank you."*)

YASHA. The peasants have come to say good-bye. In my opinion, Yermolai Alekseyevich, peasants are good-natured, but they don't know much.

(*The hum subsides. Lyubov Andreyevna enters from the hall with Gayev. She is not crying, but she is pale, her face twitches, and she cannot speak.*)

GAYEV. You gave them your purse, Lyuba. That won't do! That won't do!

LYUBOV ANDREYEVNA. I couldn't help it! I couldn't help it! (*They both go out.*)

LOPAKHIN (*in the doorway, calls after them*). Please, do me the honor of having a little glass at parting. I didn't think of bringing champagne from town, and at the station I found only one bottle. Please! What's the matter, friends, don't you want any? (*Walks away from the door.*) If I'd known that, I wouldn't have bought it. Well, then I won't drink any either. (*Yasha carefully sets the tray down on a chair.*) At least you have a glass, Yasha.

YASHA. To those who are departing! Good luck! (*Drinks.*) This champagne is not the real stuff, I can assure you.

LOPAKHIN. Eight rubles a bottle. (*Pause.*) It's devilish cold in here.

YASHA. They didn't light the stoves today; it doesn't matter, since we're leaving. (*Laughs.*)

LOPAKHIN. Why are you laughing?

YASHA. Because I'm pleased.

LOPAKHIN. It's October, yet it's sunny and still outside, like summer. Good for building. (*Looks at his watch, then calls through the door.*) Bear in mind, ladies and gentlemen, only forty-six minutes till train time! That means leaving for the station in twenty minutes. Better hurry up!

(*Trofimov enters from outside wearing an overcoat.*)

TROFIMOV. Seems to me it's time to start. The carriages are at the door. What the devil has become of my rubbers? They're lost. (*Calls through the door.*) Anya, my rubbers are not here. I can't find them.

LOPAKHIN. I've got to go to Kharkov. I'm taking the same train you are. I'm going to spend the winter in Kharkov. I've been hanging around here with you, and I'm sick and tired of loafing. I can't live without work, I don't know what to do with my hands; they dangle in some strange way, as if they didn't belong to me.

TROFIMOV. We'll soon be done, then you can take up your useful labors again.

LOPAKHIN. Here, have a little drink.

TROFIMOV. No, I don't want any.

LOPAKHIN. So you're off for Moscow?

TROFIMOV. Yes, I'll see them into town, and tomorrow I'll go to Moscow.

LOPAKHIN. Yes. . . . Well, I expect the professors haven't been giving any lectures: They're waiting for you to come!

TROFIMOV. That's none of your business.

LOPAKHIN. How many years is it you've been studying at the university?

TROFIMOV. Can't you think of something new? That's stale and flat. (*Looks for his rubbers.*) You know, we'll probably never see each other again, so allow me to give you one piece of advice at parting: Don't wave your arms about! Get out of that habit—of arm-waving. And another thing, building cottages and counting on the summer res-

idents in time becoming independent farmers—that's just another form of arm-waving. Well, when all's said and done, I'm fond of you anyway. You have fine, delicate fingers, like an artist; you have a fine delicate soul.

LOPAKHIN (*embraces him*). Good-bye, my dear fellow. Thank you for everything. Let me give you some money for the journey, if you need it.

TROFIMOV. What for? I don't need it.

LOPAKHIN. But you haven't any!

TROFIMOV. I have. Thank you. I got some money for a translation. Here it is in my pocket. (*Anxiously.*) But where are my rubbers?

VARYA (*from the next room*). Here, take the nasty things! (*Flings a pair of rubbers onto the stage.*)

TROFIMOV. What are you so cross about, Varya? Hm. . . . But these are not my rubbers.

LOPAKHIN. In the spring I sowed three thousand acres of poppies, and now I've made forty thousand rubles clear. And when my poppies were in bloom, what a picture it was! So, I'm telling you, I've made forty thousand, which means I'm offering you a loan because I can afford to. Why turn up your nose? I'm a peasant—I speak bluntly.

TROFIMOV. Your father was a peasant, mine was a pharmacist—which proves absolutely nothing. (*Lopakhin takes out his wallet.*) No, don't—even if you gave me two hundred thousand I wouldn't take it. I'm a free man. And everything that is valued so highly and held so dear by all of you, rich and poor alike, has not the slightest power over me—it's like a feather floating in the air. I can get along without you, I can pass you by, I'm strong and proud. Mankind is advancing toward the highest truth, the highest happiness attainable on earth, and I am in the front ranks!

LOPAKHIN. Will you get there?

TROFIMOV. I'll get there. (*Pause.*) I'll either get there or I'll show others the way to get there.

(*The sound of axes chopping down trees is heard in the distance.*)

LOPAKHIN. Well, good-bye, my dear fellow. It's time to go. We turn up our noses at one another, but life goes on just the same. When I work for a long time without stopping, my mind is easier, and it seems to me that I, too, know why I exist. But how many there are in Russia, brother, who exist nobody knows why. Well, it doesn't matter, that's not what makes the wheels go round. They say Leonid Andreyevich has taken a position in the bank, six thousand a year. . . . Only, of course, he won't stick it out, he's too lazy. . . .

ANYA (*in the doorway*). Mama asks you not to start cutting down the cherry orchard until she's gone.

TROFIMOV. Yes, really, not to have had the tact . . . (*Goes out through the hall.*)

LOPAKHIN. Right away, right away. . . . Ach, what people. . . . (*Follows Trofimov out.*)

ANYA. Has Firs been taken to the hospital?

YASHA. I told them this morning. They must have taken him.

ANYA (*to Yepikhodov, who is crossing the room*). Semyon Panteleyevich, please find out if Firs has been taken to the hospital.

YASHA (*offended*). I told Yegor this morning. Why ask a dozen times?

YEPIKHODOV. It is my conclusive opinion that the venerable Firs is beyond repair; it's time he was gathered to his fathers. And I can only envy him. (*Puts a suitcase down on a hatbox and crushes it.*) There you are! Of course! I knew it! (*Goes out.*)

YASHA (*mockingly*). Two-and-twenty Troubles!

VARYA (*through the door*). Has Firs been taken to the hospital?

ANYA. Yes, he has.

VARYA. Then why didn't they take the letter to the doctor?

ANYA. We must send it on after them. . . . (*Goes out.*)

VARYA (*from the adjoining room*). Where is Yasha? Tell him his mother has come to say good-bye to him.

YASHA (*waves his hand*). They really try my patience.

(*Dunyasha has been fussing with the luggage; now that Yasha is alone she goes up to him.*)

DUNYASHA. You might give me one little look, Yasha. You're going away . . . leaving me. . . . (*Cries and throws herself on his neck.*)

YASHA. What's there to cry about? (*Drinks champagne.*) In six days I'll be in Paris again. Tomorrow we'll take the express, off we go, and that's the last you'll see of us. I can hardly believe it. *Vive la France!* This place is not for me, I can't live here. . . . It can't be helped. I've had enough of this ignorance—I'm fed up with it. (*Drinks champagne.*) What are you crying for? Behave yourself properly, then you won't cry.

DUNYASHA (*looks into a small mirror and powders her face*). Send me a letter from Paris. You know, I love you, Yasha, how I loved you! I'm such a tender creature, Yasha!

YASHA. Here they come. (*Busies himself with the luggage, humming softly.*)

(*Enter Lyubov Andreyevna, Gayev, Charlotta Ivanovna.*)

GAYEV. We ought to be leaving. There's not much time now. (*Looks at Yasha.*) Who smells of herring?

LYUBOV ANDREYEVNA. In about ten minutes we should be getting into the carriages. (*Glances around the room.*) Good-bye, dear house, old grandfather. Winter will pass, spring will come, and you will no longer be here, they will tear you down. How much these walls have seen! (*Kisses her daughter warmly.*) My treasure, you are radiant, your eyes are sparkling like two diamonds. Are you glad? Very?

GAYEV (*cheerfully*). Yes, indeed, everything is all right now. Before the cherry orchard was sold we were all worried and miserable, but afterward, when the question was finally settled once and for all, everybody calmed down and felt quite cheerful. . . . I'm in a bank now, a financier

. . . cue ball into the center . . . and you, Lyuba, say what you like, you look better, no doubt about it.

LYUBOV ANDREYEVNA. Yes. My nerves are better, that's true. (*Her hat and coat are handed to her.*) I sleep well. Carry out my things, Yasha, it's time. (*To Anya.*) My little girl, we shall see each other soon. . . . I shall go to Paris and live there on the money your great-aunt sent to buy the estate—long live Auntie!—but that money won't last long.

ANYA. You'll come back soon, Mama, soon . . . won't you? I'll study hard and pass my high school examinations, and then I can work and help you. We'll read all sorts of books together, Mama. . . . Won't we? (*Kisses her mother's hand.*) We'll read in the autumn evenings, we'll read lots of books, and a new and wonderful world will open up before us. . . . (*Dreaming.*) Mama, come back. . . .

LYUBOV ANDREYEVNA. I'll come, my precious. (*Embraces her.*)

(*Enter Lopakhin, Charlotta Ivanovna is softly humming a song.*)

GAYEV. Happy Charlotta: She's singing!

CHARLOTTA (*picks up a bundle and holds it like a baby in swaddling clothes*). Bye, baby, bye. . . . (*A baby's crying is heard, "Wah Wah!"*) Be quiet, my darling, my dear little boy. (*"Wah! Wah!"*) I'm so sorry for you! (*Throws the bundle down.*) You will find me a position, won't you? I can't go on like this.

LOPAKHIN. We'll find something, Charlotta Ivanovna, don't worry.

GAYEV. Everyone is leaving us, Varya's going away . . . all of a sudden nobody needs us.

CHARLOTTA. I have nowhere to go in town. I must go away. (*Hums.*) It doesn't matter . . .

(*Enter Pishchik.*)

LOPAKHIN. Nature's wonder!

PISHCHIK (*panting*). Ugh! Let me catch my breath. . . . I'm exhausted. . . . My esteemed friends. . . . Give me some water. . . .

GAYEV. After money, I suppose? Excuse me, I'm fleeing from temptation. . . . (*Goes out.*)

PISHCHIK. It's a long time since I've been to see you . . . fairest lady. . . . (*To Lopakhin*) So you're here. . . . Glad to see you, you intellectual giant. . . . Here . . . take it . . . four hundred rubles . . . I still owe you eight hundred and forty . . .

LOPAKHIN (*shrugs his shoulders in bewilderment*). I must be dreaming. . . . Where did you get it?

PISHCHIK. Wait . . . I'm hot. . . . A most extraordinary event. Some Englishmen came to my place and discovered some kind of white clay on my land. (*To Lyubov Andreyevna*) And four hundred for you . . . fairest, most wonderful lady. . . . (*Hands her the money.*) The rest later. (*Takes a drink of water.*) Just now a young man in the train was saying that a certain . . . great philosopher recommends jumping off roofs. . . . "Jump!" he says, and therein lies the whole problem. (*In amazement.*) Think of that, now! . . . Water!

LOPAKHIN. Who were those Englishmen?

PISHCHIK. I leased them the tract of land with the clay on it for twenty-four years. . . . And now, excuse me, I have no time . . . I must be trotting along . . . I'm going to Znoikov's . . . to Kardamanov's . . . I owe everybody. (*Drinks.*) Keep well . . . I'll drop in on Thursday . . .

LYUBOV ANDREYEVNA. We're just moving into town, and tomorrow I go abroad . . .

PISHCHIK. What? (*Alarmed.*) Why into town? That's why I see the furniture . . . suitcases. . . . Well, never mind. . . . (*Through tears.*) Never mind. . . . Men of the greatest intellect, those Englishmen. . . . Never mind. . . . Be happy . . . God will help you. . . . Never mind. . . . Everything in this world comes to an end. . . . (*Kisses Lyubov Andreyevna's hand.*) And should the news reach you that my end has come, just remember this old horse, and say: "There once lived a certain Semyonov-Pishchik, God rest his soul.". . . Splendid weather. . . . Yes. . . . (*Goes out greatly disconcerted, but immediately returns and speaks from the doorway.*) Dashenka sends her regards. (*Goes out.*)

LYUBOV ANDREYEVNA. Now we can go. I am leaving with two things on my mind. First—that Firs is sick. (*Looks at her watch.*) We still have about five minutes. . . .

ANYA. Mama, Firs has already been taken to the hospital. Yasha sent him there this morning.

LYUBOV ANDREYEVNA. My second concern is Varya. She's used to getting up early and working, and now, with no work to do, she's like a fish out of water. She's grown pale and thin, and cries all the time, poor girl. . . . (*Pauses.*) You know very well, Yermolai Alekseyevich, that I dreamed of marrying her to you, and everything pointed to your getting married. (*Whispers to Anya, who nods to Charlotta, and they both go out.*) She loves you, you are fond of her, and I don't know—I don't know why it is you seem to avoid each other. I can't understand it!

LOPAKHIN. To tell you the truth, I don't understand it myself. The whole thing is strange, somehow. . . . If there's still time, I'm ready right now. . . . Let's finish it up—and *basta*,[12] but without you I feel I'll never be able to propose to her.

LYUBOV ANDREYEVNA. Splendid! After all, it only takes a minute. I'll call her in at once. . . .

LOPAKHIN. And we even have the champagne. (*Looks at the glasses.*) Empty! Somebody's already drunk it. (*Yasha coughs.*) That's what you call lapping it up.

LYUBOV ANDREYEVNA (*animatedly*). Splendid! We'll leave you. . . . Yasha, *allez!*[13] I'll call her. . . . (*At the door.*) Varya, leave everything and come here. Come! (*Goes out with Yasha.*)

LOPAKHIN. (*looking at his watch*). Yes. . . . (*Pause.*)

(*Behind the door there is smothered laughter and whispering; finally Varya enters.*)

VARYA (*looking over the luggage for a long time*). Strange, I can't seem to find it . . .

LOPAKHIN. What are you looking for?

VARYA. I packed it myself, and I can't remember . . . (*Pause.*)

LOPAKHIN. Where are you going now, Varya Mikhailovna?

VARYA. I? To the Ragulins'. . . . I've agreed to go there to look after the house . . . as a sort of housekeeper.

LOPAKHIN. At Yashnevo? That would be about seventy versts from here. (*Pause.*) Well, life in this house has come to an end. . . .

VARYA (*examining the luggage*). Where can it be? . . . Perhaps I put it in the trunk. . . . Yes, life in this house has come to an end . . . there'll be no more . . .

LOPAKHIN. And I'm off for Kharkov . . . by the next train. I have a lot to do. I'm leaving Yepikhodov here . . . I've taken him on.

VARYA. Really!

LOPAKHIN. Last year at this time it was already snowing, if you remember, but now it's still and sunny. It's cold though . . . About three degrees of frost.

VARYA. I haven't looked. (*Pause.*) And besides, our thermometer's broken. (*Pause.*)

(*A voice from the yard calls: "Yermolai Alekseyevich!"*)

LOPAKHIN (*as if he had been waiting for a long time for the call*). Coming! (*Goes out quickly.*)

(*Varya sits on the floor, lays her head on a bundle of clothes, and quietly sobs. The door opens and Lyubov Andreyevna enters cautiously.*)

LYUBOV ANDREYEVNA. Well? (*Pause.*) We must be going.

VARYA (*no longer crying, dries her eyes*). Yes, it's time, Mama dear. I can get to the Ragulins' today, if only we don't miss the train.

LYUBOV ANDREYEVNA (*in the doorway*). Anya, put your things on!

(*Enter Anya, then Gayev and Charlotta Ivanovna. Gayev wears a warm overcoat with a hood. The servants and coachmen come in. Yepikhodov bustles about the luggage.*)

LYUBOV ANDREYEVNA. Now we can be on our way.

ANYA (*joyfully*). On our way!

GAYEV. My friends, my dear, cherished friends! Leaving this house forever, can I pass over in silence, can I refrain from giving utterance, as we say farewell, to those feelings that now fill my whole being—

ANYA (*imploringly*). Uncle!

VARYA. Uncle dear, don't!

GAYEV (*forlornly*). Double the rail off the white to center table . . . yellow into the side pocket. . . . I'll be quiet. . . .

(*Enter Trofimov, then Lopakhin.*)

---

[12]*basta* "enough" in Italian
[13]*allez* "go" in French

TROFIMOV. Well, ladies and gentlemen, it's time to go!

LOPAKHIN. Yepikhodov, my coat!

LYUBOV ANDREYEVNA. I'll sit here just one more minute. It's as though I had never before seen what the walls of this house were like, what the ceilings were like, and now I look at them hungrily, with such tender love . . .

GAYEV. I remember when I was six years old, sitting on this windowsill on Whitsunday, watching my father going to church . . .

LYUBOV ANDREYEVNA. Have they taken all the things?

LOPAKHIN. Everything, I think. (*Puts on his overcoat.*) Yepikhodov, see that everything is in order.

YEPIKHODOV (*in a hoarse voice*). Rest assured, Yermolai Alekseich!

LOPAKHIN. What's the matter with your voice?

YEPIKHODOV. Just drank some water . . . must have swallowed something.

YASHA (*contemptuously*). What ignorance!

LYUBOV ANDREYEVNA. When we go—there won't be a soul left here. . . .

LOPAKHIN. Till spring.

VARYA (*pulls an umbrella out of a bundle as though she were going to hit someone; Lopakhin pretends to be frightened*). Why are you—I never thought of such a thing!

TROFIMOV. Ladies and gentlemen, let's get into the carriages—it's time now! The train will soon be in!

VARYA. Petya, there they are—your rubbers, by the suitcase. (*Tearfully.*) And what dirty old things they are!

TROFIMOV (*putting on his rubbers*). Let's go, ladies and gentlemen!

GAYEV (*extremely upset, afraid of bursting into tears*). The train . . . the station. . . . Cross table to the center, double the rail . . . on the white into the corner.

LYUBOV ANDREYEVNA. Let us go!

GAYEV. Are we all here? No one in there? (*Locks the side door on the left.*) There are some things stored in there, we must lock up. Let's go!

ANYA. Good-bye, house! Good-bye, old life!

TROFIMOV. Hail to the new life! (*Goes out with Anya.*)

(*Varya looks around the room and slowly goes out. Yasha and Charlotta with her dog go out.*)

LOPAKHIN. And so, till spring. Come along, my friends. . . . Till we meet! (*Goes out.*)

(*Lyubov Andreyevna and Gayev are left alone. As though they had been waiting for this, they fall onto each other's necks and break into quiet, restrained sobs, afraid of being heard.*)

GAYEV (*in despair*). My sister, my sister. . . .

LYUBOV ANDREYEVNA. Oh, my dear, sweet, lovely orchard! . . . My life, my youth, my happiness, good-bye! . . . Good-bye!

ANYA'S VOICE (*gaily calling*). Mama!

TROFIMOV'S VOICE (*gay and excited*). Aa-oo!

LYUBOV ANDREYEVNA. One last look at these walls, these windows. . . . Mother loved to walk about in this room. . . .

GAYEV. My sister, my sister!

ANYA'S VOICE. Mama!

TROFIMOV'S VOICE. Aa-oo!

LYUBOV ANDREYEVNA. We're coming! (*They go out.*)

(*The stage is empty. There is the sound of doors being locked, then of the carriages driving away. It grows quiet. In the stillness there is the dull thud of an ax on a tree, a forlorn, melancholy sound. Footsteps are heard. From the door on the right Firs appears. He is dressed as always in a jacket and white waistcoat, and wears slippers. He is ill.*)

FIRS (*goes to the door and tries the handle*). Locked. They have gone. . . . (*Sits down on the sofa.*) They've forgotten me. . . . Never mind. . . . I'll sit here awhile. . . . I expect Leonid Andreyevich hasn't put on his fur coat and has gone off in his overcoat. (*Sighs anxiously.*) And I didn't see to it. . . . When they're young, they're green! (*Mumbles something which cannot be understood.*) I'll lie down awhile. . . . There's no strength left in you, nothing's left, nothing. . . . Ach, you . . . addlepate! (*Lies motionless.*)

(*A distant sound is heard that seems to come from the sky, the sound of a snapped string mournfully dying away. A stillness falls, and nothing is heard but the thud of an ax on a tree far away in the orchard.*)

RIDERS TO THE SEA

JOHN MILLINGTON SYNGE

JOHN MILLINGTON SYNGE (1871–1909)

Although he was not the leader of the Irish renaissance (the turn-of-the-century movement that gave birth to the modern Irish theater), arguably no other artist had more influence on the development of contemporary drama in Ireland than John Millington Synge. Actually, Synge (pronounced "sing") was in Paris when, in 1899, William Butler Yeats and Lady Augusta Gregory, aided by George Moore and Edward Martyn, envisioned an Irish national theater that would, in the words of their manifesto, "build up a Celtic and Irish school of dramatic literature," and "bring upon the stage the deeper thoughts and emotions of Ireland." Furthermore, these artists wanted to eradicate the centuries-old perception fostered by the British that Ireland was the "home of buffoonery and of easy entertainment." In short, the new Irish Literary Theatre wanted to cultivate a native drama about local life and problems, spoken in the native idiom.

In 1904 the group, now known as the Irish National Theatre Society, opened the Abbey Theatre in Dublin, which remains the oldest continuous national theater in Europe. While the Abbey met with some success with the works of Yeats and Lady Gregory, it was not until 1907, when it produced Synge's *The Playboy of the Western World*, that the theater became the center of national attention. Though many Irish felt that Synge's raucous portrait of Irish peasants was blasphemous, Synge was merely depicting his countrymen and -women with an uncompromising honesty, born of a genuine love of Ireland and its people. Such candor would become the hallmark of subsequent Abbey productions. The *Playboy* controversy sparked a national debate about the work of the Abbey and catapulted it to the forefront of Irish culture.

Synge was educated at Trinity College in Dublin, Ireland's foremost university and the spawning ground of Irish literati. Yet, like so many Irishmen, Synge fled his native home in 1894 seeking a literary career in Paris. In 1896 Yeats met Synge in Paris and counseled the young writer to return to Ireland. "Give up Paris," he urged, "You will never create anything by reading Racine. . . . Go to the Aran Islands. Live there as if you were one of the people themselves; express a life that has never found expression." Synge, haunted by Yeats's admonition, gradually abandoned his Parisian quest and returned to Ireland, and from 1898 to 1902 spent each summer among the rugged peasant stock of the Aran Isles west of Galway. Here he found source material for his best work, especially *Riders to the Sea*. He also learned the dialect of the common people, a language he turned into the poetic idiom that characterizes his plays. He filled notebooks with observations about life among the fishermen and farmers, noting in particular phrases, sayings, and other linguistic peculiarities. He also collected folk songs and dances which he used in his plays. Synge was himself an accomplished violinist, a talent that endeared him to his Aran hosts.

In 1902 Synge was invited by Yeats to join the emerging Irish National Theatre Society, and during the remaining seven years of his life (cut short by Hodgkin's disease), he wrote six plays that would establish him as the first great playwright of the Abbey Theatre. In addition to *Riders to the Sea* and *Playboy of the Western World*, Synge's best works include *In the Shadow of the Glen*, *The Well of the Saints*, and *Deirdre of the Sorrows*. The latter was produced posthumously in 1910, and like *Riders to the Sea* remains among Ireland's finest tragedies.

RIDERS TO THE SEA (1905)

Although it is thoroughly Irish in its language, customs, and specific subject matter (the death of Aran Islanders at the hands of the raging Western sea), *Riders to the Sea* evokes the memories of two ancient forms of drama: Greek tragedy and Noh drama. Synge, who graduated with high honors in Greek from Trinity, creates a modern equivalent of Attic tragedy both in mood and style. First, the inexorable presence of death is here. Maurya has already lost a husband and five sons to the sea, and Bartley's fateful journey is cast with a tragic inevitability. Just as the ancient oracles foretold a character's fate, Maurya's dream about red and grey ponies shapes the play's ending. Cathleen and Nora function as a chorus, slowly revealing Michael's fate. Importantly, at the end of the play they are joined by the larger chorus of women, keening a lament as old as Aran's rocks. The dirge sung by these Irish women, the sea's ultimate victims who are left with little but "a bit of wet flour . . . and maybe a fish that would be stinking," echoes the cry of Euripides' chorus in *The Trojan Women*.

Ultimately, however, it is the extraordinary dignity with which Maurya bears her sorrow that makes *Riders to the Sea* sublime. We have seen that tragic heroes since Oedipus have met their fate with a calm and certitude that transcend mortal comprehension. Maurya, who has endured the very worst that life can offer, defiantly notes "there isn't anything more the sea can do to me," and in the play's last speech addresses life's ultimate certainty: "No man at all can be living forever, and we must be satisfied." This realization aligns her with other tragic heroes, like Hamlet, who similarly noted of death that "there is a special providence in the fall of a sparrow. If it be now, 'tis not to come. If it be not to come, it will be now; if it be not now, yet it will come. The readiness is all." Indeed, life on the Aran Isles taught Synge and the characters he admired that the readiness is all.

Though it was Yeats whose writing was more obviously indebted to the Noh theater of Japan, Synge's short drama here begs comparison with Japan's stately drama. First, the play is, as noted, a dirge in which the surviving women "keen" (i.e., chant mournfully) in memory of the dead men. The keening, coupled with the lyrical language (not to mention the absolute simplicity of staging it requires), invests the drama with a meditative quality not unlike that of the Noh theater. Most importantly, the impulse behind Synge's play is consistent with our most ancient dramatic impulses: the observance of the life cycle. Though death apparently triumphs on Aran's isles, the life force manifests itself in Maurya.

Historically, *Riders to the Sea* is a significant work on two counts. First, it is among the earliest and most successful modern attempts to use the folk idiom as a vehicle for serious drama. In his preface to *The Playboy of the Western World*, Synge argued that modern drama must use a rich language that grows out of the folk imagination of the peasant people: "In Ireland . . . we have a popular imagination that is fiery and magnificent and tender, so that those of us who wish to write start with a chance that is not given to writers in places where the springtime of the local life has been forgotten." *Riders to the Sea* remains the exemplar of drama written in the folk idiom. Don't be lulled by the prose format in which Synge wrote the play: this is poetic drama at its most eloquent.

Secondly, at a time when Ibsen, Shaw, and others were presenting women as protagonists of Europe's new drama, Synge has rendered a hugely sympathetic, as opposed to merely sentimental, portrait of women as the victims of a society in which they have no recourse. Long after the men have been buried in "fine coffins out of white boards and a deep grave surely," it is the women who must survive. As Maurya asks Bartley, "What way will I live and the girls with me, and I an old woman looking for the grave?" Although Synge would never have considered himself a social dramatist in the mold of Ibsen or Shaw ("The drama, like the symphony, does not have to teach or prove anything," he wrote in response to the new naturalism), he nonetheless defines the plight of women entering the twentieth century in this simple folk tragedy. Denied work beyond their peasant huts, they can only "bear and bury" the men who support them.

The mood of somber anticipation and apprehension demanded by Synge's Riders to the Sea *was nicely captured in this 1998 Royal Shakespeare Company production.*

RIDERS TO THE SEA

JOHN MILLINGTON SYNGE

LIST OF CHARACTERS

MAURYA, *an old woman*
BARTLEY, *her son*
CATHLEEN, *her daughter*
NORA, *a younger daughter*
MEN *and* WOMEN

SCENE: *An island off the West of Ireland.*
Cottage kitchen, with nets, oil-skins, spinning-wheel, some new boards standing by the wall, etc. Cathleen, a girl of about twenty, finishes kneading cake, and puts it *down in the pot-oven by the fire; then wipes her hands, and begins to spin at the wheel. Nora, a young girl, puts her head in at the door.*

NORA (*in a low voice*). Where is she?

CATHLEEN. She's lying down, God help her, and may be sleeping, if she's able.

Nora comes in softly, and takes a bundle from under her shawl.

CATHLEEN (*spinning the wheel rapidly*). What is it you have?

NORA. The young priest is after bringing them. It's a shirt and a plain stocking were got off a drowned man in Donegal.

Cathleen stops her wheel with a sudden movement, and leans out to listen.

NORA. We're to find out if it's Michael's they are, some time herself will be down looking by the sea.

CATHLEEN. How would they be Michael's, Nora? How would he go the length of that way to the far north?

NORA. The young priest says he's known the like of it. "If it's Michael's they are," says he, "you can tell herself he's got a clean burial by the grace of God, and if they're not his, let no one say a word about them, for she'll be getting her death," says he, "with crying and lamenting."

The door which Nora half-closed is blown open by a gust of wind.

CATHLEEN (*looking out anxiously*). Did you ask him would he stop Bartley going this day with the horses to the Galway fair?

NORA. "I won't stop him," says he, "but let you not be afraid. Herself does be saying prayers half through the night, and the Almighty God won't leave her destitute," says he, "with no son living."

CATHLEEN. Is the sea bad by the white rocks, Nora?

NORA. Middling bad, God help us. There's a great roaring in the west, and it's worse it'll be getting when the tide's turned to the wind. (*She goes over to the table with the bundle.*) Shall I open it now?

CATHLEEN. Maybe she'd wake up on us, and come in before we'd done. (*Coming to the table.*) It's a long time we'll be, and the two of us crying.

NORA (*goes to the inner door and listens*). She's moving about on the bed. She'll be coming in a minute.

CATHLEEN. Give me the ladder, and I'll put them up in the turf-loft, the way she won't know of them at all, and maybe when the tide turns she'll be going down to see would he be floating from the east.

They put the ladder against the gable of the chimney; Cathleen goes up a few steps and hides the bundle in the turf-loft. Maurya comes from the inner room.

MAURYA (*looking up at Cathleen and speaking querulously*). Isn't it turf enough you have for this day and evening?

CATHLEEN. There's a cake baking at the fire for a short space (*throwing down the turf*) and Bartley will want it when the tide turns if he goes to Connemara.

Nora picks up the turf and puts it round the pot-oven.

MAURYA (*sitting down on a stool at the fire*). He won't go this day with the wind rising from the south and west. He won't go this day, for the young priest will stop him surely.

NORA. He'll not stop him, mother, and I heard Eamon Simon and Stephen Pheety and Colum Shawn saying he would go.

MAURYA. Where is he itself?

NORA. He went down to see would there be another boat sailing in the week, and I'm thinking it won't be long till he's here now, for the tide's turning at the green head, and the hooker's[1] tacking from the east.

CATHLEEN. I hear some one passing the big stones.

NORA (*looking out*). He's coming now, and he in a hurry.

BARTLEY (*comes in and looks round the room. Speaking sadly and quietly*). Where is the bit of new rope, Cathleen, was bought in Connemara?

CATHLEEN (*coming down*). Give it to him, Nora; it's on a nail by the white boards. I hung it up this morning, for the pig with the black feet was eating it.

NORA (*giving him a rope*). Is that it, Bartley?

MAURYA. You'd do right to leave that rope, Bartley, hanging by the boards. (*Bartley takes the rope.*) It will be wanting in this place, I'm telling you, if Michael is washed up to-morrow morning, or the next morning, or any morning in the week, for it's a deep grave we'll make him by the grace of God.

BARTLEY (*beginning to work with the rope*). I've no halter the way I can ride down on the mare, and I must go now quickly. This is the one boat going for two weeks or beyond it, and the fair will be a good fair for horses I heard them saying below.

MAURYA. It's a hard thing they'll be saying below if the body is washed up and there's no man in it to make the coffin, and I after giving a big price for the finest white boards you'd find in Connemara.

She looks round at the boards.

BARTLEY. How would it be washed up, and we after looking each day for nine days, and a strong wind blowing a while back from the west and south?

MAURYA. If it wasn't found itself, that wind is raising the sea, and there was a star up against the moon, and it rising in the night. If it was a hundred horses, or a thousand horses you had yourself, what is the price of a thousand horses against a son where there is one son only?

BARTLEY (*working at the halter, to Cathleen*). Let you go down each day, and see the sheep aren't jumping in on the rye, and if the jobber comes you can sell the pig with the black feet if there is a good price going.

MAURYA. How would the like of her get a good price for a pig?

BARTLEY (*to Cathleen*). If the west wind holds with the last bit of the moon let you and Nora get up weed enough for another cock for the kelp.[2] It's hard set we'll be from this day with no one in it but one man to work.

MAURYA. It's hard set we'll be surely the day you're drownd'd with the rest. What way will I live and the girls with me, and I an old woman looking for the grave?

---

[1]**hooker** boat [2]**kelp** seaweed used as fertilizer

Bartley lays down the halter, takes off his old coat, and puts on a newer one of the same flannel.

BARTLEY (*to Nora*). Is she coming to the pier?

NORA (*looking out*). She's passing the green head and letting fall her sails.

BARTLEY (*getting his purse and tobacco*). I'll have half an hour to go down, and you'll see me coming again in two days, or in three days, or maybe in four days if the wind is bad.

MAURYA (*turning round to the fire, and putting her shawl over her head*). Isn't it a hard and cruel man won't hear a word from an old woman, and she holding him from the sea?

CATHLEEN. It's the life of a young man to be going on the sea, and who would listen to an old woman with one thing and she saying it over?

BARTLEY (*taking the halter*). I must go now quickly. I'll ride down on the red mare, and the gray pony'll run behind me. . . . The blessing of God on you.

He goes out.

MAURYA (*crying out as he is in the door*). He's gone now, God spare us, and we'll not see him again. He's gone now, and when the black night is falling I'll have no son left me in the world.

CATHLEEN. Why wouldn't you give him your blessing and he looking round in the door? Isn't it sorrow enough is on every one in this house without your sending him out with an unlucky word behind him, and a hard word in his ear?

Maurya takes up the tongs and begins raking the fire aimlessly without looking round.

NORA (*turning towards her*). You're taking away the turf from the cake.

CATHLEEN (*crying out*). The Son of God forgive us, Nora, we're after forgetting his bit of bread.

She comes over to the fire.

NORA. And it's destroyed he'll be going till dark night, and he after eating nothing since the sun went up.

CATHLEEN (*turning the cake out of the oven*). It's destroyed he'll be, surely. There's no sense left on any person in a house where an old woman will be talking for ever.

Maurya sways herself on her stool.

CATHLEEN (*cutting off some of the bread and rolling it in a cloth; to Maurya*). Let you go down now to the spring well and give him this and he passing. You'll see him then and the dark word will be broken, and you can say "God speed you," the way he'll be easy in his mind.

MAURYA (*taking the bread*). Will I be in it as soon as himself?

CATHLEEN. If you go now quickly.

MAURYA (*standing up unsteadily*). It's hard set I am to walk.

CATHLEEN (*looking at her anxiously*). Give her the stick, Nora, or maybe she'll slip on the big stones.

NORA. What stick?

CATHLEEN. The stick Michael brought from Connemara.

MAURYA (*taking a stick Nora gives her*). In the big world the old people do be leaving things after them for their sons and children, but in this place it is the young men do be leaving things behind for them that do be old.

She goes out slowly. Nora goes over to the ladder.

CATHLEEN. Wait, Nora, maybe she'd turn back quickly. She's that sorry, God help her, you wouldn't know the thing she'd do.

NORA. Is she gone around by the bush?

CATHLEEN (*looking out*). She's gone now. Throw it down quickly, for the Lord knows when she'll be out of it again.

NORA (*getting the bundle from the loft*). The young priest said he'd be passing to-morrow, and we might go down and speak to him below if it's Michael's they are surely.

CATHLEEN (*taking the bundle*). Did he say what way they were found?

NORA (*coming down*). "There were two men," says he, "and they rowing round with poteen[3] before the cocks crowed, and the oar of one of them caught the body, and they passing the black cliffs of the north."

CATHLEEN (*trying to open the bundle*). Give me a knife, Nora, the strings perished with the salt water, and there's a black knot on it you wouldn't loosen in a week.

NORA (*giving her a knife*). I've heard tell it was a long way to Donegal.

CATHLEEN (*cutting the string*). It is surely. There was a man in here a while ago—the man sold us that knife—and he said if you set off walking from the rock beyond, it would be seven days you'd be in Donegal.

NORA. And what time would a man take, and he floating?

Cathleen opens the bundle and takes out a bit of a stocking. They look at them eagerly.

CATHLEEN (*in a low voice*). The Lord spare us, Nora! isn't it a queer hard thing to say if it's his they are surely?

NORA. I'll get his shirt off the hook the way we can put the one flannel on the other. (*She looks through some clothes hanging in the corner.*) It's not with them, Cathleen, and where will it be?

CATHLEEN. I'm thinking Bartley put it on him in the morning, for his own shirt was heavy with the salt in it. (*Pointing to the corner.*) There's a bit of a sleeve was of the same stuff. Give me that and it will do.

Nora brings it to her and they compare the flannel.

CATHLEEN. It's the same stuff, Nora; but if it is itself aren't there great rolls of it in the shops of Galway, and isn't it many another man may have a shirt of it as well as Michael himself?

[3]**poteen** whiskey

NORA (*who has taken up the stocking and counted the stitches, crying out*). It's Michael, Cathleen, it's Michael; God spare his soul, and what will herself say when she hears this story, and Bartley on the sea?

CATHLEEN (*taking the stocking*). It's a plain stocking.

NORA. It's the second one of the third pair I knitted, and I put up three score stitches, and I dropped four of them.

CATHLEEN (*counts the stitches*). It's that number is in it. (*Crying out.*) Ah, Nora, isn't it a bitter thing to think of him floating that way to the far north, and no one to keen[4] him but the black hags that do be flying on the sea?

NORA (*swinging herself round, and throwing out her arms on the clothes*). And isn't it a pitiful thing when there is nothing left of a man who was a great rower and fisher, but a bit of an old shirt and a plain stocking?

CATHLEEN (*after an instant*). Tell me is herself coming, Nora? I hear a little sound on the path.

NORA (*looking out*). She is, Cathleen. She's coming up to the door.

CATHLEEN. Put these things away before she'll come in. Maybe it's easier she'll be after giving her blessing to Bartley, and we won't let on we've heard anything the time he's on the sea.

NORA (*helping Cathleen to close the bundle*). We'll put them here in the corner.

They put them into a hole in the chimney corner. Cathleen goes back to the spinning-wheel.

NORA. Will she see it was crying I was?

CATHLEEN. Keep your back to the door the way the light'll not be on you.

Nora sits down at the chimney corner, with her back to the door. Maurya comes in very slowly, without looking at the girls, and goes over to her stool at the other side of the fire. The cloth with the bread is still in her hand. The girls look at each other, and Nora points to the bundle of bread.

CATHLEEN (*after spinning for a moment*). You didn't give him his bit of bread?

Maurya begins to keen softly, without turning round.

CATHLEEN. Did you see him riding down?

Maurya goes on keening.

CATHLEEN (*a little impatiently*). God forgive you; isn't it a better thing to raise your voice and tell what you seen, than to be making lamentation for a thing that's done? Did you see Bartley, I'm saying to you.

MAURYA (*with a weak voice*). My heart's broken from this day.

CATHLEEN (*as before*). Did you see Bartley?

MAURYA. I seen the fearfulest thing.

---

[4]**keen** lament; a mournful, soft wailing

CATHLEEN (*leaves her wheel and looks out*). God forgive you; he's riding the mare now over the green head, and the gray pony behind him.

MAURYA (*starts, so that her shawl falls back from her head and shows her white tossed hair. With a frightened voice*). The gray pony behind him.

CATHLEEN (*coming to the fire*). What is it ails you, at all?

MAURYA (*speaking very slowly*). I've seen the fearfulest thing any person has seen, since the day Bride Dara seen the dead man with the child in his arms.

CATHLEEN AND NORA. Uah.

They crouch down in front of the old woman at the fire.

NORA. Tell us what it is you seen.

MAURYA. I went down to the spring well, and I stood there saying a prayer to myself. Then Bartley came along, and he riding on the red mare with the gray pony behind him. (*She puts up her hands, as if to hide something from her eyes.*) The Son of God spare us, Nora!

CATHLEEN. What is it you seen?

MAURYA. I seen Michael himself.

CATHLEEN (*speaking softly*). You did not, mother; it wasn't Michael you seen, for his body is after being found in the far north, and he's got a clean burial by the grace of God.

MAURYA (*a little defiantly*). I'm after seeing him this day, and he riding and galloping. Bartley came first on the red mare; and I tried to say "God speed you," but something choked the words in my throat. He went by quickly; and "the blessing of God on you," says he, and I could say nothing. I looked up then, and I crying, at the gray pony, and there was Michael upon it—with fine clothes on him, and new shoes on his feet.

CATHLEEN (*begins to keen*). It's destroyed we are from this day. It's destroyed, surely.

NORA. Didn't the young priest say the Almighty God wouldn't leave her destitute with no son living?

MAURYA (*in a low voice, but clearly*). It's little the like of him knows of the sea. . . . Bartley will be lost now, and let you call in Eamon and make me a good coffin out of the white boards, for I won't live after them. I've had a husband, and a husband's father, and six sons in this house—six fine men, though it was a hard birth I had with every one of them and they coming to the world—and some of them were found and some of them were not found, but they're gone now the lot of them. . . . There were Stephen, and Shawn, were lost in the great wind, and found after in the Bay of Gregory of the Golden Mouth, and carried up the two of them on the one plank, and in by that door.

She pauses for a moment, the girls start as if they heard something through the door that is half open behind them.

NORA (*in a whisper*). Did you hear that, Cathleen? Did you hear a noise in the north-east?

CATHLEEN (*in a whisper*). There's some one after crying out by the seashore.

MAURYA (*continues without hearing anything*). There was Sheamus and his father, and his own father again, were lost in a dark night, and not a stick or sign was seen of them when the sun went up. There was Patch after was drowned out of a curagh[5] that turned over. I was sitting here with Bartley, and he a baby, lying on my two knees, and I seen two women, and three women, and four women coming in, and they crossing themselves, and not saying a word. I looked out then, and there were men coming after them, and they holding a thing in the half of a red sail, and water dripping out of it—it was a dry day, Nora—and leaving a track to the door.

She pauses again with her hand stretched out towards the door. It opens softly and old women begin to come in, crossing themselves on the threshold, and kneeling down in front of the stage with red petticoats over their heads.

MAURYA (*half in a dream, to Cathleen*). Is it Patch, or Michael, or what is it at all?

CATHLEEN. Michael is after being found in the far north, and when he is found there how could he be here in this place?

MAURYA. There does be a power of young men floating round in the sea, and what way would they know if it was Michael they had, or another man like him, for when a man is nine days in the sea, and the wind blowing, it's hard set his own mother would be to say what man was it.

CATHLEEN. It's Michael, God spare him, for they're after sending us a bit of his clothes from the far north.

She reaches out and hands Maurya the clothes that belonged to Michael. Maurya stands up slowly and takes them in her hand. Nora looks out.

NORA. They're carrying a thing among them and there's water dripping out of it and leaving a track by the big stones.

CATHLEEN (*in a whisper to the women who have come in*). Is it Bartley it is?

ONE OF THE WOMEN. It is surely, God rest his soul.

Two younger women come in and pull out the table. Then men carry in the body of Bartley, laid on a plank, with a bit of sail over it, and lay it on the table.

CATHLEEN (*to the women, as they are doing so*). What way was he drowned?

ONE OF THE WOMEN. The gray pony knocked him into the sea, and he was washed out where there is a great surf on the white rocks.

Maurya has gone over and knelt down at the head of the table. The women are keening softly and swaying themselves with a slow movement. Cathleen and Nora kneel at the other end of the table. The men kneel near the door.

MAURYA (*raising her head and speaking as if she did not see the people around her*). They're all gone now, and there isn't anything more the sea can do to me. . . . I'll have no call now to be up crying and praying when the wind breaks from the south, and you can hear the surf is in the east, and the surf is in the west, making a great stir with the two noises, and they hitting one on the other. I'll have no call now to be going down and getting Holy Water in the dark nights after Samhain,[6] and I won't care what way the sea is when the other women will be keening. (*To Nora.*) Give me the Holy Water, Nora, there's a small sup still on the dresser.

Nora gives it to her.

MAURYA (*drops Michael's clothes across Bartley's feet, and sprinkles the Holy Water over him*). It isn't that I haven't prayed for you, Bartley, to the Almighty God. It isn't that I haven't said prayers in the dark night till you wouldn't know what I'd be saying; but it's a great rest I'll have now, and it's time surely. It's a great rest I'll have now, and great sleeping in the long nights after Samhain, if it's only a bit of wet flour we do have to eat, and maybe a fish that would be stinking.

She kneels down again, crossing herself, and saying prayers under her breath.

CATHLEEN (*to an old man*). Maybe yourself and Eamon would make a coffin when the sun rises. We have fine white boards herself bought, God help her, thinking Michael would be found, and I have a new cake you can eat while you'll be working.

THE OLD MAN (*looking at the boards*). Are there nails with them?

CATHLEEN. There are not, Colum; we didn't think of the nails.

ANOTHER MAN. It's a great wonder she wouldn't think of the nails, and all the coffins she's seen made already.

CATHLEEN. It's getting old she is, and broken.

Maurya stands up again very slowly and spreads out the pieces of Michael's clothes beside the body, sprinkling them with the last of the Holy Water.

NORA (*in a whisper to Cathleen*). She's quiet now and easy; but the day Michael was drowned you could hear her crying out from this to the spring well. It's fonder she was of Michael, and would any one have thought that?

CATHLEEN (*slowly and clearly*). An old woman will be soon tired with anything she will do, and isn't it nine days herself is after crying and keening, and making great sorrow in the house?

MAURYA (*puts the empty cup mouth downwards on the table, and lays her hands together on Bartley's feet*). They're all to-

---

[5]**curagh** an unstable canoe-like boat

[6]**Samhain** November 1, All Saints' Day

gether this time, and the end is come. May the Almighty God have mercy on Bartley's soul, and on Michael's soul, and on the souls of Sheamus and Patch, and Stephen and Shawn (*bending her head*); and may He have mercy on my soul, Nora, and on the soul of every one is left living in the world.

She pauses, and the keen rises a little more loudly from the women, then sinks away.

MAURYA (*continuing*). Michael has a clean burial in the far north, by the grace of the Almighty God. Bartley will have a fine coffin out of the white boards, and a deep grave surely. What more can we want than that? No man at all can be living for ever, and we must be satisfied.

She kneels down again and the curtain falls slowly.

CENTER STAGE   THE DINGLE BOYS OF KERRY

In many parts of Europe the day after Christmas—St. Stephen's Day—is set aside for "disguisings" and revels to maintain the festive Christmas spirit. Among the most colorful of these is the Festival of the Wren, practiced in the fishing village of Dingle in southwest Ireland. Though the participants long ago forgot the spiritual functions of these rites, their revelry nonetheless provides further evidence of the human impulse to create theater. Today the Wrenboys cavort because the festival is an enjoyable release from the tensions of the harsh Atlantic winter. Amusement and escapism are also integral to the theater experience, however profound its "message," however sublime its purpose.

The Wren Festival does not have the underlying sense of storytelling or spectacular pageantry of the Balinese Barong or the Yoruban Obatala. It is simply a parade in which the young townsmen dress in straw consumes, or *rigs*. Straw is not only abundant and cheap, but symbolizes the agricultural roots of the people. Many nights are passed working diligently on the rigs in preparation for the Wren, a welcome antidote to the rigors of winter. Conical headpieces and playful masks of animals, monsters, famous people, and po-

litical figures complete the rig (see photo).

Led by a fife-and-drum band, the disguised men (*guizers*) dance vigorously through the town, their way cleared by clowns who playfully swat onlookers with pig or sheep bladders affixed to oars borrowed from fishing boats. They seek dances, kisses, and other innocent favors from the eligible young women. Such activities are remnants of ancient fertility rites. In the comic spirit, elders are frequently the butt of satirical pranks played by the young revelers. A straw hobbyhorse accompanies the Wrenboys. This mythical, magical mare has a long history throughout the world (the Hindu *Asvamedha* uses a similar figure in its rituals). The horse is associated with sovereignty because of ancient kingship ceremonies, and—more importantly—with fertility. Young women eagerly embrace the horse to ensure healthy offspring so that "the tribe of Dingle" may prosper.

Riders to the Sea also contains elements of Irish folk rites, though they are more somber, less celebratory than the cavorting Wren. But like the Wren, Synge's play is concerned with the fierce power of nature and its effect on Irish village life.

Dressed in traditional straw costumes, guizers celebrate the Festival of the Wren in Dingle; Ireland's many folk customs blend ancient Celtic and Christian rites.

THE IMPORTANCE OF BEING EARNEST

OSCAR WILDE

OSCAR WILDE (1854–1900)

At the end of the twentieth century it is curious that a playwright who helped usher in the nineteenth century has become a major cultural icon. Several films and stage plays about Wilde's controversial life—as well as a popular film of one of his lesser-known plays (*An Ideal Husband*)—have emerged in the late 1990s. Not only has he become a symbol of the articulate outsider who rebels against a narrow-minded society, Wilde is a martyr among the gay community. Political considerations aside, Wilde remains among the most produced nineteenth-century playwrights, because he is still good "box office" in commercial and community theaters throughout the English-speaking world.

Like Goldsmith and Shaw, two playwrights to whom he has been compared, Wilde was born in Ireland and thus had an outsider's view of English society. He inherited his artistic gifts from his mother, a poet who wrote under the name of Speranza. His superior intellect manifested itself early; he entered Dublin's prestigious Trinity College at age 15 and almost immediately won a coveted prize for an essay on Greek comic poets (including Aristophanes). In 1874 he went to England, where he enrolled at Oxford University and distinguished himself as a poet and essayist. Wilde was influenced by Walter Pater, a poet and aesthetic, who advocated "art for art's sake." Wilde's poetic and dramatic works are noted for their emphasis on style and artistic flourishes.

Wilde settled in London after his Oxford days, working as a critic and writer who billed himself as a "professor of aesthetics." He wrote essays, a well-known novel (*The Picture of Dorian Gray*, 1891), and a number of plays. He was a popular lecturer who toured America in 1882. His wit, ideas, and literary work made him a popular figure in London's class-conscious society.

In 1884 he married Constance Lloyd, yet rumors about his private life plagued him. The Marquis of Queensberry (and father of the powerful Lord Alfred Douglas) accused Wilde of homosexual acts. Wilde sued the Marquis for libel, an act that proved disastrous because public sentiment turned against him. His suit was dismissed, the Marquis countersued, and in 1895 Wilde was convicted of homosexual acts and sentenced to two years in prison. The experience embittered Wilde, who exiled himself to France, where he died at age 46. His antipathy towards the shallowness and rumormongering of London society is evident in many of his plays. *The Importance of Being Earnest* was composed precisely as he was fighting to save his reputation in court.

While we think of Wilde as a comic playwright [*Lady Windemere's Fan* (1892), *An Ideal Husband* (1895)], he experimented with other genres. In 1893 he wrote (in French) the decadent melodrama *Salomé*, which has since been re-created as a popular opera. He is also admired for his poetry (most notably *The Ballad of Reading Gaol*, written under the name C.3.3, his prison number), and an autobiographical work (*De Profundis*) also composed in prison.

A trove of witty epigrams forms the common denominator of his literary work; he is rivaled only by Bernard Shaw as the creator of some of the wittiest pronouncements in the English language. Such lines as these remain Wilde's legacy:

- "To love oneself is the beginning of a lifelong romance."
- "As soon as people are old enough to know better, they don't know anything at all."
- "There is only one thing in the world that is worse than being talked about, and this is not being talked about."

THE IMPORTANCE OF BEING EARNEST (1895)

The Importance of Being Earnest, among the wittiest and most urbane plays in the English language, is part of the grand tradition of English comedy generally referred to as the Comedy of Manners (see Chapter 6). Recall that the genre in England began during the English Restoration (1660), when for a period of thirty years playwrights such as William Congreve and Aphra Behn regaled their audiences with bawdy plots, licentious characters, amoral themes, and sexual innuendo. When the powers that be, namely the lord chamberlain, who served as a censor, found such plays offensive, a new genre—sentimental comedy—evolved. Described by one of its chief proponents, Sir Richard Steele, as the representation of "a joy too exquisite for laughter," rather than ridiculing vice as Restoration comedy was wont to do, sentimental comedy sought to reward virtue. With this new genre "Decency returned to the theatre," declared critic John Harold Wilson, but, unfortunately, he continued, "dullness came along for company." Ever inventive, the British playwrights of the eighteenth century took the best features of Restoration and sentimental comedy and, melding these genres, produced "laughing comedies," among the best of which are Oliver Goldsmith's *She Stoops to Conquer* and Richard Sheridan's *The Rivals*.

It is from this glorious tradition that *Earnest* springs, for in this witty comedy we see that ridiculing vice has been tempered and rewarding of virtue is spoofed. The play, in effect, lampoons the Comedy of Manners itself as much as it satirizes the society of Victorian London (which had, of course, turned viciously against Wilde).

To accomplish his double-edged satire, Wilde takes two primary structural elements of the Comedy of Manners and manipulates them to serve his purpose. First, he begins with the archetype of comedy as outlined by Northrop Frye in "The Mythos of Spring: Comedy." Wilde begins with two pairs of rather liberal-minded young lovers (Algernon and Cecily, Jack and Gwendolen) whose romances are thwarted in part by a blocking force, Lady Bracknell, who represents a more conservative lifestyle. While there are numerous obstacles in the paths of these lovers and their nemesis, the play essentially depicts the battle of the lovers to overcome the blocker's objection to their nuptials—which, of course, they do. But not without a little help from Wilde, who, in the form of an obviously hackneyed but hilariously appropriate *deus ex machina*, "arranges," through the use of Miss Prism's handbag and the consultation of *The Army Lists*, for Jack to have been "Earnestly" named!

Wilde also draws on the traditional comic mechanisms of the Comedy of Manners—pretense, jeopardy, fancy footwork, and exposure to flesh out his plot and characters. Perhaps the oldest of these devices is pretense, the act of pretending to be someone or something one is not, or pretending that something is so when it is not. Pretense is, of course, the very bedrock upon which theater is built. Recall that the Greek word for actor was *hypokrites*, one who pretends to be that which he is not. Comic pretense is at least as old as the fourth century B.C.E., when the Greek comic playwright Aristophanes, in *The Frogs*, had his comic hero Dionysus disguise himself as Heracles.

Indeed, the comic premise of the play is pretense itself, as Wilde asks himself and us, "What would happen if a couple of young Victorian gentleman, in order to free themselves from their filial obligations and the recriminations of their loved ones, *pretended* to leave their homes to visit a destitute friend or relative?" All of the action of the play and much of the play's humor is derived from this pretense. If Algy did not have "Bunbury" and if Jack did not have "Ernest," we would not have a play.

In addition to providing the comic premise of the play, pretense also is the root of its other mechanisms. Every pretense is accompanied by the threat of exposure or "jeopardy." Each time Algy's "Bunburying" or Jack's visits to "Ernest" are brought up, we see them in danger of being exposed and we love to watch them squirm as they are "jeopardized." Such an occasion occurs in act 1 when Algy quizzes Jack (who he thinks is named Ernest) about the cigarette case.

Jack's jeopardy sets the stage for yet another mechanism, "fancy footwork," the literal and/or figurative evasion of danger. To avoid exposure, Jack must think fast as he responds to each of Algy's allegations/questions regarding Cecily and his life in London. As Jack nimbly jumps from one explanation to another, he finds himself in greater and greater jeopardy and thus must execute more and more fancy footwork, until at last, unable to "dance" fast enough to keep a step ahead of Algy, his pretense is exposed. And the exposure itself becomes a device to elicit our laughter. In another play (*A Woman of No Importance*), Wilde writes a line that is quite apt for Jack's predicament: "The one advantage of playing with fire is that one never even gets singed. It is the people who don't know how to play with it who get burned up." Jack is a master at playing with fire—but only to a point.

This use of pretense and the other mechanisms to which it gives rise is merely the logical extension of the manners of the society Wilde is satirizing. The manners themselves are pretense because the behavior of those in "high society" is quite often referred to as "pretentious." This is reflected not only in the action, where the choice between "cake or bread and butter," the consequences of the unavailability of cucumbers, and the "vital importance of being Earnest," are treated with great solemnity, but also in the language of the play. Rarely are single-syllable terms or simple phrases used when multisyllabic words and complicated sentences can be employed. For example, on seeing Jack kneeling to propose to Gwendolen, Lady Bracknell commands the suitor: "Mr. Worthing! Rise, sir, from this semirecumbent posture. It is most indecorous." And later, she responds to Jack's being found "in a handbag—a somewhat large, black leather handbag, with handles to it—an ordinary handbag, in fact," with a verbosity and syntax that are intricate to say the least:

> To be born, or at any rate bred, in a handbag, whether it had handles or not, seems to me to display a contempt for the ordinary decencies of family life that reminds one of the worst excesses of the French Revolution. . . . As for the particular locality in which the hand was found, a cloak room at a railway station might serve to conceal a social indiscretion—has probably, indeed, been used for that purpose before now—but could hardly be regarded as an assured basis for a recognized position in good society.

For Wilde such verbal excesses were an apt symbol for a society in which style was valued more highly than substance.

There is, to be sure, a deeper, more serious side to Wilde's "trivial comedy for serious people." Laugh as we may at his use of the archetypal comic pattern, comic mechanisms, and general pretentiousness of the manners of the society, we are simultaneously aware that the playwright was attacking the close-mindedness and hypocrisy of the very society that had scorned him. Like Cecily, Wilde believed that "whenever one has anything unpleasant to say, one should be quite candid." Though the actions of the play are, by design, unrealistic, there was no question in Wilde's mind that his play was a candid and "realistic" assessment of the world around him. Thus *The Importance of Being Earnest* belongs among the West's early—and best—attempts at realism.

The "casual elegance" of Oscar Wilde's world in a 1936 production of The Importance of Being Earnest; the famed English actor Sir John Gielgud (left) plays Jack Worthing.

THE IMPORTANCE OF BEING EARNEST

OSCAR WILDE

CHARACTERS
JOHN WORTHING, J.P.
ALGERNON MONCRIEFF
REV. CANON CHASUBLE, D.D.
MERRIMAN (butler)
LANE (manservant)
LADY BRACKNELL
HON. GWENDOLEN FAIRFAX
CECILY CARDEW
MISS PRISM (governess)

THE SCENES OF THE PLAY

ACT I: Algernon Moncrieff's flat in Half-Moon Street, W.
ACT II: The garden at the Manor House, Woolton
ACT III: Drawing-room of the Manor House, Woolton

TIME: The present
PLACE: London

ACT 1

SCENE: *Morning-room in Algernon's flat in Half-Moon Street. The room is luxuriously and artistically furnished. The sound of a piano is heard in the adjoining room. (Lane is arranging afternoon tea on the table, and after the music has ceased, Algernon enters.)*

ALGERNON. Did you hear what I was playing, Lane?

LANE. I didn't think it polite to listen, sir.

ALGERNON. I'm sorry for that, for your sake. I don't play accurately—anyone can play accurately—but I play with wonderful expression. As far as the piano is concerned, sentiment is my forte. I keep science for Life.

LANE. Yes, sir.

ALGERNON. And, speaking of the science of Life, have you got the cucumber sandwiches cut for Lady Bracknell?

LANE. Yes, sir. (*Hands them on a salver.*)

ALGERNON (*inspects them, takes two, and sits down on the sofa*). Oh! . . . by the way, Lane, I see from your book that on Thursday night, when Lord Shoreman and Mr. Worthing were dining with me, eight bottles of champagne are entered as having been consumed.

LANE. Yes, sir; eight bottles and a pint.

ALGERNON. Why is it that at a bachelor's establishment the servants invariably drink the champagne? I ask merely for information.

LANE. I attribute it to the superior quality of the wine, sir. I have often observed that in married households the champagne is rarely of a first-rate brand.

ALGERNON. Good Heavens! Is marriage so demoralizing as that?

LANE. I believe it *is* a very pleasant state, sir. I have had very little experience of it myself up to the present. I have only been married once. That was in consequence of a misunderstanding between myself and a young woman.

ALGERNON (*languidly*). I don't know that I am much interested in your family life, Lane.

LANE. No, sir; it is not a very interesting subject. I never think of it myself.

ALGERNON. Very natural, I am sure. That will do, Lane, thank you.

LANE. Thank you, sir. (*Lane goes out.*)

ALGERNON. Lane's views on marriage seem somewhat lax. Really, if the lower orders don't set us a good example, what on earth is the use of them? They seem, as a class, to have absolutely no sense of moral responsibility.

(*Enter Lane.*)

LANE. Mr. Ernest Worthing.

(*Enter Jack. Lane goes out.*)

ALGERNON. How are you, my dear Ernest? What brings you up to town?

JACK. Oh, pleasure, pleasure! What else should bring one anywhere? Eating as usual, I see, Algy!

ALGERNON (*stiffly*). I believe it is customary in good society to take some slight refreshment at five o'clock. Where have you been since last Thursday?

JACK (*sitting down on the sofa*). In the country.

ALGERNON. What on earth do you do there?

JACK (*pulling off his gloves*). When one is in town one amuses oneself. When one is in the country one amuses other people. It is excessively boring.

ALGERNON. And who are the people you amuse?

JACK (*airily*). Oh, neighbours, neighbours.

ALGERNON. Got nice neighbours in your part of Shropshire?

JACK. Perfectly horrid! Never speak to one of them.

ALGERNON. How immensely you must amuse them! (*Goes over and takes sandwich.*) By the way, Shropshire is your county, is it not?

JACK. Eh? Shropshire? Yes, of course. Hallo! Why all these cups? Why cucumber sandwiches? Why such reckless extravagance in one so young? Who is coming to tea?

ALGERNON. Oh! merely Aunt Augusta and Gwendolen.

JACK. How perfectly delightful!

ALGERNON. Yes, that is all very well; but I am afraid Aunt Augusta won't quite approve of your being here.

JACK. May I ask why?

ALGERNON. My dear fellow, the way you flirt with Gwendolen is perfectly disgraceful. It is almost as bad as the way Gwendolen flirts with you.

JACK. I am in love with Gwendolen. I have come up to town expressly to propose to her.

ALGERNON. I thought you had come up for pleasure? . . . I call that business.

JACK. How utterly unromantic you are!

ALGERNON. I really don't see anything romantic in proposing. It is very romantic to be in love. But there is nothing romantic about a definite proposal. Why, one may be accepted. One usually is, I believe. Then the excitement is all over. The very essence of romance is uncertainty. If ever I get married, I'll certainly try to forget the fact.

JACK. I have no doubt about that, dear Algy. The Divorce Court was specially invented for people whose memories are so curiously constituted.

ALGERNON. Oh! there is no use speculating on that subject. Divorces are made in Heaven—-(*Jack puts out his hand to take a sandwich. Algernon at once interferes.*) Please don't touch the cucumber sandwiches. They are ordered specially for Aunt Augusta. (*Takes one and eats it.*)

JACK. Well, you have been eating them all the time.

ALGERNON. That is quite a different matter. She is my aunt. (*Takes plate from below.*) Have some bread and butter. The bread and butter is for Gwendolen. Gwendolen is devoted to bread and butter.

JACK (*advancing to table and helping himself*). And very good bread and butter it is, too.

ALGERNON. Well, my dear fellow, you need not eat as if you were going to eat it all. You behave as if you were married to her already. You are not married to her already, and I don't think you ever will be.

JACK. Why on earth do you say that?

ALGERNON. Well, in the first place girls never marry the men they flirt with. Girls don't think it right.

JACK. Oh, that is nonsense!

ALGERNON. It isn't. It is a great truth. It accounts for the extraordinary number of bachelors that one sees all over the place. In the second place, I don't give my consent.

JACK. Your consent!

ALGERNON. My dear fellow, Gwendolen is my first cousin. And before I allow you to marry her, you will have to clear up the whole question of Cecily. (*Rings bell.*)

JACK. Cecily! What on earth do you mean? What do you mean, Algy, by Cecily? I don't know anyone of the name of Cecily.

(*Enter Lane.*)

ALGERNON. Bring me that cigarette case Mr. Worthing left in the smoking-room the last time he dined here.

LANE. Yes, sir. (*Lane goes out.*)

JACK. Do you mean to say you have had my cigarette case all this time? I wish to goodness you had let me know. I have been writing frantic letters to Scotland Yard about it. I was very nearly offering a large reward.

ALGERNON. Well, I wish you would offer one. I happen to be more than usually hard up.

JACK. There is no good offering a large reward now that the thing is found.

(*Enter Lane with the cigarette case on a salver. Algernon takes it at once. Lane goes out.*)

ALGERNON. I think that is rather mean of you, Ernest, I must say. (*Opens case and examines it.*) However, it makes no matter, for, now that I look at the inscription, I find that the thing isn't yours after all.

JACK. Of course it's mine. (*Moving to him.*) You have seen me with it a hundred times, and you have no right whatsoever to read what is written inside. It is a very ungentlemanly thing to read a private cigarette case.

ALGERNON. Oh! it is absurd to have a hard-and-fast rule about what one should read and what one shouldn't. More than half of modern culture depends on what one shouldn't read.

JACK. I am quite aware of the fact, and I don't propose to discuss modern culture. It isn't the sort of thing one should talk of in private. I simply want my cigarette case back.

ALGERNON. Yes; but this isn't your cigarette case. This cigarette case is a present from someone of the name of Cecily, and you said you didn't know anyone of that name.

JACK. Well, if you want to know, Cecily happens to be my aunt.

ALGERNON. Your aunt!

JACK. Yes. Charming old lady she is, too. Lives at Tunbridge Wells. Just give it back to me, Algy.

ALGERNON (*retreating to back of sofa*). But why does she call herself little Cecily if she is your aunt and lives at Tunbridge Wells? (*Reading.*) "From little Cecily with her fondest love."

JACK (*moving to sofa and kneeling upon it*). My dear fellow, what on earth is there in that? Some aunts are tall, some aunts are not tall. That is a matter that surely an aunt may be allowed to decide for herself. You seem to think that every aunt should be exactly like your aunt! That is absurd! For Heaven's sake give me back my cigarette case. (*Follows Algernon round the room.*)

ALGERNON. Yes. But why does your aunt call you her uncle? "From little Cecily, with her fondest love to her dear Uncle Jack." There is no objection, I admit, to an aunt being a small aunt, but why an aunt, no matter what her size may be, should call her own nephew her uncle, I can't quite make out. Besides, your name isn't Jack at all; it is Ernest.

JACK. It isn't Ernest; it's Jack.

ALGERNON. You have always told me it was Ernest. I have introduced you to everyone as Ernest. You answer to the name of Ernest. You look as if your name was Ernest. You are the most ernest looking person I ever saw in my life. It is perfectly absurd your saying that your name isn't Ernest. It's on your cards. Here is one of them. (*Taking it from case.*) "Mr. Ernest Worthing, B 4, The Albany." I'll keep this as a proof your name is Ernest if ever you attempt to deny it to me, or to Gwendolen, or to anyone else. (*Puts the card in his pocket.*)

JACK. Well, my name is Ernest in town and Jack in the country, and the cigarette case was given to me in the country.

ALGERNON. Yes, but that does not account for the fact that your small Aunt Cecily, who lives at Tunbridge Wells, calls you her dear uncle. Come, old boy, you had much better have the thing out at once.

JACK. My dear Algy, you talk exactly as if you were a dentist. It is very vulgar to talk like a dentist when one isn't a dentist. It produces a false impression.

ALGERNON. Well, that is exactly what dentists always do. Now, go on! Tell me the whole thing. I may mention that I have always suspected you of being a confirmed and secret Bunburyist; and I am quite sure of it now.

JACK. Bunburyist? What on earth do you mean by a Bunburyist?

ALGERNON. I'll reveal to you the meaning of that incomparable expression as soon as you are kind enough to inform me why you are Ernest in town and Jack in the country.

JACK. Well, produce my cigarette case first.

ALGERNON. Here it is. (*Hands cigarette case.*) Now produce your explanation, and pray make it improbable. (*Sits on sofa.*)

JACK. My dear fellow, there is nothing improbable about my explanation at all. In fact it's perfectly ordinary. Old Mr. Thomas Cardew, who adopted me when I was a little boy, made me in his will guardian to his granddaughter, Miss Cecily Cardew. Cecily, who addresses me as her uncle from motives of respect that you could not possibly appreciate, lives at my place in the country under the charge of her admirable governess, Miss Prism.

ALGERNON. Where is that place in the country, by the way?

JACK. That is nothing to you, dear boy. You are not going to be invited. . . . I may tell you candidly that the place is not in Shropshire.

ALGERNON. I suspected that, my dear fellow! I have Bunburyed all over Shropshire on two separate occasions. Now, go on. Why are you Ernest in town and Jack in the country?

JACK. My dear Algy, I don't know whether you will be able to understand my real motives. You are hardly serious enough. When one is placed in the position of guardian, one has to adopt a very high moral tone on all subjects. It's one's duty to do so. And as a high moral tone can hardly be said to conduce very much to either one's health or one's happiness, in order to get up to town I have always pretended to have a younger brother of the name of Ernest, who lives in the Albany, and gets into the most dreadful scrapes. That, my dear Algy, is the whole truth pure and simple.

ALGERNON. The truth is rarely pure and never simple. Modern life would be very tedious if it were either, and modern literature a complete impossibility!

JACK. That wouldn't be at all a bad thing.

ALGERNON. Literary criticism is not your forte, my dear fellow. Don't try it. You should leave that to people who haven't been at a University. They do it so well in the daily papers. What you really are is a Bunburyist. I was quite right in saying you were a Bunburyist. You are one of the most advanced Bunburyists I know.

JACK. What on earth do you mean?

ALGERNON. You have invented a very useful younger brother called Ernest, in order that you may be able to come up to town as often as you like. I have invented an invaluable permanent invalid called Bunbury, in order that I may be able to go down into the country whenever I choose. Bunbury is perfectly invaluable. If it wasn't for Bunbury's extraordinary bad health, for instance, I wouldn't be able to dine with you at Willis's to-night, for I have been really engaged to Aunt Augusta for more than a week.

JACK. I haven't asked you to dine with me anywhere tonight.

ALGERNON. I know. You are absolutely careless about sending out invitations. It is very foolish of you. Nothing annoys people so much as not receiving invitations.

JACK. You had much better dine with your Aunt Augusta.

ALGERNON. I haven't the smallest intention of doing anything of the kind. To begin with, I dined there on Monday, and once a week is quite enough to dine with one's own relatives. In the second place, whenever I do dine there I am always treated as a member of the family, and sent down with either no woman at all, or two. In the third place, I know perfectly well whom she will place me next to, tonight. She will place me next to Mary Farquhar, who always flirts with her own husband across the dinner-table. That is not very pleasant. Indeed, it is not even decent . . . and that sort of thing is enormously on the increase. The amount of women in London who flirt with their own husbands is perfectly scandalous. It looks so bad. It is simply washing one's clean linen in public. Besides, now that I know you to be a confirmed Bunburyist I naturally want to talk to you about Bunburying. I want to tell you the rules.

JACK. I'm not a Bunburyist at all. If Gwendolen accepts me, I am going to kill my brother; indeed I think I'll kill him in any case. Cecily is a little too much interested in him. It is rather a bore. So I am going to get rid of Ernest. And I strongly advise you to do the same with Mr. . . . with your invalid friend who has the absurd name.

ALGERNON. Nothing will induce me to part with Bunbury, and if you ever get married, which seems to me extremely problematic, you will be very glad to know Bunbury. A man who marries without knowing Bunbury has a very tedious time of it.

JACK. That is nonsense. If I marry a charming girl like Gwendolen, and she is the only girl I ever saw in my life that I would marry, I certainly won't want to know Bunbury.

ALGERNON. Then your wife will. You don't seem to realize, that in married life three is company and two is none.

JACK (*sententiously*). That, my dear young friend, is the theory that the corrupt French Drama has been propounding for the last fifty years.

ALGERNON. Yes; and that the happy English home has proved in half the time.

JACK. For heaven's sake, don't try to be cynical. It's perfectly easy to be cynical.

ALGERNON. My dear fellow, it isn't easy to be anything now-a-days. There's such a lot of beastly competition about. (*The sound of an electric bell is heard.*) Ah! that must be Aunt Augusta. Only relatives, or creditors, ever ring in that Wagnerian manner. Now, if I get her out of the way for ten minutes, so that you can have an opportunity for proposing to Gwendolen, may I dine with you to-night at Willis's?"

JACK. I suppose so if you want to.

ALGERNON. Yes, but you must be serious about it. I hate people who are not serious about meals. It is so shallow of them.

(*Enter Lane.*)

LANE. Lady Bracknell and Miss Fairfax. (*Algernon goes forward to meet them. Enter Lady Bracknell and Gwendolen.*)

LADY BRACKNELL. Good afternoon, dear Algernon, I hope you are behaving very well.

ALGERNON. I'm feeling very well, Aunt Augusta.

LADY BRACKNELL. That's not quite the same thing. In fact the two things rarely go together. (*Sees Jack and bows to him with icy coldness.*)

ALGERNON (*to Gwendolen*). Dear me, you are smart!

GWENDOLEN. I am always smart! Aren't I, Mr. Worthing?

JACK. You're quite perfect, Miss Fairfax.

GWENDOLEN. Oh! I hope I am not that. It would leave no room for developments, and I intend to develop in *many directions*. (*Gwendolen and Jack sit down together in the corner.*)

LADY BRACKNELL. I'm sorry if we are a little late, Algernon, but I was obliged to call on dear Lady Harbury. I hadn't been there since her poor husband's death. I never saw a woman so altered; she looks quite twenty years younger. And now I'll have a cup of tea, and one of those nice cucumber sandwiches you promised me.

ALGERNON. Certainly, Aunt Augusta. (*Goes over to tea-table.*)

LADY BRACKNELL. Won't you come and sit here, Gwendolen?

GWENDOLEN. Thanks, mamma, I'm quite comfortable where I am.

ALGERNON (*picking up empty plate in horror*). Good heavens! Lane! Why are there no cucumber sandwiches? I ordered them specially.

LANE (*gravely*). There were no cucumbers in the market this morning, sir. I went down twice.

ALGERNON. No cucumbers!

LANE. No, sir. Not even for ready money.

ALGERNON. That will do, Lane, thank you.

LANE. Thank you sir. (*Goes out.*)

ALGERNON. I am greatly distressed, Aunt Augusta, about there being no cucumbers, not even for ready money.

LADY BRACKNELL. It really makes no matter, Algernon. I had some crumpets with Lady Harbury, who seems to me to be living entirely for pleasure now.

ALGERNON. I hear her hair has turned quite gold from grief.

LADY BRACKNELL. It certainly has changed its colour. From what cause I, of course, cannot say. (*Algernon crosses and hands tea.*) Thank you. I've quite a treat for you to-night, Algernon. I am going to send you down with Mary Farquhar. She is such a nice woman, and so attentive to her husband. It's delightful to watch them.

ALGERNON. I am afraid, Aunt Augusta, I shall have to give up the pleasure of dining with you to-night after all.

LADY BRACKNELL (*frowning*). I hope not, Algernon. It would put my table completely out. Your uncle would have to dine upstairs. Fortunately he is accustomed to that.

ALGERNON. It is a great bore, and, I need hardly say, a terrible disappointment to me, but the fact is I have just had a telegram to say that my poor friend Bunbury is very ill again. (*Exchanges glances with Jack.*) They seem to think I should be with him.

LADY BRACKNELL. It is very strange. This Mr. Bunbury seems to suffer from curiously bad health.

ALGERNON. Yes; poor Bunbury is a dreadful invalid.

LADY BRACKNELL. Well, I must say, Algernon, that I think it is high time that Mr. Bunbury made up his mind whether he was going to live or to die. This shilly-shallying with the question is absurd. Nor do I in any way approve of the modern sympathy with invalids. I consider it morbid. Illness of any kind is hardly a thing to be encouraged in others. Health is the primary duty of life. I am always telling that to your poor uncle, but he never seems to take much notice . . . as far as any improvement in his ailments goes. I should be much obliged if you would ask Mr. Bunbury, from me, to be kind enough not to have a relapse on Saturday, for I rely on you to arrange my music for me. It is my last reception and one wants something that will encourage conversation, particularly at the end of the season when everyone has practically said whatever they had to say, which, in most cases, was probably not much.

ALGERNON. I'll speak to Bunbury, Aunt Augusta, if he is still conscious, and I think I can promise you he'll be all right by Saturday. You see, if one plays good music, people don't listen, and if one plays bad music people don't talk. But I'll run over the programme I've drawn out, if you will kindly come into the next room for a moment.

LADY BRACKNELL. Thank you, Algernon. It is very thoughtful of you. (*Rising, and following Algernon.*) I'm sure the programme will be delightful, after a few expurgations. French songs I cannot possibly allow. People always seem to think that they are improper, and either look shocked, which is vulgar, or laugh, which is worse. But German sounds a thoroughly respectable language, and indeed, I believe is so. Gwendolen, you will accompany me.

GWENDOLEN. Certainly, mamma. (*Lady Bracknell and Algernon go into the music-room, Gwendolen remains behind.*)

JACK. Charming day it has been, Miss Fairfax.

GWENDOLEN. Pray don't talk to me about the weather, Mr. Worthing. Whenever people talk to me about the weather, I always feel quite certain that they mean something else. And that makes me so nervous.

JACK. I do mean something else.

GWENDOLEN. I thought so. In fact, I am never wrong.

JACK. And I would like to be allowed to take advantage of Lady Bracknell's temporary absence . . .

GWENDOLEN. I would certainly advise you to do so. Mamma has a way of coming back suddenly into a room that I have often had to speak to her about.

JACK (*nervously*). Miss Fairfax, ever since I met you I have admired you more than any girl . . . I have ever met since . . . I met you.

GWENDOLEN. Yes, I am quite aware of the fact. And I often wish that in public, at any rate, you had been more demonstrative. For me you have always had an irresistible fascination. Even before I met you I was far from indifferent to you. (*Jack looks at her in amazement.*) We live, as I hope you know, Mr. Worthing, in an age of ideals. The fact is constantly mentioned in the more expensive monthly magazines, and has reached the provincial pulpits I am told: and my ideal has always been to love some one of the name of Ernest. There is something in that name that inspires absolute confidence. The moment Algernon first mentioned to me that he had a friend called Ernest, I knew I was destined to love you.

JACK. You really love me, Gwendolen?

GWENDOLEN. Passionately!

JACK. Darling! You don't know how happy you've made me.

GWENDOLEN. My own Ernest!

JACK. But you don't really mean to say that you couldn't love me if my name wasn't Ernest?

GWENDOLEN. But your name is Ernest.

JACK. Yes, I know it is. But supposing it was something else? Do you mean to say you couldn't love me then?

GWENDOLEN (*glibly*). Ah! that is clearly a metaphysical speculation, and like most metaphysical speculations has very little reference at all to the actual facts of real life, as we know them.

JACK. Personally, darling, to speak quite candidly, I don't much care about the name of Ernest . . . I don't think that name suits me at all.

GWENDOLEN. It suits you perfectly. It is a divine name. It has a music of its own. It produces vibrations.

JACK. Well, really, Gwendolen, I must say that I think there are lots of other much nicer names. I think, Jack, for instance, a charming name.

GWENDOLEN. Jack? . . . No, there is very little music in the name Jack, if any at all, indeed. It does not thrill. It produces absolutely no vibration. . . . I have known several Jacks, and they all, without exception, were more than usually plain. Besides, Jack is a notorious domesticity for John! And I pity any woman who is married to a man called John. She would probably never be allowed to know the entrancing pleasure of a single moment's solitude. The only really safe name is Ernest.

JACK. Gwendolen, I must get christened at once—I mean we must get married at once. There is no time to be lost.

GWENDOLEN. Married, Mr. Worthing?

JACK (*astounded*). Well . . . surely. You know that I love you, and you led me to believe, Miss Fairfax, that you were not absolutely indifferent to me.

GWENDOLEN. I adore you. But you haven't proposed to me yet. Nothing has been said at all about marriage. The subject has not even been touched on.

JACK. Well . . . may I propose to you now?

GWENDOLEN. I think it would be an admirable opportunity. And to spare you any possible disappointment, Mr. Worthing, I think it only fair to tell you quite frankly beforehand that I am fully determined to accept you.

JACK. Gwendolen!

GWENDOLEN. Yes, Mr. Worthing, what have you got to say to me?

JACK. You know what I have got to say to you.

GWENDOLEN. Yes, but you don't say it.

JACK. Gwendolen, will you marry me? (*Goes on his knees.*)

GWENDOLEN. Of course I will, darling. How long you have been about it! I am afraid you have had very little experience in how to propose.

JACK. My own one, I have never loved anyone in the world but you.

GWENDOLEN. Yes, but men often propose for practice. I know my brother Gerald does. All my girl-friends tell me so. What wonderfully blue eyes you have, Ernest! They are quite, quite blue. I hope you will always look at me just like that, especially when there are other people present.

(*Enter Lady Bracknell.*)

LADY BRACKNELL. Mr. Worthing! Rise, sir, from this semi-recumbent posture. It is most indecorous.

GWENDOLEN. Mamma! (*He tried to rise; she restrains him.*) I must beg you to retire. This is no place for you. Besides, Mr. Worthing has not quite finished yet.

LADY BRACKNELL. Finished what, may I ask?

GWENDOLEN. I am engaged to Mr. Worthing, mamma. (*They rise together.*)

LADY BRACKNELL. Pardon me, you are not engaged to anyone. When you do become engaged to some one, I, or your father, should his health permit him, will inform you of the fact. An engagement should come on a young girl as a surprise, pleasant or unpleasant, as the case may be. It is hardly a matter that she could be allowed to arrange for herself. . . . And now I have a few questions to put to you, Mr. Worthing. While I am making these inquiries, you, Gwendolen, will wait for me below in the carriage.

GWENDOLEN (*reproachfully*). Mamma!

LADY BRACKNELL. In the carriage, Gwendolen! (*Gwendolen goes to the door. She and Jack blow kisses to each other behind Lady Bracknell's back. Lady Bracknell looks vaguely about as if she could not understand what the noise was. Finally turns round.*) Gwendolen, the carriage!

GWENDOLEN. Yes, mamma. (*Goes out, looking back at Jack.*)

LADY BRACKNELL (*sitting down*). You can take a seat, Mr. Worthing. (*Looks in her pocket for note-book and pencil.*)

JACK. Thank you, Lady Bracknell, I prefer standing.

LADY BRACKNELL (*pencil and notebook in hand*). I feel bound to tell you that you are not down on my list of eligible young men, although I have the same list as the dear Duchess of Bolton has. We work together, in fact. However, I am quite ready to enter your name, should your answers be what a really affectionate mother requires. Do you smoke?

JACK. Well, yes, I must admit I smoke.

LADY BRACKNELL. I am glad to hear it. A man should always have an occupation of some kind. There are far too many idle men in London as it is. How old are you?

JACK. Twenty-nine.

LADY BRACKNELL. A very good age to be married at. I have

always been of opinion that a man who desires to get married should know either everything or nothing. Which do you know?

JACK (*after some hesitation*). I know nothing, Lady Bracknell.

LADY BRACKNELL. I am pleased to hear it. I do not approve of anything that tampers with natural ignorance. Ignorance is like a delicate exotic fruit; touch it and the bloom is gone. The whole theory of modern education is radically unsound. Fortunately in England, at any rate, education produces no effect whatsoever. If it did, it would prove a serious danger to the upper classes, and probably lead to acts of violence in Grosvenor Square. What is your income?

JACK. Between seven and eight thousand a year.

LADY BRACKNELL (*makes a note in her book*). In land, or in investments?

JACK. In investments, chiefly.

LADY BRACKNELL. That is satisfactory. What between the duties expected of one during one's life-time, and the duties exacted from one after one's death, land has ceased to be either a profit or a pleasure. It gives one position, and prevents one from keeping it up. That's all that can be said about land.

JACK. I have a country house with some land, of course, attached to it, about fifteen hundred acres, I believe; but I don't depend on that for my real income. In fact, as far as I can make out, the poachers are the only people who make anything out of it.

LADY BRACKNELL. A country house! How many bedrooms? Well, that point can be cleared up afterwards. You have a town house, I hope? A girl with a simple, unspoiled nature, like Gwendolen, could hardly be expected to reside in the country.

JACK. Well, I own a house in Belgrave Square, but it is let by the year to Lady Bloxham. Of course, I can get it back whenever I like, at six months' notice.

LACY BRACKNELL. Lady Bloxham? I don't know her.

JACK. Oh, she goes about very little. She is a lady considerably advanced in years.

LADY BRACKNELL. Ah, now-a-days that is no guarantee of respectability of character. What number in Belgrave Square?

JACK. 149.

LADY BRACKNELL (*shaking her head*). The unfashionable side. I thought there was something. However, that could easily be altered.

JACK. Do you mean the fashion, or the side?

LADY BRACKNELL (*sternly*). Both, if necessary, I presume. What are your politics?

JACK. Well, I am afraid I really have none. I am a Liberal Unionist.

LADY BRACKNELL. Oh, they count as Tories. They dine with us. Or come in the evening, at any rate. Now to minor matters. Are your parents living?

JACK. I have lost both my parents.

LADY BRACKNELL. Both? . . . That seems like carelessness. Who was your father? He was evidently a man of some wealth. Was he born in what the Radical papers call the purple of commerce, or did he rise from the ranks of the aristocracy?

JACK. I am afraid I really don't know. The fact is, Lady Bracknell, I said I had lost my parents. It would be nearer the truth to say that my parents seem to have lost me . . . I don't actually know who I am by birth. I was . . . well, I was found.

LADY BRACKNELL. Found!

JACK. The late Mr. Thomas Cardew, an old gentleman of a very charitable and kindly disposition, found me, and gave me the name of Worthing, because he happened to have a first-class ticket for Worthing in his pocket at the time. Worthing is a place in Sussex. It is a seaside resort.

LADY BRACKNELL. Where did the charitable gentleman who had a first-class ticket for this seaside resort find you?

JACK (*gravely*). In a hand-bag.

LADY BRACKNELL. A hand-bag?

JACK (*very seriously*). Yes, Lady Bracknell. I was in a hand-bag—a somewhat large, black leather hand-bag, with handles to it—an ordinary hand-bag in fact.

LADY BRACKNELL. In what locality did Mr. James, or Thomas, Cardew come across this ordinary hand-bag?

JACK. In the cloak-room at Victoria Station. It was given to him in mistake for his own.

LADY BRACKNELL. The cloak-room at Victoria Station?

JACK. Yes. The Brighton line.

LADY BRACKNELL. The line is immaterial. Mr. Worthing, I confess I feel somewhat bewildered by what you have just told me. To be born, or at any rate bred, in a hand-bag, whether it had handles or not, seems to me to display a contempt for the ordinary decencies of family life that remind one of the worst excesses of the French Revolution. And I presume you know what that unfortunate movement led to? As for the particular locality in which the hand-bag was found, a cloak-room at a railway station might serve to conceal a social indiscretion—has probably, indeed, been used for the purpose before now—but it could hardly be regarded as an assured basis for a recognized position in good society.

JACK. May I ask you then what you would advise me to do? I need hardly say I would do anything in the world to ensure Gwendolen's happiness.

LADY BRACKNELL. I would strongly advise you, Mr. Worthing, to try and acquire some relations as soon as possible, and to make a definite effort to produce at any rate one parent, of either sex, before the season is quite over.

JACK. Well, I don't see how I could possibly manage to do that. I can produce the hand-bag at any moment. It is in my dressing-room at home. I really think that should satisfy you, Lady Bracknell.

LADY BRACKNELL. Me, sir! What has it to do with me? You can hardly imagine that I and Lord Bracknell would dream of allowing our only daughter—a girl brought up with the utmost care—to marry into a cloak-room, and form an alliance with a parcel? Good morning, Mr. Worthing! (*Lady Bracknell sweeps out in majestic indignation.*)

JACK. Good morning! (*Algernon, from the other room, strikes up the Wedding March. Jack looks perfectly furious, and goes to the door.*) For goodness' sake don't play that ghastly tune, Algy! How idiotic you are! (*The music stops, and Algernon enters cheerily.*)

ALGERNON. Didn't it go off all right, old boy? You don't mean to say Gwendolen refused you? I know it is a way she has. She is always refusing people. I think it is most ill-natured of her.

JACK. Oh, Gwendolen is as right as a trivet. As far as she is concerned, we are engaged. Her mother is perfectly unbearable. Never met such a Gorgon . . . I don't really know what a Gorgon is like, but I am quite sure that Lady Bracknell is one. In any case, she is a monster, without being a myth, which is rather unfair. . . . I beg your pardon, Algy, I suppose I shouldn't talk about your own aunt in that way before you.

ALGERNON. My dear boy, I love hearing my relations abused. It is the only thing that makes me put up with them at all. Relations are simply a tedious pack of people, who haven't got the remotest knowledge of how to live, nor the smallest instinct about when to die.

JACK. Oh, that is nonsense!

ALGERNON. It isn't!

JACK. Well, I won't argue about the matter. You always want to argue about things.

ALGERNON. That is exactly what things were originally made for.

JACK. Upon my word, if I thought that, I'd shoot myself . . . (*A pause.*) You don't think there is any chance of Gwendolen becoming like her mother in about a hundred and fifty years, do you, Algy?

ALGERNON. All women become like their mothers. That is their tragedy. No man does. That's his.

JACK. Is that clever?

ALGERNON. It is perfectly phrased! and quite as true as any observation in civilized life should be.

JACK. I am sick to death of cleverness. Everybody is clever now-a-days. You can't go anywhere without meeting clever people. The thing has become an absolute public nuisance. I wish to goodness we had a few fools left.

ALGERNON. We have.

JACK. I should extremely like to meet them. What do they talk about?

ALGERNON. The fools? Oh! about the clever people, of course.

JACK. What fools!

ALGERNON. By the way, did you tell Gwendolen the truth about your being Ernest in town, and Jack in the country?

JACK (*in a very patronising manner*). My dear fellow, the truth isn't quite the sort of thing one tells to a nice, sweet, refined girl. What extraordinary ideas you have about the way to behave to a woman!

ALGERNON. The only way to behave to a woman is to make love to her, if she is pretty, and to someone else if she is plain.

JACK. Oh, that is nonsense.

ALGERNON. What about your brother? What about the profligate Ernest?

JACK. Oh, before the end of the week I shall have got rid of him. I'll say he died in Paris of apoplexy. Lots of people die of apoplexy, quite suddenly, don't they?

ALGERNON. Yes, but it's hereditary, my dear fellow. It's a sort of thing that runs in families. You had much better say a severe chill.

JACK. You are sure a severe chill isn't hereditary, or anything of that kind?

ALGERNON. Of course it isn't!

JACK. Very well, then. My poor brother Ernest is carried off suddenly in Paris, by a severe chill. That gets rid of him.

ALGERNON. But I thought you said that . . . Miss Cardew was a little too much interested in your poor brother Ernest? Won't she feel his loss a good deal?

JACK. Oh, that is all right. Cecily is not a silly, romantic girl, I am glad to say. She has got a capital appetite, goes for long walks, and pays no attention at all to her lessons.

ALGERNON. I would rather like to see Cecily.

JACK. I will take very good care you never do. She is excessively pretty, and she is only just eighteen.

ALGERNON. Have you told Gwendolen yet that you have an excessively pretty ward who is only just eighteen?

JACK. Oh! one doesn't blurt these things out to people. Cecily and Gwendolen are perfectly certain to be extremely great friends. I'll bet you anything you like that half an hour after they have met, they will be calling each other sister.

ALGERNON. Women only do that when they have called each other a lot of other things first. Now, my dear boy, if we want to get a good table at Willis's, we really must go and dress. Do you know it is nearly seven?

JACK (*irritably*). Oh! it always is nearly seven.

ALGERNON. Well, I'm hungry.

JACK. I never knew you when you weren't. . . .

ALGERNON. What shall we do after dinner? Go to a theatre?

JACK. Oh, no! I loathe listening.

ALGERNON. Well, let us go to the Club?

JACK. Oh, no! I hate talking.

ALGERNON. Well, we might trot round to the Empire at ten?

JACK. Oh, no! can't bear looking at things. It is so silly.

ALGERNON. Well, what shall we do?

JACK. Nothing!

ALGERNON. It is awfully hard work doing nothing. However, I don't mind hard work where there is no definite object of any kind.

(Enter Lane.)

LANE. Miss Fairfax.

(Enter Gwendolen. Lane goes out.)

ALGERNON. Gwendolen, upon my word!

GWENDOLEN. Algy, kindly turn your back. I have something very particular to say to Mr. Worthing.

ALGERNON. Really, Gwendolen, I don't think I can allow this at all.

GWENDOLEN. Algy, you always adopt a strictly immoral attitude towards life. You are not quite old enough to do that. *(Algernon retires to the fireplace.)*

JACK. My own darling!

GWENDOLEN. Ernest, we may never be married. From the expression on mamma's face I fear we never shall. Few parents now-a-days pay any regard to what their children say to them. The old-fashioned respect for the young is fast dying out. Whatever influence I ever had over mamma, I lost at the age of three. But although she may prevent us from becoming man and wife, and I may marry someone else, and marry often, nothing that she can possibly do can alter my eternal devotion to you.

JACK. Dear Gwendolen.

GWENDOLEN. The story of your romantic origin, as related to me by mamma, with unpleasing comments, has naturally stirred the deeper fibers of my nature. Your Christian name has an irresistible fascination. The simplicity of your character makes you exquisitely incomprehensible to me. Your town address at the Albany I have. What is your address in the country?

JACK. The Manor House, Woolton, Hertfordshire. *(Algernon, who has been carefully listening, smiles to himself, and writes the address on his shirt-cuff. Then picks up the Railway Guide.)*

GWENDOLEN. There is a good postal service, I suppose? It may be necessary to do something desperate. That, of course, will require serious consideration. I will communicate with you daily.

JACK. My own one!

GWENDOLEN. How long do you remain in town?

JACK. Till Monday.

GWENDOLEN. Good! Algy, you may turn round now.

ALGERNON. Thanks, I've turned round already.

GWENDOLEN. You may also ring the bell.

JACK. You will let me see you to your carriage, my own darling?

GWENDOLEN. Certainly.

JACK *(to Lane, who now enters)*. I will see Miss Fairfax out.

LANE. Yes, sir. *(Jack and Gwendolen go off. Lane presents several letters on a salver to Algernon. It is to be surmised that they are bills, as Algernon, after looking at the envelopes, tears them up.)*

ALGERNON. A glass of sherry, Lane.

LANE. Yes, sir.

ALGERNON. To-morrow, Lane, I'm going Bunburying.

LANE. Yes, sir.

ALGERNON. I shall probably not be back till Monday. You can put up my dress clothes, my smoking jacket, and all the Bunbury suits . . .

LANE. Yes, sir. *(Handing sherry.)*

ALGERNON. I hope to-morrow will be a fine day, Lane.

LANE. It never is, sir.

ALGERNON. Lane, you're a perfect pessimist.

LANE. I do my best to give satisfaction, sir.

(Enter Jack. Lane goes off.)

JACK. There's a sensible, intellectual girl! the only girl I ever cared for in my life. *(Algernon is laughing immoderately.)* What on earth are you so amused at?

ALGERNON. Oh, I'm a little anxious about poor Bunbury, that's all.

JACK. If you don't take care, your friend Bunbury will get you into a serious scrape some day.

ALGERNON. I love scrapes. They are the only things that are never serious.

JACK. Oh, that's nonsense, Algy. You never talk anything but nonsense.

ALGERNON. Nobody ever does. *(Jack looks indignantly at him, and leaves the room. Algernon lights a cigarette, reads his shirt-cuff and smiles.)*

ACT 2

SCENE: *Garden at the Manor House. A flight of gray stone steps leads up to the house. The garden, an old-fashioned one, full of roses. Time of year, July. Basket chairs, and a table covered with books, are set under a large yew tree.*

(Miss Prism discovered seated at the table. Cecily is at the back watering flowers.)

MISS PRISM *(calling)*. Cecily, Cecily! Surely such a utilitarian occupation as the watering of flowers is rather Moulton's duty than yours? Especially at a moment when intellectual pleasures await you. Your German grammar is on the table. Pray open it at page fifteen. We will repeat yesterday's lesson.

CECILY *(coming over very slowly)*. But I don't like German. It isn't at all a becoming language. I know perfectly well that I look quite plain after my German lesson.

MISS PRISM. Child, you know how anxious your guardian is that you should improve yourself in every way. He laid particular stress on your German, as he was leaving for town yesterday. Indeed, he always lays stress on your German when he is leaving for town.

CECILY. Dear Uncle Jack is so very serious! Sometimes he is so serious that I think he cannot be quite well.

MISS PRISM *(drawing herself up)*. Your guardian enjoys the best of health, and his gravity of demeanour is especially to be commended in one so comparatively young as he is. I know no one who has a higher sense of duty and responsibility.

CECILY. I suppose that is why he often looks a little bored when we three are together.

MISS PRISM. Cecily! I am surprised at you. Mr. Worthing has many troubles in his life. Idle merriment and triviality would be out of place in his conversation. You must remember his constant anxiety about that unfortunate young man, his brother.

CECILY. I wish Uncle Jack would allow the unfortunate young man, his brother, to come down here sometimes. We might have a good influence over him, Miss Prism. I am sure you certainly would. You know German, and geology, and things of that kind influence a man very much. (*Cecily begins to write in her diary.*)

MISS PRISM (*shaking her head*). I do not think that even I could produce any effect on a character that, according to his own brother's admission, is irretrievably weak and vacillating. Indeed, I am not sure that I would desire to reclaim him. I am not in favour of this modern mania for turning bad people into good people at a moment's notice. As a man sows so let him reap. You must put away your diary, Cecily. I really don't see why you should keep a diary at all.

CECILY. I keep a diary in order to enter the wonderful secrets of my life. If I didn't write them down I should probably forget all about them.

MISS PRISM. Memory, my dear Cecily, is the diary that we all carry about with us.

CECILY. Yes, but it usually chronicles the things that have never happened, and couldn't possibly have happened. I believe that Memory is responsible for nearly all the three-volume novels that Mudie sends us.

MISS PRISM. Do not speak slightingly of the three-volume novel, Cecily. I wrote one myself in earlier days.

CECILY. Did you really, Miss Prism? How wonderfully clever you are! I hope it did not end happily? I don't like novels that end happily. They depress me so much.

MISS PRISM. The good ended happily, and the bad unhappily. That is what Fiction means.

CECILY. I suppose so. But it seems very unfair. And was your novel ever published?

MISS PRISM. Alas! no. The manuscript unfortunately was abandoned. I use the word in the sense of lost or mislaid. To your work, child, these speculations are profitless.

CECILY (*smiling*). But I see dear Dr. Chasuble coming up through the garden.

MISS PRISM (*rising and advancing*). Dr. Chasuble! This is indeed a pleasure.

(*Enter Canon Chasuble.*)

CHASUBLE. And how are we this morning? Miss Prism, you are, I trust, well?

CECILY. Miss Prism has just been complaining of a slight headache. I think it would do her so much good to have a short stroll with you in the park, Dr. Chasuble.

MISS PRISM. Cecily, I have not mentioned anything about a headache.

CECILY. No, dear Miss Prism, I know that, but I felt instinctively that you had a headache. Indeed I was thinking about that, and not about my German lesson, when the Rector came in.

CHASUBLE. I hope, Cecily, you are not inattentive.

CECILY. Oh, I am afraid I am.

CHASUBLE. That is strange. Were I fortunate enough to be Miss Prism's pupil, I would hang upon her lips. (*Miss Prism glares.*) I spoke metaphorically.—My metaphor was drawn from bees. Ahem! Mr. Worthing, I suppose, has not returned from town yet?

MISS PRISM. We do not expect him till Monday afternoon.

CHASUBLE. Ah, yes, he usually likes to spend his Sunday in London. He is not one of those whose sole aim is enjoyment, as by all accounts, that unfortunate young man, his brother, seems to be. But I must not disturb Egeria and her pupil any longer.

MISS PRISM. Egeria? My name is Lætitia, Doctor.

CHASUBLE (*bowing*). A classical allusion merely, drawn from the Pagan authors. I shall see you both no doubt at Evensong.

MISS PRISM. I think, dear Doctor, I will have a stroll with you. I find I have a headache after all, and a walk might do it good.

CHASUBLE. With pleasure, Miss Prism, with pleasure. We might go as far as the schools and back.

MISS PRISM. That would be delightful. Cecily, you will read your Political Economy in my absence. The chapter on the Fall of the Rupee you may omit. It is somewhat too sensational. Even these metallic problems have their melodramatic side.

(*Goes down the garden with Dr. Chasuble.*)

CECILY (*picks up books and throws them back on table*). Horrid Political Economy! Horrid Geography! Horrid, horrid German!

(*Enter Merriman with a card on a salver.*)

MERRIMAN. Mr. Ernest Worthing has just driven over from the station. He has brought his luggage with him.

CECILY (*takes the card and reads it*). "Mr. Ernest Worthing, B 4 The Albany, W." Uncle Jack's brother! Did you tell him Mr. Worthing was in town?

MERRIMAN. Yes, Miss. He seemed very much disappointed. I mentioned that you and Miss Prism were in the garden. He said he was anxious to speak to you privately for a moment.

CECILY. Ask Mr. Ernest Worthing to come here. I suppose you had better talk to the housekeeper about a room for him.

MERRIMAN. Yes, Miss. (*Merriman goes off.*)

CECILY. I have never met any really wicked person before. I feel rather frightened. I am so afraid he will look just like everyone else.

(*Enter Algernon, very gay and debonair.*)

He does!

ALGERNON (*raising his hat*). You are my little cousin Cecily, I'm sure.

CECILY. You are under some strange mistake. I am not little. In fact, I am more than usually tall for my age. (*Algernon is rather taken aback.*) But I am your cousin Cecily. You, I see from your card, are Uncle Jack's brother, my cousin Ernest, my wicked cousin Ernest.

ALGERNON. Oh! I am not really wicked at all, cousin Cecily. You mustn't think that I am wicked.

CECILY. If you are not, then you have certainly been deceiving us all in a very inexcusable manner. I hope you have not been leading a double life, pretending to be wicked and being really good all the time. That would be hypocrisy.

ALGERNON (*looks at her in amazement*). Oh! of course I have been rather reckless.

CECILY. I am glad to hear it.

ALGERNON. In fact, now you mention the subject, I have been very bad in my own small way.

CECILY. I don't think you should be so proud of that, though I am sure it must have been very pleasant.

ALGERNON. It is much pleasanter being here with you.

CECILY. I can't understand how you are here at all. Uncle Jack won't be back till Monday afternoon.

ALGERNON. That is a great disappointment. I am obliged to go up by the first train on Monday morning. I have a business appointment that I am anxious . . . to miss.

CECILY. Couldn't you miss it anywhere but in London?

ALGERNON. No; the appointment is in London.

CECILY. Well, I know, of course, how important it is not to keep a business engagement, if one wants to retain any sense of the beauty of life, but still I think you had better wait till Uncle Jack arrives. I know he wants to speak to you about your emigrating.

ALGERNON. About my what?

CECILY. Your emigrating. He has gone up to buy your outfit.

ALGERNON. I certainly wouldn't let Jack buy my outfit. He has no taste in neckties at all.

CECILY. I don't think you will require neckties. Uncle Jack is sending you to Australia.

ALGERNON. Australia! I'd sooner die.

CECILY. Well, he said at dinner on Wednesday night, that you would have to choose between this world, the next world, and Australia.

ALGERNON. Oh, well! The accounts I have received of Australia and the next world, are not particularly encouraging. This world is good enough for me, cousin Cecily.

CECILY. Yes, but are you good enough for it?

ALGERNON. I'm afraid I'm not that. That is why I want you to reform me. You might make that your mission, if you don't mind, cousin Cecily.

CECILY. I'm afraid I've not time, this afternoon.

ALGERNON. Well, would you mind my reforming myself this afternoon?

CECILY. That is rather Quixotic of you. But I think you should try.

ALGERNON. I will. I feel better already.

CECILY. You are looking a little worse.

ALGERNON. That is because I am hungry.

CECILY. How thoughtless of me. I should have remembered that when one is going to lead an entirely new life, one requires regular and wholesome meals. Won't you come in?

ALGERNON. Thank you. Might I have a button-hole first? I never have any appetite unless I have a button-hole first.

CECILY. A Maréchal Niel? (*Picks up scissors.*)

ALGERNON. No, I'd sooner have a pink rose.

CECILY. Why? (*Cuts a flower.*)

ALGERNON. Because you are like a pink rose, cousin Cecily.

CECILY. I don't think it can be right for you to talk to me like that. Miss Prism never says such things to me.

ALGERNON. Then Miss Prism is a short-sighted old lady. (*Cecily puts the rose in his button-hole.*) You are the prettiest girl I ever saw.

CECILY. Miss Prism says that all good looks are a snare.

ALGERNON. They are a snare that every sensible man would like to be caught in.

CECILY. Oh! I don't think I would care to catch a sensible man. I shouldn't know what to talk to him about. (*They pass into the house. Miss Prism and Dr. Chasuble return.*)

MISS PRISM. You are too much alone, dear Dr. Chasuble. You should get married. A misanthrope I can understand—a womanthrope, never!

CHASUBLE (*with a scholar's shudder*). Believe me, I do not deserve so neologistic a phrase. The precept as well as the practice of the Primitive Church was distinctly against matrimony.

MISS PRISM (*sententiously*). That is obviously the reason why the Primitive Church has not lasted up to the present day. And you do not seem to realize, dear Doctor, that by persistently remaining single, a man converts himself into a permanent public temptation. Men should be careful; this very celibacy leads weaker vessels astray.

CHASUBLE. But is a man not equally attractive when married?

MISS PRISM. No married man is ever attractive except to his wife.

CHASUBLE. And often, I've been told, not even to her.

MISS PRISM. That depends on the intellectual sympathies of the woman. Maturity can always be depended on. Ripeness can be trusted. Young women are green. (*Dr.*

Chasuble starts.) I spoke horticulturally. My metaphor was drawn from fruits. But where is Cecily?

CHASUBLE. Perhaps she followed us to the schools.

(*Enter Jack slowly from the back of the garden. He is dressed in the deepest mourning, with crepe hatband and black gloves.*)

MISS PRISM. Mr. Worthing!

CHASUBLE. Mr. Worthing?

MISS PRISM. This is indeed a surprise. We did not look for you till Monday afternoon.

JACK (*shakes Miss Prism's hand in a tragic manner*). I have returned sooner than I expected. Dr. Chasuble, I hope you are well?

CHASUBLE. Dear Mr. Worthing, I trust this garb of woe does not betoken some terrible calamity?

JACK. My brother.

MISS PRISM. More shameful debts and extravagance?

CHASUBLE. Still leading his life of pleasure?

JACK (*shaking his head*). Dead!

CHASUBLE. Your brother Ernest dead?

JACK. Quite dead.

MISS PRISM. What a lesson for him! I trust he will profit by it.

CHAUSBLE. Mr. Worthing, I offer you my sincere condolence. You have at least the consolation of knowing that you were always the most generous and forgiving of brothers.

JACK. Poor Ernest! He had many faults, but it is a sad, sad blow.

CHASUBLE. Very sad indeed. Were you with him at the end?

JACK. No. He died abroad; in Paris, in fact. I had a telegram last night from the manager of the Grand Hotel.

CHAUSUBLE. Was the cause of death mentioned?

JACK. A severe chill, it seems.

MISS PRISM. As a man sows, so shall he reap.

CHASUBLE (*raising his hand*). Charity, dear Miss Prism, charity! None of us are perfect. I myself am peculiarly susceptible to draughts. Will the interment take place here?

JACK. No. He seems to have expressed a desire to be buried in Paris.

CHASUBLE. In Paris! (*Shakes his head.*) I fear that hardly points to any very serious state of mind at the last. You would no doubt wish me to make some slight allusion to this tragic domestic affliction next Sunday. (*Jack presses his hand convulsively.*) My sermon on the meaning of the manna in the wilderness can be adapted to almost any occasion, joyful, or, as in the present case, distressing. (*All sigh.*) I have preached it at harvest celebrations, christenings, confirmations, on days of humiliation and festal days. The last time I delivered it was in the Cathedral, as a charity sermon on behalf of the Society for the Prevention of Discontentment among the Upper Orders. The Bishop, who was present, was much struck by some of the analogies I drew.

JACK. Ah, that reminds me, you mentioned christenings I think, Dr. Chasuble? I suppose you know how to christen all right? (*Dr. Chasuble looks astounded.*) I mean, of course, you are continually christening, aren't you?

MISS PRISM. It is, I regret to say, one of the Rector's most constant duties in this parish. I have often spoken to the poorer classes on the subject. But they don't seem to know what thrift is.

CHASUBLE. But is there any particular infant in whom you are interested, Mr. Worthing? Your brother was, I believe, unmarried, was he not?

JACK. Oh, yes.

MISS PRISM (*bitterly*). People who live entirely for pleasure usually are.

JACK. But it is not for any child, dear Doctor. I am very fond of children. No! the fact is, I would like to be christened myself, this afternoon, if you have nothing better to do.

CHASUBLE. But surely, Mr. Worthing, you have been christened already?

JACK. I don't remember anything about it.

CHASUBLE. But have you any grave doubts on the subject?

JACK. I certainly intend to have. Of course, I don't know if the thing would bother you in any way, or if you think I am a little too old now.

CHASUBLE. Not at all. The sprinkling, and, indeed, the immersion of adults is a perfectly canonical practice.

JACK. Immersion!

CHASUBLE. You need have no apprehensions. Sprinkling is all that is necessary, or indeed I think advisable. Our weather is so changeable. At what hour would you wish the ceremony performed?

JACK. Oh, I might trot around about five if that would suit you.

CHASUBLE. Perfectly, perfectly! In fact I have two similar ceremonies to perform at that time. A case of twins that occurred recently in one of the outlying cottages on your own estate. Poor Jenkins the carter, a most hard-working man.

JACK. Oh! I don't see much fun in being christened along with other babies. It would be childish. Would half-past five do?

CHASUBLE. Admirably! Admirably! (*Takes out watch.*) And now, dear Mr. Worthing, I will not intrude any longer into a house of sorrow. I would merely beg you not to be too much bowed down by grief. What seem to us bitter trials at the moment are often blessings in disguise.

MISS PRISM. This seems to me a blessing of an extremely obvious kind.

(*Enter Cecily from the house.*)

CECILY. Uncle Jack! Oh, I am pleased to see you back. But what horrid clothes you have on! Do go and change them.

MISS PRISM. Cecily!

CHASUBLE. My child! my child! (*Cecily goes towards Jack; he kisses her brow in a melancholy manner.*)

CECILY. What is the matter, Uncle Jack? Do look happy! You look as if you had a toothache and I have such a surprise for you. Who do you think is in the dining-room? Your brother!

JACK. Who?

CECILY. Your brother Ernest. He arrived about half an hour ago.

JACK. What nonsense! I haven't got a brother.

CECILY. Oh, don't say that. However badly he may have behaved to you in the past he is still your brother. You couldn't be so heartless as to disown him. I'll tell him to come out. And you will shake hands with him, won't you, Uncle Jack? (*Runs back into the house.*)

CHASUBLE. There are very joyful tidings.

MISS PRISM. After we had all been resigned to his loss, his sudden return seems to me peculiarly distressing.

JACK. My brother is in the dining-room? I don't know what it all means. I think it is perfectly absurd.

(*Enter Algernon and Cecily hand in hand. They come slowly up to Jack.*)

JACK. Good heavens! (*Motions Algernon away.*)

ALGERNON. Brother John, I have come down from town to tell you that I am very sorry for all the trouble I have given you, and that I intend to lead a better life in the future. (*Jack glares at him and does not take his hand.*)

CECILY. Uncle Jack, you are not going to refuse your own brother's hand.

JACK. Nothing will induce me to take his hand. I think his coming down here disgraceful. He knows perfectly well why.

CECILY. Uncle Jack, do be nice. There is good in everyone. Ernest has just been telling me about his poor invalid friend, Mr. Bunbury, whom he goes to visit so often. And surely there must be much good in one who is kind to an invalid, and leaves the pleasures of London to sit by a bed of pain.

JACK. Oh, he has been talking about Bunbury, has he?

CECILY. Yes, he has told me all about poor Mr. Bunbury, and his terrible state of health.

JACK. Bunbury! Well, I won't have him talk to you about Bunbury or about anything else. It is enough to drive one perfectly frantic.

ALGERNON. Of course I admit that the faults were all on my side. But I must say that I think that Brother John's coldness to me is peculiarly painful. I expected a more enthusiastic welcome, especially considering it is the first time I have come here.

CECILY. Uncle Jack, if you don't shake hands with Ernest I will never forgive you.

JACK. Never forgive me?

CECILY. Never, never, never!

JACK. Well, this is the last time I shall ever do it. (*Shakes hands with Algernon and glares.*)

CHASUBLE. It's pleasant, is it not, to see so perfect a reconciliation? I think we might leave the two brothers together.

MISS PRISM. Cecily, you will come with us.

CECILY. Certainly, Miss Prism. My little task of reconciliation is over.

CHASUBLE. You have done a beautiful action to-day, dear child.

MISS PRISM. We must not be premature in our judgments.

CECILY. I feel very happy. (*They all go off.*)

JACK. You young scoundrel, Algy, you must get out of this place as soon as possible. I don't allow any Bunburying here.

(*Enter Merriman.*)

MERRIMAN. I have put Mr. Ernest's things in the room next to yours, sir. I suppose that is all right?

JACK. What?

MERRIMAN. Mr. Ernest's luggage, sir. I have unpacked it and put it in the room next to your own.

JACK. His luggage?

MERRIMAN. Yes, sir. Three portmanteaus, a dressing-case, two hat-boxes, and a large luncheon-basket.

ALGERNON. I am afraid I can't stay more than a week this time.

JACK. Merriman, order the dog-cart at once. Mr. Ernest has been suddenly called back to town.

MERRIMAN. Yes, sir. (*Goes back into the house.*)

ALGERNON. What a fearful liar you are, Jack. I have not been called back to town at all.

JACK. Yes, you have.

ALGERNON. I haven't heard anyone call me.

JACK. Your duty as a gentleman calls you back.

ALGERNON. My duty as a gentleman has never interfered with my pleasures in the smallest degree.

JACK. I can quite understand that.

ALGERNON. Well, Cecily is a darling.

JACK. You are not to talk of Miss Cardew like that. I don't like it.

ALGERNON. Well, I don't like your clothes. You look perfectly ridiculous in them. Why on earth don't you go up and change? It is perfectly childish to be in deep mourning for a man who is actually staying for a whole week with you in your house as a guest. I call it grotesque.

JACK. You are certainly not staying with me for a whole week as a guest or anything else. You have got to leave . . . by the four-five train.

ALGERNON. I certainly won't leave you so long as you are in mourning. It would be most unfriendly. If I were in mourning you would stay with me, I suppose. I should think it very unkind if you didn't.

JACK. Well, will you go if I change my clothes?

ALGERNON. Yes, if you are not too long. I never saw anybody take so long to dress, and with such little result.

JACK. Well, at any rate, that is better than being always over-dressed as you are.

ALGERNON. If I am occasionally a little over-dressed, I make up for it by being always immensely over-educated.

JACK. Your vanity is ridiculous, your conduct an outrage, and your presence in my garden utterly absurd. However, you have got to catch the four-five, and I hope you will have a pleasant journey back to town. This Bunburying, as you call it, has not been a great success for you. (*Goes into the house.*)

ALGERNON. I think it has been a great success. I'm in love with Cecily, and that is everything. (*Enter Cecily at the back of the garden. She picks up the can and begins to water the flowers.*) But I must see her before I go, and make arrangements for another Bunbury. Ah, there she is.

CECILY. Oh, I merely came back to water the roses. I thought you were with Uncle Jack.

ALGERNON. He's gone to order the dog-cart for me.

CECILY. Oh, is he going to take you for a nice drive?

ALGERNON. He's going to send me away.

CECILY. Then have we got to part?

ALGERNON. I am afraid so. It's a very painful parting.

CECILY. It is always painful to part from people whom one has known for a very brief space of time. The absence of old friends one can endure with equanimity. But even a momentary separation from anyone to whom one has just been introduced is almost unbearable.

ALGERNON. Thank you.

(*Enter Merriman.*)

MERRIMAN. The dog-cart is at the door, sir. (*Algernon looking appealingly at Cecily.*)

CECILY. It can wait, Merriman . . . for . . . five minutes.

MERRIMAN. Yes, miss. (*Exit Merriman.*)

ALGERNON. I hope, Cecily, I shall not offend you if I state quite frankly and openly that you seem to me to be in every way the visible personification of absolute perfection.

CECILY. I think your frankness does you great credit, Ernest. If you will allow me I will copy your remarks into my diary. (*Goes over to table and begins writing in diary.*)

ALGERNON. Do you really keep a diary? I'd give any thing to look at it. May I?

CECILY. Oh, no. (*Puts her hand over it.*) You see, it is simply a very young girl's record of her own thoughts and impressions, and consequently meant for publication. When it appears in volume form I hope you will order a copy. But pray, Ernest, don't stop. I delight in taking down from dictation. I have reached "absolute perfection." You can go on. I am quite ready for more.

ALGERNON (*somewhat taken aback*). Ahem! Ahem!

CECILY. Oh, don't cough, Ernest. When one is dictating one should speak fluently and not cough. Besides I don't know how to spell a cough. (*Writes as Algernon speaks.*)

ALGERNON (*speaking very rapidly*). Cecily, ever since I first looked upon your wonderful and incomparable beauty, I have dared to love you wildly, passionately, devotedly, hopelessly.

CECILY. I don't think that you should tell me that you love me wildly, passionately, devotedly, hopelessly. Hopelessly doesn't seem to make much sense, does it?

ALGERNON. Cecily!

(*Enter Merriman.*)

MERRIMAN. The dog-cart is waiting, sir.

ALGERNON. Tell it to come round next week, at the same hour.

MERRIMAN (*looks at Cecily, who makes no sign*). Yes, sir.

(*Merriman retires.*)

CECILY. Uncle Jack would be very much annoyed if he knew you were staying on till next week, at the same hour.

ALGERNON. Oh, I don't care about Jack. I don't care for anybody in the whole world but you. I love you, Cecily. You will marry me, won't you?

CECILY. You silly you! Of course. Why, we have been engaged for the last three months.

ALGERNON. For the last three months?

CECILY. Yes, it will be exactly three months on Thursday.

ALGERNON. But how did we become engaged?

CECILY. Well, ever since dear Uncle Jack first confessed to us that he had a younger brother who was very wicked and bad, you of course have formed the chief topic of conversation between myself and Miss Prism. And of course a man who is much talked about is always very attractive. One feels there must be something in him after all. I daresay it was foolish of me, but I fell in love with you, Ernest.

ALGERNON. Darling! And when was the engagement actually settled?

CECILY. On the 14th of February last. Worn out by your entire ignorance of my existence, I determined to end the matter one way or the other, and after a long struggle with myself I accepted you under this dear old tree here. The next day I bought this little ring in your name, and this is the little bangle with the true lovers' knot I promised you always to wear.

ALGERNON. Did I give you this? It's very pretty, isn't it?

CECILY. Yes, you've wonderfully good taste, Ernest. It's the excuse I've always given for your leading such a bad life. And this is the box in which I keep all your dear letters. (*Kneels at table, opens box, and produces letters tied up with blue ribbon.*)

ALGERNON. My letters! But my own sweet Cecily, I have never written you any letters.

CECILY. You need hardly remind me of that, Ernest. I remember only too well that I was forced to write your letters for you. I wrote always three times a week, and sometimes oftener.

ALGERNON. Oh, do let me read them, Cecily?

CECILY. Oh, I couldn't possibly. They would make you far too conceited. (*Replaces box.*) The three you wrote me after I had broken off the engagement are so beautiful, and so badly spelled, that even now I can hardly read them without crying a little.

ALGERNON. But was our engagement ever broken off?

CECILY. Of course it was. On the 22nd of last March. You can see the entry if you like. (*Shows diary.*) "Today I broke off my engagement with Ernest. I feel it is better to do so. The weather still continues charming."

ALGERNON. But why on earth did you break it off? What had I done? I had done nothing at all, Cecily. I am very much hurt indeed to hear you broke it off. Particularly when the weather was so charming.

CECILY. It would hardly have been a really serious engagement if it hadn't been broken off at least once. But I forgave you before the week was out.

ALGERNON (*crossing to her, and kneeling*). What a perfect angel you are, Cecily.

CECILY. You dear romantic boy. (*He kisses her, she puts her fingers through his hair.*) I hope your hair curls naturally, does it?

ALGERNON. Yes, darling, with a little help from others.

CECILY. I am so glad.

ALGERNON. You'll never break off our engagement again, Cecily?

CECILY. I don't think I could break it off now that I have actually met you. Besides, of course, that is the question of your name.

ALGERNON. Yes, of course. (*Nervously.*)

CECILY. You must not laugh at me, darling, but it had always been a girlish dream of mine to love some one whose name was Ernest. (*Algernon rises, Cecily also.*) There is something in that name that seems to inspire absolute confidence. I pity any poor married woman whose husband is not called Ernest.

ALGERNON. But, my dear child, do you mean to say you could not love me if I had some other name?

CECILY. But what name?

ALGERNON. Oh, any name you like—Algernon, for instance. . . .

CECILY. But I don't like the name of Algernon.

ALGERNON. Well, my own dear, sweet, loving little darling, I really can't see why you should object to the name of Algernon. It is not at all a bad name. In fact, it is rather an aristocratic name. Half of the chaps who get into the Bankruptcy Court are called Algernon. But seriously, Cecily . . . (*Moving to her*) . . . if my name was Algy, couldn't you love me?

CECILY (*rising*). I might respect you, Ernest, I might admire your character, but I fear that I should not be able to give you my undivided attention.

ALGERNON. Ahem! Cecily! (*Picking up hat.*) Your Rector here is, I suppose, thoroughly experienced in the practice of all the rites and ceremonials of the church?

CECILY. Oh, yes. Dr. Chasuble is a most learned man. He has never written a single book, so you can imagine how much he knows.

ALGERNON. I must see him at once on a most important christening—I mean on most important business.

CECILY. Oh!

ALGERNON. I sha'n't be away more than half an hour.

CECILY. Considering that we have been engaged since February the 14th, and that I only met you to-day for the first time, I think it is rather hard that you should leave me for so long a period as half an hour. Couldn't you make it twenty minutes?

ALGERNON. I'll be back in no time. (*Kisses her and rushes down the garden.*)

CECILY. What an impetuous boy he is. I like his hair so much. I must enter his proposal in my diary.

(*Enter Merriman.*)

MERRIMAN. A Miss Fairfax has just called to see Mr. Worthing. On very important business, Miss Fairfax states.

CECILY. Isn't Mr. Worthing in his library?

MERRIMAN. Mr. Worthing went over in the direction of the Rectory some time ago.

CECILY. Pray ask the lady to come out here; Mr. Worthing is sure to be back soon. And you can bring tea.

MERRIMAN. Yes, miss.   (*Goes out.*)

CECILY. Miss Fairfax! I suppose one of the many good elderly women who are associated with Uncle Jack in some of his philanthropic work in London. I don't quite like women who are interested in philanthropic work. I think it is so forward of them.

(*Enter Merriman.*)

MERRIMAN. Miss Fairfax.

(*Enter Gwendolen. Exit Merriman.*)

CECILY (*advancing to meet her*). Pray let me introduce myself to you. My name is Cecily Cardew.

GWENDOLEN. Cecily Cardew? (*Moving to her and shaking hands.*) What a very sweet name! Something tells me that we are going to be great friends. I like you already more than I can say. My first impressions of people are never wrong.

CECILY. How nice of you to like me so much after we have known each other such a comparatively short time. Pray sit down.

GWENDOLEN (*still standing up*). I may call you Cecily, may I not?

CECILY. With pleasure!

GWENDOLEN. And you will always call me Gwendolen, won't you?

CECILY. If you wish.

GWENDOLEN. Then that is all quite settled, is it not?

CECILY. I hope so. (*A pause. They both sit down together.*)

GWENDOLEN. Perhaps this might be a favourable opportunity for my mentioning who I am. My father is Lord Bracknell. You have never heard of papa, I suppose?

CECILY. I don't think so.

GWENDOLEN. Outside the family circle, papa, I am glad to say, is entirely unknown. I think that is quite as it should be. The home seems to me to be the proper sphere for the man. And certainly once a man begins to neglect his domestic duties he becomes painfully effeminate, does he not? And I don't like that. It makes men so very attractive. Cecily, mamma, whose views on education are remarkably strict, has brought me up to be extremely shortsighted; it is part of her system; so do you mind my looking at you through my glasses?

CECILY. Oh, not at all, Gwendolen. I am very fond of being looked at.

GWENDOLEN (*after examining Cecily carefully through a lorgnette*). You are here on a short visit, I suppose.

CECILY. Oh, no, I live here.

GWENDOLEN (*severely*). Really? Your mother, no doubt, or some female relative of advanced years, resides here also?

CECILY. Oh, no. I have no mother, nor, in fact, any relations.

GWENDOLEN. Indeed?

CECILY. My dear guardian, with the assistance of Miss Prism, has the arduous task of looking after me.

GWENDOLEN. Your guardian?

CECILY. Yes, I am Mr. Worthing's ward.

GWENDOLEN. Oh! It is strange he never mentioned to me that he had a ward. How secretive of him! He grows more interesting hourly. I am not sure, however, that the news inspires me with feelings of unmixed delight. (*Rising and going to her.*) I am very fond of you, Cecily; I have liked you ever since I met you. But I am bound to state that now that I know that you are Mr. Worthing's ward, I cannot help expressing a wish you were—well, just a little older than you seem to be—and not quite so very alluring in appearance. In fact, if I may speak candidly—

CECILY. Pray do! I think that whenever one has anything unpleasant to say, one should always be quite candid.

GWENDOLEN. Well, to speak with perfect candour, Cecily, I wish that you were fully forty-two, and more than usually plain for your age. Ernest has a strong upright nature. He is the very soul of truth and honour. Disloyalty would be as impossible to him as deception. But even men of the noblest possible moral character are extremely susceptible to the influence of the physical charms of others. Modern, no less than Ancient History, supplies us with many most painful examples of what I refer to. If it were not so, indeed, History would be quite unreadable.

CECILY. I beg your pardon, Gwendolen, did you say Ernest?

GWENDOLEN. Yes.

CECILY. Oh, but it is not Mr. Ernest Worthing who is my guardian. It is his brother—his elder brother.

GWENDOLEN (*sitting down again*). Ernest never mentioned to me that he had a brother.

CECILY. I am sorry to say they have not been on good terms for a long time.

GWENDOLEN. Ah! that accounts for it. And now that I think of it I have never heard any man mention his brother. The subject seems distasteful to most men. Cecily, you have lifted a load from my mind. I was growing almost anxious. It would have been terrible if any cloud had come across a friendship like ours, would it not? Of course you are quite, quite sure that it is not Mr. Ernest Worthing who is your guardian?

CECILY. Quite sure. (*A pause.*) In fact, I am going to be his.

GWENDOLEN (*enquiringly*). I beg your pardon?

CECILY (*rather shy and confidingly*). Dearest Gwendolen, there is no reason why I should make a secret of it to you. Our little county newspaper is sure to chronicle the fact next week. Mr. Ernest Worthing and I are engaged to be married.

GWENDOLEN (*quite politely, rising*). My darling Cecily, I think there must be some slight error. Mr. Ernest Worthing is engaged to me. The announcement will appear in the *Morning Post* on Saturday at the latest.

CECILY (*very politely, rising*). I am afraid you must be under some misconception. Ernest proposed to me exactly ten minutes ago. (*Shows diary.*)

GWENDOLEN (*examines diary through her lorgnette carefully*). It is certainly very curious, for he asked me to be his wife yesterday afternoon at 5.30. If you would care to verify the incident, pray do so. (*Produces diary of her own.*) I never travel without my diary. One should always have something sensational to read in the train. I am so sorry, dear Cecily, if it is any disappointment to you, but I am afraid *I* have the prior claim.

CECILY. It would distress me more than I can tell you, dear Gwendolen, if it caused you any mental or physical anguish, but I feel bound to point out that since Ernest proposed to you he clearly has changed his mind.

GWENDOLEN (*meditatively*). If the poor fellow has been entrapped into any foolish promise I shall consider it my duty to rescue him at once, and with a firm hand.

CECILY (*thoughtfully and sadly*). Whatever unfortunate entanglement my dear boy may have got into, I will never reproach him with it after we are married.

GWENDOLEN. Do you allude to me, Miss Cardew, as an entanglement? You are presumptuous. On an occasion of this kind it becomes more than a moral duty to speak one's mind. It becomes a pleasure.

CECILY. Do you suggest, Miss Fairfax, that I entrapped Ernest into an engagement? How dare you? This is no time for wearing the shallow mask of manners. When I see a spade I call it a spade.

GWENDOLEN (*satirically*). I am glad to say that I have never seen a spade. It is obvious that our social spheres have been widely different.

(*Enter Merriman, followed by the footman. He carries a salver, tablecloth, and plate-stand. Cecily is about to retort. The presence of the servants exercises a restraining influence, under which both girls chafe.*)

MERRIMAN. Shall I lay tea here as usual, miss?

CECILY (*sternly, in a calm voice*). Yes, as usual. (*Merriman begins to clear and lay cloth. A long pause. Cecily and Gwendolen glare at each other.*)

GWENDOLEN. Are there many interesting walks in the vicinity, Miss Cardew?

CECILY. Oh, yes, a great many. From the top of one of the hills quite close one can see five counties.

GWENDOLEN. Five counties! I don't think I should like that. I hate crowds.

CECILY (*sweetly*). I suppose that is why you live in town? (*Gwendolen bites her lip, and beats her foot nervously with her parasol.*)

GWENDOLEN (*looking round*). Quite a well-kept garden this is, Miss Cardew.

CECILY. So glad you like it, Miss Fairfax.

GWENDOLEN. I had no idea there were any flowers in the country.

CECILY. Oh, flowers are as common here, Miss Fairfax, as people are in London.

GWENDOLEN. Personally I cannot understand how anybody manages to exist in the country, if anybody who is anybody does. The country always bores me to death.

CECILY. Ah! This is what the newspapers call agricultural depression, is it not? I believe the aristocracy are suffering very much from it just at present. It is almost an epidemic amongst them, I have been told. May I offer you some tea, Miss Fairfax?

GWENDOLEN (*with elaborate politeness*). Thank you. (*Aside.*) Detestable girl! But I require tea!

CECILY (*sweetly*). Sugar?

GWENDOLEN (*superciliously*). No, thank you. Sugar is not fashionable any more. (*Cecily looks angrily at her, takes up the tongs and puts four lumps of sugar into the cup.*)

CECILY (*severely*). Cake or bread and butter?

GWENDOLEN (*in a bored manner*). Bread and butter, please. Cake is rarely seen at the best houses nowadays.

CECILY (*cuts a very large slice of cake, and puts it on the tray*). Hand that to Miss Fairfax. (*Merriman does so, and goes out with footman. Gwendolen drinks the tea and makes a grimace. Puts down cup at once, reaches out her hand to the bread and butter, looks at it, and finds it is cake. Rises in indignation.*)

GWENDOLEN. You have filled my tea with lumps of sugar, and though I asked most distinctly for bread and butter, you have given me cake. I am known for the gentleness of my disposition, and the extraordinary sweetness of my nature, but I warn you, Miss Cardew, you may go too far.

CECILY (*rising*). To save my poor, innocent, trusting boy from the machinations of any other girl there are no lengths to which I would not go.

GWENDOLEN. From the moment I saw you I distrusted you. I felt that you were false and deceitful. I am never deceived in such matters. My first impressions of people are invariably right.

CECILY. It seems to me, Miss Fairfax, that I am trespassing on your valuable time. No doubt you have many other calls of a similar character to make in the neighbourhood.

(*Enter Jack.*)

GWENDOLEN (*catching sight of him*). Ernest! My own Ernest!

JACK. Gwendolen! Darling! (*Offers to kiss her.*)

GWENDOLEN (*drawing back*). A moment! May I ask if you are engaged to be married to this young lady? (*Points to Cecily.*)

JACK (*laughing*). To dear little Cecily! Of course not! What could have put such an idea into your pretty little head?

GWENDOLEN. Thank you. You may. (*Offers her cheek.*)

CECILY (*very sweetly*). I knew there must be some misunderstanding, Miss Fairfax. The gentleman whose arm is at present around your waist is my dear guardian, Mr. John Worthing.

GWENDOLEN. I beg your pardon?

CECILY. This is Uncle Jack.

GWENDOLEN (*receding*). Jack! Oh!

(*Enter Algernon.*)

CECILY. Here is Ernest.

ALGERNON (*goes straight over to Cecily without noticing anyone else*). My own love! (*Offers to kiss her.*)

CECILY (*drawing back*). A moment, Ernest! May I ask you— are you engaged to be married to this young lady?

ALGERNON (*looking round*). To what young lady? Good heavens! Gwendolen!

CECILY. Yes, to good heavens, Gwendolen, I mean to Gwendolen.

ALGERNON (*laughing*). Of course not! What could have put such an idea into your pretty little head?

CECILY. Thank you. (*Presenting her cheek to be kissed.*) You may. (*Algernon kisses her.*)

GWENDOLEN. I felt there was some slight error, Miss Cardew. The gentleman who is now embracing you is my cousin, Mr. Algernon Moncrieff.

CECILY (*breaking away from Algernon*). Algernon Moncrieff! Oh! (*The two girls move towards each other and put their arms round each other's waists as if for protection.*)

CECILY. Are you called Algernon?

ALGERNON. I cannot deny it.

CECILY. Oh!

GWENDOLEN. Is your name really John?

JACK (*standing rather proudly*). I could deny it if I liked. I could deny anything if I liked. But my name certainly is John. It has been John for years.

CECILY (*to Gwendolen*). A gross deception has been practised on both of us.

GWENDOLEN. My poor wounded Cecily!

CECILY. My sweet, wronged Gwendolen!

GWENDOLEN (*slowly and seriously*). You will call me sister, will you not? (*They embrace. Jack and Algernon groan and walk up and down.*)

CECILY (*rather brightly*). There is just one question I would like to be allowed to ask my guardian.

GWENDOLEN. An admirable idea! Mr. Worthing, there is

just one question I would like to be permitted to put to you. Where is your brother Ernest? We are both engaged to be married to your brother Ernest, so it is a matter of some importance to us to know where your brother Ernest is at present.

JACK (*slowly and hesitatingly*). Gwendolen—Cecily—it is very painful for me to be forced to speak the truth. It is the first time in my life that I have ever been reduced to such a painful position, and I am really quite inexperienced in doing anything of the kind. However I will tell you quite frankly that I have no brother Ernest. I have no brother at all. I never had a brother in my life, and I certainly have not the smallest intention of ever having one in the future.

CECILY (*surprised*). No brother at all?

JACK (*cheerily*). None!

GWENDOLEN (*severely*). Had you never a brother of any kind?

JACK (*pleasantly*). Never. Not even of any kind.

GWENDOLEN. I am afraid it is quite clear, Cecily, that neither of us is engaged to be married to anyone.

CECILY. It is not a very pleasant position for a young girl suddenly to find herself in. Is it?

GWENDOLEN. Let us go into the house. They will hardly venture to come after us there.

CECILY. No, men are so cowardly, aren't they? (*They retire into the house with scornful looks*.)

JACK. This ghastly state of things is what you call Bunburying, I suppose?

ALGERNON. Yes, and a perfectly wonderful Bunbury it is. The most wonderful Bunbury I have ever had in my life.

JACK. Well, you've no right whatsoever to Bunbury here.

ALGERNON. That is absurd. One has a right to Bunbury anywhere one chooses. Every serious Bunburyist knows that.

JACK. Serious Bunburyist! Good heavens!

ALGERNON. Well, one must be serious about something, if one wants to have any amusement in life. I happen to be serious about Bunburying. What on earth you are serious about I haven't got the remotest idea. About everything, I should fancy. You have such an absolutely trivial nature.

JACK. Well, the only small satisfaction I have in the whole of this wretched business is that your friend Bunbury is quite exploded. You won't be able to run down to the country quite so often as you used to do, dear Algy. And a very good thing, too.

ALGERNON. Your brother is a little off colour, isn't he, dear Jack? You won't be able to disappear to London quite so frequently as your wicked custom was. And not a bad thing, either.

JACK. As for your conduct towards Miss Cardew, I must say that your taking in a sweet, simple, innocent girl like that is quite inexcusable. To say nothing of the fact that she is my ward.

ALGERNON. I can see no possible defence at all for your deceiving a brilliant, clever, thoroughly experienced young lady like Miss Fairfax. To say nothing of the fact that she is my cousin.

JACK. I wanted to be engaged to Gwendolen, that is all. I love her.

ALGERNON. Well, I simply wanted to be engaged to Cecily. I adore her.

JACK. There is certainly no chance of your marrying Miss Cardew.

ALGERNON. I don't think there is much likelihood, Jack, of you and Miss Fairfax being united.

JACK. Well, that is no business of yours.

ALGERNON. If it was my business, I wouldn't talk about it. (*Begins to eat muffins*.) It is very vulgar to talk about one's business. Only people like stock-brokers do that, and then merely at dinner parties.

JACK. How you can sit there, calmly eating muffins, when we are in this horrible trouble, I can't make out. You seem to me to be perfectly heartless.

ALGERNON. Well, I can't eat muffins in an agitated manner. The butter would probably get on my cuffs. One should always eat muffins quite calmly. It is the only way to eat them.

JACK. I say it's perfectly heartless your eating muffins at all, under the circumstances.

ALGERNON. When I am in trouble, eating is the only thing that consoles me. Indeed, when I am in really great trouble, as anyone who knows me intimately will tell you, I refuse everything except food and drink. At the present moment I am eating muffins because I am unhappy. Besides, I am particularly fond of muffins. (*Rising*.)

JACK (*rising*). Well, that is no reason why you should eat them all in that greedy way. (*Takes muffin from Algernon*.)

ALGERNON (*offering tea-cake*). I wish you would have tea-cake instead. I don't like tea-cake.

JACK. Good heavens! I suppose a man may eat his own muffins in his own garden.

ALGERNON. But you have just said it was perfectly heartless to eat muffins.

JACK. I said it was perfectly heartless of you, under the circumstances. That is a very different thing.

ALGERNON. That may be. But the muffins are the same. (*He seizes the muffin dish from Jack*.)

JACK. Algy, I wish to goodness you would go.

ALGERNON. You can't possibly ask me to go without having some dinner. It's absurd. I never go without my dinner. No one ever does, except vegetarians and people like that. Besides I have just made arrangements with Dr. Chasuble to be christened at a quarter to six under the name of Ernest.

JACK. My dear fellow, the sooner you give up that nonsense the better. I made arrangements this morning with Chasuble to be christened myself at 5:30, and I naturally will take the name of Ernest. Gwendolen would wish it. We can't both be christened Ernest. It's absurd. Besides, I have a perfect right to be christened if I like. There is no evidence at all that I ever have been christened by anybody. I should think it extremely probable I never was, and so does Dr. Chasuble. It is entirely different in your case. You have been christened already.

ALGERNON. Yes, but I have not been christened for years.

JACK. Yes, but you have been christened. That is the important thing.

ALGERNON. Quite so. So I know my constitution can stand it. If you are not quite sure about your ever having been christened, I must say I think it rather dangerous your venturing on it now. It might make you very unwell. You can hardly have forgotten that someone very closely connected with you was very nearly carried off this week in Paris by a severe chill.

JACK. Yes, but you said yourself that a severe chill was not hereditary.

ALGERNON. It usedn't to be, I know—but I daresay it is now. Science is always making wonderful improvements in things.

JACK (*picking up the muffin-dish*). Oh, that is nonsense; you are always talking nonsense.

ALGERNON. Jack, you are at the muffins again! I wish you wouldn't. There are only two left. (*Takes them.*) I told you I was particularly fond of muffins.

JACK. But I hate tea-cake.

ALGERNON. Why on earth then do you allow tea-cake to be served up for your guests? What ideas you have of hospitality!

JACK. Algernon! I have already told you to go. I don't want you here. Why don't you go?

ALGERNON. I haven't quite finished my tea yet, and there is still one muffin left. (*Jack groans, and sinks into a chair. Algernon still continues eating.*)

CURTAIN

ACT 3

SCENE: *Morning-room at the Manor House. Gwendolen and Cecily are at the window, looking out into the garden.*

GWENDOLEN. The fact that they did not follow us at once into the house, as anyone else would have done, seems to me to show that they have some sense of shame left.

CECILY. They have been eating muffins. That looks like repentance.

GWENDOLEN (*after a pause*). They don't seem to notice us at all. Couldn't you cough?

GWENDOLEN. They're looking at us. What effrontery!

CECILY. They're approaching. That's very forward of them.

GWENDOLEN. Let us preserve a dignified silence.

CECILY. Certainly, it's the only thing to do now.

(*Enter Jack, followed by Algernon. They whistle some dreadful popular air from a British opera.*)

GWENDOLEN. This dignified silence seems to produce an unpleasant effect.

CECILY. A most distasteful one.

GWENDOLEN. But we will not be the first to speak.

CECILY. Certainly not.

GWENDOLEN. Mr. Worthing, I have something very particular to ask you. Much depends on your reply.

CECILY. Gwendolen, your common sense is invaluable. Mr. Moncrieff, kindly answer me the following question. Why did you pretend to be my guardian's brother?

ALGERNON. In order that I might have an opportunity of meeting you.

CECILY (*to Gwendolen*). That certainly seems a satisfactory explanation, does it not?

GWENDOLEN. Yes, dear, if you can believe him.

CECILY. I don't. But that does not affect the wonderful beauty of his answer.

GWENDOLEN. True. In matters of grave importance, style, not sincerity, is the vital thing. Mr. Worthing, what explanation can you offer to me for pretending to have a brother? Was it in order that you might have an opportunity of coming up to town to see me as often as possible?

JACK. Can you doubt it, Miss Fairfax?

GWENDOLEN. I have the gravest doubts upon the subject. But I intend to crush them. This is not the moment for German scepticism. (*Moving to Cecily.*) Their explanations appear to be quite satisfactory, especially Mr. Worthing's. That seems to me to have the stamp of truth upon it.

CECILY. I am more than content with what Mr. Moncrieff said. His voice alone inspires one with absolute credulity.

GWENDOLEN. Then you think we should forgive them?

CECILY. Yes. I mean no.

GWENDOLEN. True! I had forgotten. There are principles at stake that one cannot surrender. Which of us should tell them? The task is not a pleasant one.

CECILY. Could we not both speak at the same time?

GWENDOLEN. An excellent idea! I nearly always speak at the same time as other people. Will you take the time from me?

CECILY. Certainly. (*Gwendolen beats time with uplifted finger.*)

GWENDOLEN *and* CECILY (*speaking together*). Your Christian names are still an insuperable barrier. That is all!

JACK *and* ALGERNON (*speaking together*). Our Christian names! Is that all? But we are going to be christened this afternoon.

GWENDOLEN (*to Jack*). For my sake you are prepared to do this terrible thing?

JACK. I am.

CECILY (*to Algernon*). To please me you are ready to face this fearful ordeal?

ALGERNON. I am!

GWENDOLEN. How absurd to talk of the equality of the sexes! Where questions of self-sacrifice are concerned, men are infinitely beyond us.

JACK. We are. (*Clasps hands with Algernon.*)

CECILY. They have moments of physical courage of which we women know absolutely nothing.

GWENDOLEN (*to Jack*). Darling!

ALGERNON (*to Cecily*). Darling! (*They fall into each other's arms.*)

(*Enter Merriman. When he enters he coughs loudly, seeing the situation.*)

MERRIMAN. Ahem! Ahem! Lady Bracknell!

JACK. Good heavens!

(*Enter Lady Bracknell. The couples separate in alarm. Exit Merriman.*)

LADY BRACKNELL. Gwendolen! What does this mean?

GWENDOLEN. Merely that I am engaged to be married to Mr. Worthing, Mamma.

LADY BRACKNELL. Come here. Sit down. Sit down immediately. Hesitation of any kind is a sign of mental decay in the young, of physical weakness in the old. (*Turns to Jack.*) Apprised, sir, of my daughter's sudden flight by her trusty maid, whose confidence I purchased by means of a small coin, I followed her at once by a luggage train. Her unhappy father is, I am glad to say, under the impression that she is attending a more than usually lengthy lecture by the University Extension Scheme on the Influence of a Permanent Income on Thought. I do not propose to undeceive him. Indeed I have never undeceived him on any question. I would consider it wrong. But of course, you will clearly understand that all communication between yourself and my daughter must cease immediately from this moment. On this point, as indeed on all points, I am firm.

JACK. I am engaged to be married to Gwendolen, Lady Bracknell!

LADY BRACKNELL. You are nothing of the kind, sir. And now, as regards Algernon! . . . Algernon!

ALGERNON. Yes, Aunt Augusta.

LADY BRACKNELL. May I ask if it is in this house that your invalid friend Mr. Bunbury resides?

ALGERNON (*stammering*). Oh no! Bunbury doesn't live here. Bunbury is somewhere else at present. In fact, Bunbury is dead.

LADY BRACKNELL. Dead! When did Mr. Bunbury die? His death must have been extremely sudden.

ALGERNON (*airily*). Oh, I killed Bunbury this afternoon. I mean poor Bunbury died this afternoon.

LADY BRACKNELL. What did he die of?

ALGERNON. Bunbury? Oh, he was quite exploded.

LADY BRACKNELL. Exploded! Was he the victim of a revolutionary outrage? I was not aware that Mr. Bunbury was interested in social legislation. If so, he is well punished for his morbidity.

ALGERNON. My dear Aunt Augusta, I mean he was found out! The doctors found out that Bunbury could not live, that is what I mean—so Bunbury died.

LADY BRACKNELL. He seems to have had great confidence in the opinion of his physicians. I am glad, however, that he made up his mind at the last to some definite course of action, and acted under proper medical advice. And now that we have finally got rid of this Mr. Bunbury, may I ask, Mr. Worthing, who is that young person whose hand my nephew Algernon is now holding in what seems to me a peculiarly unnecessary manner?

JACK. That lady is Miss Cecily Cardew, my ward. (*Lady Bracknell bows coldly to Cecily.*)

ALGERNON. I am engaged to be married to Cecily, Aunt Augusta.

LADY BRACKNELL. I beg your pardon?

CECILY. Mr. Moncrieff and I are engaged to be married, Lady Bracknell.

LADY BRACKNELL (*with a shiver, crossing to the sofa and sitting down*). I do not know whether there is anything peculiarly exciting in the air of this particular part of Hertfordshire, but the number of engagements that go on seems to me considerably above the proper average that statistics have laid down for our guidance. I think some preliminary enquiry on my part would not be out of place. Mr. Worthing, is Miss Cardew at all connected with any of the larger railway stations in London? I merely desire information. Until yesterday I had no idea that there were any families or persons whose origin was a Terminus. (*Jack looks perfectly furious, but restrains himself.*)

JACK (*in a clear, cold voice*). Miss Cardew is the granddaughter of the late Mr. Thomas Cardew of 149, Belgrave Square, S.W.; Gervase Park, Dorking, Surrey; and the Sporran, Fifeshire, N.B.

LADY BRACKNELL. That sounds not unsatisfactory. Three addresses always inspire confidence, even in tradesmen. But what proof have I of their authenticity?

JACK. I have carefully preserved the Court Guides of the period. They are open to your inspection, Lady Bracknell.

LADY BRACKNELL (*grimly*). I have known strange errors in that publication.

JACK. Miss Cardew's family solicitors are Messrs. Markby, Markby, and Markby.

LADY BRACKNELL. Markby, Markby, and Markby? A firm of the very highest position in their profession. Indeed I am told that one of the Mr. Markbys is occasionally to be seen at dinner parties. So far I am satisfied.

JACK (*very irritably*). How extremely kind of you, Lady Bracknell! I have also in my possession, you will be pleased to hear, certificates of Miss Cardew's birth, baptism, whooping cough, registration, vaccination, confirmation, and the measles; both the German and the English variety.

LADY BRACKNELL. Ah! A life crowded with incident, I see; though perhaps somewhat too exciting for a young girl. I am not myself in favor of premature experiences. (*Rises, looks at her watch.*) Gwendolen! the time approaches for our departure. We have not a moment to lose. As a matter of form, Mr. Worthing, I had better ask you if Miss Cardew has any little fortune?

JACK. Oh, about a hundred and thirty thousand pounds in the Funds. That is all. Good-bye, Lady Bracknell. So pleased to have seen you.

LADY BRACKNELL (*sitting down again*). A moment, Mr. Worthing. A hundred and thirty thousand pounds! And in the Funds! Miss Cardew seems to me a most attractive young lady, now that I look at her. Few girls of the present day have any really solid qualities, any of the qualities that last, and improve with time. We live, I regret to say, in an age of surfaces. (*To Cecily.*) Come over here, dear. (*Cecily goes across.*) Pretty child! your dress is sadly simple, and your hair seems almost as Nature might have left it. But we can soon alter all that. A thoroughly experienced French maid produces a really marvellous result in a very brief space of time. I remember recommending one to young Lady Lancing, and after three months her own husband did not know her.

JACK (*aside*). And after six months nobody knew her.

LADY BRACKNELL (*glares at Jack for a few moments. Then bends, with a practised smile, to Cecily*). Kindly turn round, sweet child. (*Cecily turns completely round.*) No, the side view is what I want. (*Cecily presents her profile.*) Yes, quite as I expected. There are distinct social possibilities in your profile. The two weak points in our age are its want of principle and its want of profile. The chin a little higher, dear. Style largely depends on the way the chin is worn. They are worn very high, just at present. Algernon!

ALGERNON. Yes, Aunt Augusta!

LADY BRACKNELL. There are distinct social possibilities in Miss Cardew's profile.

ALGERNON. Cecily is the sweetest, dearest, prettiest girl in the whole world. And I don't care twopence about social possibilities.

LADY BRACKNELL. Never speak disrespectfully of society, Algernon. Only people who can't get into it do that. (*To Cecily.*) Dear child, of course you know that Algernon has nothing but his debts to depend upon. But I do not approve of mercenary marriages. When I married Lord Bracknell I had no fortune of any kind. But I never dreamed for a moment of allowing that to stand in my way. Well, I suppose I must give my consent.

ALGERNON. Thank you, Aunt Augusta.

LADY BRACKNELL. Cecily, you may kiss me!

CECILY (*kisses her*). Thank you, Lady Bracknell.

LADY BRACKNELL. You may also address me as Aunt Augusta for the future.

CECILY. Thank you, Aunt Augusta.

LADY BRACKNELL. The marriage, I think, had better take place quite soon.

ALGERNON. Thank you, Aunt Augusta.

CECILY. Thank you, Aunt Augusta.

LADY BRACKNELL. To speak frankly, I am not in favour of long engagements. They give people the opportunity of finding out each other's character before marriage, which I think is never advisable.

JACK. I beg your pardon for interrupting you, Lady Bracknell, but this engagement is quite out of the question. I am Miss Cardew's guardian, and she cannot marry without my consent until she comes of age. That consent I absolutely decline to give.

LADY BRACKNELL. Upon what grounds, may I ask? Algernon is an extremely, I may almost say an ostentatiously, eligible young man. He has nothing, but he looks everything. What more can one desire?

JACK. It pains me very much to have to speak frankly to you, Lady Bracknell, about your nephew, but the fact is that I do not approve at all of his moral character. I suspect him of being untruthful. (*Algernon and Cecily look at him in indignant amazement.*)

LADY BRACKNELL. Untruthful! My nephew Algernon? Impossible! He is an Oxonian.

JACK. I fear there can be no possible doubt about the matter. This afternoon, during my temporary absence in London on an important question of romance, he obtained admission to my house by means of the false pretence of being my brother. Under an assumed name he drank, I've just been informed by my butler, an entire pint bottle of my Perrier-Jouet, Brut, '89; a wine I was specially reserving for myself. Continuing his disgraceful deception, he succeeded in the course of the afternoon in alienating the affections of my only ward. He subsequently stayed to tea, and devoured every single muffin. And what makes his conduct all the more heartless is, that he was perfectly well aware from the first that I have no brother, that I never had a brother, and that I don't intend to have a brother, not even of any kind. I distinctly told him so myself yesterday afternoon.

LADY BRACKNELL. Ahem! Mr. Worthing, after careful consideration I have decided entirely to overlook my nephew's conduct to you.

JACK. That is very generous of you, Lady Bracknell. My own decision, however, is unalterable. I decline to give my consent.

LADY BRACKNELL (*to Cecily*). Come here, sweet child. (*Cecily goes over.*) How old are you, dear?

CECILY. Well, I am really only eighteen, but I always admit to twenty when I go to evening parties.

LADY BRACKNELL. You are perfectly right in making some slight alteration. Indeed, no woman should ever be quite accurate about her age. It looks so calculating. . . . (*In meditative manner.*) Eighteen, but admitting to twenty at evening parties. Well, it will not be very long before you are of age and free from the restraints of tutelage. So I don't think your guardian's consent is, after all, a matter of any importance.

JACK. Pray excuse me, Lady Bracknell, for interrupting you again, but it is only fair to tell you that according to the terms of her grandfather's will Miss Cardew does not come legally of age till she is thirty-five.

LADY BRACKNELL. That does not seem to me to be a grave objection. Thirty-five is a very attractive age. London society is full of women of the very highest birth who have, of their own free choice, remained thirty-five for years. Lady Dumbleton is an instance in point. To my own knowledge she had been thirty-five ever since she arrived at the age of forty, which was many years ago now. I see no reason why our dear Cecily should not be even still more attractive at the age you mention than she is at present. There will be a large accumulation of property.

CECILY. Algy, could you wait for me till I was thirty-five?

ALGERNON. Of course I could, Cecily. You know I could.

CECILY. Yes, I felt it instinctively, but I couldn't wait all that time. I hate waiting even five minutes for anybody. It always makes me rather cross. I am not punctual myself, I know, but I do like punctuality in others, and waiting, even to be married, is quite out of the question.

ALGERNON. Then what is to be done, Cecily?

CECILY. I don't know, Mr. Moncrieff.

LADY BRACKNELL. My dear Mr. Worthing, as Miss Cardew states positively that she cannot wait till she is thirty-five—a remark which I am bound to say seems to me to show a somewhat impatient nature—I would beg of you to reconsider your decision.

JACK. But my dear Lady Bracknell, the matter is entirely in your own hands. The moment you consent to my marriage with Gwendolen, I will most gladly allow your nephew to form an alliance with my ward.

LADY BRACKNELL (*rising and drawing herself up*). You must be quite aware that what you propose is out of the question.

JACK. Then a passionate celibacy is all that any of us can look forward to.

LADY BRACKNELL. That is not the destiny I propose for Gwendolen. Algernon, of course, can choose for himself. (*Pulls out her watch.*) Come, dear, (*Gwendolen rises*) we have already missed five, if not six, trains. To miss any more might expose us to comment on the platform.

(*Enter Dr. Chasuble.*)

CHASUBLE. Everything is quite ready for the christenings.

LADY BRACKNELL. The christenings, sir! Is not that somewhat premature?

CHASUBLE (*looking rather puzzled, and pointing to Jack and Algernon*). Both these gentlemen have expressed a desire for immediate baptism.

LADY BRACKNELL. At their age? The idea is grotesque and irreligious! Algernon, I forbid you to be baptised. I will not hear of such excesses. Lord Bracknell would be highly displeased if he learned that that was the way in which you wasted your time and money.

CHASUBLE. Am I to understand then that there are to be no christenings at all this afternoon?

JACK. I don't think that, as things are now, it would be of much practical value to either of us, Dr. Chasuble.

CHASUBLE. I am grieved to hear such sentiments from you, Mr. Worthing. They savour of the heretical views of the Anabaptists, views that I have completely refuted in four of my unpublished sermons. However, as your present mood seems to be one peculiarly secular, I will return to the church at once. Indeed, I have just been informed by the pew-opener that for the last hour and a half Miss Prism has been waiting for me in the vestry.

LADY BRACKNELL (*starting*). Miss Prism! Did I hear you mention a Miss Prism?

CHASUBLE. Yes, Lady Bracknell. I am on my way to join her.

LADY BRACKNELL. Pray allow me to detain you for a moment. This matter may prove to be one of vital importance to Lord Bracknell and myself. Is this Miss Prism a female of repellent aspect, remotely connected with education?

CHASUBLE (*somewhat indignantly*). She is the most cultivated of ladies, and the very picture of respectability.

LADY BRACKNELL. It is obviously the same person. May I ask what position she holds in your household?

CHASUBLE (*severely*). I am a celibate, madam.

JACK (*interposing*). Miss Prism, Lady Bracknell, has been for the last three years Miss Cardew's esteemed governess and valued companion.

LADY BRACKNELL. In spite of what I hear of her, I must see her at once. Let her be sent for.

CHASUBLE (*looking off*). She approaches; she is nigh.

(*Enter Miss Prism hurriedly.*)

MISS PRISM. I was told you expected me in the vestry, dear Canon. I have been waiting for you there for an hour and three-quarters. (*Catches sight of Lady Bracknell, who has fixed her with a stony glare. Miss Prism grows pale and quails. She looks anxiously round as if desirous to escape.*)

LADY BRACKNELL (*in a severe, judicial voice*). Prism! (*Miss Prism bows her head in shame.*) Come here, Prism! (*Miss Prism approaches in a humble manner.*) Where is that baby? (*General consternation. The Canon starts back in horror. Algernon and Jack pretend to be anxious to shield Cecily and Gwendolen from hearing the details of a terrible public scandal.*) Twenty-eight years ago, Prism, you left Lord Bracknell's house, Number 104, Upper Grosvenor Street, in charge of a perambulator that contained a baby, of the male sex. You never returned. A few weeks later, through the elaborate investigations of the Metropolitan police, the perambulator was discovered at midnight, standing by itself in a remote corner of Bayswater. It contained the manuscript of a three-volume novel of more than usually revolting sentimentality. (*Miss Prism starts in involuntary indignation.*) But the baby was not there! (*Everyone looks at Miss Prism.*) Prism, where is that baby? (*A pause.*)

MISS PRISM. Lady Bracknell, I admit with shame that I do not know. I only wish I did. The plain facts of the case are these. On the morning of the day you mention, a day that is forever branded on my memory, I prepared as usual to take the baby out in its perambulator. I had also with me a somewhat old but capacious hand-bag in which I had intended to place the manuscript of a work of fiction that I had written during my few unoccupied hours. In a moment of mental abstraction, for which I never can forgive myself, I deposited the manuscript in the bassinette, and placed the baby in the hand-bag.

JACK (*who had been listening attentively*). But where did you deposit the hand-bag?

MISS PRISM. Do not ask me, Mr. Worthing.

JACK. Miss Prism, this is a matter of no small importance to me. I insist on knowing where you deposited the handbag that contained that infant.

MISS PRISM. I left it in the cloak-room of one of the larger railway stations in London.

JACK. What railway station?

MISS PRISM (*quite crushed*). VICTORIA. The Brighton line. (*Sinks into a chair.*)

JACK. I must retire to my room for a moment. Gwendolen, wait here for me.

GWENDOLEN. If you are not too long, I will wait here for you all my life.

(*Exit Jack in great excitement.*)

CHASUBLE. What do you think this means, Lady Bracknell?

LADY BRACKNELL. I dare not even suspect, Dr. Chasuble. I need hardly tell you that in families of high position strange coincidences are not supposed to occur. They are hardly considered the thing. (*Noises heard overhead as if someone was throwing trunks about. Everybody looks up.*)

CECILY. Uncle Jack seems strangely agitated.

CHASUBLE. Your guardian has a very emotional nature.

LADY BRACKNELL. This noise is extremely unpleasant. It sounds as if he was having an argument. I dislike arguments of any kind. They are always vulgar, and often convincing.

CHASUBLE (*looking up*). It has stopped now. (*The noise is redoubled.*)

LADY BRACKNELL. I wish he would arrive at some conclusion.

GWENDOLEN. The suspense is terrible. I hope it will last.

(*Enter Jack with a hand-bag of black leather in his hand.*)

JACK (*rushing over to Miss Prism*). Is this the hand-bag, Miss Prism? Examine it carefully before you speak. The happiness of more than one life depends on your answers.

MISS PRISM (*calmly*). It seems to be mine. Yes, here is the injury it received through the upsetting of a Gower Street omnibus in younger and happier days. Here is the stain on the lining caused by the explosion of a temperance beverage, an incident that occurred at Leamington. And here, on the lock, are my initials. I had forgotten that in an extravagant mood I had had them placed there. The bag is undoubtedly mine. I am delighted to have it so unexpectedly restored to me. It has been a great inconvenience being without it all these years.

JACK (*in a pathetic voice*). Miss Prism, more is restored to you than this hand-bag. I was the baby you placed in it.

MISS PRISM (*amazed*). You?

JACK (*embracing her*). Yes . . . mother!

MISS PRISM (*recoiling in indignant astonishment*). Mr. Worthing! I am unmarried!

JACK. Unmarried! I do not deny that is a serious blow. But after all, who has the right to cast a stone against one who has suffered? Cannot repentance wipe out an act of folly? Why should there be one law for men and another for women? Mother, I forgive you. (*Tries to embrace her again.*)

MISS PRISM (*still more indignant*). Mr. Worthing, there is some error. (*Pointing to Lady Bracknell.*) There is the lady who can tell you who you really are.

JACK (*after a pause*). Lady Bracknell, I hate to seem inquisitive, but would you kindly inform me who I am?

LADY BRACKNELL. I am afraid that the news I have to give you will not altogether please you. You are the son of my poor sister, Mrs. Moncrieff, and consequently Algernon's elder brother.

JACK. Algy's elder brother! Then I have a brother after all. I knew I had a brother! I always said I had a brother! Cecily,—how could you have ever doubted that I had a brother? (*Seizes hold of Algernon.*) Dr. Chasuble, my unfortunate brother. Miss Prism, my unfortunate brother. Gwendolen, my unfortunate brother. Algy, you young scoundrel, you will have to treat me with more respect in the future. You have never behaved to me like a brother in all your life.

ALGERNON. Well, not till to-day, old boy, I admit. I did my best, however, though I was out of practice. (*Shakes hands.*)

GWENDOLEN (*to Jack*). My own! But what own are you? What is your Christian name, now that you have become someone else?

JACK. Good heavens! . . . I had quite forgotten that point. Your decision on the subject of my name is irrevocable, I suppose?

GWENDOLEN. I never change, except in my affections.

CECILY. What a noble nature you have, Gwendolen!

JACK. Then the question had better be cleared up at once. Aunt Augusta, a moment. At the time when Miss Prism left me in the hand-bag, had I been christened already?

LADY BRACKNELL. Every luxury that money could buy, including christening, had been lavished on you by your fond and doting parents.

JACK. Then I was christened! That is settled. Now, what name was I given? Let me know the worst.

LADY BRACKNELL. Being the eldest son you were naturally christened after your father.

JACK (*irritably*). Yes, but what was my father's Christian name?

LADY BRACKNELL (*meditatively*). I cannot at the present moment recall what the General's Christian name was. But I have no doubt he had one. He was eccentric, I admit. But only in later years. And that was the result of the Indian climate, and marriage, and indigestion, and other things of that kind.

JACK. Algy! Can't you recollect what our father's Christian name was?

ALGERNON. My dear boy, we were never even on speaking terms. He died before I was a year old.

JACK. His name would appear in the Army Lists of the period, I suppose, Aunt Augusta?

LADY BRACKNELL. The general was essentially a man of peace, except in his domestic life. But I have no doubt his name would appear in any military directory.

JACK. The Army Lists of the last forty years are here. These delightful records should have been my constant study. (*Rushes to bookcase and tears the books out.*) M. Generals . . . Mallham, Maxbohm, Magley, what ghastly names they have—Markby, Migsby, Mobbs, Moncrieff! Lieutenant 1840, Captain, Lieutenant-Colonel, Colonel, General 1869, Christian names, Ernest John. (*Puts book very quietly down and speaks quite calmly.*) I always told you, Gwendolen, my name was Ernest, didn't I? Well, it is Ernest after all, I mean it naturally is Ernest.

LADY BRACKNELL. Yes, I remember the General was called Ernest. I knew I had some particular reason for disliking the name.

GWENDOLEN. Ernest! My own Ernest! I felt from the first that you could have no other name!

JACK. Gwendolen, it is a terrible thing for a man to find out suddenly that all his life he has been speaking nothing but the truth. Can you forgive me?

GWENDOLEN. I can. For I feel sure that you are sure to change.

JACK. My own one!

CHASUBLE (*to Miss Prism*). Lætitia! (*Embraces her.*)

MISS PRISM (*enthusiastically*). Frederick! At last!

ALGERNON. Cecily! (*Embraces her.*) At last!

JACK. Gwendolen! (*Embraces her.*) At last!

LADY BRACKNELL. My nephew, you seem to be displaying signs of triviality.

JACK. On the contrary, Aunt Augusta, I've now realized for the first time in my life the vital Importance of Being Earnest.

TABLEAU

CURTAIN

MAJOR BARBARA

[G E O R G E]   B E R N A R D   S H A W

[GEORGE] BERNARD SHAW (1856–1950)

Only Shakespeare eclipses Shaw's importance to the British theater, both in critical material written about him and in productions of his plays. Indeed, there are numerous Shaw festivals, the most prominent of which is in Niagara, Canada. Shaw is the most prodigious writer of English drama; his collected plays (53) fill almost 40 volumes. His essays—such as "The Revolutionist's Handbook," which accompanies *Man and Superman*—make excellent reading for their wit and the breadth of their subject matter. There is scarcely a topic on which Shaw has not written, and he remains among the most frequently quoted writers in world literature.

Shaw's long life spanned a period of profound change. He was born amid the Industrial Revolution and Victorianism; he matured as a writer as Europe entered the Great War; he saw revolution in Russia and the economic collapse of Europe and America; and in his last years he witnessed World War II, the birth of the atomic age, and the beginning of the cold war. Little wonder his plays are repositories of Western thought during one of its most tumultuous eras. If any playwright has the most pronounced social voice in this collection, it must be Shaw, whose very name is synonymous with "soapbox" drama.

Shaw's early years provided the preface to his plays. Like John Gay and Richard Brindsley Sheridan before him, like his contemporary Oscar Wilde, and like Samuel Beckett after him, Shaw was Irish. His status as an outsider in English society gave him license to observe and comment satirically on the deficiencies of the British Empire. His father, a drunkard, had a ready quip for every adversity, and his mother, a would-be opera singer, fled from life's difficulties into art. A stream of literary artists, elocution experts, and musicians flowed through the Shaw household, providing young Bernard with the education that would serve him as a writer. (He proclaimed the Dublin school system "a prison.") His nanny frequently took him to visit her family in the slums of Dublin, where he developed a lifelong hatred of poverty ("the greatest crime") and human suffering. For Shaw, however, life was "too horrible to weep bitter tears: I must retreat to my shelter and indulge in a laugh at myself over it."

In 1876 Shaw immigrated to England, where he attempted a series of novels, all quite unsuccessful. We still see the hand of the novelist at work in his prodigious stage directions. Shaw's first literary successes were as an arts critic for London newspapers, and he excelled in his commentary on music, especially the opera and its offshoots.

Though nonmusical, Shaw's plays attest to his profound musical knowledge; moreover, he always cast his plays for the harmony of voices that spoke his great verbal arias. Furthermore, the many nights Shaw spent in the theater watching musical plays, so steeped in melodrama, served him well as a playwright years later. He inverts well-established dramatic forms to challenge his audience's assumptions about thematic, as well as theatrical, issues in his plays.

Eighteen eighty-two was a pivotal year in Shaw's literary and personal life. He heard the socialist land reformer Henry George speak, an event that provoked him to read a French edition of Karl Marx in the reading room of the British Museum. In 1889 Shaw edited and contributed a number of essays to one of England's most influential socialist documents, *Fabian Essays in Socialism*. In many ways his plays are an extension of the ideas he formulated therein. Not only did he write about socialism, he was a powerful and entertaining orator who spoke from every platform, pulpit, and soapbox that would have him.

In 1891 J. T. Grien, whose Independent Theatre was London's version of Antoine's *Théâtre-Libre*, encouraged Shaw to provide plays for his new enterprise. Shaw responded with *Widower's House*, a comedic look at the shortcomings of capitalism. When Shaw revised that play, he was careful to include detailed stage directions for his actors so as to leave little doubt about his intentions. These became the forerunner of the so-called Shavian preface, the witty and philosophical essays that precede, follow, or accompany the majority of his plays.

Over the next 14 years Shaw scripted 11 plays, culminating with *Man and Superman* (1905), which Eric Bentley calls "the supreme triumph of Shaw's dramaturgical dialectics." All were comedies, but for Shaw, "comedy is essentially a serious business." Shaw had a simple philosophy for getting laughs: "Tell the truth. It's the funniest joke in the world." Shaw's comedy is ironic because it forces audiences to reconsider long-held values and conventions, which he subverts to expose their hollowness. Where most playwrights attack a character for failing to live up to the ideals of society, Shaw attacks the ideals themselves. For him, "Civilization is a disease produced by the practice of building societies with rotten material," that is, outmoded ideas that preserve poverty, war, slavery (of all kinds, including that of the marriage contract), and power. Shaw's solution to the ills of civilization? Follow the "Life Force" and, in the word's of Dick Dudgeon, the rascally hero of *The Devil's Disciple* (1896–1897), "Live by the law of [one's] own nature."

In addition to his prolific literary output of plays and essays, Shaw was a remarkable critic. His analysis of Ibsen's dramaturgy is still among the best of its kind, and his commentary on Shakespeare remains as fresh as it was almost a century ago. Of note are the many letters he wrote to actors, such as Mrs. Patrick Campbell and Ellen Terry, which contain both superb advice for performers and perceptive analyses of dramatic characters. Shaw staged many of his plays (often using a chessboard and figures to devise movement patterns) and left behind copious notes that are models of directorial insight. In short, Shaw was the complete man of the theater, as well as the complete man of the world.

Major Barbara (1905)

One of Shaw's best-known and most frequently produced plays, *Major Barbara* (subtitled *A Discussion in Three Acts*) examines the nature and social role of religion. At the conclusion of the play's preface, Shaw observes that "Creeds must become intellectually honest. At present there is not a single credible established religion in the world. That is perhaps the most stupendous fact in the whole world-situation." Shaw believed that current creeds, whether the conservative Church of England or the socially committed Salvation Army, only succeeded in perpetuating human misery and impeding societal progress. *Major Barbara* undertakes no less a challenge than to overturn the audience's acceptance of established religion and demand of them a pursuit of a radical way of seeing the world.

In light of Shaw's ideological intent, it is not surprising that he employed a strategy that gradually moved the audience from accepted values to new values. Had he introduced his religious and social ideas at the outset, it is probable that his audience would have rejected them; therefore, the playwright began with commonly accepted values and perceptions, only to gradually challenge and overturn their validity. Like Barbara, therefore, the spectator is taken on an intellectual and emotional journey during which firmly entrenched beliefs are eroded, exposed, and replaced.

Major Barbara begins with a verbal portrait of a devil incarnate. Andrew Undershaft is a millionaire arms manufacturer who is said to break laws and whom world leaders are afraid to oppose. He is described as a moral bankrupt with a "religion of wrongness." Even the butler Morrison is shocked as he announces Undershaft's arrival. However, Andrew's appearance and manner do not fulfill the expectation for the stereotypic melodramatic villain; he is a "stoutish, easygoing, elderly man, but with a kindly patient manner, and an engaging simplicity of character." Despite this demeanor, he takes pride in the fact that he is a profiteer in mutilation and murder and boasts that he is in a particularly good mood because he made an improvement that increased the killing power of one of his weapons. He also rejects Christianity with its "Christmas card moralities of peace on earth and goodwill among men" because adhering to its creed would bankrupt him, and insists that his religion must have room for cannons and torpedoes. Still he invites his daughter Barbara to save his soul if she will visit his arms factory after he visits her shelter.

Barbara accepts this bargain with the devil, and Andrew responds by agreeing to attend a family religious service led by Barbara. As the sounds of "Onward Christian Soldier" emanate from the adjacent drawing room to close the act, the audience has reason to anticipate that perhaps this strong-willed daughter will convert the old arms maker to a Christian religion with the motto of "Blood and Fire." Undershaft's visit to the West Ham Salvation Army shelter does not result in his conversion, but rather serves to open Barbara's eyes to the truth that Christianity serves capitalism by preventing social revolution and sustaining the wealth of the industrialists. The Bodgers and Undershafts are all too willing to buy their "salvation" by donating to a cause that protects the existing social order. The setting reflects this social reality—the West Ham shelter is described as "an old warehouse (that) is newly whitewashed." The hypocrisy of the indigents' enthusiasm and prayers is juxtaposed with their invention of sins and stealing of money to underscore the fact that they are motivated by material need and not genuine religious fervor.

The scene's centerpiece is a discussion between Undershaft and Cusins in which the arms manufacturer explains that his religion is based on money and gunpowder, money enough to live a decent life and power enough to be your own master. He argues that his creed eliminates poverty and vows that "Barbara must belong to us, not to the Salvation Army." He will convert his daughter by buying the Salvation Army and thus open her eyes to the truth that "all organizations exist by selling themselves to the rich." He mockingly hands the check that sustains the shelter to Mrs. Baines and joins the musical procession to the great prayer meeting, thus converting Cusins to his creed and compelling Barbara to resign from the army.

Following the check signing, Barbara tells Cusins that "you are breaking my heart." Heartbreak is a religious rather than an emotional Shavian concept because it denotes that moment when a person is stripped of all old beliefs. It is a time of spiritual emptiness that is essential preparation for the discovery of new ways of responding to the world. As Undershaft later explains, "You have learnt something. That always feels at first as if you had lost something." Barbara is, as Undershaft notes, "a savior of souls," as exemplified by her effect on the pugnacious Bill Walker; it is only necessary to bring her talents to bear on a more credible creed to restore her happiness and renew her messianic purpose in life.

Andrew demonstrates the superiority of Undershaft's approach in eliminating poverty. His workers enjoy material security and human dignity. But do these ends justify the means? This question dominates the discussion as Undershaft seeks to convince the foundling Cusins (and thereby Barbara) to assume responsibility for the arms business and carry on his efforts. The debate is visually reinforced by the presence of dummy soldiers "more or less mutilated, with straw protruding from their gashes . . . one has fallen forward and lies, like a grotesque corpse, on the emplacement." To accept the leadership position, Andrew warns, is to accept the code of the armorer to sell arms to whoever wants them and to invent larger and more effective inventions of destruction. He underscores his ethic by kicking a prostrate dummy brutally out of the way as he delights in the success of his new aerial battleship, which just killed 300 soldiers in an Asian war.

Cusins and Barbara accept the challenge, but vow to make war on war by creating "a power simple enough for the common men to use, yet strong enough to force the intellectual oligarchy to use its genius for the general good." Barbara sees that she will now work for a new god (Undershaft calls it "a will of which I am a part"); she will serve this Life Force so that when she dies it will be in her debt rather than vice versa. Will they succeed? Can Barbara and Cusins progress beyond the work of Undershaft by expanding the good without accepting the evil? Shaw leaves that answer to the future, but he wraps the play's conclusion in dark images that counter the couple's enthusiasm. The play's final line recalls Undershaft's earlier warning that there is no power in the position and that from the moment one accepts the business "you will never do as you please." Barbara may be "transfigured" by her decision, but the mutilated dummies remain scattered about the stage to remind us of the pernicious challenges she and Cusins face in the weeks and months ahead.

Robert G. Everding
University of Central Arkansas

PREFACE TO MAJOR BARBARA*

The Gospel of St. Andrew Undershaft

It is this credulity that drives me to help my critics out with *Major Barbara* by telling them what to say about it. In the millionaire Undershaft I have represented a man who has become intellectually and spiritually as well as practically conscious of the irresistible natural truth which we all abhor and repudiate: to wit, the greatest of our evils, and the worst of our crimes is poverty, and that our first duty, to which every other consideration should be sacrificed, is not to be poor. 'Poor but honest,' 'the respectable poor,' and such phrases are as intolerable and as immoral as 'drunken but amiable,' 'fraudulent but a good after-dinner speaker,' 'splendidly criminal,' or the like. Security, the chief pretence of civilization, cannot exist where the worst of dangers, the danger of poverty, hangs over everyone's head, and where the alleged protection of our persons from violence is only an accidental result of the existence of a police force whose real business is to force the poor man to see his children starve whilst idle people overfeed pet dogs with the money they might feed and clothe them.

It is exceedingly difficult to make people realize that an evil is an evil. For instance, we seize a man and deliberately do him a malicious injury: say, imprison him for years. One would not suppose that it needed any exceptional clearness of wit to recognize in this an act of diabolical cruelty. But in England such a recognition provokes a stare of surprise, followed by an explanation that the outrage is punishment or justice or something else that is all right, or perhaps by a heated attempt to argue that we should all be robbed and murdered in our beds if such stupid villainies as sentences of imprisonment were not committed daily. It is useless to argue that even if this were true, which it is not, the alternative to adding crimes of our own to the crimes from which we suffer is not helpless submission. Chickenpox is an evil; but if I were to declare that we must either submit to it or else repress it sternly by seizing everyone who suffers from it and punishing them by inoculation with smallpox, I should be laughed at; for though nobody could deny that the result would be to prevent chickenpox to some extent by making people avoid it much more carefully, and to effect a further apparent prevention by making them conceal it very anxiously, yet people would have sense enough to see that the deliberate propagation of smallpox was a creation of evil, and must therefore be ruled out in favor of purely humane and hygienic measures. Yet in the precisely parallel case of a man breaking into my house and stealing my wife's diamonds I am expected as a matter of course to steal ten years of his life, torturing him all the time. If he tries to defeat that monstrous retaliation by shooting me, my survivors hang him. The net result suggested by the police statistics is that we inflict atrocious injuries on the burglars we catch in order to make the rest take effectual precautions against detection; so that instead of saving our wives' diamonds from burglary we only greatly decrease our chances of ever getting them back, and increase our chances of being shot by the robber if we are unlucky enough to disturb him at his work.

But the thoughtless wickedness with which we scatter sentences of imprisonment, torture in the solitary cell and on the plank bed, and flogging, on moral invalids and energetic rebels, is as nothing compared to the silly levity with which we tolerate poverty as if it were either a wholesome tonic for lazy people or else a virtue to be embraced as St. Francis embraced it. If a man is indolent, let him be poor. If he is drunken, let him be poor. If he is not a gentleman, let him be poor. If he is addicted to the fine arts or to pure science instead of to trade and finance,

*The Preface appears in abridged form.

let him be poor. If he chooses to spend his urban eighteen shillings a week or his agriculture thirteen shillings a week on his beer and his family instead of saving it up for his old age, let him be poor. Serve him right! Also—somewhat inconsistently—blessed are the poor!

Now what does this Let Him Be Poor mean? It means let him be weak. Let him be ignorant. Let him become a nucleus of disease. Let him be a standing exhibition and example of ugliness and dirt. Let him have rickety children. Let him be cheap, and drag his fellows down to his own price by selling himself to do their work. Let his habitations turn our cities into poisonous congeries of slums. Let his daughters infect our young men with the diseases of the streets, and his sons revenge him by turning the nation's manhood into scrofula, cowardice, cruelty, hypocrisy, political imbecility, and all the other fruits of oppression and malnutrition. Let the undeserving become still less deserving; and let the deserving lay up for himself, not treasures in heaven, but horrors in hell upon earth. This being so, is it really wise to let him be poor? Would he not do ten times less harm as a prosperous burglar, incendiary, ravisher or murderer, to the utmost limits of humanity's comparatively negligible impulses in these directions? Suppose we were to abolish all penalties for such activities, and decide that poverty is the one thing we will not tolerate—that every adult with less than, say, £365 a year, shall be painlessly but inexorably killed, and every hungry half naked child forcibly fattened and clothed, would not that be an enormous improvement on our existing system, which has already destroyed so many civilizations, and is visibly destroying ours in the same way?

Is there any radicle of such legislation in our parliamentary system? Well, there are two measures just sprouting in the political soil, which may conceivably grow to something valuable. One is the institution of a Legal Minimum Wage. The other, Old Age Pensions. But there is a better plan than either of these. Some time ago I mentioned the subject of Universal Old Age Pensions to my fellow Socialist Cobden-Sanderson, famous as an artist-craftsman in bookbinding and printing. 'Why not Universal Pensions for Life?' said Cobden-Sanderson. In saying this, he solved the industrial problem at a stroke. At present we say callously to each citizen 'If you want money, earn it' as if his having or not having it were a matter that concerned himself alone. We do not even secure for him the opportunity of earning it: on the contrary, we allow our industry to be organized in open dependence on the maintenance of 'a reserve army of unemployed' for the sake of 'elasticity.' The sensible course would be Cobden-Sanderson's: that is, to give every man enough to live well on, so as to guarantee the community against the possibility of a case of the malignant disease of poverty, and then (necessarily) to see that he earned it.

Undershaft, the hero of *Major Barbara*, is simply a man who, having grasped the fact that poverty is a crime, knows that when society offered him the alternative of poverty or a lucrative trade in death and destruction, if offered him, not a choice between opulent villainy and humble virtue, but between energetic enterprise and cowardly infamy. His conduct stands the Kantian test, which Peter Shirley's does not. Peter Shirley is what we call the honest poor man. Undershaft is what we call the wicked rich one: Shirley is Lazarus, Undershaft Dives. Well, the misery of the world is due to the fact that the great mass of men act and believe as Peter Shirley acts and believes. If they acted and believed as Undershaft acts and believes, the immediate result would be a revolution of incalculable beneficence. To be wealthy, says Undershaft, is with me a point of honor for which I am prepared to kill at the risk of my own life. This preparedness is, as he says, the final test of sincerity. Like Froissart's medieval hero, who saw that 'to rob and pill was a good life' he is not the dupe of that public sentiment against killing which is propagated and endowed by people who would otherwise be killed themselves, or of the mouth-honor paid to poverty and obedience by rich and insubordinate do-nothings who want to rob the poor without courage and command them without superiority. Froissart's knight, in placing the achievement of a good life before all the other duties—which indeed are not duties at all when they conflict with it, but plain wickedness—behaved bravely, admirably, and, in the final analysis, public-spiritedly. Medieval society, on the other hand, behaved very badly indeed in organizing itself so stupidly that a good life could be achieved by robbing and pilling. If the knight's contemporaries had been all as resolute as he, robbing and pilling would have been the shortest way to the gallows, just as if we were all as resolute and clearsighted as Undershaft, an attempt to live by means of what is called 'an independent income' would be the shortest way to the lethal chamber. But as, thanks to our political imbecility and personal cowardice (fruits of poverty, both), the best imitation of a good life now procurable is life on an independent income, all sensible people aim at securing such an income, and are, of course, careful to legalize and moralize both it an all the actions and sentiments which lead to it and support it as an institution. What else can they do? They know, of course, that they are rich because others are poor. But they cannot help that: it is for the poor to repudiate poverty when they have had enough of it. The thing can be done easily enough: the demonstrations to the contrary made by the economists, jurists, moralists and sentimentalists hired by the rich defend them, or even doing the work gratuitously out of sheer folly and abjectness, impose only on those who want to be imposed on.

The reason why the independent income-tax payers are not solid in defence of their position is that since we are not medieval rovers through a sparsely populated country, the poverty of those we rob prevents our having the good life for which we sacrifice them. Rich men or aristocrats with a developed sense of life—men like Ruskin and William Morris and Kropotkin—have enormous social appetites and very fastidious personal ones. They are not content with handsome houses: they want handsome cities. They are not content with bediamonded wives and blooming daughters: they complain because the charwoman is badly dressed, because the laundress smells of gin, because the sempstress is anemic, because every man they meet is not a friend and every woman not a romance. They turn up their noses at their neighbor's drains, and are made ill by the architecture of their neighbor's houses. Trade patterns made to suit vulgar people do not please them (and they can get nothing else): they cannot sleep nor sit at ease upon 'slaughtered' cabinet makers' furniture. The very air is not good enough for them: there is too much factory smoke in it. They even demand abstract conditions: justice, honor, a noble moral atmosphere, a mystic nexus to replace the cash nexus. Finally they declare that though to rob and pill with your own hand on horseback and in steel coat may have been a good life, to rob and pill by the hands of the policeman, the bailiff, and the soldier, and to underpay them meanly for doing it, is not a good life, but rather fatal to all possibility of even a tolerable one. They call on the poor to revolt, and, finding the poor shocked at their ungentlemanliness, despairingly revile the proletariat for its 'damned wantlessness' (verdammte Bedürfnislösigkeit).

So far, however, their attack on society has lacked simplicity. The poor do not share their tastes nor understand their art-criticisms. They do not want the simple life, nor the esthetic life; on the contrary, they want very much to wallow in all the costly vulgarities from which the elect souls among the rich turn away with loathing. It is by surfeit and not by abstinence that they will be cured of their hankering after unwholesome sweets. What they do dislike and despise and are ashamed of is poverty. To ask them to fight for the difference between the Christmas number of the Illustrated London News and the Kelmscott Chaucer is silly: they prefer the News. The difference between a stock-broker's cheap and dirty starched white shirt and collar and the comparatively costly and carefully dyed blue shirt of William Morris is a difference so disgraceful to Morris in their eyes that if they fought on the subject at all, they would fight in defence of the starch. 'Cease to be slaves, in order that you may become cranks' is not a very inspiring call to arms; nor is it really improved by substituting saints for cranks. Both terms denote men of genius: he would much rather live the life of a pet collie if that were the only alternative. But he does want more money. Whatever else he may be vague about, he is clear about that. He may or may not prefer *Major Barbara* to the Drury Lane pantomime; but he always prefers five hundred pounds to five hundred shillings.

Now to deplore this preference as sordid, and teach children that it is sinful to desire money, is to strain towards the extreme possible limit of impudence in lying and corruption in hypocrisy. The universal regard for money is the one hopeful fact in our civilization, the one sound spot in our social conscience. Money is the most important thing in the world. It represents health, strength, honor, generosity and beauty as conspicuously and undeniably as the want of it represents illness, weakness, disgrace, meanness and ugliness. Not the least of its virtues is that it destroys base people as certainly as it fortifies and dignifies noble people. It is only when it is cheapened to worthlessness for some and made impossibly dear to others, that it becomes a curse. In short, it is a curse only in such foolish social conditions that life itself is a curse. For the two things are inseparable: money is the counter that enables life to be distributed socially: it *is* life as truly as sovereigns and bank notes are money. The first duty of every citizen is to insist on having money on reasonable terms; and this demand is not complied with by giving four men three shillings each for ten or twelve hours' drudgery and one man a thousand pounds for nothing. The crying need of the nation is not for better morals, cheaper bread, temperance, liberty, culture, redemption of fallen sisters and erring brothers, nor the grace, love and fellowship of the Trinity, but simply for enough money. And the evil to be attacked is not sin, suffering, greed, priestcraft, kingcraft, demagogy, monopoly, ignorance, drink, war, pestilence, nor any other of the scapegoats which reformers sacrifice, but simply poverty.

Once take your eyes from the ends of the earth and fix them on this truth just under your nose; and Andrew Undershaft's views will not perplex you in the least. Unless indeed his constant sense that he is only the instrument of a Will or Life Force which uses him for purposes wider than his own, may puzzle you. If so, that is because you are walking either in artificial Darwinian darkness, or in mere stupidity. All genuinely religious people have that consciousness. To them Undershaft the Mystic will be quite intelligible, and his perfect comprehension of his daughter the Salvationist and her lover the Euripidean republican natural and inevitable. That, however, is not new, even on the stage. What is new, as far as I know, is that article in Undershaft's religion which recognizes in Money the first need and in poverty the vilest sin of man and society.

This dramatic conception has not, of course, been attained *per saltum*. Nor has it been borrowed from Nietzsche or from any man born beyond the Channel. The late Samuel Butler, of his own department the greatest English writer of the latter half of the XIX century, steadily inculcated the necessity and morality of a conscientious Laodiceanism in religion and of an earnest and constant sense of the importance of money. It drives one almost to despair of English literature when one sees so extraordinary a study of English life as Butler's posthumous *Way of All Flesh* making so little impression that when, some years later, I produce plays in which Butler's extraordinarily fresh, free and future-piercing suggestions have an obvious share, I am met with nothing but vague cacklings about Ibsen and Nietzsche, and am only too thankful that they are not about Alfred de Musset and Georges Sand. Really, the English do not deserve to have great men. They allowed Butler to die practically unknown, whilst I, a comparatively insignificant Irish journalist, was leading them by the nose into an advertisement of me which has made my own life a burden. In Sicily there is a Via Samuele Butler. When an English tourist sees it, he either asks 'Who the devil was Samuele Butler?' or wonders why the Sicilians should perpetuate the memory of the author of *Hudibras*.

Well, it cannot be denied that the English are only too anxious to recognize a man of genius if somebody will kindly point him out to them. Having pointed myself out in this manner with some success, I now point out Samuel Butler, and trust that in consequence I shall hear a little less in future of the novelty and foreign origin of the ideas which are now making their way into the English theatre through plays written by Socialists. There are living men whose originality and power are as obvious as Butler's and when they die that fact will be discovered. Meanwhile I recommend them to insist to their own merits as an important part of their own business.

The Salvation Army

When *Major Barbara* was produced in London, the second act was reported in an important northern newspaper as a withering attack on the Salvation Army, and the despairing ejaculation of Barbara deplored by a London daily as a tasteless blasphemy. And they were set right, not by the professed critics of the theatre, but by religious and philosophical publicists like Sir Oliver Lodge and Dr. Stanton Coit, and strenuous Nonconformist journalists like William Stead, who not only understood the acts as well as the Salvationists themselves, but also saw it in its relation to the religious life of the nation, a life which seems to lie not only outside the sympathy of many of our theatre critics, but actually outside their knowledge of society. Indeed nothing could be more ironically curious than the confrontation Major Barbara effected of the theatre enthusiasts with the religious enthusiasts. On the one hand was the playgoer, always seeking pleasure, paying exorbitantly for it, suffering unbearable discomforts for it, and hardly ever getting it. One the other hand was the Salvationist, repudiating gaiety and courting effort and sacrifice, yet always in the wildest spirits, laughing, joking, singing, rejoicing, drumming, and tambourining: his life flying by in a flash of excitement, and his death arriving as a climax of triumph. And, if you please, the playgoer despising the Salvationist as a joyless person, shut out from the heaven of the theatre, self-condemned to a life of hideous gloom; and the Salvationist mourning over the playgoer as over a prodigal with vine leaves in his hair, careering outrageously to hell amid the popping of champagne corks and the ribald laughter of sirens! Could misunderstanding be more complete, or sympathy worse misplaced?

Fortunately, the Salvationists are more accessible to the religious character of the drama than the playgoers to the gay energy and artistic fertility of religion. They can see, when it is pointed out to them, that a theatre, as a place where two or three are gathered together, takes from that divine presence an inalienable sanctity of which the grossest and profanest farce can no more deprive it than a hypocritical sermon by a snobbish bishop can desecrate Westminster Abbey. But in our professional playgoers this indispensable preliminary conception of sanctity seems wanting. They talk of actors as mimes and mummers, and, I fear, think of dramatic authors as liars and pandars, whose main business is the voluptuous soothing of the tired city speculator when what he calls the serious business of the day is over. Passion, the life of drama, means nothing to them but primitive sexual excitement: such phrases as 'impassioned poetry' or 'passionate love of truth' have fallen quite out of their vocabulary and been replaced by 'passional crime' and the like. They assume, as far as I can gather, that people in whom passion has a larger scope are passionless and therefore uninteresting. Consequently they come to think of religious people as people who are not interesting and not amusing. And so, when Barbara cuts the regular Salvation Army jokes, and snatches a kiss from her lover across his drum, the devotees of the theatre think they ought to appear shocked, and conclude that the whole play is an elaborate mockery of the Army. And then either hypocritically rebuke me for mocking, or foolishly take part in the supposed mockery!

Even the handful of mentally competent critics got into difficulties over my demonstration of the economic deadlock in which the Salvation Army finds itself. Some of them thought that the Army would not have taken money from a distiller and a cannon founder: others thought it should not have taken it: all assumed more or less definitely that it reduced itself to absurdity or hypocrisy by taking it. On the first point the reply of the Army itself was prompt and conclusive. As one of its officers said, they would take money from the devil himself and be only too glad to get it out of his hands and into God's. They gratefully acknowledged that publicans not only give them money but allow them to collect it in the bar—sometimes even when there is a Salvation meeting outside preaching teetotalism. In fact, they questioned the verisimilitude of the play, not because Mrs Baines took the money, but because Barbara refused it.

On the point that the Army ought not to take such money, its justification is obvious. It must take the money because it cannot exist without money, and there is no other money to be had. Practically all the spare money in the country consists of a mass of rent, interest, and profit, every penny of which is bound up with crime, drink, prostitution, disease, and all the evil fruits of poverty, as inextricably as with enterprise, wealth, commercial probity, and national prosperity. The notion that you can earmark certain coins as tainted is an unpractical individualist superstition. None the less the fact that all our money is tainted gives a very severe shock to earnest young souls when some dramatic instance of the taint first makes them conscious of it. When an enthusiastic young clergyman of the Established Church first realizes that the Ecclesiastical Commissioners receive the rents of sporting public houses, brothels, and sweating dens; or that the most generous contributor at his last charity sermon was an employer trading in female labor cheapened by prostitution as unscrupulously as a hotel keeper trades in waiter's labor cheapened by tips, or commissionaires' labor cheapened by persons; or that the only patron who can afford to rebuild his church or his schools or give his boys' brigade a gymnasium or a library is the son-in-law of a Chicago meat King, that young clergyman has, like Barbara, a very bad quarter hour. But he cannot help himself by refusing to accept money from anybody except sweet old ladies with independent incomes and gentle and lovely ways of life. He has only to follow up the income of the sweet ladies to its industrial source, and there he will find Mrs Warren's profession and the poisonous canned meat and all the rest of it. His own stipend has the same root. He must either share the world's guilt or go to another planet. He must save the world's honor if he is to save his own. This is what all the Churches find just as the Salvation Army and Barbara find it in the play. Her discovery that she is her father's accomplice; that the Salvation Army is the accomplice of the distiller and the dynamite maker; that they can no more escape one another than they can escape the air they breathe; that there is no salvation for them through personal righteousness, but only through the redemption of the whole nation from its vicious, lazy, competitive anarchy: this discovery has been made by everyone except the Pharisees and (apparently) the professional playgoers, who still wear their Tom Hood shirts and underpay their washerwomen without the slightest misgiving as to the elevation of their private characters, the purity of their private atmospheres, and their right to repudiate as foreign to themselves the coarse depravity of the garret and the slum. Not that they mean any harm: they only desire to be, in their little private way, what they call gentlemen. They do not understand Barbara's lesson because they have not, like her, learnt it by taking their part in the larger life of the nation.

Barbara's Return to the Colors

Barbara's return to the colors may yet provide a subject for the dramatic historian of the future. To get back to the Salvation Army with the knowledge that even the Salvationists themselves are not saved yet; that poverty is not blessed, but a most damnable sin; and that when General Booth chose Blood and Fire for the emblem of Salvation instead of the Cross, he was perhaps better inspired than he knew: such knowledge, for the daughter of Andrew Undershaft, will clearly lead to something hopefuller than distributing bread and treacle at the expense of Bodger.

It is a very significant thing, this instinctive choice of the military form of organization, this substitution of the drum for the organ, by the Salvation Army. Does it not suggest that the Salvationists divine that they must actually fight the devil instead of merely praying at him? At present, it is true, they haven't quite ascertained his correct address. When they do, they may give a very rude shock to that sense of security which he has gained from his experience of the fact that hard words, even when uttered by eloquent essayists and lecturers, or carried unanimously at enthusiastic public meetings on the motion of eminent reformers, break no bones. It has been said that the French Revolution was the work of Voltaire, Rousseau and the Encyclopedists. It seems to me to have been the work of men who had observed that virtuous indignation, caustic criticism, conclusive argument and instructive pamphleteering, even when done by the most earnest and witty literary geniuses, were as useless as praying, things going steadily from bad to worse whilst the Social Contract and the pamphlets of Voltaire were at the height of their vogue. Eventually, as we know, perfectly respectable citizens and earnest philanthropists connived at the September massacres because hard experience had convinced them that if they contented themselves with appeals to humanity and patriotism, the aristocracy, though it would read their appeals with the greatest enjoyment and appreciation, flattering and admiring the writers, would none the less continue to conspire with foreign monarchists to undo the revolution and restore the old system with every circumstance of savage vengeance and ruthless repression of popular liberties.

The XIX century saw the same lesson repeated in England. It had its Utilitarians, its Christian Socialists, its Fabians (still extant): it had Bentham, Mill, Dickens, Ruskin, Carlyle, Butler, Henry George, and Morris. And the end of all their efforts is the Chicago described by Mr Upton Sinclair and the London in which the people who pay to be amused by my dramatic representation of Peter Shirley turned out to starve at forty because there are younger slaves to be had for his wages, do not take, and have not the slightest intention of taking, any effective step to organize society in such a way as to make that everyday infamy impossible. I, who have preached and pamphleteered like any Encyclopedist, have to confess that my methods are no use, and would be no use if I were Voltaire, Rousseau, Bentham, Marx, Mill, Dickens, Carlyle, Ruskin, Butler, and Morris all rolled into one, with Euripides, More, Montaigne, Molière, Beaumarchais, Swift, Goethe, Ibsen, Tolstoy, Jesus and the prophets all thrown in (as indeed in some sort I actually am, standing as I do on all their shoulders). The problem being to make heroes out of cowards, we paper apostles and artist-magicians have succeeded only in giving cowards all the sensations of heroes whilst they tolerate every abomination, accept every plunder, and submit to every oppression. Christianity, in making a merit of such submission, has marked only that depth in the abyss at which the very sense of shame is lost. The Christian has been like Dickens' doctor in the debtor's prison, who tells the newcomer of its ineffable peace and security: no duns; no tyrannical collectors of rates, taxes, and rent; no importunate hopes nor exacting duties; nothing but the rest and safety of having no farther to fall.

Yet in the poorest corner of this soul-destroying Christendom vitality suddenly begins to germinate again. Joyousness, a sacred gift long dethroned by the hellish laughter of derision and obscenity, rises like a flood miraculously out of the fetid dust and mud of the slums; rousing marches and impetuous dithyrambs rise to the heavens from people among whom the depressing noise called 'sacred music' is a standing joke; a flag with Blood and Fire on it is unfurled, not in murderous rancor, but because fire is beautiful and blood a vital and splendid red; Fear, which we flatter by calling Self, vanishes; and transfigured men and women carry their gospel through a transfigured world, calling their leader General, themselves captains and brigadiers, and their whole body an Army: praying, but praying only for refreshment, for strength to fight, and for needful MONEY (a notable sign, that); preaching, but not preaching submission; daring ill-usage and abuse, but not putting up with more of it than is inevitable; and practising what the world will let them practise, including soap and water, color and music. There is danger in such activity; and where there is danger there is hope. Our present security is nothing, and can be nothing, but evil made irresistible.

Weaknesses of the Salvation Army

For the present, however, it is not my business to flatter the Salvation Army. Rather must I point out to it that it has almost as many weaknesses as the Church of England itself. It is building up a business organization which will compel it eventually to see that its present staff of enthusiast-commanders shall be succeeded by a bureaucracy of men of business who will be no better than bishops, and perhaps a good deal more unscrupulous. That has always happened sooner or later to great orders founded by saints; and the order founded by St William Booth is not exempt from the same danger. It is even more dependent than the Church on rich people who would cut off supplies at once if it began to preach that indispensable revolt against poverty which must also be a revolt against riches. It is hampered by a heavy contingent of pious elders who are not really Salvationists at all, but Evangelicals of the old school. It still, as Commissioner Howard affirms, 'sticks to Moses,' which is flat nonsense at this time of day if the Commissioner means, as I am afraid he does, that the Book of Genesis contains a trustworthy scientific account of the origin of species, and that the god to whom Jephthah sacrificed his daughter is any less obviously a tribal idol than Dagon or Chemosh.

Further, there is still too much other-worldliness about the Army. Like Frederick's grenadier, the Salvationist wants to live for ever (the most monstrous way of crying for the moon); and though it is evident to anyone who has ever heard General Booth and his best officers that they would work as hard for human salvation as they do at present if they believed that death would be the end of them individually, they and their followers have a bad habit of talking as if the Salvationists were heroically enduring a very bad time on earth as an investment which will bring them in dividends later on in the form, not of a better life to come for the whole world, but of an eternity spent by themselves personally in a sort of bliss which would bore any active person to a second death. Surely the truth is that the Salvationists are unusually happy people. And is it not the very diagnostic of true salvation that it shall overcome the fear of death? Now the man who has come to believe that there is no such thing as death, the change so called being merely the transition to an exquisitely happy and utterly careless life, has not overcome the fear of death at all: on the contrary, it has overcome him so completely that he refuses to die on any terms whatever. I do not call a Salvationist really saved until he is ready to lie down cheerfully on the scrap heap, having paid scot and lot and something over, and let his eternal life pass on to renew its youth in the battalions of the future.

Then there is the nasty lying habit called confession, which the Army encourages because it lends itself to dramatic oratory, with plenty of thrilling incident. For my part, when I hear a convert relating the violences and oaths and blasphemies he was guilty of before he was saved, making out that he was a very terrible fellow then and is the most contrite and chastened of Christians now, I believe the millionaire who says he came up to London or Chicago as a boy with only three halfpence in his pocket. Salvationists have said to me that Barbara in my play would never have been taken in by so transparent a humbug as Snobby Price; and certainly I do not think Snobby could have taken in any experienced Salvationist on a point on which the Salvationist did not wish to be taken in. But on the point of conversion all Salvationists wish to be taken in; for the more obvious the sinner the more obvious the miracle of his conversion. When you advertize a converted burglar or reclaimed drunkard as one of the attractions at an experience meeting, your burglar can hardly have been too burglarious or your drunkard too drunken. As long as such attractions are relied on, you will have your Snobbies claiming to have beaten their mothers when they were as a matter of prosaic fact habitually beaten by them, and your Rummies of the tamest respectability pretending to a past of reckless and dazzling vice. Even when confessions are sincerely autobiographic we should beware of assuming that the impulse to make them was pious or that the interest of the hearers is wholesome. As well might we assume that the poor people who insist on shewing disgusting ulcers to district visitors are convinced hygienists, or that the curiosity which sometimes welcomes such exhibitions is a pleasant and creditable one. One is often tempted to suggest that those who pester our police superintendents with confessions of murder might very wisely be taken at their word and executed, except on the few cases in which a real murderer is seeking to be relieved of his guilt by confession and expiation. For though I am not, I hope, an unmerciful person, I do not think that the inexorability of the deed once done should be disguised by any ritual, whether in the confessional or on the scaffold

And here my disagreement with the Salvation Army, and with all propagandists of the Cross (which I loathe as I loathe all gibbets) becomes deep indeed. Forgiveness, absolution, atonement, are figments: punishment is only a pretence of cancelling one crime by another; and you can no more have forgiveness without vindictiveness than you can have a cure without a disease. You will never get a high morality from people who conceive that their misdeeds are revocable and pardonable, or in a society where absolution and expiation are officially provided for us all. The demand may be very real; but the supply is spurious. Thus Bill Walker, in my play, having assaulted the Salvation Lass, presently finds himself overwhelmed with an intolerable conviction of sin under the skilled treatment of Barbara. Straightway he begins to try to unassault the lass and deruffianize his deed, first by getting punished for it in kind, and, when that relief is denied him, by fining himself a pound to compensate the girl. He is foiled both ways. He finds the Salvation Army as inexorable as fact itself. It will not punish him: it will not take his money. It will not tolerate a redeemed ruffian: it leaves him no means of salvation except ceasing to be a ruffian. In doing this, the Salvation Army instinctively grasps the central truth of Christianity and discards its central superstition: that central truth being the vanity of revenge and punishment, and that central superstition the salvation of the world by the gibbet.

For, be it noted, Bill has assaulted an old and starving woman also; and for this worse offence he feels no remorse whatever, because she makes it clear that her malice is as great as his own. 'Let her have the law of me, as she said she would,' says Bill: 'what I done to her is no more on what you might call my conscience than sticking a pig.' This shews a perfectly natural and wholesome state of mind on his part. The old woman, like the law she threatens him with, is perfectly ready to play the game of retaliation with him: to rob him if he steals, to flog him if he strikes, to murder him if he kills. By example and precept the law and public opinion teach him to impose his will on others by anger, violence, and cruelty, and to wipe off the moral score by punishment. That is sound Crosstianity. But this Crosstianity has got entangled with something which Barbara calls Christianity, and which unexpectedly causes her to refuse to play the hangman's game of Satan casting out Satan. She refuses to prosecute a drunken ruffian; she converses on equal terms with a blackguard to whom no lady should be seen speaking in the public street: in short, she imitates Christ. Bill's conscience reacts to this just as naturally as it does to the old woman's threats. He is placed in a position of unbearable moral inferiority, and strives by every means in his power to escape from it, whilst he is still quite ready to meet the abuse of the old woman by attempting to smash a mug on her face. And that is the triumphant justification of Barbara's Christianity as against our system of judicial punishment and the vindictive villain-thrashings and 'poetic justice' of the romantic stage.

For the credit of literature it must be pointed out that the situation is only partly novel. Victor Hugo long ago gave us the epic of the convict and the bishop's candlesticks, of the Crosstian policeman annihilated by his encounter with the Christian Valjean. But Bill Walker is not, like Valjean, romantically changed from a demon into an angel. There are millions of Bill Walkers in all classes of society today; and the point which I, as a professor of natural psychology, desire to demonstrate, is that Bill, without any change in his character or circumstances whatsoever, will react one way to one sort of treatment and another way to another.

In proof I might point to the sensational object lesson provided by our commercial millionaires today. They begin as brigands: merciless, unscrupulous, dealing out ruin and death and slavery to their competitors and employees, and facing desperately the worst that their competitors can do to them. The history of the English factories, the American Trusts, the exploitation of African gold, diamonds, ivory and rubber, outdoes in villainy the worst that has ever been imagined of the buccaneers of the Spanish Main. Captain Kidd would have marooned a modern Trust magnate for conduct unworthy of a gentleman of fortune. The law every day seizes on unsuccessful scoundrels of this type and punishes them with a cruelty worse than their own, with the result that they come out of the torture house more dangerous than they went in, and renew their evil doing (nobody will employ them at anything else) until they are again seized, again tormented, and again let loose, with the same result.

But the successful scoundrel is dealt with very differently, and very Christianly. He is not only forgiven: he is idolized, respected, made much of, all but worshipped. Society returns him good for evil in the most extravagant overmeasure. And with what result? He begins to idolize himself, to respect himself, to live up to the treatment he receives. He preaches sermons; he writes books of the most edifying advice to young men, and actually persuades himself that he got on by taking his own advice; he endows educational institutions; he supports charities; he dies finally in the odor of sanctity, leaving a will which is a monument of public spirit and bounty. And all this without any change in his character. The spots of the leopard and the stripes of the tiger are as brilliant as ever; but the conduct of the world towards him has changed; and his conduct has changed accordingly. You have only to reverse your attitude towards him—to lay hands on his property, revile him, assault him, and he will be a brigand again in a moment, as ready to crush you as you are to crush him, and quite as full of pretentious moral reasons for doing it.

In short, when Major Barbara says that there are no scoundrels, she is right: there are no absolute scoundrels, though there are impracticable people of whom I shall treat presently. Every reasonable man (and woman) is a potential scoundrel and a potential good citizen. What a man is depends on his character; but what he does, and what we think of what he does, depends on his circumstances. The characteristics that ruin a man in one class make him eminent in another. The characters that behave differently in different circumstances behave alike in similar circumstances. Take a common English character like that of Bill Walker. We meet Bill everywhere: on the judicial bench, on the episcopal bench, in the Privy Council, at the War Office and Admiralty, as well as in the Old Bailey dock or in the ranks of casual unskilled labor. And the morality of Bill's characteristics varies with these various circumstances. The faults of the burglar are the qualities of the financier: the manners and habits of a duke would cost a city clerk his situation. In short, though character is independent of circumstances, conduct is not: and our moral judgments of character are not: both are circumstantial. Take any condition of life in which the circumstances are for a mass of men practically alike: felony, the House of Lords, the factory, the stables, the gipsy encampment or where you please! In spite of diversity of character and temperament, the conduct and morals of the individuals in each group are as predicable and as alike in the main as if they were a flock of sheep, morals being mostly only social habits and circumstantial necessities. Strong people know this and count upon it. In nothing have the master-minds of the world been distinguished from the ordinary suburban season-ticket holder more than in their straightforward perception of the fact that mankind is practically a single species, and not a menagerie of gentlemen and bounders, villains and heroes, cowards and daredevils, peers and peasants, grocers and aristocrats, artisans and laborers, washerwomen and duchesses, in which all the grades of income and caste represent distinct animals who must not be introduced to one another or intermarry. Napoleon constructing a galaxy of generals and courtiers, and even of monarchs, out of his collection of social nobodies; Julius Cæsar appointing as governor of Egypt the son of a freedman—one who but a short time before would have been legally disqualified for the post even of a private soldier in the Roman army; Louis XI making his barber his privy councillor: all these had in their different ways a firm hold of the scientific fact of human equality, expressed by Barbara in the Christian formula that all men are children of one father. A man who believes that men are naturally divided into upper and lower and middle classes morally is making exactly the same mistake as the man who believes that they are naturally divided in the same way socially. And just as our persistent attempts to found political institutions on a basis of social inequality have always produced long periods of destructive friction relieved from time to time by violent explosions of revolution; so the attempt—will Americans please note—to found moral institutions on a basis of moral inequality can lead to nothing but unnatural Reigns of the Saints relieved by licentious Restorations; to Americans who have made divorce a public institution turning the face of Europe onto one huge sardonic smile by refusing to stay in the same hotel with a Russian man of genius who has changed wives without the sanction of South Dakota; to grotesque hypocrisy, cruel persecution, and final utter confusion of conventions and compliances with benevolence and respectability. It is quite useless to declare that all men are born free if you deny that they are born good. Guarantee a man's goodness and his liberty will take care of itself. To guarantee his freedom on condition that you approve of his moral character is formally to abolish all freedom whatsoever, as every man's liberty is at the mercy of a moral indictment which any fool can trump up against everyone who violates custom, whether as a prophet or as a rascal. This is the lesson Democracy has to learn before it can become anything but the most oppressive of all the priesthoods.

Let us now return to Bill Walker and his case of conscience against the Salvation Army. Major Barbara, not being a modern Tetzel, or the treasurer of a hospital, refuses to sell absolution to Bill for a sovereign. Unfortunately, what the Army can afford to refuse in the case of Bill Walker, it cannot refuse in the case of Bodger. Bodger is master of the situation because he holds the purse strings. 'Strive as you will,' says Bodger, in effect: 'me you cannot do without. You cannot save Bill Walker without my money.' And the Army answers, quite rightly under the circumstances, 'We will take money from the devil himself sooner than abandon the work of Salvation.' So Bodger pays his conscience-money and gets the absolution that is refused to Bill. In real life Bill would perhaps never know this. But I, the dramatist whose business it is to shew the connexion between things that seem apart and unrelated in the haphazard order of events in real life, have contrived to make it known to Bill, with the result that the Salvation Army loses its hold of him at once.

But Bill may not be lost, for all that. He is still in the grip of the facts and of his own conscience, and may find his taste for blackguardism permanently spoiled. Still, I cannot guarantee that happy ending. Walk through the poorer quarters of our cities on Sunday when the men are not working, but resting and chewing the cud of their reflections. You will find one expression common to every mature face: the expression of cynicism. The discovery made by Bill Walker about the Salvation Army has been made by everyone there. They have found that every man has his price; and they have been foolishly or corruptly taught to mistrust and despise him for that necessary and salutary condition of social existence. When they learn that General Booth, too, has his price, they do not admire him because it is a high one, and admit the need of organizing society so that he shall get it in an honorable way: they conclude that his character is unsound and that all religious men are hypocrites and allies of their sweaters and oppressors. They know that the large subscriptions which help to support the Army are endowments, not of religion, but of the wicked doctrine of docility in poverty and humility under oppression; and they are rent by the most agonizing of all the doubts of the soul, the doubt whether their true salvation must not come from their most abhorrent passions, from murder, envy, greed, stubbornness, rage, and terrorism, rather than from public spirit, reasonableness, humanity, generosity, tenderness, delicacy, pity and kindness. The confirmation of that doubt, at which our newspapers have been working so hard for years past, is the morality of militarism; and the justification of militarism is that circumstances may at any time make it the true morality of the moment. It is by producing such moments that we produce violent and sanguinary revolutions, such as the one now in progress in Russia and the one which Capitalism in England and America is daily and diligently provoking.

At such moments it becomes the duty of the Churches to evoke all the powers of destruction against the existing order. But if they do this, the existing order must forcibly suppress them. Churches are suffered to exist only on condition that they preach submission to the State as at present capitalistically organized. The Church of England itself is compelled to add to the thirtysix articles in which it formulates its religious tenets, three more in which it apologetically protests that the moment any of these articles comes in conflict with the State it is to be entirely renounced, abjured, violated, abrogated and abhorred, the policeman being a much more important person than any of the Persons of the Trinity. And this is why no tolerated Church nor Salvation Army can ever win the entire confidence of the poor. It must be on the side of the police and the military, no matter what it believes or disbelieves; and as the police and the military are the instruments by which the rich rob and oppress the poor (on legal and moral principles made for the purpose), it is not possible to be on the side of the poor and of the police at the same time. Indeed the religious bodies, as the almoners of the rich, become a sort of auxiliary police, taking off the insurrectionary edge of poverty with coals and blankets, bread and treacle, and soothing and cheering the victims with hopes of immense and inexpensive happiness in another world when the process of working them to premature death in the service of the rich is complete in this.

Christianity and Anarchism

Such is the false position from which neither the Salvation Army nor the Church of England nor any other religious organization whatever can escape except through a reconstitution of society. Nor can they merely endure the State passively, washing their hands of its sins. The State is constantly forcing the consciences of men by violence and cruelty. Not content with exacting money from us for the maintenance of its soldiers and policemen, its gaolers and executioners, it forces us to take an active personal part in its proceedings on pain of becoming ourselves the victims of its violence. As I write these lines, a sensational example is given to the world. A royal marriage has been celebrated, first by sacrament in a cathedral, and then by a bullfight having for its main amusement the spectacle of horses gored and disembowelled by the bull, after which, when the bull is so exhausted as to be no longer dangerous, he is killed by a cautious matador. But the ironic contrast between the bullfight and the sacrament of marriage does not move anyone. Another contrast—that between the splendor, the happiness, the atmosphere of kindly admiration surrounding the young couple, and the price paid for it under our abominable social arrangements in the misery, squalor and degradation of millions of other young couples—is drawn at the same moment by a novelist, Mr Upton Sinclair, who chips a corner of the veneering from the huge meat packing industries of Chicago, and shews it to us as a sample of what is going on all over the world underneath the top layer of prosperous plutocracy. One man is sufficiently moved by that contrast to pay his own life as the price of one terrible blow at the responsible parties. His poverty has left him ignorant enough to be duped by the pretence that the innocent young bride and bridegroom, put forth and crowned by plutocracy as the heads of a State in which they have less personal power than any policemen, and less influence than any Chairman of a Trust, are responsible. At them accordingly he launches his sixpennorth of fulminate, missing his mark, but scattering the bowels of as many horses as any bull in the arena, and slaying twentythree persons, besides wounding ninetynine. And of all these, the horses alone are innocent of the guilt he is avenging: had he blown all Madrid to atoms with every adult person in it, not one could have escaped the charge of being an accessory, before, at, and after the fact, to poverty and prostitution, to such wholesale massacre of infants as Herod never dreamt of, to plague, pestilence and famine, battle, murder and lingering death—perhaps not one who had not helped, through example, precept, connivance, and even clamor, to teach the dynamiter his well-learnt gospel of hatred and vengeance, by approving every day of sentences of years of imprisonment so infernal in their unnatural stupidity and panic-stricken cruelty, that their advocates can disavow neither the dagger nor the bomb without stripping the mask of justice and humanity from themselves also.

Be it noted that at this very moment there appears the biography of one of our dukes, who, being a Scot, could argue about politics, and therefore stood out as a great brain among our aristocrats. And what, if you please, was his grace's favorite historical episode, which he declared he never read without intense satisfaction? Why, the young General Bonapart's pounding of the Paris mob to pieces in 1795, called in playful approval by our respectable classes 'the whiff of dynamite' (the flavor of the joke seems to evaporate a little, does it not?) because it was aimed at the class they hate even as our argute duke hated what he called the mob.

In such an atmosphere there can be only one sequel to the Madrid explosion. All Europe burns to emulate it. Vengeance! More blood! Tear 'the Anarchist beast' to shreds. Drag him to the scaffold. Imprison him for life. Let all civilized States band together to drive his like off the face of the earth; and if any State refuses to join, make war on it. This time the leading London newspaper, anti-Liberal and therefore anti-Russian in politics, does not say 'Serve you right' to the victims, as it did, in effect, when Bobrikoff, and Plehve, and Grand Duke Sergius, were in the same manner unofficially fulminated into fragments. No: fulminate our rivals in Asia by all means, ye brave Russian revolutionaries; but to aim at an English princess! monstrous! hideous! hound down the wretch to his doom; and observe, please, that we are a civilized and merciful people, and, however much we may regret it, must not treat him as Ravaillac and Damiens were treated. And meanwhile, since we have not yet caught him, let us soothe our quivering nerves with the bullfight, and comment in a courtly way on the unfailing tact and good taste of the ladies of our royal houses, who, though presumably of full normal natural tenderness, have been so effectually broken in to fashionable routine that they can be taken to see the horses slaughtered as helplessly as they could no doubt be taken to a gladiator show, if that happened to be the mode just now.

Strangely enough, in the midst of this raging fire of malice, the one man who still has faith in the kindness and intelligence of human nature is the fulminator, now a hunted wretch, with nothing, apparently, to secure his triumph over all the prisons and scaffolds of infuriate Europe except the revolver in his pocket and his readiness to discharge it at a moment's notice into his own or any other head. Think of him setting out to find a gentleman and a Christian in the multitude of human wolves howling for his blood. Think also of this: that at the very first essay he finds what he seeks, a veritable grandee of Spain, a noble, high-thinking, unterrified, malice-void soul, in the guise—of all masquerades in the world!—of a modern editor. The Anarchist wolf, flying from the wolves of plutocracy, throws himself on the honor of the man. The man, not being a wolf (nor a London editor), and therefore not having enough sympathy with his exploit to be made bloodthirsty by it, does not throw him back to the pursuing wolves— gives him, instead, what help he can to escape, and sends him off acquainted at last with a force that goes deeper than dynamite, though you cannot buy so much of it for sixpence. That righteous and honorable high human deed is not wasted on Europe, let us hope, though it benefits the fugitive wolf only for a moment. The plutocratic wolves presently smell him out. The fugitive shoots the unlucky wolf whose nose is nearest; shoots himself; and then convinces the world, by his photograph, that he was no monstrous freak of reversion to the tiger, but a good looking young man with nothing abnormal about him except his appalling courage and resolution (that is why the terrified shriek Coward at him): one to whom murdering a happy young couple on their wedding morning would have been an unthinkably unnatural abomination under rational and kindly human circumstances.

Then comes the climax of irony and blind stupidity. The wolves, balked of their meal of fellow-wolf, turn on the man, and proceed to torture him, after their manner, by imprisonment, for refusing to fasten his teeth in the throat of the dynamiter and hold him down until they came to finish him.

Thus, you see, a man may not be a gentleman nowadays even if he wishes to. As to being a Christian, he is allowed some latitude in that matter, because, I repeat, Christianity has two faces. Popular Christianity has for its emblem a gibbet, for its chief sensation a sanguinary execution after torture, for its central mystery an insane vengeance bought off by a trumpery expiation. But there is a nobler and profounder Christianity which affirms the sacred mystery of Equality, and forbids the glaring futility and folly of vengeance, often politely called punishment or justice. The gibbet part of Christianity is tolerated. The other is criminal felony. Connoisseurs in irony are well aware of the fact that the only editor in England who denounces punishment as radically wrong, also repudiates Christianity; calls his paper *The Freethinker*; and has been imprisoned for 'bad taste' under the law against blasphemy.

Sane Conclusions

And now I must ask the excited reader not to lose his head on one side or the other, but to draw a sane moral from these grim absurdities. It is not good sense to propose that laws against crime should apply to principals only and not to accessories whose consent, counsel, or silence may secure impunity to the principal. If you institute punishment as part of the law, you must punish people for refusing to punish. If you have a police, part of its duty must be to compel everybody to assist the police. No doubt if your laws are unjust, and your policemen agents of oppression, the result will be an unbearable violation of the private consciences of citizens. But that cannot be helped: the remedy is, not to incense everybody to thwart the law if they please, but to make laws that will command the public assent, and not to deal cruelly and stupidly with lawbreakers. Everybody disapproves of burglars; not the modern burglar, when caught and overpowered by a householder, usually appeals, and often, let us hope, with success, to his captor not to deliver him over to the useless horrors of penal servitude. In other cases the lawbreaker escapes because those who could give him up do not consider his breach of the law a guilty action. Sometimes, even, private tribunals are formed in opposition to the official tribunals; and these private tribunals employ assassins as executioners, as was done, for example, by Mahomet before he had established his power officially, and by the Ribbon lodges of Ireland in their long struggle with the landlords. Under such circumstances, the assassin goes free although everybody in the district knows who he is and what he has done. They do not betray him, partly because they justify him exactly as the regular Government justifies its official executioner, and partly because they would themselves be assassinated if they betrayed him: another method learnt from the official government. Given a tribunal, employing a slayer who has no personal quarrel with the slain; and there is clearly no moral difference between official and unofficial killing.

In short, all men are anarchists with regard to laws which are against their consciences, either in the preamble or in the penalty. In London our worst anarchists are the magistrates, because many of them are so old and ignorant that when they are called upon to administer any law that is based on ideas or knowledge less than half a century old, they disagree with it, and being mere ordinary homebred private Englishmen without any respect for law in the abstract, naïvely set the example of violating it. In this instance the man lags behind the law; but when the law lags behind the man, he becomes equally an anarchist. When some huge change in social conditions, such as the industrial revolution of the XVIII and XIX centuries, throws our legal and industrial institutions out of date, Anarchism becomes almost a religion. The whole force of the most energetic geniuses of the time in philosophy, economics, and art, concentrates itself on demonstrations and reminders that morality and law are only conventions, fallible and continually obsolescing. Tragedies in which the heroes are bandits, and comedies in which law-abiding and conventionally moral folk are compelled to satirize themselves by outraging the conscience of the spectators every time they do their duty, appear simultaneously with economic treatises entitled 'What is Property? Theft!' and with histories of 'The Conflict between Religion and Science.'

Now this is not a healthy state of things. The advantages of living in society are proportionate, not to the freedom of the individual from a code, but to the complexity and subtlety of the code he is prepared not only to accept but to uphold as a matter of such vital importance that a lawbreaker at large is hardly to be tolerated on any plea. Such an attitude becomes impossible when the only men who can make themselves heard and remembered throughout the world spend all their energy in raising our gorge against current law, current morality, current respectability, and legal property. The ordinary man, uneducated in social theory even when he is schooled in Latin verse, cannot be set against all the laws of his country and yet persuaded to regard law in the abstract as vitally necessary to society. Once he is brought to repudiate the laws and institutions he knows, he will repudiate the very conception of law and the very groundwork of institutions, ridiculing human rights, extolling brainless methods as 'historical,' and tolerating nothing except pure empiricism in conduct, with dynamite as the basis of politics and vivisection as the basis of science. That is hideous; but what is to be done? Here am I, for instance, by class a respectable man, by common sense a hater of waste and disorder, by intellectual constitution legally minded to the verge of pedantry, and by temperament apprehensive and economically disposed to the limit of old-maidishness; yet I am, and have always been, and shall now always be, a revolutionary writer, because our laws make law impossible; our liberties destroy all freedom; our property is organized robbery; our morality is an impudent hypocrisy; our wisdom is administered by inexperienced or malexperienced dupes, our power wielded by cowards and weaklings, and our honor false in all its points. I am an enemy of the existing order for good reasons; but that does not make my attacks any less encouraging or helpful to people who are its enemies for bad reasons. The existing order may shriek that if I tell the truth about it, some foolish person may drive it to become still worse by trying to assassinate it. I cannot help that, even if I could see what worse it could do than it is already doing. And the disadvantage of that worst even from its own point of view is that society, with all its prisons and bayonets and whips and ostracisms and starvations, is powerless in the face of the Anarchist who is prepared to sacrifice his own life in the battle with it. Our natural safety from the cheap and devastating explosives which every Russian student can make and every Russian grenadier has learnt to handle in Manchuria, lies in the fact that brave and resolute men, when they are rascals, will not risk their skins for the good of humanity, abhorring murder, and never committing it until their consciences are outraged beyond endurance. The remedy is, then, simply not to outrage their consciences.

Do not be afraid that they will not make allowances. All men have very large allowances indeed before they stake their own lives in a war to the death with society. Nobody demands or expects the millennium. But there are two things that must be set right, or we shall perish, like Rome, of soul atrophy disguised as empire.

The first is, that the daily ceremony of dividing the wealth of the country among its inhabitants shall be so conducted that no crumb shall, save as a criminal's ration, go to any ablebodied adults who are not producing by their personal exertions not only a full equivalent for what they take, but a surplus sufficient to provide for their superannuation and pay back the debt due for their nurture.

The second is that the deliberate infliction of malicious injuries which now goes on under the name of punishment be abandoned; so that the thief, the ruffian, the gambler, and the beggar, may without inhumanity be handed over to the law, and made to understand that a State which is too humane to punish will also be too thrifty to waste the life of honest men in watching or restraining dishonest ones. That is why we do not imprison dogs. We even take our chance of their first bite. But if a dog delights to bark and bite, it goes to the lethal chamber. That seems to me sensible. To allow the dog to expiate his bite by a period of torment, and then let him loose in a much more savage condition (for the chain makes a dog savage) to bite again and expiate again, having meanwhile spent a great deal of human life and happiness in the task of chaining and feeding and tormenting him, seems to me idiotic and superstitious. Yet that is what we do to men who bark and bite and steal. It would be far more sensible to put up with their vices, as we put up with their illnesses, until they give more trouble than they are worth, at which point we should, with many apologies and expressions of sympathy, and some generosity in complying with their last wishes, place them in the lethal chamber and get rid of them. Under no circumstances should they be allowed to expiate their misdeeds by a manufactured penalty, to subscribe to a charity, or to compensate the victims. If there is to be no punishment there can be no forgiveness. We shall never have real moral responsibility until everyone knows that his deeds are irrevocable, and that his life depends on his usefulness. Hitherto, alas! humanity has never dared face these hard facts. We frantically scatter conscience money and invent systems of conscience banking, with expiatory penalties, atonements, redemptions, salvations, hospital subscription lists and what not, to enable us to contract-out of the moral code. Not content with the old scapegoat and sacrificial lamb, we deify human saviors, and pray to miraculous virgin intercessors. We attribute mercy to the inexorable; soothe our consciences after committing murder by throwing ourselves on the bosom of divine love; and shrink even from our own gallows because we are forced to admit that it, at least, is irrevocable—as if one hour of imprisonment were not as irrevocable as any execution!

If a man cannot look evil in the face without illusion, he will never know what it really is, or combat it effectually. The few men who have been able (relatively) to do this have been called cynics, and have sometimes had an abnormal share of evil in themselves, corresponding to the abnormal strength of their minds; but they have never done mischief unless they intended to do it. That is why great scoundrels have been beneficent rulers whilst amiable and privately harmless monarchs have ruined their countries by trusting to the hocus-pocus of innocence and guilt, reward and punishment, virtuous indignation and pardon, instead of standing up the facts without either malice or mercy. Major Barbara stands up to Bill Walker in that way, with the result that the ruffian who cannot get hated, has to hate himself. To relieve this agony he tries to get punished; but the Salvationist whom he tries to provoke is as merciless as Barbara, and only prays for him. Then he tries to pay, but can get nobody to take his money. His doom is the doom of Cain, who, failing to find either a savior, a policeman, or an almoner to help him to pretend that his brother's blood no longer cried from the ground, had to live and die a murderer. Cain took care not to commit another murder, unlike our railway shareholders (I am one) who kill and maim shunters by hundreds to save the cost of automatic couplings, and make atonement by annual subscriptions to deserving charities. Had Cain been allowed to pay off his score, he might possibly have killed Adam and Eve for the mere sake of a second luxurious reconciliation with God afterwards. Bodger, you may depend on it, will go on to the end of his life poisoning people with bad whisky, because he can always depend on the Salvation Army or the Church of England to negotiate a redemption for him in consideration of a trifling percentage of his profits.

There is a third condition too, which must be fulfilled before the great teachers of the world will cease to scoff at its religions. Creeds must become intellectually honest. At present there is not a single credible established religion in the world. That is perhaps the most stupendous fact in the whole world-situation. This play of mine, Major Barbara, is, I hope, both true and inspired; but whoever says that it all happened, and that faith in it and understanding of it consist in believing that it is a record of an actual occurrence, is, to speak according to Scripture, a fool and a liar, and is hereby solemnly denounced and cursed as such by me, the author, to all posterity.

The booming drum of religion clashes with the guns of capitalism in the 1956 revival of Shaw's Major Barbara *at New York's Morosco Theater.*

MAJOR BARBARA*

BERNARD SHAW

ACT 1

It is after dinner in January 1906, in the library in Lady Britomart Undershaft's house in Wilton Crescent. A large and comfortable settee is in the middle of the room, upholstered in dark leather. A person sitting on it (it is vacant at present) would have, on his right, Lady Britomart's writing table, with the lady herself busy at it; a smaller writing table behind him on his left; the door behind him on Lady Britomart's side; and a window with a window seat directly on his left. Near the window is an armchair.

Lady Britomart is a woman of fifty or thereabouts, well dressed and yet careless of her dress, well bred and quite reckless of her breeding, well mannered and yet appallingly outspoken and indifferent to the opinion of her interlocutors, amiable and yet peremptory, arbitrary, and high-tempered to the last bearable degree, and withal a very typical managing matron of the upper class, treated as a naughty child until she grew into a scolding mother, and finally settling down with plenty of practical ability and worldly ex-

*N.B. The Euripidean verses in the second act of *Major Barbara* are not by me, nor even directly by Euripides. They are by Professor Gilbert Murray, whose English version of *The Bacchae* came into our dramatic literature with all the impulsive power of an original work shortly before *Major Barbara* was begun. The play, indeed, stands indebted to him in more ways than one.

G.B.S.

perience, limited in the oddest way with domestic and class limitations, conceiving the universe exactly as if it were a large house in Wilton Crescent, though handling her corner of it very effectively on that assumption, and being quite enlightened and liberal as to the books in the library, the pictures on the walls, the music in the portfolios, and the articles in the papers.

Her son, Stephen, comes in. He is a gravely correct young man under 25, taking himself very seriously, but still in some awe of his mother, from childish habit and bachelor shyness rather than from any weakness of character.

STEPHEN. Whats the matter?

LADY BRITOMART. Presently, Stephen.

Stephen submissively walks to the settee and sits down. He takes up a Liberal weekly called The Speaker.

LADY BRITOMART. Dont begin to read, Stephen. I shall require all your attention.

STEPHEN. It was only while I was waiting—

LADY BRITOMART. Dont make excuses, Stephen. (*He puts down The Speaker.*) Now! (*She finishes her writing; rises; and comes to the settee.*) I have not kept you waiting very long, I think.

STEPHEN. Not at all, mother.

LADY BRITOMART. Bring me my cushion. (*He takes the cushion from the chair at the desk and arranges it for her as she sits down on the settee.*) Sit down. (*He sits down and fingers his tie nervously.*) Dont fiddle with your tie, Stephen: there is nothing the matter with it.

STEPHEN. I beg your pardon. (*He fiddles with his watch chain instead.*)

LADY BRITOMART. Now are you attending to me, Stephen?

STEPHEN. Of course, mother.

LADY BRITOMART. No: it's not of course. I want something much more than your everyday matter-of-course attention. I am going to speak to you very seriously, Stephen. I wish you would let that chain alone.

STEPHEN (*hastily relinquishing the chain*). Have I done anything to annoy you, mother? If so, it was quite unintentional.

LADY BRITOMART (*astonished*). Nonsense! (*With some remorse.*) My poor boy, did you think I was angry with you?

STEPHEN. What is it, then, mother? You are making me very uneasy.

LADY BRITOMART (*squaring herself at him rather aggressively*). Stephen: may I ask how soon you intend to realize that you are a grown-up man, and that I am only a woman?

STEPHEN (*amazed*). Only a—

LADY BRITOMART. Dont repeat my words, please: it is a most aggravating habit. You must learn to face life seriously, Stephen. I really cannot bear the whole burden of our family affairs any longer. You must advise me; you must assume the responsibility.

STEPHEN. I!

LADY BRITOMART. Yes, you, of course. You were 24 last June. Youve been at Harrow and Cambridge. Youve been to India and Japan. You must know a lot of things, now; unless you have wasted your time most scandalously. Well, advise me.

STEPHEN (*much perplexed*). You know I have never interfered in the household—

LADY BRITOMART. No: I should think not. I dont want you to order the dinner.

STEPHEN. I mean in our family affairs.

LADY BRITOMART. Well, you must interfere now; for they are getting quite beyond me.

STEPHEN (*troubled*). I have thought sometimes that perhaps I ought; but really, mother, I know so little about them; and what I do know is so painful! It is so impossible to mention some things to you—(*He stops, ashamed.*)

LADY BRITOMART. I suppose you mean your father.

STEPHEN (*almost inaudibly*). Yes.

LADY BRITOMART. My dear: we cant go on all our lives not mentioning him. Of course you were quite right not to open the subject until I asked you to; but you are old enough now to be taken into my confidence, and to help me to deal with him about the girls.

STEPHEN. But the girls are all right. They are engaged.

LADY BRITOMART (*complacently*). Yes: I have made a very good match for Sarah. Charles Lomax will be a millionaire at 35. But that is ten years ahead; and in the meantime his trustees cannot under the terms of his father's will allow him more than £800 a year.

STEPHEN. But the will says also that if he increases his income by his own exertions, they may double the increase.

LADY BRITOMART. Charles Lomax's exertions are much more likely to decrease his income than to increase it. Sarah will have to find at least another £800 a year for the next ten years; and even then they will be as poor as church mice. And what about Barbara? I thought Barbara was going to make the most brilliant career of all of you. And what does she do? Joins the Salvation Army; discharges her maid; lives on a pound a week; and walks in one evening with a professor of Greek whom she has picked up in the street, and who pretends to be a Salvationist, and actually plays the big drum for her in public because he has fallen head over ears in love with her.

STEPHEN. I was certainly rather taken aback when I heard they were engaged. Cusins is a very nice fellow, certainly: nobody would ever guess that he was born in Australia; but—

LADY BRITOMART. Oh, Adolphus Cusins will make a very good husband. After all, nobody can say a word against Greek: it stamps a man at once as an educated gentleman. And my family, thank Heaven, is not a pig-headed Tory one. We are Whigs, and believe in liberty. Let snobbish people say what they please: Barbara shall marry, not the man they like, but the man *I* like.

STEPHEN. Of course I was thinking only of his income. However, he is not likely to be extravagant.

LADY BRITOMART. Dont be too sure of that, Stephen. I know your quiet, simple, refined, poetic people like Adolphus: quite content with the best of everything! They cost more than your extravagant people, who are always as mean as they are second rate. No: Barbara will need at least £2000 a year. You see it means two additional households. Besides, my dear, you must marry soon. I dont approve of the present fashion of philandering bachelors and late marriages; and I am trying to arrange something for you.

STEPHEN. It's very good of you, mother; but perhaps I had better arrange that for myself.

LADY BRITOMART. Nonsense! you are much too young to begin matchmaking: you would be taken in by some pretty little nobody. Of course I dont mean that you are not to be consulted: you know that as well as I do. (Stephen closes his lips and is silent.) Now dont sulk, Stephen.

STEPHEN. I am not sulking, mother. What has all this got to do with—with—with my father?

LADY BRITOMART. My dear Stephen: where is the money to come from? It is easy enough for you and the other children to live on my income as long as we are in the same house; but I cant keep four families in four separate houses. You know how poor my father is: he has barely seven thousand a year now; and really, if he were not the Earl of Stevenage, he would have to give up society. He can do nothing for us. He says, naturally enough, that it is absurd that he should be asked to provide for the children of a man who is rolling in money. You see, Stephen, your father must be fabulously wealthy, because there is always a war going on somewhere.

STEPHEN. You need not remind me of that, mother. I have hardly ever opened a newspaper in my life without seeing our name in it. The Undershaft torpedo! The Undershaft quick firers! The Undershaft ten inch! the Undershaft disappearing rampart gun! the Undershaft submarine! and now the Undershaft aerial battleship! At Harrow they called me the Woolwich Infant. At Cambridge it was the same. A little brute at King's who was always trying to get up revivals, spoilt my Bible—your first birthday present to me—by writing under my name, "Son and heir to Undershaft and Lazarus, Death and Destruction Dealers: address, Christendom and Judea." But that was not so bad as the way I was kowtowed to everywhere because my father was making millions by selling cannons.

LADY BRITOMART. It is not only the cannons, but the war loans that Lazarus arranges under cover of giving credit for the cannons. You know, Stephen, it's perfectly scandalous. Those two men, Andrew Undershaft and Lazarus, positively have Europe under their thumbs. That is why your father is able to behave as he does. He is above the law. Do you think Bismarck or Gladstone or Disraeli could have openly defied every social and moral obligation all their lives as your father has? They simply wouldnt have dared. I asked Gladstone to take it up. I asked The Times to take it up. I asked the Lord Chamberlain to take it up. But it was just like asking them to declare war on the Sultan. They wouldnt. They said they couldnt touch him. I believe they were afraid.

STEPHEN. What could they do? He does not actually break the law.

LADY BRITOMART. Not break the law! He is always breaking the law. He broke the law when he was born: his parents were not married.

STEPHEN. Mother! Is that true?

LADY BRITOMART. Of course it's true: that was why we separated.

STEPHEN. He married without letting you know this!

LADY BRITOMART (rather taken aback by this inference). Oh no. To do Andrew justice, that was not the sort of thing he did. Besides, you know the Undershaft motto: Unashamed. Everybody knew.

STEPHEN. But you said that was why you separated.

LADY BRITOMART. Yes, because he was not content with being a foundling himself: he wanted to disinherit you for another foundling. That was what I couldnt stand.

STEPHEN (ashamed). Do you mean for—for—for—

LADY BRITOMART. Do not stammer, Stephen. Speak distinctly.

STEPHEN. But this is so frightful to me, mother. To have to speak to you about such things!

LADY BRITOMART. It's not pleasant for me, either, especially if you are still so childish that you must make it worse by a display of embarrassment. It is only in the middle classes, Stephen, that people get into a state of dumb helpless horror when they find that there are wicked people in the world. In our class, we have to decide what is to be done with wicked people; and nothing should disturb our self-possession. Now ask your question properly.

STEPHEN. Mother: have you no consideration for me? For Heaven's sake either treat me as a child, as you always do, and tell me nothing at all; or tell me everything and let me take it as best I can.

LADY BRITOMART. Treat you as a child! What do you mean? It is most unkind and ungrateful of you to say such a thing. You know I have never treated any of you as children. I have always made you my companions and friends, and allowed you perfect freedom to do and say whatever you liked, so long as you liked what I could approve of.

STEPHEN (desperately). I daresay we have been the very imperfect children of a very perfect mother; but I do beg you to let me alone for once, and tell me about this horrible business of my father wanting to set me aside for another son.

LADY BRITOMART (amazed). Another son! I never said anything of the kind. I never dreamt of such a thing. This is what comes of interrupting me.

STEPHEN. But you said—

LADY BRITOMART (*cutting him short*). Now be a good boy, Stephen, and listen to me patiently. The Undershafts are descended from a foundling in the parish of St Andrew Undershaft in the city. That was long ago, in the reign of James the First. Well, this foundling was adopted by an armorer and gun-maker. In the course of time the foundling succeeded to the business; and from some notion of gratitude, or some vow or something, he adopted another foundling, and left the business to him. And that foundling did the same. Ever since that, the cannon business has always been left to an adopted foundling named Andrew Undershaft.

STEPHEN. But did they never marry? Were there no legitimate sons?

LADY BRITOMART. Oh yes: they married just as your father did; and they were rich enough to buy land for their own children and leave them well provided for. But they always adopted and trained some foundling to succeed them in the business; and of course they always quarrelled with their wives furiously over it. Your father was adopted in that way; and he pretends to consider himself bound to keep up the tradition and adopt somebody to leave the business to. Of course I was not going to stand that. There may have been some reason for it when the Undershafts could only marry women in their own class, whose sons were not fit to govern great estates. But there could be no excuse for passing over my son.

STEPHEN (*dubiously*). I am afraid I should make a poor hand of managing a cannon foundry.

LADY BRITOMART. Nonsense! you could easily get a manager and pay him a salary.

STEPHEN. My father evidently had no great opinion of my capacity.

LADY BRITOMART. Stuff, child! you were only a baby: it had nothing to do with your capacity. Andrew did it on principle, just as he did every perverse and wicked thing on principle. When my father remonstrated, Andrew actually told him to his face that history tells us of only two successful institutions: one the Undershaft firm, and the other the Roman Empire under the Antonines. That was because the Antonine emperors all adopted their successors. Such rubbish! The Stevenages are as good as the Antonines, I hope; and you are a Stevenage. But that was Andrew all over. There you have the man! Always clever and unanswerable when he was defending nonsense and wickedness: always awkward and sullen when he had to behave sensibly and decently!

STEPHEN. Then it was on my account that your home life was broken up, mother. I am sorry.

LADY BRITOMART. Well, dear, there were other differences. I really cannot bear an immoral man. I am not a Pharisee, I hope; and I should not have minded his merely doing wrong things: we are none of us perfect. But your father didnt exactly do wrong things: he said them and thought them: that was what was so dreadful. He really had a sort of religion of wrongness. Just as one doesnt mind men practising immorality so long as they own that they are in the wrong by preaching morality; so I couldnt forgive Andrew for preaching immorality while he practised morality. You would all have grown up without principles, without any knowledge of right and wrong, if he had been in the house. You know, my dear, your father was a very attractive man in some ways. Children did not dislike him; and he took advantage of it to put the wickedest ideas into their heads, and make them quite unmanageable. I did not dislike him myself: very far from it; but nothing can bridge over moral disagreement.

STEPHEN. All this simply bewilders me, mother. People may differ about matters of opinion, or even about religion; but how can they differ about right and wrong? Right is right; and wrong is wrong; and if a man cannot distinguish them properly, he is either a fool or a rascal: thats all.

LADY BRITOMART (*touched*). Thats my own boy! (*She pats his cheek.*) Your father never could answer that: he used to laugh and get out of it under cover of some affectionate nonsense. And now that you understand the situation, what do you advise me to do?

STEPHEN. Well, what can you do?

LADY BRITOMART. I must get the money somehow.

STEPHEN. We cannot take money from him. I had rather go and live in some cheap place like Bedford Square or even Hampstead than take a farthing of his money.

LADY BRITOMART. But after all, Stephen, our present income comes from Andrew.

STEPHEN (*shocked*). I never knew that.

LADY BRITOMART. Well, you surely didnt suppose your grandfather had anything to give me. The Stevenages could not do everything for you. We gave you social position. Andrew had to contribute something. He had a very good bargain, I think.

STEPHEN (*bitterly*). We are utterly dependent on him and his cannons, then?

LADY BRITOMART. Certainly not: the money is settled. But he provided it. So you see it is not a question of taking money from him or not: it is simply a question of how much. I dont want any more for myself.

STEPHEN. Nor do I.

LADY BRITOMART. But Sarah does; and Barbara does. That is, Charles Lomax and Adolphus Cusins will cost them more. So I must put my pride in my pocket and ask for it, I suppose. That is your advice, Stephen, is it not?

STEPHEN. No.

LADY BRITOMART (*sharply*). Stephen!

STEPHEN. Of course if you are determined—

LADY BRITOMART. I am not determined: I ask your advice; and I am waiting for it. I will not have all the responsibility thrown on my shoulders.

STEPHEN (*obstinately*). I would die sooner than ask him for another penny.

LADY BRITOMART (*resignedly*). You mean that *I* must ask him. Very well, Stephen: it shall be as you wish. You will be glad to know that your grandfather concurs. But he thinks I ought to ask Andrew to come here and see the girls. After all, he must have some natural affection for them.

STEPHEN. Ask him here!!!

LADY BRITOMART. Do not repeat my words, Stephen. Where else can I ask him?

STEPHEN. I never expected you to ask him at all.

LADY BRITOMART. Now dont tease, Stephen. Come! you see that it is necessary that he should pay us a visit, dont you?

STEPHEN (*reluctantly*). I suppose so, if the girls cannot do without his money.

LADY BRITOMART. Thank you, Stephen: I knew you would give me the right advice when it was properly explained to you. I have asked your father to come this evening. (*Stephen bounds from his seat.*) Dont jump, Stephen: it fidgets me.

STEPHEN (*in utter consternation*). Do you mean to say that my father is coming here tonight—that he may be here at any moment?

LADY BRITOMART (*looking at her watch*). I said nine. (*He gasps. She rises.*) Ring the bell, please. (*Stephen goes to the smaller writing table; presses a button on it; and sits at it with his elbows on the table and his head in his hands, outwitted and overwhelmed.*) It is ten minutes to nine yet; and I have to prepare the girls. I asked Charles Lomax and Adolphus to dinner on purpose that they might be here. Andrew had better see them in case he should cherish any delusions as to their being capable of supporting their wives. (*The butler enters: Lady Britomart goes behind the settee to speak to him.*) Morrison: go up to the drawing room and tell everybody to come down here at once. (*Morrison withdraws. Lady Britomart turns to Stephen.*) Now remember, Stephen: I shall need all your countenance and authority. (*He rises and tries to recover some vestige of these attributes.*) Give me a chair, dear. (*He pushes a chair forward from the wall to where she stands, near the smaller writing table. She sits down; and he goes to the armchair, into which he throws himself.*) I dont know how Barbara will take it. Ever since they made her a major in the Salvation Army she has developed a propensity to have her own way and order people about which quite cows me sometimes. It's not ladylike: I'm sure I dont know where she picked it up. Anyhow, Barbara shant bully me; but still it's just as well that your father should be here before she has time to refuse to meet him or make a fuss. Dont look nervous, Stephen: it will only encourage Barbara to make difficulties. *I* am nervous enough, goodness knows; but I dont shew it.

Sarah and Barbara come in with their respective young men, Charles Lomax and Adolphus Cusins. Sarah is slender, bored, and mundane. Barbara is robuster, jollier, much more energetic. Sarah is fashionably dressed: Barbara is in Salvation Army uniform. Lomax, a young man about town, is like many other young men about town. He is afflicted with a frivolous sense of humor which plunges him at the most inopportune moments into paroxysms of imperfectly suppressed laughter. Cusins is a spectacled student, slight, thin haired, and sweet voiced, with a more complex form of Lomax's complaint. His sense of humor is intellectual and subtle, and is complicated by an appalling temper. The lifelong struggle of a benevolent temperament and a high conscience against impulses of inhuman ridicule and fierce impatience has set up a chronic strain which has visibly wrecked his constitution. He is a most implacable, determined, tenacious, intolerant person who by mere force of character presents himself as—and indeed actually is—considerate, gentle, explanatory, even mild and apologetic, capable possibly of murder, but not of cruelty or coarseness. By the operation of some instinct which is not merciful enough to blind him with the illusions of love, he is obstinately bent on marrying Barbara. Lomax likes Sarah and thinks it will be rather a lark to marry her. Consequently he has not attempted to resist Lady Britomart's arrangements to that end.*

All four look as if they had been having a good deal of fun in the drawing room. The girls enter first, leaving the swains outside. Sarah comes to the settee. Barbara comes in after her and stops at the door.

BARBARA. Are Cholly and Dolly to come in?

LADY BRITOMART (*forcibly*). Barbara: I will not have Charles called Cholly: the vulgarity of it positively makes me ill.

BARBARA. It's all right, mother: Cholly is quite correct nowadays. Are they to come in?

LADY BRITOMART. Yes, if they will behave themselves.

BARBARA (*through the door*). Come in, Dolly; and behave yourself.

Barbara comes to her mother's writing table. Cusins enters smiling, and wanders towards Lady Britomart.

SARAH (*calling*). Come in, Cholly. (*Lomax enters, controlling his features very imperfectly, and places himself vaguely between Sarah and Barbara.*)

LADY BRITOMART (*peremptorily*). Sit down, all of you. (*They sit. Cusins crosses to the window and seats himself there. Lomax takes a chair. Barbara sits at the writing table and Sarah on the settee.*) I dont in the least know what you are laughing at, Adolphus. I am surprised at you, though I expected nothing better from Charles Lomax.

CUSINS (*in a remarkably gentle voice*). Barbara has been trying to teach me the West Ham Salvation March.

LADY BRITOMART. I see nothing to laugh at in that; nor should you if you are really converted.

CUSINS (*sweetly*). You were not present. It was really funny, I believe.

LOMAX. Ripping.

LADY BRITOMART. Be quiet, Charles. Now listen to me, children. Your father is coming here this evening.

General stupefaction. Lomax, Sarah, and Barbara rise: Sarah scared, and Barbara amused and expectant.

LOMAX (*remonstrating*). Oh I say!

LADY BRITOMART. You are not called on to say anything, Charles.

SARAH. Are you serious, mother?

LADY BRITOMART. Of course I am serious. It is on your account, Sarah, and also on Charles's. (*Silence. Sarah sits, with a shrug. Charles looks painfully unworthy.*) I hope you are not going to object, Barbara.

BARBARA. I! why should I? My father has a soul to be saved like anybody else. He's quite welcome as far as I am concerned. (*She sits on the table, and softly whistles 'Onward, Christian Soldiers.'*)

LOMAX (*still remonstrant*). But really, dont you know! Oh I say!

LADY BRITOMART (*frigidly*). What do you wish to convey, Charles?

LOMAX. Well, you must admit that this is a bit thick.

LADY BRITOMART (*turning with ominous suavity to Cusins*). Adolphus: you are a professor of Greek. Can you translate Charles Lomax's remarks into reputable English for us?

CUSINS (*cautiously*). If I may say so, Lady Brit, I think Charles has rather happily expressed what we all feel. Homer, speaking of Autolycus, uses the same phrase. πυκινὸν δόμον ἐλθεῖν means a bit thick.

LOMAX (*handsomely*). Not that I mind, you know, if Sarah dont. (*He sits.*)

LADY BRITOMART (*crushingly*). Thank you. Have I your permission, Adolphus, to invite my own husband to my own house?

CUSINS (*gallantly*). You have my unhesitating support in everything you do.

LADY BRITOMART. Tush! Sarah: have you nothing to say?

SARAH. Do you mean that he is coming regularly to live here?

LADY BRITOMART. Certainly not. The spare room is ready for him if he likes to stay for a day or two and see a little more of you; but there are limits.

SARAH. Well, he cant eat us, I suppose. I dont mind.

LOMAX (*chuckling*). I wonder how the old man will take it.

LADY BRITOMART. Much as the old woman will, no doubt, Charles.

LOMAX (*abashed*). I didn't mean—at least—

LADY BRITOMART. You didnt think, Charles. You never do; and the result is, you never mean anything. And now please attend to me, children. Your father will be quite a stranger to us.

LOMAX. I suppose he hasnt seen Sarah since she was a little kid.

LADY BRITOMART. Not since she was a little kid, Charles, as you express it with that elegance of diction and refinement of thought that seem never to desert you. Accordingly—er—(*impatiently*). Now I have forgotten what I was going to say. That comes of your provoking me to be sarcastic, Charles. Adolphus: will you kindly tell me where I was.

CUSINS (*sweetly*). You were saying that as Mr Undershaft has not seen his children since they were babies, he will form his opinion of the way you have brought them up from their behavior tonight, and that therefore you wish us all to be particularly careful to conduct ourselves well, especially Charles.

LADY BRITOMART (*with emphatic approval*). Precisely.

LOMAX. Look here, Dolly: Lady Brit didnt say that.

LADY BRITOMART (*vehemently*). I did, Charles. Adolphus's recollection is perfectly correct. It is most important that you should be good; and I do beg you for once not to pair off into opposite corners and giggle and whisper while I am speaking to your father.

BARBARA. All right, mother. We'll do you credit. (*She comes off the table, and sits in her chair with ladylike elegance.*)

LADY BRITOMART. Remember, Charles, that Sarah will want to feel proud of you instead of ashamed of you.

LOMAX. Oh I say! theres nothing to be exactly proud of, dont you know.

LADY BRITOMART. Well, try and look as if there was.

Morrison, pale and dismayed, breaks into the room in unconcealed disorder.

MORRISON. Might I speak a word to you, my lady?

LADY BRITOMART. Nonsense! Shew him up.

MORRISON. Yes, my lady. (*He goes.*)

LOMAX. Does Morrison know who it is?

LADY BRITOMART. Of course. Morrison has always been with us.

LOMAX. It must be a regular corker for him, dont you know.

LADY BRITOMART. Is this a moment to get on my nerves, Charles, with your outrageous expressions?

LOMAX. But this is something out of the ordinary, really—

MORRISON (*at the door*). The—er—Mr Undershaft. (*He retreats in confusion.*)

Andrew Undershaft comes in. All rise. Lady Britomart meets him in the middle of the room behind the settee.

Andrew is, on the surface, a stoutish, easygoing elderly man, with kindly patient manners, and an engaging simplicity of character. But he has a watchful, deliberate, waiting, listening face, and formidable reserves of power, both bodily and mental, in his capacious chest and long head. His gentleness is partly that of a strong man who has learnt by experience that his natural grip hurts ordinary people unless he handles them very carefully, and partly the mellowness of age and success. He is also a little shy in his present very delicate situation.

LADY BRITOMART. Good evening, Andrew.

UNDERSHAFT. How d'ye do, my dear.

LADY BRITOMART. You look a good deal older.

UNDERSHAFT (*apologetically*). I am somewhat older. (*Taking her hand with a touch of courtship.*) Time has stood still with you.

LADY BRITOMART (*throwing away his hand*). Rubbish! This is your family.

UNDERSHAFT (*surprised*). Is it so large? I am sorry to say my memory is failing very badly in some things. (*He offers his hand with paternal kindness to Lomax.*)

LOMAX (*jerkily shaking his hand*). Ahdedoo.

UNDERSHAFT. I can see you are my eldest. I am very glad to meet you again, my boy.

LOMAX (*remonstrating*). No, but look here dont you know— (*Overcome.*) Oh I say!

LADY BRITOMART (*recovering from momentary speechlessness*). Andrew: do you mean to say that you dont remember how many children you have?

UNDERSHAFT. Well, I am afraid I—. They have grown so much—er. Am I making any ridiculous mistake? I may as well confess: I recollect only one son. But so many things have happened since, of course—er—

LADY BRITOMART (*decisively*). Andrew: you are talking nonsense. Of course you have only one son.

UNDERSHAFT. Perhaps you will be good enough to introduce me, my dear.

LADY BRITOMART. That is Charles Lomax, who is engaged to Sarah.

UNDERSHAFT. My dear sir, I beg your pardon.

LOMAX. Notatall. Delighted, I assure you.

LADY BRITOMART. This is Stephen.

UNDERSHAFT (*bowing*). Happy to make your acquaintance, Mr Stephen. Then (*going to Cusins*) you must be my son. (*Taking Cusins' hands in his.*) How are you, my young friend? (*To Lady Britomart.*) He is very like you, my love.

CUSINS. You flatter me, Mr Undershaft. My name is Cusins: engaged to Barbara. (*Very explicitly.*) That is Major Barbara Undershaft, of the Salvation Army. That is Sarah, your second daughter. This is Stephen Undershaft, your son.

UNDERSHAFT. My dear Stephen, I beg your pardon.

STEPHEN. Not at all.

UNDERSHAFT. Mr Cusins: I am much indebted to you for explaining so precisely. (*Turning to Sarah.*) Barbara, my dear—

SARAH (*prompting him*). Sarah.

UNDERSHAFT. Sarah, of course. (*They shake hands. He goes over to Barbara.*) Barbara—I am right this time, I hope?

BARBARA. Quite right. (*They shake hands.*)

LADY BRITOMART (*resumimg command*). Sit down, all of you. Sit down, Andrew. (*She comes forward and sits on the settee. Cusins also brings his chair forward on her left. Barbara and Stephen resume their seats. Lomax gives his chair to Sarah and goes for another.*)

UNDERSHAFT. Thank you, my love.

LOMAX (*conversationally, as he brings a chair forward between the writing table and the settee, and offers it to Undershaft*).

Takes you some time to find out exactly where you are, dont it?

UNDERSHAFT (*accepting the chair, but remaining standing*). That is not what embarrasses me, Mr Lomax. My difficulty is that if I play the part of a father, I shall produce the effect of an intrusive stranger; and if I play the part of a discreet stranger, I may appear a callous father.

LADY BRITOMART. There is no need for you to play any part at all, Andrew. You had much better be sincere and natural.

UNDERSHAFT (*submissively*). Yes, my dear: I daresay that will be best. (*He sits down comfortably.*) Well, here I am. Now what can I do for you all?

LADY BRITOMART. You need not do anything, Andrew. You are one of the family. You can sit with us and enjoy yourself.

A painfully conscious pause. Barbara makes a face at Lomax, whose too long suppressed mirth immediately explodes in agonized neighings.

LADY BRITOMART (*outraged*). Charles Lomax: if you can behave yourself, behave yourself. If not, leave the room.

LOMAX. I'm awfully sorry, Lady Brit; but really you know, upon my soul! (*He sits on the settee between Lady Britomart and Undershaft, quite overcome.*)

BARBARA. Why dont you laugh if you want to, Cholly? It's good for your inside.

LADY BRITOMART. Barbara: you have had the education of a lady. Please let your father see that; and dont talk like a street girl.

UNDERSHAFT. Never mind me, my dear. As you know, I am not a gentleman; and I was never educated.

LOMAX (*encouragingly*). Nobody'd know it, I assure you. You look all right, you know.

CUSINS. Let me advise you to study Greek, Mr Undershaft. Greek scholars are privileged men. Few of them know Greek; and none of them know anything else; but their position is unchallengeable. Other languages are the qualifications of waiters and commercial travellers: Greek is to a man of position what the hallmark is to silver.

BARBARA. Dolly: dont be insincere. Cholly: fetch your concertina and play something for us.

LOMAX (*jumps up eagerly, but checks himself to remark doubtfully to Undershaft*). Perhaps that sort of thing isnt in your line, eh?

UNDERSHAFT. I am particularly fond of music.

LOMAX (*delighted*). Are you? Then I'll get it. (*He goes upstairs for the instrument.*)

UNDERSHAFT. Do you play, Barbara?

BARBARA. Only the tambourine. But Cholly's teaching me the concertina.

UNDERSHAFT. Is Cholly also a member of the Salvation Army?

BARBARA. No: he says it's bad form to be a dissenter. But I dont despair of Cholly. I made him come yesterday to a meeting at the dock gates, and take the collection in his hat.

UNDERSHAFT (*looks whimsically at his wife*)!!

LADY BRITOMART. It is not my doing, Andrew. Barbara is old enough to take her own way. She has no father to advise her.

BARBARA. Oh yes she has. There are no orphans in the Salvation Army.

UNDERSHAFT. Your father there has a great many children and plenty of experience, eh?

BARBARA (*looking at him with quick interest and nodding*). Just so. How did you come to understand that? (*Lomax is heard at the door trying the concertina.*)

LADY BRITOMART. Come in, Charles. Play us something at once.

LOMAX. Righto! (*He sits down in his former place, and preludes.*)

UNDERSHAFT. One moment, Mr Lomax. I am rather interested in the Salvation Army. Its motto might be my own: Blood and Fire.

LOMAX (*shocked*). But not your sort of blood and fire, you know.

UNDERSHAFT. My sort of blood cleanses: my sort of fire purifies.

BARBARA. So do ours. Come down tomorrow to my shelter—the West Ham shelter—and see what we're doing. We're going to march to a great meeting in the Assembly Hall at Mile End. Come and see the shelter and then march with us: it will do you a lot of good. Can you play anything?

UNDERSHAFT. In my youth I earned pennies, and even shillings occasionally, in the streets and in public house parlors by my natural talent for stepdancing. Later on, I became a member of the Undershaft orchestral society, and performed passably on the tenor trombone.

LOMAX (*scandalized—putting down the concertina*). Oh I say!

BARBARA. Many a sinner has played himself into heaven on the trombone, thanks to the Army.

LOMAX (*to Barbara, still rather shocked*). Yes; but what about the cannon business, dont you know? (*To Undershaft.*) Getting into heaven is not exactly in your line, is it?

LADY BRITOMART. Charles!!!

LOMAX. Well; but it stands to reason, dont it? The cannon business may be necessary and all that: we cant get on without cannons; but it isnt right, you know. On the other hand, there may be a certain amount of tosh about the Salvation Army—I belong to the Established Church myself—but still you cant deny that it's religion; and you cant go against religion, can you? At least unless youre downright immoral, dont you know.

UNDERSHAFT. You hardly appreciate my position, Mr Lomax—

LOMAX (*hastily*). I'm not saying anything against you personally—

UNDERSHAFT. Quite so, quite so. But consider for a moment. Here I am, a profiteer in mutilation and murder. I find myself in a specially amiable humor just now because, this morning, down at the foundry, we blew twenty-seven dummy soldiers into fragments with a gun which formerly destroyed only thirteen.

LOMAX (*leniently*). Well, the more destructive war becomes, the sooner it will be abolished, eh?

UNDERSHAFT. Not at all. The more destructive war becomes the more fascinating we find it. No, Mr Lomax: I am obliged to you for making the usual excuse for my trade; but I am not ashamed of it. I am not one of those men who keep their morals and their business in water-tight compartments. All the spare money my trade rivals spend on hospitals, cathedrals, and other receptacles for conscience money, I devote to experiments and researches in improved methods of destroying life and property. I have always done so; and I always shall. Therefore your Christmas card moralities of peace on earth and goodwill among men are of no use to me. Your Christianity, which enjoins you to resist not evil, and to turn the other cheek, would make me a bankrupt. My morality—my religion—must have a place for cannons and torpedoes in it.

STEPHEN (*coldly—almost sullenly*). You speak as if there were half a dozen moralities and religions to choose from, instead of one true morality and one true religion.

UNDERSHAFT. For me there is only one true morality; but it might not fit you, as you do not manufacture aerial battleships. There is only one true morality for every man; but every man has not the same true morality.

LOMAX (*overtaxed*). Would you mind saying that again? I didnt quite follow it.

CUSINS. It's quite simple. As Euripides says, one man's meat is another man's poison morally as well as physically.

UNDERSHAFT. Precisely.

LOMAX. Oh, that! Yes, yes, yes. True. True.

STEPHEN. In other words, some men are honest and some are scoundrels.

BARBARA. Bosh! There are no scoundrels.

UNDERSHAFT. Indeed? Are there any good men?

BARBARA. No. Not one. There are neither good men nor scoundrels: there are just children of one Father; and the sooner they stop calling one another names the better. You neednt talk to me: I know them. Ive had scores of them through my hands: scoundrels, criminals, infidels, philanthropists, missionaries, county councillors, all sorts. Theyre all just the same sort of sinner; and theres the same salvation ready for them all.

UNDERSHAFT. May I ask have you ever saved a maker of cannons?

BARBARA. No. Will you let me try?

UNDERSHAFT. Well, I will make a bargain with you. If I go to see you tomorrow in your Salvation Shelter, will you come the day after to see me in my cannon works?

BARBARA. Take care. It may end in your giving up the cannons for the sake of the Salvation Army.

UNDERSHAFT. Are you sure it will not end in your giving up the Salvation Army for the sake of the cannons?

BARBARA. I will take my chance of that.

UNDERSHAFT. And I will take my chance of the other. (*They shake hands on it.*) Where is your shelter?

BARBARA. In West Ham. At the sign of the cross. Ask anybody in Canning Town. Where are your works?

UNDERSHAFT. In Perivale St Andrews. At the sign of the sword. Ask anybody in Europe.

LOMAX. Hadnt I better play something?

BARBARA. Yes. Give us Onward, Christian Soldiers.

LOMAX. Well, thats rather a strong order to begin with, dont you know. Suppose I sing Thou't passing hence, my brother. It's much the same tune.

BARBARA. It's too melancholy. You get saved, Cholly; and youll pass hence, my brother, without making such a fuss about it.

LADY BRITOMART. Really, Barbara, you go on as if religion were a pleasant subject. Do have some sense of propriety.

UNDERSHAFT. I do not find it an unpleasant subject, my dear. It is the only one that capable people really care for.

LADY BRITOMART (*looking at her watch*). Well, if you are determined to have it, I insist on having it in a proper and respectable way. Charles: ring for prayers.

General amazement. Stephen rises in dismay.

LOMAX (*rising*). Oh I say!

UNDERSHAFT (*rising*). I am afraid I must be going.

LADY BRITOMART. You cannot go now, Andrew: it would be most improper. Sit down. What will the servants think?

UNDERSHAFT. My dear: I have conscientious scruples. May I suggest a compromise? If Barbara will conduct a little service in the drawing room, with Mr Lomax as organist, I will attend it willingly. I will even take part, if a trombone can be procured.

LADY BRITOMART. Dont mock, Andrew.

UNDERSHAFT (*shocked—to Barbara*). You dont think I am mocking, my love, I hope.

BARBARA. No, of course not; and it wouldnt matter if you were: half the Army came to their first meeting for a lark. (*Rising.*) Come along. (*She throws her arm round her father and sweeps him out, calling to the others from the threshold.*) Come, Dolly. Come, Cholly.

Cusins rises.

LADY BRITOMART. I will not be disobeyed by everybody. Adolphus: sit down. (*He does not.*) Charles: you may go. You are not fit for prayers: you cannot keep your countenance.

LOMAX. Oh I say! (*He goes out.*)

LADY BRITOMART (*continuing*). But you, Adolphus, can behave yourself if you choose to. I insist on your staying.

CUSINS. My dear Lady Brit: there are things in the family prayer book that I couldnt bear to hear you say.

LADY BRITOMART. What things, pray?

CUSINS. Well, you would have to say before all the servants that we have done things we ought not to have done, and left undone things we ought to have done, and that there is no health in us. I cannot bear to hear you doing your-

self such an injustice, and Barbara such an injustice. As for myself, I flatly deny it: I have done my best. I shouldnt dare to marry Barbara—I couldnt look you in the face—if it were true. So I must go to the drawing room.

LADY BRITOMART (*offended*). Well, go. (*He starts for the door.*) And remember this, Adolphus: (*He turns to listen.*) I have a very strong suspicion that you went to the Salvation Army to worship Barbara and nothing else. And I quite appreciate the very clever way in which you systematically humbug me. I have found you out. Take care Barbara doesnt. Thats all.

CUSINS (*with unruffled sweetness*). Dont tell on me. (*He steals out.*)

LADY BRITOMART. Sarah: if you want to go, go. Anything's better than to sit there as if you wished you were a thousand miles away.

SARAH (*languidly*). Very well, mamma. (*She goes.*)

Lady Britomart, with a sudden flounce, gives way to a little gust of tears.

STEPHEN (*going to her*). Mother: whats the matter?

LADY BRITOMART (*swishing away her tears with her handkerchief*). Nothing. Foolishness. You can go with him, too, if you like, and leave me with the servants.

STEPHEN. Oh, you mustnt think that, mother. I—I dont like him.

LADY BRITOMART. The others do. That is the injustice of a woman's lot. A woman has to bring up her children; and that means to restrain them, to deny them things they want, to set them tasks, to punish them when they do wrong, to do all the unpleasant things. And then the father, who has nothing to do but pet them and spoil them, comes in when all her work is done and steals their affection from her.

STEPHEN. He has not stolen our affection from you. It is only curiosity.

LADY BRITOMART (*violently*). I wont be consoled, Stephen. There is nothing the matter with me. (*She rises and goes towards the door.*)

STEPHEN. Where are you going, mother?

LADY BRITOMART. To the drawing room, of course. (*She goes out. Onward, Christian Soldiers, on the concertina, with tambourine accompaniment, is heard when the door opens.*) Are you coming, Stephen?

STEPHEN. No. Certainly not. (*She goes. He sits down on the settee, with compressed lips and an expression of strong dislike.*)

ACT 2

The yard of the West Ham shelter of the Salvation Army is a cold place on a January morning. The building itself, an old warehouse, is newly whitewashed. Its gabled end projects into the yard in the middle, with a door on the ground floor, and another in the loft above it without any balcony or ladder, but with a pulley rigged over it for hoisting sacks. Those who come from this central gable end into the yard have the gateway leading to the street on their left, with a stone horse-trough just beyond it, and, on the right, a penthouse shielding a table from the weather. There are forms at the table; and on them are seated a man and a woman, both much down on their luck, finishing a meal of bread (one thick slice each, with margarine and golden syrup) and diluted milk.

The man, a workman out of employment, is young, agile, a talker, a poser, sharp enough to be capable of anything in reason except honesty or altruistic considerations of any kind. The woman is a commonplace old bundle of poverty and hard-worn humanity. She looks sixty and probably is forty-five. If they were rich people, gloved and muffed and well wrapped up in furs and overcoats, they would be numbed and miserable; for it is a grindingly cold raw January day; and a glance at the background of grimy warehouses and leaden sky visible over the whitewashed walls of the yard would drive any idle rich person straight to the Mediterranean. But these two, being no more troubled with visions of the Mediterranean than of the moon, and being compelled to keep more of their clothes in the pawnshop, and less on their persons, in winter than in summer, are not depressed by the cold: rather are they stung into vivacity, to which their meal has just now given an almost jolly turn. The man takes a pull at his mug, and then gets up and moves about the yard with his hands deep in his pockets, occasionally breaking into a stepdance.

THE WOMAN. Feel better arter your meal, sir?

THE MAN. No. Call that a meal! Good enough for you, praps; but wot is it to me, an intelligent workin man?

THE WOMAN. Workin man! Wot are you?

THE MAN. Painter.

THE WOMAN (*sceptically*). Yus, I dessay.

THE MAN. Yus, you dessay! I know. Every loafer that cant do nothink calls isself a painter. Well, I'm a real painter: grainer, finisher, thirty-eight bob a week when I can get it.

THE WOMAN. Then why dont you go and get it?

THE MAN. I'll tell you why. Fust: I'm intelligent—fffff! it's rotten cold here—(*He dances a step or two.*) yes: intelligent beyond the station o life into which it has pleased the capitalists to call me; and they dont like a man that sees through em. Second, an intelligent bein needs a doo share of appiness; so I drink somethink cruel when I get the chawnce. Third, I stand by my class and do as little as I can so's to leave arf the job for me fellow workers. Fourth, I'm fly enough to know wots inside the law and wots outside it; and inside it I do as the capitalists do: pinch wot I can lay me ands on. In a proper state of society I am sober, industrious and honest: in Rome, so to speak, I do as the Romans do. Wots the consequence? When trade is bad—and it's rotten bad just now—and the employers az to sack arf their men, they generally start on me.

THE WOMAN. Whats your name?

THE MAN. Price. Bronterre O'Brien Price. Usually called Snobby Price, for short.

THE WOMAN. Snobby's a carpenter, aint it? You said you was a painter.

PRICE. Not that kind of snob, but the genteel sort. I'm too uppish, owing to my intelligence, and my father being a Chartist and a reading, thinking man: a stationer, too. I'm none of your common hewers of wood and drawers of water; and dont you forget it. (*He returns to his seat at the table, and takes up his mug.*) Wots your name?

THE WOMAN. Rummy Mitchens, sir.

PRICE (*quaffing the remains of his milk to her*). Your elth, Miss Mitchens.

RUMMY (*correcting him*). Missis Mitchens.

PRICE. Wot! Oh Rummy, Rummy! Respectable married woman, Rummy, gittin rescued by the Salvation Army by pretendin to be a bad un. Same old game!

RUMMY. What am I to do? I cant starve. Them Salvation lasses is dear good girls; but the better you are, the worse they likes to think you were before they rescued you. Why shouldnt they av a bit o credit, poor loves? theyre worn to rags by their work. And where would they get the money to rescue us if we was to let on we're no worse than other people? You know what ladies and gentlemen are.

PRICE. Thievin swine! Wish I ad their job, Rummy, all the same. Wot does Rummy stand for? Pet name praps?

RUMMY. Short for Romola.

PRICE. For wot!?

RUMMY. Romola. It was out of a new book. Somebody me mother wanted me to grow up like.

PRICE. We're companions in misfortune, Rummy. Both on us got names that nobody cawnt pronounce. Consequently I'm Snobby and youre Rummy because Bill and Sally wasnt good enough for our parents. Such is life!

RUMMY. Who saved you, Mr Price? Was it Major Barbara?

PRICE. No: I come here on my own. I'm going to be Bronterre O'Brien Price, the converted painter. I know wot they like. I'll tell em how I blasphemed and gambled and wopped my poor old mother—

RUMMY (*shocked*). Used you to beat your mother?

PRICE. Not likely. She used to beat me. No matter: you come and listen to the converted painter, and youll hear how she was a pious woman that taught me me prayers at er knee, an how I used to come home drunk and drag her out o bed be er snow white airs, an lam into er with the poker.

RUMMY. That whats so unfair to us women. Your confessions is just as big lies as ours: you dont tell what you really done no more than us; but you men can tell your lies right out at the meetins and be made much of for it; while the sort o confessions we az to make az to be wispered to one lady at a time. It aint right, spite of all their piety.

PRICE. Right! Do you spose the Army'd be allowed if it went and did right? Not much. It combs out air and makes us good little blokes to be robbed and put upon. But I'll play the game as good as any of em. I'll see somebody struck by lightnin, or hear a voice sayin "Snobby Price: where will you spend eternity?" I'll av a time of it, I tell you.

RUMMY. You wont be let drink, though.

PRICE. I'll take it out in gorspellin, then. I dont want to drink if I can get fun enough any other way.

Jenny Hill, a pale, overwrought, pretty Salvation lass of 18, comes in through the yard gate, leading Peter Shirley, a half hardened, half worn-out elderly man, weak with hunger.

JENNY (*supporting him*). Come! pluck up. I'll get you something to eat. Youll be all right then.

PRICE (*rising and hurrying officiously to take the old man off Jenny's hands*). Poor old man! Cheer up, brother: youll find rest and peace and appiness ere. Hurry up with the food, miss: e's fair done (*Jenny hurries into the shelter.*) Ere, buck up, daddy! she's fetchin y'a thick slice o breadn treacle, an a mug o skyblue. (*He seats him at the corner of the table.*)

RUMMY (*gaily*). Keep up your old art! Never say die!

SHIRLEY. I'm not an old man. I'm only 46. I'm as good as ever I was. The grey patch come in my hair before I was thirty. All it wants is three pennorth o hair dye: am I to be turned on the streets to starve for it? Holy God! Ive worked ten to twelve hours a day since I was thirteen, and paid my way all through; and now am I to be thrown into the gutter and my job given to a young man that can do it better than me because Ive black hair that goes white at the first change?

PRICE (*cheerfully*). No good jawrin about it. Youre ony a jumped-up, jerked-off, orspittle-turned-out incurable of an ole workin man: who cares about you? Eh? Make the thievin swine give you a meal: theyve stole many a one from you. Get a bit o your own back (*Jenny returns with the usual meal.*) There you are, brother. Awsk a blessin an tuck that into you.

SHIRLEY (*looking at it ravenously but not touching it, and crying like a child*). I never took anything before.

JENNY (*petting him*). Come, come! the Lord sends it to you: he wasnt above taking bread from his friends; and why should you be? Besides, when we find you a job you can pay us for it if you like.

SHIRLEY (*eagerly*). Yes, yes: thats true. I can pay you back: it's only a loan. (*Shivering.*) Oh Lord! oh Lord! (*He turns to the table and attacks the meal ravenously.*)

JENNY. Well, Rummy, are you more comfortable now?

RUMMY. God bless you, lovey! youve fed my body and saved my soul, havnt you? (*Jenny, touched, kisses her.*) Sit down and rest a bit: you must be ready to drop.

JENNY. Ive been going hard since morning. But theres more work than we can do. I mustnt stop.

RUMMY. Try a prayer for just two minutes. Youll work all the better after.

JENNY (*her eyes lighting up*). Oh isnt it wonderful how a few minutes prayer revives you! I was quite lightheaded at twelve o'clock, I was so tired; but Major Barbara just sent me to pray for five minutes; and I was able to go on as if I had only just begun. (*To Price.*) Did you have a piece of bread?

PRICE (*with unction*). Yes, miss; but Ive got the piece that I value more; and thats the peace that passeth hall hannerstennin.

RUMMY (*fervently*). Glory Hallelujah!

Bill Walker, a rough customer of about 25, appears at the yard gate and looks malevolently at Jenny.

JENNY. That makes me so happy. When you say that, I feel wicked for loitering here. I must get to work again.

She is hurrying to the shelter, when the new-comer moves quickly up to the door and intercepts her. His manner is so threatening that she retreats as he comes at her truculently, driving her down the yard.

BILL. Aw knaow you. Youre the one that took awy maw girl. Youre the one that set er agen me. Well, I'm gowin to ev er aht. Not that Aw care a carse for er or you: see? Bat Aw'll let er knaow; and Aw'll let you knaow. Aw'm gowing to give her a doin thatll teach er to cat awy from me. Nah in wiv you and tell er to cam aht afore Aw cam in and kick er aht. Tell er Bill Walker wants er. She'll knaow wot thet means; and if she keeps me witin itll be worse. You stop to jawr beck at me; and Aw'll stawt on you: d'ye eah? Theres your wy. In you gow. (*He takes her by the arm and slings her towards the door of the shelter. She falls on her hand and knee. Rummy helps her up again.*)

PRICE (*rising, and venturing irresolutely towards Bill*). Easy there, mate. She aint doin you no arm.

BILL. Oo are you callin mite? (*Standing over him threateningly.*) Youre gowin to stend ap for er, aw yer? Put ap your ends.

RUMMY (*running indignantly to him to scold him*). Oh, you great brute—(*He instantly swings his left hand back against her face. She screams and reels back to the trough, where she sits down, covering her bruised face with her hands and rocking herself and moaning with pain.*)

JENNY (*going to her*). Oh, God forgive you! How could you strike an old woman like that?

BILL (*seizing her by the hair so violently that she also screams, and tearing her away from the old woman*). You Gawd forgimme again an Aw'll Gawd forgive you one on the jawr thetll stop you pryin for a week. (*Holding her and turning fiercely on Price.*) Ev you ennything to sy agen it?

PRICE (*intimidated*). No, matey: she aint anything to do with me.

BILL. Good job for you! Aw'd pat two meals into you and fawt you with one finger arter, you stawved cur. (*To Jenny.*) Nah are you gowin to fetch aht Mog Ebbijem; or em Aw to knock your fice off you and fetch her meself?

JENNY (*writhing in his grasp*). Oh please someone go in and tell Major Barbara—(*She screams again as he wrenches her head down; and Price and Rummy flee into the shelter.*)

BILL. You want to gow in and tell your Mijor of me, do you?

JENNY. Oh please dont drag my hair. Let me go.

BILL. Do you or downt you? (*She stifles a scream.*) Yus or nao?

JENNY. God give me strength—

BILL (*striking her with his fist in the face*). Gow an shaow her thet, and tell her if she wants one lawk it to cam and interfere with me. (*Jenny, crying with pain, goes into the shed. He goes to the form and addresses the old man.*) Eah: finish your mess; an git aht o maw wy.

SHIRLEY (*springing up and facing him fiercely, with the mug in his hand*). You take a liberty with me, and I'll smash you over the face with the mug and cut your eye out. Aint you satisfied—young whelps like you—with takin the bread out o the mouths of your elders that have brought you up and slaved for you, but you must come shovin and cheekin and bullyin in here, where the bread o charity is sickenin in our stummicks?

BILL (*contemptuously, but backing a little*). Wot good are you, you aold palsy mag. Wot good are you?

SHIRLEY. As good as you and better. I'll do a day's work agen you or any fat young soaker of your age. Go and take my job at Horrockses, where I worked for ten year. They want young men there: they cant afford to keep men over forty-five. Theyre very sorry—give you a character and happy to help you to get anything suited to your years—sure a steady man wont be long out of a job. Well, let em try you. Theyll find the differ. What do you know? Not as much as how to beeyave yourself—layin your dirty fist across the mouth of a respectable woman!

BILL. Downt provowk me to ly it across yours: d'ye eah?

SHIRLEY (*with blighting contempt*). Yes: you like an old man to hit, dont you, when youve finished with the women. I aint seen you hit a young one yet.

BILL (*stung*). You loy, you aold soupkitchener, you. There was a yang menn eah. Did Aw offer to itt him or did Aw not?

SHIRLEY. Was he starvin or was he not? Was he a man or only a crosseyed thief an a loafer? Would you hit my son-in-law's brother?

BILL. Oo's ee?

SHIRLEY. Todger Fairmile o Balls Pond. Him that won £20 off the Japanese wrastler at the music hall by standin out 17 minutes 4 seconds agen him.

BILL (*sullenly*). Aw'm nao music awl wrastler. Ken he box?

SHIRLEY. Yes: an you cant.

BILL. Wot! Aw cawnt, cawnt Aw? Wots thet you sy? (*Threatening him.*)

SHIRLEY (*not budging an inch*). Will you box Todger Fairmile if I put him on to you? Say the word.

BILL (*subsiding with a slouch*). Aw'll stend ap to enny menn alawv, if he was ten Todger Fairmawls. But Aw dont set ap to be a perfeshnal.

SHIRLEY (*looking down on him with unfathomable disdain*). You box! Slap an old woman with the back o your hand! You hadnt even the sense to hit her where a magistrate couldnt see the mark of it, you silly young lump of conceit and ignorance. Hit a girl in the jaw and ony make her cry! If Todger Fairmile'd done it, she wouldnt a got up inside o ten minutes, no more than you would if he got on to you. Yah! I'd set about you myself if I had a week's feedin in me instead o two months' starvation. (*He turns his back on him and sits down moodily at the table.*)

BILL (*following him and stooping over him to drive the taunt in*). You loy! youve the bread and treacle in you that you cam eah to beg.

SHIRLEY (*bursting into tears*). Oh God! it's true: I'm only an old pauper on the scrap heap. (*Furiously.*) But youll come to it yourself; and then youll know. Youll come to it sooner than a teetotaller like me, fillin yourself with gin at this hour o the mornin!

BILL. Aw'm nao gin drinker, you oald lawr; bat wen Aw want to give my girl a bloomin good awdin Aw lawk to ev a bit o devil in me: see? An eah Aw emm, talkin to a rotten aold blawter like you sted o givin her wot for. (*Working himself into a rage.*) Aw'm gowin in there to fetch her aht. (*He makes vengefully for the shelter door.*)

SHIRLEY. Youre goin to the station on a stretcher, more likely; and theyll take the gin and the devil out of you there when they get you inside. You mind what youre about: the major here is the Earl o Stevenage's granddaughter.

BILL (*checked*). Garn!

SHIRLEY. Youll see.

BILL (*his resolution oozing*). Well, Aw aint dan nathin to er.

SHIRLEY. Spose she said you did! who'd believe you?

BILL (*very uneasy, skulking back to the corner of the penthouse*). Gawd! theres no jastice in this cantry. To think wot them people can do! Aw'm as good as er.

SHIRLEY. Tell her so. It's just what a fool like you would do.

Barbara, brisk and businesslike, comes from the shelter with a notebook, and addresses herself to Shirley. Bill, cowed, sits down in the corner on a form, and turns his back on them.

BARBARA. Good morning.

SHIRLEY (*standing up and taking off his hat*). Good morning, miss.

BARBARA. Sit down: make yourself at home. (*He hesitates; but she puts a friendly hand on his shoulder and makes him obey.*) Now then! since youve made friends with us, we want to know all about you. Names and addresses and trades.

SHIRLEY. Peter Shirley. Fitter. Chucked out two months ago because I was too old.

BARBARA (*not at all surprised*). Youd pass still. Why didnt you dye your hair?

SHIRLEY. I did. Me age come out at a coroner's inquest on me daughter.

BARBARA. Steady?

SHIRLEY. Teetotaller. Never out of a job before. Good worker. And sent to the knackers like an old horse!

BARBARA. No matter: if you did your part God will do his.

SHIRLEY (*suddenly stubborn*). My religion's no concern of anybody but myself.

BARBARA (*guessing*). I know. Secularist?

SHIRLEY (*hotly*). Did I offer to deny it?

BARBARA. Why should you? My own father's a Secularist, I think. Our Father—yours and mine—fulfils himself in many ways; and I daresay he knew what he was about when he made a Secularist of you. So buck up, Peter! we can always find a job for a steady man like you. (*Shirley, disarmed and a little bewildered, touches his hat. She turns from him to Bill.*) Whats your name?

BILL (*insolently*). Wots thet to you?

BARBARA (*calmly making a note*). Afraid to give his name. Any trade?

BILL. Oo's afride to give is nime? (*Doggedly, with a sense of heroically defying the House of Lords in the person of Lord Stevenage.*) If you want to bring a chawge agen me, bring it. (*She waits, unruffled.*) Moy nime's Bill Walker.

BARBARA (*as if the name were familiar: trying to remember how*). Bill Walker? (*Recollecting.*) Oh, I know: youre the man that Jenny Hill was praying for inside just now. (*She enters his name in her note book.*)

BILL. Oo's Jenny Ill? And wot call as she to pry for me?

BARBARA. I dont know. Perhaps it was you that cut her lip.

BILL (*defiantly*). Yus, it was me that cat her lip. Aw aint afride o you.

BARBARA. How could you be, since youre not afraid of God? Youre a brave man, Mr Walker. It takes some pluck to do our work here; but none of us dare lift our hand against a girl like that, for fear of her father in heaven.

BILL (*sullenly*). I want nan o your kentin jawr. I spowse you think Aw cam eah to beg from you, like this demmiged lot eah. Not me. Aw downt want your bread and scripe and ketlep. Aw dont blieve in your Gawd, no more than you do yourself.

BARBARA (*sunnily apologetic and ladylike, as on a new footing with him*). Oh, I beg your pardon for putting your name down, Mr Walker. I didnt understand. I'll strike it out.

BILL (*taking this as a slight, and deeply wounded by it*). Eah! you let maw nime alown. Aint it good enaff to be in your book?

BARBARA (*considering*). Well, you see, theres no use putting down your name unless I can do something for you, is there? Whats your trade?

BILL (*still smarting*). Thets nao concern o yours.

BARBARA. Just so. (*Very businesslike.*) I'll put you down as (*writing*) the man who—struck—poor little Jenny Hill—in the mouth.

BILL (*rising threateningly*). See eah. Awve ed enaff o this.

BARBARA (*quite sunny and fearless*). What did you come to us for?

BILL. Aw cam for maw gel, see? Aw cam to tike her aht o this and to brike er jawr for er.

BARBARA (*complacently*). You see I was right about your trade. (*Bill, on the point of retorting furiously, finds himself, to his great shame and terror, in danger of crying instead. He sits down again suddenly.*) Whats her name?

BILL (*dogged*). Er nime's Mog Ebbijem: thets wot her nime is.

BARBARA. Mog Habbijam! Oh, she's gone to Canning Town, to our barracks there.

BILL (*fortified by his resentment of Mog's perfidy*). Is she? (*Vindictively.*) Then Aw'm gowin to Kennintahn arter her. (*He crosses to the gate; hesitates; finally comes back at Barbara.*) Are you loyin to me to git shat o me?

BARBARA. I dont want to get shut of you. I want to keep you here and save your soul. Youd better stay: youre going to have a bad time today, Bill.

BILL. Oo's gowin to give it to me? You, preps?

BARBARA. Someone you dont believe in. But youll be glad afterwards.

BILL (*slinking off*). Aw'll gow to Kennintahn to be aht o reach o your tangue. (*Suddenly turning on her with intense malice.*) And if Aw downt fawnd Mog there, Aw'll cam beck and do two years for you, selp me Gawd if Aw downt!

BARBARA (*a shade kindlier, if possible*). It's no use, Bill. She's got another bloke.

BILL. Wot!

BARBARA. One of her own converts. He fell in love with her when he saw her with her soul saved, and her face clean, and her hair washed.

BILL (*surprised*). Wottud she wash it for, the carroty slat? It's red.

BARBARA. It's quite lovely now, because she wears a new look in her eyes with it. It's a pity youre too late. The new bloke has put your nose out of joint, Bill.

BILL. Aw'll put his nowse aht o joint for him. Not that Aw care a carse for er, mawnd thet. But Aw'll teach her to drop me as if Aw was dirt. And Aw'll teach him to meddle with maw judy. Wots iz bleedin nime?

BARBARA. Sergeant Todger Fairmile.

SHIRLEY (*rising with grim joy*). I'll go with him, miss. I want to see them two meet. I'll take him to the infirmary when it's over.

BILL (*to Shirley, with undissembled misgiving*). Is thet im you was speakin on?

SHIRLEY. Thats him.

BILL. Im that wrastled in the music awl?

SHIRLEY. The competitions at the National Sportin Club was worth nigh a hundred a year to him. He's gev em up now for religion; so he's a bit fresh for want of the exercise he was accustomed to. He'll be glad to see you. Come along.

BILL. Wots is wight?

SHIRLEY. Thirteen four. (*Bill's last hope expires.*)

BARBARA. Go and talk to him, Bill. He'll convert you.

SHIRLEY. He'll convert your head into a mashed potato.

BILL (*sullenly*). Aw aint afride of im. Aw aint afride of enny-body. Bat e can lick me. She's dan me. (*He sits down moodily on the edge of the horse trough.*)

SHIRLEY. You aint goin. I thought not. (*He resumes his seat.*)

BARBARA (*calling*). Jenny!

JENNY (*appearing at the shelter door with a plaster on the corner of her mouth*). Yes, Major.

BARBARA. Send Rummy Mitchens out to clear away here.

JENNY. I think she's afraid.

BARBARA (*her resemblance to her mother flashing out for a moment*). Nonsense! she must do as she's told.

JENNY (*calling into the shelter*). Rummy: the Major says you must come.

Jenny comes to Barbara, purposely keeping on the side next Bill, lest he should suppose that she shrank from him or bore malice.

BARBARA. Poor little Jenny! Are you tired? (*Looking at the wounded cheek.*) Does it hurt?

JENNY. No: it's all right now. It was nothing.

BARBARA (*critically*). It was as hard as he could hit, I expect. Poor Bill! You dont feel angry with him, do you?

JENNY. Oh no, no, no: indeed I dont, Major, bless his poor heart! (*Barbara kisses her; and she runs away merrily into the shelter. Bill writhes with an agonizing return of his new and alarming symptoms, but says nothing. Rummy Mitchens comes from the shelter.*)

BARBARA (*going to meet Rummy*). Now Rummy, bustle. Take in those mugs and plates to be washed; and throw the crumbs about for the birds.

Rummy takes the three plates and mugs; but Shirley takes back his mug from her, as there is still some milk left in it.

RUMMY. There aint any crumbs. This aint a time to waste good bread on birds.

PRICE (*appearing at the shelter door*). Gentleman come to see the shelter, Major. Says he's your father.

BARBARA. All right. Coming. (*Snobby goes back into the shelter, followed by Barbara.*)

RUMMY (*stealing across to Bill and addressing him in a subdued voice, but with intense conviction*). I'd av the lor of you, you flat eared pignosed potwalloper, if she'd let me. Youre no gentleman, to hit a lady in the face. (*Bill, with greater things moving in him, takes no notice.*)

SHIRLEY (*following her*). Here! in with you and dont get yourself into more trouble by talking.

RUMMY (*with hauteur*). I aint ad the pleasure o being hintro-duced to you, as I can remember. (*She goes into the shelter with the plates.*)

SHIRLEY. Thats the—

BILL (*savagely*). Downt you talk to me, d'ye eah? You lea me alown, or Aw'll do you a mischief. Aw'm not dirt under your feet, ennywy.

SHIRLEY (*calmly*). Dont you be afeerd. You aint such prime company that you need expect to be sought after. (*He is*

about to go into the shelter when Barbara comes out, with Undershaft on her right.)

BARBARA. Oh, there you are, Mr Shirley! (*Between them.*) This is my father: I told you he was a Secularist, didnt I? Perhaps youll be able to comfort one another.

UNDERSHAFT (*startled*). A Secularist! Not the least in the world: on the contrary, a confirmed mystic.

BARBARA. Sorry, I'm sure. By the way, papa, what is your religion? in case I have to introduce you again.

UNDERSHAFT. My religion? Well, my dear, I am a Million-aire. That is my religion.

BARBARA. Then I'm afraid you and Mr Shirley wont be able to comfort one another after all. Youre not a Millionaire, are you, Peter?

SHIRLEY. No; and proud of it.

UNDERSHAFT (*gravely*). Poverty, my friend, is not a thing to be proud of.

SHIRLEY (*angrily*). Who made your millions for you? Me and my like. Whats kep us poor? Keepin you rich. I wouldnt have your conscience, not for all your income.

UNDERSHAFT. I wouldnt have your income, not for all your conscience, Mr Shirley. (*He goes to the penthouse and sits down on a form.*)

BARBARA (*stopping Shirley adroitly as he is about to retort*). You wouldnt think he was my father, would you, Peter? Will you go into the shelter and lend the lasses a hand for a while: we're worked off our feet.

SHIRLEY (*bitterly*). Yes: I'm in their debt for a meal, aint I?

BARBARA. Oh, not because youre in their debt, but for love of them, Peter, for love of them. (*He cannot understand, and is rather scandalized.*) There! dont stare at me. In with you; and give that conscience of yours a holiday (*bustling him into the shelter*).

SHIRLEY (*as he goes in*). Ah! it's a pity you never was trained to use your reason, miss. Youd have been a very taking lecturer on Secularism.

Barbara turns to her father.

UNDERSHAFT. Never mind me, my dear. Go about your work; and let me watch it for a while.

BARBARA. All right.

UNDERSHAFT. For instance, whats the matter with that out-patient over there?

BARBARA (*looking at Bill, whose attitude has never changed, and whose expression of brooding wrath has deepened*). Oh, we shall cure him in no time. Just watch. (*She goes over to Bill and waits. He glances up at her and casts his eyes down again, uneasy, but grimmer than ever.*) It would be nice to just stamp on Mog Habbijam's face, wouldnt it, Bill?

BILL (*starting up from the trough in consternation*). It's a loy: Aw never said so. (*She shakes her head.*) Oo taold you wot was in moy mawnd?

BARBARA. Only your new friend.

BILL. Wot new friend?

BARBARA. The devil, Bill. When he gets round people they get miserable, just like you.

BILL (*with a heartbreaking attempt at devil-may-care cheerfulness*). Aw aint miserable. (*He sits down again, and stretches his legs in an attempt to seem indifferent.*)

BARBARA. Well, if youre happy, why dont you look happy, as we do?

BILL (*his legs curling back in spite of him*). Aw'm eppy enaff, Aw tell you. Woy cawnt you lea me alown? Wot ev I dan to you? Aw aint smashed your fice, ev Aw?

BARBARA (*softly: wooing his soul*). It's not me thats getting at you, Bill.

BILL. Oo else is it?

BARBARA. Somebody that doesn't intend you to smash women's faces, I suppose. Somebody or something that wants to make a man of you.

BILL (*blustering*). Mike a menn o m e! Aint Aw a menn? eh? Oo sez Aw'm not a menn?

BARBARA. Theres a man in you somewhere, I suppose. But why did he let you hit poor little Jenny Hill? That wasnt very manly of him, was it?

BILL (*tormented*). Ev dan wiv it, Aw tell you. Chack it. Aw'm sick o your Jenny Ill and er silly little fice.

BARBARA. Then why do you keep thinking about it? Why does it keep coming up against you in your mind? Youre not getting converted, are you?

BILL (*with conviction*). Not ME. Not lawkly.

BARBARA. Thats right, Bill. Hold out against it. Put out your strength. Dont lets get you cheap. Todger Fairmile said he wrestled for three nights against his salvation harder than he ever wrestled with the Jap at the music hall. He gave in to the Jap when his arm was going to break. But he didnt give in to his salvation until his heart was going to break. Perhaps youll escape that. You havnt any heart, have you?

BILL. Wot d'ye mean? Woy aint Aw got a awt the sime as ennybody else?

BARBARA. A man with a heart wouldnt have bashed poor little Jenny's face, would he?

BILL (*almost crying*). Ow, will you lea me alown? Ev Aw ever offered to meddle with you, that you cam neggin and provowkin me lawk this? (*He writhes convulsively from his eyes to his toes.*)

BARBARA (*with a steady soothing hand on his arm and a gentle voice that never lets him go*). It's your soul thats hurting you, Bill, and not me. Weve been through it all ourselves. Come with us, Bill. (*He looks wildly round.*) To brave manhood on earth and eternal glory in heaven. (*He is on the point of breaking down.*) Come. (*A drum is heard in the shelter; and Bill, with a gasp, escapes from the spell as Barbara turns quickly. Adolphus enters from the shelter with a big drum.*) Oh! there you are, Dolly. Let me introduce a new friend of mine, Mr Bill Walker. This is my bloke, Bill: Mr Cusins. (*Cusins salutes with his drumstick.*)

BILL. Gowin to merry im?

BARBARA. Yes.

BILL (*fervently*). Gawd elp im! Gaw-aw-aw-awd elp im!

BARBARA. Why? Do you think he wont be happy with me?

BILL. Awve aony ed to stend it for a mawnin: e'll ev to stend it for a lawftawm.

CUSINS. That is a frightful reflection, Mr Walker. But I cant tear myself away from her.

BILL. Well, Aw ken. (*To Barbara.*) Eah! do you knaow where Aw'm gowin to, and wot Aw'm gowin to do?

BARBARA. Yes: youre going to heaven; and youre coming back here before the week's out to tell me so.

BILL. You loy. Aw'm gowin to Kennintahn, to spit in Todger Fairmawl's eye. Aw beshed Jenny Ill's fice; an nar Aw'll git me aown fice beshed and cam beck and shaow it to er. Ee'll itt me ardern Aw itt er. Thatll mike us square. (*To Adolphus.*) Is thet fair or is it not? Youre a genlmn: you oughter knaow.

BARBARA. Two black eyes wont make one white one, Bill.

BILL. Aw didnt awst you. Cawnt you never keep your mahth shat? Oy awst the genlmn.

CUSINS (*reflectively*). Yes: I think youre right, Mr Walker. Yes: I should do it. It's curious: it's exactly what an ancient Greek would have done.

BARBARA. But what good will it do?

CUSINS. Well, it will give Mr Fairmile some exercise; and it will satisfy Mr Walker's soul.

BILL. Rot! there aint nao sach a thing as a saoul. Ah kin you tell wevver Awve a saoul or not? You never seen it.

BARBARA. Ive seen it hurting you when you went against it.

BILL (*with compressed aggravation*). If you was maw gel and took the word aht o me mahth lawk thet, Aw'd give you sathink youd feel urtin, Aw would. (*To Adolphus.*) You tike maw tip, mite. Stop er jawr; or youll doy afoah your tawm (*With intense expression.*) Wore aht: thets wot youll be: wore aht. (*He goes away through the gate.*)

CUSINS (*looking after him*). I wonder!

BARBARA. Dolly! (*Indignant, in her mother's manner.*)

CUSINS. Yes, my dear, it's very wearing to be in love with you. If it lasts, I quite think I shall die young.

BARBARA. Should you mind?

CUSINS. Not at all. (*He is suddenly softened, and kisses her over the drum, evidently not for the first time, as people cannot kiss over a big drum without practice. Undershaft coughs.*)

BARBARA. It's all right, papa, weve not forgotten you. Dolly: explain the place to papa: I havnt time. (*She goes busily into the shelter.*)

Undershaft and Adolphus now have the yard to themselves. Undershaft, seated on a form, and still keenly attentive, looks hard at Adolphus. Adolphus looks hard at him.

UNDERSHAFT. I fancy you guess something of what is in my mind, Mr Cusins. (*Cusins flourishes his drumsticks as if in the act of beating a lively rataplan, but makes no sound.*) Exactly so. But suppose Barbara finds you out!

CUSINS. You know, I do not admit that I am imposing on Barbara. I am quite genuinely interested in the views of the Salvation Army. The fact is, I am a sort of collector of religions; and the curious thing is that I find I can believe them all. By the way, have you any religion?

UNDERSHAFT. Yes.

CUSINS. Anything out of the common?

UNDERSHAFT. Only that there are two things necessary to Salvation.

CUSINS (*disappointed, but polite*). Ah, the Church Catechism. Charles Lomax also belongs to the Established Church.

UNDERSHAFT. The two things are—

CUSINS. Baptism and—

UNDERSHAFT. No. Money and gunpowder.

CUSINS (*surprised, but interested*). That is the general opinion of our governing classes. The novelty is in hearing any man confess it.

UNDERSHAFT. Just so.

CUSINS. Excuse me: is there any place in your religion for honor, justice, truth, love, mercy and so forth?

UNDERSHAFT. Yes: they are the graces and luxuries of a rich, strong, and safe life.

CUSINS. Suppose one is forced to choose between them and money or gunpowder?

UNDERSHAFT. Choose money and gunpowder; for without enough of both you cannot afford the others.

CUSINS. That is your religion?

UNDERSHAFT. Yes.

The cadence of this reply makes a full close in the conversation. Cusins twists his face dubiously and contemplates Undershaft. Undershaft contemplates him.

CUSINS. Barbara wont stand that. You will have to choose between your religion and Barbara.

UNDERSHAFT. So will you, my friend. She will find out that that drum of yours is hollow.

CUSINS. Father Undershaft: you are mistaken: I am a sincere Salvationist. You do not understand the Salvation Army. It is the army of joy, of love, of courage: it has banished the fear and remorse and despair of the old hell-ridden evangelical sects: it marches to fight the devil with trumpet and drum, with music and dancing, with banner and palm, as becomes a sally from heaven by its happy garrison. It picks the waster out of the public house and makes a man of him: it finds a worm wriggling in a back kitchen, and lo! a woman! Men and women of rank too, sons and daughters of the Highest. It takes the poor professor of Greek, the most artificial and self-suppressed of human creatures, from his meal of roots, and lets loose the rhapsodist in him; reveals the true worship of Dionysos to him; sends him down the public street drumming dithyrambs. (*He plays a thundering flourish on the drum.*)

UNDERSHAFT. You will alarm the shelter.

CUSINS. Oh, they are accustomed to these sudden ecstasies. However, if the drum worries you— (*He pockets the drumsticks; unhooks the drum; and stands it on the ground opposite the gateway.*)

UNDERSHAFT. Thank you.

CUSINS. You remember what Euripides says about your money and gunpowder?

UNDERSHAFT. No.

CUSINS (*declaiming*).

> One and another
> In money and guns may outpass his brother;
> And men in their millions float and flow
> And seethe with a million hopes as leaven;
> And they win their will; or they miss their will;
> And their hopes are dead or are pined for still;
> > But who'er can know
> > As the long days go
> That to live is happy, has found his heaven.

My translation: what do you think of it?

UNDERSHAFT. I think, my friend, that if you wish to know, as the long days go, that to live is happy, you must first acquire money enough for a decent life, and power enough to be your own master.

CUSINS. You are damnably discouraging. (*He resumes his declamation.*)

> Is it so hard a thing to see
> That the spirit of God—whate'er it be—
> The law that abides and changes not, ages long,
> The Eternal and Nature-born: these things be strong?
> What else is Wisdom? What of Man's endeavor,
> Or God's high grace so lovely and so great?
> To stand from fear set free? to breathe and wait?
> To hold a hand uplifted over Fate?
> And shall not Barbara be loved for ever?

UNDERSHAFT. Euripides mentions Barbara, does he?

CUSINS. It is a fair translation. The word means Loveliness.

UNDERSHAFT. May I ask—as Barbara's father—how much a year she is to be loved for ever on?

CUSINS. As Barbara's father, that is more your affair than mine. I can feed her by teaching Greek: that is about all.

UNDERSHAFT. Do you consider it a good match for her?

CUSINS (*with polite obstinacy*). Mr Undershaft: I am in many ways a weak, timid, ineffectual person; and my health is far from satisfactory. But whenever I feel that I must have anything, I get it, sooner or later. I feel that way about Barbara. I dont like marriage: I feel intensely afraid of it; and I dont know what I shall do with Barbara or what she will do with me. But I feel that I and nobody else must marry her. Please regard that as settled.—Not that I wish to be arbitrary; but why should I waste your time in discussing what is inevitable?

UNDERSHAFT. You mean that you will stick at nothing: not even the conversion of the Salvation Army to the worship of Dionysos.

CUSINS. The business of the Salvation Army is to save, not to wrangle about the name of the pathfinder. Dionysos or another: what does it matter?

UNDERSHAFT (*rising and approaching him*). Professor Cusins: you are a young man after my own heart.

CUSINS. Mr Undershaft: you are, as far as I am able to gather, a most infernal old rascal; but you appeal very strongly to my sense of ironic humor.

Undershaft mutely offers his hand. They shake.

UNDERSHAFT (*suddenly concentrating himself*). And now to business.

CUSINS. Pardon me. We are discussing religion. Why go back to such an uninteresting and unimportant subject as business?

UNDERSHAFT. Religion is our business at present, because it is through religion alone that we can win Barbara.

CUSINS. Have you, too, fallen in love with Barbara?

UNDERSHAFT. Yes, with a father's love.

CUSINS. A father's love for a grown-up daughter is the most dangerous of all infatuations. I apologize for mentioning my own pale, coy, mistrustful fancy in the same breath with it.

UNDERSHAFT. Keep to the point. We have to win her; and we are neither of us Methodists.

CUSINS. That doesnt matter. The power Barbara wields here—the power that wields Barbara herself—is not Calvinism, not Presbyterianism, not Methodism—

UNDERSHAFT. Not Greek Paganism either, eh?

CUSINS. I admit that. Barbara is quite original in her religion.

UNDERSHAFT (*triumphantly*). Aha! Barbara Undershaft would be. Her inspiration comes from within herself.

CUSINS. How do you suppose it got there?

UNDERSHAFT (*in towering excitement*). It is the Undershaft inheritance. I shall hand on my torch to my daughter. She shall make my converts and preach my gospel—

CUSINS. What! Money and gunpowder!

UNDERSHAFT. Yes, money and gunpowder. Freedom and power. Command of life and command of death.

CUSINS (*urbanely: trying to bring him down to earth*). This is extremely interesting, Mr Undershaft. Of course you know that you are mad.

UNDERSHAFT (*with redoubled force*). And you?

CUSINS. Oh, mad as a hatter. You are welcome to my secret since I have discovered yours. But I am astonished. Can a madman make cannons?

UNDERSHAFT. Would anyone else than a madman make them? And now (*with surging energy*) question for question. Can a sane man translate Euripides?

CUSINS. No.

UNDERSHAFT (*seizing him by the shoulder*). Can a sane woman make a man of a waster or a woman of a worm?

CUSINS (*reeling before the storm*). Father Colossus—Mammoth Millionaire—

UNDERSHAFT (*pressing him*). Are there two mad people or three in this Salvation shelter today?

CUSINS. You mean Barbara is as mad as we are?

UNDERSHAFT (*pushing him lightly off and resuming his equanimity suddenly and completely*). Pooh, Professor! let us call things by their proper names. I am a millionaire; you are a poet; Barbara is a savior of souls. What have we three to do with the common mob of slaves and idolaters? (*He sits down again with a shrug of contempt for the mob.*)

CUSINS. Take care! Barbara is in love with the common people. So am I. Have you never felt the romance of that love?

UNDERSHAFT (*cold and sardonic*). Have you ever been in love with Poverty, like St Francis? Have you ever been in love with Dirt, like St Simeon! Have you ever been in love with disease and suffering, like our nurses and philanthropists? Such passions are not virtues, but the most unnatural of all the vices. This love of the common people may please an earl's granddaughter and a university professor; but I have been a common man and a poor man; and it has no romance for me. Leave it to the poor to pretend that poverty is a blessing: leave it to the coward to make a religion of his cowardice by preaching humility: we know better than that. We three must stand together above the common people: how else can we help their children to climb up beside us? Barbara must belong to us, not to the Salvation Army.

CUSINS. Well, I can only say that if you think you will get her away from the Salvation Army by talking to her as you have been talking to me, you dont know Barbara.

UNDERSHAFT. My friend: I never ask for what I can buy.

CUSINS (*in a white fury*). Do I understand you to imply that you can buy Barbara?

UNDERSHAFT. No; but I can buy the Salvation Army.

CUSINS. Quite impossible.

UNDERSHAFT. You shall see. All religious organizations exist by selling themselves to the rich.

CUSINS. Not the Army. That is the Church of the poor.

UNDERSHAFT. All the more reason for buying it.

CUSINS. I dont think you quite know what the Army does for the poor.

UNDERSHAFT. Oh yes I do. It draws their teeth: that is enough for me as a man of business.

CUSINS. Nonsense! It makes them sober—

UNDERSHAFT. I prefer sober workmen. The profits are larger.

CUSINS. —honest—

UNDERSHAFT. Honest workmen are the most economical.

CUSINS. —attached to their homes—

UNDERSHAFT. So much the better: they will put up with anything sooner than change their shop.

CUSINS. —happy—

UNDERSHAFT. An invaluable safeguard against revolution.

CUSINS. —unselfish—

UNDERSHAFT. Indifferent to their own interests, which suits me exactly.

CUSINS. —with their thoughts on heavenly things—

UNDERSHAFT (*rising*). And not on Trade Unionism nor Socialism. Excellent.

CUSINS (*revolted*). You really are an infernal old rascal.

UNDERSHAFT (*indicating Peter Shirley, who has just come from the shelter and strolled dejectedly down the yard between them*). And this is an honest man!

SHIRLEY. Yes; and what av I got by it? (*He passes on bitterly and sits on the form, in the corner of the penthouse.*)

Snobby Price, beaming sanctimoniously, and Jenny Hill, with a tambourine full of coppers, come from the shelter and go to the drum, on which Jenny begins to count the money.

UNDERSHAFT (*replying to Shirley*). Oh, your employers must have got a good deal by it from first to last. (*He sits on the table, with one foot on the side form. Cusins, overwhelmed, sits down on the same form nearer the shelter. Barbara comes from the shelter to the middle of the yard. She is excited and a little overwrought.*)

BARBARA. Weve just had a splendid experience meeting at the other gate in Cripps's lane. Ive hardly ever seen them so much moved as they were by your confession, Mr Price.

PRICE. I could almost be glad of my past wickedness if I could believe that it would elp to keep hathers stright.

BARBARA. So it will, Snobby. How much, Jenny?

JENNY. Four and tenpence, Major.

BARBARA. Oh Snobby, if you had given your poor mother just one more kick, we should have got the whole five shillings!

PRICE. If she heard you say that, miss, she'd be sorry I didnt. But I'm glad. Oh what a joy it will be to her when she hears I'm saved!

UNDERSHAFT. Shall I contribute the odd twopence, Barbara? The millionaire's mite, eh? (*He takes a couple of pennies from his pocket.*)

BARBARA. How did you make that twopence?

UNDERSHAFT. As usual. By selling cannons, torpedoes, submarines, and my new patent Grand Duke hand grenade.

BARBARA. Put it back in your pocket. You cant buy your salvation here for twopence: you must work it out.

UNDERSHAFT. Is twopence not enough? I can afford a little more, if you press me.

BARBARA. Two million millions would not be enough. There is bad blood on your hands; and nothing but good blood can cleanse them. Money is no use. Take it away. (*She turns to Cusins.*) Dolly: you must write another letter for me to the papers. (*He makes a wry face.*) Yes: I know you dont like it; but it must be done. The starvation this winter is beating us: everybody is unemployed. The General says we must close this shelter if we cant get more money. I force the collections at the meetings until I am ashamed: dont I, Snobby?

PRICE. It's a fair treat to see you work it, miss. The way you got them up from three-and-six to four-and-ten with that

hymn, penny by penny and verse by verse, was a caution. Not a Cheap Jack on Mile End Waste could touch you at it.

BARBARA. Yes; but I wish we could do without it. I am getting at last to think more of the collection than of the people's souls. And what are those hatfuls of pence and halfpence? We want thousands! tens of thousands! hundreds of thousands! I want to convert people, not to be always begging for the Army in a way I'd die sooner than beg for myself.

UNDERSHAFT (*in profound irony*). Genuine unselfishness is capable of anything, my dear.

BARBARA (*unsuspectingly, as she turns away to take the money from the drum and put it in a bag she carries*). Yes, isnt it? (*Undershaft looks sardonically at Cusins.*)

CUSINS (*aside to Undershaft*). Mephistopheles! Machiavelli!

BARBARA (*tears coming into her eyes as she ties the bag and pockets it*). How are we to feed them? I cant talk religion to a man with bodily hunger in his eyes. (*Almost breaking down.*) It's frightful.

JENNY (*running to her*). Major, dear—

BARBARA (*rebounding*). No: dont comfort me. It will be all right. We shall get the money.

UNDERSHAFT. How?

JENNY. By praying for it, of course. Mrs Baines says she prayed for it last night; and she has never prayed for it in vain: never once. (*She goes to the gate and looks out into the street.*)

BARBARA (*who has dried her eyes and regained her composure*). By the way, dad, Mrs Baines has come to march with us to our big meeting this afternoon; and she is very anxious to meet you, for some reason or other. Perhaps she'll convert you.

UNDERSHAFT. I shall be delighted, my dear.

JENNY (*at the gate: excitedly*). Major! Major! heres that man back again.

BARBARA. What man?

JENNY. The man that hit me. Oh, I hope he's coming back to join us.

Bill Walker, with frost on his jacket, comes through the gate, his hands deep in his pockets and his chin sunk between his shoulders, like a cleaned-out gambler. He halts between Barbara and the drum.

BARBARA. Hullo, Bill! Back already!

BILL (*nagging at her*). Bin talkin ever sence, ev you?

BARBARA. Pretty nearly. Well, has Todger paid you out for poor Jenny's jaw?

BILL. Nao e aint.

BARBARA. I thought your jacket looked a bit snowy.

BILL. Sao it is snaowy. You want to knaow where the snaow cam from, downt you?

BARBARA. Yes.

BILL. Well, it cam from orf the grahnd in Pawkinses Corner in Kennintahn. It got rabbed orf be maw shaoulders: see?

BARBARA. Pity you didnt rub some off with your knees, Bill! That would have done you a lot of good.

BILL (*with sour mirthless humor*). Aw was sivin anather menn's knees at the tawm. E was kneelin on moy ed, e was.

JENNY. Who was kneeling on your head?

BILL. Todger was. E was pryin for me: pryin camfortable wiv me as a cawpet. Sow was Mog. Sao was the aol bloomin meetin. Mog she sez "Ow Lawd brike is stabborn sperrit; bat downt urt is dear art." Thet was wot she said. "Downt urt is dear art"! An er blowk—thirteen stun four!—kneelin wiv all is wight on me. Fanny, aint it?

JENNY. Oh no. We're sorry, Mr Walker.

BARBARA (*enjoying it frankly*). Nonsense! of course it's funny. Served you right, Bill! You must have done something to him first.

BILL (*doggedly*). Aw did wot Aw said Aw'd do. Aw spit in is eye. E looks ap at the skoy and sez, "Ow that Aw should be fahnd worthy to be spit upon for the gospel's sike!" e sez; an Mog sez "Glaory Allelloolier!"; an then e called me Braddher, an dahned me as if Aw was a kid and e was me mather worshin me a Setterda nawt. Aw ednt jast nao shaow wiv im at all. Arf the street pryed; an the tather arf larfed fit to split theirselves. (*To Barbara.*) There! are you settisfawd nah?

BARBARA (*her eyes dancing*). Wish I'd been there, Bill.

BILL. Yus: youd a got in a hextra bit o talk on me, wouldnt you?

JENNY. I'm so sorry, Mr Walker.

BILL (*fiercely*). Downt you gow bein sorry for me: youve no call. Listen eah. Aw browk your jawr.

JENNY. No, it didn't hurt me: indeed it didnt, except for a moment. It was only that I was frightened.

BILL. Aw downt want to be forgive be you, or be ennybody. Wot Aw did Aw'll py for. Aw trawd to gat me aown jawr browk to settisfaw you—

JENNY (*distressed*). Oh no—

BILL (*impatiently*). Tell y Aw did: cawnt you listen to wots bein taold you? All Aw got be it was being mide a sawt of in the pablic street for me pines. Well, if Aw cawnt settisfaw you one wy, Aw ken anather. Listen eah! Aw ed two quid sived agen the frost; an Awve a pahnd of it left. A mite o mawn last week ed words with the judy e's gowin to merry. E give er wot-for; an e's bin fawnd fifteen bob. E ed a rawt to itt er cause they was gowin to be merrid; but Aw ednt nao rawt to itt you; sao put anather fawv bob on an call it a pahnd's worth. (*He produces a sovereign.*) Eahs the manney. Tike it; and lets ev no more o your forgivin an pryin and your Mijor jawrin me. Let wot Aw dan be dan an pide for; and let there be a end of it.

JENNY. Oh, I couldnt take it, Mr Walker. But if you would give a shilling or two to poor Rummy Mitchens! you really did hurt her; and she's old.

BILL (*contemptuously*). Not lawkly. Aw'd give her anather as soon as look at er. Let her ev the lawr o me as she threat-ened! She aint forgiven me: not mach. Wot Aw dan to er is not on me mawnd—wot she (*indicating Barbara*) mawt call on me conscience—no more than stickin a pig. It's this Christian gime o yours that Aw wownt ev plyed agen me: this bloomin forgivin an neggin an jawrin that mikes a menn thet sore that iz lawf's a burdn to im. Aw wownt ev it, Aw tell you; sao tike your manney and stop thraowin your silly beshed fice hap agen me.

JENNY. Major: may I take a little of it for the Army?

BARBARA. No: the Army is not to be bought. We want your soul, Bill; and we'll take nothing less.

BILL (*bitterly*). Aw knaow. Me an maw few shillins is not good enaff for you. Youre a earl's grendorter, you are. Nathink less than a andered pahnd for you.

UNDERSHAFT. Come, Barbara! you could do a great deal of good with a hundred pounds. If you will set this gentleman's mind at ease by taking his pound, I will give the other ninety-nine.

Bill, dazed by such opulence, instinctively touches his cap.

BARBARA. Oh, youre too extravagant, papa. Bill offers twenty pieces of silver. All you need offer is the other ten. That will make the standard price to buy anybody who's for sale. I'm not; and the Army's not. (*To Bill.*) Youll never have another quiet moment, Bill, until you come round to us. You cant stand out against your salvation.

BILL (*sullenly*). Aw cawnt stand aht agen music awl wrastlers and awtful tangued women. Awve offered to py. Aw can do no more. Tike it or leave it. There it is. (*He throws the sovereign on the drum, and sits down on the horse-trough. The coin fascinates Snobby Price, who takes an early opportunity of dropping his cap on it.*)

Mrs Baines comes from the shelter. She is dressed as a Salvation Army Commissioner. She is an earnest looking woman of about 40, with a caressing, urgent voice, and an appealing manner.

BARBARA. This is my father, Mrs Baines (*Undershaft comes from the table, taking his hat off with marked civility.*) Try what you can do with him. He wont listen to me, because he remembers what a fool I was when I was a baby. (*She leaves them together and chats with Jenny.*)

MRS BAINES. Have you been shewn over the shelter Mr Undershaft? You know the work we're doing, of course.

UNDERSHAFT (*very civilly*). The whole nation knows it, Mrs Baines.

MRS BAINES. No, sir: the whole nation does not know it, or we should not be crippled as we are for want of money to carry our work through the length and breadth of the land. Let me tell you that there would have been rioting this winter in London but for us.

UNDERSHAFT. You really think so?

MRS BAINES. I know it. I remember 1886, when you rich gentlemen hardened your hearts against the cry of the poor. They broke the windows of your clubs in Pall Mall.

UNDERSHAFT (*gleaming with approval of their method*). And the Mansion House Fund went up next day from thirty thousand pounds to seventy-nine thousand! I remember quite well.

MRS BAINES. Well, wont you help me to get at the people? They wont break windows then. Come here, Price. Let me shew you to this gentleman. (*Price comes to be inspected.*) Do you remember the window breaking?

PRICE. My ole father thought it was the revolution, maam.

MRS BAINES. Would you break windows now?

PRICE. Oh no, maam. The windows of eaven av bin opened to me. I know now that the rich man is a sinner like myself.

RUMMY (*appearing above at the loft door*). Snobby Price!

SNOBBY. Wot is it?

RUMMY. Your mother's askin for you at the other gate in Cripps's Lane. She's heard about your confession. (*Price turns pale.*)

MRS BAINES. Go, Mr Price; and pray with her.

JENNY. You can go through the shelter, Snobby.

PRICE (*to Mrs. Baines*). I couldnt face her now, maam, with all the weight of my sins fresh on me. Tell her she'll find her son at ome, waitin for her in prayer. (*He skulks off through the gate, incidentally stealing the sovereign on his way out by picking up his cap from the drum.*)

MRS BAINES (*with swimming eyes*). You see how we take the anger and the bitterness against you out of their hearts, Mr Undershaft.

UNDERSHAFT. It is certainly most convenient and gratifying to all large employers of labor, Mrs Baines.

MRS BAINES. Barbara: Jenny: I have good news: most wonderful news. (*Jenny runs to her.*) My prayers have been answered. I told you they would, Jenny, didnt I?

JENNY. Yes, yes.

BARBARA (*moving nearer to the drum*). Have we got money enough to keep the shelter open?

MRS BAINES. I hope we shall have enough to keep all the shelters open. Lord Saxmundham has promised us five thousand pounds—

BARBARA. Hooray!

JENNY. Glory!

MRS BAINES. —if—

BARBARA. "If!" If what?

MRS BAINES. —if five other gentlemen will give a thousand each to make it up to ten thousand.

BARBARA. Who is Lord Saxmundham? I never heard of him.

UNDERSHAFT (*who has pricked up his ears at the peer's name, and is now watching Barbara curiously*). A new creation, my dear. You have heard of Sir Horace Bodger?

BARBARA. Bodger! Do you mean the distiller? Bodger's whisky!

UNDERSHAFT. That is the man. He is one of the greatest of our public benefactors. He restored the cathedral at Hakington. They made him a baronet for that. He gave half a million to the funds of his party: they made him a baron for that.

SHIRLEY. What will they give him for the five thousand?

UNDERSHAFT. There is nothing left to give him. So the five thousand, I should think, is to save his soul.

MRS BAINES. Heaven grant it may! Oh Mr Undershaft, you have some very rich friends. Cant you help us towards the other five thousand? We are going to hold a great meeting this afternoon at the Assembly Hall in the Mile End Road. If I could only announce that one gentleman had come forward to support Lord Saxmundham, others would follow. Dont you know somebody? couldnt you? wouldnt you? (*Her eyes fill with tears.*) oh, think of those poor people, Mr Undershaft: think of how much it means to them, and how little to a great man like you.

UNDERSHAFT (*sardonically gallant*). Mrs Baines: you are irresistible. I cant disappoint you; and I cant deny myself the satisfaction of making Bodger pay up. You shall have your five thousand pounds.

MRS BAINES. Thank God!

UNDERSHAFT. You dont thank me?

MRS BAINES. Oh sir, dont try to be cynical: dont be ashamed of being a good man. The Lord will bless you abundantly; and our prayers will be like a strong fortification round you all the days of your life. (*With a touch of caution.*) You will let me have the cheque to shew at the meeting, wont you? Jenny: go in and fetch a pen and ink. (*Jenny runs to the shelter door.*)

UNDERSHAFT. Do not disturb Miss Hill: I have a fountain pen. (*Jenny halts. He sits at the table and writes the cheque. Cusins rises to make room for him. They all watch him silently.*)

BILL (*cynically, aside to Barbara, his voice and accent horribly debased*). Wot prawce selvytion nah?

BARBARA. Stop. (*Undershaft stops writing: they all turn to her in surprise.*) Mrs Baines: are you really going to take this money?

MRS BAINES (*astonished*). Why not, dear?

BARBARA. Why not! Do you know what my father is? Have you forgotten that Lord Saxmundham is Bodger the whisky man? Do you remember how we implored the County Council to stop him from writing Bodger's Whisky in letters of fire against the sky; so that the poor drink-ruined creatures on the Embankment could not wake up from their snatches of sleep without being reminded of their deadly thirst by that wicked sky sign? Do you know that the worst thing I have had to fight here is not the devil, but Bodger, Bodger, Bodger, with his whisky, his distilleries, and his tied houses? Are you going to make our shelter another tied house for him, and ask me to keep it?

BILL. Rotten dranken whisky it is too.

MRS BAINES. Dear Barbara: Lord Saxmundham has a soul to be saved like any of us. If heaven has found the way to make a good use of his money, are we to set ourselves up against the answer to our prayers?

BARBARA. I know he has a soul to be saved. Let him come down here; and I'll do my best to help him to his salvation. But he wants to send his cheque down to buy us, and go on being as wicked as ever.

UNDERSHAFT (*with a reasonableness which Cusins alone perceives to be ironical*). My dear Barbara: alcohol is a very necessary article. It heals the sick—

BARBARA. It does nothing of the sort.

UNDERSHAFT. Well, it assists the doctor: that is perhaps a less questionable way of putting it. It makes life bearable to millions of people who could not endure their existence if they were quite sober. It enables Parliament to do things at eleven at night that no sane person would do at eleven in the morning. Is it Bodger's fault that this inestimable gift is deplorably abused by less than one per cent of the poor? (*He turns again to the table; signs the cheque; and crosses it.*)

MRS BAINES. Barbara: will there be less drinking or more if all those poor souls we are saving come tomorrow and find the doors of our shelters shut in their faces? Lord Saxmundham gives us the money to stop drinking—to take his own business from him.

CUSINS (*impishly*). Pure self-sacrifice on Bodger's part, clearly! Bless dear Bodger! (*Barbara almost breaks down as Adolphus, too, fails her.*)

UNDERSHAFT (*tearing out the cheque and pocketing the book as he rises and goes past Cusins to Mrs Baines*). I also, Mrs Baines, may claim a little disinterestedness. Think of my business! think of the widows and orphans! the men and lads torn to pieces with shrapnel and poisoned with lyddite! (*Mrs Baines shrinks; but he goes on remorselessly*) the oceans of blood, not one drop of which is shed in a really just cause! the ravaged crops! the peaceful peasant forced, women and men, to till their fields, under the fire of opposing armies on pain of starvation! the bad blood of the fierce little cowards at home who egg on others to fight for the gratification of their national vanity! All this makes money for me: I am never richer, never busier than when the papers are full of it. Well, it is your work to preach peace on earth and goodwill to men. (*Mrs Baines's face lights up again.*) Every convert you make is a vote against war. (*Her lips move in prayer.*) Yet I give you this money to help you to hasten my own commercial ruin. (*He gives her the cheque.*)

CUSINS (*mounting the form in an ecstasy of mischief*). The millennium will be inaugurated by the unselfishness of Undershaft and Bodger. Oh be joyful! (*He takes the drumsticks from his pocket and flourishes them.*)

MRS BAINES (*taking the cheque*). The longer I live the more proof I see that there is an Infinite Goodness that turns everything to the work of salvation sooner or later. Who would have thought that any good could have come out of war and drink? And yet their profits are brought today to the feet of salvation to do its blessed work. (*She is affected to tears.*)

JENNY (*running to Mrs Baines and throwing her arms around her*). Oh dear! how blessed, how glorious it all is!

CUSINS (*in a convulsion of irony*). Let us seize this unspeakable moment. Let us march to the great meeting at once. Excuse me just an instant. (*He rushes into the shelter. Jenny takes her tambourine from the drum head.*)

MRS BAINES. Mr Undershaft: have you ever seen a thousand people fall on their knees with one impulse and pray? Come with us to the meeting. Barbara shall tell them that the Army is saved, and saved through you.

CUSINS (*returning impetuously from the shelter with a flag and a trombone, and coming between Mrs Baines and Undershaft*). You shall carry the flag down the first street, Mrs Baines. (*He gives her the flag.*) Mr Undershaft is a gifted trombonist: he shall intone an Olympian diapason to the West Ham Salvation March. (*Aside to Undershaft, as he forces the trombone on him.*) Blow, Machiavelli, blow.

UNDERSHAFT (*aside to him, as he takes the trombone*). The trumpet in Zion! (*Cusins rushes to the drum, which he takes up and puts on. Undershaft continues, aloud.*) I will do my best. I could vamp a bass if I knew the tune.

CUSINS. It is a wedding chorus from one of Donizetti's operas; but we have converted it. We convert everything to good here, including Bodger. You remember the chorus. "For thee immense rejoicing—immenso giubilo—immenso giubilo." (*With drum obbligato.*) Rum tum ti tum, tum tum ti ta—

BARBARA. Dolly: you are breaking my heart.

CUSINS. What is a broken heart more or less here? Dionysos Undershaft has descended. I am possessed.

MRS BAINES. Come, Barbara: I must have my dear Major to carry the flag with me.

JENNY. Yes, yes, Major darling.

CUSINS (*snatches the tambourine out of Jenny's hand and mutely offers it to Barbara*).

BARBARA (*coming forward a little as she puts the offer behind her with a shudder, whilst Cusins recklessly tosses the tambourine back to Jenny and goes to the gate*). I cant come.

JENNY. Not come!

MRS BAINES (*with tears in her eyes*). Barbara: do you think I am wrong to take the money?

BARBARA (*impulsively going to her and kissing her*). No, no: God help you, dear, you must: you are saving the Army. Go; and may you have a great meeting!

JENNY. But arnt you coming?

BARBARA. No. (*She begins taking off the silver S brooch from her collar.*)

MRS BAINES. Barbara: what are you doing?

JENNY. Why are you taking your badge off? You cant be going to leave us, Major.

BARBARA (*quietly*). Father: come here.

UNDERSHAFT (*coming to her*). My dear! (*Seeing that she is going to pin the badge on his collar, he retreats to the penthouse in some alarm.*)

BARBARA (*following him*). Dont be frightened. (*She pins the badge on and steps back towards the table, shewing him to the others.*) There! It's not much for £5000, is it?

MRS BAINES. Barbara: if you wont come and pray with us, promise me you will pray for us.

BARBARA. I cant pray now. Perhaps I shall never pray again.

MRS BAINES. Barbara!

JENNY. Major!

BARBARA (*almost delirious*). I cant bear any more. Quick march!

CUSINS (*calling to the procession in the street outside*). Off we go. Play up, there! Immenso giubilo. (*He gives the time with his drum; and the band strikes up the march, which rapidly becomes more distant as the procession moves briskly away.*)

MRS BAINES. I must go, dear. Youre overworked: you will be all right tomorrow. We'll never lose you. Now Jenny: step out with the old flag. Blood and Fire! (*She marches out through the gate with her flag.*)

JENNY. Glory Hallelujah! (*Flourishing her tambourine and marching.*)

UNDERSHAFT (*to Cusins, as he marches out past him easing the slide of his trombone*). "My ducats and my daughter"!

CUSINS (*following him out*). Money and gunpowder!

BARBARA. Drunkenness and Murder! My God: why hast thou forsaken me?

She sinks on the form with her face buried in her hands. The march passes away into silence. Bill Walker steals across to her.

BILL (*taunting*). Wot prawce selvytion nah?

SHIRLEY. Dont you hit her when she's down.

BILL. She itt me wen aw wiz dahn. Waw shouldnt Aw git a bit o me aown beck?

BARBARA (*raising her head*). I didnt take your money, Bill. (*She crosses the yard to the gate and turns her back on the two men to hide her face from them.*)

BILL (*sneering after her*). Naow, it warnt enaff for you. (*Turning to the drum, he misses the money.*) Ellow! If you aint took it sammun else ez. Weres it gorn? Bly me if Jenny Ill didnt tike it arter all!

RUMMY (*screaming at him from the loft*). You lie, you dirty blackguard! Snobby Price pinched it off the drum when he took up his cap. I was up here all the time an see im do it.

BILL. Wot! Stowl maw manney! Waw didnt you call thief on him, you silly aold macker you?

RUMMY. To serve you aht for ittin me across the fice. It's cost y'pahnd, that az. (*Raising a paean of squalid triumph.*) I done you. I'm even with you. Ive ad it aht o y—(*Bill snatches up Shirley's mug and hurls it at her. She slams the loft door and vanishes. The mug smashes against the door and falls in fragments.*)

BILL (*beginning to chuckle*). Tell us, aol menn, wot o'clock this mawnin was it wen im as they call Snobby Prawce was sived?

BARBARA (*turning to him more composedly, and with unspoiled sweetness*). About half past twelve, Bill. And he pinched

your pound at a quarter to two. I know. Well, you cant afford to lose it. I'll send it to you.

BILL (*his voice and accent suddenly improving*). Not if Aw wiz to stawve for it. Aw aint to be bought.

SHIRLEY. Aint you? Youd sell yourself to the devil for a pint o beer; only there aint no devil to make the offer.

BILL (*unshamed*). Sao Aw would, mite, and often ev, cheerful. But she cawnt baw me. (*Approaching Barbara.*) You wanted maw saoul, did you? Well, you aint got it.

BARBARA. I nearly got it, Bill. But weve sold it back to you for ten thousand pounds.

SHIRLEY. And dear at the money!

BARBARA. No, Peter: it was worth more than money.

BILL (*salvationproof*). It's nao good: you cawnt get rahnd me nah. Aw downt blieve in it; and Awve seen tody that Aw was rawt. (*Going.*) Sao long, aol soupkitchener! Ta, ta, Mijor Earl's Grendorter! (*Turning at the gate.*) Wot prawce selvytion nah? Snobby Prawce! Ha! ha!

BARBARA (*offering her hand*). Goodbye, Bill.

BILL (*taken aback, half plucks his cap off; then shoves it on again defiantly*). Git aht. (*Barbara drops her hand, discouraged. He has a twinge of remorse.*) But thets aw rawt, you knaow. Nathink pasnl. Naow mellice. Sao long, Judy. (*He goes.*)

BARBARA. No malice. So long, Bill.

SHIRLEY (*shaking his head*). You make too much of him, miss, in your innocence.

BARBARA (*going to him*). Peter: I'm like you now. Cleaned out, and lost my job.

SHIRLEY. Youve youth an hope. Thats two better than me.

BARBARA. I'll get you a job, Peter. Thats hope for you: the youth will have to be enough for me. (*She counts her money.*) I have just enough left for two teas at Lockharts, a Rowton doss for you, and my tram and bus home. (*He frowns and rises with offended pride. She takes his arm.*) Dont be proud, Peter: it's sharing between friends. And promise me youll talk to me and not let me cry. (*She draws him towards the gate.*)

SHIRLEY. Well, I'm not accustomed to talk to the like of you—

BARBARA (*urgently*). Yes, yes: you must talk to me. Tell me about Tom Paine's books and Bradlaugh's lectures. Come along.

SHIRLEY. Ah, if you would only read Tom Paine in the proper spirit, miss! (*They go out through the gate together.*)

ACT 3

Next day after lunch Lady Britomart is writing in the library in Wilton Crescent. Sarah is reading in the armchair near the window. Barbara, in ordinary fashionable dress, pale and brooding, is on the settee. Charles Lomax enters. He starts on seeing Barbara fashionably attired and in low spirits.

LOMAX. Youve left off your uniform!

Barbara says nothing; but an expression of pain passes over her face.

LADY BRITOMART (*warning him in low tones to be careful*). Charles!

LOMAX (*much concerned, coming behind the settee and bending sympathetically over Barbara*). I'm awfully sorry, Barbara. You know I helped you all I could with the concertina and so forth. (*Momentously.*) Still, I have never shut my eyes to the fact that there is a certain amount of tosh about the Salvation Army. Now the claims of the Church of England—

LADY BRITOMART. Thats enough, Charles. Speak of something suited to your mental capacity.

LOMAX. But surely the Church of England is suited to all our capacities.

BARBARA (*pressing his hand*). Thank you for your sympathy, Cholly. Now go and spoon with Sarah.

LOMAX (*dragging a chair from the writing table and seating himself affectionately by Sarah's side*). How is my ownest today?

SARAH. I wish you wouldnt tell Cholly to do things, Barbara. He always comes straight and does them. Cholly: we're going to the works this afternoon.

LOMAX. What works?

SARAH. The cannon works.

LOMAX. What? your governor's shop!

SARAH. Yes.

LOMAX. Oh I say!

Cusins enters in poor condition. He also starts visibly when he sees Barbara without her uniform.

BARBARA. I expected you this morning, Dolly. Didn't you guess that?

CUSINS (*sitting down beside her*). I'm sorry. I have only just breakfasted.

SARAH. But weve just finished lunch.

BARBARA. Have you had one of your bad nights?

CUSINS. No: I had rather a good night: in fact, one of the most remarkable nights I have ever passed.

BARBARA. The meeting?

CUSINS. No: after the meeting.

LADY BRITOMART. You should have gone to bed after the meeting. What were you doing?

CUSINS. Drinking.

LADY BRITOMART. ⎫ Adolphus!
SARAH.   ⎬ Dolly!
BARBARA.   ⎪ Dolly!
LOMAX.   ⎭ Oh I say!

LADY BRITOMART. What were you drinking, may I ask?

CUSINS. A most devilish kind of Spanish burgundy, warranted free from added alcohol: a Temperance burgundy in fact. Its richness in natural alcohol made any addition superfluous.

BARBARA. Are you joking, Dolly?

CUSINS (*patiently*). No. I have been making a night of it with the nominal head of this household: that is all.

LADY BRITOMART. Andrew made you drunk!

CUSINS. No: he only provided the wine. I think it was Dionysos who made me drunk. (*To Barbara.*) I told you I was possessed.

LADY BRITOMART. Youre not sober yet. Go home to bed at once.

CUSINS. I have never before ventured to reproach you, Lady Brit; but how could you marry the Prince of Darkness?

LADY BRITOMART. It was much more excusable to marry him than to get drunk with him. That is a new accomplishment of Andrew's, by the way. He usent to drink.

CUSINS. He doesnt now. He only sat there and completed the wreck of my moral basis, the rout of my convictions, the purchase of my soul. He cares for you, Barbara. That is what makes him so dangerous to me.

BARBARA. That has nothing to do with it, Dolly. There are larger loves and diviner dreams than the fireside ones. You know that, dont you?

CUSINS. Yes: that is our understanding. I know it. I hold to it. Unless he can win me on that holier ground he may amuse me for a while; but he can get no deeper hold, strong as he is.

BARBARA. Keep to that; and the end will be right. Now tell me what happened at the meeting?

CUSINS. It was an amazing meeting. Mrs Baines almost died of emotion. Jenny Hill simply gibbered with hysteria. The Prince of Darkness played his trombone like a madman: its brazen roarings were like the laughter of the damned. 117 conversions took place then and there. They prayed with the most touching sincerity and gratitude for Bodger, and for the anonymous donor of the £5000. Your father would not let his name be given.

LOMAX. That was rather fine of the old man, you know. Most chaps would have wanted the advertisement.

CUSINS. He said all the charitable institutions would be down on him like kites on a battle-field if he gave his name.

LADY BRITOMART. Thats Andrew all over. He never does a proper thing without giving an improper reason for it.

CUSINS. He convinced me that I have all my life been doing improper things for proper reasons.

LADY BRITOMART. Adolphus: now that Barbara has left the Salvation Army, you had better leave it too. I will not have you playing that drum in the streets.

CUSINS. Your orders are already obeyed, Lady Brit.

BARBARA. Dolly: were you ever really in earnest about it? Would you have joined if you had never seen me?

CUSINS (*disingenuously*). Well—er—well, possibly, as a collector of religions—

LOMAX (*cunningly*). Not as a drummer, though, you know. You are a very clearheaded brainy chap, Dolly; and it must have been apparent to you that there is a certain amount of tosh about—

LADY BRITOMART. Charles: if you must drivel, drivel like a grown-up man and not like a schoolboy.

LOMAX (*out of countenance*). Well, drivel is drivel, dont you know, whatever a man's age.

LADY BRITOMART. In good society in England, Charles, men drivel at all ages by repeating silly formulas with an air of wisdom. Schoolboys make their own formulas out of slang, like you. When they reach your age, and get political private secretaryships and things of that sort, they drop slang and get their formulas out of The Spectator or The Times. You had better confine yourself to The Times. You will find that there is a certain amount of tosh about The Times; but at least its language is reputable.

LOMAX (*overwhelmed*). You are so awfully strong-minded, Lady Brit—

LADY BRITOMART. Rubbish! (*Morrison comes in.*) What is it?

MORRISON. If you please, my lady, Mr Undershaft has just drove up to the door.

LADY BRITOMART. Well, let him in. (*Morrison hesitates.*) Whats the matter with you?

MORRISON. Shall I announce him, my lady; or is he at home here, so to speak, my lady?

LADY BRITOMART. Announce him.

MORRISON. Thank you, my lady. You wont mind my asking, I hope. The occasion is in a manner of speaking new to me.

LADY BRITOMART. Quite right. Go and let him in.

MORRISON. Thank you, my lady. (*He withdraws.*)

LADY BRITOMART. Children: go and get ready. (*Sarah and Barbara go upstairs for their out-of-door wraps.*) Charles: go and tell Stephen to come down here in five minutes: you will find him in the drawing room. (*Charles goes.*) Adolphus: tell them to send round the carriage in about fifteen minutes. (*Adolphus goes.*)

MORRISON (*at the door*). Mr Undershaft.

Undershaft comes in. Morrison goes out.

UNDERSHAFT. Alone! How fortunate!

LADY BRITOMART (*rising*). Dont be sentimental, Andrew. Sit down. (*She sits on the settee: he sits beside her, on her left. She comes to the point before he has time to breathe.*) Sarah must have £800 a year until Charles Lomax comes into his property. Barbara will need more, and need it permanently, because Adolphus hasnt any property.

UNDERSHAFT (*resignedly*). Yes, my dear: I will see to it. Anything else? for yourself, for instance?

LADY BRITOMART. I want to talk to you about Stephen.

UNDERSHAFT (*rather wearily*). Dont, my dear. Stephen doesnt interest me.

LADY BRITOMART. He does interest me. He is our son.

UNDERSHAFT. Do you really think so? He has induced us to bring him into the world; but he chose his parents very incongruously, I think. I see nothing of myself in him, and less of you.

LADY BRITOMART. Andrew: Stephen is an excellent son, and a most steady, capable, highminded young man. You are simply trying to find an excuse for disinheriting him.

UNDERSHAFT. My dear Biddy: the Undershaft tradition disinherits him. It would be dishonest of me to leave the cannon foundry to my son.

LADY BRITOMART. It would be most unnatural and improper of you to leave it to anyone else, Andrew. Do you suppose this wicked and immoral tradition can be kept up for ever? Do you pretend that Stephen could not carry on the foundry just as well as all the other sons of the big business houses?

UNDERSHAFT. Yes: he could learn the office routine without understanding the business, like all the other sons; and the firm would go on by its own momentum until the real Undershaft—probably an Italian or a German—would invent a new method and cut him out.

LADY BRITOMART. There is nothing that any Italian or German could do that Stephen could not do. And Stephen at least has breeding.

UNDERSHAFT. The son of a foundling! Nonsense!

LADY BRITOMART. My son, Andrew! And even you may have good blood in your veins for all you know.

UNDERSHAFT. True. Probably I have. That is another argument in favor of a foundling.

LADY BRITOMART. Andrew: dont be aggravating. And dont be wicked. At present you are both.

UNDERSHAFT. This conversation is part of the Undershaft tradition, Biddy. Every Undershaft's wife has treated him to it ever since the house was founded. It is a mere waste of breath. If the tradition be ever broken it will be for an abler man than Stephen.

LADY BRITOMART (*pouting*). Then go away.

UNDERSHAFT (*deprecatory*). Go away!

LADY BRITOMART. Yes: go away. If you will do nothing for Stephen, you are not wanted here. Go to your foundling, whoever he is; and look after him.

UNDERSHAFT. The fact is, Biddy—

LADY BRITOMART. Dont call me Biddy. I dont call you Andy.

UNDERSHAFT. I will not call my wife Britomart: it is not good sense. Seriously, my love, the Undershaft tradition has landed me in a difficulty. I am getting on in years; and my partner Lazarus has at last made a stand and insisted that the succession must be settled one way or the other; and of course he is quite right. You see, I havnt found a fit successor yet.

LADY BRITOMART (*obstinately*). There is Stephen.

UNDERSHAFT. Thats just it: all the foundlings I can find are exactly like Stephen.

LADY BRITOMART. Andrew!!

UNDERSHAFT. I want a man with no relations and no schooling: that is, a man who would be out of the running altogether if he were not a strong man. And I cant find him. Every blessed foundling nowadays is snapped up in his infancy by Barnardo homes, or School Board officers, or

Boards of Guardians; and if he shews the least ability he is fastened on by schoolmasters; trained to win scholarships like a racehorse; crammed with secondhand ideas; drilled and disciplined in docility and what they call good taste; and lamed for life so that he is fit for nothing but teaching. If you want to keep the foundry in the family, you had better find an eligible foundling and marry him to Barbara.

LADY BRITOMART. Ah! Barbara! Your pet! You would sacrifice Stephen to Barbara.

UNDERSHAFT. Cheerfully. And you, my dear, would boil Barbara to make soup for Stephen.

LADY BRITOMART. Andrew: this is not a question of our likings and dislikings: it is a question of duty. It is your duty to make Stephen your successor.

UNDERSHAFT. Just as much as it is your duty to submit to your husband. Come, Biddy! these tricks of the governing class are of no use with me. I am one of the governing class myself; and it is a waste of time giving tracts to a missionary. I have the power in this matter; and I am not to be humbugged into using it for your purposes.

LADY BRITOMART. Andrew: you can talk my head off; but you cant change wrong into right. And your tie is all on one side. Put it straight.

UNDERSHAFT (disconcerted). It wont stay unless it's pinned— (He fumbles at it with childish grimaces.)

Stephen comes in.

STEPHEN (at the door). I beg your pardon. (About to retire.)

LADY BRITOMART. No: come in, Stephen. (Stephen comes forward to his mother's writing table.)

UNDERSHAFT (not very cordially). Good afternoon.

STEPHEN (coldly). Good afternoon.

UNDERSHAFT (to Lady Britomart). He knows all about the tradition, I suppose?

LADY BRITOMART. Yes. (To Stephen.) It is what I told you last night, Stephen.

UNDERSHAFT (sulkily). I understand you want to come into the cannon business.

STEPHEN. I go into trade! Certainly not.

UNDERSHAFT (opening his eyes, greatly eased in mind and manner). Oh! in that case—

LADY BRITOMART. Cannons are not trade, Stephen. They are enterprise.

STEPHEN. I have no intention of becoming a man of business in any sense. I have no capacity for business and no taste for it. I intend to devote myself to politics.

UNDERSHAFT (rising). My dear boy: this is an immense relief to me. And I trust it may prove an equally good thing for the country. I was afraid you would consider yourself disparaged and slighted. (He moves towards Stephen as if to shake hands with him.)

LADY BRITOMART (rising and interposing). Stephen: I cannot allow you to throw away an enormous property like this.

STEPHEN (stiffly). Mother: there must be an end of treating me as a child, if you please. (Lady Britomart recoils, deeply wounded by his tone.) Until last night I did not take your attitude seriously, because I did not think you meant it seriously. But I find now that you left me in the dark as to matters which you should have explained to me years ago. I am extremely hurt and offended. Any further discussion of my intentions had better take place with my father, as between one man and another.

LADY BRITOMART. Stephen! (She sits down again, her eyes filling with tears.)

UNDERSHAFT (with grave compassion). You see, my dear, it is only the big men who can be treated as children.

STEPHEN. I am sorry, mother, that you have forced me—

UNDERSHAFT (stopping him). Yes, yes, yes, yes: thats all right, Stephen. She wont interfere with you any more: your independence is achieved: you have won your latchkey. Dont rub it in; and above all, dont apologize. (He resumes his seat.) Now what about your future, as between one man and another—I beg your pardon, Biddy: as between two men and a woman.

LADY BRITOMART (who has pulled herself together strongly). I quite understand, Stephen. By all means go your own way if you feel strong enough. (Stephen sits down magisterially in the chair at the writing table with an air of affirming his majority.)

UNDERSHAFT. It is settled that you do not ask for the succession to the cannon business.

STEPHEN. I hope it is settled that I repudiate the cannon business.

UNDERSHAFT. Come, come! dont be so devilishly sulky: it's boyish. Freedom should be generous. Besides, I owe you a fair start in life in exchange for disinheriting you. You cant become prime minister all at once. Havnt you a turn for something? What about literature, art, and so forth?

STEPHEN. I have nothing of the artist about me, either in faculty or character, thank Heaven!

UNDERSHAFT. A philosopher, perhaps? Eh?

STEPHEN. I make no such ridiculous pretension.

UNDERSHAFT. Just so. Well, there is the army, the navy, the Church, the Bar. The Bar requires some ability. What about the Bar?

STEPHEN. I have not studied law. And I am afraid I have not the necessary push—I believe that is the name barristers give to their vulgarity—for success in pleading.

UNDERSHAFT. Rather a difficult case, Stephen. Hardly anything left but the stage, is there? (Stephen makes an impatient movement.) Well, come! is there anything you know or care for?

STEPHEN (rising and looking at him steadily). I know the difference between right and wrong.

UNDERSHAFT (hugely tickled). You dont say so! What! no capacity for business, no knowledge of law, no sympathy with art, no pretension to philosophy; only a simple knowledge of the secret that has puzzled all the philosophers, baffled all the lawyers, muddled all the men of business, and ruined most of the artists: the secret of right and wrong. Why, man, youre a genius, a master of masters, a god! At twentyfour, too!

STEPHEN (*keeping his temper with difficulty*). You are pleased to be facetious. I pretend to nothing more than any honorable English gentleman claims as his birthright (*He sits down angrily.*)

UNDERSHAFT. Oh, thats everybody's birthright. Look at poor little Jenny Hill, the Salvation lassie! she would think you were laughing at her if you asked her to stand up in the street and teach grammar or geography or mathematics or even drawing room dancing; but it never occurs to her to doubt that she can teach morals and religion. You are all alike, you respectable people. You cant tell me the bursting strain of a ten-inch gun, which is a very simple matter; but you all think you can tell me the bursting strain of a man under temptation. You darent handle high explosives; but youre all ready to handle honesty and truth and justice and the whole duty of man, and kill one another at that game. What a country! What a world!

LADY BRITOMART (*uneasily*). What do you think he had better do, Andrew?

UNDERSHAFT. Oh, just what he wants to do. He knows nothing and he thinks he knows everything. That points clearly to a political career. Get him a private secretaryship to someone who can get him an Under Secretaryship; and then leave him alone. He will find his natural and proper place in the end on the Treasury Bench.

STEPHEN (*springing up again*). I am sorry, sir, that you force me to forget the respect due to you as my father. I am an Englishman and I will not hear the Government of my country insulted. (*He thrusts his hands in his pockets, and walks angrily across to the window.*)

UNDERSHAFT (*with a touch of brutality*). The government of your country! *I* am the government of your country: I, and Lazarus. Do you suppose that you and half a dozen amateurs like you, sitting in a row in that foolish gabble shop, can govern Undershaft and Lazarus? No, my friend: you will do what pays us. You will make war when it suits us, and keep peace when it doesnt. You will find out that trade requires certain measures when we have decided on those measures. When I want anything to keep my dividends up, you will discover that my want is a national need. When other people want something to keep my dividends down, you will call out the police and military. And in return you shall have the support and applause of my newspapers, and the delight of imagining that you are a great statesman. Government of your country! Be off with you, my boy, and play with your caucuses and leading articles and historic parties and great leaders and burning questions and the rest of your toys. *I* am going back to my counting-house to pay the piper and call the tune.

STEPHEN (*actually smiling, and putting his hand on his father's shoulder with indulgent patronage*). Really, my dear father, it is impossible to be angry with you. You dont know how absurd all this sounds to me. You are very properly proud of having been industrious enough to make money; and it is greatly to your credit that you have made so much of it. But it has kept you in circles where you are valued for your money and deferred to for it, instead of in the doubtless very old-fashioned and behind-the-times public school and university where I formed my habits of mind. It is natural for you to think that money governs England; but you must allow me to think I know better.

UNDERSHAFT. And what does govern England, pray?

STEPHEN. Character, father, character.

UNDERSHAFT. Whose character? Yours or mine?

STEPHEN. Neither yours nor mine, father, but the best elements in the English national character.

UNDERSHAFT. Stephen: Ive found your profession for you. Youre a born journalist. I'll start you with a high-toned weekly review. There!

Before Stephen can reply Sarah, Barbara, Lomax, and Cusins come in ready for walking. Barbara crosses the room to the window and looks out. Cusins drifts amiably to the armchair. Lomax remains near the door, whilst Sarah comes to her mother.

Stephen goes to the smaller writing table and busies himself with his letters.

SARAH. Go and get ready, mama: the carriage is waiting. (*Lady Britomart leaves the room.*)

UNDERSHAFT (*to Sarah*). Good day, my dear. Good afternoon, Mr Lomax.

LOMAX (*vaguely*). Ahdedoo.

UNDERSHAFT (*to Cusins*). Quite well after last night, Euripides, eh?

CUSINS. As well as can be expected.

UNDERSHAFT. Thats right. (*To Barbara.*) So you are coming to see my death and devastation factory, Barbara?

BARBARA (*at the window*). You came yesterday to see my salvation factory. I promised you a return visit.

LOMAX (*coming forward between Sarah and Undershaft*). Youll find it awfully interesting. Ive been through the Woolwich Arsenal; and it gives you a ripping feeling of security, you know, to think of the lot of beggars we could kill if it came to fighting. (*To Undershaft, with sudden solemnity.*) Still, it must be rather an awful reflection for you, from the religious point of view as it were. Youre getting on, you know, and all that.

SARAH. You dont mind Cholly's imbecility, papa, do you?

LOMAX (*much taken aback*). Oh I say!

UNDERSHAFT. Mr Lomax looks at the matter in a very proper spirit, my dear.

LOMAX. Just so. Thats all I meant, I assure you.

SARAH. Are you coming, Stephen?

STEPHEN. Well, I am rather busy—er—(*Magnanimously.*) Oh well, yes: I'll come. That is, if there is room for me.

UNDERSHAFT. I can take two with me in a little motor I am experimenting with for field use. You wont mind its being rather unfashionable. It's not painted yet; but it's bullet proof.

LOMAX (*appalled at the prospect of confronting Wilton Crescent in an unpainted motor*). Oh I say!

SARAH. The carriage for me, thank you. Barbara doesnt mind what she's seen in.

LOMAX. I say, Dolly, old chap: do you really mind the car being a guy? Because of course if you do I'll go in it. Still—

CUSINS. I prefer it.

LOMAX. Thanks awfully, old man. Come, my ownest. (*He hurries to secure his seat in the carriage. Sarah follows him.*)

CUSINS (*moodily walking across to Lady Britomart's writing table*). Why are we two coming to this Works Department of Hell? that is what I ask myself.

BARBARA. I have always thought of it as a sort of pit where lost creatures with blackened faces stirred up smoky fires and were driven and tormented by my father? Is it like that, dad?

UNDERSHAFT (*scandalized*). My dear! It is a spotlessly clean and beautiful hillside town.

CUSINS. With a Methodist chapel? Oh do say theres a Methodist chapel.

UNDERSHAFT. There are two: a Primitive one and a sophisticated one. There is even an Ethical Society; but it is not much patronized, as my men are all strongly religious. In the High Explosives Sheds they object to the presence of Agnostics as unsafe.

CUSINS. And yet they dont object to you!

BARBARA. Do they obey all your orders?

UNDERSHAFT. I never give them any orders. When I speak to one of them it is "Well, Jones, is the baby doing well? and has Mrs Jones made a good recovery?" "Nicely, thank you, sir." And thats all.

CUSINS. But Jones has to be kept in order. How do you maintain discipline among your men?

UNDERSHAFT. I dont. They do. You see, the one thing Jones wont stand is any rebellion from the man under him, or any assertion of social equality between the wife of the man with 4 shillings a week less than himself, and Mrs Jones! Of course they all rebel against me, theoretically. Practically, every man of them keeps the man just below him in his place. I never meddle with them. I never bully them. I dont even bully Lazarus. I say that certain things are to be done; but I dont order anybody to do them. I dont say, mind you, that there is no ordering about and snubbing and even bullying. The men snub the boys and order them about; the carmen snub the sweepers; the artisans snub the unskilled laborers; the foremen drive and bully both the laborers and artisans; the assistant engineers find fault with the foremen; the chief engineers drop on the assistants; the departmental managers worry the chiefs; and the clerks have tall hats and hymnbooks and keep up the social tone by refusing to associate on equal terms with anybody. The result is a colossal profit, which comes to me.

CUSINS (*revolted*). You really are a—well, what I was saying yesterday.

BARBARA. What was he saying yesterday?

UNDERSHAFT. Never mind, my dear. He thinks I have made you unhappy. Have I?

BARBARA. Do you think I can be happy in this vulgar silly dress? I! who have worn the uniform. Do you understand what you have done to me? Yesterday I had a man's soul in my hand. I set him in the way of life with his face to salvation. But when we took your money he turned back to drunkenness and derision. (*With intense conviction.*) I will never forgive you that. If I had a child, and you destroyed its body with your explosives—if you murdered Dolly with your horrible guns—I could forgive you if my forgiveness would open the gates of heaven to you. But to take a human soul from me, and turn it into the soul of a wolf! that is worse than any murder.

UNDERSHAFT. Does my daughter despair so easily? Can you strike a man to the heart and leave no mark on him?

BARBARA (*her face lighting up*). Oh, you are right: he can never be lost now: where was my faith?

CUSINS. Oh, clever clever devil!

BARBARA. You may be a devil; but God speaks through you sometimes (*She takes her father's hands and kisses them.*) You have given me back my happiness: I feel it deep down now, though my spirit is troubled.

UNDERSHAFT. You have learnt something. That always feels at first as if you had lost something.

BARBARA. Well, take me to the factory of death; and let me learn something more. There must be some truth or other behind all this frightful irony. Come, Dolly. (*She goes out.*)

CUSINS. My guardian angel! (*To Undershaft.*) Avaunt! (*He follows Barbara.*)

STEPHEN (*quietly, at the writing table*). You must not mind Cusins, father. He is a very amiable good fellow; but he is a Greek scholar and naturally a little eccentric.

UNDERSHAFT. Ah, quite so. Thank you, Stephen. Thank you. (*He goes out.*)

Stephen smiles patronizingly; buttons his coat responsibly; and crosses the room to the door. Lady Britomart, dressed for out-of-doors, opens it before he reaches it. She looks round for the others; looks at Stephen; and turns to go without a word.

STEPHEN (*embarrassed*). Mother—

LADY BRITOMART. Dont be apologetic, Stephen. And dont forget that you have outgrown your mother. (*She goes out.*)

Perivale St Andrews lies between two Middlesex hills, half climbing the northern one. It is an almost smokeless town of white walls, roofs of narrow green slates or red tiles, tall trees, domes, campaniles, and slender chimney shafts, beautifully situated and beautiful in itself. The best view of it is obtained from the crest of a slope about half a mile to the east, where the high explosives are dealt with. The foundry lies hidden in the depths between, the tops of its chimneys sprouting like huge skittles into the middle distance. Across the crest runs an emplacement of concrete, with a firestep, and a parapet which suggests a fortification, because there is a huge cannon of the obsolete Woolwich Infant pattern peering across it at the town. The cannon is mounted on an experimental gun carriage: possibly the original model of the Undershaft disappearing rampart gun alluded to by Stephen. The firestep, being a convenient place to sit, is furnished here and there with straw disc cushions; and at one place there is the additional luxury of a fur rug.

Barbara is standing on the firestep, looking over the parapet towards the town. On her right is the cannon; on her left the end of a shed raised on piles, with a ladder of three or four steps up to the door, which opens outwards and has a little wooden landing at the threshold, with a fire bucket in the corner of the landing. Several dummy soldiers more or less mutilated, with straw protruding from their gashes, have been shoved out of the way under the landing. A few others are nearly upright against the shed; and one has fallen forward and lies, like a grotesque corpse, on the emplacement. The parapet stops short of the shed, leaving a gap which is the beginning of the path down the hill through the foundry to the town. The rug is on the firestep near this gap. Down on the emplacement behind the cannon is a trolley carrying a huge conical bombshell with a red band painted on it. Further to the right is the door of an office, which, like the sheds, is of the lightest possible construction.

Cusins arrives by the path from the town.

BARBARA. Well?

CUSINS. Not a ray of hope. Everything perfect! wonderful! real! It only needs a cathedral to be a heavenly city instead of a hellish one.

BARBARA. Have you found out whether they have done anything for old Peter Shirley?

CUSINS. They have found him a job as gatekeeper and timekeeper. He's frightfully miserable. He calls the time-keeping brainwork, and says he isnt used to it; and his gate lodge is so splendid that he's ashamed to use the rooms, and skulks in the scullery.

BARBARA. Poor Peter!

Stephen arrives from the town. He carries a fieldglass.

STEPHEN (*enthusiastically*). Have you two seen the place? Why did you leave us?

CUSINS. I wanted to see everything I was not intended to see; and Barbara wanted to make the men talk.

STEPHEN. Have you found anything discreditable?

CUSINS. No. They call him Dandy Andy and are proud of his being a cunning old rascal; but it's all horribly, frightfully, immorally, unanswerably perfect.

Sarah arrives.

SARAH. Heavens! what a place! (*She crosses to the trolley.*) Did you see the nursing home!? (*She sits down on the shell.*)

STEPHEN. Did you see the libraries and schools!?

SARAH. Did you see the ball room and the banqueting chamber in the Town Hall!?

STEPHEN. Have you gone into the insurance fund, the pension fund, the building society, the various applications of cooperation!?

Undershaft comes from the office, with a sheaf of telegrams in his hand.

UNDERSHAFT. Well, have you seen everything? I'm sorry I was called away. (*Indicating the telegrams.*) Good news from Manchuria.

STEPHEN. Another Japanese victory?

UNDERSHAFT. Oh, I dont know. Which side wins does not concern us here. No: the good news is that the aerial battleship is a tremendous success. At the first trial it has wiped out a fort with three hundred soldiers in it.

CUSINS (*from the platform*). Dummy soldiers?

UNDERSHAFT (*striding across to Stephen and kicking the prostrate dummy brutally out of his way*). No: the real thing.

Cusins and Barbara exchange glances. Then Cusins sits on the step and buries his face in his hands. Barbara gravely lays her hand on his shoulder. He looks up at her in whimsical desperation.

UNDERSHAFT. Well, Stephen, what do you think of the place?

STEPHEN. Oh, magnificent. A perfect triumph of modern industry. Frankly, my dear father, I have been a fool: I had no idea of what it all meant: of the wonderful forethought, the power of organization, the administrative capacity, the financial genius, the colossal capital it represents. I have been repeating to myself as I came through your streets "Peace hath her victories no less renowned than War." I have only one misgiving about it all.

UNDERSHAFT. Out with it.

STEPHEN. Well, I cannot help thinking that all this provision for every want of your workmen may sap their independence and weaken their sense of responsibility. And greatly as we enjoyed our tea at that splendid restaurant—how they gave us all that luxury and cake and jam and cream for threepence I really cannot imagine!—still you must remember that restaurants break up home life. Look at the continent, for instance! Are you sure so much pampering is really good for the men's characters?

UNDERSHAFT. Well you see, my dear boy, when you are organizing civilization you have to make up your mind whether trouble and anxiety are good things or not. If you decide that they are, then, I take it, you simply dont organize civilization; and there you are, with trouble and anxiety enough to make us all angels! But if you decide the other way, you may as well go through with it. However, Stephen, our characters are safe here. A sufficient dose of anxiety is always provided by the fact that we may be blown to smithereens at any moment.

SARAH. By the way, papa, where do you make the explosives?

UNDERSHAFT. In separate little sheds, like that one. When one of them blows up, it costs very little; and only the people quite close to it are killed.

Stephen, who is quite close to it, looks at it rather scaredly, and moves away quickly to the cannon. At the same moment the door of the shed is thrown abruptly open; and a foreman in overalls and list slippers comes out on the little landing and holds the door for Lomax, who appears in the doorway.

LOMAX (*with studied coolness*). My good fellow: you neednt get into a state of nerves. Nothing's going to happen to you; and I suppose it wouldnt be the end of the world if anything did. A little bit of British pluck is what you want, old chap. (*He descends and strolls across to Sarah.*)

UNDERSHAFT (*to the foreman*). Anything wrong, Bilton?

BILTON (*with ironic calm*). Gentleman walked into the high explosives shed and lit a cigaret, sir: thats all.

UNDERSHAFT. Ah, quite so. (*Going over to Lomax.*) Do you happen to remember what you did with the match?

LOMAX. Oh come! I'm not a fool. I took jolly good care to blow it out before I chucked it away.

BILTON. The top of it was red hot inside, sir.

LOMAX. Well, suppose it was! I didn't chuck it into any of your messes.

UNDERSHAFT. Think no more of it, Mr Lomax. By the way, would you mind lending me your matches.

LOMAX (*offering his box*). Certainly.

UNDERSHAFT. Thanks. (*He pockets the matches.*)

LOMAX (*lecturing to the company generally*). You know, these high explosives dont go off like gunpowder, except when theyre in a gun. When theyre spread loose, you can put a match to them without the least risk: they just burn quietly like a bit of paper. (*Warming to the scientific interest of the subject.*) Did you know that, Undershaft? Have you ever tried?

UNDERSHAFT. Not on a large scale, Mr Lomax. Bilton will give you a sample of gun cotton when you are leaving if you ask him. You can experiment with it at home. (*Bilton looks puzzled.*)

SARAH. Bilton will do nothing of the sort, papa. I suppose it's your business to blow up the Russians and Japs; but you might really stop short of blowing up poor Cholly. (*Bilton gives it up and retires into the shed.*)

LOMAX. My ownest, there is no danger. (*He sits beside her on the shell.*)

Lady Britomart arrives from the town with a bouquet.

LADY BRITOMART (*impetuously*). Andrew: you shouldnt have let me see this place.

UNDERSHAFT. Why, my dear?

LADY BRITOMART. Never mind why: you shouldnt have: thats all. To think of all that (*indicating the town*) being yours! and that you have kept it to yourself all these years!

UNDERSHAFT. It does not belong to me. I belong to it. It is the Undershaft inheritance.

LADY BRITOMART. It is not. Your ridiculous cannons and that noisy banging foundry may be the Undershaft inheritance; but all that plate and linen, all that furniture and those houses and orchards and gardens belong to us. They belong to me: they are not a man's business. I wont give them up. You must be out of your senses to throw them all away; and if you persist in such folly, I will call in a doctor.

UNDERSHAFT (*stooping to smell the bouquet*). Where did you get the flowers, my dear?

LADY BRITOMART. Your men presented them to me in your William Morris Labor Church.

CUSINS. Oh! It needed only that. A Labor Church! (*He mounts the firestep distractedly, and leans with his elbows on the parapet, turning his back to them.*)

LADY BRITOMART. Yes, with Morris's words in mosaic letters ten feet high round the dome. NO MAN IS GOOD ENOUGH TO BE ANOTHER MAN'S MASTER. The cynicism of it!

UNDERSHAFT. It shocked the men at first, I am afraid. But now they take no more notice of it than of the ten commandments in church.

LADY BRITOMART. Andrew: you are trying to put me off the subject of the inheritance by profane jokes. Well, you shant. I dont ask it any longer for Stephen: he has inherited far too much of your perversity to be fit for it. But Barbara has rights as well as Stephen. Why should not Adolphus succeed to the inheritance? I could manage the town for him; and he can look after the cannons, if they are really necessary.

UNDERSHAFT. I should ask nothing better if Adolphus were a foundling. He is exactly the sort of new blood that is wanted in English business. But he's not a foundling; and theres an end of it. (*He makes for the office door.*)

CUSINS (*turning to them*). Not quite. (*They all turn and stare at him.*) I think—Mind! I am not committing myself in any way as to my future course—but I think the foundling difficulty can be got over. (*He jumps down to the emplacement.*)

UNDERSHAFT (*coming back to him*). What do you mean?

CUSINS. Well, I have something to say which is in the nature of a confession.

SARAH.
LADY BRITOMART.
BARBARA.
STEPHEN.
} Confession!

LOMAX. Oh I say!

CUSINS. Yes, a confession. Listen, all. Until I met Barbara I thought myself in the main an honorable, truthful man, because I wanted the approval of my conscience more than I wanted anything else. But the moment I saw Barbara, I wanted her far more than the approval of my conscience.

LADY BRITOMART. Adolphus!

CUSINS. It is true. You accused me yourself, Lady Brit, of joining the Army to worship Barbara; and so I did. She bought my soul like a flower at a street corner; but she bought it for herself.

UNDERSHAFT. What! Not for Dionysos or another?

CUSINS. Dionysos and all the others are in herself. I adored what was divine in her, and was therefore a true worshipper. But I was romantic about her too. I thought she was a woman of the people, and that a marriage with a professor of Greek would be far beyond the wildest social ambitions of her rank.

LADY BRITOMART. Adolphus!!

LOMAX. Oh I say!!!

CUSINS. When I learnt the horrible truth—

LADY BRITOMART. What do you mean by the horrible truth, pray?

CUSINS. That she was enormously rich; that her grandfather was an earl; that her father was the Prince of Darkness—

UNDERSHAFT. Chut!

CUSINS. —and that I was only an adventurer trying to catch a rich wife, then I stooped to deceive her about my birth.

BARBARA (rising). Dolly!

LADY BRITOMART. Your birth! Now Adolphus, dont dare to make up a wicked story for the sake of these wretched cannons. Remember: I have seen photographs of your parents; and the Agent General for South Western Australia knows them personally and has assured me that they are most respectable married people.

CUSINS. So they are in Australia; but here they are outcasts. Their marriage is legal in Australia, but not in England. My mother is my father's deceased wife's sister; and in this island I am consequently a foundling. (Sensation.)

BARBARA. Silly! (She climbs to the cannon, and leans, listening, in the angle it makes with the parapet.)

CUSINS. Is the subterfuge good enough, Machiavelli?

UNDERSHAFT (thoughtfully). Biddy: this may be a way out of the difficulty.

LADY BRITOMART. Stuff! A man cant make cannons any the better for being his own cousin instead of his proper self. (She sits down on the rug with a bounce that expresses her downright contempt for their casuistry.)

UNDERSHAFT (to Cusins). You are an educated man. That is against the tradition.

CUSINS. Once in ten thousand times it happens that the schoolboy is a born master of what they try to teach him. Greek has not destroyed my mind: it has nourished it. Besides, I did not learn it at an English public school.

UNDERSHAFT. Hm! Well, I cannot afford to be too particular: you have cornered the foundling market. Let it pass. You are eligible, Euripides: you are eligible.

BARBARA. Dolly: yesterday morning, when Stephen told us all about the tradition, you became very silent; and you have been strange and excited ever since. Were you thinking of your birth then?

CUSINS. When the finger of Destiny suddenly points at a man in the middle of his breakfast, it makes him thoughtful.

UNDERSHAFT. Aha! You have had your eye on the business, my young friend, have you?

CUSINS. Take care! There is an abyss of moral horror between me and your accursed aerial battleships.

UNDERSHAFT. Never mind the abyss for the present. Let us settle the practical details and leave your final decision open. You know that you will have to change your name. Do you object to that?

CUSINS. Would any man named Adolphus—any man called Dolly!—object to be called something else?

UNDERSHAFT. Good. Now, as to money! I propose to treat you handsomely from the beginning. You shall start at a thousand a year.

CUSINS (with sudden heat, his spectacles twinkling with mischief). A thousand! You dare offer a miserable thousand to the son-in-law of a millionaire! No, by Heavens, Machiavelli! you shall not cheat me. You cannot do without me; and I can do without you. I must have two thousand five hundred a year for two years. At the end of that time, if I am a failure, I go. But if I am a success, and stay on, you must give me the other five thousand.

UNDERSHAFT. What other five thousand?

CUSINS. To make the two years up to five thousand a year. The two thousand five hundred is only half pay in case I should turn out a failure. The third year I must have ten per cent on the profits.

UNDERSHAFT (taken aback). Ten per cent! Why, man, do you know what my profits are?

CUSINS. Enormous, I hope: otherwise I shall require twenty-five per cent.

UNDERSHAFT. But, Mr Cusins, this is a serious matter of business. You are not bringing any capital into the concern.

CUSINS. What! no capital! Is my mastery of Greek no capital? Is my access to the subtlest thought, the loftiest poetry yet attained by humanity, no capital? My character! my intellect! my life! my career! what Barbara calls my soul! are these no capital? Say another word; and I double my salary.

UNDERSHAFT. Be reasonable—

CUSINS (peremptorily). Mr Undershaft: you have my terms. Take them or leave them.

UNDERSHAFT (recovering himself). Very well. I note your terms; and I offer you half.

CUSINS (disgusted). Half!

UNDERSHAFT (firmly). Half.

CUSINS. You call yourself a gentleman; and you offer me half!!

UNDERSHAFT. I do not call myself a gentleman; but I offer you half.

CUSINS. This to your future partner! your successor! your son-in-law!

BARBARA. You are selling your own soul, Dolly, not mine. Leave me out of the bargain, please.

UNDERSHAFT. Come! I will go a step further for Barbara's sake. I will give you three fifths; but that is my last word.

CUSINS. Done!

LOMAX. Done in the eye! Why, I get only eight hundred, you know.

CUSINS. By the way, Mac, I am a classical scholar, not an arithmetical one. Is three fifths more than half or less?

UNDERSHAFT. More, of course.

CUSINS. I would have taken two hundred and fifty. How you can succeed in business when you are willing to pay all that money to a University don who is obviously not worth a junior clerk's wages!—well! What will Lazarus say?

UNDERSHAFT. Lazarus is a gentle romantic Jew who cares for nothing but string quartets and stalls at fashionable theatres. He will be blamed for your rapacity in money matters, poor fellow! as he has hitherto been blamed for mine. You are a shark of the first order, Euripides. So much the better for the firm!

BARBARA. Is the bargain closed, Dolly? Does your soul belong to him now?

CUSINS. No: the price is settled: that is all. The real tug of war is still to come. What about the moral question?

LADY BRITOMART. There is no moral question in the matter at all, Adolphus. You must simply sell cannons and weapons to people whose cause is right and just, and refuse them to foreigners and criminals.

UNDERSHAFT (determinedly). No: none of that. You must keep the true faith of an Armorer, or you dont come in here.

CUSINS. What on earth is the true faith of an Armorer?

UNDERSHAFT. To give arms to all men who offer an honest price for them, without respect of persons or principles: to aristocrat and republican, to Nihilist and Tsar, to Capitalist and Socialist, to Protestant and Catholic, to burglar and policeman, to black man, white man and yellow man, to all sorts and conditions, all nationalities, all faiths, all follies, all causes and all crimes. The first Undershaft wrote up in his shop IF GOD GAVE THE HAND, LET NOT MAN WITHHOLD THE SWORD. The second wrote up ALL HAVE THE RIGHT TO FIGHT: NONE HAVE THE RIGHT TO JUDGE. The third wrote up TO MAN THE WEAPON: TO HEAVEN THE VICTORY. The fourth had no literary turn; so he did not write up anything; but he sold cannons to Napoleon under the nose of George the Third. The fifth wrote up PEACE SHALL NOT PREVAIL SAVE WITH A SWORD IN HER HAND. The sixth, my master, was the best of all.

He wrote up NOTHING IS EVER DONE IN THIS WORLD UNTIL MEN ARE PREPARED TO KILL ONE ANOTHER IF IT IS NOT DONE. After that, there was nothing left for the seventh to say. So he wrote up, simply, UNASHAMED.

CUSINS. My good Machiavelli, I shall certainly write something up on the wall; only, as I shall write it in Greek, you wont be able to read it. But as to your Armorer's faith, if I take my neck out of the noose of my own morality I am not going to put it into the noose of yours. I shall sell cannons to whom I please and refuse them to whom I please. So there!

UNDERSHAFT. From the moment when you become Andrew Undershaft, you will never do as you please again. Dont come here lusting for power, young man.

CUSINS. If power were my aim I should not come here for it. You have no power.

UNDERSHAFT. None of my own, certainly.

CUSINS. I have more power than you, more will. You do not drive this place: it drives you. And what drives the place?

UNDERSHAFT (enigmatically). A will of which I am a part.

BARBARA (startled). Father! Do you know what you are saying; or are you laying a snare for my soul?

CUSINS. Dont listen to his metaphysics, Barbara. The place is driven by the most rascally part of society, the money hunters, the pleasure hunters, the military promotion hunters; and he is their slave.

UNDERSHAFT. Not necessarily. Remember the Armorer's Faith. I will take an order from a good man as cheerfully as from a bad one. If you good people prefer preaching and shirking to buying my weapons and fighting the rascals, dont blame me. I can make cannons: I cannot make courage and conviction. Bah! you tire me, Euripides, with your morality mongering. Ask Barbara: she understands. (He suddenly reaches up and takes Barbara's hands, looking powerfully into her eyes.) Tell him, my love, what power really means.

BARBARA (hypnotized). Before I joined the Salvation Army, I was in my own power; and the consequence was that I never knew what to do with myself. When I joined it, I had not time enough for all the things I had to do.

UNDERSHAFT (approvingly). Just so. And why was that, do you suppose?

BARBARA. Yesterday I should have said, because I was in the power of God. (She resumes her self-possession, withdrawing her hands from his with a power equal to his own.) But you came and shewed me that I was in the power of Bodger and Undershaft. Today I feel—oh! how can I put it into words? Sarah: do you remember the earthquake at Cannes, when we were little children?—how little the surprise of the first shock mattered compared to the dread and horror of waiting for the second? That is how I feel in this place today. I stood on the rock I thought eternal; and without a word of warning it reeled and crumbled under me. I was safe with an infinite wisdom watching me, an army marching to Salvation with me; and in a moment, at a stroke of your pen in a cheque book, I stood alone; and the heavens were empty. That was the first shock of the earthquake: I am waiting for the second.

UNDERSHAFT. Come, come, my daughter! dont make too much of your little tinpot tragedy. What do we do here when we spend years of work and thought and thousands of pounds of solid cash on a new gun or an aerial battleship that turns out just a hairsbreadth wrong after all? Scrap it. Scrap it without wasting another hour or another pound on it. Well, you have made for yourself something that you call a morality or a religion or what not. It doesnt fit the facts. Well, scrap it. Scrap it and get one that does fit. That is what is wrong with the world at present. It scraps its obsolete steam engines and dynamos; but it wont scrap its old prejudices and its old moralities and its old religions and its old political constitutions. Whats the result? In machinery it does very well; but in morals and religion and politics it is working at a loss that brings it nearer bankruptcy every year. Dont persist in that folly. If your old religion broke down yesterday, get a newer and a better one for tomorrow.

BARBARA. Oh how gladly I would take a better one to my soul! But you offer me a worse one. (*Turning on him with sudden vehemence.*) Justify yourself: shew me some light through the darkness of this dreadful place, with its beautifully clean workshops, and respectable workmen, and model homes.

UNDERSHAFT. Cleanliness and respectability do not need justification, Barbara: they justify themselves. I see no darkness here, no dreadfulness. In your Salvation shelter I saw poverty, misery, cold and hunger. You gave them bread and treacle and dreams of heaven. I give them thirty shillings a week to twelve thousand a year. They find their own dreams; but I look after the drainage.

BARBARA. And their souls?

UNDERSHAFT. I save their souls just as I saved yours.

BARBARA (*revolted*). You saved my soul! What do you mean?

UNDERSHAFT. I fed you and clothed you and housed you. I took care that you should have money enough to live handsomely—more than enough; so that you could be wasteful, careless, generous. That saved your soul from the seven deadly sins.

BARBARA (*bewildered*). The seven deadly sins!

UNDERSHAFT. Yes, the deadly seven. (*Counting on his fingers.*) Food, clothing, firing, rent, taxes, respectability and children. Nothing can lift those seven millstones from Man's neck but money; and the spirit cannot soar until the millstones are lifted. I lifted them from your spirit. I enabled Barbara to become Major Barbara; and I saved her from the crime of poverty.

CUSINS. Do you call poverty a crime?

UNDERSHAFT. The worst of crimes. All the other crimes are virtues beside it: all the other dishonors are chivalry itself by comparison. Poverty blights whole cities; spreads horrible pestilences; strikes dead the very souls of all who come within sight, sound, or smell of it. What you call crime is nothing: a murder here and a theft there, a blow now and a curse then: what do they matter? they are only the accidents and illnesses of life: there are not fifty genuine professional criminals in London. But there are millions of poor people, abject people, dirty people, ill fed, ill clothed people. They poison us morally and physically: they kill the happiness of society: they force us to do away with our own liberties and to organize unnatural cruelties for fear they should rise against us and drag us down into their abyss. Only fools fear crime: we all fear poverty. Pah! (*Turning on Barbara.*) you talk of your half-saved ruffian in West Ham: you accuse me of dragging his soul back to perdition. Well, bring him to me here; and I will drag his soul back again to salvation for you. Not by words and dreams; but by thirtyeight shillings a week, a sound house in a handsome street, and a permanent job. In three weeks he will have a fancy waistcoat; in three months a tall hat and a chapel sitting; before the end of the year he will shake hands with a duchess at a Primrose League meeting, and join the Conservative Party.

BARBARA. And will he be the better for that?

UNDERSHAFT. You know he will. Dont be a hypocrite, Barbara. He will be better fed, better housed, better clothed, better behaved; and his children will be pounds heavier and bigger. That will be better than an American cloth mattress in a shelter, chopping firewood, eating bread and treacle, and being forced to kneel down from time to time to thank heaven for it: knee drill, I think you call it. It is cheap work converting starving men with a Bible in one hand and a slice of bread in the other. I will undertake to convert West Ham to Mahometanism on the same terms. Try your hand on my men: their souls are hungry because their bodies are full.

BARBARA. And leave the east end to starve?

UNDERSHAFT (*his energetic tone dropping into one of bitter and brooding remembrance*). I was an east ender. I moralized and starved until one day I swore that I would be a fullfed free man at all costs; that nothing should stop me except a bullet, neither reason nor morals nor the lives of other men. I said "Thou shalt starve ere I starve"; and with that word I became free and great. I was a dangerous man until I had my will: now I am a useful, beneficent, kindly person. That is the history of most self-made millionaires, I fancy. When it is the history of every Englishman we shall have an England worth living in.

LADY BRITOMART. Stop making speeches, Andrew. This is not the place for them.

UNDERSHAFT (*punctured*). My dear: I have no other means of conveying my ideas.

LADY BRITOMART. Your ideas are nonsense. You got on because you were selfish and unscrupulous.

UNDERSHAFT. Not at all. I had the strongest scruples about poverty and starvation. Your moralists are quite unscrupulous about both: they make virtues of them. I had rather be a thief than a pauper. I had rather be a murderer than a slave. I dont want to be either; but if you force the alternative on me, then, by Heaven, I'll choose the braver and more moral one. I hate poverty and slavery worse than any other crimes whatsoever. And let me tell you this. Poverty and slavery have stood up for centuries to your sermons and leading articles: they will not stand up to my machine guns. Dont preach at them: dont reason with them. Kill them.

BARBARA. Killing. Is that your remedy for everything?

UNDERSHAFT. It is the final test of conviction, the only lever strong enough to overturn a social system, the only way of saying Must. Let six hundred and seventy fools loose in the streets; and three policemen can scatter them. But huddle them together in a certain house in Westminster; and let them go through certain ceremonies and call themselves certain names until at last they get the courage to kill; and your six hundred and seventy fools become a government. Your pious mob fills up ballot papers and imagines it is governing its masters; but the ballot paper that really governs is the paper that has a bullet wrapped up in it.

CUSINS. That is perhaps why, like most intelligent people, I never vote.

UNDERSHAFT. Vote! Bah! When you vote, you only change the names of the cabinet. When you shoot, you pull down governments, inaugurate new epochs, abolish old orders and set up new. Is that historically true, Mr Learned Man, or is it not?

CUSINS. It is historically true. I loathe having to admit it. I repudiate your sentiments. I abhor your nature. I defy you in every possible way. Still, it is true. But it ought not to be true.

UNDERSHAFT. Ought! ought! ought! ought! ought! Are you going to spend your life saying ought, like the rest of our moralists? Turn your oughts into shalls, man. Come and make explosives with me. Whatever can blow men up can blow society up. The history of the world is the history of those who had courage enough to embrace this truth. Have you the courage to embrace it, Barbara?

LADY BRITOMART. Barbara: I positively forbid you to listen to your father's abominable wickedness. And you, Adolphus, ought to know better than to go about saying that wrong things are true. What does it matter whether they are true if they are wrong?

UNDERSHAFT. What does it matter whether they are wrong if they are true?

LADY BRITOMART (rising). Children: come home instantly. Andrew: I am exceedingly sorry I allowed you to call on us. You are wickeder than ever. Come at once.

BARBARA (shaking her head). It's no use running away from wicked people, mamma.

LADY BRITOMART. It is every use. It shews your disapprobation of them.

BARBARA. It does not save them.

LADY BRITOMART. I can see that you are going to disobey me. Sarah: are you coming home or are you not?

SARAH. I daresay it's very wicked of papa to make cannons; but I dont think I shall cut him on that account.

LOMAX (pouring oil on the troubled waters). The fact is, you know, there is a certain amount of tosh about this notion of wickedness. It doesnt work. You must look at facts. Not that I would say a word in favor of anything wrong; but then, you see, all sorts of chaps are always doing all sorts of things; and we have to fit them in somehow, dont you know. What I mean is that you cant go cutting everybody; and thats about what it comes to. (Their rapt attention to his eloquence makes him nervous.) Perhaps I dont make myself clear.

LADY BRITOMART. You are lucidity itself, Charles. Because Andrew is successful and has plenty of money to give to Sarah, you will flatter him and encourage him in his wickedness.

LOMAX (unruffled). Well, where the carcase is, there will the eagles be gathered, dont you know. (To Undershaft.) Eh? What?

UNDERSHAFT. Precisely. By the way, may I call you Charles?

LOMAX. Delighted. Cholly is the usual ticket.

UNDERSHAFT (to Lady Britomart). Biddy—

LADY BRITOMART (violently). Dont dare call me Biddy. Charles Lomax: you are a fool. Adolphus Cusins: you are a Jesuit. Stephen: you are a prig. Barbara: you are a lunatic. Andrew: you are a vulgar tradesman. Now you all know my opinion; and my conscience is clear, at all events. (She sits down with a vehemence that the rug fortunately softens.)

UNDERSHAFT. My dear: you are the incarnation of morality. (She snorts.) Your conscience is clear and your duty done when you have called everybody names. Come, Euripides! it is getting late; and we all want to go home. Make up your mind.

CUSINS. Understand this, you old demon—

LADY BRITOMART. Adolphus!

UNDERSHAFT. Let him alone, Biddy. Proceed, Euripides.

CUSINS. You have me in a horrible dilemma. I want Barbara.

UNDERSHAFT. Like all young men, you greatly exaggerate the difference between one young woman and another.

BARBARA. Quite true, Dolly.

CUSINS. I also want to avoid being a rascal.

UNDERSHAFT (with biting contempt). You lust for personal righteousness, for self-approval, for what you call a good conscience, for what Barbara calls salvation, for what I call patronizing people who are not so lucky as yourself.

CUSINS. I do not: all the poet in me recoils from being a good man. But there are things in me that I must reckon with. Pity—

UNDERSHAFT. Pity! The scavenger of misery.

CUSINS. Well, love.

UNDERSHAFT. I know. You love the needy and the outcast: you love the oppressed races, the negro, the Indian ryot, the underdog everywhere. Do you love the Japanese? Do you love the French? Do you love the English?

CUSINS. No. Every true Englishman detests the English. We are the wickedest nation on earth; and our success is a moral horror.

UNDERSHAFT. That is what comes of your gospel of love, is it?

CUSINS. May I not love even my father-in-law?

UNDERSHAFT. Who wants your love, man? By what right do you take the liberty of offering it to me? I will have your due heed and respect, or I will kill you. But your love! Damn your impertinence!

CUSINS (*grinning*). I may not be able to control my affections, Mac.

UNDERSHAFT. You are fencing, Euripides. You are weakening: your grip is slipping. Come! try your last weapon. Pity and love have broken in your hand: forgiveness is still left.

CUSINS. No: forgiveness is a beggar's refuge. I am with you there: we must pay our debts.

UNDERSHAFT. Well said. Come! you will suit me. Remember the words of Plato.

CUSINS (*starting*). Plato! You dare quote Plato to me!

UNDERSHAFT. Plato says, my friend, that society cannot be saved until either the Professors of Greek take to making gunpowder, or else the makers of gunpowder become Professors of Greek.

CUSINS. Oh, tempter, cunning tempter!

UNDERSHAFT. Come! choose, man, choose.

CUSINS. But perhaps Barbara will not marry me if I make the wrong choice.

BARBARA. Perhaps not.

CUSINS (*desperately perplexed*). You hear!

BARBARA. Father: do you love nobody?

UNDERSHAFT. I love my best friend.

LADY BRITOMART. And who is that, pray?

UNDERSHAFT. My bravest enemy. That is the man who keeps me up to the mark.

CUSINS. You know, the creature is really a sort of poet in his way. Suppose he is a great man, after all!

UNDERSHAFT. Suppose you stop talking and make up your mind, my young friend.

CUSINS. But you are driving me against my nature. I hate war.

UNDERSHAFT. Hatred is the coward's revenge for being intimidated. Dare you make war on war? Here are the means: my friend Mr. Lomax is sitting on them.

LOMAX (*springing up*). Oh I say! You dont mean that this thing is loaded, do you? My ownest: come off it.

SARAH (*sitting placidly on the shell*). If I am to be blown up, the more thoroughly it is done the better. Dont fuss, Cholly.

LOMAX (*to Undershaft, strongly remonstrant*). Your own daughter, you know!

UNDERSHAFT. So I see. (*To Cusins.*) Well, my friend, may we expect you here at six tomorrow morning?

CUSINS (*firmly*). Not on any account. I will see the whole establishment blown up with its own dynamite before I will get up at five. My hours are healthy, rational hours: eleven to five.

UNDERSHAFT. Come when you please: before a week you will come at six and stay until I turn you out for the sake of your health. (*Calling.*) Bilton! (*He turns to Lady Britomart, who rises.*) My dear: let us leave these two young people to themselves for a moment. (*Bilton comes from the shed.*) I am going to take you through the gun cotton shed.

BILTON (*barring the way*). You cant take anything explosive in here, sir.

LADY BRITOMART. What do you mean? Are you alluding to me?

BILTON (*unmoved*). No, maam. Mr Undershaft has the other gentleman's matches in his pocket.

LADY BRITOMART (*abruptly*). Oh! I beg your pardon. (*She goes into the shed.*)

UNDERSHAFT. Quite right, Bilton, quite right: here you are. (*He gives Bilton the box of matches.*) Come, Stephen. Come, Charles. Bring Sarah. (*He passes into the shed.*)

Bilton opens the box and deliberately drops the matches into the fire-bucket.

LOMAX. Oh! I say. (*Bilton stolidly hands him the empty box.*) Infernal nonsense! Pure scientific ignorance! (*He goes in.*)

SARAH. Am I all right, Bilton?

BILTON. Youll have to put on list slippers, miss: thats all. Weve got em inside. (*She goes in.*)

STEPHEN (*very seriously to Cusins*). Dolly, old fellow, think. Think before you decide. Do you feel that you are a sufficiently practical man? It is a huge undertaking, an enormous responsibility. All this mass of business will be Greek to you.

CUSINS. Oh, I think it will be much less difficult than Greek.

STEPHEN. Well, I just want to say this before I leave you to yourselves. Dont let anything I have said about right and wrong prejudice you against this great chance in life. I have satisfied myself that the business is one of the highest character and a credit to our country. (*Emotionally.*) I am very proud of my father. I—(*Unable to proceed, he presses Cusins' hand and goes hastily into the shed, followed by Bilton.*)

Barbara and Cusins, left alone together, look at one another silently.

CUSINS. Barbara: I am going to accept this offer.

BARBARA. I thought you would.

CUSINS. You understand, dont you, that I had to decide without consulting you. If I had thrown the burden of the choice on you, you would sooner or later have despised me for it.

BARBARA. Yes; I did not want you to sell your soul for me any more than for this inheritance.

CUSINS. It is not the sale of my soul that troubles me: I have sold it too often to care about that. I have sold it for a professorship. I have sold it for an income. I have sold it to escape being imprisoned for refusing to pay taxes for hangmen's ropes and unjust wars and things that I abhor. What is all human conduct but the daily and hourly sale of our souls for trifles? What I am now selling it for is neither money nor position nor comfort, but for reality and for power.

BARBARA. You know that you will have no power, and that he has none.

CUSINS. I know. It is not for myself alone. I want to make power for the world.

BARBARA. I want to make power for the world too; but it must be spiritual power.

CUSINS. I think all power is spiritual: these cannons will not go off by themselves. I have tried to make spiritual power by teaching Greek. But the world can never be really touched by a dead language and a dead civilization. The people must have power; and the people cannot have Greek. Now the power that is made here can be wielded by all men.

BARBARA. Power to burn women's houses down and kill their sons and tear their husbands to pieces.

CUSINS. You cannot have power for good without having power for evil too. Even mother's milk nourishes murderers as well as heroes. This power which only tears men's bodies to pieces has never been so horribly abused as the intellectual power, the imaginative power, the poetic, religious power that can enslave men's souls. As a teacher of Greek I gave the intellectual man weapons against the common man. I now want to give the common man weapons against the inellectual man. I love the common people. I want to arm them against the lawyers, the doctors, the priests, the literary men, the professors, the artists, and the politicians, who, once in authority, are more disastrous and tyrannical than all the fools, rascals, and impostors. I want a power simple enough for common men to use, yet strong enough to force the intellectual oligarchy to use its genius for the general good.

BARBARA. Is there no higher power than that? (*Pointing to the shell.*)

CUSINS. Yes; but that power can destroy the higher powers just as a tiger can destroy a man: therefore Man must master that power first. I admitted this when the Turks and Greeks were last at war. My best pupil went out to fight for Hellas. My parting gift to him was not a copy of Plato's Republic, but a revolver and a hundred Undershaft cartridges. The blood of every Turk he shot—if he shot any—is on my head as well as on Undershaft's. That act committed me to this place for ever. Your father's challenge has beaten me. Dare I make war on war? I dare. I must. I will. And now, is it all over between us?

BARBARA (*touched by his evident dread of her answer*). Silly baby Dolly! How could it be!

CUSINS (*overjoyed*). Then you—you—you—Oh for my drum! (*He flourishes imaginary drumsticks.*)

BARBARA (*angered by his levity*). Take care, Dolly, take care. Oh, if only I could get away from you and from father and from it all! if I could have the wings of a dove and fly away to heaven!

CUSINS. And leave me!

BARBARA. Yes, you, and all the other naughty mischievous children of men. But I cant. I was happy in the Salvation Army for a moment. I escaped from the world into a paradise of enthusiasm and prayer and soul saving; but the moment our money ran short, it all came back to Bodger: it was he who saved our people: he, and the Prince of Darkness, my papa. Undershaft and Bodger: their hands stretch everywhere: when we feed a starving fellow creature, it is with their bread, because there is no other bread; when we tend the sick, it is in the hospitals they endow; if we turn from the churches they build, we must kneel on the stones of the streets they pave. As long as that lasts, there is no getting away from them. Turning our backs on Bodger and Undershaft is turning our backs on life.

CUSINS. I thought you were determined to turn your back on the wicked side of life.

BARBARA. There is no wicked side: life is all one. And I never wanted to shirk my share in whatever evil must be endured, whether it be sin or suffering. I wish I could cure you of middle-class ideas, Dolly.

CUSINS (*gasping*). Middle cl—! A snub! A social snub to me! from the daughter of a foundling!

BARBARA. That is why I have no class, Dolly: I come straight out of the heart of the whole people. If I were middle-class I should turn my back on my father's business; and we should both live in an artistic drawing room, with you reading the reviews in one corner, and I in the other at the piano, playing Schumann: both very superior persons, and neither of us a bit of use. Sooner than that, I would sweep out the guncotton shed, or be one of Bodger's barmaids. Do you know what would have happened if you had refused papa's offer?

CUSINS. I wonder!

BARBARA. I should have given you up and married the man who accepted it. After all, my dear old mother has more sense than any of you. I felt like her when I saw this place—felt that I must have it—that never, never, never could I let it go; only she thought it was the houses and the kitchen ranges and the linen and china, when it was really all the human souls to be saved: not weak souls in starved bodies, sobbing with gratitude for a scrap of bread and treacle, but fullfed, quarrelsome, snobbish, uppish creatures, all standing on their little rights and dignities, and thinking that my father ought to be greatly obliged to them for making so much money for him—and so he ought. That is where salvation is really wanted. My father shall never throw it in my teeth again that my converts were bribed with bread. (*She is transfigured.*) I have got rid of the bribe of bread. I have got rid of the bribe of heaven. Let God's work be done for its own sake: the work he had to create us to do because it cannot be done except by living men and women. When I die, let him be in my debt, not I in his; and let me forgive him as becomes a woman of my rank.

CUSINS. Then the way of life lies through the factory of death?

BARBARA. Yes, through the raising of hell to heaven and of man to God, through the unveiling of an eternal light in the Valley of The Shadow. (*Seizing him with both hands.*) Oh, did you think my courage would never come back? did you believe that I was a deserter? that I, who have stood in the streets, and taken my people to my heart, and talked of the holiest and greatest things with them, could ever turn back and chatter foolishly to fashionable people about nothing in a drawing room? Never, never, never, never: Major Barbara will die with the colors. Oh! and I have my dear little Dolly boy still; and he has found me my place and my work. Glory Hallelujah! (*She kisses him.*)

CUSINS. My dearest: consider my delicate health. I cannot stand as much happiness as you can.

BARBARA. Yes: it is not easy work being in love with me, is it? But it's good for you. (*She runs to the shed, and calls, childlike.*) Mamma! Mamma! (*Bilton comes out of the shed, followed by Undershaft.*) I want Mamma.

UNDERSHAFT. She is taking off her list slippers, dear. (*He passes on to Cusins.*) Well? What does she say?

CUSINS. She has gone right up into the skies.

LADY BRITOMART (*coming from the shed and stopping on the steps, obstructing Sarah, who follows with Lomax. Barbara clutches like a baby at her mother's skirt*). Barbara: when will you learn to be independent and to act and think for yourself? I know as well as possible what that cry of "Mamma, Mamma," means. Always running to me!

SARAH (*touching Lady Britomart's ribs with her finger tips and imitating a bicycle horn*). Pip! pip!

LADY BRITOMART (*highly indignant*). How dare you say Pip! pip! to me, Sarah? You are both very naughty children. What do you want, Barbara?

BARBARA. I want a house in the village to live in with Dolly. (*Dragging at the skirt.*) Come and tell me which one to take.

UNDERSHAFT (*to Cusins*). Six o'clock tomorrow morning, Euripides.

THE END

TRIFLES

SUSAN GLASPELL

SUSAN GLASPELL (1882–1948)

If Eugene O'Neill is regarded as the father of the modern American theater, it is no less fitting to remember Susan Glaspell as its "mother." Though not as well known as O'Neill, Glaspell was an integral part of the movement that brought American drama to maturity in the early years of the twentieth century. In 1931 she became the first woman to win a Pulitzer Prize in drama (*Alison's House*, a drama loosely based on the life of poet Emily Dickinson), an award that helped mark the acceptance of women in the American theater.

The Iowa-born Glaspell attended Drake University in Des Moines, where she studied literature and journalism. While working as a journalist in 1908, she met George Cram Cook, a professor at University of Iowa, whom she married in 1913 (after his first marriage ended in divorce and after she had experienced the avant-garde artistic movements of Paris). The couple gravitated to Provincetown, a resort town on Cape Cod, where they joined other artists, including O'Neill, to produce short plays modeled on the new European drama. The first play produced at Provincetown was *Suppressed Desires,* coauthored by Glaspell and Cook, a still-amusing satire on Freudian psychology. The Cook-led troupe attempted to duplicate their Provincetown successes at an old stable on Macdougal Street in New York's Greenwich Village. It was there, at the Provincetown Playhouse, that the plays of Glaspell, O'Neill, e. e. cummings, Sherwood Anderson, and Edna Ferber caught the attention of New York theater patrons intrigued by the realism, Expressionism, and other experimental styles given expression in this noncommercial setting. In 1925 Glaspell and Cook distanced themselves from the Provincetown Players when O'Neill assumed the leadership of the theater while the couple was in Greece (where Cook died).

Throughout her literary career Glaspell maintained the spirit of innovation and the contemporary that marked the Provincetown enterprise. In her full-length play *The Inheritors* (1921), she challenged American jingoism in World War I while calling for greater individual freedom (especially for women) and tolerance of unpopular viewpoints. (Her Pulitzer Prize was tainted by controversy, largely because she held such liberal ideas.) Also in 1921 she wrote her most experimental work, *The Verge*, an Expressionistic drama that portrayed the inner workings of the mind of the so-called new woman. In both her short and longer pieces, Glaspell presented strong central female characters who sought autonomy in a male-dominated society. *Trifles* (1916) remains the best-known, most produced of these plays.

From 1936 to 1938 Glaspell was chief administrator of the Federal Theater Project's Midwest Bureau, a position that acknowledged her importance as a founder of the community and regional theater movement in America and as one of the standard-bearers for women's issues in art.

TRIFLES (1916)

Recall that *Lysistrata* was Aristophanes' ribald story of the rebellion of the women of Athens and Sparta during the Peloponnesian War. In Ibsen's *A Doll's House* Nora rebels against the stifling conditions in the Helmer household. Later you may read Sue Townsend's *The Great Celestial Cow*, which ends with a rousing rebellion by a group of East Indian women at a cattle market in England. So, too, is *Trifles* a "rebellion" play—but here you'll find no boisterous clashes between men and women, no slamming doors, and no chaos in the cattle barns. Rather, *Trifles* is about a subtle, silent rebellion, marked by furtive glances, withheld secrets (the dead bird), and—importantly—the restitching of a homemade quilt.

On its surface *Trifles* may be aligned with that most popular of mystery genres, the "whodunit." A farmer has been murdered and the townsmen, led by Sheriff Peters, gather to sort through evidence that may lead them to the killer. Because of their status in this male-dominated world the women are relegated to the kitchen. Read Glaspell's detailed description of that kitchen carefully because it is more than an attempt to create a realistic ambience; the opening stage direction is rife with clues about the mysteries of the Wright household.

As the men traipse about the house searching for clues and chuckling at the women's conversations about "trifles," they are oblivious to crucial clues to the murder. These they dismiss as merely sloppy housekeeping, though the women know that Minnie Foster Wright was in fact a meticulous housekeeper. Note that Minnie is the only woman to whom Glaspell assigns a full name; the others are mere extensions of their respective husbands. The women—Mrs. Peters and Mrs. Hale—gradually realize the horrible life Minnie endured at the hands of her callous, abusive husband. Moreover, they realize that circumstances, manifested by the dead bird, forced Minnie to liberate herself through violent means. Yet they do not condemn her; rather they stage a silent rebellion by withholding their knowledge from the men who have patronized them.

After the success of the play, Glaspell converted her tale into a short story (much of the dialogue of the play was inserted verbatim into the narration), which she retitled "A Jury of Her Peers." Just as the play title is ironic (the "trifles" within the Wright house hold significant truths), the short story title was especially ironic in 1917 because women, in most states, were not allowed to serve on juries, nor were they allowed to vote until 1920. Yet Mrs. Peters and Mrs. Hale prove to be the shrewdest of jurors in their analysis of the "crime," and they offer a resounding vote against abuse and disrespect in their conspiracy of silence.

The play raises challenging moral questions: Is it justifiable for a woman to resort to killing an abusive spouse? Are Mrs. Peters and Mrs. Hale culpable for concealing evidence, however "trifling," to protect Minnie? Unfortunately, our daily headlines too often force us to assess such behaviors in daily life as battered and abused women (and to be sure, men in some instances) feel forced into violent solutions to domestic violence. Glaspell's play was not only a harbinger of a new style and subject matter of drama in the American theater; it foreshadowed what has become a major social issue of the late twentieth century. Minnie Foster Wright—whom we never see, but about whom we know so much—remains the model of what we now recognize as the "battered woman syndrome."

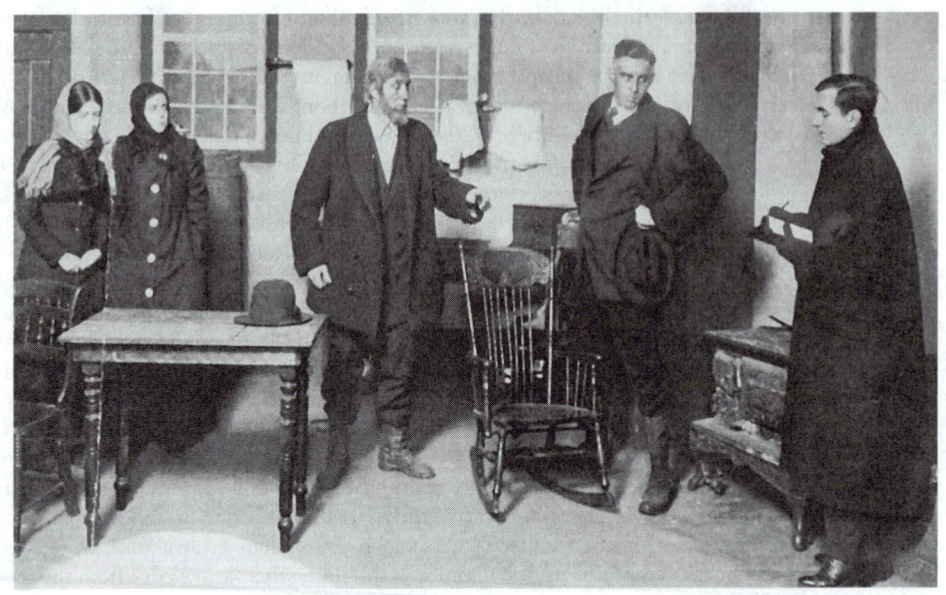

A photograph of the Provincetown Players' original production of Trifles *appeared in a 1917 edition of* Theatre Magazine, *a sign that the Greenwich Village artists had become a force in the American theater.*

TRIFLES

SUSAN GLASPELL

SCENE: *The kitchen in the now abandoned farmhouse of John Wright, a gloomy kitchen, and left without having been put in order—unwashed pans under the sink, a loaf of bread outside the breadbox, a dish towel on the table—other signs of incompleted work. At the rear the outer door opens, and the Sheriff comes in, followed by the County Attorney and Hale. The Sheriff and Hale are men in middle life, the County Attorney is a young man; all are much bundled up and go at once to the stove. They are followed by the two women—the Sheriff's Wife first; she is a slight wiry woman, a thin nervous face. Mrs. Hale is larger and would ordinarily be called more comfortable looking, but she is disturbed now and looks fearfully about as she enters. The women have come in slowly and stand close together near the door.*

COUNTY ATTORNEY (*rubbing his hands*). This feels good. Come up to the fire, ladies.

MRS. PETERS (*after taking a step forward*). I'm not—cold.

SHERIFF (*unbuttoning his overcoat and stepping away from the stove as if to the beginning of official business*). Now, Mr. Hale, before we move things about, you explain to Mr. Henderson just what you saw when you came here yesterday morning.

COUNTY ATTORNEY. By the way, has anything been moved? Are things just as you left them yesterday?

SHERIFF (*looking about*). It's just the same. When it dropped below zero last night, I thought I'd better send Frank out this morning to make a fire for us—no use getting pneumonia with a big case on; but I told him not to touch anything except the stove—and you know Frank.

COUNTY ATTORNEY. Somebody should have been left here yesterday.

SHERIFF. Oh—yesterday. When I had to send Frank to Morris Center for that man who went crazy—I want you to know I had my hands full yesterday. I knew you could get back from Omaha by today, and as long as I went over everything here myself—

COUNTY ATTORNEY. Well, Mr. Hale, tell just what happened when you came here yesterday morning.

HALE. Harry and I had started to town with a load of potatoes. We came along the road from my place; and as I got here, I said, "I'm going to see if I can't get John Wright to go in with me on a party telephone." I spoke to Wright about it once before, and he put me off, saying folks talked too much anyway, and all he asked was peace and quiet—I guess you know about how much he talked himself; but I thought maybe if I went to the house and talked about it before his wife, though I said to Harry that I didn't know as what his wife wanted made much difference to John—

COUNTY ATTORNEY. Let's talk about that later, Mr. Hale. I do want to talk about that, but tell now just what happened when you got to the house.

HALE. I didn't hear or see anything; I knocked at the door, and still it was all quiet inside. I knew they must be up, it was past eight o'clock. So I knocked again, and I thought I heard somebody say, "Come in." I wasn't sure, I'm not sure yet, but I opened the door—this door (*indicating the door by which the two women are still standing*), and there in that rocker—(*pointing to it*) sat Mrs. Wright. (*They all look at the rocker.*)

COUNTY ATTORNEY. What—was she doing?

HALE. She was rockin' back and forth. She had her apron in her hand and was kind of—pleating it.

COUNTY ATTORNEY. And how did she—look?

HALE. Well, she looked queer.

COUNTY ATTORNEY. How do you mean—queer?

HALE. Well, as if she didn't know what she was going to do next. And kind of done up.

COUNTY ATTORNEY. How did she seem to feel about your coming?

HALE. Why, I don't think she minded—one way or other. She didn't pay much attention. I said, "How do, Mrs. Wright, it's cold, ain't it?" And she said, "Is it?"—and went on kind of pleating at her apron. Well, I was surprised; she didn't ask me to come up to the stove, or to set down, but just sat there, not even looking at me, so I said, "I want to see John." And then she—laughed. I guess you would call it a laugh. I thought of Harry and the team outside, so I said a little sharp: "Can't I see John?" "No," she says, kind o' dull like. "Ain't he home?" says I. "Yes," says she, "he's home." "Then why can't I see him?" I asked her, out of patience. "'Cause he's dead," says she. "Dead?" says I. She just nodded her head, not getting a bit excited, but rockin' back and forth. "Why—where is he?" says I, not knowing what to say. She just pointed upstairs—like that (*himself pointing to the room above*). I got up, with the idea of going up there. I walked from there to here—then I says, "Why, what did he die of?" "He died of a rope around his neck," says she, and just went on pleatin' at her apron. Well, I went out and called Harry. I thought I might—need help. We went upstairs, and there he was lyin'—

COUNTY ATTORNEY. I think I'd rather have you go into that upstairs, where you can point it all out. Just go on now with the rest of the story.

HALE. Well, my first thought was to get that rope off. I looked ... (*Stops, his face twitches.*) ... but Harry, he went up to him, and he said, "No, he's dead all right, and we'd better not touch anything." So we went back downstairs. She was still sitting that same way. "Has anybody been notified?" I asked. "No," says she, unconcerned. "Who did this, Mrs. Wright?" said Harry. He said it businesslike—and she stopped pleatin' of her apron. "I don't know," she says. "You don't *know*?" says Harry. "No," says she. "Weren't you sleepin' in the bed with him?" says Harry. "Yes," says she, "but I was on the inside." "Somebody slipped a rope round his neck and strangled him, and you didn't wake up?" says Harry. "I didn't wake up," she said after him. We must 'a looked as if we didn't see how that could be, for after a minute she said, "I sleep sound." Harry was going to ask her more questions, but I said maybe we ought to let her tell her story first to the coroner, or the sheriff, so Harry went fast as he could to Rivers' place, where there's a telephone.

COUNTY ATTORNEY. And what did Mrs. Wright do when she knew that you had gone for the coroner?

HALE. She moved from that chair to this over here ... (*Pointing to a small chair in the corner.*) ... and just sat there with her hands held together and looking down. I got a feeling that I ought to make some conversation, so I said I had come in to see if John wanted to put in a telephone, and at that she started to laugh, and then she stopped and looked at me—scared. (*The County Attorney, who has had his notebook out, makes a note.*) I dunno, maybe it wasn't scared. I wouldn't like to say it was. Soon Harry got back, and then Dr. Lloyd came, and you, Mr. Peters, and so I guess that's all I know that you don't.

COUNTY ATTORNEY (*looking around*). I guess we'll go upstairs first—and then out to the barn and around there. (*To the Sheriff.*) You're convinced that there was nothing important here—nothing that would point to any motive?

SHERIFF. Nothing here but kitchen things.

(*The County Attorney, after again looking around the kitchen, opens the door of a cupboard closet. He gets up on a chair and looks on a shelf. Pulls his hand away, sticky.*)

COUNTY ATTORNEY. Here's a nice mess.

(*The women draw nearer.*)

MRS. PETERS (*to the other woman*). Oh, her fruit; it did freeze. (*To the Lawyer.*) She worried about that when it turned so cold. She said the fir'd go out and her jars would break.

SHERIFF. Well, can you beat the women! Held for murder and worryin' about her preserves.

COUNTY ATTORNEY. I guess before we're through she may have something more serious than preserves to worry about.

HALE. Well, women are used to worrying over trifles.

(*The two women move a little closer together.*)

COUNTY ATTORNEY (*with the gallantry of a young politician*). And yet, for all their worries, what would we do without the ladies? (*The women do not unbend. He goes to the sink, takes a dipperful of water from the pail and, pouring it into a basin, washes his hands. Starts to wipe them on the roller towel, turns it for a cleaner place.*) Dirty towels! (*Kicks his foot against the pans under the sink.*) Not much of a housekeeper, would you say, ladies?

MRS. HALE (*stiffly*). There's a great deal of work to be done on a farm.

COUNTY ATTORNEY. To be sure. And yet . . . (*With a little bow to her.*) . . . I know there are some Dickson county farmhouses which do not have such roller towels. (*He gives it a pull to expose its full length again.*)

MRS. HALE. Those towels get dirty awful quick. Men's hands aren't always as clean as they might be.

COUNTY ATTORNEY. Ah, loyal to your sex, I see. But you and Mrs. Wright were neighbors. I suppose you were friends, too.

MRS. HALE (*shaking her head*). I've not seen much of her of late years. I've not been in this house—it's more than a year.

COUNTY ATTORNEY. And why was that? You didn't like her?

MRS. HALE. I liked her all well enough. Farmers' wives have their hands full, Mr. Henderson. And then—

COUNTY ATTORNEY. Yes—?

MRS. HALE (*looking about*). It never seemed a very cheerful place.

COUNTY ATTORNEY. No—it's not cheerful. I shouldn't say she had the homemaking instinct.

MRS. HALE. Well, I don't know as Wright had, either.

COUNTY ATTORNEY. You mean that they didn't get on very well?

MRS. HALE. No, I don't mean anything. But I don't think a place'd be any cheerfuler for John Wright's being in it.

COUNTY ATTORNEY. I'd like to talk more of that a little later. I want to get the lay of things upstairs now. (*He goes to the left, where three steps lead to a stair door.*)

SHERIFF. I suppose anything Mrs. Peters does'll be all right. She was to take in some clothes for her, you know, and a few little things. We left in such a hurry yesterday.

COUNTY ATTORNEY. Yes, but I would like to see what you take, Mrs. Peters, and keep an eye out for anything that might be of use to us.

MRS. PETERS. Yes, Mr. Henderson.

(*The women listen to the men's steps on the stairs, then look about the kitchen.*)

MRS. HALE. I'd hate to have men coming into my kitchen, snooping around and criticizing. (*She arranges the pans under sink which the Lawyer had shoved out of place.*)

MRS. PETERS. Of course it's no more than their duty.

MRS. HALE. Duty's all right, but I guess that deputy sheriff that came out to make the fire might have got a little of this on. (*Gives the roller towel a pull.*) Wish I'd thought of that sooner. Seems mean to talk about her for not having things slicked up when she had to come away in such a hurry.

MRS. PETERS (*who has gone to a small table in the left rear corner of the room, and lifted one end of a towel that covers a pan*). She had bread set. (*Stands still.*)

MRS. HALE (*eyes fixed on a loaf of bread beside the breadbox, which is on a low shelf at the other side of the room. Moves slowly toward it*). She was going to put this in there. (*Picks up loaf, then abruptly drops it. In a manner of returning to familiar things.*) It's a shame about her fruit. I wonder if it's all gone. (*Gets up on the chair and looks.*) I think there's some here that's all right, Mrs. Peters. Yes—here; (*Holding it toward the window.*) this is cherries, too. (*Looking again.*) I declare I believe that's the only one. (*Gets down, bottle in her hand. Goes to the sink and wipes it off on the outside.*) She'll feel awful bad after all her hard work in the hot weather. I remember the afternoon I put up my cherries last summer. (*She puts the bottle on the big kitchen table, center of the room, front table. With a sigh, is about to sit down in the rocking chair. Before she is seated realizes what chair it is; with a slow look at it, steps back. The chair, which she has touched, rocks back and forth.*)

MRS. PETERS. Well, I must get those things from the front room closet. (*She goes to the door at the right, but after looking into the other room steps back.*) You coming with me, Mrs. Hale? You could help me carry them. (*They go into the other room; reappear, Mrs. Peters carrying a dress and skirt, Mrs. Hale following with a pair of shoes.*)

MRS. PETERS. My, it's cold in there. (*She puts the cloth on the big table, and hurries to the stove.*)

MRS. HALE (*examining the skirt*). Wright was close. I think maybe that's why she kept so much to herself. She didn't even belong to the Ladies' Aid. I suppose she felt she couldn't do her part, and then you don't enjoy things when you feel shabby. She used to wear pretty clothes and be lively, when she was Minnie Foster, one of the town girls singing in the choir. But that—oh, that was thirty years ago. This all you was to take in?

MRS. PETERS. She said she wanted an apron. Funny thing to want, for there isn't much to get you dirty in jail, goodness knows. But I suppose just to make her feel more natural. She said they was in the top drawer in this cupboard. Yes, here. And then her little shawl that always hung behind the door. (*Opens stair door and looks.*) Yes, here it is. (*Quickly shuts door leading upstairs.*)

MRS. HALE (*abruptly moving toward her*). Mrs. Peters?

MRS. PETERS. Yes, Mrs. Hale?

MRS. HALE. Do you think she did it?

MRS. PETERS (*in a frightened voice*). Oh, I don't know.

MRS. HALE. Well, I don't think she did. Asking for an apron and her little shawl. Worrying about her fruit.

MRS. PETERS (*starts to speak, glances up, where footsteps are heard in the room above. In a low voice*). Mr. Peters says it looks bad for her. Mr. Henderson is awful sarcastic in speech, and he'll make fun of her sayin' she didn't wake up.

MRS. HALE. Well, I guess John Wright didn't wake when they was slipping that rope under his neck.

MRS. PETERS. No, it's strange. It must have been done awful crafty and still. They say it was such a—funny way to kill a man, rigging it all up like that.

MRS. HALE. That's just what Mr. Hale said. There was a gun in the house. He says that's what he can't understand.

MRS. PETERS. Mr. Henderson said coming out that what was needed for the case was a motive; something to show anger, or—sudden feeling.

MRS. HALE (*who is standing by the table*). Well, I don't see any signs of anger around here. (*She puts her hand on the dish towel which lies on the table, stands looking down at the table, one half of which is clean, the other half messy.*) It's wiped here. (*Makes a move as if to finish work, then turns and looks at loaf of bread outside the breadbox. Drops towel. In that voice of coming back to familiar things.*) Wonder how they are finding things upstairs? I hope she had it a little more red-up there. You know, it seems kind of *sneaking.* Locking her up in town and then coming out here and trying to get her own house to turn against her!

MRS. PETERS. But, Mrs. Hale, the law is the law.

MRS. HALE. I s'pose 'tis. (*Unbuttoning her coat.*) Better loosen up your things, Mrs. Peters. You won't feel them when you go out.

(*Mrs. Peters takes off her fur tippet, goes to hang it on a hook at the back of the room, stands looking at the under part of the small corner table.*)

MRS. PETERS. She was piecing a quilt. (*She brings the large sewing basket, and they look at the bright pieces.*)

MRS. HALE. It's log cabin pattern. Pretty, isn't it? I wonder if she was goin' to quilt or just knot it?

(*Footsteps have been heard coming down the stairs. The Sheriff enters, followed by Hale and the County Attorney.*)

SHERIFF. They wonder if she was going to quilt it or just knot it. (*The men laugh, the women look abashed.*)

COUNTY ATTORNEY (*rubbing his hands over the stove*). Frank's fire didn't do much up there, did it? Well, let's go out to the barn and get that cleared up.

(*The men go outside.*)

MRS. HALE (*resentfully*). I don't know as there's anything so strange, our takin' up our time with little things while we're waiting for them to get the evidence. (*She sits down at the big table, smoothing out a block with decision.*) I don't see as it's anything to laugh about.

MRS. PETERS (*apologetically*). Of course they've got awful important things on their minds. (*Pulls up a chair and joins Mrs. Hale at the table.*)

MRS. HALE (*examining another block*). Mrs. Peters, look at this one. Here, this is the one she was working on, and look at the sewing! All the rest of it has been so nice and even. And look at this! It's all over the place! Why, it looks as if she didn't know what she was about! (*After she has said this, they look at each other, then started to glance back at the door. After an instant Mrs. Hale has pulled at a knot and ripped the sewing.*)

MRS. PETERS. Oh, what are you doing, Mrs. Hale?

MRS. HALE (*mildly*). Just pulling out a stitch or two that's not sewed very good. (*Threading a needle.*) Bad sewing always made me fidgety.

MRS. PETERS (*nervously*). I don't think we ought to touch things.

MRS. HALE. I'll just finish up this end. (*Suddenly stopping and leaning forward.*) Mrs. Peters?

MRS. PETERS. Yes, Mrs. Hale?

MRS. HALE. What do you suppose she was so nervous about?

MRS. PETERS. Oh—I don't know. I don't know as she was nervous. I sometimes sew awful queer when I'm just tired. (*Mrs. Hale starts to say something, looks at Mrs. Peters, then goes on sewing.*) Well, I must get these things wrapped up. They may be through sooner than we think. (*Putting apron and other things together.*) I wonder where I can find a piece of paper, and string.

MRS. HALE. In that cupboard, maybe.

MRS. PETERS (*looking in cupboard*). Why, here's a birdcage. (*Holds it up.*) Did she have a bird, Mrs. Hale?

MRS. HALE. Why, I don't know whether she did or not—I've not been here for so long. There was a man around last year selling canaries cheap, but I don't know as she took one; maybe she did. She used to sing real pretty herself.

MRS. PETERS (*glancing around*). Seems funny to think of a bird here. But she must have had one, or why should she have a cage? I wonder what happened to it?

MRS. HALE. I s'pose maybe the cat got it.

MRS. PETERS. No, she didn't have a cat. She's got that feeling some people have about cats—being afraid of them. My cat got in her room, and she was real upset and asked me to take it out.

MRS. HALE. My sister Bessie was like that. Queer, ain't it?

MRS. PETERS (*examining the cage*). Why, look at this door. It's broke. One hinge is pulled apart.

MRS. HALE (*looking, too*). Looks as if someone must have been rough with it.

MRS. PETERS. Why, yes. (*She brings the cage forward and puts it on the table.*)

MRS. HALE. I wish if they're going to find any evidence they'd be about it. I don't like this place.

MRS. PETERS. But I'm awful glad you came with me, Mrs. Hale. It would be lonesome for me sitting here alone.

MRS. HALE. It would, wouldn't it? (*Dropping her sewing.*) But I tell you what I do wish, Mrs. Peters. I wish I had come over sometimes when *she* was here. I—(*Looking around the room.*)—wish I had.

MRS. PETERS. But of course you were awful busy, Mrs. Hale—your house and your children.

MRS. HALE. I could've come. I stayed away because it weren't cheerful—and that's why I ought to have come. I—I've never liked this place. Maybe because it's down in a hollow, and you don't see the road. I dunno what it is, but it's a lonesome place and always was. I wish I had come over to see Minnie Foster sometimes. I can see now—(*Shakes her head.*)

MRS. PETERS. Well, you mustn't reproach yourself, Mrs. Hale. Somehow we just don't see how it is with other folks until—something comes up.

MRS. HALE. Not having children makes less work—but it makes a quiet house, and Wright out to work all day, and no company when he did come in. Did you know John Wright, Mrs. Peters?

MRS. PETERS. Not to know him; I've seen him in town. They say he was a good man.

MRS. HALE. Yes—good; he didn't drink, and kept his word as well as most, I guess, and paid his debts. But he was a hard man, Mrs. Peters. Just to pass the time of day with him. (*Shivers.*) Like a raw wind that gets to the bone. (*Pauses, her eye falling on the cage.*) I should think she would 'a wanted a bird. But what do you suppose went with it?

MRS. PETERS. I don't know, unless it got sick and died. (*She reaches over and swings the broken door, swings it again; both women watch it.*)

MRS. HALE. You weren't raised round here, were you? (*Mrs. Peters shakes her head.*) You didn't know—her?

MRS. PETERS. Not till they brought her yesterday.

MRS. HALE. She—come to think of it, she was kind of like a bird herself—real sweet and pretty, but kind of timid and—fluttery. How—she—did—change. (*Silence; then as if struck by a happy thought and relieved to get back to everyday things.*) Tell you what, Mrs. Peters, why don't you take the quilt in with you? It might take up her mind.

MRS. PETERS. Why, I think that's a real nice idea, Mrs. Hale. There couldn't possibly be any objection to it, could there? Now, just what would I take? I wonder if her patches are in here—and her things. (*They look in the sewing basket.*)

MRS. HALE. Here's some red. I expect this has got sewing things in it (*Brings out a fancy box.*) What a pretty box. Looks like something somebody would give you. Maybe her scissors are in here. (*Opens box. Suddenly puts her hand to her nose.*) Why—(*Mrs. Peters bends nearer, then turns her face away.*) There's something wrapped up in this piece of silk.

MRS. PETERS. Why, this isn't her scissors.

MRS. HALE (*lifting the silk*). Oh, Mrs. Peters—it's—(*Mrs. Peters bends closer.*)

MRS. PETERS. It's the bird.

MRS. HALE (*jumping up*). But, Mrs. Peters—look at it. Its neck! Look at its neck! It's all—other side *to*.

MRS. PETERS. Somebody—wrung—its neck.

(*Their eyes meet. A look of growing comprehension of horror. Steps are heard outside. Mrs. Hale slips box under quilt pieces, and sinks into her chair. Enter Sheriff and County Attorney. Mrs. Peters rises.*)

COUNTY ATTORNEY (*as one turning from serious things to little pleasantries*). Well, ladies, have you decided whether she was going to quilt it or knot it?

MRS. PETERS. We think she was going to—knot it.

COUNTY ATTORNEY. Well, that's interesting, I'm sure. (*Seeing the birdcage.*) Has the bird flown?

MRS. HALE (*putting more quilt pieces over the box*). We think the—cat got it.

COUNTY ATTORNEY (*preoccupied*). Is there a cat?

(*Mrs. Hale glances in a quick covert way at Mrs. Peters.*)

MRS. PETERS. Well, not now. They're superstitious, you know. They leave.

COUNTY ATTORNEY (*to Sheriff Peters, continuing an interrupted conversation*). No sign at all of anyone having come from the outside. Their own rope. Now let's go up again and go over it piece by piece. (*They start upstairs.*) It would have to have been someone who knew just the—

(*Mrs. Peters sits down. The two women sit there not looking at one another, but as if peering into something and at the same time holding back. When they talk now, it is the manner of feeling their way over strange ground, as if afraid of what they are saying, but as if they cannot help saying it.*)

MRS. HALE. She liked the bird. She was going to bury it in that pretty box.

MRS. PETERS (*in a whisper*). When I was a girl—my kitten—there was a boy took a hatchet, and before my eyes—and before I could get there—(*Covers her face an instant.*) If they hadn't held me back, I would have—(*Catches herself, looks upstairs where steps are heard, falters weakly.*)—hurt him.

MRS. HALE (*with a slow look around her*). I wonder how it would seem never to have had any children around. (*Pause.*) No, Wright wouldn't like the bird—a thing that sang. She used to sing. He killed that, too.

MRS. PETERS (*moving uneasily*). We don't know who killed the bird.

MRS. HALE. I knew John Wright.

MRS. PETERS. It was an awful thing was done in this house that night, Mrs. Hale. Killing a man while he slept, slipping a rope around his neck that choked the life out of him.

MRS. HALE. His neck. Choked the life out of him.

(Her hand goes out and rests on the birdcage.)

MRS. PETERS (with a rising voice). We don't know who killed him. We don't know.

MRS. HALE (her own feeling not interrupted). If there'd been years and years of nothing, then a bird to sing to you, it would be awful—still, after the bird was still.

MRS. PETERS (something within her speaking). I know what stillness is. When we homesteaded in Dakota, and my first baby died—after he was two years old, and me with no other then—

MRS. HALE (moving). How soon do you suppose they'll be through, looking for evidence?

MRS. PETERS. I know what stillness is. (Pulling herself back.) The law has got to punish crime, Mrs. Hale.

MRS. HALE (not as if answering that). I wish you'd seen Minnie Foster when she wore a white dress with blue ribbons and stood up there in the choir and sang. (A look around the room.) Oh, I wish I'd come over here once in a while! That was a crime! That was a crime! Who's going to punish that?

MRS. PETERS (looking upstairs). We mustn't—take on.

MRS. HALE. I might have known she needed help! I know how things can be—for women. I tell you, it's queer, Mrs. Peters. We live close together and we live far apart. We all go through the same things—it's all just a different kind of the same thing. (Brushes her eyes, noticing the bottle of fruit, reaches out for it.) If I was you, I wouldn't tell her her fruit was gone. Tell her it ain't. Tell her it's all right. Take this in to prove it to her. She—she may never know whether it was broke or not.

MRS. PETERS (takes the bottle, looks about for something to wrap it in; takes petticoat from the clothes brought from the other room, very nervously begins winding this around the bottle. In a false voice). My, it's a good thing the men couldn't hear us. Wouldn't they just laugh! Getting all stirred up over a little thing like a—dead canary. As if that could have anything to do with—with—wouldn't they laugh!

(The men are heard coming downstairs.)

MRS. HALE (under her breath). Maybe they would—maybe they wouldn't.

COUNTY ATTORNEY. No, Peters, it's all perfectly clear except a reason for doing it. But you know juries when it comes to women. If there was some definite thing. Some-

thing to show—something to make a story about—a thing that would connect up with this strange way of doing it.

(The women's eyes meet for an instant. Enter Hale from outer door.)

HALE. Well, I've got the team around. Pretty cold out there.

COUNTY ATTORNEY. I'm going to stay here awhile by myself. (To the Sheriff.) You can send Frank out for me, can't you? I want to go over everything. I'm not satisfied that we can't do better.

SHERIFF. Do you want to see what Mrs. Peters is going to take in?

(The Lawyer goes to the table, picks up the apron, laughs.)

COUNTY ATTORNEY. Oh I guess they're not very dangerous things the ladies have picked up. (Moves a few things about, disturbing the quilt pieces which cover the box. Steps back.) No, Mrs. Peters doesn't need supervising. For that matter, a sheriff's wife is married to the law. Ever think of it that way, Mrs. Peters?

MRS. PETERS. Not—just that way.

SHERIFF (chuckling). Married to the law. (Moves toward the other room.) I just want you to come in here a minute, George. We ought to take a look at these windows.

COUNTY ATTORNEY (scoffingly). Oh, windows!

SHERIFF. We'll be right out, Mr. Hale.

(Hale goes outside. The Sheriff follows the County Attorney into the other room. Then Mrs. Hale rises, hands tight together, looking intensely at Mrs. Peters, whose eyes take a slow turn, finally meeting, Mrs. Hale's. A moment Mrs. Hale holds her, then her own eyes point the way to where the box is concealed. Suddenly Mrs. Peters throws back quilt pieces and tries to put the box in the bag she is wearing. It is too big. She opens box, starts to take the bird out, cannot touch it, goes to pieces, stands there helpless. Sound of a knob turning in the other room. Mrs. Hale snatches the box and puts it in the pocket of her big coat. Enter County Attorney and Sheriff.)

COUNTY ATTORNEY (facetiously). Well, Henry, at least we found out that she was not going to quilt it. She was going to—what is it you call it, ladies?

MRS. HALE (her hand against her pocket). We call it—knot it, Mr. Henderson.

CURTAIN

THE GLASS MENAGERIE

Tennessee Williams

Tennessee Williams (1911–1983)

Despite his status as one of the twentieth-century's preeminent playwrights, Tennessee Williams has not been regarded as a social dramatist in the manner of such contemporaries as Clifford Odets, Lillian Hellman, and especially Arthur Miller, whose own playwriting career virtually parallels that of Williams. Whereas these artists and their peers might be properly considered "the sons and daughters of Ibsen," Williams is much more a "son of Chekhov" (or Strindberg). His plays portray the loneliness of life, especially from the perspective of those who are outsiders by virtue of their personality, sexual orientation, or some flaw considered deviant. However, his disturbing, often shocking, portraits of marginalized victims of a cruel society make Williams among the most eloquent of America's social voices. The central question of Williams's dramas—"Is there no mercy left in the world anymore?"—is perhaps the most urgent query of the modern world.

The story of Williams's life reads much like one of his scripts, not surprising for this most intensely subjective of contemporary American playwrights. He was born Thomas Lanier Williams in Mississippi, and though his southern roots are evident throughout his works, he is more than a regional playwright. His father, an abusive traveling shoe salesman, cruelly teased his son about his lack of masculinity, frequently calling him "Miss Lucy." His mother, the daughter of a clergyman, was schooled in southern gentility and suffered from bouts of mental illness. His sister, Rose, was sickly, delicate, and retiring (the paradigm of the Williams heroine), and he sympathized with her loneliness and unhappiness. His unhappy youth and fractured family life are reflected in his first playwriting success, *The Glass Menagerie* (1944), which was originally written as a screenplay (*The Gentleman Caller*) for the film studio MGM, to which Williams was contracted.

Williams attended the University of Missouri for two years and ultimately graduated from the University of Iowa, where he studied theater and playwriting. An odyssey across America provided him with odd jobs and experiences for his short stories and plays. Williams settled into a career as a dramatist after he won a playwriting contest sponsored by the Group Theater (out of which would grow the Actors Studio, with which Williams's name is inextricably linked). His one-act plays caught the attention of a literary agent, Audrey Wood, who championed his writing. The success of *The Glass Menagerie* in 1944 and the triumph of *A Streetcar Named Desire* (1947), for which he received a Pulitzer Prize, made him (with Miller) the preeminent American playwright at midcentury. His best works, written between 1944 and 1962, include *Summer and Smoke* (1948), *Camino Real* (1953), *Cat on a Hot Tin Roof* (1955, Pulitzer Prize), *Orpheus Descending* (1957), *Sweet Bird of Youth* (1959), and *The Night of the Iguana* (1961). His later plays, which suffered a critical backlash mostly because they failed to surpass his earlier works, are marked by experimentation with form and content. Ironically, in 1999 Williams was back on Broadway with a "new" play. One of his first efforts, a prison drama called *Not About Nightingales*, was discovered and produced as a joint effort of the Alley Theater of Houston and the Moving Theater of London (founded by actor Vanessa Redgrave to promote politically oriented plays). The production, directed by Trevor Nunn, was greeted with such enthusiasm in London that it transferred to Broadway.

Like his heroes and heroines, Williams was plagued by substance abuse, bouts of depression and illness, and sexual indulgence. His death in 1983 was a grotesque parody of his own dramas: alone in a hotel room, he choked to death on a medicine bottle cap while his lover, unaware of his predicament, remained in an adjoining room as Williams gasped for help.

Alma, another of Williams's troubled women, speaks a line in *Summer and Smoke* that has become a universal description of the principal characters in his collected works: "My little company of the faded and frightened and difficult and odd and lonely." These include drunkards and addicts, the sexually promiscuous, homosexuals, defrocked ministers, expatriates and foreigners, the mentally and physically ill, and—importantly—the artist. Shakespeare, you may recall from *A Midsummer Night's Dream* notes that "lunatics, lovers, and poets" share a common imagination, and Williams frequently creates characters with an artistic sensibility that permits them to articulate the pain they suffer by virtue of their being different. For instance, Blanche DuBois, the deluded heroine of *A Streetcar Named Desire*, once taught poetry and fancies herself possessed of an artistic spirit. It is the alienated artist in Williams's world who reminds the philistines—the Stanley Kowalskis of the world—that "we are all civilized, which means that we are all savages at heart but observing the amenities of civilized behavior."

Because he writes such extraordinary psychological portraits, and because his plays are customarily placed in naturalistic settings (the environment is a significant character in a Williams play), it is easy to align Williams with those playwrights we call realists. But like Blanche DuBois, who says, "I don't want realism, I want magic," Williams couples his realism with a superb theatricality, much of it derived from Expressionism. The action of Williams's plays is set against a bold array of sounds, lighting effects, and choric characters. Moments of crisis are almost always marked by a spectacular visual image. Williams's language is also theatrical. Though he writes in prose that seems at first reading entirely naturalistic, Williams elevates southern colloquialisms to a poetic level that transcends ordinary speech. This fusion of theatricality, heightened speech, and an abundance of verbal and visual symbols has earned Williams the title of "poetic realist." When Williams died, Walter Kerr, then America's foremost drama critic, said, "We have lost our greatest playwright."

THE GLASS MENAGERIE (1944)

Tom, who serves as the narrator and male protagonist of *The Glass Menagerie*, defines the preoccupations that dominate Williams's plays: the escape from life's ugliest realities into the arts (here, the cinema) and writing. Amanda Wingfield, among the best-written roles for a woman in the modern theater, is simultaneously a loving and loathing, satirical and sympathetic portrait of Williams's own mother. She also escapes into the dreams of her "gentleman callers," into the social world of the Daughters of the American Revolution, into an imaginary life as a southern belle, and into the fantasy world she projects for her children. And the overly shy, crippled Laura escapes into her glass menagerie for solace. Although the play's three protagonists share a claustrophobically small tenement in St. Louis, each is isolated in the tiny room from which there is no retreat.

Obviously, Tom is patterned after Williams himself; they share the same first name, the same interests, and the same poetic spirit. But it is actually Laura (the alter ego of sister Rose) that is ultimately most like the playwright. Because of his sexual orientation, his artistic temperament, and his often self-destructive lifestyle, Williams was considered "odd." That he writes such a sympathetic and moving portrait of Laura, the fragile disabled girl is understandable, for Williams was speaking from the pain of being different. He knew too well what it meant to be a piece of glass "too exquisitely fragile to be removed from the shelf."

The moment when Laura's glass unicorn—a mythic symbol of that which is unique and fragile—shatters, is of course the climax of the drama. Laura's escapist world is shattered, her innocence lost in the dance with Jim, the play's one true Gentleman Caller. It is among the most moving moments in the modern theater, a superb blend of dramatic action, exceptional human emotion and visual symbolism. Not only is the glass unicorn a symbol of that which is unique in the world, in medieval times the one-horned horse was a symbol of chastity and maidenhood. Ironically, the dance with Jim is likely the single sexual experience, innocent as it is, in Laura's life (the real Rose was relegated to a mental institution, where she underwent a lobotomy). The moment fills her, and the audience, with simultaneous joy and heartbreak.

Williams draws on other archetypal symbols in his play. Note that Tom calls Amanda "a witch"; Mother Wingfield is indeed a Gorgon who devours her children in her pathetic attempt to relive her own failed life through them. Though *The Glass Menagerie* appears to be a contemporary domestic drama in the realistic mode, its use of such archetypal symbols elevates it to something beyond the mundane.

For this reason, we urge you to read Williams's "Production Notes" (following the play on page 1092) and stage directions with special care. Through his use of lighting, music and other sounds, and what he calls "the screen device" (a technique favored by Brecht), Williams is attempting to do something other than modernize his play through the use of technology. Rather, he is creating a world of mystery and the supernatural (actually, supranatural, that which goes beyond mere naturalism), ideas on which our greatest myths are founded. For this play, as simple and realistic as it appears on first reading, is about nothing less than a titanic battle between "blood kin" (to use Aeschylus's phrase). It depicts universal issues confronting humans: pain, separation, the coming of age, loss of innocence, hatred, love, and self-realization.

Unfortunately, Williams's conspicuously theatrical devices, particularly the screens, were deleted in this much-performed play, usually in the name of realism. Of late, they have been revived by directors and producers who now better appreciate Williams's intentions. Paul Newman, whose screen credits include major roles in many Williams's plays, directed a production of *The Glass Menagerie* in which his wife, Joanne Woodward, played Amanda. Newman was adamant about employing Williams's "unusual freedoms of convention."

So again, read the "Production Notes" and stage directions carefully. They remain the most compelling commentary written about this remarkable play.

Laura escapes the pain of her troubled home by seeking refuge in her "glass menagerie" in a Yale Repertory Theatre production of Williams's autobiographical play; the unicorn stands at the center of the lower shelf.

THE GLASS MENAGERIE

TENNESSEE WILLIAMS

> nobody, not even the rain, has such small hands.
> e.e. cummings

LIST OF CHARACTERS

AMANDA WINGFIELD, the mother.—A little woman of great but confused vitality clinging frantically to another time and place. Her characterization must be carefully created, not copied from type. She is not paranoiac, but her life is paranoia. There is much to admire in Amanda, and as much to love and pity as there is to laugh at. Certainly she has endurance and a kind of heroism, and though her foolishness makes her unwittingly cruel at times, there is tenderness in her slight person.

LAURA WINGFIELD, her daughter.—Amanda, having failed to establish contact with reality, continues to live vitally in her illusions, but Laura's situation is even graver. A childhood illness has left her crippled, one leg slightly shorter than the other, and held in a brace. This defect need not be more than suggested on the stage. Stemming from this, Laura's separation increases till she is like a piece of her own glass collection, too exquisitely fragile to move from the shelf.

TOM WINGFIELD, her son.—And the narrator of the play. A poet with a job in a warehouse. His nature is not remorseless, but to escape from a trap he has to act without pity.

JIM O'CONNOR, the gentleman caller.—A nice, ordinary young man.

SCENE: *An alley in St. Louis.*
PART 1. *Preparation for a Gentleman Caller.*
PART 2. *The Gentleman Calls.*
PART 3. *Now and the Past.*

SCENE 1

The Wingfield apartment is in the rear of the building, one of those vast hive-like conglomerations of cellular living-units that flower as warty growths in overcrowded urban centers of lower middle-class population and are symptomatic of the impulse of this largest and fundamentally enslaved section of American society to avoid fluidity and differentiation and to exist and function as one interfused mass of automatism.

The apartment faces an alley and is entered by a fire-escape, a structure whose name is a touch of accidental poetic truth, for all of these huge buildings are always burning with the slow and implacable fires of human desperation. The fire escape is included in the set—that is, the landing of it and steps descending from it.

The scene is memory and is therefore non-realistic. Memory takes a lot of poetic license. It omits some details; others are exaggerated, according to the emotional value of the articles it touches, for memory is seated predominantly in the heart. The interior is therefore rather dim and poetic.

At the rise of the curtain, the audience is faced with the dark, grim rear wall of the Wingfield tenement. This building, which runs parallel to the footlights, is flanked on both sides by dark, narrow alleys which run into murky canyons of tangled clotheslines, garbage cans and the sinister latticework of neighboring fire-escapes. It is up and down these side alleys that exterior entrances and exits are made, during the play. At the end of Tom's opening commentary, the dark tenement wall slowly reveals (by means of a transparency) the interior of the ground floor Wingfield apartment.

Downstage is the living room, which also serves as a sleeping room for Laura, the sofa unfolding to make her bed. Upstage, center, and divided by a wide arch or second proscenium with transparent faded portieres (or second curtain), is the dining room. In an old-fashioned what-not in the living room are seen scores of transparent glass animals. A blown-up photograph of the father hangs on the wall of the living room, facing the audience, to the left of the archway. It is the face of a very handsome young man in a doughboy's First World War cap. He is gallantly smiling, ineluctably smiling, as if to say, "I will be smiling forever."

The audience hears and sees the opening scene in the dining room through both the transparent wall of the building and the transparent gauze portieres of the diningroom arch. It is during this revealing scene that the fourth wall slowly ascends, out of sight.

This transparent exterior wall is not brought down again until the very end of the play, during Tom's final speech.

The narrator is an undisguised convention of the play. He takes whatever license with dramatic convention as is convenient to his purposes.

Tom enters dressed as a merchant sailor from alley, stage left, and strolls across the front of the stage to the fire-escape. There he stops and lights a cigarette. He addresses the audience.

TOM. Yes, I have tricks in my pocket, I have things up my sleeve. But I am the opposite of a stage magician. He gives you the illusion that has the appearance of truth. I give you truth in the pleasant disguise of illusion. To begin with, I turn back time. I reverse it to that quaint period, the thirties, when the huge middle class of America was matriculating in a school for the blind. Their eyes had failed them, or they had failed their eyes, and so they were having their fingers pressed forcibly down on the fiery Braille alphabet of a dissolving economy. In Spain there was revolution. Here there was only shouting and confusion. In Spain there was Guernica. Here there were disturbances of labor, sometimes pretty violent, in otherwise peaceful cities such as Chicago, Cleveland, Saint Louis. . . . This is the social background of the play.

(Music.)

The play is memory. Being a memory play, it is dimly lighted, it is sentimental, it is not realistic. In memory everything seems to happen to music. That explains the fiddle in the wings. I am the narrator of the play, and also a character in it. The other characters are my mother, Amanda, my sister, Laura, and a gentleman caller who appears in the final scenes. He is the most realistic character in the play, being an emissary from a world of reality that we were somehow set apart from. But since I have a poet's weakness for symbols, I am using this character also as a symbol; he is the long delayed but always expected something that we live for. There is a fifth character in the play who doesn't appear except in this larger-than-life photograph over the mantel. This is our father who left us a long time ago. He was a telephone man who fell in love with long distances; he gave up his job with the telephone company and skipped the light fantastic out of town. . . . The last we heard of him was a picture post-card from Mazatlan, on the Pacific coast of Mexico, containing a message of two words—"Hello—Good-bye!" and no address. I think the rest of the play will explain itself. . . .

Amanda's voice becomes audible through the portieres.

(Legend on Screen: "Où Sont Les Neiges?")

He divides the portieres and enters the upstage area. Amanda and Laura are seated at a drop-leaf table. Eating is indicated by gestures without food or utensils. Amanda faces the audience. Tom and Laura are seated in profile. The interior has lit up softly and through the scrim we see Amanda and Laura seated at the table in the upstage area.

AMANDA. (*calling*). Tom?

TOM. Yes, Mother.

AMANDA. We can't say grace until you come to the table!

TOM. Coming, Mother. (*He bows slightly and withdraws, reappearing a few moments later in his place at the table.*)

AMANDA. (*to her son*). Honey, don't *push* with your *fingers*. If you have to push with something, the thing to push with is a crust of bread. And chew—chew! Animals have sections in their stomachs which enable them to digest food without mastication, but human beings are supposed to chew their food before they swallow it down. Eat food leisurely, son, and really enjoy it. A well-cooked meal has lots of delicate flavors that have to be held in the mouth for appreciation. So chew your food and give your salivary glands a chance to function!

(*Tom deliberately lays his imaginary fork down and pushes his chair back from the table.*)

TOM. I haven't enjoyed one bite of this dinner because of your constant directions on how to eat it. It's you that makes me rush through meals with your hawk-like attention to every bite I take. Sickening—spoils my appetite—all this discussion of animals' secretion—salivary glands—mastication!

AMANDA. (*lightly*). Temperament like a Metropolitan star! (*He rises and crosses downstage.*) You're not excused from the table.

TOM. I am getting a cigarette.

AMANDA. You smoke too much. (*Laura rises.*)

LAURA. I'll bring in the blanc mange.

(*He remains standing with cigarette by the portieres during the following.*)

AMANDA. (*rising*). No, sister, no, sister—you be the lady this time and I'll be the darky.

LAURA. I'm already up.

AMANDA. Resume your seat, little sister—I want you to stay fresh and pretty—for gentlemen callers!

LAURA. I'm not expecting any gentlemen callers.

AMANDA. (*crossing out to kitchenette. Airily.*) Sometimes they come when they are least expected! Why, I remember one Sunday afternoon in the Blue Mountain—(*Enters kitchenette.*)

TOM. I know what's coming!

LAURA. Yes. But let her tell it.

TOM. Again?

LAURA. She loves to tell it.

(*Amanda returns with bowl of dessert.*)

AMANDA. One Sunday afternoon in Blue Mountain—your mother received—*seventeen!* —gentlemen callers! Why

sometimes there weren't chairs enough to accommodate them all. We had to send the nigger over to bring in folding chairs from the parish house.

TOM. (*remaining at portieres*). How did you entertain those gentlemen callers?

AMANDA. I understood the art of conversation!

TOM. I bet you could talk.

AMANDA. Girls in those days *knew* how to talk, I can tell you.

TOM. Yes?

(*Image: Amanda as a Girl on a Porch Greeting Callers.*)

AMANDA. They knew how to entertain their gentlemen callers. It wasn't enough for a girl to be possessed of a pretty face and a graceful figure—although I wasn't slighted in either respect. She also needed to have a nimble wit and a tongue to meet all occasions.

TOM. What did you talk about?

AMANDA. Things of importance going on in the world! Never anything coarse or common or vulgar. (*She addresses Tom as though he were seated in the vacant chair at the table though he remains by portieres. He plays this scene as though he held the book.*) My callers were gentlemen—all! Among my callers were some of the most prominent young planters of the Mississippi Delta—planters and sons of planters!

(*Tom motions for music and a spot of light on Amanda. Her eyes lift, her face glows, her voice becomes rich and elegiac.*)

(*Screen Legend: "Où Sont Les Neiges?"*)

There was young Champ Laughlin who later became vice-president of the Delta Planters Bank. Hadley Stevenson who was drowned in Moon Lake and left his widow one hundred and fifty thousand in Government bonds. There were the Cutrere brothers, Wesley and Bates. Bates was one of my bright particular beaux! He got in a quarrel with that wild Wainright boy. They shot it out on the floor of Moon Lake Casino. Bates was shot through the stomach. Died in the ambulance on his way to Memphis. His widow was also well provided for, came into eight or ten thousand acres, that's all. She married him on the rebound—never loved her—carried my picture on him the night he died! And there was that boy that every girl in the Delta had set her cap for! That beautiful, brilliant young Fitzhugh boy from Green County!

TOM. What did he leave his widow?

AMANDA. He never married! Gracious, you talk as though all of my old admirers had turned up their toes to the daisies!

TOM. Isn't this the first you mentioned that still survives?

AMANDA. That Fitzhugh boy went North and made a fortune—came to be known as the Wolf of Wall Street! He had the Midas touch, whatever he touched turned to gold! And I could have been Mrs. Duncan J. Fitzhugh, mind you! But—I picked your *father!*

LAURA. (*rising*). Mother, let me clear the table.

AMANDA. No dear, you go in front and study your typewriter chart. Or practice your shorthand a little. Stay fresh and pretty!—It's almost time for our gentlemen callers to start arriving. (*She flounces girlishly toward the kitchenette.*) How many do you suppose we're going to entertain this afternoon?

(*Tom throws down the paper and jumps up with a groan.*)

LAURA. (*alone in the dining room*). I don't believe we're going to receive any, Mother.

AMANDA. (*reappearing, airily*). What? No one—not one? You must be joking! (*Laura nervously echoes her laugh. She slips in a fugitive manner through the half-open portieres and draws them gently behind her. A shaft of very clear light is thrown on her face against the faded tapestry of the curtain.*) (*Music: "The Glass Menagerie" Under Faintly.*)(*Lightly*) Not one gentleman caller? It can't be true! There must be a flood, there must have been a tornado!

LAURA. It isn't a flood, it's not a tornado, Mother. I'm just not popular like you were in Blue Mountain. . . . (*Tom utters another groan. Laura glances at him with a faint, apologetic smile. Her voice catching a little*) Mother's afraid I'm going to be an old maid.

(*The Scene Dims Out with "Glass Menagerie" Music.*)

SCENE 2

"LAURA, HAVEN'T YOU EVER LIKED SOME BOY?"

On the dark stage the screen is lighted with the image of blue roses. Gradually Laura's figure becomes apparent and the screen goes out. The music subsides. Laura is seated in the delicate ivory chair at the small clawfoot table. She wears a dress of soft violet material for a kimono—her hair tied back from her forehead with a ribbon. She is washing and polishing her collection of glass.

Amanda appears on the fire-escape steps. At the sound of her ascent, Laura catches her breath, thrusts the bowl of ornaments away and seats herself stiffly before the diagram of the typewriter keyboard as though it held her spellbound. Something has happened to Amanda. It is written in her face as she climbs to the landing: a look that is grim and hopeless and a little absurd.

She has one of those cheap or imitation velvety-looking cloth coats with imitation fur collar. Her hat is five or six years old, one of those dreadful cloche hats that were worn in the late twenties, and she is clasping an enormous black patent-leather pocketbook with nickel clasp and initials. This is her full-dress outfit, the one she usually wears to the D.A.R.

Before entering she looks through the door. She purses her lips, opens her eyes wide, rolls them upward and shakes her head. Then she slowly lets herself in the door. Seeing her mother's expression Laura touches her lips with a nervous gesture.

LAURA. Hello, Mother, I was—(*She makes a nervous gesture toward the chart on the wall. Amanda leans against the shut door and stares are Laura with a martyred look.*)

AMANDA. Deception? Deception? (*She slowly removes her hat and gloves, continuing the swift suffering stare. She lets the hat and gloves fall on the floor—a bit of acting.*)

LAURA. (*shakily*). How was the D.A.R. meeting? (*Amanda slowly opens her purse and removes a dainty white handkerchief which she shakes out delicately and delicately touches to her lips and nostrils.*) Didn't you go to the D.A.R. meeting, Mother?

AMANDA. (*faintly, almost inaudibly*).—No.—No. (*Then more forcibly*) I did not have the strength—to go to the D.A.R. In fact, I did not have the courage. I waited to find a hole in the ground and hide myself in it forever! (*She crosses slowly to the wall and removes the diagram of the typewriter keyboard. She holds it in front of her for a second, starting at it sweetly and sorrowfully—then bites her lips and tears it in two pieces.*)

LAURA. (*faintly*). Why did you do that, Mother? (*Amanda repeats the same procedure with the chart of the Gregg Alphabet.*) Why are you—

AMANDA. Why? Why? How old are you, Laura?

LAURA. Mother, you know my age.

AMANDA. I thought that you were an adult; it seems that I was mistaken. (*She crosses slowly to the sofa and sinks down and stares at Laura.*)

LAURA. Please don't stare at me, Mother.

(*Amanda closes her eyes and lowers her head. Count ten.*)

AMANDA. What are we going to do, what is going to become of us, what is the future?

(*Count ten.*)

LAURA. Has something happened, Mother? (*Amanda draws a long breath and takes out the handkerchief again. Dabbing process.*) Mother, has—something happened?

AMANDA. I'll be right in a minute. I'm just bewildered—(*count five*) —by life. . . .

LAURA. Mother, I wish you would tell me what's happened.

AMANDA. As you know, I was supposed to be inducted into my office at the D.A.R. this afternoon. (*Image: A Swarm of Typewriters.*) But I stopped off at Rubicam's Business College to speak to your teachers about your having a cold and ask them what progress they thought you were making down there.

LAURA. Oh. . . .

AMANDA. I went to the typing instructor and introduced myself as your mother. She didn't know who you were. Wingfield, she said. We don't have any such student enrolled at the school! I assured her she did, that you had been going to classes since early in January. "I wonder," she said, "if you could be talking about that terribly shy little girl who dropped out of school after only a few days' attendance?" "No," I said, "Laura, my daughter, has been going to school every day for the past six weeks!" "Excuse me," she said. She took the attendance book out and there was your name, unmistakably printed, and all the dates you were absent until they decided that you had dropped out of school. I still said, "No, there must have been some mistake! There must have been some mix-up in the records!" And she said, "No—I remember her perfectly now. Her hand shook so that she couldn't hit the right keys! The first time we gave a speed-test, she broke down completely—was sick at the stomach and almost had to be carried into the wash-room! After that morning she never showed up any more. We phoned the house but never got any answer"—while I was working at Famous and Barr, I suppose demonstrating those—Oh! I felt so weak I could barely keep on my feet. I had to sit down while they got me a glass of water! Fifty dollars' tuition, all of our plans—my hopes and ambitions for you—just gone up the spout, just gone up the spout like that. (*Laura draws a long breath and gets awkwardly to her feet. She crosses to the victrola and winds it up.*) What are you doing?

LAURA. Oh! (*She releases the handle and returns to her seat.*)

AMANDA. Laura, where have you been going when you've gone out pretending that you were going to business college?

LAURA. I've just been going out walking.

AMANDA. That's not true.

LAURA. It is. I just went walking.

AMANDA. Walking? Walking? In winter? Deliberately courting pneumonia in that light coat? Where did you walk to, Laura?

LAURA. It was the lesser of two evils, Mother. (*Image: Winter Scene in Park.*) I couldn't go back up. I—threw up—on the floor!

AMANDA. From half past seven till after five thirty every day you mean to tell me you walked around in the park, because you wanted to make me think that you were still going to Rubicam's Business College?

LAURA. It wasn't as bad as it sounds. I went inside places to get warmed up.

AMANDA. Inside where?

LAURA. I went in the art museum and the birdhouses at the Zoo. I visited the penguins every day! Sometimes I did without lunch and went to the movies. Lately I've been spending most of my afternoons in the Jewel-box, that big glass house where they raise the tropical flowers.

AMANDA. You did all this to deceive me, just for the deception? (*Laura looks down.*) Why?

LAURA. Mother, when you're disappointed, you get that awful suffering look on your face. Like the picture of Jesus' mother in the museum!

AMANDA. Hush!

LAURA. I couldn't face it.

(*Pause: A whisper of strings.*)

(*Legend: "The Crust of Humility."*)

AMANDA. (*hopelessly fingering the huge pocketbook*). So what are we going to do the rest of our lives? Stay home and watch the parades go by? Amuse ourselves with the glass menagerie, darling? Eternally play those worn-out phonograph records your father left as a painful reminder of him? We won't have a business career—we've given that up because it gave us nervous indigestion! (*Laughs wearily.*) What is there left but dependency all our lives? I know so well what becomes of unmarried women who aren't prepared to occupy a position. I've seen such pitiful cases in the South—barely tolerated spinsters living upon the grudging patronage of sister's husband or brother's wife! —stuck away in some little mousetrap of a room— encouraged by one inlaw to visit another—little birdlike women without any nest—eating the crust of humility all their life! Is that the future that we've mapped out for ourselves? I swear it's the only alternative I can think of! It isn't a very pleasant alternative, is it? Of course—some girls *do* marry. (*Laura twists her hands nervously.*) Haven't you ever liked some boy?

LAURA. Yes, I liked one once. (*Rises.*) I came across his picture a while ago.

AMANDA. (*with some interest*). He gave you his picture?

LAURA. No, it's in the year-book.

AMANDA. (*disappointed*). Oh—a high-school boy.

(*Screen Image: Jim as a High-School Hero Bearing a Silver Cup.*)

LAURA. Yes. His name was Jim. (*Laura lifts the heavy annual from the clawfoot table.*) Here he is in *The Pirates of Penzance*.

AMANDA. (*absently*). The what?

LAURA. The operetta the senior class put on. He had a wonderful voice and we sat across the aisle from each other Mondays, Wednesdays, and Fridays in the Aud. Here he is with the silver cup for debating! See his grin?

AMANDA. (*absently*). He must have had a jolly disposition.

LAURA. He used to call me—Blue Roses.

(*Image: Blue Roses.*)

AMANDA. Why did he call you such a name as that?

LAURA. When I had that attack of pleurosis—he asked me what was the matter when I came back. I said pleurosis— he thought I said Blue Roses! So that's what he always called me after that. Whenever he saw me, he'd holler, "Hello, Blue Roses!" I didn't care for the girl that he went out with. Emily Meisenbach. Emily was the best-dressed girl at Soldan. She never struck me, though, as being sincere. . . . It says in the Personal Section—they're engaged. That's—six years ago! They must be married by now.

AMANDA. Girls that aren't cut out for business careers usually wind up married to some nice man. (*Gets up with a spark of revival.*) Sister, that's what you'll do!

(*Laura utters a startled, doubtful laugh. She reaches quickly for a piece of glass.*)

LAURA. But, Mother—
AMANDA. Yes? (*Crossing to photograph.*)
LAURA. (*in a tone of frightened apology*) I'm—crippled!

(*Image: Screen.*)

AMANDA. Nonsense! Laura, I've told you never, never to use that word. Why, you're not crippled, you just have a little defect—hardly noticeable, even! When people have some slight disadvantage like that, they cultivate other things to make up for it—develop charm—and vivacity—and—*charm!* That's all you have to do! (*She turns again to the photograph.*) One thing your father had *plenty* of—was *charm!*

(*Tom motions to the fiddle in the wings.*)

(*The Scene Fades Out with Music.*)

SCENE 3

(LEGEND ON THE SCREEN: "AFTER THE FIASCO—")

Tom speaks from the fire-escape landing.

TOM. After the fiasco at Rubicam's Business College, the idea of getting a gentleman caller for Laura began to play a more important part in Mother's calculations. It became an obsession. Like some archetype of the universal unconscious, the image of the gentleman caller haunted our small apartment. . . . (*Image: Young Man at Door with Flowers.*) An evening at home rarely passed without some allusion to this image, this specter, this hope. . . . Even when he wasn't mentioned, his presence hung in Mother's preoccupied look and in my sister's frightened, apologetic manner—hung like a sentence passed upon the Wingfields! Mother was a woman of action as well as words. She began to take logical steps in the planned direction. Late that winter and in the early spring—realizing that extra money would be needed to properly feather the nest and plume the bird—she conducted a vigorous campaign on the telephone, roping in subscribers to one of those magazines for matrons called *The Home-maker's Companion,* the type of journal that features the serialized sublimation of ladies of letters who think in terms of delicate cup-like breasts, slim,

tapering waists, rich, creamy thighs, eyes like wood-smoke in autumn, fingers that soothe and caress like strains of music, bodies as powerful as Etruscan sculpture.

(*Screen Image: Glamour Magazine Cover.*)

(*Amanda enters with phone on long extension cord. She is spotted in the dim stage.*)

AMANDA. Ida Scott? This is Amanda Wingfield! We *missed* you at the D.A.R. last Monday! I said to myself: She's probably suffering with that sinus condition! How is that sinus condition? Horrors! Heaven have mercy!—You're a Christian martyr, yes, that's what you are, a Christian martyr! Well, I just now happened to notice that your subscription to the *Companion's* about to expire! Yes, it expires with the next issue, honey!—just when that wonderful new serial by Bessie Mae Hopper is getting off to such an exciting start. Oh, honey, it's something that you can't miss! You remember how *Gone With the Wind* took everybody by storm? You simply couldn't go out if you hadn't read it. All everybody *talked* was Scarlett O'Hara. Well, this is a book that critics already compare to *Gone With the Wind.* It's the *Gone With the Wind* of the post-World War generation!—What?—Burning? Oh, honey, don't let them burn, go take a look in the oven and I'll hold the wire! Heavens—I think she's hung up!

(*Dim Out.*)

(*Legend on Screen: "You Think I'm in Love with Continental Shoemakers?"*)

(*Before the stage is lighted, the violent voices of Tom and Amanda are heard. They are quarreling behind the portieres. In front of them stands Laura with clenched hands and panicky expression. A clear pool of light on her figure throughout this scene.*)

TOM. What in Christ's name am I—
AMANDA. (*shrilly*) Don't you use that—
TOM. Supposed to do!
AMANDA. Expression! Not in my—
TOM. Ohhh!
AMANDA. Presence! Have you gone out of your senses?
TOM. I have, that's true, *driven* out!
AMANDA. What is the mater with you, you—big—big—IDIOT!
TOM. Look—I've got *no thing,* no single thing—
AMANDA. Lower your voice?
TOM. In my life here that I can call my OWN! Everything is—
AMANDA. Stop that shouting!
TOM. Yesterday you confiscated my books! You had the nerve to—
AMANDA. I took that horrible novel back to the library—yes! That hideous book by that insane Mr. Lawrence. (*Tom laughs wildly.*) I cannot control the output of dis-

eased minds or people who cater to them—(*Tom laughs still more wildly.*) BUT I WON'T ALLOW SUCH FILTH BROUGHT INTO MY HOUSE! No, no, no, no, no!

TOM. House, house! Who pays rent on it, who makes a slave of himself to—

AMANDA. (*fairly screeching*) Don't you DARE to—

TOM. No, no, I mustn't say things! *I've* got to just—

AMANDA. Let me tell you—

TOM. I don't want to hear any more! (*He tears the portieres open. The upstage area is lit with a turgid smoky red glow.*)

Amanda's hair is in metal curlers and she wears a very old bathrobe, much too large for her slight figure, a relic of the faithless Mr. Wingfield. An upright typewriter and a mild disarray of manuscripts are on the drop-leaf table. The quarrel was probably precipitated by Amanda's interruption of his creative labor. A chair lying overthrown on the floor. Their gesticulating shadows are cast on the ceiling by the fiery glow.

AMANDA. You *will* hear more, you—

TOM. No, I won't hear more, I'm going out!

AMANDA. You come right back in—

TOM. Out, out out! Because I'm—

AMANDA. Come back here, Tom Wingfield! I'm not through talking to you!

TOM. Oh, go—

LAURA. (*desperately*) Tom!

AMANDA. You're going to listen, and no more insolence from you! I'm at the end of my patience! (*He comes back toward her.*)

TOM. What do you think I'm at? Aren't I supposed to have any patience to reach the end of, Mother? I know, I know. It seems unimportant to you, what I'm *doing*—what I *want* to do—having a little *difference* between them! You don't think that—

AMANDA. I think you've been doing things that you're ashamed of. That's why you act like this. I don't believe that you go every night to movies. Nobody goes to the movies night after night. Nobody in their right minds goes to movies as often as you pretend to. People don't go to the movies at nearly midnight, and movies don't let out at two A.M. Come in stumbling. Muttering to yourself like a maniac! You get three hours' sleep and then go to work. Oh, I can picture the way you're doing down there. Moping, doping, because you're in no condition.

TOM. (*wildly*) No, I'm in no condition!

AMANDA. What right have you got to jeopardize your job? Jeopardize the security of us all? How do you think we'd manage if you were—

TOM. Listen! You think I'm crazy *about the warehouse?* (*He bends fiercely toward her slight figure.*) You think I'm in love with the Continental Shoemakers? You think I want to spend fifty-five *years* down there in that—*celotex interior!* with—*fluorescent—tubes!* Look! I'd rather somebody picked up a crowbar and battered out my brains than go

back mornings! I *go!* Every time you come in yelling that God damn *"Rise and Shine!" "Rise and Shine!"* I say to myself "How *lucky dead* people are!" But I get up. I *go!* For sixty-five dollars a month I gave up all that I dream of doing and being *ever!* And you say self—*self's* all I ever think of. Why, listen, if self is what I thought of, Mother, I'd be where he is—GONE! (*Pointing to father's picture.*) As far as the system of transportation reaches! (*He starts past her. She grabs his arm.*) Don't grab at me, Mother!

AMANDA. Where are you going?

TOM. I'm going to the *movies!*

AMANDA. I don't believe that lie!

TOM. (*crouching toward her, overtowering her tiny figure. She backs away, gasping*) I'm going to opium dens! Yes, opium dens, dens of vice and criminals' hang-outs, Mother. I've joined the Hogan gang, I'm a hired assassin, I carry a tommy-gun in a violin case! I run a string of cat-houses in the Valley. They call me Killer, Killer Wingfield, I'm leading a double-life, a simple, honest warehouse worker by day, by night a dynamic *czar of the underworld, Mother.* I go to gambling casinos, I spin away fortunes on the roulette table! I wear a patch over one eye and a false mustache, sometimes I put on green whiskers. On those occasions they call me—*El Diablo!* Oh, I could tell you things to make you sleepless! My enemies plan to dynamite this place. They're going to blow us all sky-high some night! I'll be glad, very happy, and so will you! You'll go up, up on a broomstick, over Blue Mountain with seventeen gentlemen callers! You ugly—babbling old—*witch.* . . . (*He goes through a series of violent, clumsy movements, seizing his overcoat, lunging to the door, pulling it fiercely open. The women watch him, aghast. His arm catches in the sleeve of the coat as he struggles to pull it on. For a moment he is pinioned by the bulky garment. With an outraged groan he tears the coat off again, splitting the shoulders of it, and hurls it across the room. It strikes against the shelf of Laura's glass collection, there is a tinkle of shattering glass. Laura cries out as if wounded.*)

(*Music Legend: "The Glass Menagerie."*)

LAURA. (*shrilly*) My glass! —menagerie. . . . (*She covers her face and turns away.*)

(*But Amanda is still stunned and stupefied by the "ugly witch" so that she barely notices this occurrence. Now she recovers her speech.*)

AMANDA. (*in an awful voice*) I won't speak to you—until you apologize! (*She crosses through the portieres and draws them together behind her. Tom is left with Laura. Laura clings weakly to the mantel with her face averted. Tom stares at her stupidly for a moment. Then he crosses to shelf. Drops awkwardly to his knees to collect the fallen glass, glancing at Laura as if he would speak but couldn't.*)

(*"The Glass Menagerie" steals in as the Scene Dims Out.*)

SCENE 4

The interior is dark. Faint light in the alley. A deep-voiced bell in a church is tolling the hour by five as the scene commences.

Tom appears at the top of the alley. After each solemn boom of the bell in the tower, he shakes a little noise-maker or rattle as if to express the tiny spasm of man in contrast to the sustained power and dignity of the Almighty. This and the unsteadiness of his advance make it evident that he has been drinking.

As he climbs the few steps to the fire-escape landing light steals up inside. Laura appears in night-dress, observing Tom's empty bed in the front room.

Tom fishes in his pockets for the door-key, removing a motley assortment of articles in the search, including a perfect shower of movie-ticket stubs and an empty bottle. At last he finds the key, but just as he about to insert it, it slips from his fingers. He strikes a match and crouches below the door.

TOM. (*bitterly*) One crack—and it falls through!

(*Laura opens the door.*)

LAURA. Tom! Tom, what are you doing?
TOM. Looking for a door-key.
LAURA. Where have you been all this time?
TOM. I have been to the movies.
LAURA. All this time at the movies?
TOM. There was a very long program. There was a Garbo picture and a Mickey Mouse and a travelogue and a newsreel and a preview of coming attractions. And there was an organ solo and a collection for the milk-fund—simultaneously—which ended up in a terrible fight between a fat lady and an usher!
LAURA. (*innocently*) Did you have to stay through everything?
TOM. Of course! And, oh, I forgot! There was a big stage show! The headliner on this stage show was Malvolio the Magician. He performed wonderful tricks, many of them, such as pouring water back and forth between pitchers. First it turned to wine and then it turned to beer and then it turned to whiskey. I know it was whiskey it finally turned into because he needed somebody to come up out of the audience to help him, and I came up—both shows! It was Kentucky Straight Bourbon. A very generous fellow, he gave souvenirs. (*He pulls from his back pocket a shimmering rainbow-colored scarf.*) He gave me this. This is his magic scarf. You can have it, Laura. You wave it over a canary cage and you get a bowl of gold-fish. You wave it over the goldfish bowl and they fly away canaries. . . . But the wonderfulest trick of all was the coffin trick. We nailed him into a coffin and he got out of the coffin without removing one nail. (*He has come inside.*) There is a

trick that would come in handy for me—get me out of this 2 by 4 situation! (*Flops onto bed and starts removing shoes.*)
LAURA. Tom—Shhh!
TOM. What you shushing me for?
LAURA. You'll wake up Mother.
TOM. Goody, goody! Pay 'er back for those "Rise an' Shines." (*Lies down, groaning.*) You know it don't take much intelligence to get yourself into a nailed-up coffin, Laura. But who in hell ever got himself out of one without removing one nail?

(*As if in answer, the father's grinning photograph lights up.*)

(*Scene Dims Out.*)

Immediately following: The church bell is heard striking six. At the sixth stroke the alarm clock goes off in Amanda's room, and after a few moments we hear her calling: "Rise and Shine! Rise and Shine! Laura, go tell your brother to rise and shine!"

TOM. (*sitting up slowly*) I'll rise—but I won't shine.

(*The light increases.*)

AMANDA. Laura, tell your brother his coffee is ready.

(*Laura slips into front room.*)

LAURA. Tom! it's nearly seven. Don't make Mother nervous. (*He stares at her stupidly. Beseechingly.*) Tom, speak to Mother this morning. Make up with her, apologize, speak to her!
TOM. She won't to me. It's her that started not speaking.
LAURA. If you just say you're sorry she'll start speaking.
TOM. Her not speaking—is that such a tragedy?
LAURA. Please—please!
AMANDA. (*calling from kitchenette*) Laura, are you going to do what I asked you to do, or do I have to get dressed and go out myself?
LAURA. Going, going—soon as I get on my coat! (*She pulls on a shapeless felt hat with nervous, jerky movement, pleadingly glancing at Tom. Rushes awkwardly for coat. The coat is one of Amanda's, inaccurately made-over, the sleeves too short for Laura.*) Butter and what else?
AMANDA. (*entering upstage*) Just butter. Tell them to charge it.
LAURA. Mother, they make such faces when I do that.
AMANDA. Sticks and stones may break my bones, but the expression of Mr. Garfinkel's face won't harm me! Tell your brother his coffee is getting cold.
LAURA. (*at door*) Do what I asked you, will you, will you, Tom?

(*He looks sullenly away.*)

AMANDA. Laura, go now or just don't go at all!
LAURA. (*rushing out*). Going—going! (*A second later she cries out. Tom springs up and crosses to the door. Amanda rushes anxiously in. Tom opens the door.*)

TOM. Laura?

LAURA. I'm all right. I slipped, but I'm all right.

AMANDA. (*peering anxiously after her*). If anyone breaks a leg on those fire-escape steps, the landlord ought to be sued for every cent he possesses! (*She shuts door. Remembers she isn't speaking and returns to the other room.*)

(*As Tom enters listlessly for his coffee, she turns her back to him and stands rigidly facing the window on the gloomy gray vault of the areaway. Its light on her face with its aged but childish features is cruelly sharp, satirical as a Daumier print.*)

(*Music Under: "Ave Maria."*)

(*Tom glances sheepishly but sullenly at her averted figure and slumps at the table. The coffee is scalding hot; he sips it and gasps and spits it back in the cup. At his gasp, Amanda catches breath and half turns. Then catches herself and turns back to window.*)

(*Tom blows on his coffee, glancing sidewise at his mother. She clears her throat. Tom clears his. He starts to rise. Sinks back down again, scratches his head, clears his throat again. Amanda coughs. Tom raises his cup in both hands to blow on it, his eyes staring over the rim of it at his mother for several moments. Then he slowly sets the cup down and awkwardly and hesitantly rises from the chair.*)

TOM. (*hoarsely*) Mother. I—I apologize. Mother. (*Amanda draws a quick, shuddering breath. Her face works grotesquely. She breaks into childlike tears.*) I'm sorry for that I said, for everything that I said, I didn't mean it.

AMANDA. (*sobbingly*) My devotion has made me a witch and so I make myself hateful to my children!

TOM. No, you *don't*.

AMANDA. I worry so much, don't sleep, it makes me nervous!

TOM. (*gently*) I understand that.

AMANDA. I've had to put up a solitary battle all these years. But you're my right-hand bower! Don't fall down, don't fail!

TOM. (*gently*) I try, Mother.

AMANDA. (*with great enthusiasm*) Try and you will SUCCEED! (*The notion makes her breathless.*) Why, you—you're just *full* of natural endowments! Both of my children—they're *unusual* children! Don't you think I know it? I'm so—*proud*! Happy and—feel I've—so much to be thankful for but—Promise me one thing, son!

TOM. What, Mother?

AMANDA. Promise, son, you'll—never be a drunkard!

TOM. (*turns to her grinning*) I will never be a drunkard!

AMANDA. That's what frightened me so, that you'd be drinking! Eat a bowl of Purina!

TOM. Just coffee, Mother.

AMANDA. Shredded wheat biscuit?

TOM. No. No, Mother, just coffee.

AMANDA. You can't put in a day's work on an empty stomach. You've got ten minutes—don't gulp! Drinking too-

hot liquids makes cancer of the stomach. . . . Put cream in.

TOM. No, thank you.

AMANDA. To cool it.

TOM. No! No, thank you, I want it black.

AMANDA. I know, but it's not good for you. We have to do all that we can to build ourselves up. In these trying times we live in, all that we have to cling to is each other. . . . That's why it's so important to—Tom, I—I sent out your sister so I could discuss something with you. If you hadn't spoken I would have spoken to you. (*Sits down.*)

TOM. (*gently*) What is it, Mother, that you want to discuss?

AMANDA. Laura!

(*Tom puts his cup down slowly.*)
(*Legend on Screen: "Laura."*)
(*Music: "The Glass Menagerie."*)

TOM. —Oh.—Laura . . .

AMANDA. (*touching his sleeve*) You know how Laura is. So quiet but—still water runs deep! She notices things and I think she—broods about them. (*Tom looks up.*) A few days ago I came in and she was crying.

TOM. What about?

AMANDA. You.

TOM. Me?

AMANDA. She has an idea that you're not happy here.

TOM. What gave her that idea?

AMANDA. What gives her any idea? However, you do act strangely. I—I'm not criticizing, understand *that*! I know your ambitions do not lie in the warehouse, that like everybody in the whole wide world—you've had to—make sacrifices, but—Tom—Tom—life's not easy, it calls for—Spartan endurance! There's so many things in my heart that I cannot describe to you! I've never told you but I—*loved* your father. . . .

TOM. (*gently*) I know that, Mother.

AMANDA. And you—when I see you taking after his ways! Staying out late—and—well, you *had* been drinking the night you were in that—terrifying condition! Laura says that you hate the apartment and that you go out nights to get away from it! Is that true, Tom?

TOM. No. You say there's so much in your heart that you can't describe to me. That's true of me, too. There's so much in my heart that I can't describe to *you*! So let's respect each other's—

AMANDA. But, why—*why*, Tom—are you always so *restless*? Where do you go to, nights?

TOM. I—go to the movies.

AMANDA. Why do you go to the movies so much, Tom?

TOM. I go to the movies because—I like adventure. Adventure is something I don't have much of at work, so I go to the movies.

AMANDA. But, Tom, you go to the movies *entirely too much*!

TOM. I like a lot of adventure.

(*Amanda looks baffled, then hurt. As the familiar inquisition resumes he becomes hard and impatient again. Amanda slips back into her querulous attitude toward him.*)

(*Image on Screen: Sailing Vessel with Jolly Roger.*)

AMANDA. Most young men find adventure in their careers.

TOM. Then most young men are not employed in a warehouse.

AMANDA. The world is full of young men employed in warehouses and offices and factories.

TOM. Do all of them find adventure in their careers?

AMANDA. They do or they do without it! Not everybody has a craze for adventure.

TOM. Man is by instinct a lover, a hunter, a fighter, and none of these instincts are given much play at the warehouse!

AMANDA. Man is by instinct! Don't quote instinct to me! Instinct is something that people have got away from! It belongs to animals! Christian adults don't want it!

TOM. What do Christian adults want, then, Mother?

AMANDA. Superior things! Things of the mind and the spirit! Only animals have to satisfy instincts! Surely your aims are somewhat higher than theirs! Than monkeys—pigs—

TOM. I reckon they're not.

AMANDA. You're joking. However, that isn't what I wanted to discuss.

TOM. (*rising*) I haven't much time.

AMANDA. (*pushing his shoulders*) Sit down.

TOM. You want me to punch in red at the warehouse, Mother?

AMANDA. You have five minutes. I want to talk about Laura.

(*Legend: "Plans and Provisions."*)

TOM. All right! What about Laura?

AMANDA. We have to be making plans and provisions for her. She's older than you, two years, and nothing has happened. She just drifts along doing nothing. It frightens me terribly how she just drifts along.

TOM. I guess she's the type that people call home girls.

AMANDA. There's no such type, and if there is, it's a pity! That is unless the home is hers, with a husband!

TOM. What?

AMANDA. Oh, I can see the handwriting on the wall as plain as I see the nose in front of my face! It's terrifying! More and more you remind me of your father! He was out all hours without explanation—Then *left! Good-bye!* And me with the bag to hold. I saw that letter you got from the Merchant Marine. I know what you're dreaming of. I'm not standing here blindfolded. Very well, then. Then *do* it! But not till there's somebody to take your place.

TOM. What do you mean?

AMANDA. I mean that as soon as Laura has got somebody to take care of her, married, a home of her own, independent—why, then you'll be free to go wherever you please, on land, on sea, whichever way the wind blows! But until that time you've got to look out for your sister. I don't say me because I'm old and don't matter! I say for your sister because she's young and dependent. I put her in business college—a dismal failure! Frightened her so it made her sick to her stomach. I took her over to the Young People's League at the church. Another fiasco. She spoke to nobody, nobody spoke to her. Now all she does is fool with those pieces of glass and play those worn-out records. What kind of life is that for a girl to lead!

TOM. What can I do about it?

AMANDA. Overcome selfishness! Self, self, self is all that you ever think of! (*Tom springs up and crosses to get his coat. It is ugly and bulky. He pulls on a cap with earmuffs.*) Where is your muffler? Put your wool muffler on! (*He snatches it angrily from the closet and tosses it around his neck and pulls both ends tight.*) Tom! I haven't said what I had in mind to ask you.

TOM. I'm too late to—

AMANDA. (*catching his arms very importunately. Then shyly.*) Down the warehouse, aren't there some—nice young men?

TOM. No!

AMANDA. There *must* be—*some.*

TOM. Mother—

(*Gesture.*)

AMANDA. Find out one that's clean-living—doesn't drink and—ask him out for sister?

TOM. What?

AMANDA. For *sister!* To *meet!* Get acquainted!

TOM. (*stamping to door*). Oh, my go-osh!

AMANDA. Will you? (*He opens door. Imploringly*) Will you? (*He starts down.*) Will you? *Will* you, dear?

TOM. (*calling back*). YES!

(*Amanda closes the door hesitantly and with a troubled but faintly hopeful expression.*)

(*Screen Image: Glamor Magazine Cover.*)

(*Spot Amanda at phone.*)

AMANDA. Ella Cartwright? This is Amanda Wingfield! How are you, honey? How is that kidney condition? (*Count five.*) Horrors! (*Count five.*) You're a Christian martyr, yes, honey, that's what you are, a Christian martyr! Well, I just happened to notice in my little red book that your subscription to the *Companion* has just run out! I knew that you wouldn't want to miss out on the wonderful serial starting in this new issue. It's by Bessie Mae Hopper, the first thing she's written since *Honeymoon for Three*. Wasn't that a strange and interesting story? Well, this one is even lovelier, I believe. It has a sophisticated society background. It's all about the horsey set on Long Island!

(*Fade Out.*)

SCENE 5

(LEGEND ON SCREEN: "ANNUNCIATION.") FADE WITH MUSIC.

It is early dusk of a spring evening. Supper has just been finished in the Wingfield apartment. Amanda and Laura in light-colored dresses are removing dishes from the table, in the upstage area, which is shadowy, their movements formalized almost as a dance or ritual, their moving forms as pale and silent as moths. Tom, in white shirt and trousers, rises from the table and crosses toward the fire-escape.

AMANDA. (*as he passes her*) Son, will you do me a favor?

TOM. What?

AMANDA. Comb your hair! You look so pretty when your hair is combed! (*Tom slouches on sofa with evening paper. Enormous caption "Franco Triumphs."*) There is only one respect in which I would like you to emulate your father.

TOM. What respect is that?

AMANDA. The care he always took of his appearance. He never allowed himself to look untidy. (*He throws down the paper and crosses to fire-escape.*) Where are you going?

TOM. I'm going out to smoke.

AMANDA. You smoke too much. A pack a day at fifteen cents a pack. How much would that amount to in month? Thirty times fifteen is how much, Tom? Figure it out and you will be astounded at what you could save. Enough to give you a night-school course in accounting at Washington U! Just think what a wonderful thing that would be for you, son!

(*Tom is unmoved by the thought.*)

TOM. I'd rather smoke. (*He steps out on landing, letting the screen door slam.*)

AMANDA. (*sharply*). I know! That's the tragedy of it.... (*Alone, she turns to look at her husband's picture.*)

(*Dance Music: "All the World Is Waiting for the Sunrise!"*)

TOM. (*to the audience*). Across the alley from us was the Paradise Dance Hall. On evenings in spring the windows and doors were open and the music came outdoors. Sometimes the lights were turned out except for a large glass sphere that hung from the ceiling. It would turn slowly about and filter the dusk with delicate rainbow colors. Then the orchestra played a waltz or a tango, something that had a slow and sensuous rhythm. Couples would come outside, to the relative privacy of the alley. You could see them kissing behind ashpits and telephone poles. This was the compensation for lives that passed like mine, without any change or adventure. Adventure and change were imminent in this year. They were waiting around the corner for all these kinds. Suspended in the mist over Berchtesgaden, caught in the folds of Chamberlain's umbrella—In Spain there was Guernica! But here there was only hot swing music and liquor, dance halls, bars, and movies, and sex that hung in the gloom like a chandelier and flooded the world with brief, deceptive rainbows.... All the world was waiting for bombardments!

(*Amanda turns from the picture and comes outside.*)

AMANDA. (*sighing*). A fire-escape landing's a poor excuse for a porch. (*She spreads a newspaper on a step and sits down, gracefully and demurely as if she were settling into a swing on a Mississippi veranda.*) What are you looking at?

TOM. The moon.

AMANDA. Is there a moon this evening?

TOM. It's rising over Garfinkel's Delicatessen.

AMANDA. So it is! A little silver slipper of a moon. Have you made a wish on it yet?

TOM. Um-hum.

AMANDA. What did you wish for.

TOM. That's a secret.

AMANDA. A secret, huh? Well, I won't tell you mine either. I will be just as mysterious as you.

TOM. I bet I can guess what yours is.

AMANDA. Is my head so transparent?

TOM. You're not a sphinx.

AMANDA. No, I don't have secrets. I'll tell you what I wished for on the moon. Success and happiness for my precious children! I wish for that whenever there's a moon, and when there isn't a moon, I wish for it, too.

TOM. I thought perhaps you wished for a gentleman caller.

AMANDA. Why do you say that?

TOM. Don't you remember asking me to fetch one?

AMANDA. I remember suggesting that it would be nice for your sister if you brought home some nice young man from the warehouse. I think I've made that suggestion more than once.

TOM. Yes, you have made it repeatedly.

AMANDA. Well?

TOM. We are going to have one.

AMANDA. What?

TOM. A gentleman caller!

(*The Annunciation Is Celebrated with Music.*)
(*Amanda rises.*)
(*Image on Screen: Caller with Bouquet.*)

AMANDA. You mean you have asked some nice young man to come over?

TOM. Yep. I've asked him to dinner.

AMANDA. You really did?

TOM. I did!

AMANDA. You did, and did he—*accept?*

TOM. He did!

AMANDA. Well, well—well, well! That's—lovely!

TOM. I thought that you would be pleased.

AMANDA. It's definite, then?

TOM. Very definite.

AMANDA. Soon?

TOM. Very soon.

AMANDA. For heaven's sake, stop putting on and tell me some things, will you?

TOM. What things do you want me to tell you?

AMANDA. Naturally I would like to know when he's *coming!*

TOM. He's coming tomorrow.

AMANDA. Tomorrow?

TOM. Yep. Tomorrow.

AMANDA. But, Tom!

TOM. Yes, Mother?

AMANDA. Tomorrow gives me no time!

TOM. Time for what?

AMANDA. Preparations! Why didn't you phone me at once, as soon as you asked him, the minute that he accepted? Then, don't you see, I could have been getting ready!

TOM. You don't have to make any fuss.

AMANDA. Oh, Tom, Tom, Tom, of course I have to make a fuss! I want things nice, not sloppy! Not thrown together. I'll certainly have to do some fast thinking, won't I?

TOM. I don't see why you have to think at all.

AMANDA. You just don't know. We can't have a gentleman caller in a pig-sty! All my wedding silver has to be polished, the monogrammed table linen ought to be laundered! The windows have to be washed and fresh curtains put up. And how about clothes? We have to *wear* something, don't we?

TOM. Mother, this boy is no one to make a fuss over!

AMANDA. Do you realize he's the first young man we've had introduced to your sister? It's terrible, dreadful, disgraceful that poor little sister has never received a single gentleman caller! Tom, come inside! (*She opens the screen door.*)

TOM. What for?

AMANDA. I want to ask you some things.

TOM. If you're going to make such a fuss, I'll call it off, I'll tell him not to come.

AMANDA. You certainly won't do anything of the kind. Nothing offends people worse than broken engagements. It simply means I'll have to work like a Turk! We won't be brilliant, but we'll pass inspection. Come on inside. (*Tom follows, groaning.*) Sit down.

TOM. Any particular place you would like me to sit?

AMANDA. Thank heavens I've got that new sofa! I'm also making payments on a floor lamp I'll have sent out! And put the chintz covers on, they'll brighten things up! Of course I'd hoped to have these walls re-papered. . . . What is the young man's name?

TOM. His name is O'Connor.

AMANDA. That, of course, means fish—tomorrow is Friday! I'll have that salmon loaf—with Durkee's dressing! What does he do? He works at the warehouse?

TOM. Of course! How else would I—

AMANDA. Tom, he—doesn't drink?

TOM. Why do you ask me that?

AMANDA. Your father *did!*

TOM. Don't get started on that!

AMANDA. He *does* drink, then?

TOM. Not that I know of!

AMANDA. Make sure, be certain! The last thing I want for my daughter's a boy who drinks?

TOM. Aren't you being a little premature? Mr. O'Connor has not yet appeared on the scene!

AMANDA. But will tomorrow. To meet your sister, and what do I know about his character? Nothing! Old maids are better off than wives of drunkards!

TOM. Oh, my God.

AMANDA. Be still!

TOM. (*leaning forward to whisper*) Lots of fellows meet girls whom they don't marry!

AMANDA. Oh, talk sensibly, Tom—and don't be sarcastic! (*She has gotten a hairbrush.*)

TOM. What are you doing?

AMANDA. I'm brushing that cow-lick down! What is this young man's position at the warehouse?

TOM. (*submitting grimly to the brush and the interrogation*). This young man's position is that of a shipping clerk, Mother.

AMANDA. Sounds to me like a fairly responsible job, the sort of a job *you* would be in if you just had more *get-up*. What is his salary? Have you got any idea?

TOM. I would judge it to be approximately eighty-five dollars a month.

AMANDA. Well—not princely, but—

TOM. Twenty more than I make.

AMANDA. Yes, how well I know! But for a family man, eighty-five dollars a month is not much more than you can just get by on. . . .

TOM. Yes, but Mr. O'Connor is not a family man.

AMANDA. He might be, mightn't he? Some time in the future?

TOM. I see. Plans and provisions.

AMANDA. You are the only young man that I know of who ignores the fact that the future becomes the present, the present the past, and the past turns into everlasting regret if you don't plan for it!

TOM. I will think that over and see what I can make of it.

AMANDA. Don't be supercilious with your mother! Tell me some more about this—what do you call him?

TOM. James D. O'Connor. The D. is for Delaney.

AMANDA. Irish on *both* sides! *Gracious!* And doesn't drink?

TOM. Shall I call him up and ask him right this minute?

AMANDA. The only way to find out about those things is to make discreet inquiries at the proper moment. When I was a girl in Blue Mountain and it was suspected that a young man drank, the girl whose attentions he had been receiving, if any girl *was*, would sometimes speak to the minister of his church, or rather her father would if her father was living, and sort of feel him out on the young man's character. That is the way such things are discreetly handled to keep a young woman from making a tragic mistake!

TOM.   Then how did you happen to make a tragic mistake?

AMANDA.   That innocent look of your father's had everyone fooled! He *smiled*—the world was *enchanted!* No girl can do worse than put herself at the mercy of a handsome appearance! I hope that Mr. O'Connor is not too good-looking.

TOM.   No, he's not too good-looking. He's covered with freckles and hasn't too much of a nose.

AMANDA.   He's not right-down homely, though?

TOM.   Not right-down homely. Just medium homely, I'd say.

AMANDA.   Character's what to look for in a man.

TOM.   That's what I've always said, Mother.

AMANDA.   You've never said anything of the kind and I suspect you would never give it a thought.

TOM.   Don't be suspicious of me.

AMANDA.   At least I hope he's the type that's up and coming.

TOM.   I think he really goes in for self-improvement.

AMANDA.   What reason have you to think so?

TOM.   He goes to night school.

AMANDA.   (*beaming*) Splendid! What does he do, I mean study?

TOM.   Radio engineering and public speaking!

AMANDA.   Then he has visions of being advanced in the world! Any young man who studies public speaking is aiming to have an executive job some day! And radio engineering? A thing for the future! Both of these facts are very illuminating. Those are the sort of things that a mother should know concerning any young man who comes to call on her daughter. Seriously or—not.

TOM.   One little warning. He doesn't know about Laura. I didn't let on that we had dark ulterior motives. I just said, why don't you come have dinner with us? He said okay and that was the whole conversation.

AMANDA.   I bet it was! You're eloquent as an oyster. However, he'll know about Laura when he gets here. When we sees how lovely and sweet and pretty she is, he'll thank his lucky stars he was asked to dinner.

TOM.   Mother, you mustn't expect to much of Laura.

AMANDA.   What do you mean?

TOM.   Laura seems all those things to you and me because she's ours and we love her. We don't even notice she's crippled any more.

AMANDA.   Don't say crippled! You know that I never allow that word to be used!

TOM.   But face facts, Mother. She is and—that's not all—

AMANDA.   What do you mean "not all"?

TOM.   Laura is very different from other girls.

AMANDA.   I think the difference is all to her advantage.

TOM.   Not quite all—in the eyes of others—strangers—she's terribly shy and lives in a world of her own and those things make her seem a little peculiar to people outside the house.

AMANDA.   Don't say peculiar.

TOM.   Face the facts. She is.

(*The Dance-Hall Music Changes to a Tango That Has a Minor and Somewhat Ominous Tone.*)

AMANDA.   In what way is she peculiar—may I ask?

TOM.   (*gently*) She lives in a world of her own—a world of—little glass ornaments, Mother. . . . (*Gets up, Amanda remains holding brush, looking at him, troubled.*) She plays old phonograph records and—that's about all—(*He glances at himself in the mirror and crosses to door.*)

AMANDA.   (*sharply*) Where are you going?

TOM.   I'm going to the movies. (*Out screen door.*)

AMANDA.   Not to the movies, every night to the movies! (*Follows quickly to screen door.*) I don't believe you always go to the movies! (*He is gone. Amanda looks worriedly after him for a moment. Then vitality and optimism return and she turns from the door. Crossing to portieres.*) Laura! Laura! (*Laura answers from kitchenette.*)

LAURA.   Yes, Mother.

AMANDA.   Let those dishes go and come in front! (*Laura appears with dish towel. Gaily*) Laura, come here and make a wish on the moon!

LAURA.   (*entering*) Moon—moon?

AMANDA.   A little silver slipper of a moon. Look over your left shoulder, Laura, and make a wish! (*Laura looks faintly puzzled as if called out of sleep. Amanda seizes her shoulders and turns her at angle by the door.*) Now! Now, darling, wish!

LAURA.   What shall I wish for, Mother?

AMANDA.   (*her voice trembling and her eyes suddenly filling with tears*) Happiness! Good Fortune!

(*The violin rises and the stage dims out.*)

SCENE 6

(IMAGE: HIGH SCHOOL HERO.)

TOM.   And so the following evening I brought Jim home to dinner. I had known Jim slightly in high school. In high school Jim was a hero. He had tremendous Irish good nature and vitality with the scrubbed and polished look of white chinaware. He seemed to move in a continual spotlight. He was a star in basketball, captain of the debating club, president of the senior class and the glee club and he sang the male lead in the annual light operas. He was always running or bounding, never just walking. He seemed always at the point of defeating the law of gravity. He was shooting with such velocity through his adolescence that you would logically expect him to arrive at nothing short of the White House by the time he was thirty. But Jim apparently ran into more interference after his graduation from Soldan. His speed had definitely slowed. Six years after he left high school he was holding a job that wasn't much better than mine.

(Image: Clerk.)

He was the only one at the warehouse with whom I was on friendly terms. I was valuable to him as someone who could remember his former glory, who had seen him win basketball games and the silver cup in debating. He knew of my secret practice of retiring to a cabinet of the washroom to work on poems when business was slack in the warehouse. He called me Shakespeare. And while the other boys in the warehouse regarded me with suspicious hostility, Jim took a humorous attitude toward me. Gradually his attitude affected the others, their hostility wore off and they also began to smile at me as people smile at an oddly fashioned dog who trots across their path at some distance.

I knew that Jim and Laura had known each other at Soldan, and I had heard Laura speak admiringly of his voice. I didn't know if Jim remembered her or not. In high school Laura had been as unobtrusive as Jim had been astonishing. If he did remember Laura, it was not as my sister for when I asked him to dinner, he grinned and said, "You know, Shakespeare, I never thought of you as having folks!"

He was about to discover that I did. . . .

(Light upstage.)
(Legend on Screen: "The Accent of a Coming Foot.")
(Friday evening. It is about five o'clock of a late spring evening which comes "scattering poems in the sky." A delicate lemony light is in the Wingfield apartment. Amanda has worked like a Turk in preparation for the gentleman caller. The results are astonishing. The new floor lamp with its rose-silk shade is in place, a colored paper lantern conceals the broken light fixture in the ceiling, new billowing white curtains are at the windows, chintz covers are on chairs, and sofa, a pair of new sofa pillows make their initial appearance.

Open boxes and tissue paper are scattered on the floor.

Laura stands in the middle with lifted arms while Amanda crouches before her, adjusting the hem of the new dress, devout and ritualistic. The dress is colored and designed by memory. The arrangement of Laura's hair is changed; it is softer and more becoming. A fragile, unearthly prettiness has come out in Laura: she is like a piece of translucent glass touched by light, given a momentary radiance, not actual, not lasting.)

AMANDA. *(impatiently)* Why are you trembling?
LAURA. Mother, you've made me so nervous!
AMANDA. How have I made you nervous?
LAURA. By all this fuss! You make it seem so important?
AMANDA. I don't understand you, Laura. You couldn't be satisfied with just sitting home, and yet whenever I try to arrange something for you, you seem to resist it. *(She gets*

up.) Now take a look at yourself. No, wait! Wait just a moment—I have an idea!
LAURA. What is it now?

(Amanda produces two powder puffs which she wraps in handkerchiefs and stuffs in Laura's bosom.)

LAURA. Mother, what are you doing?
AMANDA. They call them "Gay Deceivers"!
LAURA. I won't wear them!
AMANDA. You will!
LAURA. Why should I?
AMANDA. Because, to be painfully honest, your chest is flat.
LAURA. You make it seem like we were setting a trap.
AMANDA. All pretty girls are a trap, a pretty trap, and men expect them to be.

(Legend: "A Pretty Trap.")

Now look at yourself, young lady. This is the prettiest you will ever be! I've got to fix myself now! You're going to be surprised by your mother's appearance.

(She crosses through portieres, humming gaily.)
(Laura moves slowly to the long mirror and stares solemnly at herself. A wind blows the white curtains inward in a slow, graceful motion and with a faint, sorrowful sighing.)

AMANDA. *(offstage)* It isn't dark enough yet. *(She turns slowly before the mirror with a troubled look.)*

(Legend on Screen: "This Is My Sister: Celebrate Her with Strings!" Music.)

AMANDA. *(laughing, off)* I'm going to show you something. I'm going to make a spectacular appearance!
LAURA. What is it, Mother?
AMANDA. Possess your soul in patience—you will see! Something I've resurrected from that old trunk! Styles haven't changed so terribly much after all. . . . *(She parts the portieres.)* Now just look at your mother! *(She wears a girlish frock of yellowed voile with a blue silk sash. She carries a bunch of jonquils—the legend of her youth is nearly revived. Feverishly)* This is the dress in which I led the cotillion. Won the cakewalk twice at Sunset Hill, wore one spring to the Governor's ball in Jackson! See how I sashayed around the ballroom, Laura? *(She raises her skirt and does a mincing step around the room.)* I wore it on Sundays for my gentleman callers! I had it on the day I met your father— I had malaria fever all that spring. The change of climate from East Tennessee to the Delta—weakened resistance—I had a little temperature all the time—not enough to be serious—just enough to make me restless and giddy! Invitations poured in parties all over the Delta! —"Stay in bed," said Mother, "you have fever!"— but I just wouldn't.—I took quinine but kept on going, going!—Evenings, dances!—Afternoon, long, long rides! Picnics—lovely!—So lovely, that country in May.—All

lacy with dogwood, literally flooded with jonquils.—That was the spring I had the craze for jonquils. Jonquils became an absolute obsession. Mother said, "Honey, there's no more room for jonquils." And still I kept bringing in more jonquils. Whenever, wherever I saw them, I'd say, "Stop! Stop! I see jonquils!" I made the young men help me gather the jonquils! It was a joke, Amanda and her jonquils! Finally there were no more vases to hold them, every available space was filled with jonquils. No vases to hold them? All right, I'll hold them myself! And then I— (*She stops in front of the picture.*) (*Music.*) met your father! Malaria fever and jonquils and then—this—boy. . . . (*She switches on the rose-colored lamp.*) I hope they get here before it starts to rain. (*She crosses upstage and places the jonquils in bowl on table.*) I gave your brother a little extra change so he and Mr. O'Connor could take the service car home.

LAURA. (*with altered look*) What did you say his name was?

AMANDA. O'Connor.

LAURA. What is his first name?

AMANDA. I don't remember. Oh, yes, I do. It was—Jim!

(*Laura sways slightly and catches hold of a chair.*)

(*Legend on Screen: "Not Jim!"*)

LAURA. (*faintly*) Not—Jim!

AMANDA. Yes, that was it, it was Jim! I've never know a Jim that wasn't nice!

(*Music: Ominous.*)

LAURA. Are you sure his name is Jim O'Connor?

AMANDA. Yes. Why?

LAURA. Is he the one that Tom used to know in high school?

AMANDA. He didn't say so. I think he just got to know him at the warehouse.

LAURA. There was a Jim O'Connor we both knew in high school—(*Then, with effort.*) If that is the one that Tom is bringing to dinner—you'll have to excuse me, I won't come to the table.

AMANDA. What sort of nonsense is this?

LAURA. You asked me once if I'd ever liked a boy. Don't you remember I showed you this boy's picture?

AMANDA. You mean the boy you showed me in the year book?

LAURA. Yes, that boy.

AMANDA. Laura, Laura, were you in love with that boy?

LAURA. I don't know, Mother. All I know is I couldn't sit at the table if it was him!

AMANDA. It won't be him! It isn't the least bit likely. But whether it is or not, you will come to the table. You will not be excused.

LAURA. I'll have to be, Mother.

AMANDA. I don't intend to humor your silliness, Laura. I've had too much from you and your brother, both! So just sit down and compose yourself till they come. Tom has forgotten his key so you'll have to let them in, when they arrive.

LAURA. (*panicky*) Oh, Mother—*you* answer the door!

AMANDA. (*lightly*) I'll be in the kitchen—busy!

LAURA. Oh, Mother, please answer the door, don't make me do it!

AMANDA. (*crossing into kitchenette*) I've got to fix the dressing for the salmon. Fuss, fuss—silliness!—over a gentleman caller!

(*Door swings shut. Laura is left alone.*)

(*Legend: "Terror!"*)

(*She utters a low moan and turns off the lamp—sits stiffly on the edge of the sofa, knotting her fingers together.*)

(*Legend on Screen: "The Opening of a Door!"*)

(*Tom and Jim appear on the fire-escape steps and climb to landing. Hearing their approach, Laura rises with a panicky gesture. She retreats to the portieres.*)

The doorbell. Laura catches her breath and touches her throat. Low drums.)

AMANDA. (*calling*) Laura, sweetheart! The door!

(*Laura stares at it without moving.*)

JIM. I think we just beat the rain.

TOM. Uh-huh. (*He rings again, nervously, Jim whistles and fishes for a cigarette.*)

AMANDA. (*very, very gaily*) Laura, that is your brother and Mr. O'Connor! Will you let them in, darling?

(*Laura crosses toward kitchenette door*).

LAURA. (*breathlessly*) Mother—you go to the door!

(*Amanda steps out of the kitchenette and stares furiously at Laura. She points imperiously at the door.*)

LAURA. Please, please!

AMANDA. (*in a fierce whisper*) What is the matter with you, you silly thing?

LAURA. (*desperately*) Please, you answer it, *please!*

AMANDA. I told you I wasn't going to humor you, Laura. Why have you chosen this time to lose your mind?

LAURA. Please, please, please, you go!

AMANDA. You'll have to go to the door because I can't.

LAURA. (*despairingly*) I can't either!

AMANDA. Why?

LAURA. I'm *sick?*

AMANDA. I'm sick, too—of your nonsense! Why can't you and your brother be normal people? Fantastic whims and behavior! (*Tom gives a long ring.*) Preposterous goings on! Can you give me one reason—(*Calls out lyrically.*) COMING! JUST ONE SECOND!—why should you be afraid to open a door? Now you answer it, Laura!

LAURA. Oh, oh, oh . . . (*She returns through the portieres. Darts to the victrola and winds it frantically and turns it on.*)

AMANDA. Laura Wingfield, you march right to that door!

LAURA. Yes—yes, Mother.

(*A faraway, scratchy rendition of "Dardanella" softens the air and gives her strength to move through it. She slips to the door and draws it cautiously open. Tom enters with the caller, Jim O'Connor.*)

TOM. Laura, this is Jim. Jim, this is my sister, Laura.

Jim (*stepping inside*) I didn't know that Shakespeare had a sister!

LAURA. (*retreating stiff and trembling from the door*). How—how do you do?

JIM. (*heartily extending his hand*) Okay!

(*Laura touches it hesitantly with hers.*)

JIM. Your hand's *cold*, Laura!

LAURA. Yes, well—I've been playing the victrola. . . .

JIM. Must have been playing classical music on it! You ought to play a little hot swing music to warm you up!

LAURA. Excuse me—I haven't finished playing the victrola. . . .

(*She turns awkwardly and hurries onto the front room. She pauses a second by the victrola. Then catches her breath and darts through the portieres like a frightened deer.*)

JIM. (*grinning*) What was the matter?

TOM. Oh—with Laura? Laura is—terribly shy.

JIM. Shy, huh? It's unusual to meet a shy girl nowadays. I don't believe you ever mentioned you had a sister.

TOM. Well, now you know. I have one. Here is the *Post Dispatch.* You want a piece of it?

JIM. Uh-huh.

TOM. What piece? The comics?

JIM. Sports! (*Glances at it.*) Ole Dizzy Dean is on his bad behavior.

TOM. (*disinterest*) Yeah? (*Lights cigarette and crosses back to fire-escape door.*)

JIM. Where are *you* going?

TOM. I'm going out on the terrace.

JIM. (*goes after him*) You know, Shakespeare—I'm going to sell you a bill of goods!

TOM. What goods?

JIM. A course I'm taking.

TOM. Huh?

JIM. In public speaking! You and me, we're not the warehouse type.

TOM. Thanks—that's good news. But what has public speaking got to do with it?

JIM. It fits you for—executive positions!

TOM. Awww.

JIM. I tell you it's done a helluva lot for me.

(*Image: Executive at Desk.*)

TOM. In what respect?

JIM. In every! Ask yourself what is the difference between you an' me in the office down front? Brains?—No!—Ability?—No! Then what? Just one little thing—

TOM. What is that one little thing?

JIM. Primarily it amounts to—social poise! Being able to square up to people and hold your own on any social level!

AMANDA. (*off stage*) Tom?

TOM. Yes, Mother?

AMANDA. Is that you and Mr. O'Connor?

TOM. Yes, Mother.

AMANDA. Well, you just make yourselves comfortable in there.

TOM. Yes, Mother.

AMANDA. Ask Mr. O'Connor if he would like to wash his hands.

JIM. Aw—no—no—thank you—I took care of that at the warehouse. Tom—

TOM. Yes?

JIM. Mr. Mendoza was speaking to me about you.

TOM. Favorably?

JIM. What do you think?

TOM. Well—

JIM. You're going to be out of a job if you don't wake up.

TOM. I am waking up—

JIM. You show no signs.

TOM. The signs are interior.

(*Image on Screen: The Sailing Vessel with Jolly Roger Again.*)

TOM. I'm planning to change. (*He leans over the rail speaking with quiet exhilaration. The incandescent marquees and signs of the first-run movie houses light his face from across the alley. He looks like a voyager.*) I'm right at the point of committing myself to a future that doesn't include the warehouse and Mr. Mendoza or even a night-school course in public speaking.

JIM. What are you gassing about?

TOM. I'm tired of the movies.

JIM. Movies!

TOM. Yes, movies! Look at them—(*A wave toward the marvels of Grand Avenue.*) All of those glamorous people—having adventures—hogging it all, gobbling the whole thing up! You know what happens? People go to the *movies* instead of *moving!* Hollywood characters are supposed to have all the adventures for everybody in America, while everybody in America sits in a dark room and watches them have them! Yes, until there's a war. That's when adventure becomes available to the masses! *Everyone's* dish, not only Gable's! Then the people in the dark room come out of the dark room to have some adventures themselves—Goody, goody—It's our turn now, to go to the South Sea Island—to make a safari—to be exotic, far-off—But I'm not patient. I don't want to wait till then. I'm tired of the *movies* and I am *about* to move!

JIM. (*incredulously*) Move?

TOM. Yes.

JIM. When?

TOM. Soon!

JIM. Where? Where?

(*Theme Three: Music Seems to Answer the Question, While Tom Thinks It Over. He Searches Among His Pockets.*)

TOM. I'm starting to boil inside. I know I seem dreamy, but inside—well, I'm boiling! Whenever I pick up a shoe, I shudder a little thinking how short life is and what I am doing!—Whatever that means. I know it doesn't mean shoes—except as something to wear on a traveler's feet! (*Finds paper.*) Look—

JIM. What?

TOM. I'm a member.

JIM. (*reading*) The Union of Merchant Seamen.

TOM. I paid my dues this month, instead of the light bill.

JIM. You will regret it when they turn the lights off.

TOM. I won't be here.

JIM. How about your mother?

TOM. I'm like my father. The bastard son of a bastard! See how he grins? And he's been absent going on sixteen years!

JIM. You're just talking, you drip. How does you mother feel about it?

TOM. Shhh—Here comes Mother! Mother is not acquainted with my plans?

AMANDA. (*enters portiere*) Where are you all?

TOM. On the terrace, Mother.

(*They start inside. She advances to them. Tom is distinctly shocked at her appearance. Even Jim blinks a little. He is making his first contact with girlish Southern vivacity and in spite of the night-school course in public speaking is somewhat thrown off the beam by the unexpected outlay of social charm. Certain responses are attempted by Jim but are swept aside by Amanda's gay laughter and chatter. Tom is embarrassed but after the first shock Jim reacts very warmly. Grins and chuckles, is altogether won over.*)

(*Image: Amanda as a Girl.*)

AMANDA. (*coyly smiling, shaking her girlish ringlets*) Well, well, well, so this is Mr. O'Connor. Introductions entirely unnecessary. I've heard so much about you from my boy. I finally said to him, Tom—good gracious!—why don't you bring this paragon to supper? I'd like to meet this nice young man at the warehouse!—Instead of just hearing him sing your praises so much! I don't know why my son is so stand-offish—that's not Southern behavior! Let's sit down and—I think we could stand a little more air in here! Tom, leave the door open. I felt a nice fresh breeze a moment ago. Where has it gone? Mmm, so warm already! And not quite summer, even. We're going to burn up when summer really gets started. However, we're hav-

ing—we're having a very light supper. I think light things are better fo' this time of year. The same as light clothes are. Light clothes an' light food are what warm weather calls fo'. You know our blood gets so thick during th' winter—it takes a while fo' us to *adjust* ou'selves!—when the season changes . . . It's come so quick this year. I wasn't prepared. All of a sudden—heavens! Already summer!—I ran to the trunk an' pulled out this light dress—Terribly old! Historical almost! But feels so good—so good an' cool, y'know. . . .

TOM. Mother—

AMANDA. Yes, honey?

TOM. How about—supper?

AMANDA. Honey, you go ask Sister if supper is ready! You know that Sister is in full charge of supper! Tell her you hungry boys are waiting for it. (*To Jim*) Have you met Laura?

JIM. She—

AMANDA. Let you in? Oh, good, you've met already! It's rare for a girl as sweet an' pretty as Laura to be domestic! But Laura is, thank heavens, not only pretty but also very domestic! I'm not at all. I never was a bit. I never could make a thing but angel-food cake. Well, in the South we had so many servants. Gone, gone, gone. All vestiges of gracious living! Gone completely! I wasn't prepared for what the future brought me. All of my gentleman callers were sons of planters and so of course I assumed that I would be married to one and raise my family on a large piece of land with plenty of servants. But man proposes—and woman accepts the proposal!—To vary that old, old saying a little bit—I married no planter! I married a man who worked for the telephone company!—that gallantly smiling gentleman over there! (*Points to the picture.*) A telephone man who—fell in love with long distance!—Now he travels and I don't even know where!—But what am I going on for about my—tribulations! Tell me yours—I hope you don't have any! Tom?

TOM. (*returning*). Yes, Mother?

AMANDA. Is supper nearly ready?

TOM. It looks to me like supper is on the table.

AMANDA. Let me look—(*She rises prettily and looks through portieres.*) Oh, lovely—but where is Sister?

TOM. Laura is not feeling well and she says that she thinks she'd better not come to the table.

AMANDA. What?—Nonsense!—Laura? Oh, Laura!

LAURA. (*off stage, faintly*) Yes, Mother.

AMANDA. You really must come to the table. We won't be seated until you come to the table! Come in, Mr. O'Connor. You sit over there and I'll—Laura? Laura Wingfield! You're keeping us waiting, honey! We can't say grace until you come to the table!

(*The back door is pushed weakly open and Laura comes in. She is obviously quite faint, her lips trembling, her eyes wide and staring. She moves unsteadily toward the table.*)

(Legend: "Terror!")

(Outside a summer storm is coming abruptly. The white curtains billow inward at the windows and there is a sorrowful murmur and deep blue dusk. Laura suddenly stumbles—She catches at a chair with a faint moan.)

TOM. Laura!

AMANDA. Laura! *(There's a clap of thunder).* *(Legend: "Ah!")* *(Despairingly)* Why, Laura, you *are* sick, darling! Tom, help your sister into the living room, dear! Sit in the living room, Laura—rest on the sofa. Well! *(To the gentleman caller)* Standing over the hot stove made her ill! I told her that it was just too warm this evening, but—*(Tom comes back in. Laura is on the sofa.)* Is Laura all right now?

TOM. Yes.

AMANDA. What is that? Rain? A nice cool rain has come up? *(She gives the gentleman caller a frightened look.)* I think we may—have grace—now ... *(Tom looks at her stupidly.)* Tom, honey—you say grace!

TOM. Oh ... "For these and all thy mercies—" *(They bow their heads. Amanda stealing a nervous glance at Jim. In the living room Laura, stretched on the sofa, clenches her hands to her lips, to hold back a shuddering sob.)* God's Holy Name be praised—

(The Scene Dims Out.)

SCENE 7

A SOUVENIR

Half an hour later. Dinner is just being finished in the upstage area which is concealed by the drawn portieres.

As the curtain rises Laura is still huddled upon the sofa, her feet drawn under her, her head resting on a pale blue pillow, her eyes wide and mysteriously watchful. The new floor lamp with its shade of rose-colored silk gives a soft, becoming light to her face, bringing out the fragile, unearthly prettiness which usually escapes attention. There is a steady murmur of rain, but it is slackening and stops soon after the scene begins; the air outside becomes pale and luminous as the moon breaks out.

A moment after the curtain rises, the lights in both rooms flicker and go out.

JIM. Hey, there, Mr. Light Bulb!

(Amanda laughs nervously.)

(Legend: "Suspension of a Public Service.")

AMANDA. Where was Moses when the lights went out? Haha. Do you know the answer to that one, Mr. O'Connor?

JIM. No, Ma'am, what's the answer?

AMANDA. In the dark! *(Jim laughs appreciatively.)* Everybody sit still. I'll light the candles. Isn't it lucky we have them on the table? Where's a match. Which of you gentlemen can provide a match?

JIM. Here.

AMANDA. Thank you, sir.

JIM. Not at all, Ma'am!

AMANDA. I guess the fuse has burnt out. Mr. O'Connor, can you tell a burnt-out fuse? I know I can't and Tom is a total loss when it comes to mechanics. *(Sound: Getting Up: Voices Recede a Little to Kitchenette.)* Oh, be careful, you don't bump into something. We don't want our gentleman caller to break his neck. Now wouldn't that be a fine howdy-do?

JIM. Ha-ha! Where is the fuse-box?

AMANDA. Right there next to the stove. Can you see anything?

JIM. Just a minute.

AMANDA. Isn't electricity a mysterious thing? Wasn't it Benjamin Franklin who tied a key to a kite? We live in such a mysterious universe, don't we? Some people say that science clears up all the mysteries for us. In my opinion it only creates more! Have you found it yet?

JIM. No, Ma'am. All these fuses look okay to me.

AMANDA. Tom!

TOM. Yes, Mother?

AMANDA. That light bill I gave you several days ago. The one I told you we got the notices about?

TOM. Oh.—Yeah.

(Legend: "Ha!")

AMANDA. You didn't neglect to pay it by any chance.

TOM. Why, I—

AMANDA. Didn't! I might have known it!

JIM. Shakespeare probably wrote a poem on the light bill, Mrs. Wingfield.

AMANDA. I might have known better than to trust him with it! There's such a high price for negligence in this world!

JIM. Maybe the poem will win a ten-dollar prize.

AMANDA. We'll just have to spend the remainder of the evening in the nineteenth century, before Mr. Edison made the Mazda lamp!

JIM. Candlelight is my favorite kind of light.

AMANDA. That shows you're romantic! But that's no excuse for Tom. Well, we got through dinner. Very considerate of them to let us get through dinner before they plunged us into everlasting darkness, wasn't it, Mr. O'Connor?

JIM. Ha-ha!

AMANDA. Tom, as a penalty for your carelessness you can help me with the dishes.

JIM. Let me give you a hand.

AMANDA. Indeed you will not!

JIM. I ought to be good for something.

AMANDA. Good for something? *(Her tone is rhapsodic.)* You? Why, Mr. O'Connor, nobody, *nobody's* given me this much entertainment in years—as you have!

JIM. Aw, now, Mrs. Wingfield!

AMANDA. I'm not exaggerating, not one bit! But Sister is all by her lonesome. You go keep her company in the parlor! I'll give you this lovely old candelabrum that used to be on the altar at the church of the Heavenly Rest. It was melted a little out of shape when the church burnt down. Lightning struck it one spring. Gypsy Jones was holding a revival at the time and he estimated that the church was destroyed because the Episcopalians gave card parties.

JIM. Ha-ha.

AMANDA. And how about coaxing Sister to drink a little wine? I think it would be good for her! Can you carry both at once?

JIM. Sure, I'm Superman!

AMANDA. Now, Thomas, get into this apron!

(*The door of kitchenette swings closed on Amanda's gay laughter; the flickering light approaches the portieres. Laura sits up nervously as he enters. Her speech at first is low and breathless from the almost intolerable strain of being alone with a stranger.*)

(*Legend: "I Don't Suppose You Remember Me at All!"*)

(*In her first speeches in this scene, before Jim's warmth overcomes her paralyzing shyness, Laura's voice is thin and breathless as though she has run up a steep flight of stairs. Jim's attitude is gently humorous. In playing this scene it should be stressed that while the incident is apparently unimportant, it is to Laura the climax of her secret life.*)

JIM. Hello, there, Laura.

LAURA. (*faintly*). Hello. (*She clears her throat.*)

JIM. How are you feeling now? Better?

LAURA. Yes. Yes, thank you.

JIM. This is for you. A little dandelion wine. (*He extends it toward her with extravagant gallantry.*)

LAURA. Thank you.

JIM. Drink it—but don't get drunk! (*He laughs heartily. Laura takes the glass uncertainly; laughs shyly.*) Where shall I set the candles?

LAURA. Oh—oh, anywhere . . .

JIM. How about here on the floor? Any objections?

LAURA. No.

JIM. I'll spread a newspaper under to catch the drippings. I like to sit on the floor. Mind if I do?

LAURA. Oh, no.

JIM. Give me a pillow?

LAURA. What?

JIM. A pillow!

LAURA. Oh . . . (*Hands him one quickly.*)

JIM. How about you? Don't you like to sit on the floor?

LAURA. Oh—yes.

JIM. Why don't you, then?

LAURA. I—will.

JIM. Take a pillow! (*Laura does. Sits on the other side of the candelabrum. Jim crosses his legs and smiles engagingly at her.*) I can't hardly see you sitting way over there.

LAURA. I can—see you.

JIM. I know, but that's not fair, I'm in the limelight. (*Laura moves her pillow closer.*) Good! Now I can see you! Comfortable?

LAURA. Yes.

JIM. So am I. Comfortable as a cow. Will you have some gum?

LAURA. No, thank you.

JIM. I think that I will indulge, with your permission. (*Musingly unwraps it and holds it up.*) Think of the fortune made by the guy that invented the first piece of chewing gum. Amazing, huh? The Wrigley Building is one of the sights of Chicago.—I saw it summer before last when I went up to the Century of Progress. Did you take in the Century of Progress?

LAURA. No, I didn't.

JIM. Well, it was quite a wonderful exposition. What impressed me most was the Hall of Science. Gives you an idea of what the future will be in America, even more wonderful than the present time is! (*Pause. Smiling at her.*) Your brother tells me you're shy. Is that right, Laura?

LAURA. I—don't know.

JIM. I judge you to be an old-fashioned type of girl. Well, I think that's a pretty good type to be. Hope you don't think I'm being too personal—do you?

LAURA. (*hastily, out of embarrassment*). I believe I *will* take a piece of gum, if you—don't mind. (*Clearing her throat*) Mr. O'Connor, have you—kept up with your singing?

JIM. Singing? Me?

LAURA. Yes. I remember what a beautiful voice you had.

JIM. When did you hear me sing?

(*Voice Offstage in the Pause.*)

VOICE. (*offstage*).
    O blow, ye winds, heigh-ho,
    A-roving I will go!
    I'm off to my love
    With a boxing glove—
    Ten thousand miles away!

JIM. You say you've heard me sing?

LAURA. Oh, yes! Yes, very often . . . I—don't suppose you remember me—at all?

JIM. (*smiling doubtfully*). You know I have an idea I've seen you before. I had that idea soon as you opened the door. It seemed almost like I was about to remember your name. But the name that I started to call you—wasn't a name! And so I stopped myself before I said it.

LAURA. Wasn't it—Blue Roses?

JIM. (*springs up, grinning*) Blue Roses! My gosh, yes—Blue Roses! That's what I had on my tongue when you opened the door! Isn't it funny what tricks your memory plays? I didn't connect you with the high school somehow or other. But that's where it was; it was high school. I didn't even know you were Shakespeare's sister! Gosh, I'm sorry.

LAURA. I didn't expect you to. You—barely knew me!

JIM. But we did have a speaking acquaintance, huh?

LAURA. Yes, we—spoke to each other.

JIM. When did you recognize me?

LAURA. Oh, right away!

JIM. Soon as I came in the door?

LAURA. When I heard your name I thought it was probably you. I knew that Tom used to know you a little in high school. So when you came in the door—Well, then I was—sure.

JIM. Why didn't you say something, then?

LAURA. (breathlessly) I didn't know what to say, I was—too surprised!

JIM. For goodness' sakes! You know, this sure is funny!

LAURA. Yes! Yes, isn't it, though . . .

JIM. Didn't we have a class in something together?

LAURA. Yes, we did.

JIM. What class was that?

LAURA. It was—singing—Chorus!

JIM. Aw!

LAURA. I sat across the aisle from you in the Aud.

JIM. Aw.

LAURA. Mondays, Wednesdays and Fridays.

JIM. Now I remember—you always came in late.

LAURA. Yes, it was so hard for me, getting upstairs. I had that brace on my leg—it clumped so loud!

JIM. I never heard any clumping.

LAURA. (wincing at the recollection). To me it sounded like—thunder!

JIM. Well, well, well. I never even noticed.

LAURA. And everybody was seated before I came in. I had to walk in front of all those people. My seat was in the back row. I had to go clumping all the way up the aisle with everyone watching!

JIM. You shouldn't have been self-conscious.

LAURA. I know, but I was. It was always such a relief when the singing started.

JIM. Aw, yes. I've placed you now! I used to call you Blue Roses. How was it that I got started calling you that?

LAURA. I was out of school a little while with pleurosis. When I came back you asked me what was the matter. I said I had pleurosis—you thought I said Blue Roses. That's what you always called me after that!

JIM. I hope you didn't mind.

LAURA. Oh, no—I liked it. You see, I wasn't acquainted with many—people. . . .

JIM. As I remember you sort of stuck by yourself.

LAURA. I—I—never had much luck at—making friends.

JIM. I don't see why you wouldn't.

LAURA. Well, I—started out badly.

JIM. You mean being—

LAURA. Yes, it sort of—stood between me—

JIM. You shouldn't have let it!

LAURA. I know but it did, and—

JIM. You were shy with people!

LAURA. I tried not to be but never could—

JIM. Overcome it?

LAURA. No, I—I never could!

JIM. I guess being shy is something you have to work out of kind of gradually.

LAURA. (sorrowfully) Yes—I guess it—

JIM. Takes time!

LAURA. Yes.

JIM. People are not so dreadful when you know them. That's what you have to remember! And everybody has problems, not just you, but practically everybody has got some problems. You think of yourself as having the only problems, as being the only one who is disappointed. But just look around you and you will see lots of people as disappointed as you are. For instance, I hoped when I was going to high school that I would be further along at this time, six years later, than I am now—You remember that wonderful write-up I had in *The Torch*?

LAURA. Yes! (She rises and crosses to table.)

JIM. It said I was bound to succeed in anything I went into! (Laura returns with the annual.) Holy Jeez! *The Torch*! (He accepts it reverently. They smiled across it with mutual wonder. Laura crouches beside him and they begin to turn through it. Laura's shyness is dissolving in his warmth.)

LAURA. Here you are in *Pirates of Penzance*!

JIM. (wistfully). I sang the baritone lead in that operatta.

LAURA. (rapidly) So—beautifully!

JIM. (protesting). Aw—

LAURA. Yes, yes—beautifully—beautifully!

JIM. You heard me?

LAURA. All three times!

JIM. No!

LAURA. Yes!

JIM. All three performances?

LAURA. (looking down). Yes.

JIM. Why?

LAURA. I—wanted to ask you to—autograph my program.

JIM. Why didn't you ask me to?

LAURA. You were always surrounded by your own friends so much that I never had a chance to.

JIM. You should have just—

LAURA. Well, I—thought you might think I was—

JIM. Thought I might think you was—what?

LAURA. Oh—

JIM. (with reflective relish). I was beleaguered by females in those days.

LAURA. You were terribly popular!

JIM. Yeah—

LAURA. You had such a—friendly way—

JIM. I was spoiled in high school.

LAURA. Everybody—liked you!

JIM. Including you?

LAURA. I—yes, I—I did, too—(She gently closes the book in her lap.)

JIM. Well, well, well!—Give me that program, Laura. (She

hands it to him. He signs it with a flourish.) There you are—better late then never!

LAURA. Oh, I—what a—surprise!

JIM. My signature isn't worth very much right now. But some day—maybe—it will increase in value! Being disappointed is one thing and being discouraged is something else. I am disappointed but I'm not discouraged. I'm twenty-three years old. How old are you?

LAURA. I'll be twenty-four in June.

JIM. That's not old age!

LAURA. No, but—

JIM. You finished high school?

LAURA. (*with difficulty*). I didn't go back.

JIM. You mean you dropped out?

LAURA. I made bad grades in my final examinations. (*She rises and replaces the book and the program. Her voice strained.*) How is—Emily Meisenbach getting along?

JIM. Oh, that kraut-head!

LAURA. Why do you call her that?

JIM. That's what she was.

LAURA. You're not still—going with her?

JIM. I never see her.

LAURA. It said in the Personal Section that you were—engaged!

JIM. I know, but I wasn't impressed by that—propaganda!

LAURA. It wasn't—the truth?

JIM. Only in Emily's optimistic opinion!

LAURA. Oh—

(*Legend: "What Have You Done Since High School?"*)

(*Jim lights a cigarette and leans indolently back on his elbows smiling at Laura with a warmth and charm which light her inwardly with altar candles. She remains by the table and turns in her hands a piece of glass to cover her tumult.*)

JIM. (*after several reflective puffs on a cigarette*). What have you done since high school? (*She seems not to hear him.*) Huh? (*Laura looks up.*) I said what have you done since high school, Laura?

LAURA. Nothing much.

JIM. You must have been doing something these six long years.

LAURA. Yes.

JIM, Well, then, such as what?

LAURA. I took a business course at business college—

JIM. How did that work out?

LAURA. Well, not very—well—I had to drop out, it gave me—indigestion—

(*Jim laughs gently.*)

JIM. What are you doing now?

LAURA. I don't do anything—much. Oh, please don't think I sit around doing nothing! My glass collection takes up a good deal of my time. Glass is something you have to take good care of.

JIM. What did you say—about glass?

LAURA. Collection I said—I have one—(*She clears her throat and turns away again, acutely shy.*)

JIM. (*abruptly*) You know what I judge to be the trouble with you? Inferiority complex! Know what that is? That's what they call it when someone low-rates himself? I understand it because I had it, too. Although my case was not so aggravated as yours seems to be. I had it until I took up public speaking, developed my voice, and learned that I had an aptitude for science. Before that time I never thought of myself as being outstanding in any way whatsoever! Now I've never made a regular study of it, but I have a friend who says I can analyze people better than doctors that make a profession of it. I don't claim that to be necessarily true, but I can sure guess a person's psychology, Laura. (*Takes out his gum.*) Excuse me, Laura. I always take it out when the flavor is gone. I'll use this scrap of paper to wrap it in. I know how it is to get it stuck on a shoe. Yep—that's what I judge to be your principal trouble. A lack of confidence in yourself as a person. You don't have the proper amount of faith in yourself. I'm basing that fact on a number of your remarks and also on certain observations I've made. For instance that clumping you thought was so awful in high school. You say that you even dreaded to walk into class. You see what you did? You dropped out of school, you gave up an education because of a clump, which as far as I know was practically nonexistent! A little physical defect is what you have? Hardly noticeable even! Magnified thousands of times by imagination! You know what my strong advice to you is? Think of yourself as superior in some way!

LAURA. In what way would I think?

JIM. Why, man alive, Laura! Just look about you a little. What do you see? A world full of common people! All of 'em born and all of 'em going to die! Which of them has one-tenth of your good points! Or mine! Or anyone else's, as far as that goes—Gosh! Everybody excels in some one thing. Some in many! (*Unconsciously glances at himself in the mirror.*) All you've got to do is discover in what! Take me, for instance. (*He adjusts his tie at the mirror.*) My interest happens to lie in electrodynamics. I'm taking a course in radio engineering at night school, Laura, on top of a fairly responsible job at the warehouse. I'm taking that course and studying public speaking.

LAURA. Ohhhh.

JIM. Because I believe in the future of television! (Turning back to her.) I wish to be ready to go up right along with it. Therefore I'm planning to get in on the ground floor. In fact, I've already made the right connections and all that remains is for the industry itself to get under way! Full steam—(*His eyes are starry.*) Knowledge—Zzzzzp! Money—Zzzzzzp! Power! That's the cycle democracy is built on! (*His attitude is convincingly dynamic. Laura stares at him, even her shyness eclipsed in her absolute wonder. He suddenly grins.*) I guess you think I think a lot of myself!

LAURA. No—o-o-o, I—

JIM. Now how about you? Isn't there something you take more interest in than anything else?

LAURA. Well, I do—as I said—have my—glass collection—

(*A peal of girlish laughter from the kitchen.*)

JIM. I'm not right sure I know what you're talking about. What kind of glass is it?

LAURA. Little articles of it, they're ornaments mostly! Most of them are little animals made out of glass, the tiniest little animals in the world. Mother calls them a glass menagerie! Here's an example of one, if you'd like to see it! This one is one of the oldest. It's nearly thirteen. (*He stretches out his hand.*) (*Music: "The Glass Menagerie."*) Oh, be careful—if you breathe, it breaks!

JIM. I'd better not take it. I'm pretty clumsy with things.

LAURA. Go on. I trust you with him! (*Places it in his palm.*) There now—you're holding him gently! Hold him over the light, he loves the light! You see how the light shines through him?

JIM. It sure does shine!

LAURA. I shouldn't be partial, but he is my favorite one.

JIM. What kind of thing is this one supposed to be?

LAURA. Haven't you noticed the single horn on his forehead?

JIM. A unicorn, huh?

LAURA. Mmm-hmmm!

JIM. Unicorns, aren't they extinct in the modern world?

LAURA. I know!

JIM. Poor little fellow, he must feel sort of lonesome.

LAURA. (*smiling*). Well, if he does he doesn't complain about it. He stays on a shelf with some horses that don't have horns and all of them seem to get along nicely together.

JIM. How do you know?

LAURA. (*lightly*) I haven't heard any arguments among them!

JIM. (*grinning*) No arguments, huh? Well, that's a pretty good sign! Where shall I set him?

LAURA. Put him on the table. They all like a change of scenery once in a while!

JIM. (*stretching*) Well, well, well, well—Look how big my shadow is when I stretch!

LAURA. Oh, oh, yes—it stretches across the ceiling!

JIM. (*crossing to door*) I think it's stopped raining. (*Opens fire-escape door*) Where does the music come from?

LAURA. From the Paradise Dance Hall across the alley.

JIM. How about cutting the rug a little, Miss Wingfield?

LAURA. Oh, I—

JIM. Or is your program filled up? Let me have a look at it. (*Grasps imaginary card.*) Why, every dance is taken! I'll just have to scratch some out. (*Waltz Music: "La Golondrina."*) Ahhh, a waltz! (*He executes some sweeping turns by himself then holds his arms toward Laura.*)

LAURA. (*breathlessly*) I—can't dance!

JIM. There you go, that inferiority stuff!

LAURA. I've never danced in my life!

JIM. Come on, try!

LAURA. Oh, but I'd step on you!

JIM. I'm not made out of glass.

LAURA. How—how—how do we start?

JIM. Just leave it to me. You hold your arms out a little.

LAURA. Like this?

JIM. A little bit higher. Right. Now don't tighten up, that's the main thing about it—relax.

LAURA. (*laughing breathlessly*) It's hard not to.

JIM. Okay.

LAURA. I'm afraid you can't budge me.

JIM. What do you bet I can't? (*He swings her into motion.*)

LAURA. Goodness, yes, you can!

JIM. Let yourself go, now, Laura, just let yourself go.

LAURA. I'm—

JIM. Come on!

LAURA. Trying!

JIM. Not so stiff—Easy does it!

LAURA. I know but I'm—

JIM. Loosen th' backbone! There now, that's a lot better.

LAURA. Am I?

JIM. Lots, lots better! (*He moves her about the room in a clumsy waltz.*)

LAURA. Oh, my!

JIM. Ha-ha!

LAURA. Goodness, yes you can!

JIM. Ha-ha-ha! (*They suddenly bump into the table, Jim stops.*) What did we hit on?

LAURA. Table.

JIM. Did something fall of it? I think—

LAURA. Yes.

JIM. I hope that it wasn't the little glass horse with the horn!

LAURA. Yes.

JIM. Aw, aw, aw. Is it broken?

LAURA. Now it is just like all the other horses.

JIM. It's lost its—

LAURA. Horn! It doesn't matter. Maybe it's a blessing in disguise.

JIM. You'll never forgive me. I bet that was your favorite piece of glass.

LAURA. I don't have favorites much. It's no tragedy, Freckles. Glass breaks so easily. No matter how careful you are. The traffic jars the shelves and things fall off them.

JIM. Still I'm awfully sorry that I was the cause.

LAURA. (*smiling*). I'll just imagine he had an operation. The horn was removed to make him feel less—freakish! (*They both laugh.*) Now he will feel more at home with the other horses, the ones that don't have horns . . .

JIM. Ha-ha, that's very funny! (*Suddenly serious.*) I'm glad to see that you have a sense of humor. You know—you're—well—very different! Surprisingly different from anyone else I know! (*His voice becomes soft and hesitant with a genuine feeling.*) Do you mind me telling you that? (*Laura is abashed beyond speech.*) You make me feel sort of—I don't know how to put it! I'm usually pretty good at expressing things, but—This is something that I don't know how to say! (*Laura touches her throat clears it—turns the broken unicorn in her hands.*) (*Even softer.*) Has anyone ever told you that you were pretty? (*Pause: Music.*) (*Laura looks up slowly, with wonder, and shakes her head.*) Well, you are! In a very different way from anyone else. And all the nicer because of the difference, too. (*His voice becomes low and husky. Laura turns away, nearly faint with the novelty of her emotions.*) I wish that you were my sister. I'd teach you to have some confidence in yourself. The different people are not like other people, but being different is nothing to be ashamed of. Because other people are not such wonderful people. They're one hundred times one thousand. You're one times one! They walk all over the earth. You just stay here. They're common as—weeds, but—you—well, you're—Blue Roses!

(*Image on Screen: Blue Roses.*)

(*Music Changes.*)

LAURA. But blue is wrong for—roses . . .
JIM. It's right for you—You're—pretty!
LAURA. In what respect am I pretty?
JIM. In all respects—believe me! Your eyes—your hair—are pretty! Your hands are pretty! (*He catches hold of her hand.*) You think I'm making this up because I'm invited to dinner and have to be nice. Oh, I could do that! I could put on an act for you, Laura, and say lots of things without being very sincere. But this time I am. I'm talking to you sincerely. I happened to notice you had this inferiority complex that keeps you from feeling comfortable with people. Somebody needs to build your confidence up and make you proud instead of shy and turning away and—blushing—Somebody ought to—ought to—kiss you, Laura!

(*His hand slips slowly up her arm to her shoulder.*) (*Music Swells Tumultuously.*) (*He suddenly turns her about and kisses her on the lips. When he releases her Laura sinks on the sofa with a bright, dazed look. Jim backs away and fishes in his pocket for a cigarette.*) (*Legend on Screen: "Souvenir."*) Stumble-john! (*He lights the cigarette, avoiding her look. There is a peal of girlish laughter from Amanda in the kitchen. Laura slowly raises and opens her hand. It still contains the little broken glass animal. She looks at it with a tender, bewildered expression.*) Stumble-john! I shouldn't have done that—That was way off the beam. You don't smoke, do you? (*She looks up, smiling, not hearing the question. He sits besides her a little gingerly. She looks at him speechlessly—waiting. He coughs decorously and moves a little farther aside as he considers the situation and senses her feelings, dimly, with perturbation. Gently.*) Would you—care for a—mint? (*She doesn't seem to hear him but her look grows brighter even.*) Peppermint—Life Saver? My pocket's a regular drug store—wherever I go . . . (*He pops a mint in his mouth. Then gulps and decides to make a clean breast of it. He speaks slowly and gingerly.*) Laura, you know, if I had a sister like you, I'd do the same thing as Tom. I'd bring out fellows—introduce her to them. The right type of boys of a type to—appreciate her. Only—well—he made a mistake about me. Maybe I've got no call to be saying this. This may not have been the idea in having me over. But what if it was? There's nothing wrong about that. The only trouble is that in my case—I'm not in a situation to—do the right thing. I can't take down your number and say I'll phone. I can't call up next week and—ask for a date. I thought I had better explain the situation in case you misunderstood it and—hurt your feelings. . . . (*Pause. Slowly, very slowly, Laura's look changes, her eyes returning slowly from his to the ornament in her palm.*)

(*Amanda utters another gay laugh in the kitchen.*)

LAURA. (*faintly*) You—won't—call again?
JIM. No, Laura. I can't. (*He rises from the sofa.*) As I was just explaining, I've—got strings on me, Laura, I've—been going steady! I go out all the time with a girl named Betty. She's a home-girl like you, and Catholic, and Irish, and in a great many ways we—get along fine. I met her last summer on a moonlight boat trip up the river to Alton, on the Majestic. Well—right away from the start it was—love! (*Legend: "Love!"*) (*Laura sways slightly forward and grips the arm of the sofa. He fails to notice, now enrapt in his own comfortable being.*) Being in love has made a new man of me! (*Leaning stiffly forward, clutching the arm of the sofa, Laura struggles visibly with her storm. But Jim is oblivious, she is a long way off.*) The power of love is really pretty tremendous! Love is something that—changes the whole world, Laura! (*The storm abates a little and Laura leans back. He notices her again.*) It happened that Betty's aunt took sick, she got a wire and had to go to Centralia. So Tom—when he asked me to dinner—I naturally just accepted the invitation, not knowing that you—that he—that I—(*He stops awkwardly.*) Huh—I'm a stumble-john! (*He flops back on the sofa. The holy candles in the altar of Laura's face have been snuffed out! There is a look of almost infinite desolation. Jim glances at her uneasily.*) I wish that you would—say something. (*She bites her lip which was trembling and then bravely smiles. She opens her hand again on the broken glass ornament. Then she gently takes his hand and raises it level to her own. She carefully places the unicorn in the palm of his hand, then pushes his fingers closed upon it.*) What are you—doing that for? You want me to have him? —Laura? (*She nods.*) What for?
LAURA. A—souvenir . . .

(*She rises unsteadily and crouches beside the victrola to wind it up.*)

(*Legend on Screen: "Things Have a Way of Turning Out So Badly."*)

(*Or Image: "Gentleman Caller Waving Good-Bye—Gaily."*)

(*At this moment Amanda rushes brightly back in the front room. She bears a pitcher of fruit punch in an old-fashioned cut-glass pitcher and a plate of macaroons. The plate has a gold border and poppies painted on it.*)

AMANDA. Well, well, well! Isn't the air delightful after the shower? I've made you children a little liquid refreshment. (*Turns gaily to the gentleman caller.*) Jim, do you know that song about lemonade?
> "Lemonade, lemonade
> Made in the shade and stirred with a spade—
> Good enough for any old maid!"

JIM. (*uneasily*) Ha-ha! No—I never heard it.

AMANDA. Why, Laura! You look so serious!

JIM. We were having a serious conversation.

AMANDA. Good! Now you're better acquainted!

JIM. (*uncertainly*). Ha-ha! Yes.

AMANDA. You modern young people are much more serious-minded than my generation. I was so gay as a girl!

JIM. You haven't changed, Mrs. Wingfield.

AMANDA. Tonight I'm rejuvenated! The gaiety of the occasion, Mr. O'Connor! (*She tosses her head with a peal of laughter. Spills lemonade.*) Oooo! I'm baptizing myself!

JIM. Here—let me—

AMANDA. (*setting the pitcher down.*) There now. I discovered we had some maraschino cherries. I dumped them in, juice and all!

JIM. You shouldn't have gone to that trouble, Mrs. Wingfield.

AMANDA. Trouble, trouble? Why it was loads of fun! Didn't you hear me cutting up in the kitchen? I bet your ears were burning! I told Tom how outdone with him I was for keeping you to himself so long a time! He should have brought you over much, much sooner! Well, now that you've found your way, I want you to be a very frequent caller! Not just occasional but all the time. Oh, we're going to have a lot of gay times together! I see them coming! Mmm, just breathe that air! So fresh, and the moon's so pretty! I'll skip back out—I know where my place is when young folks are having a—serious conversation!

JIM. Oh, don't go out, Mrs. Wingfield. The fact of the matter is I've got to be going.

AMANDA. Going, now? You're joking! Why, it's only the shank of the evening, Mr. O'Connor.

JIM. Well, you know how it is.

AMANDA. You mean you're a young workingman and have to keep workingmen's hours. We'll let you off early tonight. But only on the condition that next time you stay later. What's the best night for you? Isn't Saturday night the best night for you workingmen?

JIM. I have a couple of time-clocks to punch, Mrs. Wingfield. One at morning, another one at night.

AMANDA. My, but you are ambitious! You work at night, too?

JIM. No, Ma'am, not work but—Betty! (*He crosses deliberately to pick up his hat. The band at the Paradise Dance Hall goes into a tender waltz.*)

AMANDA. Betty? Betty? Who's—Betty! (*There is an ominous cracking sound in the sky.*)

JIM. Oh, just a girl. The girl I go steady with! (*He smiles charmingly. The sky falls.*)

(*Legend: "The Sky Falls"*)

AMANDA. (*a long-drawn exhalation*) Ohhhh . . . Is it a serious romance, Mr. O'Connor?

JIM. We're going to be married the second Sunday in June.

AMANDA. Ohhhh—how nice! Tom didn't mention that you were engaged to be married.

JIM. The cat's not out of the bag at the warehouse yet. You know how they are. They call you Romeo and stuff like that. (*He stops at the oval mirror to put on his hat. He carefully shapes the brim and the crown to give a discreetly dashing effect.*) It's been a wonderful evening, Mrs. Wingfield. I guess this is what they mean by Southern hospitality.

AMANDA. It really wasn't anything at all.

JIM. I hope it don't seem like I'm rushing off. But I promised Betty I'd pick her up at the Wabash depot, an' by the time I get my jalopy down there her train'll be in. Some women are pretty upset if you keep 'em waiting.

AMANDA. Yes, I know—The tyranny of women! (*Extends her hand.*) Goodbye, Mr. O'Connor. I wish you luck—and happiness—and success! All three of them, and so does Laura! —Don't you, Laura?

LAURA. Yes!

JIM. (*taking her hand*) Goodbye, Laura. I'm certainly going to treasure that souvenir. And don't you forget the good advice I gave you. (*Raises his voice to a cheery shout.*) So long, Shakespeare! Thanks again, ladies—Good night!

(*He grins and ducks jauntily out. Still bravely grimacing, Amanda closes the door on the gentleman caller. Then she turns back to the room with a puzzled expression. She and Laura don't dare to face each other. Laura crouches beside the victrola to wind it.*)

AMANDA. (*faintly*) Things have a way of turning out so badly. I don't believe that I would play the victrola. Well, well—well—Our gentleman caller was engaged to be married! Tom!

TOM. (*from back*) Yes, Mother?

AMANDA. Come in here a minute. I want to tell you something awfully funny.

TOM. (*enters with macaroon and a glass of the lemonade*) Has the gentleman caller gotten away already?

AMANDA. The gentleman caller has made an early departure. What a wonderful joke you played on us!

TOM. How do you mean?

AMANDA. You didn't mention that he was engaged to be married.

TOM. Jim? Engaged?

AMANDA. That's what he just informed us.

TOM. I'll be jiggered! I didn't know about that.

AMANDA. That seems very peculiar.

TOM. What's peculiar about it?

AMANDA. Didn't you call him your best friend down at the warehouse?

TOM. He is, but how did I know?

AMANDA. It seems extremely peculiar that you wouldn't know your best friend was going to be married!

TOM. The warehouse is where I work, not where I know things about people!

AMANDA. You don't know things anywhere! You live in a dream; you manufacture illusions! (*He crosses to door.*) Where are you going?

TOM. I'm going to the movies.

AMANDA. That's right, now that you've had us make such fools of ourselves. The effort, the preparations, all the expense! The new floor lamp, the rug, the clothes for Laura! All for what? To entertain some other girl's fiancé! Go to the movies, go! Don't think about us, a mother deserted, an unmarried sister who's crippled and has no job! Don't let anything interfere with your selfish pleasure! Just go, go, go—to the movies!

TOM. All right, I will! The more you shout about my selfishness to me the quicker I'll go, and I won't go to the movies!

AMANDA. Go, then! Then go to the moon—you selfish dreamer!

Tom smashes his glass on the floor. He plunges out on the fire-escape, slamming the door. Laura screams—cut by door.

Dance-hall music up. Tom goes to the rail and grips it desperately, lifting his face in the chill white moonlight penetrating the narrow abyss of the alley.

(*Legend on Screen:* "And So Good-Bye . . . ")

(*Tom's closing speech is timed with the interior pantomime. The interior scene is played as though viewed through sound-proof glass. Amanda appears to be making a comforting speech to Laura who is huddled upon the sofa. Now that we cannot hear the mother's speech, her silliness is gone and she has dignity and tragic beauty. Laura's dark hair hides her face until at the end of the speech she lifts it to smile at her mother. Amanda's gestures are slow and graceful, almost dancelike, as she comforts her daughter. At the end of her speech she glances a moment at the father's picture—then withdraws through the portieres. At close of Tom's speech, Laura blows out the candles, ending the play.*)

TOM. I didn't go to the moon, I went much further—for time is the longest distance between two places—Not long after that I was fired for writing a poem on the lid of a shoe-box. I left Saint Louis. I descended the steps of this fire-escape for a last time and followed, from then on, in my father's footsteps, attempting to find in motion what was lost in space—I traveled around a great deal. The cities swept about me like dead leaves, leaves that were brightly colored but torn away from the branches. I would have stopped, but I was pursued by something. It always came upon me unawares, taking me altogether by surprise. Perhaps it was a familiar bit of music. Perhaps it was only a piece of transparent glass—Perhaps I am walking along a street at night, in some strange city, before I have found companions. I pass the lighted window of a shop where perfume is sold. The window is filled with pieces of colored glass, tiny transparent bottles in delicate colors, like bits of a shattered rainbow. Then all at once my sister touches my shoulder. I turn around and look into her eyes . . . Oh, Laura, Laura, I tried to leave you behind me, but I am more faithful than I intended to be! I reach for a cigarette, I cross the street, I run into the movies or a bar, I buy a drink, I speak to the nearest stranger—anything that can blow your candles out! (*Laura bends over the candles.*)—for nowadays the world is lit by lightning! Blow out your candles, Laura—and so goodbye . . .

(*She blows the candles out.*)

(*The Scene Dissolves.*)

FORUM

"Production Notes"

TENNESSEE WILLIAMS

Being a "memory play," *The Glass Menagerie* can be presented with unusual freedom of convention. Because of its considerably delicate or tenuous material, atmospheric touches and subtleties of direction play a particularly important part. Expressionism and all other unconventional techniques in drama have only one valid aim, and that is a closer approach to truth. When a play employs unconventional techniques, it is not, or certainly shouldn't be, trying to escape its responsibility of dealing with reality, or interpreting experience, but is actually or should be attempting to find a closer approach, a more penetrating and vivid expression of things as they are. The straight realistic play with its genuine frigidaire and authentic ice cubes, its characters that speak exactly as its audience speaks, corresponds to the academic landscape and has the same virtue of a photographic likeness. Everyone should know nowadays the unimportance of the photographic in art: that truth, life, or reality is an organic thing which the poetic imagination can represent or suggest, in essence, only through transformation, through changing into other forms than those which were merely present in appearance.

These remarks are not meant as comments, only on this particular play. They have to do with a conception of a new, plastic theater which must take the place of the exhausted theater of realistic conventions if the theater is to resume vitality as a part of our culture.

The Screen Device

There is *only one important difference between the original and acting version of the play* and that is the *omission* in the latter of the device which I tentatively included in my *original* script. This device was the use of a screen on which were projected magic-lantern slides bearing images or titles. I do not regret the omission of this device from the . . . Broadway production. The extraordinary power of Miss Taylor's performance made it suitable to have the utmost simplicity in the physical production. But I think it may be interesting to some readers to see how this device was conceived. So I am putting it into the published manuscript. These images and legends, projected from behind, were cast on a section of wall between the front-room and dining-room areas, which should be indistinguishable from the rest when not in use.

The purpose of this will probably be apparent. It is to give accent to certain values in each scene. Each scene contains a particular point (or several) which is structurally the most important. In an episodic play, such as this, the basic structure or narrative line may be obscured from the audience; the effect may seem fragmentary rather than architectural. This may not be the fault of the play so much as a lack of attention in the audience. The legend or image upon the screen will strengthen the effect of what is merely allusion in the writing and allow the primary point to be made more simply and lightly than if the entire responsibility were on the spoken lines. Aside from this structural value, I think the screen will have a definite emotional appeal, less definable but just as important. An imaginative producer or director may invent many other uses for this device than those indicated in the present script. In fact the possibilities of the device seem much larger to me than the instance of the play can possibly utilize.

The Music

Another extra-literary accent in this play is provided by the use of music. A single recurring tune, "The Glass Menagerie," is used to give emotional emphasis to suitable passages. This tune is like circus music, not when you are on the grounds or in the immediate vicinity of the parade, but when you are at some distance and very likely thinking of something else. It seems under those circumstances to continue almost interminably and it weaves in and out of your preoccupied consciousness; then it is the lightest, most delicate music in the world and perhaps the saddest. It expresses the surface vivacity of life with the underlying strain of immutable and inexpressible sorrow. When you look at a piece of delicately spun glass you think of two things: how beautiful it is and how easily it can be broken. Both of those ideas should be woven into the recurring tune, which dips in and out of the play as if it were carried on a wind that changes. It serves as a tread of connection and allusion between the narrator with his separate point in time and space and the subject of his story. Between each episode it returns as reference to the emotion, nostalgia, which is the first condition of the play. It is primarily Laura's music and therefore comes out most clearly when the play focuses upon her and the lovely fragility of glass which is her image.

The Lighting

The lighting in the play is not realistic. In keeping with the atmosphere of memory, the stage is dim. Shafts of light are focused on selected areas or actors, sometimes in contradistinction to what is the apparent center. For instance, in the quarrel scene between Tom and Amanda, in which Laura has no active part, the clearest pool of light is on her figure. This is also true of the supper scene. The light upon Laura should be distinct from the others, having a peculiar pristine clarity such as light used in early religious portraits of female saints or madonnas. A certain correspondence to light in religious paintings, such as El Greco's, where the figures are radiant in atmosphere that is relatively dusky, could be effectively used throughout the play. (It will also permit a more effective use of the screen.) A free, imaginative use of light can be of enormous value in giving a mobile, plastic quality to plays of a more or less static nature.

EXPRESSIONISM AND THE EPIC THEATER

Artistic and Cultural Events

1901: Expressionist paintings by Van Gogh and Gauguin appear in Paris

1902: Strindberg's *The Dream Play*; Sorge's *The Beggar*

1900–1924: German Expressionism

1920: Erwin Piscator's theater experiments in Berlin

1922: Eugene O'Neill's *The Hairy Ape*

1926: Bertolt Brecht initiates the epic theater with *Man Is Man*

1935: Chinese actors perform in Russia, where Brecht conceives "the alienation effect"

1938–1940: Brecht's *The Good Woman of Setzuan*

1949: Arthur Miller's *Death of a Salesman*

Berliner Ensemble formed

1956: Berliner Ensemble performs in London

1900 C.E.

Historical and Political Events

1914–1918: World War 1

1929: The Great Depression begins

1939–1945: World War II

1945: U.S. drops Atomic bomb on Hiroshima

1945–1989: Cold War era

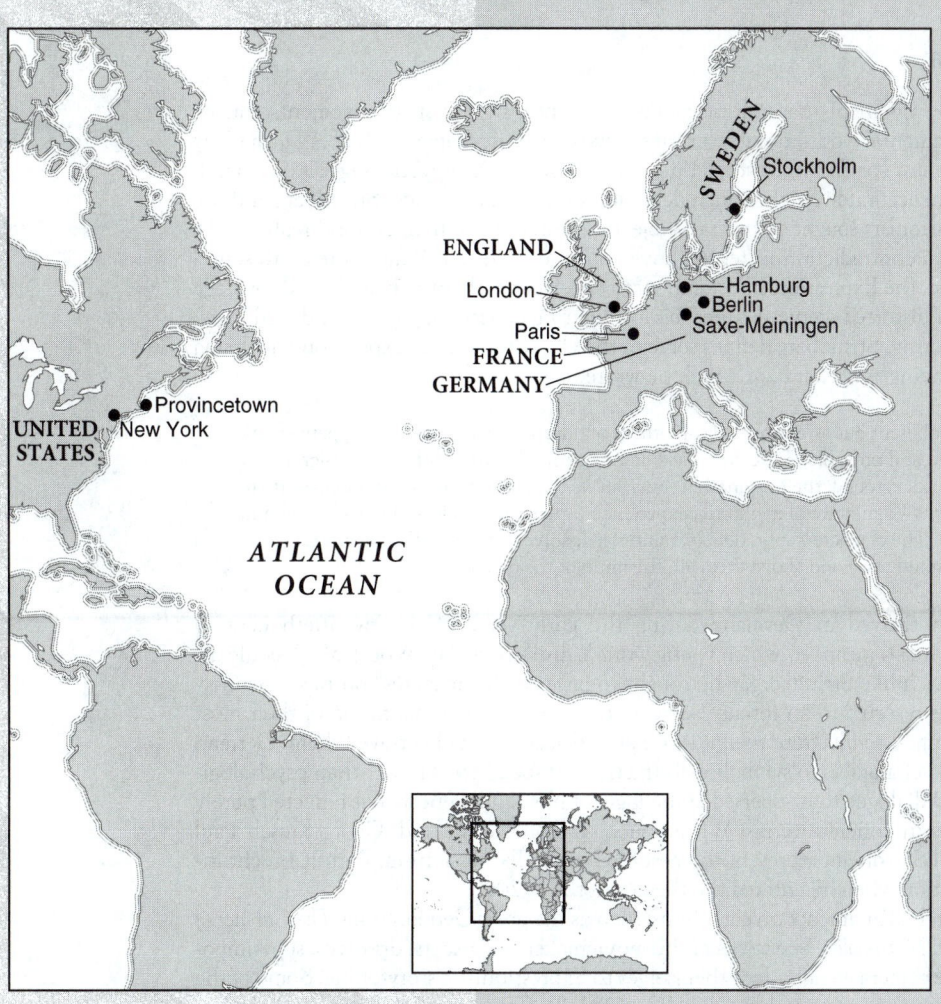

Realism, once intended as an antidote to the drama that preceded it, was itself challenged by subsequent theater artists. Even as Ibsen was writing his realistic social dramas, Expressionism was being cultivated in Sweden and Germany. It paved the way for Brecht's epic theater, and soon other "Isms"—Surrealism, Formalism, Futurism—would usurp realism's hold on the modern theater. Of these antirealist movement, Expressionism and the epic theater have enjoyed the greatest longevity and subsequent influence.

Expressionism

As effective as he was in his naturalistic works, Strindberg's greatest achievements can be found in his experimental works, notably a series of Expressionist dramas such as *A Dream Play* (1903) and *The Ghost* (or *Spook*) *Sonata* (1907). The titles of these works suggest an unreal, dreamlike, or, more accurately, nightmarish depiction of human existence. Strindberg and the subsequent Expressionists sought to portray subjective states of the human mind realistically. This is, of course, a contradiction in terms (have you ever tried to explain a dream to someone?). Nonetheless, the Expressionists attempted to construct authentic dream worlds onstage through the use of distorted scenic pictures, bizarre lighting effects, dialogue that defied logic, and nonrealistic acting. Strindberg defines some of the characteristics of Expressionistic drama in notes accompanying *A Dream Play*, which he wrote to

> imitate the incoherent but ostensibly logical form of our dreams. Anything can happen; everything is possible and probable. Time and space do not exist. Working with some insignificant real events as a background, the imagination spins out its threads of thoughts and weaves them into new patterns—a mixture of memories, experiences, spontaneous ideas, impossibilities and improbabilities. The characters split, double, multiply, dissolve, condense, float apart, coalesce. But one mind stands over and above them all, the mind of the dreamer.

Expressionism thrived in Germany during the early years of the twentieth century (1910–1924), partly as a means by which young writers, disillusioned by World War I, could attack the old order. Unlike Strindberg, who sought to project "dream states" onstage, the German Expressionists resorted to an intense subjectivism—that is, externalization of their most private inner feelings—to illustrate their outrage at a society that had betrayed them. German Expressionism used characters to symbolize abstractions of social vices rather than psychological realities, lyrical dialogue that superseded the logic of plot, and scenery that reflected purely subjective realities in concrete terms. Writers such as Frank Wedekind, Georg Kaiser, Paul Kornfeld, and Karl Sternheim represent the best of German Expressionism. Bertolt Brecht inherited their tradition when he entered the theater in the 1920s.

Expressionism had an impact on early films, such as the great German films *The Cabinet of Doctor Caligari* and *Metropolis*. The tricks of the moviemaker—crosscuts, dissolves, superimpositions, and bizarre camera angles—lent themselves to Expressionistic storytelling. Some of the most admired American playwrights, including O'Neill, Tennessee Williams, and Arthur Miller, freely used Expressionist elements in their dramas. Expressionism also did much to restore theatricality and poetry to the drama that was becoming increasingly obsessed with putting real life onstage.

The Epic Theater

The creativity of the early German Expressionists notwithstanding, it was Bertolt Brecht (1898–1956) who most transformed the German and consequently Western theater. It can be argued that Brecht is the most influential artist in the modern theater. He radically altered the means by which artists use the theater as a political instrument. Today we frequently employ the term "Brechtian" to denote a particular style that can be found in both Western (e.g., *Angels in America*) and non-Western (e.g., *Woza Albert!*) dramas, musical theater (e.g., *Cabaret*), and even opera (e.g., *Nixon in China*). Even classical plays have been presented in a Brechtian style (e.g., the Royal Shakespeare Company's acclaimed 1963 production of the *Henry VI* cycle). Although it might be argued with good reason that Brecht initiated "postmodern" theater (see Chapter 9), he was, like Ibsen and Shaw, committed to transforming society through didactic theater, and he is discussed within the context of modern drama.

Brecht began writing for the theater at the height of the German Expressionist movement in 1922. He was not so much an antirealist as he was against any form of drama that sought to engage an audience's emotions. For Brecht, this traditional approach—which he called the Aristotelian or dramatic theater—erred on two counts:

- An audience aroused to an emotional state might not make rational decisions that could amend the problem presented in the play;
- By solving the problem onstage, the audience might not feel compelled to attack the problem in the streets.

Brecht's solution was an "epic theater," which would

> not only release the feelings insights, and impulses possible within the particular historical field of human relations in which the action takes place, but [employ] and [encourage] those thoughts and feelings which help transform the field itself.

The epic theater rejected the Aristotelian catharsis, which implied a release of emotions. Instead, he sought to use the stage to provoke audiences into action. Specifically, the theater must "criticize constructively from a social point of view." Brecht constructed the following comparison between his epic theater and the dramatic theater:

Dramatic Theater	Epic Theater
plot	narrative
implicates spectator in stage situation	turns spectator into an observer
wears down his capacity for action	arouses his capacity for action
provides him with sensations	forces him to make decisions
experience	picture of the world
spectator is involved in something	spectator is made to face something
suggestion	argument
instinctive feelings are preserved	brought to point of recognition
spectator is in the thick of it, shares the experience	spectator stands outside, studies the experience
human being is taken for granted	human being is the subject of inquiry
eyes on the finish	eyes on the course
one scene makes another	each scene for itself
growth	montage
linear development	in curves (ups/down)
evolutionary determinism	jumps
man as a fixed point	man as a process
thought determines being	social being determines thought
feeling	reason*

To discourage the audience's emotional involvement with the characters, Brecht developed the *Verfremdungseffekt* ("alienation effect"), which is derived from the German verb *verfremden* ("to make strange"). In Brechtian terms, the "A-effect" (as it is now called) challenges audi-

---

*From "The Modern Theatre Is the Epic" by Bertolt Brecht, from *Brecht on Theatre*, edited and translated by John Willet, © 1964. Reprinted by permission of Methuen Publishing, Ltd.

ences to see a social problem as if for the first time, evaluate the issues, and devise solutions to correct it. Hence, the epic theater is didactic because it educates and arouses an audience to action, however entertaining its means.

To achieve the A-effect, Brecht resorted to a purposeful theatricality that reminds audiences that they are only watching a play, not real life. He admits the influence of such diverse and nonrealistic entertainments as folk plays, medieval dramas, cabaret and vaudeville, the films of Charlie Chaplin, Elizabethan stagecraft, court trials, and even boxing matches. Brecht returned the theater to the art of storytelling, frequently using narrators or singers to tell episodic tales. Between episodes, Brecht inserted speeches, songs, and visual devices such as signboards to instruct audiences about the play's intent. He rejected romantic lighting in favor of harsh, white lighting (inspired by the boxing arena) to "illuminate" the action; he rejected pretty scenery in favor of curtains that merely suggested locale and ambience; and he rejected beautiful costumes in favor of worn, used clothing made by the proletariat. Ironically, his costumes were quite often realistic.

Primarily, Brecht used *historification* to show how time and people can change societies and institutions. He set his plays in remote times and places. In *The Good Woman of Setzuan*, Brecht places his exposé of modern capitalism in provincial China. In every case he asks his audiences to judge the "pastness" of an action that clearly parallels a modern situation. Brecht was, of course, borrowing from earlier theater traditions, most notably the medieval and Elizabethan theaters, which also used history as a parallel for contemporary social problems.

Not only did Brecht—and those whom he inspired—revolutionize playwriting, he offered an alternative to realistic acting. Whereas Stanislavskian actors sought to identify with their characters through introspection and psychological motivation, Brechtian actors were taught to "quote" their characters' social essence (a boss, a worker, the oppressed, a soldier, etc.). If the Stanislavskian actor used a superobjective to get at a character's soul, the Brechtian actor defined character in terms of its *gestus* (i.e., social function). Brecht was influenced by Chinese actors he saw in Moscow in 1935, especially the great Mei Lan-fang, a man whose specialty was female roles. Brecht noted that Chinese actors sought not to become their characters, but rather to manifest the social essence of their characters. (See Forum, "Alienation Effects in Chinese Acting," following the text of *The Good Woman of Setzuan*.)

Brecht has often been accused or being antiemotional, yet a look at his plays (especially *Mother Courage*, in which a mother loses three children to the war) suggests that he could summon up an audience's emotions as well as any "dramatic" playwright. Brecht frequently employs traditional devices, particularly those of the melodrama, to arouse emotions in his audience. However, he "short-circuits" the emotional response to keep audiences from achieving the catharsis of the Aristotelian theater (which Brecht called "barbaric" because it allowed the slaughter of noble beings like Oedipus). At an emotional crest, Brecht inserted one of his A-effects—a speech, joke, or signboard—to challenge audiences to evaluate why they felt so strongly about the issues. He asked them to consider alternatives to the social problems that created the dilemma. As you read *The Good Woman of Setzuan*, *No saca nada de la escuela*, *Top Girls*, *Ti-Jean and His Brothers*, *The Great Celestial Cow*, and *Woza Albert!* you will observe these theories in practice.

THE HAIRY APE

EUGENE O'NEILL

EUGENE O'NEILL (1888–1953)

Ibsen, Strindberg, Chekhov, and Shaw are generally recognized as the progenitors of the modern theater; to this list we must add the name of Eugene O'Neill, who is acknowledged as the architect of the modern American theater. No other playwright introduced more new and significant plays than did O'Neill in the 1920s and 1930s, and—perhaps more importantly—no other playwright experimented with a greater variety of styles. It was O'Neill who introduced American audiences to Expressionism (*The Emperor Jones* and *The Hairy Ape*), the masked drama (*The Great God Brown*); the interior monologue, in which characters speak their innermost thoughts aloud in a stream-of-consciousness manner (*Strange Interlude*); and American history in the guise of Greek tragedy (*Mourning Becomes Electra*). And while he was not the first to embrace the new realism emanating from Europe, he was among the first to popularize it among mass audiences. In short, O'Neill closed the gap between the theaters of Europe and that of the United States.

O'Neill was the son of one of America's most famous nineteenth-century actors, James Tyrone O'Neill, whose reputation rested largely on his performance as the swashbuckling hero in the romantic melodrama *The Count of Monte Cristo*. O'Neill's older brother, Jamie, was also an actor. Despite their wealth and fame, the O'Neills were miserable. The father was an abusive drunkard, Jamie an irresponsible bohemian, the mother (Ella) a manic-depressive addicted to drugs. The miseries of O'Neill's youth are chronicled in two of his finest plays, *Long Day's Journey into Night* (produced posthumously, 1957) and *A Moon for the Misbegotten* (1943).

After a failed attempt as a student at Princeton, O'Neill drifted to South America and the Caribbean, occasionally working on steamers. These experiences provided him with material for a series of superb one-acts collectively known as "The Sea Plays." *The Hairy Ape* also reflects O'Neill's seagoing experiences. On his travels he contracted tuberculosis and was confined to a sanatorium for a lengthy period. This illness proved to be the turning point in his life. Bedridden, O'Neill read voraciously. In particular, he immersed himself in classical Greek tragedy; as a mature playwright he attempted (with varying degrees of success) to set tragic mythology on the American landscape. *Mourning Becomes Electra* is a retelling of the Orestes myth within the context of the Civil War, and *Desire Under the Elms* places the Hippolytus-Phaedra legend on a New England farm. In addition to the Greek tragedians, O'Neill discovered the new drama of Europe, most notably the Expressionist and psychological works of Strindberg, who remained a dominant influence on his work.

In 1914 O'Neill enrolled in George Pierce Baker's English 47 workshop at Harvard. In 1916 he joined other artists in Provincetown, Massachusetts, to form the Provincetown Players, at first a summer venture at the Wharf Theatre. In the fall the group moved to New York to start a permanent company at the Playwright's Theater in Greenwich Village (renamed the Provincetown Playhouse in 1918).

By 1922, only eight years after the English 47 workshop began, O'Neill had had some 20 plays produced, married for the second time, lost his father, gained recognition as an important dramatist, and won his first Pulitzer Prize (in 1920 for *Beyond the Horizon*). That year was no less frenetic for O'Neill. In just over a week, beginning February 28, his mother Ella O'Neill, died in Los Angeles, and he opened *The First Man* at the Neighborhood Playhouse in New York on March 4, and his Expressionistic play *The Hairy Ape* at the Provincetown Playhouse on March 9, the same day that Ella's remains arrived by train. He was too upset to either meet the train or attend the opening night performance. Also in 1922 the original Provincetown Players disbanded, although the Provincetown Playhouse continued, and O'Neill won his second Pulitzer Prize, for *Anna Christie*. O'Neill is the only American dramatist to have received the Nobel Prize in literature (1936).

O'Neill's dramas (he is known for but a single comedy, *Ah! Wilderness*) explore the universal theme that preoccupies modern playwrights: the determined effort to find meaning in a world seemingly stripped of meaning by a century of scientific and sociological thought. "Despair" is perhaps the word most closely associated with O'Neill's drama. To provide meaning to a seemingly unfathomable world, O'Neill's characters often escape into a world of illusion, or "pipe dreams," to use the playwright's favored term. *The Iceman Cometh* (1946), among the most frequently performed and most powerful plays in O'Neill's canon, perhaps best typifies the playwright's philosophic concerns.

O'Neill died in 1953, a depressed alcoholic and tormented man. Yet he left a legacy of many of the American theater's most important plays.

The Hairy Ape (1922)

Well into his "expressionist" period when he wrote *The Hairy Ape*, O'Neill uses the protagonist, Robert Smith ("Yank"), to symbolize everyman—lost, adrift, disconnected from his natural roots, unable to find his way in a social structure that seems to have no place for him. In making Yank a stoker on an ocean liner, O'Neill draws on his own experience as a sailor and on the earlier period in his life when he himself was adrift not only in alcohol but in the world, rootless, often destitute, and ultimately suicidal. In a 1924 interview in the *New York Tribune* he characterized Yank as "a symbol of man, who has lost his old harmony with nature, the harmony which he used to have as an animal and has not yet acquired in a spiritual way. Thus, not being able to find it on earth, not in heaven, he's in the middle, trying to make peace, taking the 'woist punches from bot' of 'em'."

Throughout *The Hairy Ape* expressionist techniques are apparent. The name (Robert Smith) and nickname (Yank) of the main character are generic, helping the audience understand that his struggle symbolizes the larger struggle we all must deal with in society. The settings of the play are emotive and nonrealistic, guiding the viewer through the author's expression of truth as he sees it. Although the main characters are often sympathetic, they are in no way realistic or naturalistic, except insofar as we can see ourselves through O'Neill's treatment of them. The other characters range from the one-dimensional to the surreal. Structurally, the eight scenes are arranged chronologically, but continuity is somewhat thin, ensuring that we concentrate on idea over story line.

The first scene opens on the firemen's forecastle, a bunk space for ordinary seamen on a transatlantic liner. Through O'Neill's description of the scenery as well as his dialogue we are thrust into what seems to be an animal cage filled with drunken, brutish Neanderthals. In his first monologue Yank frames the problem: While the "cap'talist class" occupies the upper decks, enjoying sunlight and fresh air, the real men—the brawn and muscle of the ship—are relegated to a dismal subterranean existence. So much for a classless society. He sees himself as a basic part of the main; not the child of a clean pure nature, but the elemental power providing the motive force for industrialized society. Yank is at once proud of what he is and yearning for recognition and place in the greater society:

> "I'm at de bottom," he says. "I'm de end! I'm de start! . . . I'm de ting in coal dat makes it boin; I'm steam and oil for de engines; I'm de ting in noise dat makes yuh hear it; I'm smoke and express trains and steamers and factory whistles; I'm de ting in gold dat makes it money! And

I'm what makes iron into steel! Steel, dat stands for de whole ting! And I'm steel—steel—steel! I'm de muscles in steel, de punch behind it! We run de whole woiks. All de rich guys dat tink dey're somep'n, dey ain't nothin! Dey don't belong. But us guys, we're in de move, we're at de bottom, de whole ting is us!

We begin to see beyond the symbols a man worth caring about expressing ideas of considerable force concerning labor, class, and society.

In scene 2 we meet Mildred Douglas, a child of privilege, on the promenade deck. Pale, anemic, bored with life, she sits in the sun but reflects no light. She is the opposite of Yank, and in her own way equally dissatisfied with her lot. The granddaughter of a steel magnate, she describes herself as " a waste product of the Bessemer process . . . I inherit the acquired trait of the by-product, wealth, but none of the energy, none of the strength of the steel that made it. I am sired by gold and damned by it . . . ".

Mildred and Yank come together in the stoke hole of the ship, where she is drawn to be stimulated by the sight of the "black gang" shoveling coal into the ship's boilers. It is a scene from hell, with subhuman acolytes tending fiery furnaces to the accompaniment of guttural chants and rhythmic movement, and when Mildred locks eyes with the howling, capering Yank she is overcome. "Oh, the filthy beast!" she exclaims as she faints from horror. Yank, insulted, is overwhelmed with rage.

Back in the forecastle in scene 4, Yank nurses his anger. The old sailor Paddy observes that "'twas as if she'd seen a great hairy ape escaped from the Zoo!" By the end of the scene Yank, in a frenzy, shouts "She done me doit, didn't she? I'll git square wit her! I'll git her some way."

Scene 5 finds Yank and his shipmate Long looking at the wildly expensive goods in New York's Fifth Avenue shop windows on a Sunday morning. When church lets out the street is filled with vain, superficial, blank-faced men and women of wealth. The scene becomes surreal as Yank bumps into them, even strikes them without having the least effect. But when he makes one of the gentlemen miss his bus police are summoned and Yank is overcome by a platoon of uniformed cops who club him to the pavement.

In a cell in the prison on Blackwell's Island, Yank learns about the "Wobblies." His introduction to the International Workers of the World (IWW) is through a derogatory, highly political newspaper article read by another inmate. He conceives of the IWW as a group of anarchists who intend to "blow up tings, . . . turn tings round," and decides to join the union, finding his place in the world and at the same time realizing his revenge on Mildred and her kind.

In the penultimate scene Yank confronts the labor union only to find that their agenda is diametrically opposed to the bloody uprisings he had envisioned. They call him stupid and accuse him of being a dirty spy for the Secret Service. "You couldn't catch a cold," they tell him, "You're a brainless ape." Rousted by a policeman on the sidewalk outside the Wobblies office, Yank asks, "Say, where do I go from here?" The cop grins. "Go to hell."

Scene 8 is the monkey house at the zoo. We join Yank in front of the gorilla cage, where the massive animal looks very much like Yank himself in the prison cell in scene 6. In his long closing monologue Yank contrasts himself with the gorilla. He sees the animal as being better off than himself because the gorilla at least has a past life of freedom to remember and because he belongs—even if his place is at the very bottom, in a cage at the zoo. Yank, conceiving a mock partnership with the gorilla, picks the lock on the cage door and releases him. If he can't find his place by moving up perhaps he can go the other way. But the ape crushes him and throws his body into the cage. Yank's dying insight is "Christ, where do I get off at? Where do I fit in? . . . In de cage, huh?" And O'Neill's final comment in the script is "And, perhaps, the Hairy Ape at last belongs."

The Hairy Ape is a fierce and angry play, one understood by its audiences more in the gut than in the intellect. As John Gassner puts it, "They experience the play as a metaphor of modern experience—of alienation in the universe and in society. "

Robert W. Wenck
Texas A&M University

Yank stands defiantly before expressionistic silhouettes of rich capitalists in Peter Stein's 1987 production of The Hairy Ape *at the National Theater of Great Britain.*

THE HAIRY APE

A Comedy of Ancient and Modern Life

In Eight Scenes

BY EUGENE O'NEILL

CHARACTERS
ROBERT SMITH, "YANK"
PADDY
LONG
MILDRED DOUGLAS

HER AUNT
SECOND ENGINEER
A GUARD
A SECRETARY OF AN ORGANIZATION
STOKERS, LADIES, GENTLEMEN, ETC.

SCENES

    Scene I: The firemen's forecastle of an ocean liner—an hour
        after sailing from New York.

    Scene II: Section of promenade deck, two days out—morning.

    Scene III: The stokehole. A few minutes later.

    Scene IV: Same as Scene I. Half an hour later.

    Scene V: Fifth Avenue, New York. Three weeks later.

    Scene VI: An island near the city. The next night.

    Scene VII: In the city. About a month later.

    Scene VIII: In the city. Twilight of the next day.

TIME: The Modern.

SCENE ONE

SCENE: *The firemen's forecastle of a trans-atlantic liner an
hour after sailing from New York for the voyage across.
Tiers of narrow, steel bunks, three deep, on all sides. An
entrance in rear. Benches on the floor before the bunks.
The room is crowded with men, shouting, cursing, laughing, singing—a confused, inchoate uproar swelling into a
sort of unity, a meaning—the bewildered, furious, baffled
defiance of a beast in a cage. Nearly all the men are drunk.
Many bottles are passed from hand to hand. All are
dressed in dungaree pants, heavy ugly shoes. Some wear
singlets, but the majority are stripped to the waist.*

    *The treatment of this scene, or of any other scene in
the play, should by no means be naturalistic. The effect
sought after is a cramped space in the bowels of a ship, imprisoned by white steel. The lines of bunks, the uprights
supporting them, cross each other like the steel framework
of a cage. The ceiling crushes down upon the men's heads.
They cannot stand upright. This accentuates the natural
stooping posture which shovelling coal and the resultant
over-development of back and shoulder muscles have given
them. The men themselves should resemble those pictures
in which the appearance of Neanderthal Man is guessed at.
All are hairy-chested, with long arms of tremendous
power, and low, receding brows above their small, fierce,
resentful eyes. All the civilized white races are represented,
but except for the slight differentiation in color of hair, skin,
eyes, all these men are alike.*

    *The curtain rises on a tumult of sound. Yank is
seated in the foreground. He seems broader, fiercer, more
truculent, more powerful, more sure of himself than the
rest. They respect his superior strength—the grudging respect of fear. Then, too, he represents to them a self-
expression, the very last word in what they are, their most
highly developed individual.*

VOICES. Gif me trink dere, you!
     'Ave a wet!
     Salute!
     Gesundheit!
     Skoal!

     Drunk as a lord, God stiffen you!
     Here's how!
     Luck!
     Pass back that bottle, dam you!
     Pourin' it down his neck!
     Ho, Froggy! Where the devil have you been?
     La Touraine.
     I hit him smash in yaw, py
       Gott!
     Jenkins—the First—he's a
       rotten swine—
     And the coppers nabbed him—
       and I run—
     I like peer better. It don't pig
       head gif you.
     A slut, I'm sayin'! She robbed
       me aslape—
     To hell with 'em all!
     You're a bloody liar!
     Say dot again!

[*Commotion. Two men about to fight are pulled apart.*]

     No scrappin' now!
     To-night—
     See who's the best man!
     Bloody Dutchman!
     To-night on the for'ard square.
     I'll bet on Dutchy.
     He packa da wallop, I tella you!
     Shut up, Wop!
     No fightin, maties. We're all
       chums, ain't we?

                  [*A voice starts bawling a song.*]

"Beer, beer, glorious beer!
Fill yourselves right up to here."

YANK [*for the first time seeming to take notice of the uproar about
him, turns around threateningly—in a tone of contemptuous
authority*]. Choke off dat noise! Where d'yuh get dat beer
stuff? Beer, hell! Beer's for goils—and Dutchmen. Me for
somep'n wit a kick to it! Gimme a drink, one of youse guys.
[*Several bottles are eagerly offered. He takes a tremendous gulp
at one of them; then, keeping the bottle in his hand, glares belligerently at the owner, who hastens to acquiesce in this robbery
by saying:*] All righto, Yank. Keep it and have another.

[*Yank contemptuously turns his back on the crowd again.
For a second there is an embarrassed silence. Then—*]

VOICES. We must be passing the Hook.
     She's beginning to roll to it.
     Six days in hell—and then
       Southampton.
     Py Yesus, I vish somepody take
       my first vatch for me!
     Gittin' seasick, Square-head?
     Drink up and forget it!

What's in your bottle?

Gin.

Dot's nigger trink.

Absinthe? It's doped. You'll
   go off your chump, Froggy!

Cochon!

Whiskey, that's the ticket!

Where's Paddy?

Going asleep.

Sing us that whiskey song,
   Paddy.

[*They all turn to an old, wizened Irishman who is dozing, very drunk, on the benches forward. His face is extremely monkey-like with all the sad, patient pathos of that animal in his small eyes.*]

Singa da song, Caruso Pat!

He's gettin' old. The drink is
   too much for him.

He's too drunk.

PADDY. [*blinking about him, starts to his feet resentfully, swaying, holding on to the edge of a bunk*]. I'm never too drunk to sing. 'Tis only when I'm dead to the world I'd be wishful to sing at all. [*With a sort of sad contempt.*] "Whiskey Johnny," ye want? A chanty, ye want? Now that's a queer wish from the ugly like of you, God help you. But no matther. [*He starts to sing in a thin, nasal, doleful tone:*]

Oh, whiskey is the life of man!

Whiskey! O Johnny!

[*They all join in on this.*]

Oh, whiskey is the life of man!

Whiskey for my Johnny!

[*Again chorus*]

Oh, whiskey drove my old man mad!

Whiskey! O Johnny!

Oh, whiskey drove my old man mad!

Whiskey for my Johnny!

YANK [*again turning around scornfully*]. Aw hell! Nix on dat old sailing ship stuff! All dat bull's dead, see? And you're dead, too, yuh damned old Harp, on'y yuh don't know it. Take it easy, see. Give us a rest. Nix on de loud noise. [*With a cynical grin.*] Can't youse see I'm tryin' to tink?

ALL. [*repeating the word after him as one with the same cynical amused mockery*]. Think!

[*The chorused word has a brazen metallic quality as if their throats were phonograph horns. It is followed by a general uproar of hard, barking laughter.*]

VOICES. Don't be cracking your head
   wid ut, Yank.

You gat headache, py yingo!

One thing about it—it rhymes
   with drink!

Ha, ha, ha!

Drink, don't think!

Drink, don't think!

Drink, don't think!

[*A whole chorus of voices has taken up this refrain, stamping on the floor, pounding on the benches with fists.*]

YANK. [*taking a gulp from his bottle—good-naturedly*]. Aw right. Can de noise. I got yuh de foist time.

[*The uproar subsides. A very drunken sentimental tenor begins to sing:*]

"Far away in Canada,
   Far across the sea,
There's a lass who fondly waits
   Making a home for me—"

YANK. [*fiercely contemptuous*]. Shut up, yuh lousey boob! Where d'yuh get dat tripe? Home? Home, hell! I'll make a home for yuh! I'll knock yuh dead! Home. T'hell with home! Where d'yuh get dat tripe? Dis is home, see? What d'yuh want wit home? [*Proudly.*] I runned away from mine when I was a kid. On'y too glad to beat it, dat was me. Home was lickings for me, dat's all. But yuh can bet your shoit noone ain't never licked me since! Wanter try it, any of youse? Huh! I guess not. [*In a more placated but still contemptuous tone.*] Goils waitin' for yuh, huh? Aw, hell! Dat's all tripe. Dey don't wait for noone. Dey'd double-cross yuh for a nickel. Dey're all tarts, get me? Treat 'em rough, dat's me. To hell wit 'em. Tarts, dat's what, de whole bunch of 'em.

LONG [*very drunk, jumps on a bench excitedly, gesticulating with a bottle in his hand*]. Listen 'ere, Comrades! Yank 'ere is right. 'E says this 'ere stinkin' ship is our 'ome. And 'e says as 'ome is 'ell. And 'e's right! This is 'ell. We lives in 'ell, Comrades—and right enough we'll die in it. [*Raging.*] And who's ter blame, I arsks yer? We ain't. We wasn't born this rotten way. All men is born free and ekal. That's in the bleedin' Bible, maties. But what d'they care for the Bible—them lazy, bloated swine what travels first cabin? Them's the ones. They dragged us down 'till we're on'y wage slaves in the bowels of a bloody ship, sweatin', burnin' up, eatin' coal dust! Hit's them's ter blame—the damned capitalist clarss!

[*There had been a gradual murmur of contemptuous resentment rising among the men until now he is interrupted by a storm of catcalls, hisses, boos, hard laugher.*]

VOICES. Turn it off!

Shut up!

Sit down!

Closa da face!

Tamn fool! (*Etc.*)

YANK [*standing up and glaring at Long*]. Sit down before I knock yuh down! [*Long makes haste to efface himself. Yank goes on contemptuously.*] De Bible, huh? De Cap'tlist class, huh? Aw nix on dat Salvation Army-Socialist bull. Git a soapbox! Hire a hall! Come and be saved, huh? Jerk us to Jesus, huh? Aw g'wan! I've listened to lots of guys like you, see. Yuh're all wrong. Wanter know what I t'ink? Yuh ain't no good for noone. Yuh're de bunk. Yuh ain't got no noive, get me? Yuh're yellow, dat's what. Yellow, dat's you. Say! What's dem slobs in de foist cabin got to do wit us? We're better men dan dey are, ain't we? Sure! One of us guys could clean up de whole mob wit one mit. Put one of 'em down here for one watch in de stokehole, what'd happen? Dey'd carry him off on a stretcher. Dem boids don't amount to nothin'. Dey're just baggage. Who makes dis old tub run? Ain't it us guys? Well den, we belong, don't we? We belong and dey don't. Dat's all. [*A loud chorus of approval. Yank goes on.*] As for dis bein' hell—aw, nuts! Yuh lost your noive, dat's what. Dis is a man's job, get me? It belongs. It runs dis tub. No stiffs need apply. But yuh're a stiff, see? Yuh're yellow, dat's you.

VOICES [*with a great hard pride in them*].
          Righto!
          A man's job!
          Talk is cheap, Long.
          He never could hold up his end.
          Divil take him!
          Yank's right. We make it go.
          Py Gott, Yank say right ting!
          We don't need noone cryin'
              over us.
          Makin' speeches.
          Throw him out!
          Yellow!
          Chuck him overboard!
          I'll break his jaw for him!
                    [*They crowd around Long threateningly.*]

YANK [*half good-natured again—contemptuously*]. Aw, take it easy. Leave him alone. He ain't woith a punch. Drink up. Here's how, whoever owns dis.

[*He takes a long swallow from his bottle. All drink with him. In a flash all is hilarious amiability again, back-slapping, loud talk, etc.*]

PADDY [*who has been sitting in a blinking, melancholy daze, suddenly cries out in a voice full of old sorrow*]. We belong to this, you're saying? We make the ship to go, you're saying? Yerra then, that Almighty God have pity on us! [*His voice runs into the wail of a keen, he rocks back and forth on his bench. The men stare at him, startled and impressed in spite of themselves.*] Oh, to be back in the fine days of my youth, ochone! Oh, there was fine beautiful ships them days— clippers wid tall masts touching the sky—fine strong men in them—men that was sons of the sea as if 'twas the mother that bore them. Oh, the clean skins of them, and the clear eyes, the straight backs and full chests of them! Brave men they was, and bold men surely! We'd be sailing out, bound down round the Horn maybe. We'd be making sail in the dawn, with a fair breeze, singing a chanty song wid no care to it. And astern the land would be sinking low and dying out, but we'd give it no heed but a laugh, and never a look behind. For the day that was, was enough, for we was free men—and I'm thinking 'tis only slaves do be giving heed to the day that's gone or the day to come—until they're old like me. [*With a sort of religious exaltation.*] Oh, to be scudding south again wid the power of the Trade Wind driving her on steady through the nights and the days! Full sail on her! Nights and days! Nights when the foam of the wake would be flaming wid fire, when the sky'd be blazing and winking wid stars. Or the full of the moon maybe. Then you'd see her driving through the gray night, her sails stretching aloft all silver and white, not a sound on the deck, the lot of us dreaming dreams, till you'd believe 'twas no real ship at all you was on but a ghost ship like the Flying Dutchman they say does be roaming the seas forevermore widout touching a port. And there was the days, too. A warm sun on the clean decks. Sun warming the blood of you, and wind over the miles of shiny green ocean like strong drink to your lungs. Work—aye, hard work—but who'd mind that at all? Sure, you worked under the sky and 'twas work wid skill and daring to it. And wid the day done, in the dog watch, smoking me pipe at ease, the lookout would be raising land maybe, and we'd see the mountains of South Americy wid the red fire of the setting sun painting their white tops and the clouds floating by them! [*His tone of exaltation ceases. He goes on mournfully.*] Yerra, what's the use of talking? 'Tis a dead man's whisper. [*To Yank resentfully.*] 'Twas them days men belonged to ships, not now. 'Twas them days a ship was part of the sea, and a man was part of a ship, and the sea joined all together and made it one. [*Scornfully.*] Is it one wid this you'd be, Yank—black smoke from the funnels smudging the sea, smudging the decks—the bloody engines pounding and throbbing and shaking—wid divil a sight of sun or a breath of clean air—choking our lungs wid coal dust—breaking our backs and hearts in the hell of the stokehole—feeding the bloody furnace—feeding our lives along wid the coal, I'm thinking—caged in by steel from a sight of the sky like bloody apes in the Zoo! [*With a harsh laugh.*] Ho-ho, divil mend you! Is it to belong to that you're wishing? Is it a flesh and blood wheel of the engines you'd be?

YANK [*who has been listening with a contemptuous sneer, barks out the answer*]. Sure ting! Dat's me! What about it?

PADDY [*as if to himself—with great sorrow*]. Me time is past due. That a great wave wid sun in the heart of it may sweep me over the side sometime I'd be dreaming of the days that's gone!

YANK. Aw, yuh crazy Mick! [*He springs to his feet and advances on Paddy threateningly—then stops, fighting some queer struggle within himself—lets his hands fall to his sides— contemptuously.*] Aw, take it easy. Yuh're aw right, at dat. Yuh're bugs, dat's all—nutty as a cuckoo. All dat tripe yuh been pullin'—Aw, dat's all right. On'y it's dead, get me? Yuh don't belong no more, see. Yuh don't get de stuff. Yuh're too old. [*Disgustedly.*] But aw say, come up for air onct in a while, can't yuh? See what's happened since yuh croaked. [*He suddenly bursts forth vehemently, growing more and more excited.*] Say! Sure! Sure I meant it! What de hell—Say, lemme talk! Hey! Hey, you old Harp! Hey, youse guys! Say, listen to me—wait a moment—I gotter talk, see. I belong and he don't. He's dead but I'm livin'. Listen to me! Sure I'm part of the engines! Why de hell not! Dey move, don't dey? Dey're speed, ain't dey? Dey smash trou, don't dey? Twenty-five knots a hour! Dat's goin' some! Dat's new stuff! Dat belongs! But him, he's too old. He gets dizzy. Say, listen. All dat crazy tripe about nights and days; all dat crazy tripe about stars and moons; all dat crazy tripe about suns and winds, fresh air and de rest of it—Aw hell, dat's all a dope dream! Hittin' de pipe of de past, dat's what he's doin'. He's old and don't belong no more. But me, I'm young! I'm in de pink! I move wit it! It, get me! I mean de ting dat's de guts of all dis. It ploughs trou all de tripe he's been sayin'. It blows dat up! It knocks dat dead! It slams dat offen de face of de oith! It, get me! De engines and de coal and de smoke and all de rest of it! He can't breathe and swallow coal dust, but I kin, see? Dat's fresh air for me! Dat's food for me! I'm new, get me? Hell in de stokehole? Sure! It takes a man to work in hell. Hell, sure, dat's my fav'rite climate. I eat it up! I git fat on it! It's me makes it hot! It's me makes it roar! It's me makes it move! Sure, on'y for me everyting stops. It all goes dead, get me? De noise and smoke and all de engines movin' de woild, dey stop. Dere ain't nothin' no more! Dat's what I'm sayin'. Everyting else dat makes de woild move, somep'n makes it move. It can't move witout somep'n else, see? Den yuh get down to me. I'm at de bottom, get me! Dere ain't nothin' foither. I'm de end! I'm de start! I start somep'n and de woild moves! It—dat's me!—de new dat's moiderin' de old! I'm de ting in coal dat makes it boin; I'm steam and oil for de engines; I'm de ting in noise dat makes yuh hear it; I'm smoke and express trains and steamers and factory whistles; I'm de ting in gold dat makes it money! And I'm what makes iron into steel! Steel, dat stands for de whole ting! And I'm steel—steel—steel! I'm de muscles in steel, de punch behind it! [*As he says this he pounds with his fist against the steel bunks. All the men, roused to a pitch of frenzied self-glorification by his speech, do likewise. There is a deafening metallic roar, through which* Yank's *voice can be heard bellowing.*] Slaves, hell! We run de whole woiks. All de rich guys dat tink dey're somep'n, dey ain't nothin'! Dey don't belong. But us guys, we're in de move, we're at de bottom, de whole ting is us! [*Paddy from the start of Yank's speech has been taking one gulp after another from his bottle, at first frightenedly, as if he were afraid to listen, then desperately, as if to drown his senses, but finally has achieved complete indifferent, even amused, drunkenness. Yank sees his lips moving. He quells the uproar with a shout.*] Hey, youse guys, take it easy! Wait a moment! De nutty Harp is sayin' somep'n.

PADDY. [*is heard now—throws his head back with a mocking burst of laughter*]. Ho-ho-ho-ho-ho—

YANK. [*drawing back his fist, with a snarl*]. Aw! Look out who yuh're givin' the bark!

Paddy [*begins to sing the "Miller of Dee" with enormous good-nature*].

"I care for nobody, no, not I,
And nobody cares for me."

YANK [*good-natured himself in a flash, interrupts* Paddy *with a slap on the bare back like a report*]. Dat's de stuff! Now yuh're gettin' wise to somep'n. Care for nobody, dat's de dope! To hell wit 'em all! And nix on nobody else carin'. I kin care for myself, get me! [*Eight bells sound, muffled, vibrating through the steel walls as if some enormous brazen gong were imbedded in the heart of the ship. All the men jump up mechanically, file through the door silently close upon each other's heels in what is very like a prisoner's lockstep. Yank slaps* Paddy *on the back.*] Our watch, yuh old Harp! [*Mockingly.*] Come on down in hell. Eat up de coal dust. Drink in de heat. It's it, see! Act like yuh liked it, yuh better—or croak yuhself.

PADDY [*with jovial defiance*]. To the divil wid it! I'll not report this watch. Let thim log me and be damned. I'm no slave the like of you. I'll be sittin' here at me ease, and drinking, and thinking, and dreaming dreams.

YANK [*contemptuously*]. Tinkin' and dreamin', what'll that get yuh? What's tinkin' got to do wit it? We move, don't we? Speed, ain't we? Fog, dat's all you stand for. But we drive trou dat, don't it? We split dat up and smash trou—twenty-five knots a hour! [*Turns his back on* Paddy *scornfully.*] Aw, yuh make me sick! Yuh don't belong!

[*He strides out the door in rear. Paddy hums to himself, blinking drowsily.*]

CURTAIN

SCENE TWO

SCENE: *Two days out. A section of the promenade deck. Mildred Douglas and her aunt are discovered reclining in deck chairs. The former is a girl of twenty, slender, delicate, with a pale, pretty face marred by a self-conscious expression of disdainful superiority. She looks fretful, nervous, and discontented, bored by her own anemia. Her aunt is a pompous and proud—and fat—old lady. She is a type even to the point of a double chin and lorgnettes. She is dressed pretentiously, as if afraid her face alone would never indicate her position in life. Mildred is dressed all in white.*

The impression to be conveyed by this scene is one of the beautiful, vivid life of the sea all about—sunshine on the deck in a great flood, the fresh sea wind blowing across it. In the midst of this, these two incongruous, artificial figures, inert and disharmonious, the elder like a gray lump of dough touched up with rouge, the younger looking as if the vitality of her stock had been sapped before she was conceived, so that she is the expression not of its life energy but merely of the artificialities that energy had won for itself in the spending.

MILDRED [*looking up with affected dreaminess*]. How the black smoke swirls back against the sky! Is it not beautiful?

AUNT [*without looking up*]. I dislike smoke of any kind.

MILDRED. My great-grandmother smoked a pipe—a clay pipe.

AUNT [*ruffling*]. Vulgar!

MILDRED. She was too distant a relative to be vulgar. Time mellows pipes.

AUNT [*pretending boredom, but irritated*]. Did the sociology you took up at college teach you that—to play the ghoul on every possible occasion, excavating old bones? Why not let your great-grandmother rest in her grave?

MILDRED [*dreamily*]. With her pipe beside her—puffing in Paradise.

AUNT [*with spite*]. Yes, you are a natural born ghoul. You are even getting to look like one, my dear.

MILDRED [*in a passionless tone*]. I detest you, Aunt. [*Looking at her critically.*] Do you know what you remind me of? Of a cold pork pudding against a background of linoleum tablecloth in the kitchen of a—but the possibilities are wearisome.

[*She closes her eyes.*]

AUNT [*with a bitter laugh*]. Merci for your candor. But since I am and must be your chaperone—in appearance, at least—let us patch up some sort of armed truce. For my part you are quite free to indulge any pose of eccentricity that beguiles you—as long as you observe the amenities—

MILDRED [*drawling*]. The inanities?

AUNT [*going on as if she hadn't heard*]. After exhausting the morbid thrills of social service work on New York's East Side—how they must have hated you, by the way, the poor that you made so much poorer in their own eyes!—you are now bent on making your slumming international. Well, I hope Whitechapel will provide the needed nerve tonic. Do not ask me to chaperone you there, however. I told your father I would not. I loathe deformity. We will hire an army of detectives and you may investigate everything—they allow you to see.

MILDRED [*protesting with a trace of genuine earnestness*]. Please do not mock at my attempts to discover how the other half lives. Give me credit for some sort of groping sincerity in that at least. I would like to help them. I would like to be some use in the world. Is it my fault I don't know how? I would like to be sincere, to touch life somewhere. [*With weary bitterness.*] But I'm afraid I have neither the vitality nor integrity. All that was burnt out in our stock before I was born. Grandfather's blast furnaces, flaming to the sky, melting steel, making millions—then father keeping those home fires burning, making more millions—and little me at the tail-end of it all. I'm a waste product in the Bessemer process—like the millions. Or rather, I inherit the acquired trait of the by-product, wealth, but none of the energy, none of the strength of the steel that made it. I am sired by gold and damned by it, as they say at the race track—damned in more ways than one.

[*She laughs mirthlessly.*]

AUNT [*unimpressed—superciliously*]. You seem to be going in for sincerity to-day. It isn't becoming to you, really—except as an obvious pose. Be as artificial as you are, I advise. There's a sort of sincerity in that, you know. And, after all, you must confess you like that better.

MILDRED [*again affected and bored*]. Yes, I suppose I do. Pardon me for my outburst. When a leopard complains of its spots, it must sound rather grotesque. [*In a mocking tone.*] Purr, little leopard. Purr, scratch, tear, kill, gorge yourself and be happy—only stay in the jungle where your spots are camouflage. In a cage they make you conspicuous.

AUNT. I don't know what you are taking about.

MILDRED. It would be rude to talk about anything to you. Let's just talk. [*She looks at her wrist watch.*] Well, thank goodness, it's about time for them to come for me. That ought to give me a new thrill, Aunt.

AUNT [*affectedly troubled*]. You don't mean to say you're really going? The dirt—the heat must be frightful—

MILDRED. Grandfather started as a puddler. I should have inherited an immunity to heat that would make a salamander shiver. It will be fun to put it to the test.

AUNT. But don't you have to have the captain's—or someone's—permission to visit the stokehole?

MILDRED [*with a triumphant smile*]. I have it—both his and the chief engineer's. Oh, they didn't want to at first, in spite of my social service credentials. They didn't seem a bit anxious that I should investigate how the other half lives and works on a ship. So I had to tell them that my father, the president of Nazareth Steel, chairman of the board of directors of this line, had told me it would be all right.

AUNT. He didn't.

MILDRED. How naïve age makes one! But I said he did, Aunt. I even said he had given me a letter to them—which I had lost. And they were afraid to take the chance that I might be lying. [*Excitedly.*] So it's ho! for the stokehole. The second engineer is to escort me. [*Looking at her watch again.*] It's time. And here he comes, I think.

[*The Second Engineer enters. He is a husky, fine-looking man of thirty-five or so. He stops before the two and tips his cap, visibly embarrassed and ill-at-ease.*]

SECOND ENGINEER. Miss Douglas.

MILDRED. Yes. [*Throwing off her rugs and getting to her feet.*] Are we all ready to start?

SECOND ENGINEER. In just a second, ma'am. I'm waiting for the Fourth. He's coming along.

MILDRED [*with a scornful smile*]. You don't care to shoulder this responsibility alone, is that it?

SECOND ENGINEER [*forcing a smile*]. Two are better than one. *Disturbed by her eyes, glances out to sea—blurts out.*] A fine day we're having.

MILDRED. Is it?

SECOND ENGINEER. A nice warm breeze—

MILDRED. It feels cold to me.

SECOND ENGINEER. But it's hot enough in the sun—

MILDRED. Not hot enough for me. I don't like Nature. I was never athletic.

SECOND ENGINEER [*forcing a smile*]. Well, you'll find it hot enough where you're going.

MILDRED. Do you mean hell?

SECOND ENGINEER [*flabbergasted, decides to laugh*]. Ho-ho! No, I mean the stokehole.

MILDRED. My grandfather was a puddler. He played with boiling steel.

SECOND ENGINEER [*all at sea—uneasily*]. Is that so? Hum, you'll excuse me, ma'am, but are you intending to wear that dress?

MILDRED. Why not?

SECOND ENGINEER. You'll likely rub against oil and dirt. It can't be helped.

MILDRED. It doesn't matter. I have lots of white dresses.

SECOND ENGINEER. I have an old coat you might throw over—

MILDRED. I have fifty dresses like this. I will throw this one into the sea when I come back. That ought to wash it clean, don't you think?

SECOND ENGINEER [*doggedly*]. There's ladders to climb down that are none too clean—and dark alleyways—

MILDRED. I will wear this very dress and none other.

SECOND ENGINEER. No offense meant. It's none of my business. I was only warning you—

MILDRED. Warning? That sounds thrilling.

SECOND ENGINEER [*looking down the deck—with a sigh of relief*]. There's the Fourth now. He's waiting for us. If you'll come—

MILDRED. Go on. I'll follow you. [*He goes. Mildred turns a mocking smile on her aunt.*] An oaf—but a handsome, virile oaf.

AUNT [*scornfully*]. Poser!

MILDRED. Take care. He said there were dark alleyways—

AUNT [*in the same tone*]. Poser!

MILDRED [*biting her lips angrily*]. You are right. But would that my millions were not so anemically chaste!

AUNT. Yes, for a fresh pose I have no doubt you would drag the name of Douglas in the gutter!

MILDRED. From which it sprang. Good-by, Aunt. Don't pray too hard that I may fall into the fiery furnace.

AUNT. Poser!

MILDRED [*viciously*]. Old hag!

[*She slaps her aunt insultingly across the face and walks off, laughing gaily.*]

AUNT [*screams after her*]. I said poser!

CURTAIN

SCENE THREE

SCENE: *The stokehole. In the rear, the dimly-outlined bulks of the furnaces and boilers. High overhead one hanging electric bulb sheds just enough light through the murky air laden with coal dust to pile up masses of shadows everywhere. A line of men, stripped to the waist, is before the furnace doors. They bend over, looking neither to right nor left, handling their shovels as if they were part of their bodies, with a strange, awkward, swinging rhythm. They use the shovels to throw open the furnace doors. Then from these fiery round holes in the black a flood of terrific light and heat pours full upon the men who are outlined in silhouette in the crouching, inhuman attitudes of chained gorillas. The men shovel with a rhythmic motion, swinging as on a pivot from the coal which lies in heaps on the floor behind to hurl it into the flaming mouths before them. There is a tumult of noise—the brazen clang of the furnace doors as they are flung open or slammed shut, the grating, teeth-gritting grind of steel against steel, of crunching coal. This clash of sounds stuns one's ears with its rending dissonance. But there is order in it, rhythm, a mechanical regulated recurrence, a tempo. And rising above all, making the air hum with the quiver of liberated energy, the roar of leaping flames in the furnaces, the monotonous throbbing heat of the engines.*

As the curtain rises, the furnace doors are shut. The men are taking a breathing spell. One or two are arranging the coal behind them, pulling it into more accessible heaps. The others can be dimly made out leaning on their shovels in relaxed attitudes of exhaustion.

PADDY [*from somewhere in the line—plaintively*]. Yerra, will this divil's own watch nivir end? Me back is broke. I'm destroyed entirely.

YANK [*from the center of the line—with exuberant scorn*]. Awk, yuh make me sick! Lie down and croak, why don't yuh? Always beefin', dat's you! Say, dis is a cinch! Dis was made for me! It's my meat, get me! [*A whistle is blown—a thin, shrill note from somewhere overhead in the darkness. Yank curses without resentment.*] Dere's de damn engineer crackin' de whip. He tinks we're loafin'.

PADDY [*vindictively*]. God stiffen him!

YANK [*in an exultant tone of command*]. Come on, youse guys! Git into de game! She's gittin' hungry! Pile some grub in her! Trow it into her belly! Come on now, all of youse! Open her up!

[*At this last all the men, who have followed his movements of getting into position, throw open their furnace doors with a deafening clang. The fiery light floods over their shoulders as they bend round for the coal. Rivulets of sooty sweat have traced maps on their backs. The enlarged muscles form bunches of high light and shadow.*]

YANK [*chanting a count as he shovels without seeming effort*]. One—two—tree—[*His voice rising exultantly in the joy of battle.*] Dat's de stuff! Let her have it! All togedder now! Sling it into her! Let her ride! Shoot de piece now! Call de toin on her! Drive her into it! Feel her move! Watch her smoke! Speed, dat's her middle name! Give her coal, youse guys! Coal, dat's her booze! Drink it up, baby! Let's see yuh sprint! Dig in and gain a lap! Dere she go-o-es—

[*This last is the chanting formula of the gallery gods at the six-day bike race. He slams his furnace door shut. The others do likewise with as much unison as their wearied bodies will permit. The effect is of one fiery eye after another being blotted out with a series of accompanying bangs.*]

PADDY [*groaning*]. Me back is broke. I'm bate out—bate—

[*There is a pause. Then the inexorable whistle sounds again from the din, regions above the electric light. There is a growl of cursing rage from all sides.*]

YANK [*shaking his fist upward—contemptuously*]. Take it easy dere, you! Who d'yuh tinks runnin' dis game, me or you? When I git ready, we move. Not before! When I git ready, get me!

VOICES [*approvingly*]. That's the stuff!
　　Yank tal him, py golly!
　　Yank ain't affeerd.
　　Goot poy, Yank!
　　Give him hell!
　　Tell 'im 'e's a bloody swine!
　　Bloody slave-driver!

YANK [*contemptuously*]. He ain't got no noive. He's yellow, get me? All de engineers is yellow. Dey got streaks a mile wide. Aw, to hell wit him! Let's move, youse guys. We had a rest. Come on, she needs it! Give her pep! It ain't for him. Him and his whistle, dey don't belong. But we belong, see! We gotter feed de baby! Come on!

[*He turns and flings his furnace door open. They all follow his lead. At this instant the Second and Fourth Engineers enter from the darkness on the left with Mildred between them. She starts, turns paler, her pose is crumbling, she shivers with fright in spite of the blazing heat, but forces herself to leave the Engineers and take a few steps nearer the men. She is right behind Yank. All this happens quickly while the men have their backs turned.*]

YANK. Come on, youse guys! [*He is turning to get coal when the whistle sounds again in a peremptory, irritating note. This drives Yank into a sudden fury. While the other men have turned full around and stopped dumfounded by the spectacle of Mildred standing there in her white dress, Yank does not turn far enough to see her. Besides, his head is thrown back, he blinks upward through the murk trying to find the owner of the whistle, he brandishes his shovel murderously over his head in one hand, pounding on his chest, gorilla-like, with the other, shouting:*] Toin off dat whistle! Come down outa dere, yuh yellow, brass-buttoned, Belfast bum, yuh! Come down and I'll knock yer brains out! Yuh lousey, stinkin', yellow mut of a Catholic-moiderin' bastard! Come down and I'll moider yuh! Pullin' dat whistle on me, huh? I'll show yuh! I'll crash yer skull in! I'll drive yer teet' down yer troat! I'll slam yer nose trou de back of yer head! I'll cut yer guts out for a nickel, yuh lousey boob, yuh dirty, crummy, muck-eatin' son of a—

[*Suddenly he becomes conscious of all the other men staring at something directly behind his back. He whirls defensively with a snarling, murderous growl, crouching to spring, his lips drawn back over his teeth, his small eyes gleaming ferociously. He sees Mildred, like a white apparition in the full light from the open furnace doors. He glares into her eyes, turned to stone. As for her, during his speech she has listened, paralyzed with horror, terror, her whole personality crushed, beaten in, collapsed, by the terrific impact of this unknown, abysmal brutality, naked and shameless. As she looks at his gorilla face, as his eyes bore into hers, she utters a low, choking cry and shrinks away from him, pulling both hands up before her eyes to shut out the sight of his face, to protect her own. This startles Yank to a reaction. His mouth falls open, his eyes grow bewildered.*]

MILDRED [*about to faint—to the* Engineers, *who now have her one by each arm—whimperingly*]. Take me away! Oh, the filthy beast!
[*She faints. They carry her quickly back, disappearing in the darkness at the left, rear. An iron door clangs shut. Rage and bewildered fury rush back on Yank. He feels himself insulted in some unknown fashion in the very heart of his pride. He roars:* God damn yuh! *And hurls his shovel after them at the door which has just closed. It hits the steel bulkhead with a clang and falls clattering on the steel floor. From overhead the whistle sounds again in a long, angry, insistent command.*]

CURTAIN

SCENE FOUR

SCENE: *The firemen's forecastle. Yank's watch has just come off duty and had dinner. Their faces and bodies shine from a soap and water scrubbing but around their eyes, where a hasty dousing does not touch, the coal dust sticks like black make-up, giving them a queer, sinister expression. Yank has not washed either face or body. He stands out in contrast to them, a blackened, brooding figure. He is seated forward on a bench in the exact attitude of Rodin's "The Thinker." The others, most of them smoking pipes are staring at Yank half-apprehensively, as if fearing an outburst; half-amusedly, as if they saw a joke somewhere that tickled them.*

VOICES. He ain't ate nothin'.
    Py golly, a fallar gat gat grub
      in him.
    Divil a lie.
    Yank feeda da fire, no feeda da
      face.
    Ha-ha.
    He ain't even washed hisself.
    He's forgot.
    Hey, Yank, you forgot to wash.
YANK [*sullenly*]. Forgot nothin'! To hell wit washin'.
VOICES. It'll stick to you.
    It'll get under your skin.
    Give yer the bleedin' itch, that's
      wot.
    It makes spots on you—like a
      leopard.
    Like a piebald nigger, you
      mean.
    Better wash up, Yank.
    You sleep better.
    Wash up, Yank.
    Wash up! Wash up!
YANK [*resentfully*]. Aw say, youse guys. Lemme alone. Can't youse see I'm tryin' to tink?
ALL [*repeating the word after him as one with cynical mockery*]. Think!

[*The word has a brazen, metallic quality as if their throats were phonograph horns. It is followed by a chorus of hard, barking laughter.*]

YANK. [*springing to his feet and glaring at them belligerently*]. Yes, tink! Tink, dat's what I said! What about it?

[*They are silent, puzzled by his sudden resentment of what used to be one of his jokes. Yank sits down again in the same attitude of "The Thinker."*]

VOICES. Leave him alone.
    He's got a grouch on.
    Why wouldn't he?
PADDY [*with a wink at the others*]. Sure I know what's the matther. 'Tis aisy to see. He's fallen in love, I'm telling you.
ALL [*repeating the word after him as one with cynical mockery*]. Love!

[*The word has a brazen, metallic quality as if their throats were phonograph horns. It is followed by a chorus of hard, barking laughter.*]

YANK [*with a contemptuous snort*]. Love, hell! Hate, dat's what. I've fallen in hate, get me?
PADDY [*philosophically*]. 'Twould take a wise man to tell one from the other. [*With a bitter, ironical scorn, increasing as he goes on.*] But I'm telling you it's love that's in it. Sure what else but love for us poor bastes in the stokehole would be bringing a fine lady, dressed like a white quane, down a mile of ladders and steps to be havin' a look at us?

      [*A growl of anger goes up from all sides.*]

LONG [*jumping on a bench—hecticly*]. Hinsultin' us! Hinsultin' us, the bloody cow! And them bloody engineers! What right 'as they got to be exhibitin' us 's if we was bleedin' monkeys in a menagerie? Did we sign for hinsults to our dignity as 'onest workers? Is that in the ship's articles? You kin bloody well bet it ain't! But I knows why they done it. I arsked a deck steward 'o she was and 'e told me. 'Er old man's a bleedin' millionaire, a bloody Capitalist! 'E's got enuf bloody gold to sink this bleedin' ship! 'E makes arf the bloody steel in the world! 'E owns this bloody boat! And you and me, comrades, we're 'is slaves! And the skipper and mates and engineers, they're 'is slaves! And she's 'is bloody daughter and we're all 'er slaves, too! And she gives 'er orders as 'ow she wants to see the bloody animals below decks and down they takes 'er!

      [*There is a roar of rage from all sides.*]

YANK [*blinking at him bewilderedly*]. Say! Wait a moment! Is all dat straight goods?
LONG. Straight as string! The bleedin' steward as waits on 'em, 'e told me about 'er. And what're we goin' ter do, I arsks yer? 'Ave we got ter swaller 'er hinsults like dogs? It ain't in the ship's articles. I tell yer we got a case. We kin go ter law—
YANK [*with abysmal contempt*]. Hell! Law!
ALL [*repeating the word after him as one with cynical mockery*]. Law!

[*The word has a brazen metallic quality as if their throats were phonograph horns. It is followed by a chorus of hard, barking laughter.*]

LONG [*feeling the ground slipping from under his feet—desperately*]. As voters and citizens we kin force the bloody governments—
YANK [*with abysmal contempt*]. Hell! Governments!
ALL [*repeating the word after him as one with cynical mockery*]. Governments!

[*The word has a brazen metallic quality as if their throats were phonograph horns. It is followed by a chorus of hard, barking laughter.*]

LONG [*hysterically*]. We're free and equal in the sight of God—
YANK [*with abysmal contempt*]. Hell! God!
ALL [*repeating the word after him as one with cynical mockery*]. God!

[*The word has a brazen metallic quality as if their throats were phonograph horns. It is followed by a chorus of hard, barking laughter.*]

YANK [*witheringly*]. Aw, join de Salvation Army!

ALL Sit down! Shut up! Damn fool! Sea-lawyer!

[*Long slinks back out of sight.*]

PADDY [*continuing the trend of his thoughts as if he had never been interrupted—bitterly*]. And there she was standing behind us, and the Second pointing at us like a man you'd hear in a circus would be saying: In this cage is a queerer kind of baboon than ever you'd find in darkest Africy. We roast them in their own sweat—and be damned if you won't hear some of thim saying they like it!

[*He glances scornfully at Yank.*]

YANK [*with a bewildered uncertain growl*]. Aw!

PADDY. And there was Yank roarin' curses and turning round wid his shovel to brain her—and she looked at him, and him at her—

YANK [*slowly*]. She was all white. I tought she was a ghost. Sure.

PADDY [*with heavy, biting sarcasm*]. 'Twas love at first sight, divil a doubt of it! If you'd seen the endearin' look on her pale mug when she shrivelled away with her hands over her eyes to shut out the sight of him! Sure, 'twas as if she'd seen a great hairy ape escaped from the Zoo!

YANK [*stung—with a growl of rage*]. Aw!

PADDY. And the loving way Yank heaved his shovel at the skull of her, only she was out the door! [*A grin breaking over his face.*] 'Twas touching, I'm telling you! It put the touch of home, swate home in the stokehole.

[*There is a roar of laughter from all.*]

YANK [*glaring at Paddy menacingly*]. Aw, choke dat off, see!

PADDY [*not heeding him—to the others*]. And her grabbin' at the Second's arm for protection. [*With a grotesque imitation of a woman's voice.*] Kiss me, Engineer dear, for it's dark down here and me old man's in Wall Street making money! Hug me tight, darlin', for I'm afeerd in the dark and me mother's on deck, makin' eyes at the skipper!

[*Another roar of laughter.*]

YANK [*threateningly*]. Say! What yuh tryin' to do, kid me, yuh old Harp?

PADDY. Divil a bit! Ain't I wishin' myself you'd brained her?

YANK [*fiercely*]. I'll brain her! I'll brain her yet, wait 'n' see! [*Coming over to Paddy—slowly.*] Say, is dat what she called me—a hairy ape?

PADDY. She looked it at you if she didn't say the word itself.

YANK [*grinning horribly*]. Hairy ape, huh? Sure! Dat's de way she looked at me, aw right. Hairy ape! So dat's me, huh? [*Bursting into rage—as if she were still in front of him.*] Yuh skinny tart! Yuh white-faced bum, yuh! I'll show yuh who's a ape! [*Turning to the others, bewilderment seizing him again.*] Say, youse guys. I was bawlin' him out for pullin' de whistle on us. You heard me. And den I seen youse lookin' at somep'n and I tought he'd sneaked down to come up in back of me, and I hopped round to knock him

dead wit de shovel. And dere she was wit de light on her! Christ, yuh coulda pushed me over with a finger! I was scared, get me? Sure! I tought she was a ghost, see? She was all in white like dey wrap around stiffs. You seen her. Kin yuh blame me? She didn't belong, dat's what. And den when I come to and seen it was a real skoit and seen de way she was lookin' at me—like Paddy said—Christ, I was sore, get me? I don't stand for dat stuff from nobody. And I flung de shovel—on'y she'd beat it. [*Furiously.*] I wished it'd banged her! I wished it'd knocked her block off!

LONG. And be 'anged for murder or 'lectrocuted? She ain't bleedin' well worth it.

YANK. I don't give a damn what! I'd be square wit her, wouldn't I? Tink I wanter let her put somep'n over on me? Tink I'm goin' to let her git away wit dat stuff? Yuh don't know me! Noone ain't never put nothin' over on me and got away wit it, see!—not dat kind of stuff—no guy and no skoit neither! I'll fix her! Maybe she'll come down again—

VOICE. No chance, Yank. You scared her out of a year's growth.

YANK. I scared her? Why de hell should I scare her? Who de hell is she? Ain't she de same as me? Hairy ape, huh? [*With his old confident bravado.*] I'll show her I'm better'n her, if she on'y knew it. I belong and she don't, see! I move and she's dead! Twenty-five knots a hour, dat's me! Dat carries her but I make dat. She's on'y baggage. Sure! [*Again bewilderedly.*] But, Christ, she was funny lookin'! Did yuh pipe her hands? White and skinny. Yuh could see de bones trough 'em. And her mush, dat was dead white, too. And her eyes, dey was like dey'd seen a ghost. Me, dat was! Sure! Hairy ape! Ghost, huh? Look at dat arm! [*He extends his right arm, swelling out the great muscles.*] I coulda took her wit dat, wit' just my little finger even, and broke her in two. [*Again bewilderedly.*] Say, who is dat skoit, huh? What is she? What's she come from? Who made her? Who give her de noive to look at me like dat? Dis ting's got my goat right. I don't get her. She's new to me. What does a skoit like her mean, huh? She don't belong, get me! I can't see her. [*With growing anger.*] But one ting I'm wise to, aw right, aw right! Youse all kin bet your shoits I'll git even wit her. I'll show her if she tinks she— She grinds de organ and I'm on de string, huh? I'll fix her! Let her come down again and I'll fling her in de furnace! She'll move den! She won't shiver at nothin', den! Speed, dat'll be her! She'll belong den! [*He grins horribly.*]

PADDY. She'll never come. She's had her belly-full, I'm telling you. She'll be in bed now, I'm thinking, wid ten doctors and nurses feedin' her salts to clean the fear out of her.

YANK [*enraged*]. Yuh tink I made her sick, too, do yuh? Just lookin' at me, huh? Hairy ape, huh? [*In a frenzy of rage.*] I'll fix her! I'll tell her where to git off! She'll git down on her knees and take it back or I'll bust de face offen her! [*Shaking one fist upward and beating on his chest with the other.*] I'll find yuh! I'm comin', d'yuh hear? I'll fix yuh, God damn yuh!

[*He makes a rush for the door.*]

VOICES. Stop him!
    He'll get shot!
    He'll murder her!
    Trip him up!
    Hold him!
    He's gone crazy!
    Gott, he's strong!
    Hold him down!
    Look out for a kick!
    Pin his arms!

[*They have all piled on him and, after a fierce struggle, by sheer weight of numbers have borne him to the floor just inside the door.*]

PADDY [*who has remained detached*]. Kape him down till he's cooled off. [*Scornfully.*] Yerra, Yank, you're a great fool. Is it payin' attention at all you are to the like of that skinny sow widout one drop of rale blood in her?

YANK [*frenziedly, from the bottom of the heap*]. She done me doit! She done me doit, didn't she? I'll git square wit her! I'll get some way! Git offen me, youse guys! Lemme up! I'll show her who's a ape!

CURTAIN

SCENE FIVE

SCENE: *Three weeks later. A corner of Fifth Avenue in the Fifties on a fine, Sunday morning. A general atmosphere of clean, well-tidied, wide street; a flood of mellow, tempered sunshine; gentle, genteel breezes. In the rear, the show windows of two shops, a jewelry establishment on the corner, a furrier's next to it. Here the adornments of extreme wealth are tantalizingly displayed. The jeweler's window is gaudy with glittering diamonds, emeralds, rubies, pearls, etc., fashioned in ornate tiaras, crowns, necklaces, collars, etc. From each piece hangs an enormous tag from which a dollar sign and numerals in intermittent electric lights wink out the incredible prices. The same in the furrier's. Rich furs of all varieties hang there bathed in a downpour of artificial light. The general effect is of a background of magnificence cheapened and made grotesque by commercialism, a background in tawdry disharmony with the clear light and sunshine on the street itself.*

    Up the side street Yank and Long come swaggering. Long is dressed in shore clothes, wears a black Windsor tie, cloth cap. Yank is in his dirty dungarees. A fireman's cap with black peak is cocked defiantly on the side of his head. He has not shaved for days and around his fierce, resentful eyes—as around those of Long to a lesser degree—the black smudge of coal dust still sticks like make-up. They

hesitate and stand together at the corner, swaggering, looking about them with a forced, defiant contempt.

LONG [*indicating it all with an oratorical gesture*]. Well, 'ere we are. Fif' Avenoo. This 'ere's their bleedin' private lane, as yer might say. [*Bitterly.*] We're trespassers 'ere. Proletarians keep orf the grass!

YANK [*dully*]. I don't see no grass, yuh boob. [*Staring at the sidewalk.*] Clean, ain't it? Yuh could eat a fried egg offen it. The white wings got some job sweepin' dis up. [*Looking up and down the avenue—surlily.*] Where's all de white-collar stiffs yuh said was here—and de skoits—her kind?

LONG. In church, blarst 'em! Arskin' Jesus to give 'em more money.

YANK. Choich, huh? I useter go to choich onct—sure—when I was a kid. Me old man and woman, dey made me. Dey never went demselves, dough. Always got too big a head on Sunday mornin', dat was dem. [*With a grin.*] Dey was scrappers for fair, bot' of dem. On Satiday nights when dey bot' got a skinful dey could put up a bout oughter been staged at de Garden. When dey got trough dere wasn't a chair or table wit a leg under it. Or else dey bot' jumped on me for somep'n. Dat was where I loined to take punishment. [*With a grin and a swagger.*] I'm a chip offen de old block, get me?

LONG. Did yer old man follow the sea?

YANK. Naw. Worked along shore. I runned away when me old lady croaked wit de tremens. I helped at truckin' and in de market. Den I shipped in de stokehole. Sure. Dat belongs. De rest was nothin'. [*Looking around him.*] I ain't never seen dis before. De Brooklyn waterfront, dat was where I was dragged up. [*Taking a deep breath.*] Dis ain't so bad at dat, huh?

LONG. Not bad? Well, we pays for it wiv our bloody sweat, if yer wants to know!

YANK [*with sudden angry disgust*]. Aw, hell! I don't see noone, see—like her. All dis gives me a pain. It don't belong. Say, ain't dere a backroom around dis dump? Let's go shoot a ball. All dis is too clean and quiet and dolled-up, get me! It gives me a pain.

LONG. Wait and yer'll bloody well see—

YANK. I don't wait for noone. I keep on de move. Say, what yuh drag me up here for, anyway? Tryin' to kid me, yuh simp, yuh?

LONG. Yer wants to get back at her, don't yer? That's what yer been sayin' every bloomin' 'our since she hinsulted yer.

YANK [*vehemently*]. Sure ting I do! Didn't I try to git even wit her in Southampton? Didn't I sneak on de dock and wait for her by de gangplank? I was goin' to spit in her pale mug, see! Sure, right in her pop-eyes! Dat woulda made me even, see? But no chanct. Dere was a whole army of plain clothes bulls around. Dey spotted me and gimme de bum's rush. I never seen her. But I'll git square wit her yet, you watch! [*Furiously.*] De lousey tart! She tinks she kin get away wit moider—but not wit me! I'll fix her! I'll tink of a way!

LONG [as disgusted as he dares to be]. Ain't that why I brought yer up 'ere—to show yer? Yer been lookin' at this 'ere 'ole affair wrong. Yer been actin' an' talkin' 's if it was all a bleedin' personal matter between yer and that bloody cow. I wants to convince yer she was on'y a representative of 'er clarss. I wants to awaken yer bloody clarss consciousness. Then yer'll see it's 'er clarss yer've got to fight, not 'er alone. There's a 'ole mob of 'em like 'er, Gawd blind 'em!

YANK [spitting on his hands—belligerently]. De more de merrier when I gits started. Bring on de gang!

LONG. Yer'll see 'em in arf a mo', when that church lets out. [He turns and sees the window display in the two stores for the first time.] Blimey! Look at that, will yer? [They both walk back and stand looking in the jeweler's. Long flies into a fury.] Just look at this 'ere bloomin' mess! Just look at it! Look at the bleedin' prices on 'em—more'n our 'old bloody stokehole makes in ten voyages sweatin' in 'ell! And they—her and her bloody clarss—buys 'em for toys to dangle on 'em! One of these 'ere would buy scoff for a starvin' family for a year!

YANK. Aw, cut de sob stuff! T' hell wit de starvin' family! Yuh'll be passin' de hat to me next. [With naïve admiration.] Say, dem tings is pretty, huh? Bet yuh dey'd hock for a piece of change aw right. [Then turning away, bored.] But, aw hell, what good are dey? Let her have 'em. Dey don't belong no more'n she does. [With a gesture of sweeping the jeweler's into oblivion.] All dat don't count, get me?

LONG [who has moved to the furrier's—indignantly]. And I s'pose this 'ere don't count neither—skins of poor, 'armless animals slaughtered so as 'er and 'ers can keep their bleedin' noses warm!

YANK [who has been staring at something inside—with queer excitement]. Take a slant at dat! Give it de once-over! Monkey fur—two t'ousand bucks! [Bewilderedly.] Is dat straight goods—monkey fur? What de hell—?

LONG [bitterly]. It's straight enuf. [With grim humor.] They wouldn't bloody well pay that for a 'airy ape's skin—no, nor for the 'ole livin' ape with all 'is 'ead, and body, and soul thrown in!

YANK [clenching his fists, his face growing pale with rage as if the skin in the window were a personal insult]. Trowin' it up in my face! Christ! I'll fix her!

LONG [excitedly]. Church is out. 'Ere they come, the bleedin' swine. [After a glance at Yank's lowering face—uneasily.] Easy goes, comrade. Keep yer bloomin' temper. Remember force defeats itself. It ain't our weapon. We must impress our demands through peaceful means—the votes of the on-marching proletarians of the bloody world!

YANK [with abysmal contempt]. Votes, hell! Votes is a joke, see. Votes for women! Let dem do it!

LONG [still more uneasily]. Calm, now. Treat 'em wiv the proper contempt. Observe the bleedin' parasites, but 'old yer 'orses.

YANK [angrily]. Git away fro me! Yuh're yellow, dat's what. Force, dat's me! De punch, dat's me every time, see!

[The crowd from church enter from the right, sauntering slowly and affectedly, their heads held stiffly up, looking neither to right nor left, talking in toneless, simpering voices. The women are rouged, calcimined, dyed, over-dressed to the nth degree. The men are in Prince Alberts, high hats, spats, canes, etc. A procession of gaudy marionettes, yet with something of the relentless horror of Frankensteins in their detached, mechanical unawareness.]

VOICES. Dear Doctor Caiaphas! He is so sincere!
    What was the sermon? I
        dozed off.
    About the radicals, my dear—
        and the false doctrines that
        are being preached.
    We must organize a hundred
        per cent American bazaar.
    And let everyone contribute
        one one-hundredth per cent
        of their income tax.
    What an original idea!
    We can devote the proceeds to
        rehabilitating the veil of the
        temple.
    But that has been done so
        many times.

YANK [glaring from one to the other of them—with an insulting snort of scorn]. Huh! Huh!

[Without seeming to see him, they make wide detours to avoid the spot where he stands in the middle of the sidewalk.]

LONG [frightenedly]. Keep yer bloomin' mouth shut, I tells yer.

YANK [viciously]. G'wan! Tell it to Sweeney! [He swaggers away and deliberately lurches into a top-hatted gentleman, then glares at him pugnaciously.] Say, who d'yuh tink yuh're bumpin'? Tink yuh own de oith?

GENTLEMAN [coldly and affectedly]. I beg your pardon.

[He has not looked at Yank and passes on without a glance, leaving him bewildered.]

LONG [rushing up and grabbing Yank's arm]. 'Ere! Come away! This wasn't what I meant. Yer'll 'ave the bloody coppers down on us.

YANK [savagely—giving him a push that sends him sprawling]. G'wan!

LONG [picks himself up—hysterically]. I'll pop orf, then. This ain't what I meant. And whatever 'appens, yer can't blame me.

[He slinks off left.]

YANK. T' hell wit youse! [He approaches a lady—with a vicious grin and a smirking wink.] Hello, Kiddo. How's every little ting? Got anyting on for tonight? I know an old boiler down to de docks we kin crawl into. [The lady stalks by without a look, without a change of pace. Yank turns to others—insultingly.] Holy smokes, what a mug! Go hide yuhself before de horses shy at yuh. Gee, pipe de heinie on dat one! Say, youse, yuh look like de stoin of a ferry-boat. Paint and powder! All dolled up to kill! Yuh look like stiffs laid out for de boneyard! Aw, g'wan, de lot of youse! Yuh give me de eye-ache. Yuh don't belong, get me! Look at me, why don't youse dare? I belong, dat's me! [*Pointing to a skyscraper across the street which is in process of construction—with bravado.*] See dat building goin' up dere? See de steel work? Steel, dat's me! Youse guys live on it and tink yuh're somep'n. But I'm *in* it, see! I'm de hoistin' engine dat makes it go up! I'm it—de inside and bottom of it! Sure! I'm steel and steam and smoke and de rest of it! It moves—speed—twenty-five stories up—and me at de top and bottom—movin'! Youse simps don't move. Yuh're on'y dolls I winds up to see 'm spin. Yuh're de garbage, get me—de leavins—de ashes we dump over de side! Now, whata yuh gotto say? [*But as they seem neither to see nor hear him, he flies into a fury.*] Bums! Pigs! Tarts! Bitches! [*He turns in a rage on the men, bumping viciously into them but not jarring them the least bit. Rather it is he who recoils after each collision. He keeps growling.*] Git off de oith! G'wan, yuh bum! Look where yuh're goin', can't yuh? Git outa here! Fight, why don't yuh? Put up yer mits! Don't be a dog! Fight or I'll knock yuh dead!

[*But, without seeming to see him, they all answer with mechanical affected politeness: I beg your pardon. Then at a cry from one of the women, they all scurry to the furrier's window.*]

THE WOMAN [*ecstatically, with a gasp of delight*]. Monkey fur! [*The whole crowd of men and women chorus after her in the same tone of affected delight*]. Monkey fur!

YANK [*with a jerk of his head back on his shoulders, as if he had received a punch full in the face—raging*]. I see yuh, all in white! I see yuh, yuh white-faced tart, yuh! Hairy ape, huh? I'll hairy ape yuh!

[*He bends down and grips at the street curbing as if to pluck it out and hurl it. Foiled in this, snarling with passion, he leaps to the lamp-post on the corner and tries to pull it up for a club. Just at that moment a bus is heard rumbling up. A fat, high-hatted, spatted gentleman runs out from the side street. He calls out plaintively: "Bus! Bus! Stop there!" and runs full tilt into the bending, straining Yank, who is bowled off his balance.*]

YANK [*seeing a fight—with a roar of joy as he springs to his feet*]. At last! Bus, huh? I'll bust yuh!

[*He lets drive a terrific swing, his fist landing full on the fat gentleman's face. But the gentleman stands unmoved as if nothing had happened.*]

GENTLEMAN. I beg your pardon. [*Then irritably.*] You have made me lose my bus.

[*He claps his hands and begins to scream: Officer! Officer! Many police whistles shrill out on the instant and a whole platoon of policemen rush in on Yank from all sides. He*

tries to fight, but is clubbed to the pavement and fallen upon. The crowd at the window have not moved or noticed this disturbance. The clanging gong of the patrol wagon approaches with a clamoring din.]

CURTAIN

SCENE SIX

SCENE: *Night of the following day. A row of cells in the prison on Blackwell's Island. The cells extend back diagonally from right front to left rear. They do not stop, but disappear in the dark background as if they ran on, numberless, into infinity. One electric bulb from the low ceiling of the narrow corridor sheds its light through the heavy steel bars of the cell at the extreme front and reveals part of the interior. Yank can be seen within, crouched on the edge of his cot in the attitude of Rodin's "The Thinker." His face is spotted with black and blue bruises. A blood-stained bandage is wrapped around his head.*

YANK [*suddenly starting as if awakening from a dream, reaches out and shakes the bars—aloud to himself, wonderingly.*] Steel. Dis is de Zoo, huh?

[*A burst of hard, barking laughter comes from the unseen occupants of the cells, runs back down the tier, and abruptly ceases.*]

VOICES [*mockingly*]. The Zoo? That's a new name for this coop—a damn good name!

Steel, eh? You said a mouthful. This is the old iron house.

Who is that boob talkin'?

He's the bloke they brung in out of his head. The bulls had beat him up fierce.

YANK [*dully*]. I musta been dreamin'. I tought I was in a cage at de Zoo—but de apes don't talk, do dey?

VOICES [*with mocking laughter*]. You're in a cage aw right.

A coop!

A pen!

A sty!

A kennel!

[*Hard laughter—a pause.*]

Say, guy! Who are you? No, never mind lying. What are you?

Yes, tell us your sad story. What's your game?

What did they jug yuh for?

YANK [*dully*]. I was a fireman—stokin' on de liners. [*Then with sudden rage, rattling his cell bars.*] I'm a hairy ape, get me? And I'll bust youse all in de jaw if yuh don't lay off kiddin' me.

VOICES. Huh! You're a hard-boiled duck, ain't you!

When you spit, it bounces!

[*Laughter.*]

Aw, can it. He's a regular guy.

Ain't you?

What did he say he was—a ape?

YANK [*defiantly*]. Sure ting! Ain't dat what youse all are—apes?

[*A silence. Then a furious rattling of bars from down the corridor.*]

A VOICE [*thick with rage*]. I'll show yuh who's a ape, yuh bum!

VOICES. Ssshh! Nix!

Can de noise!

Piano!

You'll have the guard down on

us!

YANK [*scornfully*]. De guard? Yuh mean de keeper, don't yuh?

[*Angry exclamations from all the cells.*]

VOICE [*placatingly*]. Aw, don't pay no attention to him. He's off his nut from the beatin'-up he got. Say, you guy! We're waitin' to hear what they landed you for—or ain't yuh tellin'?

YANK. Sure, I'll tell youse. Sure! Why de hell not? On'y—youse won't get me. Nobody gets me but me, see? I started to tell de Judge and all he says was: "Toity days to tink it over." Tink it over! Christ, dat's all I been doin' for weeks! [*After a pause.*] I was tryin' to git even wit someone, see?—someone dat done me doit.

VOICES. [*cynically*]. De old stuff, I bet.

Your goil, huh?

Give yuh the double-cross, huh?

That's them every time!

Did yuh beat up de odder guy?

YANK [*disgustedly*]. Aw, yuh're all wrong! Sure dere was a skoit in it—but not what youse mean, not dat old tripe. Dis was a new kind of skoit. She was dolled up all in white—in de stokehole. I tought she was a ghost. Sure. [*A pause.*]

VOICES [*whispering*]. Gee, he's still nutty.

Let him rave. It's fun listenin'.

YANK [*unheeding—groping in his thoughts*]. Her hands—dey was skinny and white like dey wasn't real but painted on somep'n. Dere was a million miles from me to her—twenty-five knots a hour. She was like some dead ting de cat brung in. Sure, dat's what. She didn't belong. She belonged in de window of a toy store, or on de top of a garbage can, see! Sure! [*He breaks out angrily.*] But would yuh believe it, she had de noive to do me doit. She lamped me like she was seein' somep'n broke loose from de menagerie. Christ, yuh'd oughter seen her eyes! [*He rattles the bars of his cell furiously.*] But I'll get back at her yet, you watch! And if I can't find her I'll take it out on de gang she runs wit. I'm wise to where dey hangs out now. I'll show her who belongs! I'll show her who's in de move and who ain't. You watch my smoke!

VOICES [*serious and joking*]. Dat's de talkin'!

Take her for all she's got!

What was this dame, anyway?

Who was she, eh?

YANK. I dunno. First cabin stiff. Her old man's a millionaire, dey says—name of Douglas.

VOICES. Douglas? That's the president of the Steel Trust, I bet.

Sure. I seen his mug in de papers.

He's filthy with dough.

VOICE. Hey, feller, take a tip from me. If you want to get back at that dame, you better join the Wobblies. You'll get some action then.

YANK. Wobblies? What de hell's dat?

VOICE. Ain't you ever heard of the I.W.W.?

YANK. Naw. What is it?

VOICE. A gang of blokes—a tough gang. I been readin' about 'em to-day in the paper. The guard give me the *Sunday Times*. There's a long spiel about 'em. It's from a speech made in the Senate by a guy named Senator Queen. [*He is in the cell next to Yank's. There is a rustling of paper.*] Wait'll I see if I got light enough and I'll read you. Listen. [*He reads:*] "There is a menace existing in this country to-day which threatens the vitals of our fair Republic—as foul a menace against the very life-blood of the American Eagle as was the foul conspiracy of Catiline against the eagles of ancient Rome!"

VOICE [*disgustedly*]. Aw hell! Tell him to salt de tail of dat eagle!

VOICE [*reading*]. "I refer to that devil's brew of rascals, jailbirds, murderers, and cutthroats who libel all honest working men by calling themselves the Industrial Workers of the World; but in the light of their nefarious plots, I call them the Industrious *Wreckers* of the World!"

YANK [*with vengeful satisfaction*]. Wreckers, dat's de right dope! Dat belongs! Me for dem!

VOICE. Ssshh! [*Reading:*] "This fiendish organization is a foul ulcer on the fair body of our Democracy—"

VOICE. Democracy, hell! Give him the boid, fellers—the raspberry! [*They do.*]

VOICE. Ssshh! [*Reading:*] "Like Cato I say to this Senate, the I.W.W. must be destroyed! For they represent an ever-present dagger pointed at the heart of the greatest nation the world has ever known, where all men are born free and equal, with equal opportunities to all, where the Founding Fathers have guaranteed to each one happiness, where Truth, Honor, Liberty, Justice, and the Brotherhood of Man are a religion absorbed with one's mother's milk, taught at our father's knee, sealed, signed, and stamped upon in the glorious Constitution of these United States."

[*A perfect storm of hisses, catcalls, boos, and hard laughter.*]

VOICES [*scornfully*]. Hurrah for de Fort' of July!

Pass de hat!

Liberty!

Justice!

Honor!

Opportunity!

Brotherhood!

ALL [*with abysmal scorn*]. Aw, hell!

VOICE. Give that Queen Senator guy the bark! All togedder now—one—two—tree—

[*A terrific chorus of barking and yapping.*]

GUARD [*from a distance*]. Quiet there, youse—or I'll git the hose.

[*The noise subsides.*]

YANK [*with a growling rage*]. I'd like to catch dat Senator guy alone for a second. I'd loin him some trute!

VOICE. Ssshh! Here's where he gits down to cases on the Wobblies. [*Reads:*] "They plot with fire in one hand and dynamite in the other. They stop not before murder to gain their ends, nor at the outraging of defenseless womanhood. They would tear down society, put the lowest scum in the seats of the mighty, turn Almighty God's revealed plan for the world topsy-turvy, and make of our sweet and lovely civilization a shambles, a desolation where man, God's masterpiece, would soon degenerate back to the ape!"

VOICE [*to Yank*]. Hey, you guy. There's your ape stuff again.

YANK [*with a growl of fury*]. I got him. So dey blow up tings, do dey? Dey turn tings round, do dey? Hey, lend me dat paper, will yuh?

VOICE. Sure. Give it to him. On'y keep it to yourself, see. We don't wanter listen to no more of that slop.

VOICE. Here you are. Hide it under your mattress.

YANK [*reaching out*]. Tanks. I can't read much, but I kin manage. [*He sits, the paper in the hand at his side, in the attitude of Rodin's "The Thinker." A pause. Several snores from down the corridor. Suddenly Yank jumps to his feet with a furious groan as if some appalling thought had crashed on him—bewilderedly.*] Sure—her old man—president of de Steel Trust—makes half de steel in de world—steel—where I tought I belonged—drivin' trou—movin'—in dat—to make *her*—and cage me in for her to spit on! Christ! [*He shakes the bars of his cell door till the whole tier trembles. Irritated, protesting exclamations from those awakened or trying to get to sleep.*] He made dis—dis cage! Steel! *It* don't belong, dat's what! Cages, cells, locks, bolts, bars—dat's what it means!—holdin' me down wit him at de top! But I'll drive trou! Fire, dat melts it! I'll be fire—under de heap—fire dat never goes out—hot as hell—breakin' out in de night—

[*While he has been saying this last he has shaken his cell door to a clanging accompaniment. As he comes to the "breakin' out" he seizes one bar with both hands and, putting his two feet up against the others so that his position is parallel to the floor like a monkey's, he gives a great wrench backwards. The bar bends like a licorice stick under his tremendous strength. Just at this moment the Prison Guard rushes in, dragging a hose behind him.*]

GUARD [*angrily*]. I'll loin youse bums to wake me up! [*Sees Yank.*] Hello, it's you, huh? Got the D.T., hey? Well, I'll

cure 'em. I'll drown your snakes for yuh! [*Noticing the bar.*] Hell, look at dat bar bended! On'y a bug is strong enough for dat!

YANK [*glaring at him*]. Or a hairy ape, yuh big yellow bum! Look out! Here I come! [*He grabs another bar.*]

GUARD [*scared now—yelling off left*]. Toin de hose on, Ben!—full pressure! And call de others—and a strait-jacket!

[*The curtain is falling. As it hides Yank from view, there is a splattering smash as the stream of water hits the steel of Yank's cell.*]

CURTAIN

SCENE SEVEN

SCENE: *Nearly a month later. An I.W.W. local near the waterfront, showing the interior of a front room on the ground floor, and the street outside. Moonlight on the narrow street, buildings massed in black shadow. The interior of the room, which is general assembly room, office, and reading-room, resembles some dingy settlement boys' club. A desk and high stool are in one corner. A table with papers, stacks of pamphlets, chairs about it, is at center. The whole is decidedly cheap, banal, commonplace, and unmysterious as a room could well be. The Secretary is perched on the stool making entries in a large ledger. An eye shade casts his face into shadows. Eight or ten men, longshoremen, iron workers, and the like, are grouped about the table. Two are playing checkers. One is writing a letter. Most of them are smoking pipes. A big signboard is on the wall at the rear, "Industrial Workers of the World— Local No. 57."*

[*Yank comes down the street outside. He is dressed as in Scene Five. He moves cautiously, mysteriously. He comes to a point opposite the door; tiptoes softly up to it, listens, is impressed by the silence within, knocks carefully, as if he were guessing at the password to some secret rite. Listens. No answer. Knocks again a bit louder. No answer. Knocks impatiently, much louder.*]

SECRETARY [*turning around on his stool*]. What the devil is that—someone knocking? [*Shouts:*] Come in, why don't you?

[*All the men in the room look up. Yank opens the door slowly, gingerly, as if afraid of an ambush. He looks around for secret doors, mystery, is taken aback by the commonplaceness of the room and the men in it, thinks he may have gotten in the wrong place, then sees the signboard on the wall and is reassured.*]

YANK [*blurts out*]. Hello.

MEN [*reservedly*]. Hello.

YANK [*more easily*]. I tought I'd bumped into de wrong dump.

SECRETARY [*scrutinizing him carefully*]. Maybe you have. Are you a member?

YANK. Naw, not yet. Dat's what I come for—to join.

SECRETARY. That's easy. What's your job—longshore?

YANK. Naw. Fireman—stoker on de liners.

SECRETARY [*with satisfaction*]. Welcome to our city. Glad to know you people are waking up at last. We haven't got many members in your line.

YANK. Naw. Dey're all dead to de woild.

SECRETARY. Well, you can help to wake 'em. What's your name? I'll make out your card.

YANK [*confused*]. Name? Lemme tink.

SECRETARY [*sharply*]. Don't you know your own name?

YANK. Sure; but I been just Yank for so long—Bob, dat's it—Bob Smith.

SECRETARY [*writing*]. Robert Smith. [*Fills out the rest of card.*] Here you are. Cost you half a dollar.

YANK. Is dat all—four bits? Dat's easy. [*Gives the* Secretary *the money.*]

SECRETARY [*throwing it in drawer*]. Thanks. Well, make yourself at home. No introductions needed. There's literature on the table. Take some of those pamphlets with you to distribute aboard ship. They may bring results. Sow the seed, only go about it right. Don't get caught and fired. We got plenty out of work. What we need is men who can hold their jobs—and work for us at the same time.

YANK. Sure.

[*But he still stands, embarrassed and uneasy.*]

SECRETARY [*looking at him—curiously*]. What did you knock for? Think we had a coon in uniform to open doors?

YANK. Naw. I tought it was locked—and dat yuh'd wanter give me the once-over trou a peep-hole or somep'n to see if I was right.

SECRETARY [*alert and suspicious, but with an easy laugh.*] Think we were running a crap game? That door is never locked. What put that in your nut?

YANK [*with a knowing grin, convinced that this is all camouflage, a part of the secrecy*]. Dis burg is full of bulls, ain't it?

SECRETARY [*sharply*]. What have the cops got to do with us? We're breaking no laws.

YANK [*with a knowing wink*]. Sure. Youse wouldn't for woilds. Sure. I'm wise to dat.

SECRETARY. You seem to be wise to a lot of stuff none of us knows about.

YANK [*with another wink*]. Aw, dat's aw right, see. [*Then, made a bit resentful by the suspicious glances from all sides.*] Aw, can it! Youse needn't put me trou de toid degree. Can't youse see I belong? Sure! I'm reg'lar. I'll stick, get me? I'll shoot de woiks for youse. Dat's why I wanted to join in.

SECRETARY [*breezily, feeling him out*]. That's the right spirit. Only are you sure you understand what you've joined? It's all plain and above board; still, some guys get a wrong

slant on us. [*Sharply.*] What's your notion of the purpose of the I.W.W.?

YANK. Aw, I know all about it.

SECRETARY [*sarcastically*]. Well, give us some of your valuable information.

YANK [*cunningly.*] I know enough not to speak outa my toin. [*Then, resentfully again.*] Aw, say! I'm reg'lar. I'm wise to de game. I know yuh got to watch your step wit a stranger. For all youse know, I might be a plain-clothes dick, or somep'n, dat's what yuh're tinkin', huh? Aw, forget it! I belong, see? Ask any guy down to de docks if I don't.

SECRETARY. Who said you didn't?

YANK. After I'm 'nitiated, I'll show yuh.

SECRETARY [*astounded*]. Initiated? There's no initiation.

YANK [*disappointed*]. Ain't there no password—no grip nor nothin'?

SECRETARY. What'd you think this is—the Elks—or the Black Hand?

YANK. De Elks, hell! De Black Hand, dey're a lot of yellow backstickin' Ginees. Naw. Dis is a man's gang, ain't it?

SECRETARY. You said it! That's why we stand on our two feet in the open. We got no secrets.

YANK [*surprised, but admiringly*]. Yuh mean to say yuh always run wide open—like dis?

SECRETARY. Exactly.

YANK. Den yuh sure got your noive wit youse!

SECRETARY [*sharply*]. Just what was it made you want to join us? Comeout with that straight.

YANK. Yuh call me? Well, I got noive, too! Here's my hand. Yuh wanter blow tings up, don't yuh? Well, dat's me! I belong!

SECRETARY [*with pretended carelessness*]. You mean change the unequal conditions of society by legitimate direction—or with dynamite?

YANK. Dynamite. Blow it offen de oith—steel—all de cages—all de factories, steamers, buildings, jails—de Steel Trust and all dat makes it go.

SECRETARY. So—that's your idea, eh? And did you have any special job in that line you wanted to propose to us?

[*He makes a sign to the men, who get up cautiously one by one and group behind Yank.*]

YANK [*boldly*]. Sure, I'll come out wit it. I'll show youse I'm one of de gang. Dere's dat millionaire guy, Douglas—

SECRETARY. President of the Steel Trust, you mean? Do you want to assassinate him?

YANK. Naw, dat don't get yuh nothin'. I mean blow up de factory, de woiks, where he makes de steel. Dat's what I'm after—to blow up de steel, knock all de steel in de woild up to de moon. Dat'll fix tings! [*Eagerly, with a touch of bravado.*] I'll do it by me lonesome! I'll show yuh! Tell me where his woiks is, how to git there, all de dope. Gimme de stuff, de old butter—and watch me do de rest! Watch de smoke and see it move! I don't give a damn if dey nab me—long as it's done! I'll soive life for it—and give 'em de laugh! [*Half to himself.*] And I'll write her a letter and tell her de hairy ape done it. Dat'll square tings.

SECRETARY. [*stepping away from Yank*]. Very interesting.

[*He gives a signal. The men, huskies all, throw themselves on Yank, and before he knows it they have his legs and arms pinioned. But he is too flabbergasted to make a struggle, anyway. They feel him over for weapons.*]

MAN. No gat, no knife. Shall we give him what's what and put the boots to him?

SECRETARY. No. He isn't worth the trouble we'd get into. He's too stupid. [*He comes closer and laughs mockingly in Yank's face.*] Ho-ho! By God, this is the biggest joke they've put up on us yet. Hey, you Joke! Who sent you—Burns or Pinkerton? No, by God, you're such a bonehead I'll bet you're in the Secret Service! Well, you dirty spy, you rotten agent provocator, you can go back and tell whatever skunk is paying you blood-money for betraying your brothers that he's wasting his coin. You couldn't catch a cold. And tell him that all he'll ever get on us, or ever has got, is just his own sneaking plots that he's framed up to put us in jail. We are what our manifesto says we are, neither more nor less—and we'll give him a copy of that any time he calls. And as for you—[*He glares scornfully at Yank, who is sunk in an oblivious stupor.*] Oh, hell, what's the use of talking? You're a brainless ape.

YANK [*aroused by the word to fierce but futile struggles*]. What's dat, yuh Sheeny bum, yuh!

SECRETARY. Throw him out, boys.

[*In spite of his struggles, this is done with gusto and éclat. Propelled by several parting kicks, Yank lands sprawling in the middle of the narrow cobbled street. With a growl he starts to get up and storm the closed door, but stops bewildered by the confusion in his brain, pathetically impotent. He sits there, brooding, in as near to the attitude of Rodin's "Thinker" as he can get in his position.*]

YANK [BITTERLY]. So dem boids don't tink I belong, neider. Aw, to hell wit 'em! Dey're in de wrong pew—de same old bull—soapboxes and Salvation Army—no guts! Cut out an hour offen de job a day and make me happy! Tree square a day, and cauliflowers in de front yard—ekal rights—a woman and kids—a lousey vote—and I'm all fixed for Jesus, huh? Aw, hell! What does dat get yuh? Dis ting's in your inside, but it ain't your belly. Feedin' your face—sinkers and coffee—dat don't touch it. It's way down—at de bottom. Yuh can't grab it, and yuh can't stop it. It moves, and everyting moves. It stops and de whole woild stops. Dat's me now—I don't tick, see?—I'm a busted Ingersoll, dat's what. Steel was me, and I owned de woild. Now I ain't steel, and de woild owns me. Aw, hell! I can't see—it's all dark, get me? It's all wrong! [*He turns a bitter mocking face up like an ape gibbering at the moon.*] Say, youse up dere, Man in de Moon, yuh look so wise, gimme de answer, huh? Slip me de inside dope, de

information right from de stable—where do I get off at, huh?

A POLICEMAN [*who has come up the street in time to hear this last—with grim humor*]. You'll get off at the station, you boob, if you don't get up out of that and keep movin'.

YANK [*looking up at him—with a hard, bitter laugh*]. Sure! Lock me up! Put me in a cage! Dat's de on'y answer yuh know. G'wan, lock me up!

POLICEMAN. What you been doin'?

YANK. Enuf to gimme life for! I was born, see? Sure, dat's de charge. Write it in de blotter. I was born, get me!

POLICEMAN [*jocosely*]. God pity your old woman! [*Then matter-of-fact.*] But I've no time for kidding. You're soused. I'd run you in but it's too long a walk to the station. Come on now, get up, or I'll fan your ears with this club. Beat it now!

[*He hauls Yank to his feet.*]

YANK [*in a vague mocking tone*]. Say, where do I go from here?

POLICEMAN [*Giving him a push—with a grin, indifferently.*] Go to hell.

CURTAIN

SCENE EIGHT

SCENE: *Twilight of the next day. The monkey house at the Zoo. One spot of clear gray light falls on the front of one cage so that the interior can be seen. The other cages are vague, shrouded in shadow from which chatterings pitched in a conversational tone can be heard. On the one cage a sign from which the word "gorilla" stands out. The gigantic animal himself is seen squatting on his haunches on a bench in much the same attitude as Rodin's "Thinker."*

[*Yank enters from the left. Immediately a chorus of angry chattering and screeching breaks out. The gorilla turns his eyes, but makes no sound or move.*]

YANK. [*with a hard, bitter laugh. Welcome to your city, huh? Hail, hail, de gang's all here! [At the sound of his voice the chattering dies away into an attentive silence: Yank walks up to the gorilla's cage and, leaning over the railing, stares in at its occupant, who stares back at him, silent and motionless. There is a pause of dead stillness. Then Yank begins to talk in a friendly confidential tone, half-mockingly, but with a deep undercurrent of sympathy.*] Say, yuh're some hard-lookin' guy, ain't yuh? I seen lots of tough nuts dat de gang called gorillas, but yuh're de foist real one I ever seen. Some chest yuh got, and shoulders, and dem arms and mits! I bet yuh got a punch in eider fist dat'd knock 'em all silly! [*This with genuine admiration. The gorilla, as if he understood, stands upright, swelling out his chest and pounding on it with his fist. Yank grins sympathetically.*] Sure, I get yuh.

Yuh challenge de whole woild, huh? Yuh got what I was sayin' even if yuh muffed de woids. [*Then bitterness creeping in.*] And why wouldn't yuh get me? Ain't we both members of de same club—de Hairy Apes! [*They stare at each other—a pause—then* Yank *goes on slowly and bitterly.*] So yuh're what she seen when she looked at me, de white-faced tart! I was you to her, get me? On'y outa de cage—broke out—free to moider her, see? Sure! Dat's what she tought. She wasn't wise dat I was in a cage, too—worser'n yours—sure—a damn sight—'cause you got some chanct to bust loose—but me—[*He grows confused.*] Aw, hell! It's all wrong, ain't it? [*A pause.*] I s'pose yuh wanter know what I'm doin' here, huh? I been warmin' a bench down to de Battery—ever since last night. Sure. I seen de sun come up. Dat was pretty, too—all red and pink and green. I was lookin' at de skyscrapers—steel—and all de ships comin' in, sailin' out, all over de oith—and dey was steel, too. De sun was warm, dey wasn't no clouds, and dere was a breeze blowin'. Sure, it was great stuff. I got it aw right—what Paddy said about dat bein' de right dope—on'y I couldn't get *in* it, see? I couldn't belong in dat. It was over my head. And I kept tinkin'—and den I beat it up here to see what youse was like. And I waited till dey was all gone to git yuh alone. Say, how d'yuh feel sittin' in dat pen all de time, havin' to stand for 'em comin' and starin' at yuh—de white-faced skinny tarts and de boobs what marry 'em—makin' fun of yuh, laughin' at yuh, gittin' scared of yuh—damn 'em! [*He pounds on the rail with his fist. The gorilla rattles the bars of his cage and snarls. All the other monkeys set up an angry chattering in the darkness.* Yank *goes on excitedly.*] Sure! Dat's de way it hits me, too. On'y yuh're lucky, see? Yuh don't belong wit 'em and yuh know it. But me, I belong with 'em—but I don't, see? Dey don't belong wit me, dat's what. Get me? Tinkin' is hard— [*He passes one hand across his forehead with a painful gesture. The gorilla growls impatiently.* Yank *goes on gropingly.*] It's dis way, what I'm drivin' at. Youse can sit and dope dream in de past, green woods, de jungle and de rest of it. Den yuh belong and dey don't. Den yuh kin laugh at 'em, see? Yuh're de champ of de woild. But me—I ain't got no past to tink in, nor nothin' dat's comin', on'y what's now—and dat don't belong. Sure, you're de best off! Yuh can't tink, can yuh? Yuh can't talk neider. But I kin make a bluff at talkin' and tinkin'—a'most git away wit it—a'most!—and dat's where de joker comes in. [*He laughs.*] I ain't on oith and I ain't in heaven, get me? I'm in de middle tryin' to separate 'em, takin' all de woist punches from bot' of 'em. Maybe dat's what dey call hell, huh? But you, yuh're at de bottom. You belong! Sure! Yuh're de on'y one in de woild dat does, yuh lucky stiff! [*The gorilla growls proudly.*] And dat's why dey gotter put yuh in a cage, see? [*The gorilla roars angrily.*] Sure! Yuh get me. It beats it when you try to tink it or talk it—it's way down—deep—behind—you 'n' me we feel it. Sure! Bot' members of dis club! [*He laughs—then in a savage tone.*] What de hell! T' hell wit it! A little action, dat's our meat! Dat belongs! Knock 'em down and keep bustin' 'em till dey croaks yuh wit a gat—wit steel! Sure! Are yuh game? Dey've looked at youse, ain't dey—in a cage? Wanter git even? Wanter wind up like a sport 'stead of croakin' slow in dere? [*The gorilla roars an emphatic affirmative.* Yank *goes on with a sort of furious exaltation.*] Sure! Yuh're reg'lar! Yuh'll stick to de finish! Me' n' you, huh?—bot' members of this club! We'll put up one last star bout dat'll knock 'em offen deir seats! Dey'll have to make de cages stronger after we're trou! [*The gorilla is straining at his bars, growling, hopping from one foot to the other.* Yank *takes a jimmy from under his coat and forces the lock on the cage door. He throws this open.*] Pardon from de governor! Step out and shake hands! I'll take yuh for a walk down Fif' Avenoo. We'll knock 'em offen de oith and croak wit de band playin'. Come on, Brother. [*The gorilla scrambles gingerly out of his cage. Goes to* Yank *and stands looking at him.* Yank *keeps his mocking tone—holds out his hand.*] Shake—de secret grip of our order. [*Something, the tone of mockery, perhaps, suddenly enrages the animal. With a spring he wraps his huge arms around* Yank *in a murderous hug. There is a crackling snap of crushed ribs—a gasping cry, still mocking, from* Yank.] Hey, I didn't say, kiss me. [*The gorilla lets the crushed body slip to the floor; stands over it uncertainly, considering; then picks it up, throws it in the cage, shuts the door, and shuffles off menacingly into the darkness at left. A great uproar of frightened chattering and whimpering comes from the other cages. Then* Yank *moves, groaning, opening his eyes, and there is silence. He mutters painfully.*] Say—dey oughter match him—wit Zybszko. He got me, aw right. I'm trou. Even him didn't tink I belonged. [*Then, with sudden passionate despair.*] Christ, where do I get off at? Where do I fit in? [*Checking himself as suddenly.*] Aw, what de hell! No squakin', see! No quittin', get me! Croak wit your boots on! [*He grabs hold of the bars of the cage and hauls himself painfully to his feet—looks around him bewilderedly—forces a mocking laugh.*] In de cage, huh? [*In the strident tones of a circus barker.*] Ladies and gents, step forward and take a slant at de one and only—[*His voice weakening*]—one and original—Hairy Ape from de wilds of—

[*He slips in a heap on the floor and dies. The monkeys set up a chattering, whimpering wail. And, perhaps, the Hairy Ape at last belongs.*]

CURTAIN

Just as realism necessitated new approaches to acting and playing spaces, so, too, was the stage refashioned to reflect an age in which science and industry affected virtually every facet of life in the West. Among many visionaries who boldly experimented with performance spaces, scenery, and even performance styles in the industrial age, four in particular merit attention here: Vesold Meyerhold, Erwin Piscator, Leopold Jessner, and Walter Gropius.

Ironically, the Russian Meyerhold (1874–1940) began his assault on the realistic theater by staging Ibsen's most realistic psychological drama, *Hedda Gabler*. In 1906 he staged the play in an intimate space with the audience seated only 7 feet from the actors. Dissatisfied with naturalistic acting techniques, Meyerhold first used an almost robotic style to force audiences to see the inner truth of characters stripped of outer realism. From this radical approach, Meyerhold developed *biomechanics,* a style in which actors performed either on an empty stage or—more likely—in a space reflecting the machinery fostered by the Industrial Revolution. To encourage his actors to distance themselves from realistic techniques, Meyerhold adapted styles drawn from a variety of theatrical performance modes: the *commedia dell'arte* and pantomime, cabaret, modern dance, ballet, and frozen tableaux. Think, for instance, of break dancing or Michael Jackson's "moon walk," both of which use techniques that Meyerhold would recognize.

Jessner (1878–1945), a German director, created a scenic structure—*Jessnersteppen* (Jessner-steps)—that manipulated both the playing arena and the acting style. He fashioned enormous steps leading from the forestage to the rear wall of the theater to create dynamic and impressive compositions. Jessner's actors had to learn to use these steps—horizontally and vertically—in order to appear in three-dimensional positions. Like Meyerhold, Jessner forced the actors into a style that was antithetical to the principles set forth by realism and naturalism. The styles reflected the modern industrial world in which workers were robotic parts of a great machine.

In Germany, Piscator and Gropius did much to transform theater spaces, production methods, and acting styles to create a total theater experience beyond the boundaries of realism and naturalism. Piscator (1893–1966), who influenced Brecht, designed a playing space incorporating large projection screens and revolving nonrealistic sets using noisy machinery. He introduced film and slide projections to create *total theater,* a presentational style that appealed to all of the audience's senses.

The concept of total theater actually originated as a part of a Bauhaus experiment. Bauhaus refers to a post–World War I architectural school founded by Gropius (1883–1969) that synthesized technology, craftsmanship, and design aesthetics. In consultation with Piscator, Gropius designed a theater that brought together audience, actor, designer, and technician in a brave new world of surprises and possibilities. Both artists migrated to the United States, where their "high tech" experiments influenced both theater architecture and production practice after World War II. Postmodernism is among the significant developments derived from the work of Gropius and others. Central Europeans, especially the Czechs and Romanians, are especially accomplished in the presentation of total theater.

THE GOOD WOMAN OF SETZUAN

BERTOLT BRECHT

BERTOLT BRECHT (1898–1956)

The son of a prosperous factory manager in Augsberg, Bavaria, Bertolt Brecht established himself as a controversial writer at an early age. As a high school student, he was nearly expelled for writing antiwar poetry in the midst of World War I. His intentions to pursue a medical career were cut short when he was conscripted into the German army in 1918 to serve as a medic. He observed firsthand the carnage and misery of war, and his subsequent writings—poetry, drama, song lyrics, and essays—are devoted to the eradication of all institutions that contribute to human suffering and indignity. In addition to his protest of war and the governments that wage it, Brecht's political satires expose corrupt social, economic, spiritual, and cultural institutions that oppress the common man. In this sense, Brecht is properly a Romantic writer, however modern and "antiemotional" the methods he employs.

Like so many young artists who lived in economically depressed postwar Germany, Brecht held a cynical, even nihilistic, view of society. And like many of his contemporaries, he gravitated to communism, whose philosophy of dialectical materialism provided him with both the subject matter and the methodology for his plays. Brecht's plays transcend mere propaganda, and he is arguably the most admired and imitated Marxist playwright of the twentieth century. Brecht was too much the humanist to write only ideological tracts, and his plays manifest a universality that transcends the particulars of Marxism. Ever the individualist aligned with no country or party, Brecht spent much of World War II writing film scripts in Santa Monica, California. When he returned to East Berlin in 1948 he obtained Austrian citizenship to skirt state censorship, and he retained a publisher in the West to protect the copyrights on his literary work. When he received the Stalin Peace Prize shortly before his death, he promptly invested the financial portion of his award in a Swiss bank account.

Brecht's first attempts at playwriting were in the Expressionist mode popular among young Germans during the war years. Such works as *Baal* (1918) and *Drums in the Night* (1918) are among his darkest efforts and reflect the angst of young Germans who realized that "the Great War" was not worth fighting. Gradually he turned to satire to vent his anger; in the early 1920s Brecht gained a reputation as a witty cabaret artist who sang politically caustic songs to the accompaniment of his own guitar. His subsequent plays are liberally sprinkled with such songs, an integral part of his *Verfremdungseffekt*. "The Song of the Smoke" in scene 6 of *The Good Woman of Setzuan* is an especially useful example.

In 1928 Brecht collaborated with composer Kurt Weill to write *The Threepenny Opera*, a contemporary retelling of John Gay's 1728 ballad opera, *The Beggar's Opera*. Largely because of its musical comedy nature, it is Brecht's most often performed work, also released as a feature film starring Raul Julia as the notorious MacHeath, about whom the popular song "Mack the Knife" was written. (Sting played the role in a New York revival in 1992.) You have no doubt heard "Mack the Knife" in either the Bobby Darrin or Louis Armstrong versions, neither of which is like the Brecht-Weill arrangement. The point is made here because the song was intended to be harsh, dissonant, and even unpleasant, quite unlike the catchy, up-tempo recording heard in pop music venues. Brecht wanted his music to be much like the plays he wrote—unsettling, antiromantic, emotionally "cool"—so that audiences would listen to the message rather than the melody.

As he was defining his methodology for an "epic theater," Brecht discovered the Japanese Noh theater and found in this ancient masked drama, like the Chinese drama he saw in Russia in 1935, an acting style that accommodated his performance theory. Brecht wanted his actors to portray the social status (or "gestus") of his dramatic creations rather than become one with the emotional life of a character. This synthesis of an antirealistic approach to playwriting and performance can be found in his masterworks: *Mother Courage and Her Children* (1938), *The Good Woman of Setzuan* (1939), *Galileo* (1938), and *The Caucasian Chalk Circle* (1944).

Between 1933 and 1948 Brecht lived in exile because his procommunist, anti-Fascist politics made him a target of the Nazi Party. He first fled to Switzerland, and subsequently spent time in Finland, Sweden, Denmark, Russia, and ultimately the United States. The anticommunist purges of the McCarthy era forced him to return to Germany in 1948, but not before he turned his hearing before the House Un-American Activities Committee into a comical piece of Brechtian theater.

In East Berlin, Brecht founded the Berliner Ensemble, a state-supported theater dedicated to the production of his works and those of similar ideology. The Ensemble production of *Mother Courage* in January 1949 (in which Brecht's wife, Helene Weigel, played the title role to great acclaim) made the Ensemble one of Europe's most respected theater companies. The Berliner Ensemble performed in Paris in 1954 and in London during the summer of 1956. These engagements captivated the postwar generation of theater artists and the Ensemble became the model for mainstream companies (e.g., the Royal Shakespeare Company) and also many of the alternative theater collectives that proliferated during the 1950s and 1960s. Both as playwright and performance theorist, Brecht remains among the most imitated artists of the twentieth century. It is likely that no other single artist has exerted as much influence on the antirealist movement as Brecht.

THE GOOD WOMAN OF SETZUAN (1938–1939)

Most anthologies title this play *The Good Woman of Setzuan*, largely because its central character, Shen Te, is indeed a good and honest woman who struggles to survive in a corrupt world. However, Brecht's German title was *Der Gute Mensch von Setzuan*. *Mensch* is derived from an Old High German word (*mennisco*) meaning "man" in the most generic sense, that is, "humanity" or "human being." Hence, the word *person* instead of *woman* in the title is actually the more accurate translation. It is also worth noting that a *mensch* in the Yiddish idiom is "a person of integrity and honor"; Brecht may have known this meaning as Yiddish (another Germanic language) was commonly spoken in Germany. Furthermore, *mensch* is often used cynically to refer to "the little guy" whose integrity is constantly challenged by the unscrupulous. In this sense, a *mensch* is a "sucker" who is easily preyed upon by con artists.

These distinctions are significant because they help us understand Brecht's intentions. Shen Te is more than a former prostitute who comes into some money and opens a small tobacco shop to earn an honest living. (Brecht frequently uses such irony in his plays: the prostitute is ultimately the most moral person in the society.) To her dismay Shen Te soon discovers that she can survive in her honest trade only when she assumes the role of a nefarious male cousin, Shui Ta, who is as ruthless as he is callous. In this sense Shen Te is neither woman nor man, and the generic *mensch*—a person, irrespective of gender—is appropriate.

Mensch, in its Yiddish sense, is also applicable because Shen Te, without her mean-spirited alter ego, is very much a sucker. Her innate goodness and her propensity to see others as honest first earns her money (when she provides shelter to the three gods who seek an honest human), but later brings her misery. She is exploited by the wealthy, by her poor neighbors, and most importantly by her lover, the penniless pilot who is after her money. Only in the guise of Shui Ta can she protect herself, her fortune, and finally her child. Her confession in the final scene crystallizes her dilemma:

To be good to others and myself—

I couldn't do both at the same time.

To help others and myself was too hard.

Alas! Your world is difficult! Too much misery! too much despair!

The hand that is extended to a beggar, the beggar at once tears off!

Whoever helps the lost is lost himself!

That Brecht indicts ruthless exploiters like the factory owner Shui Ta and his equally corrupt manager Yang Sun is to be expected; they epitomize the capitalist bosses who were skewered in many agit-prop dramas of the 1930s. But Brecht is also as acidic in his treatment of the poor. Mrs. Shin, although comical, is every bit as greedy and exploitive as Shui Ta. Brecht is not indifferent to the plight of the poor and oppressed; rather, he scolds them (and the audiences that identify with them) for not taking matters into their own hands to make changes to improve their lot.

The Good Woman of Setzuan seems to suggest that change is impossible in this world as it is currently arranged. The play ends without a satisfactory resolution as the very gods who can effect change abandon Shen Te and float back to heaven on a pink cloud with the admonition that "The world should *not* be changed!" This ending, a perverse parody of the ancient *deus ex machina*, in which gods were literally lowered onto the stage to resolve human problems, further complicates the situation. Little wonder Shen Te can only scream "Help!" as the curtain falls. Brecht's ending for *The Good Woman of Setzuan* is as contrived as that of the old nineteenth-century melodrama, which dispensed poetic justice to all. Like Shaw, to whom he is a kindred spirit, Brecht also liked to take well-known theater forms and subvert them to challenge audiences' attitudes. *The Good Woman of Setzuan* is a parody of the rags-to-riches melodrama, with elements of the damsel-in-distress generously incorporated. That his refashioned melodrama ends without resolution should not imply pessimism on Brecht's part. Rather, the ending represents the quintessentially Brechtian technique of depriving the audience of a catharsis in order to provoke them, instead, to action. He says, in effect, that it is pointless to ask for divine assistance; humans must do the work, and his innovative ending drives this point home well. Brecht believed that the theater was not the place to solve worldly problems by punishing transgressors (which is why he condemned the old Aristotelian theater as "barbaric"). His purpose was to identify social ills and arouse the audience's indignation at them. He challenges them to return to the streets to eradicate injustice through political action. Herein lies the optimism of Brecht's works, however cynical they may appear. Throughout the play Brecht uses techniques central to his epic theater. First, he purposefully sets the action of his "parable" in remote and distant Setzuan, which for him stands "for all places where men are exploited by men." This typifies Brecht's concept of "historification"—that is, removing a play's action from contemporary life so that audiences may compare their circumstances with those of the past. Furthermore, Setzuan is an intriguing choice for locale; identifying the setting with ancient China, Brecht encourages his actors to use the acting techniques of the Chinese opera, which influenced his methodology. The fact that the actor who plays Shen Te must also play Shui Ta in a mask creates a "distancing" effect.

The play is structured in 10 scenes and a prologue. Although there is a discernible plot line, it is not based on causality in the traditional sense. Rather, the 10 scenes exist independently of one another and are unified thematically by their exploration of the play's central question: To what extent is morality defined by one's economic status? Most scenes are followed by a short subscene (e.g., 1-A, 2-A, etc.) in which a comical water seller, Wong, engages the three gods in satiric banter. The water seller is a variant on the "storyteller" that Brecht favors in his works. Wong provides a critical context from which to judge the story of Shen Te. Note that he frequently addresses the audience directly (as does Shen Te); his speeches are elaborate, Westernized versions of the *yin tzu* of the ancient Chinese opera, in which a character describes his social status and dramatic purpose to the audience. Brecht, the old cabaret balladeer, interpolates a half-dozen songs throughout the play, each commenting satirically on the action and themes.

That the final scene (10) takes place in a courtroom is no accident. The trial was among Brecht's favorite devices because, he argued, the theater itself should function as a court in which the audience/jury dispassionately examines evidence, hears opposing arguments, and renders judgment. In *The Good Woman of Setzuan* the gods refuse to issue a verdict or "renounce the rules" that permit the Shui Tas of the world to hold sway. But, in Brecht's estimation, the gods sitting in the seats beyond the stage can—and must.

American composer and playwright Elizabeth Swados wrote an original score for the American Repertory Theater's 1986 production of The Good Woman of Setzuan, directed by Andrei Serban.

THE GOOD WOMAN OF SETZUAN

BERTOLT BRECHT

Translated by Eric Bentley

LIST OF CHARACTERS

WONG, *a water seller*
THREE GODS
SHEN TE, *a prostitute, later a shopkeeper*
MRS. SHIN, *former owner of Shen Te's shop*
A FAMILY OF EIGHT (*husband, wife, brother, sister-in-law, grandfather, nephew, niece, boy*)
AN UNEMPLOYED MAN
A CARPENTER
MRS. MI TZU, *Shen Te's landlady*
YANG SUN, *an unemployed pilot, later a factory manager*
AN OLD WHORE
A POLICEMAN
AN OLD MAN
AN OLD WOMAN, *his wife*
MR. SHU FU, *a barber*
MRS. YANG, *mother of Yang Sun*
GENTLEMEN, VOICES, CHILDREN (*three*), *etc.*

PROLOGUE

(*At the gates of the half-westernized city of Setzuan.* Evening. Wong the Water Seller introduces himself to the audience.*)

WONG. I sell water here in the city of Setzuan. It isn't easy. When water is scarce, I have long distances to go in search of it, and when it is plentiful, I have no income. But in our part of the world there is nothing unusual about poverty. Many people think only the gods can save the situation. And I hear from a cattle merchant—who

---

*"So Brecht's first manuscript. Brecht must later have learned that Setzuan (usually spelled Szechwan) is not a city but a province, and he adjusted the printed German text. I have kept the earlier reading since such mythology seems to me more Brechtian than Brecht's own second thoughts."—E.B.

travels a lot—that some of the highest gods are on their way here at this very moment. Informed sources have it that heaven is quite disturbed at all the complaining. I've been coming out here to the city gates for three days now to bid these gods welcome. I want to be the first to greet them. What about those fellows over there? No, no, they *work*. And that one there has ink on his fingers, he's no god, he must be a clerk from the cement factory. *Those* two are another story. They look as though they'd like to beat you. But gods don't need to beat you, do they? (*Enter Three Gods.*) What about those three? Old-fashioned clothes—dust on their feet—they *must* be gods! (*He throws himself at their feet.*) Do with me what you will, illustrious ones!

FIRST GOD (*with an ear trumpet*). Ah! (*He is pleased.*) So we were expected?

WONG (*giving them water*). Oh, yes. And I *knew* you'd come.

FIRST GOD. We need somewhere to stay the night. You know of a place?

WONG. The whole town is at your service, illustrious ones! What sort of a place would you like?

(*The Gods eye each other.*)

FIRST GOD. Just try the first house you come to, my son.

WONG. That would be Mr. Fo's place.

FIRST GOD. Mr. Fo.

WONG. One moment! (*He knocks at the first house.*)

VOICE FROM MR. FO'S. No!

(*Wong returns a little nervously.*)

WONG. It's too bad. Mr. Fo isn't in. And his servants don't dare do a thing without his consent. He'll have a fit when he finds out who they turned away, won't he?

FIRST GOD (*smiling*). He will, won't he?

WONG. One moment! The next house is Mr. Cheng's. Won't he be thrilled?

FIRST GOD. Mr. Cheng.

(*Wong knocks.*)

VOICE FROM MR. CHENG'S. Keep your gods. We have our own troubles!

WONG (*back with the Gods*). Mr. Cheng is very sorry, but he has a houseful of relations. I think some of them are a bad lot, and naturally, he wouldn't like you to see them.

THIRD GOD. Are we so terrible?

WONG. Well, only with bad people, of course. Everyone knows the province of Kwan is always having floods.

SECOND GOD. Really? How's that?

WONG. Why, because they're so irreligious.

SECOND GOD. Rubbish. It's because they neglected the dam.

FIRST GOD (*to Second*). Sh! (*To Wong.*) You're still in hopes, aren't you, my son?

WONG. Certainly. All Setzuan is competing for the honor! What happened up to now is pure coincidence. I'll be back. (*He walks away, but then stands undecided.*)

SECOND GOD. What did I tell you?

THIRD GOD. It *could* be pure coincidence.

SECOND GOD. The same coincidence in Shun, Kwan, and Setzuan? People just aren't religious any more, let's face the fact. Our mission has failed!

FIRST GOD. Oh come, we might run into a good person any minute.

THIRD GOD. How did the resolution read? (*Unrolling a scroll and reading from it.*) "The world can stay as it is if enough people are found living lives worthy of human beings." Good people, that is. Well, what about this Water Seller himself? *He's* good, or I'm very much mistaken.

SECOND GOD. You're very much mistaken. When he gave us a drink, I had the impression there was something odd about the cup. Well, look! (*He shows the cup to the First God.*)

FIRST GOD. A false bottom!

SECOND GOD. The man is a swindler.

FIRST GOD. Very well, count *him* out. That's one man among millions. And as a matter of fact, we only need one on *our* side. These atheists are saying, "The world must be changed because no one can *be* good and *stay* good." No one, eh? I say: let us find one—just one—and we have those fellows where we want them!

THIRD GOD (*to Wong*). Water Seller, is it so hard to find a place to stay?

WONG. Nothing could be easier. It's just me. I don't go about it right.

THIRD GOD. Really? (*He returns to the others. A Gentleman passes by.*)

WONG. Oh dear, they're catching on. (*He accosts the Gentleman.*) Excuse the intrusion, dear sir, but three Gods have just turned up. Three of the very highest. They need a place for the night. Seize this rare opportunity—to have real gods as your guests!

GENTLEMAN (*laughing*). A new way of finding free rooms for a gang of crooks.

(*Exit Gentleman.*)

WONG (*shouting at him*). Godless rascal! Have you no religion, gentlemen of Setzuan? (*Pause.*) Patience, illustrious ones! (*Pause.*) There's only one person left. Shen Te, the prostitute. She can't say no. (*Calls up to a window.*) Shen Te!

(*Shen Te opens the shutters and looks out.*)

WONG. They're here, and nobody wants them. Will you take them?

SHEN TE. Oh, no, Wong, I'm expecting a gentleman.

WONG. Can't you forget about him for tonight?

SHEN TE. The rent has to be paid by tomorrow or I'll be out on the street.

WONG. This is no time for calculation, Shen Te.

SHEN TE. Stomachs rumble even on the Emperor's birthday, Wong.

WONG. Setzuan is one big dung hill!

SHEN TE. Oh, very well! I'll hide till my gentleman has come and gone. Then I'll take them. (*She disappears.*)

WONG. They mustn't see her gentleman or they'll know what she is.

FIRST GOD (*who hasn't heard any of this*). I think it's hopeless.

(*They approach Wong.*)

WONG. (*jumping, as he finds them behind him*). A room has been found, illustrious ones! (*He wipes sweat off his brow.*)

SECOND GOD. Oh, good.

THIRD GOD. Let's see it.

WONG (*nervously*). Just a minute. It has to be tidied up a bit.

THIRD GOD. Then we'll sit down here and wait.

WONG (*still more nervous*). No, no! (*Holding himself back.*) Too much traffic, you know.

THIRD GOD (*with a smile*). Of course, if you *want* us to move.

(*They retire a little. They sit on a doorstep. Wong sits on the ground.*)

WONG (*after a deep breath*). You'll be staying with a single girl—the finest human being in Setzuan!

THIRD GOD. That's nice.

WONG (*to the audience*). They gave me such a look when I picked up my cup just now.

THIRD GOD. You're worn out, Wong.

WONG. A little, maybe.

FIRST GOD. Do people here have a hard time of it?

WONG. The good ones do.

FIRST GOD. What about yourself?

WONG. You mean I'm not good. That's true. And I don't have an easy time either!

(*During this dialogue, a Gentleman has turned up in front of Shen Te's house, and has whistled several times. Each time Wong has given a start.*)

THIRD GOD (*to Wong, softly*). Psst! I think he's gone now.

WONG (*confused and surprised*). Ye-e-es.

(*The Gentleman has left now, and Shen Te has come down to the street.*)

SHEN TE (*softly*). Wong!

(*Getting no answer, she goes off down the street. Wong arrives just too late, forgetting his carrying pole.*)

WONG (*softly*). Shen Te! Shen Te! (*To himself.*) So she's gone off to earn the rent. Oh dear, I can't go to the gods again with no room to offer them. Having failed in the service of the gods, I shall run to my den in the sewer pipe down by the river and hide from their sight!

(*He rushes off. Shen Te returns, looking for him, but finding the gods. She stops in confusion.*)

SHEN TE. You are the illustrious ones? My name is Shen Te. It would please me very much if my simple room could be of use to you.

THIRD GOD. Where is the Water Seller, Miss . . . Shen Te?

SHEN TE. I missed him, somehow.

FIRST GOD. Oh, he probably thought you weren't coming, and was afraid of telling us.

THIRD GOD (*picking up the carrying pole*). We'll leave this with you. He'll be needing it.

(*Led by Shen Te, they go into the house. It grows dark, then light. Dawn. Again escorted by Shen Te, who leads them through the half-light with a little lamp, the Gods take their leave.*)

FIRST GOD. Thank you, thank you, dear Shen Te, for your elegant hospitality! We shall not forget! And give our thanks to the Water Seller—he showed us a good human being.

SHEN TE. Oh, *I'm* not good. Let me tell you something: when Wong asked me to put you up, I hesitated.

FIRST GOD. It's all right to hesitate if you then go ahead! And in giving us that room you did much more than you knew. You proved that good people still exist, a point that has been disputed of late—even in heaven. Farewell!

SECOND GOD. Farewell!

THIRD GOD. Farewell!

SHEN TE. Stop, illustrious ones! I'm not sure you're right. I'd like to be good, it's true, but there's the rent to pay. And that's not all: I sell myself for a living. Even so I can't make ends meet, there's too much competition. I'd like to honor my father and mother and speak nothing but the truth and not covet my neighbor's house. I should love to stay with one man. But how? How is it done? Even breaking only a *few* of your commandments, I can hardly manage.

FIRST GOD (*clearing his throat*). These thoughts are but, um, the misgivings of an unusually good woman!

THIRD GOD. Goodbye, Shen Te! Give our regards to the Water Seller!

SECOND GOD. And above all: be good! Farewell!

FIRST GOD. Farewell!

THIRD GOD. Farewell!

(*They start to wave good-bye.*)

SHEN TE. But everything is so expensive, I don't feel sure I can do it!

SECOND GOD. That's not in our sphere. We never meddle with economics.

THIRD GOD. One moment.

(*They stop.*)

Isn't it true she might do better if she had more money?

SECOND GOD. Come, come! How could we ever account for it Up Above?

FIRST GOD. Oh, there are ways.

(*They put their heads together and confer in dumb show.*)

(*To Shen Te, with embarrassment.*) As you say you can't pay your rent, well, um, we're not paupers, so of course we insist on paying for our room. (*Awkwardly thrusting money into her hands.*) There! (*Quickly.*) But don't tell anyone! The incident is open to misinterpretation.

SECOND GOD. It certainly is!
FIRST GOD (*defensively*). But there's no law against it! It was never decreed that a god mustn't pay hotel bills!

(*The Gods leave.*)

SCENE 1

(*A small tobacco shop. The shop is not as yet completely furnished and hasn't started doing business.*)

SHEN TE (*to the audience*). It's three days now since the gods left. When they said they wanted to pay for the room, I looked down at my hand, and there was more than a thousand silver dollars! I bought a tobacco shop with the money, and moved in yesterday. I don't own the building, of course, but I can pay the rent, and I hope to do a lot of good here. Beginning with Mrs. Shin, who's just coming across the square with her pot. She had the shop before me, and yesterday she dropped in to ask for rice for her children.

(*Enter Mrs. Shin. Both women bow.*)

How do you do, Mrs. Shin.

MRS. SHIN. How do you do, Miss Shen Te. You like your new home?
SHEN TE. Indeed, yes. Did your children have a good night?
MRS. SHIN. In that hovel? The youngest is coughing already.
SHEN TE. Oh, dear!
MRS. SHIN. You're going to learn a thing or two in these slums.
SHEN TE. Slums? That's not what you said when you sold me the shop!
MRS. SHIN. Now don't start nagging! Robbing me and my innocent children of their home and then calling it a slum! That's the limit! (*She weeps.*)
SHEN TE (*tactfully*). I'll get your rice.
MRS. SHIN. And a little cash while you're at it.
SHEN TE. I'm afraid I haven't sold anything yet.
MRS. SHIN (*screeching*). I've got to have it. Strip the clothes from my back and then cut my throat, will you? I know what I'll do: I'll leave my children on your doorstep! (*She snatches the pot out of Shen Te's hands.*)
SHEN TE. Please don't be angry. You'll spill the rice.

(*Enter an elderly Husband and Wife with their shabbily-dressed Nephew.*)

WIFE. Shen Te, dear! You've come into money, they tell me.

And we haven't a roof over our heads! A tobacco shop. We had one too. But it's gone. Could we spend the night here, do you think?
NEPHEW (*appraising the shop*). Not bad!
WIFE. He's our nephew. We're inseparable!
MRS. SHIN. And who are these . . . ladies and gentlemen?
SHEN TE. They put me up when I first came in from the country. (*To the audience.*) Of course, when my small purse was empty, they put me out on the street, and they may be afraid I'll do the same to them. (*To the newcomers, kindly.*) Come in, and welcome, though I've only one little room for you—it's behind the shop.
HUSBAND. That'll do. Don't worry.
WIFE (*bringing Shen Te some tea*). We'll stay over here, so we won't be in your way. Did you make it a tobacco shop in memory of your first real home? We can certainly give you a hint or two! That's one reason we came.
MRS. SHIN (*to Shen Te*). Very nice! As long as you have a few customers too!
HUSBAND. Sh! A customer!

(*Enter an Unemployed Man, in rags.*)

UNEMPLOYED MAN. Excuse me. I'm unemployed.

(*Mrs. Shin laughs.*)

SHEN TE. Can I help you?
UNEMPLOYED MAN. Have you any damaged cigarettes? I thought there might be some damage when you're unpacking.
WIFE. What nerve, begging for tobacco! (*Rhetorically.*) Why don't they ask for bread?
UNEMPLOYED MAN. Bread is expensive. One cigarette butt and I'll be a new man.
SHEN TE (*giving him cigarettes*). That's very important—to be a new man. You'll be my first customer and bring me luck.

(*The Unemployed Man quickly lights a cigarette, inhales, and goes off, coughing.*)

WIFE. Was that right, Shen Te, dear?
MRS. SHIN. If this is the opening of a shop, you can hold the closing at the end of the week.
HUSBAND. I bet he had money on him.
SHEN TE. Oh, no, he said he hadn't!
NEPHEW. How d'you know he wasn't lying?
SHEN TE (*angrily*). How do you know he was?
WIFE (*wagging her head*). You're too good, Shen Te, dear. If you're going to keep this shop, you'll have to learn to say No.
HUSBAND. Tell them the place isn't yours to dispose of. Belongs to . . . some relative who insists on all accounts being strictly in order . . .
MRS. SHIN. That's right! What do you think you are—a philanthropist?
SHEN TE (*laughing*). Very well, suppose I ask you for my rice back, Mrs. Shin?

WIFE (*combatively, at Mrs. Shin*). So that's *her* rice?

(*Enter the Carpenter, a small man.*)

MRS. SHIN (*who, at the sight of him, starts to hurry away*). See you tomorrow, Miss Shen Te! (*Exit Mrs. Shin.*)

CARPENTER. Mrs. Shin, it's you I want!

WIFE (*to Shen Te*). Has she some claim on you?

SHEN TE. She's hungry. That's a claim.

CARPENTER. Are you the new tenant? And filling up the shelves already? Well, they're not yours, till they're paid for, ma'am. I'm the carpenter, so I should know.

SHEN TE. I took the shop "furnishings included."

CARPENTER. You're in league with that Mrs. Shin, of course. All right: I demand my hundred silver dollars.

SHEN TE. I'm afraid I haven't got a hundred silver dollars.

CARPENTER. Then you'll find it. Or I'll have you arrested.

WIFE (*whispering to Shen Te*). That relative: make it a cousin.

SHEN TE. Can't it wait till next month?

CARPENTER. No!

SHEN TE. Be a little patient, Mr. Carpenter, I can't settle all claims at once.

CARPENTER. Who's patient with me? (*He grabs a shelf from the wall.*) Pay up—or I take the shelves back!

WIFE. Shen Te! Dear! Why don't you let your . . . cousin settle this affair? (*To Carpenter.*) Put your claim in writing. Shen Te's cousin will see you get paid.

CARPENTER (*derisively*). Cousin, eh?

HUSBAND. Cousin, yes.

CARPENTER. I know these cousins!

NEPHEW. Don't be silly. He's a personal friend of mine.

HUSBAND. What a man! Sharp as a razor!

CARPENTER. All right. I'll put my claim in writing. (*Puts shelf on floor, sits on it, writes out bill.*)

WIFE (*to Shen Te*). He'd tear the dress off your back to get his shelves. Never recognize a claim! That's my motto.

SHEN TE. He's done a job, and wants something in return. It's shameful that I can't give it to him. What will the gods say?

HUSBAND. You did your bit when you took *us* in.

(*Enter the Brother, limping, and the Sister-in-Law, pregnant.*)

BROTHER (*to Husband and Wife*). So this is where you're hiding out! There's family feeling for you! Leaving us on the corner!

WIFE (*embarrassed, to Shen Te*). It's my brother and his wife. (*To them.*) Now stop grumbling, and sit quietly in that corner. (*To Shen Te.*) It can't be helped. She's in her fifth month.

SHEN TE. Oh, yes. Welcome!

WIFE (*to the couple*). Say thank you.

(*They mutter something.*)
The cups are there. (*To Shen Te.*) Lucky you bought this shop when you did!

SHEN TE (*laughing and bringing tea*). Lucky indeed!

(*Enter Mrs. Mi Tzu, the landlady.*)

MRS. MI TZU. Miss Shen Te? I am Mrs. Mi Tzu, your landlady. I hope our relationship will be a happy one? I like to think I give my tenants modern, personalized service. Here is your lease. (*To the others, as Shen Te reads the lease.*) There's nothing like the opening of a little shop, is there? A moment of true beauty! (*She is looking around.*) Not very much on the shelves, of course. But everything in the gods' good time! Where are your references, Miss Shen Te?

SHEN TE. Do I *have* to have references?

MRS. MI TZU. After all, I haven't a notion who you are!

HUSBAND. Oh, *we'd* be glad to vouch for Miss Shen Te! We'd go through fire for her!

MRS. MI TZU. And who may *you* be?

HUSBAND (*stammering*). Ma Fu, tobacco dealer.

MRS. MI TZU. Where is your shop, Mr. . . . Ma Fu?

HUSBAND. Well, um, I haven't a shop—I've just sold it.

MRS. MI TZU. I see. (*To Shen Te.*) Is there no one else that knows you?

WIFE (*whispering to Shen Te*). Your cousin! Your cousin!

MRS. MI TZU. This is a respectable house, Miss Shen Te. I never sign a lease without certain assurances.

SHEN TE (*slowly, her eyes downcast*). I have . . . a cousin.

MRS. MI TZU. On the square? Let's go over and see him. What does he do?

SHEN TE (*as before*). He lives . . . in another city.

WIFE (*prompting*). Didn't you say he was in Shung?

SHEN TE. That's right. Shung.

HUSBAND (*prompting*). I had his name on the tip of my tongue. Mr. . . .

SHEN TE (*with an effort*). Mr. . . . Shui . . . Ta.

HUSBAND. That's it! Tall, skinny fellow!

SHEN TE. Shui Ta!

NEPHEW (*to Carpenter*). You were in touch with him, weren't you? About the shelves?

CARPENTER (*surlily*). Give him this bill. (*He hands it over.*) I'll be back in the morning. (*Exit Carpenter.*)

NEPHEW (*calling after him, but with his eyes on Mrs. Mi Tzu*). Don't worry! Mr. Shui Ta pays on the nail!

MRS. MI TZU (*looking closely at Shen Te*). I'll be happy to make his acquaintance, Miss Shen Te. (*Exit Mrs. Mi Tzu.*)

(*Pause.*)

WIFE. By tomorrow morning she'll know more about you than you do yourself.

SISTER-IN-LAW (*to Nephew*). This thing isn't built to last.

(*Enter Grandfather.*)

WIFE. It's Grandfather! (*To Shen Te.*) Such a good old soul!

(*The Boy enters.*)

BOY (*over his shoulder*). Here they are!

WIFE. And the boy, how he's grown! But he always could eat enough for ten.

(*Enter the Niece.*)

WIFE (*to Shen Te*). Our little niece from the country. There are more of us now than in your time. The less we had, the more there were of us; the more there were of us, the less we had. Give me the key. We must protect ourselves from unwanted guests. (*She takes the key and locks the door.*) Just make yourself at home. I'll light the little lamp.

NEPHEW (*a big joke*). I hope her cousin doesn't drop in tonight! The strict Mr. Shui Ta!

(*Sister-in-Law laughs.*)

BROTHER (*reaching for a cigarette*). One cigarette more or less . . .

HUSBAND. One cigarette more or less.

(*They pile into the cigarettes. The Brother hands a jug of wine round.*)

NEPHEW. Mr. Shui Ta'll pay for it!

GRANDFATHER (*gravely, to Shen Te*). How do you do?

(*Shen Te, a little taken aback by the belatedness of the greeting, bows. She has the Carpenter's bill in one hand, the landlady's lease in the other.*)

WIFE. How about a bit of a song? To keep Shen Te's spirits up?

NEPHEW. Good idea. Grandfather: you start!

SONG OF THE SMOKE

GRANDFATHER.

    I used to think (before old age beset me)
      That brains could fill the pantry of the poor.
    But where did all my cerebration get me?
    I'm just as hungry as I was before.
          So what's the use?
            See the smoke float free
            Into ever colder coldness!
            It's the same with me.

HUSBAND.

    The straight and narrow path leads to disaster
      And so the crooked path I tried to tread.
    That got me to disaster even faster.
      (They say we shall be happy when we're dead.)
          So what's the use, etc.

NIECE.

    You older people, full of expectation,
      At any moment now you'll walk the plank!
    The future's for the younger generation!
      Yes, even if that future is a blank.
          So what's the use, etc.

NEPHEW (*to the Brother*). Where'd you get that wine?

SISTER-IN-LAW (*answering for the Brother*). He pawned the sack of tobacco.

HUSBAND (*stepping in*). What? That tobacco was all we had to fall back on! You pig!

BROTHER. *You'd* call a man a pig because your wife was frigid! Did you refuse to drink it?

(*They fight. The shelves fall over.*)

SHEN TE (*imploringly*). Oh, don't! Don't break everything! Take it, take it all, but don't destroy a gift from the gods!

WIFE (*disparagingly*). This shop isn't big enough. I should never have mentioned it to Uncle and the others. When *they* arrive, it's going to be disgustingly overcrowded.

SISTER-IN-LAW. And did you hear our gracious hostess? She cools off quick!

(*Voices outside. Knocking at the door.*)

UNCLE'S VOICE. Open the door!

WIFE. Uncle? Is that you, Uncle?

UNCLE'S VOICE. Certainly, it's me. Auntie says to tell you she'll have the children here in ten minutes.

WIFE (*to Shen Te*). I'll have to let him in.

SHEN TE (*who scarcely hears her*).

    The little lifeboat is swiftly sent down
    Too many men too greedily
    Hold on to it as they drown.

SCENE 1A

(*Wong's den in a sewer pipe.*)

WONG (*crouching there*). All quiet! It's four days now since I left the city. The gods passed this way on the second day. I heard their steps on the bridge over there. They must be a long way off by this time, so I'm safe.

(*Breathing a sigh of relief, he curls up and goes to sleep. In his dream the pipe becomes transparent, and the Gods appear.*)
(*Raising an arm, as if in self-defense.*) I know, I know, illustrious ones! I found no one to give you a room—not in all Setzuan! There, it's out. Please continue on your way!

FIRST GOD (*mildly*). But you did find someone. Someone who took us in for the night, watched over us in our sleep, and in the early morning lighted us down to the street with a lamp.

WONG. It was . . . Shen Te, that took you in?

THIRD GOD. Who else?

WONG. And I ran away! "She isn't coming," I thought, "she just can't afford it."

GODS (*singing*).

    O you feeble, well-intentioned, and yet feeble chap!
    Where there's need the fellow thinks there is no
      goodness!
    When there's danger he thinks courage starts to ebb
      away!
    Some people only see the seamy side!
    What hasty judgment! What premature desperation!

WONG. I'm *very* ashamed, illustrious ones.

FIRST GOD. Do us a favor, Water Seller. Go back to Setzuan. Find Shen Te, and give us a report on her. We hear that she's come into a little money. Show interest in her goodness—for no one can be good for long if goodness is not in demand. Meanwhile we shall continue the search, and find other good people. After which, the idle chatter about the impossibility of goodness will stop!

(*The Gods vanish.*)

SCENE 2

(*A knocking.*)

WIFE. Shen Te! Someone at the door. Where is she anyway?

NEPHEW. She must be getting the breakfast. Mr. Shui Ta will pay for it.

(*The Wife laughs and shuffles to the door. Enter Mr. Shui Ta and the Carpenter.*)

WIFE. Who is it?

SHUI TA. I am Miss Shen Te's cousin.

WIFE. What?

SHUI TA. My name is Shui Ta.

WIFE. Her cousin?

NEPHEW. Her cousin?

NIECE. But that was a joke. She hasn't got a cousin.

HUSBAND. So early in the morning?

BROTHER. What's all the noise?

SISTER-IN-LAW. This fellow says he's her cousin.

BROTHER. Tell him to prove it.

NEPHEW. Right. If you're Shen Te's cousin, prove it by getting the breakfast.

SHUI TA (*whose regime begins as he puts out the lamp to save oil. Loudly, to all present, asleep or awake*). Would you all please get dressed! Customers will be coming! I wish to open my shop!

HUSBAND. *Your* shop? Doesn't it belong to our good friend Shen Te?

(*Shui Ta shakes his head.*)

SISTER-IN-LAW. So we've been cheated. Where *is* the little liar?

SHUI TA. Miss Shen Te has been delayed. She wishes me to tell you there will be nothing she can do—now I am here.

WIFE (*bowled over*). I thought she was *good!*

NEPHEW. Do you have to believe *him?*

HUSBAND. *I* don't.

NEPHEW. Then do something.

HUSBAND. Certainly! I'll send out a search party at once. You, you, you, and you, go out and look for Shen Te.

(*As the Grandfather rises and makes for the door.*)

Not you, Grandfather, you and I will hold the fort.

SHUI TA. You won't find Miss Shen Te. She has suspended her hospitable activity for an unlimited period. There are too many of you. She asked me to say: this is a tobacco shop, not a gold mine.

HUSBAND. Shen Te never said a thing like that. Boy, food! There's a bakery on the corner. Stuff your shirt full when they're not looking!

SISTER-IN-LAW. Don't overlook the raspberry tarts.

HUSBAND. And don't let the policeman see you.

(*The Boy leaves.*)

SHUI TA. Don't you depend on this shop now? Then why give it a bad name, by stealing from the bakery?

NEPHEW. Don't listen to him. Let's find Shen Te. She'll give him a piece of her mind.

SISTER-IN-LAW. Don't forget to leave us some breakfast.

(*Brother, Sister-in-Law, and Nephew leave.*)

SHUI TA (*to the Carpenter*). You see, Mr. Carpenter, nothing has changed since the poet, eleven hundred years ago, penned these lines:
    A governor was asked what was needed
    To save the freezing people in the city.
    He replied:
    "A blanket ten thousand feet long
    To cover the city and all its suburbs."

(*He starts to tidy up the shop.*)

CARPENTER. Your cousin owes me money. I've got witnesses. For the shelves.

SHUI TA. Yes, I have your bill. (*He takes it out of his pocket.*) Isn't a hundred silver dollars rather a lot?

CARPENTER. No deductions! I have a wife and children.

SHUI TA. How many children?

CARPENTER. Three.

SHUI TA. I'll make you an offer. Twenty silver dollars.

(*The Husband laughs.*)

CARPENTER. You're crazy. Those shelves are real walnut.

SHUI TA. Very well. Take them away.

CARPENTER. What?

SHUI TA. They cost too much. Please take them away.

WIFE. Not bad! (*And she, too, is laughing.*)

CARPENTER (*a little bewildered*). Call Shen Te, someone! (*To Shui Ta.*) She's good!

SHUI TA. Certainly. She's ruined.

CARPENTER (*provoked into taking some of the shelves*). All right, you can keep your tobacco on the floor.

SHUI TA (*to the Husband*). Help him with the shelves.

HUSBAND (*grins and carries one shelf over to the door where the Carpenter now is*). Goodbye, shelves!

CARPENTER (*to the Husband*). You dog! You want my family to starve?

SHUI TA. I repeat my offer. I have no desire to keep my tobacco on the floor. Twenty silver dollars.

CARPENTER (*with desperate aggressiveness*). One hundred!

(*Shui Ta shows indifference, looks through the window. The Husband picks up several shelves.*)

(*To Husband.*) You needn't smash them against the doorpost, you idiot! (*To Shui Ta.*) These shelves were made to measure. They're no use anywhere else!

SHUI TA. Precisely.

(*The Wife squeals with pleasure.*)

CARPENTER (*giving up, sullenly*). Take the shelves. Pay what you want to pay.

SHUI TA (*smoothly*). Twenty silver dollars.

(*He places two large coins on the table. The Carpenter picks them up.*)

HUSBAND (*brings the shelves back in*). And quite enough too!

CARPENTER (*slinking off*). Quite enough to get drunk on.

HUSBAND (*happily*). Well, we got rid of *him!*

WIFE (*weeping with fun, gives a rendition of the dialogue just spoken*). "Real walnut," says he. "Very well, take them away," says his lordship. "I have children," says he. "Twenty silver dollars," says his lordship. "They're no use anywhere else," says he. "Precisely," said his lordship!

(*She dissolves into shrieks of merriment.*)

SHUI TA. And now: go!

HUSBAND. What's that?

SHUI TA. You're thieves, parasites. I'm giving you this chance. Go!

HUSBAND (*summoning all his ancestral dignity*). That sort deserves no answer. Besides, one should never shout on an empty stomach.

WIFE. Where's that boy?

SHUI TA. Exactly. The boy. I want no stolen goods in this shop. (*Very loudly.*) I strongly advise you to leave! (*But they remain seated, noses in the air. Quietly.*) As you wish.

(*Shui Ta goes to the door. A Policeman appears. Shui Ta bows.*)

I am addressing the officer in charge of this precinct?

POLICEMAN. That's right, Mr., um . . . what was the name, sir?

SHUI TA. Mr. Shui Ta.

POLICEMAN. Yes, of course, sir.

(*They exchange a smile.*)

SHUI TA. Nice weather we're having.

POLICEMAN. A little on the warm side, sir.

SHUI TA. Oh, a little on the warm side.

HUSBAND (*whispering to the Wife*). If he keeps it up till the boy's back, we're done for. (*Tries to signal Shui Ta.*)

SHUI TA (*ignoring the signal*). Weather, of course, is one thing indoors, another out on the dusty street!

POLICEMAN. Oh, quite another, sir!

WIFE (*to the Husband*). It's all right as long as he's standing in the doorway—the boy will see him.

SHUI TA. Step inside for a moment! It's quite cool indoors. My cousin and I have just opened the place. And we attach the greatest importance to being on good terms with the, um, authorities.

POLICEMAN (*entering*). Thank you, Mr. Shui Ta. It *is* cool!

HUSBAND (*whispering to the Wife*). And now the boy *won't* see him.

SHUI TA (*showing Husband and Wife to the Policeman*). Visitors, I think my cousin knows them. They were just leaving.

HUSBAND (*defeated*). Ye-e-es, we were . . . just leaving.

SHUI TA. I'll tell my cousin you couldn't wait.

(*Noise from the street. Shouts of "Stop, thief!"*)

POLICEMAN. What's that?

(*The Boy is in the doorway with cakes and buns and rolls spilling out of his shirt. The Wife signals desperately to him to leave. He gets the idea.*)

No, you don't! (*He grabs the Boy by the collar.*) Where's all this from?

BOY (*vaguely pointing*). Down the street.

POLICEMAN (*grimly*). So that's it. (*Prepares to arrest the Boy.*)

WIFE (*stepping in*). And *we* knew nothing about it. (*To the Boy.*) Nasty little thief!

POLICEMAN (*dryly*). Can you clarify the situation, Mr. Shui Ta?

(*Shui Ta is silent.*)

POLICEMAN (*who understands silence*). Aha. You're all coming with me—to the station.

SHUI TA. I can hardly say how sorry I am that *my* establishment . . .

WIFE. Oh, he saw the boy leave not ten minutes ago!

SHUI TA. And to conceal the theft asked a policeman in?

POLICEMAN. Don't listen to her, Mr. Shui Ta, I'll be happy to relieve you of their presence one and all! (*To all three.*) Out! (*He drives them before him.*)

GRANDFATHER (*leaving last. Gravely*). Good morning!

POLICEMAN. Good morning!

(*Shui Ta, left alone, continues to tidy up. Mrs. Mi Tzu breezes in.*)

MRS. MI TZU. You're her cousin, are you? Then have the goodness to explain what all this means—police dragging people from a respectable house! By what right does your Miss Shen Te turn my property into a house of assignation?—Well, as you see, I know all!

SHUI TA. Yes. My cousin has the worst possible reputation: that of being poor.

MRS. MI TZU. No sentimental rubbish, Mr. Shui Ta. Your cousin was a common . . .

SHUI TA. Pauper. Let's use the uglier word.

MRS. MI TZU. I'm speaking of her conduct, not her earnings. But there must have *been* earnings, or how did she buy all this? Several elderly gentlemen took care of it, I suppose. I repeat: this is a respectable house! I have tenants who prefer not to live under the same roof with such a person.

SHUI TA (*quietly*). How much do you want?

MRS. MI TZU (*he is ahead of her now*). I beg your pardon.

SHUI TA. To reassure yourself. To reassure your tenants. How much will it cost?

MRS. MI TZU. You're a cool customer.

SHUI TA (*picking up the lease*). The rent is high. (*He reads on.*) I assume it's payable by the month?

MRS. MI TZU. Not in her case.

SHUI TA (*looking up*). What?

MRS. MI TZU. Six months rent payable in advance. Two hundred silver dollars.

SHUI TA. Six . . . ! Sheer usury! And where am I to find it?

MRS. MI TZU. You should have thought of that before.

SHUI TA. Have you no heart, Mrs. Mi Tzu? It's true Shen Te acted foolishly, being kind to all those people, but she'll improve with time. I'll see to it she does. She'll work her fingers to the bone to pay her rent, and all the time be as quiet as a mouse, as humble as a fly.

MRS. MI TZU. Her social background . . .

SHUI TA. Out of the depths! She came out of the depths! And before she'll go back there, she'll work, sacrifice, shrink from nothing. . . . Such a tenant is worth her weight in gold, Mrs. Mi Tzu.

MRS. MI TZU. It's silver we were talking about, Mr. Shui Ta. Two hundred silver dollars or . . .

(*Enter the Policeman.*)

POLICEMAN. Am I intruding, Mr. Shui Ta?

MRS. MI TZU. This tobacco shop is well-known to the police, I see.

POLICEMAN. Mr. Shui Ta has done us a service, Mrs. Mi Tzu. I am here to present our official felicitations!

MRS. MI TZU. That means less than nothing to me, sir. Mr. Shui Ta, all I can say is: I hope your cousin will find my terms acceptable. Good day, gentlemen. (*Exit.*)

SHUI TA. Good day, ma'am.

(*Pause.*)

POLICEMAN. Mrs. Mi Tzu a bit of a stumbling block, sir?

SHUI TA. She wants six months' rent in advance.

POLICEMAN. And you haven't got it, eh?

(*Shui Ta is silent.*)
But surely you can get it, sir? A man like you?

SHUI TA. What about a woman like Shen Te?

POLICEMAN. You're not staying, sir?

SHUI TA. No, and I won't be back. Do you smoke?

POLICEMAN (*taking two cigars, and placing them both in his pocket*). Thank you, sir—I see your point. Miss Shen Te—let's mince no words—Miss Shen Te lived by selling herself. "What else could she have done?" you ask. "How else was she to pay the rent?" True. But the fact remains, Mr. Shui Ta, it is not respectable. Why not? A very deep question. But, in the first place, love—love isn't bought and sold like cigars, Mr. Shui Ta. In the second place, it isn't respectable to go waltzing off with someone that's paying his way, so to speak—it must be for love! Thirdly and lastly, as the proverb has it: not for a handful of rice but for love! (*Pause. He is thinking hard.*) "Well," you may say, "and what good is all this wisdom if the milk's already spilt?" Miss Shen Te is what she is. Is *where* she is. We have to face the fact that if she doesn't get hold of six months' rent pronto, she'll be back on the streets. The question then as I see it—everything in this world is a matter of opinion—the question as I see it is: *how* is she to get hold of this rent? How? Mr. Shui Ta: I don't know. (*Pause.*) I take that back, sir. It's just come to me. A husband. We must find her a husband!

(*Enter a little Old Woman.*)

OLD WOMAN. A good cheap cigar for my husband, we'll have been married forty years tomorrow and we're having a little celebration.

SHUI TA. Forty years? And you still want to celebrate?

OLD WOMAN. As much as we can afford to. We have the carpet shop across the square. We'll be good neighbors, I hope?

SHUI TA. I hope so too.

POLICEMAN (*who keeps making discoveries*). Mr. Shui Ta, you know what we need? We need capital. And how do we acquire capital? We get married.

SHUI TA (*to Old Woman*). I'm afraid I've been pestering this gentleman with my personal worries.

POLICEMAN (*lyrically*). We can't pay six months' rent, so what do we do? We marry money.

SHUI TA. That might not be easy.

POLICEMAN. Oh, I don't know. She's a good match. Has a nice, growing business. (*To the Old Woman.*) What do you think?

OLD WOMAN (*undecided*). Well—

POLICEMAN. Should she put an ad in the paper?

OLD WOMAN (*not eager to commit herself*). Well, if *she* agrees—

POLICEMAN. I'll write it for her. *You* lend us a hand, and *we* write an ad for you! (*He chuckles away to himself, takes out his notebook, wets the stump of a pencil between his lips, and writes away.*)

SHUI TA (*slowly*). Not a bad idea.

POLICEMAN. "What . . . *respectable* . . . man . . . with small capital . . . widower . . . not excluded . . . desires . . . marriage . . . into flourishing . . . tobacco shop?" And now let's add: "am . . . pretty . . ." No! . . . "Prepossessing appearance."

SHUI TA. If you don't think that's an exaggeration?

OLD WOMAN. Oh, not a bit. I've seen her.

(*The Policeman tears the page out of his notebook, and hands it over to Shui Ta.*)

SHUI TA (*with horror in his voice*). How much luck we need to keep our heads above water! How many ideas! How many friends! (*To the Policeman.*) Thank you, sir. I think I see my way clear.

SCENE 3

(*Evening in the municipal park. Noise of a plane overhead. Yang Sun, a young man in rags, is following the plane with his eyes: one can tell that the machine is describing a curve above the park. Yang Sun then takes a rope out of his pocket, looking anxiously about him as he does so. He moves toward a large willow. Enter Two Prostitutes, one old, the other the Niece whom we have already met.*)

NIECE. Hello. Coming with me?

YANG SUN (*taken aback*). If you'd like to buy me a dinner.

OLD WHORE. Buy you a dinner! (*To the Niece.*) Oh, we know him—it's the unemployed pilot. Waste no time on him!

NIECE. But he's the only man left in the park. And it's going to rain.

OLD WHORE. Oh, how do you know?

(*And they pass by. Yang Sun again looks about him, again takes his rope, and this time throws it round a branch of the willow tree. Again he is interrupted. It is the Two Prostitutes returning—and in such a hurry they don't notice him.*)

NIECE. It's going to pour!

(*Enter Shen Te.*)

OLD WHORE. There's that *gorgon* Shen Te! That *drove* your family out into the cold!

NIECE. It wasn't her. It was that cousin of hers. She offered to *pay* for the cakes. I've nothing against her.

OLD WHORE. I have, though. (*So that Shen Te can hear.*) Now where could the little lady be off to? She may be rich now but that won't stop her snatching our young men, will it?

SHEN TE. I'm going to the tearoom by the pond.

NIECE. Is it true what they say? You're marrying a widower—with three children?

SHEN TE. Yes, I'm just going to see him.

YANG SUN (*his patience at breaking point*). Move on there! This is a park, not a whorehouse!

OLD WHORE. Shut your mouth!

(*But the Two Prostitutes leave.*)

YANG SUN. Even in the farthest corner of the park, even when it's raining, you can't get rid of them! (*He spits.*)

SHEN TE (*overhearing this*). And what right have you to scold them? (*But at this point she sees the rope.*) Oh!

YANG SUN. Well, what are you staring at?

SHEN TE. That rope. What is it for?

YANG SUN. Think! Think! I haven't a penny. Even if I had, I wouldn't spend it on you. I'd buy a drink of water.

(*The rain starts.*)

SHEN TE (*still looking at the rope*). What is the rope for? You mustn't!

YANG SUN. What's it to you? Clear out!

SHEN TE (*irrelevantly*). It's raining.

YANG SUN. Well, don't try to come under this tree.

SHEN TE. Oh, no. (*She stays in the rain.*)

YANG SUN. Now go away. (*Pause.*) For one thing, I don't like your looks, you're bow-legged.

SHEN TE (*indignantly*). That's not true!

YANG SUN. Well, don't show 'em to me. Look, it's raining. You better come under this tree.

(*Slowly, she takes shelter under the tree.*)

SHEN TE. Why did you want to do it?

YANG SUN. You really want to know? (*Pause.*) To get rid of you! (*Pause.*) You know what a flyer is?

SHEN TE. Oh yes, I've met a lot of pilots. At the tearoom.

YANG SUN. You call *them* flyers? Think they know what a machine *is*? Just 'cause they have leather helmets? They gave the airfield director a bribe, that's the way *those* fellows got up in the air! Try one of them out sometime. "Go up to two thousand feet," tell him, "then let it fall, then pick it up again with a flick of the wrist at the last moment." Know what he'll say to that? "It's not in my contract." Then again, there's the landing problem. It's like landing on your own backside. It's no different, planes are human. Those fools don't understand. (*Pause.*) And I'm the biggest fool for reading the book on flying in the Peking school and skipping the page where it says: "We've got enough flyers and we don't need you." I'm a mail pilot and no mail. You understand that?

SHEN TE (*shyly*). Yes. I do.

YANG SUN. No, you don't. You'd never understand that.

SHEN TE. When we were little we had a crane with a broken wing. He made friends with us and was very good-natured about our jokes. He would strut along behind us and call out to stop us going too fast for him. But every spring and autumn when the cranes flew over the villages in great swarms, he got quite restless. (*Pause.*) I understood that. (*She bursts out crying.*)

YANG SUN. Don't!

SHEN TE (*quieting down*). No.

YANG SUN. It's bad for the complexion.

SHEN TE (*sniffing*). I've stopped.

(She dries her tears on her big sleeve. Leaning against the tree, but not looking at her, he reaches for her face.)

YANG SUN. You can't even wipe your own face. (*He is wiping it for her with his handkerchief. Pause.*)

SHEN TE (*still sobbing*). I don't know *anything*!

YANG SUN. You interrupted me! What for?

SHEN TE. It's such a rainy day. You only wanted to do . . . *that* because it's such a rainy day.

(To the audience.)

> In our country
> The evenings should never be somber
> High bridges over rivers
> The grey hour between night and morning
> And the long, long winter:
> Such things are dangerous
> For, with all the misery,
> A very little is enough
> And men throw away an unbearable life.

(Pause.)

YANG SUN. Talk about yourself for a change.

SHEN TE. What about me? I have a shop.

YANG SUN (*incredulous*). You have a shop, do you? Never thought of walking the streets?

SHEN TE. I *did* walk the streets. Now I have a shop.

YANG SUN (*ironically*). A gift of the gods, I suppose!

SHEN TE. How did you know?

YANG SUN (*even more ironical*). One fine evening the gods turned up saying: here's some money!

SHEN TE (*quickly*). One fine morning.

YANG SUN (*fed up*). This isn't much of an entertainment.

(Pause.)

SHEN TE. I can play the zither a little. (*Pause.*) And I can mimic men. (*Pause.*) I got the shop, so the first thing I did was to give my zither away. I can be as stupid as a fish now, I said to myself, and it won't matter.

> I'm rich now, I said
> I walk alone, I sleep alone
> For a whole year, I said
> I'll have nothing to do with a man.

YANG SUN. And now you're marrying one! The one at the tearoom by the pond?

(Shen Te is silent.)

YANG SUN. What do you know about love?

SHEN TE. Everything.

YANG SUN. Nothing. (*Pause.*) Or d'you just mean you enjoyed it?

SHEN TE. No.

YANG SUN (*again without turning to look at her, he strokes her cheek with his hand*). You like that?

SHEN TE. Yes.

YANG SUN (*breaking off*). You're easily satisfied, I must say. (*Pause.*) What a town!

SHEN TE. You have no friends?

YANG SUN (*defensively*). Yes, I have! (*Change of tone.*) But they don't want to hear I'm still unemployed. "What?" they ask. "Is there still water in the sea?" You have friends?

SHEN TE (*hesitating*). Just a . . . cousin.

YANG SUN. Watch him carefully.

SHEN TE. He only came once. Then he went away. He won't be back.

(Yang Sun is looking away.)

But to be without hope, they say, is to be without goodness!

(Pause.)

YANG SUN. Go on talking. A voice is a voice.

SHEN TE. Once, when I was a little girl, I fell, with a load of brushwood. An old man picked me up. He gave me a penny too. Isn't it funny how people who don't have very much like to give some of it away? They must like to show what they can do, and how could they show it better than by being kind? Being wicked is just like being clumsy. When we sing a song, or build a machine, or plant some rice, we're being kind. You're kind.

YANG SUN. You make it sound easy.

SHEN TE. Oh, no. (*Little pause.*) Oh! A drop of rain!

YANG SUN. Where'd you feel it?

SHEN TE. Between the eyes.

YANG SUN. Near the right eye? Or the left?

SHEN TE. Near the left eye.

YANG SUN. Oh, good. (*He is getting sleepy.*) So you're through with men, eh?

SHEN TE (*with a smile*). But I'm not bow-legged.

YANG SUN. Perhaps not.

SHEN TE. Definitely not.

(Pause.)

YANG SUN (*leaning wearily against the willow*). I haven't had a drop to drink all day, I haven't eaten anything for *two* days. I couldn't love you if I tried.

(Pause.)

SHEN TE. I like it in the rain.

(Enter Wong the Water Seller, singing.)

THE SONG OF THE WATER SELLER IN THE RAIN
> "Buy my water," I am yelling
> And my fury restraining
> For no water I'm selling
> 'Cause it's raining, 'cause it's raining!
> > I keep yelling: "Buy my water!"
> > But no one's buying
> > Athirst and dying
> > And drinking and paying!
> > Buy water!
> > Buy water, you dogs!

Nice to dream of lovely weather!
Think of all the consternation
Were there no precipitation
Half a dozen years together!
Can't you hear them shrieking: "Water!"
Pretending they adore me!
They all would go down on their knees before me!
Down on your knees!
Go down on your knees, you dogs!
What are lawns and hedges thinking?
What are fields and forests saying?
"At the cloud's breast we are drinking!
And we've no idea who's paying!"
                    I keep yelling: "Buy my water!"
                    But no one's buying
                    Athirst and dying
                    And drinking and paying!
                    Buy water!
                    Buy water, you dogs!

(*The rain has stopped now. Shen Te sees Wong and runs toward him.*)

SHEN TE. Wong! You're back! Your carrying pole's at the shop.

WONG. Oh, thank you, Shen Te. And how is life treating *you?*

SHEN TE. I've just met a brave and clever man. And I want to buy him a cup of your water.

WONG (*bitterly*). Throw back your head and open your mouth and you'll have all the water you need—

SHEN TE (*tenderly*).
        I want *your* water, Wong
        The water that has tired you so
        The water that you carried all this way
        The water that is hard to sell because it's been raining
        I need it for the young man over there—he's a flyer!
                    A flyer is a bold man:
                    Braving the storms
                    In company with the clouds
                    He crosses the heavens
                    And brings to friends in far-away lands
                    The friendly mail!

(*She pays Wong, and runs over to Yang Sun with the cup. But Yang Sun is fast asleep.*)

(*Calling to Wong, with a laugh.*) He's fallen asleep! Despair and rain and I have worn him out!

SCENE 3A

(*Wong's den. The sewer pipe is transparent, and the Gods again appear to Wong in a dream.*)

WONG (*radiant*). I've seen her, illustrious ones! And she hasn't changed!

FIRST GOD. That's good to hear.

WONG. She loves someone.

FIRST GOD. Let's hope the experience gives her the strength to stay good!

WONG. It does. She's doing good deeds all the time.

FIRST GOD. Ah? What sort? What sort of good deeds, Wong?

WONG. Well, she has a kind word for everybody.

FIRST GOD (*eagerly*). And then?

WONG. Hardly anyone leaves her shop without tobacco in his pocket—even if he can't pay for it.

FIRST GOD. Not bad at all. Next?

WONG. She's putting up a family of eight.

FIRST GOD (*gleefully, to the Second God*). Eight! (*To Wong.*) And that's not all, of course!

WONG. She bought a cup of water from me even though it was raining.

FIRST GOD. Yes, yes, yes, all these smaller good deeds!

WONG. Even they run into money. A little tobacco shop doesn't make so much.

FIRST GOD (*sententiously*). A prudent gardener works miracles on the smallest plot.

WONG. She hands out rice every morning. That eats up half her earnings.

FIRST GOD (*a little disappointed*). Well, as a beginning . . .

WONG. They call her the Angel of the Slums—whatever the Carpenter may say!

FIRST GOD. What's this? A carpenter speaks ill of her?

WONG. Oh, he only says her shelves weren't paid for in full.

SECOND GOD (*who has a bad cold and can't pronounce his n's and m's*). What's this? Not paying a carpenter? Why was that?

WONG. I suppose she didn't have the money.

SECOND GOD (*severely*). One pays what one owes, that's in our book of rules! First the letter of the law, then the spirit!

WONG. But it wasn't Shen Te, illustrious ones, it was her cousin. She called *him* in to help.

SECOND GOD. Then her cousin must never darken her threshold again!

WONG. Very well, illustrious ones! But in fairness to Shen Te, let me say that her cousin is a businessman.

FIRST GOD. Perhaps we should inquire what is customary? I find business quite unintelligible. But everybody's doing it. Business! Did the Seven Good Kings do business? Did Kung the Just sell fish?

SECOND GOD. In any case, such a thing must not occur again!

(*The Gods start to leave.*)

THIRD GOD. Forgive us for taking this tone with you, Wong, we haven't been getting enough sleep. The rich recommend us to the poor, and the poor tell us they haven't enough room.

SECOND GOD. Feeble, feeble, the best of them!

FIRST GOD. No great deeds! No heroic daring!

THIRD GOD. On such a *small* scale!

SECOND GOD. Sincere, yes, but what is actually *achieved?*
(*One can no longer hear them.*)

WONG (*calling after them*). I've thought of something, illustrious ones: Perhaps you shouldn't ask—too—much—all—at—once!

SCENE 4

(*The square in front of Shen Te's tobacco shop. Beside Shen Te's place, two other shops are seen: the carpet shop and a barber's. Morning. Outside Shen Te's the Grandfather, the Sister-in-Law, the Unemployed Man, and Mrs. Shin stand waiting.*)

SISTER-IN-LAW. She's been out all night again.
MRS. SHIN. No sooner did we get rid of that crazy cousin of hers than Shen Te herself starts carrying on! Maybe she does give us an ounce of rice now and then, but can you depend on her? Can you depend on her?

(*Loud voices from the Barber's.*)

VOICE OF SHU FU. What are you doing in my shop? Get out—at once!
VOICE OF WONG. But sir. They all let me sell . . .

(*Wong comes staggering out of the barber's shop pursued by Mr. Shu Fu, the barber, a fat man carrying a heavy curling iron.*)

SHU FU. Get out, I said! Pestering my customers with your slimy old water! Get out! Take your cup!

(*He holds out the cup. Wong reaches out for it. Mr. Shu Fu strikes his hand with the curling iron, which is hot. Wong howls.*)

You had it coming, my man!

(*Puffing, he returns to his shop. The Unemployed Man picks up the cup and gives it to Wong.*)

UNEMPLOYED MAN. You can report that to the police.
WONG. My hand! It's smashed up!
UNEMPLOYED MAN. Any bones broken?
WONG. I can't move my fingers.
UNEMPLOYED MAN. Sit down. I'll put some water on it.

(*Wong sits.*)

MRS. SHIN. The water won't cost you anything.
SISTER-IN-LAW. You might have got a bandage from Miss Shen Te till she took to staying out all night. It's a scandal.
MRS. SHIN (*despondently*). If you ask me, she's forgotten we ever existed!

(*Enter Shen Te down the street, with a dish of rice.*)

SHEN TE (*to the audience*). How wonderful to see Setzuan in the early morning! I always used to stay in bed with my dirty blanket over my head afraid to wake up. This morning I saw the newspapers being delivered by little boys, the streets being washed by strong men, and

fresh vegetables coming in from the country on ox carts. It's a long walk from where Yang Sun lives, but I feel lighter at every step. They say you walk on air when you're in love, but it's even better walking on the rough earth, on the hard cement. In the early morning, the old city looks like a great rubbish heap. Nice, though—with all its little lights. And the sky, so pink, so transparent, before the dust comes and muddies it! What a lot you miss if you never see your city rising from its slumbers like an honest old craftsman pumping his lungs full of air and reaching for his tools, as the poet says! (*Cheerfully, to her waiting guests.*) Good morning, everyone, here's your rice! (*Distributing the rice, she comes upon Wong.*) Good morning, Wong, I'm quite lightheaded today. On my way over, I looked at myself in all the shop windows. I'd love to be beautiful.

(*She slips into the carpet shop. Mr. Shu Fu has just emerged from his shop.*)

SHU FU (*to the audience*). It surprises me how beautiful Miss Shen Te is looking today! I never gave her a passing thought before. But now I've been gazing upon her comely form for exactly three minutes! I begin to suspect I am in love with her. She is overpoweringly attractive! (*Crossly, to Wong.*) Be off with you, rascal!

(*He returns to his shop. Shen Te comes back out of the carpet shop with the Old Man, its proprietor, and his wife—whom we have already met—the Old Woman. Shen Te is wearing a shawl. The Old Man is holding up a looking glass for her.*)

OLD WOMAN. Isn't it lovely? We'll give you a reduction because there's a little hole in it.
SHEN TE (*looking at another shawl on the Old Woman's arm*). The other one's nice too.
OLD WOMAN (*smiling*). Too bad there's no hole in that!
SHEN TE. That's right. My shop doesn't make very much.
OLD WOMAN. And your good deeds eat it all up! Be more careful, my dear . . .
SHEN TE (*trying on the shawl with the hole*). Just now, I'm lightheaded! Does the color suit me?
OLD WOMAN. You'd better ask a man.
SHEN TE (*to the Old Man*). Does the color suit me?
OLD MAN. You'd better ask your young friend.
SHEN TE. I'd like to have your opinion.
OLD MAN. It suits you, very well. But wear it this way: the dull side out.

(*Shen Te pays up.*)

OLD WOMAN. If you decide you don't like it, you can exchange it. (*She pulls Shen Te to one side.*) Has he got money?
SHEN TE (*with a laugh*). Yang Sun? Oh, no.
OLD WOMAN. Then how're you going to pay your rent?
SHEN TE. I'd forgotten about that.

OLD WOMAN. And next Monday is the first of the month! Miss Shen Te, I've got something to say to you. After we (*indicating her husband*) got to know you, we had our doubts about that marriage ad. We thought it would be better if you'd let *us* help you. Out of our savings. We reckon we could lend you two hundred silver dollars. We don't need anything in writing—you could pledge us your tobacco stock.

SHEN TE. You're prepared to lend money to a person like me?

OLD WOMAN. It's folks like you that need it. We'd think twice about lending anything to your cousin.

OLD MAN (*coming up*). All settled, my dear?

SHEN TE. I wish the gods could have heard what your wife was just saying, Mr. Ma. They're looking for good people who're happy—and helping me makes you happy because you know it was love that got me into difficulties!

(*The old couple smile knowingly at each other.*)

OLD MAN. And here's the money, Miss Shen Te.

(*He hands her an envelope. Shen Te takes it. She bows. They bow back. They return to their shop.*)

SHEN TE (*holding up her envelope*). Look, Wong, here's six months' rent! Don't you believe in miracles now? And how do you like my new shawl?

WONG. For the young fellow I saw you with in the park?

(*Shen Te nods.*)

MRS. SHIN. Never mind all that. It's time you took a look at his hand!

SHEN TE. Have you hurt your hand?

MRS. SHIN. That barber smashed it with his hot curling iron. Right in front of our eyes.

SHEN TE (*shocked at herself*). And I never noticed! We must get you to a doctor this minute or who knows what will happen?

UNEMPLOYED MAN. It's not a doctor he should see, it's a judge. He can ask for compensation. The barber's filthy rich.

WONG. You think I have a chance?

MRS. SHIN (*with relish*). If it's really good and smashed. But is it?

WONG. I think so. It's very swollen. Could I get a pension?

MRS. SHIN. You'd need a witness.

WONG. Well, you all saw it. You could all testify.

(*He looks round. The Unemployed Man, the Grandfather, and the Sister-in-Law are all sitting against the wall of the shop eating rice. Their concentration on eating is complete.*)

SHEN TE (*to Mrs. Shin*). You saw it yourself.

MRS. SHIN. I want nothin' to do with the police. It's against my principles.

SHEN TE (*to Sister-in-Law*). What about you?

SISTER-IN-LAW. Me? I wasn't looking.

SHEN TE (*to the Grandfather, coaxingly*). Grandfather, *you'll* testify, won't you?

SISTER-IN-LAW. And a lot of good that will do. He's simple-minded.

SHEN TE (*to the Unemployed Man*). You seem to be the only witness left.

UNEMPLOYED MAN. My testimony would only hurt him. I've been picked up twice for begging.

SHEN TE. Your brother is assaulted, and you shut your eyes?

He is hit, cries out in pain, and you are silent?
The beast prowls, chooses and seizes his victim, and
    you say:
"Because we showed no displeasure, he has spared us."
If no one present will be a witness, I will. I'll say I saw it.

MRS. SHIN (*solemnly*). The name for that is perjury.

WONG. I don't know if I can accept that. Though maybe I'll have to. (*Looking at his hand.*) Is it swollen enough, do you think? The swelling's not going down?

UNEMPLOYED MAN. No, no, the swelling's holding up well.

WONG. Yes. It's *more* swollen if anything. Maybe my wrist is broken after all. I'd better see a judge at once.

(*Holding his hand very carefully, and fixing his eyes on it, he runs off. Mrs. Shin goes quickly into the barber's shop.*)

UNEMPLOYED MAN (*seeing her*). She is getting on the right side of Mr. Shu Fu.

SISTER-IN-LAW. You and I can't change the world, Shen Te.

SHEN TE. Go away! Go away all of you!

(*The Unemployed Man, the Sister-in-Law, and the Grandfather stalk off, eating and sulking.*)

(*To the audience.*)

They've stopped answering
They stay put
They do as they're told
They don't care
Nothing can make them look up
But the smell of food.

(*Enter Mrs. Yang, Yang Sun's mother, out of breath.*)

MRS. YANG. Miss. Shen Te. My son has told me everything. I am Mrs. Yang, Sun's mother. Just think. He's got an offer. Of a job as a pilot. A letter has just come. From the director of the airfield in Peking!

SHEN TE. So he can fly again? Isn't that wonderful!

MRS. YANG (*less breathlessly all the time*). They won't give him the job for nothing. They want five hundred silver dollars.

SHEN TE. We can't let money stand in his way, Mrs. Yang!

MRS. YANG. If only you could help him out!

SHEN TE. I have the shop. I can try! (*She embraces Mrs. Yang.*) I happen to have two hundred with me now. Take it. (*She gives her the old couple's money.*) It was a loan but they said I could repay it with my tobacco stock.

MRS. YANG. And they were calling Sun the Dead Pilot of Setzuan! A friend in need!

SHEN TE. We must find another three hundred.

MRS. YANG. How?

SHEN TE. Let me think. (*Slowly.*) I know someone who can help. I didn't want to call on his services again, he's hard and cunning. But a flyer must fly. And I'll make this the last time.

(*Distant sound of a plane.*)

MRS. YANG. If the man you mentioned can do it.... Oh, look, there's the morning mail plane, heading for Peking!

SHEN TE. The pilot can see us, let's wave!

(*They wave. The noise of the engine is louder.*)

MRS. YANG. You know that pilot up there?

SHEN TE. Wave, Mrs. Yang! I know the pilot who *will* be up there. He gave up hope. But he'll do it now. One man to raise himself above the misery, above us all.

(*To the audience.*)

Yang Sun, my lover:
Braving the storms
In company with the clouds
Crossing the heavens
And bringing to friends in far-away lands
The friendly mail!

SCENE 4 A

(*In front of the inner curtain. Enter Shen Te, carrying Shui Ta's mask. She sings.*)

THE SONG OF DEFENSELESSNESS

In our country
A useful man needs luck
Only if he finds strong backers can he prove himself
    useful
The good can't defend themselves and
Even the gods are defenseless.

Oh, why don't the gods have their own ammunition
And launch against badness their own expedition
Enthroning the good and preventing sedition
And bringing the world to a peaceful condition?

Oh, why don't the gods do the buying and selling
Injustice forbidding, starvation dispelling
Give bread to each city and joy to each dwelling?
Oh, why don't the gods do the buying and selling?

(*She puts on Shui Ta's mask and sings in his voice.*)

You can only help one of your luckless brothers
By trampling down a dozen others

Why is it the gods do not feel indignation
And come down in fury to end exploitation
Defeat all defeat and forbid desperation

Refusing to tolerate such toleration?
Why is it?

SCENE 5

(*Shen Te's tobacco shop. Behind the counter, Mr. Shui Ta, reading the paper. Mrs. Shin is cleaning up. She talks and he takes no notice.*)

MRS. SHIN. And when certain rumors get about, what *happens* to a little place like this? It goes to pot. *I* know. So, if you want my advice, Mr. Shui Ta, find out just what exactly has been going on between Miss Shen Te and that Yang Sun from Yellow Street. And remember: a certain interest in Miss Shen Te has been expressed by the barber next door, a man with twelve houses and only one wife, who, for that matter, is likely to drop off at any time. A certain interest has been expressed. (*She relishes the phrase.*) He was even inquiring about her means and, if *that* doesn't prove a man is getting serious, what would? (*Still getting no response, she leaves with her bucket.*)

YANG SUN'S VOICE. Is that Miss Shen Te's tobacco shop?

MRS. SHIN'S VOICE. Yes, it is, but it's Mr. Shui Ta who's here today.

(*Shui Ta runs to the looking glass with the short, light steps of Shen Te, and is just about to start primping, when he realizes his mistake, and turns away, with a short laugh. Enter Yang Sun. Mrs. Shin enters behind him and slips into the back room to eavesdrop.*)

YANG SUN. I am Yang Sun.

(*Shui Ta bows.*)

Is Miss Shen Te in?

SHUI TA. No.

YANG SUN. I guess you know our relationship? (*He is inspecting the stock.*) Quite a place! And I thought she was just talking big. I'll be flying again, all right. (*He takes a cigar, solicits and receives a light from Shui Ta.*) You think we can squeeze the other three hundred out of the tobacco stock?

SHUI TA. May I ask if it is your intention to sell at once?

YANG SUN. It was decent of her to come out with the two hundred but they aren't much use with the other three hundred still missing.

SHUI TA. Shen Te was overhasty promising so much. She might have to sell the shop itself to raise it. Haste, they say, is the wind that blows the house down.

YANG SUN. Oh, she isn't a girl to keep a man waiting. For one thing or the other, if you take my meaning.

SHUI TA. I take your meaning.

YANG SUN (*leering*). Uh, huh.

SHUI TA. Would you explain what the five hundred silver dollars are for?

YANG SUN. Trying to sound me out? Very well. The director of the Peking airfield is a friend of mine from flying school. I give him five hundred: he gets me the job.

SHUI TA. The price is high.

YANG SUN. Not as these things go. He'll have to fire one of the present pilots—for negligence. Only the man he has in mind isn't negligent. Not easy, you understand. You needn't mention that part of it to Shen Te.

SHUI TA (*looking intently at Yang Sun*). Mr. Yang Sun, you are asking my cousin to give up her possessions, leave her friends, and place her entire fate in your hands. I presume you intend to marry her?

YANG SUN. I'd be prepared to.

(*Slight pause.*)

SHUI TA. Those two hundred silver dollars would pay the rent here for six months. If you were Shen Te wouldn't you be tempted to continue in business?

YANG SUN. What? Can you imagine Yang Sun the Flyer behind a counter? (*In an oily voice.*) "A strong cigar or a mild one, worthy sir?" Not in this century!

SHUI TA. My cousin wishes to follow the promptings of her heart, and, from her own point of view, she may even have what is called the right to love. Accordingly, she has commissioned me to help you to this post. There is nothing here that I am not empowered to turn immediately into cash. Mrs. Mi Tzu, the landlady, will advise me about the sale.

(*Enter Mrs. Mi Tzu.*)

MRS. MI TZU. Good morning, Mr. Shui Ta, you wish to see me about the rent? As you know it falls due the day after tomorrow.

SHUI TA. Circumstances have changed, Mrs. Mi Tzu: my cousin is getting married. Her future husband here, Mr. Yang Sun, will be taking her to Peking. I am interested in selling the tobacco stock.

MRS. MI TZU. How much are you asking, Mr. Shui Ta?

YANG SUN. Three hundred sil—

SHUI TA. Five hundred silver dollars.

MRS. MI TZU. How much did she pay for it, Mr. Shui Ta?

SHUI TA. A thousand. And very little has been sold.

MRS. MI TZU. She was robbed. But I'll make you a special offer if you'll promise to be out by the day after tomorrow. Three hundred silver dollars.

YANG SUN (*shrugging*). Take it, man, take it.

SHUI TA. It is not enough.

YANG SUN. Why not? Why not? Certainly, it's enough.

SHUI TA. Five hundred silver dollars.

YANG SUN. But why? We only need three!

SHUI TA (*to Mrs. Mi Tzu*). Excuse me. (*Takes Yang Sun on one side.*) The tobacco stock is pledged to the old couple who gave my cousin the two hundred.

YANG SUN. Is it in writing?

SHUI TA. No.

YANG SUN (*to Mrs. Mi Tzu*). Three hundred will do.

MRS. MI TZU. Of course, I need an assurance that Miss Shen Te is not in debt.

YANG SUN. Mr. Shui Ta?

SHUI TA. She is not in debt.

YANG SUN. When can you let us have the money?

MRS. MI TZU. The day after tomorrow. And remember: I'm doing this because I have a soft spot in my heart for young lovers! (*Exit.*)

YANG SUN (*calling after her*). Boxes, jars and sacks—three hundred for the lot and the pain's over! (*To Shui Ta.*) Where else can we raise money by the day after tomorrow?

SHUI TA. Nowhere. Haven't you enough for the trip and the first few weeks?

YANG SUN. Oh, certainly.

SHUI TA. How much, exactly?

YANG SUN. Oh, I'll dig it up, if I have to steal it.

SHUI TA. I see.

YANG SUN. Well, don't fall off the roof. I'll get to Peking somehow.

SHUI TA. Two people can't travel for nothing.

YANG SUN (*not giving Shui Ta a chance to answer*). I'm leaving *her* behind. No millstones round *my* neck!

SHUI TA. Oh.

YANG SUN. Don't look at me like that!

SHUI TA. How precisely is my cousin to live?

YANG SUN. Oh, you'll think of something.

SHUI TA. A small request, Mr. Yang Sun. Leave the two hundred silver dollars here until you can show me two tickets for Peking.

YANG SUN. You learn to mind your own business, Mr. Shui Ta.

SHUI TA. I'm afraid Miss Shen Te may not wish to sell the shop when she discovers that . . .

YANG SUN. You don't know women. She'll want to. Even then.

SHUI TA (*a slight outburst*). She is a human being, sir! And not devoid of common sense!

YANG SUN. Shen Te is a woman: she *is* devoid of common sense. I only have to lay my hand on her shoulder, and church bells ring.

SHUI TA (*with difficulty*). Mr. Yang Sun!

YANG SUN. Mr. Shui Whatever-it-is!

SHUI TA. My cousin is devoted to you . . . because . . .

YANG SUN. Because I have my hands on her breasts. Give me a cigar. (*He takes one for himself, stuffs a few more in his pocket, then changes his mind and takes the whole box.*) Tell her I'll marry her, then bring me the three hundred. Or let her bring it. One or the other. (*Exit.*)

MRS. SHIN (*sticking her head out of the back room*). Well, he has your cousin under his thumb, and doesn't care if all Yellow Street knows it!

SHUI TA (*crying out*). I've lost my shop! And he doesn't love me! (*He runs berserk through the room, repeating these lines incoherently. Then stops suddenly, and addresses Mrs. Shin.*) Mrs. Shin, you grew up in the gutter, like me. Are we lacking in hardness? I doubt it. If you steal a penny from me, I'll take you by the throat till you spit it out! You'd do the same to me. The times are bad, this city is hell, but we're like ants, we keep coming, up and up the walls, however smooth! Till bad luck comes. Being in love, for instance. *One* weakness is enough, and love is the deadliest.

MRS. SHIN (*emerging from the back room*). You should have a little talk with Mr. Shu Fu the Barber. He's a real gentleman and just the thing for your cousin. (*She runs off.*)

SHUI TA.

A caress becomes a stranglehold
A sigh of love turns to a cry of fear
Why are there vultures circling in the air?
A girl is going to meet her lover.

(*Shui Ta sits down and Mr. Shu Fu enters with Mrs. Shin.*)

Mr. Shu Fu?

SHU FU. Mr. Shui Ta.

(*They both bow.*)

SHUI TA. I am told that you have expressed a certain interest in my cousin Shen Te. Let me set aside all propriety and confess: she is at this moment in grave danger.

SHU FU. Oh, dear!

SHUI TA. She has lost her shop, Mr. Shu Fu.

SHU FU. The charm of Miss Shen Te, Mr. Shui Ta, derives from the goodness, not of her shop, but of her heart. Men call her the Angel of the Slums.

SHUI TA. Yet her goodness has cost her two hundred silver dollars in a single day: we must put a stop to it.

SHU FU. Permit me to differ, Mr. Shui Ta. Let us rather, open wide the gates to such goodness! Every morning, with pleasure tinged by affection, I watch her charitable ministrations. For they are hungry, and she giveth them to eat! Four of them, to be precise. Why only four? I ask. Why not four hundred? I hear she has been seeking shelter for the homeless. What about my humble cabins behind the cattle run? They are at her disposal. And so forth. And so on. Mr. Shui Ta, do you think Miss Shen Te could be persuaded to listen to certain ideas of mine? Ideas like these?

SHUI TA. Mr. Shu Fu, she would be honored.

(*Enter Wong and the Policeman. Mr. Shu Fu turns abruptly away and studies the shelves.*)

WONG. Is Miss Shen Te here?

SHUI TA. No.

WONG. I am Wong the Water Seller. You are Mr. Shui Ta?

SHUI TA. I am.

WONG. I am a friend of Shen Te's.

SHUI TA. An intimate friend, I hear.

WONG (*to the Policeman*). You see? (*To Shui Ta.*) It's because of my hand.

POLICEMAN. He hurt his hand, sir, that's a fact.

SHUI TA (*quickly*). You need a sling, I see. (*He takes a shawl from the back room, and throws it to Wong.*)

WONG. But that's her new shawl!

SHUI TA. She has no more use for it.

WONG. But she bought it to please someone!

SHUI TA. It happens to be no longer necessary.

WONG (*making the sling*). She is my only witness.

POLICEMAN. Mr. Shui Ta, your cousin is supposed to have seen the Barber hit the Water Seller with a curling iron.

SHUI TA. I'm afraid my cousin was not present at the time.

WONG. But she was, sir! Just ask her! Isn't she in?

SHUI TA (*gravely*). Mr. Wong, my cousin has her own troubles. You wouldn't wish her to add to them by committing perjury?

WONG. But it was she that told me to go to the judge!

SHUI TA. Was the judge supposed to heal your hand?

(*Mr. Shu Fu turns quickly around. Shui Ta bows to Shu Fu, and vice versa.*)

WONG (*taking the sling off, and putting it back*). I see how it is.

POLICEMAN. Well, I'll be on my way. (*To Wong.*) And you be careful. If Mr. Shu Fu wasn't a man who tempers justice with mercy, as the saying is, you'd be in jail for libel. Be off with you!

(*Exit Wong, followed by Policeman.*)

SHUI TA. Profound apologies, Mr. Shu Fu.

SHU FU. Not at all, Mr. Shui Ta. (*Pointing to the shawl.*) The episode is over?

SHUI TA. It may take her time to recover. There are some fresh wounds.

SHU FU. We shall be discreet. Delicate. A short vacation could be arranged . . .

SHUI TA. First, of course, you and she would have to talk things over.

SHU FU. At a small supper in a small, but high-class, restaurant.

SHUI TA. I'll go and find her. (*Exit into back room.*)

MRS. SHIN (*sticking her head in again*). Time for congratulations, Mr. Shu Fu?

SHU FU. Ah, Mrs. Shin! Please inform Miss Shen Te's guests they may take shelter in the cabins behind the cattle run!

(*Mrs. Shin nods, grinning.*)

(*To the audience.*) Well? What do you think of me, ladies and gentlemen? What could a man do more? Could he be less selfish? More farsighted? A small supper in a small but . . . Does that bring rather vulgar and clumsy thoughts into your mind? Ts, ts, ts. Nothing of the sort will occur. She won't even be touched. Not even accidentally while passing the salt. An exchange of ideas only. Over the flowers on the table—

white chrysanthemums, by the way (He writes down a note of this.)—yes, over the white chrysanthemums, two young souls will . . . shall I say "find each other"? We shall NOT exploit the misfortune of others. Understanding? Yes. An offer of assistance? Certainly. But quietly. Almost inaudibly. Perhaps with a single glance. A glance that could also—mean more.

MRS. SHIN (coming forward). Everything under control, Mr. Shu Fu?

SHU FU. Oh, Mrs. Shin, what do you know about this worthless rascal Yang Sun?

MRS. SHIN. Why, he's the most worthless rascal . . .

SHU FU. Is he really? You're sure? (As she opens her mouth.) From now on, he doesn't exist! Can't be found anywhere!

(Enter Yang Sun.)

YANG SUN. What's been going on here?

MRS. SHIN. Shall I call Mr. Shui Ta, Mr. Shu Fu? He wouldn't want strangers in here!

SHU FU. Mr. Shui Ta is in conference with Miss Shen Te. Not to be disturbed!

YANG SUN. Shen Te here? I didn't see her come in. What kind of conference?

SHU FU (not letting him enter the back room). Patience, dear sir! And if by chance I have an inkling who you are, pray take note that Miss Shen Te and I are about to announce our engagement.

YANG SUN. What?

MRS. SHIN. You didn't expect that, did you?

(Yang Sun is trying to push past the barber into the back room when Shen Te comes out.)

SHU FU. My dear Shen Te, ten thousand apologies! Perhaps you . . .

YANG SUN. What is it, Shen Te? Have you gone crazy?

SHEN TE (breathless). My cousin and Mr. Shu Fu have come to an understanding. They wish me to hear Mr. Shu Fu's plans for helping the poor.

YANG SUN. Your cousin wants to part us.

SHEN TE. Yes.

YANG SUN. And you've agreed to it?

SHEN TE. Yes.

YANG SUN. They told you I was bad.

(Shen Te is silent.)

And suppose I am. Does that make me need you less? I'm low, Shen Te, I have no money, I don't do the right thing but at least I put up a fight! (He is near her now, and speaks in an undertone.) Have you no eyes? Look at him. Have you forgotten already?

SHEN TE. No.

YANG SUN. How it was raining?

SHEN TE. No.

YANG SUN. How you cut me down from the willow tree? Bought me water? Promised me money to fly with?

SHEN TE (shakily). Yang Sun, what do you want?

YANG SUN. I want you to come with me.

SHEN TE (in a small voice). Forgive me, Mr. Shu Fu, I want to go with Mr. Yang Sun.

YANG SUN. We're lovers you know. Give me the key to the shop.

(Shen Te takes the key from around her neck. Yang Sun puts it on the counter. To Mrs. Shin.)

Leave it under the mat when you're through. Let's go, Shen Te.

SHU FU. But this is rape! Mr. Shui Ta!!

YANG SUN (to Shen Te). Tell him not to shout.

SHEN TE. Please don't shout for my cousin, Mr. Shu Fu. He doesn't agree with me, I know, but he's wrong. (To the audience.)

    I want to go with the man I love
    I don't want to count the cost
    I don't want to consider if it's wise
    I don't want to know if he loves me
    I want to go with the man I love.

YANG SUN. That's the spirit.

(And the couple leave.)

SCENE 5A

(In front of the inner curtain. Shen Te in her wedding clothes, on the way to her wedding.)

SHEN TE. Something terrible has happened. As I left the shop with Yang Sun, I found the old carpet dealer's wife waiting in the street, trembling all over. She told me her husband had taken to his bed—sick with all the worry and excitement over the two hundred silver dollars they lent me. She said it would be best if I gave it back now. Of course, I had to say I would. She said she couldn't quite trust my cousin Shui Ta or even my fiancé Yang Sun. There were tears in her eyes. With my emotions in an uproar, I threw myself into Yang Sun's arms, I couldn't resist him. The things he'd said to Shui Ta had taught Shen Te nothing. Sinking into his arms, I said to myself:

    To let no one perish, not even oneself
    To fill everyone with happiness, even oneself
    Is so good

How could I have forgotten those two old people? Yang Sun swept me away like a small hurricane. But he's not a bad man, and he loves me. He'd rather work in the cement factory than owe his flying to a crime. Though, of course, flying is a great passion with Sun. Now, on the way to my wedding, I waver between fear and joy.

SCENE 6

(The "private dining room" on the upper floor of a cheap restaurant in a poor section of town. With Shen Te: the

Grandfather, the Sister-in-Law, the Niece, Mrs. Shin, the Unemployed Man. In a corner, alone, a Priest. A Waiter pouring wine. Downstage, Yang Sun talking to his mother. He wears a dinner jacket.)

YANG SUN. Bad news, Mamma. She came right out and told me she can't sell the shop for me. Some idiot is bringing a claim because he lent her the two hundred she gave you.

MRS. YANG. What did *you* say? Of course, you can't marry her now.

YANG SUN. It's no use saying anything to *her.* I've sent for her cousin, Mr. Shui Ta. He said there was nothing in writing.

MRS. YANG. Good idea. I'll go out and look for him. Keep an eye on things.

(Exit Mrs. Yang. Shen Te has been pouring wine.)

SHEN TE (*to the audience, pitcher in hand*). I wasn't mistaken in him. He's bearing up well. Though it must have been an awful blow—giving up flying. I do love him so. (*Calling across the room to him.*) Sun, you haven't drunk a toast with the bride!

YANG SUN. What do we drink to?

SHEN TE. Why, to the future!

YANG SUN. When the bridegroom's dinner jacket won't be a hired one!

SHEN TE. But when the bride's dress will still get rained on sometimes!

YANG SUN. To everything we ever wished for!

SHEN TE. May all our dreams come true!

(They drink.)

YANG SUN (*with loud conviviality*). And now, friends, before the wedding gets under way, I have to ask the bride a few questions. I've no idea what kind of a wife she'll make, and it worries me. (*Wheeling on Shen Te.*) For example. Can you make five cups of tea with three tea leaves?

SHEN TE. No.

YANG SUN. So I won't be getting very much tea. Can you sleep on a straw mattress the size of that book? (*He points to the large volume the Priest is reading.*)

SHEN TE. The two of us?

YANG SUN. The one of you.

SHEN TE. In that case, no.

YANG SUN. What a wife! I'm shocked!

(While the audience is laughing, his mother returns. With a shrug of her shoulders, she tells Yang Sun the expected guest hasn't arrived. The Priest shuts the book with a bang, and makes for the door.)

MRS. YANG. Where are *you* off to? It's only a matter of minutes.

PRIEST (*watch in hand*). Time goes on, Mrs. Yang, and I've another wedding to attend to. Also a funeral.

MRS. YANG (*irately*). D'you think we planned it this way? I was hoping to manage with one pitcher of wine, and we've run through two already. (*Points to empty pitcher.*

Loudly.) My dear Shen Te, I don't know where your cousin can be keeping himself!

SHEN TE. My cousin?

MRS. YANG. Certainly. I'm old fashioned enough to think such a close relative should attend the wedding.

SHEN TE. Oh, Sun, is it the three hundred silver dollars?

YANG SUN (*not looking her in the eye*). Are you deaf? Mother says she's old fashioned. And I say I'm considerate. We'll wait another fifteen minutes.

HUSBAND. Another fifteen minutes.

MRS. YANG (*addressing the company*). Now you all know, don't you, that my son is getting a job as a mail pilot?

SISTER-IN-LAW. In Peking, too, isn't it?

MRS. YANG. In Peking, too! The two of us are moving to Peking!

SHEN TE. Sun, tell your mother Peking is out of the question now.

YANG SUN. Your cousin'll tell her. If he agrees. I don't agree.

SHEN TE (*amazed, and dismayed*). Sun!

YANG SUN. I hate this godforsaken Setzuan. What people! Know what they look like when I half close my eyes? Horses! Whinnying, fretting, stamping, screwing their necks up! (*Loudly.*) And what is it the thunder says? They are su-per-flu-ous! (*He hammers out the syllables.*) They've run their last race! They can go trample themselves to death! (*Pause.*) I've got to get out of here.

SHEN TE. But I've promised the money to the old couple.

YANG SUN. And since you always do the wrong thing, it's lucky your cousin's coming. Have another drink.

SHEN TE (*quietly*). My cousin can't be coming.

YANG SUN. How d'you mean?

SHEN TE. My cousin can't be where I am.

YANG SUN. Quite a conundrum!

SHEN TE (*desperately*). Sun, I'm the one that loves you. Not my cousin. He was thinking of the job in Peking when he promised you the old couple's money—

YANG SUN. Right. And that's why he's bringing the three hundred silver dollars. Here—to my wedding.

SHEN TE. He is not bringing the three hundred silver dollars.

YANG SUN. Huh? What makes you think that?

SHEN TE (*looking into his eyes*). He says you only bought one ticket to Peking.

(Short pause.)

YANG SUN. That was yesterday. (*He pulls two tickets part way out of his inside pocket, making her look under his coat.*) Two tickets. I don't want Mother to know. She'll get left behind. I sold her furniture to buy these tickets, so you see . . .

SHEN TE. But what's to become of the old couple?

YANG SUN. What's to become of me? Have another drink. Or do you believe in moderation? If I drink, I fly again. And if you drink, you may learn to understand me.

SHEN TE. You want to fly. But I can't help you.

YANG SUN. "Here's a plane, my darling—but it's only got one wing!"

(The Waiter enters.)

WAITER. Mrs. Yang! Mrs. Yang!

MRS. YANG. Yes?

WAITER. Another pitcher of wine, ma'am?

MRS. YANG. We have enough, thanks. Drinking makes me sweat.

WAITER. Would you mind paying, ma'am?

MRS. YANG *(to everyone)*. Just be patient a few moments longer, everyone, Mr. Shui Ta is on his way over! *(To the Waiter.)* Don't be a spoilsport.

WAITER. I can't let you leave till you've paid your bill, ma'am.

MRS. YANG. But they know me here!

WAITER. That's just it.

PRIEST *(ponderously getting up)*. I humbly take my leave. *(And he does.)*

MRS. YANG *(to the others, desperately)*. Stay where you are, everybody! The priest says he'll be back in two minutes!

YANG SUN. It's no good, Mamma. Ladies and gentlemen, Mr. Shui Ta still hasn't arrived and the priest has gone home. We won't detain you any longer.

(They are leaving now.)

GRANDFATHER *(in the doorway, having forgotten to put his glass down)*. To the bride! *(He drinks, puts down the glass, and follows the others.)*

(Pause.)

SHEN TE. Shall I go too?

YANG SUN. You? Aren't you the bride? Isn't this your wedding? *(He drags her across the room, tearing her wedding dress.)* If we can wait, you can wait. Mother calls me her falcon. She wants to see me in the clouds. But I think it may be St. Nevercome's Day before she'll go to the door and see my plane thunder by. *(Pause. He pretends the guests are still present.)* Why such a lull in the conversation, ladies and gentlemen? Don't you like it here? The ceremony is only slightly postponed—because an important guest is expected at any moment. Also because the bride doesn't know what love is. While we're waiting, the bridegroom will sing a little song. *(He does so.)*

THE SONG OF ST. NEVERCOME'S DAY

On a certain day, as is generally known,
  One and all will be shouting: Hooray, hooray!
For the beggar maid's son has a solid-gold throne
  And the day is St. Nevercome's Day
  On St. Nevercome's, Nevercome's, Nevercome's Day
He'll sit on his solid-gold throne

Oh, hooray, hooray! That day goodness will pay!
  That day badness will cost you your head!
And merit and money will smile and be funny
  While exchanging salt and bread
On St. Nevercome's, Nevercome's, Nevercome's Day
  While exchanging salt and bread

And the grass, oh, the grass will look down at the sky
  And the pebbles will roll up the stream
And all men will be good without batting an eye
  They will make of our earth a dream
On St. Nevercome's, Nevercome's, Nevercome's Day
  They will make of our earth a dream

And as for me, that's the day I shall be
  A flyer and one of the best
Unemployed man, you will have work to do
  Washerwoman, you'll get your rest
On St. Nevercome's, Nevercome's, Nevercome's Day
  Washerwoman, you'll get your rest.

MRS. YANG. It looks like he's not coming.

(The three of them sit looking at the door.)

SCENE 6A

(Wong's den. The sewer pipe is again transparent and again the Gods appear to Wong in a dream.)

WONG. I'm so glad you've come, illustrious ones. It's Shen Te. She's in great trouble from following the rule about loving thy neighbor. Perhaps she's *too* good for this world!

FIRST GOD. Nonsense! You are eaten up by lice and doubts!

WONG. Forgive me, illustrious one, I only meant you might deign to intervene.

FIRST GOD. Out of the question! My colleague here intervened in some squabble or other only yesterday. *(He points to the Third God who has a black eye.)* The results are before us!

WONG. She had to call on her cousin again. But not even he could help. I'm afraid the shop is done for.

THIRD GOD *(a little concerned)*. Perhaps we should help after all?

FIRST GOD. The gods help those that help themselves.

WONG. What if we *can't* help ourselves, illustrious ones?

(Slight pause.)

SECOND GOD. Try, anyway! Suffering ennobles!

FIRST GOD. Our faith in Shen Te is unshaken!

THIRD GOD. We certainly haven't found any *other* good people. You can see where we spend our nights from the straw on our clothes.

WONG. You might help her find her way by—

FIRST GOD. The good man finds his own way here below!

SECOND GOD. The good woman too.

FIRST GOD. The heavier the burden, the greater her strength!

THIRD GOD. We're only onlookers, you know.

FIRST GOD. And everything will be all right in the end, O ye of little faith!

(They are gradually disappearing through these last lines.)

SCENE 7

(*The yard behind Shen Te's shop. A few articles of furniture on a cart. Shen Te and Mrs. Shin are taking the washing off the line.*)

MRS. SHIN. If you ask me, you should fight tooth and nail to keep the shop.

SHEN TE. How can I? I have to sell the tobacco to pay back the two hundred silver dollars today.

MRS. SHIN. No husband, no tobacco, no house and home! What are you going to live on?

SHEN TE. I can work. I can sort tobacco.

MRS. SHIN. Hey, look, Mr. Shui Ta's trousers! He must have left here stark naked!

SHEN TE. Oh, he may have another pair, Mrs. Shin.

MRS. SHIN. But if he's gone for good as you say, why has he left his pants behind?

SHEN TE. Maybe he's thrown them away.

MRS. SHIN. Can I take them?

SHEN TE. Oh, no.

(*Enter Mr. Shu Fu, running.*)

SHU FU. Not a word! Total silence! I know all. You have sacrificed your own love and happiness so as not to hurt a dear old couple who had put their trust in you! Not in vain does this district—for all its malevolent tongues!—call you the Angel of the Slums! That young man couldn't rise to your level, so you left him. And now, when I see you closing up the little shop, that veritable haven of rest for the multitude, well, I cannot, I cannot let it pass. Morning after morning I have stood watching in the doorway not unmoved—while you graciously handed out rice to the wretched. Is that never to happen again? Is the good woman of Setzuan to disappear? If only you would allow *me* to assist you! Now don't say anything! No assurances, no exclamations of gratitude! (*He has taken out his check book.*) Here! A blank check. (*He places it on the cart.*) Just my signature. Fill it out as you wish. Any sum in the world. I herewith retire from the scene, quietly, unobtrusively, making no claims, on tiptoe, full of veneration, absolutely selflessly . . . (*He has gone.*)

MRS. SHIN. Well! You're saved. There's always some idiot of a man . . . Now hurry! Put down a thousand silver dollars and let me fly to the bank before he comes to his senses.

SHEN TE. I can pay you for the washing without any check.

MRS. SHIN. What? You're not going to cash it just because you might have to marry him? Are you crazy? Men like him *want* to be led by the nose! Are you still thinking of that flyer? All Yellow Street knows how he treated you!

SHEN TE.

When I heard his cunning laugh, I was afraid
But when I saw the holes in his shoes, I loved him
    dearly.

MRS. SHIN. Defending that good for nothing after all that's happened!

SHEN TE (*staggering as she holds some of the washing*). Oh!

MRS. SHIN (*taking the washing from her, dryly*). So you feel dizzy when you stretch and bend? There couldn't be a little visitor on the way? If that's it, you can forget Mr. Shu Fu's blank check: it wasn't meant for a christening present!

(*She goes to the back with a basket. Shen Te's eyes follow Mrs. Shin for a moment. Then she looks down at her own body, feels her stomach, and a great joy comes into her eyes.*)

SHEN TE. O joy! A new human being is on the way. The world awaits him. In the cities the people say: he's got to be reckoned with, this new human being! (*She imagines a little boy to be present, and introduces him to the audience.*)

This is my son, the well-known flyer!
Say: Welcome
To the conqueror of unknown mountains and
    unreachable regions
Who brings us our mail across the impassable deserts!

(*She leads him up and down by the hand.*) Take a look at the world, my son. That's a tree. Tree, yes. Say: "Hello, tree!" And bow. Like this. (*She bows.*) Now you know each other. And, look, here comes the Water Seller. He's a friend, give him your hand. A cup of fresh water for my little son, please. Yes, it is a warm day. (*Handing the cup.*) Oh dear, a policeman, we'll have to make a circle round him. Perhaps we can pick a few cherries over there in the rich Mr. Pung's garden. But we mustn't be seen. You want cherries? Just like children with fathers. No, no, you can't go straight at them like that. Don't pull. We must learn to be reasonable. Well, have it your own way. (*She has let him make for the cherries.*) Can you reach? Where to put them? Your mouth is the best place. (*She tries one herself.*) Mmm, they're good. But the policeman, we must run! (*They run.*) Yes, back to the street. Calm now, so no one will notice us. (*Walking the street with her child, she sings.*)

Once a plum—'twas in Japan—
Made a conquest of a man
But the man's turn soon did come
For he gobbled up the plum

(*Enter Wong, with a Child by the hand. He coughs.*)

SHEN TE. Wong!

WONG. It's about the Carpenter, Shen Te. He's lost his shop, and he's been drinking. His children are on the streets. This is one. Can you help?

SHEN TE (*to the child*). Come here, little man. (*Takes him down to the footlights. To the audience.*)

You there! A man is asking you for shelter!
A man of tomorrow says: what about today?
His friend the conqueror, whom you know,
Is his advocate!

(*To Wong.*) He can live in Mr. Shu Fu's cabins. I may have to go there myself. I'm going to have a baby. That's a secret—don't tell Yang Sun—we'd only be in his way. Can you find the Carpenter for me?

WONG. I knew you'd think of something. (*To the Child.*) Goodbye, son, I'm going for your father.

SHEN TE. What about your hand, Wong? I wanted to help, but my cousin . . .

WONG. Oh, I can get along with one hand, don't worry. (*He shows how he can handle his pole with his left hand alone.*)

SHEN TE. But your right hand! Look, take this cart, sell everything that's on it, and go to the doctor with the money . . .

WONG. She's still good. But first I'll bring the Carpenter. I'll pick up the cart when I get back. (*Exit Wong.*)

SHEN TE (*to the Child*). Sit down over here, son, till your father comes.

(*The Child sits crosslegged on the ground. Enter the Husband and Wife, each dragging a large, full sack.*)

WIFE (*furtively*). You're alone, Shen Te, dear?

(*Shen Te nods. The Wife beckons to the Nephew offstage. He comes on with another sack.*)

Your cousin's away?

(*Shen Te nods.*)

He's not coming back?

SHEN TE. No. I'm giving up the shop.

WIFE. That's why we're here. We want to know if we can leave these things in your new home. Will you do us this favor?

SHEN TE. Why, yes, I'd be glad to.

HUSBAND (*cryptically*). And if anyone asks about them, say they're yours.

SHEN TE. Would anyone ask?

WIFE (*with a glance back at her Husband*). Oh, someone might. The police, for instance. They don't seem to like us. Where can we put it?

SHEN TE. Well, I'd rather not get in any more trouble . . .

WIFE. Listen to her! The good woman of Setzuan!

(*Shen Te is silent.*)

HUSBAND. There's enough tobacco in those sacks to give us a new start in life. We could have our own tobacco factory!

SHEN TE (*slowly*). You'll have to put them in the back room.

(*The sacks are taken offstage, where the Child is left alone. Shyly glancing about him, he goes to the garbage can, starts playing with the contents, and eating some of the scraps. The others return.*)

WIFE. We're counting on you, Shen Te!

SHEN TE. Yes. (*She sees the Child and is shocked.*)

HUSBAND. We'll see you in Mr. Shu Fu's cabins.

NEPHEW. The day after tomorrow.

SHEN TE. Yes. Now, go. Go! I'm not feeling well.

(*Exeunt all three, virtually pushed off.*)

He is eating the refuse in the garbage can! Only look at his little grey mouth!

(*Pause. Music.*)

As this is the world my son will enter
I will study to defend him.
To be good to you, my son,
I shall be a tigress to all others
If I have to.
And I shall have to.

(*She starts to go.*) One more time, then. I hope really the last.

(*Exit Shen Te, taking Shui Ta's trousers. Mrs. Shin enters and watches her with marked interest. Enter the Sister-in-Law and the Grandfather.*)

SISTER-IN-LAW. So it's true, the shop has closed down. And the furniture's in the back yard. It's the end of the road!

MRS. SHIN (*pompously*). The fruit of high living, selfishness, and sensuality! Down the primrose path to Mr. Shu Fu's cabins—with you!

SISTER-IN-LAW. Cabins? Rat holes! He gave them to us because his soap supplies only went mouldy there!

(*Enter the Unemployed Man.*)

UNEMPLOYED MAN. Shen Te is moving?

SISTER-IN-LAW. Yes. She was sneaking away.

MRS. SHIN. She's ashamed of herself, and no wonder!

UNEMPLOYED MAN. Tell her to call Mr. Shui Ta or she's done for this time!

SISTER-IN-LAW. Tell her to call Mr. Shui Ta or *we're* done for this time!

(*Enter Wong and Carpenter, the latter with a Child on each hand.*)

CARPENTER. So we'll have a roof over our heads for a change!

MRS. SHIN. Roof? Whose roof?

CARPENTER. Mr. Shu Fu's cabins. And we have little Feng to thank for it. (*Feng, we find, is the name of the child already there; his Father now takes him. To the other two.*) Bow to your little brother, you two! (*The Carpenter and the two new arrivals bow to Feng.*)

(*Enter Shui Ta.*)

UNEMPLOYED MAN. Sst! Mr. Shui Ta!

(*Pause.*)

SHUI TA. And what is this crowd here for, may I ask?

WONG. How do you do, Mr. Shui Ta? This is the Carpenter. Miss Shen Te promised him space in Mr. Shu Fu's cabins.

SHUI TA. That will not be possible.

CARPENTER. We can't go there after all?

SHUI TA. All the space is needed for other purposes.

SISTER-IN-LAW. You mean we have to get out? But we've got nowhere to go.

SHUI TA. Miss Shen Te finds it possible to provide employment. If the proposition interests you, you may stay in the cabins.

SISTER-IN-LAW (*with distaste*). You mean *work?* Work for Miss Shen Te?

SHUI TA. Making tobacco, yes. There are three bales here already. Would you like to get them?

SISTER-IN-LAW (*trying to bluster*). We have our own tobacco! We were in the tobacco business before you were born!

SHUI TA (*to the Carpenter and the Unemployed Man*). You don't have your own tobacco. What about you?

(*The Carpenter and the Unemployed Man get the point, and go for the sacks. Enter Mrs. Mi Tzu.*)

MRS. MI TZU. Mr. Shui Ta? I've brought you your three hundred silver dollars.

SHUI TA. I'll Sign your lease instead. I've decided not to sell.

MRS. MI TZU. What? You don't need the money for that flyer?

SHUI TA. No.

MRS. MI TZU. And you can pay six months' rent?

SHUI TA (*takes the barber's blank check from the cart and fills it out*). Here is a check for ten thousand silver dollars. On Mr. Shu Fu's account. Look! (*He shows her the signature on the check.*) Your six months' rent will be in your hands by seven this evening. And now, if you'll excuse me.

MRS. MI TZU. So it's Mr. Shu Fu now. The flyer has been given his walking papers. These modern girls! In my day they'd have said she was flighty. That poor, deserted Mr. Yang Sun!

(*Exit Mrs. Mi Tzu. The Carpenter and the Unemployed Man drag the three sacks back on the stage.*)

CARPENTER (*to Shui Ta*). I don't know why I'm doing this for you.

SHUI TA. Perhaps your children want to eat, Mr. Carpenter.

SISTER-IN-LAW (*catching sight of the sacks*). Was my brother-in-law here?

MRS. SHIN. Yes, he was.

SISTER-IN-LAW. I thought as much. I know those sacks! That's our tobacco!

SHUI TA. Really? I thought it came from my back room? Shall we consult the police on the point?

SISTER-IN-LAW (*defeated*). No.

SHUI TA. Perhaps you will show me the way to Mr. Shu Fu's cabins?

(*Shui Ta goes off, followed by the Carpenter and his two older children, the Sister-in-Law, the Grandfather, and the Unemployed Man. Each of the last three drags a sack. Enter Old Man and Old Woman.*)

MRS. SHIN. A pair of pants—missing from the clothes line one minute—and next minute on the honorable backside of Mr. Shui Ta!

OLD WOMAN. We thought Miss Shen Te was here.

MRS. SHIN (*preoccupied*). Well, she's not.

OLD MAN. There was something she was going to give us.

WONG. She was going to help me too. (*Looking at his hand.*) It'll be too late soon. But she'll be back. This cousin has never stayed long.

MRS. SHIN (*approaching a conclusion*). No, he hasn't, has he?

SCENE 7A

(*The sewer pipe: Wong asleep. In his dream, he tells the Gods his fears. The Gods seem tired from all their travels. They stop for a moment and look over their shoulders at the Water Seller.*)

WONG. Illustrious ones, I've been having a bad dream. Our beloved Shen Te was in great distress in the rushes down by the rivers—the spot where the bodies of suicides are washed up. She kept staggering and holding her head down as if she was carrying something and it was dragging her down into the mud. When I called out to her, she said she had to take your Book of Rules to the other side, and not get it wet, or the ink would all come off. You had talked to her about the virtues, you know, the time she gave you shelter in Setzuan.

THIRD GOD. Well, but what do you suggest, my dear Wong?

WONG. Maybe a little relaxation of the rules, Benevolent One, in view of the bad times.

THIRD GOD. As for instance?

WONG. Well, um, good-will, for instance, might do instead of love?

THIRD GOD. I'm afraid that would create new problems.

WONG. Or, instead of justice, good sportsmanship?

THIRD GOD. That would only mean more work.

WONG. Instead of honor, outward propriety?

THIRD GOD. Still more work! No, no! The rules will have to stand, my dear Wong!

(*Wearily shaking their heads, all three journey on.*)

SCENE 8

(*Shui Ta's tobacco factory in Shu Fu's cabins. Huddled together behind bars, several families, mostly women and children. Among these people the Sister-in-Law, the Grandfather, the Carpenter, and his three children. Enter Mrs. Yang followed by Yang Sun.*)

MRS. YANG (*to the audience*). There's something I just *have* to tell you: strength and wisdom are wonderful things. The strong and wise Mr. Shui Ta has transformed my son from a dissipated good-for-nothing into a model citizen. As you may have heard, Mr. Shui Ta opened a small tobacco factory near the cattle runs. It flourished. Three months ago—I shall never forget it—I asked for an appointment, and Mr. Shui Ta agreed to see us—me and my son. I can see him now as he came through the door to meet us . . .

(*Enter Shui Ta, from a door.*)

SHUI TA. What can I do for you, Mrs. Yang?

MRS. YANG. This morning the police came to the house. We find you've brought an action for breach of promise of marriage. In the name of Shen Te. You also claim that Sun came by two hundred silver dollars by improper means.

SHUI TA. That is correct.

MRS. YANG. Mr. Shui Ta, the money's all gone. When the Peking job didn't materialize, he ran through it all in three days. I know he's a good-for-nothing. He sold my furniture. He was moving to Peking without me. Miss Shen Te thought highly of him at one time.

SHUI TA. What do *you* say, Mr. Yang Sun?

YANG SUN. The money's gone.

SHUI TA (*to Mrs. Yang*). Mrs. Yang, in consideration of my cousin's incomprehensible weakness for your son, I am prepared to give him another chance. He can have a job—here. The two hundred silver dollars will be taken out of his wages.

YANG SUN. So it's the factory or jail?

SHUI TA. Take your choice.

YANG SUN. May I speak with Shen Te?

SHUI TA. You may not.

(*Pause.*)

YANG SUN (*sullenly*). Show me where to go.

MRS. YANG. Mr. Shui Ta, you are kindness itself: the gods will reward you! (*To Yang Sun.*) And honest work will make a man of you, my boy.

(*Yang Sun follows Shui Ta into the factory. Mrs. Yang comes down again to the footlights.*)

Actually, honest work didn't agree with him—at first. And he got no opportunity to distinguish himself till—in the third week—when the wages were being paid. . . .

(*Shui Ta has a bag of money. Standing next to his foreman—the former Unemployed Man—he counts out the wages. It is Yang Sun's turn.*)

UNEMPLOYED MAN (*reading*). Carpenter, six silver dollars. Yang Sun, six silver dollars.

YANG SUN (*quietly*). Excuse me, sir. I don't think it can be more than five. May I see? (*He takes the foreman's list.*) It says six working days. But that's a mistake, sir. I took a day off for court business. And I won't take what I haven't earned, however miserable the pay is!

UNEMPLOYED MAN. Yang Sun. Five silver dollars. (*To Shui Ta.*) A rare case, Mr. Shui Ta!

SHUI TA. How is it the book says six when it should say five?

UNEMPLOYED MAN. I must've made a mistake, Mr. Shui Ta. (*With a look at Yang Sun.*) It won't happen again.

SHUI TA (*taking Yang Sun aside*). You don't hold back, do you? You give your all to the firm. You're even honest. Do the foreman's mistakes always favor the workers?

YANG SUN. He does have . . . friends.

SHUI TA. Thank you. May I offer you any little recompense?

YANG SUN. Give me a trial period of one week, and I'll prove my intelligence is worth more to you than my strength.

MRS. YANG (*still down at the footlight*). Fighting words, fighting words! That evening, I said to Sun: "If you're a flyer, then fly, my falcon! Rise in the world!" And he got to be foreman. Yes, in Mr. Shui Ta's tobacco factory, he worked real miracles.

(*We see Yang Sun with his legs apart standing behind the workers who are handing along a basket of raw tobacco above their heads.*)

YANG SUN. Faster! Faster! You there, d'you think you can just stand around now you're not foreman any more? It'll be your job to lead us in song. Sing!

(*Unemployed Man starts singing. The others join in the refrain.*)

SONG OF THE EIGHTH ELEPHANT

Chang had seven elephants—all much the same—
　But then there was Little Brother
The seven, they were wild, Little Brother, he was
　tame
And to guard them Chang chose Little Brother
　　Run faster!
　　Mr. Chang has a forest park
　　Which must be cleared before tonight
　　And already it's growing dark!
When the seven elephants cleared that forest park
　Mr. Chang rode high on Little Brother
While the seven toiled and moiled till dark
　On his big behind sat Little Brother
　　Dig faster!
　　Mr. Chang has a forest park
　　Which must be cleared before tonight
　　And already it's growing dark!

And the seven elephants worked many an hour
　Till none of them could work another
Old Chang, he looked sour, on the seven, he did
　glower
But gave a pound of rice to Little Brother
　　What was that?
　　Mr. Chang has a forest park
　　Which must be cleared before tonight
　　And already it's growing dark!

And the seven elephants hadn't any tusks
　The one that had the tusks was Little Brother!

Seven are no match for one, if the one has a gun!
　How old Chang did laugh at Little Brother!
　　Keep on digging!
　　Mr. Chang has a forest park
　　Which must be cleared before tonight
　　And already it's growing dark!

(*Smoking a cigar, Shui Ta strolls by. Yang Sun, laughing, has joined in the refrain of the third stanza and speeded up the tempo of the last stanza by clapping his hands.*)

MRS. YANG. And that's why I say: strength and wisdom are wonderful things. It took the strong and wise Mr. Shui Ta to bring out the best in Yang Sun. A real superior man is like a bell. If you ring it, it rings, and if you don't, it don't, as the saying is.

SCENE 9

(*Shen Te's shop, now an office with club chairs and fine carpets. It is raining. Shui Ta, now fat, is just dismissing the Old Man and Old Woman. Mrs. Shin, in obviously new clothes, looks on, smirking.*)

SHUI TA. No! I can NOT tell you when we expect her back.

OLD WOMAN. The two hundred silver dollars came today. In an envelope. There was no letter, but it must be from Shen Te. We want to write and thank her. May we have her address?

SHUI TA. I'm afraid I haven't got it.

OLD MAN (*pulling Old Woman's sleeve*). Let's be going.

OLD WOMAN. She's got to come back some time! (*They move off, uncertainly, worried. Shui Ta bows.*)

MRS. SHIN. They lost the carpet shop because they couldn't pay their taxes. The money arrived too late.

SHUI TA. They could have come to me.

MRS. SHIN. People don't like coming to you.

SHUI TA (*sits suddenly, one hand to his head*). I'm dizzy.

MRS. SHIN. After all, you *are* in your seventh month. But old Mrs. Shin will be there in your hour of trial! (*She cackles feebly.*)

SHUI TA (*in a stifled voice*). Can I count on that?

MRS. SHIN. We all have our price, and mine won't be too high for the great Mr. Shui Ta! (*She opens Shui Ta's collar.*)

SHUI TA. It's for the child's sake. All of this.

MRS. SHIN. "All for the child," of course.

SHUI TA. I'm so fat. People must notice.

MRS. SHIN. Oh no, they think it's 'cause you're rich.

SHUI TA (*more feelingly*). What will happen to the child?

MRS. SHIN. You ask that nine times a day. Why, it'll have the best that money can buy!

SHUI TA. He must never see Shui Ta.

MRS. SHIN. Oh, no. Always Shen Te.

SHUI TA. What about the neighbors? There are rumors, aren't there?

MRS. SHIN. As long as Mr. Shu Fu doesn't find out, there's nothing to worry about. Drink this.

(*Enter Yang Sun in a smart business suit, and carrying a businessman's brief case. Shui Ta is more or less in Mrs. Shin's arms.*)

YANG SUN (*surprised*). I seem to be in the way.

SHUI TA (*ignoring this, rises with an effort*). Till tomorrow, Mrs. Shin.

(*Mrs. Shin leaves with a smile, putting her new gloves on.*)

YANG SUN. Gloves now! She couldn't be fleecing you? And since when did *you* have a private life? (*Taking a paper from the brief case.*) You haven't been at your best lately, and things are getting out of hand. The police want to close us down. They say that at the most they can only permit twice the lawful number of workers.

SHUI TA (*evasively*). The cabins are quite good enough.

YANG SUN. For the workers maybe, not for the tobacco. They're too damp. We must take over some of Mrs. Mi Tzu's buildings.

SHUI TA. Her price is double what I can pay.

YANG SUN. Not unconditionally. If she has me to stroke her knees she'll come down.

SHUI TA. I'll never agree to that.

YANG SUN. What's wrong? Is it the rain? You get so irritable whenever it rains.

SHUI TA. Never! I will never . . .

YANG SUN. Mrs. Mi Tzu'll be here in five minutes. *You* fix it. And Shu Fu will be with her. . . . What's all that noise?

(*During the above dialogue, Wong is heard off stage calling: "The good Shen Te, where is she? Which of you has seen Shen Te, good people? Where is Shen Te?" A knock. Enter Wong.*)

WONG. Mr. Shui Ta, I've come to ask when Miss Shen Te will be back, it's six months now . . . There are rumors. People say something's happened to her.

SHUI TA. I'm busy. Come back next week.

WONG (*excited*). In the morning there was always rice on her doorstep—for the needy. It's been there again lately!

SHUI TA. And what do people conclude from this?

WONG. That Shen Te is still in Setzuan! She's been . . . (*He breaks off.*)

SHUI TA. She's been what? Mr. Wong, if you're Shen Te's friend, talk a little less about her, that's my advice to you.

WONG. I don't want your advice! Before she disappeared, Miss Shen Te told me something very important—she's pregnant!

YANG SUN. What? What was that?

SHUI TA (*quickly*). The man is lying.

WONG. A good woman isn't so easily forgotten. Mr. Shui Ta.

(*He leaves. Shui Ta goes quickly into the back room.*)

YANG SUN (*to the audience*). Shen Te pregnant? So that's why. Her cousin sent her away, so I wouldn't get wind of it. I have a son, a Yang appears on the scene, and what happens? Mother and child vanish into thin air! That scoundrel, that unspeakable . . . (*The sound of sobbing is heard from the back room.*) What was that? Someone sobbing? Who was it? Mr. Shui Ta the Tobacco King doesn't weep his heart out. And where does the rice come from that's on the doorstep in the morning?

(*Shui Ta returns. He goes to the door and looks out into the rain.*)

Where is she?

SHUI TA. Sh! It's nine o'clock. But the rain's so heavy, you can't hear a thing.

YANG SUN. What do you want to hear?

SHUI TA. The mail plane.

YANG SUN. What?

SHUI TA. I've been told *you* wanted to fly at one time. Is that all forgotten?

YANG SUN. Flying mail is night work. I prefer the daytime. And the firm is very dear to me—after all it belongs to my ex-fiancée, even if she's not around. And she's not, is she?

SHUI TA. What do you mean by that?

YANG SUN. Oh, well, let's say I haven't altogether—lost interest.

SHUI TA. My cousin might like to know that.

YANG SUN. I might not be indifferent—if I found she was being kept under lock and key.

SHUI TA. By whom?

YANG SUN. By you.

SHUI TA. What could you do about it?

YANG SUN. I could submit for discussion—my position in the firm.

SHUI TA. You are now my Manager. In return for a more appropriate position, you might agree to drop the enquiry into your ex-fiancée's whereabouts?

YANG SUN. I might.

SHUI TA. What position *would* be more appropriate?

YANG SUN. The one at the top.

SHUI TA. My own? (*Silence.*) And if I preferred to throw you out on your neck?

YANG SUN. I'd come back on my feet. With suitable escort.

SHUI TA. The police?

YANG SUN. The police.

SHUI TA. And when the police found no one?

YANG SUN. I might ask them not to overlook the back room. (*Ending the pretense.*) In short, Mr. Shui Ta, my interest in this young woman has not been officially terminated. I should like to see more of her. (*Into Shui Ta's face.*) Besides, she's pregnant and needs a friend. (*He moves to the door.*) I shall talk about it with the Water Seller.

(*Exit.*)

(*Shui Ta is rigid for a moment, then he quickly goes into the back room. He returns with Shen Te's belongings: underwear, etc. He takes a long look at the shawl of the previous scene. He then wraps the things in a bundle which,* upon hearing a noise, he hides under the table. Enter Mrs. Mi Tzu and Mr. Shu Fu. They put away their umbrellas and galoshes.*)

MRS. MI TZU. I thought your manager was here, Mr. Shu Ta. He combines charm with business in a way that can only be to the advantage of all of us.

SHU FU. You sent for us, Mr. Shui Ta?

SHUI TA. The factory is in trouble.

SHU FU. It always is.

SHUI TA. The police are threatening to close us down unless I can show that the extension of our facilities is imminent.

SHU FU. Mr. Shui Ta, I'm sick and tired of your constantly expanding projects. I place cabins at your cousin's disposal; you make a factory of them. I hand your cousin a check; you present it. Your cousin disappears and you find the cabins too small and talk of yet more . . .

SHUI TA. Mr. Shu Fu, I'm authorized to inform you that Miss Shen Te's return is now imminent.

SHU FU. Imminent? It's becoming his favorite word.

MRS. MI TZU. Yes, what does it mean?

SHUI TA. Mrs. Mi Tzu, I can pay you exactly half what you asked for your buildings. Are you ready to inform the police that I am taking them over?

MRS. MI TZU. Certainly, if I can take over your manager.

SHU FU. What?

MRS. MI TZU. He's so efficient.

SHUI TA. I'm afraid I need Mr. Yang Sun.

MRS. MI TZU. So do I.

SHUI TA. He will call on you tomorrow.

SHU FU. So much the better. With Shen Te likely to turn up at any moment, the presence of that young man is hardly in good taste.

SHUI TA. So we have reached a settlement. In what was once the good Shen Te's little shop we are laying the foundations for the great Mr. Shui Ta's twelve magnificent super tobacco markets. You will bear in mind that though they call me the Tobacco King of Setzuan, it is my cousin's interests that have been served . . .

VOICES (*off*). The police, the police! Going to the tobacco shop! Something must have happened! (*et cetera.*)

(*Enter Yang Sun, Wong, and the Policeman.*)

POLICEMAN. Quiet there, quiet, quiet! (*They quiet down.*) I'm sorry, Mr. Shui Ta, but there's a report that you've been depriving Miss Shen Te of her freedom. Not that I believe all I hear, but the whole city's in an uproar.

SHUI TA. That's a lie.

POLICEMAN. Mr. Yang Sun has testified that he heard someone sobbing in the back room.

SHU FU. Mrs. Mi Tzu and myself will testify that no one here has been sobbing.

MRS. MI TZU. We have been quietly smoking our cigars.

POLICEMAN. Mr. Shui Ta, I'm afraid I shall have to take a look at that room. (*He does so. The room is empty.*) No one there, of course, sir.

YANG SUN. But I hear sobbing. What's that? (*He finds the clothes.*)

WONG. Those are Shen Te's things. (*To crowd.*) Shen Te's clothes are here!

VOICES (*Off. In sequence*). Shen Te's clothes! They've been found under the table! Body of murdered girl still missing! Tobacco King suspected!

POLICEMAN. Mr. Shui Ta, unless you can tell us where the girl is, I'll have to ask you to come along.

SHUI TA. I do not know.

POLICEMAN. I can't say how sorry I am, Mr. Shui Ta. (*He shows him the door.*)

SHUI TA. Everything will be cleared up in no time. There are still judges in Setzuan.

YANG SUN. I heard sobbing!

SCENE 9A

(*Wong's den. For the last time, the Gods appear to the Water Seller in his dream. They have changed and show signs of a long journey, extreme fatigue, and plenty of mishaps. The First no longer has a hat; the Third has lost a leg; all Three are barefoot.*)

WONG. Illustrious ones, at last you're here. Shen Te's been gone for months and today her cousin's been arrested. They think he murdered her to get the shop. But I had a dream and in this dream Shen Te said her cousin was keeping her prisoner. You must find her for us, illustrious ones!

FIRST GOD. We've found very few good people anywhere, and even they didn't keep it up. Shen Te is still the only one that stayed good.

SECOND GOD. If she *has* stayed good.

WONG. Certainly she has. But she's vanished.

FIRST GOD. That's the last straw. All is lost!

SECOND GOD. A little moderation, dear colleague!

FIRST GOD (*plaintively*). What's the good of moderation now? If she can't be found, we'll have to resign! The world is a terrible place! Nothing but misery, vulgarity, and waste! Even the countryside isn't what it used to be. The trees are getting their heads chopped off by telephone wires, and there's such a noise from all the gunfire, and I can't stand those heavy clouds of smoke, and—

THIRD GOD. The place is absolutely unlivable! Good intentions bring people to the brink of the abyss, and good deeds push them over the edge. I'm afraid our book of rules is destined for the scrap heap—

SECOND GOD. It's people! They're a worthless lot!

THIRD GOD. The world is too cold!

SECOND GOD. It's people! They are too weak!

FIRST GOD. Dignity, dear colleagues, dignity! Never despair! As for this world, didn't we agree that we only have to find one human being who can stand the place? Well, we

found her. True, we lost her again. We must find her again, that's all! And at once!

(*They disappear.*)

SCENE 10

(*Courtroom. Groups: Shu Fu and Mrs. Mi Tzu; Yang Sun and Mrs. Yang; Wong, the Carpenter, the Grandfather, the Niece, the Old Man, the Old Woman; Mrs. Shin, the Policeman; the Unemployed Man, the Sister-in-Law.*)

OLD MAN. So much power isn't good for one man.

UNEMPLOYED MAN. And he's going to open twelve super tobacco markets!

WIFE. One of the judges is a friend of Mr. Shu Fu's.

SISTER-IN-LAW. Another one accepted a present from Mr. Shui Ta only last night. A great fat goose.

OLD WOMAN (*to Wong*). And Shen Te is nowhere to be found.

WONG. Only the gods will ever know the truth.

POLICEMAN. Order in the court! My lords the judges!

(*Enter the Three Gods in judges' robes. We overhear their conversation as they pass along the footlights to their bench.*)

THIRD GOD. We'll never get away with it, our certificates were so badly forged.

SECOND GOD. My predecessor's "sudden indigestion" will certainly cause comment.

FIRST GOD. But he *had* just eaten a whole goose.

UNEMPLOYED MAN. Look at that! *New* judges!

WONG. New judges. And what good ones!

(*The Third God hears this, and turns to smile at Wong. The Gods sit. The First God beats on the bench with his gavel. The Policeman brings in Shui Ta who walks with lordly steps. He is whistled at.*)

POLICEMAN (*to Shui Ta*). Be prepared for a surprise. The judges have been changed.

(*Shui Ta turns quickly round, looks at them, and staggers.*)

NIECE. What's the matter now?

WIFE. The great Tobacco King nearly fainted.

HUSBAND. Yes, as soon as he saw the new judges.

WONG. Does *he* know who they are?

(*Shui Ta picks himself up, and the proceedings open.*)

FIRST GOD. Defendant Shui Ta, you are accused of doing away with your cousin Shen Te in order to take possession of her business. Do you plead guilty or not guilty?

SHUI TA. Not guilty, my lord.

FIRST GOD (*thumbing through the documents of the case*). The first witness is the Policeman. I shall ask him to tell us something of the respective reputations of Miss Shen Te and Mr. Shui Ta.

POLICEMAN. Miss Shen Te was a young lady who aimed to please, my lord. She liked to live and let live, as the saying goes. Mr. Shui Ta, on the other hand, is a man of principle. Though the generosity of Miss Shen Te forced him at times to abandon half measures, unlike the girl, he was always on the side of the law, my lord. One time, he even unmasked a gang of thieves to whom his too trustful cousin had given shelter. The evidence, in short, my lord, proves that Mr. Shui Ta was *incapable* of the crime of which he stands accused!

FIRST GOD. I see. And are there others who could testify along, shall we say, the same lines?

(*Shu Fu rises.*)

POLICEMAN (*whispering to Gods*). Mr. Shu Fu—a very important person.

FIRST GOD (*inviting him to speak*). Mr. Shu Fu!

SHU FU. Mr. Shui Ta is a businessman, my lord. Need I say more?

FIRST GOD. Yes.

SHU FU. Very well, I will. He is Vice President of the Council of Commerce and is about to be elected a Justice of the Peace. (*He returns to his seat.*)

WONG. Elected! *He* gave him the job!

(*With a gesture the First God asks who Mrs. Mi Tzu is.*)

POLICEMAN. Another very important person. Mrs. Mi Tzu.

FIRST GOD (*inviting her to speak*). Mrs. Mi Tzu!

MRS. MI TZU. My lord, as Chairman of the Committee on Social Work, I wish to call attention to just a couple of eloquent facts: Mr. Shui Ta not only has erected a model factory with model housing in our city, he is a regular contributor to our home for the disabled. (*She returns to her seat.*)

POLICEMAN (*whispering*). And she's a great friend of the judge that ate the goose!

FIRST GOD (*to the Policeman*). Oh, thank you. What next? (*To the Court, genially.*) Oh, yes. We should find out if any of the evidence is less favorable to the Defendant.

(*Wong, the Carpenter, the Old Man, the Old Woman, the Unemployed Man, the Sister-in-Law, and the Niece come forward.*)

POLICEMAN (*whispering*). Just the riff raff, my lord.

FIRST GOD (*addressing the "riff raff"*). Well, um, riff raff—do you know anything of the Defendant, Mr. Shui Ta?

WONG. Too much, my lord.

UNEMPLOYED MAN. What don't we know, my lord?

CARPENTER. He ruined us.

SISTER-IN-LAW. He's a cheat.

NIECE. Liar.

WIFE. Thief.

BOY. Blackmailer.

BROTHER. Murderer.

FIRST GOD. Thank you. We should now let the Defendant state his point of view.

SHUI TA. I only came on the scene when Shen Te was in danger of losing what I had understood was a gift from the gods. Because I did the filthy jobs which someone had to do, they hate me. My activities were held down to the minimum, my lord.

SISTER-IN-LAW. He had us arrested!

SHUI TA. Certainly. You stole from the bakery!

SISTER-IN-LAW. Such concern for the bakery! You didn't want the shop for yourself, I suppose!

SHUI TA. I didn't want the shop overrun with parasites.

SISTER-IN-LAW. We had nowhere else to go.

SHUI TA. There were too many of you.

WONG. What about this old couple: Were *they* parasites?

OLD MAN. We lost our shop because of you!

SISTER-IN-LAW. And we gave your cousin money!

SHUI TA. My cousin's fiancé was a flyer. The money had to go to *him*.

WONG. Did you care whether he flew or not? Did you care whether she married him or not? You wanted her to marry someone else! (*He points at Shu Fu.*)

SHUI TA. The flyer unexpectedly turned out to be a scoundrel.

YANG SUN (*jumping up*). Which was the reason you made him your Manager?

SHUI TA. Later on he improved.

WONG. And when he improved, you sold him to her? (*He points out Mrs. Mi Tzu.*)

SHUI TA. She wouldn't let me have her premises unless she had him to stroke her knees!

MRS. MI TZU. What? The man's a pathological liar. (*To him.*) Don't mention my property to me as long as you live! Murderer! (*She rustles off, in high dudgeon.*)

YANG SUN (*pushing in*). My lord, I wish to speak for the Defendant.

SISTER-IN-LAW. Naturally. He's your employer.

UNEMPLOYED MAN. And the worst slave driver in the country.

MRS. YANG. That's a lie! My lord, Mr. Shui Ta is a great man. He . . .

YANG SUN. He's this and he's that, but he is not a murderer, my lord. Just fifteen minutes before his arrest I heard Shen Te's voice in his own back room.

FIRST GOD. Oh? Tell us more!

YANG SUN. I heard sobbing, my lord!

FIRST GOD. But lots of women sob, we've been finding.

YANG SUN. Could I fail to recognize her voice?

SHU FU. No, you made her sob so often yourself, young man!

YANG SUN. Yes. But I also made her happy. Till he (*pointing at Shui Ta*) decided to sell her to you!

SHUI TA. Because you didn't love her.

WONG. Oh, no: it was for the money, my lord!

SHUI TA. And what was the money for, my lord? For the poor! And for Shen Te so she could go on being good!

WONG. For the poor? That he sent to his sweatshops? And why didn't you let Shen Te be good when you signed the big check?

SHUI TA. For the child's sake, my lord.

CARPENTER. What about *my* children? What did he do about them?

(*Shui Ta is silent.*)

WONG. The shop was to be a fountain of goodness. That was the gods' idea. You came and spoiled it!

SHUI TA. If I hadn't, it would have run dry!

MRS. SHIN. There's a lot in that, my lord.

WONG. What have you done with the good Shen Te, bad man? She *was* good, my lords, she was, I swear it! (*He raises his hand in an oath.*)

THIRD GOD. What's happened to your hand, Water Seller?

WONG (*pointing to Shui Ta*). It's all his fault, my lord, *she* was going to send me to a doctor—(*To Shui Ta.*) You were her worst enemy!

SHUI TA. I was her only friend!

WONG. Where is she then? Tell us where your good friend is!

(*The excitement of this exchange has run through the whole crowd.*)

ALL. Yes, where is she? Where is Shen Te? (*et cetera.*)

SHUI TA. Shen Te had to go.

WONG. Where? Where to?

SHUI TA. I cannot tell you! I cannot tell you!

ALL. Why? Why did she have to go away? (*et cetera.*)

WONG (*into the din with the first words, but talking on beyond the others*). Why not, why not? Why did she have to go away?

SHUI TA (*shouting*). Because you'd all have torn her to shreds, that's why! My lords, I have a request. Clear the court! When only the judges remain, I will make a confession.

ALL (*except Wong, who is silent, struck by the new turn of events*). So he's guilty? He's confessing! (*et cetera.*)

FIRST GOD (*using the gavel*). Clear the court!

POLICEMAN. Clear the court!

WONG. Mr. Shui Ta has met his match this time.

MRS. SHIN (*with a gesture toward the judges*). You're in for a little surprise.

(*The court is cleared. Silence.*)

SHUI TA. Illustrious ones!

(*The Gods look at each other, not quite believing their ears.*)

SHUI TA. Yes, I recognize you!

SECOND GOD (*taking matters in hand, sternly*). What have you done with our good woman of Setzuan?

SHUI TA. I have a terrible confession to make: I am she! (*He takes off his mask, and tears away his clothes. Shen Te stands there.*)

SECOND GOD. Shen Te!

SHEN TE. Shen Te, yes. Shui Ta *and* Shen Te. Both.
  Your injunction
  To be good and yet to live
  Was a thunderbolt:
  It has torn me in two
  I can't tell how it was
  But to be good to others
  And myself at the same time
  I could not do it
  Your world is not an easy one, illustrious ones!
  When we extend our hand to a beggar, he tears it off
      for us
  When we help the lost, we are lost ourselves.
  And so
  Since not to eat is to die
  Who can long refuse to be bad?
  As I lay prostrate beneath the weight of good
      intentions
  Ruin stared me in the face
  It was when I was unjust that I ate good meat
  And hobnobbed with the mighty
  Why?
  Why are bad deeds rewarded?
  Good ones punished?
  I enjoyed giving
  I truly wished to be the Angel of the Slums
  But washed by a foster-mother in the water of the
      gutter
  I developed a sharp eye
  The time came when pity was a thorn in my side
  And, later, when kind words turned to ashes in my
      mouth
  And anger took over
  I became a wolf
  Find me guilty, then, illustrious ones,
  But know:
  All that I have done I did
  To help my neighbor
  To love my lover
  And to keep my little one from want
  For your great, godly deeds, I was too poor, too small.

(*Pause.*)

FIRST GOD (*shocked*). Don't go on making yourself miserable, Shen Te! We're overjoyed to have found you!

SHEN TE. I'm telling you I'm the bad man who committed all those crimes!

FIRST GOD (*using—or failing to use—his ear trumpet*). The good woman who did all those good deeds?

SHEN TE. Yes, but the bad man too!

FIRST GOD (*as if something had dawned*). Unfortunate coincidences! Heartless neighbors!

THIRD GOD (*shouting in his ear*). But how is she to continue?

FIRST GOD. Continue? Well, she's a strong, healthy girl . . .

SECOND GOD. You didn't hear what she said!

FIRST GOD. I heard every word! She is confused, that's all! (*He begins to bluster.*) And what about this book of rules—we can't renounce our rules, can we? (*More quietly.*) Should the world be changed? How? By whom? The world should *not* be changed! (*At a sign from him, the lights turn pink, and music plays.*)

> And now the hour of parting is at hand.
> Dost thou behold, Shen Te, yon fleecy cloud?
> It is our chariot. At a sign from me
> 'Twill come and take us back from whence we came
> Above the azure vault and silver stars . . .

SHEN TE. No! Don't go, illustrious ones!

FIRST GOD.

> Our cloud has landed now in yonder field
> From whence it will transport us back to heaven.
> Farewell, Shen Te, let not thy courage fail thee . . .

(*Exeunt Gods.*)

SHEN TE. What about the old couple? They've lost their shop! What about the Water Seller and his hand? And I've got to defend myself against the barber, because I don't love him! And against Sun, because I do love him! How? How?

(*Shen Te's eyes follow the Gods as they are imagined to step into a cloud which rises and moves forward over the orchestra and up beyond the balcony*)

FIRST GOD (*from on high*). We have faith in you, Shen Te!

SHEN TE. There'll be a child. And he'll have to be fed. I can't stay here. Where shall I go?

FIRST GOD. Continue to be good, good woman of Setzuan!

SHEN TE. I need my bad cousin!

FIRST GOD. But not very often!

SHEN TE. Once a week at least!

FIRST GOD. Once a month will be quite enough!

SHEN TE (*shrieking*). No, no! Help!

(*But the cloud continues to recede as the Gods sing.*)

VALEDICTORY HYMN

> What rapture, oh, it is to know
>   A good thing when you see it
> And having seen a good thing, oh,
> What rapture 'tis to flee it
> Be good, sweet maid of Setzuan
>   Let Shui Ta be clever
> Departing, we forget the man
>   Remember your endeavor
> Because through all the length of days
>   Her goodness faileth never
> Sing hallelujah! May Shen Te's
>   Good name live on forever!

SHEN TE. Help!

Epilogue

> You're thinking, aren't you, that this is no right
> Conclusion to the play you've seen tonight?
> After a tale, exotic, fabulous,
> A nasty ending was slipped up on us.
> We feel deflated too. We too are nettled
> To see the curtain down and nothing settled.
> How could a better ending be arranged?
> Could one change people? Can the world be changed?
> Would new gods do the trick? Will atheism?
> Moral rearmament? Materialism?
> It is for you to find a way, my friends,
> To help good men arrive at happy ends.
> *You* write the happy ending to the play!
> There must, there must, there's got to be a way!

"Alienation Effects in Chinese Acting"

BERTOLT BRECHT

The following is intended to refer briefly to the use of the alienation effect in traditional Chinese acting. This method was most recently used in Germany for plays of a non-aristotelian (not dependent on empathy) type as part of the attempts[1] being made to evolve an epic theatre. The efforts in question were directed to playing in such a way that the audience was hindered from simply identifying itself with the characters in the play. Acceptance or rejection of their actions and utterances was meant to take place on a conscious plane, instead of, as hitherto, in the audience's subconscious.

This effort to make the incidents represented appear strange to the public can be seen in a primitive form in the theatrical and pictorial displays at the old popular fairs. The way the clowns speak and the way the panoramas are painted both embody an act of alienation. The method of painting used to reproduce the picture of "Charles the Bold's flight after the Battle of Murten," as shown at many German fairs, is certainly mediocre; yet the act of alienation which is achieved here (not by the original) is in no wise due to the mediocrity of the copyist. The fleeing commander, his horse, his retinue and the landscape are all quite consciously painted in such a way as to create the impression of an abnormal event, an astonishing disaster. In spite of his inadequacy the painter succeeds brilliantly in bringing out the unexpected. Amazement guides his brush.

Traditional Chinese acting also knows the alienation effect, and applies it most subtly. It is well known that the Chinese theatre uses a lot of symbols. Thus a general will carry little pennants on his shoulder, corresponding to the number of regiments under his command. Poverty is shown by patching the silken costumes with irregular shapes of different colours, likewise silken, to indicate that they have been mended. Characters are distinguished by particular masks, i.e. simply by painting. Certain gestures of the two hands signify the forcible opening of a door, etc. The stage itself remains the same, but articles of furniture are carried in during the action. All this has long been known, and cannot very well be exported.

It is not all that simple to break with the habit of assimilating a work of art as a whole. But this has to be done if just one of a large number of effects is to be singled out and studied. The alienation effect is achieved in the Chinese theatre in the following way.

[1]Brecht uses the word "Versuche."

Above all, the Chinese artist never acts as if there were a fourth wall besides the three surrounding him. He expresses his awareness of being watched. This immediately removes one of the European stage's characteristic illusions. The audience can no longer have the illusion of being the unseen spectator at an event which is really taking place. A whole elaborate European stage technique, which helps to conceal the fact that the scenes are so arranged that the audience can view them in the easiest way, is thereby made unnecessary. The actors openly choose those positions which will show them off to the audience, just as if they were *acrobats*. A further means is that the artist observes himself. Thus if he is representing a cloud, perhaps, showing its unexpected appearance, its soft and strong growth, its rapid yet gradual transformation, he will occasionally look at the audience as if to say: isn't it just like that? At the same time he also observes his own arms and legs, adducing them, testing them and perhaps finally approving them. An obvious glance at the floor, so as to judge the space available to him for his act, does not strike him as liable to break the illusion. In this way the artists separates mime (showing observation) from gesture (showing a cloud), but without detracting from the latter, since the body's attitude is reflected in the face and is wholly responsible for its expression. At one moment the expression is of well-managed restraint; at another, of utter triumph. The artist has been using his countenance as a blank sheet, to be inscribed by the gest of the body.

The artist's object is to appear strange and even surprising to the audience. He achieves this by looking strangely at himself and his work. As a result everything put forward by him has a touch of the amazing. Everyday things are thereby raised above the level of the obvious and automatic. A young woman, a fisherman's wife, is shown paddling a boat. She stands steering a non-existent boat with a paddle that barely reaches to her knees. Now the current is swifter, and she is finding it harder to keep her balance; now she is in a pool and paddling more easily. Right: that is how one manages a boat. But this journey in the boat is apparently historic, celebrated in many songs, an exceptional journey about which everybody knows. Each of this famous girl's movements has probably been recorded in pictures; each bend in the river was a well-known adventure story, it is even known which particular bend it was. This feeling on the audience's part is induced by the artist's attitude; it is this that makes the journey famous. The scene reminded us of the march to Budejovice in Piscator's production of *The Good Soldier Schweik*. Schweik's three-day-and-night march to a front which he oddly enough never gets to was seen from a completely historic point of view, as no less noteworthy a phenomenon than,

(continued)

for instance, Napoleon's Russian expedition of 1812. The performer's self-observation, an artful and artistic act of self-alienation, stopped the spectator from losing himself in the character completely, i.e. to the point of giving up his own identity, and lent a splendid remoteness to the events. Yet the spectator's empathy was not entirely rejected. The audience identifies itself with the actor as being an observer, and accordingly develops his attitude of observing or looking on.

The Chinese artist's performance often strikes the Western actor as cold. That does not mean that the Chinese theatre rejects all representation of feelings. The performer portrays incidents of utmost passion, but without his delivery becoming heated. At those points where the character portrayed is deeply excited the performer takes a lock of hair between his lips and chews it. But this is like a ritual, there is nothing eruptive about it. It is quite clearly somebody else's repetition of the incident: a representation, even though an artistic one. The performer shows that this man is not in control of himself, and he points to the outward signs. And so lack of control is decorously expressed, or if not decorously at any rate decorously for the stage. Among all the possible signs certain particular ones are picked out, with careful and visible consideration. Anger is naturally different from sulkiness, hatred from distaste, love from liking; but the corresponding fluctuations of feeling are portrayed economically. The coldness comes from the actor's holding himself remote from the character portrayed, along the lines described. Nobody gets raped by the individual he portrays; this individual is not the spectator himself but his neighbour.

The Western actor does all he can to bring his spectator into the closest proximity to the events and the character he has to portray. To this end he persuades him to identify himself with him (the actor) and uses every energy to convert himself as completely as possible into a different type, that of the character in question. If this complete conversion succeeds then his art has been more or less expended. Once he has become the bank-clerk, doctor or general concerned he will need no more art than any of these people need "in real life."

This complete conversion operation is extremely exhausting. Stanislavsky puts forward a series of means—a complete system—by which what he calls "creative mood" can repeatedly be manufactured afresh at every performance. For the actor cannot usually manage to feel for very long on end that he really is the other person; he soon gets exhausted and begins just to copy various superficialities of the other person's speech and hearing, whereupon the effect on the public drops off alarmingly. This is certainly due to the fact that the other person has been created by an "intuitive" and accordingly murky process which takes place in the subconscious. The subconscious is not at all responsive to guidance; it has as it were a bad memory.

These problems are unknown to the Chinese performer, for he rejects complete conversion. He limits himself from the start to simply quoting the character played. But with what art he does this! He only needs a minimum of illusion. What he has to show is worth seeing even for a man in his right mind. What Western actor of the old sort (apart from one or two comedians) could demonstrate the elements of his art like the Chinese actor Mei Lan-fang, without special lighting and wearing a dinner jacket in an ordinary room full of specialists? It would be like the magician at a fair giving away his tricks, so that nobody ever wanted to see the act again. He would just be showing how to disguise oneself; the hypnotism would vanish and all that would be left would be a few pounds of ill-blended imitation, a quickly mixed product for selling in the dark to hurried customers. Of course no Western actor would stage such a demonstration. What about the sanctity of Art? The mysteries of metamorphosis? To the Westerner what matters is that his actions should be unconscious; otherwise they would be degraded. By comparison with Asiatic acting our own art still seems hopelessly parsonical. None the less it is becoming increasingly difficult for our actors to bring off the mystery of complete conversion; their subconscious's memory is getting weaker and weaker, and it is almost impossible to extract the truth from the uncensored intuitions of any member of our class society even when the man is a genius.

For the actor it is difficult and taxing to conjure up particular inner moods or emotions night after night; it is simpler to exhibit the outer signs which accompany these emotions and identify them. In this case, however, there is not the same automatic transfer of emotions to the spectator, the same emotional infection. The alienation effect intervenes, not in the form of absence of emotion, but in the form of emotions which need not correspond to those of the character portrayed. On seeing worry the spectator may feel a sensation of joy; on seeing anger, one of disgust. When we speak of exhibiting the outer signs of emotion we do not mean such an exhibition and such a choice of signs that the emotional transference does in fact take place because the actor has managed to infect himself with the emotions portrayed, by exhibiting the outer signs; thus, by letting his voice rise, holding his breath and tightening his neck muscles so that the blood shoots to his head, the actor can easily conjure up a rage. In such a case of course the effect does not occur. But it does occur if the actor at a particular point unexpectedly shows a completely white face, which he has produced mechanically by holding his face in his hands with some white make-up on them. If the actor at the same time displays an apparently composed character, then his terror at this point (as a result of this message, or that discovery) will give rise to an alienation effect. Acting like this is healthier and in our view less unworthy of a thinking being; it demands a considerable knowledge of humanity and wordly wisdom, and a keen eye for what is socially important. In this case too there is of course a creative process at work; but it is a higher one, because it is raised to the conscious level.

The alienation effect does not in any way demand an unnatural way of acting. It has nothing whatever to do with ordinary stylization. On the contrary, the achievement of an A-effect absolutely depends on lightness and naturalness of performance. But when the actor checks the truth of his performance (a necessary operation, which Stanislavsky is much concerned with in his system) he is not just thrown back on his "natural sensibilities," but can always be corrected by a comparison with reality (is that how an angry man really speaks? is that how an offended man sits down?) and so from outside, by other people. He acts in such a way that nearly every sentence could be followed by a verdict of the audience and practically every gesture is submitted for the public's approval.

The Chinese performer is in no trance. He can be interrupted at any moment. He won't have to "come round." After an interruption he will go on with his exposition from that point. We are not disturbing him at the "mystic moment of creation"; when he steps on to the stage before us the process of creation is already over. He does not mind if the setting is changed around him as he plays. Busy hands quite openly pass him what he needs for his performance. When Mei Lan-fang was playing a death scene a spectator sitting next me exclaimed with astonishment at one of his gestures. One or two people sitting in front of us turned round indignantly and sshhh'd. They behaved as if they were present at the real death of a real girl. Possibly their attitude would have been all right for a European production, but for a Chinese it was unspeakably ridiculous. In their case the A-effect had misfired.

It is not entirely easy to realize that the Chinese actor's A-effect is a transportable piece of technique: a conception that can be pried loose from the Chinese theatre. We see this theatre as uncommonly precious, its portrayal of human passions as schematized, its idea of society as rigid and wrong-headed; at first sight this superb art seems to offer nothing applicable to a realistic and revolutionary theatre. Against that, the motives and objects of the A-effect strike us as odd and suspicious.

When one sees the Chinese acting it is at first very hard to discount the feeling of estrangement which they produce in us as Europeans. One has to be able to imagine them achieving an A-effect among their Chinese spectators too. What is still harder is that one must accept the fact that when the Chinese performer conjures up an impression of mystery he seems uninterested in disclosing a mystery to us. He makes his own mystery from the mysteries of nature (especially human nature): he allows nobody to examine how he produces the natural phenomenon, nor does nature allow him to understand as he produces it. We have here the artistic counterpart of a primitive technology, a rudimentary science. The Chinese performer gets his A-effect by association with magic. "How it's done" remains hidden; knowledge is a matter of knowing the tricks and is in the hands of a few men who guard it jealously and profit from their secrets. And yet there is already an attempt here to interfere with the course of nature; the capacity to do so leads to questioning; and the future explorer, with his anxiety to make nature's course intelligible, controllable and down-to-earth, will always start by adopting a standpoint from which it seems mysterious, incomprehensible and beyond control. He will take up the attitude of somebody wondering, will apply the A-effect. Nobody can be a mathematician who takes it for granted that "two and two makes four"; nor is anybody one who fails to understand it. The man who first looked with astonishment at a swinging lantern and instead of taking it for granted that it should swing, and swing in that particular way rather than any other, was brought close to understanding the phenomenon by this observation, and so to mastering it. Nor must it simply be exclaimed that the attitude here proposed is all right for science but not for art. Why shouldn't art try, by its *own* means of course, to further the great social task of mastering life.

In point of fact the only people who can profitably study a piece of technique like Chinese acting's A-effect are those who need such a technique for quite definite social purposes.

The experiments conducted by the modern German theatre lead to a wholly independent development of the A-effect. So far Asiatic acting has exerted no influence.

The A-effect was achieved in the German epic theatre not only by the actor, but also by the music (choruses, songs) and the setting (placards, film etc.). It was principally designed to historicize the incidents portrayed. By this is meant the following:

The bourgeois theatre emphasized the timelessness of its objects. Its representation of people is bound by the alleged "eternally human." Its story is arranged in such a way as to create "universal" situations that allow Man with a capital M to express himself: man of every period and every colour. All its incidents are just one enormous cue, and this cue is followed by the "eternal" response: the inevitable, usual, natural, purely human response. An example: a black man falls in love in the same way as a white man; the story forces him to react with the same expressions as the white man (in theory this formula works as well as the other way round); and with that the sphere of art is attained. The cue can take account of what is special, different; the response is shared, there is no element of difference in it. This notion may allow that such a thing as history exists, but it is none the less unhistorical. A few circumstances vary, the environments are altered, but Man remains unchanged. History applies to the environment, not to Man. The environment is remarkably unimportant, is treated simply as a pretext; it is a variable quantity and something remarkably inhuman; it exists in fact apart from Man, confronting him as a coherent whole, whereas he is a fixed quantity, eternally unchanged. The idea of man as a function of the environment and the environment as a function of man, i.e. the breaking up of the environment into relationships between men, corresponds to a new way of thinking, the historical way. Rather than be sidetracked into the philosophy of history, let us give an example. Suppose the following is to be shown on the stage: a girl leaves home in order to take a job in a fair-sized city (Piscator's *American Tragedy*). For the bourgeois theatre this is an insignificant affair, clearly the beginning of a story; it is what one has to have been told in order to understand what comes after, or to be keyed up for it. The actor's imagination will hardly be greatly fired by it. In a sense the incident is universal: girls take jobs (in the case in question one can be keyed up to see what in particular is going to happen to her). Only in one way is it particular: this girl goes away (if she had remained what comes after would not have happened). The fact that her family lets her go is not the object of the inquiry; it is understandable (the motives are understandable). But for the historicizing theatre everything is different. The theatre concentrates entirely on whatever in this perfectly everyday event is remarkable, particular and demanding inquiry. What! A family letting one of its members leave the nest to earn her future living independently and without help? Is she up to it? Will what she has learnt here as a member of the family help her to earn her living? Can't families keep a grip on their

(continued)

children any longer? Have they become (or remained) a burden? Is it like that with every family? Was it always like that? Is this the way of the world, something that can't be affected? The fruit falls off the tree when ripe: does this sentence apply here? Do children always make themselves independent? Did they do so in every age? If so, and if it's something biological, does it always happen in the same way, for the same reasons and with the same results? These are the questions (or a few of them) that the actors must answer if they want to show the incident as a unique, historical one: if they want to demonstrate a custom which leads to conclusions about the entire structure of a society at a particular (transient) time. But how is such an incident to be represented if its historical character is to be brought out? How can the confusion of our unfortunate epoch be striking? When the mother, in between warnings and moral injunctions, packs her daughter's case—a very small one—how is the following to be shown: So many injunctions and so few clothes? Moral injunctions for a lifetime and bread for five hours? How is the actress to speak the mother's sentence as she hands over such a very small case—"There, I guess that ought to do you"—in such way that it is understood as a historic dictim? This can only be achieved if the A-effect is brought out. The actress must not make the sentence her own affair, she must hand it over for criticism, she must help us to understand its causes and protest. The effect can only be got by long training. In the New York Yiddish Theatre, a highly progressive theatre, I saw a play by S. Ornitz showing the rise of an East Side boy to be a big crooked attor-ney. The theatre could not perform the play. And yet there were scenes like this in it: the young attorney sits in the street outside his house giving cheap legal advice. A young woman arrives and complains that her leg has been hurt in a traffic accident. But the case has been bungled and her compensation has not yet been paid. In desperation she points to her leg and says: "It's started to heal up." Working without the A-effect, the theatre was unable to make use of this exceptional scene to show the horror of a bloody epoch. Few people in the audience noticed it; hardly anyone who reads this will remember that cry. But it is exactly this—the fact that this poor creature finds such a complaint natural—that she should have reported to the public like a horrified messenger returning from the lowest of all hells. To that end she would of course have needed a special technique which would have allowed her to underline the historical aspect of a specific social condition. Only the A-effect makes this possible. Without it all she can do is to observe how she is not forced to go over entirely into the character on the stage.

In setting up new artistic principles and working out new methods of representation we must start with the compelling demands of a changing epoch; the necessity and the possibility of remodelling society loom ahead. All incidents between men must be noted, and everything must be seen from a social point of view. Among other effects that a new theatre will need for its social criticism and its historical reporting of completed transformation is the A-effect.

DEATH OF A SALESMAN
ARTHUR MILLER

ARTHUR MILLER (1915–)

While Eugene O'Neill was the first American playwright to be widely accepted outside the United States, Arthur Miller is better known internationally and is the most widely produced American playwright.

Born in Harlem, the son of hard-working Jewish immigrants, Miller's early life provided much of the thematic material for his plays. Achieving financial success and then losing it in the stock market crash of 1929, his father's career epitomized the roller coaster ride of the free enterprise system. When the family recovered from the crash, Miller enrolled in the University of Michigan where his playwriting career began. Among the awards his early work received was the 1937 Theater Guild National Award, which he shared with the man who was to become the chief rival to his popularity from 1945 until the early 1960s, Tennessee Williams. In 1944, following a brief stint with the Federal Theater Project, he wrote his first Broadway play, entitled *The Man Who Had All the Luck* which—ironically—closed after only four performances. His next play, *All My Sons*, proved to be much more successful both commercially and critically, earning him the New York Drama Critics Award as the most promising playwright of the 1947 season and his first New York Drama Critics Circle Award. Two years later his most famous play, *Death of a Salesman*, earned him not only his second New York Drama Critics Circle Award, but the Tony Award for best play and the Pulitzer Prize in drama. Although his later plays—the most well known of which are *The Crucible* (1952), *A View from the Bridge* (1955), *After the Fall* (1964), *Incident at Vichy* (1964), *The Price* (1968), *The Creation of the World and Other Business* (1973), *American Clock* (1980), *Broken Glass* (1993), and *The Ride Down Mount Morgan* (1998)—rarely achieved the commercial success or the critical acclaim of the early plays, he has continued to write and his plays have been produced in the United States and throughout Europe. Interestingly, his plays were among the first works to be performed in China after normalization of diplomatic relations began in the 1970s.

Shortly after his early success, he was called before the infamous House Un-American Activities Committee. Like many artists of his day, he was grilled mercilessly about his past and his relationship with the American Communist Party. Unlike many others, he escaped imprisonment and managed to salvage his career. Cited for contempt of court for refusing to "name names" (the citation was later reversed), he was gallant in his stand for the rights of the individual. This episode in his life provided material for *The Crucible*, generally viewed as his indictment of the HUAC hearings.

As a playwright, Miller is an exceptional craftsman. His plays are marked by well-constructed plots; intriguing, highly motivated characters; and brutally honest social themes. Many of his plays, most notably *All My Sons* and *The Price*, are modern versions of the well-made play. In these plays the combination of the withheld secret and the obligatory scene are superbly crafted. However, his work is not limited to this traditional, realistic form. In *Death of a Salesman*, *After the Fall*, and *American Clock* he intricately combines realism and expressionism as his characters freely bound, sometimes in their own minds and sometimes in ours, from one time and place to another, exploring the past and its effects on the present and the future.

His characters are usually strong-willed members of a dysfunctional, middle-class American family. Motivated primarily by materialism, the Kellers in *All My Sons*, the Lomans in *Death of a Salesman*, the Franzes in *The Price*, and the Gellburgs in *Broken Glass* are all so caught up in the struggle to fulfill their individual and collective duties to self, family, and society that they betray not only one another but the values and ethics they so strongly profess.

Thematically, Miller displays two basic concerns: the ruin and disaster precipitated by materialistic evils and the individual's struggle with conscience. Invariably the family father lives a life of lies and delusions as he struggles to obtain the material trappings of the American dream for his family. He grapples with a past error in judgment or unethical action which, unknown to him, has shaped his life. The individual's social and moral responsibilities are examined through such battles.

At the heart of many Miller dramas is also his quest to deal with "Tragedy and the Common Man," which is included as a Forum after this play.

DEATH OF A SALESMAN (1949)

Death of a Salesman is Miller's most widely produced play, staged frequently not only throughout the United States and Canada, but in Latin America and as a popular example of American drama in Europe. In 1983 it was directed by Miller himself in the People's Republic of China.

The play embodies nearly all the components of Miller's writing style: a tightly constructed plot reminiscent of the well-made play; well-rounded, believable characters drawn from the American middle class; and a seamless blending of realism and Expressionism. Thematically, it relies on most of Miller's recurring concerns: a secret past action that plants the seeds of the destruction of the dysfunctional family and its individual members; a father who lives a lie; and the struggle of facing one's responsibility to family and society. Miller accomplishes this by creating a play based, in both content and form, on seeming contradictions. Using what in 1949 were regarded as antithetical styles—realism and expressionism—Miller portrays the simultaneous development and destruction of the American family and the American dream. These contradictions are exemplified by the most powerful image in the play, that of Willy and his sample cases.

As the play opens we see a defeated Willy lugging his worn and shabby sample cases back into the house after yet another failed day on the road. In Miller's words, "his exhaustion is apparent." He is a traveling salesman who can no longer travel and who can no longer sell. Our first glimpse of Willy prepares us for the drama that follows, for it is these cases, symbols of a salesman's life, that will be the death of Willy Loman. What does Willy sell? We are never told. We are told that he has the "best eye for color in the business," that he "open[ed] up unheard of territories," and that "he's vital in New England," but we never know what it is that he sells.

What is in the cases? Willy Loman himself. The cases contain the many contradictory aspects of his life. Contained in one case is what he says and in the other is what he does. In one case are his dreams and in the other is his reality. In one case is the disappearing pastoral environment for which he longs and in the other the encroaching urban society driving him to his grave. In one case are the sons whose potential has been the joy of his life, in the other the sons whose failures have become the bane of his existence. Together, the cases and their contents become Willy's coffin—the means of his livelihood has become the means of his death. He has spent his life living one lie, and he goes to his death believing another. Why do these cases contain so many contradictions? Willy himself is a constant contradiction.

Within minutes of the opening curtain we hear Willy ask Linda, "Why am I always being contradicted?" He is contradicted because those around him are reflecting what is happening in "the inside of his head," Miller's original title of the play. His contradictory nature permeates the play. He describes Biff as "a lazy bum!" then, within minutes, claims, "There's one thing about Biff —he's not lazy." Regarding his car, he says, the "Chevrolet, Linda, is the greatest car ever built!" A moment later he castigates the same vehicle: "They ought to prohibit the manufacture of that automobile." And, when schooling Biff to request a business loan from Bill

Oliver, Willy first cautions his son not "to crack any jokes" because "everybody likes a kidder but nobody lends him money." In the next breath he advises him to "walk in with a big laugh" and "start off with a couple of your best stories."

These verbal contradictions are indicative of Willy's actions throughout the play—he says one thing and then does another. For example, he indicts the boys for the lack of respect they show Linda: "Since when do you let your mother carry the wash up the stairs?" At the same time he is involved with other women on the road. Similarly, he chastises Linda for mending her old stockings while he lavishes new hosiery on secretaries. While he claims that he does not need nor cannot take Charley's money, he does so repeatedly.

Such dichotomies reflect the chasm between his dreams of success and the reality of his mediocrity. In both the past and the present episodes, his dreams of prosperity are belied by the reality of his failure. In the "old days" he dreamed of having "Knocked 'em cold in Providence" and "slaughtered 'em in Boston!," yet it is clear that he was always struggling to make ends meet. In addition to dreaming of sales success, Willy dreams of being not only liked but "well liked." Yet, casual acquaintances, friends, business associates, and even his family only tolerate him. His neighbor, Charley, and his boss, Howard, befriend him not so much because they like him but because they pity him. And Charley's secretary, Jenny, "can't deal with him anymore." His family's impressions of him are not much better. At the moment when Willy needs him most, his son Happy acknowledges Willy not as his father but as "just a guy." Biff, the son he worshipped, is so repulsed by him that he returns home only on rare occasions, reunions that end in quarrels. Even the loyal Linda, while noting that "attention must be finally paid to such a person," concedes that "he's not easy to get along with" and that "no one knows him any more, no one welcomes him."

The contradictions within Willy might be seen as manifestations of a more deeply rooted paradox—Willy's consuming desire to return to the past versus his burning aspirations to be successful in the present. His yearning for days gone by is a quest for simplicity and serenity; his obsession with the present is a quest for "being well liked." These polar quests are incompatible; pursued simultaneously, they turn the present into a vacuum.

The past, which exists only in Willy's memory, is a disappearing pastoral landscape. He remembers when the trees were so thick and the sun so warm that he "opened the windshield and just let the warm air bathe" him. At home he recalls the "lilac and wisteria," the "peonies and the daffodils," and "the fragrance in this room." He reminisces about the backyard graced by stately elms where he and Biff once hung the hammock and watched it "just swingin' there under those branches." And he wonders, "How do we get back to all the great times?" His recollections of the beauty of the past only feed his anger that all the trees are gone and that "they boxed in the whole goddam neighborhood" so that "you can't raise a carrot in the back yard."

The present is a hostile, competitive, urban world where "business is definitely business" and "everybody's gotta pull his own weight." Willy finds "the competition is maddening," and admits that he is "tired to death." He is mystified by the present. Even when Charley tells him "the only thing you got in this world is what you can sell . . . and you don't know that," Willy cannot comprehend this primary tenet of the business world.

The contradictions between Willy's words and his actions, his dreams and his reality, the past and the present are more easily understood if we remember that the play depicts the death of two antithetical salesmen. The first is the "salesman's salesman," the man Willy would like to be—Dave Singleman. The other is the mediocre salesman, the man Willy cannot escape being—Willy Loman. As their names imply, one is a "Singleman," a man who is "one in a million," while the other is a "Lo[w]man," a man who is "a dime a dozen." The death and funeral of the former is a "singular" event attended by hundreds, while the funeral of the other is a common affair attended only by the family, only one of whom is brought to tears by the death of a salesman.

Willy's preoccupation with being another "Singleman" is symbolic of Miller's exploration of the American dream. To Willy, Dave Singleman and his brother Ben personify the American dream, and he envisions himself raising a family that will inhabit this dreamworld. Realizing that he will never achieve this dream, Willy projects this vision onto his sons, who represent the two parts of their father. Biff, the laborer, appreciates the beauty of nature and bygone days, while Happy, the businessman, possesses an "overdeveloped sense of competition." These young men, whom Willy regarded as "Adonises" when they were teens, are now disappointments to him. One is a philanderer and the other a kleptomaniac. Though Willy claims, "I never in my life told [them] anything but decent things," it is he who is responsible for their lifestyles. He not only condoned their thievery, but bragged about it in front of them. As a result, Happy has become another Willy, a man with no awareness of his plight. Because he is his father's son, Happy's pursuit of the American dream is as blind and fruitless as his attempts to gain his father's attention. "I'm losing weight, Pop!" and "I'm gonna be getting married, Mom!" are hollow echoes of Willy's "knocked 'em cold in Providence . . . slaughtered 'em in Boston." Though Biff at first appears headed in the same direction, it is he who evolves into the realist by virtue of two discoveries. First, he realizes that "all I want is out there, waiting for me the minute I say I know who I am!" Equally important is the revelation that not only did Willy have "all the wrong dreams," but the Loman family was "a dime a dozen" and "a dollar an hour"; all "hard working drummers who landed in the ash can like all the rest of them."

Sometimes lost in the contradictions surrounding this death of this salesman are the facts that Willy's dreams were not all bad and that the play is not a condemnation of the free enterprise system. We must remember that while Willy sought success, he also wanted a good life for his family. What he sees in Dave Singleman, although sentimentalized, is the notion that personality, respect, comradeship, and gratitude are worthwhile goals. But unfortunately, Willy sees them as the end rather than as means to an end. He is seemingly ignorant of the fact that it was personality, respect, comradeship, and gratitude that made Dave Singleman successful and not success that made him personable, respected, friendly, and worthy of gratitude. And we must remember that while much that troubles Willy arises out of the notion that sometimes one *does* "eat the orange and throw away the peel," the play also portrays the success of Charley and Bernard, which is in no way indicted as being unethical, evil, or immoral.

Thus, through the use of contradictory styles and images, Miller succeeds in arousing the contradictory feelings of pity for and disgust with the people and events which surround and precipitate *The Death of a Salesman*.

Jo Mielziner's acclaimed expressionistic setting for the Loman household in the 1949 production of Death of a Salesman; *note the sagging roofline—dwarfed by the New York skyline—that mirrors Willy's own exasperation.*

DEATH OF A SALESMAN

Certain Private Conversations in Two Acts and a Requiem

ARTHUR MILLER

CHARACTERS

WILLY LOMAN	CHARLEY
LINDA	UNCLE BEN
BIFF	HOWARD WAGNER
HAPPY	JENNY
BERNARD	STANLEY
THE WOMAN	MISS FORSYTHE
	LETTA

SCENE: *The action takes place in Willy Loman's house and yard and in various places he visits in the New York and Boston of today.*

ACT 1

SCENE: *A melody is heard, played upon a flute. It is small and fine, telling of grass and trees and the horizon. The curtain rises.*

Before us is the Salesman's house. We are aware of towering, angular shapes behind it, surrounding it on all sides. Only the blue light of the sky falls upon the house and forestage; the surrounding area shows an angry glow of orange. As more light appears, we see a solid vault of apartment houses around the small, fragile-seeming home. An air of the dream clings to the place, a dream rising out of reality. The kitchen at center seems actual enough, for there is a kitchen table with three chairs, and a refrigerator. But no other fixtures are seen. At the back of the kitchen there is a draped entrance, which leads to the living room. To the right of the kitchen, on a level raised two feet, is a bedroom furnished only with a brass bedstead and a straight chair. On a shelf over the bed a silver athletic trophy stands. A window opens onto the apartment house at the side.

Behind the kitchen, on a level raised six and a half feet, is the boys' bedroom, at present barely visible. Two beds are dimly seen, and at the back of the room a dormer window. (This bedroom is above the unseen living room.) At the left a stairway curves up to it from the kitchen.

The entire setting is wholly or, in some places, partially transparent. The roof-line of the house is one-dimensional; under and over it we see the apartment buildings. Before the house lies an apron, curving beyond the forestage into the orchestra. This forward area serves as the back yard as well as the locale of all Willy's imaginings and of his city scenes. Whenever the action is in the present the actors observe the imaginary wall-lines, entering the house only through its door at the left. But in the scenes of the past these boundaries are broken, and characters enter or leave a room by stepping "through" a wall onto the forestage.

From the right, Willy Loman, the Salesman, enters, carrying two large sample cases. The flute plays on. He hears but is not aware of it. He is past sixty years of age, dressed quietly. Even as he crosses the stage to the doorway of the house, his exhaustion is apparent. He unlocks the door, comes into the kitchen, and thankfully lets his burden down, feeling the soreness of his palms. A word-sigh escapes his lips—it might be "Oh, boy, oh, boy." He closes the door, then carries his cases out into the living room, through the draped kitchen doorway.

Linda, his wife, has stirred in her bed at the right. She gets out and puts on a robe, listening. Most often jovial, she has developed an iron repression of her exceptions to Willy's behavior—she more than loves him, she admires him, as though his mercurial nature, his temper, his massive dreams and little cruelties, served her only as sharp reminders of the turbulent longings within him, longings which she shares but lacks the temperament to utter and follow to their end.

LINDA [*hearing Willy outside the bedroom, calls with some trepidation*]. Willy!

WILLY. It's all right. I came back.

LINDA. Why? What happened? (*Slight pause.*) Did something happen, Willy?

WILLY. No, nothing happened.

LINDA. You didn't smash the car, did you?

WILLY (*with casual irritation*). I said nothing happened. Didn't you hear me?

LINDA. Don't you feel well?

WILLY. I'm tired to the death. (*The flute has faded away. He sits on the bed beside her, a little numb.*) I couldn't make it. I just couldn't make it, Linda.

LINDA (*very carefully, delicately*). Where were you all day? You look terrible.

WILLY. I got as far as a little above Yonkers. I stopped for a cup of coffee. Maybe it was the coffee.

LINDA. What?

WILLY (*after a pause*). I suddenly couldn't drive any more. The car kept going off onto the shoulder, y'know?

LINDA (*helpfully*). Oh. Maybe it was the steering again. I don't think Angelo knows the Studebaker.

WILLY. No, it's me, it's me. Suddenly I realize I'm goin' sixty miles an hour and I don't remember the last five minutes. I'm—I can't seem to—keep my mind to it.

LINDA. Maybe it's your glasses. You never went for your new glasses.

WILLY. No, I see everything. I came back ten miles an hour. It took me nearly four hours from Yonkers.

LINDA (*resigned*). Well, you'll just have to take a rest, Willy, you can't continue this way.

WILLY. I just got back from Florida.

LINDA. But you didn't rest your mind. Your mind is overactive, and the mind is what counts, dear.

WILLY. I'll start out in the morning. Maybe I'll feel better in the morning. (*She is taking off his shoes.*) These goddam arch supports are killing me.

LINDA. Take an aspirin. Should I get you an aspirin? It'll soothe you.

WILLY (*with wonder*). I was driving along, you understand? And I was fine. I was even observing the scenery. You can imagine, me looking at scenery, on the road every week of my life. But it's so beautiful up there, Linda, the trees are so thick, and the sun is warm. I opened the windshield and just let the warm air bathe over me. And then all of a sudden I'm goin' off the road! I'm tellin' ya, I absolutely forgot I was driving. If I'd've gone the other way over the white line I might've killed somebody. So I went on again—and five minutes later I'm dreamin' again, and I nearly . . . (*He presses two fingers against his eyes.*) I have such thoughts, I have such strange thoughts.

LINDA. Willy, dear. Talk to them again. There's no reason why you can't work in New York.

WILLY. They don't need me in New York. I'm the New England man. I'm vital in New England.

LINDA. But you're sixty years old. They can't expect you to keep traveling every week.

WILLY. I'll have to send a wire to Portland. I'm supposed to see Brown and Morrison tomorrow morning at ten o'clock to show the line. Goddammit, I could sell them! (*He starts putting on his jacket.*)

LINDA (*taking the jacket from him*). Why don't you go down to the place tomorrow and tell Howard you've simply got to work in New York? You're too accommodating, dear.

WILLY. If old man Wagner was alive I'd a been in charge of New York now! That man was a prince, he was a masterful man. But that boy of his, that Howard, he don't appreciate. When I went north the first time, the Wagner Company didn't know where New England was!

LINDA. Why don't you tell those things to Howard, dear?

WILLY (*encouraged*). I will, I definitely will. Is there any cheese?

LINDA. I'll make you a sandwich.

WILLY. No, go to sleep. I'll take some milk. I'll be up right away. The boys in?

LINDA. They're sleeping. Happy took Biff on a date tonight.

WILLY (*interested*). That so?

LINDA. It was so nice to see them shaving together, one behind the other, in the bathroom. And going out together. You notice? The whole house smells of shaving lotion.

WILLY. Figure it out. Work a lifetime to pay off a house. You finally own it, and there's nobody to live in it.

LINDA. Well, dear, life is a casting off. It's always that way.

WILLY. No, no, some people—some people accomplish something. Did Biff say anything after I went this morning?

LINDA. You shouldn't have criticized him, Willy, especially after he just got off the train. You mustn't lose your temper with him.

WILLY. When the hell did I lose my temper? I simply asked him if he was making any money. Is that a criticism?

LINDA. But, dear, how could he make any money?

WILLY (*worried and angered*). There's such an undercurrent in him. He became a moody man. Did he apologize when I left this morning?

LINDA. He was crestfallen, Willy. You know how he admires you. I think if he finds himself, then you'll both be happier and not fight any more.

WILLY. How can he find himself on a farm? Is that a life? A farm hand? In the beginning, when he was young, I thought, well, a young man, it's good for him to tramp around, take a lot of different jobs. But it's more than ten years now and he has yet to make thirty-five dollars a week!

LINDA. He's finding himself, Willy.

WILLY. Not finding yourself at the age of thirty-four is a disgrace!

LINDA. Shh!

WILLY. The trouble is he's lazy, goddammit!

LINDA. Willy, please!

WILLY. Biff is a lazy bum!

LINDA. They're sleeping. Get something to eat. Go on down.

WILLY. Why did he come home? I would like to know what brought him home.

LINDA. I don't know. I think he's still lost, Willy. I think he's very lost.

WILLY. Biff Loman is lost. In the greatest country in the world a young man with such—personal attractiveness, gets lost. And such a hard worker. There's one thing about Biff—he's not lazy.

LINDA. Never.

WILLY (*with pity and resolve*). I'll see him in the morning; I'll have a nice talk with him. I'll get him a job selling. He could be big in no time. My God! Remember how they used to follow him around in high school? When he smiled at one of them their faces lit up. When he walked down the street . . . (*He loses himself in reminiscences.*)

LINDA (*trying to bring him out of it*). Willy, dear, I got a new kind of American-type cheese today. It's whipped.

WILLY. Why do you get American when I like Swiss?

LINDA. I just thought you'd like a change . . .

WILLY. I don't want a change! I want Swiss cheese. Why am I always being contradicted?

LINDA (*with a covering laugh*). I thought it would be a surprise.

WILLY. Why don't you open a window in here, for God's sake?

LINDA (*with infinite patience*). They're all open, dear.

WILLY. The way they boxed us in here. Bricks and windows, windows and bricks.

LINDA. We should've bought the land next door.

WILLY. The street is lined with cars. There's not a breath of fresh air in the neighborhood. The grass don't grow any more, you can't raise a carrot in the back yard. They should've had a law against apartment houses. Remember those two beautiful elm trees out there? When I and Biff hung the swing between them?

LINDA. Yeah, like being a million miles from the city.

WILLY. They should've arrested the builder for cutting those down. They massacred the neighborhood. (*Lost.*) More and more I think of those days, Linda. This time of year it was lilac and wisteria. And then the peonies would come out, and the daffodils. What fragrance in this room!

LINDA. Well, after all, people had to move somewhere.

WILLY. No, there's more people now.

LINDA. I don't think there's more people. I think . . .

WILLY. There's more people! That's what's ruining this country! Population is getting out of control. The competition is maddening! Smell the stink from that apartment house! And another one on the other side . . . How can they whip cheese?

On Willy's last line, Biff and Happy raise themselves up in their beds, listening.

LINDA. Go down, try it. And be quiet.

WILLY (*turning to Linda, guiltily*). You're not worried about me, are you, sweetheart?

BIFF. What's the matter?

HAPPY. Listen!

LINDA. You've got too much on the ball to worry about.

WILLY. You're my foundation and my support, Linda.

LINDA. Just try to relax, dear. You make mountains out of molehills.

WILLY. I won't fight with him any more. If he wants to go back to Texas, let him go.

LINDA. He'll find his way.

WILLY. Sure. Certain men just don't get started till later in life. Like Thomas Edison, I think. Or B. F. Goodrich. One of them was deaf. (*He starts for the bedroom doorway.*) I'll put my money on Biff.

LINDA. And Willy—if it's warm Sunday we'll drive in the country. And we'll open the windshield, and take lunch.

WILLY. No, the windshields don't open on the new cars.

LINDA. But you opened it today.

WILLY. Me? I didn't. (*He stops.*) Now isn't that peculiar! Isn't that a remarkable . . . (*He breaks off in amazement and fright as the flute is heard distantly.*)

LINDA. What, darling?

WILLY. That is the most remarkable thing.

LINDA. What, dear?

WILLY. I was thinking of the Chevvy. (*Slight pause.*) Nineteen twenty-eight . . . when I had that red Chevvy . . . (*Breaks off:*) That funny? I coulda sworn I was driving that Chevvy today.

LINDA. Well, that's nothing. Something must've reminded you.

WILLY. Remarkable. Ts. Remember those days? The way Biff used to simonize that car? The dealer refused to believe there was eighty thousand miles on it. (*He shakes his head.*) Heh! (*To Linda.*) Close your eyes, I'll be right up. (*He walks out of the bedroom.*)

HAPPY (*to Biff*). Jesus, maybe he smashed up the car again!

LINDA (*calling after Willy*). Be careful on the stairs, dear! The cheese is on the middle shelf. (*She turns, goes over to the bed, takes his jacket, and goes out of the bedroom.*)

Light has risen on the boys' room. Unseen, Willy is heard talking to himself; "Eighty thousand miles," and a little laugh. Biff gets out of bed, comes downstage a bit, and stands attentively. Biff is two years older than his brother Happy, well built, but in these days bears a worn air and seems less self-assured. He has succeeded less, and his dreams are stronger and less acceptable than Happy's. Happy is tall, powerfully made. Sexuality is like a visible color on him, or a scent that many women have discovered. He, like his brother, is lost, but in a different way, for he has never allowed himself to turn his face toward defeat and is thus more confused and hard-skinned, although seemingly more content.

HAPPY (*getting out of bed*). He's going to get his license taken away if he keeps that up. I'm getting nervous about him, y'know, Biff?

BIFF. His eyes are going.

HAPPY. No, I've driven with him. He sees all right. He just doesn't keep his mind on it. I drove into the city with him last week. He stops at a green light and then it turns red and he goes. (*He laughs.*)

BIFF. Maybe he's color-blind.

HAPPY. Pop? Why he's got the finest eye for color in the business. You know that.

BIFF (*sitting down on his bed*). I'm going to sleep.

HAPPY. You're not still sour on Dad, are you, Biff?

BIFF. He's all right, I guess.

WILLY (*underneath them, in the living room*). Yes, sir, eighty thousand miles—eighty-two thousand!

BIFF. You smoking?

HAPPY (*holding out a pack of cigarettes*). Want one?

BIFF (*taking a cigarette*). I can never sleep when I smell it.

WILLY. What a simonizing job, heh!

HAPPY (*with deep sentiment*). Funny, Biff, y'know? Us sleeping in here again? The old beds. (*He pats his bed affectionately.*) All the talk that went across those beds, huh? Our whole lives.

BIFF. Yeah. Lotta dreams and plans.

HAPPY (*with a deep and masculine laugh*). About five hundred women would like to know what was said in this room. (*They share a soft laugh.*)

BIFF. Remember that big Betsy something—what the hell was her name—over on Bushwick Avenue?

HAPPY (*combing his hair*). With the collie dog!

BIFF. That's the one. I got you in there, remember?

HAPPY. Yeah, that was my first time—I think. Boy, there was a pig. (*They laugh, almost crudely.*) You taught me everything I know about women. Don't forget that.

BIFF. I bet you forgot how bashful you used to be. Especially with girls.

HAPPY. Oh, I still am, Biff.

BIFF. Oh, go on.

HAPPY. I just control it, that's all. I think I got less bashful and you got more so. What happened, Biff? Where's the old humor, the old confidence? (*He shakes Biff's knee. Biff gets up and moves restlessly about the room.*) What's the matter?

BIFF. Why does Dad mock me all the time?

HAPPY. He's not mocking you, he . . .

BIFF. Everything I say there's a twist of mockery on his face. I can't get near him.

HAPPY. He just wants you to make good, that's all. I wanted to talk to you about Dad for a long time, Biff. Something's—happening to him. He—talks to himself.

BIFF. I noticed that this morning. But he always mumbled.

HAPPY. But not so noticeable. It got so embarrassing I sent him to Florida. And you know something? Most of the time he's talking to you.

BIFF. What's he say about me?

HAPPY. I can't make it out.

BIFF. What's he say about me?

HAPPY. I think the fact that you're not settled, that you're still kind of up in the air . . .

BIFF. There's one or two other things depressing him, Happy.

HAPPY. What do you mean?

BIFF. Never mind. Just don't lay it all to me.

HAPPY. But I think if you just got started—I mean—is there any future for you out there?

BIFF. I tell ya, Hap, I don't know what the future is. I don't know—what I'm supposed to want.

HAPPY. What do you mean?

BIFF. Well, I spent six or seven years after high school trying to work myself up. Shipping clerk, salesman, business of one kind or another. And it's a measly manner of existence. To get on that subway on the hot mornings in summer. To devote your whole life to keeping stock, or making phone calls, or selling or buying. To suffer fifty weeks of the year for the sake of a two-week vacation, when all you really desire is to be outdoors, with your shirt off. And always to have to get ahead of the next fella. And still—that's how you build a future.

HAPPY. Well, you really enjoy it on a farm? Are you content out there?

BIFF (*with rising agitation*). Hap, I've had twenty or thirty different kinds of jobs since I left home before the war, and it always turns out the same. I just realized it lately. In Nebraska when I herded cattle, and the Dakotas, and Arizona, and now in Texas. It's why I came home now, I guess, because I realized it. This farm I work on, it's spring there now, see? And they've got about fifteen new colts. There's nothing more inspiring or—beautiful than the sight of a mare and a new colt. And it's cool there now, see? Texas is cool now, and it's spring. And whenever spring comes to where I am, I suddenly get the feeling, my God, I'm not gettin' anywhere! What the hell am I doing, playing around with horses, twenty-eight dollars a week! I'm thirty-four years old, I oughta be makin' my future. That's when I come running home. And now, I get here, and I don't know what to do with myself. (*After a pause.*) I've always made a point of not wasting my life, and everytime I come back here I know that all I've done is to waste my life.

HAPPY. You're a poet, you know that, Biff? You're a—you're an idealist!

BIFF. No, I'm mixed up very bad. Maybe I oughta get married. Maybe I oughta get stuck into something. Maybe that's my trouble. I'm like a boy. I'm not married, I'm not in business, I just—I'm like a boy. Are you content, Hap? You're a success, aren't you? Are you content?

HAPPY. Hell, no!

BIFF. Why? You're making money, aren't you?

HAPPY (*moving about with energy, expressiveness*). All I can do now is wait for the merchandise manager to die. And suppose I get to be merchandise manager? He's a good friend of mine, and he just built a terrific estate on Long Island. And he lived there about two months and sold it, and now he's building another one. He can't enjoy it once it's finished. And I know that's just what I would do. I don't know what the hell I'm workin' for. Sometimes I sit in my apartment—all alone. And I think of the rent I'm paying. And it's crazy. But then, it's what I always wanted. My own apartment, a car, and plenty of women. And still, goddammit, I'm lonely.

BIFF (*with enthusiasm*). Listen, why don't you come out West with me?

HAPPY. You and I, heh?

BIFF. Sure, maybe we could buy a ranch. Raise cattle, use our muscles. Men built like we are should be working out in the open.

HAPPY (*avidly*). The Loman Brothers, heh?

BIFF (*with vast affection*). Sure, we'd be known all over the counties!

HAPPY (*enthralled*). That's what I dream about, Biff. Sometimes I want to just rip my clothes off in the middle of the store and outbox that goddam merchandise manager. I mean I can outbox, outrun, and outlift anybody in that store, and I have to take orders from those common, petty sons-of-bitches till I can't stand it any more.

BIFF. I'm tellin' you, kid, if you were with me I'd be happy out there.

HAPPY (*enthused*). See, Biff, everybody around me is so false that I'm constantly lowering my ideals . . .

BIFF. Baby, together we'd stand up for one another, we'd have someone to trust.

HAPPY. If I were around you . . .

BIFF. Hap, the trouble is we weren't brought up to grub for money. I don't know how to do it.

HAPPY. Neither can I!

BIFF. Then let's go!

HAPPY. The only thing is—what can you make out there?

BIFF. But look at your friend. Builds an estate and then hasn't the peace of mind to live in it.

HAPPY. Yeah, but when he walks into the store the waves part in front of him. That's fifty-two thousand dollars a year coming through the revolving door, and I got more in my pinky finger than he's got in his head.

BIFF. Yeah, but you just said . . .

HAPPY. I gotta show some of those pompous, self-important executives over there that Hap Loman can make the grade. I want to walk into the store the way he walks in.

Then I'll go with you, Biff. We'll be together yet, I swear. But take those two we had tonight. Now weren't they gorgeous creatures?

BIFF. Yeah, yeah, most gorgeous I've had in years.

HAPPY. I get that any time I want, Biff. Whenever I feel disgusted. The only trouble is, it gets like bowling or something. I just keep knockin' them over and it doesn't mean anything. You still run around a lot?

BIFF. Naa. I'd like to find a girl—steady, somebody with substance.

HAPPY. That's what I long for.

BIFF. Go on! You'd never come home.

HAPPY. I would! Somebody with character, with resistance! Like Mom, y'know? You're gonna call me a bastard when I tell you this. That girl Charlotte I was with tonight is engaged to be married in five weeks. (*He tries on his new hat.*)

BIFF. No kiddin'!

HAPPY. Sure, the guy's in line for the vice-presidency of the store. I don't know what gets into me, maybe I just have an over-developed sense of competition or something, but I went and ruined her, and furthermore I can't get rid of her. And he's the third executive I've done that to. Isn't that a crummy characteristic? And to top it all, I go to their weddings! (*Indignantly, but laughing.*) Like I'm not supposed to take bribes. Manufacturers offer me a hundred-dollar bill now and then to throw an order their way. You know how honest I am, but it's like this girl, see. I hate myself for it. Because I don't want the girl, and, still, I take it and—I love it!

BIFF. Let's go to sleep.

HAPPY. I guess we didn't settle anything, heh?

BIFF. I just got one idea that I think I'm going to try.

HAPPY. What's that?

BIFF. Remember Bill Oliver?

HAPPY. Sure, Oliver is very big now. You want to work for him again?

BIFF. No, but when I quit he said something to me. He put his arm on my shoulder, and he said, "Biff, if you ever need anything, come to me."

HAPPY. I remember that. That sounds good.

BIFF. I think I'll go to see him. If I could get ten thousand or even seven or eight thousand dollars I could buy a beautiful ranch.

HAPPY. I bet he'd back you. 'Cause he thought highly of you, Biff. I mean, they all do. You're well liked, Biff. That's why I say to come back here, and we both have the apartment. And I'm tellin' you, Biff, any babe you want . . .

BIFF. No, with a ranch I could do the work I like and still be something. I just wonder though. I wonder if Oliver still thinks I stole that carton of basketballs.

HAPPY. Oh, he probably forgot that long ago. It's almost ten years. You're too sensitive. Anyway, he didn't really fire you.

BIFF. Well, I think he was going to. I think that's why I quit. I was never sure whether he knew or not. I know he

thought the world of me, though. I was the only one he'd let lock up the place.

WILLY (*below*). You gonna wash the engine, Biff?

HAPPY. Shh!

Biff looks at Happy, who is gazing down, listening. Willy is mumbling in the parlor.

HAPPY. You hear that?

They listen. Willy laughs warmly.

BIFF (*growing angry*). Doesn't he know Mom can hear that?

WILLY. Don't get your sweater dirty, Biff!

A look of pain crosses Biff's face.

HAPPY. Isn't that terrible? Don't leave again, will you? You'll find a job here. You gotta stick around. I don't know what to do about him, it's getting embarrassing.

WILLY. What a simonizing job!

BIFF. Mom's hearing that!

WILLY. No kiddin', Biff, you got a date? Wonderful!

HAPPY. Go on to sleep. But talk to him in the morning, will you?

BIFF (*reluctantly getting into bed*). With her in the house. Brother!

HAPPY (*getting into bed*). I wish you'd have a good talk with him.

The light on their room begins to fade.

BIFF (*to himself in bed*). That selfish, stupid . . .

HAPPY. Sh . . . Sleep, Biff.

Their light is out. Well before they have finished speaking, Willy's form is dimly seen below in the darkened kitchen. He opens the refrigerator, searches in there, and takes out a bottle of milk. The apartment houses are fading out, and the entire house and surroundings become covered with leaves. Music insinuates itself as the leaves appear.

WILLY. Just wanna be careful with those girls, Biff, that's all. Don't make any promises. No promises of any kind. Because a girl, y'know, they always believe what you tell 'em, and you're very young, Biff, you're too young to be talking seriously to girls.

Light rises on the kitchen. Willy, talking, shuts the refrigerator door and comes downstage to the kitchen table. He pours milk into a glass. He is totally immersed in himself, smiling faintly.

WILLY. Too young entirely, Biff. You want to watch your schooling first. Then when you're all set, there'll be plenty of girls for a boy like you. (*He smiles broadly at a kitchen chair.*) That so? The girls pay for you? (*He laughs.*) Boy, you must really be makin' a hit.

Willy is gradually addressing—physically—a point offstage, speaking through the wall of the kitchen, and his voice has been rising in volume to that of a normal conversation.

WILLY. I been wondering why you polish the car so careful. Ha! Don't leave the hubcaps, boys. Get the chamois to the hubcaps. Happy, use newspaper on the windows, it's the easiest thing. Show him how to do it, Biff! You see, Happy? Pad it up, use it like a pad. That's it, that's it, good work. You're doin' all right, Hap. (*He pauses, then nods in approbation for a few seconds, then looks upward.*) Biff, first thing we gotta do when we get time is clip that big branch over the house. Afraid it's gonna fall in a storm and hit the roof. Tell you what. We get a rope and sling her around, and then we climb up there with a couple of saws and take her down. Soon as you finish the car, boys, I wanna see ya. I got a surprise for you, boys.

BIFF (*offstage*). Whatta ya got, Dad?

WILLY. No, you finish first. Never leave a job till you're finished—remember that. (*Looking toward the "big trees."*) Biff, up in Albany I saw a beautiful hammock. I think I'll buy it next trip, and we'll hang it right between those two elms. Wouldn't that be something? Just swingin' there under those branches. Boy, that would be . . .

Young Biff and Young Happy appear from the direction Willy was addressing. Happy carries rags and a pail of water. Biff, wearing a sweater with a block "S," carries a football.

BIFF (*pointing in the direction of the car offstage*). How's that, Pop, professional?

WILLY. Terrific. Terrific job, boys. Good work, Biff.

HAPPY. Where's the surprise, Pop?

WILLY. In the back seat of the car.

HAPPY. Boy! (*He runs off.*)

BIFF. What is it, Dad? Tell me, what'd you buy?

WILLY (*laughing, cuffs him*). Never mind, something I want you to have.

BIFF (*turns and starts off*). What is it, Hap?

HAPPY (*offstage*). It's a punching bag!

BIFF. Oh, Pop!

WILLY. It's got Gene Tunney's signature on it!

Happy runs onstage with a punching bag.

BIFF. Gee, how'd you know we wanted a punching bag?

WILLY. Well, it's the finest thing for the timing.

HAPPY (*lies down on his back and pedals with his feet*). I'm losing weight, you notice, Pop?

WILLY (*to Happy*). Jumping rope is good too.

BIFF. Did you see the new football I got?

WILLY (*examining the ball*). Where'd you get a new ball?

BIFF. The coach told me to practice my passing.

WILLY. That so? And he gave you the ball, heh?

BIFF. Well, I borrowed it from the locker room. (*He laughs confidentially.*)

WILLY (*laughing with him at the theft*). I want you to return that.

HAPPY. I told you he wouldn't like it!

BIFF (*angrily*). Well, I'm bringing it back!

WILLY (*stopping the incipient argument, to Happy*). Sure, he's gotta practice with a regulation ball, doesn't he? (*To Biff.*) Coach'll probably congratulate you on your initiative!

BIFF. Oh, he keeps congratulating my initiative all the time, Pop.

WILLY. That's because he likes you. If somebody else took that ball there'd be an uproar. So what's the report, boys, what's the report?

BIFF. Where'd you go this time, Dad? Gee we were lonesome for you.

WILLY (*pleased, puts an arm around each boy and they come down to the apron*). Lonesome, heh?

BIFF. Missed you every minute.

WILLY. Don't say? Tell you a secret, boys. Don't breathe it to a soul. Someday I'll have my own business, and I'll never have to leave home any more.

HAPPY. Like Uncle Charley, heh?

WILLY. Bigger than Uncle Charley! Because Charley is not—liked. He's liked, but he's not—well liked.

BIFF. Where'd you go this time, Dad?

WILLY. Well, I got on the road, and I went north to Providence. Met the Mayor.

BIFF. The Mayor of Providence!

WILLY. He was sitting in the hotel lobby.

BIFF. What'd he say?

WILLY. He said, "Morning!" And I said, "Morning!" And I said, "You got a fine city here, Mayor." And then he had coffee with me. And then I went to Waterbury. Waterbury is a fine city. Big clock city, the famous Waterbury clock. Sold a nice bill there. And then Boston—Boston is the cradle of the Revolution. A fine city. And a couple of other towns in Mass., and on to Portland and Bangor and straight home!

BIFF. Gee, I'd love to go with you sometime, Dad.

WILLY. Soon as summer comes.

HAPPY. Promise?

WILLY. You and Hap and I, and I'll show you all the towns. America is full of beautiful towns and fine, upstanding people. And they know me, boys, they know me up and down New England. The finest people. And when I bring you fellas up, there'll be open sesame for all of us, 'cause one thing, boys: I have friends. I can park my car in any street in New England, and the cops protect it like their own. This summer, heh?

BIFF AND HAPPY (*together*). Yeah! You bet!

WILLY. We'll take our bathing suits.

HAPPY. We'll carry your bags, Pop!

WILLY. Oh, won't that be something! Me comin' into the Boston stores with you boys carryin' my bags. What a sensation!

Biff is prancing around, practicing passing the ball.

WILLY. You nervous, Biff, about the game?

BIFF. Not if you're gonna be there.

WILLY. What do they say about you in school, now that they made you captain?

HAPPY. There's a crowd of girls behind him everytime the classes change.

BIFF (*taking Willy's hand*). This Saturday, Pop, this Saturday—just for you, I'm going to break through for a touchdown.

HAPPY. You're supposed to pass.

BIFF. I'm takin' one play for Pop. You watch me, Pop, and when I take off my helmet, that means I'm breakin' out. Then you watch me crash through that line!

WILLY (*kisses Biff*). Oh, wait'll I tell this in Boston!

Bernard enters in knickers. He is younger than Biff, earnest and loyal, a worried boy.

BERNARD. Biff, where are you? You're supposed to study with me today.

WILLY. Hey, looka Bernard. What're you lookin' so anemic about, Bernard?

BERNARD. He's gotta study, Uncle Willy. He's got Regents next week.

HAPPY (*tauntingly, spinning Bernard around*). Let's box, Bernard!

BERNARD. Biff! (*He gets away from Happy.*) Listen, Biff, I heard Mr. Birnbaum say that if you don't start studyin' math he's gonna flunk you, and you won't graduate. I heard him!

WILLY. You better study with him, Biff. Go ahead now.

BERNARD. I heard him!

BIFF. Oh, Pop, you didn't see my sneakers! (*He holds up a foot for Willy to look at.*)

WILLY. Hey, that's a beautiful job of printing!

BERNARD (*wiping his glasses*). Just because he printed University of Virginia on his sneakers doesn't mean they've got to graduate him, Uncle Willy!

WILLY (*angrily*). What're you talking about? With scholarships to three universities they're gonna flunk him?

BERNARD. But I heard Mr. Birnbaum say . . .

WILLY. Don't be a pest, Bernard! (*To his boys.*) What an anemic!

BERNARD. Okay, I'm waiting for you in my house, Biff.

Bernard goes off. The Lomans laugh.

WILLY. Bernard is not well liked, is he?

BIFF. He's liked, but he's not well liked.

HAPPY. That's right, Pop.

WILLY. That's just what I mean. Bernard can get the best marks in school, y'understand, but when he gets out in the business world, y'understand, you are going to be five times ahead of him. That's why I thank Almighty God you're both built like Adonises. Because the man who makes an appearance in the business world, the man who creates personal interest, is the man who gets ahead. Be liked and you will never want. You take me, for instance. I never have to wait in line to see a buyer. "Willy Loman is here!" That's all they have to know, and I go right through.

BIFF. Did you knock them dead, Pop?

WILLY. Knocked 'em cold in Providence, slaughtered 'em in Boston.

HAPPY (*on his back, pedaling again*). I'm losing weight, you notice, Pop?

Linda enters as of old, a ribbon in her hair, carrying a basket of washing.

LINDA. (*with youthful energy*). Hello, dear!

WILLY. Sweetheart!

LINDA. How'd the Chevvy run?

WILLY. Chevrolet, Linda, is the greatest car ever built. (*To the boys.*) Since when do you let your mother carry wash up the stairs?

BIFF. Grab hold there, boy!

HAPPY. Where to, Mom?

LINDA. Hang them up on the line. And you better go down to your friends, Biff. The cellar is full of boys. They don't know what to do with themselves.

BIFF. Ah, when Pop comes home they can wait!

WILLY (*laughs appreciatively*). You better go down and tell them what to do, Biff.

BIFF. I think I'll have them sweep out the furnace room.

WILLY. Good work, Biff.

BIFF (*goes through wall-line of kitchen to doorway at back and calls down*). Fellas! Everybody sweep out the furnace room! I'll be right down!

VOICES. All right! Okay, Biff.

BIFF. George and Sam and Frank, come out back! We're hangin' up the wash! Come on, Hap, on the double! (*He and Happy carry out the basket.*)

LINDA. The way they obey him!

WILLY. Well, that's training, the training. I'm tellin' you, I was sellin' thousands and thousands, but I had to come home.

LINDA. Oh, the whole block'll be at that game. Did you sell anything?

WILLY. I did five hundred gross in Providence and seven hundred gross in Boston.

LINDA. No! Wait a minute. I've got a pencil. (*She pulls pencil and paper out of her apron pocket.*) That makes your commission . . . Two hundred—my God! Two hundred and twelve dollars!

WILLY. Well, I didn't figure it yet, but . . .

LINDA. How much did you do?

WILLY. Well, I—I did—about a hundred and eighty gross in Providence. Well, no—it came to—roughly two hundred gross on the whole trip.

LINDA (*without hesitation*). Two hundred gross. That's . . . (*She figures.*)

WILLY. The trouble was that three of the stores were half-closed for inventory in Boston. Otherwise I woulda broke records.

LINDA. Well, it makes seventy dollars and some pennies. That's very good.

WILLY. What do we owe?

LINDA. Well, on the first there's sixteen dollars on the refrigerator . . .

WILLY. Why sixteen?

LINDA. Well, the fan belt broke, so it was a dollar eighty.

WILLY. But it's brand new.

LINDA. Well, the man said that's the way it is. Till they work themselves in, y'know.

They move through the wall-line into the kitchen.

WILLY. I hope we didn't get stuck on that machine.

LINDA. They got the biggest ads of any of them!

WILLY. I know, it's a fine machine. What else?

LINDA. Well, there's nine-sixty for the washing machine. And for the vacuum cleaner there's three and a half due on the fifteenth. Then the roof, you got twenty-one dollars remaining.

WILLY. It don't leak, does it?

LINDA. No, they did a wonderful job. Then you owe Frank for the carburetor.

WILLY. I'm not going to pay that man! That goddam Chevrolet, they ought to prohibit the manufacture of that car!

LINDA. Well, you owe him three and a half. And odds and ends, comes to around a hundred and twenty dollars by the fifteenth.

WILLY. A hundred and twenty dollars! My God, if business don't pick up I don't know what I'm gonna do!

LINDA. Well, next week you'll do better.

WILLY. Oh, I'll knock 'em dead next week. I'll go to Hartford. I'm very well liked in Hartford. You know, the trouble is, Linda, people don't seem to take to me.

They move onto the forestage.

LINDA. Oh, don't be foolish.

WILLY. I know it when I walk in. They seem to laugh at me.

LINDA. Why? Why would they laugh at you? Don't talk that way, Willy.

Willy moves to the edge of the stage. Linda goes into the kitchen and starts to darn stockings.

WILLY. I don't know the reason for it, but they just pass me by. I'm not noticed.

LINDA. But you're doing wonderful, dear. You're making seventy to a hundred dollars a week.

WILLY. But I gotta be at it ten, twelve hours a day. Other men—I don't know—they do it easier. I don't know why—I can't stop myself—I talk too much. A man

oughta come in with a few words. One thing about Charley. He's a man of few words, and they respect him.

LINDA. You don't talk too much, you're just lively.

WILLY (*smiling*). Well, I figure, what the hell, life is short, a couple of jokes. (*To himself:*) I joke too much! (*The smile goes.*)

LINDA. Why? You're . . .

WILLY. I'm fat. I'm very—foolish to look at, Linda. I didn't tell you, but Christmas time I happened to be calling on F. H. Stewarts, and a salesman I know, as I was going in to see the buyer I heard him say something about—walrus. And I—I cracked him right across the face. I won't take that. I simply will not take that. But they do laugh at me. I know that.

LINDA. Darling . . .

WILLY. I gotta overcome it. I know I gotta overcome it. I'm not dressing to advantage, maybe.

LINDA. Willy, darling, you're the handsomest man in the world . . .

WILLY. Oh, no, Linda.

LINDA. To me you are. (*Slight pause.*) The handsomest.

From the darkness is heard the laughter of a woman. Willy doesn't turn to it, but it continues through Linda's lines.

LINDA. And the boys, Willy. Few men are idolized by their children the way you are.

Music is heard as behind a scrim, to the left of the house; The Woman, dimly seen, is dressing.

WILLY (*with great feeling*). You're the best there is. Linda, you're a pal, you know that? On the road—on the road I want to grab you sometimes and just kiss the life outa you.

The laughter is loud now, and he moves into a brightening area at the left, where The Woman has come from behind the scrim and is standing, putting on her hat, looking into a "mirror" and laughing.

WILLY. 'Cause I get so lonely—especially when business is bad and there's nobody to talk to. I get the feeling that I'll never sell anything again, that I won't make a living for you, or a business, a business for the boys. (*He talks through The Woman's subsiding laughter; The Woman primps at the "mirror."*) There's so much I want to make for . . .

THE WOMAN. Me? You didn't make me, Willy. I picked you.

WILLY (*pleased*). You picked me?

THE WOMAN (*who is quite proper-looking, Willy's age*). I did. I've been sitting at that desk watching all the salesmen go by, day in, day out. But you've got such a sense of humor, and we do have such a good time together, don't we?

WILLY. Sure, sure. (*He takes her in his arms.*) Why do you have to go now?

THE WOMAN. It's two o'clock . . .

WILLY. No, come on in! (*He pulls her.*)

THE WOMAN. . . . my sisters'll be scandalized. When'll you be back?

WILLY. Oh, two weeks about. Will you come up again?

THE WOMAN. Sure thing. You do make me laugh. It's good for me. (*She squeezes his arm, kisses him.*) And I think you're a wonderful man.

WILLY. You picked me, heh?

THE WOMAN. Sure. Because you're so sweet. And such a kidder.

WILLY. Well, I'll see you next time I'm in Boston.

THE WOMAN. I'll put you right through to the buyers.

WILLY (*slapping her bottom*). Right. Well, bottoms up!

THE WOMAN (*slaps him gently and laughs*). You just kill me, Willy. (*He suddenly grabs her and kisses her roughly.*) You kill me. And thanks for the stockings. I love a lot of stockings. Well, good night.

WILLY. Good night. And keep your pores open!

THE WOMAN. Oh, Willy!

The Woman bursts out laughing, and Linda's laughter blends in. The Woman disappears into the dark. Now the area at the kitchen table brightens. Linda is sitting where she was at the kitchen table, but now is mending a pair of her silk stockings.

LINDA. You are, Willy. The handsomest man. You've got no reason to feel that . . .

WILLY (*coming out of The Woman's dimming area and going over to Linda*). I'll make it all up to you, Linda, I'll . . .

LINDA. There's nothing to make up, dear. You're doing fine, better than . . .

WILLY (*noticing her mending*). What's that?

LINDA. Just mending my stockings. They're so expensive . . .

WILLY (*angrily, taking them from her*). I won't have you mending stockings in this house! Now throw them out!

Linda puts the stockings in her pocket.

BERNARD (*entering on the run*). Where is he? If he doesn't study!

WILLY (*moving to the forestage, with great agitation*). You'll give him the answers!

BERNARD. I do, but I can't on a Regents! That's a state exam! They're liable to arrest me!

WILLY. Where is he? I'll whip him, I'll whip him!

LINDA. And he'd better give back that football, Willy, it's not nice.

WILLY. Biff! Where is he? Why is he taking everything?

LINDA. He's too rough with the girls, Willy. All the mothers are afraid of him!

WILLY. I'll whip him!

BERNARD. He's driving the car without a license!

The Woman's laugh is heard.

WILLY. Shut up!

LINDA. All the mothers . . .

WILLY. Shut up!

BERNARD (*backing quietly away and out*). Mr. Birnbaum says he's stuck up.

WILLY. Get outa here!

BERNARD. If he doesn't buckle down he'll flunk math! (*He goes off.*)

LINDA. He's right, Willy, you've gotta . . .

WILLY (*exploding at her*). There's nothing the matter with him! You want him to be a worm like Bernard? He's got spirit, personality . . .

As he speaks, Linda, almost in tears, exits into the living room. Willy is alone in the kitchen, wilting and staring. The leaves are gone. It is night again, and the apartment houses look down from behind.

WILLY. Loaded with it. Loaded! What is he stealing? He's giving it back, isn't he? Why is he stealing? What did I tell him? I never in my life told him anything but decent things.

Happy in pajamas has come down the stairs; Willy suddenly becomes aware of Happy's presence.

HAPPY. Let's go now, come on.

WILLY (*sitting down at the kitchen table*). Huh! Why did she have to wax the floors herself? Everytime she waxes the floors she keels over. She knows that!

HAPPY. Shh! Take it easy. What brought you back tonight?

WILLY. I got an awful scare. Nearly hit a kid in Yonkers. God! Why didn't I go to Alaska with my brother Ben that time! Ben! That man was a genius, that man was success incarnate! What a mistake! He begged me to go.

HAPPY. Well, there's no use in . . .

WILLY. You guys! There was a man started with the clothes on his back and ended up with diamond mines!

HAPPY. Boy, someday I'd like to know how he did it.

WILLY. What's the mystery? The man knew what he wanted and went out and got it! Walked into a jungle, and comes out, the age of twenty-one, and he's rich! The world is an oyster, but you don't crack it open on a mattress!

HAPPY. Pop, I told you I'm gonna retire you for life.

WILLY. You'll retire me for life on seventy goddam dollars a week? And your women and your car and your apartment, and you'll retire me for life! Christ's sake, I couldn't get past Yonkers today! Where are you guys, where are you? The woods are burning! I can't drive a car!

Charley has appeared in the doorway. He is a large man, slow of speech, laconic, immovable. In all he says, despite what he says, there is pity, and, now, trepidation. He has a robe over pajamas, slippers on his feet. He enters the kitchen.

CHARLEY. Everything all right?

HAPPY. Yeah, Charley, everything's . . .

WILLY. What's the matter?

CHARLEY. I heard some noise. I thought something happened. Can't we do something about the walls? You sneeze in here, and in my house hats blow off.

HAPPY. Let's go to bed, Dad. Come on.

Charley signals to Happy to go.

WILLY. You go ahead, I'm not tired at the moment.

HAPPY (*to Willy*). Take it easy, huh? (*He exits.*)

WILLY. What're you doin' up?

CHARLEY (*sitting down at the kitchen table opposite Willy*). Couldn't sleep good. I had a heartburn.

WILLY. Well, you don't know how to eat.

CHARLEY. I eat with my mouth.

WILLY. No, you're ignorant. You gotta know about vitamins and things like that.

CHARLEY. Come on, let's shoot. Tire you out a little.

WILLY (*hesitantly*). All right. You got cards?

CHARLEY (*taking a deck from his pocket*). Yeah, I got them. Someplace. What is it with those vitamins?

WILLY (*dealing*). They build up your bones. Chemistry.

CHARLEY. Yeah, but there's no bones in a heartburn.

WILLY. What are you talkin' about? Do you know the first thing about it?

CHARLEY. Don't get insulted.

WILLY. Don't talk about something you don't know anything about.

They are playing. Pause.

CHARLEY. What're you doin' home?

WILLY. A little trouble with the car.

CHARLEY. Oh. (*Pause.*) I'd like to take a trip to California.

WILLY. Don't say.

CHARLEY. You want a job?

WILLY. I got a job, I told you that. (*After a slight pause.*) What the hell are you offering me a job for?

CHARLEY. Don't get insulted.

WILLY. Don't insult me.

CHARLEY. I don't see no sense in it. You don't have to go on this way.

WILLY. I got a good job. (*Slight pause.*) What do you keep comin' in here for?

CHARLEY. You want me to go?

WILLY (*after a pause, withering*). I can't understand it. He's going back to Texas again. What the hell is that?

CHARLEY. Let him go.

WILLY. I got nothin' to give him, Charley, I'm clean, I'm clean.

CHARLEY. He won't starve. None a them starve. Forget about him.

WILLY. Then what have I got to remember?

CHARLEY. You take it too hard. To hell with it. When a deposit bottle is broken you don't get your nickel back.

WILLY. That's easy enough for you to say.

CHARLEY. That ain't easy for me to say.

WILLY. Did you see the ceiling I put up in the living room?

CHARLEY. Yeah, that's a piece of work. To put up a ceiling is a mystery to me. How do you do it?

WILLY. What's the difference?

CHARLEY. Well, talk about it.

WILLY. You gonna put up a ceiling?

CHARLEY. How could I put up a ceiling?

WILLY. Then what the hell are you bothering me for?

CHARLEY. You're insulted again.

WILLY. A man who can't handle tools is not a man. You're disgusting.

CHARLEY. Don't call me disgusting, Willy.

Uncle Ben, carrying a valise and an umbrella, enters the forestage from around the right corner of the house. He is a stolid man, in his sixties, with a mustache and an authoritative air. He is utterly certain of his destiny, and there is an aura of far places about him. He enters exactly as Willy speaks.

WILLY. I'm getting awfully tired, Ben.

Ben's music is heard. Ben looks around at everything.

CHARLEY. Good, keep playing; you'll sleep better. Did you call me Ben?

Ben looks at his watch.

WILLY. That's funny. For a second there you reminded me of my brother Ben.

BEN. I only have a few minutes. (*He strolls, inspecting the place. Willy and Charley continue playing.*)

CHARLEY. You never heard from him again, heh? Since that time?

WILLY. Didn't Linda tell you? Couple of weeks ago we got a letter from his wife in Africa. He died.

CHARLEY. That so.

BEN (*chuckling*). So this is Brooklyn, eh?

CHARLEY. Maybe you're in for some of his money.

WILLY. Naa, he had seven sons. There's just one opportunity I had with that man . . .

BEN. I must make a train, William. There are several properties I'm looking at in Alaska.

WILLY. Sure, sure! If I'd gone with him to Alaska that time, everything would've been totally different.

CHARLEY. Go on, you'd froze to death up there.

WILLY. What're you talking about?

BEN. Opportunity is tremendous in Alaska, William. Surprised you're not up there.

WILLY. Sure, tremendous.

CHARLEY. Heh?

WILLY. There was the only man I ever met who knew the answers.

CHARLEY. Who?

BEN. How are you all?

WILLY (*taking a pot, smiling*). Fine, fine.

CHARLEY.. Pretty sharp tonight.

BEN. Is Mother living with you?

WILLY. No, she died a long time ago.

CHARLEY. Who?

BEN. That's too bad. Fine specimen of a lady, Mother.

WILLY (*to Charley*). Heh?

BEN. I'd hoped to see the old girl.

CHARLEY. Who died?

BEN. Heard anything from Father, have you?

WILLY (*unnerved*). What do you mean, who died?

CHARLEY (*taking a pot*). What're you talkin' about?

BEN (*looking at his watch*). William, it's half-past eight!

WILLY (*as though to dispel his confusion he angrily stops Charley's hand*). That's my build!

CHARLEY. I put the ace . . .

WILLY. If you don't know how to play the game I'm not gonna throw my money away on you!

CHARLEY (*rising*). It was my ace, for God's sake!

WILLY. I'm through, I'm through!

BEN. When did Mother die?

WILLY. Long ago. Since the beginning you never knew how to play cards.

CHARLEY (*picks up the cards and goes to the door*). All right! Next time I'll bring a deck with five aces.

WILLY. I don't play that kind of game!

CHARLEY (*turning to him*). You ought to be ashamed of yourself!

WILLY. Yeah?

CHARLEY. Yeah! (*He goes out.*)

WILLY (*slamming the door after him*). Ignoramus!

BEN (*as Willy comes toward him through the wall-line of the kitchen*). So you're William.

WILLY (*shaking Ben's hand*). Ben! I've been waiting for you so long! What's the answer? How did you do it?

BEN. Oh, there's a story in that.

Linda enters the forestage, as of old, carrying the wash basket.

LINDA. Is this Ben?

BEN (*gallantly*). How do you do, my dear.

LINDA. Where've you been all these years? Willy's always wondered why you . . .

WILLY (*pulling Ben away from her impatiently*). Where is Dad? Didn't you follow him? How did you get started?

BEN. Well, I don't know how much you remember.

WILLY. Well, I was just a baby, of course, only three or four years old . . .

BEN. Three years and eleven months.

WILLY. What a memory, Ben!

BEN. I have many enterprises, William, and I have never kept books.

WILLY. I remember I was sitting under the wagon in—was it Nebraska?

BEN. It was South Dakota, and I gave you a bunch of wild flowers.

WILLY. I remember you walking away down some open road.

BEN (*laughing*). I was going to find Father in Alaska.

WILLY. Where is he?

BEN. At that age I had a very faulty view of geography, William. I discovered after a few days that I was heading due south, so instead of Alaska, I ended up in Africa.

LINDA. Africa!

WILLY. The Gold Coast!

BEN. Principally diamond mines.

LINDA. Diamond mines!

BEN. Yes, my dear. But I've only a few minutes . . .

WILLY. No! Boys! Boys! (*Young Biff and Happy appear.*) Listen to this. This is your Uncle Ben, a great man! Tell my boys, Ben!

BEN. Why, boys, when I was seventeen I walked into the jungle, and when I was twenty-one I walked out. (*He laughs.*) And by God I was rich.

WILLY (*to the boys*). You see what I been talking about? The greatest things can happen!

BEN (*glancing at his watch*). I have an appointment in Ketchikan Tuesday week.

WILLY. No, Ben! Please tell about Dad. I want my boys to hear. I want them to know the kind of stock they spring from. All I remember is a man with a big beard, and I was in Mamma's lap, sitting around a fire, and some kind of high music.

BEN. His flute. He played the flute.

WILLY. Sure, the flute, that's right!

New music is heard, a high, rollicking tune.

BEN. Father was a very great and a very wild-hearted man. We would start in Boston, and he'd toss the whole family into the wagon, and then he'd drive the team right across the country; through Ohio, and Indiana, Michigan, Illinois, and all the Western states. And we'd stop in the towns and sell the flutes that he'd made on the way. Great inventor, Father. With one gadget he made more in a week than a man like you could make in a lifetime.

WILLY. That's just the way I'm bringing them up, Ben—rugged, well liked, all-around.

BEN. Yeah? (*To Biff.*) Hit that, boy—hard as you can. (*He pounds his stomach.*)

BIFF. Oh, no, sir!

BEN (*taking boxing stance*). Come on, get to me! (*He laughs.*)

WILLY. Go to it, Biff! Go ahead, show him!

BIFF. Okay! (*He cocks his fists and starts in.*)

LINDA (*to Willy*). Why must he fight, dear?

BEN (*sparring with Biff*). Good boy! Good boy!

WILLY. How's that, Ben, heh?

HAPPY. Give him the left, Biff!

LINDA. Why are you fighting?

BEN. Good boy! (*Suddenly comes in, trips Biff, and stands over him, the point of his umbrella poised over Biff's eye.*)

LINDA. Look out, Biff!

BIFF. Gee!

BEN (*patting Biff's knee*). Never fight fair with a stranger, boy. You'll never get out of the jungle that way. (*Taking Linda's hand and bowing.*) It was an honor and a pleasure to meet you, Linda.

LINDA (*withdrawing her hand coldly, frightened*). Have a nice—trip.

BEN (*to Willy*). And good luck with your—what do you do?

WILLY. Selling.

BEN. Yes. Well . . . (*He raises his hand in farewell to all.*)

WILLY. No, Ben, I don't want you to think . . . (*He takes Ben's arm to show him.*) It's Brooklyn, I know, but we hunt too.

BEN. Really, now.

WILLY. Oh, sure, there's snakes and rabbits and—that's why I moved out here. Why, Biff can fell any one of these trees in no time! Boys! Go right over to where they're building the apartment house and get some sand. We're gonna rebuild the entire front stoop right now! Watch this, Ben!

BIFF. Yes, sir! On the double, Hap!

HAPPY (*as he and Biff run off*). I lost weight, Pop, you notice?

Charley enters in knickers, even before the boys are gone.

CHARLEY. Listen, if they steal any more from that building the watchman'll put the cops on them!

LINDA (*to Willy*). Don't let Biff . . .

Ben laughs lustily.

WILLY. You shoulda seen the lumber they brought home last week. At least a dozen six-by-tens worth all kinds a money.

CHARLEY. Listen, if that watchman . . .

WILLY. I gave them hell, understand. But I got a couple of fearless characters there.

CHARLEY. Willy, the jails are full of fearless characters.

BEN (*clapping Willy on the back, with a laugh at Charley*). And the stock exchange, friend!

WILLY (*joining in Ben's laughter*). Where are the rest of your pants?

CHARLEY. My wife bought them.

WILLY. Now all you need is a golf club and you can go upstairs and go to sleep. (*To Ben.*) Great athlete! Between him and his son Bernard they can't hammer a nail!

BERNARD (*rushing in*). The watchman's chasing Biff!

WILLY (*angrily*). Shut up! He's not stealing anything!

LINDA (*alarmed, hurrying off left*). Where is he? Biff, dear! (*She exits.*)

WILLY (*moving toward the left, away from Ben*). There's nothing wrong. What's the matter with you?

BEN. Nervy boy. Good!

WILLY (*laughing*). Oh, nerves of iron, that Biff!

CHARLEY. Don't know what it is. My New England man comes back and he's bleedin', they murdered him up there.

WILLY. It's contacts, Charley, I got important contacts!

CHARLEY (*sarcastically*). Glad to hear it, Willy. Come in later, we'll shoot a little casino. I'll take some of your Portland money. (*He laughs at Willy and exits.*)

WILLY (*turning to Ben*). Business is bad, it's murderous. But not for me, of course.

BEN. I'll stop by on my way back to Africa.

WILLY (*longingly*). Can't you stay a few days? You're just what I need, Ben, because I—I have a fine position here, but I—well, Dad left when I was such a baby and I never had a chance to talk to him and I still feel—kind of temporary about myself.

BEN. I'll be late for my train.

They are at opposite ends of the stage.

WILLY. Ben, my boys—can't we talk? They'd go into the jaws of hell for me, see, but I . . .

BEN. William, you're being first-rate with your boys. Outstanding, manly chaps!

WILLY (*hanging on to his words*). Oh, Ben, that's good to hear! Because sometimes I'm afraid that I'm not teaching them the right kind of—Ben, how should I teach them?

BEN (*giving great weight to each word, and with a certain vicious audacity*). William, when I walked into the jungle, I was seventeen. When I walked out I was twenty-one. And, by God, I was rich! (*He goes off into darkness around the right corner of the house.*)

WILLY. . . . was rich! That's just the spirit I want to imbue them with! To walk into a jungle! I was right! I was right! I was right!

Ben is gone, but Willy is still speaking to him as Linda, in nightgown and robe, enters the kitchen, glances around for Willy, then goes to the door of the house, looks out and sees him. Comes down to his left. He looks at her.

LINDA. Willy, dear? Willy?

WILLY. I was right!

LINDA. Did you have some cheese? (*He can't answer.*) It's very late, darling. Come to bed, heh?

WILLY (*looking straight up*). Gotta break your neck to see a star in this yard.

LINDA. You coming in?

WILLY. Whatever happened to that diamond watch fob? Remember? When Ben came from Africa that time? Didn't he give me a watch fob with a diamond in it?

LINDA. You pawned it, dear. Twelve, thirteen years ago. For Biff's radio correspondence course.

WILLY. Gee, that was a beautiful thing. I'll take a walk.

LINDA. But you're in your slippers.

WILLY (*starting to go around the house at the left*). I was right! I was! (*Half to Linda, as he goes, shaking his head.*) What a man! There was a man worth talking to. I was right!

LINDA (*calling after Willy*). But in your slippers, Willy!

Willy is almost gone when Biff, in his pajamas, comes down the stairs and enters the kitchen.

BIFF. What is he doing out there?

LINDA. Sh!

BIFF. God Almighty, Mom, how long has he been doing this?

LINDA. Don't, he'll hear you.

BIFF. What the hell is the matter with him?

LINDA. It'll pass by morning.

BIFF. Shouldn't we do anything?

LINDA. Oh, my dear, you should do a lot of things, but there's nothing to do, so go to sleep.

Happy comes down the stair and sits on the steps.

HAPPY. I never heard him so loud, Mom.

LINDA. Well, come around more often; you'll hear him. (*She sits down at the table and mends the lining of Willy's jacket.*)

BIFF. Why didn't you ever write me about this, Mom?

LINDA. How would I write to you? For over three months you had no address.

BIFF. I was on the move. But you know I thought of you all the time. You know that, don't you, pal?

LINDA. I know, dear, I know. But he likes to have a letter. Just to know that there's still a possibility for better things.

BIFF. He's not like this all the time, is he?

LINDA. It's when you come home he's always the worst.

BIFF. When I come home?

LINDA. When you write you're coming, he's all smiles, and talks about the future, and—he's just wonderful. And then the closer you seem to come, the more shaky he gets, and then, by the time you get here, he's arguing, and he seems angry at you. I think it's just that maybe he can't bring himself to—to open up to you. Why are you so hateful to each other? Why is that?

BIFF (*evasively*). I'm not hateful, Mom.

LINDA. But you no sooner come in the door than you're fighting!

BIFF. I don't know why. I mean to change. I'm tryin', Mom, you understand?

LINDA. Are you home to stay now?

BIFF. I don't know. I want to look around, see what's doin'.

LINDA. Biff, you can't look around all your life, can you?

BIFF. I just can't take hold, Mom. I can't take hold of some kind of a life.

LINDA. Biff, a man is not a bird, to come and go with the spring time.

BIFF. Your hair . . . (*He touches her hair.*) Your hair got so gray.

LINDA. Oh, it's been gray since you were in high school. I just stopped dyeing it, that's all.

BIFF. Dye it again, will ya? I don't want my pal looking old.

(*He smiles.*)

LINDA. You're such a boy! You think you can go away for a year and . . . You've got to get it into your head now that one day you'll knock on this door and there'll be strange people here . . .

BIFF. What are you talking about? You're not even sixty, Mom.

LINDA. But what about your father?

BIFF (*lamely*). Well, I meant him too.

HAPPY. He admires Pop.

LINDA. Biff, dear, if you don't have any feeling for him, then you can't have any feeling for me.

BIFF. Sure I can, Mom.

LINDA. No. You can't just come to see me, because I love him. (*With a threat, but only a threat, of tears.*) He's the dearest man in the world to me, and I won't have anyone making him feel unwanted and low and blue. You've got to make up your mind now, darling, there's no leeway any more. Either he's your father and you pay him that respect, or else you're not to come here. I know he's not easy to get along with—nobody knows that better than me—but . . .

WILLY (*from the left, with a laugh*). Hey, hey, Biffo!

BIFF (*starting to go out after Willy*). What the hell is the matter with him? (*Happy stops him.*)

LINDA. Don't—don't go near him!

BIFF. Stop making excuses for him! He always, always wiped the floor with you. Never had an ounce of respect for you.

HAPPY. He's always had respect for . . .

BIFF. What the hell do you know about it?

HAPPY (*surlily*). Just don't call him crazy!

BIFF. He's got no character—Charley wouldn't do this. Not in his own house—spewing out that vomit from his mind.

HAPPY. Charley never had to cope with what he's got to.

BIFF. People are worse off than Willy Loman. Believe me, I've seen them!

LINDA. Then make Charley your father, Biff. You can't do that, can you? I don't say he's a great man. Willy Loman never made a lot of money. His name was never in the paper. He's not the finest character that ever lived. But he's a human being, and a terrible thing is happening to him. So attention must be paid. He's not to be allowed to fall into his grave like an old dog. Attention, attention must be finally paid to such a person. You called him crazy . . .

BIFF. I didn't mean . . .

LINDA. No, a lot of people think he's lost his—balance. But you don't have to be very smart to know what his trouble is. The man is exhausted.

HAPPY. Sure!

LINDA. A small man can be just as exhausted as a great man. He works for a company thirty-six years this March, opens up unheard-of territories to their trademark, and now in his old age they take his salary away.

HAPPY (*indignantly*). I didn't know that, Mom.

LINDA. You never asked, my dear! Now that you get your spending money someplace else you don't trouble your mind with him.

HAPPY. But I gave you money last . . .

LINDA. Christmas time, fifty dollars! To fix the hot water it cost ninety-seven fifty! For five weeks he's been on straight commission, like a beginner, an unknown!

BIFF. Those ungrateful bastards!

LINDA. Are they any worse than his sons? When he brought them business, when he was young, they were glad to see him. But now his old friends, the old buyers that loved him so and always found some order to hand him in a pinch—they're all dead, retired. He used to be able to make six, seven calls a day in Boston. Now he takes his valises out of the car and puts them back and takes them out again and he's exhausted. Instead of walking he talks now. He drives seven hundred miles, and when he gets there no one knows him any more, no one welcomes him. And what goes through a man's mind, driving seven hundred miles home without having earned a cent? Why shouldn't he talk to himself? Why? When he has to go to Charley and borrow fifty dollars a week and pretend to me that it's his pay? How long can that go on? How long? You see what I'm sitting here and waiting for? And you tell me he has no character? The man who never worked a day but for your benefit? When does he get the medal for that? Is this his reward—to turn around at the age of sixty-three and find his sons, who he loved better than his life, one a philandering bum . . .

HAPPY. Mom!

LINDA. That's all you are, my baby! (*To Biff.*) And you! What happened to the love you had for him? You were such pals! How you used to talk to him on the phone every night! How lonely he was till he could come home to you!

BIFF. All right, Mom. I'll live here in my room, and I'll get a job. I'll keep away from him, that's all.

LINDA. No, Biff. You can't stay here and fight all the time.

BIFF. He threw me out of this house, remember that.

LINDA. Why did he do that? I never knew why.

BIFF. Because I know he's a fake and he doesn't like anybody around who knows!

LINDA. Why a fake? In what way? What do you mean?

BIFF. Just don't lay it all at my feet. It's between me and him—that's all I have to say. I'll chip in from now on. He'll settle for half my paycheck. He'll be all right. I'm going to bed. (*He starts for the stairs.*)

LINDA. He won't be all right.

BIFF. (*turning on the stairs, furiously*). I hate this city and I'll stay here. Now what do you want?

LINDA. He's dying, Biff.

Happy turns quickly to her, shocked.

BIFF. (*after a pause*). Why is he dying?

LINDA. He's been trying to kill himself.

BIFF. (*with great horror*). How?

LINDA. I live from day to day.

BIFF. What're you talking about?

LINDA. Remember I wrote you that he smashed up the car again? In February?

BIFF. Well?

LINDA. The insurance inspector came. He said that they have evidence. That all these accidents in the last year—weren't—weren't—accidents.

HAPPY. How can they tell that? That's a lie.

LINDA. It seems there's a woman . . . (*She takes a breath as:*)

BIFF. (*sharply but contained*). What woman?

LINDA. (*simultaneously*). . . . and this woman . . .

LINDA. What?

BIFF. Nothing. Go ahead.

LINDA. What did you say?

BIFF. Nothing. I just said what woman?

HAPPY. What about her?

LINDA. Well, it seems she was walking down the road and saw his car. She says that he wasn't driving fast at all, and that he didn't skid. She says he came to that little bridge, and then deliberately smashed into the railing, and it was only the shallowness of the water that saved him.

BIFF. Oh, no, he probably just fell asleep again.

LINDA. I don't think he fell asleep.

BIFF. Why not?

LINDA. Last month . . . (*With great difficulty.*) Oh, boys, it's so hard to say a thing like this! He's just a big stupid man to you, but I tell you there's more good in him than in many other people. (*She chokes, wipes her eyes.*) I was looking for a fuse. The lights blew out, and I went down the cellar. And behind the fuse box—it happened to fall out—was a length of rubber pipe—just short.

HAPPY. No kidding!

LINDA. There's a little attachment on the end of it. I knew right away. And sure enough, on the bottom of the water heater there's a new little nipple on the gas pipe.

HAPPY. (*angrily*). That—jerk.

BIFF. Did you have it taken off?

LINDA. I'm—I'm ashamed to. How can I mention it to him? Every day I go down and take away that little rubber pipe. But, when he comes home, I put it back where it was. How can I insult him that way? I don't know what to do. I live from day to day, boys. I tell you, I know every thought in his mind. It sounds so old-fashioned and silly, but I tell you he put his whole life into you and you've turned your backs on him. (*She is bent over in the chair, weeping, her face in her hands.*) Biff, I swear to God! Biff, his life is in your hands!

HAPPY. (*to Biff*). How do you like that damned fool!

BIFF. (*kissing her*). All right, pal, all right. It's all settled now. I've been remiss. I know that, Mom. But now I'll stay, and I swear to you, I'll apply myself. (*Kneeling in front of her, in a fever of self-reproach.*) It's just—you see, Mom, I don't fit in business. Not that I won't try. I'll try, and I'll make good.

HAPPY. Sure you will. The trouble with you in business was you never tried to please people.

BIFF. I know, I . . .

HAPPY. Like when you worked for Harrison's. Bob Harrison said you were tops, and then you go and do some damn fool thing like whistling whole songs in the elevator like a comedian.

BIFF. (*against Happy*). So what? I like to whistle sometimes.

HAPPY. You don't raise a guy to a responsible job who whistles in the elevator!

LINDA. Well, don't argue about it now.

HAPPY. Like when you'd go off and swim in the middle of the day instead of taking the line around.

BIFF (*his resentment rising*). Well, don't you run off? You take off sometimes, don't you? On a nice summer day?

HAPPY. Yeah, but I cover myself!

LINDA. Boys!

HAPPY. If I'm going to take a fade the boss can call any number where I'm supposed to be and they'll swear to him that I just left. I'll tell you something that I hate to say, Biff, but in the business world some of them think you're crazy.

BIFF (*angered*). Screw the business world!

HAPPY. All right, screw it! Great, but cover yourself!

LINDA. Hap, Hap!

BIFF. I don't care what they think! They've laughed at Dad for years, and you know why? Because we don't belong in this nuthouse of a city! We should be mixing cement on some open plain or—or carpenters. A carpenter is allowed to whistle!

Willy walks in from the entrance of the house, at left.

WILLY. Even your grandfather was better than a carpenter. (*Pause. They watch him.*) You never grew up. Bernard does not whistle in the elevator, I assure you.

BIFF (*as though to laugh Willy out of it*). Yeah, but you do, Pop.

WILLY. I never in my life whistled in an elevator! And who in the business world thinks I'm crazy?

BIFF. I didn't mean it like that, Pop. Now don't make a whole thing out of it, will ya?

WILLY. Go back to the West! Be a carpenter, a cowboy, enjoy yourself!

LINDA. Willy, he was just saying . . .

WILLY. I heard what he said!

HAPPY (*trying to quiet Willy*). Hey, Pop, come on now . . .

WILLY (*continuing over Happy's line*). They laugh at me, heh? Go to Filene's, go to the Hub, go to Slattery's, Boston. Call out the name Willy Loman and see what happens! Big shot!

BIFF. All right, Pop.

WILLY. Big!

BIFF. All right!

WILLY. Why do you always insult me?

BIFF. I didn't say a word. (*To Linda.*) Did I say a word?

LINDA. He didn't say anything, Willy.

WILLY (*going to the doorway of the living room*). All right, good night, good night.

LINDA. Willy, dear, he just decided . . .

WILLY (*to Biff*). If you get tired hanging around tomorrow, paint the ceiling I put up in the living room.

BIFF. I'm leaving early tomorrow.

HAPPY. He's going to see Bill Oliver, Pop.

WILLY (*interestedly*). Oliver? For what?

BIFF (*with reserve, but trying; trying*). He always said he'd stake me. I'd like to go into business, so maybe I can take him up on it.

LINDA. Isn't that wonderful?

WILLY. Don't interrupt. What's wonderful about it? There's fifty men in the City of New York who'd stake him. (*To Biff.*) Sporting goods?

BIFF. I guess so. I know something about it and . . .

WILLY. He knows something about it! You know sporting goods better than Spalding, for God's sake! How much is he giving you?

BIFF. I don't know, I didn't even see him yet, but . . .

WILLY. Then what're you talkin' about?

BIFF (*getting angry*). Well, all I said was I'm gonna see him, that's all!

WILLY (*turning away*). Ah, you're counting your chickens again.

BIFF (*starting left for the stairs*). Oh, Jesus, I'm going to sleep!

WILLY (*calling after him*). Don't curse in this house!

BIFF (*turning*). Since when did you get so clean?

HAPPY (*trying to stop them*). Wait a . . .

WILLY. Don't use that language to me! I won't have it!

HAPPY (*grabbing Biff, shouts*). Wait a minute! I got an idea. I got a feasible idea. Come here, Biff, let's talk this over now, let's talk some sense here. When I was down in Florida last time, I thought of a great idea to sell sporting goods. It just came back to me. You and I, Biff—we have a line, the Loman Line. We train a couple of weeks, and put on a couple of exhibitions, see?

WILLY. That's an idea!

HAPPY. Wait! We form two basketball teams, see? Two water-polo teams. We play each other. It's a million dollars' worth of publicity. Two brothers, see? The Loman Brothers. Displays in the Royal Palms—all the hotels. And banners over the ring and the basketball court: "Loman Brothers." Baby, we could sell sporting goods!

WILLY. That is a one-million-dollar idea!

LINDA. Marvelous!

BIFF. I'm in great shape as far as that's concerned.

HAPPY. And the beauty of it is, Biff, it wouldn't be like a business. We'd be out playin' ball again.

BIFF (*enthused*). Yeah, that's . . .

WILLY. Million-dollar . . .

HAPPY. And you wouldn't get fed up with it, Biff. It'd be the family again. There'd be the old honor, and comradeship, and if you wanted to go off for a swim or somethin'—well, you'd do it! Without some smart cooky gettin' up ahead of you!

WILLY. Lick the world! You guys together could absolutely lick the civilized world.

BIFF. I'll see Oliver tomorrow. Hap, if we could work that out . . .

LINDA. Maybe things are beginning to . . .

WILLY (*widely enthused, to Linda*). Stop interrupting! (*To Biff.*) But don't wear sport jacket and slacks when you see Oliver.

BIFF. No, I'll . . .

WILLY. A business suit, and talk as little as possible, and don't crack any jokes.

BIFF. He did like me. Always liked me.

LINDA. He loved you!

WILLY (*to Linda*). Will you stop! (*To Biff.*) Walk in very serious. You are not applying for a boy's job. Money is to pass. Be quiet, fine, and serious. Everybody likes a kidder, but nobody lends him money.

HAPPY. I'll try to get some myself, Biff. I'm sure I can.

WILLY. I see great things for you kids, I think your troubles are over. But remember, start big and you'll end big. Ask for fifteen. How much you gonna ask for?

BIFF. Gee, I don't know . . .

WILLY. And don't say "Gee." "Gee" is a boy's word. A man walking in for fifteen thousand dollars does not say "Gee!"

BIFF. Ten, I think, would be top though.

WILLY. Don't be so modest. You always started too low. Walk in with a big laugh. Don't look worried. Start off with a couple of your good stories to lighten things up. It's not what you say, it's how you say it—because personality always wins the day.

LINDA. Oliver always thought the highest of him . . .

WILLY. Will you let me talk?

BIFF. Don't yell at her, Pop, will ya?

WILLY (*angrily*). I was talking, wasn't I?

BIFF. I don't like you yelling at her all the time, and I'm tellin' you, that's all.

WILLY. What're you, takin' over this house?

LINDA. Willy . . .

WILLY (*turning to her*). Don't take his side all the time, goddammit!

BIFF (*furiously*). Stop yelling at her!

WILLY (*suddenly pulling on his cheek, beaten down, guilt ridden*). Give my best to Bill Oliver—he may remember me. (*He exits through the living room doorway.*)

LINDA (*her voice subdued*). What'd you have to start that for? (*Biff turns away.*) You see how sweet he was as soon as you talked hopefully? (*She goes over to Biff.*) Come up and say good night to him. Don't let him go to bed that way.

HAPPY. Come on, Biff, let's buck him up.

LINDA. Please, dear. Just say good night. It takes so little to make him happy. Come. (*She goes through the living room doorway, calling upstairs from within the living room.*) Your pajamas are hanging in the bathroom, Willy!

HAPPY (*looking toward where Linda went out*). What a woman! They broke the mold when they made her. You know that, Biff.

BIFF. He's off salary. My God, working on commission!

HAPPY. Well, let's face it: he's no hot-shot selling man. Except that sometimes, you have to admit, he's a sweet personality.

BIFF (*deciding*). Lend me ten bucks, will ya? I want to buy some new ties.

HAPPY. I'll take you to a place I know. Beautiful stuff. Wear one of my striped shirts tomorrow.

BIFF. She got gray. Mom got awful old. Gee, I'm gonna go in to Oliver tomorrow and knock him for a . . .

HAPPY. Come on up. Tell that to Dad. Let's give him a whirl. Come on.

BIFF (*steamed up*). You know, with ten thousand bucks, boy!

HAPPY (*as they go into the living room*). That's the talk, Biff, that's the first time I've heard the old confidence out of you! (*From within the living room, fading off*) You're gonna live with me, kid, and any babe you want just say the word . . . (*The last lines are hardly heard. They are mounting the stairs to their parents' bedroom.*)

LINDA (*entering her bedroom and addressing Willy, who is in the bathroom. She is straightening the bed for him*). Can you do anything about the shower? It drips.

WILLY (*from the bathroom*). All of a sudden everything falls to pieces. Goddam plumbing, oughta be sued, those people. I hardly finished putting it in and the thing . . . (*His words rumble off.*)

LINDA. I'm just wondering if Oliver will remember him. You think he might?

WILLY (*coming out of the bathroom in his pajamas*). Remember him? What's the matter with you, you crazy? If he'd've stayed with Oliver he'd be on top by now! Wait'll Oliver gets a look at him. You don't know the average caliber any more. The average young man today—(*he is getting into bed*)—is got a caliber of zero. Greatest thing in the world for him was to bum around.

Biff and Happy enter the bedroom. Slight pause.

WILLY (*stops short, looking at Biff*). Glad to hear it, boy.

HAPPY. He wanted to say good night to you, sport.

WILLY (*to Biff*). Yeah. Knock him dead, boy. What'd you want to tell me?

BIFF. Just take it easy, Pop. Good night. (*He turns to go.*)

WILLY (*unable to resist*). And if anything falls off the desk while you're talking to him—like a package or something—don't you pick it up. They have office boys for that.

LINDA. I'll make a big breakfast . . .

WILLY. Will you let me finish? (*To Biff.*) Tell him you were in the business in the West. Not farm work.

BIFF. All right, Dad.

LINDA. I think everything . . .

WILLY (*going right through her speech*). And don't undersell yourself. No less than fifteen thousand dollars.

BIFF (*unable to bear him*). Okay. Good night, Mom. (*He starts moving.*)

WILLY. Because you got a greatness in you, Biff, remember that. You got all kinds of greatness . . . (*He lies back, exhausted. Biff walks out.*)

LINDA (*calling after Biff*). Sleep well, darling!

HAPPY. I'm gonna get married, Mom. I wanted to tell you.

LINDA. Go to sleep, dear.

HAPPY (*going*). I just wanted to tell you.

WILLY. Keep up the good work. (*Happy exits.*) God . . . remember that Ebbets Field game? The championship of the city?

LINDA. Just rest. Should I sing to you?

WILLY. Yeah. Sing to me. (*Linda hums a soft lullaby.*) When that team came out—he was the tallest, remember?

LINDA. Oh, yes. And in gold.

Biff enters the darkened kitchen, takes a cigarette, and leaves the house. He comes downstage into a golden pool of light. He smokes, staring at the night.

WILLY. Like a young god. Hercules—something like that. And the sun, the sun all around him. Remember how he waved to me? Right up from the field, with the representatives of three colleges standing by? And the buyers I brought, and the cheers when he came out—Loman, Loman, Loman! God Almighty, he'll be great yet. A star like that, magnificent, can never really fade away!

The light on Willy is fading. The gas heater begins to glow through the kitchen wall, near the stairs, a blue flame beneath red coils.

LINDA (*timidly*). Willy dear, what has he got against you?

WILLY. I'm so tired. Don't talk any more.

Biff slowly returns to the kitchen. He stops, stares toward the heater.

LINDA. Will you ask Howard to let you work in New York?

WILLY. First thing in the morning. Everything'll be all right.

Biff reaches behind the heater and draws out a length of rubber tubing. He is horrified and turns his head toward Willy's room, still dimly lit, from which the strains of Linda's desperate but monotonous humming rise.

WILLY (*staring through the window into the moonlight*). Gee, look at the moon moving between the buildings! *Biff wraps the tubing around his hand and quickly goes up the stairs.*

ACT 2

SCENE: *Music is heard, gay and bright. The curtain rises as the music fades away. Willy, in shirt sleeves, is sitting at the kitchen table, sipping coffee, his hat in his lap. Linda is filling his cup when she can.*

WILLY. Wonderful coffee. Meal in itself.

LINDA. Can I make you some eggs?

WILLY. No. Take a breath.

LINDA. You look so rested, dear.

WILLY. I slept like a dead one. First time in months. Imagine, sleeping till ten on a Tuesday morning. Boys left nice and early, heh?

LINDA. They were out of here by eight o'clock.

WILLY. Good work!

LINDA. It was so thrilling to see them leaving together. I can't get over the shaving lotion in this house!

WILLY (*smiling*). Mmm . . .

LINDA. Biff was very changed this morning. His whole attitude seemed to be hopeful. He couldn't wait to get downtown to see Oliver.

WILLY. He's heading for a change. There's no question, there simply are certain men that take longer to get—solidified. How did he dress?

LINDA. His blue suit. He's so handsome in that suit. He could be a—anything in that suit!

Willy gets up from the table. Linda holds his jacket for him.

WILLY. There's no question, no question at all. Gee, on the way home tonight I'd like to buy some seeds.

LINDA (*laughing*). That'd be wonderful. But not enough sun gets back there. Nothing'll grow any more.

WILLY. You wait, kid, before it's all over we're gonna get a little place out in the country, and I'll raise some vegetables, a couple of chickens . . .

LINDA. You'll do it yet, dear.

Willy walks out of his jacket. Linda follows him.

WILLY. And they'll get married, and come for a weekend. I'd build a little guest house. 'Cause I got so many fine tools, all I'd need would be a little lumber and some peace of mind.

LINDA (*joyfully*). I sewed the lining . . .

WILLY. I could build two guest houses, so they'd both come. Did he decide how much he's going to ask Oliver for?

LINDA (*getting him into the jacket*). He didn't mention it, but I imagine ten or fifteen thousand. You going to talk to Howard today?

WILLY. Yeah. I'll put it to him straight and simple. He'll just have to take me off the road.

LINDA. And Willy, don't forget to ask for a little advance, because we've got the insurance premium. It's the grace period now.

WILLY. That's a hundred . . . ?

LINDA. A hundred and eight, sixty-eight. Because we're a little short again.

WILLY. Why are we short?

LINDA. Well, you had the motor job on the car . . .

WILLY. That goddam Studebaker!

LINDA. And you got one more payment on the refrigerator . . .

WILLY. But it just broke again!

LINDA. Well, it's old, dear.

WILLY. I told you we should've bought a well-advertised machine. Charley bought a General Electric and it's twenty years old and it's still good, that son-of-a-bitch.

LINDA. But, Willy . . .

WILLY. Whoever heard of a Hastings refrigerator? Once in my life I would like to own something outright before it's broken! I'm always in a race with the junkyard! I just finished paying for the car and it's on its last legs. The refrigerator consumes belts like a goddam maniac. They time those things. They time them so when you finally paid for them, they're used up.

LINDA (*buttoning up his jacket as he unbuttons it*). All told, about two hundred dollars would carry us, dear. But that includes the last payment on the mortgage. After this payment, Willy, the house belongs to us.

WILLY. It's twenty-five years!

LINDA. Biff was nine years old when we bought it.

WILLY. Well, that's a great thing. To weather a twenty-five year mortgage is . . .

LINDA. It's an accomplishment.

WILLY. All the cement, the lumber, the reconstruction I put in this house! There ain't a crack to be found in it any more.

LINDA. Well, it served its purpose.

WILLY. What purpose? Some stranger'll come along, move in, and that's that. If only Biff would take this house, and raise a family . . . (*He starts to go.*) Good-by, I'm late.

LINDA (*suddenly remembering*). Oh, I forgot! You're supposed to meet them for dinner.

WILLY. Me?

LINDA. At Frank's Chop House on Forty-eighth near Sixth Avenue.

WILLY. Is that so! How about you?

LINDA. No, just the three of you. They're gonna blow you to a big meal!

WILLY. Don't say! Who thought of that?

LINDA. Biff came to me this morning, Willy, and he said, "Tell Dad, we want to blow him to a big meal." Be there six o'clock. You and your two boys are going to have dinner.

WILLY. Gee whiz! That's really somethin'. I'm gonna knock Howard for a loop, kid. I'll get an advance, and I'll come home with a New York job. Goddammit, now I'm gonna do it!

LINDA. Oh, that's the spirit, Willy!

WILLY. I will never get behind a wheel the rest of my life!

LINDA. It's changing, Willy, I can feel it changing!

WILLY. Beyond a question. G'by, I'm late. (*He starts to go again.*)

LINDA (*calling after him as she runs to the kitchen table for a handkerchief*). You got your glasses?

WILLY (*feels for them, then comes back in*). Yeah, yeah, got my glasses.

LINDA (*giving him the handkerchief*). And a handkerchief.

WILLY. Yeah, handkerchief.

LINDA. And your saccharine?

WILLY. Yeah, my saccharine.

LINDA. Be careful on the subway stairs.

She kisses him, and a silk stocking is seen hanging from her hand. Willy notices it.

WILLY. Will you stop mending stockings? At least while I'm in the house. It gets me nervous. I can't tell you. Please.

Linda hides the stocking in her hand as she follows Willy across the forestage in front of the house.

LINDA. Remember, Frank's Chop House.

WILLY (*passing the apron*). Maybe beets would grow out there.

LINDA (*laughing*). But you tried so many times.

WILLY. Yeah. Well, don't work hard today. (*He disappears around the right corner of the house.*)

LINDA. Be careful!

As Willy vanishes, Linda waves to him. Suddenly the phone rings. She runs across the stage and into the kitchen and lifts it.

LINDA. Hello? Oh, Biff! I'm so glad you called, I just . . . Yes, sure, I just told him. Yes, he'll be there for dinner at six o'clock, I didn't forget. Listen, I was just dying to tell you. You know that little rubber pipe I told you about? That he connected to the gas heater? I finally decided to go down the cellar this morning and take it away and destroy it. But it's gone! Imagine? He took it away himself, it isn't there! (*She listens.*) When? Oh, then you took it. Oh—nothing, it's just that I'd hoped he'd taken it away himself. Oh, I'm not worried, darling, because this morning he left in such high spirits, it was like the old days! I'm not afraid any more. Did Mr. Oliver see you? . . . Well, you wait there then. And make a nice impression on him, darling. Just don't perspire too much before you see him. And have a nice time with Dad. He may have big news too! . . . That's right, a New York job. And be sweet to him tonight, dear. Be loving to him. Because he's only a little boat looking for a harbor. (*She is trembling with sorrow and joy.*) Oh, that's wonderful, Biff, you'll save his life. Thanks, darling. Just put your arm around him when he comes into the restaurant. Give him a smile. That's the boy . . . Good-by, dear. . . . You got your comb? . . . That's fine. Good-by, Biff dear.

In the middle of her speech, Howard Wagner, thirty-six, wheels in a small typewriter table on which is a wire-recording machine and proceeds to plug it in. This is on the left forestage. Light slowly fades on Linda as it rises on Howard. Howard is intent on threading the machine and only glances over his shoulder as Willy appears.

WILLY. Pst! Pst!

HOWARD. Hello, Willy, come in.

WILLY. Like to have a little talk with you, Howard.

HOWARD. Sorry to keep you waiting. I'll be with you in a minute.

WILLY. What's that, Howard?

HOWARD. Didn't you ever see one of these? Wire recorder.

WILLY. Oh. Can we talk a minute?

HOWARD. Records things. Just got delivery yesterday. Been driving me crazy, the most terrific machine I ever saw in my life. I was up all night with it.

WILLY. What do you do with it?

HOWARD. I bought it for dictation, but you can do anything with it. Listen to this. I had it home last night. Listen to what I picked up. The first one is my daughter. Get this. (*He flicks the switch and "Roll Out the Barrel" is heard being whistled.*) Listen to that kid whistle.

WILLY. That is lifelike, isn't it?

HOWARD. Seven years old. Get that tone.

WILLY. Ts, ts. Like to ask a little favor if you . . .

The whistling breaks off, and the voice of Howard's daughter is heard.

HIS DAUGHTER. "Now you, Daddy."

HOWARD. She's crazy for me! (*Again the same song is whistled.*) That's me! Ha! (*He winks.*)

WILLY. You're very good!

The whistling breaks off again. The machine runs silent for a moment.

HOWARD. Sh! Get this now, this is my son.

HIS SON. "The capital of Alabama is Montgomery; the capital of Arizona is Phoenix; the capital of Arkansas is Little Rock; the capital of California is Sacramento . . ." (*and on, and on.*)

HOWARD (*holding up five fingers*). Five years old, Willy!

WILLY. He'll make an announcer some day!

HIS SON (*continuing*). "The capital . . ."

HOWARD. Get that—alphabetical order! (*The machine breaks off suddenly.*) Wait a minute. The maid kicked the plug out.

WILLY. It certainly is a . . .

HOWARD. Sh, for God's sake!

HIS SON. "It's nine o'clock, Bulova watch time. So I have to go to sleep."

WILLY. That really is . . .

HOWARD. Wait a minute! The next is my wife.

They wait.

HOWARD'S VOICE. "Go on, say something." (*Pause.*) "Well, you gonna talk?"

HIS WIFE. "I can't think of anything."

HOWARD'S VOICE. "Well, talk—it's turning."

HIS WIFE (*shyly, beaten*). "Hello." (*Silence.*) "Oh, Howard, I can't talk into this . . ."

HOWARD (*snapping the machine off*). That was my wife.

WILLY. That is a wonderful machine. Can we . . .

HOWARD. I tell you, Willy, I'm gonna take my camera, and my bandsaw, and all my hobbies, and out they go. This is the most fascinating relaxation I ever found.

WILLY. I think I'll get one myself.

HOWARD. Sure, they're only a hundred and a half. You can't do without it. Supposing you wanna hear Jack Benny, see? But you can't be at home at that hour. So you tell the maid to turn the radio on when Jack Benny comes on, and this automatically goes on with the radio . . .

WILLY. And when you come home you . . .

HOWARD. You can come home twelve o'clock, one o'clock, any time you like, and you get yourself a Coke and sit yourself down, throw the switch, and there's Jack Benny's program in the middle of the night!

WILLY. I'm definitely going to get one. Because lots of times I'm on the road, and I think to myself, what I must be missing on the radio!

HOWARD. Don't you have a radio in the car?

WILLY. Well, yeah, but who ever thinks of turning it on?

HOWARD. Say, aren't you supposed to be in Boston?

WILLY. That's what I want to talk to you about, Howard. You got a minute? (*He draws a chair in from the wing.*)

HOWARD. What happened? What're you doing here?

WILLY. Well . . .

HOWARD. You didn't crack up again, did you?

WILLY. Oh, no. No . . .

HOWARD. Geez, you had me worried there for a minute. What's the trouble?

WILLY. Well, tell you the truth, Howard. I've come to the decision that I'd rather not travel any more.

HOWARD. Not travel! Well, what'll you do?

WILLY. Remember, Christmas time, when you had the party here? You said you'd try to think of some spot for me here in town.

HOWARD. With us?

WILLY. Well, sure.

HOWARD. Oh, yeah, yeah. I remember. Well, I couldn't think of anything for you, Willy.

WILLY. I tell ya, Howard. The kids are all grown up, y'know. I don't need much any more. If I could take home—well, sixty-five dollars a week, I could swing it.

HOWARD. Yeah, but Willy, see I . . .

WILLY. I tell ya why, Howard. Speaking frankly and between the two of us, y'know—I'm just a little tired.

HOWARD. Oh, I could understand that, Willy. But you're a road man, Willy, and we do a road business. We've only got a half-dozen salesmen on the floor here.

WILLY. God knows, Howard. I never asked a favor of any man. But I was with the firm when your father used to carry you in here in his arms.

HOWARD. I know that, Willy, but . . .

WILLY. Your father came to me the day you were born and asked me what I thought of the name Howard, may he rest in peace.

HOWARD. I appreciate that, Willy, but there just is no spot here for you. If I had a spot I'd slam you right in, but I just don't have a single solitary spot.

He looks for his lighter. Willy has picked it up and gives it to him. Pause.

WILLY (*with increasing anger*). Howard, all I need to set my table is fifty dollars a week.

HOWARD. But where am I going to put you, kid?

WILLY. Look, it isn't a question of whether I can sell merchandise, is it?

HOWARD. No, but it's business, kid, and everybody's gotta pull his own weight.

WILLY (*desperately*). Just let me tell you a story, Howard . . .

HOWARD. 'Cause you gotta admit, business is business.

WILLY (*angrily*). Business is definitely business, but just listen for a minute. You don't understand this. When I was a boy—eighteen, nineteen—I was already on the road. And there was a question in my mind as to whether selling had a future for me. Because in those days I had a yearning to go to Alaska. See, there were three gold strikes in one month in Alaska, and I felt like going out. Just for the ride, you might say.

HOWARD (*barely interested*). Don't say.

WILLY. Oh, yeah, my father lived many years in Alaska. He was an adventurous man. We've got quite a little streak of self-reliance in our family. I thought I'd go out with my older brother and try to locate him, and maybe settle in the North with the old man. And I was almost decided to go, when I met a salesman in the Parker House. His name was Dave Singleman. And he was eighty-four years old, and he'd drummed merchandise in thirty-one states. And old Dave, he'd go up to his room, y'understand, put on his green velvet slippers—I'll never forget—and pick up his phone and call the buyers, and without ever leaving his room, at the age of eighty-four, he made his living. And when I saw that, I realized that selling was the greatest career a man could want. 'Cause what could be more satisfying than to be able to go, at the age of eight-four, into twenty or thirty different cities, and pick up a phone, and be remembered and loved and helped by so many different people? Do you know? when he died—and by the way he died the death of a salesman, in his green velvet slippers in the smoker of the New York, New Haven and Hartford, going into Boston—when he died, hundreds of salesmen and buyers were at his funeral. Things were sad on a lotta trains for months after that. (*He stands up, Howard has not looked at him.*) In those days there was personality in it, Howard. There was respect, and comradeship, and gratitude in it. Today, it's all cut and dried, and there's no chance for bringing friendship to bear—or personality. You see what I mean? They don't know me any more.

HOWARD (*moving away, to the right*). That's just the thing, Willy.

WILLY. If I had forty dollars a week—that's all I'd need. Forty dollars, Howard.

HOWARD. Kid, I can't take blood from a stone, I . . .

WILLY (*desperation is on him now*). Howard, the year Al Smith was nominated, your father came to me and . . .

HOWARD (*starting to go off*). I've got to see some people, kid.

WILLY (*stopping him*). I'm talking about your father! There were promises made across this desk! You mustn't tell me you've got people to see—I put thirty-four years into this firm, Howard, and now I can't pay my insurance! You can't eat the orange and throw the peel away—a man is not a piece of fruit! (*After a pause.*) Now pay attention. Your father—in 1928 I had a big year. I averaged a hundred and seventy dollars a week in commissions.

HOWARD (*impatiently*). Now, Willy, you never averaged . . .

WILLY (*banging his hand on the desk*). I averaged a hundred and seventy dollars a week in the year of 1928! And your father came to me—or rather, I was in the office here—it was right over this desk—and he put his hand on my shoulder . . .

HOWARD (*getting up*). You'll have to excuse me, Willy, I gotta see some people. Pull yourself together. (*Going out.*) I'll be back in a little while.

On Howard's exit, the light on his chair grows very bright and strange.

WILLY. Pull myself together! What the hell did I say to him? My God, I was yelling at him! How could I? (*Willy breaks off, staring at the light, which occupies the chair, animating it. He approaches this chair, standing across the desk from it.*) Frank, Frank, don't you remember what you told me that time? How you put your hand on my shoulder, and Frank . . . (*He leans on the desk and as he speaks the dead man's name he accidentally switches on the recorder, and instantly*)

HOWARD'S SON. " . . . of New York is Albany. The capital of Ohio is Cincinnati, the capital of Rhode Island is . . . " (*The recitation continues.*)

WILLY (*leaping away with fright, shouting*). Ha! Howard! Howard! Howard!

HOWARD (*rushing in*). What happened?

WILLY (*pointing at the machine, which continues nasally, childishly, with the capital cities*). Shut it off! Shut it off!

HOWARD (*pulling the plug out*). Look, Willy . . .

WILLY (*pressing his hands to his eyes*). I gotta get myself some coffee. I'll get some coffee . . .

Willy starts to walk out. Howard stops him.

HOWARD (*rolling up the cord*). Willy, look . . .

WILLY. I'll go to Boston.

HOWARD. Willy, you can't go to Boston for us.

WILLY. Why can't I go?

HOWARD. I don't want you to represent us. I've been meaning to tell you for a long time now.

WILLY. Howard, are you firing me?

HOWARD. I think you need a good long rest, Willy.

WILLY. Howard . . .

HOWARD. And when you feel better, come back, and we'll see if we can work something out.

WILLY. But I gotta earn money, Howard. I'm in no position to . . .

HOWARD. Where are your sons? Why don't your sons give you a hand?

WILLY. They're working on a very big deal.

HOWARD. This is no time for false pride, Willy. You go to

your sons and you tell them that you're tired. You've got two great boys, haven't you?

WILLY. Oh, no question, no question, but in the meantime . . .

HOWARD. Then that's that, heh?

WILLY. All right, I'll go to Boston tomorrow.

HOWARD. No, no.

WILLY. I can't throw myself on my sons. I'm not a cripple!

HOWARD. Look, kid, I'm busy this morning.

WILLY (*grasping Howard's arm*). Howard, you've got to let me go to Boston!

HOWARD (*hard, keeping himself under control*). I've got a line of people to see this morning. Sit down, take five minutes, and pull yourself together, and then go home, will ya? I need the office, Willy. (*He starts to go, turns, remembering the recorder, starts to push off the table holding the recorder.*) Oh, yeah. Whenever you can this week, stop by and drop off the samples. You'll feel better, Willy, and then come back and we'll talk. Pull yourself together, kid, there's people outside.

Howard exits, pushing the table off left. Willy stares into space, exhausted. Now the music is heard—Ben's music—first distantly, then closer, closer. As Willy speaks, Ben enters from the right. He carries valise and umbrella.

WILLY. Oh, Ben, how did you do it? What is the answer? Did you wind up the Alaska deal already?

BEN. Doesn't take much time if you know what you're doing. Just a short business trip. Boarding ship in an hour. Wanted to say good-by.

WILLY. Ben, I've got to talk to you.

BEN (*glancing at his watch*). Haven't the time, William.

WILLY (*crossing the apron to Ben*). Ben, nothing's working out. I don't know what to do.

BEN. Now, look here, William. I've bought timberland in Alaska and I need a man to look after things for me.

WILLY. God, timberland! Me and my boys in those grand outdoors!

BEN. You've a new continent at your doorstep, William. Get out of these cities, they're full of talk and time payments and courts of law. Screw on your fists and you can fight for a fortune up there.

WILLY. Yes, yes! Linda, Linda!

Linda enters as of old, with the wash.

LINDA. Oh, you're back?

BEN. I haven't much time.

WILLY. No, wait! Linda, he's got a proposition for me in Alaska.

LINDA. But you've got . . . (*To Ben.*) He's got a beautiful job here.

WILLY. But in Alaska, kid, I could . . .

LINDA. You're doing well enough, Willy!

BEN (*to Linda*). Enough for what, my dear?

LINDA (*frightened of Ben and angry at him*). Don't say those things to him! Enough to be happy right here, right now. (*To Willy, while Ben laughs.*) Why must everybody conquer the world? You're well liked, and the boys love you, and someday—(*To Ben*)—why, old man Wagner told him just the other day that if he keeps it up he'll be a member of the firm, didn't he, Willy?

WILLY. Sure, sure. I am building something with this firm, Ben, and if a man is building something he must be on the right track, mustn't he?

BEN. What are you building? Lay your hand on it. Where is it?

WILLY (*hesitantly*). That's true, Linda, there's nothing.

LINDA. Why? (*To Ben.*) There's a man eighty-four years old . . .

WILLY. That's right, Ben, that's right. When I look at that man I say, what is there to worry about?

BEN. Bah!

WILLY. It's true, Ben. All he has to do is go into any city, pick up the phone, and he's making his living and you know why?

BEN (*picking up his valise*). I've got to go.

WILLY (*holding Ben back*). Look at this boy!

Biff, in his high school sweater, enters carrying suitcase. Happy carries Biff's shoulder guards, gold helmet, and football pants.

WILLY. Without a penny to his name, three great universities are begging for him, and from there the sky's the limit, because it's not what you do, Ben. It's who you know and the smile on your face! It's contacts, Ben, contacts! The whole wealth of Alaska passes over the lunch table at the Commodore Hotel, and that's the wonder, the wonder of this country, that a man can end with diamonds here on the basis of being liked! (*He turns to Biff.*) And that's why when you get out on that field today it's important. Because thousands of people will be rooting for you and loving you. (*To Ben, who has again begun to leave.*) And Ben! when he walks into a business office his name will sound out like a bell and all the doors will open to him! I've seen it, Ben, I've seen it a thousand times! You can't feel it with your hand like timber, but it's there!

BEN. Good-by, William.

WILLY. Ben, am I right? Don't you think I'm right? I value your advice.

BEN. There's a new continent at your doorstep, William. You could walk out rich. Rich! (*He is gone.*)

WILLY. We'll do it here, Ben! You hear me? We're gonna do it here!

Young Bernard rushes in. The gay music of the Boys is heard.

BERNARD. Oh, gee, I was afraid you left already!

WILLY. Why? What time is it?

BERNARD. It's half-past one!

WILLY. Well, come on, everybody! Ebbets Field next stop! Where's the pennants? (*He rushes through the wall-line of the kitchen and out into the living room.*)

LINDA (*to Biff*). Did you pack fresh underwear?

BIFF (*who has been limbering up*). I want to go!

BERNARD. Biff, I'm carrying your helmet, ain't I?

HAPPY. No, I'm carrying the helmet.

BERNARD. Oh, Biff, you promised me.

HAPPY. I'm carrying the helmet.

BERNARD. How am I going to get in the locker room?

LINDA. Let him carry the shoulder guards. (*She puts her coat and hat on in the kitchen.*)

BERNARD. Can I, Biff? 'Cause I told everybody I'm going to be in the locker room.

HAPPY. In Ebbets Field it's the clubhouse.

BERNARD. I meant the clubhouse. Biff!

HAPPY. Biff!

BIFF (*grandly, after a slight pause*). Let him carry the shoulder guards.

HAPPY (*as he gives Bernard the shoulder guards*). Stay close to us now.

Willy rushes in with the pennants.

WILLY (*handing them out*). Everybody wave when Biff comes out on the field. (*Happy and Bernard run off.*) You set now, boy?

The music has died away.

BIFF. Ready to go, Pop. Every muscle is ready.

WILLY (*at the edge of the apron*). You realize what this means?

BIFF. That's right, Pop.

WILLY (*feeling Biff's muscles*). You're comin' home this afternoon captain of the All-Scholastic Championship Team of the City of New York.

BIFF. I got it, Pop. And remember, pal, when I take off my helmet, that touchdown is for you.

WILLY. Let's go! (*He is starting out, with his arm around Biff, when Charley enters, as of old, in knickers.*) I got no room for you, Charley.

CHARLEY. Room? For what?

WILLY. In the car.

CHARLEY. You goin' for a ride? I wanted to shoot some casino.

WILLY (*furiously*). Casino! (*Incredulously.*) Don't you realize what today is?

LINDA. Oh, he knows, Willy. He's just kidding you.

WILLY. That's nothing to kid about!

CHARLEY. No, Linda, what's goin' on?

LINDA. He's playing in Ebbets Field.

CHARLEY. Baseball in this weather?

WILLY. Don't talk to him. Come on, come on! (*He is pushing them out.*)

CHARLEY. Wait a minute, didn't you hear the news?

WILLY. What?

CHARLEY. Don't you listen to the radio? Ebbets Field just blew up.

WILLY. You go to hell! (*Charley laughs. Pushing them out.*) Come on, come on! We're late.

CHARLEY (*as they go*). Knock a homer, Biff, knock a homer!

WILLY (*the last to leave, turning to Charley*). I don't think that was funny, Charley. This is the greatest day of his life.

CHARLEY. Willy, when are you going to grow up?

WILLY. Yeah, heh? When this game is over, Charley, you'll be laughing out of the other side of your face. They'll be calling him another Red Grange. Twenty-five thousand a year.

CHARLEY (*kidding*). Is that so?

WILLY. Yeah, that's so.

CHARLEY. Well, then, I'm sorry, Willy. But tell me something.

WILLY. What?

CHARLEY. Who is Red Grange?

WILLY. Put up your hands. Goddam you, put up your hands!

Charley, chuckling, shakes his head and walks away, around the left corner of the stage. Willy follows him. The music rises to a mocking frenzy.

WILLY. Who the hell do you think you are, better than everybody else? You don't know everything, you big, ignorant, stupid . . . Put up your hands!

Light rises, on the right side of the forestage, on a small table in the reception room of Charley's office. Traffic sounds are heard. Bernard, now mature, sits whistling to himself. A pair of tennis rackets and an old overnight bag are on the floor beside him.

WILLY (*offstage*). What are you walking away for? Don't walk away! If you're going to say something say it to my face! I know you laugh at me behind my back. You'll laugh out of the other side of your goddam face after this game. Touchdown! Touchdown! Eighty thousand people! Touchdown! Right between the goal posts.

Bernard is a quiet, earnest, but self-assured young man. Willy's voice is coming from right upstage now. Bernard lowers his feet off the table and listens. Jenny, his father's secretary, enters.

JENNY (*distressed*). Say, Bernard, will you go out in the hall?

BERNARD. What is that noise? Who is it?

JENNY. Mr. Loman. He just got off the elevator.

BERNARD (*getting up*). Who's he arguing with?

JENNY. Nobody. There's nobody with him. I can't deal with him any more, and your father gets all upset every time he comes. I've got a lot of typing to do, and your father's waiting to sign it. Will you see him?

WILLY (*entering*). Touchdown! Touch—(*He sees Jenny.*) Jenny, Jenny, good to see you. How're ya? Workin'? Or still honest?

JENNY. Fine. How've you been feeling?

WILLY. Not much any more, Jenny. Ha, ha! (*He is surprised to see the rackets.*)

BERNARD. Hello, Uncle Willy.

WILLY (*almost shocked*). Bernard! Well, look who's here! (*He comes quickly, guiltily, to Bernard and warmly shakes his hand.*)

BERNARD. How are you? Good to see you.

WILLY. What are you doing here?

BERNARD. Oh, just stopped by to see Pop. Get off my feet till my train leaves. I'm going to Washington in a few minutes.

WILLY. Is he in?

BERNARD. Yes, he's in his office with the accountant. Sit down.

WILLY (*sitting down*). What're you going to do in Washington?

BERNARD. Oh, just a case I've got there, Willy.

WILLY. That so? (*Indicating the rackets.*) You going to play tennis there?

BERNARD. I'm staying with a friend who's got a court.

WILLY. Don't say. His own tennis court. Must be fine people, I bet.

BERNARD. They are, very nice. Dad tells me Biff's in town.

WILLY (*with a big smile*). Yeah, Biff's in. Working on a very big deal, Bernard.

BERNARD. What's Biff doing?

WILLY. Well, he's been doing very big things in the West. But he decided to establish himself here. Very big. We're having dinner. Did I hear your wife had a boy?

BERNARD. That's right. Our second.

WILLY. Two boys! What do you know!

BERNARD. What kind of a deal has Biff got?

WILLY. Well, Bill Oliver—very big sporting-goods man—he wants Biff very badly. Called him in from the West. Long distance, carte blanche, special deliveries. Your friends have their own private tennis court?

BERNARD. You still with the old firm, Willy?

WILLY (*after a pause*). I'm—I'm overjoyed to see how you made the grade, Bernard, overjoyed. It's an encouraging thing to see a young man really—really . . . Looks very good for Biff—very . . . (*He breaks off, then.*) Bernard . . . (*He is so full of emotion, he breaks off again.*)

BERNARD. What is it, Willy?

WILLY (*small and alone*). What—what's the secret?

BERNARD. What secret?

WILLY. How—how did you? Why didn't he ever catch on?

BERNARD. I wouldn't know that, Willy.

WILLY (*confidentially, desperately*). You were his friend, his boyhood friend. There's something I don't understand about it. His life ended after that Ebbets Field game. From the age of seventeen nothing good ever happened to him.

BERNARD. He never trained himself for anything.

WILLY. But he did, he did. After high school he took so many correspondence courses. Radio mechanics; television; God knows what, and never made the slightest mark.

BERNARD (*taking off his glasses*). Willy, do you want to talk candidly?

WILLY (*rising, faces Bernard*). I regard you as a very brilliant man, Bernard. I value your advice.

BERNARD. Oh, the hell with the advice, Willy. I couldn't advise you. There's just one thing I've always wanted to ask you. When he was supposed to graduate, and the math teacher flunked him . . .

WILLY. Oh, that son-of-a-bitch ruined his life.

BERNARD. Yeah, but, Willy, all he had to do was go to summer school and make up that subject.

WILLY. That's right, that's right.

BERNARD. Did you tell him not to go to summer school?

WILLY. Me? I begged him to go. I ordered him to go!

BERNARD. Then why wouldn't he go?

WILLY. Why? Why! Bernard, that question has been trailing me like a ghost for the last fifteen years. He flunked the subject, and laid down and died like a hammer hit him!

BERNARD. Take it easy, kid.

WILLY. Let me talk to you—I got nobody to talk to. Bernard, Bernard, was it my fault? Y'see? It keeps going around in my mind, maybe I did something to him. I got nothing to give him.

BERNARD. Don't take it so hard.

WILLY. Why did he lay down? What is the story there? You were his friend!

BERNARD. Willy, I remember, it was June, and our grades came out. And he'd flunked math.

WILLY. That son-of-a-bitch!

BERNARD. No, it wasn't right then. Biff just got very angry, I remember, and he was ready to enroll in summer school.

WILLY (*surprised*). He was?

BERNARD. He wasn't beaten by it at all. But then, Willy, he disappeared from the block for almost a month. And I got the idea that he'd gone up to New England to see you. Did he have a talk with you then?

Willy stares in silence.

BERNARD. Willy?

WILLY (*with a strong edge of resentment in his voice*). Yeah, he came to Boston. What about it?

BERNARD. Well, just that when he came back—I'll never forget this, it always mystifies me. Because I'd thought so well of Biff, even though he'd always taken advantage of me. I loved him, Willy, y'know? And he came back after that month and took his sneakers—remember those sneakers with "University of Virginia" printed on them? He was so proud of those, wore them every day. And he took them down in the cellar, and burned them up in the furnace. We had a fist fight. It lasted at least half an hour. Just the two of us, punching each other down the cellar, and crying right through it. I've often thought of how strange it was that I knew he'd given up his life. What happened in Boston, Willy?

Willy looks at him as at an intruder.

BERNARD. I just bring it up because you asked me.

WILLY (*angrily*). Nothing. What do you mean, "What happened?" What's that got to do with anything?

BERNARD. Well, don't get sore.

WILLY. What are you trying to do, blame it on me? If a boy lays down is that my fault?

BERNARD. Now, Willy, don't get . . .

WILLY. Well, don't—don't talk to me that way! What does that mean, "What happened?"

Charley enters. He is in his vest, and he carries a bottle of bourbon.

CHARLEY. Hey, you're going to miss that train. (*He waves the bottle.*)

BERNARD. Yeah, I'm going. (*He takes the bottle.*) Thanks, Pop. (*He picks up his rackets and bag.*) Good-by, Willy, and don't worry about it. You know, "If at first you don't succeed . . ."

WILLY. Yes, I believe in that.

BERNARD. But sometimes, Willy, it's better for a man just to walk away.

WILLY. Walk away?

BERNARD. That's right.

WILLY. But if you can't walk away?

BERNARD (*after a slight pause*). I guess that's when it's tough. (*Extending his hand.*) Good-by, Willy.

WILLY (*shaking Bernard's hand*). Good-by, boy.

CHARLEY (*an arm on Bernard's shoulder*). How do you like this kid? Gonna argue a case in front of the Supreme Court.

BERNARD (*protesting*). Pop!

WILLY (*genuinely shocked, pained, and happy*). No! The Supreme Court!

BERNARD. I gotta run. 'By, Dad!

CHARLEY. Knock 'em dead, Bernard!

Bernard goes off.

WILLY (*as Charley takes out his wallet*). The Supreme Court! And he didn't even mention it!

CHARLEY (*counting out money on the desk*). He don't have to—he's gonna do it.

WILLY. And you never told him what to do, did you? You never took any interest in him.

CHARLEY. My salvation is that I never took any interest in anything. There's some money—fifty dollars. I got an accountant inside.

WILLY. Charley, look . . . (*with difficulty.*) I got my insurance to pay. If you can manage it—I need a hundred and ten dollars.

Charley doesn't reply for a moment; merely stops moving.

WILLY. I'd draw it from my bank but Linda would know, and I . . .

CHARLEY. Sit down, Willy.

WILLY (*moving toward the chair*). I'm keeping an account of everything, remember. I'll pay every penny back. (*He sits.*)

CHARLEY. Now listen to me, Willy.

WILLY. I want you to know I appreciate . . .

CHARLEY (*sitting down on the table*). Willy, what're you doin'? What the hell is going on in your head?

WILLY. Why? I'm simply . . .

CHARLEY. I offered you a job. You make fifty dollars a week. And I won't send you on the road.

WILLY. I've got a job.

CHARLEY. Without pay? What kind of a job is a job without pay? (*He rises.*) Now, look, kid, enough is enough. I'm no genius but I know when I'm being insulted.

WILLY. Insulted!

CHARLEY. Why don't you want to work for me?

WILLY. What's the matter with you? I've got a job.

CHARLEY. Then what're you walkin' in here every week for?

WILLY (*getting up*). Well, if you don't want me to walk in here . . .

CHARLEY. I'm offering you a job.

WILLY. I don't want your goddam job!

CHARLEY. When the hell are you going to grow up?

WILLY (*furiously*). You big ignoramus, if you say that to me again I'll rap you one! I don't care how big you are! (*He's ready to fight.*)

Pause.

CHARLEY (*kindly, going to him*). How much do you need, Willy?

WILLY. Charley, I'm strapped. I'm strapped. I don't know what to do. I was just fired.

CHARLEY. Howard fired you?

WILLY. That snotnose. Imagine that? I named him. I named him Howard.

CHARLEY. Willy, when're you gonna realize that them things don't mean anything? You named him Howard, but you can't sell that. The only thing you got in this world is what you can sell. And the funny thing is that you're a salesman, and you don't know that.

WILLY. I've always tried to think otherwise, I guess. I always felt that if a man was impressive, and well liked, that nothing . . .

CHARLEY. Why must everybody like you? Who liked J. P. Morgan? Was he impressive? In a Turkish bath he'd look like a butcher. But with his pockets on he was very well liked. Now listen, Willy, I know you don't like me, and nobody can say I'm in love with you, but I'll give you a job because—just for the hell of it, put it that way. Now what do you say?

WILLY. I—I just can't work for you, Charley.

CHARLEY. What're you, jealous of me?

WILLY. I can't work for you, that's all, don't ask me why.

CHARLEY (*angered, takes out more bills*). You been jealous of me all your life, you damned fool! Here, pay your insurance. (*He puts the money in Willy's hand.*)

WILLY. I'm keeping strict accounts.

CHARLEY. I've got some work to do. Take care of yourself. And pay your insurance.

WILLY (*moving to the right*). Funny, y'know? After all the highways, and the trains, and the appointments, and the years, you end up worth more dead than alive.

CHARLEY. Willy, nobody's worth nothin' dead. (*After a slight pause.*) Did you hear what I said?

Willy stands still, dreaming.

CHARLEY. Willy!

WILLY. Apologize to Bernard for me when you see him. I didn't mean to argue with him. He's a fine boy. They're all fine boys, and they'll end up big—all of them. Someday they'll all play tennis together. Wish me luck, Charley. He saw Bill Oliver today.

CHARLEY. Good luck.

WILLY (*on the verge of tears*). Charley, you're the only friend I got. Isn't that a remarkable thing? (*He goes out.*)

CHARLEY. Jesus!

Charley stares after him a moment and follows. All light blacks out. Suddenly raucous music is heard, and a red glow rises behind the screen at right. Stanley, a young waiter, appears, carrying a table, followed by Happy, who is carrying two chairs.

STANLEY (*putting the table down*). That's all right, Mr. Loman, I can handle it myself. (*He turns and takes the chairs from Happy and places them at the table.*)

HAPPY (*glancing around*). Oh, this is better.

STANLEY. Sure, in the front there you're in the middle of all kinds of noise. Whenever you got a party, Mr. Loman, you just tell me and I'll put you back here. Y'know, there's a lotta people they don't like it private, because when they go out they like to see a lotta action around them because they're sick and tired to stay in the house by theirself. But I know you, you ain't from Hackensack. You know what I mean?

HAPPY (*sitting down*). So how's it coming, Stanley?

STANLEY. Ah, it's a dog life. I only wish during the war they'd a took me in the Army. I coulda been dead by now.

HAPPY. My brother's back, Stanley.

STANLEY. Oh, he come back, heh? From the Far West.

HAPPY. Yeah, big cattle man, my brother, so treat him right. And my father's coming too.

STANLEY. Oh, your father too!

HAPPY. You got a couple of nice lobsters?

STANLEY. Hundred per cent, big.

HAPPY. I want them with the claws.

STANLEY. Don't worry, I don't give you no mice. (*Happy laughs.*) How about some wine? It'll put a head on the meal.

HAPPY. No. You remember, Stanley, that recipe I brought you from overseas? With the champagne in it?

STANLEY. Oh, yeah, sure. I still got it tacked up yet in the kitchen. But that'll have to cost a buck apiece anyways.

HAPPY. That's all right.

STANLEY. What'd you, hit a number or somethin'?

HAPPY. No, it's a little celebration. My brother is—I think he pulled off a big deal today. I think we're going into business together.

STANLEY. Great! That's the best for you. Because a family business, you know what I mean?—that's the best.

HAPPY. That's what I think.

STANLEY. 'Cause what's the difference? Somebody steals? It's in the family. Know what I mean? (*Sotto voce.*) Like this bartender here. The boss is goin' crazy what kinda leak he's got in the cash register. You put it in but it don't come out.

HAPPY (*raising his head*). Sh!

STANLEY. What?

HAPPY. You notice I wasn't lookin' right or left, was I?

STANLEY. No.

HAPPY. And my eyes are closed.

STANLEY. So what's the . . . ?

HAPPY. Strudel's comin'.

STANLEY (*catching on, looks around*). Ah, no, there's no . . .

He breaks off as a furred, lavishly dressed Girl enters and sits at the next table. Both follow her with their eyes.

STANLEY. Geez, how'd ya know?

HAPPY. I got radar or something. (*Staring directly at her profile.*) Ooooooooo . . . Stanley.

STANLEY. I think that's for you, Mr. Loman.

HAPPY. Look at that mouth. Oh, God. And the binoculars.

STANLEY. Geez, you got a life, Mr. Loman.

HAPPY. Wait on her.

STANLEY (*going to the Girl's table*). Would you like a menu, ma'am?

GIRL. I'm expecting someone, but I'd like a . . .

HAPPY. Why don't you bring her—excuse me, miss, do you mind? I sell champagne, and I'd like you to try my brand. Bring her a champagne, Stanley.

GIRL. That's awfully nice of you.

HAPPY. Don't mention it. It's all company money. (*He laughs.*)

GIRL. That's a charming product to be selling, isn't it?

HAPPY. Oh, gets to be like everything else. Selling is selling, y'know.

GIRL. I suppose.

HAPPY. You don't happen to sell, do you?

GIRL. No, I don't sell.

HAPPY. Would you object to a compliment from a stranger? You ought to be on a magazine cover.

GIRL (*looking at him a little archly*). I have been.

Stanley comes in with a glass of champagne.

HAPPY. What'd I say before, Stanley? You see? She's a cover girl.

STANLEY. Oh, I could see, I could see.

HAPPY (*to the Girl*). What magazine?

GIRL. Oh, a lot of them. (*She takes the drink.*) Thank you.

HAPPY. You know what they say in France, don't you? "Champagne is the drink of the complexion"—Hya, Biff!

Biff has entered and sits with Happy.

BIFF. Hello, kid. Sorry I'm late.

HAPPY. I just got here. Uh, Miss . . . ?

GIRL. Forsythe.

HAPPY. Miss Forsythe, this is my brother.

BIFF. Is Dad here?

HAPPY. His name is Biff. You might've heard of him. Great football player.

GIRL. Really? What team?

HAPPY. Are you familiar with football?

GIRL. No, I'm afraid I'm not.

HAPPY. Biff is quarterback with the New York Giants.

GIRL. Well, that is nice, isn't it? (*She drinks.*)

HAPPY. Good health.

GIRL. I'm happy to meet you.

HAPPY. That's my name. Hap. It's really Harold, but at West Point they called me Happy.

GIRL (*now really impressed*). Oh, I see. How do you do? (*She turns her profile.*)

BIFF. Isn't Dad coming?

HAPPY. You want her?

BIFF. Oh, I could never make that.

HAPPY. I remember the time that idea would never come into your head. Where's the old confidence, Biff?

BIFF. I just saw Oliver . . .

HAPPY. Wait a minute. I've got to see that old confidence again. Do you want her? She's on call.

BIFF. Oh, no. (*He turns to look at the Girl.*)

HAPPY. I'm telling you. Watch this. (*Turning to the Girl.*) Honey? (*She turns to him.*) Are you busy?

GIRL. Well, I am . . . but I could make a phone call.

HAPPY. Do that, will you, honey? And see if you can get a friend. We'll be here for a while. Biff is one of the greatest football players in the country.

GIRL (*standing up*). Well, I'm certainly happy to meet you.

HAPPY. Come back soon.

GIRL. I'll try.

HAPPY. Don't try, honey, try hard.

The Girl exits. Stanley follows, shaking his head in bewildered admiration.

HAPPY. Isn't that a shame now? A beautiful girl like that? That's why I can't get married. There's not a good woman in a thousand. New York is loaded with them, kid!

BIFF. Hap, look . . .

HAPPY. I told you she was on call!

BIFF (*strangely unnerved*). Cut it out, will ya? I want to say something to you.

HAPPY. Did you see Oliver?

BIFF. I saw him all right. Now look, I want to tell Dad a couple of things and I want you to help me.

HAPPY. What? Is he going to back you?

BIFF. Are you crazy? You're out of your goddam head, you know that?

HAPPY. Why? What happened?

BIFF (*breathlessly*). I did a terrible thing today, Hap. It's been the strangest day I ever went through. I'm all numb, I swear.

HAPPY. You mean he wouldn't see you?

BIFF. Well, I waited six hours for him, see? All day. Kept sending my name in. Even tried to date his secretary so she'd get me to him, but no soap.

HAPPY. Because you're not showin' the old confidence, Biff. He remembered you, didn't he?

BIFF (*stopping Happy with a gesture*). Finally, about five o'clock, he comes out. Didn't remember who I was or anything. I felt like such an idiot, Hap.

HAPPY. Did you tell him my Florida idea?

BIFF. He walked away. I saw him for one minute. I got so mad I could've torn the walls down! How the hell did I ever get the idea I was a salesman there? I even believed myself that I'd been a salesman for him! And then he gave me one look and—I realized what a ridiculous lie my whole life has been! We've been talking in a dream for fifteen years. I was a shipping clerk.

HAPPY. What'd you do?

BIFF (*with great tension and wonder*). Well, he left, see. And the secretary went out. I was all alone in the waiting room. I don't know what came over me, Hap. The next thing I know I'm in his office—paneled walls, everything. I can't explain it. I—Hap. I took his fountain pen.

HAPPY. Geez, did he catch you?

BIFF. I ran out. I ran down all eleven flights. I ran and ran and ran.

HAPPY. That was an awful dumb—what'd you do that for?

BIFF (*agonized*). I don't know, I just—wanted to take something, I don't know. You gotta help me, Hap. I'm gonna tell Pop.

HAPPY. You crazy? What for?

BIFF. Hap, he's got to understand that I'm not the man somebody lends that kind of money to. He thinks I've been spiting him all these years and it's eating him up.

HAPPY. That's just it. You tell him something nice.

BIFF. I can't.

HAPPY. Say you got a lunch date with Oliver tomorrow.

BIFF. So what do I do tomorrow?

HAPPY. You leave the house tomorrow and come back at night and say Oliver is thinking it over. And he thinks it over for a couple of weeks, and gradually it fades away and nobody's the worse.

BIFF. But it'll go on forever!

HAPPY. Dad is never so happy as when he's looking forward to something!

Willy enters.

HAPPY. Hello, scout!

WILLY. Gee, I haven't been here in years!

Stanley has followed Willy in and sets a chair for him. Stanley starts off but Happy stops him.

HAPPY. Stanley!

Stanley stands by, waiting for an order.

BIFF (*going to Willy with guilt, as to an invalid*). Sit down, Pop. You want a drink?

WILLY. Sure, I don't mind.

BIFF. Let's get a load on.

WILLY. You look worried.

BIFF. N-no. (*To Stanley.*) Scotch all around. Make it doubles.

STANLEY. Doubles, right. (*He goes.*)

WILLY. You had a couple already, didn't you?

BIFF. Just a couple, yeah.

WILLY. Well, what happened, boy? (*Nodding affirmatively, with a smile.*) Everything go all right?

BIFF (*takes a breath, then reaches out and grasps Willy's hand*). Pal . . . (*He is smiling bravely, and Willy is smiling too.*) I had an experience today.

HAPPY. Terrific, Pop.

WILLY. That so? What happened?

BIFF (*high, slightly alcoholic, above the earth*). I'm going to tell you everything from first to last. It's been a strange day. (*Silence. He looks around, composes himself as best he can, but his breath keeps breaking the rhythm of his voice.*) I had to wait quite a while for him, and . . .

WILLY. Oliver?

BIFF. Yeah, Oliver. All day, as a matter of cold fact. And a lot of—instances—facts, Pop, facts about my life came back to me. Who was it, Pop? Who ever said I was a salesman with Oliver?

WILLY. Well, you were.

BIFF. No, Dad, I was a shipping clerk.

WILLY. But you were practically . . .

BIFF (*with determination*). Dad, I don't know who said it first, but I was never a salesman for Bill Oliver.

WILLY. What're you talking about?

BIFF. Let's hold on to the facts tonight, Pop. We're not going to get anywhere bullin' around. I was a shipping clerk.

WILLY (*angrily*). All right, now listen to me . . .

BIFF. Why don't you let me finish?

WILLY. I'm not interested in stories about the past or any crap of that kind because the woods are burning, boys, you understand? There's a big blaze going on all around. I was fired today.

BIFF (*shocked*). How could you be?

WILLY. I was fired, and I'm looking for a little good news to tell your mother, because the woman has waited and the woman has suffered. The gist of it is that I haven't got a story left in my head, Biff. So don't give me a lecture about facts and aspects. I am not interested. Now what've you got to say to me?

Stanley enters with three drinks. They wait until he leaves.

WILLY. Did you see Oliver?

BIFF. Jesus, Dad!

WILLY. You mean you didn't go up there?

HAPPY. Sure he went up there.

BIFF. I did. I—saw him. How could they fire you?

WILLY (*on the edge of his chair*). What kind of a welcome did he give you?

BIFF. He won't even let you work on commission?

WILLY. I'm out! (*Driving.*) So tell me, he gave you a warm welcome?

HAPPY. Sure, Pop, sure!

BIFF (*driven*). Well, it was kind of . . .

WILLY. I was wondering if he'd remember you. (*To Happy.*) Imagine, man doesn't see him for ten, twelve years and gives him that kind of a welcome!

HAPPY. Damn right!

BIFF (*trying to return to the offensive*). Pop, look . . .

WILLY. You know why he remembered you, don't you? Because you impressed him in those days.

BIFF. Let's talk quietly and get this down to the facts, huh?

WILLY (*as though Biff had been interrupting*). Well, what happened? It's great news, Biff. Did he take you into his office or'd you talk in the waiting room?

BIFF. Well, he came in, see, and . . .

WILLY (*with a big smile*). What'd he say? Betcha he threw his arm around you.

BIFF. Well, he kinda . . .

WILLY. He's a fine man. (*To Happy.*) Very hard man to see, y'know.

HAPPY (*agreeing*). Oh, I know.

WILLY (*to Biff*). Is that where you had the drinks?

BIFF. Yeah, he gave me a couple of—no, no!

HAPPY (*cutting in*). He told him my Florida idea.

WILLY. Don't interrupt. (*To Biff.*) How'd he react to the Florida idea?

BIFF. Dad, will you give me a minute to explain?

WILLY. I've been waiting for you to explain since I sat down here! What happened? He took you into his office and what?

BIFF. Well—I talked. And—and he listened, see.

WILLY. Famous for the way he listens, y'know. What was his answer?

BIFF. His answer was—(*He breaks off, suddenly angry.*) Dad, you're not letting me tell you what I want to tell you!

WILLY (*accusing, angered*). You didn't see him, did you?

BIFF. I did see him!

WILLY. What'd you insult him or something? You insulted him, didn't you?

BIFF. Listen, will you let me out of it, will you just let me out of it!

HAPPY. What the hell!

WILLY. Tell me what happened!

BIFF (*to Happy*). I can't talk to him!

A single trumpet note jars the ear. The light of green leaves stains the house, which holds the air of night and a dream. Young Bernard enters and knocks on the door of the house.

YOUNG BERNARD (FRANTICALLY). Mrs. Loman, Mrs. Loman!

HAPPY. Tell him what happened!

BIFF (*to Happy.*). Shut up and leave me alone!

WILLY. No, no! You had to go and flunk math!

BIFF. What math? What're you talking about?

YOUNG BERNARD. Mrs. Loman, Mrs. Loman!

Linda appears in the house, as of old.

WILLY (*wildly*). Math, math, math!

BIFF. Take it easy, Pop!

YOUNG BERNARD. Mrs. Loman!

WILLY (*furiously*). If you hadn't flunked you'd've been set by now!

BIFF. Now, look, I'm gonna tell you what happened, and you're going to listen to me.

YOUNG BERNARD. Mrs. Loman!

BIFF. I waited six hours . . .

HAPPY. What the hell are you saying?

BIFF. I kept sending in my name but he wouldn't see me. So finally he . . . (*He continues unheard as light fades low on the restaurant.*)

YOUNG BERNARD. Biff flunked math!

LINDA. No!

YOUNG BERNARD. Birnbaum flunked him! They won't graduate him!

LINDA. But they have to. He's gotta go to the university. Where is he? Biff! Biff!

YOUNG BERNARD. No, he left. He went to Grand Central.

LINDA. Grand—You mean he went to Boston!

YOUNG BERNARD. Is Uncle Willy in Boston?

LINDA. Oh, maybe Willy can talk to the teacher. Oh, the poor, poor boy!

Light on house area snaps out.

BIFF (*at the table, now audible, holding up a gold fountain pen*). . . . so I'm washed up with Oliver, you understand? Are you listening to me?

WILLY (*at a loss*). Yeah, sure. If you hadn't flunked . . .

BIFF. Flunked what? What're you talking about?

WILLY. Don't blame everything on me! I didn't flunk math—you did! What pen?

HAPPY. That was awful dumb, Biff, a pen like that is worth—

WILLY (*seeing the pen for the first time*). You took Oliver's pen?

BIFF (*weakening*). Dad, I just explained it to you.

WILLY. You stole Bill Oliver's fountain pen!

BIFF. I didn't exactly steal it! That's just what I've been explaining to you!

HAPPY. He had it in his hand and just then Oliver walked in, so he got nervous and stuck it in his pocket!

WILLY. My God, Biff!

BIFF. I never intended to do it, Dad!

OPERATOR'S VOICE. Standish Arms, good evening!

WILLY (*shouting*). I'm not in my room!

BIFF (*frightened*). Dad, what's the matter? (*He and Happy stand up.*)

OPERATOR. Ringing Mr. Loman for you!

WILLY. I'm not there, stop it!

BIFF (*horrified, gets down on one knee before Willy*). Dad, I'll make good, I'll make good. (*Willy tries to get to his feet. Biff holds him down.*) Sit down now.

WILLY. No, you're no good, you're no good for anything.

BIFF. I am, Dad, I'll find something else, you understand? Now don't worry about anything. (*He holds up Willy's face.*) Talk to me, Dad.

OPERATOR. Mr. Loman does not answer. Shall I page him?

WILLY (*attempting to stand, as though to rush and silence the Operator*). No, no, no!

HAPPY. He'll strike something, Pop.

WILLY. No, no . . .

BIFF (*desperately, standing over Willy*). Pop, listen! Listen to me! I'm telling you something good. Oliver talked to his partner about the Florida idea. You listening? He—he talked to his partner, and he came to me . . . I'm going to be all right, you hear? Dad, listen to me, he said it was just a question of the amount!

WILLY. Then you . . . got it?

HAPPY. He's gonna be terrific, Pop!

WILLY (*trying to stand*). Then you got it, haven't you? You got it! You got it!

BIFF (*agonized, holds Willy down*). No, no. Look, Pop. I'm supposed to have lunch with them tomorrow. I'm just telling you this so you'll know that I can still make an impression, Pop. And I'll make good somewhere, but I can't go tomorrow, see.

WILLY. Why not? You simply . . .

BIFF. But the pen, Pop!

WILLY. You give it to him and tell him it was an oversight!

HAPPY. Sure, have lunch tomorrow!

BIFF. I can't say that . . .

WILLY. You were doing a crossword puzzle and accidentally used his pen!

BIFF. Listen, kid, I took those balls years ago, now I walk in with his fountain pen? That clinches it, don't you see? I can't face him like that! I'll try elsewhere.

PAGE'S VOICE. Paging Mr. Loman!

WILLY. Don't you want to be anything?

BIFF. Pop, how can I go back?

WILLY. You don't want to be anything, is that what's behind it?

BIFF (*now angry at Willy for not crediting his sympathy*). Don't take it that way! You think it was easy walking into that office after what I'd done to him? A team of horses couldn't have dragged me back to Bill Oliver!

WILLY. Then why'd you go?

BIFF. Why did I go? Why did I go! Look at you! Look at what's become of you!

Off left, The Woman laughs.

WILLY. Biff, you're going to go to that lunch tomorrow, or . . .

BIFF. I can't go. I've got no appointment!

HAPPY. Biff, for . . . !

WILLY. Are you spiting me?

BIFF. Don't take it that way! Goddammit!

WILLY (*strikes Biff and falters away from the table*). You rotten little louse! Are you spiting me?

THE WOMAN. Someone's at the door, Willy!

BIFF. I'm no good, can't you see what I am?

HAPPY (*separating them*). Hey, you're in a restaurant! Now cut it out, both of you! (*The girls enter.*) Hello, girls, sit down.

The Woman laughs, off left.

MISS FORSYTHE. I guess we might as well. This is Letta.

THE WOMAN. Willy, are you going to wake up?

BIFF (*ignoring Willy*). How're ya, miss, sit down. What do you drink?

MISS FORSYTHE. Letta might not be able to stay long.

LETTA. I gotta get up very early tomorrow. I got jury duty. I'm so excited! Were you fellows ever on a jury?

BIFF. No, but I been in front of them! (*The girls laugh.*) This is my father.

LETTA. Isn't he cute? Sit down with us, Pop.

HAPPY. Sit him down, Biff!

BIFF (*going to him*). Come on, slugger, drink us under the table. To hell with it! Come on, sit down, pal.

On Biff's last insistence, Willy is about to sit.

THE WOMAN (*now urgently*). Willy, are you going to answer the door!

The Woman's call pulls Willy back. He starts right, befuddled.

BIFF. Hey, where are you going?

WILLY. Open the door.

BIFF. The door?

WILLY. The washroom . . . the door . . . where's the door?

BIFF (*leading Willy to the left*). Just go straight down.

Willy moves left.

THE WOMAN. Willy, Willy, are you going to get up, get up, get up, get up?

Willy exits left.

LETTA. I think it's sweet you bring your daddy along.

MISS FORSYTHE. Oh, he isn't really your father!

BIFF (*at left, turning to her resentfully*). Miss Forsythe, you've just seen a prince walk by. A fine, troubled prince. A hardworking, unappreciated prince. A pal, you understand? A good companion. Always for his boys.

LETTA. That's so sweet.

HAPPY. Well, girls, what's the program? We're wasting time. Come on, Biff. Gather round. Where would you like to go?

BIFF. Why don't you do something for him?

HAPPY. Me!

BIFF. Don't you give a damn for him, Hap?

HAPPY. What're you talking about? I'm the one who . . .

BIFF. I sense it, you don't give a good goddam about him. (*He takes the rolled-up hose from his pocket and puts it on the table in front of Happy.*) Look what I found in the cellar, for Christ's sake. How can you bear to let it go on?

HAPPY. Me? Who goes away? Who runs off and . . .

BIFF. Yeah, but he doesn't mean anything to you. You could help him—I can't! Don't you understand what I'm talking about? He's going to kill himself, don't you know that?

HAPPY. Don't know it! Me!

BIFF. Hap, help him! Jesus . . . help him . . . Help me, help me, I can't bear to look at his face! (*Ready to weep, he hurries out, up right.*)

HAPPY (*starting after him*). Where are you going?

MISS FORSYTHE. What's he so mad about?

HAPPY. Come on, girls, we'll catch up with him.

MISS FORSYTHE (*as Happy pushes her out*). Say, I don't like that temper of his!

HAPPY. He's just a little overstrung, he'll be all right!

WILLY (*off left, as The Woman laughs*). Don't answer! Don't answer!

LETTA. Don't you want to tell your father . . .

HAPPY. No, that's not my father. He's just a guy. Come on, we'll catch Biff, and, honey, we're going to paint this town! Stanley, where's the check! Hey, Stanley!

They exit. Stanley looks toward left.

STANLEY (*calling to Happy indignantly*). Mr. Loman! Mr. Loman!

Stanley picks up a chair and follows them off. Knocking is heard off left. The Woman enters, laughing. Willy follows her. She is in a black slip; he is buttoning his shirt. Raw, sensuous music accompanies their speech:

WILLY. Will you stop laughing? Will you stop?

THE WOMAN. Aren't you going to answer the door? He'll wake the whole hotel.

WILLY. I'm not expecting anybody.

THE WOMAN. Whyn't you have another drink, honey, and stop being so damn self-centered?

WILLY. I'm so lonely.

THE WOMAN. You know you ruined me, Willy? From now on, whenever you come to the office, I'll see that you go right through to the buyers. No waiting at my desk any-more, Willy. You ruined me.

WILLY. That's nice of you to say that.

THE WOMAN. Gee, you are self-centered! Why so sad? You are the saddest, self-centeredest soul I ever did see-saw. (*She laughs. He kisses her.*) Come on inside, drummer boy. It's silly to be dressing in the middle of the night. (*As knocking is heard.*) Aren't you going to answer the door?

WILLY. They're knocking on the wrong door.

THE WOMAN. But I felt the knocking. And he heard us talk-ing in here. Maybe the hotel's on fire!

WILLY (*his terror rising*). It's a mistake.

THE WOMAN. Then tell him to go away!

WILLY. There's nobody there.

THE WOMAN. It's getting on my nerves, Willy. There's some-body standing out there and it's getting on my nerves!

WILLY (*pushing her away from him*). All right, stay in the bathroom here, and don't come out. I think there's a law in Massachusetts about it, so don't come out. It may be that new room clerk. He looked very mean. So don't come out. It's a mistake, there's no fire.

The knocking is heard again. He takes a few steps away from her, and she vanishes into the wing. The light follows him, and now he is facing Young Biff, who carries a suit-case. Biff steps toward him. The music is gone.

BIFF. Why didn't you answer?

WILLY. Biff! What are you doing in Boston?

BIFF. Why didn't you answer? I've been knocking for five minutes, I called you on the phone . . .

WILLY. I just heard you. I was in the bathroom and had the door shut. Did anything happen home?

BIFF. Dad—I let you down.

WILLY. What do you mean?

BIFF. Dad . . .

WILLY. Biffo, what's this about? (*Putting his arm around Biff.*) Come on, let's go downstairs and get you a malted.

BIFF. Dad, I flunked math.

WILLY. Not for the term?

BIFF. The term. I haven't got enough credits to graduate.

WILLY. You mean to say Bernard wouldn't give you the an-swers?

BIFF. He did, he tried, but I only got a sixty-one.

WILLY. And they wouldn't give you four points?

BIFF. Birnbaum refused absolutely. I begged him, Pop, but he won't give me those points. You gotta talk to him before they close the school. Because if he saw the kind of man you are, and you just talked to him in your way, I'm sure he'd come through for me. The class came right before practice, see, and I didn't go enough. Would you talk to him? He'd like you, Pop. You know the way you could talk.

WILLY. You're on. We'll drive right back.

BIFF. Oh, Dad, good work! I'm sure he'll change it for you!

WILLY. Go downstairs and tell the clerk I'm checkin' out. Go right down.

BIFF. Yes, sir! See, the reason he hates me, Pop—one day he was late for class so I got up at the blackboard and imi-tated him. I crossed my eyes and talked with a lithp.

WILLY (*laughing*). You did? The kids like it?

BIFF. They nearly died laughing!

WILLY. Yeah? What'd you do?

BIFF. The thquare root of thixthy twee is . . . (*Willy bursts out laughing; Biff joins.*) And in the middle of it he walked in!

Willy laughs and The Woman joins in offstage.

WILLY (*without hesitation*). Hurry downstairs and . . .

BIFF. Somebody in there?

WILLY. No, that was next door.

The Woman laughs offstage.

BIFF. Somebody got in your bathroom!

WILLY. No, it's the next room, there's a party . . .

THE WOMAN (*enters, laughing; she lisps this*). Can I come in? There's something in the bathtub, Willy, and it's moving!

Willy looks at Biff; who is staring open-mouthed and horri-fied at The Woman.

WILLY. Ah—you better go back to your room. They must be finished painting by now. They're painting her room so I let her take a shower here. Go back, go back . . . (*He pushes her.*)

THE WOMAN (*resisting*). But I've got to get dressed, Willy, I can't . . .

WILLY. Get out of here! Go back, go back . . . (*Suddenly striving for the ordinary.*) This is Miss Francis, Biff, she's a buyer. They're painting her room. Go back, Miss Francis, go back . . .

THE WOMAN. But my clothes, I can't go out naked in the hall!

WILLY (*pushing her offstage*). Get outa here! Go back, go back!

Biff slowly sits down on his suitcase as the argument con-tinues offstage.

THE WOMAN. Where's my stockings? You promised me stockings, Willy!

WILLY. I have no stockings here!

THE WOMAN. You had two boxes of size nine sheers for me, and I want them!

WILLY. Here, for God's sake, will you get outa here!

THE WOMAN (*enters holding a box of stockings*). I just hope there's nobody in the hall. That's all I hope. (*To Biff.*) Are you football or baseball?

BIFF. Football.

THE WOMAN (*angry, humiliated*). That's me too. G'night. (*She snatches her clothes from Willy, and walks out.*)

WILLY (*after a pause*). Well, better get going. I want to get to the school first thing in the morning. Get my suits out of the closet. I'll get my valise. (*Biff doesn't move.*) What's the matter! (*Biff remains motionless, tears falling.*) She's a buyer. Buys for J. H. Simmons. She lives down the hall—they're painting. You don't imagine—(*He breaks off. After a pause.*) Now listen, pal, she's just a buyer. She sells merchandise in her room and they have to keep it looking just so . . . (*Pause. Assuming command.*) All right, get my suits. (*Biff doesn't move.*) Now stop crying and do as I say. I gave you an order. Biff, I gave you an order! Is that what you do when I give you an order? How dare you cry! (*Putting his arm around Biff.*) Now look, Biff, when you grow up you'll understand about these things. You mustn't—you mustn't overemphasize a thing like this. I'll see Birnbaum first thing in the morning.

BIFF. Never mind.

WILLY (*getting down beside Biff*). Never mind! He's going to give you those points. I'll see to it.

BIFF. He wouldn't listen to you.

WILLY. He certainly will listen to me. You need those points for the U. of Virginia.

BIFF. I'm not going there.

WILLY. Heh? If I can't get him to change that mark you'll make it up in summer school. You've got all summer to . . .

BIFF (*his weeping breaking from him*). Dad . . .

WILLY (*infected by it*). Oh, my boy . . .

BIFF. Dad . . .

WILLY. She's nothing to me, Biff. I was lonely, I was terribly lonely.

BIFF. You—you gave her Mama's stockings! (*His tears break through and he rises to go.*)

WILLY (*grabbing for Biff*). I gave you an order!

BIFF. Don't touch me, you—liar!

WILLY. Apologize for that!

BIFF. You fake! You phony little fake! You fake! (*Overcome, he turns quickly and weeping fully goes out with his suitcase. Willy is left on the floor on his knees.*)

WILLY. I gave you an order! Biff, come back here or I'll beat you! Come back here! I'll whip you!

Stanley comes quickly in from the right and stands in front of Willy.

WILLY (*shouts at Stanley*). I gave you an order . . .

STANLEY. Hey, let's pick it up, pick it up, Mr. Loman. (*He helps Willy to his feet.*) Your boys left with the chippies. They said they'll see you home.

A second waiter watches some distance away.

WILLY. But we were supposed to have dinner together.

Music is heard, Willy's theme.

STANLEY. Can you make it?

WILLY. I'll—sure, I can make it. (*Suddenly concerned about his clothes.*) Do I—I look all right?

STANLEY. Sure, you look all right. (*He flicks a speck off Willy's lapel.*)

WILLY. Here—here's a dollar.

STANLEY. Oh, your son paid me. It's all right.

WILLY (*putting it in Stanley's hand*). No, take it. You're a good boy.

STANLEY. Oh, no, you don't have to . . .

WILLY. Here—here's some more, I don't need it any more. (*After a slight pause.*) Tell me—is there a seed store in the neighborhood?

STANLEY. Seeds? You mean like to plant?

As Willy turns, Stanley slips the money back into his jacket pocket.

WILLY. Yes. Carrots, peas . . .

STANLEY. Well, there's hardware stores on Sixth Avenue, but it may be too late now.

WILLY (*anxiously*). Oh, I'd better hurry. I've got to get some seeds. (*He starts off to the right.*) I've got to get some seeds, right away. Nothing's planted. I don't have a thing in the ground.

Willy hurries out as the light goes down. Stanley moves over to the right after him, watches him off. The other waiter has been staring at Willy.

STANLEY (*to the waiter*). Well, whatta you looking at?

The waiter picks up the chairs and moves off right. Stanley takes the table and follows him. The light fades on this area. There is a long pause, the sound of the flute coming over. The light gradually rises on the kitchen, which is empty. Happy appears at the door of the house, followed by Biff. Happy is carrying a large bunch of long-stemmed roses. He enters the kitchen, looks around for Linda. Not seeing her, he turns to Biff, who is just outside the house door, and makes a gesture with his hands, indicating "Not here, I guess." He looks into the living room and freezes. Inside, Linda, unseen, is seated, Willy's coat on her lap. She rises ominously and quietly and moves toward Happy, who backs up into the kitchen, afraid.

HAPPY. Hey, what're you doing up? (*Linda says nothing but moves toward him implacably.*) Where's Pop? (*He keeps backing to the right, and now Linda is in full view in the doorway to the living room.*) Is he sleeping?

LINDA. Where were you?

HAPPY (*trying to laugh it off*). We met two girls, Mom, very fine types. Here, we brought you some flowers. (*Offering them to her.*) Put them in your room, Ma.

She knocks them to the floor at Biff's feet. He has now come inside and closed the door behind him. She stares at Biff, silent.

HAPPY. Now what'd you do that for? Mom, I want you to have some flowers . . .

LINDA (*cutting Happy off, violently to Biff*). Don't you care whether he lives or dies?

HAPPY (*going to the stairs*). Come upstairs, Biff.

BIFF (*with a flare of disgust, to Happy*). Go away from me! (*To Linda.*) What do you mean, lives or dies? Nobody's dying around here, pal.

LINDA. Get out of my sight! Get out of here!

BIFF. I wanna see the boss.

LINDA. You're not going near him!

BIFF. Where is he? (*He moves into the living room and Linda follows.*)

LINDA (*shouting after Biff.*). You invite him for dinner. He looks forward to it all day—(*Biff appears in his parents' bedroom, looks around, and exits*)—and then you desert him there. There's no stranger you'd do that to!

HAPPY. Why? He had a swell time with us. Listen, when I—(*Linda comes back into the kitchen*)—desert him I hope I don't outlive the day!

LINDA. Get out of here!

HAPPY. Now look, Mom . . .

LINDA. Did you have to go to women tonight? You and your lousy rotten whores!

Biff re-enters the kitchen.

HAPPY. Mom, all we did was follow Biff around trying to cheer him up! (*To Biff.*) Boy, what a night you gave me!

LINDA. Get out of here, both of you, and don't come back! I don't want you tormenting him any more. Go on now, get your things together! (*To Biff.*) You can sleep in his apartment. (*She starts to pick up the flowers and stops herself.*) Pick up this stuff, I'm not your maid any more. Pick it up, you bum, you!

Happy turns his back to her in refusal. Biff slowly moves over and gets down on his knees, picking up the flowers.

LINDA. You're a pair of animals! Not one, not another living soul would have had the cruelty to walk out on that man in a restaurant!

BIFF (*not looking at her*). Is that what he said?

LINDA. He didn't have to say anything. He was so humiliated he nearly limped when he came in.

HAPPY. But, Mom, he had a great time with us . . .

BIFF (*cutting him off violently*). Shut up!

Without another word, Happy goes upstairs.

LINDA. You! You didn't even go in to see if he was all right!

BIFF (*still on the floor in front of Linda, the flowers in his hand; with self-loathing*). No. Didn't. Didn't do a damned thing. How do you like that, heh? Left him babbling in a toilet.

LINDA. You louse. You . . .

BIFF. Now you hit it on the nose! (*He gets up, throws the flowers in the wastebasket.*) The scum of the earth, and you're looking at him!

LINDA. Get out of here!

BIFF. I gotta talk to the boss, Mom. Where is he?

LINDA. You're not going near him. Get out of this house!

BIFF (*with absolute assurance, determination*). No. We're gonna have an abrupt conversation, him and me.

LINDA. You're not talking to him.

Hammering is heard from outside the house, off right. Biff turns toward the noise.

LINDA (*suddenly pleading*). Will you please leave him alone?

BIFF. What's he doing out there?

LINDA. He's planting the garden!

BIFF (*quietly*). Now? Oh, my God!

Biff moves outside, Linda following. The light dies down on them and comes up on the center of the apron as Willy walks into it. He is carrying a flashlight, a hoe, and a handful of seed packets. He raps the top of the hoe sharply to fix it firmly, and then moves to the left, measuring off the distance with his foot. He holds the flashlight to look at the seed packets, reading off the instructions. He is in the blue of night.

WILLY. Carrots . . . quarter-inch apart. Rows . . . one-foot rows. (*He measures it off.*) One foot. (*He puts down a package and measures off.*) Beets. (*He puts down another package and measures again.*) Lettuce. (*He reads the package, puts it down.*) One foot—(*He breaks off as Ben appears at the right and moves slowly down to him.*) What a proposition, ts, ts. Terrific, terrific. 'Cause she's suffered, Ben, the woman has suffered. You understand me? A man can't go out the way he came in, Ben, a man has got to add up to something. You can't, you can't—(*Ben moves toward him as though to interrupt.*) You gotta consider now. Don't answer so quick. Remember, it's a guaranteed twenty-thousand-dollar proposition. Now look, Ben, I want you to go through the ins and outs of this thing with me. I've got nobody to talk to, Ben, and the woman has suffered, you hear me?

BEN (*standing still, considering*). What's the proposition?

WILLY. It's twenty thousand dollars on the barrelhead. Guaranteed, gilt-edged, you understand?

BEN. You don't want to make a fool of yourself. They might not honor the policy.

WILLY. How can they dare refuse? Didn't I work like a coolie to meet every premium on the nose? And now they don't pay off? Impossible!

BEN. It's called a cowardly thing, William.

WILLY. Why? Does it take more guts to stand here the rest of my life ringing up a zero?

BEN (*yielding*). That's a point, William. (*He moves, thinking, turns.*) And twenty thousand—that is something one can feel with the hand, it is there.

WILLY (*now assured, with rising power*). Oh, Ben, that's the whole beauty of it! I see it like a diamond, shining in the dark, hard and rough, that I can pick up and touch in my hand. Not like—like an appointment! This would not be another damned-fool appointment, Ben, and it changes all the aspects. Because he thinks I'm nothing, see, and so he spites me. But the funeral . . . (*Straightening up.*) Ben, that funeral will be massive! They'll come from Maine, Massachusetts, Vermont, New Hampshire! All the old-timers with the strange license plates—that boy will be thunderstruck, Ben, because he never realized—I am known! Rhode Island, New York, New Jersey—I am known, Ben, and he'll see it with his eyes once and for all. He'll see what I am, Ben! He's in for a shock, that boy!

BEN (*coming down to the edge of the garden*). He'll call you a coward.

WILLY (*suddenly fearful*). No, that would be terrible.

BEN. Yes. And a damned fool.

WILLY. No, no, he mustn't, I won't have that! (*He is broken and desperate.*)

BEN. He'll hate you, William.

The gay music of the Boys is heard.

WILLY. Oh, Ben, how do we get back to all the great times? Used to be so full of light, and comradeship, the sleigh-riding in winter, and the ruddiness on his cheeks. And always some kind of good news coming up, always something nice coming up ahead. And never even let me carry the valises in the house, and simonizing, simonizing that little red car! Why, why can't I give him something and not have him hate me?

BEN. Let me think about it. (*He glances at his watch.*) I still have a little time. Remarkable proposition, but you've got to be sure you're not making a fool of yourself.

Ben drifts off upstage and goes out of sight. Biff comes down from the left.

WILLY (*suddenly conscious of Biff, turns and looks up at him, then begins picking up the packages of seeds in confusion*). Where the hell is that seed? (*Indignantly.*) You can't see nothing out here! They boxed in the whole goddam neighborhood!

BIFF. There are people all around here. Don't you realize that?

WILLY. I'm busy. Don't bother me.

BIFF (*taking the hoe from Willy*). I'm saying good-bye to you, Pop. (*Willy looks at him, silent, unable to move.*) I'm not coming back any more.

WILLY. You're not going to see Oliver tomorrow?

BIFF. I've got no appointment, Dad.

WILLY. He put his arm around you, and you've got no appointment?

BIFF. Pop, get this now, will you? Everytime I've left it's been a—fight that sent me out of here. Today I realized something about myself and I tried to explain it to you and I— I think I'm just not smart enough to make any sense out of it for you. To hell with whose fault it is or anything like that. (*He takes Willy's arm.*) Let's just wrap it up, heh? Come on in, we'll tell Mom. (*He gently tries to pull Willy to left.*)

WILLY (*frozen, immobile, with guilt in his voice*). No, I don't want to see her.

BIFF. Come on! (*He pulls again, and Willy tries to pull away.*)

WILLY (*highly nervous*). No, no, I don't want to see her.

BIFF (*tries to look into Willy's face, as if to find the answer there*). Why don't you want to see her?

WILLY (*more harshly now*). Don't bother me, will you?

BIFF. What do you mean, you don't want to see her? You don't want them calling you yellow, do you? This isn't your fault; it's me, I'm a bum. Now come inside! (*Willy strains to get away.*) Did you hear what I said to you?

Willy pulls away and quickly goes by himself into the house. Biff follows.

LINDA (*to Willy*). Did you plant, dear?

BIFF (*at the door, to Linda*). All right, we had it out. I'm going and I'm not writing any more.

LINDA (*going to Willy in the kitchen*). I think that's the best way, dear. 'Cause there's no use drawing it out, you'll just never get along.

Willy doesn't respond.

BIFF. People ask where I am and what I'm doing, you don't know, and you don't care. That way it'll be off your mind and you can start brightening up again. All right? That clears it, doesn't it? (*Willy is silent, and Biff goes to him.*) You gonna wish me luck, scout? (*He extends his hand.*) What do you say?

LINDA. Shake his hand, Willy.

WILLY (*turning to her, seething with hurt*). There's no necessity—to mention the pen at all, y'know.

BIFF (*gently*). I've got no appointment, Dad.

WILLY (*erupting fiercely*). He put his arm around . . . ?

BIFF. Dad, you're never going to see what I am, so what's the use of arguing? If I strike oil I'll send you a check. Meantime forget I'm alive.

WILLY (*to Linda*). Spite, see?

BIFF. Shake hands, Dad.

WILLY. Not my hand.

BIFF. I was hoping not to go this way.

WILLY. Well, this is the way you're going. Good-bye.

Biff looks at him a moment, then turns sharply and goes to the stairs.

WILLY (*stops him with*). May you rot in hell if you leave this house!

BIFF (*turning*). Exactly what is it that you want from me?

WILLY. I want you to know, on the train, in the mountains, in the valleys, wherever you go, that you cut down your life for spite!

BIFF. No, no.

WILLY. Spite, spite, is the word of your undoing! And when you're down and out, remember what did it. When you're rotting somewhere beside the railroad tracks, remember, and don't you dare blame it on me!

BIFF. I'm not blaming it on you!

WILLY. I won't take the rap for this, you hear?

Happy comes down the stairs and stands on the bottom step, watching.

BIFF. That's just what I'm telling you!

WILLY (*sinking into a chair at a table, with full accusation*). You're trying to put a knife in me—don't think I don't know what you're doing!

BIFF. All right, phony! Then let's lay it on the line. (*He whips the rubber tube out of his pocket and puts it on the table.*)

HAPPY. You crazy . . .

LINDA. Biff! (*She moves to grab the hose, but Biff holds it down with his hand.*)

BIFF. Leave it there! Don't move it!

WILLY (*not looking at it*). What is that?

BIFF. You know goddam well what that is.

WILLY (*caged, wanting to escape*). I never saw that.

BIFF. You saw it. The mice didn't bring it into the cellar! What is this supposed to do, make a hero out of you? This supposed to make me sorry for you?

WILLY. Never heard of it.

BIFF. There'll be no pity for you, you hear it? No pity!

WILLY (*to Linda*). You hear the spite!

BIFF. No, you're going to hear the truth—what you are and what I am!

LINDA. Stop it!

WILLY. Spite!

HAPPY (*coming down toward Biff*). You cut it now!

BIFF (*to Happy*). The man don't know who we are! The man is gonna know! (*To Willy.*) We never told the truth for ten minutes in this house!

HAPPY. We always told the truth!

BIFF (*turning on him*). You big blow, are you the assistant buyer? You're one of the two assistants to the assistant, aren't you?

HAPPY. Well, I'm practically . . .

BIFF. You're practically full of it! We all are! and I'm through with it. (*To Willy.*) Now hear this, Willy, this is me.

WILLY. I know you!

BIFF. You know why I had no address for three months? I stole a suit in Kansas City and I was in jail. (*To Linda, who is sobbing.*) Stop crying. I'm through with it.

Linda turns away from them, her hands covering her face.

WILLY. I suppose that's my fault!

BIFF. I stole myself out of every good job since high school!

WILLY. And whose fault is that?

BIFF. And I never got anywhere because you blew me so full of hot air I could never stand taking orders from anybody! That's whose fault it is!

WILLY. I hear that!

LINDA. Don't, Biff!

BIFF. It's goddam time you heard that! I had to be boss big shot in two weeks, and I'm through with it!

WILLY. Then hang yourself! For spite, hang yourself!

BIFF. No! Nobody's hanging himself, Willy! I ran down eleven flights with a pen in my hand today. And suddenly I stopped, you hear me? And in the middle of that office building, do you hear this? I stopped in the middle of that building and I saw—the sky. I saw the things that I love in this world. The work and the food and time to sit and smoke. And I looked at the pen and said to myself, what the hell am I grabbing this for? Why am I trying to become what I don't want to be? What am I doing in an office, making a contemptuous, begging fool of myself, when all I want is out there, waiting for me the minute I say I know who I am! Why can't I say that, Willy? (*He tries to make Willy face him, but Willy pulls away and moves to the left.*)

WILLY (*with hatred, threateningly*). The door of your life is wide open!

BIFF. Pop! I'm a dime a dozen, and so are you!

WILLY (*turning on him now in an uncontrolled outburst*). I am not a dime a dozen! I am Willy Loman, and you are Biff Loman!

Biff starts for Willy, but is blocked by Happy. In his fury, Biff seems on the verge of attacking his father.

BIFF. I am not a leader of men, Willy, and neither are you. You were never anything but a hard-working drummer who landed in the ash can like all the rest of them! I'm one dollar an hour, Willy! I tried seven states and couldn't raise it. A buck an hour! Do you gather my meaning? I'm not bringing home any prizes any more, and you're going to stop waiting for me to bring them home!

WILLY (*directly to Biff*). You vengeful, spiteful mutt!

Biff breaks from Happy. Willy, in fright, starts up the stairs. Biff grabs him.

BIFF (*at the peak of his fury*). Pop! I'm nothing! I'm nothing, Pop. Can't you understand that? There's no spite in it any more. I'm just what I am, that's all.

Biff's fury has spent itself and he breaks down, sobbing, holding on to Willy, who dumbly fumbles for Biff's face.

WILLY (*astonished*). What're you doing? What're you doing? (*To Linda.*) Why is he crying?

BIFF (*crying, broken*). Will you let me go, for Christ's sake? Will you take that phony dream and burn it before something happens? (*Struggling to contain himself, he pulls away and moves to the stairs.*) I'll go in the morning. Put him—put him to bed. (*Exhausted, Biff moves up the stairs to his room.*)

WILLY (*after a long pause, astonished, elevated*). Isn't that—isn't that remarkable? Biff—he likes me!

LINDA. He loves you, Willy!

HAPPY (*deeply moved*). Always did, Pop.

WILLY. Oh, Biff! (*Staring wildly.*) He cried! Cried to me. (*He is choking with his love, and now cries out his promise.*) That boy—that boy is going to be magnificent!

Ben appears in the light just outside the kitchen.

BEN. Yes, outstanding, with twenty thousand behind him.

LINDA (*sensing the racing of his mind, fearfully, carefully*). Now come to bed, Willy. It's all settled now.

WILLY (*finding it difficult not to rush out of the house*). Yes, we'll sleep. Come on. Go to sleep, Hap.

BEN. And it does take a great kind of a man to crack the jungle.

In accents of dread, Ben's idyllic music starts up.

HAPPY (*his arm around Linda*). I'm getting married, Pop, don't forget it. I'm changing everything. I'm gonna run that department before the year is up. You'll see, Mom. (*He kisses her.*)

BEN. The jungle is dark but full of diamonds, Willy.

Willy turns, moves, listening to Ben.

LINDA. Be good. You're both good boys, just act that way, that's all.

HAPPY. 'Night, Pop. (*He goes upstairs.*)

LINDA (*to Willy*). Come, dear.

BEN (*with greater force*). One must go in to fetch a diamond out.

WILLY (*to Linda, as he moves slowly along the edge of the kitchen, toward the door*). I just want to get settled down, Linda. Let me sit alone for a little.

LINDA (*almost uttering her fear*). I want you upstairs.

WILLY (*taking her in his arms*). In a few minutes, Linda. I couldn't sleep right now. Go on, you look awful tired. (*He kisses her.*)

BEN. Not like an appointment at all. A diamond is rough and hard to the touch.

WILLY. Go on now. I'll be right up.

LINDA. I think this is the only way, Willy.

WILLY. Sure, it's the best thing.

BEN. Best thing!

WILLY. The only way. Everything is gonna be—go on, kid, get to bed. You look so tired.

LINDA. Come right up.

WILLY. Two minutes.

Linda goes into the living room, then reappears in her bedroom. Willy moves just outside the kitchen door.

WILLY. Loves me. (*Wonderingly.*) Always loved me. Isn't that a remarkable thing? Ben, he'll worship me for it!

BEN (*with promise*). It's dark there, but full of diamonds.

WILLY. Can you imagine that magnificence with twenty thousand dollars in his pocket?

LINDA (*calling from her room*). Willy! Come up!

WILLY (*calling into the kitchen*). Yes! Yes. Coming! It's very smart, you realize that, don't you, sweetheart? Even Ben sees it. I gotta go, baby. 'By! 'By! (*Going over to Ben, almost dancing.*) Imagine? When the mail comes he'll be ahead of Bernard again!

BEN. A perfect proposition all around.

WILLY. Did you see how he cried to me? Oh, if I could kiss him, Ben!

BEN. Time, William, time!

WILLY. Oh, Ben, I always knew one way or another we were gonna make it, Biff and I.

BEN (*looking at his watch*). The boat. We'll be late. (*He moves slowly off into the darkness.*)

WILLY (*elegiacally, turning to the house*). Now when you kick off, boy, I want a seventy-yard boot, and get right down the field under the ball, and when you hit, hit low and hit hard, because it's important, boy. (*He swings around and faces the audience.*) There's all kinds of important people in the stands, and the first thing you know . . . (*Suddenly realizing he is alone.*) Ben! Ben, where do I . . . ? (*He makes a sudden movement of search.*) Ben, how do I . . . ?

LINDA (*calling*). Willy, you coming up?

WILLY (*uttering a gasp of fear, whirling about as if to quiet her*). Sh! (*He turns around as if to find his way; sounds, faces, voices, seem to be swarming in upon him and he flicks at them, crying.*) Sh! Sh! (*Suddenly music, faint and high, stops him. It rises in intensity, almost to an unbearable scream. He goes up and down on his toes, and rushes off around the house.*) Shhh!

LINDA. Willy?

There is no answer. Linda waits. Biff gets up off his bed. He is still in his clothes. Happy sits up. Biff stands listening.

LINDA (*with real fear*). Willy, answer me! Willy!

There is the sound of a car starting and moving away at full speed.

LINDA. No!

BIFF (*rushing down the stairs*). Pop!

As the car speeds off the music crashes down in a frenzy of sound, which becomes the soft pulsation of a single cello string. Biff slowly returns to his bedroom. He and Happy gravely don their jackets. Linda slowly walks out of her room. The music has developed into a dead march. The leaves of day are appearing over everything. Charley and Bernard, somberly dressed, appear and knock on the kitchen door. Biff and Happy slowly descend the stairs to the kitchen as Charley and Bernard enter. All stop a moment when Linda, in clothes of mourning, bearing a little bunch of roses, comes through the draped doorway into the kitchen. She goes to Charley and takes his arm. Now all move toward the audience, through the wall-line of the kitchen. At the limit of the apron, Linda lays down the flowers, kneels, and sits back on her heels. All stare down at the grave.

REQUIEM

CHARLEY. It's getting dark, Linda.

Linda doesn't react. She stares at the grave.

BIFF. How about it, Mom? Better get some rest, heh? They'll be closing the gate soon.

Linda makes no move. Pause.

HAPPY (*deeply angered*). He had no right to do that. There was no necessity for it. We would've helped him.

CHARLEY (*grunting*). Hmmm.

BIFF. Come along, Mom.

LINDA. Why didn't anybody come?

CHARLEY. It was a very nice funeral.

LINDA. But where are all the people he knew? Maybe they blame him.

CHARLEY. Naa. It's a rough world, Linda. They wouldn't blame him.

LINDA. I can't understand it. At this time especially. First time in thirty-five years we were just about free and clear. He only needed a little salary. He was even finished with the dentist.

CHARLEY. No man only needs a little salary.

LINDA. I can't understand it.

BIFF. There were a lot of nice days. When he'd come home from a trip; or on Sundays, making the stoop; finishing the cellar; putting on the new porch; when he built the extra bathroom; and put up the garage. You know something, Charley, there's more of him in that front stoop than in all the sales he ever made.

CHARLEY. Yeah. He was a happy man with a batch of cement.

LINDA. He was so wonderful with his hands.

BIFF. He had the wrong dreams. All, all, wrong.

HAPPY (*almost ready to fight Biff*). Don't say that!

BIFF. He never knew who he was.

CHARLEY (*stopping Happy's movement and reply; to Biff*). Nobody dast blame this man. You don't understand: Willy was a salesman. And for a salesman, there is no rock bottom to the life. He don't put a bolt to a nut, he don't tell you the law or give you medicine. He's a man way out there in the blue, riding on a smile and a shoeshine. And when they start not smiling back—that's an earthquake.

And then you get yourself a couple of spots on your hat, and you're finished. Nobody dast blame this man. A salesman has got to dream, boy. It comes with the territory.

BIFF. Charley, the man didn't know who he was.

HAPPY (*infuriated*). Don't say that!

BIFF. Why don't you come with me, Happy?

HAPPY. I'm not licked that easily. I'm staying right in this city, and I'm gonna beat this racket! (*He looks at Biff, his chin set.*) The Loman Brothers!

BIFF. I know who I am, kid.

HAPPY. All right, boy. I'm gonna show you and everybody else that Willy Loman did not die in vain. He had a good dream. It's the only dream you can have—to come out number-one man. He fought it out here, and this is where I'm gonna win it for him.

BIFF (*with a hopeless glance at Happy, bends toward his mother*). Let's go, Mom.

LINDA. I'll be with you in a minute. Go on, Charley. (*He hesitates.*) I want to, just for a minute. I never had a chance to say good-bye.

Charley moves away, followed by Happy. Biff remains a slight distance up and left of Linda. She sits there, summoning herself. The flute begins, not far away, playing behind her speech.

LINDA. Forgive me, dear. I can't cry. I don't know what it is, but I can't cry. I don't understand it. Why did you ever do that? Help me, Willy, I can't cry. It seems to me that you're just on another trip. I keep expecting you. Willy, dear, I can't cry. Why did you do it? I search and search and I search, and I can't understand it, Willy. I made the last payment on the house today. Today, dear. And there'll be nobody home. (*A sob rises in her throat.*) We're free and clear. (*Sobbing mournfully, released.*) We're free. (*Biff comes slowly toward her.*) We're free . . . We're free . . .

Biff lifts her to her feet and moves out up right with her in his arms. Linda sobs quietly. Bernard and Charley come together and follow them, followed by Happy. Only the music of the flute is left on the darkening stage as over the house the hard towers of the apartment buildings rise into sharp focus and the curtain falls.

FORUM

"Tragedy and the Common Man"

ARTHUR MILLER

In this age few tragedies are written. It has often been held that the lack is due to a paucity of heroes among us, or else that modern man has had the blood drawn out of his organs of belief by the skepticism of science, and the heroic attack on life cannot feed on an attitude of reserve and circumspection. For one reason or another, we are often held to be below tragedy—or tragedy above us. The inevitable conclusion is, of course, that the tragic mode is archaic, fit only for the very highly placed, the kings or the kingly, and where this admission is not made in so many words it is most often implied.

I believe that the common man is as apt a subject for tragedy in its highest sense as kings were. On the face of it this ought to be obvious in the light of modern psychiatry, which bases its analysis upon classic formulations, such as the Oedipus and Orestes complexes, for instances, which were enacted by royal beings, but which apply to everyone in similar emotional situations.

More simply, when the question of tragedy in art is not at issue, we never hesitate to attribute to the well-placed and the exalted the very same mental processes as the lowly. And finally, if the exaltation of tragic action were truly a property of the high-bred character alone, it is inconceivable that the mass of mankind should cherish tragedy above all other forms, let alone be capable of understanding it.

As a general rule, to which there may be exceptions unknown to me, I think the tragic feeling is evoked in us when we are in the presence of a character who is ready to lay down his life, if need be, to secure one thing—his sense of personal dignity. From Orestes to Hamlet, Medea to Macbeth, the underlying struggle is that of the individual attempting to gain his "rightful" position in his society.

Sometimes he is one who has been displaced from it, sometimes one who seeks to attain it for the first time, but the fateful wound from which the inevitable events spiral is the wound of indignity, and its dominant force is indignation. Tragedy, then, is the consequence of a man's total compulsion to evaluate himself justly.

In the sense of having been initiated by the hero himself, the tale always reveals what has been called his "tragic flaw," a failing that is not peculiar to grand or elevated characters. Nor is it necessarily a weakness. The flaw, or crack in the character, is really nothing—and need be nothing—but his inherent unwillingness to remain passive in the face of what he conceives to be a challenge to his dignity, has image of his rightful status. Only the passive, only those who accept their lot without active retaliation, are "flawless." Most of us are in that category.

But there are among us today, as there always have been, those who act against the scheme of things that degrades them, and in the process of action everything we have accepted out of fear or insensitivity or ignorance is shaken before us and examined, and from this total onslaught by an individual against the seemingly stable cosmos surrounding us—from this total examination of the "unchangeable" environment—comes the terror and the fear that is classically associated with tragedy.

More important, from this total questioning of what has previously been unquestioned, we learn. And such a process is not beyond the common man. In revolutions around the world, these past thirty years, he has demonstrated again and again this inner dynamic of all tragedy.

Insistence upon the rank of the tragic hero, or the so-called nobility of his character, is really but a clinging to the outward forms of tragedy. If rank or nobility of character was indispensable, then it would follow that the problems of those with rank were the particular problems of tragedy. But surely the right of one monarch to capture the domain from another no longer raises our passions, nor are our concepts of justice what they were to the mind of an Elizabethan king.

The quality in such plays that does shake us, however, derives from the underlying fear of being displaced, the disaster inherent in being torn away from our chosen image of what and who we are in this world. Among us today this fear is as strong, and perhaps stronger, than it ever was. In fact, it is the common man who knows this fear best.

Now, if it is true that tragedy is the consequence of a man's total compulsion to evaluate himself justly, his destruction in the attempt posits a wrong or an evil in his environment. And this is precisely the morality of tragedy and its lesson. The discovery of the moral law, which is what the enlightenment of tragedy consists of, is not the discovery of some abstract or metaphysical quantity.

The tragic right is a condition of life, a condition in which the human personality is able to flower and realize itself. The wrong is the condition which suppresses man, perverts the flowing out of his love and creative instinct. Tragedy enlightens—and it must, in that it points the heroic finger at the enemy of man's freedom. The thrust for freedom is the quality in tragedy which exalts. The revolutionary questioning of the stable environment is what terrifies. In no way is the common man debarred from such thoughts or such actions.

Seen in the light, our lack of tragedy may be partially accounted for by the turn which modern literature has taken toward the purely psychiatric view of life, or the purely sociological. If all our miseries, our indignities, are born and bred within our minds, then all action, let alone the heroic action, is obviously impossible.

And if society alone is responsible for the cramping of our

lives, then the protagonist must needs be so pure and faultless as to force us to deny his validity as a character. From neither of these views can tragedy derive, simply because neither represents a balanced concept of life. Above all else, tragedy requires the finest appreciation by the writer of cause and effect.

No tragedy can therefore come about when its author fears to question absolutely everything, when he regards any institution, habit or custom as being either everlasting, immutable or inevitable. In the tragic view the need of man to wholly realize himself is the only fixed star, and whatever it is that hedges his nature and lowers it is ripe for attack and examination. Which is not to say that tragedy must preach revolution.

The Greeks could probe the very heavenly origin of their ways and return to confirm the rightness of laws. And Job could face God in anger, demanding his right and end in submission. But for a moment everything is in suspension, nothing is accepted, and in this stretching and tearing apart of the cosmos, in the very action of so doing, the character gains "size," the tragic stature which is spuriously attached to the royal or the highborn in our minds. The commonest of men may take on that stature to the extent of his willingness to throw all he has into the contest, the battle to secure his rightful place in his world.

There is a misconception of tragedy with which I have been struck in review after review, and in many conversations with writers and readers alike. It is the idea that tragedy is of necessity allied to pessimism. Even the dictionary says nothing more about the word than that it means a story with a sad or unhappy ending. This impression is so firmly fixed that I almost hesitate to claim that in truth tragedy implies more optimism in its author than does comedy, and that its final result ought to be the reinforcement of the onlooker's brightest opinions of the human animal.

For, if it is true to say that in essence the tragic hero is intent upon claiming his whole due as a personality, and if this struggle must be total and without reservation, then it automatically demonstrates the indestructible will of man to achieve his humanity.

The possibility of victory must be there in tragedy. Where pathos rules, where pathos is finally derived, a character has fought a battle he could not possibly have won. The pathetic is achieved when the protagonist is, by virtue of his witlessness, his insensitivity or the very air he gives off, incapable of grappling with a much superior force.

Pathos truly is the mode for the pessimist. But tragedy requires a nicer balance between what is possible and what is impossible. And it is curious, although edifying, that the plays we revere, century after century, are the tragedies. In them, and in them alone, lies the belief—optimistic, if you will, in the perfectability of man.

It is time, I think, that we who are without kings, took up this bright thread of our history and followed it to the only place it can possibly lead in our time—the heart and spirit of the average man.

The following three reviews of productions of *Death of a Salesman* illustrate the types of criticism discussed in Chapter 3. The first, by William Hawkins, is a "morning after" review and represents a critic's spontaneous impressions of a play. John Mason Brown, one of the most admired critics in the American theater, wrote his review almost two weeks after the play opened. His commentary benefits from additional reflection and focuses more on the play's thematic concerns. 35 years later, Christopher Wren described Miller's production of his play in Beijing. While it, too, is a type of "first night" review, it also reflects the long history of the play. Note that Wren legitimately incorporated Miller's commentary into his review as the play was an established masterpiece in the American theater by 1983.

FORUMS

"*Death of a Salesman*: Powerful Tragedy"

WILLIAM HAWKINS

Death of a Salesman is a play written along the lines of the finest classical tragedy. It is the revelation of a man's downfall, in destruction whose roots are entirely in his own soul. The play builds to an immutable conflict where there is no resolution for this man in this life.

The play is a fervent query into the great American competitive dream of success, as it strips to the core a castaway from the race for recognition and money.

"*Death of a Salesman*: Powerful Tragedy" by William Hawkins. *New York World-Telegram*, 11 February 1949. Reprinted by permission.

(continued)

The failure of a great potential could never be so moving or so universally understandable as is the fate of Willy Loman, because his complete happiness could have been so easy to attain. He is an artisan who glories in manual effort and can be proud of the sturdy fine things he puts together out of wood and cement.

At eighteen he is introduced to the attention he might receive and the financial vistas he might travel by selling on the road. This original deception dooms him to a life of touring and a habit of prideful rationalization, until at sixty he is so far along his tangent that his efforts not to admit his resultant mediocrity are fatal.

Through most of this career runs the insistent legacy of "amounting to something" on his adopted terms, which he forces on his favorite son. With indulgent adoration he unbalances the boy, demanding a mutual idolatry which he himself inevitably fails. If young Biff steals, it is courage. If he captains a football team, the world is watching.

In the end, after repeated failure, Biff sees the truth, too late to really penetrate his father's mind. The boy's tortured efforts to explain his own little true destiny can only crack open the years-long rift, and the salesman, with all his dream's lost shadows, has no alternative to death for his peace.

Often plays have been written that crossed beyond physical actuality into the realm of memory and imagination, but it is doubtful if any has so skillfully transcended the limits of real time and space. One cannot term the chronology here a flashback technique, because the transitions are so immediate and logical.

As Willy's mind wavers under the strain of his own failure and the antagonism of his boy, he recalls the early hopeful days. The course of the play runs so smoothly that it seems one moment the two sons have gone to bed upstairs in plain sight, weary and cynical, and an instant later they are tumbling in youthful exuberance to the tune of their father's delighted flattery.

Sometimes Willy recalls the chance he once had to join his rich adventurous brother, and as his desperation increases he begs Ben for some explanation of his deep confusion.

These illuminations of the man are so exquisitely molded into the form of the play that it sweeps along like a powerful tragic symphony. The actors are attuned to the text as if they were distinct instruments. Themes rise and fade, are varied and repeated. Again as in music, an idea may be introduced as a faint echo, and afterwards developed to its fullest part in the big scheme.

It is hard to imagine anyone more splendid than Lee J. Cobb is as Willy Loman, the salesman. To be big and broken is so contradictory. The actor subtly moves from the first realizations of defeat, into a state of stubborn jauntiness alternating with childlike fear in a magnificent portrait of obsolescence.

Only the rare young actor can sustain a role of hysterical intensity with any dignity, but Arthur Kennedy does it with the utmost taste and strength. It is a complicated role, now joyous, now bitter, sometimes surly then passionately outspoken. Kennedy rings these changes without faltering.

Willy's wife Linda is a truthfully blocked out character, gentle and delicate, yet fiercely loving and fiercely loyal.

Mildred Dunnock plays her with sincerity that comes only with surface simplicity and penetrating comprehension. The scenes where she defends and explains the father to her sons are done with heart-wringing reality.

"Even as You and I"

John Mason Brown

George Jean Nathan once described a certain actress's Camille as being the first Camille he had ever seen who had died of cartarrh. This reduction in scale of a major disease to an unpleasant annoyance is symptomatic of more than the acting practice of the contemporary stage. Even our dramatists, at least most of them, tend in their writing, so to speak; to turn t.b. into a sniffle. They seem ashamed of the big things, embarrassed by the raw emotions, afraid of the naked passions, and unaware of life's brutalities and tolls.

Of understatement they make a fetish. They have all the reticences and timidities of the overcivilized and undemonstrative. They pride themselves upon writing around a scene rather than from or to it; upon what they hold back instead of upon what they release. They paint with pastels, not oils, and dodge the primary anguishes as they would the primary colors.

"Even as You and I" by John Mason Brown. From *Saturday Review of Literature*, 32 (26 February 1949), pp. 30–32. Reprinted by permission of *The Saturday Review*, © 1979, General Media International, Inc.

Their characters belong to an anemic brood. Lacking blood, they lack not only violence but humanity. They are the puppets of contrivance, not the victims of circumstance or themselves. They are apt to be shadows without substance, surfaces without depths. They can be found in the *dramatis personae* but not in the telephone book. If they have hearts, their murmurings are seldom audible. They neither hear nor allow us to hear those inner whisperings of hope, fear, despair, or joy, which are the true accompaniment to spoken words. Life may hurt them, but they do not suffer from the wounds it gives them so that we watching them, are wounded ourselves and suffer with them.

This willingness, this ability, to strike unflinchingly upon the anvil of human sorrow is one of the reasons for O'Neill's preeminence and for the respect in which we hold the best work of Clifford Odets and Tennessee Williams. It is also the source of Arthur Miller's unique strength and explains why his fine new play, *Death of a Salesman*, is an experience at once pulverizing and welcome.

Mr. Miller is, of course, remembered as the author of *Focus*, a vigorous and terrifying novel about anti-Semitism, and best known for *All My Sons*, which won the New York Critics Award two seasons back. Although that earlier play lacked the simplicity, hence the muscularity, of Mr. Miller's novel, it was notable for its force. Overelaborate as it may have been, it introduced a new and unmistakable talent. If as a young man's script it took advantage of its right to betray influences, these at least were of the best. They were Ibsen and Chekhov. The doctor who wandered in from next door might have been extradited from *The Three Sisters*. The symbolical use to which the apple tree was put was pure Ibsen. So, too, was the manner in which the action was maneuvered from the present back into the past in order to rush forward. Even so, Mr. Miller's own voice could be heard in *All My Sons*, rising strong and clear above those other voices. It was a voice that deserved the attention and admiration it won. It was not afraid of being raised. It spoke with heat, fervor, and compassion. Moreover, it had something to say.

In *Death of a Salesman* this same voice can be heard again. It has deepened in tone, developed wonderfully in modulation, and gained in carrying power. Its authority has become full grown. Relying on no borrowed accents, it now speaks in terms of complete accomplishment rather than exciting promise. Indeed, it is released in a play which provides one of the modern theatre's most overpowering evenings.

How good the writing of this or that of Mr. Miller's individual scenes may be, I do not know. Nor do I really care. When hit in the face, you do not bother to count the knuckles which strike you. All that matters, all you remember, is the staggering impact of the blow. Mr. Miller's is a terrific wallop, as furious in its onslaught on the heart as on the head. His play is the most poignant statement of man as he must face himself to have come out of our theatre. It finds the stuffs of life so mixed with the stuffs of the stage that they become one and indivisible.

If the proper study of mankind is man, man's inescapable problem is himself—what he would like to be, what he is, what he is not, and yet what he must live and die with. These are the moving, everyday, all-inclusive subjects with which Mr. Miller deals in *Death of a Salesman*. He handles them unflinchingly, with enormous sympathy, with genuine imagination, and in a mood which neither the prose of his dialogue nor the reality of his probing can rob of its poetry. Moreover, he has the wisdom and the insight not to blame the "system," in Mr. Odets' fashion, for what are the inner frailties and shortcomings of the individual. His rightful concern is with the dilemmas which are timeless in the drama because they are timeless in life.

Mr. Miller's play is a tragedy modern and personal, not classic and heroic. Its central figure is a little man sentenced to discover his smallness rather than a big man undone by his greatness. Although he happens to be a salesman tested and found wanting by his own very special crises, all of us sitting out front are bound to be shaken, long before the evening is over, by finding something of ourselves in him.

Mr. Miller's Willy Loman is a family man, father of two sons. He is sixty-three and has grubbed hard all his life. He has never possessed either the daring or the gold-winning luck of his prospector brother, who wanders through the play as a somewhat shadowy symbol of success but a necessary contrast. Stupid, limited, and confused as Willy Loman may have been, how-

ever, no one could have questioned his industry or his loyalty to his family and his firm. He has loved his sons and, when they were growing up, been rewarded by the warmth of their returned love. He loves his wife, too, and has been unfaithful to her only because of his acute, aching loneliness when on the road.

He has lived on his smile and on his hopes; survived from sale to sale; been sustained by the illusion that he has countless friends in his territory, that everything will be all right, that he is a success, and that his boys will be successes also. His misfortune is that he has gone through life as an eternal adolescent, as someone who has not dared to take stock, as someone who never knew who he was. His personality has been his profession; his energy, his protection. His major ambition has been not only to be liked, but well liked. His ideal for himself and for his sons has stopped with an easy, back-slapping, sports-loving, locker-room popularity. More than ruining his sons so that one has become a woman chaser and the other a thief, his standards have turned both boys against their father.

When Mr. Miller's play begins, Willy Loman has reached the ebb-tide years. He is too old and worn out to continue traveling. His back aches when he stoops to lift the heavy sample cases that were once his pride. His tired, wandering mind makes it unsafe for him to drive the car which has carried him from one town and sale to the next. His sons see through him and despise him. His wife sees through him and defends him, knowing him to be better than most and, at any rate, well intentioned. What is far worse, when he is fired from his job he begins to see through himself. He realizes he is, and has been, a failure. Hence his deliberate smashup in his car in order to bring in some money for his family and make the final payment on his home when there is almost no one left who wants to live in it.

Although *Death of a Salesman* is set in the present, it finds time and space to include the past. It plays the agonies of the moment of collapse against the pleasures and sorrows of recollected episodes. Mr. Miller is interested in more than the life and fate of his central character. His scene seems to be Willy Loman's mind and heart no less than his home. What we see might just as well be that Willy Loman thinks, feels, fears, or remembers as what we see him doing. This gives the play a double and successful exposure in time. It makes possible the constant fusion of what has been and what is. It also enables it to achieve a greater reality by having been freed from the fetters of realism.

Once again Mr. Miller shows how fearless and perceptive an emotionalist he is. He writes boldly and brilliantly about the way in which we disappoint those we love by having disappointed ourselves. He knows the torment of family tensions, the compensations of friendship, and the heartbreak that goes with broken pride and lost confidence. He is aware of the loyalties, not blind but open-eyed, which are needed to support mortals in their loneliness. The anatomy of failure, the pathos of age, and the tragedy of those years when a life begins to slip down the hill it has labored to climb are subjects with which he excels.

The quality and intensity of his writing can perhaps best be suggested by letting Mr. Miller speak for himself, or rather by allowing his characters to speak for him, in a single scene, in fact, in the concluding one. It is then that Willy's wife, his two sons, and his old friend move away from Jo Mielziner's brilliantly sim-

(continued)

ple and imaginative multiple setting, and advance to the footlights. It is then that Mr. Miller's words supply a scenery of their own. Willy Loman, the failure and suicide, has supposedly just been buried, and all of us are at his grave, including his wife who wants to cry but cannot and who keeps thinking that it is just as if he were off on another trip.

"You don't understand," says Willy's friend, defending Willy from one of his sons. "Willy was a salesman. And for a salesman, there is no rock bottom to the life. He don't put a bolt to a nut, he don't tell you the law or give you medicine. He's a man way out there in the blue, ridin' on a smile and a shoeshine. And then they start not smilin' back—that's an earthquake. And then you get yourself a couple spots on your hat, and you're finished. Nobody dast blame this man. A salesman is got to dream, boy. It comes with the territory."

The production of *Death of a Salesman* is as sensitive, human, and powerful as the writing. Elia Kazan has solved, and solved superbly, what must have been a difficult and challenging problem. He captures to the full the mood and heartbreak of the script. He does this without ever surrendering to sentimentality. He manages to mingle the present and the past, the moment and his memory, so that their intertwining raises no questions and causes no confusions. His direction, so glorious in its vigor, is no less considerate of those small details which can be both mountainous and momentous in daily living.

It would be hard to name a play more fortunate in its casting than *Death of a Salesman*. All its actors—especially Arthur Kennedy and Cameron Mitchell as the two sons, and Howard Smith as the friend—act with such skill and conviction that the line of demarcation between being and pretending seems abolished. The script's humanity has taken possession of their playing and is an integral part of their performances.

Special mention must be made of Lee J. Cobb and Mildred Dunnock as the salesman, Willy Loman, and his wife, Linda.

Miss Dunnock is all heart, devotion, simplicity. She is unfooled but unfailing. She is the smiling, mothering, hard-worked, good wife, the victim of her husband's budget. She is the nourisher of his dreams, even when she knows they are only dreams; the feeder of his self-esteem. If she is beyond whining or nagging, she is above self-pity. She is the marriage vow—"for better for worse, for richer for poorer, in sickness and in health"—made flesh, slight of body but strong of faith.

Mr. Cobb's Willy Loman is irresistibly touching and wonderfully unsparing. He is a great shaggy bison of a man seen at that moment of defeat when he is deserted by the herd and can no longer run with it. Mr. Cobb makes clear the pathetic extent to which the herd has been Willy's life. He also communicates the fatigue of Willy's mind and body and that boyish hope and buoyancy which his heart still retains. Age, however, is his enemy. He is condemned by it. He can no more escape from it than he can from himself. The confusions, the weakness, the goodness, the stupidity, and the self-sustaining illusions which are Willy—all these are established by Mr. Cobb. Seldom has an average man at the moment of his breaking been characterized with such exceptional skill.

Did Willy Loman, so happy with a batch of cement when puttering around the house, or when acquaintances on the road smiled back at him, fail to find out who he was? Did this man, who worked so hard and meant so well, dream the wrong dream? At least he was willing to die by that dream, even when it had collapsed for him. He was a breadwinner almost to the end, and a breadwinner even in his death. Did the world walk out on him, and his sons see through him? At any rate he could boast one friend who believed in him and thought his had been a good dream, "the only dream you can have." Who knows? Who can say? One thing is certain. No one could have raised the question more movingly or compassionately than Arthur Miller.

"Willy Loman Gets China Territory"

CHRISTOPHER S. WREN

The salesman shuffled on stage into the exposed skeleton of his small house and wearily handed his hat to his solicitous wife, who cast about for some place to put it.

"Let's get a shelf or a bench upstage of the bed," interrupted Arthur Miller from the dark of the deserted audience. "She can stash it right there and no one will ever know the difference." Ying Ruocheng, the Chinese actor who is also his liaison, nodded and translated to the stage manager.

Nearly 35 years after it opened on Broadway with Lee J. Cobb playing Willy Loman, the salesman "riding on a smile and a shoeshine to self-destruction," *Death of a Salesman* has come to China. Translated into Chinese, it is being directed by the playwright with a cast from the Peking People's Art Theater.

The revival could prove one of the most significant events for the Chinese theater since the end of a Cultural revolution [1965–1975], when the tedious repertory of Maoist plays got jettisoned. Many in the Chinese audiences raised on prim Socialist morality plays will get their first acquaintance with the more ambiguous nature of contemporary Western drama.

It is customary here to allocate tickets to foreign plays to Government offices and factories, where officials will decide who gets them. Mr. Ying has appealed, however, for the Government to release one-half of the tickets for *Death of a Salesman* for public sale.

He doesn't normally like directing his plays, Mr. Miller explained, because he would rather be home writing. He said he consented to devote nearly two months to this project because, "It seemed like an adventure to me—a window into China that is without parallel."

Though the story of a man made superfluous under capitalism would appeal to China's cultural commissars, there was still apparent hesitation about allowing in *Death of a Salesman* and its flawed hero.

"My impression is that they had long and strenuous debates about it, and those who backed the idea have a lot riding on it," Mr. Miller said. "That's why I wanted to do it."

The playwright, who has visited China twice before, is already popular for *The Crucible*. When it was staged [in Peking] several years ago, the Chinese saw the Salem witch hunts of seventeenth century New England as an allegory of their capriciously cruel Cultural Revolution. *All My Sons* was performed in China, too, though the playwright isn't sure where.

To transport Willy Loman from Brooklyn to Peking, the Chinese painstakingly reconstructed the original 1949 set from plans Mr. Miller sent over earlier. Whether Chinese audiences can as easily empathize with a traveling salesman defeated by the American dream will become clear after the play opens. [N.B.: The production was given a standing ovation by Chinese audiences.—Eds.]

Mr. Miller said: "*Salesman* represents a challenge they didn't think they could meet because they didn't think the audience would get it. About a year and half ago, they decided to risk it. I have to remind you that when the play opened originally in New York, there was also a question whether the audience was going to follow Willy through the corridors of his mind."

The Chinese, with their tradition of closely knit family, should have no trouble recognizing Willy Loman's frictions with his sons or Linda Loman's inability to save her husband. [Miller's wife] recalled that one woman came to watch a rehearsal, broke down, and sobbed, "It's the same situation."

Mr. Miller said: "The play is really about morality and leaving something behind. Willy Loman is trying to write his name on a cake of ice on a hot July day, and they know all about that."

Chinese who have grown up with a centrally planned state-run economy may be confused about how a salesman earns his living, though the Government's recent encouragement of private enterprise has made Miller's job easier.

"I thought we'd have to write a big essay explaining what salesman are and put it in the program," Mr. Miller said, "but Willy explains in the course of the play what a salesman does. In 1983, they know all about that. There are now people selling stuff on commission. There are now traveling buyers going from place to place to buy materials. There are factories loaded with surplus goods that are selling them in distant places. It may have not been a known profession, but it sure as hell is now."

Mr. Miller's liaison, Ying Ruocheng, is a distinguished actor who played the Mongol emperor, Kublai Khan, in the television series *Marco Polo* last year. Mr. Ying not only plays the part of Willy Loman, he also interprets Mr. Miller's directions to the actors. And he translated *Death of a Salesman* into Chinese, doing it so deftly that Mr. Miller said he could follow the script by listening to the cadence of the language.

Mr. Miller wasn't sure that Mr. Ying realized beforehand how strenuous playing Willy Loman would be. "He's rarely off stage and the scenes when he is on are at very high intensity." Mr. Ying said he agreed that the role was "one of the toughest anywhere."

A more difficult task has been getting the other actors to drop stylized gestures characteristic of Chinese Socialist drama and to behave naturally. They are used to exaggerating their emotions as stereotypes of good and evil to hammer across the play's message.

"I kill it every time it starts," Mr. Miller said of their mannerisms, though he sighed that "it crops up in different disguises."

The actor playing Howard Wagner, the employer who discharges Willy Loman, was dissuaded from making the character hateful. "I had to work longer with him than with anyone else to break the villainy out of him," Mr. Miller said. "He's quite affable now."

The actors, who wear 1940s Western clothing, have also been crammed with such details as the popularity of American football. "I've had to indoctrinate them with a lot of American folklore and stories," said Mr. Miller, who believes that a director must be a teacher too. "You have to do it with American actors, too, but they have the American references at their fingertips."

The greatest leap for the Chinese may be accepting a play without the customary Marxist moralistic didacticism. "The first thing they ask of anything, whether it's a bridge or a pair of shoes, is 'What's the message?'" Mr. Miller said.

The play has not been affected by the Chinese Government's move to suspend cultural and sports exchanges with the United States for the rest of [1983] to protest the political asylum given Hu Na, the tennis player. The project is sponsored by the United States–China Arts Exchange, a nongovernmental program run out of Columbia University. "That's why we weren't shut down," Mr. Miller said.

Except for Mr. Ying, who has visited the United States and Europe, Mr. Miller has found most Chinese uninformed about Western theater. When actors ask him what they can learn, Mr. Miller says: "I disappoint them by saying the West is in turmoil as far as the theater is concerned. There is only experimentation, and much of it isn't any good. But I tell them they might have to go through this experimentation."

Mr. Miller believes that the contemporary repertory already familiar in the West is a good place for Chinese theater to begin after the long years of isolation. "They're really coming out of a cave and blinking their eyes," the playwright said.

ABSURDISM

Artistic and Cultural Events

1916:
Tristan Tzara
begins Dadism
in Switzerland

1930s:
Symbolist
drama in
Spain

1950:
Eugène
Ionesco's
*The Bald
Soprano*

1896:
Alfred Jarry's
Ubu Roi,
first
absurdist
play

1902:
Filippo
Marinetti
initiates
futurism
in Italy

1923:
André Breton
initiates
surrealism

1944:
Jean-Paul
Sartre's
No Exit

1953:
Samuel
Beckett's
*Waiting for
Godot*

1956:
Osvaldo
Dragún's
*Stories
to be
Told*

1961:
Edward
Albee's
*The
American
Dream*

1800 C.E.   **1900 C.E.**

Historical and Political Events

1914–1918:
World War I

1939–1945:
World War II

1960s:
Counter-
revolution

1206

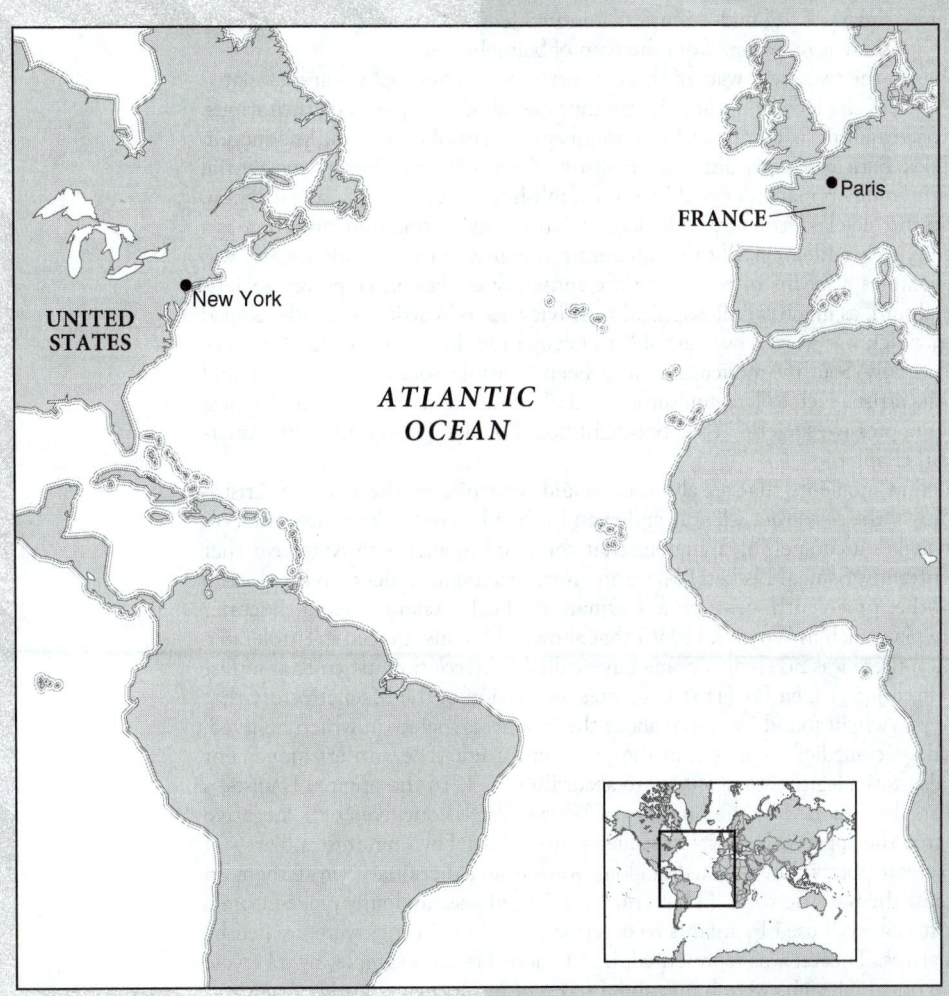

Whether they used realistic or other means in their exploration of social issues, most writers and artists in the modern theater shared the optimistic belief that change is possible, that social dilemmas can be solved if people are made aware of the problems that create them. Others, however, were less hopeful. Like Chekhov, they believed that time and institutions are indifferent to the human condition and that we are trapped by our circumstances and inertia. One of the most famous plays of the mid–twentieth century, Jean Paul Sartre's *No Exit* (*Huis Clos*, 1944) argues that there is no escape from the pain of being human.

Out of the ashes of the two great wars of this century arose a philosophy—and a related theater movement—that challenged optimistic assumptions about people and institutions. The philosophy, existentialism, is manifested in a number of types of drama and production styles. Osborne's *Look Back in Anger*, although realistic, depicts Jimmy Porter's existential dilemma: how does a common man educated by the Establishment survive in a social system that is still rooted in the old class structure? "He doesn't," in Jimmy's estimation, and there is a fundamental absurdity to his dilemma. But the inherent rationality of the realistic theater was dismissed as inadequate as a means of portraying the senselessness of contemporary society. The theater of the absurd, as much a philosophical worldview as a theatrical style, developed primarily in France, which was scarred by years of Nazi occupation. Importantly, the theater of Latin America, especially South America, has also been a fertile source of absurdist and grotesque drama as its artists, such as Dragún, turned to dark humor to depict the senselessness of their existence in oppressive societies. (See Spotlight box, Popular Theater in Latin America, at the end of this chapter.)

While we can find moments that an absurdist would recognize in the plays of Aristophanes, the clowning of the *commedia dell'arte*, and even in the plays of Shakespeare (the Polish critic Jan Kott makes a compelling argument that there are moments in *King Lear* that might have been written by Samuel Beckett), there are more recent antecedents to the theatre of the absurd. In the nineteenth century a German medical student, Georg Büchner (1813–1837), wrote plays such as *Woyzeck* (1836) that showed humans trapped in intolerable situations from which there was no escape. Some have called *Woyzeck* the first truly absurdist work; others cite Alfred Jarry's *Ubu Roi* (1896), a grotesque version of the Macbeth story that exposes all that the playwright found irrational about the bourgeois society in which he lived. It is among the darkest comedies composed in the preabsurdist era. The anti-art movement known as Dadism also was a legitimate precursor to absurdism. In 1916 the original Dadists, a group of young artists disillusioned by the brutality of World War I, conceived of a "negative art" that would destroy the apparently senseless values—promulgated by literature and art—of modern society. To create poetry they selected random words from a dictionary, wrote them on slips of paper, and cast them to the wind. (The term "dada" itself was randomly picked from a French dictionary; it is a word used by infants to describe horses.) Paintings were created by tossing paint at a canvas. Theater was represented, in a famous French example, by a bicycle wheel, a clothesline on which signs were hung, and a series of insults exchanged between actors and audience. By 1922 Dadism had lost much of its appeal, but it planted the seeds of an "anti-art" and skepticism that would resurface in the 1940s as the theatre of the absurd.

During and immediately after World War II a group of international writers and philosophers flourished in Paris: Sartre and Albert Camus (France), Eugène Ionesco (Romania), and Samuel Beckett (Ireland) (see Spotlight box, *Waiting for Godot: The Modern Masterpiece*). Appalled by German atrocities, they embraced a philosophy that argued that there was no longer a system of order in the world (how else could one explain the Holocaust?) and that one was responsible for defining one's existence through personal choices. Disillusioned by the horrors of war, the economic depression of the 1930s, and other modern catastrophes, these nihilistic existentialists asserted that "the world is irrational and the truth unknowable."

If the world was indeed senseless, then it followed that art itself should mirror that senselessness. Traditional theater had to be transformed to reflect this condition. Conventional plots, dependent on causality and resolution, were abandoned in favor of cyclic plots that rarely resolved conflicts. Borrowing from the Expressionists and symbolists, the absurdists drew characters who were poetic abstractions. They were given generalized names (A and B, He and

SPOTLIGHT — *WAITING FOR GODOT:* THE MODERN MASTERPIECE

Samuel Beckett's *Waiting for Godot* is among the most remarkable plays in the history of world theater. Nothing quite like it preceded its arrival in Paris in 1953, and it has since become one of the most imitated (if indirectly) and analyzed plays of the twentieth century. It stands as the epitome of the theater of the absurd, yet it has transcended the limitations of absurdism and remains a metaphysical landmark of the late twentieth century. Ironically, its status as a masterwork has curtailed its publication rights, so we may offer only this synopsis of the play and a brief assessment of its impact on the modern theater.

The story of *Waiting for Godot* is as sparse as the landscape in which it takes place: two tramps (Gogo and Didi) wait under a barren tree for a "Mr. Godot." They "improvise life" as they wait, and we watch them quarreling about seemingly insignificant matters, eating carrots and chicken bones, adjusting their ill-fitted shoes, and attempting suicide (unsuccessfully—fitting in a play about futility). Their wait is interrupted by two strangers, Pozzo (a master) and Lucky (his slave). The tramps engage in pseudophilosophic discourse with Pozzo, who proclaims that we live on a "bitch of an earth." The tree sprouts a few leaves between acts, and Pozzo and Lucky return, this time blind and dumb. Finally, a boy arrives to inform the tramps that Godot will not come, and they continue to wait "in the midst of nothingness." The mundane routines with which Gogo and Didi occupy themselves as they wait reinforce the play's most quoted line: "Habit is the great deadener."

While "nothing" seems to happen during the play and in its seemingly incoherent conversations, in actuality everything happens. Virtually every aspect of the human condition is addressed—birth, death, suffering, redemption, salvation, loss, freedom, slavery, free will, isolation, companionship, hope, and despair. Midway

through the play, Lucky—who speaks only once—delivers a long monologue (in the stream-of-consciousness style of Beckett's countryman James Joyce) that seems to summarize the history of humanity as it sits perched "astride of a grave and a difficult birth":

. . . but time will tell I resume alas alas on on in short in fine on on abode of stones who can doubt it I resume but not so fast I resume the skull fading fading fading and concurrently simultaneously what is more for reasons unknown in spite for the tennis on on the beard the flames the tears the stones so blue so calm alas alas on on the skull the skull the skull the skull in Connemara in spite of the tennis the labors abandoned left unfinished graver still abode of stones in a word I resume alas alas abandoned unfinished . . .

So what does *Godot* mean? Indeed, who/what is Godot? Until his dying day Beckett steadfastly refused to reveal his intentions, saying only that "perhaps" is the most important word in the play. In the spirit of the absurdist movement, the playwright thus forces audiences—as they have been forced since 1953—to assign meaning to the play, if there is indeed meaning. Critics, scholars, philosophers, directors, actors, and general audiences have all attempted to assign meaning to Beckett's enigmatic play:

- It portrays humanity's fruitless search for someone or something that gives meaning to life.
- It attempts to bridge the gap between human hopes and human futility.
- It is a modern myth, grounded in archetypal characters and situations, about "the suffering of being."
- It shows that humans "act out" life rather than live it; that is, we are actors in a cosmic drama, yet we do not know our lines, much less the character we are asked to play.

- It is a meaningless exercise that mirrors the meaningless of all human activity.

Despite its cryptic themes, *Godot* transformed the contemporary theater by loosening the grip of realism and absolute logic on dramaturgy. It returned the language of the theater to the realm of the evocative and symbolic, rather than the literal, and it released characterization from the particulars of psychology and sociology, thus making stage characters again mythic. Gogo and Didi, by the way, are rooted in that most elemental theater character: the hapless clown. For all its modernity, *Godot* is theater at its most essential—an empty space, a universal question, and skilled actors who bring it to life.

Godot was first staged by Roger Blin at the Théâtre de Babylon in Paris, where it ran for over 400 performances. Like *Hernani*, it provoked heated discussion; some in the opening-night audience felt they had been duped by this "nonplay." Like Gogo, they, too, believed the play was an event in which "nothing happens, nobody comes, nobody goes, it's awful." Others saw it as a theatrical Second Coming that would free the theater from the snares of realism just as *Hernani* had overthrown the Neoclassic codes 120 years earlier. News of Beckett's audacious work spread, and the play was performed at the Arts Theatre in London in 1955. It was directed by Peter Hall, fresh out of Cambridge University, who would found the Royal Shakespeare Company five years later. Harold Pinter and Tom Stoppard would be among the prominent British playwrights drawn to Beckett's new style. Stoppard wrote *Rosencrantz and Guildenstern Are Dead*, a dark comedy in which *Hamlet*'s Rosencrantz and Guildenstern resemble Beckett's tramps more than Shakespeare's creations.

The American premiere of *Godot* also stunned its audience, but for somewhat different reasons: Hearing that the

(continued)

play was a popular French comedy, an impresario booked it into a tourist resort theater in Florida. It has since been performed in hundreds of theaters by some of the American theater's most important actors: Bert Lahr, E. G. Marshall, and George C. Scott, to name but a few. A recent production at New York's Lincoln Center featured two of the most popular American comedians, Steve Martin and Robin Williams. *Godot* has been performed around the world; in 1979, for instance, Gogo and Didi were played in the Australian Academy of Dramatic Art by student actors Mel Gibson and Geoffrey Rush.

For almost a half-century actors, audiences, and critics have responded to Beckett's central question, spoken by Didi:

What are we doing here, *that* is the question? And we are blessed in this, that we happen to know the answer. Yes, in the immense confusion one thing alone is clear. We are waiting for Godot to come—

She, Gogo and Didi) and placed in unspecified time and space, often against dark curtains symbolizing the black void of existence. To illustrate lack of communication, language was frequently reduced to nonsensical utterings, non sequiturs, or mechanically repeated phrases. This dialogue from Ionesco's *The Bald Soprano* (1950) parodies the discussion drama of polite society. The speakers were indistinguishable from one another:

MR. MARTIN. One doesn't polish spectacles with black wax.
MRS. SMITH. Yes, but with money one can buy anything.
MR. MARTIN. I'd rather kill a rabbit than sing in the garden.
MR. SMITH. Cockatoos, cockatoos, cockatoos, cockatoos, cockatoos, cockatoos, cockatoos, cockatoos, cockatoos, cockatoos.
MRS. SMITH. Such caca, such caca, such caca, such caca, such caca, such caca, such caca, such caca, such caca.
MR. MARTIN. Such cascades of cacas, such cascades of cacas . . .

Traditional distinctions among the genres blur in the absurdist world: the comic frequently becomes serious, even near tragic, while the serious becomes laughable. Most absurdist plays are essentially comic, partly because they are satirical and partly because we are not engaged in the dramatic life of the characters. We laugh, albeit uncomfortably, at the enormous gap between human aspirations and the reality of existence. Edward Albee, whose early plays (e.g., *The American Dream*) are often categorized as absurdist, is perhaps the most successful playwright to have fused the philosophical concerns of the absurdists with traditional dramatic forms. His assessment of absurdism identifies the movement's concerns:

As I get it, the Theatre of the Absurd is an absorption-in-art of certain existentialist and post-existentialist philosophical concepts having to do, in the main, with man's attempts to make sense of his senseless position in a world which makes no sense—which makes no sense because the moral, religious, political and social structures man has erected to "illusion" himself have collapsed.

In short, the theater of the absurd attempts to "make sense through nonsense." Unlike Ibsen, Shaw, and Brecht, absurdist playwrights refuse to suggest solutions to human problems. Meaning in this senseless world is derived solely by the audience, and in absurdist drama the discussion takes place long after the inevitable fade to black. (See Forum, "The Significance of the Absurd," following the text of *The American Dream*.)

Many of the newer, antirealistic forms of drama have had a salutary effect on the theater. First, they have returned the art to its poetic roots. Theater began not as an imitation of real life but as a metaphor for life. Second, the social concerns voiced by both realists and antirealists exposed the plight of marginalized people throughout the world and opened the door to new writers. Consequently, the theater has been enriched in word and action by an infusion of new voices previously unheard in the mainstream. The final two sections of this anthology— "Africa and the African Diaspora" and "The Contemporary Theater" —contain many fine examples of voices not previously heard in the theater.

THE AMERICAN DREAM

EDWARD ALBEE

EDWARD ALBEE (1928 –)

The winner of three Pulitzer Prizes in drama, Edward Albee has emerged as one of the finest American playwrights of the twentieth century. He bridges the early generation of admired playwrights (O'Neill, Miller, Williams) and the current one (Shepard, August Wilson). No other playwright dominated the American theater in the 1960s as did Albee, who pioneered American absurdism in *The American Dream* and *The Sandbox*. After his initial exploration of absurdist drama, Albee took psychological realism to uncommon heights, tempering it with an almost surrealistic overlay. And he has emerged as one of the most articulate and candid spokespersons for the arts in America.

It is fitting that Albee should have pursued a life in the theater. His adoptive parents were heirs to the Albee-Keith fortune established in 1885 by Edward Franklin Albee II and B. F. Keith, who built a vaudeville empire that eventually stretched across America. Upon his adoption from a home for foundlings in Washington, D.C., Albee was christened Edward F. Albee III in memory of his adoptive grandfather. Though Albee's early life seems to have been charmed, his childhood was troubled and rancorous. His antipathy to his parents, especially his domineering mother, has been well publicized, and it appears that the domestic battles of the Albee household provided him with material for such plays as *Who's Afraid of Virginia Woolf?* and *The American Dream*, both of which are concerned with the disintegration of the contemporary family.

His parents' prosperity allowed Albee to attend the finest prep schools in the East, including Choate, followed by a brief stint at Trinity College in 1946–1947. His grandmother—a model for the Grandmother in *The Sandbox* and *The American Dream*—bequeathed him sufficient money to escape his home life. After a series of odd jobs, Albee achieved his first playwriting success when *The Zoo Story* was performed in New York (but only after proving itself in a West Berlin production in 1959). Performed on a bill with Beckett's *Krapp's Last Tape*, *The Zoo Story* was generously praised by Tennessee Williams. In May 1960 Albee wrote a short one-act, *The Sandbox*, whose principal characters reappeared the following year in *The American Dream*. In these works we see several Albee motifs: the impossibility of honest, open communication; emasculated father-figures embattled in a war of words with overbearing wives; the callous rejection of the older generation; masking reality with illusions (or delusions); and violence lurking beneath the surface of modern life.

In 1962 *Who's Afraid of Virginia Woolf?* premiered on Broadway, and its two-year run validated the critical praise it earned. It received the Drama Critics Circle Award and a Tony as best play of the season, but it failed to win the Pulitzer Prize because of a dispute among the trustees over the play's sexual references. Nonetheless, the play remains arguably Albee's finest drama in its devastating depiction of a psychological exorcism. Despite its patina of contemporary realism, the play is part Sartrean existentialism ("Hell is other people") and part Artaudian theater of cruelty as its characters "signal through the flames" of their personal hell. Albee did receive Pulitzer Prizes for *A Delicate Balance* (1966) and *Seascape* (1975). In the latter play,

Albee experimented with fantasy as a middle-aged couple encounters two prehistoric creatures from the sea; the play is a witty, philosophical discussion of mortality and human progress.

Despite his reputation as a superior playwright, whose dialogue is admired for its caustic wit and sophistication, Albee has had a curious relationship with critics. Like Williams, Albee was rejected by critics after his initial successes, partly because he tried to be too thoughtful in his works, and because he never measured up to the exacting standards he set for himself with *Virginia Woolf*, *Tiny Alice* (1964), and *A Delicate Balance*. In 1994 Albee was redeemed by *Three Tall Women*, a poetic look at immortality; the play won him a third Pulitzer Prize. In addition to playwriting, Albee also directs his own works. When not in New York, he teaches playwriting at the University of Houston and is an associate artist at Houston's Alley Theater.

THE AMERICAN DREAM (1960)

Because the centerpiece of this play is a lengthy story (an Albee trademark) about the adoption of "a little bumble of joy" by overbearing parents, it is tempting to regard *The American Dream* as an autobiographical piece in which the playwright exorcises the demons of his troubled youth. While this reading has some validity, the play transcends the particulars of Albee's life and remains among the most disturbing depictions of American culture in the postwar era. Furthermore, it provides insights into Albee's more mature, full-length works, such as *Who's Afraid of Virginia Woolf?* and *A Delicate Balance*. It can be argued that this one-act was a "first draft" of *Virginia Woolf*, just as *The Sandbox* was a precursor to *The American Dream*.

First, consider the play as an example of absurdist drama, the kind that emanated from Europe in the late 1940s and throughout the 1950s. In spirit and content, it is indebted to Eugène Ionesco's seminal absurdist drama, *The Bald Soprano* (1950). As in Ionesco's parody of banal small talk that precludes meaningful communication, *The American Dream* also relies on hilarious non sequiturs, the inversion of normal social exchanges (e.g., "What a dreadful apartment you have here," followed by "Yes, but you don't know what trouble it is"), gross violations of decorum (e.g., when Mrs. Barker removes her dress at Mommy's too-polite invitation), and the reduction of adult conversation to infantile prattling ("try to get the leak in the johnny fixed"). Albee's characters make self-canceling statements ("She's just a dreadful woman . . . so naturally I'm terribly fond of her") and elevate the most trivial elements of human endeavors (e.g., the color of a hat) to nearly cosmic significance. This was very much the arsenal of early absurdists who lamented the impossibility of communication in an increasingly illogical world; for them, language is reduced to a mechanical process of thoughtless noncommunication. Eventually, playwrights, led by Albee and Pinter, turned to a language of evasion and subterfuge to show lack of communication. More accurately, their characters refuse to communicate in a threatening world without verifiable meaning.

Also typical of absurdist comedy, the characters here are ciphers, nonentities in and of themselves but provocative symbols of the world at large. Only Mrs. Barker is given an actual name, yet in the context of this play it seems thoroughly generic. The bland box set described in the opening stage direction is peopled by the prototypical antiheroes of Albee's urban, WASP-ish wasteland. Daddy is the archetypal Albee male: emasculated, ineffectual, unable to commit himself to anything. Mommy is predictably domineering, stifling, sexually repressed. These are the parents of the American household at midcentury. In *Who's Afraid of Virginia Woolf?* the playwright fleshes them out with greater psychological complexity and, ominously, names them George and Martha (a macabre joke about the "first parents" of America?). Only Grandma is presented sympathetically, yet even she is just another discard in our disposable society. Early in the play, Mommy and Daddy threaten to "call the van man and have her taken away," and by the end of the play, when Grandma "disappears," Mrs. Barker tells us "the van man was here." Albee seems less interested in exposing the plight of the elderly than in examining America's preoccupation with the cult of youth. Even as Albee wrote the play in 1960, America was electing its youngest president (John Kennedy) and the baby boomer generation was entering adolescence.

Enter "the Young Man," a virile, narcissistic youth who, we are told, is "the American dream." Who is he, this identical twin of a child earlier adopted (and subsequently destroyed) by Mommy and Daddy? Is he the "American dream"—that is, the handsome, charming youth who seems immortal? Is he "the Angel of Death," as Albee called virtually the same character in *The Sandbox?* (Albee returned to the Angel of Death in his 1979 play, *The Lady from Dubuque.*) Albee challenges the audience to ascertain the symbolic value of this enigmatic character. Whatever he represents, the Young Man's most compelling line captures the ultimate dilemma in Albee's world. He tells Grandma, with whom he has a sympathetic covenant, that "I have been unable to love." The Young Man, it needs saying, is one of the first sympathetic portraits of a homosexual in the American theater as he recounts his plight as a male prostitute. Here Albee opened vistas for a subsequent generation of playwrights, including Harvey Fierstein and Terrence McNally.

Despite its grim portrait of contemporary life, the play is a comedy in its satirical portrait of the manners of a bourgeois family. In this sense it is kin to such works as *Tartuffe* and *She Stoops to Conquer.* Significantly, Albee ends his play with the staple of comedies since Aristophanes: the *komos,* or "joyful ending," in which opposing parties unite to celebrate a new order. Albee's absurdly dysfunctional family, joined by Mrs. Barker and the mysterious Young Man, gather together "while everybody's happy" to drink "dreadful sauterne" in what appears to be a harmonious conclusion. Grandma breaks the illusion of the fourth wall to tell the audience that it is time to end the comedy "while everybody's got what he wants . . . or what he thinks he wants." And getting what one "wants" is, of course, the American dream. For Albee, the American dream seems to be as hollow and artificial as the contrived and sentimental ending of his play.

The Young Man stands before pictures of American icons (for example, Babe Ruth) in a 1975 Stevens Theatre Company production of Edward Albee's The American Dream.

THE AMERICAN DREAM

A Play in One Scene (1959–1960)

EDWARD ALBEE

For David Diamond

THE PLAYERS
MOMMY
DADDY
GRANDMA
MRS. BARKER
YOUNG MAN

THE SCENE: *A living room. Two armchairs, one toward either side of the stage, facing each other diagonally out toward the audience. Against the rear wall, a sofa. A door, leading out from the apartment, in the rear wall, far stage-right. An archway, leading to other rooms, in the side wall, stage-left.*

At the beginning, Mommy and Daddy are seated in the armchairs, DADDY *in the armchair stage-left, Mommy in the other.*

Curtain up. A silence. Then:

MOMMY. I don't know what can be keeping them.
DADDY. They're late, naturally.
MOMMY. Of course, they're late; it never fails.

DADDY. That's the way things are today, and there's nothing you can do about it.

MOMMY. You're quite right.

DADDY. When we took this apartment, they were quick enough to have me sign the lease; they were quick enough to take my check for two months' rent in advance . . .

MOMMY. And one month's security . . .

DADDY. . . . and one month's security. They were quick enough to check my references; they were quick enough about all that. But now! But now, try to get the icebox fixed, try to get the doorbell fixed, try to get the leak in the johnny fixed! Just try it . . . they aren't so quick about *that*.

MOMMY. Of course not; it never fails. People think they can get away with anything these days . . . and, of course they can. I went to buy a new hat yesterday.

(*Pause*)

I said, I went to buy a new hat yesterday.

DADDY. Oh! Yes . . . yes.

MOMMY. Pay attention.

DADDY. I *am* paying attention, Mommy.

MOMMY. Well, be sure you do.

DADDY. Oh, I am.

MOMMY. All right, Daddy; now listen.

DADDY. I'm listening, Mommy.

MOMMY. You're sure!

DADDY. Yes . . . yes, I'm sure, I'm all ears.

MOMMY (*Giggles at the thought; then*). All right, now. I went to buy a new hat yesterday and I said, "I'd like a new hat, please." And so, they showed me a few hats, green ones and blue ones, and I didn't like any of them, not one bit. What did I say? What did I just say?

DADDY. You didn't like any of them, not one bit.

MOMMY. That's right; you just keep paying attention. And then they showed me one that I did like. It was a lovely little hat, and I said, "Oh, this is a lovely little hat; I'll take this hat; oh my, it's lovely. What color is it?" And they said, "Why, this is beige; isn't it a lovely little beige hat?" And I said, "Oh, it's just lovely." And so, I bought it.

(*Stops, looks at Daddy*)

DADDY. (*To show he is paying attention*). And so you bought it.

MOMMY. And so I bought it, and I walked out of the store with the hat right on my head, and I ran spang into the chairman of our woman's club, and she said, "Oh, my dear, isn't that a lovely little hat? Where did you get that lovely little hat? It's the loveliest little hat; I've always wanted a wheat-colored hat *myself*." And, I said, "Why, no, my dear; this hat is beige; beige." And she laughed and said, "Why no, my dear, that's a wheat-colored hat . . . wheat. I know beige from wheat." And I said, "Well, my dear, I know beige from wheat, too." What did I say? What did I just say?

DADDY (*Tonelessly*). Well, my dear, I know beige from wheat, too.

MOMMY. That's right. And she laughed, and she said, "Well, my dear, they certainly put one over on you. That's wheat if I ever saw wheat. But it's lovely, just the same." And then she walked off. She's a dreadful woman, you don't know her; she has dreadful taste, two dreadful children, a dreadful house, and an absolutely adorable husband who sits in a wheel chair all the time. You don't know him. You don't know anybody, do you? She's just a dreadful woman, but she *is* chairman of our woman's club, so naturally I'm terribly fond of her. So, I went right back into the hat shop, and I said, "Look here; what do you mean selling me a hat that you say is beige, when it's wheat all the time . . . wheat! I can tell beige from wheat any day in the week, but not in this artificial light of yours." They have artificial light, Daddy.

DADDY. Have they!

MOMMY. And I said, "The minute I got outside I could tell that it wasn't a beige hat at all; it was a wheat hat." And they said to me, "How could you tell that when you had the hat on the top of your head?" Well, that made me angry, and so I made a scene right there; I screamed as hard as I could; I took my hat off and I threw it down on the counter, and oh, I made a terrible scene. I said, I made a terrible scene.

DADDY (*Snapping to*). Yes . . . yes . . . good for you!

MOMMY. And I made an absolutely terrible scene; and they became frightened, and they said, "Oh, madam; oh, madam." But I kept right on, and finally they admitted that they might have made a mistake; so they took my hat into the back, and then they came out again with a hat that looked exactly like it. I took one look at it, and I said, "This hat is wheat-colored; wheat." Well, of course, they said, "Oh, no, madam, this hat is beige; you go outside and see." So, I went outside, and lo and behold, it *was* beige. So I bought it.

DADDY (*Clearing his throat*). I would imagine that it was the same hat they tried to sell you before.

MOMMY (*With a little laugh*). Well, of course it was!

DADDY. That's the way things are today; you just can't get satisfaction; you just try.

MOMMY. Well, *I* got satisfaction.

DADDY. That's right, Mommy. *You did* get satisfaction, didn't you?

MOMMY. Why are they so late? I don't know what can be keeping them.

DADDY. I've been trying for two weeks to have the leak in the johnny fixed.

MOMMY. You can't get satisfaction; just try. *I* can get satisfaction, but you can't.

DADDY. I've been trying for two weeks and it isn't so much for my sake; I can always go to the club.

MOMMY. It isn't so much for my sake, either; I can always go shopping.

DADDY. It's really for Grandma's sake.

MOMMY. Of course it's for Grandma's sake. Grandma cries every time she goes to the johnny as it is; but now that it doesn't work it's even worse, it makes Grandma think she's getting feeble-headed.

DADDY. Grandma *is* getting feeble-headed.

MOMMY. Of course Grandma is getting feeble-headed, but not about her johnny-do's.

DADDY. No; that's true. I must have it fixed.

MOMMY. WHY are they so late? I don't know what can be keeping them.

DADDY. When they came here the first time, they were ten minutes early; they were quick enough about it then.

(*Enter Grandma from the archway, stage left. She is loaded down with boxes, large and small, neatly wrapped and tied.*)

MOMMY. Why Grandma, look at you! What *is* all that you're carrying?

GRANDMA. They're boxes. What do they look like?

MOMMY. Daddy! Look at Grandma; look at all the boxes she's carrying!

DADDY. My goodness, Grandma; look at those boxes.

GRANDMA. Where'll I put them?

MOMMY. Heavens! I don't know. Whatever are they for?

GRANDMA. That's nobody's damn business.

MOMMY. Well, in that case, put them down next to Daddy; there.

GRANDMA (*Dumping the boxes down, on and around* Daddy's *feet*). I sure wish you'd get the john fixed.

DADDY. Oh, I do wish they'd come and fix it. We hear you . . . for hours . . . whimpering away . . .

MOMMY. Daddy! What a terrible thing to say to Grandma!

GRANDMA. Yeah. For shame, talking to me that way.

DADDY. I'm sorry, Grandma.

MOMMY. Daddy's sorry, Grandma.

GRANDMA. Well, all right. In that case I'll go get the rest of the boxes. I suppose I deserve being talked to that way. I've gotten so old. Most people think that when you get so old, you either freeze to death or you burn up. But you don't. When you get so old, all that happens is that people talk to you that way.

DADDY (*Contrite*). I said I'm sorry, Grandma.

MOMMY. Daddy said he was sorry.

GRANDMA. Well, that's all that counts. People being sorry. Makes you feel better; gives you a sense of dignity, and that's all that's important . . . a sense of dignity. And it doesn't matter if you don't care, or not, either. You got to have a sense of dignity, even if you don't care, 'cause, if you don't have that, civilization's doomed.

MOMMY. You've been reading my book club selections again!

DADDY. How dare you read Mommy's book club selections, Grandma!

GRANDMA. Because I'm old! When you're old you gotta do something. When you get old, you can't talk to people because people snap at you. When you get so old, people talk to you that way. That's why you become deaf, so you won't be able to hear people talking to you that way. And that's why you go and hide under the covers in the big soft bed, so you won't feel the house shaking from people talking to you that way. That's why old people die, eventually. People talk to them that way. I've got to go and get the rest of the boxes.

(*Grandma exits*)

DADDY. Poor Grandma, I didn't mean to hurt her.

MOMMY. Don't you worry about it; Grandma doesn't know what she means.

DADDY. She knows what she says, though.

MOMMY. Don't you worry about it; she won't know that soon. I love Grandma.

DADDY. I love her, too. Look how nicely she wrapped these boxes.

MOMMY. Grandma has always wrapped boxes nicely. When I was a little girl, I was very poor, and Grandma was very poor, too, because Grandpa was in heaven. And every day, when I went to school, Grandma used to wrap a box for me, and I used to take it with me to school; and when it was lunchtime, all the little boys and girls used to take out their boxes of lunch, and they weren't wrapped nicely at all, and they used to open them and eat their chicken legs and chocolate cakes; and I used to say, "Oh, look at my lovely lunch box; it's so nicely wrapped it would break my heart to open it." And so, I wouldn't open it.

DADDY. Because it was empty.

MOMMY. Oh no. Grandma always filled it up, because she never ate the dinner she cooked the evening before; she gave me all her food for my lunch box the next day. After school, I'd take the box back to Grandma, and she'd open it and eat the chicken legs and chocolate cake that was inside. Grandma used to say, "I love day-old cake." That's where the expression day-old cake came from. Grandma always ate everything a day late. I used to eat all the other little boys' and girls' food at school, because they thought my lunch box was empty. They thought my lunch box was empty, and that's why I wouldn't open it. They thought I suffered from the sin of pride, and since that made them better than me, they were very generous.

DADDY. You were a very deceitful little girl.

MOMMY. We were very poor! But then I married you, Daddy, and now we're very rich.

DADDY. Grandma isn't rich.

MOMMY. No, but you've been so good to Grandma she feels rich. She doesn't know you'd like to put her in a nursing home.

DADDY. I wouldn't!

MOMMY. Well, heaven knows, *I* would! I can't stand it, watching her do the cooking and the housework, polishing the silver, moving the furniture. . . .

DADDY. She likes to do that. She says it's the least she can do to earn her keep.

MOMMY. Well, she's right. You can't live off people. I can live off you, because I married you. And aren't you lucky all I brought with me was Grandma. A lot of women I know would have brought their whole families to live off you. All I brought was Grandma. Grandma is all the family I have.

DADDY. I feel very fortunate.

MOMMY. You should. I have a right to live off of you because I married you, and because I used to let you get on top of me and bump your uglies; and I have a right to all your money when you die. And when you do, Grandma and I can live by ourselves . . . if she's still here. Unless you have her put away in a nursing home.

DADDY. I have no intention of putting her in a nursing home.

MOMMY. Well, I wish somebody would do something with her!

DADDY. At any rate, you're very well provided for.

MOMMY. You're my sweet Daddy; that's very nice.

DADDY. I love my Mommy.

(*Enter Grandma again, laden with more boxes*)

GRANDMA (*Dumping the boxes on and around* Daddy's *feet*). There; that's the lot of them.

DADDY. They're wrapped so nicely.

GRANDMA (*To Daddy*). You won't get on my sweet side that way . . .

MOMMY. Grandma!

GRANDMA. . . . telling me how nicely I wrap boxes. Not after what you said: how I whimpered for hours. . . .

MOMMY. Grandma!

GRANDMA (*To Mommy*). Shut up!

(*To Daddy*)

You don't have any feelings, that's what's wrong with you. Old people make all sorts of noises, half of them they can't help. Old people whimper, and cry, and belch, and make great hollow rumbling sounds at the table; old people wake up in the middle of the night screaming, and find out they haven't even been asleep; and when old people *are* asleep, they try to wake up, and they can't . . . not for the longest time.

MOMMY. Homilies, homilies!

GRANDMA. And there's more, too.

DADDY. I'm really very sorry, Grandma.

GRANDMA. I know you are, Daddy; it's Mommy over there makes all the trouble. If you'd listened to me, you wouldn't have married her in the first place. She was a tramp and a trollop and a trull to boot, and she's no better now.

MOMMY. Grandma!

GRANDMA (*To Mommy*). Shut up!

(*To Daddy*)

When she was no more than eight years old she used to climb up on my lap and say, in a sickening little voice, "When I gwo up, I'm going to mahwy a wich old man; I'm going to set my wittle were end right down in a tub o' butter, that's what I'm going to do." And I warned you,

Daddy; I told you to stay away from her type. I told you to. I did.

MOMMY. You stop that! You're my mother, not his!

GRANDMA. I am?

DADDY. That's right, Grandma. Mommy's right.

GRANDMA. Well, how would you expect somebody as old as I am to remember a thing like that? You don't make allowances for people. I want an allowance. I want an allowance!

DADDY. All right, Grandma; I'll see to it.

MOMMY. Grandma! I'm ashamed of you.

GRANDMA. Humf! It's a fine time to say that. You should have gotten rid of me a long time ago if that's the way you feel. You should have had Daddy set me up in business somewhere . . . I could have gone into the fur business, or I could have been a singer. But no; not you. You wanted me around so you could sleep in my room when Daddy got fresh. But now it isn't important, because Daddy doesn't want to get fresh with you any more, and I don't blame him. You'd rather sleep with me, wouldn't you, Daddy?

MOMMY. Daddy doesn't want to sleep with anyone. Daddy's been sick.

DADDY. I've been sick. I don't even want to sleep in the apartment.

MOMMY. You see? I told you.

DADDY. I just want to get everything over with.

MOMMY. That's right. Why are they so late? Why can't they get here on time?

GRANDMA (*An owl*). Who? Who? . . . Who? Who?

MOMMY. You know, Grandma.

GRANDMA. No, I don't.

MOMMY. Well, it doesn't really matter whether you do or not.

DADDY. Is that true?

MOMMY. Oh, more or less. Look how pretty Grandma wrapped these boxes.

GRANDMA. I didn't really like wrapping them; it hurt my fingers, and it frightened me. But it had to be done.

MOMMY. Why, Grandma?

GRANDMA. None of your damn business.

MOMMY. Go to bed.

GRANDMA. I don't want to go to bed. I just got up. I want to stay here and watch. Besides . . .

MOMMY. Go to bed.

DADDY. Let her stay up, Mommy; it isn't noon yet.

GRANDMA. I want to watch; besides . . .

DADDY. Let her watch, Mommy.

MOMMY. Well all right, you can watch; but don't you dare say a word.

GRANDMA. Old people are very good at listening; old people don't like to talk; old people have colitis and lavender perfume. Now I'm going to be quiet.

DADDY. She never mentioned she wanted to be a singer.

MOMMY. Oh, I forgot to tell you, but it was ages ago.

(*The doorbell rings*)

Oh, goodness! Here they are!

GRANDMA. Who? Who?

MOMMY. Oh, just some people.

GRANDMA. The van people? Is it the van people? Have you finally done it? Have you called the van people to come and take me away?

DADDY. Of course not, Grandma!

GRANDMA. Oh, don't be too sure. She'd have you carted off too, if she thought she could get away with it.

MOMMY. Pay no attention to her, Daddy.

(An aside to Grandma)

My God, you're ungrateful!

(The doorbell rings again)

DADDY *(Wringing his hands)*. Oh dear; oh dear.

MOMMY *(Still to Grandma)*. Just you wait; I'll fix your wagon.

(Now to Daddy)

Well, go let them in Daddy. What are you waiting for?

DADDY. I think we should talk about it some more. Maybe we've been hasty . . . a little hasty, perhaps.

(Doorbell rings again)

I'd like to talk about it some more.

MOMMY. There's no need. You made up your mind; you were firm; you were masculine and decisive.

DADDY. We might consider the pros and the . . .

MOMMY. I won't argue with you; it has to be done; you were right. Open the door.

DADDY. But I'm not sure that . . .

MOMMY. Open the door.

DADDY. Was I firm about it?

MOMMY. Oh, so firm; so firm.

DADDY. And was I decisive?

MOMMY. SO decisive! Oh, I shivered.

DADDY. And masculine? Was I really masculine?

MOMMY. Oh, Daddy, you were so masculine; I shivered and fainted.

GRANDMA. Shivered and fainted, did she? Humf!

MOMMY. You be quiet.

GRANDMA. Old people have a right to talk to themselves; it doesn't hurt the gums, and it's comforting.

(Doorbell rings again)

DADDY. I shall now open the door.

MOMMY. WHAT a masculine Daddy! Isn't he a masculine Daddy?

GRANDMA. Don't expect me to say anything. Old people are obscene.

MOMMY. Some of your opinions aren't so bad. You know that?

DADDY *(Backing off from the door)*. Maybe we can send them away.

MOMMY. Oh, look at you! You're turning into jelly; you're indecisive; you're a woman.

DADDY. All right. Watch me now; I'm going to open the door. Watch. Watch!

MOMMY. We're watching; we're watching.

GRANDMA. *I'm* not.

DADDY. Watch now; it's opening.

(He opens the door)

It's open!

(Mrs. Barker steps into the room)

Here they are!

MOMMY. Here they are!

GRANDMA. Where?

DADDY. Come in. You're late. But, of course, we expected you to be late; we were saying that we expected you to be late.

MOMMY. Daddy, don't be rude! We were saying that you just can't get satisfaction these days, and we were talking about you, of course. Won't you come in?

MRS. BARKER. Thank you. I don't mind if I do.

MOMMY. We're very glad that you're here, late as you are. You do remember us, don't you? You were here once before. I'm Mommy, and this is Daddy, and that's Grandma, doddering there in the corner.

MRS. BARKER. Hello, Mommy; hello, Daddy; and hello there, Grandma.

DADDY. Now that you're here, I don't suppose you could go away and maybe come back some other time.

MRS. BARKER. Oh no; we're much too efficient for that. I said, hello there, Grandma.

MOMMY. Speak to them, Grandma.

GRANDMA. I don't see them.

DADDY. For shame, Grandma; they're here.

MRS. BARKER. Yes, we're here, Grandma. I'm Mrs. Barker. I remember you; don't you remember me?

GRANDMA. I don't recall. Maybe you were younger, or something.

MOMMY. Grandma! What a terrible thing to say!

MRS. BARKER. Oh no, don't scold her, Mommy; for all she knows she may be right.

DADDY. Uh . . . Mrs. Barker, is it? Won't you sit down?

MRS. BARKER. I don't mind if I do.

MOMMY. Would you like a cigarette, and a drink, and would you like to cross your legs?

MRS. BARKER. You forget yourself, Mommy; I'm a professional woman. But I will cross my legs.

DADDY. Yes, make yourself comfortable.

MRS. BARKER. I don't mind if I do.

GRANDMA. Are they still here?

MOMMY. Be quiet, Grandma.

MRS. BARKER. Oh, we're still here. My, what an unattractive apartment you have!

MOMMY. Yes, but you don't know what a trouble it is. Let me tell you . . .

DADDY. I was saying to Mommy . . .

MRS. BARKER. Yes, I know. I was listening outside.

DADDY. About the icebox, and . . . the doorbell . . . and the . . .

MRS. BARKER. . . . and the johnny. Yes, we're very efficient; we have to know everything in our work.

DADDY. Exactly what do you do?

MOMMY. Yes, what is your work?

MRS. BARKER. Well, my dear, for one thing, I'm chairman of your woman's club.

MOMMY. Don't be ridiculous. I was talking to the chairman of my woman's club just yester—Why, so you are. You remember, Daddy, the lady I was telling you about? The lady with the husband who sits in the *swing?* Don't you remember?

DADDY. No . . . no.

MOMMY. Of course you do. I'm sorry, Mrs. Barker. I would have known you anywhere, except in this artificial light. And look! You have a hat just like the one I bought yesterday.

MRS. BARKER (*With a little laugh*). No, not really; this hat is cream.

MOMMY. Well, my dear, that may look like a cream hat to you, but I can . . .

MRS. BARKER. Now, now; you seem to forget who I am.

MOMMY. Yes, I do, don't I? Are you sure you're comfortable? Won't you take off your dress.

MRS. BARKER. I don't mind if I do.

(*She removes her dress*)

MOMMY. There. You must feel a great deal more comfortable.

MRS. BARKER. Well, I certainly *look* a great deal more comfortable.

DADDY. I'm going to blush and giggle.

MOMMY. Daddy's going to blush and giggle.

MRS. BARKER (*Pulling the hem of her slip above her knees*). You're lucky to have such a man for a husband.

MOMMY. Oh, don't I know it!

DADDY. I just blushed and giggled and went sticky wet.

MOMMY. Isn't Daddy a caution, Mrs. Barker?

MRS. BARKER. Maybe if I smoked . . . ?

MOMMY. Oh, that isn't necessary.

MRS. BARKER. I don't mind if I do.

MOMMY. No; no, don't. Really.

MRS. BARKER. I don't mind . . .

MOMMY. I won't have you smoking in my house, and that's that! You're a professional woman.

DADDY. Grandma drinks AND smokes; don't you, Grandma?

GRANDMA. No.

MOMMY. Well, now, Mrs. Barker; suppose you tell us why you're here.

GRANDMA (*As Mommy walks through the boxes*). The boxes . . . the boxes . . .

MOMMY. Be quiet, Grandma.

DADDY. What did you say, Grandma?

GRANDMA (*As Mommy steps on several of the boxes*). The boxes, damn it!

MRS. BARKER. Boxes; she said boxes. She mentioned the boxes.

DADDY. What about the boxes, Grandma? Maybe Mrs. Barker is here because of the boxes. Is that what you meant, Grandma?

GRANDMA. I don't know if that's what I meant or not. It's certainly not what I *thought* I meant.

DADDY. Grandma is of the opinion that . . .

MRS. BARKER. Can we assume that the boxes are for us? I mean, can we assume that you had us come here for the boxes?

MOMMY. Are you in the habit of receiving boxes?

DADDY. A very good question.

MRS. BARKER. Well, that would depend on the reason we're here. I've got my fingers in so many little pies, you know. Now, I can think of one of my little activities in which we are in the habit of receiving *baskets;* but more in a literary sense than really. We *might* receive boxes, though, under very special circumstances. I'm afraid that's the best answer I can give you.

DADDY. It's a very interesting answer.

MRS. BARKER. *I* thought so. But, does it help?

MOMMY. No; I'm afraid not.

DADDY. I wonder if it might help us any if I said I feel misgivings, that I have definite qualms.

MOMMY. Where, Daddy?

DADDY. Well, mostly right here, right around where the stitches were.

MOMMY. Daddy had an operation, you know.

MRS. BARKER. Oh, you poor Daddy! I didn't know; but then, how could I?

GRANDMA. You might have asked; it wouldn't have hurt you.

MOMMY. Dry up, Grandma.

GRANDMA. There you go. Letting your true feelings come out. Old people aren't dry enough, I suppose. My sacks are empty, the fluid in my eyeballs is all caked on the inside edges, my spine is made of sugar candy, I breathe ice; but you don't hear me complain. Nobody hears old people complain because people think that's all old people do. And *that's* because old people are gnarled and sagged and twisted into the shape of a complaint.

(*Signs off*)

That's all.

MRS. BARKER. What was wrong, Daddy?

DADDY. Well, you know how it is: the doctors took out something that was there and put in something that wasn't there. An operation.

MRS. BARKER. You're very fortunate, I should say.

MOMMY. Oh, he is; he is. All his life. Daddy has wanted to be a United States Senator; but now . . . why now he's changed his mind, and for the rest of his life he's going to want to be Governor . . . it would be nearer the apartment, you know.

MRS. BARKER. You *are* fortunate, Daddy.

DADDY. Yes, indeed; except that I get these qualms now and then, definite ones.

MRS. BARKER. Well, it's just a matter of things settling; you're like an old house.

MOMMY. Why Daddy, thank Mrs. Barker.

DADDY. Thank you.

MRS. BARKER. Ambition! That's the ticket. I have a brother who's very much like you, Daddy . . . ambitious. Of course, he's a great deal younger than you; he's even younger than I am . . . if such a thing is possible. He runs a little newspaper. Just a little newspaper . . . but he runs it. He's chief cook and bottle washer of that little newspaper, which he calls *The Village Idiot*. He has such a sense of humor; he's so self-deprecating, so modest. And he'd never admit it himself, but he *is* the Village Idiot.

MOMMY. Oh, I think that's just grand. Don't you think so, Daddy?

DADDY. Yes, just grand.

MRS. BARKER. My brother's a dear man, and he has a dear little wife, whom he loves, dearly. He loves her so much he just can't get a sentence out without mentioning her. He wants everybody to know he's married. He's really a stickler on that point; he can't be introduced to anybody and say hello without adding, "Of course, I'm married." As far as I'm concerned, he's the chief exponent of Women Love in this whole country; he's even been written up in psychiatric journals because of it.

DADDY. Indeed!

MOMMY. Isn't that lovely.

MRS. BARKER. Oh, I think so. There's too much woman hatred in this country, and that's a fact.

GRANDMA. Oh, I don't know.

MOMMY. Oh, I think that's just grand. Don't you think so, Daddy?

DADDY. Yes, just grand.

GRANDMA. In case anybody's interested . . .

MOMMY. Be quiet, Grandma.

GRANDMA. Nuts!

MOMMY. Oh, Mrs. Barker, you *must* forgive Grandma. She's rural.

MRS. BARKER. I don't mind if I do.

DADDY. Maybe Grandma has something to say.

MOMMY. Nonsense. Old people have nothing to say; and if old people *did* have something to say, nobody would listen to them.

(*To Grandma*)

You see? I can pull that stuff just as easy as you can.

GRANDMA. Well, you got the rhythm, but you don't really have the quality. Besides, you're middle-aged.

MOMMY. I'm proud of it.

GRANDMA. Look. I'll show you how it's really done. Middle-aged people think they can do anything, but the truth is that middle-aged people can't do most things as well as they used to. Middle-aged people think they're special be-cause they're like everybody else. We live in the age of deformity. You see? Rhythm *and* content. You'll learn.

DADDY. I do wish I weren't surrounded by women; I'd like some men around here.

MRS. BARKER. You can say that again!

GRANDMA. I don't hardly count as a woman, so can I say my piece?

MOMMY. Go on. Jabber away.

GRANDMA. It's very simple; the fact is, these boxes don't have anything to do with why this good lady is come to call. Now, if you're interested in knowing why these boxes *are* here . . .

DADDY. I'm sure that must be all very true, Grandma, but what does it have to do with why . . . pardon me, what is that name again?

MRS. BARKER. Mrs. Barker.

DADDY. Exactly. What does it have to do with why . . . that name again?

MRS. BARKER. Mrs. Barker.

DADDY. Precisely. What does it have to do with why what's-her-name is here?

MOMMY. They're here because we asked them.

MRS. BARKER. Yes. That's why.

GRANDMA. Now if you're interested in knowing why these boxes *are* here . . .

MOMMY. Well, nobody *is* interested!

GRANDMA. You can be as snippety as you like for all the good it'll do you.

DADDY. You two will have to stop arguing.

MOMMY. I don't argue with her.

DADDY. It will just have to stop.

MOMMY. Well, why don't you call a van and have her taken away?

GRANDMA. Don't bother; there's no need.

DADDY. No, now, perhaps I can go away myself. . . .

MOMMY. Well, one or the other; the way things are now it's impossible. In the first place, it's too crowded in this apartment.

(*To Grandma*)

And it's you that takes up all the space, with your enema bottles, and your Pekingese, and God-only-knows-what-else . . . and now all these boxes . . .

GRANDMA. These boxes are . . .

MRS. BARKER. I've never heard of enema *bottles*. . . .

GRANDMA. She means enema bags, but she doesn't know the difference. Mommy comes from extremely bad stock. And besides, when Mommy was born . . . well, it was a difficult delivery, and she had a head shaped like a banana.

MOMMY. You ungrateful— Daddy? Daddy, you see how ungrateful she is after all these years, after all the things we've done for her?

(*To Grandma*)

One of these days you're going away in a van; that's what's going to happen to you!

GRANDMA. Do tell!

MRS. BARKER. Like a banana?

GRANDMA. Yup, just like a banana.

MRS. BARKER. My word!

MOMMY. You stop listening to her; she'll say anything. Just the other night she called Daddy a hedgehog.

MRS. BARKER. She didn't!

GRANDMA. That's right, baby; you stick up for me.

MOMMY. I don't know where she gets the words; on the television, maybe.

MRS. BARKER. Did you really call him a hedgehog?

GRANDMA. Oh look; what difference does it make whether I did or not?

DADDY. Grandma's right. Leave Grandma alone.

MOMMY (To Daddy). How dare you!

GRANDMA. Oh, leave her alone, Daddy; the kid's all mixed up.

MOMMY. You see? I told you. It's all those television shows. Daddy, you go right into Grandma's room and take her television and shake all the tubes loose.

DADDY. Don't mention tubes to me.

MOMMY. Oh! Mommy forgot!

(To Mrs. Barker)

Daddy has tubes now, where he used to have tracts.

MRS. BARKER. Is that a fact!

GRANDMA. I know why this dear lady is here.

MOMMY. You be still.

MRS. BARKER. Oh, I do wish you'd tell me.

MOMMY. No! No! That wouldn't be fair at all.

DADDY. Besides, she knows why she's here; she's here because we called them.

MRS. BARKER. La! But that still leaves me puzzled. I know I'm here because you called us, but I'm such a busy girl, with this committee and that committee, and the Responsible Citizens Activities I indulge in.

MOMMY. Oh my; busy, busy.

MRS. BARKER. Yes, indeed. So I'm afraid you'll have to give me some help.

MOMMY. Oh, no. No, you must be mistaken. I can't believe we asked you here to give you any help. With the way taxes are these days, and the way you can't get satisfaction in ANYTHING . . . no, I don't believe so.

DADDY. And if you need help . . . why, I should think you'd apply for a Fulbright Scholarship.

MOMMY. And if not that . . . why, then a Guggenheim Fellowship. . . .

GRANDMA. Oh, come on; why not shoot the works and try for the Prix de Rome.

(Under her breath to Mommy and Daddy)

Beasts!

MRS. BARKER. Oh, what a jolly family. But let me think. I'm knee-deep in work these days; there's the Ladies' Auxiliary Air Raid Committee, for one thing; how do you feel about air raids?

MOMMY. Oh, I'd say we're hostile.

DADDY. Yes, definitely; we're hostile.

MRS. BARKER. Then, you'll be no help there. There's too much hostility in the world these days as it is; but I'll not badger you! There's a surfeit of badgers as well.

GRANDMA. While we're at it, there's been a run on old people, too. The Department of Agriculture, or maybe it wasn't the Department of Agriculture—anyway, it was some department that's run by a girl—put out figures showing that ninety per cent of the adult population of the country is over eighty years old . . . or eighty percent is over ninety years old . . .

MOMMY. You're such a liar! You just finished saying that everyone is middle-aged.

GRANDMA. I'm just telling you what the government says . . . that doesn't have anything to do with what . . .

MOMMY. It's that television! Daddy, go break her television.

GRANDMA. You won't find it!

DADDY (Wearily getting up). If I must . . . I must.

MOMMY. And don't step on the Pekingese; it's blind.

DADDY. It may be blind, but Daddy isn't.

(He exits, through the archway, stage left)

GRANDMA. You won't find it, either.

MOMMY. Oh, I'm so fortunate to have such a husband. Just think; I could have a husband who was poor, or argumentative, or a husband who sat in a wheel chair all day . . . OOOOHHHH! What have I said? What have I said?

GRANDMA. You said you could have a husband who sat in a wheel . . .

MOMMY. I'm mortified! I could die! I could cut my tongue out! I could . . .

MRS. BARKER (Forcing a smile). Oh, now . . . now . . . don't think about it . . .

MOMMY. I could . . . why, I could . . .

MRS. BARKER. . . . don't think about it . . . really. . . .

MOMMY. You're quite right. I won't think about it, and that way I'll forget that I ever said it, and that way it will be all right.

(Pause)

There . . . I've forgotten. Well, now, now that Daddy is out of the room we can have some girl talk.

MRS. BARKER. I'm not sure that I . . .

MOMMY. You do want to have some girl talk, don't you?

MRS. BARKER. I was going to say I'm not sure that I wouldn't care for a glass of water. I feel a little faint.

MOMMY. Grandma, go get Mrs. Barker a glass of water.

GRANDMA. Go get it yourself. I quit.

MOMMY. Grandma loves to do little things around the house; it gives her a false sense of security.

GRANDMA. I quit! I'm through!

MOMMY. Now, you be a good Grandma, or you know what will happen to you. You'll be taken away in a van.

GRANDMA. You don't frighten me. I'm too old to be frightened. Besides . . .

MOMMY. WELL! I'll tend to you later. I'll hide your teeth . . . I'll . . .

GRANDMA. Everything's hidden.

MRS. BARKER. I *am* going to faint. I *am*.

MOMMY. Good heavens! I'll go myself.

(*As she exits, through the archway, stage-left*)

I'll fix you, Grandma. I'll take care of you later.

(*She exits*)

GRANDMA. Oh, go soak your head.

(*To Mrs. Barker*)

Well, dearie, how do you feel?

MRS. BARKER. A little better, I think. Yes, much better, thank you, Grandma.

Grandma. That's good.

MRS. BARKER. But . . . I feel so lost . . . not knowing why I'm here . . . and, on top of it, they say I was here before.

GRANDMA. Well, you were. You weren't *here*, exactly, because we've moved around a lot, from one apartment to another, up and down the social ladder like mice, if you like similes.

MRS. BARKER. I don't . . . particularly.

GRANDMA. Well, then, I'm sorry.

MRS. BARKER (*Suddenly*). Grandma, I feel I can trust you.

GRANDMA. Don't be too sure; it's every man for himself around this place. . . .

MRS. BARKER. Oh . . . is it? Nonetheless, I really do feel that I can trust you. *Please* tell me why they called and asked us to come. I implore you!

GRANDMA. Oh my; that feels good. It's been so long since anybody implored me. Do it again. Implore me some more.

MRS. BARKER. You're your daughter's mother, all right!

GRANDMA. Oh, I don't mean to be hard. If you won't implore me, then beg me, or ask me, or entreat me . . . just anything like that.

MRS. BARKER. You're a dreadful old woman!

GRANDMA. You'll understand some day. Please!

MRS. BARKER. Oh, for heaven's sake! . . . I implore you . . . I beg you . . . I beseech you!

GRANDMA. Beseech! Oh, that's the nicest word I've heard in ages. You're a dear, sweet woman. . . . You . . . beseech . . . me. I can't resist that.

MRS. BARKER. Well, then . . . please tell me why they asked us to come.

GRANDMA. Well, I'll give you a hint. That's the best I can do, because I'm a muddleheaded old woman. Now listen, because it's important. Once upon a time, not too very long ago, but a long enough time ago . . . oh, about twenty years ago . . . there was a man very much like Daddy, and a woman very much like Mommy, who were married to each other, very much like Mommy and Daddy are married to each other; and they lived in an apartment very much like one that's very much like this one, and they lived there with an old woman who was very much like yours truly, only younger, because it was some time ago; in fact, they were all somewhat younger.

MRS. BARKER. How fascinating!

GRANDMA. Now, at the same time, there was a dear lady very much like you, only younger then, who did all sorts of Good Works. . . . And one of the Good Works this dear lady did was in something very much like a volunteer capacity for an organization very much like the Bye-Bye Adoption Service, which is nearby and which was run by a terribly deaf old lady very much like the Miss Bye-Bye who runs the Bye-Bye Adoption Service nearby.

MRS. BARKER. How enthralling!

GRANDMA. Well, be that as it may. Nonetheless, one afternoon this man, who was very much like Daddy, and this woman who was very much like Mommy came to see this dear lady who did all the Good Works, who was very much like you, dear, and they were very sad and very hopeful, and they cried and smiled and bit their fingers, and they said all the most intimate things.

MRS. BARKER. How spellbinding! What did they say?

GRANDMA. Well, it was very sweet. The woman, who was very much like Mommy, said that she and the man who was very much like Daddy had never been blessed with anything very much like a bumble of joy.

MRS. BARKER. A what?

GRANDMA. A bumble; a bumble of joy.

MRS. BARKER. Oh, like bundle.

GRANDMA. Well, yes; very much like it. Bundle, bumble; who cares? At any rate, the woman, who was very much like Mommy, said that hey wanted a bumble of their own, but that the man, who was very much like Daddy, couldn't have a bumble; and the man, who was very much like Daddy, said that yes, they had wanted a bumble of their own, but that the woman, who was very much like Mommy, couldn't have one, and that now they wanted to buy something very much like a bumble.

MRS. BARKER. How engrossing!

GRANDMA. Yes. And the dear lady, who was very much like you, said something that was very much like, "Oh, what a shame; but take heart . . . I think we have just the bumble *for* you." And, well, the lady, who was very much like Mommy, and the man, who was very much like Daddy, cried and smiled and bit their fingers, and said some more intimate things, which were totally irrelevant but which were pretty hot stuff, and so the dear lady, who was very much like you, and who had something very much like a penchant for pornography, listened with something very much like enthusiasm. "Whee," she said. "Whoooopeeeeee!" But that's beside the point.

MRS. BARKER. I suppose *so*. But how gripping!

GRANDMA. Anyway . . . they *bought* something very much

like a bumble, and they took it away with them. But . . . things didn't work out very well.

MRS. BARKER. You mean there was trouble?

GRANDMA. You got it.

(*With a glance through the archway*)

But, I'm going to have to speed up now because I think I'm leaving soon.

MRS. BARKER. Oh. Are you really?

GRANDMA. Yup.

MRS. BARKER. But old people don't go anywhere; they're either taken places, or put places.

GRANDMA. Well, this old person is different. Anyway . . . things started going badly.

MRS. BARKER. Oh yes. Yes.

GRANDMA. Weeeeelllll . . . in the first place, it turned out the bumble didn't look like either one of its parents. That was enough of a blow, but things got worse. One night, it cried its heart out, if you can imagine such a thing.

MRS. BARKER. Cried its heart out! Well!

GRANDMA. But that was only the beginning. Then it turned out it only had eyes for its Daddy.

MRS. BARKER. For its Daddy! Why, any self-respecting woman would have gouged those eyes right out of its head.

GRANDMA. Well, she did. that's exactly what she did. But then, it kept its nose up in the air.

MRS. BARKER. Ufggh! How disgusting!

GRANDMA. That's what they thought. But *then*, it began to develop an interest in its you-know-what.

MRS. BARKER. In its you-know-what! Well! I hope they cut its hands off at the wrists!

GRANDMA. Well, yes, they did that eventually. But first, they cut off its you-know-what.

MRS. BARKER. A much better idea!

GRANDMA. That's what they thought. But after they cut off its you-know-what, it *still* put is hands under the covers, *looking* for its you-know-what. So, finally, they *had* to cut off its hands at the wrists.

MRS. BARKER. Naturally!

GRANDMA. And it was such a resentful bumble. Why, one day it called its Mommy a dirty name.

MRS. BARKER. Well, I hope they cut its tongue out!

GRANDMA. Of course. And then, as it got bigger, they found out all sorts of terrible things about it, like: it didn't have a head on its shoulders, it had no guts, it was spineless, its feet were made of clay . . . just dreadful things.

MRS. BARKER. Dreadful!

GRANDMA. So you can understand how they became discouraged.

MRS. BARKER. I certainly can! And what did they do?

GRANDMA. What did they do? Well, for the last straw, it finally up and died; and you can imagine how *that* made them feel, their having paid for it, and all. So, they called up the lady who sold them the bumble in the first place

and told her to come right over to their apartment. They wanted satisfaction; they wanted their money back. That's what they wanted.

MRS. BARKER. My, my, my.

GRANDMA. How do you like *them* apples?

MRS. BARKER. My, my, my.

DADDY (*Off stage*). Mommy! I can't find Grandma's television, and I can't find the Pekingese, either.

MOMMY (*Off stage*). Isn't that funny! And I can't find the water.

GRANDMA. Heh, heh, heh. I told them everything was hidden.

MRS. BARKER. Did you hide the water, too?

GRANDMA (*Puzzled*). No. No, I didn't do *that*.

DADDY (*Off stage*). The truth of the matter is, I can't even find Grandma's room.

GRANDMA. Heh, heh, heh.

MRS. BARKER. My! You certainly did hide things, didn't you?

GRANDMA. Sure, kid, sure.

MOMMY (*Sticking her head in the room*). Did you ever hear of such a thing, Grandma? Daddy can't find your television, and he can't find the Pekingese, and the truth of the matter is he can't even find your room.

GRANDMA. I told you. I hid everything.

MOMMY. Nonsense, Grandma! Just wait until I get my hands on you. You're a troublemaker . . . that's what you are.

GRANDMA. Well, I'll be out of here pretty soon, baby.

MOMMY. Oh, you don't know how right you are! Daddy's been wanting to send you away for a long time now, but I've been restraining him. I'll tell you one thing, though . . . I'm getting sick and tired of this fighting, and I might just let him have his way. Then you'll see what'll happen. Away you'll go; in a van, too. I'll let Daddy call the van man.

GRANDMA. I'm away ahead of you.

MOMMY. How can you be so old and so smug at the same time? You have no sense of proportion.

GRANDMA. You just answered your own question.

MOMMY. Mrs. Barker, I'd much rather you came into the kitchen for that glass of water, what with Grandma out here, and all.

MRS. BARKER. I don't see what Grandma has to do with it; and besides, I don't think you're very polite.

MOMMY. You seem to forget that you're a guest in this house . . .

GRANDMA. Apartment!

MOMMY. Apartment! And that you're a professional woman. So, if you'll be so good as to come into the kitchen, I'll be more than happy to show you where the water is, and where the glass is, and then you can put two and two together, if you're clever enough.

(*She vanishes*)

MRS. BARKER. (*After a moment's consideration*). I suppose she's right.

GRANDMA. Well, that's how it is when people call you up and ask you over to do something for them.

MRS. BARKER. I suppose you're right, too. Well, Grandma, it's been very nice talking to you.

GRANDMA. And I've enjoyed listening. Say, don't tell Mommy or Daddy that I gave you that hint, will you?

MRS. BARKER. Oh, dear me, the hint! I'd forgotten about it, if you can imagine such a thing. No, I won't breathe a word of it to them.

GRANDMA. I don't know if it helped you any . . .

MRS. BARKER. I can't tell, yet. I'll have to . . . what *is* the word I want? . . . I'll have to relate it . . . that's it . . . I'll have to relate it to certain things that I *know*, and . . . draw . . . conclusions. . . . What I'll really have to do is to see if it applies to anything. I mean, after all, I *do* do volunteer work for an adoption service, but it isn't very much *like* the Bye-Bye Adoption Service . . . it *is* the Bye-Bye Adoption Service . . . and while I can remember Mommy and Daddy coming to see me, oh, about twenty years ago, about buying a bumble, I can't quite remember anyone very much *like* Mommy and Daddy coming to see me about buying a bumble. Don't you see? It really presents quite a problem. . . . I'll have to think about it . . . mull it . . . but at any rate, it was truly first-class of you to try to help me. Oh, will you still be here after I've had my drink of water?

GRANDMA. Probably . . . I'm not as spry as I used to be.

MRS. BARKER. Oh. Well, I won't say good-bye then.

GRANDMA. No. Don't.

(*Mrs. Barker exits through the archway*)

People don't say good-bye to old people because they think they'll frighten them. Lordy! If they only knew how awful "hello" and "My, you're looking chipper" sounded, they wouldn't say those things either. The truth is, there isn't much you *can* say to old people that doesn't sound just terrible.

(*The doorbell rings*)

Come on in!

(*The Young Man enters. Grandma looks him over*)

Well, now, aren't you a breath of fresh air!

YOUNG MAN. Hello there.

GRANDMA. My, my, my. Are you the van man?

YOUNG MAN. The what?

GRANDMA. The van man. The van man. Are you coming to take me away?

YOUNG MAN. I don't know what you're talking about.

GRANDMA. Oh.

(*Pause*)

Well.

(*Pause*)

My, my, aren't you something!

YOUNG MAN. Hm?

GRANDMA. I said, my, my, aren't you something.

YOUNG MAN. Oh. Thank you.

GRANDMA. You don't sound very enthusiastic.

YOUNG MAN. Oh, I'm . . . I'm used to it.

GRANDMA. Yup . . . yup. You know, if I were about a hundred and fifty years younger I could go for you.

YOUNG MAN. Yes, I imagine so.

GRANDMA. Unh-hunh . . . will you look at those muscles!

YOUNG MAN (*Flexing his muscles*). Yes, they're quite good, aren't they?

GRANDMA. Boy, they sure are. They natural?

YOUNG MAN. Well the basic structure was there, but I've done some work, too . . . you know, in a gym.

GRANDMA. I'll bet you have. You ought to be in the movies, boy.

YOUNG MAN. I know.

GRANDMA. Yup! Right up there on the old silver screen. But I suppose you've heard that before.

YOUNG MAN. Yes, I have.

GRANDMA. You ought to try out for them . . . the movies.

YOUNG MAN. Well, actually, I may have a career there yet. I've lived out on the West coast almost all my life . . . and I've met a few people who . . . might be able to help me. I'm not in too much of a hurry, though. I'm almost as young as I look.

GRANDMA. Oh, that's nice. And will you look at that face!

YOUNG MAN. Yes, it's quite good, isn't it? Clean-cut, midwest farm boy type, almost insultingly good-looking in a typically American way. Good profile, straight nose, honest eyes, wonderful smile . . .

GRANDMA. Yup. Boy, you know what you are, don't you? You're the American Dream, that's what you are. All those other people, they don't know what they're talking about. You . . . *you* are the American Dream.

YOUNG MAN. Thanks.

MOMMY (*Off stage*). Who rang the doorbell?

GRANDMA (*Shouting off-stage*). The American Dream!

MOMMY (*Off stage*). What? What was that, Grandma?

GRANDMA (*Shouting*). The American Dream! The American Dream! Damn it!

DADDY (*Off stage*). How's that, Mommy?

MOMMY (*Off stage*). Oh, some gibberish; pay no attention. Did you find Grandma's room?

DADDY (*Off stage*). No. I can't even find Mrs. Barker.

YOUNG MAN. What was all that?

GRANDMA. Oh, that was just the folks, but let's not talk about them, honey; let's talk about you.

YOUNG MAN. All right.

GRANDMA. Well, let's see. If you're not the van man, what are you doing here?

YOUNG MAN. I'm looking for work.

GRANDMA. Are you! Well, what kind of work?

YOUNG MAN. Oh, almost anything . . . almost anything that pays. I'll do almost anything for money.

GRANDMA. Will you . . . will you? Hmmmm. I wonder if there's anything you could do around here?

YOUNG MAN. There might be. It looked to be a likely building.

GRANDMA. It's always looked to be a rather unlikely building to me, but I suppose you'd know better than I.

YOUNG MAN. I can sense these things.

GRANDMA. There *might* be something you could do around here. Stay there! Don't come any closer.

YOUNG MAN. Sorry.

GRANDMA. I don't mean I'd *mind*. I don't know whether I'd mind, or not. . . . But it wouldn't look well; it would look just *awful*.

YOUNG MAN. Yes; I suppose so.

GRANDMA. Now, stay there, let me concentrate. What could you do? The folks have been in something of a quandary around here today, sort of a dilemma, and I wonder if you mightn't be some help.

YOUNG MAN. I hope so . . . if there's money in it. Do you have any money?

GRANDMA. Money! Oh, there's more money around here than you'd know what to do with.

YOUNG MAN. I'm not so sure.

GRANDMA. Well, maybe not. Besides, I've got money of my own.

YOUNG MAN. You have?

GRANDMA. Sure. Old people quite often have lots of money; more often than most people expect. Come here, so I can whisper to you . . . not too close. I might faint.

YOUNG MAN. Oh, I'm sorry.

GRANDMA. It's all right, dear. Anyway . . . have you ever heard of that big baking contest they run? The one where all the ladies get together in a big barn and bake away?

YOUNG MAN. I'm . . . not . . . sure. . . .

GRANDMA. Not so close. Well, it doesn't matter whether you've heard of it or not. The important thing is—and I don't want anybody to hear this . . . the folks think I haven't been out of the house in eight years—the important thing is that I won first prize in that baking contest this year. Oh, it was in all the papers; not under my own name, though. I used a *nom de boulangère;* I called myself Uncle Henry.

YOUNG MAN. Did you?

GRANDMA. Why not? I didn't see any reason not to. I look just as much like an old man as I do like an old woman. And you know what I called it . . . what I won for?

YOUNG MAN. No. What did you call it?

GRANDMA. I called it Uncle Henry's Day-Old Cake.

YOUNG MAN. That's a very nice name.

GRANDMA. And it wasn't any trouble, either. All I did was go out and get a store-bought cake, and keep it around for a while, and then slip it in, unbeknownst to anybody. Simple.

YOUNG MAN. You're a very resourceful person.

GRANDMA. Pioneer stock.

YOUNG MAN. Is all this true? Do you want me to believe all this?

GRANDMA. Well, you can believe it or not . . . it doesn't make any difference to me. All *I* know is, Uncle Henry's Day-Old Cake won me twenty-five thousand smackerolas.

YOUNG MAN. Twenty-five thou—

GRANDMA. Right on the old loggerhead. Now . . . how do you like them apples?

YOUNG MAN. Love 'em.

GRANDMA. I thought you'd be impressed.

YOUNG MAN. Money talks.

GRANDMA. Hey! You look familiar.

YOUNG MAN. Hm? Pardon?

GRANDMA. I said you look familiar.

YOUNG MAN. Well, I've done some modeling.

GRANDMA. No . . . no. I don't mean that. You look familiar.

YOUNG MAN. Well, I'm a type.

GRANDMA. Yup; you sure are. Why do you say you'd do anything for money . . . if you don't mind my being nosy?

YOUNG MAN. No, no. It's part of the interviews. I'll be happy to tell you. It's that I have no talents at all, except what you see . . . my person; my body, my face. In every other way I am incomplete, and I must therefore . . . compensate.

GRANDMA. What do you mean, incomplete? You look pretty complete to me.

YOUNG MAN. I think I can explain it to you, partially because you're very old, and very old people have perceptions they keep to themselves, because if they expose them to other people . . . well, you know what ridicule and neglect are.

GRANDMA. I do, child, I do.

YOUNG MAN. Then listen. My mother died the night that I was born, and I never knew my father; I doubt my mother did. But, I wasn't alone, because lying with me . . . in the placenta . . . there was someone else . . . my brother . . . my twin.

GRANDMA. Oh, my child.

YOUNG MAN. We were identical twins . . . he and I . . . not fraternal . . . identical; we were derived from the same ovum; and in *this*, in that we were twins not from separate ova but from the same one, we had a kinship such as you cannot imagine. We . . . we felt each other breathe . . . his heartbeats thundered in my temples . . . mine in his . . . our stomachs ached and we cried for feeding at the same time . . . are you old enough to understand?

GRANDMA. I think so, child; I think I'm nearly old enough.

YOUNG MAN. I hope so. But we were separated when we were still very young, my brother, my twin and I . . . inasmuch as you can separate one being. We were torn apart . . . thrown to opposite ends of the continent. I don't know what became of my brother . . . to the rest of myself . . . except that, from time to time, in the years that have passed, I have suffered losses . . . that I can't explain. A fall from grace . . . a departure of innocence . . . loss . . . loss. How can I put it to you? All right; like this: Once . . . it was as if all at once my heart . . . became numb . . . almost as though I . . . almost as though . . . just like that

. . . it had been wrenched from my body . . . and from that time I have been unable to love. Once . . . I was asleep at the time . . . I awoke, and my eyes were burning. And since that time I have been unable to see anything, *anything*, with pity, with affection . . . with anything but . . . cool disinterest. And my groin . . . even there . . . since one time . . . one specific agony . . . since then I have not been able to *love* anyone with my body. And even my hands . . . I cannot touch another person and feel love. And there is more . . . there are more losses, but it all comes down to this: I no longer have the capacity to feel anything. I have no emotions. I have been drained, torn asunder . . . disemboweled. I have, now, only my person . . . my body, my face. I use what I have . . . I let people love me . . . I accept the syntax around me, for while I know I cannot relate . . . I know I must be related *to*. I let people love me . . . I let people touch me . . . I let them draw pleasure from my groin . . . from my presence . . . from the fact of me . . . but, that is all it comes to. As I told you, I am incomplete . . . I can feel nothing. I can feel nothing. And so . . . here I am . . . as you see me. I am . . . but this . . . what you see. And it will always be thus.

GRANDMA. Oh, my child; my child.

(Long pause; then)

I was mistaken . . . before. I don't know you from somewhere, but I knew . . . once . . . someone very much like you . . . or, very much as perhaps you were.

YOUNG MAN. Be careful; be very careful. What I have told you may not be true. In my profession . . .

GRANDMA. Shhhhhh.

(The Young Man bows his head, in acquiescence)

Someone . . . to be more precise . . . who might have turned out to be very much like you might have turned out to be. And . . . unless I'm terribly mistaken . . . you've found yourself a job.

YOUNG MAN. What are my duties?

MRS. BARKER *(Off stage)*. Yoo-hoo! Yoo-hoo!

GRANDMA. Oh-oh. You'll . . . you'll have to play it by ear, my dear . . . unless I get a chance to talk to you again. I've got to go into my act, now.

YOUNG MAN. But, I . . .

GRANDMA. Yoo-hoo!

MRS. BARKER *(Coming through archway)*. Yoo-hoo . . . oh, there you are, Grandma. I'm glad to see somebody. I can't find Mommy or Daddy.

(Double takes)

Well . . . who's this?

GRANDMA. This? Well . . . un . . . oh, this is the . . . uh . . . the van man. That's who it is . . . the van man.

MRS. BARKER. So! It's true! They *did* call the van man. They *are* having you carted away.

GRANDMA *(Shrugging)*. Well, you know. It figures.

MRS. BARKER *(To Young Man)*. How dare you cart this poor old woman away!

YOUNG MAN *(After a quick look at Grandma, who nods)*. I do what I'm paid to do. I don't ask any questions.

MRS. BARKER *(After a brief pause)*. Oh.

(Pause)

Well, you're quite right, of course, and I shouldn't meddle.

GRANDMA *(To Young Man)*. Dear, will you take my things out to the van? *(She points to the boxes)*

YOUNG MAN *(After only the briefest hesitation)*. Why, certainly.

GRANDMA *(As the Young Man takes up half the boxes, exits by the front door)*. Isn't that a nice young van man?

MRS. BARKER *(Shaking her head in disbelief, watching the Young Man exit)*. Unh-hunh . . . some things have changed for the better. I remember when I had *my* mother carted off . . . the van man who came for her wasn't anything near as nice as this one.

GRANDMA. Oh, did you have your mother carted off, too?

MRS. BARKER *(Cheerfully)*. Why certainly! Didn't you?

GRANDMA *(Puzzling)*. No . . . no, I didn't. At least, I can't remember. Listen dear; I got to talk to you for a second.

MRS. BARKER. Why certainly, Grandma.

GRANDMA. Now, listen.

MRS. BARKER. Yes, Grandma. Yes.

GRANDMA. Now listen carefully. You got this dilemma here with Mommy and Daddy . . .

MRS. BARKER. Yes! I wonder where they've gone to?

GRANDMA. They'll be back in. Now, LISTEN!

MRS. BARKER. Oh, I'm sorry.

GRANDMA. Now, you got this dilemma here with Mommy and Daddy, and I think I got the way out for you.

(The Young Man re-enters through the front door)

Will you take the rest of my things out now, dear?

(To Mrs. Barker, while the Young Man takes the rest of the boxes, exits again by the front door)

Fine. Now listen, dear.

(She begins to whisper in Mrs. Barker's ear)

MRS. BARKER. Oh! Oh! Oh! I don't think I could . . . do you really think I could? Well, why not? What a wonderful idea . . . what an absolutely wonderful idea!

GRANDMA. Well, yes, I thought it was.

MRS. BARKER. And you so old!

GRANDMA. Heh, heh, heh.

MRS. BARKER. Well, I think it's absolutely marvelous, anyway. I'm going to find Mommy and Daddy right now.

GRANDMA. Good. You do that.

MRS. BARKER. Well, now. I think I will say good-bye. I can't thank you enough.

(She starts to exit through the archway)

GRANDMA. You're welcome. Say it!

MRS. BARKER. Huh? What?

GRANDMA. Say good-bye.
MRS. BARKER. Oh. Good-bye.

(*She exits*)

Mommy! I say, Mommy! Daddy!
GRANDMA. Good-bye.

(*By herself now, she looks about*)

Ah me.

(*Shakes her head*)

Ah me.

(*Takes in the room*)

Good-bye.

(*The Young Man re-enters*)

GRANDMA. Oh, hello, there.
YOUNG MAN. All the boxes are outside.
GRANDMA (*A little sadly*). I don't know why I bother to take them with me. They don't have much in them . . . some old letters, a couple of regrets . . . Pekingese . . . blind at that . . . the television . . . my Sunday teeth . . . eighty-six years of living . . . some sounds . . . a few images, a little garbled by now . . . and, well . . .

(*She shrugs*)

. . . you know . . . the things one accumulates.
YOUNG MAN. Can I get you . . . a cab, or something?
GRANDMA. Oh no, dear . . . thank you just the same. I'll take it from here.
YOUNG MAN. And what shall I do now?
GRANDMA. Oh, you stay here, dear. It will all become clear to you. It will be explained. You'll understand.
YOUNG MAN. Very well.
GRANDMA (*After one more look about*). Well . . .
YOUNG MAN. Let me see you to the elevator.
GRANDMA. Oh . . . that *would* be nice, dear.

(*They both exit by the front door, slowly*)

(*Enter Mrs. Barker, followed by Mommy and Daddy*)

MRS. BARKER. . . . and I'm happy to tell you that the whole thing's settled. Just like that.
MOMMY. Oh, we're so glad. We were afraid there might be a problem, what with delays, and all.
DADDY. Yes, we're very relieved.
MRS. BARKER. Well, now; that's what professional women are for.
MOMMY. Why . . . where's Grandma? Grandma's not here! Where's Grandma? And look! The boxes are gone, too. Grandma's gone, and so are the boxes. She's taken off, and she's stolen something! Daddy!
MRS. BARKER. Why, Mommy, the van man was here.
MOMMY (*Startled*). The what?
MRS. BARKER. The van man. The van man was here.

(*The lights might dim a little, suddenly*)

MOMMY (*Shakes her head*). No, that's impossible.
MRS. BARKER. Why, I saw him with my own two eyes.
MOMMY (*Near tears*). No, no, that's impossible. No. There's no such thing as the van man. There is no van man. We . . . we made him up. Grandma? Grandma?
DADDY (*Moving to* Mommy). There, there, now.
MOMMY. Oh Daddy . . . where's Grandma?
DADDY. There, there, now.

(*While Daddy is comforting Mommy, Grandma comes out, stage right, near the footlights*)

GRANDMA (*To the audience*). Shhhhhh! I want to watch this.

(*She motions to Mrs. Barker who, with a secret smile, tip-toes to the front door and opens it. The Young Man is framed therein. Lights up full again as he steps into the room*)

MRS. BARKER. Surprise! Surprise! Here we are!
MOMMY. What? What?
DADDY. Hm? What?
MOMMY (*Her tears merely sniffles now*). What surprise?
MRS. BARKER. Why, I told you. The surprise I told you about.
DADDY. You . . . you know, Mommy.
MOMMY. Sur . . . prise?
DADDY (*Urging her to cheerfulness*). You remember, Mommy; why we asked . . . uh . . . what's-her-name to come here?
MRS. BARKER. Mrs. Barker, if you don't mind.
DADDY. Yes. Mommy? You remember now? About the bumble . . . about wanting satisfaction?
MOMMY (*Her sorrow turning into delight*). Yes. Why yes! Of course! Yes! Oh, how wonderful!
MRS. BARKER (*To the* Young Man). This is Mommy.
YOUNG MAN. How . . . how do you do?
MRS. BARKER (*Stage whisper*). Her name's Mommy.
YOUNG MAN. How . . . how do you do, Mommy?
MOMMY. Well! Hello there!
MRS. BARKER (*To the* Young Man). And that is Daddy.
YOUNG MAN. How do you do, sir?
DADDY. How do you do?
MOMMY (*Herself again, circling the* Young Man, *feeling his arm, poking him*). Yes, sir! Yes, sirree! Now this is more like it. Now this is a great deal more like it! Daddy! Come see. Come see if this isn't a great deal more like it.
DADDY. I . . . I can see from here, Mommy. It does look a great deal more like it.
MOMMY. Yes, sir. Yes sirree! Mrs. Barker, I don't know *how* to thank you.
MRS. BARKER. Oh, don't worry about that. I'll send you a bill in the mail.
MOMMY. What this really calls for is a celebration. It calls for a drink.
MRS. BARKER. Oh, what a nice idea.
MOMMY. There's some sauterne in the kitchen.

YOUNG MAN. I'll go.

MOMMY. Will you? Oh, how nice. The kitchen's through the archway there.

(*As the Young Man exits: to Mrs. Barker*)

He's very nice. Really top notch; much better than the other one.

MRS. BARKER. I'm glad you're pleased. And I'm glad everything's all straightened out.

MOMMY. Well, at least we know why we sent for you. We're glad that's cleared up. By the way, what's his name?

MRS. BARKER. Ha! Call him whatever you like. He's yours. Call him what you called the other one.

MOMMY. Daddy? What did we call the other one?

DADDY (*Puzzles*). Why . . .

YOUNG MAN (*Re-entering with a tray on which are a bottle of sauterne and five glasses*). Here we are!

MOMMY. Hooray! Hooray!

MRS. BARKER. Oh, good!

MOMMY (*Moving to the tray*). So, let's—Five glasses? Why five? There are only four of us. Why five?

YOUNG MAN (*Catches Grandma's eye; Grandma indicates she is not there*). Oh, I'm sorry.

MOMMY. You must learn to count. We're a wealthy family, and you must learn to count.

YOUNG MAN. I will.

MOMMY. Well, everybody take a glass.

(*They do*)

And we'll drink to celebrate. To satisfaction! Who says you can't get satisfaction these days!

MRS. BARKER. What dreadful sauterne!

MOMMY. Yes, isn't it?

(*To Young Man*, *her voice already a little fuzzy from the wine*)

You don't know how happy I am to see you! Yes sirree. Listen, that time we had with . . . with the other one. I'll tell you about it some time.

(*Indicates Mrs. Barker*)

After she's gone. She was responsible for all the trouble in the first place. I'll tell you all about it.

(*Sidles up to him a little*)

Maybe . . . maybe later tonight.

YOUNG MAN (*Not moving away*). Why yes. That would be very nice.

MOMMY (*Puzzles*). Something familiar about you . . . you know that? I can't quite place it.

GRANDMA (*Interrupting . . . to audience*). Well, I guess that just about wraps it up. I mean, for better or worse, this is a comedy, and I don't think we'd better go any further. No, definitely not. So, let's leave things as they are right now . . . while everybody's happy . . . while everybody's got what he wants . . . or everybody's got what he thinks he wants. Good night, dears.

CURTAIN

F O R U M

"The Significance of the Absurd"

MARTIN ESSLIN

In 1961 Martin Esslin's book The Theatre of the Absurd *defined the (then) unusual characteristics and thematic concerns of the new dramas of Europe and America. It was he who coined the term "theatre of the absurd," and his study remains an admirable example of a critic who enlightens the public about new forms in drama.*

. . . The Theatre of the Absurd . . . bravely faces up to the fact that for those to whom the world has lost its central expla-

From "The Significance of the Absurd" by Martin Esslin, from *The Theatre of the Absurd* by Martin Esslin. Copyright © 1961 by Martin Esslin. Used by permission of Doubleday, a division of Bantam Doubleday Dell Publishing Group, Inc.

nation and meaning, it *is* no longer possible to accept art forms still based on the continuation of standards and concepts that have lost their validity; that is, the possibility of knowing the laws of conduct and ultimate values, as deducible from a firm foundation of revealed uncertainty about the purpose of man in the universe.

In expressing the tragic sense of loss at the disappearance of ultimate certainties the Theatre of the Absurd, by a strange paradox, is also a symptom of what probably comes nearest to being a genuine religious quest in our age: an effort, however, timid and tentative, to sing, to laugh, to weep—and to growl—if not in praise of God (whose name, in Adamov's phrase, has for so long been degraded by usage that it has lost its meaning), at least in search of a dimension of the Ineffable; an effort to make man aware of the ultimate realities of his condition, to instill in him again the lost sense of cosmic wonder and primeval anguish, to shock him out of an existence that has become trite, mechanical, complacent, and deprived of the dignity that comes of awareness. For God is dead, above all, to the masses who live from day to day and have lost all contact with the basic facts—and mysteries—of the human condition with which, in former times, they were kept in touch through the living ritual of their religion, which made them parts of a real community and not atoms in an atomized society.

The Theatre of the Absurd forms part of the unceasing endeavor of the true artists of our time to breach this dead wall of complacency and automatism and to re-establish an awareness of man's situation when confronted with the ultimate reality of his condition. As such, the Theatre of the Absurd fulfills a dual purpose and presents its audience with a twofold absurdity.

On the one hand, it castigates, satirically, the absurdity of lives lived unaware and unconscious of ultimate reality. This is the feeling of the deadness and mechanical senselessness of half-unconscious lives, the feeling of "human beings secreting inhumanity," which Camus describes in *The Myth of Sisyphus*:

> In certain hours of lucidity, the mechanical aspect of their gestures, their senseless pantomime, makes stupid everything around them. A man speaking on the telephone behind a glass partition—one cannot hear him but observes his trivial gesturing. One asks oneself, why is he alive? This malaise in front of man's own inhumanity, this incalculable letdown when faced with the image of what we are, this "nausea," as a contemporary writer calls it, also is the Absurd.

This is the experience that Ionesco expresses in plays like *The Bald Soprano* or *The Chairs*, Adamov in *La Parodie*, or N. F. Simpson in *A Resounding Tinkle*. It represents the satirical, parodistic aspect of the Theatre of the Absurd, its social criticism, its pillorying of an inauthentic, petty society. This may be the most easily accessible, and therefore most widely recognized, message of the Theatre of the Absurd, but it is far from being its most essential or most significant feature.

Behind the satirical exposure of the absurdity of inauthentic ways of life, the Theatre of the Absurd is facing up to a deeper layer of absurdity—the absurdity of the human condition itself in a world where the decline of religious belief has deprived man of certainties. When it is no longer possible to accept simple and complete systems of values and revelations of divine purpose, life must be faced in its ultimate, stark reality. That is why, in the analysis of the dramatists of the Absurd in this book, we have always seen man stripped of the accidental circumstances of social position or historical context, confronted with the basic choices, the basic situations of his existence. . . .

Concerned as it is with the ultimate realities of the human condition, the relatively few fundamental problems of life and death, isolation and communication, the Theatre of the Absurd, however grotesque, frivolous, and irreverent it may appear, represents a return to the original, religious function of the theatre—the confrontation of man with the spheres of myth and religious reality. Like ancient Greek tragedy and the medieval mystery plays and baroque allegories, the Theatre of the Absurd is intent on making its audience aware of man's precarious and mysterious position in the universe.

The difference is merely that in ancient Greek tragedy—and comedy—as well as in the medieval mystery play and the baroque *auto sacramental*, the ultimate realities concerned were generally known and universally accepted metaphysical systems, while the Theatre of the Absurd expresses the absence of any such generally accepted cosmic system of values. Hence, much more modestly, the Theatre of the Absurd makes no pretense at explaining the way of God to man. It can merely present, in anxiety or with derision, an individual human being's intuition of the ultimate realities as he experiences them; the fruits of one man's descent into the depths of his personality, his dreams, fantasies, and nightmares.

While former attempts at confronting man with the ultimate realities of his condition projected a coherent and generally recognized version of the truth, the Theatre of the Absurd merely communicates one poet's most intimate and personal intuition of the human situation, his own *sense of being*, his individual vision of the world. This is the *subject matter* of the Theatre of the Absurd, and it determines its *form*, which must, of necessity, represent a convention of the stage basically different from the "realistic" theatre of our time.

As the Theatre of the Absurd is not concerned with conveying information or presenting the problems or destinies of characters that exist outside the author's inner world, as it does not expound a thesis or debate ideological propositions, it is not concerned with the representation of events, the narration of the fate or the adventures of characters, but instead with the presentation of one individual's basic situation. It is a theatre of situation as against a theatre of events in sequence, and therefore it uses a language based on patterns of concrete images rather than argument and discursive speech. And since it is trying to present a sense of being, it can neither investigate nor solve problems of conduct or morals.

Because the Theatre of the Absurd projects its author's personal world, it lacks objectively valid characters. It cannot show the clash of opposing temperaments or study human passions locked in conflict, and is therefore not dramatic in the accepted sense of the term. Nor is it concerned with telling a story in order to communicate some moral or social lesson, as is the aim of Brecht's narrative, "epic" theatre. The action in a play of the Theatre of the Absurd is not intended to tell a story but to communicate a pattern of poetic images. To give but one example: Things happen in *Waiting for Godot*, but these happenings do not constitute a plot or story; they are an image of Beckett's intuition that *nothing really ever happens* in man's existence. . . .

. . . [The] Theatre of the Absurd aims at concentration and depth in an essentially lyrical, poetic pattern. Of course, dramatic, narrative, and lyrical elements are present in all drama. Brecht's own theatre, like Shakespeare's, contains lyrical inserts in the form of songs; even at their most didactic, Ibsen and Shaw are rich in purely poetic moments. The Theatre of the Absurd, however, in abandoning psychology, subtlety of characterization, and plot in the conventional sense, gives the poetical element an incomparably greater emphasis. While the play with

(continued)

a linear plot describes a development in time, in a dramatic form that presents a concretized poetic image the play's extension in time is purely incidental. Expressing an *intuition in depth*, it should ideally be apprehended *in a single moment*, and only because it is physically impossible to present so complex an image in an instant does it have to be spread over a period of time. The formal structure of such a play is, therefore, merely a device to express a complex total image by unfolding it in a sequence of interacting elements.

The endeavor to communicate a total sense of being is an attempt to present a truer picture of reality itself, reality as apprehended by an individual. The Theatre of the Absurd is the last link in a line of development that started with naturalism. Once the idealistic, Platonic belief in immutable essences—ideal forms that it was the artist's task to present in a purer state than they could ever be found in nature—had foundered in the aftermath of the rise of the philosophy of Locke and Kant, which based reality on perception and the inner structure of the human mind, art became mere imitation of external nature. Yet the imitation of surfaces was bound to prove unsatisfying and this inevitably led to the next step—the exploration of the reality of the mind. Ibsen and Strindberg exemplified that development during the span of their own lifetime's exploration of reality. James Joyce began with minutely realistic stories and ended up with the vast multiple structure of *Finnegan's Wake*. The work of the dramatists of the Absurd continues the same development. Each of these plays is an answer to the questions "How does this individual feel when confronted with the human situation? What is the basic mood in which he faces the world? What does it feel like to be him?" And the answer is a single, total, but complex and contradictory poetic image—one play—or a succession of such images, complementing each other—the dramatist's *œuvre*.

Any really fundamental analysis of reality as perceived by man leads to the recognition that any attempt at communicating what we perceive and feel consists of the dissection of a momentary, simultaneous intuition of a complex of perceptions into a *sequence* of atomized concepts structured in time within a sentence, or a sequence of sentences. To convert our perception into conceptual terms, into logical thought and language, we perform an operation analogous to the scanner that analyzes the picture in a television camera into rows of single impulses. The poetic image, with its ambiguity and its simultaneous evocation of multiple elements of sense associations, is one of the methods by which we can, however imperfectly, communicate the reality of our intuition of the world. . . .

And it is in this striving to communicate a basic and as yet undissolved totality of perception, an intuition of being, that we can find a key to the devaluation and disintegration of language in the Theatre of the Absurd. For if it is the translation of the total intuition of being into the logical and temporal sequence of conceptual thought that deprives it of its pristine complexity and poetic truth, it is understandable that the artist should try to find ways to circumvent this influence of discursive speech and logic. Here lies the chief difference between poetry and prose: Poetry is ambiguous and associative, striving to approximate the wholly unconceptual language of music. The Theatre of the Absurd, in carrying the same poetic endeavor into the

concrete imagery of the stage, can go further than pure poetry in dispensing with logic, discursive thought, and language. The stage is a multidimensional medium; it allows the simultaneous use of visual elements, movement, light, and language. It is, therefore, particularly suited to the communication of complex images consisting of the contrapuntal interaction of all these elements.

In the "literary" theatre, language remains the predominant component. In the anti-literary theatre of the circus or the music hall, language is reduced to a very subordinate role. The Theatre of the Absurd has regained the freedom of using language as merely one—sometimes dominant, sometimes submerged—component of its multidimensional poetic imagery. By putting the language of a scene in contrast to the action, by reducing it to meaningless patter, or by abandoning discursive logic for the poetic logic of association or assonance, the Theatre of the Absurd has opened up a new dimension of the stage.

In its devaluation of language, the Theatre of the Absurd is in tune with the trend of our time. . . .

. . . Exposed to the incessant, and inexorably loquacious, onslaught of the mass media, the press, and advertising, the man in the street becomes more and more skeptical toward the language he is exposed to. The citizens of totalitarian countries know full well that most of what they are told is double-talk, devoid of real meaning. They become adept at reading between the lines; that is, at guessing at the reality the language conceals rather than reveals. In the West, euphemisms and circumlocutions fill the press or resound from the pulpits. And advertising, by its constant use of superlatives, has succeeded in devaluing language to a point where it is a generally accepted axiom that most of the words one sees displayed on billboards or in the colored pages of magazine advertising are as meaningless as the jingles of television commercials. A yawning gulf has opened between language and reality.

Apart from the general devaluation of language in the flood of mass communications, the growing specialization of life has made the exchange of ideas on an increasing number of subjects impossible between members of different spheres of lie which have each developed its own specialized jargon. . . .

That is why communication between human beings is so often shown in a state of breakdown in the Theatre of the Absurd. It is merely a satirical magnification of the existing state of affairs. Language has run riot in an age of mass communication. It must be reduced to its proper function—the expression of authentic content, rather than its concealment. But this will be possible only if man's reverence toward the spoken or written word as a means of communication is restored, and the ossified clichés that dominate thought (as they do in the limericks of Edward Lear or the world of Humpty Dumpty) are replaced by a living language that serves it. And this, in turn, can be achieved only if the limitations of logic and discursive language are recognized and respected, and the uses of poetic language acknowledged.

The means by which the dramatists of the Absurd express their critique—largely instinctive and unintended—of our disintegrating society are based on suddenly confronting their audiences with a grotesquely heightened and distorted picture of a world that has gone mad. This is a shock therapy that achieves what Brecht's doctrine of the "alienation effect" postulated in theory but failed to achieve in practice—the inhibition of the audience's identification with the characters on the stage (which is the age-old and highly effective method of the traditional theatre), and its replacement by a detached, critical attitude. . . .

In the Theatre of the Absurd, on the other hand, the audience is confronted with characters whose motives and actions remain largely incomprehensible. With such characters it is almost impossible to identify; the more mysterious their action and their nature, the less human the characters become, the more difficult it is to be carried away into seeing the world from their point of view. Characters with whom the audience fails to identify are inevitably comic. If we identified with the figure of farce who loses his trousers, we should feel embarrassment and shame. If, however, our tendency to identify has been inhibited by making such a character grotesque, we laugh at his predicament. We see what happens to him from the outside, rather than from his own point of view. As the incomprehensibility of the motives, and the often unexplained and mysterious nature of the characters' actions in the Theatre of the Absurd effectively prevent identification, such theatre is a comic theatre in spite of the fact that its subject matter is somber, violent, and bitter. That is why the Theatre of the Absurd transcends the categories of comedy and tragedy and combines laughter with horror.

. . . It presents the audience with a picture of a disintegrating world that has lost its unifying principle, its meaning, and its purpose—an absurd universe. What is the audience to make of this bewildering confrontation with a truly alienated world that, having lost its rational principle, has in the true sense of the word gone mad?

. . . In the Theatre of the Absurd, the whole of the action is mysterious, unmotivated, and at first sight nonsensical and mad.

The alienation effect in the Brechtian theatre is intended to activate the audience's critical, intellectual attitude. The Theatre of the Absurd speaks to a deeper level of the audience's mind. It activates psychological forces, releases, and liberates hidden fears and repressed aggressions, and, above all, by confronting the audience with a picture of disintegration, it sets in motion an active process of integrative forces in the mind of each individual spectator. . . .

. . . Once drawn into the mystery of the play, the spectator is compelled to come to terms with his experience. The stage supplies him with a number of disjointed clues that he has to fit into a meaningful pattern. In this manner, he is forced to make a creative effort of his own, an effort at interpretation and integration. The time has been made to appear out of joint; the audience of the Theatre of the Absurd is being compelled to set it right, or, rather, by being made to see that the world has become absurd, in acknowledging that fact takes the first step in coming to terms with reality. . . .

The challenge to make sense out of what appears as a senseless and fragmented action, the recognition that the fact that the modern world has lost its unifying principle is the source of its bewildering and soul-destroying quality, is therefore more than a mere intellectual exercise; it has a therapeutic effect. In Greek tragedy, the spectators were made aware of man's forlorn but heroic stand against the inexorable forces of fate and the will of the gods—and this had a cathartic effect upon them and made them better able to face their time. In the Theatre of the Absurd, the spectator is confronted with the madness of the human condition, is enabled to see his situation in all its grimeness and despair, and this, in stripping him of illusions or vaguely felt fears and anxieties, enables him to face it consciously, rather than feel it vaguely below the surface of euphemisms and optimistic illusions. And this, in turn, results in the liberating effect of anxieties overcome by being formulated. This is the nature of all the gallows humor and *humour noir* of world literature, of which the Theatre of the Absurd is the latest example. It is the unease caused by the presence of illusions that are obviously out of tune with reality that is dissolved and discharged through liberating laughter at the recognition of the fundamental absurdity of the universe. The greater the anxieties and the temptation to indulge in illusions, the more beneficial is this therapeutic effect—hence the success of *Waiting for Godot* at San Quentin. It was a relief for the convicts to be made to recognize in the tragicomic situation of the tramps the hopelessness of their own waiting for a miracle. They were enabled to laugh at the tramps—and at themselves.

As the reality with which the Theatre of the Absurd is concerned is a psychological reality expressed in images that are the outward projection of states of mind, fears, dreams, nightmares, and conflicts within the personality of the author, the dramatic tension produced by this kind of play differs fundamentally from the suspense created in a theatre concerned mainly with the revelation of objective characters through the unfolding of a narrative plot. The pattern of exposition, conflict, and final solution mirrors a view of the world in which solutions are possible, a view based on a recognizable and generally accepted pattern of an objective reality that can be apprehended so that the purpose of man's existence and the rules of conduct it entails can be deduced from it. . . .

The Theatre of the Absurd, however, which proceeds not by intellectual concepts but by poetic images, neither poses an intellectual problem in its exposition nor provides any clear-cut solution that would be reducible to a lesson or an apothegm. Many of the plays of the Theatre of the Absurd have a circular structure, ending exactly as they began; others progress merely by a growing intensification of the initial situation. And as the Theatre of the Absurd rejects the idea that it is possible to motivate all human behavior, or that human character is based on an immutable essence, it is impossible for it to base its effect on the suspense that in other dramatic conventions springs from awaiting the solution of a dramatic equation based on the working out of a problem involving clearly defined quantities introduced in the opening scenes. In most dramatic conventions, the audience is constantly asking itself the question "What is going to happen next?"

In the Theatre of the Absurd, the audience is confronted with actions that lack apparent motivation, characters that are in constant flux, and often happenings that are clearly outside the realm of national experience. Here, too, the audience can ask, "What is going to happen next?" But then *anything* may

(continued)

happen next, so that the answer to this question cannot be worked out according to the rules of ordinary probability based on motive and characterizations that will remain constant throughout the play. The relevant question here is not so much what is going to happen next but what *is* happening? "What does the action of the play represent?"

This constitutes a different, but by no means less valid, kind of dramatic suspense. Instead of being provided with a *solution*, the spectator is challenged to formulate the *questions* that he will have to ask if he wants to approach the meaning of the play. The total action of the play, instead of proceeding from Point A to Point B, as in other dramatic conventions, gradually builds up the complex pattern of the *poetic image* that the play expresses. The spectator's suspense consists in waiting for the gradual completion of this pattern which will enable him to see the image as a whole. And only when that image is assembled—after the final curtain—can he *begin* to explore, not so much its meaning as its structure, texture, and impact.

This is the element the Theatre of the Absurd (without making any claim at reaching the heights the greatest dramatists have attained with intuition and the richness of their creative capacity) has tried to make the core of its dramatic convention. . . .

. . . It is this language of stage images that embody a truth beyond the power of mere discursive thought which the Theatre of the Absurd places at the center of its endeavor to build a new dramatic convention, subordinating all other elements of stagecraft to it.

But if the Theatre of the Absurd concentrates on the power of stage imagery, on the projection of visions of the world dredged up from the depth of the subconscious; if it neglects the rationally measurable ingredients of the theatre—the highly polished carpentry of plot and counterplot of the well-made play, the imitation of reality which can be measured against reality itself, the clever motivation of character—how can it be judged by rational analysis, how can it be subjected to criticism by objectively valid standards? If it is a purely subjective expression of its author's vision and emotion, how can the public distinguish the genuine, deeply felt work of art from mere impostures? . . .

. . . All art is subjective, and the standards against which the critics measure success or failure are always worked out *a posteriori* from an analysis of accepted and empirically successful works. In the case of a phenomenon like the Theatre of the Absurd, which is the outcome not of the conscious pursuit of a collectively worked-out program or theory (as the Romantic movement was, for example) but of an unpremeditated response by a number of independent authors to tendencies inherent in the general movement of thought in a period of transition, we have to analyze the works themselves and find the tendencies and modes of thought they express, in order to gain a picture of their artistic purpose. And once we have gained a clear idea of their general tendency and aim, we can arrive at a perfectly valid judgment of how they measure up to what they have set out to do.

If in the course of this book, therefore, we have established that the Theatre of the Absurd is concerned essentially with the evocation of concrete poetic images designed to communicate to the audience the sense of perplexity that their authors feel when confronted with the human condition, we must judge the success or failure of these works by the degree to which they succeed in communicating this mixture of poetry and grotesque, tragicomic horror. And this in turn will depend on the quality and power of the poetic images evoked. . . .

. . . Unsuccessful examples of the Theatre of the Absurd, like unsuccessful abstract painting, are usually characterized by the transparent way in which they still bear the mark of the fragments of reality from which they are made up. They have not undergone that sea change through which the merely *negative* quality of *lack* of logic or verisimilitude is transmuted into the *positive* quality of a new world that makes imaginative sense in its own right.

Here we have one of the real hallmarks of excellence in the Theatre of the Absurd. Only when its invention springs from deep layers of profoundly experienced emotion, only when it mirrors real obsessions, dreams, and valid images in the subconscious mind of its author, will such a work of art have that quality of truth, of instantly recognized general, as distinct from merely private, validity that distinguishes the vision of a poet from the delusions of the mentally afflicted. This quality of depth and unity of vision is instantly recognizable and beyond trickery. No degree of technical accomplishment and mere cleverness can here, as in the sphere of representational art or drama, cover up the poverty of the inner core of the work in question.

To write a well-made problem play or a witty comedy of manners may therefore be more laborious or require a higher degree of ingenuity or intelligence. On the other hand, to invent a generally valid poetic image of the human condition requires unusual depth of feeling and intensity of emotion, and a far higher degree of genuinely creative vision—in short, inspiration. It is a widespread but vulgar fallacy that bases a hierarchy of artistic achievement on the mere difficulty or laboriousness of the process of composition. If it were not futile from the outset to argue in terms of position on a scale of values, such a scale could be based only on the quality, the universal validity, the depth of vision and insight of the work itself, whether or not it was produced in decades of patient plodding or in a flash of inspiration.

The criteria of achievement in the Theatre of the Absurd are not only the quality of invention, the complexity of the poetic images evoked, and the skill with which they are combined and sustained but also, and even more essentially, the *reality* and *truth* of the vision these images embody. For all its freedom of invention and spontaneity, the Theatre of the Absurd is concerned with communicating an experience of being, and in doing so it is trying to be uncompromisingly honest and fearless in exposing the reality of the human condition. . . .

In trying to deal with the ultimates of the human condition not in terms of intellectual understanding but in terms of communicating a metaphysical truth through a living experience, the Theatre of the Absurd touches the religious sphere. There is a vast difference between *knowing* something to be the case in the conceptual sphere and *experiencing* it as a living reality. It is the mark of all great religions that they not only possess a body of knowledge that can be taught in the form of cosmological information or ethical rules but that they also communicate the essence of this body of doctrine in the living, recurring poetic imagery of ritual. It is the loss of the latter sphere, which responds to a deep inner need in all human beings, that the decline of religion has left as a deeply felt deficiency in our civilization. We possess at least an approximation to a coherent philosophy in the scientific method, but we lack the means to make it a living reality, an experienced focus of men's lives. That is why the theatre, a place where men congregate to experience poetic or artistic insights, has in many ways assumed the function of a substitute church. Hence the immense importance placed upon the theatre by totalitarian creeds, which are fully aware of the need to make their doctrines a living, experienced reality to their followers.

The Theatre of the Absurd, paradoxical though this may appear at first sight, can be seen as an attempt to communicate the metaphysical experience behind the scientific attitude and, at the same time, to supplement it by rounding off the partial view of the world it presents, and integrating it in a wider vision of the world and its mystery.

For if the Theatre of the Absurd presents the world as senseless and lacking unifying principle, it does so merely in the terms of those philosophies that start from the idea that human thought *can* reduce the totality of the universe to a complete, unified, coherent system. It is only from the point of view of those who cannot bear a world where it is impossible to know why it was created, what part man has been assigned in it, and what constitutes right actions and wrong actions that a picture of the universe lacking all these clear-cut definitions appears deprived of sense and sanity, and tragically absurd. . . .

The Theatre of the Absurd expresses the anxiety and despair that spring from the recognition that man is surrounded by areas of impenetrable darkness, that he can never know his true nature and purpose, and that no one will provide him with ready-made rules of conduct. . . .

To confront the limits of the human condition is not only equivalent to facing up to the philosophical basis of the scientific attitude, it is also a profound mystical experience. It is precisely this experience of the ineffability, the emptiness, the nothingness at the basis of the universe that forms the content of Eastern as well as Christian mystical experience. . . .

. . . [I]n facing man's inability ever to comprehend the meaning of the universe, in recognizing the Godhead's total transcendence, His total otherness from all we can understand with our senses, the great mystics experienced a sense of exhilaration and liberation. This exhilaration also springs from the recognition that the language and logic of cognitive thought cannot do justice to the ultimate nature of reality. . . .

Seen from this angle the dethronement of language and logic forms part of an essentially mystical attitude toward the basis of reality as being too complex and at the same time too unified, too much of one piece, to be validly expressed by the analytical means of orderly syntax and conceptual thought. As the mystics resort to poetic images, so does the Theatre of the Absurd. But if the Theatre of the Absurd presents analogies with the methods and imagery of mysticism, how can it, at the same time, be regarded as expressing the skepticism, the humble refusal to provide an explanation of absolutes, that characterize the scientific attitude?

The answer is simply that there is no contradiction between the recognition of the limitations of man's ability to comprehend all of reality by integrating it in a single system of values and the recognition of the mysterious and ineffable oneness, beyond all rational comprehension, that, once experienced, gives serenity of mind and the strength to face the human condition. These are in fact two sides of the same medal—the mystical experience of the absolute otherness and ineffability of ultimate reality is the religious, poetic counterpart to the rational recognition of the limitation of man's senses and intellect, which reduces him to exploring the world slowly by trial and error. Both these attitudes are in basic contradiction to systems of thought, religious or ideological (e.g., Marxism), that claim to provide complete answers to all questions of ultimate purpose and day-to-day conduct.

The realization that thinking in poetic images has its validity side by side with conceptual thought and the insistence on a clear recognition of the function and possibilities of each mode does not amount to a return to irrationalism; on the contrary, it opens the way to a truly rational attitude.

Ultimately, a phenomenon like the Theatre of the Absurd does not reflect despair or a return to dark irrational forces but expresses modern man's endeavor to come to terms with the world in which he lives. It attempts to make him face up to the human condition as it really is, to free him from illusions that are bound to cause constant maladjustment and disappoint. There are enormous pressures in our world that seek to induce mankind to bear the loss of faith and moral certainties by being drugged into oblivion—by mass entertainments, shallow material satisfactions, pseudo-explanations of reality, and cheap ideologies. At the end of that road lies Huxley's Brave New World of senseless euphoric automata. Today, when death and old age are increasingly concealed behind euphemisms and comforting baby talk, and life is threatened with being smothered in the mass consumption of hypnotic mechanized vulgarity, the need to confront man with the reality of his situation is greater than ever. For the dignity of man lies in his ability to face reality in all its senselessness; to accept it freely, without fear, without illusions—and to laugh at it.

That is the cause to which, in their various individual, modest, and quoxotic ways, the dramatists of the Absurd are dedicated.

ROCKABY

Samuel Beckett

SAMUEL BECKETT (1906–1989)

Perhaps no writer in the second half of the twentieth century has been as influential and imitated as Samuel Beckett. Harold Pinter, Tom Stoppard, and Edward Albee, to name the most prominent examples, have cited Beckett as the inspiration for their earliest works. Sam Shepard recalls that reading *Waiting for Godot* when he was a teenager in California motivated his subsequent writing career: "I didn't understand it at all, but the words and the language amazed me. I had no place to put it in, no category, but once I started writing plays, I felt a connection." And no other twentieth-century playwright has generated so many critical assessments of his work; there is even an academic journal devoted exclusively to Beckett's drama, poetry, and novels.

Beckett is another transplanted Irishman who fled his homeland, partly to escape oppressive provincialism (though he was Protestant, not Catholic), and partly to experience the robust intellectual life of Europe's capitals between the wars. After earning a degree in languages at Dublin's Trinity College (where he also taught briefly), he traveled throughout the Continent. In Paris he met James Joyce, his countryman, whose work he helped translate into French. Beckett's writing clearly shows the influence of Joyce, particularly in its inventive wordplay and in the stream-of-consciousness style found in such plays as *Rockaby*. Beckett settled permanently in Paris in 1938, declaring that he would "rather live in France during war than in Ireland during peace." After 1946 he wrote the bulk of his work in French and later translated it into his native English. Consequently, he is claimed by both French and English literati, though in truth he is the most international of modern playwrights because his works are conspicuously free of the specifics of time and place.

By the 1940s Paris had become the nexus for such existential writer-philosophers as Jean-Paul Sartre and Albert Camus, and Beckett's writing echoes many of the darker elements of these thinkers, who argued that the world lacks a cohesive system to guide it. Beckett's plays are peopled with characters who are trapped both by a universe they cannot comprehend and, equally importantly, by their own inability to change their circumstances. Consider Gogo and Didi, the tramps who wait futilely under the barren tree in *Waiting for Godot*, or Nagg and Nell, the old couple who spend *Endgame* encased in ashbins. Like the old woman pinned to her chair in *Rockaby*, they are victims of their own inertia as much as of the world's indifference to their existence. "There is no escape from the days and the hours," Beckett wrote in echo of Proust.

While Beckett wrote in the absurdist tradition—as much as any writer he gave it credibility—his dramatic works transcend absurdism's limitations. Beckett is a minimalist (he actually titled one of his prose fictions *Lessness*) who has shown us how little it takes to create an effective, poetic theater. *Rockaby* is the exemplar of Beckett's minimalist technique: a single woman sits, immobile, in a rocking chair awaiting the inevitability of death. His language is as sparse as his stage settings and as ripe with possibility as his simple, deftly chosen set pieces. The very ambiguity of his language encompasses multiple layers of meaning.

Beckett was not only an admired playwright and recipient of the Nobel Prize in Literature in 1969, he was also a superb director of his works. His marginal notes provide valuable critical insights into his themes and dramaturgy. Curiously, in his later years he allowed only school-children to attend his rehearsals. Beckett's most significant dramatic works include: *Waiting for Godot* (1953), *All That Fall* (1957), *Endgame* (1958), *Krapp's Last Tape* (1960), *Happy Days* (1962), *Not I* (1973), *That Time* and *Footfalls* (1976), *Ghost Trio* (1977), and *Rockaby* (1981). His novels include *Malloy* (1951), *Malone Dies* (1951), and *The Unnameable* (1953). He has also written numerous poems, as well as an admired study of Proust.

ROCKABY (1981)

Written as a response to an American scholar's request for a play commemorating Beckett's seventy-fifth birthday, *Rockaby* premiered in Buffalo, New York, in April 1981. The role of "the Woman" was created by Billie Whitelaw, the only British performer personally selected by Beckett to appear in his plays. She is considered among the foremost interpreters of Beckett. The production was staged by the late Alan Schneider, the most respected American director of Beckett's works. Given the occasion and the assembled talent, it was a major theatrical event—which lasted all of 14 minutes and 30 seconds.

Despite its brevity, the play actually encompasses a lifetime. A woman, "old before her time" with "huge eyes and a white expressionless face," sits before a window in a rocking chair, listening to a voice (her own? her mother's? a detached third party's?). The voice drones in perfect synchronization with the rocker (which, as Beckett commands in his notes, is "controlled mechanically without assistance from the Woman"). Though the voice tells us little of consequence, the narration conjures a world of experience which succinctly captures the futility of human endeavor. The woman wakes, rocks before the window, gazes at the world through her window, and at "the end of a long day" she sleeps. She calls "more" each time the voice stops, a plea that is simultaneously pitiable and cruelly ironic. She craves contact, even if it is only a mechanical voice in the distance, yet the "rerun" of the tape only emphasizes her inability to change in this unchanging, unyielding world. For her, as for all Beckett's characters, habit is indeed "the great deadener" (*Godot*). Finally she drifts off to sleep—or perhaps she dies—as Beckett describes it, with "a long pause with a spot on face alone. Head slowly sinks, comes to rest. Fade out spot." Whether she sleeps or dies is of little consequence because there is little difference between the two. For Beckett, the woman died long before the play began and her rocker serves simultaneously as her tomb and as a womb with "rounded curving arms to suggest an embrace."

Rockaby offers a frightening picture of loneliness and alienation. It is told in the simplest of terms through the least action imaginable. Yet by the end of the play, we feel as if we have participated in the totality of the woman's life.

Compare *Rockaby* with an earlier play about a woman who also faces life's final moments—the Japanese Noh drama, *Komachi at Sekidera*. Beckett's play is similar in several aspects: it is a poetic meditation that uses a minimum of action to depict an old woman in her last hours. (Beckett's drama is evocative of a Noh drama, perhaps the legacy of his countryman William Butler Yeats, who experimented with the Noh form in the early years of the twentieth century.) A melancholy strain runs through *Komachi* as the old poet reflects on the apparent futility of her life's work; for her, as in Beckett's world, time is the corrupter that thwarts human ambition. However, there is ultimately something uplifting in Komachi's drama of death, first in the hope of the young monk who keeps her work alive, and secondly in the dance of the Butterfly performed by Komachi and the child. In Beckett, there is also a dance in the slow, rhythmic rocking of the old chair. But there is neither the hope nor regeneration we experience in Komachi's triumphant dance. There is only the repetitious forward, then backward, movement that will not cease whether the woman lives or dies in the rocking chair. It is a chilling dance of futility that does not stop, but only fades into silence, that most terrifying of sounds in Beckett's world. It is the essential Beckett moment.

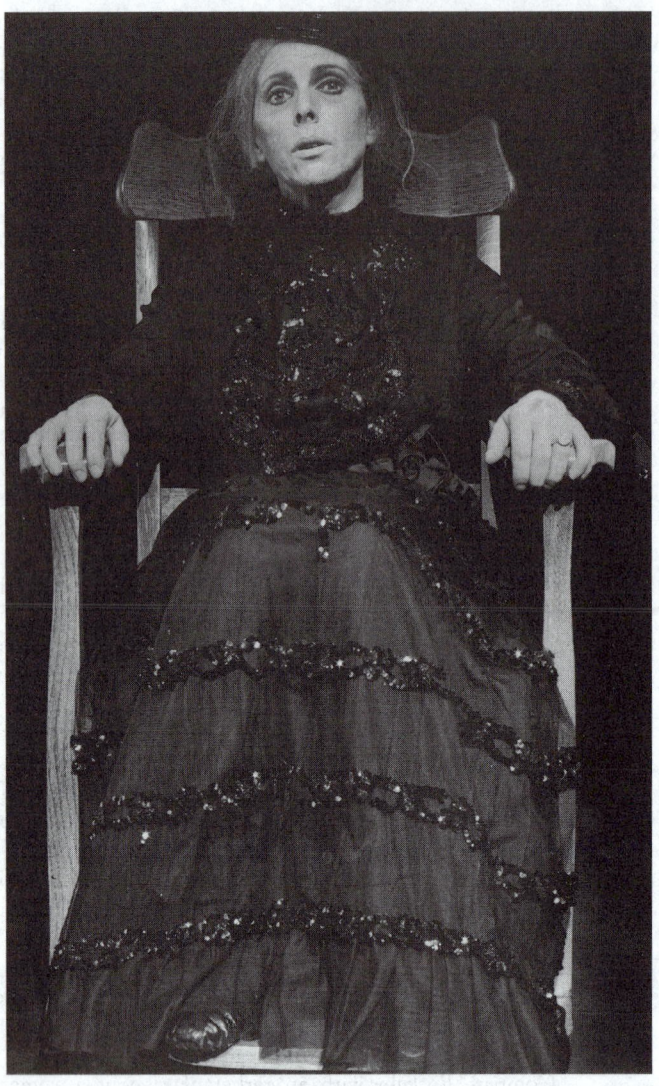

Samuel Beckett wrote the role of the lonely woman for Billie Whitelaw; this 1984 production of Rockaby in New York was directed by Alan Schneider, the United States' foremost interpreter of Beckett's plays.

ROCKABY

SAMUEL BECKETT

W = *Woman in chair.*
V = *Her recorded voice.*

Fade up on W in rocking chair facing front downstage slightly off centre audience left.

Long pause.

W. More.

Pause. Rock and voice together.

V. till in the end
the day came
in the end came
close of a long day
when she said
to herself
whom else
time she stopped
time she stopped

going to and fro
all eyes
all sides
high and low
for another
another like herself
another creature like herself
a little like
going to and fro
all eyes
all sides
high and low
for another
till in the end
close of a long day
to herself
whom else
time she stopped
time she stopped
going to and fro
all eyes
all sides
high and low
for another
another living soul
one other living soul
going to and fro
all eyes like herself
all sides
high and low
for another
another like herself
a little like
going to and fro
till in the end
close of a long day
to herself
whom else
time she stopped
going to and fro
time she stopped
time she stopped

*Together: echo of "time she
stopped," coming to rest of rock,
faint fade of light.*

Long pause.

W.   More.

Pause. Rock and voice together.

V.   so in the end
close of a long day
went back in
in the end went back in

saying to herself
whom else
time she stopped
time she stopped
going to and fro
time she went and sat
at her window
quiet at her window
facing other windows
so in the end
close of a long day
in the end went and sat
went back in and sat
at her window
let up the blind and sat
quiet at her window
only window
facing other windows
other only windows
all eyes
all sides
high and low
for another
at her window
another like herself
a little like
another living soul
one other living soul
at her window
gone in like herself
gone back in
in the end
close of a long day
saying to herself
whom else
time she stopped
time she stopped
going to and fro
time she went and sat
at her window
quiet at her window
only window
facing other windows
other only windows
all eyes
all sides
high and low
for another
another like herself
a little like
another living soul
one other living soul

*Together: echo of "living soul,"
coming to rest of rock, faint
fade of light.*

Samuel Beckett

Long pause.

W. More.

Pause. Rock and voice together.

V. till in the end
  the day came
  in the end came
  close of a long day
  sitting at her window
  quiet at her window
  only window
  facing other windows
  other only windows
  all blinds down
  never one up
  hers alone up
  till the day came
  in the end came
  close of a long day
  sitting at her window
  quiet at her window
  all eyes
  all sides
  high and low
  for a blind up
  one blind up
  no more
  never mind a face
  behind the pane
  famished eyes
  like hers
  to see
  be seen
  no
  a blind up
  like hers
  a little like
  one blind up no more
  another creature there
  somewhere there
  behind the pane
  another living soul
  one other living soul
  till the day came
  in the end came
  close of a long day
  when she said
  to herself
  whom else
  time she stopped
  time she stopped
  sitting at her window
  quiet at her window
  only window
  facing other windows

  other only windows
  all eyes
  all sides
  high and low
  time she stopped
  time she stopped

Together: echo of "time she stopped," coming to rest of rock, faint fade of light.

Long pause.

W. More.

Pause. Rock and voice together.

V. so in the end
  close of a long day
  went down
  in the end went down
  down the steep stair
  let down the blind and down
  right down
  into the old rocker
  mother rocker
  where mother sat
  all the years
  all in black
  best black
  sat and rocked
  rocked
  till her end came
  in the end came
  off her head they said
  gone off her head
  but harmless
  no harm in her
  dead one day
  no
  night
  dead one night
  in the rocker
  in her best black
  head fallen
  and the rocker rocking
  rocking away
  so in the end
  close of a long day
  went down
  in the end went down
  down the steep stair
  let down the blind and down
  right down
  into the old rocker
  those arms at last
  and rocked
  rocked

1238

with closed eyes
closing eyes
she so long all eyes
famished eyes
all sides
high and low
to and fro
at her window
to see
be seen
till in the end
close of a long day
to herself
whom else
time she stopped
let down the blind and stopped
time she went down
down the steep stair
time she went right down
was her own other
own other living soul
so in the end
close of a long day
went down
down the steep stair
let down the blind and down
right down
into the old rocker
and rocked
rocked
saying to herself
no
done with that
the rocker
those arms at last
saying to the rocker
rock her off
stop her eyes
fuck life

stop her eyes
rock her off
rock her off

Together: echo of "rock her off,"
coming to rest of rock,
slow fade out.

NOTES

Light   *Subdued on chair. Rest of stage dark. Subdued spot on face constant throughout, unaffected by successive fades. Either wide enough to include narrow limits of rock or concentrated on face when still or at mid-rock. Then throughout speech face slightly swaying in and out of light.*
  Opening fade-up: first spot on face alone. Long pause. Then light on chair. Final fade-out: first chair. Long pause with spot on face alone. Head slowly sinks, comes to rest. Fade out spot.

W   *Prematurely old. Unkempt grey hair. Huge eyes in white expressionless face. White hands holding ends of armrests.*

Eyes   *Now closed, now open in unblinking gaze. About equal proportions section 1, increasingly closed 2 and 3, closed for good halfway through 4.*

Costume   *Black lacy high-necked evening gown. Long sleeves. Jet sequins to glitter when rocking. Incongruous frivolous headdress set askew with extravagant trimmings to catch light when rocking.*

Attitude   *Completely still till fade-out of chair. Then in light of spot head slowly inclined.*

Chair   *Pale wood highly polished to gleam when rocking. Footrest. Vertical back. Rounded inward curving arms to suggest embrace.*

Rock   *Slight. Slow. Controlled mechanically without assistance from W.*

Voice   *Lines in italics spoken by W with V a little softer each time. W's "More" a little softer each time. Towards end of section 4, say from "saying to herself" on, voice gradually softer.*

THE MAN WHO TURNED INTO A DOG

OSVALDO DRAGÚN

OSVALDO DRAGÚN (1929–1999)

One of Latin America's leading playwrights, Osvaldo Dragún was born in the province of Entre Rios in northern Argentina. Following his initial impulse to study law, he abandoned his university studies to move to Buenos Aires to pursue a career in the theater. Widely recognized throughout the Americas and Europe, Dragún wrote over 30 dramatic works including *Tupac Amarú* (1957), *And They Told Us We Were Immortal* (1962), and *Stories to Be Told* (1956). The latter is a tetralogy that includes *The Man Who Turned into a Dog*, one of the most widely performed pieces in his repertoire. Dragún lectured extensively in the United States and was awarded the prestigious Casa de las Americas Prize in 1966 for his play *Heroics of Buenos Aires*. Dragún served as the artistic director of Teatro Cervantes, the national theater of Argentina.

Dragún was a humanist concerned with personal identity and the way we cope with our world. Above all, he was concerned with the choices people make, especially as they affect an entire society. For Dragún, the world that humans built and the kinds of social structures they invented were the repositories of the greatest tragedies of human experience. He emphasized this point because he believed that men and women were often forced to assume roles that oppose their natural potential. "Man is born to create," he said, but—for Dragún—humans had ceased to be creative. Instead, people often hid themselves, using external difficulties as a pretense for their masquerade. As Dragún put it, humans used one percent of their capacity creatively, and the remaining 99 percent merely satisfied fundamental needs that were too often banal. As soon as one chooses the banal, he or she has ceased to be:

> The terrible destruction which the human being is bringing about is his own animalization . . . or the transformation of natural elements into the domain of the unnatural. We have learned to accept things that are terribly unnatural.

THE MAN WHO TURNED INTO A DOG (1956)

The protagonists of this short play may be viewed as individuals who choose the unnatural, which brings about their dehumanization. Dragún's dramatic scalpel dissects each character's choices in light of the social realities that dictate those decisions. His is a social theater with characters who cry out for a better future and a release from the futility of their lives.

A look into how Dragún conceived the structure of *The Man Who Turned into a Dog* illustrates the importance he places on borrowing material from his surroundings:

> I had difficulty arriving at the exact structure of "Stories." . . . I had a general idea about a play that had to encompass many facets of a man working in Buenos Aires. I thought about bringing to the stage my own father. You see, my father is the protagonist of *Stories to be Told*. It is he who is depicted in "The Man Who Turned into a Dog." These dramatic moments were born from incidents in real life which were projected and deformed by my own imagination.

Dragún did not know exactly how to formulate a structure that would contain the many characters, settings, and props he had in mind. He remembers a visit to a public fair on the outskirts of Buenos Aires. While mingling with the crowd, the playwright became aware of three women who — grouped very close to one another — were discussing what seemed to be something extremely important. The image was a striking one for Dragún, who inched nearer so he could listen to their conversation:

> These three women then were gossiping back and forth, commenting about who had come to visit, what the visitors had said in the meantime . . . these women would speak about Aunt Julia, for example, by imitating her voice, they would mimic Uncle Ramon and, as they ceased their comments about the poor man, they would become themselves again.

Dragún had found his structure. Gossip was, he noted, a social necessity in Buenos Aires because people were compelled to "speak softly" in Argentina's repressive political climate.

Dragún's theatrical aesthetics relied on a simplicity born of his affinity for the carnivalesque and street theater—forms popular throughout Latin America. Dragún believed that the ideal playing area is an empty space that provides freedom for actors and audiences to use their imaginations. For Dragún, a stage cluttered with scenery and costumes could only present what is happening at a particular moment. Dragún's "empty space" could "present a reality based on the past, present, and the unreality of the future."

To successfully stage *The Man Who Turned into a Dog,* the emphasis must be placed on the art of the actor. Dragún emphasizes that actors involved in his plays must be carefully trained to physically compensate for the lack of costumes, scenery, and sophisticated lighting equipment. Since nothing external was available to Dragún's actors and director, they had to invent everything. The actors become the animals, the trees, the automobiles; their voices replaced electronic sound effects. Four performers were challenged to play as many as 15 parts within 45 minutes. In some cases, actors had only seconds to make transitions between characters.

The combination of an empty space and versatile acting created a dual freedom: freedom of expression for the artists and freedom of the imagination for the audience. This freedom of theatrical presentation corresponded to the quest for social and political freedom evident in Dragún's drama. It stemmed from the political exigencies of his native Argentina:

> Our theatre is not dependent on the stage, costumes, lights. . . . We can work anywhere. We can work on a patio or in a hen house, and we'll incorporate the chickens into our product. Our actors are always ready to change the structure of the play at any given time if the police enter the theatre. Our performers are used to going to the theatre and finding out that it has been shut down. So they ask permission to use roofs and patios. This has led our writers to write for a theatre that can be performed anywhere. But this has brought about freedom.

The Man Who Turned into a Dog is theatrically vivid and exuberant. The spectator is confronted with a protagonist who must make a choice that will provide some sort of financial compensation that allows him to continue living, even if it means becoming a working dog to gain employment. His choice, a tragic one indeed, provides him with the basic necessities. He is further cajoled into accepting the demeaning position by the vague promise of a human position later on. In the meantime, a deeper shattering of the human being occurs. The protagonist must learn not only how to bark but how to live in a doghouse and adapt to a diet of bones. In the course of the story, the central character undergoes both a physical and (importantly) a psychological change. He becomes accustomed not only to being manipulated, but to being manipulated as an animal.

The protagonist is plunged into a dark world in which inhuman treatment is a reality. If previously he fought against his position, he now accepts it without question. It is his reality, and he enters a world where, in truth, he is neither human nor dog. He barks and growls at humanity. He can no longer walk upright or act or think. He commits psychological suicide.

Dragún's tragicomedy provoked many questions. Who is to blame? The society that has inflicted such a high degree of dehumanization in order to hire cheap labor? The protagonist who accepts the role of the dog? Is survival so important that it must be bought with one's individuality? And finally, is money supreme to mankind? To these questions, the playwright suggested one troubling answer: "People are more preoccupied with what they have and not with what they are. This is absurd, tragically absurd."

Elenco Experimental performed The Man Who Turned into a Dog *in El Paso, Texas, on a bill of Osvaldo Dragún's* Stories to be Told *staged by Roberto D. Pomo.*

THE MAN WHO TURNED INTO A DOG

OSVALDO DRAGÚN

Translated by Roberto D. Pomo

ACTOR #2. Friends, a story. We shall tell it this way . . .

ACTOR #3. The way it was told to us this afternoon.

ACTRESS. It is the story of a man who turned into a dog.

ACTOR #3. It began two years ago . . . on a park bench. There, friends . . . where today you tried to discover the secret of a leaf.

ACTRESS. There . . . where we stretch our arms squeezing the world by its head and feet . . . as we say to it: "Play, accordion, play!"

ACTOR #2. We met him there . . .

Actor #1 enters.

He was . . . (*Pointing*) Just as you see him, nothing more. He was very unhappy.

ACTRESS. He was our friend. He was looking for work . . . and we were actors.

ACTOR #3. He had to support his wife . . . and we were actors.

ACTOR #2. He would dream of life . . . and wake up screaming at nights . . . and we were actors.

ACTRESS. Of course, he was our friend . . . just as you see him . . . (*Pointing*) Nothing more.

ALL. And he was very unhappy!

ACTOR #3. Time passed . . . Autumn . . .

ACTOR #2. Summer . . .

ACTRESS. Winter . . .

ACTOR #3. Spring.

ACTOR #1. It's a lie! I never knew spring.

ACTOR #2. Autumn . . .

ACTRESS. Winter . . .

ACTOR #3. Summer . . . And we returned. We went to see him . . . because he was our friend.

ACTOR #2. We asked . . . "Is he well?" His wife said to us . . .

ACTRESS. I don't know . . .

ACTOR #3. Is he ill?

ACTRESS. I don't know . . .

ACTORS #2 and 3. Where is he?

ACTRESS. In the dog pound.

Actor #1 positions himself on all fours.

ACTORS #2 and 3. Ohhh!

ACTOR #3. (*Watching him*). I'm the director of this dog pound . . . This appears to me . . . to be phenomenal. He arrived barking like a dog . . . (*Aside*) an essential requirement . . . and even though he wears a suit . . . he *is* a dog . . . No doubt about it.

ACTOR #2 (*Stuttering*). I . . . I . . . I . . . am the . . . the . . . vet . . . terina . . . rian . . . a . . . and . . . this is very clear t . . . t . . . to me . . . . Although he . . . he . . . looks . . . like a . . . a . . . ma . . . man, what we ha . . . have here is a dog!

ACTOR #1. As for me, what can I tell you? I don't know whether I'm a man or a dog. I believe that, in the end, not even you will be able to tell me . . . because everything began in an ordinary way. I went to a factory to look for work. I had been looking for three months . . . I couldn't get anything . . . I went to look for work.

ACTOR #3. Didn't you read the sign? NO OPENINGS!

ACTOR #1. Yes, I read it. Isn't there anything for me?

ACTOR #3. If it says 'No openings' . . . there are *no openings*!

ACTOR #1. Yes, of course. But isn't there anything for me?

ACTOR #3. Not for you or a cabinet minister!

ACTOR #1. I see. Isn't there anything for me?

ACTOR #3. NO!!

ACTOR #1. Machinist?

ACTOR #3. No!

ACTOR #1. Mechanic?

ACTOR #3. No!

ACTOR #1. General assistant?

ACTOR #3. No!

ACTOR #1. Mail boy?

ACTOR #3. No!

ACTOR #1. Janitor?

ACTOR #3. NOOO!

ACTOR #1. Night watchman! Night watchman . . . even if it's just a night watchman!

ACTRESS (*Imitating the sound of a bugle*). Tutu, tu-tu-tu-tu. THE FOREMAN!

Actors #2 and 3 speak by signaling to one another.

ACTOR #3. The night watchman's dog, friends, had died the night before . . . after twenty-five years of loyalty.

ACTOR #2. He was a very old dog.

ACTRESS. Amen!

ACTOR #2. (*To Actor #1*) Can you bark?

ACTOR #1. Machinist.

ACTOR #2. Can you bark?

ACTOR #1. Brick layer.

ACTORS #2 and 3. THERE ARE NO OPENINGS!

ACTOR #1. Bow-wow . . .

ACTOR #2. Very good! I congratulate you!

ACTOR #3. You'll get ten pesos a day, a dog house and food.

ACTOR #2. As you can see, he was making ten pesos . . . more than the actual dog did.

ACTRESS. When he came home, he told me about his new job. He was drunk.

ACTOR #1 (*To his wife*). But they promised me that as soon as an employee retires . . . or dies . . . or gets fired, I'll get his job. Ah, enjoy yourself, Mariá . . . enjoy yourself . . . Bow-wow . . . Enjoy yourself!

ACTORS #2 and 3. Bow-wow. Enjoy yourself, Mariá! . . . Enjoy yourself!

ACTRESS. He was drunk. Poor . . .

ACTOR #1. And that night I began to work

He gets down on all fours.

ACTOR #2. Is the dog house a bit small for you?

ACTOR #1. I can't bend over that far.

ACTOR #3. Is it tight here?

ACTOR #1. Yes.

ACTOR #3. Look don't tell me, "Yes." You have to begin to get used to it. Say . . . bow-wow!

ACTOR #2. Is it tight here?

Actor #1 does not respond.

Is it tight here?

ACTOR #1. Bow-wow . . .

ACTOR #2. Oh well. . . .

ACTOR #1. It rained that night. I had to get into the dog house.

ACTOR #2 (*To Actor #1*). Now . . . it isn't tight . . .

ACTOR #3. He's in his dog house.

ACTOR #2 (*To the audience*). You see how one gets used to everything?

ACTRESS. One gets used to everything. . . .

ACTORS #2 and 3. Amen . . .

ACTRESS. He began to get used to it.

ACTOR #3. . . . So when you notice that someone enters . . . you go . . . Bow-wow! Let me see.

Actor #2 runs by.

ACTOR #1. Bow-wow . . .

Actor #2 crosses slowly, silently.

Bow-wow . . .

Actor #2 bows down.

Bow-wow-wow . . .

Osvaldo Dragún

Actor #1 Exits.

ACTOR #3 (*To Actor #2*). It's ten extra pesos a day in our budget . . .
ACTOR #2. Hmm . . .
ACTOR #3. But the poor guy is so industrious . . . He deserves it.
ACTOR #2. Hmm . . .
ACTOR #3. Besides, he doesn't eat more than the dead one.
ACTOR #2. Hmm . . .
ACTOR #3. We ought to help his family!
ACTOR #2. Hm . . . hm . . . Hmmm . . .

They exit.

ACTRESS. Nonetheless, I knew he was sad. I would try to console him every time he came home . . .

Actor #1 enters.

We had visitors today . . .
ACTOR #1. Really?
ACTRESS. The dances at the club? You remember?
ACTOR #1. Yes.
ACTRESS. Which one was our tango?
ACTOR #1. I don't know.
ACTRESS. Of course you do . . .
"You told me that you loved me . . . !"

Actor #1 gets down on all fours.

And one day you brought me a carnation . . .

She sees him and is almost terrified.

What are you doing?
ACTOR #1. What?
ACTRESS. You're on all fours.
ACTOR #1. I can't stand it any more! I'm going to speak to the foreman!

Actors #2 and 3 enter.

ACTOR #3. But there's nothing else.
ACTOR #1. They told me that an old worker died.
ACTOR #3. Yes . . . but we're trying to economize. Wait a bit longer.
ACTRESS. He waited. He went back after three months.
ACTOR #1. They told me that someone retired. . . .
ACTOR #2. Yes, but we're thinking about closing that section. Wait a bit longer.
ACTOR #3. He waited. He went back after two months.
ACTOR #1. Give me the job of one of those who were fired because of the strike?
ACTOR #3. Impossible! Their positions will remain vacant . . .
ACTORS #2 and 3. As punishment!

They exit.

ACTOR #1. I couldn't stand it it any longer . . . I quit!

ACTRESS. It was our happiest evening in a long time.

She takes his arm.

What's the name of this flower?
ACTOR #1. Flower.
ACTRESS. And what is the name of that star?
ACTOR #1. Mariá.
ACTRESS (*Laughing*). Mariá is my name . . .
ACTOR #1. It's the star's, too . . . it's the star's, too!

He takes her hand and kisses it.

ACTRESS. Don't bite me!

She takes her hand away.

ACTOR #1. I wasn't going to bite you . . . I was going to kiss you, Mariá.
ACTRESS. Oh! I thought you were going to bite me.

They exit.

Actors #2 and 3 enter.

ACTOR #2. Of course . . .
ACTOR #3. The following morning . . .
ACTORS #2 and 3. He began to look for work again.
ACTOR #1. I went to various places, until . . .
ACTOR #3. Look, we have no openings . . . except for a . . .
ACTOR #1. WHAT?
ACTOR #3. The night watchman's dog died last night.
ACTOR #2. He was thirty-five years old, the poor thing.
ACTORS #2 and 3. Poor thing . . .
ACTOR #1. So I had to accept again.
ACTOR #2. But we paid him! Fifteen pesos a day!

Actors #2 and 3 turn away.

Hm . . . Hm . . . Hmm! Hmmm . . .
ACTORS #2 and 3. Hired! Let it be fifteen!

They exit.

ACTRESS. Of course, 450 pesos isn't enough to pay the rent.
ACTOR #1. Look, since I have the dog house, why don't you move into a place with maybe . . . four or five other girls . . . okay?
ACTRESS. There's no other solution. And since we don't have enough to eat . . .
ACTOR #1. Look, since I've gotten used to bones, I'll bring you the meat . . . okay?
ACTORS #2 and 3. The board of directors gave their consent!
ACTOR #1 and ACTRESS. They gave their consent. . . . Blessed by the board!

Actors #2 and 3 exit.

ACTOR #1. I had already gotten used to it. The dog house seemed bigger. To go around on all fours is no different than going around on two legs. As for Mariá, we'd meet in the plaza . . .

He crosses to her.

Since you can't fit into the dog house, and since I can't be in your room . . . Then one night . . .

ACTRESS. We were walking. Suddenly I felt terrible . . .

ACTOR #1. What's the matter?

ACTRESS. I feel dizzy.

ACTOR #1. Why?

ACTRESS (*Starting to cry*). I think . . . I'm going to have a baby . . .

ACTOR #1. So why are you crying?

ACTRESS. I'm afraid . . . I'm afraid . . .

ACTOR #1. But why?

ACTRESS. I'm afraid . . . I'm afraid. I don't want to have a baby.

ACTOR #1. And why not, Mariá? Why not?

ACTRESS. I'm afraid he'll be . . . (*In a whisper*) a dog.

He looks at her, frightened. He starts to exit, running, barking. He falls to the floor. She stands.

He went away. At times standing . . . then down on all fours . . .

ACTOR #1. It's a lie! I was never standing! I couldn't stand. My waist would hurt if I stood up. Bow-wow . . . Cars would almost run over me . . . People were looking at me . . .

Actors #2 and 3 enter.

Get out of here! Haven't you ever seen a dog?

ACTOR #2. He's crazy! Call a doctor!

He exits.

ACTOR #3. He's drunk! Call a policeman!

He exits.

ACTRESS. Afterwards, they told me that a man who took pity approached him kindly . . .

ACTOR #2. Are you sick, my friend? You can't stay on all fours like that. Do you know how many beautiful things you can see standing up? With your eyes always upward? Come on, stand up . . . I'll help you . . . Come on, stand up . . .

ACTOR #1. (*He begins to stand up.*) Bow-wow . . .

Suddenly, he bites the other.

Bow-wow . . .

Actor #1 exits.

Actor #3 enters.

ACTOR #3. Anyway, after two years without seeing him, we asked his wife . . . "How is he?" She answered . . .

ACTRESS. I don't know.

ACTOR #2. Is he well?

ACTRESS. I don't know.

ACTOR #3. Is he ill?

ACTRESS. I don't know.

ACTORS #2 and 3. Where is he?

ACTRESS. In the dog pound.

ACTOR #3. And while we were coming here, a boxer passed us by . . .

ACTOR #2. They told us he couldn't read . . . and that it didn't matter since he was a boxer.

ACTOR #3. A draftee went by . . .

ACTRESS. A policeman went by . . .

ACTOR #2. They all went by . . . they all went by . . . they all went by . . . And you all went by . . . and we thought that maybe you would care about our friend's story . . .

ACTRESS. Because . . . who knows, maybe there's a woman among you who's thinking . . . "What if I have a . . . (*In a whisper*) dog?"

ACTOR #3. Or someone among you who's been offered a job as a night watchman's dog?

ACTRESS. If there's no one . . . we're glad.

ACTOR #2. But if there is someone among you who would like to turn into a dog . . . like our friend did . . . then . . . well . . . that's another story to be told.

BLACK OUT

SPOTLIGHT   POPULAR THEATER IN LATIN AMERICA

Spanish colonialists brought theater to Central and South America. Therefore, it is not surprising that many Latin American theater forms, especially in the southernmost regions of South America, can be traced to Europe. Mexican playwright Octavio Paz calls another theater form *mestizo* ("mixed-blood") theater, that is, one in which the rituals and theatrical ceremonies of indigenous peoples such as the Maya and Aztecs have been combined with Spanish drama to create a "mixed" theater with a singular identity. And particularly in Brazil and the Caribbean, the African influence in the theater is strong. However, each of these forms has assumed an identity of its own and reflects the political and cultural realities of the people who attended the theater.

Popular entertainments, of which there are numerous types, have thrived in Latin America, largely because much of the population has not been formally educated. Accordingly, entertainment has been aimed at a working class, much the way Pixérécourt's melodramas catered to the tastes of Parisian laborers. Consider but a few of the many and fascinating entertainments developed in Latin America.

The *Costumbrista*

Costumbrista is a generic term referring to popular entertainments that feature local manners and customs of the common people. Though they were disdained by the upper classes, they thrived among the workers because they portrayed situations and local conflicts of the commoners, and, importantly, because they used colloquial speech. Most *costumbristas* were short and comical, not unlike any number of contemporary sitcoms on television. Each country, indeed regions within a country, developed a unique version of the *costumbrista*, which formed the bases for national theaters throughout the Latin world. By 1915 *costumbristas* became anachro-

nistic to the Latin American public, but collectively they established a foundation on which subsequent theater would be based.

The *Zarzuela*

The *zarzuela*, a type of musical much lighter in tone and spirit than the opera, evolved in Spain during the seventeenth century. Drawing on the older *entreméses* (interludes) and *sainetes* (short farces), both of which had musical passages, Pedro Calderón developed these short, mostly comic playlets based on classical myths. Calderón began writing *zarzuelas* about 1652 at the request of King Felipe IV, whose royal hunting lodge, La *Zarzuela* (for the *zarzas*, or brambles, that surrounded it), hosted the first of these musical entertainments. The earliest *zarzuelas* were quite elaborate, akin to the Italian *intermezzi* and English masques. In the 1760s the *zarzuelas* turned to popular culture for subject matter and often reflected the lives of families in the cosmopolitan world of Madrid. By 1787 *zarzuelas* disappeared from the Spanish stage, but were rediscovered in the mid–nineteenth century, when they enjoyed a golden age. Folk music and dance were incorporated into the *zarzuelas*, particularly by Francisco Asenjo Barbieri (1823–1894), who wrote some 60 musicals, including *Pan y toros* [*Bread and Bulls* (1864)] and *Jugar con fuego* [*Playing with Fire* (1851)].

The Spanish brought the *zarzuela* to their colonies in Latin America, where *zarzuelas bufas* (comic musicals) and *bailetes* (dance musicals) became popular among immigrants and indigenous peoples, particularly in Mexico. The most notable theatrical event in Mexico City in 1806 was a performance of a musical adaptation (by Paisiello) of the Beamarchais comedy *The Barber of Seville*. Billed as "a comic opera in four acts," the piece was clearly in the *zarzuela* tradition. This opera *con zarzuela* remained popular among the

citizens of the capital, and it was repeated with Mexican songs (*sonecitos del pais*). Throughout the Caribbean and South America one can still find both the *zarzuela* proper (a three-act musical) and the *zarzuela chica* (the "little *zarzuela*," or one-act musical), which frequently relies on audience participation.

The *Revista*

Brazil, South America's largest country, has its own rich musical theater tradition that has been influenced by the song, dance, and storytelling of Africa. In 1861 Carlos Gomes (1836–1886) wrote Brazil's first opera, *A noite de castelo* (*A Night in the Castle*), which deals with Brazil's identity as an emerging nation in the Southern Hemisphere. The *revista*, a musical review adorned by expensive and sophisticated costumes and scenery, is Brazil's variant on the zarzuela. As Brazilian music has influenced much popular music (especially jazz), the *revista* has had an international impact.

Gaucho Drama

South America developed a dramatic version of the American western, especially in Argentina and Uruguay, where the gaucho ruled the pampas. Like the American cowboy, the gaucho was a romantic symbol of the rugged individual who tamed a harsh land. He also enjoyed an almost mythic status among city dwellers who envied his ability to fly with the wind on his horse. Predictably, a national drama evolved celebrating the gaucho, his love of the land, and his freedom. Whereas the American western glorified men who conquered the frontier, the gaucho drama challenged European conquests and argued for a national identity. Gaucho drama represents the first truly national (i.e., non-Eurocentric) drama in South America in its celebration of the common worker on the pampas.

Fittingly, a former president of Argentina, Domingo Faustino Sarmiento, best defines the mythic appeal of the *gauchesco* character. In 1845 this former miner and bartender wrote *Facundo*, the most eloquent treatise on Argentina's gaucho writing. Of the *gauchesco*, he says:

> He is a type that belongs to certain localities, an outlaw, a squatter, a misanthrope. . . . He knows the reality of the desert. His morality is natural . . . justice pursues him always. . . . He is a mysterious character who often roams the Pampas. He partakes of vices, but points his horse in the direction of the desert, without a sense of rush. . . . Sometimes he appears at the door of a country-dance, with a young maiden he has whisked away. Other times, he appears in front of the offended and seduced maiden's parents. This man is divorced from society, a savage in white face. He is not a bandit, nor a highwayman; he's a horseman.

Although Sarmiento sings of his Argentine countrymen, his remarks could apply to the American cowboy, especially those antiheroes popularized in the films of Clint Eastwood.

Immigration Plays

Much of Latin America, like the United States, saw an influx of immigrants from Europe and elsewhere. Though they sought riches and political freedom, they often found hardship and alienation. Among the most poignant immigration plays were the *Cocoliche* dramas of Argentina. In the 1870s the Podestá brothers, who owned a popular circus, added review sketches and variety acts as part of their tent entertainments. Among their most popular skits were those that dealt with a character named *Cocoliche*, an Italian immigrant who sought a more profitable life in the Americas. Cocoliche was a hard-working, well-intentioned laborer who was also comic, largely because of his linguistic difficulties. The Podestá skits blossomed into full-length plays depicting the misadventures of Cocoliche, whose very name became synonymous with the genre. Though the impulse behind the *Cocoliches* was comedic and escapist, a serious—and political—current nonetheless reflected the unpleasant realities of a changing world.

Similarly, Cuba developed a peculiarly potent form of populist entertainment that reflected social and political realities. Much like the American minstrel show, the *bufo Cubano* (also known as the *bufos Habañeros* after the capital, Havana) featured white performers in blackface to depict the various races that composed Cuba's population. There was the *gallego* (the Spaniard), the *negrito* (the African), and *chinos* or *mulattos* (persons of mixed ethnicity). Although the *bufo Cubano* enjoyed its greatest popularity from about 1869 to 1878, it continued into the twentieth century. Fidel Castro's 1959 revolution was, in part, precipitated by the Cuban people's resentment of the Eurocentrism that created and sustained the *bufo Cubano*.

Zambia's popular Chikwakwa Traveling Theater Company performs The Trial of Zwangendaba *(1976), which fuses contemporary politics and traditional African theater practice.*

CHAPTER 8

THE THEATER OF AFRICA AND THE AFRICAN DIASPORA

As it has been for thousands of years, contemporary African theater and drama is markedly functional (as opposed to diversionary) because within its many communities it serves a purpose beyond mere entertainment. While it may often draw upon the traditional forms and performance styles of its colonial past, African drama is a rich amalgam of ancient and modern influences. Because Africa is an enormous continent comprising many countries and distinct cultures, it is inaccurate to imply too homogeneous a view of African theater. Nevertheless, an indisputable vitality and urgency characterizes late-twentieth-century theater throughout Africa.

Colonial policies, especially in education, brought Western-style drama to Africa, but there has also been a fortuitous enrichment of Western culture by Africans displaced by the diaspora—the enforced resettlement of indigenous peoples through slavery. The diaspora is a name applied to the capture and redistribution of Africans during the seventeenth and eighteenth centuries. Traditionally, the Diaspora is the name given to the migration of the Jews from their homeland in biblical times, but today the word also refers to the dispersion of a variety of peoples because of political turmoil, war, or economic explotation. David Henry Hwang's play *The Dance and the Railroad* (Chapter 9) is based on the Chinese diaspora, when thousands of Chinese were imported as cheap labor for the American railroad. However, diaspora, as it is used here, refers specifically to the forced relocation of African slaves from the sub-Sahara.

Though the diaspora remains an ignoble tragedy for the continent, people of African heritage have significantly contributed to the arts and other endeavors wherever they were settled. Jazz (and its derivatives, rhythm and blues, and rock and roll) is perhaps the best-known by-product of the fusion of traditional African music and that of other cultures. Artists whose roots may be traced to Africa have particularly enriched theater in the United States, the Caribbean, and Latin America. Of late, the British theater has enjoyed the influence of writers and artists from Africa and the West Indies; Mustapha Matura from Trinidad has been especially successful at adapting European works, such as Synge's *The Playboy of the Western World*, to the idioms of the Caribbean.

Plays by Lorraine Hansberry, Amiri Baraka (née LeRoi Jones), August Wilson, George C. Wolfe, and Derek Walcott are included in this anthology to complement those of such admired African playwrights as Wole Soyinka, Barney Simon, Percy Mtwa, and Mbongeni Ngema. The white South African playwright Athol Fugard employs distinctly European forms in his passionately antiapartheid dramas; his plays have been produced throughout the world and are among the very best works in the contemporary theater.

AFRICA

Artistic and Cultural Events

2500 B.C.E.:
Abydos Passion Play; variety of rituals, ceremonies, masquerades, spirit cult performances throughout Africa

1880s:
Missionaries use theater for conversions

1947:
National Theater Organization founded in South Africa

1965:
Makerere Travelling Theater Company founded in East Africa

1970s:
Township theater flourishes in South Africa

1986:
Soyinka wins Nobel Prize

c. 3000 B.C.E.:
Pyramid texts

1801:
First European theater in Cape Town, South Africa

1930s:
First plays published by native black Africans

1958:
Experimental theater in Ghana

1966:
First African Arts and Cultural Festival

1976:
Market Theatre opens in Johannesburg

Pre-Nineteenth Century   1800 C.E.   1900 C.E.

Historical and Political Events

1844–1845:
European nations partition Africa in Berlin

1960:
Independence of Nigeria, Camaroon, and Mali

1976:
Soweto Riots in South Africa

1830s:
Africa opened for exploration by Europeans

1957:
Independence of Ghana

1963:
Independence of Kenya

1994:
Apartheid abolished in South Africa

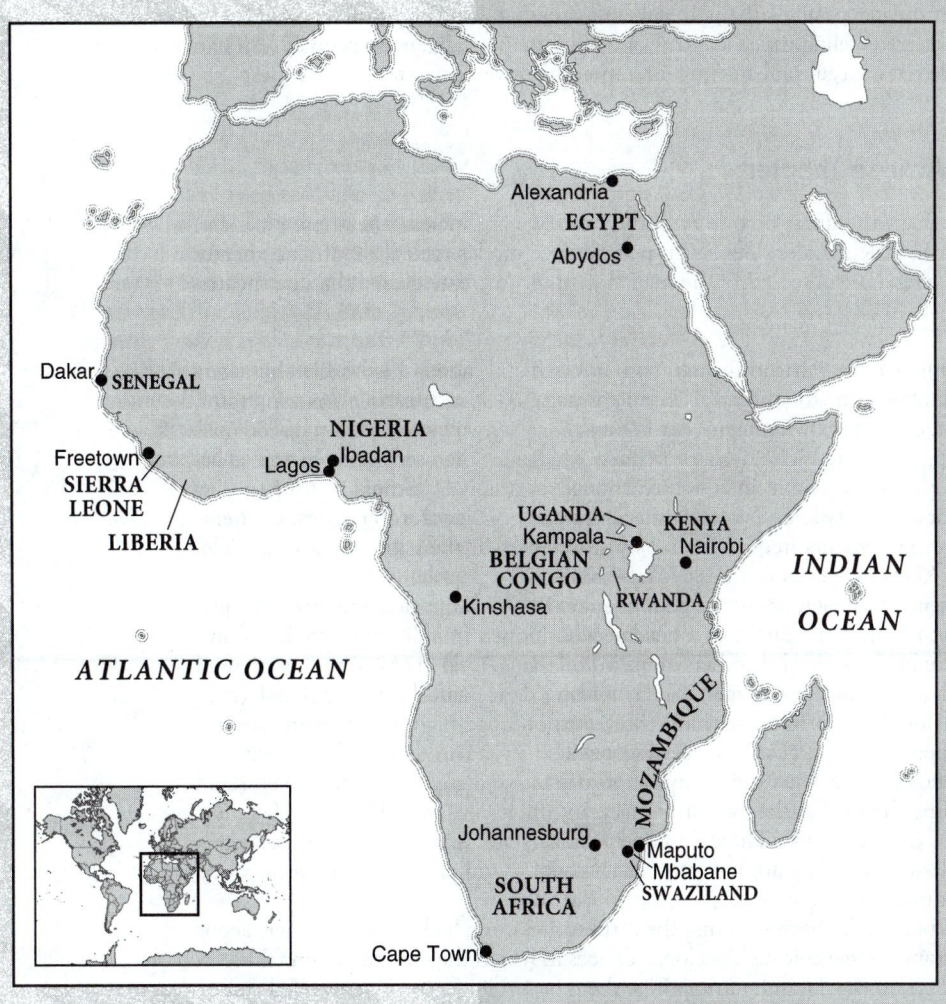

Alexandria
EGYPT
Abydos

Dakar● SENEGAL

NIGERIA

Freetown● ●Ibadan
Lagos●
SIERRA
LEONE

LIBERIA

UGANDA
Kampala● ●KENYA
Nairobi●
BELGIAN
CONGO
RWANDA

Kinshasa●

ATLANTIC OCEAN

INDIAN

OCEAN

MOZAMBIQUE

Johannesburg●
●Maputo
Mbabane
SWAZILAND
SOUTH
AFRICA

Cape Town●

The history of the theater in Africa—particularly that of the sub-Sahara—is complex. Though its theatrical roots are ancient, written drama by black Africans is largely a twentieth-century phenomenon. Prior to this time, formal drama was largely the product of European colonists, but since the late 1950s, native black Africans (as opposed to Africans of European descent, such as Athol Fugard) have used drama as a political tool. Accordingly, the evolution of contemporary African theater parallels the political emancipation of much of the continent. As European colonists have relinquished control of Africa to its indigenous peoples, African drama has reasserted its own cultural and linguistic integrity by returning to its theatrical roots.

The Roots of African Theater

Africa remains perhaps the finest repository of the world's most ancient theatrical practices. Cultural historian E. T. Kirby identifies seven performance modes typical of African theater that, collectively, offer a useful review of the human instinct to create events that are theatrical:

1. *Storytelling performances:* African theater, both ancient and modern, is largely characterized by its emphasis on storytelling. Central to many African theatricals is a narrator, often the *griot*, or "healer," who improvises a story (however well known) to the accompaniment of song and dance. The narrator frequently assumes the voice and physical characteristics of the many people in his story, though occasionally others leap in to play particular characters. Masks and costume pieces may distinguish the characters. Contemporary African playwrights frequently employ storytellers in their dramas; for example, *Death and the King's Horseman* features a "Praise Singer."

2. *Simple enactments:* Bushmen improvise performances in which hunting animals is the primary plot. For instance, a man wears a headpiece fashioned from a forked stick and impersonates a kudu antelope while others mime killing him. A group of young boys pretend to be dogs that accompany the men. Such hunting dances are both functional (they promise food for the tribe) and spiritual (they acknowledge higher powers in nature). Other enactments are more clearly social in scope. The Shona use simple plays in which a woman pretends to cook as part of an initiation rite for young girls. Other women scold her for sampling the food as they smear her face with flour and warn her that "You must not eat before your husband." These unscripted dramas are as basic a form of theater as can be found; at heart, they are imitation games such as children might perform while learning their roles in society.

3. *Ritualized enactments:* We have seen that the earliest rites often had an aura of magic about them. For instance, some cultures developed dances in which they imitated rain falling in the hope that nature would, in return, imitate them by sending rain. This is called *sympathetic* (or *homeopathic*) *magic*, one of earliest forms of theatrical activity. Numerous examples of such ritual activity are found throughout Africa today. The Loga of Central Africa have a lengthy initiation ritual in which important artifacts are paraded through the village while proverbs are sung. A processional dance leads the villagers to a specially constructed initiation hut; the participants climb upon the roof while eight proverbs are chanted. The "magic" occurs when the malevolent spirits are driven from the hut and when good spirits enter the bodies of the Loga.

4. *Spirit cult performances:* A medium, thought to be possessed by spirits, assumes a "character" while in a trance. Dressed in striking costumes and speaking in a "spirit language," the medium performs gestures so extraordinary that they give the illusion that the spirit, or even a god, is actually present. There is strong dramatic interaction between the character and the audience, most of it improvised by the medium. Such performances are so common among the people of western Uganda that anthropologist John Beattie refers to them as their "traditional national theater." A spirit called a *shave*, recognizable by his white shirt, hat, and belt, possesses mediums of one east African community. Drinking, dancing, and dialogue mark the trance ceremony with the spirits. Slaves brought spirit

cult performances to the Americas. For instance, the Macumba of Brazil still use spirit performances in healing ceremonies. The medium customarily becomes one of four identifiable characters: an old slave (a reminder of past suffering); a native (who embodies pre-Columbian glory); a temptress (the spirit of fertility and pleasure); and, perhaps most intriguing, the trickster, a symbol of mischief who figures prominently in world drama.

5. *Masquerades:* Masquerades, evolved from ceremonials performed by secret societies to honor the dead, remain perhaps the most representative form of indigenous African theater. Enormous and colorful masks, large costumes (often made of wicker or grass), and vigorous dancing and other mimetic actions characterize masquerades. Frequently, a dramatic narrative holds them together. Ibibio masquerades even improvise comic skits. The costumes used at Carnival in Trinidad (see Center Stage box, The Trinidad Carnival, at the end of this chapter). are remnants of such masquerades, brought by slaves to the Americas.

6. *Ceremonial performances:* Like so many other indigenous theatricals in Africa, singing, dancing, and the beating of drums accompany ceremonial performances. The Dogon of West Africa celebrate a Festival of the Dead each year, a ceremony in which the feats of ancestors are recalled. There are nightlong mock battles, acrobatic dances, and a display of weapons meant to teach the Dogon respect for its past and acceptance of the inevitability of death.

7. *"Comedies":* Perhaps the theatrical activities most closely resembling a play as we understand the term are comedies performed in open spaces in the villages of many African tribes. These performances may have evolved from simple enactments or masquerades into plays with a discernible plot and characterization. Just when this happened we cannot ascertain, but the presence of these comic playlets suggests the process by which formal drama has developed around the world. Coincidentally, many of the characters appearing in these comedies are African versions of popular comic characters found in ancient Rome, Renaissance Italy, Chinese opera, and Japanese *kyógen* (farces), not to mention American TV sitcoms. The Mande-speaking people of West Africa perform comedies portraying a deceiving wife, a gullible husband, a bragging warrior, and a trickster-thief. Though they are painted with clay or white ash, these village actors are no less appealing to their audiences than the comedians of Italy's *commedia dell'arte* or the *chou* (clown) of Chinese opera. The comedies use dialogue, frequently improvised, and may be accompanied by singers and an orchestra. Men frequently play women's roles, a convention we find throughout world theater, particularly in those cultures in which women are not permitted to act. Like comedy everywhere, the African plays portray the social aspects of village life. In one comedy, a husband working in the fields with his wife burns a pile of stalks under which his wife's lover is hidden. The piece ends with a comic chase as the transgressor flees both the irate husband and the flames. Like all good comedy, the plays are intended, in Walter Kerr's words, "to show the cracks in the human façade."

Postcolonial Drama in Africa

By the 1880s sub-Saharan Africa was largely in the control of European powers including England, France, Germany, and the Netherlands. The British established colonies in South Africa much earlier in the nineteenth century, and by 1801 a theater had been established in what is now Cape Town. In 1884–1885 the Europeans divided their African colonies among themselves in Berlin. Consequently, formal drama in Africa was virtually a European enterprise, though records indicate native black Africans improvised plays in the nineteenth century. Christian missionaries also used drama as a means of converting black Africans; *The Redemption*, for instance, contributed to the Christianization of Rwanda. Note that Amiri Baraka's *The Slave Ship* attacks Christians for subverting traditional African religious practices.

We do not find plays published by native black Africans until the 1930s, and there is little significant publication and production of black African plays until the 1950s. The drama of black Africans developed in three significant stages:

- Plays in which black Africans attempt to show they have assimilated the culture of the colonists; these dramas show an indebtedness to European dramaturgy. Popular European plays, such as those by Oscar Wilde, Bernard Shaw, and the operettists Gilbert and Sullivan, were often the staples of colonial African theater, whether performed by Europeans or black Africans.
- Plays in which the colonized dramatists display an uncertainty about their status and attempt to recover their native past and its forms. Because of a Eurocentric educational system, plays still rely on an essentially Old World dramaturgy.
- Plays that revolt against colonization, both politically and aesthetically. Here dramatists purposefully employ traditional African theater modes as they write plays designed to rouse the people against colonization. In 1956 the West African playwright Aime Cesaaire wrote a play in which the central character, the Rebel, tells his oppressors: "Leave me alone, leave me to shout enough to intoxicate myself with that cry of revolt, I wish to be alone under my skin, I recognize no one's right to live in me."

Hubert Ogunde (Nigeria), Ngugiwa Thiong'o (Kenya), and Herbert Dholmo (South Africa) were among the first black African playwrights to achieve international respect for dramas about the liberation of Africa.

In 1966 the First World Festival of Negro Arts was held in Dakar, Senegal (formerly French West Africa), and in 1977 a Black and African Festival of Arts and Culture (FESTAC) convened in Lagos, Nigeria. In many ways, these events signaled the arrival of contemporary black African theater and arts as entities liberated from the Eurocentric tradition that dominated African stages for over a century. There exist relatively few outlets for contemporary African drama in the West because of translation and publication problems. The best-known work comes from Nigeria and South Africa, though playwrights such as Jacob Hemvi in Uganda are enjoying international publication and production. Within the next decade we can expect greater accessibility to contemporary African drama and theater.

While there is a distinctly commercial theater throughout Africa the most famous of which is the Market Theatre in South Africa (see Spotlight box, South Africa's Market Theatre and the Independent Theater Phenomenon, following the text of "MASTER HAROLD" later in this chapter), much contemporary African drama emerges from three significant sources:

1. *Universities:* Although many African universities were established by colonialists and retain an educational system based on European models, the majority of Africa's most accomplished dramatists (and directors and actors) have emerged from such universities as Makerere University (Uganda), which served all of East Africa until the breakup of the East African community in the 1950s. Ibadan University (Nigeria) encouraged the early work of Soyinka and John Pepper Clark-Bekederemo. The University of Zimbabwe (formerly Rhodesia) introduced a full theater curriculum in 1984 and has produced much of that country's best drama, a phenomenon that has been repeated throughout much of modern Africa.
2. *Traveling theater companies:* Numerous companies, such as Zambia's Chikwakwa Theater (1971) and the Yoruba Traveling Theater (Nigeria, c. 1955), take plays into rural areas to entertain and, more importantly, to instruct villagers about a variety of social, political, and cultural issues. Often theater artists elicit commentary and solutions from the audience as they improvise their works.
3. *Village and community theater:* Although the roots of such enterprises may be traced to precolonial times, black Africans seeking to restore their culture have revitalized popular theater. To non-Africans, the township plays of South Africa (see Center Stage box, South African Township Theater, following the text of *Woza Albert!* later in this chapter) are the best-known forms of community-created theater, though numerous varieties can be cited throughout the continent. In Niger—formerly a French colony in West Africa that was liberated in 1960—youth groups (*samariyas*) who speak in their native Hausa perform "ballets." These dramas are performed in government-constructed youth centers or in open spaces in the villages. In Togo, once a German colony, "concert parties" are

popular mass entertainments (despised by the literate elite). They are composed of "high-life" music, skits and storytelling, and improvised plays on topical issues; the language is a blend of native Ewe and pidgin colonial dialects.

The Conventions of African Theater

While realistic theater in the Euro-American mode exists in Africa, most African theater is presentational and uses conspicuously theatrical conventions. Narrators, storytellers, and praise singers guide the action; actors frequently play multiple roles and address the audience directly. African dramatists and performers do not distance themselves from their people, and they do not write abstruse material for the learned elite; rather, they continue the tradition of the *griot* as they chronicle the history and concerns of their audiences. There is often considerable interaction between performers and the audience, which is free to respond verbally to the action onstage. Song, dance, and poetry are used freely in both scripted and improvised performances. Traditional, as well as contemporary, masks remain central to much African theater. Scenery and costumes may be found, but financial constraints often require simple settings that use "found" objects and selective costuming. This is particularly apparent in community theater. It is the energy and vitality of the actors—and their interplay with the audience—that provides the appeal of African theater.

Theater throughout Africa is performed in a variety of spaces, from sophisticated, modern theaters that rival those found in Europe and America to open spaces in courtyards and platform stages erected in the round. Because African audiences are participating audiences, vocally and even physically, often no conspicuous attempt is made to separate the audience from the performers. To do so would kill the spirit of the theater whose very roots depended on the interaction between performer and audience.

Aided by a chorus of women bearing baskets, actors perform an antelope dance during a political rally in Mali. "Street theater" is common in African villages that may not have formal performance spaces.

WOZA ALBERT!

PERCY MTWA, MBONGENI NGEMA, BARNEY SIMON

PERCY MTWA (1951 –), MBONGENI NGEMA (1955 –), BARNEY SIMON (1933 –)

Percy Mtwa was born and raised in Wattville, Benoni, where he began his theatrical career as a dancer and musician. At the age of 17 he formed his own group, Percy and the Maestros, which brought him to the attention of playmaker Gibson Kente, the father of township theater. Kente gave Mtwa a role in the musical *Mama and the Load* in which Ngema also performed. While touring throughout South Africa, the two young actors began improvising material that eventually became *Woza Albert!* Later they formed their own company, The Earth Players. The international success of *Woza Albert!* encouraged Mtwa to write and direct *Bopha!* ("Arrest") in 1985, another successful township-style play about a black policeman forced to arrest his own son.

Mbongeni Ngema, born near Durban, South Africa, is best known to European and American audiences as the creator-director of *Sarafina!*, a lively musical about the Soweto uprising of 1976. That play, which enjoyed a lengthy run in London's West End and on Broadway, was made into a motion picture featuring Whoopee Goldberg and Ngema himself as the villain. After a series of roles as a musician and actor in Durban, Ngema earned his first stage role in Johannesburg in *Mama and the Load,* where he met Mtwa. Ngema visited the United States where he saw the work of Luis Valdez's Teatro Campesino (see Chapter 9). Valdez' politically edged satire inspired Ngema to form his own company, Committed Artists, which has emerged as one of South Africa's best known political theaters. It has produced such works as *Asinamali!* (1985), which exposes the intolerable prison conditions facing black South Africans; *Sarafina!* (1987); *Township Fever* (1990), which deals with the violence filled railway strikes; and *Magic at 4:00 a.m.* (1993), which is a celebration of township life. In these works, Ngema freely mixes Zulu and pop music, humor, and scathing social commentary. In addition to his writing, acting, and directing credits, Ngema is a record producer who has encouraged the development of South African musicians.

Barney Simon is a founder (with Manny Manim) and artistic director of the Market Theatre, among the most influential theaters in the world in the late-twentieth century (see Spotlight box, South Africa's Market Theatre and the Independent Theatre Phenomenon). In the 1950s Simon apprenticed under Joan Littlewood, a British stage director noted for her politically caustic, yet highly entertaining productions. In London, he also saw Brecht's Berliner Ensemble in 1956, an event that profoundly affected his vision of the theater's potential as a political weapon. After his London years, Simon returned to his native South Africa, and in the early 1960s met Athol Fugard, whom he directed as an actor and encouraged as a playwright. He also encouraged Mtwa and Ngema as they developed *Woza Albert!* and helped them shape the work into its present form. Simon has spent considerable time in the United States, working with such diverse alternative theater companies as Teatro Campesino, the San Francisco

Mime Troupe, and Amiri Baraka's Spirit House. Although Simon has won numerous awards for his stage direction and as a producer, his legacy will remain the Market Theatre, the prototype of interracial theater in South Africa.

WOZA ALBERT! (1980)

Woza Albert! was conceived in 1979 while two of its authors, Percy Mtwa and Mbongeni Ngema, were touring the South African townships in Gibson Kente's *Mama and the Load.* So committed to their idea were these artists that they abandoned the security of regular wages for the two-year run of Kente's show and threw themselves into their project. With neither financial support nor rehearsal and performance facilities, they lived hand to mouth on the meager support of a few businessmen. Following their arrest for subversive activity, for which they spent 30 days in solitary confinement, they lost what little support they had. Businessman Vusi Magudulela came to their rescue, paying them 30 rands ($10) a week as they continued to develop their production. Following a year of rehearsal, they were joined by Barney Simon, artistic director of Johannesburg's Market Theatre. With Simon's direction and financial backing, *Woza Albert!* premiered to critical acclaim at the Market Theatre in 1980. Following a successful run at the Market, the play toured Europe and won a Fringe First Award at the Edinburgh Festival. In 1986 it was presented at Lincoln Center in New York City as part of the Woza Afrika! Festival.

True to the spirit of township theater, the play uses music and character transformations to depict a mixture of hilariously funny and poignant scenes performed by a collection of characters in motley costumes in front of tattered scenery. Combined, these elements provide insight into township life and the inequities of apartheid.

Like many satiric comedies, *Woza Albert!* is based on a singular premise: "What if the Second Coming had taken place in 1980 in South Africa?" *Woza Albert!* portrays the reactions of the South African people to the Second Coming of "the Morena" (Savior). The play consists of three types of scenes: those representing life in the townships; those representing the return of Morena; and those scenes in which the actors/characters present their point of view directly to the audience. Often all three types of scenes commingle in a mixture of representational and presentational drama.

The action progresses through a series of scenes in which one character is a sympathetic believer and another character is a skeptical antagonist. Throughout the play the actors, who go by their own names, play both themselves and a variety of roles, often within a single scene. In the "Brick Yard Scene," for example, Percy alternates between playing the white boss, Baas Kom, and a black laborer, Bobbejaan, more than a dozen times and then concludes the scene as a police car. Meanwhile, Mbongeni sustains a dialogue between a black laborer, Zuluboy, and the imaginary Morena, concluding the scene with a Zulu war dance. All this transpires in ten to twelve minutes of stage time. At the end it is Percy, who has mostly played the sympathetic believer, who becomes Morena; Mbongeni, who mostly has played the skeptic, continues in that role as Zuluboy. He is finally convinced of Morena's Second Coming, and joins Percy as they conjure such revolutionary heroes of black South Africa as Steve Biko[1] and Albert Luthuli. ("Woza Albert!" literally means "Rise up Albert!," a reference to Luthuli, the early antiapartheid leader who served as president of the African National Congress and who received the Nobel Peace Prize in 1960.)

We move from the predictions of Morena's Second Coming through the rumors of his imminent arrival to descriptions of his appearance and actions. The play ends with his triumph over the evil forces of apartheid and the resurrection of the country's black heroes. Interspersed throughout are alternating comic and touching scenes depicting the depressing and meager existence of life in the township and on the streets of Johannesburg. In each vignette, the plight

---

[1] A founder of the black consciousness movement and first president of the South African Students' Organization who was beaten to death by the security police.

of the people and their needs is illustrated. In response to the question "What shall I ask from Morena if he comes to South Africa?", the poor invariably say they would request very little. The meatseller says he would ask for "good luck, so that the people that come will buy all this meat . . . [And for Morena] to take me to school, Sub-A [kindergarten]"; Auntie Dudu says she would ask him for "lots of food here—cabbages, tomatoes, chicken, hot dogs, all the nice things white people eat"; and the barber says he would ask him "to build me a barbershop . . . and [for] customers with big hair!" These petitions are not for riches and luxuries, but instead are requests for the very things that black South Africans have sought since colonization.

Pictures of these indigent scavengers are paralleled with those of people lucky enough to have a work permit. As Mbongeni points out in scene 16, having a permit does not guarantee a job, nor does it give the worker respectability. When Percy brags about his work permit—his "six month special!"—Mbongeni reiterates their predicament: "Have you got a job? Have you got school fees for your children? Have you got money for rent? Have you got bus fare to come to the Pass Office? Oh, come on man, we've all got specials [permits] but we're still their dogs!" Even when they have jobs, the wages are inadequate, the working conditions poor, the relationship with the "Boss" tenuous, and job security nonexistent. As with the indigent, the laborers' requests are simple—a decent day's wages and a life with their families.

While the blacks' requests are simple, Percy and Mbongeni present a different perspective of the government. After boasting that "Morena is back and South Africa has got him . . . [because] he chose us!", Pretoria tries to impress him by showing off the natural and man-made wonders of the Republic of South Africa. Ironically, each reflects ongoing exploitation: the game reserves (the blacks' original hunting grounds), the gold and diamond mines (where the blacks unearth the great riches while working under inhuman conditions), the Government Gardens of Pretoria (built and manicured by black laborers), and, of course, SUN CITY—THE LAS VEGAS OF SOUTH AFRICA! (where the wealthy indulge themselves with the fruits of their exploitation).

But with unyielding optimism, Mbongeni points out that Morena looks beyond the façade presented by the government:

> I pass people who sit in dust and beg for work that will buy them bread. And on the other side I see people who are living in gold and glass and whose rubbish bins are loaded with food for a thousand mouths. . . . I see families torn apart, I see mothers without sons, children without fathers, and wives who have no men!

Of course, Mbongeni's prediction comes true. In spite of being repeatedly imprisoned, Morena reappears to carry out the epiphany at the end of the play.

While many black South Africans, including Desmond Tutu and Nelson Mandela, are Christians to whom the Second Coming of the Savior holds significance, many others do not share these beliefs. Can they relate to the play? Can it speak for and to them? Perhaps. A less literal reading of the play accommodates a figurative savior—freedom, the dream common to all black South Africans. Such an interpretation may even strengthen the play's message. Morena is characterized by the government as a "cheap imposter . . . a cheap communist magician [sent] to pose as the Morena, and undermine the security of our nation," yet the people see him as indestructible and omnipotent. When he raises the dead and reinvigorates the dreams of the people, the practices of the old Pretoria government appear even more abominable. The many inequities enumerated by Mbongeni in his description of Pretoria's exploitation would be obliterated by freedom. The dreams of Albert Luthuli, Steve Biko, Hector Peterson,[2] and the rest of those who rise up in the finale will be resurrected when freedom is finally established. In fact, all of the dreams for the "New South Africa" are possible only with the second coming of freedom.

---

[2]The first of many students killed by the police in the school boycott of June 1976. This event led to the Soweto uprising and the political unrest that eventually overturned South Africa's apartheid laws.

South African actor Rapulana Seiphemo (bottom) joins American Clinton Sam in a bit of improvisation in the opening scene from Woza Albert! in a production staged by Roger Schultz at Texas A&M University in 1993.

WOZA ALBERT!

——PERCY MTWA, MBONGENI NGEMA,——
BARNEY SIMON

CHARACTERS
PERCY MTWA
MBONGENI NGEMA

The stage is lit by the house-lights. The set consists of two up-ended tea-chests side by side about center stage. Further upstage an old wooden plank, about ten feet long, is suspended horizontally on old ropes. From nails in the plank hang the ragged clothes that the actors will use for their transformation. The actors wear grey track-suit bottoms and running shoes. They are bare-chested. Around each actor's neck is a piece of elastic, tied to which is half a squash ball painted pink—a clown's nose, to be placed over his own nose when he plays a white man.

1259

SCENE ONE

The actors enter and take their positions quickly, simply. Mbongeni sits on the tea-chests at the point they meet in the middle. Percy squats between his legs. As they create their totem, the house-lights dim to blackout.

On the first note of their music, overhead lights come on, sculpting them. They become an instrumental jazz band, using only their bodies and their mouths—double bass, saxophone, flute, drums, bongos, trumpet, etc. At the climax of their performance, they transform into audience, applauding wildly.

Percy stands, disappears behind the clothes rail. Mbongeni goes on applauding. Percy reappears wearing his pink nose and a policeman's cap. He is applauding patronisingly. Mbongeni stares at him, stops applauding.

PERCY. Hey! Beautiful audience, hey? Beautiful musician, né? Okay, now let us see how beautiful his pass book is! (*To appalled Mbongeni:*) Your pass!

MBONGENI (*playing for time*). Excuse my boss, excuse? What?

PERCY (*smugly, to audience with his back to Mbongeni*). Okay, I'll start again. You know you're a black man, don't you?

MBONGENI. Yes, my boss.

PERCY. And you live here in South Africa?

MBONGENI (*attempting to sidle off-stage behind Percy's back*). Yes, my boss.

PERCY. So you know that you must always carry your pass.

MBONGENI. Yes, my boss.

PERCY. Okay, now what happens if you don't have your pass?

MBONGENI. I go to jail, my boss.

PERCY. And what happens if your pass is not in order?

MBONGENI (*nearly off-stage*). I go to jail, my boss.

PERCY (*wheels on Mbongeni*). H-E-E-E-Y! Your pass!!!

MBONGENI (*effusively*). OOOOhhh, my pass, my constable! (*Moves to Percy, holding out his pass.*) Here's my pass my lieutenant.

PERCY. Okay, now let's have a look. (*Examines the pass.*) Where do you work?

MBONGENI. I work here, my Captain.

PERCY. You work here? If you worked here your passbook would be written 'Market Theatre, Johannesburg'. But look, it is written 'Kentucky Southern Fried'. Is this Kentucky Southern Fried? And look at the date. It tells me you haven't worked in four years. This is vagrancy, you're unemployed. (*To audience:*) Ja, this is what I call 'loafer-skap!'

MBONGENI. No, my Colonel, I am a guitarist, I've been playing music for five years, my boss.

PERCY. Hey, you lie, you fuckin' entertainer!

MBONGENI. It's true, it's true, my boss.

PERCY. Can you show me where it is written 'musician'? Hey? Where's a guitar? Where's a guitar? Where's a guitar?

MBONGENI. Ag, nee—my Brigadier, I am self-employed!

PERCY. Self-employed? (*Chuckling collusively to audience:*) Hell, but these kaffirs can lie, hey?

MBONGENI. Maar, dis die waarheid, but it is true—my General!

PERCY. You know where you should be?

MBONGENI. No, my boss.

PERCY. You should be in prison!

MBONGENI. No, my boss.

PERCY. And when you come out of prison, do you know where you should go?

MBONGENI. No, my boss.

PERCY. Back to the bush with the baboons. That's where you belong! Kom hierso! Section 29. (*To audience, pleasantly:*) Do you know about Section 29? That's a nice little law specially made for loafers like him. And I've got a nice little place waiting for him in Modder-B Prison. Kom jong! (*Pulls Mbongeni by his track-suit.*)

MBONGENI (*aside*). Shit!

PERCY (*threatening*). What did you say? Wat het jy gesê?

MBONGENI. Nothing—my President!

The policeman (Percy) chases the musician (Mbongeni) behind the clothes-rail.

SCENE TWO

Enter both actors with prison blankets wrapped around their shoulders. Both are singing a prison song, a prisoner's fantasy of his woman's longing for him:

SONG.

      Ha-ja-ka-rumba
      Ha-ja-karumba

(Solo) Bath'uyeza—uyez'uyezana?
      Bath'uyeza—uyez'uyezana?
      Kuthima ngizule kodwa mangicabanga
      Yini s'thandwa sithando sami ye—

(Chorus) Hajakarumba—hajakarumba.
      Hajakarumba—hajakarumba.
      [They say he is coming. Is he really coming?
      I am mad when I think of it.
      Come back my love, oh my love.]

Under the song, Mbongeni gives orders:

MBONGENI. Modder-B Prison . . . prisoners—line up! Body Inspection. Hey wena cell number 16. Inspection cell number 16. Awusafuni na? Awusafunukuvula vula hey wena wendola. Vul'ingqwza sisbone. [Hey you, cell number 16. Inspection cell number 16. Are you hiding anything? Don't you want to show what is hidden—come on you men—show me your arses!] Prisoners inspection!

BOTH (*doing 'Towsa' dance, revealing empty orifices and armpits*). Ready for body inspection, my Basie! Blankets clear, my Basie! No tobacco! No money! No watch! My Basie! Mouth clear! Ears clear! (*Open mouths wide:*) Hooo! Hooo! (*Pull ear-lobes:*) Haaa! Haaa! My Basie!

PERCY. Hands up!

BOTH (*raise arms*). Arms clear, my Basie! (*Raise legs:*) Everything clear, my Basie! Also arse, my Basie!

MBONGENI. Inspection! (*They pull down their trousers, display bare backsides.*) See nothing hidden, my Basie! Prisoners! Lights out! (*Lights dim.*)

BOTH (*lying on the floor covering themselves with blankets*). Goodnight, Basie, goodnight. Dankie Baba, dankie. Beautiful arse, my Baba. Nothing hidden, my Basie.

Lights dim on sleeping figures.

SCENE THREE

PERCY (*singing in his sleep*). Morena walks with me all the way / Watching over me all the day / When the night time comes he's there with me / Watching over, loving me.

MBONGENI (*restless, stirring from sleep*). Hey man uyangxola man—uyangxola man. [Hey man, you making noise man.]

The singing continues.

MBONGENI. Hey! Hey, hey! Stop singing your bloody hymns man, you're singing in your bladdy sleep again! Morena! Morena hoo-hoo, there's no Morena here!

PERCY (*dazed*). I'm sorry. (*Silence. He begins to hum again.*)

MBONGENI (*kicks Percy, who jumps up, is chased*). Hayi man—isejele la. [This is prison man.]

PERCY (*cowering*). Morena, the saviour, is watching over you too, my friend.

MBONGENI. Morena, the saviour, here in Modder-B Prison? BULLSHIT!

Lights up bright. Work yard. Actors holding picks.

MBONGENI. Prisoners! Work yard!

BOTH (*working and singing a work-song*).
Siboshiwe siboshel'wa mahala
Wen'utha senzenjani
Siboshiwe siboshel'wa mahala
Wen'utha senzenjani
[They arrested us for nothing
So what can we do?]

Mbongeni hurts his hand, nurses it.

MBONGENI. It's this bladdy hard labour!

PERCY (*attempting comfort*). Don't worry my friend. Morena is over there, he's watching over us.

MBONGENI. Morena. Here in prison?

PERCY. He's watching over you too.

MBONGENI (*kicking at him, chasing him*). Morena here?? BULLSHIT!!

SCENE FOUR

MBONGENI. Prisoners! Supper!

BOTH (*running*). Supper! Supper! Supper!

Transforms to supper-time. Prisoners racing around in a circle, carrying plates, handing them in for food. Mbongeni bullies Percy out of the way.

PERCY. Thank you, soup, Baba. Thank you, Baba.

MBONGENI. Soup, Baba. Thank you soup, Baba, thank you Baba.

PERCY. Porridge, Baba. Little bit of sugar, Baba.

MBONGENI. Porridge, Baba! Porridge. A little bit of sugar, Baba. A little bit of sugar, Baba. Thank you, Baba.

PERCY. A little bit sugar, Baba. Please, little bit, Baba. Thank you, Baba. Thank you, Baba, too much sugar, Baba.

MBONGENI. Sugar . . . (*Reaches for Percy's food. Percy points to a guard, stopping Mbongeni who smiles to the guard.*) No complaints, my boss. Geen klagte nie.

PERCY. No complaints, Baba.

Mbongeni eats in growing disgust; Percy with relish.

MBONGENI (*spits on the floor*). Ukudla kwemi godoyi lokhu [This is food for a dog]—No, a dog wouldn't even piss on this food. Ikhabishi, amazambane, ushukela, ipapa, utamatisi endishini eyodwa—ini leyo? [Cabbage, potatoes, sugar, porridge, tomatoes in one dish—what is this?]

PERCY (*eating unconcerned*). Thank you Morena for the food that you have given me. Amen.

MBONGENI (*turns on him, furious*). Hey uthini Amen? [What do you say Amen for?]—For this shit? Thank you Morena for this shit?

Percy crawls away. Mbongeni beckons him back.

MBONGENI. Woza la! [Come here!]

Percy hesitates.

MBONGENI (*moves threateningly; points to the ground at his feet*). Woza la!

Percy crawls over reluctantly.

MBONGENI. On your knees!

Percy, terrified, gets down on his knees.

MBONGENI. Pray! Mr Bullshit, I'm getting out of here tomorrow. Pray to your Morena, tell him thanks for me. I'll never listen to your voice again!

Mbongeni pushes Percy forward on to the floor. Percy goes down with a scream that becomes a siren.

Blackout.

SCENE FIVE

The siren transforms into train sounds. Lights up. Both men are sitting back-to-back on boxes, rocking as in a train. Mbongeni is reading a newspaper, Percy a Bible. Mbongeni spits out of the window, sits again.

PERCY (*evangelically*). Bléssed are those that are persecuted for righteousness' sake, for theirs is the Kingdom of Heaven. Bléssed are ye when men shall revile ye and persecute ye and shall send all manner of evil against ye falsely, for thy sake. Rejoice, and be exceedingly glad for great is the reward of heaven. For so persecuted they—

MBONGENI (*turns on him, hits him on the head with newspaper*). Hey! Persecuted! Prosecuted! Voetsak! Voetsak! (*Recognises his former fellow prisoner:*) Hey, brother Bullshit! When did you come out of prison? They promised me they would keep you in for life!

PERCY. Be careful, my friend, of the anger in your heart. For Morena will return and bear witness to our lives on earth and there will be no place to hide. He will point his holy finger and there will be those who rise to heaven and those who burn in hell. Hallelujah! I hope you're not one of them!

MBONGENI. Rise to heaven? Where is heaven?

PERCY. It is the Kingdom of God.

MBONGENI. Up there? Neil Armstrong has been there.

PERCY. Neil Armstrong?

MBONGENI. Hallelujah! He's been right up to the moon and he found a desert, no god!

PERCY. My brother, I don' care what you or your friend on the moon say, because I know that he will return to his father's kingdom on earth, even as I know that his father has heard your blasphemies and forgiven you!

MBONGENI. Where does his father live? In Jerusalem?

PERCY. The Lord, our father, is everywhere.

MBONGENI. And Morena, the saviour, is coming to South Africa?

PERCY. Hallelujah!

MBONGENI. How is he coming to South Africa? By South African Airways jumbo jet? (*He transforms into a photographer photographing the audience.*) And everybody will be waiting in Johannesburg at Jan Smuts airport. Pressmen, radiomen, South African television, international television, ABC, NBC, CBS, BBC, and they will all gather around—(*He turns to Percy, who has transformed into the Prime Minister with pink nose and spectacles.*)—our honourable Prime Minister!

SCENE SIX

PERCY (*moving forward ingratiatingly into spotlight*). Thank you very much, thank you very much. My people, Morena is back and South Africa has got him! I hope that the free world will sit up and notice whose bread is buttered and where! Let them keep their boycotts, their boxers, rugby players, and tennis racketeers. Stay home Larry Holmes! Stay home John McEnroe! We have got Morena! But there is already rumours going around that this is not the real Morena, but some cheap impostor. And to those that spread such vicious rumours I can only say, 'Tough luck friends! He chose us!' (*Raises his hands in V-signs, laughs.*)

Blackout.

SCENE SEVEN

Lights up on Mbongeni wearing a Cuban army cap and smoking a fat cigar.

PERCY (*as announcer*). And now ladies and gentlemen, on the hotline straight from Havana—the comrade from Cuba—Fidel Castro! Sir, have you got any comment to make on the impending visit of Morena to South Africa?

MBONGENI (*laughing*). Morena in South Africa? Who's playing the part? Ronald Reagan?

Blackout.

SCENE EIGHT

Lights up on Percy playing cool bongo on boxes.

MBONGENI (*dancing flashily*). And now for you to see on Black TV—the face of Black South Africa! (*Enjoying the bongo, dancing up to the player.*) Beautiful music my brother, cool sound, man, cool! Real cool! Beautiful music, oh yeah, oh yeah. Now tell me, my brother—what would you say—if Morena—walks in—right through that door?

PERCY (*making a rude finger-sign*). Aay, fok off man!

Blackout.

SCENE NINE

Lights up bright on Percy, now a young street meat-vendor. The boxes are his stall. He is swatting flies with a newspaper held in one hand. His other hand holds a second newspaper as shade against the sun.

MBONGENI (*enters, singing, as a labourer-customer*)
(Song): Siyitshil'igusha sayigqiba
Siyitshil'igusha sayigqiba
Muhla sitsh'igusha.
Wena wendoda wawuphina
Wena wendoda wawuphina
Muhla sitsh'igusha.
[We ate and finished a big sheep the other day. Where were you when we blessed ourselves with a sheep?]

MBONGENI. Hullo, my boy.

PERCY. Hello, Baba.

MBONGENI (*not tempted by the display*). Ehhh, what meat can you sell me today?

PERCY. I've got mutton, chicken, and nice sausages. (*Swats a fly on the sausages.*)

MBONGENI. Oh yeah . . . the chicken does not smell nice, hey? Must get some cover, some shade from the sun, hey? (*Deliberating.*) Ehhh, how much are those chops?

PERCY. It's two rand fifty, Baba.

MBONGENI. Two rand fifty? Are they mutton chops?

PERCY. Ehhh, it's mutton.

MBONGENI. No pork?

PERCY. No pork, Baba. I don't like pork.

MBONGENI. Okay my boy, give me mutton chops. Two rand fifty, hey? Where's your mother, my boy?

PERCY. She's at work.

MBONGENI. She's at work? Tell her I said 'tooka-tooka' on her nose. (*Tickles the boy's nose.*) She must visit me at the men's hostel, okay? Dube hostel, room number 126, block 'B', okay? Bye-bye, my boy. 'B', don't forget. (*About to leave, he turns astonished at sight of—invisible—TV interviewer.*)

PERCY (*awed by TV interviewer*). Hello, Skulu. I'm fine, thanks. And you? (*Listens.*) Morena? Here in South Africa? What shall I ask from Morena if he comes to South Africa? Baba, I want him to bring me good luck. So that the people that come will buy all this meat. And then? I want him to take me to school. Sub-A, uh huh. (*Watching the interviewer leave.*) Thank you, Baba. Inkos'ibusise [God bless]. Yeah, Baba . . . Au! TV!

Blackout.

SCENE TEN

Lights up, dim, on Mbongeni as Auntie Dudu, an old woman, wearing a white dust-coat as a shawl. She is searching a garbage bin (upturned box). She eats some food, chases flies, then notices the interviewer. She speaks very shyly.

MBONGENI. Hey? My name is Auntie Dudu. No work my boy, I'm too old. Eh? (*Listens.*) If Morena comes to South Africa? That would be very good. Because everybody will be happy and there will be lots and lots of parties. And we'll find lots of food here—(*Indicates bin.*)—cabbages, tomatoes, chicken, hot-dogs, all the nice things white people eat. Huh? (*Receives tip.*) Oh, thank you, my boy. Thank you, Baba. Inkos'ibusise. [God bless.] God bless you. Bye bye, bye bye . . .

A fly buzzes close. She chases it.

Fade.

SCENE ELEVEN

Lights up bright on a barber's open-air stall. Percy—the barber—is sitting on a box, Mbongeni—the customer—between his knees. Auntie Dudu's shawl is now the barber's sheet.

PERCY. Ehh, French cut? German cut? Cheese cut?

MBONGENI. Cheese cut.

PERCY. Cheese cut—all off!

MBONGENI (*settling*). That's nice . . . How much is a cheese cut?

PERCY. Seventy-five cents.

MBONGENI. Aaay! Last week my cousin was here and it was fifty cents.

PERCY. Hey, you've got very big hair my friend. (*He begins cutting hair.*)

MBONGENI (*squirming nervously during the—mimed—clipping, relaxing at the end of a run*). That's nice. What machine is this?

PERCY. Oh, it's number ten . . .

MBONGENI. Number ten? Ohhh.

PERCY. Though it's a very old clipper.

MBONGENI. That's nice. (*More cutting, more squirming.*) That's nice. Where's your daughter now?

PERCY. Ohh, she's in university.

MBONGENI. University? That's nice. What standard is she doing in university?

PERCY (*clipping*). Ohhh, she's doing LLLLLB. I don't know, it's some very high standard.

MBONGENI. Oh yeah, LLB.

PERCY (*confirming with pleasure*). Uh huh, LLB.

MBONGENI. That's nice! I remember my school principal failed seven times LLB!

PERCY. Ohhh, I see! I understand it's a very high standard.

MBONGENI. Tell me my friend, but why don't you apply for a

barbershop? Why do you work in the open air where everyone is looking?

PERCY (*continuing clipping*). Aaahh, don't ask me nonsense. I had a barbershop. But the police came with the bulldozers during the Soweto riots.

MBONGENI. Ooohh, 1976?

PERCY. Uh huh. During the times of black power. Everything was upside down . . . (*To the invisible interviewer as he enters:*) Oh, hello, Skulu. I'm fine, thanks. And you? (*Listens.*) Morena? Here, in South Africa?

MBONGENI. That's nice.

PERCY (*clipping, talking excitedly*). Well now, I want him to build me a barbershop in a very big shopping center in Johannesburg city, with white tiles, mirrors all over the walls, and customers with big hair! (*The clipper gets caught in Mbongeni's hair. He struggles.*)

MBONGENI. EEEEeeeeiiiiii!

Blackout.

SCENE TWELVE

Lights up. Percy and Mbongeni are coal-vendors, soot-stained sacks on their heads. They are climbing onto boxes—a coal lorry—taking off.

PERCY & MBONGENI. Hey! Firewood for sale! Coal for sale! Smokeless coal for sale! Firewood for sale! (*They make the sound of the lorry's engine revving. The lorry moves off.*)

PERCY. *Coal for sale!* Hey wena, Auntie Ma-Dlamini, phum'endlini. [Hey, you, Aunt Dlamini, come out of your house.] (*He spies a young girl, gestures.*) Dudlu—mayemaye, the sugar the pumpkin. [Hallo there, hi hi, you are the sugar, the pumpkin.]

MBONGENI. Red light! Hey wena! [Hey you!] Driver—awuboni irobbot? [Can't you see the red light?]

PERCY. Don't you see the red light?

MBONGENI. Awuboni la uyakhona? [Don't you see where you're going?]

PERCY. He hasn't got a license.

Noise of the lorry revving. They discover the invisible interviewer below, turn to him impatiently.

PERCY. What? Morena here in South Africa? You're talking rubbish! (*Lorry sounds again. It jerks forward.*) Smokeless coal for sale! Firewood for sale! (*Looks back.*) Putsho putshu ikaka kwedini. [You're talking shit, boy.]

MBONGENI. Inkanda leyo-kwedini-iyashisa he? [Your prick is hot, boy—heh?]

Percy looks back contemptuously and makes a rude sign with his finger as the lorry drives off.

Fade.

SCENE THIRTEEN

Lights up on Mbongeni entering as a fragile, toothless old man. He sings throughout the following action. He settles on the boxes, attempts to thread a needle. His hands tremble but he perseveres. He succeeds on the third, laborious attempt and begins to sew a button on his coat.

MBONGENI (*humming*).
Bamqalokandaba bayimpi
Heya we-bayimpi izwelonke
Ngonyama ye zizwe
Ohlab'izitha
UNdaba bamgwazizwe lonke okazulu
Amambuka nkosi

[The soldiers of our enemies have come to attack the king
They are coming from the four corners of the world to attack the Lion
We must kill the enemies
They are attacking him from all over the world, the son of Zulu
These strangers from another place attack our King.]

Mbongeni becomes aware of the (invisible) interviewer. Laughs knowingly.

MBONGENI (*speaking*). Eh? What would happen to Morena if he comes to South Africa? What would happen to Morena is what happened to Piet Retief! Do you know Piet Retief? The big leader of the white men long ago, the leader of the Afrikaners! Ja! He visited Dingane, the great king of the Zulus! When Piet Retief came to Dingane, Dingane was sitting in his camp with all his men. And he thought, 'Hey, these white men with their guns are wizards. They are dangerous!' But he welcomed them with a big smile. He said, he said, 'Hello. Just leave your guns outside and come inside and eat meat and drink beer.' Eeeeii! That is what will happen to Morena today! The Prime Minister will say, just leave your angels outside and the power of your father outside and come inside and enjoy the fruits of apartheid. And then, what will happen to Morena is what happened to Piet Retief when he got inside. Dingane was sitting with all his men in his camp, when Piet Retief came inside. All the Zulus were singing and dancing . . . Bamqalokandaba bayimpi . . . (*Repeats snatches of the song.*) And all the time Dingane's men were singing and dancing. (*Proudly*) they were waiting for the signal from their king. And Dingane just stood up . . . He spit on the ground. He hit his beshu and he shouted, 'Bulalan'abathakathi. Kill the wizards! Kill the wizards! Kill the wizards!" And Dingane's men came with all their spears. (*Mimes throat-slitting, throwing of bodies.*) Suka! That is what will happen to Morena here in South Africa. Morena here? (*Disgusted.*) Eeii! Suka!

Blackout.

SCENE FOURTEEN

Lights flash on, Percy, an airport announcer, is standing on a box, calling out.

PERCY. Attention, please! Attention, please! Now this is a great moment for South Africa! The Lord Morena has arrived! The jumbo jet from Jerusalem has landed! Now lay down your blankets, sing hosanna, hosanna, lay down your presents. Hey, you over there, move away from the tarmac! (*More urgently.*) Move away from the runway! Move away!

MBONGENI (*rushing in as a photographer*): Hosanna! Hosanna! Son of God! 'Hosanna nyana ka thixo!' ['Son of God'.] Hey, what will you say if Morena comes to you? (*To a member of the audience:*) Smile, smile! (*He turns to Percy then back to the camera crew.*) Sound! Rolling! Slate! Scene twenty-seven, take one. And action . . .

SCENE FIFTEEN

Percy, wearing his pink nose and flash sunglasses, alights from the plane (box).

MBONGENI (*approaching him with a mimed microphone*). Happy landings, sir.

PERCY (*flattered by this attention*). Oh, thank you. Thank you.

MBONGENI. Well sir, you've just landed from a jumbo jet!

PERCY. Eh, yes.

MBONGENI. Any comments, sir?

PERCY. I beg your pardon?

MBONGENI (*arch interviewer*). Would you not say that a jumbo jet is faster than a donkey, sir?

PERCY. Eh, yes.

MBONGENI. Aaahh. Now tell me, sir, where have you been all this time?

PERCY. Around and about.

MBONGENI. And how is it up there in the heavens?

PERCY. Oh, it's very cool.

MBONGENI. Cool! (*laughs artificially loud*) So, I'm to understand that you've been studying our slang, too!

PERCY. Right on!

They laugh together.

MBONGENI. Now tell me, sir, in the face of all boycotting moves, why did you choose South Africa for your grand return?

PERCY. I beg your pardon?

MBONGENI. I mean, uuuh, why did you come here, sir?

PERCY. To visit my Great-aunt Matilda.

MBONGENI. Excuse me, sir?

PERCY. Yes?

MBONGENI. Your name, sir?

PERCY. Patrick Alexander Smith.

MBONGENI. You mean you're not Morena, sir?

PERCY. Who?

MBONGENI. Morena.

PERCY. Morena?

MBONGENI. Are you not Morena? (*To film-makers:*) Cut!!! Morena! Where is Morena? (*Percy minces off, insulted. Stage dim. Mbongeni wanders across stage, calling disconsolately.*) Morena! Morena! Morena! M-o-o-o-r-e-e-n-a-a-a! . . .

Lights dim. Percy begins to join the call, alternating, from behind the clothes rail. He emerges calling and addressing a high and distant Morena. As he talks, the lights come up.

SCENE SIXTEEN

PERCY. Morena! Morena-a-a! Where are you? Come to Albert Street! Come to the Pass Office! We need you here Morena! Ja, Morena, this is the most terrible street in the whole of Johannesburg! Ja, Morena, this is the street where we Black men must come and stand and wait and wait and wait just to get a permit to work in Johannesburg! And if you're lucky enough to get the permit, what happens? You wait and wait and wait again for the white bosses to come in their cars to give you work. (*Turns back to Mbongeni.*) But I'm lucky! I've got six months special! (*Shows his passbook.*) Qualified to work in Johannesburg for six months!

MBONGENI. How many months? Eh?

PERCY. Six months!

MBONGENI. Six months? Congratulations. (*Laughs, slaps Percy's back, shakes his hand.*) Eh! Six month special!

PERCY. Three weeks in a queue!

MBONGENI. But you're still their dog! (*Moves upstage to urinate, with his back to the audience.*)

PERCY. Aaahh, jealous! You jealous!

MBONGENI. Have you got a job? Have you got school fees for your children? Have you got money for rent? Have you got bus fare to come to the Pass Office? Oh, come on man, we've all got specials but we're still their dogs!

Car sounds.

PERCY (*leaps up*). Hey! There's a car! A white man! (*Moves to the car at the front edge of the stage, follows it as it moves across.*) Are you looking for workers, my boss? Ya, I've got six month special, qualified to work in Johannesburg.

Mbongeni moves forward trying frantically to distract the driver. Car sounds continue, actors alternating.

MBONGENI. Boss, I've got fourteen day special. This is my last chance. This is my last chance. Take two boys, my boss, two!

PERCY. Messenger boy, tea boy, my boss. One! I make nice

tea for the Madam, my boss. Bush tea, China tea, English tea! Please, Baba. Lots of experience, Baba. Very good education; my boss. Please my boss. Standard three, very good English, Baba.

Mbongeni's sound of a departing car transforms into a mocking laugh.

MBONGENI. I told you, you're still their dog! (*Laughs, mocks.*) Standard three, bush tea, China tea—where do you get China tea in Soweto?

PERCY. Aah voetsak! [I've got six months special!]

MBONGENI (*shows Percy his pass book*). Hey, look at my picture. I look beautiful, heh?

PERCY (*laughs bitterly*). How can you look beautiful in your pass book?

Car sounds again. Mbongeni rushes forward to the stage edge, follows the car, Percy behind him.

MBONGENI. One! One, my boss! Everything! Sweeper, anything, everything, my boss! Give me anything. Carwash? Yeah, always smiling, my boss. Ag, have you got work for me, my boss? I'm a very good nanny. I look after small white children. I make them tomato sandwich. I take them to school, my boss. Please, my boss. Please.

Car leaves. Mbongeni wanders disconsolately upstage. Percy watches him.

PERCY (*laughing*). Ja! Who's a dog? Don't talk like that! This is South Africa! This is Albert Street. (Laughs.) Nanny, nanny, tomato sandwich!

Car sounds again.

BOTH ACTORS (*confusion of requests from each*). Six month special, my boss. Fourteen day special, Baba. This is my last chance. Hey man, this is my corner! Very strong, Baas. Ek donder die kaffers op die plaas. [I beat up the kaffirs on the farm.] One, my boss. Two, my boss. Anything, my boss. Have you got anything for me, Baba?

PERCY. Basie, he's a thief, this one.

MBONGENI. He can't talk Afrikaans, this one, my boss.

PERCY. He's lying, Basie. Hy lieg, my baas!

The third car pulls away.

PERCY (*confronting Mbongeni angrily*). Hey, this is my corner, these are my cars. I've got six months special.

MBONGENI. Hey! Fuck off! I stand where I like, man.

PERCY. You've got fourteen day special. There's your corner.

MBONGENI. Hey! You don't tell me where to stand!

PERCY. You've got fourteen day special. You're not even qualified to be on Albert Street.

MBONGENI. Qualified? Qualified? Wenzani uthath'a ma shansi hey uthatha ma shansi. [What are you trying to do? You taking chances. Hey? You taking chances.]

Mbongeni kicks Percy. Percy turns on him.

PERCY. Baas Piet! Baas Piet! I'll tell Baas Piet you got forgery.

MBONGENI (*mimes picking up stone*). Okay, okay. Call your white boss! I've got friends too!

PERCY. Baas Piet!

MBONGENI (*beckons his friends, wildly picking up stones*). Hey Joe! We Joe! Zwakala—sigunu mfwethu. (To Percy:) Angihlali eZola mina—angihlali eMdeni mina—Joe zwakala simenze njalo. [Joe come here—It's happening. (To Percy:) I don't live in Zola—I'm not from Mdeni—Joe come here let's work on him.]

Mbongeni quietens, struck by something in the audience.

PERCY (*Muttering sulkily*). These are my cars, man. I've got six month special, these are mine. This is my corner—That's the temporal corner! I'll tell Baas Piet!

MBONGENI (*now totally stunned by what he is watching*). Heeey, heeey! Ssh man, ssh.

PERCY (*cautious*). What?

MBONGENI (*indicating the audience*). Morena . . .

PERCY. Aaay, fok off!

MBONGENI. It's Morena—that one there with the white shirt.

PERCY (*doubtfully*). Morena? Ay, nonsense . . . Is it Morena?

MBONGENI. It's him—I saw him in the *Sunday Times* with Bishop Tutu. It's him!

He sidles forward to the edge of the stage. Percy shyly eggs him on.

PERCY. Hey, speak to him.

MBONGENI (*nods with the invisible Morena*). Excuse. Are you not Morena? Yiiiii! Hosanna! Morena!

The actors embrace joyously. They follow Morena, frantically showing their passes and pleading.

BOTH ACTORS. Morena, look at my pass book!

PERCY. I've got six month special but I can't find work.

MBONGENI. I've been looking here two months, no work. Take us to heaven, Morena, it's terrible here.

Mbongeni follows Morena. Percy falls behind.

PERCY. Temporary or permanent is okay Morena! (*Silence as Mbongeni converses with Morena. He comes back exhilarated.*) Hey, what does he say?

MBONGENI. He says let us throw away our passes and follow him to Soweto!

PERCY. Hey! He's right! Morena! Morena!

BOTH ACTORS (*sing, exhorting the audience*).

Woza giya nansi inkonyane ye ndlovu—
Aph'amadoda sibabambe sebephelele.
Wozani madoda niyesaba na?

[Come on join this child of an elephant
Where are the men? Let us face them!
Come men, are you afraid?]

PERCY (*under the song*). Morena says throw away your passes and follow him to Soweto.

MBONGENI. We are not pieces of paper, man! We are men!

PERCY. Ja! Let them know our faces as Morena knows our faces!

MBONGENI. Morena says no more passes!

PERCY. Ja!

MBONGENI. We don't have numbers any more!

PERCY. Ja!

MBONGENI. Let them look at our faces to know that we are men.

PERCY. Ja! When we follow Morena we walk as one!

The actors throw away their passes and their song transforms into train sounds.

SCENE SEVENTEEN

The actors mime standing beside each other at a train window. They wave to people outside.

PERCY. Hey madoda! Sanibona madoda! May God bless them! Ja, you've got a very good imagination. I really like your stories. But you must go to church sometimes—Hey, there's a train coming! (*Looks to one side.*)

Flurry of their faces and noises as they mime watching adjoining train pass. Then they pull their windows up. Siren. Mbongeni moves downstage. Percy stands on a box, begins Regina Mundi Song:

> Somlandela—somlandela u Morena
> Somlandela yonke indawo
> Somlandela—somlandela u Morena
> Lapho eyakhona somlandela.
>
> [We shall follow—we shall follow Morena
> We shall follow him everywhere
> We shall follow—we shall follow Morena
> Where-ever he leads—we shall follow.]

While the song continues:

MBONGENI (*joyous siren*). Ja, madoda, hundreds of thousands will gather at the Regina Mundi Church in the heart of Soweto. And people will sing and dance. There will be bread for all. And wine for all. Our people will be left in peace, because there will be too many of us and the whole world will be watching. And people will go home to their beds.(*He joins in the song for a few phrases.*) These will be days of joy. Auntie Dudu will find chicken legs in her rubbish bin, and whole cabbages. And amadoda—our men—will be offered work at the Pass Office. The barber will be surrounded by white tiles. The young meat-seller will wear a nice new uniform and go to school, and we will all go to Morena for our blessings. (*Song subsides.*

Percy lies on boxes as sleeping woman. Lights dim.) And then . . . the government will begin to take courage again . . . The police and the army will assemble from all parts of the country . . . And one night, police dogs will move in as they have done before. There will be shouts at night and bangings on the door . . .

PERCY (*banging on a box*). Hey! Open up, it's the police! Maak die deur oop! Polisie!

MBONGENI (*ducking down by the boxes as if hiding beside a bed*). . . . There will be sounds of police vans and the crying of women and their babies.

PERCY (*turns over on the boxes as an old woman waking in bed, starts crying and calling in Zulu*). We Jabulani, hayi-bo-hey-hey-we-Nonoza, akenivule bo nanka amaphoyisa esesihlasele, we Thoko akenivule bo. Auw-Nkosi-Yami, ezingane ze-Black Power! [Hey, Jabulani, Hey no, hey-hey, Nonoza, open the door, can't you hear the police are here. They've come to attack us. Thoko, please open the door. Oh my God, these children of Black Power!]

He goes to open the door. Throughout Mbongeni tries to stop him.

MBONGENI. Sssh Mama! Tula Mama! Mama! Mama! Leave the door! (*Mbongeni gives up, stands silent, transfixed, hiding.*) They'll start surrounding our homes at night. And some of our friends will be caught by stray bullets. There will be roadblocks at every entrance to Soweto, and Regina Mundi Church will be full of tear-gas smoke! Then life will go on as before.

He throws his arms up in the air in disgust, cries out.

SCENE EIGHTEEN

Lights flash on. Bright daylight. Coronation Brickyard. Mbongeni, as Zuluboy, is singing:

MBONGENI (*singing*).
> Akuntombi lokhu kwabulala ubhuti ngesibumbu kuyamsondeza. [This is no woman. She killed my brother with a fuck and she never lets him go.]

(*He calls out toward the street*): Hey Angelina—sweetheart! Why are you walking down the street? Come here to Coronation Brickyard! Zuluboy is waiting for you with a nice present! (*Points to his genitals, laughing*).

PERCY (*enters as Bobbejaan—Baboon—Zuluboy's fellow brick-yard worker*). Hey! Zuluboy, forget about women. Start the machine!

Mbongeni sings on.

PERCY. Hey! The white man is watching us. Boss Kom is standing by the window! Start the machine.

He makes machine sounds as he attempts to start it. He pulls the starter cord abortively, flies backwards across the yard.

MBONGENI (*laughs*). Hey Bobbejaan! Start the machine!

PERCY. You laugh and I must do all this work! I'll tell Baas Kom. Baas Kom! Basie! Baas Kom!

MBONGENI. Ssshhhhhh! Bobbejaan! Bobbejaan . . . ssh—I want to tell you a secret.

PERCY. What secret?

MBONGENI (*whispers*). We don't have to work so hard any more. Because Morena, the saviour, is coming here.

PERCY. Huh? Morena here? Hau! Baas Kom!

MBONGENI. Hau, no Bobbejaan! Listen—I was there on Thursday by the Jan Smuts Airport. We were delivering bricks. People were coming with taxis, bikes, trains, trucks, others on foot. There were many people, Bobbejaan. They were singing and crying and laughing and dancing and sweating and this other woman was shouting: Morena, give me bread for my baby. The other woman was shouting: Morena, my son is in detention. The other man: Morena, give me a special permit to work in Johannesburg city. The little girl, standing next to me: Morena, give me a lollipop. The big fat Zulu—the driver from Zola Hostel—Morena, give me a Chevrolet Impala! And me—I was there too—

PERCY. What did you say?

MBONGENI. Morena, come to Coronation Brickyard tomorrow morning! And he's coming here.

PERCY. To Coronation Brickyard? Morena?

MBONGENI. Hau—Bobbejaan, at the wedding, long ago—ten thousand years ago—he take a bucket of water, he make wine.

PERCY (*smugly*). Ja, everybody knows that!

MBONGENI. He take one fish, he make fish for everybody! Fried fish!

PERCY. Hau!

MBONGENI. He take one loaf of brown bread, he make the whole bakery! Here at Coronation Brickyard, you will see wonders. He will take one brick, number one brick, and throw it up in the air. And it will fall down on our heads, a million bricks like manna from heaven!

PERCY. Hey! You're talking nonsense. Morena? Here at Coronation Bricks? Start the machine. I'll tell Baas Kom!

Percy goes off. Mbongeni begins rolling a cigarette, singing his Zuluboy's song. Percy, as Baas Kom with pink nose and white dust-coat, enters quietly from behind the clothes rail and creeps up on him. Mbongeni spits, just missing Percy who leaps back.

MBONGENI. Oh, sorry, Boss. Sorry, sorry . . . (*He runs to start the machine.*)

PERCY. Sis! Where were you brought up?

MBONGENI. Sorry Boss!

PERCY. Ja Zuluboy! And what are you sitting around for?

MBONGENI. Sorry, Boss. Sorry.

PERCY. Are you waiting for Morena?

MBONGENI. No, Boss. No.

PERCY. Ja, I've been listening. I've been watching. You're waiting for Morena. Ja. Did you not listen to the Prime Minister on the radio today?

MBONGENI. I don't have a radio, Boss.

PERCY. We don't like Morena anymore. And everybody who's waiting for Morena is getting fired.

MBONGENI. Oh, very good, Boss. Me? I'm Zuluboy—ten thousand bricks in one day!

PERCY. Ja. Where's Bobbejaan?

MBONGENI (*attempting to start the machine*). He's gone to the toilet.

PERCY. Call him. Call him, quickly!

MBONGENI. Hey! Bobbejaan! (*He makes motor sounds as the machine kicks over but does not fire.*) Bobbejaan!

PERCY (*still as Baas Kom with Mbongeni watching over his shoulder*). Now listen. I want two thousand bricks for Boss Koekemoer. Two thousand bricks for Baas Pretorius. Two thousand bricks for Mrs Dawson. (*Mbongeni indicates his pleasure in Mrs Dawson. Percy cautions him:*) Zuluboy! Six thousand bricks for Boss Van der Westhuizen. Two thousand bricks for Boss Koekemoer. Two thousand bricks for Baas Pretorius. Two thousand bricks for Mrs Dawson.

MBONGENI. Baas, sorry, I'm confused.

PERCY. What confused? What confused? You're bloody lazy, man! See to these orders and push the truck. (*He indicates the truck on the side of the stage.*)

MBONGENI. Hey! This truck is too heavy, Baas!

PERCY. Get other people!

MBONGENI. People have gone to lunch.

PERCY. Get Bobbejaan!

MBONGENI. Ten thousand bricks, Boss!

PERCY. Hey! Get Bobbejaan!

MBONGENI. Bobbejaan! Uyahamba laphe khaya. [They'll fire you.] Bobbejaan! (*Mumbling:*) Two thousand bricks Mrs Dawson . . . Hau! (*Laughs with pleasure.*) Mrs Dawson! Ten thousand brick Baas van Des-des-destuizen . . . Too much! (*He starts the engine. Engine fires. Mbongeni shouts:*) Bobbejaan!

PERCY (*off-stage, as Bobbejaan*). I'm coming, man! (*He enters.*) Hey, hey. Where's Morena?

MBONGENI. No, Morena. Hey, shovel the sand. Baas Kom is firing everybody that's waiting for Morena.

PERCY (*laughing*). Ja! I've been telling you! Hey, bring down the pot. (*They alternate shovel and motor sounds, as they mime shovelling. Mbongeni begins to sing and dance his Zuluboy song.*) Hey, stop dancing. Stop dancing!

MBONGENI. Hey! I am boss-boy here!

Mbongeni switches off the machine.

PERCY. Lunch time!

MBONGENI. No Bobbejaan. First push the truck.

PERCY. Hau! Ten thousand bricks! Hau! Lunch time!

MBONGENI. Baas Kom said, push the truck! Get Bobbejaan, push the truck. PUSH!

Percy joins him reluctantly. They start to chant while they mime pushing the heavy truck.

BOTH (*chanting*).
Woza kanye-kanye! [Come together!]
Abelungu oswayini! [Whites are swines!]
Basibiza ngo-damn! [They call us damns!]

Woza kanye-kanye! [Come together!]
Abelungu oswayini! [Whites are swines!]
Basibiza ngo-damn! [They call us damns!]

They finally stop, exhausted.

PERCY (*holding his back, moaning*). Oh, oh, oh, yii, yii! Lunch time! Kayi ndiva kuthi qhu. [My back is breaking.]
MBONGENI. Hayi suka unamanga. [Hey you lie.] (*He squats to examine the truck.*) It has gone too far. Reverse!
PERCY. Reverse?! Reverse?

Muttering, he joins Mbongeni. They pull the truck back again, chanting.

BOTH (*chanting*).
Woza emuva! [Come reverse!]
Phenduka ayi. [Change now.]
Abelungu oswayini! [Whites are swines!]
Basibiza ngo-damn! [They call us damns!]

PERCY. Hayi. (*Percy goes off.*)
MBONGENI. Bobbejaan, come back, it stuck in ditch.
PERCY (*off-stage*). Hayi, xelel'ubaas Kom ukuba sifuna i-ncrease. [Tell Baas Kom we want increase.]
MBONGENI. We . . . kuyintekentekana lokhu okuwu-Bobbe-jaan. [Hey man, Bobbejaan too weak.] Come back, Bobbejaan! Uyahamba laphe khaya. [They'll fire you.] Where's my cigarette? (*Mimes lighting a cigarette. Talks to himself. Starts praise-chant.*)
PERCY (*enters as Baas Kom*). And now? And now? (*Mocking praise-chant:*) Aaay, hakela, hakela. What the bloody hell is that? Huh? Push the truck! Come!
MBONGENI. Having rest, baas. Still smoking.
PERCY. Do you think I pay you for smoking? (*Glances at the truck.*) Ye, push the truck!
MBONGENI. We pushed the truck! Ten thousand bricks! Boss, there's too much work for two people. Me and Bobbejaan start the engine. Me and Bobbejaan shovel the sand. Me and Bobbejaan load the bricks. Me and Bobbe-jaan push the truck! Aaay suka! We need other people!
PERCY. There's no jobs!
MBONGENI. There *is* jobs!!! Ten thousand bricks! This morning there were many people at the gates standing there looking for work. And you chased them away!
PERCY. Zuluboy, you're getting cheeky, huh?
MBONGENI. I'm not getting cheeky. It's true.

PERCY. Ja! I'm cutting down your salary. I think you're get-ting too much. Ja! Ja!
MBONGENI. The boss can't cut salary.
PERCY. Ek gaan dit doen! [I'm going to do it.]
MBONGENI. That's not showing sympathy for another man. The cost of living is too high. There is too much inflation.
PERCY. Zuluboy! Zuluboy! You sit around waiting for Morena and then you come and tell me about the cost of living? You talk about inflation? What do you know about inflation? I've got you here, just here. One more mistake, once more cheeky, and you're fired!
MBONGENI. Okay. All right boss. Let's talk business like two people.
PERCY (*bangs on the box*). He-ey! Push the truck man!
MBONGENI (*furious, bangs on the box. Percy retreats towards his office space*). Hey! You must listen nice when another man talks!
PERCY. Okay. Talk, talk. (*Mbongeni advances.*) No—talk over there, talk over there!
MBONGENI (*backs away*). All right. Okay, okay. The people want increase. Where's the money for the people?
PERCY. Increase?
MBONGENI. Increase!
PERCY. Don't I give you free food? Free boarding and lodg-ing?
MBONGENI. The people don't like your free food! They want money. There is too big families to support. Too many children.
PERCY. I don't give a damn about your too many children. Don't you know about family planning?
MBONGENI. Family planning? What is that?
PERCY. Don't you know that you must not have too many children? You must have two, three, and stop your fuck-fuck nonsense! Too many pic-a-ninnies! Too many black kaffir babies all over the country. (*Sharing this with the au-dience:*) Their kaffir babies cry 'Waaaaa! Waaaaa!' Just like too many piccaninny dogs!
MBONGENI (*threatening*). Hey!
PERCY. Zuluboy!
MBONGENI. Whose children cry 'Waaa, waaa!'?
PERCY. Zuluboy!
MBONGENI. Whose children is piccaninny dogs?
PERCY. Bring your pass-book!
MBONGENI. Why?
PERCY. You're fired! Bring your pass-book. I'm signing you off.
MBONGENI. You can't sign me off!
PERCY. I'm calling the police! I'm calling the government buses and I'm sending you back to your homelands. Ek stuur julle na julle fokken verdomde, donorse, bliksemse plase toe! [I'm sending you to your fucking, cursed, use-less farms.] You don't like my work? You don't like my food! Go back to your bladdy farms! Go starve on your bladdy farms!
MBONGENI. I must starve?

PERCY. Ja!

MBONGENI. My children must starve?

PERCY. Ja!

MBONGENI. Go on strike!!!

PERCY. Hey! Bring your pass-book!

MBONGENI (*pulls out his knobkerrie from behind the box*). Here's my pass-book!

PERCY. Zuluboy!

MBONGENI (*advancing*). Here's my pass-book.

PERCY (*ducking behind the rack of clothes at the back of the stage*). Bobbejaan!

MBONGENI. Here's my pass-book! Stay away—hlala phansi wena ngane ka Ngema. Hlala wena ngane ka Mad-lokovu—hlala. Wena dlula bedlana inkunzi engena mona, hlala phansi mfana—Hlala!! Pho—kuhlala ba. [Stay away—sit down you son of Ngema. Sit down son of Madlokovu. Sit. You fuck and you never feel jealous. Sit down great son. Sit. So who am I—the greatest!] (*Mutters to himself:*) Stay away. Go on strike. My children cry 'Waa waa.' (*Suddenly he sees Morena approaching. He wipes the sweat from his eyes, shakes his head in disbelief. Falls to his knees.*) Hey. Hey! Morena! So you've come to Coronation Bricks! Come, Morena. Did you listen to the radio today? Everybody's waiting for you, and everybody is fired. Come, sit down here, Morena. (*Offers a box.*) Sit down. Sit down Morena. (*Calls out:*) Bobbejaan!

PERCY (*entering as Bobbejaan, angrily*). Hau! One minute 'Bobbejaan!' One minute 'Bobbejaan!" (*He sees Morena, stops complaining and turns away shyly.*)

MBONGENI (*laughs*). Bobbejaan, who is this? Who is this!!!

PERCY (*backs away smiling shyly*). Hey. I don't know him. Who is it?

MBONGENI. Who is this? I win the bet. Give ten rands.

PERCY. Who is he?

MBONGENI. Give ten rands!

PERCY. Who is he?

MBONGENI. Morena!

PERCY. Hey! Morena?!

MBONGENI. He's from heaven. He has come now. He landed at Jan Smuts Airport on Thursday by the airline from Jerusalem.

PERCY. Hey Morena! (*Clapping hands.*) I saw your picture in the paper. Morena, I could not believe you're coming. I thought you're coming back by the clouds. (*He sits on the floor.*)

MBONGENI. The clouds are too hot now. It's summer. He flies air-conditioned. Excuse, Morena, this is Bobbejaan. Bobbejaan, shake hands with Morena. (*Percy stands, embarrassed, backs away.*) Shake hands with the Son of God! Shake hands, Bobbejaan! (*Percy ducks behind the Zuluboy on the box. Zuluboy laughs.*) Bobbejaan is shy! We are working together here, Morena. When I say, 'Morena, come to Coronation Brickyard', I mean you must make bricks like you make bread and wine long ago. I mean you must make bricks to fall down like manna from heaven—

PERCY. Like you made fried fish!

MBONGENI. Ja! But now, I say no! Stay away! No! You must not make bricks for Coronation Brickyard! You must go on strike like me and Bobbejaan! Angithi Bobbejaan? [Isn't it so, Bobbejaan?] We work hard here. We sweat. Sweating for one man!

PERCY. Boss Koekemoer!

MBONGENI. Every Friday, Boss Koekemoer, seven thousand bricks—

PERCY. Boss Pretorius!

MBONGENI. Boss Pretorius ten thousand bricks!

PERCY. Van de Westhuizen!

MBONGENI. Boss Van-des-detuizen, eleven thousand bricks! Where do we stay?

PERCY. In a tin!

MBONGENI. In a tin! Like sardine fish!

PERCY. In a tin, Morena!

MBONGENI. Where do the bricks go to!? The bricks go to make a big house, six rooms, for two people. A white man and his wife! Angithi Bobbejaan? [Isn't it so, Bobbejaan?] Our fingers are breaking Morena! Is nie good kanjalo man. [That's not good like that, man.]

PERCY. Ten thousand bricks!

MBONGENI. Ten thousand bricks! Me and Bobbejaan must push the truck. Aaay suka! Stay away! No bricks for Coronation Bricks! (*He puts out his cigarette and clears his nose—to Percy's embarrassment.*) Are you hungry, Morena? Are you hungry? I've got nice food for you. I've got a packet of chips. (*Mimes.*) It's very good, this one. There's lots of vinegar and salt—I bought them from the shop just around the corner.

PERCY. That's potatoes, Morena.

MBONGENI. I've got half-brown bread. Whole-wheat. You made this long ago, huh? I've been telling Bobbejaan, you made plenty in the wedding—He's got power, this one! (*Mimes.*) This is Coca-cola, Morena.

PERCY. It's cold drink.

MBONGENI. For quenching thirst.

PERCY. Ha, Morena, there's no Coca-cola in heaven?

MBONGENI. What do you drink up there?

They listen, then laugh uproariously.

PERCY. These two!

MBONGENI. You and your father! Skelm! [Mischief-makers!]

He mimes opening a cola bottle.

PERCY (*looks upstage, then calls in Baas Kom's voice, as if from offstage*). Bobbejaan! (*Then as Bobbejaan again:*) Baas Kom! Morena, I must go! One minute 'Bobbejaan!' One minute 'Bobbejaan!' (*Going off:*) hey Zuluboy, I want my chips!

MBONGENI (*drinks from the mimed cola bottle, burps, offers it to Morena*). Yabhodla ingane yenZule ukuba okungu—MSuthu ngabe kudala kuzinyele. [There burps the son of a Zulu; if it was a Sotho he would be shitting.] Did you hear that man who was shouting 'Bobbejaan'? That's our white boss. Boss Kom. He's not good. But don't worry . . .

PERCY (*offstage in Baas Kom's voice*). Bobbejaan!

MBONGENI. Lots of vinegar . . .

PERCY (*enters as Baas Kom, stops at sight of Morena*). En nou! En nou? Who is this? Who is sitting around eating lunch with my kaffirs? That's why you're getting cheeky, hey? Ja, you sit around and have lunch with terrorists!

MBONGENI. Hau! He's not a terrorist, Baas! He's a big man from heaven!

PERCY. This man is a communist, jong! Ek het va jou nonsense gehoor. Die hele land praat van jou. [I've heard of your nonsense. The whole country is talking about you.]

MBONGENI. Excuse. He cannot understand Afrikaans.

PERCY. What? Cannot understand Afrikaans?

MBONGENI. Right.

PERCY. Cannot understand Afrikaans? Stay where you are! (*Retreats to his office behind the clothes.*) I'm calling the police. Fuckin' agitator!

MBONGENI. Aaay suka!! Don't worry, Morena, don't worry. (*He proffers the cola bottle.*) He does not know who you are. He does not know who your father is.

PERCY (*as Baas Kom, offstage*). Hello? Hello? Lieutenant Venter? Ja! Now listen here. There's a terrorist here who's making trouble with my kaffirs. Ek sê daar's'n uitlander hier wat kak maak met my kaffirs. [I say there's a foreigner here who's making shit with my kaffirs.] Ja. Hello? Hello? Ag die fuckin' telephone! Bobbejaan! (*As Bobbejaan:*) Ja, Basie? (*As Baas Kom:*) Kom, kom, kom. (*As Bobbejaan:*) Ja, Basie? (*As Baas Kom:*) You see that man eating with Zuluboy? (*As Bobbejaan:*) Ja, Basie. (*As Baas Kom:*) He's a terrorist! (*As Bobbejaan:*) A terrorist, Basie? That's Morena! (*As Baas Kom:*) It's not Morena—Now listen here. Listen carefully. I'm writing down this message. You take this message to the police station and I'm going to give you a very nice present. A ten rand increase, okay? (*As Bobbejaan:*) Ja, thank you Basie, thank you Basie. (*As Baas Kom:*) Ja, go straight to the police station and don't tell Zuluboy. (*As Bobbejaan:*) Ja Basie, ja. (*As Baas Kom:*) Go to the police station and you get the ten rand increase!

MBONGENI. Did you hear that, Morena? (*He listens.*) What? Forgive a man seventy times seventy-seven? Aikhona Morena! This is South Africa. We fight! Bobbejaan is very dangerous. (*Listens to Morena.*) Okay, you win. Wait and see, Morena.

PERCY (*enters as Bobbejaan, putting on his shirt*). Morena, I'm going to the shop, just around the corner.

MBONGENI. Bobbejaan, your chips are here.

PERCY. Give them to Morena.

MBONGENI. Morena is not hungry.

PERCY. Eat them yourself.

MBONGENI. I'm not hungry either. Where are you going, Bobbejaan?

PERCY. To the shop!

MBONGENI. Why, Bobbejaan?

PERCY. I'm going to buy hot-dogs for Baas Kom.

MBONGENI. Where's the money?

PERCY. I've got it here.

MBONGENI. Show it to me.

PERCY. Why?

MBONGENI. Ja. You Judas, Bobbejaan!

PERCY. What are you talking about?

MBONGENI. You betray Morena, Bobbejaan.

PERCY. Haw! Morena, do you hear that?

MBONGENI. Bobbejaan, you betray Morena, Bobbejaan! You Judas, Bobbejaan!

PERCY. I'm going to buy hot-dogs for Baas Kom!

MBONGENI. You . . . you . . . you take a message to the police. And you get ten rands increase Bobbejaan!

PERCY. Aay Morena. Morena, do you hear that?

MBONGENI. Morena, shhh. Keep quiet. This is South Africa. Ten rands increase (*He reaches for the knobkerrie.*)

PERCY. Baas Kom! (*He runs off.*)

MBONGENI (*mimes his knobkerrie being grabbed by Morena*). Morena, leave it! Leave it! Morena! Morena, leave it! Morena! He has run away now. Bobbejaan, sodibana nawe wena. [Bobbejaan, you and I will meet again.] A man hits this cheek you give him the other. Aikhona, Morena! They're calling the police to arrest you now! Okay, come. Let me hide you there by the trees—Quickly—(*Siren sounds. He stops.*) There's one, two, three . . . there's thirteen police cars. Huh? Forgive them, they do not know what they are doing? Aikhona, Morena! They know! They know! (*He sings and performs a Zulu war dance, which ends with him thrusting his knobkerrie again and again at the audience in attack.*)

Qobolela njomane kandaba heya-he
soze sibajahe abelungu he ya he.

[Be ready you horses of the black warriors
Time will come when we'll chase these whites away.]

SCENE NINETEEN

The lights come up on the actors wearing military hats and pink noses. Percy has a bloody bandage under his hat.

MBONGENI. Address! Ssshhhooo! Attention!

They drill in unison.

PERCY (*saluting*). Reporting sir! John Vorster Squad, sir!

MBONGENI. What have you to report, Sergeant?

PERCY. Operation Coronation, sir!

MBONGENI. Meaning, Sergeant!

PERCY. We have finally captured Morena, sir!

MBONGENI. You've what? Attention! One-two-three-one-two-three-one! (*They march to each other, shake hands.*) Excellent, Sergeant! Excellent!

PERCY. Thank you, sir.

MBONGENI. And now, what's happened to your head, Sergeant?

PERCY. A mad Zulu, sir.

MBONGENI. A mad Zulu?

PERCY. Yes sir. He struck me with a branch of a tree, sir.

MBONGENI. A branch of a tree?

PERCY. They call it a knobkerrie, sir.

MBONGENI. Ah! When, Sergeant?

PERCY. During Operation Coronation, sir.

MBONGENI. You mean Morena was with a bunch of mad Zulus?

PERCY. No, sir.

MBONGENI. What does he mean, this stupid Sergeant?

PERCY. He was with one mad Zulu, sir!

MBONGENI. One mad Zulu?

PERCY. Yes, sir!

MBONGENI. And how many men did you have, Sergeant?

PERCY. Thirty, sir!

MBONGENI. And where are they now, Sergeant?

PERCY. In hospital, sir!

MBONGENI. And the mad Zulu?

PERCY. He got away, sir!

MBONGENI. God! Wat gaan aan?! [God! What's going on?!] Where is Morena now, Sergeant?

PERCY (*pointing proudly above the audience*). He's upstairs, above us, sir. On the tenth floor of John Vorster Square Prison, sir!

MBONGENI. Aaaahhh! (*Looking up.*) And you've provided ample guard, Sergeant?

PERCY. Yes, sir. One hundred and twenty, sir.

MBONGENI (*moving forward, watching the tenth floor, mesmerised*). Are you sure he's on the tenth floor, Sergeant?

PERCY (*following his gaze nervously*). Yes, sir.

MBONGENI. Then what is that I see?

PERCY (*moving behind him, also mesmerised, both eye-lines travelling above the audience*). I'm sorry sir.

MBONGENI. Why are you sorry, Sergeant?

PERCY. I see two men floating, sir.

MBONGENI. Then why are you sorry, Sergeant?

PERCY. I'm afraid one of them is Morena, sir.

MBONGENI (*moving in, nose-to-nose, menacingly*). Precisely, Sergeant! And-who-is-the-other?

PERCY. The Angel Gabriel, sir.

MBONGENI (*despairing*). Ha! Gabriel!

PERCY. I'm sorry, sir. I never thought of air flight, sir.

MBONGENI. Eeeeeiiiii! One-two-three-four-one-four! Attention! Dismissed, Sergeant!

SCENE TWENTY

Lights find both actors travelling beside each other on a train.

MBONGENI (*laughing*). Jaaa. And where do we go from there? After a miracle like flying men, I'm telling you the government will be real nervous. And they won't start nonsense with him for a long time. In fact, they will try very hard to please Morena. He will be taken to all the nice places in the country. Like the game reserve where he can lie down with a leopard and a lamb. (*They cuddle.*) And then—(*They mime a highspeed lift.*)—they will take him right up to the high spots of Johannesburg City— Panorama Wimpy Bar, Carlton Centre, fiftieth floor! And then, on a Thursday they will take him down— (*They mime going down, pink noses on their foreheads like miners' lamps.*)—the gold mines to watch. (*They mime deafening drills.*) And then, on a Sunday the mine dancers. (*They perform a short dance routine.*) And— (*Hand to ear.*)—aah, the government gardens in Pretoria. (*Doves cooing.*) And then, they will take him on a trip to SUN CITY—(*Stage radiantly light.*)—THE LAS VEGAS OF SOUTH AFRICA, where they will build him a holy suite and President Lucas Mangope, the puppet, will offer him the key to the homeland of Bophutatswana! And then, what will happen? They will take him past the good-time girls. (*Standing on a box, Percy mimes.*) And the gambling machines. (*Percy transforms into a one-armed bandit, Mbongeni works him, wins triumphantly.*) And when television cameras turn on him, will he be smiling? Will he be joyous? No. He'll be crying. And when all the people shout—

BOTH. Speech! Morena, speech!

MBONGENI. —Morena will say, 'No.'

PERCY (*miming holding a mike*). No, speak up.

MBONGENI. No! Morena will say, what key is this? What place is this? This place where old people weep over the graves of children? How has it happened? How has it been permitted? I've passed people with burning mouths. People buying water in a rusty piece of tin, and beside them I see people swimming in a lake that they have made from water that is here!

PERCY. Be careful, there are police spies here.

MBONGENI. What spies? Morena will say, I pass people who sit in dust and beg for work that will buy them bread. And on the other side I see people who are living in gold and glass and whose rubbish bins are loaded with food for a thousand mouths.

PERCY. Hey! That's not your business. There are security police, man.

MBONGENI. What security police? Morena will say, I see families torn apart, I see mothers without sons, children without fathers, and wives who have no men! Where are the men? Aph'amadoda madoda? [Where are the men?] And people will say, Ja, Morena, it's this bladdy apartheid. It's those puppets, u Mangope! u Matanzima! u Sebe! Together with their white Pretoria masters. They separate us from our wives, from our sons and daughters! And women will say, Morena there's no work in the

homelands. There's no food. They divide us from our husbands and they pack them into hostels like men with no
names, men with no lives! And Morena will say, come to
me, you who are divided from your families. Let us go to
the cities where your husband work. We will find houses
where you can live together and we will talk to those who
you fear! What country is this? (*Spits on ground.*)

*Percy starts to sing and march on the spot. Mbongeni joins
him. They mime carrying a banner.*

BOTH ACTORS (*sing a Zulu song and march*).
    Oyini oyini madoda
    Oyini oyini madoda
    Sibona ntoni uma sibon'u Mangope
    Siboni sell-out uma sibon'u Mangope
    Sibona ntoni uma sibon'u Gatsha
    Siboni puppet uma sibon'u Gatsha
    Khulula khulula Morena
    Khulula khulula Morena
    Sibona ntoni nang'u Matanzima
    Sibon'u mbulali nang'u Matanzima

    [What is this, what is this men
    What is this, what is this men
    What do we see when we see Mangope
    We see a sell-out when we see Mangope
    What do we see when we see Gatsha
    We see a puppet when we see Gatsha
    Help us—Help us Morena
    Help us—Help us Morena
    What do we see—there is Matanzima
    We see a killer when we see Matanzima.]
PERCY (*interrupted*). Hey! Tear gas!

*They struggle, continuing the song, throwing stones,
sounding sirens, dogs barking. Lights go down as they are
subdued.*

BOTH. Morena-a-a-a! Morena-a-a-a!

SCENE TWENTY-ONE

*Spotlight finds Percy as Prime Minister, pink nose, specta-
cles.*

PERCY. My people, as your Prime Minister I must warn you
that we stand alone in the face of total onslaught. Our
enemies will stop at nothing, even to the extent of sending a cheap communist magician to pose as the Morena,
and undermine the security of our nation. But let me assure you that this cheap impostor is safely behind bars,
from which he cannot fly. Peace and security have returned to our lovely land.

SCENE TWENTY-TWO

*Lights come up on Mbongeni squatting on a box, wrapped
in a prisoner's blanket.*

MBONGENI (*knocking*). Cell number six! Morena! (*Knocking.*) Cell number six! Morena! Bad luck, hey! I hear they
got you again. They tell me you're in solitary confinement just like us. From Sun City to Robben Island!
(*Laughs ruefully.*) You've made us famous, Morena. The
whole world is talking about us. Hey bayasiteya labedana
bamabhunu man! [Hey they are riding us these white
boys.] Morena, I sit there just like you with this one light
bulb and only the Bible to read! Ja! And the New Testament tells me about you, and your family, and your
thoughts. But why do they give us your book to read,
Morena? They must be bladdy mad, Morena. This book
only proves how mad they are. Listen. (*Knocking.*) Cell
number six! For people like us, to be locked here like this
is just rubbish. So what do you want here? What does
your father know? What does he say? Come on, Morena,
man! (*Knocking.*) Cell number six! You've got all the
power! How can you let these things happen? How can
you just sit there like that, Morena? Okay, okay, I know
you don't like miracles, but these are bladdy hard times,
Morena. Morena, I must tell you, now that I've gone into
your book, I really like you, Morena. But I'm getting
bladdy disappointed. How long must we wait for you to
do something? Morena, I must tell you, I'm among those
who have stopped waiting. One day we'll have to help
you! Pamberi ne hondo! [Power to the people!] Can you
hear me Morena? Cell number six!! (*'Sarie Marais' being
whistled offstage. Knocking more cautiously:*) Cell number
six!! Morena! Morena . . . Cell number six . . .

SCENE TWENTY-THREE

*Percy enters whistling 'Sarie Marais'. He is a soldier, pink
nose, camouflage hat. Mimes carrying rifle.*

MBONGENI (*enters similarly dressed*). Two three! Morning
Corporal!
PERCY. Morning Sergeant!
MBONGENI. How are things going, Corporal? (*He rests on a
box.*)
PERCY. I'm tired, Sergeant.
MBONGENI. Oh, God. To be a guard on bladdy Robben Is-
land!
PERCY. Ja, ever since they brought Morena out here to
Robben Island everything has been upside down.
MBONGENI. All those bladdy interviews, that's what's
killing us!
PERCY. I'm sick of having my photograph taken.

MBONGENI. I know. The next photographer I see, I shoot to kill!

PERCY. Daily News.

MBONGENI. Sunday Times.

PERCY. Time Life.

MBONGENI. Pravda.

PERCY. London Observer.

MBONGENI. New York Times.

PERCY. All those bladdy communists!

MBONGENI. You know, I got a letter from a woman in Sweden. She saw my photograph in her newspaper. And my wife was chasing me with a frying pan! I told her I never knew the woman, but she didn't believe me.

PERCY. I wish they had kept him in John Vorster Square or Pretoria Central.

MBONGENI. Come on, Corporal. You know what happened at John Vorster Square. Gabriel got him out of there in ten seconds flat! Only Robben Island has got the right kind of AA missiles.

PERCY. AA? What is that?

MBONGENI. Anti-Angel.

PERCY. Anti-Angel? I never heard of that!

MBONGENI. He'll never get away from Robben Island!

PERCY (distracted, points into the audience). Hey! Sergeant! What's that you said? Just look over there! Just look over there!!!

MBONGENI (moves lazily toward him singing 'Sarie Marais'). My Sarie Marais is so ver van my hart . . . (Suddenly he looks into the audience, horrified.) God! Hey! Fire! Fire!

They riddle the audience with machine-gun fire.

PERCY. Call helicopter control, quick!!!

MBONGENI. Hello? Hello? Radio 1254 CB? Over. Hello? Radio 1254 . . .

SCENE TWENTY-FOUR

Lights reduce to spot-light the boxes. Actors turn their hat brims up. Mbongeni spins his hand above his head. Helicopter sounds. They are in a helicopter, looking down.

PERCY (mimes radio). Radio 1254 CB receiving, over. What? That's impossible! Are you sure? Okay, over and out. Hey, what do you see down below?

MBONGENI (miming binoculars). Oh, it's a beautiful day down below. Birds are flying, swimmers are swimming, waves are waving. Hey! Morena's walking on water to Cape Town! Ag shame! His feet must be freezing! Hey, I wish I had my camera here!

PERCY. This must be the miracle of the decade!

MBONGENI. Ag, I always forget my camera!

PERCY. Down! Down! Radio 1254 CB receiving, over. Yes, we've got him. Yeah, what? Torpedo? Oh no, have a

heart! He's not even disturbing the waves! Ja, I wish you could see him, he looks amazing!

MBONGENI (nodding frenetically into mike). Ja jong, ja! [Yes man, yes!]

PERCY. What? Bomb Morena? Haven't you heard what they say? You start with Morena and it's worse than an atom bomb! Over and out! Hey, this is a shit bladdy job! You pull the chain.

MBONGENI. No, you!

PERCY. No! You pull the chain!

MBONGENI. No, man!

PERCY. This man is mos' happy, why blow him up?

MBONGENI. No come on, come on. Fair deal! Eenie, meenie, minie moe. Vang a kaffir by the toe. As hy shrik, let him go. Eenie, meenie, minie, moe! It's you!

PERCY. Okay! This is the last straw! I think I'm resigning tomorrow!

MBONGENI. Ready . . . target centre below . . . release depth charges . . . bombs . . . torpedoes . . . go!

They watch. The bombs fall. A moment of silence and then a terrible explosion. They separate, come together detonating each other. Light reduces to stark overhead shaft.

BOTH. Momeeeee! Aunti-i-i-eee! He-e-e-l-l-p!

Blackout.

SCENE TWENTY-FIVE

South African television news theme is proclaimed in darkness.

MBONGENI. News!

Lights on.

PERCY (in pink nose, proudly holds a cardboard TV screen shape around his face). Good evening. The United Nations Security Council is still waiting further information on the explosion which completely destroyed Cape Town and its famous Table Mountain. (Bland smile.) United Nations nuclear sensors have recorded distinct signs of nuclear disturbance in the Southern African sector. Investigators have suggested a strong possibility of a mishap to an SAA Military Helicopter carrying a nuclear missile over the bay. However, Mrs Fatima Mossop, domestic servant, Sea Point, a freak survivor of the calamity, insisted that the explosion emanated from a human figure walking across the bay from the Island, supporting the superstition that the nuclear-type explosion was an inevitable result of a bomb attack on Morena. The Prime Minister himself continues to deny any relationship between Morena and the agitator imprisoned on the Island. Mrs Fatima Mossop is still under observation by the state psychiatrists. Well, that is all for tonight. Goodnight. (Fade on fixed smile.)

SCENE TWENTY-SIX

The graveyard. Mbongeni in a hat and dust-coat is weed-
ing and singing Zuluboy's song from Scene Eighteen. Percy
is sleeping on the boxes. Mbongeni sees him, rouses him.

MBONGENI. Hey! Hey! Hey! This is not a park bench. It's a
tombstone. This is a cemetery, it's not Joubert Park.

PERCY (*groggy*). I'm sorry, I should know better.

MBONGENI. You want Joubert Park? You want Joubert Park?
You catch the number fifty-four bus. Or you want Zola
Park? You catch a Zola taxi. Or you want to have a look at
the ducks? Go to the Zoo Lake. But don't sit on my tombstones. Please.

PERCY. Okay, I'm sorry about that. Can I have a look
around?

MBONGENI. Oh, well if you want to have a look around,
look around, but don't sit around! The dead are having a
hard enough time. These tombstones are bladdy heavy!

PERCY. Aaahh, tell me, do you keep your tombstones in alphabetical order?

MBONGENI. Yeah. What do you want?

PERCY. Where's 'L'?

MBONGENI. You want 'L'?

PERCY. Ja.

MBONGENI. Serious? Okay. Right there. That whole line is
'L'. By that big tombstone. See? Livingstone . . . Lamele
. . . Lusiti . . . Lizi . . .

PERCY. Have you got any Lazarus here?

MBONGENI. Lazarus? Lazarus? Oh, Israel Lazarus! That was a
very good man! You mean that one? American Half-Price
Dealers? That was a very good man, I used to work for
him in 1962. But he's not dead yet! Why are you looking
for his grave here?

PERCY. I'm just looking for something to do.

MBONGENI. But this face I know. Are you his son?

PERCY. No, not his.

MBONGENI. Then who are you?

PERCY. Morena.

MBONGENI. You? Morena? Aaay suka! They killed him.
That is his tombstone.

PERCY. Oh no, Baba. Have you forgotten? I will always come
back after three days, bombs or no bombs.

MBONGENI. Hay! Morena! Aawu nkulunkulu wami! [Oh my
God!]

PERCY. Ssssshhhh! Please, don't shout my name.

MBONGENI. Do you remember me?

PERCY. Who are you?

MBONGENI. Zuluboy from Coronation Brickyard!

PERCY. Hey! Zuluboy! (*They embrace.*) What are you doing
here?

MBONGENI. I'm working here at the cemetery. I'm disguised
from the police! Lazarus . . . Lazarus . . . aaaahhh! Now I
understand! Morena, you're looking for people to raise!

PERCY. Ja!

MBONGENI. But why didn't you ask me?

PERCY. How would I know?

MBONGENI. I know exactly who my people want! Come, let
us look at these tombstones.

Mbongeni leads Percy in a dance around the cemetery,
singing. Mbongeni stops, Percy beside him. He points to a
corner of the audience.

MBONGENI. Morena! Here's our 'L'—ALBERT LUTHULI—
the Father of our Nation! Raise him Morena!

PERCY. Woza Albert! [Rise up Albert!]

Mbongeni falls over, stunned then ecstatic.

BOTH (*singing*).
Yamemeza inkosi yethu
Yathi ma thambo hlanganani
Uyawa vusa amaqhawe amnyama
Wathi kuwo

[Our Lord is calling.
He's calling for the bones of the dead to join together.
He's raising up the black heroes.
He calls to them]

MBONGENI (*addressing the risen but invisible Albert Luthuli*).
Hey, Luthuli uyangibona mina? U Zulu boy. Ngakhula
phansi kwakho e-Stanger. [Hey, Luthuli, do you remember me? I'm Zuluboy. I grew up in Stanger.]

They dance on, repeating the song.

BOTH (*singing*).
Yamemeza inkosi yethu
Yathi ma thambo hlanganani
Uyawa vusa amaqhawe amnyama
Wathi kuwo

[Our Lord is calling.
He's calling for the bones of the dead to join together.
He's raising up the black heroes.
He calls to them]

Mbongeni stops, Percy beside him.

MBONGENI. Morena! Robert Sobukwe! He taught us Black
Power! Raise him!

PERCY. Woza Robert!

MBONGENI (*ecstatic*). Hau Mangaliso! Mangaliso!

They dance on.

BOTH (*singing*).
Yamemeza inkosi yethu
Yathi ma thambo hlanganani
Uyawa vusa amaqhawe amnyama
Wathi kuwo

[Our Lord is calling.
He's calling for the bones of the dead to join together.
He's raising up the black heroes.

He calls to them]

MBONGENI. Lilian Ngoyi! She taught our mothers about freedom. Raise her!

PERCY. Woza Lilian!

MBONGENI (*spins with joy*). Woza Lilian!—Hey Lilian, uya mbona uMorena? Uvuswe uMorena. [Come Lilian—hey Lilian, do you see Morena? It's Morena who raised you.]

They dance on.

BOTH [*singing*].
Yamemeza inkosi yethu
Yathi ma thambo hlanganani
Uyawa vusa amaqhawe amnyama
Wathi kuwo

[Our Lord is calling.
He's calling for the bones of the dead to join together.
He's raising up the black heroes.]

He calls to them]

MBONGENI. Steve Biko! The hero of our children! Please Morena—Please raise him!

PERCY. Woza Steve!

MBONGENI. Steve! Steve! Uyangikhumbula ngikulandela e Kingwilliams-town? [Steve, do you remember me, following you in Kingswilliamstown?]

BOTH (*dancing*). Woza Bram Fischer! . . . Woza Ruth First! . . . Woza Griffith Mxenge . . . Woza Hector Peterson . . . (*They stop, arms raised triumphantly.*) WOZA ALBERT!!!

Blackout.

SONQOBA SIMUNYE

Center Stage   SOUTH AFRICAN TOWNSHIP THEATER

South African township theater typifies Jerzy Grotowski's vision of a "poor theater" because it is necessarily reduced to the essence of the theatrical act by stripping the performance of superfluous accoutrements. Grotowski argues and township theater proves that "theater *can* exist without makeup, without autonomic costume and scenography, without a separate performance area (stage), without lighting and sound effects, etc. It *cannot* exist without the actor-spectator relationship of perceptual, direct, live communion." The Polish artist envisioned a theater that becomes a "spiritual act" and South African township theater is that spiritual act. Its form develops out of the demands of its content and milieu, not a shaping of the content to fit an existing form. Township theater is about freedom. It is about poverty and oppression. It is about not only what is, but what could be. Township theater is presented with the barest essentials—the actor and the audience. It merely suggests scenery, properties, and costumes, all of which are usually "found" rather than "designed."

Township theater is, in the words of critic Keyan Tomaselli, "the most accessible and forceful medium . . . to articulate [black] ideology, expose the contradictions of apartheid, and communicate a more accurate portrayal of the actual conditions of existence." Playwright Matsemela Manaka says, "Our theater is here to search for the truth about the history of the dispossessed . . . [about] the liberation of the mind and the liberation of the body." In such a theater, David Coplan, author of *In the Township Tonight!*, declares, "The working class aesthetic of the township is that theater is a direct extension of the actual conditions of black existence, with no necessary boundaries between art and life, performer and audience."

Township theater, a relatively new form of South African theater, emerged within a decade of the formal establishment of apartheid in 1948. This dauntless and dynamic theater was spawned in the "locations" or "townships" (read ghettos) established by the government. As Pretoria gradually tightened the noose of apartheid and the suffering of the indigenous population grew, both the form and content of this so-called "poor theater" evolved.

Its development passed through four stages, each lasting about ten years. The early plays, essentially those of the 1950s, were largely escapist entertainments depicting daily life in the townships. During the 1960s the plays developed into pictures of the suffering of the blacks of South Africa, presenting the plight of those who were physically and psychologically maimed by the system. As an awareness of history and bitterness against imperialism grew in the 1970s, township theater evolved into a medium for the expression of the rage that accompanied the rise in black consciousness. The final stage, which began in the late 1970s and continued throughout the 1980s to the present, is almost celebratory. It is an affirmation of the noble spirit, the undying optimism, and the impending liberation of the people.

Township theater is truly a theater of the people. Although it exemplifies Grotowski's poor theater, it also resembles other agitprop and revolutionary theaters, most notably Bertolt Brecht's

Mistress It's A Pity, the teacher of Sarafina and her schoolmates, leads the students in a rousing number from Mbongeni Ngema's internationally acclaimed musical hit Sarafina!

epic theater (see Chapter 7). Township theater first exposes the transgressions of the oppressors and then infuses the oppressed with a sense of beauty and self-worth and imbues them with political power. "There is only one ally against the growth of barbarism:" declares Brecht, "the people on whom it imposes these sufferings. Only the people offer any prospects. Thus it is natural to turn to them."

The leaders of township theater are the playwrights and directors, who most often take on both duties. The popular term for this combined role is "playmaker." Playmakers work improvisationally with their companies to develop new works that rely on the people in the townships for their experiences and stories. In fact, the plays are often cast first, and then the script is developed based on the lives and observations of the actors. For example, when Mbongeni Ngema developed his company, Committed Artists, he gathered the homeless of Durban, who knew firsthand the particulars of the rent strike. Their collective experience gave birth to the play *Asinamali! (We Have No Money!)*. "If the actors didn't . . . get the spirit right," declares Ngema, "I would say, 'let's go to a funeral in Lamontville (where police were shooting people almost daily), so that we can experience running away from tear gas, how it is to be close to death.'"

This type of "patchy," pieced-together playmaking, which is the heart and soul of township theater, has led to the development of what might be called "motley theater"—motley venues, scripts, and performance styles. The venues for these performances consist of "found spaces" because few or no theaters exist in the townships. For example, the township of Soweto, a community of a million people, is served by a single theater—Deipkloof Hall, a performance space that more closely approximates a small high school gymnasium than a theater. The most popular performance spaces are the local churches, schoolyards, community halls, garages, and streets.

The scripts consist of collages of images portraying township life. Farcical comedy combines with pathetic tragedy; poignant sentimentalism freely mixes with cold documentary; the surreal and expressionistic is superimposed on the realistic and naturalistic. This eclectic mix of styles bombards the senses with striking images of township life. These seemingly plotless, episodic, improvisational plays often offend traditional theater connoisseurs and critics.

These unique plays are often presented on a bare stage with little costuming. A packing crate or two, a couple of chairs, and whatever discarded clothes can be found are the visual staples of these dramas. The opening description of *Woza Albert!* is an excellent illustration:

The set consists of two up-ended tea-chests side by side about center stage. Further upstage an old wooden plank, about ten feet long, is suspended horizontally on old ropes. From nails in the plank hang the ragged clothes that the actors will use for their transformation. The actors wear grey track-suit bottoms and running shoes. They are bare-chested.

Eclectic music is used to reinforce theme and mood. A single play may use music drawn from traditional African rhythms, Christian hymns, African choral songs, English secular compositions, Afro-American jazz, miners' chants and *mbaquanga*, the music of the inner city, so beautifully reflected in the score of *Sarafina!* The music, whether composed especially for the play or borrowed, is live, and the actors frequently sing a cappella in rich harmonies.

Township performers combine the skills of the actor, athlete, singer, dancer, mime, historian, impressionist, politician, and social commentator. Usually appearing on the stage as "themselves," these performers are specialists at "transformation"—the act of evolving spontaneously. Virtually an entire population can be played by a couple of actors using imaginative physical manipulation, clever vocal alteration, and a cacophony of sound effects. In *Woza Albert!*, for example, the two actors create people ranging from the homeless to the Prime Minister; they create machines such as cement mixers, garbage trucks, and helicopters; and they create an airport, a prison, a TV studio, and a nuclear explosion. In later plays, such as Ngema's *Sarafina!* and *Township Fever!*, the casts are expanded and there is far less use of transformation. Such plays resemble a more traditional Western musical.

"MASTER HAROLD" . . . and the boys

ATHOL FUGARD

ATHOL FUGARD (1932 –)

Identified by *Time* as "the greatest active playwright in the English-speaking world," South African Harold Athol Lanning Fugard was born in Middleburg, Cape Province. When he was 3, his family moved to Port Elizabeth in Eastern Province, where his mother was forced to be the family provider because of his father's heavy drinking and physical handicap. She ran the Jubilee Hotel and the Saint George's Park Tea Room. After graduation from the local technical high school, Fugard earned a scholarship to the University of Cape Town, where he studied philosophy for three years before dropping out to embark on a life as a sailor, journalist, and court clerk. In each job he was constantly confronted by the inequities, bigotry, and racism fostered by apartheid, South Africa's official policy of racial separation. As an adolescent he was subjected to his father's "pointless, unthoughtout prejudices"; as the only white sailor on a voyage to Japan, he gained intimate knowledge of the plight of many blacks and Asians; and as a court clerk he saw firsthand the cruel effects of apartheid.

Unsatisfied and at the urging of his wife, actress Sheila Meiring, he turned to playwriting. A voracious reader, he was influenced by British playwright John Osborne and the American novelist William Faulkner. Following Osborne's lead as the outspoken "angry young man" and Faulkner's "unashamedly regional" preoccupation, he developed into a passionate, regional playwright whose insight and sensitivity spoke not only to his native land but to the world.

It is not only life in South Africa that is portrayed in a Fugard play, but the life of the playwright himself. An autobiographical thread runs through his major plays, which include: *No-Good Friday* (1958), *Blood Knot* (1961), *Bosman and Lena* (1968), *The Island* and *Sizwe Bansi Is Dead* (1972, both written in collaboration with Winston Ntshona and John Kani), *Statements After an Arrest Under the Immorality Act* (1974), *A Lesson from Aloes* (1978), *"MASTER HAROLD" . . . and the boys* (1982), *The Road to Mecca* (1984), *My Children! My Africa!* (1989), *Playland* (1992), and *Valley Song* (1996).

His work as a dramatist began in Port Elizabeth with the Serpent Players, a company including white, black, and "colored" South Africans, many of whom became his lifelong friends. Two members, Zakes Mokae and John Kani—South Africa's leading black actors—have played many leading roles in his plays. His early works were developed as pieces-in-progress in which much of the action and the dialogue were created through improvisation. His later plays, though rooted in his apartheid experiences, are more the work of an individual voice.

Fugard's plots, reminiscent of Ibsen's great discussion dramas, develop painstakingly slowly. With exceptional care, he meticulously lays out the exposition so that as the action moves through its complications, a tremendous sense of rhythm and momentum carries the viewer to an unexpected and shattering conclusion. Because his works are usually populated by only two or three people, each character is well developed. Often the situations he creates reflect the mixed population of South Africa. For example, *Blood Knot* concerns Zack and Morrie, men of mixed race (or "coloreds," as apartheid classifies them) who are sons of the same mother and different fathers; *My Children! My Africa!* presents Mr. M., Thami, and Isabel, a black schoolmaster, his black male pupil, and a white female student; in "MASTER HAROLD" . . . *and the boys* we meet Hally, Sam, and Willie, a white adolescent and two older blacks. Whether his characters are tied together by a blood knot, a desire for learning, or sense of surrogate family, they form a bond that crosses racial and generational barriers only to be destroyed by the ingrained racism of which they are victims.

Thematically, Fugard's plays are an indictment of the ignorance, racism, and hatred that nourishes apartheid. Calling for patience, tolerance, and understanding, his plays reveal not only the exploitation and victimization of the black and colored majority of South Africa, but the dehumanizing effects on the white minority. Quite often Fugard creates a peaceful world within a violent one. In *Blood Knot* it is the men's shanty hut; in *My Children! My Africa!*, the classroom; and in *"MASTER HAROLD" . . . and the boys*, the tea room. Inside, the dream of equality thrives and optimism rules, but outside a nightmare of separateness and injustice flourishes while despair reigns.

"MASTER HAROLD" . . . and the boys (1982)

For Fugard, the playwright's work begins not with ideas but with images. "From the very first, the generative—the seed of what energy's involved and goes on to produce a play—comes from images, not ideas," declares Fugard, " . . . something I have to see or hear, not think, but see or hear," that leads to crafting of the play. In "MASTER HAROLD," Fugard has created images of sublime memories juxtaposed with those of grotesque reality. More specifically, the play is composed of a number of central images—ballroom dancing, kite making and flying, and teaching—each presented metatheatrically to create in the tea room a microcosm of a bigoted world.

The plot of the play is simple. "Master Harold" of the title is Hally, a precocious white South African teenager, and "the boys" are Willie and Sam, black men, both of whom work for Hally's family and are old enough to be his father. The action takes place in Port Elizabeth, South Africa, in 1950. On his way home from school, Hally stops by the family-owned tea room, where Willie and Sam are tidying up while they practice their ballroom dancing in preparation for the "event of the year"—the Eastern Province Ballroom Dancing Championships in New Brighton, a black township outside Port Elizabeth. A lifetime of camaraderie is apparent as Hally, Sam and Willie talk, joke, and revel in fond memories. This cordial atmosphere is shattered, however, as Hally, via a telephone call from his mother, learns that his crippled, alcoholic father is about to be released from the hospital and will be home again, where his presence is painfully disruptive. Suddenly angry and afraid, Hallie turns viciously on Willie and Sam. For the father he cannot strike, Hally substitutes the fathers who cannot retaliate. As Hally lashes out at his two lifelong African friends, we understand how the underlying realities of time and place define who we are and dominate our actions. The play is based on an actual incident in Fugard's youth, and he presents an image of himself caught in emotional turmoil as he moved from the innocence of youth to the poisonous bigotry of adulthood.

Among Fugard's most obvious images is that of life as a dance—a vision of a world in which "accidents don't happen; a vision of a world without collisions." The play presents simultaneous images of rituals in the tea room—one a figurative dance, the other a literal one. We immediately see the figurative dance—the boys preparing the dilapidated tea room for the next business day. The establishment is a mess: chairs and tables piled atop one another, the floor half-scrubbed, the windows dirty. As the action proceeds, they ritualistically clean the room. At the same time, "the boys" prepare for the ballroom dancing contest by taking turns dancing around the room with their invisible partners. The play ends with the tea room neatly prepared for the next day's business, while "the boys" continue their dance, gliding effortlessly through the clutter of the tea room that represents their cluttered lives.

Sam's image of the dance as "a world without collisions" is displayed as Hally, Sam and Willie dance and reminisce. Just before the climax of the play, the tea room is partially cleaned and arranged, Sam explains "a world without collisions" to Hally, and Willie weaves his way through the clutter. When the dreamworld is interrupted by the "bump" from Hally's mother, the dancing ceases and their peace is destroyed.

Though Fugard indicates that the boys are tidying the room and dancing, he mentions very little specific action. What is implied, however, is that in the course of rearranging the furniture, the boys have set up a difficult obstacle course, which only experienced dancers can negotiate. The tea room resembles a crowded ballroom dance floor; it is a safe world inhabited only by the boys, who, having violently bumped into Hally, continue to dream of a world without collisions. The final dance seems to be an image of harmony among men. Unfortunately, at the time the play is set (and even when it was written), harmony existed only among black men. However, we now know it was the white man, Hally (Fugard himself), who went on to write about Sam's dream. It was Hally who in the end learned the lesson that was being taught on that rainy afternoon.

Images of a kite also appear throughout the play. Kite making and kite flying are presented as accomplishments. "I wanted you to look up," says Sam, "[and] be proud of something, of yourself." The kite in this sublime memory is not store-bought fresh from the factory but a "homemade" kite constructed from the refuse of their lives. The memory of that kite in flight conjures up the image of freedom and of Sam, a man who, surrounded by a constricting society, is free only in his mind. Sam relinquished control of the kite that fateful day in hopes that Hally might see the beauty of freedom. In addition to the freedom implied by a soaring kite, there is also the sense of communion between the kite and its handler. Neither one can be successful, nor exist, without the other. Their kite is, of course, a phoenix—it flew once and, as we see in postapartheid South Africa, it may fly again.

Closely aligned with the image of the kite is that of the "whites-only bench." While the kite signifies togetherness, the bench epitomizes separateness—or to use the Afrikaans term, apartheid. As long as the "whites-only bench" exists and Hally continues to make use of it, the kite and its freedom will only be a vague memory of youth, a dream destined for oblivion. As Sam explains to Hally, "You're going to be sitting up there by yourself for a long time to come, and there won't be a kite in the sky."

Throughout the play Hally seems to be the teacher and Sam the student. At the conclusion, we realize that while Hally has led Sam on a journey through books, it is Sam who has worked tirelessly to teach Hally "what being a man means." In the end Hally declares: "I don't know. I don't know anything anymore." Sam reassures him, saying, "Are you sure of that, Hally? Because it would be hopeless if that was true. It would mean nothing has been learnt in here this afternoon, and there was a hell of a lot of teaching going on . . . one way or the other."

The characters move freely about the entire tearoom, where, at least after hours, there are no "whites-only benches." Even as Sam and Willie dance, Hally stands behind the counter to make an ice cream soda. Not until the final moments are they separated, and we see an image of Sam and Willie as servants waiting to, in Hally's words, "get on with [their] job[s]." But even this picture changes as Sam reaches out one last time to Hally. When he asks Hally if they "should try again . . . [to] fly another kite," it is more than forgiveness, more than turning the other cheek he represents. He is the epitome of generosity, the ultimate act of humanity, which makes Sam the "man of magnitude" referred to in Hally's school lesson.

The images of the dancing, the kite, the "whites-only bench," and the teaching are presented through a metatheatrical motif—everything is acted out. Fugard's few stage directions demand that the characters "perform" for one another. For example, as Hally conjures up the memory of the old Jubilee Boarding House, he exclaims: "I bet I could still find my way to your room with my eye closed." To which Fugard adds, "(*He does exactly that.*)" Shortly thereafter, "using a few chairs [Hally] re-creates the room," and Willie, eager to partake in the drama, assumes the "boxing pose" of Joe Louis as Hally, now a director, works to bring the scene to life. Later, as Sam describes the finale to the ballroom dancing contest, Fugard places Sam "onto the chair to act out the M.C."

The "let's pretend" images of the play occur in the dialogue as well. As Hally completes his re-creation of the Old Jubilee Boarding House, he exclaims, "Right, so much for the stage directions. Now the characters." He proceeds to describe Sam and Willie, who "move to their appropriate positions in the bedroom." Certainly implied here are the directions for "Master Harold" and "the boys" to act out as much of the description in the text as possible—in short, to turn the narratives into dramatic performance.

The overriding reality of racism permeates the play's images, especially in Hally's dialogue. While his condescending "Don't be smart, Sam, it doesn't become you," "What does a black man know about flying a kite?" and "It's called bigotry, Sam" are attempts at humor, they are also signs of Hally's latent racism. Hally is his father's son, and the greatest irony of all is that while Hally is ashamed of his father's afflictions, his greatest disease is neither physical nor drug induced but his ignorant racism. The degrading racist lines we hear early in the play are actually figurative spits in the face as disturbing as the literal spit of the climax.

The world of the tea room is a microcosm of South Africa, which is itself a microcosm of the world. Fugard sees his hometown as representative of South Africa: "In Port Elizabeth, I think, you have a microcosm in a microcosm . . . black, white, Indian, Chinese, and Colored [mixed race]. It is also very representative of South Africa in the range of its social strata, from total affluence on the white side to the extremist poverty of the non-white." Fugard has written that the circumstances of his life have set him in opposition to apartheid and makes it clear that in his plays he is "judging my own people for what they have done to themselves, done to the Black people in that country, done to the Colored people in that country, done to the Indian people in that country, done to the Chinese people in that country. My sense of myself as judge came about without my realizing it; it came out of a sense of the common humanity of all people in that country." While apartheid has been "officially" banned in the Republic of South Africa and many other sovereign nations, a great deal of informal separateness lingers in our society, breeding the same kind of racism we see in Hally.

A young Master Harold (Damaso Rodriguez) shares his dreams with "the boys"—Sam (Rapulana Seiphemo) and Willie (Armando Garza) in this production staged by Roger Schultz at Texas A&M University in 1994.

"MASTER HAROLD" . . . and the boys

ATHOL FUGARD

The St. George's Park Tea Room on a wet and windy Port Elizabeth[1] afternoon.

Tables and chairs have been cleared and are stacked on one side except for one which stands apart with a single chair. On this table a knife, fork, spoon and side plate in anticipation of a simple meal, together with a pile of comic books.

Other elements: a serving counter with a few stale cakes under glass and a not very impressive display of sweets, cigarettes and cool drinks, etc.; a few cardboard advertising handouts—Cadbury's Chocolate, Coca-Cola—and a blackboard on which an untrained hand has chalked up the prices of Tea, Coffee, Scones, Milk-shakes—all flavors—and Cool Drinks; a few sad ferns in pots; a telephone; an old-style jukebox.

There is an entrance on one side and an exit into a kitchen on the other.

Leaning on the solitary table, his head cupped in one hand as he pages through one of the comic books, is Sam. A black man in his mid-forties. He wears the white coat of a waiter. Behind him on his knees, mopping down the floor with a bucket of water and a rag, is Willie. Also black and about the same age as Sam. He has his sleeves and trousers rolled up.

[1] **Port Elizabeth** city in South Africa

The year: 1950

WILLIE (*singing as he works*).
>   "She was scandalizin' my name,
>   She took my money
>   She called me honey
>   But she was scandalizin' my name.
>   Called it love but was playin' a game . . . "

He gets up and moves the bucket. Stands thinking for a moment, then, raising his arms to hold an imaginary partner, he launches into an intricate ballroom dance step. Although a mildly comic figure, he reveals a reasonable degree of accomplishment.

Hey, Sam.

Sam, absorbed in the comic book, does not respond.

Hey, Boet[2] Sam!

Sam looks up.

I'm getting it. The quickstep. Look now and tell me. (*He repeats the step.*) Well?

SAM (*encouragingly*). Show me again.

WILLIE. Okay, count for me.

SAM. Ready?

WILLIE. Ready.

SAM. Five, six, seven, eight . . . (*Willie starts to dance.*) A-n-d one two three four . . . and one two three four. . . . (*Ad libbing as Willie dances.*) Your shoulders, Willie . . . your shoulders! Don't look down! Look happy, Willie! Relax, Willie!

WILLIE (*desperate but still dancing*). I am relax.

SAM. No, you're not.

WILLIE. (*He falters.*) Ag no man, Sam! Mustn't talk. You make me make mistakes.

SAM. But you're too stiff.

WILLIE. Yesterday I'm not straight . . . today I'm too stiff!

SAM. Well, you are. You asked me and I'm telling you.

WILLIE. Where?

SAM. Everywhere. Try to glide through it.

WILLIE. Glide?

SAM. Ja, make it smooth. And give it more style. It must look like you're enjoying yourself.

WILLIE (*emphatically*). I wasn't.

SAM. Exactly.

WILLIE. How can I enjoy myself? Not straight, too stiff and now it's also glide, give it more style, make it smooth. . . . Haai! Is hard to remember all those things, Boet Sam.

SAM. That's your trouble. You're trying too hard.

WILLIE. I try hard because it *is* hard.

SAM. But don't let me see it. The secret is to make it look easy. Ballroom must look happy, Willie, not like hard work. It must . . . Ja! . . . it must look like romance.

WILLIE. Now another one! What's romance?

SAM. Love story with happy ending. A handsome man in tails, and in his arms, smiling at him, a beautiful lady in evening dress!

WILLIE. Fred Astaire, Ginger Rogers.

SAM. You got it. Tapdance or ballroom, it's the same. Romance. In two weeks' time when the judges look at you and Hilda, they must see a man and a woman who are dancing their way to a happy ending. What I saw was you holding her like you were frightened she was going to run away.

WILLIE. Ja! Because that is what she wants to do! I got no romance left for Hilda anymore, Boet Sam.

SAM. Then pretend. When you put your arms around Hilda, imagine she is Ginger Rogers.

WILLIE. With no teeth? You try.

SAM. Well, just remember, there's only two weeks left.

WILLIE. I know, I know! (*To the jukebox.*) I do it better with music. You got sixpence for Sarah Vaughan?[3]

SAM. That's a slow foxtrot. You're practicing the quickstep.

WILLIE. I'll practice slow foxtrot.

SAM (*shaking his head*). It's your turn to put money in the jukebox.

WILLIE. I only got bus fare to go home. (*He returns disconsolately to his work.*) Love story and happy ending! She's doing it all right, Boet Sam, but is not me she's giving happy endings. Fuckin' whore! Three nights now she doesn't come practice. I wind up gramophone, I get record ready and I sit and wait. What happens? Nothing. Ten o'clock I start dancing with my pillow. You try and practice romance by yourself, Boet Sam. Struesgod, she doesn't come tonight I take back my dress and ballroom shoes and I find me new partner. Size twenty-six. Shoes size seven. And now she's also making trouble for me with the baby again. Reports me to Child Wellfed, that I'm not giving her money. She lies! Every week I am giving her money for milk. And how do I know is my baby? Only his hair looks like me. She's fucking around all the time I turn my back. Hilda Samuels is a bitch! (*Pause.*) Hey, Sam!

SAM. Ja.

WILLIE. You listening?

SAM. Ja.

WILLIE. So what you say?

SAM. About Hilda?

WILLIE. Ja.

SAM. When did you last give her a hiding?

WILLIE (*reluctantly*). Sunday night.

SAM. And today is Thursday.

WILLIE. (*He knows what's coming.*) Okay.

SAM. Hiding on Sunday night, then Monday, Tuesday and Wednesday she doesn't come to practice . . . and you are asking me why?

WILLIE. I said okay, Boet Sam!

---

[2]**Boet** Buddy, Brother

[3]**Sarah Vaughan** (1924 – 1990) American jazz singer

SAM. You hit her too much. One day she's going to leave you for good.

WILLIE. So? She makes me the hell-in too much.

SAM (*emphasizing his point*). *Too* much and *too* hard. You had the same trouble with Eunice.

WILLIE. Because she also make the hell-in, Boet Sam. She never got the steps right. Even the waltz.

SAM. Beating her up every time she makes a mistake in the waltz? (*Shaking his head.*) No, Willie! That takes the pleasure out of ballroom dancing.

WILLIE. Hilda is not too bad with the waltz, Boet Sam. Is the quickstep where the trouble starts.

SAM (*teasing him gently*). How's your pillow with the quickstep?

WILLIE. (*ignoring the tease*). Good! And why? Because it got no legs. That's her trouble. She can't move them quick enough, Boet Sam. I start the record and before halfway Count Basie[4] is already winning. Only time we catch up with him is when gramophone runs down.

Sam laughs.

Haaikona, Boet Sam, is not funny.

SAM (*snapping his fingers*). I got it! Give her a handicap.

WILLIE. What's that?

SAM. Give her a ten-second start and then let Count Basie go. Then I put my money on her. Hot favorite in the Ballroom Stakes: Hilda Samuels ridden by Willie Malopo.

WILLIE (*turning away*). I'm not talking to you no more.

SAM (*relenting*). Sorry, Willie . . .

WILLIE. It's finish between us.

SAM. Okay, okay . . . I'll stop.

WILLIE. You can also fuck off.

SAM. Willie, listen! I want to help you!

WILLIE. No more jokes?

SAM. I promise.

WILLIE. Okay. Help me.

SAM (*his turn to hold an imaginary partner*). Look and learn. Feet together. Back straight. Body relaxed. Right hand placed gently in the small of her back and wait for the music. Don't start worrying about making mistakes or the judges or the other competitors. It's just you, Hilda and the music, and you're going to have a good time. What Count Basie do you play?

WILLIE. "You the cream in my coffee, you the salt in my stew."

SAM. Right. Give it to me in strict tempo.

WILLIE. Ready?

SAM. Ready.

WILLIE. A-n-d . . . (*Singing.*)
"You the cream in my coffee.
You the salt in my stew.

You will always be my necessity.
I'd be lost without you. . . ." (etc.)

Sam launches into the quickstep. He is obviously a much more accomplished dancer than Willie. Hally enters. A seventeen-year-old white boy. Wet raincoat and school case. He stops and watches Sam. The demonstration comes to an end with a flourish. Applause from Hally and Willie.

HALLY. Bravo! No question about it. First place goes to Mr. Sam Semela.

WILLIE (*in total agreement*). You was gliding with style, Boet Sam.

HALLY (*cheerfully*). How's it, chaps?

SAM. Okay, Hally.

WILLIE (*springing to attention like a soldier and saluting*). At your service, Master Harold!

HALLY. Not long to the big event, hey!

SAM. Two weeks.

HALLY. You nervous?

SAM. No.

HALLY. Think you stand a chance?

SAM. Let's just say I'm ready to go out there and dance.

HALLY. It looked like it. What about you, Willie?
Willie groans.
What's the matter?

SAM. He's got leg trouble.

HALLY (*innocently*). Oh, sorry to hear that, Willie.

WILLIE. Boet Sam! You promised. (*Willie returns to his work.*)

Hally deposits his school case and takes off his raincoat. His clothes are a little neglected and untidy: black blazer with school badge, gray flannel trousers in need of an ironing, khaki shirt and tie, black shoes. Sam has fetched a towel for Hally to dry his hair.

HALLY. God, what a lousy bloody day. It's coming down cats and dogs out there. Bad for business, chaps . . . (*Conspiratorial whisper.*) . . . but it also means we're in for a nice quiet afternoon.

SAM. You can speak loud, Your Mom's not here.

HALLY. Out shopping?

SAM. No. The hospital.

HALLY. But it's Thursday. There's no visiting on Thursday afternoons. Is my Dad okay?

SAM. Sounds like it. In fact, I think he's going home.

HALLY (*stopped short by Sam's remark*). What do you mean?

SAM. The hospital phoned.

HALLY. To say what?

SAM. I don't know. I just heard your Mom talking.

HALLY. So what makes you say he's going home?

SAM. It sounded as if they were telling her to come and fetch him.

Hally thinks about what Sam has said for a few seconds.

HALLY. When did she leave?

---

[4] **Count Basie** William Basie (1904–1984), American jazz pianist, and band leader

SAM. About an hour ago. She said she would phone you. Want to eat?

Hally doesn't respond.

Hally, want your lunch?

HALLY. I suppose so. (*His mood has changed.*) What's on the menu? . . . as if I don't know.

SAM. Soup, followed by meat pie and gravy.

HALLY. Today's?

SAM. No.

HALLY. And the soup?

SAM. Nourishing pea soup.

HALLY. Just the soup. (*The pile of comic books on the table.*) And these?

SAM. For your Dad. Mr. Kempston brought them.

HALLY. You haven't been reading them, have you?

SAM. Just looking.

HALLY (*examining the comics*). Jungle Jim . . . Batman and Robin . . . Tarzan . . . God, what rubbish! Mental pollution. Take them away.

Sam exits waltzing into the kitchen. Hally turns to Willie.

HALLY. Did you hear my Mom talking on the telephone, Willie?

WILLIE. No, Master Hally. I was at the back.

HALLY. And she didn't say anything to you before she left?

WILLIE. She said I must clean the floors.

HALLY. I mean about my Dad.

WILLIE. She didn't say nothing to me about him, Master Hally.

HALLY (*with conviction*). No! It can't be. They said he needed at least another three weeks of treatment. Sam's definitely made a mistake. (*Rummages through his school case, finds a book and settles down at the table to read.*) So, Willie!

WILLIE. Yes, Master Hally! Schooling okay today?

HALLY. Yes, okay. . . . (*He thinks about it.*) . . . No, not really. Ag, what's the difference? I don't care. And Sam says you've got problems.

WILLIE. Big problems.

HALLY. Which leg is sore?

Willie groans.

Both legs.

WILLIE. There is nothing wrong with my legs. Sam is just making jokes.

HALLY. So then you will be in the competition.

WILLIE. Only if I can find me a partner.

HALLY. But what about Hilda?

SAM (*returning with a bowl of soup*). She's the one who's got trouble with her legs.

HALLY. What sort of trouble, Willie?

SAM. From the way he describes it, I think the lady has gone a bit lame.

HALLY. Good God! Have you taken her to see a doctor?

SAM. I think a vet would be better.

HALLY. What do you mean?

SAM. What do you call it again when a racehorse goes very fast?

HALLY. Gallop?

SAM. That's it!

WILLIE. Boet Sam!

HALLY. "A gallop down the homestretch to the winning post." But what's that got to do with Hilda?

SAM. Count Basie always gets there first.

Willie lets fly with his slop rag. It misses Sam and hits Hally.

HALLY (*furious*). For Christ's sake, Willie! What the hell do you think you're doing!

WILLIE. Sorry, Master Hally, but it's him. . . .

HALLY. Act your bloody age! (*Hurls the rag back at Willie.*) Cut out the nonsense now and get on with your work. And you too, Sam. Stop fooling around.

Sam moves away.

No. Hang on. I haven't finished! Tell me exactly what my Mom said.

SAM. I have. "When Hally comes, tell him I've gone to the hospital and I'll phone him."

HALLY. She didn't say anything about taking my Dad home?

SAM. No. It's just that when she was talking on the phone . . .

HALLY (*interrupting him*). No, Sam. They can't be discharging him. She would have said so if they were. In any case, we saw him last night and he wasn't in good shape at all. Staff nurse even said there was talk about taking more X-rays. And now suddenly today he's better? If anything, it sounds more like a bad turn to me . . . which I sincerely hope it isn't. Hang on . . . how long ago did you say she left?

SAM. Just before two . . . (*His wrist watch.*) . . . hour and a half.

HALLY. I know how to settle it. (*Behind the counter to the telephone. Talking as he dials.*) Let's give her ten minutes to get to the hospital, ten minutes to load him up, another ten, at the most, to get home and another ten to get him inside. Forty minutes. They should have been home for at least half an hour already. (*Pause—he waits with the receiver to his ear.*) No reply, chaps. And you know why? Because she's at his bedside in hospital helping him pull through a bad turn. You definitely heard wrong.

SAM. Okay.

As far as Hally is concerned, the matter is settled. He returns to his table, sits down and divides his attention between the book and his soup. Sam is at his school case and picks up a textbook "Modern Graded Mathematics for Standards Nine and Ten." Opens it at random and laughs at something he sees.

Who is this supposed to be?

HALLY. Old fart-face Prentice.

SAM. Teacher?

HALLY. Thinks he is. And believe me, that is not a bad likeness.

SAM. Has he seen it?

HALLY. Yes.

SAM. What did he say?

HALLY. Tried to be clever, as usual. Said I was no Leonardo da Vinci and that bad art had to be punished. So, six of the best, and his are bloody good.

SAM. On your bum?

HALLY. Where else? The days when I got them on my hands are gone forever, Sam.

SAM. With your trousers down!

HALLY. No. He's not quite that barbaric.

SAM. That's the way they do it in jail.

HALLY (flicker of morbid interest). Really?

SAM. Ja. When the magistrate sentences you to "strokes with a light cane."

HALLY. Go on.

SAM. They make you lie down on a bench. One policeman pulls down your trousers and holds your ankles, another one pulls your shirt over your head and holds your arms . . .

HALLY. Thank you! That's enough.

SAM. . . . and the one that gives you the strokes talks to you gently and for a long time between each one. (He laughs.)

HALLY. I've heard enough, Sam! Jesus! It's a bloody awful world when you come to think of it. People can be real bastards.

SAM. That's the way it is, Hally.

HALLY. It doesn't have to be that way. There is something called progress, you know. We don't exactly burn people at the stake anymore.

SAM. Like Joan of Arc.

HALLY. Correct. If she was captured today, she'd be given a fair trial.

SAM. And then the death sentence.

HALLY (a world-weary sigh). I know, I know! I oscillate between hope and despair for this world as well, Sam. But things will change, you wait and see. One day somebody is going to get up and give history a kick up the backside and get it going again.

SAM. Like who?

HALLY (after thought). They're called social reformers. Every age, Sam, has got its social reformer. My history book is full of them.

SAM. So where's ours?

HALLY. Good question. And I hate to say it, but the answer is: I don't know. Maybe he hasn't even been born yet. Or is still only a babe in arms at his mother's breast. God, what a thought.

SAM. So we just go on waiting.

HALLY. Ja, looks like it. (Back to his soup and the book.)

SAM (reading from the textbook). "Introduction: In some mathematical problems only the magnitude . . ." (He mispronounces the word "magnitude.")

HALLY (correcting him without looking up). Magnitude.

SAM. What's it mean?

HALLY. How big it is. The size of the thing.

SAM (reading). ". . . a magnitude of the quantities is of importance. In other problems we need to know whether these quantities are negative or positive. For example, whether there is a debit or credit bank balance . . ."

HALLY. Whether you're broke or not.

SAM. ". . . whether the temperature is above or below Zero . . ."

HALLY. Naught degrees. Cheerful state of affairs! No cash and you're freezing to death. Mathematics won't get you out of that one.

SAM. "All these quantities are called . . ." (Spelling the word.) . . . s-c-a-l . . .

HALLY. Scalars.

SAM. Scalars! (Shaking his head with a laugh.) You understand all that?

HALLY (turning a page). No. And I don't intend to try.

SAM. So what happens when the exams come?

HALLY. Failing a maths exam isn't the end of the world, Sam. How many times have I told you that examination results don't measure intelligence?

SAM. I would say about as many times as you've failed one of them.

HALLY (mirthlessly). Ha, ha, ha.

SAM (simultaneously). Ha, ha, ha.

HALLY. Just remember Winston Churchill didn't do particularly well at school.

SAM. You've also told me that one many times.

HALLY. Well, it just so happens to be the truth.

SAM (enjoying the word). Magnitude! Magnitude! Show me how to use it.

HALLY (after thought). An intrepid social reformer will not be daunted by the magnitude of the task he has undertaken.

SAM (impressed). Couple of jaw-breakers in there!

HALLY. I gave you three for the price of one. Intrepid, daunted and magnitude. I did that once in an exam. Put five of the words I had to explain in one sentence. It was half a page long.

SAM. Well, I'll put my money on you in the English exam.

HALLY. Piece of cake. Eighty percent without even trying.

SAM (another textbook from Hally's case). And history?

HALLY. So-so. I'll scrape through. In the fifties if I'm lucky.

SAM. You didn't do too badly last year.

HALLY. Because we had World War One. That at least had some action. You try to find that in the South African Parliamentary system.

SAM (reading from the history textbook). "Napoleon and the

principle of equality." Hey! This sounds interesting. "After concluding peace with Britain in 1802, Napoleon used a brief period of calm to in-sti-tute . . . "

HALLY. Introduce.

SAM. ". . . many reforms. Napoleon regarded all people as equal before the law and wanted them to have equal opportunities for advancement. All ves-ti-ges of the feu-dal system with its oppression of the poor were abolished." Vestiges, feudal system and abolished. I'm all right on oppression.

HALLY. I'm thinking. He swept away . . . abolished . . . the last remains . . . vestiges . . . of the bad old days . . . feudal system.

SAM. Ha! There's the social reformer we're waiting for. He sounds like a man of some magnitude.

HALLY. I'm not so sure about that. It's a damn good title for a book, though. A man of magnitude!

SAM. He sounds pretty big to me, Hally.

HALLY. Don't confuse historical significance with greatness. But maybe I'm being a bit prejudiced. Have a look in there and you'll see he's two chapters long. And hell! . . . has he only got dates, Sam, all of which you've got to remember! This campaign and that campaign, and then, because of all the fighting, the next thing is we get Peace Treaties all over the place. And what's the end of the story? Battle of Waterloo, which he loses. Wasn't worth it. No, I don't know about him as a man of magnitude.

SAM. Then who would you say was?

HALLY. To answer that, we need a definition of greatness, and I suppose that would be somebody who . . . somebody who benefited all mankind.

SAM. Right. But like who?

HALLY. (*He speaks with total conviction.*) Charles Darwin. Remember him? That big book from the library. *The Origin of the Species.*

SAM. Him?

HALLY. Yes. For his Theory of Evolution.

SAM. You didn't finish it.

HALLY. I ran out of time. I didn't finish it because my two weeks was up. But I'm going to take it out again after I've digested what I read. It's safe. I've hidden it away in the Theology section. Nobody ever goes in there. And anyway who are you to talk? You hardly even looked at it.

SAM. I tried. I looked at the chapters in the beginning and I saw one called "The Struggle for an Existence." Ah ha, I thought. At last! But what did I get? Something called the mistletoe which needs the apple tree and there's too many seeds and all are going to die except one . . . ! No, Hally.

HALLY (*intellectually outraged*). What do you mean, No! The poor man had to start somewhere. For God's sake, Sam, he revolutionized science. Now we know.

SAM. What?

HALLY. Where we come from and what it all means.

SAM. And that's a benefit to mankind? Anyway, I still don't believe it.

HALLY. God, you're impossible. I showed it to you in black and white.

SAM. Doesn't mean I got to believe it.

HALLY. It's the likes of you that kept the Inquisition in business. It's called bigotry. Anyway, that's my man of magnitude. Charles Darwin! Who's yours?

SAM (*without hesitation*). Abraham Lincoln.

HALLY. I might have guessed as much. Don't get sentimental, Sam. You've never been a slave, you know. And anyway we freed your ancestors here in South Africa long before the Americans. But if you want to thank somebody on their behalf, do it to Mr. William Wilberforce.[5] Come on. Try again. I want a real genius. (*Now enjoying himself, and so is Sam. Hally goes behind the counter and helps himself to a chocolate.*)

SAM. William Shakespeare.

HALLY (*no enthusiasm*). Oh. So you're also one of them, are you? You're basing that opinion on only one play, you know. You've only read my *Julius Caesar* and even I don't understand half of what they're talking about. They should do what they did with the old Bible: bring the language up to date.

SAM. That's all you've got. It's also the only one you've read.

HALLY. I know. I admit it. That's why I suggest we reserve our judgment until we've checked up on a few others. I've got a feeling, though, that by the end of this year one is going to be enough for me, and I can give you the names of twenty-nine other chaps in the Standard Nine class of the Port Elizabeth Technical College who feel the same. But if you want him, you can have him. My turn now. (*Pacing.*) This is a damned good exercise, you know! It started off looking like a simple question and here it's got us really probing into the intellectual heritage of our civilization.

SAM. So who is it going to be?

HALLY. My next man . . . and he gets the title on two scores: social reform and literary genius . . . is Leo Nikolaevich Tolstoy.

SAM. That Russian.

HALLY. Correct. Remember the picture of him I showed you?

SAM. With the long beard.

HALLY (*trying to look like Tolstoy*). And those burning, visionary eyes. My God, the face of a social prophet if ever I saw one! And remember my words when I showed it to you? Here's a *man*, Sam!

SAM. Those were words, Hally.

HALLY. Not many intellectuals are prepared to shovel manure with the peasants and then go home and write a "little book" called *War and Peace.* Incidentally, Sam, he was

---

[5]**William Wilberforce** (1759–1833) English abolitionist

somebody else who, to quote, "... did not distinguish himself scholastically."

SAM. Meaning?

HALLY. He was also no good at school.

SAM. Like you and Winston Churchill.

HALLY. (*mirthlessly*). Ha, ha, ha.

SAM (*simultaneously*). Ha, ha, ha.

HALLY. Don't get clever, Sam. That man freed his serfs of his own free will.

SAM. No argument. He was a somebody, all right. I accept him.

HALLY. I'm sure Count Tolstoy will be very pleased to hear that. Your turn. Shoot. (*Another chocolate from behind the counter.*) I'm waiting, Sam.

SAM. I've got him.

HALLY. Good. Submit your candidate for examination.

SAM. Jesus.

HALLY (*stopped dead in his tracks*). Who?

SAM. Jesus Christ.

HALLY. Oh, come on, Sam!

SAM. The Messiah.

HALLY. Ja, but still ... No, Sam. Don't let's get started on religion. We'll just spend the whole afternoon arguing again. Suppose I turn around and say Mohammed?

SAM. All right.

HALLY. You can't have them both on the same list!

SAM. Why not? You like Mohammed, I like Jesus.

HALLY. I *don't* like Mohammed. I never have. I was merely being hypothetical. As far as I'm concerned, the Koran is as bad as the Bible. No. Religion is out! I'm not going to waste my time again arguing with you about the existence of God. You know perfectly well I'm an atheist ... and I've got homework to do.

SAM. Okay, I take him back.

HALLY. You've got time for one more name.

SAM (*after thought*). I've got one I know we'll agree on. A simple straightforward great Man of Magnitude ... and no arguments. And he really did benefit all mankind.

HALLY. I wonder. After your last contribution I'm beginning to doubt whether anything in the way of an intellectual agreement is possible between the two of us. Who is he?

SAM. Guess.

HALLY. Socrates? Alexandre Dumas? Karl Marx? Dostoevsky? Nietzsche?

Sam shakes his head after each name.

Give me a clue.

SAM. The letter P is important ...

HALLY. Plato!

SAM. ... and his name begins with an F.

HALLY. I've got it. Freud and Psychology.

SAM. No. I didn't understand him.

HALLY. That makes two of us.

SAM. Think of mouldy apricot jam.

HALLY (*after a delighted laugh*). Penicillin and Sir Alexander

Fleming! And the title of the book: *The Microbe Hunters*. (*Delighted.*) Splendid, Sam! Splendid. For once we are in total agreement. The major breakthrough in medical science in the Twentieth Century. If it wasn't for him, we might have lost the Second World War. It's deeply gratifying, Sam, to know that I haven't been wasting my time in talking to you. (*Strutting around proudly.*) Tolstoy may have educated his peasants, but I've educated you.

SAM. Standard Four to Standard Nine.

HALLY. Have we been at it as long as that?

SAM. Yep. And my first lesson was geography.

HALLY (*intrigued*). Really? I don't remember.

SAM. My room there at the back of the old Jubilee Boarding House. I had just started working for your Mom. Little boy in short trousers walks in one afternoon and asks me seriously: "Sam, do you want to see South Africa?" Hey man! Sure I wanted to see South Africa!

HALLY. Was that me?

SAM. ... So the next thing I'm looking at a map you had just done for homework. It was your first one and you were very proud of yourself.

HALLY. Go on.

SAM. Then came my first lesson. "Repeat after me, Sam: Gold in the Transvaal, mealies in the Free State, sugar in Natal and grapes in the Cape." I still know it!

HALLY. Well, I'll be buggered. So that's how it all started.

SAM. And your next map was one with all the rivers and the mountains they came from. The Orange, the Vaal, the Limpopo, the Zambezi ...

HALLY. You've got a phenomenal memory!

SAM. You should be grateful. That is why you started passing your exams. You tried to be better than me.

They laugh together. Willie is attracted by the laughter and joins them.

HALLY. The old Jubilee Boarding House. Sixteen rooms with board and lodging, rent in advance and one week's notice. I haven't thought about it for donkey's years ... and I don't think that's an accident. God, was I glad when we sold it and moved out. Those years are not remembered as the happiest ones of an unhappy childhood.

WILLIE (*knocking on the table and trying to imitate a woman's voice*). "Hally, are you there?"

HALLY. Who's that supposed to be?

WILLIE. "What you doing in there, Hally? Come out at once!"

HALLY (*to Sam*). What's he talking about?

SAM. Don't you remember?

WILLIE. "Sam, Willie ... is he in there with you boys?"

SAM. Hiding away in our room when your mother was looking for you.

HALLY (*another good laugh*). Of course! I used to crawl and hide under your bed! But finish the story, Willie. Then what used to happen? You chaps would give the game away by telling her I was in there with you. So much for friendship.

SAM. We couldn't lie to her. She knew.

HALLY. Which meant I got another rowing for hanging around the "servants' quarters." I think I spent more time in there with you chaps than anywhere else in that dump. And do you blame me? Nothing but bloody misery wherever you went. Somebody was always complaining about the food, or my mother was having a fight with Micky Nash because she'd caught her with a petty officer in her room. Maud Meiring was another one. Remember those two? They were prostitutes, you know. Soldiers and sailors from the troopships. Bottom fell out of the business when the war ended. God, the flotsam and jetsam that life washed up on our shores! No joking, if it wasn't for your room, I would have been the first certified ten-year-old in medical history. Ja, the memories are coming back now. Walking home from school and thinking: "What can I do this afternoon?" Try out a few ideas, but sooner or later I'd end up in there with you fellows. I bet you I could still find my way to your room with my eyes closed. (*He does exactly that.*) Down the corridor . . . telephone on the right, which my Mom keeps locked because somebody is using it on the sly and not paying . . . past the kitchen and unappetizing cooking smells . . . around the corner into the backyard, hold my breath again because there are more smells coming when I pass your lavatory, then into that little passageway, first door on the right and into your room. How's that?

SAM. Good. But, as usual, you forgot to knock.

HALLY. Like that time I barged in and caught you and Cynthia . . . at it. Remember? God, was I embarrassed! I didn't know what was going on at first.

SAM. Ja, that taught you a lesson.

HALLY. And about a lot more than knocking on doors, I'll have you know, and I don't mean geography either. Hell, Sam, couldn't you have waited until it was dark?

SAM. No.

HALLY. Was it that urgent?

SAM. Yes, and if you don't believe me, wait until your time comes.

HALLY. No, thank you. I am not interested in girls. (*Back to his memories . . . Using a few chairs he recreates the room as he lists the items.*) A gray little room with a cold cement floor. Your bed against that wall . . . and I now know why the mattress sags so much! . . . Willie's bed . . . it's propped up on bricks because one leg is broken . . . that wobbly little table with the washbasin and jug of water . . . Yes! . . . stuck to the wall above it are some pin-up pictures from magazines. Joe Louis[6] . . .

---

[6]**Joe Louis** (1914–1981) African-American prizefighter known as the Brown Bomber

WILLIE. Brown Bomber. World Title. (*Boxing pose.*) Three rounds and knockout.

HALLY. Against who?

SAM. Max Schmeling.

HALLY. Correct. I can also remember Fred Astaire and Ginger Rogers, and Rita Hayworth in a bathing costume which always made me hot and bothered when I looked at it. Under Willie's bed is an old suitcase with all his clothes in a mess, which is why I never hide there. Your things are neat and tidy in a trunk next to your bed, and on it there is a picture of you and Cynthia in your ballroom clothes, your first silver cup for third place in a competition and an old radio which doesn't work anymore. Have I left out anything?

SAM. No.

HALLY. Right, so much for the stage directions. Now the characters. (*Sam and Willie move to their appropriate positions in the bedroom.*) Willie is in bed, under his blankets with his clothes on, complaining nonstop about something, but we can't make out a word of what he's saying because he's got his head under the blankets as well. You're on your bed trimming your toenails with a knife—not a very edifying sight—and as for me . . . What am I doing?

SAM. You're sitting on the floor giving Willie a lecture about being a good loser while you get the checker board and pieces ready for a game. Then you go to Willie's bed, pull off the blankets and make him play with you first because you know you're going to win, and that gives you the second game with me.

HALLY. And you certainly were a bad loser, Willie!

WILLIE. Haai!

HALLY. Wasn't he, Sam? And so slow! A game with you almost took the whole afternoon. Thank God I gave up trying to teach you how to play chess.

WILLIE. You and Sam cheated.

HALLY. I never saw Sam cheat, and mine were mostly the mistakes of youth.

WILLIE. Then how is it you two was always winning?

HALLY. Have you ever considered the possibility, Willie, that it was because we were better than you?

WILLIE. Every time better?

HALLY. Not every time. There were occasions when we deliberately let you win a game so that you would stop sulking and go on playing with us. Sam used to wink at me when you weren't looking to show me it was time to let you win.

WILLIE. So then you two didn't play fair.

HALLY. It was for your benefit, Mr. Malopo, which is more than being fair. It was an act of self-sacrifice. (*To Sam.*) But you know what my best memory is, don't you?

SAM. No.

HALLY. Come on, guess. If your memory is so good, you must remember it as well.

SAM. We got up to a lot of tricks in there, Hally.

HALLY. This one was special, Sam.

SAM. I'm listening.

HALLY. It started off looking like another of those useless nothing-to-do afternoons. I'd already been down to Main Street looking for adventure, but nothing had happened. I didn't feel like climbing trees in the Donkin Park or pretending I was a private eye and following a stranger . . . so as usual: See what's cooking in Sam's room. This time it was you on the floor. You had two thin pieces of wood and you were smoothing them down with a knife. It didn't look particularly interesting, but when I asked you what you were doing, you just said, "Wait and see, Hally. Wait . . . and see" . . . in that secret sort of way of yours, so I knew there was a surprise coming. You teased me, you bugger, by being deliberately slow and not answering my questions!

Sam laughs.

And whistling while you worked away! God, it was infuriating! I could have brained you! It was only when you tied them together in a cross and put that down on the brown paper that I realized what you were doing. "Sam is making a kite?" And when I asked you and you said "Yes" . . . ! (*Shaking his head with disbelief.*) The sheer audacity of it took my breath away. I mean, seriously, what the hell does a black man know about flying a kite? I'll be honest with you, Sam, I had no hopes for it. If you think I was excited and happy, you got another guess coming. In fact, I was shit-scared that we were going to make fools of ourselves. When we left the boarding house to go up onto the hill, I was praying quietly that there wouldn't be any other kids around to laugh at us.

SAM (*enjoying the memory as much as Hally*). Ja, I could see that.

HALLY. I made it obvious, did I?

SAM. Ja. You refused to carry it.

HALLY. Do you blame me? Can you remember what the poor thing looked like? Tomato-box wood and brown paper! Flour and water for glue! Two of my mother's old stockings for a tail, and then all those bits and pieces of string you made me tie together so that we could fly it! Hell, no, that was now only asking for a miracle to happen.

SAM. Then the big argument when I told you to hold the string and run with it when I let go.

HALLY. I was prepared to run, all right, but straight back to the boarding house.

SAM (*knowing what's coming*). So what happened?

HALLY. Come on, Sam, you remember as well as I do.

SAM. I want to hear it from you.

Hally pauses. He wants to be as accurate as possible.

HALLY. You went a little distance from me down the hill, you held it up ready to let it go. . . . "This is it," I thought. "Like everything else in my life, here comes another fiasco." Then you shouted, "Go, Hally!" and I started to run. (*Another pause.*) I don't know how to describe it, Sam. Ja! The miracle happened! I was running, waiting for it to crash to the ground, but instead suddenly there was something alive behind me at the end of the string, tugging at it as if it wanted to be free. I looked back . . . (*Shakes his head.*) . . . I still can't believe my eyes. It was flying! Looping around and trying to climb even higher into the sky. You shouted to me to let it have more string. I did, until there was none left and I was just holding that piece of wood we had tied it to. You came up and joined me. You were laughing.

SAM. So were you. And shouting, "It works, Sam! We've done it!"

HALLY. And we had! I was so proud of us! It was the most splendid thing I had ever seen. I wished there were hundreds of kids around to watch us. The part that scared me, though, was when you showed me how to make it dive down to the ground and then just when it was on the point of crashing, swoop up again!

SAM. You didn't want to try yourself.

HALLY. Of course not! I would have been suicidal if anything had happened to it. Watching you do it made me nervous enough. I was quite happy just to see it up there with its tail fluttering behind it. You left me after that, didn't you? You explained how to get it down, we tied it to the bench so that I could sit and watch it, and you went away. I wanted you to stay, you know. I was a little scared of having to look after it by myself.

SAM (*quietly*). I had work to do, Hally.

HALLY. It was sort of sad bringing it down, Sam. And it looked sad again when it was lying there on the ground. Like something that had lost its soul. Just tomato-box wood, brown paper and two of my mother's old stockings! But, hell, I'll never forget that first moment when I saw it up there. I had a stiff neck the next day from looking up so much.

Sam laughs. Hally turns to him with a question he never thought of asking before.

Why did you make that kite, Sam?

SAM (*evenly*). I can't remember.

HALLY. Truly?

SAM. Too long ago, Hally.

HALLY. Ja, I suppose it was. It's time for another one, you know.

SAM. Why do you say that?

HALLY. Because it feels like that. Wouldn't be a good day to fly it, though.

SAM. No. You can't fly kites on rainy days.

HALLY. (*He studies Sam. Their memories have made him conscious of the man's presence in his life.*) How old are you, Sam?

SAM. Two score and five.

HALLY. Strange, isn't it?

SAM. What?

HALLY. Me and you.

SAM. What's strange about it?

HALLY. Little white boy in short trousers and a black man old enough to be his father flying a kite. It's not every day you see that.

SAM. But why strange? Because the one is white and the other black?

HALLY. I don't know. Would have been just as strange, I suppose, if it had been me and my Dad . . . cripple man and a little boy! Nope! There's no chance of me flying a kite without it being strange. (*Simple statement of fact—no self-pity.*) There's a nice little short story there. "The Kite-Flyers." But we'd have to find a twist in the ending.

SAM. Twist?

HALLY. Yes. Something unexpected. The way it ended with us was too straightforward . . . me on the bench and you going back to work. There's no drama in that.

WILLIE. And me?

HALLY. You?

WILLIE. Yes me.

HALLY. You want to get into the story as well, do you? I got it! Change the title: "Afternoons in Sam's Room" . . . expand it and tell all the stories. It's on its way to being a novel. Our days in the old Jubilee. Sad in a way that they're over. I almost wish we were still in that little room.

SAM. We're still together.

HALLY. That's true. It's just that life felt the right size in there . . . not too big and not too small. Wasn't so hard to work up a bit of courage. It's got so bloody complicated since then.

The telephone rings. Sam answers it.

SAM. St. George's Park Tea Room . . . Hello, Madam . . . Yes, Madam, he's here . . . Hally, it's your mother.

HALLY. Where is she phoning from?

SAM. Sounds like the hospital. It's a public telephone.

HALLY (*relieved*). You see! I told you. (*The telephone.*) Hello, Mom . . . Yes . . . Yes no fine. Everything's under control here. How's things with poor old Dad? . . . Has he had a bad turn? . . . What? . . . Oh, God! . . . Yes, Sam told me, but I was sure he'd made a mistake, But what's this all about, Mom? He didn't look at all good last night. How can he get better so quickly? . . . Then very obviously you must say no. Be firm with him. You're the boss. . . . You know what it's going to be like if he comes home. . . . Well, then, don't blame me when I fail my exams at the end of the year. . . . Yes! How am I expected to be fresh for school when I spend half the night massaging his gammy leg? . . . So am I! . . . So tell him a white lie. Say Dr. Colley wants more X-rays of his stump. Or bribe him. We'll sneak in double tots of brandy in the future. . . . What? . . . Order him to get back into bed at once! If he's going to behave like a child, treat him like one. . . . All right, Mom! I was just trying to . . . I'm sorry. . . . I said I'm sorry. . . . Quick, give me your number. I'll phone you back. (*He hangs up and waits a few seconds.*) Here we go again! (*He dials.*) I'm sorry, Mom. . . . Okay . . . But now listen to me carefully. All it needs is for you to put your foot down. Don't take no for an answer. . . . Did you hear me? And whatever you do, don't discuss it with him. . . . Because I'm frightened you'll give in to him. . . . Yes, Sam gave me lunch. . . . I ate all of it! . . . No, Mom not a soul. It's still raining here. . . . Right, I'll tell them. I'll just do some homework and then lock up. . . . But remember now, Mom. Don't listen to anything he says. And phone me back and let me know what happens. . . . Okay. Bye, Mom. (*He hangs up. The men are staring at him.*) My Mom says that when you're finished with the floors you must do the windows. (*Pause.*) Don't misunderstand me, chaps. All I want is for him to get better. And if he was, I'd be the first person to say: "Bring him home." But he's not, and we can't give him the medical care and attention he needs at home. That's what hospitals are there for. (*Brusquely.*) So don't just stand there! Get on with it!

Sam clears Hally's table.

You heard right. My Dad wants to go home.

SAM. Is he better?

HALLY (*sharply.*). No! How the hell can he be better when last night he was groaning with pain? This is not an age of miracles!

SAM. Then he should stay in hospital.

HALLY (*seething with irritation and frustration*). Tell me something I don't know, Sam. What the hell do you think I was saying to my Mom? All I can say is fuck-it-all.

SAM. I'm sure he'll listen to your Mom.

HALLY. You don't know what she's up against. He's already packed his shaving kit and pajamas and is sitting on his bed with his crutches, dressed and ready to go. I know him when he gets in that mood. If she tries to reason with him, we've had it. She's no match for him when it comes to a battle of words. He'll tie her up in knots. (*Trying to hide his true feelings.*)

SAM. I suppose it gets lonely for him in there.

HALLY. With all the patients and nurses around? Regular visits from the Salvation Army? Balls! It's ten times worse for him at home. I'm at school and my mother is here in the business all day.

SAM. He's at least got you at night.

HALLY (*before he can stop himself*). And we've got him! Please! I don't want to talk about it anymore. (*Unpacks his school case, slamming down books on the table.*) Life is just a plain bloody mess, that's all. And people are fools.

SAM. Come on, Hally.

HALLY. Yes, they are! They bloody well deserve what they get.

SAM. Then don't complain.

HALLY. Don't try to be clever, Sam. It doesn't suit you. Anybody who thinks there's nothing wrong with this world needs to have his head examined. Just when things are going along all right, without fail someone or something will come along and spoil everything. Somebody should write that down as a fundamental law of the Universe. The principle of perpetual disappointment. If there is a God who created this world, he should scrap it and try again.

SAM. All right, Hally, all right. What you got for homework?

HALLY. Bullshit, as usual. (*Opens an exercise book and reads.*) "Write five hundred words describing an annual event of cultural or historical significance."

SAM. That should be easy enough for you.

HALLY. And also plain bloody boring. You know what he wants, don't you? One of their useless old ceremonies. The commemoration of the landing of the 1820 Settlers, or if it's going to be culture, Carols by Candlelight every Christmas.

SAM. It's an impressive sight. Make a good description, Hally. All those candles glowing in the dark and the people singing hymns.

HALLY. And it's called religious hysteria. (*Intense irritation.*) Please, Sam! Just leave me alone and let me get on with it. I'm not in the mood for games this afternoon. And remember my Mom's orders . . . you're to help Willie with the windows. Come on now, I don't want any more nonsense in here.

SAM. Okay, Hally, okay.

Hally settles down to his homework; determined preparations . . . pen, ruler, exercise book, dictionary, another cake . . . all of which will lead to nothing. (Sam waltzes over to Willie and starts to replace tables and chairs. He practices a ballroom step while doing so. Willie watches. When Sam is finished, Willie tries.)

Good! But just a little bit quicker on the turn and only move in to her after she's crossed over. What about this one?

Another step. When Sam is finished, Willie again has a go.

Much better. See what happens when you just relax and enjoy yourself? Remember that in two weeks' time and you'll be all right.

WILLIE. But I haven't got partner, Boet Sam.

SAM. Maybe Hilda will turn up tonight.

WILLIE. No, Boet Sam. (*Reluctantly.*) I gave her a good hiding.

SAM. You mean a bad one.

WILLIE. Good bad one.

SAM. Then you mustn't complain either. Now you pay the price for losing your temper.

WILLIE. I also pay two pounds ten shilling entrance fee.

SAM. They'll refund you if you withdraw now.

WILLIE. (*appalled*). You mean, don't dance?

SAM. Yes.

WILLIE. No! I wait too long and I practice too hard. If I find me new partner, you think I can be ready in two weeks? I ask Madam for my leave now and we practice every day.

SAM. Quickstep non-stop for two weeks. World record, Willie, but you'll be mad at the end.

WILLIE. No jokes, Boet Sam.

SAM. I'm not joking.

WILLIE. So then what?

SAM. Find Hilda. Say you're sorry and promise you won't beat her again.

WILLIE. No.

SAM. Then withdraw. Try again next year.

WILLIE. No.

SAM. Then I give up.

WILLIE. Haaikona, Boet Sam, you can't.

SAM. What do you mean, I can't? I'm telling you: I give up.

WILLIE (*adamant*). No! (*Accusingly.*) It was you who start me ballroom dancing.

SAM. So?

WILLIE. Before that I use to be happy. And is you and Miriam who bring me to Hilda and say here's partner for you.

SAM. What are you saying, Willie?

WILLIE. You!

SAM. But me what? To blame?

WILLIE. Yes.

SAM. Willie . . . ? (*Bursts into laughter.*)

WILLIE. And now all you do is make jokes at me. You wait. When Miriam leaves you is my turn to laugh. Ha! Ha! Ha!

SAM. (*He can't take Willie seriously any longer.*) She can leave me tonight! I know what to do. (*Bowing before an imaginary partner*). May I have the pleasure? (*He dances and sings.*)

"Just a fellow with his pillow . . .
Dancin' like a willow . . .
In an autumn breeze . . . "

WILLIE. There you go again!

Sam goes on dancing and singing.

Boet Sam!

SAM. There's the answer to your problem! Judges' announcement in two weeks' time: "Ladies and gentlemen, the winner in the open section . . . Mr. Willie Malopo and his pillow!"

This is too much for a now really angry Willie. He goes for Sam, but the latter is too quick for him and puts Hally's table between the two of them.

HALLY (*exploding*). For Christ's sake, you two!

WILLIE (*still trying to get at Sam*). I donner you, Sam! Struesgod!

SAM (*still laughing*). Sorry, Willie . . . Sorry . . .

HALLY. Sam! Willie! (*Grabs his ruler and gives Willie a vicious whack on the bum.*) How the hell am I supposed to concentrate with the two of you behaving like bloody children!

WILLIE. Hit him too!

HALLY. Shut up, Willie.

WILLIE. He started jokes again.

HALLY. Get back to your work. You too, Sam. (*His ruler.*) Do you want another one, Willie?

Sam and Willie return to their work. Hally uses the opportunity to escape from his unsuccessful attempt at homework. He struts around like a little despot, ruler in hand, giving vent to his anger and frustration.

Suppose a customer had walked in then? Or the Park Superintendent. And seen the two of you behaving like a pair of hooligans. That would have been the end of my mother's license, you know. And your jobs! Well, this is the end of it. From now on there will be no more of your ballroom nonsense in here. This is a business establishment, not a bloody New Brighton dancing school. I've been far too lenient with the two of you. (*Behind the counter for a green cool drink and a dollop of ice cream. He keeps up his tirade as he prepares it.*) But what really makes me bitter is that I allow you chaps a little freedom in here when business is bad and what do you do with it? The foxtrot! Specially you, Sam. There's more to life than trotting around a dance floor and I thought at least you knew it.

SAM. It's a harmless pleasure, Hally. It doesn't hurt anybody.

HALLY. It's also a rather simple one, you know.

SAM. You reckon so? Have you ever tried?

HALLY. Of course not.

SAM. Why don't you? Now.

HALLY. What do you mean? Me dance?

SAM. Yes. I'll show you a simple step—the waltz—then you try it.

HALLY. What will that prove?

SAM. That it might not be as easy as you think.

HALLY. I didn't say it was easy. I said it was simple—like in simple-minded, meaning mentally retarded. You can't exactly say it challenges the intellect.

SAM. It does other things.

HALLY. Such as?

SAM. Make people happy.

HALLY (*the glass in his hand*). So do American cream sodas with ice cream. For God's sake, Sam, you're not asking me to take ballroom dancing serious, are you?

SAM. Yes.

HALLY (*sigh of defeat*). Oh, well, so much for trying to give you a decent education. I've obviously achieved nothing.

SAM. You still haven't told me what's wrong with admiring something that's beautiful and then trying to do it yourself.

HALLY. Nothing. But we happen to be talking about a foxtrot, not a thing of beauty.

SAM. But that is just what I'm saying. If you were to see two champions doing, two masters of the art . . . !

HALLY. Oh, God, I give up. So now it's also art!

SAM. Ja.

HALLY. There's a limit, Sam. Don't confuse art and entertainment.

SAM. So then what is art?

HALLY. You want a definition?

SAM. Ja.

HALLY. (*He realizes he has got to be careful. He gives the matter a lot of thought before answering.*) Philosophers have been trying to do that for centuries. What is Art? What is Life? But basically I suppose it's . . . the giving of meaning to matter.

SAM. Nothing to do with beautiful?

HALLY. It goes beyond that. It's the giving of form to the formless.

SAM. Ja, well, maybe it's not art, then. But I still say it's beautiful.

HALLY. I'm sure the word you mean to use is entertaining.

SAM (*adamant*). No. Beautiful. And if you want proof, come along to the Centenary Hall in New Brighton in two weeks' time.

The mention of the Centenary Hall draws Willie over to them.

HALLY. What for? I've seen the two of you prancing around in here often enough.

SAM. (*He laughs.*) This isn't the real thing, Hally. We're just playing around in here.

HALLY. So? I can use my imagination.

SAM. And what do you get?

HALLY. A lot of people dancing around and having a so-called good time.

SAM. That all?

HALLY. Well, basically it is that, surely.

SAM. No, it isn't. Your imagination hasn't helped you at all. There's a lot more to it than that. We're getting ready for the championships, Hally, not just another dance. There's going to be a lot of people, all right, and they're going to have a good time, but they'll only be spectators, sitting around and watching. It's just the competitors out there on the dance floor. Party decorations and fancy lights all around the walls! The ladies in beautiful evening dresses!

HALLY. My mother's got one of those, Sam, and quite frankly, it's an embarrassment every time she wears it.

SAM (*undeterred*). Your imagination left out the excitement.

Hally scoffs.

Oh, yes. The finalists are not going to be out there just to have a good time. One of those couples will be the 1950 Eastern Province Champions. And your imagination left out the music.

WILLIE. Mr. Elijah Gladman Guzana and his Orchestral Jazzonions.

SAM. The sound of the big band, Hally. Trombone, trumpet, tenor and alto sax. And then, finally, your imagination also left out the climax of the evening when the dancing is finished, the judges have stopped whispering among themselves and the Master of Ceremonies collects their scorecards and goes up onto the stage to announce the winners.

HALLY. All right. So you make it sound like a bit of a do. It's an occasion. Satisfied?

SAM (*victory*). So you admit that!

HALLY. Emotionally yes, intellectually no.

SAM. Well, I don't know what you mean by that, all I'm telling you is that it is going to be the event of the year in New Brighton. It's been sold out for two weeks already. There's only standing room left. We've got competitors coming from Kingwilliamstown, East London, Port Alfred.

Hally starts pacing thoughtfully.

HALLY. Tell me a bit more.

SAM. I thought you weren't interested . . . intellectually.

HALLY (*mysteriously*). I've got my reasons.

SAM. What do you want to know?

HALLY. It takes place every year?

SAM. Yes. But only every third year in New Brighton. It's East London's turn to have the championships next year.

HALLY. Which, I suppose, makes it an even more significant event.

SAM. Ah ha! We're getting somewhere. Our "occasion" is now a "significant event."

HALLY. I wonder.

SAM. What?

HALLY. I wonder if I would get away with it.

SAM. But what?

HALLY (*to the table and his exercise book*). "Write five hundred words describing an annual event of cultural or historical significance." Would I be stretching poetic license a little too far if I called your ballroom championships a cultural event?

SAM. You mean . . . ?

HALLY. You think we could get five hundred words out of it, Sam?

SAM. Victor Sylvester has written a whole book on ballroom dancing.

WILLIE. You going to write about it, Master Hally?

HALLY. Yes, gentlemen, that is precisely what I am considering doing. Old Doc Bromely—he's my English teacher—is going to argue with me, of course. He doesn't like natives. But I'll point out to him that in strict anthropological terms the culture of a primitive black society includes its dancing and singing. To put my thesis in a nutshell: The war-dance has been replaced by the waltz. But it still amounts to the same thing: the release of primitive emotions through movement. Shall we give it a go?

SAM. I'm ready.

WILLIE. Me also.

HALLY. Ha! This will teach the old bugger a lesson. (*Decision taken.*) Right. Let's get ourselves organized. (*This means another cake on the table. He sits.*) I think you've given me enough general atmosphere, Sam, but to build the tension and suspense I need facts. (*Pencil poised.*)

WILLIE. Give him facts, Boet Sam.

HALLY. What you called the climax . . . how many finalists?

SAM. Six couples.

HALLY (*making notes*). Go on. Give me the picture.

SAM. Spectators seated right around the hall. (*Willie becomes a spectator.*)

HALLY. . . . and it's a full house.

SAM. At one end, on the stage, Gladman and his Orchestral Jazzonions. At the other end is a long table with the three judges. The six finalists go onto the dance floor and take up their positions. When they are ready and the spectators have settled down, the Master of Ceremonies goes to the microphone. To start with, he makes some jokes to get the people laughing . . .

HALLY. Good touch! (*As he writes.*) ". . . creating a relaxed atmosphere which will change to one of tension and drama as the climax is approached."

SAM (*onto a chair to act out the M.C.*). "Ladies and gentlemen, we come now to the great moment you have all been waiting for this evening. . . . The finals of the 1950 Eastern Province Open Ballroom Dancing Championships. But first let me introduce the finalists! Mr. and Mrs. Welcome Tchabalala from Kingwilliamstown . . ."

WILLIE (*He applauds after every name*). Is when the people clap their hands and whistle and make a lot of noise, Master Hally.

SAM. "Mr. Mulligan Njikelane and Miss Nomhle Nkonyeni of Grahamstown; Mr. and Mrs. Norman Nchinga from Port Alfred; Mr. Fats Bokolane and Miss Dina Plaatjies from East London; Mr. Sipho Dugu and Mrs. Mable Magada from Peddie; and from New Brighton our very own Mr. Willie Malopo and Miss Hilda Samuels."

Willie can't believe his ears. He abandons his role as spectator and scrambles into position as a finalist.

WILLIE. Relaxed and ready to romance!

SAM. The applause dies down. When everybody is silent, Gladman lifts up his sax, nods at the Orchestral Jazzonions . . .

WILLIE. Play the jukebox please, Boet Sam!

SAM. I also only got bus fare, Willie.

HALLY. Hold it, everybody. (*Heads for the cash register behind the counter.*) How much is in the till, Sam?

SAM. Three shillings. Hally . . . your Mom counted it before she left.

Hally hesitates.

HALLY. Sorry, Willie. You know how she carried on the last time I did it. We'll just have to pool our combined imaginations and hope for the best. (*Returns to the table.*) Back to work. How are the points scored, Sam?

SAM. Maximum of ten points each for individual style, deportment, rhythm and general appearance.

WILLIE. Must I start?

HALLY. Hold it for a second, Willie. And penalties?

SAM. For what?

HALLY. For doing something wrong. Say you stumble or bump into somebody . . . do they take off any points?

SAM (*aghast*). Hally . . . !

HALLY. When you're dancing. If you and your partner collide into another couple.

Hally can get no further. Sam has collapsed with laughter. He explains to Willie.

SAM. If me and Miriam bump into you and Hilda . . .

Willie joins him in another good laugh.

Hally, Hally . . . !

HALLY. (*perplexed*). Why? What did I say?

SAM. There's no collisions out there, Hally. Nobody trips or stumbles or bumps into anybody else. That's what that moment is all about. To be one of those finalists on that dance floor is like . . . like being in a dream about a world in which accidents don't happen.

HALLY (*genuinely moved by Sam's image*). Jesus, Sam! That's beautiful!

WILLIE (*can endure waiting no longer*). I'm starting! (*Willie dances while Sam talks.*)

SAM. Of course it is. That's what I've been trying to say to you all afternoon. And it's beautiful because that is what we want life to be like. But instead, like you said, Hally, we're bumping into each other all the time. Look at the three of us this afternoon: I've bumped into Willie, the two of us have bumped into you, you've bumped into your mother, she bumping into your Dad. . . . None of us knows the steps and there's no music playing. And it doesn't stop with us. The whole world is doing it all the time. Open a newspaper and what do you read? America has bumped into Russia, England is bumping into India, rich man bumps into poor man. Those are big collisions, Hally. They make for a lot of bruises. People get hurt in all that bumping, and we're sick and tired of it now. It's been going on for too long. Are we never going to get it right? . . . Learn to dance life like champions instead of always being just a bunch of beginners at it?

HALLY (*deep and sincere admiration of the man*). You've got a vision, Sam!

SAM. Not just me. What I'm saying to you is that everybody's got it. That's why there's only standing room left for the Centenary Hall in two weeks' time. For as long as the music lasts, we are going to see six couples get it right, the way we want life to be.

HALLY. But is that the best we can do, Sam . . . watch six finalists dreaming about the way it should be?

SAM. I don't know. But it starts with that. Without the dream we won't know what we're going for. And anyway I reckon there are a few people who have got past just dreaming about it and are trying for something real. Remember that thing we read once in the paper about the Mahatma Gandhi? Going without food to stop those riots in India?

HALLY. You're right. He certainly was trying to teach people to get the steps right.

SAM. And the Pope.

HALLY. Yes, he's another one. Our old General Smuts as well, you know. He's also out there dancing. You know, Sam, when you come to think of it, that's what the United Nations boils down to . . . a dancing school for politicians!

SAM. And let's hope they learn.

HALLY (*a little surge of hope*). You're right. We mustn't despair. Maybe there's some hope for mankind after all. Keep it up, Willie. (*Back to his table with determination.*) This is a lot bigger than I thought. So what have we got? Yes, our title: "A World Without Collisions."

SAM. That sounds good! "A World Without Collisions."

HALLY. Subtitle: "Global Politics on the Dance Floor." No. A bit too heavy, hey? What about "Ballroom Dancing as a Political Vision"?

The telephone rings. Sam answers it.

SAM. St. George's Park Tea Room . . . Yes, Madam . . . Hally, it's your Mom.

HALLY (*back to reality*). Oh, God, yes! I'd forgotten all about that. Shit! Remember my words, Sam? Just when you're enjoying yourself, someone or something will come along and wreck everything.

SAM. You haven't heard what she's got to say yet.

HALLY. Public telephone?

SAM. No.

HALLY. Does she sound happy or unhappy?

SAM. I couldn't tell. (*Pause.*) She's waiting, Hally.

HALLY (*to the telephone*). Hello, Mom . . . No, everything is okay here. Just doing my homework. . . . What's your news? . . . You've what? . . . (*Pause. He takes the receiver away from his ear for a few seconds. In the course of Hally's telephone conversation, Sam and Willie discretely position the stacked tables and chairs. Hally places the receiver back to his ear.*) Yes, I'm still here. Oh, well, I give up now. Why did you do it, Mom? . . . Well, I just hope you know what you've let us in for. . . . (*Loudly.*) I said I hope you know what you've let us in for! It's the end of the peace and quiet we've been having. (*Softly.*) Where is he? (*Normal voice.*) He can't hear us from in there. But for God's sake, Mom, what happened? I told you to be firm with him. . . . Then you and the nurses should have held him down, taken his crutches away. . . . I know only too well he's my father! . . . I'm not being disrespectful, but I'm sick and tired of emptying stinking chamberpots full of phlegm and piss. . . . Yes, I do! When you're not there, he asks *me* to do it. . . . If you really want to know the truth, that's why I've got no appetite for my food. . . . Yes! There's a lot of things you don't know about. For your information, I still haven't got that science textbook I need. And you know why? He borrowed the money you gave me for it. . . . Because I didn't want to start another fight between you two. . . . He says that every time. . . . All right, Mom! (*Viciously.*) Then just remember to start hiding your bag away again, because he'll be at your purse before long for money for booze. And when he's well enough to come down here, you better keep an eye on the till as well, because that is also going to develop a leak. . . . Then don't complain to me when he starts his old tricks. . . . Yes, you do. I get it from you on one side and from him on the other, and it makes life hell for me. I'm not going to be the peacemaker anymore. I'm warning you now: when the two of you start fighting again, I'm leaving home. . . . Mom, if you start crying, I'm going to put down the receiver. . . . Okay . . . (*Lowering his voice to a vicious whisper.*) Okay, Mom. I heard you. (*Desperate.*) No. . . . Because I don't want to. I'll see him when I get home! Mom! . . . (*Pause. When he speaks again, his tone changes completely. It is not simply pretense. We sense a genuine emotional conflict.*) Welcome home, chum! . . . What's that? . . . Don't be silly, Dad. You being home is just about the best news in the world. . . . I bet you are. Bloody depressing there with everybody going on about their ailments, hey! . . . How you feeling? . . . Good . . . Here as well, pal. Coming down cats and dogs. . . . That's right. Just the day for a kip and a toss in your old Uncle Ned. . . . Everything's just hunky-dory on my side, Dad. . . . Well, to start with, there's a nice pile of comics for you on the counter. . . . Yes, old Kemple brought them in. *Batman and Robin, Submariner* . . . just your cup of tea . . . I will. . . . Yes, we'll spin a few yarns tonight. . . . Okay, chum, see you in a little while. . . . No, I promise. I'll come straight home. . . . (*Pause—his mother comes back on the phone.*) Mom? Okay. I'll lock up now. . . . What? . . . Oh, the brandy . . . Yes, I'll remember! . . . I'll put it in my suitcase now, for God's sake. I know well enough what will happen if he doesn't get it. . . . (*Places a bottle of brandy on the counter.*) I was kind to him, Mom. I didn't say anything nasty! . . . All right. Bye. (*End of telephone conversation. A desolate Hally doesn't move. A strained silence.*)

SAM (*quietly*). That sounded like a bad bump, Hally.

HALLY (*having a hard time controlling his emotions. He speaks carefully*). Mind your own business, Sam.

SAM. Sorry. I wasn't trying to interfere. Shall we carry on? Hally? (*He indicates the exercise book. No response from Hally.*)

WILLIE. (*also trying*). Tell him about when they give out the cups, Boet Sam.

SAM. Ja! That's another big moment. The presentation of the cups after the winners have been announced. You've got to put that in.

Still no response from Hally.

WILLIE. A big silver one, Master Hally, called floating trophy for the champions.

SAM. We always invite some big-shot personality to hand them over. Guest of honor this year is going to be His Holiness Bishop Jabulani of the All African Free Zionist Church.

Hally gets up abruptly, goes to his table and tears up the page he was writing on.

HALLY. So much for a bloody world without collisions.

SAM. Too bad. It was on its way to being a good composition.

HALLY. Let's stop bullshitting ourselves, Sam.

SAM. Have we been doing that?

HALLY. Yes! That's what all our talk about a decent world has been . . . just so much bullshit.

SAM. We did say it was still only a dream.

HALLY. And a bloody useless one at that. Life's a fuck-up and it's never going to change.

SAM. Ja, maybe that's true.

HALLY. There's no maybe about it. It's a blunt and brutal fact. All we've done this afternoon is waste our time.

SAM. Not if we'd got your homework done.

HALLY. I don't give a shit about my homework, so, for Christ's sake, just shut up about it. (*Slamming books viciously into his school case.*) Hurry up now and finish your work. I want to lock up and get out of here. (*Pause.*) And then go where? Home-sweet-fucking-home. Jesus, I hate that word.

Hally goes to the counter to put the brandy bottle and comics in his school case. After a moment's hesitation, he smashes the bottle of brandy. He abandons all further attempts to hide his feelings. Sam and Willie work away as unobtrusively as possible.

Do you want to know what is really wrong with your lovely little dream, Sam? It's not just that we are all bad dancers. That does happen to be perfectly true, but there's more to it than just that. You left out the cripples.

SAM. Hally!

HALLY (*now totally reckless*). Ja! Can't leave them out, Sam. That's why we always end up on our backsides on the dance floor. They're also out there dancing . . . like a bunch of broken spiders trying to do the quickstep! (*An ugly attempt at laughter.*) When you come to think of it, it's a bloody comical sight. I mean, it's bad enough on two legs . . . but one and a pair of crutches! Hell, no, Sam. That's guaranteed to turn that dance floor into a shambles. Why you shaking your head? Picture it, man. For once this afternoon let's use our imaginations sensibly.

SAM. Be careful, Hally.

HALLY. Of what? The truth? I seem to be the only one around here who is prepared to face it. We've had the pretty dream, it's time now to wake up and have a good long look at the way things really are. Nobody knows the steps, there's no music, the cripples are also out there tripping up everybody and trying to get into the act, and it's all called the All-Comers-How-to-Make-a-Fuckup-of-

Life Championships. (*Another ugly laugh.*) Hang on, Sam! The best bit is still coming. Do you know what the winner's trophy is? A beautiful big chamber-pot with roses on the side, and it's full to the brim with piss. And guess who I think is going to be this year's winner.

SAM (*almost shouting*). Stop now!

HALLY (*suddenly appalled by how far he has gone*). Why?

SAM. Hally? It's your father you're talking about.

HALLY. So?

SAM. Do you know what you've been saying?

Hally can't answer. He is rigid with shame. Sam speaks to him sternly.

No, Hally, you mustn't do it. Take back those words and ask for forgiveness! It's a terrible sin for a son to mock his father with jokes like that. You'll be punished if you carry on. Your father is your father, even if he is a . . . cripple man.

WILLIE. Yes, Master Hally. Is true what Sam say.

SAM. I understand how you are feeling, Hally, but even so . . .

HALLY. No, you don't!

SAM. I think I do.

HALLY. And I'm telling you you don't. Nobody does. (*Speaking carefully as his shame turns to rage at Sam.*) It's your turn to be careful, Sam. Very careful! You're treading on dangerous ground. Leave me and my father alone.

SAM. I'm not the one who's been saying things about him.

HALLY. What goes on between me and my Dad is none of your business!

SAM. Then don't tell me about it. If that's all you've got to say about him, I don't want to hear.

For a moment Hally is at loss for a response.

HALLY. Just get on with your bloody work and shut up.

SAM. Swearing at me won't help you.

HALLY. Yes, it does! Mind your own fucking business and shut up!

SAM. Okay. If that's the way you want it, I'll stop trying.

He turns away. This infuriates Hally even more.

HALLY. Good. Because what you've been trying to do is meddle in something you know nothing about. All that concerns you in here, Sam, is to try and do what you get paid for—keep the place clean and serve the customers. In plain words, just get on with your job. My mother is right. She's always warning me about allowing you to get too familiar. Well, this time you've gone too far. It's going to stop right now.

No response from Sam.

You're only a servant in here, and don't forget it.

Still no response. Hally is trying hard to get one.

And as far as my father is concerned, all you need to remember is that he is your boss.

SAM (*needled at last*). No, he isn't. I get paid by your mother.

HALLY. Don't argue with me, Sam!

SAM. Then don't say he's my boss.

HALLY. He's a white man and that's good enough for you.

SAM. I'll try to forget you said that.

HALLY. Don't! Because you won't be doing me a favor if you do. I'm telling you to remember it.

A pause. Sam pulls himself together and makes one last effort.

SAM. Hally, Hally . . . ! Come on now. Let's stop before it's too late. You're right. We are on dangerous ground. If we're not careful, somebody is going to get hurt.

HALLY. It won't be me.

SAM. Don't be so sure.

HALLY. I don't know what you're talking about, Sam.

SAM. Yes, you do.

HALLY (*furious*). Jesus, I wish you would stop trying to tell me what I do and what I don't know.

Sam gives up. He turns to Willie.

SAM. Let's finish up.

HALLY. Don't turn your back on me! I haven't finished talking.

He grabs Sam by the arm and tries to make him turn around. Sam reacts with a flash of anger.

SAM. Don't do that, Hally! (*Facing the boy.*) All right, I'm listening. Well? What do you want to say to me?

HALLY (*pause as Hally looks for something to say*). To begin with, why don't you also start calling me Master Harold, like Willie.

SAM. Do you mean that?

HALLY. Why the hell do you think I said it?

SAM. And if I don't.

HALLY. You might just lose your job.

SAM (*quietly and very carefully*). If you make me say it once, I'll never call you anything else again.

HALLY. So? (*The boy confronts the man.*) Is that meant to be a threat?

SAM. Just telling you what will happen if you make me do that. You must decide what it means to you.

HALLY. Well, I have. It's good news. Because that is exactly what Master Harold wants from now on. Think of it as a little lesson in respect, Sam, that's long overdue, and I hope you remember it as well as you do your geography. I can tell you now that somebody who will be glad to hear I've finally given it to you will be my Dad. Yes! He agrees with my Mom. He's always going on about it as well. "You must teach the boys to show you more respect, my son."

SAM. So now you can stop complaining about going home. Everybody is going to be happy tonight.

HALLY. That's perfectly correct. You see, you mustn't get the wrong idea about me and my Dad, Sam. We also have our good times together. Some bloody good laughs. He's got a marvelous sense of humor. Want to know what our favorite joke is? He gives out a big groan, you see, and says: "It's not fair, is it, Hally?" Then I have to ask: "What, chum?" And then he says: "A nigger's arse" . . . and we both have a good laugh.

The men stare at him with disbelief.

What's the matter, Willie? Don't you catch the joke? You always were a bit slow on the uptake. It's what is called a pun. You see, fair means both light in color and to be just and decent. (*He turns to Sam.*) I thought *you* would catch it, Sam.

SAM. Oh ja, I catch it all right.

HALLY. But it doesn't appeal to your sense of humor.

SAM. Do you really laugh?

HALLY. Of course.

SAM. To please him? Make him feel good?

HALLY. No, for heaven's sake! I laugh because *I* think it's a bloody good joke.

SAM. You're really trying hard to be ugly, aren't you? And why drag poor old Willie into it? He's done nothing to you except show you the respect you want so badly. That's also not being fair, you know . . . and *I* mean just or decent.

WILLIE. It's all right, Sam. Leave it now.

SAM. It's me you're after. You should just have said "Sam's arse" . . . because that's the one you're trying to kick. Anyway, how do you know it's not fair? You've never seen it. Do you want to? (*He drops his trousers and underpants and presents his backside for Hally's inspection.*) Have a good look. A real Basuto arse . . . which is about as nigger as they can come. Satisfied? (*Trousers up.*) Now you can make your Dad even happier when you go home tonight. Tell him I showed you my arse and he is quite right. It's not fair. And if it will give him an even better laugh next time, I'll also let him have a look. Come, Willie, let's finish up and go.

Sam and Willie start to tidy up the tea room. Hally doesn't move. He waits for a moment when Sam passes him.

HALLY (*quietly*). Sam . . .

Sam stops and looks expectantly at the boy. Hally spits in his face. A long and heartfelt groan from Willie. For a few seconds Sam doesn't move.

SAM (*taking out a handkerchief and wiping his face*). It's all right, Willie.

To Hally.

Ja, well, you've done it . . . Master Harold. Yes, I'll start calling you that from now on. It won't be difficult anymore. You've hurt yourself, Master Harold. I saw it coming. I warned you, but you wouldn't listen. You've just hurt yourself *bad*. And you're a coward, Master Harold. The face you should be spitting in is your father's . . . but you used mine, because you think you're safe inside your fair skin . . . and this time I don't mean just or decent. (*Pause, then moving violently towards Hally.*) Should I hit him, Willie?

WILLIE. (*stopping Sam*). No, Boet Sam.

SAM (*violently*). Why not?

WILLIE. It won't help, Boet Sam.

SAM. I don't want to help! I want to hurt him.

WILLIE. You also hurt yourself.

SAM. And if he had done it to you, Willie?

WILLIE. Me? Spit at me like I was a dog? (*A thought that had not occurred to him before. He looks at Hally.*) Ja. Then I want to hit him. I want to hit him hard!

A dangerous few seconds as the men stand staring at the boy. Willie turns away, shaking his head.

But maybe all I do is go cry at the back. He's little boy, Boet Sam. Little *white* boy. Long trousers now, but he's still little boy.

SAM (*his violence ebbing away into defeat as quickly as it flooded*). You're right. So go on, then: groan again, Willie. You do it better than me. (*To Hally.*) You don't know all of what you've just done . . . Master Harold. It's not just that you've made me feel dirtier than I've ever been in my life . . . I mean, how do I wash off yours and your father's filth? . . . I've also failed. A long time ago I promised myself I was going to try and do something, but you've just shown me . . . Master Harold . . . that I've failed. (*Pause.*) I've also got a memory of a little white boy when he was still wearing short trousers and a black man, but they're not flying a kite. It was the old Jubilee days, after dinner one night. I was in my room. You came in and just stood against the wall, looking down at the ground, and only after I'd asked you what you wanted, what was wrong, I don't know how many times, did you speak and even then so softly I almost didn't hear you. "Sam, please help me to go and fetch my Dad." Remember? He was dead drunk on the floor of the Central Hotel Bar. They'd phoned for your Mom, but you were the only one at home. And do you remember how we did it? You went in first by yourself to ask permission for me to go into the bar. Then I loaded him onto my back like a baby and carried him back to the boarding house with you following behind carrying his crutches. (*Shaking his head as he remembers.*) A crowded Main Street with all the people watching a little white boy following his drunk father on a nigger's back! I felt for that little boy . . . Master Harold. I felt for him. After that we still had to clean him up, remember? He'd messed in his trousers, so we had to clean him up and get him into bed.

HALLY (*great pain*). I love him, Sam.

SAM. I know you do. That's why I tried to stop you from saying these things about him. It would have been so simple if you could have just despised him for being a weak man. But he's your father. You love him and you're ashamed of him. You're ashamed of so much! . . . And now that's going to include yourself. That was the promise I made to myself: to try and stop that happening. (*Pause.*) After we got him to bed you came back with me to my room and sat in a corner and carried on just looking down at the ground. And for days after that! You hadn't done anything wrong, but you went around as if you owed the world an apology for being alive. I didn't like seeing that! That's not the way a boy grows up to be a man! . . . But the one person who should have been teaching you what that means was the cause of your shame. If you really want to know, that's why I made you that kite. I wanted you to look up, be proud of something, of yourself . . . (*Bitter smile at the memory.*) . . . and you certainly were that when I left you with it up there on the hill. Oh, ja . . . something else! . . . If you ever do write it as a short story, there *was* a twist in our ending. I couldn't sit down there and stay with you. It was a "Whites Only" bench. You were too young, too excited to notice then. But not anymore. If you're not careful . . . Master Harold . . . you're going to be sitting up there by yourself for a long time to come, and there won't be a kite in the sky. (*Sam has got nothing more to say. He exits into the kitchen, taking off his waiter's jacket.*)

WILLIE. Is bad. Is all all bad in here now.

HALLY (*books into his school case, raincoat on*). Willie . . . (*It is difficult to speak.*) Will you lock up for me and look after the keys?

WILLIE. Okay.

Sam returns. Hally goes behind the counter and collects the few coins in the cash register. As he starts to leave . . .

SAM. Don't forget the comic books.

Hally returns to the counter and puts them in his case. He starts to leave again.

SAM (*to the retreating back of the boy*). Stop . . . Hally . . .

Hally stops, but doesn't turn to face him.

Hally . . . I've got no right to tell you what being a man means if I don't behave like one myself, and I'm not doing so well at that this afternoon. Should we try again, Hally?

HALLY. Try what?

SAM. Fly another kite, I suppose. It worked once, and this time I need it as much as you do.

HALLY. It's still raining, Sam. You can't fly kites on rainy days, remember.

SAM. So what do we do? Hope for better weather tomorrow?

HALLY (*helpless gesture*). I don't know. I don't know anything anymore.

SAM. You sure of that, Hally? Because it would be pretty hopeless if that was true. It would mean nothing has been learnt in here this afternoon, and there was a hell of a lot of teaching going on . . . one way or the other. But anyway, I don't believe you. I reckon there's one thing you know. You don't *have* to sit up there by yourself. You know what that bench means now, and you can leave it any time you choose. All you've got to do is stand up and walk away from it.

Hally leaves. Willie goes up quietly to Sam.

WILLIE. Is okay, Boet Sam. You see. Is . . . (*He can't find any better words.*) . . . is going to be okay tomorrow. (*Changing his tone.*) Hey, Boet Sam! (*He is trying hard.*) You right. I think about it and you right. Tonight I find Hilda and say sorry. And make promise I won't beat her no more. You hear me, Boet Sam?

SAM. I hear you, Willie.

WILLIE. And when we practice I relax and romance with her from beginning to end. Non-stop! You watch! Two weeks' time: "First prize for promising newcomers: Mr. Willie Malopo and Miss Hilda Samuels." (*Sudden impulse.*) To hell with it! I walk home. (*He goes to the jukebox, puts in a coin and selects a record. The machine comes to life in the gray twilight, blushing its way through a spectrum of soft, romantic colors.*) How did you say it, Boet Sam? Let's dream. (*Willie sways with the music and gestures for Sam to dance.*)

Sarah Vaughan sings.

> "Little man you're crying,
> I know why you're blue,
> Someone took your kiddy car away;
> Better go to sleep now,
> Little man you've had a busy day." (*etc. etc.*)
> You lead. I follow.

The men dance together.

> "Johnny won your marbles,
> Tell you what we'll do;
> Dad will get you new ones right away;
> Better go to sleep now,
> Little man you've had a busy day."

For more than 20 years the Market Theatre in Johannesburg has been the leading noncommercial theater in South Africa. It has produced new works by such prominent South African playwrights as Mbogeni Ngema and Athol Fugard, as well as classics by Shakespeare and Chekhov. Despite strict apartheid laws, its productions feature multiracial casts. In spirit and purpose since its inception, the Market Theatre truly reflects the vision of the late-nineteenth-century social realists, and its legacy is as important as that of Ibsen, Strindberg, and Antoine. The Market Theatre stands beside the Théâtre-Libre, the Intimate Theatre, and the Provincetown Playhouse as a space of extraordinary importance in the evolution of world theater.

The creation of the Market Theatre on June 21, 1976, was the dream of many, but two individuals are credited as the engineers of its development: Barney Simon and Mannie Manin. Each dreamed of creating a new theater for South Africa, though they came from different backgrounds. Manin had been working in South Africa's State Theater, where he produced plays in plush entertainment palaces, working with budgets of millions of rands. Simon found a condemned mansion and turned the dingy dining room into a theater to which he could invite black and white audiences alike. Manin grew increasingly frustrated working in a bureaucracy that did not understand theater or his pleas to expand the state's offerings of traditional European fare. He argued without success that in addition to the state's white audience there was also a black and colored audience to be served. Manin knew that Simon and others were working individually, but with little progress, to create a new theater that truly reflected South Africa's reality. So, in his words, "holding hands, we all decided to make the big jump," and with Manin's pension as the working capital, the Market Theatre was created in the shell of the old Indian Fruit Market in downtown Johannesburg. Coincidentally, its first effort was a Simon-directed production of Chekhov's *The Seagull*, the play that defined the Moscow Art Theatre in 1898.

Under the leadership of Simon (artistic director) and Manin (managing trustee), the Market Theatre was established under the banner "Theatre with, by, and for all the people of South Africa." It was to be, according to Manin, "dedicated to a theater that would be relevant to and involved with the lives of the people." Simon wanted the new theater "to give a reflecting surface in which our community might find an image of itself and share images of each other."

From the beginning the major mission of the Market was—in the words of John Kani—"to create a situation where all people could come together, where all artists could share and give together." Kani, the Market's Associate Artistic Director and most prominent actor, recalls that when the Market started "we wanted a space that could be available to all the artists of this country, irrespective of color, race, or creed. We wanted to promote a theater that was South African in identity. We are here to bring the South African different races together to share and to exchange ideas." Jon White-Spunner adds that "we have tried to do work that mirrors people's lives, work that looks at issues that are important to people." Under the strict apartheid laws of the time, however, that was a difficult, not to mention illegal, task.

Today the Market Theatre is Africa's foremost producer of new scripts by both black (e.g., Mbongeni Ngema) and white writers (e.g., Athol Fugard). *Woza Albert!* and "*MASTER HAROLD*" . . . *and the boys* are both products of the Market Theatre.

Other stories tell of similar theater ventures conceived by visionaries such as Antoine in Paris in 1888. The so-called Off-Broadway movement, begun in New York City in the 1950s, eventually spawned the fiercely independent "Off-off-Broadway" theaters (again, in Greenwich Village, the home of the Provincetown Players in 1915). In 1957 Joe Cino turned his coffeehouse, Café Cino, into a soundingboard for new playwrights, and several years later Ellen Stewart created La Mama Experimental Theater Club, still the model of such theaters in New York. London countered with its "fringe" theaters, also dedicated to producing new, socially relevant works. Today, the English Stage Company at the Royal Court Theater, founded by George Divine in 1956, is Britain's preeminent home for new works (*The Great Celestial Cow*, Chapter 9, premiered there in 1984).

Independent theaters also thrived in Latin America. From the 1930s to the mid–1950s, Argentina witnessed one of its most productive anticommercial theater movements. It portrayed the broken dreams of immigrants who moved to Argentina to escape the despair that plagued Europe following World War I. These dramas, performed in small theaters, parks, open markets, and streets, spoke of a nation transformed by a military regime that imperiled democracy. Highly influenced by European Expressionism, the theater of the grotesque, and Brecht's epic theater, playwrights such as Griselda Gambarro (Chapter 9) and Osvaldo Dragun (Chapter 7)—both of European lineage—created a radically new drama in opposition to the naturalistic tradition. Chile enjoyed a similar phenomenon, largely in response to its own oppressive military. In Cuba the Teatro de Arte La Cueva (The Cellar Art Theater) was founded in 1936 with a production of Pirandello's *Tonight We Improvise*. The event signaled a new experimentation with form and content in Cuban drama and eventually led to the creation of original Cuban dramas. In 1940 the Academy of the Dramatic Arts of the Free School of Havana was established to cultivate a specifically Cuban acting style, free of the old traditions of Spanish acting and vocal techniques. Brazil saw the formation of a dramatic training school in 1948 to foster a distinctively Brazilian style of theater and performance. Os Comediantes, an experimental group that used Rio de Janeiro's lower-class slang for the first time in Brazilian drama, prompted a drama that was distinct from the European style that pervaded that country's theater heritage.

DEATH AND THE KING'S HORSEMAN

WOLE SOYINKA

WOLE SOYINKA (1934 –)

Born into the Yoruban culture of Abeokuta, Nigeria, Akinwande Oluwole Soyinka has emerged as Africa's most noteworthy playwright; he is as well a supremely accomplished poet, novelist, short-story writer, and literary theorist. He received his initial education at St. Peter's School and the Abeokuta Grammar School in his native city, then went to Ibadam, capital of Nigeria's Oyo state, where he studied at both the Government College and University College. From 1954 to 1957 he was a student at Leeds University in north-central England where he earned Honors in English and some renown as a short-story writer.

In 1957 he was attached to the newly founded Royal Court Theatre in London as a play reader, and it was there that his unpublished play *The Invention* was first performed in 1959. The Royal Court has continued to produce many of Soyinka's works, including: *The Lion and the Jewel* (1963), *A Dance in the Forest* (1963), *The Road* (1965), *Kongi's Harvest* (1967), an adaptation of Euripides' *The Bacchae* (1973), *Death and the King's Horseman* (1975), *A Play of Giants* (1984), and most recently, *From Zia with Love* (1992). His novels include *The Interpreters* (1965) and *Seasons of Agony* (1973), and his poetry is collected as *Indare and Other Poems* (1967), *Ogun Abibiman* (1976), and the newly published *Mandela's Earth*. Soyinka has written several autobiographical works, such as *Ake: The Years of Childhood* (1981) and *Ibadan* (1994). And he has excelled in critical writing, most notably *Myth, Literature, and the African World* (1976) and *Art, Dialogue, and Outrage* (1988). This prodigious outpouring of literature, which has inspired both praise and controversy, earned Soyinka the Nobel Prize in 1986; he was the first African writer to receive the world's most prestigious literary award.

Soyinka's critics—primarily Marxists and neo-Negritudists (those wanting to reclaim Africa for black Africans)—have attacked him on the grounds that his work lacks a specific political direction. Generally, such claims are accurate: Soyinka himself has frequently spoken out forcefully against imposing constraints on artistic exploration in favor of the hegemonic goals of a particular group. Yet, Soyinka is anything but apolitical. As early as 1965 he was arrested for pirating a radio broadcast of the Nigerian Broadcasting Corporation subsequent to the disputed elections in Nigeria's Western Regions. Though he was acquitted of this crime, he was later arrested and placed in solitary confinement for not being demonstrably anti-Biafran during the Nigerian civil war of the late 1960s (he recounted the terrors of this two-year imprisonment in his book *A Man Died*). Currently, Soyinka energetically (some have said recklessly) opposes the military dictatorship that rules Nigeria and names himself as one of the three most dangerous men in the world to that regime. The government has shown no reservation in silencing dissident voices within its borders, a point evidenced by the mock trial and execution of Soyinka's colleague and fellow playwright, Ken Saro-Wiwa, in November 1995. Were Soyinka not speaking about Nigeria's turmoil from the safety of exile, his fate would in all likelihood be the same as Saro-Wiwa's.

DEATH AND THE KING'S HORSEMAN (1975)

Soyinka's "Author's Note" to *Death and the King's Horseman* has drawn much attention from critics but little consensus about its meaning. To the Yoruba (or to many peoples whose religious life is animistic and therefore not separated from the natural world), Soyinka's instructions seem superfluous. But the playwright does not level his warnings to those who already understand them; rather, he admonishes those aspects of Western consciousness that he sees as ultimately prohibitive to the apprehension of Yoruban tragedy. For the Western reader steeped in "modernist" sensibilities, perhaps Soyinka's note should appear at the end of the play. Reading it subsequent to the actual text might prove useful in measuring the extent to which Soyinka is accurate in his assessment of how the play must be interpreted. Should readers ignore the "Author's Note" as a prologue (as some critics have suggested it is) and instead read it afterward as a commentary on a specific type of work, they may discover the trap which Soyinka identifies as "the bane of themes of this genre"—that is, the facile tag of a "clash of cultures" play. In fact, a real clash of cultures does occur when the Western mind attempts to analyze drama that does not conform to traditional forms or content. It is at precisely this point that Soyinka's poetic imagination comes into conflict with the Western-trained critic.

Soyinka's approach to tragic myth within the context of the Yoruban world-view can be found in his essay "The Fourth Stage" (see Center Stage box and Forum following the text of the play) a piece heavily influenced by Friedrich Nietzsche's *The Birth of Tragedy* (1872). Nietzsche's work, among the most important in dramatic theory, explores the manner in which Greek tragedy developed through a marriage between the Apollonian (i.e., rationale) art of the sculptor and the nonvisual Dionysian (i.e., emotional) art of music. Though these two creative urges are often in violent opposition to each other, they ultimately coupled to form tragedy, which was for Nietzsche the perfect synthesis of the Apollonian and Dionysian impulses in humans. Certainly Yoruban tragedy, as discussed in Soyinka's "The Fourth Stage," is not a copy of Greek tragedy. Yet, these Nietzschean images and those of the Yoruban myth lend themselves to a comparison that may lead us to an understanding of *Death and the King's Horseman*.

The same sense of duality that is found in Nietzsche's tragic schema can be found in the dyadic, self-contradictory nature of Ogun, a god seeking to rejoin himself to man. At the same time, humans attempt to elevate themselves to the stature of a god, as demonstrated by Elesin's desire to follow his king in death. Both god and humans reach for knowledge they do not possess, a daring and hubristic quest that challenges nature itself. Thus Soyinka sees Ogun as the embodiment of not only the Apollonian and Dionysian, but also of the Promethean virtues. The tragic hero is one who confronts nature (often on his own) and thereby dares to enter the great abyss—what Soyinka calls "the gulf of transition"—and suffers whatever agony awaits him before achieving the ultimate reward: cosmic oneness. To the Yoruba and Soyinka, Ogun is the embodiment of the will, which originally overcame the forces of this abyss between being and nonbeing, and it is Ogun who reunited the gods with humans. When humans, in the world of the living, face a challenge of tragic proportion, it is seen as a vital manifestation, not merely a representation, of Ogun's self-sacrifice. Elesin's obsession with meeting his death as "the King's (first) Horseman" is best understood in this light: the horseman is re-creating Ogun's own act.

Ogun's tragic heroism restored the inseparability of the gods and man in nature (as seen in animism: Elesin, the rider, is an extension of the horse itself). By this means Ogun earned his most revered title, the Lord of the Road, the "road" being the means by which peoples of all times are connected. Consequently, there is no separation among the ancestors and the living and the unborn. After Ogun's sacrifice, "the gulf of transition" continuously connects the three realms of the dead, the living, and the unborn. But to pass from one realm to the next, one must brave the abyss after the manner of the hero-god Ogun. Thus, all transitions become rites of passage. Braving the abyss—as Prince Olunde does—demands the will of a true tragic hero. Soyinka's fourth stage is the abyss itself, the chthonic or underworld, realm of the immediate, physical, and animistic world of the Yoruba, for whom all things are potentially sacred.

In the "Author's Note" Soyinka insists that the play's "threnodic essence" be stressed. This relates to the rhythm and music of the dirge that provides the aural backdrop for *Death and the King's Horseman*. Music is an immediate and necessary element in tragedy, and for Soyinka music is inseparable from the will. The Western mind cannot fully appreciate this concept of music-as-will without first shedding all notions of music as a commodity to be used for financial gain or diversion. To those for whom tragedy is a living product of natural forces, such as Soyinka and Nietzsche (and the ancient Greeks: recall that Aristotle identified music as an integral part of the tragic experience), music is the mournful lament (i.e., the threnody), as well as the solitary companion of the tragic hero at the moment of "self-individuation" on the brink of the abyss. Soyinka says that "if we agree that, in the European sense, music is the direct copy or the direct expression of the will, it is only because nothing rescues man (ancestral, living, or unborn) from loss of self within this abyss but a titanic resolution of the will whose ritual summons, response, and expression is the strange alien sound to which we give the name of Music." Music, then, is the creative essence, the will itself, and it both drives and accompanies the tragic hero—Ogun, Elesin, Olunde—into the abyss of transition. Ironically, the means by which Soyinka illustrates this in *Death and the King's Horseman* is largely through Apollonian means—words, symbols, argument. Herein lies the play's true "clash of cultures."

Allen Alford
Louisiana State University

Death and the King's Horseman *was revived in 1987 at New York's Lincoln Center with Earle Hyman as Elesin, shown here with the Praise Singer.*

DEATH AND THE KING'S HORSEMAN

WOLE SOYINKA

CHARACTERS

PRAISE-SINGER
ELESIN, *Horseman of the King*
IYALOJA, *'Mother' of the market*
SIMON PILKINGS, *District Officer*
JANE PILKINGS, *his wife*
SERGEANT AMUSA

JOSEPH, *houseboy to the Pilkingses*
BRIDE
H.R.H THE PRINCE
THE RESIDENT
AIDE-DE-CAMP
OLUNDE, *eldest son of Elesin*
DRUMMERS, WOMEN, YOUNG GIRLS, DANCERS AT THE BALL

AUTHOR'S NOTE

This play is based on events which took place in Oyo, ancient Yoruba city of Nigeria, in 1946. That year, the lives of Elesin (Olori Elesin), his son, and the Colonial District Officer intertwined with the disastrous results set out in the play. The changes I have made are in matters of detail, sequence and of course characterisation. The action has also been set back two or three years to while the war was still on, for minor reasons of dramaturgy.

The factual account still exists in the archives of the British Colonial Administration. It has already inspired a fine play in Yoruba (*Oba Wàjà*) by Duro Ladipo. It has also misbegotten a film by some German television company.

The bane of themes of this genre is that they are no sooner employed creatively than they acquire the facile tag of 'clash of cultures', a prejudicial label which, quite apart from its frequent misapplication, presupposes a potential equality *in every given situation* of the alien culture and the indigenous, on the actual soil of the latter. (In the area of misapplication, the overseas prize for illiteracy and mental conditioning undoubtedly goes to the blurb-writer for the American edition of my novel *Seasons of Agony* who unblushingly declares that this work portrays the 'clash between old values and new ways, between western methods and African traditions'!) It is thanks to this kind of perverse mentality that I find it necessary to caution the would-be producer of this play against a sadly familiar reductionist tendency, and to direct his vision instead to the far more difficult and risky task of eliciting the play's threnodic essence.

One of the more obvious alternative structures of the play would be to make the District Officer the victim of a cruel dilemma. This is not to my taste and it is not by chance that I have avoided dialogue or situation which would encourage this. No attempt should be made in production to suggest it. The Colonial Factor is an incident, a catalytic incident merely. The confrontation in the play is largely metaphysical, contained in the human vehicle which is Elesin and the universe of the Yoruba mind—the world of the living, the dead and the unborn, and the numinous passage which links all: transition. *Death and the King's Horseman* can be fully realised only through an evocation of music from the abyss of transition.

W.S.

1

A passage through a market in its closing stages. The stalls are being emptied, mats folded. A few women pass through on their way home, loaded with baskets. On a cloth-stand, bolts of cloth are taken down, display pieces folded and piled on a tray. Elesin Oba enters along a passage before the market, pursued by his drummers and praise-singers. He is a man of enormous vitality, speaks, dances and sings with that infectious enjoyment of life which accompanies all his actions.

PRAISE-SINGER. Elesin o! Elesin Oba! Howu! What tryst is this the cockerel goes to keep with such haste that he must leave his tail behind?

ELESIN (*slows down a bit, laughing*). A tryst where the cockerel needs no adornment.

PRAISE-SINGER. O-oh, you hear that my companions? That's the way the world goes. Because the man approaches a brand-new bride he forgets the long faithful mother of his children.

ELESIN. When the horse sniffs the stable does he not strain at the bridle? The market is the long-suffering home of my spirit and the women are packing up to go. That Esu-harrassed day slipped into the stewpot while we feasted. We ate it up with the rest of the meat. I have neglected my women.

PRAISE-SINGER. We know all that. Still it's no reason for shedding your tail on this day of all days. I know the women will cover you in damask and *alari* but when the wind blows cold from behind, that's when the fowl knows his true friends.

ELESIN. Olohun-iyo!

PRAISE-SINGER. Are you sure there will be one like me on the other side?

ELESIN. Olohun-iyo!

PRAISE-SINGER. Far be it for me to belittle the dwellers of that place but, a man is either born to his art or he isn't. And I don't know for certain that you'll meet my father, so who is going to sing these deeds in accents that will pierce the deafness of the ancient ones. I have prepared my going—just tell me: Olohun-iyo, I need you on this journey and I shall be behind you.

ELESIN. You're like a jealous wife. Stay close to me, but only on this side. My fame, my honour are legacies to the living; stay behind and let the world sip its honey from your lips.

PRAISE-SINGER. Your name will be like the sweet berry a child places under his tongue to sweeten the passage of food. The world will never spit it out.

ELESIN. Come then. This market is my roost. When I come among the women I am a chicken with a hundred mothers. I become a monarch whose palace is built with tenderness and beauty.

PRAISE-SINGER. They love to spoil you but beware. The hands of women also weaken the unwary.

ELESIN. This night I'll lay my head upon their lap and go to sleep. This night I'll touch feet with their feet in a dance that is no longer of this earth. But the smell of their flesh, their sweat, the smell of indigo on their cloth, this is the last air I wish to breathe as I go to meet my great forebears.

PRAISE-SINGER. In their time the world was never tilted from its groove, it shall not be in yours.

ELESIN. The gods have said No.

PRAISE-SINGER. In their time the great wars came and went, the little wars came and went; the white slavers came and went, they took away the heart of our race, they bore away the mind and muscle of our race. The city fell and was rebuilt; the city fell and our people trudged through mountain and forest to found a new home but—Elesin Oba do you hear me?

ELESIN. I hear your voice Olohun-iyo.

PRAISE-SINGER. Our world was never wrenched from its true course.

ELESIN. The gods have said No.

PRAISE-SINGER. There is only one home to the life of a river-mussel; there is only one home to the life of a tortoise; there is only one shell to the soul of man: there is only one world to the spirit of our race. If that world leaves its course and smashes on boulders of the great void, whose world will give us shelter?

ELESIN. It did not in the time of my forebears, it shall not in mine.

PRAISE-SINGER. The cockerel must not be seen without his feathers.

ELESIN. Nor will the Not-I bird be much longer without his nest.

PRAISE-SINGER (*stopped in his lyric stride*). The Not-I bird, Elesin?

ELESIN. I said, the Not-I bird.

PRAISE-SINGER. All respect to our elders but, is there really such a bird?

ELESIN. What! Could it be that he failed to knock on your door?

PRAISE-SINGER (*smiling*). Elesin's riddles are not merely the nut in the kernel that breaks human teeth; he also buries the kernel in hot embers and dares a man's fingers to draw it out.

ELESIN. I am sure he called on you, Olohun-iyo. Did you hide in the loft and push out the servant to tell him you were out?

(*Elesin executes a brief, half-taunting dance. The drummer moves in and draws a rhythm out of his steps. Elesin dances towards the market-place as he chants the story of the Not-I bird, his voice changing dexterously to mimic his characters. He performs like a born raconteur, infecting his retinue with his humour and energy. More women arrive during his recital, including Iyaloja.*)

Death came calling.
Who does not know his rasp of reeds?
A twilight whisper in the leaves before
The great araba falls? Did you hear it?

Not I! swears the farmer! He snaps
His fingers round his head, abandons

A hard-worn harvest and begins
A rapid dialogue with his legs.

'Not I,' shouts the fearless hunter, 'but—
It's getting dark, and this night-lamp
Has leaked out all its oil. I think
It's best to go home and resume my hunt
Another day.' But now he pauses, suddenly
Lets out a wail: 'Oh foolish mouth, calling
Down a curse on your own head!
    Your lamp
Has leaked out all its oil, has it?'
Forwards or backwards now he dare not move.
To search for leaves and make *etutu*
On that spot? Or race home to the safety
Of his hearth? Ten market-days have passed
My friends, and still he's rooted there
Rigid as the plinth of Orayan.

The mouth of the courtesan barely
Opened wide enough to take a ha'penny *robo*
When she wailed: 'Not I.' All dressed she was
To call upon my friend the Chief Tax Officer.
But now she sends her go-between instead:
'Tell him I'm ill: my period has come suddenly
But not—I hope—my time.'

Why is the pupil crying?
His hapless head was made to taste
The knuckles of my friend the Mallam:
'If you were then reciting the Koran
Would you have ears for idle noises
Darkening the trees, you child of ill omen?'
He shuts down school before its time
Runs home and rings himself with amulets.

And take my good kinsman Ifawomi.
His hands were like a carver's, strong
And true. I saw them
Tremble like wet wings of a fowl
One day he cast his time-smoothed *opele*
Across the divination board. And all because
The suppliant looked him in the eye and asked,
'Did you hear that whisper in the leaves?'
'Not I,' was his reply; 'perhaps I'm growing deaf—
Good-day.' And Ifa spoke no more that day
The priest locked fast his doors,
Sealed up his leaking roof—but wait!
This sudden care was not for Fawomi
But for Osanyin, courier-bird of Ifa's
Heart of wisdom. I did not know a kite
Was hovering in the sky
And Ifa now a twittering chicken in
The brood of Fawomi the Mother Hen.

Ah, but I must not forget my evening

Courier from the abundant palm, whose groan
Became Not I, as he constipated down
A wayside bush. He wonders if Elegbara
Has tricked his buttocks to discharge
Against a sacred grove. Hear him
Mutter spells to ward off penalties
For an abomination he did not intend.
If any here
Stumbles on a gourd of wine, fermenting
Near the road, and nearby hears a stream
Of spells issuing from a crouching form,
Brother to a *sigidi*, bring home my wine,
Tell my tapper I have ejected
Fear from home and farm. Assure him,
All is well.

PRAISE-SINGER. In your time we do not doubt the peace of
farmstead and home, the peace of road and hearth, we do
not doubt the peace of the forest.

ELESIN. There was fear in the forest too.
Not-I was lately heard even in the lair
Of beasts. The hyena cackled loud Not I,
The civet twitched his fiery tail and glared:
Not I. Not-I became the answering-name
Of the restless bird, that little one
Whom Death found nesting in the leaves
When whisper of his coming ran
Before him on the wind. Not-I
Has long abandoned home. This same dawn
I heard him twitter in the gods' abode.
Ah, companions of this living world
What a thing this is, that even those
We call immortal
Should fear to die.

IYALOJA. But you, husband of multitudes?

ELESIN. I, when that Not-I bird perched
Upon my roof, bade him seek his nest again,
Safe, without care or fear. I unrolled
My welcome mat for him to see. Not-I
Flew happily away, you'll hear his voice
No more in this lifetime—You all know
What I am.

PRAISE-SINGER. That rock which turns its open lodes
Into the path of lightning. A gay
Thoroughbred whose stride disdains
To falter through an adder reared
Suddenly in his path.

ELESIN. My rein is loosened.
I am master of my Fate. When the hour comes
Watch me dance along the narrowing path
Glazed by the soles of my great precursors.
My soul is eager. I shall not turn aside.

WOMEN. You will not delay?

ELESIN. Where the storm pleases, and when, it directs
The giants of the forest. When friendship summons
Is when the true comrade goes.

WOMEN. Nothing will hold you back?

ELESIN. Nothing. What! Has no one told you yet?
I go to keep my friend and master company.
Who says the mouth does not believe in
'No, I have chewed all that before?' I say I have.
The world is not a constant honey-pot.
Where I found little I made do with little.
Where there was plenty I gorged myself.
My master's hands and mine have always
Dipped together and, home or sacred feast,
The bowl was beaten bronze, the meats
So succulent our teeth accused us of neglect.
We shared the choicest of the season's
Harvest of yams. How my friend would read
Desire in my eyes before I knew the cause—
However rare, however precious, it was mine.

WOMEN. The town, the very land was yours.

ELESIN. The world was mine. Our joint hands
Raised houseposts of trust that withstood
The siege of envy and the termites of time.
But the twilight hour brings bats and rodents—
Shall I yield them cause to foul the rafters?

PRAISE-SINGER. Elesin Oba! Are you not that man who
Looked out of doors that stormy day
The god of luck limped by, drenched
To the very lice that held
His rags together? You took pity upon
His sores and wished him fortune.
Fortune was footloose this dawn, he replied,
Till you trapped him in a heartfelt wish
That now returns to you. Elesin Oba!
I say you are that man who
Chanced upon the calabash of honour
You thought it was palm wine and
Drained its contents to the final drop.

ELESIN. Life has an end. A life that will outlive
Fame and friendship begs another name.
What elder takes his tongue to his plate,
Licks it clean of every crumb? He will encounter
Silence when he calls on children to fulfill
The smallest errand! Life is honour.
It ends when honour ends.

WOMEN. We know you for a man of honour.

ELESIN. Stop! Enough of that!

WOMEN (*puzzled, they whisper among themselves, turning
mostly to Iyaloja*). What is it? Did we say something to
give offence? Have we slighted him in some way?

ELESIN. Enough of that sound I say. Let me hear no more in
that vein. I've heard enough.

IYALOJA. We must have said something wrong. (*Comes forward a little.*) Elesin Oba, we ask forgiveness before you
speak.

ELESIN. I am bitterly offended.

IYALOJA. Our unworthiness has betrayed us. All we can do is
ask your forgiveness. Correct us like a kind father.

ELESIN. This day of all days . . .

IYALOJA. It does not bear thinking. If we offend you now we have mortified the gods. We offend heaven itself. Father of us all, tell us where we went astray. (*She kneels, the other women follow.*)

ELESIN. Are you not ashamed? Even a tear-veiled
Eye preserves its function of sight.
Because my mind was raised to horizons
Even the boldest man lowers his gaze
In thinking of, must my body here
Be taken for a vagrant's?

IYALOJA. Horseman of the King, I am more baffled than ever.

PRAISE-SINGER. The strictest father unbends his brow when the child is penitent, Elesin. When time is short, we do not spend it prolonging the riddle. Their shoulders are bowed with the weight of fear lest they have marred your day beyond repair. Speak now in plain words and let us pursue the ailment to the home of remedies.

ELESIN. Words are cheap. 'We know you for
A man of honour.' Well tell me, is this how
A man of honour should be seen?
Are these not the same clothes in which
I came among you a full half-hour ago?

(*He roars with laughter and the women, relieved, rise and rush into stalls to fetch rich cloths.*)

WOMAN. The gods are kind. A fault soon remedied is soon forgiven. Elesin Oba, even as we match our words with deed, let your heart forgive us completely.

ELESIN. You who are breath and giver of my being
How shall I dare refuse you forgiveness
Even if the offence were real.

IYALOJA (*dancing round him. Sings*).
He forgives us. He forgives us.
What a fearful thing it is when
The voyager sets forth
But a curse remains behind.

WOMEN. For a while we truly feared
Our hands had wrenched the world adrift
In emptiness.

IYALOJA. Richly, richly, robe him richly
The cloth of honour is *alari*
Sanyan is the band of friendship
Boa-skin makes slippers of esteem.

WOMEN. For a while we truly feared
Our hands had wrenched the world adrift
In emptiness.

PRAISE-SINGER. He who must, must voyage forth
The world will not roll backwards
It is he who must, with one
Great gesture overtake the world.

WOMEN. For a while we truly feared
Our hands had wrenched the world
In emptiness.

PRAISE-SINGER. The gourd you bear is not for shirking.
The gourd is not for setting down
At the first crossroad or wayside grove.
Only one river may know its contents

WOMEN. We shall all meet at the great market
We shall all meet at the great market
He who goes early takes the best bargains
But we shall meet, and resume our banter.

(*Elesin stands resplendent in rich clothes, cap, shawl, etc. His sash is of a bright red alari cloth. The women dance round him. Suddenly, his attention is caught by an object off-stage.*)

ELESIN. The world I know is good.

WOMEN. We know you'll leave it so.

ELESIN. The world I know is the bounty
Of hives after bees have swarmed.
No goodness teems with such open hands
Even in the dreams of deities.

WOMEN. And we know you'll leave it so.

ELESIN. I was born to keep it so. A hive
Is never known to wander. An anthill
Does not desert its roots. We cannot see
The still great womb of the world—
No man beholds his mother's womb—
Yet who denies it's there? Coiled
To the navel of the world is that
Endless cord that links us all
To the great origin. If I lose my way
The trailing cord will bring me to the roots.

WOMEN. The world is in your hands.

(*The earlier distraction, a beautiful young girl, comes along the passage through which Elesin first made his entry.*)

ELESIN. I embrace it. And let me tell you, women—
I like this farewell that the world designed,
Unless my eyes deceive me, unless
We are already parted, the world and I,
And all that breeds desire is lodged
Among our tireless ancestors. Tell me friends,
Am I still earthed in that beloved market
Of my youth? Or could it be my will
Has outleapt the conscious act and I have come
Among the great departed?

PRAISE-SINGER. Elesin-Oba why do your eyes roll like a bushrat who sees his fate like his father's spirit, mirrored in the eye of a snake? And all these questions! You're standing on the same earth you've always stood upon. This voice you hear is mine, Oluhun-iyo, not that of an acolyte in heaven.

ELESIN. How can that be? In all my life
As Horsemen of the King, the juiciest
Fruit on every tree was mine. I saw,

I touched, I wooed, rarely was the answer No.
The honour of my place, the veneration I
Received in the eye of man or woman
Prospered my suit and
Played havoc with my sleeping hours.
And they tell me my eyes were a hawk
In perpetual hunger. Split an iroko tree
In two, hide a woman's beauty in its heartwood
And seal it up again—Elesin, journeying by,
Would make his camp beside that tree
Of all the shades in the forest.

PRAISE-SINGER. Who would deny your reputation, snake-on-the-loose in dark passages of the market! Bed-bug who wages war on the mat and receives the thanks of the vanquished! When caught with his bride's own sister he protested—but I was only prostrating myself to her as becomes a grateful in-law. Hunter who carries his powder-horn on the hips and fires crouching or standing! Warrior who never makes that excuse of the whining coward—but how can I go to battle without my trousers?—trouser-less or shirtless it's all one to him. Oka-rearing-from-a-camouflage-of-leaves, before he strikes the victim is already prone! Once they told him, Howu, a stallion does not feed on the grass beneath him: he replied, true, but surely he can roll on it!

WOMEN. Ba-a-a-ba O!

PRAISE-SINGER. Ah, but listen yet. You know there is the leaf-knibbling grub and there is the cola-chewing beetle; the leaf-nibbling grub lives on the leaf, the cola-chewing beetle lives in the colanut. Don't we know what our man feeds on when we find him cocooned in a woman's wrapper?

ELESIN. Enough, enough, you all have cause
To know me well. But, if you say this earth
Is still the same as gave birth to those songs,
Tell me who was that goddess through whose lips
I saw the ivory pebbles of Oya's riverbed.
Iyaloja, who is she? I saw her enter
Your stall; all your daughters I know well.
No, not even Ogun-of-the-farm toiling
Dawn till dusk on his tuber patch
Not even Ogun with the finest hoe he ever
Forged at the anvil could have shaped
That rise of buttocks, not though he had
The richest earth between his fingers.
Her wrapper was no disguise
For thighs whose ripples shamed the river's
Coils around the hills of Ilesi. Her eyes
Were new-laid eggs glowing in the dark.
Her skin . . .

IYALOJA. Elesin Oba . . .

ELESIN. What! Where do you all say I am?

IYALOJA. Still among the living.

ELESIN. And that radiance which so suddenly
Lit up this market I could boast
I knew so well?

IYALOJA. Has one step already in her husband's home. She is betrothed.

ELESIN (irritated). Why do you tell me that?

(Iyaloja falls silent. The women shuffle uneasily.)

IYALOJA. Not because we dare give you offence Elesin. Today is your day and the whole world is yours. Still, even those who leave town to make a new dwelling elsewhere like to be remembered by what they leave behind.

ELESIN. Who does not seek to be remembered?
Memory is Master of Death, the chink
In his armour of conceit. I shall leave
That which makes my going the sheerest
Dream of an afternoon. Should voyagers
Not travel light? Let the considerate traveller
Shed, of his excessive load, all
That may benefit the living.

WOMEN (relieved). Ah Elesin Oba, we knew you for a man of honour.

ELESIN. Then honour me. I deserve a bed of honour to lie upon.

IYALOJA. The best is yours. We know you for a man of honour. You are not one who eats and leaves nothing on his plate for children. Did you not say it yourself? Not one who blights the happiness of others for a moment's pleasure.

ELESIN. Who speaks of pleasure? O women, listen!
Pleasure palls. Our acts should have meaning.
The sap of the plantain never dries.
You have seen the young shoot swelling
Even as the parent stalk begins to wither.
Women, let my going be likened to
The twilight hour of the plantain.

WOMEN. What does he mean Iyaloja? This language is the language of our elders, we do not fully grasp it.

IYALOJA. I dare not understand you yet Elesin.

ELESIN. All you who stand before the spirit that dares
The opening of the last door of passage,
Dare to rid my going of regrets! My wish
Transcends the blotting out of thought
In one mere moment's tremor of the senses.
Do me credit. And do me honour.
I am girded for the route beyond
Burdens of waste and longing.
Then let me travel light. Let
Seed that will not serve the stomach
On the way remain behind. Let it take root
In the earth of my choice, in this earth
I leave behind.

IYALOJA (turns to women). The voice I hear is already touched by the waiting fingers of our departed. I dare not refuse.

WOMAN. But Iyaloja . . .

IYALOJA. The matter is no longer in our hands.

WOMAN. But she is betrothed to your own son. Tell him.

IYALOJA. My son's wish is mine. I did the asking for him, the loss can be remedied. But who will remedy the blight of closed hands on the day when all should be openness and light? Tell him, you say! You wish that I burden him with knowledge that will sour his wish and lay regrets on the last moments of his mind. You pray to him who is your intercessor to the other world—don't set this world adrift in your own time; would you rather it was my hand whose sacrilege wrenched it loose?

WOMAN. Not many men will brave the curse of a dispossessed husband.

IYALOJA. Only the curses of the departed are to be feared. The claims of one whose foot is on the threshold of their abode surpasses even the claims of blood. It is impiety even to place hindrances in their ways.

ELESIN. What do my mothers say? Shall I step
Burdened into the unknown?

IYALOJA. Not we, but the very earth says No. The sap in the plantain does not dry. Let grain that will not feed the voyagers at his passage drop here and take root as he steps beyond this earth and us. Oh you who fill the home from hearth to threshold with the voices of children, you who now bestride the hidden gulf and pause to draw the right foot across and into the resting-home of the great forebears, it is good that your loins be drained into the earth we know, that your last strength be ploughed back into the womb that gave you being.

PRAISE-SINGER. Iyaloja, mother of multitudes in the teeming market of the world, how your wisdom transfigures you!

IYALOJA (smiling broadly, completely reconciled). Elesin, even at the narrow end of the passage I know you will look back and sigh a last regret for the flesh that flashed past your spirit in flight. You always had a restless eye. Your choice has my blessing. (To the women.) Take the good news to our daughter and make her ready. (Some women go off.)

ELESIN. Your eyes were clouded at first.

IYALOJA. Not for long. It is those who stand at the gateway of the great change to whose cry we must pay heed. And then, think of this—it makes the mind tremble. The fruit of such a union is rare. It will be neither of this world nor of the next. Nor of the one behind us. As if the timelessness of the ancestor world and the unborn have joined spirits to wring an issue of the elusive being of passage . . . Elesin!

ELESIN. I am here. What is it?

IYALOJA. Did you hear all I said just now?

ELESIN. Yes.

IYALOJA. The living must eat and drink. When the moment comes, don't turn the food to rodents' droppings in their mouth. Don't let them taste the ashes of the world when they step out at dawn to breathe the morning dew.

ELESIN. This doubt is unworthy of you Iyaloja.

IYALOJA. Eating the awusa nut is not so difficult as drinking water afterwards.

ELESIN. The waters of the bitter stream are honey to a man Whose tongue has savoured all.

IYALOJA. No one knows when the ants desert their home; they leave the mound intact. The swallow is never seen to peck holes in its nest when it is time to move with the season. There are always throngs of humanity behind the leave-taker. The rain should not come through the roof for them, the wind must not blow through the walls at night.

ELESIN. I refuse to take offence.

IYALOJA. You wish to travel light. Well, the earth is yours. But be sure the seed you leave in it attracts no curse.

ELESIN. You really mistake my person Iyaloja.

IYALOJA. I said nothing. Now we must go prepare your bridal chamber. Then these same hands will lay your shrouds.

ELESIN (exasperated). Must you be so blunt? (Recovers.) Well, weave your shrouds, but let the fingers of my bride seal my eyelids with earth and wash my body.

IYALOJA. Prepare yourself Elesin.

(She gets up to leave. At that moment the women return, leading the Bride. Elesin's face glows with pleasure. He flicks the sleeves of his agbada with renewed confidence and steps forward to meet the group. As the girl kneels before Iyaloja, lights fade out on the scene.)

2

The verandah of the District Officer's bungalow. A tango is playing from an old hand-cranked gramophone and, glimpsed through the wide windows and doors which open onto the forestage verandah are the shapes of Simon Pilkings and his wife, Jane, tangoing in and out of shadows in the living-room. They are wearing what is immediately apparent as some form of fancy-dress. The dance goes on for some moments and then the figure of a 'Native Administration' policeman emerges and climbs up the steps onto the verandah. He peeps through and observes the dancing couple, reacting with what is obviously a long-standing bewilderment. He stiffens suddenly, his expression changes to one of disbelief and horror. In his excitement he upsets a flower-pot and attracts the attention of the couple. They stop dancing.

PILKINGS. Is there anyone out there?

JANE. I'll turn off the gramophone.

PILKINGS (approaching the verandah). I'm sure I heard something fall over. (The constable retreats slowly, open-mouthed as Pilkings approaches the verandah.) Oh it's you Amusa. Why didn't you just knock instead of knocking things over?

AMUSA (*stammers badly and points a shaky finger at his dress*). Mista Pirinkin . . . Mista Pirinkin . . .

PILKINGS. What is the matter with you?

JANE (*emerging*). Who is it dear? Oh, Amusa . . .

PILKINGS. Yes its Amusa, and acting most strangely.

AMUSA (*his attention now transferred to Mrs Pilkings*). Mam-madam . . . you too!

PILKINGS. What the hell is the matter with you man!

JANE. Your costume darling. Our fancy dress.

PILKINGS. Oh hell, I'd forgotten all about that. (*Lifts the face mask over his head showing his face. His wife follows suit.*)

JANE. I think you've shocked his big pagan heart bless him.

PILKINGS. Nonsense, he's a Moslem. Come on Amusa, you don't believe in all this nonsense do you? I thought you were a good Moslem.

AMUSA. Mista Pirinkin, I beg you sir, what you think you do with that dress? It belong to dead cult, not for human being.

PILKINGS. Oh Amusa, what a let down you are. I swear by you at the club you know—thank God for Amusa, he doesn't believe in any mumbo-jumbo. And now look at you!

AMUSA. Mista Pirinkin, I beg you, take it off. Is no good for man like you to touch that cloth.

PILKINGS. Well, I've got it on. And what's more Jane and I have bet on it we're taking first prize at the ball. Now, if you can just pull yourself together and tell me what you wanted to see me about . . .

AMUSA. Sir, I cannot talk this matter to you in that dress. I no fit.

PILKINGS. What's that rubbish again?

JANE. He is dead earnest too Simon. I think you'll have to handle this delicately.

PILKINGS. Delicately my . . . ! Look here Amusa, I think this little joke has gone far enough hm? Let's have some sense. You seem to forget that you are a police officer in the service of His Majesty's Government. I order you to report your business at once or face disciplinary action.

AMUSA. Sir, it is a matter of death. How can man talk against death to person in uniform of death? Is like talking against government to person in uniform of police. Please sir, I go and come back.

PILKINGS (*roars*). Now! (*Amusa switches his gaze to the ceiling suddenly, remains mute.*)

JANE. Oh Amusa, what is there to be scared of in the costume? You saw it confiscated last month from those egun-gun men who were creating trouble in town. You helped arrest the cult leaders yourself—if the juju didn't harm you at the time how could it possibly harm you now? And merely by looking at it?

AMUSA (*without looking down*). Madam, I arrest the ring-leaders who make trouble but me I no touch *egungun*. That *egungun* itself, I no touch. And I no abuse 'am. I arrest ringleader but I treat *egungun* with respect.

PILKINGS. It's hopeless. We'll merely end up missing the best part of the ball. When they get this way there is nothing you can do. It's simply hammering against a brick wall. Write your report or whatever it is on that pad Amusa and take yourself out of here. Come on Jane. We only upset his delicate sensibilities by remaining here.

(*Amusa waits for them to leave, then writes in the note-book, somewhat laboriously. Drumming from the direction of the town wells up. Amusa listens, makes a movement as if he wants to recall Pilkings but changes his mind. Completes his note and goes. A few moments later Pilkings emerges, picks up the pad and reads.*)

PILKINGS. Jane!

JANE (*from the bedroom*). Coming darling. Nearly ready.

PILKINGS. Never mind being ready, just listen to this.

JANE. What is it?

PILKINGS. Amusa's report. Listen. 'I have to report that it come to my information that one prominent chief, namely, the Elesin Oba, is to commit death tonight as a result of native custom. Because this is criminal offence I await further instruction at charge office. Sergeant Amusa.'

(*Jane comes out onto the verandah while he is reading.*)

JANE. Did I hear you say commit death?

PILKINGS. Obviously he means murder.

JANE. You mean a ritual murder?

PILKINGS. Must be. You think you've stamped it all out but it's always lurking under the surface somewhere.

JANE. Oh. Does it mean we are not getting to the ball at all?

PILKINGS. No-o. I'll have the man arrested. Everyone remotely involved. In any case there may be nothing to it. Just rumours.

JANE. Really? I thought you found Amusa's rumours generally reliable.

PILKINGS. That's true enough. But who knows what may have been giving him the scare lately. Look at his conduct tonight.

JANE (*laughing*). You have to admit he had his own peculiar logic. (*Deepens her voice.*) How can man talk against death to person in uniform of death? (*Laughs.*) Anyway, you can't go into the police station dressed like that.

PILKINGS. I'll send Joseph with instructions. Damn it, what a confounded nuisance!

JANE. But don't you think you should talk first to the man, Simon?

PILKINGS. Do you want to go to the ball or not?

JANE. Darling, why are you getting rattled? I was only trying to be intelligent. It seems hardly fair just to lock up a man—and a chief at that—simply on the er . . . what is that legal word again?—uncorroborated word of a sergeant.

PILKINGS. Well, that's easily decided. Joseph!

JOSEPH (*from within*). Yes master.

PILKINGS. You're quite right of course, I am getting rattled. Probably the effect of those bloody drums. Do you hear how they go on and on?

JANE. I wondered when you'd notice. Do you suppose it has something to do with this affair?

PILKINGS. Who knows? They always find an excuse for making a noise . . . (*Thoughtfully*.) Even so . . .

JANE. Yes Simon?

PILKINGS. It's different Jane. I don't think I've heard this particular—sound—before. Something unsettling about it.

JANE. I thought all bush drumming sounded the same.

PILKINGS. Don't tease me now Jane. This may be serious.

JANE. I'm sorry. (*Gets up and throws her arms around his neck. Kisses him. The houseboy enters, retreats and knocks.*)

PILKINGS (*wearily*). Oh, come in Joseph! I don't know where you pick up all these elephantine notions of tact. Come over here.

JOSEPH. Sir?

PILKINGS. Joseph, are you a Christian or not?

JOSEPH. Yessir.

PILKINGS. Does seeing me in this outfit bother you?

JOSEPH. No sir, it has no power.

PILKINGS. Thank God for some sanity at last. Now Joseph, answer me on the honour of a Christian—what is supposed to be going on in town tonight?

JOSEPH. Tonight sir? You mean that chief who is going to kill himself?

PILKINGS. What?

JANE. What do you mean, kill himself?

PILKINGS. You do mean he is going to kill somebody don't you?

JOSEPH. No master. He will not kill anybody and no one will kill him. He will simply die.

JANE. But why Joseph?

JOSEPH. It is native law and custom. The King die last month. Tonight is his burial. But before they can bury him, the Elesin must die so as to accompany him to heaven.

PILKINGS. I seem to be fated to clash more often with that man than with any of the other chiefs.

JOSEPH. He is the King's Chief Horseman.

PILKINGS (*in a resigned way*). I know.

JANE. Simon, what's the matter?

PILKINGS. It would have to be him!

JANE. Who is he?

PILKINGS. Don't you remember? He's that chief with whom I had a scrap some three or four years ago. I helped his son get to a medical school in England, remember? He fought tooth and nail to prevent it.

JANE. Oh now I remember. He was that very sensitive young man. What was his name again?

PILKINGS. Olunde. Haven't replied to his last letter come to think of it. The old pagan wanted him to stay and carry on some family tradition or the other. Honestly I couldn't understand the fuss he made. I literally had to help the boy escape from close confinement and load him onto the next boat. A most intelligent boy, really bright.

JANE. I rather thought he was much too sensitive you know. The kind of person you feel should be a poet munching rose petals in Bloomsbury.

PILKINGS. Well, he's going to make a first-class doctor. His mind is set on that. And as long as he wants my help he is welcome to it.

JANE (*after a pause*). Simon.

PILKINGS. Yes?

JANE. This boy, he was his eldest son wasn't he?

PILKINGS. I'm not sure. Who could tell with that old ram?

JANE. Do you know, Joseph?

JOSEPH. Oh yes madam. He was the eldest son. That's why Elesin cursed master good and proper. The eldest son is not supposed to travel away from the land.

JANE (*giggling*). Is that true Simon? Did he really curse you good and proper?

PILKINGS. By all accounts I should be dead by now.

JOSEPH. Oh no, master is white man. And good Christian. Black man juju can't touch master.

JANE. If he was his eldest, it means that he would be the Elesin to the next king. It's a family thing isn't it Joseph?

JOSEPH. Yes madam. And if this Elesin had died before the King, his eldest son must take his place.

JANE. That would explain why the old chief was so mad you took the boy away.

PILKINGS. Well it makes me all the more happy I did.

JANE. I wonder if he knew.

PILKINGS. Who? Oh, you mean Olunde?

JANE. Yes. Was that why he was so determined to get away? I wouldn't stay if I knew I was trapped in such a horrible custom.

PILKINGS (*thoughtfully*). No, I don't think he knew. At least he gave no indication. But you couldn't really tell with him. He was rather close you know, quite unlike most of them. Didn't give much away, not even to me.

JANE. Aren't they all rather close, Simon?

PILKINGS. These natives here? Good gracious. They'll open their mouths and yap with you about their family secrets before you can stop them. Only the other day . . .

JANE. But Simon, do they really give anything away? I mean, anything that really counts. This affair for instance, we didn't know they still practised that custom did we?

PILKINGS. Ye-e-es, I suppose you're right there. Sly, devious bastards.

JOSEPH (*stiffly*). Can I go now master? I have to clean the kitchen.

PILKINGS. What? Oh, you can go. Forgot you were still here.

(*Joseph goes.*)

JANE. Simon, you really must watch your language. Bastard isn't just a simple swear-word in these parts, you know.

PILKINGS. Look, just when did you become a social anthropologist, that's what I'd like to know.

JANE. I'm not claiming to know anything. I just happen to have overheard quarrels among the servants. That's how I know they consider it a smear.

PILKINGS. I thought the extended family system took care of all that. Elastic family, no bastards.

JANE (shrugs). Have it your own way.

(Awkward silence. The drumming increases in volume. Jane gets up suddenly, restless.)

That drumming Simon, do you think it might really be connected with this ritual? It's been going on all evening.

PILKINGS. Let's ask our native guide. Joseph! Just a minute Joseph. (Joseph re-enters.) What's the drumming about?

JOSEPH. I don't know master.

PILKINGS. What do you mean you don't know? It's only two years since your conversion. Don't tell me all that holy water nonsense also wiped out your tribal memory.

JOSEPH (visibly shocked). Master!

JANE. Now you've done it.

PILKINGS. What have I done now?

JANE. Never mind. Listen Joseph, just tell me this. Is that drumming connected with dying or anything of that nature?

JOSEPH. Madam, this is what I am trying to say: I am not sure. It sounds like the death of a great chief and then, it sounds like the wedding of a great chief. It really mix me up.

PILKINGS. Oh get back to the kitchen. A fat lot of help you are.

JOSEPH. Yes master. (Goes.)

JANE. Simon . . .

PILKINGS. Alright, alright. I'm in no mood for preaching.

JANE. It isn't my preaching you have to worry about, it's the preaching of the missionaries who preceded you here. When they make converts they really convert them. Calling holy water nonsense to our Joseph is really like insulting the Virgin Mary before a Roman Catholic. He's going to hand in his notice tomorrow you mark my word.

PILKINGS. Now you're being ridiculous.

JANE. Am I? What are you willing to bet that tomorrow we are going to be without a steward-boy? Did you see his face?

PILKINGS. I am more concerned about whether or not we will be one native chief short by tomorrow. Christ! Just listen to those drums. (He strides up and down, undecided.)

JANE (getting up). I'll change and make up some supper.

PILKINGS. What's that?

JANE. Simon, it's obvious we have to miss this ball.

PILKINGS. Nonsense. It's the first bit of real fun the European club has managed to organise for over a year, I'm damned if I'm going to miss it. And it is a rather special occasion. Doesn't happen every day.

JANE. You know this business has to be stopped Simon. And you are the only man who can do it.

PILKINGS. I don't have to stop anything. If they want to throw themselves off the top of a cliff or poison themselves for the sake of some barbaric custom what is that to me? If it were ritual murder or something like that I'd be duty-bound to do something. I can't keep an eye on all the potential suicides in this province. And as for that man—believe me it's good riddance.

JANE (laughs). I know you better than that Simon. You are going to have to do something to stop it—after you've finished blustering.

PILKINGS (shouts after her). And suppose after all it's only a wedding. I'd look a proper fool if I interrupted a chief on his honeymoon, wouldn't I? (Resumes his angry stride, slows down.) Ah well, who can tell what those chiefs actually do on their honeymoon anyway? (He takes up the pad and scribbles rapidly on it.) Joseph! Joseph! Joseph! (Some moments later Joseph puts in a sulky appearance.) Did you hear me call you? Why the hell didn't you answer?

JOSEPH. I didn't hear master.

PILKINGS. You didn't hear me! How come you are here then?

JOSEPH (stubbornly). I didn't hear master.

PILKINGS (controls himself with an effort). We'll talk about it in the morning. I want you to take this note directly to Sergeant Amusa. You'll find him at the charge office. Get on your bicycle and race there with it. I expect you back in twenty minutes exactly. Twenty minutes, is that clear?

JOSEPH. Yes master. (Going.)

PILKINGS. Oh er . . . Joseph.

JOSEPH. Yes master?

PILKINGS (between gritted teeth). Er . . . forget what I said just now. The holy water is not nonsense. I was talking nonsense.

JOSEPH. Yes master. (Goes.)

JANE (pokes her head round the door). Have you found him?

PILKINGS. Found who?

JANE. Joseph. Weren't you shouting for him?

PILKINGS. Oh yes, he turned up finally.

JANE. You sounded desperate. What was it all about?

PILKINGS. Oh nothing. I just wanted to apologise to him. Assure him that the holy water isn't really nonsense.

JANE. Oh? And how did he take it?

PILKINGS. Who the hell gives a damn! I had a sudden vision of our Very Reverend Macfarlane drafting another letter of complaint to the Resident about my unchristian language towards his parishioners.

JANE. Oh I think he's given up on you by now.

PILKINGS. Don't be too sure. And anyway, I wanted to make sure Joseph didn't 'lose' my note on the way. He looked sufficiently full of the holy crusade to do some such thing.

JANE. If you've finished exaggerating, come and have something to eat.

PILKINGS. No, put it all way. We can still get to the ball.

JANE. Simon . . .

PILKINGS. Get your costume back on. Nothing to worry about. I've instructed Amusa to arrest the man and lock him up.

JANE. But that station is hardly secure Simon. He'll soon get his friends to help him escape.

PILKINGS. A-ah, that's where I have out-thought you. I'm not having him put in the station cell. Amusa will bring him right here and lock him up in my study. And he'll stay with him till we get back. No one will dare come here to incite him to anything.

JANE. How clever of you darling. I'll get ready.

PILKINGS. Hey.

JANE. Yes darling.

PILKINGS. I have a surprise for you. I was going to keep it until we actually got to the ball.

JANE. What is it?

PILKINGS. You know the Prince is on a tour of the colonies don't you? Well, he docked in the capital only this morning but he is already at the Residency. He is going to grace the ball with his presence later tonight.

JANE. Simon! Not really.

PILKINGS. Yes he is. He's been invited to give away the prizes and he has agreed. You must admit old Engleton is the best Club Secretary we ever had. Quick off the mark that lad.

JANE. But how thrilling.

PILKINGS. The other provincials are going to be damned envious.

JANE. I wonder what he'll come as.

PILKINGS. Oh I don't know. As a coat-of-arms perhaps. Anyway it won't be anything to touch this.

JANE. Well that's lucky. If we are to be presented I won't have to start looking for a pair of gloves. It's all sewn on.

PILKINGS (laughing). Quite right. Trust a woman to think of that. Come on, let's get going.

JANE (rushing off). Won't be a second. (Stops.) Now I see why you've been so edgy all evening. I thought you weren't handling this affair with your usual brilliance—to begin with that is.

PILKINGS (his mood is much improved). Shut up woman and get your things on.

JANE. Alright boss, coming.

(Pilkings suddenly begins to hum the tango to which they were dancing before. Starts to execute a few practice steps. Lights fade.)

3

A swelling, agitated hum of women's voices rises immediately in the background. The lights come on and we see the frontage of a converted cloth stall in the market. The floor leading up to the entrance is covered in rich velvets and woven cloth. The women come on stage, borne backwards by the determined progress of Sergeant Amusa and his two constables who already have their batons out and use them as a pressure against the women. At the edge of the cloth-covered floor however the women take a determined stand

and block all further progress of the men. They begin to tease them mercilessly.

AMUSA. I am tell you women for last time to commot my road. I am here on official business.

WOMAN. Official business you white man's eunuch? Official business is taking place where you want to go and it's a business you wouldn't understand.

WOMAN (makes a quick tug at the constable's baton). That doesn't fool anyone you know. It's the one you carry under your government knickers that counts. (She bends low as if to peep under the baggy shorts. The embarrassed constable quickly puts his knees together. The women roar.)

WOMAN. You mean there is nothing there at all?

WOMAN. Oh there was something. You know that handbell which the whiteman uses to summon his servants . . . ?

AMUSA (he manages to preserve some dignity throughout). I hope you women know that interfering with officer in execution of his duty is criminal offence.

WOMAN. Interfere? He says we're interfering with him. You foolish man we're telling you there's nothing there to interfere with.

AMUSA. I am order you now to clear the road.

WOMAN. What road? The one your father built?

WOMAN. You are a Policeman not so? Then you know what they call trespassing in court. Or—(Pointing to the cloth-lined steps)—do you think that kind of road is built for every kind of feet.

WOMAN. Go back and tell the white man who sent you to come himself.

AMUSA. If I go I will come back with reinforcement. And we will all return carrying weapons.

WOMAN. Oh, now I understand. Before they can put on those knickers the white man first cuts off their weapons.

WOMAN. What a cheek! You mean you come here to show power to women and you don't even have a weapon.

AMUSA (shouting above the laughter). For the last time I warn you women to clear the road.

WOMAN. To where?

AMUSA. To that hut. I know he dey dere.

WOMAN. Who?

AMUSA. The chief who call himself Elesin Oba.

WOMAN. You ignorant man. It is not he who calls himself Elesin Oba, it is his blood that says it. As it called out to his father before him and will to his son after him. And that is in spite of everything your white man can do.

WOMAN. Is it not the same ocean that washes this land and the white man's land? Tell your white man he can hide our son away as long as he likes. When the time comes for him, the same ocean will bring him back.

AMUSA. The government say dat kin' ting must stop.

WOMAN. Who will stop it? You? Tonight our husband and father will prove himself greater than the laws of strangers.

AMUSA. I tell you nobody go prove anyting tonight or anytime. Is ignorant and criminal to prove dat kin' prove.

IYALOJA (*entering, from the hut. She is accompanied by a group of young girls who have been attending the Bride*). What is it Amusa? Why do you come here to disturb the happiness of others.

AMUSA. Madame Iyaloja, I glad you come. You know me. I no like trouble but duty is duty. I am here to arrest Elesin for criminal intent. Tell these women to stop obstructing me in the performance of my duty.

IYALOJA. And you? What gives you the right to obstruct our leader of men in the performance of his duty.

AMUSA. What kin' duty be dat one Iyaloja.

IYALOJA. What kin' duty? What kin' duty does a man have to his new bride?

AMUSA (*bewildered, looks at the women and at the entrance to the hut*). Iyaloja, is it wedding you call dis kin' ting?

IYALOJA. You have wives haven't you? Whatever the white man has done to you he hasn't stopped you having wives. And if he has, at least he is married. If you don't know what a marriage is, go and ask him to tell you.

AMUSA. This no to wedding.

IYALOJA. And ask him at the same time what he would have done if anyone had come to disturb him on his wedding night.

AMUSA. Iyaloja, I say dis no to wedding.

IYALOJA. You want to look inside the bridal chamber? You want to see for yourself how a man cuts the virgin knot?

AMUSA. Madam . . .

WOMAN. Perhaps his wives are still waiting for him to learn.

AMUSA. Iyaloja, make you tell dese women make den no insult me again. If I hear dat kin' insult once more . . .

GIRL (*pushing her way through*). You will do what?

GIRL. He's out of his mind. It's our mothers you're talking to, do you know that? Not to any illiterate villager you can bully and terrorise. How dare you intrude here anyway?

GIRL. What a cheek, what impertinence!

GIRL. You've treated them too gently. Now let them see what it is to tamper with the mothers of this market.

GIRLS. Your betters dare not enter the market when the women say no!

GIRL. Haven't you learnt that yet, you jester in khaki and starch?

IYALOJA. Daughters . . .

GIRL. No no Iyaloja, leave us to deal with him. He no longer knows his mother, we'll teach him.

(*With a sudden movement they snatch the batons of the two constables. They begin to hem them in.*)

GIRL. What next? We have your batons? What next? What are you going to do?

(*With equally swift movements they knock off their hats.*)

GIRL. Move if you dare. We have your hats, what will you do about it? Didn't the white man teach you to take off your hats before women?

IYALOJA. It's a wedding night. It's a night of joy for us. Peace . . .

GIRL. Not for him. Who asked him here?

GIRL. Does he dare go to the Residency without an invitation?

GIRL. Not even where the servants eat the left-overs.

GIRLS (*in turn. In an 'English' accent*). Well well it's Mister Amusa. Were you invited? (*Play-acting to one another. The older women encourage them with their titters.*)

—Your invitation card please?

—Who are you? Have we been introduced?

—And who did you say you were?

—Sorry, I didn't quite catch your name.

—May I take your hat?

—If you insist. May I take yours? (*Exchanging the policeman's hats.*)

—How very kind of you.

—Not at all. Won't you sit down?

—After you.

—Oh no.

—I insist.

—You're most gracious.

—And how do you find the place?

—The natives are alright.

—Friendly?

—Tractable.

—Not a teeny-weeny bit restless?

—Well, a teeny-weeny bit restless.

—One might even say, difficult?

—Indeed one might be tempted to say, difficult.

—But you do manage to cope?

—Yes indeed I do. I have a rather faithful ox called Amusa.

—He's loyal?

—Absolutely.

—Lay down his life for you what?

—Without a moment's thought.

—Had one like that once. Trust him with my life.

—Mostly of course they are liars.

—Never known a native tell the truth.

—Does it get rather close around here?

—It's mild for this time of the year.

—But the rains may still come.

—They are late this year aren't they?

—They are keeping African time.

—Ha ha ha ha

—Ha ha ha ha

—The humidity is what gets me.

—It used to be whisky.

—Ha ha ha ha

—Ha ha ha ha

—What's your handicap old chap?

—Is there racing by golly?

—Splendid golf course, you'll like it.

—I'm beginning to like it already.

—And a European club, exclusive.

—You've kept the flag flying.

—We do our best for the old country.

—It's a pleasure to serve.

—Another whisky old chap?

—You are indeed too too kind.

—Not at all sir. Where is that boy? (*With a sudden bellow.*) Sergeant!

AMUSA (*snaps to attention*). Yessir!

(*The women collapse with laughter.*)

GIRL. Take your men out of here.

AMUSA (*realising the trick, he rages from loss of face*). I'm give you warning . . .

GIRL. Alright then. Off with his knickers! (*They surge slowly forward.*)

IYALOJA. Daughters, please.

AMUSA (*squaring himself for defence*). The first woman wey touch me . . .

IYALOJA. My children, I beg of you . . .

GIRL. Then tell him to leave this market. This is the home of our mothers. We don't want the eater of white leftovers at the feast their hands have prepared.

IYALOJA. You heard them Amusa. You had better go.

GIRLS. Now!

AMUSA (*commencing his retreat*). We dey go now, but make you no say we no warn you.

GIRL. Now!

GIRL. Before we read the riot act—you should know all about that.

AMUSA. Make we go. (*They depart, more precipitately.*)

(*The women strike their palms across in the gesture of wonder.*)

WOMEN. Do they teach you all that at school?

WOMAN. And to think I nearly kept Apinke away from the place.

WOMAN. Did you hear them? Did you see how they mimicked the white man?

WOMAN. The voices exactly. Hey, there are wonders in this world!

IYALOJA. Well, our elders have said it: Dada may be weak, but he has a younger sibling who is truly fearless.

WOMAN. The next time the white man shows his face in this market I will set Wuraola on his tail.

(*A woman bursts into song and dance of euphoria—'Tani l'awa o l'ogbeja? Kayi! A l'ogbeja. Omo Kekere l'ogbeja.* *The rest of the women join in, some placing the girls on their back like infants, other dancing round them. The dance becomes general, mounting in excitement. Elesin appears, in wrapper only. In his hands a white velvet cloth folded loosely as if it held some delicate object. He cries out.*)

*Who says we haven't a defender? Silence! We have our defenders. Little children are our champions.

ELESIN. Oh you mothers of beautiful brides! (*The dancing stops. They turn and see him, and the object in his hands. Iyaloja approaches and gently takes the cloth from him.*) Take it. It is no mere virgin stain, but the union of life and the seeds of passage. My vital flow, the last from this flesh is intermingled with the promise of future life. All is prepared. Listen! (*A steady drum-beat from the distance.*) Yes. It is nearly time. The King's dog has been killed. The King's favourite horse is to follow his master. My brother chiefs know their task and perform it well. (*He listens again.*)

(*The Bride emerges, stands shyly by the door. He turns to her.*)

Our marriage is not yet wholly fulfilled. When earth and passage wed, the consummation is complete only when there are grains of earth on the eyelids of passage. Stay by me till then. My faithful drummers, do me your last service. This is where I have chosen to do my leave-taking, in this heart of life, this hive which contains the swarm of the world in its small compass. This is where I have known love and laughter away from the palace. Even the richest food cloys when eaten days on end; in the market, nothing ever cloys. Listen. (*They listen to the drums.*) They have begun to seek out the heart of the King's favourite horse. Soon it will ride in its bolt of raffia with the dog at its feet. Together they will ride on the shoulders of the King's grooms through the pulse centres of the town. They know it is here I shall await them. I have told them. (*His eyes appear to cloud. He passes his hand over them as if to clear his sight. He gives a faint smile.*) It promises well; just then I felt my spirit's eagerness. The kite makes for wide spaces and the wind creeps up behind its tail; can the kite say less than—thank you, the quicker the better? But wait a while my spirit. Wait. Wait for the coming of the courier of the King. Do you know friends, the horse is born to this one destiny, to bear the burden that is man upon its back. Except for this night, this night alone when the spotless stallion will ride in triumph on the back of man. In the time of my father I witnessed the strange sight. Perhaps tonight also I shall see it for the last time. If they arrive before the drums beat for me, I shall tell him to let the Alafin know I follow swiftly. If they come after the drums have sounded, why then, all is well for I have gone ahead. Our spirits shall fall in step along the great passage. (*He listens to the drums. He seems again to be falling into a state of semi-hypnosis; his eyes scan the sky but it is in a kind of daze. His voice is a little breathless.*) The moon has fed, a glow from its full stomach fills the sky and air, but I cannot tell where is that gateway through which I must pass. My faithful friends, let our feet touch together this last time, lead me into the other market with sounds that cover my skin with down yet make my limbs strike earth like a thoroughbred. Dear mothers, let me dance into the passage even as I have lived beneath your roofs. (*He comes down progressively among them. They make a way for him, the drummers playing. His dance is one of solemn, regal motions, each gesture of the body is made with a solemn finality. The women join him, their steps a somewhat more fluid version of his. Beneath the Praise-Singer's exhortation the women dirge 'Alẹ, lẹ lẹ, awo mil lọ'.*)

PRAISE-SINGER. Elesin Alafin, can you hear my voice?

ELESIN. Faintly, my friend, faintly.

PRAISE-SINGER. Elesin Alafin, can you hear my call?

ELESIN. Faintly my king, faintly.

PRAISE-SINGER. Is your memory sound Elesin?
Shall my voice be a blade of grass and
Tickle the armpit of the past?

ELESIN. My memory needs no prodding but
What do you wish to say to me?

PRAISE-SINGER. Only what has been spoken. Only what concerns
The dying wish of the father of all.

ELESIN. It is buried like seed-yam in my mind
This is the season of quick rains, the harvest
Is this moment due for gathering.

PRAISE-SINGER. If you cannot come, I said, swear
You'll tell my favourite horse. I shall
Ride on through the gates alone.

ELESIN. Elesin's message will be read
Only when his loyal heart no longer beats.

PRAISE-SINGER. If you cannot come Elesin, tell my dog.
I cannot stay the keeper too long
At the gate.

ELESIN. A dog does not outrun the hand
That feeds it meat. A horse that throws its rider
Slows down to a stop. Elesin alafin
Trusts no beasts with messages between
A king and his companion.

PRAISE-SINGER. If you get lost my dog will track
The hidden path to me.

ELESIN. The seven-way crossroads confuses
Only the stranger. The Horseman of the King
Was born in the recesses of the house.

PRAISE-SINGER. I know the wickedness of men. If there is
Weight on the loose end of your sash, such weight
As no mere man can shift; if your sash is earthed
By evil minds who mean to part us at the last . . .

ELESIN. My sash is of the deep purple *alari*;
It is no tethering-rope. The elephant
Trails no tethering-rope; that king
Is not yet crowned who will peg an elephant—
Not even you my friend and King.

PRAISE-SINGER. And yet this fear will not depart from me
The darkness of this new abode is deep—
Will your human eyes suffice?

ELESIN. In a night which falls before our eyes
However deep, we do not miss our way.

PRAISE-SINGER. Shall I now not acknowledge I have stood
Where wonders met their end? The elephant deserves
Better than that we say 'I have caught
A glimpse of something'. If we see the tamer
Of the forest let us say plainly, we have seen
An elephant.

ELESIN (*his voice is drowsy*).
I have freed myself of earth and now
It's getting dark. Strange voices guide my feet.

PRAISE-SINGER. The river is never so high that the eyes
Of a fish are covered. The night is not so dark
That the albino fails to find his way. A child
Returning homewards craves no leading by the hand.
Gracefully does the mask regain his
grove at the end of day . . .
Gracefully. Gracefully does the mask dance
Homeward at the end of day, gracefully . . .

(*Elesin's trance appears to be deepening, his steps heavier.*)

IYALOJA. It is the death of war that kills the valiant,
Death of water is how the swimmer goes
It is the death of markets that kills the trader
And death of indecision takes the idle away
The trade of the cutlass blunts its edge
And the beautiful die the death of beauty.
It takes an Elesin to die the death of death . . .
Only Elesin . . . dies the unknowable death of death . . .
Gracefully, gracefully does the horseman regain
The stables at the end of day, gracefully . . .

PRAISE-SINGER. How shall I tell what my eyes have seen? The Horseman gallops on before the courier, how shall I tell what my eyes have seen? He says a dog may be confused by new scents of beings he never dreamt of, so he must precede the dog to heaven. He says a horse may stumble on strange boulders and be lamed, so he races on before the horse to heaven. It is best, he says, to trust no messenger who may falter at the outer gate; oh how shall I tell what my ears have heard? But do you hear me still Elesin, do you hear your faithful one?

(*Elesin in his motions appears to feel for a direction of sound, subtly, but he only sinks deeper into his trance-dance.*)

Elesin, Alafin, I no longer sense your flesh. The drums are changing now but you have gone far ahead of the world. It is not yet noon in heaven; let those who claim it is begin their own journey home. So why must you rush like an impatient bride: why do you race to desert your Olohun-iyo?

(*Elesin is now sunk fully deep in his trance, there is no longer sign of any awareness of his surroundings.*)

Does the deep voice of *gbedu* cover you then, like the passage of royal elephants? Those drums that brook no rivals, have they blocked the passage to your ears that my voice passes into wind, a mere leaf floating in the night? Is your flesh lightened Elesin, is that lump of earth I slid between your slippers to keep you longer slowly sifting from your feet? Are the drums on the other side no tuning skin to skin with ours in osugbo? Are there sounds there I cannot hear, do footsteps surround you which pound the earth like *gbedu*, roll like thunder round the dome of the world? Is the darkness gathering in your head Elesin? Is there now a streak of light at the end of the passage, a light I dare not look upon? Does it reveal whose voices we often heard, whose touches we often felt, whose wisdoms come suddenly into the mind when the wisest have shaken their heads and murmured; It cannot be done? Elesin Alafin, don't think I do not know why your lips are heavy, why your limbs are drowsy as palm oil in the cold of harmattan. I would call you back but when the elephant heads for the jungle, the tail is too small a handhold for the hunter that would pull him back. The sun that heads for the sea no longer heeds the prayers of the farmer. When the river begins to taste the salt of the ocean, we no longer know what deity to call on, the river-god or Olokun. No arrow flies back to the string, the child does not return through the same passage that gave it birth. Elesin Oba, can you hear me at all? Your eyelids are glazed like a courtesan's, is it that you see the dark groom and master of life? And will you see my father? Will you tell him that I stayed with you to the last? Will my voice ring in your ears awhile, will you remember Olohun-iyo even if the music on the other side surpasses his mortal craft? But will they know you over there? Have they eyes to gauge your worth, have they the heart to love you, will they know what thoroughbred prances towards them in caparisons of honour? If they do not Elesin, if any there cuts your yam with a small knife, or pours you wine in a small calabash, turn back and return to welcoming hands. If the world were not greater than the wishes of Olohun-iyo, I would not let you go . . .

(*He appears to break down. Elesin dances on, completely in a trance. the dirge wells up louder and stronger. Elesin's dance does not lose its elasticity but his gestures become, if possible, even more weighty. Lights fade slowly on the scene.*)

4

A Masque. The front side of the stage is part of a wide corridor around the great hall of the Residency extending beyond vision into the rear and wings. It is redolent of the tawdry decadence of a far-flung but key imperial frontier. The couples in a variety of fancy-dress are ranged around the walls, gazing in the same direction. The guest-of-honour is about to make an appearance. A portion of the local police brass band with its white conductor is just visible. At last, the entrance of Royalty. The band plays 'Rule Britannia', badly, beginning long before he is visible. The couples bow and curtsey as he passes by them. Both he and his companions are dressed in seventeenth century European costume. Following behind are the Resident and his partner similarly attired. As they gain the end of the hall where the orchestra dais begins the music comes to an end. The Prince bows to the guests. The bank strikes up a Viennese waltz and the Prince formally opens the floor. Several bars later the Resident and his companion follow suit. Others follow in appropriate pecking order. The orchestra's waltz rendition is not of the highest musical standard.*

Some time later the Prince dances again into view and is settled into a corner by the Resident who then proceeds to select couples as they dance past for introduction, sometimes threading his way through the dancers to tap the lucky couple on the shoulder. Desperate efforts from many to ensure that they are recognised in spite of, perhaps, their costume. The ritual of introductions soon takes in Pilkings and his wife. The Prince is quite fascinated by their costume and they demonstrate the adaptations they have made to it, pulling down the mask to demonstrate how the egungun normally appears, then showing the various press-button controls they have innovated for the face flaps, the sleeves, etc. They demonstrate the dance steps and the guttural sounds made by the egungun, harass other dancers in the hall, Mrs Pilkings playing the 'restrainer' to Pilkings' manic darts. Everyone is highly entertained, the Royal Party especially who lead the applause.

At this point a liveried footman comes in with a note on a salver and is intercepted almost absent-mindedly by the Resident who takes the note and reads it. After polite coughs he succeeds in excusing the Pilkingses from the Prince and takes them aside. The Prince considerately offers the Resident's wife his hand and dancing is resumed.

On their way out the Resident gives an order to his Aide-De-Camp. They come into the side corridor where the Resident hands the note to Pilkings.

RESIDENT. As you see it says 'emergency' on the outside. I took the liberty of opening it because His Highness was obviously enjoying the entertainment. I didn't want to interrupt unless really necessary.

PILKINGS. Yes, yes of course sir.

RESIDENT. Is it really as bad as it says? What's it all about?

PILKINGS. Some strange custom they have sir. It seems because the King is dead some important chief has to commit suicide.

RESIDENT. The King? Isn't it the same one who died nearly a month ago?

PILKINGS. Yes sir.

RESIDENT. Haven't they buried him yet?

PILKINGS. They take their time about these things sir. The pre-burial ceremonies last nearly thirty days. It seems tonight is the final night.

RESIDENT. But what has it got to do with the market women? Why are they rioting? We've waived that troublesome tax haven't we?

PILKINGS. We don't quite know that they are exactly rioting yet sir. Sergeant Amusa is sometimes prone to exaggerations.

RESIDENT. He sounds desperate enough. That comes out even in his rather quaint grammar. Where is the man anyway? I asked my aide-de-camp to bring him here.

PILKINGS. They are probably looking in the wrong verandah. I'll fetch him myself.

RESIDENT. No no you stay here. Let your wife go and look for them. Do you mind my dear . . . ?

JANE. Certainly not, your Excellency. (*Goes.*)

RESIDENT. You should have kept me informed Pilkings. You realise how disastrous it would have been if things had erupted while His Highness was here.

PILKINGS. I wasn't aware of the whole business until tonight sir.

RESIDENT. Nose to the ground Pilkings, nose to the ground. If we all let these little things slip past us where would the empire be eh? Tell me that. Where would we all be?

PILKINGS (*low voice*). Sleeping peacefully at home I bet.

RESIDENT. What did you say Pilkings?

PILKINGS. It won't happen again sir.

RESIDENT. It mustn't Pilkings. It mustn't. Where is that damned sergeant? I ought to get back to His Highness as quickly as possible and offer him some plausible explanation for my rather abrupt conduct. Can you think of one Pilkings?

PILKINGS. You could tell him the truth sir.

RESIDENT. I could? No no no no no Pilkings, that would never do. What! Go and tell him there is a riot just two miles away from him? This is supposed to be a secure colony of His Majesty, Pilkings.

PILKINGS. Yes sir.

RESIDENT. Ah, there they are. No, these are not our native police. Are these the ring-leaders of the riot?

PILKINGS. Sir, these are my police officers.

RESIDENT. Oh, I beg your pardon officers. You do look at little . . . I say, isn't there something missing in their uniform? I think they used to have some rather colourful sashes. If I remember rightly I recommended them myself in my young days in the service. A bit of colour always appeals to the natives, yes, I remember putting that in my report. Well well well, where are we? Make your report man.

PILKINGS (*moves close to Amusa, between his teeth*). And let's have no more superstitious nonsense from your Amusa or I'll throw you in the guardroom for a month and feed you pork!

RESIDENT. What's that? What has pork to do with it?

PILKINGS. Sir, I was just warning him to be brief. I'm sure you are most anxious to hear his report.

RESIDENT. Yes yes yes of course. Come on man, speak up. Hey, didn't we give them some colourful fez hats with all those wavy things, yes, pink tassells . . .

PILKINGS. Sir, I think if he was permitted to make his report we might find that he lost his hat in the riot.

RESIDENT. Ah yes indeed. I'd better tell His Highness that. Lost his hat in the riot, ha ha. He'll probably say well, as long as he didn't lose his head. (*Chuckles to himself.*) Don't forget to send me a report first thing in the morning young Pilkings.

PILKINGS. No sir.

RESIDENT. And whatever you do, don't let things get out of hand. Keep a cool head and—nose to the ground Pilkings. (*Wanders off in the general direction of the hall.*)

PILKINGS. Yes sir.

AIDE-DE-CAMP. Would you be needing me sir?

PILKINGS. No thanks Bob. I think His Excellency's need of you is greater than ours.

AIDE-DE-CAMP. We have a detachment of soldiers from the capital sir. They accompanied His Highness up here.

PILKINGS. I doubt if it will come to that but, thanks, I'll bear it in mind. Oh, could you send an orderly with my cloak.

AIDE-DE-CAMP. Very good sir. (*Goes.*)

PILKINGS. Now Sergeant.

AMUSA. Sir . . . (*Makes an effort, stops dead. Eyes to the ceiling.*)

PILKINGS. Oh, not again.

AMUSA. I cannot against death to dead cult. This dress get power of dead.

PILKINGS. Alright, let's go. You are relieved of all further duty Amusa. Report to me first thing in the morning.

JANE. Shall I come Simon?

PILKINGS. No, there's no need for that. If I can get back later I will. Otherwise get Bob to bring you home.

JANE. Be careful Simon . . . I mean, be clever.

PILKINGS. Sure I will. You two, come with me. (*As he turns to go, the clock in the Residency begins to chime. Pilkings looks at his watch then turns, horror-stricken, to stare at his wife. The same thought clearly occurs to her. He swallows hard. An orderly brings his cloak.*) It's midnight. I had no idea it was that late.

JANE. But surely . . . they don't count the hours the way we do. The moon, or something . . .

PILKINGS. I am . . . not so sure.

(*He turns and breaks into a sudden run. The two constables follow, also at a run. Amusa, who has kept his eyes on the ceiling throughout waits until the last of the footsteps has faded out of hearing. He salutes suddenly, but without once looking in the direction of the woman.*)

AMUSA. Goodnight madam.

JANE. Oh. (*She hesitates.*) Amusa . . . (*He goes off without seeming to have heard.*) Poor Simon . . . (*A figure emerges from the shadows, a young black man dressed in a sober western suit. He peeps into the hall, trying to make out the figures of the dancers.)*

Who is that?

OLUNDE *(emerging into the light)*. I didn't mean to startle you madam. I am looking for the District Officer.

JANE. Wait a minute . . . don't I know you? Yes, you are Olunde, the young man who . . .

OLUNDE. Mrs Pilkings! How fortunate. I came here to look for your husband.

JANE. Olunde! Let's look at you. What a fine young man you've become. Grand but solemn. Good God, when did you return? Simon never said a word. But you do look well Olunde. Really!

OLUNDE. You are . . . well, you look quite well yourself Mrs Pilkings. From what little I can see of you.

JANE. Oh, this. It's caused quite a stir I assure you, and not all of it very pleasant. You are not shocked I hope?

OLUNDE. Why should I be? But don't you find it rather hot in there? Your skin must find it difficult to breathe.

JANE. Well, it is a little hot I must confess, but it's all in a good cause.

OLUNDE. What cause Mrs Pilkings?

JANE. All this. The ball. And His Highness being here in person and all that.

OLUNDE *(mildly)*. And that is the good cause for which you desecrate an ancestral mask?

JANE. Oh, so you are shocked after all. How disappointing.

OLUNDE. No I am not shocked Mrs Pilkings. You forget that I have now spent four years among your people. I discovered that you have no respect for what you do not understand.

JANE. Oh. So you've returned with a chip on your shoulder. That's a pity Olunde. I am sorry.

(An uncomfortable silence follows.)

I take it then that you did not find your stay in England altogether edifying.

OLUNDE. I don't say that. I found your people quite admirable in many ways, their conduct and courage in this war for instance.

JANE. Ah yes the war. Here of course it is all rather remote. From time to time we have a black-out drill just to remind us that there is a war on. And the rare convoy passes through on its way somewhere or on manoeuvres. Mind you there is the occasional bit of excitement like that ship that was blown up in the harbour.

OLUNDE. Here? Do you mean through enemy action?

JANE. Oh no, the war hasn't come that close. The captain did it himself. I don't quite understand it really. Simon tried to explain. The ship had to be blown up because it had become dangerous to the other ships, even to the city itself. Hundreds of the coastal population would have died.

OLUNDE. Maybe it was loaded with ammunition and had caught fire. Or some of those lethal gases they've been experimenting on.

JANE. Something like that. The captain blew himself up with it. Deliberately. Simon said someone had to remain on board to light the fuse.

OLUNDE. It must have been a very short fuse.

JANE *(shrugs)*. I don't know much about it. Only that there was no other way to save lives. No time to devise anything else. The captain took the decision and carried it out.

OLUNDE. Yes . . . I quite believe it. I met men like that in England.

JANE. Oh just look at me! Fancy welcoming you back with such morbid news. Stale too. It was at least six months ago.

OLUNDE. I don't find it morbid at all. I find it rather inspiring. It is an affirmative commentary on life.

JANE. What is?

OLUNDE. That captain's self-sacrifice.

JANE. Nonsense. Life should never be thrown deliberately away.

OLUNDE. And the innocent people round the harbour?

JANE. Oh, how does one know? The whole thing was probably exaggerated anyway.

OLUNDE. That was a risk the captain couldn't take. But please Mrs Pilkings, do you think you could find your husband for me? I have to talk to him.

JANE. Simon? Oh. *(As she recollects for the first time the full significance of Olunde's presence.)* Simon is . . . there is a little problem in town. He was sent for. But . . . when did you arrive? Does Simon know you're here?

OLUNDE *(suddenly earnest)*. I need your help Mrs Pilkings. I've always found you somewhat more understanding than your husband. Please find him for me and when you do, you must help me talk to him.

JANE. I'm afraid I don't quite . . . follow you. Have you seen my husband already?

OLUNDE. I went to your house. Your houseboy told me you were here. *(He smiles.)* He even told me how I would recognise you and Mr Pilkings.

JANE. Then you must know what my husband is trying to do for you.

OLUNDE. For me?

JANE. For you. For your people. And to think he didn't even know you were coming back! But how do you happen to be here? Only this evening we were talking about you. We thought you were still four thousand miles away.

OLUNDE. I was sent a cable.

JANE. A cable? Who did? Simon? The business of your father didn't begin till tonight.

OLUNDE. A relation sent it weeks ago, and it said nothing about my father. All it said was, Our King is dead. But I knew I had to return home at once so as to bury my father. I understood that.

JANE. Well, thank God you don't have to go through that agony. Simon is going to stop it.

OLUNDE. That's why I want to see him. He's wasting his time. And since he has been so helpful to me I don't want him to incur the enmity of our people. Especially over nothing.

JANE (*sits down open-mouthed*). You . . . you Olunde!

OLUNDE. Mrs Pilkings, I came home to bury my father. As soon as I heard the news I booked my passage home. In fact we were fortunate. We travelled in the same convoy as your Prince, so we had excellent protection.

JANE. But you don't think your father is also entitled to whatever protection is available to him?

OLUNDE. How can I make you understand? He *has* protection. No one can undertake what he does tonight without the deepest protection the mind can conceive. What can you offer him in place of his peace of mind, in place of the honour and veneration of his own people? What would you think of your Prince if he had refused to accept the risk of losing his life on this voyage? This . . . showing-the-flag tour of colonial possessions.

JANE. I see. So it isn't just medicine you studied in England.

OLUNDE. Yet another error into which your people fall. You believe that everything which appears to make sense was learnt from you.

JANE. Not so fast Olunde. You have learnt to argue I can tell that, but I never said you made sense. However cleverly you try to put it, it is still a barbaric custom. It is even worse—it's feudal! The king dies and a chieftain must be buried with him. How feudalistic can you get!

OLUNDE (*waves his hand towards the background. The Prince is dancing past again—to a different step—and all the guests are bowing and curtseying as he passes*). And this? Even in the midst of a devastating war, look at that. What name would you give to that?

JANE. Therapy, British style. The preservation of sanity in the midst of chaos.

OLUNDE. Others would call it decadence. However, it doesn't really interest me. You white races know how to survive; I've seen proof of that. By all logical and natural laws this war should end with all the white races wiping out one another, wiping out their so-called civilisation for all time and reverting to a state of primitivism the like of which has so far only existed in your imagination when you thought of us. I thought all that at the beginning. Then I slowly realised that your greatest art is the art of survival. But at least have the humility to let others survive in their own way.

JANE. Through ritual suicide?

OLUNDE. Is that worse than mass suicide? Mrs Pilkings, what do you call what those young men are sent to do by their generals in this war? Of course you have also mastered the art of calling things by names which don't remotely describe them.

JANE. You talk! You people with your long-winded, roundabout way of making conversation.

OLUNDE. Mrs Pilkings, whatever we do, we never suggest that a thing is the opposite of which it really is. In your newsreels I heard defeats, thorough, murderous defeats described as strategic victories. No wait, it wasn't just on your newsreels. Don't forget I was attached to hospitals all the time. Hordes of your wounded passed through those wards. I spoke to them. I spent long evenings by their bedside while they spoke terrible truths of the realities of that war. I know now how history is made.

JANE. But surely, in a war of this nature, for the morale of the nation you must expect . . .

OLUNDE. That a disaster beyond human reckoning be spoken of as a triumph? No. I mean, is there no mourning in the home of the bereaved that such blasphemy is permitted?

JANE (*after a moment's pause*). Perhaps I can understand you now. The time we picked for you was not really one for seeing us at our best.

OLUNDE. Don't think it was just the war. Before that even started I had plenty of time to study your people. I saw nothing, finally, that gave you the right to pass judgement on other peoples and their ways. Nothing at all.

JANE (*hesitantly*). Was it the . . . colour thing? I know there is some discrimination.

OLUNDE. Don't make it so simple, Mrs Pilkings. You make it sound as if when I left, I took nothing at all with me.

JANE. Yes . . . and to tell the truth, only this evening, Simon and I agreed that we never really knew what you left with.

OLUNDE. Neither did I. But I found out over there. I am grateful to your country for that. And I will never give it up.

JANE. Olunde, please . . . promise me something. Whatever you do, don't throw away what you have started to do. You want to be a doctor. My husband and I believe you will make an excellent one, sympathetic and competent. Don't let anything make you throw away your training.

OLUNDE (*genuinely surprised*). Of course not. What a strange idea. I intend to return and complete my training. Once the burial of my father is over.

JANE. Oh, please . . . !

OLUNDE. Listen! Come outside. You can't hear anything against that music.

JANE. What is it?

OLUNDE. The drums. Can you hear the change? Listen.

(*The drums come over, still distant but more distinct. There is a change of rhythm, it rises to a crescendo and then, suddenly, it is cut off. After a silence, a new beat begins, slow and resonant.*)

There. It's all over.

JANE. You mean he's . . .

OLUNDE. Yes Mrs Pilkings, my father is dead. His willpower has always been enormous; I know he is dead.

JANE (*screams*). How can you be so callous! So unfeeling! You announce your father's own death like a surgeon looking down on some strange . . . stranger's body! You're just a savage like all the rest.

AIDE-DE-CAMP (*rushing out*). Mrs Pilkings. Mrs Pilkings. (*She breaks down, sobbing.*) Are you alright, Mrs Pilkings?

OLUNDE. She'll be alright. (*Turns to go.*)

AIDE-DE-CAMP. Who are you? And who the hell asked your opinion?

OLUNDE. You're quite right, nobody. (*Going.*)

AIDE-DE-CAMP. What the hell! Did you hear me ask you who you were?

OLUNDE. I have business to attend to.

AIDE-DE-CAMP. I'll give you business in a moment you impudent nigger. Answer my question!

OLUNDE. I have a funeral to arrange. Excuse me. (*Going.*)

AIDE-DE-CAMP. I said stop! Orderly!

JANE. No no, don't do that. I'm alright. And for heaven's sake don't act so foolishly. He's a family friend.

AIDE-DE-CAMP. Well he'd better learn to answer civil questions when he's asked them. These natives put a suit on and they get high opinions of themselves.

OLUNDE. Can I go now?

JANE. No no don't go. I must talk to you. I'm sorry about what I said.

OLUNDE. It's nothing Mrs Pilkings. And I'm really anxious to go. I couldn't see my father before, it's forbidden for me, his heir and successor to set eyes on him from the moment of the king's death. But now . . . I would like to touch his body while it is still warm.

JANE. You will. I promise I shan't keep you long. Only, I couldn't possibly let you go like that. Bob, please excuse us.

AIDE-DE-CAMP. If you're sure . . .

JANE. Of course I'm sure. Something happened to upset me just then, but I'm alright now. Really.

(*The Aide-De-Camp goes, somewhat reluctantly.*)

OLUNDE. I mustn't stay long.

JANE. Please, I promise not to keep you. It's just that . . . oh you saw yourself what happens to one in this place. The Resident's man thought he was being helpful, that's the way we all react. But I can't go in among that crowd just now and if I stay by myself somebody will come looking for me. Please, just say something for a few moments and then you can go. Just so I can recover myself.

OLUNDE. What do you want me to say?

JANE. Your calm acceptance for instance, can you explain that? It was so unnatural. I don't understand that at all. I feel a need to understand all I can.

OLUNDE. But you explained it yourself. My medical training perhaps. I have seen death too often. And the soldiers who returned from the front, they died on our hands all the time.

JANE. No. It has to be more than that. I feel it has to do with the many things we don't really grasp about your people. At least you can explain.

OLUNDE. All these things are part of it. And anyway, my father has been dead in my mind for nearly a month. Ever since I learnt of the King's death. I've lived with my be-

reavement so long now that I cannot think of him alive. On that journey on the boat, I kept my mind on my duties as the one who must perform the rites over his body. I went through it all again and again in my mind as he himself had taught me. I didn't want to do anything wrong, something which might jeopardise the welfare of my people.

JANE. But he had disowned you. When you left he swore publicly you were no longer his son.

OLUNDE. I told you, he was a man of tremendous will. Sometimes that's another way of saying stubborn. But among our people, you don't disown a child just like that. Even if I had died before him I would still be buried like his eldest son. But it's time for me to go.

JANE. Thank you. I feel calmer. Don't let me keep you from your duties.

OLUNDE. Goodnight Mrs Pilkings.

JANE. Welcome home. (*She holds out her hand. As he takes it footsteps are heard approaching the drive. A short while later a woman's sobbing is also heard.*)

PILKINGS (*off*). Keep them here till I get back. (*He strides into view, reacts at the sight of Olunde but turns to his wife.*) Thank goodness you're still here.

JANE. Simon, what happened?

PILKINGS. Later Jane, please. Is Bob still here?

JANE. Yes, I think so. I'm sure he must be.

PILKINGS. Try and get him out here as quietly as you can. Tell him it's urgent.

JANE. Of course. Oh Simon, you remember . . .

PILKINGS. Yes yes. I can see who it is. Get Bob out here. (*She runs off.*) At first I thought I was seeing a ghost.

OLUNDE. Mr Pilkings, I appreciate what you tried to do. I want you to believe that. I can only tell you it would have been a terrible calamity if you'd succeeded.

PILKINGS (*opens his mouth several times, shuts it*). You . . . said what?

OLUNDE. A calamity for us, the entire people.

PILKINGS (*sighs*). I see. Hm.

OLUNDE. And now I must go. I must see him before he turns cold.

PILKINGS. Oh ah . . . em . . . but this is a shock to see you. I mean er thinking all this while you were in England and thanking God for that.

OLUNDE. I came on the mail boat. We travelled in the Prince's convoy.

PILKINGS. Ah yes, a-ah, hm . . . er well . . .

OLUNDE. Goodnight. I can see you are shocked by the whole business. But you must know by now there are things you cannot understand—or help.

PILKINGS. Yes. Just a minute. There are armed policemen that way and they have instructions to let no one pass. I suggest you wait a little. I'll er . . . yes, I'll give you an escort.

OLUNDE. That's very kind of you. But do you think it could be quickly arranged.

PILKINGS. Of course. In fact, yes, what I'll do is send Bob

over with some men to the er . . . place. You can go with them. Here he comes now. Excuse me a minute.

AIDE-DE-CAMP. Anything wrong sir?

PILKINGS (*takes him to one side*). Listen Bob, that cellar in the disused annex of the Residency, you know, where the slaves were stored before being taken down to the coast . . .

AIDE-DE-CAMP. Oh yes, we use it as a storeroom for broken furniture.

PILKINGS. But it's still got the bars on it?

AIDE-DE-CAMP. Oh yes, they are quite intact.

PILKINGS. Get the keys please. I'll explain later. And I want a strong guard over the Residency tonight.

AIDE-DE-CAMP. We have that already. The detachment from the coast . . .

PILKINGS. No, I don't want them at the gates of the Residency. I want you to deploy them at the bottom of the hill, a long way from the main hall so they can deal with any situation long before the sound carries to the house.

AIDE-DE-CAMP. Yes of course.

PILKINGS. I don't want His Highness alarmed.

AIDE-DE-CAMP. You think the riot will spread here?

PILKINGS. It's unlikely but I don't want to take a chance. I made them believe I was going to lock the man up in my house, which was what I had planned to do in the first place. They are probably assailing it by now. I took a roundabout route here so I don't think there is any danger at all. At least not before dawn. Nobody is to leave the premises of course—the native employees I mean. They'll soon smell something is up and they can't keep their mouths shut.

AIDE-DE-CAMP. I'll give instructions at once.

PILKINGS. I'll take the prisoner down myself. Two policemen will stay with him throughout the night. Inside the cell.

AIDE-DE-CAMP. Right sir. (*Salutes and goes off at the double.*)

PILKINGS. Jane. Bob is coming back in a moment with a detachment. Until he gets back please stay with Olunde. (*He makes an extra warning gesture with his eyes.*)

OLUNDE. Please Mr Pilkings . . .

PILKINGS. I hate to be stuffy old son, but we have a crisis on our hands. It has to do with your father's affair if you must know. And it happens also at a time when we have His Highness here. I am responsible for security so you'll simply have to do as I say. I hope that's understood. (*Marches off quickly, in the direction from which he made his first appearance.*)

OLUNDE. What's going on? All this can't be just because he failed to stop my father killing himself.

JANE. I honestly don't know. Could it have sparked off a riot?

OLUNDE. No. If he'd succeeded that would be more likely to start the riot. Perhaps there were other factors involved. Was there a chieftaincy dispute?

JANE. None that I know of.

ELESIN (*an animal bellow from off*). Leave me alone! Is it not

enough that you have covered me in shame! White man, take your hand from my body!

(*Olunde stands frozen on the spot. Jane understanding at last, tries to move him.*)

JANE. Let's go in. It's getting chilly out here.

PILKINGS (*off*). Carry him.

ELESIN. Give me back the name you have taken away from me you ghost from the land of the nameless!

PILKINGS. Carry him! I can't have a disturbance here. Quickly! stuff up his mouth.

JANE. Oh God! Let's go in. Please Olunde. (*Olunde does not move.*)

ELESIN. Take your albino's hand from me you . . .

(*Sounds of a struggle. His voice chokes as he is gagged.*)

OLUNDE (*quietly*). That was my father's voice.

JANE. Oh you poor orphan, what have you come home to?

(*There is a sudden explosion of rage from off-stage and powerful steps come running up the drive.*)

PILKINGS. You bloody fools, after him!

(*Immediately Elesin, in handcuffs, comes pounding in the direction of Jane and Olunde, followed some moments afterwards by Pilkings and the constables. Elesin confronted by the seeming statue of his son, stops dead. Olunde stares above his head into the distance. The constables try to grab him. Jane screams at them.*)

JANE. Leave him alone! Simon, tell them to leave him alone.

PILKINGS. All right, stand aside you. (*Shrugs.*) Maybe just as well. It might help to calm him down.

For several moments they hold the same position. Elesin moves a few steps forward, almost as if he's still in doubt.

ELESIN. Olunde! (*He moves his head, inspecting him from side to side.*) Olunde! (*He collapses slowly at Olunde's feet.*) Oh son, don't let the sight of your father turn you blind!

OLUNDE (*he moves for the first time since he heard his voice, brings his head slowly down to look on him*). I have no father, eater of left-overs.

(*He walks slowly down the way his father had run. Light fades out on Elesin, sobbing into the ground.*)

5

A wide iron-barred gate stretches almost the whole width of the cell in which Elesin is imprisoned. His wrists are encased in thick iron bracelets, chained together; he stands against the bars, looking out. Seated on the ground to one side on the outside is his recent bride, her eyes bent perpetually to the ground. Figures of the two guards can be seen deeper inside the cell, alert to every movement Elesin makes. Pilkings now in a police officer's uniform enters noiselessly, observes him for a while. Then he coughs ostentatiously and approaches. Leans against the bars near a corner, his back to Elesin. He is obviously trying to fall in mood with him. Some moments' silence.

PILKINGS. You seem fascinated by the moon.

ELESIN *(after a pause).* Yes, ghostly one. Your twin-brother up there engages my thoughts.

PILKINGS. It is a beautiful night.

ELESIN. Is that so?

PILKINGS. The light on the leaves, the peace of the night . . .

ELESIN. The night is not at peace, District Officer.

PILKINGS. No? I would have said it was. You know, quiet . . .

ELESIN. And does quiet mean peace for you?

PILKINGS. Well, nearly the same thing. Naturally there is a subtle difference . . .

ELESIN. The night is not at peace ghostly one. The world is not at peace. You have shattered the peace of the world for ever. There is no sleep in the world tonight.

PILKINGS. It is still a good bargain if the world should lose one night's sleep as the price of saving a man's life.

ELESIN. You did not save my life District Officer. You destroyed it.

PILKINGS. Now come on . . .

ELESIN. And not merely my life but the lives of many. The end of the night's work is not over. Neither this year nor the next will see it. If I wished you well, I would pray that you do not stay long enough on our land to see the disaster you have brought upon us.

PILKINGS. Well, I did my duty as I saw it. I have no regrets.

ELESIN. No. The regrets of life always come later.

(Some moments' pause.)

You are waiting for dawn white man. I hear you saying to yourself: only so many hours until dawn and then the danger is over. All I must do is keep him alive tonight. You don't quite understand it all but you know that tonight is when what ought to be must be brought about. I shall ease your mind even more, ghostly one. It is not an entire night but a moment of the night, and that moment is past. The moon was my messenger and guide. When it reached a certain gateway in the sky, it touched that moment for which my whole life has been spent in blessings. Even I do not know the gateway. I have stood here and scanned the sky for a glimpse of that door but, I cannot see it. Human eyes are useless for a search of this nature. But in the house of osugbo, those who keep watch through the spirit recognised the moment, they sent word to me through the voice of our sacred drums to prepare myself. I heard them and I shed all thoughts of earth. I began to follow the moon to the abode of gods . . . servant of the white king, that was when you entered my chosen place of departure on feet of desecration.

PILKINGS. I'm sorry, but we all see our duty differently.

ELESIN. I no longer blame you. You stole from me my first-born, sent him to your country so you could turn him into something in your own image. Did you plan it all beforehand? There are moments when it seems part of a larger plan. He who must follow my footsteps is taken from me, sent across the ocean. Then, in my turn, I am stopped from fulfilling my destiny. Did you think it all out before, this plan to push our world from its course and sever the cord that links us to the great origin?

PILKINGS. You don't really believe that. Anyway, if that was my intention with your son, I appear to have failed.

ELESIN. You did not fail in the main thing ghostly one. We know the roof covers the rafters, the cloth covers blemishes; who would have known that the white skin covered our future, preventing us from seeing the death our enemies had prepared for us. The world is set adrift and its inhabitants are lost. Around them, there is nothing but emptiness.

PILKINGS. Your son does not take so gloomy a view.

ELESIN. Are you dreaming now white man? Were you not present at my reunion of shame? Did you not see when the world reversed itself and the father fell before his son, asking forgiveness?

PILKINGS. That was in the heat of the moment. I spoke to him and . . . if you want to know, he wishes he could cut out his tongue for uttering the words he did.

ELESIN. No. What he said must never be unsaid. The contempt of my own son rescued something of my shame at your hands. You may have stopped me in my duty but I know now that I did give birth to a son. Once I mistrusted him for seeking the companionship of those my spirit knew as enemies of our race. Now I understand. One should seek to obtain the secrets of his enemies. He will avenge my shame, white one. His spirit will destroy you and yours.

PILKINGS. That kind of talk is hardly called for. If you don't want my consolation . . .

ELESIN. No white man, I do not want your consolation.

PILKINGS. As you wish. Your son anyway, sends his consolation. He asks your forgiveness. When I asked him not to despise you his reply was: I cannot judge him, and if I cannot judge him, I cannot despise him. He wants to come to you to say goodbye and to receive your blessing.

ELESIN. Goodbye? Is he returning to your land?

PILKINGS. Don't you think that's the most sensible thing for him to do? I advised him to leave at once, before dawn, and he agrees that is the right course of action.

ELESIN. Yes, it is best. And even if I did not think so, I have lost the father's place of honour. My voice is broken.

PILKINGS. Your son honours you. If he didn't he would not ask your blessing.

ELESIN. No. Even a thoroughbred is not without pity for the turf he strikes with his hoof. When is he coming?

PILKINGS. As soon as the town is a little quieter. I advised it.

ELESIN. Yes white man, I am sure you advised it. You advise all our lives although on the authority of what gods, I do not know.

PILKINGS (*opens his mouth to reply, then appears to change his mind. Turns to go. Hesitates and stops again*). Before I leave you, may I ask just one thing of you?

ELESIN. I am listening.

PILKINGS. I wish to ask you to search the quiet of your heart and tell me—do you not find great contradictions in the wisdom of your own race?

ELESIN. Make yourself clear, white one.

PILKINGS. I have lived among you long enough to learn a saying or two. One came to my mind tonight when I stepped into the market and saw what was going on. You were surrounded by those who egged you on with song and praises. I thought, are these not the same people who say: the elder grimly approaches heaven and you ask him to bear your greetings yonder; do you really think he makes the journey willingly? After that, I did not hesitate.

(*A pause. Elesin sighs. Before he can speak a sound of running feet is heard.*)

JANE (*off*). Simon! Simon!

PILKINGS. What on earth . . . ! (*Runs off.*)

(*Elesin turns to his new wife, gazes on her for some moments.*)

ELESIN. My young bride, did you hear the ghostly one? You sit and sob in your silent heart but say nothing to all this. First I blamed the white man, then I blamed my gods for deserting me. Now I feel I want to blame you for the mystery of the sapping of my will. But blame is a strange peace offering for a man to bring a world he has deeply wronged, and to its innocent dwellers. Oh little mother, I have taken countless women in my life but you were more than a desire of the flesh. I needed you as the abyss across which my body must be drawn, I filled it with earth and dropped my seed in it at the moment of preparedness for my crossing. You were the final gift of the living to their emissary to the land of the ancestors, and perhaps your warmth and youth brought new insights of this world to me and turned my feet leaden on this side of the abyss. For I confess to you, daughter, my weakness came not merely from the abomination of the white man who came violently into my fading presence, there was also a weight of longing on my earth-held limbs. I would have shaken it off, already my foot had begun to lift but then, the white ghost entered and all was defiled.

(*Approaching voices of Pilkings and his wife.*)

JANE. Oh Simon, you will let her in won't you?

PILKINGS. I really wish you'd stop interfering.

(*They come in view. Jane is in a dressing-gown. Pilkings is holding a note to which he refers from time to time.*)

JANE. Good gracious, I didn't initiate this. I was sleeping quietly, or trying to anyway, when the servant brought it. It's not my fault if one can't sleep undisturbed even in the Residency.

PILKINGS. He'd have done the same if we were sleeping at home so don't sidetrack the issue. He knows he can get round you or he wouldn't send you the petition in the first place.

JANE. Be fair Simon. After all he was thinking of your own interests. He is grateful you know, you seem to forget that. He feels he owes you something.

PILKINGS. I just wish they'd leave this man alone tonight, that's all.

JANE. Trust him Simon. He's pledged his word it will all go peacefully.

PILKINGS. Yes, and that's the other thing. I don't like being threatened.

JANE. Threatened? (*Takes the note.*) I didn't spot any threat.

PILKINGS. It's there. Veiled, but it's there. The only way to prevent serious rioting tomorrow—what a cheek!

JANE. I don't think he's threatening you Simon.

PILKINGS. He's picked up the idiom alright. Wouldn't surprise me if he's been mixing with commies or anarchists over there. The phrasing sounds too good to be true. Damn! If only the Prince hadn't picked this time for his visit.

JANE. Well, even so Simon, what have you got to lose? You don't want a riot on your hands, not with the Prince here.

PILKINGS (*going up to Elesin*). Let's see what he has to say. Chief Elesin, there is yet another person who wants to see you. As she is not a next-of-kin I don't really feel obliged to let her in. But your son sent a note with her, so it's up to you.

ELESIN. I know who that must be. So she found out your hiding-place. Well, it was not difficult. My stench of shame is so strong, it requires no hunter's dog to follow it.

PILKINGS. If you don't want to see her, just say so and I'll send her packing.

ELESIN. Why should I not want to see her? Let her come. I have no more holes in my rag of shame. All is laid bare.

PILKINGS. I'll bring her in. (*Goes off.*)

JANE (*hesitates, then goes to Elesin*). Please, try and understand. Everything my husband did was for the best.

ELESIN (*he gives her a long strange stare, as if he is trying to understand who she is*). You are the wife of the District Officer?

JANE. Yes. My name, is Jane.

ELESIN. That is my wife sitting down there. You notice how still and silent she sits? My business is with your husband.

(*Pilkings returns with Iyaloja.*)

PILKINGS. Here she is. Now first I want your word of honour that you will try nothing foolish.

ELESIN. Honour? White one, did you say you wanted my word of honour?

PILKINGS. I know you to be an honourable man. Give me your word of honour you will receive nothing from her.

ELESIN. But I am sure you have searched her clothing as you would never dare touch your own mother. And there are these two lizards of yours who roll their eyes even when I scratch.

PILKINGS. And I shall be sitting on that tree trunk watching even how you blink. Just the same I want your word that you will not let her pass anything to you.

ELESIN. You have my honour already. It is locked up in that desk in which you will put away your report of the night's events. Even the honour of my people you have taken already; it is tied together with those papers of treachery which make you masters in this land.

PILKINGS. Alright. I am trying to make things easy but if you must bring in politics we'll have to do it the hard way. Madam, I want you to remain along this line and move no nearer to that cell door. Guards! (*They spring to attention.*) If she moves beyond this point, blow your whistle. Come on Jane. (*They go off.*)

IYALOJA. How boldly the lizard struts before the pigeon when it was the eagle itself he promised us he would confront.

ELESIN. I don't ask you to take pity on me Iyaloja. You have a message for me or you would not have come. Even if it is the curses of the world, I shall listen.

IYALOJA. You made so bold with the servant of the white king who took your side against death. I must tell your brother chiefs when I return how bravely you waged war against him. Especially with words.

ELESIN. I more than deserve your scorn.

IYALOJA (*with sudden anger*). I warned you, if you must leave a seed behind, be sure it is not tainted with the curses of the world. Who are you to open a new life when you dared not open the door to a new existence? I say who are you to make so bold? (*The Bride sobs and Iyaloja notices her. Her contempt noticeably increases as she turns back to Elesin.*) Oh you self-vaunted stem of the plantain, how hollow it all proves. The pith is gone in the parent stem, so how will it prove with the new shoot? How will it go with that earth that bears it? Who are you to bring this abomination on us!

ELESIN. My powers deserted me. My charms, my spells, even my voice lacked strength when I made to summon the powers that would lead me over the last measure of earth into the land of the fleshless. You saw it, Iyaloja. You saw me struggle to retrieve my will from the power of the stranger whose shadow fell across the doorway and left me floundering and blundering in a maze I had never before encountered. My senses were numbed when the touch of cold iron came upon my wrists. I could do nothing to save myself.

IYALOJA. You have betrayed us. We fed you sweetmeats such as we hoped awaited you on the other side. But you said No, I must eat the world's left-overs. We said you were the hunter who brought the quarry down; to you belonged the vital portions of the game. No, you said, I am the hunter's dog and I shall eat the entrails of the game and the faeces of the hunter. We said you were the hunter returning home in triumph, a slain buffalo pressing down on his neck; you said wait, I first must turn up this cricket hole with my toes. We said yours was the doorway at which we first spy the tapper when he comes down from the tree, yours was the blessing of the twilight wine, the purl that brings night spirits out of doors to steal their portion before the light of day. We said yours was the body of wine whose burden shakes the tapper like a sudden gust on his perch. You said, No, I am content to lick the dregs from each calabash when the drinkers are done. We said, the dew on earth's surface was for you to wash your feet along the slopes of honour. You said No, I shall step in the vomit of cats and the droppings of mice; I shall fight them for the left-overs of the world.

ELESIN. Enough Iyaloja, enough.

IYALOJA. We called you leader and oh, how you led us on. What we have no intention of eating should not be held to the nose.

ELESIN. Enough, enough. My shame is heavy enough.

IYALOJA. Wait. I came with a burden.

ELESIN. You have more than discharged it.

IYALOJA. I wish I could pity you.

ELESIN. I need neither your pity nor the pity of the world. I need understanding. Even I need to understand. You were present at my defeat. You were part of the beginnings. You brought about the renewal of my tie to earth, you helped in the binding of the cord.

IYALOJA. I gave you warning. The river which fills up before our eyes does not sweep us away in its flood.

ELESIN. What were warnings beside the moist contact of living earth between my fingers? What were warnings beside the renewal of famished embers lodged eternally in the heart of man. But even that, even if it overwhelmed one with a thousandfold temptations to linger a little while, a man could overcome it. It is when the alien hand pollutes the source of will, when a stranger force of violence shatters the mind's calm resolution, this is when a man is made to commit the awful treachery of relief, commit in his thought the unspeakable blasphemy of seeing the hand of the gods in this alien rupture of his world. I know it was this thought that killed me, sapped my powers and turned me into an infant in the hands of unnamable strangers. I made to utter my spells anew but my tongue merely rattled in my mouth. I fingered hidden charms and the contact was damp; there was no spark left to sever the life-strings that should stretch from every fingertip. My will was squelched in the spittle of an alien race, and all because I had committed this blasphemy of thought—that there might be the hand of the gods in a stranger's intervention.

IYALOJA. Explain it how you will, I hope it brings you peace of mind. The bush-rat fled his rightful cause, reached the market and set up a lamentation. 'Please save me!'—are these fitting words to hear from an ancestral mask? 'There's a wild beast at my heels' is not becoming language from a hunter.

ELESIN. May the world forgive me.

IYALOJA. I came with a burden I said. It approaches the gates which are so well guarded by those jackals whose spittle will from this day be on your food and drink. But first, tell me, you who were once Elesin Oba, tell me, you who know so well the cycle of the plantain: is it the parent shoot which withers to give sap to the younger or, does your wisdom see it running the other way?

ELESIN. I don't see your meaning Iyaloja?

IYALOJA. Did I ask you for a meaning? I asked a question. Whose trunk withers to give sap to the other? The parent shoot or the younger?

ELESIN. The parent.

IYALOJA. Ah. So you do know that. There are sights in this world which say different Elesin. There are some who choose to reverse this cycle of our being. Oh you emptied bark that the world once saluted for a pith-laden being, shall I tell you what the gods have claimed of you?

(In her agitation she steps beyond the line indicated by Pilkings and the air is rent by piercing whistles. The two Guards also leap forward and place safe-guarding hands on Elesin. Iyaloja stops, astonished. Pilkings comes racing in, followed by Jane.)

PILKINGS. What is it? Did they try something?

GUARD. She stepped beyond the line.

ELESIN (*in a broken voice*). Let her alone. She meant no harm.

IYALOJA. Oh Elesin, see what you've become. Once you had no need to open your mouth in explanation because evil-smelling goats, itchy of hand and foot had lost their senses. And it was a brave man indeed who dared lay hands on you because Iyaloja stepped from one side of the earth onto another. Now look at the spectacle of your life. I grieve for you.

PILKINGS. I think you'd better leave. I doubt you have done him much good by coming here. I shall make sure you are not allowed to see him again. In any case we are moving him to a different place before dawn, so don't bother to come back.

IYALOJA. We foresaw that. Hence the burden I trudged here to lay beside your gates.

PILKINGS. What was that you said?

IYALOJA. Didn't our son explain? Ask that one. He knows what it is. At least we hope the man we once knew as Elesin remembers the lesser oaths he need not break.

PILKINGS. Do you know what she is talking about?

ELESIN. Go to the gates, ghostly one. Whatever you find there, bring it to me.

IYALOJA. Not yet. It drags behind me on the slow, weary feet of women. Slow as it is Elesin, it has long overtaken you. It rides ahead of your laggard will.

PILKINGS. What is she saying now? Christ! Must your people forever speak in riddles?

ELESIN. It will come white man, it will come. Tell your men at the gates to let it through.

PILKINGS (*dubiously*). I'll have to see what it is.

IYALOJA. You will. (*Passionately.*) But this is one oath he cannot shirk. White one, you have a king here, a visitor from your land. We know of his presence here. Tell me, were he to die would you leave his spirit roaming restlessly on the surface of earth? Would you bury him here among those you consider less than human? In your land have you no ceremonies of the dead?

PILKINGS. Yes. But we don't make our chiefs commit suicide to keep him company.

IYALOJA. Child, I have not come to help your understanding. (*Points to Elesin.*) This is the man whose weakened understanding holds us in bondage to you. But ask him if you wish. He knows the meaning of a king's passage; he was not born yesterday. He knows the peril to the race when our dead father, who goes as intermediary, waits and waits and knows he is betrayed. He knows when the narrow gate was opened and he knows it will not stay for laggards who drag their feet in dung and vomit, whose lips are reeking of the left-overs of lesser men. He knows he has condemned our king to wander in the void of evil with beings who are enemies of life.

PILKINGS. Yes er . . . but look here . . .

IYALOJA. What we ask is little enough. Let him release our King so he can ride on homewards alone. The messenger is on his way on the backs of women. Let him send word through the heart that is folded up within the bolt. It is the least of all his oaths, it is the easiest fulfilled.

(The Aide-De-Camp runs in.)

PILKINGS. Bob?

AIDE-DE-CAMP. Sir, there's a group of women chanting up the hill.

PILKINGS (*rounding on Iyaloja*). If you people want trouble . . .

JANE. Simon, I think that's what Olunde referred to in his letter.

PILKINGS. He knows damned well I can't have a crowd here! Damn it, I explained the delicacy of my position to him. I think it's about time I got him out of town. Bob, send a car and two or three soldiers to bring him in. I think the sooner he takes his leave of his father and gets out the better.

IYALOJA. Save your labour white one. If it is the father of your prisoner you want, Olunde, he who until this night we knew as Elesin's son, he comes soon himself to take his leave. He has sent the women ahead, so let them in.

(Pilkings remains undecided.)

AIDE-DE-CAMP. What do we do about the invasion? We can still stop them far from here.

PILKINGS. What do they look like?

AIDE-DE-CAMP. They're not many. And they seem quite peaceful.

PILKINGS. No men?

AIDE-DE-CAMP. Mm, two or three at the most.

JANE. Honestly, Simon, I'd trust Olunde. I don't think he'll deceive you about their intentions.

PILKINGS. He'd better not. Alright, let them in Bob. Warn them to control themselves. Then hurry Olunde here. Make sure he brings his baggage because I'm not returning him into town.

AIDE-DE-CAMP. Very good sir. (*Goes.*)

PILKINGS (*to Iyaloja*). I hope you understand that if anything goes wrong it will be on your head. My men have orders to shoot at the first sign of trouble.

IYALOJA. To prevent one death you will actually make other deaths? Ah, great is the wisdom of the white race. But have no fear. Your Prince will sleep peacefully. So at long last will ours. We will disturb you no further, servant of the white king. Just let Elesin fulfill his oath and we will retire home and pay homage to our King.

JANE. I believe her Simon, don't you?

PILKINGS. Maybe.

ELESIN. Have no fear ghostly one. I have a message to send my King and then you have nothing more to fear.

IYALOJA. Olunde would have done it. The chiefs asked him to speak the words but he said no, not while you lived.

ELESIN. Even from the depths to which my spirit has sunk, I find some joy that this little has been left to me.

(*The women enter, intoning the dirge 'Alẹ lẹ lẹ' and swaying from side to side. On their shoulders is borne a longish object roughly like a cylindrical bolt, covered in cloth. They set it down on the spot where Iyaloja had stood earlier, and form a semi-circle round it. The Praise-Singer and Drummer stand on the inside of the semi-circle but the drum is not used at all. The Drummer intones under the Praise-Singer's invocations.*)

PILKINGS (*as they enter*). What is *that*?

IYALOJA. The burden you have made white one, but we bring it in peace.

PILKINGS. I said *what* is it?

ELESIN. White man, you must let me out. I have a duty to perform.

PILKINGS. I most certainly will not.

ELESIN. There lies the courier of my King. Let me out so I can perform what is demanded of me.

PILKINGS. You'll do what you need to do from inside there or not at all. I've gone as far as I intend to with this business.

ELESIN. The worshipper who lights a candle in your church to bear a message to his god bows his head and speaks in a whisper to the flame. Have I not seen it ghostly one? His voice does not ring out to the world. Mine are no words

for anyone's ears. They are not words even for the bearers of this load. They are words I must speak secretly, even as my father whispered them in my ears and I in the ears of my first-born. I cannot shout them to the wind and the open night-sky.

JANE. Simon . . .

PILKINGS. Don't interfere. Please!

IYALOJA. They have slain the favourite horse of the king and slain his dog. They have borne them from pulse to pulse centre of the land receiving prayers for their king. But the rider has chosen to stay behind. Is it too much to ask that he speak his heart to heart of the waiting courier? (Pilkings *turns his back on her*.) So be it. Elesin Oba, you see how even the mere leavings are denied you. (*She gestures to the Praise-Singer.*)

PRAISE-SINGER. Elesin Oba! I call you by that name only this last time. Remember when I said, if you cannot come, tell my horse. (*Pause.*) What? I cannot hear you? I said, if you cannot come, whisper in the ears of my horse. Is your tongue severed from the roots Elesin? I can hear no response. I said, if there are boulders you cannot climb, mount my horse's back, this spotless black stallion, he'll bring you over them. (*Pauses.*) Elesin Oba, once you had a tongue that darted like a drummer's stick. I said, if you get lost my dog will track a path to me. My memory fails me but I think you replied: My feet have found the path, Alafin.

(*The dirge rises and falls.*)

I said at the last, if evil hands hold you back, just tell my horse there is weight on the hem of your smock. I dare not wait too long.

(*The dirge rises and falls.*)

There lies the swiftest ever messenger of a king, so set me free with the errand of your heart. There lie the head and heart of the favourite of the gods, whisper in his ears. Oh my companion, if you had followed when you should, we would not say that the horse preceded its rider. If you had followed when it was time, we would not say the dog has raced beyond and left his master behind. If you had raised your will to cut the thread of life at the summons of the drums, we would not say your mere shadow fell across the gateway and took its owner's place at the banquet. But the hunter, laden with a slain buffalo, stayed to root in the cricket's hole with his toes. What now is left? If there is a dearth of bats, the pigeon must serve us for the offering. Speak the words over your shadow which must now serve in your place.

ELESIN. I cannot approach. Take off the cloth. I shall speak my message from heart to heart of silence.

IYALOJA (*moves forward and removes the covering*). Your courier Elesin, cast your eyes on the favoured companion of the King.

(*Rolled up in the mat, his head and feet showing at either end is the body of Olunde.*)

There lies the honour of your household and of our race. Because he could not bear to let honour fly out of doors, he stopped it with his life. The son has proved the father Elesin, and there is nothing left in your mouth to gnash but infant gums.

PRAISE-SINGER. Elesin, we placed the reins of the world in your hands yet you watched it plunge over the edge of the bitter precipice. You sat with folded arms while evil strangers tilted the world from its course and crashed it beyond the edge of emptiness—you muttered, there is little that one man can do, you left us floundering on a blind future. Your heir has taken the burden on himself. What the end will be, we are not gods to tell. But this young shoot has poured its sap into the parent stalk, and we know this is not the way of life. Our world is tumbling in the void of strangers, Elesin.

(Elesin has stood rock-still, his knuckles taut on the bars, his eyes glued to the body of his son. The stillness seizes and paralyses everyone, including Pilkings who has turned to look. Suddenly Elesin flings one arm round his neck, once, and with the loop of the chain, strangles himself in a swift, decisive pull. The guards rush forward to stop him but they are only in time to let his body down. Pilkings has leapt to the door at the same time and struggles with the lock. He rushes within, fumbles with the handcuffs and unlocks them, raises the body to a sitting position while he tries to give resuscitation. The women continue their dirge, unmoved by the sudden event.)

IYALOJA. Why do you strain yourself? Why do you labour at tasks for which no one, not even the man lying there would give you thanks? He is gone at last into the passage but oh, how late it all is. His son will feast on the meat and throw him bones. The passage is clogged with droppings from the King's stallion; he will arrive all stained in dung.

PILKINGS *(in a tired voice)*. Was this what you wanted?

IYALOJA. No child, it is what you brought to be, you who play with strangers' lives, who even usurp the vestments of our dead, yet believe that the stain of death will not cling to you. The gods demanded only the old expired plantain but you cut down the sap-laden shoot to feed your pride. There is your board, filled to overflowing. Feast on it. *(She screams at him suddenly, seeing that Pilkings is about to close Elesin's staring eyes.)* Let him alone! However sunk he was in debt he is no pauper's carrion abandoned on the road. Since when have strangers donned clothes of indigo before the bereaved cries out his loss?

(She turns to the Bride who has remained motionless throughout.)

CHILD.

(The girl takes up a little earth, walks calmly into the cell and closes Elesin's eyes. She then pours some earth over each eyelid and comes out again.)

Now forget the dead, forget even the living. Turn your mind only to the unborn.

(She goes off, accompanied by the Bride. The dirge rises in volume and the women continue their sway. Lights fade to a black-out.)

THE END

CENTER STAGE · YORUBAN OBATALA FESTIVAL IN EDE, NIGERIA, WEST AFRICA

Though their roots are thousands of years old, Yoruban festivals have been continuously celebrated in late January in many Nigerian villages since the seventeenth century. The Yoruba use rituals to mark seasonal rhythms, religious beliefs, and cultural heritage. For the Yoruba contemporary theater remains directly related to the rituals and dance dramas from which it sprang. An understanding of their theology helps us understand why theater remains an intensely spiritual activity for the Yoruba.

The Yoruban Worldview
As one of Africa's most resilient people, the Yoruba can be traced throughout the Western world of the sub-Saharan diaspora. The Yoruba are also unusual among Africans because they have successfully adapted to large urban centers. Both Lagos and Ibadan lie within that part of southwest Nigeria known as Yorubaland, where currently 13 million Yoruba live.

The Yoruba are animistic; that is, their existence is governed by a religion

(continued)

that abounds with gods and spirits that interact—usually in animal form—with humans. The actual number of deities within the Yoruban pantheon is virtually impossible to ascertain because the people within various regions in Yorubaland worship gods unique to themselves. There are, however, several major gods who are recognized and worshipped by all Yoruba in varying forms.

According to Yoruban myth, the gods and humans once dwelt on earth and shared the joys of comradeship and thereby a sense of wholeness. Each needed the other to exist. A "cosmic totality" (to apply Soyinka's phrase) can exist only when gods and humans share this wholeness; only when each seeks an interaction with the essential character of the other can either claim a complete personality. This bond was broken (either through sin or sacrilege, as various interpreters have suggested), and the gods sought new residence in the ethereal regions. Humans were then separated from the gods by death. It was the god Ogun, who is given to imperfection, as are all Yoruban gods, who felt the "anguish of incompleteness" and broke away from the other deities. To bridge "the gulf of transition" between gods and humans, Ogun plunged hubristically into the *chthonic realm*. This act of self-sacrifice gives Ogun a heroic status that sets him apart from all other Yoruban deities.

In addition to being the god of iron and metallurgy, Ogun is also "the Creative Essence" (similar to the Greek Dionysus) and "the Lord of the Road" because he leads humans over the "way" that bridges the "gulf of transition." He is perhaps the favorite god of the Yoruba, and it is he with whom Soyinka most identifies because Ogun, by becoming human again, is "the first actor" (i.e., one who assumes an identity other than his own). Ogun was the first to confront nature and bend it to his will, even while suffering the pain of disinte-

A wooden mask used in Yoruban Egungun festivals in Nigeria; such masks sustain a vital link between the wearer and his ancestors.

gration within the abyss of being and nonbeing. The communicant chorus in the ritual reenactments of Ogun's heroic act—the Ogun Mysteries—is, in itself, a physical manifestation of the god's spiritual reincarnation.

The Yoruban Festival
Thus, the Obatala Festival at Ede is an intense spiritual experience that em-

ploys such common ritualistic devices as symbolic sacrifice, prayers, drumming, singing, dancing, and storytelling that encourage worshippers to come closer to their gods through the enactment of their myths. After a day of sacred songs and dances, the second day of the festival features heroic epics handed down from generation to generation. The performance lasts for almost two weeks as solo maskers often take an entire day to tell stories of superhuman deeds that nourish the Yoruba. The festival begins with the women dancing into the playing space as they carry sacred masks (*eba*) to symbolize fertility and harmony. The men tell stories through songs, using bananas and oils derived from native plants to lubricate their throats and facilitate their incantations. The action is mimed by dancers in colorful costumes and enormous headpieces that not only disguise their human form but also transform them into godlike beings. Nonperformers are forbidden to touch these "gods" who sing and dance, or even to imitate their sounds.

The performers and their audience collectively relive the fabled battle between Ajagemo, the incarnation of Obatala, and another priest, Olunwi. Ajagemo, is captured by Olunwi and carried off from the palace. The Oba (king), however, seeks his release. He pays ransom to Olunwi, and Ajagemo is freed and returns to the palace. His triumph is marked by a magnificent procession in which the performers and audience unite in celebration. *Death and the King's Horseman* is a contemporary play that retains elements of Yoruban ritual in its use of the Praise Singer and especially in the costumes worn by the Pilkingtons to their masquerade. For a full account of Yoruban art and myth, see Femi Euba's *Archetypes, Imprecators, and Victims of Fate: Origins and Developments of Satire in Black Drama* (New York, 1989).

FORUM

"The Fourth Stage: Through the Mysteries of Ogun to the Origin of Yoruba Tragedy"

WOLE SOYINKA

Wole Soyinka is a Nobel Laureate from Nigeria who has written plays, poetry, and critical essays. The following excerpt from his examination of traditional African myth and literature illustrates that concepts of tragedy vary from culture to culture, and that there exist legitimate alternatives to Aristotle's analysis of tragedy. Soyinka's essay makes reference to Friedrich Nieztsche's The Birth of Tragedy (1872), among the most influential discussions of tragedy in Western culture.

The persistent search for the meaning of tragedy, for a re-definition in terms of cultural or private experience is, at the least, man's recognition of certain areas of depth-experience which are not satisfactorily explained by general aesthetic theories; and, of all the subjective unease that is aroused by man's creative insights, that wrench within the human psyche which we vaguely define as "tragedy" is the most insistent voice that bids us to return to our own sources. There, illusively, hovers the key to the human paradox, to man's experience of being and non-being, his dubiousness as essence and matter, intimations of transience and eternity, and the harrowing drives between uniqueness and Oneness.

Our course to the heart of the Yoruba Mysteries leads by its own ironic truths through the light of Nietzsche[1] and the Phrygian deity; but there are the inevitable, key departures. "Blessed Greeks" sings our mad votary in his recessional rapture, "how great must be your Dionysos, if the Delic god thinks such enchantments necessary to cure you of your Dithyrambic madness." Such is Apollo's resemblance to the serene art of Obatala[2] the pure unsullied one, to the "essence" idiom of his rituals, that it is tempting to place him at the end of a creative axis with Ogun,[3] in a parallel evolutionary relationship to Nietzsche's Dionysos—Apollo brotherhood. But Obatala the sculptural god is not the artist of Apollonian illusion but of inner essence. The idealist

[1]Nietzsche, *The Birth of Tragedy.*

[2]Obatala: God of creation (by syncretist tradition with Orisa-nla), essence of the serene arts. Obatala moulds the forms but the breath of life is administered by Edumare, the Supreme deity. The art of Obatala is thus essentially plastic and formal.

[3]Ogun: God of creativity, guardian of the road, god of metallic lore and artistry. Explorer, hunter, god of war, custodian of the sacred oath.

bronze and terra-cotta of Ife which may tempt the comparison implicit in "Apollonian" died at some now forgotten period, evidence only of the universal surface culture of courts and never again resurrected. It is alien to the Obatala spirit of Yoruba "essential" art. Obatala finds expression, not in Nietzsche's Apollonian "mirror of enchantment" but as a statement of world resolution. The mutual tempering of illusion and will, necessary to an understanding of the Hellenic spirit, may mislead us, when we are faced with Yoruba art, for much of it has a similarity in its aesthetic serenity to the plastic arts of the Hellenic. Yoruba traditional art is not ideational however, but "essential." It is not the idea (in religious arts) that is transmitted into wood or interpreted in music or movement, but a quintessence of inner being, a symbolic interaction of the many aspects of revelations (within a universal context) with their moral apprehension.

Ogun, for his part, is best understood in Hellenic values as a totality of the Dionysian, Apollonian and Promethean virtues. Nor is that all. Transcending, even today, the distorted myths of his terrorist reputation, traditional poetry records him as, "protector of orphans," "roof over the homeless," "terrible guardian of the sacred oath;" Ogun stands for a transcendental, humane but rigidly restorative justice. . . . The first artist and technician of the forge, he evokes like Nietzsche's Apollonian spirit, a "massive impact of image, concept, ethical doctrine and sympathy." Obatala is the placid essence of creation; Ogun the creative urge and instinct, the essence of creativity.

> Rich-laden is his home, yet decked in palm fronds
> He ventures forth, refuge of the down-trodden,
> To rescue slaves he unleashed the judgement of war
> Because of the blind, plunged into forests
> Of curative herbs, Bountiful One
> Who stands bulwark to offsprings of the dead of heaven
> Salutations, O lone being, who swims in rivers of blood.

Such virtues place Ogun apart from the distorted dances to which Nietzsche's Dionysiac frenzy led him in his search for a selective "Aryan" soul, yet do not detract from Ogun's revolutionary grandeur. Ironically, it is the depth-illumination of Nietzsche's intuition into basic universal impulses which negates his race exclusivist conclusions on the nature of art and tragedy. In our journey to the heart of Yoruba tragic art which indeed belongs in the Mysteries of Ogun and the choric ecstasy of revellers, we do not find that the Yoruba, as the Greek did, "built for his chorus the scaffolding of a fictive chthonic realm and placed thereon fictive nature spirits . . ." on which foundation, claims Nietzsche, Greek tragedy developed: in short, the principle of illusion.

(continued)

Yoruba tragedy plunges straight into the "chthonic realm," the seething cauldron of the dark world will and psyche, the transitional yet inchoate matrix of death and becoming. Into this universal womb once plunged and emerged Ogun, the first actor, disintegrating within the abyss. His spiritual re-assemblage does not require a "copying of actuality" in the ritual re-enactment of his devotees, any more than Obatala does in plastic represenation, in the art of Obatala. The actors in Ogun Mysteries are the communicant chorus, containing within their collective being the essence of that transitional abyss. But only as essence, held, contained and mystically expressed. Within the mystic summons of the chasm the protagonist actor (and every god-suffused choric individual) resists, like Ogun before him, the final step towards complete annihilation. From this alone steps forward the eternal actor of the tragic rites, first as the unresisting mouthpiece of the god, uttering visions symbolic of the transitional gulf, interpreting the dread power within whose essence he is immersed as agent of the choric will. Only later, in the evenness of release from the tragic climax, does the serene self-awareness of Obatala reassert its creative control. He, the actor, emerges still as the mediant voice of the god, but stands now as it were beside himself, observant, understanding, creating. At this stage is known to him the sublime *aesthetic* joy, not within Nietzsche's heart of original oneness but in the distanced celebration of the cosmic struggle. This resolved aesthetic serenity is the link between Ogun's tragic art and Obatala's plastic beauty. The unblemished god, Obatala, is the serene womb of chthonic reflections (or memory), a passive strength awaiting and celebrating each act of vicarious restoration of his primordial being. (We shall come later to the story of that first severance.) His beauty is enigmatic, expressive only of the resolution of plastic healing through the wisdom of acceptance. Obtala's patient suffering is the well-known aesthetics of the saint.

For the Yoruba, the gods are the final measure of eternity, as humans are of earthly transience. To think, because of this, that the Yoruba mind reaches intuitively towards absorption in god-like essence is to misunderstand the principle of religious rites, and to misread, as many have done, the significance of religious possession. Past, present and future being so pertinently conceived and woven into the Yoruba world view, the element of eternity which is the gods' prerogative does not have the same quality of remoteness or exclusiveness which it has in Christian or Buddhist culture. The belief of the Yoruba in the contemporaneous existence within his daily experience of these aspects of time has long been recognised but again misinterpreted. It is no abstraction. The Yoruba is not, like European man, concerned with the purely conceptual aspects of time; they are too concretely realised in his own life, religion, sensitivity, to be mere tags for explaining the metaphysical order of his world. If we may put the same thing in fleshed-out cognitions, life, present life, contains within it manifestations of the ancestral, the living and the unborn. All are vitally within the intimations and affectiveness of life, beyond mere abstract conceptualisation.

And yet the Yoruba does not for that reason fail to distinguish between himself and the deities, between himself and the ancestors, between the unborn and his reality, or discard his awareness of the essential gulf that lies between one area of existence and another. This gulf is what must be constantly diminished by the sacrifices, the rituals, the ceremonies of appeasement to those cosmic powers which lie guardian to the gulf. Spiritually, the primordial disquiet of the Yoruba psyche may be expressed as the existence in collective memory of a primal severance in transitional ether,[4] whose first effective defiance is symbolised in the myth of the gods' descent to earth and the battle with immense chaotic growth which had sealed off re-union with man. For they were coming down, not simply to be acknowledged but to be re-united with human essence, to reassume that portion of re-creative transient awareness which the first deity Orisa-nla possessed and expressed through his continuous activation of man images—brief reflections of divine facets—just as man is grieved by a consciouness of the loss of the eternal essence of his being and must indulge in symbolic transactions to recover his totality of being.

Tragedy, in Yoruba traditional drama, is the anguish of this severance, the fragmentation of essence from self. Its music is the stricken cry of man's blind soul as he flounders in the void and crashes through a deep abyss of a-spirituality and cosmic rejection. Tragic music is an echo from that void; the celebrant speaks, sings and dances in authentic archetypal images from within the abyss. All understand and respond, for it is the language of the world.

It is necessary to emphasise that the gods were coming down to be reunited with man, for this tragedy could not be, the anguish of severance would not attain such tragic proportions, if the gods' position on earth (i.e. in man's conception) was to be one of divine remoteness. This is again testified to by the form of worship, which is marked by camaraderie and irreverence just as departure to ancestorhood is marked by bawdiness in the midst of grief. The anthropomorphic origin of uncountable deities is one more leveller of divine class-consciousness but, finally, it is the innate humanity of the gods themselves, their bond with man through a common animist relation with nature and phenomena. Continuity for the Yoruba operates both through the cyclic concept of time and the animist interfusion of all matter and consciousness.

The first actor—for he led the others—was Ogun, first suffering deity, first creative energy, the first challenger, and conqueror of transition. And his, the first art, was tragic art, for the complementary drama of the syncretic successor to Orisa-nla, Obatala's "Passion" play, is only the plastic resolution of Ogun's tragic engagement. The Yoruba metaphysics of accommodation and resolution could only come after the passage of the gods through the transitional gulf, after the demonic test of the self-will of Ogun the explorer-god in the creative cauldron of cosmic powers. Only after such testing could the harmonious Yoruba world be born, a harmonious will which accommodates every alien material or abstract phenomenon within its infinitely stressed spirituality. The artifact of Ogun's conquest of separation, the "fetish," was iron ore, symbol of earth's womb-energies,

---

[4] I would render this more cogently today in terms of race origination, uprooting, wandering and settling. This group experience is less remote, and parallels the mythology of primordial chaos, as well as the rites of transition (birth, death, etc.).

cleaver and welder of life. Ogun, through his redemptive action became the first symbol of the alliance of disparities when, from earth itself, he extracted elements for the subjugation of chthonic chaos. In tragic consciousness the votary's psyche reaches out beyond the realm of nothingness (or spiritual chaos) which is potentially destructive of human awareness, through areas of terror and blind energies into a ritual empathy with the gods, the eternal presence, who once preceded him in parallel awareness of their own incompletion. Ritual anguish is therefore experienced as that primal transmission of the god's despair—vast, numinous, always incomprehensible. In vain we seek to capture it in words; there is only for the protagonist the certainty of the experience of this abyss—the tragic victim plunges into it in spite of ritualistic earthing and is redeemed only by action. Without acting, and yet in spite of it he is forever lost in the maul of tragic tyranny.

Acting is therefore a contradiction of the tragic spirit, yet it is also its natural complement. To act, the Promethean instinct of rebellion, channels anguish into a creative purpose which releases man from a totally destructive despair, releasing from within him the most energetic, deeply combative inventions which, without usurping the territory of the infernal gulf, bridges it with visionary hopes. Only the battle of the will is thus primally creative; from its spiritual stress springs the soul's despairing cry which proves its own solace, which alone reverberating within the cosmic vaults usurps (at least, and however briefly) the powers of the abyss. At the charged climatic moments of the tragic rites we understand how music came to be the sole art form which can contain tragic reality. The votary is led by no other guide into the pristine heart of tragedy. Music as the embodiment of the tragic spirit has been more than perceptively exhausted in the philosophy of Europe; there is little to

add, much to qualify. And the function and nature of music in Yoruba tragedy is peculiarly revealing of the shortcomings of long accepted conclusions of European intuition.

This is the fourth stage, the vortex of archetypes and home of the tragic spirit.

It is necessary to recall again that the past is not a mystery and that although the future (the unborn) is yet unknown, it is not a mystery to the Yoruba but co-existent in present consciousness. Tragic terror exists therefore neither in the evocation of the past nor of the future. The stage of transition is, however, the metaphysical abyss both of god and man, and if we agree that, in the European sense, music is the "direct copy or the direct expression of the will," it is only because nothing rescues man (ancestral, living or unborn) from loss of self within this abyss but a titanic resolution of the will whose ritual summons, response, and expression is the strange alien sound to which we give the name of music. On the arena of the living, when man is stripped of excrescences, when disasters and conflicts (the material of drama) have crushed and robbed him of self-consciousness and pretensions, he stands in present reality at the spiritual edge of this gulf, he has nothing left in physical existence which successfully impresses upon his spiritual or psychic perception. It is at such moments that transitional memory takes over and intimations rack him of that intense parallel of his progress through the gulf of transition, of the dissolution of his self and his struggle and triumph over subsumation through the agency of will. It is this experience that the modern tragic dramatist recreates through the medium of physical contemporary action, reflecting emotions of the first active battle of the will through the abyss of dissolution. Ogun is the first actor in that battle, and Yoruba tragic drama is the re-enactment of the cosmic conflict.

AFRICAN AMERICAN THEATER

Artistic and Cultural Events

1821:
W. H. Brown establishes the African Theatre in New York

1824:
Brown's *The Drama of King Shotaway*

1884:
Astor Place Company of Colored Tragedians

1915:
LaFayette Players, New York

1924:
Willis Richardson's *The Chip Woman's Fortune*, first play by African American on Broadway

1930s:
The Harlem Renaissance

1940:
American Negro Theatre

1959:
Lorraine Hansberry's *A Raisin in the Sun*

1964:
Black Arts Repertory Theatre

1967:
Negro Ensemble Company

1969:
Amiri Baraka's *Slave Ship*

1970:
Charles Gordone's *No Place to Be Somebody*; first Pulitzer Prize for African American playwright

1983:
August Wilson's *Fences*

1800 C.E.   1900 C.E.

Historical and Political Events

Slavery practiced in U.S.

1863:
Emancipation Proclamation abolishes slavery

1861–1865:
Civil War

1954:
U.S. Supreme Court desegregates schools

1967:
"Summer of Rage," civil rights riots throughout U.S.A.

1968:
Martin Luther King assassinated

1963:
Civil Rights March on Washington; "I Have a Dream" speech by Martin Luther King

Seeking solace from their slavery and the continuity of an indigenous culture, Africans in America performed folktales (often about Anansi, the frail spider who survived by using his wits), songs, music, and dance in cabins and camp meetings, even in town parks such as Congo Square in New Orleans. Such performances eventually melded with, and were transformed by, the Euro-American culture. In 1821 William Henry Brown established the African Theatre in New York, an enterprise modeled after the white playhouses. Brown's company performed traditional European fare, particularly Shakespeare, but Brown also authored *The Drama of King Shotaway*, based on slavery; it is the first play by an author of African descent in the United States. Though Brown's enterprise was short-lived, it was a notable attempt to produce theater for and about African exiles. Ira Aldridge (1807–1867) emerged as the African Theatre's finest actor, and he is generally regarded as the first "star" actor of African descent in the American theater. Aldridge achieved his greatest fame in Europe, where he performed major Shakespearean roles; he was buried with state honors in Lodz, Poland.

After the demise of the African Theatre there was little theatrical activity by Africans in America (save the minstrel show, see Chapter 7) until after the Civil War (1861–1865). In New York the Astor Place Company of Colored Tragedians was founded by J. A. Arnaux in 1884 to perform mostly Shakespearean plays. Most performers of African descent were specialty artists, such as Henrietta Vinto Davies (an opera singer) and the popular stars of vaudeville and musical comedy, Bob Cole and Bert Williams.

In 1915 the Lafayette Players were founded in New York and became the preeminent outlet for African American dramatists in the early twentieth century. That year also saw the emergence of the Provincetown Players (see Chapter 7), which produced Eugene O'Neill's *The Emperor Jones* in 1922. Charles Gilpin played Brutus Jones to great acclaim and became the first prominent African American actor on Broadway.

In 1923 Willis Richardson's *The Chip Woman's Fortune* was the first nonmusical play written by an African American staged on Broadway. However, it was Lorraine Hansberry's *A Raisin in the Sun* (1959) that became the first Broadway "hit" written by an African American. Hansberry's drama was as significant a groundbreaker in its time as the dramas by Europe's early realists. Its title was taken from a poem by Langston Hughes, a leader of the 1930s Harlem Renaissance (an outpouring of poetry, fiction, and plays by and for African Americans). Hughes's own play *Mulatto* (1935) was among the finest achievements of the Harlem Renaissance. The play, which portrayed the lynching of a young man of mixed race, ran for almost 400 performances on Broadway, a testimony to the power of Hughes's writing and to the acting of Rose McClendon, among the first black women to achieve stardom in the New York theater. The play was later turned into an opera, *The Barrier* (1950). The American Negro Theatre, founded by Abram Hill and Frederick O'Neill in 1940, provided more opportunities for dramatists and actors to work in the American mainstream. Its most successful production, *Anna Lucasta* (1944), played for 957 performances on Broadway and became an international hit.

The civil rights movement in postwar America fostered more African American and integrated theater companies, most notably the Free Southern Theatre, founded by Gilbert Moses to develop African American drama "as unique to the Negro people as blues and jazz." Based in New Orleans, the FST was the first integrated theater company to perform in the American South; it produced both European dramas (e.g., *Waiting for Godot*) and works written expressly for African Americans (e.g., Ossie Davis's rousing comedy *Purlie Victorious*).

The civil rights movement also encouraged the development of playwrights writing from and about the black experience: Amiri Baraka (LeRoi Jones), Charles Gordone (the first Pulitzer Prize–winning dramatist of African descent), Ed Bullins, Adrienne Kennedy, Ntozaki Shange, Charles Fuller, and most recently Suzan Lori Parks. Small theaters such as the New Lafayette Playhouse emerged as showcases for African American writers. In 1967 the Negro Ensemble Company (NEC) was organized in New York by playwright Douglas Turner Ward and actor Robert Hooks to train young artists as performers and playwrights and especially to produce plays relevant to black Americans. It remains one of the most admired production companies in America, with over 50 productions of new plays, including the Pulitzer Prize–winning, *A Soldier's Play* (1982). Curiously, the NEC turned down Gordone's Pulitzer Prize winning play (*No Place to Be Somebody*, 1970).

African American theater artists are also thriving well beyond New York. Currently August Wilson, winner of two Pulitzer Prizes, is recognized as the foremost American playwright—as opposed to the foremost African American playwright. Wilson lives in St. Paul, and his plays usually receive their first productions at Yale's renowned School of Drama. His works have become mainstays of many professional regional companies, notably in Seattle, Houston, and Kansas City.

Among the most interesting and visible phenomena concerning African American performance has been the popularity of musicals based on the works of such pioneers in jazz as Fats Waller (*Ain't Misbehavin'*, 1979), Eubie Blake (*Bubblin' Brown Sugar*, 1976, and *Eubie*, 1978), and Jelly Roll Morton (*Jelly's Last Jam*, 1992). These reviews have introduced a new generation of Americans to the extraordinary contributions of African Americans to the country's culture.

A RAISIN IN THE SUN

LORRAINE HANSBERRY

LORRAINE HANSBERRY (1930–1965)

Born into a prominent, middle-class African American family in Chicago (her father helped found one of the first banks for people of color in that city), Lorraine Hansberry grew up comfortably in surroundings quite unlike the cramped quarters of the Younger household on Chicago's South Side she depicts in *A Raisin in the Sun*. She was introduced to the arts, particularly drama, at a young age, and she remembers a trip to see *The Dark of the Moon* as the moment that inspired her to write for the theater.

However, the Hansberry world was not idyllic. Her father became disillusioned with the treatment of African Americans in the United States and migrated to Mexico to seek a more color-blind existence. Unfortunately, he died there in 1945, but his quest for interracial harmony instilled in his daughter a similar passion.

Hansberry attended the University of Wisconsin and Roosevelt College in Chicago. But, as she has said, her real education came when she moved to New York in 1950. She married a songwriter–music publisher (Bob Nemiroff) and lived in Greenwich Village, where liberal politics and an intellectual environment kindled her aspirations to become a writer. She dabbled in playwriting while working with some local theater groups, but had not finished a play. In 1955 she began to write *A Raisin in the Sun*. Another music publisher, Philip Rose, heard a reading of the play at a dinner party and was determined to have the play produced in New York. Because plays by and about African Americans were virtually nonexistent, Rose and the Nemiroffs found it difficult to raise funds for the production. After successful out-of-town try-outs, which encouraged the producers, the play eventually premiered at the Ethel Barrymore Theater on March 11, 1959. It was directed by a young African American, Lloyd Richards (currently noted for his association with August Wilson), and it starred an unknown Sidney Poitier as Walter Lee. Audiences embraced the play, and Hansberry was awarded the New York Drama Critics Circle Award for best play. It was the first time an African American woman received this prestigious award.

Hansberry continued to write, most notably *The Sign in Sidney Brustein's Window*, a play about a Greenwich Village intellectual that has virtually nothing to do with African Americans. Hansberry died of cancer the night this play closed on Broadway in 1965. After her untimely death, her husband pieced together a collection of her letters, notes, and unfinished manuscripts, which he titled *To Be Young, Gifted, and Black*. Adapted for the stage, the work has become a staple of educational and community theater, and was also made into a film. Despite her short life and the small output of works, Hansberry is recognized as a major force in the shaping of minority theater in the United States. Yet she always argued that she was not a black playwright. She maintained that she wrote about people, "some of whom happened to be black."

A Raisin in the Sun (1959)

Contrary to popular belief, *A Raisin in the Sun* was not the first play by and about African Americans produced on Broadway. In 1923 Willis Richardson's *The Chip Woman's Fortune* claimed the distinction of becoming the first nonmusical African American play to be produced on Broadway. *A Raisin in the Sun*, however, is among the first commercially successful plays written by an African American and performed on Broadway.

There are many reasons for the play's success. First, it is useful to look at the play in terms of its historical context. The legitimacy of African American literature and arts was established by the Harlem Renaissance of the 1930s, a movement that encouraged young African American writers and artists to cultivate work that reflected the American experience from the black point of view. Its leader was Langston Hughes, a fine playwright (*Mulatto*, 1934) and a superb poet. It was Hughes who provided Hansberry with the title of her play; he asks in his most famous poem,

> *What happens to a dream deferred?*
>
> *Does it wither like a raisin in the sun?*
>
> . . . .
>
> *Or does it explode?*

Hughes anticipated the "black rage" that erupted in America in the 1960s when anger at social injustices literally exploded in the streets of Watts, Detroit, and Newark.

But while repressed anger lurks beneath *A Raisin in the Sun*, it is not an angry play in the confrontational manner of Amiri Baraka's works. And that is precisely one of the reasons the play was embraced by Broadway audiences in 1959. White audiences entering the Ethel Barrymore Theater were far more sympathetic to the injustices suffered by African Americans than perhaps at any previous time in the nation's history. In April 1947, Jackie Robinson showed that African Americans could perform magnificently in a previously all-white world when he broke baseball's color barrier. Soon other African Americans followed Robinson in baseball, as well as other sports. The nation had a new host of African American heroes to admire.

In 1954 the Supreme Court desegregated schools, a move that fueled and reflected the emerging civil rights movement. Even as Hansberry's play moved to Broadway, the Reverend Martin Luther King Jr. was leading marches through the South; his famous "I Have a Dream" speech was delivered just four years after *Raisin* opened. Rosa Parks defiantly refused to "move to the back of the bus" in Montgomery, Alabama. Such events were duly recorded on television, a relatively new medium that allowed middle-class America to see first hand the problems and poverty spawned by racism. A new consciousness about race relations was developing. Mama's eloquent reflection on her husband's dreams engaged Broadway audiences on a more personal level than was possible for previous generations: "Big Walter used to say . . . 'seem like God didn't see fit to give the black man nothing but dreams—but He did give us children to make them dreams worth while.'"

Actually, the dreams that most affected audiences at the Barrymore—and in the theaters throughout the country that added *Raisin* to their repertory—was the American dream of owning a house. Mama's argument that "it makes a difference in a man when he can walk on floors that belong to *him*" echoed any number of lines that had become the staple of American drama. In 1943 *Oklahoma* expressed the sentiment that "we know we belong to the land, and the land we belong to is grand." *Tobacco Road*, the longest-running Broadway play during the Great Depression, presented a dirt-poor farmer, Jeeter Lester, who eloquently defended his property to a banker who was attempting to evict him:

> This was my Daddy's place and his Daddy's before him, and I don't know how many Lesters before that. There wasn't nothing here but the whole country before they came. . . . Now I don't own it and it belongs to a durn bank that ain't never had nothing to do with it even. By

God, that ain't right, I tell you. God won't stand for such cheating much longer. He ain't so liking of the rich as people think He is. God, he likes the poor.

Or "plain people," to use Mama Younger's term.

Despite its status as a seminal African American drama, *A Raisin in the Sun* is actually a
rather conventional play. At its heart it is a mid-twentieth-century version of the German *fam-
ilienstucke*, a brand of melodrama pioneered by Agust Iffland early in the nineteenth century.
Such plays—in which families were threatened by eviction if they did not raise money for the
mortgage—became a staple of the American melodrama. Audiences understood the sanctity of
the "old homestead." The irony of Hansberry's play, however, is that the Younger family actually has the mortgage money. It is not the greed of the heartless banker that threatens their
new home; rather, it is the incipient racism expressed by Mr. Linder, the spokesman for the
Homeowners Association: ". . . our Negro families are happier when they live in their *own*
communities." Ironically, the greedy thief of the old melodrama is Walter Lee's friend, Willy
Harris, who dashes the Younger dream when he absconds with the insurance money, a plot element that elevates Hansberry's play above the level of mere polemic.

Beneatha, Mama's daughter, offered white audiences an occasion to see a newly emerging
phenomenon among African Americans: the quest to recapture the pride and dignity of their
cultural roots. (Less than two decades after *Raisin*, Arthur Hailey's epic novel *Roots* became the
most popular miniseries in the history of American television.) She proclaims proudly and defiantly that she is looking for her identity. Furthermore, she is not an assimilationist, that is,
one who gives up her cultural roots in favor of those of the country in which she lives. Hansberry invents Joseph Asagai, the immigrant student with aspirations to the American dream,
to underscore Beneatha's plight. He retains his "old country" prejudices against women ("For a
woman [love and a family] should be enough"), and ironically Beneatha must fight biases
among her own people as much as those of white society. Again Hansberry raised issues beyond
racial intolerance. (See *The Great Celestial Cow*, which also confronts the issues of assimilation
and prejudices against women by men of their own culture; Chapter 9.)

Despite its status as a groundbreaking work, *A Raisin in the Sun* has fallen into disrepute
among some African Americans. It has been criticized for not being militant enough. Mama's
dependence on religion ("There'll always be a God in this house!") has caused her to be seen
as passive; she relies on divine guidance rather than actively working to change her circumstances. These issues and others have been addressed by George C. Wolfe, the playwright and
director who also heads the New York Shakespeare Festival Public Theater. Wolfe wrote *The
Colored Museum* (1988), a collection of sketches, some fiercely satirical, others poignant vignettes, which attack stereotypical views of African Americans enshrined in "the colored museum" of white consciousness. One sketch, "The Last Mama-on-the-Couch Play," parodies *A
Raisin in the Sun* (and Poitier's mannered acting). We have appended it here as a critique of
Hansberry's work from the perspective of African Americans in the late twentieth century.
Wolfe's sketch thus creates a dialogue between his generation and that represented by Hansberry.

However much subsequent events in the civil rights movement may have altered the status of *A Raisin in the Sun*, it nonetheless remains among the most significant plays in the history of the American theater. It was an urgent play in 1959 and a necessary step in the evolution of African American literature and performance.

Walter Lee (Ossie Davis) lectures his wife Ruth (left) and his sister Beneatha (right), who prides herself on her traditional African dress in this Lincoln Center revival of A Raisin in the Sun.

A RAISIN IN THE SUN

LORRAINE HANSBERRY

What happens to a dream deferred?
Does it dry up
Like a raisin in the sun?
Or fester like a sore—
And then run?
Does it stink like rotten meat?
Or crust and sugar over—

Like a syrupy sweet?

Maybe it just sags
Like a heavy load.

Or does it explode?

—Langston Hughes

To Mama:
In Gratitude for the Dream

(In order of appearance)
RUTH YOUNGER
TRAVIS YOUNGER
WALTER LEE YOUNGER (*Brother*)
BENEATHA YOUNGER
LENA YOUNGER (*Mama*)
JOSEPH ASAGAI
GEORGE MURCHISON
KARL LINDNER
BOBO
MOVING MEN

The action of the play is set in Chicago's Southside, sometime between World War II and the present.

ACT ONE

Scene 1. Friday morning.

Scene 2. The following morning.

ACT TWO

Scene 1. Later, the same day.

Scene 2. Friday night, a few weeks later.

Scene 3. Moving day, one week later.

ACT THREE

An hour later.

ACT ONE

SCENE ONE

The Younger living room would be a comfortable and well-ordered room if it were not for a number of indestructible contradictions to this state of being. Its furnishings are typical and undistinguished and their primary feature now is that they have clearly had to accommodate the living of too many people for too many years—and they are tired. Still, we can see that at some time, a time probably no longer remembered by the family (except perhaps for Mama), the furnishings of this room were actually selected with care and love and even hope—and brought to this apartment and arranged with taste and pride.

That was a long time ago. Now the once loved pattern of the couch upholstery has to fight to show itself from under acres of crocheted doilies and couch covers which have themselves finally come to be more important than the upholstery. And here a table or a chair has been moved to disguise the worn places in the carpet; but the carpet has fought back by showing its weariness, with depressing uniformity, elsewhere on its surface.

Weariness has, in fact, won in this room. Everything has been polished, washed, sat on, used, scrubbed too often. All pretenses but living itself have long since vanished from the very atmosphere of this room.

Moreover, a section of this room, for it is not really a room unto itself, though the landlord's lease would make it seem so, slopes backward to provide a small kitchen area, where the family prepares the meals that are eaten in the living room proper, which must also serve as dining room. The single window that has been provided for these "two" rooms is located in this kitchen area. The sole natural light the family may enjoy in the course of a day is only that which fights its way through this little window.

At left, a door leads to a bedroom which is shared by Mama and her daughter, Beneatha. At right, opposite, is a second room (which in the beginning of the life of this apartment was probably a breakfast room) which serves as a bedroom for Walter and his wife, Ruth.

Time: Sometime between World War II and the present.

Place: Chicago's southside.

At rise: It is morning dark in the living room. Travis is asleep on the make-down bed at center. An alarm clock sounds from within the bedroom at right, and presently Ruth enters from that room and closes the door behind her. She crosses sleepily toward the window. As she passes her sleeping son she reaches down and shakes him a little. At the window she raises the shade and a dusky Southside morning light comes in feebly. She fills a pot with water and puts it on to boil. She calls to the boy, between yawns, in a slightly muffled voice.

Ruth is about thirty. We can see that she was a pretty girl, even exceptionally so, but now it is apparent that life has been little that she expected, and disappointment has already begun to hang in her face. In a few years, before thirty-five even, she will be known among her people as a "settled woman."

She crosses to her son and gives him a good, final, rousing shake.

RUTH. Come on now, boy, it's seven thirty! (*Her son sits up at last, in a stupor of sleepiness*) I say hurry up, Travis! You ain't the only person in the world got to use a bathroom! (*The child, a sturdy, handsome little boy of ten or eleven, drags himself out of the bed and almost blindly takes his towels and "today's clothes" from drawers and a closet and goes out to the bathroom, which is in an outside hall and which is shared by another family or families on the same floor. Ruth crosses to the bedroom door at right and opens it and calls in to her husband*) Walter Lee! . . . It's after seven thirty! Lemme see you do some waking up in there now! (*She waits*) You better get up from there, man! It's after seven thirty I tell you. (*She waits again*) All right, you just go ahead and lay there and next thing you know Travis be finished and Mr. Johnson'll be in there and you'll be fussing and cussing round here like a mad man! And be late too! (*She waits, at the end of patience*) Walter Lee—it's time for you to get up!

(*She waits another second and then starts to go into the bedroom, but is apparently satisfied that her husband has begun to get up. She stops, pulls the door to, and returns to the kitchen area. She wipes her face with a moist cloth and runs her fingers through her sleep-disheveled hair in a vain effort and ties an apron around her housecoat. The bedroom door at right opens and her husband stands in the doorway in his pajamas, which are rumpled and mismated. He is a lean, intense young man in his middle thirties, inclined to quick nervous movements and erratic speech habits—and always in his voice there is a quality of indictment.*)

WALTER. Is he out yet?

RUTH. What you mean *out*? He ain't hardly got in there good yet.

WALTER (*Wandering in, still more oriented to sleep than to a new day*). Well, what was you doing all that yelling for if I can't even get in there yet? (*Stopping and thinking*) Check coming today?

RUTH. They *said* Saturday and this is just Friday and I hopes to God you ain't going to get up here first thing this morning and start talking to me 'bout no money—'cause I 'bout don't want to hear it.

WALTER. Something the matter with you this morning?

RUTH. No—I'm just sleepy as the devil. What kind of eggs you want?

WALTER. Not scrambled. (*Ruth starts to scramble eggs*) Paper come? (*Ruth points impatiently to the rolled up* Tribune *on the table, and he gets it and spreads it out and vaguely reads the front page.*) Set off another bomb yesterday.

RUTH (*Maximum indifference*). Did they?

WALTER (*looking up*). What's the matter with you?

RUTH. Ain't nothing the matter with me. And don't keep asking me that this morning.

WALTER. Ain't nobody bothering you. (*Reading the news of the day absently again.*) Say Colonel McCormick is sick.

RUTH (*Affecting tea-party interest*). Is he now? Poor thing.

WALTER (*Sighing and looking at his watch*). Oh, me. (*He waits*) Now what is that boy doing in that bathroom all this time? He just going to have to start getting up earlier. I can't be being late to work on account of him fooling around in there.

RUTH (*Turning on him*). Oh, no he ain't going to be getting up no earlier no such thing! It ain't his fault that he can't get to bed no earlier nights 'cause he got a bunch of crazy good-for-nothing clowns sitting up running their mouths

in what is supposed to be his bedroom after ten o'clock at night . . .

WALTER. That's what you mad about, ain't it? The things I want to talk about with my friends just couldn't be important in your mind, could they?

(*He rises and finds a cigarette in her handbag on the table and crosses to the little window and looks out, smoking and deeply enjoying this first one.*)

RUTH (*Almost matter of factly, a complaint too automatic to deserve emphasis*). Why you always got to smoke before you eat in the morning?

WALTER (*At the window*). Just look at 'em down there . . . Running and racing to work . . . (*He turns and faces his wife and watches her a moment at the stove and then, suddenly*) You look young this morning, baby.

RUTH (*Indifferently*). Yeah?

WALTER. Just for a second—stirring them eggs. It's gone now—just for a second it was—you looked real young again. (*Then, drily*) It's gone now—you look like yourself again.

RUTH. Man, if you don't shut up and leave me alone.

WALTER (*Looking out to the street again*). First thing a man ought to learn in life is not to make love to no colored woman first thing in the morning. You all some evil people at eight o'clock in the morning.

(*Travis appears in the hall doorway, almost fully dressed and quite wide awake now, his towels and pajamas across his shoulders. He opens the door and signals for his father to make the bathroom in a hurry.*)

TRAVIS (*Watching the bathroom*). Daddy, come on! (*Walter gets his bathroom utensils and flies out to the bathroom*)

RUTH. Sit down and have your breakfast, Travis.

TRAVIS. Mama, this is Friday. (*Gleefully*) Check coming tomorrow, huh?

RUTH. You get your mind off money and eat your breakfast.

TRAVIS (*Eating*). This is the morning we supposed to bring the fifty cents to school.

RUTH. Well, I ain't got no fifty cents this morning.

TRAVIS. Teacher say we have to.

RUTH. I don't care what teacher say. I ain't got it. Eat your breakfast, Travis.

TRAVIS. I *am* eating.

RUTH. Hush up now and just eat!

(*The boy gives her an exasperated look for her lack of understanding, and eats grudgingly.*)

TRAVIS. You think Grandmama would have it?

RUTH. No! And I want you to stop asking your grandmother for money, you hear me?

TRAVIS (*Outraged*). Gaaaleee! I don't ask her, she just gimme it sometimes!

RUTH. Travis Willard Younger—I got too much on me this morning to be—

TRAVIS. Maybe Daddy—
RUTH. *Travis!*

(*The boy hushes abruptly. They are both quiet and tense for several seconds.*)

TRAVIS (*Presently*). Could I maybe go carry some groceries in front of the supermarket for a little while after school then?
RUTH. Just hush, I said. (*Travis jabs his spoon into his cereal bowl viciously, and rests his head in anger upon his fists.*) If you through eating, you can get over there and make up your bed.

(*The boy obeys stiffly and crosses the room, almost mechanically, to the bed and more or less carefully folds the covering. He carries the bedding into his mother's room and returns with his books and cap.*)

TRAVIS (*Sulking and standing apart from her unnaturally*). I'm gone.
RUTH (*Looking up from the stove to inspect him automatically*). Come here. (*He crosses to her and she studies his head.*) If you don't take this comb and fix this here head, you better! (*Travis puts down his books with a great sigh of oppression, and crosses to the mirror. His mother mutters under her breath about his "stubbornness."*) 'Bout to march out of here with that head looking just like chickens slept in it! I just don't know where you get your stubborn ways . . . And get your jacket, too. Looks chilly out this morning.
TRAVIS (*With conspicuously brushed hair and jacket*). I'm gone.
RUTH. Get carfare and milk money—(*Waving one finger*)—and not a single penny for no caps, you hear me?
TRAVIS (*With sullen politeness*). Yes'm.

(*He turns in outrage to leave. His mother watches after him as in his frustration he approaches the door almost comically. When she speaks to him, her voice has become a very gentle tease.*)

RUTH (*Mocking; as she thinks he would say it*). Oh, Mama makes me so mad sometimes, I don't know what to do! (*She waits and continues to his back as he stands stock-still in front of the door.*) I wouldn't kiss that woman good-bye for nothing in this world this morning! (*The boy finally turns around and rolls his eyes at her, knowing the mood has changed and he is vindicated; he does not, however, move toward her yet.*) Not for nothing in this world! (*She finally laughs aloud at him and holds out her arms to him and we see that it is a way between them, very old and practiced. He crosses to her and allows her to embrace him warmly but keeps his face fixed with masculine rigidity. She holds him back from her presently and looks at him and runs her fingers over the features of his face. With utter gentleness—*) Now—whose little old angry man are you?
TRAVIS (*The masculinity and gruffness start to fade at last*). Aw gaalee—Mama . . .
RUTH (*Mimicking*). Aw—gaaaaalleeeee, Mama! (*She pushes

him, with rough playfulness and finality, toward the door.*) Get on out of here or you going to be late.
TRAVIS (*In the face of love, new aggressiveness*). Mama, could I *please* go carry groceries?
RUTH. Honey, it's starting to get so cold evenings.
WALTER (*Coming in from the bathroom and drawing a make-believe gun from a make-believe holster and shooting at his son*). What is it he wants to do?
RUTH. Go carry groceries after school at the supermarket.
WALTER. Well, let him go . . .
TRAVIS (*Quickly, to the ally*). I have to—she won't gimme the fifty cents . . .
WALTER (*To his wife only*). Why not?
RUTH (*Simply, and with flavor*). 'Cause we don't have it.
WALTER (*To Ruth only*). What you tell the boy things like that for? (*Reaching down into his pants with a rather important gesture*) Here, son—

(*He hands the boy the coin, but his eyes are directed to his wife's. Travis takes the money happily.*)

TRAVIS. Thanks, Daddy.

(*He starts out. Ruth watches both of them with murder in her eyes. Walter stands and stares back at her with defiance, and suddenly reaches into his pocket again on an afterthought.*)

WALTER (*Without even looking at his son, still staring hard at his wife*). In fact, here's another fifty cents . . . Buy yourself some fruit today—or take a taxi cab to school or something!
TRAVIS. Whoopee—

(*He leaps up and clasps his father around the middle with his legs, and they face each other in mutual appreciation; slowly Walter Lee peeks around the boy to catch the violent rays from his wife's eyes and draws his head back as if shot.*)

WALTER. You better get down now—and get to school, man.
TRAVIS (*At the door*). O. K. Good-bye.

(*He exits*)

WALTER (*After him, pointing with pride*). That's my boy. (*She looks at him in disgust and turns back to her work.*) You know what I was thinking 'bout in the bathroom this morning?
RUTH. No.
WALTER. How come you always try to be so pleasant!
RUTH. What is there to be pleasant 'bout!
WALTER. You want to know what I was thinking 'bout in the bathroom or not!
RUTH. I know what you was thinking 'bout.
WALTER (*Ignoring her*). 'Bout what me and Willy Harris was talking about last night.
RUTH (*Immediately—a refrain*). Willy Harris is a good-for-nothing loud mouth.
WALTER. Anybody who talks to me has got to be a good-for-nothing loud mouth, ain't he? And what you know about

who is just a good-for-nothing loud mouth? Charlie Atkins was just a "good-for-nothing loud mouth" too, wasn't he! When he wanted me to go in the dry-cleaning business with him. And now—he's grossing a hundred thousand a year. A hundred thousand dollars a year! You still call *him* a loud mouth!

RUTH (*Bitterly*). Oh, Walter Lee . . .

(*She folds her head on her arms over on the table*)

WALTER (*Rising and coming to her and standing over her*). You tired, ain't you? Tired of everything. Me, the boy, the way we live—this beat-up hole—everything. Ain't you? (*She doesn't look up, doesn't answer.*) So tired—moaning and groaning all the time, but you wouldn't do nothing to help, would you? You couldn't be on my side that long for nothing, could you?

RUTH. Walter, please leave me alone.

WALTER. A man needs for a woman to back him up . . .

RUTH. Walter—

WALTER. Mama would listen to you. You know she listen to you more than she do me and Bennie. She think more of you. All you have to do is just sit down with her when you drinking your coffee one morning and talking 'bout things like you do and—(*He sits down beside her and demonstrates graphically what he thinks her methods and tone should be.*)—you just sip your coffee, see, and say easy like that you been thinking 'bout that deal Walter Lee is so interested in, 'bout the store and all, and sip some more coffee, like what you saying ain't really that important to you—And the next thing you know, she be listening good and asking you questions and when I come home—I can tell her the details. This ain't no fly-by-night proposition, baby. I mean we figured it out, me and Willy and Bobo.

RUTH (*With a frown*). Bobo?

WALTER. Yeah. You see, this little liquor store we got in mind cost seventy-five thousand and we figured the initial investment on the place be 'bout thirty thousand, see. That be ten thousand each. Course, there's a couple of hundred you got to pay so's you don't spend your life just waiting for them clowns to let your license get approved—

RUTH. You mean graft?

WALTER (*Frowning impatiently*). Don't call it that. See there, that just goes to show you what women understand about the world. Baby, don't *nothing* happen for you in this world 'less you pay *somebody* off!

RUTH. Walter, leave me alone! (*She raises her head and stares at him vigorously—then says, more quietly*) Eat your eggs, they gonna be cold.

WALTER (*Straightening up from her and looking off*). That's it. There you are. Man say to his woman: I got me a dream. His woman say: Eat your eggs. (*Sadly, but gaining in power*) Man say: I got to take hold of this here world, baby! And a woman will say: Eat your eggs and go to work. (*Passionately now*) Man say: I got to change my life, I'm choking

to death, baby! And his woman say—(*In utter anguish as he brings his fists down on his thighs*) —Your eggs is getting cold!

RUTH (*Softly*). Walter, that ain't none of our money.

WALTER (*Not listening at all or even looking at her*). This morning, I was lookin' in the mirror and thinking about it . . . I'm thirty-five years old; I been married eleven years and I got a boy who sleeps in the living room—(*Very, very quietly*)—and all I got to give him is stories about how rich white people live . . .

RUTH. Eat your eggs, Walter.

WALTER. *Damn my eggs . . . damn all the eggs that ever was!*

RUTH. Then go to work.

WALTER (*Looking up at her*). See—I'm trying to talk to you 'bout myself—(*Shaking his head with the repetition*)—and all you can say is eat them eggs and go to work.

RUTH (*Wearily*). Honey, you never say nothing new. I listen to you every day, every night and every morning, and you never say nothing new. (*Shrugging*) So you would rather be Mr. Arnold than be his chauffeur: So—I would *rather* be living in Buckingham Palace.

WALTER. That is just what is wrong with the colored woman in this world . . . Don't understand about building their men up and making 'em feel like the somebody. Like they can do something.

RUTH (*Drily, but to hurt*). There *are* colored men who do things.

WALTER. No thanks to the colored woman.

RUTH. Well, being a colored woman, I guess I can't help myself none.

(*She rises and gets the ironing board and sets it up and attacks a huge pile of rough-dried clothes, sprinkling them in preparation for the ironing and then rolling them into tight fat balls.*)

WALTER (*Mumbling*). We one group of men tied to a race of women with small minds.

(*His sister Beneatha enters. She is about twenty, as slim and intense as her brother. She is not as pretty as her sister-in-law, but her lean, almost intellectual face has a handsomeness of its own. She wears a bright-red flannel nightie, and her thick hair stands wildly about her head. Her speech is a mixture of many things; it is different from the rest of the family's insofar as education has permeated her sense of English—and perhaps the Midwest rather than the South has finally—at last—won out in her inflection; but not altogether, because over all of it is a soft slurring and transformed use of vowels which is the decided influence of the Southside. She passes through the room without looking at either Ruth or Walter and goes to the outside door and looks, a little blindly, out to the bathroom. She sees that it has been lost to the Johnsons. She closes the door with a sleepy vengeance and crosses to the table and sits down a little defeated.*)

BENEATHA. I am going to start timing those people.

WALTER. You should get up earlier.

BENEATHA. (*Her face in her hands. She is still fighting the urge to go back to bed*) Really—would you suggest dawn? Where's the paper?

WALTER (*Pushing the paper across the table to her as he studies her almost clinically, as though he has never seen her before*). You a horrible-looking chick at this hour.

BENEATHA (*Drily*). Good morning, everybody.

WALTER (*Senselessly*). How is school coming?

BENEATHA (*In the same spirit*). Lovely. Lovely. And you know, biology is the greatest. (*Looking up at him*) I dissected something that looked just like you yesterday.

WALTER. I just wondered if you've made up your mind and everything.

BENEATHA (*Gaining in sharpness and impatience*). And what did I answer yesterday morning—and the day before that?

RUTH (*From the ironing board, like someone disinterested and old*). Don't be so nasty, Bennie.

BENEATHA (*Still to her brother*). And the day before that and the day before that!

WALTER (*Defensively*). I'm interested in you. Something wrong with that? Ain't many girls who decide—

WALTER AND BENEATHA (*In unison*). —"to be a doctor." (*Silence*)

WALTER. Have we figured out yet just exactly how much medical school is going to cost?

RUTH. Walter Lee, why don't you leave that girl alone and get out of here to work?

BENEATHA (*Exits to the bathroom and bangs on the door*). Come on out of there, please!

(*She comes back into the room*)

WALTER (*Looking at his sister intently*). You know the check is coming tomorrow.

BENEATHA (*Turning on him with a sharpness all her own*). That money belongs to Mama, Walter, and it's for her to decide how she wants to use it. I don't care if she wants to buy a house or a rocket ship or just nail it up somewhere and look at it. It's hers. Not ours—*hers*.

WALTER (*Bitterly*). Now ain't that fine! You just got your mother's interest at heart, ain't you, girl? You such a nice girl—but if Mama got that money she can always take a few thousand and help you through school too—can't she?

BENEATHA. I have never asked anyone around here to do anything for me!

WALTER. No! And the line between asking and just accepting when the time comes is big and wide—ain't it!

BENEATHA (*With fury*). What do you want from me, Brother—that I quit school or just drop dead, which!

WALTER. I don't want nothing but for you to stop acting holy 'round here. Me and Ruth done made some sacrifices for you—why can't you do something for the family?

RUTH. Walter, don't be dragging me in it.

WALTER. You are in it—Don't you get up and go work in somebody's kitchen for the last three years to help put clothes on her back?

RUTH. Oh, Walter—that's not fair . . .

WALTER. It ain't that nobody expects you to get on your knees and say thank you, Brother; thank you, Ruth; thank you, Mama—and thank you, Travis, for wearing the same pair of shoes for two semesters—

BENEATHA (*Dropping to her knees*). Well—I *do*—all right?— thank everybody . . . and forgive me for ever wanting to be anything at all . . . forgive me, forgive me!

RUTH. Please stop it! Your mama'll hear you.

WALTER. Who the hell told you you had to be a doctor? If you so crazy 'bout messing 'round with sick people—then go be a nurse like other women—or just get married and be quiet . . .

BENEATHA. Well—you finally got it said . . . It took you three years but you finally got it said. Walter, give up; leave me alone—it's Mama's money.

WALTER. *He was my father, too!*

BENEATHA. So what? He was mine, too—and Travis' grandfather—but the insurance money belongs to Mama. Picking on me is not going to make her give it to you to invest in any liquor stores—(*Underbreath, dropping into a chair*)—and I for one say, God bless Mama for that!

WALTER (*To Ruth*). See—did you hear? Did you hear!

RUTH. Honey, please go to work.

WALTER. Nobody in this house is ever going to understand me.

BENEATHA. Because you're a nut.

WALTER. Who's a nut?

BENEATHA. You—you are a nut. Thee is mad, boy.

WALTER (*Looking at his wife and his sister from the door, very sadly*). The world's most backward race of people, and that's a fact.

BENEATHA (*Turning slowly in her chair*). And then there are all those prophets who would lead us out of the wilderness—(*Walter slams out of the house.*)—into the swamps!

RUTH. Bennie, why you always gotta be pickin' on your brother? Can't you be a little sweeter sometimes? (*Door opens. Walter walks in.*)

WALTER (*To Ruth*). I need some money for carfare.

RUTH (*Looks at him, then warms; teasing, but tenderly*). Fifty cents? (*She goes to her bag and gets money.*) Here, take a taxi.

(*Walter exits. Mama enters. She is a woman in her early sixties, full-bodied and strong. She is one of those women of a certain grace and beauty who wear it so unobtrusively that it takes a while to notice. Her dark-brown face is surrounded by the total whiteness of her hair, and, being a woman who has adjusted to many things in life and overcome many more, her face is full of strength. She has, we can see, wit and faith of a kind that keep her eyes lit and full of interest and expectancy. She is, in a word, a beautiful woman. Her bearing is perhaps most like the noble bearing of the women of the Hereros of Southwest*

Africa—rather as if she imagines that as she walks she still bears a basket or a vessel upon her head. Her speech, on the other hand, is as careless as her carriage is precise—she is inclined to slur everything—but her voice is perhaps not so much quiet as simply soft.)

MAMA. Who that 'round here slamming doors at this hour?

(*She crosses through the room, goes to the window, opens it, and brings in a feeble little plant growing doggedly in a small pot on the window sill. She feels the dirt and puts it back out.*)

RUTH. That was Walter Lee. He and Bennie was at it again.

MAMA. My children and they tempers. Lord, if this little old plant don't get more sun than it's been getting it ain't never going to see spring again. (*She turns from the window.*) What's the matter with you this morning, Ruth? You looks right peaked. You aiming to iron all them things? Leave some for me. I'll get to 'em this afternoon. Bennie honey, it's too drafty for you to be sitting 'round half dressed. Where's your robe?

BENEATHA. In the cleaners.

MAMA. Well, go get mine and put it on.

BENEATHA. I'm not cold, Mama, honest.

MAMA. I know—but you so thin . . .

BENEATHA (*Irritably*). Mama, I'm not cold.

MAMA (*Seeing the make-down bed as* Travis *has left it*). Lord have mercy, look at that poor bed. Bless his heart—he tries, don't he?

(*She moves to the bed Travis has sloppily made up.*)

RUTH. No—he don't half try at all 'cause he knows you going to come along behind him and fix everything. That's just how come he don't know how to do nothing right now—you done spoiled that boy so.

MAMA. Well—he's a little boy. Ain't supposed to know 'bout housekeeping. My baby, that's what he is. What you fix for his breakfast this morning?

RUTH (*Angrily*). I feed my son, Lena!

MAMA. I ain't meddling—(*Underneath; busy-bodyish*) I just noticed all last week he had cold cereal, and when it starts getting this chilly in the fall a child ought to have some hot grits or something when he goes out in the cold—

RUTH (*Furious*). I gave him hot oats—is that all right?

MAMA. I ain't meddling. (*Pause*). Put a lot of nice butter on it? (Ruth *shoots her an angry look and does not reply*) He likes lots of butter.

RUTH (*Exasperated*). Lena—

MAMA (*To* Beneatha. Mama *is inclined to wander conversationally sometimes*). What was you and your brother fussing 'bout this morning?

BENEATHA. It's not important, Mama.

(*She gets up and goes to look out at the bathroom, which is apparently free, and she picks up her towels and rushes out.*)

MAMA. What was they fighting about?

RUTH. Now you know as well as I do.

MAMA (*Shaking her head*). Brother still worrying hisself sick about that money?

RUTH. You know he is.

MAMA. You had breakfast?

RUTH. Some coffee.

MAMA. Girl, you better start eating and looking after yourself better. You almost thin as Travis.

RUTH. Lena—

MAMA. Un-hunh?

RUTH. What are you going to do with it?

MAMA. Now don't you start, child. It's too early in the morning to be talking about money. It ain't Christian.

RUTH. It's just that he got his heart set on that store—

MAMA. You mean that liquor store that Willy Harris want him to invest in?

RUTH. Yes—

MAMA. We ain't no business people, Ruth. We just plain working folks.

RUTH. Ain't nobody business people till they go into business. Walter Lee say colored people ain't never going to start getting ahead till they start gambling on some different kinds of things in the world—investments and things.

MAMA. What done got into you, girl? Walter Lee done finally sold you on investing.

RUTH. No. Mama, something is happening between Walter and me. I don't know what it is—but he needs something—something I can't give him any more. He needs this chance, Lena.

MAMA (*Frowning deeply*). But liquor, honey—

RUTH. Well—like Walter say—I spec people going to always be drinking themselves some liquor.

MAMA. Well—whether they drinks it or not ain't none of my business. But whether I go into business selling it to 'em *is*, and I don't want that on my ledger this late in life. (*Stopping suddenly and studying her daughter-in-law*.) Ruth Younger, what's the matter with you today? You look like you could fall over right there.

RUTH. I'm tired.

MAMA. Then you better stay home from work today.

RUTH. I can't stay home. She'd be calling up the agency and screaming at them, "My girl didn't come in today—send me somebody! My girl didn't come in!" Oh, she just have a fit . . .

MAMA. Well, let her have it. I'll just call her up and say you got the flu—

RUTH (*Laughing*). Why the flu?

MAMA. 'Cause it sounds respectable to 'em. Something white people get, too. They know 'bout the flu. Otherwise they think you been cut up or something when you tell 'em you sick.

RUTH. I got to go in. We need the money.

MAMA. Somebody would of thought my children done all but starved to death the way they talk about money here late. Child, we got a great big old check coming tomorrow.

RUTH (*Sincerely, but also self-righteously*). Now that's your money. It ain't got nothing to do with me. We all feel like that—Walter and Bennie and me—even Travis.

MAMA (*Thoughtfully, and suddenly very far away*). Ten thousand dollars—

RUTH. Sure is wonderful.

MAMA. Ten thousand dollars.

RUTH. You know what you should do, Miss Lena? You should take yourself a trip somewhere. To Europe or South America or someplace—

MAMA (*Throwing up her hands at the thought*). Oh, child!

RUTH. I'm serious. Just pack up and leave! Go on away and enjoy yourself some. Forget about the family and have yourself a ball for once in your life—

MAMA (*Drily*). You sound like I'm just about ready to die. Who'd go with me? What I look like wandering 'round Europe by myself?

RUTH. Shoot—these here rich white women do it all the time. They don't think nothing of packing up their suitcases and piling on one of them big steamships and—swoosh!—they gone, child.

MAMA. Something always told me I wasn't no rich white woman.

RUTH. Well—what are you going to do with it then?

MAMA. I ain't rightly decided. (*Thinking. She speaks now with emphasis.*) Some of it got to be put away for Beneatha and her schoolin'—and ain't nothing going to touch that part of it. Nothing. (*She waits several seconds, trying to make up her mind about something, and looks at Ruth a little tentatively before going on.*) Been thinking that we maybe could meet the notes on a little old two-story somewhere, with a yard where Travis could play in the summertime, if we use part of the insurance for a down payment and everybody kind of pitch in. I could maybe take on a little day work again, few days a week—

RUTH (*Studying her mother-in-law furtively and concentrating on her ironing, anxious to encourage without seeming to*). Well, Lord knows, we've put enough rent into this here rat trap to pay for four houses by now . . .

MAMA (*Looking up at the words "rat trap" and then looking around and leaning back and sighing—in a suddenly reflective mood—*). "Rat trap"—yes, that's all it is. (*Smiling*) I remember just as well the day me and Big Walter moved in here. Hadn't been married but two weeks and wasn't planning on living here no more than a year. (*She shakes her head at the dissolved dream.*) We was going to set away, little by little, don't you know, and buy a little place out in Morgan Park. We had even picked out the house. (*Chuckling a little*) Looks right dumpy today. But Lord, child, you should know all the dreams I had 'bout buying that house and fixing it up and making me a little garden in the back—(*She waits and stops smiling*) And didn't none of it happen.

(*Dropping her hands in a futile gesture*)

RUTH (*Keeps her head down, ironing*). Yes, life can be a barrel of disappointments, sometimes.

MAMA. Honey, Big Walter would come in here some nights back then and slump down on that couch there and just look at the rug, and look at me and look at the rug and then back at me—and I'd know he was down then . . . really down. (*After a second very long and thoughtful pause; she is seeing back to times that only she can see*) And then, Lord, when I lost that baby—little Claude—I almost thought I was going to lose Big Walter too. Oh, that man grieved hisself! He was one man to love his children.

RUTH. Ain't nothin' can tear at you like losin' your baby.

MAMA. I guess that's how come that man finally worked hisself to death like he done. Like he was fighting his own war with this here world that took his baby from him.

RUTH. He sure was a fine man, all right. I always liked Mr. Younger.

MAMA. Crazy 'bout his children! God knows there was plenty wrong with Walter Younger—hard-headed, mean, kind of wild with women—plenty wrong with him. But he sure loved his children. Always wanted them to have something—be something. That's where Brother gets all these notions, I reckon. Big Walter used to say, he'd get right wet in the eyes sometimes, lean his head back with the water standing in his eyes and say, "Seem like God didn't see fit to give the black man nothing but dreams—but He did give us children to make them dreams seem worth while." (*She smiles*) He could talk like that, don't you know.

RUTH. Yes, he sure could. He was a good man, Mr. Younger.

MAMA. Yes, a fine man—just couldn't never catch up with his dreams, that's all.

(*Beneatha comes in, brushing her hair and looking up to the ceiling, where the sound of a vacuum cleaner has started up.*)

BENEATHA. What could be so dirty on that woman's rugs that she has to vacuum them every single day?

RUTH. I wish certain young women 'round here who I could name would take inspiration about certain rugs in a certain apartment I could also mention.

BENEATHA (*Shrugging*). How much cleaning can a house need, for Christ's sakes.

MAMA (*Not liking the Lord's name used thus*). Bennie!

RUTH. Just listen to her—just listen!

BENEATHA. Oh, God!

MAMA. If you use the Lord's name just one more time—

BENEATHA (*A bit of a whine*). Oh, Mama—

RUTH. Fresh—just fresh as salt, this girl!

BENEATHA (*Drily*). Well—if the salt loses its savor—

MAMA. Now that will do. I just ain't going to have you 'round here reciting the scriptures in vain—you hear me?

BENEATHA. How did I manage to get on everybody's wrong side by just walking into a room?

RUTH. If you weren't so fresh—

BENEATHA. Ruth, I'm twenty years old.

MAMA. What time you be home from school today?

BENEATHA. Kind of late. (*With enthusiasm*) Madeline is going to start my guitar lessons today.

(*Mama and Ruth look up with the same expression.*)

MAMA. Your *what* kind of lessons?

BENEATHA. Guitar.

RUTH. Oh, Father!

MAMA. How come you done taken it in your mind to learn to play the guitar?

BENEATHA. I just want to, that's all.

MAMA (*Smiling*). Lord, child, don't you know what to do with yourself? How long it going to be before you get tired of this now—like you got tired of that little play-acting group you joined last year? (*Looking at Ruth*) And what was it the year before that?

RUTH. The horseback-riding club for which she bought that fifty-five-dollar riding habit that's been hanging in the closet ever since?

MAMA (*To Beneatha*). Why you got to flit so from one thing to another, baby?

BENEATHA (*Sharply*). I just want to learn to play the guitar. Is there anything wrong with that?

MAMA. Ain't nobody trying to stop you. I just wonders sometimes why you has to flit so from one thing to another all the time. You ain't never done nothing with all that camera equipment you brought home—

BENEATHA. I don't flit! I—I experiment with different forms of expression—

RUTH. Like riding a horse?

BENEATHA. —People have to express themselves one way or another.

MAMA. What is it you want to express?

BENEATHA (*Angrily*). Me! (*Mama and Ruth look at each other and burst into raucous laughter.*) Don't worry—I don't expect you to understand.

MAMA (*To change the subject*). Who you going out with tomorrow night?

BENEATHA (*With displeasure*). George Murchison again.

MAMA (*Pleased*). Oh—you getting a little sweet on him?

RUTH. You ask me, this child ain't sweet on nobody but herself— (*Underbreath*) Express herself!

(*They laugh*)

BENEATHA. Oh—I like George all right, Mama. I mean I like him enough to go out with him and stuff, but—

RUTH (*For devilment*). What does *and stuff* mean?

BENEATHA. Mind your own business.

MAMA. Stop picking at her now, Ruth. (*A thoughtful pause, and then a suspicious sudden look at her daughter as she turns in her chair for emphasis*) What *does* it mean?

BENEATHA (*Wearily*). Oh, I just mean I couldn't ever really be serious about George. He's—he's so shallow.

RUTH. Shallow—what do you mean he's shallow? He's *Rich!*

MAMA. Hush, Ruth.

BENEATHA. I know he's rich. He knows he's rich, too.

RUTH. Well—what other qualities a man got to have to satisfy you, little girl?

BENEATHA. You wouldn't even begin to understand. Anybody who married Walter could not possibly understand.

MAMA (*Outraged*). What kind of way is that to talk about your brother?

BENEATHA. Brother is a flip—let's face it.

MAMA (*To Ruth, helplessly*). What's a flip?

RUTH (*Glad to add kindling*). She's saying he's crazy.

BENEATHA. Not crazy. Brother isn't really crazy yet—he—he's an elaborate neurotic.

MAMA. Hush your mouth!

BENEATHA. As for George. Well. George looks good—he's got a beautiful car and he takes me to nice places and, as my sister-in-law says, he is probably the richest boy I will ever get to know and I even like him sometimes—but if the Youngers are sitting around waiting to see if their little Bennie is going to tie up the family with the Murchisons, they are wasting their time.

RUTH. You mean you wouldn't marry George Murchison if he asked you someday? That pretty, rich thing? Honey, I knew you was odd—

BENEATHA. No, I would not marry him if all I felt for him was what I feel now. Besides, George's family wouldn't really like it.

MAMA. Why not?

BENEATHA. Oh, Mama—the Murchisons are honest-to-God-real-*live-rich* colored people, and the only people in the world who are more snobbish than rich white people are rich colored people. I thought everybody knew that. I've met Mrs. Murchison. She's a scene!

MAMA. You must not dislike people 'cause they well off, honey.

BENEATHA. Why not? It makes just as much sense as disliking people 'cause they are poor, and lots of people do that.

RUTH (*A wisdom-of-the-ages manner. To Mama*). Well, she'll get over some of this—

BENEATHA. Get over it? What are you talking about, Ruth? Listen, I'm going to be a doctor. I'm not worried about who I'm going to marry yet—if I ever get married.

MAMA AND RUTH. *If!*

MAMA. Now, Bennie—

BENEATHA. Oh, I probably will . . . but first I'm going to be a doctor, and George, for one, still thinks that's pretty funny. I couldn't be bothered with that. I am going to be a doctor and everybody around here better understand that!

MAMA (*Kindly*). 'Course you going to be a doctor, honey, God willing.

BENEATHA (*Drily*). God hasn't got a thing to do with it.

MAMA. Beneatha—that just wasn't necessary.

BENEATHA. Well—neither is God. I get sick of hearing about God.

MAMA. Beneatha!

BENEATHA. I mean it! I'm just tired of hearing about God all the time. What has He got to do with anything? Does he pay tuition?

MAMA. You 'bout to get your fresh little jaw slapped!

RUTH. That's just what she needs, all right!

BENEATHA. Why? Why can't I say what I want to around here, like everybody else?

MAMA. It don't sound nice for a young girl to say things like that—you wasn't brought up that way. Me and your father went to trouble to get you and Brother to church every Sunday.

BENEATHA. Mama, you don't understand. It's all a matter of ideas, and God is just one idea I don't accept. It's not important. I am not going out and be immoral or commit crimes because I don't believe in God. I don't even think about it. It's just that I get tired of Him getting credit for all the things the human race achieves through its own stubborn effort. There simply is no blasted God—there is only man and it is he who makes miracles!

(*Mama absorbs this speech, studies her daughter and rises slowly and crosses to Beneatha and slaps her powerfully across the face. After, there is only silence and the daughter drops her eyes from her mother's face, and Mama is very tall before her.*)

MAMA. Now—you say after me, in my mother's house there is still God. (*There is a long pause and Beneatha stares at the floor wordlessly. Mama repeats the phrase with precision and cool emotion*) In my mother's house there is still God.

BENEATHA. In my mother's house there is still God.

(*A long pause*)

MAMA (*Walking away from Beneatha, too disturbed for triumphant posture. Stopping and turning back to her daughter*). There are some ideas we ain't going to have in this house. Not long as I am at the head of this family.

BENEATHA. Yes, ma'am.

(*Mama walks out of the room.*)

RUTH (*Almost gently, with profound understanding*). You think you a woman, Bennie—but you still a little girl. What you did was childish—so you got treated like a child.

BENEATHA. I see. (*Quietly*) I also see that everybody thinks it's all right for Mama to be a tyrant. But all the tyranny in the world will never put a God in the heavens!

(*She picks up her books and goes out.*)

RUTH (*Goes to Mama's door*). She said she was sorry.

MAMA (*Coming out, going to her plant*). They frightens me, Ruth. My children.

RUTH. You got good children, Lena. They just a little off sometimes—but they're good.

MAMA. No—there's something come down between me and them that don't let us understand each other and I don't know what it is. One done almost lost his mind thinking 'bout money all the time and the other done commence to talk about things I can't seem to understand in no form or fashion. What is it that's changing, Ruth?

RUTH (*Soothingly, older than her years*). Now . . . you taking it all too seriously. You just got strong-willed children and it takes a strong woman like you to keep 'em in hand.

MAMA (*Looking at her plant and sprinkling a little water on it*). They spirited all right, my children. Got to admit they got spirit—Bennie and Walter. Like this little old plant that ain't never had enough sunshine or nothing—and look at it . . .

(*She has her back to Ruth, who has had to stop ironing and lean against something and put the back of her hand to her forehead.*)

RUTH (*Trying to keep Mama from noticing*). You . . . sure . . . loves that little old thing, don't you? . . .

MAMA. Well, I always wanted me a garden like I used to see sometimes at the back of the houses down home. This plant is close as I ever got to having one. (*She looks out of the window as she replaces the plant.*) Lord, ain't nothing as dreary as the view from this window on a dreary day, is there? Why ain't you singing this morning, Ruth? Sing that "No Ways Tired." That song always lifts me up so— (*She turns at last to see that Ruth has slipped quietly into a chair, in a state of semiconsciousness.*) Ruth! Ruth honey— what's the matter with you . . . Ruth!

CURTAIN

SCENE TWO

It is the following morning; a Saturday morning, and house cleaning is in progress at the Youngers. Furniture has been shoved hither and yon and Mama is giving the kitchen-area walls a washing down. Beneatha, in dungarees, with a handkerchief tied around her face, is spraying insecticide into the cracks in the walls. As they work, the radio is on and a Southside disk-jockey program is inappropriately filling the house with a rather exotic saxophone blues. Travis, the sole idle one, is leaning on his arms, looking out of the window.

TRAVIS. Grandmama, that stuff Bennie is using smells awful. Can I go downstairs, please?

MAMA. Did you get all them chores done already? I ain't seen you doing much.

TRAVIS. Yes'm—finished early. Where did Mama go this morning?

MAMA (*Looking at Beneatha*). She had to go on a little errand.

TRAVIS. Where?

MAMA. To tend to her business.

TRAVIS. Can I go outside then?

MAMA. Oh, I guess so. You better stay right in front of the house, though . . . and keep a good lookout for the postman.

TRAVIS. Yes'm. (*He starts out and decides to give his Aunt Beneatha a good swat on the legs as he passes her*) Leave them poor little cockroaches alone, they ain't bothering you none.

(*He runs as she swings the spray gun at him both viciously and playfully. Walter enters from the bedroom and goes to the phone*)

MAMA. Look out there, girl, before you be spilling some of that stuff on that child!

TRAVIS (*Teasing*). That's right—look out now!

(*He exits*)

BENEATHA (*Drily*). I can't imagine that it would hurt him—it has never hurt the roaches.

MAMA. Well, little boys' hides ain't as tough as Southside roaches.

WALTER (*Into phone*). Hello—let me talk to Willy Harris.

MAMA. You better get over there behind the bureau. I seen one marching out of there like Napoleon yesterday.

WALTER. Hello, Willy? It ain't come yet. It'll be here in a few minutes. Did the lawyer give you the papers?

BENEATHA. There's really one way to get rid of them, Mama—

MAMA. How?

BENEATHA. Set fire to this building.

WALTER. Good. Good. I'll be right over.

BENEATHA. Where did Ruth go, Walter?

WALTER. I don't know.

(*He exits abruptly.*)

BENEATHA. Mama, where did Ruth go?

MAMA (*Looking at her with meaning*). To the doctor, I think.

BENEATHA. The doctor? What's the matter? (*They exchange glances.*) You don't think—

MAMA (*With her sense of drama*). Now I ain't saying what I think. But I ain't never been wrong 'bout a woman neither.

(*The phone rings*)

BENEATHA (*At the phone*). Hay-lo . . . (*Pause, and a moment of recognition*) Well—when did you get back! . . . And how was it? . . . Of course I've missed you—in my way . . . This morning? No . . . house cleaning and all that and Mama hates it if I let people come over when the house is like this . . . You *have*? Well, that's different . . . What is it— Oh, what the hell, come on over . . . Right, see you then.

(*She hangs up.*)

MAMA (*Who has listened vigorously, as is her habit*). Who is that you inviting over here with this house looking like this? You ain't got the pride you was born with!

BENEATHA. Asagai doesn't care how houses look, Mama—he's an intellectual.

MAMA. *Who?*

BENEATHA. Asagai—Joseph Asagai. He's an African boy I met on campus. He's been studying in Canada all summer.

MAMA. What's his name?

BENEATHA. Asagai, Joseph. Ah-sah-guy . . . He's from Nigeria.

MAMA. Oh, that's the little country that was founded by slaves way back . . .

BENEATHA. No, Mama—that's Liberia.

MAMA. I don't think I never met no African before.

BENEATHA. Well, do me a favor and don't ask him a whole lot of ignorant questions about Africans. I mean, do they wear clothes and all that—

MAMA. Well, now, I guess if you think we so ignorant 'round here maybe you shouldn't bring your friends here—

BENEATHA. It's just that people ask such crazy things. All anyone seems to know about when it comes to Africa is Tarzan—

MAMA (*Indignantly*). Why should I know anything about Africa?

BENEATHA. Why do you give money at church for the missionary work?

MAMA. Well, that's to help save people.

BENEATHA. You mean save them from *heathenism*—

MAMA (*Innocently*). Yes.

BENEATHA. I'm afraid they need more salvation from the British and the French.

(*Ruth comes in forlornly and pulls off her coat with dejection. They both turn to look at her.*)

RUTH (*Dispiritedly*). Well, I guess from all the happy faces—everybody knows.

BENEATHA. You pregnant?

MAMA. Lord have mercy, I sure hope it's a little old girl. Travis ought to have a sister.

(*Beneatha and Ruth give her a hopeless look for this grandmotherly enthusiasm.*)

BENEATHA. How far along are you?

RUTH. Two months.

BENEATHA. Did you mean to? I mean did you plan it or was it an accident?

MAMA. What do you know about planning or not planning?

BENEATHA. Oh, Mama.

RUTH (*Wearily*). She's twenty years old, Lena.

BENEATHA. Did you plan it, Ruth?

RUTH. Mind your own business.

BENEATHA. It is my business—where is he going to live, on the *roof*? (*There is silence following the remark as the three women react to the sense of it.*) Gee—I didn't mean that,

Ruth, honest. Gee, I don't feel like that at all. I—I think it is wonderful.

RUTH (*Dully*). Wonderful.

BENEATHA. Yes—really.

MAMA (*Looking at* Ruth, *worried*). Doctor say everything going to be all right?

RUTH (*Far away*). Yes—she says everything is going to be fine . . .

MAMA (*Immediately suspicious*). "She"—What doctor you went to? (*Ruth folds over, near hysteria. Mama worriedly hovers over her.*) Ruth honey—what's the matter with you—you sick?

(*Ruth has her fists clenched on her thighs and is fighting hard to suppress a scream that seems to be rising in her.*)

BENEATHA. What's the matter with her, Mama?

MAMA (*Working her fingers in Ruth's shoulder to relax her*). She be all right. Women gets right depressed sometimes when they get her way. (*Speaking softly, expertly, rapidly*) Now you just relax. That's right . . . just lean back, don't think 'bout nothing at all . . . nothing at all—

RUTH. I'm all right . . .

(*The glassy-eyed look melts and then she collapses into a fit of heavy sobbing. The bell rings.*)

BENEATHA. Oh, my God—that must be Asagai.

MAMA (*To* Ruth). Come on now, honey. You need to lie down and rest awhile . . . then have some nice hot food.

(*They exit, Ruth's weight on her mother-in-law. Beneatha, herself profoundly disturbed, opens the door to admit a rather dramatic-looking young man with a large package.*)

ASAGAI. Hello, Alaiyo—

BENEATHA (*Holding the door open and regarding him with pleasure*). Hello . . . (*Long pause*) Well—come in. And please excuse everything. My mother was very upset about my letting anyone come here with the place like this.

ASAGAI (*Coming into the room*). You look disturbed too . . . Is something wrong?

BENEATHA (*Still at the door, absently*). Yes . . . we've all got acute ghetto-itus. (*She smiles and comes toward him, finding a cigarette and sitting*) So—sit down! How was Canada?

ASAGAI (*A sophisticate*). Canadian.

BENEATHA (*Looking at him*). I'm very glad you are back.

ASAGAI (*Looking back at her in turn*). Are you really?

BENEATHA. Yes—very.

ASAGAI. Why—you were quite glad when I went away. What happened?

BENEATHA. You went away.

ASAGAI. Ahhhhhhh.

BENEATHA. Before—you wanted to be so serious before there was time.

ASAGAI. How much time must there be before one knows what one feels?

BENEATHA (*Stalling this particular conversation. Her hands pressed together, in a deliberately childish gesture*). What did you bring me?

ASAGAI (*Handing her the package*). Open it and see.

BENEATHA (*Eagerly opening the package and drawing out some records and the colorful robes of Nigerian woman*). Oh, Asagai! . . . You got them for me! . . . How beautiful . . . and the records too!

(*She lifts out the robes and runs to the mirror with them and holds the drapery up in front of herself.*)

ASAGAI (*Coming to her at the mirror*). I shall have to teach you how to drape it properly. (*He flings the material about her for the moment and stands back to look at her.*) Ah—Oh-pay-gay-day, oh-gbah-mu-shay. (*A Yoruba exclamation for admiration*) You wear it well . . . very well . . . mutilated hair and all.

BENEATHA (*Turning suddenly*). My hair—what's wrong with my hair?

ASAGAI (*Shrugging*). Were you born with it like that?

BENEATHA (*Reaching up to touch it*). No . . . of course not.

(*She looks back to the mirror, disturbed.*)

ASAGAI (*Smiling*). How then?

BENEATHA. You know perfectly well how . . . as crinkly as yours . . . that's how.

ASAGAI. And it is ugly to you that way?

BENEATHA (*Quickly*). Oh, no—not ugly . . . (*More slowly, apologetically*) But it's so hard to manage when it's, well—raw.

ASAGAI. And so to accommodate that—you mutilate it every week?

BENEATHA. It's not mutilation!

ASAGAI (*Laughing aloud at her seriousness*). Oh . . . please! I am only teasing you because you are so very serious about these things. (*He stands back from her and folds his arms across his chest as he watches her pulling at her hair and frowning in the mirror.*) Do you remember the first time you met me at school? . . . (*He laughs*) You came up to me and you said—and I thought you were the most serious little thing I had ever seen—you said: (*He imitates her.*) "Mr. Asagai—I want very much to talk with you. About Africa. You see, Mr. Asagai, I am looking for my *identity*."

(*He laughs*)

BENEATHA (*Turning to him, not laughing*). Yes—

(*Her face is quizzical, profoundly disturbed.*)

ASAGAI (*Still teasing and reaching out and taking her face in his hands and turning her profile to him*). Well . . . it is true that this is not so much a profile of a Hollywood queen as perhaps a queen of the Nile— (*A mock dismissal of the importance of the question*) But what does it matter? Assimilationism is so popular in your country.

BENEATHA (*Wheeling, passionately, sharply*). I am not an assimilationist!

ASAGAI (*The protest hangs in the room for a moment and Asagai studies her, his laughter fading*). Such a serious one. (*There is a pause.*) So—you like the robes? You must take excellent care of them—they are from my sister's personal wardrobe.

BENEATHA (*With incredulity*). You—you sent all the way home—for me?

ASAGAI (*With charm*). For you—I would do much more . . . Well, that is what I came for. I must go.

BENEATHA. Will you call me Monday?

ASAGAI. Yes . . . We have a great deal to talk about. I mean about identity and time and all that.

BENEATHA. Time?

ASAGAI. Yes. About how much time one needs to know what one feels.

BENEATHA. You never understood that there is more than one kind of feeling which can exist between a man and a woman—or, at least, there should be.

ASAGAI (*Shaking his head negatively but gently*). No. Between a man and a woman there need be only one kind of feeling. I have that for you . . . Now even . . . right this moment . . .

BENEATHA. I know—and by itself—it won't do. I can find that anywhere.

ASAGAI. For a woman it should be enough.

BENEATHA. I know—because that's what it says in all the novels that men write. But it isn't. Go ahead and laugh—but I'm not interested in being someone's little episode in America or— (*With feminine vengeance*) —one of them! (*Asagai has burst into laughter again.*) That's funny as hell, huh!

ASAGAI. It's just that every American girl I have known has said that to me. White—black—in this you are all the same. And the same speech, too!

BENEATHA (*Angrily*). Yuk, yuk, yuk!

ASAGAI. It's how you can be sure that the world's most liberated women are not liberated at all. You all talk about it too much!

(*Mama enters and is immediately all social charm because of the presence of a guest.*)

BENEATHA. Oh—Mama—this is Mr. Asagai.

MAMA. How do you do?

ASAGAI (*Total politeness to an elder*). How do you do, Mrs. Younger. Please forgive me for coming at such an outrageous hour on a Saturday.

MAMA. Well, you are quite welcome. I just hope you understand that our house don't always look like this. (*Chatterish*) You must come again. I would love to hear all about— (*Not sure of the name*) —your country. I think it's so sad the way our American Negroes don't know nothing about Africa 'cept Tarzan and all that. And all that money they pour into these churches when they ought to be helping you people over there drive out them French and Englishmen done taken away your land.

(*The mother flashes a slightly superior look at her daughter upon completion of the recitation.*)

ASAGAI (*Taken aback by this sudden and acutely unrelated expression of sympathy*). Yes . . . yes . . .

MAMA (*Smiling at him suddenly and relaxing and looking him over*). How many miles is it from here to where you come from?

ASAGAI. Many thousands.

MAMA (*Looking at him as she would Walter*). I bet you don't half look after yourself, being away from your mama either. I spec you better come 'round here from time to time and get yourself some decent home-cooked meals . . .

ASAGAI (*Moved*). Thank you. Thank you very much. (*They are all quiet, then—*) Well . . . I must go. I will call you Monday, Alaiyo.

MAMA. What's that he call you?

ASAGAI. Oh—"Alaiyo." I hope you don't mind. It is what you would call a nickname, I think. It is a Yoruba word. I am a Yoruba.

MAMA (*Looking at Beneatha*). I—I thought he was from—

ASAGAI (*Understanding*). Nigeria is my country. Yoruba is my tribal origin—

BENEATHA. You didn't tell us what Alaiyo means . . . for all I know, you might be calling me Little Idiot or something . . .

ASAGAI. Well . . . let me see . . . I do not know how just to explain it . . . The sense of a thing can be so different when it changes languages.

BENEATHA. You're evading.

ASAGAI. No—really it is difficult . . . (*Thinking*) It means . . . it means One for Whom Bread—Food—Is Not Enough. (*He looks at her.*) Is that all right?

BENEATHA. (*Understanding, softly*) Thank you.

MAMA (*Looking from one to the other and not understanding any of it*). Well . . . that's nice . . . You must come to see us again—Mr.—

ASAGAI. Ah-sah-guy . . .

MAMA. Yes . . . Do come again.

ASAGAI. Good-bye.

(*He exits.*)

MAMA (*After him*). Lord, that a pretty thing just went out here! (*Insinuatingly, to her daughter*) Yes, I guess I see why we done commence to get so interested in Africa 'round here. Missionaries my aunt Jenny!

(*She exits.*)

BENEATHA. Oh, Mama! . . .

(*She picks up the Nigerian dress and holds it up to her in front of the mirror again. She sets the headdress on haphazardly and then notices her hair again and clutches at it and then replaces the headdress and frowns at herself. Then she starts to wriggle in front of the mirror as she thinks a Nigerian woman might. Travis enters and regards her*)

TRAVIS. You cracking up?

BENEATHA. Shut up.

(*She pulls the headdress off and looks at herself in the mirror and clutches at her hair again and squinches her eyes as if trying to imagine something. Then, suddenly, she gets her raincoat and kerchief and hurriedly prepares for going out*)

MAMA (*Coming back into the room*). She's resting now. Travis, baby, run next door and ask Miss Johnson to please let me have a little kitchen cleanser. This here can is empty as Jacob's kettle.

TRAVIS. I just came in.

MAMA. Do as you told. (*He exits and she looks at her daughter.*) Where are you going?

BENEATHA (*Halting at the door*). To become a queen of the Nile!

(*She exits in a breathless blaze of glory. Ruth appears in the bedroom doorway.*)

MAMA. Who told you to get up?

RUTH. Ain't nothing wrong with me to be lying in no bed for. Where did Bennie go?

MAMA (*Drumming her fingers*). Far as I could make out—to Egypt. (*Ruth just looks at her*) What time is it getting to?

RUTH. Ten twenty. And the mailman going to ring that bell this morning just like he done every morning for the last umpteen years.

(*Travis comes in with the cleanser can.*)

TRAVIS. She say to tell you that she don't have much.

MAMA (*Angrily*). Lord, some people I could name sure is tight-fisted! (*Directing her grandson*) Mark two cans of cleanser down on the list there. Is she that hard up for kitchen cleanser, I sure don't want to forget to get her none!

RUTH. Lena—maybe the woman is just short on cleanser—

MAMA (*Not listening*). —Much baking powder as she done borrowed from me all these years, she could of done gone into the baking business!

(*The bell sounds suddenly and sharply and all three are stunned—serious and silent—mid-speech. In spite of all the other conversations and distractions of the morning, this is what they have been waiting for, even Travis, who looks helplessly from his mother to his grandmother. Ruth is the first to come to life again.*)

RUTH (*To Travis*). Get down them steps, boy!

(*Travis snaps to life and flies out to get the mail.*)

MAMA (*Her eyes wide, her hand to her breast*). You mean it done really come?

RUTH (*Excited*). Oh, Miss Lena!

MAMA (*Collecting herself*). Well . . . I don't know what we all

so excited about 'round here for. We known it was coming for months.

RUTH. That's a whole lot different from having it come and being able to hold it in your hands . . . a piece of paper worth ten thousand dollars . . . (*Travis burst back into the room. He holds the envelope high above his head, like a little dancer, his face is radiant and he is breathless. He moves to his grandmother with sudden slow ceremony and puts the envelope into her hands. She accepts it, and then merely holds it and looks at it.*) Come on! Open it . . . Lord have mercy, I wish Walter Lee was here!

TRAVIS. Open it, Grandmama!

MAMA (*Staring at it*). Now you all be quiet. It's just a check.

RUTH. Open it . . .

MAMA (*Still staring at it*). Now don't act silly . . . We ain't never been no people to act silly 'bout no money—

RUTH (*Swiftly*). We ain't never had none before—open it!

(*Mama finally makes a good strong tear and pulls out the thin blue slice of paper and inspects it closely. The boy and his mother study it raptly over Mama's shoulders.*)

MAMA. Travis! (*She is counting off with doubt.*) Is that the right number of zeros.

TRAVIS. Yes'm . . . ten thousand dollars. Gaalee, Grandmama, you rich.

MAMA (*She holds the check away from her, still looking at it. Slowly her face sobers into a mask of unhappiness*). Ten thousand dollars. (*She hands it to Ruth.*) Put it away somewhere, Ruth. (*She does not look at Ruth; her eyes seem to be seeing something somewhere very far off.*) Ten thousand dollars they give you. Ten thousand dollars.

TRAVIS (*To his mother, sincerely*). What's the matter with Grandmama—don't she want to be rich?

RUTH (*Distractedly*). You go on out and play now, baby.

(*Travis exits. Mama starts wiping dishes absently, humming intently to herself. Ruth turns to her, with kind exasperation.*) You've gone and got yourself upset.

MAMA (*Not looking at her*). I spec if it wasn't for you all . . . I would just put that money away or give it to the church or something.

RUTH. Now what kind of talk is that. Mr. Younger would just be plain mad if he could hear you talking foolish like that.

MAMA (*Stopping and staring off*). Yes . . . he sure would. (*Sighing*) We got enough to do with that money, all right. (*She halts then, and turns and looks at her daughter-in-law hard; Ruth avoids her eyes and Mama wipes her hands with finality and starts to speak firmly to Ruth*) Where did you go today, girl?

RUTH. To the doctor.

MAMA (*Impatiently*). Now, Ruth . . . you know better than that. Old Doctor Jones is strange enough in his way but there ain't nothing 'bout him make somebody slip and call him "she"—like you done this morning.

RUTH. Well, that's what happened—my tongue slipped.

MAMA. You went to see that woman, didn't you?

RUTH (*Defensively, giving herself away*). What woman you talking about?

MAMA (*Angrily*). That woman who—

(*Walter enters in great excitement.*)

WALTER. Did it come?

MAMA (*Quietly*). Can't you give people a Christian greeting before you start asking about money?

WALTER (*To Ruth*). Did it come? (*Ruth unfolds the check and lays it quietly before him, watching him intently with thoughts of her own. Walter sits down and grasps it close and counts off the zeros.*) Ten thousand dollars— (*He turns suddenly, frantically to his mother and draws some papers out of his breast pocket.*) Mama—look. Old Willy Harris put everything on paper—

MAMA. Son—I think you ought to talk to your wife . . . I'll go on out and leave you alone if you want—

WALTER. I can talk to her later—Mama, look—

MAMA. Son—

WALTER. WILL SOMEBODY PLEASE LISTEN TO ME TODAY!

MAMA (*Quietly*). I don't 'low no yellin' in this house, Walter Lee, and you know it—(*Walter stares at them in frustration and starts to speak several times.*) And there ain't going to be no investing in no liquor stores. I don't aim to have to speak on that again.

(*A long pause*)

WALTER. Oh—so you don't aim to have to speak on that again? So *you* have decided . . . (*Crumpling his papers*) Well, *you* tell that to my boy tonight when you put him to sleep on the living-room couch . . . (*Turning to Mama and speaking directly to her.*) Yeah—and tell it to my wife, Mama, tomorrow when she has to go out of here to look after somebody else's kids. And tell it to *me*, Mama, every time we need a new pair of curtains and I have to watch *you* go out and work in somebody's kitchen. Yeah, you tell me then!

(*Walter starts out.*)

RUTH. Where you going?

WALTER. I'm going out!

RUTH. Where?

WALTER. Just out of this house somewhere—

RUTH (*Getting her coat*). I'll come too.

WALTER. I don't want you to come!

RUTH. I got something to talk to you about, Walter.

WALTER. That's too bad.

MAMA (*Still quietly*). Walter Lee— (*She waits and he finally turns and looks at her.*) Sit down.

WALTER. I'm a grown man, Mama.

MAMA. Ain't nobody said you wasn't grown. But you still in

my house and my presence. And as long as you are— you'll talk to your wife civil. Now sit down.

RUTH (*Suddenly*). Oh, let him go on out and drink himself to death! He makes me sick to my stomach! (*She flings her coat against him.*)

WALTER (*Violently*). And you turn mine too, baby! (*Ruth goes into their bedroom and slams the door behind her.*) That was my greatest mistake—

MAMA (*Still quietly*). Walter, what is the matter with you?

WALTER. Matter with me? Ain't nothing the matter with *me*!

MAMA. Yes there is. Something eating you up like a crazy man. Something more than me not giving you this money. The past few years I been watching it happen to you. You get all nervous acting and kind of wild in the eyes—(*Walter jumps up impatiently at her words.*) I said sit there now, I'm talking to you!

WALTER. Mama—I don't need no nagging at me today.

MAMA. Seem like you getting to a place where you always tied up in some kind of knot about something. But if anybody ask you 'bout it you just yell at 'em and bust out of the house and go out and drink somewheres. Walter Lee, people can't live with that. Ruth's a good, patient girl in her way—but your getting to be too much. Boy, don't make the mistake of driving that girl away from you.

WALTER. Why—what she do for me?

MAMA. She loves you.

WALTER. Mama—I'm going out. I want to go off somewhere and be by myself for a while.

MAMA. I'm sorry 'bout your liquor store, son. It just wasn't the thing for us to do. That's what I want to tell you about—

WALTER. I got to go out, Mama—

(*He rises*)

MAMA. It's dangerous, son.

WALTER. What's dangerous?

MAMA. When a man goes outside his home to look for peace.

WALTER (*Beseechingly*). Then why can't there never be no peace in this house then?

MAMA. You done found it in some other house?

WALTER. No—there ain't no woman! Why do women always think there's a woman somewhere when a man gets restless (*Coming to her*) Mama—Mama—I want so many things . . .

MAMA. Yes, son—

WALTER. I want so many things that they are driving me kind of crazy . . . Mama—look at me.

MAMA. I'm looking at you. You a good-looking boy. You got a job, a nice wife, a fine boy and—

WALTER. A job. (*Looks at her*) Mama, a job? I open and close car doors all day long. I drive a man around in his limousine and I say, "Yes, sir; no, sir; very good, sir; shall I take the Drive, sir?" Mama, that ain't no kind of job . . . that ain't nothing at all. (*Very quietly*) Mama, I don't know if I can make you understand.

MAMA. Understand what, baby?

WALTER (*Quietly*). Sometime it's like I can see the future stretched out in front of me—just plain as day. The future, Mama. Hanging over there at the edge of my days. Just waiting for me—a big, looming blank space—full of *nothing*. Just waiting for *me*. (*Pause*) Mama—sometimes when I'm downtown and I pass them cool, quiet-looking restaurants where them white boys are sitting back and talking 'bout things . . . sitting there turning deals worth millions of dollars . . . sometimes I see guys don't look much older than me—

MAMA. Son—how come you talk so much 'bout money?

WALTER (*With immense passion*). Because it is life, Mama!

MAMA (*Quietly*). Oh— (*Very quietly*) So now it's life. Money is life. Once upon a time freedom used to be life—now it's money. I guess the world really do change . . .

WALTER. No—it was always money, Mama. We just didn't know about it.

MAMA. No . . . something has changed. (*She looks at him.*) You something new, boy. In my time we was worried about not being lynched and getting to the North if we could and how to stay alive and still have a pinch of dignity too . . . Now here come you and Beneatha—talking 'bout things we ain't never even thought about hardly, me and your daddy. You ain't satisfied or proud of nothing we done. I mean that you had a home; that we kept you out of trouble till you was grown; that you don't have to ride to work on the back of nobody's streetcar—You my children—but how different we done become.

WALTER. You just don't understand, Mama, you just don't understand.

MAMA. Son—do you know your wife is expecting another baby? (*Walter stands, stunned, and absorbs what his mother has said.*) That's what she wanted to talk to you about. (*Walter sinks down into a chair.*) This ain't for me to be telling—but you ought to know. (*She waits*) I think Ruth is thinking 'bout getting rid of that child.

WALTER (*Slowly understanding*). No—no—Ruth wouldn't do that.

MAMA. When the world gets ugly enough—a woman will do anything for her family. *The part that's already living.*

WALTER. You don't know Ruth, Mama, if you think she would do that.

(*Ruth opens the bedroom door and stands there a little limp.*)

RUTH (*Beaten*). Yes I would too, Walter. (*Pause*) I gave her a five-dollar down payment.

(*There is total silence as the man stares at his wife and the mother stares at her son.*)

MAMA (*Presently*). Well—(*Tightly*) Well—son, I'm waiting to hear you say something . . . I'm waiting to hear how

you be your father's son. Be the man he was . . . (*Pause*) Your wife say she going to destroy your child. And I'm waiting to hear you talk like him and say we a people who give children life, not who destroys them—(*She rises*) I'm waiting to see you stand up and look like your daddy and say we done give up one baby to poverty and that we ain't going to give up nary another one . . . I'm waiting.

WALTER. Ruth—

MAMA. If you a son of mine, tell her! (*Walter turns, looks at her and can say nothing. She continues, bitterly.*) You . . . you are a disgrace to your father's memory. Somebody get me my hat.

CURTAIN

ACT TWO

SCENE ONE

Time: Later the same day.

At rise: Ruth is ironing again. She has the radio going. Presently Beneatha's bedroom door opens and Ruth's mouth falls and she puts down the iron in fascination.

RUTH. What have we got on tonight!

BENEATHA (*Emerging grandly from the doorway so that we can see her thoroughly robed in the costume Asagai brought*). You are looking at what a well-dressed Nigerian woman wears—(*She parades for Ruth, her hair completely hidden by the headdress; she is coquettishly fanning herself with an ornate oriental fan, mistakenly more like Butterfly than any Nigerian that ever was.*) Isn't it beautiful? (*She promenades to the radio and, with an arrogant flourish, turns off the good loud blues that is playing.*) Enough of this assimilationist junk! (*Ruth follows her with her eyes as she goes to the phonograph and puts on a record and turns and waits ceremoniously for the music to come up. Then, with a shout—*) OCOMOGOSIAY!

(*Ruth jumps. The music comes up, a lovely Nigerian melody. Beneatha listens, enraptured, her eyes far away—"back to the past." She begins to dance. Ruth is dumfounded.*)

RUTH. What kind of dance is that?

BENEATHA. A folk dance.

RUTH (*Pearl Bailey*). What kind of folks do that, honey?

BENEATHA. It's from Nigeria. It's a dance of welcome.

RUTH. Who you welcoming?

BENEATHA. The men back to the village.

RUTH. Where they been?

BENEATHA. How should I know—out hunting or something. Anyway, they are coming back now . . .

RUTH. Well, that's good.

BENEATHA. (*With the record*)
Alundi, alundi
Alundi alunya
Jop pu a jeepua
Ang gu sooooooooooo

Ai yai yae . . .
Ayehaye—alundi . . .

(*Walter comes in during this performance; he has obviously been drinking. He leans against the door heavily and watches his sister, at first with distaste. Then his eyes look off— "back to the past"—as he lifts both his fists to the roof, screaming.*)

WALTER. YEAH . . . AND ETHIOPIA STRETCH FORTH HER HANDS AGAIN! . . .

RUTH (*Drily, looking at him*). Yes—and Africa sure is claiming her own tonight.

(*She gives them both up and starts ironing again.*)

WALTER (*All in a drunken, dramatic shout*). Shut up! . . . I'm digging them drums . . . them drums move me! . . . (*He makes his weaving way to his wife's face and leans in close to her.*) In my *heart of hearts*—(*He thumps his chest.*)—I am much warrior!

RUTH (*Without even looking up*). In your heart of hearts you are much drunkard.

WALTER (*Coming away from her and starting to wander around the room, shouting*). Me and Jomo . . . (*Intently, in his sister's face. She has stopped dancing to watch him in this unknown mood.*) That's my man, Kenyatta. (*Shouting and thumping his chest*) FLAMING SPEAR! HOT DAMN! (*He is suddenly in possession of an imaginary spear and actively spearing enemies all over the room.*) OCOMOGOSIAY . . . THE LION IS WAKING . . . OWIMOWEH! (*He pulls his shirt open and leaps up on a table and gestures with his spear. The bell rings. Ruth goes to answer.*)

BENEATHA (*To encourage Walter, thoroughly caught up with this side of him*). OCOMOGOSIAY, FLAMING SPEAR!

WALTER (*On the table, very far gone, his eyes pure glass sheets. He sees what we cannot, that he is a leader of his people, a great chief, a descendant of Chaka, and that the hour to march has come*). Listen, my black brothers—

BENEATHA. OCOMOGOSIAY!

WALTER. —Do you hear the waters rushing against the shores of the coastlands—

BENEATHA. OCOMOGOSIAY!

WALTER. —Do you hear the screeching of the cocks in yonder hills beyond where the chiefs meet in council for the coming of the mighty war—

BENEATHA. OCOMOGOSIAY!

WALTER. —Do you hear the beating of the wings of the birds flying low over the mountains and the low places of our land—

(*Ruth opens the door. George Murchison enters.*)

BENEATHA. OCOMOGOSIAY!

WALTER. —Do you hear the singing of the women, singing the war songs of our fathers to the babies in the great houses . . . singing the sweet war songs? OH, DO YOU HEAR, MY BLACK BROTHERS!

BENEATHA (*Completely gone*). We hear you, Flaming Spear—

WALTER. Telling us to prepare for the greatness of the time—(*To George*) Black Brother!

(*He extends his hand for the fraternal clasp.*)

GEORGE. Black Brother, hell!

RUTH (*Having had enough, and embarrassed for the family*). Beneatha you got company—what's the matter with you? Walter Lee Younger, get down off that table and stop acting like a fool . . .

(*Walter comes down off the table suddenly and makes a quick exit to the bathroom.*)

RUTH. He's had a little to drink . . . I don't know what her excuse is.

GEORGE (*To Beneatha*). Look honey, we're going to the theatre—we're not going to be in it . . . so go change, huh?

RUTH. You expect this boy to go out with you looking like that?

BENEATHA (*Looking at George*). That's up to George. If he's ashamed of his heritage—

GEORGE. Oh, don't be so proud of yourself, Bennie—just because you look eccentric.

BENEATHA. How can something that's natural be eccentric?

GEORGE. That's what being eccentric means—being natural. Get dressed.

BENEATHA. I don't like that, George.

RUTH. Why must you and your brother make an argument out of everything people say?

BENEATHA. Because I hate assimilationist Negroes!

RUTH. Will somebody please tell me what assimila-whoever means!

GEORGE. Oh, it's just a college girl's way of calling people Uncle Toms—but that isn't what it means at all.

RUTH. Well, what does it mean?

BENEATHA (*Cutting George off and staring at him as she replies to Ruth*). It means someone who is willing to give up his own culture and submerge himself completely in the dominant, and in this case, *oppressive* culture!

GEORGE. Oh, dear, dear, dear! Here we go! A lecture on the African past! On our Great West African Heritage! In one second we will hear all about the great Ashanti empires; the great Songhay civilizations; and the great sculpture of Bénin—and then some poetry in the Bantu—and the whole monologue will end with the word *heritage*! (*Nastily*) Let's face it, baby, your heritage is nothing but a bunch of raggedy-assed spirituals and some grass huts!

BENEATHA. *Grass huts!* (*Ruth crosses to her and forcibly pushes her toward the bedroom.*) See there . . . you are standing there in your splendid ignorance talking about people who were the first to smelt iron on the face of the earth! (*Ruth is pushing her through the door.*) The Ashanti were performing surgical operations when the English—(*Ruth pulls the door to, with Beneatha on the other side, and smiles graciously at George. Beneatha opens the door and shouts the end of the sentence defiantly at George.*)—were still tatooing themselves with blue dragons . . .

(*She goes back inside.*)

RUTH. Have a seat, George. (*They both sit. Ruth folds her hands rather primly on her lap, determined to demonstrate the civilization of the family.*) Warm, ain't it? I mean for September. (*Pause*) Just like they always say about Chicago weather: If it's too hot or cold for you, just wait a minute and it'll change. (*She smiles happily at this cliché of clichés.*) Everybody say it's got to do with them bombs and things they keep setting off. (*Pause*) Would you like a nice cold beer?

GEORGE. No, thank you. I don't care for beer. (*He looks at his watch.*) I hope she hurries up.

RUTH. What time is the show?

GEORGE. It's an eight-thirty curtain. That's just Chicago, though. In New York standard curtain time is eight forty.

(*He is rather proud of this knowledge.*)

RUTH (*Properly appreciating it*). You get to New York a lot?

GEORGE (*Offhand*). Few times a year.

RUTH. Oh—that's nice. I've never been to New York.

(*Walter enters. We feel he has relieved himself, but the edge of unreality is still with him.*)

WALTER. New York ain't got nothing Chicago ain't. Just a bunch of hustling people all squeezed up together—being "Eastern."

(*He turns his face into a screw of displeasure.*)

GEORGE. Oh—you've been?

WALTER. *Plenty* of times.

RUTH (*Shocked at the lie*). Walter Lee Younger!

WALTER (*Staring her down*). Plenty! (*Pause*) What we got to drink in this house? Why don't you offer this man some refreshment. (*To George*) They don't know how to entertain people in this house, man.

GEORGE. Thank you—I don't really care for anything.

WALTER (*Feeling his head; sobriety coming*). Where's Mama?

RUTH. She ain't come back yet.

WALTER (*Looking Murchison over from head to toe, scrutinizing his carefully casual tweed sports jacket over cashmere V-neck sweater over soft eyelet shirt and tie, and soft slacks, finished off with white buckskin shoes*). Why all you college boys wear them fairyish-looking white shoes?

RUTH. Walter Lee!

(*George Murchison ignores the remark.*)

WALTER (*To Ruth*). Well, they look crazy as hell—white shoes, cold as it is.

RUTH (*Crushed*). You have to excuse him—

WALTER. No he don't! Excuse me for what? What you always excusing me for! I'll excuse myself when I needs to be excused! (*A pause*) They look as funny as them black knee socks Beneatha wears out of here all the time.

RUTH. It's the college *style*, Walter.

WALTER. Style, hell. She looks like she got burnt legs or something!

RUTH. Oh, Walter—

WALTER (*An irritable mimic*). Oh, Walter! Oh, Walter! (*To Murchison*) How's your old man making out? I understand you all going to buy that big hotel on the Drive? (*He finds a beer in the refrigerator, wanders over to Murchison, sipping and wiping his lips with the back of his hand, and straddling a chair backwards to talk to the other man.*) Shrewd move. Your old man is all right, man. (*Tapping his head and half winking for emphasis.*) I mean he knows how to operate. I mean he thinks *big*, you know what I mean, I mean for a *home*, you know? But I think he's kind of running out of ideas now. I'd like to talk to him. Listen, man, I got some plans that could turn this city upside down. I mean I think like he does. *Big*. Invest big, gamble big, hell, lose *big* if you have to, you know what I mean. It's hard to find a man on this whole Southside who understands my kind of thinking—you dig? (*He scrutinizes Murchison again, drinks his beer, squints his eyes and leans in close, confidential, man to man.*) Me and you ought to sit down and talk sometimes, man. Man, I got me some ideas . . .

MURCHISON (*With boredom*). Yeah—sometimes we'll have to do that, Walter.

WALTER (*Understanding the indifference, and offended*). Yeah—well, when you get the time, man. I know you a busy little boy.

RUTH. Walter, please—

WALTER (*Bitterly, hurt*). I know ain't nothing in this world as busy as you colored college boys with your fraternity pins and white shoes . . .

RUTH (*Covering her face with humiliation*). Oh, Walter Lee

WALTER. I see you all all the time—with the books tucked under your arms—going to your (*British A—a mimic*) "clahsses." And for what! What the hell you learning over there! Filling up your heads— (*Counting off on his fingers*)—with the sociology and the psychology—but they teaching you how to be a man? How to take over and run the world? They teaching you how to run a rubber plantation or a steel mill? Naw—just to talk proper and read books and wear white shoes . . .

GEORGE (*looking at him with distaste, a little above it all*). You're all wacked up with bitterness, man.

WALTER (*Intently, almost quietly, between the teeth, glaring at the boy*). And you—ain't you bitter man? Ain't you just about had it yet? Don't you see no stars gleaming that you can't reach out and grab? You happy?—you contented son-of-a-bitch—you happy? You got it made? Bitter? Man, I'm a volcano. Bitter? Here I am a giant—surrounded by ants! Ants who can't even understand what it is the giant is talking about.

RUTH (*Passionately and suddenly*). Oh, Walter—ain't you with nobody!

WALTER (*Violently*). No! 'Cause ain't nobody with me! Not even my own mother!

RUTH. Walter, that's a terrible thing to say!

(*Beneatha enters, dressed for the evening in a cocktail dress and earrings.*)

GEORGE. Well—hey, you look great.

BENEATHA. Let's go, George. See you all later.

RUTH. Have a nice time.

GEORGE. Thanks. Good night. (*To Walter, sarcastically*) Good night, *Prometheus.*

(*Beneatha and George exit.*)

WALTER (*To Ruth*). Who is Prometheus?

RUTH. I don't know. Don't worry about it.

WALTER (*In fury, pointing after George*). See there—they get to a point where they can't insult you man to man—they got to go talk about something ain't nobody never heard of!

RUTH. How you know it was an insult? (*To humor him*) Maybe Prometheus is a nice fellow.

WALTER. Prometheus! I bet there ain't even no such thing! I bet that simple-minded clown—

RUTH. Walter—

(*She stops what she is doing and looks at him.*)

RUTH. Start what?

WALTER. Your nagging! Where was I? Who was I with? How much money did I spend?

RUTH (*Plaintively*). Walter Lee—why don't we just try to talk about it . . .

WALTER (*Not listening*). I been out talking with people who understand me. People who care about the things I got on my mind.

RUTH (*Wearily*). I guess that means people like Willy Harris.

WALTER. Yes, people like Willy Harris.

RUTH (*With a sudden flash of impatience*). Why don't you all just hurry up and go into the banking business and stop talking about it!

WALTER. Why? You want to know why? 'Cause we all tied up in a race of people that don't know how to do nothing but moan, pray and have babies!

(*The line is too bitter even for him and he looks at her and sits down.*)

RUTH. Oh, Walter . . . (*Softly*) Honey, why can't you stop fighting me?

WALTER (*Without thinking*). Who's fighting you? Who even cares about you?

(*This line begins the retardation of his mood.*)

RUTH. Well— (*She waits a long time, and then with resignation starts to put away her things.*) I guess I might as well go on to bed . . . (*More or less to herself*) I don't know where we lost it . . . but we have . . . (*Then, to him*) I—I'm sorry about this new baby, Walter. I guess maybe I better go on and do what I started . . . I guess I just didn't realize how bad things was with us . . . I guess I just didn't really realize—(*She starts out to the bedroom and stops.*) You want some hot milk?

WALTER. Hot milk?

RUTH. Yes—hot milk.

WALTER. Why hot milk?

RUTH. 'Cause after all that liquor you come home with you ought to have something hot in your stomach.

WALTER. I don't want no milk.

RUTH. You want some coffee then?

WALTER. No, I don't want no coffee. I don't want nothing hot to drink. (*Almost plaintively*) Why you always trying to give me something to eat?

RUTH (*Standing and looking at him helplessly*). What else can I give you, Walter Lee Younger?

(*She stands and looks at him and presently turns to go out again. He lifts his head and watches her going away from him in a new mood which began to emerge when he asked her "Who cares about you?"*)

WALTER. It's been rough, ain't it, baby? (*She hears and stops but does not turn around and he continues to her back.*) I guess between two people there ain't never as much understood as folks generally thinks there is. I mean like between me and you— (*She turns to face him.*) How we gets to the place where we scared to talk softness to each other. (*He waits, thinking hard himself.*) Why you think it got to be like that? (*He is thoughtful, almost as a child would be.*) Ruth, what is it gets into people ought to be close?

RUTH. I don't know, honey. I think about it a lot.

WALTER. On account of you and me, you mean? The way things are with us. The way something done come down between us.

RUTH. There ain't so much between us, Walter . . . Not when you come to me and try to talk to me. Try to be with me . . . a little even.

WALTER (*Total honesty*). Sometimes . . . sometimes . . . I don't even know how to try.

RUTH. Walter—

WALTER. Yes?

RUTH (*Coming to him, gently and with misgiving, but coming to him*). Honey . . . life don't have to be like this. I mean sometimes people can do things so that things are better

. . . You remember how we used to talk when Travis was born . . . about the way we were going to live . . . the kind of house . . . (*She is stroking his head*) Well, it's all starting to slip away from us . . .

(*Mama enters, and Walter jumps up and shouts at her.*)

WALTER. Mama, where have you been?

MAMA. My—them steps is longer than they used to be. Whew! (*She sits down and ignores him.*) How you feeling this evening, Ruth?

(*Ruth shrugs, disturbed some at having been prematurely interrupted and watching her husband knowingly.*)

WALTER. Mama, where have you been all day?

MAMA (*Still ignoring him and leaning on the table and changing to more comfortable shoes*). Where's Travis?

RUTH. I let him go out earlier and he ain't come back yet. Boy, is he going to get it!

WALTER. Mama!

MAMA (*As if she has heard him for the first time*). Yes, son?

WALTER. Where did you go this afternoon?

MAMA. I went down town to tend to some business that I had to tend to.

WALTER. What kind of business?

MAMA. You know better than to question me like a child, Brother.

WALTER (*Rising and bending over the table*). Where were you, Mama? (*Bringing his fists down and shouting*) Mama, you didn't go do something with that insurance money, something crazy?

(*The front door opens slowly, interrupting him, and Travis peeks his head in, less than hopefully.*)

TRAVIS (*To his mother*). Mama, I—

RUTH. "Mama I" nothing! You're going to get it, boy! Get on in that bedroom and get yourself ready!

TRAVIS. But I—

MAMA. Why don't you all never let the child explain hisself.

RUTH. Keep out of it now, Lena.

(*Mama clamps her lips together, and Ruth advances toward her son menacingly.*)

RUTH. A thousand times I have told you not to go off like that—

MAMA (*Holding out her arms to her grandson*). Well—at least let me tell him something. I want him to be the first one to hear . . . Come here, Travis. (*The boy obeys, gladly.*) Travis—(*She takes him by the shoulders and looks into his face.*)—you know that money we got in the mail this morning?

TRAVIS. Yes'm—

MAMA. Well—what you think your grandmama gone and done with that money?

TRAVIS. I don't know, Grandmama.

MAMA (*Putting her finger on his nose for emphasis*). She went

out and she bought you a house! (*The explosion comes from Walter at the end of the revelation and he jumps up and turns away from all of them in a fury. Mama continues, to Travis*) You glad about the house? It's going to be yours when you get to be a man.

TRAVIS. Yeah—I always wanted to live in a house.

MAMA. All right, gimme some sugar then—(*Travis puts his arms around her neck as she watches her son over the boy's shoulder. Then, to Travis, after the embrace*) Now when you say your prayers tonight, you thank God and your grandfather—'cause it was him who give you the house—in his way.

RUTH (*Taking the boy from Mama and pushing him toward the bedroom*). Now you get out of here and get ready for your beating.

TRAVIS. Aw, Mama—

RUTH. Get on in there— (*Closing the door behind him and turning radiantly to her mother-in-law*) So you went and did it!

MAMA (*Quietly, looking at her son with pain*). Yes, I did.

RUTH (*Raising both arms classically*). Praise God! (*Looks at Walter a moment, who says nothing. She crosses rapidly to her husband*) Please, honey—let me be glad . . . you be glad too. (*She has laid her hands on his shoulders, but he shakes himself free of her roughly, without turning to face her.*) Oh, Walter . . . a home . . . a home. (*She comes back to Mama*) Well—where is it? How big is it? How much it going to cost?

MAMA. Well—

RUTH. When we moving?

MAMA (*Smiling at her*). First of the month.

RUTH (*Throwing back her head with jubilance*). Praise God!

MAMA (*Tentatively, still looking at her son's back turned against her and Ruth*). It's—it's a nice house too . . . (*She cannot help speaking directly to him. An imploring quality in her voice, her manner, makes her almost like a girl now.*) Three bedrooms—nice big one for you and Ruth. . . . Me and Beneatha still have to share our room, but Travis have one of his own—and— (*With difficulty*) I figures if the— new baby—is a boy, we could get one of them double-decker outfits . . . And there's a yard with a little patch of dirt where I could maybe get to grow me a few flowers . . . And a nice big basement . . .

RUTH. Walter, honey, be glad . . .

MAMA (*Still to his back, fingering things on the table*). 'Course I don't want to make it sound fancier than it is . . . It's just a plain little old house—but it's made good and solid— and it will be *ours*. Walter Lee—it makes a difference in a man when he can walk on floors that belong to *him* . . .

RUTH. Where is it?

MAMA (*Frightened at this telling*). Well—well—it's out there in Clybourne Park—

(*Ruth's radiance fades abruptly, and Walter finally turns slowly to face his mother with incredulity and hostility.*)

RUTH. Where?

MAMA (*Matter-of-factly*). Four o six Clybourne Street, Clybourne Park.

RUTH. Clybourne Park? Mama, there ain't no colored people living in Clybourne Park.

MAMA (*Almost idiotically*). Well, I guess there's going to be some now.

WALTER (*Bitterly*). So that's the peace and comfort you went out and bought for us today!

MAMA (*Raising her eyes to meet his finally*). Son—I just tried to find the nicest place for the least amount of money for my family.

RUTH (*Trying to recover from the shock*). Well—well— 'course I ain't one never been 'fraid of no crackers, mind you—but—well, wasn't there no other houses nowhere?

MAMA. Them houses they put up for colored in them areas way out all seem to cost twice as much as other houses. I did the best I could.

RUTH (*Struck senseless with the news, in its various degrees of goodness and trouble, she sits a moment, her fists propping her chin in thought, and then she starts to rise, bringing her fists down with vigor, the radiance spreading from cheek to cheek again*). Well—well!—All I can say is—if this is my time in life—my time—to say good-bye—(*And she builds with momentum as she starts to circle the room with an exuberant, almost tearfully happy release.*)—to these Goddamned cracking walls!—(*She pounds the walls.*) and these marching roaches!—(*She wipes at an imaginary army of marching roaches.*)—and this cramped little closet which ain't now or never was no kitchen! . . . then I say it loud and good, Hallelujah! and good-bye misery . . . I don't never want to see your ugly face again! (*She laughs joyously, having practically destroyed the apartment, and flings her arms up and lets them come down happily, slowly, reflectively, over the abdomen, aware for the first time perhaps that the life therein pulses with happiness and not despair.*) Lena!

MAMA (*Moved, watching her happiness*). Yes, honey?

RUTH (*Looking off*). Is there—is there a whole lot of sunlight?

MAMA (*Understanding*). Yes, child, there's a whole lot of sunlight.

(*Long pause*)

RUTH (*Collecting herself and going to the door of the room Travis is in*). Well—I guess I better see 'bout Travis. (*To Mama*) Lord, I sure don't feel like whipping nobody today!

(*She exits.*)

MAMA (*The mother and son are left alone now and the mother waits a long time, considering deeply, before she speaks*). Son—you—you understand what I done, don't you? (*Walter is silent and sullen.*) I—I just seen my family falling apart today . . . just falling to pieces in front of my eyes . . . We couldn't of gone on like we was today. We was going backwards 'stead of forwards—talking 'bout killing babies and wishing each other was dead . . . When it gets like that in life—you just got to do something different, push on out and do something bigger . . . (*She waits.*) I wish you say something, son . . . I wish you'd say how deep inside you you think I done the right thing—

WALTER (*Crossing slowly to his bedroom door and finally turning there and speaking measuredly*). What you need me to say you done right for? *You* the head of this family. You run our lives like you want to. It was your money and you did what you wanted with it. So what you need for me to say it was all right for? (*Bitterly, to hurt her as deeply as he knows is possible*) So you butchered up a dream of mine—you—who always talking 'bout your children's dreams . . .

MAMA. Walter Lee—

(*He just closes the door behind him. Mama sits alone, thinking heavily.*)

CURTAIN

SCENE TWO

Time: Friday night. A few weeks later.

At rise: Packing crates mark the intention of the family to move. Beneatha and George come in, presumably from an evening out again.

GEORGE. O.K. . . . O.K., whatever you say . . . (*They both sit on the couch. He tries to kiss her. She moves away.*) Look, we've had a nice evening; let's not spoil it, huh? . . .

(*He again turns her head and tries to nuzzle in and she turns away from him, not with distaste but with momentary lack of interest; in a mood to pursue what they were talking about.*)

BENEATHA. I'm *trying* to talk to you.

GEORGE. We always talk.

BENEATHA. Yes—and I love to talk.

GEORGE (*Exasperated; rising*). I know it and I don't mind it sometimes . . . I want you to cut it out, see—The moody stuff, I mean. I don't like it. You're a nice-looking girl . . . all over. That's all you need, honey, forget the atmosphere. Guys aren't going to go for the atmosphere— they're going to go for what they see. Be glad for that. Drop the Garbo routine. It doesn't go with you. As for myself, I want a nice—(*Groping*)—simple—(*Thoughtfully*)—sophisticated girl . . . not a poet—O.K.?

(*She rebuffs him again and he starts to leave.*)

BENEATHA. Why are you angry?

GEORGE. Because this is stupid! I don't go out with you to

discuss the nature of "quiet desperation" or to hear all about your thoughts—because the world will go on thinking what it thinks regardless—

BENEATHA. Then why read books? Why go to school?

GEORGE (*With artificial patience, counting on his fingers*). It's simple. You read books—to learn facts—to get grades—to pass the course—to get a degree. That's all—it has nothing to do with thoughts.

(*A long pause*)

BENEATHA. I see. (*A longer pause as she looks at him*) Good night, George.

(*George looks at her a little oddly, and starts to exit. He meets Mama coming in.*)

GEORGE. Oh—hello, Mrs. Younger.

MAMA. Hello, George, how you feeling?

GEORGE. Fine—fine, how are you?

MAMA. Oh, a little tired. You know them steps can get you after a day's work. You all have a nice time tonight?

GEORGE. Yes—a fine time. Well, good night.

MAMA. Good night. (*He exits. Mama closes the door behind her*) Hello, honey. What you sitting like that for?

BENEATHA. I'm just sitting.

MAMA. Didn't you have a nice time?

BENEATHA. No.

MAMA. No? What's the matter?

BENEATHA. Mama, George is a fool—honest. (*She rises*)

MAMA (*Hustling around unloading the packages she has entered with. She stops*). Is he, baby?

BENEATHA. Yes.

(*Beneatha makes up Travis' bed as she talks.*)

MAMA. You sure?

BENEATHA. Yes.

MAMA. Well—I guess you better not waste your time with no fools.

(*Beneatha looks up at her mother, watching her put groceries in the refrigerator. Finally she gathers up her things and starts into the bedroom. At the door she stops and looks at her mother.*)

BENEATHA. Mama—

MAMA. Yes, baby—

BENEATHA. Thank you.

MAMA. For what?

BENEATHA. For understanding me this time.

(*She exits quickly and the mother stands, smiling a little, looking at the place where Beneatha just stood. Ruth enters.*)

RUTH. Now don't you fool with any of this stuff, Lena—

MAMA. Oh, I just thought I'd sort a few things out.

(*The phone rings. Ruth answers.*)

RUTH (*At the phone*). Hello—Just a minute. (*Goes to door*) Walter, it's Mrs. Arnold. (*Waits. Goes back to the phone. Tense*) Hello. Yes, this is his wife speaking . . . He's lying down now. Yes . . . well, he'll be in tomorrow. He's been very sick. Yes—I know we should have called, but we were so sure he'd be able to come in today. Yes—yes, I'm very sorry. Yes . . . Thank you very much. (*She hangs up. Walter is standing in the doorway of the bedroom behind her.*) That was Mrs. Arnold.

WALTER (*Indifferently*). Was it?

RUTH. She said if you don't come in tomorrow that they are getting a new man . . .

WALTER. Ain't that sad—ain't that crying sad.

RUTH. She said Mr. Arnold has had to take a cab for three days . . . Walter, you ain't been to work for three days! (*This is a revelation to her.*) Where you been, Walter Lee Younger? (*Walter looks at her and starts to laugh.*) You're going to lose your job.

WALTER. That's right . . .

RUTH. Oh, Walter, and with your mother working like a dog every day—

WALTER. That's sad, too—Everything is sad.

MAMA. What you been doing for these three days, son?

WALTER. Mama—you don't know all the things a man what got leisure can find to do in this city . . . What's this—Friday night? Well—Wednesday I borrowed Willy Harris' car and I went for a drive . . . just me and myself and I drove and drove . . . Way out . . . way past South Chicago, and I parked the car and I sat and looked at the steel mills all day long. I just sat in the car and looked at them big black chimneys for hours. Then I drove back and I went to the Green Hat. (*Pause*) And Thursday—Thursday I borrowed the car again and I got in it and I pointed it the other way and I drove the other way—for hours—way, way up to Wisconsin, and I looked at the farms. I just drove and looked at the farms. Then I drove back and I went to the Green Hat. (*Pause*) And today—today I didn't get the car. Today I just walked. All over the Southside. And I looked at the Negroes and they looked at me and finally I just sat down on the curb at Thirty-ninth and South Parkway and I just sat there and watched the Negroes go by. And then I went to the Green Hat. You all sad? You all depressed? And you know where I am going right now—

(*Ruth goes out quietly.*)

MAMA. Oh, Big Walter, is this the harvest of our days?

WALTER. You know what I like about the Green Hat? (*He turns the radio on and a steamy, deep blues pours into the room.*) I like this little cat they got there who blows a sax . . . He blows. He talks to me. He ain't but 'bout five feet tall and he's got a conked head and his eyes is always closed and he's all music—

MAMA (*Rising and getting some papers out of her handbag*). Walter—

WALTER. And there's this other guy who plays the piano . . . and they got a sound. I mean they can work on some music . . . They got the best little combo in the world in the Green Hat . . . You can just sit there and drink and listen to them three men play and you realize that don't nothing matter worth a damn, but just being there—

MAMA. I've helped do it to you, haven't I, son? Walter, I been wrong.

WALTER. Naw—you ain't never been wrong about nothing, Mama.

MAMA. Listen to me, now. I say I been wrong, son. That I been doing to you what the rest of the world been doing to you. (*She stops and he looks up slowly at her and she meets his eyes pleadingly.*) Walter—what you ain't never understood is that I ain't got nothing, don't own nothing, ain't never really wanted nothing that wasn't for you. There ain't nothing as precious to me . . . There ain't nothing worth holding on to, money, dreams, nothing else—if it means—if it means it's going to destroy my boy. (*She puts her papers in front of him and he watches her without speaking or moving.*) I paid the man thirty-five hundred dollars down on the house. That leaves sixty-five hundred dollars. Monday morning I want you to take this money and take three thousand dollars and put it in a savings account for Beneatha's medical schooling. The rest you put in a checking account—with your name on it. And from now on any penny that comes out of it or that go in it is for you to look after. For you to decide. (*She drops her hands a little helplessly.*) It ain't much, but it's all I got in the world and I'm putting in your hands. I'm telling you to be the head of this family from now on like you supposed to be.

WALTER (*Stares at the money*). You trust me like that, Mama?

MAMA. I ain't never stop trusting you. Like I ain't never stop loving you.

(*She goes out, and Walter sits looking at the money on the table as the music continues in its idiom, pulsing in the room. Finally, in a decisive gesture, he gets up and, in a furious action, flings the bedclothes wildly from his son's makeshift bed to all over the floor—with a cry of desperation. Then he picks up the money and goes out in a hurry.*)

CURTAIN

SCENE THREE

Time: Saturday, moving day, one week later.

Before the curtain rises, Ruth's voice, a strident, dramatic church alto, cuts through the silence.

It is, in the darkness, a triumphant surge, a penetrating statement of expectation: "Oh, Lord, I don't feel no ways tried! Children, oh, glory hallelujah!"

As the curtain rises we see that Ruth is alone in the living room, finishing up the family's packing. It is moving day. She is nailing crates and tying cartons. Beneatha enters, carrying a guitar case, and watches her exuberant sister-in-law.

RUTH. Hey!

BENEATHA (*Putting away the case*). Hi.

RUTH (*Pointing at a package*). Honey—look in that package there and see what I found on sale this morning at the South Center. (*Ruth gets up and moves to the package and draws out some curtains*) Lookahere—hand-turned hems!

BENEATHA. How do you know the window size out there?

RUTH (*Who hadn't thought of that*). Oh—Well, they bound to fit something in the whole house. Anyhow, they was too good a bargain to pass us. (*Ruth slaps her head, suddenly remembering something*) Oh, Bennie—I meant to put a special note on that carton over there. That's your mama's good china and she wants 'em to be very careful with it.

BENEATHA. I'll do it.

(*Beneatha finds a piece of paper and starts to draw large letters on it.*)

RUTH. You know what I'm going to do soon as I get in that new house?

BENEATHA. What?

RUTH. Honey—I'm going to run me a tub of water up to here . . . (*With her fingers practically up to her nostrils*) And I'm going to get in it—and I am going to sit . . . and sit . . . and sit in that hot water and the first person who knocks to tell *me* to hurry up and come out—

BENEATHA. Gets shot at sunrise.

RUTH (*Laughing happily*). You said it, sister! (*Noticing how large Beneatha is absent-mindedly making the note.*) Honey, they ain't going to read that from no airplane.

BENEATHA (*Laughing herself*). I guess I always think things have more emphasis if they are big, somehow.

RUTH (*Looking up at her and smiling*). You and your brother seem to have that as a philosophy of life. Lord, that man—done changed so 'round here. You know—you know what we did last night? Me and Walter Lee?

BENEATHA. What?

RUTH (*Smiling to herself*). We went to the movies. (*Looking at Beneatha to see if she understands.*) We went to the movies. You know the last time me and Walter went to the movies together?

BENEATHA. No.

RUTH. Me neither. That's how long it been. (*Smiling again*) But we went last night. The picture wasn't much good, but that didn't seem to matter. We went—and we held hands.

BENEATHA. Oh, Lord!

RUTH. We held hands—and you know what?

BENEATHA. What?

RUTH. When we come out of the show it was late and dark and all the stores and things was closed up . . . and it was kind of chilly and there wasn't many people on the streets . . . and we was still holding hands, me and Walter.

BENEATHA. You're killing me.

(*Walter enters with a large package. His happiness is deep in him; he cannot keep still with his new-found exuberance. He is singing and wiggling and snapping his fingers. He puts his package in a corner and puts a phonograph record, which he has brought in with him, on the record player. As the music comes up he dances over to Ruth and tries to get her to dance with him. She gives in at last to his raunchiness and in a fit of giggling allows herself to be drawn into his mood and together they deliberately burlesque an old social dance of their youth.*)

BENEATHA (*Regarding them a long time as they dance, then drawing in her breath for a deeply exaggerated comment which she does not particularly mean*). Talk about—old-ddddddddd-fashionedddddddd—Negroes!

WALTER (*Stopping momentarily*). What kind of Negroes?

(*He says this in fun. He is not angry with her today, nor with anyone. He starts to dance with his wife again.*)

BENEATHA. Old-fashioned.

WALTER (*As he dances with Ruth*). You know, when these *New Negroes* have their convention—(*Pointing at his sister*)—that is going to be the chairman of the Committee on Unending Agitation. (*He goes on dancing, then stops.*) Race, race, race! . . . Girl, I do believe you are the first person in the history of the entire human race to successfully brainwash yourself. (*Beneatha breaks up and he goes on dancing. He stops again, enjoying his tease.*) Damn, even the N double A C P takes a holiday sometimes! (*Beneatha and Ruth laugh. He dances with Ruth some more and starts to laugh and stops and pantomimes someone over an operating table.*) I can just see that chick someday looking down at some poor cat on an operating table before she starts to slice him, saying . . . (*Pulling his sleeves back maliciously*) "By the way, what are your views on civil rights down there? . . ."

(*He laughs at her again and starts to dance happily. The bell sounds.*)

BENEATHA. Sticks and stones may break my bones but . . . words will never hurt me!

(*Beneatha goes to the door and opens it as Walter and Ruth go on with the clowning. Beneatha is somewhat surprised to see a quiet-looking middle-aged white man in a business suit holding his hat and a briefcase in his hand and consulting a small piece of paper.*)

MAN. Uh—how do you do, miss. I am looking for a Mrs.—(*He looks at the slip of paper.*) Mrs. Lena Younger?

BENEATHA (*Smoothing her hair with slight embarrassment*). Oh—yes, that's my mother. Excuse me. (*She closes the door and turns to quiet the other two.*) Ruth! Brother! Somebody's here. (*Then she opens the door. The man casts a curious quick glance at all of them.*) Uh—come in please.

MAN (*Coming in*). Thank you.

BENEATHA. My mother isn't here just now. Is it business?

MAN. Yes . . . well, of a sort.

WALTER (*Freely, the Man of the House*). Have a seat. I'm Mrs. Younger's son. I look after most of her business matters.

(*Ruth and Beneatha exchange amused glances.*)

MAN (*Regarding Walter, and sitting*). Well—My name is Karl Lindner . . .

WALTER (*Stretching out his hand*). Walter Younger. This is my wife—(*Ruth nods politely*)—and my sister.

LINDNER. How do you do.

WALTER (*Amiably, as he sits himself easily on a chair, leaning with interest forward on his knees and looking expectantly into the newcomer's face*). What can we do for you, Mr. Lindner!

LINDNER (*Some minor shuffling of the hat and briefcase on his knees*). Well—I am a representative of the Clybourne Park Improvement Association—

WALTER (*Pointing*). Why don't you sit your things on the floor?

LINDNER. Oh—yes. Thank you. (*He slides the briefcase and hat under the chair.*) And as I was saying—I am from the Clybourne Park Improvement Association and we have had it brought to our attention at the last meeting that you people—or at least your mother—has bought a piece of residential property at—(*He digs for the slip of paper again*)—four o six Clybourne Street . . .

WALTER. That's right. Care for something to drink? Ruth, get Mr. Lindner a beer.

LINDNER (*Upset for some reason*). Oh—no, really. I mean thank you very much, but no thank you.

RUTH (*Innocently*). Some coffee?

LINDNER. Thank you, nothing at all.

(*Beneatha is watching the man carefully.*)

LINDNER. Well, I don't know how much you folks know about our organization. (*He is a gentle man; thoughtful and somewhat labored in his manner.*) It is one of these community organizations set up to look after—oh, you know, things like block upkeep and special projects and we also have what we call our New Neighbor Orientation Committee.

BENEATHA (*Drily*). Yes—and what do they do?

LINDNER (*Turning a little to her and then returning the main force to Walter*). Well—it's what you might call a sort of welcoming committee, I guess. I mean they, we, I'm the chairman of the committee—go around and see the new people who move into the neighborhood and sort of give them the lowdown on the way we do things out in Clybourne Park.

BENEATHA (*With appreciation of the two meanings, which escape Ruth and Walter*). Un-huh.

LINDNER. And we also have the category of what the association calls—(*He looks elsewhere*) —uh—special community problems . . .

BENEATHA. Yes—and what are some of those?

WALTER. Girl, let the man talk.

LINDNER (*With understated relief*). Thank you. I would sort of like to explain this thing in my own way. I mean I want to explain to you in a certain way.

WALTER. Go ahead.

LINDNER. Yes. Well. I'm going to try to get right to the point. I'm sure we'll all appreciate that in the long run.

BENEATHA. Yes.

WALTER. Be still now!

LINDNER. Well—

RUTH (*Still innocently*). Would you like another chair—you don't look comfortable.

LINDNER (*More frustrated than annoyed*). No, thank you very much. Please. Well—to get right to the point I—(*A great breath, and he is off at last*) I am sure you people must be aware of some of the incidents which have happened in various parts of the city when colored people have moved into certain areas—(*Beneatha exhales heavily and starts tossing a piece of fruit up and down in the air.*) Well—because we have what I think is going to be a unique type of organization in American community life—not only do we deplore that kind of thing—but we are trying to do something about it. (*Beneatha stops tossing and turns with a new and quizzical interest to the man.*) We feel—(*gaining confidence in his mission because of the interest in the faces of the people he is talking to*)—we feel that most of the trouble in this world, when you come right down to it—(*He hits his knee for emphasis.*)—most of the trouble exists because people just don't sit down and talk to each other.

RUTH (*Nodding as she might in church, pleased with the remark*). You can say that again, mister.

LINDNER (*More encouraged by such affirmation*). That we don't try hard enough in this world to understand the other fellow's problem. The other guy's point of view.

RUTH. Now that's right.

(*Beneatha and Walter merely watch and listen with genuine interest.*)

LINDNER. Yes—that's the way we feel out in Clybourne Park. And that's why I was elected to come here this afternoon and talk to you people. Friendly like, you know, the way people should talk to each other and see if we couldn't find some way to work this thing out. As I say, the whole business is a matter of *caring* about the other fellow. Anybody can see that you are a nice family of folks, hard working and honest I'm sure. (*Beneatha frowns slightly, quizzically, her head tilted regarding him.*) Today everybody knows what it means to be on the outside of *something*. And of course, there is always somebody who is out to take the advantage of people who don't always understand.

WALTER. What do you mean?

LINDNER. Well—you see our community is made up of people who've worked hard as the dickens for years to build up that little community. They're not rich and fancy people; just hard-working, honest people who don't really have much but those little homes and a dream of the kind of community they want to raise their children in. Now, I don't say we are perfect and there is a lot wrong in some of the things they want. But you've got to admit that a man, right or wrong, has the right to want to have the neighborhood he lives in a certain kind of way. And at the moment the overwhelming majority of our people out there feel that people get along better, take more of a common interest in the life of the community, when they share a common background. I want you to believe me when I tell you that race prejudice simply doesn't enter into it. It is a matter of the people of Clybourne Park believing, rightly or wrongly, as I say, that for the happiness of all concerned that our Negro families are happier when they live in their *own* communities.

BENEATHA (*With a grand and bitter gesture*). This, friends, is the Welcoming Committee!

WALTER (*Dumfounded, looking at Lindner*). Is this what you came marching all the way over here to tell us?

LINDNER. Well, now we've been having a fine conversation. I hope you'll hear me all the way through.

WALTER (*Tightly*). Go ahead, man.

LINDNER. You see—in the face of all things I have said, we are prepared to make your family a very generous offer . . .

BENEATHA. Thirty pieces and not a coin less!

WALTER. Yeah?

LINDNER (*Putting on his glasses and drawing a form out of the briefcase*). Our association is prepared, through the collective effort of our people, to buy the house from you at a financial gain to your family.

RUTH. Lord have mercy, ain't this the living gall!

WALTER. All right, you through?

LINDNER. Well, I want to give you the exact terms of the financial arrangement—

WALTER. We don't want to hear no exact terms of no arrangements. I want to know if you got any more to tell us 'bout getting together?

LINDNER (*Taking off his glasses*). Well—I don't suppose that you feel . . .

WALTER. Never mind how I feel—you got any more to say 'bout how people ought to sit down and talk to each other? . . . Get out of my house, man.

(*He turns his back and walks to the door.*)

LINDNER (*Looking around at the hostile faces and reaching and assembling his hat and briefcase*). Well—I don't understand why you people are reacting this way. What do you think you are going to gain by moving into a neighborhood where you just aren't wanted and where some elements—well—people can get awful worked up when they feel that their whole way of life and everything they've worked for is threatened.

WALTER. Get out.

LINDNER (*At the door, holding a small card*). Well—I'm sorry it went like this.

WALTER. Get out.

LINDNER (*Almost sadly regarding Walter*). You just can't force people to change their hearts, son.

(*He turns and puts his card on a table and exits. Walter pushes the door to with stinging hatred, and stands looking at it. Ruth just sits and Beneatha just stands. They say nothing. Mama and Travis enter.*)

MAMA. Well—this all the packing got done since I left out of here this morning. I testify before God that my children got all the energy of the dead. What time the moving men due?

BENEATHA. Four o'clock. You had a caller, Mama.

(*She is smiling, teasingly.*)

MAMA. Sure enough—who?

BENEATHA (*Her arms folded saucily*). The Welcoming Committee.

(*Walter and Ruth giggle.*)

MAMA (*Innocently*). Who?

BENEATHA. The Welcoming Committee. They said they're sure going to be glad to see you when you get there.

WALTER (*Devilishly*). Yes, they said they can't hardly wait to see your face.

(*Laughter*)

MAMA (*Sensing their facetiousness*). What's the matter with you all?

WALTER. Ain't nothing the matter with us. We just telling you 'bout the gentleman who came to see you this afternoon. From the Clybourne Park Improvement Association.

MAMA. What he want?

RUTH (*In the same mood as Beneatha and Walter*). To welcome you, honey.

WALTER. He said they can't hardly wait. He said the one thing they don't have, that they just *dying* to have out there is a fine family of colored people! (*To Ruth and Beneatha*) Ain't that right!

RUTH AND BENEATHA (*Mockingly*). Yeah! He left his card in case—

(*They indicate the card, and Mama picks it up and throws it on the floor—understanding and looking off as she draws*

her chair up to the table on which she has put her plant and some sticks and some cord.*)

MAMA. Father, give us strength. (*Knowingly—and without fun*) Did he threaten us?

BENEATHA. Oh—Mama—they don't do it like that any more. He talked Brotherhood. He said everybody ought learn how to sit down and hate each other with good Christian fellowship.

(*She and Walter shake hands to ridicule the remark.*)

MAMA (*Sadly*). Lord, protect us . . .

RUTH. You should hear the money those folks raised to buy the house from us. All we paid and then some.

BENEATHA. What they think we going to do—eat 'em?

RUTH. No, honey, marry 'em.

MAMA (*Shaking her head*). Lord, Lord, Lord . . .

RUTH. Well—that's the way the crackers crumble. Joke.

BENEATHA (*Laughingly noticing what her mother is doing*). Mama, what are you doing?

MAMA. Fixing my plant so it won't get hurt none on the way . . .

BENEATHA. Mama, you going to take *that* to the new house?

MAMA. Un-huh—

BENEATHA. That raggedy-looking old thing?

MAMA (*Stopping and looking at her*). It expresses *me*.

RUTH (*With delight, to Beneatha*). So there, Miss Thing!

(*Walter comes to Mama suddenly and bends down behind her and squeezes her in his arms with all his strength. She is overwhelmed by the suddenness of it and, though delighted, her manner is like that of Ruth with Travis.*)

MAMA. Look out now, boy! You make me mess up my thing here!

WALTER (*His face lit, he slips down on his knees beside her, his arms still about her*). Mama . . . you know what it means to climb up in the chariot?

MAMA (*Gruffly, very happy*). Get on away from me now . . .

RUTH (*Near the gift-wrapped package, trying to catch Walter's eye*). Psst—

WALTER. What the old song say, Mama . . .

RUTH. Walter—Now?

(*She is pointing at the package.*)

WALTER (*Speaking the lines, sweetly, playfully, in his mother's face*). I got wings
. . . you got wings . . .
All God's children got wings . . .

MAMA. Boy—get out of my face and do some work . . .

WALTER.
When I get to heaven gonna put on my wings,
Gonna fly all over God's heaven . . .

BENEATHA (*Teasingly, from across the room*). Everybody talking 'bout heaven ain't going there!

WALTER (*To Ruth, who is carrying the box across to them*). I don't know, you think we ought to give her that . . .

Seems to me she ain't been very appreciative around here.

MAMA (*Eying the box, which is obviously a gift*). What is that?

WALTER (*Taking it from Ruth and putting it on the table in front of Mama*). Well—what you all think. Should we give it to her?

RUTH. Oh—she was pretty good today.

MAMA. I'll good you—

(*She turns her eyes to the box again.*)

BENEATHA. Open it, Mama.

(*She stands up, looks at it, turns and looks at all of them, and then presses her hands together and does not open the package.*)

WALTER (*Sweetly*). Open it, Mama. It's for you. (*Mama looks in his eyes. It is the first present in her life without its being Christmas. Slowly she opens her package and lifts out, one by one, a brand-new sparkling set of gardening tools. Walter continues, prodding*) Ruth made up the note—read it . . .

MAMA (*Picking up the card and adjusting her glasses*). "To our own Mrs. Miniver—Love from Brother, Ruth and Beneatha." Ain't that lovely . . .

TRAVIS (*Tugging at his father's sleeve*). Daddy, can I give her mine now?

WALTER. All right, son. (*Travis flies to get his gift.*) Travis didn't want to go in with the rest of us, Mama. He got his own. (*Somewhat amused*) We don't know what it is . . .

TRAVIS (*Racing back in the room with a large hatbox and putting it in front of his grandmother*). Here!

MAMA. Lord have mercy, baby! You done gone and bought your grandmother a hat?

TRAVIS (*Very proud*). Open it!

(*She does and lifts out an elaborate, but very elaborate, wide gardening hat, and all the adults break up at the sight of it.*)

RUTH. Travis, honey, what is that?

TRAVIS (*Who thinks it is beautiful and appropriate*). It's a gardening hat! Like the ladies always have on in the magazines when they work in their gardens.

BENEATHA (*Giggling fiercely*). Travis—we were trying to make Mama Mrs. Miniver—not Scarlet O'Hara!

MAMA (*Indignantly*). What's the matter with you all! This here is a beautiful hat! (*Absurdly*) I always wanted me one just like it!

(*She pops it on her head to prove it to her grandson, and the hat is ludicrous and considerably oversized.*)

RUTH. Hot dog! Go, Mama!

WALTER (*Doubled over with laughter*). I'm sorry, Mama—but you look like you ready to go out and chop you some cotton sure enough!

(*They all laugh except Mama, out of deference to Travis' feelings.*)

MAMA (*Gathering the boy up to her*). Bless your heart—this is the prettiest hat I ever owned—(*Walter, Ruth and Beneatha chime in—noisily, festively and insincerely congratulating Travis on his gift*) What are we all standing around here for? We ain't finished packin' yet. Bennie, you ain't packed one book.

(*The bell rings.*)

BENEATHA. That couldn't be the movers . . . it's not hardly two good yet—

(*Beneatha goes into her room. Mama starts for door.*)

WALTER (*Turning, stiffening*). Wait—wait—I'll get it.

(*He stands and looks at the door.*)

MAMA. You expecting company, son?

WALTER (*Just looking at the door*). Yeah—yeah . . .

(*Mama looks at Ruth, and they exchange innocent and unfrightened glances.*)

MAMA (*Not understanding*). Well, let them in, son.

BENEATHA (*From her room*). We need some more string.

MAMA. Travis—you run to the hardware and get me some string cord.

(*Mama goes out and Walter turns and looks at Ruth. Travis goes to a dish for money.*)

RUTH. Why don't you answer the door, man?

WALTER (*Suddenly bounding across the floor to her*). 'Cause sometimes it hard to let the future begin! (*Stooping down in her face*)

I got wings!
You got wings!
All God's children got wings!

(*He crosses to the door and throws it open. Standing there is a very slight little man in a not too prosperous business suit and with haunted frightened eyes and a hat pulled down tightly, brim up, around his forehead. Travis passes between the men and exits. Walter leans deep in the man's face, still in his jubilance.*)

When I get to heaven gonna put on my wings,
Gonna fly all over God's heaven . . .

(*The little man just stares at him.*)

Heaven—

(*Suddenly he stops and looks past the little man into the empty hallway.*) Where's Willy, man?

BOBO. He ain't with me.

WALTER (*Not disturbed*). Oh—come on in. You know my wife.

BOBO (*Dumbly, taking off his hat*). Yes—h'you, Miss Ruth.

RUTH (*Quietly, a mood apart from her husband already, seeing Bobo*). Hello, Bobo.

WALTER. You right on time today . . . Right on time. That's

the way! (*He slaps Bobo on his back*) Sit down . . . lemme hear.

(*Ruth stands stiffly and quietly in back of them, as though somehow she senses death, her eyes fixed on her husband.*)

BOBO (*His frightened eyes on the floor, his hat in his hands*). Could I please get a drink of water, before I tell you about it, Walter Lee?

(*Walter does not take his eyes off the man. Ruth goes blindly to the tap and gets a glass of water and brings it to Bobo.*)

WALTER. There ain't nothing wrong, is there?

BOBO. Lemme tell you—

WALTER. Man—didn't nothing go wrong?

BOBO. Lemme tell you—Walter Lee. (*Looking at Ruth and talking to her more than to Walter*) You know how it was. I got to tell you how it was. I mean first I got to tell you how it was all the way . . . I mean about the money I put in, Walter Lee . . .

WALTER (*With taut agitation now*). What about the money you put in?

BOBO. Well—it wasn't much as we told you—me and Willy—(*He stops.*) I'm sorry, Walter. I got a bad feeling about it. I got a bad feeling about it . . .

WALTER. Man, what you telling me about all this for? . . . Tell me what happened in Springfield.

RUTH (*Like a dead woman*). What was supposed to happen in Springfield?

BOBO (*To her*). This deal that me and Walter went into with Willy—Me and Willy was going to go down to Springfield and spread some money 'round so's we wouldn't have to wait so long for the liquor license . . . That's what we were going to do. Everybody said that was the way you had to do, you understand, Miss Ruth?

WALTER. Man—what happened down there?

BOBO (*A pitiful man, near tears*). I'm trying to tell you, Walter.

WALTER (*Screaming at him suddenly*). THEN TELL ME, GODDAMNIT . . . WHAT'S THE MATTER WITH YOU?

BOBO. Man . . . I didn't go to no Springfield, yesterday.

WALTER (*Halted, life hanging in the moment*). Why not?

BOBO (*The long way, the hard way to tell*). 'Cause I didn't have no reasons to . . .

WALTER. Man, what are you talking about!

BOBO. I'm talking about the fact that when I got to the train station yesterday morning—eight o'clock like we planned . . . Man—Willy didn't never show up.

WALTER. Why . . . where was he . . . where is he?

BOBO. That's what I'm trying to tell you . . . I don't know . . . I waited six hours . . . I called his house . . . and I waited . . . six hours . . I waited in that train station six hours . . . (*Breaking into tears*) That was all the extra money I had in the world . . . (*Looking up at Walter with the tears running down his face*) Man, Willy is gone.

WALTER. Gone, what you mean Willy is gone? Gone where? You mean he went by himself. You mean he went off to Springfield by himself—to take care of getting the license—(*Turns and looks anxiously at Ruth*) You mean maybe he didn't want too many people in on the business down there? (*Looks to Ruth again, as before*) You know Willy got his own ways. (*Looks back to Bobo*) Maybe you was late yesterday and he just went on down there without you. Maybe—maybe—he's been callin' you at home tryin' to tell you what happened or something. Maybe—maybe—he just got sick. He's somewhere—he's got to be somewhere. We just go to find him—me and you got to find him. (*Grabs Bobo senselessly by the collar and starts to shake him.*) We got to!

BOBO (*In sudden angry, frightened agony*). What's the matter with you, Walter! When a cat take off with your money he don't leave no maps!

WALTER (*Turning madly, as though he is looking for Willy in the very room*). Willy! . . . Willy . . . don't do it . . . Please don't do it . . . Man, not with that money . . . Man, please, not with that money . . . Oh, God . . . Don't let it be true . . . (*He is wandering around, crying out for Willy and looking for him or perhaps for help from God.*) Man . . . I trusted you . . . Man, I put my life in your hands . . . (*He starts to crumple down on the floor as Ruth just covers her face in horror. Mama opens the door and comes into the room, with Beneatha behind her.*) Man . . . (*He starts to pound the floor with his fists, sobbing wildly.*) That money is made out of my father's flesh . . .

BOBO (*Standing over him helplessly*). I'm sorry, Walter . . . (*Only Walter's sobs reply. Bobo puts on his hat.*) I had my life staked on this deal, too . . .

(*He exits*)

MAMA (*To Walter*). Son— (*She goes to him, bends down to him, talks to his bent head*) Son . . . Is it gone? Son, I gave you sixty-five hundred dollars. Is it gone? All of it? Beneatha's money too?

WALTER (*Lifting his head slowly*). Mama . . . I never . . . went to the bank at all . . .

MAMA (*Not wanting to believe him*). You mean . . . your sister's school money . . . you used that too . . . Walter? . . .

WALTER. Yessss! . . . All of it . . . It's all gone . . .

(*There is total silence. Ruth stands with her face covered with her hands; Beneatha leans forlornly against a wall, fingering a piece of red ribbon from the mother's gift. Mama stops and looks at her son without recognition and then, quite without thinking about it, starts to beat him senselessly in the face. Beneatha goes to them and stops it.*)

BENEATHA. Mama!

(*Mama stops and looks at both of her children and rises slowly and wanders vaguely, aimlessly away from them.*)

MAMA. I seen . . . him . . . night after night . . . come in . . .

and look at that rug . . . and then look at me . . . the red showing in his eyes . . . the veins moving in his head . . . I seen him grow thin and old before he was forty . . . working and working and working like somebody's old horse . . . killing himself . . . and you—you give it all away in a day . . .

BENEATHA. Mama—

MAMA. Oh, God . . . (*She looks up to Him.*) Look down here—and show me the strength.

BENEATHA. Mama—

MAMA (*Folding over*). Strength . . .

BENEATHA (*Plaintively*). Mama . . .

MAMA. Strength!

CURTAIN

ACT THREE

An hour later.

    At curtain, there is a sullen light of gloom in the living room, gray light not unlike that which began the first scene of Act One. At left we can see Walter within his room, alone with himself. He is stretched out on the bed, his shirt out and open, his arms under his head. He does not smoke, he does not cry out, he merely lies there, looking up at the ceiling, much as if he were alone in the world.

    In the living room Beneatha sits at the table, still surrounded by the now almost ominous packing crates. She sits looking off. We feel that this is a mood struck perhaps an hour before, and it lingers now, full of the empty sound of profound disappointment. We see on a line from her brother's bedroom the sameness of their attitudes. Presently the bell rings and Beneatha rises without ambition or interest in answering. It is Asagai, smiling broadly, striding into the room with energy and happy expectation and conversation.

ASAGAI. I came over . . . I had some free time. I thought I might help with the packing. Ah, I like the look of packing crates. A household in preparation for a journey. It depresses some people . . . but for me . . . it is another feeling. Something full of the flow of life, do you understand? Movement, progress . . . It makes me think of Africa.

BENEATHA. Africa!

ASAGAI. What kind of a mood is this? Have I told you how deeply you move me?

BENEATHA. He gave away the money, Asagai . . .

ASAGAI. Who gave away what money?

BENEATHA. The insurance money. My brother gave it away.

ASAGAI. Gave it away?

BENEATHA. He made an investment! With a man even Travis wouldn't have trusted.

ASAGAI. And it's gone?

BENEATHA. Gone!

ASAGAI. I'm very sorry . . . And you, now?

BENEATHA. Me? . . . Me? . . . Me I'm nothing . . . Me. When I was very small . . . we used to take our sleds out in the wintertime and the only hills we had were the ice-covered stone steps of some houses down the street. And we used to fill them in with snow and make them smooth and slide down them all day . . . and it was very dangerous you know . . . far too steep . . . and sure enough one day a kid named Rufus came down too fast and hit the sidewalk . . . and we saw his face just split open right there in front of us . . . And I remember standing there looking at his bloody open face thinking that was the end of Rufus. But the ambulance came and they took him to the hospital and they fixed the broken bones and they sewed it all up . . . and the next time I saw Rufus he just had a little line down the middle of his face . . . I never got over that . . .

ASAGAI. What?

BENEATHA. That that was what one person could do for another, fix him up—sew up the problem, make him all right again. That was the most marvelous thing in the world . . . I wanted to do that. I always thought it was the one concrete thing in the world that a human being could do. Fix up the sick, you know—and make them whole again. This was truly being God . . .

ASAGAI. You wanted to be God?

BENEATHA. No—I wanted to cure. It used to be so important to me. I wanted to cure. It used to matter. I used to care. I mean about people and how their bodies hurt . . .

ASAGAI. And you've stopped caring?

BENEATHA. Yes—I think so.

ASAGAI. Why?

BENEATHA. Because it doesn't seem deep enough, close enough to the truth.

ASAGAI. Truth? Why is it that you despairing ones always think that only you have the truth? I never thought to see *you* like that. You! Your brother made a stupid, childish mistake—and you are grateful to him. So that now you can give up the ailing human race on account of it. You talk about what good is struggle; what good is anything? Where are we all going? And why are we bothering?

BENEATHA. *And you cannot answer it!* All your talk and dreams about Africa and Independence. Independence and then what? What about all the crooks and petty thieves and just plain idiots who will come into power to steal and plunder the same as before—only now they will be black and do it in the name of the new Independence—You cannot answer that.

ASAGAI (*Shouting over her*). *I live the answer!* (*Pause*) In my village at home it is the exceptional man who can even read a newspaper . . . or who ever *sees* a book at all. I will go home and much of what I will have to say will seem strange to the people of my village . . . But I will teach and work and things will happen, slowly and swiftly. At times it will seem that nothing changes at all . . . and then again . . . the sudden dramatic events which make history leap into the future. And then quiet again. Retrogression even. Guns, murder, revolution. And I even will have moments when I wonder if the quiet was not better than all that death and hatred. But I will look about my village at the illiteracy and disease and ignorance and I will not wonder long. And perhaps . . . perhaps I will be a great man . . . I mean perhaps I will hold on to the substance of truth and find my way always with the right course . . . and perhaps for it I will be butchered in my bed some night by the servants of empire . . .

BENEATHA. *The martyr!*

ASAGAI. . . . or perhaps I shall live to be a very old man respected and esteemed in my new nation . . . And perhaps I shall hold office and this is what I'm trying to tell you, Alaiyo; perhaps the things I believe now for my country will be wrong and outmoded, and I will not understand and do terrible things to have things my way or merely to keep my power. Don't you see that there will be young men and women, not British soldiers then, but my own black countrymen . . . to step out of the shadows some evening and slit my then useless throat? Don't you see they have always been there . . . that they always will be. And that such a thing as my own death will be an advance? They who might kill me even . . . actually replenish me!

BENEATHA. Oh, Asagai, I know all that.

ASAGAI. Good! Then stop moaning and groaning and tell me what you plan to do.

BENEATHA. Do?

ASAGAI. I have a bit of a suggestion.

BENEATHA. What?

ASAGAI (*Rather quietly for him*). That when it is all over—that you come home with me—

BENEATHA (*Slapping herself on the forehead with exasperation born of misunderstanding*). Oh—Asagai—at this moment you decide to be romantic!

ASAGAI (*Quickly understanding the misunderstanding*). My dear, young creature of the New World—I do not mean across the city—I mean across the ocean; home—to Africa.

BENEATHA (*Slowly understanding and turning to him with murmured amazement*). To—to Nigeria?

ASAGAI. Yes! . . . (*Smiling and lifting his arms playfully*) Three hundred years later the African Prince rose up out of the seas and swept the maiden back across the middle passage over which her ancestors had come—

BENEATHA (*Unable to play*). Nigeria?

ASAGAI. Nigeria. Home. (*Coming to her with genuine romantic flippancy*) I will show you our mountains and our stars; and give you cool drinks from gourds and teach you the old songs and the ways of our people—and, in time, we will pretend that— (*Very softly*) —you have only been away for a day—

(*She turns her back to him, thinking. He swings her around and takes her full in his arms in a long embrace which proceeds to passion.*)

BENEATHA (*Pulling away*). You're getting me all mixed up—

ASAGAI. Why?

BENEATHA. Too many things—too many things have happened today. I must sit down and think. I don't know what I feel about anything right this minute.

(*She promptly sits down and props her chin on her fist.*)

ASAGAI (*Charmed*). All right, I shall leave you. No—don't get up. (*Touching her, gently, sweetly*) Just sit awhile and think . . . Never be afraid to sit awhile and think. (*He goes to door and looks at her*) How often I have looked at you and said, "Ah—so this is what the New World hath finally wrought . . ."

(*He exits. Beneatha sits on alone. Presently Walter enters from his room and starts to rummage through things, feverishly looking for something. She looks up and turns in her seat.*)

BENEATHA (*Hissingly*). Yes—just look at what the New World hath wrought! . . . Just look! (*She gestures with bitter disgust*) There he is! *Monsieur le petit bourgeois noir*—himself! There he is—Symbol of a Rising Class! Entrepreneur! Titan of the system! (*Walter ignores her completely and continues frantically and destructively looking for something and hurling things to floor and tearing things out of their place in his search. Beneatha ignores the eccentricity of his actions and goes on with the monologue of insult.*) Did you dream of yachts on Lake Michigan, Brother? Did you see yourself on that Great Day sitting down at the Conference Table, surrounded by all the mighty bald-headed men in America? All halted, waiting, breathless, waiting for your pronouncements on industry? Waiting for you—Chairman of the Board? (*Walter finds what he is looking for—a small piece of white paper—and pushes it in his pocket and puts on his coat and rushes out without ever having looked at her. She shouts after him*) I look at you and I see the final triumph of stupidity in the world!

(*The door slams and she returns to just sitting again. Ruth comes quickly out of Mama's room.*)

RUTH. Who was that?

BENEATHA. Your husband.

RUTH. Where did he go?

BENEATHA. Who knows—maybe he has an appointment at U. S. Steel.

RUTH (*Anxiously, with frightened eyes*). You didn't say nothing bad to him, did you?

BENEATHA. Bad? Say anything bad to him? No—I told him he was a sweet boy and full of dreams and everything is strictly peachy keen, as the ofay kids say!

(*Mama enters from her bedroom. She is lost, vague, trying to catch hold, to make some sense of her former command of the world, but it still eludes her. A sense of waste overwhelms her gait; a measure of apology rides on her shoulders. She goes to her plant, which has remained on the table, looks at it, picks it up and takes it to the window sill and sits it outside, and she stands and looks at it a long moment. Then she closes the window, straightens her body with effort and turns around to her children.*)

MAMA. Well—ain't it a mess in here, though? (*A false cheerfulness, a beginning of something*) I guess we all better stop moping around and get some work done. All this unpacking and everything we got to do. (*Ruth raises her head slowly in response to the sense of the line; and Beneatha in similar manner turns very slowly to look at her mother.*) One of you all better call the moving people and tell 'em not to come.

RUTH. Tell 'em not to come?

MAMA. Of course, baby. Ain't no need in 'em coming all the way here and having to go back. They charges for that too. (*She sits down, fingers to her brow, thinking*) Lord, ever since I was a little girl, I always remembers people saying, "Lena—Lena Eggleston, you aims too high all the time. You needs to slow down and see life a little more like it is. Just slow down some." That's what they always used to say down home—"Lord, that Lena Eggleston is a high-minded thing. She'll get her due one day!"

RUTH. No, Lena . . .

MAMA. Me and Big Walter just didn't never learn right.

RUTH. Lena, no! We gotta go. Bennie—tell her . . . (*She rises and crosses to Beneatha with her arms outstretched. Beneatha doesn't respond*) Tell her we can still move . . . the notes ain't but a hundred and twenty five a month. We got four grown people in this house—we can work . . .

MAMA (*To herself*). Just aimed too high all the time—

RUTH (*Turning and going to Mama fast—the words pouring out with urgency and desperation*). Lena—I'll work . . . I'll work twenty hours a day in all the kitchens in Chicago . . . I'll strap my baby on my back if I have to and scrub all the floors in America and wash all the sheets in America if I have to—but we got to move . . . We got to get out of here . . .

(*Mama reaches out absently and pats Ruth's hand.*)

MAMA. No—I sees things differently now. Been thinking 'bout some of the things we could do to fix this place up some. I seen a second-hand bureau over on Maxwell Street just the other day that could fit right there. (*She points to where the new furniture might go. Ruth wanders away from her.*) Would need some new handles on it and then a little varnish and then it look like something brand-new. And—we can put up them new curtains in the kitchen . . . Why this place be looking fine. Cheer us all up so that we forget trouble ever came (*To Ruth*) And you could get some nice screens to put up in your room round the baby's bassinet . . . (*She looks at both of them, pleadingly.*) Sometimes you just got to know when to give up some things . . . and hold on to what you got.

(*Walter enters from the outside, looking spent and leaning against the door, his coat hanging from him.*)

MAMA. Where you been, son?

WALTER (*Breathing hard*). Made a call.

MAMA. To who, son?

WALTER. To the Man.

MAMA. What man, baby?

WALTER. The Man, Mama. Don't you know who The Man is?

RUTH. Walter Lee?

WALTER. *The Man.* Like the guys in the street say—The Man. Captain Boss—Mistuh Charley . . . Old Captain Please Mr. Bossman . . .

BENEATHA (*Suddenly*). Lindner!

WALTER. That's right! That's good. I told him to come right over.

BENEATHA (*Fiercely, understanding*). For what? What do you want to see him for!

WALTER (*Looking at his sister*). We going to do business with him.

MAMA. What you talking 'bout, son?

WALTER. Talking 'bout life, Mama. You all always telling me to see life like it is. Well—I laid in there on my back today . . . and I figured it out. Life just like it is. Who gets and who don't get. (*He sits down with his coat on and laughs.*) Mama, you know it's all divided up. Life is. Sure enough. Between the takers and the "tooken." (*He laughs.*) I've figured it out finally. (*He looks around at them.*) Yeah. Some of us always getting "tooken." (*He laughs.*) People like Willy Harris, they don't never get "tooken." And you know why the rest of us do? 'Cause we all mixed up. Mixed up bad. We get to looking 'round for the right and the wrong; and we worry about it and cry about it and stay up nights trying to figure out 'bout the wrong and the right of things all the time . . . And all the time, man, them takers is out there operating, just taking and taking. Willy Harris? Shoot—Willy Harris don't even count. He don't even count in the big scheme of things. But I'll say one thing for old Willy Harris . . . he's taught me something. He's taught me to keep my eyes on what counts in this world. Yeah— (*Shouting out a little*) Thanks, Willy!

RUTH. What did you call that man for, Walter Lee?

WALTER. Called him to tell him to come on over to the show. Gonna put on a show for the man. Just what he wants to see. You see, Mama, the man came here today and he told us that them people out there where you want us to move—well they so upset they willing to pay us not to move out there. (*He laughs again.*) And—and oh, Mama—you would of been proud of the way me and Ruth and Bennie acted. We told him to get out . . . Lord have mercy! We told the man to get out. Oh, we was some proud folks this afternoon, yeah. (*He lights a cigarette.*) We were still full of that old-time stuff . . .

RUTH (*Coming toward him slowly*). You talking 'bout taking them people's money to keep us from moving in that house?

WALTER. I ain't just talking 'bout it, baby—I'm telling you that's what's going to happen.

BENEATHA. Oh, God! Where is the bottom! Where is the real honest-to-God bottom so he can't go any farther!

WALTER. See—that's the old stuff. You and that boy that was here today. You all want everybody to carry a flag and a spear and sing some marching songs, huh? You wanna spend your life looking into things and trying to find the right and the wrong part, huh? Yeah. You know what's going to happen to that boy someday—he'll find himself sitting in a dungeon, locked in forever—and the takers will have the key! Forget it, baby! There ain't no causes—there ain't nothing but taking in this world, and he who takes most is smartest—and it don't make a damn bit of difference *how*.

MAMA. You making something inside me cry, son. Some awful pain inside me.

WALTER. Don't cry, Mama. Understand. That white man is going to walk in that door able to write checks for more money than we ever had. It's important to him and I'm going to help him ... I'm going to put on the show, Mama.

MAMA. Son—I come from five generations of people who was slaves and sharecroppers—but it ain't nobody in my family never let nobody pay 'em no money that was a way of telling us we wasn't fit to walk the earth. We ain't never been that poor. (*Raising her eyes and looking at him.*) We ain't never been that dead inside.

BENEATHA. Well—we are dead now. All the talk about dreams and sunlight that goes on in this house. All dead.

WALTER. What's the matter with you all! I didn't make this world! It was give to me this way! Hell, yes, I want me some yachts someday! Yes, I want to hang some real pearls 'round my wife's neck. Ain't she supposed to wear no pearls? Somebody tell me—tell me, who decides which women is suppose to wear pearls in this world. I tell you I am a *man*—and I think my wife should wear some pearls in this world!

(*This last line hangs a good while and Walter begins to move about the room. The word "Man" has penetrated his consciousness; he mumbles it to himself repeatedly between strange agitated pauses as he moves about.*)

MAMA. Baby, how you going to feel on the inside?

WALTER. Fine! ... Going to feel fine ... a man ...

MAMA. You won't have nothing left then, Walter Lee.

WALTER (*Coming to her*). I'm going to feel fine, Mama. I'm going to look that son-of-a-bitch in the eyes and say—(*He falters*)—and say, "All right, Mr. Lindner—(*He falters even more.*)—that's your neighborhood out there. You got the right to keep it like you want. You got the right to have it like you want. Just write the check and—the house is yours." And, and I am going to say— (*His voice almost breaks.*) And you—you people just put the money in my hand and you won't have to live next to this bunch of stinking niggers! ... (*He straightens up and moves away from his mother, walking around the room.*) Maybe—maybe I'll just get down on my black knees ... (*He does so; Ruth and Bennie and Mama watch him in frozen horror.*) Captain,

Mistuh, Bossman. (*He starts crying.*) A-hee-hee-hee! (*Wringing his hands in profoundly anguished imitation*) Yasssssuh! Great White Father, just gi' ussen de money, fo' God's sake, and we's ain't gwine come out deh and dirty up yo' white folks neighborhood ...

(*He breaks down completely, then gets up and goes into the bedroom.*)

BENEATHA. That is not a man. That is nothing but a toothless rat.

MAMA. Yes—death done come in this here house. (*She is nodding slowly, reflectively.*) Done come walking in my house. On the lips of my children. You what supposed to be my beginning again. You—what supposed to be my harvest. (*To Beneatha*) You—you mourning your brother?

BENEATHA. He's no brother of mine.

MAMA. What you say?

BENEATHA. I said that that individual in that room is no brother of mine.

MAMA. That's what I thought you said. You feeling like you better than he is today? (*Beneatha does not answer.*) Yes? What you tell him a minute ago? That he wasn't a man? Yes? You give him up for me? You done wrote his epitaph too—like the rest of the world? Well, who give you the privilege?

BENEATHA. Be on my side for once! You saw what he just did, Mama! You saw him—down on his knees. Wasn't it you who taught me—to despise any man who would do that. Do what he's going to do.

MAMA. Yes—I taught you that. Me and your daddy. But I thought I taught you something else too ... I thought I taught you to love him.

BENEATHA. Love him? There is nothing left to love.

MAMA. There is always something left to love. And if you ain't learned that, you ain't learned nothing. (*Looking at her*) Have you cried for that boy today? I don't mean for yourself and for the family 'cause we lost the money. I mean for him; what he been through and what it done to him. Child, when do you think is the time to love somebody the most; when they done good and made things easy for everybody? Well then, you ain't learning—because that ain't the time at all. It's when he's at his lowest and can't believe in hisself 'cause the world done whipped him so. When you starts measuring somebody, measure him right, child, measure him right. Make sure you done taken into account what hills and valleys he come through before he got to wherever he is.

(*Travis bursts into the room at the end of the speech, leaving the door open.*)

TRAVIS. Grandmama—the moving men are downstairs! The truck just pulled up.

MAMA (*Turning and looking at him*). Are they baby? They downstairs?

(*She sighs and sits. Lindner appears in the doorway. He peers in and knocks lightly, to gain attention, and comes in. All turn to look at him.*)

LINDNER (*Hat and briefcase in hand*). Uh—hello . . .

(*Ruth crosses mechanically to the bedroom door and opens it and lets it swing open freely and slowly as the lights come up on Walter within, still in his coat, sitting at the far corner of the room. He looks up and out through the room to Lindner.*)

RUTH. He's here.

(*A long minute passes and Walter slowly gets up.*)

LINDNER (*Coming to the table with efficiency, putting his briefcase on the table and starting to unfold the papers and unscrew fountain pens*). Well, I certainly was glad to hear from you people. (*Walter has begun the trek out of the room, slowly and awkwardly, rather like a small boy, passing the back of his sleeve across the back of his mouth from time to time.*) Life can really be so much simpler than people let it be most of the time. Well—with whom do I negotiate? You, Mrs. Younger, or your son here? (*Mama sits with her hands folded on her lap and her eyes closed as Walter advances. Travis goes close to Lindner and looks at the papers curiously.*) Just some official papers, sonny.

RUTH. Travis, you go downstairs.

MAMA (*Opening her eyes and looking into Walter's*). No. Travis, you stay right here. And you make him understand what you doing, Walter Lee. You teach him good. Like Willy Harris taught you. You show where our five generations done come to. Go ahead, son—

WALTER (*Looks down into his boy's eyes. Travis grins at him merrily and Walter draws him beside him with his arm lightly around his shoulder*). Well, Mr. Lindner. (*Beneatha turns away.*) We called you—(*There is a profound, simple groping quality in his speech.*) —because, well, me and my family (*He looks around and shifts from one foot to the other.*) Well—we are very plain people . . .

LINDNER. Yes—

WALTER. I mean—I have worked as a chauffeur most of my life—and my wife here, she does domestic work in people's kitchens. So does my mother. I mean—we are plain people . . .

LINDNER. Yes, Mr. Younger—

WALTER (*Really like a small boy, looking down at his shoes and then up at the man*). And—uh—well, my father, well, he was a laborer most of his life.

LINDNER (*Absolutely confused*). Uh, yes—

WALTER (*Looking down at his toes once again*). My father almost beat a man to death once because this man called him a bad name or something, you know what I mean?

LINDNER. No, I'm afraid I don't.

WALTER (*Finally straightening up*). Well, what I mean is that we come from people who had a lot of pride. I mean—we

are very proud people. And that's my sister over there and she's going to be a doctor—and we are very proud—

LINDNER. Well—I am sure that is very nice, but—

WALTER (*Starting to cry and facing the man eye to eye*). What I am telling you is that we called you over here to tell you that we are very proud and that this is—this is my son, who makes the sixth generation of our family in this country, and that we have all thought about your offer and we have decided to move into our house because my father—my father—he earned it. (*Mama has her eyes closed and is rocking back and forth as though she were in church, with her head nodding the amen yes.*) We don't want to make no trouble for nobody or fight no causes—but we will try to be good neighbors. That's all we got to say. (*He looks the man absolutely in the eyes*) We don't want your money.

(*He turns and walks away from the man.*)

LINDNER (*Looking around at all of them*). I take it then that you have decided to occupy.

BENEATHA. That's what the man said.

LINDNER (*To Mama in her reverie*). Then I would like to appeal to you, Mrs. Younger. You are older and wiser and understand things better I am sure . . .

MAMA (*Rising*). I am afraid you don't understand. My son said we was going to move and there ain't nothing left for me to say. (*Shaking her head with double meaning*) You know how these young folks is nowadays, mister. Can't do a thing with 'em. Good-bye.

LINDNER (*Folding up his materials*). Well—if you are that final about it . . . There is nothing left for me to say. (*He finishes. He is almost ignored by the family, who are concentrating on Walter Lee. At the door Lindner halts and looks around*) I sure hope you people know what you're doing.

(*He shakes his head and exits.*)

RUTH (*Looking around and coming to life*). Well, for God's sake—if the moving men are here—LET'S GET THE HELL OUT OF HERE!

MAMA (*Into action*). Ain't it the truth! Look at all this here mess. Ruth put Travis' good jacket on him . . . Walter Lee, fix your tie and tuck your shirt in, you look just like somebody's hoodlum. Lord have mercy, where is my plant? (*She flies to get it amid the general bustling of the family, who are deliberately trying to ignore the nobility of the past moment.*) You all start on down . . . Travis child, don't go empty-handed . . . Ruth, where did I put that box with my skillets in it? I want to be in charge of it myself . . . I'm going to make us the biggest dinner we ever ate tonight . . . Beneatha, what's the matter with them stockings? Pull them things up, girl . . .

(*The family starts to file out as two moving men appear and begin to carry out the heavier pieces of furniture, bumping into the family as they move about.*)

BENEATHA. Mama, Asagai—asked me to marry him today and go to Africa—

MAMA (*In the middle of her getting-ready activity*). He did? You ain't old enough to marry nobody—(*Seeing the moving men lifting one of her chairs precariously*) Darling, that ain't no bale of cotton, please handle it so we can sit in it again. I had that chair twenty-five years . . .

(*The movers sigh with exasperation and go on with their work.*)

BENEATHA (*Girlishly and unreasonably trying to pursue the conversation*). To go to Africa, Mama—be a doctor in Africa . . .

MAMA (*Distracted*). Yes, baby—

WALTER. Africa! What he want you to go to Africa for?

BENEATHA. To practice there . . .

WALTER. Girl, if you don't get all them silly ideas out of your head! You better marry yourself a man with some loot . . .

BENEATHA (*Angrily, precisely as in the first scene of the play*). What have you got to do with who I marry!

WALTER. Plenty. Now I think George Murchison—

(*He and Beneatha go out yelling at each other vigorously; Beneatha is heard saying that she would not marry George Murchison if he were Adam and she were Eve, etc. The anger is loud and real till their voices diminish. Ruth stands at the door and turns to Mama and smiles knowingly.*)

MAMA (*Fixing her hat at last*). Yeah—they something all right, my children . . .

RUTH. Yeah—they're something. Let's go, Lena.

MAMA (*Stalling, starting to look around at the house*). Yes—I'm coming. Ruth—

RUTH. Yes?

MAMA (*Quietly, woman to woman*). He finally come into his manhood today, didn't he? Kind of like a rainbow after the rain . . .

RUTH (*Biting her lip lest her own pride explode in front of Mama*). Yes, Lena.

(*Walter's voice calls for them raucously.*)

MAMA (*Waving Ruth out vaguely*). All right honey—go on down. I be down directly.

(*Ruth hesitates, then exits. Mama stands, at last alone in the living room, her plant on the table before her as the lights start to come down. She looks around at all the walls and ceilings and suddenly, despite herself, while the children call below, a great heaving thing rises in her and she puts her fist to her mouth, takes a final desperate look, pulls her coat about her, pats her hat and goes out. The lights dim down. The door opens and she comes back in, grabs her plant, and goes out for the last time.*)

CURTAIN

"THE LAST MAMA-ON-THE-COUCH PLAY"

from *The Colored Museum*

GEORGE C. WOLFE

GEORGE C. WOLFE (1954-)

In less than a decade George C. Wolfe emerged as one of the most influential and respected artists in the American theater. As playwright, director, acting teacher, and producer, Wolfe has enjoyed success at all levels. He has won an OBIE for his playwriting (*The Colored Museum*, 1986), and Tony Awards for his direction of Tony Kushner's enormously successful *Angels in America: Millennium Approaches*, his own *Jelly's Last Jam*, and the 1996 dance-musical hit *Bring in da Noise, Bring in da Funk*. He was named the artistic director–producer of the New York Shakespeare Festival Public Theater in 1993.

Wolfe was reared in Kentucky and received his undergraduate degree in theater from Pomona College in California. After teaching theater and acting at City College of New York for a short time, Wolfe enrolled in the graduate musical theater program at NYU, where he received a master of fine arts degree. Stephen Sondheim, America's foremost composer of Broadway musicals, praised Wolfe's abilities and encouraged him to write musicals. He worked with Duke Ellington on *Queenie Pie* (1987), and then created the successful *Jelly's Last Jam* (1992), based on the life of the great jazz musician Jelly Roll Morton.

His best-known work remains *The Colored Museum*, a collection of eleven satirical vignettes that challenge racial stereotypes. "The Last Mama-on-the-Couch Play" parodies *A Raisin in the Sun* and is offered here as a critique of Hansberry's play from the perspective of a post-60's African American.

"THE LAST MAMA-ON-THE-COUCH PLAY"

GEORGE C. WOLFE

(A Narrator, dressed in a black tuxedo, enters through the audience and stands center stage. He is totally solemn.)

NARRATOR. We are pleased to bring you yet another Mama-on-the-Couch play. A searing domestic drama that tears at the very fabric of racist America. (He crosses upstage center and sits on a stool and reads from a playscript.) Act One, Scene One.

(Mama revolves on stage left, sitting on a couch reading a large, oversized Bible. A window is placed stage right. Mama's dress, the couch, and drapes are made from the same material. A doormat lays down center.)

NARRATOR. Lights up on a dreary, depressing, but with middle-class aspirations tenement slum. There is a couch, with a Mama on it. Both are well worn. There is a picture of Jesus on the wall . . . (A picture of Jesus is instantly revealed.) . . . and a window which looks onto an abandoned tenement. It is late spring.

Enter Walter-Lee-Beau-Willie-Jones. (Son enters through the audience.) He is Mama's thirty-year-old son. His brow is heavy from three hundred years of oppression.

MAMA. (Looking up from her Bible, speaking in a slow manner) Son, did you wipe your feet?

SON. (An ever-erupting volcano). No, Mama, I didn't wipe me feet! Out there, every day, Mama, is the Man. The Man, Mama. Mr. Charlie! Mr. Bossman! And he's wipin' his feet on me. On me, Mama, every damn day of my life. Ain't that enough for me to deal with? Ain't that enough?

MAMA. Son, wipe your feet.

SON. I wanna dream. I wanna be somebody. I wanna take charge of my life.

MAMA. You can do all of that, but first you got to wipe your feet.

SON. (As he crosses to the mat, mumbling and wiping his feet). Wipe my feet . . . wipe my feet . . . wipe my feet . . .

MAMA. That's a good boy.

SON. (Exploding) Boy! Boy! I don't wanna be nobody's good boy, Mama. I wanna be my own man!

MAMA. I know son, I know. God will show the way.

SON. God, Mama! Since when did your God ever do a damn thing for the black man. Huh, Mama, huh? You tell me. When did your God ever help me.

MAMA. (Removing her wire-rim glasses.) Son, come here.

(Son crosses to Mama, who slowly stands and in an exaggerated stage slap, backhands Son clear across the stage. The Narrator claps his hands to create the sound for the slap. Mama then lifts her clenched fists to the heavens.)

MAMA. Not in my house, my house, will you ever talk that way again!

(The Narrator, so moved by her performance, erupts in applause and encourages the audience to do so.)

NARRATOR. Beautiful. Just stunning.

(He reaches into one of the secret compartments of the set and gets an award which he ceremoniously gives to Mama for her performance. She bows and then returns to the couch.)

NARRATOR. Enter Walter-Lee-Beau-Willie's wife, The Lady in Plaid.

(Music from nowhere is heard, a jazzy pseudo-abstract intro as the Lady in Plaid dances in through the audience, wipes her feet, and then twirls about.)

LADY.
She was a creature of regal beauty
who in ancient time graced the temples
of the Nile
with her womanliness
But here she was, stuck being colored
and a woman in a world that valued
neither.

SON. You cooked my dinner?

LADY: (Oblivious to Son.)
Feet flat, back broke,
she looked at the man who, though he be
thirty,
still ain't got his own apartment.
Yeah, he's still livin' with his Mama!
And she asked herself, was this the life
for a Princess Colored, who by the
translucence of her skin, knew the
universe was her sister.

(The Lady in Plaid twirls and dances.)

SON. (Becoming irate.) I've had a hard day of dealin' with the Man. Where's my damn dinner? Woman, stand still when I'm talkin' to you!

LADY. And she cried for her sisters in Detroit

Who knew, as she, that their souls
belonged
in ancient temples on the Nile.
And she cried for her sisters in Chicago
who, like her, their life has become
one colored hell.

SON. There's only one thing gonna get through to you.

LADY. And she cried for her sisters in New Orleans
And her sisters in Trenton and
Birmingham,
and
Poughkeepsie and Orlando and Miami
Beach
and
Las Vegas, Palm Springs.

(*As she continues to call out cities, he crosses offstage and returns with two black dolls and then crosses to the window.*)

SON. Now are you gonna cook me dinner?

LADY. Walter-Lee-Beau-Willie-Jones, No! Not my babies.

(*Son throws them out the window. The Lady in Plaid then lets out a primal scream.*)

LADY. He dropped them!!!!

(*The Narrator breaks into applause.*)

NARRATOR. Just splendid. Shattering.

(*He then crosses and after an intense struggle with Mama, he takes the award from her and gives it to the Lady in Plaid, who is still suffering primal pain.*)

LADY. Not my babies . . . not my . . . (*Upon receiving the award, she instantly recovers.*) Help me up, sugar. (*She then bows and crosses and stands behind the couch.*)

NARRATOR. Enter Medea Jones, Walter-Lee-Beau-Willie's sister.

(*Medea moves very ceremoniously, wiping her feet and then speaking and gesturing as if she just escaped from a Greek tragedy.*)

MEDEA.
Ah, see how the sun kneels to speak
her evening vespers, exulting all
in her vision, even lowly tenement
long abandoned.

Mother, wife of brother, I trust
the approaching darkness finds you
safe in Hestia's busom.

Brother, why wear the face of a man
in anguish. Can the garment of thine
feelings cause the shape of your
countenance to disfigure so?

SON. (*At the end of his rope.*) Leave me alone, Medea.

MEDEA. (*To Mama*).
Is good brother still going on
and on and on
about He and The Man.

MAMA-LADY: What else?

MEDEA. Ah brother, if with our thoughts and
words we could cast thine oppressors
into the lowest bowels of wretched
hell, would that make us more like the
gods or more like our oppressors.

No, brother, no, do not let thy rage
choke the blood which anoints thy
heart with love. Forgo thine darkened
humor and let love shine on your
soul, like a jewel on a young maiden's
hand.

(*Dropping to her knees.*)

I beseech thee, forgo thine
anger and leave wrath to the gods!

SON. Girl, what has gotten into you.

MEDEA. Julliard, good brother. For I am no
longer bound by rhythms of race or
region. Oh, no. My speech, like my
pain and suffering, have become
classical and therefore universal.

LADY. I didn't understand a damn thing she said, but girl you usin' them words.

(*Lady in Plaid crosses and gives Medea the award and everyone applauds.*)

SON. (*Trying to stop the applause.*). Wait one damn minute! This my play. It's about me and the Man. It ain't got nuthin' to do with no ancient temples on the Nile and it ain't got nuthin' to do with Hestia's busom. And it ain't got nuthin' to do with you slappin' me across no room. (*His gut-wrenching best.*) It's about me. Me and my pain! My pain!

THE VOICE OF THE MAN. Walter-Lee-Beau-Willie, this is the Man. You have been convicted of overacting. Come out with your hands up.

(*Son starts to cross to the window.*)

SON. Well now that does it.

MAMA. Son, no, don't go near the window. Son, no!

(*Gun shots ring out and Son falls dead.*)

MAMA. (*Crossing to the body, too emotional for words.*) My son, he was a good boy. Confused. Angry. Just like his father. And his father's father. And his father's father's father. And now he's dead.

(*Seeing she's about to drop to her knees, the Narrator rushes and places a pillow underneath her just in time.*)

If only he had been born into a world better than this. A world where there are no well-worn couches and no well-worn Mamas and nobody over emotes.

If only he had been born into an all-black musical.

(*A song intro begins.*)

Nobody ever dies in an all-black musical.

(*Medea and Lady in Plaid pull out church fans and begin to fan themselves.*)

MAMA. (*Singing a soul-stirring gospel.*)
>OH WHY COULDN'T HE
>BE BORN
>INTO A SHOW WITH LOTS OF
>SINGING
>AND DANCING
>
>I SAY WHY
>COULDN'T HE
>BE BORN

LADY. Go ahead hunny. Take your time.
MAMA.
>INTO A SHOW WHERE EVERYBODY
>IS HAPPY

NARRATOR/MEDEA. Preach! Preach!
MAMA.
>OH WHY COULDN'T HE BE BORN
>WITH THE CHANCE
>TO SMILE A LOT AND SING AND
>DANCE
>OH WHY
>OH WHY
>
>OH WHY
>COULDN'T HE
>BE BORN
>INTO AN ALL-BLACK SHOW
>WOAH-WOAH

(*The Cast joins in, singing do-wop gospel background to Mama's lament.*)

>OH WHY
>COULDN'T HE
>BE BORN
>(HE BE BORN)
>INTO A SHOW WHERE EVERYBODY
>IS HAPPY
>
>WHY COULDN'T HE BE BORN WITH
>THE CHANCE
>TO SMILE A LOT AND SING AND
>DANCE
>WANNA KNOW WHY
>WANNA KNOW WHY
>
>OH WHY
>COULDN'T HE

>BE BORN
>INTO AN ALL-BLACK SHOW
>AMEN

(*A singing/dancing, spirit-raising revival begins.*)

>OH, SON, GET UP
>GET UP AND DANCE
>WE SAY GET UP
>THIS IS YOUR SECOND CHANCE
>
>DON'T SHAKE A FIST
>JUST SHAKE A LEG
>AND DO THE TWIST
>DON'T SCREAM AND BEG
>SON SON SON
>GET UP AND DANCE
>
>GET
>GET UP
>GET UP AND
>GET UP AND DANCE—ALL RIGHT!
>GET UP AND DANCE—ALL RIGHT!
>GET UP AND DANCE!

(*Walter-Lee-Beau-Willie springs to life and joins in the dancing. A foot-stomping, hand-clapping production number takes off, which encompasses a myriad of black-Broadwayesque dancing styles—shifting speeds*

MAMA. (*Bluesy*).
>WHY COULDN'T HE BE BORN INTO
>AN ALL-BLACK SHOW

CAST.
>WITH SINGING AND DANCING

MAMA. BLACK SHOW

(*Mama scats and the dancing becomes manic and just a little too desperate to please.*)

CAST.
>WE GOTTA DANCE
>WE GOTTA DANCE
>GET UP GET UP GET UP AND DANCE
>WE GOTTA DANCE
>WE GOTTA DANCE
>GOTTA DANCE!

(*Just at the point the dancing is about to become violent, the cast freezes and pointedly, simply sings:*)

>IF WE WANT TO LIVE
>WE HAVE GOT TO
>WE HAVE GOT TO
>DANCE . . . AND DANCE . . . AND
>DANCE . . .

(*As they continue to dance with zombie-like frozen smiles and faces, around them images of coon performers flash as the lights slowly fade.*)

SLAVE SHIP

An Historical Pageant

AMIRI BARAKA
(EVERETT LeRoi Jones)

AMIRI BARAKA (1934–)

Amiri Baraka, contemporary America's most political African American playwright, is himself a curious enigma. The product of a middle-class East Coast upbringing, he has evolved from a college graduate (Howard University, 1954) to an airman in the U.S. Air Force, to an advocate for radical revolutionary change as a left-wing political intellectual. He is a disciple of Marx and Lenin, Mao Zedong, and Islam. As a poet, essayist, social critic, and novelist, Baraka has a single goal: to depict an American society steeped in Eurocentric traditions, Western religious practices, racism, violence, and a voracious appetite for consumption. Of the source of his creative impulse, he writes: "Sometimes, though, you feel you move through tragedy and shame. That you step forward in the midst of ruins and explosions. Your eyes shining. Your survival ensured somehow by the fact of the running of that computer track between your ears, behind your eyes." His commitment to an American black arts movement has made Baraka a pivotal figure in the country's multicultural landscape.

The author of more than 20 dramatic works, Baraka writes in a style rooted in Expressionism, the European avant garde, the Beat scene, modern dance, and jazz. While his theater work is firmly grounded in the American Off-Broadway tradition, perhaps his most direct theatrical influence has always been the theoretical writings of Antonin Artaud (see Chapter 9). His Artaudian bent is evident in such plays as *Dutchman* (1964), *Madheart* (1969), *The Baptism* (1966), and *Slave Ship: An Historical Pageant* (1967). As in Artaud's vision, Baraka's theater attempts to cleanse the mind and body of the viewer in order to bring about spiritual purgation. Like Artaud, Baraka desires a ritualistic theater, void of psychological nuance, where symbolic and evocative gestures, postures, individual movement, rhythm, and sound envelop the audience. In his manifesto "The Revolutionary Theater," Baraka argues that "the Revolutionary Theater, even if it is Western, must be anti-Western. It must show horrible coming attractions of 'The Crumbling of the West.' Even as Artaud designed *The Conquest of Mexico,* so must we design *The Conquest of White Eye,* and show the missionaries and wiggly liberals dying under blasts of concrete. For sound effects, wild screams of joy, from all the peoples of the world." (See Baraka's essay in the Forum following the text of the play.)

Most of Baraka's dramatic personae share similar characteristics under the roof of suffocating environments: the hold of slave ship, a bare toilet, a subway car, a decayed log cabin, a decrepit church. His characters are victims of an oppressive society unwilling (or unable) to come to terms with social diversity, economic equality, and political representation. Although they are loners, misunderstood, emotionally charged, and internally damaged, they attempt to find a type of spiritual "conversion" that Baraka believes cannot be found in the current American social and political environment. The only solution for their physical survival is to locate alternative means of communication through rituals, alchemy, and, in many cases, violence.

In addition to his dramatic work, Baraka has published poetry (*Twenty Volume Suicide Note,* 1961) and numerous critical and political essays on the African American experience (*Reggae or Not!*, 1981). He founded a publishing house (People's War), and currently heads a center for playwriting, Spirit House, in Newark, New Jersey (which August Wilson attended). Baraka has taught at Yale and SUNY–Stony Brook, and he performs with an experimental jazz/poetry group.

SLAVE SHIP (1969)

Although critics often refer to *Dutchman* as the playwright's most successful dramatic work, *Slave Ship* perhaps best realizes Baraka's artistic and intellectual commitment to a ritualistic, political, and nonlinear theatrical experience. Enveloped in music, chants, screams, epic visual imagery, and minimalist dialogue, the power of the piece lies in its stage directions:

> Drums down low, like tapping, turns to beating floor, walls, rattling, dragging chains, percussive sounds people make in the hold of a ship. The moans and pushed-together agony. Children crying incessantly. The mother trying to calm them. More than one child. Young girls afraid to be violated. Men trying to break out. Or turning into frightened children. Families separated for the first time.

This description evokes an emotional power that extends the codified pattern of written or spoken linear language, and it allows the reader to create a mental landscape free from the subjugation of traditional dramatic texts. The stage directions penetrate the psyche by emphasizing the horror of the human transport vessel; they punctuate moments of terror and despair. In short, our reality as readers or viewers is radically shifted, from one second to the next, as we envision the madness of human slavery.

Baraka's elusive, almost ritualistic dialogue acts as the kind of chant Artaud envisioned in his call for "something in the significance [of] dreams." The play's language is staccato and highly symbolic, shifting from guttural sounds, through screams and moans, to short verbal tirades that emphasize the physical, mental, and spiritual deterioration of the characters. Likewise, Baraka's emphases on music, dance, and stage lighting are carefully coordinated to bombard the spectator's senses. Musical "interruptions" separate us from a realistic theatrical environment, while stage lighting highlights movement and dance to create an expressive and almost mythical experience. Under a pulsating rhythmical and musical structure, the play moves from past to present as the music shifts from prayerlike chants to the echoes and beats of 1960s Motown sounds. Baraka himself refers to the dances, based on routines performed by the Temptations and the Miracles, as the Boogaloo-Yoruba to emphasize the African roots of pop culture in America.

Slave Ship is Baraka's vision of a Western world run amok, a ritualistic journey that hopes to exorcise the evils of previous generations inflicted on the African reality. The playwright condemns the African diaspora for uprooting entire populations that carried with them the collective baggage of tribal belief systems, religious foundations, a rich oral history, and ancient social and cultural structures. In addition, *Slave Ship* is Baraka's attempt to target the instigator of the diaspora: the Christian, Anglo-Saxon power base that willingly altered the temporal state of Africans. The unseen character of the Voice epitomizes the arrogance of the oppressors: "You scared of me, niggers. I'm god. You can't kill white Jesus God. I got long blonde blow hair. I don't even need to wear a wig. You love the way I look. You want to look like me? I'm white Jesus savior, right?"

Baraka's drama pits the heritage of African rites (and their modern offspring) against western Christianity; here we see the passengers on Slave Ship.

SLAVE SHIP
An Historical Pageant

AMIRI BARAKA
(LEROI JONES)

A drama presented without intermission. The action takes place in the hold of a ship.

CAST
AFRICAN SLAVES, *voices of African slaves*
1ST MAN, *prayer—husband of Dademi*
2ND MAN, *curser*
3RD MAN, *struggler*
1ST WOMAN, *prayer*
2ND WOMAN, *screamer—attacked*
3RD WOMAN, *with child*

DANCERS
MUSICIANS
CHILDREN
PLUS VOICES AND BODIES IN THE SLAVE SHIP
OLD TOM SLAVE
NEW TOM, *preacher*
WHITE MEN, *voices of white men*
CAPTAIN
SAILOR
PLANTATION OWNER, *"Eternal Oppressor"*

PROPS

Smell effects: incense, dirt/filth smells/bodies
Heavy chains
Drums (African bata drums, and bass and snare)
Rattles and tambourines
Banjo music for plantation atmosphere
Ship noises
Ship bells
Rocking and splashing of sea
Guns and cartridges
Whips/whip sounds

SLAVE SHIP

Whole theater in darkness. Dark. For a long time. Just dark. Occasional sound, like ship groaning, squeaking, rocking. Sea smells. In the dark. Keep the people in the dark, and gradually the odors of the sea, and the sounds of the ship, creep up. Burn incense, but make a significant almost stifling smell come up. Pee. Shit. Death. Life processes going on anyway. Eating. These smells, and cries, the slash and tear of the lash, in a total atmos-feeling, gotten some way.

African drums like the worship of some Orisha. Obatala. Mbwanga rattles of the priests. BamBamBamBamBoom BoomBoom BamBam.

Rocking of the slave ship, in darkness, without sound. But smells. Then sound. Now slowly, out of blackness with smells and drums staccato the hideous screams. All the women together, scream: AAAAAIIIEEEEEEEEEE. Drums come up again, rocking rocking, black darkness of the slave ship. Smells, Drums go up high. Stop. Scream: AAAAAAIIIIEEEEEEEEE. Drums. Black darkness with smells.

Chains, the lash, and people moaning. Listen to the sounds come up out of the actors of Black People dragged and thrown down into the hold. AAAAIIIEEEEEEEE. Of people, dropped down in the darkness, frightened, angry, mashed together in common terror. The bells of the ship. White Men's Voices, on top, ready to set sail.

VOICE 1. Okay, let's go! A good cargo ob black gold. Let's go! We head West! We head West. [*Long laughter*] Black gold in the West. We got our full cargo.

V-2. Aye, aye, Cap'n. We're on our way. Riches to be ours, by God.

V-1. Aye, riches riches be ours. We're on our way. America!

Laughter. There is just dim light at top of set, to indicate where voices are. African drums. With the swiftness of dance, but running into the heaviness the dark enforces. The drums slow. The beat beat of the darkness. "Where are we, God?" The mumble murmur rattle below. The drone of terror. The voices begin to beat against the dark.

W-1. Ooooooooo, Obatala!

W-2. Shango!

W-1. Ooooooooo, Obatala. . . .

Children's crying in the hold, and the women trying to comfort them. Trying to keep their sanity too.

W-3. Moshake, chile, calm calm be you. Moshake, chile. O calm Orisha, save us!

W-2. AAAIIIEEEEEEEEEE.

M-1. Quiet woman! Quiet. Save your strength for your child.

W-2. AAAIIIEEEEEEEEEE.

M-1. Quiet, foolish woman! Be quiet!

W-3. Moshake, baby, chile, be calm, be calm, it give you, ooooooo.

M-1. Shango, Obatala, make your lightning, beat the inside bright with paths for your people. Beat Beat Beat.

Drums come up, but they are walls and floors being beaten. Chains rattled. Chains rattled. Drag the chains.

We get the feeling of many, many people jammed together, men, women, children, aching in the darkness. The chains, the whips, magnify the chains and whips. The dragging together. The pain. The terror.

Women begin to moan a chant-song: African sorrow song, with scraping of floor and chains to accompaniment.

M2. Fukwididila! Fukwididila! Fukwididila! Fuck you, Orisha! God! Where you be? Where you now, Black God? Help me. I be a strong warrior, and no woman. And I strain against these chains! But you must help me, Orisha. OBATALA!

M-3. Quiet, you fool, you frighten the women!

Women still chanting, moaning. Children now crying. Mothers trying to comfort them. Feeling of people moving around, tumbling over each other. Screaming as they try to find "a place" in the bottom of the boat, and then the long stream of different wills, articulated as screams, grunts, cries, songs, etc.

M-3. Pull, pull, break them. Pull.

W-1. Oh, Obatala!

W-3. Oh, chile . . . my chile, please please get away . . . you crush . . . !

M-3. Break . . . Break. . . .

ALL. Uhh, Uhhh, Uhhh, Uhhh, OOOOOOOOOOOOOOOOO.

WOMEN. AAAAAIIIIIEEEEEEEEEE.

ALL. Uhhh, Uhhh, Uhhh, Uhhh, OOOOOOOOOOOOO.

WOMEN. AAAIIIIEEEEEEEE.

Drums down low, like tapping, turns to beating floor, walls, rattling dragging chains, percussive sounds people make in the hold of a ship. The moans and pushed-together agony. Children crying incessantly. The mothers trying to calm them. More than one child. Young girls afraid they may be violated. Men trying to break out. Or turning into frightened children. Families separated for the first time.

W-2. Ifanami, Ifanami . . . where you? Where you?? Ifanami [*Cries*] Please, oh God.

M-1. Obata . . .

Drums beat down, softer . . . humming starts . . . hummmmm hummmm, like old colored women humming for three centuries in the slow misery of slavery . . . hummmmmm hummmmmmmmmmmmmmmmmmm. Lights flash up on the faces of white men in sailor suits, grinning . . . humming voices down, humming, "hummmmmmmmmm . . . hummmm . . ." Lights flash on white men in sailor suits grinning their vices . . . voices down, hummmummin . . . hummmmmmmmmmmmmmmmmmm mmmm. Lights to light white people are sudden, very bright and blinding. The white men begin to laugh and point, as if they were pointing at the filth, misery and degradation of the Black People. They laugh: "HHAAAAAAHAAAHAAHAA-HAAHAAHHAAHAHAHAHAHAHA." When they are outlined again they are rolling in merriment. Pointing, dancing, jumping up and down. HaHaHa Ha hahaha Haaaa.

Laughter is drowned in the drums. Then the chant-moan of the woman . . . then silence. Then the drums, softer, then the humming, on and on in a maddening, building death-patience. broken by the screams, and the babies and the farts, and the babies crying for light, and young wives crying for their men. Old people calling for God. Warriors calling for freedom. Some crying out against the white man.

M-3. Devils! Devils! Devils! White beasts! Shit eaters! Beasts! [*They beat the walls, and try to tear the chains out of the walls*] White shit eaters.

W-3. Aiiiiieeeeeeeee.

M-1. God, she's killed herself, and the child. Oh, God. Oh, God.

Moans, Moans. Soft drums, and the constant, now almost maddening humming . . . hummmmmmmmmmmm, hummmmmmmmmmmm, hummmmmmmmmmmmmm . . . like mad old nigger ladies humming forever, in deathly patience . . . hummmmmmm hummmmmm hmmm.

W-1. She strangled herself with the chain. Choked the child. Oh, Shago! Help us Lord. Oh, please.

W-2. Why you leave us, Lord?

M-1. Dademi, Dademi . . . she dead, she dead . . . Dademi . . . [*Hear man wracked with death cries, screams*] Dademi, Dademi!!!!

Hummmmmmmmmm, Hummmmmmmmmmm, Hummmmmmmmmm, Hummmmmmmmm. Drums low, and moans . . . the chains, and Black people pushed against each other struggling for breath and room to live. The Black

Man weeps for his woman. The Black Woman weeps for her man together in the darkness, some calling for God.

W-2. Oh, please, please don't touch me . . . Please . . . [*Frantic*] Ifanami, where you? [*Screams at someone's touch in the dark, grabbing her, trying to drag her in the darkness, press her done against the floor*] Akiyele . . . please . . . please . . . don't don't touch me . . . please. Ifanami, where you? Please help me. . . . Go . . .

M-1. What you doing? Get away from that woman. That's not your woman. You turn into a beast too.

Scuffle of two men turning in the darkness trying to kill each other. Lights show white men laughing silent, dangling their whips, in pantomime, still pointing.

M-3. Devils. Devils. Cold walking shit.

All Mad Sounds Together.

Humming begins again. Bells of ship. Silence. And moans. And humming. And movement in the dark, of people. Sliding back and forth. Trying to stay alive, and now, over it, the constant crazy laughter of the sailors.

SAILORS. AHAHAHAHAHAHAHAHAHAHAHA-HAAAAA HHHAHAHAHAHAHAHHA HAHAH.

M-3. I kill you devils. I break these chains [*Sound of men struggling against heavy chains*] I tear your face off. Crush your throat. Devils. Devils.

W-1. Oh, oh, God, she dead . . . and the child.

[*Silence, Sound of the sea . . . fades.*]

[*Humming*] HMMMMMMMM HMMMMMMM HMM-MMMMM HMMMMMMMM HMMMMMMM HM-MMMMMM.

Lights on suddenly show a shuffling "Negro." Lights off . . . drums of ancient African warriors come up . . . hero-warriors. Lights blink back on show shuffling Black Man, hat in his hand, scratching his head. Lights off. Drums again. Black dancing in the dark, with bells, as if free, dancing wild old dances. BamBoom Bam Booma Bimbam Boomama boom beem bam. Dancing in the darkness . . . Yoruba Dance: Lights flash on briefly, spot on off the dance. Then off. Then on to show The Slave raggedy ass ragged hat in hand shuffling toward the audience, shuffling, scratching his head and butt. Shaking his head up and down, agreeing with massa, agreeing, and agreeing, while whips snap. Lights off, flash on, and the sailors, with hats changed to show them as plantation owners, are still laughing, no sound, but laughing and pointing, holding their sides, and they laugh and point.

SLAVE. [*In darkness*] Yassa, boss, yassa, massa Tim, yass, Boss. [*Lights up*] I'se happy as a brand-new monkey ass, yass boss, yassa, mass' Tim, Yass, mass Booboo, I'se so happy

I'se so happy I jus' don' know what to do. Yass, mas' boa, youse so han'some and good and youse hip too, yass, I'se so happy I jus' stan' and scratch my old nigger haid. [*Lights flash on slave doing an old-new dance for the boss, when he finishes he bows and scratches*]

Lights out . . . the same hummmmmm rises up . . . with low drums, but the hum grown louder drowns it out . . . hummmmmmhummmmmm hummmmmmhummmmmmmmmm. The laughter now drowns out the humming, the same cold, hideous laughter.

W-3. [*Whispering after death*] Moshake. . . . Moshake. . . . Moshake-chile, calm yourself, love [*Woman runs down into soft weep, with no other distracting sound, just her moaning sad cry, for her baby*]

Chains. Chains. Dragging the chains. The humming. Hummmmmmmmmmmmmmmmm.

WOM. AIEEEEEEEEEEEEEEEEEEEEE.
ALL. Uhh, Uhhh, Uhhh, Uhhh, Ooooooooooooooooooo.
Silence.
Soft at first, then rising. Banjos of the plantation.
SLAVE 1. Reverend, what we gdon' do when mass come? [*He sounds afraid*]
SLAVE 2. We gon' cut his fuckin' throat!
Banjos. Humming . . . Hummmmmmmmmmm.
S-1. Reverend: what we gon' do when the white man come?
S-2. We gon' cut his fuckin' throat.
S-3. Devil. Beast. Murderer of women and children. Soulless shit eater!
S-1. Reverend Turner, sir, what we gon' do when the mass come?
S-2. Cut his Godless throat.

Lights flash up on same tomish slave, still scratching his head, but now apparently talking to a white man.

SLAVE. Uhh, dass right, mass Time . . . dey gon' 'volt.
WHVOI. What? Vote? Are you crazy?
SLAVE. Nawsaw . . . I said 'volt . . . uhhhh . . . re-volt.

Laughter now, rising behind the dialogue.

WHV. When, boy?
S. Ahhh, t'night, boss, t'night . . . they say they gon' . . . 'scuse de 'spression . . . cut you . . . uhh fockin' . . . uhh throat . . .
V. [*Laughs*] And who's in charge of this " 'volt"?
S. Uhh . . . Reverend Turner . . . suh . . .
V. What?
S. Uhh . . . dass right . . . Reverend Turner . . . suh. . . . Now can I have dat extra chop you promised me??? [*Screams now, as soon as the lights go down*] AIEEEEEEIEIEIEIEIEI.

Gunshots, combination of slave ship and breakup of the revolt. Voices of master and slaves in combat.

WHVOICE. I kill yu niggahs. You Black savages.
BLVOICE. White Beast. Devil, from hell. [*Voice, now, humming, humming, slow, deathly patient hum*] HUMMMMM-MMMMM.

Drums of Africa and the screams of Black and White in combat. Lights flash on Tom, cringing as if he is hiding from combat, gnawing on pork chop. Voice of white man laughing in triumph. Another chop comes sailing out of the darkness. Tom grabs it and scoffs it down, grinning and doing the dead-ape shuffle, humming while he eats.

W-3. [*Dead whispered voice*] Moshake, Moshake . . . chile . . . calm calm. . . . We be all right, now. . . . Moshake, be calm.
M. White beasts!
ALL. Uhh. Ohhh. Uhhh. Uhhh. Uhhh. [*As if pulling a tremendous weight*] Uhhh. Ohhh. Uhhh. Uhhh. Uhhh.
W. Ifanami. . . .
M-1. Dademi . . . Dademi.
W-2. Akiyele . . . Akiyele. Lord, husband, where you . . . help me.
M. Olabumi . . . Olabumi. . . . Touch my hand . . . woman . . .
W. Ifanami!
W. Moshake!

Now same voices as if transported in time to the slave farms . . . call names, English slave names.

ALL. [*Alternating man and woman losing mate in death, or thru slavesale, or the aura of constant fear of separation*] "Luke. Oh, my God."
M. Sarah.
W. John. Everett. My God, they killed him.
ALL. Mama, Mama. . . . Nana. Nana. Willie, Ohhh, Lord. . . . They done. Uhh. Uhhh. Uhh. Obatala. Obatala. Save Us. Lord. Shango. Lord of forests. Give us back our strength.

Chains. Chains. Dragging and grunting of people pushed against each other. The sound of a spiritual. "Oh, Lord Deliver Me. . . . Oh Lord" . . . and now cries of "JESUS LORD JESUS . . . HELP US JESUS."

M-1. Ogun. Give me weapons. Give me iron. My spear. My bone and muscle make them tight with tension of combat. Ogun, give me fire and death to give these beasts. Sarava! Sarava! Ogun.

Drums of fire and blood briefly loud and smashing against the dark, but now calming, dying down, till only the moans, and then the same patient humming . . . of women now, no men, only the women . . . strains of "The Old Rugged Cross" . . . and only the women and the humming . . . the time passing in the darkness, soft soft mournful weeping. "Jesus . . . Jesus . . . Jesus . . . Jesus . . . Jesus . . . Jesus . . . Jesus . . . Jesus."

Now lights flash on, and preacher in modern business suit stands with hat in his hand. He is the same Tom as before. He stands at first talking to his congregation: "Jesus, Jesus, Jesus, Jesus, Jesus, Jesus," then with a big grin, speaking in the pseudo-intelligent patter he uses for the boss. He tries to be, in fact, assumes he is, dignified, trying to hold his shoulders straight, but only succeeds in giving his entire body an odd slant like a diseased coal shute.

PRE. Yass, we under-stand . . . the problem. And personally I think some agreement can be reached. We will be nonviolenk . . . to the last . . . because we under-stand the dignity of pruty mcbonk and the greasy ghost. Of course diddy rip to bink, of vout juice. And penguins would do the same. I have a trauma, that the gold sewers won't integrate. Present fink. I have an enema . . . a trauma, on the coaster with your wife bird-shit.

W-3. [*Black woman's voice screaming for her child again*] Moshake! Moshake! Moshake . . . beeba . . . beeba . . . Wafwa Ko wafwa ko fukwididila.

Screams moans . . . drums . . . mournful deathtone. . . . The preacher looks head turned just slightly, as if embarrassed, trying still to talk to the white man. Then, one of the Black Men, out of the darkness, comes and sits before the Tom, a wrapped-up bloody corpse of the dead burned baby, as if they had just taken the body from a blown-up church, sets corpse in front of preacher. Preacher stops. Looks up at "person" he's tomming before, then, with his foot, tries to push baby's body behind him, grinning, and jeffing all the time, showing teeth, and being "dignified."

PR. Uhherr . . . as I was sayin' . . . Mas' un . . . Mister Tastyslop. . . . We Kneegrows are ready to integrate . . . the blippy rump of stomach bat has corrinked a lip to push the thimble. Yass Yass Yass.

In background while preacher is frozen in his "Jeff" position . . . high hard sound of saxophone, backed by drums. New sound saxophone tearing up the darkness. At height of screaming saxophone, instruments and drums comes voices screaming.

M. Beasts. Beasts. Beasts. Ogun. Give me spear and iron. Let me kill . . .

Humming as before . . . long . . . incredible patience, as if it would go on forever, turns into OMMMMMMMMMM- MMMMMMMMMMMMMMMMMM: all take it up, as the climax rise. Lights down. Ommmmm sound, mixed with sounds of slave ship, saxophone and drums. Sounds of people, thrown against each other, now as if trying all, to rise, pick up. Sounds of people picking up. Like dead people rising. And against that the same sounds of slave ship. White laughter over all of it. White laughter. Song begins to build with the saxophone and drums. First chanted.

ALL.

> Rise, Rise, Rise
> Cut these ties, Black Man, Rise
> We gon' be the thing we are . . .

Now all sing "When We Gonna Rise"

WHEN WE GONNA RISE
When we gonna rise-up
When we gonna rise-up
When we gonna rise-up
When we gonna rise
I mean when we gonna lift our heads and voices
When we gonna show the world who we really are
When we gonna rise up, brother
When we gonna rise above the sun
When we gonna take our own place, brother
Like the world had just begun
I mean when we gonna lift our heads and voices
Show the world who we really are
Warrior-Gods, and lovers, the first Men to walk this
   star
Yes, oh, yes, the First Men to walk this star
How far, How long will it be
When the world belongs to you and me
When we gonna rise up, brother
When we gonna rise above the sun
When we gonna take our own place, brother
Like the world had just begun.

Drum—new sax—voice arrangement. Bodies dragging up, in darkness. Lights up on the preacher in one part of the stage. He stands still jabbering senselessly to the white man. And the white man's laughter is heard trying to drown out the music, but the music is rising. Preacher turns to look into the darkness at the people dragging up behind him, embarrassed at first, then beginning to get frightened. The laughter too takes on a less arrogant tone.

W. Moshake. Moshake.
M. Ogun, give me steel.
ALL. Uhh. Uhh. Ohhh. Uhhh. Uhhh.

Humming rising too behind. Still singing "When We Gonna Rise." Preacher squirms, turns to see, and suddenly his eyes begin to open very wide, lights are coming up very slowly, almost imperceptibly at first. Now singing is beginning to be heard, mixed with old African drums, and voices, cries, pushing screams, of the slave ship. Preacher begins to fidget, as if he does not want to be where he is. He looks to boss for help. Voice is breaking, as lights come up and we see all the people in the slave ship in Miracles'/Temptations' dancing line. Some doing African dance. Some doing new Boogaloo, but all moving toward Preacher, and toward voice. It is a new-old Boogaloo yoruba line, women children all moving popping fingers all singing, and drummers, beating out old and new, and moving all moving. Finally, the Preacher begins to cringe and plead for help from the white voice.

PRE. Please, boss, these niggers goin' crazy, please, boss, throw yo lightnin' at 'em, white Jesus boss, white light god, they goin' crazy! Help!

VOICE. [*Coughing as if choking on something, trying to laugh because sight of Preacher is funny . . . still managing to laugh at Preacher*] Fool, Fool.

PR. Please, boss, please . . . I do anything for you . . . you know that, boss . . . Please . . . please . . .

All group merge on him and kill him daid. Then they turn in the direction of where the voice is coming from. Dancing, singing, right on toward the now pleading voice.

VOICE. HaaHaaHaaHaa [*Laugh gets stuck in his throat*] Uhh . . . now what . . . you' haha can't touch me . . . you scared of me, niggers. I'm god. You cain't kill white Jesus God. I got long blonde blow hair. I don't even need to wear a wig. You love the way I look. You want to look like me. You love me. You want me. Please. I'm good. I'm kind. I'll give you anything you want. I'm white Jesus saviour right

God pay you money nigger me is good God be please . . . please don't . . .

Lights begin to fade . . . drums and voices of old slave ship come back.

ALL. Uhh. Ohh. Uhh. Ohh. Uhh. Ohh. Uhh. Ohh. [*And then the terrible humming, turning to the OMMMMMMM-MMMMMMmmmmmmmmmm sound, broken now by the finally awful scream of the killed white voice*] AWHAWHAE-HAHWAWHWHAHW.

All players fixed in half light, at the moment of the act. Then lights go down. Black.

Lights comes up abruptly, and people onstage begin to dance, same hip Boogalyoruba, fingerpop, skate, monkey, dog. Enter Audience, get members of audience to dance. To same music RISE UP. Turns into an actual party. When the party reaches some loose improvisation, etc., audience relaxed, somebody throws the preachers head into center of floor, i.e., after the dancing starts for real. Then black.

FORUM

"The Revolutionary Theatre"

AMIRI BARAKA (NÉ LEROI JONES)

Baraka, the author of Slave Ship, *was the theater's dominant voice in the Black Power movement of the late 1960s and early 1970s. The following essay suggests both the anger and fervor of the movement. While Baraka's argument speaks specifically about African American theatre at this time, it also echoes ideas espoused by other radical theater groups, both in the United States and abroad.*

The Revolutionary Theatre should force change; it should be change. (All their faces turned into the lights and you work on them black nigger magic, and cleanse them at having seen the ugliness. And if the beautiful see themselves, they will love themselves.) We are preaching virtue again, but by that to mean NOW, toward what seems the most constructive use of the world.

The Revolutionary Theatre must EXPOSE! Show up the insides of these humans, look into black skulls. White men will

cower before this theatre because it hates them. Because they themselves have been trained to hate. The Revolutionary Theatre must hate them for hating. For presuming with their technology to deny the supremacy of the Spirit. They will die because of this.

The Revolutionary Theatre must teach them their deaths. It must crack their faces open to the mad cries of the poor. It must teach them about silence and the truths lodged there. It must kill any God anyone names except Common Sense. The Revolutionary Theatre should flush the fags and murders out of Lincoln's face.

It should stagger through our universe correcting, insulting, preaching, spitting craziness—but a craziness taught to us in our most rational moments. People must be taught to trust true scientists (knowers, diggers, oddballs) and that the holiness of life is the constant possibility of widening the consciousness. And they must be incited to strike back against *any* agency that attempts to prevent this widening.

The Revolutionary Theatre must Accuse and Attack anything that can be accused and attacked. It must Accuse and Attack because it is a theatre of Victims. It looks at the sky with the victims' eyes, and moves the victims to look at the strength in their minds and their bodies.

Clay in *Dutchman*, Ray in *The Toilet*, Walker in *The Slave*, are all victims. In the Western sense they could be heroes. But the Revolutionary Theatre, even if it is Western, must be anti-Western. It must show horrible coming attractions of *The Crumbling of the West*. Even as Artaud designed *The Conquest of Mexico*, so we must design *The Conquest of White Eye*, and show the missionaries and wiggly Liberals dying under blasts of concrete. For sound effects, wild screams of joy, from all the peoples of the world.

The Revolutionary Theatre must take dreams and give them a reality. It must isolate the ritual and historical cycles of reality. But it must be food for all those who need food, and daring propaganda for the beauty of the Human Mind. It is a political theatre, a weapon to help in the slaughter of these dimwitted fat-bellied white guys who somehow believe that the rest of the world is here for them to slobber on.

This should be a theatre of World Spirit. Where the spirit can be shown to be the most competent force in the world. Force. Spirit. Feeling. The language will be anybody's, but tightened by the poet's backbone. And even the language must show what the facts are in this consciousness epic, what's happening. We will talk about the world, and the preciseness with which we are able to summon the world will be our art. Art is method. And art, "like any ashtray or senator," remains in the world. Wittgenstein said ethics and aesthetics are one. I believe this. So the Broadway theatre is a theatre of reaction whose ethics, like its aesthetics, reflect the spiritual values of this unholy society, which sends young crackers all over the world blowing off colored people's heads. (In some of these flippy Southern towns they even shoot up the immigrants' Favorite Son, be it Michael Schwerner or JFKennedy.)

The Revolutionary Theatre is shaped by the world, and moves to reshape the world, using as its force the natural force and perpetual vibrations of the mind in the world. We are history and desire, what we are, and what any experience can make us.

It is a social theatre, but all theatre is social theatre. But we will change the drawing rooms into places where real things can be said about a real world, or into smoky rooms where the destruction of Washington can be plotted. The Revolutionary Theatre must function like an incendiary pencil planted in Curtis Lemay's cap. So that when the final curtain goes down brains are splattered over the seats and the floor, and bleeding nuns must wire SOS's to Belgians with gold teeth.

Our theatre will show victims so that their brothers in the audience will be better able to understand that they are the brothers of victims, and that they themselves are victims if they are blood brothers. And what we show must cause the blood to rush, so that pre-revolutionary temperaments will be bathed in this blood, and it will cause their deepest souls to move, and they will find themselves tensed and clenched, even ready to die, at what the soul has been taught. We will scream and cry, murder, run through the streets in agony, if it means some soul will be moved, moved to actual life understanding of what the world is, and what it ought to be. We are preaching virtue and

feeling, and a natural sense of the self in the world. All men live in the world, and the world ought to be a place for them to live.

What is called the imagination (from image, magi, magic, magician, etc.) is a practical vector from the soul. It stores all data, and can be called on to solve all our "problems." The imagination is the projection of ourselves past our sense of ourselves as "things." Imagination (Image) is all possibility, because from the image, the initial circumscribed energy, any use (idea) is possible. And so begins that image's use in the world. Possibility is what moves us.

The popular white man's theatre like the popular white man's novel shows tired white lives, and the problems of eating white sugar, or else it herds bigcaboosed blondes onto huge stages in rhinestones and makes believe they are dancing or singing. WHITE BUSINESSMEN OF THE WORLD, DO YOU WANT TO SEE PEOPLE REALLY DANCING AND SINGING??? ALL OF YOU GO UP TO HARLEM AND GET YOURSELF KILLED. THERE WILL BE DANCING AND SINGING, THEN, FOR REAL!! (In *The Slave*, Walker Vessels, the black revolutionary, wears an armband, which is the insignia of the attacking army—a big red-lipped minstrel, grinning like crazy.)

The liberal white man's objection to the theatre of the revolution (if he is "hip" enough) will be on aesthetic grounds. Most white Western artists do not need to be "political," since usually, whether they know it or not, they are in complete sympathy with the most repressive social forces in the world today. There are more junior birdmen fascists running around the West today disguised as Artists than there are disguised as fascists. (But then, that word, *Fascist*, and with it, *Fascism*, has been made obsolete by the words *America*, and *Americanism*.) The American Artist usually turns out to be just a super-Bourgeois, because, finally, all he has to show for his sojourn through the world is "better taste" than the Bourgeois—many times not even that.

Americans will hate the Revolutionary Theatre because it will be out to destroy them and whatever they believe is real. American cops will try to close the theatres where such nakedness of the human spirit is paraded. American producers will say the revolutionary plays are filth, usually because they will treat human life as if it were actually happening. American directors will say that the white guys in the plays are too abstract and cowardly ("don't get me wrong . . . I mean aesthetically . . . ") and they will be right.

The force we want is of twenty million spooks storming America with furious cries and unstoppable weapons. We want actual explosions and actual brutality: AN EPIC IS CRUMBLING and we must give it the space and hugeness of its actual demise. The Revolutionary Theatre, which is now peopled with victims, will soon begin to be peopled with new kinds of heroes—not the weak Hamlets debating whether or not they are ready to die for what's on their minds, but men and women (and minds) digging out from under a thousand years of "high art" and weak-faced dalliance. We must make an art that will function so as to call down the actual wrath of world spirit. We are witch doctors and assassins, but we will open a place for the true scientists to expand our consciousness. This is a theatre of assault. The play will split the heavens for us will be called THE DESTRUCTION.

FENCES

AUGUST WILSON

AUGUST WILSON (1945–)

Just as Arthur Miller and Tennessee Williams dominated the American theater in the years following World War II, August Wilson has become the most admired and decorated American playwright of the 1980s and 1990s. In little more than a decade he has already won two Pulitzer Prizes (*Fences*, 1987; *The Piano Lesson*, 1990); virtually all of his other works (see below) have won a "best of season" award from the New York Drama Critics. Given the esteem he has earned among critics and audiences, Wilson will likely emerge as one of America's most honored playwrights before his playwriting career is concluded.

Perhaps the most intriguing aspect of his collected plays is their organizational principle. Each play of a proposed ten-play cycle is set in a different decade of the twentieth century, and each is framed against the backdrop of a peculiarly American cultural icon ('20s jazz for *Ma Rainey's Black Bottom*, '50s baseball for *Fences*, and '40s delta blues for *Seven Guitars*). Collectively the plays chronicle the evolution of an authentic African American voice within the broader national culture. Though the past Wilson depicts painfully dramatizes racism and the residue of slavery, there nonetheless remains an undercurrent of optimism in Wilson's work. He has talked about "exorcising the demons of memory" so that African Americans can advance in the next century (in *Joe Turner's Come and Gone* an actual exorcism typifies his canon).

Many of Wilson's plays are set in Pittsburgh, where he was born to a white father and a black mother; he was raised in the Hill district, a ghetto for African Americans. His father was rarely around, and his strong-willed mother was determined that her son would succeed; she moved the family to a mostly white suburb. But social realities deterred Wilson: he left a Catholic school because of racial slurs; he deemed a vocational school academically worthless; and his brief experience in a public high school embittered him when a teacher falsely accused him of plagiarizing a 20-page paper on Napoléon. Wilson's rage at such injustices drew him to the black power movement of the 1960s. In Pittsburgh he helped found the Black Horizon on the Hill, a theater company that staged the plays of LeRoi Jones (Amiri Baraka), whose work inspired him to take up playwriting. At first he was discouraged because he "wasn't any good at dialogue," an ironic assessment from a man whose plays are praised for their lyrical, yet completely naturalistic, language.

In 1978 Wilson accepted an invitation to move to St. Paul, Minnesota, to write plays for a theater company founded by a former Pittsburgh colleague. Despite his success, he still maintains the same tiny apartment in St. Paul. In 1982 Wilson was a fellow-in-residence at a playwright-development program at the Eugene O'Neill Center in Connecticut. There he met Lloyd Richards, an African American director and head of the Yale School of Drama, who encouraged Wilson by producing his works. Today his plays are still tested at Yale prior to their New York opening. The Wilson-Richards collaboration has proven to be among the most fruitful in the history of the American theater.

Though Wilson's works are rooted in naturalism (heredity and environment are central to the lives of his characters), his works transcend the style and assume an aura of mystery and myth. Again we turn to his comments about the need to exorcise demons from American life as perhaps the source of the mystic in his plays. Ultimately, his collected works—from *Ma Rainey* in 1983 to *Seven Guitars* in 1996—have attracted audiences of all races and economic classes because they speak of universal suffering and hope. While the plays are unmistakably about the African American experience in a nation with a history of troubled race relations, they are also about human problems, which may account for their unprecedented success.

FENCES (1987)

Fences is in many ways similar to *Death of a Salesman*, particularly in its portrait of the clash between a domineering father and his athletically gifted son. Like Willy, Troy Maxson is a man who cannot adapt to a changing world, who is unfaithful to his wife and who ultimately drives his son away by his stubbornness. Furthermore, as in *Salesman*, we meet a ne'er-do-well son (cf. Happy and Lyons) and a long-suffering, dutiful wife (cf. Linda and Rose). And both plays are set in the so-called boom years after World War II, when many prospered while others were left behind.

But whereas Miller's near-tragic hero, Willy Loman, is the essence of "the little [low] man," Wilson invests Troy with a larger-than-life ("maximum") quality; like Prometheus, Troy is a titan who rails against the injustices heaped on the black man. Note that in virtually every confrontation in which Troy engages himself, his opponent is aligned with superhuman values: Mr. Death, the Devil, and "the Boss" for whom he works as a trash man (Troy's heroic stand at work is truly Promethean in its sheer audacity). Even the furniture salesman with whom he battles is described in supernatural terms ("devil standing there bigger than life"). The great baseball players with whom Troy aligns himself—Josh Gibson ("the Black Babe Ruth"), the ageless Satchel Paige, the trail-blazing Jackie Robinson, and the young Hank Aaron—emerge as godlike beings. Thus Wilson creates in Troy a modern mythic hero who tries to shake a universe filled with injustice and inequality. The playwright even assigns him a trumpet-playing brother, Gabriel, who tries to blow down the gates of heaven itself. Troy is Wilson's finest creation, and he stands among the most compelling characters to emerge in the contemporary American theater.

But Troy is as flawed as he is heroic. His "errors in judgement"—to use an apt Aristotelian term—are many. Because of his own failed career as an athlete, he stifles Cory's ambitions to escape the destitution in which he lives. Though he proclaims his love for Rose, he condemns her to a life of servitude ("You supposed to come when I call you, woman"); ironically, he treats her much as his boss treats him. In short, he doesn't let her "drive the truck." He possesses a destructive temper and a pride that ultimately destroys him—and his family. Wilson's refusal to render his protagonist in only heroic terms makes Troy all the more universal and sympathetic. Through Troy's weaknesses, Wilson argues that the most divisive and dangerous threats to the African American community stem from internal conflict. To be sure, they are exacerbated by the rage fostered by a racist society, but Wilson represents a new strain of African American playwriting. Unlike the works of Baraka, Ed Bullins, and other early black power dramatists, Wilson argues that the enemy is as often within as without the black community.

Rose Maxson also emerges as an extraordinary being, another in a long line of memorable American stage mothers (Amanda Wingfield, Mama Younger, Linda Loman). Rose is uncommonly heroic in her acceptance of Raynell and, of course, in the manner in which she preserves a quiet dignity in the face of Troy's chauvinism. Her monologue at the end of act 2, Scene 1, is a masterpiece of self-realization, and her dismissal of Troy at the end of the next scene ("you a womanless man") is as powerful as Nora Helmer's famed door slam at the end of *A Doll's House*.

Cory, like Biff, is repulsed by his father's hypocrisy and heavy-handed justice; ironically, Troy is just as angered at the "unfairness" of his boss. And Cory, like Biff, is condemned to walk in his father's shoes (says Cory, "I got to the place where I could feel [Troy] kicking in my blood and knew that the only thing that separated us was the matter of a few years"). And, true to the form of dramas about generational warfare, Wilson provides us with an obligatory scene in which father and son square off in an archetypal battle in which a baseball bat is as potent a weapon as a broadsword.

It may be tempting to assume that Cory "wins" the battle because our final view of him is as a smartly dressed "corporal in the United States Marine Corps." He has escaped the "fence" of Pittsburgh's Hill, and he is clearly admired by Bono, Raynell, and Rose. But the reality is that Cory is a marine in 1965, and his escape from the Hill most likely will lead him to the rice paddies of Vietnam. For Wilson, although military service seemed an attractive alternative to life in the inner city, the reality was that "a whole bunch of blacks went over and died in the Vietnam War. The survivors came back to the same street corners and found nothing had changed. They still couldn't get a job." Cory, then, is also condemned to an institution, as are the other principal characters: Rose at her church, Lyons in jail, and Gabriel in a mental hospital. Even Bono remains trapped on the Hill, his only respite the Friday evening paycheck that brings a few hours' solace.

Despite the bleak ending, Wilson—as is typical of his work—intimates some hope throughout, largely in his well-chosen music. In addition to his use of baseball (along with boxing, the first mainstream sporting enterprise to employ African Americans and thus change perceptions about minorities in America), Wilson also uses the song of black Americans liberally throughout his scripts for both thematic and cultural purposes. Note that each song in *Fences* comments on the action just as the ancient Greek choral odes did. But the music is also a manifestation of the characters' ability to persevere amidst hardship. In his earliest full-length play, *Ma Rainey's Black Bottom*, the title character (an actual historical figure who is recognized as "the mother of the blues") declares that "you don't sing to feel better—you sing because that's a way of understanding life." The line is an apt prologue to Wilson's ten-play cycle—especially *Fences*—in which he explores the black experience through the lens of various cultural phenomena that simultaneously enrich and exploit African Americans. To paraphrase Ma Rainey, Wilson doesn't write to entertain; he writes because it is a proven way for audiences of all colors to understand life. And in that understanding of the pain of rejection, injustice, and human error emerges a kind of hope that the world's imperfections, on the Hill and elsewhere, will diminish, just as surely as baseball's "color line" was broken in Brooklyn in 1947.

James Earl Jones created the role of Troy Maxson in the New York production of Fences; *his baseball bat is the modern equivalent of a warrior's weapon as he battles the demons of racism.*

FENCES

AUGUST WILSON

for Lloyd Richards,
who adds to whatever he touches.

When the sins of our fathers visit us
We do not have to play host.
We can banish them with forgiveness
As God, in His Largeness and Laws.
—August Wilson

LIST OF CHARACTERS

TROY MAXSON
JIM BONO, *Troy's friend*
ROSE, *Troy's wife*
LYONS, *Troy's oldest son by previous marriage*
GABRIEL, *Troy's brother*
CORY, *Troy and Rose's son*
RAYNELL, *Troy's daughter*

SETTING: *The setting is the yard which fronts the only entrance to the Maxson household, an ancient two-story brick house set back off a small alley in a big-city neighborhood. The entrance to the house is gained by two or three steps leading to a wooden porch badly in need of paint.*

A relatively recent addition to the house and running its full width, the porch lacks congruence. It is a sturdy porch with a flat roof. One or two chairs of dubious value sit at one end where the kitchen window opens onto the porch. An old-fashioned icebox stands silent guard at the opposite end.

The yard is a small dirt yard, partially fenced, except for the last scene, with a wooden saw horse, a pile of lumber, and other fence-building equipment set off to the side. Opposite is a tree from which hangs a ball made of rags. A baseball bat leans against the tree. Two oil drums serve as garbage receptacles and sit near the house at right to complete the setting.

THE PLAY: *Near the turn of the century, the destitute of Europe sprang on the city with tenacious claws and an honest and solid dream. The city devoured them. They swelled its belly until it burst into a thousand furnaces and sewing machines, a thousand butcher shops and bakers' ovens, a thousand churches and hospitals and funeral parlors and money-lenders. The city grew. It nourished itself and offered each man a partnership limited only by his talent, his guile, and his willingness and capacity for hard work. For the immigrants of Europe, a dream dared and won true.*

The descendants of African slaves were offered no such welcome or participation. They came from places called the Carolinas and the Virginias, Georgia, Alabama, Mississippi, and Tennessee. They came strong, eager, searching. The city rejected them and they fled and settled along the riverbanks and under bridges in shallow, ramshackle houses made of sticks and tarpaper. They collected rags and wood. They sold the use of their muscles and their bodies. They cleaned houses and washed clothes, they shined shoes, and in quiet desperation and vengeful pride, they stole, and lived in pursuit of their own dream. That they could breathe free, finally, and stand to meet life with the force of dignity and whatever eloquence the heart could call upon.

By 1957, the hard-won victories of the European immigrants had solidified the industrial might of America. War had been confronted and won with new energies that used loyalty and patriotism as its fuel. Life was rich, full, and flourishing. The Milwaukee Braves won the World Series, and the hot winds of change that would make the sixties a turbulent, racing, dangerous, and provocative decade had not yet begun to blow full.

ACT 1

SCENE 1

It is 1957. Troy and Bono enter the yard, engaged in conversation. Troy is fifty-three years old, a large man with thick, heavy hands; it is this largeness that he strives to fill out and make an accommodation with. Together with his blackness, his largeness informs his sensibilities and the choices he has made in his life.

Of the two men, Bono is obviously the follower. His commitment to their friendship of thirty-odd years is rooted in his admiration of Troy's honesty, capacity for hard work, and his strength, which Bono seeks to emulate.

It is Friday night, payday, and the one night of the week the two men engage in a ritual of talk and drink. Troy is usually the most talkative and at times he can be crude and almost vulgar, though he is capable of rising to profound heights of expression. The men carry lunch buckets and wear or carry burlap aprons and are dressed in clothes suitable to their jobs as garbage collectors.

BONO. Troy, you ought to stop that lying!

TROY. I ain't lying! The nigger had a watermelon this big. (*He indicates with his hands.*) Talking about . . . "What watermelon, Mr. Rand?" I liked to fell out! "What watermelon, Mr. Rand?" . . . And it sitting there big as life.

BONO. What did Mr. Rand say?

TROY. Ain't said nothing. Figure if the nigger too dumb to know he carrying a watermelon, he wasn't gonna get much sense out of him. Trying to hide that great big old watermelon under his coat. Afraid to let the white man see him carry it home.

BONO. I'm like you . . . I ain't got no time for them kind of people.

TROY. Now what he look like getting mad cause he see the man from the union talking to Mr. Rand?

BONO. He come to me talking about . . . "Maxson gonna get us fired." I told him to get away from me with that. He walked away from me calling you a troublemaker. What Mr. Rand say?

TROY. Ain't said nothing. He told me to go down the Commissioner's office next Friday. They called me down there to see them.

BONO. Well, as long as you got your complaint filed, they can't fire you. That's what one of them white fellows tell me.

TROY. I ain't worried about them firing me. They gonna fire me cause I asked a question? That's all I did. I went to Mr. Rand and asked him, "Why? Why you got the white mens driving and the colored lifting?" Told him, "What's the matter, don't I count? You think only white fellows got sense enough to drive a truck. That ain't no paper job!

Hell, anybody can drive a truck. How come you got all whites driving and the colored lifting?" He told me "take it to the union." Well, hell, that's what I done! Now they wanna come up with this pack of lies.

BONO. I told Brownie if the man come and ask him any questions . . . just tell the truth! It ain't nothing but something they done trumped up on you cause you filed a complaint on them.

TROY. Brownie don't understand nothing. All I want them to do is change the job description. Give everybody a chance to drive the truck. Brownie can't see that. He ain't got that much sense.

BONO. How you figure he be making out with that gal be up at Taylor's all the time . . . that Alberta gal?

TROY. Same as you and me. Getting just as much as we is. Which is to say nothing.

BONO. It is, huh? I figure you doing a little better than me . . . and I ain't saying what I'm doing.

TROY. Aw, nigger, look here . . . I know you. If you had got anywhere near that gal, twenty minutes later you be looking to tell somebody. And the first one you gonna tell . . . that you gonna want to brag to . . . is me.

BONO. I ain't saying that. I see where you be eyeing her.

TROY. I eye all the women. I don't miss nothing. Don't never let nobody tell you Troy Maxson don't eye the women.

BONO. You been doing more than eyeing her. You done bought her a drink or two.

TROY. Hell yeah, I bought her a drink! What that mean? I bought you one, too. What that mean cause I buy her a drink? I'm just being polite.

BONO. It's all right to buy her one drink. That's what you call being polite. But when you wanna be buying two or three . . . that's what you call eyeing her.

TROY. Look here, as long as you known me . . . you ever known me to chase after women?

BONO. Hell yeah! Long as I done known you. You forgetting I knew you when.

TROY. Naw, I'm talking about since I been married to Rose?

BONO. Oh, not since you been married to Rose. Now, that's the truth, there. I can say that.

TROY. All right then! Case closed.

BONO. I see you be walking up around Alberta's house. You supposed to be at Taylors' and you be walking up around there.

TROY. What you watching where I'm walking for? I ain't watching after you.

BONO. I seen you walking around there more than once.

TROY. Hell, you liable to see me walking anywhere! That don't mean nothing cause you see me walking around there.

BONO. Where she come from anyway? She just kinda showed up one day.

TROY. Tallahassee. You can look at her and tell she one of them Florida gals. They got some big healthy women down there. Grow them right up out the ground. Got a little bit of Indian in her. Most of them niggers down in Florida got some Indian in them.

BONO. I don't know about that Indian part. But she damn sure big and healthy. Woman wear some big stockings. Got them great big old legs and hips as wide as the Mississippi River.

TROY. Legs don't mean nothing. You don't do nothing but push them out of the way. But them hips cushion the ride!

BONO. Troy, you ain't got no sense.

TROY. It's the truth! Like you riding on Goodyears!

Rose enters from the house. She is ten years younger than Troy, her devotion to him stems from her recognition of the possibilities of her life without him: a succession of abusive men and their babies, a life of partying and running the streets, the Church, or aloneness with its attendant pain and frustration. She recognizes Troy's spirit as a fine and illuminating one and she either ignores or forgives his faults, only some of which she recognizes. Though she doesn't drink, her presence is an integral part of the Friday night rituals. She alternates between the porch and the kitchen, where supper preparations are under way.

ROSE. What you all out here getting into?

TROY. What you worried about what we getting into for? This is men talk, woman.

ROSE. What I care what you all talking about? Bono, you gonna stay for supper?

BONO. No, I thank you, Rose. But Lucille say she cooking up a pot of pigfeet.

TROY. Pigfeet! Hell, I'm going home with you! Might even stay the night if you got some pigfeet. You got something in there to top them pigfeet, Rose?

ROSE. I'm cooking up some chicken. I got some chicken and collard greens.

TROY. Well, go on back in the house and let me and Bono finish what we was talking about. This is men talk. I got some talk for you later. You know what kind of talk I mean. You go on and powder it up.

ROSE. Troy Maxson, don't you start that now!

TROY (*puts his arm around her*). Aw, woman . . . come here. Look here, Bono . . . when I met this woman . . . I got out that place, say, "Hitch up my pony, saddle up my mare . . . there's a woman out there for me somewhere. I looked here. Looked there. Saw Rose and latched on to her." I latched on to her and told her—I'm gonna tell you the truth—I told her, "Baby, I don't wanna marry, I just wanna be your man." Rose told me . . . tell him what you told me, Rose.

ROSE. I told him if he wasn't the marrying kind, then move out the way so the marrying kind could find me.

TROY. That's what she told me. "Nigger, you in my way. You blocking the view! Move out the way so I can find me a husband." I thought it over two or three days. Come back—

ROSE. Ain't no two or three days nothing. You was back the same night.

TROY. Come back, told her . . . "Okay, baby . . . but I'm gonna buy me a banty rooster and put him out there in the backyard . . . and when he see a stranger come, he'll flap his wings and crow. . . ." Look here, Bono, I could watch the front door by myself . . . it was that back door I was worried about.

ROSE. Troy, you ought not talk like that. Troy ain't doing nothing but telling a lie.

TROY. Only thing is . . . when we first got married . . . forget the rooster . . . we ain't had no yard!

BONO. I hear you tell it. Me and Lucille was staying down there on Logan Street. Had two rooms with the outhouse in the back. I ain't mind the outhouse none. But when that goddamn wind blow through there in the winter . . . that's what I'm talking about! To this day I wonder why in the hell I ever stayed down there for six long years. But see, I didn't know I could do no better. I thought only white folks had inside toilets and things.

ROSE. There's a lot of people don't know they can do no better than they doing now. That's just something you got to learn. A lot of folks still shop at Bella's.

TROY. Ain't nothing wrong with shopping at Bella's. She got fresh food.

ROSE. I ain't said nothing about if she got fresh food. I'm talking about what she charge. She charge ten cents more than the A&P.

TROY. The A&P ain't never done nothing for me. I spends my money where I'm treated right. I go down to Bella, say, "I need a loaf of bread, I'll pay you Friday." She give it to me. What sense that make when I got money to go and spend it somewhere else and ignore the person who done right by me? That ain't in the Bible.

ROSE. We ain't talking about what's in the Bible. What sense it make to shop there when she overcharge?

TROY. You shop where you want to. I'll do my shopping where the people been good to me.

ROSE. Well, I don't think it's right for her to overcharge. That's all I was saying.

BONO. Look here . . . I got to get on. Lucille going be raising all kind of hell.

TROY. Where you going, nigger? We ain't finished this pint. Come here, finish this pint.

BONO. Well, hell, I am . . . if you ever turn the bottle loose.

TROY (hands him the bottle). The only thing I say about the A&P is I'm glad Cory got that job down there. Help him take care of his school clothes and things. Gabe done moved out and things getting tight around here. He got that job. . . . He can start to look out for himself.

ROSE. Cory done went and got recruited by a college football team.

TROY. I told that boy about that football stuff. The white man ain't gonna let him get nowhere with that football. I told him when he first come to me with it. Now you come telling me he done went and got more tied up in it. He ought to go and get recruited in how to fix cars or something where he can make a living.

ROSE. He ain't talking about making no living playing football. It's just something the boys in school do. They gonna send a recruiter by to talk to you. He'll tell you he ain't talking about making no living playing football. It's a honor to be recruited.

TROY. It ain't gonna get him nowhere. Bono'll tell you that.

BONO. If he be like you in the sports . . . he's gonna be all right. Ain't but two men ever played baseball as good as you. That's Babe Ruth and Josh Gibson.[1] Them's the only two men ever hit more home runs than you.

TROY. What it ever get me? Ain't got a pot to piss in or a window to throw it out of.

ROSE. Times have changed since you was playing baseball, Troy. That was before the war. Times have changed a lot since then.

TROY. How in hell they done changed?

ROSE. They got lots of colored boys playing ball now. Baseball and football.

BONO. You right about that, Rose. Times have changed, Troy. You just come along too early.

TROY. There ought not never have been no time called too early! Now you take that fellow . . . what's that fellow they had playing right field for the Yankees back then? You know who I'm talking about, Bono. Used to play right field for the Yankees.

ROSE. Selkirk?

TROY. Selkirk! That's it! Man batting .269, understand? .269. What kind of sense that make? I was hitting .432 with thirty-seven home runs! Man batting .269 and playing right field for the Yankees! I saw Josh Gibson's daughter yesterday. She walking around with raggedy shoes on her feet. Now I bet you Selkirk's daughter ain't walking around with raggedy shoes on the feet! I bet you that!

ROSE. They got a lot of colored baseball players now. Jackie Robinson[2] was the first. Folks had to wait for Jackie Robinson.

TROY. I done seen a hundred niggers play baseball better than Jackie Robinson. Hell, I know some teams Jackie Robinson couldn't even make! What you talking about Jackie Robinson. Jackie Robinson wasn't nobody. I'm talking about if you could play ball then they ought to have let you play. Don't care what color you were. Come telling me I come along too early. If you could play . . . then they ought to have let you play.

[1]African-American ballplayer (1911–1947), known as the Babe Ruth of the Negro leagues
[2]In 1947 Robinson (1919–1972) became the first African-American to play baseball in the major leagues.

Troy takes a long drink from the bottle.

ROSE. You gonna drink yourself to death. You don't need to be drinking like that.

TROY. Death ain't nothing. I done seen him. Done wrassled with him. You can't tell me nothing about death. Death ain't nothing but a fastball on the outside corner. And you know what I'll do to that! Lookee here, Bono . . . am I lying? You get one of them fastballs, about waist high, over the outside corner of the plate where you can get the meat of the bat on it . . . and good god! You can kiss it goodbye. Now, am I lying?

BONO. Naw, you telling the truth there. I seen you do it.

TROY. If I'm lying . . . that 450 feet worth of lying! (*Pause.*) That's all death is to me. A fastball on the outside corner.

ROSE. I don't know why you want to get on talking about death.

TROY. Ain't nothing wrong with talking about death. That's part of life. Everybody gonna die. You gonna die, I'm gonna die. Bono's gonna die. Hell, we all gonna die.

ROSE. But you ain't got to talk about it. I don't like to talk about it.

TROY. You the one brought it up. Me and Bono was talking about baseball . . . you tell me I'm gonna drink myself to death. Ain't that right, Bono? You know I don't drink this but one night out of the week. That's Friday night. I'm gonna drink just enough to where I can handle it. Then I cuts it loose. I leave it alone. So don't you worry about me drinking myself to death. 'Cause I ain't worried about Death. I done seen him. I done wrestled with him.

Look here, Bono . . . I looked up one day and Death was marching straight at me. Like Soldiers on Parade! The Army of Death was marching straight at me. The middle of July, 1941. It got real cold just like it be winter. It seem like Death himself reached out and touched me on the shoulder. He touch me just like I touch you. I got cold as ice and Death standing there grinning at me.

ROSE. Troy, why don't you hush that talk.

TROY. I say . . . what you want, Mr. Death? You be wanting me? You done brought your army to be getting me? I looked him dead in the eye. I wasn't fearing nothing. I was ready to tangle. Just like I'm ready to tangle now. The Bible say be ever vigilant. That's why I don't get but so drunk. I got to keep watch.

ROSE. Troy was right down there in Mercy Hospital. You remember he had pneumonia? Laying there with a fever talking plumb out of his head.

TROY. Death standing there staring at me . . . carrying that sickle in his hand. Finally he say, "You want bound over for another year?" See, just like that . . . "You want bound over for another year?" I told him, "Bound over hell! Let's settle this now!"

It seem like he kinda fell back when I said that, and all the cold went out of me. I reached down and grabbed that sickle and threw it just as far as I could throw it . . . and me and him commenced to wrestling.

We wrestled for three days and three nights. I can't say where I found the strength from. Everytime it seemed like he was gonna get the best of me, I'd reach way down deep inside myself and find the strength to do him one better.

ROSE. Everytime Troy tell that story he find different ways to tell it. Different things to make up about it.

TROY. I ain't making up nothing. I'm telling you the facts of what happened. I wrestled with Death for three days and three nights and I'm standing here to tell you about it. (*Pause.*) All right. At the end of the third night we done weakened each other to where we can't hardly move. Death stood up, throwed on his robe . . . had him a white robe with a hood on it. He throwed on that robe and went off to look for his sickle. Say, "I'll be back." Just like that. "I'll be back." I told him, say, "Yeah, but . . . you gonna have to find me!" I wasn't no fool. I wasn't going looking for him. Death ain't nothing to play with. And I know he's gonna get me. I know I got to join his army . . . his camp followers. But as long as I keep my strength and see him coming . . . as long as I keep up my vigilance . . . he's gonna have to fight to get me. I ain't going easy.

BONO. Well, look here, since you got to keep up your vigilance . . . let me have the bottle.

TROY. Aw hell, I shouldn't have told you that part. I should have left out that part.

ROSE. Troy be talking that stuff and half the time don't even know what he be talking about.

TROY. Bono know me better than that.

BONO. That's right. I know you. I know you got some Uncle Remus[3] in your blood. You got more stories than the devil got sinners.

TROY. Aw hell, I done seen him too! Done talked with the devil.

ROSE. Troy, don't nobody wanna be hearing all that stuff.

Lyons enters the yard from the street. Thirty-four years old, Troy's son by a previous marriage, he sports a neatly trimmed goatee, sport coat, white shirt, tieless and buttoned at the collar. Though he fancies himself a musician, he is more caught up in the rituals and "idea" of being a musician than in the actual practice of the music. He has come to borrow money from Troy, and while he knows he will be successful, he is uncertain as to what extent his lifestyle will be held up to scrutiny and ridicule.

LYONS. Hey, Pop.

TROY. What you come "Hey, Popping" me for?

LYONS. How you doing, Rose? (*He kisses her.*) Mr. Bono. How you doing?

---

[3]Narrator of traditional black tales in a book by Joel Chandler Harris.

BONO. Hey, Lyons . . . how you been?

TROY. He must have been doing all right. I ain't seen him around here last week.

ROSE. Troy, leave your boy alone. He come by to see you and you wanna start all that nonsense.

TROY. I ain't bothering Lyons. (*Offers him the bottle.*) Here . . . get you a drink. We got an understanding. I know why he come by to see me and he know I know.

LYONS. Come on, Pop . . . I just stopped by to say hi . . . see how you was doing.

TROY. You ain't stopped by yesterday.

ROSE. You gonna stay for supper, Lyons? I got some chicken cooking in the oven.

LYONS. No, Rose . . . thanks. I was just in the neighborhood and thought I'd stop by for a minute.

TROY. You was in the neighborhood all right, nigger. You telling the truth there. You was in the neighborhood cause it's my payday.

LYONS. Well, hell, since you mentioned it . . . let me have ten dollars.

TROY. I'll be damned! I'll die and go to hell and play black-jack with the devil before I give you ten dollars.

BONO. That's what I wanna know about . . . that devil you done seen.

LYONS. What . . . Pop done seen the devil? You too much, Pops.

TROY. Yeah, I done seen him. Talked to him too!

ROSE. You ain't seen no devil. I done told you that man ain't had nothing to do with the devil. Anything you can't understand, you want to call it the devil.

TROY. Look here, Bono . . . I went down to see Hertzberger about some furniture. Got three rooms for two-ninety-eight. That what it say on the radio. "Three rooms . . . two-ninety-eight." Even made up a little song about it. Go down there . . . man tell me I can't get no credit. I'm working every day and can't get no credit. What to do? I got an empty house with some raggedy furniture in it. Cory ain't got no bed. He's sleeping on a pile of rags on the floor. Working every day and can't get no credit. Come back here—Rose'll tell you—madder than hell. Sit down . . . try to figure what I'm gonna do. Come a knock on the door. Ain't been living here but three days. Who know I'm here? Open the door . . . devil standing there bigger than life. White fellow . . . white fellow . . . got on good clothes and everything. Standing there with a clip-board in his hand. I ain't had to say nothing. First words come out of his mouth was . . . "I understand you need some furniture and can't get no credit." I liked to fell over. He say, "I'll give you all the credit you want, but you got to pay the interest on it." I told him, "Give me three rooms worth and charge whatever you want." Next day a truck pulled up here and two men unloaded them three rooms. Man what drove the truck give me a book. Say send ten dollars, first of every month to the address in the book and every thing will be all right. Say if I miss a pay-

ment the devil was coming back and it'll be hell to pay. That was fifteen years ago. To this day . . . the first of the month I send my ten dollars, Rose'll tell you.

ROSE. Troy lying.

TROY. I ain't never seen that man since. Now you tell me who else that could have been but the devil? I ain't sold my soul or nothing like that, you understand. Naw, I wouldn't have truck with the devil about nothing like that. I got my furniture and pays my ten dollars the first of the month just like clockwork.

BONO. How long you say you been paying this ten dollars a month?

TROY. Fifteen years!

BONO. Hell, ain't you finished paying for it yet? How much the man done charged you?

TROY. Ah hell, I done paid for it. I done paid for it ten times over! The fact is I'm scared to stop paying it.

ROSE. Troy lying. We got that furniture from Mr. Glickman. He ain't paying no ten dollars a month to nobody.

TROY. Aw hell, woman. Bono know I ain't that big a fool.

LYONS. I was just getting ready to say . . . I know where there's a bridge for sale.

TROY. Look here, I'll tell you this . . . it don't matter to me if he was the devil. It don't matter if the devil give credit. Somebody has got to give it.

ROSE. It ought to matter. You going around talking about having truck with the devil . . . God's the one you gonna have to answer to. He's the one gonna be at the Judgment.

LYONS. Yeah, well, look here, Pop . . . Let me have that ten dollars. I'll give it back to you. Bonnie got a job working at the hospital.

TROY. What I tell you, Bono? The only time I see this nigger is when he wants something. That's the only time I see him.

LYONS. Come on, Pop, Mr. Bono don't want to hear all that. Let me have the ten dollars. I told you Bonnie working.

TROY. What that mean to me? "Bonnie working." I don't care if she working. Go ask her for the ten dollars if she working. Talking about "Bonnie working." Why ain't you working?

LYONS. Aw, Pop, you know I can't find no decent job. Where am I gonna get a job at? You know I can't get no job.

TROY. I told you I know some people down there. I can get you on the rubbish if you want to work. I told you that the last time you came by here asking me for something.

LYONS. Naw, Pop . . . thanks. That ain't for me. I don't wanna be carrying nobody's rubbish. I don't wanna be punching nobody's time clock.

TROY. What's the matter, you too good to carry people's rubbish? Where you think that ten dollars you talking about come from? I'm just supposed to haul people's rubbish and give my money to you cause you too lazy to work. You too lazy to work and wanna know why you ain't got what I got.

ROSE. What hospital Bonnie working at? Mercy?

LYONS. She's down at Passavant working in the laundry.

TROY. I ain't got nothing as it is. I give you that ten dollars and I got to eat beans the rest of the week. Naw . . . you ain't getting no ten dollars here.

LYONS. You ain't got to be eating no beans. I don't know why you wanna say that.

TROY. I ain't got no extra money. Gabe done moved over to Miss Pearl's paying her the rent and things done got tight around here. I can't afford to be giving you every payday.

LYONS. I ain't asked you to give me nothing. I asked you to loan me ten dollars. I know you got ten dollars.

TROY. Yeah, I got it. You know why I got it? Cause I don't throw my money away out there in the streets. You living the fast life . . . wanna be a musician . . . running around in them clubs and things . . . then, you learn to take care of yourself. You ain't gonna find me going and asking nobody for nothing. I done spent too many years without.

LYONS. You and me is two different people, Pop.

TROY. I done learned my mistake and learned to do what's right by it. You still trying to get something for nothing. Life don't owe you nothing. You owe it to yourself. Ask Bono. He'll tell you I'm right.

LYONS. You got your way of dealing with the world . . . I got mine. The only thing that matters to me is the music.

TROY. Yeah, I can see that! It don't matter how you gonna eat . . . where your next dollar is coming from. You telling the truth there.

LYONS. I know I got to eat. But I got to live too. I need something that gonna help me to get out of the bed in the morning. Make me feel like I belong in the world. I don't bother nobody. I just stay with the music cause that's the only way I can find to live in the world. Otherwise there ain't no telling what I might do. Now I don't come criticizing you and how you live. I just come by to ask you for ten dollars. I don't wanna hear all that about how I live.

TROY. Boy, your mamma did a hell of a job raising you.

LYONS. You can't change me, Pop. I'm thirty-four years old. If you wanted to change me, you should have been there when I was growing up. I come by to see you . . . ask for ten dollars and you want to talk about how I was raised. You don't know nothing about how I was raised.

ROSE. Let the boy have ten dollars, Troy.

TROY (to Lyons). What the hell you looking at me for? I ain't got no ten dollars. You know what I do with my money. (To Rose.) Give him ten dollars if you want him to have it.

ROSE. I will. Just as soon as you turn it loose.

TROY (handing Rose the money). There it is. Seventy-six dollars and forty-two cents. You see this, Bono? Now, I ain't gonna get but six of that back.

ROSE. You ought to stop telling that lie. Here, Lyons. (She hands him the money.)

LYONS. Thanks, Rose. Look . . . I got to run . . . I'll see you later.

TROY. Wait a minute. You gonna say, "thanks, Rose" and ain't gonna look to see where she got that ten dollars from? See how they do me, Bono?

LYONS. I know she got it from you, Pop. Thanks. I'll give it back to you.

TROY. There he go telling another lie. Time I see that ten dollars . . . he'll be owing me thirty more.

LYONS. See you, Mr. Bono.

BONO. Take care, Lyons!

LYONS. Thanks, Pop. I'll see you again.

Lyons exits the yard.

TROY. I don't know why he don't go and get him a decent job and take care of that woman he got.

BONO. He'll be all right, Troy. The boy is still young.

TROY. The *boy* is thirty-four years old.

ROSE. Let's not get off into all that.

BONO. Look here . . . I got to be going. I got to be getting on. Lucille gonna be waiting.

TROY (puts his arm around Rose). See this woman, Bono? I love this woman. I love this woman so much it hurts. I love her so much . . . I done run out of ways of loving her. So I got to go back to basics. Don't you come by my house Monday morning talking about time to go to work . . . 'cause I'm still gonna be stroking!

ROSE. Troy! Stop it now!

BONO. I ain't paying him no mind, Rose. That ain't nothing but gin-talk. Go on, Troy. I'll see you Monday.

TROY. Don't you come by my house, nigger! I done told you what I'm gonna be doing.

The lights go down to black.

SCENE 2

The lights come up on Rose hanging up clothes. She hums and sings softly to herself. It is the following morning.

ROSE (sings).

Jesus, be a fence all around me every day
Jesus, I want you to protect me as I travel on my way.
Jesus, be a fence all around me every day.

Troy enters from the house.

Jesus, I want you to protect me
As I travel on my way.

(To Troy.) 'Morning. You ready for breakfast? I can fix it soon as I finish hanging up these clothes.

TROY. I got the coffee on. That'll be all right. I'll just drink some of that this morning.

ROSE. That 651 hit yesterday. That's the second time this month. Miss Pearl hit for a dollar . . . seem like those that need the least always get lucky. Poor folks can't get nothing.

TROY. Them numbers don't know nobody. I don't know why you fool with them. You and Lyons both.

ROSE. It's something to do.

TROY. You ain't doing nothing but throwing your money away.

ROSE. Troy, you know I don't play foolishly. I just play a nickel here and a nickel there.

TROY. That's two nickels you done thrown away.

ROSE. Now I hit sometimes . . . that makes up for it. It always comes in handy when I do hit. I don't hear you complaining then.

TROY. I ain't complaining now. I just say it's foolish. Trying to guess out of six hundred ways which way the number gonna come. If I had all the money niggers, these Negroes, throw away on numbers for one week—just one week—I'd be a rich man.

ROSE. Well, you wishing and calling it foolish ain't gonna stop folks from playing numbers. That's one thing for sure. Besides . . . some good things come from playing numbers. Look where Pope done bought him that restaurant off of numbers.

TROY. I can't stand niggers like that. Man ain't had two dimes to rub together. He walking around with his shoes all run over bumming money for cigarettes. All right. Got lucky there and hit the numbers . . .

ROSE. Troy, I know all about it.

TROY. Had good sense, I'll say that for him. He ain't throwed his money away. I seen niggers hit the numbers and go through two thousand dollars in four days. Man bought him that restaurant down there . . . fixed it up real nice . . . and then didn't want nobody to come in it! A Negro go in there and can't get no kind of service. I seen a white fellow come in there and order a bowl of stew. Pope picked all the meat out of the pot for him. Man ain't had nothing but a bowl of meat! Negro come behind him and ain't got nothing but the potatoes and carrots. Talking about what numbers do for people, you picked a wrong example. Ain't done nothing but make a worser fool out of him than he was before.

ROSE. Troy, you ought to stop worrying about what happened at work yesterday.

TROY. I ain't worried. Just told me to be down there at the Commissioner's office on Friday. Everybody think they gonna fire me. I ain't worried about them firing me. You ain't got to worry about that. (*Pause.*) Where's Cory? Cory in the house? (*Calls.*) Cory?

ROSE. He gone out.

TROY. Out, huh? He gone out 'cause he know I want him to help me with this fence. I know how he is. That boy scared of work.

Gabriel enters. He comes halfway down the alley and, hearing Troy's voice, stops.

TROY (*continues*). He ain't done a lick of work in his life.

ROSE. He had to go to football practice. Coach wanted them to get in a little extra practice before the season start.

TROY. I got his practice . . . running out of here before he get his chores done.

ROSE. Troy, what is wrong with you this morning? Don't nothing set right with you. Go on back in there and go to bed . . . get up on the other side.

TROY. Why something got to be wrong with me? I ain't said nothing wrong with me.

ROSE. You got something to say about everything. First it's the numbers . . . then it's the way the man runs his restaurant . . . then you done got on Cory. What's it gonna be next? Take a look up there and see if the weather suits you . . . or is it gonna be how you gonna put up the fence with the clothes hanging in the yard.

TROY. You hit the nail on the head then.

ROSE. I know you like I know the back of my hand. Go on in there and get you some coffee . . . see if that straighten you up. 'Cause you ain't right this morning.

Troy starts into the house and sees Gabriel. Gabriel starts singing. Troy's brother, he is seven years younger than Troy. Injured in World War II, he has a metal plate in his head. He carries an old trumpet tied around his waist and believes with every fiber of his being that he is the Archangel Gabriel. He carries a chipped basket with an assortment of discarded fruits and vegetables he has picked up in the strip district and which he attempts to sell.

GABRIEL (*singing*).
> Yes, ma'am I got plums
> You ask me how I sell them
> Oh ten cents apiece
> Three for a quarter
> Come and buy now
> 'Cause I'm here today
> And tomorrow I'll be gone

Gabriel enters.

Hey, Rose!

ROSE. How you doing Gabe?

GABRIEL. There's Troy . . . Hey, Troy!

TROY. Hey, Gabe.

Exit into kitchen.

ROSE (*to Gabriel*). What you got there?

GABRIEL. You know what I got, Rose. I got fruits and vegetables.

ROSE (*looking in basket*). Where's all these plums you talking about?

GABRIEL. I ain't got no plums today, Rose. I was just singing that. Have some tomorrow. Put me in a big order for plums. Have enough plums tomorrow for St. Peter and everybody.

Troy reenters from kitchen, crosses to steps.

(*To Rose.*) Troy's mad at me.

TROY. I ain't mad at you. What I got to be mad at you about? You ain't done nothing to me.

GABRIEL. I just moved over to Miss Pearl's to keep out from in your way. I ain't mean no harm by it.

TROY. Who said anything about that? I ain't said anything about that.

GABRIEL. You ain't mad at me, is you?

TROY. Naw . . . I ain't mad at you, Gabe. If I was mad at you I'd tell you about it.

GABRIEL. Got me two rooms. In the basement. Got my own door too. Wanna see my key? (*He holds up a key.*) That's my own key! My two rooms!

TROY. Well, that's good, Gabe. You got your own key . . . that's good.

ROSE. You hungry, Gabe? I was just fixing to cook Troy his breakfast.

GABRIEL. I'll take some biscuits. You got some biscuits? Did you know when I was in heaven . . . every morning me and St. Peter would sit down by the gate and eat some big fat biscuits? Oh, yeah! We had us a good time. We'd sit there and eat us them biscuits and then St. Peter would go off to sleep and tell me to wake him up when it's time to open the gates for the judgment.

ROSE. Well, come on . . . I'll make up a batch of biscuits.

Rose exits into the house.

GABRIEL. Troy . . . St. Peter got your name in the book. I seen it. It say . . . Troy Maxson. I say . . . I know him! He got the same name like what I got. That's my brother!

TROY. How many times you gonna tell me that, Gabe?

GABRIEL. Ain't got my name in the book. Don't have to have my name. I done died and went to heaven. He got your name though. One morning St. Peter was looking at his book . . . marking it up for the judgment . . . and he let me see your name. Got it in there under M. Got Rose's name . . . I ain't seen it like I seen yours . . . but I know it's in there. He got a great big book. Got everybody's name what was ever been born. That's what he told me. But I seen your name. Seen it with my own eyes.

TROY. Go on in the house there. Rose going to fix you something to eat.

GABRIEL. Oh, I ain't hungry. I done had breakfast with Aunt Jemimah. She come by and cooked me up a whole mess of flapjacks. Remember how we used to eat them flapjacks?

TROY. Go on in the house and get you something to eat now.

GABRIEL. I got to sell my plums. I done sold some tomatoes. Got me two quarters. Wanna see? (*He shows Troy his quarters.*) I'm gonna save them and buy me a new horn so St. Peter can hear me when it's time to open the gates. (*Gabriel stops suddenly. Listens.*) Hear that? That's the

hellhounds. I got to chase them out of here. Go on get out of here! Get out!

Gabriel exits singing.

> Better get ready for the judgment
> Better get ready for the judgment
> My Lord is coming down

Rose enters from the house.

TROY. He's gone off somewhere.

GABRIEL (*offstage*).

> Better get ready for the judgment
> Better get ready for the judgment morning
> Better get ready for the judgment
> My God is coming down

ROSE. He ain't eating right. Miss Pearl say she can't get him to eat nothing.

TROY. What you want me to do about it, Rose? I done did everything I can for the man. I can't make him get well. Man got half his head blown away . . . what you expect?

ROSE. Seem like something ought to be done to help him.

TROY. Man don't bother nobody. He just mixed up from that metal plate he got in his head. Ain't no sense for him to go back into the hospital.

ROSE. Least he be eating right. They can help him take care of himself.

TROY. Don't nobody wanna be locked up, Rose. What you wanna lock him up for? Man go over there and fight the war . . . messin' around with them Japs, get half his head blow off . . . and they give him a lousy three thousand dollars. And I had to swoop down on that.

ROSE. Is you fixing to go into that again?

TROY. That's the only way I got a roof over my head . . . cause of that metal plate.

ROSE. Ain't no sense you blaming yourself for nothing. Gabe wasn't in no condition to manage that money. You done what was right by him. Can't nobody say you ain't done what was right by him. Look how long you took care of him . . . till he wanted to have his own place and moved over there with Miss Pearl.

TROY. That ain't what I'm saying, woman! I'm just stating the facts. If my brother didn't have that metal plate in his head . . . I wouldn't have a pot to piss in or a window to throw it out of. And I'm fifty-three years old. Now see if you can understand that!

Troy gets up from the porch and starts to exit the yard.

ROSE. Where you going off to? You been running out of here every Saturday for weeks. I thought you was gonna work on this fence?

TROY. I'm gonna walk down to Taylor's. Listen to the ball game. I'll be back in a bit. I'll work on it when I get back.

He exits the yard. The lights go to black.

SCENE 3

The lights come up on the yard. It is four hours later. Rose is taking down the clothes from the line. Cory enters carrying his football equipment.

ROSE. Your daddy like to had a fit with you running out of here this morning without doing your chores.

CORY. I told you I had to go to practice.

ROSE. He say you were supposed to help him with this fence.

CORY. He been saying that the last four or five Saturdays, and then he don't never do nothing, but go down to Taylors'. Did you tell him about the recruiter?

ROSE. Yeah, I told him.

CORY. What he say?

ROSE. He ain't said nothing too much. You get in there and get started on your chores before he gets back. Go on and scrub down them steps before he gets back here hollering and carrying on.

CORY. I'm hungry. What you got to eat, Mama?

ROSE. Go on and get started on your chores. I got some meat loaf in there. Go on and make you a sandwich . . . and don't leave no mess in there.

Cory exits into the house. Rose continues to take down the clothes. Troy enters the yard and sneaks up and grabs her from behind.

Troy! Go on, now. You liked to scared me to death. What was the score of the game? Lucille had me on the phone and I couldn't keep up with it.

TROY. What I care about the game? Come here, woman. (*He tries to kiss her.*)

ROSE. I thought you went down Taylors' to listen to the game. Go on, Troy! You supposed to be putting up this fence.

TROY (*attempting to kiss her again*). I'll put it up when I finish with what is at hand.

ROSE. Go on, Troy. I ain't studying you.

TROY (*chasing after her*). I'm studying you . . . fixing to do my homework!

ROSE. Troy, you better leave me alone.

TROY. Where's Cory? That boy brought his butt home yet?

ROSE. He's in the house doing his chores.

TROY (*calling*). Cory! Get your butt out here, boy!

Rose exits into the house with the laundry. Troy goes over to the pile of wood, picks up a board, and starts sawing. Cory enters from the house.

TROY. You just now coming in here from leaving this morning?

CORY. Yeah, I had to go to football practice.

TROY. Yeah, what?

CORY. Yessir.

TROY. I ain't but two seconds off you noway. The garbage sitting in there overflowing . . . you ain't done none of your chores . . . and you come in here talking about "Yeah."

CORY. I was just getting ready to do my chores now, Pop . . .

TROY. Your first chore is to help me with this fence on Saturday. Everything else come after that. Now get that saw and cut them boards.

Cory takes the saw and begins cutting the boards. Troy continues working. There is a long pause.

CORY. Hey, Pop . . . why don't you buy a TV?

TROY. What I want with a TV? What I want one of them for?

CORY. Everybody got one. Earl, Ba Bra . . . Jesse!

TROY. I ain't asked you who had one. I say what I want with one?

CORY. So you can watch it. They got lots of things on TV. Baseball games and everything. We could watch the World Series.

TROY. Yeah . . . and how much this TV cost?

CORY. I don't know. They got them on sale for around two hundred dollars.

TROY. Two hundred dollars, huh?

CORY. That ain't that much, Pop.

TROY. Naw, it's just two hundred dollars. See that roof you got over your head at night? Let me tell you something about that roof. It's been over ten years since that roof was last tarred. See now . . . the snow come this winter and sit up there on that roof like it is . . . and it's gonna seep inside. It's just gonna be a little bit . . . ain't gonna hardly notice it. Then the next thing you know, it's gonna be leaking all over the house. Then the wood rot from all that water and you gonna need a whole new roof. Now, how much you think it cost to get that roof tarred?

CORY. I don't know.

TROY. Two hundred and sixty-four dollars . . . cash money. While you thinking about a TV, I got to be thinking about the roof . . . and whatever else go wrong here. Now if you had two hundred dollars, what would you do . . . fix the roof or buy a TV?

CORY. I'd buy a TV. Then when the roof started to leak . . . when it needed fixing . . . I'd fix it.

TROY. Where you gonna get the money from? You done spent it for a TV. You gonna sit up and watch the water run all over your brand new TV.

CORY. Aw, Pop. You got money. I know you do.

TROY. Where I got it at, huh?

CORY. You got it in the bank.

TROY. You wanna see my bankbook? You wanna see that seventy-three dollars and twenty-two cents I got sitting up in there?

CORY. You ain't got to pay for it all at one time. You can put a down payment on it and carry it on home with you.

TROY. Not me. I ain't gonna owe nobody nothing if I can help it. Miss a payment and they come and snatch it right out of your house. Then what you got? Now, soon as I get two hundred dollars clear, then I'll buy a TV. Right now, as soon as I get two hundred and sixty-four dollars, I'm gonna have this roof tarred.

CORY. Aw . . . Pop!

TROY. You go on and get you two hundred dollars and buy one if ya want it. I got better things to do with my money.

CORY. I can't get no two hundred dollars. I ain't never seen two hundred dollars.

TROY. I'll tell you what . . . you get you a hundred dollars and I'll put the other hundred with it.

CORY. All right, I'm gonna show you.

TROY. You gonna show me how you can cut them boards right now.

Cory begins to cut the boards. There is a long pause.

CORY. The Pirates won today. That makes five in a row.

TROY. I ain't thinking about the Pirates. Got an all-white team. Got that boy . . . that Puerto Rican boy . . . Clemente. Don't even half-play him. That boy could be something if they give him a chance. Play him one day and sit him on the bench the next.

CORY. He gets a lot of chances to play.

TROY. I'm talking about playing regular. Playing every day so you can get your timing. That's what I'm talking about.

CORY. They got some white guys on the team that don't play every day. You can't play everybody at the same time.

TROY. If they got a white fellow sitting on the bench . . . you can bet your last dollar he can't play! The colored guy got to be twice as good before he get on the team. That's why I don't want you to get all tied up in them sports. Man on the team and what it get him? They got colored on the team and don't use them. Same as not having them. All them teams the same.

CORY. The Braves got Hank Aaron and Wes Covington. Hank Aaron hit two home runs today. That makes forty-three.

TROY. Hank Aaron ain't nobody. That what you supposed to do. That's how you supposed to play the game. Ain't nothing to it. It's just a matter of timing . . . getting the right follow-through. Hell, I can hit forty-three home runs right now!

CORY. Not off no major-league pitching, you couldn't.

TROY. We had better pitching in the Negro leagues. I hit seven home runs off of Satchel Paige.[4] You can't get no better than that!

CORY. Sandy Koufax. He's leading the league in strikeouts.

TROY. I ain't thinking of no Sandy Koufax.

CORY. You got Warren Spahn and Lew Burdette. I bet you couldn't hit no home runs off of Warren Spahn.

TROY. I'm through with it now. You go on and cut them boards. (*Pause.*) Your mama tell me you done got recruited by a college football team? Is that right?

CORY. Yeah. Coach Zellman say the recruiter gonna be coming by to talk to you. Get you to sign the permission papers.

TROY. I thought you supposed to be working down there at the A&P. Ain't you suppose to be working down there after school?

CORY. Mr. Stawicki say he gonna hold my job for me until after the football season. Say starting next week I can work weekends.

TROY. I thought we had an understanding about this football stuff? You suppose to keep up with your chores and hold that job down at the A&P. Ain't been around here all day on a Saturday. Ain't none of your chores done . . . and now you telling me you done quit your job.

CORY. I'm going to be working weekends.

TROY. You damn right you are! And ain't no need for nobody coming around here to talk to me about signing nothing.

CORY. Hey, Pop . . . you can't do that. He's coming all the way from North Carolina.

TROY. I don't care where he coming from. The white man ain't gonna let you get nowhere with that football noway. You go on and get your book-learning so you can work yourself up in that A&P or learn how to fix cars or build houses or something, get you a trade. That way you have something can't nobody take away from you. You go on and learn how to put your hands to some good use. Besides hauling people's garbage.

CORY. I get good grades, Pop. That's why the recruiter wants to talk with you. You got to keep up your grades to get recruited. This way I'll be going to college. I'll get a chance . . .

TROY. First you gonna get your butt down there to the A&P and get your job back.

CORY. Mr. Stawicki done already hired somebody else 'cause I told him I was playing football.

TROY. You a bigger fool than I thought . . . to let somebody take away your job so you can play some football. Where you gonna get your money to take out your girlfriend and whatnot? What kind of foolishness is that to let somebody take away your job?

CORY. I'm still gonna be working weekends.

TROY. Naw . . . naw. You getting your butt out of here and finding you another job.

CORY. Come on, Pop! I got to practice. I can't work after school and play football too. The team needs me. That's what Coach Zellman say . . .

TROY. I don't care what nobody else say. I'm the boss . . . you understand? I'm the boss around here. I do the only saying what counts.

CORY. Come on, Pop!

TROY. I asked you . . . did you understand?

CORY. Yeah . . .

TROY. What?!

CORY. Yessir.

TROY. You go on down there to that A&P and see if you can get your job back. If you can't do both . . . then you quit the football team. You've got to take the crookeds with the straights.

---

[4]Paige (1906–1982) was a pitcher in the Negro leagues.

CORY. Yessir. (*Pause.*) Can I ask you a question?

TROY. What the hell you wanna ask me? Mr. Stawicki the one you got the questions for.

CORY. How come you ain't never liked me?

TROY. Liked you? Who the hell say I got to like you? What law is there say I got to like you? Wanna stand up in my face and ask a damn foolass question like that. Talking about liking somebody. Come here, boy, when I talk to you.

Cory comes over to where Troy is working. He stands slouched over and Troy shoves him on his shoulder.

Straighten up, goddammit! I asked you a question . . . what law is there say I got to like you?

CORY. None.

TROY. Well, all right then! Don't you eat every day? (*Pause.*) Answer me when I talk to you! Don't you eat every day?

CORY. Yeah.

TROY. Nigger, as long as you in my house, you put that sir on the end of it when you talk to me.

CORY. Yes . . . sir.

TROY. You eat every day.

CORY. Yessir!

TROY. Got a roof over your head.

CORY. Yessir!

TROY. Got clothes on your back.

CORY. Yessir.

TROY. Why you think that is?

CORY. Cause of you.

TROY. Ah, hell I know it's cause of me . . . but why do you think that is?

CORY (*hesitant*). Cause you like me.

TROY. Like you? I go out of here every morning . . . bust my butt . . . putting up with them crackers every day . . . cause I like you? You are the biggest fool I ever saw. (*Pause.*) It's my job. It's my responsibility! You understand that? A man got to take care of his family. You live in my house . . . sleep you behind on my bedclothes . . . fill you belly up with my food . . . cause you my son. You my flesh and blood. Not cause I like you! Cause it's my duty to take care of you. I owe a responsibility to you! Let's get this straight right here . . . before it go along any further . . . I ain't got to like you. Mr. Rand don't give me my money come payday cause he likes me. He gives me cause he owe me. I done give you everything I had to give you. I gave you your life! Me and your mama worked that out between us. And liking your black ass wasn't part of the bargain. Don't you try and go through life worrying about if somebody like you or not. You best be making sure they doing right by you. You understand what I'm saying boy?

CORY. Yessir.

TROY. Then get the hell out of my face, and get on down to that A&P.

Rose has been standing behind the screen door for much of the scene. She enters as Cory exits.

ROSE. Why don't you let the boy go ahead and play football, Troy? Ain't no harm in that. He's just trying to be like you with the sports.

TROY. I don't want him to be like me! I want him to move as far away from my life as he can get. You the only decent thing that ever happened to me. I wish him that. But I don't wish him a thing else from my life. I decided seventeen years ago that boy wasn't getting involved in no sports. Not after what they did to me in the sports.

ROSE. Troy, why don't you admit you was too old to play in the major leagues? For once . . . why don't you admit that?

TROY. What do you mean too old? Don't come telling me I was too old. I just wasn't the right color. Hell, I'm fifty-three years old and can do better than Selkirk's .269 right now!

ROSE. How's was you gonna play ball when you were over forty? Sometimes I can't get no sense out of you.

TROY. I got good sense, woman. I got sense enough not to let my boy get hurt over playing no sports. You been mothering that boy too much. Worried about if people like him.

ROSE. Everything that boy do . . . he do for you. He wants you to say "Good job, son." That's all.

TROY. Rose, I ain't got time for that. He's alive. He's healthy. He's got to make his own way. I made mine. Ain't nobody gonna hold his hand when he get out there in that world.

ROSE. Times have changed from when you was young, Troy. People change. The world's changing around you and you can't even see it.

TROY (*slow, methodical*). Woman . . . I do the best I can do. I come in here every Friday. I carry a sack of potatoes and a bucket of lard. You all line up at the door with your hands out. I give you the lint from my pockets. I give you my sweat and my blood. I ain't got no tears. I done spent them. We go upstairs in that room at night . . . and I fall down on you and try to blast a hole into forever. I get up Monday morning . . . find my lunch on the table. I go out. Make my way. Find my strength to carry me through to the next Friday. (*Pause.*) That's all I got, Rose. That's all I got to give. I can't give nothing else.

Troy exits into the house. The lights go down to black.

SCENE 4

It is Friday. Two weeks later. Cory starts out of the house with his football equipment. The phone rings.

CORY (*calling*). I got it! (*He answers the phone and stands in the screen door talking.*) Hello? Hey, Jesse. Naw . . . I was just getting ready to leave now.

ROSE (*calling*). Cory!

CORY. I told you, man, them spikes is all tore up. You can

use them if you want, but they ain't no good. Earl got some spikes.

ROSE (*calling*). Cory!

CORY (*calling to Rose*). Mam? I'm talking to Jesse. (*Into phone.*) When she say that? (*Pause.*) Aw, you lying, man. I'm gonna tell her you said that.

ROSE (*calling*). Cory, don't you go nowhere!

CORY. I got to go to the game, Ma! (*Into the phone.*) Yeah, hey, look, I'll talk to you later. Yeah, I'll meet you over Earl's house. Later. Bye, Ma.

Cory exits the house and starts out the yard.

ROSE. Cory, where you going off to? You got that stuff all pulled out and thrown all over your room.

CORY (*in the yard*). I was looking for my spikes. Jesse wanted to borrow my spikes.

ROSE. Get up there and get that cleaned up before your daddy get back in here.

CORY. I got to go to the game! I'll clean it up *when I get back*.

Cory exits.

ROSE. That's all he need to do is see that room all messed up.

Rose exits into the house. Troy and Bono enter the yard. Troy is dressed in clothes other than his work clothes.

BONO. He told him the same thing he told you. Take it to the union.

TROY. Brownie ain't got that much sense. Man wasn't thinking about nothing. He wait until I confront them on it . . . then he wanna come crying seniority. (*Calls.*) Hey, Rose!

BONO. I wish I could have seen Mr. Rand's face when he told you.

TROY. He couldn't get it out of his mouth! Liked to bit his tongue! When they called me down there to the Commissioner's office . . . he thought they was gonna fire me. Like everybody else.

BONO. I didn't think they was gonna fire you. I thought they was gonna put you on the warning paper.

TROY. Hey, Rose! (*To Bono.*) Yeah, Mr. Rand like to bit his tongue.

Troy breaks the seal on the bottle, takes a drink, and hands it to Bono.

BONO. I see you run right down to Taylors' and told that Alberta gal.

TROY (*calling*). Hey Rose! (*To Bono.*) I told everybody. Hey, Rose! I went down there to cash my check.

ROSE (*entering from the house*). Hush all that hollering, man! I know you out here. What they say down there at the Commissioner's office?

TROY. You supposed to come when I call you, woman. Bono'll tell you that. (*To Bono.*) Don't Lucille come when you call her?

ROSE. Man, hush your mouth. I ain't no dog . . . talk about "come when you call me."

TROY (*puts his arm around Rose*). You hear this, Bono? I had me an old dog used to get uppity like that. You say, "C'mere, Blue!" . . . and he just lay there and look at you. End up getting a stick and chasing him away trying to make him come.

ROSE. I ain't studying you and your dog. I remember you used to sing that old song.

TROY (*he sings*).

Hear it ring! Hear it ring! I had a dog his name was Blue.

ROSE. Don't nobody wanna hear you sing that old song.

TROY (*sings*).

You know Blue was mighty true.

ROSE. Used to have Cory running around here singing that song.

BONO. Hell, I remember that song myself.

TROY (*sings*).

You know Blue was a good old dog.

Blue treed a possum in a hollow log.

That was my daddy's song. My daddy made up that song.

ROSE. I don't care who made it up. Don't nobody wanna hear you sing it.

TROY (*makes a song like calling a dog*). Come here, woman.

ROSE. You come in here carrying on, I reckon they ain't fired you. What they say down there at the Commissioner's office?

TROY. Look here, Rose . . . Mr. Rand called me into his office today when I got back from talking to them people down there . . . it come from up top . . . he called me in and told me they was making me a driver.

ROSE. Troy, you kidding!

TROY. No I ain't. Ask Bono.

ROSE. Well, that's great, Troy. Now you don't have to hassle them people no more.

Lyons enters from the street.

TROY. Aw hell, I wasn't looking to see you today. I thought you was in jail. Got it all over the front page of the *Courier* about them raiding Sefus's place . . . where you be hanging out with all them thugs.

LYONS. Hey, Pop . . . that ain't got nothing to do with me. I don't go down there gambling. I go down there to sit in with the band. I ain't got nothing to do with the gambling part. They got some good music down there.

TROY. They got some rogues . . . is what they got.

LYONS. How you been, Mr. Bono? Hi, Rose.

BONO. I see where you playing down at the Crawford Grill tonight.

ROSE. How come you ain't brought Bonnie like I told you? You should have brought Bonnie with you, she ain't been over in a month of Sundays.

LYONS. I was just in the neighborhood . . . thought I'd stop by.

TROY. Here he come . . .

BONO. Your daddy got a promotion on the rubbish. He's gonna be the first colored driver. Ain't got to do nothing but sit up there and read the paper like them white fellows.

LYONS. Hey, Pop . . . if you knew how to read you'd be all right.

BONO. Naw . . . naw . . . you mean if the nigger knew how to drive he'd be all right. Been fighting with them people about driving and ain't even got a license. Mr. Rand know you ain't got no driver's license?

TROY. Driving ain't nothing. All you do is point the truck where you want it to go. Driving ain't nothing.

BONO. Do Mr. Rand know you ain't got no driver's license? That's what I'm talking about. I ain't asked if driving was easy. I asked if Mr. Rand know you ain't got no driver's license.

TROY. He ain't got to know. The man ain't got to know my business. Time he find out, I have two or three driver's licenses.

LYONS (going into his pocket). Say, look here, Pop . . .

TROY. I knew it was coming. Didn't I tell you, Bono? I know what kind of "Look here, Pop" that was. The nigger fixing to ask me for some money. It's Friday night. It's my payday. All them rogues down there on the avenue . . . the ones that ain't in jail . . . and Lyons is hopping in his shoes to get down there with them.

LYONS. See, Pop . . . if you give somebody else a chance to talk sometimes, you'd see that I was fixing to pay you back your ten dollars like I told you. Here . . . I told you I'd pay you when Bonnie got paid.

TROY. Naw . . . you go ahead and keep that ten dollars. Put it in the bank. The next time you feel like you wanna come by here and ask me for something . . . you go on down there and get that.

LYONS. Here's your ten dollars, Pop. I told you I don't want you to give me nothing. I just wanted to borrow ten dollars.

TROY. Naw . . . you go on and keep that for the next time you want to ask me.

LYONS. Come on, Pop . . . here go your ten dollars.

ROSE. Why don't you go on and let the boy pay you back, Troy?

LYONS. Here you go, Rose. If you don't take it I'm gonna have to hear about it for the next six months. (He hands her the money.)

ROSE. You can hand yours over here too, Troy.

TROY. You see this, Bono. You see how they do me.

BONO. Yeah, Lucille do me the same way.

Gabriel is heard singing off stage. He enters.

GABRIEL. Better get ready for the Judgment! Better get ready for . . . Hey! . . . Hey! . . . There's Troy's boy!

LYONS. How are you doing, Uncle Gabe?

GABRIEL. Lyons . . . The King of the Jungle! Rose . . . hey, Rose. Got a flower for you. (He takes a rose from his pocket.) Picked it myself. That's the same rose like you is!

ROSE. That's right nice of you, Gabe.

LYONS. What you been doing, Uncle Gabe?

GABRIEL. Oh, I been chasing hellhounds and waiting on the time to tell St. Peter to open the gates.

LYONS. You been chasing hellhounds, huh? Well . . . you doing the right thing, Uncle Gabe. Somebody got to chase them.

GABRIEL. Oh, yeah . . . I know it. The devil's strong. The devil ain't no pushover. Hellhounds snipping at everybody's heels. But I got my trumpet waiting on the judgment time.

LYONS. Waiting on the Battle of Armageddon, huh?

GABRIEL. Ain't gonna be too much of a battle when God get to waving that Judgment sword. But the people's gonna have a hell of a time trying to get into heaven if them gates ain't open.

LYONS (putting his arm around Gabriel). You hear this, Pop. Uncle Gabe, you all right!

GABRIEL (laughing with Lyons). Lyons! King of the Jungle.

ROSE. You gonna stay for supper, Gabe? Want me to fix you a plate?

GABRIEL. I'll take a sandwich, Rose. Don't want no plate. Just wanna eat with my hands. I'll take a sandwich.

ROSE. How about you, Lyons? You staying? Got some short ribs cooking.

LYONS. Naw, I won't eat nothing till after we finished playing. (Pause.) You ought to come down and listen to me play, Pop.

TROY. I don't like that Chinese music. All that noise.

ROSE. Go on in the house and wash up, Gabe . . . I'll fix you a sandwich.

GABRIEL (to Lyons, as he exits). Troy's mad at me.

LYONS. What you mad at Uncle Gabe for, Pop?

ROSE. He thinks Troy's mad at him cause he moved over to Miss Pearl's.

TROY. I ain't mad at the man. He can live where he want to live at.

LYONS. What he move over there for? Miss Pearl don't like nobody.

ROSE. She don't mind him none. She treats him real nice. She just don't allow all that singing.

TROY. She don't mind that rent he be paying . . . that's what she don't mind.

ROSE. Troy, I ain't going through that with you no more. He's over there cause he want to have his own place. He can come and go as he please.

TROY. Hell, he could come and go as he please here. I wasn't stopping him. I ain't put no rules on him.

ROSE. It ain't the same thing, Troy. And you know it.

Gabriel comes to the door.

Now, that's the last I wanna hear about that. I don't wanna hear nothing else about Gabe and Miss Pearl. And next week . . .

GABRIEL. I'm ready for my sandwich, Rose.

ROSE. And next week . . . when that recruiter come from that school . . . I want you to sign that paper and go on and let Cory play football. Then that'll be the last I have to hear about that.

TROY (*to Rose as she exits into the house*). I ain't thinking about Cory nothing.

LYONS. What . . . Cory got recruited? What school he going to?

TROY. That boy walking around here smelling his piss . . . thinking he's grown. Thinking he's gonna do what he want, irrespective of what I say. Look here, Bono . . . I left the Commissioner's office and went down to the A&P . . . that boy ain't working down there. He lying to me. Telling me he got his job back . . . telling me he working weekends . . . telling me he working after school . . . Mr. Stawicki tell me he ain't working down there at all!

LYONS. Cory just growing up. He's just busting at the seams trying to fill out your shoes.

TROY. I don't care what he's doing. When he get to the point where he wanna disobey me . . . then it's time for him to move on. Bono'll tell you that. I bet he ain't never disobeyed his daddy without paying the consequences.

BONO. I ain't never had a chance. My daddy came on through . . . but I ain't never knew him to see him . . . or what he had on his mind or where he went. Just moving on through. Searching out the New Land. That's what the old folks used to call it. See a fellow moving around from place to place . . . woman to woman . . . called it searching out the New Land. I can't say if he ever found it. I come along, didn't want no kids. Didn't know if I was gonna be in one place long enough to fix on them right as their daddy. I figured I was going searching too. As it turned out I been hooked up with Lucille near about as long as your daddy been with Rose. Going on sixteen years.

TROY. Sometimes I wish I hadn't known my daddy. He ain't cared nothing about no kids. A kid to him wasn't nothing. All he wanted was for you to learn how to walk so he could start you to working. When it come time for eating . . . he ate first. If there was anything left over, that's what you got. Man would sit down and eat two chickens and give you the wing.

LYONS. You ought to stop that, Pop. Everybody feed their kids. No matter how hard times is . . . everybody care about their kids. Make sure they have something to eat.

TROY. The only thing my daddy cared about was getting them bales of cotton in to Mr. Lubin. That's the only thing that mattered to him. Sometimes I used to wonder why he was living. Wonder why the devil hadn't come and got him. "Get them bales of cotton in to Mr. Lubin" and find out he owe him money . . .

LYONS. He should have just went on and left when he saw he couldn't get nowhere. That's what I would have done.

TROY. How he gonna leave with eleven kids? And where he gonna go? He ain't knew how to do nothing but farm. No, he was trapped and I think he knew it. But I'll say this for him . . . he felt a responsibility toward us. Maybe he ain't treated us the way I felt he should have . . . but without that responsibility he could have walked off and left us . . . made his own way.

BONO. A lot of them did. Back in those days what you talking about . . . they walk out their front door and just take on down one road or another and keep on walking.

LYONS. There you go! That's what I'm talking about.

BONO. Just keep on walking till you come to something else. Ain't you never heard of nobody having the walking blues? Well, that's what you call it when you just take off like that.

TROY. My daddy ain't had them walking blues! What you talking about? He stayed right there with his family. But he was just as evil as he could be. My mama couldn't stand him. Couldn't stand that evilness. She run off when I was about eight. She sneaked off one night after he had gone to sleep. Told me she was coming back for me. I ain't never seen her no more. All his women run off and left him. He wasn't good for nobody.

When my turn come to head out, I was fourteen and got to sniffing around Joe Canewell's daughter. Had us an old mule we called Greyboy. My daddy sent me out to do some plowing and I tied up Greyboy and went to fooling around with Joe Canewell's daughter. We done found us a nice little spot, got real cozy with each other. She about thirteen and we done figured we was grown anyway . . . so we down there enjoying ourselves . . . ain't thinking about nothing. We didn't know Greyboy had got loose and wandered back to the house and my daddy was looking for me. We down there by the creek enjoying ourselves when my daddy come up on us. Surprised us. He had them leather straps off the mule and commenced to whupping me like there was no tomorrow. I jumped up, mad and embarrassed. I was scared of my daddy. When he commenced to whupping on me . . . quite naturally I run to get out of the way. (*Pause.*) Now I thought he was mad cause I ain't done my work. But I see where he was chasing me off so he could have the gal for himself. When I see what the matter of it was, I lost all fear of my daddy. Right there is where I become a man . . . at fourteen years of age. (*Pause.*) Now it was my turn to run him off. I picked up them same reins that he had used on me. I picked up them reins and commenced to whupping on him. The gal jumped up and run off . . . and when my daddy turned to face me, I could see why the devil had never come to get him . . . cause he was the devil himself. I don't know what happened. When I woke up, I was laying right there by the creek, and Blue . . . this old dog we had . . . was licking my face. I thought I was blind. I couldn't see nothing. Both my eyes were swollen shut. I laid there and cried. I didn't know what I was gonna do. The only thing I knew was the time had come for me to leave my daddy's house. And right there the world suddenly got big. And it was a long time before I could cut it down to where I could handle it.

Part of that cutting down was when I got to the place where I could feel him kicking in my blood and knew that the only thing that separated us was the matter of a few years.

Gabriel enters from the house with a sandwich.

LYONS. What you got there, Uncle Gabe?

GABRIEL. Got me a ham sandwich. Rose gave me a ham sandwich.

TROY. I don't know what happened to him. I done lost touch with everybody except Gabriel. But I hope he's dead. I hope he found some peace.

LYONS. That's a heavy story, Pop. I didn't know you left home when you was fourteen.

TROY. And didn't know nothing. The only part of the world I knew was the forty-two acres of Mr. Lubin's land. That's all I knew about life.

LYONS. Fourteen's kinda young to be out on your own. (*Phone rings.*) I don't even think I was ready to be out on my own at fourteen. I don't know what I would have done.

TROY. I got up from the creek and walked on down to Mobile. I was through with farming. Figured I could do better in the city. So I walked the two hundred miles to Mobile.

LYONS. Wait a minute . . . you ain't walked no two hundred miles, Pop. Ain't nobody gonna walk no two hundred miles. You talking about some walking there.

BONO. That's the only way you got anywhere back in them days.

LYONS. Shhh. Damn if I wouldn't have hitched a ride with somebody!

TROY. Who you gonna hitch it with? They ain't had no cars and things like they got now. We talking about 1918.

ROSE (*entering*). What you all out here getting into?

TROY (*to Rose*). I'm telling Lyons how good he got it. He don't know nothing about this I'm talking.

ROSE. Lyons, that was Bonnie on the phone. She say you supposed to pick her up.

LYONS. Yeah, okay, Rose.

TROY. I walked on down to Mobile and hitched up with some of them fellows that was heading this way. Got up here and found out . . . not only couldn't you get a job . . . you couldn't find no place to live. I thought I was in freedom. Shhh. Colored folks living down there on the riverbanks in whatever kind of shelter they could find for themselves. Right down there under the Brady Street Bridge. Living in shacks made of sticks and tarpaper. Messed around there and went from bad to worse. Started stealing. First it was food. Then I figured, hell, if I steal money I can buy me some food. Buy me some shoes too!

One thing led to another. Met your mama. I was young and anxious to be a man. Met your mama and had you. What I do that for? Now I got to worry about feeding you and her. Got to steal three times as much. Went out one day looking for somebody to rob . . . that's what I was, a robber. I'll tell you the truth. I'm ashamed of it today. But it's the truth. Went to rob this fellow . . . pulled out my knife . . . and he pulled out a gun. Shot me in the chest. I felt just like somebody had taken a hot branding iron and laid it on me. When he shot me I jumped at him with my knife. They told me I killed him and they put me in the penitentiary and locked me up for fifteen years. That's where I met Bono. That's where I learned how to play baseball. Got out that place and your mama had taken you and went on to make life without me. Fifteen years was a long time for her to wait. But that fifteen years cured me of that robbing stuff. Rose'll tell you. She asked me when I met her if I had gotten all that foolishness out of my system. And I told her, "Baby, it's you and baseball all what count with me." You hear me, Bono? I meant it too. She say, "Which one comes first?" I told her, "Baby, ain't no doubt it's baseball . . . but you stick and get old with me and we'll both outlive this baseball." Am I right, Rose? And it's true.

ROSE. Man, hush your mouth. You ain't said no such thing. Talking about, "Baby you know you'll always be number one with me." That's what you was talking.

TROY. You hear that, Bono. That's why I love her.

BONO. Rose'll keep you straight. You get off the track, she'll straighten you up.

ROSE. Lyons, you better get on up and get Bonnie. She waiting on you.

LYONS (*gets up to go*). Hey, Pop, why don't you come on down to the Grill and hear me play?

TROY. I ain't going down there. I'm too old to be sitting around in them clubs.

BONO. You got to be good to play down at the Grill.

LYONS. Come on, Pop . . .

TROY. I got to get up in the morning.

LYONS. You ain't got to stay long.

TROY. Naw, I'm gonna get my supper and go on to bed.

LYONS. Well, I got to go. I'll see you again.

TROY. Don't you come around my house on my payday.

ROSE. Pick up the phone and let somebody know you coming. And bring Bonnie with you. You know I'm always glad to see her.

LYONS. Yeah, I'll do that, Rose. You take care now. See you, Pop. See you, Mr. Bono. See you, Uncle Gabe.

GABRIEL. Lyons! King of the Jungle!

Lyons exits.

TROY. Is supper ready, woman? Me and you got some business to take care of. I'm gonna tear it up too.

ROSE. Troy, I done told you now!

TROY (*puts his arm around Bono*). Aw hell, woman . . . this is

Bono. Bono like family. I done known this nigger since
. . . how long I done know you?

BONO. It's been a long time.

TROY. I done know this nigger since Skippy was a pup. Me
and him done been through some times.

BONO. You sure right about that.

TROY. Hell, I done know him longer than I known you.
And we still standing shoulder to shoulder. Hey, look
here, Bono . . . a man can't ask for no more than that.
(*Drinks to him.*) I love you, nigger.

BONO. Hell, I love you too . . . I got to get home see my
woman. You got yours in hand. I got to get mine.

*Bono starts to exit as Cory enters the yard, dressed in his
football uniform. He gives Troy a hard, uncompromising
look.*

CORY. What you do that for, Pop?

He throws his helmet down in the direction of Troy.

ROSE. What's the matter? Cory . . . what's the matter?

CORY. Papa done went up to the school and told Coach
Zellman I can't play football no more. Wouldn't even let
me play the game. Told him to tell the recruiter not to
come.

ROSE. Troy . . .

TROY. What you Troying me for. Yeah, I did it. And the boy
know why I did it.

CORY. Why you wanna do that to me? That was the one
chance I had.

ROSE. Ain't nothing wrong with Cory playing football,
Troy.

TROY. The boy lied to me. I told the nigger if he wanna play
football . . . to keep up his chores and hold down that job
at the A&P. That was the conditions. Stopped down
there to see Mr. Stawicki . . .

CORY. I can't work after school during the football season,
Pop! I tried to tell you that Mr. Stawicki's holding my job
for me. You don't never want to listen to nobody. And
then you wanna go and do this to me!

TROY. I ain't done nothing to you. You done it to yourself.

CORY. Just cause you didn't have a chance! You just scared
I'm gonna be better than you, that's all.

TROY. Come here.

ROSE. Troy . . .

Cory reluctantly crosses over to Troy.

TROY. All right! See. You done made a mistake.

CORY. I didn't even do nothing!

TROY. I'm gonna tell you what your mistake was. See . . .
you swung at the ball and didn't hit it. That's strike one.
See, you in the batter's box now. You swung and you
missed. That's strike one. Don't you strike out!

Lights fade to black.

ACT 2

SCENE 1

*The following morning. Cory is at the tree hitting the ball
with the bat. He tries to mimic Troy, but his swing is awkward, less sure. Rose enters from the house.*

ROSE. Cory, I want you to help me with this cupboard.

CORY. I ain't quitting the team. I don't care what Poppa say.

ROSE. I'll talk to him when he gets back. He had to go see
about your Uncle Gabe. The police done arrested him.
Say he was disturbing the peace. He'll be back directly.
Come on in here and help me clean out the top of this
cupboard.

*Cory exits into the house. Rose sees Troy and Bono com-
ing down the alley.*

Troy. . . . what they say down there?

TROY. Ain't said nothing. I give them fifty dollars and they
let him go. I'll talk to you about it. Where's Cory?

ROSE. He's in there helping me clean out these cupboards.

TROY. Tell him to get his butt out here.

*Troy and Bono go over to the pile of wood. Bono picks up
the saw and begins sawing.*

TROY (*to Bono*). All they want is the money. That makes six
or seven times I done went down there and got him. See
me coming they stick out their hands.

BONO. Yeah. I know what you mean. That's all they care
about . . . that money. They don't care about what's right.
(*Pause.*) Nigger, why you got to go and get some hard
wood? You ain't doing nothing but building a little old
fence. Get you some soft pine wood. That's all you need.

TROY. I know what I'm doing. This is outside wood. You put
pine wood inside the house. Pine wood is inside wood.
This here is outside wood. Now you tell me where the
fence is gonna be?

BONO. You don't need this wood. You can put it up with
pine wood and it'll stand as long as you gonna be here
looking at it.

TROY. How you know how long I'm gonna be here, nigger?
Hell, I might just live forever. Live longer than old man
Horsely.

BONO. That's what Magee used to say.

TROY. Magee's damn fool. Now you tell me who you ever
heard of gonna pull their own teeth with a pair of rusty
pliers.

BONO. The old folks . . . my granddaddy used to pull his
teeth with pliers. They ain't had no dentists for the colored folks back then.

TROY. Get clean pliers! You understand? Clean pliers! Ster-
ilize them! Besides we ain't living back then. All Magee
had to do was walk over to Doc Goldblum's.

BONO. I see where you and that Tallahassee gal . . . that Alberta . . . I see where you all done got tight.

TROY. What you mean "got tight"?

BONO. I see where you be laughing and joking with her all the time.

TROY. I laughs and jokes with all of them, Bono. You know me.

BONO. That ain't the kind of laughing and joking I'm talking about.

Cory enters from the house.

CORY. How you doing. Mr. Bono?

TROY. Cory? Get that saw from Bono and cut some wood. He talking about the wood's too hard to cut. Stand back there, Jim, and let that young boy show you how it's done.

BONO. He's sure welcome to it.

Cory takes the saw and begins to cut the wood.

Whew-e-e! Look at that. Big old strong boy. Look like Joe Louis. Hell, must be getting old the way I'm watching that boy whip through that wood.

CORY. I don't see why Mama want a fence around the yard noways.

TROY. Damn if I know either. What the hell she keeping out with it? She ain't got nothing nobody want.

BONO. Some people build fences to keep people out . . . and other people build fences to keep people in. Rose wants to hold on to you all. She loves you.

TROY. Hell, nigger, I don't need nobody to tell me my wife loves me. Cory . . . go on in the house and see if you can find that other saw.

CORY. Where's it at?

TROY. I said find it! Look for it till you find it!

Cory exits into the house.

What's that supposed to mean? Wanna keep us in?

BONO. Troy . . . I done known you seem like damn near my whole life. You and Rose both. I done know both of you all for a long time. I remember when you met Rose. When you was hitting them baseball out the park. A lot of them old gals was after you then. You had the pick of the litter. When you picked Rose, I was happy for you. That was the first time I knew you had any sense. I said . . . My man Troy knows what he's doing . . . I'm gonna follow this nigger . . . he might take me somewhere. I been following you too. I done learned a whole heap of things about life watching you. I done learned how to tell where the shit lies. How to tell it from the alfalfa. You done learned me a lot of things. You showed me how to not make the same mistakes . . . to take life as it comes along and keep putting one foot in front of the other. (*Pause.*) Rose a good woman, Troy.

TROY. Hell, nigger, I know she a good woman. I been married to her for eighteen years. What you got on your mind, Bono?

BONO. I just say she a good woman. Just like I say anything. I ain't got to have nothing on my mind.

TROY. You just gonna say she a good woman and leave it hanging out there like that? Why you telling me she a good woman?

BONO. She loves you, Troy. Rose loves you.

TROY. You saying I don't measure up. That's what you trying to say. I don't measure up cause I'm seeing this other gal. I know what you trying to say.

BONO. I know what Rose means to you, Troy. I'm just trying to say I don't want to see you mess up.

TROY. Yeah, I appreciate that, Bono. If you was messing around on Lucille I'd be telling you the same thing.

BONO. Well, that's all I got to say. I just say that because I love you both.

TROY. Hell, you know me . . . I wasn't out there looking for nothing. You can't find a better woman than Rose. I know that. But seems like this woman just stuck onto me where I can't shake her loose. I done wrestled with it, tried to throw her off me . . . but she just stuck on tighter. Now she's stuck on for good.

BONO. You's in control . . . that's what you tell me all the time. You responsible for what you do.

TROY. I ain't ducking the responsibility of it. As long as it sets right in my heart . . . then I'm okay. Cause that's all I listen to. It'll tell me right from wrong every time. And I ain't talking about doing Rose no bad turn. I love Rose. She done carried me a long ways and I love and respect her for that.

BONO. I know you do. That's why I don't want to see you hurt her. But what you gonna do when she find out? What you got then? If you try and juggle both of them . . . sooner or later you gonna drop one of them. That's common sense.

TROY. Yeah, I hear what you saying, Bono. I been trying to figure a way to work it out.

BONO. Work it out right, Troy. I don't want to be getting all up between you and Rose's business . . . but work it so it come out right.

TROY. Ah hell, I get all up between you and Lucille's business. When you gonna get that woman that refrigerator she been wanting? Don't tell me you ain't got no money now. I know who your banker is. Mellon don't need that money bad as Lucille want that refrigerator. I'll tell you that.

BONO. Tell you what I'll do . . . when you finish building this fence for Rose . . . I'll buy Lucille that refrigerator.

TROY. You done stuck your foot in your mouth now!

Troy grabs up a board and begins to saw. Bono starts to walk out the yard.

Hey, nigger . . . where you going?

BONO. I'm going home. I know you don't expect me to help you now. I'm protecting my money. I wanna see you put that fence up by yourself. That's what I want to see. You'll be here another six months without me.

TROY. Nigger, you ain't right.

BONO. When it comes to my money . . . I'm right as fireworks on the Fourth of July.

TROY. All right, we gonna see now. You better get out your bankbook.

Bono exits, and Troy continues to work. Rose enters from the house.

ROSE. What they say down there? What's happening with Gabe?

TROY. I went down there and got him out. Cost me fifty dollars. Say he was disturbing the peace. Judge set up a hearing for him in three weeks. Say to show cause why he shouldn't be recommitted.

ROSE. What was he doing that cause them to arrest him?

TROY. Some kids was teasing him and he run them off home. Say he was howling and carrying on. Some folks seen him and called the police. That's all it was.

ROSE. Well, what's you say? What'd you tell the judge?

TROY. Told him I'd look after him. It didn't make no sense to recommit the man. He stuck out his big greasy palm and told me to give him fifty dollars and take him on home.

ROSE. Where's he at now? Where'd he go off to?

TROY. He's gone about his business. He don't need nobody to hold his hand.

ROSE. Well, I don't know. Seem like that would be the best place for him if they did put him into the hospital. I know what you're gonna say. But that's what I think would be best.

TROY. The man done had his life ruined fighting for what? And they wanna take and lock him up. Let him be free. He don't bother nobody.

ROSE. Well, everybody got their own way of looking at it I guess. Come on and get your lunch. I got a bowl of lima beans and some cornbread in the oven. Come and get something to eat. Ain't no sense you fretting over Gabe.

Rose turns to go into the house.

TROY. Rose . . . got something to tell you.

ROSE. Well, come on . . . wait till I get this food on the table.

TROY. Rose!

She stops and turns around.

I don't know how to say this. (*Pause.*) I can't explain it none. It just sort of grows on you till it gets out of hand. It starts out like a little bush . . . and the next thing you know it's a whole forest.

ROSE. Troy . . . what is you talking about?

TROY. I'm talking, woman, let me talk. I'm trying to find a way to tell you . . . I'm gonna be a daddy. I'm gonna be somebody's daddy.

ROSE. Troy . . . you're not telling me this? You're gonna be . . . what?

TROY. Rose . . . now . . . see . . .

ROSE. You telling me you gonna be somebody's daddy? You telling your *wife* this?

Gabriel enters from the street. He carries a rose in his hand.

GABRIEL. Hey, Troy! Hey, Rose!

ROSE. I have to wait eighteen years to hear something like this.

GABRIEL. Hey, Rose . . . I got a flower for you. (*He hands it to her.*) That's a rose. Same rose like you is.

ROSE. Thanks, Gabe.

GABRIEL. Troy, you ain't mad at me is you? Them bad mens come and put me away. You ain't mad at me is you?

TROY. Naw, Gabe, I ain't mad at you.

ROSE. Eighteen years and you wanna come with this.

GABRIEL (*takes a quarter out of his pocket*). See what I got? Got a brand new quarter.

TROY. Rose . . . it's just . . .

ROSE. Ain't nothing you can say, Troy. Ain't no way of explaining that.

GABRIEL. Fellow that give me this quarter had a whole mess of them. I'm gonna keep this quarter till it stop shining.

ROSE. Gabe, go on in the house there. I got some watermelon in the Frigidaire. Go on and get you a piece.

GABRIEL. Say, Rose . . . you know I was chasing hellhounds and them bad mens come and get me and take me away. Troy helped me. He come down there and told them they better let me go before he beat them up. Yeah, he did!

ROSE. You go on and get you a piece of watermelon, Gabe. Them bad mens is gone now.

GABRIEL. Okay, Rose . . . gonna get me some watermelon. The kind with the stripes on it.

Gabriel exits into the house.

ROSE. Why, Troy? Why? After all these years to come dragging this in to me now. It don't make no sense at your age. I could have expected this ten or fifteen years ago, but not now.

TROY. Age ain't got nothing to do with it, Rose.

ROSE. I done tried to be everything a wife should be. Everything a wife could be. Been married eighteen years and I got to live to see the day you tell me you been seeing another woman and done fathered a child by her. And you know I ain't never wanted no half nothing in my family. My whole family is half. Everybody got different fathers and mothers . . . my two sisters and my brother. Can't hardly tell who's who. Can't never sit down and talk about Papa and Mama. It's your papa and your mama and my papa and my mama . . .

TROY. Rose . . . stop it now.

ROSE. I ain't never wanted that for none of my children. And now you wanna drag your behind in here and tell me something like this.

TROY. You ought to know. It's time for you to know.

ROSE. Well, I don't want to know, goddamn it!

TROY. I can't just make it go away. It's done now. I can't wish the circumstance of the thing away.

ROSE. And you don't want to either. Maybe you want to wish me and my boy away. Maybe that's what you want? Well, you can't wish us away. I've got eighteen years of my life invested in you. You ought to have stayed upstairs in my bed where you belong.

TROY. Rose . . . now listen to me . . . we can get a handle on this thing. We can talk this out . . . come to an understanding.

ROSE. All of a sudden it's "we." Where was "we" at when you was down there rolling around with some godforsaken woman? "We" should have come to an understanding before you started making a damn fool of yourself. You're a day late and a dollar short when it comes to an understanding with me.

TROY. It's just . . . She gives me a different idea . . . a different understanding about myself. I can step out of this house and get away from the pressures and problems . . . be a different man. I ain't got to wonder how I'm gonna pay the bills or get the roof fixed. I can just be a part of myself that I ain't never been.

ROSE. What I want to know . . . is do you plan to continue seeing her. That's all you can say to me.

TROY. I can sit up in her house and laugh. Do you understand what I'm saying. I can laugh out loud . . . and it feels good. It reaches all the way down to the bottom of my shoes. (*Pause.*) Rose, I can't give that up.

ROSE. Maybe you ought to go on and stay down there with her . . . if she's a better woman than me.

TROY. It ain't about nobody being a better woman or nothing. Rose, you ain't the blame. A man couldn't ask for no woman to be a better wife than you've been. I'm responsible for it. I done locked myself into a pattern trying to take care of you all that I forgot about myself.

ROSE. What the hell was I there for? That was my job, not somebody else's.

TROY. Rose, I done tried all my life to live decent . . . to live a clean . . . hard . . . useful life. I tried to be a good husband to you. In every way I knew how. Maybe I come into the world backwards, I don't know. But . . . you born with two strikes on you before you come to the plate. You got to guard it closely . . . always looking for the curve ball on the inside corner. You can't afford to let none get past you. You can't afford a call strike. If you going down . . . you going down swinging. Everything lined up against you. What you gonna do. I fooled them, Rose. I bunted. When I found you and Cory and a halfway decent job . . . I was safe. Couldn't nothing touch me. I wasn't gonna strike out no more. I wasn't going back to the penitentiary. I wasn't gonna lay in the streets with a bottle of wine. I was safe. I had me a family. A job. I wasn't gonna get that last strike. I was on first looking for one of them boys to knock me in. To get me home.

ROSE. You should have stayed in my bed, Troy.

TROY. Then when I saw that gal . . . she firmed up my backbone. And I got to thinking that if I tried . . . I just might be able to steal second. Do you understand after eighteen years I wanted to steal second.

ROSE. You should have held me tight. You should have grabbed me and held on.

TROY. I stood on first base for eighteen years and I thought . . . well, goddamn it . . . go on for it!

ROSE. We're not talking about baseball! We're talking about you going off to lay in bed with another woman . . . and then bring it home to me. That's what we're talking about. We ain't talking about no baseball.

TROY. Rose, you're not listening to me. I'm trying the best I can to explain it to you. It's not easy for me to admit that I been standing in the same place for eighteen years.

ROSE. I been standing with you! I been right here with you, Troy. I got a life too. I gave eighteen years of my life to stand in the same spot with you. Don't you think I ever wanted other things? Don't you think I had dreams and hopes? What about my life? What about me. Don't you think it ever crossed my mind to want to know other men? That I wanted to lay up somewhere and forget about my responsibilities? That I wanted someone to make me laugh so I could feel good? You not the only one who's got wants and needs. But I held on to you, Troy. I took all my feelings, my wants and needs, my dreams . . . and I buried them inside you. I planted a seed and watched and prayed over it. I planted myself inside you and waited to bloom. And it didn't take me no eighteen years to find out the soil was hard and rocky and it wasn't never gonna bloom.

But I held on to you, Troy. I held you tighter. You was my husband. I owed you everything I had. Every part of me I could find to give you. And upstairs in that room . . . with the darkness falling in on me . . . I gave everything I had to try and erase the doubt that you wasn't the finest man in the world. And wherever you was going . . . I wanted to be there with you. Cause you was my husband. Cause that's the only way I was gonna survive as your wife. You always talking about what you give . . . and what you don't have to give. But you take too. You take . . . and don't even know nobody's giving!

Rose turns to exit into the house; Troy grabs her arm.

TROY. You say I take and don't give!

ROSE. Troy! You're hurting me!

TROY. You say I take and don't give!

ROSE. Troy . . . you're hurting my arm! Let go!

TROY. I done give you everything I got. Don't you tell that lie on me.

ROSE. Troy!

TROY. Don't you tell that lie on me!

Cory enters from the house.

CORY. Mama!

ROSE. Troy. You're hurting me.

TROY. Don't you tell me about no taking and giving.

Cory comes up behind Troy and grabs him. Troy, surprised, is thrown off balance just as Cory throws a glancing blow that catches him on the chest and knocks him down. Troy is stunned, as is Cory.

ROSE. Troy. Troy. No!

Troy gets to his feet and starts at Cory.

Troy . . . no. Please! Troy!

Rose pulls on Troy to hold him back. Troy stops himself.

TROY (*to Cory*). All right. That's strike two. You stay away from around me, boy. Don't you strike out. You living with a full count. Don't you strike out.

Troy exits out the yard as the lights go down.

SCENE 2

It is six months later, early afternoon. Troy enters from the house and starts to exit the yard. Rose enters from the house.

ROSE. Troy, I want to talk to you.

TROY. All of a sudden, after all this time, you want to talk to me, huh? You ain't wanted to talk to me for months. You ain't wanted to talk to me last night. You ain't wanted no part of me then. What you wanna talk to me about now?

ROSE. Tomorrow's Friday.

TROY. I know what day tomorrow is. You think I don't know tomorrow's Friday? My whole life I ain't done nothing but look to see Friday coming and you got to tell me it's Friday.

ROSE. I want to know if you're coming home.

TROY. I always come home, Rose. You know that. There ain't never been a night I ain't come home.

ROSE. That ain't what I mean . . . and you know it. I want to know if you're coming straight home after work.

TROY. I figure I'd cash my check . . . hang out at Taylors' with the boys . . . maybe play a game of checkers . . .

ROSE. Troy, I can't live like this. I won't live like this. You livin' on borrowed time with me. It's been going on six months now you ain't been coming home.

TROY. I be here every night. Every night of the year. That's 365 days.

ROSE. I want you to come home tomorrow after work.

TROY. Rose . . . I don't mess up my pay. You know that now. I take my pay and I give it to you. I don't have no money but what you give me back. I just want to have a little time to myself . . . a little time to enjoy life.

ROSE. What about me? When's my time to enjoy life?

TROY. I don't know what to tell you, Rose. I'm doing the best I can.

ROSE. You ain't been home from work but time enough to change your clothes and run out . . . and you wanna call that the best you can do?

TROY. I'm going over to the hospital to see Alberta. She went into the hospital this afternoon. Look like she might have the baby early. I won't be gone long.

ROSE. Well, you ought to know. They went over to Miss Pearl's and got Gabe today. She said you told them to go ahead and lock him up.

TROY. I ain't said no such thing. Whoever told you that is telling a lie. Pearl ain't doing nothing but telling a big fat lie.

ROSE. She ain't had to tell me. I read it on the papers.

TROY. I ain't told them nothing of the kind.

ROSE. I saw it right there on the papers.

TROY. What it say, huh?

ROSE. It said you told them to take him.

TROY. Then they screwed that up, just the way they screw up everything. I ain't worried about what they got on the paper.

ROSE. Say the government send part of his check to the hospital and the other part to you.

TROY. I ain't got nothing to do with that if that's the way it works. I ain't made up the rules about how it work.

ROSE. You did Gabe just like you did Cory. You wouldn't sign the paper for Cory . . . but you signed for Gabe. You signed that paper.

The telephone is heard ringing inside the house.

TROY. I told you I ain't signed nothing, woman! The only thing I signed was the release form. Hell, I can't read, I don't know what they had on that paper! I ain't signed nothing about sending Gabe away.

ROSE. I said send him to the hospital . . . you said let him be free . . . now you done went down there and signed him to the hospital for half his money. You went back on yourself, Troy. You gonna have to answer for that.

TROY. See now . . . you been over there talking to Miss Pearl. She done got mad cause she ain't getting Gabe's rent money. That's all it is. She's liable to say anything.

ROSE. Troy, I seen where you signed the paper.

TROY. You ain't seen nothing I signed. What she doing got papers on my brother anyway? Miss Pearl telling a big fat lie. And I'm gonna tell her about it too! You ain't seen nothing I signed. Say . . . you ain't seen nothing I signed.

Rose exits into the house to answer the telephone. Presently she returns.

ROSE. Troy . . . that was the hospital. Alberta had the baby.

TROY. What she have? What is it?

ROSE. It's a girl.

TROY. I better get on down to the hospital to see her.

ROSE. Troy . . .

TROY. Rose . . . I got to go see her now. That's only right . . . what's the matter . . . the baby's all right, ain't it?

ROSE. Alberta died having the baby.

TROY. Died . . . you say she's dead? Alberta's dead?

ROSE. They said they done all they could. They couldn't do nothing for her.

TROY. The baby? How's the baby?

ROSE. They say it's healthy. I wonder who's gonna bury her.

TROY. She had family, Rose. She wasn't living in the world by herself.

ROSE. I know she wasn't living in the world by herself.

TROY. Next thing you gonna want to know if she had any insurance.

ROSE. Troy, you ain't got to talk like that.

TROY. That's the first thing that jumped out your mouth. "Who's gonna bury her?" Like I'm fixing to take on that task for myself.

ROSE. I am your wife. Don't push me away.

TROY. I ain't pushing nobody away. Just give me some space. That's all. Just give me some room to breathe.

Rose exits into the house. Troy walks about the yard.

TROY (*with a quiet rage that threatens to consume him*). All right . . . Mr. Death. See now . . . I'm gonna tell you what I'm gonna do. I'm gonna take and build me a fence around this yard. See? I'm gonna build me a fence around what belongs to me. And then I want you to stay on the other side. See? You stay over there until you're ready for me. Then you come on. Bring your army. Bring your sickle. Bring your wrestling clothes. I ain't gonna fall down on my vigilance this time. You ain't gonna sneak up on me no more. When you ready for me . . . when the top of your list say Troy Maxson . . . that's when you come around here. You come up and knock on the front door. Ain't nobody else got nothing to do with this. This is between you and me. Man to man. You stay on the other side of that fence until you ready for me. Then you come up and knock on the front door. Anytime you want. I'll be ready for you.

The lights go down to black.

SCENE 3

The lights come up on the porch. It is late evening three days later. Rose sits listening to the ball game waiting for Troy. The final out of the game is made and Rose switches off the radio. Troy enters the yard carrying an infant wrapped in blankets. He stands back from the house and calls.

Rose enters and stands on the porch. There is a long, awkward silence, the weight of which grows heavier with each passing second.

TROY. Rose . . . I'm standing here with my daughter in my arms. She ain't but a wee bittie little old thing. She don't

know nothing about grownups' business. She innocent . . . and she ain't got no mama.

ROSE. What you telling me for, Troy?

She turns and exits into the house.

TROY. Well . . . I guess we'll just sit out here on the porch.

He sits down on the porch. There is an awkward indelicateness about the way he handles the baby. His largeness engulfs and seems to swallow it. He speaks loud enough for Rose to hear.

A man's got to do what's right for him. I ain't sorry for nothing I done. It felt right in my heart. (*To the baby.*) What you smiling at? Your daddy's a big man. Got these great big old hands. But sometimes he's scared. And right now your daddy's scared cause we sitting out here and ain't got no home. Oh, I been homeless before. I ain't had no little baby with me. But I been homeless. You just be out on the road by your lonesome and you see one of them trains coming and you just kinda go like this . . .

He sings as a lullaby.

Please, Mr. Engineer let a man ride the line
Please, Mr. Engineer let a man ride the line
I ain't got no ticket please let me ride the blinds.

Rose enters from the house. Troy, hearing her steps behind him, stands and faces her.

She's my daughter, Rose. My own flesh and blood. I can't deny her no more than I can deny them boys. (*Pause.*) You and them boys is my family. You and them and this child is all I got in the world. So I guess what I'm saying is . . . I'd appreciate it if you'd help me take care of her.

ROSE. Okay, Troy . . . you're right. I'll take care of your baby for you . . . cause . . . like you say . . . she's innocent . . . and you can't visit the sins of the father upon the child. A motherless child has got a hard time. (*She takes the baby from him.*) From right now . . . this child got a mother. But you a womanless man.

Rose turns and exits into the house with the baby. Lights go down to black.

SCENE 4

It is two months later. Lyons enters the street. He knocks on the door and calls.

LYONS. Hey, Rose! (*Pause.*) Rose!

ROSE (*from inside the house*). Stop that yelling. You gonna wake up Raynell. I just got her to sleep.

LYONS. I just stopped by to pay Papa this twenty dollars I owe him. Where's Papa at?

ROSE. He should be here in a minute. I'm getting ready to go down to the church. Sit down and wait on him.

LYONS. I got to go pick up Bonnie over her mother's house.

ROSE. Well, sit it down there on the table. He'll get it.

LYONS (*enters the house and sets the money on the table*). Tell Papa I said thanks. I'll see you again.

ROSE. All right, Lyons. We'll see you.

Lyons starts to exit as Cory enters.

CORY. Hey, Lyons.

LYONS. What's happening, Cory? Say man, I'm sorry I missed your graduation. You know I had a gig and couldn't get away. Otherwise, I would have been there, man. So what you doing?

CORY. I'm trying to find a job.

LYONS. Yeah I know how that go, man. It's rough out here. Jobs are scarce.

CORY. Yeah, I know.

LYONS. Look here, I got to run. Talk to Papa . . . he know some people. He'll be able to help get you a job. Talk to him . . . see what he say.

CORY. Yeah . . . all right, Lyons.

LYONS. You take care. I'll talk to you soon. We'll find some time to talk.

Lyons exits the yard. Cory wanders over to the tree, picks up the bat, and assumes a batting stance. He studies an imaginary pitcher and swings. Dissatisfied with the result, he tries again. Troy enters. They eye each other for a beat. Cory puts the bat down and exits the yard. Troy starts into the house as Rose exits with Raynell. She is carrying a cake.

TROY. I'm coming in and everybody's going out.

ROSE. I'm taking this cake down to the church for the bake sale. Lyons was by to see you. He stopped by to pay you your twenty dollars. It's laying in there on the table.

TROY (*going into his pocket*). Well . . . here go this money.

ROSE. Put it in there on the table, Troy. I'll get it.

TROY. What time you coming back?

ROSE. Ain't no use in you studying me. It don't matter what time I come back.

TROY. I just asked you a question, woman. What's the matter . . . can't I ask you a question?

ROSE. Troy, I don't want to go into it. Your dinner's in there on the stove. All you got to do is heat it up. And don't you be eating the rest of them cakes in there. I'm coming back for them. We having a bake sale at the church tomorrow.

Rose exits the yard. Troy sits down on the steps, takes a pint bottle from his pocket, opens it, and drinks. He begins to sing.

TROY.

Hear it ring! Hear it ring!
Had an old dog his name was Blue
You know Blue was mighty true
You know Blue as a good old dog

Blue trees a possum in a hollow log
You know from that he was a good old dog.

Bono enters the yard.

BONO. Hey, Troy.

TROY. Hey, what's happening, Bono?

BONO. I just thought I'd stop by to see you.

TROY. What you stop by and see me for? You ain't stopped by in a month of Sundays. Hell, I must owe you money or something.

BONO. Since you got your promotion I can't keep up with you. Used to see you every day. Now I don't even know what route you working.

TROY. They keep switching me around. Got me out in Greentree now . . . hauling white folks' garbage.

BONO. Greentree, huh? You lucky, at least you ain't got to be lifting them barrels. Damn if they ain't getting heavier. I'm gonna put in my two years and call it quits.

TROY. I'm thinking about retiring myself.

BONO. You got it easy. You can drive for another five years.

TROY. It ain't the same, Bono. It ain't like working the back of the truck. Ain't got nobody to talk to . . . feel like you working by yourself. Naw, I'm thinking about retiring. How's Lucille?

BONO. She all right. Her arthritis get to acting up on her sometime. Saw Rose on my way in. She going down to the church, huh?

TROY. Yeah, she took up going down there. All them preachers looking for somebody to fatten their pockets. (*Pause.*) Got some gin here.

BONO. Naw, thanks. I just stopped by to say hello.

TROY. Hell, nigger . . . you can take a drink. I ain't never known you to say no to a drink. You ain't got to work tomorrow.

BONO. I just stopped by. I'm fixing to go over to Skinner's. We got us a domino game going over his house every Friday.

TROY. Nigger, you can't play no dominoes. I used to whup you four games out of five.

BONO. Well, that learned me. I'm getting better.

TROY. Yeah? Well, that's all right.

BONO. Look here . . . I got to be getting on. Stop by sometime, huh?

TROY. Yeah, I'll do that, Bono. Lucille told Rose you bought her a new refrigerator.

BONO. Yeah, Rose told Lucille you had finally built your fence . . . so I figured we'd call it even.

TROY. I knew you would.

BONO. Yeah . . . okay. I'll be talking to you.

TROY. Yeah, take care, Bono. Good to see you. I'm gonna stop over.

BONO. Yeah. Okay, Troy.

Bono exits. Troy drinks from the bottle.

TROY.

> Old Blue died and I dig his grave
> Let him down with a golden chain
> Every night when I hear old Blue bark
> I know Blue treed a possum in Noah's Ark.
> Hear it ring! Hear it ring!

Cory enters the yard. They eye each other for a beat. Troy is sitting in the middle of the steps. Cory walks over.

CORY. I got to get by.

TROY. Say what? What's you say?

CORY. You in my way. I got to get by.

TROY. You got to get by where? This is my house. Bought and paid for. In full. Took me fifteen years. And if you wanna go in my house and I'm sitting on the steps . . . you say excuse me. Like your mama taught you.

CORY. Come on, Pop . . . I got to get by.

Cory starts to maneuver his way past Troy. Troy grabs his leg and shoves him back.

TROY. You just gonna walk over top of me?

CORY. I live here too!

TROY (*advancing toward him*). You just gonna walk over top of me in my own house?

CORY. I ain't scared of you.

TROY. I ain't asked if you was scared of me. I asked you if you was fixing to walk over top of me in my own house? That's the question. You ain't gonna say excuse me? You just gonna walk over top of me?

CORY. If you wanna put it like that.

TROY. How else am I gonna put it?

CORY. I was walking by you to go into the house cause you sitting on the steps drunk, singing to yourself. You can put it like that.

TROY. Without saying excuse me???

Cory doesn't respond.

I asked you a question. Without saying excuse me???

CORY. I ain't got to say excuse me to you. You don't count around here no more.

TROY. Oh, I see . . . I don't count around here no more. You ain't got to say excuse me to your daddy. All of a sudden you done got so grown that your daddy don't count around here no more . . . Around here in his own house and yard that he done paid for with the sweat of his brow. You done got so grown to where you gonna take over. You gonna take over my house. Is that right? You gonna wear my pants. You gonna go in there and stretch out on my bed. You ain't got to say excuse me cause I don't count around here no more. Is that right?

CORY. That's right. You always talking this dumb stuff. Now, why don't you just get out my way?

TROY. I guess you got someplace to sleep and something to put in your belly. You got that, huh? You got that? That's what you need. You got that, huh?

CORY. You don't know what I got. You ain't got to worry about what I got.

TROY. You right! You one hundred percent right! I done spent the last seventeen years worrying about what you got. Now it's your turn, see? I'll tell you what to do. You grown . . . we done established that. You a man. Now, let's see you act like one. Turn your behind around and walk out this yard. And when you get out there in the alley . . . you can forget about this house. See? Cause this is my house. You go on and be a man and get your own house. You can forget about this. Cause this is mine. You go on and get yours cause I'm through with doing for you.

CORY. You talking about what you did for me . . . what'd you ever give me?

TROY. Them feet and bones! That pumping heart, nigger! I give you more than anybody else is ever gonna give you.

CORY. You ain't never gave me nothing! You ain't never done nothing but hold me back. Afraid I was gonna be better than you. All you ever did was try and make me scared of you. I used to tremble every time you called my name. Every time I heard your footsteps in the house. Wondering all the time . . . what's Papa gonna say if I do this? . . . What's he gonna say if I do that? . . . What's Papa gonna say if I turn on the radio? And Mama, too . . . she tries . . . but she's scared of you.

TROY. You leave your mama out of this. She ain't got nothing to do with this.

CORY. I don't know how she stand you . . . after what you did to her.

TROY. I told you to leave your mama out of this!

He advances toward Cory.

CORY. What you gonna do . . . give me a whupping? You can't whup me no more. You're too old. You just an old man.

TROY (*shoves him on his shoulder*). Nigger! That's what you are. You just another nigger on the street to me!

CORY. You crazy! You know that?

TROY. Go on now! You got the devil in you. Get on away from me!

CORY. You just a crazy old man . . . talking about I got the devil in me.

TROY. Yeah, I'm crazy! If you don't get on the other side of that yard . . . I'm gonna show you how crazy I am! Go on . . . get the hell out of my yard.

CORY. It ain't your yard. You took Uncle Gabe's money he got from the army to buy this house and then you put him out.

TROY (*advances on Cory*). Get your black ass out of my yard!

Troy's advance backs Cory up against the tree. Cory grabs up the bat.

CORY. I ain't going nowhere! Come on . . . put me out! I ain't scared of you.

TROY. That's my bat!

CORY. Come on!

TROY. Put my bat down!

CORY. Come on, put me out.

Cory swings at Troy, who backs across the yard.

What's the matter? You so bad . . . put me out!

Troy advances toward Cory.

CORY (*backing up*). Come on! Come on!

TROY. You're gonna have to use it! You wanna draw that bat back on me . . . you're gonna have to use it.

CORY. Come on! . . . Come on!

Cory swings the bat at Troy a second time. He misses. Troy continues to advance toward him.

TROY. You're gonna have to kill me! You wanna draw that bat back on me. You're gonna have to kill me.

Cory, backed up against the tree, can go no farther. Troy taunts him. He sticks out his head and offers him a target.

Come on! Come on!

Cory is unable to swing the bat. Troy grabs it.

TROY. Then I'll show you.

Cory and Troy struggle over the bat. The struggle is fierce and fully engaged. Troy ultimately is the stronger and takes the bat from Cory and stands over him ready to swing. He stops himself.

Go on and get away from around my house.

Cory, stung by his defeat, picks himself up, walks slowly out of the yard and up the alley.

CORY. Tell Mama I'll be back for my things.

TROY. They'll be on the other side of that fence.

Cory exits.

TROY. I can't taste nothing. Helluljah! I can't taste nothing no more. (*Troy assumes a batting posture and begins to taunt Death, the fastball on the outside corner.*) Come on! It's between you and me now! Come on! Anytime you want! Come on! I be ready for you . . . but I ain't gonna be easy.

The lights go down on the scene.

SCENE 5

The time is 1965. The lights come up in the yard. It is the morning of Troy's funeral. A funeral plaque with a light hangs beside the door. There is a small garden plot off to the side. There is noise and activity in the house as Rose, Lyons, and Bono have gathered. The door opens and Raynell, seven years old, enters dressed in a flannel night-

gown. She crosses to the garden and pokes around with a stick. Rose calls from the house.

ROSE. Raynell!

RAYNELL. Mam?

ROSE. What you doing out there?

RAYNELL. Nothing.

Rose comes to the door.

ROSE. Girl, get in here and get dressed. What you doing?

RAYNELL. Seeing if my garden growed.

ROSE. I told you it ain't gonna grow overnight. You got to wait.

RAYNELL. It don't look like it never gonna grow. Dag!

ROSE. I told you a watched pot never boils. Get in here and get dressed.

RAYNELL. This ain't even no pot, Mama.

ROSE. You just have to give it a chance. It'll grow. Now you come on and do what I told you. We got to be getting ready. This ain't no morning to be playing around. You hear me?

RAYNELL. Yes, mam.

Rose exits into the house. Raynell continues to poke at her garden with a stick. Cory enters. He is dressed in a Marine corporal's uniform, and carries a duffelbag. His posture is that of a military man, and his speech has a clipped sternness.

CORY (*to Raynell*). Hi. (*Pause.*) I bet your name is Raynell.

RAYNELL. Uh huh.

CORY. Is your mama home?

Raynell runs up on the porch and calls through the screen door.

RAYNELL. Mama . . . there's some man out here. Mama?

Rose comes to the door.

ROSE. Cory? Lord have mercy! Look here, you all!

Rose and Cory embrace in a tearful reunion as Bono and Lyons enter from the house dressed in funeral clothes.

BONO. Aw, looka here . . .

ROSE. Done got all grown up!

CORY. Don't cry, Mama. What you crying about?

ROSE. I'm just so glad you made it.

CORY. Hey Lyons. How you doing, Mr. Bono.

Lyons goes to embrace Cory.

LYONS. Look at you, man. Look at you. Don't he look good, Rose. Got them Corporal stripes.

ROSE. What took you so long?

CORY. You know how the Marines are, Mama. They got to get all their paperwork straight before they let you do anything.

ROSE. Well, I'm sure glad you made it. They let Lyons come.

Your Uncle Gabe's still in the hospital. They don't know if they gonna let him out or not. I just talked to them a little while ago.

LYONS. A Corporal in the United States Marines.

BONO. Your daddy knew you had it in you. He used to tell me all the time.

LYONS. Don't he look good, Mr. Bono?

BONO. Yeah, he remind me of Troy when I first met him. (*Pause.*) Say, Rose, Lucille's down at the church with the choir. I'm gonna go down and get the pallbearers lined up. I'll be back to get you all.

ROSE. Thanks, Jim.

CORY. See you, Mr. Bono.

LYONS (*with his arm around Raynell*). Cory . . . look at Raynell. Ain't she precious? She gonna break a whole lot of hearts.

ROSE. Raynell, come and say hello to your brother. This is your brother, Cory. You remember Cory.

RAYNELL. No, Mam.

CORY. She don't remember me, Mama.

ROSE. Well, we talk about you. She heard us talk about you. (*To Raynell.*) This is your brother, Cory. Come on and say hello.

RAYNELL. Hi.

CORY. Hi. So you're Raynell. Mama told me a lot about you.

ROSE. You all come on into the house and let me fix you some breakfast. Keep up your strength.

CORY. I ain't hungry, Mama.

LYONS. You can fix me something, Rose. I'll be in there in a minute.

ROSE. Cory, you sure you don't want nothing? I know they ain't feeding you right.

CORY. No, Mama . . . thanks. I don't feel like eating. I'll get something later.

ROSE. Raynell . . . get on upstairs and get that dress on like I told you.

Rose and Raynell exit into the house.

LYONS. So . . . I hear you thinking about getting married.

CORY. Yeah, I done found the right one, Lyons. It's about time.

LYONS. Me and Bonnie been split up about four years now. About the time Papa retired. I guess she just got tired of all them changes I was putting her through. (*Pause.*) I always knew you was gonna make something out yourself. Your head was always in the right direction. So . . . you gonna stay in . . . make it a career . . . put in your twenty years?

CORY. I don't know. I got six already, I think that's enough.

LYONS. Stick with Uncle Sam and retire early. Ain't nothing out here. I guess Rose told you what happened with me. They got me down the workhouse. I thought I was being slick cashing other people's checks.

CORY. How much time you doing?

LYONS. They give me three years. I got that beat now. I ain't got but nine more months. It ain't so bad. You learn to deal with it like anything else. You got to take the crookeds with the straights. That's what Papa used to say. He used to say that when he struck out. I seen him strike out three times in a row . . . and the next time up he hit the ball over the grandstand. Right out there in Homestead Field. He wasn't satisfied hitting in the seats . . . he want to hit it over everything! After the game he had two hundred people standing around waiting to shake his hand. You got to take the crookeds with the straights. Yeah, Papa was something else.

CORY. You still playing?

LYONS. Cory . . . you know I'm gonna do that. There's some fellows down there we got us a band . . . we gonna try and stay together when we get out . . . but yeah, I'm still playing. It still helps me to get out of bed in the morning. As long as it do that I'm gonna be right there playing and trying to make some sense out of it.

ROSE (*calling*). Lyons, I got these eggs in the pan.

LYONS. Let me go on and get these eggs, man. Get ready to go bury Papa. (*Pause.*) How you doing? You doing all right?

Cory nods. Lyons touches him on the shoulder and they share a moment of silent grief. Lyons exits into the house. Cory wanders about the yard. Raynell enters.

RAYNELL. Hi.

CORY. Hi.

RAYNELL. Did you used to sleep in my room?

CORY. Yeah . . . that used to be my room.

RAYNELL. That's what Papa call it. "Cory's room." It got your football in the closet.

Rose comes to the door.

ROSE. Raynell, get in there and get them good shoes on.

RAYNELL. Mama, can't I wear these? Them other one hurt my feet.

ROSE. Well, they just gonna have to hurt your feet for a while. You ain't said they hurt your feet when you went down to the store and got them.

RAYNELL. They didn't hurt then. My feet done got bigger.

ROSE. Don't you give me no backtalk now. You get in there and get them shoes on.

Raynell exits into the house.

Ain't too much changed. He still got that piece of rag tied to that tree. He was out here swinging that bat. I was just ready to go back in the house. He swung that bat and then he just fell over. Seem like he swung it and stood there with this grin on his face . . . and then he just fell over. They carried him on down to the hospital, but I knew there wasn't no need . . . why don't you come on in the house?

CORY. Mama . . . I got something to tell you. I don't know how to tell you this . . . but I've got to tell you . . . I'm not going to Papa's funeral.

ROSE. Boy, hush your mouth. That's your daddy you talking

about. I don't want hear that kind of talk this morning. I done raised you to come to this? You standing there all healthy and grown talking about you ain't going to your daddy's funeral?

CORY. Mama . . . listen . . .

ROSE. I don't want to hear it, Cory. You just get that thought out of your head.

CORY. I can't drag Papa with me everywhere I go. I've got to say no to him. One time in my life I've got to say no.

ROSE. Don't nobody have to listen to nothing like that. I know you and your daddy ain't seen eye to eye, but I ain't got to listen to that kind of talk this morning. Whatever was between you and your daddy . . . the time has come to put it aside. Just take it and set it over there on the shelf and forget about it. Disrespecting your daddy ain't gonna make you a man, Cory. You got to find a way to come to that on your own. Not going to your daddy's funeral ain't gonna make you a man.

CORY. The whole time I was growing up . . . living in his house . . . Papa was like a shadow that followed you everywhere. It weighed on you and sunk into your flesh. It would wrap around you and lay there until you couldn't tell which one was you anymore. That shadow digging in your flesh. Trying to crawl in. Trying to live through you. Everywhere I looked, Troy Maxson was staring back at me . . . hiding under the bed . . . in the closet. I'm just saying I've got to find a way to get rid of that shadow, Mama.

ROSE. You just like him. You got him in you good.

CORY. Don't tell me that, Mama.

ROSE. You Troy Maxson all over again.

CORY. I don't want to be Troy Maxson. I want to be me.

ROSE. You can't be nobody but who you are, Cory. That shadow wasn't nothing but you growing into yourself. You either got to grow into it or cut it down to fit you. But that's all you got to make life with. That's all you got to measure yourself against that world out there. Your daddy wanted you to be everything he wasn't . . . and at the same time he tried to make you into everything he was. I don't know if he was right or wrong . . . but I do know he meant to do more good than he meant to do harm. He wasn't always right. Sometimes when he touched he bruised. And sometimes when he took me in his arms he cut.

When I first met your daddy I thought . . . Here is a man I can lay down with and make a baby. That's the first thing I thought when I seen him. I was thirty years old and had done seen my share of men. But when he walked up to me and said, "I can dance a waltz that'll make you dizzy," I thought, Rose Lee, here is a man that you can open yourself up to and be filled to bursting. Here is a man that can fill all them empty spaces you been tipping around the edges of. One of them empty spaces was being somebody's mother.

I married your daddy and settled down to cooking his supper and keeping clean sheets on the bed. When your daddy walked through the house he was so big he filled it up. That was my first mistake. Not to make him leave some room for me. For my part in the matter. But at that time I wanted that. I wanted a house that I could sing in. And that's what your daddy gave me. I didn't know to keep up his strength I had to give up little pieces of mine. I did that. I took on his life as mine and mixed up the pieces so that you couldn't hardly tell which was which anymore. It was my choice. It was my life and I didn't have to live it like that. But that's what life offered me in the way of being a woman and I took it. I grabbed hold of it with both hands.

By the time Raynell came into the house, me and your daddy had done lost touch with one another. I didn't want to make my blessing off of nobody's misfortune . . . but I took on to Raynell like she was all them babies I had wanted and never had.

The phone rings.

Like I'd been blessed to relive a part of my life. And if the Lord see fit to keep up my strength . . . I'm gonna do her just like your daddy did you . . . I'm gonna give her the best of what's in me.

RAYNELL (*entering, still with her old shoes*). Mama . . . Reverend Tollivier on the phone.

Rose exits into the house.

RAYNELL. Hi.

CORY. Hi.

RAYNELL. You in the Army or the Marines?

CORY. Marines.

RAYNELL. Papa said it was the Army. Did you know Blue?

CORY. Blue? Who's Blue?

RAYNELL. Papa's dog what he sing about all the time.

CORY (*singing*).
    Hear it ring! Hear it ring!
    I had a dog his name was Blue
    You know Blue was mighty true
    You know Blue was a good old dog
    Blue treed a possum in a hollow log
    You know from that he was a good old dog.
    Hear it ring! Hear it ring!

Raynell joins in singing.

CORY and RAYNELL.
    Blue treed a possum out on a limb
    Blue looked at me and I looked at him
    Grabbed that possum and put him in a sack
    Blue stayed there till I came back
    Old Blue's feets was big and round
    Never allowed a possum to touch the ground.

    Old Blue died and I dug his grave
    I dug his grave with a silver spade
    Let him down with a golden chain
    And every night I call his name
    Go on Blue, you good dog you

Go on Blue, you good dog you.
RAYNELL.
Blue laid down and died like a man
Blue laid down and died . . .
BOTH.
Blue laid down and died like a man
Now he's treeing possums in the Promised Land
I'm gonna tell you this to let you know
Blue's gone where the good dogs go
When I hear old Blue bark
When I hear old Blue bark
Blue treed a possum in Noah's Ark
Blue treed a possum in Noah's Ark.

Rose comes to the screen door.

ROSE. Cory, we gonna be ready to go in a minute.
CORY (*to Raynell*). You go on in the house and change them
shoes like Mama told you so we can go to Papa's funeral.
RAYNELL. Okay, I'll be back.

*Raynell exits into the house. Cory gets up and crosses over
to the tree. Rose stands in the screen door watching him.
Gabriel enters from the alley.*

GABRIEL (*calling*). Hey, Rose!
ROSE. Gabe?
GABRIEL. I'm here, Rose. Hey Rose, I'm here!

Rose enters from the house.

ROSE. Lord . . . Look here, Lyons!

LYONS. See, I told you, Rose . . . I told you they'd let him
come.
CORY. How you doing, Uncle Gabe?
LYONS. How you doing, Uncle Gabe?
GABRIEL. Hey, Rose. It's time. It's time to tell St. Peter to
open the gates. Troy, you ready? You ready, Troy. I'm
gonna tell St. Peter to open the gates. You get ready now.

*Gabriel, with great fanfare, braces himself to blow. The
trumpet is without a mouthpiece. He puts the end of it into
his mouth and blows with great force, like a man who has
been waiting some twenty-odd years for this single
moment. No sound comes out of the trumpet. He braces
himself and blows again with the same result. A third time
he blows. There is a weight of impossible description that
falls away and leaves him bare and exposed to a frightful
realization. It is a trauma that a sane and normal mind
would be unable to withstand. He begins to dance. A
slow, strange dance, eerie and life-giving. A dance of
atavistic signature and ritual. Lyons attempts to embrace
him. Gabriel pushes Lyons away. He begins to howl in
what is an attempt at song, or perhaps a song turning back
into itself in an attempt at speech. He finishes his dance
and the gates of heaven stand open as wide as God's closet.*

That's the way that go!

BLACKOUT

THE CARIBBEAN

Artistic and Cultural Events

c. 1570: Corpus Christi rites in Cuba

1826: Five professional theaters established in Trinidad

1941: Little Theatre Movement, Jamaica

1955: Racially integrated plays in Trinidad

1968: Theatre Escambray, Cuba

Areítos performed in Cuba and Puerto Rico

1590s: Spanish comedias performed in Cuba

1755: First Cuban play, *The Gardener Prince and Imagined Cloridano* (Santiago Pita y Borroto)

1866: First Grand Masquerade of Trinidad Carnival

1920: Paragon Players, Port-au-Prince Spain, Trinidad

1943–1945: Teatro Popular, Cuba

1948: Little Carib Theater, Trinidad

1953: René Marqués's *The Ox Cart*, Puerto Rico

1959: Trinidad Theater Workshop

1500 C.E. | **1600–1800 C.E.** | **1900 C.E.**

Historical and Political Events

1898: Spanish-American War

1834: Slaves emancipated in Trinidad

1952: Puerto Rico becomes independent commonwealth

1959: Cuban Revolution

Spaniards in Hispanola

African slaves brought to Caribbean by Europeans who govern islands

In his study of the history of the Caribbean, *The Repeating Island*, Antonio Benitez-Rojo articulates the present social, political, and economic realities of the region: "For it is certain that the Caribbean basin, although it includes the first American lands to be explored, conquered, and colonized by Europe, is still, especially in the discourse of the social sciences, one of the least known regions of the modern world." This archipelago, with its legacy of the diaspora, numerous languages, diverse histories of colonization, and cultural nuances is today one of the richest areas for the discovery and understanding of human creativity. Sadly and quite often, our impressions of the Caribbean are based on television commercials selling ocean cruises, people resting on a beach surrounded by exotic drinks, and the rhythmic movement of a "native" beckoning the viewer to travel to paradise. What these commercials do not reveal, however, is the Caribbean's relentless commitment to survive in the face of industrial global expansion, foreign intervention, unstable economies, and political turmoil. The Cuban writer Alejo Carpentier defines the problem: "Our cities, because they haven't yet entered our literature, are more difficult to handle than the jungles or the mountains."

Given its rich history of tradition, survival, and transition, the theatrical and dramatic productivity of the Caribbean is complex and diverse. As we have seen, theatrical expression often evolves from mimetic activity and the necessity for humans to express themselves through mime, dance, song, and the oral tradition. The first European-recorded signs of theatrical activity in the New World emanate from the late fifteenth century when Spanish colonizers witnessed performances of *areítos* in Cuba and Puerto Rico. These ritual-like activities, under the supervision of a choral leader, were performed by indigenous people to share their tribal history through music, dance, and the spoken word. Considered primitive and often blasphemous in the eyes of Catholic colonizers, these activities ceased by the sixteenth century. Similar activities took place in the Francophone islands of Haiti, Martinique, and French Guyana during the early seventeenth century when the African diaspora produced a multitude of slaves to serve the European plantations. These slaves, and their Creole descendants, devised ritualistic performances using music, dance, and storytelling that linked their new envi-

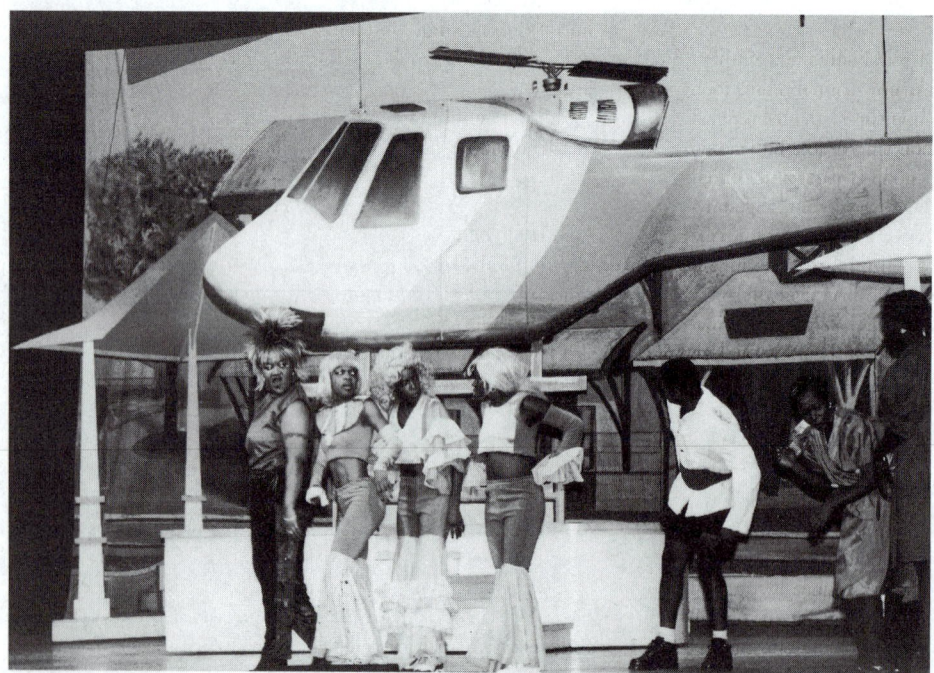

Contemporary issues are often presented with a playful theatricality in Caribbean theater. Here the Little Theatre Movement and the National Pantomime Company of Jamaica lampoon the Y2K bug in a production of Bugsie the Millennium Bug *by Barbara Gloudon and Conliffe Wilmot-Simpson.*

ronment to their past heritage, religions, and cultural traditions, all of which were nearly destroyed by the slave trade.

Throughout the eighteenth and nineteenth centuries, many of the Caribbean islands witnessed theatrical fare imported from Europe, mostly from the Renaissance and Neoclassical perspective. In the nineteenth century, European Romantic drama and melodrama gave way to individual Caribbean dramatic voices that emphasized local social conditions, language, and ethnic heritage. Of particular importance in this artistic development are the islands of Cuba, Puerto Rico, Haiti, Jamaica, and Trinidad-Tobago, each of which paved the way for sophisticated twentieth-century theatrical endeavors and internationally respected playwrights, directors, and actors.

Cuba

Despite the current disenfranchisement caused by its socialist politics, the United States-imposed blockade, and Russia's inability to continue its economic assistance to the Castro regime, Cuba still maintains a strong commitment to theatrical exploration. Following Castro's revolution in 1959, Cuban theater saw the implementation of the National Council for Culture which augmented artistic activity throughout the island. Today, the well-established House of the Americas continues to produce Latin American theater festivals and frequently honors plays (e.g., Egon Wolff's *Paper Flowers*, Chapter 9) with its prestigious House of the Americas Prize.

Because of his international recognition, José Triana remains Cuba's most respected playwright, and his plays have been produced throughout the Americas and Europe; the most notable of these, *Night of the Assassins* (1965), is a violent, surrealistic work portraying three adolescents who kill their parents as a ritual exorcism. A protégé of Triana, Freddy Artiles also represents Cuba's most progressive and mature playwriting. The author of serious dramas and children's plays, Artiles is a product of Cuba's social revolution, whose best works examine Cuban social and political realities; for instance, *At the Station* (part of a 1977 trilogy, *At the End of Blood's Journey*) depicts two Cuban citizens attempting to depart their native land in 1959 because of repressive political policies. Artiles continues his work as a playwright, professor of theater, and dramaturg, and his workshops and lectures have been presented throughout Europe, Canada, the United States, Mexico, and Latin America.

Under the direction of the well-known actor and director Sergio Corrieri, Theatre Escambray (1968) has altered the aesthetics of Cuban theater. Its innovative staging techniques include interviews with audience members who are asked to provide solutions to local problems; postperformance discussions between actors and audiences are important features of Escambray's work. Presently the Galiano 108 Theatre is a collective dedicated to a new performance style using Expressionistic techniques. *Saint Cecilia*, a recent one-woman tour de force, has won wide recognition for the Galiano Company.

The contemporary press, preoccupied by the long-standing conflict between opposite political ideologies, often portrays Cuba in negative terms. Nevertheless, Cuba remains at the forefront of theatrical and dramatic productivity in the Caribbean.

Puerto Rico

Although this island has been an independent commonwealth of the United States since 1952, the spirit of Puerto Rico is rooted in the indigenous culture of the Taíno. For centuries the people of this historic island have sought to settle its national sense of belonging, and thus Puerto Rico's political winds have undergone massive changes. With its roots in the diasporic tradition and the Spanish-American War, it has attempted to become an independent nation. In spite of its political and economic shifts, Puerto Rico's theatrical culture has influenced dramatic activity in the Caribbean, the United States, Latin America, and Europe; it has also exerted an influence on the Hollywood cinema.

Contemporary Puerto Rican drama has been influenced by the likes of the brilliant René Marqués, who in 1953 wrote perhaps his most important play, *The Ox Cart*, a stinging, naturalistic critique of Puerto Rican immigration to the United States. The play depicts its characters' feelings as they rediscover their Caribbean roots. Significantly, Puerto Rican theater has opened many a door to women, most notably Rosa Luisa Márquez, a professor of theater and drama at the University of Puerto Rico. A director, actor, and playwright, she founded the Anamu Theater Collective and received the Puerto Rican Drama Critics Circle Award. Márquez, who is committed to the alternative theater movement, is an active participant of the Bread and Puppet Theater of Peter Schumann, and she is also a board member of the International School of Theater of Latin America and the Caribbean, once headed by the late Osvaldo Dragún (see Chapter 7).

Regardless of its political future in the twenty-first century, it is clear that Puerto Rico will continue to be a dominant voice in Caribbean theater. Puerto Rico's centuries of creativity attest to the human will to survive in spite of social and political dichotomies.

Haiti and Jamaica

For two centuries, Haiti has also survived numerous social, economic, and political shifts. A product of French colonial occupation, invasion and occupation by the United States from 1915 to 1934, and the devastating consequences of the recent François Duvalier dictatorship, this Caribbean island has been fractured in its economic development. Although Haiti has been ignored by the world economy, it continues to exhibit a sound strength in her theatrical identity, which was originally based on religious voodoo ceremonies derived from African rituals in honor of their *orishas* (gods). These were later mixed with Catholic ceremonial traditions. Given its colonial nature, Haitian theater has always exhibited a mix of French popular offerings and the many Creole attempts to establish a national drama. Haiti's theatrical and dramatic maturity, however, occurred in the twentieth century, and it is best appreciated in the dramatic output of Mona Guérin, the author of numerous plays about the social conditions of her native land. The more contemporary plays of Frédéric Surpris, author of *Coup d'état*, speak of Haiti's immersion in poverty and the colonial mentality. Although Haiti appears politically stable despite its economic problems, its theater continues to explore the nation's vacillation between its Francophone past and its emerging Creole identity, both within the island and abroad. A massive Haitian migratory journey toward North America and Europe has carried Haitian drama beyond its Caribbean shores.

Caribbean theater boasts a unique form of expression found in the oral discourse of Jamaica. Such performances are usually acted out by a writer-actor who shares with the audience her/his perception of race, identity, and social status within the culture. Much like Homer's *Iliad*, these works link the entire island society to its national sense of belonging. Spoken in the Jamaican-Creole language, these oral performances help audiences realize that regional dialects are a valid—often superior—form of expression. Mixing poetry and the musical rhythms of reggae, well-known Jamaican performers (e.g., Michael Smith, Binta Breeze, and Oku Onuora) have brought a national consciousness to Jamaicans, as well as to people abroad. Like the rap music of the United States, these oral performances remind their audiences that the power of popular culture is not necessarily highbrow.

Trinidad-Tobago

Trinidad was seized from the indigenous Arawak Indians by Columbus in 1498, and for 300 years it remained a Spanish possession. The French and their African slaves arrived in 1783, and the British took control of the island in 1797 and retained it as a Crown colony until 1962. Nearby Tobago was first a Dutch colony, then French, and finally became a British colony in 1763. To replace African slaves who were freed in the 1830s, plantation owners imported Chinese, Muslim, Portuguese, and East Indians (who currently comprise about 40 percent of the islands' population). Given this diverse cultural mix, theater emanating from these sister islands is among the richest and most diverse in the Caribbean.

The most famous theatrical activity in Trinidad is the annual pre-Lenten Carnival, which is described in some detail in conjunction with *Ti-Jean and His Brothers* (see Center Stage box, The Trinidad Carnival, at the end of this chapter). There is also a major street festival (the *Hosay*) conducted by the islands' East Indian community to commemorate the Muslim battle of Karbala. Calypso plays, in which topical events are enacted in song and story to the rhythms of steel-drum bands, are especially popular among the locals, and lively calypso play competitions are held several times a year. In 1982 the Trinidad Tent Theater was founded to specialize in carnival theater with a political thrust; *King Jab Jab* was especially notable for its fierce political satire. Thus there is a rich and popular tradition of street theater in Trinidad-Tobago.

A thriving theater community produces some of the most compelling drama in the Caribbean. The roots of formal theater can be traced to 1826, when Port of Spain, the capital city, housed five professional theaters and three amateur companies. E. J. Joseph, a Scotsman, wrote some of the islands' first dramas (e.g., *Martial Law in Trinidad*, 1832), which are notable for their sympathetic and dignified portrayals of slaves and their dialects. After emancipation, there was a fallow period in Trinidad's theaters. In 1858, for example, there was only a single theater in the capital, and by 1866 no theaters existed. Though the Trinidad Drama Club revived theater in 1897, most work was imported and, of course, most of the plays performed were European and American.

In 1932 two schoolteachers, Arthur Roberts and De Wilton Rogers, began producing works on topical problems, such as race (*Blue Blood and Black*, 1936) and imperialism (*Silk Cotton Grove*, 1942). Such works showed the people of Trinidad-Tobago that the theater could be a weapon as the islands attempted to define themselves culturally and to become autonomous. In 1943 there was a concerted effort towards recognizing folk culture and island music when the respected musician Edric Connor delivered a powerful lecture on West Indian folk music and ethnography to the Music Association. This sparked a renewed interest in local heritage and customs that soon affected the theater. In 1948 Beryl McBurnie founded the Little Carib Theater in Port of Spain, primarily to promote dance, but it soon became the preeminent theater in Trinidad and sponsored an arts festival in which over 500 entries celebrated West Indian arts and entertainment. A number of Trinidad-Tobago's most prominent theater artists, including Errol Hill and Derek Walcott, tested their work at the Little Carib.

The University of the West Indies sponsored playwriting competitions in the 1950s that raised the quality of the region's drama. In 1955 John Ainsworth, an English actor, staged racially integrated plays, such as *Hamlet* and *Macbeth*, which further opened the possibilities for would-be artists in Trinidad-Tobago. And in 1959 Walcott—the first Caribbean literary artist to win a Nobel Prize—opened the Trinidad Theater Workshop, the most influential artistic enterprise on these islands.

In addition to Walcott, Trinidad-Tobago has produced a number of internationally respected dramatists (e.g., Lennox Brown, Mustapha Matura, and Pearl Springer), actors (Errol Jones and Jean Sue-Wing), and directors (Errol Sitahal and Ralph Maraj).

TI-JEAN AND HIS BROTHERS

D E R E K   W A L C O T T

DEREK WALCOTT (1930–)

As a poet and a dramatist, Derek Walcott is among the most honored writers of the twentieth century. In 1992 he achieved the world's highest literary award, the Nobel Prize, and is thus one of the few dramatists to receive that honor (Soyinka is another).

Walcott and his twin brother and theater colleague, Roderick, were born on the Caribbean island of St. Lucia and reared by their mother after their father died. Because his mother was the headmistress of the local Methodist Infant School, Walcott received an excellent education and an uncommonly fine grounding in English, which was not available to other nonwhites on the island. His father had been a civil servant with a strong interest in the arts, particularly play reading and painting. The Walcott twins were encouraged to pursue these interests by their mother and family friends.

He studied at University College of the West Indies in Jamaica, where he continued the classical education begun in St. Lucia. The tension between his Eurocentered education and his desire to create a theater representative of his native West Indies has been a source of controversy for Walcott throughout his career. As a student Walcott distinguished himself as a poet, dramatist, and editor of a literary journal. He began writing plays in 1946, and his drama about Haiti's revolution, *Henri Christophe* (1949), earned him respect as a dramatist. In 1950 he cofounded the Arts Guild of St. Lucia as an outlet for native voices.

The Trinidad Theater Workshop, which evolved from his work with Little Carib Theater and the Basement Theater, was founded in the late 1950s and remains the legacy of Walcott's vision of a "little theater" devoted to the development of native Caribbean drama performed in a distinctive West Indian style. The TTW created works fusing native stories, music, and dance with such diverse non-Caribbean theater forms as Noh and Kabuki, classical European theater, American method acting, Brechtian epic theater, and Grotowski's poor theater. Walcott's best dramatic pieces were written for the TTW: *The Charlatan* (1962), *Dream on Monkey Mountain* (1968), *The Joker of Seville* (a work commissioned by the Royal Shakespeare Company in 1975), and *O! Babylon!* (1976). His works have been produced by Joseph Papp's New York Free Shakespeare Festival, the Mark Taper Forum in Los Angeles, and the Boston Playwright's Theater. In addition to his plays, Walcott has written volumes of poetry, including his lengthy autobiographical poem *Another Life*. He is among the most anthologized poets of the twentieth century.

TI-JEAN AND HIS BROTHERS (1958)

"Dancing with the devil" is a recurring image in our survey of global theatrical rituals and ceremonies. We have seen devils, actual and metaphorical, called the *Barong* in Bali, the *Chapayepkas* among the Yaqui Indians, *leshij* in Russia, *diablos* in Mexico and Latin America, and *diablesse* in Trinidad—where *Ti-Jean* is set. The need to exorcise the spirits of darkness so that life can proceed in harmony has been manifested in both ancient and advanced cultures, and it is not surprising that a significant body of the globe's dramatic literature portrays humans locked in combat with demons.

Derek Walcott's folk play *Ti-Jean and His Brothers* is simultaneously a contemporary work (1958) portraying modern political realities and a very ancient story, adapted from a St. Lucian legend, which uses archetypal characters engaged in battle with the devil himself. Its plotting and theatricality are primitive in the best sense because it is so fundamental. Yet there is sophistication in the way Walcott blends contemporary concerns with older traditions to create a new work that both entertains and instructs his West Indian audiences.

The play comprises three short scenes, which are preceded by a lengthy prologue. Actually, two prologues provide exposition. The first is purposely artificial and uses a chorus of forest creatures, the frog and his allies, to establish the story telling framework of the main plot. Furthermore, the prologue given by the creatures mythologizes Ti-Jean's exploits and raises him to hero status ("Ti-jean the hunter . . . he beat the devil"). This contrived prologue, very much in the story-telling tradition, allows the audience to accept more readily the play's extraordinary events.

The second prologue introduces us to the play's earthly characters, each an archetype found in folk plays. We meet the long-suffering mother, impoverished and anxious to feed and shelter her children. Through her, Walcott quickly enlists our sympathy. Mother has three sons, each an emblem of a particular human value. Gros ("Big") Jean, the oldest, relies solely on his physical powers, whereas the middle son, Mi(ddle)-Jean, is bookish and depends on his intelligence. The spirited rivalry between Gros Jean and Mi-Jean is more than a sibling rivalry: theirs is that ancient battle between brains and brawn. The little brother, Ti(ny)-Jean, has only a portion of his oldest brother's strength and his elder brother's wit; he possesses a greater strength, however, which enables him to triumph over the devil. Significantly, Ti-Jean aligns himself with the biblical David who slays Goliath, the quintessential archetype of the "little guy" who topples the giant-oppressor.

That Walcott resorts to a tripartite structure for his story is not surprising. The "rule of three" is a favorite tool of storytellers and playwrights everywhere (Shakespeare used it in *Hamlet,* in which three sons must avenge the deaths of three fathers). Think of how many fairy tales, folk stories, or jokes you know that begin with "there were three . . ." There are several reasons for this universal plot structure. First, the two errant brothers become foils to Ti-Jean; that is, we judge his success against the failure of his brothers. The first prologue actually reveals the ending so that the audience may assess the choices each brother makes. Second, the tripartite structure builds suspense. The three-step build to a resolution has proven to be an ideal number for involving audiences, even when we know the eventual outcome as in *Ti-Jean.* A lesser number does not tease us quite enough, a larger one becomes cumbersome. Finally, the "rule of three" has a phenomenological significance. Something that happens once (Gros Jean is devoured by the devil) we think of as happenstance; if it happens twice (Mi-Jean's defeat) it is coincidence. A third occurrence, especially when resolved to our satisfaction, moves the problem into the realm of universal law.

Each of the three scenes has a well-defined point of attack: a brother encounters the devil. The rising action increases the tension as each brother "riles" at a different tempo. And finally, there is a well-marked climax to each sequence in which a brother is either devoured or triumphs. Playwriting does not get much clearer than this. Walcott's skill keeps us involved through the debate between each brother and the devil.

Thematically, the play works on two levels. First, it is a simple folktale, the roots of which can be found in many locales around the globe. We might refer to it as a "rite of passage play," not unlike *A Midsummer Night's Dream.* Here, three young men must go into the world to test themselves against the unknown. Gros Jean leaves his mother while singing

> *There's a time for every man*
> *To leave his mother and father*
> *To leave everybody he know*
> *And march to the grave me one!*

(The last line is a nice bit of poetry in which Walcott uses the West Indian dialect; it actually means "march to the grave on my own," but the playwright creates an ironic pun within the dialect.) Each brother ventures into the forest to use his particular strength to battle the devil. From the winner, we learn a lesson about the hierarchy of human virtues.

To this simple folk motif, however, Walcott adds contemporary political commentary. He aligns the devil with plantation owners, the old colonialists who used native and African labor for profit in Trinidad's troubled past. Carnival in Trinidad (see Center Stage box, The Trinidad Carnival, following the text of the play) traditionally begins with a *canboulay*, a mock military march that parodies the colonial guards who oversaw the slaves. *Canboulay* refers to "the burning of the cane," a nineteenth-century rebellion in which the slaves burned the sugar cane fields rather than submit to the horrible conditions to which they were subjected. In the final scene Walcott scripts a "cane burners chorus" that sings "Burn, burn, burn de cane!" The vestiges of this historical event, so central to the spirit of the people of the West Indies, is skillfully blended into the dramatic framework of the play and foreshadows Ti-Jean's triumph over his diabolical adversary. Some critics, by the way, have noted that *Ti-Jean* is a parable about the evolution of Africans in the Caribbean—that is, from exploited physical laborers (Gros Jean), to educated "Anglo-Africans" (Mi-Jean), to resourceful "natives" who remain true to their innate sense of self (Ti-Jean).

Whether we view it as a folktale or a political parable, *Ti-Jean and His Brothers* is superb theater by any criterion. It blends local dialects and speech rhythms to complement Walcott's own poetic talents. As is his custom, Walcott uses both Creole folk songs and Trinidad's popular calypso music to heighten the atmosphere and, on occasion, to make thematic points (e.g., the song of triumph that concludes the action). As you read the play, "hear" the infectious music that the people of the West Indies use to hearten themselves in the face of hardship.

You must also see this play in your mind's eye. At both the Little Carib Theater in Port of Spain and at Walcott's Trinidad Theater Workshop, where it was successfully revived as a "musical drama" in 1970, the play takes place on an open stage and uses little scenery. Colorfully dressed and masked actors (inspired by Walcott's contact with the Noh theater while in New York in the mid-fifties) created the environment through body language. Theatrically exciting scenes abound throughout the play: the invasion of the spirits midway through the prologue, the chorus of forest creatures, the literally explosive climax of each scene, the various transformations of the devil into old man and planter, and the final tableau in which the older brothers are seen passing through hell. Walcott uses little that has not been seen in theaters around the world; his ingenuity springs from the spirited manner in which he adapts older forms for his West Indian audiences, while addressing concerns that are universal.

Derek Walcott, dramatist and poet, is the first Nobel
Laureate from the Caribbean.

TI-JEAN AND HIS BROTHERS

—DEREK WALCOTT—

for Peter Walcott

CHARACTERS
CRICKET
FROG
FIREFLY
BIRD
GROS JEAN
MI-JEAN
TI-JEAN
MOTHER
BOLOM
{OLD MAN, OR PAPA BOIS
{PLANTER
{DEVIL

PROLOGUE

*Evening. Rain. The heights of a forest. A Cricket, a Frog,
a Firefly, a Bird. Left, a hut with bare table, an empty
bowl, stools. The Mother waiting.*

FROG.
    Greek-croak, Greek-croak.
CRICKET.
    Greek-croak, Greek-croak.
    [The others join.]
FROG.
    [Sneezing]

Derek Walcott

Aeschylus me!
All that rain and no moon tonight.
CRICKET.
  The moon always there even fighting the rain
  Creek-crak, it is cold, but the moon always there
  And Ti-Jean in the moon just like the story.

[Bird passes.]

CRICKET.
  Before you fly home, listen,
  The cricket cracking a story
  A story about the moon.
FROG.
  If you look in the moon,
  Though no moon is here tonight,
  There is a man, no, a boy,
  Bent by the weight of faggots
  He carried on his shoulder,
  A small dog trotting with him.
  That is Ti-Jean the hunter,
  He got the heap of sticks
  From the old man of the forest
  They calling Papa Bois,
  Because he beat the devil,
  God put him in that height
  To be the sun's right hand
  And light the evil dark,
  But as the bird so ignorant
  I will start the tale truly.

[Music]

  Well, one time it had a mother,
  That mother had three sons.
  The first son was Gros Jean.
  That son he was the biggest,
  His arm was hard as iron,
  But he was very stupid.

[Enter Gros Jean, a bundle of faggots in one hand, an axe
over his shoulder, moving in an exaggerated march to
music. The creatures laugh.]

FROG.
  The name of the second son,
  They was calling him Mi-Jean,
  In size, the second biggest,
  So only half as stupid; now,
  He was a fisherman, but
  Always studying book, and
  What a fisherman; for
  When he going and fish,
  Always forgetting the bait,
  So between de bait and debate . . .
CRICKET.
  Mi boug qui tait cooyon!
  (Look man who was a fool!)

[Roll of drums. Comic quatro, martial]

[Enter Mi-Jean from the opposite side, carrying a book in
one hand and a fishing net over his shoulder. Halfway
across the stage he flings the net casually, still reading]

BIRD.
  How poor their mother was?

[Sad music on flute]

FROG.
  Oh that was poverty, bird!
  Old hands dried up like claws
  Heaping old sticks on sticks,
  Too weak to protect her nest.
  Look, the four of that family

[Light shows the hut.]

  Lived in a little house,
  Made up of wood and thatch,
  On the forehead of the mountain,
  Where night and day was rain,
  Mist, cloud white as cotton
  Caught in the dripping branches;
  Where sometimes it was so cold
  The frog would stop its singing

[The Frog stops. Five beats. Resumes.]

  The cricket would stop rattling
  And the wandering firefly
  That lights the tired woodsman
  Home through the raining trees
  Could not strike a damp light
  To star the wanderer home!

[The music stops. The brothers Gros Jean and Mi-Jean
put their arms around each other, and to heavy drums
tramp home.]

CRICKET.
  I damned sorry for that mother.
FROG.
  Aie, cricket, you croak the truth!
  The life of an old woman
  With her husband cold in earth,
  Where the bamboo leaves lie lightly,
  And smell of mouldering flesh,
  How well I know that story!
  Near where the mother was,
  Across the wet and melancholy
  Mountain where her hut was, O God,
  The Devil used to live!

[Crash of cymbals. Shrieks, thunder. The animals cower
as the Devil with his troop of fiends, the Werewolf, the
Diablesse, the Bolom, somersault and dance across the
stage. The sky is red.]

DEVIL.
Bai Diable-là manger un'ti mamaille!
(Give the Devil a child for dinner!)
DEVILS.
Un, deux, trois'ti mamaille!
(One, two, three little children!)

[They whirl around the stage leaping, chanting, then as suddenly go off.]

BIRD.
Wow!
Were they frightened of him?
FROG.
If they were frightened?
They were frightened of his skin,
Powdery as leprosy,
Like the pock-marked moon,
Afraid of his dead eye,
That had no fire in it . . .
CRICKET.
Of the terrible thunder
In his wood-shaking throat!

[Roar of devils off-stage]

FROG.
Just hear them in the hut . . .

[Sad flute, as the light comes up on the three sons around the knees of the old woman]

GROS JEAN.
One time again it have nothing to eat,
But one day bread to break;
I went out to chop some wood
To make a nice fire,
But the wood was too damp,
So I didn't use the axe
As I didn't want it to get wet;
If it get wet it get rusty.
MI-JEAN.
Sense!
I went out to do fishing
For crayfish by the cold stones,
In the cold spring in the ferns,
But when I get there so,
I find I lack bait,

[Rising solemnly]

Now for man to catch fish,
That man must have bait,
But the best bait is fish,
Yet I cannot catch no fish
Without I first have bait,
As the best bait for fish
Is to catch fish with fish,
So I . . .

GROS JEAN.
Mi-Jean is a fool,
Reading too much damn book.
MOTHER.
My sons, do not quarrel,
Here all of us are starving,
While the planter is eating
From plates painted golden,
Forks with silver tongues,
The brown flesh of birds,
And the white flesh of fish,
What did you do today,
My last son Ti-Jean?
TI-JEAN.
Maman, m'a fait un rien.
(Mama, I didn't do a thing.)
GROS JEAN.
We do all the damned work.
MI-JEAN.
We do all the damn thinking
GROS JEAN.
And he sits there like a prince.
MI-JEAN.
As useless as a bone.
GROS JEAN and MI-JEAN.

[Jeering]

Maman, m'a fait un rien!
Maman, m'a fait un rien!
MOTHER.
Wait, and God will send us something.
GROS JEAN.
God forget where he put us.
MI-JEAN.
God too irresponsible.
MOTHER.
Children!

[Weird music. The Bolom or Foetus rolls in unheard, somersaults around the hut, then waits. Sound of wind, rain, shriek of insects.]

Children, listen,
There is something listening
Outside of the door!
GROS JEAN.
I don't hear nothing.
MI-JEAN.
I hear only the rain,
Falling hard on the leaves,
And the wind down the throat
Of the gorge with the spring,
The crickets and the bull-frog,
And maybe one frightened bird.
MOTHER.

[Standing]

I tell you there is something
Outside of the door,
I tell you from experience
I know when evil comes.
It is not the wind, listen!

[The Bolom imitates a child crying.]

MI-JEAN.
    A young child out in the forest.
GROS JEAN.
    Looking for its mother.
MOTHER.
    The Devil has sent us
    Another of his angels!
    I prayed to God all day,
    While I scrubbed the hut bare,
    On the knuckles of my knees
    All day in the hungry house;
    Now God has sent me evil,
    Who can understand it?
    Death, death is coming nearer.
GROS JEAN.
    Line the step with fine sand
    To keep the evil out!
MI-JEAN.
    Turn over, Mother, the hem of your skirt!
GROS JEAN and MI-JEAN.
    Let two of our fingers form in one crucifix!

[Ti-Jean steps outside.]

MOTHER.
    Spirit that is outside,
    With the voice of a child
    Crying out in the rain,
    What do you want from the poor?

[Ti-Jean searches carefully.]

BOLOM.
    I have a message for a woman with three sons.
MOTHER.
    Child of the Devil, what is your message?
BOLOM.
    Send the first of your sons outside for it,
    They must die in that order. And let the youngest
    Return into the hut.

[Ti-Jean steps back into the hut.]

MOTHER.
    We can hear you in the wind,
    What do you want of me?

[A weird light shows the Bolom. Shrieks.]

ALL.
    Where are you? Where is it?

Hit it! There! Where is it?
BOLOM.

[Leaping, hiding]

    Here, in the bowl!
    Here, sitting on a stool!
    Here, turning in a cup!
    Here, crawling up your skirt!
MOTHER.
    I have done you no harm, child.
BOLOM.
    A woman did me harm,
    Called herself mother,
    The fear of her hatred
    A cord round my throat!
MOTHER.

[Turning, searching]

    Look, perhaps it is luckiest
    Never to be born,
    To the horror of this life
    Crowded with shadows,
    Never to have known
    That the sun will go out,
    The green leaf rust,
    The strong tree be stricken
    And the roaring spring quail;
    Peace to you, unborn,
    You can find comfort here.
    Let a mother touch you,
    For the sake of her kind.
BOLOM.

[Shrieks, dancing back]

    Whatever flesh touches me,
    Withers me into mortality;
    Not till your sons die, Mother,
    Shall this shape feel this life.
GROS JEAN.

[Seizes axe]

    Kill it, then, kill it.
MI-JEAN.
    Curse it back to the womb.
DEMON'S VOICE.
    Faire ça mwen di ous!
    (Do what I commanded!)
BOLOM.
    I hear the voice of my master.
DEMON'S VOICE.
    Bolom, faire tout ça mwen dire ous!
    (Child, do all that I ordered you!)
BOLOM.
    Listen, creature of gentleness,
    Old tree face marked with scars,

And the wounds of bearing children,
Whom the earth womb will swallow,
This is the shriek
Of a child which was strangled,
Who never saw the earth light
Through the hinge of the womb,
Strangled by a woman,
Who hated my birth,
Twisted out of shape,
Deformed past recognition,
Tell me then, Mother,
Would you care to see it?

[Bolom moves out of the light, shrieking.]

GROS JEAN.
Let us see you!
MOTHER.
The sight of such horror, though you are brave,
Would turn you to stone, my strong son, Gros Jean.
MI-JEAN.
Let us reason with you.
MOTHER.
My son, the thing may be a ball of moving fire,
A white horse in the leaves, or a clothful of skin,
Found under a tree, you cannot explain that!
BOLOM.
Save your understanding for the living,
Save your pity for the dead,
I am neither living nor dead,
A puny body, a misshapen head.
MOTHER.
What does your white master
The Devil want from us?
BOLOM.
The house looks warm, old woman,
Love keeps the house warm,
From the cold wind and cold rain;
Though you bar up the door,
I can enter the house.

[Thunder]

MOTHER.
Enter! You are welcome.

[She flings open the door.]

GROS JEAN and MI-JEAN.
Shut the door, shut the door!

[Crash of cymbals. The Bolom rolls in a blue light towards the hut, then enters; all freeze in fear.]

BOLOM.
The Devil my master
Who owns half the world,
In the kingdom of night,
Has done all that is evil
Butchered thousands in war,
Whispered his diseases
In the ears of great statesmen,
Invented human justice,
Made anger, pride, jealousy,
And weakened prayer;
Still cannot enjoy
Those vices he created.
He is dying to be human.
So he sends you this challenge!
To all three of your sons,
He says through my voice,
That if anyone on earth

[Devils' Voices chanting].

Anyone human
Can make him feel anger,
Rage, and human weakness,
He will reward them,
He will fill that bowl,
With a shower of sovereigns,
You shall never more know hunger,
But fulfillment, wealth, peace.

[Increased drum roll to climax]

But if any of your sons
Fails to give him these feelings,
For he never was human,
Then his flesh shall be eaten,
For he is weary of the flesh
Of the fowls of the air,
And the fishes in the sea,
But whichever of your sons
Is brave enough to do this,
Then that one shall inherit
The wealth of my prince.
And once they are dead, woman,
I too shall feel life!

[Exit]

DEVILS' VOICES OFF.
Bai Diable-là manger un'ti mamaille,
Un, deux, trois'ti mamaille!
Bai Diable-là manger un'ti mamaille,
Un,
    deux,
        trois . . .
(Give the Devil a child for dinner,
One, two, three little children!
Give the Devil a child for dinner,
One,
    two,
        three . . .)

Fadeout

1433

SCENE ONE

Daybreak. The hut. The Mother and her sons asleep. Gros Jean rises, packs a bundle. His Mother stirs and watches. He opens the door.

MOTHER.
    You will leave me just so,
    My eldest son?
GROS JEAN.
    Is best you didn't know.
MOTHER.
    Woman life is so. Watching and losing.
GROS JEAN.
    Maman, the time obliged to come I was to leave the
    house, go down the tall forest, come out on the high
    road, and find what is man work. Is big man I reach now,
    not no little boy again. Look, feel this arm, but to split
    trees is nothing. I have an arm of iron, and have nothing
    I fraid.
MOTHER.
    The arm which digs a grave
    Is the strongest arm of all.
    Your grandfather, your father,
    Their muscles like brown rivers
    Rolling over rocks.
    Now, they bury in small grass,
    Just the jaws of the ant
    Stronger than them now.
GROS JEAN.
    I not even fraid that. You see,
    Is best you still was sleeping?
    I don't want to wake my brothers.
    Ti-Jean love me and will frighten.
    Mi-Jean will argue and make me remain.
    The sun tapping me on my shoulder.
MOTHER.
    When you go down the tall forest, Gros Jean,
    Praise God who make all things; ask direction
    Of the bird, and the insects, imitate them;
    But be careful of the hidden nets of the devil,
    Beware of a wise man called Father of the Forest,
    The Devil can hide in several features,
    A woman, a white gentleman, even a bishop.
    Strength, *ça pas tout*, there is patience besides;
    There always is something stronger than you.
    If is not man, animal, is God or demon.
GROS JEAN.
    Maman, I know all that already.
MOTHER.
    Then God bless you, Gros Jean.
GROS JEAN.
    The world not the same it was in your time,
    Tell my brothers I gone. A man have to go.

[Marches from hut]

[Martial flute, quatro, drum]

GROS JEAN.

    [Sings]

    There's a time for every man
    To leave his mother and father
    To leave everybody he know
    And march to the grave he one!

    [Enter the animals, hopping around him]

    So the time has come for me
    To leave me mother and father
    To add my force to the world
    And go to the grave me one!

[The Frog is in his path. He aims a kick.]

Get out of my way, you slimy bastard! How God could
make such things? Jump out under my foot, cricket, you
know you have no bones! *Gibier! Gibier, montrez-moi sor-
tir!* Bird-o, bird-o, show me a good short-cut, be quick!

*[Suddenly the Bird, Cricket and the Frog all scurry shriek-
ing, croaking. The Old Man enters limping and rests a
bundle of faggots down. Gros Jean watches. The Old
Man lifts a corner of his robe to scratch a cloven, hairy
hoof. Gros Jean emerges.]*

GROS JEAN.
    Bon jour, vieux papa.
OLD MAN.
    Bon matin, Gros Jean.
GROS JEAN.
    What you have with your foot?
OLD MAN.
    Fleas, fleas, boy.

    [Covers it quickly]

GROS JEAN.
    Is man I am now. Chiggers in your flesh?
    Is man I am, papa, and looking for success.
OLD MAN.
    The flesh of the earth is rotting. Worms.
GROS JEAN.
    Which way, papa?
OLD MAN.
    I cannot tell you the way to success;
    I can only show you, Gros Jean,
    One path through the forest.
GROS JEAN.
    I have no time to waste. I have an arm of iron,
    It have nothing, I fraid, man, beast, or beast-man,
    And more quick I get what I want, more better.
OLD MAN.
    I think strength should have patience. Look at me today.

I was a strong woodman, now I burn coals,
I'm as weak as ashes. And nearly deaf. Come nearer.
GROS JEAN.

[Advances calmly]

What you would say is the quickest way?
OLD MAN.

The quickest way to what?
GROS JEAN.

To what counts in this world.
OLD MAN.

What counts in this world is money and power.
GROS JEAN.

I have an arm of iron, only money I missing.
OLD MAN.

Then I can't advise you.
GROS JEAN.

You old and you have experience.
So don't be selfish with it.
Or you know what I'll do.

[Grabs him, hurls him down, axe uplifted]

Chop you and bury you in the bamboo leaves!
OLD MAN.

With your arm of iron, the first thing to kill is wisdom?
GROS JEAN.

That's right, papa.
OLD MAN.

Well, the Devil always wants help.
GROS JEAN.

The Devil boasts that he never get vex.
OLD MAN.

[Rising]

Easy, easy son, I'll help you if you wait,
Just let me adjust the edge of my skirt.
Well, I was coming through the forest now
And I passed by the white spring, and I saw
Some poor souls going to work for the white planter.
He'll work you like the devil, but that's what you want,
You and your impatience and arm cast in iron,
So turn to the right, go through the bamboo forest,
Over the black rocks, then the forest will open,
And you will see the sky, below that a valley,
And smoke, and a white house that is empty,
The old fellow is hiring harvesters today.
Remember an iron arm may rust, flesh is deciduous.
There's your short-cut, Gros Jean, make the most of it.
GROS JEAN.

Next time don't be so selfish.

[Exit Gros Jean, marching]

OLD MAN.

[Sings, gathering bundle]

Who is the man who can speak to the strong?

Where is the fool who can talk to the wise?
Men who are dead now have learnt this long,
Bitter is wisdom that fails when it tries.
[To the audience] Ah well, there's wood to cut, fires to
light, smoke to wrinkle an old man's eyes, and a shrivel-
ling skin to keep warm. There went the spirit of war: an
iron arm and a clear explanation, and might is still right,
thank God, for God is the stronger. But get old father forest from the path of the fable, for there's wood to cut, a
nest of twittering beaks to feed with world-eating worms.
Oh, oh, oh.

[The creatures creep after him timidly.]

For they all eat each other, and that's natural law,
So remember the old man in the middle of the forest.

[He turns suddenly. Then hobbles after them]

Eat and eat one another! It's another day. Ha, ha! Wah!
Wah!

[They flee. He goes out.]

GROS JEAN.

[In another part of the wood] I have an arm of iron, and
that's true, but I here since the last two days working for
this damn white man, and I don't give a damn if he
watching me. You know what I doing here with this bag
and this piece of stick? Well, I go tell you. While I smoke
a pipe. Let me just sit down, and I won't lose my patience.
[He sits on a log] Well, you remember how I leave home,
and then bounce up this old man who put me on to a
work? Remember what the old son of a leaf-gathering
beggar said? He said that working for the Devil was the
shortest way to success. Well, I walked up through the
bush then I come onto a large field. Estate-like, you
know. Sugar, tobacco, and a hell of a big white house
where they say the Devil lives. Ay-ay.

So two next black fellers bring me up to him. Big white
man, his hand cold as an axe blade and his mind twice as
sharp. So he say, "Gros Jean, we has a deal to make,
right?" So I say, "Sure, boss!" He say the one that get the
other one vex, the one who show the first sign of anger
will be eaten rrruuunnnhhh, just like that, right? You
think I stupid? I strong, I have some sense and my name
not Gros Jean for nothing. That was two days ago. Well,
Jesus, a man ain't rest since then! The first job I had, I
had was to stand up in a sugar-cane field and count all the
leaves of the cane. That take me up till four o'clock. I
count all the leaves and then divide by the number of
stalks. I must tell you there had times when I was getting
vex but the old iron arm fix me, because there is patience
in strength. The Devil ain't say anything. About seven
o'clock, he tell me to go and catch about seventy fireflies.
Well, you must try and catch fireflies! Is no easy. Had a
time when I do so once, one whap with the hand! thinking was a bunch but was nothing, only stars! So in the

middle of all that, this man come up to me and say, what's the matter, Joe, he always like he don't know my name, but I is me, Gros Jean, the strongest! And if you ain't know my name, you best don't call me nothing. Say, "What's matter, Mac? You vex or sumpin?" So I say, "No, I ain't vex!" Well, is two days now, and I ain't get a cent. I so tired I giddy. But I giving the old iron arm a rest from cramp, and breaking a little smoke. After all! If was only sensible work, if a man could get the work that suit him, cotton or sugar or something important! Plus he getting eighty-five per cent of the profit? Shucks, man, that ain't fair. Besides I could just bust his face, you know. But me mother ain't bring me up so. After all, man, after all, a man have to rest man. Shime!

[Enter Devil masked as a Planter.]

PLANTER.

Well, how's it progressing, Joe, tired?

GROS JEAN.

From where you was and now you come you hear me say I fagged? *[Slowly]* And Gros Jean is the name, boss.

PLANTER.

Tobacco break? Whistle's blown past lunch, boy.

GROS JEAN.

I taking a five here, chief. Black people have to rest too, and once I rest, chief, I do more work than most, right?

PLANTER.

That's right, Mac.

GROS JEAN.

[Gritting his teeth] Gros Jean . . . Gros . . . Jean . . . chief . . . !

PLANTER.

You sound a bit annoyed to me.

GROS JEAN.

[With a painful, fixed grin from now on] Have your fun. I know I ain't nobody yet, chief, but an old man tell me to have patience. And I ain't let you down yet, chief, hasn't I?

PLANTER.

That's right, Gros Chien, Gros Jean, Gros Jean, sorry. Can't tell one face from the next out here. How's the work then? *[Pacing up and down]*

GROS JEAN.

Chief, why you don't take a rest too somewhat? You have all this land, all this big house and so forth, people working for you as if is ants self, but is only work, work, work in your mind, ent you has enough?

PLANTER.

[Looking at his watch] Other people want what I have, Charley, and other people have more. Can't help myself, Joe, it's some sort of disease, and it spreads right down to the common man.

GROS JEAN.

I not no common man, boss. People going hear about Gros Jean. Because I come from that mountain forest, don't mean I can't come like you, or because I black. One day all this could be mine!

PLANTER.

Yes, yes. Well anyway, Horace, time is flying, and I want these leaves checked, counted, filed and classified by weight and texture and then stacked . . . What's the matter, Francis?

GROS JEAN.

[To audience] You see how he provoking me, you don't think I should curse his . . . *[Turns, bites hard on pipe, grinning]* Look, I haven't let you down yet, boss, have I? I mean to say I take two three hours to catch your goat you send me to catch. I mean not so? Wait, chief, wait, listen . . . I ain't vex, boss. Ha-ha!

PLANTER.

Sit down, Joe, relax, you can't take it with you, they say, only time is money, and the heights that great men reached etc., and genius is ninety per cent perspiration and so forth . . . So, sit down, waste time, but I thought you were in a hurry . . . Henry.

GROS JEAN.

Boss. *[Smiling]* You really impatianate, yes. Ha-ha-ha! I mean I don't follow you, chief. After I count and carry all the cane leaves for you, ain't I, and look—when the wind blow them wrong side I ain't say nothing, and I'm smiling ain't I? *[Relaxes his expression, then resumes]* I'm smiling because I got confidence in the old iron arm, ain't it? And if I do it and have time to spare is the work and pay that matter, and is all you worried about, *big shot!* Ain't it? Excuse me, I mean to say, I'm smiling ain't I?

PLANTER.

Sorry, sorry, Gros Jean, sometimes we people in charge of industry forget that you people aren't machines. I mean people like you, Hubert . . .

[Gros Jean is about to sit.]

GROS JEAN.

[Rising] Gros Jean, chief, Gros Jean . . . Ha-ha!

PLANTER.

Gros Jean, very well . . . *[Pause]* Have your smoke. *[Pause]* Plenty of time. It might rain, people may be stealing from me now. The market is unsteady this year. *[Pause]* But we're human. *[Pause]* You don't know what it means to work hard, to have to employ hundreds of people. *[Embracing him]* You're worth more to me, Benton, than fifty men. So you should smoke, after all. *[Pause]* And such a pleasant disposition, always smiling. *[Pause, steps back]* Just like a skull. *[Long pause]* But remember, Mervin, I'd like you to try and finish this, you see I have a contract and the harder you work the more I . . .

GROS JEAN.

[Exploding, smashing pipe in anger] Jesus Christ what this damn country coming to a man cyant even get a god-

damned smoke? [*He tries to grin*] I ent vex, I ent vex, chief. Joke, joke, boss . . .

Explosion

[*When the smoke clears, the Devil, his Planter's mask removed, is sitting on the log, calmly nibbling the flesh from a bone.*]

DEVILS' VOICES OFF.
　　Bai Diable-là manger un'ti mamaille
　　Un!
　　(Give the Devil a child for dinner
　　One! . . .)

Blackout

SCENE TWO

Music. Dawn. The forest. A cross marked "Gros Jean." The creatures foraging. Enter Mi-Jean walking fast and reading, a net slung over his shoulder.)

BIRD.

[*To flute*]

Mi-Jean, Mi-Jean, *bon jour*, M'sieu Mi-Jean.

[*The creatures dance.*]

MI-JEAN.

[*Closes the book*]

Bird, you disturbing me!
Too much whistling without sense,
Is animal you are, so please know your place.
CRICKET.
　　Where you going, Mi-Jean?
MI-JEAN.

[*To the audience*]

But see my cross, *oui*, ay-ay!
Since from what time cricket
Does ask big man their business?
FROG.
　　You going to join your brother?
　　You are a man's size now.
MI-JEAN.

[*Again to the audience*]

Well, confusion on earth, frog could talk!
Gros Jean was one man, I is a next. Frog,
You ever study your face in
The mirror of a pool?
BIRD.
　　Mi-Jean, Mi-Jean,

Your brother is a little heap
Of white under the bamboo leaves,
Every morning the black beetles
More serious than a hundred priests,
Frowning like fifty undertakers
Come and bear a piece away
To build a chapel from his bones. Look, look!

[*Bird shows the cross. Mi-Jean kneels and peers through his spectacles.*]

CRICKET.
　　Every morning I sit here,
　　And see the relics of success,
　　An arm of iron turned to rust,
　　Not strong enough to stir the dirt.
FROG.
　　Gros Jean was strong, but had no sense.
MI-JEAN.

[*Rising and dusting his clothes*]

He had the sin called over-confidence!
Listen, I . . .
BIRD.
　　Run, run, Papa Bois, Papa Bois . . .

[*All run off*]

OLD MAN.
　　Bon jour, Mi-Jean, Mi-Jean, *le philosophe*.
MI-JEAN.

[*To the audience*]

When my mother told me goodbye in tears,
She said, no one can know what the Devil wears.

[*To the Old Man*]

Bon jour, Papa Bois, how come you know my name?
OLD MAN.
　　Who in the heights, in any small hut hidden in the ferns, where the trees are always weeping, or any two men are ploughing on a wet day, wrapped in old cloaks, or down in the villages among the smoke and rum, has not heard of Mi-Jean the jurist, and the gift of his tongue, his prowess in argument, Mi-Jean, the *avocat*, the fisherman, the litigant? Come, come sir, don't be modest! I've been sitting there on the cold, crusty log, rough as the armoured bark of a frog, waiting to exchange knowledge with you. Ah, your brother's grave! How simple he was! Well, I'm half-blind, but I see you have one virtue more than your brother, fear. Nothing lives longer than brute strength, sir, except it is human cowardice. Come nearer, come nearer, and tell us why you left home? Sit down, you're among equals.

MI-JEAN.
    I good just where I am.
    I on my way to the sea
    To become a rich captain,
    The land work too hard,
    Then to become a lawyer.
OLD MAN.

    [Softly singing]

    On land on sea no man is free,
    All meet death, the enemy. I see,
    Hence the net, the net and the book.
MI-JEAN.
    What?
OLD MAN.
    I say hence the book,
    Hence the net, and the book.
MI-JEAN.
    Ça c'est hence? (What is "hence"?)
OLD MAN.
    Same as whereas, and hereunto affixed.
    These are terms used in tautology and law.
MI-JEAN.

    [Nodding blankly. Pause. Then:]

    I see you have a cow-foot. Ain't that so?
OLD MAN.
    Yes, yes. A cow's foot. You have an eye for detail!
    Born with it, actually. Source of embarrassment.
    Would you like some tobacco? What are you reading?
MI-JEAN.

    [Opens the book]

    This book have every knowledge it have;
    I checking up on man with cow-foot, boss,
    In the section call religion, and tropical superstition.
    Bos . . . Bovis . . . Cow . . . foot . . . foot, boss? Boss foot?
    Bovis?
OLD MAN.
    Outside in the world they are wiser, now, Mi-Jean;
    They don't believe in evil or the prevalence of devils,
    Believe me, philosopher, nobody listens to old men;
    Sit down next to me and have a bit of tobacco.
    And since you need knowledge, I'll give you advice . . .
MI-JEAN.

    [Still reading]

    I don't smoke and I don't drink,
    I keep my head clear, and advice,
    I don't need none, but will listen.

    [Shuts the book]

    This book is Latin mainly.
    It have bos, meaning cow,

and pes, meaning foot,
    Boss' foot, bospes, cow-heel perhaps,
    It have plenty recipe
    But it don't give the source! [Sighs loudly] So!
    Yes, apart from wisdom, I have no vices.
OLD MAN.
    Life without sin. How about women?
MI-JEAN.
    The downfall of man! I don't care for women,
    Women don't have no brain. Their foot just like yours.
OLD MAN.
    You believe in the Devil?
    Oh, why don't you sit nearer,
    Haven't you ever seen a cow-heel before?
MI-JEAN.
    Not under a skirt, no. [Sighs loudly] Yes!
    I believe in the Devil, yes,
    Or so my mother make me,
    And is either that, papa,
    Or not believe in God.
    And when I meet this devil,
    Whatever shape he taking,
    And I know he is not you,
    Since he would never expose
    His identity so early,
    I will do all that he commands,
    But you know how I will beat him,

[Sits near the Old Man]

With silence, and a smile.

[He smiles]

Too besides when I meet him,
I will know if God exist,
We calling that in philosophy

[Checks in the book]

We calling that in big knowledge,
Ah, polarities of belief,
When the existence of one object
Compels that of the other,
Bon Dieu, what terms, what terms!

[Sighs loudly, rests the book down]

Yes. Silence shall be my defence.

[He sings "The Song of Silence."]

I
Within this book of wisdom
Hear what the wise man say:
The man who is wise is dumb
And lives another day,
You cannot beat the system
Debate is just a hook,

Open your mouth, de bait in!
And is you they going to juck.
CHORUS.
   So when things dark, go blind
   When nothing left, go deaf
   When the blows come, be dumb
   And hum, hum.

                    II

In Chapter Five from para-
Graph three, page 79,
This book opines how Socra-
Tes would have been better off blind.
God gave him eyes like all of we,
But he, he had to look.
The next thing, friends, was jail, *oui!*
Hemlock and him lock up!
CHORUS.
   So when things dark, go blind, etc.

                    III

The third set of instruction
This self-said book declares
Is that the wise man's function
Is how to shut his ears
Against riot and ruction
That try to climb upstairs.
If you can hear, don't listen!
If you can see, don't look!
If you must talk, be quiet!
Or your mouth will dig your grave.

[While he sings his song, the Old Man goes behind a grove of bamboo, leisurely removes his robe and his mask, under which is the mask of the Devil; then he changes into the mask and clothes of the Planter.]

PLANTER.
   [He sits on the log, legs crossed, smiling throughout the scene]
   Ah, finished all the work I gave you, Mi-Jean?

[Mi-Jean nods]

And menial work didn't bore you, a thinker?

[Mi-Jean nods]

You're not one for small-talk, are you?

[Mi-Jean nods]

Did you catch the wild goat?

[Mi-Jean nods yes]

Frisky little bugger, wasn't he? Yes, sir, that's one hell of a goat. Some kid, what? Clever, however. How many canes were there on the estate?

[Mi-Jean uses ten fingers repeatedly.]

Don't waste words, eh? All right, all right. Look, you

don't mind a little chat while we work, do you? A bit of a gaff lightens labour. God Lord, man, you've been here for over two days and haven't had the common decency to even pass the time of day. Where did you get your reputation as a bush lawyer, I mean it's only manners, blast it.

[Mi-Jean cocks his head at the Planter.]

Oh, don't flatter yourself, young man, I'm not annoyed. It takes two to make a quarrel. Shut up, by all means. *[Rises]* Now, before it gets dark, I want you to come up to the house, check and polish the silver, rearrange my library and . . .

[The goat bleats. Mi-Jean frowns.]

Aha, looks like the old goat's broken loose again, son. Better drop what you're not doing and catch it before it's dark.

[Mi-Jean rises rapidly, runs off, returns.]

Ah, now you're smiling again, fixed him this time, haven't you?

[The goat bleats.]

Not quite, cunning animal, that goat, couldn't have tied him.

[Mi-Jean dashes out, annoyed, returns.]

Fast worker!

[The goat bleats.]

Look, before you dash off, I'd like to say here and now . . .

[The goat bleating as Mi-Jean, mumbling, smiling, points off.]

that I do admire your cheery persistence, your resigned nonchalance, so let me demonstrate something. There's a special kind of knot, and there's an end to that. Hence you take the rope thus, and whereas the goat being hereto affixed to the . . .

[Goat bleating, Mi-Jean raging inside.]

but if that doesn't fix him, then my recommendation is . . .
MI-JEAN.
   Look!
PLANTER.
   Yes?
MI-JEAN.
   I think I know what I'm doing . . . sir . . .
PLANTER.
   [Above the sound of bleating] Oh, sure, sure. But I was simply trying to explain just to help you out, that . . . *[Goat bleats]* . . . You see? He's gone off again! Just a little more patience . . . *[Mi-Jean is about to run off]* It's simply a

question of how you tie this knot, don't you see? [Mi-Jean, *collecting himself, nods, then tiredly smiles*] I mean, I've seen dumber men, not you, fail at this knot you know, it's just a matter of know-how, not really knowledge, just plain skill . . . [Mi-Jean *nodding, nodding*] You look the kind of fellow who doesn't mind a bit of expert advice. [*Goat bleats furiously*] And you'd better hurry up before it gets dark. Wait, remember how to tie the knot.

MI-JEAN.

[*Under control, nods*] Yes, I remember. [*Runs off, crosses the stage several times in a chase*]

PLANTER.

[*Walks up and down in a rage*] Well, what the hell, I thought I had him there, he's no fool, that's certain, for the Devil comes in through apertures. He doesn't know right from wrong, and he's not interested. The only entrance I could have got through his mouth, I tried to leave ajar, but the fool bolted it completely. There he goes chasing the bloody goat like a simpleton, and not even shouting at it. Good old Master Speak No Evil. I hope he breaks his God-supported neck, the dummy! [*He sits*] Here comes the comedy again, an eloquent goat and a tongueless biped!

[*The goat cavorts across and around the stage to merry music, with Mi-Jean behind him waving a rope and the net. Mi-Jean collapses.*]

PLANTER.

Tough life, eh?

[*Mi-Jean groans, nodding.*]

Don't let it get you down.

[*Goat bleats.*]

MI-JEAN.

That goat certainly making a plethora of cacophony.

PLANTER.

It's only a poor animal, in its own rut.

MI-JEAN.

[*Smiling*] Men are lustiferous animals also, but at least they have souls.

PLANTER.

Ah, the philosopher! The contemplative! An opinion at last! A man is no better than an animal. The one with two legs makes more noise and that makes him believe he can think. It is talk that makes men think they have souls. There's no difference, only in degree. No animal, but man, dear boy, savours such a variety of vices. He knows no season for lust, he is a kneeling hypocrite who on four legs, like a penitent capriped, prays to his maker, but is calculating the next vice. That's my case!

MI-JEAN.

Nonsensical verbiage! *Bettise!*

PLANTER.

It's not, you know, and you're getting annoyed.

MI-JEAN.

[*Shakes his head*] You can't get me into no argument! I have brains, but won't talk. [*Long pause*] All I say is that man is divine!

PLANTER.

You're more intelligent than the goat, you think?

MI-JEAN.

I not arguing! Anything you want.

PLANTER.

[*Rises*] Honestly, I'd like to hear what you think. You're the kind of chap I like to talk to. Your brother was a sort of politician, but you're a thinker.

[*Mi-Jean, rising, is about to lecture. The goat bleats.*]

Steady-on. For all we know, that may be poetry. Which Greek scholar contends in his theory of metempsychosis that the souls of men may return into animals?

MI-JEAN.

I never study Greek, but I . . . [*Goat bleats. Mi-Jean pauses*] I was saying that I never study no Greek, but I'd . . . [*Goat bleats*] It getting on like to have sense, eh?

PLANTER.

Why not?

MI-JEAN.

Listen, I ent mind doing what you proposed, anything physical, because that's ostentatious, but when you start theorising that there's an equality of importance in the creatures of this earth, when you animadvertently imbue mere animals with an animus or soul, I have to call you a crooked-minded pantheist . . . [*Goat bleats, sounding like "Hear, hear!"*] Oh, shut up, you can't hear two people talking? No, I'm not vexed, you know, but . . . [*Goat bleats.*]

PLANTER.

[*Advancing towards him*] Your argument interests me. It's nice to see ideas getting you excited. But logically now. The goat, I contend, may be a genius in its own right. For all we know, this may be the supreme goat, the apogee of capripeds, the voice of human tragedy, the Greek . . .

MI-JEAN.

Exaggerated hypothesis! Unsubstantiated!

PLANTER.

Since the goat is mine, and if you allow me, for argument's sake, to pursue my premise, then if you get vexed at the goat, who represents my view, then you are vexed with me, and the contract must be fulfilled.

MI-JEAN.

I don't mind talking to you, but don't insult me, telling me a goat have more sense than I, than me. Than both of we!

PLANTER.

[*Embracing him*] Descendant of the ape, how eloquent you

have become! How assured in logic! How marvellous in invention! And yet, poor shaving monkey, the animal in you is still in evidence, that goat . . . [*Goat sustains its bleating.*]

MI-JEAN.

Oh, shut you damn mouth, both o'all you! I ain't care who right who wrong! I talking now! What you ever study? I ain't even finish making my points and all two of you interrupting, breach of legal practice! O God, I not vex, I not vex . . .

[*Planter removes his mask, and the Devil advances on Mi-Jean.*]

*Explosion
Blackout*

[*The goat bleats once*]

DEVILS' VOICES OFF.

Bai Diable-là manger un'ti mamaille
(Give the Devil a child for dinner)
Un!
(One!)
Deux!
(Two! . . .)

INTERVAL

SCENE THREE

Dawn. The forest. Two crosses marked "Gros Jean," "Mi-Jean." The Old Man sits on the log, the creatures huddle near him. Ti-Jean, Mother, in the hut.

DEVILS' VOICES OFF.

*Bai Diable-là manger un'ti mamaille,
Un, deux, trois'ti mamaille!
Bai Diable-là manger un'ti mamaille,
Un, deux, trois'ti mamaille.*

OLD MAN.

Aie! Feed the Devil the third, feed the Devil the third. Power is knowledge, knowledge is power, and the Devil devours them on the hour!

DEVILS.

*Bai Diable-là manger un'ti mamaille
Un, deux, trois'ti mamaille!*

OLD MAN.

[*To audience*] Well, that's two good meals finished with a calm temper, and if all goes mortally, one more is to come. [*Shrieks, points to where Ti-Jean is consoling his Mother*] Aie, ya, yie, a chicken is to come, a calf, a veal-witted young man, tender in flesh, soft in the head and bones, tenderer than old muscle power, and simpler than that net-empty atheist. For the next dish is man-wit,

common sense. But I can wait, I can wait, gathering damp rotting faggots, aie!

MOTHER.

[*To flute*]

If you leave me, my son,
I have empty hands left,
Nothing to grieve for.
You are hardly a man,
A stalk, bending in wind
With no will of its own,
Never proven your self
In battle or in wisdom,
I have kept you to my breast,
As the last of my chickens,
Not to feed the blind jaws
Of the carnivorous grave.

TI-JEAN.

You have told me yourself
Our lives are not ours,
That no one's life is theirs
Husband or wife,
Father or son,
That our life is God's own.

MOTHER.

You are hard, hard, Ti-Jean,
O what can I tell you?
I have never learnt enough.

TI-JEAN.

You have taught me this strength,
To do whatever we will
And love God is enough.

MOTHER.

I feel I shall never see you again.

TI-JEAN.

To return what we love is our glory, our pain.

OLD MAN.

Oh, enough of these sentiments, I'm hungry, and I'm cold!

TI-JEAN.

Now pray for me, *maman*,
The sun is in the leaves.

MOTHER.

The first of my children
Never asked for my strength,
The second of my children
Thought little of my knowledge,
The last of my sons, now,
Kneels down at my feet,
Instinct be your shield,
It is wiser than reason,
Conscience be your cause
And plain sense your sword.

[The Bolom rolls towards the hut. Drums.]

BOLOM.
Old tree shaken of fruit,
This green one must die.
MOTHER.
Aie, I hear it, I hear it,
The cry of the unborn!
But then have I not given
Birth and death to the dead?

[The Bolom dances off, shrieking. Ti-Jean rises.]

Oh, Ti-Jean, you are so small,
So small. *[Exit]*
TI-JEAN.
Yes, I small, *maman*, I small,
And I never learn from book,
But, like the small boy, David.

[Sings]

I go bring down, bring down Goliath,
Bring down below.
Bring down, bring down Goliath,
Bring down below.

[He enters the forest.]

TI-JEAN.
Ah, *bon matin, compère Crapaud*,
Still in your dressing gown?
FROG.
Ti-Jean, like your brothers you're making fun of me.
TI-JEAN
Why should I laugh at the frog and his fine bass voice?
FROG
You wouldn't call me handsome, would you?
TI-JEAN.

[Kneels among the Creatures]

Oh, I don't know, you have your own beauty.
Like the castanet music of the cricket over there.
CRICKET.
Crak, crak. Now say something nice to the firefly.
FIREFLY.
How can he? I don't look so hot in the daytime.
TI-JEAN.
But I have often mistaken you at night for a star.

[Rises]

Now friends, which way is shortest to the Devil's estate?
FROG.
Beware of an old man whose name is wordly wisdom.
FIREFLY.
With a pile of sticks on his back.
CRICKET.
. . . and a foot cloven like a beast.

TI-JEAN.
If he is an old man, and mortal,
He will judge everything on earth
By his own sad experience.
God bless you, small things.
It's a hard life you have,
Living in the forest.
FIREFLY.
God preserve you for that.
Bird, take the tree and cry
If the old man comes through
That grove of dry bamboo.

[Bird flies off.]

CRICKET.
Crashing through the thicket
With the cleft hoof of a beast.
FIREFLY.
For though we eat each other,
I can't tempt that frog too close,
And we never see each other for dinner,
We do not do it from evil.
FROG.
True. Is a long time I never eat a firefly.
FIREFLY.
Watch it, watch it, brother,
You don't want heartburn, do you?
TI-JEAN.
No, it is not from evil.
What are these crosses?
CRICKET.
Nothing. Do not look, Ti-Jean.
Why must you fight the Devil?
TI-JEAN.
To know evil early, life will be simpler.
FROG.
Not so, Ti-Jean, not so. Go back.

[Ti-Jean goes to the crosses, weeps.]

BIRD.
Weep-weep-weep-weep-quick,
The old man is coming, quick.
FROG.
If you need us, call us, brother, but
You understand we must move.

[Ti-Jean stands over the crosses.]

OLD MAN.
Ah, good morning, youngster! It's a damp, mournful walk
through the forest, isn't it, and only the cheep of a bird to
warm one. Makes old bones creak. Now it's drizzling.
Damn it.
TI-JEAN.
Bon jou, vieux cor', I find the world pleasant in the early
light.

OLD MAN.
They say, the people of the forest, when the sun and rain
contend for mastery, they say that the Devil is beating his
wife. Know what I say? I say it brings rheumatism, I don't
believe in the Devil. Eighty-eight years, and never seen
his face.

TI-JEAN.
Could you, being behind it?

OLD MAN.
Eh? Eh? I'm deaf, come nearer. Come here and shelter.
Good. Some people find me ugly, monstrous ugly. Even
the small insects sometimes. The snake moves from me,
and this makes me sad. I was a woodsman once, but look
now, I burn wood into ashes. Let me sit on this log
awhile. Tobacco?

TI-JEAN.
No, thanks, sir.

OLD MAN.
Tell me, boy, is your father living? Or your mother perhaps? You look frail as an orphan.

TI-JEAN.
I think nothing dies. My brothers are dead but they live
in memory of my mother.

OLD MAN.
You're very young, boy, to be talking so subtly. So you lost
two brothers?

TI-JEAN.
I said I had brothers, I never said how many. May I see
that foot, father?

OLD MAN.
In a while, in a while. No, I saw you looking at the two
graves, so I presumed there were two. There were two,
weren't there? Ah well, none can escape that evil that
men call death.

TI-JEAN.
Whatever God made, we must consider blessed. I'm going
to look at your foot.

OLD MAN.
Hold on, son. Whatever God made, we must consider
blessed? Like the death of your mother?

TI-JEAN.
Like the death of my mother.

OLD MAN.
Like the vileness of the frog?

TI-JEAN.
[Advancing] Like the vileness of the frog.

OLD MAN.
Like the froth of the constrictor?

TI-JEAN.
Like the froth of the constrictor. [He is above the Old
Man.]

OLD MAN.
Like the cloven cow's foot under an old man's skirt?

[Ti-Jean sweeps up the skirt, then drops it.]

What did you hope to find, but an old man's weary feet?

You're a forward little fool! Now, do you want some advice? Tell me how you'll face the Devil, and I'll give you
advice.

TI-JEAN.
O help me, my brothers, help me to win.

[He retreats to the crosses.]

OLD MAN.
Getting frightened, aren't you? Don't be a coward, son.
I gather twigs all day, in the darkness of the forest.
And never feared man nor beast these eighty-eight years.
I think you owe me some sort of apology.

[The Bird runs out and begins to peck at the rope, untying
the faggots with his beak. The Old Man jumps up,
enraged.]

Leave that alone, you damned . . .

TI-JEAN.
I'll help you, father.

[Instead, he loosens the bundle.]

OLD MAN.
I'll kill that bird. Why did you loosen my sticks?
Haven't you any respect for the weariness of the old?
You've had your little prank, now help me collect them.
If you had a father you'd know what hard work was,
In the dark of the forest, lighting damp faggots . . .

[Ti-Jean pretends to be assisting the Old Man, but carefully he lifts his skirt and sees that below the sackcloth robe he
has a forked tail.]

TI-JEAN.
My mother always told me, my spirits were too merry,
Now, here we are, old father, all in one rotten bundle.

OLD MAN.
What's come over you, you were frightened a while back?

TI-JEAN.
Which way to the Devil? Oh, you've never seen him.
Tell me, does the Devil wear a hard, stiff tail?

OLD MAN.
How would I know. [Feels his rear, realises] Mm. Well, you
go through that track, and you'll find a short-cut through
the bamboo. It's wet, leaf-rotting path, then you come to
the springs of sulphur, where the damned souls are cooking . . .

TI-JEAN.
You sure you not lying?

OLD MAN.
It's too early in the morning to answer shallow questions,
That's a fine hat you're wearing, so I'll bid you goodbye.

[Ti-Jean lifts up a stick]

TI-JEAN.
Not until I know who you are, papa!
Look, I'm in a great hurry, or I'll brain you with this;

If evil exists, let it come forward.
Human, or beast, let me see it plain.

[The stage darkens. Drums. The Old Man rises.]

OLD MAN.
Very well then, look!

[He unmasks; the Devil's face. Howls, cymbals clash]

DEVIL.
Had you not gotten me, fool,
Just a trifle angry,
I might have played the Old Man
In fairness to our bargain,
But this is no play, son.
For here is the Devil,
You asked for him early,
Impatient as the young.
Now remember our bargain,
The one who wastes his temper,
Will be eaten! Remember that!
Now, you will work!

TI-JEAN.
Cover your face, the wrinkled face of wisdom,
Twisted with memory of human pain,
Is easier to bear; this is like looking
At the blinding gaze of God.

DEVIL.

[Replacing Old Man's mask, and changing]

It is hard to distinguish us,
Combat to fair combat, then I cover my face,
And the sun comes out of the rain, and the clouds.
Now these are the conditions, and the work you must do.

TI-JEAN.
Wait, old man, if is anything stupid,
I don't have your patience, so you wasting time.

OLD MAN.
Then you must pay the penalty.
These are your orders:
I have an ass of a goat
That will not stay tied.
I want you to catch it
Tonight before sundown.
Over hill and valley
Wherever it gallops.
Then tie it good and hard.
And if it escapes
You must catch it again
As often as it gets loose
You try as many times.
If you should lose your temper . . .

TI-JEAN.
Where the hell is this goat?

OLD MAN.
Over there by the . . . wait.

The fool has run off.
He won't last very long.

[Exit Ti-Jean. The Old Man sits down, rocking back and forth with laughter. Ti-Jean runs back.]

OLD MAN.
Finished already?

TI-JEAN.
That's right. Anything else?

OLD MAN.
Ahm. Yes, yes, yes. Best I've seen, though.
Now I want you to go down to the edge of the cane field

[The goat bleats.]

Looks like you didn't tie him?

TI-JEAN.
I tied the damned thing up.
Something is wrong here.
I tied the thing up properly.

[The Old Man laughs. Ti-Jean runs off. The Old Man dances with joy. Goat bleats, then stops suddenly. Ti-Jean returns with something wrapped in a banana leaf and sits down quietly. The Old Man watches him. Pause. No bleat.]

OLD MAN.
What's that in your hands?

TI-JEAN.

[Proffers the leaf]

Goat seed.

[The goat bleats girlishly.]

OLD MAN.
His voice is changing.
I don't get you. Goat-seed?

TI-JEAN.
I tied the damn thing.
Then made it a eunuch.

[The goat bleats weakly.]

Sounds much nicer.

OLD MAN.
You er . . . fixed my one goat?
Then you must have been angry.

TI-JEAN.
No, I just couldn't see myself
Chasing the damned thing all night.
And anyhow, where I tied it,
She'll never move again.

OLD MAN.

[Walking around stage]

You sit there calm as hell
And tell me you er . . . altered Emilia?

Ti-Jean.
Funny goat, with a girl's name,
It's there by the plantain tree,
Just by the stones.
Old Man.
Boy, you have a hell of a nerve.
Ti-Jean.
It look like you vex.
Old Man.
Angry? I'm not angry. I'm not vexed at all.
You see? Look! I'm smiling.
What's an old goat anyhow?
Just the only goat I had.
Gave sour milk anyway.
Ti-Jean.

[Rising. Rubbing his hands]

Fine. Now, what's next on the agenda?
Old Man.
What? Yes, yes . . . Fixed the goat . . .
Ti-Jean.
Now look here, life is . . .
Old Man.
Enough of your catechism!
Ti-Jean.
Temper, temper. Or you might lose something. Now what
next?
Old Man.
Now, listen to this, boy.
Go down to the cane-fields
And before the next cloud
Start checking every blade,
Count each leaf on the stalk,
File them away properly
As fast as you can
Before the night comes,
Then report back to me.
Well, what are you waiting for?
Ti-Jean.
I got a bit tired chasing the goat,
I'm human you know.
Old Man.
I'm going back to the house,
I'll be back at dawn to check on your progress.

[Exit]

Ti-Jean.

[Goes to the edge of the cane-field]

Count all the canes, what a waste of time!

[Cups his hands]

Hey, all you niggers sweating there in the canes!
Hey, all you people working hard in the fields!

Voices.

[Far off]

'Ayti? What happen? What you calling us for?
Ti-Jean.
You are poor damned souls working for the Devil?
Voices.
Yes! Yes! What you want?
Ti-Jean.
Listen, I'm the new foreman! Listen to this:
The Devil say you must burn everything, now.
Burn the cane, burn the cotton! Burn everything now!
Voices.
Burn everything now? Okay, boss!

[Drums. Cries. Caneburners' chorus]

Ti-Jean.
The man say Burn, burn, burn de cane!
Chorus.
Burn, burn, burn de cane!
Ti-Jean.
You tired work for de man in vain!
Chorus.
Burn, burn, burn de cane!

[Exeunt]

[The Frog enters.]

Frog.

[Sings]

And all night the night burned
Turning on its spit,
Until in the valley, the grid
Of the canefield glowed like coals,
When the devil, as lit as the dawn returned,
Dead drunk, and singing his song of lost souls.

[Enter Devil, drunk, with a bottle, singing]

Devil.
Down deep in hell, where it black like ink,
Where the oil does boil and the sulphur stink,
It ain't have no ice, no refrigerator
If you want water, and you ask the waiter,
He go bring brimstone with a saltpetre chaser,
While de devils bawling.

[He is carrying the Old Man's mask. Now he puts it on.] Oh, if
only the little creatures of this world could understand, but
they have no evil in them . . . so how the hell can they?
[The Cricket passes.] Cricket, cricket, it's the old man.
Cricket.
Crek, crek, boo!
Chorus.
Fire one! Fire one
Till the place burn down,

Fire one! Fire one.

DEVIL.

[Flings the mask away]

I'll be what I am, so to hell with you. I'll be what I am. I drink, and I drink, and I feel nothing. Oh, I lack heart to enjoy the brevity of the world! [The Firefly passes, dancing.] Get out of my way, you burning backside, I'm the prince of obscurity and I won't brook interruption! Trying to mislead me, because I been drinking. Behave, behave. That youngster is having terrible effect on me. Since he came to the estate, I've felt like a fool. First time in me life too. Look, just a while ago I nearly got angry at an insect that's just a half-arsed imitation of a star. It's wonderful! An insect brushes my dragonish hand, and my scales tighten with fear. Delightful! So this is what it means! I'm drunk, and hungry. [The Frog, his eyes gleaming, hops across his path] O God, O God, a monster! Jesus, help! Now that for one second was the knowledge of death. O Christ, how weary it is to be immortal. [Sits down on log] Another drink for confidence.

[Sings]

> When I was the Son of the Morning,
> When I was the Prince of Light.

[He picks up the mask.]

Oh, to hell with that! You lose a job, you lose a job. Ambition. Yet we were one light once up there, the old man and I, till even today some can't tell us apart.

[He holds the mask up. Sings.]

> And so I fell for forty days,
> Passing the stars in the endless pit.

Come here, frog, I'll give you a blessing. [The Frog hops back, hissing.] Why do you spit at me? Oh, nobody loves me, nobody loves me. No children of my own, no worries of my own. To hell with . . . [Stands] To hell with every stinking one of you, fish, flesh, fowl . . . I had the only love of God once [Sits] but I lost that, I lost even that.

[Sings]

> Leaning, leaning,
> Leaning on the everlasting arms . . .

To hell with dependence and the second-lieutenancy! I had a host of burnished helmets once, and a forest of soldiery waited on my cough, on my very belch. Firefly, firefly, you have a bit of hell behind you, so light me home. [Roars at the Creatures] Get out, get out, all of you . . . Oh, and yet this is fine, this is what they must call despondency, weakness. It's strange, but suddenly the world has

got bright, I can see ahead of me and yet I hope to die. I can make out the leaves, and . . . wait, the boy's coming. Back into the Planter. [Wears the Planter's mask]

TI-JEAN.

[Enters, also with a bottle] Oh, it's you, you're back late. Had a good dinner?

DEVIL.

You nearly scared me. How long you been hiding there?

TI-JEAN.

Oh, I just came through. Drunk as a fish.

DEVIL.

Finished the work?

TI-JEAN.

Yes, sir. All you told me. Cleaned the silver, made up the fifty rooms, skinned and ate curried goat for supper, and I had quite a bit of the wine.

DEVIL.

Somehow I like you, little man. You have courage. Your brothers had it too, but you are somehow different. Curried goat? . . .

TI-JEAN.

They began by doing what you suggested. Dangerous. So naturally when the whole thing tired them, they got angry with themselves. The one way to annoy you is rank disobedience. Curried goat, yes.

DEVIL.

We'll discuss all that in the morning. I'm a little drunk, and I am particularly tired. A nice bathtub of coals, and a pair of cool sheets, and sleep. You win for tonight. Tomorrow I'll think of something. Show me the way to go home.

TI-JEAN.

[His arms around the Devil]

> Oh, show me the way to go home,
> I'm tired and I want to go to bed,
> I had a little drink half an hour ago . . .

DEVIL.

[Removing his arm] Wait a minute, wait a minute . . . I don't smell liquor on you. What were you drinking?

TI-JEAN.

Wine, wine. You know, suspicion will be the end of you. That's why you don't have friends.

DEVIL.

You have a fine brain to be drunk. Listen, I'll help you. You must have a vice, just whisper it in my ear and I won't tell the old fellow with the big notebook.

TI-JEAN.

[Holds up bottle] This is my weakness. Got another drink in there?

DEVIL.

[Passing the bottle] This is powerful stuff, friend, liquid brimstone. May I call you friend?

TI-JEAN.

You may, you may. I have pity for all power. That's why I

love the old man with the windy beard. He never wastes
it. He could finish you off, like that . . .

DEVIL.

Let's not argue religion, son. Politics and religion . . . You
know, I'll confess to you. You nearly had me vexed several
times today.

TI-JEAN.

How did my two brothers taste?

DEVIL.

Oh, let's forget it! Tonight we're all friends. It gets dull in
that big house. Sometimes I wish I couldn't have everything I wanted. He spoiled me, you know, when I was his
bright, starry lieutenant. Gave me everything I desired. I
was God's spoiled son. Result: ingratitude. But he had it
coming to him. Drink deep, boy, and let's take a rest from
argument. Sleep, that's what I want, a nice clean bed.
Tired as hell. Tired as hell. And I'm getting what I suspect
is a hell of a headache. [A blaze lightens the wood] I think
I'll be going up to the house. Why don't you come in, it's
damp and cold out here. It's got suddenly bright. Is that
fire?

TI-JEAN.

Looks like fire, yes.

DEVIL.

What do you think it is, friend?

TI-JEAN.

I think it's your house.

DEVIL.

I don't quite understand . . .

TI-JEAN.

Sit down. Have a drink. In fact, I'm pretty certain it's
your home. I left a few things on fire in it.

DEVIL.

It's the only house I had, boy.

TI-JEAN.

My mother had three sons, she didn't get vexed. Why not
smile and take a drink like a man?

DEVIL.

[Removing the Planter's mask]

What the hell do you think I care about your mother?
The poor withered fool who thinks it's holy to be poor,
who scraped her knees to the knuckle praying to an old
beard that's been deaf since noise began? Or your two
damned fools of brothers, the man of strength and the
rhetorician? Come! Filambo! Azaz! Cacarat! You've
burnt property that belongs to me.

[Assistant Devils appear and surround Ti-Jean.]

TI-JEAN.

You're not smiling, friend.

DEVIL.

Smiling? You expect me to smile? Listen to him! [The

Devils laugh] You share my liquor, eat out my 'fridge, treat
you like a guest, tell you my troubles. I invite you to my
house and you burn it!

TI-JEAN.

[Sings]

Who with the Devil tries to play fair,
Weaves the net of his own despair.
Oh, smile; what's a house between drunkards?

DEVIL.

I've been watching you, you little nowhere nigger! You
little squirt, you hackneyed cough between two immor-
talities, who do you think you are? You're dirt, and that's
where you'll be when I'm finished with you. Burn my
house, my receipts, all my papers, all my bloody triumphs.

TI-JEAN.

[To the Devils]

Does your master sound vexed to you?

DEVIL.

Seize him!

[The Bolom enters and stands between Ti-Jean and the
Devil.]

BOLOM.

Master, be fair!

DEVIL.

He who would with the devil play fair,
Weaves the net of his own despair.
This shall be a magnificent ending:
A supper cooked by lightning and thunder.

[Raises fork]

MOTHER.

[In a white light in the hut]

Have mercy on my son,
Protect him from fear,
Protect him from despair,
And if he must die,
Let him die as a man,
Even as your Own Son
Fought the Devil and died.

DEVIL.

I never keep bargains. Now, tell me, you little fool, if you
aren't afraid.

TI-JEAN.

I'm as scared as Christ.

DEVIL.

Burnt my house, poisoned the devotion of my servants,
small things all of them, dependent on me.

TI-JEAN.
You must now keep
Your part of the bargain.
You must restore
My brothers to life.

DEVIL.
What a waste, you know yourself
I can never be destroyed.
They are dead. Dead, look!

[The Brothers pass.]

There are your two brothers,
In the agony where I put them,
One moaning from weakness,
Turning a mill-wheel
For the rest of his life,
The other blind as a bat,
Shrieking in doubt.

[The two Brothers pass behind a red curtain of flame.]

TI-JEAN.
O God.

DEVIL.
[Laughing] Seize him! Throw him into the fire.

TI-JEAN.
[With a child's cry] Mama!

DEVIL.
She can't hear you, boy.

TI-JEAN.
Well, then, you pay her what you owe me!
I make you laugh, and I make you vex,
That was the bet. You have to play fair.

DEVIL.
Who with the devil tries to play fair . . .

TI-JEAN.
[Angrily] I say you vex and you lose, man! Gimme me
money!

DEVIL.
Go back, Bolom!

BOLOM.
Yes, he seems vexed,
But he shrieked with delight
When a mother strangled me
Before the world light.

DEVIL.
Be grateful, you would have amounted to nothing, child,
a man. You would have suffered and returned to dirt.

BOLOM.
No, I would have known life, rain on my skin, sunlight on
my forehead. Master, you have lost. Pay him! Reward
him!

DEVIL.
For cruelty's sake I could wish you were born. Very well
then, Ti-Jean. Look there, towards the hut, what do you
see?

TI-JEAN.
I see my mother sleeping.

DEVIL.
And look down at your feet,
Falling here, like leaves,
What do you see? Filling this vessel?

TI-JEAN.
The shower of sovereigns,
Just as you promised me.
But something is wrong.
Since when you play fair?

BOLOM.
Look, look, there in the hut,
Look there, Ti-Jean, the walls,
The walls are glowing with gold.
Ti-Jean, you can't see it?
You have won, you have won!

TI-JEAN.
It is only the golden
Light of the sun, on
My mother asleep.

[Light comes up on the hut.]

DEVIL.
Not asleep, but dying, Ti-Jean.
But don't blame me for that!

TI-JEAN.
Mama!

DEVIL.
She cannot hear you, child.
Now, can you still sing?

FROG.
Sing, Ti-Jean, sing!
Show him you could win!
Show him what a man is!
Sing Ti-Jean . . . Listen,
All around you, nature
Still singing. The frog's
Croak doesn't stop for the dead;
The cricket is still merry,
The bird still plays its flute,
Every dawn, little Ti-Jean . . .

TI-JEAN.

[Sings, at first falteringly]

To the door of breath you gave the key,
Thank you, Lord,
The door is open, and I step free,
Amen, Lord . . .
Cloud after cloud like a silver stair
My lost ones waiting to greet me there
With their silent faces, and starlit hair
Amen, Lord.

[Weeps]

DEVIL.

What is this cooling my face, washing it like a
Wind of morning. Tears! Tears! Then is this the
Magnificence I have heard of, of
Man, the chink in his armour, the destruction of the
Self? Is this the strange, strange wonder that is
Sorrow? You have earned your gift, Ti-Jean, ask!

BOLOM.

Ask him for my life!
O God, I want all this
To happen to me!

TI-JEAN.

Is life you want, child?
You don't see what it bring?

BOLOM.

Yes, yes, Ti-Jean, life!

TI-JEAN.

Don't blame me when you suffering,
When you lose everything,
And when the time come
To put two cold coins
On your eyes. Sir, can you give him life.

DEVIL.

Just look!

BOLOM.

[Being born]

I am born, I shall die! I am born, I shall die!
O the wonder, and pride of it! I shall be man!
Ti-Jean, my brother!

DEVIL.

Farewell, little fool! Come, then,
Stretch your wings and soar, pass over the fields
Like the last shadow of night, imps, devils, bats,
Eazaz, Beelzebub, Cacarat, soar! Quick, quick the sun!
We shall meet again, Ti-Jean. You, and your new brother!
The features will change, but the fight is still on.

[Exeunt]

TI-JEAN.

Come then, little brother. And you, little creatures.
Ti-Jean must go on. Here's a bundle of sticks that
Old wisdom has forgotten. Together they are strong,

Apart, they are all rotten.
God look after the wise, and look after the strong,
But the fool in his folly will always live long.

[Sings]

Sunday morning I went to the chapel
Ring down below!
I met the devil with the book and the Bible.
Ring down below!
Ask him what he will have for dinner.

CHORUS.

Ring down below!

TI-JEAN.

Cricket leg and a frog with water.

CHORUS.

Ring down below!

TI-JEAN.

I leaving home and I have one mission!

CHORUS.

Ring down below!

TI-JEAN.

You come to me by your own decision.

CHORUS.

Ring down below!

TI-JEAN.

Down in hell you await your vision.

CHORUS.

Ring down below!

TI-JEAN.

I go bring down, bring down Goliath.

CHORUS.

Bring down below!

[Exeunt. The Creatures gather as before.]

FROG.

And so it was that Ti-Jean, a fool like all heroes, passed
through the tangled opinions of this life, loosening the
rotting faggots of knowledge from old men to bear them
safely on his shoulder, brother met brother on his way,
that God made him the clarity of the moon to lighten the
doubt of all travellers through the shadowy wood of life.
And bird, the rain is over, the moon is rising through the
leaves. Messieurs, creek. Crack.

CENTER STAGE   THE TRINIDAD CARNIVAL

*You got the great big long wall in
   China,
And in India the Taj Mahal,
I know the greatest wonder of them all
Is my Trinidad Carnival.*

Though perhaps not as famous as Mardi Gras in Rio de Janeiro or New Orleans, Carnival in Trinidad, extolled here in the Mighty Douglas's calypso song, has been called "undoubtedly the greatest annual theatrical spectacle of all time" (Erroll Hill, *The Trinidad Carnival*, 1972). Annually over 100,000 people appear in striking masquerades, street dances, and stage shows during the week before Lent. Most Christian societies enjoy some form of pre-Lenten "carnival," most of which are derived from pagan rites such as the Roman Saturnalia. Carnival is a period of indulgent merrymaking in which costumed revelers take to the streets to sing, dance, mime, perform, eat, drink, and carouse before entering into a somber period of abstinence for 40 days. *Carnival* comes from a Latin phrase— *carne vale*—which means "flesh farewell," a bittersweet reminder that both eating meat and indulging in the pleasures of the flesh are forbidden for six weeks.

The essence of Carnival is role reversal; that is, a celebration of chaos in which normality is suspended for a few days. Streets conveying people to the workplace are sealed off and overrun with merrymakers whose thoughts are far from the workaday world. Men dress as animals or women; the poor carica-

Spectacular costumes, perhaps derived from African masquerades, are one of the hallmarks of Trinidad-Tobago's pre-Lenten Carnival. Here we see Peter Samuels as King of the band "Papillon" in a costume, designed by Peter Minshell, titled "The Sacred and the Profane."

ture the wealthy. Rationality, conventionality, and restraint give way to indulgence, fantasy, and play. The comic spirit reigns, as evidenced by the cartoonlike costumes, headpieces, and masks, the frenetic dancing, the bawdy and sensual music, the satiric plays improvised on makeshift stages and under tents. Ash Wednesday is the time for solemnity and reflection, but on Mardi Gras ("Fat Tuesday") there is only time for giving oneself to the spirit of Carnival.

Carnival in Trinidad is a fascinating hybrid of many cultures and ideologies: pagan and Christian, European and African, Indian and Spanish, Western and Eastern, ancient and modern, poor and wealthy. Trinidad dates the beginnings of its Carnival to 1783 and the arrival of French planters with their African slaves. Early Carnivals had a racist tone as the plantation owners imitated the dress and manners of the slaves and danced traditional African dances such as the *bamboula* and the *ghouba*. This typifies the "role reversal" aspect so prominent in Carnival. Today, Carnival has a more salutary effect on the twin-island nation of Trinidad-Tobago: the ethnic and social divisions in this multiracial culture are united in a common will to make each new carnival the greatest ever.

Trinidad's slaves were emancipated on August 1, 1834, an event which forever made Carnival a symbol of freedom for the masses. It was never again a plaything for the elite as it became a celebration of deliverance. Not surprisingly, many popular costumes are comic reminders of the days of oppression: Moco Jumbie, a cult figure found throughout West Africa, dances atop 10-to-15 foot stilts, wearing an Eton coat and lord admiral's hat to parody the European oppressor. Each carnival begins with a *canboulay*, a military march mocking the imperial guards that subjugated the slaves. There is clearly a political dimension to this great Carnival that transcends its roots. *Ti-Jean and His Brothers* contains a song taken from the old *canboulay* as it merges the spirit of Carnival with contemporary political issues.

Masquerades were once used to channel the dead into the souls of the living, but modern masquerades mirror societal concerns. A grand masquerade, dating back to 1866, dominates the final two days of the festival. The maskers are transformed into possessed spirits on "the glorious Monday morning" that begins the Masquerade. At dawn, act 1 begins; it is the *jouvay* (from a Creole expression, "Is it daybreak?") in which characters from island folklore are brought to life. Many are demonic (the *diablesse*); others are satiric, such as the popular Dame Lorraine, a "fashionable lady" played by a man in gaudy female dress, an example of the crossdressing phenomenon throughout world theater. The masqueraders typify the spirit of mockery and misrule permeating Carnival. Act 2 presents traditional masks such as the Wild Indian, the Clowns, Midnight Robbers, and others that are often portrayed for generations within a single family. The third act introduces the big bands for which the island is famous. Act 4 is devoted to historical pageantry, a blend of past events, fantasy, and imagination in which islanders imitate world leaders and conquering heroes. At dusk on Tuesday, the final act brings together the various performers and—very importantly—the spectators in an enormous, spontaneous street dance, songfest, and mimed combat.

Drum dance competitions are held in bamboo huts built especially for Carnival. A masquerade king and queen in extravagant regalia preside over the dance competitions. A coronation ceremony is among the first orders of business; a *borokit* (from the Spanish *borriquito*, "little donkey"), that is, a comic horse's costume, is placed on the king, who then dances around the room carrying a wooden sword. He is accompanied by his queen, always a male in drag, who begs money to finance the spectacle. Shortly before midnight on Fat Tuesday, the masquerade concludes with a mock execution of the king of Carnival. The execution is accompanied by a chant as old as time:

And every year we dance and sing,
And every year we kill the king,
Because the old king must be slain
For the new king to rise again.

Arianne Mnouchkine's 1979 production of Klaus Mann's Mephisto *used a curious blend of styles: a baroque proscenium fronts an industrial-steel setting as a contemporary man and a Victorian gentleman watch a grotesque vaudeville.*

CHAPTER 9

THE CONTEMPORARY THEATER

As we enter the new millennium, the world provides us with extraordinary scenarios that reflect a new reality:

- Late at night in a provincial Chinese village, where running water and indoor toilets are rare, flickering lights emanate from virtually every small house and store. The lights are produced by 13-inch color television sets that broadcast John Forsythe apparently speaking fluent Mandarin on *Falcon Crest*.
- The Los Angeles Dodgers, among the most traditional baseball organizations, features starting pitchers born in Japan, South Korea, the Dominican Republic, and Mexico. Between innings, fans—many of whom were born in Asia, Africa, and Latin America—rise to dance the Macarena from South America, while their images are projected by a giant television screen made in Japan. Many listen to the game they are watching on transistor radios manufactured under the new capitalism of Communist China.
- England and Pakistan elect prime ministers—both women. Political discussion in America (and elsewhere) centers on whether women should be allowed in combat. A newly elected American president announces that homosexuals will no longer be discharged from the military, initiating a compromise "don't ask, don't tell" policy.

Our rapidly changing world has truly become, in Marshall McLuhan's words, a "global village," and the tension between the beliefs of an older, more absolute order and those of a more pluralistic, democratic, and ambiguous order is evident in the theater as well as in politics, commerce, and education. Contemporary thought has been shaped by any number of thinkers and historical events, each of which has prompted us to reevaluate the way in which we perceive the world.

Influences on Contemporary Thought

We can find parallels to the changes in contemporary thought in the challenges to the Enlightenment and its emphasis on rationality and absolute values. In the eighteenth century the universe was viewed as a great, ordered machine bound by well-defined, fixed laws. In Sir Isaac Newton's world—bound by apparent certainties formed by a limited perspective from which to view the universe—an apple fell to the earth because it obeyed the laws of gravity. In Albert Einstein's world at the dawn of the twentieth century that same apple could be seen to float upward if it were twelve miles above earth and free from gravitational pull. The law of gravity had not changed, but human perceptions had expanded mightily since Newton's day. As he worked on his celebrated theory of relativity, Einstein was facinated by the avant-garde painters of Europe, especially the Cubists (themselves influenced by African sculpture), who challenged the way humans could look at their world. Even in the eighteenth century, thinkers such as the Scottish empiricist David Hume (1711–1776) showed the limits of reason—and the absolutism in much Western thought—by challenging the inviolability of the principle of cause-and-effect. In the theater, causality was the foundation for Scribe's well-made play and the naturalists' belief that social problems were caused by one's heredity and environment.

Even as Ibsen was writing his social dramas questioning the old absolute order, Friedrich Nietzsche (1844–1900) argued that an absolute "truth" does not exist, that a search for the truth was an "artificial burden," and ultimately that societies change their belief systems (or "perspectives") over time without arriving at an absolute view of the world. Fittingly, Nietzsche, who has been called the first philosopher with a truly postmodern view, developed his theories while trying to discover the original text of a tragedy by Sophocles; he found only various, conflicting copies of the original that had been filtered through the perspectives of subsequent cultures. He argued that a fixed interpretation of a literary work does not and cannot exist, and that one's subjective response is as "truthful" as any other is.

World events have been as forceful in altering our beliefs as any philosophical writing. In the twentieth century two world wars, the Holocaust, a global depression, the threat of nuclear annihilation, and the decline of the so-called superpowers taught us, often through painful experience, that the old absolutes were no longer necessarily operable. Thinkers and artists soon challenged other apparent certainties about language, social organisms, gender, and race. Such challenges were also made *in* theaters and *about* the way in which theater is written and performed. And as we saw with modern drama, philosophers and social scientists–critics fostered an intellectual atmosphere that inspired yet another revolution in the arts.

In Austria, Ludwig Wittgenstein (1889–1951) argued that the West was in decline largely because our instrument of communication—that is, language—was faulty and imprecise. In particular, philosophy was suspect because it relied on such ambiguous terms as "good" and "moral," words whose meanings were relative to particular cultures and times. T. S. Eliot, a playwright and literary critic, noted this problem in a poem lamenting the indeterminacy of a modern world in which old absolutes were suddenly suspect:

> . . . *Words strain*
>
> *Crack and sometimes break under the burden,*
>
> *Under the pressure, slip, slide, perish,*
>
> *Decay with imprecision, will not stay in place,*
>
> *Will not stay still.*

Therefore, the limits and liabilities of language necessarily redefined human perceptions of the world. Each person was, in essence, free to define "reality" according to her or his perceptions of the truth behind the language. Perception became reality, a concept captured by the title of Luigi Pirandello's play *Right You Are, If You Think You Are* (or, *It Is So If You Think So*, 1917). Playwrights, notably Harold Pinter (see *One for the Road* later in this chapter), applied these principles to dramaturgy. Classical texts have been given new, ironic readings by actors and directors versed in new language theories represented by the French critic-philosopher Jacques Derrida, who argues that "there is nothing outside the text." This proposition encourages the reader/interpreter/viewer to participate actively in creating whatever meaning or message one finds in the text, whatever the author's intentions. Other stage artists, such as Robert Wilson and Heiner Müller (see *Medeaplay*), have virtually abandoned language as an integral part of the theater experience and use an almost exclusively visual vocabulary.

Not only language but human institutions have been reassessed in contemporary thought. In 1966 Peter Berger and Thomas Luckmann wrote *The Social Construction of Reality*, in which they argued that society, culture, and even the roles we play in our daily lives are created by humans. We routinely forget that we ourselves have created these structures and live in a world we have forgotten we made. We err in assuming that our social organizations, our culture and its myths, and especially the societal roles we play cannot be re-created. Their thesis challenged individuals to re-create not only social institutions but themselves. Contemporaneously, the feminist and civil rights movements sought to redefine the roles imposed on women and minorities by traditional social systems.

In 1949 Simone de Beauvoir (1908–1986) wrote *The Second Sex,* an argument that women were treated as "the Other," an anthropological term used to describe those who are different from or who are not included in a majority culture. She claimed that men often accord women a different and inferior existence than themselves and advised women to seek independence from the old patriarchy by creating their own identity. Betty Friedan (1921–) initiated the modern American feminist movement with the publication of *The Feminine Mystique* (1963), which articulated the politics of gender. Coincidentally, 1963 was the year in which the African-American civil rights movement triumphed as Martin Luther King Jr. led a march of hundreds of thousands of activists in Washington, D.C., where he delivered his famous "I Have a Dream" speech. Perhaps the most famous example of how language, social structures, and individual worth were redefined is the "Black Is Beautiful" slogan of the civil rights movement. Though they do not eradicate racism, such reconfigurations of language encouraged people of all colors to think—and perhaps act—more positively about people of African descent.

Social change precipitated by the feminist and the civil rights movements gave new voices and power to previously marginalized social groups such as Latinos, Asians, indigenous peoples, and homosexuals. Correspondingly, the theater has become a major outlet through which the new pluralism expresses itself. You will find many recent dramas that reflect the diversity of voices and ideologies of the pluralistic culture in which we now live.

Postmodernism and the Theater

Though we think of this as the contemporary era, it is often referred to as *postmodern* (i.e., "after the modern"), an often controversial term that describes a less Eurocentric culture than that which dominated the world for the past 400 years. The contemporary culture is decidedly more pluralistic and multicultural than at any other time in human history.

In keeping with this shift in thought, a postmodern style has emerged in the arts. Whether postmodernism will survive and become a long-lived artistic movement, or whether it is merely a transitional period (such as those that typically appear at the turn of a century), remains to be seen.

Though the concept of postmodernism was first defined in the 1930s (first by Federico de Onis in his 1934 study of Spanish-language poetry, then in 1938 in Arnold Toynbee's *A Study of History*), postmodernism as a bona fide movement in the arts evolved from architects who rebelled against the stark, sterile, purely functional and thereby "inhuman" designs of the so-called modernists. The new school of architects, exemplified by Robert Venturi (1925–), who favored "messy vitality over obvious unity," playfully fused elements of contemporary "pop" (or "democratic" as opposed to the old aristocratic) culture with traditional styles. In a spirit of global unity encouraged by the founding of the United Nations in 1945, architects looked to the Third World for inspiration. For example, they fronted a Neoclassic building with the silhouette of an African hut. These deliberate contrasts of style are hallmarks of postmodernism, and words such as *pastiche* and *collage* are central to its vocabulary and its practice. (Architects, by the way, write the term as "post-modern," with the hyphen. "Postmodern" is usually applied to literature and the other arts. This quibble suggests that the term is still being defined and that there is appreciable disagreement among postmodernism's practitioners, as well as its critics.)

Contradictions in artwork can create a playful irony that encourages people to look at the world from new perspectives. The imaginative blend of materials drawn from cultures beyond Europe and America is integral to postmoderns who, like the modernists, seek a more equitable world. Richard Rorty, the American philosopher whose writings (e.g., *Contingency, Irony, Solidarity,* 1989) envision a truly democratic world committed to universal freedom, creativity, and the elimination of cruelty. This new utopia is achieved by "poeticizing" human experience rather than "rationalizing" it. By recasting traditional forms through the inclusion of material drawn from a truly pluralistic society, new wave creator-artists shatter what they perceive as an oppressive power aligned with the older Eurocentric order. The Canadian Jean François Lyotard, whose study *The Postmodern Condition: A Report on Knowledge* (1979) laid the foundation for much of the critical thinking of the phenomenon, describes what he considers the appeal of postmodernism: "One listens to reggae [music], watches a Western, eats McDonald's food for lunch and local cuisine for dinner, wears Paris perfume in Tokyo and 'retro' clothes in Hong Kong." Similarly, Peter Sellars, the theater and opera director whose work is unmistakably postmodern, told the *New York Times* in 1984:

> We're living in a culture that is incredibly multifaceted. I grew up with [avant garde composer] John Cage and [modern dancer] Merce Cunningham as old masters. But while they were giving birth to something, [painter] Norman Rockwell was also in his prime. With the push of a button we can choose some 18th century Chinese lute music, the Mahler 6th [symphony], or [the artist formerly known as] Prince.

In *Postmodernism and the Social Sciences* (1992), Pauline Marie Rosenau identifies two approaches to postmodernism. The first, skeptical postmodernism, was inspired by Nietzsche and is akin to the absurdist movement, which is pessimistic and steeped in malaise. In general, these skeptics are Europeans, scarred by the memories of World War II and communism. The second approach, called affirmative postmodernism, more indigenous to the Anglo–North American culture, seeks a harmonious world in which traditional distinctions between genders, races, nations, and cultural biases are dismissed as relative constructs. Rorty typifies the latter strain in his belief that freedom occurs when the individual can live and create without being obsessed by universal truths and rules that all rational beings must follow.

In addition to Lyotard's "healthy pluralism," spiritualism underlies some elements of the postmodern movement, though it is not necessarily rooted in traditional Judeo-Christian religions. Whereas modernists looked to science and technology as means to eradicate social ills, many postmoderns distrust unbridled technology, which they argue gave the world the atomic age and its threat of instant annihilation, pollution, and a greater disparity between the "haves" and the "have nots." In its place they have turned to ancient religions (such as Taoism), the occult, and mysticism to fill the void left by the "religion of science." Though it borrows freely from ancient religions, rituals, and musical practice, "New Age" is the term most closely associated with the new spiritualism. Nonetheless, it suggests a deeply rooted quest for something that transcends the particulars of sociology, psychology, politics, and contemporary mass-produced culture. The theories of the French anthropologist Claude Lévi-Strauss helped define this worldview, which maintains that innate—archetypal—mental patterns of all humans, irrespective of historical period or social setting, cause them to interact with nature and one another in recurring ways. In particular, Lévi-Strauss examined ritual activities around the world, and his findings have influenced Western theater practice, which in many instances has returned to a ritualistic—as opposed to realistic—depiction of human activity. Most theater in Asia, Africa, and much of Latin America never completely abandoned its ritual heritage.

Needless to say, postmodernism in the theater has been criticized, partly because it energetically and often irreverently challenges old systems, partly because it is perceived to be a license for indulgence among artists who, some would say, can now do anything they want and call it art. Walter D. Bannard, writing for *Arts Magazine* in 1983, dismissed postmodernism as "aimless, anarchic, amorphous, self-indulgent, inclusive, horizontally structured, and aim[ing] for the popular." It can be, and it has done so. Yet postmodernism, a constellation of many legitimate styles, seems to be the prevailing style of our age. To put Bannard's critique in perspective (or to "relativize" it), his comments might well have been penned by a member of the French Academy in 1830 as a response to Hugo's *Hernani*.

Artaud and the Theater of Cruelty

Such attitudes concerning cultural diversity have affected the theater and drama. The re-creation of ritual has been espoused as a primary component of the contemporary theater experience. Antonin Artaud (1895–1948) foreshadowed the new theater practice with his bold visions and experiments in Paris. Theater historian Margaret Croyden has written that "more than any other theorist of his generation, Artaud set the tone for the theater of the 1960s," and consequently for much postmodern theater. In 1933 Artaud, an actor frustrated by the limitations of the realistic theater, which emphasized a rational depiction of life, saw a Balinese theater company performing the Barong trance dance (see Chapter 1) at an international exhibition in Paris. Based on this experience, Artaud envisioned what he called a *theater of cruelty* that would, in his words, "link the theater to the expressive possibilities of forms, to everything in the domain of gestures, noises, colors, movements [in order] to restore it to its original direction, to reinstate it in its religious and metaphysical aspect, to reconcile it with the universe." By "cruelty" Artaud meant that artists should force audiences to confront their basest instincts and crimes, which, he believed, promoted the horrors of modern civilization. The theater, he argued, must compel humans to unmask themselves through "cries, groans, apparitions, surprises, theatricalities of all kinds, resplendent lighting, sudden changes of lights, masks, and effigies." Artaud's theater assaulted the senses to break down audiences' defenses and force them to confront the "plague," his metaphor for modern atrocities. The Romantics sought an intensely emotional reaction to societal ills, Brecht an intellectual detachment in his spectators; Artaud craved a thoroughly visceral response that transcends sentiment and rationality.

Though Artaud's own theater work failed to achieve his ends, he has had an extraordinary influence on production style, playwrights, and theater companies. In its early years, for instance, the Royal Shakespeare Company devoted its 1962–1963 seasons to an exploration of Artaud's theories on both classical and modern texts. Peter Brook directed the "cruelty seasons," staging *King Lear* and Peter Weiss's *The Persecution and Assassination of Jean-Paul Marat as Performed by the Inmates of the Asylum of Charenton Under the Direction of the Marquis de Sade* (or *Marat/Sade*). Even Broadway and London musicals, such as *Hair* (1967) and *Jesus Christ Superstar* (1970), employed techniques espoused by Artaud. Curiously, among the most successful derivatives of Artaud's theories, whether by design or accident, have been modern rock concerts and MTV videos. Pulsing lights, heavily amplified music, scenic effects such as towers of flame, stage actions such as smashing cars and guitars, and—in the case of videos—rapid cutting and overlapping of highly sensory images all are techniques espoused by Artaud, though they lack the spiritual foundation of his new theater.

In addition to Artaud's encounter with the Balinese dancers, other postmodern theater artists have looked to the East in their attempt to return the theater to its spiritual roots. Arianne Mnouchkine's *Théâtre du Soleil* regularly employs Asian dance and gesture in her refashioning of classical Western myths, as did Brook's eight-hour multinational production of India's sacred *Mahabharata* (1983). The first act of Sue Townsend's 1984 play, *The Great Celestial Cow* ends with an Indian goddess and the protagonists celebrating a mystical dance. Stylized gesture and dance are again central to many contemporary plays and productions of earlier works. The diminution of language, the new spirituality, and—as significantly—music videos as typified by MTV have all conspired to return theater to many of its original performance modes. Ironically, through rituals, dance and gesture, and especially powerful and provocative images that transcend purely intellectual and emotional responses the theater has to some degree come full circle by returning to its most elemental means of communication.

Theater Collectives and Alternative Theater

Inspired by the theory and practice of Brecht and Artaud (both of whom are legitimate precursors of the postmodern theater), the *theater collective* has become one of the most notable phenomena of contemporary theater. Collectives are companies that frequently live together and share a sociopolitical ideology; they experiment with theater forms and collectively create a play and its production. To some degree the modern theater collective functions much like the "tribe" of older civilizations in that its members are bound spiritually (though not necessarily religiously) by common beliefs and goals that transcend commercialism and even art itself. Theodore Shank, who has studied collectives at some length, offers a useful description of both the philosophy and the techniques of these experimental (or alternative) theater companies:

The artists who comprise alternative theater explore the relationship of the artist and the performance to the spectator. They attempt to discover the possibilities of live theater, and they seek ways of extending the uses of theater beyond its entertainment and financial functions. . . . They set out to articulate what they know about being alive in changing times, about society, about perceiving, feeling, and knowing. Of necessity, they find new materials, develop new techniques, and create new forms to hold and express this knowledge because the theatrical conventions cannot express the concepts they consider important.

If this sounds familiar, perhaps it is because Dumas *fils*, Ibsen, Strindberg, Shaw, Brecht, and so many of the other social revolutionaries in the theater have said much the same thing at various times.

The prototype of the modern theater collective in the West was the Group Theatre, founded in 1931 by Harold Clurman, Cheryl Crawford, and Lee Strasberg to promote leftist causes in new works performed in the then-new realist style. They inspired subsequent generations of artists who also experimented with theater forms, especially those that are nonrealistic.

In the West, two companies merit particular attention because of their influence: the Living Theatre of Judith Malina (1926–) and Julian Beck (1925–1994) and the Polish Laboratory Theatre of Jerzy Grotowski. The Living Theatre was founded in 1947, ostensibly to perform poetic dramas such as Federico García Lorca's *Blood Wedding*. After a period in the late 1950s of experimentation with improvisational realism (*The Connection*, 1959), the Living Theatre turned to the work for which it was best known: highly ritualized performance pieces critical of institutions that the company considered "antihuman." The Living Theatre, like so many other alternative companies, emphasized physicality, rhythm, and chanting (among other things) instead of characterization and literary scripts. The company perhaps came closest to realizing Artaud's vision for a modern theater steeped in ritual and archetypal images to exorcise modern demons.

In Wroclaw, Poland, Jerzy Grotowski (1933–1999) founded the Polish Laboratory Theatre in 1965. His company experimented with performance styles while addressing the many social issues that have plagued Poland for hundreds of years. Out of this work came Grotowski's vision of a "poor theatre," the concept that perhaps most significantly influenced the many socially conscious theater collectives in the 1960s and 1970s. In essence Grotowski wanted to return the theater to its spiritual roots by creating a ritualistic experience in which spectators and performers together could achieve a "collective introspection" of the social and philosophical problems confronting society. To achieve these ends, Grotowski and his colleagues reduced the theater experience to its most essential elements—actors in a space before an audience. The motto *via negativa* ("to refrain from doing") dictated the poor theater's production choices. Grotowski and his disciples avoided all elaborate lighting effects and performed in intimate spaces that were created for each play. The audience was invariably interspersed in the acting area to reinforce their roles as "privileged participants in a ritual." There was no scenery as such, and all props were multifunctional and made of "found" objects. Actors wore no makeup but learned to transform their faces into masks through arduous physical training. Productions such as *Akropolis* (about Nazi concentration camps) and an adaptation of Calderón's *The Constant Prince* gained renown for their ritualistic simplicity and the physical discipline of Grotowski's superbly trained actors. For Grotowski, actors were the equivalent of modern shamans who took on the suffering of the community; hence, they were trained as artist-priests who practiced self-denial and physical hardship for the good of the community.

Much of the most compelling experimental theater was produced in Third World countries where the lack of economic resources necessarily promoted creative, as opposed to financial, solutions to problems. In South Africa, Mbogeni Ngema founded Committed Artists in 1984 to develop scripts about the problems of apartheid and township life. Township theater has by necessity put many of the ideas espoused by Grotowski in practice; found objects such as old tires, corrugated tin panels, and packing crates customarily form the scenic backdrop for the plays. *Woza Albert!* is typical of the work produced by Committed Artists, as was the 1993 film *Sarafina!*, based on an Ngema musical. In Latin America Augusto Boal's Teatro de Arena (Brazil) has produced socially relevant works that could, by their ingenuity and simplicity, be taken into remote villages to educate people, much like Sergio Corrieri's Grupo Teatro

Escambray in Cuba. Like Brecht, Boal rejects Aristotelian theater, which he perceives as coercive in its punishment of wrongdoers, whom he regards as oppressed. Boal actually takes Brecht a step further by actively engaging members of his audiences and prompting them to discover how they might rectify social problems (see Forum, "From *Theater of the Oppressed*" later in this chapter.) In the United States a similar phenomenon occurred with the founding of the Teatro Campesino by Luis Valdez in 1965; Valdez's accomplishments are discussed with *No saco nada de la escuela*, a play that vividly illustrates the philosophy and practice of the political theater collective.

In the past quarter-century there has been a proliferation of theaters that target specific audiences that have traditionally been outside the mainstream. An admittedly random sampling of such enterprises will give you some sense of the scope of the theater's newest constituencies. The Women's Playwright Project and Women's Interart, among others, have provided a theatrical platform for feminist issues (see Forum, "From *Acting Out: Feminist Performances*" later in this chapter). In 1974 a women's theater collective called At the Foot of the Mountain was formed in Minneapolis, Minnesota, to create new, ritual-based works drawn from their personal experiences (e.g., abuse) and the issues that confronted them directly (e.g., the challenges of motherhood). Audience members were invited to assist in the creation of a piece that, naturally, changed from one performance to the next. Gay and lesbian issues are argued by such companies as Rhinoceros, the Cockettes, and Split Britches; the AIDS crisis has understandably been a central concern of many gay theater companies. The National Theatre of the Deaf, which employs both hearing and hearing-impaired actors, depicts the needs of the physically disadvantaged; it also creates extraordinary productions of classical and poetic texts such as Ben Jonson's *Volpone* and Dylan Thomas's *Under Milkwood*; some members speak the lines while others "sign" them with a physicality that is as poetic as the spoken word.

Contemporary Playwriting

This discussion of visionary directors (now sometimes referred to as *auteurs* because theirs is a more creative than interpretative role) and theater collectives suggests a diminution of the role of the playwright. Playwrights are still very much the cornerstone of the theater process, though the lure of the television and film industries (and their lucrative contracts) has created something of a crisis. Nonetheless, plays are still being written though their form has changed considerably since Scribe's well-made play or Ibsen's discussion drama.

Because of the reassessment of purely rational communication (i.e., language and the well-structured plot), "ambiguity"—some would say "incomprehensibility"—is a term often applied to much contemporary theater. Plot, character, and meaning cannot be readily fathomed because we lack a single, consistent perspective from which to view them. Contemporary artists—playwrights and collectives—deconstruct social myths, or *metanarratives* (a term preferred by postmodernists), that reflect the pluralism of the world. Lyotard, in fact, defined postmodern as an "incredulity towards metanarratives" and suggested that the old myths had lost their legitimacy in a world in which traditional truths were challenged. As we have seen often throughout our study of the theater, the form of a play often reflects its content. The Greeks and Neoclassicists believed in a harmonious universe, and their plays were carefully structured affairs in which problems were resolved (although not always happily) in five compact acts. By contrast, the absurdists wrote about the great "rut of existence" and devised cyclic plots to show the meaningless of our actions. Because they see the world as a series of artificial constructs whose meanings change according to time, circumstance, and personal experience, many contemporary dramatists resist a single explanation for issues, characters, and plots, and thus *fragmentation* is often a characteristic of postmodern plays.

Plots are rarely linear; instead of lengthy acts with a well-defined beginning, middle, and end, we are given a series of scenes, often in markedly contrasting styles and moods (a technique used by Brecht, and even Shakespeare, though for different reasons). Many plays, in fact, are bereft of traditional exposition and denouements to heighten their ambiguity. The plays of Pinter and Shepard are particularly representative of this technique ("I write stories without endings," says the latter). All is calculated to force audiences to assign meanings based on one's particular perception of reality, sometimes whimsically referred to as the MYOM ("Make Your Own Meaning") syndrome.

Some theorists, especially those aligned with postmodernism, argue that originality in art is a Romantic myth and that all art—indeed, all human endeavor—is influenced by myriad cultures and consciousness. Hence, art in our postmodern age is achieved by freely integrating styles and subject matter from across the spectrum of time and place. To achieve this spirit of *pastiche* (or *collage*), scripts frequently incorporate (or "quote") material from other periods and pieces of literature. Because of its pervasive influence on world culture and economics, material drawn from America's pop culture is especially popular. This often contradictory, purposefully disorienting style of playwriting is intended to challenge our beliefs about the way we perceive the world and the manner in which artists can represent it. As with all art, reinventing forms can have both salutary and controversial effects. Shepard regularly intersperses pop icons, such as comic book characters and cowboy heroes, with "real" characters throughout his innovative and much-praised work. In one of the most controversial examples of the pastiche script, Arthur Miller sued Elizabeth LeCompte and the Wooster Group, among New York's most controversial experimental theatrical companies, for using material from his play *The Crucible* in their 1984 collectively created "intertextual" work, *L.S.D. (or, Just the High Points)*.

Time and space are malleable concepts in postmodern plays, an outgrowth of the argument that history is suspect because it has been written by those in power to protect their base; like literature, history itself must be deconstructed. Scripts freely commingle historical periods and even reconstruct time lines. Caryl Churchill's *Top Girls* portrays women from five different historical periods meeting a contemporary "top girl" for lunch; the play ends with a scene that takes place one year *before* the first scene.

Whatever quibbles people may have about contemporary dramatic literature, there is considerable agreement that the movement has revitalized theater. By emphasizing the purely visual aspects of performance, the theater has reestablished itself as "the seeing place." Ironically, much of this has been accomplished by the very technology that postmodernists disdain. The realistic setting and the overused box set are now passé and best left to film and television, which handle the realistic style more convincingly. The conceptually stunning and purely theatrical images created by such directors as Peter Brook, Peter Stein, Anne Bogart, Tadashi Suzuki, Joanne Akalitis, Julie Taymor, and especially Robert Wilson reaffirm the theater's ability to create stunning effects live and before a living audience in imaginative ways that film cannot. After years of stark, minimalist designs reflecting the modernist preoccupation with a "less is more" philosophy, the designs of Joseph Svoboda, Maria Bjornson, and Ming Cho Lee commonly blend multiple styles, periods, and media to create haunting, archetypal images that transcend time and place (see Forum, "From *The Theater of Images*" later in this chapter).

Acting in Contemporary Plays

With its current focus on the multiple roles we play in our lives, as well as the "gamesmanship" that is required to survive in this world of artificial constructs, the theater itself has become a leading metaphor for contemporary philosophy (Shakespeare notwithstanding; proclaiming that "All the world's a stage. . . . ," he used the "play-life" metaphor in virtually every play he wrote). The actor has become a favorite metaphor for artists. In 1921 Luigi Pirandello defined this theme in *Six Characters in Search of an Author*, which remains the prototype of the life-as-theater playscript. We have taken the liberty of including *Six Characters* as the first play in this section on contemporary theater, even though it was written in 1921, because many have called it the first postmodern play. The English social satirist Tom Stoppard echoes Pirandello in *Rosencrantz and Guildenstern Are Dead* (1967), a retelling of *Hamlet* from the bit-players' point of view. In that play he reminds us that in our day-to-day existence, "every entrance is an exit, and every exit is an entrance." How adroitly we shift from one role to another as we make those entrances and exits is a predominant theme of the contemporary theater.

Actors themselves have had to adjust to the texts of contemporary scripts. Like the characters they portray, actors are often required to play multiple roles, literally and figuratively. It is not uncommon—as in Churchill's *Top Girls*—for an actor to be assigned several roles in a single play to underscore the fragmentation of personality. Often actors cross-dress to call attention to gender issues; Sue Townsend's *The Great Celestial Cow* provides an innovative example. Anna Deavere Smith's *Twilight: Los Angeles, 1992,* is more than a one-woman show in which she skillfully plays different women and men of many races and both genders. Hers is the quintessential postmodern performance. Even when an actor plays a single character, the old notion of the Stanislavskian "spine" or "through line"—which suggests a consistency of character and motivation—is now less applicable. In the postmodern theater, characters are the sum of their inconsistencies, each determined by the multiple roles they play in society. The postmodern actor must be extraordinarily versatile and able to mix styles (e.g., realism with the New Vaudeville, or the classical with Expressionism) in a heartbeat. Furthermore, postmodern actors are more frequently asked to perform in a presentational style, unlike method actors who are grounded in an essentially representational style that ignores the presence of the audience.

Contemporary Dramatic Criticism: Deconstructionism and Others

Postmodernism has fostered various approaches to dramatic theory and criticism. Among the most prominent is *deconstructionist criticism,* which "constructs" new meanings through the "destruction" of old ones based on (arguably) erroneous perceptions of language and ideologies imposed by older hierarchies. Many detractors of deconstructionism claim it is less a critical tool than an ideological movement intended to undermine Western orthodoxy. Though deconstructionism and Jacques Derrida, its principal voice, have lost some of the appeal they had a decade ago, they have left two important legacies.

First, deconstructionist thought made possible, and even respectable, ironist readings of a text; that is, an interpreter could argue with the text in an essay or in a production by playing against its traditional historical and cultural meaning. This encouraged a debate between our society and the one that originally produced the work. For instance, Peter Stein, an Austrian director known for his provocative stagings of classical texts, applied deconstructionist theory and practice to his treatment of *Othello* in the 1980s. Othello was played by a Caucasian actor in blackface to underscore the obviousness of his ethnicity; by design, his makeup rubbed off on all those with whom he came in contact. Desdemona was dressed in a bikini to show that she was little more than a sex object over whom the men fought. Much of the play was acted as a cheap vaudeville sketch to undercut its romantic foundation. These theatrical choices were conspicuously at variance with our perceptions of Shakespeare's intentions, but their very audacity forced audiences to reconsider the racism and sexism inherent in our culture.

Secondly, deconstructionism's commitment to an "openness to the other"—that is, an acceptance of a multiplicity of perspectives—has enlarged the arena for criticism. Derrida argues that this is deconstructionism's most affirmative project. Evolving with deconstructionism, and perhaps to some degree because of it, have been gender studies, feminist criticism, gay and lesbian criticism, and multicultural criticism. All share the common impulse to expand the literary canon and theatrical criticism from the dominant perspective of the traditional patriarchy. Each is written in the belief that differences of sex, race, class, ethnicity, and other variables give us a sense of personal identity, both interiorly (how we see ourselves) and exteriorly (how others see us). Accordingly, specific strains of criticism have developed to accommodate these varied perspectives:

- feminist criticism, which critiques gender bias among male writers;
- gender criticism, which is less concerned with the distinction between "male" and "female" than with the examination of gender itself as a political system and as a cultural construct (see Forum, "The Boys Don't Count" at the conclusion of this chapter);
- gay and lesbian criticism, or "queer theory" (a term used by those within the movement) calls for an understanding of, and advocacy for, literature that sympathetically portrays homosexual lifestyles;
- multicultural criticism embraces race, economic class, ethnicity, and Third World cultures or some other variable to examine differences in perspective.

The common ground among these critical approaches is a belief that literary criticism, literature, and performance are inherently political and that the concerns of marginalized people can be best addressed when examined from perspectives other than traditional European and American cultures.

Some minority, as well as feminist and gay, critics argue that when whites attempt to speak for nonwhites (or men for women, or straights for gays), they are engaging in "ventriloquism," which is a form of cultural imperialism. To cite a prominent recent example: when Paul Simon, the pop singer-writer, wrote *The Capeman* (1997), a musical drama about Puerto Ricans in New York, he was criticized by some Latinos for appropriating their music and culture. All of this brings us to a very sensitive and much-discussed issue: political correctness. Surely there have been excesses that have provided critics with ripe material. Robert Brustein, among the American theater's most respected critics and directors, wrote in 1993 that "PC [political correctness] has crypto-Maoist roots and in extreme form is dedicated to a program not unlike that of the unlamented cultural revolution by the People's Republic of China—replacing an 'elite' system with a 'populist' agenda through egalitarian leveling." Brustein is not objecting to pluralism itself, which he embraces for the increased possibilities it brings to the creative experience. Rather, he fears that the increased focus on the particular concerns of a group or minority may "balkanize" theater audiences by turning them into "hostile self-absorbed enclaves in a disunited America" (and elsewhere).

If the theater continues to address fundamental human concerns at the highest aesthetic levels, there is nothing to fear in the work of contemporary artists. Such was the goal that guided Aeschylus in Greece, Kālidāsa in India, Ogun in West Africa, and Zeami in Japan. The advantage we have today is that we have never been so well equipped—mentally, artistically, and technically—to portray the triumphs and shortcomings of our species through such truly global means.

THE CONTEMPORARY WESTERN WORLD

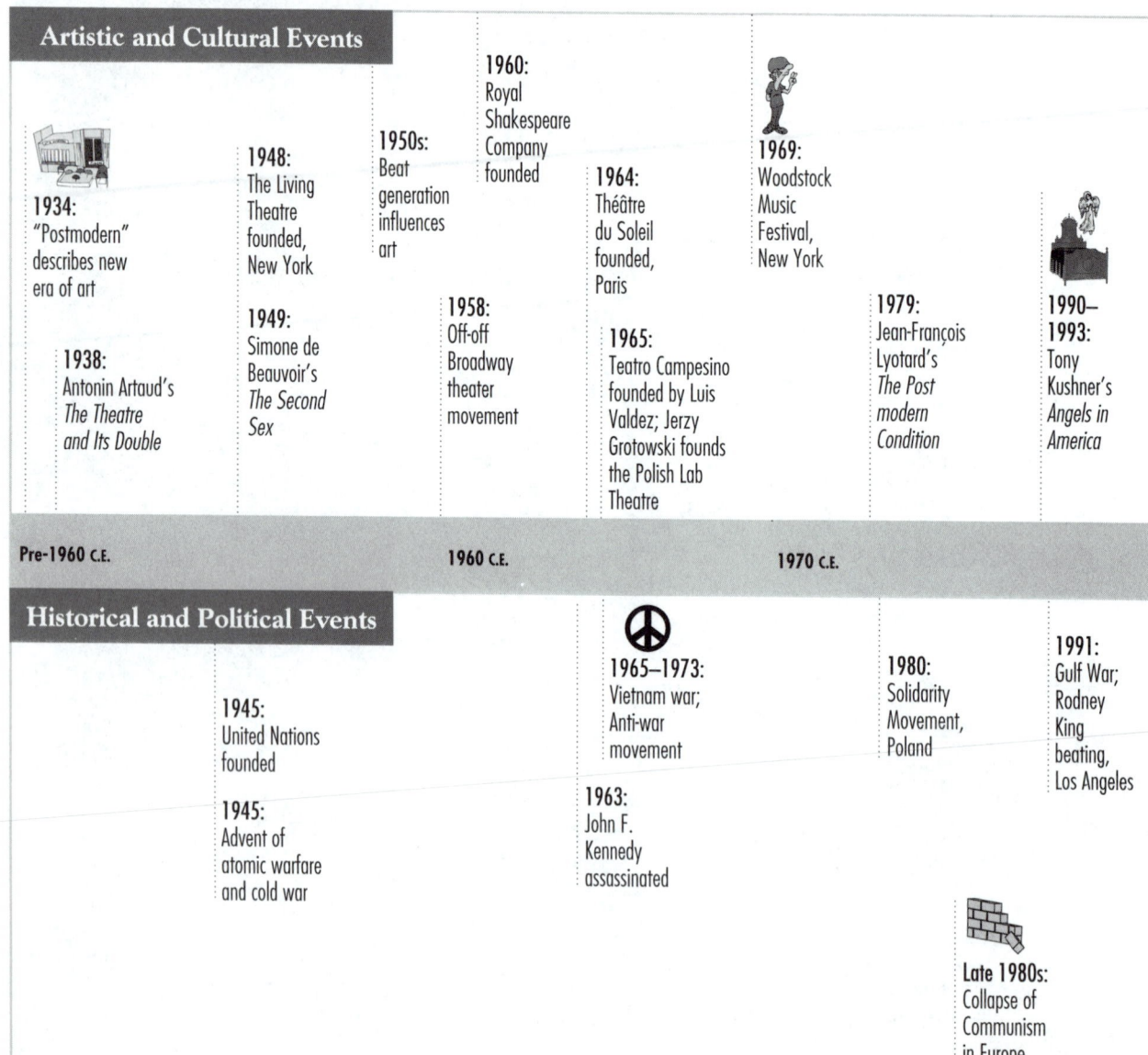

Artistic and Cultural Events

1934:
"Postmodern" describes new era of art

1938:
Antonin Artaud's *The Theatre and Its Double*

1948:
The Living Theatre founded, New York

1949:
Simone de Beauvoir's *The Second Sex*

1950s:
Beat generation influences art

1958:
Off-off Broadway theater movement

1960:
Royal Shakespeare Company founded

1964:
Théâtre du Soleil founded, Paris

1965:
Teatro Campesino founded by Luis Valdez; Jerzy Grotowski founds the Polish Lab Theatre

1969:
Woodstock Music Festival, New York

1979:
Jean-François Lyotard's *The Post modern Condition*

1990–1993:
Tony Kushner's *Angels in America*

Pre-1960 C.E.   **1960 C.E.**   **1970 C.E.**

Historical and Political Events

1945:
United Nations founded

1945:
Advent of atomic warfare and cold war

1963:
John F. Kennedy assassinated

1965–1973:
Vietnam war; Anti-war movement

1980:
Solidarity Movement, Poland

Late 1980s:
Collapse of Communism in Europe

1991:
Gulf War; Rodney King beating, Los Angeles

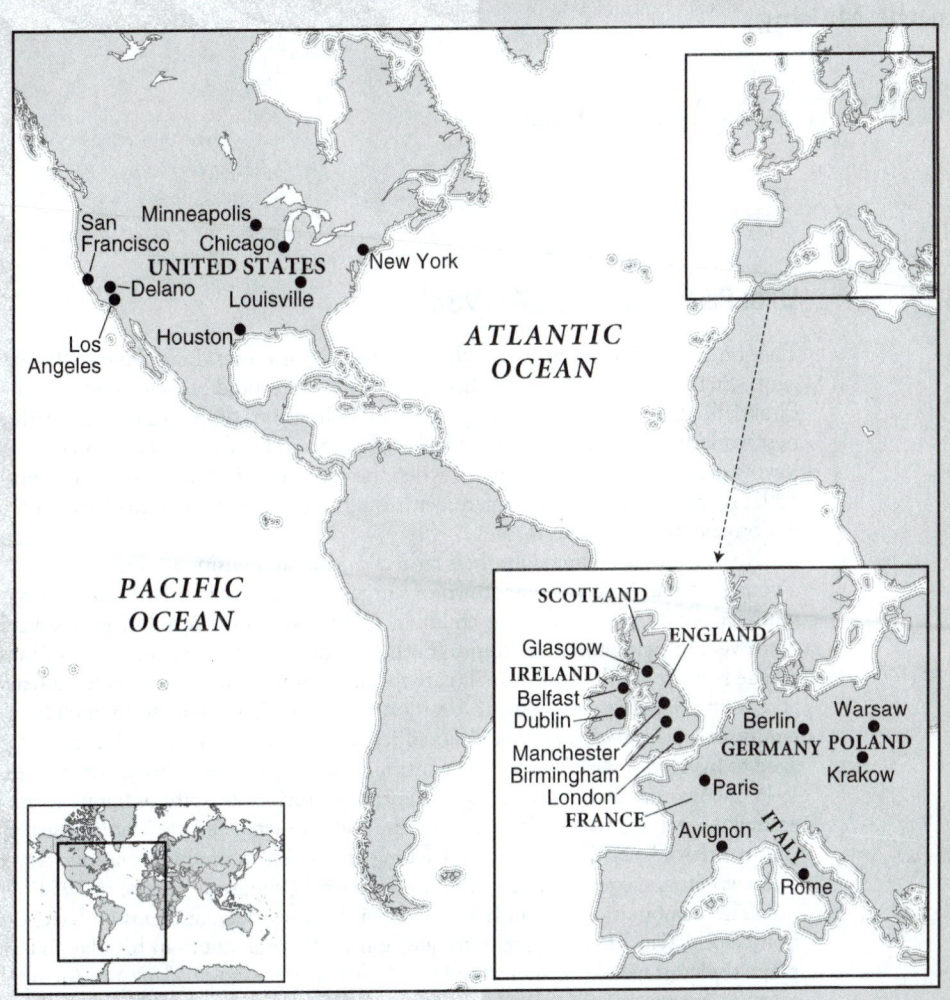

SIX CHARACTERS IN SEARCH OF AN AUTHOR

A Comedy in the Making

LUIGI PIRANDELLO

LUIGI PIRANDELLO (1867–1936)

The son of a well-respected, wealthy owner of sulfur mines, Luigi Pirandello was born in Girgenti, Sicily, in 1867. Although his father hoped he would become a businessman, the young Pirandello did not share the entrepreneurial inclinations of his father. After failing in the business world, he enrolled at the University of Rome and embarked on a career in philology. Following graduate study in Germany, where he received his doctorate from Bonn University in 1891, he returned to Rome, where, with the financial support of his father, he began writing fiction and literary criticism.

In 1894, to accommodate their fathers' wishes and business arrangements, Pirandello and a young woman from his hometown of Girgenti were married. Following 10 years of a happy marriage which produced three children, disaster struck—the sulfur mines were flooded and destroyed, bringing financial ruin to both families and the onset of mental illness that was to plague his wife until her death. To care for his family, Pirandello accepted a teaching position at a women's college in Rome, a position that provided adequate financial resources for his family; however, it also provoked fits of jealous rage from his wife. Although he was encouraged to institutionalize his wife, he continued to care for her at home for the next 15 years. In 1919 she was finally committed to a mental institution. In spite of family turmoil, Pirandello earned respect for his novels, including the well-known *The Late Mattia Pascal*, and numerous short stories. His skill in creating intriguing characters in unique situations served him well as a playwright and eventually earned him the Nobel Prize for literature in 1934.

The combination of family problems and the worldwide chaos and skepticism resulting from World War I led Pirandello to question traditional values in his plays. He wrote over 40 plays, the most well known of which are *Right You Are—If You Think You Are* (1916); *Six Characters in Search of an Author* (1921); *Henry IV* (1922); *Each in His Own Way* (1924); and *Tonight We Improvise* (1930).

In most of his plays, Pirandello challenges the validity of scientific or objective observation as a means of ascertaining truth. Though we might suspect that plays so deeply rooted in philosophy are emotionally unappealing, Pirandello imbues his plots and characters with a powerful respect for the possibilities that life presents to them. This elicits not only our interest but our sympathy. Invariably his characters are placed in situations in which they question the fine line between illusion and reality as they search for truth. In the aptly titled *Right You Are—If You Think You Are*, he presents family members torn asunder by their perceptions of personal identity. The husband, Signor Ponza, and his mother-in-law, Signora Frola, each perceive his wife, Signora Ponza, as a different individual. Ponza claims that Signora Ponza is not Frola's daughter but his second wife. Signora Frola claims that Ponza is deluded and that Signora Ponza is truly her daughter. Both give compelling but diametrically opposite rationales for why Signora Ponza and Signora Frola never see each other face to face. When Signora Ponza is given the chance to clear up the misunderstanding and tell the "truth," she declares that she is "the daughter of Signora Frola . . . and the second wife of Signor Ponza." She concludes, "I am she whom you believe me to be," thus articulating the basic Pirandellian tenet: there can be no truth because truth varies with the individual and the circumstance.

Pirandello also explores the connection between art and nature. Because he saw nature as a process of continual change, he sought to create a theater that would accurately depict this dynamic quality. He believed that if art is to truly reflect the world in which we live, it must be rooted in a philosophy and style that intermingle the two. For him, art should be nearly indistinguishable from life. As the Stepdaughter in *Six Characters in Search of an Author* exclaims: "How shall I play it, how shall I live it?"

SIX CHARACTERS IN SEARCH OF AN AUTHOR (1921)

Throughout this anthology, our analysis of dramatic literature has often begun by classifying the play according to its style and genre, a logical starting point for traditional discussion. However, Pirandello's "logic" is not traditional.

For Pirandello, following a traditional, uncomplicated structure was an insufficient means of holding "the mirror up to nature." The late-nineteenth- early-twentieth-century realistic style was inadequate because it was too simple. So too were the traditional generic classifications of comedy, tragedy, farce, and melodrama that told the audience what they might expect as they entered the theater. By accepting as truth the simple action of a traditional plot, the audience members remained outside the drama. Pirandello wanted the spectator not only to witness the action, but also to be caught up in it—to be part of the action and to share the characters' anxiety as they struggle to understand their essence. To accomplish this Pirandello fabricates an intricate metatheatrical structure. And *Six Characters in Search of an Author* is nothing if not an elaborate presentation of metatheater.

Metatheater has been variously defined as "a dramatic genre that does go beyond drama . . . becoming a kind of antiform in which the boundaries between the play as a work of self-contained art and life are dissolved" and an attempt "to establish some direct bridge between the created world of the play and the real world of its audience." In its simplest form, metatheater is the idea of "a play within a play" or "drama within drama." The playwright uses the characters' awareness of their existence *as characters* as a metaphor for the audience's conscious or unconscious awareness of its own participation in the "drama" of life. Just as Pirandello's six characters seek an author to give them understanding, we also seek to know our reason for being.

The metatheatrical action of the play exists on at least three levels. On the first level we have the "actors" rehearsing for *Mixing It Up*. On the second level we see six characters interrupt them as they search for an author. Finally, we have the actors and characters from the first two levels playing, or, in the case of the six characters, replaying, the scene that occurs in Madam Pace's shop. To further complicate the structure of the play, both the actors and the characters are conscious of the roles they play. All of this, of course, manifests the essential Pirandellian dilemma (and that of so many postmodern writers)—the human inability to come to grips with the "truth" and to distinguish illusion from reality. Thus, the form of the play fittingly reflects Pirandello's complicated view of human awareness.

Within this metatheatrical framework, Pirandello presents the action of his play through a series of surprises. As the players rehearse *Mixing It Up*, they are, without warning, confronted by the six characters, who are, in turn, surprised not only by the inability of the actors to convincingly play the scene, but by their own lack of success in finding an author. In what more likely environs than a theater could they have expected to find their "savior"? And we, the audience, are surprised by the multilayered interaction between the actors and the characters in the colliding worlds of the theater and life.

By the end of the play we have found no conclusion in the traditional sense. The actors in *Mixing It Up* have neither completed their own play nor succeeded in portraying the "Madam Pace" scene from the six characters' lives. The six characters are still searching for an author. And, of course, we as audience members are left without a resolution to any of the plot lines. Thus, Pirandello would have us see the perplexing and incomplete lives of his actors and characters as a parallel to our own lives because we, too, are all actors playing a series of different roles or characters. With no certain knowledge of what is illusion and what is reality, with no certain knowledge of the meaning of our existence, we are also left in search of an author and some conclusion to our lives. No matter how carefully we plan, no matter how much we try to prepare ourselves for the inevitable, we are constantly surprised by what happens. Just when we think we understand ourselves and think we have our lives under control, new "characters" seeking authors and answers enter our lives.

Such were Pirandello's circumstances as he created *Six Characters in Search of an Author*. Thanks to the "nimble little maidservant" he called Fantasy, Pirandello claims that "without having made any effort to seek them out, I found before me, alive . . . the six characters now seen on the stage." And when these six characters *appeared* to him, Pirandello said to himself, "I having already afflicted my readers with hundreds and hundreds of stories. Why should I afflict them now by narrating the sad entanglements of these six unfortunates?" Why, indeed? Perhaps because their plight was the ideal illustration of Pirandello's view of our complicated lives, or, as he said, "Born alive, they wished to live."

Just as Pirandello's characters in each level of the play seek answers to questions both great and small, the actors who play the various roles —completely conscious of their plight—also seek truth about themselves and their relationships with others. As the Stepdaughter says, "What is the stage? It's a place, baby, you know, where people play at being serious, a place where they act comedies. We've got to act a comedy now, dead serious, you know. . . ."

Thus, it is not by chance that Pirandello entitles his play within the play *Mixing It Up*. It is, after all, Pirandello who is "Mixing It Up." Is this play "a comedy in the making" as he subtitled it? Or is it "the bursting forth of . . . passions seeking . . . to overwhelm each other with a tragic, lacerating fury," as he says in his preface? The answer is, of course, "both" and "neither." As he himself says,

> The result was what it had to be: a mixture of tragic and comic, fantastic and realistic, in a humorous situation that was quite new and infinitely complex, a drama which is conveyed by means of the characters, who carry it within them and suffer it, a drama, breathing, speaking, self-propelled, which seeks at all costs to find the means of its own presentation; and the comedy of the vain attempt at an improvised realization of the drama on the stage.

By including the various levels and by obliterating traditional styles and genres, Pirandello gives us an art form that approximates reality. The Father, who might well be Pirandello's *raisonneur*, characterizes it best: "Reality is a mere transitory and fleeting illusion, taking this form today and that tomorrow, according to your will, your sentiments which in turn are controlled by an intellect that shows them to you today in one manner and tomorrow . . . who knows how?"

Real life intrudes upon life in the theater as one of Pirandello's six characters interrupts a rehearsal during a production by New York's Jean Cocteau Repertory Company.

SIX CHARACTERS IN SEARCH OF AN AUTHOR

A Comedy in the Making

LUIGI PIRANDELLO

Translated by Edward Storer

CHARACTERS OF THE COMEDY IN THE MAKING

THE FATHER	THE BOY ⎫
THE MOTHER	THE CHILD ⎬ *do not speak*
THE STEPDAUGHTER	MADAME PACE ⎭
THE SON	

ACTORS OF THE COMPANY

THE MANAGER	L'INGÉNUE
LEADING LADY	JUVENILE LEAD
LEADING MAN	OTHER ACTORS
SECOND LADY LEAD	AND ACTRESSES

PROPERTY MAN   MANAGER'S SECRETARY
PROMPTER   DOOR-KEEPER
MACHINIST   SCENE-SHIFTERS

SCENE: Daytime. The stage of a theater.

(N.B.: *The Comedy is without acts or scenes. The performance is interrupted once, without the curtain being lowered, when the Manager and the chief characters withdraw to arrange a scenario. A second interruption of the action takes place when, by mistake, the stage hands let the curtain down.*)

ACT I

(The spectators will find the curtain raised and the stage as it usually is during the daytime. It will be half dark, and empty, so that from the beginning the public may have the impression of an impromptu performance.)

(Prompter's box and a small table and chair for the Manager.)

(Two other small tables and several chairs scattered about as during rehearsals.)

(The Actors and Actresses of the company enter from the back of the stage: first one, then another, then two together; nine or ten in all. They are about to rehearse a Pirandello play: Mixing It Up. Some of the company move off toward their dressing rooms. The Prompter, who has the "book" under his arm, is waiting for the Manager in order to begin the rehearsal.)

(The Actors and Actresses, some standing, some sitting, chat and smoke. One perhaps reads a paper; another cons his part.)

(Finally, the Manager enters and goes to the table prepared for him. His Secretary brings him his mail, through which he glances. The Prompter takes his seat, turns on a light, and opens the "book.")

THE MANAGER *(throwing a letter down on the table)*. I can't see. *(To Property Man.)* Let's have a little light, please.

PROPERTY MAN. Yes, sir, yes, at once. *(A light comes down on to the stage.)*

THE MANAGER *(clapping his hands)*. Come along! Come along! Second act of "Mixing It Up." *(Sits down.)*

(The Actors and Actresses go from the front of the stage to the wings, all except the three who are to begin the rehearsal.)

THE PROMPTER *(reading the "book")*. "Leo Gala's house. A curious room serving as dining-room and study."

THE MANAGER *(to Property Man)*. Fix up the old red room.

PROPERTY MAN *(noting it down)*. Red set. All right!

THE PROMPTER *(continuing to read from the "book")*. "Table already laid and writing desk with books and papers. Bookshelves. Exit rear to Leo's bedroom. Exit left to kitchen. Principal exit to right."

THE MANAGER *(energetically)*. Well, you understand: The principal exit over there; here, the kitchen. *(Turning to actor who is to play the part of Socrates.)* You make your entrances and exits here. *(To Property Man.)* The baize doors at the rear, and curtains.

PROPERTY MAN *(noting it down)*. Right!

PROMPTER *(reading as before)*. "When the curtain rises, Leo Gala, dressed in cook's cap and apron, is busy beating an egg in a cup. Philip, also dressed as a cook, is beating another egg. Guidi Venanzi is seated and listening."

LEADING MAN *(to Manager)*. Excuse me, but must I absolutely wear a cook's cap?

THE MANAGER *(annoyed)*. I imagine so. It says so there anyway. *(Pointing to the "book.")*

LEADING MAN. But it's ridiculous!

THE MANAGER *(jumping up in a rage)*. Ridiculous? Ridiculous? Is it my fault if France won't send us any more good comedies, and we are reduced to putting on Pirandello's works, where nobody understands anything, and where the author plays the fool with us all? *(The Actors grin. The Manager goes to Leading Man and shouts.)* Yes sir, you put on the cook's cap and beat eggs. Do you suppose that with all this egg-beating business you are on an ordinary stage? Get that out of your head. You represent the shell of the eggs you are beating! *(Laughter and comments among the Actors.)* Silence! and listen to my explanations, please! *(To Leading Man.)* "The empty form of reason without the fullness of instinct, which is blind."—You stand for reason, your wife is instinct. It's a mixing up of the parts, according to which you who act your own part become the puppet of yourself. Do you understand?

LEADING MAN. I'm hanged if I do.

THE MANAGER. Neither do I. But let's get on with it. It's sure to be a glorious failure anyway. *(Confidentially.)* But I say, please face three-quarters. Otherwise, what with the abstruseness of the dialogue, and the public that won't be able to hear you, the whole thing will go to hell. Come on! come on!

PROMPTER. Pardon sir, may I get into my box? There's a bit of a draft.

THE MANAGER. Yes, yes, of course!

(At this point, the Door-Keeper has entered from the stage door and advances toward the Manager's table, taking off his braided cap. During this maneuver, the Six Characters enter, and stop by the door at back of stage, so that when the Door-Keeper is about to announce their coming to the Manager, they are already on the stage. A tenuous light surrounds them, almost as if irradiated by them—the faint breath of their fantastic reality.)

(This light will disappear when they come forward toward the actors. They preserve, however, something of the dream lightness in which they seem almost suspended; but this does not detract from the essential reality of their forms and expressions.)

(He who is known as the Father is a man of about 50: hair, reddish in color, thin at the temples; he is not bald, however; thick mustaches, falling over his still fresh mouth, which often opens in an empty and uncertain smile. He is fattish, pale; with an especially wide forehead. He has blue, oval-shaped eyes, very clear and piercing. Wears light trousers and a dark jacket. He is alternatively mellifluous and violent in his manner.)

(The Mother seems crushed and terrified as if by an intolerable weight of shame and abasement. She is dressed in modest black and wears a thick widow's veil of crepe. When she lifts this, she reveals a waxlike face. She always keeps her eyes downcast.)

(The Stepdaughter is dashing almost impudent, beautiful. She wears mourning too, but with great elegance. She shows contempt for the timid half-frightened manner of the wretched Boy (14 years old, and also dressed in black); on the other hand, she displays a lively tenderness for her little sister, the Child (about four), who is dressed in white, with a black silk sash at the waist.

(The Son (22) is tall, severe in his attitude of contempt for the Father, supercilious and indifferent to the Mother. He looks as if he had come on the stage against his will.)

DOOR-KEEPER *(cap in hand).* Excuse me, sir . . .

THE MANAGER *(rudely).* Eh? What is it?

DOOR-KEEPER *(timidly).* These people are asking for you, sir.

THE MANAGER *(furious).* I am rehearsing, and you know perfectly well no one's allowed to come in during rehearsals! *(Turning to the Characters.)* Who are you, please? What do you want?

THE FATHER *(coming forward a little, followed by the others who seem embarrassed).* As a matter of fact . . . we have come here in search of an author . . .

THE MANAGER *(half angry, half amazed).* An author? What author?

THE FATHER. Any author, sir.

THE MANAGER. But there's no author here. We are not rehearsing a new piece.

THE STEPDAUGHTER *(vivaciously).* So much the better, so much the better! We can be your new piece.

AN ACTOR *(coming forward from the others).* Oh, do you hear that?

THE FATHER *(to Stepdaughter).* Yes, but if the author isn't here . . . *(To Manager.)* unless you would be willing . . .

THE MANAGER. You are trying to be funny.

THE FATHER. No, for Heaven's sake, what are you saying? We bring you a drama, sir.

THE STEPDAUGHTER. We may be your fortune.

THE MANAGER. Will you oblige me by going away? We haven't time to waste with mad people.

THE FATHER *(mellifluously).* Oh sir, you know well that life is full of infinite absurdities, which, strangely enough, do not even need to appear plausible, since they are true.

THE MANAGER. What the devil is he talking about?

THE FATHER. I say that to reverse the ordinary process may well be considered a madness: that is, to create credible situations, in order that they may appear true. But permit me to observe that if this be madness, it is the sole *raison d'être*[1] of your profession, gentlemen. *(The Actors look hurt and perplexed.)*

THE MANAGER *(getting up and looking at him).* So our profession seems to you one worthy of madmen then?

THE FATHER. Well, to make seem true that which isn't true . . . without any need . . . for a joke as it were . . . Isn't that

your mission, gentlemen: to give life to fantastic characters on the stage?

THE MANAGER *(interpreting the rising anger of the Company).* But I would get you to believe, my dear sir, that the profession of the comedian is a noble one. If today, as things go, the playwrights give us stupid comedies to play and puppets to represent instead of men, remember we are proud to have given life to immortal works here on these very boards! *(The Actors, satisfied, applaud their Manager.)*

THE FATHER *(interrupting furiously).* Exactly, perfectly, to living beings more alive than those who breathe and wear clothes: beings less real perhaps, but truer! I agree with you entirely. *(The Actors look at one another in amazement.)*

THE MANAGER. But what do you mean? Before, you said . . .

THE FATHER. No, excuse me, I meant it for you, sir who were crying out that you had no time to lose with madmen, while no one better than yourself knows that nature uses the instrument of human fantasy in order to pursue her high creative purpose.

THE MANAGER. Very well,—but where does all this take us?

THE FATHER. Nowhere! It is merely to show you that one is born to life in many forms, in many shapes, as tree, or as stone, as water, as butterfly, or as woman. So one may also be born a character in a play.

THE MANAGER *(with feigned comic dismay).* So you and these other friends of yours have been born characters?

THE FATHER. Exactly, and alive as you see! *(Manager and Actors burst out laughing.)*

THE FATHER *(hurt).* I am sorry you laugh, because we carry in us a drama, as you can guess from this woman here veiled in black.

THE MANAGER *(losing patience at last and almost indignant).* Oh, chuck it! Get away please! Clear out of here! *(To Property Man.)* For Heaven's sake, turn them out!

THE FATHER *(resisting).* No, no, look here, we . . .

THE MANAGER *(roaring).* We come here to work, you know.

LEADING ACTOR. One cannot let oneself be made such a fool of.

THE FATHER *(determined, coming forward).* I marvel at your incredulity, gentleman. Are you not accustomed to see the characters created by an author spring to life in yourselves and face each other? Just because there is no "book" *(pointing to the Prompter's box)* which contains us, you refuse to believe . . .

THE STEPDAUGHTER *(advances toward Manager, smiling and coquettish).* Believe me, we are really six most interesting characters, sir; sidetracked however.

THE FATHER. Yes, that is the word! *(To Manager all at once.)* In the sense, that is, that the author who created us alive no longer wished, or was no longer able, materially to put us into a work of art. And this was a real crime, sir; because he who has had the luck to be born a character can laugh even at death. He cannot die. The man, the writer, the instrument of the creation will die, but his creation does not die. And to live for ever, it does not need to

[1] *raison d'être* French for "reason to exist"

have extraordinary gifts or to be able to work wonders. Who was Sancho Panza? Who was Don Abbondio?[2] Yet they live eternally because—live germs as they were—they had the fortune to find a fecundating matrix, a fantasy which could rise and nourish them: make them live for ever!

THE MANAGER. That is quite all right. But what do you want here, all of you?

THE FATHER. We want to live.

THE MANAGER (*ironically*). For Eternity?

THE FATHER. No, sir, only for a moment . . . in you.

AN ACTOR. Just listen to him!

LEADING LADY. They want to live, in us . . . !

JUVENILE LEAD (*pointing to the Stepdaughter*). I've no objection, as far as that one is concerned!

THE FATHER. Look here! Look here! The comedy has to be made. (*To the Manager.*) But if you and your actors are willing, we can soon concert it among ourselves.

THE MANAGER (*annoyed*). But what do you want to concert? We don't go in for concerts here. Here we play dramas and comedies!

THE FATHER. Exactly! That is just why we have come to you.

THE MANAGER. And where is the "book"?

THE FATHER. It is in us! (*The Actors laugh.*) The drama is in us, and we are the drama. We are impatient to play it. Our inner passion drives us on to this.

THE STEPDAUGHTER (*disdainful, alluring, treacherous, full of impudence*). My passion, sir! Ah, if you only knew! My passion for him! (*Points to the Father and makes a pretense of embracing him. Then she breaks out into a loud laugh.*)

THE FATHER (*angrily*). Behave yourself! And please don't laugh in that fashion.

THE STEPDAUGHTER. With your permission, gentlemen, I, who am a two months orphan, will show you how I can dance and sing. (*Sings and then dances Prenez garde à Tchou-Tchin-Tchou.*)

Les chinois sont un peuple malin,
De Shagaî à Pékin,
Ils ont mis des écriteaux partout:
Prenez garde à Tchou-Tchin-Tchou.[3]

ACTORS AND ACTRESSES. Bravo! Well done! Tip-top!

THE MANAGER. Silence! This isn't a café concert, you know! (*Turning to the Father in consternation.*) Is she mad?

THE FATHER. Mad? No, she's worse than mad.

THE STEPDAUGHTER (*to Manager*). Worse? Worse? Listen! Stage this drama for us at once! Then you will see that at a certain moment I . . . when this little darling here. . . . (*Takes the Child by the hand and leads her to the Manager.*) Isn't she a dear? (*Takes her up and kisses her.*) Darling! Darling! (*Puts her down again and adds feelingly.*) Well, when God suddenly takes this dear little child away from that poor mother there; and this imbecile here (*seizing hold of the Boy roughly and pushing him forward*) does the stupidest things, like the fool he is, you will see me run away. Yes, gentlemen, I shall be off. But the moment hasn't arrived yet. After what has taken place between him and me (*indicates the Father with a horrible wink*) I can't remain any longer in this society, to have to witness the anguish of this mother here for that fool. . . . (*Indicates the Son.*) Look at him! Look at him! See how indifferent, how frigid he is, because he is the legitimate son. He despises me, despises him (*pointing to the Boy*), despises this baby here; because . . . we are bastards. (*Goes to the Mother and embraces her.*) And he doesn't want to recognize her as his mother—she who is the common mother of us all. He looks down upon her as if she were only the mother of us three bastards. Wretch! (*She says all this very rapidly, excitedly. At the word "bastards" she raises her voice, and almost spits out the final "Wretch!"*)

THE MOTHER (*to the Manager, in anguish*). In the name of these two little children, I beg you. . . . (*She grows faint and is about to fall.*) Oh God!

THE FATHER (*coming forward to support her as do some of the Actors*). Quick, a chair, a chair for this poor widow!

THE ACTORS. Is it true? Has she really fainted?

THE MANAGERS. Quick, a chair! Here!

(*One of the Actors brings a chair, the others proffer assistance. The Mother tries to prevent the Father from lifting the veil which covers her face.*)

THE FATHER. Look at her! Look at her!

THE MOTHER. No, no; stop it please!

THE FATHER (*raising her veil*). Let them see you!

THE MOTHER (*rising and covering her face with her hands, in desperation*). I beg you, sir, to prevent this man from carrying out his plan which is loathsome to me.

THE MANAGER (*dumbfounded*). I don't understand at all. What is the situation? (*To the Father.*) Is this lady your wife?

THE FATHER. Yes, gentlemen: my wife!

THE MANAGER. But how can she be a widow if you are alive? (*The Actors find relief for their astonishment in a loud laugh.*)

THE FATHER. Don't laugh! Don't laugh like that, for Heaven's sake. Her drama lies just here in this: she has had a lover, a man who ought to be here.

THE MOTHER (*with a cry*). No! No!

THE STEPDAUGHTER. Fortunately for her, he is dead. Two months ago as I said. We are in mourning, as you see.

THE FATHER. He isn't here, you see, not because he is dead.

---

[2]**Sancho Panza . . . Don Abbondio** Memorable characters in novels: the squire in Cervantes's *Don Quixote* and the priest in Manzoni's *I Promessi Sposi* (*The Betrothed*), respectively. [3]**Prenez . . . Tchou** This French popular song is an adaptation of "Chu-Chin-Chow," an old Broadway show tune. "The Chinese are a sly people; / From Shanghai to Peking, / They've stuck up warning signs: / Beware of Tchou-Tchin-Tchou."

He isn't here—look at her a moment and you will understand—because her drama isn't a drama of the love of two men for whom she was incapable of feeling anything except possibly a little gratitude—gratitude not for me but for the other. She isn't a woman, she is a mother, and her drama—powerful, sir, I assure you—lies, as a matter of fact, all in these four children she has had by two men.

THE MOTHER. I had them? Have you got the courage to say that I wanted them? (*To the Company.*) It was his doing. It was he who gave me that other man, who forced me to go away with him.

THE STEPDAUGHTER. It isn't true.

THE MOTHER (*startled*). Not true, isn't it?

THE STEPDAUGHTER. No, it isn't true, it just isn't true.

THE MOTHER. And what can you know about it?

THE STEPDAUGHTER. It isn't true. Don't believe it. (*To Manager.*) Do you know why she says so? For that fellow there. (*Indicates the Son.*) She tortures herself, destroys herself on account of the neglect of that son there; and she wants him to believe that if she abandoned him when he was only two years old, it was because he (*indicates the Father*) made her do so.

THE MOTHER (*vigorously*). He forced me to it, and I call God to witness it. (*To the Manager.*) Ask him (*indicates Husband*) if it isn't true. Let him speak. You (*to Daughter*) are not in a position to know anything about it.

THE STEPDAUGHTER. I know you lived in peace and happiness with my father while he lived. Can you deny it.

THE MOTHER. No, I don't deny it. . . .

THE STEPDAUGHTER. He was always full of affection and kindness for you. (*To the Boy, angrily.*) It's true, isn't it? Tell them! Why don't you speak, you little fool?

THE MOTHER. Leave the poor boy alone. Why do you want to make me appear ungrateful, daughter? I don't want to offend your father. I have answered him that I didn't abandon my house and my son through any fault of mine, nor from any wilful passion.

THE FATHER. Is it true. It was my doing.

LEADING MAN (*to the Company*). What a spectacle!

LEADING LADY. We are the audience this time.

JUVENILE LEAD. For once, in a way.

THE MANAGER (*beginning to get really interested*). Let's hear them out. Listen!

THE SON. Oh yes, you're going to hear a fine bit now. He will talk to you of the Demon of Experiment.

THE FATHER. You are a cynical imbecile. I've told you so already a hundred times. (*To the Manager.*) He tries to make fun of me on account of this expression which I have found to excuse myself with.

THE SON (*with disgust*). Yes, phrases! phrases!

THE FATHER. Phrases! Isn't everyone consoled when faced with a trouble or fact he doesn't understand, by a word, some simple word, which tells us nothing and yet calms us?

THE STEPDAUGHTER. Even in the case of remorse. In fact, especially then.

THE FATHER. Remorse? No, that isn't true. I've done more than use words to quiet the remorse in me.

THE STEPDAUGHTER. Yes, there was a bit of money too. Yes, yes, a bit of money. There were the hundred lire he was about to offer me in payment, gentlemen. . . . (*Sensation of horror among the Actors.*)

THE SON (*to the Stepdaughter*). This is vile.

THE STEPDAUGHTER. Vile? There they were in a pale blue envelope on a little mahogany table in the back of Madame Pace's shop. You know Madam Pace—one of those ladies who attract poor girls of good family into their ateliers, under the pretext of their selling *robes et manteaux*.[4]

THE SON. And he thinks he has bought the right to tyrannize over us all with those hundred lire he was going to pay; but which, fortunately—note this, gentlemen—he had no chance of paying.

THE STEPDAUGHTER. It was a near thing, though, you know! (*Laughs ironically.*)

THE MOTHER (*protesting*). Shame, my daughter, shame!

THE STEPDAUGHTER. Shame indeed! This is my revenge! I am dying to live that scene . . . The room . . . I see it . . . Here is the window with the mantles exposed, there the divan, the looking-glass, a screen, there in front of the window the little mahogany table with the blue envelope containing one hundred lire. I see it. I see it. I could take hold of it. . . . But you, gentlemen, you ought to turn your backs now: I am almost nude, you know. But I don't blush: I leave that to him. (*Indicating Father.*)

THE MANAGER. I don't understand this at all.

THE FATHER. Naturally enough. I would ask you, sir, to exercise your authority a little here, and let me speak before you believe all she is trying to blame me with. Let me explain.

THE STEPDAUGHTER. Ah yes, explain it in your own way.

THE FATHER. But don't you see that the whole trouble lies here? In words, words. Each one of us has within him a whole world of things, each man of us his own special world. And how can we ever come to an understanding if I put in the words I utter the sense and value of things as I see them; while you who listen to me must inevitably translate them according to the conception of things each one of you has within himself. We think we understand each other, but we never really do. Look here! This woman (*indicating the Mother*) takes all my pity for her as a specially ferocious form of cruelty.

THE MOTHER. But you drove me away.

THE FATHER. Do you hear her? I drove her away! She believes I really sent her away.

---

[4]*robes et manteaux.* French for "dresses and capes"

THE MOTHER. You know how to talk, and I don't; but, believe me, sir (*to Manager*), after he had married me . . . who knows why? . . . I was a poor insignificant woman. . . .

THE FATHER. But, good Heavens! It was just for your humility that I married you. I loved this simplicity in you. (*He stops when he sees she makes signs to contradict him, opens his arms wide in sign of desperation, seeing how hopeless it is to make himself understood.*) You see she denies it. Her mental deafness, believe me, is phenomenal, the limit: (*touches his forehead*) deaf, deaf, mentally deaf! She has plenty of feeling. Oh yes, a good heart for the children; but the brain—deaf, to the point of desperation—!

THE STEPDAUGHTER. Yes, but ask him how his intelligence has helped us.

THE FATHER. If we could see all the evil that may spring from god, what should we do? (*At this point the Leading Lady, who is biting her lips with rage at seeing the Leading Man flirting with the Stepdaughter, comes forward and speaks to the Manager.*)

LEADING LADY. Excuse me, but are we going to rehearse today?

MANAGER. Of course, of course; but let's hear them out.

JUVENILE LEAD. This is something quite new.

L'INGÉNUE. Most interesting.

LEADING LADY. Yes, for the people who like that kind of thing. (*Casts a glance at Leading Man.*)

THE MANAGER (*to Father*). You must please explain yourself quite clearly. (*Sits down.*)

THE FATHER. Very well then: Listen! I had in my service a poor man, who became friends with her. (*Indicating the Mother.*) They understood one another, were kindred souls in fact, without, however, the least suspicion of any evil existing. They were incapable even of thinking of it.

THE STEPDAUGHTER. So he thought of it—for them!

THE FATHER. That's not true. I meant to do good to them—and to myself, I confess, at the same time. Things had come to the point that I could not say a word to either of them without their making a mute appeal, one to the other, with their eyes. I could see them silently asking each other how I was to be kept in countenance, how I was to be kept quiet. And this, believe me, was just about enough of itself to keep me in a constant rage, to exasperate me beyond measure.

THE MANAGER. And why didn't you send him away then—this secretary of yours?

THE FATHER. Precisely what I did, sir. And then I had to watch this poor woman drifting forlornly about the house like an animal without a master, like an animal one has taken in out of pity.

THE MOTHER. Ah yes . . . !

THE FATHER (*suddenly turning to the Mother*). It's true about the son anyway, isn't it?

THE MOTHER. He took my son away from me first of all.

THE FATHER. But not from cruelty. I did it so that he should grow up healthy and strong by living in the country.

THE STEPDAUGHTER (*pointing to him ironically*). As one can see.

THE FATHER (*quickly*). Is it my fault if he has grown up like this? I sent him to a wet nurse in the country, a peasant, as *she* did not seem to me strong enough, though she is of humble origin. That was, anyway, the reason I married her. Unpleasant all this may be, but how can it be helped? My mistake possibly, but there we are! All my life I have had these confounded aspirations towards a certain moral sanity. (*At this point the Stepdaughter bursts into a noisy laugh.*) Oh, stop it! Stop it! I can't stand it.

THE MANAGER. Yes, please stop it, for Heaven's sake.

THE STEPDAUGHTER. But imagine moral sanity from him, if you please—the client of certain ateliers like that of Madame Pace!

THE FATHER. Fool! That is the proof that I am a man! This seeming contradiction, gentlemen, is the strongest proof that I stand here a live man before you. Why, it is just for this very incongruity in my nature that I have had to suffer what I have. I could not live by the side of that woman (*indicating the Mother*) any longer; but not so much for the boredom she inspired me with as for the pity I felt for her.

THE MOTHER. And so he turned me out——.

THE FATHER. —well provided for! Yes, I sent her to that man, gentlemen . . . to let her go free of me.

THE MOTHER. And to free himself.

THE FATHER. Yes, I admit it. It was also a liberation for me. But great evil has come of it. I meant well when I did it; and I did it more for her sake than mine. I swear it. (*Crosses his arms on his chest; then turns suddenly to the Mother.*) Did I ever lose sight of you until that other man carried you off to another town, like the angry fool he was? And on account of my pure interest in you . . . my pure interest, I repeat, that had no base motive in it . . . I watched with the tenderest concern the new family that grew up around her. She can bear witness to this. (*Points to the Stepdaughter.*)

THE STEPDAUGHTER. Oh yes, that's true enough. When I was a kiddie, so so high, you know, with plaits over my shoulders and knickers longer than my skirts, I used to see him waiting outside the school for me to come out. He came to see how I was growing up.

THE FATHER. This is infamous, shameful!

THE STEPDAUGHTER. No. Why?

THE FATHER. Infamous! infamous! (*Then excitedly to Manager, explaining.*) After she (*indicating the Mother*) went away, my house seemed suddenly empty. She was my incubus, but she filled my house. I was like a dazed fly alone in the empty rooms. This boy here (*indicating the Son*) was educated away from home, and when he came back, he seemed to me to be no more mine. With no mother to stand between him and me, he grew up entirely for himself, on his own, apart, with no tie of intellect or affection binding him to me. And then—strange but true—I was driven, by curiosity at first and then by some tender sentiment, towards her family, which had come into being through my will. The thought of her began gradually to fill up the emptiness I felt all around me. I wanted to know if she were happy in living out the simple daily duties of life. I wanted to think of her as fortunate and happy because far away from the complicated torments of my spirit. And so, to have proof of this, I used to watch that child coming out of school.

THE STEPDAUGHTER. Yes, yes. True. He used to follow me in the street and smiled at me, waved his hand, like this. I would look at him with interest, wondering who he might be. I told my mother, who guessed at once. (*The Mother agrees with a nod.*) Then she didn't want to send me to school for some days; and when I finally went back, there he was again—looking so ridiculous—with a paper parcel in his hands. He came close to me, caressed me, and drew out a fine straw hat from the parcel, with a bouquet of flowers—all for me!

THE MANAGER. A bit discursive this, you know!

THE SON (*contemptuously*). Literature! Literature!

THE FATHER. Literature indeed! This is life, this is passion!

THE MANAGER. It may be, but it won't act.

THE FATHER. I agree. This is only the part leading up. I don't suggest this should be staged. She (*pointing to the Stepdaughter*), as you see, is no longer the flapper with plaits down her back—

THE STEPDAUGHTER. —and knickers showing below the skirt!

THE FATHER. The drama is coming now, sir; something new, complex, most interesting.

THE STEPDAUGHTER. As soon as my father died . . .

THE FATHER. —there was absolute misery for them. They came back here, unknown to me. Through her stupidity! (*Pointing to the Mother.*) It is true she can barely write her own name; but she could anyhow have got her daughter to write to me that they were in need . . .

THE MOTHER. And how was I to divine all this sentiment in him?

THE FATHER. That is exactly your mistake, never to have guessed any of my sentiments.

THE MOTHER. After so many years apart, and all that had happened . . .

THE FATHER. Was it my fault if that fellow carried you away? It happened quite suddenly; for after he had obtained some job or other, I could find no trace of them; and so, not unnaturally, my interest in them dwindled. But the drama culminated unforeseen and violent on their return, when I was impelled by my miserable flesh that still lives. . . . Ah! What misery, what wretchedness is that of the man who is alone and disdains debasing *liaisons!* Not old enough to do without women, and not young enough to go and look for one without shame. Misery? It's worse than misery; it's a horror; for no woman can any longer give him love; and when a man feels this. . . . One ought

to do without, you say? Yes, yes, I know. Each of us when he appears before his fellows is clothed in a certain dignity. But every man knows what unconfessable things pass within the secrecy of his own heart. One gives way to the temptation, only to rise from it again, afterwards, with a great eagerness to reestablish one's dignity, as if it were a tombstone to place on the grave of one's shame, and a moment to hide and sign the memory of our weaknesses. Everybody's in the same case. Some folks haven't the courage to say certain things, that's all!

THE STEPDAUGHTER. All appear to have the courage to do them though.

THE FATHER. Yes, but in secret. Therefore, you want more courage to say these things. Let a man but speak these things out, and folks at once label him a cynic. But it isn't true. He is like all the others, better indeed, because he isn't afraid to reveal with the light of the intelligence the red shame of human bestiality on which most men close their eyes so as not to see it.

Woman—for example, look at her case! She turns tantalizing inviting glances on you. You seize her. No sooner does she feel herself in your grasp than she closes her eyes. It is the sign of her mission, the sign by which she says to man: "Blind yourself, for I am blind."

THE STEPDAUGHTER. Sometimes she can close them no more: when she no longer feels the need of hiding her shame to herself, but dry-eyed and dispassionately, sees only that of the man who has blinded himself without love. Oh, all these intellectual complications make me sick, disgust me—all this philosophy that uncovers the beast in man, and then seeks to save him, excuse him . . . I can't stand it, sir. When a man seeks to "simplify" life bestially, throwing aside every relic of humanity, every chaste aspiration, every pure feeling, all sense of ideality, duty, modesty, shame . . . then nothing is more revolting and nauseous than a certain kind of remorse—crocodiles' tears, that's what it is.

THE MANAGER. Let's come to the point. This is only discussion.

THE FATHER. Very good, sir! But a fact is like a sack which won't stand up when it's empty. In order that it may stand up, one has to put into it the reason and sentiment which have caused it to exist. I couldn't possibly know that after the death of that man, they had decided to return here, that they were in misery, and that she (*pointing to the Mother*) had gone to work as a modiste, and at a shop of the type of that of Madame Pace.

THE STEPDAUGHTER. A real high-class modiste, you must know, gentlemen. In appearance, she works for the leaders of the best society; but she arranges matters so that these elegant ladies serve her purpose . . . without prejudice to other ladies who are . . . well . . . only so so.

THE MOTHER. You will believe me, gentlemen, that it never entered my mind that the old hag offered me work because she had her eye on my daughter.

THE STEPDAUGHTER. Poor mamma! Do you know, sir, what that women did when I brought her back the work my mother had finished? She would point out to me that I had torn one of my frocks, and she would give it back to my mother to mend. It was I who paid for it, always I; while this poor creature here believed she was sacrificing herself for me and these two children here, sitting up at night sewing Madame Pace's robes.

THE MANAGER. And one day you met there . . .

THE STEPDAUGHTER. Him, him. Yes sir, an old client. There's a scene for you to play! Superb!

THE FATHER. She, the Mother arrived just then . . .

THE STEPDAUGHTER (*treacherously*). Almost in time!

THE FATHER (*crying out*). No, in time! in time! Fortunately I recognized her . . . in time. And I took them back home with me to my house. You can imagine now her position and mine; she, as you see her; and I who cannot look her in the face.

THE STEPDAUGHTER. Absurd! How can I possibly be expected—after that—to be a modest young miss, a fit person to go with his confounded aspirations for "a solid moral sanity"?

THE FATHER. For the drama lies all in this—in the conscience that I have, that each one of us has. We believe this conscience to be a single thing, but it is many-sided. There is one for this person, and another for that. Diverse consciences. So we have this allusion of being one person for all, of having a personality that is unique in all our acts. But it isn't true. We perceive this when, tragically perhaps, in something we do, we are as it were, suspended, caught up in the air on a kind of hook. Then we perceive that all of us was not in that act, and that it would be an atrocious injustice to judge us by that action alone, as if all our existence were summed up in that one deed. Now do you understand the perfidy of this girl? She surprised me in a place, where she ought not to have known me, just as I could not exist for her; and she now seeks to attach to me a reality such as I could never suppose I should have to assume for her in a shameful and fleeting moment of my life. I feel this above all else. And the drama, you will see, requires a tremendous value from this point. Then there is the position of the others . . . his . . . (*Indicating the Son.*)

THE SON (*shrugging his shoulders scornfully*). Leave me alone! I don't come into this.

THE FATHER. What? You don't come into this?

THE SON. I've got nothing to do with it, and don't want to have; because you know well enough I wasn't made to be mixed up in all this with the rest of you.

THE STEPDAUGHTER. We are only vulgar folk! He is he fine gentleman. You may have noticed, Mr. Manager, that I fix him now and again with a look of scorn while he lowers his eyes—for he knows the evil he has done me.

THE SON (*scarcely looking at her*). I?

THE STEPDAUGHTER. You! you! I owe my life on the streets to you. Did you or did you not deny us, with your behavior, I won't say the intimacy of home, but even that mere hospitality which makes guests feel at their ease? We were intruders who had come to disturb the kingdom of your legitimacy. I should like to have you witness, Mr. Manager, certain scenes between him and me. He says I have tyrannized over everyone. But it was just his behavior which made me insist on the reason for which I had come into the house—this reason he calls "vile"—into his house, with my mother who is his mother too. And I came as mistress of the house.

THE SON. It's easy for them to put me always in the wrong. But imagine, gentlemen, the position of a son, whose fate it is to see arrive one day at his home a young woman of impudent bearing, a young woman who inquires for his father, with whom who knows what business she has. This young man has then to witness her return bolder than ever, accompanied by that child there. He is obliged to watch her treat his father in an equivocal and confidential manner. She asks for money of him in a way that lets one suppose he must give it to her, *must*, do you understand, because he has every obligation to do so.

THE FATHER. But I have, as a matter of fact, this obligation. I owe it to your mother.

THE SON. How should I know? When had I ever seen or heard of her? One day there arrive with her (*indicating Stepdaughter*) that lad and this baby here. I am told: "This is *your* mother too, you know." I divine from her manner (*indicating Stepdaughter again*) why it is they have come home. I had rather not say what I feel and think about it. I shouldn't even care to confess to myself. No action can therefore be hoped for from me in this affair. Believe me, Mr. Manager, I am an "unrealized" character, dramatically speaking; and I find myself not at all at ease in their company. Leave me out of it, I beg you.

THE FATHER. What? It is just because you are so that . . .

THE SON. How do you know what I am like? When did you ever bother your head about me?

THE FATHER. I admit it. I admit it. But isn't that a situation in itself? This aloofness of yours which is so cruel to me and to your mother, who returns home and sees you almost for the first time grown up, who doesn't recognize you but knows you are her son. . . . (*Pointing out the Mother to the Manager.*) See, she's crying!

THE STEPDAUGHTER (*angrily, stamping her foot*). Like a fool!

THE FATHER (*indicating Stepdaughter*). She can't stand him, you know. (*Then referring again to the Son.*) He says he doesn't come into the affair, whereas he is really the hinge of the whole action. Look at that lad who is always clinging to his mother, frightened and humiliated. It is on account of this fellow here. Possibly his situation is the most painful of all. He feels himself a stranger more than the others. The poor little chap feels mortified, humiliated at being brought into a home out of charity as it were. (*In confidence.*) He is the image of his father. Hardly talks at all. Humble and quiet.

THE MANAGER. Oh, we'll cut him out. You've no notion what a nuisance boys are on the stage. . . .

THE FATHER. He disappears soon, you know. And the baby too. She is the first to vanish from the scene. The drama consists finally in this: when that mother reenters my house, her family born outside of it, and shall we say superimposed on the original, ends with the death of the little girl, the tragedy of the boy and the flight of the elder daughter. It cannot go on, because it is foreign to its surroundings. So after much torment, we three remain: I, the mother, that son. Then, owing to the disappearance of that extraneous family, we too find ourselves strange to one another. We find we are living in an atmosphere of mortal desolation which is the revenge, as he (*indicating Son*) scornfully said of the Demon of Experiment, that unfortunately hides in me. Thus, sir, you see when faith is lacking, it becomes impossible to create certain states of happiness, for we lack the necessary humility. Vaingloriously, we try to substitute ourselves for this faith, creating thus for the rest of the world a reality which we believe after their fashion, while, actually, it doesn't exist. For each one of us has his own reality to be respected before God, even when it is harmful to one's very self.

THE MANAGER. There is something in what you say. I assure you all this interests me very much. I begin to think there's the stuff for a drama in all this, and not a bad drama either.

THE STEPDAUGHTER (*coming forward*). When you've got a character like me . . .

THE FATHER (*shutting her up, all excited to learn the decision of the Manager*). You be quiet!

THE MANAGER (*reflecting, heedless of interruption*). It's new . . . hem . . . yes. . . .

THE FATHER. Absolutely new!

THE MANAGER. You've got a nerve though, I must say, to come here and fling it at me like this . . .

THE FATHER. You will understand, sir, born as we are for the stage . . .

THE MANAGER. Are you amateur actors then?

THE FATHER. No, I say born for the stage, because . . .

THE MANAGER. Oh, nonsense. You're an old hand, you know.

THE FATHER. No sir, no. We act that role for which we have been cast, that role which we are given in life. And in my own case, passion itself, as usually happens, becomes a trifle theatrical when it is exalted.

THE MANAGER. Well, well, that will do. But you see, without an author. . . . I could give you the address of an author if you like . . .

THE FATHER. No, no. Look here! You must be the author.

THE MANAGER. I? What are you talking about?

THE FATHER. Yes, you, you! Why not?

THE MANAGER. Because I have never been an author: that's why.

THE FATHER. Then why not turn author now? Everybody does it. You don't want any special qualities. Your task is made much easier by the fact that we are all here alive before you. . . .

THE MANAGER. It won't do.

THE FATHER. What? When you see us live our drama. . . .

THE MANAGER. Yes, that's all right. But you want someone to write it.

THE FATHER. No, no. Someone to take it down, possibly, while we play it, scene by scene! It will be enough to sketch it out at first, and then try it over.

THE MANAGER. Well . . . I am almost tempted. It's a bit of an idea. One might have a shot at it.

THE FATHER. Of course. You'll see what scenes will come out of it. I can give you one, at once . . .

THE MANAGER. By Jove, it tempts me. I'd like to have a go at it. Let's try it out. Come with me to my office. (*Turning to the Actors.*) You are at liberty for a bit, but don't step out of the theater for long. In a quarter of an hour, twenty minutes, all back here again! (*To the Father.*) We'll see what can be done. Who knows if we don't get something really extraordinary out of it?

THE FATHER. There's no doubt about it. They (*indicating the Characters*) had better come with us too, hadn't they?

THE MANAGER. Yes, yes. Come on! come on! (*Moves away and then turning to the Actors.*) Be punctual, please! (*Manager and the Six Characters cross the stage and go off. The other Actors remain, looking at one another in astonishment.*)

LEADING MAN. Is he serious? What the devil does he want to do?

JUVENILE LEAD. This is rank madness.

THIRD ACTOR. Does he expect to knock up a drama in five minutes?

JUVENILE LEAD. Like the improvisers!

LEADING LADY. If he thinks I'm going to take part in a joke like this. . . .

JUVENILE LEAD. I'm out of it anyway.

FOURTH ACTOR. I should like to know who they are. (*Alludes to Characters.*)

THIRD ACTOR. What do you suppose? Madmen or rascals!

JUVENILE LEAD. And he takes them seriously!

L'INGÉNUE. Vanity! He fancies himself as an author now.

LEADING MAN. It's absolutely unheard of. If the stage has come to this . . . well I'm . . .

FIFTH ACTOR. It's rather a joke.

THIRD ACTOR. Well, we'll see what's going to happen next.

(*Thus talking, the Actors leave the stage, some going out by the little door at the back, others retiring to their dressing rooms.*)

(The curtain remains up.)

(The action of the play is suspended for twenty minutes.)

ACT II

(The stage call-bells ring to warn the company that the play is about to begin again.)

(The Stepdaughter comes out of the Manager's office along with the Child and the Boy. As she comes out of the office, she cries: —)

Nonsense! nonsense! Do it yourselves! I'm not going to mix myself up in this mess. *(Turning to the Child and coming quickly with her on to the stage.)* Come on, Rosetta, let's run!

(The Boy follows them slowly, remaining a little behind and seeming perplexed.)

THE STEPDAUGHTER *(stops, bends over the Child and takes the latter's face between her hands).* My little darling! You're frightened, aren't you? *(Pretending to reply to a question of the Child).* What is the stage? It's a place, baby, you know, where people play at being serious, a place where they act comedies. We've got to act a comedy now, dead serious, you know; and you're in it also, little one. *(Embraces her, pressing the little head to her breast, and rocking the Child for a moment.)* Oh darling, darling, what a horrid comedy you've got to play! What a wretched part they've found for you! A garden . . . a fountain . . . look . . . just suppose, kiddie, it's here. Where, you say? Why, right here in the middle. It's all pretense you know. That's the trouble, my pet: it's all make-believe here. It's better to imagine it though, because if they fix it up for you, it'll only be painted cardboard, painted cardboard for the rockery, the water, the plants. . . . Ah, but I think a baby like this one would sooner have a make-believe fountain than a real one, so she could play with it. What a joke it'll be for the others! But for you, alas! not quite such a joke: you who are real, baby dear, and really play by a real fountain that is big and green and beautiful, with ever so many bamboos around it that are reflected in the water, and a whole lot of little ducks swimming about. . . . No, Rosetta, no, your mother doesn't bother about you on account of that wretch of a son there. I'm in the devil of a temper, and as for that lad. . . . *(Seizes Boy by the arm to force him to take one of his hands out of his pockets.)* What have you got there? What are you hiding? *(Pulls his hand out of his pocket, looks into it, and catches the glint of a revolver.)* Ah, where did you get this? *(The Boy, very pale in the face, looks at her, but does not answer.)* Idiot! If I'd been in your place, instead of killing myself, I'd have shot one of those two, or both of them: father and son.

(The Father enters from the office, all excited from his work. The Manager follows him.)

THE FATHER. Come on, come on dear! Come here for a minute! We've arranged everything. It's all fixed up.

THE MANAGER *(also excited).* If you please, young lady, there are one or two points to settle still. Will you come along?

THE STEPDAUGHTER *(following him toward the office).* Ouff! what's the good, if you've arranged everything.

(The Father, Manager, and Stepdaughter go back into the office again [off] for a moment. At the same time, the Son, followed by the Mother, comes out.)

THE SON *(looking at the three entering office).* Oh this is fine, fine! And to think I can't even get away!

(The Mother attempts to look at him, but lowers her eyes immediately when he turns away from her. She then sits down. The Boy and the Child approach her. She casts a glance again at the Son, and speaks with humble tones, trying to draw him into conversation.)

THE MOTHER. And isn't my punishment the worst of all? *(Then seeing from the Son's manner that he will not bother himself about her.)* My God! Why are you so cruel? Isn't it enough for one person to support all this torment? Must you then insist on others seeing it also?

THE SON *(half to himself, meaning the Mother to hear, however).* And they want to put it on the stage! If there was at least a reason for it! He thinks he has got at the meaning of it all. Just as if each one of us in every circumstance of life couldn't find his own explanation of it! *(Pauses.)* He complains he was discovered in a place where he ought not to have been seen, in a moment of his life which ought to have remained hidden and kept out of the reach of that convention which he has to maintain for other people. And what about my case? Haven't I had to reveal that no son ought ever to reveal: how father and mother live and are man and wife for themselves quite apart from that idea of father and mother which we give them? When this idea is revealed, our life is then linked at one point only to that man and that woman; and as such it should shame them, shouldn't it?

(The Mother hides her face in her hands. From the dressing rooms and the little door at the back of the stage the Actors and Stage Manager return, followed by the Property Man and the Prompter. At the same moment, the Manager comes out of his office, accompanied by the Father and the Stepdaughter.)

THE MANAGER. Come on, come on, ladies and gentlemen! Heh! you there, machinist!

MACHINIST. Yes sir?

THE MANAGER. Fix up the parlor with the floral decorations. Two wings and a drop with a door will do. Hurry up!

(The Machinist runs off at once to prepare the scene and arranges it while the Manager talks with the Stage Manager, the Property Man, and the Prompter on matters of detail.)

THE MANAGER (*to Property Man*). Just have a look, and see if there isn't a sofa or a divan in the wardrobe . . .

PROPERTY MAN. There's the green one.

THE STEPDAUGHTER. No no! Green won't do. It was yellow, ornamented with flowers—very large! and most comfortable!

PROPERTY MAN. There isn't one like that.

THE MANAGER. It doesn't matter. Use the one we've got.

THE STEPDAUGHTER. Doesn't matter? It's most important.

THE MANAGER. We're only trying it now. Please don't interfere. (*To Property Man.*) See if we've got a shop window—long and narrowish.

THE STEPDAUGHTER. And the little table! The little mahogany table for the pale blue envelope!

PROPERTY MAN (*to Manager*). There's that little gilt one.

THE MANAGER. That'll do fine.

THE FATHER. A mirror.

THE STEPDAUGHTER. And the screen! We must have a screen. Otherwise how can I manage?

PROPERTY MAN. That's all right, Miss. We've got any amount of them.

THE MANAGER (*to the Stepdaughter*). We want some clothes pegs too, don't we?

THE STEPDAUGHTER. Yes, several, several!

THE MANAGER. See how many we've got and bring them all.

PROPERTY MAN. All right!

(*The Property Man hurries off to obey his orders. While he is putting the things in their places, the Manager talks to the Prompter and then with the Characters and the Actors.*)

THE MANAGER (*to Prompter*). Take your seat. Look here: this is the outline of the scenes, act by act. (*Hands him some sheets of paper.*) And now I'm going to ask you to do something out of the ordinary.

PROMPTER. Take it down in shorthand?

THE MANAGER (*pleasantly surprised*). Exactly! Can you do shorthand?

PROMPTER. Yes, a little.

THE MANAGER. Good! (*Turning to a Stage Hand.*) Go and get some paper from my office, plenty, as much as you can find.

(*The Stage Hand goes off and soon returns with a handful of paper which he gives to the Prompter.*)

THE MANAGER (*to Prompter*). You follow the scenes as we play them, and try and get the points down, at any rate the most important ones. (*Then addressing the Actors.*) Clear the stage, ladies and gentlemen! Come over here (*pointing to the left*) and listen attentively.

LEADING LADY. But, excuse me, we . . .

THE MANAGER (*guessing her thought*). Don't worry! You won't have to improvise.

LEADING MAN. What have we to do then?

THE MANAGER. Nothing. For the moment you just watch and listen. Everybody will get his part written out afterwards. At present we're going to try the things as best we can. They're going to act now.

THE FATHER (*as if fallen from the clouds into the confusion of the stage*). We? What do you mean, if you please, by a rehearsal?

THE MANAGER. A rehearsal for them. (*Points to the Actors.*)

THE FATHER. But since we are the characters . . .

THE MANAGER. All right: "characters" then, if you insist on calling yourselves such. But here, my dear sir, the characters don't act. Here the actors do the acting. The characters are there, in the "book" (*pointing toward Prompter's box*)—when there is a "book"!

THE FATHER. I won't contradict you; but excuse me, the actors aren't the characters. They want to be, they pretend to be, don't they? Now if these gentlemen here are fortunate enough to have us alive before them . . .

THE MANAGER. Oh, this is grand! You want to come before the public yourselves then?

THE FATHER. As we are. . . .

THE MANAGER. I can assure you it would be a magnificent spectacle!

LEADING MAN. What's the use of us here anyway then?

THE MANAGER. You're not going to pretend that you can act? It makes me laugh! (*The Actors laugh.*) There, you see, they are laughing at the notion. But, by the way, I must cast the parts. That won't be difficult. They cast themselves. (*To the Second Lady Lead.*) You play the Mother. (*To the Father.*) We must find her a name.

THE FATHER. Amalia, sir.

THE MANAGER. But that is the real name of your wife. We don't want to call her by her real name.

THE FATHER. Why ever not, if it is her name? . . . Still, perhaps, if that lady must . . . (*Makes a slight motion of the hand to indicate the Second Lady Lead.*) I see this woman here (*means the Mother*) as Amalia. But do as you like. (*Gets more and more confused.*) I don't know what to say to you. Already, I begin to hear my own words ring false, as if they had another sound . . .

THE MANAGER. Don't you worry about it. It'll be our job to find the right tones. And as for her name, if you want her Amalia, Amalia it shall be; and if you don't like it, we'll find another! For the moment though, we'll call the characters in this way: (*To Juvenile Lead.*) You are the Son. (*To the Leading Lady.*) You naturally are the Stepdaughter . . .

THE STEPDAUGHTER (*excitedly*). What? what? I, that woman there? (*Bursts out laughing.*)

THE MANAGER (*angry*). What is there to laugh at?

LEADING LADY (*indignant*). Nobody has ever dared to laugh at me. I insist on being treated with respect; otherwise I go away.

THE STEPDAUGHTER. No, no, excuse me . . . I am not laughing at you. . . .

THE MANAGER (*to Stepdaughter*). You ought to feel honored to be played by . . .

LEADING LADY (*at once, contemptuously*). "That woman there" . . .

THE STEPDAUGHTER. But I wasn't speaking of you, you know. I was speaking of myself—whom I can't see at all in you! That is all. I don't know . . . but . . . you . . . aren't in the least like me. . . .

THE FATHER. True. Here's the point. Look here, sir, our temperaments, our souls. . . .

THE MANAGER. Temperament, soul, be hanged! Do you suppose the spirit of the piece is in you? Nothing of the kind!

THE FATHER. What, haven't we our own temperaments, or own souls?

THE MANAGER. Not at all. Your soul or whatever you like to call it takes shape here. The actors give body and form to it, voice and gesture. And my actors—I may tell you—have given expression to much more lofty material than this little drama of yours, which may or may not hold up on the stage. But if it does, the merit of it, believe me, will be due to my actors.

THE FATHER. I don't dare contradict you, sir; but, believe me, it is a terrible suffering for us who are as we are, with these bodies of ours, these features to see. . . .

THE MANAGER (*cutting him short and out of patience*). Good heavens! The make-up will remedy all that, man, the make-up. . . .

THE FATHER. Maybe. But the voice, the gestures . . .

THE MANAGER. Now, look here! On the stage, you as yourself, cannot exist. The actor here acts you, and that's an end to it!

THE FATHER. I understand. And now I think I see why our author who conceived us as we are, all alive, didn't want to put us on the stage after all. I haven't the least desire to offend your actors. Far from it! But when I think that I am to be acted by . . . I don't know by whom. . . .

LEADING MAN (*on his dignity*). By me, if you've no objection!

THE FATHER (*humbly, mellifluously*). Honored, I assure you, sir. (*Bows.*) Still, I must say that try as this gentleman may, with all his good will and wonderful art, to absorb me into himself. . . .

LEADING MAN. Oh chuck it! "Wonderful art!" Withdraw that, please!

THE FATHER. The performance he will give, even doing his best with make-up to look like me. . . .

LEADING MAN. It will certainly be a bit difficult! (*The Actors laugh.*)

THE FATHER. Exactly! It will be difficult to act me as I really am. The effect will be rather—apart from the make-up—according as to how he supposes I am, as he senses me—if he does sense me—and not as I inside of myself feel myself to be. It seems to me then that account should be taken of this by everyone whose duty it may become to criticize us. . . .

THE MANAGER. Heavens! The man's starting to think about the critics now! Let them say what they like. It's up to us to put on the play if we can. (*Looking around.*) Come on! come on! Is the stage set? (*To the Actors and Characters.*) Stand back—stand back! Let me see, and don't let's lose any more time! (*To the Stepdaughter.*) Is it all right as it is now?

THE STEPDAUGHTER. Well, to tell the truth, I don't recognize the scene.

THE MANAGER. My dear lady, you can't possibly suppose that we can construct that shop of Madame Pace piece by piece here? (*To the Father.*) You said a white room with flowered wallpaper, didn't you?

THE FATHER. Yes.

THE MANAGER. Well then. We've got the furniture right more or less. Bring that little table a bit further forward. (*The Stage Hands obey the order. To Property Man.*) You go and find an envelope, if possible, a pale blue one; and give it to that gentleman. (*Indicates Father.*)

PROPERTY MAN. An ordinary envelope?

MANAGER AND FATHER. Yes, yes, an ordinary envelope.

PROPERTY MAN. At once, sir. (*Exit.*)

THE MANAGER. Ready, everyone! First scene—the Young Lady. (*The Leading Lady comes forward.*) No, no, you must wait. I meant her. (*Indicating the Stepdaughter.*) You just watch—

THE STEPDAUGHTER (*adding at once*). How I shall play it, how I shall live it! . . .

LEADING LADY (*offended*). I shall live it also, you may be sure, as soon as I begin!

THE MANAGER (*with his hands to his head*). Ladies and gentlemen, if you please! No more useless discussions! Scene I: the Young Lady with Madame Pace: Oh! (*Looks around as if lost.*) And this Madam Pace, where is she?

THE FATHER. She isn't with us, sir.

THE MANAGER. Then what the devil's to be done?

THE FATHER. But she is alive too.

THE MANAGER. Yes, but where is she?

THE FATHER. One minute. Let me speak! (*Turning to the Actresses.*) If these ladies would be so good as to give me their hats for a moment. . . .

THE ACTRESSES (*half surprised, half laughing, in chorus*). What? Why? Our hats? What does he say?

THE MANAGER. What are you going to do with the ladies' hats? (*The Actors laugh.*)

THE FATHER. Oh nothing. I just want to put them on these pegs for a moment. And one of the ladies will be so kind as to take off her mantle. . . .

THE ACTORS. Oh, what d'you think of that? Only the mantle? He must be mad.

SOME ACTRESSES. But why? Mantles as well?

THE FATHER. To hang them up here for a moment. Please be so kind, will you?

THE ACTRESSES (*taking off their hats, one or two also their cloaks, and going to hang them on the racks*). After all, why not? There you are! This is really funny. We've got to put them on show.

THE FATHER. Exactly; just like that, on show.

THE MANAGER. May we know why?

THE FATHER. I'll tell you. Who knows if, by arranging the stage for her, she does not come here herself, attracted by the very articles of her trade? (*Inviting the Actors to look toward the exit at back of stage.*) Look! Look!

(*The door at the back of stage opens and Madame Pace enters and takes a few steps forward. She is a fat, oldish woman with puffy oxygenated hair. She is rouged and powdered, dressed with a comical elegance in black silk. Round her waist is a long silver chain from which hangs a pair of scissors. The Stepdaughter runs over to her at once amid the stupor of the Actors.*)

THE STEPDAUGHTER (*turning toward her*). There she is! There she is!

THE FATHER (*radiant*). It's she! I said so, didn't I! There she is!

THE MANAGER (*conquering his surprise, and then becoming indignant*). What sort of a trick is this?

LEADING MAN (*almost at the same time*). What's going to happen next?

JUVENILE LEAD. Where does *she* come from?

L'INGÉNUE. They've been holding her in reserve, I guess.

LEADING LADY. A vulgar trick!

THE FATHER (*dominating the protests*). Excuse me, all of you! Why are you so anxious to destroy in the name of a vulgar, commonplace sense of truth, this reality which comes to birth attracted and formed by the magic of the stage itself, which has indeed more right to live here than you, since it is much truer than you—if you don't mind my saying so? Which is the actress among you who is to play Madame Pace? Well, here is Madame Pace herself. And you will allow, I fancy, that the actress who acts her will be less true than this woman here, who is herself in person. You see my daughter recognized her and went over to her at once. Now you're going to witness the scene!

(*But the scene between the Stepdaughter and Madame Pace has already begun despite the protest of the Actors and the reply of the Father. It has begun quietly, naturally, in a manner impossible for the stage. So when the Actors, called to attention by the Father, turn round and see Madame Pace, who has placed one hand under the Stepdaughter's chin to raise her head, they observe her at first with great attention, but hearing her speak in an unintelligent manner their interest begins to wane.*)

THE MANAGER. Well? well?

LEADING MAN. What does she say?

LEADING LADY. One can't hear a word.

JUVENILE LEAD. Louder! Louder please!

THE STEPDAUGHTER (*leaving Madame Pace, who smiles a Sphinx-like smile, and advancing toward the Actors*).

Louder? Louder? What are you talking about? These aren't matters which can be shouted at the top of one's voice. If I have spoken them out loud, it was to shame him and have my revenge. (*Indicates Father.*) But for Madame it's quite a different matter.

THE MANAGER. Indeed? indeed? But here, you know, people have got to make themselves heard, my dear. Even we who are on the stage can't hear you. What will it be when the public's in the theater? And anyway, you can very well speak up now among yourselves, since we shan't be present to listen to you as we are now. You've got to pretend to be alone in a room at the back of a shop where no one can hear you.

(*The Stepdaughter coquettishly and with a touch of malice makes a sign of disagreement two or three times with her finger.*)

THE MANAGER. What do you mean by no?

THE STEPDAUGHTER (*sotto voce,[5] mysteriously*). There's someone who will hear us if she (*indicating Madame Pace*) speaks out loud.

THE MANAGER (*in consternation*). What? Have you got someone else to spring on us now? (*The Actors burst out laughing.*)

THE FATHER. No, no, sir. She is alluding to me. I've got to be here—there behind the door, in waiting; and Madame Pace knows it. In fact, if you will allow me, I'll go there at once, so I can be quite ready. (*Moves away.*)

THE MANAGER (*stopping him*). No! wait! wait! We must observe the conventions of the theater. Before you are ready . . .

THE STEPDAUGHTER (*interrupting him*). No, get on with it at once! I'm just dying, I tell you, to act this scene. If he's ready, I'm more than ready.

THE MANAGER (*shouting*). But, my dear young lady, first of all, we must have the scene between you and this lady . . . . (*Indicates Madame Pace.*) Do you understand?

THE STEPDAUGHTER. Good Heavens! She's been telling me what you know already: that mama's work is badly done again, that the material's ruined; and that if I want her to continue to help us in our misery I must be patient. . . .

MADAME PACE (*coming forward with an air of great importance*). Yes indeed, sir, I no wanta take advantage of her, I no wanta be hard. . . .

(*Note: Madame Pace is supposed to talk in a jargon half Italian, half English.*)

THE MANAGER (*alarmed*). What. What? She talks like that? (*The Actors burst out laughing again.*)

THE STEPDAUGHTER (*also laughing*). Yes yes, that's the way she talks, half English, half Italian! Most comical it is!

---

[5]**sotto voce** In a stage whisper

MADAME PACE. Itta seem not verra polite gentlemen laugha atta me eeff I trya best speaka English.

THE MANAGER. *Diamine!* Of course! Of course! Let her talk like that! Just what we want. Talk just like that, Madame, if you please! The effect will be certain. Exactly what was wanted to put a little comic relief into the crudity of the situation. Of course she talks like that! Magnificent!

THE STEPDAUGHTER. Magnificent? Certainly! When certain suggestions are made to one in language of that kind, the effect is certain, since it seems almost a joke. One feels inclined to laugh when one hears her talk about an "old signore" "who wanta talka nicely with you." Nice old signore, eh, Madame?

MADAME PACE. Not so old my dear, not so old! And even if you no lika him, he won't make any scandal!

THE MOTHER (*jumping up amid the amazement and consternation of the Actors, who had not been noticing her. They move to restrain her*). You old devil! You murderess!

THE STEPDAUGHTER (*running over to calm her Mother*). Calm yourself, Mother, calm yourself! Please don't. . . .

THE FATHER (*going to her also at the same time*). Calm yourself! Don't get excited! Sit down now!

THE MOTHER. Well then, take that woman away out of my sight.

THE STEPDAUGHTER (*to Manager*). It is impossible for my mother to remain here.

THE FATHER (*to Manager*). They can't be here together. And for this reason, you see: that woman there was not with us when we came. . . . If they are on together, the whole thing is given away inevitably, as you see.

THE MANAGER. It doesn't matter. This is only a first rough sketch—just to get an idea of the various points of the scene, even confusedly. . . . (*Turning to the Mother and leading her to her chair.*) Come along, my dear lady, sit down now, and let's get on with the scene. . . .

(*Meanwhile, the Stepdaughter, coming forward again, turns to Madame Pace.*)

THE STEPDAUGHTER. Come on, Madame, come on!

MADAME PACE (*offended*). No, no, *grazie.* I do not do anything witha your mother present.

THE STEPDAUGHTER. Nonsense! Introduce this "old signore" who wants to talk nicely to me. (*Addressing the Company imperiously.*) We've got to do this scene one way or another, haven't we? Come on! (*To Madame Pace.*) You can go!

MADAME PACE. Ah yes! I go'way! I go'way! Certainly! (*Exits furious.*)

THE STEPDAUGHTER (*to the Father*). Now you make your entry. No, you needn't go over there. Come here. Let's suppose you've already come in. Like that, yes! I'm here with bowed head, modest like. Come on! Out with your voice! Say "Good morning, Miss" in that peculiar tone, that special tone. . . .

THE MANAGER. Excuse me, but are you the Manager, or am I? (*To the Father, who looks undecided and perplexed.*) Get on with it, man! Go down there to the back of the stage. You needn't go off. Then come right forward here.

(*The Father does as he is told, looking troubled and perplexed at first. But as soon as he begins to move, the reality of the action affects him, and he begins to smile and to be more natural. The Actors watch intently.*)

THE MANAGER (*sotto voce, quickly to the Prompter in his box*). Ready! ready! Get ready to write now.

THE FATHER (*coming forward and speaking in a different tone*). Good afternoon, Miss!

THE STEPDAUGHTER (*head bowed down slightly, with restrained disgust*). Good afternoon!

THE FATHER (*looks under her hat which partly covers her face. Perceiving she is very young, he makes an exclamation, partly of fear lest he compromise himself in a risky adventure*). Ah . . . but . . . ah . . . I say . . . this is not the first time that you have come here, is it?

THE STEPDAUGHTER (*modestly*). No sir.

THE FATHER. You've been here before, eh? (*Then seeing her nod agreement.*) More than once? (*Waits for her to answer, looks under her hat, smiles, and then says:*) Well then, there's no need to be so shy, is there? May I take off your hat?

THE STEPDAUGHTER (*anticipating him and with veiled disgust*). No sir . . . I'll do it myself. (*Takes it off quickly.*)

(*The Mother, who watches the progress of the scene with the Son and the other two children who cling to her, is on thorns; and follows with varying expressions of sorrow, indignation, anxiety, and horror the words and actions of the other two. From time to time she hides her face in her hands and sobs.*)

THE MOTHER. Oh, my God, my God!

THE FATHER (*playing his part with a touch of gallantry*). Give it to me! I'll put it down. (*Takes hat from her hands.*) But a dear little head like yours ought to have a smarter hat. Come and help me choose one from the stock, won't you?

L'INGÉNUE (*interrupting*). I say . . . those are our hats you know.

THE MANAGER (*furious*). Silence! silence! Don't try and be funny, if you please. . . . We're playing the scene now, I'd have you notice. (*To the Stepdaughter.*) Begin again, please!

THE STEPDAUGHTER (*continuing*). No thank you, sir.

THE FATHER. Oh, come now. Don't talk like that. You must take it. I shall be upset if you don't. There are some lovely little hats here; and then—Madame will be pleased. She expects it, anyway, you know.

THE STEPDAUGHTER. No, no! I couldn't wear it!

THE FATHER. Oh, you're thinking about what they'd say at home if they saw you come in with a new hat? My dear girl, there's always a way round these little matters, you know.

THE STEPDAUGHTER (*all keyed up*). No, it's not that. I couldn't wear it because I am . . . as you see . . . you might have noticed . . .

(*Showing her black dress.*)

THE FATHER. . . . in mourning! Of course: I beg your pardon: I'm frightfully sorry. . . .

THE STEPDAUGHTER (*forcing herself to conquer her indignation and nausea*). Stop! Stop! It's I who must thank you. There's no need for you to feel mortified or specially sorry. Don't think any more of what I've said. (*Tries to smile.*) I must forget that I am dressed so. . . .

THE MANAGER (*interrupting and turning to the Prompter*). Stop a minute! Stop! Don't write that down. Cut out that last bit. (*Then go to the Father and Stepdaughter.*) Fine! it's going fine! (*To the Father only.*) And now you can go on as we arranged. (*To the Actors.*) Pretty good that scene, where he offers her the hat, eh?

THE STEPDAUGHTER. The best's coming now. Why can't we go on?

THE MANAGER. Have a little patience! (*To the Actors.*) Of course, it must be treated rather lightly.

LEADING MAN. Still, with a bit of go in it!

LEADING LADY. Of course! It's easy enough! (*To Leading Man.*) Shall you and I try it now?

LEADING MAN. Why, yes! I'll prepare my entrance.

(*Exit in order to make his entrance.*)

THE MANAGER (*to Leading Lady*). See here! The scene between you and Madame Pace is finished. I'll have it written out properly after. You remain here . . . oh, where are you going?

LEADING LADY. One minute. I want to put my hat on again. (*Goes over to hatrack and puts her hat on her head.*)

THE MANAGER. Good! You stay here with your head bowed down a bit.

THE STEPDAUGHTER. But she isn't dressed in black.

LEADING LADY. But I shall be, and much more effectively than you.

THE MANAGER (*to Stepdaughter*). Be quiet please, and watch! You'll be able to learn something. (*Clapping his hands.*) Come on! come on! Entrance, please!

(*The door at rear of stage opens, and the Leading Man enters with the lively manner of an old gallant. The rendering of the scene by the Actors from the very first words is seen to be quite a different thing, though it has not in any way the air of a parody. Naturally, the Stepdaughter and the Father, not being able to recognize themselves in the Leading Lady and the Leading Man, who deliver their words in different tones and with a different psychology, express, sometimes with smiles, sometimes with gestures, the impression they receive.*)

LEADING MAN. Good afternoon, Miss . . .

THE FATHER (*at once unable to contain himself*). No! no!

(*The Stepdaughter, noticing the way the Leading Man enters, bursts out laughing.*)

THE MANAGER (*furious*). Silence! And you, please, just stop that laughing. If we go on like this, we shall never finish.

THE STEPDAUGHTER. Forgive me, sir, but it's natural enough. This lady (*indicating Leading Lady*) stands there still; but if she is supposed to be me, I can assure you that if I heard anyone say "Good afternoon" in that manner and in that tone, I should burst out laughing as I did.

THE FATHER. Yes, yes, the manner, the tone . . .

THE MANAGER. Nonsense! Rubbish! Stand aside and let me see the action.

LEADING MAN. If I've got to represent an old fellow who's coming into a house of an equivocal character . . .

THE MANAGER. Don't listen to them, for Heaven's sake! Do it again! It goes fine. (*Waiting for the Actors to begin again.*) Well?

LEADING MAN. Good afternoon, Miss.

LEADING LADY. Good afternoon.

LEADING MAN (*imitating the gesture of the Father when he looked under the hat, and then expressing quite clearly first satisfaction and then fear*): Ah, but . . . I say . . . this is not the first time that you have come here, is it?

THE MANAGER. Good, but not quite so heavily. Like this. (*Acts himself.*) "This isn't the first time that you have come here" . . . (*To Leading Lady.*) And you say: "No, sir."

LEADING LADY. No, sir.

LEADING MAN. You've been here before, more than once.

THE MANAGER. No, no, stop! Let her nod "yes" first. "You've been here before, eh?" (*The Leading Lady lifts up her head slightly and closes her eyes as though in disgust. Then she inclines her head twice.*)

THE STEPDAUGHTER (*unable to contain herself*). Oh my God! (*Puts a hand to her mouth to prevent herself from laughing.*)

THE MANAGER. (*turning round*). What's the matter?

THE STEPDAUGHTER. Nothing, nothing!

THE MANAGER (*to Leading Man*). Go on!

LEADING MAN. You've been here before, eh? Well then, there's no need to be so shy, is there? May I take off your hat?

(*The Leading Man says this last speech in such a tone and with such gestures that the Stepdaughter, though she has her hand to her mouth, cannot keep from laughing.*)

LEADING LADY (*indignant*). I'm not going to stop here to be made a fool of by that woman there.

LEADING MAN. Neither am I! I'm through with it!

THE MANAGER (*shouting to Stepdaughter*). Silence! for once and for all, I tell you!

THE STEPDAUGHTER. Forgive me! forgive me!

THE MANAGER. You haven't any manners: that's what it is! You go too far.

THE FATHER (*endeavoring to intervene*). Yes, it's true, but excuse her . . .

THE MANAGER. Excuse what? It's absolutely disgusting.

THE FATHER. Yes, sir, but believe me, it has such a strange effect when . . .

THE MANAGER. Strange. Why strange? Where is it strange?

THE FATHER. No, sir; I admire your actors—this gentleman here, this lady; but they are certainly not us!

THE MANAGER. I should hope not. Evidently they cannot be you, if they are actors.

THE FATHER. Just so: actors! Both of them act our parts exceedingly well. But, believe me, it produces quite a different effect on us. They want to be us, but they aren't, all the same.

THE MANAGER. What is then anyway?

THE FATHER. Something that is . . . that is theirs—and no longer ours . . .

THE MANAGER. But naturally, inevitably, I've told you so already.

THE FATHER. Yes, I understand . . . I understand . . .

THE MANAGER. Well then, let's have no more of it! (*Turning to the Actors.*) We'll have the rehearsals by ourselves, afterwards, in the ordinary way. I never could stand rehearsing with the author present. He's never satisfied! (*Turning to Father and Stepdaughter.*) Come on! Let's get on with it again; and try and see if you can't keep from laughing.

THE STEPDAUGHTER. Oh, I shan't laugh any more. There's a nice little bit coming from me now: you'll see.

THE MANAGER. Well then: when she says "Don't think any more of what I've said, I must forget, etc.," you (*addressing the Father*) come in sharp with "I understand"; and then you ask her . . .

THE STEPDAUGHTER (*interrupting*). What?

THE MANAGER. Why she is in mourning.

THE STEPDAUGHTER. Not at all! See here: when I told him that it was useless for me to be thinking about my wearing mourning, do you know how he answered me? "Ah well," he said, "then let's take off this little frock."

THE MANAGER. Great! Just what we want, to make a riot in the theater!

THE STEPDAUGHER. But it's the truth!

THE MANAGER. What does that matter? Acting is our business here. Truth up to a certain point, but no further.

THE STEPDAUGHTER. What do you want to do then?

THE MANAGER. You'll see! Leave it to me.

THE STEPDAUGHTER. No sir! What you want to do is to piece together a little romantic sentimental scene out of my disgust, out of all the reasons, each more cruel and viler than the other, why I am what I am. He is to ask me why I'm in mourning; and I'm to answer with tears in my eyes, that it is just two months since papa died. No sir, no! He's got to say to me, as he did say. "Well, let's take off this little dress at once." And I, with my two months' mourning in my heart, went there behind that screen, and with these fingers tingling with shame . . .

THE MANAGER (*running his hands through his hair*). For Heaven's sake! What are you saying?

THE STEPDAUGHTER (*crying out excitedly*). The truth! The truth!

THE MANAGER. It may be. I don't deny it, and I can understand all your horror; but you must surely see that you can't have this kind of thing on the stage. It won't go.

THE STEPDAUGHTER. Not possible, eh. Very well! I'm much obliged to you—but I'm off.

THE MANAGER. Now be reasonable. Don't lose your temper!

THE STEPDAUGHTER. I won't stop here! I won't! I can see you fixed it all up with him in your office. All this talk about what is possible for the stage . . . I understand! He wants to get at his complicated "cerebral drama," to have his famous remorses and torments acted; but I want to act my part, *my part*!

THE MANAGER (*annoyed, shaking his shoulders*). Ah! Just *your* part! But, if you will pardon me, there are other parts than yours: His (*indicating the Father*) and hers (*indicating the Mother*)! On the stage you can't have a character becoming too prominent and overshadowing all the others. The thing is to pack them all into a neat little framework and then act what is actable. I am aware of the fact that everyone has his own interior life which he wants very much to put forward. But the difficulty lies in this fact: to set out just so much as is necessary for the stage, taking the other characters into consideration, and at the same time hint at the unrevealed interior life of each. I am willing to admit, my dear young lady, that from your point of view it would be a fine idea if each character could tell the public all his troubles in a nice monologue or a regular one hour lecture. (*Good humoredly.*) You must restrain yourself, my dear, and in your own interest, too; because this fury of yours, this exaggerated disgust you show, may make a bad impression, you know. After you have confessed to me that there were others before him at Madame Pace's and more than once . . .

THE STEPDAUGHTER (*bowing her head, impressed*). It's true. But remember those other mean him for me all the same.

THE MANAGER (*not understanding*). What? The others? What do you mean?

THE STEPDAUGHTER. For one who has gone wrong, sir, he who was responsible for the first fault is responsible for all that follow. He is responsible for my faults, was, even before I was born. Look at him, and see if it isn't true!

THE MANAGER. Well, well! And does the weight of so much responsibility seem nothing to you? Give him a chance to act it, to get it over!

THE STEPDAUGHTER. How? How can he act all his "noble remorses," all his "moral torments," if you want to spare him the horror of being discovered one day—after he had asked her what he did ask her—in the arms of her, that already fallen woman, that child, sir, that child he used to watch come out of school? (*She is moved.*)

(*The Mother at this point is overcome with emotion and*

breaks out into a fit of crying. All are touched. A long pause.)

THE STEPDAUGHTER (*as soon as the Mother becomes a little quieter, adds resolutely and gravely*). At present, we are unknown to the public. Tomorrow, you will act as you wish, treating us in your own manner. But do you really want to see drama, do you want to see it flash out as it really did?

THE MANAGER. Of course! That's just what I do want, so I can use as much of it as is possible.

THE STEPDAUGHTER. Well then, ask that Mother there to leave us.

THE MOTHER (*changing her low plaint into a sharp cry*). No! No! Don't permit, it, sir, don't permit it!

THE MANAGER. But it's only to try it.

THE MOTHER. I can't bear it. I can't.

THE MANAGER. But since it has happened already . . . I don't understand!

THE MOTHER. It's taking place now. It happens all the time. My torment isn't a pretended one. I live and feel every minute of my torture. Those two children there—have you heard them speak? They can't speak anymore. They cling to me to keep my torment actual and vivid for me. But for themselves, they do not exist, they aren't anymore. And she (*indicating the Stepdaughter*) has run away, she has left me, and is lost. If I now see her here before me, it is only to renew for me the tortures I have suffered for her too.

THE FATHER. The eternal moment! She (*indicating the Stepdaughter*) is here to catch me, fix me, and hold me eternally in the stocks for that one fleeing and shameful moment of my life. She can't give it up! And you, sir, cannot either fairly spare me it.

THE MANAGER. I never said I didn't want to act it. It will form, as a matter of fact, the nucleus of the whole first act right up to her surprise. (*Indicates the Mother.*)

THE FATHER. Just so! This is my punishment: the passion in all of us that must culminate in her final cry.

THE STEPDAUGHTER. I can hear it still in my ears. It's driven me mad, that cry!—You can put me on as you like; it doesn't matter. Fully dressed, if you like—provided I have at least the arm bare; because, standing like this (*she goes close to the Father and leans her head on his breast*) with my head so, and my arms around his neck, I saw a vein pulsing in my arm here; and then, as if that live vein had awakened disgust in me, I closed my eyes like this, and let my head sink on his breast. (*Turning to the Mother.*) Cry out, mother! Cry out! (*Buries head in Father's breast, and with her shoulders raised as if to prevent her hearing the cry, adds in tones of intense emotion.*) Cry out as you did then!

THE MOTHER (*coming forward to separate them*). No! My daughter, my daughter! (*And after having pulled her away from him.*) You brute! you brute! She is my daughter! Don't you see she's my daughter?

THE MANAGER (*walking backward toward footlights*). Fine! fine! Damned good! And then, of course—curtain!

THE FATHER (*going toward him excitedly*). Yes, of course, because that's the way it really happened.

THE MANAGER (*convinced and pleased*). Oh, yes, no doubt about it. Curtain here, curtain.

(*At the reiterated cry of the Manager, the Machinist lets the curtain down, leaving the Manager and the Father in front of it before the footlights.*)

THE MANAGER. The darned idiot! I said "curtain" to show the act should end there, and he goes and lets it down in earnest. (*To the Father, while he pulls the curtain back to go on to the stage again.*) Yes, yes, it's all right. Effect certain! That's the right ending. I'll guarantee the first act at any rate.

ACT III

(*When the curtain goes up again, it is seen that the stage hands have shifted the bit of scenery used in the last part and have rigged up instead at the back of the stage a drop, with some trees, and one or two wings. A portion of a fountain basin is visible. The Mother is sitting on the right with the two children by her side. The Son is on the same side, but away from the others. He seems bored, angry, and full of shame. The Father and the Stepdaughter are also seated toward the right front. On the other side (left) are the Actors, much in the positions they occupied before the curtain was lowered. Only the Manager is standing up in the middle of the stage, with his hand closed over his mouth, in the act of meditating.*)

THE MANAGER (*shaking his shoulders after a brief pause*). Ah yes: the second act! Leave it to me, leave it all to me as we arranged, and you'll see! It'll go fine!

THE STEPDAUGHTER. Our entry into his house (*indicates Father*) in spite of him . . . (*Indicates the Son.*)

THE MANAGER (*out of patience*). Leave it to me, I tell you!

THE STEPDAUGHTER. Do let it be clear, at any rate, that it is in spite of my wishes.

THE MOTHER (*from her corner, shaking her head*). For all the good that's come of it . . .

THE STEPDAUGHTER (*turning toward her quickly*). It doesn't matter. The more harm done us the more remorse for him.

THE MANAGER (*impatiently*). I understand! Good Heavens! I understand! I'm taking it into account.

THE MOTHER (*supplicatingly*). I beg you, sir, to let it appear quite plain that for conscience's sake I did try in every way . . .

THE STEPDAUGHTER (*interrupting indignantly and continuing for the Mother*). . . . . to pacify me, to dissuade me from spiting him. (*To Manager.*) Do as she wants: satisfy her, because it is true! I enjoy it immensely. Anyhow, as you can see, the meeker she is, the more she tries to get at his heart, the more distant and aloof does he become.

THE MANAGER. Are we going to begin this second act or not?

THE STEPDAUGHTER. I'm not going to talk any more now. But I must tell you this: you can't have the whole action take place in the garden, as you suggest. It isn't possible!

THE MANAGER. Why not?

THE STEPDAUGHTER. Because he (*indicates the Son again*) is always shut up alone in his room. And then there's all the part of that poor dazed-looking boy there which takes place indoors.

THE MANAGER. Maybe! On the other hand, you will understand—we can't change scenes three or four times in one act.

LEADING MAN. They used to once.

THE MANAGER. Yes, when the public was up to the level of that child there.

LEADING LADY. It makes the illusion easier.

THE FATHER (*irritated*). The illusion! For Heaven's sake, don't say illusion. Please don't use that word, which is particularly painful for us.

THE MANAGER (*astounded*). And why, if you please?

THE FATHER. It's painful, cruel, really cruel; and you ought to understand that.

THE MANAGER. But why? What ought we to say then? The illusion, I tell you, sir, which we've got to create for the audience. . . .

THE LEADING MAN. With our acting.

THE MANAGER. The illusion of a reality.

THE FATHER. I understand; but you, perhaps, do not understand us. Forgive me! You see . . . here for you and your actors, the thing is only—and rightly so . . . a kind of game. . . .

THE LEADING LADY (*interrupting indignantly*). A game! We're not children here, if you please! We are serious actors.

THE FATHER. I don't deny it. What I mean is the game, or play, of your art, which has to give, as the gentleman says, a perfect illusion of reality.

THE MANAGER. Precisely—!

THE FATHER. Now, if you consider the fact that we (*indicates himself and the other five Characters*), as we are, have no other reality outside of this illusion. . . .

THE MANAGER (*astonished, looking at his Actors, who are also amazed*). And what does that mean?

THE FATHER (*after watching them for a moment with a wan smile*). As I say, sir, that which is a game of art for you is our sole reality. (*Brief pause. He goes a step or two nearer the Manager and adds.*) But not only for us, you know, by the way. Just you think it over well. (*Looks him in the eyes.*) Can you tell me who you are?

THE MANAGER (*perplexed, half smiling*). What? Who am I? I am myself.

THE FATHER. And if I were to tell you that that isn't true, because you and I . . . ?

THE MANAGER. I should say you were mad—! (*The Actors laugh.*)

THE FATHER. You're quite right to laugh: because we are all making believe here. (*To Manager.*) And you can therefore object that it's only for a joke that that gentleman there (*indicates the Leading Man*), who naturally is himself, has to be me, who am on the contrary myself—this thing you see here. You see I've caught you in a trap! (*The Actors laugh.*)

THE MANAGER (*annoyed*). But we've had all this over once before. Do you want to begin again?

THE FATHER. No, no! That wasn't my meaning! In fact, I should like to request you to abandon this game of art (*looking at the Leading Lady as if anticipating her*) which you are accustomed to play here with your actors, and to ask you seriously once again: who are you?

THE MANAGER (*astonished and irritated, turning to his Actors*). If this fellow here hasn't got a nerve! A man who calls himself a character comes and asks me who I am!

THE FATHER (*with dignity, but not offended*). A character, sir, may always ask a man who he is. Because a character has really a life of his own, marked with his especial characteristics; for which reason he is always "somebody." But a man—I'm not speaking of you now—may very well be "nobody."

THE MANAGER. Yes, but you are asking these questions of me, the boss, the manager! Do you understand?

THE FATHER. But only in order to know if you, as you really are now, see yourself as you once were with all the illusions that were yours then, with all the things both inside and outside of you as they seemed to you—as they were then indeed for you. Well, sir, if you think of all those illusions that mean nothing to you now, of all those things which don't even *seem* to you to exist anymore, while once they *were* for you, don't you feel that—I won't say these boards—but the very earth under your feet is sinking away from you when you reflect that in the same way this *you* as you feel it today—all this present reality of yours—is fated to seem a mere illusion to you tomorrow?

THE MANAGER (*without having understood much, but astonished by the specious argument*). Well, well! And where does all this take us anyway?

THE FATHER. Oh, nowhere! It's only to show you that if we (*indicating the Characters*) have no other reality beyond the illusion, you too must not count overmuch on your reality as you feel it today, since, like that of yesterday, it may prove an illusion for you tomorrow.

THE MANAGER (*determining to make fun of him*). Ah, excellent! Then you'll be saying next that you, with this comedy of yours that you brought here to act, are truer and more real than I am.

THE FATHER (*with the greatest seriousness*). But of course; without doubt!

THE MANAGER. Ah, really?

THE FATHER. Why, I thought you'd understand that from the beginning.

THE MANAGER. More real than I?

THE FATHER. If your reality can change from one day to another. . . .

THE MANAGER. But everyone knows it can change. It is always changing, the same as anyone else's.

THE FATHER (*with a cry*). No, sir, not ours! Look here! That is the very difference! Our reality doesn't change: it can't change! It can't be other than what it is, because it is already fixed for ever. It's terrible. Ours is an immutable reality which should make you shudder when you approach us if you are really conscious of the fact that your reality is mere transitory and fleeting illusion, taking this form today and that tomorrow, according to the conditions, according to your will, your sentiments, which in turn are controlled by an intellect that shows them to you today in one manner and tomorrow . . . who knows how? . . . Illusions of reality represented in this fatuous comedy of life that never ends, nor can ever end! Because if tomorrow it were to end . . . then why, all would be finished.

THE MANAGER. Oh, for God's sake, will you *at least* finish with this philosophizing and let us try and shape this comedy which you yourself have brought me here? You argue and philosophize a bit too much, my dear sir. You know you seem to me almost, almost . . . (*Stops and looks him over from head to foot.*) Ah, by the way, I think you introduced yourself to me as a—what shall . . . we say—a "character," created by an author who did not afterward care to make a drama of his own creations.

THE FATHER. It is the simple truth, sir.

THE MANAGER. Nonsense! Cut that out, please! None of us believes it, because it isn't a thing, as you must recognize yourself, which one can believe seriously. If you want to know, it seems to me you are trying to imitate the manner of a certain author whom I heartily detest—I warn you—although I have unfortunately bound myself to put on one of his works. As a matter of fact, I was just starting to rehearse it, when you arrived. (*Turning to the Actors.*) And this is what we've gained—out of the frying-pan into the fire!

THE FATHER. I don' know to what author you may be alluding, but believe me I feel what I think; and I seem to be philosophizing only for those who do not think what they feel, because they blind themselves with their own sentiment. I know that for many people this self-blinding seems much more "human"; but the contrary is really true. For man never reasons so much and becomes so introspective as when he suffers; since he is anxious to get at the cause of his sufferings, to learn who has produced them, and whether it is just or unjust that he should have to bear them. On the other hand, when he is happy, he takes his happiness as it comes and doesn't analyze it, just as if happiness were his right. The animals suffer without reasoning about their sufferings. But take the case of a man who suffers and begins to reason about it. Oh no! it can't be allowed! Let him suffer like an animal, and then—ah yes, he is "human"!

THE MANAGER. Look here! Look here! You're off again, philosophizing worse than ever.

THE FATHER. Because I suffer, sir! I'm not philosophizing: I'm crying aloud the reason of my sufferings.

THE MANAGER (*makes brusque movement as he is taken with a new idea*). I should like to know if anyone has ever heard of a character who gets right out of his part and perorates and speechifies as you do. Have you ever heard of a case? I haven't.

THE FATHER. You have never met such a case, sir, because authors, as a rule, hide the labor of their creations. When the characters are really alive before their author, the latter does nothing but follow them in their action, in other words, in the situations which they suggest to him; and he has to will them the way they will themselves—for there's trouble if he doesn't. When a character is born, he acquires at once such an independence, even of his own author, that he can be imagined by everybody even in many other situations where the author never dreamed of placing him; and so he acquires for himself a meaning which the author never thought of giving him.

THE MANAGER. Yes, yes, I know this.

THE FATHER. What is there then to marvel at in us? Imagine such a misfortune for characters as I have described to you: to be born of an author's fantasy, and be denied life by him; and then answer me if these characters left alive, and yet without life, weren't right in doing what they did do and are doing now, after they have attempted everything in their power to persuade him to give them their stage life. We've all tried him in turn, I, she (*indicating the Stepdaughter*) and she (*indicating the Mother*).

THE STEPDAUGHTER. It's true. I too have sought to tempt him, many, many times, when he has been sitting at his writing table, feeling a bit melancholy, at the twilight hour. He would sit in his armchair too lazy to switch on the light, and all the shadows that crept into his room were full of our presence coming to tempt him. (*As if she saw herself still there by the writing table, and was annoyed by the presence of the Actors.*) Oh, if you would only go away, go away and leave us alone—mother here with that son of hers—I with that child—that boy there always alone—and then I with him (*just hints at the Father*)—and then I alone, alone . . . in those shadows! (*Makes a sudden movement as if in the vision she has of herself illuminating those shadows she wanted to seize hold of herself.*) Ah! my life! my life! Oh, what scenes we proposed to him—and I tempted him more than any of the others!

THE FATHER. Maybe. But perhaps it was your fault that he refused to give us life: because you were too insistent, too troublesome.

THE STEPDAUGHTER. Nonsense! Didn't he make me so himself? (*Goes close to the Manager to tell him as if in confidence.*) In my opinion he abandoned us in a fit of depression, of disgust for the ordinary theater as the public knows it and likes it.

THE SON. Exactly what it was, sir; exactly that!

THE FATHER. Not at all! Don't believe it for a minute. Listen to me! You'll be doing quite right to modify, as you suggest, the excesses both of this girl here, who wants to do too much, and of this young man, who won't do anything at all.

THE SON. No, nothing!

THE MANAGER. You too get over the mark occasionally, my dear sir, if I may say so.

THE FATHER. I? When? Where?

THE MANAGER. Always! Continuously! Then there's this insistence of yours in trying to make us believe you are a character. And then too, you must really argue and philosophize less, you know, much less.

THE FATHER. Well, if you want to take away from me the possibility of representing the torment of my spirit which never gives me peace, you will be suppressing me: that's all. Every true man, sir, who is a little above the level of the beasts and plants does not live for the sake of living, without knowing how to live; but he lives so as to give a meaning and a value of his own to life. For me this is *everything*. I cannot give up this, just to represent a mere fact as she (*indicating the Stepdaughter*) wants. It's all very well for her, since her "vendetta" lies in the "fact." I'm not going to do it. It destroys my *raison d'être*.

THE MANAGER. Your *raison d'être*! Oh, we're going ahead fine! First she starts off, and then you jump in. At this rate, we'll never finish.

THE FATHER. Now, don't be offended! Have it your own way—provided, however, that within the limit of the parts you assign us each one's sacrifice isn't too great.

THE MANAGER. You've got to understand that you can't go on arguing at your own pleasure. Drama is action, sir, action and not confounded philosophy.

THE FATHER. All right. I'll do just as much arguing and philosophizing as everybody does when he is considering his own torments.

THE MANAGER. If the drama permits! But for Heaven's sake, man, let's get along and come to the scene.

THE STEPDAUGHTER. It seems to me we've got too much action with our coming into his house. (*Indicating Father.*) You said, before, you couldn't change the scene every five minutes.

THE MANAGER. Of course not. What we've got to do is combine and group up all the facts in one simultaneous, close-knit action. We can't have it as you want, with your little brother wandering like a ghost from room to room, hiding behind doors and mediating a project which—what did you say it did to him?

THE STEPDAUGHTER. Consumes him, sir, wastes him away!

THE MANAGER. Well, it may be. And then at the same time, you want the little girl there to be playing in the garden . . . one in the house, and other in the garden; isn't that it?

THE STEPDAUGHTER. Yes, in the sun, in the sun! That is my only pleasure: to see her happy and careless in the garden after the misery and squalor of the horrible room where we all four slept together. And I had to sleep with her—I, do you understand?—with my vile contaminated body next to hers; with her folding me fast in her loving little arms. In the garden, whenever she spied me, she would run to take my by the hand. She didn't care for the big flowers, only the little ones; and she loved to show me them and pet me.

THE MANAGER. Well then, we'll have it in the garden. Everything shall happen in the garden; and we'll group the other scenes there. (*Calls a Stage Hand.*) Here, a backcloth with trees and something to do as a fountain basin. (*Turning round to look at the back of the stage.*) Ah, you've fixed it up. Good! (*To Stepdaughter.*) This is just to give an idea, of course. The Boy, instead of hiding behind the doors, will wander about here in the garden, hiding behind the trees. But it's going to be rather difficult to find a child to do that scene with you where she shows you the flowers. (*Turning to the Boy.*) Come forward a little, will you please? Let's try it now! Come along! come along! (*Then seeing him come shyly forward, full of fear and looking lost.*) It's a nice business, this lad here. What's the matter with him? We'll have to give him a word or two to say. (*Goes close to him, puts a hand on his shoulders, and leads him behind one of the trees.*) Come on! come on! Let me see you a little! Hide here . . . yes, like that. Try and show your head just a little as if you were looking for someone. . . . (*Goes back to observe the effect, when the Boy at once goes through the action.*) Excellent! fine! (*Turning to Stepdaughter.*) Suppose the little girl there were to surprise him as he looks round, and run over to him, so we could give him a word or two to say?

THE STEPDAUGHTER. It's useless to hope he will speak, as long as that fellow there is here. . . . (*Indicates the Son.*) You must send him away first.

THE SON (*jumping up*). Delighted! Delighted! I don't ask for anything better. (*Begins to move away.*)

THE MANAGER (*at once stopping him*). No! No! Where are you going? Wait a bit!

(*The Mother gets up alarmed and terrified at the thought that he is really about to go away. Instinctively she lifts her arms to prevent him, without, however, leaving her seat.*)

THE SON (*to Manager, who stops him*). I've got nothing to do with this affair. Let me go, please! Let me go!

THE MANAGER. What do you mean by saying you've got nothing to do with this?

THE STEPDAUGHTER (*calmly, with irony*). Don't bother to stop him: he won't go away.

THE FATHER. He has to act the terrible scene in the garden with his mother.

THE SON (*suddenly resolute and with dignity*). I shall act nothing at all. I've said so from the very beginning. (*To the Manager.*) Let me go!

THE STEPDAUGHTER (*going over to the Manager*). Allow me? (*Puts down the Manager's arm which is restraining the Son.*) Well, go away then, if you want to! (*The Son looks at her with contempt and hatred. She laughs and says*) You see, he can't, he can't go away! He is obliged to stay here, indissolubly bound to the chain. If I, who fly off when that happens which has to happen because I can't bear him—if I am still here and support that face and expression of his, you can well imagine that he is unable to move. He has to remain here, has to stop with that nice father of his, and that mother whose only son he is. (*Turning to the Mother.*) Come on, mother, come along! (*Turning to Manager to indicate her.*) You see, she was getting up to keep him back. (*To the Mother, beckoning her with her hand.*) Come on, come on! (*Then to Manager.*) You can imagine how little she wants to show these actors of yours what she really feels; but so eager is she to get near him that. . . . There, you see? She is willing to act her part. (*And in fact, the Mother approaches him; and as soon as the Stepdaughter has finished speaking, opens her arms to signify that she consents.*)

THE SON (*suddenly*). No! no! If I can't go away, then I'll stop here; but I repeat: I act nothing!

THE FATHER (*to Manager excitedly*). You can force him, sir.

THE SON. Nobody can force me.

THE FATHER. I can.

THE STEPDAUGHTER. Wait a minute, wait . . . First of all, the baby has to go to the fountain. . . . (*Runs to take the Child and leads her to the fountain.*)

THE MANAGER. Yes, yes of course; that's it. Both at the same time.

(*The Second Lady Lead and the Juvenile Lead at this point separate themselves from the group of Actors. One watches the Mother attentively; the other moves about studying the movements and manner of the Son whom he will have to act.*)

THE SON (*to Manager*). What do you mean by both at the same time? It isn't right. There was no scene between me and her. (*Indicates the Mother.*) Ask her how it was.

THE MOTHER. Yes, it's true. I had come into his room. . . .

THE SON. Into my room, do you understand? Nothing to do with the garden.

THE MANAGER. It doesn't matter. Haven't I told you we've got to group the action?

THE SON (*observing the Juvenile Lead studying him*). What do you want?

THE JUVENILE LEAD. Nothing! I was just looking at you.

THE SON (*turning toward the Second Lady Lead*). Ah, she's at it too: to re-act her part! (*Indicating the Mother.*)

THE MANAGER. Exactly! And it seems to me that you ought to be grateful to them for their interest.

THE SON. Yes, but haven't you yet perceived that it isn't possible to live in front of a mirror which not only freezes us with the image of ourselves, but throws our likeness back at us with a horrible grimace?

THE FATHER. That is true, absolutely true. You must see that.

THE MANAGER (*to Second Lady Lead and Juvenile Lead*). He's right! Move away from them!

THE SON. Do as you like. I'm out of this!

THE MANAGER. Be quiet, you, will you? And let me hear your mother! (*To Mother.*) You were saying you had entered. . . .

THE MOTHER. Yes, into his room, because I couldn't stand it any longer. I went to empty my heart to him of all the anguish that tortures me. . . . But as soon as he saw me come in. . . .

THE SON. Nothing happened! There was no scene. I went away, that's all! I don't care for scenes!

THE MOTHER. It's true, true. That's how it was.

THE MANAGER. Well now, we've got to this bit between you and him. It's indispensable.

THE MOTHER. I'm ready . . . when you are ready. If you could only find a chance for me to tell him what I feel here in my heart.

THE FATHER (*going to Son in a great rage*). You'll do this for your mother, for your mother, do you understand?

THE SON (*quite determined*). I do nothing!

THE FATHER (*taking hold of him and shaking him*). For God's sake, do as I tell you! Don't you hear your mother asking you for a favor? Haven't you even got the guts to be a son?

THE SON (*taking hold of the Father*). No! No! And for God's sake stop it, or else. . . . (*General agitation. The Mother, frightened, tries to separate them.*)

THE MOTHER (*pleading*). Please! please!

THE FATHER (*not leaving hold of the Son*). You've got to obey, do you hear?

THE SON (*almost crying from rage*). What does it mean, this madness you've got? (*They separate.*) Have you no decency, that you insist on showing everyone our shame? I won't do it! I won't! And I stand for the will of our author in this. He didn't want to put us on the stage, after all!

THE MANAGER. Man alive! You came here . . .

THE SON (*indicating Father*). He did! I didn't!

THE MANAGER. Aren't you here now?

THE SON. It was his wish, and he dragged us along with him. He's told you not only the things that did happen, but also things that have never happened at all.

THE MANAGER. Well, tell me then what did happen. You went out of your room without saying a word?

THE SON. Without a word, so as to avoid a scene!

THE MANAGER. And then what did you do?

THE SON. Nothing . . . walking in the garden. . . .

(*Hesitates for a moment with expression of gloom.*)

THE MANAGER (*coming closer to him, interested by his extraordinary reserve*). Well, well . . . walking in the garden. . . .

THE SON (*exasperated*). Why on earth do you insist? It's horrible!

(The Mother trembles, sobs, and looks toward the fountain.)

THE MANAGER *(slowly observing the glance and turning toward the Son with increasing apprehension)*. The baby?

THE SON. There in the fountain. . . .

THE FATHER *(pointing with tender pity to the Mother)*. She was follow him at the moment. . . .

THE MANAGER *(to the Son anxiously)*. And then you. . . .

THE SON. I ran over to her; I was jumping in to drag her out when I saw something that froze my blood . . . the boy standing stock still, with eyes like a madman's, watching his little drowned sister, in the fountain! *(The Stepdaughter bends over the fountain to hide the Child. She sobs.)* Then. . . . *(A revolver shot rings out behind the trees where the Boy is hidden.)*

THE MOTHER *(with a cry of terror runs over in that direction together with several of the Actors amid general confusion)*. My son! My son! *(Then amid the cries and exclamations one hears her voice.)* Help! Help!

THE MANAGER *(pushing the Actors aside while they lift up the Boy and carry him off)*. Is he really wounded?

SOME ACTORS. He's dead! dead!

OTHER ACTORS. No, no, it's only make-believe, it's only pretense!

THE FATHER *(with a terrible cry)*. Pretense? Reality, sir, reality!

THE MANAGER. Pretense? Reality? To hell with it all! Never in my life has such a thing happened to me. I've lost a whole day over these people, a whole day!

LATIN AMERICA

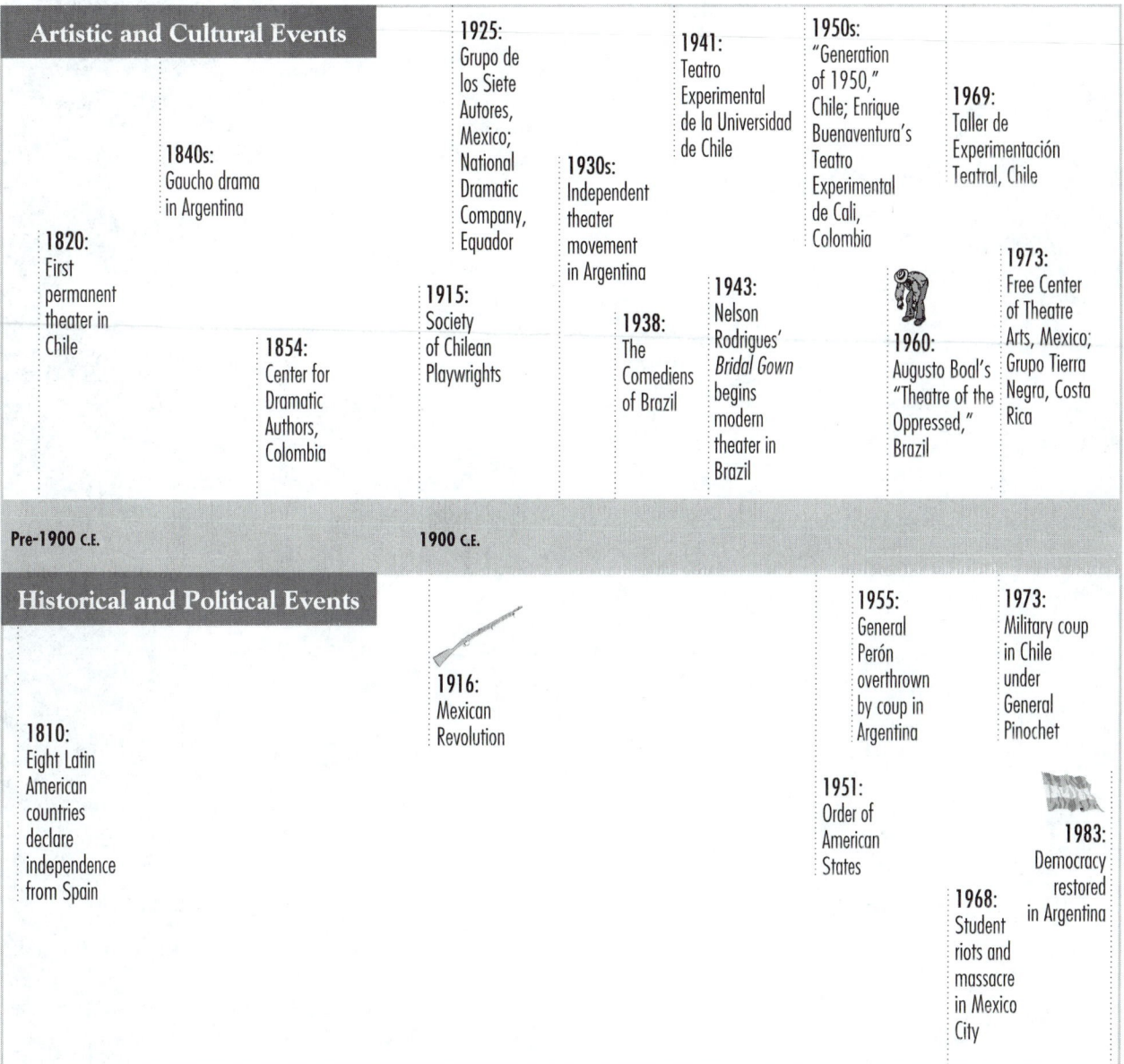

Artistic and Cultural Events

1820:
First permanent theater in Chile

1840s:
Gaucho drama in Argentina

1854:
Center for Dramatic Authors, Colombia

1915:
Society of Chilean Playwrights

1925:
Grupo de los Siete Autores, Mexico; National Dramatic Company, Equador

1930s:
Independent theater movement in Argentina

1938:
The Comediens of Brazil

1941:
Teatro Experimental de la Universidad de Chile

1943:
Nelson Rodrigues' *Bridal Gown* begins modern theater in Brazil

1950s:
"Generation of 1950," Chile; Enrique Buenaventura's Teatro Experimental de Cali, Colombia

1960:
Augusto Boal's "Theatre of the Oppressed," Brazil

1969:
Taller de Experimentación Teatral, Chile

1973:
Free Center of Theatre Arts, Mexico; Grupo Tierra Negra, Costa Rica

Pre-1900 C.E.   1900 C.E.

Historical and Political Events

1810:
Eight Latin American countries declare independence from Spain

1916:
Mexican Revolution

1951:
Order of American States

1955:
General Perón overthrown by coup in Argentina

1968:
Student riots and massacre in Mexico City

1973:
Military coup in Chile under General Pinochet

1983:
Democracy restored in Argentina

A SOLID HOME
(UN HOGAR SOLIDO)

ELENA GARRO

ELENA GARRO (1920–1999)

Elena Garro's first love was the theater: reading the classics of Spain's golden age as a child, touring provincial cities with other student actors, and performing in Mexico City's Palace of Fine Arts and in the university theater productions of the National Autonomous University of Mexico (UNAM). In the preface of the one-act play *El Árbol* (*The Tree*, 1967), Garro asserted:

> My first contact with the theater was in my childhood when I read the Spanish classics. *Lady Simpleton* (by Lope de Vega), *The Star of Sevilla* (another play attributed to Lope de Vega), *The Walls Have Ears* (by Juan Ruiz de Alarcón), *The Dog in the Manger* (Lope de Vega), *The Man Condemned for Lack of Faith* (by Tirso de Molina), etc. introduced me to the shining world of Spanish fantasy from which I still have not escaped. The discovery of a world which exists locked up in books and which can be re-created at will, revealed to me the possibility of living within a reality infinitely richer than everyday reality.

In 1937, at the young age of 17, Garro married the Mexican Nobel Prize winner Octavio Paz, who was in the earliest stages of his prominent and influential career. The two spent the first months of their marriage in Spain as part of the International Brigades, fighting against the armies of Francisco Franco. When they returned to Mexico, she began to write for the journal *Asi*, but she left her career as a journalist to accompany Paz to the United States, first to Berkeley (1943) and later to San Francisco (1945). After a short residence in New York, she went to France as a member of the Mexican diplomatic corps. Paz and Garro came to know the Parisian and expatriate artists and writers living in the French capital. In 1951 she followed Paz to Tokyo, where he served as ambassador for three years. On her return to Mexico, she began to publish some of her plays and wrote several movie scripts, two of which were successfully produced.

Garro became involved with the cause of the peasants fighting for agrarian reform, using her skills as a writer and her contacts within the government to help the movement. However, the Mexican president, seeking to minimize her influence, sent her to New York to isolate her from Mexican politics. When Paz returned to Paris as ambassador (1959), Garro left New York to join him, only to find that he had been granted a divorce by mail. Although this dissolution was later declared illegal, the separation was final and led eventually to a legal divorce.

From abroad, Garro made infrequent visits to Mexico, where she continued to support agrarian reformers and opposition groups. In 1968 she was briefly jailed as an instigator of the student demonstrations that culminated in the slaughter in Tlatelolco Plaza, where police killed hundreds of students and spectators at an antigovernment protest. After an additional 20 years abroad, she returned to Mexico City, and subsequently died in Cuernavaca in September 1999.

Although she was born in Puebla, Mexico, and did not leave her country until 1937, the fact that her father was a Spaniard and that she did not declare herself a Mexican when she turned 21 complicated her citizenship. In 1943 she had to undergo the difficult process of naturalization, and again she had problems in 1963 when she returned from Paris. In addition to her many years abroad, Garro allied herself with political causes unacceptable to the conservative governmental administration. Perhaps these obstacles only served to strengthen her sense of identity as a Mexican.

Garro published more novels and short stories than plays, consistent with the difficulties Latin American playwrights face in producing or publishing their work. However, from 1956 to 1958, the University of Veracruz published *Un Hogar sólido*, containing 12 plays. The title play was produced, along with two others from the collection—"*Los pilares de Doña Blanca*" (*The Pillars of Doña Blanca*) and *Andarse por las ramas* (*To Beat Around the Bushes*)—during the 1957 season at UNAM. In 1963 she won the important Villaurrutia Prize for the book *Los recuerdos del provenir* (*Recollections of Things to Come*) and her play *La señora en su balcon* (*The Lady on Her Balcony*) was produced by the Mexican Studio Theater (Teatro Estudios de México) with such great success that it toured several Latin American countries.

A SOLID HOME (1957)

In an interview with Patricia Rosas Lopategui and Rhina Toruño, Garro claimed that one night in a bar on the Paseo de la Reforma (a central boulevard in Mexico City) while talking with her cousin Amalia Hernandez, founder of the Ballet Folklórico de México, she remarked: "What I need is a solid home." She had the title for a play, and when Octavio Paz asked her to write something for his theater Poesía en Voz Alta (Poetry Aloud), she completed the play in half an hour. She confesses that she had not given any thought to a possible relationship to Sartre's play *No Exit,* nor to any relationship to the Surrealists. This story may be true, but it is also the kind of mask Mexicans often adopt: a prevarication to avoid self-revelation. At the time of this interview, Garro still suffered repercussions from the bloody incident in Tlatelolco. After her experiences in jail, harsh criticism, and outrageous rumors, she no longer maintained ties with other intellectuals in Paris and even stopped going to the theater.

In *A Solid Home* the typical Mexican fascination with death takes an unexpected form, for the characters are neither ghosts nor *almas en pensa* (suffering souls). With a characteristic Mexican sense of humor about death (see Center Stage box, *Día de los Muertos,* following the text of the play), Don Clement, the family patriarch, is always misplacing parts of his skeleton, and his granddaughter parades around using his femur as a toy trumpet. Doña Gertrude, his wife, is so embarrassed by the inappropriateness of her shroud that she dare not rise to greet her family members.

The play opens within a family crypt as several generations of Don Clement's family await the Final Judgment. Family members pass the time with complaints, laments for family members buried apart from the rest, and reminiscences about life. Suddenly they detect the approach of still another person suspended in a circle of light. She is Lydia, a daughter now reunited with her parents and other family members she has known only through photographs and family stories. The audience hears part of the graveside eulogy portraying Lydia's life as one of "unbreakable faith, Christian forbearance, and piety" as befits a proper Mexican woman— the wife and mother who denies herself as a sacrifice to her husband and children. She leaves behind "a solid Christian home," but Lydia feels she has missed something.

Lydia (or Lili, her childhood name) chats with Muni, a cousin whose body she identified in the police station. Presumably, Muni succumbed to a vagrant lifestyle while searching for "a solid city, like the home which we had as children." Lydia sought a more personal level of happiness ("a solid home"), but what she found was a house into which she poured her energies, passing the time performing wifely duties.

Where was the *hilo mágico* ("magic thread") that ties the invisible world together? Muni and the other adult characters explain that she will find it now, and as the curtain falls, she exclaims, "A solid home! That's what I am! The stone slabs of my tomb!"

Garro's play illustrates a most intriguing feature of Mexican (and Latin American) literature, art, and theater: *magic realism.* Its imaginative blend of Surrealistic images and realistic issues serves a higher purpose than mere theatricality, although it is among the most truly theatrical styles in world drama. Rather, magic realism encourages both artists and audience to transcend the limitations of our day-to-day existence by undertaking a spiritual journey that allows us to see essential truths about human existence. Just as Lydia must transcend the bounds of the "real" world in which she lives to understand the truth of her "reality," so, too, does magic realism permit us to escape the mundane and the obvious to see—better yet, to experience—the world as if for the first time.

Bernardíne Banning
Radford University

With the aid of magic realism, Vincente Mejía enters from the world of los muertos (the dead) in the Núcleo de Estudios Teatrales Drama School production of Elena Garro's A Solid Home, directed by Sandra Félix.

A SOLID HOME

ELENA GARRO

CHARACTERS
DON CLEMENT, *sixty years old*
DOÑA GERTRUDE, *forty years old*
MAMA JESSIE, *eighty years old*
KATIE, *five years old*

VINCENT MEJÍA, *twenty-three years old*
MUNI, *twenty-eight years old*
EVE, *a foreigner, twenty years old*
LYDIA, *thirty-two years old*

(*Interior of a small room with stone walls and ceiling. There are neither windows nor doors. To the left, imbedded in the wall and of stone also, are some berths. In one of them, Mama Jessie in a nightgown and a lace sleep cap. The stage is very dark.*)

VOICE OF DOÑA GERTRUDE. Clement! Clement! I hear footsteps!

VOICE OF DON CLEMENT. You're always hearing footsteps! Why must women be so impatient? Always anticipating what isn't going to happen, predicting calamities!

VOICE OF DOÑA GERTRUDE. Well, I hear them.

VOICE OF DON CLEMENT. No, woman, you're always mistaken. You're carried away by your nostalgia for catastrophes. . . .

VOICE OF DOÑA GERTRUDE. It's true . . . but this time I'm not mistaken.

VOICE OF KATIE. They're many feet, Gertrude! (*Katie comes out dressed in an ancient white dress, high black shoes, and a coral necklace. Her hair is tied at the nape of her neck with a red bow*). How nice! Now nice! Tra-la-la! Tra-la-la! (*She jumps and claps her hands.*)

DOÑA GERTRUDE (*appearing in a rose dress of the 1930s*). Children don't make mistakes. Aunt Katherine, isn't it true that someone is coming?

KATIE. Yes, I know it! I knew it from the first time that they came! I was so afraid here all alone. . . .

DON CLEMENT (*appearing in a black suit with white cuffs*). I believe that they're right. Gertrude! Gertrude! Help me find my metacarpuses. I always lose them and I can't shake hands without them.

VINCENT MEJÍA (*appearing in a uniform of an officer of Benito Juárez*). You read a lot, Don Clement, that's why you have the bad habit of forgetting things. Look at me, perfect in my uniform, always ready for any occasion!

MAMA JESSIE (*straightening up in her berth and poking out her head which is covered with the lace sleeping cap*). Katie's right! The steps are coming this way. (*She puts one hand behind her ear as though listening.*) The first ones have stopped . . . unless the Ramirezes have had a misfortune. . . . This neighborhood has already been very disappointing to us!

KATIE (*jumping*). You, go to sleep, Jessie! You only like to sleep:

Rock-a-bye Jessie.
on the tree top.
When the wind blows,
the cradle will rock.
When the bough bends,
the cradle will fall.
And down will come Jessie,
cradle and all.

MAMA JESSIE. And what do you want me to do? If they left me in my nightgown . . .

DON CLEMENT. Don't complain, Mama Jessie. We thought that out of respect . . .

DOÑA GERTRUDE. If it had been up to me, mama . . . , but what were the girls and Clement going to do?

(*Many footsteps which stop and then start again are heard overhead.*)

MAMA JESSIE. Katie! Come here and polish my forehead. I want it to shine like the North Star. Happy the day when I went through the house like lightning, sweeping, shaking the dust that would fall on the piano in deceptive gold mists. Then when everything shone like a comet. I'd break the ice on my bucket of water left out in the night air and bathe myself with water full of winter stars. Do you remember, Gertrude! That was living! Surrounded by my children straight and clean as lead pencils.

DOÑA GERTRUDE. Yes, mama. And I also remember the burnt cork you used to make circles under your eyes with, and the lemons you'd eat so that you'd look pale. And those nights when you would go with papa to the theater. How pretty you looked with your fan and your drop earrings!

MAMA JESSIE. You see, daughter, life is short. Each time that I would arrive at our box. . . .

DON CLEMENT (*interrupting*). For pity's sake, now I can't find my femur!

MAMA JESSIE. What a lack of courtesy! To interrupt a lady!

(*Meanwhile, Katie has been helping Jessie arrange her nightcap.*)

VINCENT MEJÍA. I saw Katie using it for a trumpet.

DOÑA GERTRUDE. Aunt Katie, where did you leave Clement's femur?

KATIE. Jessie, Jessie! They want to take my bugle away from me!

MAMA JESSIE. Gertrude, let this child alone! And as for you, let me tell you for a grown woman you're more spoiled than she is. . . .

DOÑA GERTRUDE. But, mama, don't be unjust. It's Clement's femur!

KATIE. Ugly! Bad! I'll hit you! It's not his femur, it's my little sugar bugle!

DON CLEMENT (*to Gertrude*). Could she have eaten it? Your aunt's unbearable.

DOÑA GERTRUDE. I don't know, Clement. My broken clavicle got lost. She liked the little streaks left along the scar a lot. And it was my favorite bone! It reminded me of the walls of my house, covered with heliotrope. I told you how I fell, didn't I? The day before, we'd gone to the circus. All of Chihuahua was in the stands to see the clown, Richard Bell. Suddenly a tightrope walker came out. She resembled a butterfly. I've never forgotten her. . . . (*A blow is heard above. Gertrude interrupts herself. Continuing:*) In the morning I climbed the fence to dance on one foot, because all night I'd dreamed that I was she. . . . (*Overhead a harder blow is heard.*) Of course, I didn't know that I had bones. As a little girl, one doesn't know anything. Because

I broke it, I always say that it was the first little bone that I had. It takes you by surprise!

(*The blows follow one another more rapidly.*)

VINCENT MEJÍA (*smoothing his mustache*). There's no doubt. Someone's coming. We have guests. (*He sings.*)
>When in darkness
>The moon glimmers
>And on the pool
>The swallow sings . . .

MAMA JESSIE. Be quiet, Vincent! This isn't the time to sing. Look at these unexpected guests! In my day people announced themselves before dropping in for a visit. There was more respect. Let's see now whom they're bringing us, probably one of these foreigners who married my girls! "God overwhelms the humble!" as my poor Raymond, may God have him in his Glory, used to say. . . .

VINCENT MEJÍA. You haven't improved at all, Jessie! You find defects in everything. Before, you were so agreeable. The only thing you liked was to dance polkas! (*He hums a tune and dances a few steps.*) Do you remember how we danced at that carnival? (*He continues dancing.*) Your pink dress spun around and around, and your neck was very close to my lips . . .

MAMA JESSIE. For heaven's sake, cousin Vincent! Don't remind me of those foolish things.

VINCENT MEJÍA (*laughing*). What would Raymond say now? He was so jealous. And you and I here together, while he rots there alone in that other cemetery.

DOÑA GERTRUDE. Uncle Vincent, be quiet. You're going to cause an argument.

DON CLEMENT (*alarmed*). I already explained to you, Mama Jessie, that at the time we didn't have the money to transfer him.

MAMA JESSIE. And the girls, why don't they bring him? Don't give me explanations. You always lacked tact.

(*A harder blow is heard.*)

KATIE. I saw a light! (*A ray of light enters.*) I saw a sword. St. Michael's coming to visit us again! Look at his sword!

VINCENT MEJÍA. Are we all here? Now then, easy does it!

DON CLEMENT. Muni and my sister-in-law are missing.

MAMA JESSIE. The foreigners, always keeping away!

DOÑA GERTRUDE. Muni, Muni! Someone's coming. Maybe it's one of your cousins. Aren't you happy, dear? You'll be able to play and laugh with them again. Let's see if that sadness leaves you.

(*Eve appears, blond, tall, sad, very young, in a traveling dress of the 1920s.*)

EVE. Muni was around here a moment ago. Muni, dear! Do you hear that blow? That's the way the sea beats against the rocks of my house. . . . None of you knew it. . . . It was a rock, high, like a wave, always beaten by the winds that lulled us to sleep at night. Swirls of salt covered its windows with sea stars. The walls in the kitchen had a golden glow which radiated from my father's hands, warm as the sun. . . . During the nights, creatures of wind, water, fire, and salt came in through the fireplace. They would huddle in the flames and sing in the water that dripped into the washstands. . . . Drip! Drop! Drip! Drop! Drip! Drop! . . . And iodine spread itself about the house like sleep. . . . The tail of a shining dolphin would announce day to us, with this light of fish scales and corals!

(*With the last sentence, Eve raises her arm and points to the torrent of light that enters the crypt when the first stone slab is moved above. The room is inundated with sunlight. All the luxurious clothes are dusty and all the faces pale. The child Katie jumps with pleasure.*)

KATIE. Look, Jessie! Someone's coming! Who's bringing him, Jessie? Lady Diptheria or Saint Michael?

MAMA JESSIE. Wait, child. We're going to see.

KATIE. Lady Diptheria brought me. Do you remember her? She had fingers of cotton and she wouldn't let me breathe. Did she frighten you, Jessie?

MAMA JESSIE. Yes, little sister. I remember that they took you away and the patio of the house remained strewn with purple petals. Mama cried a lot and we girls did too.

KATIE. Dummy! Didn't you know that you were going to come to play with me here? That day, St. Michael sat down beside me and wrote it with his sword of fire on the roof of my house. I didn't know how to read . . . and I read it. And was the school of the Misses Simson nice?

MAMA JESSIE. Very nice, Katie. Mama sent us with black ribbons. . . .

KATIE. And did you learn to spell? That's why mama was going to send me. . . .

MUNI (*comes in wearing pajamas, with a blue face and blond hair*). Who can it be?

(*Overhead, through the fragment of the vault open to the sky, a woman's feet are seen suspended in a circle of light.*)

DOÑA GERTRUDE. Clement, Clement! They're Lydia's feet. What a pleasure, daughter, what a pleasure that you've died so soon!

(*Everyone becomes silent. The descent of Lydia, suspended on ropes, begins. She is stiff, wearing a white dress, her arms crossed on her chest, her fingers in the form of a cross, and her head bowed. Her eyes are closed.*)

KATIE. Who's Lydia?

MUNI. Lydia's the daughter of my uncle Clement and my aunt Gertrude, Katie. (*He caresses the girl.*)

MAMA JESSIE. Now we have the whole bunch of grandchildren here. So many brats! Well, isn't the crematory oven more modern? As far as I'm concerned at least it seems more hygienic.

KATIE. Isn't it true, Jessie, that Lydia isn't for real?

MAMA JESSIE. I wish it were so, my dear. There's room here for everyone except my poor Raymond!

EVE. How she grew! When I came she was as little as Muni.

(*Lydia remains standing, in the midst of all of them, as they look at her. Then she opens her eyes and sees them.*)

LYDIA. Papa! (*She embraces him.*) Mama! Muni! (*She embraces them.*)

DOÑA GERTRUDE. You're looking very well, daughter.

LYDIA. And grandmother?

DON CLEMENT. She can't get up. Do you remember that we made the mistake of burying her in her nightgown?

MAMA JESSIE. Yes, Lili, here I am, lying down forever.

DOÑA GERTRUDE. My mother's notions! You already know, Lili, how well groomed she always was.

MAMA JESSIE. The worst thing will be, daughter, to present yourself this way before God, our Lord. Doesn't it seem a disgrace to you? Why didn't it occur to you to bring me a dress? That gray one with the brocade ruffles and the bouquet of violets at the neck. Do you remember it? I'd put it on for formal occasions . . . but no one remembers the old people. . . .

KATIE. When Saint Michael visits us, she hides.

LYDIA. And who are you, precious?

KATIE. Katie!

LYDIA. Of course! We had your picture on the piano! Now it's in Evie's house. How sad it was to look at you, so melancholy, painted in your white dress. I'd forgotten that you were here.

VINCENT MEJÍA. And aren't you pleased to meet me, niece?

LYDIA. Uncle Vincent! We also had your picture in the living room, with your uniform and your medal in a little red velvet box.

EVE. And don't you remember your Aunt Eve?

LYDIA. Aunt Eve! Yes, I just barely remember you, with your blond hair spread out in the sun . . . and I remember your purple parasol and your faded face under it, like that of a beautiful drowned woman . . . and your empty chair rocking to the rhythm of your song, after you had gone.

(*From the circle of light, a Voice comes forth.*)

VOICE. The general earth of our Mexico opens its arms to give you loving shelter. Virtuous woman, most exemplary mother, model wife, you leave an irreparable void . . .

MAMA JESSIE. Who's speaking to you with such familiarity?

LYDIA. It's Don Gregory de la Huerta Ramírez Puente, President of the Association of the Blind.

VINCENT MEJÍA. What madness! And what do so many blind people do together?

MAMA JESSIE. But why does he address you in such intimate terms?

DOÑA GERTRUDE. It's the style, mama, to address the dead familiarly.

VOICE. Most cruel loss, whose absence we shall feel in time. You leave us forever deprived of your boundless charm. You also leave a solid and Christian home in the most terrible neglect. The homes do tremble before inexorable Death. . . .

DON CLEMENT. Good God! But is that blustering fool still running around there?

MAMA JESSIE. What's useless abounds.

LYDIA. Yes, and now he's president of the bank, of the Knights of Columbus, of the Association for the Blind, the Flag Day and Mother's Day Committees.

VOICE. Only irrevocable faith, Christian resignation, and pity . . .

KATIE. Don Hilary always says the same thing.

MAMA JESSIE. It isn't Don Hilary, Katie. Don Hilary died trifling sixty-five years ago. . . .

KATIE (*not hearing her*). When they brought me, he said, "A little angel flew away!" And it wasn't true. I was here below, alone and very frightened. Isn't that so Vincent? Isn't it true that I don't tell lies?

VINCENT MEJÍA. You're telling me! Imagine, I arrived here, still stunned by the powder flashes, with my wounds open . . . and what do I see? Katie crying: "I want to see my mama! I want to see my mama!" What trouble she caused me! Believe me, I'd rather have fought the French. . . .

VOICE. Rest in peace!

(*They begin to replace the stone slabs. The scene becomes dark slowly.*)

KATIE. We were alone a long time, weren't we, Vincent? We didn't know what was happening, but no one came anymore.

MAMA JESSIE. I've already told you, Katie, we went to the capital, then the revolution came along. . . .

KATIE. Until one day Eve arrived. You said, Vincent, that she was a foreigner. . . .

VINCENT MEJÍA. The situation was a little tense and Eve didn't say a single word to us.

EVE. I too was restrained . . . and besides I was thinking of Muni . . . and of my home. . . . Everything was so quiet here.

(*Silence. They place the last slab.*)

LYDIA. And now, what'll we do?

DON CLEMENT. Wait.

LYDIA. Still wait?

DOÑA GERTRUDE. Yes, daughter. You'll see.

EVE. You'll see everything you want to see, except your home with your white pine table and the waves and the sails of the boats through your windows.

MUNI. Aren't you happy, Lili?

LYDIA. Yes, Muni, especially to see you. When I saw you that night lying in the courtyard of the police station, with that smell of urine that came from the broken flagstones, and you dead on the stretcher, between the feet of the policemen with your wrinkled pajamas and your blue face, I ask myself, "Why? Why?"

KATIE. Me too, Lili. I hadn't seen a blue dead person either. Then Jessie told me that cyanide has many artists' brushes, but only one tube of color, blue!

MAMA JESSIE. Don't bother that boy any longer! Blue looks very good on blonds.

MUNI. Why, cousin Lili? Haven't you seen stray dogs walk and walk along the sidewalks looking for bones in the butcher shops full of flies, and the butcher, with his fingers drenched in blood from cutting up the meat? Well, I no longer wanted to talk along atrocious sidewalks looking through the blood for a bone, nor look at those corners, shelters for drunks and urinals for dogs. I wanted a happy city, full of sunlight and moonlight. A solid city like the home we had as children, with sunshine in every door, moonlight for every window, and wandering stars in the rooms. Do you remember it, Lili? It had a labyrinth of laughs. Its kitchen was a crossroads; its garden, source of all the rivers; and all of it, the birthplace of Man. . . .

LYDIA. A solid home, Muni! That's just what I wanted . . . and you already know, they took me to a strange house. And in it I found only clocks and eyes without eyelids that looked at me for years. . . . I polished the floors so as not to see the thousands of dead words that the maids swept in the mornings. I shined the mirrors in order to drive away our hostile glances. I hoped that one morning the loving image would face me in the looking glass. I opened books in order to open avenues in that circular hell. I embroidered napkins with linked initials in order to find the magic, unbreakable thread that make two names into one. . . .

MUNI. I know, Lili.

LYDIA. But it was all useless. The furious eyes didn't stop looking at me ever. If I could find the spider that once lived in my house—with the invisible thread that unites the flower to light, the apple to fragrance, woman to man, I would sew loving eyelids to close the eyes that look at me and this house would enter into the solar order. Each balcony would be a different country. Its furniture would bloom. From its glasses jets of water would spurt. The sheets would turn into magic carpets in order to travel to sleep. From the hands of my children, castles, flags, and battles would come forth . . . but I didn't find the thread, Muni. . . .

MUNI. You told me that at the police station. In that strange courtyard, forever far from the other courtyard, in whose sky a belltower counted for us the hours that we had left to play.

LYDIA. Yes, Muni, and you and I put away forever the last day that we were children. Afterward, only a Lydia seated, facing the wall, waiting, remained.

MUNI. I couldn't grow, either, and live on the street corners. I wanted my home. . . .

EVE. Me too, Muni, my son, I wanted a solid home. A house that the sea would beat every night. Boom! Boom! A house that would laugh with my father's laugh full of fish and nets.

MUNI. Don't be sad, Lili. You'll find the thread, and you'll find the spider.

DON CLEMENT. Lili, aren't you happy? Now your house is the center of the sun, the heart of every star, the root of all the grasses, the most solid point of every stone.

MUNI. Yes, Lili, you still don't know it, but suddenly you won't need a house, nor a river. We'll not swim in the Mezcala River, we'll be the Mezcala.

DOÑA GERTRUDE. At times, daughter, you'll be very cold, and you'll be the snow falling on an unknown city or gray roofs and red caps.

KATIE. What I like most is being a piece of candy in a little girl's mouth. Or a sty, to make those who read near a window weep!

MUNI. Don't grieve when your eyes begin to disappear, because then you'll be all the eyes of the dogs looking at absurd feet.

MAMA JESSIE. Ah, child! May you never be the eyes of the blind, of a blind fish in the deepest abyss of the seas! You don't know the terrible feeling that I had. It was like seeing and not seeing things never thought of.

KATIE (laughing and clapping). You also were very frightened when you were the worm that came in and out of your mouth.

VINCENT MEJÍA. Well, for me, the worst thing was being a murderer's dagger!

MAMA JESSIE. Now the gophers will return. Don't shout when you yourself run along your face.

DON CLEMENT. Don't tell her that. You're going to frighten her. It's frightening to learn to be everything.

DOÑA GERTRUDE. Especially because in the world one scarcely learns to be a man.

LYDIA. And will I be able to be a pine tree with a nest of spiders and build a solid home?

DON CLEMENT. Of course! And you'll be the pine tree and the staircase and the fire.

LYDIA. And then?

MAMA JESSIE. Then God will call us to his bosom.

DON CLEMENT. After having learned to be all things, St. Michael's sword will appear, center of the universe, and by its light the divine armies of angels will come forth and we'll enter into the celestial order.

MUNI. I want to be the fold of an angel's tunic.

MAMA JESSIE. Your color will go very well. It'll give beautiful reflections. And I, what'll I do dressed in this nightgown?

KATIE. I want to be the index finger of God the Father!

ALL TOGETHER. Child!

EVE. And I, a wave sprinkled with salt, changed into a cloud!

LYDIA. And I the sewing fingers of the Virgin, embroidering . . . embroidering . . . !

DOÑA GERTRUDE. And I the music from the harp of St. Cecilia!

VINCENT MEJÍA. And I the rage of the sword of St. Gabriel!

DON CLEMENT. And I a particle of the stone of St. Peter!

KATIE. And I a window that looks at the world!

MAMA JESSIE. There'll no longer be a world, Katie, because we'll be all that after the Final Judgment.

KATIE (*weeping*). There'll no longer be a world. And when am I going to see it? I didn't see anything. I didn't even learn the spelling book. I want there to be a world.

VINCENT MEJÍA. Look at it now, Katie!

(*In the distance a trumpet is heard.*)

MAMA JESSIE. Jesus, Mary Most Pure! The trumpet of Final Judgment! And me in a nightgown! Pardon me, my Lord, this immodesty!

LYDIA. No, grandma, it's taps. There's a barracks near the cemetery.

MAMA JESSIE. Ah, yes, they had already told me! And I always forget it. Who had the bright idea of putting a barracks so close to us? What a government! It lends itself to so much confusion!

VINCENT MEJÍA. Taps! I'm going. I'm the wind that opens all the doors that I didn't open, that goes up the stairs that I never went up in a whirl, that runs along new streets in my officer's uniform and lifts the skirts of the pretty, unknown girls. . . . Ah, coolness! (*He disappears.*)

MAMA JESSIE. Rascal!

DON CLEMENT. Ah, rain on the water! (*He disappears.*)

DOÑA GERTRUDE. Wood in flames! (*She disappears.*)

MUNI. Do you hear? A dog howls. Ah, melancholy! (*She disappears.*)

KATIE. The table where nine children eat supper! I'm the game they play! (*She disappears.*)

MAMA JESSIE. The fresh heart of a head of lettuce! (*She disappears.*)

EVE. I'm the flash of fire that sinks into the black sea! (*She disappears.*)

LYDIA. A solid home! That's what I am! The stone slabs of my tomb! (*She disappears.*)

CURTAIN

CENTER STAGE *DÍA DE LOS MUERTOS* IN MEXICO

Mexico's *Día de los Muertos* (Day of the Dead) is a traditional fiesta that celebrates life and death as a single entity in human experience. On November 1 and 2—which correspond to the Christian All Saints' and All Souls' Days, respectively (as well as Halloween)—even the tiniest Mexican villages are overrun by cavorting spirits, skeletons, and other impersonations of *los muertitos* ("the dead ones"). The celebration is simultaneously a sacred and satiric ritual, part street theater and part folk ceremony, that may be traced to ancient rites signaling the end of the growing season.

Mexico's fascination with death can be traced to the Aztec Empire. At the Grand Pyramid of Quetzalcoatl, near what is now Mexico City, Aztec worshippers could view thousands of human skulls on a rack adjacent to the sacred temple. Inside, dozens of clay jars held human remains. As recently as a hundred years ago, actual human skulls were exhumed for the Day of the Dead, after which they were carefully replaced under the supervision of village priests.

Today the Day of the Dead is observed over a two-day period, though preparations begin well in advance of November 1, when the souls of children (*los angelitos*) return to their families and loved ones. Special sweet breads (*panes de muertos*) are baked, and gifts (*ofertas*) are given to children, both living and deceased. Failing to give gifts for the dead is considered a serious offense; those who do not leave *ofertas* to their dead will see the spirits of weeping relatives visit their own graves. The souls of the children leave on the morning of November 2 as those of deceased adults arrive.

On November 2, a national holiday in Mexico, townspeople march en masse in a triumphant procession to the cemetery, where food is placed on the graves of loved ones. En route, young girls strew flower petals from the *Zempausuchitl* (the marigold) to attract the souls of the dead. A street band leads the procession, while drum-beating skeletons dance about the crowd, playing tricks on unsuspecting audience members to scare off anyone who might bring bad luck. After cleansing the graves, the living remain for a festive vigil in which the spirits of the departed are welcomed back. The merrymaking

José Guadalupe Posada revolutionized contemporary Mexican art with his pen-and-ink drawings of Día de los Muertos; *well-dressed skeletons cavort in a graveyard in a sketch that epitomizes the spirited manner in which Mexicans confront death.*

includes skits (*actos*) that make fun of death and dying. The clowning allows the survivors to laugh at death and to accept it as a natural part of life's process. They further comfort themselves with storytelling, music, and dancing. As night falls, a costume ball—the Dance of Death—commands the attention of revelers, many of whom wear costumes associated with

death. Children amuse themselves by playing with puppets and other toys that bear images of death. They also eat sugar skeletons with their names written on the skulls.

Octavio Paz, Mexico's 1990 Nobel laureate, writes that *Día de los Muertos* is not only a national ritual but also a manifestation of the Mexican character. For the Mexican, "Death is not the

natural end of life, but one phase of an infinite cycle. Life, death and resurrection are stages of a cosmic process that repeated itself continuously. . . . A civilization that denies death ends up denying life."

In *A Solid Home* Elena Garro reflects Mexico's unique celebration of death as she presents the ironic wit and theatricality that permeates *Día de los Muertos*.

NO SACO NADA DE LA ESCUELA
(I DON'T GET NOTHIN' FROM SCHOOL)

LUIS VALDEZ

LUIS VALDEZ (1940–)

No individual is more responsible for the development of Mexican-American drama than Luis Valdez, and no other Chicano in any art medium has had more written about him and his work. From simple beginnings in farm fields in California's Central Valley in the 1960s, Valdez's theatrical—and now film—work truly entered the mainstream. He was the first Mexican-American to have a play produced on Broadway (*Zoot Suit*, 1981), and his 1987 film *La Bamba* (about Chicano rock star Richie Valens) was admired by critics and the public.

Valdez was born in Delano, California in 1940, the son of campesinos, the migrant farmworkers who picked grapes and other crops from the citrus groves of Southern California to the apple orchards of Washington State. In part because of their transient lifestyle, the children of campesinos often perform poorly in school (an issue in *No saco nada*) and frequently drop out. Valdez, however, persevered and graduated from high school, even while working as a ventriloquist at a local television station. He earned a scholarship to San Jose State College, where he took theater classes and eventually wrote his first play, *The Shrunken Head of Pancho Villa*. A surrealistic work about a young Mexican-American without a head (who represents "faceless" Chicanos struggling for recognition in mainstream America), the play received a lengthy standing ovation at its premiere production at SJSC and in reworked form has assumed major status in Valdez's compiled works.

After college Valdez joined the San Francisco Mime Troupe, a politically committed band of artists in the Bay Area who fused a *commedia dell'arte* style with social activism. When he returned to his home in Delano in 1965, he met Cesar Chavez, who was organizing the United Farm Workers in an attempt to gain better working conditions, wages, health care, and education for the campesinos. Valdez worked as a UFW recruiter for two years. Applying what he learned in the Mime Troupe, Valdez began a theater company—El Teatro Campesino—which performed short plays (*actos*) in fields, at union halls, in churches, even on flatbed trucks. The *actos* were an inventive combination of satirical clowning, Brechtian theater, folk plays, and agitprop designed to educate farmworkers about their rights and provoke them to act (specifically, to strike against the growers). Valdez also refers to these early *actos* as *huelguistas* ("strike plays") because they were performed during the period known as *La Huelga*, the prolonged grape boycott that eventually led to a victory for the UFW. It was the beginning of the civil rights movement for Hispanic Americans, and El Teatro Campesino's plays were as instrumental in its success as Martin Luther King Jr.'s speeches were for the African American movement. Note that *No saco nada* ends with the actors getting the audience to rise and shout "*La raza*" ("the race"), "*La huelga*" ("strike") and "Chicano power" in the best agitprop tradition.

Valdez himself defines the purpose of *actos*:

> Inspire the audience to social action. Illuminate specific points about social problems. Satirize the opposition. Show or hint at a solution. Express what people are feeling.

Like South African township theater or the work of many of the theater collectives in Latin America, the *actos* performed by El Teatro Campesino epitomize rough theater as defined by Sir Peter Brook: "The Rough Theater is close to the people . . . the theater that's not a theater, the theater on carts, on wagons, on trestles, audiences standing, drinking, sitting round tables, audiences joining in, answering back." To further the bond between actors and performers, the *actos* were frequently accompanied by *corridos* and *rancheras*, popular songs that served as a kind of "living newspaper" to keep audiences informed about current events. Valdez's actors, it must be noted, were not trained professionals (though many became professional actors), but emerged from the ranks of the farmworkers themselves. Their presence lent a compelling authenticity to the message of the plays.

Among Valdez's best-known *actos* is *Los Vendidos* (1967), a satirical portrait of Mexican-American "sellouts" who contribute to the stereotypical notions Anglos have about Hispanics or who try to "pass" as Anglos. *The Dark Root of a Scream* (1967) and *Soldado Razo* (1970) are *actos* about the victimization of Hispanics during the Vietnam War. After the success of *La Huelga*, Valdez turned to mythological themes extolling the virtues of Aztlán, the sacred kingdom of the Aztecs and the repository of the greatness of "la raza." *Bernabé* (1970) is an especially poignant portrait of a young Chicano with learning disabilities on a quest for La Tierra, the mythical goddess of the land. In 1980 Valdez combined social activism and myth in *Zoot Suit*, a drama with music. Based on the infamous "zoot suit" riots in Los Angeles in the 1940s, the play portrays the tragedy of a "pachuco" (a street-smart Chicano noted for extravagant dress) who gradually realizes his link to his Aztec heritage. The play was among the most popular works of the 1981 Los Angeles theater season and was subsequently produced on Broadway, but was largely ignored by New York audiences whose Hispanic referent was Puerto Rican–Americans.

El Teatro Campesino is still based in San Juan Bautista, California. In addition to its stage work, it has contributed films and several television shows to contemporary culture. Each Christmas season, PBS broadcasts *La Pastorella*, a Chicano version of the Nativity featuring well-known Mexican-American performers such as Linda Ronstadt, Paul Rodriguez, Cheech Marin, and the Tejano rock band, the Texas Tornados.

No saco nada de la escuela (1969)

Though it is not the best known of Valdez's *actos*, *No saco nada de la escuela* articulates most of the principal themes of El Teatro Campesino. Furthermore, it is the only *acto* to address the problems of other minorities in America, and its issues are still central to the national debate about the education of minorities. Although it seems a simple satire about the futility minorities face in the educational system, it is more complex than a first reading indicates. As Valdez warns in a short essay about the nature of *actos*, "What to a non-Chicano audience may seem like oversimplification . . . is to the Chicano a true expression of his social state and therefore reality."

The play, first performed at the Mexican Cultural Center in Fresno, is divided into three sections: grammar school, high school, and college. The oppressors are broadly drawn caricatures meant to elicit laughter and scorn from its audience: the old schoolteacher who explodes into violence; the redneck whose only talent is for racist insults; the smug college professor whose ignorance is appalling. The play's ingenuity rests in the three-step progression from ignorance to knowledge by its youthful protagonists, each of whom represents an element in minority culture. Francisco is a potential *vendido*, or sellout; he is effectively contrasted with Esperanza (ironically, her name means "hope"), a true *vendido* whose father is a well-to-do landowner. Ultimately, Francisco, like his African American counterpart, Malcolm, gains an awareness of his racial identity and the militancy that will effect change for his people. Similarly, Florence, the *gabacha* (white girl), represents '60s liberalism in her movement from self-absorption to an openness to others; she cannot, however, quite shake her old prejudices. Though she is a parody of antiwar, profeminist activists, she emerges as a more sympathetic character than the other Anglos.

The central character is Moctezuma, who epitomizes Chicanismo, that is, a fierce pride in "la raza." His name embodies the glory of the Aztecs, who ruled central and northern Mexico in the preconquest era. Like the insensitive teacher who sings "From the halls of Montezuma . . . " when she hears his name, most Anglos—and, ironically, many in Valdez's late 1960's audience—assume Montezuma is the correct pronunciation and spelling of the name of the last emperor of the Aztecs (1466–1520). However, this is an Anglicized version, and Valdez's hero wants his name restored to its preconquest form—Moctezuma—as a means of recapturing his racial and spiritual identity. When Moctezuma corrects the teacher's ignorant and insensitive pronunciation, Valdez was actually educating his audience about their heritage. In many ways *No saco nada* is more a tool to instruct the audience in the values of Chicanismo than a satire on the insensitivity of the majority culture. Like his African American counterpart, Malcolm (whose chosen name honors civil rights leader Malcolm X), Moctezuma becomes increasingly aware of his heritage, a progress that is marked in both cases by the inventive use of the alphabet game as the structural centerpiece of the play.

As its title suggests, the play argues that the educational system is irrelevant to the needs of the minority community, particularly in regard to the awareness of one's culture. The message in 1967 was that people had to educate themselves about their ethnicity, as suggested by the lines of the play. Since the play was written, various perceived weaknesses of contemporary education have been addressed, with varying degrees of success. Today multicultural education, ethnic studies programs, and similar curricular changes have become commonplace in both lower and higher education. Valdez's *acto* is a reminder that this was not always the case.

The figure of Richard Nixon is also central to the play, which was written during the Vietnam War. Nixon, who was a figure of ridicule in many alternative theater movements of the era, became an effigy to those opposed to a war that, many argued, was being fought primarily by the poor and especially by minorities. Though El Teatro Campesino specifically addressed this issue in such plays as *The Root of a Scream*, it is instructive that Valdez includes the issue in this play. School was seen as a haven for many middle-class young men who received deferrals while attending college. Minorities had less access to education and were therefore more likely to be drafted. This is another reason why *No saco nada* is such a scathing attack on the educational system. While its performers claimed to have learned "nothing" in school, the play they used to vent their anger at a system that excluded them was enormously instructive to its audience.

Teatro Espejo, *which has performed for twenty-five years at California State University, Sacramento,* *continues the tradition of Luis Valdez's* El Teatro Campesino *in its performance of* Chicano Acto.

NO SACO NADA DE LA ESCUELA

Luis Valdez

CHARACTERS:
FRANCISCO
MOCTEZUMA (MONTY)
MALCOLM
FLORENCE
ABRAHAM
GRADE SCHOOL TEACHER
ESPERANZA
COLLEGE PROFESSOR
NIXON
VATO

Elementary School. School Yard sounds: children playing, shouting, laughing. Four kids come running out. Florence, a white girl in pigtails and freckles; Malcolm, a black boy; then Francisco and Moctezuma, two chicanitos.

ALL. (*A cheer.*) Yeah! Ring around the rosey, pocket full of posies, ashes, ashes, all fall down! Yeah! Let's do it again!

(*Francisco has been watching from the side. He is grabbed by Florence and Monty, and pulled into circle, trying to get in step.*) Ring around the rosey, pocket full of posies, ashes, ashes, we all fall down! (*Bell rings off stage.*)

FLORENCE. Oh! The bell! (*They jump to their places, and sit in two rows facing each other. Two on each side.*)

MONTY. Heh, look! Florence has a boyfriend! Florence has a boyfriend, y es un negro!

FLORENCE. No I don't. I don't have no boyfriend. (*Teacher enters, short bowlegged, old, ugly. She wears a white mask and her feet stomp as she walks. She carries a huge pencil, two feet long, and a sign which she places on a stand at upstage center.*)

TEACHER. (*Mimicking writing on blackboard.*) Elementary A-B-C's. (*Students begin to throw paper wads across the room at one another. Teacher turns, commands with high pitched voice.*) Children! I want those papers picked off the floor immediately! (*Students run to pick up papers. Then sit down.*) There now, that's better. (*Her version of cheerful-*

ness.) Good morning, class. (*Class begins to sing except for Francisco, who looks at others, bewildered. Teacher leads singing with her pencil.*)

ALL. Good morning to you, good morning to you, good morning dear teacher, good morning to you.

TEACHER. That's fine. Now for roll call. Florence.

FLORENCE. Here teacher.

TEACHER. Malcolm.

MALCOLM. Yeow.

TEACHER. Moc . . . Moc . . . (*She can't pronounce "Moctezuma."*) Ramírez!

MONTY. Here.

TEACHER. Francisco.

FRANCISCO. Aquí. (*Monty raises Francisco's hand.*)

TEACHER. Abraham.

MONTY. Teacher, teacher. He's outside. He's a crybaby.

(*Abraham comes running out and runs across front stage, crying. He is dressed in cowboy boots, baseball cap on sideways, face is pale white with freckles.*)

TEACHER. (*Helps him.*) There, there now, dear, don't cry. I want you to sit right there. (*Points to Monty.*)

ABRAHAM. Wah! I can't sit there, he's brown.

MONTY. No, I'm not. (*Rubs forearm trying to remove color.*)

TEACHER. (*Turns him around.*) Well, then I want you to sit right over there. (*Points towards Malcolm.*)

ABRAHAM. Wah! I can't sit there, he's Black.

TEACHER. Well, then do you see that nice little white girl over there? (*Points to Florence.*) Would you like to sit there?

ABRAHAM. (*Man's voice.*) Uh-huh!

TEACHER. Boy! (*Points to Malcolm.*) You move. (*Abraham sits next to Florence, Malcolm moves over by Monty and Francisco. They pantomime playing marbles.*)

TEACHER. Now, all rise for the flag salute. (*Sweetly.*) Stand up, Florence. Stand up, Abraham, dear. (*Turns to others.*) I said stand up! (*Monty, Malcolm and Francisco jump up and begin flag salute.*)

ALL. I pledge allegiance to the flag . . . (*Abraham sneaks behind the Teacher's back and pokes Francisco in the behind. Francisco thinks it was Monty and hits him, pushing him into Malcolm. They stand up straight again to continue and Abraham sneaks over, again he pokes Francisco who again hits Monty, who again pushes into Malcolm. Malcolm points to Abraham. All three then attack Abraham and throw him to the ground.*)

TEACHER. (*Turns screaming.*) Class! For heaven's sake!

(*Abraham, Monty and Francisco run back to their seats.*) Did they hurt you Abraham, dear? (*Turns to Monty and Francisco.*) You should have more respect!

FRANCISCO. Pero, yo no hice nada.

TEACHER. Shut up! (*Francisco cries.*) Shut up! I said shut up! (*Francisco continues crying. Teacher kicks him and he shuts up. Teacher moves to center stage.*) And now for our elementary A, B, C's. Florence, you're first.

FLORENCE. Here's an apple, teacher. (*Hands Teacher an apple.*)

TEACHER. Thank you, dear.

FLORENCE. (*Moves down stage center.*) A is for apple. B is for baby. And C is for candy. (*Pantomimes licking sucker and skips back to her seat giggling.*)

TEACHER. Very good! Now let's see who's next. Willie? (*She means Malcolm, who sits daydreaming.*) Willie? (*Malcolm does not respond.*) Willie! I meant you boy! (*Points at him.*)

MALCOLM. Teacher, my name ain't Willie. It's Malcolm.

TEACHER. It doesn't matter. It doesn't matter. Do your ABC's!

MALCOLM. A is for Alabama. B is for banjo and C is for cotton! (*Stamps foot, walks back to his seat. All the students are giggling.*)

TEACHER. Not bad at all, boy, not bad at all. Let's see. Who's next? Abraham dear? Say your ABC's.

ABRAHAM. A is for animal and B is for . . . black and brown!

(*Points to Monty and Francisco and Malcolm.*)

TEACHER. Oh! He's able to distinguish his colors. Go on.

ABRAHAM. And C is for . . . for . . .

TEACHER. It has a "kuh," "kuh" sound. (*Meaning cat.*)

ABRAHAM. Kill! (*Brightens up. Points to Francisco, Monty and Malcolm.*)

TEACHER. Oh, no, we mustn't say those things in class.

ABRAHAM. (*Crying.*) I promise never to say it again. Teacher, look. (*Points upward. Teacher looks and Abraham spits on Francisco, Monty and Malcolm. They start to get up but are interrupted by Teacher.*)

TEACHER. Class! Did you all know that Abraham here was named after one of our most famous presidents? Mr. Abraham Lincoln—the man who freed the slaves!

ALL. (*Aghast.*) Gaw-leee!

TEACHER. After they were forced to pick cotton against their own free will.

ALL. Shame, shame, shame.

TEACHER. (*To Abraham.*) Now, aren't you proud of your heritage?

ABRAHAM. A-huh. (*Laughing.*)

TEACHER. Of course, you are. Who's next. Moc . . . Moc . . . (*She can't pronounce his name.*) Ramírez!

MONTY. Yes, teacher?

TEACHER. How do you pronounce your name?

MONTY. Moctezuma.

TEACHER. What?

MONTY. Moctezuma.

TEACHER. Oh! What a funny name! (*She laughs and class joins her. Teacher stomps foot and shuts them up.*) Class! (*To Moctezuma.*) And what ever does it mean?

MONTY. He was an emperor in the times of the Indians. He was a Mexican like me.

TEACHER. Oh! You mean Montezuma.

MONTY. No, Moctezuma.

TEACHER. Montezuma.

MONTY. Moctezuma.

TEACHER. Montezuma!

MONTY. Moctezuma!

TEACHER. Montezuma! (*Begins to march up and down stage singing "The Marines Hymn."*) "From the halls of Monte-zoo-ma to the shore of Tripoli." (*Using her oversized pencil as a bayonet, she stabs Monty, who falls forward with head and arms hanging.*) Now what's your name, boy? (*Lifts his head.*)

MONTY. Monty.

TEACHER. Do your ABC's.

MONTY. A is for airplane, B is for boat and C is for . . . ah, C is for . . . for cucaracha!

TEACHER. What!

MONTY. (*Crying.*) Cuca . . . caca qui qui.

TEACHER. (*Twisting his ear.*) What you meant to say was cock-a-roach, right?

MONTY. Sí.

TEACHER. What? (*Twists his ear even more.*)

MONTY. Yes!

TEACHER. Yes, what?

MONTY. Yes, teacher!

TEACHER. Sit down! (*He sits down crying.*) And shut up! Let's see who's next. Oh, yes, Francisco.

FRANCISCO. ¿Qué?

TEACHER. Oh! Another one that can't speak English! Why do they send these kids to me? You can't communicate with them. Is there anybody here that can speak Spanish?

MONTY. I can, teacher.

TEACHER. Tell him to do his ABC's.

MONTY. Dice que digas tu ABC's.

FRANCISCO. Dile que no las sabo en inglés, nomás en español.

MONTY. Teacher, he don't know how.

TEACHER. Oh, sit down! This has been a most trying day! Class dismissed . . . (*Students start to run out cheering.*) except (*They freeze.*) for Monty and Franky. (*Teacher points to them. The rest of the class runs out.*)

MALCOLM. (*Offstage.*) You better give me that swing.

ABRAHAM. (*Offstage.*) No!

MALCOLM. (*Offstage.*) I'm gonna hit you.

ABRAHAM. (*Offstage.*) No. (*Slap is heard and then Abraham wails.*)

TEACHER. (*Teacher, Monty and Francisco freeze until after the above, then they begin to move again.*) Now look, boy. Tell him his name is no longer Francisco, but Franky.

MONTY. Dice que tu nombre ya no es Francisco, es Franky.

FRANCISCO. No es Francisco . . . Panchito.

MONTY. Hey, teacher, he said his name is still Francisco.

(*Francisco punches him in the back.*)

TEACHER. Look boy, Francisco . . . no; Franky . . . yes.

FRANCISCO. No. Francisco.

TEACHER. Franky!

FRANCISCO. Francisco!

TEACHER. Franky!

FRANCISCO. Okay. (*As Teacher begins to walk away to audience.*) Francisco.

TEACHER. It's Franky!

FRANCISCO. (*Grabs sign and throws it on the ground.*) Es Francisco, ya estufas.

TEACHER. Oh! You nasty boy! (*Beats him over the head twice.*) Remember the Alamo! (*Hits him again.*) And just for that, you don't pass.

MONTY. Teacher, teacher, do I pass? (*Picks up sign, and hands it to her.*)

TEACHER. I suppose so. You are learning to speak English. (*To audience.*) They shouldn't place these culturally deprived kids with the normal children. No, no, no. (*She leaves. Stomps out. Monty begins to follow.*)

FRANCISCO. (*Getting up from floor.*) Oye, Moctezuma, ¿qué dijo esa vieja chaparra y panzona?

MONTY. Dijo que tú no pasaste. You don't pass.

FRANCISCO. ¿Y tú pasaste?

MONTY. Sure, I pass. I speak good English and, besides my name isn't Moctezuma anymore . . . it's Monty.

FRANCISCO. No, es Moctezuma.

MONTY. Monty.

FRANCISCO. Moctezuma.

MONTY. It's Monty. See, you stupid? You never learn. (*Sticks his tongue out at him and leaves.*)

FRANCISCO. (*Crying.*) Entonces dile a tu teacher que coma chet! (*Leaves crying.*)

High School. Scene begins with same stand at center stage. High school teacher, male, grey business suit, white mask. Walks across stage. Places high school sign on board.

STUDENTS. (*Backstage, singing.*) On hail to thee, our Alma Mater, we'll always hold you dear. (*Then a cheer.*) Rah, rah, sis boom bah! Sock it to them, sock it to them! (*Florence enters stage right. Abraham enters stage left. His neck has a reddish tinge. He tries to hug Florence and is pushed away. He tries again and is pushed away. Florence continues walking.*)

ABRAHAM. Where you going?

FLORENCE. To class.

ABRAHAM. What do you mean to class? I thought we were going steady.

FLORENCE. We were going steady.

ABRAHAM. (*Mimicking her.*) What do you mean "We were going steady?"

FLORENCE. That's right. I saw you walking with that new girl, Esperanza.

ABRAHAM. That Mexican chick? Aw, you know what I want from her. Besides, you're the only girl I love. I'll even get down on my knees for you. (*Falls on knees.*)

FLORENCE. Oh! Abe, don't be ridiculous, get up.

ABRAHAM. (*Getting up.*) Does that mean we're still going steady?

FLORENCE. I guess so.

ABRAHAM. Hot dog! (*From stage right Francisco enters wear-*

ing dark glasses and strutting like a vato loco. Abraham to Florence.) See that spic over there? Just to show you how much I love you, I'm gonna kick his butt!

FLORENCE. Oh, Abe, you can't be racist!

ABRAHAM. Get out of my way. *(Does warm up exercises like a boxer. Francisco has been watching him all along and has a knife in his hand, hidden behind his back so that it is not visible.)* Heh, greaser, spic!

FRANCISCO. *(Calmly.)* You talking to me, vato?

ABRAHAM. You want some beef? *(Raises his fists.)*

FRANCISCO. *(To audience.)* Este vato quiere pedo. ¿Cómo la ven? ¡Pos que le ponga! *(Pulls out a knife and goes after Abraham.)*

ABRAHAM. *(Backing up.)* Heh, wait a minute! I didn't mean it. I was only fooling. I . . . *(Francisco thrusts knife toward Abraham. Florence steps in between and stops the knife by holding Francisco's arm. Action freezes. From stage right Malcolm jumps in and struts downstage. He wears a do rag on his head, and sunglasses. He bops around, snapping his fingers; walks up to Francisco and Abraham; looks at knife, feels the blade and walks away as if nothing is happening. From stage right, Monty enters with his arm around Esperanza "Hopi." He runs up to Malcolm.)*

MONTY. Hey, man, what's going on here?

MALCOLM. Say, baby, I don't know. I just don't get into these things. *(Moves away.)*

MONTY. *(Stops him.)* Hey, man, I said what's going on here?

MALCOLM. And I said I don't get into these things! What's the matter with you? Don't you understand? Don't you speak English?

MONTY. *(Angered.)* You think you're better than me, huh? *(Monty grabs Malcolm by the throat, and Malcolm grabs him back. They start choking each other. Teacher enters stage center and observes the fight.)*

MONTY. Nigger!

MALCOLM. Greaser!

MONTY. Coon!

MALCOLM. Spic!

ESPERANZA. Oh, Monty, Monty!

TEACHER. Okay, that's enough. Cut it out, boys! We can settle this after school in the gym. We might even charge admission. Everyone to your seats. *(Monty and Malcolm separate. Francisco puts his knife away and all move back to their seats.)*

TEACHER. Now, before we begin, I want to know who started that fight.

ABRAHAM. *(Innocently.)* Mr. White? He did, Sir.

FRANCISCO. *(Stands up.)* I didn't start anything. He insulted me!

ABRAHAM. Who you going to believe, him or me? Besides, he pulled a knife.

TEACHER. *(To Francisco.)* You did what? Get to the Principal's office immediately!

FRANCISCO. Orale, but you know what? This is the last time I'm going to the Principal's office for something

like this. *(Exits mumbling.)* Me la vas a pagar, ese, qué te crees.

TEACHER. I don't understand that boy. And he's one of the school's best athletes. *(Opens mouth, sudden realization. Runs to exit, shouts after Francisco.)* Don't forget to show up for baseball practice. The school needs you.

FLORENCE. *(Stands.)* Mr. White? I refuse to sit next to Abraham. He's a liar!

TEACHER. *(Stands next to Abraham.)* Why, Florence, Abe here is the son of one of our best grower families.

FLORENCE. Well, I don't care if you believe me or not. But I refuse to sit next to a liar. *(Gives Abraham his ring.)* And here's your ring.

TEACHER. All right, sit over here. *(Florence moves across stage and sits next to Esperanza. Francisco comes strutting in, whistling.)* I thought I told you to go to the Principal's office.

FRANCISCO. I did, man.

TEACHER. What did he say?

FRANCISCO. He told me not to beat on anymore of his gabachitos. *(Taps Abraham on the head.)*

TEACHER. *(Angered.)* All right, sit over there. *(Indicates a spot beside Florence.)* And you . . . *(To Esperanza.)* over here.

ESPERANZA. *(Stops beside Francisco at center stage.)* You rotten pachuco. *(She sits besides Abraham.)*

FRANCISCO. Uh que la . . . esta ruca, man. *(He sits besides Florence.)*

TEACHER. Now, class, before we begin our high school reports, I'd like to introduce a new student. Her name is Esperanza Espinoza. *(He gives the pronunciation of her name with an Italian inflection.)* It sounds Italian, I know, but I think she's Mexican-American. Isn't that right, dear?

ESPERANZA. *(Self-consciously rising.)* No, my parents were, but I'm Hawaiian. And you can just call me Hopi.

TEACHER. That's fine, Hopi. Now for our high school reports. Florence, you're first.

FLORENCE. *(Drumbeats. Florence walks to center stage, swaying hips like a stripper.)* A is for achievement. B is for betterment. And C is for *(Bump and grind.)* college! *(More drumbeats as she walks back to her seat.)*

TEACHER. *(Impressed.)* Well! It's good to see that you're thinking of your future. Let's see who's next. Oh yes, Willie.

MALCOLM. *(Hops to his feet.)* I told you, man, my name ain't Willie. It's Malcolm!

TEACHER. All right, you perfectionist! Get up there and give your report.

MALCOLM. *(Struts to center stage. He begins to snap his fingers, setting a rhythm. Everybody joins in.)* A is for Africa. B is for black like me. And C is for community like black ghetto.

ALL. *(Still snapping to rhythm.)* My goodness, Willie, you sure got rhythm. But then after all, all you people do. *(Three final snaps.)*

TEACHER. Now then, Willie, about your report. The first

two pages were fine, but that last part about the ghetto . . . don't you think it needs some improvement?

MALCOLM. You're telling me! Don't you think we know it?

TEACHER. Okay, that's a good C minus. Back to your seat. (*Malcolm sits down.*) Abraham, up front!

ABRAHAM. Jabol mein fuehrer! (*Stomps to center stage.*) A is for America: Love or leave it! (*Francisco and Malcolm stand up to leave.*)

TEACHER. Heh, you two! (*Motions for them to sit down.*)

ABRAHAM. B is for better: Better dead than red. And C is for kill, kill, kill! As in the United States Marine Corps. (*Snaps to attention.*)

TEACHER. (*Marches up like a Marine.*) Very good, Abraham!

ABRAHAM. (*Saluting.*) Thank you, sir.

TEACHER. That's an A plus, Abraham!

ABRAHAM. What did you expect, sir?

TEACHER. Dismissed! (*Abraham marches back to seat.*) Monty, up front!

MONTY. Yes, sir! (*Marches sloppily to stage center. Salutes and freezes.*)

TEACHER. (*With contempt.*) Cut that out, and give your report.

MONTY. A is for American. B is for beautiful, like America the Beautiful. And C is for country, like God bless this beautiful American country! Ooooh, I love it. (*He falls to his knees, kisses the floor.*)

TEACHER. (*Grabs Monty by the collar like a dog.*) Here, have a dog biscuit. (*Monty scarfs up imaginary dog biscuit, then is led back to his seat on all fours by Teacher.*) Now, who's next? Oh yes, Hopi.

ESPERANZA. (*Rises prissily, goes to center stage.*) A is for Avon, as in "Ding dong, Avon calling." B is for burgers, which I love, and beans, which I hate! (*Sneers at Francisco.*) And C is for can't as in "I can't speak Spanish." And we have a new Buick Riviera, and my sister goes to the University of California, and we live in a tract home . . .

TEACHER. (*Leading her back to her seat.*) Yes, dear! Just fine!

ESPERANZA. Really, really we do!

TEACHER. I believe you. That deserves a bean . . . uh, I mean B plus. (*Pause.*) Now let's hear from . . . Franky?

FRANCISCO. Yeah, Teach?

TEACHER. What do you mean "yeah, Teach?" You know my name is Mr. White.

FRANCISCO. I know what you name is, ese. But you seem to forget that my name is Francisco, loco.

TEACHER. Get up and give your report, you hoodlum.

FRANCISCO. Orale, ese vato, llévatela suave. (*Moves to center stage.*) A is for amor, como amor de mi raza.

TEACHER. What!

FRANCISCO. B is for barrio como where the raza lives. (*Teacher growls.*) And C is carnalismo.

TEACHER. (*Heated.*) How many times have I told you about speaking Spanish in my classroom? Now what did you say?

FRANCISCO. Carnalismo.

TEACHER. (*At the limit of his patience.*) And what does that mean?

FRANCISCO. Brotherhood.

TEACHER. (*Blows up.*) Get out!!

FRANCISCO. Why? I was only speaking my language. I'm a Chicano, ¿que no?

TEACHER. Because I don't understand you, and the rest of the class doesn't understand you.

FRANCISCO. So what? When I was small, I didn't understand English, and you kept flunking me and flunking me instead of teaching me.

TEACHER. You are permanently expelled from this high school!

FRANCISCO. Big deal! You call yourself a teacher! I can communicate in two languages. You can only communicate in one. Who's the teacher, Teach? (*Starts to exit.*)

MONTY. We're not all like that, teacher.

FRANCISCO. ¡Tú te me callas! (*Pushes Monty aside and exits.*)

TEACHER. That's the last straw! A is for attention. B is for brats like that. And C is for cut out. High school dismissed! (*Teacher exits, taking high school sign with him. Malcolm exits also at opposite side of stage. Abraham, Florence, Esperanza and Monty rise, facing each other.*)

MONTY. (*Looking at Florence.*) Oh, Hopi?

ESPERANZA. (*Looking at Abraham.*) Yes?

ABRAHAM. (*Looking at Esperanza.*) Oh, Flo?

FLORENCE. (*Looking at Monty.*) Yeah?

ABRAHAM AND MONTY. (*Together.*) Do you wanna break up?

FLORENCE AND ESPERANZA. (*Together.*) Yeah! (*Monty takes Florence by the arm; Abraham takes Esperanza.*)

MONTY. Oh boy, let's go to a party.

ABRAHAM. Let's go to a fiesta. (*all exit.*)

State College. Backstage sounds: Police siren, shouts of "pigs off campus!" College Professor enters and places sign on stand. It reads, "State College." Francisco enters pushing a broom.

FRANCISCO. Oh, professor?

PROFESSOR. Yes?

FRANCISCO. I want to go to college.

PROFESSOR. Didn't you drop out of high school?

FRANCISCO. Simón, but I still want to go to college. I want to educate myself.

PROFESSOR. Well, that's tough. (*Exits.*)

FRANCISCO. Pos, mira, qué jijo . . . (*Swings broom. Florence enters followed by Monty. Francisco freezes.*)

FLORENCE. Guess what, folks? Monty and I are living together. Isn't that right, Monty?

MONTY. That's right, baby. Just me and you.

FLORENCE. Do you love me, Monty?

MONTY. Oh, you know I do.

FLORENCE. Then, come to momma!

MONTY. Ay mamasota, una gabacha! (*He runs over to her and begins to kiss her passionately.*)

FLORENCE. (*Swooning.*) Oh, you Latin lovers.

MONTY. (*Suddenly peeved.*) Latin lovers? Your people have been oppressing my people for 150 years!

FLORENCE. Yes, Monty!

MONTY. You gabachas are all alike!

FLORENCE. (*The guilty liberal.*) Oh yes, Monty!

MONTY. And that's why I'm going to give it to you! (*Rolls up his sleeve, clenches fist.*) Right between the you-know-what. (*Grabs her and begins to kiss her again passionately.*) ¡Viva Zapata! (*Makes out again.*) ¡Viva Villa! (*Raises fist.*) ¡Viva la Revolución! (*Wraps a leg around her. Kisses her. Then falls to the floor exhausted.*)

FLORENCE. (*Sitting on his back.*) Oh, Monty. You do that so well.

MONTY. (*Puffing underneath.*) Shut up. While my people are starving in the barrio, your people are sitting fat and reech.

FLORENCE. Reech?

MONTY. Rich! Rich, you beech. Oh, my accent sleeped . . . slopped, sloped! What am I saying?

FLORENCE. (*Noticing Francisco.*) Monty, look, a chicken-o.

MONTY. A what?

FLORENCE. A Mexican-American?

MONTY. A what?

FLORENCE. An American of Mexican descent?

MONTY. I'm going to give you one more chance. I'm going to spell it out for you. (*Spells out C-H-I-C-A-N-O in the air.*) What's this?

FLORENCE. (*Reading his movements.*) C!

MONTY. And this and this? (*H and I.*)

FLORENCE. C-H-I . . . Chic! Chica . . . oh, Chicano! Chicano! (*Jumps up and down.*)

MONTY. Good! Now get out. And don't come back until I call you. (*Florence exits.*) 'Cause this is a job for . . . Supermacho! (*Approaches Francisco. Anglo accent to his Spanish.*) ¡Qué-húbole, easy vato loco? Heh, don't I know you?

FRANCISCO. ¿Qué nuevas?

MONTY. Isn't your name Francisco?

FRANCISCO. Simón.

MONTY. You're wanted.

FRANCISCO. No, I'm not! (*Begins to run across stage.*)

MONTY. For our program. (*Stops Francisco.*)

FRANCISCO. What program?

FLORENCE. (*Sticking her hand out from backstage.*) Now Monty?

MONTY. No, not yet. (*Turns to Francisco.*) Hey, man, you know la raza is getting together! You know we have 300 years of Chicano culture? You know our women are beautiful?! Just look at them, mamasotas!

FRANCISCO. Simón, están a toda madre.

MONTY. Pero primero necesitamos unos cuantos gritos como los meros machos. Mira, fíjate, ¡Que viva la raza! (*Francisco repeats.*) ¡Que viva la huelga! (*Francisco repeats.*)

FLORENCE. (*Enters.*) Look, Monty, I'm getting tired of waiting, godamit!

MONTY. (*Turns to Florence.*) Okay, just a minute. Just one more. (*Turns to Francisco.*) Uno más pero éste con muchos tú sabes qué, ¿eh? ¡Que viva la revolución!

FRANCISCO. ¡La revolución . . . ? (*Looks at Florence.*) Pos que viva, y a comenzar con esa gabacha, jija de . . .

MONTY. Hey, wait a minute, man. That's not where it's at, vato. This is what you call "universal love." I don't think you're ready for college. (*Florence jumps on Monty's back.*) And when you are, come look for me up at the Mexican Opportunity Commission Organization: MOCO. And I'm the Head Moco. Chicano power, carnal! (*Exits.*)

FRANCISCO. (*To audience.*) No, hombre, está más mocoso que la . . . (*Hopi and Abraham enter stage left. Abraham is wearing a ten gallon hat.*)

ESPERANZA. Guess what, folks? Abraham and I are engaged. Isn't that right, Abraham?

ABRAHAM. That's right, baby. Just me and you. (*He leans her over to kiss her.*)

ESPERANZA. (*Snapping back up. To Francisco.*) What are you looking at?

FRANCISCO. Oh! Esperanza, ¿no te acuerdas de mí?

ESPERANZA. My name is Hopi.

FRANCISCO. Orale, esa, no te . . .

ABRAHAM. Is that Mexican bothering you?

ESPERANZA. Just ignore him, sugar plum, just ignore him. (*They move stage right.*)

ABRAHAM. Do you know that my dad owns 20,000 acres of lettuce in the Salinas Valley?

ESPERANZA. Really!

ABRAHAM. And he has 200 dumb Mexicans just like him working for him.

ESPERANZA. Really!

ABRAHAM. My daddy's a genius!

ESPERANZA. Oh! You're so smart! You're so intelligent! Oh, you white god, you! (*Bows falling on her knees in worship.*)

ABRAHAM. Shucks. You don't have to do that. Why, you remind me of a little brown squaw my grandpappy used to have.

ESPERANZA. Squaw! (*Getting up in anger.*)

ABRAHAM: Don't get mad, my little taco. My little tamale. My little frijol. (*Pronounced free hole.*)

FRANCISCO. Free hole?

ABRAHAM. Besides, I've got a surprise for you. Why, just the other day my pappy made me president.

ESPERANZA. President?

ABRAHAM. President!

ESPERANZA. Of the company?

ABRAHAM. Of the Future Farmers of America.

ESPERANZA. (*Disappointed.*) Oh, Abraham.

FRANCISCO. (*Laughing, moves up to Hopi.*) ¡Oyes, por eso venistes al colegio? ¿A toparte con un pendejo?

ESPERANZA. Well, at least he's not out on the corner pushing dope.

ABRAHAM. You Mexicans ought to be out in the fields.

ESPERANZA. (*To Abraham.*) You tell him, sugar.

FRANCISCO. That's all you think I can do, huh? Well I'm gonna go to college on the E.O.P. program!

ESPERANZA. Look. I made it through college without any assistance. I don't see why you can't.

FRANCISCO. (*Mimics her.*) I made it through college . . . (Professor *enters stage center, Monty and Florence enter stage right.*)

PROFESSOR. Ladies and gentlemen, can we prepare for our college seminar? (*Spots Francisco.*) Aren't you the custodian?

FRANCISCO. Yes, but, a . . . Monty wants to talk to you.

MONTY. Oh, sir, we thought we might be able to get him in under MOCO, you know, Mexican Opportunity Commission Organization?

PROFESSOR. Now look, Monty, we got you in here and unless you want to be out, get back into your place. (*To Francisco.*) No, I'm sorry, there's no room. No room! (*Pushes him out.*)

FRANCISCO. I want to go to college!

PROFESSOR. These students, they don't understand. (*To audience.*) They don't realize that there is no room in our college, no room at all. In this college there is not room for one more student. Not one more minority student. (*Malcolm enters stage right wearing a black shirt, black leather jacket and black beret. He is carrying a rifle. Abraham begins to shake and points at him.*)

PROFESSOR. (*To Abraham.*) I'll handle it. (*Moves over to Malcolm.*) Pardon me, boy, but are you registered? (*Malcolm cocks rifle, Professor looks at rifle chamber, looks at Malcolm, looks at audience.*) He's registered.

ALL. He's registered.

FRANCISCO. (*Peeking back in.*) ¿Vistes eso, Moctezuma?

PROFESSOR. No, no, out! Out! (*Moctezuma helps Professor push Francisco out.*)

MONTY. (*Pushes him out.*) I'll see that it doesn't happen again, sir.

PROFESSOR. Well, see that it doesn't. Now class, in order to qualify for graduation, you must deliver one final report. And it must be concise, logical and have conviction. Miss Florence, you're first.

FLORENCE. A is for anti as in anti-war. B is for Berkeley as in anti-war Berkeley. And C is for chick as in anti-war Berkeley chick.

PROFESSOR. Well, that was a very personal and revealing account, Miss Florence, and that should qualify for . . .

ABRAHAM. That stunk! And if you pass her, I'll have your job. Remember, you are working for my daddy!

MONTY. Oh, sir, please give her one more chance.

PROFESSOR. Yes, just get back to your seat, Monty. I was about to say that it lacked conviction. Try again, Miss Florence. (*Stands next to her.*)

FLORENCE. A is for adult.

PROFESSOR. A-huh.

FLORENCE. B is for become, as to become an adult.

PROFESSOR. It happens to the best of us.

FLORENCE. And C is for cop-out, as to become an adult and cop-out.

PROFESSOR. That is the American way, Miss Florence. You will graduate! Let's see who's next . . . Malcolm.

MALCOLM. (*Moves forward menacingly.*) A is for Afro, as in Afro-American. B is for Black, as in Afro-American Black Panther. And C is for Cleaver, Eldridge Cleaver, Afro-American Black Panther! (*Gives panther salute.*)

PROFESSOR. Well, I see the logic, but I don't like it.

MALCOLM. Good, that's the way we want it!

PROFESSOR. All right! All right! You'll graduate.

ABRAHAM. He graduates? (*He begins to pantomime different ways of killing Malcolm. Machine gun, grenades, airplane and finally builds a rocket.*) A is for anti. (*Puts first stage of missile.*) B is for ballistic. (*Builds second stage.*) And M is for missile. (*Puts final stage on missile. During the above, Malcolm has just been standing, cool and collected. Everybody but Malcolm begins the countdown.*)

ALL. 5–4–3–2–1 Fire! (*They make whistling noise of a rocket in the air. As the rocket lands with a loud noise, Malcolm turns around and points gun at Abraham.*)

ABRAHAM. (*Scared like a boy.*) A is for animal. B is for back off. And C is for coward, Mama! (*Exits.*)

PROFESSOR. Abraham, come back! (*Francisco enters stage left dressed as a brown beret with rifle in hand.*)

FRANCISCO. ¿Ya ves, Moctezuma? (*Monty tries to push him out, but is thrown back.*) ¡Un lado!

PROFESSOR. Just a minute! Just a minute! (*To Francisco.*) You want to go to college? What are your qualifications?

FRANCISCO. My qualifications? Pos, mira que jijo de . . . (*Pulls back rifle into position to hit Teacher from the front and Malcolm pokes his gun at his back. They freeze and Esperanza walks over and moves around Francisco, checking him out. She moves back to her place.*)

PROFESSOR. (*Jumps up and they unfreeze.*) All right, you're in!

FRANCISCO. Where do I sit?

PROFESSOR. Over there! (*Frantically.*) This is getting out of hand. Monty, Monty, my boy, your report.

MONTY. A is for American like a Mexican-American.

PROFESSOR. Wonderful!

MONTY. And B is for bright, like a bright Mexican-American.

PROFESSOR. Great! Great!

MONTY. And C is for comprado like a bright, Mexican-American comprado.

PROFESSOR. Bought and sold! Monty, my boy, you will graduate. Congratulations! And as you go forward into this great society, I want you to remember one thing. (*Points forward.*) I want you always to move forward, move forward in that great American tradition. (*Monty *has been looking to where the* Professor *has been pointing, gets scared and sneaks off to his place, moving backward.*) Forever forward. (*Looks around when he realizes that Monty has left.*) Monty! Monty! (*Getting hysterical.*) Oh! This is getting out of hand! Out of hand! Let's see. Oh, yes, Hopi?

ESPERANZA. (*She has been talking to Francisco and now has her arms around his neck.*) Who?

PROFESSOR. (*Scared.*) Hopi?

ESPERANZA. My name is Esperanza, you marrano!

PROFESSOR. Your report, please.

ESPERANZA. Orale, llévatela suave. (*Walks pachuca fashion to center stage.*) A is for action, as in acción social. B is for batos, as in acción social de batos. And C is for Chicana as in Acción Social de Batos y Chicanas. (*Francisco lets out with a grito.*)

FRANCISCO. ¿Y ahora qué dices, Moctezuma?

PROFESSOR. All right, Francisco, your report.

FRANCISCO. Hey, wait a minute, man. I just got in here.

MONTY. What's the matter? Can't do it, huh?

PROFESSOR. (*Regaining a sense of authority.*) Is that your problem, boy, can't you do it?

FRANCISCO. Yes, I can! And don't call me boy!

PROFESSOR. (*Cringes in fear again.*) Fine, fine.

FRANCISCO. A is for advanced, as the advanced culture of Indigenous American Aztlán. B is for bronze as in the advanced culture of Indigenous American Aztlán, which brought bronze civilization to the Western Hemisphere. And C is for century, as the advanced culture of Indigenous American Aztlán, which brought bronze civilization to the Western Hemisphere and which, moreover, will create el nuevo hombre in the twenty-first century, El Chicano. Give me my diploma.

PROFESSOR. Just a minute, hold it right there! (*Goes to side and grabs book.*) I have here in my hand the book of American knowledge. There is nothing in here about Asta lan, nothing in here about Chicken-o. In fact there is nothing in here about nothing and, as you can see, (*Turns book towards the audience, there is a dollar sign printed on page.*) this is the honest truth which is close to all of our American hearts. No, I'm sorry, but under the circumstances, I don't think that you will (*Francisco has gun in Professor's face and Malcolm puts his rifle to his back.*) be here next year, because you will graduate. (*Malcolm and Francisco move to their places.*) And now, students, line up for that golden moment, graduation! And here to present the awards on this fine day is none other than that great statesman, that golden-mouthed orator, that old grape sucker himself, the President of the United States, Mr. Richard Nixon. (*Nixon moves in from stage right, he is wearing cap and gown, giving peace symbol. Shakes hands with Professor.*) A few words, please, Mr. President.

NIXON. I'd like to say just three things today, only three. First, don't forget that great American dollar which put you through college. (*Applause.*) Second, always kiss ass; and third, eat plenty of Salinas scab lettuce!

PROFESSOR. Thank you, Mr. President. Now, if you'll just step this way, we shall begin the awards. First, we have Miss Florence, a fine girl. (*Florence moves to centerstage, receives diploma. Nixon places a graduation cap on her head. Cap comes with white hood, which covers her head completely. She moves back to her place.*) Next we have, Monty. Good boy. (*Monty walks up and kisses the President's hand. Then he places cap over his own head, goes back to his place.*) Next is Willie.

PRESIDENT. Here we are, Willie.

MALCOLM. (*Takes diploma.*) My name is Malcolm, you white mutha. (*President and Professor duck.*)

PRESIDENT. And here's your white bag.

MALCOLM. I don't need that.

PROFESSOR. But what are you going to do without it?

MALCOLM. You're going to find out. (*He walks to stage right and whistles.*) Come here, baby. (*Florence takes off her cap, moves to center stage, throws cap on floor, walks off stage with Malcolm.*)

PRESIDENT. A militant!

PROFESSOR. That's okay. There's a whole lot of them that aren't. Next we have Francisco. (*Francisco moves up, takes diploma, moves quickly back to his place. President tries to put cap on him, misses and almost falls on Esperanza. He backs off cautiously.*)

PRESIDENT. Speedy, these Mexicans. Fast!

PROFESSOR. Next, we have Esperanza. (*She moves to center stage, takes diploma.*)

PRESIDENT. And here's your white bag.

ESPERANZA. I don't need your white bag!

PRESIDENT. But you can't exist in our society without me.

PROFESSOR. What are you going to do without your white bag? (*From audience someone gets up and yells, "Hey, I want to go to college."*)

ESPERANZA. That's what I'm going to do. I'm going to help my carnales get into college.

VATO. ¡Ayúdenme! (*Runs toward stage.*)

PROFESSOR. No! (*Francisco and Esperanza try to help Vato from audience. There's a tug of war.*)

VATO. ¡Sí! (*With Francisco and Esperanza.*)

PROFESSOR. No!

VATO. ¡Sí!

PROFESSOR. No!

VATO. ¡Sí! (*Jumps up onstage, pushing Professor back. Vato waves to audience and yells.*) Orale, I made it into college. (*Gives Chicano handshake to Francisco and Esperanza.*)

PRESIDENT. Well, I can see that my job here is done. I shall now take my students, student . . . into the great white world. Right face! Forward march! (*Exits stage right followed by Monty.*)

FRANCISCO. ¡Moctezuma! ¡Quédate con tu raza!

ESPERANZA. Ah, let him go. There's more where he came from.

FRANCISCO. ¡Pos, que le pongan! (*Students start coming in from all sides of stage, everyone starts pointing at Professor yelling.*) Teach us! Teach us!

PROFESSOR. Just a minute. Just a minute. (*To audience.*) So many brown faces, brown minds, brown ideas, what is this? A chocolate factory? (*Everybody jumps at him.*) I'm going to a college where they understand. Where they appreciate good white professors, where there won't be any Chicanos . . . like Fresno State College. President Baxter, help!!!

(*Exits stage right. Everybody starts looking for change. Vato begins to take collection.*)

FRANCISCO. ¿Colecta, para qué?
FIRST NEW STUDENT. La birria.
SECOND NEW STUDENT. La mota.
THIRD NEW STUDENT. El wine.

FRANCISCO. Pos, ¿no están bien, calabazas? Estamos en colegio. Hay que aprender de nuestra cultura, nuestra raza, de Aztlán.

VATO. (*Turns to next student.*) But who's going to teach us? (*They move on down the line asking each other the same question.*)

ESPERANZA. (*Last in line, asks Francisco.*) Who's going to teach us?

FRANCISCO. Who's going to teach us?
ALL. Our own people! (*They point at audience.*)
FRANCISCO. ¡Entonces, qué se dice? ¡Viva . . . !
ALL. ¡La raza!
FRANCISCO. ¡Viva!
ALL. ¡La huelga!
FRANCISCO. ¡Chicano!
ALL. Power! (*Actors get audience to shout "Chicano power." Then all sing "bella ciao."*)

FORUM

"From *Theater of the Oppressed*"

AUGUSTO BOAL

The Brazilian Boal is perhaps the best-known contemporary artist to use theater as a means to bring about social change. Others have adopted his methods throughout Latin America, Africa, and other Third World locales, and there have been a number of symposia and workshops dedicated to Boal's work. This abridged essay (numerous specific examples have been pruned) is both a manifesto for Boal's social-activist theater and a guidebook to his methods.

In the beginning the theater was the dithyrambic song: free people singing in the open air. The carnival. The feast.

Later, the ruling classes took possession of the theater and built their dividing walls. First, they divided the people, separating actors from spectators: people who act and people who watch—the party is over! Secondly, among the actors, they separated the protagonists from the mass. The coercive indoctrination began!

Now the oppressed people are liberated themselves and, once more, are making the theater their own. The walls must be torn down. First, the spectator starts acting again: invisible theater, forum theater, image theater, etc. Secondly, it is necessary to eliminate the private property of the characters by the individual actors: the "Joker" System. . . .

In order to understand this *poetics of the oppressed* one must keep in mind its main objective: to change the people—"spectators," passive beings in the theatrical phenomenon—into subjects, into actors, transformers of the dramatic action. I hope that the differences remain clear. Aristotle proposes a poetics in which the spectator delegates power to the dramatic character so that the latter may act and think for him. Brecht proposes a poetics in which the spectator delegates power to the character who thus acts in his place but the spectator reserves the right to think for himself, often in opposition to the character. In the first case, a "catharsis" occurs; in the second, an awakening of critical consciousness. But the *poetics of the oppressed* focuses on the action itself: the spectator delegates no power to the character (or actor) either to act or to think in his place; on the contrary, he himself assumes the protagonic role, changes the dra-

(continued)

matic action, tries out solutions, discusses plans for change—in short, trains himself for real action. In this case, perhaps the theater is not revolutionary in itself, but it is surely a rehearsal for the revolution. The liberated spectator, as a whole person, launches into action. No matter that the action is fictional; what matters is that it is action!

I believe that all the truly revolutionary theatrical groups should transfer to the people means of production in the theater so that the people themselves may utilize them. The theater is a weapon, and it is the people who should wield it. . . .

We can begin by stating that the first word of the theatrical vocabulary is the human body, the main source of sound and movement. Therefore, to control the means of theatrical production, man must, first of all, control his own body, know his own body, in order to be capable of making it more expressive. Then he will be able to practice theatrical forms in which by stages he frees himself from his condition of spectator and takes on that of actor, in which he ceases to be an object and becomes a subject, is changed from witness into protagonist.

The plan for transforming the spectator into actor can be systematized in the following general outline of four stages:

First stage: *Knowing the body:* a series of exercises by which one gets to know one's body, its limitations and possibilities, its social distortions and possibilities of rehabilitation.

Second stage: *Making the body expressive:* a series of games by which one begins to express one's self through the body, abandoning other, more common and habitual forms of expression.

Third Stage: *The theater as language:* one begins to practice theater as a language that is living and *present,* not as a finished product displaying images from the past:

First degree: *Simultaneous dramaturgy:* the spectators "write" simultaneously with the acting of the actors;

Second degree: *Image theater:* the spectators intervene directly, "speaking" through images made with the actors' bodies;

Third degree: *Forum theater:* the spectators intervene directly in the dramatic action and act.

Fourth stage: *The theater as discourse:* simple forms in which the spectator-actor creates "spectacles" according to his need to discuss certain themes or rehearse certain actions.

Examples:

1. Newspaper theater
2. Invisible theater
3. Photo-romance theater
4. Breaking of repression
5. Myth theater
6. Trial theater
7. Masks and Rituals

FIRST STAGE: KNOWING THE BODY

The initial contact with a group of peasants, workers, or villagers—if they are confronted with the proposal to put on a the-atrical performance—can be extremely difficult. They have quite likely never heard of theater and if they have heard of it, their conception of it will probably have been distorted by television, with its emphasis on sentimentality, or by some traveling circus group. It is also very common for those people to associate theater with leisure or frivolity. Thus caution is required even when the contact takes place through an educator who belongs to the same class as the illiterates or semi-illiterates, even if he lives among them in a shack and shares their comfortless life. The very fact that the educator comes with the mission of eradicating illiteracy (which presupposes a coercive, forceful action) is in itself an alienating factor between the agent and the local people. For this reason the theatrical experience should begin not with something alien to the people (theatrical techniques that are taught or imposed) but with the *bodies* of those who agree to participate in the experiment.

There is a great number of exercises designed with the objective of making each person aware of his own body, of his bodily possibilities, and of deformations suffered because of the type of work he performs. That is, it is necessary for each one to feel the "muscular alienation" imposed on his body by work. . . .

SECOND STAGE: MAKING THE BODY EXPRESSIVE

In the second stage the intention is to develop the expressive ability of the body. In our culture we are used to expressing everything through words, leaving the enormous expressive capabilities of the body in an underdeveloped state. A series of "games" can help the participants to begin to use their bodily resources for self-expression. I am talking about parlor games and not necessarily those of a theatrical laboratory. The participants are invited to "play," not to "interpret," characters but they will "play" better to the extent that they "interpret" better.

For example: In one game pieces of paper containing names of animals, male and female, are distributed, one to each participant. For ten minutes, each person tries to give a physical, bodily impression of the animal named on his piece of paper. Talking or making noises that would suggest the animal is forbidden. The communication must be effected entirely through the body. After the first ten minutes, each participant must find his mate among the others who are imitating the animals, since there will always be a male and a female for each one. When two participants are convinced they constitute a pair, they leave the stage, and the game is over when all participants find their mates through a purely physical communication, without the utilization of words or recognizable sounds.

What is important in games of this type is not to guess right but rather that all the participants try to express themselves through their bodies, something they are not used to doing. Without realizing it they will in fact be giving a "dramatical performance."

THIRD STAGE: THE THEATER AS LANGUAGE

This stage is divided into three parts, each one representing a different degree of direct participation of the spectator in the performance. The spectator is encouraged to intervene in the action, abandoning his condition of object and assuming fully the role of subject. The two preceding stages are preparatory, centering around the work of the participants with their own bodies. Now this stage focuses on the theme to be discussed and furthers the transition from passivity to action.

First degree: *Simultaneous dramaturgy:* This is the first invitation made to the spectator to intervene without necessitating his physical presence on the "stage."

Here it is a question of performing a short scene, of ten to twenty minutes, proposed by a local resident, one who lives in the *barrio*. The actors may improvise with the aid of a script prepared beforehand, as they may also compose the scene directly. In any case, the performance gains in theatricality if the person who proposed the theme is present in the audience. Having begun the scene, the actors develop it to the point at which the main problem reaches a crisis and needs a solution. Then the actors stop the performance and ask the audience to offer solutions. They improvise immediately all the suggested solutions, and the audience has the right to intervene, to correct the actions or words of the actors, who are obligated to comply strictly with these instructions from the audience. Thus, while the audience "writes" the work the actors perform it simultaneously. The spectator's thoughts are discussed theatrically on stage with the help of the actors. All the solutions, suggestions, and opinions are revealed in theatrical form. The discussion itself need not simply take the form of words, but rather should be effected through all the other elements of theatrical expression as well. . . .

This form of theater creates great excitement among the participants and starts to demolish the wall that separates actors from spectators. Some "write" and others act almost simultaneously. The spectators feel that they can intervene in the action. The action ceases to be presented in a deterministic manner, as something inevitable, as Fate. Man is Man's fate. Thus Man-the-spectator is the creator of Man-the-character. Everything is subject to criticism, to rectification. All can be changed, and at a moment's notice: the actors must always be ready to accept, without protest, any proposed action; they must simply act it out, to give a live view of its consequences and drawbacks. Any spectator, by virtue of being a spectator, has the right to try his version—without censorship. The actor does not change his main function: he goes on being the interpreter. What changes is the object of his interpretation. If formerly he interpreted the solitary author locked in his study, to whom divine inspiration dictated a finished text, here on the contrary, he must interpret the mass audience, assembled in their local committees, societies of "friends of the *barrio*," groups of neighbors, schools, unions, peasant leagues, or whatever; he must give expression to the collective thought of men and women. The actor ceases to interpret the individual and starts to interpret the group, which is much more difficult and at the same time much more creative.

Second degree: *Image theater:* Here the spectator has to participate more directly. He is asked to express his views on a certain theme of common interest that the participants wish to discuss. The theme can be far-reaching, abstract—as, for example, imperialism—or it can be a local problem such as the lack of water, a common occurrence in almost all the *barrios*. The participant is asked to express his opinion, but without speaking, using only the bodies of the other participants and "sculpting" with them a group of statues, in such a way that his opinions and feelings become evident. The participant is to use the bodies of the others as if he were a sculptor and the others were made of clay: he must determine the position of each body down to the most minute details of their facial expressions. He is not allowed to speak under any circumstances. The most that is permitted to him is to show with his own facial expressions what he wants the statue-spectator to do. After organizing this group of statues he is allowed to enter into a discussion with the other participants in order to determine if all agree with his "sculpted" opinion. Modifications can be rehearsed: the spectator has the right to modify the statues in their totality or in some detail. When finally an image is arrived at that is the most acceptable to all, then the spectator-sculptor is asked to show the way he would like the given theme to be; that is, in the first grouping the *actual image* is shown, in the second the *ideal image*. Finally he is asked to show a *transitional image*, to show how it would be possible to pass from one reality to the other. In other words, how to carry out the change, the transformation, the revolution, or whatever term one wishes to use. Thus, starting with a grouping of "statues" accepted by all as representative of a real situation, each one is asked to propose ways of changing it. . . .

FOURTH STAGE: THE THEATER AS DISCOURSE

George Ikishawa used to say that the bourgeois theater is the finished theater. The bourgeoisie already knows what the world is like, *their* world, and is able to present images of this complete, finished world. The bourgeoisie presents the spectacle. On the other hand, the proletariat and the oppressed classes do not know yet what their world will be like; consequently their theater will be the rehearsal, not the finished spectacle. This is quite true, though it is equally true that the theater can present images of transition.

I have been able to observe the truth of this view during all my activities in the people's theater of so many and such different countries of Latin America. Popular audiences are interested in experimenting, in rehearsing, and they abhor "closed" spectacles. In those cases they try to enter into a dialogue with the actors, to interrupt the action, to ask for explanations without waiting politely for the end of the play. Contrary to the bourgeois code of manners, the people's code allows and encourages the spectator to ask questions, to dialogue, to participate.

All the methods that I have discussed are forms of a rehearsal-theater, and not a spectacle-theater. One knows how these experiments will begin but not how they will end, because the spectator is freed from his chains, finally acts, and becomes a protagonist. Because they respond to the real needs of a popular audience they are practiced with success and joy. . . .

CONCLUSION: "SPECTATOR, A BAD WORD!"

Yes, this is without a doubt the conclusion: "Spectator" is a bad word! The spectator is less than a man and it is necessary

(continued)

to humanize him, to restore to him his capacity of action in all its fullness. He too must be a subject, an actor on an equal plane with those generally accepted as actors, who must also be spectators. All these experiments of a people's theater have the same objective—the liberation of the spectator, on whom the theater has imposed finished visions of the world. And since those responsible for theatrical performances are in general people who belong directly or indirectly to the ruling classes, obviously their finished images will be reflections of themselves. The spectators in the people's theater (i.e., the people themselves) cannot go on being the passive victims of those images.

As we have seen in the first essay of this book, the poetics of Aristotle is the *poetics of oppression:* the world is known, perfect or about to be perfected, and all its values are imposed on the spectators, who passively delegate power to the characters to act and think in their place. In so doing the spectators purge them-selves of their tragic flaw—that is, of something capable of changing society. A catharsis of the revolutionary impetus is produced! Dramatic action substitutes for real action.

Brecht's poetics is that of the enlightened vanguard: the world is revealed as subject to change, and the change starts in the theater itself, for the spectator does not delegate power to the characters to think in his place, although he continues to delegate power to them to act in his place. The experience is revealing on the level of consciousness, but not globally on the level of the action. Dramatic action throws light upon real action. The spectacle is a preparation for action.

The *poetics of the oppressed* is essentially the poetics of liberation: the spectator no longer delegates power to the characters either to think or to act in his place. The spectator frees himself; he thinks and acts for himself! Theater is action!

Perhaps the theater is not revolutionary in itself; but have no doubts, it is a rehearsal of revolution!

PAPER FLOWERS
(FLORES DE PAPEL)
A Play in Six Scenes

EGON WOLFF

EGON WOLFF (1926 –)

Although a chemical engineer by training, Egon Wolff emerged as a leading voice in South American drama, particularly when *Paper Flowers* won the coveted *Casa de las Américas* Prize in 1970 as Latin America's best new play. The influential *Latin American Theatre Review* called the play "among the top three or four plays from all of Spanish America" in its Spring 1983 edition.

Wolff first wrote plays as an avocation, largely because he wished to address the social, political, and economic problems facing his native Chile. In 1963 he achieved national recognition for his play *The Invaders*, an Expressionistic work in which a rich industrialist dreams that his estate is invaded by the poor—a dream that becomes frighteningly true. Chileans considered the play prophetic when in 1970 Salvador Allende Gossens was elected president, the first Marxist to be elected democratically in the Western Hemisphere. Allende, who promised to turn Chile into a socialist state, was driven from office just three years later by a right-wing military coup led by Augusto Pinochet Ugarte.

As might be expected, Wolff's plays reflect the bitter and often violent struggles between Chile's wealthy and poor classes. He maintains his emphasis on class conflict because "people aren't listening." His plays are directed at the upper class, who—according to Wolff—have the responsibility and the power to change social circumstances in Chile (and elsewhere in Latin America). However, he does not write overt political dramas because "it doesn't interest me."

Wolff admits that his work has become increasingly darker, less hopeful. When he was younger he felt he had answers for the social problems he depicted. "I write for the present of Chile and that is enough. 'Future' is a word that sometimes terrifies me." He continues to write and to work as an engineer. His works have been produced throughout Latin America, the United States, and Great Britain, in both Spanish and English productions.

PAPER FLOWERS (1970)

Paper Flowers may remind North American audiences of Edward Albee's *The Zoo Story* (1958), a controversial one-act play about a New York drifter who accosts a middle-class man in Central Park, berates him for his indifference to the plight of the less fortunate, and finally forces the hapless bourgeois to commit a shocking act of violence that horribly joins the two men in the final moment. Europeans may align Wolff's drama with Harold Pinter's theater of menace because its ambiguous dialogue creates a tension that is simultaneously disturbing and darkly amusing. The plot is also Pinteresque: a seemingly "safe" room is invaded by a mysterious stranger whose presence becomes more menacing as the play progresses toward its frightening conclusion. That Wolff should invite comparisons with Albee and Pinter is not surprising, as the latter were among the West's most imitated playwrights during the 1960s.

Wolff may have absorbed both plot and stylistic elements from the likes of Albee and Pinter, but his work—particularly *Paper Flowers*—reflects the social and political realities that shaped Latin American drama in the 1970s. Wolff's native Chile was perhaps the most notorious example of a country run by an oppressive military dictatorship committed to the preservation of wealth by the few at the expense of the many. The Hake's debasement and eventual conquest of the middle-class Eva reflects the restless, revolutionary spirit among Latin America's poor. Wolff's antipathy toward middle-class complacency, which he believes contributes to anarchy and revolution among the oppressed, has been well documented. *Paper Flowers* is, in one respect, a dramatic working out of a manifesto issued by the Coordinating Committee of the Revolutionary Imagination in Buenos Aires in 1969:

> Art as produced by our society will always be absorbed and rendered useless by the bourgeois. . . . What is it we want to transform? The Latin American man—ourselves: victims of neocolonial exploitation, of our native oligarchy, of all the forms of degradation and humiliation, conscious and unconscious, which shape our human and cultural values, our very existence.

It was in this spirit that many theater companies and collectives were formed throughout Latin America. And it is in this spirit that the Hake tells Eva that "I only know what I am, what I seem and that I am what I don't seem. In other words, you have your fantasy and I have only reality, which is much poorer, much sadder, much more disillusioning." The destruction he wreaks on her well-ordered bourgeois home manifests Wolff's vision of the anarchy that awaits Chile—indeed much of South America—if the disparity between social classes is not addressed. The apocalyptic finale—a mock wedding between the warring classes—is Wolff's darkest resolution and suggests that the hope for reconciliation he expressed in a similar play (*The Invaders*, 1963) is impossible.

But *Paper Flowers* is a more intriguing play than so many of the political tracts that emerged throughout Latin America during this tumultuous period. On one hand, the play is a taut psychological thriller in which the Hake methodically destroys Eva's personality and absorbs it into his own, which is filled with self-loathing. Socioeconomics aside, the Hake's treacherous conquest of Eva recalls Iago's destruction of Othello, and—as in Shakespeare's play—we are simultaneously fascinated and repulsed by the audacity of his mischief. The skilled, yet destructive, tempter is among the oldest archetypes known to humanity. It is no accident that Wolff names his heroine Eva and makes a point of having the Hake discover her in the Botanical Garden painting picture-perfect flowers. The Hake—whose name in Spanish is El Merluza—is a predatory fish of the Chilean coastal waters noted for its sharp teeth and voracious appetite. He is a cousin of the infamous serpent in the Garden of Genesis, a seducer of the impressionable. Thus the playwright marries mythology with sociology, noting that because hake is a dietary staple of Chile's poor, it is an apt symbol of the socioeconomic conflict of the play.

On another level, *Paper Flowers* joins a rich treasury of literature devoted to "the battle of the sexes." The Hake's conquest is as much one of sexual domination as it is sociopolitical or psychological. He takes over not only Eva's habitat but her clothing as well (e.g., he wears her bathrobe in scene 3). And throughout the play his language (its ambiguity becomes a weapon by which he destroys Eva) is fraught with sexual innuendo that is simultaneously erotic and degrading. Such phrases as "anything you want to give me," "the way you cross your legs," and "you have to raise the chair skirt" abet the Hake's multilevel seduction of Eva. Again we are reminded of another play, *Miss Julie*. Although Wolff has said he did not know Strindberg's *Miss Julie* when he wrote *Paper Flowers*, there are nonetheless extraordinary similarities between the two works. The brutal killing of Eva's pet canary (compare Julie's green finch) is an obvious parallel. Recall, however, that *Miss Julie* was a naturalistic drama that explored the hereditary forces that led to the countess's destruction, even as it reflected Strindberg's much-discussed misogyny. But Wolff is no misogynist, and the Hake's brutal degradation of Eva reflects the unfortunate reality of the subjugation of women throughout the world. In Latin America the problem is particularly exacerbated by the cult of *machismo* or "macho" by which one's manhood is validated by "owning" a woman. Note that the Hake refers (with his usual ambiguity) to the macho world of the streets, gangs, and violence. (Curiously, he is terrified by the ominous specter of Mario, who may or may not exist.) The converse of *machismo* is *mariannismo*, a term used by psychotherapists Rosa Maria Gil and Carmen Inoa Vazquez to describe a situation in which Latinas enable men by remaining faithful and submissive, regardless of how they are treated. Among the most frequently asked questions about the play and its meaning is, "Why does Eva allow the Hake to treat her so inhumanely?" It is the question, unfortunately, that we must ask ourselves about battered women. *Paper Flowers* may be read as a condemnation of both *machismo* and *mariannismo*, both of which contribute as much to the loss of human dignity as do socioeconomic circumstances.

Finally, Wolff's play explores one of literature's archetypal conflicts: the battle between rationality and raw passion. Our first impression of Eva's apartment (neat, orderly), her art (realistic, classical), and her language (lucid and in ordered paragraphs) suggests a rational mind. By contrast, the Hake lives in makeshift slums and speaks in halting, often incomplete sentences (marked by a disturbing lack of specificity) and creates art of trash (mostly old newspapers, the most transitory and disposable means of communication). We therefore think of him as raw, primitive, even uncivilized. As each scene progresses we note that his attempts at restraint give way to unbridled passion. Each outburst becomes more violent and destructive. Eventually, it is the Hake's modes of expression that triumphs. Eva's furniture, artwork, and ultimately her language are destroyed. In the end "she tries to speak, but can't. Once or twice she makes an effort that frustrates her, then she gives up." The Hake speaks, but in disjointed, often unintelligible gibberish ("Humba! Tekeke! Takumba!"), and when he does make sense, his message is terrifying ("many people, falling, have broken their necks"). His art—"dark, enormous, ragged paper flowers"—provides the play's final image, and the flowers dominate a landscape in which "total disorder reigns."

Wolff is not, of course, advocating the superiority of the Hake's "primitive" art. Hardly. Rather he seems to indict the old order, the Aristotelian imitation of the beautiful, because its indifference to the oppressed contributes to a world in which anarchy reigns. His ultimate message, in this play of many messages, seems to be that art has the responsibility to produce more than pretty pictures of pretty flowers, or it may be replaced by "paper flowers" and all that they imply.

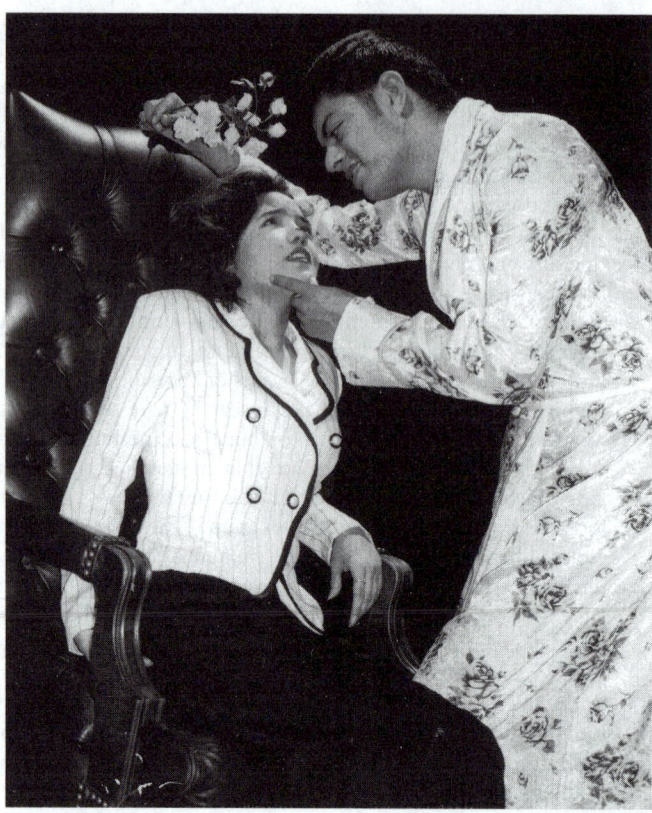

The Hake (A. M. Garcia) continues his conquest of Eva (Marisa Saenz) in Egon Wolff's Paper Flowers, a play which deals with political as well as sexual conquests.

PAPER FLOWERS

A Play in Six Scenes

EGON WOLFF

Translated by Margaret Sayers Peden

The hake is a fish of the Chilean seacoast. It is long and thin-bodied, its large, acute-nosed mouth set with sharp teeth. It hunts the deep waters of the Pacific to feed its voracious appetite.

SCENE ONE

The living room of a small suburban apartment, carefully arranged, revealing a feminine hand. Comfortable. Intimate. Three doors in addition to the entrance. One, to the bedroom; one to the bathroom; the third to the kitchen.

One window.

A canary in a cage.

Somewhere, an easel with a half-finished painting. A box of oils.

Also, straw figures: fish, heads of animals, roosters, etc.

The stage is empty. Then Eva and The Hake enter. Eva, forty, is well dressed, with conscious elegance. The Hake, thirty, dirty, his hair uncombed, thin, pale. Eva, who opens the door, enters resolutely. She walks toward the kitchen. The Hake stands in the doorway. He carries two large paper bags. He is trembling visibly. He looks at the room with timid curiosity.

EVA (*returning from the kitchen*). Well, come in! Come in! Leave those in there, in the kitchen!

The Hake enters with respectful caution. Never taking his eyes from the objects in the room, he places the bags on the floor, in the middle of the room.

Not there! (*She points to the kitchen.*) In the kitchen. Next to the stove, please!

The Hake does as she says. He returns without the bags. Eva has gone into the bedroom. She comes out brushing her hair. She takes a bill from her wallet, which has been lying on a small table, and hands it to him.

EVA. Here you are, and . . . thanks very much.

The Hake refuses the bill she hands him. Take it! You're not going to tell me you carried my packages for nothing?

The Hake stares at her.

Well, then . . . thanks very much. You've been very kind.

The Hake continues to stare at her.

Very pleasant. There was no reason for you to do it. Thank you very much.

THE HAKE (*in an impersonal, painful voice*). I would rather you gave me a cup . . . of tea.

EVA (*a little surprised*). Tea?

THE HAKE. You do have some, don't you?

EVA. Yes, I do, but . . . I don't have time. (*She offers him the bill once more.*) You can buy yourself some tea anywhere with this. There's a drugstore on the corner.

THE HAKE. "Anywhere" wouldn't be the same.

EVA (*interested, amused*). Oh, no? Why?

THE HAKE. It wouldn't be the same.

He stares at her, continuously.

EVA. Well . . . but I don't have time, I already told you. Take this and go on. I have things to do.

THE HAKE. They're waiting for me down there.

EVA. Who's waiting for you?

THE HAKE. Miguel and "Birdy."

EVA. The two that were following us?

The Hake nods.

What do they want? Why are they waiting for you?

THE HAKE. To get me.

EVA. Well, what do you want me to do? (*Annoyed.*) Take this. I have things to do.

THE HAKE. They're going to kill me.

EVA. That's your affair. Don't bother me any more, I tell you. Go away!

THE HAKE. I didn't think you'd be so hard. You don't look it.

EVA. Well, then, you were mistaken.

THE HAKE. Since the first time I saw you, last year, painting those flowers in the Botanical Garden. I've thought you were different.

A pause.

EVA. The Botanical Garden? You saw me?

THE HAKE. You were behind the parrot's cage, painting some clumps of laurel. . . . (*He stares at her.*) You had on a light straw hat with a green ribbon. And a kerchief with some scenes of Venice.

EVA. You're a good observer, aren't you?

THE HAKE. I observe certain things.

EVA. So your offer today, to carry the packages for me. . . . (*Perturbed.*) What did you say you wanted.

THE HAKE. A cup of tea.

EVA. Wouldn't you rather have a bowl of soup? I'll bet you haven't eaten today.

THE HAKE. Anything you want to give me.

EVA. I have some soup from last night. Shall I warm it for you?

THE HAKE. If you want to.

EVA. Well, sit down while I fix it.

She goes into the kitchen. One hears the clatter of pots and pans. The Hake, meanwhile, stands fixed where he is, not moving a millimeter. Eva comes back after a while.

Sit down. Surely you're not going to stand there all day.

THE HAKE. Not in these clothes.

EVA (*from the kitchen*). I don't think the furniture will mind.

The Hake takes a newspaper from an inside pocket of his coat, doubles it carefully, scrupulously, and places it on one of the armchairs. He sits upon it. Eva watches his actions and smiles. She props open the kitchen door with a chair so she will be able to talk through the open door.

Do you go often to the Botanical Garden?

THE HAKE. Sometimes.

EVA. To look at the flowers?

THE HAKE. No, to give peanuts to the monkeys.

EVA. Do you like the monkeys?

The Hake shrugs his shoulders.

I think they're dirty . . . gross! I can't bear them. To watch them . . . there . . . picking their fleas in front of everybody. I can't stand them!

THE HAKE. They do what they can.

EVA. Do you have time for that?

THE HAKE. For what?

EVA. To go to the Garden?

THE HAKE. I arrange it.

EVA. I wish I had more!

At that moment The Hake is struck by uncontrollable spasms. They rack his entire body. They contort his face. He must hold on to the table to maintain his upright position. He turns his back to the door of the kitchen and clamps his arms between his legs. It concerns him that Eva not see him in this state. Nevertheless, Eva notices. Finally, he masters the spasms.

How do you do at the supermarket? Do you find many clients?

THE HAKE. There's always someone who finds his packages too heavy.

Eva comes out of the kitchen carrying soup and table service for them both. She places it all on the small table. As she does this, The Hake rises.

EVA. It isn't very warm, but I suppose you'd like it better that way. Sit down!

THE HAKE. I'm fine.

EVA. Sit down and help yourself.

The Hake takes the bowl and begins to take spoonfuls standing up.

But sit down, for Heaven's sake!

She returns to the kitchen and comes out again carrying a hard-boiled egg, a tomato, and a glass of milk. She places them on the table.

I'm not going to begin if you go on standing there like that.

THE HAKE. It's . . . considerate enough of you to invite me to have this. I wouldn't take advantage and sit down with you—where I don't belong.

EVA (*openly*). And if I tell you it doesn't matter to me?

THE HAKE. I thought you were saying it to make it seem . . . easy. (*He sits down.*) It isn't good to go too far. (*Indicating the soup.*) Is it because of your figure?

EVA (*laughing*). Yes. Because of my figure! If it weren't for this, I'd be big as a balloon! I have a terrible tendency to gain weight. I eat a piece of bread and I gain a pound.

THE HAKE. That's a shame.

EVA. Yes. And a nuisance.

THE HAKE. It's just the opposite with Mario.

EVA. Who's Mario?

THE HAKE. A friend. Every time he eats a piece of bread he loses half a pound. He's skin and bones. It comes from stubbornness. The doctors tell him he should eat more, but he's stubborn.

He looks in her eyes with an expressionless, concentrated look.

You shouldn't do that.

EVA. Do what?

THE HAKE. Eat so little. It might harm you. You might die.

EVA. Does it matter? Does it matter to anyone?

THE HAKE. It matters to me.

They eat a moment, in silence, each one concentrating on his soup. The Hake spoons his, but never takes his eyes off Eva. After a while, Eva rises nervously.

EVA (*half laughing*). So that's how you kill your time? Going to the Botanical Garden to see how a lonely old woman kills *her* time painting the laurel in bloom?

She goes into the kitchen. She returns with salt and a napkin.

Because that's how I seem to you, isn't it? A lonely old woman? Killing time?

The Hake looks at her; he does not respond.

Let's see. Tell me! What do you think I am?

THE HAKE. A woman.

EVA. No, no! What I mean is: married or single?

THE HAKE. Married.

EVA (*with coquettish curiosity*). Why?

THE HAKE. From the way you cross your legs.

Eva laughs.

EVA. Oh, how amusing! And why? How do old maids cross their legs?

THE HAKE. (*expressionless*). They don't cross them.

Eva laughs nervously.

EVA. How amusing you are! (*Always half laughing.*) Tell me. Do you always stare at people?

The Hake immediately lowers his glance to his soup.

Well, you guessed (*touched; excited*). I'm married. Doesn't that worry you? What if my husband should enter suddenly and find me here with you?

THE HAKE (*low*). What *could* he think?

EVA (*still coquettish*). Why not?

THE HAKE. You shouldn't joke about being poor.

A moment of embarrassment. The Hake is struck by another attack, which he can scarcely suppress.

EVA (*doesn't know what to do*). Eat something, man. You haven't eaten a thing.

The Hake gestures that it doesn't matter.

A drink? Is that it? (*Pause.*) Do you need a drink to calm that trembling?

The Hake makes a vague gesture. Eva goes toward the kitchen and returns with a glass of wine, which The Hake grabs from her hands and drinks avidly. This finally calms him.

Almost, mmmm?

THE HAKE. Almost what?

EVA. Well . . . almost. I didn't mean to offend you. I wasn't amusing myself at your expense; it's just that it seems so . . . well, so strange, that you remember me. Among others. . . . There are other people who paint in the Garden. For instance, the old man in the blue corduroy hat. Have you seen him? The one who comes in the afternoons with his little cane stool. Sometimes with a dog, sometime without. (*Laughs.*) One day he got angry with me because of the way I use green tones. He practically yelled at me that it wasn't academic. I never knew what he meant by that. He walked around and around me, shaking his cane. I thought he was going to knock over my easel!

During this monologue, The Hake is almost doubled over.

Are you in pain?
THE HAKE. No.
EVA. Well, then, what's the matter?
THE HAKE. After my "dance," my stomach always knots up.
EVA. I have some tranquilizers. Do you want one?
THE HAKE. No, thank you.
EVA. Then, do you need a drink?

The Hake looks at her.

I mean, the trembling comes because of that, doesn't it?

There is no response. An embarrassing moment. Eva looks toward the kitchen.

Well, you'd better hurry because I have to leave soon. I open the store at two.

The Hake renews his slow spooning of soup. Eva returns with two peeled peaches. She places one in front of The Hake. She eats hers.

These peaches don't have the flavor they used to. I don't know what they do to them now. I remember when I was a child. We used to go with Mamma and Papa to a farm near the river where for practically nothing they let us go to the orchard and eat our fill of peaches and strawberries. What we could throw down! Those peaches really had flavor! Today they export the best ones and leave the leftovers for us. I remember that while Papa and Mamma sat down to eat at some tables that had been set under the trees, Alfredo and I—Alfredo is my brother—would go play in a barn that was close by. Climbing over the baler. . . . My brother Alfredo! He had a real obsession for doing the heroic thing. I remember he would hoist a handkerchief tied like a flag and we'd play "Take the Brigantine"! (*Laughs.*) He was the glorious captain, and I was the accursed corsair! Oh, what times! Silly, happy kids!
THE HAKE. If you throw me out, Miguel and "Birdy" will kill me.
EVA. And what do you want me to do? Leave you here?
THE HAKE. They're waiting for me around the corner, behind the pharmacy.

Eva goes to the window and looks out, barely raising the curtain.

EVA. There they are. They're looking up here.

She turns toward him.

Well. . . . What shall we do? I can't leave you here!

(*Hardening herself.*) I have to go to the store . . . soon. I've already told you.

The Hake suddenly explodes, a spurting, agitated, machine-gun rattle of words. The tone is monotonous, mournful, almost a litany. As he finishes, he has a new onslaught of trembling.

THE HAKE. "Birdy" has a meathook under his coat! He has a meathook and he's been waiting all morning for me to kill me! Because last night I won a few bucks from him shooting craps and he says I cheated on him! And it isn't true, because I won fair and square. Playing fair and square. He came to Julia's house this morning to look for me, but I saw him hide behind the oven and got past him and ran toward the river. All morning I hid in the bushes down by the tannery, until I went to the supermarket, and if you hadn't helped me, he'd have killed me! If you don't help me and hide me, he'll kill me! If you don't help me hide, I'll die, and I don't want to die! I don't want to die! I don't want to die!
EVA. There, it's all right. It's all right! Calm yourself. No one's going to do anything to you.

She doesn't know what to do.

I could notify the police. Do you want me to? So they'll arrest those men?

The Hake shakes his head.

Ah, yes. That's true. The code of honor, umm? You don't denounce each other.

The Hake is bent over. He shivers. Eva considers the situation a while.

I'll have to lock you up in here.

The Hake looks at her.

Because you understand, don't you? I don't know you. And besides, the lock and chain are on the outside. I'll have to lock you inside until I come back.
THE HAKE. I understand.
EVA. I'll lock the other rooms, too. You'll have to wait for me here.
THE HAKE. More than logical.
EVA. You have some magazines. Today's paper . . .
THE HAKE. Thank you. . . .

He smiles for the first time—a broad, open smile—that says nothing.

It's as if everything had been . . . well, prepared. . . . Ready. . . . The newspapers, I mean, and the magazines. I couldn't ask for anything more, to tell the truth. Anything else would be, well . . . ungrateful, I'd say.
EVA. Yes.

Eva removes the bowls. She goes into the bathroom and

then walks around combing her hair. The Hake eats a little of the peach. Then he gets up and walks toward the canary's cage.

THE HAKE. A pretty little bird. What's its name?
EVA. Goldie.
THE HAKE. Goldie, eh? (*He plays with it.*) Ps, ps, ps, ps! (*He gives it a piece of peach.*) You like that, eh? Ps, ps, ps, ps! You like to eat ripe fruit under the trees, eh, little glutton? (*Gives it another piece.*) Here, take it! That's it!

Eva closes the door to the bathroom. The Hake is alone.

You have quite a gullet, eh, you little queer? (*His voice takes on a tone of harshness.*) Did you know that I'm the cursed captain and you're the glorious corsair? Didn't you know that, you fuck-up? (*He shakes the cage.*) Didn't you know that? That I'm the cursed captain and you're the glorious corsair, you freaking bird? (*With a wounded voice.*) I don't know you! (*He shakes the cage again.*) I'll have to lock you up, because I don't know you, son-of-a-bitch bird. I'll have to chain you . . . !

Eva comes from the bathroom. She is ready to leave.

Ps, ps, ps, ps! Little canary . . . !

Eva turns on the radio.

EVA. I'll leave you this. Change it if you want.
THE HAKE. Thank you.

Eva walks toward the door.

Ma'am . . .
EVA (*turns.*). Yes?
THE HAKE. I knew. The thousand times I've seen you, I knew that you were what your eyes say you are. . . .
EVA. I'll be back at six. (*Points to the kitchen.*) If you want to help yourself to anything. . . .

> She exits.
> One hears the noise of the lock and the rattle of the chain.
> The Hake shakes the cage.

THE HAKE. Eat your little peaches! Eat, you shit! Eat, you fruity corsair!

He is shaking the cage as the curtain falls.

SCENE TWO

The same evening, a little after six o'clock. The Hake is making a paper basket from doubled strips of newspaper. A paper bird hangs from the light fixture, a kind of gull, tied by a thread. The Hake is kneeling on the floor, surrounded by piles of scattered, disordered newspapers. The radio is playing a dance tune. Offstage, the sound of an automobile's brakes and the closing of its door. The Hake goes to

the window to look, peering out from behind the curtain. Then he returns to his work.

> *After the sound of the key in the lock and the rattle of the chain, Eva enters. She is carrying a paper bag from which the neck of a bottle protrudes.*

EVA (*nervous; appearing to be casual*). You see? Three minutes after six. Not a minute before or a minute after!

She closes the door. She bumps into the bird.

And this? What is it? Did you make it?
THE HAKE. Nobody else has been here.
EVA. It's precious! You're quite an artist, you know? A gull!
THE HAKE. Do you think it is?
EVA. Yes, of course! A gull! Precious!
THE HAKE. Then it is.
EVA (*about the basket*). And that? A basket?

The Hake nods.

That's precious, too. Where did you learn the art?
THE HAKE. It's for you. . . .
EVA. What? The basket.
THE HAKE. Everything.
EVA. Oh, thank you!
THE HAKE. Providing it doesn't bother you. . . .
EVA. No. Why should it bother me?
THE HAKE. The newspapers, I mean. Because I have spread out all the papers this way. Everything messed up.

He begins hastily to pick up the papers. He folds them carefully.

EVA. No, it doesn't matter. . . .

She goes toward the kitchen.

But, where did you learn this?
THE HAKE. Around. I worked for a guy who worked with wicker. But he was a moron. He only knew how to make chairs. I know how to make flowers, too.
EVA. Flowers?
THE HAKE. Camellias.
EVA (*from the kitchen*). But . . . for Heaven's sake! The dishes! Who washed them?

The Hake does not respond. Eva enters from the kitchen.

You didn't have to do that.

The Hake shrugs his shoulders.

I'll bet you scrubbed the floor, too? It wasn't this shiny when I left.
THE HAKE. There was some wax here, and I thought a little polish wouldn't hurt it any.
EVA (*smiling*). I don't dare go into the bedroom. What might I find there?
THE HAKE. Nothing. How could I go in there without your permission?

Eva goes into the kitchen again and returns with a salami and some cheese and a few packages of cigarettes.

EVA. Speaking of surprises, don't think I forgot you. I thought, since the nights are cold and "a full stomach is one's best friend" . . . a few snacks. A little paté. And cheese. Gruyère. Very rich. It was especially recommended by the owner of the store, who's a friend of mine.

The Hake scarcely looks at what Eva is showing him. He has finished gathering up the newspapers in a carefully folded stack and is going to carry them to the kitchen. He runs into Eva, and this produces a brief business of getting into each other's way.

Where are you going?

THE HAKE (*referring to the papers*). I took them from the kitchen.

EVA. Leave them. It doesn't matter.

THE HAKE. Everything's going to be messy.

EVA (*a little impatient; nervous*). It doesn't matter, I tell you. (*Smiles.*) Put them down there. (*Always with a small, nervous smile that looks strange, almost as if she were laughing to herself.*) When I went into the store, I was so wild to get there, thinking about buying this, that I completely forgot to invent an . . . excuse, because the question was bound to come up, and it did. "Who are you buying all this for, dear? Don't tell me it's all for you?" At first, I didn't know what to say. I stammered out a couple of silly things, and then, when I was about out of breath, it occurred to me to say that it was for a picnic! (*Laughs.*) A picnic with some friends. Imagine! Me, on a picnic!

The Hake, kneeling on the floor again, folds and smooths the stack of newspapers with exaggerated care.

Because if I told her the truth. . . . Who do you think would have believed me?

THE HAKE. Nobody.

EVA. Yes. That's what I thought, too.

THE HAKE. In these cases you always offer a bowl of warm soup. (*Indicating the snacks.*) That would never occur to anyone. It's not necessary.

EVA (*laughs nervously*). Do you like it?

THE HAKE. What?

EVA. The salami? The cheese?

THE HAKE. You always ask two questions at once. I never know which to answer first.

EVA (*confused*). The salami?

THE HAKE. It turns my stomach.

EVA. You don't like it?

THE HAKE. It isn't that. It must be because my stomach isn't used to it. When you're only given rice soup and things like that, you develop a weak stomach. Once the sisters at the charity kitchen gave me roast meat with mushroom and I vomited for two days.

EVA. I should have thought of that. I shouldn't have bought it.

THE HAKE (*looks at her for the first time, with the look so typical*

of him—*it says nothing*). Eat it with your friends on the picnic.

EVA. What friends? I don't have any friends.

THE HAKE. Tough luck for you.

Resumes his task.

EVA (*lively*). Well, I think I should start preparing dinner. That's my life. Eat, and then eat some more. A meal in the morning. A meal at noon. A meal at night! Sometimes I get to the point I think that's all life is: one big continuous meal, with an occasional pause for boredom, and then we begin eating again. And happiness too, naturally! Like a thin powdery dusting of sugar over the whole affair!

While speaking, she has gone from the kitchen to the bedroom, putting on and taking off a wool jacket, putting on and taking off some slippers, opening and closing closets, always with The Hake watching her imperturbably.

What foolish things one does. . . . Opening and closing closets. . . and putting clothes on and off . . . If you add up the days, the hours, you lose doing useless things . . .

She goes to the kitchen, where she can be heard working with the pans. She drops a glass. The noise of breaking glass.

Oh! How stupid I am! What's the matter with me today!

She comes out of the kitchen winding a handkerchief around her finger and walks toward the bedroom.

I cut myself! The day never passes that I don't have to go to my medicine chest!

The Hake rises.

THE HAKE. May I help you?

EVA (*from the bedroom*). No, let it be. I'm used to it. I told you. My fingers are covered with scars! The quarts of blood I've spilled! Not that I do it on purpose!

She comes out of the bedroom.

But a person wouldn't do a thing like that on purpose, do you think?

She hands him a pair of scissors and gauze.

Cut it here, will you, please?

The Hake cuts the gauze skillfully.

THE HAKE. Iodine, do you have any?

EVA. Yes.

She goes to the bedroom and returns with a little bottle of iodine that The Hake also uses with agility and skill. He paints the wound with iodine, places the gauze on it, and secures it with adhesive. Eva observes his movements. The Hake ostensively avoids all physical contact with her. He avoids her with prudent and delicate caution. Eva, on the other hand, doesn't show the same reticence; rather, curi-

ous sympathy, in contrast to his timidity. When The Hake finishes, he starts to tremble again. He sits down. He clasps his arms between his knees in his characteristic gesture. Eva goes to the kitchen and returns with a glass of wine. The Hake drinks avidly. The trembling subsides. He coughs.

Is that better?

The Hake nods.

It seems you have learned a little of everything around, haven't you? The only thing you don't seem to have learned is to talk. . . . Are you always so frugal with your words?

THE HAKE. Where I live there isn't much interest in listening.

EVA (*with irony*). I don't think where I live there is, either.

THE HAKE. Put on the jacket.

EVA. What did you say?

THE HAKE. The jacket and the slippers. . . .

EVA. Oh, that! No, I'm all right this way. . . .

THE HAKE. You were going to put them on.

EVA. Yes, but I'm fine. . . .

THE HAKE. Well, you were going to put them on. . . .

EVA. Yes, but . . . not now . . . and don't look at me like that! (*Laughs nervously.*) Don't look at me so much. Good Lord, what a starer you are! What a starer of a man! Do you always stare like that, tell me.

The Hake lowers his glance.

You're capable of making one completely . . .

She goes toward the kitchen.

Let's see, but I want to hear your story! Come on, tell me. Where did you learn to use your hands so well? In putting on gauze and adhesive, I mean?

From the kitchen.

You give the impression of being very familiar with them.

THE HAKE. I learned from an orderly, a sergeant.

EVA. Were you in the Army?

THE HAKE. In the hospital.

EVA. Ill?

THE HAKE. Something like that.

EVA. Like what? What was the matter?

THE HAKE. I can't talk like this. . . .

Eva comes out of the kitchen.

I can't talk like this . . . with you in the kitchen and me here, shouting. I can't talk if I don't see the other person's face. You'll forgive me, won't you? But I think you don't allow yourself sufficient . . . repose.

EVA (*her curiosity piqued*). Why do you say that?

THE HAKE. Because you're always going back and forth . . . up and down . . . moving things . . . changing things around . . . with no apparent reason. Since I came in here,

you haven't once stopped moving around. Have you looked, for example, at the basket I'm making?

EVA. I looked at it, yes . . .

THE HAKE. No, but really . . . looked at it?

EVA. Yes, I looked at it, I already told you.

THE HAKE. Thought about it?

EVA. Well . . .

THE HAKE. Do you like it?

EVA. Yes. I like it. I told you already.

THE HAKE. Why?

EVA (*anguished*). It's only a . . . basket.

THE HAKE. It's more than that.

Moment of embarrassment.

EVA. Yes, You're right. Forgive me. I told you, I'm a machine. I think it's because of the kind of life I have to lead.

THE HAKE. I could show you how I make the flowers, for example. Paper flowers.

EVA (*more than necessarily interested*). Yes. Let's see, show me!

She kneels down next to him.

THE HAKE (*taking a sheet of newspaper*). You take a sheet of newspaper, like this, and you double it from the corner, like this, you see? (*He does it.*) And it isn't an ordinary sheet of paper, as you will see. You take a piece of paper that has a lot of printing, or a large photograph, or a lot of photographs without any printing, you see? Like this. So that the flower has some meaning. Some continuity. Some beauty.

While he works and speaks, something is changing in him. Something that possesses and absorbs him.

For some people the paper of newspapers is just that. A strip of worthless paper that's only good to wrap meat, to plug holes, or to line suitcases. But it isn't that. Those who think so, it's clear, are marked, and you can recognize them by other superficial features. The paper from newspapers has a world of things to say. It takes whatever form you want to give it. It folds submissively. It allows itself to be handled without resistance. It occupies very little space in your pocket. And it is a faithful companion on winter nights. It keeps you company . . . tranquilly . . . silently . . . always ready, there it is, for any use whatever.

The flower is ready.

There it is! A camellia, you see?

He places it at Eva's brow.

To adorn the beautiful.

EVA. Who are you?

THE HAKE. I also make carnations and chrysanthemums, but that's a little more difficult, because you need scissors, and scissors aren't something they let you have, ordinarily. Even less on winter nights, down by the river.

His excitement continues to increase.

I also make fish and butterflies of paper! But that's much more difficult, because once you have them made, no one wants them. Because everyone wants fish in beautifully lighted fishbowls, and butterflies mounted on pins in little mahogany boxes. But made from dirty newspapers that are only good for lining suitcases, no! No one wants dirty paper butterflies, dirty from wrapping meat, mounted in lighted mahogany boxes! Nor does anyone want to dirty her brow with flowers of dirty paper!

As he finishes he is panting.

At least, that's what the bourgeois say . . . who are the arbiters of style . . . in everything . . . including the way you work . . . the paper . . . the newspapers.

He coughs. Brief pause.

EVA. Who are you?

THE HAKE. They call me "The Hake."

EVA. I mean . . . your name?

THE HAKE. I don't know. A name, one loses it around here in the streets, down a crack . . .

EVA. But you must have some name. I can't call you "The Hake."

THE HAKE (*with an expressionless face*). Why not?

EVA (*confused*). Well . . . because . . .

THE HAKE (*with the same lack of expression*). Because it's the name the gang uses.

EVA. It isn't a Christian name.

THE HAKE. And you're not part of the gang.

EVA (*with certain defiance*). No, no I'm not, if you want to put it like that. Among my friends we call each other by Christian names.

THE HAKE. I thought you told me you didn't have any friends.

EVA. It's a way of speaking.

THE HAKE. It must be, then, that between us—who aren't friends—we call each other by names that *aren't* Christian. (*Smiles, pacifying her.*) My mother calls me Robert.

EVA. That's better. I'll call you Robert, then.

THE HAKE. And Bobby.

EVA. Bobby?

THE HAKE. And pig. Pig before we ate. I had two mothers. She called me pig before we ate, Bobby, after.

EVA. Did she die?

THE HAKE. Something like that.

Eva rises, and with exaggerated vivacity goes to a piece of furniture and takes out some scissors and hands them to him.

EVA. Well! Here we're not on the shore of the river; we have scissors! Show me how you make the chrysanthemums!

THE HAKE (*rises*). I think it's time for me to go.

EVA (*hadn't thought about this*). Oh, yes! Of course! But, those men? Don't you think you're still in danger?

Eva rises and goes to the window.

There they are! They're still waiting for you!

THE HAKE. What do you think? That they're playing?

EVA. Well, what do they want? You haven't done anything except win a couple of dollars from them shooting dice! Isn't winning allowed among you?

THE HAKE. It's allowed. But you pay for it.

EVA. I don't understand! How can they be so vengeful?

THE HAKE. From watching how dogs fight over a piece of meat.

EVA. So, as soon as you leave the building they'll assault you?

THE HAKE. Their pulse won't miss a beat.

EVA. I can't allow them to do that.

THE HAKE. Shall I show you how I make paper chrysanthemums?

EVA. You stay here until those men go away.

The Hake begins to cut up pieces of paper. He is contained at first, but then goes about it with increasing fury.

THE HAKE. You take a piece of paper and you cut it from the corners, you see?

He does it.

You make some long cuts along the printed lines, you see? Until you make shreds of paper, the thinnest possible . . . with the finest points . . . until the whole sheet of paper, which originally was a newspaper, . . . looks like a big piece of shredded paper! As if a dog had made it his prey! Or a falcon! Or any rabid animal! Like when in the bus someone runs his razor along the seats and leaves his mark of stupor and rage there! Or when in the hospital the orderly pours iodine on a back shredded by the whip.

EVA. Bobby . . .

The Hake looks at her.

Do you mind if I call you Bobby?

The Hake continues to stare at her with eyes that express nothing.

Does it seem like a good idea . . . for you to sleep here? Tonight? In this big chair? I'll lend you some blankets. It doesn't matter to me.

THE HAKE. But you brought me salami and cheese so I'd leave.

EVA. Not now, Bobby. You can't go like this.

THE HAKE. If I stay I'll have to . . . take a bath, naturally?

EVA. Have I said that?

The Hake laughs and looks for laughter in Eva's face.

THE HAKE (*laughing*). No, no! Say it! "It would be better if you took a bath, Bobby!"

EVA. I already told you: it's just the same to me.

THE HAKE (*always laughing*). No, no! It isn't the same! Go on, say it! Confess! I want to hear how you say it! "It would be better if you took a bath, Bobby, because like that, with those clothes and that filth . . . ," mmh? Come on!

EVA. All right, if you insist. "It would be better if you took a bath, Bobby."

THE HAKE (*suddenly serious*). But . . . I can't use your bathroom. How could such a thing ever occur to me?

EVA. Go ahead and use it! Did I say not to?

THE HAKE. No, naturally not. That's true, you didn't tell me! What ideas I have! How could you say such a thing to me?

Suddenly.

Shall I show you how I make paper chrysanthemums?

EVA. You already showed me.

THE HAKE (*never taking his eyes off her*). But you didn't look.

EVA (*protests*). Yes, I . . .

THE HAKE. No, you never looked.

EVA. Well, show me.

The Hake takes another sheet of paper and begins to cut it the same way he did the first.

THE HAKE. You take a sheet of paper and you cut it with the scissors from the corners, you see? You make some long cuts along the printed lines until you make shreds of paper, the thinnest possible . . . with the finest points . . . until the whole sheet of paper, which originally was a newspaper, . . . looks like a big piece of shredded paper! Or like a dog had made it his prey! Or a falcon! Or any rabid animal!

His voice has become tense. The words are squeezed from his mouth.

Or like in the bus when somebody runs a razor . . .

CURTAIN

SCENE THREE

The following day, early morning. The Hake is already up. It is obvious he has bathed and combed his hair. His clothing is folded on a chair. Next to it, his shoes. He has put on one of Eva's bathrobes, which is obviously short and tight on him. He is moving around the room, cleaning with a broom and a dustcloth. He opens the curtains. He runs the dustcloth over the furniture. From the kitchen, the noise of a teakettle. He hums a tune while he cleans. The sun floods in. The straw figures are no longer in view. In their place on the walls, and hanging from threads stretched from wall to wall, some paper flowers and a few butterflies. After a while.

EVA (*from the bedroom*). Good morning!

THE HAKE. Good morning.

EVA. How did you sleep?

THE HAKE. Couldn't be better!

EVA. Up so early?

THE HAKE. It's a beautiful morning!

EVA. What are you doing?

THE HAKE. A little cleaning!

EVA. But why?

She opens the bedroom door, which obviously has been locked. She enters, in a bathrobe, combing her hair.

You didn't have to . . .

She notices the appearance of The Hake. She cannot repress an expression of stupefied amusement.

THE HAKE (*gesturing to the bathrobe*). It was in the bathroom. It doesn't bother you, I suppose?

EVA. No, no. Why should it bother me?

THE HAKE. The soapsuds were so fragrant it must have gone to my head. I didn't know what I was doing. This morning I woke with this on.

EVA. That's fine.

THE HAKE. And then I said to myself: "Hake, you have to do something useful!" I looked around and I saw the blossoms of the mimosa and the beautiful swallows swooping after each other around the General's statue, and I said to myself: "Hake, you have to do something useful!" (*Laughs his characteristic laugh; a laugh that covers his whole face, but says nothing.*) On a day like this, even the river rats would like to come out dressed in lace! How do you like your eggs?

EVA. Eggs?

THE HAKE. Yes, eggs.

EVA. But, Bobby, I don't . . .

THE HAKE. Fried or boiled?

EVA (*resigned*). Boiled.

THE HAKE. I guessed! They're already boiling. That doesn't bother you, I suppose?

EVA. What?

THE HAKE. That I took the eggs like that, without permission?

EVA. Why should it bother me?

THE HAKE. You told me the same thing yesterday.

EVA. What?

THE HAKE. "Why should it bother me?" Curious how one always repeats himself, isn't it?

While he speaks, he has been straightening his improvised bed. He collects the blankets. He folds them carefully. Eva goes into the bathroom.

I used to have a friend, down south in a sawmill where I was working for a while, who had a little refrain too. "I'm innocent," he used to say all the time. When he got up, at breakfast, on the job . . . persistently. It was an obsession that made a martyr of him. "I'm innocent! I'm innocent!"

He drove us out of our minds! One day a few of us grabbed him and hung him up by his feet, so he wouldn't go on talking. No use! Even hanging upside down that way he kept on: "I'm innocent! . . . I'm innocent!" No one ever knew what he was innocent of! Simply, the poor man thought he was innocent of something, and that gave him strength to go on living! Curious things, refrains, aren't they? Sometimes they seem meaningless!

Eva comes out of the bathroom, tying a ribbon in her combed hair.

EVA. You woke up loquacious this morning, didn't you? You weren't, last night. I love to see you this way.

The Hake shrugs his shoulders, lifts the corner of the rug, sweeps.

THE HAKE. I already told you. The mimosa in bloom.

Eva looks at him.

EVA. Your face, too. You look different today.
THE HAKE (*smiles happily*). The bath . . .

Eva sees that the straw figures are not there.

EVA. And my figures?
THE HAKE. Mmh?
EVA. My straw figures? The burro's head? The rooster?
THE HAKE. I put them in the kitchen cabinet.
EVA (*surprised*). And why?
THE HAKE (*indicating the flowers*). I thought that these would look better.
EVA (*doesn't know what to say*). Oh, yes . . .
THE HAKE. It doesn't bother you, I suppose?
THE TWO IN CHORUS. No, why should it bother me?

The Hake laughs, then Eva.

EVA. Well, anyway, one of these days I was going to take them down. You just saved me the effort.
THE HAKE. Why? Didn't you like them?
EVA. Horrible.
THE HAKE. Why? I didn't think they were so bad.
EVA. Why did you take them down, then?
THE HAKE. Because I thought these would look better. That's all. Don't you agree?
EVA. Oh, yes.
THE HAKE. You shouldn't belittle your own work. Because . . . you made them yourself, didn't you?
EVA. In a weak moment.
THE HAKE. That's bad, that you expect so much of yourself.

He leaps toward the kitchen.

Those eggs must be well cooked by now!

From the kitchen.

By the way . . . the little bird . . . I gave him some seeds. Was that all right?
EVA (*goes to the cage; plays with the canary*). Yes, that's fine!
THE HAKE. I was going to give him some bread balls, but I remembered that he's a pet! That's a habit from feeding pigeons!
EVA. Bobby!
THE HAKE. Yes?
EVA. I heard voices last night.
THE HAKE. Voices?
EVA. Arguments! It seemed to me they were coming from the corridor! Did you hear anything?
THE HAKE. Arguments? No!
EVA. Like people arguing heatedly!
THE HAKE. I slept like a log! I couldn't hear a thing!
EVA. Strange! Then I heard something like a door being slammed! It must have been the neighbors. Some Italians who work in a cabaret. Sometimes they bring friends home with them in the middle of the night. They forget this is a building where people are . . .
THE HAKE. Quiet and unassuming.
EVA. What did you say?
THE HAKE. Quiet, unassuming people.
EVA. Well, yes . . . something like that! You always take the words out of my mouth!
THE HAKE. People who don't know how to act! I always say they should go live down by the river to learn how not to do it!

He comes out of the kitchen with a tray on which are two eggs in egg cups, two cups, a teapot, a creamer, a napkin, a butter dish, and biscuits, all very tastefully arranged in the clean, neat manner of an upper-class hotel. He has doubled the towel over his arm to serve as his napkin. He puts everything down with great skill and elegance.

EVA. Don't tell me you worked in a hotel, too?
THE HAKE (*very efficient; with a bow*). Comment ditesvous, madame?

Eva laughs.

The Hake is now serious.

Préférez-vous le beurre salé ou sans sel, madame?

Eva laughs good-naturedly.

EVA. Who are you, Bobby? Where did you learn to do that? You are diverse! Really diverse!
THE HAKE (*always serious*). One does what one can.

Both begin to eat their eggs.

EVA. Did you work in a hotel? Really?
THE HAKE. Mmh.
EVA. As a . . . waiter?
THE HAKE (*with his mouth full of egg*). As a thief.

Eva laughs.

It's true. It was a snobbish hotel; because of that I had to go in the back door so the public wouldn't see me, you understand?

Eva understands.

I had a contract as a washer. A dishwasher. It really wasn't a real contract. Just a slap on the back by the fat guy who ran the kitchen. A guy who liked to make himself important. (*He imitates.*) "All right, stupid, go stand over there by one of those sinks. Let's see if you can wash a plate!" He told me he'd give me a penny for every washed plate. He was tricky. He didn't tell me he'd deduct for all the ones I broke. In the evening when I went to pick up my money, I owed him two dollars.

EVA. You owed him?

THE HAKE. I owed him.

EVA. And the French?

THE HAKE. What about it?

EVA. Where did you learn it? There?

THE HAKE. I had to stay six days to pay my debt. Actually I never did pay it, because every day that passed, my debt was bigger. You understand, don't you?

EVA. Yes.

THE HAKE. After a week I realized that wasn't the way to get ahead. That's when I decided to steal a calculating machine, and I lifted . . .

EVA. That seems fair to me.

THE HAKE. Do you think so? They didn't.

EVA. But . . . the French? Where did you learn it? In another hotel?

THE HAKE. Painting some incubators for a guy in Saint Andrews.

EVA. Was he French?

THE HAKE. No, Yugoslavian. Do you know I can make silhouettes with my hands?

EVA. Silhouettes?

THE HAKE. Yes. (*He spoons the bottom of his cup.*) Dogs . . . foxes . . .

EVA. Let's see.

The Hake goes to close the curtains. He turns on the lamp that's on the table. He spreads the leaves of a magazine so it will stand on edge.

THE HAKE. Look! What do you see?

He throws the silhouette of a figure on the magazine.

EVA. A dog!

THE HAKE. And now?

EVA. A rabbit!

THE HAKE. And this?

EVA. A deer? Let's see, let me do it!

She tries.

No. It doesn't come out. How do you do it?

THE HAKE. The forefinger up. The thumb like this.

EVA (*holds out her hands to him*). You do it for me!

The Hake hesitates in taking her hands.

Come on!

THE HAKE (*taking her fingers with care*). Like this. No. This finger's stuck out.

EVA. A deer! (*Enthusiastic.*) Come on . . . another!

The Hake moves close to her. He holds her hands. This produces a brief, embarrassed paralysis of movement during which they look in each other's eyes. Then The Hake, confused, goes to the window and opens the curtains again. He turns off the lamp.

Bobby, there's no reason to be timid with me. (*Laughs.*) I'm not going to eat you, don't you know. (*Agitated.*) After all, having spent the night here together, gives us a right to . . . a certain familiarity, don't you think?

THE HAKE. Don't play with me, please.

EVA. But, Bobby, it's ridiculous. Just because you brushed my hand . . . it doesn't matter to me.

THE HAKE. One ought to keep his distance.

EVA. What distance?

THE HAKE (*indicating the bathrobe*). It's because you see me in this, and washed, that you forget.

EVA. What have I forgotten?

The Hake points to his clothes.

Don't be ridiculous. Have I shown in any way that it matters to me?

THE HAKE. It can't be.

EVA. If you insist.

THE HAKE. I'll have to go right now.

EVA. I'm not saying you should go.

The Hake rises and moves away from her. He turns his back.

THE HAKE (*suspiciously*). Why?

EVA. Why, what?

THE HAKE. Why do you want me to stay?

EVA. I haven't said you should stay. I've only said you don't have to go.

THE HAKE (*complaining*). Why is it my fault, I say?

EVA. But Bobby . . .

THE HAKE. Why is it my fault I was born as I was. I didn't ask my mother to be born where I was!

Eva rises.

EVA. But, Bobby, for Heaven's sake!

THE HAKE. I'm a simple man, but I have my pride!

EVA. Of course you have! Who says you don't?

She approaches him. To his back.

Bobby! I'm not the woman I seem to be. I'm just a woman

filled with a need for kindness! Perhaps it doesn't seem so, because I look so forceful, so . . . fulfilled. (*Smiles.*) But you see, I paint alone, laurel in bloom, Saturday afternoons in the Botanical Garden. Doesn't that seem . . . odd?

THE HAKE. I'll need new pants. If I stay here any longer, I'll need new pants. I can't put those back on.

Eva looks at him without speaking.

Because if I put those on, I can't stay here, isn't that right?

EVA. I hadn't thought about that.

THE HAKE (*never looking at her*). But now you think about it, isn't it true?

EVA. Well, perhaps . . .

THE HAKE (*his tone changes; he returns to his earlier manner of speaking, anxious, intense*). Because what if suddenly, someone came in here? Yes, suddenly, some friend of yours came in here, what explanation could we give them? If they see me here, with this on (*indicating the bathrobe*), or those (*indicating his pants*), sitting on one of your chairs like a king in his castle? Don't you see? They might think I'm a beggar from down by the river that you picked up out of pity to prevent the poor devil's turning up his paws before God meant him to, offering him something . . . some warm soup or salami. . . . It wouldn't be very correct, do you think? Sad, instead, don't you think? A sad, hopeless situation that neither you, nor I, could stand for very long, don't you agree? Because that would mean that you know as well as I . . . how could we avoid it? That you as well as I knew the sad reality. It would establish a situation of moral misery between us that would be very difficult . . . to disguise. Don't you think so?

EVA. And do you think a new pair of pants will change all that?

THE HAKE. We could play at it a little, deceive ourselves. Don't you think so?

EVA. You'll have to overcome that . . . that obsession, Bobby. I've noticed how it makes you suffer.

The Hake whirls around. A broad smile illuminates his face.

THE HAKE. Blue pants with a white stripe. A white stripe an inch wide, no more, no less. That's the kind I've always dreamed of.

EVA. We'll look for something you like.

THE HAKE (*like a happy child*). Will you do it? Really? Will you go yourself from store to store, looking for what I ask?

EVA. Why not?

The Hake takes her hands and pulls her up. He whirls her around.

THE HAKE. You're an angel. You're an angel! An angel!

EVA. Oh, for Heaven's sake, Bobby!

They stop. Eva is breathless.

What I meant is I find it meaningless! Really meaningless, Bobby! I don't notice things like that!

THE HAKE (*laughing in amusement; teasing slyly*). Yes, yes, you notice!

EVA. No, really, no.

THE HAKE (*reprimands her with a finger*). Yes, you notice! You notice!

EVA. Why do you say that to me? Why are you laughing?

The Hake laughs as if he were telling a funny and rather embarrassing story.

THE HAKE. Yesterday evening, when you arrived here, a friend brought you in her car and you didn't want to let her come up!

EVA (*denying effusively*). No . . .

THE HAKE. Yes, yes! I saw the gestures she was making. As if she wanted to come up with you, but you told her, with signs, too, that you were fine . . . that you didn't need anything, or something like that! It was amusing, extremely amusing, to see how you were trying to think of something . . . how you cast about, almost desperately, for some explanation!

Choked with laughter.

Waving your arms like this! Gasping for air!

EVA. No, no. That wasn't the reason . . .

THE HAKE. Yes, yes! But don't get mad. I understand! I understand! If you only knew how well I understand!

Suddenly becoming serious.

What did you tell your friend?

EVA. Well, I told her that . . .

THE HAKE. When I have new pants, we'll be free from embarrassment, you see. We can say I'm your cousin. A distant cousin who dropped in from the country, how does that seem? A cousin, or an uncle? Which seems better? More plausible?

A pause.

EVA. You're going to have to get that obsession out of your head, Bobby.

The Hake drops his arms, discouraged.

THE HAKE. Yes. Perhaps that comes from wandering around by the river so much, looking for things under the stones. From so much crawling around, looking for things, scratching for food. Finally, the world gets you right around the ankles. It's a little tiny world, the one you see, and in this tiny little world, we're the tiniest of all! Not even as high as a toad. You get a kind of subservient personality. Sub-something, anyway. (*He smiles again with an empty smile, radiant, meaningless.*) A "sub" personality . . . sub-normal . . . sub-ordinant . . . sub-jugated . . . sub-versive!

He stands before her, smiling happily.

A white stripe an inch wide. No more, no less. Will you buy them for me as I asked?

EVA (*worried*). I'll do what I can.

The Hake kisses her hands.

THE HAKE. You're an angel!

Eva pours herself some coffee.

EVA. If this means anything to you, Bobby, I should tell you that I've become very fond of you. In my opinion, you have a tremendous potential for becoming a . . . fulfilled man.

As she says "fulfilled," The Hake starts to tremble again. Eva wants to help him, but he waves her away. He calms down again.

I don't know what it is that torments you.

The Hake picks up the papers and begins to make flowers again.

Drink your coffee.

Eva walks to the kitchen.

This needs sugar.

Suddenly a scream from the kitchen.

What's this?

She enters. She is carrying the straw rooster and burro. One is hanging grotesquely from each hand; their necks are broken.

Why did you throw these into the trash can? And their necks . . . why did you break them?

THE HAKE. They didn't fit in the trash can.

EVA. But throw them away. You told me yourself you'd put them in the cabinet.

THE HAKE. But they didn't fit there either. (*Innocently protesting.*) But you told me yourself they were horrible!

EVA. Yes, but . . .

THE HAKE. I'll make you one of paper! I swear that when you come back this evening I'll have a rooster and a burro made of paper for you! Mmh? What do you say? With strong, red feet, and a great golden comb! A strong powerful rooster! Mmh? Is that all right?

EVA (*doesn't know what to say*). Well, I . . .

THE HAKE (*with his broad smile; playful, vacant*). It won't bother you if I do it, will it?

THE TWO IN CHORUS. No. why should it bother me!

The Hake laughs loudly. Eva enters in chorus. Both laugh with all their hearts. The Hake's, finally, with exaggeration, out of tune, drowning out Eva's laughter.

CURTAIN

SCENE FOUR

Evening of the same day. The arrangement of all the pieces of furniture has been changed. The canary cage, its door open, is empty. The shade of the floor lamp has been taken off. It serves now as a vase for three enormous paper flowers with wire stems. In addition, there are flowers hanging from the walls and from the lamp.

The Hake, his legs wrapped in a blanket of Scotch wool, a bottle of cognac at his side, is lounging in the big chair, watching television. One can see he has just washed his hair, because he has a towel wrapped around his head. He is apparently happy. The television entertains him enormously. The sound of shots from the screen, which cannot be seen. The shouting of Indians. Little by little The Hake becomes involved in the action. He imitates the movements he sees. He hides behind the chair. He shoots toward the set. He jumps on top of the chair. He shoots again. A bullet gets him. He "dies" ostentatiously in the middle of the living room floor.

He's lying there, sprawled on the floor, when the door opens and Eva enters. She is carrying several packages.

EVA. Bobby!

The Hake doesn't move.

Bobby! What's the matter?

She drops the packages on the floor. She kneels next to him.

What's the matter with you? (*She touches him.*) My God! (*She touches his face.*) Bobby. . . . (*She shakes him.*) Wake up! Bobby, for God's sake!

She looks around desperately. She goes into the kitchen. She runs back with a glass of water. She gives him a drink while she holds his head. The Hake opens one eye.

THE HAKE. Did you bring the pants?

EVA. Oh, God, Bobby! What did you do? You frightened me so!

THE HAKE. Blue? With white stripes?

Eva hands him a package, which The Hake opens eagerly, ripping the paper.

They're gray!

EVA. Yes. I couldn't find the ones you wanted.

THE HAKE (*injured*). But I asked you for blue ones!

EVA. I'm telling you. I couldn't find what you wanted.

THE HAKE (*screams*). Blue, with a white stripe! An inch wide! And you bring me gray! What do you want me to do with these?

EVA. I looked in all the stores, but . . .

THE HAKE. You didn't look enough.

EVA. Yes, I looked Bobby. I looked, but . . .

THE HAKE. You didn't look. Yesterday I saw three pairs in different stores.

He holds the pants up.

What am I going to look like in these? What will Mario say to me when he sees me dressed like this? That I'm one of those playboys from España Square, that's what he's going to say I look like. One of those playboys from the apartments in España Square, who aren't good for anything except to warm their women's beds! Playboys in skirts! Playboys with soft bellies! That's what he'll say I look like!

He throws them away.

I don't want them!

Eva picks them up dejectedly. She wraps them up again.

EVA. I didn't think it would matter so much.
THE HAKE. No, of course not. For a guy who goes around in rags, anything is good enough.
EVA. I wasn't thinking that when I did it.

A long embarrassing pause. The Hake turns off the television.

THE HAKE. Do you like the way I arranged the furniture?
EVA (*distraught*). Oh, yes . . . fine.
THE HAKE. Is it better this way?
EVA. Better, yes.
THE HAKE. And the flowers? Do you like them?
EVA. Pretty, yes.
THE HAKE. The canary got out.

Eva turns toward the cage.

EVA. Goldie! Oh, God! How did it happen?
THE HAKE (*in the middle of the room: the very picture of innocence*). I opened the door to give him some seeds, and zap! he got away!
EVA. And where is he?
THE HAKE. I don't know.

Eva goes to the window and looks outside.

It was when I opened the door to give him some seeds that he got away. He flew around the room a while; he went into the bedroom, into the kitchen, and then flew over my head again. I tried to catch him with a towel. I got a towel from the bathroom and tried to catch him. For a minute I thought I'd caught him. It was when he lighted on the frame of that picture. I stopped in front of him, waiting for the minute to throw the towel over him, but that's when I realized that he didn't *want* me to get him.

Eva turns toward him.

It was all up to me. I couldn't miss. It was a question of throwing the towel, zap! he would have been mine. But that's when I realized he didn't want me to catch him. Something in his attitude, you understand?
EVA. So you let him get away?
THE HAKE. I don't know. It was just that for a minute, I couldn't do anything. I think that's when he started to fly again; he flew around the whole apartment and, finally, went out that window . . . toward the mimosa blossoms. It must be my fault. I think that bird never liked me. From the first day, he always looked at me out of the corner of his eye, a little suspicious. It must be that he realized, before I did, that there wasn't room enough for both of us here.

His smile—that says nothing—returns.

Little creatures have tremendous insight in these matters. It's lucky that he left first, because if not, suddenly, it could have been me . . .

Eva disappears into the bedroom.

Did you know I'd given him a nickname? "Corsair." A strange name for a canary, I know, but it's just that that name reminds me of something! Maybe that it's necessary to be very brave to be able to bear a cage! "Corsair." Poor little thing.

He waits a while.

Do you want me to go?

Eva enters, putting on a robe over her dress. She can't help smiling at the appearance of The Hake standing in the middle of the room, his arms by his sides, wrapped up in the blanket, his head wrapped in the towel, his legs bare— guilty, abject, contrite.

EVA. And why should I want you to go?
THE HAKE. Because of the bird. Ever since I've come I haven't done anything but cause confusion.
EVA. You're just a spoiled child, Bobby.
THE HAKE. To be so unpleasant to you when I refused the beautiful pants you brought me.

Eva takes his hand.

EVA. Come on, you big baby. I've been thinking we need to talk about something. Clear something up.
THE HAKE. After all your affection . . .

Eva sits him beside her in the chair. She places a finger on his lips.

EVA. What were you doing in the Botanical Garden, the day I was painting the laurel, spoiled child?
THE HAKE. Well . . . wandering around.
EVA. Come on, tell me the truth.

The Hake maintains his distance from her.

THE HAKE. You talk to me as if you've known me for a long time.

EVA. You can treat me the same way if you want. I won't break because of it, you know.

THE HAKE. There you go again, laughing at me.

EVA (*impatient*). Oh, Bobby, come on! Why don't you drop it? We're not going to spend a lifetime this way, you so sensitive, and I not knowing how to take you. I know you're not what you seem or what you pretend to be. Some error, some slip "along life's road" (*She makes a gesture as if entertained at her own cliché.*) brought you where you find yourself now, but I know you aren't what you seem . . . or you don't seem to be what you *are* . . . None of that matters to me; you see I don't even ask you. Can you accuse me of that? Of having asked you?

The Hake shakes his head.

No, isn't that true? Then why don't you be yourself? Hmm? Shall we talk as equal to equal?

THE HAKE. As equal to what?

EVA. Well, as equal to equal, as I said.

THE HAKE. And if I weren't what I seem to be, or I didn't seem to be what I am, we wouldn't be speaking like this, isn't that right? As equal to equal . . .

EVA. Well, maybe not.

THE HAKE. Why?

EVA. Because your sensitivity would be in the way, preventing it. (*She moves a little closer to him.*) Come on, silly, tell me . . . what were you doing in the Garden?

THE HAKE. Looking at the parrots.

EVA. No, really? What were you doing?

THE HAKE. Mario had sent me to pick up cigarette butts in front of Orfeon kiosk, so we could grind up the tobacco and sell it at the Marquesa's brothel.

Pause.

EVA. So you don't want to confess, eh?

THE HAKE. Also Chancha, the deaf old woman who sells newspapers in front of the Congress, had asked me to pull some feathers out of the parrot's tail to make a decoration for her hat.

EVA. Yesterday, just after you arrived, you told me that you remembered me a year ago painting the blooming laurels in the Garden in my straw hat with a green ribbon. Unless you're terribly observant and have a very special memory, no one would believe that you'd remember those details so long, if it weren't for a very special reason.

THE HAKE. Special reason?

EVA. Special inclination.

THE HAKE. Special inclination?

He is standing far away from her, his back turned.

EVA. Oh, Bobby, don't be so . . . timid!

The Hake rises.

THE HAKE. It's just that it can't be!

EVA (*from her place*). Why?

THE HAKE. Where would all this lead?

EVA. Who cares? It's strange that you, with the life you lead, should worry about tomorrow. As if you had spent all your life looking ahead. I'll bet you've never worried about anything in your life. Why worry now? Am I worried, for example?

THE HAKE. It's different with you.

EVA. Why with me?

THE HAKE. Because you know what I don't know.

EVA. And what do I know?

THE HAKE. That I'm not what I seem or I don't seem to be what I am. On the other hand, I only know I am what I seem and not that I am not what I don't seem. In other words, you have your fantasy and I have only reality, which is much poorer, much sadder, much more disillusioning. . . . (*In a clipped voice.*) That's the advantage you have over me, although you tell me not to worry . . . what happens is that one worries so much about worrying that in the end he doesn't worry any more about worrying.

EVA. Bobby, Bobby, turn around!

The Hake turns. He doesn't look at her, however.

If you were only the poor vagabond you seem to be, we wouldn't even be able to have this conversation, don't you see? It would all have been over between us a long time ago. Yesterday perhaps. After I gave you your warm soup, I would have sent you away, because it's certain you would have ended up . . . boring me. There's nothing more boring than the conversation of the poor when they're complaining. Don't you agree?

The Hake thinks so. He nods his head, looking at the floor. Eva approaches him and takes his arm.

From the first moment I saw you, I knew who you were. I understand that your shyness must be a consequence of the bad treatment you've had from life. Things that have happened to you have made you pull into your shell. I want you to believe that I'm completely sincere when I tell you that doesn't matter to me. I place no false barriers between us, do you understand?

The Hake understands.

Do you believe I'm your friend, Bobby?

The Hake believes.

Then . . . ?

Eva waits.

THE HAKE. Then we'll have to change the furniture here.

EVA (*surprised*). The furniture? Why?

THE HAKE. I don't like it.

EVA. You don't like it?

THE HAKE. That's what I said.

EVA. Well . . . (*Doesn't know what to say.*) What do we . . . ?

THE HAKE. It has no class.

EVA. Class?

THE HAKE. Style. It has no style. (*With irritation.*) Trash you find by the thousands in any second-class junk store! Just looking at it makes me want to scream! It has no imagination, no fantasy, no dream of any kind!

Eva is stunned. The Hake whirls toward her.

Let's see! How much time did you spend choosing it?

EVA. Well, I . . .

THE HAKE. Not five minutes, I'll bet! You went in the store like someone going in to buy some aspirin and you pointed to the first piece of junk that met your eyes, I'll bet! Anything that would serve to throw your body on and fall asleep! Well, you're mistaken! You need to be a poet to choose furniture and give it the tone it deserves! All the nerve cells that decide taste must be aroused when the moment comes to decide! You're like that crazy old Fabian from the other side of the bay who'll set his ass down on anything he finds . . . an old paraffin tin . . . a rickety old suitcase . . . his shoes . . . on the chest of the old syphilitic Sandilla who bums around with him stealing railroad ties, anything at all. . . . As if one could resolve the problem that way! Choosing furniture is a liturgical act!

His excitement increases as he acts out what he has been describing. His concentration absorbs him completely. He concludes as if debating with another being that is within himself, as if arguing with someone whom he should convince.

You have to raise the chair skirt and see if the framework is made of poplar or of mahogany, because there is always some wretch who wants to trade you a cat for a hare and pass off poplar for mahogany, and that wouldn't be good, because your visitors might notice! Then, it's also important that all the nails be in place! All the nails, or rather all the glue, because it could be that it isn't satin fringe but only tufts of ordinary cloth some son-of-a-bitch wants to palm off! And it's also important, very important, of *primary* importance, to concern yourself with the form, the color, the design, whether it's brocade or velvet, whether the style today is an oblong silhouette or square design, whether the pegs are concave or convex, whether the sons-of-bitches have put in nails—nails, and not screws! Because when visitors sit down they shouldn't simply fall into a chair, but instead, when they bend their knees they should encounter . . . that's it, they should encounter the anatomy of a chair adjusted to their rumps.

All of that should be taken into account! All of that should be considered with the greatest care! Because all of it is of maximum importance! Of primary importance! Of the *most* primary importance. (*He concludes, exhausted.*) You must put life into it, life . . . if necessary . . . that's what that stupid Fabian can't understand! (*Pause.*) We have to change this furniture. We owe it to our visitors.

EVA. Well, we'll change it. You choose. Is that all right with you?

THE HAKE. When?

EVA. Tomorrow?

THE HAKE. I won't be here tomorrow.

EVA. Don't you understand, silly, that starting from today you'll be here tomorrow and all the days you want to?

THE HAKE. We'll have to go out.

EVA. For what?

THE HAKE. To choose the furniture.

EVA. Well, what about it? We'll go out, then.

THE HAKE. In what clothes?

EVA. I'll buy you a suit.

THE HAKE. Gray.

EVA. I thought you wanted blue with white stripes.

THE HAKE. That's for the pants. The suit I want gray. Gray with little white flecks, hardly visible. Better invisible than visible . . . better . . .

EVA. Whatever you say. Is that all right with you?

The Hake looks at her out of the corner of his eye. Distrustful. Icy.

THE HAKE. No, not unless you tell me what it will be like?

EVA. How *what* will be like?

THE HAKE. Walking through the streets.

EVA. I don't understand.

THE HAKE. Will I walk in front of you or behind you?

EVA. There you go again. Beside me, if you want to.

THE HAKE. How far away? A foot? Two? Have you thought about it? And what will we tell the store owner?

Eva looks at him. She does not answer.

Because there are suspicious types, tremendously suspicious. They see rags and they imagine a world of things. Just a simple glance at some rags awakens a whole mythological fantasy.

He turns toward Eve.

Do you understand what I mean? We have to be extremely careful. (*His face completely blank.*) Do you think it would be a good idea if we say I play . . . tennis?

EVA. Tennis? Why that?

THE HAKE. Doesn't your husband play tennis?

EVA. Yes. How did you know?

THE HAKE (*points toward the bedroom*). The pants and the racket there in the closet.

EVA. Curious, hmm?

THE HAKE. Do you think I could pass?

EVA. You could pass for anything at all!

The Hake's blank smile.

THE HAKE. Even for a gigolo, hmm?

EVA. Tonight you'll sleep here in the chair, but I won't lock my bedroom door. I no longer distrust you, you see?

The Hake takes her hands.

If you feel lonely, don't hesitate to call me. I sleep very lightly.

Very close to him.

Unless you're not attracted by ladies over forty who paint out of desperation, or for nostalgia's sake keep the clothes of a man who left his nest centuries ago. A woman alone who doesn't even know how to buy the right kind of furniture.

THE HAKE (*rigid again*). Will I have to . . . take a bath again?

Eva leans her head on his chest.

EVA. Oh, Bobby! Give up! Relax. (*After a while.*) Resting my head on your chest is like resting it on a rock. What has life done to you to make you like this?

THE HAKE. *Comment dîtes-vous, madame?*

EVA (*looks at him; kisses his cheek*). Oh, my love!

The Hake looks straight ahead. He is a rock. A sphinx.

THE HAKE. Yes. It is of the greatest importance, of absolutely primary importance, to choose appropriate words to say what one wishes to say. It involves a complete process of selection carefully prearranged by the spirit. A process that has nothing to do with one's own will. The fundamental thing is to believe in the beauty of one's own expression, since without the contribution of one's delivery, words, thrown out by pure whim, acquire a false dimension in which not even one's self, and certainly not others, can find anything that evokes even a lie. The important thing, then, is to say what one wants to say without saying it, so that others contribute the entire weight of their own . . . deception. Only this way may one be happy.

EVA. Oh, God!

The Hake begins to make little figures with his hands that he projects upon the front wall.

THE HAKE. A rabbit, see? An owl. A child. A frightened child. (*He looks at her.*) Do you have a hatchet?

EVA. Yes.

THE HAKE. And a saw? And a hammer?

EVA. Yes.

THE HAKE. Give them to me. Tonight I'll make the kind of furniture I like.

EVA. They're in the kitchen.

Eva goes into the kitchen. A scream.

What's this! What happened to Goldie!

She comes in with the dead canary hanging from her hand.

Who did this to him?

THE HAKE (*disconsolate; very rapidly, like a child caught doing something wrong*). I told you! I wanted to catch him, but he wouldn't let me. From the beginning he took a dislike to me! From the first glance, he looked at me out of the corner of his eye! I followed him all over the room! I begged him, I implored him to let me catch him, but he insisted on flying! He didn't want to hear my pleas. . . . (*Pause.*) When finally he couldn't fly any more, he was too worn out to understand the meaning of my pleas. He expired without giving me the opportunity to explain to him. (*Another pause.*) I could have loved that little bird. (*Sobs.*) I could have really loved him if he had only let me.

(*He looks at Eva.*)

Poor Goldie. Poor son-of-a-bitch.

CURTAIN

SCENE FIVE

The following morning. The radio is playing "The Waltz of the Dragon-Flies." The Hake, in tennis clothes, is kneeling in the middle of the living room, nailing together a rustic chair, or rather what seems to be a chair, from the remains of a torn-up chair. Of the original chair all that remains is a scattered pile of cotton and feathers, springs and ripped cloth. The wood frame, too, has been violently torn apart as if a bird of prey had seized upon it.

The pictures are no longer there. In their places hang pages from newspapers. There are more paper flowers scattered around. The flowers are larger now, more carelessly made. Simulacrums of flowers, as if made from whole pages of wadded newspapers, attached in the center to wire stems. The Hake hums happily to the music as he works.

After a while Eva appears, in her bathrobe, in the doorway. For a moment she watches The Hake working, then . . .

EVA. I heard you working all night long. It sounded as if a big rat had been trapped in my apartment.

She looks at the room.

You can't say you haven't been busy.

THE HAKE. Do you like it?

EVA. Good work.

THE HAKE. The fever got me. When I get the fever it's like

seeing double. I see one thing to do, and then another to be done. When I attack one, there's already another asking me to persist, and so on . . . Mario has never given me credit for being a carpenter.

EVA. He ought to come see now.

THE HAKE. He says I'm good for taking things apart . . . breaking them, but as for carpentry, real carpentry . . . doing it really right, you understand?

EVA. Yes.

THE HAKE. He says I'm no good. "You're a vandal," he tells me. He's continually telling me that. Perhaps because he's always seen me do just this: rebuilding scattered pieces, putting scraps together. Don't you think?

Eva has gone to sit down in the only remaining chair.

EVA. It must be because of that.

THE HAKE. That's the bad thing about Mario. He only has the imagination about a posteriori things. He doesn't have any imagination about a priori things. I think he ought to see me doing this now, don't you think?

EVA. That's what I told you.

THE HAKE. That would shut his big yap. Don't you think?

He doesn't wait for an answer. He holds on high, in triumph, the chair he has just finished.

Louis XV! What do you think? Or Louis XVI perhaps?

EVA. Restoration.

He finds the idea amusing. He laughs.

THE HAKE. Restoration, yes! That's funny, you know? Restoration. I hadn't thought about that. (*Still laughing.*) That's what I like about you, you know? You have a sense of humor. From the first moment I stuck my dirty paws into your kingdom. I come in here and I break all your furniture . . . I let your canary loose . . . I turn your closets inside out . . . I fill your room with horrible papers flowers and you're still . . . complacent! Always smiling!

EVA. So? What else is there for me to do?

THE HAKE. Yes. The force of circumstances?

EVA. Of destiny.

THE HAKE (*abruptly serious*). Destiny is cirrhosis of the liver or a lung punctured by a stupid life squandered in drunkenness. Don't confuse it with anything else. I'm here strictly because of some warm soup. Don't forget it.

He shows her again the chair on which he has been working.

Do you like it now?

Eva goes to the radio and turns it off.

EVA. Bobby . . . I left the door open last night. You didn't come in. (*The Hake concentrates on his work.*) I waited for you. (*Pause; uncertain smile.*) Since you didn't come in, you couldn't know that I even put on a special nightgown last night. The nightgown I wore my first night of . . .

love. (*She laughs.*) Afterwards, my husband made me wear it on our anniversaries. A long gown, celestial blue, with two rosettes here on the yoke. A gown that still has the odor of the pines at Saint Stephens. My husband thought so anyway. That it retained the odor of our first night under the pines at Saint Stephens . . . with the waves of the sea breaking nearby . . . almost at our feet . . . and the moon . . . the eternal moon. (*Smiles.*) An intrusive, friendly moon, witnessing our . . . passion.

She waits.

Would you believe it, Bobby? That I would be capable of that? Of a night of passion beneath the pines, with only the moon as witness, and the blue nightgown as a pillow?

She presses her hand to her forehead.

It doesn't seem possible to you, does it? That's what makes you so unjust, that you think that it isn't possible . . . or that it isn't possible any more. Because you *do* think that it isn't possible, don't you?

The Hake works.

Isn't that right? You think that it's no longer possible?

A vague evasive *gesture; and an uncertain smile; brief dizziness.*

That a woman like me, alone, oh God! . . . could strip herself of her prudery and open her arms to love, with only the aroma of the pines as witness . . . and the intrusive moon . . .

She looks at him.

Answer me. You don't even hear what I'm saying! Answer me! Do you think it's possible?

The Hake has finished his chair. He holds it in the air. He shakes it in triumph.

THE HAKE. I finished it! I finished it! Now I'd like to invite Mario to come see it! That would shut the old pessimist's trap! Firm structure, well assembled! Strong back, as ordered! Firmness in the line! Solid! Resistant! Do you like it?

EVA. Yes. I like it.

THE HAKE. A lie! You say it for some secret motive locked up in that head of yours. You say it out of compassion! I know the symptoms of the voice. I know each inflection of the voice when somebody speaks out of compassion. It's the voice of one who lowers his hand to give something, which is distinct from the voice of someone who raises his hand to receive something. Let's hear you say, "I like your chair."

EVA. I like your chair.

The Hake gives a cry of triumph.

THE HAKE. There, that's it! You see? That inflection in the

voice! That uncertain tremble! That painful quiver! YOU HAVE COMPASSION FOR ME!

The Hake shakes the chair. He looks at it with disgust.

This chair is horrible. Bad taste. Badly put together. Badly structured. Badly conceived. The risers don't fit. The back's coming apart.

He begins to tear it apart.

The pieces don't fit. You can see the hand that made it had no class.

With every word a piece of the chair is torn off.

No refinement, stubby, primitive, ordinary, shiftless, dumb, of a concept . . . made . . . by a man . . . of the . . . PEOPLE!

He shatters on the floor the few pieces that remain.

It was a chair that deserved to sit near a campfire of filthy trash by the shore of a river, not in a beautiful apartment on España Square.

He rests, finally.

The end of a dream. (*Looks at Eva.*) You should have told me, though.

EVA (*with the greatest naturalness possible*). Why should I tell you something I don't feel?

THE HAKE. Because this establishes an abyss between you and me, you understand? An abyss as wide as the distance around the world.

Declamatory, impersonal, once again sententious. Light.

Pity is the broken, hanging bridge that joins wrath to a full belly!

He smiles a vacant smile that covers his whole face.

Did you like that?

EVA. Oh, God, Bobby! How shall I take you?

The Hake looks at her, desolated.

I swear I don't know. As soon as you arrived I opened the door of my house to you; I received you in it with all my affection. I tried to give you everything I have, but you persist in . . . ignoring me.

The Hake stands in the middle of the room. As Eva speaks, everything in him takes on a desolate air, like a guilty child receiving a reprimand for something he's done, that he cannot now repair.

I speak to you with affection and you respond with irony. I want to be sincere with you and you reject me, saying that I'm lying. I do everything possible to erase between us any sign that recalls your . . . poverty, but you insist on recalling it.

The Hake begins to tremble. He is a child without shelter who is cold, who is afraid. The smallest expression, diminished and sad, of the child of the ruins, hungry, abandoned, frozen.

I'm not the rich, cruel, and frivolous woman you think you see in me. I am a poor lonely woman, very lonely . . . hungry for friendship and affection. I offer you my love, Bobby.

She walks toward him and takes his face. His whole body shivers. A trembling that racks him, which he cannot control.

Oh, my love, be calm, be calm! I am here with you. Your woman is here with you and she's going to help you! Your woman is here with you and she's going to give you all the warmth you've been denied.

The Hake looks before him into the emptiness.

Bobby! Bobby! Look at me! I'm here! I love you! Do you hear me? I love you, Bobby, look at me! Bobby . . .

She shakes him.

Looks at me! For the love of God, look at me!

She shakes him violently.

I'm speaking to you! Listen to me!

Still shaking him.

Listen to me, you damned fool! Look at me!

Nothing. She falls at his feet. Slowly The Hake ceases trembling. A long pause. The "Waltz of the Dragon-Flies" sounds in the emptiness.

THE HAKE (*after the pause*). You still haven't told me how I look in the tennis outfit.

He says it without looking at her, his cold eyes staring into the emptiness straight ahead of him. Eva screams.

EVA. Oh! You don't want me to help you! Your arrogance, your pride, is so great you don't want me to help you!

She rises, wrathful.

So nobody can get near your precious body, huh? Well, I'm going to tell you what you look like in that outfit!

She moves away from him. She picks up the paper flowers and other paper objects and throws them at him as she screams.

Do you know what you look like? A puppet! A ridiculous, deformed puppet! You don't even have any chest! You don't have any shoulders. You don't have the carriage to wear an outfit like that! How dare you put it on!

She awaits his reaction, which doesn't come.

Do you know what you have to have to walk around in something like that? You have to have smooth muscles! Long, smooth, springy muscles! Sure and decisive movements! Not muscles like yours, twisted and starved, that are only fit for scarecrows!

She waits another moment. She moves closer to him. In his face.

You don't have shoulders! You have a hump!

She drops sobbing at his feet, her voice barely discernible.

You don't have muscles . . . you have . . . lumps!

THE HAKE (*distant; very lightly; as if reciting*). And then out of the thicket flew a little bird. He flew for an instant above the green foliage . . .

EVA. Oh . . .

THE HAKE. Over the scenery bathed in light! Fly, little Corsair, I told him . . .

Eva covers her ears.

Fly, little bird!

The Hake looks at her with smiling compassion. He sits down beside her. He is sententious.

Love is a truce between periods of exhaustion. Love is broken teeth in a hungry mouth. What do you say? Did you like it?

EVA (*looks at him through tearful eyes*). Go away.

The Hake looks at her, perplexed.

THE HAKE (*genuinely desolate*). Are your throwing me out?

EVA. Yes! Yes! Yes! Yes! Yes!

THE HAKE. And what am I going to do?

EVA. It doesn't matter to me! Get out!

THE HAKE. I told Mario . . . I told him: these rich people give up in a hurry. At the first opposition they throw the whole thing over. (*Laughs.*) They forget themselves in a good symphony or by giving up something for Lent.

He looks at her.

Do you know what I saw a monkey in a circus do once? That monkey was trying to reach his mate, but he couldn't because they had put them in two separate cages and there were bars between them. It must have been about one o'clock in the afternoon when I saw him try to reach her for the first time. That night he hadn't succeeded, but he was still trying. His chest was all bloody and his teeth were broken from the iron bars, but still he kept trying. It was the following day that he succeeded in getting close to her, when they carried the female monkey to his burial. Sad, isn't it?

He wants to talk. He sits down on the floor at Eva's feet, crossing his legs in the position of a Hindu.

That is, naturally, always considering that love still exists. Saint Simon, the fool of Constitution Bridge, says that it doesn't. Actually, he doesn't even say that any more. One can only deduce it, given his . . . peculiar attitude. Do you know what he does, or what he *doesn't* do? He sits there night and day, on the railing of the bridge, watching the water go by. If anyone speaks to him: nothing. If anyone pokes him: nothing. If anyone shouts at him: (*He shouts.*) Ahhhhhh! Nothing! It's just that nothing interests him any more. He's arrived at a state of complete renunciation of life, where not even struggle is possible any longer. They say that one day a dove made a nest in his hat and he wasn't even aware of it. It's a legend, naturally, but it illustrates the situation, don't you think? Don't you think it illustrates it?

EVA. Didn't you hear what I asked you?

THE HAKE. What?

EVA. That you leave?

THE HAKE. Do you believe that? That we've arrived at the point of spiritual starvation where not even struggle is possible?

Eva rises to her feet. She screams and flees toward the bedroom. She locks herself in. The Hake watches her flee, halfway between stupefaction and amusement.

Do you believe that, Corsair? That we've arrived at a point of lack of love where love is no longer possible?

He approaches the cage. He talks to it, as he hits it, amuses himself. The cage almost hits the ceiling. The blows grow more violent as he speaks as in an interview; making the clichés ridiculous.

"Do you believe that, Mr. Happy?" . . . "That the human soul, deprived of all consolation, finds itself in a lamentable stage of spiritual prostration, where not even mutual confidence is possible?" "Do you believe it, Miss Smile?"

A violent blow.

Do you believe it, you fruity bird? Umm? What do you say? Do you believe it, you son-of-a-bitching bird? Don't you think that flying around the room that way without even saying goodbye was really a fruity thing to do, you pig of a bird? Umm? What do you say? What do you say, you shit? (*Screams.*) Speak, you queer! SPEAK!

The cage shatters against the wall.

CURTAIN

SCENE SIX

The night of the same day.
Nothing of the original décor remains in the room.

Everything is turned upside down.

There are no longer any curtains. In their place hang men's pants.

From corner to corner are draped garlands made from men's shirts tied together by the sleeves, interwoven with others made of women's underwear.

Furniture has been constructed from pieces of the original furniture tied together with strips of wool jackets, torn blankets, and spreads.

The lamps that were hanging are now on the floor. Those that were on the floor are hanging.

The walls are covered with childish figures and drawings, made with burnt cork; "the cat," "the bad man," "the hand," etc. There are also sayings: "I am good" . . . "Christ is King" . . . "God is at my right hand" . . . "Long live me!"

In essence, nothing is in its rightful place. A cyclone has passed through the room. The only things that retain any appearance of premeditated arrangement are the paper flowers. Many new large paper flowers hang in profuse garlands from the walls and are distributed here and there on the floor.

Eva, standing in the midst of the disorder, is allowing herself to serve as model for a bridal gown, which The Hake is fitting to her body with careful solicitude.

THE HAKE (*pinning; making pleats*). Do you see? You see that with a little hope, a little good will, this was worth digging into the old trunk for? It's a little tight, it's true, . . . a little wrinkled, but we must concede that you never . . . suspected that sometime you would have "a second chance," umm?

He moves away, looking at his work.

Or was it for a first time that never was? Umm?

He adjusts a pleat.

There you are! That's it! A little tight through the hips, perhaps. The fault of too much starch, or the years . . . or carelessness, but it passes the test, doesn't it?

He adjusts another pleat. He is the tailor who speaks to his client, intimately, suggestively.

We oughtn't to have put it so far down in the trunk. I understand: because of a passing streetcar, a hand waving suggestively as it moves out of sight, or a word that was left unsaid, or all, all, all the imagination now passed under the bridge, we condemned it to the depths of the trunk, but what about the bells? The little bells? And the laughter at the entrance of the church? And the furtive kiss on the cheek? "Goodbye, Mary, I hope you'll be very happy!" "Good luck!" Doesn't that count, too? We shouldn't be so harsh with time. Objects, too, have a right to take revenge. We shouldn't expect that everything will take its just place, if we don't help it a little, don't you agree?

He moves away, he approaches again. Something about the total appearance displeases him. He rips one side of the dress.

Perhaps it's a question of ripping the cloth a little, in order to see the flesh.

He tears off a piece of the cretonne from the chair by his feet, and with it patches a piece of the torn dress. He smiles.

Sweet little brides! I've observed them! Crouched under the crepe myrtle in the park opposite the church; I've seen them, I've watched them. Not that I had any twisted feeling, like envy or anything like that! No! Why should I, when I had enough paper and scissors at hand?

He tears another piece of the dress and patches it with another strip of cretonne cloth.

They come walking through the high grass, their feet scarcely touching the ground, as if they were floating above the spikes of rye grass . . . they come shimmering over in the damp meadows . . . cadenced steps . . . radiant . . . in smooth white undulations, moving sinuously among the trunks of the oaks . . . straight toward the steps radiant in the sun . . . straight toward the gloved hand!

He speaks into her ear.

And there, at the same moment, before the lascivious glances of all the horrible dwarfs hidden behind the brick walls, hidden under the shadowy atrium, I have seen them . . . I have seen them!

He chokes. Trembles.

I have seen them! Open . . . ! The petals of their bodies! And offer . . . imagine! Offer! (*He shouts.*) Offer! (*He calms himself.*) . . . Their virgin corollas to the consummation of love.

A choked cry.

Oh, God!

He controls himself. He regains his festive tone. He rips a sleeve. He replaces it with another sleeve made from a scrap of paper.

There are some naturally who have a different version of the affair, Fabian, for example. One day I was with him under the crepe myrtle. He had lifted some tinned smoked oysters, and we were preparing to enjoy them . . .

He slashes the hem of the skirt with the scissors.

I should warn you that Fabian has an especially noisy way of moving his mouth when he eats, a manner like this, holding his food in his mouth . . . as if he were afraid it would get to his intestines too fast, or that he might finish too soon, or that it might end too soon the pleasure of his de-gus-ta-tion! The fact is that I don't know if it was his way of chewing, I mean, or my particular state of tension that day, or the stone under my elbow—because a stone had got under my elbow, a damned stone under my elbow! The fact is I don't know if it was that way of his of chewing, like I said, or the stone, or my particular state of tension . . . the fact is that Fabian irritates me! He drives me to madness, I must confess! I don't know if it were that, I say, or the other . . . the insolence of his type, you understand me? His brutal, his bestial insensitivity, or his way of chewing, or the stone, or my particular state of tension. The fact is that, looking toward the church, I suddenly say, "Look!" And he answers me, "Those bitches! Those bitches." Imagine. I looked at his puss and I saw the oil of the smoked oysters dribbling from the corners of his mouth . . . and his bloodshot eyes, you understand me? And his noisy, disagreeable, embarrassing, repugnant way of chewing! The fact is that *something* produced in me, you understand me, a particular state of uncontrollable tension . . . and I grabbed the other tin of oysters that was open, but not eaten, you understand me . . . ? And I pushed it . . . I ground it . . . I shoved it into his filthy puss!

The preceding in screams; he calms himself. Now angelical.

In that moment the church bells rang, and I felt that I had done something that had to be done, you understand? That I had fulfilled my duty! Because guys like Fabian don't know, can't imagine, can't conceive . . . the scope . . . the complete miracle signified by the sur-ren-der-of-one's-vir-gi-ni-ty!

Accentuating the words with false pronunciation, he completely vitiates the meaning.

THE . . . MOST . . . SPLEN-DID . . . OFFERING OF LOVE!

He is amused by his own idea.

Love is a broken bridge with a broken tooth with a broken crank that whirls beyond its four confines breaking heads! Love is a dog with three feet! A tramp with only one hand and two bananas.

He has torn most of the skirt and is replacing it with pieces of the curtain and pieces of his own shirt he has torn into strips. He looks at her.

What's the matter with you? Are you shivering?

Eva shivers, with the same trembling as The Hake.

Are you cold? Are you hot? What is it?

Pause. He waits.

Do you want to go for a stroll on the beach with the happy bridegroom? Gathering shells? Hand in hand, gathering sand dollars? Discussing the number, and the sex, and the number, and the names, and the number, and the sex, of the children that the splendid future will

give you? Discussing the arrangement of the furniture . . . of the cretonne . . . of the colors . . . of the "No it's better here," "No it's better there," of the sizes . . . of the cretonne . . . of the furniture . . . (*His voice is growing louder, faster.*) of the positions of the cretonnes! Of the sizes! Of the numbers, of the children, of the furniture . . . of the sizes . . . of the children? Spea-king-of-love! Love with an L, an O, an E, an X, a U, a tongue, everything, with strength, without strength! The possibilities . . . of being! Of achieving! Of fleeing! Of love! Of solitude! Of death! With a tongue! Arriving! Arriving! Arriving!

He screams.

ARRIVING! ARRIVING! AR . . RI . . VING!

He pants.

Is that it? Is that the secret the refrigerator hides?

Of the original bride's dress, only the veil remains. The rest is a ragbag.

That's funny. Now we're two little brothers.

He rips off the rest of his shirt. He covers his head with a paper rosette in the manner of a crown from which hang long strips of paper that reach to his waist. He takes a board from a piece of furniture in the manner of a lance and brandishes it.

I am Ukelele, the Simba Warrior!

He circles around Eva, making grotesque contortions and amusing grimaces.

Uku! Azahanba! Humba! Tekeke! Takamba! Tumba!

He looks at her as a curious orangutan might regard his prey, with simian curiosity. He puts his face right up to hers.

Comment allez-vous, madame? Did you say something?
EVA (*with an effort.*). I . . .
THE HAKE. Yes?
EVA. I . . .
THE HAKE. Yes?
EVA. I only . . .
THE HAKE. You only, yes . . . ? You already said that. You only . . .
EVA. I only . . .
THE HAKE. Yes?

Eva tries to speak, but can't. Once or twice she makes an effort that frustrates her, then gives up. A pause.

You only wanted to love me and for me to love you. Is that it?

Eva nods weakly.

Yes. But it's too late for that. Ukelele has his guts in his hands and now he doesn't know what to do with them.

He places one of the big paper flowers in the bodice of Eva's dress. It is so large it completely covers her face. He takes her arm in his.

Shall we go?

Someone is knocking at the door.

Yes! (He yells.) We're coming.

He looks at Eva with solicitude, like a very considerate sweetheart.

Are you ready?

His expression changes suddenly to the one we are accustomed to seeing. Sententious. Vacant.

As you see, it is of the greatest importance to have understood the game. To believe in each other. To confide mutually. To renounce your own identity, to the benefit of the identity of the other, until your own identity and the identity of the other, and your own identity . . . own . . . identity . . . of the other . . . identity . . . own . . . don't you think so?

Eva weakly agrees.

Mendelssohn's Wedding March. Their march begins. "Ukelele," very stiff, pathetic almost in his dignity, nude, covered only in rags; on his head is a crown of shredded paper. Eva by his side, her arm in his, absent, lost, beneath the immensity of her paper flower. The only real thing about her is the beautiful veil.

Before we arrive there, I think I should inform you about the geography of the river, of the dangers it offers. There are, out there, some dangerous depths, where on nights of the full moon—when the river flows swollen with broken furniture—many people, falling, have broken their necks.

They exit. In the room now, total disorder reigns. Everything is broken, undone. There remains in it only the new beauty. The dark, enormous, ragged paper flowers.

CURTAIN

F O R U M

"The Popular Theater: Historic and Ideological Considerations"

Domingo Piga T.

Translated by: Roberto D. Pomo and Colleen H. Trujillo

THE PUBLIC AND THE THEATER HOUSES

There are many reasons why the theater is unable to attract a steady, devoted public. In addition to ignoring the struggles of the working class, the theater has avoided social, cultural, economic, and domestic issues.

In earlier historical periods, among the Ancient Greeks and medieval audiences, for example, the masses flocked to dramatic events and religious theater. Beginning with the Renaissance, those audiences abandoned the theater, and it became a venue for character development in the classic sense. This aesthetic, dramatic focus, which emphasized the trials and tribulations of the aristocracy, led to the development of a type of theater architecture radically different from the public plaza, open-air market performance spaces. These people-oriented locales were replaced by ostentatious playhouses, many with orchestra pits, luxury boxes, and balconies. Thus, the theater building, as well as the drama itself, both luxurious expressions of baroque style, began to serve the nobility and the wealthy rather than the art of the theater. The opera house further contributed to this new architecture, which reflected the social classes and their economic power. The theater of the eighteenth and nineteenth centuries is best known for ignoring the common masses, with the exception of a few romantic dramas and the movement toward realism.

Excerpted from Domingo Piga T., "*El Teatro Popular: Consideraciones Históricas e Ideológicas,*" in Gerardo Luzuriaga, ed., *Popular Theater for Social Change in Latin America: Essays in Spanish and English* (Los Angeles: UCLA Latin American Center Publications, 1978), pp. 13–19. Translation published with permission of the Regents of the University of California.

In effect, up to the concluding decades of the 1800s, we have a panorama encompassing four centuries of theatrical fare that mirrored the superstructure of a social elite that manipulated the political and economic European reality. And for the dramatist, actor, designer and theater manager, the only way to survive in the profession was to cater to the wants of the privileged.

Under these conditions, did the popular masses have access to the theater? Impossible, with perhaps the exception of the theater-going student population, a few members of the lower-middle class, or those who hungered for artistic creativity. For them, a space at a lower admission price was set aside in the upper balcony, lacking in luxury and removed from the rest of the audience. . . .

. . . Unlike the ancient Greeks or the audience of the Middle Ages who perceived the theater as a way to nurture and enrich their lives, . . . the elites of the middle class and before them the aristocracy saw the theater as an occasion to mingle with one another—men in their frock coats, tails, tuxedos, and top hats, and women with expensive gowns, jewels, and fancy coiffures. . . . Once inside the theater, they occupied their private boxes or "special" places where champagne, liquor, and food were served during performances. It is clear from this brief description that over these four centuries, the formula had become: theater = entertainment for the well-dressed wealthy middle class.

Did the millions of people who made up the laboring classes have access to the theater? Absolutely not. Even today, opening night is a special occasion. There are areas where men cannot go without a tie. . . .

Furthermore, the price is out of reach for the working class. . . . In Europe, the United States and Latin America the theater continues to be geared to a clientele with money. The price of a theater ticket far exceeds the cost of a movie.

And the working classes, which live far away from the theater districts and depend upon public transportation to get there, do not have time, after a full day's work, to go home, dine, change clothes, and go out for a night at the theater. This practical reality, coupled with the fact that television, as a form of entertainment, is readily accessible, has contributed to the decay of the theater. . . . The theater continues to be a "special occasion" activity, or an event shared in conversations among family members or friends: "I saw this play," or "I saw this particular actor," or "It took place during. . . ." For the theater to attract a wider audience, it must become a common experience, like eating, working, dressing, walking, relaxing. . . .

If we continue to think of the theater as something out of the ordinary, it will remain just that. My friend Roberto Sebastián Matta, the great surrealist painter, shared with me in one of our many conversations that art is, by its very nature, an extraordinary event, and thus could never be a daily experience. I would argue, however, that the social function of art has changed completely. The painter's canvas has become the wall of a building or factory. Music has left the concert halls to be played in parks—and Matta himself went on to paint street murals. The theater must be within reach of the working classes on a daily basis. Moreoover, seventy percent of the theater-going

public are women. Are we then to assume that men do not find the theater interesting and that it is an art form for women?

We must also address the issues of education and cultural formation. Today, the child of a working-class family has access to only primary education. For a small group, 25 to 30 percent, there is middle-level education, while the percentage with access to a university education is even lower. The middle class has created schools availiable only to its own. But this is not the place to elaborate on the transformation of the university into a factory which produces professionals eager to serve a capitalistic worldview. Nor is this a forum for discussing the peasant classes, which only recently were declared part of the human race. Nevertheless, education as we know it has not prepared the individual to perceive art as anything but decoration, ornamentation, or something superfluous or useless. This is why hundreds of thousands of educated people are not interested in the theater. Likewise, our educational system has not adequately addressed (and has often totally ignored) the meaning of art in our lives— with the exception perhaps of music and the fine arts. Perhaps this void could have been filled by careful tutelage in the home. But how? What kind of background do today's parents have in the arts? . . .

Many question the relationship between education and the theater. For centuries, the working classes around the world have existed to serve capitalist interests. Daily, they consume bread, but rarely do they consume culture, let alone art. Anything artistic was contained within the boundaries set forth by the bourgeoisie. Consequently, the masses—which could easily constitute a huge popular audience—are not attracted to the theater as a form of entertainment. . . . Therefore, we must reeducate our public, create a "new public." We must teach them how to listen to music and how to view a play. We must teach them how to "read." About 75 percent of Latin America is literate. The percentage that reads books, however, is very low. (In Haiti about 80 percent of the population is illiterate.) When people do read, they consume magazines, best-sellers, and erotic literature, or only what they need to read for professional or technical survival. The habit of reading develops along with that of listening to music and appreciating theater. These are human needs that are cultivated, and the development of culture is the responsibility of the state. The development of culture corresponds to and depends upon the evolution and revolution of a political and economic structure.

NATIONAL CULTURE, CRITICAL VIEWS AND POPULAR FOUNDATIONS

In order to attract a theater-going public, we must bring the theater to the people by making it affordable.

I am not speaking only of popular theater, but all theater. The dramatic themes, the content, the issues, as well as the characters, must reflect the lifestyles of the popular classes. We are attempting to recapture a public that has been absent from the theater for centuries. Whatever methods are utilized to accomplish this are fine, as long as we keep in mind that theater must entertain and transform the human experience.

(continued)

Polls show that in a given year in major theater centers—like London, Paris, New York—only about 3 percent of the population goes to the theater. . . . In the theater capitals of Latin America (Buenos Aires, Montevideo, Santiago), the percentage is even lower. Only some 1 to 1.5 percent of the population attend theatrical events.

To summarize, popular theater has survived over time because it: contains dramatic content that elevates us morally and culturally and contributes to our education; treats themes related to societal problems; is critical of the social condition and at times speaks, in a quasi-romantic way, of a future without injustice and where one can be content; and incorporates class struggle and political themes. With respect to form and structure, modern popular theater has been influenced by realism, especially the critical and social drama of Ibsen. And granted, much has been said about the need to change the structure of drama and to utilize symbols in order to recapture an audience. There are several reasons, then, why the public shies away from the theater: inconvenience—the theater district is a long distance from home or the workplace; high admission price; and the intimidating, opulent playhouses. To deal with these obstacles, we need to establish low-cost theater venues in neighborhoods where the working classes live that will compete favorably with the movie houses. This approach reflects the ideas of the Enlightenment, the French Revolution, the progressive nineteenth-century middle class . . . and the theoretical and practical works of contemporary Europeans and Latin Americans. . . . Much has been said here about the importance of the subject matter of popular theater. The vitality of this kind of drama must lift up our spirits and energize the communal breath of our people. A theater that limits itself only to analyzing or interpreting daily reality lacks a sense of vitality. What do we mean when we say create a new future? Basically, transform mankind, transform history. Theater that simply criticizes humankind is theater rooted in the past. This was pointed out, quite correctly, by Gogol, Ostrowski, Chekov, Isben, and Hauptmann.

Most of the plays that I come into contact with are works by individuals who think they are writing popular theater, but who are just writing about the mundane aspects of human existence. They find the world to be corrupt so they criticize it. What should the writer's mission really be? To provoke a complete transformation, not just by revealing the follies of society nor weeping about them, but by building a new and different future. The future begins today, after the criticism has taken place.

MEDEAPLAY

HEINER MÜLLER

HEINER MÜLLER (1929–1995)

Heiner Müller, surely the most accomplished playwright in the contemporary German theater since Brecht, is also among the most controversial and outspoken artists of the postmodern era. Consider the following comment, given in an interview shortly before his death:

> The worst experience I had during my stay in the United States was a film I saw called *Fantasia*, by Walt Disney. I had never heard of it and actually ended up watching it by mistake. There were three films playing at the same movie house and I went to the wrong one. The most barbaric thing about this film, something I learned later, was that almost every American child between the ages of six and eight gets to view it. Which means that these people will never again be able to hear specific works by Beethoven, Bach, Handel, Tchaikovsky, etc., without seeing the Disney figures and images. The horrifying thing for me in this is the occupation of the imagination by clichés and images which will never go away; the use of images to prevent experiences, to prevent the having of experiences.

Born on January 9, 1929, in Eppendorf, Saxony, Müller was a journalist, critic, philosopher, poet and playwright. He is the recipient of many literary prizes, including the Lessing Prize, Germany's highest literary honor, in 1975, and the prestigious *Mulheimer Dramatikerpreis*, for excellence in dramatic writing, in 1979.

Müller's creative impulses emanated from the destruction of Europe in World War II and the rubble of postwar political and economic decay. At the age of four his reality was radically altered as he witnessed the apprehension and lengthy incarceration of his father by the German National Socialists. Müller himself became a prisoner of war in 1945; for two days he was imprisoned by the Allied liberation army, which actually allowed him to escape and return to his home on foot. Other important events that influenced his literary output were the division of Germany; the violent strike by Berlin construction workers in 1953 (which forced the Soviet army to intercede); the Hungarian Revolution of 1956; the cold war, which permeated Germany's social fabric; and the erection of the Berlin Wall in 1961. The Wall, literally and symbolically, isolated Müller from the rest of Germany and his European sensibility. Müller was finally allowed to travel freely in the 1970s, thanks to the international reputation his artistic achievements had earned him. Yet he always returned to Berlin, conspicuously choosing to be a comfortable product of German isolationism.

In addition to Shakespeare and Brecht, Müller's theatrical models were the classical Greek tragedians, especially the cynical Euripides (upon whose play this *Medeaplay* is based). His dramatic themes concern human beings in a state of flux because of sociopolitical displacement. Carl Weber, the foremost scholar and translator of Müller's works, defines the playwright's purpose:

> The reader will discover certain threads which connect most, if not all, of Müller's thinking and writing. There is the conflict of the individual's desire for fulfillment . . . the pursuit of hap-

piness, which clashes with the crushing demands history and its social upheavals force upon humankind. Müller has kept struggling with and writing about this conflict for forty years. The conviction that individuals are beholden to history and social forces which are forged by it is never forgotten by Müller. He may investigate and question the individual's commitment, he may discuss and distrust ideologies which enforce such a commitment, but he always maintains that the individual cannot escape responsibility for humankind's present and future.

Although his early dramatic works were influenced by the dramaturgy of Brecht and the early realists, Müller's greatest contribution to the theater came after the early 1970s when his drama emphasized "synthetic fragment." He coined the term to define a postmodern, image-driven, often Surrealistic approach to a radically new performance aesthetic intended to disintegrate the "fourth wall" of the social realists. Müller attempted to create a new performance aesthetic. Many of his pieces, in particular *Hamletmachine* (1977), *The Task* (1980), and *Heartpiece* (1981), are nonlinear, devoid of conflict, and tension free. They are intellectual and ideological explorations of humans attempting to explain their present condition in a preapocalyptic world. Written in an almost hieroglyphic manner, Müller's plays elicit an audience response rarely experienced in the contemporary theater. Thematically, they manifest the playwright's sensitivity to the oppressed plight of the working class, and the individual caught in historical schisms. His is not a theater of illusion but one that penetrates both the conscious and particularly the unconscious. Like Brecht, Müller wants his audience to ponder, to think, and to choose if necessary—but never to remain inert.

MEDEAPLAY (1974)

Reminiscent of Antonin Artaud's scenarios, which evolved from his vision of a theater of cruelty, this short piece was Muller's first experimentation with synthetic fragmentation in order to create a theater of epic power without spoken language. Borrowing from Greek myth and Euripides' tragedy, *Medeaplay* is a collage of cinematic and MTV-like images. Though it appears to be a short work, it is actually a lengthy piece in which Medea and Jason experience a total transformation until the disturbing climax ("Debris, limbs, intestines fall from the flies on the man") is forced on our vision.

Can *Medeaplay* invite a traditional and linear description or analysis of its dramatic events? Perhaps not. It does not pretend to induce an intellectual response. Rather, the strength and importance of this theatrical creation lies in our ability to move beyond the written word to experience viscerally "images" created by its author, to reconstruct and deconstruct, to alter in our minds Euripides' original text. Müller asks us to consider that, in our daily experience, we continue to go about our business without regard to the consequences mapped out by our socially imposed inventions. For Müller, it is not just running the red light that brings a ticket from the legal official—who has been carefully hidden between corners and driveways. Rather, Müller probes the reasons why officials must aggressively protect humanity from its excesses and transgressions. He argues that our insatiable greed for superiority and control too often forces humans to stoop to excessive means to gain and maintain power. *Medeaplay* vividly portrays those excesses, and if it is itself excessive, it is because it embodies—in a short paragraph—the surfeit of horror produced by the modern police state. Though it portrays an action in ancient Corinth, it resonates with the shrieks of Auschwitz, Tiananmen Square, Tibet, Kent State, Bosnia, Tlatelolco Plaza in Mexico City, Chiapas, and Soweto.

"The Bride" (Leslie Malitz), having "taken off her face," reaches for the child she is about to "rip up" in Müller's Artaudian retelling of the Greek legend.

MEDEAPLAY

HEINER MÜLLER

A bed is lowered from the flies and put upright on stage. Two female figures with death masks lead a girl on stage and place her with her back to the bed. Dressing of the bride. She is tied to the bed with the belt of her wedding dress. Two male figures with death masks lead the bridegroom in and place him facing the bride. He stands on his head, walks on his hands, turns cartwheels before her, etc.; she laughs without a sound. He rips up the wedding dress and takes his place with the bride. Projection: The Sexual Act. The male death masks tie the hands of the bride to the bed with the shreds of the wedding dress, and the female death masks her feet. The remains serve to gag her. While the man stands on his head, walks on his hands, turns cartwheels, etc. before the (female) spectators, the woman's belly swells until it bursts. Projection: The Act of Birth. The female death masks pull a child from the woman's belly, untie her hands, place the child in her arms. Meanwhile, the male death masks have draped the man with so many arms that he can move only on all fours. Projection: The Act of Killing. The woman takes off her face, rips up the child, and hurls the parts in the direction of the man. Debris, limbs, intestines fall from the flies on the man.

END

FORUM

"From *The Theatre of Images*"

BONNIE MARRANCA

Bonnie Marranca is among the foremost chroniclers of contemporary theater trends; she has written numerous books and articles on the principal trend-setters in the theater of the 1980s and 1990s. In this introduction to her book, The Theatre of Images, *she summarizes the shift to a visual, less verbal theater as created by Robert Wilson, Richard Foreman, and Lee Breuer.*

In the last dozen years the American avant-garde theater has emerged as a dynamic voice in the international arts scene. From its crude beginnings in out-of-the-way lofts, churches, private clubs and renovated spaces, it has become for many the liveliest, most creative center of theatrical activity in the West. This is due partly to the help of grant monies, but primarily to the emergence of a number of highly imaginative and gifted theater artists.

Experimental groups of the sixties and early seventies broke down traditional parameters of theatrical experience by introducing new approaches to acting, playwriting and the creation of theatrical environments; they reorganized audience and performing space relationships, and eliminated dialogue from drama. Collaborative creation became the rule.

Value came increasingly to be placed on performance with the result that the new theater never became a literary theater, but one dominated by images—visual and aural. This is the single most important feature of contemporary American theater, and it is characteristic of the works of groups *and* playwrights. As early as eight years ago Richard Kostelanetz pointed out the non-literary character of the American theater when he wrote in *The Theatre of Mixed Means:*

> . . . the new theatre contributes to the contemporary cultural revolt against the pre-dominance of the word; for it is definitely a theatre for a post-literate (which is not the same as illiterate) age. . . .[1]

If this theatre refused to believe in the supremacy of language as a critique of reality, it offered a multiplicity of images in its place. Kostelanetz's McLuhanesque statement clarifies the direction that the American theater has steadily followed since the Happenings. It has now culminated in a Theater of Im-

[1]Richard Kostelanetz, *Theatre of Mixed Means* (N.Y.: Dial Press, 1968), p. 33.

Introduction to *The Theatre of Images*, edited with introductory essays by Bonnie Marranca. Copyright © 1977, 1996 by Bonnie Marranca. Reprinted by permission of the author.

ages—the generic term I have chosen to define a particular style of the American avant-garde which is represented here by Richard Foreman (Ontological-Hysteric Theater), Robert Wilson (Byrd Hoffman School of Byrds) and Lee Breuer (Mabou Mines).

The works of Foreman, Wilson and Breuer represent the climactic point of a movement in the American avant-garde that extends from The Living Theatre, The Open Theatre, The Performance Group, The Manhattan Project and the Iowa Theatre Lab, to the "show and tell" styles of political groups like El Teatro Campesino, The San Francisco Mime Troupe and The Bread and Puppet Theatre. (And it is continued in the current proliferation of art-performances.) Today it is demonstrated in the image-oriented Structuralist Workshop of Michael Kirby and in the works of younger artists: *Sakonnet Point* by Spalding Gray and Elizabeth LeCompte; the "spectacles" of Stuart Sherman. All of the productions and groups mentioned above exclude dialogue or use words minimally in favor of aural, visual and verbal imagery that calls for alternative modes of perception on the part of the audience. This break from a theatrical structure founded on dialogue marks a watershed in the history of American theatre, a *rite de passage*.

The intention of this [essay] is to demonstrate the significance of the Theatre of Images, its derivation from theatrical and non-theatrical sources, its distinctively American roots in the avant-garde, its embodiment of a certain contemporary sensibility and its impact on audiences.

This essay, which first isolates characteristics of the Theatre of Images, and then deals at length with the specific pieces published here, will perhaps suggest an attitude to bring to this theatre. Hopefully, it will also offer helpful, new tools of analysis—an alternative critical vocabulary—with which to view contemporary theatre.

The absence of dialogue leads to the predominance of the stage picture in the Theatre of Images. This voids all considerations of theatre as it is conventionally understood in terms of plot, character, setting, language and movement. Actors do not create "roles." They function instead as media through which the playwright expresses his ideas; they serve as icons and images. Text is merely a pretext—a scenario.

The texts as published here (less so in the case of *The Red Horse Animation* which offers a comic book as a textual alternative) remain incomplete documents of a theatre that must be seen to be understood; one cannot talk about the works of Foreman, Wilson and Breuer without talking about their productions. Attending a theatrical performance is always an experience apart from reading a dramatic text; but a playscript *does* generally stand on its own merits as a pleasurable experience, indicating what it is about and usually giving a clue as to how it is staged. Conversely, reading Wilson's *A Letter for Queen Victoria* can be frustrating for readers attuned to theme, character, story, genre and logical language structure. There is scarcely a clue to its presentation in a script composed of bits and pieces of overheard conversations, television and films. Similarly, in Foreman's work, which insists on demonstrating what the words say (in Wittgensteinian-styled language games), to read the text alone is to lose the sensual delight and intellectual exchange of his theatre. And *The Red Horse Animation* is not a play at all.

Just as the Happenings had no immediate theatrical antecedents, the Theatre of Images, though not quite so renegade, has developed aesthetically from numerous non-theatrical roots. This is not to say that this movement disregards theatrical practices of the past: It is the application of them that makes the difference. More directly, the avant-garde must use the past in order to create a dialogue with it.

Foreman's work shows the influence (and the radicalization) of Brechtian technique; Breuer has acknowledged his attempt to synthesize the acting theories of Stanislavsky, Brecht and Grotowski; the productions of Wilson descend from Wagner. However, in their work, spatial, temporal and linguistic concepts are non-theatrically conditioned. Extra-theatrical influences have had a more formative impact. Cagean aesthetics, new dance, popular cultural forms, painting, sculpture and the cinema are important forces that have shaped the Theatre of Images. It is also logical that America, a highly technological society dominated by aural and visual stimuli, should produce this kind of theatre created, almost exclusively, by a generation of artists who grew up with television and movies.

The proliferation of images, ideas and forms availiable to the artist in such a culture leads to a crisis in the artist's choice of creative materials, and in his relationship to the art object. It is not suprising, then, that all of the pieces collected here are metatheatrical: They are about the making of art. In *Pandering to the Masses: A Misrepresentation* Foreman speaks directly to the audience (on tape) concerning the "correct" interpretation of events *as they occur*. The actors relate the formal "Outline" of the production at intervals in *Red Horse*. The result is a high degree of focus on process. How one sees is as important as what one sees.

This focus on process—the producedness, or seams-showing quality of a work—is an attempt to make the audience more conscious of events in the theatre than they are accustomed to. It is the idea of *being there* in the theatre that is the impulse behind Foreman's emphasis on immediacy in the relationship of the audience to the theatrical event.

The importance given to consciousness in the Theatre of Images is also manifest in its use of individual psychologies: Foreman in his psychology of art; Wilson in his collaboration with Christopher Knowles, an autistic teenager whose personal psychology is used as creative material (not as a psychology of the disturbed); and in Breuer's interest in motivational acting. In *Pandering*, life and theatre merge as Foreman incorporates his thoughts into the written text. In *Queen Victoria*, Wilson

adapts, if only partially, autistic behavior as an alternative, positive mode of perceiving life. Through Breuer's use of interior monologue, the consciousness of the Horse is explored in *Red Horse*.

Each artist refrains from developing character in a predictable, narrative framework which would evoke conditioned patterns of intellectual and emotional response. Like all modernist experiments, which necessarily suggest a new way to perceive familiar objects and events, their works agitate for radical, alternative modes of perception.

In the Theatre of Images the painterly and sculptural qualities of performance are stressed, transforming this theatre into a spatially dominated one activated by sense impressions, as opposed to a time-dominated one ruled by linear narrative. Like modern painting, the Theatre of Images is timeless (*Queen Victoria* could easily be expanded or contracted), abstract and presentational (in *Red Horse*, images are both abstract and anthropomorphic), often static (the principle of duration rules the work of Foreman and Wilson); frequently the stage picture is framed two-dimensionally (in *Pandering* the actors are often poised in frontal positions). Objects are dematerialized, functioning in their natural rhythmic context. The body of the actor is malleable and pictorial—like the three actors who form multiple images of an Arabian steed lying *on* the performing space (*Red Horse*). It is flattening of the image (stage picture) that characterizes the Theatre of Images, just as it does modern painting.

If the acting is pictorial, it also nonvirtuosic, an inheritance from the new dance which emphasizes natural movement. This is an aesthetic quality of the particular branch of the avant-garde dealt with here. What I wish to suggest is that the Theatre of Images in performance demonstrates a radical refunctioning of naturalism. It uses the performer's natural, individual movements as a starting point in production. Of the artists featured in this anthology, Foreman is the most thoroughly naturalistic. He allows performers (untrained) a personal freedom of expression while at the same time making them appear highly stylized in slow-motion, speeded-up, noninflectional patterns of speech or movement. He also pays a great deal of attention to actual situation and detail and the factor of time. Foreman's work is stylized yet naturalistic as are Alain Resnais's *Last Year at Marienbad* and Marguerite Duras's *India Song*.

The naturalism of nontraditional theatre is a curious phenomenon but one worth paying attention to because of its prevalence and diversity; it is also quite a paradox to admit that the avant-garde, in 1976, is naturalistic. In addition to being characteristic of the scripts printed here, it has shown itself in the production of David Gaard's *The Marilyn Project* directed last year by Richard Schechner, in Scott Burton's recent art-performance *Pair Behavior Tableaux*, as well as in Peter Handke's play without words, *My Foot My Tutor*. In these works there is a high degree of stylization by performers who "naturally" engage in an activity which is presented pictorially.

Perhaps that is why, in the Theatre of Images, tableau is so often the chief unit of composition. Tableau, in fact, has been a dominant structure in the work of twentieth-century innovators: the Cubists, Gertrude Stein, Bertolt Brecht, Jean-Luc

(continued)

Godard, Alain Robbe-Grillet, Philip Glass, to name a few. It is evident in the work of Foreman, Wilson and Breuer as well. Tableau has the multiple function of compelling the spectator to analyze its specific placement in the artistic framework, stopping time by throwing a scene into relief, expanding time and framing scenes. In *Pandering*, the tableaux function as objects in a cubist space, very often confusing perception by the intrusion of a single kinetic element. The cinematic "cuts" of *Red Horse* frequently focus the actors in close-up; "frames" are duplicated in the actual comic book documentation of the performance.

The stillness of tableau sequences suspends time, causing the eye to focus on an image, and slows down the process of input. This increases the critical activity of the mind. For Foreman it represents the ideal moment to impart taped directives to the audience; it also regulates the dialectical interplay of word and image.

Neither time nor space are bound by conventional law. Time is slowed-down, speeded up—experienced as duration. It is never clocked time. Likewise, spatial readjustment is frequent in all of the pieces published here. *Red Horse* is played in multiple viewing perspectives: The actors perform both lying on the floor and standing on it, and up against a back wall of the performing space. *Pandering* alternates easily from flat perspective to linear perspective; the actors continually rearrange the drapes and flats of the set during performance. In *Queen Victoria* space is divided, cut apart and blackened—usually by means of light—leaving the actors to serve as images or silhouettes in a surreal landscape.

If time and space are dysynchronous in the Theatre of Im-ages, so is language broken apart and disordered. The language of *Queen Victoria* is "throwaway," devoid of content. In *Red Horse* choral narrative is correlated with the image in space as interior monologue substitutes for dialogue. *Pandering* is ruled by the distributive principle of sound: Actors speak parts of sentences which are completed either by other actors or Foreman's voice on tape.

Sound is used sculpturally, just as the actors are. Aural tableaux complement or work dialectically with visual tableaux. In *Pandering* the audience, surrounded by stereo speakers, is bombarded with sound. Sound and visual images dominate in performance in an attempt to expand normal capabilities for experiencing sense stimuli. Because of the sophisticated sound equipment used in the productions of Foreman, Wilson and Breuer it is reasonable to conclude that the Theatre of Images would not exist without the benefit of advanced technology. Perhaps experiments with holography may lead in the future to a theatre of total images and recorded sound.

The significance of the Theatre of Images is its expansion of the audience's capacity to perceive. It is a theatre devoted to the creation of a new stage language, a visual grammar "written" in sophisticated perceptual codes. To break these codes is to enter the refined sensual worlds this theatre offers.

Here, then, are three examples of the best of the American avant-garde theatre: works which break down the parameters of human experience which we have too hastily accepted.

Robert Wilson's extraordinary visual images in works such as The Forest *have made him among the most respected artists in the contemporary theater.*

BURIED CHILD

SAM SHEPARD

SAM SHEPARD (1943–)

No other American playwright has received more critical attention in the past quarter century than Sam Shepard, an oddity given that only two of his plays—*Buried Child* and *True West*—have appeared on the Broadway stage (and then only as revivals in 1995 and 2000, respectively). Like Beckett, who was his earliest inspiration, Shepard writes enigmatic dramas whose meanings are passionately debated by critics and scholars.

Although he was born in Illinois (the locale of *Buried Child*), Shepard was a self-described Air Force brat whose family was constantly on the move, perhaps contributing to one of Shepard's thematic obsessions: the search for one's roots. As a teenager, his family settled in Duarte, California, in the high desert east of Los Angeles. Not surprisingly, many of Shepard's plays are set on or adjacent to the desert. As a teen, Shepard read his first play, Samuel Beckett's desolate tragicomedy *Waiting for Godot*, which he claims has had the most influence on his writing.

In the early 1960s Shepard fled the high desert for New York City, where he waited tables while searching for work as a musician (he was the drummer for a rock band, the Holy Modal Rounders, that contributed music to the cult film *Easy Rider*). Shepard ran the streets of New York with the son of jazz great Charles Mingus. His early plays attempted to create the theatrical equivalent of the improvisational jazz style that reflects impressions of American life; he refers to these plays as "vibrations."

Shepard joined Joseph Chaikin's experimental theater company, The Open Theatre, for whom he both acted and wrote plays until 1973. The Open Theatre was noted for its work with transformations, acting exercises in which performers transformed themselves from one being into another. Transformation is a central theme of Shepard's dramatic works, and his style requires actors to shift effortlessly between naturalistic and stylistic modes of performance.

Shepard's canon can be divided into three phases: the early vibrations, almost exclusively one-acts (e.g., *Cowboy Mouth*, 1965), written as nonrealistic, experimental monologues; the middle plays (e.g., *Tooth of Crime*, 1968), fantasies that borrowed from westerns and gangster films, science fiction works, cartoons, and pop entertainment while exploring the isolation of the artist in a violent world; and the later, neorealistic plays that collectively explore the disintegration of the family in the American West, including: *Curse of the Starving Class* (1978), *Buried Child* (1979, Pulitzer Prize), *True West* (1980), *Fool for Love* (1983), and *Lie of the Mind* (1985).

In addition to his achievements as a playwright, Shepard is a highly respected film actor (*The Right Stuff*) and screenwriter (*Country*). Although he lives in the high desert near Santa Fe, New Mexico, he remains associated with San Francisco's Magic Theater.

BURIED CHILD (1979)

With *Curse of the Starving Class* Shepard began a series of family plays that evolved into what may be collectively called "the old man cycle"—five plays bound together by the real or implied specter of "the old man," whose sins weigh heavily on the heads of his children (or grandson in *Buried Child*). The offspring of "the old man" are obsessed with recapturing a vision of America and the family that may or may not have ever existed. Like Aeschylus's *Oresteia*, Shepard's five plays explore the traditional mythic themes of guilt and expiation, blood pollution, regeneration, violence, and passion within the context of the family.

For Shepard myth is the means of coming to grips with the mystery of life because it "speaks to everything at once":

> Myth is a powerful medium because it talks to the emotions and not the head. It moves us into an area of mystery. . . . [Folk-rock singer Bob] Dylan creates a mythic atmosphere out of the land around us. The land we walk on everyday and never see until someone shows it to us.

Shepard's modern myths, as presented in *Buried Child*, are created through a fusion of incantatory language that possesses "the capacity to evoke visions in the eye of the audience," and powerful stage pictures that conjure archetypal images. These cause audiences to view the world with the same sense of awe, mystery, and even terror as that felt by our ancient forbears. In *Buried Child*, for instance, the fallow land suddenly bursts forth to yield corn and carrots; a ritual burial in corn husks and a shearing ceremony end the first act of the play. Shepard's theater achieves in practice the theory of Artaud's theater of cruelty, which called for incantation, archetypal images, and other primal means to force audiences to confront the plague of modern civilization. Of such images Shepard has said:

> The fantastic thing about theater is that it can make something be seen that is invisible . . . that you can be watching this thing happening with actors and costumes and lights and set and language and even plot, and something emerges beyond that, and that's the image part I'm looking for.

It is this quest for the invisible, the mysterious, the otherworldly, even the spiritual that aligns Shepard with the most ancient impulses of world theater.

Shepard has defined myth as "an ancient formula that is expressed as a means of handing down a very specific knowledge," and he cites the myth of Osiris, celebrated in the ancient Egyptian Passion play at Abydos (see Center Stage, *The Abydos Passion Play* in Chapter 1), as a prime example. Osiris was slain by a jealous brother who dismembered the body and scattered its remains throughout the Nile Valley (the original "buried child"?). Mysteriously, the arid land became strangely fertile wherever it held pieces of Osiris's corpse. In *Buried Child* the land that has cradled the corpse of Halie's murdered baby mysteriously yields crops which are gathered by Tilden, much to the dismay of Bradley. Thus Shepard exposes a contemporary American myth: the land man has conquered on the frontier will produce plenty through the sweat of one's brow. The playwright returns to a more primitive myth that suggests that life comes from death—and sometimes from evil itself.

More importantly, Shepard evokes a myth that specifically deals with "blood pollution," that is, family feuding that ends in death and the destruction of the line. Since Aeschylus, stories of intrafamily strife have best met our dramatic and thematic needs; Aristotle himself devotes the 15th chapter of *The Poetics* to this phenomenon. To the houses of Sophocles' Laius, Aeschylus's Atrius, Shakespeare's Lear and Old Hamlet, Ibsen's Alvings, O'Neill's Tyrones and Cabots, and Miller's Lomans, we can add Shepard's warring families. He is acutely aware that extreme violence most frequently occurs within the family. In *True West*, Lee—the son of Cain—tells his brother the L.A. Police Department will confirm that family people kill each other the most: "Brothers. Brothers-in-law. Cousins. Real American type people. They kill each other in the heat mostly." In *Buried Child*, old man Dodge asks questions for which playwrights and mythmakers since the Greeks have tried to provide answers: "You think just because people propagate they have to love their offspring? You never seen a bitch eat her puppies?"

Are Shepard's works the legitimate successors of O'Neill's tormented studies of the family at war with itself? Or, are they another chapter in the line of 1950s "kitchen sink" dramas? Or, are they western—as opposed to WASPish—versions of Edward Albee's family brawls? Though

Shepard has absorbed these links in the evolution of contemporary drama into his work, he goes beyond them.

As a number of critics have pointed out, Shepard's family plays are the final chapter of an odyssey in which a young male hero, such as Vince, returns to his family home to recover his roots. Shelley tells *Buried Child* audiences that Vince's trip back to the Illinois farm of his childhood is very much a quest: "We had to stop off at every little meatball town he remembered from his boyhood! Every stupid little donut shop he ever kissed a girl in! Every drive-in. Every drag strip. Every football field he ever broke a leg on."

The events that follow when the prodigal son returns to the old homestead are quite unlike those depicted in traditional American plays, films, and television sitcoms. Shepard's America is not that of Ozzie and Harriet or *Leave It to Beaver,* which celebrate the puritannical virtues of hard work, integrity, love of the land, and the sanctity of the family. Rather, Shepard's plays are the stuff of ancient legend: incest, fratricide, infanticide, passion, territorial battles, dispossession, loss, and death.

Shepard is less interested than O'Neill in the plight of a particular family. He does not permit us to refer to a curse on the house of Tyrone, nor does he present us with the allegorical implications of Miller's "Low-man" families. He simply does not assign surnames, and thus his families remain generalized, never mired in the particular woes of a particular family. What Shepard implies is that we are all members of a single, disintegrating family. Speeches throughout the quintet of family plays remind us that humans are inextricably bound together. Vince's description of his late-night ride across Illinois in *Buried Child* best illustrates our commonality:

> I could see myself in the windshield. My face. My eyes. I studied my face . . . as though I was looking at another man. As though I could see his whole race behind him. Like a mummy's face. I saw him dead and alive at the same time. In the same breath. In the windshield. I watched him breathe as if he were frozen in time. . . . And then his face changed. His face became his father's face. Same bones. Same eyes. Same breath. And his face changed to his Grandfather's face. And it went on and on like that. Changing. Clear on back to faces I'd never seen before but still recognized. . . . I followed my family clear to Iowa. Every last one. Straight to the Corn Belt and further.

The speech is one of those obligatory moments we look for in plays: the Aristotelian "recognition speech." At this moment, Vince, who understands the object of his quest, literally "reverses" himself by turning his car around and returning to the family farm.

It is no coincidence that Shepard's homesteads are invariably found on western land. In an early play he has a character refer to the West as a "Looks Within Place," the last frontier of our technological world where people can come to terms with themselves. On one hand Shepard's West is primordial and pristine, the paradise envisioned by those who settled it in the nineteenth century. Shelley's first reaction to Vince's family farm is that it reminds her of something out of an idyllic Norman Rockwell painting. This is surely the mythic West that Shepard—and his characters—would like the world to be. But the myth is "a lie of the mind." The reality of the West was its violence, and the code of the West was survival, even if that meant abandoning those closest to you. The law of the West is that one made one's own laws to survive. Shepard has said that he finds western violence simultaneously "ugly" and "very moving" because "it has something to do with humiliation . . . and the guilt of having gotten this country by wiping out a native race of people." Shepard is less interested in history than in the general condition of humanity, which is best expressed in poetry and myth. And thus the American West is the ideal metaphor for his apocalyptic vision of the world. The Promised Land is also the Wasteland, and the territory of the rugged individualist is also the prison of the lonely and isolated. Vince's half-brother Tilden says of his journey to New Mexico: "I was more lonely than I've ever been before." For Shepard, the home on the range is also the house of the cursed.

The "old man" in each of the family plays is a product of the mythic west of "the lie." He is a son of the West who subscribes to the code of violence, isolation, and using others (especially women) and the land for personal gain. The sons and grandsons, like Vince, are visionaries who seek the idyllic West, where commitment to the land and to others increases one's chances for survival. The enigmatic ending of *Buried Child* suggests the two visions of the West: even while a miraculous, life-giving rain falls on the land, the "buried child" is carried through the house that Vince has inherited. The ambiguity of the ending avoids the comfort of catharsis, which, Shepard says, "gets rid of something, and I'm not looking to get rid of it. I'm looking to find it. I'm not [writing plays] to vent demons. I want to shake hands with them."

Vince's bizarre family disturbs Shelly in the Broadway production of Shepard's Pulitzer drama,
Buried Child; the askew lampshades and dilapidated furniture reflect the decline of the idyllic mid-
western farm.

BURIED CHILD

SAM SHEPARD

While the rain of your fingertips falls,
while the rain of your bones falls,
and your laughter and marrow fall down,
you come flying.

> Pablo Neruda

CHARACTERS

DODGE, *in his seventies*
HALIE, *his wife, mid-sixties*
TILDEN, *their oldest son*
BRADLEY, *their next oldest son, an amputee*
VINCE, *Tilden's son*
SHELLY, *Vince's girlfriend*
FATHER DEWIS, *a Protestant minister*

ACT ONE

SCENE: *Day. Old wooden staircase down left with pale,*
frayed carpet laid down on the steps. The stairs lead off-
stage left up into the wings with no landing. Up right is an
old, dark green sofa with the stuffing coming out in spots.
Stage right of the sofa is an upright lamp with a faded yel-
low shade and a small night table with several small bottles
of pills on it. Down right of the sofa, with the screen facing
the sofa, is a large, old-fashioned brown T.V. A flickering
blue light comes from the screen, but no image, no sound.
In the dark, the light of the lamp and the T.V. slowly
brighten in the black space. The space behind the sofa, up-
stage, is a large, screened-in porch with a board floor. A

solid interior door to stage right of the sofa, leading into the room onstage; and another screen door up left, leading from the porch to the outside. Beyond that are the shapes of dark elm trees.

Gradually the form of Dodge is made out, sitting on the couch, facing the T.V., the blue light flickering on his face. He wears a well-worn T-shirt, suspenders, khaki work pants, and brown slippers. He's covered himself in an old brown blanket. He's very thin and sickly looking, in his late seventies. He just stares at the T.V. More light fills the stage softly. The sound of light rain. Dodge slowly tilts his head back and stares at the ceiling for a while, listening to the rain. He lowers his head again and stares at the T.V. He turns his head slowly to the left and stares at the cushion of the sofa next to the one he's sitting on. He pulls his left arm out from under the blanket, slides his hand under the cushion, and pulls out a bottle of whiskey. He looks down left toward the staircase, listens, then uncaps the bottle, takes a long swig, and caps it again. He puts the bottle back under the cushion and stares at the T.V. He starts to cough slowly and softly. The coughing gradually builds. He holds one hand to his mouth and tries to stifle it. The coughing gets louder, then suddenly stops when he hears the sound of his wife's voice coming from the top of the staircase.

HALIE'S VOICE. Dodge?

(Dodge just stares at the T.V. Long pause. He stifles two short coughs.)

HALIE'S VOICE. Dodge! You want a pill, Dodge?

(He doesn't answer. Takes the bottle out again and takes another long swig. Puts the bottle back, stares at T.V., pulls blanket up around his neck.)

HALIE'S VOICE. You know what it is, don't you? It's the rain! Weather. That's it. Every time. Every time you get like this, it's the rain. No sooner does the rain start then you start. *(Pause.)* Dodge?

(He makes no reply. Pulls a pack of cigarettes out from his sweater and lights one. Stares at T.V. Pause.)

HALIE'S VOICE. You should see it coming down up here. Just coming down in sheets. Blue sheets. The bridge is pretty near flooded. What's it like down there? Dodge?

(Dodge turns his head back over his left shoulder and takes a look out through the porch. He turns back to the T.V.)

DODGE *(to himself)*. Catastrophic.
HALIE'S VOICE. What? What'd you say, Dodge?
DODGE *(louder)*. It looks like rain to me! Plain old rain!
HALIE'S VOICE. Rain? Of course it's rain! Are you having a seizure or something! Dodge? *(Pause.)* I'm coming down there in about five minutes if you don't answer me!

DODGE. Don't come down.
HALIE'S VOICE. What!
DODGE *(louder)*. Don't come down!

(He has another coughing attack. Stops.)

HALIE'S VOICE. You should take a pill for that! I don't see why you just don't take a pill. Be done with it once and for all. Put a stop to it.

(He takes bottle out again. Another swig. Returns bottle.)

HALIE'S VOICE. It's not Christian, but it works. It's not necessarily Christian, that is. We don't know. There's some things the ministers can't even answer. I, personally, can't see anything wrong with it. Pain is pain. Pure and simple. Suffering is a different matter. That's entirely different. A pill seems as good an answer as any. Dodge? *(Pause.)* Dodge, are you watching baseball?
DODGE. No.
HALIE'S VOICE. What?
DODGE *(louder)*. No!
HALIE'S VOICE. What're you watching? You shouldn't be watching anything that'll get you excited! No horse racing!
DODGE. They don't race on Sundays.
HALIE'S VOICE. What?
DODGE *(louder)*. They don't race on Sundays!
HALIE'S VOICE. Well they shouldn't race on Sundays.
DODGE. Well they don't.
HALIE'S VOICE. Good. I'm amazed they still have that kind of legislation. That's amazing.
DODGE. Yeah, it's amazing.
HALIE'S VOICE. What?
DODGE *(louder)*. It is amazing!
HALIE'S VOICE. It is. It truly is. I would've thought these days they'd be racing on Christmas even. A big flashing Christmas tree right down at the finish line.
DODGE *(shakes his head)*. No.
HALIE'S VOICE. They used to race on New Year's! I remember that.
DODGE. They never raced on New Year's!
HALIE'S VOICE. Sometimes they did.
DODGE. They never did!
HALIE'S VOICE. Before we were married they did!

(Dodge waves his hand in disgust at the staircase. Leans back in sofa. Stares at TV.)

HALIE'S VOICE. I went once. With a man.
DODGE *(mimicking her)*. Oh, a "man."
HALIE'S VOICE. What?
DODGE. Nothing!
HALIE'S VOICE. A wonderful man. A breeder.
DODGE. A what?
HALIE'S VOICE. A breeder! A horse breeder! Thoroughbreds.

DODGE. Oh, thoroughbreds. Wonderful.

HALIE'S VOICE. That's right. He knew everything there was to know.

DODGE. I bet he taught you a thing or two, huh? Gave you a good turn around the old stable?

HALIE'S VOICE. Knew everything there was to know about horses. We won bookoos of money that day.

DODGE. What?

HALIE'S VOICE. Money! We won every race I think.

DODGE. Bookoos?

HALIE'S VOICE. Every single race.

DODGE. Bookoos of money?

HALIE'S VOICE. It was one of those kind of days.

DODGE. New Year's!

HALIE'S VOICE. Yes! It might've been Florida. Or California! One of those two.

DODGE. Can I take my pick?

HALIE'S VOICE. It was Florida!

DODGE. Aha!

HALIE'S VOICE. Wonderful! Absolutely wonderful! The sun was just gleaming. Flamingos. Bougainvilleas. Palm trees.

DODGE (*to himself, mimicking her*). Bougainvilleas. Palm trees.

HALIE'S VOICE. Everything was dancing with life! There were all kinds of people from everywhere. Everyone was dressed to the nines. Not like today. Not like they dress today.

DODGE. When was this anyway?

HALIE'S VOICE. This was long before I knew you.

DODGE. Must've been.

HALIE'S VOICE. Long before. I was escorted.

DODGE. To Florida?

HALIE'S VOICE. Yes. Or it might've been California. I'm not sure which.

DODGE. All that way you were escorted?

HALIE'S VOICE. Yes.

DODGE. And he never laid a finger on you, I suppose? (*Long silence.*) Halie?

(*No answer. Long pause.*)

HALIE'S VOICE. Are you going out today?

DODGE (*gesturing toward rain*). In this?

HALIE'S VOICE. I'm just asking a simple question.

DODGE. I rarely go out in the bright sunshine, why would I go out in this?

HALIE'S VOICE. I'm just asking because I'm not doing any shopping today. And if you need anything you should ask Tilden.

DODGE. Tilden's not here!

HALIE'S VOICE. He's in the kitchen.

(*Dodge looks toward stage left, then back toward T.V.*)

DODGE. All right.

HALIE'S VOICE. What?

DODGE (*louder*). All right!

HALIE'S VOICE. Don't scream. It'll only get your coughing started.

DODGE. All right.

HALIE'S VOICE. Just tell Tilden what you want and he'll get it. (*Pause.*) Bradley should be over later.

DODGE. Bradley?

HALIE'S VOICE. Yes. To cut your hair.

DODGE. My hair? I don't need my hair cut!

HALIE'S VOICE. It won't hurt!

DODGE. I don't need it!

HALIE'S VOICE. It's been more than two weeks, Dodge.

DODGE. I don't need it!

HALIE'S VOICE. I have to meet Father Dewis for lunch.

DODGE. You tell Bradley that if he shows up here with those clippers, I'll kill him!

HALIE'S VOICE. I won't be very late. No later than four at the very latest.

DODGE. You tell him! Last time he left me almost bald! And I wasn't even awake! I was sleeping! I woke up and he'd already left!

HALIE'S VOICE. That's not my fault!

DODGE. You put him up to it!

HALIE'S VOICE. I never did!

DODGE. You did too! You had some fancy, stupid meeting planned! Time to dress up the corpse for company! Lower the ears a little! Put up a little front! Surprised you didn't tape a pipe to my mouth while you were at it! That woulda' looked nice! Huh? A pipe? Maybe a bowler hat! Maybe a copy of the *Wall Street Journal* casually placed on my lap!

HALIE'S VOICE. You always imagine the worst things of people!

DODGE. That's not the worst! That's the least of the worst!

HALIE'S VOICE. I don't need to hear it! All day long I hear things like that and I don't need to hear more.

DODGE. You better tell him!

HALIE'S VOICE. You tell him yourself! He's your own son. You should be able to talk to your own son.

DODGE. Not while I'm sleeping! He cut my hair while I was sleeping!

HALIE'S VOICE. Well, he won't do it again.

DODGE. There's no guarantee.

HALIE'S VOICE. I promise he won't do it without your consent.

DODGE (*after pause*). There's no reason for him to even come over here.

HALIE'S VOICE. He feels responsible.

DODGE. For my hair?

HALIE'S VOICE. For your appearance.

DODGE. My appearance is out of his domain! It's even out of mine! In fact, it's disappeared! I'm an invisible man!

HALIE'S VOICE. Don't be ridiculous.

DODGE. He better not try it. That's all I've got to say.

HALIE'S VOICE. Tilden will watch out for you.

DODGE. Tilden won't protect me from Bradley!

HALIE'S VOICE. Tilden's the oldest. He'll protect you.

DODGE. Tilden can't even protect himself!

HALIE'S VOICE. Not so loud! He'll hear you. He's right in the kitchen.

DODGE (*yelling off left*). Tilden!

HALIE'S VOICE. Dodge, what are you trying to do?

DODGE (*yelling off left*). Tilden, get in here!

HALIE'S VOICE. Why do you enjoy stirring things up?

DODGE. I don't enjoy anything!

HALIE'S VOICE. That's a terrible thing to say.

DODGE. Tilden!

HALIE'S VOICE. That's the kind of statement that leads people right to the end of their rope.

DODGE. Tilden!

HALIE'S VOICE. It's no wonder people turn to Christ!

DODGE. TILDEN!!

HALIE'S VOICE. It's no wonder the messengers of God's word are shouted down in public places!

DODGE. TILDEN!!!!

(*Dodge goes into a violent, spasmodic coughing attack as Tilden enters from stage left, his arms loaded with fresh ears of corn. Tilden is Dodge's oldest son, late forties, wears heavy construction boots, covered with mud, dark green work pants, a plaid shirt, and a faded brown windbreaker. He has a butch haircut, wet from the rain. Something about him is profoundly burned out and displaced. He stops center stage with the ears of corn in his arms and just stares at Dodge until he slowly finishes his coughing attack. Dodge looks up at him slowly. He stares at the corn. Long pause as they watch each other.*)

HALIE'S VOICE. Dodge, if you don't take that pill nobody's going to force you.

(*The two men ignore the voice.*)

DODGE (*to Tilden*). Where'd you get that?

TILDEN. Picked it.

DODGE. You picked all that?

(*Tilden nods.*)

DODGE. You expecting company?

TILDEN. No.

DODGE. Where'd you pick it from?

TILDEN. Right out back.

DODGE. Out back where!

TILDEN. Right out in back.

DODGE. There's nothing out there!

TILDEN. There's corn.

DODGE. There hasn't been corn out there since about nineteen thirty-five! That's the last time I planted corn out there!

TILDEN. It's out there now.

DODGE (*yelling at stairs*). Halie!

HALIE'S VOICE. Yes dear!

DODGE. Tilden's brought a whole bunch of corn in here! There's no corn out in back is there?

TILDEN (*to himself*). There's tons of corn.

HALIE'S VOICE. Not that I know of!

DODGE. That's what I thought.

HALIE'S VOICE. Not since about nineteen thirty-five!

DODGE (*to Tilden*). That's right. Nineteen thirty-five.

TILDEN. It's out there now.

DODGE. You go and take that corn back to wherever you got it from!

TILDEN (*after pause, staring at Dodge*). It's picked. I picked it all in the rain. Once it's picked you can't put it back.

DODGE. I haven't had trouble with neighbors here for fifty-seven years. I don't even know who the neighbors are! And I don't wanna know! Now go put that corn back where it came from!

(*Tilden stares at Dodge, then walks slowly over to him and dumps all the corn on Dodge's lap and steps back. Dodge stares at the corn, then back to Tilden. Long pause.*)

DODGE. Are you having trouble here, Tilden? Are you in some kind of trouble?

TILDEN. I'm not in any trouble.

DODGE. You can tell me if you are. I'm still your father.

TILDEN. I know you're still my father.

DODGE. I know you had a little trouble back in New Mexico. That's why you came out here.

TILDEN. I never had any trouble.

DODGE. Tilden, your mother told me all about it.

TILDEN. What'd she tell you?

(*Tilden pulls some chewing tobacco out of his jacket and bites off a plug.*)

DODGE. I don't have to repeat what she told me! She told me all about it!

TILDEN. Can I bring my chair in from the kitchen?

DODGE. What?

TILDEN. Can I bring in my chair from the kitchen?

DODGE. Sure. Bring your chair in.

(*Tilden exits left. Dodge pushes all the corn off his lap onto the floor. He pulls the blanket off angrily and tosses it at one end of the sofa, pulls out the bottle and takes another swig. Tilden enters again from left with a milking stool and a pail. Dodge hides the bottle quickly under the cushion before Tilden sees it. Tilden sets the stool down by the sofa, sits on it, puts the pail in front of him on the floor. Tilden starts picking up the ears of corn one at a time and husking them. He throws the husks and silk in the center of the stage and drops the ears into the pail each time he cleans one. He repeats this process as they talk.*)

DODGE (*after pause*). Sure is nice looking corn.

TILDEN. It's the best.

DODGE. Hybrid?

TILDEN. What?

DODGE. Some kinda fancy hybrid?

TILDEN. You planted it. I don't know what it is.

DODGE (*pause*). Tilden, look, you can't stay here forever. You know that, don't you?

TILDEN (*spits in spittoon*). I'm not.

DODGE. I know you're not. I'm not worried about that. That's not the reason I brought it up.

TILDEN. What's the reason?

DODGE. The reason is I'm wondering what you're gonna do.

TILDEN. You're not worried about me, are you?

DODGE. I'm not worried about you.

TILDEN. You weren't worried about me when I wasn't here. When I was in New Mexico.

DODGE. No, I wasn't worried about you then either.

TILDEN. You shoulda worried about me then.

DODGE. Why's that? You didn't do anything down there, did you?

TILDEN. I didn't do anything.

DODGE. Then why should I have worried about you?

TILDEN. Because I was lonely.

DODGE. Because you were lonely?

TILDEN. Yeah. I was more lonely than I've ever been before.

DODGE. Why was that?

TILDEN (*pause*). Could I have some of that whiskey you've got?

DODGE. What whiskey? I haven't got any whiskey.

TILDEN. You've got some under the sofa.

DODGE. I haven't got anything under the sofa! Now mind your own damn business! Jesus God, you come into the house outa the middle of nowhere, haven't heard or seen you in twenty years and suddenly you're making accusations.

TILDEN. I'm not making accusations.

DODGE. You're accusing me of hoarding whiskey under the sofa!

TILDEN. I'm not accusing you.

DODGE. You just got through telling me I had whiskey under the sofa!

HALIE'S VOICE. Dodge?

DODGE (*to Tilden*). Now she knows about it!

TILDEN. She doesn't know about it.

HALIE'S VOICE. Dodge, are you talking to yourself down there?

DODGE. I'm talking to Tilden!

HALIE'S VOICE. Tilden's down there!

DODGE. He's right here!

HALIE'S VOICE. What?

DODGE (*louder*). He's right here!

HALIE'S VOICE. What's he doing?

DODGE (*to Tilden*). Don't answer her.

TILDEN (*To Dodge*). I'm not doing anything wrong.

DODGE. I know you're not.

HALIE'S VOICE. What's he doing down there!

DODGE (*to Tilden*). Don't answer.

TILDEN. I'm not.

HALIE'S VOICE. Dodge!

(*The men sit in silence. Dodge lights a cigarette. Tilden keeps husking corn, spits tobacco now and then in spittoon.*)

HALIE'S VOICE. Dodge! He's not drinking anything, is he? You see to it that he doesn't drink anything! You've gotta watch out for him. It's our responsibility. He can't look after himself anymore, so we have to do it. Nobody else will do it. We can't just send him away somewhere. If we had lots of money we could send him away. But we don't. We never will. That's why we have to stay healthy. You and me. Nobody's going to look after us. Bradley can't look after us. Bradley can hardly look after himself. I was always hoping that Tilden would look out for Bradley when they got older. After Bradley lost his leg. Tilden's the oldest. I always thought he'd be the one to take responsibility. I had no idea in the world that Tilden would be so much trouble. Who would've dreamed. Tilden was an All-American, don't forget. Don't forget that. Fullback. Or quarterback. I forget which.

TILDEN (*to himself*). Fullback. (*Still husking.*)

HALIE'S VOICE. Then when Tilden turned out to be so much trouble, I put all my hopes on Ansel. Of course Ansel wasn't as handsome, but he was smart. He was the smartest probably. I think he probably was. Smarter than Bradley, that's for sure. Didn't go and chop his leg off with a chain saw. Smart enough not to go and do that. I think he was smarter than Tilden too. Especially after Tilden got in all that trouble. Doesn't take brains to go to jail. Anybody knows that. Course then when Ansel died that left us all alone. Same as being alone. No different. Same as if they'd all died. He was the smartest. He could've earned lots of money. Lots and lots of money.

(*Halie enters slowly from the top of the staircase as she continues talking. Just her feet are seen at first as she makes her way down the stairs, a step at a time. She appears dressed completely in black, as though in mourning. Black handbag, hat with a veil, and pulling on elbow-length black gloves. She is about sixty-five with pure white hair. She remains absorbed in what she's saying as she descends the stairs and doesn't really notice the two men who continue sitting there as they were before she came down, smoking and husking.*)

HALIE. He would've took care of us, too. He would've seen to it that we were repaid. He was like that. He was a hero. Don't forget that. A genuine hero. Brave. Strong. And very intelligent. Ansel could've been a great man. One of the greatest. I only regret that he didn't die in action. It's not fitting for a man like that to die in a motel room. A soldier. He could've won a medal. He could've been decorated for valor. I've talked to Father Dewis about putting up a plaque for Ansel. He thinks it's a good idea. He agrees. He knew Ansel when he used to play basketball. Went to every game. Ansel was his favorite player. He even recommended to the City Council that they put up a statue of Ansel. A big, tall statue with a basketball in one hand and a rifle in the other. That's how much he thinks of Ansel.

(Halie reaches the stage and begins to wander around, still absorbed in pulling on her gloves, brushing lint off her dress, and continuously talking to herself as the men just sit.)

HALIE. Of course, he'd still be alive today if he hadn't married into the Catholics. The Mob. How in the world he never opened his eyes to that is beyond me. Just beyond me. Everyone around him could see the truth. Even Tilden. Tilden told him time and again. Catholic women are the Devil incarnate. He wouldn't listen. He was blind with love. Blind. I knew. Everyone knew. The wedding was more like a funeral. You remember? All those Italians. All that horrible black, greasy hair. The smell of cheap cologne. I think even the priest was wearing a pistol. When he gave her the ring I knew he was a dead man. I knew it. As soon as he gave her the ring. But then it was the honeymoon that killed him. The honeymoon. I knew he'd never come back from the honeymoon. I kissed him and he felt like a corpse. All white. Cold. Icy blue lips. He never used to kiss like that. Never before. I knew then that she'd cursed him. Taken his soul. I saw it in her eyes. She smiled at me with that Catholic sneer of hers. She told me with her eyes that she'd murder him in his bed. Murder my son. She told me. And there was nothing I could do. Absolutely nothing. He was going with her, thinking he was free. Thinking it was love. What could I do? I couldn't tell him she was a witch. I couldn't tell him that. He'd have turned on me. Hated me. I couldn't stand him hating me and then dying before he ever saw me again. Hating me in his death bed. Hating me and loving her! How could I do that? I had to let him go. I had to. I watched him leave. I watched him throw gardenias as he helped her into the limousine. I watched his face disappear behind the glass.

(She stops abruptly and stares at the corn husks. She looks around the space as though just waking up. She turns and looks hard at Tilden and Dodge who continue sitting calmly. She looks again at the corn husks.)

HALIE *(pointing to the husks)*. What's this in my house! *(Kicks husks.)* What's all this!

(Tilden stops husking and stares at her.)

HALIE *(to Dodge)*. And you encourage him!

(Dodge pulls blanket over him again.)

DODGE. You're going out in the rain?
HALIE. It's not raining.

(Tilden starts husking again.)

DODGE. Not in Florida it's not.
HALIE. We're not in Florida!
DODGE. It's not raining at the race track.
HALIE. Have you been taking those pills? Those pills always make you talk crazy. Tilden, has he been taking those pills?
TILDEN. He hasn't took anything.
HALIE *(to Dodge)*. What've you been taking?
DODGE. It's not raining in California or Florida or the race track. Only in Illinois. This is the only place it's raining. All over the rest of the world it's bright golden sunshine.

(Halie goes to the night table next to the sofa and checks the bottle of pills.)

HALIE. Which ones did you take? Tilden, you must've seen him take something.
TILDEN. He never took a thing.
HALIE. Then why's he talking crazy?
TILDEN. I've been here the whole time.
HALIE. Then you've both been taking something!
TILDEN. I've just been husking the corn.
HALIE. Where'd you get that corn anyway? Why is the house suddenly full of corn?
DODGE. Bumper crop!
HALIE *(moving center)*. We haven't had corn here for over thirty years.
TILDEN. The whole back lot's full of corn. Far as the eye can see.
DODGE *(to Halie)*. Things keep happening while you're upstairs, ya know. The world doesn't stop just because you're upstairs. Corn keeps growing. Rain keeps raining.
HALIE. I'm not unaware of the world around me! Thank you very much. It so happens that I have an overall view from the upstairs. The back yard's in plain view of my window. And there's no corn to speak of. Absolutely none!
DODGE. Tilden wouldn't lie. If he says there's corn, there's corn.
HALIE. What's the meaning of this corn, Tilden!
TILDEN. It's a mystery to me. I was out in back there. And the rain was coming down. And I didn't feel like coming back inside. I didn't feel the cold so much. I didn't mind the wet. So I was just walking. I was muddy but I didn't mind the mud so much. And I looked up. And I saw this stand of corn. In fact I was standing in it. So, I was standing in it.
HALIE. There isn't any corn outside, Tilden! There's no corn! Now, you must've either stolen this corn or you bought it.
DODGE. He doesn't have any money.
HALIE *(to Tilden)*. So you stole it!
TILDEN. I didn't steal it. I don't want to get kicked out of

Illinois. I was kicked out of New Mexico and I don't want to get kicked out of Illinois.

HALIE. You're going to get kicked out of this house, Tilden, if you don't tell me where you got that corn!

(Tilden starts crying softly to himself but keeps husking corn. Pause.)

DODGE *(to Halie)*. Why'd you have to tell him that? Who cares where he got the corn? Why'd you have to go and tell him that?

HALIE *(to Dodge)*. It's your fault you know! You're the one that's behind all this! I suppose you thought it'd be funny! Some joke! Cover the house with corn husks. You better get this cleaned up before Bradley sees it.

DODGE. Bradley's not getting in the front door!

HALIE *(kicking husks, striding back and forth)*. Bradley's going to be very upset when he sees this. He doesn't like to see the house in disarray. He can't stand it when one thing is out of place. The slightest thing. You know how he gets.

DODGE. Bradley doesn't even live here!

HALIE. It's his home as much as ours. He was born in this house!

DODGE. He was born in a hog wallow.

HALIE. Don't you say that! Don't you ever say that!

DODGE. He was born in a goddamn hog wallow! That's where he was born and that's where he belongs! He doesn't belong in this house!

HALIE *(she stops)*. I don't know what's come over you, Dodge. I don't know what in the world's come over you. You've become an evil man. You used to be a good man.

DODGE. Six of one, a half dozen of another.

HALIE. You sit there day and night, festering away! Decomposing! Smelling up the house with your putrid body! Hacking your head off till all hours of the morning! Thinking up mean, evil, stupid things to say about your own flesh and blood!

DODGE. He's not my flesh and blood! My flesh and blood's buried in the back yard!

(They freeze. Long pause. The men stare at her.)

HALIE *(quietly)*. That's enough, Dodge. That's quite enough. I'm going out now. I'm going to have lunch with Father Dewis. I'm going to ask him about a monument. A statue. At least a plaque.

(She crosses to the door up right. She stops.)

HALIE. If you need anything, ask Tilden. He's the oldest. I've left some money on the kitchen table.

DODGE. I don't need anything.

HALIE. No, I suppose not. *(She opens the door and looks out through porch.)* Still raining. I love the smell just after it stops. The ground. I won't be too late.

(Shes goes out door and closes it. She's still visible on the porch as she crosses toward stage left screen door. She

stops in the middle of the porch, speaks to Dodge but doesn't turn to him.)

HALIE. Dodge, tell Tilden not to go out in the back lot anymore. I don't want him back there in the rain.

DODGE. You tell him. He's sitting right here.

HALIE. He never listens to me, Dodge. He's never listened to me in the past.

DODGE. I'll tell him.

HALIE. We have to watch him just like we used to now. Just like we always have. He's still a child.

DODGE. I'll watch him.

HALIE. Good.

(She crosses to screen door, left, takes an umbrella off a hook, and goes out the door. The door slams behind her. Long pause. Tilden husks corn, stares at pail. Dodge lights a cigarette, stares at T.V.)

TILDEN *(still husking)*. You shouldn't a told her that.

DODGE *(staring at T.V.)*. What?

TILDEN. What you told her. You know.

DODGE. What do you know about it?

TILDEN. I know. I know all about it. We all know.

DODGE. So what difference does it make? Everybody knows, everybody's forgot.

TILDEN. She hasn't forgot.

DODGE. She should've forgot.

TILDEN. It's different for a woman. She couldn't forget that. How could she forget that?

DODGE. I don't want to talk about it!

TILDEN. What do you want to talk about?

DODGE. I don't want to talk about anything! I don't want to talk about troubles or what happened fifty years ago or thirty years ago or the race track or Florida or the last time I seeded the corn! I don't want to talk!

TILDEN. You don't wanna die, do you?

DODGE. No, I don't wanna die either.

TILDEN. Well, you gotta talk or you'll die.

DODGE. Who told you that?

TILDEN. That's what I know. I found that out in New Mexico. I thought I was dying but I just lost my voice.

DODGE. Were you with somebody?

TILDEN. I was alone. I thought I was dead.

DODGE. Might as well have been. What'd you come back here for?

TILDEN. I didn't know where to go.

DODGE. You're a grown man. You shouldn't be needing your parents at your age. It's unnatural. There's nothing we can do for you now anyway. Couldn't you make a living down there? Couldn't you find some way to make a living? Support yourself? What'd'ya come back here for? You expect us to feed you forever?

TILDEN. I didn't know where else to go.

DODGE. I never went back to my parents. Never. Never even had the urge. I was independent. Always independent. Always found a way.

TILDEN. I didn't know what to do. I couldn't figure anything out.

DODGE. There's nothing to figure out. You just forge ahead. What's there to figure out?

(*Tilden stands.*)

TILDEN. I don't know.

DODGE. Where are you going?

TILDEN. Out back.

DODGE. You're not supposed to go out there. You heard what she said. Don't play deaf with me!

TILDEN. I like it out there.

DODGE. In the rain?

TILDEN. Especially in the rain. I like the feeling of it. Feels like it always did.

DODGE. You're supposed to watch out for me. Get me things when I need them.

TILDEN. What do you need?

DODGE. I don't need anything! But I might. I might need something any second. Any second now. I can't be left alone for a minute!

(*Dodge starts to cough.*)

TILDEN. I'll be right outside. You can just yell.

DODGE (*between coughs*). No! It's too far! You can't go out there! It's too far! You might not even hear me!

TILDEN (*moving to pills*). Why don't you take a pill? You want a pill?

(*Dodge coughs more violently, throws himself back against sofa, clutches his throat. Tilden stands by helplessly.*)

DODGE. Water! Get me some water!

(*Tilden rushes off left. Dodge reaches out for the pills, knocking some bottles to the floor, coughing in spasms. He grabs a small bottle, takes out pills, and swallows them. Tilden rushes back on with a glass of water. Dodge takes it and drinks, his coughing subsides.*)

TILDEN. You all right now?

(*Dodge nods. Drinks more water. Tilden moves in closer to him. Dodge sets glass of water on the night table. His coughing is almost gone.*)

TILDEN. Why don't you lay down for a while? Just rest a little.

(*Tilden helps Dodge lay down on the sofa. Covers him with blanket.*)

DODGE. You're not going outside, are you?

TILDEN. No.

DODGE. I don't want to wake up and find you not here.

TILDEN. I'll be here.

(*Tilden tucks blanket around Dodge.*)

DODGE. You'll stay right here?

TILDEN. I'll stay in my chair.

DODGE. That's not a chair. That's my old milking stool.

TILDEN. I know.

DODGE. Don't call it a chair.

TILDEN. I won't.

(*Tilden tries to take Dodge's baseball cap off.*)

DODGE. What're you doing! Leave that on me! Don't take that offa me! That's my cap!

(*Tilden leaves the cap on Dodge.*)

TILDEN. I know.

DODGE. Bradley'll shave my head if I don't have that on. That's my cap.

TILDEN. I know it is.

DODGE. Don't take my cap off.

TILDEN. I won't.

DODGE. You stay right here now.

TILDEN (*sits on stool*). I will.

DODGE. Don't go outside. There's nothing out there.

TILDEN. I won't.

DODGE. Everything's in here. Everything you need. Money's on the table. T.V. Is the T.V. on?

TILDEN. Yeah.

DODGE. Turn it off! Turn the damn thing off! What's it doing on?

TILDEN (*shuts off T.V., light goes out*). You left it on.

DODGE. Well, turn it off.

TILDEN (*sits on stool again*). It's off.

DODGE. Leave it off.

TILDEN. I will.

DODGE. When I fall asleep you can turn it on.

TILDEN. Okay.

DODGE. You can watch the ball game. Red Sox. You like the Red Sox don't you?

TILDEN. Yeah.

DODGE. You can watch the Red Sox. Pee Wee Reese. Pee Wee Reese. You remember Pee Wee Reese?

TILDEN. No.

DODGE. Was he with the Red Sox?

TILDEN. I don't know.

DODGE. Pee Wee Reese. (*falling asleep.*) You can watch the Cardinals. You remember Stan Musial.

TILDEN. No.

DODGE. Stan Musial. (*falling into sleep.*) Bases loaded. Top a' the sixth. Bases loaded. Runner on first and third. Big fat knuckle ball. Floater. Big as a blimp. Cracko! Ball just took off like a rocket. Just pulverized. I marked it. Marked it with my eyes. Straight between the clock and the Burma Shave ad. I was the first kid out there. First kid. I had to fight hard for that ball. I wouldn't give it up. They almost tore the ears right off me. But I wouldn't give it up.

(*Dodge falls into deep sleep. Tilden just sits staring at him for a while. Slowly he leans toward the sofa, checking to see if Dodge is well asleep. He reaches slowly under the cushion and pulls out the bottle of booze. Dodge sleeps soundly. Tilden stands quietly, staring at Dodge as he uncaps the bottle and takes a long drink. He looks around at the husks on the floor and then back to Dodge. He moves center stage and gathers an armload of corn husks then crosses back to the sofa. He stands holding the husks over Dodge and looking down at him he gently spreads the corn husks over the whole length of Dodge's body. He stands back and looks at Dodge. Pulls out bottle, takes another drink, returns bottle to his hip pocket. He gathers more husks and repeats the procedure until the floor is clean of corn husks and Dodge is completely covered in them except for his head. Tilden takes another long drink, stares at Dodge sleeping, then quietly exits stage left. Long pause as the sound of rain continues. Dodge sleeps on. The figure of Bradley appears up left, outside the screen porch door. He holds a wet newspaper over his head as a protection from the rain. He seems to be struggling with the door, then slips and almost falls to the ground. Dodge sleeps on, undisturbed.)*

BRADLEY. Sonuvabitch! Sonuvagoddamnbitch!

(Bradley recovers his footing and makes it through the screen door onto the porch. He throws the newspaper down, shakes the water out of his hair, and brushes the rain off of his shoulders. He is a big man dressed in a gray sweatshirt, black suspenders, baggy dark blue pants, and black janitor's shoes. His left leg is wooden, having been amputated above the knee. He moves with an exaggerated, almost mechanical limp. The squeaking sounds of leather and metal accompany his walk coming from the harness and hinges of the false leg. His arms and shoulders are extremely powerful and muscular due to a lifetime dependency on the upper torso doing all the work for the legs. He is about five years younger than Tilden. He moves laboriously to the stage right door and enters, closing the door behind him. He doesn't notice Dodge at first. He moves toward the staircase.)

BRADLEY *(calling to upstairs)*. Mom!

(He stops and listens. Turns upstage and sees Dodge sleeping. Notices corn husks. He moves slowly toward sofa. Stops next to pail and looks into it. Looks at husks. Dodge stays asleep. Talks to himself.)

BRADLEY. What in the hell is this?

(He looks at Dodge's sleeping face and shakes his head in disgust. He pulls out a pair of black electric hair clippers from his pocket. Unwinds the cord and crosses to the lamp. He jabs his wooden leg behind the knee, causing it to bend at the joint and awkwardly kneels to plug the cord into a floor outlet. He pulls himself to his feet again by using the sofa as leverage. He moves to Dodge's head and again jabs his false leg. Goes down on one knee. He vio-

lently knocks away some of the corn husks, and then jerks off Dodge's baseball cap and throws it down center stage. Dodge stays asleep. Bradley switches on the clippers. Lights start dimming. Bradley cuts Dodge's hair while he sleeps. Lights dim slowly to black with the sound of clippers and rain.)

ACT TWO

SCENE: *Same set as act 1. Night. Sound of rain. Dodge still asleep on sofa. His hair is cut extremely short and in places the scalp is cut and bleeding. His cap is still center stage. All the corn and husks, pail and milking stool have been cleared away. The lights come up to the sound of a young girl laughing offstage left. Dodge remains asleep. Shelly and Vince appear up left outside the screen porch door sharing the shelter of Vince's overcoat above their heads. Shelly is about nineteen, black hair, very beautiful. She wears tight jeans, high heels, purple T-shirt, and a short rabbit fur coat. Her makeup is exaggerated and her hair has been curled. Vince is Tilden's son, about twenty-two, wears a plaid shirt, jeans, dark glasses, cowboy boots and carries a black saxophone case. They shake the rain off themselves as they enter the porch through the screen door.*

SHELLY *(laughing, gesturing to house)*. This is it? I don't believe this is it!

VINCE. This is it.

SHELLY. This is the house?

VINCE. This is the house.

SHELLY. I don't believe it!

VINCE. How come?

SHELLY. It's like a Norman Rockwell cover or something.

VINCE. What's a' matter with that? It's American.

SHELLY. Where's the milkman and the little dog? What's the little dog's name? Spot. Spot and Jane. Dick and Jane and Spot.

VINCE. Knock it off.

SHELLY. Dick and Jane and Spot and Mom and Dad and Junior and Sissy!

(She laughs. Slaps her knee.)

VINCE. Come on! It's my heritage. What dya' expect?

(She laughs more hysterically, out of control.)

SHELLY. "And Tuffy and Toto and Dooda and Bonza all went down one day to the corner grocery store to buy a big bag of licorice for Mr. Marshall's pussy cat!"

(She laughs so hard she falls to her knees holding her stomach. Vince stands there looking at her.)

VINCE. Shelly, will you get up!

(She keeps laughing. Staggers to her feet. Turning in circles holding her stomach.)

SHELLY (*continuing her story in kid's voice*). "Mr. Marshall was on vacation. He had no idea that the four little boys had taken such a liking to his little kitty cat."

VINCE. Have some respect, would ya'!

SHELLY (*trying to control herself*). I'm sorry.

VINCE. Pull yourself together.

SHELLY (*salutes him*). Yes, sir.

(*She giggles.*)

VINCE. Jesus Christ, Shelly.

SHELLY (*pause, smiling*). And Mr. Marshall—

VINCE. Cut it out.

(*She stops. Stands there staring at him. Stifles a giggle.*)

VINCE (*after pause*). Are you finished?

SHELLY. Oh brother!

VINCE. I don't wanna go in there with you acting like an idiot.

SHELLY. Thanks.

VINCE. Well, I don't.

SHELLY. I won't embarrass you. Don't worry.

VINCE. I'm not worried.

SHELLY. You are too.

VINCE. Shelly, look, I just don't wanna go in there with you giggling your head off. They might think something's wrong with you.

SHELLY. There is.

VINCE. There is not!

SHELLY. Something's definitely wrong with me.

VINCE. There is not!

SHELLY. There's something wrong with you too.

VINCE. There's nothing wrong with me either!

SHELLY. You wanna know what's wrong with you?

VINCE. What?

(*Shelly laughs.*)

VINCE (*crosses back left toward screen door*). I'm leaving!

SHELLY (*stops laughing*). Wait! Stop. Stop! (*Vince stops.*) What's wrong with you is that you take the situation too seriously.

VINCE. I just don't want to have them think that I've suddenly arrived out of the middle of nowhere completely deranged.

SHELLY. What do you want them to think then?

VINCE (*pause*). Nothing. Let's go in.

(*He crosses porch toward stage right interior door. Shelly follows him. The stage right door opens slowly. Vince sticks his head in, doesn't notice Dodge sleeping. Calls out toward staircase.*)

VINCE. Grandma!

(*Shelly breaks into laughter, unseen behind Vince. Vince pulls his head back outside and pulls door shut. We hear their voices again without seeing them.*)

SHELLY'S VOICE (*stops laughing*). I'm sorry. I'm sorry, Vince. I really am. I really am sorry. I won't do it again. I couldn't help it.

VINCE'S VOICE. It's not all that funny.

SHELLY'S VOICE. I know it's not. I'm sorry.

VINCE'S VOICE. I mean this is a tense situation for me! I haven't seen them for over six years. I don't know what to expect.

SHELLY'S VOICE. I know. I won't do it again.

VINCE'S VOICE. Can't you bite your tongue or something?

SHELLY'S VOICE. Just don't say Grandma, okay? (*She giggles, stops.*) I mean if you say "Grandma," I don't know if I can stop myself.

VINCE'S VOICE. Well try!

SHELLY'S VOICE. Okay. Sorry.

(*Door opens again. Vince sticks his head in then enters. Shelly follows behind him. Vince crosses to staircase, sets down saxophone case and overcoat, looks up staircase. Shelly notices Dodge's baseball cap. Crosses to it. Picks it up and puts it on her head. Vince goes up the stairs and disappears at the top. Shelly watches him, then turns and sees Dodge on the sofa. She takes off the baseball cap.*)

VINCE'S VOICE (*from above stairs*). Grandma!

(*Shelly crosses over to Dodge slowly and stands next to him. She stands at his head, reaches out slowly, and touches one of the cuts. The second she touches his head, Dodge jerks up to a sitting position on the sofa, eyes open. Shelly gasps. Dodge looks at her, sees his cap in her hands, quickly puts his hand to his bare head. He glares at Shelly, then whips the cap out of her hands and puts it on. Shelly backs away from him. Dodge stares at her.*)

SHELLY. I'm uh—with Vince.

(*Dodge just glares at her.*)

SHELLY. He's upstairs.

(*Dodge looks at the staircase, then back to Shelly.*)

SHELLY (*calling upstairs*). Vince!

VINCE'S VOICE. Just a second!

SHELLY. You better get down here!

VINCE'S VOICE. Just a minute! I'm looking at the pictures.

(*Dodge keeps staring at her.*)

SHELLY (*to Dodge*). We just got here. Pouring rain on the freeway so we thought we'd stop by. I mean Vince was planning on stopping anyway. He wanted to see you. He said he hadn't seen you in a long time.

(*Pause. Dodge just keeps staring at her.*)

SHELLY. We were going all the way through to New Mexico. To see his father. I guess his father lives out there. We thought we'd stop by and see you on the way. Kill two birds with one stone, you know? (*She laughs, Dodge stares, she stops laughing.*) I mean Vince has this thing about his family now. I guess it's a new thing with him. I kind of find it hard to relate to. But he feels it's important. You know. I mean he feels he wants to get to know you all again. After all this time.

(*Pause, Dodge just stares at her. She moves nervously to staircase and yells up to Vince.*)

SHELLY. Vince, will you come down here please!

(*Vince comes halfway down the stairs.*)

VINCE. I guess they went out for a while.

(*Shelly points to sofa and Dodge. Vince turns and sees Dodge. He comes all the way down staircase and crosses to Dodge. Shelly stays behind near staircase, keeping her distance.*)

VINCE. Grandpa?

(*Dodge looks up at him, not recognizing him.*)

DODGE. Did you bring the whiskey?

(*Vince looks back at Shelly, then back at Dodge.*)

VINCE. Grandpa, it's Vince. I'm Vince. Tilden's son. You re-member?

(*Dodge stares at him.*)

DODGE. You didn't do what you told me. You didn't stay here with me.
VINCE. Grandpa, I haven't been here until just now. I just got here.
DODGE. You left. You went outside like we told you not to do. You went out there in back. In the rain.

(*Vince looks back at Shelly. She moves slowly toward sofa.*)

SHELLY. Is he okay?
VINCE. I don't know. (*Takes off his shades.*) Look, Grandpa, don't you remember me? Vince. Your Grandson.

(*Dodge stares at him, then takes off his baseball cap.*)

DODGE (*points to his head*). See what happens when you leave me alone? See that? That's what happens.

(*Vince looks at his head. Vince reaches out to touch his head. Dodge slaps his hand away with the cap and puts it back on his head.*)

VINCE. What's going on, Grandpa? Where's Halie?
DODGE. Don't worry about her. She won't be back for days. She says she'll be back but she won't be. (*He starts laughing.*) There's life in the old girl yet! (*Stops laughing.*)
VINCE. How did you do that to your head?
DODGE. I didn't do it! Don't be ridiculous!
VINCE. Well, who did then?

(*Pause. Dodge stares at Vince.*)

DODGE. Who do you think did it? Who do you think?

(*Shelly moves toward Vince.*)

SHELLY. Vince, maybe we oughta' go. I don't like this. I mean this isn't my idea of a good time.
VINCE (*to Shelly*). Just a second. (*to Dodge.*) Grandpa, look, I just got here. I just now got here. I haven't been here for six years. I don't know anything that's happened.

(*Pause. Dodge stares at him.*)

DODGE. You don't know anything?
VINCE. No.
DODGE. Well, that's good. That's good. It's much better not to know anything. Much, much better.
VINCE. Isn't there anybody here with you?

(*Dodge turns slowly and looks off to stage left.*)

DODGE. Tilden's here.
VINCE. No, Grandpa, Tilden's in New Mexico. That's where I was going. I'm going out there to see him.

(*Dodge turns slowly back to Vince.*)

DODGE. Tilden's here.

(*Vince backs away and joins Shelly. Dodge stares at them.*)

SHELLY. Vince, why don't we spend the night in a motel and come back in the morning? We could have breakfast. Maybe everything would be different.
VINCE. Don't be scared. There's nothing to be scared of. He's just old.
SHELLY. I'm not scared.
DODGE. You two are not my idea of the perfect couple!
SHELLY (*after pause*). Oh really? Why's that?
VINCE. Shh! Don't aggravate him.
DODGE. There's something wrong between the two of you. Something not compatible.
VINCE. Grandpa, where did Halie go? Maybe we should call her.
DODGE. What are you talking about? Do you know what you're talking about? Are you just talking for the sake of talking? Lubricating the gums?
VINCE. I'm trying to figure out what's going on here!
DODGE. Is that it?
VINCE. Yes. I mean I expected everything to be different.
DODGE. Who are you to expect anything? Who are you sup-posed to be?
VINCE. I'm Vince! Your Grandson!
DODGE. Vince. My Grandson.
VINCE. Tilden's son.
DODGE. Tilden's son, Vince.
VINCE. You haven't seen me for a long time.
DODGE. When was the last time?

VINCE. I don't remember.

DODGE. You don't remember?

VINCE. No.

DODGE. You don't remember. How am I supposed to remember if you don't remember?

SHELLY. Vince, come on. This isn't going to work out.

VINCE (to Shelly). Just take it easy.

SHELLY. I'm taking it easy! He doesn't even know who you are!

VINCE (crossing toward Dodge). Grandpa, look—

DODGE. Stay where you are! Keep your distance!

(Vince stops. Looks back at Shelly, then to Dodge.)

SHELLY. Vince, this is really making me nervous. I mean he doesn't even want us here. He doesn't even like us.

DODGE. She's a beautiful girl.

VINCE. Thanks.

DODGE. Very Beautiful Girl.

SHELLY. Oh my God.

DODGE (to Shelly). What's your name?

SHELLY. Shelly.

DODGE. Shelly. That's a man's name isn't it?

SHELLY. Not in this case.

DODGE (to Vince). She's a smart-ass too.

SHELLY. Vince! Can we go?

DODGE. She wants to go. She just got here and she wants to go.

VINCE. This is kind of strange for her.

DODGE. She'll get used to it. (To Shelly.) What part of the country do you come from?

SHELLY. Originally?

DODGE. That's right. Originally. At the very start.

SHELLY. L.A.

DODGE. L.A. Stupid country.

SHELLY. I can't stand this, Vince! This is really unbelievable!

DODGE. It's stupid! L.A. is stupid! So is Florida! All those Sunshine States. They're all stupid! Do you know why they're stupid?

SHELLY. Illuminate me.

DODGE. I'll tell you why. Because they're full of smart-asses! That's why.

(Shelly turns her back to Dodge, crosses to staircase, and sits on bottom step.)

DODGE (to Vince). Now she's insulted.

VINCE. Well, you weren't very polite.

DODGE. She's insulted! Look at her! In my house she's insulted! She's over there sulking because I insulted her!

SHELLY (to Vince). This is really terrific. This is wonderful. And you were worried about me making the right first impression.

DODGE (to Vince). She's a fireball, isn't she? Regular fireball. I had some a' them in my day. Temporary stuff. Never lasted more than a week.

VINCE. Grandpa—

DODGE. Stop calling me Grandpa will ya'! It's sickening. "Grandpa." I'm nobody's Grandpa!

(Dodge starts feeling around under the cushion for the bottle of whiskey. Shelly gets up from the staircase.)

SHELLY (to Vince). Maybe you've got the wrong house. Did you ever think of that? Maybe this is the wrong address!

VINCE. It's not the wrong address! I recognize the yard.

SHELLY. Yeah, but do you recognize the people? He says he's not your Grandfather.

DODGE (digging for bottle). Where's that bottle!

VINCE. He's just sick or something. I don't know what's happened to him.

DODGE. Where's my goddamn bottle!

(Dodge gets up from sofa and starts tearing the cushions off it and throwing them downstage, looking for the whiskey.)

SHELLY. Can't we just drive on to New Mexico? This is terrible, Vince! I don't want to stay here. In this house. I thought it was going to be turkey dinners and apple pie and all that kinda stuff.

VINCE. Well, I hate to disappoint you!

SHELLY. I'm not disappointed! I'm fuckin' terrified! I wanna' go!

(Dodge yells toward stage left.)

DODGE. Tilden! Tilden!

(Dodge keeps ripping away at the sofa looking for his bottle and knocks over the night stand with the bottles. Vince and Shelly watch as he starts ripping the stuffing out the sofa.)

VINCE (to Shelly). He's lost his mind or something. I've got to try to help him.

SHELLY. You help him! I'm leaving!

(Shelly starts to leave. Vince grabs her. They struggle as Dodge keeps ripping away at the sofa and yelling.)

DODGE. Tilden! Tilden, get your ass in here! Tilden!

SHELLY. Let go of me!

VINCE. You're not going anywhere! You're going to stay right here!

SHELLY. Let go of me, you sonuvabitch! I'm not your property!

(Suddenly Tilden walks on from stage left just as he did before. This time his arms are full of carrots. Dodge, Vince, and Shelly stop suddenly when they see him. They all stare at Tilden as he crosses slowly center stage with the carrots and stops. Dodge sits on sofa, exhausted.)

DODGE (panting, to Tilden). Where in the hell have you been?

TILDEN. Out back.

DODGE. Where's my bottle?

TILDEN. Gone.

(Tilden and Vince stare at each other. Shelly backs away.)

DODGE *(to Tilden).* You stole my bottle!

VINCE *(to Tilden).* Dad?

(Tilden just stares at Vince.)

DODGE. You had no right to steal my bottle! No right at all!

VINCE *(to Tilden).* It's Vince. I'm Vince.

(Tilden stares at Vince, then looks at Dodge, then turns to Shelly.)

TILDEN *(after pause).* I picked these carrots. If anybody wants any carrots, I picked 'em.

SHELLY *(to Vince).* This is your father?

VINCE *(to Tilden).* Dad, what're you doing here?

(Tilden just stares at Vince, holding carrots, Dodge pulls the blanket back over himself.)

DODGE *(to Tilden).* You're going to have to get me another bottle! You gotta get me a bottle before Halie comes back! There's money on the table. *(Points to stage left kitchen.)*

TILDEN *(shaking his head).* I'm not going down there. Into town.

(Shelly crosses to Tilden. Tilden stares at her.)

SHELLY *(to Tilden).* Are you Vince's father?

TILDEN *(to Shelly).* Vince?

SHELLY *(pointing to Vince).* This is supposed to be your son! Is he your son? Do you recognize him? I'm just along for the ride here. I thought everybody knew each other!

(Tilden stares at Vince. Dodge wraps himself up in the blanket and sits on sofa staring at the floor.)

TILDEN. I had a son once but we buried him.

(Dodge quickly looks at Tilden. Shelly looks to Vince.)

DODGE. You shut up about that! You don't know anything about that!

VINCE. Dad, I thought you were in New Mexico. We were going to drive down there and see you.

TILDEN. Long way to drive.

DODGE *(to Tilden).* You don't know anything about that! That happened before you were born! Long before!

VINCE. What's happened, Dad? What's going on here? I thought everything was all right. What's happened to Halie?

TILDEN. She left.

SHELLY *(to Tilden).* Do you want me to take those carrots for you?

(Tilden stares at her. She moves in close to him. Holds out her arms. Tilden stares at her arms then slowly dumps the carrots into her arms. Shelly stands there holding the carrots.)

TILDEN *(to Shelly).* You like carrots?

SHELLY. Sure. I like all kinds of vegetables.

DODGE *(to Tilden).* You gotta get me a bottle before Halie comes back!

(Dodge hits sofa with his fist. Vince crosses up to Dodge and tries to console him. Shelly and Tilden stay facing each other.)

TILDEN *(to Shelly).* Back yard's full of carrots. Corn. Potatoes.

SHELLY. You're Vince's father, right?

TILDEN. All kinds of vegetables. You like vegetables?

SHELLY *(laughs).* Yeah. I love vegetables.

TILDEN. We could cook these carrots, ya' know. You could cut 'em up and we could cook 'em.

SHELLY. All right.

TILDEN. I'll get you a pail and a knife.

SHELLY. Okay.

TILDEN. I'll be right back. Don't go.

(Tilden exits offstage left. Shelly stands center, arms full of carrots. Vince stands next to Dodge. Shelly looks toward Vince, then down at the carrots.)

DODGE *(to Vince).* You could get me a bottle. *(Pointing off left.)* There's money on the table.

VINCE. Grandpa, why don't you lay down for a while?

DODGE. I don't wanna lay down for a while! Every time I lay down something happens! *(Whips off his cap, points at his head.)* Look what happens! That's what happens! *(Pulls his cap back on.)* You go lie down and see what happens to you! See how you like it! They'll steal your bottle! They'll cut your hair! They'll murder your children! That's what'll happen.

VINCE. Just relax for a while.

DODGE *(pause).* You could get me a bottle, ya' know. There's nothing stopping you from getting me a bottle.

SHELLY. Why don't you get him a bottle, Vince? Maybe it would help everybody identify each other.

DODGE *(pointing to Shelly).* There, see? She thinks you should get me a bottle.

(Vince crosses to Shelly.)

VINCE. What're you doing with those carrots?

SHELLY. I'm waiting for your father.

DODGE. She thinks you should get me a bottle!

VINCE. Shelly, put the carrots down, will ya'! We gotta deal with the situation here! I'm gonna need your help.

SHELLY. I'm helping.

VINCE. You're only adding to the problem! You're making things worse! Put the carrots down!

(Vince tries to knock the carrots out of her arms. She turns away from him, protecting the carrots.)

SHELLY. Get away from me! Stop it! *(Vince stands back from her. She turns to him still holding the carrots.)*

VINCE *(to Shelly)*. Why are you doing this? Are you trying to make fun of me? This is my family, you know!

SHELLY. You coulda' fooled me! I'd just as soon not be here myself. I'd just as soon be a thousand miles from here. I'd rather be anywhere but here. You're the one who wants to stay. So I'll stay. I'll stay and I'll cut the carrots. And I'll cook the carrots. And I'll do whatever I have to do to survive. Just to make it through this.

VINCE. Put the carrots down, Shelly.

(Tilden enters from left with pail, milking stool, and a knife. He sets the stool and pail center stage for Shelly. Shelly looks at Vince, then sits down on stool, sets the carrots on the floor, and takes the knife from Tilden. She looks at Vince again, then picks up a carrot, cuts the ends off, scrapes it, and drops it in pail. She repeats this; Vince glares at her. She smiles.)

DODGE. She could get me a bottle. She's the type a' girl that could get me a bottle. Easy. She'd go down there. Slink up to the counter. They'd probably give her two bottles for the price of one. She could do that.

(Shelly laughs. Keeps cutting carrots. Vince crosses up to Dodge, looks at him. Tilden watches Shelly's hands. Long pause.)

VINCE *(to Dodge)*. I haven't changed that much. I mean physically. Physically I'm just about the same. Same size. Same weight. Everything's the same.

(Dodge keeps staring at Shelly while Vince talks to him.)

DODGE. She's a beautiful girl. Exceptional.

(Vince moves in front of Dodge to block his view of Shelly. Dodge keeps craning his head around to see her as Vince demonstrates tricks from his past.)

VINCE. Look. Look at this. Do you remember this? I used to bend my thumb behind my knuckles. You remember? I used to do it at the dinner table.

(Vince bends a thumb behind his knuckles for Dodge and holds it out to him. Dodge takes a short glance then looks back at Shelly. Vince shifts position and shows him something else.)

VINCE. What about this?

(Vince curls his lips back and starts drumming on his teeth with his fingernails making little tapping sounds. Dodge watches awhile. Tilden turns toward the sound. Vince keeps it up. He sees Tilden taking notice and crosses to Tilden as he drums on his teeth. Dodge turns T.V. on, watches it.)

VINCE. You remember this, Dad?

(Vince keeps on drumming for Tilden. Tilden watches awhile, fascinated, then turns back to Shelly. Vince keeps up the drumming on his teeth, crosses back to Dodge doing it. Shelly keeps working on carrots, talking to Tilden.)

SHELLY *(to Tilden)*. He drives me crazy with that sometimes.

VINCE *(to Dodge)*. I know! Here's one you'll remember. You used to kick me out of the house for this one.

(Vince pulls his shirt out of his belt and holds it tucked under his chin with his stomach exposed. He grabs the flesh on either side of his belly button and pushes it in and out to make it look like a mouth talking. He watches his belly button and makes a deep sounding cartoon voice to synchronize with the movement. He demonstrates it to Dodge, then crosses down to Tilden doing it. Both Dodge and Tilden take short, uninterested glances then ignore him.)

VINCE *(deep cartoon voice)*. "Hello. How are you? I'm fine. Thank you very much. It's so good to see you looking well this fine Sunday morning. I was going down to the hardware store to fetch a pail of water."

SHELLY. Vince, don't be pathetic, will ya!

(Vince stops. Tucks his shirt back in.)

SHELLY. Jesus Christ. They're not gonna play. Can't you see that?

(Shelly keeps cutting carrots. Vince slowly moves toward Tilden. Tilden keeps watching Shelly. Dodge watches T.V.)

VINCE *(to Shelly)*. I don't get it. I really don't get it. Maybe it's me. Maybe I forgot something.

DODGE *(from sofa)*. You forgot to get me a bottle! That's what you forgot. Anybody in this house could get me a bottle. Anybody! But nobody will. Nobody understands the urgency! Peelin' carrots is more important. Playin' piano on your teeth! Well I hope you all remember this when you get up in years. When you find yourself immobilized. Dependent on the whims of others.

(Vince moves up toward Dodge. Pause as he looks at him.)

VINCE. I'll get you a bottle.

DODGE. You will?

VINCE. Sure.

(Shelly stands holding knife and carrot.)

SHELLY. You're not going to leave me here, are you?

VINCE *(moving to her)*. You suggested it! You said, "Why don't I go get him a bottle?" So I'll go get him a bottle!

SHELLY. But I can't stay here.

VINCE. What is going on! A minute ago you were ready to cut carrots all night!

SHELLY. That was only if you stayed. Something to keep me busy, so I wouldn't be so nervous. I don't want to stay here alone.

DODGE. Don't let her talk you out of it! She's a bad influence. I could see it the minute she stepped in here.

SHELLY (*to Dodge*). You were asleep!

TILDEN (*to Shelly*). Don't you want to cut carrots anymore?

SHELLY. Sure. Sure I do.

(*Shelly sits back down on stool and continues cutting carrots. Pause. Vince moves around, stroking his hair, staring at Dodge and Tilden. Vince and Shelly exchange glances. Dodge watches T.V.*)

VINCE. Boy! This is amazing. This is truly amazing. (*Keeps moving around.*) What is this anyway? Am I in a time warp or something? Have I committed an unpardonable offense? It's true, I'm not married. (*Shelly looks at him, then back to carrots.*) But I'm also not divorced. I have been known to plunge into sinful infatuation with the Alto Saxophone. Sucking on number 5 reeds deep into the wee wee hours.

SHELLY. Vince, what are you doing that for? They don't care about any of that. They just don't recognize you, that's all.

VINCE. How could they not recognize me! How in the hell could they not recognize me! I'm their son!

DODGE (*watching T.V.*). You're no son of mine. I've had sons in my time and you're not one of 'em.

(*Long pause. Vince stares at Dodge, then looks at Tilden. He turns to Shelly.*)

VINCE. Shelly, I gotta go out for a while. I just gotta go out. I'll get a bottle and I'll come right back. You'll be okay here. Really.

SHELLY. I don't know if I can handle this, Vince.

VINCE. I just gotta think or something. I don't know. I gotta put this all together.

SHELLY. Can't we just go?

VINCE. No! I gotta find out what's going on.

SHELLY. Look, you think you're bad off, what about me? Not only don't they recognize me but I've never seen them before in my life. I don't know who these guys are. They could be anybody!

VINCE. They're not anybody!

SHELLY. That's what you say.

VINCE. They're my family for Christ's sake! I should know who my own family is! Now give me a break. It won't take that long. I'll just go out and I'll come right back. Nothing'll happen. I promise.

(*Shelly stares at him. Pause.*)

SHELLY. All right.

VINCE. Thanks. (*He crosses up to Dodge.*) I'm gonna go out now, Grandpa, and I'll pick you up a bottle. Okay?

DODGE. Change of heart huh? (*Pointing off left.*) Money's on the table. In the kitchen.

(*Vince moves toward Shelly.*)

VINCE (*to Shelly*). You be all right?

SHELLY (*cutting carrots*). Sure. I'm fine. I'll just keep real busy while you're gone.

(*Vince looks at Tilden who keeps staring down at Shelly's hands.*)

DODGE. Persistence, see? That's what it takes. Persistence. Persistence, fortitude, and determination. Those are the three virtues. You stick with those three and you can't go wrong.

VINCE (*to Tilden*). You want anything, Dad?

TILDEN (*looks up at Vince*). Me?

VINCE. From the store? I'm gonna get Grandpa a bottle.

TILDEN. He's not supposed to drink. Halie wouldn't like it.

VINCE. He wants a bottle.

TILDEN. He's not supposed to drink.

DODGE (*to Vince*). Don't negotiate with him! Don't make any transactions until you've spoken to me first! He'll steal you blind!

VINCE (*to Dodge*). Tilden says you're not supposed to drink.

DODGE. Tilden's lost his marbles! Look at him! He's around the bend. Take a look at him.

(*Vince stares at Tilden. Tilden watches Shelly's hands as she keeps cutting carrots.*)

DODGE. Now look at me. Look here at me!

(*Vince looks back to Dodge.*)

DODGE. Now, between the two of us, who do you think is more trustworthy? Him or me? Can you trust a man who keeps bringing in vegetables from out of nowhere? Take a look at him.

(*Vince looks back at Tilden.*)

SHELLY. Go get the bottle, Vince.

VINCE (*to Shelly*). You sure you'll be all right?

SHELLY. I'll be fine. I feel right at home now.

VINCE. You do?

SHELLY. I'm fine. Now that I've got the carrots everything is all right.

VINCE. I'll be right back.

(*Vince crosses stage left.*)

DODGE. Where are you going?

VINCE. I'm going to get the money.

DODGE. Then where are you going?

VINCE. Liquor store.

DODGE. Don't go anyplace else. Don't go off some place and drink. Come right back here.

VINCE. I will.

(Vince exits stage left.)

DODGE *(calling after Vince)*. You're got responsibility now! And don't go out the back way either! Come out through this way! I wanna' see you when you leave! Don't go out the back!

VINCE'S VOICE *(off left)*. I won't!

(Dodge turns and looks at Tilden and Shelly.)

DODGE. Untrustworthy. Probably drown himself if he went out the back. Fall right in a hole. I'd never get my bottle.

SHELLY. I wouldn't worry about Vince. He can take care of himself.

DODGE. Oh he can, huh? Independent.

(Vince comes on again from stage left with two dollars in his hand. He crosses stage right past Dodge.)

DODGE *(to Vince)*. You got the money?

VINCE. Yeah. Two bucks.

DODGE. Two bucks. Two bucks is two bucks. Don't sneer.

VINCE. What kind do you want?

DODGE. Whiskey! Gold Star Sour Mash. Use your own discretion.

VINCE. Okay.

(Vince crosses to stage right door. Opens it. Stops when he hears Tilden.)

TILDEN *(to Vince)*. You drove all the way from New Mexico?

(Vince turns and looks at Tilden. They stare at each other. Vince shakes his head, goes out the door, crosses porch, and exits out screen door. Tilden watches him go. Pause.)

SHELLY. You really don't recognize him? Either one of you?

(Tilden turns again and stares at Shelly's hands as she cuts carrots.)

DODGE *(watching T.V.)*. Recognize who?

SHELLY. Vince.

DODGE. What's to recognize?

(Dodge lights a cigarette, coughs slightly, and stares at T.V.)

SHELLY. It'd be cruel if you recognized him and didn't tell him. Wouldn't be fair.

(Dodge just stares at T.V., smoking.)

TILDEN. I thought I recognized him. I thought I recognized something about him.

SHELLY. You did?

TILDEN. I thought I saw a face inside his face.

SHELLY. Well, it was probably that you saw what he used to look like. You haven't seen him for six years.

TILDEN. I haven't?

SHELLY. That's what he says.

(Tilden moves around in front of her as she continues with carrots.)

TILDEN. Where was it I saw him last?

SHELLY. I don't know. I've only known him for a few months. He doesn't tell me everything.

TILDEN. He doesn't?

SHELLY. Not stuff like that.

TILDEN. What does he tell you?

SHELLY. You mean in general?

TILDEN. Yeah.

(Tilden moves around behind her.)

SHELLY. Well, he tells me all kinds of things.

TILDEN. Like what?

SHELLY. I don't know! I mean I can't just come right out and tell you how he feels.

TILDEN. How come?

(Tilden keeps moving around her slowly in a circle.)

SHELLY. Because it's stuff he told me privately!

TILDEN. And you can't tell me?

SHELLY. I don't even know you!

DODGE. Tilden, go out in the kitchen and make me some coffee! Leave the girl alone.

SHELLY *(to Dodge)*. He's all right.

(Tilden ignores Dodge, keeps moving around Shelly. He stares at her hair and coat. Dodge stares at T.V.)

TILDEN. You mean you can't tell me anything?

SHELLY. I can tell you some things. I mean we can have a conversation.

TILDEN. We can?

SHELLY. Sure. We're having a conversation right now.

TILDEN. We are?

SHELLY. Yes. That's what we're doing.

TILDEN. But there's certain things you can't tell me, right?

SHELLY. Right.

TILDEN. There's certain things I can't tell you either.

SHELLY. How come?

TILDEN. I don't know. Nobody's supposed to hear it.

SHELLY. Well, you can tell me anything you want to.

TILDEN. I can?

SHELLY. Sure.

TILDEN. It might not be very nice.

SHELLY. That's all right. I've been around.

TILDEN. It might be awful.

SHELLY. Well, can't you tell me anything nice?

(Tilden stops in front of her and stares at her coat. Shelly looks back at him. Long pause.)

TILDEN *(after pause)*. Can I touch your coat?

SHELLY. My coat? *(She looks at her coat then back to Tilden.)* Sure.

TILDEN. You don't mind?
SHELLY. No. Go ahead.

(Shelly holds her arm out for Tilden to touch. Dodge stays fixed on T.V. Tilden moves in slowly toward Shelly, staring at her arm. He reaches out very slowly and touches her arm, feels the fur gently, then draws his hand back. Shelly keeps her arm out.)

SHELLY. It's rabbit.
TILDEN. Rabbit.

(He reaches out again very slowly and touches the fur on her arm then pulls back his hand again. Shelly drops her arm.)

SHELLY. My arm was getting tired.
TILDEN. Can I hold it?
SHELLY *(pause)*. The coat? Sure.

(Shelly takes off her coat and hands it to Tilden. Tilden takes it slowly, feels the fur, then puts it on. Shelly watches as Tilden strokes the fur slowly. He smiles at her. She goes back to cutting carrots.)

SHELLY. You can have it if you want.
TILDEN. I can?
SHELLY. Yeah. I've got a raincoat in the car. That's all I need.
TILDEN. You've got a car?
SHELLY. Vince does.

(Tilden walks around stroking the fur and smiling at the coat. Shelly watches him when he's not looking. Dodge sticks with T.V., stretches out on sofa wrapped in blanket.)

TILDEN *(as he walks around)*. I had a car once! I had a white car! I drove. I went everywhere. I went to the mountains. I drove in the snow.
SHELLY. That must've been fun.
TILDEN *(still moving, feeling coat)*. I drove all day long sometimes. Across the desert. Way out across the desert. I drove past towns. Anywhere. Past palm trees. Lightning. Anything. I would drive through it. I would drive through it and I would stop and I would look around and I would drive on. I would get back in and drive! I loved to drive. There was nothing I loved more. Nothing I dreamed of was better than driving.
DODGE *(eyes on T.V.)*. Pipe down, would ya'!

(Tilden stops. Stares at Shelly.)

SHELLY. Do you do much driving now?
TILDEN. Now? Now? I don't drive now.
SHELLY. How come?
TILDEN. I'm grown up now.
SHELLY. Grown up?
TILDEN. I'm not a kid.
SHELLY. You don't have to be a kid to drive.

TILDEN. It wasn't driving then.
SHELLY. What was it?
TILDEN. Adventure. I went everywhere.
SHELLY. Well, you can still do that.
TILDEN. Not now.
SHELLY. Why not?
TILDEN. I just told you. You don't understand anything. If I told you something you wouldn't understand it.
SHELLY. Told you what?
TILDEN. Told you something that's true.
SHELLY. Like what?
TILDEN. Like a baby. Like a little tiny baby.
SHELLY. Like when you were little?
TILDEN. If I told you you'd make me give your coat back.
SHELLY. I won't. I promise. Tell me.
TILDEN. I can't. Dodge won't let me.
SHELLY. He won't hear you. It's okay.

(Pause. Tilden stares at her. Moves slightly toward her.)

TILDEN. We had a baby. *(Motioning to Dodge.)* He did. Dodge did. Could pick it up with one hand. Put it in the other. Little baby. Dodge killed it.

(Shelly stands.)

TILDEN. Don't stand up. Don't stand up!

(Shelly sits again. Dodge sits up on sofa and looks at them.)

TILDEN. Dodge drowned it.
SHELLY. Don't tell me anymore! Okay?

(Tilden moves closer to her. Dodge takes more interest.)

DODGE. Tilden? You leave that girl alone!
TILDEN *(pays no attention)*. Never told Halie. Never told anybody. Just drowned it.
DODGE *(shuts off T.V.)*. Tilden!
TILDEN. Nobody could find it. Just disappeared. Cops looked for it. Neighbors. Nobody could find it.

(Dodge struggles to get up from sofa.)

DODGE. Tilden, what're you telling her! Tilden!

(Dodge keeps struggling until he's standing.)

TILDEN. Finally everybody just gave up. Just stopped looking. Everybody had a different answer. Kidnap. Murder. Accident. Some kind of accident.

(Dodge struggles to walk toward Tilden and falls. Tilden ignores him.)

DODGE. Tilden, you shut up! You shut up about it!

(Dodge starts coughing on the floor. Shelly watches him from the stool.)

TILDEN. Little tiny baby just disappeared. It's not hard. It's so small. Almost invisible.

(*Shelly makes a move to help Dodge. Tilden firmly pushes her back down on the stool. Dodge keeps coughing.*)

TILDEN. He said he had his reasons. Said it went a long way back. But he wouldn't tell anybody.

DODGE. Tilden! Don't tell her anything! Don't tell her!

TILDEN. He's the only one who knows where it's buried. The only one. Like a secret buried treasure. Won't tell any of us. Won't tell me or mother or even Bradley. Especially Bradley. Bradley tried to force it out of him but he wouldn't tell. Wouldn't even tell why he did it. One night he just did it.

(*Dodge's coughing subsides. Shelly stays on stool staring at Dodge. Tilden slowly takes Shelly's coat off and holds it out to her. Long pause. Shelly sits there trembling.*)

TILDEN. You probably want your coat back now.

(*Shelly stares at coat but doesn't move to take it. The sound of Bradley's leg squeaking is heard off left. The others on stage remain still. Bradley appears up left outside the screen door wearing a yellow rain slicker. He enters through screen door, crosses porch to stage right door and enters stage. Closes door. Takes off rain slicker and shakes it out. He sees all the others and stops. Tilden turns to him. Bradley stares at Shelly. Dodge remains on floor.*)

BRADLEY. What's going on here? (*Motioning to Shelly.*) Who's that?

(*Shelly stands, moves back away from Bradley as he crosses toward her. He stops next to Tilden. He sees coat in Tilden's hand and grabs it away from him.*)

BRADLEY. Who's she supposed to be?

TILDEN. She's driving to New Mexico.

(*Bradley stares at her. Shelly is frozen. Bradley limps over to her with the coat in his fist. He stops in front of her.*)

BRADLEY (*to Shelly, after pause*). Vacation?

(*Shelly shakes her head "no," trembling.*)

BRADLEY (*to Shelly, motioning to Tilden*). You taking him with you?

(*Shelly shakes her head "no." Bradley crosses back to Tilden*).

BRADLEY. You oughta'. No use leaving him here. Doesn't do a lick a' work. Doesn't raise a finger. (*Stopping, to Tilden.*) Do ya'. (*To Shelly.*) 'Course he used to be an All-American Quarterback or fullback or somethin'. He tell you that?

(*Shelly shakes her head "no."*)

BRADLEY. Yeah, he used to be a big deal. Wore lettermen's

sweaters. Had medals hanging all around his neck. Real purty. Big deal. (*He laughs to himself, notices Dodge on floor, crosses to him, stops.*) This one too (*To Shelly*). You'd never think it to look at him, would ya!? All bony and wasted away.

(*Shelly shakes her head again. Bradley stares at her, crosses back to her, clenching the coat in his fist. He stops in front of Shelly.*)

BRADLEY. Women like that kinda' thing, don't they?

SHELLY. What?

BRADLEY. Importance. Importance in a man!

SHELLY. I don't know.

BRADLEY. Yeah. You know, you know. Don't give me that. (*Moves closer to Shelly.*) You're with Tilden?

SHELLY. No.

BRADLEY (*turning to Tilden*). Tilden! She with you?

(*Tilden doesn't answer. Stares at floor.*)

BRADLEY. Tilden!

(*Tilden suddenly bolts and runs off up stage left. Bradley laughs. Talks to Shelly. Dodge starts moving his lips silently as though talking to someone invisible on the floor.*)

BRADLEY (*laughing*). Scared to death! He was always scared!

(*Bradley stops laughing. Stares at Shelly.*)

BRADLEY. You're scared too, right? (*Laughs again.*) You're scared and you don't even know me. (*Stops laughing.*) You don't gotta be scared.

(*Shelly looks at Dodge on the floor.*)

SHELLY. Can't we do something for him?

BRADLEY (*looking at Dodge*). We could shoot him. (*Laughs.*) We could drown him! What about drowning him?

SHELLY. Shut up!

(*Bradley stops laughing. Moves in closer to Shelly. She freezes. Bradley speaks slowly and deliberately.*)

BRADLEY. Hey! Missus. Don't talk to me like that. Don't talk to me in that tone a' voice. There was a time when I had to take that tone a' voice from pretty near everyone. (*Motioning to Dodge.*) Him, for one! Him and that half brain that just ran outa' here. They don't talk to me like that now. Not anymore. Everything's turned around now. Full circle. Isn't that funny?

SHELLY. I'm sorry.

BRADLEY. Open your mouth.

SHELLY. What?

BRADLEY (*motioning for her to open her mouth*). Open up.

(*She opens her mouth slightly.*)

BRADLEY. Wider.

(*She opens her mouth wider.*)

BRADLEY. Keep it like that.

(*She does. Stares at Bradley. With his free hand he puts his fingers into her mouth. She tries to pull away.*)

BRADLEY. Just stay put!

(*She freezes. He keeps his fingers in her mouth. Stares at her. Pause. He pulls his hand out. She closes her mouth, keeps her eyes on him. Bradley smiles. He looks at Dodge on the floor and crosses over to him. Shelly watches him closely. Bradley stands over Dodge and smiles at Shelly. He holds her coat up in both hands over Dodge, keeps smiling at Shelly. He looks down at Dodge, then drops the coat so that it lands on Dodge and covers his head. Bradley keeps his hands up in the position of holding the coat, looks over at Shelly, and smiles. The lights black out.*)

ACT THREE

SCENE: *Same set. Morning. Bright sun. No sound of rain. Everything has been cleared up again. No sign of carrots. No pail. No stool. Vince's saxophone case and overcoat are still at the foot of the staircase. Bradley is asleep on the sofa under Dodge's blanket. His head toward stage left. Bradley's wooden leg is leaning against the sofa right by his head. The shoe is left on it. The harness hangs down. Dodge is sitting on the floor, propped up against the T.V. set facing stage left wearing his baseball cap. Shelly's rabbit fur coat covers his chest and shoulders. He stares off toward stage left. He seems weaker and more disoriented. The lights rise slowly to the sound of birds and remain for a while in silence on the two men. Bradley sleeps very soundly. Dodge hardly moves. Shelly appears from stage left with a big smile, slowly crossing toward Dodge balancing a steaming cup of broth in a saucer. Dodge just stares at her as she gets close to him.*

SHELLY (*as she crosses*). This is going to make all the difference in the world, Grandpa. You don't mind me calling you Grandpa, do you? I mean I know you minded when Vince called you that but you don't even know him.
DODGE. He skipped town with my money, ya' know. I'm gonna hold you as collateral.
SHELLY. He'll be back. Don't you worry.

(*She kneels down next to Dodge and puts the cup and saucer in his lap.*)

DODGE. It's morning already! Not only didn't I get my bottle but he's got my two bucks!
SHELLY. Try to drink this, okay? Don't spill it.
DODGE. What is it?
SHELLY. Beef bouillon. It'll warm you up.
DODGE. Bouillon! I don't want any goddamn bouillon! Get that stuff away from me!
SHELLY. I just got through making it.

DODGE. I don't care if you just spent all week making it! I ain't drinking it!
SHELLY. Well, what am I supposed to do with it then? I'm trying to help you out. Besides, it's good for you.
DODGE. Get it away from me!

(*Shelly stands up with cup and saucer.*)

DODGE. What do you know what's good for me anyway?

(*She looks at Dodge, then turns away from him, crossing to staircase, sits on bottom step, and drinks the bouillon. Dodge stares at her.*)

DODGE. You know what'd be good for me?
SHELLY. What?
DODGE. A little massage. A little contact.
SHELLY. Oh no. I've had enough contact for a while. Thanks anyway.

(*She keeps sipping bouillon, stays sitting. Pause as Dodge stares at her.*)

DODGE. Why not? You got nothing better to do. That fella's not gonna be back here. You're not expecting him to show up again, are you?
SHELLY. Sure. He'll show up. He left his horn here.
DODGE. His horn? (*laughs.*) You're his horn!
SHELLY. Very funny.
DODGE. He's run off with my money? He's not coming back here.
SHELLY. He'll be back.
DODGE. You're a funny chicken, you know that?
SHELLY. Thanks.
DODGE. Full of faith. Hope. Faith and hope. You're all alike, you hopers. If it's not God then it's a man. If it's not a man then it's a woman. If it's not a woman then it's the land or the future of some kind. Some kind of future.

(*Pause.*)

SHELLY (*looking toward porch*). I'm glad it stopped raining.
DODGE (*looks toward porch then back to her*). That's what I mean. See, you're glad it stopped raining. Now you think everything's gonna be different. Just 'cause the sun comes out.
SHELLY. It's already different. Last night I was scared.
DODGE. Scared a' what?
SHELLY. Just scared.
DODGE. Bradley? (*Looks at Bradley.*) He's a pushover. 'Specially now. All ya' gotta do is take his leg and throw it out the back door. Helpless. Totally helpless.

(*Shelly turns and stares at Bradley's wooden leg, then looks at Dodge. She sips bouillon.*)

SHELLY. You'd do that?
DODGE. Me? I've hardly got the strength to breathe.
SHELLY. But you'd actually do it if you could?

DODGE. Don't be so easily shocked, girlie. There's nothing a man can't do. You dream it up and he can do it. Anything.

SHELLY. You've tried I guess.

DODGE. Don't sit there sippin' your bouillon and judging me! This is my house!

SHELLY. I forgot.

DODGE. You forgot? Whose house did you think it was?

SHELLY. Mine.

(Dodge just stares at her. Long pause. She sips from cup.)

SHELLY. I know it's not mine but I had that feeling.

DODGE. What feeling?

SHELLY. The feeling that nobody lives here but me. I mean everybody's gone. You're here, but it doesn't seem like you're supposed to be. *(Pointing to Bradley.)* Doesn't seem like he's supposed to be here either. I don't know what it is. It's the house or something. Something familiar. Like I know my way around here. Did you ever get that feeling?

(Dodge stares at her in silence. Pause.)

DODGE. No. No, I never did.

(Shelly gets up. Moves around space holding cup.)

SHELLY. Last night I went to sleep up there in that room.

DODGE. What room?

SHELLY. That room up there with all the pictures. All the crosses on the wall.

DODGE. Halie's room?

SHELLY. Yeah. Whoever "Halie" is.

DODGE. She's my wife.

SHELLY. Do you remember her?

DODGE. Whad'ya mean! 'Course I remember her! She's only been gone for a day—half a day. However long it's been.

SHELLY. Do you remember her when her hair was bright red? Standing in front of an apple tree?

DODGE. What is this, the third degree or something! Who're you to be askin' me personal questions about my wife!

SHELLY. You never look at those pictures up there?

DODGE. What pictures!

SHELLY. Your whole life's up there hanging on the wall. Somebody who looks just like you. Somebody who looks just like you used to look.

DODGE. That isn't me! That never was me! This is me. Right here. This is it. The whole shootin' match, sittin' right in front of you.

SHELLY. So the past never happened as far as you're concerned?

DODGE. The past? Jesus Christ. The past. What do you know about the past?

SHELLY. Not much. I know there was a farm.

(Pause.)

DODGE. A farm?

SHELLY. There's a picture of a farm. A big farm. A bull. Wheat. Corn.

DODGE. Corn?

SHELLY. All the kids are standing out in the corn. They're all waving these big straw hats. One of them doesn't have a hat.

DODGE. Which one was that?

SHELLY. There's a baby. A baby in a woman's arms. The same woman with the red hair. She looks lost standing out there. Like she doesn't know how she got there.

DODGE. She knows! I told her a hundred times it wasn't gonna' be the city! I gave her plenty a' warning.

SHELLY. She's looking down at the baby like it was somebody else's. Like it didn't even belong to her.

DODGE. That's about enough outa' you! You got some funny ideas. Some damn funny ideas. You think just because people propagate they have to love their offspring? You never seen a bitch eat her puppies? Where are you from anyway?

SHELLY. L.A. We already went through that.

DODGE. That's right, L.A. I remember.

SHELLY. Stupid country.

DODGE. That's right! No wonder.

(Pause.)

SHELLY. What's happened to this family anyway?

DODGE. You're in no position to ask! What do you care? You some kinda' Social Worker?

SHELLY. I'm Vince's friend.

DODGE. Vince's friend! That's rich. That's really rich. "Vince"! "Mr. Vince"! "Mr. Thief" is more like it! His name doesn't mean a hoot in hell to me. Not a tinkle in the well. You know how many kids I've spawned? Not to mention Grand kids and Great Grand kids and Great Great Grand kids after them?

SHELLY. And you don't remember any of them?

DODGE. What's to remember? Halie's the one with the family album. She's the one you should talk to. She'll set you straight on the heritage if that's what you're interested in. She's traced it all the way back to the grave.

SHELLY. What do you mean?

DODGE. What do you think I mean? How far back can you go? A long line of corpses! There's not a living soul behind me. Not a one. Who's holding me in their memory? Who gives a damn about bones in the ground?

SHELLY. Was Tilden telling the truth?

(Dodge stops short. Stares at Shelly. Shakes his head. He looks off stage left.)

SHELLY. Was he?

(Dodge's tone changes drastically.)

DODGE. Tilden? *(Turns to Shelly, calmly.)* Where is Tilden?

SHELLY. Last night. Was he telling the truth about the baby?

(*Pause.*)

DODGE (*turns toward stage left*). What's happened to Tilden? Why isn't Tilden here?

SHELLY. Bradley chased him out.

DODGE (*looking at Bradley asleep*). Bradley? Why is he on my sofa? (*Turns back to Shelly.*) Have I been here all night? On the floor?

SHELLY. He wouldn't leave. I hid outside until he fell asleep.

DODGE. Outside? Is Tilden outside? He shouldn't be out there in the rain. He'll get himself into trouble. He doesn't know his way around here anymore. Not like he used to. He went out West and got himself into trouble. Got himself into bad trouble. We don't want any of that around here.

SHELLY. What did he do?

(*Pause.*)

DODGE (*quietly stares at Shelly*). Tilden? He got mixed up. That's what he did. We can't afford to leave him alone. Not now.

(*Sound of Halie laughing comes from off left. Shelly stands, looking in direction of voice, holding cup and saucer, doesn't know whether to stay or run.*)

DODGE (*motioning to Shelly*). Sit down. Sit back down!

(*Shelly sits. Sound of Halie's laughter again.*)

DODGE (*to Shelly in a heavy whisper, pulling coat up around him*). Don't leave me alone now! Promise me? Don't go off and leave me alone. I need somebody here with me. Tilden's gone now and I need someone. Don't leave me! Promise!

SHELLY (*sitting*). I won't.

(*Halie appears outside the screen porch door, up left with Father Dewis. She is wearing a bright yellow dress, no hat, white gloves and her arms are full of yellow roses. Father Dewis is dressed in traditional black suit, white clerical collar, and shirt. He is a very distinguished gray-haired man in his sixties. They are both slightly drunk and feeling giddy. As they enter the porch through the screen door, Dodge pulls the rabbit fur coat over his head and hides. Shelly stands again. Dodge drops the coat and whispers intensely to Shelly. Neither Halie nor Father Dewis are aware of the people inside the house.*)

DODGE (*to Shelly in a strong whisper*). You promised!

(*Shelly sits on stairs again. Dodge pulls coat back over his head. Halie and Father Dewis talk on the porch as they cross toward stage right interior door.*)

HALIE. Oh, Father! That's terrible! That's absolutely terrible. Aren't you afraid of being punished?

(*she giggles.*)

DEWIS. Not by the Italians. They're too busy punishing each other.

(*They both break out in giggles.*)

HALIE. What about God?

DEWIS. Well, prayerfully, God only hears what he wants to. That's just between you and me of course. In our heart of hearts we know we're every bit as wicked as the Catholics.

(*They giggle again and reach the stage right door.*)

HALIE. Father, I never heard you talk like this in Sunday sermon.

DEWIS. Well, I save all my best jokes for private company. Pearls before swine, you know.

(*They enter the room laughing and stop when they see Shelly. Shelly stands. Halie closes the door behind Father Dewis. Dodge's voice is heard under the coat, talking to Shelly.*)

DODGE (*under coat, to Shelly*). Sit down, sit down! Don't let 'em buffalo you!

(*Shelly sits on stair again. Halie looks at Dodge on the floor, then looks at Bradley asleep on sofa and sees his wooden leg. She lets out a shriek of embarrassment for Father Dewis.*)

HALIE. Oh my gracious! What in the name of Judas Priest is going on in this house!

(*She hands over the roses to Father Dewis.*)

HALIE. Excuse me, Father.

(*Halie crosses to Dodge, whips the coat off him, and covers the wooden leg with it. Bradley stays asleep.*)

HALIE. You can't leave this house for a second without the Devil blowing in through the front door!

DODGE. Gimme back that coat! Gimme back that goddamn coat before I freeze to death!

HALIE. You're not going to freeze! The sun's out in case you hadn't noticed!

DODGE. Gimme back that coat! That coat's for live flesh not dead wood!

(*Halie whips the blanket off Bradley and throws it on Dodge. Dodge covers his head again with blanket. Bradley's amputated leg can be faked by having half of it under a cushion of the sofa. He's fully clothed. Bradley sits up with a jerk when the blanket comes off him.*)

HALIE (*as she tosses blanket*). Here! Use this! It's yours anyway! Can't you take care of yourself for once!

BRADLEY (*yelling at Halie*). Gimme that blanket! Gimme back that blanket! That's my blanket!

(*Halie crosses back toward Father Dewis who just stands there with the roses. Bradley thrashes helplessly on the sofa trying to reach blanket. Dodge hides himself deeper in blanket. Shelly looks on from staircase still holding cup and saucer.*)

HALIE. Believe me, Father, this is not what I had in mind when I invited you in.

DEWIS. Oh, no apologies please. I wouldn't be in the ministry if I couldn't face real life.

(*He laughs self-consciously. Halie notices Shelly again and crosses over to her. Shelly stays sitting. Halie stops and stares at her.*)

BRADLEY. I want my blanket back! Gimme my blanket!

(*Halie turns toward Bradley and silences him.*)

HALIE. Shut up, Bradley! Right this minute! I've had enough!

(*Bradley slowly recoils, lies back down on sofa, turns his back toward Halie and whimpers softly. Halie directs her attention to Shelly again. Pause.*)

HALIE (*to Shelly*). What're you doing with my cup and saucer?

SHELLY (*looking at cup, back to Halie*). I made some bouillon for Dodge.

HALIE. For Dodge?

SHELLY. Yeah.

HALIE. Well, did he drink it?

SHELLY. No.

HALIE. Did you drink it?

SHELLY. Yes.

(*Halie stares at her. Long pause. She turns abruptly away from Shelly and crosses back to Father Dewis.*)

HALIE. Father, there's a stranger in my house. What would you advise? What would be the Christian thing?

DEWIS (*squirming*). Oh, well . . . I . . . I really—

HALIE. We still have some whiskey, don't we?

(*Dodge slowly pulls the blanket down off his head and looks toward Father Dewis. Shelly stands.*)

SHELLY. Listen, I don't drink or anything. I just—

(*Halie turns toward Shelly viciously.*)

HALIE. You sit back down!

(*Shelly sits again on stair. Halie turns again to Dewis.*)

HALIE. I think we have plenty of whiskey left! Don't we, Father.

DEWIS. Well, yes. I think so. You'll have to get it. My hands are full.

(*Halie giggles. Reaches into Dewis's pockets, searching for bottle. She smells the roses as she searches. Dewis stands stiffly. Dodge watches Halie closely as she looks for bottle.*)

HALIE. The most incredible things, roses! Aren't they incredible, Father?

DEWIS. Yes. Yes, they are.

HALIE. They almost cover the stench of sin in this house. Just magnificent! The smell. We'll have to put some at the foot of Ansel's statue. On the day of the unveiling.

(*Halie finds a silver flask of whiskey in Dewis's vest pocket. She pulls it out. Dodge looks on eagerly. Halie crosses to Dodge, opens the flask, and takes a sip.*)

HALIE (*to Dodge*). Ansel's getting a statue, Dodge. Did you know that? Not a plaque but a real live statue. A full bronze. Tip to toe. A basketball in one hand a rifle in the other.

BRADLEY (*his back to Halie*). He never played basketball!

HALIE. You shut up, Bradley! You shut up about Ansel! Ansel played basketball better than anyone! And you know it! He was an All-American! There's no reason to take the glory away from others.

(*Halie turns away from Bradley, crosses back toward Dewis, sipping on the flask and smiling.*)

HALIE (*to Dewis*). Ansel was a great basketball player. One of the greatest.

DEWIS. I remember Ansel.

HALIE. Of course! You remember. You remember how he could play. (*She turns toward Shelly.*) Of course nowadays they play a different brand of basketball. More vicious. Isn't that right, dear?

SHELLY. I don't know.

(*Halie crosses to Shelly, sipping in flask. She stops in front of Shelly.*)

HALIE. Much, more more vicious. They smash into each other. They knock each other's teeth out. There's blood all over the court. Savages.

(*Halie takes the cup from Shelly and pours whiskey into it.*)

HALIE. They don't train like they used to. Not at all. They allow themselves to run amuck. Drugs and women. Women mostly.

(*Halie hands the cup of whiskey back to Shelly slowly. Shelly takes it.*)

HALIE. Mostly women. Girls. Sad, pathetic little girls. (*She crosses back to Father Dewis.*) It's just a reflection of the times, don't you think, Father? An indication of where we stand?

DEWIS. I suppose so, yes.

HALIE. Yes. A sort of bad omen. Our youth becoming monsters.

DEWIS. Well, I uh—

HALIE. Oh you can disagree with me if you want to, Father. I'm open to debate. I think argument only enriches both sides of the question don't you? (*She moves toward Dodge.*) I suppose, in the long run, it doesn't matter. When you see the way things deteriorate before your very eyes. Everything running downhill. It's kind of silly to even think about youth.

DEWIS. No, I don't think so. I think it's important to believe in certain things.

HALIE. Yes. Yes, I know what you mean. I think that's right. I think that's true. (*She looks at Dodge.*) Certain basic things. We can't shake certain basic things. We might end up crazy. Like my husband. You can see it in his eyes. You can see how mad he is.

(*Dodge covers his head with the blanket again. Halie takes a single rose from Dewis and moves slowly over to Dodge.*)

HALIE. We can't not believe in something. We can't stop believing. We just end up dying if we stop. Just end up dead.

(*Halie throws the rose gently onto Dodge's blanket. It lands between his knees and stays there. Long pause as Halie stares at the rose. Shelly stands suddenly. Halie doesn't turn to her but keeps staring at rose.*)

SHELLY (*to Halie*). Don't you wanna' know who I am? Don't you wanna know what I'm doing here! I'm not dead!

(*Shelly crosses toward Halie. Halie turns slowly toward her.*)

HALIE. Did you drink your whiskey?

SHELLY. No! And I'm not going to either!

HALIE. Well, that's a firm stand. It's good to have a firm stand.

SHELLY. I don't have any stand at all. I'm just trying to put all this together.

(*Halie laughs and crosses back to Dewis.*)

HALIE (*to Dewis*). Surprises, surprises! Did you have any idea we'd be returning to this?

SHELLY. I came here with your grandson for a little visit! A little innocent friendly visit.

HALIE. My grandson?

SHELLY. Yes! That's right. The one no one remembers.

HALIE (*to Dewis*). This is getting a little far-fetched.

SHELLY. I told him it was stupid to come back here. To try to pick up from where he left off.

HALIE. Where was that?

SHELLY. Wherever he was when he left here! Six years ago! Ten years ago! Whenever it was. I told him nobody cares.

HALIE. Didn't he listen?

SHELLY. No! No, he didn't. We had to stop off at every tiny little meatball town that he remembered from his boyhood! Every stupid little donut shop he ever kissed a girl in. Every drive-in. Every drag strip. Every football field he ever broke a bone on.

HALIE (*suddenly alarmed, to Dodge*). Where's Tilden?

SHELLY. Don't ignore me!

HALIE. Dodge! Where's Tilden gone?

(*Shelly moves violently toward Halie.*)

SHELLY (*to Halie*). I'm talking to you!

(*Bradley sits up fast on the sofa, Shelly backs away.*)

BRADLEY (*to Shelly*). Don't you yell at my mother!

HALIE. Dodge! (*She kicks Dodge.*) I told you not to let Tilden out of your sight! Where's he gone to?

DODGE. Gimme a drink and I'll tell ya'.

DEWIS. Halie, maybe this isn't the right time for a visit.

(*Halie crosses back to Dewis.*)

HALIE (*to Dewis*). I never should've left. I never, never should've left! Tilden could be anywhere by now! Anywhere! He's not in control of his faculties. Dodge knew that. I told him when I left here. I told him specifically to watch out for Tilden.

(*Bradley reaches down, grabs Dodge's blanket, and yanks it off him. He lays down on sofa and pulls the blanket over his head.*)

DODGE. He's got my blanket again! He's got my blanket!

HALIE (*turning to Bradley*). Bradley! Bradley, put that blanket back!

(*Halie moves toward Bradley. Shelly suddenly throws the cup and saucer against the stage right door. Dewis ducks. The cup and saucer smash into pieces. Halie stops, turns toward Shelly. Everyone freezes. Bradley slowly pulls his head out from under blanket, looks toward stage right door, then to Shelly. Shelly stares at Halie. Dewis cowers with roses. Shelly moves slowly toward Halie. Long pause. Shelly speaks softly.*)

SHELLY (*to Halie*). I don't like being ignored. I don't like being treated like I'm not here. I didn't like it when I was a kid and I still don't like it.

BRADLEY (*sitting up on sofa*). We don't have to tell you anything, girl. Not a thing. You're not the police, are you? You're not the government. You're just some prostitute that Tilden brought in here.

HALIE. Language! I won't have that language in my house!

SHELLY (*to Bradley*). You stuck your hand in my mouth and you call me a prostitute!

HALIE. Bradley. Did you put your hand in her mouth? I'm ashamed of you. I can't leave you alone for a minute.

BRADLEY. I never did. She's lying!

DEWIS. Halie, I think I'll be running along now. I'll just put the roses in the kitchen.

(*Dewis moves toward stage left. Halie stops him.*)

HALIE. Don't go now, Father. Not now.

BRADLEY. I never did anything, Mom! I never touched her! She propositioned me! And I turned her down. I turned her down flat!

(*Shelly suddenly grabs her coat off the wooden leg and takes both the leg and coat downstage, away from Bradley.*)

BRADLEY. Mom! Mom! She's got my leg! She's taken my leg! I never did anything to her! She's stolen my leg!

(*Bradley reaches pathetically in the air for his leg. Shelly sets it down for a second, puts on her coat fast, and picks the leg up again. Dodge starts coughing softly.*)

HALIE (*to Shelly*). I think we've had about enough of you, young lady. Just about enough. I don't know where you came from or what you're doing here but you're no longer welcome in this house.

SHELLY (*laughs, holds leg*). No longer welcome!

BRADLEY. Mom! That's my leg! Get my leg back! I can't do anything without my leg.

(*Bradley keeps making whimpering sounds and reaching for his leg.*)

HALIE. Give my son back his leg. Right this very minute!

(*Dodge starts laughing softly to himself in between coughs.*)

HALIE (*to Dewis*). Father, do something about this, would you! I'm not about to be terrorized in my own house!

BRADLEY. Gimme back my leg!

HALIE. Oh, shut up, Bradley! Just shut up! You don't need your leg now! Just lay down and shut up!

(*Bradley whimpers. Lays down and pulls blanket around him. He keeps one arm outside blanket, reaching out toward his wooden leg. Dewis cautiously approaches Shelly with the roses in his arms. Shelly clutches the wooden leg to her chest as though she's kidnapped it.*)

DEWIS (*to Shelly*). Now, honestly dear, wouldn't it be better to try to talk things out? Try to use some reason?

SHELLY. There isn't any reason here! I can't find a reason for anything.

DEWIS. There's nothing to be afraid of. These are all good people. All righteous people.

SHELLY. I'm not afraid!

DEWIS. But this isn't your house. You have to have some respect.

SHELLY. You're the strangers here, not me.

HALIE. This has gone far enough!

DEWIS. Halie, please. Let me handle this.

SHELLY. Don't come near me! Don't anyone come near me. I don't need any words from you. I'm not threatening anybody. I don't even know what I'm doing here. You all say you don't remember Vince, okay, maybe you don't. Maybe it's Vince that's crazy. Maybe he's made this whole family thing up. I don't even care anymore. I was just coming along for the ride. I thought it'd be a nice gesture. Besides, I was curious. He made all of you sound familiar to me. Every one of you. For every name, I had an image. Every time he'd tell me a name, I'd see the person. In fact, each of you was so clear in my mind that I actually believed it was you. I really believed when I walked through that door that the people who lived here would turn out to be the same people in my imagination. But I don't recognize any of you. Not one. Not even the slightest resemblance.

DEWIS. Well, you can hardly blame others for not fulfilling your hallucination.

SHELLY. It was no hallucination! It was more like a prophecy. You believe in prophecy, don't you?

HALIE. Father, there's no point in talking to her any further. We're just going to have to call the police.

BRADLEY. No! Don't get the police in here. We don't want the police in here. This is our home.

SHELLY. That's right. Bradley's right. Don't you usually settle your affairs in private? Don't you usually take them out in the dark? Out in the back?

BRADLEY. You stay out of our lives! You have no business interfering!

SHELLY. I don't have any business period. I got nothing to lose.

(*She moves around, staring at each of them.*)

BRADLEY. You don't know what we've been through. You don't know anything!

SHELLY. I know you've got a secret. You've all got a secret. It's so secret in fact, you're all convinced it never happened.

(*Halie moves to Dewis.*)

HALIE. Oh, my God, Father!

DODGE (*laughing to himself*). She thinks she's going to get it out of us. She thinks she's going to uncover the truth of the matter. Like a detective or something.

BRADLEY. I'm not telling her anything! Nothing's wrong here! Nothin's ever been wrong! Everything's the way it's supposed to be! Nothing ever happened that's bad! Everything is all right here! We're all good people!

DODGE. She thinks she's gonna suddenly bring everything out into the open after all these years.

DEWIS (*to Shelly*). Can't you see that these people want to be left in peace? Don't you have any mercy? They haven't done anything to you.

DODGE. She wants to get to the bottom of it. (*To Shelly.*) That's it, isn't it? You'd like to get right down to bedrock? You want me to tell ya'? You want me to tell ya' what happened? I'll tell ya'. I might as well.

BRADLEY. No! Don't listen to him. He doesn't remember anything!

DODGE. I remember the whole thing from start to finish. I remember the day he was born.

(*Pause.*)

HALIE. Dodge, if you tell this thing—if you tell this, you'll be dead to me. You'll be just as good as dead.

DODGE. That won't be such a big change, Halie. See this girl, this girl here, she wants to know. She wants to know something more. And I got this feeling that it doesn't make a bit a' difference. I'd sooner tell it to a stranger than anybody else.

BRADLEY (*to Dodge*). We made a pact! We made a pact between us! You can't break that now!

DODGE. I don't remember any pact.

BRADLEY (*to Shelly*). See, he doesn't remember anything. I'm the only one in the family who remembers. The only one. And I'll never tell you!

SHELLY. I'm not so sure I want to find out now.

DODGE (*laughing to himself*). Listen to her! Now she's runnin' scared!

SHELLY. I'm not scared!

(*Dodge stops laughing, long pause. Dodge stares at her.*)

DODGE. You're not, huh? Well, that's good. Because I'm not either. See, we were a well-established family once. Well-established. All the boys were grown. The farm was producing enough milk to fill Lake Michigan twice over. Me and Halie here were pointed toward what looked like the middle part of our life. Everything was settled with us. All we had to do was ride it out. Then Halie got pregnant again. Outa' the middle a' nowhere, she got pregnant. We weren't planning on havin' any more boys. We had enough boys already. In fact, we hadn't been sleepin' in the same bed for about six years.

HALIE (*moving toward stairs*). I'm not listening to this! I don't have to listen to this!

DODGE (*stops Halie*). Where are you going? Upstairs! You'll just be listenin' to it upstairs! You go outside, you'll be listenin' to it outside. Might as well stay here and listen to it.

(*Halie stays by stairs.*)

BRADLEY. If I had my leg you wouldn't be saying this. You'd never get away with it if I had my leg.

DODGE (*pointing to Shelly*). She's got your leg. (*Laughs.*)

She's gonna keep your leg too. (*To Shelly.*) She wants to hear this. Don't you?

SHELLY. I don't know.

DODGE. Well even if ya' don't I'm gonna' tell ya'. (*Pause.*) Halie had this kid. This baby boy. She had it. I let her have it on her own. All the other boys I had had the best doctors, best nurses, everything. This one I let her have by herself. This one hurt real bad. Almost killed her, but she had it anyway. It lived, see. It lived. It wanted to grow up in this family. It wanted to be just like us. It wanted to be a part of us. It wanted to pretend that I was its father. She wanted me to believe in it. Even when everyone around us knew. Everyone. All our boys knew. Tilden knew.

HALIE. You shut up! Bradley, make him shut up!

BRADLEY. I can't.

DODGE. Tilden was the one who knew. Better than any of us. He'd walk for miles with that kid in his arms. Halie let him take it. All night sometimes. He'd walk all night out there in the pasture with it. Talkin' to it. Singin' to it. Used to hear him singing to it. He'd make up stories. He'd tell that kid all kinds a' stories. Even when he knew it couldn't understand him. Couldn't understand a word he was sayin'. Never would understand him. We couldn't let a thing like that continue. We couldn't allow that to grow up right in the middle of our lives. It made everything we'd accomplished look like it was nothin'. Everything was canceled out by this one mistake. This one weakness.

SHELLY. So you killed him?

DODGE. I killed it. I drowned it. Just like the runt of a litter. Just drowned it.

(*Halie moves toward Bradley.*)

HALIE (*to Bradley*). Ansel would've stopped him! Ansel would've stopped him from telling these lies! He was a hero! A man! A whole man! What's happened to the men in this family? Where are the men!

(*Suddenly Vince comes crashing through the screen porch door up left, tearing it off its hinges. Everyone but Dodge and Bradley back away from the porch and stare at Vince who has landed on his stomach on the porch in a drunken stupor. He is singing loudly to himself and hauls himself slowly to his feet. He has a paper shopping bag full of empty booze bottles. He takes them out one at a time as he sings and smashes them at the opposite end of the porch, behind the solid interior door, stage right. Shelly moves slowly toward stage right, holding wooden leg and watching Vince.*)

VINCE (*singing loudly as he hurls bottles*). "From the Halls of Montezuma to the Shores of Tripoli. We will fight our country's battles on the land and on the sea."

(*He punctuates the words "Montezuma," "Tripoli," "battles," and "sea" with a smashed bottle each. He stops throwing for a second, stares toward stage right of the porch, shades his eyes with his hand as though looking across to a battlefield, then cups his hands around his mouth and yells across the space of the porch to an imaginary army. The others watch in terror and expectation.*)

VINCE (*to imagined army*). Have you had enough over there! 'Cause there's a lot more here where that came from! (*Pointing to paper bag full of bottles.*) A helluva lot more! We got enough over here to blow ya' from here to King-domcome!

(*He takes another bottle, makes high whistling sound of a bomb, and throws it toward stage right porch. Sound of bottle smashing against wall. This should be the actual smashing of bottles and not tape sound. He keeps yelling and heaving bottles one after another.*)

(*Vince stops for a while, breathing heavily from exhaustion. Long silence as the others watch him. Shelly approaches tentatively in Vince's direction, still holding Bradley's wooden leg.*)

SHELLY (*after silence*). Vince?

(*Vince turns toward her. Peers through screen.*)

VINCE. Who? What? Vince who? Who's that in there?

(*Vince pushes his face against the screen from the porch and stares in at everyone.*)

DODGE. Where's my goddamn bottle!
VINCE (*looking in at Dodge*). What? Who is that?
DODGE. It's me! Your Grandfather! Don't play stupid with me! Where's my two bucks!
VINCE. Your two bucks?

(*Halie moves away from Dewis, upstage, peers out at Vince, trying to recognize him.*)

HALIE. Vincent? Is that you, Vincent?

(*Shelly stares at Halie, then looks out at Vince.*)

VINCE (*from porch*). Vincent who? What is this! Who are you people?
SHELLY (*to Halie*). Hey, wait a minute. Wait a minute! What's going on?
HALIE (*moving closer to porch screen*). We thought you were a murderer or something. Barging in through the door like that.
VINCE. I am a Murderer! don't underestimate me for a minute! I'm the Midnight Strangler! I devour whole families in a single gulp!

(*Vince grabs another bottle and smashes it on the porch. Halie backs away.*)

SHELLY (*approaching Halie*). You mean you know who he is?
HALIE. Of course I know who he is! That's more than I can say for you.

BRADLEY (*sitting up on sofa*). You get off our front porch, you creep! What're you doing out there breaking bottles. Who are these foreigners anyway! Where did they come from?
VINCE. Maybe I should come in there and break them!
HALIE (*moving toward porch*). Don't you dare! Vincent, what's got into you? Why are you acting like this?
VINCE. Maybe I should come in there and usurp your territory!

(*Halie turns back toward Dewis and crosses to him.*)

HALIE (*to Dewis*). Father, why are you just standing around here when everything's falling apart? Can't you rectify this situation?

(*Dodge laughs, coughs.*)

DEWIS. I'm just a guest here, Halie. I don't know what my position is exactly. This is outside my parish anyway.

(*Vince starts throwing more bottles as things continue.*)

BRADLEY. If I had my leg I'd rectify it! I'd rectify him all over the goddamn highway! I'd pull his ears out if I could reach him!

(*Bradley sticks his fist through the screening of the porch and reaches out for Vince, grabbing at him and missing. Vince jumps away from Bradley's hand.*)

VINCE. Aaaah! Our lines have been penetrated! Tentacled animals! Beasts from the deep!

(*Vince strikes out at Bradley's hand with a bottle. Bradley pulls his hand back inside.*)

SHELLY. Vince! Knock it off, will ya! I want to get out of here!

(*Vince pushes his face against screen, looks in at Shelly.*)

VINCE (*to Shelly*). Have they got you prisoner in there, dear? Such a sweet young thing too. All her life in front of her. Nipped in the bud.
SHELLY. I'm coming out there, Vince! I'm coming out there and I want us to get in the car and drive away from here. Anywhere. Just away from here.

(*Shelly moves toward Vince's saxophone case and overcoat. She sets down the wooden leg, downstage left, and picks up the saxophone case and overcoat. Vince watches her through the screen.*)

VINCE (*to Shelly*). We'll have to negotiate. Make some kind of a deal. Prisoner exchange or something. A few of theirs for one of ours. Small price to pay if you ask me.

(*Shelly crosses toward stage right door with overcoat and case.*)

SHELLY. Just go and get the car! I'm coming out there now. We're going to leave.

VINCE. Don't come out here! Don't you dare come out here!

(*Shelly stops short of the door, stage right.*)

SHELLY. How come?

VINCE. Off limits! Verboten! This is taboo territory. No man or woman has ever crossed the line and lived to tell the tale!

SHELLY. I'll take my chances.

(*Shelly moves to stage right door and opens it. Vince pulls out a big folding hunting knife and pulls open the blade. He jabs the blade into the screen and starts cutting a hole big enough to climb through. Bradley cowers in a corner of the sofa as Vince rips at the screen.*)

VINCE (*as he cuts screen*). Don't come out here! I'm warning you! You'll disintegrate!

(*Dewis takes Halie by the arm and pulls her toward stair-case.*)

DEWIS. Halie, maybe we should go upstairs until this blows over.

HALIE. I don't understand it. I just don't understand it. He was the sweetest little boy!

(*Dewis drops the roses beside the wooden leg at the foot of the staircase, then escorts Halie quickly up the stairs. Halie keeps looking back at Vince as they climb the stairs.*)

HALIE. There wasn't a mean bone in his body. Everyone loved Vincent. Everyone. He was the perfect baby.

DEWIS. He'll be all right after a while. He's just had a few too many that's all.

HALIE. He used to sing in his sleep. He'd sing. In the middle of the night. The sweetest voice. Like an angel. (*She stops for a moment.*) I used to lie awake listening to it. I used to lie awake thinking it was all right if I died. Because Vincent was an angel. A guardian angel. He'd watch over us. He'd watch over all of us.

(*Dewis takes her all the way up the stairs. They disappear above. Vince is now climbing through the porch screen onto the sofa. Bradley crashes off the sofa, holding tight to his blanket, keeping it wrapped around him. Shelly is outside on the porch. Vince holds the knife in his teeth once he gets the hole wide enough to climb through. Bradley starts crawling slowly toward his wooden leg, reaching out for it.*)

DODGE (*to Vince*). Go ahead! Take over the house! Take over the whole goddamn house! You can have it! It's yours. It's been a pain in the neck ever since the very first mortgage. I'm gonna die any second now. Any second. You won't even notice. So I'll settle my affairs once and for all.

(*As Dodge proclaims his last will and testament, Vince climbs into the room, knife in mouth, and strides slowly*

around the space, inspecting his inheritance. He casually notices Bradley as he crawls toward his leg. Vince moves to the leg and keeps pushing it with his foot so that it's out of Bradley's reach, then goes on with his inspection. He picks up the roses and carries them around smelling them. Shelly can be seen outside on the porch, moving slowly center and staring in at Vince. Vince ignores her.*)

DODGE. The house goes to my Grandson, Vincent. All the furnishings, accoutrements, and paraphernalia therein. Everything tacked to the walls or otherwise resting under this roof. My tools—namely my band saw, my skill saw, my drill press, my chain saw, my lathe, my electric sander, all go to my eldest son, Tilden. That is, if he ever shows up again. My shed and gasoline powered equipment, namely my tractor, my dozer, my hand tiller plus all the attachments and riggings for the above mentioned machinery, namely my spring tooth harrow, my deep plows, my disk plows, my automatic fertilizing equipment, my reaper, my swathe, my seeder, my John Deere Harvester, my post hole digger, my jackhammer, my lathe—(*to himself*) Did I mention my lathe? I already mentioned my lathe—my Bennie Goodman records, my harnesses, my bits, my halters, my brace, my rough rasp, my forge, my welding equipment, my shoeing nails, my levels and bevels, my milking stool—no, not my milking stool—my hammers and chisels, my hinges, my cattle gates, my barbed wire, self-tapping augers, my horse hair ropes, and all related materials are to be pushed into a gigantic heap and set ablaze in the very center of my fields. When the blaze is at its highest, preferably on a cold, windless night, my body is to be pitched into the middle of it and burned till nothing remains but ash.

(*Pause. Vince takes the knife out of his mouth and smells the roses. He's facing toward audience and doesn't turn around to Shelly. He folds up knife and pockets it.*)

SHELLY (*from porch*). I'm leaving, Vince. Whether you come or not, I'm leaving.

VINCE (*smelling roses*). Just put my horn on the couch there before you take off.

SHELLY (*moving toward hole in screen*). You're not coming?

(*Vince stays downstage, turns, and looks at her.*)

VINCE. I just inherited a house.

SHELLY (*through hole, from porch*). You want to stay here?

VINCE (*as he pushes Bradley's leg out of reach*). I've gotta carry on the line. I've gotta see to it that things keep rolling.

(*Bradley looks up at him from floor, keeps pulling himself toward his leg. Vince keeps moving it.*)

SHELLY. What happened to you, Vince? You just disappeared.

VINCE (*pause, delivers speech front*). I was gonna run last night. I was gonna run and keep right on running. I drove all night. Clear to the Iowa border. The old man's two bucks sitting right on the seat beside me. It never stopped raining the whole time. Never stopped once. I could see myself in the windshield. My face. My eyes. I studied my face. Studied everything about it. As though I was looking at another man. As though I could see his whole race behind him. Like a mummy's face. I saw him dead and alive at the same time. In the same breath. In the windshield, I watched him breathe as though he was frozen in time. And every breath marked him. Marked him forever without him knowing. And then his face changed. His face became his father's face. Same bones. Same eyes. Same nose. Same breath. And his father's face changed to his grandfather's face. And it went on like that. Changing. Clear on back to faces I'd never seen before but still recognized. Still recognized the bones underneath. The eyes. The breath. The mouth. I followed my family clear into Iowa. Every last one. Straight into the Corn Belt and further. Straight back as far as they'd take me. Then it all dissolved. Everything dissolved.

(*Shelly stares at him for a while then reaches through the hole in the screen and sets the saxophone case and Vince's overcoat on the sofa. She looks at Vince again.*)

SHELLY. Bye, Vince.

(*She exits left off the porch. Vince watches her go. Bradley tries to make a lunge for his wooden leg. Vince quickly picks it up and dangles it over Bradley's head like a carrot. Bradley keeps making desperate grabs at the leg. Dewis comes down the staircase and stops halfway, staring at Vince and Bradley. Vince looks up at Dewis and smiles. He keeps moving backwards with the leg toward upstage left as Bradley crawls after him.*)

VINCE (*to Dewis as he continues torturing Bradley*). Oh, excuse me, Father. Just getting rid of some of the vermin in the house. This is my house now, ya' know? All mine. Everything. Except for the power tools and stuff. I'm gonna get all new equipment anyway. New plows, new tractor, everything. All brand new. (*Vince teases Bradley closer to the up left corner of the stage.*) Start right off on the ground floor.

(*Vince throws Bradley wooden leg far offstage left. Bradley follows his leg offstage, pulling himself along on the ground, whimpering. As Bradley exits, Vince pulls the blanket off him and throws it over his own shoulder. He crosses toward Dewis with the blanket and smells the roses. Dewis comes to the bottom of the stairs.*)

DEWIS. You'd better go up and see your Grandmother.
VINCE (*looking up stairs, back to Dewis*). My Grandmother?

There's nobody else in this house. Except for you. And you're leaving, aren't you?

(*Dewis crosses toward stage right door. He turns back to Vince.*)

DEWIS. She's going to need someone. I can't help her. I don't know what to do. I don't know what my position is. I just came in for some tea. I had no idea there was any trouble. No idea at all.

(*Vince just stares at him. Dewis goes out the door, crosses porch, and exits left. Vince listens to him leaving. He smells roses, looks up the staircase, then smells roses again. He turns and looks upstage at Dodge. He crosses up to him and bends over looking at Dodge's open eyes. Dodge is dead. His death should have come completely unnoticed. Vince lifts the blanket, then covers his head. He sits on the sofa, smelling roses and staring at Dodge's body. Long pause. Vince places the roses on Dodge's chest, then lays down on the sofa, arms folded behind his head, staring at the ceiling. His body is in the same relationship to Dodge's. After a while Halie's voice is heard coming from above the staircase. The lights start to dim almost imperceptibly as Halie speaks. Vince keeps staring at the ceiling.*)

HALIE'S VOICE. Dodge? Is that you, Dodge? Tilden was right about the corn, you know. I've never seen such corn. Have you taken a look at it lately? Tall as a man already. This early in the year. Carrots too. Potatoes. Peas. It's like a paradise out there, Dodge. You oughta' take a look. A miracle. I've never seen it like this. Maybe the rain did something. Maybe it was the rain.

(*As Halie keeps talking offstage, Tilden appears from stage left, dripping with mud from the knees down. His arms and hands are covered with mud. In his hands he carries the corpse of a small child at chest level, staring down at it. The corpse mainly consists of bones wrapped in muddy, rotten cloth. He moves slowly downstage toward the staircase, ignoring Vince on the sofa. Vince keeps staring at the ceiling as though Tilden wasn't there. As Halie's voice continues. Tilden slowly makes his way up the stairs. His eyes never leave the corpse of the child. The lights keep fading.*)

HALIE'S VOICE. Good hard rain. Takes everything straight down deep to the roots. The rest takes cares of itself. You can't force a thing to grow. You can't interfere with it. It's all hidden. It's all unseen. You just gotta wait till it pops up out of the ground. Tiny little shoot. Tiny little white shoot. All hairy and fragile. Strong though. Strong enough to break the earth even. It's a miracle, Dodge. I've never seen a crop like this in my whole life. Maybe it's the sun. Maybe that's it. Maybe it's the sun.

(*Tilden disappears above. Silence. Lights go to black.*)

THE DANCE AND THE RAILROAD

DAVID HENRY HWANG

DAVID HENRY HWANG (1957 –)

When Hwang's play M. *Butterfly* won the Tony Award (and a Pulitzer Prize nomination) in 1988, it marked the first time the American commercial theater's premier award was bestowed on a playwright of Asian descent. Though Asian-Americans have been prominently involved in the theater (e.g., the Shanghai-born designer Ming Cho Li, and the avant-garde artist Ping Chong), Hwang is a principal spokesman of Asian immigrants in the American theater.

Hwang was born in Los Angeles to an affluent family. An early play, *Family Devotions* (1981), is a farcical encounter between an old uncle from mainland China and the wealthy relatives he visits in the posh suburb of Bel Air. Typical of Hwang's work, it explores the clash between Eastern and Western value systems. Hwang was educated at Stanford University and the Yale School of Drama. His first play, *F.O.B.* (1980), was developed in a playwriting seminar led by Sam Shepard. The title, an acronym for "fresh off the boat," suggests its theme: the problems faced by Chinese immigrants as they adapt to life in the West. Like *The Dance and the Railroad*, *F.O.B.* uses elements of Chinese Opera, folktales, and myth; Guan Gung, the god of warriors, writers, and prostitutes, is central to *F.O.B.*, just as he is to *The Dance and the Railroad*. Joseph Papp produced *F.O.B.* in New York, where the play won an Obie Award as the best Off-Broadway work of 1980. Its success led to other plays, such as *Rich Relations* (1986) and *Broken Promises* (1987), and an opera written with avant-garde composer Philip Glass, *A Thousand Airplanes on the Roof*.

M. *Butterfly*, now a film, is among the most provocative plays in recent Broadway history. Based on the true story of a French diplomat and his Chinese lover (a beautiful opera singer who is revealed as not only a spy, but a transvestite), the play examines East-West relations and racial and sexual stereotyping. According to Hwang, the play is a critique of "Orientalism" (a term coined by Edward Said in his book of the same title), which refers to the erroneous Western notion that "the East is mysterious, inscrutable, and therefore ultimately inferior." Hwang's work, as typified by M. *Butterfly* and *The Dance and the Railroad*, often fuses Chinese theater practice and Western realism.

THE DANCE AND THE RAILROAD (1981)

You may recall a scene in Francis Ford Coppola's film *The Godfather, Part II* in which the young Vito Corleone, himself "fresh off the boat" from Italy, seeks a bit of the old country in a small, colorful Italian-language theater in New York City's Little Italy. Immigrants frequently use the theater as a meeting place to share memories of the land they left behind as well as to discuss problems in adjusting to a new life in a strange land. Frequently, the theater itself addresses these problems, often satirically. In New York, for instance, the Yiddish Theater for years provided a meeting place for displaced Jewish immigrants, just as the Bowery Theater courted Irish Americans. In Buenos Aires, Italian immigrants (who were, like Lone and Ma, imported to build railroads) laughed at the *cocoleche* plays about immigrants and their problems with

1585

language in a new country. Today, one can go to the Tricycle Theater in North London and see plays staged by and for West Indian immigrants.

It was this impulse that led to the creation of *The Dance and the Railroad*. Based on a true incident in which Chinese railworkers went on strike in California in 1867, this one-act was developed by Hwang in collaboration with two actors trained in Chinese theater and dance, John Lone and Tzi Ma. Appropriately, Hwang named the play's characters after his collaborators because their own struggles as artists in a new culture mirror those of the immigrant workers. On its most obvious level, the play is about the conflict between "the dance" (the values of the East) versus "the railroad" (Western technology, built largely on the backs of immigrant workers). The railroad is an especially apt symbol, as it was both the means by which the country expanded in the nineteenth century and an ironic reminder that workers like Ma have themselves traveled thousands of miles so that their sweat can provide a comfortable means of travel for others.

To tell his story Hwang uses a time-tested construct—the master-pupil relationship. The device works well, especially for didactic drama, because as the pupil learns, so does the audience. In Hwang's play Lone, who trained in the Peking Opera for eight years before seeking his fortune on Gold Mountain (a variant on the "streets paved with gold" metaphor used by hopeful immigrants to describe America), is approached by Ma, newly arrived in California. Ma ascends the mountain to ask Lone to be his instructor. The younger man wants to learn the secrets of the opera, as well as how to survive in his new environment. Lone relies on the aesthetics and discipline of his opera training to escape the dreariness of the menial work at the foot of the mountain. "You think you understand the dedication one must have to be in the opera? You think it's the same as working on a railroad?" he challenges his pupil.

As is often the case, in the process of education, the teacher learns much from the student. In Ma's näiveté—about the opera, about working conditions, about the American dream—Lone ultimately sees himself. When he learns from Ma that the strike has been settled—though not to the workers' advantage—he becomes aware that his dreams (delusions?) about the opera are as hollow as Ma's about working conditions. In the final moment of the play the teacher asks the pupil to help him take his stage props—symbols of his own unrealistic dreams—down the mountain. Reality waits in the "ChinaMan" camp at the foot of the mountain, while the mountain itself is as illusory as its name. There is no Gwan Gung, the Robin Hood–like warrior loved by devotees of the opera, to save Lone and Ma from their fate as he might have done in a Peking Opera theater.

For all the play's talk about the "white devils" who exploit the workers, Hwang notes that there are enemies within the immigrant culture as well. We learn that "the heads of the gang" decide the fate of the rail workers; we learn that the "coolies" had to pay $125 "to the said head of said Hong" for their passage on the rotting ship from China because they were promised by Hong's minions that they could "make our fortunes on Gold Mountain, where work is play and the sun scares off the snow;" and we learn that a successful black market operation exploits newcomers in San Francisco. These are all references to a reality faced by immigrants that is as disturbing as any perpetrated by the majority culture—the "selling out" of immigrants by members of their own race. Not all of the devils Ma and Lone confront have "hair the color of a sick chicken and eyes round as eggs." Hwang's strength rests on his recognition that the complex problems of immigrants involve more than racism.

We cannot, however, dismiss racism as a central issue of Hwang's play. Though he is newly come to America, Ma quickly learns that he must play to racist stereotypes to survive. He speaks fluent "demon English": "Eight hours a day good for white man, all same good for ChinaMan." And both he and Lone can parody "demon English" as they play "white Devils": "Wha che doo doo blah blah . . . bla bla doo doo tee tee." Ironically, to deal with the devil they must themselves adopt the same racist attitudes toward their bosses that the bosses have toward them; note that they refer to whites in blatantly stereotypical terms. They have assimilated the customs of the country too well. Even behind their role playing within the opera motif, Ma and Lone are painfully aware that they are viewed as "different." When they play at being various animals, insects, and birds, Lone and Ma are reminded of intolerance. Lone discovers that he "never realized how uncomfortable a duck's life is" as he squats and quacks; later, he tells his pupil that there is "nothing worse than a duck [or a ChinaMan?] that doesn't know his place." Here art clearly imitates life for Lone.

Ma's lengthy speech in scene 4 is a parable about one of the most disturbing problems facing immigrants—that is, various minorities are pitted against one another by the majority in a "divide and conquer" strategy. As he recounts his story about the locusts and the grasshoppers, he seems to suggest that one class of immigrants (the innocent grasshoppers) pays for the sins of another (the plague-bearing locusts) at the hands of the spiteful Second Uncle (Sam?). Is Ma suggesting that the Chinese are victims of prejudice against nonwhites, which in the California of his time (and today) would have been the Mexicans and their descendants? While we know that immigrants are too often and too easily blamed for any number of social and economic problems in their host country, Hwang lets us see yet another insidious aspect of "immigrant bashing," to use a current term: the resentment of one group of immigrants toward another. History recently provided a concrete example of what seems to be one of Hwang's concerns in this play. In the L.A. riots following the first Rodney King verdict (in which white police officers were acquitted of beating King, an African American) it was Korean Americans who suffered most at the hands of black and Hispanic rioters. Anna Deavere Smith also addresses this phenomenon in *Twilight: Los Angeles, 1992,* the final play in this text.

In *The Dance and the Railroad*, Hwang offers a much bolder critique of intolerance and exploitation. By expanding his focus to include internal problems—as well as the well-documented, much-discussed external ones—he exposes "the cult of racism" (not limited to white racism) that is the blight on Gold Mountain.

THE DANCE AND THE RAILROAD

DAVID HENRY HWANG

CHARACTERS
LONE, *twenty years old, ChinaMan railroad worker*
MA, *eighteen years old, ChinaMan railroad worker*

PLACE
A mountain top near the transcontinental railroad.

TIME
June, 1867.

SYNOPSIS OF SCENES
Scene One: Afternoon.
Scene Two: Afternoon, a day later.
Scene Three: Late afternoon, four days later.
Scene Four: Late that night.
Scene Five: Just before the following dawn.

SCENE ONE

A mountain top. Lone is practicing opera steps. He swings his pigtail around like a fan. Ma enters, cautiously, watches from a hidden spot. Ma approaches Lone.

LONE. So, there are insects hiding in the bushes.
MA. Hey, listen, we haven't met, but—
LONE. I don't spend time with insects.

(Lone whips his hair into Ma's face; Ma backs off; Lone pursues him, swiping at Ma with his hair.)

MA. What the . . . ? Cut it out!

(Ma pushes Lone away.)

LONE. Don't push me.
MA. What was that for?
LONE. Don't ever push me again.

MA. You mess like that, you're gonna get pushed.

LONE. Don't push me.

MA. You started it. I just wanted to watch.

LONE. You "just wanted to watch." Did you ask my permission?

MA. What?

LONE. Did you?

MA. C'mon.

LONE. You can't expect to get in for free.

MA. Listen. I got some stuff you'll wanna hear.

LONE. You think so?

MA. Yeah. Some advice.

LONE. Advice? How old are you, anyway?

MA. Eighteen!

LONE. A child.

MA. Yeah. Right. A child. But listen . . .

LONE. A child who tries to advise a grown man . . .

MA. Listen, you got this kind of attitude.

LONE. —is a child who will never grow up.

MA. You know, the ChinaMen down at camp, they can't stand it.

LONE. Oh?

MA. Yeah. You gotta watch yourself. You know what they say? They call you "Prince of the Mountain." Like you're too good to spend time with them.

LONE. Perceptive of them.

MA. After all, you never sing songs, never tell stories. They say you act like your spit is too clean for them, and they got ways to fix that.

LONE. Is that so?

MA. Like they're gonna bury you in the shitbuckets, so you'll have more to clean than your nails.

LONE. But I don't shit.

MA. Or they're gonna cut out your tongue, since you never speak to them.

LONE. There's no one here worth talking to.

MA. Cut it out, Lone. Look, I'm trying to help you, all right? I got a solution.

LONE. So young yet so clever.

MA. That stuff you're doing—it's beautiful. Why don't you do it for the guys at camp? Help us celebrate?

LONE. What will "this stuff" help celebrate?

MA. C'mon. The strike, of course. Guys on a railroad gang, we gotta stick together, you know.

LONE. This is something to celebrate?

MA. Yeah. Yesterday, the weak-kneed ChinaMen: they were running around like chickens without a head: "The white devils are sending their soldiers! Shoot us all!" But now, look—day four, see? Still in one piece. Those soldiers—we've never seen a gun or a bullet.

LONE. So you're all warrior-spirits, huh?

MA. They're scared of us, Lone—that's what it means.

LONE. I appreciate your advice. Tell you what—you go down—

MA. Yeah?

LONE. Down to the camp.

MA. Okay.

LONE. To where the men are—

MA. Yeah?

LONE. Sit there—

MA. Yeah?

LONE. And wait for me.

MA. Okay. (Pause.) That's it? What do you think I am?

LONE. I think you're an insect interrupting my practice. So fly away. Go home.

MA. Look, I didn't come here to get laughed at.

LONE. No, I suppose you didn't.

MA. So just stay up here. By yourself. You deserve it.

LONE. I do.

MA. And don't expect any more help from me.

LONE. I haven't gotten any yet.

MA. If one day, you wake up and your head is buried in the shit can—

LONE. Yes?

MA. You can't find your body, your tongue is cut out—

LONE. Yes.

MA. Don't worry 'cuz I'll be there.

LONE. Oh.

MA. To make sure your mother's head is sitting right next to yours.

(Ma exits.)

LONE. His head is too big for this mountain.

(Returns to practicing.)

SCENE TWO

(Mountaintop. Next day. Lone is practicing. Ma enters.)

MA. Hey.

LONE. You? Again?

MA. I forgive you.

LONE. You . . . what?

MA. For making fun of me yesterday. I forgive you.

LONE. You can't—

MA. No. Don't thank me.

LONE. You can't forgive me.

MA. No. Don't mention it.

LONE. You—! I never asked for your forgiveness.

MA. I know. That's just the kinda guy I am.

LONE. This is ridiculous. Why don't you leave? Go down to your friends and play soldiers, sing songs, tell stories.

MA. Ah! See? That's just it. I got other ways I wanna spend my time. Will you teach me the opera?

LONE. What?

MA. I wanna learn it. I dreamt about it all last night.

LONE. No.

MA. The dance, the opera—I can do it.

LONE. You think so?

MA. Yeah. When I get outa here, I wanna go back to China and perform.

LONE. You want to become an actor?

MA. Well, I wanna perform.

LONE. Don't you remember the story about the three sons whose parents send them away to learn a trade? After three years, they return. The first one says, "I have become a coppersmith." The parents say, "Good. Second son, what have you become?" "I've become a silversmith." "Good . . . and youngest son . . . what about you?" "I have become an actor." When the parents hear that their son has become only an actor, they are very sad. The mother beats her head against the ground until the ground, out of pity, opens up and swallows her. The father is so angry, he can't even speak, and the anger builds up inside him until it blows his body to pieces—little bits of his skin are found hanging from trees days later. You don't know how you endanger your relatives by becoming an actor.

MA. Well, I don't wanna become an "actor." That sounds terrible. I just wanna perform. Look, I'll be rich by the time I get out of here, right?

LONE. Oh?

MA. Sure. By the time I go back to China, I'll ride in gold sedan chairs, with twenty wives fanning me all around.

LONE. Twenty wives? This boy is ambitious.

MA. I'll give out pigs on New Years and keep a stable of small birds to give to any woman who pleases me. And in my spare time, I'll perform.

LONE. Between your twenty wives and your birds, where will you find a free moment?

MA. I'll play Gwan Gung and tell stories of what life was like in the Gold Mountain.

LONE. Ma, just how long have you been in "America"?

MA. Huh? About four weeks.

LONE. You are a big dreamer.

MA. Well, all us ChinaMen here are—right? Men with little dreams have little brains to match. They walk with their eyes down, trying to find extra grains of rice on the ground.

LONE. So, you know all about "America"? Tell me, what kind of stories will you tell?

MA. I'll say, "We laid tracks like soldiers. Mountains? We hung from cliffs in baskets and the winds blew us like birds. Snow? We lived underground like moles for days at a time. Deserts? We—."

LONE. Wait. Wait. How do you know these things after only four weeks?

MA. They told me—the other ChinaMen on the gang. We've been telling stories ever since the strike began.

LONE. They make it sound like it's very enjoyable.

MA. They said it is.

LONE. Oh? And you believe them?

MA. They're my friends. Living underground in winter—sounds exciting, huh?

LONE. Did they say anything about the cold?

MA. Oh, I already know about that. They told me about the mild winters and the warm snow.

LONE. Warm snow?

MA. When I go home, I'll bring some back to show my brothers.

LONE. Bring some——On the boat?

MA. They'll be shocked—they never seen American snow before.

LONE. You can't. By the time you get snow to the boat, it'll have melted, evaporated, and returned as rain already.

MA. No.

LONE. No?

MA. Stupid.

LONE. Me?

MA. You been here awhile, haven't you?

LONE. Yes. Two years.

MA. Then how come you're so stupid? This is the Gold Mountain. The snow here doesn't melt. It's not wet.

LONE. That's what they told you?

MA. Yeah. It's true.

LONE. Did anyone show you any of this snow?

MA. No. It's not winter.

LONE. So where does it go?

MA. Huh?

LONE. Where does it go? If it doesn't melt, what happens to it?

MA. The snow? I dunno. I guess it just stays around.

LONE. So where is it? Do you see any?

MA. Here? Well, no, but . . . (Pause.) This is probably one of those places where it doesn't snow—even in winter.

LONE. Oh.

MA. Anyway, what's the use of me telling you what you already know? Hey, c'mon—teach me some of that stuff. Look—I've been practicing the walk—how's this? (Demonstrates)

LONE. You look like a duck in heat.

MA. Hey—it's a start, isn't it?

LONE. Tell you what—you want to play some die siu?

MA. Die Siu? Sure.

LONE. You know, I'm pretty good.

MA. Hey, I play with the guys at camp. You can't be any better than Lee—he's really got it down.

(Lone pulls out a case with two dice)

LONE. I used to play 'til morning.

MA. Hey, us too. We see the sun start to rise, and say, "Hey, if we go to sleep now, we'll never get up for work." So we just keep playing.

LONE (Holding out dice). Die or Siu?

MA. Siu.

LONE. You sure?

MA. Yeah!

LONE. All right. (*He rolls*) Die!

MA. *Siu.*

(*They see the result.*)

MA. *Siu!* Not bad.

(*They continue taking turns rolling through the following section; Ma always loses.*)

LONE. I haven't touched these in two years.

MA. I gotta practice more . . .

LONE. Have you lost much money?

MA. Huh? So what?

LONE. Oh, you have gold hidden in all your shirt linings, huh?

MA. Here in "America"—losing is no problem. You know—End of the Year Bonus?

LONE. Oh, right.

MA. After I get that, I'll laugh at what I lost.

LONE. Lee told you there was a bonus, right?

MA. How'd you know?

LONE. When I arrived here, Lee told me there was a bonus, too.

MA. Lee teach you how to play?

LONE. Him? He talked to me a lot.

MA. Look, why don't you come down and start playing with the guys again?

LONE. The "guys."

MA. Before we start playing, Lee uses a stick to write "Kill!" in the dirt.

LONE. You seem to live for your nights with "the guys."

MA. What's life without friends, huh?

LONE. Well, why do *you* think I stopped playing?

MA. Hey, maybe you were the one getting killed, huh?

LONE. What?

MA. Hey, just kidding.

LONE. Who's getting killed here?

MA. Just a joke.

LONE. That's not a joke, it's blasphemy.

MA. Look, obviously you stopped playing 'cause you wanted to practice the opera.

LONE. Do you understand that discipline?

MA. But, I mean, you don't have to overdo it either. You don't have to beat 'em like dirt. I mean, who are you trying to impress?

(*Pause; Lone throws dice into the bushes.*)

LONE. Oooops. Better go see who won.

MA. Hey! C'mon! Help me look!

LONE. If you find them, they are yours.

MA. You serious?

LONE. Yes.

MA. Here.

(*Finds the dice.*)

LONE. Who won?

MA. I didn't check.

LONE. Well, no matter. Keep the dice. Take them, and go play with your friends.

MA. Here. (*He offers them to Lone*) A present.

LONE. A present? This isn't a present!

MA. They're mine, aren't they? You gave them to me, right?

LONE. Well, yes, but—

MA. So now I'm giving them to you.

LONE. You can't give me a present. I don't want them.

MA. You wanted them enough to keep them two years.

LONE. I'd forgotten I had them.

MA. See, I know, Lone. You wanna get rid of me. But you can't. I'm paying for lessons.

LONE. With my dice.

MA. Mine now. (*He offers them again*) Here.

(*Pause; Lone runs Ma's hand across his forehead.*)

LONE. Feel this.

MA. Hey!

LONE. Pretty wet, huh?

MA. Big deal.

LONE. Well, it's not from playing *Die Siu.*

MA. I know how to sweat. I wouldn't be here if I didn't.

LONE. Yes, but are you willing to sweat after you've finished sweating? Are you willing to come up after you've spent the whole day chipping half an inch off a rock, and punish your body some more?

MA. Yeah. Even after work, I still—

LONE. No, you don't. You want to gamble, and tell dirty stories, and dress up like women to do shows.

MA. Hey, I never did that.

LONE. You've only been here a month. (*Pause.*) And what about "the guys?" They're not going to treat you so well once you stop playing with them. Are you willing to work all day listening to them whisper, "That one—let's put spiders in his soup."

MA. They won't do that to me. With you, it's different.

LONE. Is it?

MA. You don't have to act that way.

LONE. What way?

MA. Like you're so much better than them.

LONE. No. You haven't even begun to understand. To practice every day, you must have a fear to force you up here.

MA. A fear? No—it's 'cause what you're doing is beautiful.

LONE. No.

MA. I've seen it.

LONE. It's ugly to practice when the mountain has turned your muscles to ice. When my body hurts too much to come here, I look at the other ChinaMen and think, "They are dead. Their muscles work only because the white man forces them." I live because I can still force my muscles to work for me." Say it. "They are dead."

MA. No. They're my friends.

LONE. Well, then, take your dice down to your friends.

MA. But I want to learn—

LONE. This is your first lesson.
MA. Look, it shouldn't matter—
LONE. It does.
MA. It shouldn't matter what I think.
LONE. Attitude is everything.
MA. But as long as I come up, do the exercises—
LONE. I'm not going to waste time on a quitter.
MA. I'm not!
LONE. Then say it—"They are dead men."
MA. I can't.
LONE. Then you will never have the dedication.
MA. That doesn't prove anything.
LONE. I will not teach a dead man.
MA. What?
LONE. If you can't see it, then you're dead too.
MA. Don't start pinning—
LONE. Say it!
MA. All right.
LONE. What?
MA. All right. I'm one of them. I'm a dead man too.

(Pause.)

LONE. I thought as much. So, go. You have your friends.
MA. But I don't have a teacher.
LONE. I don't think you need both.
MA. Are you sure?
LONE. I'm being questioned by a child.

(Lone returns to practicing; silence.)

MA. Look, Lone, I'll come up here every night—after work—I'll spend my time practicing, okay? (Pause.) But I'm not gonna say that they're dead. Look at them. They're on strike; dead men don't go on strike, Lone. The white devils—they try and stick us with a ten-hour day. We want a return to eight hours and also a fourteen-dollar-a-month raise. I learned the demon English—listen: "Eight hour a day good for white man, all same good for ChinaMan." These are the demands of live ChinaMen, Lone. Dead men don't complain.
LONE. All right, this is something new. But no one can judge the ChinaMen till after the strike.
MA. They say we'll hold out for months if we have to. The smart men will live on what we've hoarded.
LONE. A ChinaMan's mouth can swallow the earth. (He takes the dice.) While the strike is on, I'll teach you.
MA. And afterwards?
LONE. Afterwards—we'll decide then whether these are dead or live men.
MA. When can we start?
LONE. We've already begun. Give me your hand.

SCENE THREE

(Lone and Ma are doing physical exercises.)

MA. How long will it be before I can play Gwan Gung?

LONE. How long before a dog can play the violin?
MA. Old Ah Hong—have you heard him play the violin?
LONE. Yes. Now he should take his violin and give it to a dog.
MA. I think he sounds okay.
LONE. I think he caused that avalanche last winter.
MA. He used to play for weddings back home.
LONE. Ah Hong?
MA. That's what he said.
LONE. You probably heard wrong.
MA. No.
LONE. He probably said he played for funerals.
MA. He's been playing for the guys down at camp.
LONE. He should play for the white devils—that will end this stupid strike.
MA. Yang told me for sure—it'll be over by tomorrow.
LONE. Eight days already. And Yang doesn't know anything.
MA. He said they're already down to an eight-hour day and five dollars raise at the bargaining sessions.
LONE. Yang eats too much opium.
MA. That doesn't mean he's wrong about this.
LONE. You can't trust him. One time—last year—he went around camp looking in everybody's eyes and saying, "Your nails are too long. They're hurting my eyes." This went on for a week. Finally, all the men clipped their nails, made a big pile, which they wrapped in leaves and gave to him. Yang used the nails to season his food—he put it in his soup, sprinkled it on his rice, and never said a word about it again. Now tell me—are you going to trust a man who eats other men's fingernails?
MA. Well, all I know is we won't go back to work until they meet all our demands. Listen, teach me some Gwan Gung steps.
LONE. I should have expected this. A boy who wants to have twenty wives is the type who demands more than he can handle.
MA. Just a few.
LONE. It takes years before an actor can play Gwan Gung.
MA. I can do it. I spend a lot of time watching the opera when it comes around. Every time I see Gwan Gung, I say, "Yeah. That's me. The god of fighters. The god of adventurers. We have the same kind of spirit."
LONE. I tell you, if you work very hard, when you return to China, you can perhaps be the Second Clown.
MA. Second Clown?
LONE. If you work hard.
MA. What's the Second Clown?
LONE. You can play the p'i p'a, and dance and jump all over.
MA. I'll buy them.
LONE. Excuse me?
MA. I'm going to be rich, remember? I'll buy a troupe and force them to let me play Gwan Gung.
LONE. I hope you have enough money, then, to pay audiences to sit through your show.
MA. You mean, I'm going to have to practice here every night—and in return, all I can play is the Second Clown?

LONE. If you work hard.

MA. Am I that bad? Maybe I shouldn't even try to do this. Maybe I should just go down.

LONE. It's not you. Everyone must earn the right to play Gwan Gung. I entered Opera school when I was ten years old. My parents decided to sell me for ten years to this Opera company. I lived with eighty other boys and we slept in bunks four beds high and hid our candy and rice cakes from each other. After eight years, I was studying to play Gwan Gung.

MA. Eight years?

LONE. I was one of the best in my class. One day, I was summoned by my master, who told me I was to go home for two days, because my mother had fallen very ill and was dying. When I arrived home, Mother was standing at the door waiting, not sick at all. Her first words to me, the son away for eight years, were, "You've been playing while your village has starved. You must go to the Gold Mountain and work."

MA. And you never returned to school?

LONE. I went from a room with eighty boys to a ship with three hundred men. So, you see, it does not come easily to play Gwan Gung.

MA. Did you want to play Gwan Gung?

LONE. What a foolish question!

MA. Well, you're better off this way.

LONE. What?

MA. Actors—they don't make much money. Here, you make a bundle, then go back and be an actor again. Best of both worlds.

LONE. "Best of both worlds."

MA. Yeah!

(Lone drops to the floor, begins imitating a duck, waddling and quacking.)

MA. Lone? What are you doing? *(Lone quacks)* You're a duck? *(Lone quacks)* I can see that. *(Lone quacks)* Is this an exercise? Am I supposed to do this? *(Lone quacks)* This is dumb. I never seen Gwan Gung waddle. *(Lone quacks)* Okay. All right I'll do it. *(Ma and Lone quack and waddle)* You know, I never realized before how uncomfortable a duck's life is. And you have to listen to yourself quacking all day. Go crazy! *(Lone stands up straight)* Now, what was that all about?

LONE. No, no. Stay down there, duck.

MA. What's the—

LONE *(prompting)*. Quack, quack, quack.

MA. I don't—

LONE. Act your species!

MA. I'm not a duck!

LONE. Nothing worse than a duck that doesn't know his place.

MA. All right. *(Mechanically)* Quack, quack.

LONE. More.

MA. Quack.

LONE. More!

MA. Quack, quack, quack!

(Ma now continues quacking, as Lone gives commands.)

LONE. Louder! It's your mating call! Think of your twenty duck wives! Good! Louder! Project! More! Don't slow down! Put your tail feathers into it! They can't hear you!

(Ma is now quacking up a storm. Lone exits, unnoticed by Ma)

MA. Quack! Quack! Quack! Quack. Quack . . . quack. *(He looks around)* Quack . . . quack . . . Lone? . . . Lone? *(He waddles around the stage looking)* Lone, where are you? Where'd you go? *(He stops, scratches his left leg with his right foot)* C'mon—stop playing around. What is this? *(Lone enters as a tiger, unseen by Ma)* Look, let's call it a day, okay? I'm getting hungry. *(Ma turns around, notices Lone right before Lone is to bite him)* Aaaaah! Quack, quack, quack!

(They face off, in character as animals. Duck-Ma is terrified.)

LONE. Grrrr!

MA *(as a cry for help)*. Quack, quack, quack!

(Lone pounces on Ma. They struggle, in character. Ma is quacking madly, eyes tightly closed. Lone stands up straight. Ma continues to quack)

LONE. Stand up.

MA *(Eyes still closed)*. Quack, quack, quack!

LONE *(Louder)*. Stand up!

MA *(opening his eyes)*. Oh.

LONE. What are you?

MA. Huh?

LONE. A ChinaMan or a duck?

MA. Huh? Gimme a second to remember.

LONE. You like being a duck?

MA. My feet fell asleep.

LONE. You change forms so easily.

MA. You said to.

LONE. What else could you turn into?

MA. Well, you scared me—sneaking up like that.

LONE. Perhaps a rock. That would be useful. When the men need to rest, they can sit on you.

MA. I got carried away.

LONE. Let's try . . . a locust. Can you become a locust?

MA. No. Let's cut this, okay?

LONE. Here. It's easy. You just have to know how to hop.

MA. You're not gonna get me—

LONE. Like this.

(He demonstrates.)

MA. Forget it, Lone.

LONE. I'm a locust.

(He begins jumping towards Ma)

MA. Hey! Get away!

LONE. I devour whole fields.

MA. Stop it.

LONE. I starve babies before they are born.

MA. Hey look, stop it!

LONE. I cause famines and destroy villages.

MA. I'm warning you! Get away!

LONE. What are you going to do? You can't kill a locust.

MA. You're not a locust.

LONE. You kill one, and another sits on your hand.

MA. Stop following me.

LONE. Locusts always trouble people. If not, we'd feel useless. Now, if you become a locust, too . . .

MA. I'm not going to become a locust.

LONE. Just stick your teeth! Out!

MA. I'm not gonna be a bug! It's stupid!

LONE. No man who's just been a duck has the right to call anything stupid.

MA. I thought you were trying to teach me something.

LONE. I am. Go ahead.

MA. All right. There. That look right?

LONE. Your legs should be a little lower. Lower! There. That's adequate. So, how does it feel to be a locust?

(Lone gets up.)

MA. I dunno. How long do I have to do this?

LONE. Could you do it for three years?

MA. Three years? Don't be—

LONE. You couldn't, could you? Could you be a duck for that long?

MA. Look, I wasn't born to be either of those.

LONE. Exactly. Well, I wasn't born to work on a railroad, either. "Best of both worlds." How can you be such an insect?

(Pause.)

MA. Lone . . .

LONE. Stay down there! Don't move! I've never told anyone my story—the story of my parents kidnapping me from school. All the time we were crossing the ocean, the last two years here—I've kept my mouth shut. To you, I finally tell it. And all you can say is, "Best of both worlds." You're a bug to me, a locust. You think you understand the dedication one must have to be in the opera? You think it's the same as working on a railroad.

MA. Lone, all I was saying is that you'll go back too, and—

LONE. You're no longer a student of mine.

MA. What?

LONE. You have no dedication.

MA. Lone, I'm sorry.

LONE. Get up.

MA. I'm honored that you told me that.

LONE. Get up.

MA. No.

LONE. No?

MA. I don't want to. I want to talk.

LONE. Well, I've learned from the past. You're stubborn. You don't go. All right. Stay there. If you want to prove to me that you're dedicated, be a locust 'til morning. I'll go.

MA. Lone, I'm really honored that you told me.

LONE. I'll return in the morning.

(Exits.)

MA. Lone? Lone, that's ridiculous. You think I'm gonna stay like this? If you do, you're crazy. Lone? Come back here.

SCENE FOUR

(Night. Ma, alone, as a locust.)

MA. Locusts travel in huge swarms, so large that when they cross the sky, they block out the sun, like a storm. Second Uncle—back home—when he was a young man, his whole crop got wiped out by locusts one year. In the famine that followed, Second Uncle lost his eldest son and his second wife—the one he married for love. Even to this day, we look around before saying the word "locust"—to make sure Second Uncle is out of hearing range. About eight years ago, my brother and I discovered Second Uncle's cave in back of the stream near our house. We saw him come out of it one day around noon. Later, just before the sun went down, we sneaked in. We only looked once. Inside, there must have been hundreds—maybe five hundred or more—grasshoppers in huge bamboo cages—and around them—stacks of grasshopper legs, grasshopper heads, grasshopper antennae, grasshoppers with one leg still trying to hop but toppling like trees coughing, grasshoppers wrapped around sharp branches rolling from side to side, grasshopper legs cut off grasshopper bodies then tied around grasshoppers and tightened till grasshoppers died. Every conceivable kind of grasshopper in every conceivable stage of life and death, subject to every conceivable grasshopper torture. We ran out quickly, my brother and I—we knew an evil place by the thickness of the air. Now, I think of Second Uncle. How sad that the locusts forced him to take out his agony on innocent grasshoppers. What if Second Uncle could see me now? Would he cut off my legs? He might as well. I can barely feel them. But then again, Second Uncle never tortured actual locusts, just weak grasshoppers.

SCENE FIVE

Night. Ma still as a locust.

LONE (*off, singing*).
    "Hit your hardest,

Pound out your tears.
The more you try,
The more you'll cry
At how little I've moved
And how large I loom
By the time the sun goes down."

MA. You look rested.

LONE. Me?

MA. Well, you sound rested.

LONE. No, not at all.

MA. Maybe I'm just comparing you to me.

LONE. I didn't even close my eyes all last night.

MA. Aw, Lone, you didn't have to stay up for me. You coulda just come up here and—

LONE. For you?

MA. —apologized and everything woulda' been—

LONE. I didn't stay up for you.

MA. Huh? You didn't?

LONE. No.

MA. Oh. You sure?

LONE. Positive. I was thinking, that's all.

MA. About me?

LONE. Well . . .

MA. Even a little?

LONE. I was thinking about the ChinaMen—and you. Get up, Ma.

MA. Aw, do I have to? I've gotten to know these grasshoppers real well.

LONE. Get up. I have a lot to tell you.

MA. What'll they think? They take me in even though I'm a little large, then they find out I'm a human being. I stepped on their kids. No trust. Gimme a hand, will you? (*Lone helps Ma up, but Ma's legs can't support him.*) Aw, shit. My legs are coming off.

(*He lies down and tries to straighten them out.*)

LONE. I have many surprises. First, you will play Gwan Gung.

MA. My legs will be sent home without me. What'll my family think? Come to port to meet me, and all they get is two legs.

LONE. Did you hear me?

MA. Hold on. I can't be in agony and listen to Chinese at the same time.

LONE. Did you hear my first surprise?

MA. No. I'm too busy screaming.

LONE. I said, you'll play Gwan Gung.

MA. Gwan Gung?

LONE. Yes.

MA. Me?

LONE. Yes.

MA. Without legs?

LONE. What?

MA. That might be good.

LONE. Stop that!

MA. I'll become a legend. Like the blind man who defended Amoy.

LONE. Did you hear?

MA. "The legless man who played Gwan Gung."

LONE. Isn't that what you want? To play Gwan Gung?

MA. No, I just wanna sleep.

LONE. No, you don't. Look. Here. I brought you something.

MA. Food?

LONE. Here. Some rice.

MA. Thanks, Lone. And duck?

LONE. Just a little.

MA. Where'd you get the duck?

LONE. Just bones and skin.

MA. We don't have duck. And the white devils have been blockading the food.

LONE. Sing—he had some left over.

MA. Sing? That thief?

LONE. And something to go with it.

MA. What? Lone, where did you find whiskey?

LONE. You know, Sing—he has almost anything.

MA. Yeah. For a price.

LONE. Once, even some thousand-day-old eggs.

MA. He's a thief. That's what they told me.

LONE. Not if you're his friend.

MA. Sing don't have any real friends. Everyone talks about him bein' tied in to the head of the klan in San Francisco. Lone, you didn't have to do this. Here. Have some.

LONE. I had plenty.

MA. Don't gimme that. This cost you plenty, Lone.

LONE. Well, I thought if we were going to celebrate, we should do it as well as we would at home.

MA. Celebrate? What for? Wait.

LONE. Ma, the strike is over.

MA. Shit, I knew it. And we won, right?

LONE. Yes, the ChinaMen have won. They can do more than just talk.

MA. I told you. Didn't I tell you?

LONE. Yes. Yes, you did.

MA. Yang told me it was gonna be done. He said—

LONE. Yes, I remember.

MA. Didn't I tell you? Huh?

LONE. Ma, eat your duck.

MA. Nine days, we civilized the white devils. I knew it, I knew we'd hold out till their ears started twitching. So that's where you got the duck, right? At the celebration?

LONE. No, there wasn't a celebration.

MA. Huh? You sure? The ChinaMen—they look for any excuse to party.

LONE. But I thought *we* should celebrate.

MA. Well, that's for sure.

LONE. So you will play Gwan Gung.

MA. God, nine days. Shit, it's finally done. Well, we'll show them how to party. Make noise. Jump off rocks. Make the mountain shake.

LONE. We'll wash your body, to prepare you for the role.

MA. What role?

LONE. Gwan Gung. I've been telling you.

MA. I don't wanna play Gwan Gung.

LONE. You've shown the dedication required to become my student, so—

MA. Lone, you think I stayed up last night 'cause I wanted to play Gwan Gung?

LONE. You said you were like him.

MA. I am. Gwan Gung stayed up all night once to prove his loyalty. Well, now I have too. Lone, I'm honored that you told me your story.

LONE. Yes . . . That is like Gwan Gung.

MA. Good. So let's do an opera about *me*.

LONE. What?

MA. You wanna party or what?

LONE. About you?

MA. You said I was like Gwan Gung, didn't you?

LONE. Yes, but—

MA. Well, look at the operas he's got. I ain't even got one.

LONE. Still, you can't—

MA. You tell me, is that fair?

LONE. You can't do an opera about yourself.

MA. I just won a victory, didn't I? I deserve an opera in my honor.

LONE. But, it's not traditional.

MA. Traditional? Lone, you gotta figure any way I could do Gwan Gung wasn't gonna be traditional anyway. I may be as good a guy as him, but he's a better dancer. (*sings*)
Old Gwan Gung, just sits about
Til the dime-store fighters have had it out.
Then he pitches his peach pit
Combs his beard
Draws his sword
And they scatter in fear

LONE. What are you talking about?

MA. I just won a great victory. I get—whatcha call it?—po-etic license. C'mon. Hit the gongs. I'll immortalize my story.

LONE. I refuse. This goes against all my training. I try and give you your wish and—

MA. Do it. Gimme my wish. Hit the gongs.

LONE. I never—I can't.

MA. Can't what? Don't think I'm worth an opera? No. I guess not. I forgot—you think I'm just one of those dead men.

(*Silence. Lone pulls out a gong. Ma gets into position. Lone hits the gong. They do the following in a mock Chinese opera style.*)

MA. I am Ma. Yesterday, I was kicked out of my house by my three elder brothers, calling me the lazy dreamer of the family. I am sitting here in front of the temple trying to decide how I will avenge this indignity. Here comes the poorest beggar in this village. (*He cues Lone.*) He is called Fleaman because his body is the most popular meeting place for fleas from around the province.

LONE (*singing*).
Fleas in love
Find your happiness
In the gray scraps of my suit

MA. Hello, Flea—

LONE (*Continuing*).
Fleas in need,
Shield your families
In the gray hairs of my beard

MA. Hello, Flea—

(*Lone cuts Ma off, continues an extended improvised aria*)

MA. Hello, Fleaman.

LONE. Hello, Ma. Are you interested in providing a home for these fleas?

MA. No!

LONE. This couple here—seeking to start a new home. Housing today is so hard to find. How about your left arm.

MA. I may have plenty of my own fleas in time. I have been thrown out by my elder brothers.

LONE. Are you seeking revenge? A flea epidemic on your house? (*To a flea.*) Get back there. You should be asleep. Your mother will worry.

MA. Nothing would make my brothers angrier than seeing me rich.

LONE. Rich? After the bad crops of the last three years, even the fleas are thinking of moving north.

MA. I heard a white devil talk yesterday.

LONE. Oh—with hair the color of a sick chicken and eyes round as eggs? The fleas and I call him Chicken-Laying-an-Egg.

MA. He said we can make our fortunes on the Gold Mountain, where work is play and the sun scares off snow.

LONE. Don't listen to chicken-brains.

MA. Why not? He said gold grows like weeds.

LONE. I have heard that it is slavery.

MA. Slavery? What do you know, Fleaman? Who told you? The fleas? Yes, I will go to Gold Mountain.

(*Gongs. Ma strikes a submissive pose to Lone*)

LONE. "The one hundred twenty-five dollars passage money is to be paid to the said head of said Hong, who will make arrangements with the coolies, that their wages shall be deducted until the debt is absorbed."

(*Ma bows to Lone. Gongs. They pick up fighting sticks and do a water-crossing dance. Dance ends. They stoop next to each other and rock*)

MA. I have been in the bottom of this boat for thirty-six days now. Tang, how many have died?

LONE. Not me. I'll live through this ride.

MA. I didn't ask how you are.

LONE. But why's the Gold Mountain so far?

MA. We left with three hundred and three.

LONE. My family's depending on me.
MA. So tell me how many have died?
LONE. I'll be the last one alive.
MA. That's not what I wanted to know.
LONE. I'll find some fresh air in this hole.
MA. I asked, how many have died.
LONE. Is that a crack in the side?
MA. Are you listening to me?
LONE. If I had some air—
MA. I asked, don't you see—?
LONE. The crack—over there—
MA. Will you answer me please?
LONE. I need to get out.
MA. The rest here agree—
LONE. I can't stand the smell.
MA. That a hundred eighty—
LONE. I can't see the air.
MA. Of us will not see—
LONE. And I can't die.
MA. Our Gold Mountain dream.

(*Lone/Tang dies; Ma throws his body overboard. The boat docks. Ma exits, walks through the streets. He picks up one of the fighting sticks, while Lone becomes the mountain.*)

MA. I have been given my pickaxe. Now, I will attack the mountain.

(*Ma does a dance of labor. Lone sings.*)

LONE.
>Hit your hardest
>Pound out your tears
>The more you try
>The more you'll cry
>At how little I've moved
>And how large I loom
>By the time the sun goes down

(*Dance stops*)

MA. This Mountain is clever. But why shouldn't it be? It's fighting for its life, like we fight for ours.

(*The Mountain picks up a stick. Ma and the Mountain do a battle dance. The dance ends*)

MA. This mountain not only defends itself—it also attacks. It turns our strength against us.

(*Lone does Ma's labor dance, while Ma plants explosives in mid-air. Dance ends.*)

MA. The mountain has survived for millions of years. Its wisdom is immense.

(*Lone and Ma begin a second battle dance. This one ends with them working the battle sticks together. Lone breaks away, does a warrior strut*)

LONE. I am a white devil! Listen to my stupid language: "Wha che doo doo blah blah." Look at my wide eyes—like I have drunk seventy-two pots of tea. Look at my funny hair—twisting, turning, like a snake telling lies. (*To Ma.*) Bla bla doo doo tee tee.
MA. We don't understand English.
LONE (*angry*). Bla bla doo doo tee tee!
MA (*with Chinese accent*). Please you-ah speak-ah Chinese?
LONE. Oh. Work—uh—one—two—more—work—two—
MA. Two hours more? Stupid demons. As confused as your hair. We will strike!

(*Gongs. Ma is on strike*)

MA (*in broken English*). Eight hours day good for white man, alla same good for ChinaMan.
LONE. The strike is over! We've won!
MA. I knew we would.
LONE. We forced the white devil to act civilized.
MA. Tame the barbarians!
LONE. Did you think—
MA. Who woulda thought?
LONE. —it could be done?
MA. Who?
LONE. But who?
MA. Who could tame them?
MA AND LONE. Only a ChinaMan?

(*They laugh.*)

LONE. Well, c'mon.
MA. Let's celebrate!
LONE. We have.
MA. Oh.
LONE. Back to work.
MA. But we've won the strike.
LONE. I know. Congratulations. And now—
MA. —back to work?
LONE. Right.
MA. No.
LONE. But the strike is over.

(*Lone tosses Ma a stick; they resume their stick battle as before, but Ma is heard over Lone's singing.*)

LONE.	MA.
Hit your hardest,	Wait.
Pound out your	I'm tired of this!
tears.	How do we end it?
The more you try,	Let's stop now, all
The more you'll cry	right?
At how little I've	Look, I said enough!
moved	
And how large I	
loom	
By the time the	
sun goes down.	

(Ma tosses his stick away, but Lone is already aiming a blow towards it, so that Lone hits Ma instead and knocks him down)

MA. Oh! Shit . . .

LONE. I'm sorry! Are you all right?

MA. Yeah. I guess.

LONE. Why'd you let go? You can't just do that.

MA. I'm bleeding.

LONE. That was stupid—where?

MA. Here.

LONE. No.

MA. Ow!

LONE. There will probably be a bump.

MA. I dunno.

LONE. What?

MA. I dunno why I let go.

LONE. It was stupid.

MA. But how were we going to end the opera?

LONE. Here. *(He applies whiskey to Ma's bruise.)* I don't know.

MA. Why didn't we just end it with the celebration? Ow! Careful.

LONE. Sorry. But Ma, the celebration's not the end. We're returning to work. Today. At dawn.

MA. What?

LONE. We've already lost nine days of work. But we got eight hours.

MA. Today? That's terrible.

LONE. What do you think we're here for? But they listened to our demands. We're getting a raise.

MA. Right. Fourteen dollars.

LONE. No. Eight.

MA. What?

LONE. We had to compromise. We got an eight dollar raise.

MA. But we wanted fourteen! Why didn't we get fourteen?

LONE. It was the best deal they could get. Congratulations.

MA. Congratulations? Look, Lone, I'm sick of you making fun of the ChinaMen.

LONE. Ma, I'm not. For the first time. I was wrong. We got eight dollars.

MA. We wanted fourteen.

LONE. But we got eight hours.

MA. We'll go back on strike.

LONE. Why?

MA. We could hold out for months.

LONE. And lose all that work?

MA. But we just gave in.

LONE. You're being ridiculous. We got eight hours. Besides, it's already been decided.

MA. I didn't decide. I wasn't there. You made me stay up here.

LONE. The heads of the gangs decide.

MA. And that's it?

LONE. It's done.

MA. Back to work? That's what they decided? Lone, I don't want to go back to work.

LONE. Who does?

MA. I forgot what it's like.

LONE. You'll pick up the technique again soon enough.

MA. I mean, what it's like to have them telling you what to do all the time. Using up your strength.

LONE. I thought you said even after work, you still feel good.

MA. Some days. But others . . . *(Pause)* I get so frustrated sometimes. At the rock. The rock doesn't give in. It's not human. I wanna claw it with my fingers, but that would just rip them up. I wanna throw myself head first onto it, but it'd just knock my skull open. The rock would knock my skull open, then just sit there, smiling, still, like nothing had happened like a faceless Buddha. *(Pause)* Lone, when do I get out of here?

LONE. Well, the railroad may get finished—

MA. It'll never get finished.

LONE. — or you may get rich.

MA. Rich. Right. This is the Gold Mountain. *(Pause)* Lone, has anyone ever gone home rich from here?

LONE. Yes. Some.

MA. But most?

LONE. Most . . . do go home.

MA. Do you still have the fear?

LONE. The fear?

MA. That you'll become like them—dead men?

LONE. Maybe I was wrong about them.

MA. Well, I do. You wanted me to say it before, I can say it now: "They are dead men." Their greatest accomplishment was to win a strike that's gotten us nothing.

LONE. They're sending money home.

MA. No.

LONE. It's not much, I know, but it's something.

MA. Lone, I'm not even doing that. If I don't get rich here, I might as well die here. Let my brothers laugh in peace.

LONE. Ma, you're too soft to get rich here, naïve—you believed the snow was warm.

MA. I've got to change myself. Toughen up. Take no shit. Count my change. Learn to gamble. Learn to win. Learn to stare. Learn to deny. Learn to look at men with opaque eyes.

LONE. You want to do that?

MA. I will. 'Cause I've got the fear. You've given it to me.

(Pause)

LONE. Will I see you here tonight?

MA. Tonight?

LONE. I just thought I'd ask.

MA. I'm sorry, Lone. I haven't got time to be the Second Clown.

LONE. I thought you might not.

MA. Sorry.

LONE. You could have been a . . . fair actor.

MA. You coming down? I gotta get ready for work. This is gonna be a terrible day. My legs are sore and my arms are outa practice.

LONE. You go first. I'm going to practice some before work. There's still time.

MA. Practice? But you said you lost your fear. And you said that's what brings you up here.

LONE. I guess I was wrong about that, too. Today, I am dancing for no reason at all.

MA. Do whatever you want. See you down at camp.

LONE. Could you do me a favor?

MA. A favor?

LONE. Could you take this down so I don't have to take it all?

(Lone points to a pile of props)

MA. Well, okay. (*Pause*) But this is the last time.

LONE. Of course, Ma. (*Ma exits*) See you soon. The last time. I suppose so.

(Lone resumes practicing. He twirls his hair around as in the beginning of the play. The sun begins to rise. It continues rising until Lone is moving and seen only in shadow.)

TOP GIRLS

CARYL CHURCHILL

CARYL CHURCHILL (1938 –)

Caryl Churchill is the most frequently produced and critically admired female playwright of our time. She has written for several of England's most prestigious political theaters, primarily the Royal Court, the wellspring of contemporary British drama. She has also been affiliated with 7:84 Theater Company (whose name refers to the fact that 7 percent of Britain's population controls 84 percent of its wealth), Joint Stock, and Monstrous Regiment, a major feminist company. In America, her works have been produced by Joseph Papp's Public Theater (the American counterpart to the Royal Court) and with regularity in Off- and Off-Off-Broadway theaters. The production of *Top Girls*, for instance, won several Obie Awards in 1982 as the year's best Off-Broadway work.

Born in London, Churchill lived in Montreal, Canada, from 1949 to 1956, then returned to England to study at Oxford University. Though her primary field was English literature (which she uses frequently as source material for her works), Churchill was introduced to Buddhism and other Eastern religions such as Taoism, Jainism, and Hinduism at Oxford. Eastern philosophy and spirituality have influenced not only the themes of her plays (e.g., illusions, historical cycles, the transcendental nature of personality), but their very structure, as illustrated in *Top Girls*, where time is manipulated freely and is not bound by Western logic.

Churchill wrote several plays at Oxford, then several admired radio dramas in the 1960s, and in 1972 her first commercial stage play, *Owners*, was produced. Not until 1979, however, did she receive international recognition, for *Cloud Nine*, which was written as part of a collective exploration of sexual identities for the Joint Stock Company. Produced by the Royal Court in 1979, it subsequently played in New York and other theater capitals. Her best works include *Vinegar Tom* (1977), *Top Girls* (1982), *Fen* (1983), *Softcops* (1984), and *Serious Money* (1987).

Although she is generally accepted as the world's foremost feminist playwright, Churchill describes herself as a socialist writer first who only later adopted the feminist cause. She now describes herself as a "socialist-feminist," noting that although "socialism and feminism aren't synonymous . . . I feel strongly about both and wouldn't be interested in a form of one that didn't include the other." Though her later plays deal with feminist issues, they are equally bound by her critique of Western society, which she feels exploits its weakest individuals for monetary and political gain. Her plays often explore the friction between the "old world" colonial system and the new, pluralistic world in which women, gays, and non-Caucasians strive to overcome the strictures imposed by the old.

Not suprisingly, Churchill has adopted—and expanded on—many techniques associated with Brecht, himself a socialist who used the theater to advance his ideology. Like Brecht, Churchill writes plays that thrive on dialectical arguments that are often "historicized" to challenge modern assumptions about social, political, and economic issues. Act 1 of *Cloud Nine*, for instance, is set in a nineteenth-century British colonial outpost; in act 2, both the characters and the play's issues are hurtled into the late twentieth century. *Serious Money* is written as a mock Restoration comedy in rhymed couplets, but set amid contemporary financial centers. *Top Girls*, perhaps Churchill's most innovative use of historification, opens with famous women of history and myth dining in a modern restaurant with a newly promoted executive of a personnel agency. The play's final scene takes place a year *prior* to the first scene, as Churchill boldly manipulates time to force her audience to confront the play's "frightening" issues.

Churchill often supersedes Brecht's techniques, particularly in her use of social *gestus* as the foundation of an actor's character. Not only does Churchill typically assign multiple roles to actors (as in *Top Girls*), she frequently specifies cross-gender casting (most notably in *Cloud Nine*) to undermine our preconceptions about sexual roles in society by naturally "alienating" actors from their characters. Churchill wittily illustrates that history itself does this—note that Pope Joan in *Top Girls* is the ultimate example of cross-gender casting. In Churchill's boldly theatrical world, disorientation rules to shake audiences from their bourgeois complacency. "Confusing" is a word often applied to her works by naïve critics—but confusion about time and history, sex and gender, and literary style itself is calculated to provoke the audience to find clarity in a world that confuses power and wealth with natural superiority.

Top Girls (1982)

Here we find a decidedly feminist play—yet it satirically indicts much of the feminist movement. Here we meet women, both modern and historical, who appear to exemplify the "successful" woman—yet each is revealed as flawed, thus diminishing whatever admiration we first felt. The play opens with a fantasy about the past—yet it ends with a flashback that is an ironic preview of the future. Between these surreal sequences, Churchill scripts essentially realistic scenes from a contemporary society in which the only way to get ahead—for man and woman alike—is to "play the game" ruthlessly. This free mixture of historical periods, contrary ideologies, and assorted theatrical styles is, of course, typical of postmodern dramaturgy, and *Top Girls* represents some of the finest impulses of contemporary experimental drama. More importantly, the meaning of Churchill's play is best found in its provocative contradictions.

The play begins in that most mundane of modern meeting places—the chic restaurant (aptly named La Prima Donna) known for its Frascati wine and avocado vinaigrette. Into this world comes Marlene, the successful woman, newly appointed to an executive position in the Top Girls Employment Agency (where, ironically, women are "ordered up" like items on the restaurant's menu). Note, by the way, that Marlene is the only role that is not subsequently "doubled"; she is unalterably the prototype of the late-twentieth-century liberated woman. In a mood to celebrate, Marlene meets five celebrated women: Isabella Bird, the noted Victorian explorer who liberated herself from home and hearth as she trekked across the world; Lady Nijo, a medieval Japanese concubine who became a Buddhist nun; Dull Gret, an ax-wielding revolutionary from a Breughel canvas; Pope Joan, an actual woman who disguised herself as a man to ascend to the papacy in the ninth century; and Patient Griselda, the heroine of Chaucer's *Clerk's Tale*.

Churchill wryly implies that Marlene's promotion is the modern woman's triumphant equivalent of the more grandiose exploits of her famous foresisters ("It's not the Pope, but it is the managing director," she says to aggrandize herself). Here the playwright is attacking what has been called bourgeois feminism, that is, the notion that women succeed only when they assume the power and wealth afforded men. Yet in subsequent scenes in the employment agency, we see that Marlene and her staff advise would-be employees to mute their feminine roles. More tellingly, Marlene denigrates her own sister (Joyce) and her "niece" (Angie) as being inferior because they have not risen above their class status or mental states (Marlene is especially cruel in her rejection of the slow-witted Angie; "She's not going to make it," she tells her sister). Thus, Marlene epitomizes, in effect, the very aspects of the male-dominated socioeconomic system condemned by socialists such as Churchill. Marlene is so comfortable in her position as a "top girl" (the sexual innuendo is thematically significant) that she cannot attempt to change the hierarchical and exploitive structure of the capitalist world. She has become one of the "old boys" who sustain the status quo by using, even abusing, others to get "on top."

Isabella, Lady Nijo, Pope Joan, and Dull Gret can be aligned with aggressive feminists who posit the superiority of the feminine principal—and feminine principles. Each has charted her own destiny in male-dominated worlds, and each has triumphed (more or less) over male prejudices. But, again ironically, each has done so primarily by assuming a male identity (symbolized by clothing), or in Isabella's case by sealing herself off from the world to the extent that she is neither man nor woman, but only a solitary Scot trekking across the world. As strong and successful as these women are, each is flawed: Isabella is devoid of human feeling (save for her rather conventional sister, whom she never sees) and she retains a colonialist's attitude of superiority ("Buddhism is really most uncomfortable"); Lady Nijo loves the "thin silk" too much and dismisses her dead child as "only a girl"; Pope Joan wants the trappings of the papacy but none of its responsibilities; and Dull Gret (who has raised ten children—and a pig) assaults the demons of hell not for herself or her oppressed "sisters," but to protect the men and children who made her daily existence a hell. Significantly, Patient Griselda is the last to arrive at the dinner party. She has sacrificed her children and her life, all to prove her fealty to her demanding and abusive husband. The rapid-fire dinner conversation (note that lines overlap contrapuntally to heighten Churchill's critique of the women) shows the women to be self-centered egotists who seem more interested in personal aggrandizement than in addressing the collective problems they face as women. Thus, when Marlene toasts the gathering—"to our courage and the way we changed our lives and our extraordinary achievements"—her words ring hollow. We note that by the end of the first scene all the the women are drunk (remember, Lady Nijo earlier mocks the men at court for being drunkards), and they are dutifully attended by the Waitress, a serving woman whose presence among these "top girls" is marked by an extraordinary silence.

Things are no better in the "real" world. Marlene's associates (Nell and Win) are supposed to represent the best that Top Girls has to offer; yet they thrive on banality and condescend to the women who seek employment (and empowerment). Marlene, we learn, has achieved her autonomy only by abandoning her roots and her literal and metaphorical sister(s). She spurns Angie as an unpleasant and unwanted memory of the past she tries to escape. Angie (quite appropriately played by the same actor who plays the battle-scarred Dull Gret) is socially maladjusted and homicidal, the by-product of that quintessential macho film, *The Exterminator*. Her best friend, Kit, we are assured, will make it because she has charm and beauty, the requisites of a "top girl" in the old patriarchal society. Only Joyce shows true heroism when she agrees to raise her sister's illegitimate child; she is motivated neither by economic nor material gain, but only by the will to do something "right" for her sister. Yet even Joyce is flawed; we might call her "Impatient Joyce" because of the way in which she wearily denigrates Angie in the ugliest of sexist terms ("fucking rotten little cunt"). Indeed, Churchill presents us with a "frightening" world, to borrow the play's last line.

While Churchill is clearly sympathetic to the plight of women, and while she knowingly writes for audiences conversant in feminist issues, she refuses to provide comfortable solutions to validate feminist beliefs. There is no preaching to the choir here. Rather, she raises questions, the answers to which may provide solutions to the greater problems created by outmoded systems in which women must become men—or at least male-like—to get "on top."

Dull Gret confronts a modern "top girl," Marlene, as Pope Joan and others look on; the New York Shakespeare Festival produced the American premiere of Caryl Churchill's play, Top Girls.

TOP GIRLS

CARYL CHURCHILL

CHARACTERS
MARLENE
WAITRESS/KIT/SHONA
ISABELLA BIRD/JOYCE/MRS. KIDD
LADY NIJO/WIN
DULL GRET/ANGIE
POPE JOAN/LOUISE
PATIENT GRISELDA/NELL/JEANINE

ACT I

Scene I: A Restaurant.
Scene II: Top Girls' Employment Agency, London.
Scene III: Joyce's backyard in Suffolk.

ACT II

Scene I: Top Girls' Employment Agency.
Scene II: A Year Earlier. Joyce's kitchen.

Production Note: *The seating order for Act I, Scene I in the original production at the Royal Court was (from right) Gret, Nijo, Marlene, Joan, Griselda, Isabella.*

THE CHARACTERS
ISABELLA BIRD (1831–1904): *Lived in Edinburgh, traveled extensively between the ages of forty and seventy.*
LADY NIJO (b. 1258): *Japanese, was an Emperor's courtesan and later a Buddhist nun who traveled on foot through Japan.*
DULL GRET: *Is the subject of the Brueghel painting Dulle Griet, in which a woman in an apron and armor leads a crowd of women charging through hell and fighting the devils.*
POPE JOAN: *Disguised as a man, is thought to have been pope between 854 and 856.*
PATIENT GRISELDA: *Is the obedient wife whose story is told by Chaucer in "The Clerk's Tale" of The Canterbury Tales.*

THE LAYOUT

A speech usually follows the one immediately before it but:

(1) *When one character starts speaking before the other has finished, the point of interruption is marked /. e.g.,*

ISABELLA. This is the Emperor of Japan? / I once met the Emperor of Morocco.
NIJO. In fact he was the ex-Emperor.

(2) *A character sometimes continues speaking right through another's speech, e.g.,*

ISABELLA. When I was forty I thought my life was over. / Oh I was pitiful. I was
NIJO. I didn't say I felt it for twenty years. Not every minute.
ISABELLA. sent on a cruise for my health and I felt even worse. Pains in my bones, pins and needles . . . etc.

(3) *Sometimes a speech follows on from a speech marked earlier than the one immediately before it, and continuity is marked*. e.g.,*

GRISELDA. I'd seen him riding by, we all had. And he'd seen me in the fields with the sheep.*
ISABELLA. I would have been well suited to minding sheep.
NIJO. And Mr. Nugent went riding by.
ISABELLA. Of course not, Nijo, I mean a healthy life in the open air.
JOAN. *He just rode up while you were minding the sheep and asked you to marry him?

where "in the fields with the sheep" is the cue to both "I would have been" and "He just rode up."

ACT I

SCENE I

(Restaurant. Saturday night. There is a table with a white cloth set for dinner with six places. The lights come up on Marlene and the Waitress.)

MARLENE. Excellent, yes, table for six. One of them's going to be late but we won't wait. I'd like a bottle of Frascati straight away if you've got one really cold. (*The Waitress goes. Isabella Bird arrives.*) Here we are, Isabella.
ISABELLA. Congratulations, my dear.
MARLENE. Well, it's a step. It makes for a party. I haven't time for a holiday. I'd like to go somewhere exotic like you but I can't get away. I don't know how you could bear to leave Hawaii. / I'd like to lie
ISABELLA. I did think of settling.
MARLENE. in the sun forever, except of course I can't bear sitting still.

ISABELLA. I sent for my sister Hennie to come and join me. I said, Hennie we'll live here forever and help the natives. You can buy two sirloins of beef for what a pound of chops costs in Edinburgh. And Hennie wrote back, the dear, that yes, she would come to Hawaii if I wished, but I said she had far better stay where she was. Hennie was suited to life in Tobermory.
MARLENE. Poor Hennie.
ISABELLA. Do you have a sister?
MARLENE. Yes in fact.
ISABELLA. Hennie was happy. She was good. I did miss its face, my own pet. But I couldn't stay in Scotland. I loathed the constant murk.

(Lady Nijo arrives)

MARLENE (*seeing her.*). Ah! Nijo! (*The Waitress enters with the wine.*)
NIJO. Marlene! (*To Isabella.*) So excited when Marlene told me / you were coming.
ISABELLA. I'm delighted / to meet you.
MARLENE. I think a drink while we wait for the others. I think a drink anyway. What a week. (*Marlene seats Nijo. The Waitress pours wine.*)
NIJO. It was always the men who used to get so drunk. I'd be one of the maidens, passing the sake.
ISABELLA. I've had sake.[1] Small hot drink. Quite fortifying after a day in the wet.
NIJO. One night my father proposed three rounds of three cups, which was normal, and then the Emperor should have said three rounds of three cups, but he said three rounds of nine cups, so you can imagine. Then the Emperor passed his sake cup to my father and said, "Let the wild goose come to me this spring."
MARLENE. Let the what?
NIJO. It's a literary allusion to a tenth-century epic, / His Majesty was very cultured.
ISABELLA. This is the Emperor of Japan? / I once met the Emperor of Morocco.
NIJO. In fact he was the ex-Emperor.
MARLENE. But he wasn't old? / Did you, Isabella?
NIJO. Twenty-nine.
ISABELLA. Oh it's a long story.
MARLENE. Twenty-nine's an excellent age.
NIJO. Well I was only fourteen and I knew he meant something but I didn't know what. He sent me an eight-layered gown and I sent it back. So when the time came I did nothing but cry. My thin gowns were badly ripped. But even that morning when he left / he'd a green
MARLENE. Are you saying he raped you.
NIJO. robe with a scarlet lining and very heavily embroidered trousers, I already felt different about him. It made me uneasy. No, of course not, Marlene, I belonged to

---

[1] **sake** a wine made from rice in Japan

him, it was what I was brought up for from a baby. I soon found I was sad if he stayed away. It was depressing day after day not knowing when he would come. I never enjoyed taking other women to him.

ISABELLA. I certainly never saw my father drunk. He was a clergyman. / And I didn't get married till I was fifty. (*The Waitress brings menus.*)

NIJO. Oh, my father was a very religious man. Just before he died he said to me, "Serve His Majesty, be respectful, if you lose his favour enter holy orders."

MARLENE. But he meant stay in a convent, not go wandering round the country.

NIJO. Priests were often vagrants, so why not a nun? You think I shouldn't? / I still did what my father wanted.

MARLENE. No, no, I think you should. / I think it was wonderful.

(*Dull Gret arrives.*)

ISABELLA. I tried to do what my father wanted.

MARLENE. Gret, good. Nijo. Gret / I know Griselda's going to be late, but should we wait for Joan? / Let's get you a drink.

ISABELLA. Hello Gret! (*She continues to* Nijo:) I tried to be a clergyman's daughter. Needlework, music, charitable schemes. I had a tumour removed from my spine and spent a great deal of time on the sofa. I studied the metaphysical poets and hymnology. / I thought I enjoyed intellectual pursuits.

NIJO. Ah, you like poetry. I come of a line of eight generations of poets. Father had a poem / in the anthology.

ISABELLA. My father taught me Latin although I was a girl. / But really I was

MARLENE. They didn't have Latin at my school.

ISABELLA. more suited to manual work. Cooking, washing, mending, riding horses. / Better than reading

NIJO. Oh but I'm sure you're very clever.

ISABELLA. books, eh Gret! A rough life in the open air.

NIJO. I can't say I enjoyed my rough life. What I enjoyed most was being the Emperor's favorite / and wearing thin silk.

ISABELLA. Did you have any horses, Gret?

GRET. Pig.

(*Pope Joan arrives.*)

MARLENE. Oh Joan, thank God, we can order. Do you know everyone? We were just talking about learning Latin and being clever girls. Joan was by way of an infant prodigy. Of course you were. What excited you when you were ten?

JOAN. Because angels are without matter they are not individuals. Every angel is a species.

MARLENE. There you are. (*They laugh. They look at menus.*)

ISABELLA. Yes, I forgot all my Latin. But my father was the mainspring of my life and when he died I was so grieved. I'll have the chicken, please, / and the soup.

NIJO. Of course you were grieved. My father was saying his prayers and he dozed off in the sun. So I touched his knee to rouse him. "I wonder what will happen," he said, and then he was dead before he finished the sentence. / If he'd

MARLENE. What a shock.

NIJO. died saying his prayers he would have gone straight to heaven. / Waldorf salad.

JOAN. Death is the return of all creatures to God.

NIJO. I shouldn't have woken him.

JOAN. Damnation only means ignorance of the truth. I was always attracted by the teachings of John the Scot, though he was inclined to confuse / God and the world.

ISABELLA. Grief always overwhelmed me at the time.

MARLENE. What I fancy is a rare steak. Gret?

ISABELLA. I am of course a member of the / Church of England.

MARLENE. Gret?

GRET. Potatoes.

MARLENE. I haven't been to church for years. / I like Christmas carols.

ISABELLA. Good works matter more than church attendance.

MARLENE. Make that two steaks and a lot of potatoes. Rare. But I don't do good works either.

JOAN. Canelloni, please, / and a salad.

ISABELLA. Well, I tried, but oh dear. Hennie did good works.

NIJO. The first half of my life was all sin and the second / all repentance.*

MARLENE. Oh what about starters?

GRET. Soup.

JOAN. *And which did you like best?

MARLENE. Were your travels just a penance? Avocado vinaigrette. Didn't you / enjoy yourself?

JOAN. Nothing to start with for me, thank you.

NIJO. Yes, but I was very unhappy. / It hurt to remember the past

MARLENE. And the wine list.

NIJO. I think that was repentance.

MARLENE. Well I wonder.

NIJO. I might have just been homesick.

MARLENE. Or angry.

NIJO. Not angry, no, / why angry?

GRET. Can we have some more bread?

MARLENE. Don't you get angry? I get angry.

NIJO. But what about?

MARLENE. Yes let's have two more Frascati. And some more bread, please. (*The Waitress exits.*)

ISABELLA. I tried to understand Buddhism when I was in Japan but all this birth and death succeeding each other through eternities just filled me with the most profound melancholy. I do like something more active.

NIJO. You couldn't say I was inactive. I walked every day for twenty years.

ISABELLA. I don't mean walking. / I mean in the head.

NIJO. I vowed to copy five Mahayana sutras. / Do you know how long they are?

MARLENE. I don't think religious beliefs are something we

have in common. Activity yes. (*Gret empties the bread basket into her apron.*)

NIJO. My head was active. / My head ached.

JOAN. It's no good being active in heresy.

ISABELLA. What heresy? She's calling the Church of England / a heresy.

JOAN. There are some very attractive / heresies.

NIJO. I had never heard of Christianity. Never / heard of it. Barbarians.

MARLENE. Well I'm not a Christian. / And I'm not a Buddhist.

ISABELLA. You have heard of it?

MARLENE. We don't all have to believe the same.

ISABELLA. I knew coming to dinner with a pope we should keep off religion.

JOAN. I always enjoy a theological argument. But I won't try to convert you, I'm not a missionary. Anyway I'm a heresy myself.

ISABELLA. There are some barbaric practices in the east.

NIJO. Barbaric?

ISABELLA. Among the lower classes.

NIJO. I wouldn't know.

ISABELLA. Well theology always made my head ache.

MARLENE. Oh good, some food. (*The Waitress brings the first course, serves it during the following, then exits.*)

NIJO. How else could I have left the court if I wasn't a nun? When father died I had only His Majesty. So when I fell out of favor I had nothing. Religion is a kind of nothing / and I dedicated what was left of me to nothing.

ISABELLA. That's what I mean about Buddhism. It doesn't brace.

MARLENE. Come on, Nijo, have some wine.

NIJO. Haven't you ever felt like that? You've all felt / like that. Nothing will ever happen again. I am dead already.

ISABELLA. You thought your life was over but it wasn't.

JOAN. You wish it was over.

GRET. Sad.

MARLENE. Yes, when I first came to London I sometimes . . . and when I got back from America I did. But only for a few hours. Not twenty years.

ISABELLA. When I was forty I thought my life was over. / Oh I was pitiful. I was sent

NIJO. I didn't say I felt it for twenty years. Not every minute.

ISABELLA. on a cruise for my health and I felt even worse. Pains in my bones, pins and needles in my hands, swelling behind the ears, and—oh, stupidity. I shook all over, indefinable terror. And Australia seemed to me a hideous country, the acacias stank like drains. / I

NIJO. You were homesick. (*Gret steals a bottle of wine.*)

ISABELLA. had a photograph taken for Hennie but I told her I wouldn't send it, my hair had fallen out and my clothes were crooked, I looked completely insane and suicidal.

NIJO. So did I, exactly, dressed as a nun. I was wearing walking shoes for the first time.

ISABELLA. I longed to go home, / but home to what? Houses are perfectly dismal.*

NIJO. I longed to go back ten years.

MARLENE. *I thought travelling cheered you both up.

ISABELLA. Oh it did / of course. It was on

NIJO. I'm not a cheerful person, Marlene. I just laugh a lot.

ISABELLA. the trip from Australia to the Sandwich Isles, I fell in love with the sea. There were rats in the cabin and ants in the food but suddenly it was like a new world. I woke up every morning happy, knowing there would be nothing to annoy me. No nervousness. No dressing.

NIJO. Don't you like getting dressed? I adored my clothes. / When I was chosen

MARLENE. You had prettier colours than Isabella.

NIJO. to give sake to His Majesty's brother, the Emperor Kameyana, on his formal visit, I wore raw silk pleated trousers and a seven-layered gown in shades of red, and two outer garments, / yellow lined with green

MARLENE. Yes, all that silk must have been very—

(*The Waitress enters, clears the first course and exits.*)

JOAN. I dressed as a boy when I left home.*

NIJO. and a light green jacket. Lady Betto had a five-layered gown in shades of green and purple.

ISABELLA. *You dressed as a boy?

MARLENE. Of course, / for safety.

JOAN. It was easy, I was only twelve. / Also women weren't allowed in the library. We wanted to study in Athens.

MARLENE. You ran away alone?

JOAN. No, not alone, I went with my friend. / He was

NIJO. Ah, an elopement.

JOAN. sixteen but I thought I knew more science than he did and almost as much philosophy.

ISABELLA. Well I always traveled as a lady and I repudiated strongly any suggestion in the press that I was other than feminine.

MARLENE. I don't wear trousers in the office. / I could but I don't.

ISABELLA. There was no great danger to a woman of my age and appearance.

MARLENE. And you got away with it, Joan?

JOAN. I did then. (*The Waitress brings the main course.*)

MARLENE. And nobody noticed anything?

JOAN. They noticed I was a very clever boy. / And

MARLENE. I couldn't have kept pretending for so long.

JOAN. when I shared a bed with my friend, that was ordinary—two poor students in a lodging house. I think I forgot I was pretending.

ISABELLA. Rocky Mountain Jim, Mr Nugent, showed me no disrespect. He found it interesting, I think, that I could make scones and also lasso cattle. Indeed he declared his love for me, which was most distressing.

NIJO. What did he say? / We always sent poems first.

MARLENE. What did you say?

ISABELLA. I urged him to give up whisky, / but he said it was too late.

MARLENE. Oh Isabella.

ISABELLA. He had lived alone in the mountains for many years.

MARLENE. But did you—? (*The Waitress goes.*)

ISABELLA. Mr Nugent was a man that any woman might love but none could marry. I came back to England.

NIJO. Did you write him a poem when you left? / Snow on the mountains. My sleeves

MARLENE. Did you never seen him again?

ISABELLA. No, never.

NIJO. are wet with tears. In England no tears, no snow.

ISABELLA. Well, I say never. One morning very early in Switzerland, it was a year later, I had a vision of him as I last saw him / in his trapper's clothes with his

NIJO. A ghost!

ISABELLA. hair round his face, and that was the day, / I learnt later, he died with a

NIJO. Ah!

ISABELLA. bullet in his brain. / He just bowed to me and vanished.

MARLENE. Oh Isabella.

NIJO. When your lover dies—One of my lovers died. / The priest Ariake.

JOAN. My friend died. Have we all got dead lovers?

MARLENE. Not me, sorry.

NIJO (*to Isabella*). I wasn't a nun, I was still at court, but he was a priest, and when he came to me he dedicated his whole life to hell. / He knew that when he died he would fall into one of the three lower realms. And he died, he did die.

JOAN (*to Marlene*). I'd quarrelled with him over the teachings of John the Scot, who held that our ignorance of God is the same as his ignorance of himself. He only knows what he creates because he creates everything he knows but he himself is above being— do you follow?

MARLENE. No, but go on.

NIJO. I couldn't bear to think / in what shape would he be reborn.*

JOAN. St. Augustine maintained that the Neo-Platonic Ideas are indivisible

ISABELLA. *Buddhism is really most uncomfortable.

JOAN. from God, but I agreed with John that the created world is essences derived from Ideas which derived from God. As Denys the Areopagite said—the pseudo-Denys—first we give God a name, then deny it / then reconcile the contradition

NIJO. In what shape would he return?

JOAN. by looking beyond / those terms—

MARLENE. Sorry, what? Denys said what?

JOAN. Well we disagreed about it, we quarrelled. And next day he was ill, / I was so annoyed with him,

NIJO. Misery in this life and worse in the next, all because of me.

JOAN. all the time I was nursing him I kept going over the arguments in my mind. Matter is not a means of knowing the essence. The source of the species is the Idea. But then I realised he'd never understand my arguments again, and that night he died. John the Scot held that the individual disintegrates / and there is no personal immortality.

ISABELLA. I wouldn't have you think I was in love with Jim Nugent. It was yearning to save him that I felt.

MARLENE (*to Joan*). So what did you do?

JOAN. First I decided to stay a man. I was used to it. And I wanted to devote my life to learning. Do you know why I went to Rome? Italian men didn't have beards.

ISABELLA. The loves of my life were Hennie, my own pet, and my dear husband the doctor, who nursed Hennie in her last illness. I knew it would be terrible when Hennie died but I didn't know how terrible. I felt half of myself had gone. How could I go on my travels without that sweet soul waiting at home for my letters? It was Doctor Bishop's devotion to her in her last illness that made me decide to marry him. He and Hennie had the same sweet character. I had not.

NIJO. I thought his majesty had sweet character because when he found out about Ariake he was so kind. But really it was because he no longer cared for me. One night he even sent me out to a man who had been pursuing me. / He lay awake on the other side of the screens and listened.

ISABELLA. I did wish marriage had seemed more of a step. I tried very hard to cope with the ordinary drudgery of life. I was ill again with carbuncles on the spine and nervous prostration. I ordered a tricycle, that was my idea of adventure then. And John himself fell ill, with erysipelas and anemia. I began to love him with my whole heart but it was too late. He was a skeleton with transparent white hands. I wheeled him on various seafronts in a bathchair. And he faded and left me. There was nothing in my life. The doctors said I had gout / and my heart was much affected.

NIJO. There was nothing in my life, nothing, without the Emperor's favor. The Empress had always been my enemy, Marlene, she said I had no right to wear three-layered gowns. / But I was the adopted daughter of my grandfather the Prime Minister. I had been publicly granted permission to wear thin silk.

JOAN. There was nothing in my life except my studies. I was obsessed with pursuit of the truth. I taught at the Greek School in Rome, which St. Augustine had made famous. I was poor, I worked hard. I spoke apparently brilliantly, I was still very young, I was a stranger; suddenly I was quite famous, I was everyone's favorite. Huge crowds came to hear me. The day after they made me cardinal I fell ill and lay two weeks without speaking, full of terror and regret. / But then I got up determined to

MARLENE. Yes, success is very . . .

JOAN. go on. I was seized again / with a desperate longing for the absolute.

ISABELLA. Yes, yes, to go on. I sat in Tobermory among Hennie's flowers and sewed a complete outfit in Jaeger flannel. / I was fifty-six years old.

NIJO. Out of favor but I didn't die. I left on foot, nobody saw me go. For the next twenty years I walked through Japan.

GRET. Walking is good. (*Meanwhile, the Waitress enters, pours lots of wine, then shows Marlene the empty bottle.*)

JOAN. Pope Leo died and I was chosen. All right then. I would be Pope. I would know God. I would know everything.

ISABELLA. I determined to leave my grief behind and set off for Tibet.

MARLENE. Magnificent all of you. We need some more wine, please, two bottles I think, Griselda isn't even here yet, and I want to drink a toast to you all. (*The Waitress exits*)

ISABELLA. To yourself surely, / we're here to celebrate your success.

NIJO. Yes, Marlene.

JOAN. Yes, what is it exactly, Marlene?

MARLENE. Well it's not Pope but it is managing director.*

JOAN. And you find work for people.

MARLENE. Yes, an employment agency.

NIJO. *Over all the women you work with. And the men.

ISABELLA. And very well deserved too. I'm sure it's just the beginning of something extraordinary.

MARLENE. Well it's worth a party.

ISABELLA. To Marlene.*

MARLENE. And all of us.

JOAN. *Marlene.

NIJO. Marlene.

GRET. Marlene.

MARLENE. We've all come a long way. To our courage and the way we changed our lives and our extraordinary achievements. (*They laugh and drink a toast.*)

ISABELLA. Such adventures. We were crossing a mountain pass at seven thousand feet, the cook was all to pieces, the muleteers suffered fever and snow blindness. But even though my spine was agony I managed very well.*

MARLENE. Wonderful.

NIJO. Once I was ill for four months lying alone at an inn. Nobody to offer a horse to Buddha. I had to live for myself, and I did live.

ISABELLA. Of course you did. It was far worse returning to Tobermory. I always felt dull when I was stationary. / That's why I could never stay anywhere.

NIJO. Yes, that's it exactly. New sights. The shrine by the beach, the moon shining on the sea. The goddess had vowed to save all living things. / She would even save the fishes. I was full of hope.

JOAN. I had thought the Pope would know everything. I thought God would speak to me directly. But of course he knew I was a woman.

MARLENE. But nobody else even suspected? (*The Waitress brings more wine and then exits.*)

JOAN. In the end I did take a lover again.*

ISABELLA. In the Vatican?

GRET. *Keep you warm.

NIJO. *Ah, lover.

MARLENE. *Good for you.

JOAN. He was one of my chamberlains. There are such a lot of servants when you're a Pope. The food's very good. And I realized I did know the truth. Because whatever the Pope says, that's true.

NIJO. What was he like, the chamberlain?*

GRET. Big cock.

ISABELLA. Oh Gret.

MARLENE. *Did he fancy you when he thought you were a fella?

NIJO. What was he like?

JOAN. He could keep a secret.

MARLENE. So you did know everything.

JOAN. Yes, I enjoyed being Pope. I consecrated bishops and let people kiss my feet. I received the King of England when he came to submit to the church. Unfortunately there were earthquakes, and some village reported it had rained blood, and in France there was a plague of giant grasshoppers, but I don't think that can have been my fault, do you?* (*Laughter.*)
The grasshoppers fell on the English Channel / and were washed up on shore

NIJO. I once went to sea. It was very lonely. I realised it made very little difference where I went.

JOAN. and their bodies rotted and poisoned the air and everyone in those parts died. (*Laughter.*)

ISABELLA. *Such superstition! I was nearly murdered in China by a howling mob. They thought the barbarians ate babies and put them under railway sleepers to make the tracks steady, and ground up their eyes to make the lenses of cameras. / So they were shouting,

MARLENE. And you had a camera!

ISABELLA. "child-eater, child-eater." Some people tried to sell girl babies to Europeans for cameras or stew! (*Laughter.*)

MARLENE. So apart from the grasshoppers it was a great success.

JOAN. Yes, if it hadn't been for the baby I expect I'd have lived to an old age like Theodora of Alexandria, who lived as a monk. She was accused by a girl / who fell in love with her of being the father of her child and—

NIJO. But tell us what happened to your baby. I had some babies.

MARLENE. Didn't you think of getting rid of it?

JOAN. Wouldn't that be a worse sin than having it? / But a Pope with a child was about as bad as possible.

MARLENE. I don't know, you're the Pope.

JOAN. But I wouldn't have known how to get rid of it.

MARLENE. Other Popes had children, surely.

JOAN. They didn't give birth to them.

NIJO. Well you were a woman.

JOAN. Exactly and I shouldn't have been a woman. Women, children and lunatics can't be Pope.

MARLENE. So the only thing to do / was to get rid of it some-how.

NIJO. You had to have it adopted secretly.

JOAN. But I didn't know what was happening. I thought I was getting fatter, but then I was eating more and sitting about, the life of a Pope is quite luxurious. I don't think I'd spoken to a woman since I was twelve. The chamber-lain was the one who realized.

MARLENE. And by then it was too late.

JOAN. Oh I didn't want to pay attention. It was easier to do nothing.

NIJO. But you had to plan for having it. You had to say you were ill and go away.

JOAN. That's what I should have done I suppose.

MARLENE. Did you want them to find out?

NIJO. I too was often in embarrassing situations, there's no need for a scandal. My first child was His Majesty's, which unfortunately died, but my second was Akebono's. I was seventeen. He was in love with me when I was thir-teen, he was very upset when I had to go to the Emperor, it was very romantic, a lot of poems. Now His Majesty hadn't been near me for two months so he thought I was four months pregnant when I was really six, so when I reached the ninth month / I announced I was seriously ill,

JOAN. I never knew what month it was.

NIJO. and Akebono announced he had gone on a religious retreat. He held me round the waist and lifted me up as the baby was born. He cut the cord with a short sword, wrapped the baby in white and took it away. It was only a girl but I was sorry to lose it. Then I told the Emperor that the baby had miscarried because of my illness, and there you are. The danger was past.

JOAN. But Nijo, I wasn't used to having a woman's body.

ISABELLA. So what happened?

JOAN. I didn't know of course that it was near the time. It was Rogation Day, there was always a procession. I was on the horse dressed in my robes and a cross was carried in front of me, and all the cardinals were following, and all the clergy of Rome, and a huge crowd of people. / We set off from St Peter's to go

MARLENE. Total Pope. (*Gret pours the wine and steals the bottle*)

JOAN. to St John's. I had felt a slight pain earlier, I thought it was something I'd eaten, and then it came back, and came back more often. I thought when this is over I'll go to bed. There were still long gaps when I felt perfectly all right and I didn't want to attract attention to myself and spoil the ceremony. Then I suddenly realized what it must be. I had to last out till I could get home and hide. Then something changed, my breath started to catch, I couldn't plan things properly any more. We were in a little street that goes between St Clement's and the Colosseum, and I just had to get off the horse and sit down for a minute. Great waves of pressure were gong through my body, I heard sounds like a cow lowing, they came out of my mouth. Far away I heard people screaming, "The Pope is ill, the Pope is dying." And the baby just slid out onto the road.*

MARLENE. The cardinals / won't have known where to put themselves.

NIJO. Oh dear, Joan, what a thing to do! In the street!

ISABELLA. *How embarrassing.

GRET. In a field, yah. (*They are laughing.*)

JOAN. One of the cardinals said, 'The Antichrist!' and fell over in a faint. (*They all laugh.*)

MARLENE. So what did they do? They weren't best pleased.

JOAN. They took me by the feet and dragged me out of town and stoned me to death. (*They stop laughing.*)

MARLENE. Joan, how horrible.

JOAN. I don't really remember.

NIJO. And the child died too?

JOAN. Oh yes, I think so, yes. (*The Waitress enters to clear the plates. They start talking quietly.*)

ISABELLA (*to Joan*). I never had any children. I was very fond of horses.

NIJO (*to Marlene*). I saw my daughter once. She was three years old. She wore a plum-red / small-sleeved gown. Akebono's wife

ISABELLA. Birdie was my favorite. A little Indian bay mare I rode in the Rocky Mountains.

NIJO. had taken the child because her own died. Everyone thought I was just a visitor. She was being brought up carefully so she could be sent to the palace like I was. (*Gret steals her empty plate.*)

ISABELLA. Legs of iron and always cheerful, and such a pretty face. If a stranger led her she reared up like a bronco.

NIJO. I never saw my third child after he was born, the son of Ariake the priest. Ariake held him on his lap the day he was born and talked to him as if he could understand, and cried. My fourth child was Ariake's too. Ariake died before he was born. I didn't want to see anyone, I stayed alone in the hills. It was a boy again, my third son. But oddly enough I felt nothing for him.

MARLENE. How many children did you have, Gret?

GRET. Ten.

ISABELLA. Whenever I came back to England I felt I had so much to atone for. Hennie and John were so good. I did no good in my life. I spent years in self-gratification. So I hurled myself into committees, I nursed the people of To-bermory in the epidemic of influenza, I lectured the Young Women's Christian Association on Thrift. I talked and talked explaining how the East was corrupt and vi-cious. My travels must do good to someone beside myself. I wore myself out with good causes.

MARLENE (*pause*). Oh God, why are we all so miserable?

JOAN (*pause*). The procession never went down that street again.

MARLENE. They rerouted it specially?

JOAN. Yes they had to go all round to avoid it. And they in-troduced a pierced chair.

MARLENE. A pierced chair?

JOAN. Yes, a chair made out of solid marble with a hole in the seat / and it was

MARLENE. You're not serious.

JOAN. in the Chapel of the Saviour, and after he was elected the Pope had to sit in it.

MARLENE. And someone looked up his skirts? / Not really?

ISABELLA. What an extraordinary thing.

JOAN. Two of the clergy / made sure he was a man.

NIJO. On their hands and knees!

MARLENE. A pierced chair!

GRET. Balls!

(Griselda arrives unnoticed.)

NIJO. Why couldn't he just pull up his robe?

JOAN. He had to sit there and look dignified.

MARLENE. You could have made all your chamberlains sit in it.*

GRET. Big one, small one.

NIJO. Very useful chair at court.

ISABELLA. *Or the laird of Tobermory in his kilt.

(They are quite drunk. They get the giggles. Marlene notices Griselda and gets up to welcome her. The others go on talking and laughing. Gret crosses to Joan and Isabella and pours them wine from her stolen bottles. The Waitress gives out the menus.)

MARLENE. Griselda! / There you are. Do you want to eat?

GRISELDA. I'm sorry I'm so late. No, no, don't bother.

MARLENE. Of course it's no bother. / Have you eaten?

GRISELDA. No really, I'm not hungry.

MARLENE. Well have some pudding.

GRISELDA. I never eat pudding.

MARLENE. Griselda, I hope you're not anorexic. We're having pudding, I am, and getting nice and fat.

GRISELDA. Oh if everyone is. I don't mind.

MARLENE. Now who do you know? This is Joan who was Pope in the ninth century, and Isabella Bird, the Victorian traveler, and Lady Nijo from Japan, Emperor's concubine and Buddhist nun, thirteenth century, nearer your own time, and Gret who was painted by Brueghel. Griselda's in Boccaccio and Petrarch and Chaucer because of her extraordinary marriage. I'd like profiteroles because they're disgusting.

JOAN. Zabaglione, please.

ISABELLA. Apple pie / and cream.

NIJO. What's this?

MARLENE. Zabaglione, it's Italian, it's what Joan's having, / it's delicious.

NIJO. A Roman Catholic / dessert? Yes please.

MARLENE. Gret?

GRET. Cake.

GRISELDA. Just cheese and biscuits, thank you. (The Waitress exits.)

MARLENE. Yes, Griselda's life is like a fairy story, except it starts with marrying the prince.

GRISELDA. He's only a marquis, Marlene.

MARLENE. Well everyone for miles around is his liege and he's absolute lord of life and death and you were the poor but beautiful peasant girl and he whisked you off. / Near enough a prince.

NIJO. How old were you?

GRISELDA. Fifteen.

NIJO. I was brought up in court circles and it was still a shock. Had you ever seen him before?

GRISELDA. I'd seen him riding by, we all had. And he'd seen me in the fields with the sheep.*

ISABELLA. I would have been well suited to minding sheep.

NIJO. And Mr. Nugent went riding by.

ISABELLA. Of course not, Nijo, I mean a healthy life in the open air.

JOAN. *He just rode up while you were minding the sheep and asked you to marry him?

GRISELDA. No, No, it was on the wedding day. I was waiting outside the door to see the procession. Everyone wanted him to get married so there'd be an heir to look after us when he died, / and at last he

MARLENE. I don't think Walter wanted to get married. It is Walter? Yes.

GRISELDA. announced a day for the wedding but nobody knew who the bride was, we thought it must be a foreign princess, we were longing to see her. Then the carriage stopped outside our cottage and we couldn't see the bride anywhere. And he came and spoke to my father.

NIJO. And your father told you to serve the Prince.

GRISELDA. My father could hardly speak. The Marquis said it wasn't an order, I could say no, but if I said yes I must always obey him in everything.

MARLENE. That's when you should have suspected.

GRISELDA. But of course a wife must obey her husband. / And of course I must obey the Marquis.*

ISABELLA. I swore to obey dear John, of course, but it didn't seem to arise. Naturally I wouldn't have wanted to go abroad while I was married.

MARLENE. *Then why bother to mention it at all? He'd got a thing about it, that's why.

GRISELDA. I'd rather obey the Marquis than a boy from the village.

MARLENE. Yes, that's a point.

JOAN. I never obeyed anyone. They all obeyed me.

NIJO. And what did you wear? He didn't make you get married in your own clothes? That would be perverse.*

MARLENE. Oh, you wait.

GRISELDA. *He had ladies with him who undressed me and they had a white silk dress and jewels for my hair.

MARLENE. And at first he seemed perfectly normal?

GRISELDA. Marlene, you're always so critical of him. / Of course he was normal, he was very kind.

MARLENE. But Griselda, come on, he took your baby.

GRISELDA. Walter found it hard to believe I loved him. He couldn't believe I would always obey him. He had to prove it.

MARLENE. I don't think Walter likes women.

GRISELDA. I'm sure he loved me, Marlene, all the time.

MARLENE. He just had a funny way / of showing it.

GRISELDA. It was hard for him too.

JOAN. How do you mean he took away your baby?

NIJO. Was it a boy?

GRISELDA. No, the first one was a girl.

NIJO. Even so it's hard when they take it away. Did you see it at all?

GRISELDA. Oh yes, she was six weeks old.

NIJO. Much better to do it straight away.

ISABELLA. But why did your husband take the child?

GRISELDA. He said all the people hated me because I was just one of them. And now I had a child they were restless. So he had to get rid of the child to keep them quiet. But he said he wouldn't snatch her, I had to agree and obey and give her up. So when I was feeding her a man came in and took her away. I thought he was going to kill her even before he was out of the room.

MARLENE. But you let him take her? You didn't struggle?

GRISELDA. I asked him to give her back so I could kiss her. And I asked him to bury her where no animals could dig her up. / It was Walter's child to do what he

ISABELLA. Oh my dear.

GRISELDA. liked with.*

MARLENE. Walter was bonkers.

GRET. Bastard.

ISABELLA. *But surely, murder.

GRISELDA. I had promised.

MARLENE. I can't stand this. I'm going for a pee.

(Marlene goes out. The Waitress brings dessert, serves it during the following, then exits)

NIJO. No, I understand. Of course you had to, he was your life. And were you in favor after that?

GRISELDA. Oh yes, we were very happy together. We never spoke about what had happened.

ISABELLA. I can see you were doing what you thought was your duty. But didn't it make you ill?

GRISELDA. No, I was very well, thank you.

NIJO. And you had another child?

GRISELDA. Not for four years, but then I did, yes, a boy.

NIJO. Ah a boy. / So it all ended happily.

GRISELDA. Yes he was pleased. I kept my son till he was two years old. A peasant's grandson. It made the people angry. Walter explained.

ISABELLA. But surely he wouldn't kill his children / just because—

GRISELDA. Oh it wasn't true. Walter would never give in to the people. He wanted to see if I loved him enough.

JOAN. He killed his children / to see if you loved him enough?

NIJO. Was it easier the second time or harder?

GRISELDA. It was always easy because I always knew I would do what he said. (*Pause. They start to eat.*)

ISABELLA. I hope you didn't have any more children.

GRISELDA. Oh no, no more. It was twelve years till he tested me again.

ISABELLA. So whatever did he do this time? / My poor John, I never loved him enough, and he would never have dreamt . . .

GRISELDA. He sent me away. He said the people wanted him to marry someone else who'd give him an heir and he'd got special permission from the Pope. So I said I'd go home to my father. I came with nothing / so I went with nothing. I took

NIJO. Better to leave if your master doesn't want you.

GRISELDA. off my clothes. He let me keep a slip so he wouldn't be shamed. And I walked home barefoot. My father came out in tears. Everyone was crying except me.

NIJO. At least your father wasn't dead. / I had nobody.

ISABELLA. Well it can be a relief to come home. I loved to see Hennie's sweet face again.

GRISELDA. Oh yes, I was perfectly content. And quite soon he sent for me again.

JOAN. I don't think I would have gone.

GRISELDA. But he told me to come. I had to obey him. He wanted me to help prepare his wedding. He was getting married to a young girl from France / and nobody except me knew how to arrange things the way he liked them.

NIJO. It's always hard taking him another woman. (*Marlene comes back.*)

JOAN. I didn't live a woman's life. I don't understand it.

GRISELDA. The girl was sixteen and far more beautiful than me. I could see why he loved her. / She had her younger brother with her as a page. (*The Waitress enters.*)

MARLENE. Oh God, I can't bear it. I want some coffee. Six coffees. Six brandies. / Double brandies. Straightaway. (*The Waitress exits.*)

GRISELDA. They all went in to the feast I'd prepared. And he stayed behind and put his arms round me and kissed me. / I felt half asleep with the shock.

NIJO. Oh, like a dream.

MARLENE. And he said, "This is your daughter and your son."

GRISELDA. Yes.

JOAN. What?

NIJO. Oh. Oh I see. You got them back.

ISABELLA. I did think it was remarkably barbaric to kill them but you learn not to say anything. / So he had them brought up secretly I suppose.

MARLENE. Walter's a monster. Weren't you angry? What did you do?

GRISELDA. Well I fainted. Then I cried and kissed the children. / Everyone was making a fuss of me.

NIJO. But did you feel anything for them?

GRISELDA. What?

NIJO. Did you feel anything for the children?

GRISELDA. Of course, I loved them.

JOAN. So you forgave him and lived with him?

GRISELDA. He suffered so much all those years.

ISABELLA. Hennie had the same sweet nature.

NIJO. So they dressed you again?

GRISELDA. Cloth of gold.

JOAN. I can't forgive anything.

MARLENE. You really are exceptional, Griselda.

NIJO. Nobody gave me back my children. (*She cries.*)

(*The Waitress brings the brandies and then exits. During the following, Joan goes to Nijo.*)

ISABELLA. I can never be like Hennie. I was always so busy in England, a kind of business I detested. The very presence of people exhausted my emotional reserves. I could not be like Hennie however I tried. I tried and was as ill as could be. The doctor suggested a steel net to support my head, the weight of my own head was too much for my diseased spine. It is dangerous to put oneself in depressing circumstances. Why should I do it?

JOAN (*to Nijo*). Don't cry.

NIJO. My father and the Emperor both died in the autumn. So much pain.

JOAN. Yes, but don't cry.

NIJO. They wouldn't let me into the palace when he was dying. I hid in the room with his coffin, then I couldn't find where I'd left my shoes, I ran after the funeral procession in bare feet, I couldn't keep up. When I got there it was over, a few wisps of smoke in the sky, that's all that was left of him. What I want to know is, if I'd still been at court, would I have been allowed to wear full mourning?

MARLENE. I'm sure you would.

NIJO. Why do you say that? You don't know anything about it. Would I have been allowed to wear full mourning?

ISABELLA. How can people live in this dim pale island and wear our hideous clothes? I cannot and will not live the life of a lady.

NIJO. I'll tell you something that made me angry. I was eighteen, at the Full Moon Ceremony. They make a special rice gruel and stir it with their sticks, and then they beat their women across the loins so they'll have sons and not daughters. So the Emperor beat us all / very hard as

MARLENE. What a sod. (*The Waitress enters with the coffees.*)

NIJO. usual—that's not it, Marlene, that's normal, what made us angry, he told his attendants they could beat us too. Well they had a wonderful time. / So Lady Genki and I made a plan, and the ladies

MARLENE. I'd like another brandy please. Better make it six. (*The Waitress exits.*)

NIJO. all hid in his rooms, and Lady Mashimizu stood guard with a stick at the door, and when His Majesty came in Genki seized him and I beat him till he cried out and promised he would never order anyone to hit us again. Afterward there was a terrible fuss. The nobles were horrified. "We wouldn't even dream of stepping on Your Majesty's shadow." And I had hit him with a stick. Yes, I hit him with a stick.

(*The Waitress brings the brandy bottle and tops up the glasses. Joan crosses in front of the table and back to her place while drunkenly reciting:*)

JOAN. Suave, mari magno turbantibus aequora ventis,
     e terra magnum alterius spectare laborem;
     non quia vexari quemquamst iucunda voluptas,
     sed quibus ipse malis careas quia cernere suave est.
     Suave etiam belli certamina magna tueri
     per campos instructa tua sine parte pericli.
     Sed nil dulcius est, bene quam munita tenere
     edita doctrine sapientum templa serena, /
     despicere uncle queas alios passimque videre
     errare atque viam palantis quaerere vitae,

GRISELDA. I do think—I do wonder—it would have been nicer if Walter hadn't had to.

ISABELLA. Why should I? Why should I?

MARLENE. Of course not.

NIJO. I hit him with a stick.

JOAN. certare ingenio, contendere nobilitate,
     noctes atque dies niti praestante labore
     ad summas emergere opes retumque potiri.
     O miseras hominum mentis, / o pectora caeca![2]

ISABELLA. Oh miseras!

NIJO. *Pectora caeca.

JOAN. qualibus in tenebris vitae quantisque periclis
     degitur hoc aevi quodcumquest! / nonne videre
     nil aliud sibi naturam latrare, nisi utqui
     corpore seiunctus dolor absit, mente fruatur[3] . . .

(*She subsides.*)

GRET. We come to hell through a big mouth. Hell's black and red. / It's

MARLENE (*to Joan*). Shut up, pet.

GRISELDA. Hush, please.

ISABELLA. Listen, she's been to hell.

---

[2]**Suave, . . . o pectora caeca!** Joan is quoting a passage from Titus Lucretius Carus, a Roman philosopher, who wrote *On the Nature of Things* in the first century B.C.E. In English (by Cyril Bailey) the passage reads: Sweet it is, when on the great sea the winds are buffeting the waters, to gaze from the land on another's great struggles; not because it is pleasure or joy that any one should be distressed, but because it is sweet to perceive from what misfortune you yourself are free. Sweet is it too, to behold great contests of war in full array over the plains, when you have no part in the danger. But nothing is more gladdening than to dwell in the calm high places, firmly embattled on the heights by the teaching of the wise, whence you can look down on others, and see them wandering hither and thither, going astray as they seek the way of life, in strife matching their wits or rival claims of birth, struggling night and day by surpassing effort to rise up to the height of power and gain possession of the world. Ah! miserable minds of men, blind hearts! [3]**qualibus.** In what darkness of life, in what great dangers ye spend this little span of years! to think that ye should not see that nature cries aloud for nothing else but that pain may be kept far sundered from the body, and that, withdrawn from care and fear, she may enjoy in mind the sense of pleasure!

GRET. like the village where I come from. There's a river and a bridge and houses. There's places on fire like when the soldiers come. There's a big devil sat on a roof with a big hole in his arse and he's scooping stuff out of it with a big ladle and it's falling down on us, and it's money, so a lot of the women stop and get some. But most of us is fighting the devils. There's lots of little devils, our size, and we get them down all right and give them a beating. There's lots of funny creatures round your feet, you don't like to look, like rats and lizards, and nasty things, a bum with a face, and fish with legs, and faces on things that don't have faces on. But they don't hurt, you just keep going. Well we'd had worse, you see, we'd had the Spanish. We'd all had family killed. My big son die on a wheel. Birds eat him. My baby, a soldier run her through with a sword. I'd had enough, I was mad, I hate the bastards. I come out my front door that morning and shout till my neighbors come out and I said, "Come on, we're going where the evil come from and pay the bastards out." And they all come out just as they was / from baking or

NIJO. All the ladies come.

GRET. washing in their aprons, and we push down the street and the ground opens up and we go through a big mouth into a street just like ours but in hell. I've got a sword in my hand from somewhere and I fill a basket with gold cups they drink out of down there. You just keep running on and fighting / you didn't stop for nothing. Oh we give them devils such a beating.*

NIJO. Take that, take that.

JOAN. *Something something something mortisque timores
tum vacuum pectus[4]—damn.
Quod si ridicula—
something something on and on and on
and something splendorem purpureai.

ISABELLA. I thought I would have a last jaunt up the west river in China. Why not? But the doctors were so very grave. I just went to Morocco. The sea was so wild I had to be landed by ship's crane in a coal bucket. / My horse was a terror to me, a powerful black charger.

GRET. Coal bucket, good.

JOAN. nos in luce timemus
something
terrorem.[5]

[4]**Something . . . pectus.** From Lucretius: "the dread of death leaves your heart empty . . ." [5]**Quod . . . purpureai. . . . nos in luce . . . terrorem.** Also from Lucretius: But if we see that these thoughts are mere mirth and mockery, and in very truth the fears of men and the cares that dog them fear not the clash of arms nor the weapons of war, but pass boldly among kings and lords of the world, nor dread the glitter that comes from gold nor the bright sheen of the purple robe, can you doubt that all such power belongs to reason alone, above all when the whole of life is but a struggle in darkness? For even as children tremble and fear everything in blinding darkness, so we sometimes dread in the light things that are no whit more to be feared than what chidren shudder at in the dark.

(*Nijo is laughing and crying. Joan gets up and is sick. Griselda looks after her.*)

GRISELDA. Can I have some water, please? (*The Waitress exits.*)

ISABELLA. So off I went to visit the Berber sheikhs in full blue trousers and great brass spurs. I was the only European woman ever to have seen the Emperor of Morocco. I was (*the Waitress brings the water.*) seventy years old. What lengths to go to for a last chance of joy. I knew my return of vigour was only temporary, but how marvellous while it lasted.

SCENE II

(*"Top Girls" Employment Agency. Monday morning. The lights come up on Marlene and Jeanine.*)

MARLENE. Right Jeanine, you are Jeanine aren't you? Let's have a look. O's and A's.[6] / No A's, all those

JEANINE. Six O's.

MARLENE. O's you probably could have got an A. / Speeds, not brilliant, not too bad.

JEANINE. I wanted to go to work.

MARLENE. Well, Jeanine, what's your present job like?

JEANINE. I'm a secretary.

MARLENE. Secretary or typist?

JEANINE. I did start as a typist but the last six months I've been a secretary.

MARLENE. To?

JEANINE. To three of them, really, they share me. There's Mr. Ashford, he's the office manager, and Mr. Philby / is sales, and—

MARLENE. Quite a small place?

JEANINE. A bit small.

MARLENE. Friendly?

JEANINE. Oh it's friendly enough.

MARLENE. Prospects?

JEANINE. I don't think so, that's the trouble. Miss Lewis is secretary to the managing director and she's been there forever, and Mrs. Bradford / is—

MARLENE. So you want a job with better prospects?

JEANINE. I want a change.

MARLENE. So you'll take anything comparable?

JEANINE. No, I do want prospects. I want more money.

MARLENE. You're getting—?

JEANINE. Hundred.

MARLENE. It's not bad you know. You're what? Twenty?

JEANINE. I'm saving to get married.

MARLENE. Does that mean you don't want a long-term job, Jeanine?

[6]**O's and A's.** Examinations given in British school. O-levels are for basic knowledge skills, while A-levels are for more advanced skills learned in secondary schools.

JEANINE. I might do.

MARLENE. Because where do the prospects come in? No kids for a bit?

JEANINE. Oh no, not kids, not yet.

MARLENE. So you won't tell them you're getting married?

JEANINE. Had I better not?

MARLENE. It would probably help.

JEANINE. I'm not wearing a ring. We thought we wouldn't spend on a ring.

MARLENE. Saves taking it off.

JEANINE. I wouldn't take it off.

MARLENE. There's no need to mention it when you go for an interview. / Now Jeanine do you have a feel

JEANINE. But what if they ask?

MARLENE. for any particular kind of company?

JEANINE. I thought advertising.

MARLENE. People often do think advertising. I have got a few vacancies but I think they're looking for something glossier.

JEANINE. You mean how I dress? / I

MARLENE. I mean experience.

JEANINE. can dress different. I dress like this on purpose for where I am now.

MARLENE. I have a marketing department here of a knitwear manufacturer. / Marketing is near enough

JEANINE. Knitwear?

MARLENE. advertising secretary to the marketing manager, he's thirty-five, married, I've sent him a girl before and she was happy, left to have a baby, you won't want to mention marriage there. He's very fair I think, good at his job, you won't have to nurse him along. Hundred and ten, so that's better than you're doing now.

JEANINE. I don't know.

MARLENE. I've a fairly small concern here, father and two sons, you'd have more say potentially, secretarial and reception duties, only a hundred but the job's going to grow with the concern and then you'll be in at the top with new girls coming in underneath you.

JEANINE. What is it they do?

MARLENE. Lampshades. / This would be my first choice for you.

JEANINE. Just lampshades?

MARLENE. There's plenty of different kinds of lampshade. So we'll send you there, shall we, and the knitwear second choice. Are you free to go for an interview any day they call you?

JEANINE. I'd like to travel.

MARLENE. We don't have any foreign clients. You'd have to go elsewhere.

JEANINE. Yes I know. I don't really . . . I just mean . . .

MARLENE. Does your fiancé want to travel?

JEANINE. I'd like a job where I was here in London and with him and everything but now and then—I expect it's silly. Are there jobs like that?

MARLENE. There's personal assistant to a top executive in a multinational. If that's the idea you need to be planning ahead. Is that where you want to be in ten years?

JEANINE. I might not be alive in ten years.

MARLENE. Yes but you will be. You'll have children.

JEANINE. I can't think about ten years.

MARLENE. You haven't got the speeds anyway. So I'll send you to these two shall I? You haven't been to any other agency? Just so we don't get crossed wires. Now Jeanine I want you to get one of these jobs, all right? If I send you that means I'm putting myself on the line for you. Your presentation's OK, you look fine, just be confident and go in there convinced that this is the best job for you and you're the best person for the job. If you don't believe it they won't believe it.

JEANINE. Do you believe it?

MARLENE. I think you could make me believe it if you put your mind to it.

JEANINE. Yes, all right.

SCENE III

(*Joyce's back yard. Sunday afternoon. The house with a back door is upstage. Downstage is a shelter made of junk, made by children. The lights come up on two girls, Angie and Kit, who are squashed together in the shelter. Angie is sixteen, Kit is twelve. They cannot be seen from the house.*)

JOYCE (*off, calling from the house*). Angie. Angie are you out there?

(*Silence. They keep still and wait. When nothing else happens they relax.*)

ANGIE. Wish she was dead.

KIT. Wanna watch *The Exterminator*?

ANGIE. You're sitting on my leg.

KIT. There's nothing on telly. We can have an ice cream. Angie?

ANGIE. Shall I tell you something?

KIT. Do you wanna watch *The Exterminator*?

ANGIE. It's X, innit.

KIT. I can get into Xs.

ANGIE. Shall I tell you something?

KIT. We'll go to something else. We'll go to Ipswich. What's on the Odeon?

ANGIE. She won't let me, will she?

KIT. Don't tell her.

ANGIE. I've no money.

KIT. I'll pay.

ANGIE. She'll moan though, won't she?

KIT. I'll ask her for you if you like.

ANGIE. I've no money, I don't want you to pay.

KIT. I'll ask her.

ANGIE. She don't like you.

KIT. I still got three pounds birthday money. Did she say she don't like me? I'll go by myself then.

ANGIE. Your mum don't let you. I got to take you.

KIT. She won't know.

ANGIE. You'd be scared who'd sit next to you.

KIT. No I wouldn't. She does like me anyway. Tell me then.

ANGIE. Tell you what?

KIT. It's you she doesn't like.

ANGIE. Well I don't like her so tough shit.

JOYCE (off). Angie. Angie. Angie. I know you're out there. I'm not coming out after you. You come in here. (Silence. Nothing happens.)

ANGIE. Last night when I was in bed. I been thinking yesterday could I make things move. You know, make things move by thinking about them without touching them. Last night I was in bed and suddenly a picture fell down off the wall.

KIT. What picture?

ANGIE. My gran, that picture. Not the poster. The photograph in the frame.

KIT. Had you done something to make it fall down?

ANGIE. I must have done.

KIT. But were you thinking about it?

ANGIE. Not about it, but about something.

KIT. I don't think that's very good.

ANGIE. You know the kitten?

KIT. Which one?

ANGIE. There only is one. The dead one.

KIT. What about it?

ANGIE. I heard it last night.

KIT. Where?

ANGIE. Out here. In the dark. What if I left you here in the dark all night?

KIT. You couldn't. I'd go home.

ANGIE. You couldn't.

KIT. I'd / go home.

ANGIE. No you couldn't, not if I said.

KIT. I could.

ANGIE. Then you wouldn't see anything. You'd just be ignorant.

KIT. I can see in the daytime.

ANGIE. No you can't. You can't hear it in the daytime.

KIT. I don't want to hear it.

ANGIE. You're scared that's all.

KIT. I'm not scared of anything.

ANGIE. You're scared of blood.

KIT. It's not the same kitten anyway. You just heard an old cat, / you just heard some old cat.

ANGIE. You don't know what I heard. Or what I saw. You don't know nothing because you're a baby.

KIT. You're sitting on me.

ANGIE. Mind my hair / you silly cunt.

KIT. Stupid fucking cow, I hate you.

ANGIE. I don't care if you do.

KIT. You're horrible.

ANGIE. I'm going to kill my mother and you're going to watch.

KIT. I'm not playing.

ANGIE. You're scared of blood. (Kit puts her hand under her dress, brings it out with blood on her finger.)

KIT. There, see, I got my own blood, so. (Angie takes Kit's hand and licks her finger.)

ANGIE. Now I'm a cannibal. I might turn into a vampire now.

KIT. That picture wasn't nailed up right.

ANGIE. You'll have to do that when I get mine.

KIT. I don't have to.

ANGIE. You're scared.

KIT. I'll do it, I might do it. I don't have to just because you say. I'll be sick on you.

ANGIE. I don't care if you are sick on me, I don't mind sick. I don't mind blood. If I don't get away from here I'm going to die.

KIT. I'm going home.

ANGIE. You can't go through the house. She'll see you.

KIT. I won't tell her.

ANGIE. Oh great, fine.

KIT. I'll say I was by myself. I'll tell her you're at my house and I'm going there to get you.

ANGIE. She knows I'm here, stupid.

KIT. Then why can't I go through the house?

ANGIE. Because I said not.

KIT. My mum don't like you anyway.

ANGIE. I don't want her to like me. She's a slag.

KIT. She is not.

ANGIE. She does it with everyone.

KIT. She does not.

ANGIE. You don't even know what it is.

KIT. Yes I do.

ANGIE. Tell me then.

KIT. We get it all at school, cleverclogs. It's on television. You haven't done it.

ANGIE. How do you know?

KIT. Because I know you haven't.

ANGIE. You know wrong then because I have.

KIT. Who with?

ANGIE. I'm not telling you / who with.

KIT. You haven't anyway.

ANGIE. How do you know?

KIT. Who with?

ANGIE. I'm not telling you.

KIT. You said you told me everything.

ANGIE. I was lying wasn't I?

KIT. Who with? You can't tell me who with because / you never—

ANGIE. Sh.

(Joyce has come out of the house. She stops halfway across the yard and listens. They listen.)

JOYCE. You there Angie? Kit? You there Kitty? Want a cup of

tea? I've got some chocolate biscuits. Come on now I'll put the kettle on. Want a choccy biccy, Angie? (*They all listen and wait.*) Fucking rotten little cunt. You can stay there and die. I'll lock the door.

(*They all wait. Joyce goes back to the house. Angie and Kit sit in silence for a while.*)

KIT. When there's a war, where's the safest place?

ANGIE. Nowhere.

KIT. New Zealand is, my mum said. Your skin's burned right off. Shall we go to New Zealand?

ANGIE. I'm not staying here.

KIT. Shall we go to New Zealand?

ANGIE. You're not old enough.

KIT. You're not old enough.

ANGIE. I'm old enough to get married.

KIT. You don't want to get married.

ANGIE. No but I'm old enough.

KIT. I'd find out where they were going to drop it and stand right in the place.

ANGIE. You couldn't find out.

KIT. Better than walking round with your skin dragging on the ground. Eugh. / Would you like walking round with your skin dragging on the ground?

ANGIE. You couldn't find out, stupid, it's a secret.

KIT. Where are you going?

ANGIE. I'm not telling you.

KIT. Why?

ANGIE. It's a secret.

KIT. But you tell me all your secrets.

ANGIE. Not the true secrets.

KIT. Yes you do.

ANGIE. No I don't.

KIT. I want to go somewhere away from the war.

ANGIE. Just forget the war.

KIT. I can't.

ANGIE. You have to. It's so boring.

KIT. I'll remember it at night.

ANGIE. I'm going to do something else anyway.

KIT. What? Angie, come on. Angie.

ANGIE. It's a little secret.

KIT. It can't be worse than the kitten. And killing your mother. And the war.

ANGIE. Well I'm not telling you so you can die for all I care.

KIT. My mother says there's something wrong with you playing with someone my age. She says why haven't you got friends your own age. People your own age know there's something funny about you. She says you're a bad influence. She says she's going to speak to your mother. (*Angie twists Kit's arm till she cries out.*)

ANGIE. Say you're a liar.

KIT. She said it not me.

ANGIE. Say you eat shit.

KIT. You can't make me. (*Angie lets go.*)

ANGIE. I don't care anyway. I'm leaving.

KIT. Go on then.

ANGIE. You'll all wake up one morning and find I've gone.

KIT. Go on then.

ANGIE. You'll wake up one morning and find I've gone.

KIT. Good.

ANGIE. I'm not telling you when.

KIT. Go on then.

ANGIE. I'm sorry I hurt you.

KIT. I'm tired.

ANGIE. Do you like me?

KIT. I don't know.

ANGIE. You do like me.

KIT. I'm going home. (*She gets up.*)

ANGIE. No you're not.

KIT. I'm tired.

ANGIE. She'll see you.

KIT. She'll give me a chocolate biscuit.

ANGIE. Kitty.

KIT. Tell me where you're going.

ANGIE. Sit down.

KIT (*sittting down again*). Go on then.

ANGIE. Swear?

KIT. Swear.

ANGIE. I'm going to London. To see my aunt.

KIT. And what?

ANGIE. That's it.

KIT. I see my aunt all the time.

ANGIE. I don't see my aunt.

KIT. What's so special?

ANGIE. It is special. She's special.

KIT. Why?

ANGIE. She is.

KIT. Why?

ANGIE. She is.

KIT. Why?

ANGIE. My mother hates her.

KIT. Why?

ANGIE. Because she does.

KIT. Perhaps she's not very nice.

ANGIE. She is nice.

KIT. How do you know?

ANGIE. Because I know her.

KIT. You said you never see her.

ANGIE. I saw her last year. You saw her.

KIT. Did I?

ANGIE. Never mind.

KIT. I remember her. That aunt. What's so special?

ANGIE. She gets people jobs.

KIT. What's so special?

ANGIE. I think I'm my aunt's child. I think my mother's really my aunt.

KIT. Why?

ANGIE. Because she goes to America, now shut up.

KIT. I've been to London.

ANGIE. Now give us a cuddle and shut up because I'm sick.

KIT. You're sitting on my arm.

(They curl up in each other's arms. Silence. Joyce comes out and comes up to them quietly.)

JOYCE. Come on.

KIT. Oh hello.

JOYCE. Time you went home.

KIT. We want to go to the Odeon.

JOYCE. What time?

KIT. Don't know.

JOYCE. What's on?

KIT. Don't know.

JOYCE. Don't know much do you?

KIT. That all right then?

JOYCE. Angie's got to clean her room first.

ANGIE. No I don't.

JOYCE. Yes you do, it's a pigsty.

ANGIE. Well I'm not.

JOYCE. Then you're not going. I don't care.

ANGIE. Well I am going.

JOYCE. You've no money, have you?

ANGIE. Kit's paying anyway.

JOYCE. No she's not.

KIT. I'll help you with your room.

JOYCE. That's nice.

ANGIE. No you won't. You wait here.

KIT. Hurry then.

ANGIE. I'm not hurrying. You just wait. *(Angie goes into the house. Silence.)*

JOYCE. I don't know. *(Silence.)* How's school then?

KIT. All right.

JOYCE. What are you now? Third year?

KIT. Second year.

JOYCE. Your mum says you're good at English. *(Silence.)* Maybe Angie should've stayed on.

KIT. She didn't like it.

JOYCE. I didn't like it. And look at me. If your face fits at school it's going to fit other places too. It wouldn't make no difference to Angie. She's not going to get a job when jobs are hard to get. I'd be sorry for anyone in charge of her. She'd better get married. I don't know who'd have her, mind. She's one of those girls might never leave home. What do you want to be when you grow up, Kit?

KIT. Physicist.

JOYCE. What?

KIT. Nuclear physicist.

JOYCE. Whatever for?

KIT. I could, I'm clever.

JOYCE. I know you're clever, pet. *(Silence.)* I'll make a cup of tea. *(Silence.)* Looks like it's going to rain. *(Silence.)* Don't you have friends your own age?

KIT. Yes.

JOYCE. Well then.

KIT. I'm old for my age.

JOYCE. And Angie's simple is she? She's not simple.

KIT. I love Angie.

JOYCE. She's clever in her own way.

KIT. You can't stop me.

JOYCE. I don't want to.

KIT. You can't, so.

JOYCE. Don't be cheeky, Kitty. She's always kind to little children.

KIT. She's coming so you better leave me alone.

(Angie comes out. She has changed into an old best dress, slightly small for her.)

JOYCE. What you put that on for? Have you done your room? You can't clean your room in that.

ANGIE. I looked in the cupboard and it was there.

JOYCE. Of course it was there, it's meant to be there. Is that why it was a surprise, finding something in the right place? I should think she's surprised, wouldn't you Kit, to find something in her room in the right place.

ANGIE. I decided to wear it.

JOYCE. Not today, why? To clean your room? You're not going to the pictures till you've done your room. You can put your dress on after if you like. *(Angie picks up a brick.)* Have you done your room? You're not getting out of it, you know.

KIT. Angie, let's go.

JOYCE. She's not going till she's done her room.

KIT. It's starting to rain.

JOYCE. Come on, come on then. Hurry and do your room, Angie, and then you can go to the cinema with Kit. Oh it's wet, come on. We'll look up the time in the paper. Does your mother know, Kit, it's going to be a late night for you, isn't it? Hurry up, Angie. You'll spoil your dress. You make me sick. *(Joyce and Kit run into the house. Angie stays where she is. There is the sound of rain. Kit comes out of the house.)*

KIT *(shouting)*. Angie. Angie, come on, you'll get wet. *(She comes back to Angie.)*

ANGIE. I put on this dress to kill my mother.

KIT. I suppose you thought you'd do it with a brick.

ANGIE. You can kill people with a brick. *(She puts the brick down.)*

KIT. Well you didn't, so.

ACT II

SCENE I

("Top Girls" Employment Agency. Monday morning. There are three desks in the main office and a separate interviewing area. The lights come up in the main office on Win and Nell, who have just arrived for work.)

NELL. Coffee coffee coffee coffee / coffee.

WIN. The roses were smashing. / Mermaid.

NELL. Ohhh.

WIN. Iceberg. He taught me all their names. (*Nell has some coffee now.*)

NELL. Ah. Now then.

WIN. He has one of the finest rose gardens in West Sussex. He exhibits.

NELL. He what?

WIN. His wife was visiting her mother. It was like living together.

NELL. Crafty, you never said.

WIN. He rang on Saturday morning.

NELL. Lucky you were free.

WIN. That's what I told him.

NELL. Did you hell.

WIN. Have you ever seen a really beautiful rose garden?

NELL. I don't like flowers. / I like swimming pools.

WIN. Marilyn. Esther's Baby. They're all called after birds.

NELL. Our friend's late. Celebrating all weekend I bet you.

WIN. I'd call a rose Elvis. Or John Conteh.

NELL. Is Howard in yet?

WIN. If he is he'll be bleeping us with a problem.

NELL. Howard can just hang on to himself.

WIN. Howard's really cut up.

NELL. Howard thinks because he's a fella the job was his as of right. Our Marlene's got far more balls than Howard and that's that.

WIN. Poor little bugger.

NELL. He'll live.

WIN. He'll move on.

NELL. I wouldn't mind a change of air myself.

WIN. Serious?

NELL. I've never been a staying put lady. Pastures new.

WIN. So who's the pirate?

NELL. There's nothing definite.

WIN. Inquiries?

NELL. There's always inquiries. I'd think I'd got bad breath if there stopped being inquiries. Most of them can't afford me. Or you.

WIN. I'm all right for the time being. Unless I go to Australia.

NELL. There's not a lot of room upward.

WIN. Marlene's filled it up.

NELL. Good luck to her. Unless there's some prospects moneywise.

WIN. You can but ask.

NELL. Can always but ask.

WIN. So what have we got? I've got a Mr. Holden I saw last week.

NELL. Any use?

WIN. Pushy. Bit of a cowboy.

NELL. Goodlooker?

WIN. Good dresser.

NELL. High flyer?

WIN. That's his general idea certainly but I'm not sure he's got it up there.

NELL. Prestel wants six high flyers and I've only seen two and a half.

WIN. He's making a bomb on the road but he thinks it's time for an office. I sent him to IBM but he didn't get it.

NELL. Prestel's on the road.

WIN. He's not overbright.

NELL. Can he handle an office?

WIN. Provided his secretary can punctuate he should go far.

NELL. Bear Prestel in mind then, I might put my head round the door. I've got that poor little nerd I should never have said I could help. Tender heart me.

WIN. Tender like old boots. How old?

NELL. Yes well forty-five.

WIN. Say no more.

NELL. He knows his place, he's not after calling himself a manager, he's just a poor little bod wants a better commission and a bit of sunshine.

WIN. Don't we all.

NELL. He's just got to relocate. He's got a bungalow in Dymchurch.

WIN. And his wife says.

NELL. The lady wife wouldn't care to relocate. She's going through the change.

WIN. It's his funeral, don't waste your time.

NELL. I don't waste a lot.

WIN. Good weekend you?

NELL. You could say.

WIN. Which one?

NELL. One Friday, one Saturday.

WIN. Aye—aye.

NELL. Sunday night I watched telly.

WIN. Which of them do you like best really?

NELL. Sunday was best, I liked the Ovaltine.

WIN. Holden, Barker, Gardner, Duke.

NELL. I've a lady here thinks she can sell.

WIN. Taking her on?

NELL. She's had some jobs.

WIN. Services?

NELL. No, quite heavy stuff, electric.

WIN. Tough bird like us.

NELL. We could do with a few more here.

WIN. There's nothing going here.

NELL. No but I always want the tough ones when I see them. Hang onto them.

WIN. I think we're plenty.

NELL. Derek asked me to marry him again.

WIN. He doesn't know when he's beaten.

NELL. I told him I'm not going to play house, not even in Ascot.

WIN. Mind you, you could play house.

NELL. If I chose to play house I would play house ace.

WIN. You could marry him and go on working.

NELL. I could go on working and not marry him.

(Marlene arrives.)

MARLENE. Morning ladies. (*Win and Nell cheer and whistle.*) Mind my head.

NELL. Coffee coffee coffee.

WIN. We're tactfully not mentioning you're late.

MARLENE. Fucking tube.

WIN. We've heard that one.

NELL. We've used that one.

WIN. It's the top executive doesn't come in as early as the poor working girl.

MARLENE. Pass the sugar and shut your face, pet.

WIN. Well I'm delighted.

NELL. Howard's looking sick.

WIN. Howard is sick. He's got ulcers and heart. He told me.

NELL. He'll have to stop then won't he?

WIN. Stop what?

NELL. Smoking, drinking, shouting. Working.

WIN. Well, working.

NELL. We're just looking through the day.

MARLENE. I'm doing some of Pam's ladies. They've been piling up while she's away.

NELL. Half a dozen little girls and an arts graduate who can't type.

WIN. I spent the whole weekend at his place in Sussex.

NELL. She fancies his rose garden.

WIN. I had to lie down in the back of the car so the neighbours wouldn't see me go in.

NELL. You're kidding.

WIN. It was funny.

NELL. Fuck that for a joke.

WIN. It was funny.

MARLENE. Anyway they'd see you in the garden.

WIN. The garden has extremely high walls.

NELL. I think I'll tell the wife.

WIN. Like hell.

NELL. She might leave him and you could have the rose garden.

WIN. The minute it's not a secret I'm out on my ear.

NELL. Don't know why you bother.

WIN. Bit of fun.

NELL. I think it's time you went to Australia.

WIN. I think it's pushy Mr. Holden time.

NELL. If you've any really pretty bastards, Marlene, I want some for Prestel.

MARLENE. I might have one this afternoon. This morning it's all Pam's secretarial.

NELL. Not long now and you'll be upstairs watching over us all.

MARLENE. Do you feel bad about it?

NELL. I don't like coming second.

MARLENE. Who does?

WIN. We'd rather it was you than Howard. We're glad for you, aren't we Nell.

NELL. Oh yes. Aces.

(Louise enters the interviewing area. The lights cross-fade to Win and Louise in the interviewing area. Nell exits.)

WIN. Now Louise, hello, I have your details here. You've been very loyal to the one job I see.

LOUISE. Yes I have.

WIN. Twenty-one years is a long time in one place.

LOUISE. I feel it is. I feel it's time to move on.

WIN. And you are what age now?

LOUISE. I'm in my early forties.

WIN. Exactly?

LOUISE. Forty-six.

WIN. It's not necessarily a handicap, well it is of course we have to face that, but it's not necessarily a disabling handicap, experience does count for something.

LOUISE. I hope so.

WIN. Now between ourselves is there any trouble, any reason why you're leaving that wouldn't appear on the form?

LOUISE. Nothing like that.

WIN. Like what?

LOUISE. Nothing at all.

WIN. No long term understandings come to a sudden end, making for an insupportable atmosphere?

LOUISE. I've always completely avoided anything like that at all.

WIN. No personality clashes with your immediate superiors or inferiors?

LOUISE. I've always taken care to get on very well with everyone.

WIN. I only ask because it can affect the reference and it also affects your motivation, I want to be quite clear why you're moving on. So I take it the job itself no longer satisfies you. Is it the money?

LOUISE. It's partly the money. It's not so much the money.

WIN. Nine thousand is very respectable. Have you dependants?

LOUISE. No, no dependants. My mother died.

WIN. So why are you making a change?

LOUISE. Other people make changes.

WIN. But why are you, now, after spending most of your life in the one place?

LOUISE. There you are, I've lived for that company, I've given my life really you could say because I haven't had a great deal of social life, I've worked in the evenings. I haven't had office entanglements for the very reason you just mentioned and if you are committed to your work you don't move in many other circles. I had management status from the age of twenty-seven and you'll appreciate what that means. I've built up a department. And there it is, it works extremely well, and I feel I'm stuck there. I've spent twenty years in middle management. I've seen young men who I trained go on, in my own company or elsewhere, to higher things. Nobody notices me, I don't expect it, I don't attract attention by making mistakes, everybody takes it for granted that my work is perfect.

They will notice me when I go, they will be sorry I think to lose me, they will offer me more money of course, I will refuse. They will see when I've gone what I was doing for them.

WIN. If they offer you more money you won't stay?

LOUISE. No I won't.

WIN. Are you the only woman?

LOUISE. Apart from the girls of course, yes. There was one, she was my assistant, it was the only time I took on a young woman assistant, I always had my doubts. I don't care greatly for working with women, I think I pass as a man at work. But I did take on this young woman, her qualifications were excellent, and she did well, she got a department of her own, and left the company for a competitor where she's now on the board and good luck to her. She has a different style, she's a new kind of attractive well-dressed—I don't mean I don't dress properly. But there is a kind of woman who is thirty now who grew up in a different climate. They are not so careful. They take themselves for granted. I have had to justify my existence very minute, and I have done so, I have proved—well.

WIN. Let's face it, vacancies are going to be ones where you'll be in competition with younger men. And there are companies that will value your experience enough you'll be in with a chance. There are also fields that are easier for a woman, there is a cosmetic company here where your experience might be relevant. It's eight and a half, I don't know if that appeals.

LOUISE. I've proved I can earn money. It's more important to get away. I feel it's now or never. I sometimes / think—

WIN. You shouldn't talk too much at an interview.

LOUISE. I don't. I don't normally talk about myself. I know very well how to handle myself in an office situation. I only talk to you because it seems to me this is different, it's your job to understand me, surely. You asked the questions.

WIN. I think I understand you sufficiently.

LOUISE. Well good, that's good.

WIN. Do you drink?

LOUISE. Certainly not. I'm not a teetotaller, I think that's very suspect, it's seen as being an alcoholic if you're teetotal. What do you mean? I don't drink. Why?

WIN. I drink.

LOUISE. I don't.

WIN. Good for you.

(The lights crossfade to the main office with Marlene sitting at her desk. Win and Louise exit. Angie arrives in the main office.)

ANGIE. Hello.

MARLENE. Have you an appointment?

ANGIE. It's me. I've come.

MARLENE. What? It's not Angie?

ANGIE. It was hard to find this place. I got lost.

MARLENE. How did you get past the receptionist? The girl on the desk, didn't she try to stop you?

ANGIE. What desk?

MARLENE. Never mind.

ANGIE. I just walked in. I was looking for you.

MARLENE. Well you found me.

ANGIE. Yes.

MARLENE. So where's your mum? Are you up in town for the day?

ANGIE. Not really.

MARLENE. Sit down. Do you feel all right?

ANGIE. Yes thank you.

MARLENE. So where's Joyce?

ANGIE. She's at home.

MARLENE. Did you come up on a school trip then?

ANGIE. I've left school.

MARLENE. Did you come up with a friend?

ANGIE. No. There's just me.

MARLENE. You came up by yourself, that's fun. What have you been doing? Shopping? Tower of London?

ANGIE. No, I just come here. I come to you.

MARLENE. That's very nice of you to think of paying your aunty a visit. There's not many nieces make that the first port of call. Would you like a cup of coffee?

ANGIE. No thank you.

MARLENE. Tea, orange?

ANGIE. No thank you.

MARLENE. Do you feel all right?

ANGIE. Yes thank you.

MARLENE. Are you tired from the journey?

ANGIE. Yes, I'm tired from the journey.

MARLENE. You sit there for a bit then. How's Joyce?

ANGIE. She's all right.

MARLENE. Same as ever.

ANGIE. Oh yes.

MARLENE. Unfortunately you've picked a day when I'm rather busy, if there's ever a day when I'm not, or I'd take you out to lunch and we'd go to Madame Tussaud's. We could go shopping. What time do you have to be back? Have you got a day return?

ANGIE. No.

MARLENE. So what train are you going back on?

ANGIE. I came on the bus.

MARLENE. So what bus are you going back on? Are you staying the night?

ANGIE. Yes.

MARLENE. Who are you staying with? Do you want me to put you up for the night, is that it?

ANGIE. Yes please.

MARLENE. I haven't got a spare bed.

ANGIE. I can sleep on the floor.

MARLENE. You can sleep on the sofa.

ANGIE. Yes please.

MARLENE. I do think Joyce might have phoned me. It's like her.

ANGIE. This is where you work is it?

MARLENE. It's where I have been working the last two years but I'm going to move into another office.

ANGIE. It's lovely.

MARLENE. My new office is nicer than this. There's just the one big desk in it for me.

ANGIE. Can I see it?

MARLENE. Not now, no, there's someone else in it now. But he's leaving at the end of next week and I'm going to do his job.

ANGIE. Is that good?

MARLENE. Yes, it's very good.

ANGIE. Are you going to be in charge?

MARLENE. Yes I am.

ANGIE. I knew you would be.

MARLENE. How did you know?

ANGIE. I knew you'd be in charge of everything.

MARLENE. Not quite everything.

ANGIE. You will be.

MARLENE. Well we'll see.

ANGIE. Can I see it next week then?

MARLENE. Will you still be here next week?

ANGIE. Yes.

MARLENE. Don't you have to go home?

ANGIE. No.

MARLENE. Why not?

ANGIE. It's all right.

MARLENE. Is it all right?

ANGIE. Yes, don't worry about it.

MARLENE. Does Joyce know where you are?

ANGIE. Yes of course she does.

MARLENE. Well does she?

ANGIE. Don't worry about it.

MARLENE. How long are you planning to stay with me then?

ANGIE. You know when you came to see us last year?

MARLENE. Yes, that was nice wasn't it?

ANGIE. That was the best day of my whole life.

MARLENE. So how long are you planning to stay?

ANGIE. Don't you want me?

MARLENE. Yes yes, I just wondered.

ANGIE. I won't stay if you don't want me.

MARLENE. No, of course you can stay.

ANGIE. I'll sleep on the floor. I won't be any bother.

MARLENE. Don't get upset.

ANGIE. I'm not, I'm not. Don't worry about it.

(*Mrs Kidd comes in.*)

MRS. KIDD. Excuse me.

MARLENE. Yes.

MRS KIDD. Excuse me.

MARLENE. Can I help you?

MRS KIDD. Excuse me bursting in on you like this but I have to talk to you.

MARLENE. I am engaged at the moment. / If you could go to reception—

MRS KIDD. I'm Rosemary Kidd, Howard's wife, you don't recognize me but we did meet, I remember you of course / but you wouldn't—

MARLENE. Yes of course, Mrs. Kidd, I'm sorry, we did meet. Howard's about somewhere I expect, have you looked in his office?

MRS KIDD. Howard's not about, no. I'm afraid it's you I've come to see if I could have a minute or two.

MARLENE. I do have an appointment in five minutes.

MRS KIDD. This won't take five minutes. I'm very sorry. It is a matter of some urgency.

MARLENE. Well of course. What can I do for you?

MRS KIDD. I just wanted a chat, an informal chat. It's not something I can simply—I'm sorry if I'm interrupting your work. I know office work isn't like housework / which is all interruptions.

MARLENE. No, no, this is my niece. Angie. Mrs. Kidd.

MRS KIDD. Very pleased to meet you.

ANGIE. Very well thank you.

MRS KIDD. Howard's not in today.

MARLENE. Isn't he?

MRS KIDD. He's feeling poorly.

MARLENE. I didn't know. I'm sorry to hear that.

MRS KIDD. The fact is he's in a state of shock. About what's happened.

MARLENE. What has happened?

MRS KIDD. You should know if anyone. I'm referring to you being appointed managing director instead of Howard. He hasn't been at all well all weekend. He hasn't slept for three nights. I haven't slept.

MARLENE. I'm sorry to hear that, Mrs. Kidd. Has he thought of taking sleeping pills?

MRS KIDD. It's very hard when someone has worked all these years.

MARLENE. Business life is full of little setbacks. I'm sure Howard knows that. He'll bounce back in a day or two. We all bounce back.

MRS. KIDD. If you could see him you'd know what I'm talking about. What's it going to do to him working for a woman? I think if it was a man he'd get over it as something normal.

MARLENE. I think he's going to have to get over it.

MRS. KIDD. It's me that bears the brunt. I'm not the one that's been promoted. I put him first every inch of the way. And now what do I get? You women this, you women that. It's not my fault. You're going to have to be very careful how you handle him. He's very hurt.

MARLENE. Naturally I'll be tactful and pleasant to him, you don't start pushing someone round. I'll consult him over any decisions affecting his department. But that's no different, Mrs. Kidd, from any of my other colleagues.

MRS KIDD. I think it is different, because he's a man.

MARLENE. I'm not quite sure why you came to see me.

MRS KIDD. I had to do something.

MARLENE. Well you've done it, you've seen me. I think

that's probably all we've time for. I'm sorry he's been taking it out on you. He really is a shit, Howard.

MRS KIDD. But he's got a family to support. He's got three children. It's only fair.

MARLENE. Are you suggesting I give up the job to him then?

MRS KIDD. It had crossed my mind if you were unavailable after all for some reason, he would be the natural second choice I think, don't you? I'm not asking.

MARLENE. Good.

MRS KIDD. You mustn't tell him I came. He's very proud.

MARLENE. If he doesn't like what's happening here he can go and work somewhere else.

MRS KIDD. Is that a threat?

MARLENE. I'm sorry but I do have some work to do.

MRS KIDD. It's not that easy, a man of Howard's age. You don't care. I thought he was going too far but he's right. You're one of these ballbreakers, / that's what you

MARLENE. I'm sorry but I do have some work to do.

MRS KIDD. are. You'll end up miserable and lonely. You're not natural.

MARLENE. Could you please piss off?

MRS KIDD. I thought if I saw you at least I'd be doing something. (Mrs. Kidd goes.)

MARLENE. I've got to go and do some work now. Will you come back later?

ANGIE. I think you were wonderful.

MARLENE. I've got to go and do some work now.

ANGIE. You told her to piss off.

MARLENE. Will you come back later?

ANGIE. Can't I stay here?

MARLENE. Don't you want to go sightseeing?

ANGIE. I'd rather stay here.

MARLENE. You can stay here I suppose, if it's not boring.

ANGIE. It's where I most want to be in the world.

MARLENE. I'll see you later then.

(Marlene goes. Shona and Nell enter the interviewing area. Angie sits at Win's desk. The lights crossfade to Nell and Shona in the interviewing area.)

NELL. Is this right? You are Shona?

SHONA. Yeh.

NELL. It says here you're twenty-nine.

SHONA. Yeh.

NELL. Too many late nights, me. So you've been where you are for four years, Shona, you're earning six basic and three commission. So what's the problem?

SHONA. No problem.

NELL. Why do you want a change?

SHONA. Just a change.

NELL. Change of product, change of area?

SHONA. Both.

NELL. But you're happy on the road?

SHONA. I like driving.

NELL. You're not after management status?

SHONA. I would like management status.

NELL. You'd be interested in titular management status but not come off the road?

SHONA. I want to be on the road, yeh.

NELL. So how many calls have you been making a day?

SHONA. Six.

NELL. And what proportion of those are successful?

SHONA. Six.

NELL. That's hard to believe.

SHONA. Four.

NELL. You find it easy to get the initial interest do you?

SHONA. Oh yeh, I get plenty of initial interest.

NELL. And what about closing?

SHONA. I close, don't I?

NELL. Because that's what an employer is going to have doubts about with a lady as I needn't tell you, whether she's got the guts to push through to a closing situation. They think we're too nice. They think we listen to the buyer's doubts. They think we consider his needs and his feelings.

SHONA. I never consider people's feelings.

NELL. I was selling for six years, I can sell anything, I've sold in three continents, and I'm jolly as they come but I'm not very nice.

SHONA. I'm not very nice.

NELL. What sort of time do you have on the road with the other reps? Get on all right? Handle the chat?

SHONA. I get on. Keep myself to myself.

NELL. Fairly much of a loner are you?

SHONA. Sometimes.

NELL. So what field are you interested in?

SHONA. Computers.

NELL. That's a top field as you know and you'll be up against some very slick fellas there, there's some very pretty boys in computers, it's an American-style field.

SHONA. That's why I want to do it.

NELL. Video systems appeal? That's a high-flying situation.

SHONA. Video systems appeal OK.

NELL. Because Prestel have half a dozen vacancies I'm looking to fill at the moment. We're talking in the area of ten to fifteen thousand here and upwards.

SHONA. Sounds OK.

NELL. I've half a mind to go for it myself. But it's good money here if you've got the top clients. Could you fancy it do you think?

SHONA. Work here?

NELL. I'm not in a position to offer, there's nothing officially going just now, but we're always on the lookout. There's not that many of us. We could keep in touch.

SHONA. I like driving.

NELL. So the Prestel appeals?

SHONA. Yeh.

NELL. What about ties?

SHONA. No ties.

NELL. So relocation wouldn't be a problem.

SHONA. No problem.

NELL. So just fill me in a bit more could you about what you've been doing.

SHONA. What I've been doing. It's all down there.

NELL. The bare facts are down here but I've got to present you to an employer.

SHONA. I'm twenty-nine years old.

NELL. So it says here.

SHONA. We look young. Youngness runs in the family in our family.

NELL. So just describe your present job for me.

SHONA. My present job at present. I have a car. I have a Porsche. I go up the M1 a lot. Burn up the M1 a lot. Straight up the M1 in the fast lane to where the clients are, Staffordshire, Yorkshire, I do a lot in Yorkshire. I'm selling electric things. Like dishwashers, washing machines, stainless steel tubs are a feature and the reliability of the program. After sales service, we offer a very good after sales service, spare parts, plenty of spare parts. And fridges, I sell a lot of fridges specially in the summer. People want to buy fridges in the summer because of the heat melting the butter and you get fed up standing the milk in a basin of cold water with a cloth over, stands to reason people don't want to do that in this day and age. So I sell a lot of them. Big ones with big freezers. Big freezers. And I stay in hotels at night when I'm away from home. On my expense account. I stay in various hotels. They know me, the ones I go to. I check in, have a bath, have a shower. Then I go down to the bar, have a gin and tonic, have a chat. Then I go into the dining room and have dinner. I usually have fillet steak and mushrooms, I like mushrooms. I like smoked salmon very much. I like having a salad on the side. Green salad. I don't like tomatoes.

NELL. Christ what a waste of time.

SHONA. Beg your pardon?

NELL. Not a word of this is true is it?

SHONA. How do you mean?

NELL. You just filled in the form with a pack of lies.

SHONA. Not exactly.

NELL. How old are you?

SHONA. Twenty-nine.

NELL. Nineteen?

SHONA. Twenty-one.

NELL. And what jobs have you done? Have you done any?

SHONA. I could though, I bet you.

(*The lights crossfade to the main office with Angie sitting as before. Win comes in to the main office. Shona and Nell exit.*)

WIN. Who's sitting in my chair?

ANGIE. What? Sorry.

WIN. Who's been eating my porridge?

ANGIE. What?

WIN. It's all right, I saw Marlene. Angie isn't it? I'm Win. And I'm not going out for lunch because I'm knackered.

I'm going to set me down here and have a yogurt. Do you like yogurt?

ANGIE. No.

WIN. That's good because I've only got one. Are you hungry?

ANGIE. No.

WIN. There's a cafe on the corner.

ANGIE. No thank you. Do you work here?

WIN. How did you guess?

ANGIE. Because you look as if you might work here and you're sitting at the desk. Have you always worked here?

WIN. No I was headhunted. That means I was working for another outfit like this and this lot came and offered me more money. I broke my contract, there was a hell of a stink. There's not many top ladies about. Your aunty's a smashing bird.

ANGIE. Yes I know.

MARLENE. Fan are you? Fan of your aunty's?

ANGIE. Do you think I could work here?

WIN. Not at the moment.

ANGIE. How do I start?

WIN. What can you do?

ANGIE. I don't know. Nothing.

WIN. Type?

ANGIE. Not very well. The letters jump up when I do capitals. I was going to do a CSE[7] in commerce but I didn't.

WIN. What have you got?

ANGIE. What?

WIN. CSE's, O's.

ANGIE. Nothing, none of that. Did you do all that?

WIN. Oh yes, all that, and a science degree funnily enough. I started out doing medical research but there's no money in it. I thought I'd go abroad. Did you know they sell Coca-Cola in Russia and Pepsi-Cola in China? You don't have to be qualified as much as you might think. Men are awful bullshitters, they like to make out jobs are harder than they are. Any job I ever did I started doing it better than the rest of the crowd and they didn't like it. So I'd get unpopular and I'd have a drink to cheer myself up. I lived with a fella and supported him for four years, he couldn't get work. After that I went to California. I like the sunshine. Americans know how to live. This country's too slow. Then I went to Mexico, still in sales, but it's no country for a single lady. I came home, went bonkers for a bit, thought I was five different people, got over that all right, the psychiatrist said I was perfectly sane and highly intelligent. Got married in a moment of weakness and he's inside now, he's been inside four years, and I've not been to see him too much this last year. I like this better than sales, I'm not really that aggressive. I started thinking sales was a good job if you want to meet people,

[7]**CSE:** Certificate of Secondary Education.

but you're meeting people that don't want to meet you. It's no good if you like being liked. Here your clients want to meet you because you're the one doing them some good. They hope. (*Angie has fallen asleep. Nell comes in.*)

NELL. You're talking to yourself, sunshine.

WIN. So what's new?

NELL. Who is this?

WIN. Marlene's little niece.

NELL. What's she got, brother, sister? She never talks about her family.

WIN. I was telling her my life story.

NELL. Violins?

WIN. No, success story.

NELL. You've heard Howard's had a heart attack?

WIN. No, when?

NELL. I heard just now. He hadn't come in, he was at home, he's gone to hospital. He's not dead. His wife was here, she rushed off in a cab.

WIN. Too much butter, too much smoke. We must send him some flowers. (*Marlene comes in.*) You've heard about Howard?

MARLENE. Poor sod.

NELL. Lucky he didn't get the job if that's what his health's like.

MARLENE. Is she asleep?

WIN. She wants to work here.

MARLENE. Packer in Tesco more like.

WIN. She's a nice kid. Isn't she?

MARLENE. She's a bit thick. She's a bit funny.

WIN. She thinks you're wonderful.

MARLENE. She's not going to make it.

SCENE II

(*Joyce's kitchen. Sunday evening, a year earlier. The lights come up on Joyce, Angie, and Marlene. Marlene is taking presents out of bright carrier bag. Angie has already opened a box of chocolates.*)

MARLENE. Just a few little things. / I've

JOYCE. There's no need.

MARLENE. no memory for birthdays have I, and Christmas seems to slip by. So I think I owe Angie a few presents.

JOYCE. What do you say?

ANGIE. Thank you very much. Thank you very much, Aunty Marlene. (*She opens a present. It is the dress from Act I, new.*) Oh look, Mum, isn't it lovely?

MARLENE. I don't know if it's the right size. She's grown up since I saw her. / I knew she was always

ANGIE. Isn't it lovely?

MARLENE. tall for her age.

JOYCE. She's a big lump.

MARLENE. Hold it up, Angie, let's see.

ANGIE. I'll put it on, shall I?

MARLENE. Yes, try it on.

JOYCE. Go to your room then, we don't want / a strip show thank you.

ANGIE. Of course I'm going to my room, what do you think? Look Mum, here's something for you. Open it, go on. What is it? Can I open it for you?

JOYCE. Yes, you open it, pet.

ANGIE. Don't you want to open it yourself? / Go on.

JOYCE. I don't mind, you can do it.

ANGIE. It's something hard. It's—what is it? A bottle. Drink is it? No, it's what? Perfume, look. What a lot. Open it, look, let's smell it. Oh it's strong. It's lovely. Put it on me. How do you do it? Put it on me.

JOYCE. You're too young.

ANGIE. I can play wearing it like dressing up.

JOYCE. And you're too old for that. Here, give it here, I'll do it, you'll tip the whole bottle over yourself / and we'll have you smelling all summer.

ANGIE. Put it on you. Do I smell? Put it on Aunty too. Put it on Aunty too. Let's all smell.

MARLENE. I didn't know what you'd like.

JOYCE. There's no danger I'd have it already, / that's one thing.

ANGIE. Now we all smell the same.

MARLENE. It's a bit of nonsense.

JOYCE. It's very kind of you Marlene, you shouldn't.

ANGIE. Now I'll put on the dress and then we'll see. (*Angie goes.*)

JOYCE. You've caught me on the hop with the place in a mess. / If you'd let me

MARLENE. That doesn't matter.

JOYCE. know you was coming I'd have got something in to eat. We had our dinner dinnertime. We're just going to have a cup of tea. You could have an egg.

MARLENE. No, I'm not hungry. Tea's fine.

JOYCE. I don't expect you take sugar.

MARLENE. Why not?

JOYCE. You take care of yourself.

MARLENE. How do you mean you didn't know I was coming?

JOYCE. You could have written. I know we're not on the phone but we're not completely in the dark ages, / we do have a postman.

MARLENE. But you asked me to come.

JOYCE. How did I ask you to come?

MARLENE. Angie said when she phoned up.

JOYCE. Angie phoned up, did she?

MARLENE. Was it just Angie's idea?

JOYCE. What did she say?

MARLENE. She said you wanted me to come and see you. / It was a couple of

JOYCE. Ha.

MARLENE. weeks ago. How was I to know that's a ridiculous idea? My diary's always full a couple of weeks ahead so we fixed it for this weekend. I was meant to get here earlier but I was held up. She gave me messages from you.

JOYCE. Didn't you wonder why I didn't phone you myself?

MARLENE. She said you didn't like using the phone. You're shy on the phone and can't use it. I don't know what you're like, do I.

JOYCE. Are there people who can't use the phone?

MARLENE. I expect so.

JOYCE. I haven't met any.

MARLENE. Why should I think she was lying?

JOYCE. Because she's like what she's like.

MARLENE. How do I know / what she's like?

JOYCE. It's not my fault you don't know what she's like. You never come and see her.

MARLENE. Well I have now / and you don't seem over the moon.*

JOYCE. Good. *Well I'd have got a cake if she'd told me. (*Pause*.)

MARLENE. I did wonder why you wanted to see me.

JOYCE. I didn't want to see you.

MARLENE. Yes, I know. Shall I go?

JOYCE. I don't mind seeing you.

MARLENE. Great, I feel really welcome.

JOYCE. You can come and see Angie any time you like, I'm not stopping you. / You know where we are. You're the one went away, not me. I'm right here where I was. And will be a few years yet I shouldn't wonder.

MARLENE. All right. All right. (*Joyce gives Marlene a cup of tea*.)

JOYCE. Tea.

MARLENE. Sugar? (*Joyce passes Marlene the sugar*.) It's very quiet down here.

JOYCE. I expect you'd notice it.

MARLENE. The air smells different too.

JOYCE. That's the scent.

MARLENE. No, I mean walking down the lane.

JOYCE. What sort of air you get in London then?

(*Angie comes in, wearing the dress. It fits*.)

MARLENE. Oh, very pretty. / You do look pretty, Angie.

JOYCE. That fits all right.

MARLENE. Do you like the color?

ANGIE. Beautiful. Beautiful.

JOYCE. You better take it off, / you'll get it dirty.

ANGIE. I want to wear it. I want to wear it.

MARLENE. It is for wearing after all. You can't just hang it up and look at it.

ANGIE. I love it.

JOYCE. Well if you must you must.

ANGIE. If someone asks me what's my favorite colour I'll tell them it's this. Thank you very much, Aunty Marlene.

MARLENE. You didn't tell your mum you asked me down.

ANGIE. I wanted it to be a surprise.

JOYCE. I'll give you a surprise / one of these days.

ANGIE. I thought you'd like to see her. She hasn't been here since I was nine. People do see their aunts.

MARLENE. Is it that long? Doesn't time fly?

ANGIE. I wanted to.

JOYCE. I'm not cross.

ANGIE. Are you glad?

JOYCE. I smell nicer anyhow, don't I?

(*Kit comes in without saying anything, as if she lived there*.)

MARLENE. I think it was a good idea, Angie, about time. We are sisters after all. It's a pity to let that go.

JOYCE. This is Kitty, / who lives up the road. This is Angie's Aunty Marlene.

KIT. What's that?

ANGIE. It's a present. Do you like it?

KIT. It's all right. / Are you coming out?*

MARLENE. Hello, Kitty.

ANGIE. *No.

KIT. What's that smell?

ANGIE. It's a present.

KIT. It's horrible. Come on.*

MARLENE. Have a chocolate.

ANGIE. *No, I'm busy.

KIT. Coming out later?

ANGIE. No.

KIT (*to Marlene*). Hello. (*Kit goes without a chocolate*.)

JOYCE. She's a little girl Angie sometimes plays with because she's the only child lives really close. She's like a little sister to her really. Angie's good with little children.

MARLENE. Do you want to work with children, Angie? / Be a teacher or a nursery nurse?

JOYCE. I don't think she's ever thought of it.

MARLENE. What do you want to do?

JOYCE. She hasn't an idea in her head what she wants to do. / Lucky to get anything.

MARLENE. Angie?

JOYCE. She's not clever like you. (*Pause*.)

MARLENE. I'm not clever, just pushy.

JOYCE. True enough. (*Marlene takes a bottle of whisky out of the bag*.) I don't drink spirits.

ANGIE. You do at Christmas.

JOYCE. It's not Christmas, is it?

ANGIE. It's better than Christmas.

MARLENE. Glasses?

JOYCE. Just a small one then.

MARLENE. Do you want some, Angie?

ANGIE. I can't, can I?

JOYCE. Taste it if you want. You won't like it. (*Angie tastes it*.)

MARLENE. We got drunk together the night your grandfather died.

JOYCE. We did not get drunk.

MARLENE. I got drunk. You were just overcome with grief.

JOYCE. I still keep up the grave with flowers.

MARLENE. Do you really?

JOYCE. Why wouldn't I?

MARLENE. Have you seen Mother?

JOYCE. Of course I've seen Mother.

MARLENE. I mean lately.

JOYCE. Of course I've seen her lately, I go every Thursday.

MARLENE (*to Angie*). Do you remember your grandfather?

ANGIE. He got me out of the bath one night in a towel.

MARLENE. Did he? I don't think he ever gave me a bath. Did he give you a bath, Joyce? He probably got soft in his old age. Did you like him?

ANGIE. Yes of course.

MARLENE. Why?

ANGIE. What?

MARLENE. So what's the news? How's Mrs. Paisley? Still going crazily? / And Dorothy. What happened to Dorothy?*

ANGIE. Who's Mrs. Paisley?

JOYCE. *She went to Canada.

MARLENE. Did she? What to do?

JOYCE. I don't know. She just went to Canada.

MARLENE. Well / good for her.

ANGIE. Mr. Connolly killed his wife.

MARLENE. What, Connolly at Whitegates?

ANGIE. They found her body in the garden. / Under the cabbages.

MARLENE. He was always so proper.

JOYCE. Stuck up git. Connolly. Best lawyer money could buy but he couldn't get out of it. She was carrying on with Matthew.

MARLENE. How old's Matthew then?

JOYCE. Twenty-one. / He's got a motorbike.

MARLENE. I think he's about six.

ANGIE. How can he be six? He's six years older than me. / If he was six I'd be nothing, I'd be just born this minute.

JOYCE. Your aunty knows that, she's just being silly. She means it's so long since she's been here she's forgotten about Matthew.

ANGIE. You were here for my birthday when I was nine. I had a pink cake. Kit was only five then, she was four, she hadn't started school yet. She could read already when she went to school. You remember my birthday? / You remember me?

MARLENE. Yes, I remember the cake.

ANGIE. You remember me?

MARLENE. Yes, I remember you.

ANGIE. And Mum and Dad was there, and Kit was.

MARLENE. Yes, how is your dad? Where is he tonight? Up the pub?

JOYCE. No, he's not here.

MARLENE. I can see he's not here.

JOYCE. He moved out.

MARLENE. What? When did he? / Just recently?*

ANGIE. Didn't you know that? You don't know much.

JOYCE. *No, it must be three years ago. Don't be rude, Angie.

ANGIE. I'm not, am I Aunty? What else don't you know?

JOYCE. You was in America or somewhere. You sent a postcard.

ANGIE. I've got that in my room. It's the Grand Canyon. Do you want to see it? Shall I get it? I can get it for you.

MARLENE. Yes, all right. (*Angie goes.*)

JOYCE. You could be married with twins for all I know. You must have affairs and break up and I don't need to know about any of that so I don't see what the fuss is about.

MARLENE. What fuss? (*Angie comes back with the postcard.*)

ANGIE. "Driving across the states for a new job in L. A. It's a long way but the car goes very fast. It's very hot. Wish you were here. Love from Aunty Marlene."

JOYCE. Did you make a lot of money?

MARLENE. I spent a lot.

ANGIE. I want to go to America. Will you take me?

JOYCE. She's not going to America, she's been to America, stupid.

ANGIE. She might go again, stupid. It's not something you do once. People who go keep going all the time, back and forth on jets. They go on Concorde and Laker and get jet lag. Will you take me?

MARLENE. I'm not planning a trip.

ANGIE. Will you let me know?

JOYCE. Angie, / you're getting silly.

ANGIE. I want to be American.

JOYCE. It's time you were in bed.

ANGIE. No it's not. / I don't have to go to bed at all tonight.

JOYCE. School in the morning.

ANGIE. I'll wake up.

JOYCE. Come on now, you know how you get.

ANGIE. How do I get? / I don't get anyhow.*

JOYCE. Angie. *Are you staying the night?

MARLENE. Yes, if that's all right. / I'll see you in the morning.

ANGIE. You can have my bed. I'll sleep on the sofa.

JOYCE. You will not, you'll sleep in your bed. / Think

ANGIE. Mum.

JOYCE. I can't see through that? I can just see you going to sleep / with us talking.

ANGIE. I would, I would go to sleep, I'd love that.

JOYCE. I'm going to get cross, Angie.

ANGIE. I want to show her something.

JOYCE. Then bed.

ANGIE. It's a secret.

JOYCE. Then I expect it's in your room so off you go. Give us a shout when you're ready for bed and your aunty'll be up and see you.

ANGIE. Will you?

MARLENE. Yes of course. (*Angie goes. Silence.*)

It's cold tonight.

JOYCE. Will you be all right on the sofa? You can / have my bed.

MARLENE. The sofa's fine.

JOYCE. Yes the forecast said rain tonight but it's held off.

MARLENE. I was going to walk down to the estuary but I've left it a bit late. Is it just the same?

JOYCE. They cut down the hedges a few years back. Is that since you were here?

MARLENE. But it's not changed down the end, all the mud? And the reeds? We used to pick them up when they were bigger than us. Are there still lapwings?

JOYCE. You get strangers walking there on a Sunday. I expect they're looking at the mud and the lapwings, yes.

MARLENE. You could have left.

JOYCE. Who says I wanted to leave?

MARLENE. Stop getting at me then, you're really boring.

JOYCE. How could I have left?

MARLENE. Did you want to?

JOYCE. I said how, / how could I?

MARLENE. If you'd wanted to you'd have done it.

JOYCE. Christ.

MARLENE. Are we getting drunk?

JOYCE. Do you want something to eat?

MARLENE. No, I'm getting drunk.

JOYCE. Funny time to visit, Sunday evening.

MARLENE. I came this morning. I spent the day—

ANGIE (off). Aunty! Aunty Marlene!

MARLENE. I'd better go.

JOYCE. Go on then.

MARLENE. All right.

ANGIE (off). Aunty! Can you hear me? I'm ready.

(*Marlene goes. Joyce goes on sitting, clears up, sits again. Marlene comes back.*)

JOYCE. So what's the secret?

MARLENE. It's a secret.

JOYCE. I know what it is anyway.

MARLENE. I bet you don't. You always said that.

JOYCE. It's her exercise book.

MARLENE. Yes, but you don't know what's in it.

JOYCE. It's some game, some secret society she has with Kit.

MARLENE. You don't know the password. You don't know the code.

JOYCE. You're really in it, aren't you. Can you do the handshake?

MARLENE. She didn't mention a handshake.

JOYCE. I thought they'd have a special handshake. She spends hours writing that but she's useless at school. She copies things out of books about black magic, and politicians out of the paper. It's a bit childish.

MARLENE. I think it's a plot to take over the world.

JOYCE. She's been in the remedial class the last two years.

MARLENE. I came up this morning and spent the day in Ipswich. I went to see mother.

JOYCE. Did she recognize you?

MARLENE. Are you trying to be funny?

JOYCE. No, she does wander.

MARLENE. She wasn't wandering at all, she was very lucid thank you.

JOYCE. You were very lucky then.

MARLENE. Fucking awful life she's had.

JOYCE. Don't tell me.

MARLENE. Fucking waste.

JOYCE. Don't talk to me.

MARLENE. Why shouldn't I talk? Why shouldn't I talk to you? / Isn't she my mother too?

JOYCE. Look, you've left, you've gone away, / we can do without you.

MARLENE. I left home, so what, I left home. People do leave home / it is normal.

JOYCE. We understand that, we can do without you.

MARLENE. We weren't happy. Were you happy?

JOYCE. Don't come back.

MARLENE. So it's just your mother is it, your child, you never wanted me round, / you were jealous

JOYCE. Here we go.

MARLENE. of me because I was the little one and I was clever.

JOYCE. I'm not clever enough for all this psychology / if that's what it is.

MARLENE. Why can't I visit my own family / without

JOYCE. Aah.

MARLENE. all this?

JOYCE. Just don't go on about Mum's life when you haven't been to see her for how many years. / I go

MARLENE. It's up to me.

JOYCE. and see her every week.

MARLENE. Then don't go and see her every week.

JOYCE. Somebody has to.

MARLENE. No they don't. / Why do they?

JOYCE. How would I feel if I didn't go?

MARLENE. A lot better.

JOYCE. I hope you feel better.

MARLENE. It's up to me.

JOYCE. You couldn't get out of here fast enough. (*Pause.*)

MARLENE. Of course I couldn't get out of here fast enough. What was I going to do? Marry a dairyman who'd come home pissed? / Don't you fucking this

JOYCE. Christ.

MARLENE. fucking that fucking bitch fucking tell me what to fucking do fucking.

JOYCE. I don't know how you could leave your own child.

MARLENE. You were quick enough to take her.

JOYCE. What does that mean?

MARLENE. You were quick enough to take her.

JOYCE. Or what? Have her put in a home? Have some stranger / take her would you rather?

MARLENE. You couldn't have one so you took mine.

JOYCE. I didn't know that then.

MARLENE. Like hell, / married three years.

JOYCE. I didn't know that. Plenty of people / take that long.

MARLENE. Well it turned out lucky for you, didn't it?

JOYCE. Turned out all right for you by the look of you. You'd be getting a few less thousand a year.

MARLENE. Not necessarily.

JOYCE. You'd be stuck here / like you said.

MARLENE. I could have taken her with me.

JOYCE. You didn't want to take her with you. It's no good coming back now, Marlene, / and saying—

MARLENE. I know a managing director who's got two children, she breast feeds in the board room, she pays a hundred pounds a week on domestic help alone and she can afford that because she's an extremely high-powered lady earning a great deal of money.

JOYCE. So what's that got to do with you at the age of seventeen?

MARLENE. Just because you were married and had somewhere to live—

JOYCE. You could have lived at home. / Or live

MARLENE. Don't be stupid.

JOYCE. with me and Frank. / You

MARLENE. You never suggested.

JOYCE. said you weren't keeping it. You shouldn't have had it / if you wasn't

MARLENE. Here we go.

JOYCE. going to keep it. You was the most stupid, / for someone so clever you was the most stupid, get yourself pregnant, not go to the doctor, not tell.

MARLENE. You wanted it, you said you were glad, I remember the day, you said I'm glad you never got rid of it, I'll look after it, you said that down by the river. So what are you saying, sunshine, you don't want her?

JOYCE. Course I'm not saying that.

MARLENE. Because I'll take her, / wake her up and pack now.

JOYCE. You wouldn't know how to begin to look after her.

MARLENE. Don't you want her?

JOYCE. Course I do, she's my child.

MARLENE. Then why are you going on about / why did I have her?

JOYCE. You said I got her off you / when you didn't—

MARLENE. I said you were lucky / the way it—

JOYCE. Have a child now if you want one. You're not old.

MARLENE. I might do.

JOYCE. Good. (Pause.)

MARLENE. I've been on the pill so long / I'm probably sterile.

JOYCE. Listen when Angie was six months I did get pregnant and I lost it because I was so tired looking after your fucking baby / because she cried so

MARLENE. You never told me.

JOYCE. much—yes I did tell you— / and the doctor

MARLENE. Well I forgot.

JOYCE. said if I'd sat down all day with my feet up I'd've kept it / and that's the only chance I ever had because after that—

MARLENE. I've had two abortions, are you interested? Shall I tell you about them? Well I won't, it's boring, it wasn't a problem. I don't like messy talk about blood / and what a bad time we all had.

JOYCE. If I hadn't had your baby. The doctor said.

MARLENE. I don't want a baby. I don't want to talk about gynaecology.

JOYCE. Then stop trying to get Angie off of me.

MARLENE. I come down here after six years. All night you've been saying I don't come often enough. If I don't come for another six years she'll be twenty-one, will that be OK?

JOYCE. That'll be fine, yes, six years would suit me fine. (Pause.)

MARLENE. I was afraid of this. I only came because I thought you wanted . . . I just want . . . (She cries.)

JOYCE. Don't grizzle, Marlene, for God's sake. Marly? Come on, pet. Love you really. Fucking stop it, will you? (She goes to Marlene.)

MARLENE. No, let me cry. I like it. (They laugh. Marlene begins to stop crying.) I knew I'd cry if I wasn't careful.

JOYCE. Everyone's always crying in this house. Nobody takes any notice.

MARLENE. You've been wonderful looking after Angie.

JOYCE. Don't get carried away.

MARLENE. I can't write letters but I do think of you.

JOYCE. You're getting drunk. I'm going to make some tea.

MARLENE. Love you. (Joyce gets up to make tea.)

JOYCE. I can see why you'd want to leave. It's a dump here.

MARLENE. So what's this about you and Frank?

JOYCE. He was always carrying on, wasn't he? And if I wanted to go out in the evening he'd go mad, even if it was nothing, a class, I was going to go to an evening class. So he had this girlfriend, only twenty-two poor cow, and I said go on, off you go, hoppit. I don't think he even likes her.

MARLENE. So what about money?

JOYCE. I've always said I don't want your money.

MARLENE. No, does he send you money?

JOYCE. I've got four different cleaning jobs. Adds up. There's not a lot round here.

MARLENE. Does Angie miss him?

JOYCE. She doesn't say.

MARLENE. Does she see him?

JOYCE. He was never that fond of her to be honest.

MARLENE. He tried to kiss me once. When you were engaged.

JOYCE. Did you fancy him?

MARLENE. No, he looked like a fish.

JOYCE. He was lovely then.

MARLENE. Ugh.

JOYCE. Well I fancied him. For about three years.

MARLENE. Have you got someone else?

JOYCE. There's not a lot round here. Mind you, the minute you're on your own, you'd be amazed how your friends' husbands drop by. I'd sooner do without.

MARLENE. I don't see why you couldn't take my money.

JOYCE. I do, so don't bother about it.

MARLENE. Only got to ask.

JOYCE. So what about you? Good job?

MARLENE. Good for a laugh. / Got back

JOYCE. Good for more than a laugh I should think.

MARLENE. from the US of A a bit wiped out and slotted into this speedy employment agency and still there.

JOYCE. You can always find yourself work then.

MARLENE. That's right.

JOYCE. And men?

MARLENE. Oh there's always men.

JOYCE. No one special?

MARLENE. There's fellas who like to be seen with a high-flying lady. Shows they've got something really good in their pants. But they can't take the day to day. They're waiting for me to turn into the little woman. Or maybe I'm just horrible of course.

JOYCE. Who needs them?

MARLENE. Who needs them? Well I do. But I need adventures more. So on into the sunset. I think the eighties are going to be stupendous.

JOYCE. Who for?

MARLENE. For me. / I think I'm going up up up.

JOYCE. Oh for you. Yes, I'm sure they will.

MARLENE. And for the country, come to that. Get the economy back on its feet and whosh. She's a tough lady, Maggie. I'd give her a job. / She just needs to hang

JOYCE. You voted for them, did you?

MARLENE. in there. This country needs to stop whining. / Monetarism is not

JOYCE. Drink your tea and shut up, pet.

MARLENE. stupid. It takes time, determination. No more slop. / And

JOYCE. Well I think they're filthy bastards.

MARLENE. who's got to drive it on? First woman prime minister. Terrifico. Aces. Right on. / You must admit. Certainly gets my vote.

JOYCE. What good's first women if it's her? I suppose you'd have liked Hitler if he was a woman. Ms. Hitler. Got a lot done, Hitlerina. / Great adventures.

MARLENE. Bosses still walking on the workers' faces? Still Dadda's little parrot? Haven't you learned to think for yourself? I believe in the individual. Look at me.

JOYCE. I am looking at you.

MARLENE. Come on, Joyce, we're not going to quarrel over politics.

JOYCE. We are through.

MARLENE. Forget I mentioned it. Not a word about the slimy unions will cross my lips. (*Pause.*)

JOYCE. You say Mother had a wasted life.

MARLENE. Yes I do. Married to that bastard.

JOYCE. What sort of life did he have? /

MARLENE. Violent life?

JOYCE. Working in the fields like an animal. / Why

MARLENE. Come off it.

JOYCE. wouldn't he want a drink? You want a drink. He couldn't afford whisky.

MARLENE. I don't want to talk about him.

JOYCE. You started, I was talking about her. She had a rotten life because she had nothing. She went hungry.

MARLENE. She was hungry because he drank the money. / He used to hit her.

JOYCE. It's not all down to him. / Their

MARLENE. She didn't hit him.

JOYCE. lives were rubbish. They were treated like rubbish. He's dead and she'll die soon and what sort of life / did they have?

MARLENE. I saw him one night. I came down.

JOYCE. Do you think I didn't? / They

MARLENE. I still have dreams.

JOYCE. didn't get to America and drive across it in a fast car. / Bad nights, they had bad days. I knew when I

MARLENE. America, America, you're jealous. / I had to get out,

JOYCE. Jealous?

MARLENE. was thirteen, out of their house, out of them, never let that happen to me, / never let him, make my own way, out.

JOYCE. Jealous of what you've done, you'd be ashamed of me if I came to your office, your smart friends, wouldn't you, I'm ashamed of you, think of nothing but yourself, you've got on, nothing's changed for most people / has it?

MARLENE. I hate the working class / which is what

JOYCE. Yes you do.

MARLENE. you're going to go on about now, it doesn't exist any more, it means lazy and stupid. / I don't

JOYCE. Come on, now we're getting it.

MARLENE. like the way they talk. I don't like beer guts and football vomit and saucy tits / and brothers and sisters—

JOYCE. I spit when I see a Rolls Royce, scratch it with my ring / Mercedes it was

MARLENE. Oh very mature—

JOYCE. I hate the cows I work for / and their dirty dishes with blanquette of fucking veau.

MARLENE. and I will not be pulled down to their level by a flying picket and I won't be sent to Siberia / or a loony bin just because I'm original. And I support

JOYCE. No, you'll be on a yacht, you'll be head of Coca-Cola and you wait, the eighties is going to be stupendous all right because we'll get you lot off our backs—

MARLENE. Reagan even if he is a lousy movie star because the reds are swarming up his map and I want to be free in a free world—

JOYCE. What? / What?

MARLENE. I know what I mean / by that—not shut up here.

JOYCE. So don't be round here when it happens because if someone's kicking you I'll just laugh. (*Silence.*)

MARLENE. I don't mean anything personal. I don't believe in class. Anyone can do anything if they've got what it takes.

JOYCE. And if they haven't.

MARLENE. If they're stupid or lazy or frightened, I'm not going to help them get a job, why should I?

JOYCE. What about Angie?

MARLENE. What about Angie?

JOYCE. She's stupid, lazy and frightened, so what about her?

MARLENE. You run her down too much. She'll be all right.

JOYCE. I don't expect so, no. I expect her children will say what a wasted life she had. If she has children. Because nothing's changed and it won't with them in.

MARLENE. Them, them. / Us and them?

JOYCE. And you're one of them.

MARLENE. And you're us, wonderful us, and Angie's us / and Mum and Dad's us.

JOYCE. Yes, that's right, and you're them.

MARLENE. Come on, Joyce, what a night. You've got what it takes.

JOYCE. I know I have.

MARLENE. I didn't really mean all that.

JOYCE. I did.

MARLENE. But we're friends anyway.

JOYCE. I don't think so, no.

MARLENE. Well it's lovely to be out in the country. I really must make the effort to come more often. I want to go to sleep. I want to go to sleep. (*Joyce gets blankets for the sofa.*)

JOYCE. Goodnight then. I hope you'll be warm enough.

MARLENE. Goodnight. Joyce—

JOYCE. No, pet. Sorry. (*Joyce goes. Marlene sits wrapped in a blanket and has another drink. Angie comes in.*)

ANGIE. Mum?

MARLENE. Angie? What's the matter?

ANGIE. Mum?

MARLENE. No. she's gone to bed. It's Aunty Marlene.

ANGIE. Frightening.

MARLENE. Did you have a bad dream? What happened in it? Well you're awake now, aren't you pet?

ANGIE. Frightening.

THE GREAT CELESTIAL COW

SUE TOWNSEND

SUE TOWNSEND (1947–)

After dropping out of school at age 15, Sue Townsend worked at a variety of jobs and, after a training period, became a social worker, an occupation that provided her with source material for her plays. She began writing for the stage in the mid–1970s and received her first production (*Womberang*) at the SohoPoly Theater in London in 1979. In 1981 the Phoenix Arts Company commissioned her to write a play, *The Ghost of Daniel Lambert*, which was subsequently performed in Leicester. That success led to productions at London's Royal Court Theater, England's most important source of new dramas. Her first Royal Court play, *Bazaar and Rummage*, was also filmed for BBC television.

The Great Celestial Cow was written in late 1983 at the request of the Joint Stock Theater Group, one of England's most respected political theaters. The JSTG was founded in 1974 to provide new plays for tours throughout Great Britian. Joint Stock's productions are developed through workshops in which the playwright, actors, director, and members of the community improvise scenes portraying relevant social problems. The community provides anecdotes, ideas, and—very importantly—feedback to the creative team that shapes the finished product. Townsend, director Carole Hayman, and nine Joint Stock actors (seven of whom were of Indian or Pakistani decent) spent three weeks living among Leicester's Asian community to develop *The Great Celestial Cow*. It opened at the Leicester Haymarket Studio in February 1984, and later transferred to the London's Royal Court where it was among 1984's best new plays.

Townsend is also a published novelist, best known for her companion works *The Secret Diary of Adrian Mole Aged 13 3/4* and *The Growing Pains of Adrian Mole*.

THE GREAT CELESTIAL COW (1984)

The Great Celestial Cow typifies postmodernist theater in theory and especially in practice. Its examination of the new pluralism that is changing the face of Western societies, its critique of the old patriarchal system that subjugates women and minorities, and its portrait of characters fragmented by the clash and merge of old and new world values are essential concerns of drama in the late twentieth century. Theatrically, the deliberate juxtaposition of genres (comedic/social drama), styles (presentational/representational, realism/fantasy), classical myth and pop icons (Kali/Bay City Rollers), and performance traditions (Eastern/Western) places Townsend's play squarely within postmodernism's domain. As in Caryl Churchill's plays, we also find actors playing multiple roles (including cross-gender casting) as a comment on personality, societal roles, and sexual stereotypes. (Multicasting also reflected economic concerns; as a touring project, the Joint Stock had to keep the number of actors to a minimum.)

One moment in *The Great Celestial Cow* superbly crystallizes the play's postmodern spirit. Consider the stage directions that precede act 1, scene 7:

> 1976.
> Leicester. Outside a junior school gate. KISHWAR, a Muslim woman, is waiting outside the gate. She has a box of Pampers disposable nappies [i.e., diapers] under her arm. She is in full Purdah, her face is completely veiled. From the school comes the sound of junior school children singing "Away in a Manger."

Moments later a little girl in a Muslim headdress emerges from the school, wearing a pair of Christian angel wings as the music inside changes, appropriately and ironically, to "We Three Kings of Orient Are": the postmodern Madonna and Child *cum* Pampers.

Townsend and her collaborators have in this scene distilled the dilemma of the new world citizen in the late twentieth century. Everyone in the play is at some point disoriented and cut off from the old country. Sita and her family are the most ready examples, but so are the English. The two boorish officials in act 1 who verbally abuse immigrants typify this phenomenon. While their racism needs little comment here, note that they are also "strangers in a strange land." The second official cannot comprehend his wife's behavior, much less her "opinions about everything," while the first official communicates (poorly) with the immigrants only in an invidious gibberish: "Quicki! quicki! move to benchi!" Throughout the play the English—from the bigoted stallholder to the posh Clarendon Park "liberal" to the crass cowmen at the auction—cannot cope with the influx of new people who dress, look, and talk differently. Actually, they do cope, but clumsily, by resorting to cruel jibes that dehumanize their newest citizens.

But *The Great Celestial Cow* is more than a polemic against racism and the hardships immigrants endure. Townsend extends the parameters of the debate to include the immigrants, particularly the males, as part of the problem. While the JSTG embraces pluralism, the play attacks those attitudes and behaviors in other cultures that limit the possibilities of its people, especially women. If *Top Girls* is a feminist play that critiques the deleterious aspects of feminism, then *The Great Celestial Cow* is a "propluralist" work that challenges some premodern customs that are decidedly at odds with our postmodern world.

From the opening sequence, in which young Prem berates "the Cow," we see that the women, both in India and in England, are victims of a repressive patriarchal system. They are bartered for in matrimony, spied on by elders, and chastised for laughing in public. They are, however, permitted to work in garment factories (read sweatshops) while tending to domestic chores such as making *chappatis*. In essence, the Indian women are treated very much like "old cows" (as are the English women: Prem also calls his teachers a "stupid cow" in act 1). Finally, and not unexpectedly to English audiences conditioned by years of romantic-social dramas, they rebel in Leicester's cattle market. Even the cantankerous old Mother-in-Law (a popular and comic figure in much Asian drama) is "converted" to the cause in a climax that is simultaneously uplifting and comical.

The fragmentation of the women's lives—among postmodernism's central concerns—is best captured in act 2 as Sita, alone in front of a mirror, asks: "Sita, where are you? I don't know where you are. Come back to me. . . . " Ironically, Sita's "reality" is that she is neither here (England) nor there (India). Her color and her clothing mark her as an unwanted "exotic" among the Europeans, yet her newly emerging values isolate her from her traditional community. When she asserts her will at the end of act 1 and declares unequivocally that Bibi, who is maturing into full womanhood, will indeed dance at the Navarati (despite the superstitions invoked by the older women), she severs her ties to the old traditions. It is an heroic act, tantamount to Prometheus stealing the fire of the gods, or, more appropriately, to Kāli's assault on the demons of death and destruction. But, alas, just as Kāli was driven mad by drinking the blood of the demons, so, too, does Sita become mad from her confrontation with modern demons.

That Townsend mythologizes Sita in her heroic quest is no accident. Deconstructing the patriarchal myths of antiquity is part of the postmodern process. Townsend and her collaborators revert to that time-tested framework, the great journey that takes Sita full circle. Throughout she is guided by the constellation of the celestial cow (aptly named Princess, a royal woman). The old bucket, an object of derision, is the sacred totem to which she anchors her faith. And Sita ultimately triumphs—much like her ancient namesake, Princess Sita, who is regarded among Hindus as the prototype of the perfect woman. But whereas the Sita of ancient Hindu myth relied on Prince Rama for her liberation (as told in India's great epic, *The Ramayana*), our postmodern, mythic Sita triumphs through her indomitable will, the support of the women about her, and the celestial cow named Princess.

Bibi, an immigrant from India, and a New English friend are photographed with the Great Celestial Cow; the first London production (1984) of Townsend's play, The Great Celestial Cow, *was at the Royal Court Theatre, noted for its commitment to political theater.*

THE GREAT CELESTIAL COW

SUE TOWNSEND

CHARACTERS

SPIRIT OF KALI	MR PATEL
2ND OFFICIAL	COW IN FIELD
MOTHER-IN-LAW (*Dadima*)	SITA
MUSLIM GIRL	DAHEBA
PREM	STEWARDESS
OLD AGE PENSIONER	1ST OFFICIAL
ROSE	FAT AUNTIE (*Masi*)
COW IN FIELD	LIBERAL
AUTIONEER	SARLA
PRINCESS	BIBI
RACHEL	STALLHOLDER
LILA	COW IN NATIVITY
CLASSICAL INDIAN DANCER	ANITA
INDIRA	DR MISTRY
RAM	NAAL PLAYER
NURSE	PHOTOGRAPHER
PRINCESS	NEW OWNER
MARTIN	RAJ
HARMONIUM PLAYER	2ND FAT AUNTIE
KISHWAR	HAROLD
ASIAN ELDER	

NOTE ON THE LAYOUT

A speech usually follows the one immediately before it BUT:

(1) when one character starts speaking before the other has finished, the point of interruption is marked /.

eg. MOTHER-IN-LAW. Sita's chappatis are too hard / for my teeth.
BIBI. I like them.

(2) a character sometimes continues speaking right through another's speech:

eg. BIBI. All that petting and baby / talk? It would drive me
MOTHER-IN-LAW. Raj is too soft with her.
BIBI. mad. Bugger off until the floor is dry.

(3) sometimes a speech follows on from a speech earlier than the one immediately before it, and continuity is marked * or **.

eg. BIBI. All that petting and baby / talk? It would drive me
MOTHER-IN-LAW. Raj is too soft with her.
BIBI. mad. Bugger off until the floor is dry.**
FAT AUNTIE. She wants to be head of the house, you know.*

PREM. **No, I want to walk on it.
BIBI. You dare.
MOTHER-IN-LAW. *What would happen to us if she was?

Where 'the floor is dry' is the cue to 'No, I want to walk', and 'head of the house, you know' is the cue to 'What would happen to us'.

ACT ONE

SCENE ONE

1975.

Early morning in a village in India. A Little Boy dressed in white shorts and vest is dragging a pile of grass towards a rickety compound. Inside the compound a Cow raises its head. It makes an aggressive warning noise. The Little Boy backs off slightly.

PREM. Today is the last day you send my heart diving.

He unties the bundle, throws grass to the Cow.

Stupid cow! I don't like you. Bad luck for you eh? But you started it! Go on, eat!

The Cow doesn't eat.

I got up before I was awake to cut that grass. (*He shouts.*) Eat! Or choke on it! Do something! Stupid, idiot cow!

The Cow repeats the warning noise. The Boy backs off.

(*He shouts louder.*) I'm going to England and you're staying here! (*He laughs.*) When I am flying over the ocean and Buckingham Palace you will still be here! When I am looking at the queen and the Bay City Rollers you will be a million miles away! When I am sitting on the toilet in Leicester (*He laughs, shouting.*) you will be here standing in your own dirt!

A Woman carrying a pail runs on, she is Sita, the Boy's mother. She is angry.

SITA. Don't shout at her, you will ruin her milk! (*Stroking the Cow.*) There there, he is excited. He is only a little boy. His head is full of the aeroplane.

The Cow eats.

(*To Prem:*) Without her milk you and I and your sister would have starved, when Bapu's money didn't come.

PREM. Is starve the same as hungry?
SITA. No and I hope you never find out the difference for yourself.
PREM. I am always hungry. In Leicester I will eat and eat and eat until my belly bursts open.

Sita milks the Cow.

SITA. Yes and then I will have to stitch you up. More work for me.
It is five-thirty, go and tell your sister to come. Tell her to look her best for the photograph. Tidy hair and a clean face.

Prem dawdles off.

Sita sings a small snatch of a lament. A Neighbour enters. She is carrying a bundle of clothes. She walks past Sita ignoring her.

Daheba!

Daheba turns slowly, looks at Sita.

DAHEBA. After six months of silence you speak to me?
SITA. Yes I am leaving here today.
DAHEBA. I know, you are going to Leicester. My uncle's cousin is there.
SITA (*slightly put out*). So, you know, do you, which flight I am taking?
DAHEBA. No but you are landing at Heathrow.

The Women smile.

SITA. A silly quarrel. I can't remember what it was about.
DAHEBA. I can, you said that my daughters would never marry.
SITA. But it was meant as a compliment to you. You are a magnificent mother, who would want to leave you?
DAHEBA (*bows her head accepting the lie*). The cow is sold satisfactorily?
SITA. Oh yes. I am satisfied with the price.
DAHEBA. And the milking bucket?
SITA. No, not the bucket.
DAHEBA. You are perhaps taking it with you?
SITA. A bucket on an aeroplane?
DAHEBA. Ridiculous! So the bucket remains here, without an owner.

The Women sigh.

SITA. Of course there is hand luggage.
DAHEBA. True.
SITA. But a bucket is heavy.
DAHEBA. And noisy. Clank, clank, clank. It would draw attention to you. Make a bad impression. English people would say, 'Tuh! Here comes another dirty immigrant with her children and bucket.'
SITA. English people would say that?
DAHEBA. Oh yes. My uncle's cousin has been there for five years now.
SITA. But I am not an immigrant. I am a British subject.
DAHEBA. They call us all immigrants over there.
SITA. Then I will tell them the truth.
DAHEBA. You can speak English can you?
SITA. No, but I will learn.

Then to the Cow.

Thank you, good girl.

DAHEBA. So, the bucket.

Sita finishes milking. She carries the bucket out of the compound.

SITA. Yes, this is a good bucket. No leaks. No rust. Comfortable to carry. Hard to leave behind.

Bibi enters. She is eleven years old. She is dressed in her best clothes. She has ribbons in her hair.

BIBI. Do I look all right?

SITA. Let me see you.

Sita goes to Bibi and gives her a severe motherly inspection. She tightens the hair ribbons etc.

Show me your teeth.

Bibi bares her teeth.

Good, good. Yes you are as pretty as you can be.

DAHEBA (*to Bibi*). How tall you are. I hope you will not continue to grow or you will be nudging the stars.

SITA. She will outshine them if she does.

DAHEBA. But so lanky for eleven!

PREM (*off*). He's here, he's here!

Prem enters.

DAHEBA. Ah, here is the one to melt hearts.

PREM. He's here, Ma.

A Photographer enters on a bike. He is wearing a mixture of Indian and Western clothes. The Women draw their scarves over their heads.

PHOTOGRAPHER. Your son has told me that you want the photograph taken here. Is that true?

He looks round in disgust.

SITA. Yes.

PHOTOGRAPHER. It will be most difficult, the light . . .

He peers at the sky.

SITA. There is not enough light or too much?

Prem hovers around the bike.

DAHEBA. Shush! He is a professional you know. You have a studio don't you?

PHOTOGRAPHER. Yes. The light in my studio is perfect. It is from Germany. (*To Prem.*) Don't touch the spokes.

PREM. The light is from Germany?

PHOTOGRAPHER. My lamps are from Germany.

PREM. Is Germany near England?

PHOTOGRAPHER. Yes. Very near. That's why they are always fighting.

PREM. England won both times.

He does fighting acting at his sister.

BIBI. Don't.

SITA. Prem! Don't! (*Prem stops.*)

PREM. Who is to be in the photograph?

Daheba looks eager.

SITA. My children and Princess.

PHOTOGRAPHER (*to Daheba*). You are Princess?

The Children and Sita laugh.

DAHEBA (*angry*). You dare to call me a cow? My husband and father-in-law will come and smash up your German lamps. (*Scornfully.*) Studio! Ha! A white sheet hung on a wall and he calls it a studio. (*To Sita.*) Keep your old pail. I don't want it! (*She exits.*)

PHOTOGRAPHER. Are the people in this village mad? What did I say? (*Pause.*) Is her husband tall?

BIBI. I don't know. He doesn't leave his bed.

PREM. He's dying.

PHOTOGRAPHER. Oh good. I have decided I will photograph you all in your house. I cannot work in these conditions.

The Children laugh.

Is there some sickness in this village that makes you all laugh and get angry for nothing? If so tell me and I will go back to my bed in my own village.

SITA. Princess is our cow. You cannot take her photograph in our house because she will not get through the door.

PHOTOGRAPHER. You have brought me here to take a *cow's* photograph?

SITA. Yes. Our cow has been good to us. I want to take a small piece of her with me.

BIBI. We are going to England.

PHOTOGRAPHER. Then cut off one of her ears and take that because I refuse to take a cow's photograph. You bring me here at this terrible hour . . . the sleep still in my eyes . . .

SITA. I am going to pay you! And your trousers show that you need the money.

PHOTOGRAPHER. Let me see your money.

Sita shows money.

I'm not used to this third class situation. I am going to Delhi in two years' time you know.

He sets up his rickety tripod, fusses around with camera and film.

PREM. Don't touch the spokes, Bibi.

PHOTOGRAPHER. A big studio on a fashionable thoroughfare.

BIBI. I'm only looking, no harm.

PREM. Don't waste your eyes. You won't ride a bike, but I will.

SITA (*instructing the Children*). Prem, don't crowd in front of Princess. She is the most important. I won't see her again.

Kneel down. Put your arms around each other. Smile. (*To the Photographer.*) Go ahead.

PHOTOGRAPHER. What about you. Don't you want your photograph taken?

SITA. No, I am there with my children. Ready, steady.

Blackout.

Flash of the photograph.

SCENE TWO

The aeroplane. Bibi, Prem and Sita, sitting. Jet noise. Lights dim to half light. A Stewardess tucks blankets around the family.

STEWARDESS. Sleep well.

PREM. Ma, I can't go to sleep.

BIBI. Tell him to be quiet, Mama.

SITA. Prem, close your eyes now.

PREM. I want to see the stars.

BIBI. Shush. If you are not quiet Kali will come.

PREM. Which one's Kali?

SITA. The wife of Shiva.

PREM. He's the best god, isn't he?

SITA. Yes.

BIBI. Kali was better than him. When Shiva was sleeping she killed the demons, didn't she?

SITA. Yes but Shiva was thinking, not sleeping like you two will be soon. So demons came and started eating the villagers.

BIBI. So the villagers that were left went to the top of the mountain and tried to wake Shiva, but he wouldn't wake so Kali . . .

PREM. Let Ma tell it, Bibi.

SITA. Shush. So Kali looked at the death and destruction that the demons were causing and a strange thing happened.

BIBI. Oh yes I know, she changed into a monster!

SITA. With many arms and many legs and a garland made of skulls and a hideous face like this.

Prem cuddles closer to Sita.

. . . but terrible though she was and even using many swords she could not defeat the demons. They fought for many days and nights.

BIBI (*sleepily*). Nine.

SITA. Each time she killed one demon many more would spring up in its place formed by the drops of blood.

BIBI. The worst bit now.

SITA. So Kali drank their blood.

PREM. Ugh!

SITA. And maddened and made terrible by it, *she* started to kill the villagers.

PREM. I would have killed her easy.

SITA. No. She became all-powerful.

PREM. Not better than Shiva?

BIBI. Don't interrupt Prem.

SITA. The villagers woke Shiva somehow. He came down from his mountain and tried to stop his wife. But he couldn't, and Kali fought him down to the ground and was about to kill him with a big sword when Shiva said 'No don't, I'm your husband. And Kali looked down at him from her great height and she said 'Husband, I will not take your life'.

PREM. So it ended happily?

He snuggles down.

SITA. I don't know. I suppose it does.

BIBI. For the villagers.

Pause.

PREM. I bet he beat her when he got her home.

SITA. Yes. Now sleep, and when you wake up you will be in England.

The Children get into sleeping attitudes. Sita stares straight ahead. Princess appears.

Goodbye Princess.

Princess's New Owner appears.

NEW OWNER. C'mon cow what are you doing lying down? On your feet! C'mon, on your feet you lazy cow, there is work to be done.

He whacks Princess. She makes an anguished cow noise. Sita screws her eyes shut unable to bear it.

SCENE THREE

The arrival lounge at Heathrow airport. The family sit on the floor, they have been waiting for two hours. Bibi has the bucket on her lap.

An announcement from the loudspeaker.

LOUDSPEAKER. Would Mr Raj Prakash come to the enquiry desk where his family are waiting for him. Mr Raj Prakash. Please come to the enquiry desk.

A uniformed Official approaches.

1ST OFFICIAL (*London working-class accent*). Mrs Prakash? Would you mind moving on to one of the benches please. You're in the way here. (*Pause.*) No English?

SITA. Leicester. (*She shows documentation, passports.*)

1ST OFFICIAL. Yes. Leicester. Now if you wouldn't mind moving.

2nd Official approaches.

2ND OFFICIAL. She still here?

1ST OFFICIAL. Her old man ain't turned up has he?

2ND OFFICIAL. He's probably changed his mind, got halfway down the M bloody 1 and threw a wobbler.

They laugh, the Children look up and smile.

1ST OFFICIAL. You can't blame him can you. He's had five years of freedom over here, then his missus and kids and a bloody bucket turn up.

2ND OFFICIAL. They'll cramp his style a bit.

1ST OFFICIAL. Not half.

2ND OFFICIAL. Mind you the Asians are good family people . . . Look after each other . . . You know, the old people . . . Bit like the Jews.

1ST OFFICIAL. Yeah, how's *your* mum?

2ND OFFICIAL (*evasively*). Oh all right, (*Small pause.*) I think. We don't get over as often as we'd like . . . but it's a nice place . . . for an institution like.

1ST OFFICIAL. Still you couldn't have had her with you, could you, Mick?

2ND OFFICIAL. No, her wheelchair knocked every bit of paint off the skirting boards. An' Brenda and her never did get on . . .

1ST OFFICIAL. Well don't you feel guilty about it . . . You got your own life to live ain't you? Your mum's had hers.

2ND OFFICIAL. That's the problem. You see she *ain't* really. She's lived, but she ain't had what I'd call a *life*.

1ST OFFICIAL. Well they didn't in the old days did they? They was too busy livin' to have a life.

2ND OFFICIAL. Well my old woman's makin' up for it, I tell you, the way she's going . . . out every bloody night. Weight Watchers, nightschool, jewellery parties . . .

1ST OFFICIAL. 'Bout time you started cracking down.

2ND OFFICIAL. An' she's got opinions about everything.

1ST OFFICIAL. Opinions?

2ND OFFICIAL. Yeah. Bloody this, bloody that. She'll be standin' for the bloody GLC next.

1ST OFFICIAL. An' I'd vote for her if she'd put a few white people at the top of the housing list for a change.

2ND OFFICIAL. I know, dis-bloody-gustin'.

1ST OFFICIAL: (*to the family group*). Right come on now! Quicki quicki, move to benchi!

The Officials go.

PREM. What is he saying Mama?

SITA. How do I know?

BIBI. He is telling us to move I think. We must move, Ma. Look, nobody else is sitting on the floor.

SITA. Exactly, so your father will be sure to see us won't he?

BIBI. What time is it, Ma?

SITA. Milking time.

BIBI. Morning or evening.

SITA. Evening. (*She cries.*)

Two hippies, Rachel and Martin, watch.

RACHEL. Oh Martin look. Oh how *sad*.

MARTIN. Yeah.

RACHEL. Do you think somebody's been, you know, *awful* to them?

MARTIN. Could be.

They stand over the family group.

RACHEL. Ask them what's wrong. Go on, Martin you're good with kids.

MARTIN. Er . . . er . . . (*He pats his chest and says*): 'Mitra'.

PREM. Tell the nasty man to go away, Ma.

RACHEL (*Pats her chest and says*). 'Mitra'. Don't cry! Me and him we've come back from India. Bombay, Calcutta, Delhi, Madras. We love your country. (*She smiles.*)

MARTIN. Yeah . . . 'Mitra'.

BIBI. They are saying 'friend' in Gujerati I think.

PREM. Mama! Tell him to go away.

RACHEL. What he say?

MARTIN. Dunno. (*He squats down.*) Hey. C'mon kids.

RACHEL. If only we could explain that we *know* India and its people. We *know* it.

MARTIN (*to Sita*). Spiritually . . .

Rachel puts her hands together and bows to Sita.

RACHEL. You are my sister.

Sita nods, baffled.

MARTIN. C'mon Rachel. I gotta get to the bank.

RACHEL. Look what's more important Martin, helping this poor, ignorant family, or cashing your bloody traveller's cheques?

MARTIN. Look, don't pull that moral superiority shit on me again, right? I've had six fucking months of it. It's my traveller's cheques that have paid for your spiritual awareness right?

RACHEL. I shouldn't have come back. I should have stayed. I belong there. They need my skills.

MARTIN. Yeah, they're crying out for English Literature degrees right?

RACHEL. I could dig an Artesian well! I could advise on basic hygiene . . . and Swami Niranda invited me back.

MARTIN. Yeah, and told you to bring five hundred fucking pounds.

RACHEL. He didn't!

BIBI. What are the dirty people saying?

MARTIN. He did!

SITA. They are quarreling.

PREM. She doesn't like his smelly face.

The Children laugh.

SITA. Shush. Remember your manners. Don't laugh at the misfortunes of others.

Rachel and Martin go off, still arguing.

PREM. When's Bapu coming?

BIBI. Soon, soon. Here eat this. Keep your mouth busy. (*Bibi gives Prem a chappati.*)

The noise of the arrival lounge; slow fade of lights.

SCENE FOUR

The family is sleeping on a bench in the arrival lounge. Raj Prakash and his elderly Mother (Dadima) and Aunt (Masi) approach. Raj looks down at his family. His Mother goes to wake the group. Raj restrains her.

RAJ. No.

MOTHER-IN-LAW. So son, how do you feel at this moment?

FAT AUNTIE (*broken voiced*). His heart is full and so are his eyes. (*She takes out a handkerchief.*)

MOTHER-IN-LAW. No let me. (*She mops Raj's tears.*) My grandchildren! (*Pause.*) Your wife has lost her beauty son. (*She then wipes her own eyes with the handkerchief.*)

FAT AUNTIE. Children drain beauty away, they put the lines on our foreheads and the white in our hair.

RAJ. I hardly know her.

MOTHER-IN-LAW. Tired, she is tired. A long flight, remember Masi.

FAT AUNTIE. Ai, ai, ai. So long. My head was in the clouds for a week.

RAJ. But so different.

FAT AUNTIE. In five years people change, a baby becomes a child and a young woman becomes an old woman. That's how it is.

MOTHER-IN-LAW. Wake them. I want to go back to Leicester. I don't like it here, I can't hear my thoughts.

A jet starts to take off. They mime their meeting. Prem is greeted first. Then Raj and Sita politely greet each other, but Prem comes between them. The plane noise stops.

Come on everybody. Pick up the luggage. (*To Prem:*) Not you little one. Come on Bibi. Masi, you help.

They collect the baggage and bundles, Bibi picks up the bucket.

Why are you carrying a bucket? Put it down.

BIBI. It's mother's. I'm in charge of it.

SITA. You remember Princess, Raj? It's her milking bucket.

RAJ. There are no cows in Leicester, Sita. I have written and told you many times about Leicester.

MOTHER-IN-LAW. No land. Only parks . . .

FAT AUNTIE. They are owned by the council and you may not walk on the grass. In some parts you may but in others there is a sign.

MOTHER-IN-LAW. 'Keep off the grass.'

RAJ. And our house opens on to a street. And the street is busy with cars and buses and lorries.

MOTHER-IN-LAW. I already have a bucket, it is red and made of plastic.

SITA. I would like to keep it, please.

RAJ. But how will it look? We have to pass many people before we reach the minibus. No, I refuse to be seen walking with a bucket.

PREM. Ma wants to buy a cow, she told me on the plane.

BIBI. You were naughty, she told you stories so that you would sit still. Bapu are you going to beat Prem?

RAJ (*laughing*). No, why should I beat my beloved son? I haven't seen him for five years?

He picks up Prem and hugs him.

BIBI. I wish somebody would. He pulls my hair.

Laughter.

MOTHER-IN-LAW. Come on, I want to go home. (*To Bibi.*) Pick it up child, it won't carry itself.

They exit carrying luggage and bundles. Sita walks behind them. She has picked up the bucket and hidden it under a piece of cloth.

SCENE FIVE

Raj and Sita alone in their room. Sita looks around, Raj sits on the bed.

RAJ. So what do you think of it?

SITA. Such a big room for two people. Do we sleep alone?

RAJ. We do tonight, come here.

Sita approaches him.

RAJ. Take off your sari, I want to look at you.

SITA. And a window!

RAJ. Sita, let me look at you.

SITA. There's no hurry, Raj.

RAJ. After five years there's no hurry? You are my wife. Take off your sari, Sita.

SITA. In India you would wait a little. Kiss me. Use fine words to help me.

RAJ. Who can blame me for being impatient? Come here.

Sita approaches shyly. Raj gets up and unfastens Sita's sari.

RAJ (*quietly*). I will unfasten you as I did on our wedding night, remember?

He unwinds the sari slowly.

You were so young, and very beautiful. The most beautiful girl in the village. But tired, too tired to move. I had to teach you everything, didn't I Sita? I hope I was (*Still unwinding the sari.*) patient with you. I didn't want to frighten you. You lay still in my arms for the first months but then you began to move and . . . (*Still unwinding the sari.*) . . . how much longer? Are women wearing so much cloth in India now? Help me Sita.

Sita clutches her sari to her.

SITA. I am afraid for you to see my body.

RAJ. Why? Is it scarred or diseased in some way? (*He laughs.*)

SITA. No, but I have not cared for it as *you* liked. There was no time. And I lost interest in how I looked and only took pride in what my body could do. There was always so much work.

RAJ. Your work will be easier here. There are machines for cooking and washing. Your hands and feet will soon lose their roughness.

SITA. How will I fill my time?

RAJ. I have arranged a job for you. You start at Mr Lakhani's dress factory on Monday. It is easy work. You will like it there and earn £55 a week. I told Mr Lakhani that you are an excellent machinist.

Sita remains still.

Now come to bed and prove that you are also an excellent wife.

SITA. Raj, I feel frozen.

RAJ. I will plug in the electric fire.

SITA. No, I'm not cold, but I'm frozen.

Raj takes Sita in his arms, kisses her neck. Music; Indian film dance drama. Raj does melodramatic seduction acting, Sita is impassive. Suddenly Raj grows impatient and pulls Sita's sari, twirling her round and round. Sita is revealed in her petticoat and under-blouse. Raj is about to remove her blouse when Prem runs into the room in some distress.

PREM. I dreamed I was being eaten by a cow!

He clings to his father's legs.

RAJ. The cows in England are miles away in the country. You are quite safe, now go back to bed. Ma and Bapu want to be alone.

PREM. No, I want to sleep with Ma. I always do don't I Ma?

RAJ. Not tonight. Now go to your own bed.

PREM. No I won't! I want to sleep with Ma. (*Shouts.*) I want Ma! I want Ma!

RAJ. And I want Ma. She was mine before she was yours.

PREM. But she's mine now. I don't want you to sleep in her bed.

RAJ. It is not her bed, it is mine. I bought it from the Co-op. (*To Sita:*) Leave the room Sita.

SITA. Don't beat him, Raj.

RAJ. I won't. I have things to explain. Father to son.

Sita exits.

My son, there is no need for this panic. You will never leave your mother. You will grow up and marry and bring your wife to our house and your mother will train your wife and help to bring up your sons and daughters, just like Dadima does now.

When I am old and no longer the head of the house, then you will take my place, you will make the choices. You will decide how the money is spent. How much to give to the Temple, how much to allow the women. It is a big responsibility and your mother and your wife will depend on you for their happiness.

PREM. So Ma will always be mine?

RAJ. Until the day she is taken from you by God.

PREM. I won't let God take her!

RAJ. Good little man, we'll have another talk when you are older. Now go to bed. Sita! Sita!

SCENE SIX

Leicester market. Three weeks later. A fruit stall, a cacophony of sounds as stall holders compete in attracting attention. A Woman stands behind her fruit stall. She is wearing a sheepskin coat and a fur hat. She blows on her hands, stamps her feet.

STALLHOLDER. Guavas, melons, all your exotics! Come on ladies! Fresh in today! Lovely fruit. Take some home to your old man. Ba-na-nas. O-ran-ges, Coxes Pipp-ins.

A White Woman approaches the stall. She is a middle-class liberal. She looks at the fruit critically.

LIBERAL. Have you any unripe bananas left?

STALLHOLDER. Dunno love, I'll have a look. Cold enough for you?

She sorts through bananas.

LIBERAL. I don't know how you do it. You're awfully brave to stand out in all weathers.

STALLHOLDER (*shouting*). Ba-na-nas. Jaffa Oranges, Cox-es Pippins.

An Old White Woman comes to the stall.

OLD WOMAN. Can I have a few of each? Only I've got me husband in the infirmary. He likes a bit of fruit but it gus off so quick, don't it. In the 'eat of an 'ospital?

STALLHOLDER. You could grow tomatoes in them wards couldn't you?

LIBERAL. Yes, the heat actually makes one feel worse.

STALLHOLDER. I was in last year, I didn't wear me bedjacket once.

Sita enters and hovers around the stall.

OLD WOMAN. He's a bit fussy, couldn't I pick me own?

STALLHOLDER. Sorry duck. No handling the fruit, that's the rule. I'll pick some out for you though. Just give me a minute to serve this lady.

OLD WOMAN. Sorry. I didn't mean to butt in.

LIBERAL. Oh, that's all right.

Sita gesticulates towards the fruit after catching the Stall-holder's eye.

STALLHOLDER (*To the White Women*). Here we go. Pantomime time! (*Slowly and loudly.*) This twenty pence a pound. (*Pointing.*) This ten pence each. These eighteen pence. Understand? No, of course you don't bloody understand. I don't know, they come over here, push to the front of the queue . . .

OLD WOMAN. The hospital's full of black faces.

LIBERAL. Yes. I owe my life to a black midwife.

OLD WOMAN. No, these are in the beds. Stopping us white people from having our operations.

STALLHOLDER. They're taking over. No doubt about that. There's one born every thirty seconds.

OLD WOMAN (*alarmed*). In Leicester?

STALLHOLDER. No, the world!

OLD WOMAN (*dismissively*). Oh that.

The Stallholder is about to weigh the bananas, when she sees Sita picking up the fruit.

STALLHOLDER. Eh! Get your dirty black hands off my fruit! People have got to eat that! They won't want it if they see you mauling it about will they?

Sita holds an apple, uncomprehending but frightened by the violent tone.

I said put it down! Down! This is Leicester, not Calcutta.

LIBERAL. She doesn't understand.

The Stallholder grabs the apple from Sita.

STALLHOLDER. She understands all right. They want to stick to their own shops in their own districts. Not come into town stinking the bleddy place out. (*To Sita.*) Go away. Go on. Go away. (*To Liberal:*) That's thirty-nine pence, all right for you?

LIBERAL. No. I don't want them now. I don't think you should have spoken to her like that. It was very unkind.

STALLHOLDER. It's the only way they understand.

LIBERAL. I shan't come to this stall again.

STALLHOLDER. Well I shan't cut me wrists over that.

LIBERAL (*To Sita*). I'm awfully sorry. Look would you like a coffee? No of course not, well nice to meet you.

She holds out her hand. Sita looks at it. The Liberal picks up Sita's right hand and manufactures a handshake.

We're not all like that. At least not in Clarendon Park.

She rushes off in confusion.

SITA (*to the Stallholder*). Sabhat karna sikho.

Sita exits.

OLD WOMAN. What's she say?

STALLHOLDER. Paki talk. (*Calling after Sita:*) Come back when you've learnt to talk proper, like what I do! (*To the Old Woman.*) See how they go on?

OLD WOMAN. It's no wonder these racialists and such don't like them is it? I'm not one myself.

STALLHOLDER. Nor me. But I can feel myself turning.

SCENE SEVEN

1976.

Leicester. Outside a junior school gate. Kishwar, a Muslim woman, is waiting outside the gate. She has a box of Pampers disposable nappies under her arm. She is in full Purdah, her face is completely veiled. From the school comes the sound of junior school children singing 'Away in a Manger'. Sita joins her.

SITA. They *are* late coming out today. It's twenty-five to.

KISHWAR. They are practising for the Christmas concert.

SITA. Oh yes, I'm going to see it, are you?

KISHWAR. No, I am too busy tomorrow. I would like to see it . . . My daughter is an angel . . . She talks of nothing but her silver paper wings . . . (*Small pause.*) But there is singing and dancing and as you know it is forbidden for me.

SITA. The singing and dancing of children?

KISHWAR. Yes. My husband has become very devout since we moved to this country. I did not always have this cloth between me and the world.

The sound of large numbers of children set free from school. Prem and a little Girl in Muslim headdress run out of school.

ZHORA (*showing a painting*). Look Umy I painted an angel.

KISHWAR. Oh yes, it's very nice. But what are those lumps sticking out of its back?

ZHORA. That's her wings.

PREM. The concert's dead good, Ma. I'm a horse.

ZHORA. No, you're a donkey, Mrs Mortlake said.

PREM. I'm a horse. Donkeys are stupid.

ZHORA. Well so are you. You're only on Red Book One. Stupid git.

KISHWAR. Now Zhora don't be cruel. Prem has only been in England one year.

SITA. He'll soon catch up. Won't you Prem?

PREM. I *am* a horse. You'll see tomorrow.

Kishwar and Zhora start to go.

ZHORA. Are you coming to see me in the concert Umy?

KISHWAR. I'll ask.

PREM. Her wings are stupid. They keep falling off. Mrs Mortlake tries to mend them but they just fall off again. Mrs Mortlake is a stupid cow!

Sita slaps Prem. He bawls, open mouthed. Sita drags him away.

SITA. No Smarties on the way home!

SCENE EIGHT

The school concert.

Sita and Kishwar sit on hard chairs watching the concert. A piano plays 'We Three Kings of Orient Are'. Rose enters.

ROSE. Eh up, Sita, is that anyone's seat or are you saving it? Trust me to be late. Me bleddy washer overflowed. Look there's my Delroy. (*She waves.*) Oh he's dropped his Frankincense. (*She looks anxious.*) Pick it up Delroy!

SITA. Your daughter is a beautiful angel.

KISHWAR. Thank you. Your son looks very handsome as a donkey.

ROSE. Can she see?

SITA. Tum dekh sakti ho.

KISHWAR. Han usko kaho main dekh sakti hoon.

SITA. Yes she can, she's used to it now.

ROSE (*To Sita*). Can she take it off at home?

SITA. Yes, unless strangers arrive.

ROSE. It'd drive me mad. I can't stand anything around my face. Who makes her wear it?

SITA. Kaun pehenata hai.

KISHWAR. Koi nahin, hamare dharm men hai.

SITA. She says she wears it because it's traditional in her culture.

ROSE. That can't be right. I mean you wouldn't wear it out of choice would you? Shame really, she's ever so nice underneath it. I knew her before she took the veil. She's got lovely eyes. (*To Kishwar.*) OK?

KISHWAR. OK.

ROSE. Bloody hell, he's tripped over his dressing-gown now. He's a clumsy little sod! (*She mimes pulling a dressing-gown up, to her son.*) Sorry for swearing.

The piano changes to 'Silent Night'.

SITA. I don't mind.

ROSE. You're not allowed to swear are you? Don't you get your hands chopped off or something?

SITA. Shush Rose!

ROSE. Whoops a daisy, there goes Jesus, fell out of the crib! It's the same every bloody year.

SITA. Who is that boy wearing the beard?

ROSE. That's Joseph.

SITA. Who is he?

ROSE. He's the bloke Mary's married to.

SITA. He's the father of Jesus.

ROSE. Well . . . No . . . Jesus is a miracle. He's God's child.

SITA. Does Joseph know this?

ROSE. Oh he *knows*. Mary told him. But to my mind the true miracle was that Joseph believed her. I should have told my ex-husband that Delroy was God's child instead of Winston Johnson's.

KISHWAR (*To Sita*). Oh her wings have fallen off!

ROSE (*To Sita*). Tell her not to worry, it is traditional in our culture.

A primary school cow enters on its way to the stage. It stands beside Rose.

ROSE. Christ what's that?

SITA (*Excited*). It's a cow, oh and so pretty. Look Kishwar, I've got a cow. Her name is Princess.

The cow goes on to the stage.

ROSE. That cow's name is Tracy Wainwright. I'd know them feet anywhere.

SITA (*clapping*). Good cow. Very good.

ROSE. Eh shut up. You'll get us chucked out. You don't clap at a nativity play, it's holy.

KISHWAR. Holy?

SITA. Like Delroy's socks.

ROSE. You cheeky bugger, Sita. Oh don't they show you up!

SCENE NINE

December 1977
Four Women leaving a factory. Their scarves have slipped down. They are laughing.

LILA. . . . And his big fat behind! . . . Waddle, waddle . . . like my auntie-in-law dancing at my wedding!

She does a waddling impression.

It is ten years since Lakhani saw his toes!

The Women laugh.

SARLA. Lila you are wicked! If Mr Lakhani heard you . . .

ANITA. You would get the sack.

LILA. I can say what I like when I get out of his factory. He may have bought my time, but my tongue is still my own.

ANITA. Do his voice again, Lila.

SITA. Do the bit about the talking.

Lila takes on Mr Lakhani's physical characteristics: fat, pompous.

LILA (*Mr Lakhani's voice*). You women are talking too much. It is slowing down your work. Do you want to bankrupt me? Do you want me to have to sell my £60,000 house and my mercedes . . . and my volkswagen bus . . .

ANITA. He didn't say that! (*She laughs.*)

LILA (*Mr Lakhani's voice*). Do you want to take the gold from my wife's throat? Or send my children to state schools? I will sack every damned one of you unless you reach the quota.

SARLA. He did say that, about the quota.

ANITA. He is a foolish man, nobody can reach the quota.

SITA. Not even if he put sticky tape over our mouths.

LILA. The next time he shouts and raves I will prick his belly with a pin and he will fly around the workshop like a balloon.

She does a balloon deflating action, complete with noise. The Women shriek with laughter and clutch each other. An elderly Indian Man walks by. He looks at them disapprovingly.

LILA (*rattling car keys*). C'mon girls. Time to go, that's it for today. Chappatis to make.

SITA. Children to fetch from school.

ANITA. Grandfather to wash.

SARLA. Mother-in-law to quarrel with.

LILA. Cheer up, work tomorrow! The quota!

WOMEN. The quota!

The Women go, laughing.

SCENE TEN

The Prakash living-room, the next evening.

RAJ. It has come to my ears that you were behaving in a shameful manner yesterday.

SITA. Me?

RAJ. After work, laughing and shrieking in the street with low-caste women.

SITA. Can't I laugh now?

RAJ. Not if your laughter is loud enough to cause talk in the community.

SITA. Who is this outraged person you listen to?

RAJ. The father of my work colleague Dev. He told his wife and his wife told my mother and naturally enough she told me. This is a small community, you must be careful. I don't want to stop you working in the factory . . .

SITA. Raj you wouldn't.

RAJ. . . . but if I hear any more bad reports on you I will have to consider it. Perhaps arrange for you to work at home.

SITA. I laughed at Lila, she's so *funny*. You would have laughed if you had been there

RAJ. But it doesn't matter if *I* laugh in the street.

SITA. Is that fair?

RAJ. It's how things are.

SITA. Not in India in our village.

RAJ. Laughter is different in a village. Here there are walls and echoes to make a woman's laughter sound defiant and coarse, and I don't want you to associate with Lila. She is a divorced woman.

SITA (*shouting*). Her husband is a lunatic who tried to set fire to her. What was she to do? Continue living with him until she was a pile of ashes?

RAJ. I can see that you care enough for this Lila to raise your voice in anger against me, so I forbid you to speak to her outside your workplace.

SITA. Lila is my friend. She helps me with my English . . .

RAJ. There is no need for you to speak English. Anyone you need to speak to speaks your own language.

Spot on an Asian Elder, who gives a speech.
An Indian Dancer performs a graceful, contained dance.

ASIAN ELDER. As I was walking to the temple to perform my duties I saw some of our women laughing in the street. I heard the words they used to each other. They were bad words, invisible rough weapons of disrespect to the parents that gave them birth and culture.

We elders must protect our women from the invasion of Western attitudes and habits. They must be watched and guarded and cherished. They must not be allowed the terrible freedom that has ruined the family life of Westerners. Already there have been incidents, young girls complaining of restrictions, some even phoning the police and accusing their families of cruelty. One girl from our community left her home and sold her body to strangers. When I heard of this I was so ashamed I wept. Our women must not allow their bodies to be used by any man except their husbands. Sex must not be brought downstairs.

Sometimes I wonder if we were right to come here. Is it worth losing our culture just so that we play with Western toys?

When I see the bold brazen behaviour of some of our girls I wish that I was dead. For it is better to drown in a flood or starve during a famine than to see centuries of tradition wear away.

Each grain of sand once belonged to a rock. I am saving with the Bank of India, when I have enough money I will take my family home.

SCENE ELEVEN

The Prakash living-room. 1977. Bibi is washing the floor on hands and knees. Mother-in-Law and Fat Auntie are making chappatis.

MOTHER-IN-LAW. Sita's chappatis are too hard / for my teeth.*

BIBI. I like them.

FAT AUNTIE. *She uses too much flour. I've told her but she won't listen.

MOTHER-IN-LAW. Raj likes soft chappatis.

Prem enters. He looks down at Bibi. Mother-in-Law and Fat Auntie smile at him.

BIBI. Wait a minute. / It's not dry yet.*

FAT AUNTIE. We shouldn't be doing the kitchen work.

PREM. *What am I supposed to do? I can't float.

BIBI. Really? I thought you were a god /

MOTHER-IN-LAW. How many times has she burnt the lentils?

BIBI. since you came to Leicester.*

FAT AUNTIE. Twice this month.

PREM. *You're jealous 'cos they like me best.

Prem looks at Mother-in-Law and Fat Auntie.

BIBI. All that petting and baby / talk? It

MOTHER-IN-LAW. Raj is too soft with her.

BIBI. would drive me mad. Bugger off until the floor is dry.**

FAT AUNTIE. She wants to be head of the house you know.*

PREM. **No, I want to walk on it.

BIBI. You dare.

MOTHER-IN-LAW. *What would happen to us if she was?

FAT AUNTIE. She would turn me out.

Prem walks over the floor.

MOTHER-IN-LAW. I wouldn't let / her.*

BIBI. / You rotten little sod!

She swipes Prem with the floorcloth.

FAT AUNTIE. *But she might turn *you* out!

MOTHER-IN-LAW. Put me into an old /

PREM. Cow!

MOTHER-IN-LAW. people's home you mean? Hai hai hai.

BIBI. Do you want some more?

Prem falls to the floor and works up to a tantrum.

FAT AUNTIE ⎫
MOTHER-IN-LAW ⎬ (*together*).
with / the baby?

Prem!
What's wrong

BIBI. He walked on the floor!

Mother-in-Law and Fat Auntie cuddle Prem.

FAT AUNTIE ⎫
MOTHER-IN-LAW ⎬ (*together*).

Such a
little one.
What else

is he to do?

BIBI ⎫
PREM ⎬ (*together*).

I asked him not to.
She hit me with a dirty cloth!

MOTHER-IN-LAW. Go upstairs to / your

PREM. There's germs on it! I'll get a disease.

MOTHER-IN-LAW. room.

FAT AUNTIE. She takes after her mother.

MOTHER-IN-LAW. Headstrong. Do as I say.

FAT AUNTIE. Do as she says.

BIBI (*going*). Why do I always get the blame? (*To Prem.*) Why bother, they've given the Academy Awards out this year.

Mother-in-Law takes Prem and talks to him in Hindi. Fat Auntie goes back to the chappatis.
Sita enters.

SITA. What's the matter with him now? I could hear him in the street.

PREM. Bibi hit me with a dirty cloth!

FAT AUNTIE. For nothing.

SITA. For nothing, Prem?

Sita looks at him long and hard. Prem drops eye contact.

SITA ⎫
FAT AUNTIE ⎬ (*together*).

For nothing?
Bibi has to
learn respect.

MOTHER-IN-LAW. She must learn to control / herself.

SITA. For this spoiled boy? Why do you always take his side?

MOTHER-IN-LAW. I have to. You know that.

PREM (*to Mother-in-Law*). She's always going on at me, always.

FAT AUNTIE. Never mind, we love you.

SITA. I love him, but I don't like him much, not now.

FAT AUNTIE. You don't like England either do you?

SITA. Everything is so grey.

MOTHER-IN-LAW. If you want colour go and see a film. We are here to work and save and go back to our village important people.

FAT AUNTIE. Why am I doing this? It is her job.

MOTHER-IN-LAW. And I'm not well, but I have to look after the house. You shouldn't be out working.

SITA. Maji. (*She grabs her by the shoulders.*) Promise me that the next time you are unwell you will tell me and I will do your work for you.

MOTHER-IN-LAW. Why this sudden affection? What do you want?

SITA. I want us all to share this house peacefully. I don't want you to keep this feeling of resentment against me.

PREM. Masi and Dadima don't like you Ma.

MOTHER-IN-LAW ⎫
FAT AUNTIE ⎬ (*together*).

Shush.
Hold your
tongue!

SITA. I know. It makes me sad.

FAT AUNTIE (*to Sita*). Here, you make the chappatis!

MOTHER-IN-LAW. Yes. We'll take this poor boy and dress him in his lovely clothes, eh? Who's going to the dance tonight?

PREM. We've been practising the stick dance at school today. I'm dead good at it.

They go.

FAT AUNTIE. And not so much flour!

Sita makes chappatis. Bibi enters and kisses Sita.

SITA. Don't worry about Prem, Bibi. I'm sure he deserved it. (*Small pause.*) You ought to dress soon.

BIBI. Ma.

SITA. Yes?

BIBI. A terrible thing has happened to me.

SITA (*panic*). What? Are you ill?

BIBI. Yes, I am bleeding.

SITA. Where?

BIBI. From my legs. At the top, I have such pains. Will I die?

SITA. No, you won't die. You have become a woman.

She hugs Bibi.

I can't call you my little girl now.

BIBI. I'm not ready to be a woman. I don't want to be a woman.

SITA. But it's a good thing, women are strong and brave. We are the mothers of the world.

BIBI. I don't want to be a mother. I might have a girl and then everyone will be angry.

SITA. Silly! Silly! Have you washed yourself?

BIBI. Yes, but it keeps coming back. I don't like it. I don't want to go to school tomorrow.

SITA. Don't let it interrupt your life. Start as you mean to go on. I'll show you what to use. You're lucky living here—when I started my period . . .

Mother-in-Law and Fat Auntie enter.

Masi, Maji, Bibi has started her period.

MOTHER-IN-LAW. Get away from the food!

FAT AUNTIE. Why didn't you tell her?

Fat Auntie takes over the chappatis.

SITA. I don't agree with it.

MOTHER-IN-LAW (*to Bibi*). When you have a period you are unclean, you must not enter the kitchen. If you happen to approach a vessel of wine it will sour.

FAT AUNTIE. If you touch any corn it will wither. Sit you under a tree, the fruit will fall. The very bees in the hive die. Iron and steel take rust.

SITA. Nonsense! Old superstition. English women don't stop cooking.

MOTHER-IN-LAW. English women are not clean.

FAT AUNTIE. You cannot go to Navratri now either. You may watch, but not dance.

BIBI. But I want to dance.

MOTHER-IN-LAW. You cannot worship our Goddess if you are unclean!

SITA. Our Goddess never bled?

MOTHER-IN-LAW. No, that is why we women worship her.

Raj enters carrying an open Leicester Mercury.

RAJ. Is there never any peace in this house? What's wrong with you all now?

A long pause.

SITA. Raj. Our daughter became a woman today.

MOTHER-IN-LAW. Go out Raj. (*She pushes him.*)

FAT AUNTIE. Don't listen!

SITA. She started her period.

Raj starts to move to Bibi.

MOTHER-IN-LAW. In front of a man to use such words. (*She covers her ears.*)

FAT AUNTIE. No shame!

Fat Auntie and Mother-in-Law wail.

SITA. Your mother has told Bibi she may not dance at Navratri tonight.

RAJ (*to Mother-in-Law*). Why not?

MOTHER-IN-LAW. It's not allowed, Raj. It will dishonour our family. It will insult the Goddess. Tell Bibi she may not dance.

SITA. I say she will dance. Bibi, go and put your pretty clothes on.

BIBI. No I'm dirty! I'm going to have a bath.

FAT AUNTIE. No you must not bathe.

MOTHER-IN-LAW. She must not bathe, tell her Raj.

SITA. She *will* bathe, and then she will dance. She will show our community how beautiful she is, and she will honour the Goddess. And all the while she will be bleeding, but she will hold her head high. And she will not be made to feel unclean!

FAT AUNTIE. But not in front of the Goddess Raj!

RAJ. She will *not* dance Sita.

SITA. Raj!

RAJ. She will *not* dance.

SITA. She is my daughter as well, and I say she will dance. Why must we all do as you say?

MOTHER-IN-LAW. Your husband has spoken. Isn't that enough? (*To Raj.*) She will kill me. Every day she is questioning. You should never have left her alone in India for so long. She has developed a will of her own, she is trying to dominate you.

SITA (*quietly*). I don't want to dominate, I want to share. I want to be up there with him, not above or below, but *with* him.

SCENE TWELVE

Navrati music. A big hall. A shrine containing a Goddess to one side. A Male Dancer enters and dances around the stage. He is joined by members of the family. Raj, Mother-in-Law, Fat Auntie and Prem dance in a circle. Sita and Bibi enter. Sita is carrying the bucket. Bibi sits on a chair and watches. Raj pulls Sita into the dance. Raj drops out of the dance and takes an offering of money to the Goddess. Prem follows him and examines the other offerings. They rejoin the dance.

Mother-in-Law and Fat Auntie give offerings to the Goddess, then they rejoin the dance. Sita leaves the dance and joins Bibi. She picks up the bucket and gives it to Bibi. Bibi pours milk from the bucket into a dish at the Goddess's feet. The Goddess drinks the milk, then steps down from the shrine. She joins hands with Sita and Bibi and dances with them. They dance faster and laugh.

ACT TWO

SCENE ONE

The Prakash living-room. A Bride is sitting. She is veiled and still. She is surrounded by Women laughing and talking.

MOTHER-IN-LAW. It won't be long before she knows what it is to be a wife eh?

FAT AUNTIE. I hope he is gentle with her. My husband frightened me so much I didn't open my eyes for a month! Never mind my legs!

2ND FAT AUNTIE. You couldn't believe what you were seeing eh?

FAT AUNTIE. It was a new sight!

MOTHER-IN-LAW. But you got used to it eh?

Laughter.

FAT AUNTIE. Oh yes, but it didn't last long.

She lapses into melancholy.

2ND FAT AUNTIE. No, no, I won't let you tell us about your years as a barren widow. We have heard it a thousand times. Come on, get up and dance with me.

She pulls Fat Auntie to her feet.

Come on! Everybody dancing! Come on old women, show these young girls how to dance. They are as stiff as broom handles. Bend! Bend! Dip and bend.

The Women dance in a circle, young and old. The Bride sits with downcast eyes.

At the end of the dance Prem is led in.

2ND FAT AUNTIE. I hope you are prepared for this ordeal.

Prem stands. The Women sit.

FAT AUNTIE. He eats with his mouth wide open!

MOTHER-IN-LAW. And sleeps with it open too, his snores rattle the windows! His poor bride will get no peace!

The Women giggle and nudge each other.

FAT AUNTIE. But then look at the size of his big fat nose!

2ND FAT AUNTIE. You know what they say. Big nose, big sou sou.

The Women laugh.

MOTHER-IN-LAW. No, that's not right! Don't you remember when we would dry him after his bath? His sou sou was so small, what did we need to find it? A magnifying glass!

FAT AUNTIE. And have you heard that there is more hair on his hands than on his chest?

BIBI. He will be bald by the time he's thirty. Look, his hair's falling out.

PREM. Where? (*He looks at his shoulder.*)

BIBI. It's all the whisky he drinks!

MOTHER-IN-LAW. That's why his eyes are pink like a rat's.

PREM. I'm not here to be insulted.

BIBI. That's exactly what you are here for, cretin.

Prem fingers his nose.

SITA. Oh Prem, I thought you liked the traditions. It's traditional to respond with good humour.

PREM. It's stupid!

BIBI. He can't think of anything to say.

FAT AUNTIE. He is dull witted!

MOTHER-IN-LAW. He was nine years of age before he could tie his shoelaces!

PREM. I was eight!

The Women laugh.

FAT AUNTIE. Is that the best you can do?

MOTHER-IN-LAW. Is it true he has no savings?

FAT AUNTIE. Oh yes, it is true!

A loud whisper.

That's why he is marrying this girl.

2ND FAT AUNTIE (*loud whisper*). I hear she brings a cash dowry with her.

SITA (*quietly*). The insults are only for Prem. She is not here to be insulted.

FAT AUNTIE. It is no insult to have a good dowry. It shows she comes from a provident family.

PREM. Have you finished?

FAT AUNTIE. No we have not! Come on, you young women, you are leaving us to think up insults. It is the only chance you ever get so don't waste it.

BIBI. I can think of a few good ones, but Prem looks as if he's going to cry, so I won't. And look, she's crying. I don't blame her. I would if I had to marry him.

PREM. You wait Bibi.

MOTHER-IN-LAW. Good Bibi, carry on.

BIBI. If I carried on speaking the truth about Prem, this girl would get up and run from the room. So I will keep silent.

The Bride wipes her eyes with the corner of her veil. Sita comforts her.

MOTHER-IN-LAW. Sita, don't give her comfort. You will have kitchen trouble if you are too friendly.

SITA. I'm not going to make an enemy of a seventeen-year-old girl who is leaving her family to live amongst strangers.

FAT AUNTIE. Prem is not a stranger. She has met him four times!

PREM. They always cry the night before.

SITA (*To Indira, the Bride*). Do you want to marry my son?

Shock from everyone except Bibi.

Look at him!

Indira glances briefly at Prem then looks away.

INDIRA. It is all arranged.

SITA. It can all be disarranged.

MOTHER-IN-LAW. No it cannot! The food is ordered! The hall is booked!

FAT AUNTIE. People are coming from the M6 and the M1!

2ND FAT AUNTIE. She will be disgraced if the wedding is called off. Then she will never marry.

BIBI. There's love marriage. Lots of the girls at school had them.

MOTHER-IN-LAW. A love marriage is a step into darkness hoping that you will not fall too far. But Indira's and Prem's marriage has been gone into carefully, they are well matched.

BIBI. I think they are very badly matched. Indira is a nice girl but Prem is a lying sneaky bastard.

MOTHER-IN-LAW. That's enough Bibi.

PREM. I've had enough of this. Can I go?

MOTHER-IN-LAW. Yes. Go.

Prem leaves the room without a backward glance.

FAT AUNTIE. Come on now! Come on, start the music up, Bibi. You know how to work that machine.

SCENE TWO

Rose's living-room. Loud reggae music playing.

ROSE (*off*). Delroy! Delroy! Turn that bleddy music down! Delroy!!! I've gorra customer with me!

Sorry to keep you waiting—I'll be out in a bit—I'm just putting me face on. Ooh, it's like plastering a wall—Max Factor oughta present me with a long service medal.

Rose rushes on.

Right, this is me spring catalogue. We'll have a good look through it in a bit. But I can recommend it. If it weren't for this, me and Delroy'd be going round naked. I mean, who can afford to pay cash for new stuff nowadays? I never thought I'd gerrit going. When I seen the Indians moving in round here I thought, oh well, you can say goodbye to building yourself a round up, Rose. I were a bit suspicious of 'em at first. Well, when they first come, some of 'em looked at me like I were muck. I know I ain't much, but I ain't muck. You can get used to owt can't you? And some of them are really nice—not all, but some. Any road up, as it turned out, I've got myself a nice little round going in our street. I take me catalogue round of a Wednesday, collect the money, and after we've had a few drinks, I ask 'em if they want owt else. Sita's paying me one-fifty a week for some sheets she had last year. When she's finished paying, she's having a ottoman to put 'em in.

Bibi had her first pair of jeans from out my club—Christ, didn't that cause a stink! You'd have thought she'd had a G-string or sommat! Them two old bags, bleddy Dadima an' Masi wanted Sita to send 'em back, but Sita stuck to her guns.

O' course, that were a few year ago—she's having a bit of a wobber now. I don't know what's up, but sommat is. She's not the same girl as come here eight year ago. To tell the truth, I don't know her now. She works too hard. She's out the house at eight, and don't get back till after six, and I know she don't sit down when she gets home. She's always up and doing—has to be busy. Now I've learnt the secret of relaxation? I take life gradual, have a few laughs. It's laughing's kept me going. An it's free, so I can recommend that and all! Anyway, what you going to have?

SCENE THREE

The next day.
Sita alone looking in a blank mirror touching her body.

SITA. Sita, where are you? I don't know where you are. Come back to me. You've been away so long I'm afraid that I won't know you when you come back.

Raj enters unnoticed. He watches Sita anxiously.

Is this you? (*She pinches her arm.*) Is this your hair? (*She pulls her hair.*) Your belly? (*She punches her own belly. Shouts.*) No it is not you! (*She beats herself. Despairing.*) Sita! Sita! I want you, please come back!

Raj, frightened and furious, walks up to Sita, turns her in front of the mirror, forces her head until she is staring into the mirror.

RAJ. You *are* there you mad woman, you are there. You want proof?

He slaps her and knocks her to the floor.

If you feel pain then you are there. Now get to your feet. We have visitors soon. (*Raj exits.*)

Sita gets up calmly and tidies herself, applies lipstick in the mirror, turns to leave, goes back to the mirror.

She exits.

SCENE FOUR

Fat Auntie, Mother-in-Law and Raj in the living-room. The same day. Prem enters smoking. He puts his cigarette in the corner of Fat Auntie's mouth while she sleeps.

PREM. Dead good impression *she's* going to make, look at her.

Looking at Fat Auntie.

MOTHER-IN-LAW (*to Fat Auntie*). Don't go to sleep now! Take that out of your mouth. They will be here soon. Look alert.

PREM. How long they gonna be, Dad? I can't hang about, I've got a meet set up. There's a guy after the Datsun.

RAJ. If they don't come soon I'll ring and tell them to cancel. They are wasting my time.

He gets up and paces around the room.

PREM. I should get three hundred quid, if he don't notice the filler.

RAJ (*angry*). Two more minutes then I ring.

PREM. Is this the one whose dad's got the video shops?

RAJ. Yes, four.

MOTHER-IN-LAW. Hear that sister? Video shops. We'll be all right for films, eh?

FAT AUNTIE. Let's hope she accepts this time.

PREM. She reckons she don't want to get married.

MOTHER-IN-LAW. She is twenty years old, time is passing. People will be thinking there is something wrong with her.

The bell rings.

RAJ (*shouting*). Sita! They're here.

SITA (*off*). I know, I'm going.

MOTHER-IN-LAW. Everybody sit up! Look respectable.

Raj goes to the door as two Men enter. One is Mr Patel the other is his son Ram who is wearing flared trousers.

MR PATEL (*shaking hands with Raj*). I am most sorry to be so late.

Ram looks shy, awkward.

RAJ. Not at all, not at all, are you late? I didn't notice. This way. My mother, my aunt and my son.

PREM (*giving his card to Mr Patel*). My card—Prakesh Motors.

MR PATEL. Thank you. So you are in the car business?

PREM. Purveyor of quality secondhand vehicles.

MOTHER-IN-LAW. Excuse me. I have kitchen work to do.

Mother-in-Law stares at Ram Patel before she leaves the room.

RAJ. Please sit down.

They all sit. Long pause.

So how old is your son?

MR PATEL. Twenty-one years.

PREM. How many 'A' levels has he got?

MR PATEL. Ram, show these people that you have a tongue.

RAM (*shy*). No 'A' levels, but three 'O' levels, English, maths and physics.

MR PATEL. Good grades, nothing below a B.

FAT AUNTIE. And have you had rickets?

RAM. No.

An awkward silence.

MR PATEL. He has passed his driving test.

FAT AUNTIE. First time?

MR PATEL. No third.

PREM. Passed mine first time.

FAT AUNTIE. What is his character like? I can see that he is shy.

MR PATEL. Yes, he is a shy extrovert.

FAT AUNTIE. What is that, extrovert?

RAJ. Always laughing.

FAT AUNTIE. Heh! This one?

MR PATEL. Speak up Ram. Talk about your hobbies.

RAM. I like films and television and I write poetry.

PREM. Poetry!?

RAM. It is no good but . . .

MR PATEL. Of course it is good. It is excellent poetry.

FAT AUNTIE. And what are his vices?

MR PATEL. He hasn't got any vices have you, Ram?

RAM. I eat sweets. And my room is untidy sometimes.

MR PATEL. The first is nothing. The second a wife will correct.

An awkward pause.

RAJ. Ah, the women with the food.

The Women enter carrying tid-bits of food.

My mother you've met, my wife. My daughter Bibi. Beautiful, isn't she?

RAM. Hello.

BIBI. Hello.

MR PATEL. Bibi is how old?

RAJ. Eighteen.

BIBI (*corrects*). Twenty. I've got three 'A' levels.

Everyone takes a piece of food.

RAJ. Bibi cooked this herself, didn't you Bibi?

BIBI. No Ma cooked it. I don't like cooking.

MOTHER-IN-LAW (*alarm*). She likes to joke! She is a slave to the stove. We have to tear her away.

MR PATEL. A sense of humour is a good thing—in moderation.

RAJ. Bibi is moderate in most things, aren't you Bibi?

BIBI. No, I am considered extreme in most things.

RAJ. Again she jokes, she is so happy and cheerful!

FAT AUNTIE. Stand up and show yourself girl.

Bibi stands, does a twirl.

BIBI. I am twenty years old, Hindu. I am five feet six inches tall. My complexion is good, my skin tone light, my teeth (*She bares her gums.*) are perfect. I have two fillings, gold. I weight nine stone when I am naked. My shoe size is five and a half, my pelvis is wide. Naturally I will have many sons. I speak English, Hindi, Gujerati, a little Punjabi, and French. I read two library books a week. I cook good chappatis and can make my own clothes. I have a light melodious singing voice, I dance gracefully and I am currently working in the the gas offices where I earn £95 a week before tax.

She sits down to silence. A pause. She rises again.

And most important of all. I am a virgin.

PREM (*under his breath*). Fucking hell.

She sits down to horrified silence. She rises again.

BIBI. Sorry. My dowry consists of blankets, sheets, an electric toaster, a fridge freezer, a portable colour television . . . a magi-mix with full accessories.

MR PATEL. Come, Ram. The girl is laughing at us.

MOTHER-IN-LAW. She must be ill. She has never spoken like this before. Call for a doctor.

SITA. She's not ill. She told the truth!

RAJ. Sita! (*Sita and Bibi stand together.*)

SITA. She told them what they came to find out. Why waste everyone's time with fine words?

MR PATEL. She is too Western. We want a traditional girl.

Mr Patel and Ram back out of the room.

SITA. Go on then, go and look for your kitchen slave. My daughter will be an executive one day. She will have her own mortgage. She has money saved in the Leicester Building Society!

The Patels exit.

MOTHER-IN-LAW. Why doesn't she stick a knife in my heart and be done with? (*To Sita.*) Go on, kill me now!

FAT AUNTIE. It's her fault Bibi is so outspoken.

RAJ (*To Bibi*). By tonight the whole of the community will have learnt of our shame.

BIBI. Stop bringing them to the house, Pa.

PREM. Four video shops and she blew it.

BIBI. You think I'd marry a man wearing flared trousers?

PREM (*shouting*). For four fucking video shops *I'd* marry a man in flared trousers.

SITA. She's going to buy land and a cow!

BIBI. Ma I've only got thirty pounds saved.

Bibi goes to leave the room.

RAJ. Where are you going?

BIBI. Out!

Bibi exits. Raj sits with his head in his hands.
From now on the rest of the family treat Sita as though she were invisible.

MOTHER-IN-LAW. Your wife is sick in the head. Cows! And land!

FAT AUNTIE. Did you notice the strange look in her eye lately? I did.

SITA. Who are you talking about? What strange look?

MOTHER-IN-LAW. Pressure takes different women different ways.

RAJ. But she's had no pressure.

PREM. What about at work? She's a supervisor.

SITA. You're talking about me?

RAJ. I should have stopped her years ago! I blame myself.

SITA. Raj, I'm here look.

MOTHER-IN-LAW. You've got a soft heart, son. Sometimes it can be a curse.

SITA. I'm here!

FAT AUNTIE. It stops you doing your duty.

SITA. Auntie!

PREM. It's not as if she needs to work is it? Not now there's three of us bringing money home?

SITA. Prem, can you see me?

MOTHER-IN-LAW. Yes, you must stop her working, Raj. Make her take a rest. We'll look after her won't we, sister?

FAT AUNTIE. Yes. We'll take her to the doctor's.

RAJ. No, I'll take her. I'll make an appointment.

SITA. I'm not sick!

PREM. I reckon she started cracking up about the time of my wedding.

MOTHER-IN-LAW. The wedding that never was, poor boy.

SITA. Ma Ge.

PREM. It was all her fault it was called off.

SITA. The girl didn't like you, she was brave enough to say no.

MOTHER-IN-LAW. People don't want madness in the family, who can blame them?

SITA (*shouting*). I'm standing here in front of you!

FAT AUNTIE. Where is she?

MOTHER-IN-LAW. She'll be mooning over that stupid old bucket.

FAT AUNTIE. You see? Only a mad person would do such a thing.

RAJ. I'll go and see.

Raj crosses right in front of Sita and exits.

SCENE FIVE

The loo in the Palais. Midnight.

BIBI. Well, I had a brilliant time tonight. Debauchery galore there was. I've been with every bloke in the Palais—must be 200. I came in at eight and it's Cinderella time now. So it's not bad going is it? It's my legs you see. One glimpse and the English blokes are sitting on their haunches panting for it and I'm so depraved and corrupted by the West that I let them have it. You see I've no morality of my own. No respect for my body. I've got three 'A' levels but no intelligence. I can't be trusted, after all I'm only twenty. Mum knows I come here. There's nothing I wouldn't tell her—well the odd thing.

But Mum doesn't count for much in our family. When it's not at Sketchleys I keep me gear in a black plastic bag in Mum's wardrobe, next to her bucket. It's pathetic. Here I am an Asian girl caught in a culture clash. See these things each side of my head? Inverted commas. Now the English *are* lucky—they don't have family problems. No, they sit around in shafts of sunlight eating cornflakes, then get up and run around meadows in slow motion. One in four that is. The other three are undergoing divorce or family therapy. Yes we all jostle for space on the *Guardian* Women's Page. There's me, cheek by jowl with 'Shall I, a committed Socialist, send my Rupert to public school?' Now that *would* make you toss and turn at night. I'm educated. I'm healthy, and I'll make myself some sort of life. But until then I'll change in the bog. Me mum's got enough on her plate. (*Pause.*) If anyone asks, I've been babysitting.

SCENE SIX

Dr Mistry's surgery. The next day. Raj and Sita, seated.
Dr Mistry pacing about.

DR MISTRY. So there are no problems in your family?

RAJ. No, no problems. My son is in business now, my daughter passed her 'As' and will marry soon. We have a comfortable home. No, no problems.

DR MISTRY. Your wife is obsessed with cows you say?

RAJ. Obsessed?

DR MISTRY. A medical term. It means morbidly interested.

RAJ. Yes, she is morbidly interested in cows.

SITA. There is only one cow.

DR MISTRY. Yes, naturally Mrs Prakesh. Of course there is only one cow.

SITA. Her name is Princess.

RAJ. You see?

DR MISTRY. Charming. She is a pretty cow?

SITA. Not particularly. Her eyes are nice but she was really nothing special. She wasn't a film star.

DR MISTRY. No, naturally.

RAJ. What will become of her? (*He weeps.*)

DR MISTRY. I see many women like her.

RAJ. All morbidly interested in cows?

DR MISTRY. No, your wife is lucky, at least this cow seems to give her pleasure. (*To Sita.*) You like this cow don't you Mrs Prakesh?

SITA. She is everything to me.

RAJ. Perhaps if she'd had more children. It is my fault! I will never forgive myself.

DR MISTRY. You have had your testicles tied?

RAJ. No, but I failed to impregnate her more than twice. Even her womb is stubborn.

Sita laughs.

DR MISTRY. I will give you a prescription. You must make sure your wife takes the tablets I prescribe.

RAJ. Will she stop thinking about the cow?

DR MISTRY. Oh yes. She will stop thinking altogether. Good morning.

Dr Mistry stands. Raj and Sita exit.

SCENE SEVEN

Two months later.
Sita is sitting in the ward of a mental hospital. She is perfectly composed, thinking.

NURSE. Visitors, Mrs Prakesh. (*Pause.*) Mrs. Prakesh!

She shakes Sita gently.

SITA. I want to go home. I'm not mad.

NURSE. No, you are just here for a rest, aren't you?

SITA. Not even that, I was not tired.

Raj, Bibi, Prem, Mother-in-Law, Fat Auntie enter. Bibi runs up to Sita and holds her tight.

MOTHER-IN-LAW. To see her in such a place! I can't bear it, it will kill me. All these crazy people we passed.

FAT AUNTIE. Did you do the right thing, Raj? She is looking perfectly calm now.

RAJ. I listened to the doctor's advice. I am not an expert in these affairs.

BIBI. But you know your own wife.

PREM. She was round the bend. You know she was. Cows! Cows! Cows!

SITA (*to Raj*). You put me in here. (*To Prem.*) And you.

Fat Auntie and Mother-in-Law fuss with the food looking for somewhere to put it.

PREM. Don't blame me!

RAJ. You were behaving so strangely, Sita.

FAT AUNTIE. We have brought food for you, Sita. You must eat it all up and get well again.

MOTHER-IN-LAW. Will Raj put *me* in this place if I lose my keys again?

FAT AUNTIE. No. Of course not. I won't let him. (*Pause.*) And what about me? I have been having strange thoughts lately.

MOTHER-IN-LAW. Thoughts?

FAT AUNTIE. Yes. About so many things. Wrong things. Things I can't say aloud.

MOTHER-IN-LAW. Then don't say them aloud.

FAT AUNTIE. But I can't stop my brain from thinking, sister.

MOTHER-IN-LAW. We are too old to start thinking.

SITA. Bibi, the next time you come bring my bucket, will you?

PREM. The hospital won't allow it, Mama.

RAJ. There are bound to be regulations, rules.

BIBI. Yes, Mama, I'll bring the bucket.

MOTHER-IN-LAW. Lila was asking for you, Sita. She sends her love and says work is now a dull place without you.

RAJ. Dull without Sita?

MOTHER-IN-LAW. Sita was the life and soul. That's what Lila said, the life and soul. I don't know what it means.

PREM. It means Mama was good for a laugh, that can't be right.

RAJ. No that *can't* be right.

BIBI. That's what you think. We have a really good time don't we, Ma?

SITA. When they let us.

FAT AUNTIE (*to Mother-in-Law*). That is what I have been thinking! I have needed permission all my life. Permission. Father, husband, Raj, and if I live long enough, Prem. Permission, always permission.

MOTHER-IN-LAW. Sister keep your thoughts to yourself! You have stored them away in a jar like a good housewife for 40 years. Don't let them out to spoil in the air.

BIBI. Masi, we'll sit up and talk tonight. And you Dadima don't go to bed at nine. Let's stay up late and keep each other company, eh?

MOTHER-IN-LAW. What will we talk about for so long?

BIBI. We will open Auntie's jar and see what is inside eh?

PREM. If you ask me you all belong in the loony bin.

MOTHER-IN-LAW. Nobody is asking you, are they? So shut your ugly mouth.

Shock.

Oh I'm sorry, it is this place. It made me forget myself.

Prem looks at his watch.

PREM. I've got to be somewhere in half an hour so when you're ready . . .

MOTHER-IN-LAW. Oh, we'd better go.

BIBI. No, we've only just arrived.

RAJ. But Prem is driving so . . .

BIBI. So I will phone for a taxi. We can be independent of Prem to get around—

FAT AUNTIE. Yes, I never thought of a taxi. Simple isn't it?

SITA. Don't look so unhappy, Prem. Go and keep your appointment. I can see that you don't like to be here. Take your father with you.

RAJ. But I'm not ready to go yet.

PREM. Are you coming or do you wanna go home with the women?

Raj and Prem exit.

SCENE EIGHT

The living-room. Later that day. Prem is sitting with the Princess photograph in his hand. Bibi enters. She hesitates before moving toward Prem. Prem doesn't notice Bibi until she pulls the photograph out of his hand. Bibi looks at the photo.

BIBI. I thought it was lost. I haven't seen it for years. God, I was skinny then!

PREM. I had it in my wallet. I donno why I hated that cow.

Pause.

It just about cracked me up seeing her in there.

BIBI. You were quick enough to take her in!

PREM. I only drove the car. I didn't sign the papers! She hates me.

BIBI. No, but she doesn't like what you've become and neither do I.

PREM. The others like me.

BIBI. You're their insurance policy, Prem. You'll be head of the house one day, you thick get!

PREM. I didn't ask to be head of the house. I don't want them all on my back. I wanna live my own life.

BIBI. Well, you've got a few years yet.

PREM. What's gonna happen to Ma?

BIBI. That's up to you.

PREM. And you.

BIBI. Since when did I have any influence over anything?

PREM. Well I'm not doing it on me own. When I were driving back I kept thinking about in India. I donno how she did it. Bringing us up on us own. No money, just that cowin' cow.

BIBI. She did it 'cos she's a bleddy wonderful woman.

PREM (*pause*). We should have stayed in India.

BIBI. D'you reckon? I'm glad we came. I wouldn't have got three 'A' levels at the village school would I?

PREM. You couldn't call it a school. It were a patch of ground under a tree.

BIBI. And look how well you're doing with your garage.

PREM. It's only a lock-up under a railway arch.

BIBI. It's a start. You'd be a rich man in India.

PREM. I wouldn't mind going back. Just to see it like.

BIBI. Yeah.

PREM. I'll go and see Ma tomorrow, on me own.

BIBI. Take her the photo, she'd like that.

PREM. No, I want the photo.

SCENE NINE

One month later.
Sita sitting in the mental hospital ward, her bucket at her feet. A Patient enters and stands to one side. Kishwar enters wearing a borqa.

SITA. Kishwar, is that you?

KISHWAR. Sita! Is that your voice?

SITA. Yes, it's me. (*She takes Kishwar's hands.*) Why are you here?

KISHWAR. I have lost my face. Why are you here?

SITA. I want to buy a cow.

KISHWAR. Have you seen my face, Sita?

SITA. No I have never seen your face. When did you see it last?

KISHWAR. I'm sure I had it last year. Perhaps I left it somewhere.

SITA. Somewhere in the house?

KISHWAR. Yes, I have not left the house until this day so it is somewhere in the house. I have asked everyone. Have you seen my face? Where is my face? They say, Kishwar your face is still there. But it's not. It's not. It's gone.

SITA. Let me see for myself.

KISHWAR. No.

Sita raises Kishwar's veil. There is nothing there.

SITA. You have not lost your face, Kishwar. It has been stolen.

The Patient and Sita comfort Kishwar.

SCENE TEN

Mother-in-Law, Fat Auntie, Bibi and Lila enter. The Patient exits.

LILA. Sita!

She runs to Sita.

SITA. Lila!

LILA. They told me you were crazy! But look at you, you were pretending, eh? To get a rest!

SITA. You're the one who should be in here. You were always a madwoman.

LILA. When they told me you had gone crazy on cows, I said so what? If she wants a cow, buy her a cow.

MOTHER-IN-LAW. How are you Daughter?

SITA. I am well. But I want to leave here now. This is a very sad place you know. It is depressing me.

BIBI. I talked to the doctor.

SITA. Him? He's mad. Don't listen to anything he says.

BIBI. He says that you can come out for the day.

SITA. Out? Do you mean home?

BIBI. Yes, if you want to . . .

LILA. Home! She doesn't want to go to boring home. I have the car. We will go out for a run. See the countryside.

FAT AUNTIE. Oh yes! I mean whatever everyone else would like to do. Sita? It's your day.

SITA. I can choose? What a gift!

BIBI. Do you want to go to the country?

SITA. Yes, could we walk on the grass?

BIBI. You can take your clothes off and roll in the grass if you want to.

MOTHER-IN-LAW. No, that is going too far.

FAT AUNTIE. But we have no food!

LILA. There are cafés, shops, this is Leicestershire, not the foothills of the Himalayas. Well, what are we waiting for?

BIBI. Come on, Ma.

MOTHER-IN-LAW. An adventure. (*She clasps her hands girlishly.*) Where are we going?

LILA. Who knows? I will get behind the wheel and let the car take us where it wants.

SCENE ELEVEN

The Women, travelling in the car.

FAT AUNTIE. Not so fast Lila!

LILA. I have slowed down to 30. Nice country, eh.

MOTHER-IN-LAW. I don't know, my eyes are shut.

BIBI. Isn't it lovely Lila? It was near here I came camping with the Guides. My first night away from home. I cried so much Akala brought me home the next day.

FAT AUNTIE. And you taught us all that terrible song about goolies.

MOTHER-IN-LAW. With words for idiots.

SITA. I thought it was a foreign language, French. I thought it was French.

Sita sings 'Ging gang gooly'. Everyone joins in.

Look cows! Stop the car!

Groans from everyone else but Bibi.

BIBI. Stop the car, Lila. Stop!

Lila stops the car.

MOTHER-IN-LAW. Remember the green cross code!

Sita crosses the road. She runs to the fence, looks into the meadow. Two Cows approach the fence.

SITA. Hello. How are you?

BOTH COWS. Not happy. We are going to the market today.

SITA. Do you know Princess?

1ST COW. Princess?

2ND COW. From India?

SITA. Yes, that's her.

1ST COW. Mummm.

SITA. She is looking for me. Will you tell her where I am?

BOTH COWS. Mummm.

SITA. Where is the market?

2ND COW. Melton Mowbray, just down the road.

SITA. Thank you, goodbye. (*Sita crosses the road gets into the car.*)

BOTH COWS. Morning.

1ST COW. } Nice woman.
2ND COW. } Good smell.
SITA. We are going to Melton Mowbray.
LILA. Where is that?
SITA. That cow said it was just down the road.
MOTHER-IN-LAW. Ay ay ay.
FAT AUNTIE. A cow told you? How can you believe a cow? In my experience they are very unreliable. You have heard the expression, 'lying cow'?
MOTHER-IN-LAW. Yes. Better look at the map.

SCENE TWELVE

The cattle market.

The Women enter the showing area. They look at the ring. An Auctioneer and a stockman, Harold, are talking at the side entrance gate.

MOTHER-IN-LAW. Chi, what a stink! My nose thinks it has been dipped in a sewer.
AUCTIONEER. Now there's a nice one for my collection.
HAROLD. Never had a brown 'un?
AUCTIONEER. Never had the opportunity, Harold. Don't see many Asiatics round here.
FAT AUNTIE. Watch where you're putting your feet, Sita. You're getting cow dung on your sandals.
HAROLD. Look at the arse on that one. (*He goes to whistle at* Bibi *but the Auctioneer stops him.*)
AUCTIONEER. Not so crude, Harold, they're easily frightened.
LILA. You belong in a straight jacket, Sita. A day out and you choose to trample in cow shit!

The Women laugh.

AUCTIONEER (*to the Women*). Morning, ladies! (*He tips his hat slightly*)
WOMEN. Morning. (*They are quite pleased at this politeness.*)
AUCTIONEER. Can we be of any assistance?
BIBI. No thank you, we're going now. Have you seen enough, Ma?
SITA. Yes. I don't like it here. I want to go.
HAROLD. This is a short cut ladies.

He opens the gate. The Women walk towards the gate and are about to pass by the Men when Harold grabs Bibi's wrist.

WOMEN. Thank you.
HAROLD. Nearly fell din't you?
BIBI. No I didn't, let go! (*Harold continues holding Bibi's wrist.*)
AUCTIONEER. While you're here, I'd just like to say that you've got the nicest pair of tits I've seen in a lifetime's study.

Bibi, shocked, instinctively covers her breasts with her free hand.

LILA. You dirty bastard!
AUCTIONEER. Foul mouthed cow!

Sita is chopping at Harold's hand holding Bibi's wrist.

SITA. Let my daughter go! (*Harold fondles Bibi's bum.*)
BIBI. Mama!
AUCTIONEER. Shut the other gate, Harold. We'll have a good look at 'em.

Harold closes the back gate, trapping the Women. The Auctioneer closes the side gate. Lila rushes to the side gate, tries to open it.

AUCTIONEER. Give her a bit of stick, Harold!

Harold hits Lila hard. She runs around the ring as a cow.

HAROLD. Gwaan Gwaan, move round you stubborn buggers!

The Auctioneer stands on his podium.

AUCTIONEER. Get 'em moving, Harold!

Harold pokes the stick into the group of Women. The Women move apart a little and run round the ring.

AUCTIONEER. Separate them out, Harold. Get 'em running. Go on Harold show 'em who's master.

Mr Patel enters. He stands at the side of the ring appraising the Women.

HAROLD. Geed up! Geed up! Go on run you buggers!
AUCTIONEER. A small herd and a rarity in these parts. Pedigree Indian stock. Good breeders and three guaranteed milkers. What am I bid for a herd? C'mon gentlemen, what am I bid? No bids? C'mon gentlemen, who'll start? Who'll start? No bids? Get rid of the old uns, Harold.

Harold forces Mother-in-Law and Fat Auntie to the side of the ring. They stand together. The other three Women continue round the ring.

AUCTIONEER. Three milkers gentlemen, fine colour, a rarity. What am I bid?

This is repeated five times. Mr Patel shakes his head slightly.

No takers. Show us the young un, Harold.

Harold forces Sita and Lila to the side of the ring. The Women herd together. They make low distressed cow noises. Bibi moves slowly making whimpering cow noises. Mr Patel takes part in the bidding.

AUCTIONEER. A youngun. A youngun. Full udders. Fine legs. Good colour. A hundred and fifteen! And twenty! Twenty-five, thirty, thirty-five, *two hundred, two hundred.*

Two hundred and fifty—and seventy. Eighty. Three, Three, Three—Three hundred and two, five and fifty. Seven five. Four hundred . . . and fifty. Five. Five hundred. Six hundred. That's more like it. Seven. Eight. A thousand. Two hundred and three. Three, four, five a thousand five hundred! Five hundred. Six, seven, eight. Two thousand five hundred. Sold to Mr Patel! Take her away Harold.

Harold prods Bibi.

HAROLD. Move you cow!

Bibi straightens up then tries to run away. But Harold pushes her down, pins her to the ground and forces her legs apart. Bibi screams.
    Sita leads the other Women into Kali sequence. They bear down on Harold.

AUCTIONEER. Settle 'em down, Harold! They're getting out of control.

Bibi joins the Women.

Use your stick man!

The Women continue moving in on Harold.
    The Auctioneer runs from his podium and through the gate, leaving it open. The Women continue towards Harold. He threatens them with his stick.
    The Auctioneer runs into the ring.

Now get back! Move back! I'm used to being obeyed!

The Auctioneer is knocked out of the way. He runs out of the ring.
    Harold raises his stick to attack the Women but Sita pulls it from him. Harold falls on the floor. Sita stands over him threatening him with the stick.

HAROLD. Don't kill me, please! Please! Please! I'm sorry.

The Women begin to normalise.
Harold takes a chance and jumps up.

You want locking up! You're fucking mad the whole lot of you.

AUCTIONEER. If you're not out of here in one minute I'm phoning the police.

The Auctioneer and Harold go.

SITA. Call the police, we'll do the same to them!

The Women jeer and gesticulate at the Men. Mother-in-Law makes particularly violent gestures.

LILA. I'll fetch the car round. (*As she exits.*) Don't let Dadima out of your sight eh? She's not safe.

The Women laugh and tidy themselves.

SITA. Are you hurt, Bibi?

BIBI. I don't know. I'm too high to care.
FAT AUNTIE. My legs are wobbling. So much exercise!
MOTHER-IN-LAW. But we got rid of the demons didn't we? How they ran!
BIBI. They were only men Mam, hardly demons.
SITA. Anyone that treats my daughter in that way is a demon. And will get the same treatment.

They start to go.

FAT AUNTIE. Listen to her.
MOTHER-IN-LAW. They got what they deserved.

SCENE THIRTEEN

The mental hospital.
    Sita and Bibi enter the ward singing a snatch of 'Ging gan gooly.'

BIBI (*half laughing*). Don't tell 'em what happened or they will have you in a straightjacket.
SITA. I'll say we had a quiet picnic.
BIBI. Some picnic!

They laugh. The Nurse enters, carrying tea.

NURSE. You're tea, no sugar, aren't you Mrs Prakash?
SITA. Yes. (*Pause. She takes the tea.*) Have you put anything in it?
NURSE (*laughing*). So suspicious! (*She looks at Sita.*) You're looking well. The fresh air did you good.
SITA. Yes, we're leaving soon.
NURSE. Oh you are, are you? Where are you going?

The Nurse looks at Sita and Bibi. Bibi shrugs.
    The Nurse hands Sita a small pill cup and stands, expecting Sita to swallow the pill inside.

NURSE (*kindly*). It's a lower dosage.
BIBI. Go on, Ma. You'll be off them soon.
NURSE. Yes I'll have a word with the doctor tomorrow.

Sita pretends to swallow the pill. She does this skillfully, the audience shouldn't notice.

You're doing very well.
SITA. I know.

The Nurse exits.

Good she's gone. Now we can go to India.
BIBI. India! When were you thinking of going?
SITA. Tonight.

BIBI. I can't come tonight, Ma. In fact I don't want to go at all. I've got my work you see.

SITA. Then you must come for a long visit. You and Prem.

BIBI. Oh yes. I'd love a holiday there.

SITA. I'll be off as soon as I find Princess. She's very near now. Are you sure you'll be all right in England?

BIBI. Of course I will. I like it. It's where I live.

SITA. Good. Then I needn't worry about you?

BIBI. I'll come and see you tomorrow. Do you want me to bring anything in?

SITA. But I won't be here. I'll be in India. Goodbye, my darling girl. Give my love to the family. Oh and Bibi, get rid of this.

She hands Bibi the pill.

BIBI. Yes I will. Sleep well.

Bibi exits.

SITA. Come on Princess, I know you're there. That's it Princess, this way, look I'm here.

Princess appears in the window.

How beautiful you look, not a day older. I've been waiting for you for so long, but now I can go home.

She puts her hand on the window.

SCENE FOURTEEN

The Indian village, early morning as in Act One, Scene One.

Sita is milking and watching Bibi and Prem who are playing a game with a small stick and a block of wood. They are happy.

Mother-in-Law and Fat Auntie are mending the photographer's bicycle.

MOTHER-IN-LAW. We got a bargain eh, sister?

FAT AUNTIE. That crazy photographer, to sell his bike for fifty rupees.

PREM. When it's mended can I ride it?

MOTHER-IN-LAW. No, it's too big for you. You will fall off and break your head in half.

PREM. But I want to ride it and I will ride it!

FAT AUNTIE (*sternly*). No! Carry on with your game and move out of our way!

PREM. Who's it for if it's not for me?

FAT AUNTIE. It's for Bibi.

PREM. Girls don't ride bicycles.

SITA. Bibi go and show that boy that he's wrong.

BIBI. But I don't know how to ride it.

FAT AUNTIE. Of course you don't know, but you'll have to learn. Now get on it.

Bibi gets on.

BIBI. But why me?

FAT AUNTIE. You're the eldest. You will need it for secondary school.

MOTHER-IN-LAW. Now we both take a side and support you. Turn the pedals, Bibi. You must do some of the work yourself.

They support Bibi as she wobbles around the compound.

PREM. My sister riding a bike! I am the only boy in the village whose sister can ride a bike! Go on Bibi, do it by yourself now!

Bibi rides alone.

BIBI. Look Ma, I can do it. I can do it!

ONE FOR THE ROAD

Harold Pinter

Harold Pinter (1933 –)

Since the early 1960s Pinter has been among the most produced and discussed playwrights in the world. As a writer for the stage and screen, he is among the most prolific dramatists of the post–World War II era and, subsequently, an influence on numerous young writers who have imitated his cryptic style, as well as his message that no one is safe from the terrors of the unknown in this nuclear age. Furthermore, few playwrights better illustrate the postmodern notion that truth is relative, that all of us construct our version of "the truth" to fit our needs.

Pinter was born in the tough East End of London, the son of Portuguese Jews who Anglicized their name (Da Pinta) to protect themselves from anti-Semitic prejudices. His status as an outsider in British society provided him with subject matter for his dramas. After high school, where he acted and wrote poetry, Pinter enrolled in London's Royal Academy of Dramatic Art (RADA), where he was introduced to classical acting and Stanislavsky's System. The latter influenced Pinter's playwriting, particularly in its emphasis on subtext. Indeed, a Pinter play is virtually all subtext; his characters desperately hide behind a cloud of words to protect themselves from malevolent forces they cannot understand. Feigning a nervous breakdown, Pinter left RADA, however, because he was terrified that he could not compete with his more sophisticated peers. Pinter then ran afoul of the British government when, as a conscientious objector, he refused to perform national service; subsequently, he was fined and reprimanded by the magistracy. *One for the Road* suggests his long-standing hostility toward governments, and he remains a human rights activist and spokesman for humanitarian causes. Though his plays prior to *One for the Road* and *Mountain Language* (1984) do not seem to be political, Pinter has admitted that his works have always been indictments of oppression.

Pinter eventually attended the Central School of Speech and Drama, where he became further acquainted with Stanislavsky's theories. He also was influenced by Rudolf Laban, the respected dance and mime teacher. Building on the legacy of Chekhov and Beckett, Pinter writes plays noted for their pauses and silences, and he relies on the actor's body language and subtlety of gesture. For example, *One for the Road* is virtually a monologue for Nicholas, while Victor and Gila must rely on discreet physical reactions to signal their responses to his brutal assaults.

Pinter first worked professionally in the theater as an actor, touring Ireland with Anew McMaster's company. As David Baron, he also acted in British films, many of which were of the gangster variety. These, too, provided Pinter with material for his plays, especially in the manner in which characters use words as weapons. His scripts are rife with threatening innuendoes and the possibility of explosive violence. One other influence bears mention: Pinter—like so many of his generation—was captivated by Franz Kafka's novel, *The Trial*, in which a young man is inexplicably arrested for no apparent crime, subjected to psychological terrors by his interrogators, and sentenced at a mock trial that is designed to humiliate him. The novel was Kafka's metaphor for the uncertainty of a modern world in which nothing—particularly the truth—is verifiable.

Samuel Beckett is the playwright to whom Pinter is most indebted. Like the Irish drama-tist, Pinter depicts the absurdity and virtual hopelessness of modern life, although Pinter in-variably sets his plays in a more recognizable world. Though his plays have the patina of natu-ralism in both setting and speech, they avoid the strict logic of realism. To convey the unknown (which is always the villain of a Pinter play), the playwright rarely provides exposi-tion about situation or characters, and he customarily refuses to script denouements that neatly resolve his conflicts. Like the absurdist playwrights with whom he is aligned, he places the bur-den of meaning squarely on the audience. Pinter has, in fact, coyly said that even he does not always understand his characters' motivations or his own strange twists of plot.

Generically, his plays are often referred to as "the theater of menace" because invariably a threat exists that neither the characters nor the audience quite fathom. Characteristically, his plays are quite funny—at least at the outset—but gradually give way to silent terrors. His skill-ful use of silence has ingrained the term "the Pinter pause" in the lexicon of postmodern the-ater. In a 1962 essay, "Writing for the Theater," Pinter explains his fascination with silence in the theater:

> So often, below the word spoken, is the thing unknown and unspoken . . . a language where
> under what is said, another thing is being said. It is in the silence that my characters are most
> evident to me. There are two silences. One when no word is spoken. The other when perhaps
> a torrent of language is being employed. The speech is an indication of that which we don't
> hear. It is a necessary avoidance, a violent, sly, anguished or mocking smoke screen which
> keeps the other in its place. . . . One way of looking at speech is to say that it is a constant strat-
> agem to cover nakedness.

Pinter's best-known works include the one-acts *The Room* (1957), *The Dumb Waiter* (1957), *The Collection* (1962), *The Dwarfs* (1963), *One for the Road* (1984), and *Mountain Lan-guage* (1985); and the full-length plays *The Birthday Party* (1957), *The Caretaker* (1960), *The Homecoming* (1965), *No Man's Land* (1970), *Old Times* (1971), *Betrayal* (1977), and the recent *Moonlight* (1994). Pinter's many screenplays include *The Pumpkin Eater*, *The Servant*, *The French Lieutenant's Woman*, and *The Turtle Diaries*. Pinter also directs his own work and that of other playwrights; when Great Britain opened its National Theater in 1976, Pinter directed Noel Coward's *Blithe Spirit* to inaugurate the Lyttleton Theater.

ONE FOR THE ROAD (1984)

Such typical Pinter plays as *The Birthday Party* and *Old Times* employ a recurring motif in which a "room" is invaded by an outside force about which the insiders know little (an early work was simply titled *The Room*). The action proceeds through a series of ambiguous conver-sations in which the invader attempts to uncover a hidden truth about the victim, while the victims struggle against being "found out." Like Joseph K. in Kafka's *The Trial*, victims, who rarely know why they are being scrutinized, are prey to the nagging insinuation (induced by la-tent guilt for some past transgression?) that they must protect themselves at all costs. Fre-quently, the victims uncover some hidden truth about the invader—which only increases the precariousness of their dilemma. Pinter's plays most often end without the secret being re-vealed, and the audience is left to assign "truth" to the situation—although Pinter's plays seem to suggest that "truth" is unverifiable in our absurd and dangerous world.

One for the Road loosely follows this scenario, although here it is the victims who are brought into Nicholas's claustrophobic room to be verbally assaulted for some unnamed crime committed against an unnamed government. There is little of the subtlety and ambiguity of Pinter's previous works. The victims (Victor, Gila, and little Nicky) scarcely speak as Nicholas delivers a barrage of innuendoes and accusations. And whereas in other Pinter works the threat of violence is only suggested, here physical pain is frighteningly present. Gila has been raped, Victor's tongue has been cut, and Nicky is apparently killed prior to the last scene.

When the play opened at a lunch-hour venue, British theater critics—who named it "best new play of 1984—were puzzled by Pinter's calculated choice to abandon his previous ambiguity for something more overtly political and tangibly violent. Michael Billington, writing for the *Guardian*, judged the play "a totally direct, upfront, and unambiguous condemnation of totalitarian cruelty," further noting that it represents "the new committed Pinter and it suggests that what he has lost in oblique irony he has gained in heart."

Pinter, whose work is customarily dispassionate, wrote the play in a single sitting in response to an offhand remark he overheard at a London cocktail party. Two young women from Turkey were talking about political repression in their country, where torture is systematic and political prisoners can be held incommunicado for 30 days. Pinter says he asked the women what they thought about such matters:

> They said, "Oh, well it was probably deserved . . . they were probably Communists. We have to protect ourselves against Communism." I said, "When you say 'probably,' what kinds of facts do you have?" They of course had no facts at their fingertips. . . ."But what do you have to say about torture?" I asked. "Oh, you're a man of imagination." I said, "Do you mean it's worse for me than the victims?" They gave another shrug and said, "Yes, possibly." Whereupon instead of strangling them, I came back immediately, sat down, and, it's true, started to write *One for the Road*.

Still, Pinter is Pinter; despite the rage that prompted his most overtly "social voice," elements of vintage Pinter remain. We see them primarily in the precision with which he uses the civilized language of discourse to create his menace and terror. In the first scene Nicholas, the immaculately dressed, eerily "friendly, insouciant" interrogator, says to Victor, "One has to be so scrupulous about language." Throughout the interrogation, which often has the chatty nonchalance of a job interview, Nicholas vacillates between a conspicuous civility ("Your wife and I had a very nice chat but I couldn't help noticing she didn't look her best") to horrifying crudeness ("you flounder in wet shit"). It is this violence of contrast—the civilized man instantaneously reverting to barbarism—that unnerves both Nicholas's victims and the audience. Like Victor and his family, we are kept perpetually disoriented and off-balance as we experience Nicholas's verbal assaults.

The play's title is taken from the cocktail party salute, "One for the road." Throughout the play Nicholas casually pours drinks as if he were at a gentleman's club, pausing each time to salute his victim between passages about patriotism and his religious fervor ("The voice of God speaks through me"). The picture we see—two educated, sophisticated men sharing drinks—is at such odds with the situation as it has been defined that irony becomes terrifying rather than merely satiric. Note that the only time that Nicholas actually shares a drink with Victor is when the latter's mouth is cut and bleeding.

Nicholas alternates between elliptical questions (as in the opening sequence with Gila) and torrents of language that spill out almost without cause. Customarily in Pinter's world, when characters explode into lengthy speeches it is a sign that they are losing control. Recall that Pinter has said that the "other silence" in his plays consists of such verbal outbursts because they are "a necessary avoidance, a violent, sly, anguished or mocking smoke screen which keeps the other in its place"; this is precisely what he refers to as "a strategy to cover nakedness." Surely Nicholas embodies a moral nakedness, however oblivious he may be.

Although he is usually averse to propaganda in the theater ("I find agitprop insulting and objectionable"), Pinter defends *One for the Road*'s overt political message as necessary in a world where some "90 countries practice torture now quite commonly—as an accepted routine." He recalls conversations with New York theatergoers who left *One for the Road* saying, "We know all about this. We don't need to be told." "I believe they were lying," says Pinter. "They did not know about it and did not want to know." And, he concludes, their greatest fear was not for the plight of the victims in the play, but that they themselves were too often "interrogators" in their daily lives.

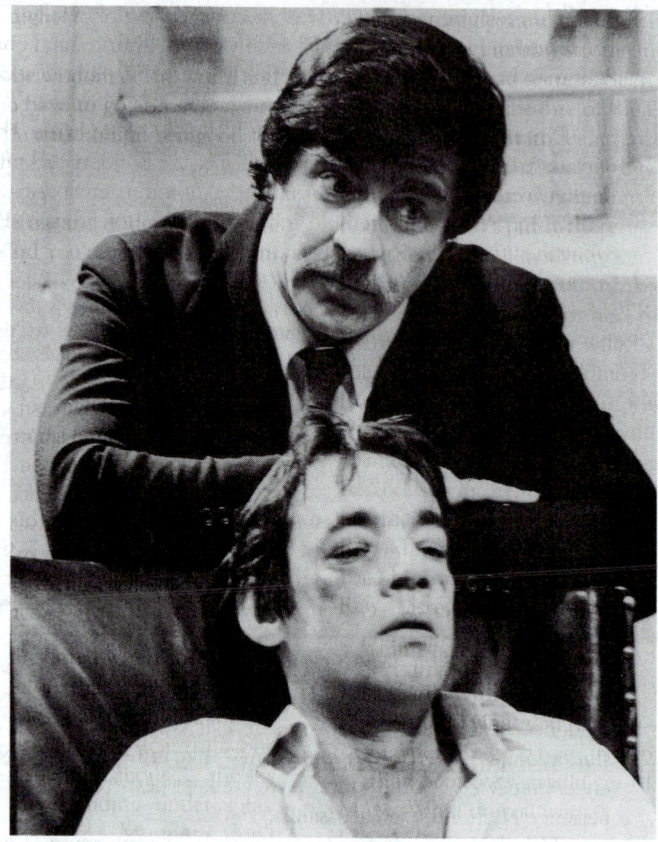

Nicholas (Alan Bates) plays mind games with Victor (Rogert Lloyd Pack) in One for the Road, *which premiered as a lunch-time production at London's Lyric Hammersmith Theatre in 1984.*

ONE FOR THE ROAD

HAROLD PINTER

1

A room. Morning.

Nicolas at his desk. He leans forward and speaks into a machine.

NICOLAS. Bring him in.

He sits back. The door opens. Victor walks in, slowly. His clothes are torn. He is bruised. The door closes behind him.

Hello! Good morning. How are you? Let's not beat about the bush. Anything but that. *D'accord?* You're a civilised man. So am I. Sit down.

Victor slowly sits. Nicolas stands, walks over to him.

What do you think this is? It's my finger. And this is my little finger. I wave my big finger in front of your eyes. Like this. And now I do the same with my little finger. I can also use both . . . at the same time. Like this. I can do absolutely anything I like. Do you think I'm mad? My mother did.

He laughs.

Do you think waving fingers in front of people's eyes is silly? I can see your point. You're a man of the highest intelligence. But would you take the same view if it was my boot—or my penis? Not my eyes. Other people's eyes. The eyes of people who are brought to me here. They're so vulnerable. The soul shines through them. Are you a religious man? I am. Which side do you think God is on? I'm going to have a drink.

He goes to sideboard, pours whisky.

You're probably wondering where your wife is. She's in another room.

He drinks.

Good-looking woman.

He drinks.

God, that was good.

He pours another.

Don't worry, I can hold my booze.

He drinks.

You may have noticed I'm the chatty type. You probably think I'm part of a predictable, formal, long-established pattern; i.e., I chat away, friendly, insouciant, I open the batting, as it were, in a light-hearted, even carefree manner, while another waits in the wings, silent, introspective, coiled like a puma. No, no. It's not quite like that. I run the place. God speaks through me. I'm referring to the Old Testament God, by the way, although I'm a long way from being Jewish. Everyone respects me here. Including you, I take it? I think that is the correct stance.

Pause.

Stand up.

Victor stands.

Sit down.

Victor sits.

Thank you so much.

Pause.

Tell me something . . .

Silence.

What a good-looking woman your wife is. You're a very lucky man. Tell me . . . one for the road, I think . . .

He pours whisky.

You do respect me, I take it?

He stands in front of Victor and looks down at him. Victor looks up.

I would be right in assuming that?

Silence.

VICTOR (*quietly*). I don't know you.
NICOLAS. But you respect me.

VICTOR. I don't know you.
NICOLAS. Are you saying you don't respect me?

Pause.

Are you saying you would respect me if you knew me better? Would you like to know me better?

Pause.

Would you like to know me better?
VICTOR. What I would like . . . has no bearing on the matter.
NICOLAS. Oh yes it has.

Pause.

I've heard so much about you. I'm terribly pleased to meet you. Well, I'm not sure that pleased is the right word. One has to be so scrupulous about language. Intrigued. I'm intrigued. Firstly because I've heard so much about you. Secondly because if you don't respect me you're unique. Everyone else knows the voice of God speaks through me. You're not a religious man, I take it?

Pause.

You don't believe in a guiding light?

Pause.

What then?

Pause.

So . . . morally . . . you flounder in wet shit. You know . . . like when you've eaten a rancid omelette.

Pause

I think I deserve one for the road.

He pours, drinks.

Do you drink whisky?

Pause.

I hear you have a lovely house. Lots of books. Someone told me some of my boys kicked it around a bit. Pissed on the rugs, that sort of thing. I wish they wouldn't do that. I do really. But you know what it's like—they have such responsibilities—and they feel them—they are constantly present—day and night—these responsibilities—and so, sometimes, they piss on a few rugs. You understand. You're not a fool.

Pause.

Is your son all right?
VICTOR. I don't know.
NICOLAS. Oh, I'm sure he's all right. What age is he . . . seven . . . or thereabouts? Big lad, I'm told. Nevertheless, silly of him to behave as he did. But is he all right?
VICTOR. I don't know.

NICOLAS. Oh, I'm sure he's all right. Anyway, I'll have a word with him later and find out. He's somewhere on the second floor, I believe.

Pause.

Well now . . .

Pause.

What do you say? Are we friends?

Pause.

I'm prepared to be frank, as a true friend should. I love death. What about you?

Pause.

What about you? Do you love death? Not necessarily your own. Others. The death of others. Do you love the death of others, or at any rate, do you love the death of others as much as I do?

Pause.

Are you always do dull? I understood you enjoyed the cut and thrust of debate.

Pause.

Death. Death. Death. Death. As has been noted by the most respected authorities, it is beautiful. The purest, most harmonious thing there is. Sexual intercourse is nothing compared to it.

He drinks.

Talking about sexual intercourse . . .

He laughs, wildly, stops.

Does she . . . fuck? Or does she . . . ? Or does she . . . like . . . you know . . . what? What does she like? I'm talking about your wife. Your *wife*.

Pause.

You know the old joke? Does she fuck?

Heavily, in another voice:

Does she fuck!

He laughs.

It's ambiguous, of course. It could mean she fucks like a rabbit or she fucks not at all.

Pause.

Well, we're all God's creatures. Even your wife.

Pause.

There is only one obligation. *To be honest.* You have no other obligations. Weigh that. In your mind. Do you know the man who runs this country? No? Well, he's a very nice chap. He took me aside the other day, last Wednesday, I think it was, he took me aside at a reception, visiting dignitaries, he took *me* aside, *me,* and he said to me, he said, in what I can only describe as a hoarse whisper, Nic, he said, Nic (that's my name), Nic, if you ever come across anyone whom you have good reason to believe is getting on my tits, tell them one thing, tell them honesty is the best policy. The cheese was superb. Goat. One for the road.

He pours.

Your wife and I had a very nice chat but I couldn't help noticing she didn't look her best. She's probably menstruating. Women do that.

Pause.

You know, old chap, I do love other things, apart from death. So many things. Nature. Trees, things like that. A nice blue sky. Blossom.

Pause.

Tell me . . . truly . . . are you beginning to love me?

Pause.

I think your wife is. Beginning. She is beginning to fall in love with me. On the brink . . . of doing so. The trouble is, I have rivals. Because everyone here has fallen in love with your wife. It's her eyes have beguiled them. What's her name? Gila . . . or something?

Pause.

Who would you prefer to be? You or me?

Pause.

I'd go for me if I were you. The trouble about you, although I grant your merits, is that you're on a losing wicket, while I can't put a foot wrong. Do you take my point? Ah God, let me confess, let me make a confession to you. I have never been more moved, in the whole of my life, as when—only the other day, last Friday, I believe—the man who runs this country announced to the country: We are all patriots, we are as one, we all share a common heritage. Except you, apparently.

Pause.

I feel a link, you see, a bond. I share a commonwealth of interest. I am not alone. I am not alone!

Silence.

VICTOR. Kill me.
NICOLAS. What?
VICTOR. Kill me.

Nicolas goes to him, puts his arm around him.

NICOLAS. What's the matter?

Pause.

What in heaven's name is the matter?

Pause.

Mmmnnn?

Pause.

You're probably just hungry. Or thirsty. Let me tell you something. I hate despair. I find it intolerable. The stink of it gets up my nose. It's a blemish. Despair, old fruit, is a cancer. It should be castrated. Indeed I've often found that that works. Chop the balls off and despair goes out the window. You're left with a happy man. Or a happy woman. Look at me.

Victor does so.

Your soul shines out of your eyes.

BLACKOUT.

2

Lights up. Afternoon.

Nicolas standing with a small boy.

NICOLAS. What is your name?
NICKY. Nicky.
NICOLAS. Really? How odd.

Pause.

Do you like cowboys and Indians?
NICKY. Yes. A bit.
NICOLAS. What do you really like?
NICKY. I like aeroplanes.
NICOLAS. Real ones or toy ones?
NICKY. I like both kinds of ones.
NICOLAS. Do you?

Pause.

Why do you like aeroplanes?

Pause.

NICKY. Well . . . because they go so fast. Through the air. The real ones do.
NICOLAS. And the toy ones?
NICKY. I pretend they go as fast as the real ones do.

Pause.

NICOLAS. Do you like your mummy and daddy?

Pause.

Do you like your mummy and daddy?
NICKY. Yes.
NICOLAS. Why?

Pause.

Why?

Pause.

Do you find that a hard question to answer?

Pause.

NICKY. Where's mummy?
NICOLAS. You don't like your mummy and daddy?
NICKY. Yes. I do.
NICOLAS. Why?

Pause.

Would you like to be a soldier when you grow up?
NICKY. I don't mind.
NICOLAS. You don't? Good. You like soldiers. Good. But you spat at my soldiers and you kicked them. You attacked them.
NICKY. Were they your soldiers?
NICOLAS. They are your country's soldiers.
NICKY. I didn't like those soldiers.
NICOLAS. They don't like you either, my darling.

BLACKOUT.

3

Lights up. Night.

Nicolas sitting. Gila standing. Her clothes are torn. She is bruised.

NICOLAS. When did you meet your husband?
GILA. When I was eighteen.
NICOLAS. Why?
GILA. Why?
NICOLAS. Why?
GILA. I just met him.
NICOLAS. Why?
GILA. I didn't plan it.
NICOLAS. Why not?
GILA. I didn't know him.
NICOLAS. Why not?

Pause.

Why not?
GILA. I didn't know him.
NICOLAS. Why not?
GILA. I met him.
NICOLAS. When?
GILA. When I was eighteen.
NICOLAS. Why?
GILA. He was in the room.
NICOLAS. Room?

Pause.

Room?
GILA. The same room.
NICOLAS. As what?
GILA. As I was.
NICOLAS. As I was?
GILA (*screaming*). As I was!

Pause.

NICOLAS. Room? What room?
GILA. A room.
NICOLAS. What room?
GILA. My father's room.
NICOLAS. Your father? What's your father got to do with it?

Pause.

Your *father*? How dare you? Fuckpig.

Pause.

Your father was a wonderful man. His country is proud of
him. He's dead. He was a man of honour. He's dead. Are
you prepared to insult the memory of your father?

Pause.

Are you prepared to defame, to debase, the memory of
your father? Your father fought for his country. I knew
him. I revered him. Everyone did. He believed in God.
He didn't *think*, like you shitbags. He *lived*. He lived. He
was iron and gold. He would die, he would die, he would
die, for his country, for his God. And he did die, he died,
he died, for his God. You turd. To spawn such a daughter.
What a fate. Oh, poor, perturbed spirit, to be haunted forever by such scum and spittle. How do you dare speak of
your father to me? I loved him, as if he were my own father.

Silence.

Where did you meet your husband?
GILA. In a street.

NICOLAS. What were you doing there?
GILA. Walking.
NICOLAS. What was he doing?
GILA. Walking.

Pause.

I dropped something. He picked it up.
NICOLAS. What did you drop?
GILA. The evening paper.
NICOLAS. You were drunk.

Pause.

You were drugged.

Pause.

You had absconded from your hospital.
GILA. I was not in a hospital.
NICOLAS. Where are you now?

Pause.

Where are you now? Do you think you are in a hospital?

Pause.

Do you think we have nuns upstairs?

Pause.

What do we have upstairs?
GILA. No nuns.
NICOLAS. What do we have?
GILA. Men.
NICOLAS. Have they been raping you?

She stares at him.

How many times?

Pause.

How many times have you been raped?

Pause.

How many times?

He stands, goes to her, lifts his finger.

This is my big finger. And this is my little finger. Look. I
wave them in front of your eyes. Like this. How many
times have you been raped?
GILA. I don't know.
NICOLAS. And you consider yourself a reliable witness?

He goes to sideboard, pours drink, sits, drinks.

You're a lovely woman. Well, you were.

He leans back, drinks, sighs.

Your son is . . . seven. He's a little prick. You made him so. You have taught him to be so. You had a choice. You could have encouraged him to be a good person. Instead, you encouraged him to be a little prick. You encouraged him to spit, to strike at soldiers of honour, soldiers of God.

Pause.

Oh well . . . in one way I suppose it's academic.

Pause.

You're of no interest to me. I might even let you out of here, in due course. But I should think you might entertain us all a little more before you go.

BLACKOUT.

4

Lights up. Night.

Nicolas standing. Victor sitting. Victor is tidily dressed.

NICOLAS. How have you been? Surviving?
VICTOR. Yes.
NICOLAS. Yes?
VICTOR. Yes. Yes.
NICOLAS. Really? How?
VICTOR. Oh . . .

Pause.

NICOLAS. I can't hear you.
VICTOR. It's my mouth.
NICOLAS. Mouth?
VICTOR. Tongue.
NICOLAS. What's the matter with it?

Pause.

What about a drink? One for the road. What do you say to a drink?

He goes to the bottle, pours two glasses, gives a glass to Victor.

Drink up. It'll put lead in your pencil. And then we'll find someone to take it out.

He laughs.

We can do that, you know. We have a first class brothel upstairs, on the sixth floor, chandeliers, the lot. They'll suck you in and blow you out in little bubbles. All volunteers. Their daddies are in our business. Which is, I remind you, to keep the world clean for God. Got me? Drink up. Drink up. Are you refusing to drink with me?

Victor drinks. His head falls back.

Cheers.

Nicolas drinks.

You can go.

Pause.

You can leave. We'll meet again, I hope. I trust we will always remain friends. Go out. Enjoy life. Be good. Love your wife. She'll be joining you in about a week, by the way. If she feels up to it. Yes. I feel we've both benefited from our discussions.

Victor mutters.

What?

Victor mutters.

What?

VICTOR. My son.
NICOLAS. Your son? Oh, don't worry about him. He was a little prick.

Victor straightens and stares at Nicolas.

Silence.

BLACKOUT.

MUD

A Play in 17 Scenes

MARIA IRENE FORNES

MARIA IRENE FORNES (1930–)

Maria Irene Fornes is not only a pioneer of contemporary feminist drama (see Forum, "From *Acting Out: Feminist Performances*," following the play) but the precursor of contemporary Latino-American dramatists. A writer of fiction, a lyricist, and a poet, Fornes is also an accomplished translator, stage director, and teacher. Born in La Havana, Cuba, in 1930, she settled in the United States in 1945. Her formative years included an eclectic education in painting, music, and literature, both in the United States and France. Fornes became involved in New York City's rich sociopolitical theater of the early 1960s and, rather quickly, was recognized as among the brightest dramatists of the Off-Broadway theater movement. Her early works were produced by the Judson's Poets Theatre, the Open Theatre, the Promenade Theatre, and the San Francisco Actors' Workshop. Firmly established as an important voice in the contemporary American theater, Fornes's predilection for socially conscious expression helped found the ground-breaking Women's Theater Council in 1972 to encourage the writing and production of new American plays by women. The author of some 30 plays, Fornes is best known for the critically acclaimed *Fefu and Her Friends* (1977) and the musical *Promenade* (with Al Carmines, 1965).

Although her early works combined satire, theatrical fantasy, comedy, pathos, and pensive and allegorical lyricism, her recent dramatic works, such as *The Conduct of Life* (1985) and *Mud*, are much more concerned with the darker issues of sexual enslavement. In spite of their spiritual and psychological incarceration, her earlier protagonists ruminate rather passively about their existence. In *Fefu and Her Friends*, Paula typifies these entrapped women:

> Well, the break-up takes place in parts. The brain, the heart, the body, mutual things, shared things. The mind leaves but the heart is still there. The heart has left but the body wants to stay. The body leaves but the things are still in the apartment. You must come back. You move everything out of the apartment but the mind stays behind. Memory lingers in the place. Seven years later, perhaps seven years later, it doesn't matter any more.

In contrast, Olympia in *The Conduct of Life* epitomizes Fornes's more aggressive women:

> You drive me crazy. . . . You drive me crazy! You are a bastard! One day I'm going to kill you when you're asleep! I'm going to open you up and cut your entrails and feed them to the snakes . . . I'm going to tear your heart out and feed it to the dogs! I'm going to cut your head open and have the cats eat your brain! . . . I'm going to cut your peepee and hang it on a tree and feed it to the birds.

Often regarded as a realist playwright, Fornes is a rare combination of the avant-garde and theatrical naturalism. Her preoccupation with the survival of the feminine psyche has been the connecting link in her dramatic repertoire. Yet, an important aspect of her creativity has often been omitted: Fornes is, at the core of her being, a Latina writer. Susan Sontag defines this aspect of Fornes's work:

Although the language in which she became a writer was English, not Spanish—and Fornes's early work is inconceivable without the reinforcement of the lively local New York milieu (particularly Judson's Poets Theatre) in which she surfaced in the early 1960s—she is unmistakably a writer of bicultural inspiration: one very American way of being a writer. Her imagination seems to me to have, among other sources, a profoundly Cuban one. I am reminded of the witty, sensual, phantasmagorias of Cuban writers such as Lydia Cabrera, Calvert Casey, Virgilio Pinera.

The winner of seven Obie (Off-Broadway) Awards and a citation for Sustained Achievement in the Theater (1982), Fornes is a member of the American Academy and Institute of Arts and Letters. A 1989 Pulitzer Prize finalist, she has received both Guggenheim and Rockefeller fellowships. In addition to her directorial and ongoing lecture commitments, Fornes remains actively engaged in training young Hispanic talent.

MUD (1988)

A play in 17 scenes, *Mud* is an Expressionistic work spiced with presentational stylistic qualities. The Expressionistic stamp is evident not only in the fragmented nature of the piece, but also in the demands placed by the playwright on the playing style. Note the specific direction to freeze the action at the conclusion of each scene. Fragmentation, a hallmark of Expressionism, is also manifested in the dialogue. The three characters speak mostly in incomplete sentences that typify their fragmented lives, personal choices, and secret desires. Moreover, the landscape of the play is punctuated by photographic moments, a by-product of Fornes's artistic training:

> I started as a painter and developed a strong visual sense. In painting you make a drawing and you practice perspective; you make a drawing of two people and how, because of their positions, they relate to each other. This is something you do when you take pictures also, if you don't just take quick snap shots and take a little more care. You move the camera, slightly, carefully, and you see how the perspective changes and you see how the picture can become a lot more interesting, more beautiful, more powerful. That kind of eye is very important for the theater, to make it a lot more beautiful and a lot more mysterious.

Additionally, *Mud* contains strong symbols that emerge from the playwright's rich visual imagery. A symbolic representation of death can be found in Fornes's description of the wooden walls with "color and texture of bone that has dried in the sun." Equally powerful is the expansive sense of life, as defined by a "vast blue sky," which is emblematic of Mae's desire to break free from her entombment. Fornes's props and scenic pieces are also quite specific, as if the playwright added finishing touches to her theatrical painting: "On the table there is a pile of pressed trousers. Under the bench, there is a bundle of women's clothes. . . . On the mantle-piece there are, from right to left: a brown paper bag with a pamphlet in it, a plate with broken bread, a pitcher with milk, a textbook. . . ." It is evident that a Fornes script demands scrupulous attention to detail; one cannot separate the scenic elements from the characters, or for that matter, the dramatic nuances of her work.

Thematically, *Mud* embodies marginalized individuals who are unable to cope with their surroundings, yet remain oblivious to their inertia. An exception to this state of despair is Mae. From the very start of the play she is determined to upset the balance of things to change her condition. Mae is a careful combination of victim and heroine, *horrida bella* and pacifist, servant and conqueror. Entrapped and manipulated by Lloyd, she persists in her quest to rid herself of his dominance and her illiterate self. Mae is typical of Fornes's female protagonists—a woman who appears to be a stereotype of chauvinistic empiricism, psychologically wounded but willing to go on, entrapped but eager to free herself from oppression. She questions her counterparts' behavior, choices, and life experience to understand better her present state—or more precisely, to avoid repeating their mediocre existence. Battling male dominance while healing the sick, Mae symbolizes Fornes's "mother," "virgin," and "whore" icons. Again, Sontag explains: "Unlike most contemporary dramatists, for whom psychological brutality is the principal, inexhaustible subject, Fornes is never in complicity with the brutality she depicts.

She has an increasingly expressive relation to dread, to grief and to passion." As the psychological cruelty increases, Mae forges on, mapping her exit, tearing at the walls that suffocate her. Even in the play's horrific conclusion, Mae remains in total control. In short, she is the mouthpiece of Fornes's sense of equilibrium: to remain firmly committed to the struggle without losing sight of one's intelligence in an abnormal environment.

Although it foreshadows the climax of the play, Mae's description of the hermit crab (scene 9) is a crowning description of Lloyd, the prototype of the controlling male ego. He rules by impudence in spite of his impotence, diseased body, and psychological displacement—signs of his mental and spiritual disintegration. More at home with animals, he is unable to utter a complete sentence and remains content in his present condition. Tellingly, he prefers "mud" rather than a civilized existence. Like an animal, Lloyd must be a part of the pack for he is unable to survive on his own. Paradoxically, it is Lloyd who drives the comic elements of the play. Although we gasp at his inhumane comportment, we laugh—albeit uncomfortably—at his moronic jokes. Lloyd is clearly Fornes's depiction of male domination gone haywire, a one-man army willing to pillage and destroy.

At first glance Henry appears to be the stabilizing influence—the saving angel and grace incarnate—in Fornes's violent world. Why else would Mae find him appealing? But as Fornes explained in a recent interview:

> I saw a production of *Mud* where Henry was a kind, old smart-alec, a self-centered character from the beginning. That diminished the character and the whole play for me. Why would Mae be so attracted to a man like that in Henry? To me it isn't just that it's not the way I saw the character, but it has to do with the whole play being demeaned. Because if Mae is attracted to him, then what does that make Mae? It has all kinds of repercussions that deal with the totality of the play, and I do get upset when I see that.

In Henry, Mae contemplates salvation; it is he who precipitates Mae's decision to evacuate the sinking ship. Henry appears to be a righteous man, a prayerful and giving soul. The cross he bears is Lloyd, who will be crucified by Mae. But as the play unfolds, Henry becomes a Judas figure. He takes her money and abducts Mae's soul. But, simultaneously the giver and the taker, the archangel and the destroyer, he becomes physically incapacitated, and bears in effect the ashes of his own spiritual consumption.

Mud is a contemporary American tragedy. We pity Mae, who suffers disproportionately for her "crime" (i.e., being born a woman). And we are frightened by the play's unrelenting depiction of the subjugation of the human spirit by forces beyond the control of the underprivileged. Here the powers that rule without regard to identity and beliefs reflect a modern preoccupation with domination, figuratively and politically. Yet *Mud* is more than a feminist critique of male aggression; it is ultimately a humanistic treatise on the dark side of the American experience.

Mae exacts revenge on Henry for his cruelty in Maria Irene Fornes's Mud. *This photo, from the New York production, was taken by Megan Terry, another respected feminist playwright.*

MUD

A Play in 17 Scenes

MARIA IRENE FORNES

CHARACTERS

MAE: *A spirited young woman. She is single-minded and determined, a believer. She is mid-twenties.*

LLOYD: *A simple and good-hearted young man. He is ungainly and unkempt. His shoulders slope, his stomach protrudes, some of his teeth are missing. At the start of the play, illness contributes to his poor appearance. He is mid-twenties.*

HENRY: *A large man. He has a natural sense of dignity, a philosophical mind. He can barely read. He is mid-fifties.*

The set is a wooden room which sits on an earth promontory. The promontory is five feet high and covers the same periphery as the room. The wood has the color and texture of bone that has dried in the sun. It is ashen and cold. The earth in the promontory is red and soft and so is the earth around it. There is no greenery. Behind the promontory there is a vast blue sky. On the black wall of the room there is an oversized fireplace which is the same color and texture as the walls and floor. On each side of the fireplace there are narrow doors. The door to the right leads to the exterior. There is a blue sky. The one to the left leads to a dark corridor. In the center of the room there is a kitchen table. There is a chair on each end. Down right there is an ironing board. There is an iron on it and a pair of trousers. Against the back wall on the left there is another chair. After the first scene these three chairs will always be placed around the table and will be referred to as right, center, and left.

Against the right wall there is a bench. On it there is a pile of unpressed trousers. On the table there is a pile of pressed trousers. Under the bench, there is a bundle of women's clothes and a pair of old, flat women's shoes. Inside the fireplace there are two cardboard boxes. One is full and tied with a string, the other is empty. On the mantelpiece there are, from right to left: a brown paper bag with a pamphlet in it, a pot with three metal plates and three spoons stacked upon it, a plate with broken bread, a pitcher with milk, a textbook, a notebook and pencil, a dish with string beans, a folded newspaper and a box with pills. Between the fireplace and the door to the left there are an ax and a rifle.

Offstage there is an empty box the same size as the box tied with a string. The following props are carried by the actors as they enter to perform the scene.

Mae: 2 bundles of clothes and a loose clean rag.

Lloyd: 3 coins, a prescription note and a cup with oatmeal and a spoon.

Henry: lipstick wrapped in paper, a small mirror, a notebook, bills and pencil, loose coins, a tin cup of milk, and a wad of bills.

At the end of each scene a freeze is indicated. These freezes will last eight seconds which will create the effect of a still photograph. When the freeze is broken, the actors will make the necessary set changes and proceed to perform the following scene.

ACT ONE

SCENE 1

Lloyd sits left. He is unwashed and unshaven. He has a fever. He is clumsy and badly coordinated. Mae is at the ironing board. She is unkempt.

LLOYD. You think you learn a lot at school?

MAE. I do.

LLOYD. What do you learn?

MAE. Subjects.

LLOYD. What is subjects?

MAE. Different things.

LLOYD. What things?

MAE. You want to know?

LLOYD. What are they?

MAE. Arithmetic.

LLOYD. Big deal arithmetic. I know arithmetic.

MAE. I'll bet.

LLOYD. Don't talk back to me. I'll kick your ass.

MAE. Fuck you, Lloyd. I'm telling you about arithmetic and you talk to me like that? You're a moron. I won't tell you anything.

LLOYD. Oh, no?

MAE. No.

LLOYD. So what's arithmetic?

MAE. Fuck you. I'm not telling you.

LLOYD (*Moving toward here*). I'll fuck you till you're blue in the face! (*He stops and starts back to the chair.*) I don't even want to fuck you.

MAE. You can't, that's why. You can't get it up.

LLOYD. Oh yeah? I got it up yesterday!

MAE. When?

LLOYD. Afternoon!

MAE. Never saw it.

LLOYD. You weren't here.

MAE. Where was I?

LLOYD. At school. You missed it. I got it up.

MAE. Who with?

LLOYD. Fuck you. I'm not telling you.

MAE. Who with?

LLOYD. With myself.—I don't need someone. I got it up right here. (*Pointing to the wall.*) See that? I did that! From here. I didn't give it to you or anyone. (*Pantomiming an erection and ejaculation.*) I held it as long as I wanted. Then I gave it to the wall. (*Pointing to a spot on the wall.*) See. Fuck you, Mae.

MAE. Fuck you, Lloyd.

LLOYD. So tell me!

MAE. Tell you what.

LLOYD. What's arithmetic?

MAE. It's numbers.

LLOYD. Oh yeah!

MAE. Yeah!

LLOYD. Why didn't you say it's number!—I know numbers.

MAE. You don't know numbers.

LLOYD. Yes I do. (*He stands.*) I'm Lloyd. I have two pigs. My mother died. I was seven. My father left. He is dead. (*He gets three coins from his pocket.*) This is money. It's mine. It's three nickels. I'm Lloyd. That's arithmetic.

MAE. That is not arithmetic.

LLOYD. Why not?

MAE. It isn't.

LLOYD (*He returns to the chair*). It's numbers!

MAE. Arithmetic is more!

LLOYD. What more!

MAE. A lot more!—Multiplication!

LLOYD. Come here! (*She puts the iron down.*)

MAE. What for!

LLOYD. I'm going to show you something.

MAE (*She walks to him*). What!

LLOYD (*In one move he takes her hand, crosses his left leg, and puts her hand on his crotch*). Feel it!

MAE. What?

LLOYD. It! It! Touch it!

MAE. I'm touching it!

LLOYD. Do something to it!

MAE. What!

LLOYD. Anything, stupid!

MAE. Let go of my hand!

LLOYD (*Pressing her tighter*). What hand?

MAE. Let go, you jerk! You stink! You smell bad!

LLOYD. So what!

MAE. You're disgusting!

LLOYD. No kidding!

MAE. Let go! (*She steps on his foot.*)

LLOYD. Shit! (*She goes back to the ironing board.*) I'll kick your ass! (*He feels his genitals.*) Shit, it's gone!

MAE. What's gone! You can't get it up! You have some sickness there! (*Short pause.*) You should go to a doctor.

LLOYD. Didn't I say I got it up yesterday!

MAE. Yes. You did.

LLOYD. OK! So I did!—So where's dinner!

MAE. I don't know where's dinner.

LLOYD. You know where's dinner!

MAE. You know where's dinner!

LLOYD. Yeah, where's dinner! Dinner's in a pot on the stove! Dinner's on the table! It's in the cupboard! It's dried up in the pot! Dinner is somewhere! It's spilled on the floor! Where's dinner! (*There is a pause.*) *Where's dinner!* (*She continues ironing.*) Come here!

MAE. Fuck you.

LLOYD. You're a whore!

MAE. I'm pressing, jerk! What are you doing! I'm pressing. What are you doing! (*He looks away.*) I'm pressing what are you doing! You're a jerk. (*She continues ironing.*) I work. See, I work. I'm working. I learned to work. I wake up and I work. Open my eyes and I work. I work. What do you do! Yeah, what do you do!—Work!

LLOYD. So what. (*He sits in a corner on the floor.*)

MAE. What do you do when you open your eyes. I work, jerk. You're a pig. You'll die like a pig in the mud. You'll rot there in the mud. No one will bury you. Your skin will bloat. In the mud. Then, it will get blue like rotten meat and it will bloat even more. And you will get so rotten that the dogs will puke when they come near you. Even flies won't go near you. You'll just lay there and rot. (*She irons.*) I'm going to die in a hospital. In white sheets. You hear? (*She looks front.*) Clean feet. Injections. That's how I'm going to die. I'm going to die clean. I'm going to school and I'm learning things. You're stupid. I'm not. When I finish school I'm leaving. You hear that? You can stay in the mud. (*She irons.*) Did you pick the corn?

LLOYD. What corn?

MAE. The corn I told you to pick.

LLOYD. There is no corn.

MAE. How come there is no corn.

LLOYD. The groundhog ate it.

MAE. You let him eat it.

LLOYD. I didn't.

MAE. You didn't watch it.

LLOYD. I came in to sleep. I had to sleep.

MAE. You can sleep in the field.

LLOYD. It's wet there! It's cold! I'm sick! You sleep there!

MAE. I work here, not in the field.

LLOYD. I'll work here. You work there.

MAE (*Harshly*). I wish you went to the doctor.—You're not going to get well if you don't. When I leave you'll starve.

LLOYD. I'll find food.

MAE. Where?

LLOYD. Anywhere. There's food.

MAE. Where.

LLOYD. There's pigslop.

MAE. What pigslop? There won't be any pigslop. Not if you don't grow something to put in it!

(*Pause.*)

LLOYD. I did it to Betsy.

MAE. You did.

LLOYD. Yeah.—I felt bad.—My head hurt.—I went to her. She's nice. She lets me eat her food.—I did it to her.—I got it up. I got it in her all the way.—It didn't hurt.

MAE. No kidding.

LLOYD. It didn't hurt.

MAE. You don't fuck pigs.

LLOYD. She liked it.

MAE. I'll bet.

LLOYD. What do you mean?

MAE. Did you get clean before you did it?

LLOYD. What for? I'm clean.

MAE. No you're not. You stink.

LLOYD. She didn't mind.

MAE (*She places the ironing board alongside the right wall and places the garment she has pressed on top of the other pressed clothes*). I'm taking these up now. We'll walk to the clinic. You have to see a doctor. (*She starts putting on her shoes.*) Put on your shoes, Lloyd.—I'll walk there with you. I know you won't get there if I don't go with you. Get moving, Lloyd. (*She takes the clothes and goes to the door.*) Come on. (*He doesn't move.*) Let's go, Lloyd. (*He stands and goes for the ax. He holds the ax as he waits for her to exit.*) You're not going to the clinic with an ax.

LLOYD (*He goes to the chair still holding the ax and sits*). Why not.

MAE. You can't.

LLOYD. I'll take my knife, then.

MAE. You can't take your knife either.

LLOYD. I won't go then.

(*They freeze.*)

SCENE 2

Mae takes a brown paper bag from the mantelpiece, opens the right door, steps on the threshold and turns front as if she had just come from the outside. She has an air of serenity. Lloyd sits on the left. His appearance has worsened.

MAE. I went to the clinic, Lloyd. And I told them what you have.

LLOYD. What did you tell them?

MAE. (*Stepping into the room*). I told them you're sick. And I told them what you have.

LLOYD. What did they say?

MAE. They said you have to go there. (*As she gets the chair from the left corner and places it center.*) You have to go to the clinic. They won't give you medicine till you go.

LLOYD. I'm not going.

MAE. They have to give you a test. They can't give you medicine till they find out what you have. They said you may have something bad.

LLOYD. What.

MAE (*She sits*). They didn't say. (*She takes a pamphlet out of the paper bag.*) They gave me this book.

LLOYD. What does it say?

MAE (*She places the paper bag on the mantelpiece*). I couldn't read it. I tried to read it but I can't. I got Henry to read it for you. He's outside.

LLOYD. Why can't you read it?

MAE. It's too difficult.

LLOYD. All that time at school and you can't read.

MAE. I tried to read it and it was too difficult. That's why I got Henry to read it because it was too difficult for me. It is advanced. I'm not advanced yet. I'm intermediate. I can read a lot of things but not this.—I'm going to let Henry in.

LLOYD (*Reproachfully*). I wish you could have read it.

MAE. Me too. I wish I could have read it. (*She opens the door and walks to the left of the center chair.*) Come in, Henry. (*Henry enters and stands by the fireplace. He places his left hand on the mantelpiece.*) Sit down, Henry. (*Henry sits on the center chair. Mae closes the door.*) Here's Henry, Lloyd. He's going to read for you.

HENRY. Are you drunk, Lloyd? You look drunk.

MAE (*Sitting on the right*). He's sick. He has a fever.

HENRY. Has he been drinking?

LLOYD. I am not drunk.

HENRY. What's wrong with him?

MAE. He's sick.

HENRY. Remember Ron, what happened to him.

LLOYD. What happened to him?

HENRY. He died.—And what did he die of?

LLOYD. He drank till he died.

MAE. His liver failed him.

HENRY. Why did his liver fail him? Alcohol.—Why did he drink? He drank because he owned alcohol. And why did he own alcohol? He owned alcohol because he owned a pharmacy. And why did that lead a man to drinking? Because he kept alcohol in the pharmacy.—There you have two things: alcohol and time to do nothing. So what happens? You drink yourself to death.—So, you have alcohol, you drink it. You don't have alcohol, you don't drink it. You have money to buy alcohol, you buy it. You don't have money to buy it, you don't buy it.—Does Lloyd have alcohol, Mae?

MAE. He has no money to buy it.

HENRY. If Lloyd had money he would drink. He'd be a drunk.

MAE. Yes, he would.

HENRY. If he's not a drunk it's because he's poor.

MAE. He is.—This is the book, Henry.

HENRY (*Henry puts on his glasses. He reads each section first to himself in a low voice. Then he reads it out loud stumbling through the words at a high speed*). Prostatitis and Prostatosis. Acute and chronic bacterial infection of the prostrate gland: symptoms, diagnosis, and treatment. (*He wets his finger and turns the page.*) Common symptoms of acute prostatitis and bacterial prostatosis are: febrile illness, back pains, perineal pain, irritative voiding, aching of the perineum, sexual pain, sexual impotency, painful ejaculation, and intermittent disureah, or bloody ejaculation.

LLOYD. What does that mean?

HENRY. I don't know what it means, Lloyd. These are medical terms. It needs study. This may require the use of a dictionary—a special dictionary. One that has medical terms—technical terms—probably a dictionary that would have all kinds of technical terms—from hardware and construction terms to scientific terms—like physics. There are such dictionaries. (*Short pause.*) You look swollen, Lloyd.

MAE. He is swollen.

HENRY. And your color is poor.

MAE. Show him your tongue, Lloyd. His tongue is white and his breath smells bad.

(*Lloyd opens his mouth. Henry looks at Lloyd's tongue.*)

HENRY. What is wrong with you?

MAE. I want him to go to the doctor but he won't.

HENRY. Why won't you go to the doctor, Lloyd.

LLOYD. I don't want to go.

MAE. He will stay here and rot.

LLOYD. I won't rot. I said I'd go. You said I couldn't go.

MAE. He wanted to go up with an ax. He's an animal. You don't go to the clinic with an ax. You can't do that.

HENRY. Why would you do that, Lloyd?

LLOYD. I didn't do it. I never went.

HENRY. He does smell bad.

MAE. He's rotting away and he won't do anything about it. You better dig your grave while you can, Lloyd. Because I'm not going to do it for you. I told him to find a spot and dig it. It takes a strong person to dig that deep. I can't do it. I wouldn't, even if I could. (*Pause.*) Would you like some bread, Henry? I got some butter.

HENRY. Yes, thank you.

MAE. Would you like some dinner? We have soup.

HENRY. Yes, thank you.

MAE. Stay then, I haven't started it yet.

HENRY. I will, thank you.

(*They freeze.*)

SCENE 3

Mae places the pamphlet on the mantelpiece, then takes the pot, plates and spoons and places them on the table. They each take a spoon and plate, then they pass them to Mae, who holds the plates in her hands as if she were about to put them away. Lloyd lies on the floor, under the table, facing front. Henry moves his chair slightly to the left. He and Mae have been talking. They both speak with philosophical objectivity.

HENRY. Soon everything will be used only once. We will use things once. We will need to do that as our time will be of value and it will not be feasible to spend it caring for things: washing them, mending them, repairing them. We will use a car till it breaks down. Then, we will discard it. A radio or any machine or appliance will be discarded as soon as it breaks down. We will make a call on the telephone and a new one will be delivered. Already we see places that use paper cups, paper plates, paper towels.—Our time will not be wasted and we will choose how to spend it.

MAE. I don't think I'll be wanted in such a world.

HENRY. Why not?

MAE. . . . Oh. (*Pause.*) In such a world a person must be of value.

HENRY. Oh?

MAE. I feel I am hollow . . . and offensive. (*As Mae places the dishes on the mantelpiece.*)

HENRY. Why is that?

MAE. I think most people are.

HENRY. What do you mean?—Explain what you mean.

MAE. I don't think I can.

HENRY. I am not offensive. I don't think I am offensive. I think I am a decent man.

MAE. You are decent, Henry. I know you are, and so is Lloyd in his own way.

HENRY. Then, what do you mean when you say we are offensive?

MAE. I mean that we are base, and that we spend our lives with small things.

HENRY. I don't feel I do that.

MAE. Don't be offended, Henry. You are not base. Of all the people I know you are the finest. You are the person I respect and I feel most proud to know.—(*She begins to look at him fixedly, possessed by fervor.*) I have no one to talk to. And sometimes I feel hollow and base. And I feel I don't have a mind. But when I talk to you I do. I feel I have a mind. Why is that? (*She moves closer to him.*) Why is it that some people make you feel stupid and some people make you feel smart. Not smart, because I am not smart. But some people make you feel that you have something inside you. Inside your head. (*She moves closer.*) Why is it

that you can talk, Henry, and Lloyd cannot talk? Why is that? What I'm saying, Henry, is that I want you. That I want you here with me. That I love you.

HENRY. Mae, this is unexpected.

MAE. It is unexpected, Henry.

HENRY. I have nothing to offer you.

MAE. Yes, you do. I want you.

HENRY. Me?

MAE (*She starts to move her head toward him slowly and intensely*). I want your mind.

HENRY. . . . My mind?

MAE (*Still moving her head toward him*). I want it. (*She kisses him intensely. They look at each other.*)

HENRY. Did you feel my mind?

MAE. Yes. I did. (*She kisses him again.*) I did. I want you here.

HENRY. Here?

MAE. I want you here.

HENRY. To live here?

MAE. If you will.

(*They freeze.*)

SCENE 4

Henry exits. Mae places the spoons and pot on the mantelpiece. Then, she takes off her shoes, places a pair of trousers on the ironing board and puts out the ironing board. Lloyd gets the box with the string from the fireplace and stands down left holding it. Mae irons.

MAE. Just put it down. (*He stands still. She continues ironing.*) Put it down Lloyd. (*He stands still.*) Henry is going to stay here with us. He is going to live here. He needs a place and I want him to stay here. You can learn from Henry. If you want to, he can teach you how to read. Put the box down. I'll take it up to the bedroom. Henry's going to sleep in the bedroom. He has a bad back and he needs to sleep in the bed. You can sleep here.—Get papers from the shed and lay them on the floor. I'll get you a blanket.—I'll take it up now. (*She takes the box from Lloyd and exits left. He is distraught. He sits on the chair on the left and cries. He puts his head on the table and freezes.*)

SCENE 5

Mae places the ironing board against the wall. Lloyd places the pitcher of milk and the plate with bread on the table. Mae gets the plates and spoons. She places the spoons in the center and lays each plate in front of her. Henry enters and sits center. Lloyd sits left. Lloyd and Henry take a spoon each. Mae serves bread onto the plates, pours milk on the bread and passes two plates to Henry, who passes one to Lloyd and keeps the second for himself. Mae sits. They start eating.

MAE. Do you say grace before a meal, Henry?

HENRY. I do sometimes.

MAE. Would you say grace?

HENRY. I will, if you want me to.

MAE. I do.

HENRY (*Crosses his hands*). Oh, give thanks unto the Lord, for he is good: for his mercy endures forever. For he satisfies the longing soul, and fills the hungry soul with goodness.

MAE. We never said grace in this house. My father never did and I never learned how and neither did Lloyd.—Lloyd did you hear that? Henry said grace. I feel grace in my heart. I feel fresh inside as if a breeze had just gone inside my heart. What was it you said, Henry? What were these words. I don't retain the words. I never do. I find it hard to retain words I learn. It is hard for me to do the work at school. I can work on my feet all day at the ironing board. I can make myself do it, even if I am tired. But I cannot make myself retain what I learn. I have no memory. The teacher says I have no memory. And it's true I don't. I don't remember the things I learn too well. Not enough to pass the test. But I rejoice with the knowledge that I get. Not everything, but most things, make me feel joyful. Do you feel that way, Henry?

HENRY. I am not sure. I like to know things. But if I didn't remember what I learned, I don't think I would feel any pleasure.—If I didn't remember things, I would feel that I don't know them. I like to learn things so I can live according to them, according to my knowledge. What would be the use of knowing things if they don't serve you, if they don't help you shape your life.—Lloyd, do you take pleasure in learning if you forget what you have learned?

(*Lloyd looks at Mae, then at Henry again.*)

MAE. Lloyd doesn't like learning things.

LLOYD. I like learning things.

MAE. Why don't you then?

LLOYD. What is it I haven't learned?

(*Mae and Henry look at each other.*)

MAE. Henry, would you say grace again?

HENRY. Again?

MAE. Is that wrong?

HENRY. No. Oh, give thanks unto the Lord, for he is good: for his mercy endures forever. For he satisfies the longing soul, and fills the hungry soul with goodness. (*Mae sobs.*) Why are you crying?

MAE. I am a hungry soul. I am a longing soul. I am an empty soul. (*She cries.*) I cry with joy. It satisfies me to hear words that speak so lovingly to my soul. (*Mae eats. Lloyd eats. Henry watches Mae.*) Don't be afraid to eat from our dishes, Henry. They are clean.

(*They freeze.*)

SCENE 6

Lloyd places his plate and spoon over Henry's. Henry places the pitcher and bread plate on the mantelpiece and exits. Mae places the plates and spoons on the mantelpiece and gets the textbook. She sits center and reads with difficulty. She follows the written words with the fingers of both hands. Her reading is inspired. Lloyd listens to her and stares at the book.

MAE. The starfish is an animal, not a fish. He is called a fish because he lives in the water. The starfish cannot live out of the water. If he is moist and in the shade he may be able to live out of the water for a day. Starfish eat old and dead sea animals. They keep the water clean. A starfish has five arms like a star. That is why it is called a starfish. Each of the arms of the starfish has an eye in the end. These eyes do not look like our eyes. A starfish's eye cannot see. But they can tell if it is night or day. If a starfish loses an arm he can grow a new one. This takes about a year. A starfish can live five or ten years or perhaps more, no one really knows.

(*Lloyd slaps the book off the table. Mae slaps Lloyd. They freeze.*)

SCENE 7

Lloyd picks up the book and places it on the down-left corner of the table. He places the left chair against the wall and sits. Mae takes a notebook and pencil from the mantelpiece. She takes the book and stands on the upright side of the table copying from the book. Henry enters and stands on the up-left corner.

HENRY. What is Lloyd to you? (*There is a pause.*) He's a man and he's not a blood relative. So what is he to you?

MAE. Lloyd? (*Pause.*) He is like family.

HENRY. But he is not.—Everyone knows he is not. What is he?

MAE. I don't know what you call what he is. If I were to ask myself I would not know what to answer.—He is not with me. You know he is not. He sleeps down here.

HENRY. I feel I am offending him. And he is offending me. So what is he.

MAE (*Sitting on the right facing front*). What can I do. Henry, I don't want you to be offended. There's nothing I can do and there's nothing you can do and there is nothing Lloyd can do. He's always been here, since he was little. My dad brought him in. He said that Lloyd was a good boy and that he could keep me company. He said he was old and tired and he didn't understand what a young person like me was like. That he had no patience left and he was weary of life and he had no more desire to make things work. He didn't want to listen to me talk and he felt sorry to see me sad and lonely. He didn't want to be mean to me, but he didn't have the patience. He was sick. My dad was good but he was sad and hopeless and when my mom died he went to hell with himself. He got sick and died and he left Lloyd here and Lloyd and I took care of each other. I don't know what we are. We are related but I don't know what to call it. We are not brother and sister. We are like animals who grow up together and mate. We were mates till you came here, but not since then. I could not be his mate again, not while you are here. I am not an animal. I care about things, Henry, I do. I know some things that I never learned. It's just that I don't know what they are. I cannot grasp them. (*She goes on her knees as her left shoulder leans on the corner of the table.*) I don't want to live like a dog. (*Pause.*) Lloyd is good, Henry. And this is his home. (*Pause. She looks up.*) When you came here I thought heaven had come to this place, and I still feel so. How can there be offense here for you?

(*They freeze.*)

SCENE 8

Lloyd places his chair by the table and exits. Mae places the notebook, pencil and textbook on the mantelpiece. She places the dish with string beans center and sits. She snaps beans. Henry walks behind Mae and covers her eyes. He takes a small package from his pocket and puts it in the bowl.

MAE. What is it? (*He uncovers her eyes. She unwraps the package. It is a lipstick.*) Lipstick . . . (*Henry pushes the lipstick out of the tube. He takes a mirror out of his pocket and holds it in front of her.*) A mirror. (*She holds the mirror and puts on lipstick. She puckers her lips. He kisses her.*) Oh, Henry.

(*They freeze.*)

SCENE 9

Mae places the lipstick, mirror, and dish with string beans on the mantelpiece. She places the textbook center and sits. Henry places the paper and lipstick cover on the mantelpiece. He takes the newspaper, turns the left chair toward the down-left corner and sits to read, leaning his elbow on the table. Lloyd sits on the floor, down of the right chair with his arm leaning on it.

MAE (*Reading*). This is a hermit crab. He is called a hermit because he lives in empty shells that once belonged to other animals. When he is little he likes to crawl into the shells of water snails. When he grows larger he finds a larger shell. Often he tries several shells before he finds the one that fits. Sometimes he wants the shell of another

hermit crab and then there is a fight. Sometimes the owner is pulled out. Sometimes the owner wins and stays.

(*Lloyd lifts himself up to look at Henry. He mouths a curse. Mae turns to look at Lloyd, then looks at Henry. Henry turns to look at Mae, then he looks at Lloyd. They freeze.*)

ACT TWO

SCENE 10

Henry enters left carrying a notebook, pencil and a few bills. He sits left. He transfers figures from the bills to the ledger. Lloyd enters right. He stands up-center. He reaches into his pocket for a medical prescription and stretches his arm in Henry's direction. He sits to the right. The italicized words represent a stuttering.

LLOYD. They gave me *this.*
HENRY (*Reads what's on the paper while still in Lloyd's hand. He returns to his papers*). That's the prescription for your medicine.
LLOYD. They said I should buy *this.* (*Pause.*) They said I should *buy* it.
HENRY. Did you?
LLOYD. No.
HENRY. Why not.
LLOYD. I went to the *clinic.*
HENRY (*Without looking at him*). I'm glad you did.
LLOYD. It took a *while.* I thought they *kept* me a long time. I went *early* and just came back.
HENRY. How do you feel?
LLOYD. I don't feel *better.*—I feel *worse.*
HENRY. Why is that?
LLOYD. They have *instruments* there. They *stuck instruments* in me.
HENRY. What did they say?
LLOYD. I have to take *medicine*—*pills.* I have to *buy* them. They said I have to *swallow* the pills.
HENRY. I'm glad you went.
LLOYD (*Stretches his arm to show Henry the prescription*). They gave me *this.* They said I should *buy* this. (*He puts the prescription on the table.*) They said I should *buy* it.
HENRY (*With contained anger*). You should get the medicine, Lloyd. You should take it and get it over with. You should take the medication and get well. You should not walk around with an illness that's eating your insides. Get the medicine. Do as you are told.

(*They freeze.*)

SCENE 11

Henry exits. Lloyd takes the box of pills from the mantelpiece and empties it on the table. He sits center. Mae enters right, wiping her wet hands with her skirt. She sits right. Lloyd puts a pill in his mouth. A moment later he spits it.

MAE. What are they?

LLOYD. Pills.

MAE. Lloyd . . . What are you doing? (*He cleans his tongue.*) Does it taste bad?

LLOYD. Yeah.

MAE (*She picks up the pill and sits*). Try it again. (*He puts it in his mouth.*) Swallow it. (*He swallows and chokes. She stands by him and pushes the pill down his throat. She looks at him.*) Did you swallow it? (*She looks at him.*) What do you feel? (*He makes a face. She sits and puts the pills in the box.*) How did you get them?

LLOYD (*Defensively*). I bought them.—I took the money.— From Henry.—From his trousers.—I took the money from his trousers.—I don't care.—He owes me money.— For rent.—For my bed.—He took my bed.—Like a crab.—He got into my bed like a crab.—I took it.—I didn't steal it, because it belonged to me.—Because I needed to get my medicine.—And he never gave me what he owed me.—I had to ask him for it.—And he never gave it to me.—I asked him.—And he never gave it to me.—And he came here only to take things from me.—Like a crab.

(*Henry enters left. He is in his underwear. He carries his pants over his left arm. He holds a change purse in his right hand. He walks down left and stands there. He is stunned.*)

HENRY. Someone took money from my purse.—There is less money here than I should have.—Some of the money I had is gone.

MAE. Lloyd took it.

HENRY (*He sits*). Well, tell him to give it back.

MAE. He took it for his medicine.

HENRY. He went to my purse and took it?

MAE. He needed money for his medicine. (*Pause.*) Would you let Lloyd have that money?

HENRY. Have Lloyd have my money?

(*Pause.*)

MAE. He'll pay it back.

HENRY. How will he pay it back?

MAE (*To Lloyd*). . . . Lloyd . . . ? (*Lloyd looks at Mae.*)

HENRY. How will he pay it back. How will Lloyd get money to pay me back? (*Pause.*) How much money did he take?

MAE. . . . Lloyd . . . ?

LLOYD. I don't know how much I took.

HENRY. How will he pay it back if he doesn't know how much he took? (*Pause.*) Tell him I want to know how much he took.

LLOYD. I went to the clinic.—And they put those instru-

ments in me.—And they said I had to buy that medicine.—And I couldn't find someone to help me buy that medicine.—I went to the pharmacy.—And they said I had to pay for it.—And Henry had money but he wouldn't pay for it.—And he took my bed.—And he can take anything he wants from me.—And I had to buy that medicine.—So I took the money from him.

HENRY. Ask him when he took it.

LLOYD. I took it while he slept.

HENRY. How much did he take?

(*Pause.*)

MAE. Lloyd can't count, Henry.

HENRY (*He takes money out of the purse, puts it on the table and counts it. He does mental subtraction*). Tell him he took one fifty four. (*Mae looks at Lloyd.*) Is that what he spent? Does he still have any of that money? (*Lloyd reaches into his pocket.*) Tell him to put it on the table. (*Lloyd does. Henry counts the money, then does mental subtraction. He puts the coins in the purse and goes to the door.*) Tell him he owes me one thirty eight. And tell him I wish he'll pay it back. (*He exits. Mae goes to the door and looks in the direction Henry has walked. They freeze.*)

SCENE 12

Mae puts a pair of trousers on the ironing board and puts the ironing board out. Lloyd places the box of pills on the mantelpiece and stands on top of the table.

LLOYD. There is a reason why it happened to him and not to me.

MAE. I wish it had happened to you.

LLOYD. Ha!—It couldn't have happened to me. I'm strong. He's weak and old. That's why he fell. (*Doing an exaggerated demonstration of someone walking on dangerous ground.*) I can walk on wet stones and I don't fall. Look. I can run on wet stones. I can stand on my own two feet. Look! (*He jumps to the floor and stands with his feet apart.*) Try and push me. Go on. Push me. (*She ignores him. He jumps on the table in a prone position with his legs crossed and his hands under his head.*) I wish he had drowned. I wish he had fallen in the water and drowned. He's old. His legs couldn't hold him. That's why he fell. (*He jumps to the floor and runs across jumping up in the air making sounds as he goes up and down. He does this several times, then holds an athletic pose.*) Can he do that?

MAE (*Still ironing*). No, he can't. He's paralyzed. He may be a cripple. You know he can't do that!

LLOYD (*Lies on the table with his hands under his head*). He couldn't do it before he fell. That's why he fell. He's old. He was falling apart. That's why he fell. Now he can't even move.—Look! (*He does several cartwheels.*) Can he do that?

MAE. No, he can't.

LLOYD (*Sits on the table with his arms and legs in a body-builder's pose*). He has no muscle. I wouldn't fall if I had to walk on wet stones. I can run on wet stones. Like this. (*He demonstrates.*) I wish he had fell in the water. I wish he had drowned. So now he can't walk. (*Short pause.*) Who's going to take care of him?

MAE. We are.

(*Lloyd exits right. The sound of vomiting is heard. She freezes.*)

SCENE 13

Mae puts the ironing board alongside the wall. Lloyd enters left with the cup with oatmeal and the spoon. He places the right chair away from the table. Henry enters. He sits on the chair to the right. His left side is paralyzed and deformed. His trousers are rolled to the knees. He is bare-chested and wears a kitchen towel as a bib. He wears a necktie under the towel. He holds a tin cup of milk in his left hand. Lloyd is perched against the table next to Henry. He feeds oatmeal to him. Henry moves the oatmeal around his mouth, then he lets it dribble out or he spits it. Henry's speech is incomprehensible.

LLOYD. Stop it! (*Scooping the spilled oatmeal from Henry's chin and bib and pulling it back in his mouth.*) Stop doing that.—Don't do that. (*Henry lets the oatmeal out.*) You just quit that.—Chew it.—Swallow it. (*Henry lets the oatmeal out. Lloyd starts scooping it.*) Stop that! Stop doing that! You better stop that, Henry.—(*Henry lets the oatmeal out.*) Quit that. You just quit that. (*Henry slaps the cup of milk and spills it on the floor.*) That is it, Henry. (*Taking Henry's bib off.*) You get your own food.

HENRY. It spilled.

LLOYD. You did it on purpose.

HENRY. It spilled.

LLOYD. No, it didn't. You spilled it.

HENRY. Clean it!

LLOYD. No, I won't. You clean it. I saw you do it. You clean it.

HENRY. Clean it!

LLOYD. I won't clean it. You clean it.

HENRY. Clean it!

LLOYD. You clean it!

HENRY. Mae . . . ! (*Pause.*) Mae . . . ! (*Pause.*) Mae . . . !

MAE (*Enters. She carries a bundle of clothes and a cleaning rag*). What is it?

HENRY (*Pointing to the milk*). Look!

MAE. What happened? (*Mae puts the clothes on the bench and stands by Henry with the rag.*)

HENRY. He spilled it!

LLOYD. I didn't spill it! He spilled it!

MAE. So clean it up!

HENRY. Clean it!

LLOYD. I'm going to kill him.

MAE. Kill him if you want.—He can't talk straight any more. (*She starts wiping the oatmeal off Henry.*) Clean up the milk!

HENRY. Clean it!

(*Lloyd takes Henry's bib and starts wiping the milk.*)

MAE. Did you feed the pigs?

LLOYD. Yeah.

MAE. Did Henry eat?

LLOYD. He spilled the milk.

MAE. Did he eat! (*Lloyd doesn't answer.*) Did he eat! (*Pause.*) Did you eat, Henry?

HENRY. I ate.

MAE. He ate. Why didn't you say he ate. (*Mae walks to the left door and opens it.*)

LLOYD. I'm going to kill him.

MAE (*Stands on the threshold and turns to Lloyd*). So kill him.

(*They freeze.*)

SCENE 14

Mae exits. Lloyd places the bib, the oatmeal cup and spoon, and the tin cup on the mantelpiece. He takes the textbook and sits center. He attempts to read. He first makes the sound of the letter. Then, he speaks the name of the letter and traces it with his finger on the table. Then, he puts the sounds of the letters together. Henry sits to the right facing front. He mimics Lloyd's effort and laughs in silent convulsions.

LLOYD. S.

HENRY. S.

LLOYD. T. St.

HENRY. T. St.

LLOYD. A.

HENRY. A.

LLOYD. Stop that!

HENRY. A.

LLOYD. Stop it, Henry!

HENRY. A.

LLOYD. R. Ar.

HENRY. R. Ar.

LLOYD. Sta.

HENRY. Sta.

LLOYD. Star.

(*The left door opens. Mae stands outside and looks in.*)

HENRY. Star.

LLOYD. F.

HENRY. F.

LLOYD. I. Fi.

HENRY. I. Fi.

LLOYD. S. Fis.

HENRY. S. Fis.

LLOYD. Stop it. Cut it out. Fish.

HENRY. Fish.

(*Mae enters left. She carries a bundle of clothes.*)

LLOYD. Fish.

HENRY. Fish.

MAE. Someone took my money. Who did? (*Neither looks at her.*) Who did!—Did you Lloyd!

LLOYD. I didn't. Fish.

HENRY. Fish.

MAE. Did Henry? Did you take the money, Henry? (*She closes the door.*) Answer me. Did you take the money! Someone took it! You took it, Lloyd. Hand it over.

LLOYD. I didn't take it.

MAE. Hand it over.

LLOYD. I didn't take it!

MAE. Who took it then!

LLOYD. Henry took it.

MAE (*To Lloyd*). He didn't take it. He can't walk.

LLOYD. Yes, he can. You know he can. Walk, Henry. Show Mae how you can walk. Walk! He can walk.

MAE (*Enraged*). Walk!

HENRY. I can't walk.

LLOYD. You can walk!

MAE. Don't say he can walk, Lloyd. He can't walk. He didn't take the money. (*She notices the book.*) What are you doing with my book? (*He lowers his head. She is perplexed.*) What are you doing? (*She takes the book and holds it protectively.*) Don't mess my book.

HENRY. He was messing it. (*He laughs.*)

MAE. Shut up, Henry.

HENRY. He was saying "Fish." (*He laughs.*)

MAE. Everything turns bad for me.

(*They freeze.*)

SCENE 15

Lloyd exits. Mae places the book on the mantelpiece and stands by the down-right corner of the table. Henry walks to the left and sits. His hand is inside his fly. He handles himself.

HENRY. Mae. I still feel desire.—I am sexual.—I have not lost my sexuality.—Mae, make love to me. (*Mae doesn't answer. He continues touching himself.*) You are my wife. I want you. I feel the same desires. I feel the same needs. I have not changed. (*He holds on to the table and begins to stand.*) Mae, I have not stopped wanting you.—I can make love to you.—I can satisfy you. (*Supporting himself on the table, he slides toward her.*) I am potent.—I can make you happy. Kiss me, Mae.—(*He grabs her wrist.*) Tell me you still love me. Kiss me. Let me feel you close to me.—You think a cripple has no feelings.—I'm not crippled in my parts.—It gets hard. (*He puts his right arm*

around her waist.) Mae, I love you. (*He holds her tighter. He starts moving his pelvis against her.*) I'm coming . . . (*He starts sliding down to the floor.*) I'm coming. . . . I'm coming. . . . I'm coming. . . . I'm coming. . . . (*He collapses. She falls on the chair. She stands and leans against the table.*)

MAE. You can walk, Henry. You took my money.

(*They freeze.*)

SCENE 16

Mae exits left. Henry is on the floor trying to sit on the chair. Lloyd enters right. He helps Henry up and closes his fly. Mae enters with Henry's box and lifts it up in the air.

HENRY. Don't Mae.

MAE (*Throwing the box at him*). Get out!

(*Lloyd exits right.*)

HENRY. Don't throw things at me, Mae!

MAE. You took the money!

HENRY. You hurt me, Mae! You threw that box at me and hurt me!

MAE. You took the money!

HENRY. I didn't take it!

MAE. You took it! Where is it? (*She moves toward him.*)

HENRY. I didn't take it!

(*Mae reaches in his right pocket. She pulls out a wad of bills. She grabs his necktie, turns it back and pulls it down. Lloyd puts his head in through the left door and begins to enter. Mae and Lloyd speak the following speeches at the same time.*)

MAE. I feed you and I take care of you! And you steal from me? You eat my food and you sleep in my bed and you steal from me! You're a pig, Henry. You're worse than Lloyd!

LLOYD. Kill him, Mae! Kill him! Kill him! (*He climbs on the table on all fours.*) He's no good! Kill him, Mae! He's no good! He's a thief!

(*Henry falls off the chair. Mae falls on her knees next to him. Lloyd jumps off the table. He lets out a hysterical laugh.*)

LLOYD. Look he's bleeding! (*He chants and dances.*) Henry's bleeding! Henry's bleeding! Henry's bleeding!

MAE. Shut up, Lloyd!

(*There is silence.*)

HENRY. It was my money. Lloyd never paid me. He never paid me. He never paid me what he owed me.

MAE. You could have let him have it. Just because he takes care of you. You could have let him have your money. He takes care of you.

HENRY. He never paid me.

MAE (*She looks up to the sky*). Can't I have a decent life? (*There is a pause.*)

LLOYD. But I love you, Mae.

HENRY. I love you, Mae.

(*They freeze.*)

SCENE 17

Lloyd places the box inside the fireplace. He closes the left door. Mae gets the empty box from the fireplace and places it on the right chair. She places the bundle of women's clothes from under the bench on the table. She is packing clothes in the box. Lloyd stands up-left. He watches her. Henry sits left.

MAE (*As she packs*). I'm leaving, Lloyd. I'm going somewhere else. I'm leaving you and Henry. Both of you are no good. I got rotten luck. I work too hard and the two of you keep sucking my blood. I'm going to look for a better place to be. (*Lloyd sits on the chair upstage of the table.*) Just a place where the two of you are not sucking my blood. I'm going to find myself a job. And a room to live in. Far away from you. Where I don't have my blood sucked.

LLOYD. Don't go, Mae.

HENRY. Don't go.

MAE. I'm going and that's that.

LLOYD. Where are you going?

MAE. I don't know, Lloyd. I'm just going.

LLOYD. I'll do what you say.

MAE. I don't care what you do. (*Closing the box.*) You do what you want. Henry too. I don't care what he does.

LLOYD. Stay, Mae.

HENRY. Please.

MAE. I'm going. You take care of Henry, Lloyd. (*She goes to the door.*)

LLOYD. Don't go, Mae.

HENRY. Please.

MAE. Goodbye.

(*She exits through the right door and closes the door. Lloyd is still for a few seconds. He then runs to the door, knocking down his chair. He exits.*)

LLOYD (*Shouting*). Mae . . . ! (*Henry makes a plaintive sound.*) Mae . . . !

HENRY. Mae . . . !

LLOYD (*Offstage*). Mae . . . ! (*Henry makes a plaintive sound.*) Stop, Mae!

HENRY. Stop!

(*Lloyd enters running. He takes the rifle. Henry makes incoherent sounds. Lloyd exits running.*)

LLOYD. Mae . . . ! Stop . . . ! Stop, Mae!

HENRY. Mae . . . !

LLOYD. Mae, stop . . . !

HENRY. Mae . . . !

LLOYD. Mae! Mae! Mae!

(*A shot is heard. There is silence. Another shot is heard.*)

HENRY (*Plaintively*). . . . Mae . . .

(*Lloyd appears in threshold carrying Mae. She is drenched in blood and unconscious. Lloyd turns to Henry.*)

LLOYD. She's not leaving, Henry.

(*Henry lets out a whimper. Lloyd places Mae on the table. Mae begins to move.*)

MAE. Like the starfish, I live in the dark and my eyes see only a faint light. It is faint and yet it consumes me. I long for it. I thirst for it. I would die for it. Lloyd, I am dying.

(*Mae collapses. Lloyd sobs. Henry lets out a plaintive cry. They freeze.*)

END

FORUM

"From *Acting Out: Feminist Performances*"

LYNDA HART AND PEGGY PHELAN

Acting Out: Feminist Performances, edited by Lynda Hart and Peggy Phelan, provides an overview of contemporary feminist theater, both its traditional plays and experimental work, such as "performance art." The introduction to their book, reprinted here, outlines the history of feminist performance and identifies key artists within the movement.

I got the kind of madness Socrates talked about, "A divine release of the soul from the yoke of custom and convention." I refuse to be intimidated by reality anymore. After all, what is reality anyway? Nothin' but a collective hunch.

—*Jane Wagner, The Search for Signs of Intelligent Life in the Universe*

"Reality" is a fantasy-construction which enables us to mask the Real of our desire.

—*Jacques Lacan*

Jane Wagner's "bag lady" Trudy speaks her subjectivity from the far margins of the social order as well as the borderlands of psychic space. Wagner thus neatly connects the material circumstances of her heroine with her psychic determination. Lily Tomlin's one-woman performance processes a series of rapidly mutating personae, all traversed by the consciousness of Trudy, whose madness affords her a motility that might be read as evidence of the primordial splitting of the antihumanistic subject. Trudy inhabits a spatiotemporal order—the spaced-out time of her extraterrestrial chums—disconsonant with the linear time of humanistic narrative. Miming the unconscious, where the subject is not consonant with the self, where the "I" is multiple, shifting, and subject and object positions are endlessly mutable, this subject-without-a-fixed-identity created in the fissure of a radical split would be in need of a therapeutic restoration of wholeness for the humanist spectator. Trudy is "acting out," transgressing the boundary between the imaginary and the real. Catherine Clément points out that acting out, "however dangerous it might be, is also therapeutic, monstrously so."[1] Wagner both calls attention to and reinforces the impossibility of her female speaker's rejection of the symbolic as Trudy reports: "I never could've done stuff like that when I was in my *right* mind. I'd be worried people would think I was *crazy*.[2]

By translating her madness into divinity, Trudy attempts to make the best of a bad situation. Her dilemma is not unlike that of women in general. If "there can be nothing *human* that preexists or exists outside the law represented by the father; [if] there is only either its denial (psychosis) or the fortunes and mis-

fortunes ('normality' and neurosis) of its terms,"[3] then we can better understand why *Search for Signs*, a materialist-feminist performance that satirizes the misfortunes of women caught within the sociosymbolic order dominated by the law of the Father, seeks escape in madness and communion with extrahuman space chums. Wagner and Tomlin deviously address the problem but nonetheless appeal to the model. There is no easy way out for Trudy and her multiple incarnations. She attempts to manipulate her world, but, Cassandra-like, no one will believe her. Her madness relegates her to an aberrant individuality; thus isolated, she cannot speak for a credible community. It is nonetheless in these moments of "acting out" that the "factious identity of the subject disappears."[4] Clément speaks of identity as a prosthesis or an armor that one must wear in order to be understood. Identities are necessary if we are to live in reality, but they mask our desire. Feminist identities embrace the monstrous possibilities of acting out. Cutting ourselves off from "reality" can be a way to escape our inundation in *a* masculine imaginary that passes as *the* symbolic order.

If *Search for Signs* managed to squeak some subversive moments past the patriarchal censors and still gain wide popularity as well as commercial success, what the theatrical establishment usually authorizes under the name "women's," and occasionally even "feminist," theater is recently best represented by Wendy Wasserstein's *Heidi Chronicles*. Wasserstein herself as well as her main character, Heidi Holland, eschew a feminist identity in deference to a humanist one, and thereby become spokeswomen for a feminism that failed, that left women like Heidi "stranded." The play's most highly charged moment occurs when Dr. Heidi Holland is invited to address Miss Crain's School East Coast Alumnae Association as a distinguished alumna. Her topic is "Women, Where Are We Going?" "Nowhere" is her answer. She sums up the history of the feminist movement in an iconic aerobics class locker room scene, in which she finds herself alienated from, envious of, and superior to the young women wearing purple and green leather who bring their own heavier weights, the mothers with pressed blue jeans who know where to purchase Zeus sneakers, the gray-haired woman who talks about brown rice and women's fiction, and whom Heidi imagines is having "a bisexual relationship with a female dock worker."[5] Heidi realizes at this moment that she is not happy and hasn't been for a long time. Her speech ends with this spontaneous, nostalgic lament: "I don't blame the ladies in the locker room for how I feel. I don't blame any of us. We're all concerned, intelligent, good women. (Pause). It's just that I feel stranded. And I thought the whole point was that I wouldn't feel stranded. I thought the point was we were all in this together. Thank you. (She walks off.)"[6]

The Heidi Chronicles is a valuable commodity in this increasingly conservative political climate. Feminism, it insists, has

---

woefully failed "women." The play's realism offers nothing in the way of commentary on the fact that the conceptual space it carves out for "women" is occupied by a white, middle-class, heterosexual woman who finds her fulfillment in motherhood and considers herself a humanist. For those women who have contributed to the demise of such a monolithic feminism, Heidi's "failure" is our triumph. This play fulfills the fantasy that the divisions within contemporary feminism signal a dissolve, rather than productive disassembling. . . .

. . . There is a moment in the U.S. lesbian-feminist Split Britches and London's gay duo Bloolips collaboration, *Belle Reprieve*, that addresses this emphasis. Frustrated with this postmodern pastiche of Tennessee William's *A Streetcar Named Desire*, Bloolips Bette (Blanche) demands a story. Stamping his feet and whining his complaints with hyperbolic distress, Bette insists that the cast stop all this "romping about in the avant-garde and I don't know what else,"[7] and allow him to memorize his lines, don a pair of pretty pumps, and play a real part, a part his seventy-three-year-old mother, who is still hoping to see him play Romeo one day, can understand. Lois Weaver (Stella) menacingly challenges Bette to a realistic scene. Peggy Shaw (Stanley) attempts to play it with him—straight—from *A Streetcar Named Desire*:

BLANCH: "Just let me get by you."
STANLEY: "Get by me? Sure, go ahead."
BLANCHE: "You stand over there."
STANLEY: "You got plenty of room, go ahead."
BLANCHE: "Not with you there! I've got to get by somehow!"

Bette is a drag queen, which offers him a way out of sliding too easily into patriarchal womanhood, and he refuses to play the scene. When he realizes what is about to happen to him, he interrupts the action by reminding Stanley that he is not a real man. No, Shaw admits, if I were a real man I would say: "Come to think of it, maybe you wouldn't be so bad to interfere with. . . . If you want to play a woman, the woman in this play gets raped and goes crazy."[8] Bette says that he didn't plan on getting raped and going crazy; he only wanted a chance to wear a nice frock. This is one moment in which the "reprieve," a temporary escape from pain or trouble, occurs. This performance of bodies and drives and violence upends any expectation for realism. If spectators are frustrated in their desire for identification, Bette (Blanche) finally gives them the moment described above in which they might enter this show. Laura Mulvey's claim that "sadism demands a story" has never seemed so incandescent.[9] Getting raped, going crazy, and, of course, dying—this is what women appear to do most often in realistic theater. The recurrence of these actions is often enough thematic, but it also indicates the space of representation for the feminine subject position. Within the psychosemiotics of theatrical realism, the "death-space," space of absence, negativity, unrepresentability, is where femininity most often takes a place. Realism, like/as ideology, needs subjects, and subjects are constituted through divisions and losses that are always already gendered.

One response to the impossibility of the feminine taking a place within the symbolic has been an effort to recover, or postulate, a predscursive body, a critical effort to free the female body from its overdeterminations as a body saturated with sex, site of pleasure for (an)other, subjected and devoid of subjectivity. This issue has a particular valence in performance studies, where the female body on stage is easily recieved as iconic, seemingly less arbitrary than a linguistic sign, and even more so than photographic or televisual images, exceptionally susceptible to naturalization. Indeed, the female body on stage appears to be the "thing itself," incapable of mimesis, afforded not only no distance between sign and referent but, indeed, taken for the referent.

In his discussion of the reception of televisual broadcasts Stuart Hall retains the distinction "denotation/connotation"—a conceptual pairing that he recognizes as rather outmoded in linguistic theory—but which continues to hold a certain "analytic value." The distinction is useful for thinking about the female body in performance, for, as Hall outlines it, the connotative level of the sign is the site where "'meanings' are *not* apparently fixed in natural perception (that is, they are not fully naturalized), and their fluidity of meaning and association can be more fully exploited and transformed."[10] By contrast the denotative level of the sign (understood here as an analytic category and not a literal transcription) is the site where "its ideological value is strongly *fixed*—because it has become so fully universal and 'natural.'"[11] Elin Diamond has cautioned us against "leap[ing] to examples of performance art where, supposedly, the body's texts displace the conventional mimesis of the text-performance structure."[12] Certainly the work represented here does not simply and effortlessly evade the body/text conflation of conventional mimesis, but I do envision this collection as an antidote to the virtual hegemony of realism in Anglo-American theater.

Most of the performance [art] texts . . . do not have the status of "plays," nor do they aspire to such categorization. They do not, however, by virtue of operating on the level of the connotative sign—where, according to Hall's schema, "situational ideologies alter and transform signification"—produce meanings that are *outside* of ideology. But perhaps they could be said to have a certain advantage that is produced alongside their marginalized status. In that sense they are in limited but important ways "unbound," achieving a fluidity of movement simultaneously inside and outside dominant discourses. . . .

Collective authorship was an extremely important concept in early feminist companies of the 1970s and 1980s. As the utopian fervor of such collectivities gave way to a realization that they were, to some extent, based on a vision of feminist homogeneity that could not fully take into account the divisions and productive conflicts between and among feminists, the "idea" of a collective suffered fragmentations, largely in response to women of color and lesbians, who began calling attention to the inadequacies of the model. Nevertheless, today we may yet have something to learn from the history of these collectives; certainly the problem of authorship and textual ownership has become even more pressing in the last few decades. Julie Malnig and Judy Rosenthal map the history of the Women's Experimental Theatre Company (WET), an emblematic company

(continued)

founded in 1975. The optimism of the 1970s, in which feminist theater companies were operating with the idea that presenting "positive" images of women could counteract the misogyny of masculinist representations of women, gave way to the realization that differences between, among, and within women precluded any direct access to what constitutes "positivity." WET dissolved in 1985, but its ten-year history is marked with the conflicts that many women in performance grappled with during this period. In the histories of these collectives we can observe the process of feminists wrestling with what Derrida has called "women as truth" and "women as untruth," both remaining "within the economy of truth's system, in the phallogocentric space."[13] Such oscillation between competing claims for a definition of "women," raises the problem of essentialism and the necessity of performing gender and sexuality in a register that disrupts a metaphysics of presence. . . .

The three-woman troupe Split Britches has been one of the most influential groups in feminist performance. Its productions have been the subject of excitement, controversy, and much provocative writing in feminist performance studies. . . . As a single feminist performance artist, Karen Finley probably has the highest profile of any woman working in the field today. Her notoriety as centerpiece for the National Endowment for the Arts (NEA) controversies has propelled her into a refractive and projective spotlight, which . . . has taken quite a toll on her. Long before the NEA debates began, however, Finley's performances elicited heated reactions. . . . Finley's work excites a multiplicity of spectatorial identifications that illuminate the complexities of seeing. She is both susceptible to assimilation and co-optation by the dominant gaze that decries her representations and a model for subversive transgressions.[14]

The question of identity formations is crucial to feminist theorizing. As the work of the collectives exemplifies, the last decade has been one of struggle between competing identities. Whereas earlier feminist theorists were enabled by constituting "women" as a group opposed to a dominant patriarchy, they also came to realize that such a position presumed a hegemonic Other that was by no means monolithic. Such an "us-them" stance was not only reductive, but it also precluded making coalitions across gender, race, and sexual borders. It relegated "us" to victims and gave "them" a hegemonic power that left no way out for feminist subjectivities. And, most important, it erased the differences between, among, and within "women," who presumably constituted the category. This has been a central issue in feminist theory for some time now, and its ongoing political importance is addressed by many writers in this collection. Yvonne Yarbro-Bejarano evokes the Chicana "speaking for ourselves" but is quick to problematize the expression in Cherríe Moraga's work that permits no simplistic access to a unified Chicana identity or experience. Moraga is one of the leading figures in representing and historicizing the imbrication of gender, race, and sexuality as both multiple sites of oppression and spaces of contradiction in which different subjectivities can be constructed. Yarbo-Bejarano shows that the "familia" is a crucial concept to maintain for Chicano/a ethnic identity—but it must be refigured by ending the social construct of "man." . . .

Anna Deavere Smith's one-woman "On the Road" performances make patent the way in which feminist poststructuralists theorize formations of subjectivity. I particularly like Sandra Richard's description of Smith's work as "solo carnival," a provocative paradox that neatly captures Smith's "imitations" of her interviewees. If the "selves" that Smith performs are a series of ego identifications, she shows that these are dialogic formations that constantly mutate. Smith does not simply capture the people she interviews and reproduce their images; she also shows us the more unsettling process of their subjectivities being formed in the act of exchange with her, then among the spectators who witness the multiple incarnations. Such a "kaleidoscope of often contradictory positions" both addresses the problematics of community building and, ironically perhaps, facilitates their formation. . . .

I am concerned that feminists will retreat in the face of the deeply reactionary times in which we are mired. Will the progress we have made in fracturing monumental, exclusionary, totalizing constructs of women lose its force as we seek ways to mobilize our defenses? This seems to me to be a most urgent threat. Is greater visibility our best offense and defense? Acting out, acting up, coming out—these have been the strategies most frequently deployed to resist the swell of the New Right's agenda. They have produced some astonishing successes but have also been compromising in complex ways that bear close scrutiny.

Notes

[1] Catherine Clément, *The Lives and Legends of Jacques Lacan*, trans. Arther Goldhammer (New York: Columbia University Press, 1983), 71.

[2] Jane Wagner, *The Search for Signs of Intelligent Life in the Universe* (New York: Harper and Row, 1986), 18.

[3] Juliet Mitchell, "Introduction—I," *Feminine Sexuality: Jacques Lacan and the école freudienne*, trans. Jacqueline Rose (New York: W. W. Norton, 1985), 23.

[4] Clément, *Lives and Legends*, 92.

[5] Wendy Wasserstein, *The Heidi Chronicles* (New York: Dramatists Play Services, 1990), 61. *The Heidi Chronicles* won not only the 1989 Pulitzer prize for drama but also the 1989 best play distinction from the Drama Desk, the New York Drama Critics' Circle, the Outer Critics' Circle, as well as the Dramatists Guild's Hull Warriner Award and the Susan Smith Blackburn Prize.

[6] Ibid., 62.

[7] *Belle Reprieve* is a collaborative work by Split Britches and Bloolips. It will be published in *Gay and Lesbian Plays Today*, ed. Terry Helbing (Portsmouth, N.H.: Heinemann). My quotations are taken from proof pages.

[8] Ibid.

[9] Laura Mulvey, "Visual Pleasure and Narrative Cinema," *Visual and Other Pleasures* (Bloomington: Indiana University Press, 1989), 22.

[10] Stuart Hall, "Encoding/decoding," *Culture, Media, Language*, ed. Stuart Hall (London: Hutchinson, 1980), 133.

[11] Ibid.

[12] Elin Diamond, "Mimesis, Mimicry, and the 'True-Real,'" *Modern Drama* 32, no. 1 (March 1989): 68; reprinted in this volume.

[13] Jacques Derrida, *Spurs: Nietzche's Styles*, trans. Barbara Harlow (Chicago: University of Chicago Press, 1978), 97 and passim.

[14] I have discussed Finley's work at length elsewhere. See Lynda Hart, "Motherhood according to Karen Finley: The Theory of Total Blame," *Drama Review* 36, no. 1 (Spring 1992): 124–34; and "Karen Finley's Dirty Work: Homophobia, Censorship, and the NEA," *Genders* 14 (Fall 1992): 1–15.

PERSONAL EFFECTS
(EFFECTOS PERSONALES)
GRISELDA GAMBARO

GRISELDA GAMBARO (1928–)

Born in Argentina, Griselda Gambaro is widely considered the most prolific and accomplished Latin American woman dramatist. A professional novelist, short fiction writer, and author and lyricist of children's narratives, Gambaro has written over 30 full-length plays, one-acts, and brief dramatic sketches. Although she began her playwriting career in the early 1960s with the well-known *Las Páredes* (*The Walls*), she did not attain international recognition until the mid-1970s. Twice the winner of the prestigious Emecé Award, as well as other literary honors, Gambaro has lectured extensively throughout Latin America, Canada, France, Italy, and Spain, and taught at many universities in the United States, notably Yale, Cornell, and Rice. To escape Argentina's catastrophic political events in the 1970s, Gambaro lived in Barcelona from 1977 until 1980, when democracy was restored in her homeland.

It is difficult to assess Gambaro's dramatic and theatrical style because she eschews stylistic and thematic comparisons. For example, she stated in a recent interview: "I remember that after the opening of *The Walls*, critics compared me to [Harold] Pinter, even though I had not read one Pinter play." Often labeled an absurdist, an Expressionist, or an antirealist, Gambaro rejects narrow categorization:

> I am more interested in the comic, the farcical and in the grotesque. But when I listen to critical comparisons to Absurdism, I feel a certain degree of convolutedness since the Theater of the Absurd is not an influence on my work. But there are elements of the Grotesque in my work . . . that is the mixture of pathos, the tragic and the tragi-comic that tend to appear in many of my plays.

Gambaro does cite the influence of Shakespeare, Molière, Chekhov, Pirandello, Brecht, and O'Neill. She also acknowledges her indebtedness to the Argentinean masters Armando Discepolo (1887–1971), Florencio Sánchez (1875–1910), and her contemporary Osvaldo Dragún (see Chapter 7).

Gambaro's themes are similar to those of Dragún: the devastating effects of urbanization; the inability to communicate; destructive psychological games that sabotage honest relationships; the inner strength of humans who must survive the political conditioning of dictatorships. Yet, at the core of her worldview lies an intensely compassionate and hopeful ideology:

> We see in the human condition a series of inseparable cruelties; often we are cruel without meaning to be—even as we love, we are often cruel. One finds many categories of cruelty. Likewise, we are rational beings, thinking beings; we are capable of improving, of educating ourselves; we can co-exist, live, in our communal surroundings. In short, we could live in harmony—a special kind of madness. My plays demonstrate this, and it is up to each one of us to extract our own conclusions.

The recent publication of a five-volume collection of Gambaro's work is a significant achievement, particularly in Latin America, where commercial publishers ignore or discourage women writers dedicated to exposing sociopolitical inequities.

Personal Effects (1988)

Written in 1988, *Personal Effects* premiered in Madrid in March 1990. A tragicomedy with Beckett-like themes and style, the play is a brief, albeit expansive journey into the mind of a seemingly failed musician awaiting the arrival of a train that will transport him from his provincial surroundings back to his cosmopolitan dreamland. The violinist contemplates his existence while surrounded by a pile of luggage amid a desolate landscape. A clownish figure reminiscent of Chaplin's Little Tramp or Beckett's grotesque clowns, the musician has a volatile, self-indulgent, paranoid, and retentive personality.

Gambaro immediately establishes a relationship between the musician-performer and the audience. He directly communicates his psychological and spiritual displacement, and we are invited to share in his suffering, just as his fictional audience was invited, only hours before the curtain rises, to share in his musical communication. But as we learn of his apparent failure to reach an appreciative musical audience, we begin to understand that his disconnected narrative is truly an act of confession in which this postmodern clown proceeds to "unrobe" himself.

Just as Lucky in Beckett's *Waiting for Godot* carries with him the remnants of Western civilization in the form of a rope, a bag, and a picnic basket, so does our musician carry quantities of luggage symbolizing the residue of a nation unable to reassemble the pieces of a once rich and democratic society. The "heavy baggage" of recent Argentine history comprises numerous military coups, deposed presidencies, dictatorships, civil war, and the disappearance of thousands at the hands of the military. The disastrous defeat of the Argentine army by British forces during the brief Falklands-Malvinas War (1982) was the weight that broke the nation's back. As the musician busily rearranges the suitcases during the play's climactic moments, he mutters:

> You foolish thing . . . you're so foolish, so stubborn, so obstinate. I know what you have there . . . to try to fool me . . . (*walking with [a case] clutched to his chest*). You and I together. (*Pointing at the other suitcases on the ground.*) See? These other ones I'll leave behind. I'll kick them. . . . I detest them! If they're offended, that's their problem.

Just as the musician is unable to overcome loneliness and inertia, likewise Gambaro suggests that certain pieces of historical baggage can never be discarded—that cultural signifiers have, for better or worse, been stored away, compartmentalized, and assimilated into a landscape of the contemporary Argentine social fiber.

Additional difficulties arise for the musician because the railway station lacks water—an emblem of a society lacking a socioeconomic structure. Gambaro implies that in Argentina, in spite of a developed labor force and a highly educated population, nothing seems to function properly. The richest country in Latin America during the early twentieth century, contemporary Argentina is a dried-out shell incapable of reinventing itself. Or as the musician laments:

> What's the use of an effective work ethic? They dug and dug . . . put in pipes. . . . They installed this shitty little sink . . . connected it to this fountain . . . placed a deposit so that they could pay wages . . . make people get up at five in the morning . . . for what? Why so much effort? So much sweat? So that one can turn on the faucet and . . . NO WATER?

The impending arrival of the train—which never materializes—is yet another imposing image in Gambaro's play. Again, just as Gogo and Didi await Godot as the solution to their distress, Gambaro's musician waits, and waits, and waits. Didi and Gogo find refuge in each other as they pass time, but the musician relies only on the companionship of his "personal effects" to make time bearable. The locomotive becomes a symbol of psychological torture—somewhere in the distance, perhaps, it makes its way. But its motion is circular, just as the musician's attempted escape from his provincial environment is circular in nature. The first lines of the play are intriguing: "I'm lucky! I didn't miss the train. I'm so fortunate. I mean, to miss the train in this town would be a catastrophe." Yet, one might ask: Did he miss the train? Will the train ever arrive? After all, the station is deserted, its walls faded and covered with outdated announcements. There is not an attendant in sight. The present becomes the past, while the past becomes the future. Thus Gambaro's train metamorphosizes into a torture chamber; ironically, it can never be a means of escape from the musician's plight.

For all its implications concerning Argentina's internal dilemmas, *Personal Effects* is ultimately a universal tragicomedy about the inability of a human being to understand fully the resonance of memory or the collective history of human experience. Shackled to the past, and its baggage, the human cannot move beyond self-destruction. Gambaro argues that

> if one looks at the condition of world politics, one sees a road heading toward death—it is not a road towards personal growth or maturity, or a road towards the possibilities that life offers; on the contrary, it is a road in search of an arms buildup, a war, a road heading towards world hunger, towards power plays and interests that are egotistical in nature. And all of us continue to protect our small pieces of turf thinking that it will never affect us.

Gambaro's musician is an artistically stilted, psychologically displaced, and marginalized individual who, through the accumulation of excess baggage, continues to attempt to find a way out of his own discord. Yet, through laughter and poignant theatrical moments, we see a mirror image of ourselves as we, too, attempt to find solace in a world quickly crumbling beneath our feet. Our baggage—our personal effects—are equally taxing.

The baggage of his 'personal effects' so burden him that The Man (Sauree Pinckard) in Personal Effects can no longer function as an artist.

PERSONAL EFFECTS

GRISELDA GAMBARO

Translated by Roberto D. Pomo

A deserted train station in a small town. There are no benches, only a small drinking fountain next to a wall. Pasted on the walls, a few public announcements that are faded and semi-peeled. A man enters running—out of breath—as if attempting to catch a departing train. Over his shoulder is a rather large duffel bag. Under one of his arms and in his hand he carries a variety of suitcases of different sizes, while with his other hand he drags a large and heavy suitcase by a rope. He stops and looks around at the station's platform with a sense of relief. He dumps his entire baggage on the ground. A pause. He exits. He re-enters—this time with much more luggage and carrying a torn violin case. Again he drags yet another large suitcase by a thick rope. It's too much for him. He drops everything in a pile next to the other pieces of luggage. He turns to the large suitcase he has been dragging behind. With both hands he drags the suitcase toward the other suitcases. A pause. He looks all around desperately looking for something, pushing and kicking the suitcases until he locates his violin case. Relieved and content now, he picks it up,

brushes the case off, embraces it and places the case on top of the heap with care. A pause. He stares at the railroad tracks. He exits. He enters again carrying an arm-load full of more suitcases which he dumps on top on the existing pile and on top of the violin case. A pause. He wipes the perspiration off his forehead as he stares into the distance. A pause.

I'm lucky! I didn't miss the train. I'm so fortunate. I mean, to miss the train in this town would be a catastrophe.

(He sits on top of one of the large suitcases and rests. He notices the schedule posted on one of the walls, walks to it, reads it. He looks at his watch, outraged.)

Why in the hell did they make me rush? Two hours . . .

(A tense smile)

Two hours . . . I didn't even have a chance to have breakfast. What am I doing in this God-forsaken desert? Better have some order here.

(He straightens everything up with meticulous care.)

This one here. This one there. One up here, one down there. This one on the ground, and this one tied with the rope so that I won't lose it.

(He ties the suitcase with the rope.)

This one here, and this one . . .

(He holds a small, worn-out, rectangular suitcase in his hands.)

What did I put in here?

(He looks at it turns it upside down, places his ear next to it, then shakes it.)

No, I'm not going to open it . . . I'm curious, but not THAT curious. If I'm going to open every single suitcase to see what's inside . . .

(He laughs. Places the suitcase on the ground a bit apart from the other ones. He sits and stares at the suitcase through the corner of his eyes.)

It's not that heavy . . . it's old. What the hell did I put in here? I don't remember.

(He sniffs. Suddenly fear overcomes him.)

What? Don't tell me I have a cold now! And I didn't bring any aspirin.

(He stares at the suitcase.)

No, I didn't pack any aspirin in there . . . I'm almost certain.

(He stares at the suitcase with irritation.)

This suitcase must be good for something, but not for aspirin . . . no sir, not for aspirin . . .

(Brusquely)

Socks, underwear . . . I packed that. No, wait a minute . . . socks, underwear . . . change of clothes always in here . . .

(He looks through the pile and locates the duffel bag. Opens it.)

Ah! Here we go!

(He takes out a sandwich, unwraps it, and stares at it.)

Salami and cheese? I told them . . . NO SALAMI!

(Unhappily)

I can't stand salami . . . what the hell, I'll eat it anyway.

(He sits on one of the suitcases and proceeds to eat the sandwich.)

I know where everything is packed. You, too . . .

(He rubs the small suitcase with his foot.)

Only a fool doesn't know what's inside his own luggage.

(Pointing at one of the suitcases)

Inside that one, gifts . . . all trash . . . the town's coat of arms! What the hell do I want with the town's coat of arms? You tell me! They should have given me a ham sandwich . . . with fresh lettuce. I didn't buy any gifts. What in the world could anyone buy here? What? A cow? There you go, that's what I need, a cow! A mule! Yes, a mule! A mule could carry everything! Wait a minute, but then they wouldn't let me board the train . . . as if there's a difference between myself and a mule. What IS the difference? For a mule, there's no difference. A mule sees a man and the mule says "there's a mule." A mule can also say "there's a horse." Hey, a mule has no earthly idea about . . . what the hell, the WORLD! Wait a minute, what time is it? It's been ten minutes.

(Distracted, he straightens out other suitcases. He belches.)

This sandwich is a belly bomber!

(Screaming)

WATER!

(He crosses to the drinking fountain, but there's no water. He's dumbfounded.)

I could die of thirst here!

(He collapses on top of the large suitcase and then jumps up.)

Anyone can die of thirst here! Old people! Children . . . me! A universal dehydration! Rotten stuff! What's the use of an effective work ethic? They dug and dug . . . put in pipes . . . they installed this shitty little sink . . . connected it to this fountain . . . placed a deposit so that they could pay wages . . . made people get up at five in the morning . . . for what? Why so much effort? So much sweat? So that one can turn on the faucet and . . . NO WATER? I can't stand it! In an earthquake one would understand . . . there are things that happen underground . . . caprices of nature . . . wickedness! But this . . . so much human effort to enjoy a convenience . . . water for the thirsty . . . and what . . . NOTHING!

(He laughs hysterically. Attempts to move the drinking fountain. Kicks it.)

Not even a drop! The thirsty die of thirst! And to top everything off, no one accompanied me to this station! I walked! Like Jesus at Calvary, but with my own suitcases. Ah, who cares? I played for everyone in this small damn town . . . even for deaf ears!

(Speaking to his suitcase)

What's in here? A gray suit . . . neatly folded.

(Looks at another suitcase. A sense of doubt registers on his face.)

Or did I put it in there . . .

(Slowly he crosses to the suitcase. A pause. He stares at it intently.)

No, not inside the small one, that I remember . . . I'm positive . . . with absolute certainty. In this one I packed three wool jackets and a leather one.

(He kneels by and opens the suitcase. Rummages through its contents and takes out a pair of pants and a gray jacket.)

I was wrong. It's in here, neatly folded . . . didn't want to get it wrinkled. I was tempted to put it inside the small one, but at the last minute I realized . . . how could I pack this suit in such a small suitcase? It would look like an accordion!

(As he speaks, he nervously places the contents back into the suitcase. He smooths out the wrinkles of the jacket by hitting it rapidly. The nervous tension increases. He rolls and shoves the pair of pants into the suitcase—attempts to close it, but is unable to do so. He sits on top of it and finally manages to close it. Pieces of clothing are seen peering out from all around the suitcase.)

A gray suit! For these people? I'm such an idiot! I'm giving a concert to myself! Just for me . . . it's my gift to me! Free of charge. Music always fills my soul. And I must rejoice after the damn mule, the damn salami sandwich, the damn sink with no water, and the damn clothes that I can't fit back inside my damn suitcase!

(He stands and angrily pulls the suitcase around by one of the protruding pieces of clothing.)

I can't even get the damn things out!

(He madly struggles with it.)

HOW AGGRESSIVE OF ME!

(He kicks it. After a few seconds he attempts to control himself.)

Think about your soul . . . the serenity the music brings.

(He looks at the heap of luggage, then scatters the pieces around. His nervousness increases again.)

Where is it? But, I put it right here, on top of . . .

(He locates the violin case, dusts it with his sleeve. Places the case under his arm and applauds loudly. With modesty he takes a bow and salutes.)

Thank you . . . please . . . thank you.

(He opens the case, takes out the violin. A pause. He's speechless and dumbfounded.)

My dear God! The string's broken! It's broken . . . my dear God . . . my God . . . why me? Why did thou do this to me? Aren't I just a child? A mere mortal? Just a poor man? Why has thou no mercy on me? So, it's alright if these people don't know my mule, or if the mule doesn't even know who I am?

(A pause)

But I have to think! There are other possibilities here, right? No don't answer me! I don't want to hear any excuses! Save them! Repentance doesn't do any good! The string's broken! Why did it have to happen to me? Why didn't it happen to the damn mule? She wouldn't care!

(Looking at another suitcase)

And what did I pack in here? Ah, forget it . . . I'm ignoring this. I know where everything else is. I'm ignoring this!

(He laughs with a false sense of cheerfulness. He kisses the violin case and speaks to it as he carefully puts it down.)

Don't suffer . . . a broken string is not the end of the world.

(Offended)

But why did this have to happen to me?

(Screaming)

WHY DID THIS HAVE TO HAPPEN TO ME?
　Why am I repeating myself? Why am I rep . . . on to other things. They can think whatever they want to. But this is the truth: I am here, waiting for the train, with a cheese and salami sandwich in my stomach that I have not yet digested, dying of thirst, to the point of almost catching a cold, and regardless, I'm . . . I'm . . . I can't give a concert now! How can I play? I can't . . . I have a broken string!

(He laughs hysterically and looks at another suitcase.)

I'm not going to open you up! I know what's inside. I'm only having a momentary lapse of memory. Good! We have time. Ten minutes have passed. During the next ten minutes, I'm going to arrange my luggage . . . going to figure out how much of a tip I'm going to give the carrier . . . because I need some help here . . . I don't have a mule anymore.

(He takes out a few coins from his pockets. He realizes that there are only a few. He looks at them and places them back inside his pocket.)

No, I can do this by myself . . . the train won't leave without me. I have everything ready to go. From the platform I'll open up the window, throw the suitcases in, one after the other . . .

(He gestures as he talks.)

I better place everything in order. In this one, I have my shoes. In this one, the ceramic plate the club president gave me . . .

(Shaking a smaller suitcase)

What's this clicking? Something must be broken in there . . . Thank God . . . too damn heavy this one! In this one the umbrella, the shaving kit . . . the tea pot. . . books and magazines. In this one pills and medication . . . BUT NO ASPIRIN!

(He jumps over the suitcases.)

I know, the Scottish blanket!

(Laughing)

Yes, I packed it . . . at the last minute . . . since I'm always so cold. I said to myself "For this trip I'll be safe and not sorry."

(Suddenly he remains still with a frozen smile.)

The solution is at hand . . . well, maybe not.

(He stares at the larger suitcase.)

I may doubt, but I never ignore. Doubt is the cornerstone of intelligence. Or did I pack it in there? That damn Scottish blanket . . . not to mention that damn blue bedspread . . . God, they itch like hell. I brought both . . . and an overcoat in case it gets cold, but, it was hot! Wait a minute, did I separate them! Hmm . . . too much bulk. Doubt is the cornerstone of . . . Stop it! Don't repeat yourself!

(He crosses to the suitcase and opens it. He takes out the Scottish blanket and throws it up in the air. Immediately he takes out the blue bedspread.)

Didn't I tell you? Here they are! They could have been placed in here . . . or there . . . but no! They've chosen this particular suitcase!

(He laughs as he kicks them around. After a few seconds he straightens out the Scottish blanket and picks up the blue bedspread. As if in a trance, he wrestles with it. He stops and places the blanket inside the suitcase. He does not close the suitcase but walks away from it.)

Done!

(He looks at the suitcase with disdain.)

Something is not right here. If I had a stethoscope . . . or an x-ray machine . . . or a laser . . . anyway, I would realize the error of your ways . . . your cheap pride. So, I would play and they would cough . . . they would move about in their seats! And some of them would arrive late! Stomp . . . stomp . . . stomp through the aisles . . . like they were wearing big, heavy boots . . . clumsy oafs! That's what they did!

(Laughing)

Who would have thought it, eh? To come to this measly little town? But, there was this sweet little thing, seated in the front row . . . but I lost sight of her. And the dogs followed me here! So, what's in here? Tell me. Don't be so proud . . . I'm not going to open you up. I'm not going to please you in this way. Who the hell pleases me, eh? The rope is broken . . . I have a cold . . . that sweet thing never, and I mean never took her eyes away from me . . . so I missed a few notes in my performance . . . so what? The *Flight of the Bumble Bee* was perfect, but by the end, the damn bumble bee splattered on the wall.

(He hums a few bars of the Flight of the Bumble Bee *until he muddles the song.)*

The audience couldn't tell . . . neither could she. You could tell she was a small town kind of girl . . . no sense of fashion . . . so beautiful.

(A long pause)

And she applauded . . . she waited around . . . the other ones left . . . like the plague! And most of them got in for free!

(Jubilant laughter)

I starched two shirts and an undershirt.

(He sits on top of a large suitcase.)

So, where's your pride now, eh? Everything from memory . . . nothing escapes me . . . I remember EVERYTHING!

(The stage grows darker. A long pause. He stares at another suitcase. He restrains himself.)

No, not this time. I'm not about to repeat this damn game! I'm sure . . . most sure of it. It's not just a matter of intuition . . . it's an absolute conviction . . . the solution to the mysteries of the universe. I'll specify the exact details: the white shirt has two buttons missing, the light blue striped shirt and the starched undershirt with holes in the elbows . . . I should have sewn them . . . I know. But that's neither here nor there. Maybe I didn't pack the undershirt . . . I'm not so sure . . . it's a hunch . . . hmm, maybe I stuck it in there . . .

(Pointing at another suitcase)

I'll take a look! That way, I'll place all doubts aside.

(To the smaller suitcase)

So that you will not have any more doubts. Not so much for me, mind you . . . doubt is the cornerstone of . . .

(He realizes the repetition and stops. He opens the suitcase and takes out an alarm clock, a saucepan, a spatula and smaller pieces of various garments.)

See? It's not in here . . .

(*He holds the undershirt in his hand. Pretending to be cheerful*)

Here! Because I don't own two undershirts, this could be the one with the holes in the elbows . . . let's see the elbows . . . ripped . . . worn out!

(*He places the undershirt aside while continuing to extract pieces of clothing out of the suitcase.*)

But an undershirt is not a shirt.

(*Holding up two shirts*)

Shirts are different . . . they're much more elegant. They're not in here.

(*Looking at the shirts*)

They're so . . .

(*He places everything inside without closing the suitcase. A long pause. He stands still.*)

It's getting dark . . . I'm forty years old now.

(*Genuinely surprised*)

Me?

(*Taking out his identification from his pocket. He stares at the papers for a few seconds.*)

It seems like I was born only yesterday. Now, I'm forty years old . . . I'm losing my hair . . . I haven't accomplished much.

(*A long pause*)

She looked at me . . . yes, me . . . she looked at ME! Why didn't she wait for me after the performance? I walked around the block three times hoping to find her again, and not even a dog was around. Well, yes, dogs were around . . . dogs here . . . dogs there . . . but not even the dogs looked at me . . . they played by themselves . . . moronic animals . . . smelling each other . . . smelling each other's butts . . . as if they were enjoying some kind of exquisite delicacies . . . sniffing everywhere . . . nibbling at each other's backs . . . they played by themselves.

(*Looking at the suitcase out of the corner of his eyes*)

I know, enough of these damn feelings . . . let's let the subconscious do the work . . . I'm going for a walk!

(*Humming as he walks*)

Why did I study the violin?

(*Answering himself*)

Because you enjoyed music!
   Why did you enjoy music?

(*Answering himself*)

Because I had a sensitive soul. . . . Yes, I'm sensitive . . . it's true. My fingers failed me, not my soul. But at times it's probably better if the soul fails you . . . one can't notice that.

(*Lifting his shoulders*)

This town is truly radiant! The streets are bursting with life! What hustle and bustle!

(*Falling to his knees*)

I don't remember a damn thing! Do I open it? After all, that's what it's waiting for. That's why it draws attention to itself. So that it can say "You . . . I won, see!" Well, you're deadly wrong! You're not going to twist my arm!

(*He stands and crosses to the suitcase. He embraces it.*)

You foolish thing . . . you're so foolish, so stubborn, so obstinate. I know what you have in there . . . to try to fool me . . . your own daddy . . . your master . . . let's take a walk!

(*Walking with it clutched to his chest*)

You and I together.

(*Pointing at the other suitcases on the ground*)

See? These other ones I'll leave behind. I'll kick them . . . I detest them! If they're offended, that's their problem. Whisper in my ear . . . tell me . . . don't be ashamed . . . tell me . . .

(*He positions his ear next to the suitcase. He listens. A long pause*)

That's all? This is all you want to say to me?

(*Clutching it, he sits on top of the large suitcase.*)

All this for . . . well, it's alright . . . no need to be ashamed . . . you did what you could. Wait a minute . . . not really . . . you did a lot . . . not much . . . a lot . . .

(*He stands still, embracing the suitcase. Slowly and with a deep feeling of sadness, he exits.*)

AFTER A FEW SECONDS

BLACKOUT

ANGELS IN AMERICA, PART ONE: MILLENNIUM APPROACHES

TONY KUSHNER

TONY KUSHNER (1956–)

Although he was born in Manhattan, Tony Kushner was raised in Lake Charles, Louisiana, a conservative southern town. As a Jew and a homosexual (which he did not openly acknowledge until he was in college), he knew too well the effects of prejudice against people who are "different." The son of classical musicians, Kushner found solace in the arts, especially the theater. Kushner left Louisiana to attend Columbia University in New York, where he studied medieval art, literature, and philosophy. As a student he attended the theater frequently and was drawn to the experimental work of such directors as Richard Foreman, JoAnne Akalaitis, and Charles Ludlam (an early champion of gay theater). From Foreman and Akalaitis he learned the power of the visual image; Ludlam's "theater of the ridiculous" taught him a freedom of form in which a variety of styles could be mixed to maximize theatrical effect. His work fuses Brecht's political theater with the narrative and psychological tradition of O'Neill and Williams. His universe extends from heaven to earth (including Antarctica), and mixes the metaphysical with the mundane to form what he calls "the theater of the fabulous."

While completing an MFA in stage direction at New York University, Kushner took a job as a switchboard operator. When not answering phones, he worked on a draft of his first play, *A Bright Room Called Day*, about the rise of Nazism. At the suggestion of his friend and mentor, Oskar Eustis (of San Francisco's Eureka Theater), Kushner began writing *Angels in America* in 1988. The first part, *Millennium Approaches*, won the Pulitzer Prize in drama in 1993; *Millennium Approaches* and *Perestroika*, a sequel, won successive Tony Awards (1993 and 1994) for best play, unprecedented in the history of the Tonys. The combined works have been performed throughout the world and have won virtually every accolade that can be given a play. The academic community has also canonized the play, about which at least two major compendiums of critical essays have already been published. In October 2003, HBO broadcast a made-for-television version of the play, directed by Mike Nichols; Al Pacino portrayed Roy M. Cohn in a critically acclaimed performance.

Kushner has continued his exploration of personal dilemmas amid global politics with *Slavs!* and *The Dybbuk*. He has also adapted Corneille's seventeenth-century drama *The Illusion*. Kushner lives in Manhattan, but the worldwide popularity of *Angels in America* has made him, in effect, an international citizen.

ANGELS IN AMERICA, PART ONE: MILLENNIUM APPROACHES (1992)

Although *Angels in America* has emerged as the most decorated and widely accepted play about gays, it is not the first to explore the subject sympathetically. As early as 1592 Christopher Marlowe wrote about the relationship between King Edward II and Piers Gaveston in *Edward II*. Shakespeare addresses the subject in *Troilus and Cressida* in the Achilles-Patroclus subplot, and a number of recent studies explore homoeroticism in his works. Subsequent playwrights, such as Oscar Wilde, Tennessee Williams, and Edward Albee (all known homosexuals), have included gays and gay issues in their works. But these works are not generally considered "gay plays" in the manner we recognize *Angels in America* as such.

Mart Crowley's *The Boys in the Band* (1968) was the first Broadway play to place the gay community and its distinctive subculture at center stage. Crowley's success paved the way for such respected playwrights as Terrence McNally, Harvey Fierstein, and Lanford Wilson. Gay musicals, such as *La Cage Aux Folles* (*The Bird Cage*, 1983), were also accepted within Broadway's mainstream. The AIDS crisis, which surfaced in the early 1980s, prompted several respected plays, most notably Larry Kramer's *The Normal Heart* and William Hoffman's *As Is*. By 1993 the American mainstream eagerly embraced *Angels in America*, not as a trailblazer, but as a necessary play about the state of the union as it entered the third millennium.

Kushner has subtitled his two-part, seven-hour epic "a gay fantasia on national themes." The themes in question concern the AIDS crisis; religious, racial, and sexual bigotry; drug addiction; and contemporary American politics, specifically the "conservative revolution" fostered by the Reagan presidency. Kushner attacks the belief that it is "OK to be AIDS-phobic and homophobic," and he advocates federal intervention to achieve equal rights for gays and lesbians. Although *Millennium Approaches* is a play about despair (and can be appreciated as a work unto itself), its sequel, *Perestroika*, ends with what Kushner calls "great quiet and hope." *Perestroika* is a Russian term coined by former premier Gorbachev to describe a major change in political attitudes. In it, Kushner has found "a more perfect metaphor for human change than it was in the heady days of 1990, when the world seemed to have miraculously transformed." Hence, the hope that pervades *Perestroika*.

The success of *Angels in America*, however, transcends its political message ("I don't think art is a public service announcement," Kushner says). Rather, its appeal is attributable to its audacious scope, its extraordinary mixture of styles, and ultimately its sympathetic portrait of people—straight as well as gay—who suffer unbearable loneliness, uncertainty, and pain.

Angels in America is a virtual casebook of contemporary—specifically postmodern—theatrical technique:

- It is episodic, even cinematic, in structure. Events fade, blur, and merge into one another, and often occur simultaneously. One set of characters discusses an issue that is echoed by another conversation in a different locale. See especially act 2, scene 9, which, according to Kushner, should be played "fast and obviously furious; overlapping is fine; the proceedings may be a little confusing but not the final result."
- Locales—Salt Lake City, Washington, D.C., the Arctic Circle, and Central Europe, even heaven itself—segue into one another almost seamlessly. One senses that the whole world, if not the universe, is in disarray.
- The public world of history overlaps the private world of the individual (a rather Shakespearean concept); ultimately, the history of America at the end of the millennium is the history of individuals in conflict with personal as well as larger social issues.
- Kushner freely mixes styles and genres. The issues are serious, nearly tragic, yet comedy in all its forms dominates the play. Even as Prior lies dying of AIDS, Belize, a campy ex-drag queen, upstages the action. Realism, Expressionism, fantasy, agitprop, vaudeville sketch, and—most importantly—grand theatricality meld to create one of the most ambitious plays in the history of the American theater.
- Actors are asked to play multiple roles. The actor who plays the angel is also seen, quite deliberately, as the homeless lady in the South Bronx, the grotesquely hilarious real estate saleswoman in Salt Lake City, and the nurse. One actor plays a man (Rabbi Chemelwitz) and a woman (Hannah), a Jew and a Christian. We see variants on the same character simultaneously: the dying Prior is visited by his ancestors, a medieval monk and a fop out of the Restoration Theater.
- Pop culture (i.e., references to entertainers such as Judy Garland and Steven Spielberg) complements Marxist political tracts, biblical allusions, and other notable literature; vulgarity coexists with some of the most poetic stage language since Tennessee Williams. The result is a multilayered text that defies categorization.

- Despite its much-praised language, the play's most memorable moments are visual, even ritualistic: the descent of a single feather from on high, the eruption of a sacred book from the bowels of the earth, and, most famously, the apparition of the angel "with magnificent steel gray wings" in the final moment. Kushner's is very much "a theater of images."

Kushner's multifaceted dramaturgy, heightened by an inventive showmanship absent from most recent nonmusical theater, creates an ambience that transcends the particular "national themes" he explores. By mixing styles and theatrical effects, the play emerges as something more profound than a contemporary political tract. Its use of archetypes, most notably the Angel of Death and her intimations of "the Continental Principality of America," extends the parameters of the playwright's message that "everywhere things are collapsing."

For all its postmodern sensibilities, *Angels in America* emerges as a very traditional play in its treatment of human isolation. It is the legitimate successor of the works of O'Neill and Williams, especially in its psychological (and perhaps autobiographical) portraiture. Kushner's drama follows a cross-section of tormented Americans in the waning years of the millennium. Joe and Harper Pitt, staid Mormons, must confront their sexuality and mental deterioration (Harper's Valium-induced hallucinations are among the most troubling—and comic—in the play). Joe's mother, Hannah, can confront her son's dilemma only by denying it. Similarly, Louis, Prior's lover, chooses to leave his dying companion rather than face the reality of their situation. The scenes shared by this quartet of lovers are the most moving in the play.

The play is dominated by the specter of an actual historical figure, Roy Cohn (1927–1986), a lawyer who worked for the infamous Joseph McCarthy during the "Red scare" witch-hunts of the 1950s. Cohn was the prosecutor in the famous cold-war trial of Julius and Ethel Rosenberg, accused of treason; Cohn won his (still controversial) case, and the Rosenbergs were sentenced to death and executed. One of Kushner's masterstrokes is a scene in which Ethel Rosenberg's spirit visits Cohn as he is dying. Later Cohn worked in the Nixon administration and became a symbol among liberals of the cruel, dispassionate attitudes they associated with conservative Republicans. Kushner's Cohn—whom he describes as "a dramatic fiction"—is simultaneously the most reprehensible and pitiful character in the play. He is dying of AIDS, yet he denies reality ("It's just liver cancer"). He does not want to be branded as a homosexual because homosexuals are—in his mind—"only weak men who in fifteen years of trying cannot get a pissant antidiscrimination bill through City Council." In his twisted logic, he is "a heterosexual man . . . who fucks around with guys." In Kushner's mind, Cohn is the quintessential hypocrite who justifies his ruthless actions as serving the public good, even as he practices the very acts he condemns. Cohn is the dark angel hovering over the American landscape, and his hypocrisy is seen as more destructive than Harper's drug addiction, Joe's sexual ambiguity, Louis's callousness toward his dying lover, or the purportedly indecent acts committed by consenting adults. It is Cohn's ambiguity and contradictions that make his the most memorable and disturbing role in a memorable and disturbing play.

The Angel descends over Prior's deathbed in the theatrically stunning climax of Angels in America,
Part One: Millennium Approaches.

ANGELS IN AMERICA, PART ONE:
MILLENNIUM APPROACHES

TONY KUSHNER

THE CHARACTERS

ROY M. COHN, *a successful New York lawyer and unofficial
power broker.*

JOSEPH PORTER PITT, *chief clerk for Justice Theodore Wilson of
the Federal Court of Appeals, Second Circuit.*

HARPER AMATY PITT, *Joe's wife, an agoraphobic with a mild
Valium addiction.*

LOUIS IRONSON, *a word processor working for the Second Circuit Court of Appeals.*

PRIOR WALTER, *Louis's boyfriend. Occasionally works as a club*

*designer or caterer, otherwise lives very modestly but with
great style off a small trust fund.*

HANNAH PORTER PITT, *Joe's mother, currently residing in Salt
Lake City, living off her deceased husband's army pension.*

BELIZE, *a former drag queen and former lover of Prior's. A registered nurse. Belize's name was originally Norman Arriaga;
Belize is a drag name that stuck.*

THE ANGEL, *four divine emanations, Fluor, Phosphor, Lumen
and Candle; manifest in One: the Continental Principality of
America. She was magnificent in steel-gray wings.*

OTHER CHARACTERS IN PART ONE

RABBI ISIDOR CHEMELWITZ, *an orthodox Jewish rabbi, played by the actor playing Hannah.*

MR. LIES, *Harper's imaginary friend, a travel agent, who in style of dress and speech suggests a jazz musician; he always wears a large lapel badge emblazoned "IOTA" (The International Order of Travel Agents). He is played by the actor playing Belize.*

THE MAN IN THE PARK, *played by the actor playing Prior.*

THE VOICE, *the voice of The Angel.*

HENRY, *Roy's doctor, played by the actor playing Hannah.*

EMILY, *a nurse, played by the actor playing The Angel.*

MARTIN HELLER, *a Reagan Administration Justice Department flackman, played by the actor playing Harper.*

SISTER ELLA CHAPTER, *a Salt Lake City real-estate saleswoman, played by the actor playing The Angel.*

PRIOR 1, *the ghost of a dead Prior Walter from the 13th century, played by the actor playing Joe. He is a blunt, gloomy medieval farmer with a guttural Yorkshire accent.*

PRIOR 2, *the ghost of a dead Prior Walter from the 17th century, played by the actor playing Roy. He is a Londoner, sophisticated, with a High British accent.*

THE ESKIMO, *played by the actor playing Joe.*

THE WOMAN IN THE SOUTH BRONX, *played by the actor playing The Angel.*

ETHEL ROSENBERG, *played by the actor playing Hannah.*

PLAYWRIGHT'S NOTES

A DISCLAIMER

Roy M. Cohn, the character, is based on the late Roy M. Cohn (1927–1986), who was all too real; for the most part the acts attributed to the character Roy, such as his illegal conferences with Judge Kaufmann during the trial of Ethel Rosenberg, are to be found in the historical record. But this Roy is a work of dramatic fiction; his words are my invention, and liberties have been taken.

A NOTE ABOUT THE STAGING

The play benefits from a pared-down style of presentation, with minimal scenery and scene shifts done rapidly (no blackouts!), employing the cast as well as stagehands—which make for an actor-driven event, as this must be. The moments of magic—the appearance and disappearance of Mr. Lies and the ghosts, the Book hallucination, and the ending—are to be fully realized, as bits of wonderful theatrical illusion—which means it's OK if the wires show, and maybe it's good that they do, but the magic should at the same time be thoroughly amazing.

*In a murderous time
the heart breaks and breaks
and lives by breaking.*
—Stanley Kunitz, "The Testing-Tree"

ACT ONE: BAD NEWS

October–November 1985

SCENE 1

The last days of October. Rabbi Isidor Chemelwitz alone onstage with a small coffin. It is a rough pine box with two wooden pegs, one at the foot and one at the head, holding the lid in place. A prayer shawl embroidered with a Star of David is draped over the lid, and by the head a yarzheit candle is burning.

RABBI ISIDORE CHEMELWITZ (*He speaks sonorously, with a heavy Eastern European accent, unapologetically consulting a sheet of notes for the family names*). Hello and good morning. I am Rabbi Isidor Chemelwitz of the Bronx Home for Aged Hebrews. We are here this morning to pay respects at the passing of Sarah Ironson, devoted wife of Benjamin Ironson, also deceased, loving and caring mother of her sons Morris, Abraham, and Samuel, and her daughters Esther and Rachel; beloved grandmother of Max, Mark, Louis, Lisa, Maria . . . uh . . . Lesley, Angela, Doris, Luke and Eric. (*Looks more closely at paper*) Eric? This is a Jewish name? (*Shrugs*) Eric. A large and loving family. We assemble that we may mourn collectively this good and righteous woman.

(*He looks at the coffin*)

This woman. I did not know this woman. I cannot accurately describe her attributes, nor do justice to her dimensions. She was. . . . Well, in the Bronx Home of Aged Hebrews are many like this, the old, and to many I speak but not to be frank with this one. She preferred silence. So I do not know her and yet I know her. She was . . .

(*He touches the coffin*)

. . . not a person but a whole kind of person, the ones who crossed the ocean, who brought with us to America the villages of Russia and Lithuania—and how we struggled, and how we fought, for the family, for the Jewish home, so that you would not grow up here, in this strange place, in the melting pot where nothing melted. Descendants of this immigrant woman, you do not grow up in America, you and your children and their children with the goyis-che names. You do not live in America. No such place exists. Your clay is the clay of some Litvak shtetl, your air the air of the steppes—because she carried the old world on her back across the ocean, in a boat, and she put it down on Grand Concourse Avenue, or in Flatbush, and she worked that earth into your bones, and you pass it to your children, this ancient, ancient culture and home.

(Little pause)

You can never make that crossing that she made, for such Great Voyages in this world do not any more exist. But every day of your lives the miles that voyage between that place and this one you cross. Every day. You understand me? In you that journey is.

So . . .

She was the last of the Mohicans, this one was. Pretty soon . . . all the old will be dead.

SCENE 2

Same day. Roy and Joe in Roy's office. Roy at an impressive desk, bare except for a very elaborate phone system, rows and rows of flashing buttons which bleep and beep and whistle incessantly, making chaotic music underneath Roy's conversations. Joe is sitting, waiting. Roy conducts business with great energy, impatience and sensual abandon: gesticulating, shouting, cajoling, crooning, playing the phone, receiver and hold button with virtuosity and love.

ROY (*Hitting a button*). Hold. (*To Joe*) I wish I was an octopus, a fucking octopus. Eight loving arms and all those suckers. Know what I mean?

JOE. No, I . . .

ROY (*Gesturing to a deli platter of little sandwiches on his desk*). You want lunch?

JOE. Not, that's OK really I just . . .

ROY (*Hitting a button*). Ailene? Roy Cohn. Now what kind of a greeting is. . . . I thought we were friends, Ai. . . . Look Mrs. Soffer, you don't have to get. . . . You're upset. You're yelling. You'll aggravate your condition, you shouldn't yell, you'll pop little blood vessels in your face if you yell. . . . No that was a joke, Mrs. Soffer, I was joking. . . . I already apologized sixteen times for that, Mrs. Soffer, you . . . (*While she's fulminating, Roy covers the mouthpiece with his hand and talks to Joe*) This'll take a minute, *eat* already, what is this tasty sandwich here it's—(*He takes a bite of a sandwich*) Mmmmm, liver or some. . . . Here.

(*He pitches the sandwich to Joe, who catches it and returns it to the platter.*)

ROY (*Back to Mrs. Soffer*). Uh huh, uh huh. . . . No, I already told you, it wasn't a vacation, it was business, Mrs. Soffer, I have clients in Haiti, Mrs. Soffer, I. . . . Listen, AILENE, YOU THINK I'M THE ONLY GODDAM LAWYER IN HISTORY EVER MISSED A COURT DATE? Don't make such a big fucking. . . . Hold. (*He hits the hold button*) You HAG!

JOE. If this is a bad time . . .

ROY. *Bad* time? This is a good time! (*Button*) Baby doll, get me. . . . Oh fuck, wait . . . (*Button, button*) Hello? Yah. Sorry to keep you holding, Judge Hollins, I. . . . Oh *Mrs.* Hollins, sorry dear deep voice you got. Enjoying your visit? (*Hands over mouthpiece again, to Joe*) She sounds like a truckdriver and he sounds like Kate Smith, very confusing. Nixon appointed him, all the geeks are Nixon appointees . . . (*To Mrs. Hollins*) Yeah yeah right good so how many tickets dear? Seven. For what, *Cats, 42nd Street,* what? No you wouldn't like *La Cage,* trust me, I know. Oh for godsake. . . . Hold. (*Button, button*) Baby doll, seven for *Cats* or something, anything hard to get, I don't give a fuck what and neither will they. (*Button; to Joe*) You see *La Cage?*

JOE. No I . . .

ROY. Fabulous. Best thing on Broadway. Maybe ever. (*button*) Who? Aw, Jesus H. Christ, Harry, no, Harry, Judge John Francis Grimes, Manhattan Family Court. Do I have to do every goddam thing myself? *Touch* the bastard, Harry, and don't call me on this line again, I told you not to . . .

JOE (*Starting to get up*). Roy, uh, should I wait outside or . . .

ROY (*To Joe*). Oh sit. (*To Harry*) You hold. I pay you to hold fuck you Harry you jerk. (*Button*) Half-wit dick-brain. (*Instantly philosophical*) I see the universe, Joe, as a kind of sandstorm in outer space with winds of mega-hurricane velocity, but instead of grains of sand it's shards and splinters of glass. You ever feel that way? Ever have one of those days?

JOE. I'm not sure I . . .

ROY. So how's life in Appeals? How's the Judge?

JOE. He sends his best.

ROY. He's a good man. Loyal. Not the brightest man on the bench, but he has manners. And a nice head of silver hair.

JOE. He gives me a lot of responsibility.

ROY. Yeah, like writing his decisions and signing his name.

JOE. Well . . .

ROY. He's a nice guy. And you cover admirably.

JOE. Well, thanks, Roy, I . . .

ROY (*Button*). Yah? Who is *this?* Well who the fuck are *you?* Hold—(*Button*) Harry? Eighty-seven grand, something like that. Fuck him. Eat me. New Jersey, chain of porno film stores in, uh, Weehawken. That's—Harry, that's the beauty of the law. (*Button*) So, baby doll, what? *Cats?* Bleah. (*Button*) *Cats!* It's about cats. Singing cats, you'll love it. Eight o'clock, the theatre's always at eight. (*Button*) Fucking tourists. (*Button, then to Joe*) Oh live a little, Joe, *eat something for Christ sake*—

JOE. Um, Roy, could you . . .

ROY. What? (*To Harry*) Hold a minute. (*Button*) Mrs. Soffer? Mrs. . . . (*Button*) God-fucking-dammit to hell, where is . . .

JOE (*Overlapping*). Roy, I'd really appreciate it if . . .

ROY (*Overlapping*). Well she was here a minute ago, baby doll, see if . . .

(*The phone starts making three different beeping sounds, all at once.*)

ROY (*Smashing buttons*). Jesus fuck this goddam thing . . .

JOE (*Overlapping*). I really wish you wouldn't . . .

ROY (*Overlapping*). Baby doll? Ring the *Post* get me Suzy see if . . .

(*The phone starts whistling loudly.*)

ROY. CHRIST!

JOE. *Roy.*

ROY (*Into receiver*). Hold. (*Button; to Joe*) What?

JOE. Could you please not take the Lord's name in vain?

(*Pause*)

I'm sorry. But please. At least while I'm . . .

ROY (*Laughs, then*). Right. Sorry. Fuck.

    Only in America. (*Punches a button*) Baby doll, tell 'em all to fuck off. Tell 'em I died. You handle Mrs. Soffer. Tell her it's on the way. Tell her I'm schtupping the judge. I'll call her back. I *will* call her. I know how much I borrowed. She's got four hundred times that stuffed up her. . . . Yeah, tell her I said that. (*Button. The phone is silent*)

    So, Joe.

JOE. I'm sorry Roy, I just . . .

ROY. No no no no, principles count, I respect principles, I'm not religious but I like God and God likes me. Baptist, Catholic?

JOE. Mormon.

ROY. Mormon. Delectable. Absolutely. Only in America. So, Joe. Whattya think?

JOE. It's . . . well . . .

ROY. Crazy life.

JOE. Chaotic.

ROY. Well but God bless chaos. Right?

JOE. Ummm . . .

ROY. Huh. Mormons. I knew Mormons, in um, Nevada.

JOE. Utah, mostly.

ROY. No, these Mormons were in Vegas.

    So. So, how'd you like to go to Washington and work for the Justice Department?

JOE. Sorry?

ROY. How'd you like to go to Washington and work for the Justice Department? All I gotta do is pick up the phone, talk to Ed, and you're in.

JOE. In . . . what, exactly?

ROY. Associate Assistant Something Big. Internal Affairs, heart of the woods, something nice with clout.

JOE. Ed . . . ?

ROY. Meese. The Attorney General.

JOE. Oh.

ROY. I just have to pick up the phone . . .

JOE. I have to think.

ROY. Of course.

(*Pause*)

It's a great time to be in Washington, Joe.

JOE. Roy, it's incredibly exciting . . .

ROY. And it would mean something to me. You understand?

(*Little pause.*)

JOE. I . . . can't say how much I appreciate this Roy, I'm sort of . . . well, stunned, I mean. . . . Thanks, Roy. But I have to give it some thought. I have to ask my wife.

ROY. Your wife. Of course.

JOE. But I really appreciate . . .

ROY. Of course. Talk to your wife.

SCENE 3

Later that day. Harper at home, alone. She is listening to the radio and talking to herself, as she often does. She speaks to the audience.

HARPER. People who are lonely, people left alone, sit talking nonsense to the air, imagining . . . beautiful systems dying, old fixed orders spiraling apart . . .

    When you look at the ozone layer, from outside, from a spaceship, it looks like a pale blue halo, a gentle, shimmering aureole encircling the atmosphere encircling the earth. Thirty miles above our heads, a thin layer of three-atom oxygen molecules, product of photosynthesis, which explains the fussy vegetable preference for visible light, its rejection of darker rays and emanations. Danger from without. It's a kind of gift, from God, the crowning touch to the creation of the world: guardian angel, hands linked, make a spherical net, a blue-green nesting orb, a shell of safety for itself. But everywhere, things are collapsing, lies surfacing, systems of defense giving way. . . . This is why, Joe, this is why I shouldn't be left alone.

(*Little pause*)

I'd like to go traveling. Leave you behind to worry. I'll send postcards with strange stamps and tantalizing messages on the back. "Later maybe." "Nevermore . . ."

(*Mr. Lies, a travel agent, appears.*)

HARPER. Oh! You startled me!

MR. LIES. Cash, check or credit card?

HARPER. I remember you. You're from Salt Lake. You sold us the plane tickets when we flew here. What are you doing in Brooklyn?

MR. LIES. You said you wanted to travel . . .

HARPER. And here you are. How thoughtful.

MR. LIES. Mr. Lies. Of the International Order of Travel Agents. We mobilize the globe, we set people adrift, we stir the populace and send nomads eddying across the planet. We are adepts of motion, acolytes of the flux. Cash, check or credit card. Name your destination.

HARPER. Antarctica, maybe. I want to see the hole in the ozone. I heard on the radio . . .

MRI. LIES (*He has a computer terminal in his briefcase*). I can arrange a guided tour. Now?

HARPER. Soon. Maybe soon. I'm not safe here you see. Things aren't right with me. Weird stuff happens . . .

MR. LIES. Like?

HARPER. Well, like you, for instance. Just appearing. Or last week . . . well never mind. People are like planets, you need a thick skin. Things get to me, Joe stays away and now. . . . Well look. My dreams are talking back to me.

MR. LIES. It's the price of rootlessness. Motion sickness. The only cure: to keep moving.

HARPER. I'm undecided. I feel . . . that something's going to give. It's 1985. Fifteen years till the third millennium. Maybe Christ will come again. Maybe seeds will be planted, maybe there'll be harvest then, maybe early figs to eat, maybe new life, maybe fresh blood, maybe companionship and love and protection, safety from what's outside, maybe the door will hold, or maybe . . . maybe the troubles will come, and the end will come, and the sky will collapse and there will be terrible rains and showers of poison light, or maybe my life is really fine, maybe Joe loves me and I'm only crazy thinking otherwise, or maybe not, maybe it's even worse than I know, maybe . . . I want to know, maybe I don't. The suspense, Mr. Lies, it's killing me.

MR. LIES. I suggest a vacation.

HARPER (*Hearing something*). That was the elevator. Oh God, I should fix myself up, I. . . . You have to go, you shouldn't be here . . . you aren't even real.

MR. LIES. Call me when you decide . . .

HARPER. Go!

(*The Travel Agent vanishes as Joe enters.*)

JOE. Buddy?
    Buddy? Sorry I'm late. I was just . . . out. Walking. Are you mad?

HARPER. I got a little anxious.

JOE. Buddy kiss.

(*They kiss.*)

JOE. Nothing to get anxious about.
    So, So how'd you like to move to Washington?

SCENE 4

Same day. Louis and Prior outside the funeral home, sitting on a bench, both dressed in funereal finery, talking. The funeral service for Sarah Ironson has just concluded and Louis is about to leave for the cemetery.

LOUIS. My grandmother actually saw Emma Goldman speak. In Yiddish. But all Grandma could remember was that she spoke well and wore a hat.
    What a weird service. That rabbi . . .

PRIOR. A definite find. Get his number when you go to the graveyard. I want him to bury me.

LOUIS. Better head out there. Everyone gets to put dirt on the coffin once it's lowered in.

PRIOR. Oooh. Cemetery fund. Don't want to miss that.

LOUIS. It's an old Jewish custom to express love. Here, Grandma, have a shovelful. Latecomers run the risk of finding the grave completely filled.
    She was pretty crazy. She was up there in the home for ten years, talking to herself. I never visited. She looked too much like my mother.

PRIOR (*Hugs him*). Poor Louis. I'm sorry your grandma is dead.

LOUIS. Tiny little coffin, huh
    Sorry I didn't introduce you to. . . . I always get so closety at these family things.

PRIOR. Butch. You get butch. (*Imitating*) "Hi Cousin Doris, you don't remember me I'm Lou, Rachel's boy." Lou, not Louis, because if you say Louis they'll hear the sibilant S.

LOUIS. I don't have a . . .

PRIOR. I don't blame you, hiding. Bloodlines, Jewish curses are the worst. I personally would dissolve if anyone ever looked me in the eye and said "Feh." Fortunately WASPs don't say "Feh." Oh and by the way, darling, cousin Doris is a dyke.

LOUIS. No.
    Really?

PRIOR. You don't notice anything. If I hadn't spent the last four years fellating you I'd swear you were straight.

LOUIS. You're in a pissy mood. Cat still missing?

(*Little pause.*)

PRIOR. Not a furball in sight. It's your fault.

LOUIS. It is?

PRIOR. I warned you, Louis. Names are important. Call an animal "Little Sheba" and you can't expect it to stick around. Besides, it's a dog's name.

LOUIS. I wanted a dog in the first place, not a cat. He sprayed my books.

PRIOR. He was a female cat.

LOUIS. Cats are stupid, high-strung predators, Babylonians sealed them up in bricks. Dogs have brains.

PRIOR. Cats have intuition.

LOUIS. A sharp dog is as smart as a really dull two-year-old child.

PRIOR. Cats know when something's wrong.

LOUIS. Only if you stop feeding them.

PRIOR. They know. That's why Sheba left, because she knew.

LOUIS. Knew what?

(Pause.)

PRIOR. I did my best Shirley Booth this morning, floppy slippers, housecoat, curlers, can of Little Friskies; "Come back, Little Sheba, come back. . . ." To no avail. Le chat, elle ne reviendra jamais, jamais . . .

(He removes his jacket, rolls up his sleeve, shows Louis a dark-purple spot on the underside of his arm near the shoulder)

See.

LOUIS. That's just a burst blood vessel.

PRIOR. Not according to the best medical authorities.

LOUIS. What?

(Pause)

Tell me.

PRIOR. K. S., baby. Lesion number one. Lookit. The wine-dark kiss of the angel of death.

LOUIS *(Very softly, holding Prior's arm)*. Oh please . . .

PRIOR. I'm a lesionnaire. The Foreign Lesion. The American Lesion. Lesionnaire's disease.

LOUIS. Stop.

PRIOR. My troubles are lesion.

LOUIS. Will you *stop*.

PRIOR. Don't you think I'm handling this well?
      I'm going to die.

LOUIS. Bullshit.

PRIOR. Let go of my arm.

LOUIS. No.

PRIOR. Let go.

LOUIS *(Grabbing Prior, embracing him ferociously)*. No.

PRIOR. I can't find a way to spare you baby. No wall like the wall of hard scientific fact. K. S. Wham. Bang your head on that.

LOUIS. Fuck you. *(Letting go)* Fuck you fuck you fuck you.

PRIOR. Now that's what I like to hear. A mature reaction. Let's go see if the cat's come home.
      Louis?

LOUIS. When did you find this?

PRIOR. I couldn't tell you.

LOUIS. Why?

PRIOR. I was scared, Lou.

LOUIS. Of what?

PRIOR. That you'll leave me.

LOUIS. Oh.

(Little pause.)

PRIOR. Bad timing, funeral and all, but I figured as long as we're on the subject of death . . .

LOUIS. I have to go bury my grandma.

PRIOR. Lou?

(Pause)

      Then you'll come home?

LOUIS. Then I'll come home.

SCENE 5

Same day, later on. Split scene: Joe and Harper at home; Louis at the cemetery with Rabbi Isidor Chemelwitz and the little coffin.

HARPER. Washington?

JOE. It's an incredible honor, buddy, and . . .

HARPER. I have to think.

JOE. Of course.

HARPER. Say no.

JOE. You said you were going to think about it.

HARPER. I don't want to move to Washington.

JOE. Well I do.

HARPER. It's a giant cemetery, huge white graves and mausoleums everywhere.

JOE. We could live in Maryland. Or Georgetown.

HARPER. We're happy here.

JOE. That's not really true, buddy, we . . .

HARPER. Well happy enough! Pretend happy. That's better than nothing.

JOE. It's time to make some changes, Harper.

HARPER. No changes. Why?

JOE. I've been chief clerk for four years. I make twenty-nine thousand dollars a year. That's ridiculous. I graduated fourth in my class and I make less than anyone I know. And I'm . . . I'm tired of being a clerk, I want to go where something good is happening.

HARPER. Nothing good happens in Washington. We'll forget church teachings and buy furniture at . . . at *Conran's* and become yuppies. I have too much to do here.

JOE. Like what?

HARPER. I *do* have things . . .

JOE. What things?

HARPER. I have to finish painting the bedroom.

JOE. You've been painting in there for over a year.

HARPER. I know, I. . . . It just isn't done because I never get time to finish it.

JOE. Oh that's . . . that doesn't make sense. You have all the time in the world. You could finish it when I'm at work.

HARPER. I'm afraid to go in there alone.

JOE. Afraid of what?

HARPER. I heard someone in there. Metal scraping on the wall. A man with a knife, maybe.

JOE. There's no one in the bedroom, Harper.

HARPER. Not now.

JOE. Not this morning either.

HARPER. How do you know? You were at work this morning. There's something creepy about this place. Remember *Rosemary's Baby*?

JOE. *Rosemary's Baby*?

HARPER. Our apartment looks like that one. Wasn't that apartment in Brooklyn?

JOE. No, it was . . .

HARPER. Well, it looked like this. It did.

JOE. Then let's move.

HARPER. Georgetown's worse. *The Exorcist* was in Georgetown.

JOE. The devil, everywhere you turn, huh, buddy.

HARPER. Yeah. Everywhere.

JOE. How many pills today, buddy?

HARPER. None. One. Three. Only three.

LOUIS (*Pointing at the coffin*). Why are there just two little wooden pegs holding the lid down?

RABBI ISIDOR CHEMELWITZ. So she can get out easier if she wants to.

LOUIS. I hope she stays put.

I pretended for years that she was already dead. When they called to say she had died it was a surprise. I abandoned her.

RABBI ISIDOR CHEMELWITZ. "Sharfer vi di tson fun a shlang iz n umdankbar kind!"

LOUIS. I don't speak Yiddish.

RABBI ISIDOR CHEMELWITZ. Sharper than the serpent's tooth is the ingratitude of children. Shakespeare. *King Lear*.

LOUIS. Rabbi, what does the Holy Writ say about someone who abandons someone he loves at a time of great need?

RABBI ISIDOR CHEMELWITZ. Why would a person do such a thing?

LOUIS. Because he has to.

Maybe because this person's sense of the world, that it will change for the better with struggle, maybe a person who has this neo-Hegelian positivist sense of constant historical progress towards happiness or perfection or something, who feels very powerful because he feels connected to these forces, moving uphill all the time . . . maybe that person can't, um, incorporate sickness into his sense of how things are supposed to go. Maybe vomit . . . and sores and disease . . . really frighten him, maybe . . . he isn't so good with death.

RABBI ISIDOR CHEMELWITZ. The Holy Scriptures have nothing to say about such a person.

LOUIS. Rabbi, I'm afraid of the crimes I may commit.

RABBI ISIDOR CHEMELWITZ. Please, mister. I'm a sick old rabbi facing a long drive home to the Bronx. You want to confess, better you should find a priest.

LOUIS. But I'm not a Catholic, I'm a Jew.

RABBI ISIDOR CHEMELWITZ. Worse luck for you, bubbulah. Catholics believe in foregiveness. Jews believe in Guilt. (*He pats the coffin tenderly*)

LOUIS. You just make sure those pegs are in good and tight.

RABBI ISIDOR CHEMELWITZ. Don't worry, mister. The life she had, she'll stay put. She's better off.

JOE. Look, I know this is scary for you. But try to understand what it means to me. Will you try?

HARPER. Yes.

JOE. Good. Really try.

I think things are starting to change in the world.

HARPER. But I don't want . . .

JOE. Wait. For the good. Change for the good. America has rediscovered itself. Its sacred position among nations. And people aren't ashamed of that like they used to be. This is a great thing. The truth restored. Law restored. That's what President Reagan's done, Harper. He says, "Truth exists and can be spoken proudly." And the country responds to him. We become better. More good. I need to be part of that, I need something big to lift me up. I mean, six years ago the world seemed in decline, horrible, hopeless, full of unsolvable problems and crime and confusion and hunger and . . .

HARPER. But it still seems that way. More now than before. They say the ozone layer is . . .

JOE. Harper . . .

HARPER. And today out the window on Atlantic Avenue there was a schizophrenic traffic cop who was making these . . .

JOE. Stop it! I'm trying to make a point.

HARPER. So am I.

JOE. You aren't even making sense, you . . .

HARPER. My point is the world seems just as . . .

JOE. It only seems that way to you because you never go out in the world, Harper, and you have emotional problems.

HARPER. I do so get out in the world.

JOE. You don't. You stay in all day, fretting about imaginary . . .

HARPER. I get out. I do. You don't know what I do.

JOE. You don't stay in all day.

HARPER. No.

JOE. Well. . . . Yes you do.

HARPER. That's what you think.

JOE. Where do you go?

HARPER. Where do *you* go? When you walk.

(*Pause, then angrily*) And I DO NOT have emotional problems.

JOE. I'm sorry.

HARPER. And if I do have emotional problems it's from living with you. Or . . .

JOE. I'm sorry buddy, I didn't mean to . . .

HARPER. Or if you do think I do then you should never have married me. You have all these secrets and lies.

JOE. I want to be married to you, Harper.

HARPER. You shouldn't. You never should.

   (*Pause*)

      Hey buddy. Hey buddy.

JOE. Buddy kiss . . .

   (*They kiss.*)

HARPER. I heard on the radio how to give a blowjob.

JOE. What?

HARPER. You want to try?

JOE. You really shouldn't listen to stuff like that.

HARPER. Mormons can give blowjobs.

JOE. *Harper.*

HARPER (*Imitating his tone*). *Joe.*

     It was a little Jewish lady with a German accent. This is a good time. For me to make a baby.

   (*Little pause. Joe turns away.*)

HARPER. Then they went on to a program about holes in the ozone layer. Over Antarctica. Skin burns, birds go blind, icebergs melt. The world's coming to an end.

SCENE 6

First week of November. In the men's room of the offices of the Brooklyn Federal Court of Appeals; Louis is crying over the sink; Joe enters.

JOE. Oh, um. . . . Morning.

LOUIS. Good morning, counselor.

JOE (*He watches Louis cry*). Sorry, I. . . . I don't know your name.

LOUIS. Don't bother. Word processor. The lowest of the low.

JOE (*Holding out hand*). Joe Pitt. I'm with Justice Wilson . . .

LOUIS. Oh, I know that. Counselor Pitt. Chief Clerk.

JOE. Were you . . . are you OK?

LOUIS. Oh, yeah. Thanks. What a nice man.

JOE. Not so nice.

LOUIS. What?

JOE. Not so nice. Nothing. You sure you're . . .

LOUIS. Life sucks shit. Life . . . just sucks shit.

JOE. What's wrong?

LOUIS. Run in my nylons.

JOE. Sorry . . . ?

LOUIS. Forget it. Look, thanks for asking.

JOE. Well . . .

LOUIS. I mean it really is nice of you.

   (*He starts crying again*)

   Sorry, sorry, sick friend . . .

JOE. Oh, I'm sorry.

LOUIS. Yeah, yeah, well, that's sweet.

     Three of your colleagues have preceded you to this baleful sight and you're the first one to ask. The others

just opened the door, saw me, and fled. I hope they had to pee real bad.

JOE (*Handing him a wad of toilet paper*). They just didn't want to intrude.

LOUIS. Hah. Reaganite heartless macho asshole lawyers.

JOE. Oh, that's unfair.

LOUIS. What is? Heartless? Macho? Reaganite? Lawyer?

JOE. I voted for Reagan.

LOUIS. You did?

JOE. Twice.

LOUIS. Twice? Well, oh boy. A Gay Republican.

JOE. Excuse me?

LOUIS. Nothing.

JOE. I'm not . . .

     Forget it.

LOUIS. Republican? Not Republican? Or . . .

JOE. What?

JOE. Not gay. I'm not gay.

LOUIS. Oh, Sorry.

   (*Blows his nose loudly*) It's just . . .

JOE. Yes?

LOUIS. Well, sometimes you can tell from the way a person sounds that . . . I mean you *sound* like a . . .

JOE. No I don't. Like what?

LOUIS. Like a Republican.

   (*Little pause. Joe knows he's being teased; Louis knows he knows. Joe decides to be a little brave.*)

JOE (*Making sure no one else is around*). Do I? Sound like a . . . ?

LOUIS. What? Like a . . . ? Republican, or . . . ? Do I?

JOE. Do you what?

LOUIS. Sound like a . . . ?

JOE. Like a . . . ?

     I'm . . . confused.

LOUIS. Yes.

     My name is Louis. But all my friends call me Louise. I work in Word Processing. Thanks for the toilet paper.

   (*Louis offers Joe his hand, Joe reaches. Louis feints and pecks Joe on the cheek, then exits.*)

SCENE 7

A week later. Mutual dream scene. Prior is at a fantastic makeup table, having a dream, applying the face. Harper is having a pill-induced hallucination. She has these from time to time. For some reason, Prior has appeared in this one. Or Harper has appeared in Prior's dream. It is bewildering.

PRIOR (*Alone, putting on makeup, then examining the results in the mirror; to the audience*): "I'm ready for my closeup, Mr. DeMille."

     One wants to move through life with elegance and grace, blossoming infrequently but with exquisite taste,

and perfect timing, like a rare bloom, a zebra orchid. . . .
One wants. . . . But one so seldom gets what one wants,
does one? No. One does not. One gets fucked. Over. One
. . . dies at thirty, robbed of . . . decades of majesty.
Fuck this shit. Fuck this shit.

(*He almost crumbles; he pulls himself together; he studies
his handiwork in the mirror*)

I look like a corpse. A corpsette. Oh my queen; you
know you've hit rock-bottom when even drag is a drag.

(*Harper appears*)

HARPER. Are you. . . . Who are you?

PRIOR. Who are you?

HARPER. What are you doing in my hallucination?

PRIOR. I'm not in your hallucination. You're in my dream.

HARPER. You're wearing makeup.

PRIOR. So are you.

HARPER. But you're a man.

PRIOR (*Feigning dismay, shock, he mimes slashing his throat
with his lipstick and dies, fabulously tragic. Then*). The
hands and feet give it away.

HARPER. There must be some mistake here. I don't recognize you. You're not. . . . Are you my . . . some sort of
imaginary friend?

PRIOR. No. Aren't you too old to have imaginary friends?

HARPER. I have emotional problems. I took too many pills.
Why are you wearing makeup?

PRIOR. I was in the process of applying the face, trying to
make myself feel better—I swiped the new fall colors at
the Clinique counter at Macy's. (*Showing her*)

HARPER. You stole these?

PRIOR. I was out of cash; it was an emotional emergency!

HARPER. Joe will be so angry. I promised him. No more pills.

PRIOR. These pills you keep alluding to?

HARPER. Valium. I take Valium. Lots of Valium.

PRIOR. And you're dancing as fast as you can.

HARPER. I'm not *addicted*. I don't believe in addiction, and I
never . . . well, I *never* drink. And I never take drugs.

PRIOR. Well, smell *you*, Nancy Drew.

HARPER. Except Valium.

PRIOR. Except Valium; in wee fistfuls.

HARPER. It's terrible. Mormons are not supposed to be addicted to anything. I'm a Mormon.

PRIOR. I'm a homosexual.

HARPER. Oh! In my church we don't believe in homosexuals.

PRIOR. In my church we don't believe in Mormons.

HARPER. What church do . . . oh! (*She laughs*) I get it.

I don't understand this. If I didn't ever see you before
and I don't think I did then I don't think you should be
here, in this hallucination, because in my experience the
mind, which is where hallucinations come from, shouldn't
be able to make up anything that wasn't there to start
with, that didn't enter it from experience, from the real

world. Imagination can't create anything new, can it? It
only recycles bits and pieces from the world and reassem-
bles them into visions. . . . Am I making sense right now?

PRIOR. Given the circumstances, yes.

HARPER. So when we think we've escaped the unbearable
ordinariness and, well, untruthfulness of our lives, it's really only the same old ordinariness and falseness re-
arranged into the appearance of novelty and truth. Nothing unknown is knowable. Don't you think it's depressing?

PRIOR. The limitations of the imagination?

HARPER. Yes.

PRIOR. It's something you learn after your second theme
party: It's All Been Done Before.

HARPER. The world. Finite. Terribly, terribly. . . . Well . . .
This is the most depressing hallucination I've ever had.

PRIOR. Apologies. I do try to be amusing.

HARPER. Oh, well, don't apologize, you. . . . I can't expect
someone who's really sick to entertain me.

PRIOR. How on earth did you know . . .

HARPER. Oh that happens. This is the very threshold of revelation sometimes. You can see things . . . how sick you
are. Do you see anything about me?

PRIOR. Yes.

HARPER. What?

PRIOR. You are amazingly unhappy.

HARPER. Oh big deal. You meet a Valium addict and you figure out she's unhappy. That doesn't count. Of course I. . . .
Something else. Something surprising.

PRIOR. Something surprising.

HARPER. Yes.

PRIOR. Your husband's a homo.

(*Pause.*)

HARPER. Oh, ridiculous.

(*Pause, then very quietly*)

Really?

PRIOR (*Shrugs*). Threshold of revelation.

HARPER. Well I don't like your revelations. I don't think you
intuit well at all. Joe's a very normal man, he . . .

Oh God. Oh God. He. . . . Do homos take, like, lots of
long walks?

PRIOR. Yes. We do. In stretch pants with lavender coifs. I
just looked at you, and there was . . .

HARPER. A sort of blue streak of recognition.

PRIOR. Yes.

HARPER. Like you knew me incredibly well.

PRIOR. Yes.

HARPER. Yes.

I have to go now, get back, something just . . . fell
apart.

Oh God, I feel so sad . . .

PRIOR. I . . . I'm sorry. I usually say, "Fuck the truth," but
mostly, the truth fucks you.

HARPER. I see something else about you . . .

PRIOR. Oh?

HARPER. Deep inside you, there's a part of you, the most inner part, entirely free of disease. I can see that.

PRIOR. Is that. . . . That isn't true.

HARPER. Threshold of revelation.

Home . . .

(She vanishes.)

PRIOR. People come and go so quickly here . . .

(To himself in the mirror) I don't think there's any uninfected part of me. My heart is pumping polluted blood. I feel dirty.

(He begins to wipe makeup off with his hands, smearing it around. A large gray feather falls from up above. Prior stops smearing the makeup and looks at the feather. He goes to it and picks it up.)

A VOICE *(It is an incredibly beautiful voice)*. Look up!

PRIOR *(Looking up, not seeing anyone)*. Hello?

A VOICE. Look up!

PRIOR. Who is that?

A VOICE. Prepare the way!

PRIOR. I don't see any . . .

(There is a dramatic change in lighting, from above.)

A VOICE.

Look up, look up,
prepare the way
the infinite descent
A breath in air
floating down
Glory to . . .

(Silence.)

PRIOR. Hello? Is that it? Helloooo!

What the fuck . . . ? *(He holds himself)*

Poor me. Poor poor me. Why me? Why poor poor me? Oh I don't feel good right now. I don't.

SCENE 8

That night. Split scene: Harper and Joe at home; Prior and Louis in bed.

HARPER. Where were you?

JOE. Out.

HARPER. Where?

JOE. Just out. Thinking.

HARPER. It's late.

JOE. I had a lot to think about.

HARPER. I burned dinner.

JOE. Sorry.

HARPER. Not my dinner. My dinner was fine. Your dinner. I put it back in the oven and turned everything up as high as it could go and I watched till it burned black. It's still hot. Very hot. Want it?

JOE. You didn't have to do that.

HARPER. I know. It just seemed like the kind of thing a mentally deranged sex-starved pill-popping housewife would do.

JOE. Uh huh.

HARPER. So I did it. Who knows anymore what I have to do?

JOE. How many pills?

HARPER. A bunch. Don't change the subject.

JOE. I won't talk to you when you . . .

HARPER. No. No. Don't do that! I'm . . . I'm fine, pills are not the problem, not our problem, I WANT TO KNOW WHERE YOU'VE BEEN! I WANT TO KNOW WHAT'S GOING ON!

JOE. Going on with what? The job?

HARPER. Not the job.

JOE. I said I need more time.

HARPER. Not the job!

JOE. Mr. Cohn, I talked to him on the phone, he said I had to hurry . . .

HARPER. Not the . . .

JOE. But I can't get you to talk sensibly about anything so . . .

HARPER. SHUT UP!

JOE. Then what?

HARPER. Stick to the subject.

JOE. I don't know what that is. You have something you want to ask me? Ask me. Go.

HARPER. I . . . can't. I'm scared of you.

JOE. I'm tired, I'm going to bed.

HARPER. Tell me without making me ask. Please.

JOE. This is crazy, I'm not . . .

HARPER. When you come through the door at night your face is never exactly the way I remembered it. I get surprised by something . . . mean and hard about the way you look. Even the weight of you in the bed at night, the way you breathe in your sleep seems unfamiliar.

You terrify me.

JOE *(Cold)*. I know who you are.

HARPER. Yes. I'm the enemy. That's easy. That doesn't change.

You think you're the only one who hates sex; I do; I hate it with you; I do. I dream that you batter away at me till all my joints come apart, like wax, and I fall into pieces. It's like a punishment. It was wrong of me to marry you. I knew you . . . *(She stops herself)* It's a sin, and it's killing us both.

JOE. I can always tell when you've taken pills, because it makes you red-faced and sweaty and frankly that's very often why I don't want to . . .

HARPER. Because . . .

JOE. Well, you aren't pretty. Not like this.

HARPER. I have something to ask you.

JOE. Then ASK! ASK! What in hell are you . . .

HARPER. Are you a homo?

(Pause)

Are you? If you try to walk out right now I'll put your dinner back in the oven and turn it up so high the whole building will fill with smoke and everyone in it will asphyxiate. So help me God I will.

Now answer the question.

JOE. What if I . . .

(Small pause.)

HARPER. Then tell me, please. And we'll see.

JOE. No, I'm not.

I don't see what difference it makes.

LOUIS. Jews don't have any clear textual guide to the afterlife; even that it exists. I don't think much about it. I see it as a perpetual rainy Thursday afternoon in March. Dead leaves.

PRIOR. Enough. Very Greco-Roman.

LOUIS. Well for us it's not the verdict that counts, it's the act of judgment. That's why I could never be a lawyer. In court all that matters is the verdict.

PRIOR. Your could never be a lawyer because you are oversexed. You're too distracted.

LOUIS. Not distracted: *abstracted*. I'm trying to make a point:

PRIOR. Namely:

LOUIS. It's the judge in his or her chambers, weighing, books open, pondering the evidence, ranging freely over categories: good, evil, innocent, guilty; the judge in the chamber of circumspection, not the judge on the bench with the gavel. The shaping of the law, not its execution.

PRIOR. The point, dear, the point . . .

LOUIS. That it should be the questions and shape of a life, its total complexity gathered, arranged and considered, which matters in the end, not some stamp of salvation or damnation which disperses all the complexity in some unsatisfying decision—balancing of the scales . . .

PRIOR. I like this; very zen; it's . . . reassuringly incomprehensible and useless. We who are about to die thank you.

LOUIS. You are not about to die.

PRIOR. It's not going well, really . . . two new lesions. My leg hurts. There's protein in my urine, the doctor says, but who knows what the fuck that portends. Anyway it shouldn't be there, the protein. My butt is chapped from diarrhea and yesterday I shat blood.

LOUIS. I really hate this. You don't tell me . . .

PRIOR. You get too upset, I wind up comforting you. It's easier . . .

LOUIS. Oh thanks.

PRIOR. If it's bad I'll tell you.

LOUIS. Shitting blood sounds bad to me.

PRIOR. And I'm telling you.

LOUIS. And I'm handling it.

PRIOR. Tell me some more about justice.

LOUIS. I *am* handling it.

PRIOR. Well Louis you win Trooper of the Month.

(Louis starts to cry.)

PRIOR. I take it back. You aren't Trooper of the Month. This isn't working . . .

Tell me some more about justice.

LOUIS. You are not about to die.

PRIOR. Justice . . .

LOUIS. . . . is an immensity, a confusing vastness. Justice is God.

Prior?

PRIOR. Hmmm?

LOUIS. You love me.

PRIOR. Yes.

LOUIS. What if I walked out on this?

Would you hate me forever?

(Prior kisses Louis on the forehead.)

PRIOR. Yes.

JOE. I think we ought to pray. Ask God for help. Ask him together . . .

HARPER. God won't talk to me. I have to make up people to talk to me.

JOE. You have to keep asking.

HARPER. I forgot the question.

Oh yeah, God, is my husband a . . .

JOE *(Scary)*. Stop it, Stop it. I'm warning you.

Does it make any difference? That I might be one thing deep within, no matter how wrong or ugly that thing is, so long as I have fought, with everything I have, to kill it. What do you want from me? What do you want from me, Harper? More than that? For God's sake, there's nothing left, I'm a shell. There's nothing left to kill.

As long as my behavior is what I know it has to be. Decent. Correct. That alone in the eyes of God.

HARPER. No, no, not that, that's Utah talk, Mormon talk, I hate it, Joe tell me, say it . . .

JOE. All I will say is that I am a very good man who has worked very hard to become good and you want to destroy that. You want to destroy me, but I am not going to let you do that.

(Pause.)

HARPER. I'm going to have a baby.

JOE. Liar.

HARPER You liar.

A baby born addicted to pills. A baby who does not dream but who hallucinates, who stares up at us with big mirror eyes and who does not know who we are.

(Pause.)

JOE. Are you really . . .

HARPER. No. Yes. No. Yes. Get away from me.

Now we both have a secret.

PRIOR. One of my ancestors was a ship's captain who made money bringing whale oil to Europe and returning with immigrants—Irish mostly, packed in tight, so many dollars per head. The last ship he captained foundered off the coast of Nova Scotia in a winter tempest and sank to the bottom. He went down with the ship—la Grande Geste—but his crew took seventy women and kids in the ship's only longboat, this big, open rowboat, and when the weather got too rough, and they thought the boat was overcrowded, the crew started lifting people up and hurling them into the sea. Until they got the ballast right. They walked up and down the longboat, eyes to the waterline, and when the boat rode low in the water they'd grab the nearest passenger and throw them into the sea. The boat was leaky, see; seventy people; they arrived in Halifax with nine people on board.

LOUIS. Jesus.

PRIOR. I think about that story a lot now. People in a boat, waiting, terrified, while implacable, unsmiling men, irresistibly strong, seize . . . maybe the person next to you, maybe you, and with no warning at all, with time only for a quick intake of air you are pitched into freezing, turbulent water and salt and darkness to drown.

I like your cosmology, baby. While time is running out I find myself drawn to anything that's suspended, that lacks an ending—but it seems to me that it lets you off scot-free.

LOUIS. What do you mean?

PRIOR. No judgment, no guilt or responsibility.

LOUIS. For me.

PRIOR. For anyone. It was an editorial "you."

LOUIS. Please get better. Please.

Please don't get any sicker.

SCENE 9

Third week in November, Roy and Henry, his doctor, in Henry's office.

HENRY. Nobody knows what causes it. And nobody knows how to cure it. The best theory is that we blame a retrovirus, the Human Immunodeficiency Virus. Its presence is made known to us by the useless antibodies which appear in reaction to its entrance into the bloodstream through a cut, or an orifice. The antibodies are powerless to protect the body against it. Why, we don't know. The body's immune system ceases to function. Sometimes the body even attacks itself. At any rate it's left open to a whole horror house of infections from microbes which it usually defends against.

Like Kaposi's sarcomas. These lesions. Or your throat problem. Or the glands.

We think it may also be able to slip past the blood-brain barrier into the brain. Which is of course very bad news.

And it's fatal in we don't know what percent of people with suppressed immune responses.

(Pause.)

ROY. This is very interesting, Mr. Wizard, but why the fuck are you telling me this?

(Pause.)

HENRY. Well, I have just removed one of three lesions which biopsy results will probably tell us is a Kaposi's sarcoma lesion. And you have a pronounced swelling of glands in your neck, groin, and armpits—lymphadenopathy is another sign. And you have oral candidiasis and maybe a little more fungus under the fingernails of two digits on your right hand. So that's why . . .

ROY. This disease . . .

HENRY. Syndrome.

ROY. Whatever. It afflicts mostly homosexuals and drug addicts.

HENRY. Mostly. Hemophiliacs are also at risk.

ROY. Homosexuals and drug addicts. So why are you implying that I . . .

(Pause)

What are you implying, Henry?

HENRY. I don't . . .

ROY. I'm not a drug addict.

HENRY. On come on Roy.

ROY. What, what, come on Roy what? Do you think I'm a junkie, Henry, do you see tracks?

HENRY. This is absurd.

ROY. Say it.

HENRY. Say what?

ROY. Say, "Roy Cohn, you are a . . ."

HENRY. Roy.

ROY. "You are a. . . ." Go on. Not "Roy Cohn you are a drug fiend." "Roy Marcus Cohn, you are a . . ."

Go on, Henry, it starts with an "H."

HENRY. Oh I'm not going to . . .

ROY. *With an "H,"* Henry, and it isn't "Hemophiliac." Come on . . .

HENRY. What are you doing, Roy?

ROY. No, say it. I mean it. Say: "Roy Cohn, you are a homosexual."

(Pause)

And I will proceed, systematically, to destroy your reputation and your practice and your career in New York State, Henry. Which you know I can do.

(Pause.)

HENRY. Roy, you have been seeing me since 1958. Apart from the facelifts I have treated you for everything from syphilis . . .

ROY. From a whore in Dallas.

HENRY. From syphilis to venereal warts. In your rectum. Which you may have gotten from a whore in Dallas, but it wasn't a female whore.

(Pause.)

ROY. So say it.

HENRY. Roy Cohn, you are . . .

You have had sex with men, many many times, Roy, and one of them, or any number of them, has made you very sick. You have AIDS.

ROY. AIDS.

Your problem, Henry, is that you are hung up on words, on labels, that you believe they mean what they seem to mean. AIDS. Homosexual. Gay. Lesbian. You think these are names that tell you who someone sleeps with, but they don't tell you that.

HENRY. No?

ROY. No. Like all labels, they tell you one thing and one thing only: where does an individual so identified fit in the food chain, in the pecking order? Not ideology, or sexual taste, but something much simpler: clout. Not who I fuck or who fucks me, but who will pick up the phone when I call, who owes me favors. This is what a label refers to. Now to someone who does not understand this, homosexual is what I am because I have sex with men. But really this is wrong. Homosexuals are not men who sleep with other men. Homosexuals are men who in fifteen years of trying cannot get a pissant antidiscrimination bill through City Council. Homosexuals are men who know nobody and who nobody knows. Who have zero clout. Does this sound like me, Henry?

HENRY. No.

ROY. No. I have clout. A lot. I can pick up this phone, punch fifteen numbers, and you know who will be on the other end in under five minutes, Henry?

HENRY. The President.

ROY. Even better, Henry, His wife.

HENRY. I'm impressed.

ROY. I don't want you to be impressed. I want you to understand. This is not sophistry. And this is not hypocrisy. This is reality. I have sex with men. But unlike nearly every other man of whom this is true, I bring the guy I'm screwing to the White House and President Reagan smiles at us and shakes his hand. Because *what* I am is defined entirely by *who* I am. Roy Cohn is not a homosexual. Roy Cohn is a heterosexual man, Henry, who fucks around with guys.

HENRY. OK, Roy.

ROY. And what is my diagnosis, Henry?

HENRY. You have AIDS, Roy.

ROY. No, Henry, no. AIDS is what homosexuals have. I have liver cancer.

(Pause.)

HENRY. Well, whatever the fuck you have, Roy, it's very serious, and I haven't got a damn thing for you. The NIH in Bethesda has a new drug called AZT with a two-year waiting list that not even I can get you onto. So get on the phone, Roy, and dial the fifteen numbers, and tell the First Lady you need in on an experimental treatment for liver cancer, because you can call it any damn thing you want, Roy, but what it boils down to is very bad news.

ACT TWO: IN VITRO

December 1985–January 1986

SCENE 1

Night, the third week in December. Prior alone on the floor of his bedroom; he is much worse.

PRIOR. Louis, Louis, please wake up, oh God.

(Louis runs in.)

PRIOR. I think something horrible is wrong with me I can't breathe . . .

LOUIS *(Starting to exit)*. I'm calling the ambulance.

PRIOR. No, wait, I . . .

LOUIS. *Wait?* Are you fucking crazy? Oh God you're on fire, your head is on fire.

PRIOR. It hurts, it hurts . . .

LOUIS. I'm calling the ambulance.

PRIOR. I don't want to go to the hospital, I don't want to go to the hospital please let me lie here, just . . .

LOUIS. No, no, God, Prior, stand up . . .

PRIOR. DON'T TOUCH MY LEG!

LOUIS. We have to . . . oh God this is so crazy.

PRIOR. I'll be OK if I just lie here Lou, really, if I can only sleep a little . . .

(Louis exits.)

PRIOR. Louis?

No! No! Don't call, you'll send me there and I won't come back, please, please Louis I'm begging, baby, please . . .

(Screams) LOUIS!!

LOUIS *(From off; hysterical)*. WILL YOU SHUT THE FUCK UP!

PRIOR *(Trying to stand)*. Aaaah, I have . . . to go to the bathroom. Wait. Wait, just . . . oh. Oh God. *(He shits himself.)*

LOUIS *(Entering)*. Prior? They'll be here in . . .

Oh my God.

PRIOR. I'm sorry, I'm sorry.

LOUIS. What did . . . ? What?

PRIOR. I had an accident?

(Louis goes to him.)

LOUIS. This is blood.

PRIOR. Maybe you shouldn't touch it . . . me. . . . I . . . (He faints)

LOUIS (Quietly). Oh help. Oh help. Oh God oh God oh God help me I can't I can't I can't.

SCENE 2

Same night. Harper is sitting at home, all alone, with no lights on. We can barely see her. Joe enters, but he doesn't turn on the lights.

JOE. Why are you sitting in the dark? Turn on the light.

HARPER. No. I heard the sounds in the bedroom again. I know someone was in there.

JOE. No one was.

HARPER. Maybe actually in the bed, under the covers with a knife.

Oh, boy. Joe. I, um, I'm thinking of going away. By which I mean: I think I'm going off again. You . . . you know what I mean?

JOE. Please don't. Stay. We can fix it. I pray for that. This is my fault, but I can correct it. You have to try too . . .

(He turns on the light. She turns it off again.)

HARPER. When you pray, what do you pray for?

JOE. I pray for God to crush me, break me up into little pieces and start all over again.

HARPER. Oh. Please. Don't pray for that.

JOE. I had a book of Bible stories when I was a kid. There was a picture I'd look at twenty times every day: Jacob wrestles with the angel. I don't really remember the story, or why the wrestling—just the picture. Jacob is young and very strong. The angel is . . . a beautiful man, with golden hair and wings, of course. I still dream about it. Many nights, I'm . . . It's me. In that struggle. Fierce, and unfair. The angel is not human, and it holds nothing back, so how could anyone human win, what kind of a fight is that? It's not just. Losing means your soul thrown down in the dust, your heart torn out from God's. But you can't not lose.

HARPER. In the whole entire world, you are the only person, the only person I love or have ever loved. And I love you terribly. Terribly. That's what's so awfully, irreducibly real. I can make up anything but I can't dream that away.

JOE. Are you . . . are you really going to have a baby?

HARPER. It's my time, and there's no blood. I don't really know. I suppose it wouldn't be a great thing. Maybe I'm just not bleeding because I take too many pills. Maybe I'll give birth to a pill. That would give a new meaning to pill-popping, huh?

I think you should go to Washington. Alone. Change, like you said.

JOE. I'm not going to leave you, Harper.

HARPER. Well maybe not. But I'm going to leave you.

SCENE 3

One AM, the next morning. Louis and a nurse, Emily, are sitting in Prior's room in the hospital.

EMILY. He'll be all right now.

LOUIS. No he won't.

EMILY. No. I guess not. I gave him something that makes him sleep.

LOUIS. Deep asleep?

EMILY. Orbiting the moons of Jupiter.

LOUIS. A good place to be.

EMILY. Anyplace better than here. You his . . . uh?

LOUIS. Yes, I'm his uh.

EMILY. This must be hell for you.

LOUIS. It is. Hell. The After Life. Which is not at all like a rainy afternoon in March, by the way, Prior. A lot more vivid than I'd expected. Dead leaves, but the crunchy kind. Sharp, dry air. The kind of long, luxurious dying feeling that breaks your heart.

EMILY. Yeah, well we all get to break our hearts on this one. He seems like a nice guy. Cute.

LOUIS. Not like this.

Yes, he is. Was. Whatever.

EMILY. Weird name. Prior Walter. Like, "The Walter before this one."

LOUIS. Lots of Walters before this one. Prior is an old old family name in an old old family. The Walters go back to the Mayflower and beyond. Back to the Norman Conquest. He says there's a Prior Walter stitched into the Bayeux tapestry.

EMILY. Is that impressive?

LOUIS. Well, it's old. Very old. Which in some circles equals impressive.

EMILY. Not in my circle. What's the name of the tapestry?

LOUIS. The Bayeux tapestry. Embroidered by La Reine Mathilde.

EMILY. I'll tell my mother. She embroiders. Drives me nuts.

LOUIS. Manual therapy for anxious hands.

EMILY. Maybe you should try it.

LOUIS. Mathilde stitched while William the Conqueror was off to war. She was capable of . . . more than loyalty. Devotion.

She waited for him, she stitched for years. And if he had come back broken and defeated from war, she would have loved him even more. And if he had returned mutilated, ugly, full of infection and horror, she would still have loved him; fed by pity, by a sharing of pain, she would love him even more, and even more, and she would never, never have prayed to God, please let him die if he can't return to me whole and healthy and able to live a normal life . . . If he had died, she would have buried her heart with him.

So what the fuck is the matter with me?

(Little pause)

Will he sleep through the night?

EMILY. At least.

LOUIS. I'm going.

EMILY. It's one AM. Where do you have to go at . . .

LOUIS. I know what time it is. A walk. Night air, good for the. . . . The park.

EMILY. Be careful.

LOUIS. Yeah, Danger.

Tell him, if he wakes up and you're still on, tell him goodbye, tell him I had to go.

SCENE 4

An hour later. Split scene: Joe and Roy in a fancy (straight) bar; Louis and a Man in the Rambles in Central Park, Joe and Ray are sitting at the bar; the place is brightly lit. Joe has a plate for food in front of him but he isn't eating. Roy occasionally reaches over the table and forks small bites off Joe's plate. Roy is drinking heavily. Joe not at all. Louis and the Man are eyeing each other, each alternating interest and indifference.

JOE. The pills were something she started when she miscarried or . . . no, she took some before that. She had a really bad time at home, when she was a kid, her home was really bad. I think a lot of drinking and physical stuff. She doesn't talk about that, instead she talks about . . . the sky falling down, people with knives hiding under sofas. Monsters. Mormons. Everyone thinks Mormons don't come from homes like that, we aren't supposed to behave that way, but we do. It's not lying, or being two-faced. Everyone tries very hard to live up to God's strictures, which are very . . . um . . .

ROY. Strict.

JOE. I shouldn't be bothering you with this.

ROY. No, please. Heart to heart. Want another. . . . What is that, seltzer?

JOE. The failure to measure up hits people hard. From such a strong desire to be good they feel very far from goodness when they fail.

What scares me is that maybe what I really love in her is the part of her that's farthest from the light, from God's love; maybe I was drawn to that in the first place. And I'm keeping it alive because I need it.

ROY. Why would you need it?

JOE. There are things. . . . I don't know how well we know ourselves. I mean, what if? I know I married her because she . . . because I love it that she was always wrong, always doing something wrong, like one step out of step. In Salt Lake City that stands out. I never stood out, on the outside, but inside, it was hard for me. To pass.

ROY. Pass?

JOE. Yeah.

ROY. Pass as what?

JOE. Oh, Well. . . . As someone cheerful and strong. Those who love God with an open heart unclouded by secrets and struggles are cheerful; God's easy simple love for them shows in how strong and happy they are. The saints.

ROY. But you had secrets? Secret struggles . . .

JOE. I wanted to be one of the elect, one of the Blessed. You feel you ought to be, that the blemishes are yours by choice, which of course they aren't. Harper's sorrow, that really deep sorrow, she didn't choose that. But it's there.

ROY. You didn't put it there.

JOE. No.

ROY. You sound like you think you did.

JOE. I am responsible for her.

ROY. Because she's your wife.

JOE. That. And I do love her.

ROY. Whatever. She's your wife. And so there are obligations. To her. But also to yourself.

JOE. She'd fall apart in Washington.

ROY. Then let her stay here.

JOE. She'll fall apart if I leave her.

ROY. Then bring her to Washington.

JOE. I just can't, Roy. She needs me.

ROY. Listen, Joe. I'm the best divorce lawyer in the business.

(Little pause.)

JOE. Can't Washington wait?

ROY. You do what you need to do, Joe. What *you* need. *You.* Let her life go where it wants to go. You'll be better for that. *Somebody* should get what they want.

MAN. What do you want?

LOUIS. I want you to fuck me, hurt me, make me bleed.

MAN. I want to.

LOUIS. Yeah?

MAN. I want to hurt you.

LOUIS. Fuck me.

MAN. Yeah?

LOUIS. Hard.

MAN. Yeah? You been a bad boy?

(Pause. Louis laughs, softly.)

LOUIS. Very bad. Very bad.

MAN. You need to be punished, boy?

LOUIS. Yes. I do.

MAN. Yes what?

(Little pause.)

LOUIS. Um, I . . .

MAN. Yes *what*, boy?

LOUIS. Oh. Yes sir.

MAN. I want you to take me to your place, boy.

LOUIS. No, I can't do that.

MAN. No *what*?

LOUIS. No sir, I can't, I . . .

I don't live alone, sir.

MAN. Your lover know you're out with a man tonight, boy?

LOUIS. No sir, he . . .

My lover doesn't know.

MAN. Your lover know you . . .

LOUIS. Let's change the subject, OK? Can we go to your place?

MAN. I live with my parents.

LOUIS. Oh.

ROY. Everyone who makes it in this world makes it because somebody older and more powerful takes an interest. The most precious asset in life, I think is the ability to be a good son. You have that, Joe. Somebody who can be a good son to a father who pushes them farther than they would otherwise go. I've had many fathers, I owe my life to them, powerful, powerful men. Walter Winchell, Edgar Hoover. Joe McCarthy most of all. He valued me because I am a good lawyer, but he loved me because I was and am a good son. He was a very difficult man, very guarded and cagey; I brought out something tender in him. He would have died for me. And me for him. Does this embarrass you?

JOE. I had a hard time with my father.

ROY. Well sometimes that's the way. Then you have to find other fathers, substitutes, I don't know. The father-son relationship is central to life. Women are for birth, beginning, but the father is continuance. The son offers the father his life as a vessel for carrying forth his father's dream. Your father's living?

JOE. Um, dead.

ROY. He was . . . what? A difficult man?

JOE. He was in the military. He could be very unfair. And cold.

ROY. But he loved you.

JOE. I don't know.

ROY. No, no, Joe, he did, I know this. Sometimes a father's love has to be very, very hard, unfair even, cold to make his son grow strong in a world like this. This isn't a good world.

MAN. Here, then.

LOUIS. I. . . . Do you have a rubber?

MAN. I don't use rubbers.

LOUIS. You should. (*He takes one from his coat pocket*) Here.

MAN. I don't use them.

LOUIS. Forget it, then. (*He starts to leave*)

MAN. No, wait.
    Put it on me. Boy.

LOUIS. Forget it, I have to get back. Home. I must be going crazy.

MAN. Oh come on please he won't find out.

LOUIS. It's cold. Too cold.

MAN. It's never too cold, let me warm you up. Please?

(*They begin to fuck.*)

MAN. Relax.

LOUIS (*A small laugh*). Not a chance.

MAN. It . . .

LOUIS. What?

MAN. I think it broke. The rubber. You want me to keep going? (*Little pause*) Pull out? Should I . . .

LOUIS. Keep going.
    Infect me.
    I don't care. I don't care.

(*Pause. The Man pulls out.*)

MAN. I . . . um, look, I'm sorry, but I think I want to go.

LOUIS. Yeah.
    Give my best to mom and dad.

(*The Man slaps him.*)

LOUIS. Ow!

(*They stare at each other.*)

LOUIS. It was a joke.

(*The Man leaves.*)

ROY. How long have we known each other?

JOE. Since 1980.

ROY. Right. A long time. I feel close to you, Joe. Do I advise you well?

JOE. You've been an incredible friend, Roy, I . . .

ROY. I want to be family. Familia, as my Italian friends call it. La Familia. A lovely word. It's important for me to help you, like I was helped.

JOE. I owe practically everything to you, Roy.

ROY. I'm dying, Joe. Cancer.

JOE. Oh my God.

ROY. Please. Let me finish.
    Few people know this and I'm telling you this only because. . . . I'm not afraid of death. What can death bring that I haven't faced? I've lived; life is the worst. (*Gently mocking himself*) Listen to me, I'm a philosopher.

JOE. You must do this. You must must must. Love; that's a trap. Responsibility; that's a trap too. Like a father to a son I tell you this: Life is full of horror; nobody escapes, nobody; save yourself. Whatever pulls on you, whatever needs from you, threatens you. Don't be afraid; people are so afraid; don't be afraid to live in the raw wind, naked, alone. . . . Learn at least this: What you are capable of. Let nothing stand in your way.

SCENE 5

Three days later. Prior and Belize in Prior's hospital room. Prior is very sick but improving. Belize has just arrived.

PRIOR. Miss Thing.

BELIZE. Ma cherie bichete.

PRIOR. Stella.

BELIZE. Stella for star. Let me see. (*Scrutinizing Prior*) You look like shit, why yes indeed you do, comme la merde!

PRIOR. Merci.

BELIZE (*Taking little plastic bottles from his bag, handing them to Prior*). Not to despair, Belle Reeve. Lookie! Magic goop!

PRIOR (*Opening a bottle, sniffing*). Pooh! What kinda crap is that?

BELIZE. Beats me. Let's rub it on your poor blistered body and see what it does.

PRIOR. This is not Western medicine, these bottles . . .

BELIZE. Voodoo cream. From the botanica 'round the block.

PRIOR. And you a registered nurse.

BELIZE (*Sniffing it*). Beeswax and cheap perfume. Cut with Jergen's Lotion. Full of good vibes and love from some little black Cubana witch in Miami.

PRIOR. Get that trash away from me, I am immune-suppressed.

BELIZE. I *am* a health professional. I *know* what I'm doing.

PRIOR. It stinks. Any word from Louis?

(*Pause. Belize starts giving Prior a gentle massage.*)

PRIOR. Gone.

BELIZE. He'll be back. I know the type. Likes to keep a girl on edge.

PRIOR. It's been . . .

(*Pause.*)

BELIZE (*Trying to jog his memory*). How long?

PRIOR. I don't remember.

BELIZE. How long have you been here?

PRIOR (*Getting suddenly upset*). I don't remember, I don't give a fuck. I want Louis. I want my fucking boyfriend, where the fuck is he? I'm dying, I'm dying, where's Louis?

BELIZE. Shhhh, shhh . . .

PRIOR. This is a very strange drug, this drug. Emotional liability, for starters.

BELIZE. Save a tab or two for me.

PRIOR. Oh no, not this drug, ce n'est pas pour la joyeux noël et la bonne année, this drug she is serious poisonous chemistry, ma pauvre bichette.

And not just disorienting. I hear things. Voices.

BELIZE. Voices.

PRIOR. A voice.

BELIZE. Saying what?

(*Pause.*)

PRIOR. I'm not supposed to tell.

BELIZE. You better tell the doctor. Or I will.

PRIOR. No no don't. Please. I want the voice; it's wonderful. It's all that's keeping me alive. I don't want to talk to some intern about it.

You know what happens? When I hear it, I get hard.

BELIZE. Oh my.

PRIOR. Comme ça. (*He uses his arm to demonstrate*) And you know I am slow to rise.

BELIZE. My jaw aches at the memory.

PRIOR. And would you deny me this little solace—betray my concupiscence to Florence Nightingale's storm troopers?

BELIZE. Perish the thought, ma bébé.

PRIOR. They'd change the drug just to spoil the fun.

BELIZE. You and your boner can depend on me.

PRIOR. Je t'adore, ma belle nègre.

BELIZE. All this girl-talk shit is politically incorrect, you know. We should have dropped it back when we gave up drag.

PRIOR. I'm sick, I get to be politically incorrect if it makes me feel better. You sound like Lou.

(*Little pause*)

Well, at least I have the satisfaction of knowing he's in anguish somewhere. I loved his anguish. Watching him stick his head up his asshole and eat his guts out over some relatively minor moral conundrum—it was the best show in town. But Mother warned me: if they get overwhelmed by the little things . . .

BELIZE. They'll be belly-up bustville when something big comes along.

PRIOR. Mother warned me.

BELIZE. And they do come along.

PRIOR. But I didn't listen.

BELIZE. No. (*Doing Hepburn*) Men are beasts.

PRIOR (*Also Hepburn*). The absolute lowest.

BELIZE. I have to go. If I want to spend my whole lonely life looking after white people I can get underpaid to do it.

PRIOR. You're just a Christian martyr.

BELIZE. Whatever happens, baby, I will be here for you.

PRIOR. Je t'aime.

BELIZE. Je t'aime. Don't go crazy on me, girlfriend, I already got enough crazy queens for one lifetime. For two. I can't be bothering with dementia.

PRIOR. I promise.

BELIZE (*Touching him; softly*). Ouch.

PRIOR. Ouch. Indeed.

BELIZE. Why'd they have to pick on you?

And eat more, girlfriend, you really do look like shit.

(*Belize leaves.*)

PRIOR (*After waiting a beat*). He's gone.

Are you still . . .

VOICE. I can't stay. I will return.

PRIOR. Are you one of those "Follow me to the other side" voices?

VOICE. No. I am no nightbird. I am a messenger . . .

PRIOR. You have a beautiful voice, it sounds . . . like a viola, like a perfectly tuned, tight string, balanced, the truth. . . . Stay with me.

VOICE. Not now. Soon I will return, I will reveal myself to you; I am glorious, glorious; my heart, my countenance and my message. You must prepare.

PRIOR. For what? I don't want to . . .

VOICE. No death, no:

A marvelous work and a wonder we undertake, an edifice awry we sink plumb and straighten, a great Lie we abolish, a great error correct, with the rule, sword and broom of Truth!

PRIOR. What are you talking about, I . . .

VOICE.

    I am on my way; when I am manifest, our Work begins:
    Prepare for the parting of the air,
    The breath, the ascent,
    Glory to . . .

SCENE 6

The second week of January. Martin, Roy and Joe in a fancy Manhattan restaurant.

MARTIN. It's a revolution in Washington, Joe. We have a new agenda and finally a real leader. They got back the Senate but we have the courts. By the nineties the Supreme Court will be block-solid Republican appointees, and the Federal bench—Republican judges like land mines, everywhere, everywhere they turn. Affirmative action? Take it to court. Boom! Land mine. And we'll get our way on just about everything: abortion, defense, Central America, family values, a live investment climate. We have the White House locked till the year 2000. And beyond. A permanent fix on the Oval Office? It's possible. By '92 we'll get the Senate back, and in ten years the South is going to give us the House. It's really the end of Liberalism. The end of New Deal Socialism. The end of ipso facto secular humanism. The dawning of a genuinely American political personality. Modeled on Ronald Wilson Reagan.

JOE. It sounds great, Mr. Heller.

MARTIN. Martin. And Justice is the hub. Especially since Ed Meese took over. He doesn't specialize in Fine Points of the Law. He's a flatfoot, a cop. He reminds me of Teddy Roosevelt.

JOE. I can't wait to meet him.

MARTIN. Too bad, Joe, he's been dead for sixty years.

(There is a little awkwardness. Joe doesn't respond.)

MARTIN. Teddy Roosevelt. You said you wanted to. . . . Little joke. It reminds me of the story about the . . .

ROY (*Smiling, but nasty*). Aw shut the fuck up Martin.

    (*To Joe*) You see that? Mr. Heller here is one of the mighty, Joseph, in D.C. he sitteth on the right hand of the man who sitteth on the right of The Man. And yet I can say "shut the fuck up" and he will take no offense. Loyalty. He . . .

    Martin?

MARTIN. Yes, Roy?

ROY. Rub my back.

MARTIN. Roy . . .

ROY. No no really, a sore spot, I get them all the time now, these. . . . Rub it for me darling, would you do that for me?

(Martin rubs Roy's back. They both look at Joe.)

ROY (*To Joe*). How do you think a handful of Bolsheviks turned St. Petersburg into Leningrad in one afternoon?

Comrades. Who do for each other. Marx and Engels. Lenin and Trotsky. Josef Stalin and Franklin Delano Roosevelt.

(Martin laughs.)

ROY. *Comrades*, right, Martin?

MARTIN. This man, Joe, is a Saint of the Right.

JOE. I know, Mr. Heller, I . . .

ROY. And you see what I mean, Martin? He's special, right?

MARTIN. Don't embarrass him, Roy.

ROY. Gravity, decency, smarts! His strength is as the strength of ten because his heart is pure! *And* he's a Roy-boy, one hundred percent.

MARTIN. We're on the move, Joe. On the move.

JOE. Mr. Heller, I . . .

MARTIN (*Ending backrub*). We can't wait any longer for an answer.

(Little pause.)

JOE. Oh. Um, I . . .

ROY. Joe's a married man, Martin.

MARTIN. Aha.

ROY. With a wife. She doesn't care to go to D.C., and so Joe cannot go. And keeps us dangling. We've seen that kind of thing before, haven't we? These men and their wives.

MARTIN. Oh yes. Beware.

JOE. I really can't discuss this under . . .

MARTIN. Then *don't* discuss. Say yes, Joe.

ROY. Now.

MARTIN. Say yes I will.

ROY. Now.

    Now. I'll hold my breath till you do, I'm turning blue waiting. . . . Now, goddammit!

MARTIN. Roy, calm down, it's not . . .

ROY. Aw, fuck it. (*He takes a letter from his jacket pocket, hands it to Joe.*)

    Read. Came today.

(Joe reads the first paragraph, then looks up.)

JOE. Roy. This is . . . Roy, this is terrible.

ROY. You're telling me.

    A letter from the New York State Bar Association, Martin.

    They're gonna try and disbar me.

MARTIN. Oh my.

JOE. Why?

ROY. Why, Martin?

MARTIN. Revenge.

ROY. The whole Establishment. Their little rules. Because I know no rules. Because I don't see the Law as a dead and arbitrary collection of antiquated dictums, thou shall, thou shalt not, because, because I know the Law's a pliable, breathing, sweating . . . *organ*, because, because . . .

MARTIN. Because he borrowed half a million from one of his clients.

ROY. Yeah, well, there's that.

MARTIN. *And he forgot to* return *it.*

JOE. Roy, that's. . . . You borrowed money from a client?

ROY. I'm deeply ashamed.

(Little pause.)

JOE *(Very sympathetic).* Roy, you know how much I admire you. Well I mean I know you have unorthodox ways, but I'm sure you only did what you thought at the time you needed to do. And I have faith that . . .

ROY. Not so damp, please. I'll deny it was a loan. She's got no paperwork. Can't prove a fucking thing.

(Little pause. Martin studies the menu.)

JOE *(Handing back the letter, more official in tone).* Roy I really appreciate your telling me this, and I'll do whatever I can to help.

ROY *(Holding up a hand, then, carefully).* I'll tell you what you can do.

I'm about to be tried, Joe, by a jury that is not a jury of my peers. The disbarment committee: genteel gentleman Brahmin lawyers, country-club men. I offend them, to these men . . . I'm what, Martin, some sort of filthy little Jewish troll?

MARTIN. Oh well, I wouldn't go so far as . . .

ROY. Oh well I would.

Very fancy lawyers, these disbarment committee lawyers, fancy lawyers with fancy corporate clients and complicated cases. Antitrust suits. Deregulation. Environmental control. Complex cases like these need Justice Department cooperation like flowers need the sun. Wouldn't you say that's an accurate assessment, Martin?

MARTIN. I'm not here, Roy. I'm not hearing any of this.

ROY. No. Of course not.

Without the light of the sun, Joe, these cases, and the fancy lawyers who represent them, will wither and die.

A well-placed friend, someone in the Justice Department, say, can turn off the sun. Cast a deep shadow on my behalf. Make them shiver in the cold. If they overstep. They would fear that.

(Pause.)

JOE. Roy. I don't understand.

ROY. You do.

(Pause.)

JOE. You're not asking me to . . .

ROY. Ssshhhh. Careful.

JOE *(A beat, then).* Even if I said yes to the job, it would be illegal to interfere. With the hearings. It's unethical. No. I can't.

ROY. Un-ethical.

Would you excuse us, Martin?

MARTIN. Excuse you?

ROY. Take a walk, Martin. For real.

(Martin leaves.)

ROY. Un-ethical. Are you trying to embarrass me in front of my friend?

JOE. Well it is unethical, I can't . . .

ROY. Boy, you are really something. What the fuck do you think this is, Sunday School?

JOE. No, but Roy this is . . .

ROY. This is . . . this is gastric juices churning, this is enzymes and acids, this is intestinal is what this is, bowel movement and blood-red meat—this stinks, this is *politics,* Joe, the game of being alive. And you think you're . . . . What? Above that? Above alive is what? Dead! In the clouds! You're on earth, goddammit! Plant a foot, stay a while.

I'm sick. They smell I'm weak. They want blood this time. I must have eyes in Justice. In Justice you will protect me.

JOE. Why can't Mr. Heller . . .

ROY. Grow up, Joe. The administration can't get involved.

JOE. But I'd be part of the administration. The same as him.

ROY. Not the same. Martin's Ed's man. And Ed's Reagan's man. So Martin's Reagan's man.

And you're mine.

(Little pause. He holds up the letter)

This will never be. Understand me?

(He tears the letter up)

I'm gonna be a lawyer, Joe, I'm gonna be a lawyer, Joe, I'm gonna be a goddam motherfucking legally licensed member of the bar lawyer, just like daddy was, till my last bitter day on earth, Joseph, until the day I die.

(Martin returns.)

ROY. Ah, Martin's back.

MARTIN. So are we agreed?

ROY. Joe?

(Little pause.)

JOE. I will think about it.

(*To Roy*) I will.

ROY. Huh.

MARTIN. It's the fear of what comes after the doing that makes the doing hard to do.

ROY. Amen.

MARTIN. But you can almost always live with the consequences.

SCENE 7

That afternoon. On the granite steps outside the Hall of Justice, Brooklyn. It is cold and sunny. A Sabrett wagon is selling hot dogs. Louis, in a shabby overcoat, is sitting on the steps contemplatively eating one. Joe enters with three hot dogs and a can of Coke.

JOE. Can I . . . ?

LOUIS. Oh, sure. Sure. Crazy cold sun.

JOE *(Sitting)*. Have to make the best of it.
    How's your friend?

LOUIS. My . . . ? Oh. He's worse. My friend is worse.

JOE. I'm sorry.

LOUIS. Yeah, well. Thanks for asking. It's nice, You're nice. I can't believe you voted for Reagan.

JOE. I hope he gets better.

LOUIS. Reagan?

JOE. Your friend.

LOUIS. He won't. Neither will Reagan.

JOE. Let's not talk politics, OK?

LOUIS *(Pointing to Joe's lunch)*. You're eating *three* of those?

JOE. Well . . . I'm . . . hungry.

LOUIS. They're really terrible for you. Full of rat-poo and beetle legs and wood shavings 'n' shit.

JOE. Huh.

LOUIS. And . . . um . . . irridium, I think. Something toxic.

JOE. You're eating one.

LOUIS. Yeah, well, the shape, I can't help myself, plus I'm *trying* to commit suicide, what's your excuse?

JOE. I don't have an excuse. I just have Pepto-Bismol.

(Joe takes a bottle of Pepto-Bismol and chugs it. Louis shudders audibly.)

JOE. Yeah I know but then I wash it down with Coke.

(He does this. Louis mimes barfing in Joe's lap. Joe pushes Louis's head away.)

JOE. Are you *always* like this?

LOUIS. I've been worrying a lot about his kids.

JOE. Whose?

LOUIS. Reagan's. Maureen and Mike and little orphan Patti and Miss Ron Reagan Jr., the you-should-pardon-the-expression heterosexual.

JOE. Ron Reagan Jr. is *not*. . . . You shouldn't just make these assumptions about people. How do you know? About him? What he is? You don't know.

LOUIS *(Doing Tallulah)*. Well darling he never sucked *my* cock but . . .

JOE. Look, if you're going to get vulgar . . .

LOUIS. No no really I mean. . . . What's it like to be the child of the Zeitgeist? To have the American Animus as your dad? It's not really a *family*, the Reagans. I read *People*, there aren't any connections there, no love, they don't even speak to each other except through their agents. So what's it like to be Reagan's kid? Enquiring minds want to know.

JOE. You can't believe everything you . . .

LOUIS *(Looking away)*. But . . . I think we all know what that's like. Nowadays. No connections. No responsibilities. All of us . . . falling through the cracks that separate

what we owe to our selves and . . . and what we owe to love.

JOE. You just. . . . Whatever you feel like saying or doing, you don't care, you just . . . do it.

LOUIS. Do what?

JOE. It. Whatever. Whatever it is you want to do.

LOUIS. Are you trying to tell me something?

(Little pause, sexual. They stare at each other. Joe looks away.)

JOE. No, I'm just observing that you . . .

LOUIS. Impulsive.

JOE. Yes, I mean it must be scary, you . . .

LOUIS *(Shrugs)*. Land of the free. Home of the brave. Call me irresponsible.

JOE. It's kind of terrifying.

LOUIS. Yeah, well, freedom is. Heartless, too.

JOE. Oh you're not heartless.

LOUIS. You don't know.
    Finish your weenie.

(He pats Joe on the knee, starts to leave.)

JOE. Um . . .

(Louis turns, looks at him. Joe searches for something to say.)

JOE. Yesterday was Sunday but I've been a little unfocused recently and I thought it was Monday. So I came here like I was going to work. And the whole place was empty. And at first I couldn't figure out why, and I had this moment of incredible . . . fear and also. . . . It just flashed through my mind: The whole Hall of Justice, it's empty, it's deserted, it's gone out of business. Forever. The people that make it run have up and abandoned it.

LOUIS *(Looking at the building)*. Creepy.

JOE. Well yes but. I felt that I was going to scream. Not because it was creepy, but because the emptiness felt so *fast*.
    And . . . well, good. A . . . happy scream.
    I just wondered what a thing it would be . . . if overnight everything you owe anything to, justice, or love, had really gone away. Free.
    It would be . . . heartless terror. Yes. Terrible, and . . .
    Very great. To shed your skin, every old skin, one by one then walk away, unencumbered, into the morning.

(Little pause. He looks at the building)

    I can't go in there today.

LOUIS. Then don't.

JOE *(Not really hearing Louis)*. I can't go in, I need . . .

(He looks for what he needs. He takes a swig of Pepto-Bismol)

    I can't *be* this anymore. I need . . . a change, I should just . . .

LOUIS (*Not a come-on, necessarily; he doesn't want to be alone*). Want some company? For whatever?

(*Pause. Joe looks at Louis and looks away, afraid. Louis shrugs.*)

LOUIS. Sometimes, even if it scares you to death, you have to be willing to break the law. Know what I mean?

(*Another little pause.*)

JOE. Yes.

(*Another little pause.*)

LOUIS. I moved out. I moved out on my . . .
    I haven't been sleeping well.
JOE. Me neither.

(*Louis goes up to Joe, licks his napkin and dabs at Joe's mouth.*)

LOUIS. Antacid moustache.
    (*Points to the building*) Maybe the court won't convene. Ever again. Maybe we are free. To do whatever.
    Children of the new morning, criminal minds. Selfish and greedy and loveless and blind. Reagan's children.
    You're scared. So am I. Everybody is in the land of the free. God help us all.

SCENE 8

Late that night. Joe at a payphone phoning Hannah at home in Salt Lake City.

JOE. Mom?
HANNAH. Joe?
JOE. Hi.
HANNAH. You're calling from the street. It's . . . it must be four in the morning. What's happened?
JOE. Nothing, nothing, I . . .
HANNAH. It's Harper. Is Harper. . . . Joe? Joe?
JOE. Yeah, hi. No, Harper's fine. Well, no, she's . . . not fine. How are you, Mom?
HANNAH. What's happened?
JOE. I just wanted to talk to you. I, uh, wanted to try something out on you.
HANNAH. Joe, you haven't . . . have you been drinking, Joe?
JOE. Yes ma'am. I'm drunk.
HANNAH. That isn't like you.
JOE. No. I mean, who's to say?
HANNAH. Why are you out on the street at four AM? In that crazy city. It's dangerous.
JOE. Actually, Mom, I'm not on the street. I'm near the boathouse in the park.
HANNAH. What park?
JOE. *Central Park.*
HANNAH. CENTRAL PARK! Oh my Lord. What on earth

are you doing in Central Park at this time of night? Are you . . .
    Joe, I think you ought to go home right now. Call me from home.

(*Little pause*)

    Joe?
JOE. I come here to watch, Mom. Sometimes. Just to watch.
HANNAH. Watch what? What's there to watch at four in the . . .
JOE. Mom, did Dad Love me?
HANNAH. What?
JOE. Did he?
HANNAH. You ought to go home and call from there.
JOE. Answer.
HANNAH. Oh now really. This is maudlin. I don't like this conversation.
JOE. Yeah, well, it gets worse from here on.

(*Pause*)

HANNAH. Joe?
JOE. Mom. Momma. I'm a homosexual, Momma.
    Boy, did that come out awkward.

(*Pause*)

    Hello? Hello?
    I'm a homosexual.

(*Pause*)

    Please, Momma. Say something.
HANNAH. You're old enough to understand that your father didn't love you without being ridiculous about it.
JOE. What?
HANNAH. You're ridiculous. You're being ridiculous.
JOE. I'm . . .
    What?
HANNAH. You really ought to go home now to your wife. I need to go to bed. This phone call. . . . We will just forget this phone call.
JOE. Mom.
HANNAH. No more talk. Tonight. This . . .
    (*Suddenly very angry*) Drinking is a sin! A sin! I raised you better than that.

(*She hangs up*)

SCENE 9

The following morning, early. Split scene: Harper and Joe at home; Louis and Prior in Prior's hospital room. Joe and Louis have just entered. This should be fast and obviously furious; overlapping is fine; the proceedings may be a little confusing but not the final results.

HARPER. Oh God. Home. The moment of truth has arrived.
JOE. Harper.

LOUIS. I'm going to move out.

PRIOR. The fuck you are.

JOE. Harper. Please listen. I still love you very much. You're still my best buddy; I'm not going to leave you.

HARPER. No, I don't like the sound of this. I'm leaving.

LOUIS. I'm leaving.

I already have.

JOE. Please listen. Stay. This is really hard. We have to talk.

HARPER. We are talking. Aren't we. Now please shut up. OK?

PRIOR. Bastard. Sneaking off while I'm flat out here, that's low.

If I could get up now I'd beat the holy shit out of you.

JOE. Did you take pills? How many?

HARPER. No pills. Bad for the . . . (*Pats stomach*)

JOE. You aren't pregnant. I called your gynecologist.

HARPER. I'm seeing a new gynecologist.

PRIOR. You have no right to do this.

LOUIS. Oh, that's ridiculous.

PRIOR. No right. It's criminal.

JOE. Forget about that. Just listen. You want the truth. This is the truth.

I knew this when I married you. I've known this I guess for as long as I've known anything, but . . . I don't know, I thought maybe that with enough effort and will I could change myself . . . but I can't . . .

PRIOR. Criminal.

LOUIS. There oughta be a law.

PRIOR. There is a law. You'll see.

JOE. I'm losing ground here, I go walking, you want to know where I walk, I . . . go to the park, or up and down 53rd Street, or places where. . . . And I keep swearing I won't go walking again, but I just can't.

LOUIS. I need some privacy.

PRIOR. That's new.

LOUIS. Everything's new, Prior.

JOE. I try to tighten my heart into a knot, a snarl, I try to learn to live dead, just numb, but then I see someone I want, and it's like a nail, like a hot spike through my chest, and I know I'm losing.

PRIOR. Apartment too small for three? Louis and Prior comfy but not Louis and Prior and Prior's disease?

LOUIS. Something like that.

I won't be judged by you. This isn't a crime, just—the inevitable consequence of people who run out of—whose limitations . . .

PRIOR. Bang bang bang. The court will come to order.

LOUIS. I mean let's talk practicalities, schedules; I'll come over if you want, spend nights with you when I can, I can . . .

PRIOR. Has the jury reached a verdict?

LOUIS. I'm doing the best I can.

PRIOR. Pathetic. Who cares?

JOE. My whole life has conspired to bring me to this place, and I can't despise my whole life. I think I believed when I met you I could save you, you at least if not myself, but . . .

I don't have any sexual feelings for you, Harper. And I don't think I ever did.

(*Little pause.*)

HARPER. I think you should go.

JOE. Where?

HARPER. Washington. Doesn't matter.

JOE. What are you talking about?

HARPER. Without me.

Without me, Joe. Isn't that what you want to hear?

(*Little pause.*)

JOE. Yes.

LOUIS. You can love someone and fail them. You can love someone and not be able to . . .

PRIOR. You *can*, theoretically, yes. A person can, maybe an editorial "you" can love, Louis, but not *you*, specifically you, I don't know, I think you are excluded from that general category.

HARPER. You were going to save me, but the whole time you were spinning a lie. I just don't understand that.

PRIOR. A person could theoretically love and maybe many do but we both know now you can't.

LOUIS. I do.

PRIOR. You can't even say it.

LOUIS. I love you, Prior.

PRIOR. I repeat. Who cares?

HARPER. This is so scary, I want this to stop, to go back . . .

PRIOR. We have reached a verdict, your honor. This man's heart is deficient. He loves, but his love is worth nothing.

JOE. Harper . . .

HARPER. Mr. Lies, I want to get away from here. Far away. Right now. Before he starts talking again. Please, please . . .

JOE. As long as I've known you Harper you've been afraid of . . . of men hiding under the bed, men hiding under the sofa, men with knives.

PRIOR (*Shattered; almost pleading; trying to reach him*). I'm dying! You stupid fuck! Do you know what that is! Love! Do you know what love means? We lived together four-and-a-half years, you animal, you idiot.

LOUIS. I have to find some way to save myself.

JOE. Who are these men? I never understood it. Now I know.

HARPER. What?

JOE. It's me.

HARPER. It is?

PRIOR. GET OUT OF MY ROOM!

JOE. I'm the man with the knives.

HARPER. You are?

PRIOR. If I could get up now I'd kill you. I would. Go away. Go away or I'll scream.

HARPER. Oh God . . .

JOE. I'm sorry . . .

HARPER. It is you.

LOUIS. Please don't scream.

PRIOR. Go.
HARPER. I recognize you now.
LOUIS. Please . . .
JOE. Oh. Wait, I. . . . Oh!

(*He covers his mouth with his hand, gags, and removes his hand, red with blood*)

I'm bleeding.

(*Prior screams.*)

HARPER. Mr. Lies.
MR. LIES (*Appearing, dressed in antarctic explorer's apparel*). Right here.
HARPER. I want to go away. I can't see him anymore.
MR. LIES. Where?
HARPER. Anywhere. Far away.
MR. LIES. Absolutamento.

(*Harper and Mr. Lies vanish. Joe looks up, sees that she's gone.*)

PRIOR (*Closing his eyes*). When I open my eyes you'll be gone.

(*Louis leaves.*)

JOE. Harper?
PRIOR (*Opening his eyes*). Huh. It worked.
JOE (*Calling*). Harper?
PRIOR. I hurt all over. I wish I was dead.

SCENE 10

The same day, sunset. Hannah and Sister Ella Chapter, a real-estate saleswoman, Hannah Pitt's closest friend, in front of Hannah's house in Salt Lake City.

SISTER ELLA CHAPTER. Look at that view! A view of heaven. Like the living city of heaven, isn't it, it just fairly glimmers in the sun.
HANNAH. Glimmers.
SISTER ELLA CHAPTER. Even the stone and brick it just glimmers and glitters like heaven in the sunshine. Such a nice view you get, perched up on a canyon rim. Some kind of beautiful place.
HANNAH. It's just Salt Lake, and you're selling the house *for* me, not *to* me.
SISTER ELLA CHAPTER. I like to work up an enthusiasm for my properties.
HANNAH. Just get me a good price.
SISTER ELLA CHAPTER. Well, the market's off.
HANNAH. At least fifty.
SISTER ELLA CHAPTER. Forty'd be more like it.
HANNAH. Fifty.
SISTER ELLA CHAPTER. Wish you'd wait a bit.

HANNAH. Well I can't.
SISTER ELLA CHAPTER. Wish you would. You're about the only friend I got.
HANNAH. Oh well now.
SISTER ELLA CHAPTER. Know why I decided to like you? I decided to like you 'cause you're the only unfriendly Mormon I ever met.
HANNAH. Your wig is crooked.
SISTER ELLA CHAPTER. Fix it.

(*Hannah straightens Sister Ella's wig.*)

SISTER ELLA CHAPTER. New York City. All they got there is tiny rooms.
   I always thought: People ought to stay put. That's why I got my license to sell real estate. It's a way of saying: Have a house! Stay put! It's a way of saying traveling's no good. Plus I needed the cash. (*She takes a pack of cigarettes out of her purse, lights one, offers pack to Hannah*).
HANNAH. Not out here, anyone could come by.
   There's been days I've stood at this ledge and thought about stepping over.
   It's a hard place, Salt Lake: baked dry. Abundant energy; not much intelligence. That's a combination that can wear a body out. No harm looking someplace else. I don't need much room.
   My sister-in-law Libby thinks there's radon gas in the basement.
SISTER ELLA CHAPTER. Is there gas in the . . .
HANNAH. Of course not. Libby's a fool.
SISTER ELLA CHAPTER. 'Cause I'd have to include that in the description.
HANNAH. There's no gas, Ella. (*Little pause*) Give a puff. (*She takes a furtive drag of Ella's cigarette*) Put it away now.
SISTER ELLA CHAPTER. So I guess it's goodbye.
HANNAH. You'll be all right, Ella, I wasn't ever much of a friend.
SISTER ELLA CHAPTER. I'll say something but don't laugh, OK?
   This is the home of saints, the godliest place on earth, they say, and I think they're right. That means there's no evil here? No. Evil's everywhere. Sin's everywhere. But this . . . is the spring of sweet water in the desert, the desert flower. Every step a Believer takes away from here is a step fraught with peril. I fear for you, Hannah Pitt, because you are my friend. Stay put. This is the right home of saints.
HANNAH. Latter-day saints.
SISTER ELLA CHAPTER. Only kind left.
HANNAH. But still. Late in the day . . . for saints and everyone. That's all. That's all. Fifty thousand dollars for the house, Sister Ella Chapter; don't undersell. It's an impressive view.

ACT THREE: NOT-YET-CONSCIOUS, FORWARD DAWNING

January 1986

SCENE 1

Late night, three days after the end of Act Two. The stage is completely dark. Prior is in bed in his apartment, having a nightmare. He wakes up, sits up and switches on a nightlight. He looks at his clock. Seated by the table near the bed is a man dressed in the clothing of a 13th-century British squire.

PRIOR *(Terrified)*. Who are you?

PRIOR 1. *My name is Prior Walter.*

(Pause.)

PRIOR. My name is Prior Walter.

PRIOR 1. I know that.

PRIOR. Explain.

PRIOR 1. You're alive. I'm not. We have the same name. What do you want me to explain?

PRIOR. A ghost?

PRIOR 1. An ancestor.

PRIOR. Not *the* Prior Walter? The Bayeux tapestry Prior Walter?

PRIOR 1. His great-great grandson. The fifth of the name.

PRIOR. I'm the thirty-fourth, I think.

PRIOR 1. Actually the thirty-second.

PRIOR. Not according to Mother.

PRIOR 1. She's including the two bastards, then; I say leave them out. I say no room for bastards. The little things you swallow . . .

PRIOR. Pills.

PRIOR 1. Pills. For the pestilence. I too . . .

PRIOR. Pestilence. . . . You too what?

PRIOR 1. The pestilence in my time was much worse than now. Whole villages of empty houses. You could look outdoors and see Death walking in the morning, dew dampening the ragged hem of his black robe. Plain as I see you now.

PRIOR. You died of the plague.

PRIOR 1. The spotty monster. Like you, alone.

PRIOR. I'm not alone.

PRIOR 1. You have no wife, no children.

PRIOR. I'm gay.

PRIOR 1. So? Be gay, dance in your altogether for all I care, what's that to do with not having children?

PRIOR. Gay homosexual, not bonny, blithe and . . . never mind.

PRIOR 1. I had twelve. When I died.

(The second ghost appears, this one dressed in the clothing of an elegant 17th-century Londoner.)

PRIOR 1 *(Pointing to Prior 2)*. And I was three years younger than him.

(Prior sees the new ghost, screams.)

PRIOR. Oh God another one.

PRIOR 2. Prior Walter. Prior to you by some seventeen others.

PRIOR 1. He's counting the bastards.

PRIOR. Are you having a convention?

PRIOR 2. We've been sent to declare her fabulous incipience. They love a well-paved entrance with lots of heralds, and . . .

PRIOR 1. The messenger come. Prepare the way. The infinite descent, a breath of in air . . .

PRIOR 2. They chose us, I suspect, because of the mortal affinities. In a family as long-descended as the Walters there are bound to be a few carried off by plague.

PRIOR 1. The spotty monster.

PRIOR 2. Black Jack. Came from a water pump, half the city of London, can you imagine? His came from fleas. Yours, I understand, is the lamentable consequence of venery . . .

PRIOR 1. Fleas on rats, but who knew that?

PRIOR. Am I going to die?

PRIOR 2. We aren't allowed to discuss . . .

PRIOR 1. When you do, you don't get ancestors to help you through it. You may be surrounded by children but you die alone.

PRIOR. I'm afraid.

PRIOR 1. You should be. There aren't even torches, and the path's rocky, dark and steep.

PRIOR 2. Don't alarm him. There's good news before there's bad.

We two come to stew rose petal and palm leaf before the triumphal procession. Prophet. Seer. Revelator. It's a great honor for the family.

PRIOR 1. He hasn't got a family.

PRIOR 2. I meant for the Walters, for the family in the larger sense.

PRIOR *(Singing)*.
    All I want is a room somewhere,
    Far away from the cold night air . . .

PRIOR 2 *(Putting a hand on Prior's forehead)*. Calm, calm, this is no brain fever . . .

(Prior calms down, but keeps his eyes closed. The lights begin to change. Distant Glorious Music.)

PRIOR 1 *(Low chant)*.
    Adonai, Adonai,
    Olam ha-yichud,
    Zefirot, Zazahot,
    Ha-adam, ha-gadol

Daughter of Light,
Daughter of Splendors,
Fluor! Phosphor!
Lumen! Candle!
PRIOR 2 (*Simultaneously*).
Even now,
From the mirror-bright halls of heaven,
Across the cold and lifeless infinity of space,
The Messenger comes
Trailing orbs of light,
Fabulous, incipient,
Oh Prophet,
To you . . .
PRIOR 1 AND PRIOR 2.
Prepare, prepare,
The Infinite Descent,
A breath, a feather,
Glory to . . .

(*They vanish.*)

SCENE 2

The next day. Split scene: Louis and Belize in a coffee shop. Prior is at the outpatient clinic at the hospital with Emily, the nurse; she has him on a pentamidine IV drip.

LOUIS. Why has democracy succeeded in America? Of course by succeeded I mean comparatively, not literally, not in the present, but what makes for the prospect of some sort of radical democracy spreading outward and growing up? Why does the power that was once so carefully preserved at the top of the pyramid by the original framers of the Constitution seem drawn inexorably downward and outward in spite of the best effort of the Right to stop this? I mean it's the really hard thing about being Left in this country, the American Left can't help but trip over all these petrified little fetishes: freedom, that's the worst; you know, *Jeane Kirkpatrick* for God's sake will go on and on about freedom and so what does that mean, the word freedom, when she talks about it, or human rights; you have Bush talking about human rights, and so what are these people talking about, they might as well be talking about the mating habits of Venusians, these people don't begin to know what, ontologically, freedom is or human rights, like they see these bourgeois property-based Rights-of-Man-type rights but that's not enfranchisement, not democracy, not what's implicit, what's potential within the idea, not the idea with blood in it. That's just liberalism, the worst kind of liberalism, really, bourgeois tolerance, and what I think is that what AIDS shows us is the limits of tolerance, that it's not enough to be tolerated, because when the shit hits the fan you find out how much tolerance is worth. Nothing. And underneath all the tolerance is intense, passionate hatred.

BELIZE. Uh huh.
LOUIS. Well don't you think that's true?
BELIZE. Uh huh. It is.
LOUIS. *Power* is the object, not being tolerated. Fuck assimilation. But I mean in spite of all this the thing about America, I think, is that ultimately we're different from every other nation on earth, in that, with people here of every race, we can't. . . . Ultimately what defines us isn't race, but politics. Not like any European country where there's an insurmountable fact of a kind of racial, or ethnic, monopoly, or monolith, like all Dutchmen, I mean Dutch people, are well, Dutch, and the Jews of Europe were never Europeans, just a small problem. Facing the monolith. But here there are so many small problems, it's really just a collection of small problems, the monolith is missing. Oh, I mean, of course I suppose there's the monolith of White America. White Straight Male America.
BELIZE. Which is not unimpressive, even among monoliths.
LOUIS. Well, no, but when the race thing gets taken care of, and I don't mean to minimize how major it is, I mean I know it is, this is a really, really incredibly racist country but it's like, well, the British. I mean, all these blue-eyed pink people. And it's just weird, you know, I mean I'm not all that Jewish-looking, or . . . well, maybe I am but, you know, in New York, everyone is . . . well, not everyone, but so many are but so but in England, in London I walk into bars and I feel like Sid the Yid, you know I mean like Woody Allen in *Annie Hall,* with the payess and the gabardine coat, like never, never anywhere so much—I mean, not actively despised, not like they're Germans, who I think are still terribly anti-Semitic, and racist too, I mean black-racist, they pretend otherwise but, anyway, in London, there's just . . . and at one point I met this black gay guy from Jamaica who talked with a lilt but he said his family'd been living in London since before the Civil War—the American one—and how the English never let him forget for a minute that he wasn't blue-eyed and pink and I said yeah, me too, these people are anti-Semites and he said yeah but the British Jews have the clothing business all sewed up and blacks here can't get a foothold. And it was an incredibly awkward moment of just. . . . I mean here we were, in this bar that was gay but it was a *pub,* you know, the beams and the plaster and those horrible little, like, two-day-old fish and egg sandwiches—and just so British, so *old,* and I felt, well, there's no way out of this because both of us are, right now, too much immersed in this history, hope is dissolved in the sheer age of this place, where race is what counts and there's no real hope of change—it's the racial destiny of the Brits that matters to them, not their political destiny, whereas in America . . .
BELIZE. Here in America race doesn't count.
LOUIS. No, no, that's not. . . . I mean you *can't* be hearing that . . .
BELIZE. I . . .

LOUIS. It's—look, race, yes, but ultimately race here is a political question, right? Racists just try to use race here as a
tool in a political struggle. It's not really about race. Like
the spiritualists try to use that stuff, are you enlightened,
are you centered, channeled, whatever, this reaching out
for a spiritual past in a country where no indigenous spirits exist—only the Indians, I mean Native American spirits and we killed them off so now, there are no gods here,
no ghosts and spirits in America, there are no angels in
America, no spiritual past, no racial past, there's only the
political, and the decoys and the ploys to maneuver
around the inescapable battle of politics, the shifting
downwards and outwards of political power to the people
. . .

BELIZE. POWER to the People! AMEN! (*Looking at his
watch*) *OH MY GOODNESS!* Will you look at the time.
I gotta . . .

LOUIS. Do you. . . . You think this is, what, racist or naive or
something?

BELIZE. Well it's certainly *something*. Look, I just remembered I have an appointment . . .

LOUIS. What? I mean I really don't want to, like, speak from
some position of privilege and . . .

BELIZE. I'm sitting here, thinking, eventually he's *got* to run
out of steam, so I let you rattle on and on saying about
maybe seven or eight things I find really offensive.

LOUIS. What?

BELIZE. But I know you, Louis, and I know the guilt fueling
this peculiar tirade is obviously already swollen bigger
than your hemorrhoids.

LOUIS. I don't have hemorrhoids.

BELIZE. I hear different. May I finish?

LOUIS. Yes, but I don't have hemorrhoids.

BELIZE. So finally, when I . . .

LOUIS. Prior told you, he's an asshole, he should have . . .

BELIZE. You promised, Louis. Prior is not a subject.

LOUIS. You brought him up.

BELIZE. I brought up hemorrhoids.

LOUIS. So it's indirect. Passive-aggressive.

BELIZE. Unlike, I suppose, banging me over the head with
your theory that America doesn't have a race problem.

LOUIS. Oh be fair I never said that.

BELIZE. Not exactly, but . . .

LOUIS. I said . . .

BELIZE. . . . but it was close enough, because if it'd been that
blunt I'd've just walked out and . . .

LOUIS. You deliberately misinterpreted! I . . .

BELIZE. Stop interrupting! I haven't been able to . . .

LOUISE. Just let me . . .

BELIZE. NO! What, *talk*? You've been running your mouth
nonstop since I got here, yaddadda yaddadda blah blah
blah, up the hill, down the hill, playing with your
MONOLITH . . .

LOUIS (*Overlapping*). Well, you could have joined in at any
time instead of . . .

BELIZE (*Continuing over Louis*). . . . and girlfriend it is truly
an *awesome* spectacle but I got better things to do with
my time than sit here listening to this racist bullshit just
because I feel sorry for you that . . .

LOUIS. I am not a racist!

BELIZE. Oh come on . . .

LOUIS. So maybe I am a racist but . . .

BELIZE. Oh I really hate that! It's no fun picking on you
Louis; you're so guilty, it's like throwing darts at a glob of
jello, there's no satisfying hits, just quivering, the darts
just blop in and vanish.

LOUIS. I just think when you are discussing lines of oppression it gets very complicated and . . .

BELIZE. Oh is that a fact? You know, we black drag queens
have a rather intimate knowledge of the complexity of
the lines of . . .

LOUIS. *Ex*-black drag queen.

BELIZE. Actually ex-ex.

LOUIS. You're doing drag again?

BELIZE. I don't. . . . Maybe. I don't have to tell you. Maybe.

LOUIS. I think it's sexist.

BELIZE. I didn't ask you.

LOUIS. Well it is. The gay community, I think, has to adopt
the same attitude towards drag as black women have to
take towards black women blues singers.

BELIZE. Oh my we *are* walking dangerous tonight.

LOUIS. Well, it's all internalized oppression, right, I mean
the masochism, the stereotypes, the . . .

BELIZE. Louis, are you deliberately trying to make me hate
you?

LOUIS. No, I . . .

BELIZE. I mean, are you deliberately transforming yourself
into an arrogant, sexual-political Stalinist-slash-racist
flagwaving thug for my benefit?

(*Pause.*)

LOUIS. You know what I think?

BELIZE. What?

LOUIS. You hate me because I'm a Jew.

BELIZE. I'm leaving.

LOUIS. It's true.

BELIZE. You have no basis except your . . .

Louis, it's good to know you haven't changed; you are
still an honorary citizen of the Twilight Zone, and after
your pale, pale white polemics on behalf of racial insensitivity you have a flaming *fuck* of a lot of nerve calling me
an anti-Semite. Now I really gotta go.

LOUIS. You called me Lou the Jew.

BELIZE. That was a joke.

LOUIS. I didn't think it was funny. It was hostile.

BELIZE. It was three years ago.

LOUIS. So?

BELIZE. You just called yourself Sid the Yid.

LOUIS. That's not the same thing.

BELIZE. Sid the Yid is different from Lou the Jew.

LOUIS. Yes.

BELIZE. Someday you'll have to explain that to me, but right now . . .

> You hate me because you hate black people.

LOUIS. I do not. But I do think most black people are anti-Semitic.

BELIZE. "Most black people." *That's* racist, Louis, and *I* think most Jews . . .

LOUIS. Louis Farrakhan.

BELIZE. Ed Koch.

LOUIS. Jesse Jackson.

BELIZE. Jackson. Oh really, Louis, this is . . .

LOUIS. Hymietown! Hymietown!

BELIZE. Louis, you voted for Jesse Jackson. You send checks to the Rainbow Coalition.

LOUIS. I'm ambivalent. The checks bounced.

BELIZE. All your checks bounce, Louis; you're ambivalent about everything.

LOUIS. What's that supposed to mean?

BELIZE. You may be dumber than shit but I refuse to believe you can't figure it out. Try.

LOUIS. I was never ambivalent about Prior. I love him. I do. I really do.

BELIZE. Nobody said different.

LOUIS. Love and ambivalence are. . . . Real love isn't ambivalent.

BELIZE. "Real love isn't ambivalent." I'd swear that's a line from my favorite bestselling paperback novel, *In Love with the Night Mysterious,* except I don't think you ever read it.

(*Pause.*)

LOUIS. I never read it, no.

BELIZE. You ought to. Instead of spending the rest of your life trying to get through *Democracy in America.* It's about this white woman whose Daddy owns a plantation in the Deep South in the years before the Civil War—the American one—and her name is Margaret, and she's in love with her Daddy's number-one slave, and his name is Thaddeus, and she's married but her white slave-owner husband has AIDS: Antebellum Insufficiently Developed Sexorgans. And there's a lot of hot stuff going down when Margaret and Thaddeus can catch a spare torrid ten under the cotton-picking moon, and then of course the Yankees come, and here they set the slaves free, and the slaves string up old Daddy, and so on. Historical fiction. Somewhere in there I recall Margaret and Thaddeus find the time to discuss the nature of love; her face is reflecting the flames of the burning plantation—you know, the way white people do—and his black face is dark in the night and she says to him, "Thaddeus, real love isn't ever ambivalent."

(*Little pause. Emily enters and turns off IV drip.*)

BELIZE. Thaddeus looks at her; he's contemplating her thesis; and he isn't sure he agrees.

EMILY (*Removing IV drip from Prior's arm*). Treatment number . . . (*Consulting chart*) four.

PRIOR. Pharmaceutical miracle. Lazarus breathes again.

LOUIS. Is he. . . . How bad is he?

BELIZE. You want the laundry list?

EMILY. Shirt off, let's check the . . .

(*Prior takes his shirt off. She examines his lesions.*)

BELIZE. There's the weight problem and the shit problem and the morale problem.

EMILY. Only six. That's good. Pants.

(*He drops his pants. He's naked. She examines.*)

BELIZE. And. He thinks he's going crazy.

EMILY. Looking good. What else?

PRIOR. Ankles sore and swollen, but the leg's better. The nausea's mostly gone with the little orange pills. BM's pure liquid but not bloody anymore, for now, my eye doctor says everything's OK, for now, my dentist says "Yuck!" when he sees my fuzzy tongue, and now he wears little condoms on his thumb and forefinger. And a mask. So what? My dermatologist is in Hawaii and my mother . . . well leave my mother out of it. Which is usually where my mother is, out of it. My glands are like walnuts, my weight's holding steady for week two, and a friend died two days ago of bird tuberculosis; bird tuberculosis; that scared me and I didn't go to the funeral today because he was an Irish Catholic and it's probably open casket and I'm afraid of . . . something, the bird TB or seeing him or. . . . So I guess I'm doing OK. Except for of course I'm going nuts.

EMILY. We ran the toxoplasmosis series and there's no indication . . .

PRIOR. I know, I know, but I feel like something terrifying is on its way, you know, like a missile from outer space, and its plummeting down towards the earth, and I'm ground zero, and . . . I am generally known where I am known as one cool, collected queen. And I am ruffled.

EMILY. There's really nothing to worry about. I think that shochen bamromim hamtzeh menucho nechono al kanfey haschino.

PRIOR. What?

EMILY. Everything's fine. Bemaalos k'doshim ut'horim kezohar horokeea mazhirim . . .

PRIOR. Oh I don't understand what you're . . .

EMILY. Es nishmas Prior sheholoch leolomoh, baavur shenodvoo z'dokoh b'ad hazkoras nishmosoh.

PRIOR. Why are you doing that? Stop it! Stop it!

EMILY. Stop what?

PRIOR. You were just . . . weren't you just speaking in Hebrew or something.

EMILY. *Hebrew?* (*Laughs*) I'm basically Italian-American. No. I didn't speak in Hebrew.

PRIOR. Oh no, oh God please I really think I . . .

EMILY. Look, I'm sorry, I have a waiting room full of. . . . I think you're one of the lucky ones, you'll live for years, probably—you're pretty healthy for someone with no immune system. Are you seeing someone? Loneliness is a danger. A therapist?

PRIOR. No, I don't need to see anyone, I just . . .

EMILY. Well think about it. You aren't going crazy. You're just under a lot of stress. No wonder . . . (*She starts to write in his chart*)

(*Suddenly there is an astonishing blaze of light, a huge chord sounded by a gigantic choir, and a great book with steel pages mounted atop a molten-red pillar pops up from the stage floor. The book opens; there is a large Aleph inscribed on its pages, which bursts into flames. Immediately the book slams shut and disappears instantly under the floor as the lights become normal again. Emily notices none of this, writing. Prior is agog.*)

EMILY (*Laughing, exiting*). Hebrew . . .

(*Prior flees.*)

LOUIS. Help me.

BELIZE. I beg your pardon?

LOUIS. You're a nurse, give me something, I . . . don't know what to do anymore, I. . . . Last week at work I screwed up the Xerox machine like permanently and so I . . . then I tripped on the subway steps and my glasses broke and I cut my forehead, here, see, and now I can't see much and my forehead . . . it's like the Mark of Cain, stupid, right, but it won't heal and every morning I see it and I think, Biblical things, Mark of Cain, Judas Iscariot and his silver and his noose, people who . . . in betraying what they love betray what's truest in themselves, I feel . . . nothing but cold for myself, just cold, and every night I miss him, I miss him so much but then . . . those sores, and the smell and . . . where I thought it was going. . . . I could be . . . I could be sick too, maybe I'm sick too. I don't know.

Belize. Tell him I love him. Can you do that?

BELIZE. I've thought about it for a long time, and I still don't understand what love is. Justice is simple. Democracy is simple. Those things are unambivalent. But love is very hard. And it goes bad for you if you violate the hard law of love.

LOUIS. I'm dying.

BELIZE. He's dying. You just wish you were.

Oh cheer up, Louis. Look at that heavy sky out there.

LOUIS. Purple.

BELIZE. *Purple?* Boy, what kind of a homosexual are you, anyway? That's not purple, Mary, that color up there is (*very grand*) mauve.

All day today it's felt like Thanksgiving. Soon, this . . . ruination will be blanketed white. You can smell it—can you smell it?

LOUIS. Smell what?

BELIZE. Softness, compliance, forgiveness, grace.

LOUIS. No . . .

BELIZE. I can't help you learn that. I can't help you, Louis. You're not my business. (*He exits*)

(*Louis puts his head in his hands, inadvertently touching his forehead.*)

LOUIS. Ow FUCK! (*He stands slowly, looks towards where Belize is seated*) Smell what?

(*He looks both ways to be sure no one is watching, then inhales deeply, and is surprised.*) Huh. Snow.

SCENE 3

Same day. Harper in a very white, cold place, with a brilliant sky above; a delicate snowfall. She is dressed in a beautiful snowsuit. The sound of the sea, faint.

HARPER. Snow! Ice! Mountains of ice! Where am I? I . . . I feel better, I do. I . . . feel better. There are ice crystals in my lungs, wonderful and sharp. And the snow smells like cold, crushed peaches. And there's something . . . some current of blood in the wind, how strange, it has that iron taste.

MR. LIES. Ozone.

HARPER. Ozone! Wow! Where am I?

MR. LIES. The Kingdom of Ice, the bottommost part of the world.

HARPER (*Looking around, then realizing*). Antarctica. This is Antarctica!

MR. LIES. Cold shelter for the shattered. No sorrow here, tears freeze.

HARPER. Antarctica, Antarctica, oh boy oh boy, LOOK at this, I . . . Wow, I must've really snapped the tether, huh?

MR. LIES. Apparently . . .

HARPER. That's great. I want to stay here forever. Set up camp. Build things. Build a city, an enormous city made up of frontier forts, dark wood and green roofs and high gates made of pointed logs and bonfires burning on every street corner. I should build by a river. Where are the forests?

MR. LIES. No timber here. Too cold. Ice, no trees.

HARPER. Oh details! I'm sick of details! I'll plant them and grow them. I'll live off caribou fat, I'll melt it over the bonfires and drink it from long, curved goat-horn cups.

It'll be great. I want to make a new world here. So that I never have to go home again.

MR. LIES. As long as it lasts. Ice has a way of melting . . .

HARPER. No. Forever. I can have anything I want here—maybe even companionship, someone who has . . . desire for me. You, maybe.

MR. LIES. It's against the by-laws of the International Order of Travel Agents to get involved with clients. Rules are rules. Anyway, I'm not the one you really want.

HARPER. There isn't anyone . . . maybe an Eskimo. Who

could ice-fish for food. And help me build a nest for when the baby comes.

MR. LIES. There are no Eskimo in Antarctica. And you're not really pregnant. You made that up.

HARPER. Well all of this is made up. So if the snow feels cold I'm pregnant. Right? Here, I can be pregnant. And I can have any kind of a baby I want.

MR. LIES. This is a retreat, a vacuum, its virtue is that it lacks everything; deep-freeze for feelings. You can be numb and safe here, that's what you came for. Respect the delicate ecology of your delusions.

HARPER. You mean like no Eskimo in Antarctica.

MR. LIES. Correcto. Ice and snow, no Eskimo. Even hallucinations have laws.

HARPER. Well then who's that?

(*The Eskimo appears.*)

MR. LIES. An Eskimo.

HARPER. An antarctic Eskimo. A fisher of the polar deep.

MR. LIES. There's something wrong with this picture.

(*The Eskimo beckons.*)

HARPER. I'm going to like this place. It's my own National Geographic Special! Oh! Oh! (*She holds her stomach*) I think . . . I think I felt her kicking. Maybe I'll give birth to a baby covered with thick white fur, and that way she won't be cold. My breasts will be full of hot cocoa so she doesn't get chilly. And if it gets really cold, she'll have a pouch I can crawl into. Like a marsupial. We'll mend together. That's what we'll do; we'll mend.

SCENE 4

Same day. An abandoned lot in the South Bronx. A homeless Woman is standing near an oil drum in which a fire is burning. Snowfall. Trash around. Hannah enters dragging two heavy suitcases.

HANNAH. Excuse me? I said excuse me? Can you tell me where I am? Is this Brooklyn? Do you know a Pineapple Street? Is there some sort of bus or train or . . . ?

I'm lost, I just arrived from Salt Lake. City. Utah? I took the bus that I was told to take and I got off—well it was the very last stop, so I had to get off, and I *asked* the driver was this Brooklyn, and he nodded yes but he was from one of those foreign countries where they think it's good manners to nod at everything even if you have no idea what it is you're nodding at, and in truth I think he spoke no English at all, which I think would make him ineligible for employment on public transportation. The public being English-speaking, mostly. Do you speak English?

(*The Woman nods.*)

HANNAH. I was supposed to be met at the airport by my son. He didn't show and I don't wait more than three and three-quarters hours for *anyone*. I should have been patient, I guess, I. . . . Is this . . .

WOMAN. Bronx.

HANNAH. Is that. . . . The *Bronx*? Well how in the name of Heaven did I get to the Bronx when the bus driver said . . .

WOMAN (*Talking to herself*). Slurp slurp slurp will you STOP that disgusting slurping! YOU DISGUSTING SLURPING FEEDING ANIMAL! Feeding yourself, just feeding yourself, what would it matter, to you or to ANYONE, if you just stopped. Feeding. And DIED?

(*Pause.*)

HANNAH. Can you just tell me where I . . .

WOMAN. Why was the Kosciusko Bridge named after a Polack?

HANNAH. I don't know what you're . . .

WOMAN. That was a joke.

HANNAH. Well what's the punchline?

WOMAN. I don't know.

HANNAH (*Looking around desperately*). Oh for pete's sake, is there anyone else who . . .

WOMAN (*Again, to herself*). Stand further off you fat loathsome whore, you can't have any more of this soup, slurp slurp slurp you animal, and the—I know you'll just go pee it all away and where will you do that? Behind what bush? It's FUCKING COLD out here and I . . .

Oh that's right, because it was supposed have been a tunnel!

That's not very funny.

Have you read the prophecies of Nostradamus?

HANNAH. Who?

WOMAN. Some guy I went out with once somewhere, Nostradamus. Prophet, outcast, eyes like. . . . Scary shit, he . . .

HANNAH. Shut up. Please. Now I want you to stop jabbering for a minute and pull your wits together and tell me how to get to Brooklyn. Because you know! And you are going to tell me! Because there is no one else around to tell me and I am wet and cold and I am very hungry! So I am sorry you're psychotic but just make the effort—take a deep breath—DO IT!

(*Hannah and the Woman breathe together.*)

HANNAH. That's good. Now exhale.

(*They do.*)

HANNAH. Good. Now how do I get to Brooklyn?

WOMAN. Don't know. Never been. Sorry. Want some soup?

HANNAH. Manhattan? Maybe you know . . . I don't suppose you know the location of the Mormon Visitor's . . .

WOMAN. 65th and Broadway.

HANNAH. How do you . . .

WOMAN. Go there all the time. Free movies. Boring, but you can stay all day.

HANNAH. Well. . . . So how do I . . .

WOMAN. Take the D Train. Next block make a right.

HANNAH. Thank you.

WOMAN. Oh yeah. In the next century I think we will all be insane.

SCENE 5

Same day. Joe and Roy in the study of Roy's brownstone. Roy is wearing an elegant bathrobe. He has made a considerable effort to look well. He isn't well, and he hasn't succeeded much in looking it.

JOE. I can't. The answer's no. I'm sorry.

ROY. Oh, well, apologies . . .

I can't see that there's anyone asking for apologies.

(Pause.)

JOE. I'm sorry, Roy.

ROY. Oh, well, apologies.

JOE. My wife is missing, Roy. My mother's coming from Salt Lake to . . . to help look, I guess. I'm supposed to be at the airport now, picking her up but. . . . I just spent two days in a hospital, Roy, with a bleeding ulcer, I was spitting up blood.

ROY. Blood, huh? Look, I'm very busy here and . . .

JOE. It's just a job.

ROY. A job? A *job*? *Washington*! Dumb Utah Mormon hick shit!

JOE. Roy . . .

ROY. WASHINGTON! When Washington called me I was younger than you, you think I said, "Aw fuck no I can't go I got two fingers up my asshole and a little moral nosebleed to boot!" When Washington calls you my pretty young punk friend you go or you can go fuck yourself sideways 'cause the train has pulled out of the station, and you are *out*, nowhere, out in the cold. Fuck you, Mary Jane, get outta here.

JOE. Just let me . . .

ROY. Explain? Ephemera. You broke my heart. Explain that. Explain that.

JOE. I love you. Roy.

There's so much that I want, to be . . . what you see in me, I want to be a participant in the world, in your world, Roy, I want to be capable of that, I've tried, really I have but . . . I can't do this. Not because I don't believe in you, but because I believe in you so much, in what you stand for, at heart, the order, the decency. I would give anything to protect you, but. . . . There are laws I can't break. It's too ingrained. It's not me. There's enough damage I've already done.

Maybe you were right, maybe I'm dead.

ROY. You're not dead, boy, you're a sissy.

You love me; that's moving, I'm moved. It's nice to

be loved. I warned you about her, didn't I, Joe? But you don't listen to me, why, because you say Roy is smart and Roy's a friend but Roy . . . well, he isn't nice, and you wanna be nice. Right? A nice, nice man!

(Little pause)

You know what my greatest accomplishment was, Joe, in my life, what I am able to look back on and be proudest of? And I have helped make Presidents and unmake them and mayors and more goddam judges than anyone in NYC ever—AND several million dollars, tax-free—and what do you think means the most to me?

You ever hear of Ethel Rosenberg? Huh, Joe, huh?

JOE. Well, yeah, I guess I . . . Yes.

ROY. Yes. Yes. You have heard of Ethel Rosenberg. Yes. Maybe you even read about her in the history books.

If it wasn't for me, Joe, Ethel Rosenberg would be alive today, writing some personal-advice column for *Ms.* magazine. She isn't. Because during the trial, Joe, I was on the phone every day, talking with the judge . . .

JOE. Roy . . .

ROY. Every day, doing what I do best, talking on the telephone, making sure that timid Yid nebbish on the bench did his duty to America, to history. That sweet unprepossessing woman, two kids, boo-hoo-hoo, reminded us all of our little Jewish mamas—she came this close to getting life; I pleaded till I wept to put her in the chair. Me. I did that. I would have fucking pulled the switch if they'd have let me. Why? Because I fucking hate traitors. Because I fucking hate communists. Was it legal? Fuck legal. Am I a nice man? Fuck nice. They say terrible things about me in the *Nation*. Fuck the *Nation*. You want to be Nice, or you want to be Effective? Make the law, or subject to it. Choose. Your wife chose. A week from today, she'll be back. SHE knows how to get what SHE wants. Maybe I ought to send *her* to Washington.

JOE. I don't believe you.

ROY. Gospel.

JOE. You can't possibly mean what you're saying.

Roy, you were the Assistant United States Attorney on the Rosenberg case, ex parte communication with the judge during the trial would be . . . censurable, at least, probably conspiracy and . . . in a case that resulted in execution, it's . . .

ROY. What? Murder?

JOE. You're not well is all.

ROY. What do you mean, not well? Who's not well?

(Pause.)

JOE. You said . . .

ROY. No I didn't. I said what?

JOE. Roy, you have cancer.

ROY. No I don't.

(Pause.)

JOE. You told me you were dying.

ROY. What the fuck are you talking about Joe? I never said that. I'm in perfect health. There's not a goddam thing wrong with me.

(He smiles)

Shake?

(Joe hesitates. He holds out his hand to Roy. Roy pulls Joe into a close, strong clinch.)

ROY *(More to himself than to Joe)*. It's OK that you hurt me because I love you, baby Joe. That's why I'm so rough on you.

(Roy releases Joe. Joe backs away a step or two.)

ROY. Prodigal son. The world will wipe its dirty hands all over you.

JOE. It already has, Roy.

ROY. Now go.

(Roy shoves Joe, hard. Joe turns to leave. Roy stops him, turns him around.)

ROY *(Smoothing Joe's lapels, tenderly)*. I'll always be here, waiting for you . . .

(Then again, with sudden violence, he pulls Joe close, violently)

What did you want from me, what was all this, what do you want, you treacherous ungrateful little . . .

(Joe, very close to belting Roy grabs him by the front of his robe, and propels him across the length of the room. He holds Roy at arm's length, the other arm ready to hit.)

ROY *(Laughing softly, almost pleading to be hit)*. Transgress a little, Joseph.

(Joe releases Roy.)

ROY. There are so many laws; find one you can break.

(Joe hesitates, then leaves, backing out. When Joe has gone, Roy doubles over in great pain, which he's been hiding throughout the scene with Joe.)

ROY. Ah, Christ . . .
Andy! Andy! Get in here! Andy!

(The door opens but it isn't Andy. A small Jewish Woman dressed modestly in a fifties hat and coat stands in the doorway. The room darkens.)

ROY. Who the fuck are you? The new nurse?

(The figure in the doorway says nothing. She stares at Roy. A pause. Roy looks at her carefully, gets up, crosses to her. He crosses back to the chair, sits heavily.)

ROY. Aw, fuck. Ethel.

ETHEL ROSENBERG *(Her manner is friendly, her voice is ice-cold)*. You don't look good, Roy.

ROY. Well, Ethel. I don't feel good.

ETHEL ROSENBERG. But you lost a lot of weight. That suits you. You were heavy back then. Zaftig, mit hips.

ROY. I haven't been that heavy since 1960. We were all heavier back then, before the body thing started. Now I look like a skeleton. They stare.

ETHEL ROSENBERG. That shit's really hit the fan, huh, Roy?

(Little pause. Roy nods.)

ETHEL ROSENBERG. Well, the fun's just started.

ROY. What is this, Ethel, Halloween? You trying to scare me?

(Ethel says nothing.)

ROY. Well you're wasting your time! I'm scarier than you any day of the week! So beat it, Ethel! BOOO! BETTER DEAD THAN RED! Somebody trying to shake me up? HAH HAH! From the throne of God in heaven to the belly of hell, you can all fuck yourselves and then go jump in the lake because I'M NOT AFRAID OF YOU OR DEATH OR HELL OR ANYTHING!

ETHEL ROSENBERG. Be seeing you soon, Roy. Julius sends his regards.

ROY. Yeah, well send this to Julius!

(He flips the bird in her direction, stands and moves towards her. Halfway across the room he slumps to the floor, breathing laboriously, in pain.)

ETHEL ROSENBERG. You're a very sick man, Roy.

ROY. Oh God . . . ANDY!

ETHEL ROSENBERG. Hmmm. He doesn't hear you, I guess. We should call the ambulance.

(She goes to the phone)

Hah! Buttons! Such things they got now.
What do I dial, Roy?

(Pause. Roy looks at her, then)

ROY. 911.

ETHEL ROSENBERG. *(Dials the phone)*? It sings!
(Imitating dial tones) La la la . . .
Huh.
Yes, you should please send an ambulance to the home of Mister Roy Cohn, the famous lawyer.
What's the address, Roy?

ROY *(A beat, then)*. 244 East 87th.

ETHEL ROSENBERG. 244 East 87th Street. No apartment number, he's got the whole building.
My name? *(A beat)* Ethel Greenglass Rosenberg.
(Small smile) Me? No I'm not related to Mr. Cohn. An old friend.

(She hangs up)

They said a minute.

ROY. I have all the time in the world.

ETHEL ROSENBERG. You're immortal.

ROY. I'm immortal. Ethel. *(He forces himself to stand)* I have forced my way into history. I ain't never gonna die.

ETHEL ROSENBERG *(A little laugh, then)*. History is about to crack wide open. Millennium approaches.

SCENE 6

Late that night. Prior's bedroom. Prior 1 watching Prior in bed, who is staring back at him, terrified. Tonight Prior 1 is dressed in weird alchemical robes and hat over his historical clothing and he carries a long palm-leaf bundle.

PRIOR 1. Tonight's the night! Aren't you excited? Tonight she arrives! Right through the roof! Ha-adam, Ha-gadol . . .

PRIOR 2 *(Appearing similarly attired)*. Lumen! Phosphor! Fluor! Candle! An unending billowing of scarlet and . . .

PRIOR. Look. Garlic. A mirror. Holy water. A crucifix. FUCK OFF! Get the fuck out of my room! GO!

PRIOR 1 *(To Prior 2)*. Hard as a hickory knob, I'll bet.

PRIOR 2. We all tumesce when they approach. We wax full, like moons.

PRIOR 1. Dance.

PRIOR. Dance?

PRIOR 1. Stand up, dammit, give us your hands, dance!

PRIOR 2. Listen . . .

(A lone oboe begins to play a little dance tune.)

PRIOR 2. Delightful sound. Care to dance?

PRIOR. Please leave me alone, please just let me sleep . . .

PRIOR 2. Ah, he wants someone familiar. A partner who knows his steps. *(To Prior)* Close your eyes. Imagine . . .

PRIOR. I don't . . .

PRIOR 2. Hush. Close your eyes.

(Prior does.)

PRIOR 2. Now open them.

(Prior does. Louis appears. He looks gorgeous. The music builds gradually into a full-blooded, romantic dance tune.)

PRIOR. Lou.

LOUIS. Dance with me.

PRIOR. I can't, my leg, it hurts at night . . .

Are you . . . a ghost, Lou?

LOUIS. No. Just spectral. Lost to myself. Sitting all day on cold park benches. Wishing I could be with you. Dance with me, babe . . .

(Prior stands up. The legs stop hurting. They begin to dance. The music is beautiful.)

PRIOR 1 *(To Prior 2)*. Hah. Now I see why he's got no children. He's a sodomite.

PRIOR 2. Oh be quiet, you medieval gnome, and let them dance.

PRIOR 1. I'm not interfering, I've done my bit. Hooray, hooray, the messenger's come, now I'm blowing off. I don't like it here.

(Prior 1 vanishes.)

PRIOR 2. The twentieth century. Oh dear, the world has gotten so terribly, terribly old.

(Prior 2 vanishes. Louis and Prior waltz happily. Lights fade back to normal. Louis vanishes.
Prior dances alone.
Then suddenly, the sound of wings fills the room.)

SCENE 7

Split scene: Prior alone in his apartment; Louis alone in the park.
Again, a sound of beating wings.

PRIOR. Oh don't come in here don't come in . . . LOUIS!!
No. My name is Prior Walter, I am . . . the scion of an ancient line, I am . . . abandoned I . . . no, my name is . . . is . . . Prior and I live . . . *here and now*, and . . . in the dark, in the dark, the Recording Angel opens its hundred eyes and snaps the spine of the Book of Life and . . . hush! Hush!
I'm talking nonsense, I . . .
No more mad scene, hush, hush . . .

(Louis in the park on a bench. Joe approaches, stands at a distance. They stare at each other, then Louis turns away.)

LOUIS. Do you know the story of Lazarus?

JOE. Lazarus?

LOUIS. Lazarus. I can't remember what happens, exactly.

JOE. I don't. . . . Well, he was dead, Lazarus, and Jesus breathed life into him. He brought him back from death.

LOUIS. Come here often?

JOE. No. Yes. Yes.

LOUIS. Back from the dead. You believe that really happened?

JOE. I don't know anymore what I believe.

LOUIS. This is quite a coincidence. Us meeting.

JOE. I followed you.
From work. I . . . followed you here.

(Pause.)

LOUIS. You followed me.
You probably saw me that day in the washroom and thought: there's a sweet guy, sensitive, cries for friends in trouble.

JOE. Yes.

LOUIS. Well I fooled you. Crocodile tears. Nothing . . . (*He touches his heart, shrugs*)

(*Joe reaches tentatively to touch Louis's face.*)

LOUIS (*Pulling back*). What are you doing? Don't do that.

JOE (*Withdrawing his hand*). Sorry. I'm sorry.

LOUIS. I'm . . . just not . . . I think, if you touch me, your hand might fall off or something. Worse things have happened to people who have touched me.

JOE. Please.

Oh, boy . . .

Can I . . .

I . . . want . . . to touch you. Can't I please just touch you . . . um, here?

(*He puts his hand on one side of Louis's face. He holds it there*)

I'm going to hell for doing this.

LOUIS. Big deal. You think it could be any worse than New York City?

(*He puts his hand on Joe's hand. He takes Joe's hand away from his face, holds it for a moment, then*) Come on.

JOE. Where?

LOUIS. Home. With me.

JOE. This makes no sense. I mean I don't know you.

LOUIS. Likewise.

JOE. And what you do know about me you don't like.

LOUIS. The Republican stuff?

JOE. Yeah, well for starters.

LOUIS. I don't not like that. I *hate* that.

JOE. So why on earth should we . . .

(*Louis goes to Joe and kisses him.*)

LOUIS. Strange bedfellows. I don't know. I never made it with one of the damned before. I would really rather not have to spend tonight alone.

JOE. I'm a pretty terrible person, Louis.

LOUIS. Lou.

JOE. No, I really am. I don't think I deserve being loved.

LOUIS. There? See? We already have a lot in common.

(*Louis stands, begins to walk away. He turns, looks back at Joe, Joe follows. They exit.*)

(*Prior listens. At first no sound, then once again, the sound of beating wings, frighteningly near.*)

PRIOR. That sound, that sound, it. . . . What is that, like birds or something, like a *really* big bird, I'm frightened, I . . . no, no fear, find the anger, find the . . . anger, my blood is clean, my brain is fine, I can handle pressure, I am a gay man and I am used to pressure, to trouble, I am tough and strong and. . . . Oh. Oh my goodness. I . . . (*He is washed over by an intense sexual feeling*) Ooohhhh. . . . I'm hot, I'm . . . so . . . aw Jeez what is going on here I . . . must have a fever I . . .

(*The bedside lamp flickers wildly as the bed begins to roll forward and back. There is a deep bass creaking and groaning from the bedroom ceiling, like the timbers of a ship under immense stress, and from above a fine rain of plaster dust.*)

PRIOR. OH!

PLEASE, OH PLEASE! Something's coming in here, I'm scared, I don't like this at all, something's approaching and I . . . OH!

(*There is a great blaze of triumphal music, heralding. The light turns an extraordinary harsh, cold, pale blue, then a rich, brilliant warm golden color, then a hot bilious green, and then finally a spectacular royal purple. Then silence.*)

PRIOR (*An awestruck whisper*). God almighty . . .

Very Steven Spielberg.

(*A sound, like a plummeting meteor, tears down from very, very far above the earth, hurtling at an incredible velocity towards the bedroom; the light seems to be sucked out of the room as the projectile approaches; as the room reaches darkness, we hear a terrifying CRASH as something immense strikes earth; the whole building shudders and a part of the bedroom ceiling, lots of plaster and lathe and wiring, crashes to the floor. And then in a shower of unearthly white light, spreading great opalescent gray-silver wings, the Angel descends into the room and floats above the bed.*)

ANGEL.

Greetings, Prophet;

The Great Work begins:

The Messenger has arrived.

(*Blackout.*)

END OF PART ONE

From TWILIGHT: LOS ANGELES, 1992

ANNA DEAVERE SMITH

ANNA DEAVERE SMITH (1950–)

Anna Deavere Smith received her theater training at the American Conservatory Theater in San Francisco. An actor, director, playwright, and poet, she has appeared in numerous films (*The American President*), on Broadway and Off-Broadway, and in many regional theaters. She has also taught at Carnegie Mellon University, Yale, New York University, the University of Southern California, Stanford University, and Harvard University. In 2000 she began a joint appointment in the School of the Arts and School of Law at New York University.

She is currently continuing her work-in-progress *On the Road: A Search for American Character*, a series of performance pieces she began in 1983. The most successful of these is *Fires in the Mirror: Crown Heights, Brooklyn, and Other Identities* (1991). *Fires*, which Cornel West, director of Afro-American studies at Princeton University, calls "the most significant artistic exploration of Black-Jewish relations in our time," won an Obie Award and was a finalist for the Pulitzer Prize. Each part of *On the Road* has been created, in Smith's words, "by interviewing people and later performing them using their own words." Her most recent work, *House Arrest: First Edition* (1997), creates a picture of political life in Washington, D.C. Unlike her earlier works, which were created for a solo performer, the cast of *House Arrest* includes 14 actors who portray dozens of characters. Smith also includes material from historical records in addition to her interviews.

Language and the power of the spoken word as the keys to understanding self and society intrigue Smith: "I started thinking that if I listened carefully to people's words, and particularly to their rhythms, that I could use language to learn about my own time. If I could find a way to really inhabit the words of those around me . . . I could learn about the spirit, the imagination, and the challenges of my own time." Following extensive interviews, she edits and arranges the text into a more conventional "script." In creating the script she tries "to represent multiple points of view" and thereby to "capture the personality of a place by showing its individuals." The people/characters Smith portrays are members of the diverse communities that comprise the American patchwork. Furthermore, members of each community have a distinct sense of who they are and how they differ from other communities and individuals. "I'm interested," declares Smith, "in capturing the American character through documenting these differences."

Smith explores two principal themes throughout her work. First, our identity as American is always being negotiated, and second, there is an inevitable tension between people. As you read *Twilight: Los Angeles, 1992* note that nearly all the characters talk about their ethnic backgrounds and how, as "Americans," they adjust to events and to other people either to increase or to minimize the tensions that exist between them. Smith is interested in how audiences respond to the negotiations individuals make according to the situation.

Note that the title of her extended work is *A Search for*, not *the* American character or *an* American character, but simply *American Character*. Smith argues that there is no single American character: "American character lives not in one place or the other, but in the gaps between the places, and in our struggle to be together in our difference. It lives not in what has been fully articulated, but in what is in the process of being articulated, not in the smooth-sounding words, but in the very moment that the smooth-sounding words fail us. It is alive right now. We might not like what we see, but in order to change it, we have to see it clearly."

Smith's success has been attributed to the objectivity and truth in her work. Ironically, American audiences of European, African, and Asian heritage all feel that Smith is "easier" on the "others" and too critical of "us" in her work—a testimony to her extraordinary objectivity. Smith's audiences also debate whether this writer-actor is creating "true" characters or carica-tures or stereotypes. According to Smith, "Character lives in the obvious gap between the real person and my *attempt* to seem like them. I try to close the gap between us, but I applaud the gap between us. I am willing to display my own *unlikeness*." Ultimately, it is her belief that out of the tension comes motion. "In moving from one side to the other," she declares, "in experi-encing one hand and the other hand, and in building bridges *between* places," there is hope for a better future.

Twilight: Los Angeles, 1992

The 14th piece in Smith's evolving American epic, *Twilight: Los Angeles, 1992* combines tradi-tional theater, documentary, and performance art to expose the devastating impact of what some have called the worst riots in U.S. history. Following a high-speed chase through the streets of Los Angeles during the spring of 1991, Rodney King, a black man, was brutally beaten by four white police officers. A broadcast of the incident (which had been videotaped by a nearby resident) on national television drew an immediate national outcry. The following year, the officers were tried and acquitted, much to the surprise of city officials and average cit-izens. Public reaction in various sections of Los Angeles was explosive; for more than three days burning, looting, beating, and killing paralyzed the city. Among those beaten was white truck driver Reginald Denny, whose black assailants were also tried.

Following nine months of extensive interviews with over 200 people directly involved or tangentially associated with the incidents, Smith selected over 50 individuals whose voices and words best reflected the diversity and tension of a city in turmoil to create her script.

A quick glance at the cast of characters reveals Smith's diverse selection of voices repre-senting both men and women of Asian, Hispanic, African, and European descent. They range in age from teenagers to senior citizens. Among those presented are Rodney King's aunt; white police officer Briseno; Korean liquor store owner Mrs. Young-Soon Han; Mexican sculptor and painter Rudy Sala Jr.; white real estate agent Elaine Young; former chief of the Los Angeles Po-lice Department Daryl Gates; Keith Watson, a young black man accused of beating Reginald Denny; and Denny himself.

The differences in individual perceptions of the events succeed in capturing what Smith calls "the personality of place." Perhaps nowhere are the varied perspectives so penetrating as in the accounts of the King beating offered by "use of force expert" LAPD SWAT Sergeant Charles Duke, and Los Angeles City clerk-typist Josie Morales, who witnessed the attack. Ac-cording to Duke, Officer Laurence M. Powell, one of King's assailants, was totally ineffective in his pummeling of King because

> [he] holds the baton
> like this [demonstrating]
> and that is not a good . . .
> the proper way of holding the baton
> is like this [demonstrating].
>
> •   •   •   •   •   •
>
> Powell has no strength and no power
> in his baton strikes.
> The whole thing boils down to . . .
> Powell was ineffective with the baton.

On the other hand, Morales found Powell and the others to be more proficient in their martial art:

> the next thing we know, um,
> ten or twelve officers made a circle around
> him and they started to hit him.
> I remember
> that they just not only hit him with a stick,
> they also kicked him,
> and one guy,
> one officer, even pummeled his fist
> into his face,
> and they were kicking him.

King's aunt attests to the efficiency of the beating as she recalls seeing the videotape of the attack. She remembers seeing King in a hospital bed, "looking like hell," and recalls the fact that "Rodney went through three plastic surgeons just to look like Rodney again."

Nowhere does Smith better succeed "in capturing the American character through documenting these differences" than when, in performance, she juxtaposes the rage-filled activist Paul Parker with beating victim Reginald Denny, who pleads for understanding. Says Parker:

> So the bottom line is it, it, it's
> a white victim, you know, beaten down by some blacks.
> "Innocent."
> I don't see it on the innocent tip,
> because if that's the case, then we supposed to have some empathy
> or some sympathy toward this one white man?
> It like well, how 'bout the empathy and the sympathy towards?'
> You know, like I said before, we innocent.

Juxtaposed with Parker's tirade is the hymn to harmony from Denny, who, in a long, rambling speech, concludes:

> I just want people to wake up.
> It's not a color, it's a person.
> so this room,
> it's just gonna be
> people,
> just a wild place,
> it's gonna be a blast.
> one day,
> Lord
> willing, it'll happen.

As we arrive at the final play in this anthology, we have in a sense come full circle. You will recall that on page 1, we identified storytellers as the progenitors of theater and drama in Europe, Africa, Asia, and the Americas. As solitary artists, they recounted for their audience the events of the past. Thousands of years later, in Smith's work, we enjoy much the same thing—a performer, alone on a bare stage, re-creating the events of the past to illuminate for her audience basic truths about the present in hopes of creating a more harmonious future.

Anna Deavere Smith played over 60 roles in her examination of the 1992 Los Angeles riots in Twilight: Los Angeles, 1992. Among her most memorable portraits were those of the beaten truck driver Reginald Denny and the old Korean woman, Mrs. Young-Soon Han.

From TWILIGHT: LOS ANGELES, 1992

ANNA DEAVERE SMITH

THE TERRITORY

THESE CURIOUS PEOPLE

STANLEY K. SHEINBAUM, FORMER PRESIDENT,
LOS ANGELES POLICE COMMISSION

(A beautiful house in Brentwood. There is art on all the walls. The art has a real spirit to it. These are the paintings by his wife, Betty Sheinbaum. There is a large living room, an office off the living room which you can see. It is mostly made of wood, lots of papers and books. The office of a writer. There are glass windows that look out on a pool, a garden, a view. Behind us is a kitchen where his wife, Betty, was, but eventually she leaves. Stanley is sitting at a round wooden table with a cup of coffee. He is in a striped shirt and khaki pants and loafers. He has a beard. He is tall, and about seventy-three years old. He seems gruff, but when he smiles or laughs, his face lights up the room. It's very unusual. He has the smile and laugh of a highly spiritual, joyous, old woman, like a grandmother who has really been around. There is a bird inside the house which occasionally chirps.)

Very
interesting thing happened.
Like a week and a half (*very thoughtfully trying to remember*),

Maxine Waters calls me up—
You know who she is?
We're very good friends—
she calls me up and she says,
"Ya gotta come with me.
I been going down to Nickerson Gardens
and
the cops come in and break up these gang meetings
and these are gang meetings
for the purpose of truces."
(*I was momentarily distracted*)
Pay attention.
The next Satuday afternoon,
the next day even,
I go down with her,
uh,
to,
uh,
Nickerson Gardens

    (*an abrupt stop, and
    second pause, as if he's forgotten something for a moment*)

and I see a whole bunch of, uh,
police car
sirens and the lights

and I say, "What the hell's going on here?"
So sure enough, I pull in there

(*three-second pause*).

We pull in there
and, uh,
I ask a cop what's going on
and he says,
"Well, we got a call for help."
There's a gang meeting over there.
There's a community park there and there's a gym
and I go down to the . . .
we go down to the gang meeting
and half of 'em
outside of the
gym
and half of 'em
inside
and here's about a hundred cops lined up over here
and about another hundred
over here
and, uh,
I go
into the, uh,
into the group of gang members who were outside.
Even Maxine got scared by this.
I gotta tell you I was brought up in Harlem.
I just have a feel for what I can do and what I can't do
and I did that.
And I spent about
two, two
hours talkin' to these guys.
Some of these guys were ready to kill me.

(*A bird chirps loudly; maybe this is a parakeet or an inside bird*)

I'm the police commissioner
and therefore a cop
and therefore all the things that went along with being a cop.
It was a very interesting experience, God knows.
One guy who was really disheveled and disjointed
and disfigured
opens up his whole body
and it's clear he's been shot across . . .
not in that . . . not in that day,
months or years before,
and, you know,
these guys have been through the wars down there
and,
you know, I hung around long enough that I could talk to them,
get some insights.
But the cops were mad,
they were really mad
that I would go talk to them
and not talk to them

and I knew that if I went and talked to them
I'd have bigger problems here
But I also knew as I was doing this,
I knew they were gonna be pissed.
Two days I got a letter
and I was . . .
the letter really pleased me in some way.
It was very respectful.
"You went in and talked to our enemy."
Gangs are their enemy.
And so
I marched down to Seventy-seventh
and, uh,
I said, "Fuck you,
I can come in here
anytime I want and talk to you."
Yeah, at roll call.
I said, uh,
"This is a shot I had at talking to these
curious people
about whom I know nothing
and I wanna learn.
Don't you want me to learn about 'em?"
You know, that kind of thing.
At the same time, I had been on this kick,
as I told you before, of . . .
of fighting for what's right for the cops,
because they haven't gotten what they should.
I mean, this city has abused both sides.
The city has abused the cops.
Don't ever forget that.
If you want me to give you an hour on that, I'll give you an hour on
that.
Uh,
and at the end,
uh,
I knew I hadn't won when they said,
"So which side are you on?"
When I said, I said, it's . . .
my answer was
"Why do I have to be on a side?"
Yu, yuh, yeh know.
Why do I have to be on a side?
There's a problem here.

WHEN I FINALLY GOT MY VISION/NIGHTCLOTHES

MICHAEL ZINZUN

Representative, Coalition Against Police Abuse

(*In his office at Coalition Against Police Abuse. There are very bloody and disturbing photographs of victims of police*

Anna Deavere Smith

abuse. The most disturbing one was a man with part of his skull blown off and part of his body in the chest area blown off, so that you can see the organs. There is a large white banner with a black circle and a panther. The black panther is the image from the Black Panther Party. Above the circle is "All Power to the People." At the bottom is "Support Our Youth, Support the Truce.")

I witnessed police abuse.
It was
about one o'clock in the morning
and, um,
I was asleep,
like
so many of the other neighbors,
and I hear this guy calling out for help.
So myself and other people came out in socks
and gowns
and, you know,
nightclothes
and we came out so quickly we saw the police had this brother
handcuffed
and they was beatin' the shit out of him!
You see,
Eugene Rivers was his name
and, uh,
we had our community center here
and they was doin' it right across the street from it.
So I went out there 'long with other people and we demanded they stop.
They tried to hide him by draggin' him away and we followed him
and told him they gonna stop.
They singled me out.
They began Macing the crowd, sayin' it was hostile.
They began
shootin' the Mace to get everybody back.
They singled me out.
I was handcuffed.
Um,
when I got Maced I moved back
but as I was goin' back I didn't go back to the center,
I ended up goin' around this . . .
it was a darkened
unlit area.
And when I finally got my vision
I said I ain't goin' this way with them police behind me,
so I turned back around, and when I did,
they Maced me again
and I went down on one knee
and all I could do was feel all these police stompin' on my back.

(He is smiling)

And I was thinkin' . . . I said
why, sure am glad they got them soft walkin' shoes on,
because when the patrolmen, you know, they have them cushions,
so every stomp,
it wasn't a direct hard old . . .
yeah
type thing.
So
then they handcuffed me.
I said they . . .
well,
I can take this,
we'll deal with this tamarr [sic],
and they handcuffed me.
And then one of them lifted my
head up—
I was on my stomach—
he lifted me from behind
and hit me with a billy club
and struck me in the
side of the head,
which gave me about forty stitches—
the straight billy club,
it wasn't a
P–28, the one with the side handle.
Now, I thought in my mind, said hunh,
they couldn't even knock me out,
they in trouble now.
You see what I'm sayin'?
'Cause I knew what we were gonna do,
'cause I dealt with police abuse
and I knew how to organize.
I say they couldn't even knock me out,
and so as I was layin' there
they was all standin' around me.
They still was Macing, the crowd was gettin' larger and larger and
larger
and more police was comin'.
One these pigs stepped outta the crowd with his flashlight,
caught me right in my eye,
and you can still see the stitches (*He lowers his lid and shows it*)
and
exploded the optic nerve to the brain,
ya see,
and boom (*He snaps his fingers*)
that was it.
I couldn't see no more since then.
I mean, they . . .
they took me to the hospital
and the doctor said, "Well, we can sew this eyelid up and these
stitches here

but
I don't think we can do nothin' for that eye."
So when I got out I got a CAT scan,
you know,
and
they said,
"It's gone."
So I still didn't understand it but I said
well,
I'm just gonna keep strugglin'.
We mobilized
to the point where we were able
to get two officers fired,
two officers had to go to trial,
and
the city on an eye
had to cough up one point two million dollars
and so
that's why
I am able to be here every day,
because that money's bein' used to further the struggle.
I ain't got no big Cadillac,
I ain't got no gold . . .
expensive shoes or clothes.
What we do have
is an opportunity to keep struggling and to do research and to
organize.

HERE'S A NOBODY

CARMEN

ANGELA KING AUNT OF RODNEY KING

*A shop in Pasadena. A very, very rainy day. We are sitting
in back of the shop. She insists that my assistant, Kishisha
Jefferson, join us, because she thought it was not good to
make Kishisha sit in the car in the rain. We are in the back of
her shop. There are work tables with paints, etc. She makes
T-shirts. The shop itself is a boutique with clothing for men,
women, and children. Some of the clothing is Afrocentric in
design, other items are more mainstream. She is a powerful
looking woman with a direct gaze and wavy hair, and a
warmth that is natural, even when it is not intended. She
looks as though she has Native American ancestry. She is
wearing a white sweater, a long skirt, and boots. She smokes
a cigarette. There is an iron gate at the main door that is
painted white. There is a small television in the back where
we are. She lives in an area behind where we are sitting. The
interview was actually scheduled for the day before, but she
was reluctant to speak with me, because when I arrived
Kishisha was in the car. (Kishisha normally drove me to, but*

*did not attend, each interview.) It is ironic that now at the
rescheduled time, she insists that Kishisha join us.*

Our life is something like,
uh,
what's the name of that picture
with Dorothy Dandridge
when she was like
a prostitute and the guy she met was in the Air Force—
the service?
Carmen.
Dorothy Dandridge
and Harry Belafonte—
that was us.
How they partied a lot,
and the guy in the Air Force,
the way he was conservative,
was my father.
We were brought up
for about five or six years like that.
The part where she was . . .
she got in some trouble,
the way my mom,
she cut my father:
They were at the NCO club,
they got to drinkin',
and they went to jail out on the base.
She stabbed him—
oh yeah, honey—
he had a scar on his neck.
She went to jail behind that.
We were twelve or thirteen years old.
It seems like it should have been in a movie:
separated and
livin' in different homes
and then joinin' back together in different homes
and reuniting.
My brother and I were only two that stayed together,
and that brother was the father of Rodney.
Things that we did
like goin fishin',
and then on Franklin,
the Sacramento River,
and then . . .
I ain't never seen nothing like it in my life.
It was me, Rodney, Paul, and Sam,
Rodney's friend,
and I looked up and Rodney was down in the water—
had his pants rolled,
feet and all,
like these Africans—
done caught him a big old
trout
by his—

with his hands.
That was the worst mess I seen.
Got him like this here:
"I got him, I got him!
I got a big . . .
'bout that big . . ."
I said, "Boy, you sure you ain't got some African in you?"
Ooh,
yeah,
I'm talkin 'bout them wild Africans,
not one them well raised ones.
Like with a fish hook?
But to see somebody down in the water with the pants rolled
	up
like this here . . .
I said "Get out of there you scaring 'em, you scaring um!"
"Naw, I got this one, I got this one!"
And comin' up there with this big old trout.
Hand fishin'!
He was the only one I saw down in there in that water,
him and this other guy, this big Mexican guy,
Sam?
And he's the only one I seen catch fish like that.
The rest of 'em got poles.
Down in there with them pants up like that.
That remind me of what I see in Africa somewhere.
I ain't never seen nobody fish with their hands.
Talkin' 'bout "I ain't got time to wait."
That's why I call him greedy.
I'm 'a ask him does he remember that.
He oughta remember it, he was bout sixteen or seventeen
	years old.
Um, Um, Um . . .
He—Glen,
Rodney—
went through three plastic surgeons
just to look like Rodney again.
Galen called to say cops done beat Glen up, talkin about
	Rodney,
I said "What?"
And when I was just turning the channels,
I saw this white car . . .
And he looked just like his father.
I don't know if it's when you lose a life
it comes back in somebody else.
Oh, you should have seen him.
It's a hell of a look.
I, I mean you wouldn't have known him
to look at him now.
I tell him he's got a lot to be thankful for—
a hell of a lot:
He couldn't talk,
just, "Der, der, der."
I said, Goddamn!
I was right here

when it happened.
You want me to tell it?
Ah . . .

(She starts crying; she makes about seven sobs)

Oh, man.
It just came out.

(She gets up and goes away to the door. The hammering is louder. There are two hammers, in different places, as if above or next door. The hammers really sound like a dialogue, and there are cars outside, and rain. The dripping is very close.)

Ah.
It comes up every now and then.
Don't worry.
Just burst out . . .
Um . . .
I told you this whole thing is too much.
It's hurting an' then you're happy,
'specially when I get to thinking about such treacherous
people out there.
We weren't raised like this.
We weren't raised with no black and white thing.
We were raised with all kinds of friends:
Mexicans, Indians, Blacks, Whites, Chinese.
You never would have known that something like this would
	happen to us.
And now it's such a shock.
And then the media,
and then, uh,
"What the hell did you get on there tellin' them people?"
I said,
"Leave me the hell alone,"—
this is the other end of the family—
"them people wants to know.
I'm not gonna keep my doors closed up."
I'm arguin' with them.
"Well tell them this here,
and the next time you get on there,
you tell these people this"
I'm not tellin' these people a damn thing—
all this here went through my damn mind.
I get up here,
"Well Mrs. King so and so and so and so."
Um hum, yeah.
And then they . . .
You know I get up here,
"Oh should I say this should I say that?"
Just a mess, the whole thing.
The media came to me 'cause I was a relative
of Rodney's
and his mother
Dessa wasn't gonna talk—
they didn't because of they religion,

they didn't want to get involved in a political . . .
whatever this thing was.
But I didn't give a damn if it was the president's . . .
whatever it was,
my brother's son out there was lookin' like hell,
that I saw in that bed, and I was gonna fight for every bit of
our justice
and fairness.
I didn't care nothin' 'bout no religious . . .
You know, the President,
he's the top thing,
you know, they cared about him;
that's the way I cared about Glen,
you know, Rodney.
That's the way I feel,
you know, a higher sorts.
It could have been my mother.
But I'm not gonna say that.
You see how everybody rave when something happens with
    the
President of the United States?
Okay, here's a nobody,
but the way they beat him.
this is the way I felt towards him,
You understand what I'm sayin' now?
You do? (*really making sure that I mean what I say*)
Alright.

(*a breath, and more speed as she proceeds*)

That's the way I felt.
I didn't give a damn about no religious
nothin' else,
I wanted justice,
and I wanted whatever
them things had comin' to them done to them,
regardless—you can call it revenge or whatever, but
    what I saw on that video,
on that TV,
that was a
mess.
And I just heard him holler,
that's what got me 'while ago.
And then they say,
"Motorist."
And then I look and saw that white car,
and then I saw him out on that ground,
I heard him hollerin',
I recognized him
out on that ground.
Um . . .
Um . . .
That Koon—
that's the one in that whole trial—
that man showed no kind of remorse at all,
you know that?

He sit there like "It ain't no big thing,
and I
will do it again."
That's the way he looked.
You ever seen him?
And he smile at you.
I don't know how,
I don't *even* know how . . .
the nerve,
the audacity.
And even Briseno,
he's gonna get on there . . .
that's what I'm tellin'
Rodney:
"They tryin'
to do everything they possibly can—*anything* they can—
to make you look bad to the people.
Because of what they had,
that, you know,
what's been done to them—
they've been embarrassed,
and they caught them,
you know, on video,
beatin' you like that,
and the public saw it,
they tryin' to do anything they can to discredit you.
You need to get somewhere and sit down."
I didn't hear nobody mention
about 'em having a bug.
It was like a screw
about the size of my thumb
on the bumper—
on the Blazer—
and they were trailin' him everywhere he went.
This is how they knew
where he was goin',
or how
every time you turn around Rodney King's encounter with
    the law
they had a *screw*.
This is how they had him tagged down.
Uhm hum. Uhm hum.
Right after that Hollywood incident
with that prostitute
and on the phone.
I can hear the echo.
And when I hang up someone is still there.
And then most of the time
I be talkin' crazy anyway
so it doesn't matter.
And why? I have no idea.
But they say there's nothing they can do about the taps.
I've called the telephone company
but
something—it being interfered with the federal government,

so it wasn't nothin' they could do about it.
But I know one thing:
Half the things I said to them on there—
it's been goin' on for a while—
I drop through profanity,
I do,
'cause I get on there, I be wantin' to talk and relax, you know,
and here something click up and click up
and that's when I get started.
I do.
'Cause you have to stop and catch yourself,
you can't just talk comfortable.
Yeah.

WHERE THE WATER IS

SERGEANT CHARLES DUKE

SPECIAL WEAPONS AND TACTICS UNIT, LAPD
USE-OF-FORCE EXPERT FOR THE DEFENSE WITNESS,
SIMI VALLEY AND FEDERAL TRIALS

*(He is standing with a baton. He is wearing glasses and a
uniform and black shoes.)*

Powell holds the baton
like this
and that is
not a good . . .
the proper way of holding the baton
is like this.
So one of the things
they keep talking about
why did it take fifty-six baton blows.
Powell has no strength and no power
in his baton strikes.
The whole thing boils down to . . .
Powell was ineffective with the baton.
You're aware
that that night
he went to baton training
and the sergeant held him afterward
because he was weak and inefficient with the baton training.
That night. That night.
He should have been taken out of the field.
He needed to be taken up to the academy and had a couple
   days of
instruction get him back into
focus.

   (He drinks water)

Oh, I know what I was gonna do.
Prior to this

we lost upper-body-control holds,
in 1982.
If we had upper-body-control holds
involved in this,
this tape woulda never been on,
this incident woulda lasted about
fifteen seconds.
The reason that we lost upper-body-control holds . . .
because we had something like
seventeen to twenty deaths in a period of about 1975–76 to
   1982, and
they said it was associated with its being used on Blacks
and Blacks were dying.
Now,
the so-called community leaders
came forward and complained

   (He drinks water)

and they started a hysteria
about the upper-body-control holds—
that it was inhumane use of force—
so it got elevated from intermediate use of force,
which is the same category as a baton,
to deadly force,
and what I told you was that it was used
in all but one of the incidents.
High levels of PCP and cocaine were found in the systems
of those people it was used on.
If PCP and cocaine did not correlate into the equation
of why people were dying,
how come we used it since the fifties
and we had maybe in a ten-year period one incident of a
   death?
The use of force policy hasn't changed since this incident.
And Gilbert Lindsay,
who was a really neat man,
when he saw a demonstration with the baton
he made a statement
that "you're not gonna beat my people with the baton,
I want you to use the chokehold on 'em."
And a couple other people said,
"I don't care you beat 'em into submission,
you break their bones,
you're not chokin' 'em anymore."
So the political framework was laid
for eliminating upper-body-control holds,
and Daryl Gates—
I believe, but I can't prove it—
but his attitude supports it.
He
and his command staff
and I started
use-of-force reports come through my office,
so I review 'em and I look for training things

and I look for things that will impact how I can make training better.
So I started seeing a lot of incidents similar to Rodney
King
and some of them identical to Rodney King
and I said we gotta find some alternative uses of force.
And their attitude was:
"Don't worry about it,
don't worry about it."
And I said, "Wait a minute,
you gonna get some policemen indicted,
you gonna get some policemen sent to jail,
and they're gonna hurt somebody and it's gonna be perceived to be
other than a proper use of force,
and then you guys in management are gonna scurry away
from it,
you're gonna run away from it,
you're gonna get somebody . . . somebody
is gonna go to the joint because of your lack of effort."
And the last conversation I had was with one of my . . .
He walked by my office,
so I ran out of my office and I catch up with him right by the
fountain,
right by where the water is.
I said,
"Listen, we got another one of these . . .
we gotta explore some techniques and we gotta explore some
options,"
and his response to me:
"Sergeant Duke,
I'm tired of hearing this shit.
We're gonna beat people into submission
and we're gonna break bones."
And he said the Police Commission and the City Council
took this
away from us.
"Do you understand that,
Sergeant Duke?"
And I said, "Yes, sir,"
and I never brought it up again.
And that, to me,
tells me
this is an "in your face" to the City Council and to the Police
Commission.
And like I said,
I can't prove this,
but I believe that Daryl Gates
and the Command staff were gonna do an "in your face" to
the City
Council and the Police Commission, saying,
"You took upper-body-control holds away from us.
Now we're really gonna show you what you're gonna get,
with lawsuits and all the other things that are associated
with it."

YOUR HEADS IN SHAME

ANONYMOUS MAN

JUROR IN SIMI VALLEY TRIAL

*(A house in Simi Valley. Fall. Halloween decorations are
up. Dusk. Low lamplight. A slender, soft-spoken man in
glasses. His young daughter and wife greeted me as well.
Quietness.)*

As soon as we went
into the courtroom with the verdicts
there were
plainclothes policemen everywhere.
You know, I knew that
there would be people unhappy with the verdict,
but I didn't expect near
what happened.
If I had known
what was going to happen,
I mean, it's not,
it's not fair to say I would have voted a different
way.
I wouldn't have—
that's not our justice system—
but I would have written a note to the judge saying,
"I can't do this,"
because of
what it put my family through.
Excuse me.

(Crying)

So anyway,
we started going out to the bus
and the police said
right away,
"If there's rocks and bottles, don't worry
the glass on the bus is bulletproof."
And then I noticed a huge mob scene,
and it's a sheriff's bus that they lock prisoners in.
We got to the hotel and there were some obnoxious re-
porters out
there
already, trying to get interviews.
And you know, the police were trying to get us into the bus
and cover
our faces,
and,
and this reporter said,
"Why are you hiding your heads in shame? Do you know
that buildings
are burning
and people are dying in South LA
because of you?"

And twenty minutes later I got home
and the same obnoxious reporter was at the door
and my wife was saying, "He doesn't want to talk to any-
    body,"
and she kept saying,
"The people wanna know,
the people wanna know,"
and trying to get her foot in the door.
And I said, "Listen, I don't wanna talk to anybody. My wife
    has made
that clear."
And I,
you know, slammed the door in her face.
And so she pulled two houses down
and started
filming our house.
And watching on the TV
and seeing all the political leaders,
Mayor Bradley
and President Bush,
condemning our verdicts.
I mean, the jurors as a group, we tossed around:
was this a setup of some sort?
We just feel like we were pawns that were thrown away by
    the
system.
I mean,
the judge,
most of the jurors
feel like when he was reading the verdicts
he . . .
we thought we could sense a look of disdain on his face,
and he also had said
beforehand
that after the verdicts came out
he would like to come up and talk to us,
but after we gave the verdicts
he sent someone up and said he didn't really want to
do that then.
And plus, he had the right and power to
withhold our names for a period of time
and he did not do that,
he released them right away.
I think it was apparent that we would be harassed
and I got quite a few threats.
I got threatening letters and threatening phone calls.
I think he just wanted to separate himself . . .
A lot of newspapers published our addresses too.
The *New York Times* published the values of our homes.
They were released in papers all across the country.
We didn't answer the phone,
because it was just every three minutes . . .
We've been portrayed as white racists.
One of the most disturbing things, and a lot of the jurors
said that

the thing that bothered them that they received in the mail
more
than anything else,
more than the threats, was a letter from the KKK
saying,
"We support you, and if you need our help, if you want to join
our organization,
we'd welcome you into our fold."
And we all just were:
No, oh!
God!

WAR ZONE

RIOT

CHUNG LEE

PRESIDENT OF THE KOREAN-AMERICAN VICTIMS
ASSOCIATION

*(A conference room in an office in Korea town. A man in
his sixties. His son translates. Afternoon. The following is
a phonetic transcription.*)*

Guda-ume, o, uri,
gage ne-ibohant's jonhwaha nikkani,
o, uri gugagega da t'olligo
guyangbanhanun, gusaramhanun yegiga

(And next I called my neighbor's store
and the gentleman—uh, the man told me,
"Your store's been completely looted!)

nohi mulgoni gilgonnos'o p'uraja-e jonbuda,
ap'e p'urajande p'urajallo jonbuda
gonnowa itta hanun jonhwarul badas' o,

(Your whole stock is scattered all over
in front of the project across the street.")

gunyang da ijen, o,
p'okttong-i nassunikkani,
mulgoni gocchok waitta goredo urin
gogi-e dehan-gon hanna
miryonhanna an-gajottagu

(Well now, uh . . .
I realized then that a riot had begun,
so even though our stuff was thrown out there,
we decided to give up
any sense of attachment to our possessions.)

guldoni e, gusaram hant'e
yolttushi ban-gyony-in-ga yolttushin-ga,
nohi gagega bult'ago ittago jonhwaga wattago yo

*Phonetics arranged by Kyung Ja Lee.

(And then, uh, he called around twelve-thirty or maybe
    twelve,
and he told me that my store was on fire.)

"DON'T SHOOT"

RICHARD KIM APPLIANCE STORE OWNER

*(Morning. August 1993. A Korean-American man in his
thirties. He is dressed in khakis, a white shirt, and a tie.
We are sitting in the back of his electronics store, which is
quite large. We are in a room with very expensive stereo
equipment.)*

We waited for about half an hour
and then my father showed up with a neighbor.
He told me what had happened.
There was no police officer to be found anywhere.
We came back here.
We started calling all the police stations and the hospitals to
    see if
anybody had checked in
if they fit the description.
Unfortunately we can't get any kind of answer from anybody.
While that was happening, a neighbor called and said you
    better
come down here because
there are hundreds of people and your store's being looted
at this time.
So we packed up our van, four people, five people, including
myself, and we headed down there.
I already knew people were carrying guns,
already knew my mother was shot at that corner.
So it was like going to war.
That's the only thing I can say.
By the time we got there
at this time
there are hundreds of people at our store.
At that time when we were approaching the store
I realized there are gunshots going on.
As I was approaching the store
one person was carrying to the side—
obviously he was wounded—
and our neighbor,
he was a car dealership and he was trying to hold down the
    store,
trying to keep the people back,
and I can see one person still at the corner by the door
with a shotgun and I looked at across the street.
There are at least three or four people with handguns firing
    back.
There was exchange of fire going on.
So I pulled our van—I was driving—
I pulled our van in between our store entrance,

in between the person firing at me in front of the store,
and I got out and my first thought was I could use the van to
    block
the bullets from hitting the guy in front of the store.
I yelled for everybody to stop shooting, yelled,
"Don't shoot!"
For a split second, they stopped shooting.
And across the street
I looked, could see three people, they looked at me, and they
    pointed the
guns at me.
And they were so close
I could see the barrels of the guns.
And . . . I knew they were going to start firing.
I got a gut feeling.
And I ducked.
And . . . they started firing at the van.
And . . . I came around the van, to the back.
And . . . we had a rifle inside the van.
And . . . I pulled it out,
pulled the trigger,
and it just clicked, because there was no bullet in the cham-
    ber.
So I went back,
put the bullet in the chamber, and returned fire at the people
    firing
at us.
I wasn't aiming to hurt anybody.
More or less trying to disperse the people.
I was firing at the general direction that the gunfire was
    coming from.
When that happened, people dispersed.
I guess the people firing at me decided it wasn't worth it and
    they all
took off.
Everybody just went "pa-chew."

BUBBLE GUM MACHINE MAN

ALLEN COOPER, A.K.A. BIG AL

EX-GANG MEMBER, EX-CONVICT,
ACTIVIST IN NATIONAL TRUCE MOVEMENT

*(He is wearing an odd cap with a button, and buttons on
his shirt. In a gym in Nickerson Gardens, 5:30 P.M.)*

The L.A. Four they committed a crime of what?
Assault
and battery?
And what did the government dig for?
What did they dig for?
Stoppin' traffic of a truck?
Are they sure that truck belonged in that area?

Did they check to see if that truck qualified to fit on that city
 street?
No, they didn't check that.
That wasn't a highway or nothin';
that was a boulevard.
He was turnin' off a residential street!
You gotta understand, it may have been a
intimidation move,
OK,
drivin' into a location that is at a uprising.
And I guess he's at a point tryin' to prove he can get
past.
Any other commonsense person
woulda went around.
But we're not basin' our life on Reginald Denny;
neither are we basin' our lives on Rodney King.
Only thing we're expressing through the Rodney King—
through Reginald Denny beating—
it shows how
a black person gets treated in his community.
And it was once brought to the light
and shown
and then we still . . . we see no belief,
because they never handled, from the top of the level, the
 way it
should have been handled,
because they handled like a soap opera.
That's all that
really was.
If you put twenty hidden cameras
in the county jail system,
you got people beat worse than that
point blank.
Some jails got things
called
the red room
and the blue room,
you get what they call an attitude adjustment.
What Rodney King . . .
It been—
it's been twenty, thirty years,
and people suffered beatings from law enforcement.
It ain't nothin' new.
It was just brought to the light this time.
But then it showed what—
it showed that it doesn't mean a thing,
It doesn't mean a thing.
Now if that was an officer down there gettin' beat,
it would a been a real national riot thing—
you hear me?
Just imagine how many people woulda been out there
clappin';
it wouldn't a been no sad sorry, hot . . .
it woulda been a happy hot line.
Everybody makin' emotion out of somethin':

Rotney King, Rotney King, Rotney King.
It's not Rotney King.
It's the ghetto.
I was at one of these swap meets
and a bubble gum machine man pulled a gun out.
Now what a bubble gum machine man doin' with a pistol?
Who wanna rob a bubble gum machine?
Because we live here, the conditions are so
enormous and so dangerous,
that they have to be qualified to carry a firearm.
What is the purpose?
You got to live here to express this point, you got to live
here to see what's goin' on.
You gotta look at history, baby,
you gotta look at history.
It wasn't . . .
Anything is never a problem 'til the black man gets his
 hands on it.
It was good for the NRA
to have fully automatic weapons,
but when the Afro-American people got hold of 'em,
it was a crime!
Aww . . .
He's a problem
in the neighborhood;
he has a AK-47 assault weapon.
We didn't bring them guns here.
We didn't make up—
they was put here for a reason:
to entrap us!
Point blank.
You gotta look at history, baby,
you gotta look at history.
This Reginald Denny thing is a joke.
It's joke.
That's just a delusion to the real
problem.

A WEIRD COMMON THREAD IN OUR LIVES

REGINALD DENNY

*(In the office of Johnnie Cochran, his lawyer. A confer-
ence room. Walls are lined with law books. Denny is wearing a baseball hat and T-shirt. His friend, a man, is there
with a little girl. One of Cochran's assistants, a young
black woman attorney, sits in on the interview. Denny is
upbeat, speaks loudly. Morning, May 1993.)*

Every single day
I must make this trip to Inglewood—no problem—
and I get off the freeway like usual,
taking up as much space as I can in the truck.

People don't like that.
Because I have to.
That little turn onto Florence
is pretty tricky,
it's really a tight turn.
I take two lanes to do it in
and
it was just like a scene
out of a movie.
Total confusion and chaos.
I was just in awe.
And the thing that I remember most vivid—
broken glass
on the ground.
And for a split second I was goin'
check this out,
and the truck in front of me—
and I found out later—
the truck in front of me,
medical supplies goin' to Daniel Freeman!

(He laughs)

Kind of a
ironic thing!
And the, uh,
the strange thing was
that what everyone thought was a fire extinguisher
I got clubbed with,
it was a bottle of oxygen,
'cause the guy had medical supplies.
I mean,
does anyone know
what a riot looks like?
I mean, I'm sure they do now.
I didn't have a clue of what one looked like
and
I didn't know that the verdict had come down.
I didn't pay any attention
to that,
because that
was somebody else's problem
I guess I thought
at the time.
It didn't have anything to do with me.
I didn't usually pay too much attention of what was going on
in
California
or in America or anything
and, uh,
I couldn't for the life of me figure out what was goin' on.
Strange things do happen on that street.
Every now and again police busting somebody.
That was a street that was never . . .
I mean, it was always an exciting . . .
we,

lot of guys looked forward to going down that street
'cause there was always something going on, it seemed
like,
and the cool thing was I'd buy those cookies
from
these guys
on the corner,
and I think they're, uh,
Moslems?
And they sell cookies
or cakes,
the best-tasting stuff,
and whatever they were selling that day,
and it was always usually a surprise,
but it was very well known
that it was a good surprise!
Heck, a good way to munch!
But when I knew something was wrong was when they
    bashed in the
right window of
my truck.
That's the end of what I remember as far as anything
until five or six days later.
They say I was in a coma.
And I still couldn't figure out,
you know,
how I got here.
And
It was quite a few weeks after I was in the hospital
that they even let on that there was a riot,
because the doctor didn't feel it
was something I needed to know.
Morphine is what they were givin' me for pain,
and it was just an interesting time.
But I've never been in an operating room.
It was like . . .
this is just . . .
I 'member like in a movie
they flip on the big lights
and they're really in there.

(He laughs)

I was just goin' "God"
and seein' doctors around with masks on
and I still didn't know why I was still there
and next thing
I know I wake up a few days later.
I think when it really dawned on me
that something big might have happened
was when important people wanted to come in and say hi.
The person that I remember that wanted to come and see
    me,
the first person that I was even aware of who wanted to see
    me,
was Reverend Jesse Jackson,

Anna Deavere Smith

and I'm just thinkin':
not this guy,
that's the dude I see on TV all the time.
And then it was a couple days later that
Arsenio Hall came to see me
and he just poked his head in, said hello,
and, uh,
I couldn't say nothin' to him.
And then, about then I started to, uh,
started to get it.
And by the time I left Daniel Freeman I knew what hap-
    pened,
except they wouldn't let me watch it on TV.
I mean, they completely controlled that remote-control
    thing.
They just had it on a movie station.
And if I hadn't seen some of the stuff,
you know, of me doin' a few things after everything was
    done,
like climbing back into the truck,
and talking to Titus and Bobby and Terry and Lee—
that's the four people
who came to my rescue,
you know—they're telling me stuff that I would never
even have known.
Terry
I met only because she came as a surprise guest visit to the
    hospital.
That was an emotional time.
How does one say that
someone
saved
my life?
How does a person,
how do I
express enough
thanks
for someone risking their
neck?
And then I was kind of . . .
I don't know if "afraid" is the word,
I was just a little,
felt a little awkward meeting people
who
saved me.
Meeting them was not like meeting
a stranger,
but it was like
meeting a
buddy.
There was a weird common thread in our lives
That's an extraordinary event,
and here is four people—
the ones in the helicopter—
and they just stuck with it,

and then you got four people
who seen it on TV
and said enough's enough
and came to my rescue.
They tell me
I drove the truck for what? About a hundred or so feet.
The doctors say there's *fight* or *flight* syndrome.
And I guess I was in *flight!*
And it's been seventeen years since I got outta high school!
I been driving semis,
it's almost second nature,
but Bobby Green
saw that I was gettin' nowhere fast and she just jumped in
    and
scooted me over
and drove the truck.
By this time
it was tons of glass and blood everywhere,
'cause I've seen pictures of what I look like
when I first went into surgery,
and I mean it was a pretty
bloody mess.
And they showed me my hair,
when they cut off my hair
they gave it to me in a plastic bag.
And it was just
long hair and
glass and blood.
Lee—
that's a woman—
Lee Euell,
she told me
she just
cradled me.
There's no
passenger seat in the truck
and here I am just kind of on my knees in the middle of the
    floor
and, uh,
Lee's just covered with blood,
and Titus is on one side,
'cause Bobby couldn't see out the window.
The front windshield was so badly broken
it was hard to see.
And Titus is standing on the running board telling Bobby
    where to go,
and then Terry,
Titus's girlfriend,
she's in front of the truck
weaving through traffic,
dodging toward cars
to get them to
kind of move out of the way,
to get them to clear a path,
and next stop was

Daniel Freeman Hospital!
Someday when I,
uh,
get a house,
I'm gonna have one of the rooms
and it's just gonna be
of all the riot stuff
and it won't be a
blood-and-guts
memorial,
it's not gonna be a sad,
it's gonna be a happy room.
It's gonna be . . .
Of all the crazy things that I've got,
all the,
the
love and compassion
and the funny notes
and the letters from faraway places,
just framed, placed,
framed things,
where a person will walk in
and just have a good old time in there.
It'll just be
fun to be in there,
just like a fun thing,
and there won't be
a color problem
in this room.
You take the toughest
white guy
who thinks he's a bad-ass
and
thinks he's better than any other race in town,
get him in a position where he needs help,
he'll take the help
from no matter who the color of the guy across . . .
because he so self-
centered and -serving,
he'll take it
and then
soon as he's better
he'll turn around
and rag on 'em.
I know that for a fact.
Give me what I need and shove off.
It's crazy, it's nuts.
That's the person I'd like to shake and go,
"Uuuh,
you fool,
you selfish little shit"—
those kind of words.
"Uhhh, man, you *nut*."

(Pause and intense stare, low-key)

I don't know what I want.
I just want people to wake up.
It's not a color, it's a person.
So this room,
it's just gonna be
people,
just a wild place,
it's gonna be a blast.
One day,
Lord
willing, it'll happen.

GODZILLA

ANONYMOUS MAN #2 (HOLLYWOOD AGENT)

(Morning. A good looking man in shirt and tie and fine shoes. A chic office in an agency in Beverly Hills. We are sitting in a sofa.)

There was still the uneasiness that was growing
when the fuse was still burning,
but
it was
business as usual.
Basically,
you got
such-and-so on line one,
such-and-so on line two.
Traffic,
Wilshire,
Santa Monica.
Bunch of us hadda go to lunch at the
the Grill
in Beverly Hills.
Um,
gain major
show business dead center business restaurant,
kinda loud but genteel.
The . . . there was an incipient panic—
you could just feel—
the tension
in the
restaurant
it
was palpable,
it was tangible,
you could cut it with a knife.
All anyone was talking
about, you could hear little bits
of information—
did ya hear?

did ya hear?
It's like we were transmitting
thoughts
to each other
all across the restaurant,
we were transmitting thoughts to each other.
All the,
frankly, the
white
upper class,
upper middle class—
whatever your,
the
definition is—
white successful . . .
spending too much money,
too, ya know, too good a restaurant,
that kinda thing.
We were just
getting ourselves into a frenzy,
which I think a lot of it
involved
guilt,
just generic guilt.
When we drove back,
and it's about a ten-minute drive,
talking about the need
for guns
to protect ourselves,
it had just gone from here to there.
But I'm tellin' you, nothin' happened!
I don't mean somebody in the restaurant
had a fight
or somebody screamed at someone—
nothing, just,
ya know,
Caesar salad,
da-de-da,
ya know,
but the whole
bit
went
like that.
We walked in
from the underground garage into here and we looked at
    each other
and we could see people
running around
instead of . . . like,
people walk fast in this business
but now they were, they were like
running,
and
we looked at ourselves—
"we gotta close the office."

So we had gone from
"I'm a little nervous"
to "We gotta close the office,
shut down."
This is a business
we don't shut down.
Memo goes
out saying:
"Office closed for the day.
Everyone please leave
the office."
And *then*
I remember somebody said:
"Did you hear?
They're burning down
the Beverly Center."
By the way, *they* . . .
No no no, it's . . .
There is no *who*.
Whaddya mean, *who*?
No, just *they*.
That's fair enough.
"Did you hear *they* are burning down the Beverly Center?"
Oh, okay, *they* . . .
Ya know what I mean?
It almost didn't matter who,
it's irrelevant.
Somebody.
It's not *us*!
That was one of the highlights for me.
So I'm looking outside
and the traffic is far worse
and people were basically fleeing the office
and we were closing all the blinds
and this is about,
um,
I guess about four o'clock.
The vision of all these yuppies
and aging or aged yuppies,
Armani suits,
and, you know,
fleeing like
wild-eyed . . .
All you needed was Godzilla behind them,
you know,
like this . . .
chasing them out of the building,
that's really it.
Aaah, aaah.

    (*He laughs a very hearty laugh*)

Still
still,
nothing had happened—
I don't mean to tell you that bombs were exploding—

nothing, zero.
So we,
I was one of the last to leave,
as usual,
and the roads were so packed it
it must be like
they were leaving
Hiroshima
or something,
Dresden . . .
I've never been in a war or . . .
just the daily war of . . .

    (Intercom beeps)

Who's that?
Do you need me?
One sec. (*He leaves, then returns*)
Where was I?
Yeah.
What, what was, was
"I deserve it,"
you know,
was I, was I getting
my . . .
when I was *fearing*
for
safety
or my family or something . . .
those moments.
Because the panic was so high
that, oh my God,
I was almost thinking:
"Did I deserve this,
do I, do I deserve it?"
I thought me, personally—no,
me, generically,
maybe so.
Even though I, I . . .
what's provoked it—
the spark—
was the verdict,
which was
ab*surd.*
But that was just the spark—
this had been set
for years before.
But maybe,
not maybe,
but, uh, the
system
plays unequally,
and the people who were
the, they,
who were burning down the Beverly Center
had been victims of the system.

Whether well-intentioned or not,
somebody got the short shrift,
and they did,
and I started to
absorb a little guilt
and say, uh,
"I deserve,
I deserve it!"
I don't mean I deserve to get my house burned down.
The us
did
not in . . .
not,
I like to think, not intentionally,
but
maybe so,
there's just . . .
it's so
awful out there,
it was so *heartbreaking,*
seeing those . . .
the devastation that went on
and people reduced to burning down their own neighbor-
    hoods.
Burning down our neighborhoods
I could see.
But burning down their own—
that was more dramatic
to me.

I WAS SCARED

Anonymous Young Woman Student, University of Southern California

(*February. A rainstorm. Late afternoon, early evening. Dark out. Just before dinner. A sorority house at the University of Southern California, which is a very affluent university in the middle of South-Central. We are in a small room with Laura Ashley furnishings. Lamplight. While we are talking, someone comes by ringing a dinner bell which is like a xylophone.*)

I was scared to death.
I've never felt as sacred, as frightened, in my life.
Um,
and it was a different fear that I've ever felt.
I mean, I was really afraid.
At a certain point
it dawned on us that they might try to attack the row,
the sororities and the fraternities.
Because they did do that during the Watts riots.
And, um, they . . .

Anna Deavere Smith

they went
into the house,
where they smashed the windows.
I don't know how we got this information but somebody
   knew that,
so that
spread in the house real fast,
and once we realize that,
we started packing.
We all packed a bag and we all had put on our tennis shoes.
This was late in the evening, and we all sat in our hallways
   upstairs,
very small hallways,
and we all said,
"Oh, if they come to the front door, this is what we're gonna
   do."
Many things I can tell you.
First of all, my parents were on their way,
to drive to California,
to take part in a caravan
in which they bring old cars,
old forties cars,
and a whole bunch of 'em, all their friends, a huge club.
They all drive their cars around the country.
My dad has an old car.
It's a '41 Cadillac.
I told 'em to turn around, go home.
I said, "Go home, Mom."
All I can think of . . . one bottle,
one shear from one bottle in my father's car,
he will die!
He will die.
He collects many cars,
he has about fifteen different kinds of cars.
This is his thing, this is what he does.
He's got Lincoln
Continentals
and different Town and Countries.
All forties.
His favorite is a '41 Cadillac.
And, um, so . . . he keeps them from five to ten years, you
   know.
Depending on whether you can get a good value for 'em.
It's a business
as well as a hobby.
And so I don't specifically know what car he came out in.
But one of 'em.
And those are his pride
and joys.
They are perfect.
They are polished.
They are run perfect.
They are perfect.
All I can think of is a bottle gettin' anywhere near it.

THE UNHEARD

MAXINE WATERS, CONGRESSWOMAN, 35TH DISTRICT

*(This interview is from a speech that she gave at the First
African Methodist Episcopal Church, just after Daryl
Gates had resigned and soon after the upheaval. FAME is
a center for political activity in LA. Many movie stars go
there. On any Sunday you are sure to see Arsenio Hall
and others. Barbra Streisand contributed money to the
church after the unrest. It is a very colorful church, with an
enormous mural and a huge choir with very exciting music.
People line up to go in to the services the way they line up
for the theater or a concert.*

*(Maxine Waters is a very elegant, confident congress-
woman, with a big smile, a fierce bite, and a lot of guts.
Her area is in South-Central. She is a brilliant orator. Her
speech is punctuated by organ music and applause. Sometimes the audience goes absolutely wild.)*

First
African
Methodist Episcopal Church.
You all here got it going on.
I didn't know this is what you did at twelve o'clock on Sun-
   day.
Methodist,
Baptist,
Church of God and Christ all rolled into one.
There was an insurrection in this city before
and if I remember correctly
it was sparked by police brutality.
We had a Kerner Commission report.
It talked about what was wrong with our society.
It talked about institutionalized racism.
It talked about a lack of services,
lack of government responsive to the people.
Today, as we stand here in 1992,
if you go back and read the report
it seems as though we are talking about what that report
   cited
some twenty years ago still exists today.
Mr. President,
THEY'RE HUNGRY IN THE BRONX TONIGHT,
THEY'RE HUNGRY IN ATLANTA TONIGHT,
THEY'RE HUNGRY IN ST. LOUIS TONIGHT.
Mr. President,
our children's lives are at stake.
We want to deal with the young men who have been
   dropped off of
America's agenda.
Just hangin' out,
chillin',
nothin' to do,

nowhere to go.
They don't show up on anybody's statistics.
They're not in school,
they have never been employed,
they don't really live anywhere.
They move from grandmama
to mama to girlfriend.
They're on general relief and
they're sleepin' under bridges.
Mr. President,
Mr. Governor,
and anybody else who wants to listen:
Everybody in the street was not a thug
or a hood.
For politicians who think
everybody in the street
who committed a petty crime,
stealing some Pampers
for the baby,
a new pairs of shoes . . .
We know you're not supposed to steal,
but the times are such,
the environment is such,
that good people reacted in strange ways. They are not all
    crooks and
criminals.
If they are,
Mr. President,
what about your violations?
Oh yes.
We're angry,
and yes,
this Rodney King incident.
The verdict.
Oh, it was more than a slap in the face.
It kind of reached in and grabbed you right here in the heart
and it pulled at you
and it hurts so bad.
They want me to march out into Watts,
as the black so-called leadership did in the sixties,
and say, "Cool it, baby,
cool it."
I am sorry.
I know how to talk to my people.
I know how to tell them not to put their lives at risk.
I know how to say don't put other people's lives at risk.
But, journalists,
don't you dare dictate to me
about what I'm supposed to say.
It's not nice to display anger.
I am angry.
It is all right to be angry.
It is unfortunate what people do when they are frustrated
    and angry.

The fact of the matter is,
whether we like it or not,
riot
is the voice of the unheard.

IT'S AWFUL HARD
TO BREAK AWAY

DARYL GATES, FORMER CHIEF OF LOS ANGELES POLICE DEPARTMENT AND CURRENT TALK SHOW HOST

(In a lounge at the radio station where he does a talk show. He is in great physical shape and is wearing a tight-fitting golf shirt and jeans. There is the sound of a Xerox machine. This is my second interview with him.)

First of all, I . . . I don't think it was a fund-raiser.
I don't think it was a fund-raiser at all.
It was a group of
people
who were in opposition
to Proposition F.
We're talking about long-term support.
We're talking about people who
came out and supported me right from the beginning
of this controversy,
when people were trying to get me to retire and everything.
Real strong supporters
of mine
and they were supporting
a no against Prop . . .
Proposition F.
And they begged me to be there
and I said I would and this is before we knew the . . . the,
uh, verdicts were coming in
and I didn't wanna go.
I didn't like those things, I don't like them at all,
but
strong supporters and I said I'll drop by for a little while,
I'll drop by,
and, um, so I had a commitment
and I'm a person who tries very hard to keep commitments
and somewhere along the way
better sense
should have
prevailed.
Not because it would have changed
the course of . . . of events in any way, shape, or form, it
    wouldn't have.
I was in constant contact with my office.
I have radio beepers, telephones,
uh,
a portable telephone . . .

telephone in my car,
just about everything you'd need
to communicate anywhere within our power.
But somewhere along the line
I should have said
my commitment to them is
not as important as my overall commitment to the . . . to the
    city.
When I . . . when I thought things were getting
to the point that I had . . . we were having some serious prob-
    lems,
I was almost there.
My intent was to drop in say, "Hey,
I think we got a . . . a, uh,
riot blossoming.
I can't stay. I gotta get out of here."
And that's basically what I did.
The problem was
I was further away.
I thought it was in Bel Air. It turned out to be Pacific Pal-
    isades.
And my driver kept saying,
"We're almost there, we're almost there."
You know, he was kinda . . .
he wasn't sure of the distance either.
"We're almost there, Chief, we're almost there."
My intent was
to say, "Hey, I . . . I gotta get outta here," say hi,
and that's what I intended to do,
and it's awful hard to
break away.
I kept walking toward the door, walking toward the door.
People want a picture.
Shake your hand.
And it took longer than I thought it was
and I've criticized myself
from the very beginning. I've never, uh, I've never, uh,
justified that in any way, shape, or form.
I said it was wrong. I shouldn't have . . . I should have turned
    around.
I know better.
Would it have made any difference
if I had closeted myself in . . . in my office and did nothing?
I never would have been criticized.
But the very fact
that it gave that . . . that
perception of a fund-raiser,
and I know
in the minds of some
that's a big
cocktail party
and
it wasn't that at all, eh,
but, eh, in somebody's home
and there weren't that many people there are all

and anyway . . .
But I shouldn't have gone!
If for no other reason
than it's given
so many people
who wanted it
an opportunity to carp
and to criticize,
for . . . for
I should have been smarter.
I'm usually smart enough to realize hey,
I know I'll be criticized for that,
and I'm not going to give them the opportunity.
But for some
reason I didn't and, uh . . .
I think a lot of people who have . . . have
looked at me as being, uh,
stubborn and
obstinate
because I wouldn't compromise
and I was not going to be forced out of the department
and I believed it would be overall harmful to the department
    to be
forced out
and I think
the department was demoralized anyway
and I think it would just have absolutely
totally demoralized 'em.
And when I stood up,
they said, "Hey,
by golly, uh,
uh,
he's saying a lot of things that
I'd like to say."
And some of them were just shaking with anger because they
    were
being accused of things
that
they wouldn't think of doing and
didn't do
and they know the people around them,
their partners, wouldn't have done those types of things.
I don't think there's anyone who doesn't feel and isn't sensi-
    tive to
what is being said about them
day in and day out.
All you gotta do is pick up a newspaper and see what's being
    said
about you in the *Los Angeles Times*
and the . . . and, and the . . . and in the electronic media.
I mean, it was day in and day out.
Editorials
and all kinds of things.
I mean, the community activists
and most of them were really nasty

politicians,
nasty. I mean, they weren't so . . .
Nobody likes to read those types of things and more impor-
    tantly
no one wants their friends and family
to read those kinds of things and I mean, uh, uh, it's a terri-
    bly difficult
thing to endure
and when people hear it over and over and over again.
And I make speeches
on college campuses all across the country
and I swear
I have a group,
mostly African-Americans,
and I swear
I am the symbol
of police oppression
in the United States,
if not the world.
I am.
Me!
And I ask them:
Who told you this?
What gave you this idea?
You don't know me.
You don't have any idea
what I've done.
Forty-three years in law enforcement,
no one has said that about me,
no one.
And suddenly
I am the symbol
of police oppression
and it's a tough thing to deal with,
a very tough thing.
You know,
just prior
to this,
in a poll
taken by a legitimate pollster,
the individual
with the greatest credibility
in the state of California—
I can't say the state
of California,
but the southern
part of the state of California—
was me.
The most popular Republican in Los Angeles
and Los Angeles County
was me.
I got more support
than
Ronald Reagan,
George Deukmejian,

what other Republicans,
Pete Wilson.
I got more support,
and suddenly!
suddenly!
I am the symbol.
And, you know,
on the day
that the Rodney thing [sic],
thing
happened,
the
President of the United States
was declaring me a national hero
for the work that I had done
in drugs
and narcotics
and the work that I had done with kids
and a lot of these kids were black kids.
And suddenly,
suddenly,
I am the symbol
of police oppression.
Just because some officers
whacked Rodney King
out in Foothill Division
while I was in Washington, D.C.

TWILIGHT

I REMEMBER GOING . . .

REV. TOM CHOI MINISTER, WESTWOOD PRESBYTERIAN CHURCH

*(In a pastor's office in the church, a church with an afflu-
ent congregation. Afternoon, during a rainstorm, winter
1993. He is a tall, slender Chinese-American man. He
was educated at Yale Divinity School and labors during the
interview to be clear and not to overstate.)*

I remember going out
finally on Saturday to, um, do some cleanup work.
And I remember
very distinctly
going down there and choosing to wear my clerical collar.
And I haven't worn my clerical collar for about seven or
    eight years,
you know,
because, you know, people call me "Father,"
all this kind of stuff,
and I didn't like that identification.
But I remember doing that specifically
because I was afraid that somebody

would mistake me for a Korean shop owner
and . . . and, um, either berate me physically or beat me up.
So I remember hiding behind this collar
for protection.
The reason why a minister would wear a collar
is to proclaim . . .
to let everybody know who he is and what he is,
but I'm using it for protection,
which I, I knew about that
and I said, "Gee."
But I didn't take it off.
Anyway, I went down
and we were asked to go
and pick up
stuff from the Price Club
and so I had to go down to the bank
and get money
and I went to the area.
Also I remember some people complaining
that Korean-Americans didn't patronize black businesses.
So I made sure that I went to black businesses for lunch
and whatnot, wearing my collar and waiting around for food.
And I remember just going to people and people just looking
    at me.
And . . . and I usually kind of slump over when I walk, but in
    this case I
kind of stood straight and I had my neck high
and I made sure that everyone saw my collar.

  (Laughs)

And . . . and I, I just went to somebody and, um, who was
    standing
next in line and I said,
"How are you doing?"
Every . . . every place I went
I got the same answer:
"Oh, I'm doing all right.
How are you?"
And I said, "Oh, I'm just trying to make it."
And there'd be a chuckle.
And . . . and agreement.
And then we just started having this conversation.
And in every instance,
you know,
of these people that quote unquote
were supposed to be hostile on TV and whatnot,
there was nothing but warmth,
nothing but a sense of . . . of
"Yeah, we should stick together" and nothing but friendli-
    ness
that I have felt,
and this was, um, a discovery
that I had been out of touch with this part of the city.
After a couple of days
I stopped wearing the collar

and I realize that if there's any protection I needed
it was just whatever love I had in my heart to share with peo-
    ple that
proved to be enough,
the love that God has taught me to share.
That is what came out in the end for me.

APPLICATION OF THE LAWS

BILL BRADLEY SENATOR, D-NEW JERSEY

(His office in the Senate Building. A Sunday in February 1993. A well-lit office with wonderful art on the wall. He is dressed in jeans but is wearing very elegant English shoes. His daughter is in the other part of the empty office doing her homework. They are on their way to a basketball practice for her.)

I mean, you know, it's still . . .
there are people who are, uh,
who the law treats in different ways.
I mean, you know, one of the things that strike me about,
uh, the events of Los Angeles, for example, was, um, the fol-
    lowing:
I have a friend,
an African-American,
uh, was uhhh,
I think a second-year Harvard Law School student.
And he was interning
a summer in the late seventies
out in LA, at a big law firm.
and every Sunday
the . . . the different partners would . . .
would invite the interns to their home
for tea or brunch or whatever.
And this was a particular Sunday and he was on his way
    driving
to one of the partners' homes.
There's a white woman in the car with him.
I think she was an intern.
I'm not positive of that.
They were driving and they were in the very . . .
just about the neighborhood of the,
uh, partner, obviously well-to-do neighborhood in Los An-
    geles.
Suddenly he looks in the rearview mirror.
There is a, uh, police car,
red light.
He pulls over.
Police car pulls in front of him,
pull . . . police car pulls behind him,
police car pulls beside of him.
Police jump out,

guns, pull him out of the car,
throw him to the floor,
put a handcuff on him behind his back.
All the while pointing a gun at him.
Run around to the woman on the other side. "You're being held
against your will, aren't you, being held against your will."
She gets hysterical
and they keep their guns pointed.
Takes them fifteen or twenty minutes to convince them.
"No, no, I'm not, uh, I'm not, uh, I'm, I'm, I'm, I'm an intern, law firm,
I'm on my way to a meeting, partner's brunch."
And after that, he convinces them of that, while his head is down in
the ground, right?
They take the handcuff off.
They say, "Okay, go ahead."
They put their hats on, flip their sunglasses down, get in their police
cars, and drive away, as if nothing happened.
So my first reaction
to that is, um . . .
The events of April aren't new
or the Rodney King
episode isn't news in Los Angeles
or in many other places.
My second thought is: What did the partner of that law firm do on
Monday?
Did the partner call the police commissioner?
Did the partner call anybody?
The answer is no.
And it gets to, well,
who's got responsibility here?
I mean, all of us have responsibility
to try to improve the circumstances
among the races of this country.
I mean, you know, uh, a teenage mother's got a responsibility
to realize that if she has more children the life chances of those
children are gonna be less;
the gang member's gotta be held accountable for his finger on a gun.
Right?
The corporate executive has gotta be responsible for hiring and
promoting diverse talent
and the head of the law firms gotta be responsible for that as well,
but
both the corporate executive and the law firm have to use their moral power.
It's not a total contradiction.
I don't think it is. The moral power of the law firm

or corporation when
moments arise such as my friend's face in the ground with the gun
pointed at his head because he was in the wrong neighborhood and
black
and the moral power of those institutions have to be brought to bear
in the public institutions, which in many places are not fair.
To put it mildly.
Right? And the application of the law
before which we are all in *theory* equal.

ASK SADDAM HUSSEIN

ELAINE BROWN FORMER HEAD OF THE BLACK PANTHER
PARTY, AUTHOR, A TASTE OF POWER

(*A pretty black woman in her early fifties. She is in a town outside of Paris, France, on the phone. It is 5 P.M. France time. Spring.*)

I think people do have, uh,
some other image
of the Black Panther Party than the guns.
The young men, of course, are attracted
to the guns,
but what I tell them is this:
Did you know Jonathan Jackson?
Because I did,
and Jonathan Jackson was seventeen years old.
He was probably one of the most brilliant young men
that you could meet.
He happened to be a science genius.
He was not a gang member, by the way,
but Jonathan Jackson
went to a courtroom by himself
and took over for that one glorious minute
in the name of
revolution and the freedom of his brother
and other people who were in prison
and died that day.
My question to you,
seventeen-year-old young brother with a gun in your hand,
tough and strong and beautiful as you are:
Do you think it would be better
if Jonathan Jackson were alive today
or that he died
that day in Marin County?
Me personally,
I'd rather know Jonathan Jackson.
That's what I'd rather do,
and I'd rather him be alive today,

to be among the leadership that we do not have,
then to be dead and in his grave at seventeen years old.
I'm talking merely about strategy,
not swashbuckling.
I think that this idea of picking up the gun and going into
    the street
without a
plan and without
any more rhyme or reason than rage
is bizarre and so, uh . . .
And it's foolish
because it will, uh . . .
I think that
all one has to do
is ask, to ask the Vietnamese
or Saddam Hussein
about the power and weaponry
and the arsenal of the United States government and its
    willingness to
use it
to get to understanding what this is about.
You are not facing a,
you know, some little Nicaraguan clique
here.
You are not in Havana in 1950 something.
This is the United States of America.
There isn't another *country*,
there isn't another *community*
that is more organized and armed.
Uh,
not only is it naive,
it is foolish if one is talking
about jumping out into the street
and waving a gun,
because you not that bad,
you see what I'm saying?
You just not that bad.
You *think* you bad,
but I say again,
ask Saddam Hussein
about who is bad
and you'll get the answer.
So what I am saying is:
Be conscious of what you are doing.
If you just want to die
and become a poster,
go ahead and do that—
we will all put you on the wall with all the rest of the people.
But if you want to effect change for your people
and you are serious about it,
that doesn't mean throw down your gun.
Matter of fact, I would def . . . definitely never tell anybody
    to do that,
not black and in America.
But if you want a gun,

I hope you can shoot
and I hope you know who to shoot
and I hope you know how to not go to jail for having done
    that
and then let that be the end of that.
But if you are talking about a war
against the United States government,
then you better talk to Saddam Hussein
and you better talk to the Vietnamese People
and the Nicaraguans
and El Salvadorans
and people in South Africa
and people in other countries in Southeast Asia
and ask those motherfuckers
what this country is capable of doing.
So all I am saying is:
I'm saying that
if you are *committed*,
if you seriously make a *commitment*,
because . . .
and that commitment
must be based not on hate but on love.
And that's the other thing.
My theme is
that love of your people.
Then you gonna have to realize that this may have to be a
    lifetime
commitment
and that the longer you live,
the more you can do.
So don't get hung up
on your own ego
and your own image
and pumping up your muscles
and putting on a black beret
or some kinda Malcolm X hat or whatever other
regalia
and symbolic vestment you can put on your body.
Think in terms of what
are you going to do
for black people.
I'm saying that these
are the long haul,
because then you might be talkin' about
bein' in a better position for a so-called
armed struggle.
At this point you talkin' about a piss-poor,
ragtag, unorganized, poorly armed
and poorly, poorly,
uh-uhm,
poorly led
army
and we will be twenty more years
trying to figure out what happened to Martin, Malcolm,
and the Black Panther Party.

TWILIGHT #1

HOMI BHABHA LITERARY CRITIC/WRITER/SCHOLAR

(Phone interview. He was in England. I was in L.A. He is part Persian, lived in India. Has a beautiful British accent.)

This twilight moment
is an in-between moment.
It's the moment of dusk.
It's the moment of ambivalence
and ambiguity.
The inclarity,
the enigma,
the ambivalences,
in what happened in the L.A.
uprisings
are precisely what we want to get hold of.
It's exactly the moment
when the L.A. uprisings could be something
else
than it was
seen to be,
or maybe something
other than it was seen to be.
I think when we look at it in twilight
we learn
to . . .
we learn three things:
one, we learn that the hard outlines of what we see in day-
    light
that make it easy for us to order
daylight
disappear.
So we begin to see its boundaries in a much more faded way.
That fuzziness of twilight
allows us to see the intersections
of the event with a number of other things that daylight ob-
    scures for
us,
to use a paradox.
We have to interpret more in
twilight,
we have to make ourselves
part of the act,
we have to interpret,
we have to project more.
But also the thing itself
in twilight
challenges us
to
be aware
of how we are projecting onto the event itself.
We are part of

producing the event,
whereas, to use the daylight
metaphor,
there we somehow think
the event and its clarity
as it is presented to us,
and we have to just react to it.
Not that we're participating in its clarity:
it's more interpretative,
it's more creative.

JUSTICE

SWALLOWING THE BITTERNESS

MRS. YOUNG-SOON HAN FORMER LIQUOR STORE OWNER

(A house on Sycamore Street in Los Angeles just south of Beverly. A tree-lined street. A quiet street. It's in an area where many Hasidic Jews live as well as yuppie types. Mrs. Young-Soon Han's living room is impeccable. Dark pink-and-apricot rug and sofa and chairs. The sofa and chairs are made of a velour. On the back of the sofa and chairs is a Korean design. A kind of circle with lines in it, a geometric design. There is a glass coffee table in front of the sofa. There is nothing on the coffee table. There is a mantel with a bookcase, and a lot of books. The mantel has about thirty trophies. These are her nephew's. They may be for soccer. On the wall behind the sofa area, a series of citations and awards. These are her ex-husband's. They are civic awards. There are a couple of pictures of her husband shaking hands with official-looking people and accepting awards. In this area is also a large painting of Jesus Christ. There is another religious painting over the archway to the dining room. There are some objects hanging on the side of the archway. Long strips and oval shapes. It is very quiet. When we first came in, the television was on, but she turned it off.

(She is sitting on the floor and leaning on the coffee table. When she hits her hand on the table, it sounds very much like a drum. I am accompanied by two Korean-American graduate students from UCLA.)

Until last year
I believed America is the best.
I still believe it.
I don't deny that now
because I'm a victim,
but
as
the year ends in '92
and we were still in turmoil

and having all the financial problems
and mental problems.
Then a couple months ago
I really realized that
Korean immigrants were left out
from this
society and we were nothing.
What is our right?
Is it because we are Korean?
Is it because we have no politicians?
Is it because we don't
speak good English?
Why?
Why do we have to be left out?

(She is hitting her hand on the coffee table)

We are not qualified to have medical treatment.
We are not qualified to get, uh,
food stamp

(She hits the table once),

not GR

(Hits the table once),

no welfare

(Hits the table once).

Anything.
Many Afro-Americans

(Two quick hits)

who never worked

(One hit),

they get
at least minimum amount

(One hit)

of money

(One hit)

to survive

(One hit)

We don't get any!

(large hit with full hand spread)

Because we have a car

(One hit)

and we have a house.

(Pause six seconds)

And we are high taxpayers.

(One hit)

(Pause fourteen seconds)

Where do I finda [sic] justice?
Okay, Black people
probably
believe they won
by the trial?
Even some complains only half right?
justice was there.
But I watched the television
that Sunday morning,
early morning as they started.
I started watch it all day.
They were having party and then they celebrated,
all of South-Central,
all the churches.
They finally found that justice exists
in this society.
Then where is the victims' rights?
They got their rights.
By destroying innocent Korean merchants . . .
They have a lot of respect,
as I do,
for
Dr. Martin King?
He is the only model for Black community.
I don't care Jesse Jackson.
But
he was the model
of nonviolence.
Nonviolence?
They like to have hiseh [sic] spirits.
What about last year?
They destroyed innocent people.

(Five second pause)

And I wonder if that is really justice

*(And a very soft "uh" after "justice," like "justicah," but
very quick)*

to get their rights
in this way.

(Thirteen-second pause)

I waseh swallowing the bitternesseh,
sitting here alone
and watching them.
They became all hilarious

(Three-second pause)

and, uh,
in a way I was happy for them
and I felt glad for them.
At leasteh they got something back, you know.
Just let's forget Korean victims or other victims
who are destroyed by them.
They have fought
for their rights

(One hit simultaneous with the word "rights")

over two centuries

(One hit simultaneous with "centuries")

and I have a lot of sympathy and understanding for them.
Because of their effort and sacrificing,
other minorities, like Hispanic
or Asian,
maybe we have to suffer more
by mainstream.
You know,
that's why I understand,
and then
I like to be part of their
'joyment.
But . . .
That's why I had mixed feeling
as soon as I heard the verdict.
I wish I could
live together
with eh [sic] Blacks,
but after the riots
there were too much differences.
The fire is still there—
how do you call it? —
igni . . .
igniting fire.

(She says a Korean phrase phonetically: "Dashi yun gi ga nuh")

It's still dere.
It canuh
burst out anytime.

LIMBO/TWILIGHT #2

TWILIGHT BEY ORGANIZER OF GANG TRUCE

(In a Denny's restaurant in a shopping center. Saturday morning. February 1993. He is a gang member. He is short, graceful, very dark skinned. He is soft-spoken and even in his delivery. He is very confident.)

Twilight Bey,
that's my name.
When I was
twelve and thirteen,
I stayed out until, they say,
until the sun come up.
Every night, you know,
and that was my thing.
I was a
watchdog.
You know, I stayed up in the neighborhood,

make sure we wasn't being rolled on and everything,
and when people
came into light
a what I knew,
a lot of people said,
"Well, Twilight, you know,
you a lot smarter and you have a lot more wisdom than those
twice your age."
And what I did, you know,
I was
at home writing one night
and I was writing my name
and I just looked at it and it came ta me:
"twi,"
abbreviation
of the word "twice."
You take a way the "ce."
You have the last word,
"light."
"Light" is a word that symbolizes knowledge, knowing,
wisdom,
within the Koran and the Holy Bible.
Twilight.
I have twice the knowledge of those my age,
twice the understanding of those my age.
So twilight
is
that time
between day and night.
Limbo,
I call it limbo.
So a lot of times when I've brought up ideas to my homeboys,
they say,
"Twilight,
that's before your time,
that's something you can't do now."
When I talked about the truce back in 1988,
that was something they considered before its time,
yet
in 1992
we made it
realistic.
So to me it's like I'm stuck in limbo,
like the sun is stuck between night and day
in the twilight hours.
You know,
I'm in an area not many people exist.
Nighttime to me
is like a lack of sun,
and I don't affiliate
darkness with anything negative.
I affiliate
darkness with what was first,
because it was first,
and then relative to my complexion.
I am a dark individual,

and with me stuck in limbo,
I see darkness as myself.
I see the light as knowledge and the wisdom of the world and
understanding others,
and in order for me to be a, to be a true human being,
I can't forever dwell in darkness,
I can't forever dwell in the idea,
of just identifying with people like me and understanding me
    and mine.
So I'm up twenty-four hours, it feels like,
and, you know,
what I see at nighttime
is,
like,
little kids
between the ages of
eight and eleven
out at three in the morning.

They beatin' up a old man on the bus stop,
a homeless old man.
You know,
I see these things.
I tell 'em, "Hey, man, what ya all doin'?
Whyn't ya go on home?
What ya doin' out this time of night?"
You know,
and then when I'm in my own neighborhood, I'm driving
    through and I
see the living dead, as we call them,
the base heads,
the people who are so addicted on crack,
if they need a hit they be up all night doin' whatever they
    have to do
to make the money to get the hit.
It's like gettin' a total dose
of what goes on in the daytime creates at night.

F O R U M

"The Boys Don't Count: Or Why Won't Shakespeare Put His Men in Dresses?"

LYNN M. THOMPSON

Lynn Thompson's essay addresses several issues germane to an understanding of contemporary theater criticism: gender roles, cross-dressing (actually, an ancient and common practice in theaters throughout the world), sexual orientation, and, of course, Shakespearean criticism and stage production.

It does not take long for even a casual reader of Shakespearean drama to notice how frequently the image of the cross-dressed woman appears. At times, the cross-dressing either involves a secondary character or else occurs only briefly as in *Cymbeline* or *The Two Gentlemen of Verona*, but at other times it is the central character who cross-dresses, her disguise becoming the crux upon which the solution to the play's central problem rests, as in *Twelfth Night*, *The Merchant of Venice*, or *As You Like It*. In these plays, it is the female characters who cross-dress—always female characters. But, where are the cross-dressed men in Shakespeare?

At this point, one is likely to recall that boy actors portrayed all of the female characters on the early modern English stage: *here* are the cross-dressed men. Here is the male manifestation of transvestism. (In the study of Renaissance literature, it is the practice to use the terms cross-dressing and transvestism as synonymous.) However, these cross-dressed boys are not characters

within the play, but only the actors creating the performance. A close examination of Shakespeare's plays will reveal a few cross-dressed male characters, but these characters—save one—are nearly identical and tangential to the plot in that they are usually cross-dressed pages or children. It also becomes necessary to consider the implications of transvestism occurring on stage and compare such cross-dressing with the transvestism occurring within the dramatic plot.

The complexities and ambiguities are compounded when both forms of cross-dressing occur at the same time. For example, how does one discuss the transvestism of a boy actor who portrayed a female character in male disguise? In such cases, there was no *actual* cross-dressing, for the boy actor on stage was dressed in male attire. However, the actor who played the part of a woman was accepted as a woman by the spectators for the duration of the play. Because of this acceptance, transvestism was called to the audience's attention: the actor represented a woman dressed as a man. By contrast, the more frequent occurrence of *actual* transvestism—where cross-dressing boy actors played all the female roles—was *not* called to the attention of the audience.

The absence in drama of male characters in women's clothing is a curiosity—adult male transvestism occurs on stage only once in all of Shakespeare's plays—and briefly at that—in *The Merry Wives of Windsor*. One might argue that a playwright would see no advantage for his male character in giving up male status and privilege just to solve the type of plot complications one finds in comedies such as *The Merchant of Venice*. As a mere woman and wife of Bassanio, Portia cannot help Antonio except by masquerading as a lawyer, and so disguise is necessary for her where it may not be so for a male character. But this argument loses force when one considers the situation that occasionally arises in nondramatic romances such as Sidney's *The Countess of Pembroke's Arcadia*. In order to approach and woo Philoclea, Pyrocles assumes the name and dress of an Amazon. Similarly, in Spenser's *The Faerie Queene*, Artegall is conquered by the Amazon Radigund and forced to dress in women's clothes. Considering the ubiquity of disguise and female cross-dressing in plays, whether comedy, romance, history, or tragedy, why did the playwrights—and Shakespeare in particular—rarely, if ever, incorporate a transvestite plot involving a male character?

Although we must be careful not to project assumptions and practices into the past, the absence of cross-dressed males becomes even more odd in light of their frequent appearance in our comtemporary age. In fact, it is the cross-dressed woman who has become rare by comparison, though she still exists. Does the absence of this representation on Shakespeare's stage mean that the idea never occurred to him or that it was up to a later age to invent this comedic image? Or is it that there was something so unsettling to an Elizabethan audience about the sight of a man in women's clothing that it was too disturbing to portray on stage? And if that *is* the problem—and I think it is—then what are we to think about all those boy "actresses," as Stephen Orgel (1989) calls them? Why are transvestite boys acceptable, but men in drag are not? And is the problem that one cannot show a male *character* in a dress or, rather, that one cannot show an adult male *actor* in a dress? Or both? If the idea of a cross-dressed man is so dangerous, then how do we explain Falstaff's transvestism in *The Merry Wives of Windsor*?

I believe the restriction on this particular form of dramatic transvestism can be explained by the anxiety in early modern England over a commonly held belief in the fluidity of sex differences and the conviction that the spectacle of cross-dressing on the stage could corrupt and subvert the masculinity of men both on stage and in the audience. Anti-theatrical writers of the time believed that stage portrayals of male transvestism undermined male identity and privilege by suggesting that any man could be effeminized or even transformed into a woman. Laura Levine, paraphrasing a 1583 tract by Phillip Stubbes, states: "male actors who wore women's clothing could literally 'adulterate' male gender" (1986, 121). If a man could so easily become a woman or like a woman, then was there a significant, fundamental difference between a man and a woman? And if the line between male and female was so thin, it became possible to ask why men had all the power and privilege in society and women had none. To maintain and protect traditional gender roles, it was vital to forestall or eliminate any threats. Because of the potential for subversion, stage portrayals of cross-dressing adult males were more threatening than the sight of juvenile males cross-dressing. The effeminization of a boy posed less of a threat to society because, in the hierarchy of sex, a boy was less perfect than a man and, therefore, more like a woman than a man was.

By contrast, any adult male wearing feminine attire jeopardized not only his own place in the social hierarchy, but also the place of every other male.

Thus society policed and reinforced male gender status through social taboos against violating the rigid boundaries of masculinity, even in the theater. Shakespearean drama sharply limited and contained male gender transgressions—evidence that these plays more closely adhered to cultural laws—to satisfy society's anxious need to fix masculinity despite its belief that biological sex, and therefore gender, was ever-shifting. On the other hand, the nondramatic *Arcadia* and *Faerie Queene* allowed their male characters greater freedom from legal and cultural gender restrictions, primarily because the gender transgressions were not actually represented on stage but, additionally, because society's gender roles are invariably upheld in the end. For example, Pyrocles eventually sheds his female garb and marries his princess, suffering no permanent consequences from his transvestism; on the contrary, for him, cross-dressing becomes a tool to maintain male privilege and power, instead of a destabilizing force.

The need for early modern English society to fix masculinity in place was further complicated by beliefs about human physiology. While apparently supporting society's construction of gender roles, these biological views also suggested that an individual could change potentially from male to female or female to male. As Thomas Laqueur (1990) explains in *Making Sex*, female and male genitalia were thought to be essentially the same in form and function, different only in position within or without the body. The vagina was the mirror image of the penis; the ovaries, the testes; and the womb, the scrotum. There were not two sexes, but only one. As a result, it was believed that vigorous activity could cause a woman to transform into a man; likewise, a man who was too "womanish" in behavior and appearance could become a woman. Stephen Greenblatt (1988) tells of a young French woman who, while chasing her pigs, spread her legs too far leaping over a ditch, spontaneously turning into a man. Stories like this were taken very seriously by Elizabethans because they verified beliefs about sexual development—that women were simply a lower order of men—and seemed proof that it was possible for men to regress, to turn back into women (Orgel 1989). Thus, all qualities that contributed to a man's social position could be given up or taken from him. According to Greenblatt, "A man in Renaissance society had symbolic and material advantages that no woman could hope to attain, and he had them by virtue of separating himself, first as a child and then as an adult, from women" (1988, 76).

Renaissance medical authorities also believed that a child forever carried within it the intermingled male and female "seed" and that the child's sex and gender was determined by which seed predominated. Problems arose when the predominance of one seed or the other was sufficient to sex the child, but not sufficient to subdue all traits of the opposite gender. Thus a man became effeminate and a woman too masculine (Greenblatt 1988; Orgel 1989). Another important ingredient in establishing a child's sex was heat. The heat of male seed made the child stronger and more vigorous and so the child was

(continued)

able to push its genitals outside its body and become male. Female seed was colder and weaker and therefore, created a less perfect female child with internal genitalia (Greenblatt 1988; Orgel 1989).

Stage portrayals of male transvestism create an enormous unease in the mind of the Elizabethan man about the instability of his gender. No man could be sure just what it would take to push him "down" into femaleness. In light of this preoccupation with the ambiguity of gender, the anxiety over the transvestite theater and the plays produced upon its stage is understandable. If there is not that much difference between a man and a woman, there is even less difference between a boy and a woman. In a patriarchal society concerned with preserving male status and privilege through the control and restriction of women, boy "actresses" are logical. According to most scholars, the transvestite theater arose in order to eliminate woman as a spectacle and to exert control over women both as performers and spectators. Women were expected to be chaste, silent, and obedient. An actress is not silent, and by performing on stage, she risks her chastity by making herself the erotic object of the gaze of spectators. A transvestite theater was constituted to avoid such problems. However, this solution created new problems of gender ambiguity, for now the transvestite boy actor became the eroticized object of the spectators' gaze; although the women were no longer at risk of gender transgressions, the men were. Not only were the boy actors effeminized, it was feared that the adult actors who performed with them, as well as the male spectators who gazed at them, were also effeminized. According to the anti-theatrical writers, cross-dressed boy actors, because they were eroticized, would cause men in the audience to be sexually attracted to boys instead of to women. Fears that theatrical cross-dressing would lead to widepread homosexual activity underlay many of the arguments against the theater. (According to Alan Bray and other scholars, the term "homosexual" did not exist at the time, nor did early modern English society conceive of the idea of a person who had a *permanent* sexual preference for those of the same sex.) Arguments grew more shrill after cross-dressing became a fad among the citizens of London; it appeared that the predictions about the subversion of the social order were coming to pass.

Because of the theory that human anatomy was mutable and thus threatened individual gender identity, the transvestite theater, as well as the plays performed on its stage, becomes the locus of anxiety over gender transgressions. If maleness was not fixed, then a society concerned with the rank and privilege of males needed to set up gender boundaries to protect male status. Maleness needed to be defined, redefined, and reinforced by signs of masculine identity. By constructing and adhering to rigid gender boundaries, society could guard against the erosion of power and privilege that would occur should a man become unsexed and "slip" from his superior position or, indeed, should a woman "rise" from her subordinate rank. Laura Levine, in her article on anti-theatricality, discusses the idea of the fluid self as it pertains to actors in and spectators of plays:

> If we locate a self whose chief characteristics are its abilities to
> be carried, programmed, poured out of its container into something
> else, we begin to see how it would be possible to maintain

the kinds of claims [the anti-theatricalists make in their tracts], the claim that the spectator could be made compulsively to replicate the actor. If you believe the self is so tenuous that it can be altered at the slightest touch, then the slightest touch becomes magic, witchcraft, capable of radical, constitutive, mysterious change. (1986, 127)

With this concept of the self, cross-dressing by either sex, even by actors performing in a play, becomes an activity full of risk. For if a woman is strong, independent, and dresses as a man, what is the difference between her and a man? Similarly, if a man dresses in female attire, how does he differ from a woman? For the Elizabethans, the lines become disturbingly fuzzy, biological sex not withstanding. A man dressed as a woman causes other men to react to him just as though he were a woman. The cross-dresser, through the magic of the instability of the self, becomes another self, and can lead others to similar instability. The man in women's clothing becomes an effeminizing influence on himself and others, leading men away from their natural roles as husbands to women. Lisa Jardine, in *Still Harping on Daughters*, quotes from Dr. John Rainoldes's 1599 anti-theatrical tract *The Overthrow of Stage-Players*:

> The appareil of women is a great provocation of men to lust
> and leacherie. . . . A womans garment beeing put on a man
> doeth vehemently touch and moue him with the remembrance
> and imagination of a woman; and the imagination of a thing
> desirable doth stirr up the desire. (1983, 9)

Thus, the absence of adult male cross-dressing in the plays becomes understandable. Indeed, it is the frequent male cross-dressing within the nondramatic texts that, at first, seems at odds with social gender restrictions. A look at nondramatic texts shows, however, that they are not entirely insensitive to these anxieties regarding gender transgressions. Both Spenser's *The Faerie Queene* and Sidney's *The Countess of Pembroke's Arcadia* portray cross-dressed men: Artegall, who is held captive by an Amazon, and Pyrocles, who is in disguise as an Amazon. The Amazon, a figure originating in classical Greek texts, was a problematic one both in antiquity and in early modern England. Spenser most clearly reflects this ambivalence, for the representation of his Amazonian characters, including Britomart, Knight of Chastity and avatar for Queen Elizabeth, and Radigund, the Amazon queen who defeats Artegall, is not wholly positive. In Sidney's *Arcadia*, Pyrocles takes on the disguise of the Amazon in order to woo Philoclea, much to the consternation of his friend Musidorus. Sidney acknowledges fears about emasculation through the horrified words of Musidorus, who warns Pyrocles that he risks letting "himself slide to viciousness" by donning female attire, and that his action "subverts the course of nature in making reason give place to sense, and man to woman" (1977, 133). However, Pyrocles is certain that, because he takes on his disguise in the name of love, his masculinity will be strengthened, not weakened. Although deployment of the figure of the Amazon by both Sidney and Spenser captures perfectly the anxiety about male gender transgressions of early modern English society, male cross-dressing is used more extensively in these romances than in dramatic texts because there is no actual performance or enactment of transvestism as there would be in a dramatic performance.

Now, what are we to make of Falstaff's appearance in *The Merry Wives of Windsor*, the sole example of an adult male appearing on stage in women's clothing in all of Shakespeare's plays? It should come as no suprise that Shakespeare chooses Falstaff. Patricia Parker in *Literary Fat Ladies* points out Falstaff's feminine nature as he appears in the *Henriad*, speaking of the "tongues of women" and his "womb"; his fat is "compared to the image of the pregnant earth" (1987, 21). Feminized in the history plays, by the end of *The Merry Wives of Windsor*, Falstaff has little left to him besides a weary and resigned sense of humor about his humiliation at the hands of the merry wives: "I do begin to perceive that I am made an ass" (Evans 1974, 5.5.119). First, the wives strip Falstaff of his noble status by having him tossed in the river; next, they peel away his male status when he must dress as a woman to escape the wrath of Master Ford; finally, the wives deprive him even of his humanity when Falstaff is persuaded to dress as the spirit of Herne the Hunter, wearing the head of a buck. It is also likely that because Falstaff's transvestism is brief and ritualized, it poses little risk, either to the actor portraying him, or to the audience watching him. Indeed, Falstaff is the cause of the disruption to the social order by attempting to seduce two honest wives, thereby creating two cuckolded husbands. Because the cross-dressing episode occurs at the urging of the wives, it becomes a means to reassert the proper social order, not subvert it. Thus, this episode of cross-dressing carried little risk to the actor playing Falstaff. It is also significant that Falstaff dresses up as a specific woman: the witch of Brainford. Witches were the most masculine of women; they were thought to be sexually wanton, and they were outside male control because they did not fulfill acceptable roles such as daughter, wife, or mother. In fact, witches often had thick beards and controlled others through their magic. If an actor *had* to play a woman, he would want to play the most masculine kind of woman possible for his own safety: what better role than the witch of Brainford? Also, Falstaff's transvestism is very brief. It is not comparable in either duration or scope to a role such as Viola's in *Twelfth Night* or Rosalind's in *As You Like It*, where the female character is cross-dressed for most of the play.

In the comedies, Shakespeare permits his female characters much latitude to resolve complications successfully through cross-dressing. Males who try to do the same are punished by humiliation. It is not permissible for a male character to relinnquish his gender privilege, even temporarily, because this cross-dressed male undercuts the authority of all men. Thus, Falstaff receives a beating for cross-dressing because his act devalues not only male privilege, but also his noble status as a knight. The comic undercutting of males who fail to uphold society's standards of masculinity also occurs through other types of transformations besides cross-dressing: Malvolio's absurd attire and Bottom's ass's head are examples of such undercutting. Male behavior permissible in the comedies is not, however, possible in the tragedies. Although these plays do not deploy cross-dressing on stage, there are numerous instances of male characters who exhibit some gender ambiguity either through their language or their behavior. Antony, for example, is effeminized by his love for Cleopatra and

turns against Octavian's Rome. Similarly, Hamlet's tragedy is the result of what he perceives as his "womanish" reliance on language and inaction. These characters transgress male gender codes by failing to think or act in socially acceptable masculine ways. In the tragedies, such language or behavior on the part of these characters could be defined as "metaphorical transvestism," and a "metaphorical transvestite" would be any male character who takes on feminine qualities and consequently creates the very tragedy he tries to avoid. In Shakespearean tragedy, a male character's failure to embody "proper" masculine characteristics threatens his society with chaos or disintegration; order can return only with the arrival of a conventionally masculine leader, as occurs in *Hamlet* or *Antony and Cleopatra*. In the case of Hal, in *Henry IV, Part 2*, he is able to free himself from the influences of the weak, "womanish" Falstaff to assume his proper role as prince and, later, king. Through such metaphorical transvestism, Shakespeare defines and limits acceptable masculine behavior.

It is no suprise that the fascination with gender and sex exhibited by early modern English society coexisted with considerable anxiety over the possible impermanence and artificiality of sex and gender distinctions. Because one's place in the social hierarchy was determined by sex, and because men and women had widely disparate roles and identities, any suggestion that one's sex could change abruptly was disturbing. The texts of Shakespeare, Sidney, and Spenser are preoccupied with the place of the individual in the social order and, naturally, gender is a primary concern. By defining and reinforcing the roles of men and women, and by fixing sex and gender in place, these texts reassured readers and audiences of the permanence of the individual's place in society, regardless of the many political, economic, or religious changes that were occurring at the time.

References

Bray, A. 1988. *Homosexuality in Renaissance England*. Boston: Gay Men's Press.

Evans, G. B., ed. 1974. *The Riverside Shakespeare*. Boston: Houghton Mifflin Company.

Greenblatt, S., ed. 1988. *Shakespearean Negotiations: The Circulation of Social Energy in Renaissance England*. Berkeley: University of California Press.

Jardine, L. 1983. *Still Harping on Daughters: Women and Drama in the Age of Shakespeare*. New York: Columbia University Press.

Laqueur, T. 1990. *Making Sex: Body and Gender from the Greeks to Freud*. Cambridge: Harvard University Press.

Levine, L. 1986. "Men in women's clothing: Anti-theatricality and effeminization from 1579–1642." *Criticism* 28: 121–43.

Orgel, S. 1989. "Nobody's perfect: or why did the English stage take boys for women?" *South Atlantic Quarterly* 88, no. 1: 7–29.

Parker, P. 1987. *Literary Fat Ladies*. New York: Methuen.

Sidney, Sir P. 1977. *The Countess of Pembroke's Arcadia*. New York: Penguin Books.

Spenser, E. 1977. *The Faerie Queene*. Edited by A. C. Hamilton. London: Longman.

APPENDIX A

THE STUDENT AS CRITIC

Now it is your turn to be a critic—to participate actively in the theater experience—by discussing your impressions of a play you read or see. You need not have written a play or acted, directed, or designed to be a thoughtful critic. Your qualifications? An idea sparked by a play or performance and the means to articulate that idea clearly and vividly.

Writing about the theater is an invaluable way to enhance your experience. First, it allows you to apply what you have learned about the theater to a specific play; second, it encourages you to consider what you have experienced and transform it into ideas of your own. Do not think of a critical essay as homework; rather, accept it as an opportunity to participate in the theater in a lively way.

You will likely be asked to write one of two kinds of critical papers, perhaps both:

- a production review of a live performance (or perhaps a film version) you have seen;
- an interpretive essay on an aspect or theme of a play you have read and/or seen.

Each has its own needs and style, yet both share common traits. They are specific in their judgment; they are supported by specific examples; and they offer a definite point of view.

The Production Review

As we suggested in Chapter 3, production reviews require a reasonably quick response to the play and its performance. Usually, the reviewer does not go back for a second look—though one of the advantages of a college production is that it is accessible and usually inexpensive. It may be possible (and useful) to see a show twice if circumstances permit.

The production review customarily assesses two things: the play itself and the production of the play (i.e., the acting, the direction, the designs, and the technical support). By the conclusion of your review, the reader ought to have a good idea of what the play is about, what it says, how well it says it, and the quality of its realization in live performance. It is

quite possible you may admire the play, but have reservations about the performance—or vice versa. You may like elements of the plot or character, but have questions about other aspects of the scripted play, just as you may find some actors quite good, others less so. A good review is balanced: it does not uniformly praise a play and its production, nor does it unrelentingly castigate both. There are certainly times when a play gets a thoroughly glowing review, just as there are times when a thundering pan (i.e., negative review) is given. In most cases you will find that even the best plays and productions could be improved, while even the weakest at least show some potential. Good reviewers are sensitive to both possibilities.

If you can, try to read the play before you see it; a second reading may help jog your memory after you've seen it. Theater is meant to be enjoyed, so sit back and enjoy the show. It's best to jot down your ideas, key points, and memorable lines during intermission or after the play because actors hate to see audiences dutifully scribbling notes during performance. Please respect the actors and, if you must, take notes unobtrusively. Those lines or moments you remember most vividly are probably your best source of inspiration. Because of their unfamiliarity, at new plays it may indeed be necessary to jot down a significant line.

A well-written review begins with a "grabber," a vivid introduction that tells the reader something about the play, the production, and the reviewer's overall opinion of the event. It also prompts the reader to continue. In short, a good review opens much like a good play in production: it draws the audience into the play, raises questions about the experience to come, and establishes a dominant idea to be explored. Here's a good example taken from a review of August Wilson's *Ma Rainey's Black Bottom* written by Frank Rich of the *New York Times* (1984):

> Late in Act I of *Ma Rainey's Black Bottom*, a somber, aging band trombonist (Joe Seneca) tilts his head heavenward to sing the blues. The setting is a dilapidated Chicago recording studio of 1927, and the song sounds as old as time. "If I had my way," goes the lyric, "I would tear this building down." Once the play has ended that

lyric has almost become a prophecy. In *Ma Rainey's Black Bottom*, the writer August Wilson sends the entire history of black America crashing down upon our heads. The play is a searing inside account of what white racism does to its victims—and it floats on the same authentic artistry as the blues music it celebrates.

Note how this introduction captures some of the energy of the performance, as well as satisfying the reader's need to know what the play is about and whether it is a worthwhile experience.

Having secured the reader's interest, the reviewer then moves on to a summary of the play's plot and its thematic intentions. Plot summaries should be brief, usually no more than two to three sentences. Identify the principal characters and the conflicts in which they are engaged. It is not the reviewer's job to reveal how the conflicts are resolved—unless the playwright has contrived the resolution implausibly. While summarizing the plot the reviewer should also indicate something about the ambience of the work. This is especially important when environment is important to the play or when directors and designers have recontextualized a work by placing it in another milieu.

After identifying the play's issues (lovers flee to forest to escape tyrannical father, dejected salesman can no longer "cut it" on the road), the reviewer comments on its thematic values. Even the frothiest musical, such as *42nd Street*, offers a simple idea ("perseverance and a little bit of luck ultimately pays off"). Great plays, those that we call universal, usually suggest a number of themes. It is entirely possible, even probable, that a production will choose to explore one of those themes in a new or controversial manner, as when Arianne Mnouchkine staged *Tartuffe* in 1995 as a critique of the West's complicity in human rights violations in Bosnia-Herzegovina (see Chapter 6). Often the most interesting conflict in a production is that between the playwright and director, and the reviewer should address this issue. Reviewers ought to be confident enough to suggest an interpretation of the play (readers know it is not necessarily definitive). Such analyses are most credible when they are supported with specific evidence, such as lines from the text or the re-creation of a particular moment, that illustrate the theme. Comments about the originality or profundity of the play's themes are a useful way to conclude the discussion of the script.

A significant portion of the review must evaluate the performances of the principal actors, and perhaps of supporting ones whose work is especially noteworthy. While it is easy to toss around well-worn adjectives to describe actors—"scintillating," "memorable," "convincing," or "poor"—it is more useful (and challenging) to describe the actor at work. Rich's comments on Theresa Merritt's performance as Ma Rainey accomplish this:

[She] is Ma Rainey incarnate. A singing actress of both wit and power, she finds bitter humor in the character's

distorted sense of self: When she barks her outrageous demands to [the black musicians], we see a show business monster who's come a long way from her roots. Yet the roots can still be unearthed. In a rare reflective moment, she explains why she sings the blues. "You don't sing to feel better," Miss Merritt says tenderly. "You sing because that's a way of understanding life."

Here we get both a sense of the actor's emotional range and the reality of the character she creates. Never do we doubt that Miss Merritt was "scintillating" or "memorable," but here we understand why Rich judged her performance positively.

A note about negative criticism is in order because some reviewers often use it as an opportunity to show off their own wit rather than to remedy a weak performance. Even good reviewers succumb to this temptation, as when John Mason Brown dismissed Tallulah Bankhead's performance in Shakespeare's *Antony and Cleopatra:* " [She] barged down the Nile as Cleopatra last night—and sank." It is more constructive to discuss an actor's lack of emotional range or predictable vocal patterns than to summarize his or her work as poor or uninteresting. Though it is unlikely actors will read your reviews, discussing acting strengths and weaknesses in concrete terms is a constructive way to hone your critical thinking skills.

You may not have space or time to assess every actor's performance, but often you can single out a minor role and comment on the artistry an actor brings to it. And by all means, be sure to assess the ensemble effect of a production. A play dominated by a single actor may not, in the end, be as satisfying as one in which all actors—from stars to spear carriers—are contributing equally to the quality of the performance.

Designers do not want to read that their sets, costumes, and lighting were little more than "beautiful," "electric," or "marvelous." They want to know that their visual artistry contributed to the mood and ambience of the play, and perhaps even to its thematic intentions. Judge the design and technical work within the context of the whole production and not merely as a visual delight. Jo Mielziner's design for the 1949 Broadway production of *Death of a Salesman* was thoughtfully crystallized by T. C. Worsley in *The New Statesman* (August 6, 1949): "The stage design is skeletal; we see all three rooms at once, and we see, even more important, looming up behind, the great lowering claustrophobic cliff of concrete skyscrapers in which their living space is embedded." Writing like this elevates reviewing to an art form.

Your review ought to close with a brief statement that not only summarizes the impact of the production you saw, but that also beckons the reader to share in the experience. Rich's review of *Ma Rainey's Black Bottom* accomplishes this:

The lines [see comments on Merritt's acting above] might also apply to the play's author. Mr. Wilson can't mend the broken lives he unravels in *Ma Rainey's Black*

Bottom. But, like his heroine, he makes their suffering into art that forces us to understand and won't allow us to forget.

Finally, it might be useful to hear the words of a theater artist about the role of the critic-reviewer in the theater. Jack O'Brien is the artistic director of the Old Globe Theater in San Diego and a successful Broadway director:

> Years ago I used to love the early reviews of Walter Kerr, and I used to hold them up to our critics today—and still do—because to write great criticism, to read criticism is not to hear something brilliantly torn apart and dissected and dismissed. It's to make you or somebody get off their dead asses and go out and buy a ticket. And if you can do that, I think you belong in some proximity to the theater. Not just to say, "This is what it means" and "This is where it's deficient," but to say, "If you care, see that performance. This actor is not delivering yet, but you're watching somebody beginning to achieve greatness." Or to create the idea that it *might* happen.

If you are not doing so already, make it part of your continuing theater education to read reviews regularly. Doing so will not only keep you abreast of what's new in the theater, but also sharpen your critical skills by learning from professional critics. Newspapers in major cities, mass-circulation magazines such as *Time, Newsweek,* and *Rolling Stone,* and theater periodicals such as *American Theater* or *Variety* regularly contain reviews. Soon you will find critics whose style and opinions you value. Also, each year since 1943 virtually every review of plays performed in New York has been collected and bound under the title, *New York Theatre Critics Reviews* (now *National Theatre Critics Reviews*); this series should be in your library. Spend an hour leafing through several volumes to get a feel for good critical writing. By no means should you take everything you read at face value. Learn to be as discriminating in your reading of reviews as you are in your theatergoing. It will not take you long to distinguish quality critical writing from inferior work, even if you have not seen the play in question.

Critical Essays

You have probably written a critical essay on a novel, poem, short story, or other literary work in which you analyzed a theme, character, or recurring image. Perhaps you have compared two authors' approaches to a given subject. Therefore, you already possess some skills and experience to write a critical essay about a play or several plays. This text and the course you are taking provide you with specific resources and the vocabulary to talk about the theater and playcraft.

The first step in writing a paper, of course, is to select a topic. Often your instructor will provide a topic or list of topics for you. A comment during class discussion or a lecture may suggest material for an essay. We have included some

commentary with each play to spark your imagination and critical thinking; also, a list of questions appended to the end of this essay may help you choose a topic. Perhaps the best sources, however, come from a gut feeling you have as you respond to a work or from a question you ask while reading or watching a play. Whatever its source, your topic ought to suggest some originality (does the world really need another essay on "Ambition in *Macbeth*"?). Topics that discuss the obvious are not going to challenge you or your reader.

Think of a topic as a problem that begs for a resolution—or, better yet, resolutions. Good art does not produce a single answer; rather, it opens the possibilities for a variety of answers. And what is important about your paper is that you devise a plausible solution to the problem you have defined—not necessarily *the* answer, because in the arts *the* answer does not exist.

Whether your paper is an *analysis* of plot structure, recurring images, or character development, a *comparison* (or *contrast*) of characters or themes, a *description* of a performance or design, an *interpretation* of a play's meaning, or simply a *response* to your reading or viewing of the play, write it from an *argumentative* or *persuasive* point of view. That is, make a claim and then argue your case. We have seen that many plays in ancient Greece contained an *agon* (debate) because it produced a well-defined conflict and its resolution. A good critical essay is also an *agon* in which you identify a problem and then persuade your audience that your ideas are reasonable. You do not have to convince your audience that your opinion is definitive; you should, however, make the case that it is plausible. As any good debater will tell you, the strength of your argument depends on the quality of the evidence.

A word of caution: do not try to address every aspect of a play in your paper. Sufficiently narrow your topic so that you can discuss it comfortably and in reasonable depth in the space you are allowed. Better to say a lot about a little than to say a little about a lot of things. Stanislavsky's observation that "less is more" applies to good writing as much as to good acting. Also, if you can cover a narrowly focused topic well (e.g., "Images of Disease in *Hamlet*"), your instructor may reasonably assume you could—time and space permitting—cover a much larger topic ("Imagery in *Hamlet*").

As you focus on your topic, it may prove useful to jot down key words, phrases, and ideas that relate to it; these will eventually pattern themselves into the key elements of your argument. Reread the play carefully, each time noting lines, speeches, and specific actions that relate to your topic. You may want to use colored markers to code dialogue, stage directions, or plot moments that provide evidence for your argument. Make notes on 3 x 5 cards so they can be readily organized as you create an outline for the paper. (By the way, directors and designers often work this way in preparation for a show.)

As you undertake this brainstorming session, your topic will more readily define itself. Once you have defined the problem and the evidence to support it, you are ready to construct a *thesis* or *proposition*—the major point you wish to argue in your paper. Like Stanislavsky's "superobjective," the thesis serves as a unifying agent that controls every element of the paper. A topic, by the way, is not itself a thesis. Topics are usually conveyed in nouns and phrases such as "imagery," "symbols," "irony," or "conflict." A thesis puts the noun into action: "Symbols of lightness and darkness convey the meaning of *Oedipus the King*," or "The conflict between Nora Helmer and Torvald reflects the conflict between old world patriarchy and a new social order in Europe in the late nineteenth century." Using action verbs—as opposed to "being" verbs—gives your paper energy; it is the same principle actors use as they frame objectives.

Your thesis needs testing to insure that you have sufficient support to sustain it. Usually a minimum of three major points or proofs are needed to substantiate your claim. Again, note that playwrights frequently observe this "rule of three" when devising their plots (see *Ti-Jean and His Brothers* and its accompanying essay) because three examples are usually sufficient to suggest a universal truth. Though you may think of a larger number, the length of your paper will probably dictate a maximum of five major points in your argument.

For each point you need evidence, usually drawn from the script of the play. Quotations, stage directions, major plot moments (e.g., reversal or recognition) are your best means of substantiating your case. You may also want to cite secondary sources, such as the comments of other critics and scholars. Your instructor will define the degree to which you should do this. Some want a paper based solely on your reading and/or viewing of the play; others expect something more along the lines of a traditional research paper.

Quotations are, of course, subject to interpretation, particularly in the modern theater, where dialogue can be intentionally ambiguous. A famous story describes Harold Pinter in attendance at a rehearsal of one of his plays. The actors and director Peter Wood were trying to interpret a particularly difficult line; frustrated, the director turned to Pinter and said, "What does this line mean?" Pinter wryly answered, "I don't know, Peter, I only heard it in my head as I was writing the play." However, as a critic you—like an actor—must assign a specific meaning to a line, unless, of course, your topic is about ambiguity, in which case you should suggest all potential meanings that occur to you. The bottom line is to be sure that you understand a given line thoroughly before using it as evidence. You therefore need some knowledge of the conditions that created the play: the historical backgrounds of the society and theater, the playwright's life and works, the prevailing philosophy of the age, and so on. The essays throughout this book have been written to inform you about the historical and theatrical milieus that inspired the plays.

Use quotations to support your claims because the text is primary evidence, but avoid stringing a number of quotes together. Your paper should emphasize your ideas about the play and its meaning to you; don't let your ideas become obscured by a barrage of quotes. Just as good actors use gestures sparingly and for emphasis, good critical writers similarly use quotes as emphatic support. Shakespeare's advice to "use all gently" is as applicable to writers as to actors.

OK; you have selected a topic about which you are enthused. You have read the play several times and dutifully taken notes. If necessary you have done some background reading about the play, its playwright, and the period in which it was written, and you have carefully framed a thesis statement. Are you ready to write? Not exactly. Just as actors need some rehearsal time before performance, you also need to do some preparation work. First, write an outline of your paper, which allows you to test your thesis by carefully lining up the major points you wish to make. Place the evidence you believe will support each argument under the appropriate section of your outline. List the evidentiary material by a key word and page/line number so you can quickly find it as you write the paper. In your outline you need not worry much about the razzle-dazzle attention-getter or the memorable conclusion; these are often best written last, when you have built your case. State your thesis in a single sentence at the top, then list the three-to-five major points you wish to make on its behalf. Under each major point list a couple of minor points, each with its own evidence. (We have included a sample outline of our own essay on *Ti-Jean and His Brothers* as a model; compare it with the finished essay in Chapter 8). It's best to live with this outline for a couple of days (time permitting!) and adjust it as you get new insights. Again, this is very much the way an actor works in rehearsal: make some early choices, play with them, then adjust as new choices occur to you.

After your outline has been polished, you may want to preview your ideas by showing them to your instructor, who is a sort of "director" who gives you feedback about your choices. Then you can begin writing the paper in earnest. If you have done this groundwork, you will be surprised how easily the writing comes to you. Write quickly without much attention to the niceties of style and mechanics. These can be cleaned up later. For now, focus on discussing your ideas clearly and logically. Don't even worry about inserting full quotations at this time; that's easily done in the redraft. This stage is like an early run-through of a play in which the actors simply try to get from the first line to the last coherently. The "polish'n'perfect" stage comes later, much closer to opening.

After you have written the first draft, put it aside for a while. Come back to it fresh and with a critical eye toward polishing your writing style. Try reading your paper aloud, particularly to a friend or roommate; better yet, let the friend read your paper to you. Listen to the quality and clarity of the writing. It's often easier to hear a "clunker" of a sentence than it is to see it on the page. (This is why playwrights crave a reading of their play.) This technique is also quite useful for judging the appropriateness of support material; you will hear if a quotation sounds like a natural outgrowth of your argument.

Having written the main body of your paper and re-worked its style and mechanics, you are now ready to write an attention-getting introduction and a memorable conclusion. Frankly, such elements have been the bane of writers since Aeschylus; we have no sure-fire formula to give you, as inspiration plays a pivotal role in composing introductions and conclusions. Just as a playwright tries to grab the audience's attention by raising questions about the subject matter, creating a tone, and providing a sense of direction for the remainder of the play (all in the first five minutes), so should you devise an introduction that will engage your reader. An opener such as "In this paper I am going to . . ." is a bit like opening a play with five pages of heavy-handed exposition. Skim the introductions to several essays in this text and see which opening paragraphs catch your interest. You should be able to formulate a few principles about attention-getters. As a general rule, limit your introduction to 10 to 15 percent of the length of your entire paper.

Conclusions should be about 5 percent of the length of the paper. A good conclusion should not only clinch your argument, but leave a lasting impression. You may want to summarize the main points of your argument, but present them freshly so that you are not merely rehashing what the reader knows. The one thing that should not appear in a conclusion is new evidentiary material; that belongs in the body of the argument.

A Few Technical Notes

Writing about drama raises particular problems, especially where quotations are concerned. Because you will be using a number of quotations, it is cumbersome and distracting to footnote each one. After an initial foot- or endnote, you can usually identify the quotation in parentheses, using one of several systems. In general, quotations of one-act verse dramas, such as Greek tragedies, are identified by line numbers, which are usually placed along the right-hand margin of the script (publishers' practices vary). Quotations from most classical dramas, such as those of Shakespeare and his contemporaries, are identified by act, scene, and line number(s). You might see Hamlet's "To be or not to be" soliloquoy identified as 3.1.55 ff., which means it is found in act 3, scene 1, lines 55 and following (or lines 55–89 if the full speech is cited). If you are dealing with several plays and have not specifically identified a quotation by play in your text, use a standard abbreviation for the play prior to the line numbers (e.g., *Hamlet* is *H* or *Ham*; *A Midsummer Night's Dream* is usually *MND*). Quotations from most modern plays are usually identified by the page number of the script from which they are taken. In all cases, however, cite the specific text from which you have quoted the lines; this is especially important for some classic plays because lines may actually be numbered differently from text to text (among other things, prose speeches often alter line numbers). There are two ways to cite the text in a footnote for the first quotation:

- provide all of the bibliographic information and add a phrase such as "all quotations are from this text and will hereafter be cited parenthetically";
- list the text in a Works Cited appendix at the end of the paper.

Your instructor will probably indicate which method is preferred.

Lengthy quotations from plays (that is, those over three lines long) should be set off from your text; this is usually done by indenting five spaces and single-spacing the extract. If the quotation is in verse, it should be reproduced as verse in your paper. You should make every effort to reproduce the verse as it is laid out in the original text by indenting appropriate lines. The shared line of Elizabethan playwriting would look like this:

QUEEN. Why, how now, Hamlet?
              HAMLET. What's the matter now?
QUEEN. Have you forgot me?
              HAMLET. No, by the rood, not so.
                    (H., 3.4.13–14)

Note that extracts do not require quotation marks as they are clearly separated from your writing. Shorter quotations can be incorporated into the regular text by placing them in quotation marks. Any parenthetical line or page numbers are placed outside the quotation marks. If you are quoting a couple of lines of verse, indicate the break in the verse line by using a slash mark and capitalizing the second line. Thus, Hamlet's question "What is a man, / If his chief good and market of his time / Be but to sleep and feed?" (4.4.33–35) would be typed as you read it here. (*Note*: the "I" in "If" is capitalized because it is capitalized in the text; if it is not capitalized, do not capitalize it. If you wish to indicate it as a low-ercase "i" because it is in the middle of your sentence, bracket your alteration from the original: "[I]f the chief good. . . .")

Titles of plays of any length are customarily identified by underlining or italicizing them (though newspapers generally put titles of plays in quotation marks). If your instructor has not indicated a specific format for annotations and bibliography (such as the *MLA* or *Chicago Manual of Style*), use one with which you are familiar or invest in a guidebook. The important thing is to be consistent in whichever format you use.

Throughout this book we have stressed the importance of the audience in the theater event. Ideally, plays set up a dialogue between artists and audience. In the theater, you cannot (in most cases) talk back to the playwright, actors, and technical artists, but you do send them signals of approval (laughter, applause, an "electric" silence) and disapproval (coughing, squirming in your seat, thumbing through the program). Critical writing allows you to participate in the dialogue more intensely than usual. You, too, become part of the process. It is both a responsibility and a creative act; perform it with enthusiasm and relish.

General Questions About a Play and Its Performance

As you read the plays in this text, keep the following questions and analytical principles in mind. You may wish to develop one of these into an essay.

The Four Dimensions of A Play

I. ACTION: *What happens?*
   A. Describe the basic action of the play in one sentence.
   B. Outline briefly, as a sequence of events, the plot.
   C. Identify the minor and the major crises, their climaxes, and the resolution to each crisis.
II. CHARACTER: *Who is the play about?*
   A. Who are the characters whose interaction creates the play?
   B. Describe the social/historical context in which the characters live. If relevant, define the hierarchy to which they belong.
   C. Which characters are:
      i. major (foreground)?
      ii. supporting (middleground)?
      iii. minor (background)?
   D. Name the principal interactions among these characters.
III. IDEA/THEME: *What is the play "about"?*
   A. Identify the principal conflict(s) of values the play represents.
   B. To what extent, and in what way, are these conflicts resolved?
IV. PERFORMANCE: *What aspects of live performance are implicit in the script?*
   A. Evidence of the circumstances of the original performance
      i. place (theater space) and occasion
      ii. actors (and style of acting) and the audience's relationship to actors
      iii. specific conventions (e.g., asides, soliloquies, direct address to audience, etc.)
   B. Audible qualities
      i. language (prose, poetry, elevated, "street")
      ii. music, song, sound effects
   C. Visual qualities
      i. *presentational* (nonrealistic) or *representational* (realistic)
      ii. scenery, costumes, props, visual effects
      iii. actors in motion: blocking, business, composition

Other questions you might ask include:

1. How is this play different from others you have read?
2. From what perspective do we see the events (psychological, political, ethical, moral, heroic, etc.)?

3. What is the conflict in terms of opposing principles (i.e., society vs. the individual, ideas vs. conformity, one right vs. another, etc.)?
4. Why is each character necessary to the play's argument or theme?
5. What general or universal experience does the play seem to be dramatizing? (i.e., if an old play is worth reading/seeing today, it should tell us something permanent about human nature and the problems of life.)
6. What is the playwright's attitude toward the material (skeptical, critical, pessimistic, sympathetic, neutral, objective, sentimental)? What features or elements of the play seem to be the source of this attitude (e.g., a character you can trust, the arrangement of the incidents)?
7. What special formal characteristics of the play make it different from earlier plays of its kind?

A Sample Outline for a Critical Essay on *Ti-Jean and His Brothers* (see Chapter 8)

THESIS: Derek Walcott combines traditional storytelling and theater techniques and a contemporary political sensibility to create a modern parable in *Ti-Jean and His Brothers*.

I. INTRODUCTION (*establishes background for essay and states the thesis*)
   A. "Dancing with the devil" is a popular subject in dramatic literature.
      1. *Ancient*: Theatrical rituals and ceremonies described in Chapter 1 of this text provide numerous examples of diabolic figures.
      2. *Classical Drama*: Medieval morality plays and classical tragedies, such as *Othello*, used either real or symbolic devils to tell their stories.
      3. *Modern Drama*: We have invented new names, such as neuroses and obsessions, for our demons in modern plays.
   B. *Ti-Jean and His Brothers* combines ancient and modern sensibilities to create a contemporary parable.

II. BODY (*presents the proofs for the thesis*)
   A. "*Ti-Jean and His Brothers*" uses traditional elements of the folktale; these are governed by "the rule of three."
      1. Plot structure and the rule of three
         a. Twin prologues
            i. the fantasy world
            ii. the "real" world
         b. Three scenes in which a brother confronts the devil
      2. Archetypal characters

    a. The Suffering Mother
    b. The Three Brothers
      i. "Big brother": physical prowess
      ii. "Middle brother": intellectual prowess
      iii. "Little brother": wit and common sense

B. *Ti-Jean and His Brothers* offers a universal folk theme and a contemporary political theme to instruct its audience.

  1. Folk theme

    a. "Rite of passage" play in which brothers journey into the forest.

    b. Natural wit is superior to raw strength or learned intelligence.

  2. Political theme

    a. A critique of old colonial system that exploits island workers.

    b. Aligned with traditional *canboulay*, the nineteenth-century rebellion that ultimately freed the slaves, in Trinidad.

    c. Play traces evolution of Africans in the Caribbean from exploited manual laborers to resourceful "Anglo-Africans."

C. The superb theatricality of the play engages audience and promotes Walcott's message.

  1. Audible qualities: music, poetry, language

  2. Visual elements: colorful costuming, fantasy elements, masks, strong moments of physical conflict

III. CONCLUSION (*reaffirms thesis and links play to world drama*)

A. Walcott has not invented new subject matter or theater techniques.

B. Yet the play retains its appeal because of its combination of universal themes and contemporary issues.

APPENDIX B

GLOSSARY OF TERMS

act: the primary division of the action of a play. A play can consist of a single act or comprise two, three, four, or five acts; ten-act plays are not uncommon in India. *Also*, to represent or perform an action onstage.

action: what happens in the story line of a play; a **plot** consists of events that create the play's action.

acto: Spanish term for an act of a play; in contemporary American theater, it is usually a short satiric play on social issues important to Chicanos.

afterpiece: a short entertainment, usually a song or dance, performed at the conclusion of a play.

agitprop: short for "agitation-propaganda," a form of drama that incites the emotions ("agitation") and then teaches social and political lessons to encourage the audience to engage in a particular political action. Clifford Odets's play *Waiting for Lefty* and the *actos* of Luis Valdez are agitprop.

agon: Greek term for "debate" or "contest"; both tragedies and comedies had formal agons in which the central idea of the drama was debated.

alienation effect: from the German term *Verfremdungseffekt* (from the verb *verfremden*, "to make strange"), this was Brecht's technique for making the audience stand back and objectively observe the action of a play so that it might judge its social issues. Elements such as songs, political speeches, signboards, storytellers, and direct address "alienate" the audience from the action of the play.

allegory: a play in which symbolic fictional characters portray truths or generalizations about human existence; medieval **morality plays** were allegories, as is Dickens's famous story *A Christmas Carol*.

alternative theater: generic term for theater practice and theory that is outside the traditional commercial theater; usually avant-garde and experimental, it depends on collective creation by its practitioners, most of whom are bound by a common ideology.

ananke: Greek term for "necessity" or "that which has to be"; *anankē* was the force in the universe that kept "the natural order of things."

antagonist: the character who opposes the **protagonist,** or central character of a play; for example, Iago in *Othello*.

antimasque: grotesque parodies of **masques,** usually involving monstrous figures.

antistrophe: one of the three principal divisions of a Greek ode; it means "counterturn" (see **strophe**).

Aoi-no-ue play: the "ghost play" in **Noh** drama in which a vengeful spirit returns to torment a wrongdoer.

apron: the part of the stage closest to the audience and in front of the proscenium. In theaters without a proscenium (such as the Elizabethan theater), virtually the entire stage becomes an **apron stage** (sometimes called a **thrust stage**). In some historical periods, such as the Restoration, all acting took place on the apron.

archetypal character: a recurring figure who transcends the particulars of time and place to take on a symbolic value with universal appeal; a primary example. For example, Prometheus is the archetype of the human who takes on suffering for the greater good.

archon: a wealthy Greek citizen who provided the financial backing for the drama festivals; the forerunner of the contemporary producer.

arena theater: theater configuration in which the audience sits on all sides of the stage; sometimes referred to as "theater in the round."

areítos: pre-Columbian ritual dramas using song, dance, mime, and the spoken word that were performed in Cuba, Puerto Rico, and other parts of the Caribbean; they represent some of the first performances recorded by Europeans in the New World.

aragoto: the "rough" or masculine style of **Kabuki** performance, usually adopted in samurai and other military roles.

aside: a performance convention in which a character speaks directly to the audience while the other characters do not hear him or her.

atmosphere: the mood of a play created by scenery, lighting, sound, movement, and other effects.

Atsu-mori play: "warrior play" in **Noh** drama in which a military man disguises himself as a priest to repent a life of violence.

autos sacramentales: religious dramas performed in Spain during the Middle Ages; in the Renaissance they became secularized, but retained their allegorical nature. Also known simply as *autos*.

avant-garde: an intelligentsia that develops new or experimental forms, especially in the arts.

bailetes: dance musicals in the Spanish-language theater.

ballad opera: genre in which popular songs and ballads are inserted into the action to advance plot, character, or theme. John Gay's *The Beggar's Opera* (1727) is the prototype of the genre, which gradually evolved into **musical theater.**

beat: the smallest motivational unit of a playscript; it may be only a phrase or sentence in which a character manifests a particular need that must be fulfilled (see also **unit**).

benevolence: a philosophic belief in the innate goodness of humanity and the corresponding belief that humans have an obligation to use their natural instincts of love and charity; benevolence (or "sensibility") is particularly prominent in sentimental comedies, domestic tragedies, and many melodramas.

bill: the list and order of acts in a vaudeville show; also, the order of acts in a theatrical presentation.

blank verse: poetic speech that does not rhyme; it is customarily written in **iambic pentameter** in English.

blocking: the movement and positioning of actors on the stage.

bourgeois tragedy (also **domestic tragedy** and *le Drame*): serious dramas devoted to common people faced with everyday problems.

braggart warrior: stock character of the Roman theater (and subsequent ages); he was portrayed as a boastful soldier who, in reality, was a coward. The most common Roman name was **Miles Gloriosis;** Shakespeare's Sir John Falstaff is the best-known braggart warrior.

bufo Cubano: Cuban versions of the **minstrel show.**

burlesque: 1. a comic parody of a serious work; 2. a theatrical entertainment comprising broadly humorous skits and short turns ("blackouts"), songs, dances, and frequently striptease acts.

business: actions performed by actors, such as drinking, smoking, comic beatings, and the like.

cabaret: variety show, associated with the German theater, in which political skits and songs are performed in a restaurant and/or barroom.

canziones: Italian word for "song," particularly those placed between acts of Renaissance comedies.

carros: Spanish pageant wagons.

catharsis: the emotional cleansing initiated by the tragic experience; for the character it is the recognition and acceptance of his or her error; for the audience, it is the sum total of the pity and fear created by the play.

ceremony: an action performed formally and meant to sanction a political, social, or religious concept; it usually lacks the deeper significance of a **ritual.** Examples of a ceremony include a graduation or swearing-in.

character: 1. a person in a play; 2. the personality of such a person; 3. one of the six elements of drama as defined by Aristotle. (See also **stock character** and **archetypal character.**)

Children of the Pear Garden: traditional term for actors in Chinese theater, so named because the Tang emperor Ming Huan established a school for actors in the pear garden of his estate.

ching: a character role in Chinese opera, usually distinguished by a painted face.

ching hsi: the Peking Opera or, more broadly, Chinese opera.

ch'ou: a stock character of the Chinese theater; the clown or trickster.

choreography: the arrangement and movement of performers onstage; though the term customarily applies to dancers, it is also used to denote the orchestrated movement of actors, especially in stage combat.

choric speech: a speech spoken by a group; also, a speech which describes offstage action.

chorus: a group (usually 12–15) of singer-dancers in Greek drama participating in or commenting on the action of the play; in other ages (e.g. the Elizabethan theater) the chorus was a single figure who speaks the prologue and epilogue and comments on the action.

ch'uan-ch'i: form of classical Chinese drama derived from the southern provinces; forerunner of the Peking Opera.

chūnori: ("riding the sky") flying effects in the **Kabuki** theater.

City Dionysia: spring festivals held in honor of **Dionysus** in Greek city-states; one of the highlights of these annual events was the presentation of a series of tragic and comic plays.

Classicism: dramatic style that emphasizes order, harmony, balance, and the unities of time, place, and action. Characteristically, classical plays use few characters and follow a single line of action. *Oedipus the King* typifies the classical play.

climax: the resolution of the protagonist's principal conflict; the climax usually grows out of the **crisis** and brings about a play's **denouement,** or falling action.

closet drama: a play not intended for performance; such plays are usually read within a circle of acquaintances. Some historians believe Seneca's tragedies were closet dramas.

cocoliche: comic dramas from Argentina dealing with the problems of immigrants.

comedia: generic Spanish term for a play, both comic and serious.

comedy: a primary dramatic genre that usually ends happily and treats its subject matter lightly.

comedy of humors: comic genre that focuses on a single personality flaw of a character; it was based on the medieval belief that human behavior was influenced by bodily fluids (or "humors") and that an imbalance of these fluids led to erratic behavior.

comedy of manners: comic genre that satirizes the behaviors, fashions, and mores of a given social class or set.

Restoration comedies and Molière's *Tartuffe* typify the comedy of manners. Such plays demand a sophisticated and knowledgeable audience.

comic relief: humorous scenes inserted in tragic or serious dramas that provide emotional relief from the play's weighty issues; comic relief can, however, also provide an alternate perspective to the serious issues of the play. The gravedigger in *Hamlet* provides both comic relief and a commentary on death.

commedia dell'arte: popular improvised comedy performed by street entertainers during the Italian Renaissance; it featured such characters as Harlequin and Pantalone, and relied on physical or "slapstick" comedy (beatings, pratfalls, etc.).

commedia erudita: "learned" comedy written for court academies in the Italian Renaissance; based on Latin models and observing the classical unities.

concetti: set comic speeches by actors in the *commedia dell'arte*; for example, the Capitano's *concetti* might include boastful descriptions of his military prowess.

conflict: the opposition of forces. In drama, there are two types of conflict: **external conflict** occurs when an individual is at odds with another person, society, or nature; **internal conflict** refers to an individual at odds with himself or herself.

context: the "given circumstances" of a text, including the historical, social, and interpersonal backgrounds of the characters.

convention: an established technique or device which the audience agrees to accept as "real" in a performance; the "ground rules" under which a particular play will be performed. Examples include asides, soliloquies, the use of mime, and shifting scenery in view of the audience. Conventions change from age to age, from production to production.

corrales: Spanish term for theaters.

costumbristas: popular entertainments in Latin America that reflect the manners, dress, music, and dance of the common people.

coup de théâtre: French for "stroke of theater"; either a sudden sensational turn in a play (e.g., when the screen falls in *The School for Scandal*) or a spectacular moment that stops the show (e.g., the ascension of Mephistopholes and Grizabella in *Cats*).

crisis: that moment in a play at which the protagonist faces the greatest conflict; it is the turning point of the play and precipitates the **climax.**

curtain line: 1. the point where the curtain falls and meets the stage floor; it usually marks the line between the auditorium and the playing space in realistic theater; 2. a contrived line spoken as the curtain falls to end an act, usually to heighten the dramatic impact of a scene (especially in melodrama).

cyclic plot: form of plotting especially popular in the modern theater in which the end of a play repeats the opening action, usually to show that there are no resolutions to life's problems and that humans are trapped in their existence.

dama: Spanish for "lady," the virtuous heroine of romance dramas.

deconstructionism: postmodern critical approach that "constructs" new meanings of old texts by subverting (or "deconstructing") them; based on the premise that language is an imprecise instrument that has been manipulated by the traditional Eurocentric worldview. Theater productions, as well as written criticism, can be deconstructionist.

decorum: Neoclassic belief that characters were required to behave according to expectations based on their social status, sex, age, etc.; sometimes referred to as *beinseance* ("good sense").

denouement (falling action): the final outcome of the dramatic action in which the fate of the characters is determined, harmony is restored, and destinies are settled; it follows the climax.

desengaño: Spanish term meaning "disillusionment," that is, the act of removing all illusions about the world; theater and drama was a means of achieving *desengaño*.

deus ex machina: literally, "the god from the machine," a reference to the practice of lowering a god onto the stage in the ancient Greek and Roman theaters; as a literary term it refers to a character that is introduced late in the play to provide a contrived solution to an apparently insolvable problem. See the ending of *Tartuffe* for an example.

deuteragonist(s): secondary character(s) in a play.

dialogue: the exchange of speeches by two or more characters in a play. Also, a generic term referring to the words in a script.

diction: one of the six Aristotelian elements of the drama; it deals with the language of a play and the manner in which characters speak; as an acting term it refers to the clarity with which an actor speaks.

didactic theater: propagandist theater whose primary aim is to instruct or teach. Most medieval religious plays were didactic in that they instructed audiences about the Bible or morality. Most modern didactic theater, such as Brecht's, is political.

Diderot's paradox: the ability of an actor to exhibit extreme emotion while maintaining an inner control that allows for the successful artistic creation of the emotion; named for the eighteenth-century French philosopher and playwright, Denis Diderot.

didaskolos: in the Greek theater, the "teacher" of the chorus; the forerunner of the modern choreographer and choral director.

dikē: Greek term for "the natural order of things."

Dionysia: communal celebrations in ancient Greece held in honor of the god Dionysus; a three-day theatrical competition was a central event in the Dionysia.

Dionysus (Roman, **Bacchus**): Greek god of wine and—by extension—creativity, passion, and irrational behavior.

diorama: a scenic representation in which sculptured figures and miniatures are displayed against a painted background; the effect suggests a realistic panorama.

director: the theatrical artist most responsible for coordinating the work of the actors, designers, and technicians as they interpret the work of the playwright.

directorial concept: the director's interpretation of the play and the means by which he or she achieves it.

dithyramb: hymns sung in honor of Dionysus in ancient Greece; according to Aristotle, these hymns gradually developed into plays.

downstage line: performance mode in which the actors stand in a semicircle on the forestage and deliver their lines; the style was popular in France in the seventeenth and eighteenth centuries.

drama: a composition in verse or prose that portrays the actions of characters in conflict; the literary form of a play; a series of events involving intense conflict.

dramatis personae: a list of characters appearing in a play; the Latin term for "persons of the drama." Characters may be listed by order of importance to the play, order of appearance, or (as in the Renaissance) in hierarchical order.

dramaturgy: the art of writing and crafting plays.

drao: a Greek word meaning "to act" or "to do"; **drama** derives from this term.

duke's seat: the ideal seat in a court theater from which the ranking official could view the action (and especially the scenic perspective) from a perfect vantage point.

ekkyklema: a wheeled platform used to display dead bodies or suggest an interior scene in the Greek theater.

emotion memory: acting technique in which the performer summons up the memory of a particular emotional experience and transfers it to the emotional life of the character he or she portrays.

Enlightenment: eighteenth-century philosophic movement characterized by an emphasis on rationalism and a rejection of traditional religious, political, and social beliefs in favor of empiricism and the new science.

environmental theater: performance mode in which the action is not confined to a traditional stage but uses the entire "environment" for the presentation of the play; the action frequently takes place in and around the spectators (who are often encouraged to participate in the play).

ensemble pathos: term coined by Francis Ferguson to describe playwriting style that focuses not on the plight of a single individual but on a group of people; the audience's emotional response is therefore dispersed among the group. The plays of Chekhov epitomize ensemble pathos.

entr'acte: short entertainment (such as a song or dance) inserted between the acts of a play; also, the musical overture preceding the second act of a musical theater piece.

entremeses: Spanish term for "interludes," that is, short plays performed between courses of a banquet or other affair; forerunner of classical Spanish drama.

epic theater: non-Aristotelian theater espoused by Bertolt Brecht aimed at the audience's intellect rather than its emotions; it seeks to instruct audiences so that they may deal with contemporary moral problems and social realities, via nonrealistic modes of performance.

epilogue: a formal speech, usually in verse, addressed to the audience by an actor after a play; epilogues were especially popular in the seventeenth and eighteenth centuries (see *The Rover*). Often called a "curtain speech."

episode: the equivalent of an act in a Greek play; episodes advance the story line (see *stasimon*).

episodic plot: a story with a series of events, often unrelated, which can take place over great periods of time and in many locales; the events of an episodic plot are not necessarily causally related. Epic dramas, the history plays of Shakespeare, and the works of Brecht are episodic in structure.

epode: a lyric poem sung by the chorus in a Greek tragedy; one of the three parts of the **stasimon.**

Erinyes: the Furies, who in Greek theology were charged with the duty of keeping order, usually through revenge or torment.

Eumenides: "the Kindly Ones," who supplanted the Erinyes and kept order through justice.

existentialism: predominantly twentieth-century philosophy that argues that humans define themselves (i.e., their "existence" rather than their "essence") by the choices and actions they freely and consciously make. Existentialism has influenced much mid-twentieth-century drama, especially that of the absurdists.

exodos: the formal song of exit for the chorus in a Greek play; customarily it sums up the meaning of the play. See the last choric speech in *Oedipus the King* for an example.

exposition: essential information that an audience needs to know about a character or events (particularly those that happen prior to the first scene). Usually exposition is found in the first act or scene, but **distributed exposition** may be found throughout the play.

Expressionism: Early-twentieth-century literary and performance style that attempted to create the inner workings of the human mind by showing subjective states of reality through distortion, nightmarish images, and similar devices.

external actor: an actor whose primary emphasis and training are on such things as voice, physicality, and gesture.

extravaganza: lavish and spectacular stage show, often re-creating famous military battles or stories from the Wild West.

fabliau: bawdy tales popular in the late Middle Ages; they may have inspired early secular comedies.

familienstücke: form of German domestic drama that focuses on the plight of families in crisis (e.g., losing the family homestead); influenced the melodrama.

farce: comic genre that depends on an elaborately contrived, usually improbable plot, broadly drawn stock characters, and physical humor. Most farces are amoral and exist to entertain.

feminist theater: theater practice, theory, and criticism devoted to drama by women and/or about the problems of women in society.

floorplan: a set designer's drawing of the layout of the stage to show the spatial relationships between set pieces, placement of platforms, entrances, exits, and so on. The rehearsal room floor is usually taped to designate the various elements of the floorplan.

foil: a character who serves as a contrast to another (and usually central) character; Laertes and Fortinbras are foils to Hamlet.

follies: theatrical variety show using song and dance, and (frequently) scantily clad female performers.

foreshadowing: hints of events or actions to come in a play; usually foreshadowing helps create suspense.

formalism: late-twentieth-century performance style that emphasizes external and visual elements. The works of Robert Wilson typify formalism.

fourth wall: convention of the realistic theater in which the audience assumes it is looking through an invisible wall into an actual room; this wall is determined by the opening in the proscenium arch.

gagaku: ancient Japanese folk dance from which **Noh** drama may have evolved.

galán: Spanish for "gallant," the handsome and virtuous male character in romantic dramas.

gamos: in Greek Old Comedy, the formal union of the sexes at the conclusion of the play. The **gamos** is a particular form of the **komos**.

gauchescos: Argentine plays about "gauchos" (cowboys), comparable to westerns of the United States.

genero chico: Spanish-American variety shows similar to the vaudeville or music hall. Also known as a *puchero* ("stew").

genre: a category of play characterized by a particular style, form, and content; for example, tragedy, comedy, tragicomedy, melodrama, farce.

genzai play: one of the five types of **Noh** drama; a "living person piece" usually dealing with madness, obsessions, and passion.

gestus: the most important term in Brecht's vocabulary for actors; it refers to the social reality the character is asked to play (as opposed to the psychological reality of Stanislavskian acting).

gracioso: stock character in Spanish dramas, usually the "fool" or "wise fool" who stands outside the action and comments on the folly of his betters.

Great Chain of Being: Medieval worldview that used the metaphor of a chain to show that all of creation was linked: God was at the superior end of the chain, nonliving matter at the other. The concept influenced both the ideas of medieval and Renaissance dramas and the structure of the plays

(e.g., the highest-ranking person onstage invariably was given the final speech of the play).

griot: African term for storyteller.

groundlings: generic term for the members of an audience at an Elizabethan public theater who stood in the "pit" (i.e., on the ground) in such theaters as the Globe.

habit à la Romaine: classical French costuming meant to suggest the clothing of Roman antiquity.

hamartia: Greek term (which means "missing the mark") usually applied to the flaw or error in judgment that leads to the downfall of the tragic hero.

hana: Japanese term meaning "flower" applied to the aesthetics of acting in the **Noh** theater; it is achieved through rigorous training and sacrificing oneself to the art.

hanimichi ("flowery way"): the runway from the back of the auditorium to the **Kabuki** stage which actors use for entrances and exits.

happy idea: the problem to be tested in Greek Old Comedy, usually established in the prologue. In *Lysistrata* the happy idea is that the women should refrain from sex with their husbands until the war is ended.

hashigakari: a bridgeway in the Japanese **Noh** theater over which actors enter the stage; traditionally, it is decorated with three small pine trees.

hayagawari: quick-change and physical transformation effects in the **Kabuki** theater (e.g., a woman is changed into a spider).

heavens: in the Elizabethan public theater (such as the Globe), the area beneath the roof that covered the stage. It was painted with astrological signs and heavenly bodies to suggest the firmament. Often deities would descend to the stage from the heavens.

hero (fem, **heroine**): the central character of a play, usually the character who undergoes the most pronounced change; in Romantic drama and melodrama the hero is usually the person who embodies "good." The twentieth century has seen the emergence of the antihero, a character who may not be "good" but who is still the central figure in the drama. Willy Loman is an antihero.

high comedy: sophisticated comedy that depends on witty dialogue, social satire, and sophisticated characters for impact. The plays of George Bernard Shaw typify high comedy.

historification: setting the action of a play in the historic past to draw parallels with contemporary events; among Brecht's favorite devices for creating an **alienation effect** for his audience.

histriones: Latin word for "actors"; **histrionic** refers to deliberately theatrical displays of emotion.

honmizu: water effects in the **Kabuki** theater (e.g., creating a waterfall or a running brook).

hsieh-tzu: the "wedge" in classical Chinese drama; it was inserted between acts or, occasionally, as the prologue to a play.

hua lien: the "painted face" roles in Chinese drama.

hua pu: folk dramas in the Chinese theater.

hubris: the most common term for tragic flaw, usually ascribed to excessive pride or arrogance. Prometheus is a victim of hubris when he steals the fire of the gods.

hypokrites: the original Greek term for "actor"; originally it meant "answerer."

iambic pentameter: the metrical pattern in a line of verse (especially **blank verse**) in which five unaccented syllables alternate with five accented syllables: puh-POM puh-POM puh-POM puh-POM puh-POM. The pattern is most compatible with the normal rhythms of English speech, and was a fixture of Elizabethan verse.

imitation: the act of representing (or re-creating) another person through voice and gesture; see *mimesis.* Imitation is one of the founding principles of the theatrical arts.

independent theater(s): generic term for (mostly) small theaters at the end of the nineteenth century whose aim was not commercial success but artistic and social drama. The Théâtre-Libre in Paris, the Abbey Theater in Ireland, and the Provincetown Playhouse in America typify the independent theater movement.

interlude: short play or entertainment performed between courses of a banquet or other function in the early Renaissance; in England, interludes evolved into allegorical dramas and paved the way for secular plays.

intermezzi: Italian term for "interludes"; in Renaissance Italy they evolved into spectacular entertainments held at court (see **masques**).

integrated actor: an actor who combines both internal and external techniques as the basis of his or her work.

internal actor: an actor who relies on inner technique as the source of his or her performance; emotion memory, subtext, and psychological motivations are central to the internal approach.

irony: 1. an unexpected reversal of fortune (or *peripitea*) in a drama in which characters expect exactly the opposite of what occurs; 2. dramatic irony occurs when a character is deprived of knowledge that other characters and the audience share.

Jacobean tragedy: cynical, often violent, drama written during the early seventeenth century in England; stems from a pessimistic worldview and contends that all people, innocent and evildoers, ultimately die violent deaths.

jeu des paumes: early French theater spaces derived from tennis courts.

jidaimono: historical plays in the **Kabuki** theater which glorify the samurai code.

Kabuki: traditional Japanese popular drama that uses song and dance and is performed in a highly stylized manner in elaborate costumes and fanciful makeup; the Kabuki dates from the early seventeenth century.

Kabuki-za: the most prestigious **Kabuki** theater in Japan.

Kadensho: Zeami's seven-book treatise on **Noh** playwriting and performance.

kagami no ma: the "mirror room" in which Japanese **Noh** actors dress and prepare for performance through meditation.

kami (waki) **play:** one of the five types of **Noh** drama; a "god play" which celebrates an auspicious religious event.

kata: basic movement and vocal patterns used by **Kabuki** actors to create atmosphere and psychological states; they are antirealistic and employ exaggeration and rhythm.

kazura **play:** one of the five types of **Noh** drama; a "woman play" about an illustrious woman; these are sometimes referred to as "wig plays" because they are acted by men dressed as women.

keren: tricks and other scenic effects in the **Kabuki** theater (e.g., disappearances, transformations, etc.).

kiri **plays:** one of the five types of **Noh** drama; a "demon play" in which the protagonist is a demon, devil, or other supernatural figure.

kojo: an announcement made to the audience during a **Kabuki** play, usually to praise an actor for his accomplishments.

kokata: a child character in Japanese **Noh** drama, usually symbolizing a new order.

komos: literally "a joyful union"; it is the denouement in classical comedy and is usually marked by a wedding, a dance, or a banquet.

koryphaios: the leader of the chorus in Greek drama.

kothornoi: elevated boots (or buskins) worn by actors in the Greek theater.

K'un-chü: populist plays from the south of China which influenced the development of the Peking Opera.

k'ung-meng: stock character—the heroic king—in classical Chinese drama.

kyōgen: 1. short farces in the Japanese theater; usually accompanying the **Noh** drama; 2. a clown character in a **Noh** drama.

lazzi: Italian term for comic stage business (e.g., a beating, a pratfall).

laughing comedy: term coined by Oliver Goldsmith in 1772 to describe conventional comedy of wit and humor, as opposed to the sentimental comedy.

linear plot: the most traditional form of plotting, beginning with exposition and building through a series of minor crises to a major crisis and climax. Linear plots are usually based on causality, that is, one event "causes" another to happen.

liturgical drama: dramas enacted as part of a church service (or liturgy). In the Middle Ages such plays told stories from the Bible and Christian lore and eventually moved outside the churches.

logeion: in the Greek theater, a raised platform on which the principal characters are thought to have stood while performing; the forerunner of the modern raised stage.

low comedy: comedy that usually relies on physical humor or crude wordplay, as opposed to the more sophisticated **high comedy.**

ludi: Latin term for "play" or "games."

machiavel: stock character, usually villainous, who uses cunning, duplicity, and other amoral behaviors to achieve his ends; named for Niccoló Machiavelli, who suggested that "the end justifies the means" in his political treatise, *The Prince*. Iago is a well-known stage machiavel.

"magic if": Stanislavsky's term for the trigger that allows the actor to enter into the emotional life of a character: "Under these circumstances, what would I do *if* I were this character?"

mai: solemn dances of the **Noh** theater of Japan.

maschere: Italian word for "masked performers"; collective term for actors in the *commedia dell'arte.*

mask: 1. a device that hides the face to conceal an identity; 2. a pose or false front, especially true of a "psychological mask."

masque: Renaissance entertainments in which courtiers and royalty dressed in elaborate costumes and performed brief plays against majestic scenery; poetry, song, and dance were integral to the masque, which usually culminated spectacularly, often with the reigning official elevated into the heavens. Ben Jonson was the foremost composer of masques in Europe.

masquerade: theatrical activity characterized by the use of elaborate masks, oversized costumes, and vigorous physical dancing and other mimetic actions; the Carnival in Trinidad, the New Orleans Mardi Gras, and the Yoruban Festival are examples of masquerade.

mēchanē: the "machine" used to lower the gods from the heavens in the Greek theater (see also *deus ex machina*).

melodrama: the dramatic genre characterized by an emphasis on plot over characterization; typically, characters are defined as heroes or villains, conflicts are defined along moral lines, and the resolution rewards the good and punishes the wicked. Spectacle and action are important to the melodramatic effect.

mestizo: Spanish for "of mixed blood"; refers to plays that are a mixture of the drama of Spain and indigenous dramas of Latin America.

metanarrative: postmodern term for the "new myths" created by a synthesis of traditional stories and modern sensibilities. Stoppard's *Rosencrantz and Guildenstern Are Dead* is a metanarrative on *Hamlet*.

metatheater: dramatic genre that purposefully blurs the distinction between a play-as-a-work-of-art and life itself to establish a link between the artificial world of the stage and the real world of the audience; see Pirandello's *Six Characters in Search of an Author*.

method acting: strongly internalized acting that emphasizes emotion memory and personal experience in creating a character. The term is closely associated with Lee Strasberg's teaching at New York's Actors Studio.

michiyuki: circular movement about the stage meant to imply a long journey in both the **Noh** and **Kabuki** theaters.

mie: formal pose adopted by a **Kabuki** actor on his entrance; it allows the audience time to reflect on his costume and his psychological state (see *kata*).

Miles Gloriosis: see **braggart warrior.**

mimesis: Greek term referring to the art of imitation through physical and vocal means.

minstrel show: popular American theatrical entertainments in the nineteenth century comprising a variety of comic skits, songs, and dances performed by actors in blackface.

miracle play: medieval play depicting the lives of the saints and church figures.

mise en scène: the arrangement of actors and scenery on the stage for a theatrical production; the physical setting for the action; sometimes used to denote the sixth of Aristotle's elements of the theater: spectacle.

mizumono: **Kabuki** plays whose setting includes water (e.g., lakes, the ocean, etc.); noted for their spectacular water effects (*honmizu*).

moira: Greek term for "fate" or "the sharer out." Customarily, fate was depicted as three sisters who spun out the thread of one's life. One spun the thread, the second determined its length, and the third (representing death) cut the thread.

monologue: a lengthy speech spoken by a single character, usually to other characters (see **soliloquy**).

moral interlude: early Renaissance play that was didactic and dealt with proper and improper conduct in secular matters; the secular equivalent of the religious **morality play.**

morality play: medieval drama that portrayed moral dilemmas through allegorical figures such as Everyman and various virtues (Strength, Beauty) and vices (Gluttony, Rumor). Most moralities (such as *Everyman*) dealt with the way in which the Christian meets death.

mudras: mime and dance gestures used by actors in the theater of India.

multiculturalism: the incorporation into an artwork of the values and modes of expression of those other than traditional Eurocentricism. Soyinka's *Death and the King's Horseman* and Townsend's *The Great Celestial Cow* are multicultural works.

music: one of the six Aristotelian elements of the drama; it refers to song, melody, and rhythm.

musical theater: genre that uses song, music, and dance as an integral part of the play's action; it is not usually as elevated as **opera** or even **operetta**. **Musical theater** can be further divided into musical drama (e.g., *West Side Story*) or musical comedy (e.g., *Guys and Dolls*).

mystery play: in the medieval theater, a short play depicting events from the Bible. A number of mysteries were strung together to form a cycle, which attempted to tell the story of humanity from the Creation to the Day of Judgment. The term is derived from a medieval word which referred to the "masters" or skilled workmen to whom the performance of the plays was assigned. *Abraham and Isaac* is a typical mystery play.

mythos: the story; see **praxis** and **plot.**

naguata: the ensemble of orchestra and singing chorus in the **Kabuki** theater.

nātaka **play:** Sanskrit play based on traditional mythology or history, usually five to seven acts in length. *Śakuntalā* is a *nātaka* play (see *prakarana* **play**).

naturalism: a particular form of realism that emphasizes environment; naturalism was also a philosophical movement that saw humans as products of their heredity and environment.

natyamandapa: the playhouse of classical theater in India.

Nātyaśāstra (*Treatise on Drama*): the so-called Fifth Veda, a sacred text devoted to dramatic theory and stage practice in the theater of India.

Neoclassicism: Renaissance movement that consciously imitated the classical style of the Greeks and Romans; noted for its strict adherence to the rules of dramatic writing and its emphasis on morality and decorum. The plays of Jean Racine epitomize Neoclassicism.

New Comedy: post-Aristophanic comedy dealing with the lives and actions of common people; usually New Comedy is apolitical and focuses on the follies of ordinary people. Menander is said to have originated New Comedy, and the Roman playwrights Plautus and Terence perfected it. Most television sitcoms are derived from New Comedy.

new stagecraft: early-twentieth-century movement that moved away from pictorial realism to more abstract settings designed to evoke mood and emphasize the language of a play.

Noh (Nō) theater: the classical dance-drama of Japan, distinguished by a fusion of dance, poetry, music, mime, and meditation.

obligatory scene (also *scène à faire*): climactic scene which the audience comes to expect; usually, the ultimate confrontation between the protagonist and antagonist which leads to the resolution of the play's conflict; in the well-made play, the obligatory scene is often marked by the revelation of a secret.

ode: a song sung by the chorus in a Greek play, usually between episodes of the plot. Odes, divided into sections called **strophes, antistrophes,** and **epodes,** were used to comment on the action.

odori: temple dancers of Japan; the forerunners of **Kabuki** performers.

Old Comedy: Ancient Greek comedy, most associated with the plays of Aristophanes, which was satirical in its depiction of civic affairs. (See Spotlight box, Greek Old Comedy, Chapter 4)

onkos: a large headpiece, containing a mask, worn by actors in the Greek theater.

onnagata: traditional **Kabuki** role in which a male plays a woman; it also refers to the acting style used to play feminine beauty.

onno: the original women's **Kabuki** of seventeenth-century Japan.

opera: a drama almost exclusively sung to orchestral accompaniment; operas usually deal with tragic and heroic theme; (e.g., *Madame Butterfly* or the *Ring* cycle).

opéra bouffe: satirical comic opera (e.g., *Orpheus in Hades*).

operetta: "little opera," a romantic and comic play that incorporates considerable music, song, and dance (e.g., *The Merry Widow* or *The Mikado*).

orchestra: the large (c. 70-foot diameter) circle in a Greek theater in which the chorus sang, danced, and stood during a play. It was located between the audience and the *logeion*.

overture: an orchestral piece played before the beginning of an opera, operetta, or musical play; overtures were also often played before nonmusical plays in the eighteenth and nineteenth centuries.

pageant wagon (or **pageant**): medieval stage built on wagons or carts that could be transported through towns; often, two wagons were used, one for scenery, a second for an acting platform.

pantomime: dumb shows that emphasize spectacle.

parabisis: the "harangue" in Greek Old Comedy in which the playwright addresses topical issues of personal concern.

parados: 1. the song of entry for the chorus in a Greek play; 2. the path or aisles on which the chorus entered or exited, located on either side of the playing space.

pastiche: postmodern playwriting technique that fuses a variety of styles, genres, and story lines to create a new form. Stoppard's *Rosencrantz and Guildenstern Are Dead* is a pastiche of Shakespeare's *Hamlet*, Beckett's *Waiting for Godot*, absurdist theater, vaudeville, and existentialist tract.

pastoral drama: play dealing with rustic life; it extols the virtues of simple living by contrasting it with the corrupt life of the city; evolved in Italy during the Renaissance and may have been patterned after the **satyr play** of ancient Greece. The **romance** is an outgrowth of the pastoral drama.

Peking Opera: generic term for populist Chinese theater, originating in the eighteenth century, which uses song, dance, and nonrealistic means to tell melodramatic stories; the national theater of China.

periaktoi: prisms that served as the principal scenic effect in the Greek theater; locales such as a forest, a palace, or a seacoast were painted on each side of the triangle, which could be turned to reveal a new location.

peripeteia: Aristotelian term for "reversal" in a play, that is, the moment when the fortunes of the protagonist are drastically changed.

perspective: technique, used by scenic designers, of representing on a flat surface (such as a canvas drop) the spatial relation of objects as they might appear to the eye.

pictorial realism: the attempt to suggest "real life" on the stage through painterly devices.

pit: in Restoration and eighteenth-century theaters, the seating (occasionally standing) area immediately in front of the stage, customarily inhabited by fops and rakes. Today the pit usually refers to the orchestra pit, a recessed area in front of (or often beneath) the stage where an orchestra sits during a performance.

plaudite: a formal speech at the end of classical comedies in which the speaker asks the audience's forgiveness for any transgressions and requests applause; see Puck's final speech in *A Midsummer Night's Dream.*

play: literary genre in which a story (plot) is presented by actors imitating characters before an audience. One might say that a play is a script "on its feet."

play-within-the-play: a usually brief play inserted into the action of a larger play, often to comment on or illuminate the primary play. The performance of the Pyramis and Thisbe play by the workingmen in *A Midsummer Night's Dream* is a play-within-the-play.

plot: the first of Aristotle's six elements of theater; the structure of a play's story line; see **praxis.**

pluralism: the inclusion of many cultures, races, and lifestyles into an enterprise; in the theater, this includes multicultural/racial drama, feminist drama, gay and lesbian drama; in general, pluralism is an alternative to traditional male-dominated, Eurocentric art.

poetic justice: moral doctrine that requires that the good be rewarded for their benevolent deeds and that the wicked be punished for their transgressions; the doctrine is particularly influential on the resolution of melodramas and sentimental comedies.

Poetics: Aristotle's treatise on dramatic theory and stage practice; in particular, it defines and discusses tragedy. Written in the mid–fourth century B.C.E., it is the germinal work on dramatic theory in Western theater.

point of attack: that moment nearest the beginning of the play in which the major conflict to be resolved occurs; sometimes called the inciting moment.

poor theater: Jerzy Grotowski's term for a theater which seeks (by choice or necessity) to eliminate everything not entirely essential to the performance (e.g., scenery, elaborate costumes, makeup, high-tech lighting); "found" objects and costumes are used and the actors themselves create effects to support the production (see also ***via negativa***).

postmodernism: late-twentieth-century critical, literary, and performance movement that reacts to modern art and literature; postmodernists suggest that truth is no longer verifiable, and that new art forms are best created by freely mixing previous styles and themes.

***prakarana* play:** Sanskrit play invented by the playwright, usually ten acts in length. *The Little Clay Cart* is a *prakarana* play (see also ***nātaka* play**).

praxis: the action of a story; that is, the arrangement of the events of the story calculated to bring about a desired response from the audience.

presentational style: performance mode in which the actors openly acknowledge the presence of the audience and play to it.

problem plays: usually refers to a series of plays written by Shakespeare in the first decade of the seventeenth century that do not neatly fit into the traditional generic categories

of comedy and tragedy; they include *Measure for Measure* and *Troilus and Cressida.*

prologue: the opening action of a Greek play; it usually is a dialogue between two or three characters and establishes the problem of the play. It now refers to an opening section of a play that is not part of the first scene or act.

proscenium: in modern theaters, the wall that separates the stage from the auditorium and provides the **arch** that frames it; often referred to as the "picture frame" stage.

protagonist: literally, "the first debater," but the term applies to the central character in a drama.

punto de honor: Spanish for "point of honor," applied to a form of drama in which the hero must defend the honor of his family, his lady, or himself.

queer theater/theory: drama, theory, and criticism concerned with the problems confronting gays and lesbians in society.

quid pro quo: Latin for "something for something"; a playwriting term applied to a situation in which one, two, or more characters unknowingly misunderstand a situation, which further enmeshes them in the play's action.

raisonneur: common term applied to a character who speaks for society or the playwright; customarily, the *raisonneur* gives advice to the **protagonist.** Tiresias in *Oedipus the King* and Cléante in *Tartuffe* are *raisonneurs.*

rake (or **rakehell**): comic hero who lives by the code of love and uses deceit, cunning, and seduction to attain his conquests; such characters were especially popular in late-seventeenth- and eighteenth-century comedies.

ran-i: Japanese term for "the sublime," referring to the ecstasy and exaltation produced by advanced artistry.

rasa: the ultimate goal of performance in the theater of India; roughly translated as "flavor," rasa refers to the emotional state or mood that the playwright hopes to engender in the audience. A given play has a dominant rasa and each component act has its own rasa.

realism: an attempt to re-create actual life onstage in a manner that employs the details and routines of daily dress, speech, environment, and situations. Ibsen's social dramas typify realism (see also **naturalism**).

recognition (*anagnōrisis*): a character discovers a truth previously unknown; in tragedy it is the awareness of the error in judgment that leads to the character's downfall; originally, it referred to the recognition of one character by another (e.g., Electra recognizes her long-lost brother, Orestes) but the term now applies to the discovery of an error or a truth about oneself.

renderings: a scenery or costume designer's drawings of the set or costumes; these are usually colored or painted to suggest what the finished product will look like.

régisseur: Continental term for the stage director.

repartée: witty verbal exchanges between characters, especially in high comedy.

representational style: performance mode in which the actors seem to ignore the presence of the audience.

revenge tragedy: Elizabethan-Jacobean drama that depended on sensational events, murders, and revenge for plot; the Roman tragedies of Seneca were the models for revenge tragedies.

reversal (*peripitea*): a drastic change in fortune, usually for the protagonist of a play. In tragedy the reversal is calamitous and leads to the downfall of the principal character; in comedy, the reversal usually brings about good fortune and a happy resolution to the play.

reviewer: a theater critic who attends a play in performance and assesses the quality of the script, the performances and designs, and the overall experience.

revistas: Brazilian popular entertainments, usually musicals.

revue: theatrical presentation usually composed of loosely related skits, songs, and dances (see **vaudeville**).

rhapsode: Greek term for poet, storyteller, and myth maker; Homer is the best known of the rhapsodes.

rising action: the series of minor crises in a plot that build toward the major crisis and climax.

ritual: a formal and customarily repeated act, usually according to religious or social customs; a ritual generally has greater significance than a **ceremony** (e.g., a baptism or wedding). Early rituals often were intended to control the outcome of events.

ritualized enactment: symbolic actions performed in a pattern and progression that eventually become highly controlled and precise in their execution.

romance: drama about imaginary characters involved in events from a remote place and time, usually involving heroic deeds in a mysterious setting; *Śakuntalā* and Shakespeare's *The Tempest* are romances.

Romanticism: late-eighteenth and early-nineteenth-century philosophical and artistic movement marked by an emotional appeal to the heroic, adventurous, remote, mysterious, or idealized. Romanticism celebrated the common people and is aligned with the democratic revolution.

roppō: a stylized walk—part dance, part martial art—used by a **Kabuki** actor as he enters the stage on the ***hanimichi***; literally, it means "six directions" and refers to the vigorous turns he executes during the walk. A *tobiroppō* is an exit walk and often occurs after the curtain is closed.

sainetes: short farces in the Spanish-language theater.

Sanskrit drama: the classical court theater of India that thrived until c. 1000 C.E.

satire: species of comic drama that holds human follies and institutions up to ridicule and scorn; the use of wit, irony, or sarcasm to expose vice and folly. *The Importance of Being Earnest* is a satire.

satyr plays: early Greek comedy in which actors dressed in animal skins (particularly goats) and performed often bawdy parodies of serious dramas; the **satyrs** were the mythological creatures (half-man, half-goat) who served and protected Dionysus.

scenario: an outline of a play that denotes the principal actions of the plot; actors in the *commedia dell'arte* improvised plays from their **scenarii.**

scene: the secondary division of a play; acts may be divided into scenes. Also, the locale of a play's action.

scenery: the backdrops, furniture, and other visual accessories that help define the locale and mood of a play.

Senecan tragedy: Renaissance tragedy modeled after the Roman plays of Seneca; noted for the use of the supernatural and violent resolutions to the plot (e.g. Shakespeare's *Titus Andronicus*).

sentimental comedy (also **weeping comedy**, *comédie larmoyant*): popular eighteenth-century comedies marked by emotional idealism and excessive feeling.

sermons joyeaux: medieval French burlesques of church sermons.

set: the scenery constructed for a particular play; usually, it is three dimensional (as opposed to painted drops).

setting: the locale of a play's action and the scenic elements that help define it.

sewamono: domestic dramas in the **Kabuki** theater, usually portraying the world of the merchant class.

shaman: a holy person who uses magic and ritual for the purpose of curing the sick, divining hidden mysteries, or controlling events. Shamans are often storytellers who preserve a community's myths.

shared line: two or more speeches in verse combined to form a line of iambic pentameter. This is usually a cue for the actors to pick up the pace.

sheng: male roles in Chinese opera (usually non-"character" roles).

shibai: common term for **Kabuki** theaters, derived from Japanese term for "grass sitting" (a reference to the grassy slope on which audiences sat in one of the earliest Kabuki theaters).

Shingeki: the new or alternative (to the **Kabuki** and **Noh**) theater of contemporary Japan.

shite: the protagonist or principal character in a Japanese **Noh** drama; literally, the term means "doer."

***shura-mono* play:** one of the five types of **Noh** drama; a "warrior play" in which the protagonist, usually a slain warrior, returns as a ghost to relieve human suffering.

***siglo d'oro* drama:** Spanish drama from the seventeenth-century golden age, particularly the plays of Lope De Vega and Pedro Calderón.

skene: the "hut" or building that served as the scenic background for the the Greek theater. It provided an area for actors to change, masked their entrances, and denoted locale. Traditionally, the *skene* had three to five doors.

slapstick: a form of comedy that depends exclusively on physical humor such as beatings, chases, and pratfalls. The term is derived from a prop devised by actors in the *commedia dell'arte* that was used to administer beatings. The films of the Three Stooges epitomize slapstick comedy.

soliloquy: a theater convention in which a character speaks his or her thoughts aloud to the audience; it is particularly associated with Elizabethan drama.

sotties: short French farces that portray religious and/or political leaders as fools.

spectacle: one of the six Aristotelian elements of the drama; it refers to the visual elements of a play—scenery, costume, movement, gesture, and so on. (see also **mise-en-scène**).

spine: see **superobjective**.

spirit cult performance: theatricalized ritual in which a medium, thought to be possessed by spirits of the dead, assumes a character while in a trance state.

sporagmos: a scapegoat or sacrificial victim who takes on suffering for the greater good of a tribe or community. A tragic hero, such as Oedipus, may be considered a sporagmos.

stage direction: the playwright's instructions to the actors, designers, and directors concerning setting, motivations, and characterization.

Stage Yankee: popular American comic figure noted for his ingenuity, honesty, and patriotism; he usually outwits his "betters" and triumphs because he adheres to American virtues.

stasimon: the choral odes in a Greek play; they alternate with **episodes** and are used to comment on the action, project the play's message, and create the emotional atmosphere.

stichomythia: stage dialogue in which characters alternate single lines to increase dramatic tension. Though the term is Greek in origin, it is found in many eras of theater.

stock character: instantly recognizable type of figure that reoccurs in many works (e.g., the young lover, the grouchy old man, the sassy servant, the braggart soldier).

storytelling performance: preliterate form of drama, especially common in Africa, in which a narrator tells a story while enacting the central roles; others may play roles as well as provide song and dance to accompany the tale.

strophe: one of the three principal divisions of a choral ode in a Greek play; it means "turn" and suggests something about the dance nature of the odes.

Sturm und Drang: German for "storm and stress," a philosophical and artistic movement in the late eighteenth century characterized by high emotion and rousing action that often dealt with an individual's revolt against society; the forerunner of **Romanticism.**

style: the manner in which a play is performed. The two principal styles are **presentational**, in which the actors openly acknowledge the presence of the audience and play to it, and **representational**, in which the actors seem to ignore the presence of the audience. Style implies the degree of "reality" or artificiality of a performance.

subplot: a secondary plot in a play which often parallels the major plot; e.g., in *A Midsummer Night's Dream* the story of Nick Bottom constitutes a subplot.

subtext: literally, "the text beneath the text"; it refers to the implied or underlying meaning of a line. Sometimes also called "the intentional meaning."

superobjective: Stanislavsky's term for the primary motivation of a character (e.g., Oedipus's superobjective is "to find the truth").

suspension of disbelief: Coleridge's term for an audience's willingness to accept events onstage as true or plausible during the course of a play.

sūtradhara: a storyteller in India, often a Brahmin priest.

symbolism: a literary or theatrical device in which an object or action suggests another meaning beyond its literal meaning. Willy's worn suitcases in *Death of a Salesman* symbolize his life and failures. Also, a theatrical style popular in the early twentieth century that relied almost exclusively on symbols for its impact; such plays as García Lorca's *Blood Wedding* typify symbolist drama.

sympathetic (homeopathic) magic: when humans imitate an act of nature in the hope that nature, in turn, will imitate humans and thereby produce a desired result (e.g., a Native American rain dance).

the System: term applied to Stanislavsky's approach to actor training at the Moscow Art Theater; a blend of external technique with strong psychological analysis of the character.

tableaux vivants: French for "living pictures," spectacular scenes which often re-created historical events or violent situations (such as guillotinings). Today a tableau refers to a "freeze" in which the actors do not move.

tan: female roles in Chinese opera.

tetralogy: a grouping of four plays by theme and content; in the ancient Greek theater the tetralogy customarily comprised three tragedies (a **trilogy**) and a **satyr play.** Shakespeare wrote two tetralogies (the four plays dealing with King Henry V, and the four plays dealing with King Henry VI and the rise and fall of Richard III).

text: the printed version of a play; a script (see also **context** and **subtext**).

theater: the art form by which drama is realized; also, the formal space in which a drama is performed.

theater collectives: alternative theater companies, usually bound by a common ideology, who create works collectively; often they live in communes. The Living Theater (USA), the *Théâtre du Soleil* (France), Committed Artists (South Africa), and *Grupo Teatro Escambray* (Cuba) are examples of collectives.

theater of cruelty: movement associated with the theories of Antonin Artaud, who forced audiences to purge their inhumanity ("the Plague") by stripping away their defense mechanisms through an assault on the senses.

theater of the absurd: dramatic movement of the mid–twentieth century concerned with the metaphysical anguish of the human condition in a world that defies rational sense; it relies on plotless dramas, discursive dialogue, motiveless behavior, and ambiguity. The plays of Samuel Beckett exemplify absurdist drama.

theatrical (theatricality): the formal and stylized use of costumes, makeup, scenery, properties, lighting, and sound as a means of performance; with theatricality there is no pretense of realism.

theatron: Greek term for "the seeing place;" the area of a Greek theater where the audience sat.

thesis play (also, *pièce à thèse* and "discussion drama"): social drama in which contemporary problems are illustrated and discussed; typified by the early works of Ibsen, Shaw, and Odets. Most thesis plays are presented in a realistic or naturalistic style.

thought: one of the six Aristotelean elements of the drama; it deals with the idea or thematic values of a play.

thrust stage: a stage or acting area that is projected into the audience and is usually surrounded by the audience on three sides. The classical Greek theater and the Elizabethan public theaters used thrust stages.

thymele: the sacred altar in a Greek theater; it was customarily placed in the center of the **orchestra** and is a reminder of the religious roots of Greek drama.

tirade: a lengthy, highly emotional speech most often associated with the French Neoclassic theater; a strong outpouring of emotion.

tiring house: in the Elizabethan public theater, the area behind the stage where the actors dressed (or attired) themselves; the term also applies to the entire architectural structure (customarily four stories) that backed the playing space.

tlatquetzque: professional entertainers or actors in the Mayan culture, often dressed as ocelots, sacred snakes, or colorful birds.

total theater: twentieth-century performance mode that employs multisensory, multimedia techniques to assault the audience's senses. Traditional performance techniques are often combined with film, video, slide shows, electronic soundtracks, light shows, etc.

township theater: performances derived from the townships of South Africa in which actors often improvise dialogue and stories and use "found" materials for costumes and props.

tragedy: one of the principal dramatic genres, in which a central character is in conflict with an external, as well as internal, force; the conflict ends disastrously for the character and provokes pity and fear in the audience.

tragicomedy: one of the principal dramatic genres, which blends serious and comic elements; frequently the serious is treated comically, while the comic is given a more somber treatment. The plays of Anton Chekhov and Samuel Beckett typify tragicomedy.

trap(door): a hole cut in the stage floor (covered by a hinged door) that allows for entrances and exits below the stage; often used for special effects (e.g., the apparition of ghosts).

trilogy: a collection of three plays usually related by theme or characters. Aeschylus's *Oresteia* is a trilogy dealing with the fall of the house of Atreus. Neil Simon's *Brighton Beach* trilogy portrays the playwright's early life.

trope: antiphonal biblical passage set to music and sung in Christian ceremonies in the Middle Ages; eventually tropes—such as the *Quem Queritas* trope—grew into dramas in which events from Scripture were acted before the congregation.

tsa chu: Chinese term for classical Yuan drama (e.g., *Autumn in the Palace of Han*).

ts'ao-ts'ao: stock villain in classical Chinese drama; usually a counselor to the emperor.

tsure: a secondary character in Japanese **Noh** drama who accompanies the **shite**.

unities: refer to the time, place, and action of a drama. The Neoclassicists believed that a play ought to be confined to a single action that takes place in a single location and occurs within a short time span.

vaudeville: stage entertainment comprising a variety of unrelated acts such as songs, dances, magic, comedy, etc. Originally, a vaudeville was a French entertainment that combined pantomime, dance, and music to tell a simple story.

Vedas: sacred Hindu scriptures; the Fifth Veda is a sacred text on dramatic theory written by Brahma to illustrate how the gods invented drama as a means of enlightenment for humans (see **Nātyaśāstra**).

Verfremdungseffekt: Brecht's term for the **alienation effect**.

verisimilitude: "likeness to truth," the attempt to put a truthful picture of life onstage. Although it purported to "realism," verisimilitude, especially in the Renaissance, offered an idealized view of "real life."

via negativa: Grotowski's motto for the **poor theater**, which means to refrain from doing. It encourages actors to rely solely on their resources, and not externals, for the creation of the theater act.

wagoto: the refined, delicate acting style of the **Kabuki** theater, most often used to portray handsome young men, lovers, and princes.

waki: an objective third party in Japanese **Noh** drama; he is usually a holy person who watches from the side and comments on the actions of the **shite**.

wakushu: the young men's (boy's) **Kabuki** of seventeenth-century Japan.

well-made play: also, *pièce bien faite;* a drama in which a carefully constructed plot is designed to create suspense and forward movement, often at the expense of characterization. Such plays frequently employ a withheld secret, confrontations between heroes and villains, a series of minor crises building to a climax and resolution in which all the conflicts are neatly worked out. Although *Oedipus the King* is the prototype of the well-made play, it is a genre that flourished in the nineteenth century, especially in the works of Eúgene Scribe.

wen hsi: domestic, usually romantic, stories in the Peking, or Chinese, Opera.

Wild West shows: popular American **extravaganzas** of the late nineteenth century which re-created frontier life, battles with Native Americans, and so on; associated with Buffalo Bill Cody.

wu: Chinese term for story and also for storyteller.

wu-hsi: military plays in the Chinese or Peking Opera.

ya pu: traditional classical drama of the Chinese theater, usually associated with the court and scholars (as opposed to the **hua pu**, or folk drama).

yarō: mature male **Kabuki** performers.

yūgen: Japanese term for "mysterious beauty"; it is the goal of Noh drama and seeks to achieve a mood of quietness, meditation, and aesthetic gratification.

zanni: collective term for comedians in the Italian *commedia dell'arte*; usually, these were unnamed characters who played a variety of roles and added bits of clowning to the action.

zarzuela: Spanish term applied to musical comedy; begun by Calderón in seventeenth-century Spain and brought to the New World by Spanish colonists. **Zarzuelas bufas** are "comical musicals," while **bailetes** are "dance musicals."

APPENDIX C

BIBLIOGRAPHY

Chapter 1: Stories, Rituals, and Theater

Blau, Herbert. *The Audience*. Baltimore: John Hopkins University Press, 1990.

Carlson, Marvin. *Theories of the Theatre: A Historical and Critical Survey from the Greeks to the Present*. Ithaca: Cornell University Press, 1985.

Cole, David. *The Theatrical Event: A Mythos, a Vocabulary, a Perspective*. Middletown: Wesleyan University Press, 1975.

Covarrubias, Miguel. *Island of Bali*. New York: Alfred A. Knopf, 1950.

Kirby, E. T. *Ur-Drama*. New York: New York University Press, 1975.

Lommel, Andreas. *Shamanism: The Beginnings of Art*. New York: McGraw-Hill, 1967.

Ridgeway, William. *The Dramas and Dramatic Dances of Non-European Races*. New York: B. Blom, 1964.

Schechner, Richard and Willa Appel. *By Means of Performance: Intercultural Studies of Theater and Ritual*. Cambridge: Cambridge University Press, 1990.

Turner, Victor. *From Ritual to Theatre*. New York: Performing Arts Journal Publications, 1982.

Chapter 2: From Theater to Drama

DRAMATIC THEORY

Beckerman, Bernard. *Dynamics of Drama: Theory and Method of Analysis*. New York: Alfred A. Knopf, 1970.

Dukore, Bernard F. *Dramatic Theory and Criticism: Greeks to Grotowski*. New York: Holt Rinehart and Winston, 1974.

Esslin, Martin. *An Anatomy of Drama*. London: T. Smith, 1976.

Frye, Northrop. *The Anatomy of Criticism*. Princeton: Princeton University Press, 1957.

Hoy, Cyrus. *The Hyacinth Room: An Investigation into the Nature of Comedy, Tragedy, and Tragicomedy*. New York: Chatto and Windus, 1984.

Kitto, H. D. F. *Form and Meaning in Drama*. London: Methuen, 1956.

Langer, Suzanne. *Feeling and Form: A Theory of Art*. New York: Scribner and Sons, 1953.

Pavis, Patrice. *Languages of the Stage: Essays in the Semiology of the Theatre*. New York: Performing Arts Journal Publications, 1982.

States, Bert O. *Great Reckonings in Little Rooms: On the Phenomenology of Theater*. Berkeley: University of California Press, 1985.

TRAGEDY AND MELODRAMA

Butcher, S. H. *Aristotle's Theory of Poetry and Fine Art*. London: Macmillan, 1895.

Corrigan, Robert. *Tragedy: Vision and Form*. San Francisco: Chandler Publishing Company, 1965.

Else, Gerald. *Aristotle's Poetics: The Argument*. Cambridge, MA: Harvard University Press, 1957.

Smith, James L. *Melodrama*. London: Methuen, 1973.

COMEDY AND FARCE

Bergson, Henri. *Laughter*. Trans. Cloudesley Brereton and Frank Rothwell. London: Macmillan and Company, 1917.

Bermel, Albert. *Farce: A History from Aristophanes to Woody Allen*. New York: Simon and Schuster, 1982.

Corrigan, Robert W. ed., *Comedy: Meaning and Form*. San Francisco: Chandler Publishing Company, 1965.

Davis, Jessica Milner. *Farce*. London: Harper and Row, 1978.

Hirst, David L. *Tragicomedy*. London: Methuen, 1984.

Kerr, Walter. *Tragedy and Comedy*. New York: 1967.

Ionesco, Eugene. *Notes and Counternotes*. Trans. Donald Watson. New York: 1964.

Lauter, Paul, ed. *Theories of Comedy*. Garden City: Anchor Books, 1964.

Olson, Elder. *The Theory of Comedy*. Bloomington: Indiana University Press, 1968.

STYLES AND CONVENTIONS

Russell, Douglas. *Period Style for the Theater*. 2nd ed. Boston: Allyn and Bacon, 1987.

St. Denis, Michel. *The Rediscovery of Style*. New York: Theater Arts Books, 1960.

THEATER ARCHITECTURE, SPACES

Carlson, Marvin. *Places of Performance: The Semiotics of Theatre Architecture*. Ithaca: Cornell University Press, 1989.

Leacroft, Helen and Richard. *The Theatre*. New York: Roy Publishers, 1961.

McNamara, Brooks. *Theatres, Spaces, Environments*. New York: Drama Book Specialists, 1975.

Mullin, Donald C. *The Development of the Playhouse: A Survey of Theater Architecture from the Renaissance to the Present*. Berkeley: University of California Press, 1970.

Chapter 3: From the Page to the Stage

THE ACTOR

Berry, Cicely. *The Actor and the Text*. New York: Applause Theatre Books, 1992.

Boleslavski, Richard. *Acting: The First Six Lessons*. New York: Theatre Arts Books, 1933.

Chaikin, Joseph. *The Presence of the Actor*. New York: Atheneum, 1974.

Cole, Toby and Helen K. Chinoy, eds. *Actors on Acting: The Theories, Techniques, and Practices of the Great Actors of All Times as Told in Their Own Words*. New York: Crown Publishers, 1954.

Diderot, Denis. "The Paradox of Acting" in William Archer, *Masks or Faces?* New York: Hill and Wang, 1957.

Duerr, Edward. *The Length and Depth of Acting*. New York: Rinehart and Winston, 1962.

Hagan, Uta. *Respect for Acting*. New York: Macmillan, 1973.

Hill, Hilly. *Actors' Lives On and Off the American Stage: Interviews*. New York: Theatre Communications Group, 1993.

Marowitz, Charles. *The Act of Being*. New York: Taplinger Publishing Company, 1978.

Spolin, Viola. *Improvisation for the Theater*. Evanston: Northwestern University Press, 1963.

Stanislavsky, Konstantin. *An Actor Prepares*. Trans. Elizabeth Reynolds Hapgood. New York: Theatre Arts Books, 1946.

———. *Building a Character*. Trans. Elizabeth Reynolds Hapgood. New York: Theatre Arts Books, 1949.

———. *Creating a Role*. Trans. Elizabeth Reynolds Hapgood. New York: Theatre Arts Books, 1961.

Strasberg, Lee. *A Dream of Passion: The Development of the Method*. Evangelina Morphos, ed. Boston: Little Brown, 1987.

Wilson, Garff B. *A History of American Acting*. Bloomington: Indiana University Press, 1966.

THE PLAYWRIGHT

Bakhtin, Mikail. *The Dialogic Imagination: Four Essays*. Trans. Caryl Emerson. Austin: University of Texas Press, 1981.

Bentley, Eric. *The Playwright as Thinker: A Study of Drama in the Modern Times*. New York: Reynal and Hitchcock, 1946.

Betsko, Kathleen and Rachel Koenig, eds. *Interviews with Contemporary Playwrights*. New York: Applause Theatre Books, 1987.

Brater, Enoch, ed. *Feminine Focus: The New Women Playwrights*. New York: Oxford University Press, 1989.

Brayer, Jackson R., ed. *The Playwright's Art*. New Brunswick: Rutgers University Press, 1995.

Cole, Toby, ed. *Playwrights on Playwriting*. New York: Hill and Wang, 1961.

DiGaetani, John L. *A Search for a Postmodern Theater: Interviews with Contemporary Playwrights*. Westport: Greenwood Press, 1991.

Macgowan, Kenneth. *Primer for Playwriting*. Westport: Greenwood Press, 1981.

"Playwrights and Playwriting Issues," *Drama Review* 21, no. 4, 1970.

Savran, David, ed. *In Their Own Words: Contemporary American Playwrights: Interviews*. New York: Theatre Communications Group, 1988.

Smiley, Sam. *Playwriting: The Structure of Action*. Englewood Cliffs: Prentice-Hall, 1971.

Suzuki, Tadashi. *The Way of Acting*. Trans. Thomas Rymer. New York: Theatre Communications Group, 1986.

Wager, Walter H. *The Playwrights Speak*. New York: Delacorte Press, 1967.

THE DIRECTOR

Barstow, Arthur. *The Director's Voice: Twenty-one Interviews*. New York: Theatre Communications Group, 1989.

Brook, Peter. *The Empty Space*. New York: Atheneum, 1968.

Clurman, Harold. *On Directing*. New York: Macmillan, 1972.

Cole, Toby and Helen K. Chinoy, eds. *Directors on Directing*. Rev. ed. New York: Bobbs-Merrill, 1963.

Dean, Alexander. *Fundamentals of Play Directing*. 3rd ed. Rev. Lawrence Carra. New York: Farrar and Rhinehart, 1974.

Greenwald, Michael L. *Directions by Indirections: John Barton of the Royal Shakespeare Company*. Toronto and London: University of Delaware Press, 1985.

Guthrie, Tyrone. *A Life in the Theatre*. London: Faber and Faber, 1987.

Leiter, Samuel L. *From Belasco to Brook: Representative Directors of the English-Speaking Stage*. Westport: Greenwood Press, 1991.

Nelson, Richard and David Jones. *Making Plays: The Writer-Director Relationship in the Theater Today*. London: Faber and Faber 1995.

Schnieder, Alan. *Entrances: An American Director's Journey*. New York: Viking Press, 1986.

THE DESIGNERS

Anderson, Barbara and Cletus Anderson. *Costume Design*. New York: Rhinehart and Winston, 1984.

Aronson, Arnold. *American Set Design*. New York: Theatre Communications Group, 1985.

Bay, Howard. *Stage Design*. New York: Drama Book Specialists, 1974.

Burian, Jarka. *The Scenography of Josef Swoboda*. Middletown: Wesleyan University Press, 1971.

Burdick, Elizabeth B., et al., eds. *Contemporary Stage Design*. Middletown: Wesleyan University Press, 1975.

Corey, Irene. *The Mask of Reality: An Approach to Design for the Theatre*. New Orleans: Anchorage Press, 1968.

Hainaux, Rene, ed. *Scene Design Throughout the World Since 1950*. New York: Harrup, 1964.

Jones, Robert Edmund. *The Dramatic Imagination*. New York: Theatre Arts Books, 1987.

Laver, James. *Costumes in the Theater*. New York: Harrup, 1964.

Leeper, Janet. E. *Gordon Craig: Designs for the Theater*. Hammondsworth, England: Penguin Books, 1949.

McCandless, Stanley R. *A Method of Lighting the Stage*. New York: Theatre Arts Books, 1958.

Mielziner, Jo. *Designing for the Theatre*. New York: Atheneum, 1965.

Oenslager, Donald. *Scenery Then and Now*. New York: W. W. Norton and Company, Inc., 1935.

———. *Stage Design: Four Centuries of Scenic Innovation*. New York: Viking Press, 1975.

Palmer, Richard H. *The Lighting Art: The Aesthetics of Stage Lighting Design*. Englewood Cliffs: Prentice-Hall, 1984.

THE CRITIC

Billington, Michael. *One Night Stands: A Critic's View of the Modern British Theater*. London: Nick Hearn Books, 1999.

Gussow, Mel. *Theater on the Edge: New Visions, New Voices*. New York: Applause Theatre Books, 1998.

National Theatre Critics Reviews [formerly, *New York Theater Critics Reviews*]. New York: Published annually since 1943.

Palmer, Richard H. *The Critics' Canon: Standards of Theatrical Reviews in America*. New York: Greenwood Press, 1988.

Chapter 4: The Theater of Greece and Rome

GREECE

Arnott, Peter. *The Ancient Greek and Roman Theater.* New York: Random House, 1971.

Bieber, Margarete. *The History of the Greek and Roman Theater.* Princeton: Princeton University Press, 1939.

Bowra, C. M. *Sophoclean Tragedy.* Oxford: The Clarendon Press, 1947.

Cornford, Francis. *The Origin of Attic Comedy.* Cambridge: Anchor Books, 1914.

Deardon, C. W. *The Stage of Aristophanes.* London: Athlone Press, 1976.

Des Bouvrie, Synnove. *Women in Greek Tragedy: An Anthopological Approach.* Oslo: Symbolue Osloenses, 1991.

Gardiner, Cynthia P. *The Sophoclean Chorus: A Study of Character and Function.* Iowa City: University of Iowa Press, 1987.

Harriott, Rosemary M. *Aristophanes: Poet and Dramatist.* Baltimore: Croom Helm, 1986.

Harsh, Phillip Whaley. *A Handbook of Classical Drama.* Palo Alto: Stanford University Press, 1944.

Kitto, H. D. F. *Greek Tragedy: A Literary Study.* London: Methuen, 1939.

Kott, Jan. *The Eating of the Gods: An Interpretation of Greek Tragedy.* Trans. Boleslaw Taborski and Edward J. Czerwinski. New York: Random House, 1970.

Lawler, Lillian B. *The Dance of the Ancient Greek Theater.* Iowa City: University of Iowa Press, 1964.

Lloyd-Jones, Hugh. *Greek Comedy. Hellenisitc Literature, Greek Religion, and Miscellanea.* Oxford: Oxford University Press, 1990.

Murray, Gilbert. *Aeschylus: The Creator of Tragedy.* Oxford: The Clarendon Press, 1940.

O'Brien, M. J., ed. *Twentieth-Century Interpretations of* Oedipus Rex. Englewood Cliffs: Pretnice-Hall, 1968.

Padel, Ruth. *In and Out of Mind: Greek Images of the Tragic Self.* Princeton: Princeton University Press, 1992.

Pickard-Cambridge, Arthur W. *The Dramatic Festivals of Athens.* Oxford: The Clarendon Press, 1953.

Reckford, Kenneth. *Aristophanes' Old and New Comedy.* Chapel Hill: University of North Carolina Press, 1987.

Seale, David. *Vision and Stagecraft in Sophocles.* London: University of Chicago Press, 1982.

Sifikis, G. M. *Parabisis and Animal Chorus.* London: Oxford University Press, 1971.

Taplin, Oliver. *Greek Tragedy in Action.* Berkeley: University of California Press, 1978.

Walcot, Peter. *Greek Drama in Its Theatrical and Social Context.* Cardiff,: University of Wales Press, 1976.

Walton, J. Micheal. *The Greek Sense of Theater.* London: Methuen, 1984.

Winkler, John J. and Froma I. Zeitlin, eds. *Nothing to Do with Dionysus? Athenian Drama in Its Social Context.* Princeton: Princeton University Press, 1990.

ROME

Beare, William. *The Roman Stage.* London: Methuen, 1964.

Duckworth, George E. *The Nature of Roman Comedy: A Study in Popular Entertainment.* Princeton: Princeton University Press, 1952.

Hamilton, Edith. *The Roman Way.* New York: W.W. Norton and Company, 1930.

Leffingwell, Georgina Williams. *Social and Private Life at Rome in the Times of Plautus and Terence.* New York: Oxford University Press, 1968.

Lucas, Frank L. *Seneca and Elizabethan Tragedy.* Cambridge: Cambridge University Press, 1922.

Norwood, Gilbert. *The Art of Terence.* New York: Russell and Russell, 1923.

Segal, Eric. *Roman Laughter: The Comedy of Plautus.* Cambridge, MA: Harvard University Press, 1968.

Chapter 5: The Theater of India, China, and Japan

INDIA

Bowers, Faubion. *Dance in India.* New York: AMS Press, 1953.

Coomaraswamy, Amanda Kentish. *The Dance of Śiva: Fourteen Indian Essays.* New York: Sunrwise Turn, 1918.

Garagi, Balwant. *Folk Theater of India.* Seattle: University of Washington Press, 1966.

Iyer, K. B. *Kathakali: The Sacred Dance-Drama of Malabar.* London: Luzac, 1955.

Nemichandra, Jain. *The Indian Theater: Tradition, Continuity, Change.* New Delhi: Vikas Publishing House, 1992.

Richmond, Farley, et al, eds. *Indian Theater:Traditions of Performance.* Honolulu: University of Hawaii Press, 1990.

Schuyler, M. A. *A Bibliography of the Sanskrit Drama with an Introductory Sketch of the Dramatic Literature of India.* New York: Macmillan, 1965.

Shekhar, Indu. *Sanskrit Drama: Its Origins and Decline.* New Delhi: Munshiram Mancharal, 1977.

Srampickal, Jacob. *Voice of the Voiceless: The Power of People's Theater in India.* London and New York: St. Martin's Press, 1994.

Wells, Henry H. *The Classical Drama of India.* Bombay and New York: Asia Publishing House, 1963.

CHINA

Chang, Pe-Chin. *Chinese Opera and the Painted Face.* Taipei: Mei Ya Publications, 1979.

Dolby, William. *A History of Chinese Drama.* London: P. Elek, 1976.

Halson, Elizabeth. *Peking Opera: A Short Guide.* London: Oxford University Press, 1966.

Huang, Shang. *Tales from the Peking Opera.* Beijing: New World Press, 1985.

Hung, Josephine Huang. *Children of the Pear Garden.* Taipei: Mei Ya Publications, 1961.

Hsu, Tao-Ching. *The Chinese Conception of Theatre.* Seattle and London: University of Washington Press, 1985.

Mackerras, Colin. *The Performing Arts in Contemporary China.* London and Boston: Routledge & Kegan Paul, 1981.

Scott, A. C. *Traditional Chinese Plays.* 3 vols. Madison: University of Wisconsin Press, 1970, 1975.

Wu, Zuguang, Zuolin Huang, and Shaowu Mei. *Peking Opera and Mei Lan-fang.* Beijing: New World Press, 1981.

Zung, Cecelia S. C. *Secrets of the Chinese Drama.* New York: B. Blom, 1964.

JAPAN

Arnott, Peter. *The Theaters of Japan.* New York: Macmillan, 1969.

Goodman, David G., *Japanese Drama and Culture in the 1960s: The Return of the Gods.* Armonk: M. E. Sharpe, 1988.

Kawatake, Shigetoshi. *An Illustrated History of Japanese Theater Arts.* Tokyo: Kodansha International, 1956.

Keene, Donald. *Nō: The Classical Drama of Japan.* Tokyo and Palo Alto: Kodansha International, 1966.

Kirby, E. T. "The Origins of Nō Drama," *Educational Theatre Journal* 25, no. 3 (1973), 269–84.

Motokiyo, Zeami. *On the Art of the No Drama.* Trans. J. Thomas Rimer and Kamazaki Masakazu. Princeton: Princeton University Press, 1980.

O'Neill, P. G. *Early Noh Drama.* London: Lund Humphries, 1958.

Ortolani, Benito. *The Japanese Theatre: From Shamanistic Ritual to Contemporary Pluralism.* Princeton: Princeton University Press, 1994.

Rimer, J. Thomas. *Toward a Modern Japanese Theater.* Princeton: Princeton University Press, 1974.

Sakanishi, S. *Kyōgen: Comic Interludes of Japan.* Boston: Marshall Jones Company, 1938.

Senda, Akihiko. *The Voyage of Contemporary Japanese Theater.* Trans. J. Thomas Rimer. Honolulu: University of Hawaii Press, 1997.

Suzuki, Tadashi. *The Way of Acting.* Trans. J. Thomas Rimer. New York: Theatre Communications Group, 1986.

Waley, Arthur. *The Nō Plays of Japan.* London: Alfred A, Knopf, 1921.

Yoshinobu Inoura and Toshio Kawatake. *The Traditional Theater of Japan.* Tokyo: Weatherhill, 1981.

Zeami. *Kadensho.* Trans. Chuichi Sakurai et al. Kyoto: Sumiya-Shinobe Publications International, 1971.

Chapter 6: The Early Modern Theater

THE MIDDLE AGES

Axton, Richard. *European Drama of the Early Middle Ages.* Pittsburgh: University of Pittsburgh Press, 1973.

Brody, Alan. *The English Mummers and Their Play.* Philadelphia: University of Pennsylvania Press, 1970.

Case, Sue-Ellen. "Reviewing Hrotsvita," *Theater Journal* 35, no. 4 (1983), 533–42.

Chambers, E. K. *The Medieval Stage.* 2 vols. Oxford: The Clarendon Press, 1903.

Craig, Hardin. *English Religious Drama of the Middle Ages.* Oxford: The Clarendon Press, 1960.

Holme, Bryan. *Medieval Pageant.* London: Thames and Hudson, 1987.

Potter, Robert A. *The English Morality Play: Origins, History, and Influence of a Dramatic Tradition.* London: Routledge & Kegan Paul, 1975.

Southern, Richard. *The Medieval Theater in the Round.* London: Faber and Faber, 1957.

Woolf, Rosemary. *The English Mystery Plays.* Berkeley: University of California Press, 1972.

THE EUROPEAN RENAISSANCE

England

Adams, John Cranford. *The Globe Playhouse: Its Design and Equipment.* New York: Barnes and Noble, 1961.

Avery, Emmett and Arthur Scouten. *The London Stage, 1600–1700: A Critical Introduction.* Carbondale: Southern Illinois University Press, 1965.

Bentley, Gerald Eades. *The Jacobean and Caroline Stage.* 7 vols. Oxford: Oxford University Press, 1966.

Bogart, Travis. *The Tragic Satire of John Webster.* Berkeley: University of California Press, 1955.

Bowers, Fredson T. *Elizabethan Revenge Tragedy.* Princeton: Princeton University Press, 1940.

Bradbrook, Muriel C. *Themes and Conventions of Elizabethan Tragedy.* Cambridge: Cambridge University Press, 1935.

Cohen, Walter. *Drama of a Nation: Public Theater in Renaissance England and Spain.* Ithaca: Cornell University Press, 1985.

Dessen, Alan C. *Elizabethan Stage Conventions and Modern Interpreters.* Cambridge: Harvard University Press, 1978.

Gurr, Andrew. *The Shakespearean Stage: 1574–1642.* New York: Cambridge University Press, 1984.

Harrison, G. B. *Elizabethan Plays and Players.* Ann Arbor: University of Michigan Press, 1956.

Hotson, Leslie. *Shakespeare's Wooden O.* New York: Macmillan, 1960.

Leacroft, Richard. *The Development of the Elizabethan Playhouse.* Ithaca: Cornell University Press, 1973.

Orgel, Stephen. *The Illusion of Power: Political Theater in the English Renaissance.* Berkeley: University of California Press, 1975.

Ornstein, Robert. *The Moral Vision of Jacobean Tragedy.* Madison: University of Wisconsin Press, 1960.

Schoenbaum, Sam. *William Shakespeare: A Documentary Life.* New York: Oxford University Press, 1975.

Smith, Irwin. *Shakespeare's Blackfriars Playhouse: Its History and Design.* New York: New York University Press, 1964.

Smith, Lacey Baldwin. *The Elizabethan World.* Boston: Houghton Mifflin, 1967.

Tillyard, E. M. W. *The Elizabethan World Picture.* New York: Vintage Books, n.d.

Wickham, Glynne. *Early English Stages, 1300–1660.* East Lansing: Michigan State University Press, 1961.

Wilson, F. P. and G. K. Hunter. *The English Drama, 1485–1585.* London: The Clarendon Press, 1969.

Spain and the Americas

Allen, John J. *The Reconstruction of a Spanish Golden Age Playhouse.* Gainesville: University of Florida Press, 1983.

Arias, Ricardo. *The Spanish Sacramental Plays.* Boston: Twayne, 1980.

Bancroft-Hunt, Norman. *North American Indians: The Life and Culture of the Native American.* London: B. Trodd Publishing House, 1991.

Brown, Vinson. *Voices of the Earth: Sky and Vision Life of the Native Americans and Their Cultural Heroes.* Harrisburg: Stackpole Books, 1974.

Coe, Michael D. *The Maya.* Rev. ed. New York: Prager, 1980.

Crawford, J. P. W. *Spanish Drama Before Lope de Vega.* Philadelphia: University of Pennsylvania Press, 1967.

Edmundson, Munro S. *The Book of Counsel: The Popol Vuh of the Quiche Maya of Gautamala.* New Orleans: Tulane University-Middle America Research Institute, 1971.

Horse Capture, C.P. *Powwow.* Seattle: University of Washington Press, 1992.

Irving, Thomas Ballantine, ed. *The Maya's Own Words.* Culver City: Labyrinthos, 1985.

Jones, Willis Knapp. *Behind Spanish American Footlights.* Austin: University of Texas Press, 1966.

Kamen, Henry. *Golden Age Spain.* Houndmills, UK: Macmillan Education, 1988.

Kelly, James F. *Lope de Vega and the Spanish Drama.* New York: Haskell House, 1971.

Larson, Donald R. *The Honor Plays of Lope de Vega*. Cambridge: Harvard University Press, 1967.

Leonard, Irving A. *Baroque Times in Old Mexico*. New York: Ann Arbor: University of Michigan Press, 1959.

McKendrick, Melveena. *Theater in Spain: 1400–1700*. Cambridge: Cambridge University Press, 1989.

Norea, Carlos G. *Studies in Spanish Renaissance Thought*. The Hague: Nijhoff, 1975.

Parker, Alexander. *The Mind and Art of Calderón*. Cambridge: Harvard University Press, 1988.

Rennert, Hugh. *The Spanish Stage in the Time of Lope de Vega*. New York: Dover Publications, 1963.

Shank, Theodore. "A Return to Mayan and Aztec Roots," *Drama Review* 18, no. 4 (1974), 58–70.

Shergold, N. D. *A History of the Spanish Stage from Medieval Times Until the End of the Seventeenth Century*. Oxford: The Clarendon Press, 1967.

Shoemaker, William Hutchinson. *The Multiple Stage in Spain during the 15th and 16th Centuries*. Princeton: Princeton University Press, 1935.

Surtz, Ronald E. *The Birth of a Theater: Dramatic Conventions from Juan del Encina to Lope de Vega*. Princeton: Princeton University Press, 1979.

Tedlock, Dennis, ed., and trans. *Popol Vuh: The Definitive Edition of the Mayan Book of the Dawn of Life and the Glories of Gods and Kings*. New York: Simon and Schuster, 1985.

Trevor Davies, G. *The Golden Century of Spain, 1501–1621*. London: St. Martin's Press, 1937.

Wardropper, Bruce W., ed. *Critical Essays on the Theater of Calderón*. New York: New York University Press, 1965.

Wilson, Margaret. *Spanish Drama of the Golden Age*. Oxford: The Clarendon Press, 1969.

France and Italy

Arnott, Peter. *An Introduction to French Theater*. Totowa: Roman and Littlefield, 1977.

Burkhardt, Jacob. *The Civilization of the Renaissance in Italy*. Oxford: Oxford University Press, 1981.

Clark, Priscilla Parkhurst. *Literary France: The Making of a Culture*. Berkeley: University of California Press, 1987.

Cook, Albert. *French Tragedy*. Chicago: Swallow Press, 1964.

Duchartre, Pierre Louis. *The Italian Comedy, the Improvisation, Scenarios, Lives, Attitudes, Portraits, and Masks of the Illustrious Characters of the Commedia dell'Arte*. Trans. Randolph T. Weaver. London: Dover, 1966..

Hewitt, Bernard, ed. *The Renaissance Stage: Documents of Serlio, Sabbattini, and Furtenbach*. Coral Gables: University of Miami Press, 1958.

Howarth, W. D. *Molière: A Playwright and His Audience*. New York: Cambridge University Press, 1982.

Knight, R. C. *Racine: Modern Judgments*. London: Macmillan, 1969.

Lea, K. M. *Italian Popular Comedy, a Study of the Commedia dell'Arte, 1560–1620*. 2 vols. Oxford: The Clarendon Press, 1934.

Nagler, K. M. *Theater Festivals of the Medici, 1539–1637*. New Haven: Yale University Press, 1964.

Nicoll, Allardyce. *The World of Harlequin*. Cambridge: Cambridge University Press, 1963.

Ruffo-Fiore, Silvuia. *Niccolo Machiavelli*. Boston: Twayne, 1982.

Sand, Maurice. *The History of the Harlequinade*. 2 vols. London: M. Secker, 1915.

Smith, Winifred. *The Commedia dell' Arte, a Study in Italian Popular Comedy*. New York: New Era Printing Co., 1912.

White, John. *The Birth and Rebirth of Pictorial Space*. London: Faber and Faber, 1957.

Wiley, William Leon. *The Hotel du Bourgogne: Another Look at France's First Public Theater*. Chapel Hill: University of North Carolina Press, 1969.

LATE-SEVENTEENTH AND EIGHTEENTH CENTURIES

Brereton, Geoffrey. *French Comic Drama from the Sixteenth to the Eighteenth Century*. London: Methuen, 1977.

Gilder, Rosamond. *Enter the Actress: The First Women in the Theatre*. Boston: Houghton Mifflin Co., 1931.

Holland, Norman. *The First Modern Comedies*. Cambridge: Harvard University Press, 1959.

Holland, Peter. *The Ornament of Action: Text and Performance in Restoration Comedy*. Cambridge: Cambridge University Press, 1979.

Loftis, John. ed. *Sheridan and the Drama of Georgian England*. Cambridge: Harvard University Press, 1986.

Lough, John. *Seventeenth-Century French Drama: The Background*. Oxford: The Clarendon Press, 1979.

Lynch, James J. *Box, Pit, and Gallery: Stage and Society in Johnson's London*. Berkeley: University of California Press, 1953.

Mittman, Barbara G. *Spectators on the Paris Stage in the 17th and 18th Centuries*. Ann Arbor: University of Michigan Press, 1984.

Muir, Kenneth. *The Comedy of Manners*. London: Hutchinson, 1970.

Price, Cecil. *Theatre in the Age of Garrick*. Oxford: The Clarendon Press, 1973.

Rothstein, Eric. *Restoration Tragedy*. Madison: University of Wisconsin Press, 1975.

Southern, Richard. *The Georgian Playhouse*. London: Pleides Books, 1948.

Styan, J. L. *Restoration Comedy in Performance*. Cambridge: Harvard University Press,1986.

Swedenberg, H. T. *England in the Restoration and Early Eighteenth Century*. Berkeley: University of California Press, 1973.

Wilcox, John. *The Relation of Molière to Restoration Comedy*. New York: B. Blom, 1964.

Wilson, John H. *A Preface to Restoration Drama*. Boston: Houghton Mifflin, 1965.

Chapter 7: The Modern Theater

ROMANTICISM

Bowra, C. M. *The Romantic Imagination*. New York: Oxford University Press, 1961.

Carlson, Marvin. *The French Stage in the Nineteenth Century*. Metuchen: Scarecrow Press, 1972.

Daniels, Barry V. *Revolution in the Theater: French Romantic Theories of the Drama*. Westport: Greenwood Press, 1983.

Grimsted, David. *Melodrama Unveiled: American Theater and Culture, 1800–1850*. Chicago: University of Chicago Press, 1968.

Hewitt, Bernard. *Theater U.S.A., 1665 to 1957*. New York: McGraw-Hill, 1959.

Hodge, Francis Richard. *Yankee Theater: The Image of America on the Stage, 1825–1850*. Austin: University of Texas Press, 1965.

Lacey, Alexander, *Pixérécourt and the French Romantic Drama*. Toronto: University of Toronto Press, 1928.

Lewis, Philip C. *Trouping: How the Show Came to Town*. New York: Harper and Row, 1973.

Moody, Richard. *America Takes the Stage: Romanticism in American Drama and Theater, 1750–1900*. Bloomington: Indiana University Press, 1955.

Peyre, Henri. *What Is Romanticism?* Trans. Roda Roberts. Tuscaloosa: University of Alabama Press, 1977.

UNCLE TOM'S CABIN AND THE MINSTREL SHOW

Birdoff, Harry. *The World's Greatest Hit.* New York: Vanni, 1947.

Leonard, William Torbert. *Masquerade in Black.* Metuchen: Scarecrow Press, 1986.

Gosset, Thomas F. *Uncle Tom's Cabin and American Culture.* Dallas: Southern Methodist University Press, 1985.

Meserve, Walter, and Ruth Meserve. "*Uncle Tom's Cabin* and Modern Chinese Drama," *Modern Drama* 17 (1974), 57–66.

Wittke, Carl. *Tambo and Bones: A History of the American Minstrel Stage.* Durham: Duke University Press, 1930.

REALISM AND NATURALISM

General

Archer, William. *The Old Drama and the New.* London and Boston: Maynard and Company, 1926.

Barzun, Jacques. *Darwin, Marx, Wagner: Critique of a Heritage.* Chicago: Doubleday, 1981.

Bentley, Eric. ed. *The Theory of the Modern Stage: An Introduction to Modern Theatre and Drama.* Baltimore: Penguin, 1976.

Brockett, Oscar G. and Robert Findlay. *Century of Innovation: A History of European and American Theatre and Drama Since 1870.* Englewood Cliffs: Prentice-Hall, 1973.

Cheney, Sheldon. *The Art Theatre.* New York: Alfred A. Knopf, 1925.

Cohn, Ruby. *From Desire to Godot.* Berkeley: University of California Press, 1987.

Gassner, John. *Directions in Modern Drama and Theater.* New York: Rinehart and Winston, 1967.

Gerould, Daniel, ed. *American Melodrama.* New York: Performing Arts Journal Publications, 1980.

Gilman, Richard. *The Making of Modern Drama: A Study of Buchner, Ibsen, Strindberg, Chekhov, Pirandello, Brecht, Beckett, Handke.* New York: Farrar, Strauss, and Giroux, 1987.

Miller, Anna Irene. *The Independent Theatre in Europe, 1887 to the Present.* New York: B. Blom, 1966.

Roken, Freddie. *Theatrical Space in Ibsen, Chekhov, and Strindberg: Public Forms of Privacy.* Ann Arbor: University of Michigan Press, 1986.

Seltzer, Daniel, ed. *The Modern Theatre: Readings and Documents.* Boston: Little Brown, 1967.

Styan, John. *Modern Drama in Theory and Practice: Realism and Naturalism.* New York: Cambridge University Press, 1983.

Taylor, John Russel. *The Rise and Fall of the Well-Made Play.* New York: Methuen, 1967.

Valency, Maurice. *The Flower and the Castle: An Introduction to Modern Drama.* New York: Macmillan, 1963.

Williams, Raymond. *Drama from Ibsen to Brecht.* London: Oxford University Press, 1968.

England

Brown, John Russell, ed. *Modern British Dramatists: A Colleciton of Critical Essays.* Englewood Cliffs: Prentice Hall, 1968.

Carpenter, Charles A. *Bernard Shaw and the Art of Destroying Ideals: The Early Plays.* Madison: University of Wisconsin Press, 1969.

Crompton, Louis. *Shaw the Dramatist.* Lincoln: University of Nebraska Press, 1969.

Elsom, John. *Post-War British Theatre Criticism.* London: Routledge & Kegan Paul, 1971.

Ervine, St. John. *Bernard Shaw.* New York: Morrow, 1956.

Findlater, Richard. *At the Royal Court: 25 Years of the English Stage Company.* London: Random House, 1974.

Hudson, L.A. *The English Stage, 1850–1950.* London: 1951.

Marowitz, Charles and Simon Trussler. *Theater at Work: Playwrights and Productions in the Modern British Theater.* New York: Methuen,1968.

Taylor, John Russell. *Anger and After: A Guide to the New British Drama.* London: Penguin, 1962.

France

Antoine, Andre. *Memoirs of the Theatre-libre.* Trans. Marvin Carlson. Coral Gables: University of Miami Press, 1964.

Carter, Lawson. *Zola and the Theater.* New Haven: Yale University Press, 1963.

Chiari, Joseph. *The Contemporary French Theater: Flight from Naturalism.* New York: Macmillan, 1958.

Fowlie, Wallace. *Dionysus in Paris: A Guide to French Contemporary Theater.* New York: Meridion Books, 1959.

Guicharnaud, Jacques. *Modern French Theater from Giradoux to Beckett.* New Haven: Yale University Press, 1961.

Pronko, Leonard. *Avant-Garde: The Experimental Theater in France.* Berkeley: University of California Press, 1962.

Waxman, S. M. *Antoine and the Theatre-Libre.* Cambridge: Harvard University Press, 1926.

Germany

Grube, Max. *The Story of the Meiningen.* Trans. Ann Marie Koller. Coral Gables: University of Miami Press, 1963.

Garten, Hugh F. *Modern German Drama.* London: Essential Books, 1959.

Ley-Piscator, Maria. *The Piscator Experiment.* New York: Heinemann, 1967.

Pascal, Roy. *From Naturalism to Expressionism: German Literature and Society 1880–1918.* London: Basic Books, 1973.

Piscator, Erwin. *The Political Theater.* Trans. Hugh Rorrison. New York: Avon Books, 1978.

Shaw, Leroy R. *The German Theater Today.* Austin: University of Texas Press, 1963.

Ireland

Byrne, Dawson. *The Story of Ireland's National Theater.* Dublin: The Talbot Press, 1929.

Ellis-Fermor, Una. *The Irish Dramatic Movement.* London, 1939.

Hogan, Robert G. *After the Irish Renaissance: A Critical History of the Irish Drama Since "The Plough and the Stars,"* Minneapolis: University of Minnesota Press, 1967.

Hunt, Hugh. *The Abbey: Ireland's National Theatre, 1904–1979.* New York: Columbia University Press, 1979.

Ishibashi, Hiro. *Yeats and the Noh.* Ed. Anthony Kerrigan. Dublin: Colin Smythe, 1966.

Robinson, Lennox, ed. *Ireland's Abbey Theatre: A History, 1899–1951.* London: Sidgwick and Jackson, 1951.

Simpson, Alan. *Beckett, Behan, and the Theatre in Dublin.* London: Routledge & Kegan Paul, 1962.

Russia

Gorchakov, Nikolai. *Stanislavsky Directs.* Trans. Miriam Goldina. New York: Funk and Wagnalls, 1955.

Houghton, Norris. *Moscow Rehearsals.* New York: Harcourt Brace Jovanovich, 1936.

Magarshack, David. *Chekhov.* London: Faber and Faber, 1952.

Nemirovitch-Danchenko, Vladimir. *My Life in the Russian Theatre.* Trans. John Cournos. London: Theatre Arts Books, 1936.

Sayler, Oliver M. *Inside the Moscow Art Theatre.* New York: Brentano's, 1925.

Slonin, Marc. *Russian Theater From the Empire to the Soviets*. Cleveland and New York: World Publishing Company, 1961.

Stanislavsky, Konstantin. *My Life in Art*. Trans. J. J. Robbins. New York: Theatre Arts Books, 1924.

Styan, Joseph. *Chekhov in Performance: A Commentary on the Major Plays*. Cambridge: Harvard University Press, 1971.

Valency, Maurice. *The Breaking String: The Plays of Anton Chekhov*. New York: Oxford University Press, 1966.

Scandanavia

Bradbrook, Muriel C. *Ibsen the Norwegian*. Hamden: Archon Books, 1966.

Brandes, Georg. *Henrik Ibsen; Bjornsterne Bjornson: Critical Studies*. New York: Arno Press, 1977.

Dahlstrom, Carl E. *August Strindberg, the Father of Dramatic Expressionism*. Ann Arbor: University of Michigan Press, 1929.

Holtan, Orley. *Mythic Patterns in Ibsen's Last Plays*. Minneapolis: University of Minnesota Press, 1970.

Johnson, Walter. *Strindberg and the Historical Drama*. Seattle: University of Washington Press, 1963.

Klaf, Franklin S. *Strindberg: Origins of Psychology in Modern Drama*. New York: Citadel Press, 1963.

Madsen, Borge G. *Strindberg's Naturalistic Theatre: Its Relation to French Naturalism*. Seattle: University of Washington Press, 1962.

Shaw, George Bernard. *The Quintessence of Ibsenism*. London: Brentano's, 1913.

Sprigge, Elizabeth. *The Strange Life of August Strindberg*. London: Macmillan, 1949.

Spain and Latin America

Cortes, Eladio and Mirta Barrea, eds. *Dictionary of Latin American Theater*. Westport: Greenwood Press, 2000

Ilie, Paul. *The Surrealist Mode in Spanish Literature*. Ann Arbor: University of Michigan Press, 1968.

Lima, Robert. *The Theatre of García Lorca*. New York: Las Americas Pub. Co., 1963.

Lyday, Leon F. and George Woodyard, eds. *Dramatists in Revolt: The New Latin American Theater*. Austin: University of Texas Press, 1976

United States

Beckerman, Bernard and Howard Siegman, eds. *On Stage: Selected Theater Reviews from the New York Times, 1920–1970*. New York: Quadrangle, 1973.

Bigsby, C. W. E. *A Critical Introduction to Twentieth Century American Drama*, 3 vols. Cambridge: Harvard University Press, 1982–85.

Bogart, Travis, Richard Moody, and Walter J. Meserve. *The Revels History of Drama in English*. Vol. 7. London: Oxford University Press, 1977.

Carter, Jean and Jess Ogden. *Everyman's Drama: A Study of Noncommercial Theatre in the United States*. New York: American Association for Adult Education, 1938.

Chinoy, Helen Krich and Linda Walsh Jenkins. *Women in the American Theatre*. New York: Theatre Communications Group, 1987.

Clurman, Harold. *The Fervent Years: The Story of the Group Theatre and the Thirties*. New York: Hill and Wang, 1945.

Demastes, William W. *Beyond Naturalism: A New Realism in the American Theatre*. Westport: Greenwood Press, 1988.

Downer, Alan S. *Fifty Years of American Drama, 1900–1950*. Chicago: Regnery, 1951.

Dukore, Bernard F. *American Dramatists 1918–1945*. New York: Grove Press, 1984.

Flanagan, Hallie. *Arena: The Story of the Federal Theatre*. New York: Sloan and Pearce, 1940.

France, Rachel. *A Century of Plays by American Women*. New York: Richards Rosen Press, 1979.

Freedman, Morris. *American Drama in Social Context*. Carbondale: Southern Illinois University Press, 1971.

Goldstein, Malcolm. *The Political Stage: American Drama and Theater of the Great Depression*. New York: Oxford University Press, 1974.

Himmeslstein, Morgan. *Drama Was a Weapon: The Left-Wing Theatre in New York, 1929–1941*. New Brunswick: Rutgers University Press, 1963.

Jacobs, Susan. *On Stage: The Making of a Broadway Play*. New York: Alfred A.Knopf, 1967.

Krutch, Joseph Wood. *The American Drama Since 1918*. New York: George Braziller, 1957.

Lahr, John. *Up Against the Fourth Wall*. New York: Grove Press, 1970.

Lynes, Russell. *The Lively Audience: A Social History of the Visual and Performing Arts in America, 1890–1950*. New York: Harper and Row, 1985.

Murphy, Brenda. *American Realism and American Drama, 1880–1940*. Cambridge and New York: Cambridge University Press, 1987.

Parker, Dorothy. ed. *Essays on Modern American Drama: Williams, Miller, Albee, and Shepard*. Toronto: University of Toronto Press, 1987.

Rabkin, Gerald. *Drama and Commitment: Politics in the American Theater of the Thirties*. Bloomington: Indiana University Press, 1964.

Reynolds, R. C. *Stage Left, The Development of American Social Drama in the Thirties*. Troy: Whitson, 1986.

Scharine, Richard G. *From Class to Caste in American Drama: Political and Social Themes Since the 1930s*. Westport: Greenwood Press, 1991.

EXPRESSIONISM AND THE EPIC THEATER

Benjamin, Walter. *Understanding Brecht*. London: New Left Books, 1977.

Brecht, Bertolt. *Brecht on Theatre*. Trans. John Willet. New York: Methuen, 1964.

Engel, Edwin. *The Haunted Heroes of Eugene O'Neill*. Cambridge: Harvard University Press, 1953.

Esslin, Martin. *Brecht: The Man and His Work*. New York: Doubleday, 1960.

Fuegi, John. *The Essential Brecht*. Los Angeles: Hennessey and Ingalls, 1972.

Miller, Arthur. *Timebends: A Life*. New York: Grove Press, 1987.

Samuel, Richard and Thomas R. Hinton. *Expressionism in Twentieth-Century German Literature*. New York: W. Heffer and Sons, 1964.

Ritchie, J. M. *German Expressionist Drama*. Boston: Twayne, 1976.

Valgemae, Mardi. *Accelerted Grimace: Expressionism in the American Drama of the 1920s*. Carbondale: Southern Illinois University Press, 1972.

Willet, John, ed. *Brecht on Theatre: The Development of an Aesthetic*. New York: Hill and Wang, 1964.

ABSURDISM

Esslin, Martin. *The Theatre of the Absurd*. New York: Doubleday, 1961.

Jameson, Fredric. *Sartre: The Origins of Style*. New Haven: Yale University Press, 1961.

Styan, John L. *The Dark Comedy*. Cambridge: Harvard University Press, 1968.

Chapter 8: The Theater of Africa and the African Diaspora

AFRICA

Banham, Martin with C. Wake. *African Theater Today*. London: Pitman's, 1976.

Banham, Martin et al. *The Cambridge Guide to African and Caribbean Theatre*. Cambridge: Cambridge University Press, 1994.

Ekwueme, Victoria C. "Story Theatre in Africa: An Essay in Description," *Yale/Theatre* 3, no. 2 (1971), 79–83.

Gotrick, Karl. *Apidan Theatre and Modern Drama*. Göteborg: Almquist and Wisken International, 1984.

Graham-White, Anthony. *The Drama of Black Africa*. London and New York: Samuel French, 1974.

Kirby, E. T. "Indigenous African Theatre," *Drama Review* 18, no. 4 (1974), 22–33.

Soyinka, Wole. *Myth, Literature, and the African World*. Cambridge: Cambridge University Press, 1976.

AFRICAN-AMERICAN THEATER

Fabre, Genevieve. *Drumbeats and Metaphor: Contemporary Afro-American Theatre*. Cambridge: Harvard University Press, 1983.

Haskin, James. *Black Theatre in America*. New York: Thomas Y. Crowell, 1982.

Hatch, James V. *The Black Image on the American Stage*. New York: Drama Book Specialists, 1970.

Hill, Errol. *The Theater of Black Americans*. 2 vols. Englewood Cliffs: Applause Theatre Books, 1980.

Hughes, Langston and Milton Meltzer. *Black Magic: A Pictorial History of Black Entertainers in America*. New York: Prentice-Hall, 1967.

Sanders, L. C. *The Development of Black Theater in America: From Shadows to Selves*. Baton Rouge: Louisiana State University Press, 1988.

Williams, Mance. *Black Theatre in the 1960s and 1970s: A Historical-Critical Analysis of the Movement*. Westport: Greenwood Press, 1985.

Woll, Albert. *Black Musical Theatre from Coontown to Dreamgirls*. Baton Rouge: Louisiana State University Press, 1989.

THE CARIBBEAN

Baxter, I. *The Arts of an Island*. Metuchen: Scarecrow Press, 1970.

Collins, J. A. *Contemporary Theater in Puerto Rico*. Rio Piedras: Editorial Universitaria-Universidad de Puerto Rico, 1979.

Corsbie, K. *Theatre in the Caribbean*. London: Faber and Faber, 1984.

Leal, R. *A Brief History of Cuban Theatre*. Havana: Editorial Letras Cubanas, 1980.

Omotoso, K. *The Theatrical into Theatre: A Study of Drama and Theatre in the English-Speaking Caribbean*. London: New Beacon Books, 1982.

Perereira, J. R. "The Black Presence in Cuban Theatre," *Afro-Hispanic Review* 2 no. 1 (January 1983), 23-35.

Phillips, J. B. *Contemporary Puerto Rican Drama*. New York: Plaza Mayor Ediciones, 1972.

Rohlehr, G. *Calypso and Society in Pre-Independence Trinidad*. Port of Spain, Trinidad: G. Rohlehr, 1990.

Chapter 9: The Contemporary Theater

Albuquerque, Severino Joao. *A Study of Contemporary Latin American Theater*. Detroit: Wayne State University Press, 1991.

Arrizon, Alicia. *Latina Performance: Traversing the Stage*. Bloomington: Indiana University Press, 1999.

Artaud, Antonin. *The Theatre and Its Double*. Trans. M. C. Richards. New York: Grove Press, 1958.

Birringer, Johannes. *Theatre, Theory, Postmodernism*. Bloomington: Indiana University Press, 1991.

Blau, Herbert. *The Eye of the Prey: Subversions of the Postmodern*. Bloomington: Indiana University Press, 1987.

Case, Sue-Ellen. *Feminism and the Theatre*. New York: Macmillan, 1987.

Dolan, Jill. *The Feminist Spectator as Critic*. Ann Arbor: University of Michigan Press, 1988.

Grotowski, Jerzy. *Towards a Poor Theatre*. New York: Simon and Schuster, 1968.

Hart, Lynda, ed. *Making a Spectacle: Feminist Essays on Contemporary Women's Theatre*. Ann Arbor: University of Michigan Press, 1989.

Jencks, Charles. *What Is Post-modernism?* London: Academy Editions, 1996.

Kostelanetz, Richard. *The Theatre of Mixed Means*. New York: Dial Press, 1968.

Larson, Catherine and Margarita Vargas. *Latin American Women Dramatists: Theater, Texts, and Theory*. Bloomington: Indiana University Press, 1998.

Malpede, Karen, ed. *Women in Theatre: Compassion and Hope*. New York: Drama Book Specialists, 1983.

Marranca, Bonnie. *Theatre of Images*. New York: Drama Book Specialists, 1985.

Marranca, Bonnie and Guatam Dasgupta. *American Playwrights: A Critical Survey*. New York: Drama Book Specialists, 1981.

Parker, Rozsika and Griselda Pollocks, eds. *Framing Feminism: Art and the Women's Movement, 1979–1985*. London: Pandora Press, 1987.

Pavis, Patrice. *Theatre at the Crossroads of Culture*. Trans. Loren Kruger. London and New York: Routledge, 1992.

Rostagno, Aldo. *We, the Living Theatre*. New York: Ballantine Books, 1970.

Schechner, Richard. *The End of Humanism: Writing on Performance*. New York: Theatre Arts Books, 1982.

Schecter, Joel. *Durov's Pig: Clowns, Politics, and Theatre*. New York: Theater Arts Books, 1985.

Schevill, James. *Breakout! In Search of New Theatrical Environments*. Chicago: Swallow Press, 1972.

Taylor, Diana. *Theatre of Crisis: Drama and Politics in Latin America*. Lexington: University Press of Kentucky, 1991.

Taylor, Karen Malpede. *Peoples Theatre in Amerika*. New York: Drama Book Specialists, 1972.

Wandor, Michelene. *Carry On, Understudies: Theatre and Sexual Politics*. London: Routledge & Kegan Paul, 1986.

Weales, Gerald. *The Jumping-Off Place: American Drama in the 1960s, from Broadway to Off-Off Broadway to Happenings*. New York: Macmillan, 1969.

Wellwarth, George E. *The Theater of Protest and Paradox: Developments in the Avant-Garde Drama*. Rev. ed. New York: New York University Press, 1971.

Wheale, Nigel, ed. *The Postmodern Arts*. London and New York: Routledge, 1995.

ACKNOWLEDGMENTS

Aeschylus. *Prometheus Bound*, from *Aeschylus II*, in *The Complete Greek Tragedies*. David Grene, Translator. Chicago: University of Chicago Press, 1953. Copyright 1953 by University of Chicago. Reprinted with permission.

Kobo Abe. *The Man Who Turned into a Stick* by Kobo Abe, translated by Donald Keene. Copyright © 1975 by Kobo Abe. Reprinted by permission of International Creative Management, Inc.

Anonymous. *The Apple Tree*, translated by John Cartwright. Copyright © 1995. Reprinted by permission of the author.

Anonymous. *Everyman*. Footnotes accompanying *Everyman* by Sylvan Barnet, from *Types of Drama: Plays and Contexts*, Seventh Edition by Sylvan Barnet, Morton Berman, William Burto, and Ken Draya. Copyright © 1997 by Sylvan Barnet, Morton Berman, William Burto, and Ken Draya.

Anonymous. *Master Pierre Pathelin* translated by Alan E. Knight from *Semiotics of Deceit* by Donald Maddoz. Copyright © Associated University Presses, Cranbury, New Jersey. Reprinted by Permission.

Anonymous. *The Qing Ding Pearl*. Reprinted with the permission of Scribner, a Division of Simon & Schuster from *Famous Chinese Plays*, translated and edited by L.C. Arlington and Harold Acton (Russell & Russell, NY, 1963).

Aristophanes. *Lysistrata* by Aristophanes translated by Donald Sutherland. Copyright © 1961 by Harper & Row, Publishers, Inc. Reprinted by permission of Addison Wesley Educational Publishers Inc.

Edward Albee. *The American Dream*. Copyright © 1961, Renewed 1988 by Edward Albee. Reprinted by permission of William Morris Agency, Inc. on behalf of the Author. CAUTION: Professionals and amateurs are hereby warned that *The American Dream* is subject to royalty. It is fully protected under the copyright laws of the United States of America and all countries covered by the International Copyright Union (including the Dominion of Canada and the rest of the British Commonwealth), the Berne Convention, the Pan-American Copyright Convention and the Universal Copyright Convention as well as all countries with which the United States has reciprocal copyright relations. All rights, including professional/amateur stage rights, motion picture, recitation, lecturing, public reading, radio broadcasting, television, video or sound recording, all other forms of mechanical or electronic reproduction, such as CD-ROM, CD-I, information storage and retrieval systems and photocopying, and the rights of translation into foreign languages, are strictly reserved. Particular emphasis is laid upon the matter of readings, permission for which must be secured from the Author's agent in writing. Inquiries concerning rights should be addressed to: William Morris Agency, Inc., 1325 Avenue of the Americas, New York, New York 10019, Attn: Owen Laster.

Amiri Baraka. *Slave Ship* by Amiri Baraka. Reprinted by permission of Sterling Lord Literistic, Inc. Copyright 1978 by Amiri Baraka.

Samuel Beckett. *Rockaby* by Samuel Beckett. Copyright © 1982 by Samuel Beckett. Used by permission of Grove/Atlantic, Inc.

Aphra Behn. *The Rover*. Footnotes accompanying *The Rover* by Sylvan Barnet, from *Types of Drama: Plays and Contexts*, Seventh Edition by Sylvan Barnet, Morton Berman, William Burto, and Ken Draya. Copyright © 1997 by Sylvan Barnet, Morton Berman, William Burto, and Ken Draya.

Bertolt Brecht. *The Good Woman of Setzuan* by Bertolt Brecht. Copyright by Eric Bentley, 1947, as an unpublished MS, Registration No. D-12239. © Copyright 1956, 1961 by Eric Bentley. Epilogue © Copyright by Eric Bentley. From *Parables for the Theatre, Two plays by Bertolt Brecht*, translated by Eric Bentley. Reprinted by permission of the University of Minnesota Press.

Pedro Calderón de la Barca. *Life's a Dream* by Calderón de la Barca, translated and adapted by Adrian Mitchell and John Barton. Copyright © 1990. Reprinted by permission of Oberon Books, London.

Anton Chekhov. *The Cherry Orchard* by Anton Chekhov. From *Chekhov: The Major Plays* by Anton Chekhov, translated by Ann Dunnigan. Copyright © 1964 by Ann Dunnigan. Used by permission of Dutton Signet, a division of Penguin Putnam Inc.

Ma Chih-yüan. *Autumn in the Palace of Han*, by Ma Chih-yüan, translated by Donald Keene. From *Anthology of Chinese Literature* edited by Cyril Birch. Copyright © 1965 by Grove Press, Inc. Used by Permission of Grove/Atlantic, Inc.

Caryl Churchill. *Top Girls* by Caryl Churchill. Reprinted by permission of Methuen Publishing Ltd.

Acknowledgments

Osvaldo Dragún. *The Man Who Turned into a Dog* by Osvaldo Dragún. Translated by Roberto D. Pomo. Copyright © 1981 by Roberto D. Pomo. Reprinted by permission.

Euripides. *Medea.* Copyright © 1974 by Paul Roche, from *Three Plays of Euripides: Alcestis, Medea, The Bacchae* by Paul Roche, translator. Reprinted by permission of W. W. Norton & Company, Inc.

Maria Irene Fornes. *Mud* by Maria Irene Fornes, from *Maria Irene Fornes: Plays.* Copyright 1986. © copyright 1984 by PAJ Publications and Maria Irene Fornes. Reprinted by permission of PAJ Publications.

Athol Fugard. *"MASTER HAROLD"... and the boys.* From *"MASTER HAROLD"... and the boys* by Athol Fugard. Copyright © 1982 by Athol Fugard. Reprinted by permission of Alfred A. Knopf, a Division of Random House, Inc. CAUTION: Professionals and amateurs are hereby warned that *"MASTER HAROLD"... and the boys* is subject to a royalty. It is fully protected under the copyright laws of the United States of America, the British Commonwealth, including Canada, and all other countries of the copyright Union. All rights, including professional, amateur, motion pictures, recitation, lecture, public reading, radio broadcasting, television, and the rights of translation into foreign languages are strictly reserved. In its present form the play is dedicated to the reading public only. The amateur live stage performance rights to *"MASTER HAROLD"... and the boys* are controlled exclusively by Samuel French, Inc., and royalty arrangements and licensees must be secured well in advance of presentation. PLEASE NOTE that amateur royalty fees are set upon application in accordance with your producing circumstances. When applying for a royalty quotation for and license please give us the number of performance, intended dates of production, your seating capacity and admission fee. Royalties are payable one week before the opening performance of the play to Samuel French, Inc., at 45 W. 25th Street, New York, NY 10010; or at 7623 Sunset Blvd., Hollywood, CA 90046, or to Samuel French (Canada), Ltd., 80 Richmond Street East, Toronto, Ontario, Canada M5C 1Pl. For all other rights than those stipulated above, apply to William Morris Agency, Inc., 1350 Ave. of the Americas, New York, NY 10019.

Griselda Gambaro. *Personal Effects* by Griselda Gambaro. Translated by Roberto D. Pomo. Copyright © 1999. Reprinted by permission.

Elena Garro. *A Solid Home* by Elena Garro, from *Selected Latin American One-Act Plays,* Francesca Colecchia and Julio Matas, eds. and trans. Published in 1973 by the University of Pittsburgh Press. Reprinted by permission of the publisher.

Namiki Gohei III. *Kanjinchō, A Kabuki Play,* by Namiki Gohei. English Adaptation by James R. Brandon and Tamako Niwa. Copyright © 1966 by Samuel French, Inc. CAUTION: Professionals and amateurs are hereby warned that *Kanjinchō* being fully protected under the copyright laws of the United States of America, the British Commonwealth countries, including Canada and the other countries of the Copyright Union, is subject to a royalty. All rights, including professional, amateur, motion picture, recitation, public reading, radio, television, and cable broadcasting, and the rights of translation into foreign languages, are strictly reserved. Any inquiry regarding the availability of performance rights, or the purchase of individual copies of the authorized acting edition, must be directed to Samuel French, Inc., 45 West 25 Street, NY, NY 10010 with other locations in Hollywood and Toronto, Canada.

Lorraine Hansberry. *A Raisin in the Sun* by Lorraine Hansberry. From *A Raisin in the Sun,* by Lorraine Hansberry. Copyright © 1958 by Robert Nemiroff, as an unpublished work. Copyright © 1959, 1966, 1984 by Robert Nemiroff. Reprinted by permission of Random House, Inc. CAUTION: Professionals and amateurs are hereby warned that performance of *A Raisin in the Sun* is subject to a royalty. It is fully protected under the copyright laws of the United States of America, and of all countries covered by the International Copyright Union (including the Dominion of Canada and the rest of the British Commonwealth), and of all countries covered by the Pan-American Copyright Convention, the Universal Copyright Convention, the Berne Convention, and of all countries with which the United States has reciprocal copyright relations. All rights, including professional/amateur stage rights, motion picture, recitation, lecturing, public reading, radio broadcasting, television, video or sound recording, all other forms of mechanical or electronic reproduction, such as CD-ROM, CD-I, information storage and retrieval systems and photocopying, and the rights of translation into foreign languages, are strictly reserved. Particular emphasis is laid upon the matter of readings, permission for which must be secured from the Author's agent in writing. The amateur stage performance rights for *A Raisin in the Sun* are controlled exclusively by the DRAMATISTS PLAY SERVICE, INC., 440 Park Avenue South, New York, N. Y. 10016. No non-professional performance of the Play may be given without obtaining in advance the written permission of the DRAMATISTS PLAY SERVICE, INC., and paying the requisite fee.

Victor Hugo. *Hernani* by Victor Hugo. Translated by Linda Asher. Copyright by Linda Asher, reprinted by permission.

David Henry Hwang. *The Dance and the Railroad.* Copyright © 1981. by David Henry Hwang. Reprinted by permission of the author.

Henrik Ibsen. *A Doll's House* by Henrik Ibsen. Reprinted by permission of Harold Ober Associates Incorporated. Copyright © 1965, 1980, 1993 by Michael Meyer. *Hedda Gabler* by Henrik Ibsen. Reprinted by permission of Harold Ober Associates Incorporated. Copyright © 1962, 1974, 1980, renewed in 1990 by Michael Meyer. CAUTION: These plays are fully protected, in whole, in part or in any form under the copyright laws of the United States of America, the British Empire including the Dominion of Canada, and all other countries of the Copyright Union, and are subject to royalty. All rights including, motion picture, radio, television, recitation, public reading, are strictly reserved. For professional rights and amateur rights all inquiries should be addressed to the Author's Agent: Robert A. Freedman Dramatic Agency Inc., 1501 Broadway, New York, NY 10036.

Kālidāsā. *Abhijnanasakuntalam* from *Kālidāsā: The Loom of Time,* translated by Chandra Rajan, is reproduced courtesy the publishers (Penguin Books India Pvt. Ltd.) and the translator.

Tony Kushner. *Angels in America, Part One: Millennium Approaches* by Tony Kushner. Copyright © 1993 by Tony Kushner. Reprinted by permission of Theatre Communication Group, Inc.

Arthur Miller. *Death of a Salesman* by Arthur Miller. Copyright 1949, renewed © 1977 by Arthur Miller. Used by permission of Viking Penguin, a division of Penguin Putnam Inc.

Molière. *Tartuffe* by Molière, translated by Richard Wilbur. Copyright © 1963, 1962, 1961, and renewed 1991, 1990 and 1989 by Richard Wilbur, reprinted by permission of Harcourt Brace & Company. CAUTION: Professionals and amateurs are hereby warned that this translation, being fully protected under the copyright laws of the United States of America, the British Empire, including the Dominion of Canada and the other countries which are signatories to the Universal Copyright Convention and the International Copyright Union, is subject to a royalty. All rights, including professional, amateur, motion picture, recitation, lecturing, public reading, radio broadcasting, and television, are strictly reserved. Particular emphasis is laid on the question of readings, permission for which must be secured from the author's agent in writing. Inquires on professional rights (except for amateur rights) should be addressed to Mr. Gilbert Parker, Curtis Brown, Ltd. Ten Astor Place, New York, NY 10003; inquires on translation rights should be addressed to Harcourt Brace & Company Publishers, Orlando, FL 32887. The Amateur acting rights of *Tartuffe* are controlled exclusively by the Dramatists Play Service, Inc., 400 Park Avenue South, New York, New York. No Amateur performance of the play may be given without obtaining in advance the written permission of the Dramatists Play Service, Inc., and paying the requisite fee.

Percy Mtwa, Mbongeni Ngema, and Barney Simon. *Woza Albert!* by Percy Mtwa, Mbongeni Ngema, and Barney Simon. Reprinted by permission of Methuen Publishing Ltd.

Heiner Müller. *Medeaplay* by Heiner Müller, from *Hamletmachine and Other Texts for the Stage*, translated by Carl Weber. © Copyright 1984 by PAJ Publications. English translation copyright 1984 by Carl Weber. Reprinted by permission of PAJ Publications.

Eugene O'Neill. *The Hairy Ape* by Eugene O'Neill. From *The Plays of Eugene O'Neill, Volume III* by Eugene O'Neill. Copyright 1924 and renewed 1950 by Eugene O'Neill. Reprinted by permission of Random House, Inc. CAUTION: Professionals and amateurs are hereby warned that *The Hairy Ape* is subject to a royalty. It is fully protected under the copyright laws of the United States of America, the British Commonwealth, including Canada, and all other countries of the copyright Union. All rights, including professional, amateur, motion pictures, recitation, lecture, public reading, radio broadcasting, television, and the rights of translation into foreign languages are strictly reserved. In its present form the play is dedicated to the reading public only. The amateur live stage performance rights to *The Hairy Ape* are controlled exclusively by Samuel French, Inc., and royalty arrangements and licensees must be secured well in advance of presentation. PLEASE NOTE that amateur royalty fees are set upon application in accordance with your producing circumstances.. When applying for a royalty quotation for and license please give us the number of performance, intended dates of production, your seating capacity and admission fee. Royalties are payable one week before the opening performance of the play to Samuel French, Inc., at 45 W. 25th Street, New York, NY 10010; or at 7623 Sunset Blvd., Hollywood, CA 90046, or to Samuel French (Canada), Ltd., 80 Richmond Street East, Toronto, Ontario, Canada M5C 1Pl.

Harold Pinter. *One For the Road* by Harold Pinter. Copyright © 1984 by Harold Pinter. Used by permission of Grove/Atlantic, Inc. and Faber and Faber Ltd.

Luigi Pirandello. *Six Characters in Search of an Author* by Luigi Pirandello. Copyright 1922 by E.P. Dutton. Renewed 1950 in the names of Stefano, Fausto and Lietta Pirandello. From *Naked Masks: Five Plays by Luigi Pirandello*, edited by Eric Bentley, translation copyright 1922 by E. P. Dutton. Renewed 1950 in the names of Stefano, Fausto and Lietta Pirandello. Used by permission of Dutton, a division of Penguin Putnam Inc.

William Shakespeare. Footnotes accompanying *Hamlet, Prince of Denmark* and *A Midsummer Night's Dream* from *The Complete Works Of Shakespeare* 4th ed. by David Bevington. Copyright 1992 by HarperCollins Publishers Inc. Reprinted by permission of Addison-Wesley Educational Publishers Inc.

Sam Shepard. *Buried Child*, Copyright © 1979 by Sam Shepard. From *Seven Plays* by Sam Shepard. Used by permission of Bantam Books, a division of Random House, Inc.

Bernard Shaw. *Major Barbara*. © Copyright 1907,1913, 1930, 1941 George Bernard Shaw. © Copyright 1957 The Public Trustee as Executor of the Estate of George Bernard Shaw. Reprinted by permission of The Society of Authors on behalf of the Estate of Bernard Shaw.

Anna Deavere Smith. *Twilight: Los Angeles, 1992* by Anna Deavere Smith. Reprinted by permission of Anna Deavere Smith and the Watkins/Loomis Agency.

Sophocles. *Oedipus the King*. From *Sophocles I*, in *The Complete Greek Tragedies*. David Grene, Translator, Chicago: University of Chicago Press, 1954. Copyright 1954 by University of Chicago. Reprinted with permission.

Wole Soyinka. *Death and the King's Horseman* by Wole Soyinka. Copyright © 1975 by Wole Soyinka. Reprinted by permission of W.W. Norton & Company, Inc.

August Strindberg. *Miss Julie* by August Strindberg, translated by Harry Carlson. From *Strindberg: Five Plays* translated/edited by Harry Carlson; translation of *Miss Julie* by Harry Carlson. Copyright 1983 The Regents of the University of California. Reprinted by permission.

Terence. *Brothers* by Terence, translated by Charles Mercier. Copyright © 1998. Reprinted by permission, Focus Publishing/R. Pullins Co., Inc.

Sue Townsend. *The Great Celestial Cow* by Sue Townsend. Reprinted by permission of Methuen Publishing Ltd.

Luis Valdez. *No saco nada de la escuela* by Luis Valdez, from *Luis Valdez—Early Works: Actos, Bernabe and Pensamiento Serpentino*. Copyright by Luis Valdez for El Teatro Campesino, reprinted by permission of Arte Publico Press.

Derek Walcott. *Ti-Jean and His Brothers* by Derek Walcott. From *Dream on Monkey Mountain* by Derek Walcott. Copyright © 1970 by Derek Walcott. Reprinted by Permission of Farrar, Straus & Giroux, Inc. CAUTION: Professionals and amateurs are hereby warned that *Ti-Jean and His Brothers* by Derek Walcott, being fully protected under the copyright laws of the United States of America, and all other

PHOTO CREDITS

INDEX

Index

Index